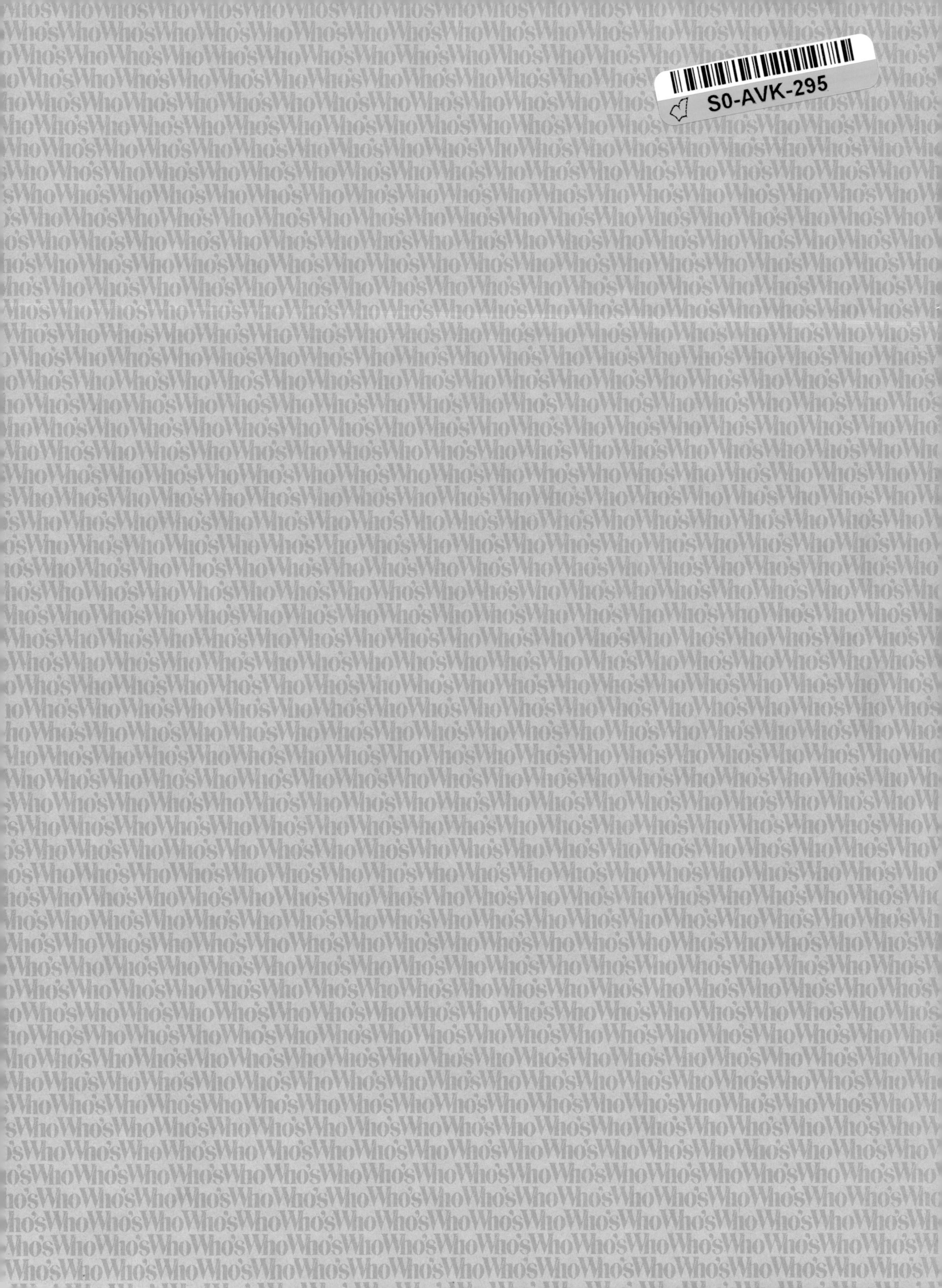

S0-AVK-295

Who's Who in the West®

Biographical Titles Currently Published by Marquis Who's Who

Who's Who in America
Who's Who in America Junior & Senior High School Version
Who Was Who in America
  Historical Volume (1607–1896)
  Volume I (1897–1942)
  Volume II (1943–1950)
  Volume III (1951–1960)
  Volume IV (1961–1968)
  Volume V (1969–1973)
  Volume VI (1974–1976)
  Volume VII (1977–1981)
  Volume VIII (1982–1985)
  Volume IX (1985–1989)
  Volume X (1989–1993)
  Index Volume (1607–1993)
Who's Who in the World
Who's Who in the East
Who's Who in the Midwest
Who's Who in the South and Southwest
Who's Who in the West
Who's Who in American Education
Who's Who in American Law
Who's Who in American Nursing
Who's Who of American Women
Who's Who of Emerging Leaders in America
Who's Who in Finance and Industry
Who's Who in Medicine and Healthcare
Who's Who in Science and Engineering
Index to Marquis Who's Who Publications
The *Official* ABMS Directory of Board Certified Medical Specialists

Who's Who in the West®

1996–1997

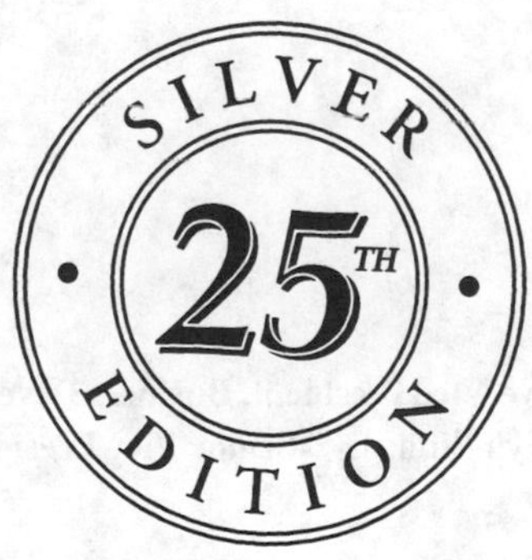

Including Alaska, Arizona, California, Colorado, Hawaii, Idaho, Montana, Nevada, New Mexico, Oregon, Utah, Washington, and Wyoming; and in Canada, the provinces of Alberta, British Columbia, and Saskatchewan, and the Northwest and Yukon Territories.

121 Chanlon Road
New Providence, NJ 07974 U.S.A.

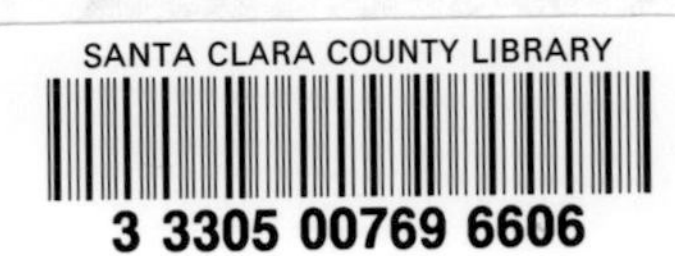

Who'sWho in the West®

Marquis Who's Who

Published by Marquis Who's Who, A Reed Reference Publishing Company.

Library of Congress Catalog Card Number 49-48186
International Standard Book Number 0-8379-0926-0 (Classic Edition)
0-8379-0927-9 (Deluxe Edition)

Manufactured in the United States of America

Table of Contents

Preface

The Silver 25th Edition of *Who's Who in the West* is our most recent compilation of biographical information on men and women of distinction whose influence is concentrated in the western region of North America. Such individuals are of reference interest locally, and to a degree, nationally.

The volume contains approximately 23,300 names from the western region of the United States including Alaska, Arizona, California, Colorado, Hawaii, Idaho, Montana, Nevada, New Mexico, Oregon, Utah, Washington, and Wyoming. Also included are the Canadian provinces of Alberta, British Columbia, and Saskatchewan, and the Northwest and Yukon Territories. In some instances, persons who do not reside in the western region of the United States or Canada have also been included as Biographees. They appear in this edition because they have made significant professional or civic contributions to this region. Reviewed, revised, and amended, the Silver 25th Edition offers current coverage of a broad range of Westerners based on position or individual achievement.

The persons sketched in this volume represent virtually every important field of endeavor. Included are executives and officials in government, business, education, medicine, religion, the press, law, and other fields. This edition also includes significant contributors in such areas as contemporary art, music, and science.

In most cases, Biographees have furnished their own data, thus assuring a high degree of accuracy. In some cases where individuals failed to supply information, Marquis staff members compiled the data through careful, independent research. Sketches compiled in this manner are denoted by an asterisk. As in previous editions, Biographees were given the opportunity to review prepublication proofs of their sketches to make sure they were correct.

The question is often asked, "How do people get into a Marquis Who's Who volume?" Name selection is based on one fundamental principle: reference value.

Biographees of *Who's Who in the West* can be classified in two basic categories: (1) Persons who are of regional reference importance to colleagues, librarians, researchers, scholars, the media, historians, biographers, participants in business and civic affairs, and others with specific or general inquiry needs; (2) Individuals of national reference interest who are also of such regional or local importance that their inclusion in the book is essential.

In the editorial evaluation that resulted in the ultimate selection of the names appearing in this directory, an individual's desire to be listed was not sufficient reason for inclusion; rather it was the person's achievement that ruled. Similarly, neither wealth nor social position was a criterion; only occupational stature or achievement in a field within the western region of North America influenced selection.

A new feature in the Silver 25th Edition of *Who's Who in the West* is a Professional Index. Within the index, each Biographee is listed by occupation, and under each occupational category, names are listed alphabetically by country, state, and city. This reference tool will make it easier than ever for interested readers to find Biographees in any given profession or location.

Marquis Who's Who editors exercise the utmost care in preparing each biographical sketch for publication. Occasionally, however, errors occur. Users of this directory are requested to draw the attention of the publisher to any errors found so that corrections can be made in a subsequent edition.

The Silver 25th Edition of *Who's Who in the West* carries on the tradition of excellence established in 1899 with the publication of the first edition of *Who's Who in America*. The essence of that tradition is reflected in our continuing effort to produce reference works that are responsive to the needs of their users throughout the world.

Board of Advisors

Marquis Who's Who gratefully acknowledges the following distinguished individuals who have made themselves available for review, evaluation, and general comment with regard to the publication of the Silver 25th Edition of Marquis *Who's Who in the West*. The advisors have enhanced the reference value of this edition by the nomination of outstanding individuals for inclusion. However, the Board of Advisors, either collectively or individually, is in no way responsible for the final selection of names, or for the accuracy or comprehensiveness of the biographical information or other material contained herein.

Standards of Admission

The foremost consideration in selecting Biographees for Marquis *Who's Who in the West* is the extent of an individual's reference interest. Such reference interest is judged on either of two factors: (1) the position of responsibility held, or (2) the level of achievement attained by the individual.

Admissions based on the factor of position include:

Members of the U.S. Congress

Federal judges

Governors of states covered by this volume

Premiers of Canadian provinces covered by this volume

State attorneys general

Judges of state and territorial courts of highest appellate jurisdiction

Mayors of major cities

Heads of major universities and colleges

Heads of leading philanthropic, educational, cultural, and scientific institutions and associations

Chief ecclesiastics of the principal religious denominations

Principal officers of national and international business

Admission for individual achievement is based on objective qualitative criteria. To be selected, a person must have attained conspicuous achievement.

Key to Information

[1] ASHTON, HARDY AMES, [2] lawyer; **[3]** b. Topeka, Aug. 3, 1934; **[4]** s. Samuel Taylor and Barbara (Hanson) A.; **[5]** m. Nancy Richardson, June 20, 1955; **[6]** children: Marilyn Ashton Heim, Barbara Anne, William Marc. **[7]** BA, Pa. State U., 1955; JD, Syracuse U.,1960. **[8]** Bar: Calif.1960, U.S. Supreme Ct. 1968. **[9]** Assoc. Prine, Belden and Coates, Sacramento, 1960-67; mem. Johnson, Randolph, Sikes and Bord, Sacramento, 1967—, ptnr., 1969-74, sr. ptnr., 1974—; **[10]** legal cons. Sacramento Urban League. **[11]** Author: Urban Renewal and the Law, 1975, Changes in California Zoning Laws: A Perspective, 1987. **[12]** Commr. Sutter County Park Dist., 1971-78; mem. planning com. Arroyo Seco Redevel. Project, Sacramento, 1980—; bd. dirs. Hargrave Inst. **[13]** Served with U.S. Army, 1956-57. **[14]** Named Man of the Yr., Sacramento C. of C., 1986. **[15]** Mem. ABA, Calif. Bar Assn., Sacramento Bar Assn., Am. Judicature Soc., Order of Coif. Clubs: Twelve Trees Country, Tuesday Luncheon. Lodge: Lions (Sacramento). **[16]** Democrat. **[17]** Episcopalian. **[18]** Home: 3080 Grant St Sacramento CA 95814 **[19]** Office: Johnson Randolph Sikes & Bord 10 Saint Paul St Sacramento CA 95822

KEY

[1] Name
[2] Occupation
[3] Vital statistics
[4] Parents
[5] Marriage
[6] Children
[7] Education
[8] Professional certifications
[9] Career
[10] Career related
[11] Writings and creative works
[12] Civic and political activities
[13] Military
[14] Awards and fellowships
[15] Professional and association memberships, clubs and lodges
[16] Political affiliation
[17] Religion
[18] Home address
[19] Office address

Table of Abbreviations

The following abbreviations and symbols are frequently used in this book.

*An asterisk following a sketch indicates that it was researched by the Marquis Who's Who editorial staff and has not been verified by the Biographee.

A Associate (used with academic degrees only)
AA, A.A. Associate in Arts, Associate of Arts
AAAL American Academy of Arts and Letters
AAAS American Association for the Advancement of Science
AACD American Association for Counseling and Development
AACN American Association of Critical Care Nurses
AAHA American Academy of Health Administrators
AAHP American Association of Hospital Planners
AAHPERD American Alliance for Health, Physical Education, Recreation, and Dance
AAS Associate of Applied Science
AASL American Association of School Librarians
AASPA American Association of School Personnel Administrators
AAU Amateur Athletic Union
AAUP American Association of University Professors
AAUW American Association of University Women
AB, A.B. Arts, Bachelor of
AB Alberta
ABA American Bar Association
ABC American Broadcasting Company
AC Air Corps
acad. academy, academic
acct. accountant
acctg. accounting
ACDA Arms Control and Disarmament Agency
ACHA American College of Hospital Administrators
ACLS Advanced Cardiac Life Support
ACLU American Civil Liberties Union
ACOG American College of Ob-Gyn
ACP American College of Physicians
ACS American College of Surgeons
ADA American Dental Association
a.d.c. aide-de-camp
adj. adjunct, adjutant
adj. gen. adjutant general
adm. admiral
adminstr. administrator
adminstrn. administration
adminstrv. administrative
ADN Associate's Degree in Nursing
ADP Automatic Data Processing
adv. advocate, advisory
advt. advertising
AE, A.E. Agricultural Engineer
A.E. and P. Ambassador Extraordinary and Plenipotentiary
AEC Atomic Energy Commission
aero. aeronautical, aeronautic
aerodyn. aerodynamic
AFB Air Force Base
AFL-CIO American Federation of Labor and Congress of Industrial Organizations
AFTRA American Federation of TV and Radio Artists
AFSCME American Federation of State, County and Municipal Employees
agr. agriculture
agrl. agricultural
agt. agent
AGVA American Guild of Variety Artists
agy. agency
A&I Agricultural and Industrial
AIA American Institute of Architects
AIAA American Institute of Aeronautics and Astronautics
AIChE American Institute of Chemical Engineers
AICPA American Institute of Certified Public Accountants
AID Agency for International Development
AIDS Acquired Immune Deficiency Syndrome
AIEE American Institute of Electrical Engineers
AIM American Institute of Management
AIME American Institute of Mining, Metallurgy, and Petroleum Engineers
AK Alaska
AL Alabama
ALA American Library Association
Ala. Alabama
alt. alternate
Alta. Alberta
A&M Agricultural and Mechanical
AM, A.M. Arts, Master of
Am. American, America
AMA American Medical Association
amb. ambassador
A.M.E. African Methodist Episcopal
Amtrak National Railroad Passenger Corporation
AMVETS American Veterans of World War II, Korea, Vietnam
ANA American Nurses Association
anat. anatomical
ANCC American Nurses Credentialing Center
ann. annual
ANTA American National Theatre and Academy
anthrop. anthropological
AP Associated Press
APA American Psychological Association
APGA American Personnel Guidance Association
APHA American Public Health Association
APO Army Post Office
apptd. appointed
Apr. April
apt. apartment
AR Arkansas
ARC American Red Cross
arch. architect
archeol. archeological
archtl. architectural
Ariz. Arizona
Ark. Arkansas
ArtsD, ArtsD. Arts, Doctor of
arty. artillery
AS American Samoa
AS Associate in Science
ASCAP American Society of Composers, Authors and Publishers
ASCD Association for Supervision and Curriculum Development
ASCE American Society of Civil Engineers
ASHRAE American Society of Heating, Refrigeration, and Air Conditioning Engineers
ASME American Society of Mechanical Engineers
ASNSA American Society for Nursing Service Administrators
ASPA American Society for Public Administration
ASPCA American Society for the Prevention of Cruelty to Animals
assn. association
assoc. associate
asst. assistant
ASTD American Society for Training and Development
ASTM American Society for Testing and Materials
astron. astronomical
astrophys. astrophysical
ATLA Association of Trial Lawyers of America
ATSC Air Technical Service Command
AT&T American Telephone & Telegraph Company
atty. attorney
Aug. August
AUS Army of the United States
aux. auxiliary
Ave. Avenue
AVMA American Veterinary Medical Association
AZ Arizona
AWHONN Association of Women's Health Obstetric and Neonatal Nurses

B. Bachelor
b. born
BA, B.A. Bachelor of Arts
BAgr, B.Agr. Bachelor of Agriculture
Balt. Baltimore
Bapt. Baptist
BArch, B.Arch. Bachelor of Architecture
BAS, B.A.S. Bachelor of Agricultural Science
BBA, B.B.A. Bachelor of Business Administration
BBB Better Business Bureau
BBC British Broadcasting Corporation
BC, B.C. British Columbia

BCE, B.C.E. Bachelor of Civil Engineering
BChir, B.Chir. Bachelor of Surgery
BCL, B.C.L. Bachelor of Civil Law
BCLS Basic Cardiac Life Support
BCS, B.C.S. Bachelor of Commercial Science
BD, B.D. Bachelor of Divinity
bd. board
BE, B.E. Bachelor of Education
BEE, B.E.E. Bachelor of Electrical Engineering
BFA, B.F.A. Bachelor of Fine Arts
bibl. biblical
bibliog. bibliographical
biog. biographical
biol. biological
BJ, B.J. Bachelor of Journalism
Bklyn. Brooklyn
BL, B.L. Bachelor of Letters
bldg. building
BLS, B.L.S. Bachelor of Library Science
BLS Basic Life Support
Blvd. Boulevard
BMI Broadcast Music, Inc.
BMW Bavarian Motor Works (Bayerische Motoren Werke)
bn. battalion
B.&O.R.R. Baltimore & Ohio Railroad
bot. botanical
BPE, B.P.E. Bachelor of Physical Education
BPhil, B.Phil. Bachelor of Philosophy
br. branch
BRE, B.R.E. Bachelor of Religious Education
brig. gen. brigadier general
Brit. British, Brittanica
Bros. Brothers
BS, B.S. Bachelor of Science
BSA, B.S.A. Bachelor of Agricultural Science
BSBA Bachelor of Science in Business Administration
BSChemE Bachelor of Science in Chemical Engineering
BSD, B.S.D. Bachelor of Didactic Science
BSEE Bachelor of Science in Electrical Engineering
BSN Bachelor of Science in Nursing
BST, B.S.T. Bachelor of Sacred Theology
BTh, B.Th. Bachelor of Theology
bull. bulletin
bur. bureau
bus. business
B.W.I. British West Indies

CA California
CAA Civil Aeronautics Administration
CAB Civil Aeronautics Board
CAD-CAM Computer Aided Design-Computer Aided Model
Calif. California
C.Am. Central America
Can. Canada, Canadian
CAP Civil Air Patrol
capt. captain
cardiol. cardiological
cardiovasc. cardiovascular
CARE Cooperative American Relief Everywhere
Cath. Catholic
cav. cavalry
CBC Canadian Broadcasting Company
CBI China, Burma, India Theatre of Operations
CBS Columbia Broadcasting Company
C.C. Community College
CCC Commodity Credit Corporation
CCNY City College of New York
CCRN Critical Care Registered Nurse
CCU Cardiac Care Unit
CD Civil Defense
CE, C.E. Corps of Engineers, Civil Engineer
CEN Certified Emergency Nurse
CENTO Central Treaty Organization
CEO chief executive officer
CERN European Organization of Nuclear Research
cert. certificate, certification, certified
CETA Comprehensive Employment Training Act
CFA Chartered Financial Analyst
CFL Canadian Football League
CFO chief financial officer
CFP Certified Financial Planner
ch. church
ChD, Ch.D. Doctor of Chemistry
chem. chemical
ChemE, Chem.E. Chemical Engineer
ChFC Chartered Financial Consultant
Chgo. Chicago
chirurg. chirurgical
chmn. chairman
chpt. chapter
CIA Central Intelligence Agency
Cin. Cincinnati
cir. circle, circuit
CLE Continuing Legal Education
Cleve. Cleveland
climatol. climatological
clin. clinical
clk. clerk
C.L.U. Chartered Life Underwriter
CM, C.M. Master in Surgery
CM Northern Mariana Islands
CMA Certified Medical Assistant
cmty. community
CNA Certified Nurse's Aide
CNOR Certified Nurse (Operating Room)
C.&N.W.Ry. Chicago & North Western Railway
CO Colorado
Co. Company
COF Catholic Order of Foresters
C. of C. Chamber of Commerce
col. colonel
coll. college
Colo. Colorado
com. committee
comd. commanded
comdg. commanding
comdr. commander
comdt. commandant
comm. communications
commd. commissioned
comml. commercial
commn. commission
commr. commissioner
compt. comptroller
condr. conductor
Conf. Conference
Congl. Congregational, Congressional
Conglist. Congregationalist
Conn. Connecticut
cons. consultant, consulting
consol. consolidated
constl. constitutional
constn. constitution
constrn. construction
contbd. contributed
contbg. contributing
contbn. contribution
contbr. contributor
contr. controller
Conv. Convention
COO chief operating officer
coop. cooperative
coord. coordinator
CORDS Civil Operations and Revolutionary Development Support
CORE Congress of Racial Equality
corp. corporation, corporate
corr. correspondent, corresponding, correspondence
C.&O.Ry. Chesapeake & Ohio Railway
coun. council
CPA Certified Public Accountant
CPCU Chartered Property and Casualty Underwriter
CPH, C.P.H. Certificate of Public Health
cpl. corporal
CPR Cardio-Pulmonary Resuscitation
C.P.Ry. Canadian Pacific Railway
CRT Cathode Ray Terminal
C.S. Christian Science
CSB, C.S.B. Bachelor of Christian Science
C.S.C. Civil Service Commission
CT Connecticut
ct. court
ctr. center
ctrl. central
CWS Chemical Warfare Service
C.Z. Canal Zone

D. Doctor
d. daughter
DAgr, D.Agr. Doctor of Agriculture
DAR Daughters of the American Revolution
dau. daughter
DAV Disabled American Veterans
DC, D.C. District of Columbia
DCL, D.C.L. Doctor of Civil Law
DCS, D.C.S. Doctor of Commercial Science
DD, D.D. Doctor of Divinity
DDS, D.D.S. Doctor of Dental Surgery
DE Delaware
Dec. December
dec. deceased
def. defense
Del. Delaware
del. delegate, delegation
Dem. Democrat, Democratic
DEng, D.Eng. Doctor of Engineering
denom. denomination, denominational
dep. deputy
dept. department
dermatol. dermatological
desc. descendant
devel. development, developmental
DFA, D.F.A. Doctor of Fine Arts
D.F.C. Distinguished Flying Cross
DHL, D.H.L. Doctor of Hebrew Literature
dir. director
dist. district
distbg. distributing
distbn. distribution
distbr. distributor
disting. distinguished
div. division, divinity, divorce
DLitt, D.Litt. Doctor of Literature
DMD, D.M.D. Doctor of Dental Medicine
DMS, D.M.S. Doctor of Medical Science
DO, D.O. Doctor of Osteopathy
docs. documents
DON Director of Nursing
DPH, D.P.H. Diploma in Public Health
DPhil, D.Phil. Doctor of Philosophy
D.R. Daughters of the Revolution
Dr. Drive, Doctor
DRE, D.R.E. Doctor of Religious Education
DrPH, Dr.P.H. Doctor of Public Health, Doctor of Public Hygiene
D.S.C. Distinguished Service Cross
DSc, D.Sc. Doctor of Science

DSChemE Doctor of Science in Chemical Engineering
D.S.M. Distinguished Service Medal
DST, D.S.T. Doctor of Sacred Theology
DTM, D.T.M. Doctor of Tropical Medicine
DVM, D.V.M. Doctor of Veterinary Medicine
DVS, D.V.S. Doctor of Veterinary Surgery

E, E. East
ea. eastern
E. and P. Extraordinary and Plenipotentiary
Eccles. Ecclesiastical
ecol. ecological
econ. economic
ECOSOC Economic and Social Council (of the UN)
ED, E.D. Doctor of Engineering
ed. educated
EdB, Ed.B. Bachelor of Education
EdD, Ed.D. Doctor of Education
edit. edition
editl. editorial
EdM, Ed.M. Master of Education
edn. education
ednl. educational
EDP Electronic Data Processing
EdS, Ed.S. Specialist in Education
EE, E.E. Electrical Engineer
E.E. and M.P. Envoy Extraordinary and Minister Plenipotentiary
EEC European Economic Community
EEG Electroencephalogram
EEO Equal Employment Opportunity
EEOC Equal Employment Opportunity Commission
E.Ger. German Democratic Republic
EKG Electrocardiogram
elec. electrical
electrochem. electrochemical
electrophys. electrophysical
elem. elementary
EM, E.M. Engineer of Mines
EMT Emergency Medical Technician
ency. encyclopedia
Eng. England
engr. engineer
engring. engineering
entomol. entomological
environ. environmental
EPA Environmental Protection Agency
epidemiol. epidemiological
Episc. Episcopalian
ERA Equal Rights Amendment
ERDA Energy Research and Development Administration
ESEA Elementary and Secondary Education Act
ESL English as Second Language
ESPN Entertainment and Sports Programming Network
ESSA Environmental Science Services Administration
ethnol. ethnological
ETO European Theatre of Operations
Evang. Evangelical
exam. examination, examining
Exch. Exchange
exec. executive
exhbn. exhibition
expdn. expedition
expn. exposition
expt. experiment
exptl. experimental
Expy. Expressway
Ext. Extension

F.A. Field Artillery
FAA Federal Aviation Administration
FAO Food and Agriculture Organization (of the UN)
FBA Federal Bar Association
FBI Federal Bureau of Investigation
FCA Farm Credit Administration
FCC Federal Communications Commission
FCDA Federal Civil Defense Administration
FDA Food and Drug Administration
FDIA Federal Deposit Insurance Administration
FDIC Federal Deposit Insurance Corporation
FE, F.E. Forest Engineer
FEA Federal Energy Administration
Feb. February
fed. federal
fedn. federation
FERC Federal Energy Regulatory Commission
fgn. foreign
FHA Federal Housing Administration
fin. financial, finance
FL Florida
Fl. Floor
Fla. Florida
FMC Federal Maritime Commission
FNP Family Nurse Practitioner
FOA Foreign Operations Administration
found. foundation
FPC Federal Power Commission
FPO Fleet Post Office
frat. fraternity
FRS Federal Reserve System
FSA Federal Security Agency
Ft. Fort
FTC Federal Trade Commission
Fwy. Freeway

G-1 (or other number) Division of General Staff
GA, Ga. Georgia
GAO General Accounting Office
gastroent. gastroenterological
GATE Gifted and Talented Educators
GATT General Agreement on Tariffs and Trade
GE General Electric Company
gen. general
geneal. genealogical
geod. geodetic
geog. geographic, geographical
geol. geological
geophys. geophysical
geriat. geriatrics
gerontol. gerontological
G.H.Q. General Headquarters
GM General Motors Corporation
GMAC General Motors Acceptance Corporation
G.N.Ry. Great Northern Railway
gov. governor
govt. government
govtl. governmental
GPO Government Printing Office
grad. graduate, graduated
GSA General Services Administration
Gt. Great
GTE General Telephone and Electric Company
GU Guam
gynecol. gynecological

HBO Home Box Office
hdqs. headquarters
HEW Department of Health, Education and Welfare
HHD, H.H.D. Doctor of Humanities
HHFA Housing and Home Finance Agency
HHS Department of Health and Human Services
HI Hawaii
hist. historical, historic
HM, H.M. Master of Humanities
HMO Health Maintenance Organization
homeo. homeopathic
hon. honorary, honorable
Ho. of Dels. House of Delegates
Ho. of Reps. House of Representatives
hort. horticultural
hosp. hospital
H.S. High School
HUD Department of Housing and Urban Development
Hwy. Highway
hydrog. hydrographic

IA Iowa
IAEA International Atomic Energy Agency
IATSE International Alliance of Theatrical and Stage Employees and Moving Picture Operators of the United States and Canada
IBM International Business Machines Corporation
IBRD International Bank for Reconstruction and Development
ICA International Cooperation Administration
ICC Interstate Commerce Commission
ICCE International Council for Computers in Education
ICU Intensive Care Unit
ID Idaho
IEEE Institute of Electrical and Electronics Engineers
IFC International Finance Corporation
IGY International Geophysical Year
IL Illinois
Ill. Illinois
illus. illustrated
ILO International Labor Organization
IMF International Monetary Fund
IN Indiana
Inc. Incorporated
Ind. Indiana
ind. independent
Indpls. Indianapolis
indsl. industrial
inf. infantry
info. information
ins. insurance
insp. inspector
insp. gen. inspector general
inst. institute
instl. institutional
instn. institution
instr. instructor
instrn. instruction
instrnl. instructional
internat. international
intro. introduction
IRE Institute of Radio Engineers
IRS Internal Revenue Service
ITT International Telephone & Telegraph Corporation

JAG Judge Advocate General
JAGC Judge Advocate General Corps
Jan. January
Jaycees Junior Chamber of Commerce
JB, J.B. Jurum Baccalaureus

JCB, J.C.B. Juris Canoni Baccalaureus
JCD, J.C.D. Juris Canonici Doctor, Juris Civilis Doctor
JCL, J.C.L. Juris Canonici Licentiatus
JD, J.D. Juris Doctor
jg. junior grade
jour. journal
jr. junior
JSD, J.S.D. Juris Scientiae Doctor
JUD, J.U.D. Juris Utriusque Doctor
jud. judicial

Kans. Kansas
K.C. Knights of Columbus
K.P. Knights of Pythias
KS Kansas
K.T. Knight Templar
KY, Ky. Kentucky

LA, La. Louisiana
L.A. Los Angeles
lab. laboratory
L.Am. Latin America
lang. language
laryngol. laryngological
LB Labrador
LDS Latter Day Saints
LDS Church Church of Jesus Christ of Latter Day Saints
lectr. lecturer
legis. legislation, legislative
LHD, L.H.D. Doctor of Humane Letters
L.I. Long Island
libr. librarian, library
lic. licensed, license
L.I.R.R. Long Island Railroad
lit. literature
litig. litigation
LittB, Litt.B. Bachelor of Letters
LittD, Litt.D. Doctor of Letters
LLB, LL.B. Bachelor of Laws
LLD, L.L.D. Doctor of Laws
LLM, L.L.M. Master of Laws
Ln. Lane
L.&N.R.R. Louisville & Nashville Railroad
LPGA Ladies Professional Golf Association
LPN Licensed Practical Nurse
LS, L.S. Library Science (in degree)
lt. lieutenant
Ltd. Limited
Luth. Lutheran
LWV League of Women Voters

M. Master
m. married
MA, M.A. Master of Arts
MA Massachusetts
MADD Mothers Against Drunk Driving
mag. magazine
MAgr, M.Agr. Master of Agriculture
maj. major
Man. Manitoba
Mar. March
MArch, M.Arch. Master in Architecture
Mass. Massachusetts
math. mathematics, mathematical
MATS Military Air Transport Service
MB, M.B. Bachelor of Medicine
MB Manitoba
MBA, M.B.A. Master of Business Administration
MBS Mutual Broadcasting System
M.C. Medical Corps
MCE, M.C.E. Master of Civil Engineering
mcht. merchant
mcpl. municipal
MCS, M.C.S. Master of Commercial Science
MD, M.D. Doctor of Medicine
MD, Md. Maryland
MDiv Master of Divinity
MDip, M.Dip. Master in Diplomacy
mdse. merchandise
MDV, M.D.V. Doctor of Veterinary Medicine
ME, M.E. Mechanical Engineer
ME Maine
M.E.Ch. Methodist Episcopal Church
mech. mechanical
MEd., M.Ed. Master of Education
med. medical
MEE, M.E.E. Master of Electrical Engineering
mem. member
meml. memorial
merc. mercantile
met. metropolitan
metall. metallurgical
MetE, Met.E. Metallurgical Engineer
meteorol. meteorological
Meth. Methodist
Mex. Mexico
MF, M.F. Master of Forestry
MFA, M.F.A. Master of Fine Arts
mfg. manufacturing
mfr. manufacturer
mgmt. management
mgr. manager
MHA, M.H.A. Master of Hospital Administration
M.I. Military Intelligence
MI Michigan
Mich. Michigan
micros. microscopic, microscopical
mid. middle
mil. military
Milw. Milwaukee
Min. Minister
mineral. mineralogical
Minn. Minnesota
MIS Management Information Systems
Miss. Mississippi
MIT Massachusetts Institute of Technology
mktg. marketing
ML, M.L. Master of Laws
MLA Modern Language Association
M.L.D. Magister Legnum Diplomatic
MLitt, M.Litt. Master of Literature, Master of Letters
MLS, M.L.S. Master of Library Science
MME, M.M.E. Master of Mechanical Engineering
MN Minnesota
mng. managing
MO, Mo. Missouri
moblzn. mobilization
Mont. Montana
MP Northern Mariana Islands
M.P. Member of Parliament
MPA Master of Public Administration
MPE, M.P.E. Master of Physical Education
MPH, M.P.H. Master of Public Health
MPhil, M.Phil. Master of Philosophy
MPL, M.P.L. Master of Patent Law
Mpls. Minneapolis
MRE, M.R.E. Master of Religious Education
MRI Magnetic Resonance Imaging
MS, M.S. Master of Science
MS, Ms. Mississippi
MSc, M.Sc. Master of Science
MSChemE Master of Science in Chemical Engineering
MSEE Master of Science in Electrical Engineering
MSF, M.S.F. Master of Science of Forestry
MSN Master of Science in Nursing
MST, M.S.T. Master of Sacred Theology
MSW, M.S.W. Master of Social Work
MT Montana
Mt. Mount
MTO Mediterranean Theatre of Operation
MTV Music Television
mus. museum, musical
MusB, Mus.B. Bachelor of Music
MusD, Mus.D. Doctor of Music
MusM, Mus.M. Master of Music
mut. mutual
MVP Most Valuable Player
mycol. mycological

N. North
NAACOG Nurses Association of the American College of Obstetricians and Gynecologists
NAACP National Association for the Advancement of Colored People
NACA National Advisory Committee for Aeronautics
NACDL National Association of Criminal Defense Lawyers
NACU National Association of Colleges and Universities
NAD National Academy of Design
NAE National Academy of Engineering, National Association of Educators
NAESP National Association of Elementary School Principals
NAFE National Association of Female Executives
N.Am. North America
NAM National Association of Manufacturers
NAMH National Association for Mental Health
NAPA National Association of Performing Artists
NARAS National Academy of Recording Arts and Sciences
NAREB National Association of Real Estate Boards
NARS National Archives and Record Service
NAS National Academy of Sciences
NASA National Aeronautics and Space Administration
NASP National Association of School Psychologists
NASW National Association of Social Workers
nat. national
NATAS National Academy of Television Arts and Sciences
NATO North Atlantic Treaty Organization
NATOUSA North African Theatre of Operations, United States Army
nav. navigation
NB, N.B. New Brunswick
NBA National Basketball Association
NBC National Broadcasting Company
NC, N.C. North Carolina
NCAA National College Athletic Association
NCCJ National Conference of Christians and Jews
ND, N.D. North Dakota
NDEA National Defense Education Act
NE Nebraska
NE, N.E. Northeast
NEA National Education Association
Nebr. Nebraska
NEH National Endowment for Humanities
neurol. neurological
Nev. Nevada
NF Newfoundland

NFL National Football League
Nfld. Newfoundland
NG National Guard
NH, N.H. New Hampshire
NHL National Hockey League
NIH National Institutes of Health
NIMH National Institute of Mental Health
NJ, N.J. New Jersey
NLRB National Labor Relations Board
NM New Mexico
N.Mex. New Mexico
No. Northern
NOAA National Oceanographic and Atmospheric Administration
NORAD North America Air Defense
Nov. November
NOW National Organization for Women
N.P.Ry. Northern Pacific Railway
nr. near
NRA National Rifle Association
NRC National Research Council
NS, N.S. Nova Scotia
NSC National Security Council
NSF National Science Foundation
NSTA National Science Teachers Association
NSW New South Wales
N.T. New Testament
NT Northwest Territories
nuc. nuclear
numis. numismatic
NV Nevada
NW, N.W. Northwest
N.W.T. Northwest Territories
NY, N.Y. New York
N.Y.C. New York City
NYU New York University
N.Z. New Zealand

OAS Organization of American States
ob-gyn obstetrics-gynecology
obs. observatory
obstet. obstetrical
occupl. occupational
oceanog. oceanographic
Oct. October
OD, O.D. Doctor of Optometry
OECD Organization for Economic Cooperation and Development
OEEC Organization of European Economic Cooperation
OEO Office of Economic Opportunity
ofcl. official
OH Ohio
OK Oklahoma
Okla. Oklahoma
ON Ontario
Ont. Ontario
oper. operating
ophthal. ophthalmological
ops. operations
OR Oregon
orch. orchestra
Oreg. Oregon
orgn. organization
orgnl. organizational
ornithol. ornithological
orthop. orthopedic
OSHA Occupational Safety and Health Administration
OSRD Office of Scientific Research and Development
OSS Office of Strategic Services
osteo. osteopathic
otol. otological
otolaryn. otolaryngological

PA, Pa. Pennsylvania
P.A. Professional Association
paleontol. paleontological
path. pathological
PBS Public Broadcasting System
P.C. Professional Corporation
PE Prince Edward Island
pediat. pediatrics
P.E.I. Prince Edward Island
PEN Poets, Playwrights, Editors, Essayists and Novelists (international association)
penol. penological
P.E.O. women's organization (full name not disclosed)
pers. personnel
pfc. private first class
PGA Professional Golfers' Association of America
PHA Public Housing Administration
pharm. pharmaceutical
PharmD, Pharm.D. Doctor of Pharmacy
PharmM, Pharm.M. Master of Pharmacy
PhB, Ph.B. Bachelor of Philosophy
PhD, Ph.D. Doctor of Philosophy
PhDChemE Doctor of Science in Chemical Engineering
PhM, Ph.M. Master of Philosophy
Phila. Philadelphia
philharm. philharmonic
philol. philological
philos. philosophical
photog. photographic
phys. physical
physiol. physiological
Pitts. Pittsburgh
Pk. Park
Pky. Parkway
Pl. Place
P.&L.E.R.R. Pittsburgh & Lake Erie Railroad
Plz. Plaza
PNP Pediatric Nurse Practitioner
P.O. Post Office
PO Box Post Office Box
polit. political
poly. polytechnic, polytechnical
PQ Province of Quebec
PR, P.R. Puerto Rico
prep. preparatory
pres. president
Presbyn. Presbyterian
presdl. presidential
prin. principal
procs. proceedings
prod. produced (play production)
prodn. production
prodr. producer
prof. professor
profl. professional
prog. progressive
propr. proprietor
pros. atty. prosecuting attorney
pro tem. pro tempore
PSRO Professional Services Review Organization
psychiat. psychiatric
psychol. psychological
PTA Parent-Teachers Association
ptnr. partner
PTO Pacific Theatre of Operations, Parent Teacher Organization
pub. publisher, publishing, published
pub. public
publ. publication
pvt. private

quar. quarterly
qm. quartermaster
Q.M.C. Quartermaster Corps
Que. Quebec

radiol. radiological
RAF Royal Air Force
RCA Radio Corporation of America
RCAF Royal Canadian Air Force
RD Rural Delivery
Rd. Road
R&D Research & Development
REA Rural Electrification Administration
rec. recording
ref. reformed
regt. regiment
regtl. regimental
rehab. rehabilitation
rels. relations
Rep. Republican
rep. representative
Res. Reserve
ret. retired
Rev. Reverend
rev. review, revised
RFC Reconstruction Finance Corporation
RFD Rural Free Delivery
rhinol. rhinological
RI, R.I. Rhode Island
RISD Rhode Island School of Design
Rlwy. Railway
Rm. Room
RN, R.N. Registered Nurse
roentgenol. roentgenological
ROTC Reserve Officers Training Corps
RR Rural Route
R.R. Railroad
rsch. research
rschr. researcher
Rt. Route

S. South
s. son
SAC Strategic Air Command
SAG Screen Actors Guild
SALT Strategic Arms Limitation Talks
S.Am. South America
san. sanitary
SAR Sons of the American Revolution
Sask. Saskatchewan
savs. savings
SB, S.B. Bachelor of Science
SBA Small Business Administration
SC, S.C. South Carolina
SCAP Supreme Command Allies Pacific
ScB, Sc.B. Bachelor of Science
SCD, S.C.D. Doctor of Commercial Science
ScD, Sc.D. Doctor of Science
sch. school
sci. science, scientific
SCLC Southern Christian Leadership Conference
SCV Sons of Confederate Veterans
SD, S.D. South Dakota
SE, S.E. Southeast
SEATO Southeast Asia Treaty Organization
SEC Securities and Exchange Commission
sec. secretary
sect. section
seismol. seismological
sem. seminary
Sept. September
s.g. senior grade
sgt. sergeant
SHAEF Supreme Headquarters Allied Expeditionary Forces
SHAPE Supreme Headquarters Allied Powers in Europe
S.I. Staten Island

S.J. Society of Jesus (Jesuit)
SJD Scientiae Juridicae Doctor
SK Saskatchewan
SM, S.M. Master of Science
SNP Society of Nursing Professionals
So. Southern
soc. society
sociol. sociological
S.P.Co. Southern Pacific Company
spkr. speaker
spl. special
splty. specialty
Sq. Square
S.R. Sons of the Revolution
sr. senior
SS Steamship
SSS Selective Service System
St. Saint, Street
sta. station
stats. statistics
statis. statistical
STB, S.T.B. Bachelor of Sacred Theology
stblzn. stabilization
STD, S.T.D. Doctor of Sacred Theology
std. standard
Ste. Suite
subs. subsidiary
SUNY State University of New York
supr. supervisor
supt. superintendent
surg. surgical
svc. service
SW, S.W. Southwest
sys. system

TAPPI Technical Association of the Pulp and Paper Industry
tb. tuberculosis
tchg. teaching
tchr. teacher
tech. technical, technology
technol. technological
tel. telephone
Tel. & Tel. Telephone & Telegraph
telecom. telecommunications
temp. temporary
Tenn. Tennessee
Ter. Territory
Ter. Terrace
TESOL Teachers of English to Speakers of Other Languages
Tex. Texas
ThD, Th.D. Doctor of Theology
theol. theological
ThM, Th.M. Master of Theology
TN Tennessee
tng. training
topog. topographical
trans. transaction, transferred
transl. translation, translated
transp. transportation
treas. treasurer
TT Trust Territory
TV television
TVA Tennessee Valley Authority
TWA Trans World Airlines
twp. township
TX Texas
typog. typographical

U. University
UAW United Auto Workers
UCLA University of California at Los Angeles
UDC United Daughters of the Confederacy
U.K. United Kingdom
UN United Nations
UNESCO United Nations Educational, Scientific and Cultural Organization
UNICEF United Nations International Children's Emergency Fund
univ. university
UNRRA United Nations Relief and Rehabilitation Administration
UPI United Press International
U.P.R.R. United Pacific Railroad
urol. urological
U.S. United States
U.S.A. United States of America
USAAF United States Army Air Force
USAF United States Air Force
USAFR United States Air Force Reserve
USAR United States Army Reserve
USCG United States Coast Guard
USCGR United States Coast Guard Reserve
USES United States Employment Service
USIA United States Information Agency
USMC United States Marine Corps
USMCR United States Marine Corps Reserve
USN United States Navy
USNG United States National Guard
USNR United States Naval Reserve
USO United Service Organizations
USPHS United States Public Health Service
USS United States Ship
USSR Union of the Soviet Socialist Republics
USTA United States Tennis Association
USV United States Volunteers
UT Utah

VA Veterans Administration
VA, Va. Virginia
vet. veteran, veterinary
VFW Veterans of Foreign Wars
VI, V.I. Virgin Islands
vice pres. vice president
vis. visiting
VISTA Volunteers in Service to America
VITA Volunteers in Technical Assistance
vocat. vocational
vol. volunteer, volume
v.p. vice president
vs. versus
VT, Vt. Vermont

W, W. West
WA Washington (state)
WAC Women's Army Corps
Wash. Washington (state)
WATS Wide Area Telecommunications Service
WAVES Women's Reserve, US Naval Reserve
WCTU Women's Christian Temperance Union
we. western
W. Ger. Germany, Federal Republic of
WHO World Health Organization
WI Wisconsin
W.I. West Indies
Wis. Wisconsin
WSB Wage Stabilization Board
WV West Virginia
W.Va. West Virginia
WWI World War I
WWII World War II
WY Wyoming
Wyo. Wyoming

YK Yukon Territory
YMCA Young Men's Christian Association
YMHA Young Men's Hebrew Association
YM & YWHA Young Men's and Young Women's Hebrew Association
yr. year
YT, Y.T. Yukon Territory
YWCA Young Women's Christian Association

zool. zoological

Alphabetical Practices

Names are arranged alphabetically according to the surnames, and under identical surnames according to the first given name. If both surname and first given name are identical, names are arranged alphabetically according to the second given name.

Surnames beginning with De, Des, Du, however capitalized or spaced, are recorded with the prefix preceding the surname and arranged alphabetically under the letter D.

Surnames beginning with Mac and Mc are arranged alphabetically under M.

Surnames beginning with Saint or St. appear after names that begin Sains, and are arranged according to the second part of the name, e.g. St. Clair before Saint Dennis.

Surnames beginning with Van, Von, or von are arranged alphabetically under the letter V.

Compound surnames are arranged according to the first member of the compound.

Many hyphenated Arabic names begin Al-, El-, or al-. These names are alphabetized according to each Biographee's designation of last name. Thus Al-Bahar, Neta may be listed either under Al- or under Bahar, depending on the preference of the listee.

Also, Arabic names have a variety of possible spellings when transposed to English. Spelling of these names is always based on the practice of the Biographee. Some Biographees use a Western form of word order, while others prefer the Arabic word sequence.

Similarly, Asian names may have no comma between family and given names, but some Biographees have chosen to add the comma. In each case, punctuation follows the preference of the Biographee.

Parentheses used in connection with a name indicate which part of the full name is usually deleted in common usage. Hence Chambers, E(lizabeth) Anne indicates that the usual form of the given name is E. Anne. In such a case, the parentheses are ignored in alphabetizing and the name would be arranged as Chambers, Elizabeth Anne. However, if the name is recorded Chambers, (Elizabeth) Anne, signifying that the entire name Elizabeth is not commonly used, the alphabetizing would be arranged as though the name were Chambers, Anne. If an entire middle or last name is enclosed in parentheses, that portion of the name is used in the alphabetical arrangement. Hence Chambers, Elizabeth (Anne) would be arranged as Chambers, Elizabeth Anne.

Where more than one spelling, word order, or name of an individual is frequently encountered, the sketch has been entered under the form preferred by the Biographee, with cross-references under alternate forms.

Who'sWho in the West®

Biographies

AADAHL, JORG, business executive; b. Trondheim, Norway, June 16, 1937; came to U.S., 1966; s. Ottar P. and Gurli (Lockra) A.; MS in Mech. Engring., Tech. U. Norway, 1961; MBA, U. San Francisco, 1973; m. Inger R. Holst, July 13, 1973; children: Erik, Nina. Rsch. fellow Tech. U. Norway, Trondheim, 1961-62; mgr. arc welding devel. NAG, Oslo, 1964-66; mfg. engr. Varian Assocs., Palo Alto, Calif., 1966-67; bus. mgr. United Airlines, San Francisco, 1974-75, sr. systems analyst, 1977-81; strategic planning specialist Magnex Corp., San Jose, 1981-82; cons. in mgmt., 1982-84; founder, pres. Safeware, Inc., San Mateo, Calif., 1984—; dir. Safeware Sys.Ltd., U.K., 1990—. Developer Safechem Hazardous Chem. Mgmt. Sys. Recipient Cert. of Honor, San Francisco Bd. Suprs., 1973. Mem. Leif Erikson League (pres. 1973), Norwegian Soc. Profl. Engrs. Club: Young Scandinavians (v.p. 1971), Environment and Safety Data Exch. (founding mem., dir.). Author: Strength Analysis, Welded Structures, 1967; contbr. articles in various fields to profl. jours.; editor Nordic Highlights, 1972. Office: Safeware Inc 999 Baker Way San Mateo CA 94404-1566

AAGAARD, EARLA GARDNER, psychiatrist; b. Java, Dec. 5, 1922; came to U.S., 1937; d. J. Earl and Ethel (Swing) Gardner; m. Carl M.J. Aagaard, Mar. 13, 1943; children: Carla, Earl, Victor, Lola. BA, Pacific Union Coll., 1941; MD, Loma Linda U., 1945. Intern L.A. County Gen. Hosp., 1945-46; resident Childrens Hosp., San Francisco, 1947-48, Mendocino State Hosp., Talmadge, Calif., 1949-52, Langley-Porter Clinic, San Francisco, 1952-54; pvt. practice psychiatry Ukiah, Calif., 1955—. Mem. Am. Psychiat. Assn. (life). Home: 1101 W Clay St Ukiah CA 95482-4606 Office: Aagaard Med Corp 207 S Pine St Ukiah CA 95482-4822

AALTO, MADELEINE, library director. BA, Wellesley Coll., 1964; BLS, U. Toronto, 1967. Clerical asst. Toronto Pub. Libr., 1964-66, children's libr. Parkdale br., 1968-69, collection libr. Spaced Out libr., 1969-73, br. head Annette St. br., 1973-74, coord. adult svcs., 1974-75; chief libr. East York Pub. Libr., 1975-84, Greater Victoria Pub. Libr., 1984-88; dir. Vancouver (B.C.) Pub. Libr., Can., 1988—. Contbr. intro. to A Geography for Children (Philippe du Fresnoy), 1968. Recipient Commerative medal 125th Anniversary Confederation Can., 1993. Mem. B.C. Libr. Assn. Office: Vancouver Pub Lib, 350 W Georgia St, Vancouver, BC Canada V6B 6B1

AAMODT, TERRIE DOPP, history and English educator; b. Clarkston, Wa., Nov. 30, 1954; d. Matthew Alexander and Janice Arlene (Horner) Dopp; m. Larry Duane Aamodt, June 20, 1982; children: Erica Janelle, Alex Kristian. BA in History and English, Columbia Union Coll., 1976; MA in English, Coll. William and Mary, 1978; PhD in Am. Studies, Boston U., 1986. Publ. coord. Loma Linda (Calif.) U. Med. Ctr., 1978-79; from instr. to assoc. prof. Walla Walla Coll., College Place, Wash., 1979-92, prof. English and History, 1992—. Author: Bold Venture: A History of Walla Walla College, 1992 (Bronze award Coun. for Advancement and Support of Edn. 1993). Coach Fellowship Christian Athletes, College Place, 1989-90, 92; asst. coach Little League, Redlands, Calif., 1979. Named Disting. Faculty Lectr. Walla Walla Coll., 1994; recipient Burlington No. award for excellence in teaching, 1988. Mem. MLA, Am. Studies Assn., Orgn. Am. Historians. Adventist. Office: Walla Walla Coll 204 S College Ave College Place WA 99324-1139

AARON, BUD, systems analyst; b. White Sulphur Springs, Mont., Apr. 27, 1927; m. Dina Aaron, Jan. 10, 1960; children: Alex, Roy, Erica, Bill. Owner Microkits, 1963-67; prodn. mgr. Ednl. Computer Products, 1967-68, mfg. rep., 1968-69; instr. Control Data Inst., 1969-70; supr. ICL, Kidsgrove, England, 1970-73; tech. writer Philips Small Computers, Fontenay aux Rose, France, 1973-74; designer, developer computer programs Hughes, JPL. Lawrence Livermore Labs. and others, 1974-76; programmer, mgr., sales BusinessMaster, Carlsbad, Calif., 1976-86; mgr., writer, programmer The Aaron Group, Oceanside, Calif., 1986—.

AARON, ROY HENRY, lawyer, business consultant; b. Los Angeles, Apr. 8, 1929; s. Samuel Arthur and Natalie (Krakauer) A.; m. Theresa Gesas, Dec. 20, 1953; 1 child, Jill. BA, U. Calif.-Berkeley, 1951; LLB, U. So. Calif., 1956. Bar: Calif. 1957. Mem. Pacht, Ross, Warne, Bernhard & Sears, Inc., L.A., 1957-79, of counsel, 1979-83; sr. v.p., gen. counsel Plitt Theatres, Inc. and Plitt Theatre Holdings, Inc., L.A., 1978-80, pres., COO, 1980-85; pres. Plitt Entertainment Group, Inc., L.A., 1985—; pres., chief exec. officer Showscan Corp., L.A., 1985-93; lectr. Calif. Continuing Edn. of Bar; lectr. continuing legal edn. Loyola U. Law Sch., Los Angeles. Mem. editorial bd. U. So. Calif. Law Rev., 1954-56. Trustee, mem. exec. com. Vista Del Mar Child-Care Svc., 1968-80, Reiss-Davis Child Study Ctr., 1977-80, Plitt So. Theaters Inc. Employees Trust; mem. adv. bd. dirs. Rape Treatment Ctr. of Santa Monica Hosp.; pres. UCLA Royce Two Seventy, 1986-88; UCLA Bd. Visitors, UCLA Found., pres.-elect, 1995-96, bd. dirs., trustee. Fellow Am. Bar Found. (life), L.A. County Bar Found. (life); mem. ABA, State Bar Calif., L.A. County Bar Assn. (trustee 1977-83, v.p. 1979-80, pres. 1982-83), Beverly Hills Bar Assn., U. So. Calif. Law Alumni Assn., Legion Lex, Found. Motion Picture Pioneers (bd. dirs.), Am. Judicature Soc., Order of Coif, Chancery Club L.A.

AARON, SHIRLEY MAE, tax consultant; b. Covington, La., Feb. 28, 1935; d. Morgan and Pearl (Jenkins) King; m. Richard L. King, Feb. 16, 1952 (div. Feb. 1965); children: Deborah, Richard, Roberta, Keely; m. Michael A. Aaron, Nov. 27, 1976 (dec. July 1987). Adminstrv. asst. South Central Bell, Covington, La., 1954-62; acct. Brown & Root, Inc., Houston, 1962-75; timekeeper Alyeska Pipeline Co., Fairbanks, Alaska, 1975-77; adminstrv. asst. Boeing Co., Seattle, 1979-93; pres. Aaron Enterprises, Seattle, 1977—; owner Gabriel's Dinner Club, La., 1993—. Contbr.: Who's Cooking What in America by Phyllis Hanes, 1993. Bd. dirs. Burien 146 Homeowners Assn., Seattle, 1979—, pres., 1980-83. Mem. NAFE. Avocation: singing, art. Home: 131 Gerard St Mandeville LA 70448-5808

AASE, JON MORTON, dysmorphologist, pediatrics educator; b. Eau Claire, Wis., July 15, 1936; s. Maurice Ferdinand and Lorraine (Moe) A.; m. Kathleen Frances Doherty, July 17, 1982; children: Lara Kirsten, Nicholas Edward Jonathan, Caitlin Mariele. BA, Pomona Coll., 1958; MD, Yale U., 1962. Diplomate Am. Bd. Pediatrics. Straight pediatric intern U. Minn. Hosps., Mpls., 1962-63; resident U. Wash. Sch. Medicine, Seattle, 1963-65, sr. fellow dysmorphology unit dept. pediatrics, 1967-69, clin. instr., 1969-74; chief resident Children's Orthopedic Hosp., Seattle, 1964; pvt. practice, Anchorage, 1969-74; asst. prof. U. N.Mex. Sch. Medicine, Albuquerque, 1974-77, assoc. prof., dir. div. dysmorphology, 1977-90, mem. faculty senate sch. medicine, 1978-80, clin. prof. pediat., 1994—; pvt. practice Albuquerque, 1990—; dep. dir. Wash.-Alaska Regional Med. Program, Anchorage, 1969-71; cons. Alaska Native Svc., USPHS, 1969-74, Indian Health Svc., 1979—; assoc. in med. sci. Wash.-Alaska-Mont.-Idaho program U. Alaska, Fairbanks, 1971-74; med. cons. Alaska satellite biomed. communication project Lister Hill Ctr. for Biomed. Communications, Bethesda, Md., 1972-74; program dir. Alaska March of Dimes Svc. Project, Anchorage, 1972-74; vis. prof. Fitzsimons Army Med. Ctr., 1988, U. Hawaii, 1989, also others. Author: Diagnostic Dysmorphology: An approach to the child with congenital abnormalities, 1990; also articles. Acting surgeon USPHS, 1965-67. Recipient William C. and Katherine K. Adamson Scholars award Inst. for Child Devel., Hackensack (N.J.) Med. Ctr., 1990; grantee Nat. Found., 1972-74, 75-78, 80-82, Regional Med. Program Health Care Delivery grantee, 1974-75, Nat. Arthritis, Metabolism and Digestive Diseases, 1978-82, Maternal Child Health, 1985-89, Ctrs. for Disease Control, 1991—. Fellow Am. Acad. Pediatrics; mem. Teratology Soc., Internat. Dermatoglyphics Assn., Western Soc. for Pediatric Rsch., Mountain States Regional Genetic Svcs. Network (steering com.), Alpha Omega Alpha. Office: PO Box 30652 Albuquerque NM 87190-0652

AASEN, EUGENE NELS, workers' compensation underwriting manager; b. Seattle, Nov. 28, 1952; s. Paul Holden and Pearl Mathilda (Lanson) A.; m. Alison Hedquist, Aug. 30, 1983 (div. Jan. 23, 1985); 1 child, Daniel Erik. BS in Econs. and Bus. Adminstrn., Idaho State U., 1982. CPCU. Office mgr. N.Y. Life Ins. Co., Colorado Springs, 1977-85, Phoenix Mut. Life Ins. Co., Denver, 1985-86; workers compensation underwriting mgr. Farmers Ins. Group, L.A., 1986—; loaned exec. United Way, Colorado Springs, 1987-88; project bus. cons. Jr. Achievement, Colorado Springs, 1984-85. Home: 3963 Frandon Ct Simi Valley CA 93063-2838 Office: Farmers Ins Group 4700 Wilshire Blvd Los Angeles CA 90010-3853

ABARBANELL, GAYOLA HAVENS, financial planner; b. Chgo., Oct. 21, 1939; d. Leonard Milton and Lillian Love (Leviten) Havens; m. Burton J. Abarbanell, June 1, 1965 (div. 1972); children: Jeffrey J. and Dena Reddick Lamb. Student, UCLA, 1975; student, San Joaquin Coll. Law, 1976-77. Cert. fin. planner; lic. real estate rep., Calif.; lic. life ins. broker, Calif., Wash., Nev., N.Y., Ill.; lic. securities broker. Postal clk. Van Nuys, Calif., 1966-69; regional mgr. Niagara Cyclo Massage, Fresno, Calif., 1969-72; owner, mgr. AD Enterprises, Fresno, 1970-72; agt., field supr. Equitable of Iowa, Fresno, 1972-73; rep. Ciba Pharms., Fresno, 1973-75; owner, operator Creativity Unltd., Fresno, 1975-76; registered fin. advisor Univ. Securities Corp., L.A., 1976-83, Fin. Network Investment Corp., L.A., 1983—; lectr. seminars for civic orgns.; mem. adv. bd. Fin. Network, Torrance, Calif., 1985-88. Co-author: Guidelines to Feminist Consciousness Raising, 1985. Mem. bus. adv. bd. of 2d careers. Recipient award Women in Ins., 1972. Mem. Bus. and Profl. Assn., L.A. Internat. Assn. Fin. Planners (bd. dirs. 1993-94), Inst. Cert. Fin. Planners, So. Calif. Socially Responsible Investment Profls., ACLU, NOW (nat. consciousness raising coord. 1975-76), Gay Acad. Union, Nat. Gay Task Force, Culver City C. of C., Internat. Assn. Fin. Planners, Social Investment Forum, Rotary (founding mem. L.A. Westside Sunrise Club sgt. at arms 1990-91, community svc. chair 1991-94, v.p. 1992-93, found. chair 1993-94). Democrat. Jewish. Home: 57124 Mono Wind Way North Fork CA 93643-9797 Office: Fin Network Investment Corp 5625 Green Valley Cir Apt 103 Culver City CA 90230-7120

ABBOTT, ANTON DWIGHT, aerospace engineer; b. Indpls., Aug. 28, 1936; s. Horace Emerson and Evelyn (Goff) A.; m. Janet Mavis Kyseth, June 27, 1964; children: Steven, Douglas. BS in Aero. Engring., Purdue U., 1958, MS in Indsl. Adminstrn., 1965. Mgr. systems definition Aerospace Corp., San Bernardino, Calif., 1965-68; dir. advanced projects Aerospace Corp., Los Angeles, 1968-75; prin. dir. Eastern tech. div. Aerospace Corp., Washington, 1975-82; prin. dir. Space Transp. Plans and Architecture Aerospace Corp., Los Angeles, 1982-90; prin. dir. Design Engring. Aerospace Corp., L.A., 1990-92; gen. mgr. Bus. Mgmt. Aerospace Corp., L.A., 1992—. Patentee in field. Fellow AIAA (assoc.); mem. AAAS, Purdue U. Gimlet Club. Home: 1825 Via Estudillo Palos Verdes Peninsula CA 90274-1907

ABBOTT, CHARLES FAVOUR, JR., lawyer; b. Sedro-Woolley, Wash., Oct. 12, 1937; s. Charles Favour and Violette Doris (Boulter) A.; m. Oranee Harward Sept. 19, 1958; children: Patricia, Stephen, Nelson, Cynthia, Lisa, Alyson. BA in Econs., U. Wash., 1959, JD, 1962. Bar: Calif. 1962, Utah 1981. Law clk. Judge M. Oliver Koelsch, U.S. Ct. Appeals (9th cir.), San Francisco, 1963; assoc. Jones, Hatfield & Abbott, Escondido, Calif., 1964; pvt. practice, Escondido, 1964-77, Provo, Utah, 1983-93; of counsel Meuller & Abbott, Escondido, 1977—; ptnr. Abbott, Thorn & Hill, Provo, 1981-83, Abbott & Abbott, Provo, 1993—. Mem. Utah Bar Assn., Calif. Bar Assn., U.S. Supreme Ct. Bar Assn., Assn. Trial Lawyers Am. Mem. Ch. of Jesus Christ of Latter Day Saints. Editorial bd. Wash. Law Rev. and State Bar Assn. Jour., 1961-62; author: How to Do Your Own Legal Work, 1976, 2d edit., 1981, How to Win in Small Claims Court, 1981, How to be Free of Debt in 24 Hours, 1981, How to Hire the Best Lawyer at the Lowest Fee, 1981, The Lawyers' Inside Method of Making Money, 1979, The Millionaire Mindset, 1987, How to Make Big Money in the Next 30 Days, 1989, Business Legal Manual and Forms, 1990, How To Make Millions in Marketing, 1990, Telemarketing Training Course, 1990, How To Form A Corporation In Any State, 1990, The Complete Asset Protection Plan, 1990; weekly columnist The Daily Herald; contbr. articles to profl. jours. Home: 2830 Marrcrest North Cir Provo UT 84604-3830 Office: 100 West 40 S Provo UT 84601

ABBOTT, GREGORY B., pharmaceutical executive; b. 1948. BA, Yale U., 1970; JD, U. Denver, 1973. Atty. Holme, Roberts & Owen, Denver, 1974-86; with Synergen Inc., Boulder, Colo., 1986—. Office: Synergen Inc 1885 33rd St Boulder CO 80301-2505*

ABBOTT, JOHN RODGER, electrical engineer; b. L.A., Aug. 2, 1933; s. Carl Raymond and Helen Catherine (Roche) A.; m. Theresa Andrea McQuaide, Apr. 20, 1968. BS with honors, UCLA, 1955; MSEE, U. So. Calif., 1957. Registered profl. engr., Calif.; cert. tchr. Calif. Advanced study engr. Lockheed Missile Systems, L.A., 1955-56; radar systems engr. Hughes Aircraft Co., L.A., 1956-59; devel. engr. Garrett Airesearch Co., L.A., 1959-63, instr. in-plant tng. program, 1962-63; asst. project engr. Litton Industries, L.A., 1963; space power systems engr. TRW Systems, L.A., 1963-65; engr. specialist L.A. Dept. Water and Power, 1965-92; engr. specialist Abtronix, 1992—; frequency coordination chmn. Region X, Utilities Telecommunications Coun., 1977-79, sec.-treas. Utilities Telecommunication Coun., 1979-80; instr. amateur radio course L.A. City Schs., Birmingham High Sch., Van Nuys, Calif., 1965-66, Los Feliz Elem. Sch., Hollywood, Calif., 1990—. Contbr. articles to profl. jours. Mem. IEEE, Am. Radio Relay League (Pub. Svc. award 1971), Tau Beta Pi. Office: Abtronix PO Box 220066 Santa Clarita CA 91322-0066

ABBOTT, KEITH EUGENE, lawyer, consultant; b. Wichita, Kans., Feb. 11, 1949; s. Robert E. Abbott and Dorothy E. (Thompson) McDermott; (div. Nov. 1987); children: Jessica Jeanne, Dana Jeanne, Kellie Jeanne. AA, Aims Coll., 1975; BA, U. No. Colo., 1978; JD, Ohio No. U., 1980. Bar: Colo. 1982, U.S. Dist. Ct. Colo. 1982. Freelance landman oil and gas Greeley, Colo., 1981-83; atty. JRC Oil, Greeley, 1981-83; pres. RA Resources, Inc., Greeley, 1983-87, also bd. dirs.; ptnr. law firm Varallo, Abbott & Dugan, P.C., Greeley, 1987-89; bd. dirs. First No. Savs. & Loan, Greeley, 1984-87. Rep. precinct chmn., Greeley, 1985-88. Served with USN, 1967-70, Vietnam.p. Mem. ABA, Colo. Bar Assn., Weld County Bar Assn., Rotary (bd. dirs., pres. Greeley Centennial chpt. 1990-91. Office: 710 11th Ave Ste 110 Greeley CO 80631-3200

ABBOTT, PATTI MARIE, middle school educator; b. Lewistown, Mont., Mar. 15, 1942; d. Vernal Hall and Marquerite (Cowen) A. BS, Ea. Mont. Coll., 1963, MS, 1968; postgrad. in adminstrn., Mont. State U., 1980. Tchr. Sch. Dist. No. 1, Glendive, Mont., 1964; tchr. Billings (Mont.) Pub. Schs., 1964—, pub. rels. rep., 1983-87. Contbr. articles to profl. jours. Resource person Girl Scouts U.S., Billings, 1973—, cadet leader, 1976-79; resource person Campfire Girls, Billings, 1978—; vol. Heart Fund, Am. Cancer Soc., Birth Defects Found., 1976—; v.p. Sweet Adelines, Billings, 1981-83. Named Tchr. of Yr., Masonic Order, Billings, 1985, 86. Mem. NEA, ASCD, AAUW (sec. Billings chpt. 1985-87, scholar 1987, essay chairperson 1992-93), Am. Bus. Women's Assn. (pres. Billings chpt. 1980-82, Woman of Yr. award 1980), Harmony Club (pres. 1986-87), Rebeccas, Eagles, Alpha Delta Kappa (mem. internat. exec. bd., grand historian, grand v.p. 1983-87, grand pres. 1993—). Home: 701 Torch Dr Billings MT 59102-5925 Office: Lewis and Clark Jr High 1315 Lewis Ave Billings MT 59102-4237

ABBOTT, ROBERT CARL, management company executive; b. Riverside, Calif., Oct. 20, 1955; s. Orville Hancock and Erna Adella (Sparber) Whitney; m. Diane Alicia Sallstrom, Aug. 5, 1978; children: Ryan Christian, Aaron Matthew, Kalen James. MBA, Century U., 1993. Ordained to ministry Calvary Grace Christian, 1976; firefighter, Wash., Emergency Med. Tech., first aid instr. and survival instr. Affirmative action officer State of Wash., Spokane, Wash., 1976-77; personnel supr. Key Tronic Corp., Spokane, 1977-80; personnel mgr. ISC Systems Corp., Spokane, 1980-84; fire chief Millwood Fire Dept., Millwood, Wash., 1982-88; pres. and CEO Total Mgmt. Systems, Inc., Millwood, 1984-88; gen. mgr. Ptarmigan Village, Whitefish, Mont., 1988-91, Unitech Composites, Inc., Hayden Lake, Idaho, 1991-93; CEO Total Mgmt Sys., Rathdrum, Idaho, 1993-94; dir. staffing and employee devel. N.W. Natural Gas Co., 1994—; bd. dirs. Jans Touch, Hayden Lake, Idaho; cons. Total Mgmt. Systems, Spokane. Mem. Gov.'s Com. of Vet. Bus., Washington, 1983-84; chmn. Whitefish Fire Svcs. Area Commn., 1989-91; mem. CAP. Named Most Influential for the Year, Millwood Fire Dept., 1984. Mem. Millwood Fire Assn., Inland Empire Emergency Svcs. Assn. (pres.). Christian. Home: 17957 S Greenfield Dr Oregon City OR 97045-7848 Office: Total Mgmt Sys 17957 S Greenfield Dr Oregon City OR 97045-7848

ABBOTT, ROBERT T., pharmaceutical company executive; b. 1947. Graduate, McGill U., Montreal, Can., PhD in Pathology, 1973. WithBio Sci. Labs. Divsn. Dow Chem. Co., Indpls., 1974-83; bus. mgr. Oncogen, Seattle, 1983-84; with NeoRxCorp., Seattle, 1984-90; founder, pres., CEO. Viagene, Inc., San Diego, 1990—. Office: Viagene Inc 11055 Roselle St San Diego CA 92121-1204*

ABBRESCIA, JOSEPH LEONARD, artist, educator; b. Bronx, N.Y., Oct. 1, 1936; s. John and Elizabeth (Mollicone) A.; m. Suzanne Carole Berkheiser, Apr. 20, 1963; children: Joseph Antonio, Anthony John. Artist, lectr., demonstrator, workshop facilitator. Exhibited in one-man shows at Ace Powell Art Gallery, Kalispell, Mont., 1975, Tex. Art Gallery, Dallas, 1982, 84, Driscol Gallery, Beaver Creek, Colo., 1988, Newman Gallery, Boston, 1988, others; group shows include Finley Point Gallery, Helena, Mont., Hockaday Ctr. for the Arts, Kalispell, Mus. of Native Am. Cultures, Spokane, Holter Mus., Helena, Miller Gallery, Cin., also shows in Whitefish, Mont., Scottsdale, Ariz., Catalina Island, Calif., Tucson, Kansas City, Mo., Casper, Wyo., others. Named Artist of Yr., Am. Royal Western Art Assn., 1984; recipient awards for art. Home and Studio: 12 1st Ave W Kalispell MT 59901-4440

ABBRUZZESE, CARLO ENRICO, physician, writer, educator; b. Rome, Italy, May 28, 1923; came to U.S., 1951, naturalized, 1959; s. Aurelio and Maria (Sbriccoli) A.; m. Silvia Ramirez-Lemus; children: Marco A., Carlo M., Eric L., Christopher E., Romana S. Liceo-Ginnasio, Dante Alighieri, Roma, 1935-43; Facoltà di Medicina e Chirurgia, Università di Roma, 1943-49; DSc, London Inst. Applied Rsch., 1973. Lic. med. dr. Italy, European Community, Calif. Resident in tropical subtropical diseases U. Rome, 1950-51; intern Woman's and Highland Park Gen. hosps., Detroit, 1951-53; resident in family practice Saratoga Gen. Hosp., Detroit, Columbus Hosp., Newark, 1953-57; gen. practice occupational and sport medicine Rome, 1949-51, Oakland, Calif., 1958-75, Santa Ana, Calif., 1975-84; dir. emergency and outpatient depts. Drs. Hosp. Santa Ana, Calif., 1975-77; dir. North Bristol Family Med. Clinic, Rsch. and Diagnostic Lab. Author: Storia della Psicologia, 1949, Roma, L'ascoltazione Stetoscopica del cuore, RCA italiana, 1953, L'ascoltazione stetoscopica, 1955, 56, 83, 86, Roma, 1986, Esercitazioni di diagnostica ascoltatoria, 1983, 86; founder, pub., editor-in-chief ESDNA, Rome, 1983, ESDI, Rome, 1986; pub. Med. Newsletter, 1987; contbr. articles to profl. jours. Founder, leader polit. youth movements, Rome, 1943-47; co-founder, nat. chmn. U.S. divorce reforms orgns., 1975; UN rep. on violation of due process and domestic human rights, 1977; active Nat. Italian Am. Found. Decorated Commendatore di Merito, 1950, Gran Croce Merito del Lavoro, Internat. Bus. Corp., 1981; Fulbright fellow, 1951-53. Fellow Am. Acad. Family Physicians; mem. AMA, Calif. Med. Assn., Orange County Med. Assn., Ordine dei Medici di Roma, Società Italiana di Chirurgia, Union Am. Physicians, Am. Acad. Family Practice (co-founder). Office: 316 N Bristol St Santa Ana CA 92703-3811

ABDALJABBAR, ABDALHAMEED A., educational administrator; b. Falluja, Iraq, July 1, 1941; came to U.S., 1982; s. Abdullah A. Abdaljabbar and Baseirra (Saleh) Mustafah; m. Amal Abdalrazak, Feb. 1, 1971; children: Bushra, Nagam, Azaheer. BA, Almustansyriah U., Baghdad, Iraq, 1967; MA, Baghdad U., 1977; EdD, U. No. Colo., 1989. Tchr. Ramadi (Iraq) Sch. Dist., 1968-73, Baghdad-Risafa Sch. Dist., 1973-77; lectr. Mosel (Iraq) U., 1977-82; prin. Granada Sch., Santa Clara, Calif., 1991-93, 1993-94, dir. curriculum and staff devel., 1994—. Postdoctoral fellow U. No. Colo., 1990-91. Home: 1000 Kiely Blvd Apt 116 Santa Clara CA 95051-4819

ABDOU, IKRAM ESCANDAR, engineering consultant; b. Beni Suef, Egypt, Apr. 22, 1948; came to U.S., 1975; s. Escandar Abdou and Amira Armanious; m. Mona Yanni, June 5, 1987; children: Irene, John. BS, Cairo U., 1970, MS, 1973; PhD, U. So. Calif., 1978. Asst. lectr. Cairo U., 1970-75; rsch. asst. U. So. Calif., L.A., 1975-78; postdoctoral fellow IBM Rsch. Lab., San Jose, Calif., 1978-80; sr. engr. Aydin Computer Systems, Ft. Washington, Pa., 1980-83; asst. prof. engring. U. Del., Newark, 1983-88; staff engr. Martin Marietta Electronic Systems, Orlando, Fla., 1989-93; sr. rsch. engr. SRI Internat., Menlo Park, Calif., 1993—; cons. in field. Scholar Egyptian Ministry Edn., 1962-65, Cairo U., 1965-70; grantee U. Del. Rsch. Found., 1984-85, Bethlehem Steel, 1985. Mem. IEEE (sr.), Sigma Xi, Eta Kappa Nu. Mem. Coptic Orthodox Christian Ch. Avocations: reading, music, traveling. Home: 1790 Lark Ln Sunnyvale CA 94087-4827 Office: SRI Internat 333 Ravenswood Ave Menlo Park CA 94025-3453

ABDUL, CORINNA GAY, software engineer, consultant; b. Honolulu, Aug. 10, 1961; d. Daniel Lawrence and Katherine Yoshie (Kanada) A. BS in Computer Sci., U. Hawaii, 1984. With computer support for adminstrv. and fiscal svcs. U. Hawaii, Honolulu, 1982-84; mem. tech. staff II test systems and software engr. dept. of Space & Tech. Group TRW Inc., Redondo Beach, Calif., 1985-89; systems software engr. II, Sierra On-Line, Inc., Oakhurst, Calif., 1989-90; sr. programmer, analyst Decision Rsch. Corp., Honolulu, 1990-92; ind. computer cons. Honolulu, 1992-94; computer cons. Wailuku, Hawaii, 1994—. Home: 1825 Anapuni St Apt 201 Honolulu HI 96822-3208

ABE, GREGORY, microbiologist; b. L.A., Nov. 25, 1954; s. Mabel (Tsumori) A. AA, L.A. Valley Coll., 1978; PharmD, U. So. Calif., 1988; BS, Calif. State U., L.A., 1990. Men's asst. tennis coach, Calif. State U., L.A., 1990—. Mem. Am. Soc. Microbiology, So. Calif. Soc. Microbiology, Calif. Faculty Assn., Intercollegiate Tennis Assn. Office: Calif State U LA 5151 State University Dr Los Angeles CA 90032-4221

ABEL, MARK JEFFREY, electrical engineer, communications researcher; b. Cleve., May 30, 1957; married; 2 children. BSEE summa cum laude, U.

Mich., 1979; MSEE, Stanford U., 1980. Mem. tech. staff AT&T Bell Labs., Naperville, Ill., 1979-83; staff engr. Siemens AG, Munich, Germany, 1983-85; mem. rsch. staff Xerox PARC-NW, Portland, Oreg., 1985-87; MTS, rsch. sci., mgr. U.S. West Advanced Technologies, Portland, Englewood and Boulder, Colo, 1987-91; mgr., sr. staff engr. Intel Corp., Hillsboro, Oreg., 1991—; bd. dirs. Multimedia Commn. Forum; chair, founder MMCF Transport Svcs. Interface Working Group, 1993—; mem. tech. adv. bd. Oreg. Advanced Computing Inst., 1991-92; vis. rschr. NW Regional Ednl. Lab., Portland, 1990-91; invited del. comm. People's Republic China, 1987. Co-holder several patents. Co-founder, mem. Lake Oswego Citizen Traffic Adv. Com., 1990-92; spkr. engrng. career K-12 students, 1980—; bd. dirs. Forest Highlands Neighborhood Assn., 1991-92. Mem. IEEE, ACM. Office: Intel Corp MS JF2-52 5200 NE Elam Young Pky Hillsboro OR 97124-6463

ABEL, RICHARD EUGENE, book publishing consultant; b. Great Falls, Mont., July 7, 1925; s. Ernest E. and Anna (Rempel) A.; m. Katherine F. Ferguson, Dec. 14, 1947; children: Katherine A. Hawkins, Corinne A. Bacher. BA, Reed Coll., 1948. Founder, pres. Richard Abel & Co., Inc., Portland, Oreg., 1960-74, Internat. Book Svcs., Portland, Oreg., 1967-79; co-founder, pres. Rsch. Studies Press, Portland, Oreg., 1976-78, Dilithiam Press Inc., Portland, Oreg., 1977-79; founder, pres. Timber Press Inc., Portland, Oreg., 1978-89, Dioscorides Press, Inc., Portland, Oreg., 1980-89, Amadeus Press, Inc., Portland, Oreg., 1983-89; book trade cons. Richard Abel Consultant, Portland, Oreg., 1989—. Contbr. articles to Publishers Rsch. Quar., Logos and others. Bd. dirs. Oreg. Mus. Sci. and Industry, Portland, 1971-74, Oreg. Sch. of Arts and Crafts, Portland, 1978-80, Oreg. State Bd. Forestry, Salem, 1976-80; chmn. Gov.'s Task Force on Small Woodlands, Salem, 1978-79. Mem. AAAS. Home: 1730 SW 90th Ave Portland OR 97225-6509

ABELS, ROBERT FREDERICK, tax consultant; b. West Palm Beach, Fla., Nov. 18, 1926; s. John Frederick and Nelly (Bulfin) A.; m. Shirley Mae Larsen, May 31, 1953; children: Robert Frederick, Steven John, Richard Alan. Student, U. S.C., 1946-47; ed. flight tng. program, Naval Air Sta., Pensacola, Fla., 1947-49; BS, U. S.C., Pensacola Naval Air Sta., Fla., 1946-47, 49; MBA in Finance, U. West Fla., 1971. Enlisted USN, 1944, commd. ensign, 1949, advanced through grades to comdr., 1963, radar operator PT boats, 1945-46, radar and radio operator PT Boats World War II; aviator USN, Republic of Korea, 1950, 51, 53, Pensacola, Fla., Vietnam, 1962-63, 65-66; ret. USN, 1969; tchr. math. and bus. Skyline H.S., Lemon Grove, Calif., 1971-83; ind. tax cons. Sun City West, Ariz., 1971—; past ptnr., salesman area real estate co.; enrolled agent IRS, Washington, 1984. Decorated Bronze Star, Air medal, Commendation medal; Vietnamese Cross Gallantry. Mem. Nat. Assn. Enrolled Agts., Inland Soc. Tax. Cons., Nat. Assn. Tax Consultors. Republican. Lutheran. Office: 20411 N Wintergreen Dr Sun City West AZ 85375-5458

ABENDROTH, KATHI JUDKINS, archivist; b. Seattle, Aug. 20, 1937; d. John Ronald and Eleanor Louise (Geary) Judkins; m. Raymond Orie Abendroth, Mar. 19, 1955; children: Ron, Don, Scott, Susan. Pres., archivist, rschr. Judkins Family Assn., Seattle, 1985—, editor, publisher, 1985-87, 89—; editor, publisher Holy Angels Acad. Alumnae Assn., Seattle, 1994—. Pres. Adams Grade Sch. PTA, Seattle, 1970-71; pack leader, den mother Boy Scouts Am., Seattle. Mem. N.H. Soc. Genealogists, Maine Genealogy Soc. Roman Catholic. Home and Office: 1538 NW 60th St Seattle WA 98107-2328

ABENDROTH, KENT ALLEN, broadcast engineer, electronic engineer; b. Portland, Oreg., May 18, 1943; s. Telore William and Dorothy Hellen (Moorhead) A.; m. Irene A. Brady, July 9, 1963 (div. Jan. 1969); m. Sandra Ann Jensen, June 10, 1972; children: Crystal Kay, Amy Lynn. Assoc. in Gen. Studies with honors, Everett Community Coll., 1981. Lic. FCC gen. radiotelephone; cert. sr. broadcast engr. Engr./announcer KIHR Radio, Hood River, Oreg., 1963-65; electronics technician Rodgers Organ Co., Hillsboro, Oreg., 1972-73; tech. svcs. mgr. WR Communications, Seattle, 1974-79; ptnr. Cascade Computerware Co., Everett, Wash., 1979-84; sr. mfg. engr. John Fluke Mfg. Co., Everett, Wash., 1979-84; network dir. World Radio Network, McAllen, Tex., 1984-88; dir. engrng. Enterprise Network, Billings, Mont., 1988—; owner Electronics Unltd., Billings, 1992—. Developer electronic device; contbr. articles to profl. jours. Founding mem. Bellingham (Wash.) Christian Singles, 1970-71; spl. rep. HCJB World Radio, Colorado Springs, Colo., 1979—; mem. Yellowstone Creationism Com., Billings, 1991—. With USN, 1965-71. Recipient Outstanding Communications award Civil Air Patrol, 1973; cited in book Mount Hood-Complete History, 1975. Mem. Soc. Broadcast Engrs., CAP (comdr. 1989-93, Commendation, 1991, 94), Yellowstone Amateur Radio Club, Beartooth Mountain Rescue Unit, Absaroka Search Dogs. Republican. Evangelical. Home: 839 Lynch Dr Billings MT 59105-4149 Office: Enterprise Network PO Box 30455 Billings MT 59107-0455

ABERBACH, JOEL DAVID, political science educator, author; b. New York City, June 19, 1940; s. Isidore and Miriam (Meltzer) A.; m. Joan F. Gross, June 17, 1962; Children: Ian Mark, Amy Joyce, Matthew Daniel, Rachel Ann. AB, Cornell U., 1961; MA, Ohio State U., 1963, Yale U., 1965; PhD, Yale U., 1967. Asst. prof. U. Mich., Ann Arbor, 1967-72; research scientist U. Mich., 1967-88, assoc. prof., 1972-78, prof., 1978-88; sr. fellow Brookings Inst., Washington, 1977-80; dir. Ctr. for Am. Politics and Pub. Policy, UCLA, 1988; prof. UCLA, 1986—; cons. Commn. on the Op. of the Senate, Washington, 1976, U.S. Office of Pers. Mgmt., Washington, 1983, Nat. Pub. Radio, Washington, 1983-84, U.S. Gen. Acctg. Office, 1990—. Author: Keeping a Watchful Eye, 1990; co-author: Race in the City, 1973, Bureaucrats and Politicians in Western Democracies, 1981. Del. Mich. Dem. Conv., Detroit, 1972; editorial bd. Congress and the Presidency, Washington, 1981—, Governance, Oxford, Eng., 1987—. Research grantee Nat. Sci. Found., Washington, 1969-73, 1978-81, 1986-89, 1993-98. Fellow Brookings Inst., Ctr. for Advanced Study in Behavioral Scis.; mem. Am. Polit. Sci. Assn., Am. Sociol. Assn. (com. on viable constitutionalism, exec. bd., 1993—), Rsch. Com. on Structure and Orgn. Govt. of Internat. Polit. Sci. Assn. (exec. bd. 1985-89, co-chmn. 1989—), Phi Beta Kappa. Jewish. Home: 10453 Colina Way Los Angeles CA 90077-2041 Office: UCLA 4289 Bunche Hall Los Angeles CA 90024

ABERCROMBIE, NEIL, congressman; s. G. Don and Vera June (Giersdorf) A.; m. Nancie Ellen Caraway, July 18, 1981; BA Union Coll., 1959, MA U. Hawaii, 1964, PhD in Am. Studies, 1974; Mem. Hawaii state legislature, 1974-86; elected to U.S. Congress, 1986, 91—, mem. armed svcs., ranking minority mem. Resources subcom. on Energy & Mineral Resources; mem. Nat. Security Coun., Honolulu City Coun., 1988-90. Democrat. Address: US Ho of Reps 1233 Longworth Washington DC 20515-1101*

ABERLE, DAVID FRIEND, anthropologist, educator; b. St. Paul, Nov. 23, 1918; s. David Winfield and Lisette (Friend) A.; m. Eleanor Kathleen Gough, Sept. 5, 1955 (dec. Sept. 1990); 1 son. A.B. summa cum laude, Harvard U., 1940; Ph.D. in Anthropology, Columbia U., 1950; postgrad., U. N.Mex., summers 1938-40, No. Ariz. U., summers 1971, 73, Harvard U., 1946-47. Instr. dept. social rels. Harvard U., Cambridge, Mass., 1947-50, rsch. assoc. Sch. Pub. Health, 1948-50; vis. assoc. prof. Page Sch., Johns Hopkins U., Balt., 1950-52; assoc. prof., then prof. dept. sociology and dept. anthropology U. Mich., Ann Arbor, 1952-60; fellow Ctr. Advanced Study in Behavioral Scis., Stanford, Calif., 1955-56; Simon vis. prof. and hon. research assoc. dept. social anthropology Manchester U., Eng., 1960-61; prof., chmn. dept. anthropology Brandeis U., Waltham, Mass., 1961-63; prof. dept. anthropology U. Oreg., Eugene, 1963-67; prof. dept. anthropology and sociology U. B.C., Vancouver, Can., 1967-83, prof. emeritus, 1983—; cons. Inst. Devel. Anthropology, Inc., Binghamton, N.Y., 1978-79; cons. to attys. Navajo Tribe, 1976-77; disting. lectr. at ann. meeting Am. Anthrop. Assn., 1986. Author: The Peyote Religion Among the Navaho, 1966, (with Isidore Dyen) Lexical Reconstruction, the Case of the Proto-Athapaskan Kinship System, 1974; contbr. articles on anthropological theory and Navajo Indians to scholarly jours.; rev. editor: Am. Anthropologist, 1952-55. Served with U.S. Army, 1942-46. Recipient Social Sci. Research Council Demobilization award, 1946; Harvard U. Nat. scholar; NIMH grantee; USPHS grantee; Wenner-Gren Found. grantee, 1954-63; NSF grantee, 1965-72; Can. Council grantee, 1969-77; Social Scis. and Humanities Research Council Can., 1978-80, 84-86. Fellow Royal Soc. Can., Royal Anthropol. Inst. of Gt. Britain and Ireland; mem. Am. Anthropol. Assn. (mem. panel on Navajo-Hopi land dispute 1973-95), Am. Sociol. Assn., Soc. Applied Anthropology, Am. Ethnol. Assn., Can. Anthropology Soc., Phi Beta Kappa. Jewish. Office: U BC Dept Anthropology, 6303 NW Marine Dr, Vancouver, BC Canada V6T 2B2

ABERNATHY, SHIELDS B., allergist, immunologist, internist; b. Bronxville, N.Y., Mar. 14, 1951; m. Leslie Abernathy; children: Amelia, Camille, Lant. BA, Ohio Wesleyan U., 1973; MS, Harvard U., 1975; MD, Med. Coll. Pa., 1979. Diplomate Am. Bd. Internal Medicine, Am. Bd. Allergy and Immunology, eligible Am. Preventive Medicine, Nat. Bd. Med. Examiners; Qualified Med. Examiner Calif.; Fed. Aviation Med. Examiner; ACLS Am. Heart Assn. Intern in internal medicine L.A. County/U. So. Calif. Med. Ctr., L.A., 1979-80; resident in internal medicine Hosp. of Good Samaritan, L.A., 1980-81; resident UCLA Wadsworth VA Med. Ctr., 1981-82, fellow allergy and immunology, 1982-84; instr. pub. edn. programs; rschr. in field. Fellow Am. Coll. Allergy and Immunology, Am. Acad. Allergy and Immunology; mem. Am. Med. Health Assn., Am. Pub. Health Assn. (internat. health sect.). Office: 1050 Las Tablas Rd Ste 3 Templeton CA 93465-9792

ABERNATHY, VICKI MARIE, nurse; b. L.A., Feb. 14, 1949; d. James David and Margaret Helen (Quider) Abernathy; m. Dirk Klaus Ernst Wiese, Aug. 15, 1968 (div. 1973); 1 child, Zoe Erde. Student, U. Calif., Riverside, 1966-67, L.A. City Coll., 1968-69; AA in Nursing, Riverside City Coll., 1971-74. RN, Calif.; cert. med.-surg. nurse; cert. ACLS. Staff nurse Riverside (Calif.) County Hosp., 1974, Oceanside (Calif.) Community Hosp., 1974-76; with Scripps Hosp., Encinitas, Calif., 1976—, ambulatory surgery unit and endoscopy coord., 1981-94, staff nurse short stay unit, 1994—. Mem. ACLU, Calif. Nurses Assn., San Diego Zool. Soc. Democrat.

ABERNETHY, ROBERT JOHN, real estate developer; b. Indpls., Feb. 28, 1940; s. George Lawrence and Helen Sarah (McLandress) A. BA, Johns Hopkins U., 1962; MBA, Harvard U., 1968; cert. in Real Estate Fin. and Constrn., UCLA, 1974. Asst. to chief scientist Phoenix missile program Hughes Aircraft Co., L.A., 1968-69, asst. program mgr. Iroquois night fighter and night tracker program, 1969-71, asst. to contr. space and communication group, 1971-72, contr. tech. div., 1972-74; pres. Am. Standard Devel. Co., L.A., 1974—; bd. dirs., chmn. audit com. Storage Equities, Glendale, Calif., Marathon Nat. Bank, L.A., L.A. Bancorp, Met. Water Dist., L.A., Met. Transp. Authority, L.A. County; pres. Self Svc. Storage Assn., San Francisco, 1978-83. Asst. to dep. campaign mgr. Humphrey for Pres., Washington, 1968; commr. L.A. Planning Commn., 1984-88, L.A. Telecomm. Commn., 1992-93; vice chmn. L.A. Econ. Devel. Coun., 1988-93; chmn. Ctr. for Study Dem. Inst., Santa Barbara, Calif., 1986—; bd. dirs. Met. Transp. Authority L.A. County, World Children's Transplant Fund, Pacific Coun. on Internat. Policy; adv. bd. mem. Peabody Conservatory, 1992—, Nitse Sch. Advanced Internat. Studies, 1993—; mem. bd. visitors Davidson Coll.; bd. dirs. L.A. Theatre Ctr., 1986-92, also YMCA; trustee Johns Hopkins U., 1991—; mem. L.A. Com. on Fgn. Rels. Lt. USNR, 1962-66. Mem. So. Calif. Planning Congress (bd. dirs.), Parker Found. (bd. dirs.), Californian Club, St. Francis Yacht Club, Jonathan Club, Calif. Yacht Club, Alpha Lambda. Home: 5800 W Century Blvd Los Angeles CA 90009-5600 Office: Am Standard Devel Co 5221 W 102nd St Los Angeles CA 90045-6001

ABEYTA, JOSE REYNATO, retired pharmacist, state legislator, cattle rancher; b. Blanco, N.Mex., July 18, 1927; s. Jose Porfirio and Carmen (Sandoval) A.; m. Margarita M. Ledoux, Nov. 24, 1950; children: Carolyn, Georgean, Gary, Diana. BS in Pharmacy, U. N.Mex., 1951. Registered pharmacist. Staff pharmacist Western Drug Co., Las Vegas, N.Mex., 1951-53, Duran Ctrl. Drug, Albuquerque, 1953-63, Linder Drug, Springer, N.Mex., 1981-82, Springer Drug, 1985-90, Walgreen Drug Co., Las Vegas, 1990-92; owner, mgr. Best Drug Co., Albuquerque, 1963-80; chief pharmacist Northeastern Regional Hosp., Las Vegas, 1982-85; ret., 1992; mem. N.Mex. Ho. of Reps., 1992—; vice-chmn. Bernalillo Alcohol Treatment Bd., 1972-74. Mem. Albuquerque City Coun., 1974-80. With U.S. Army, 1945-47. Mem. Nat. Assn. Retail Druggists, N.Mex. Pharm. Assn. (Ernie Welch award for Outstanding Profl. and Cmty. Svc. 1994), Am. Soc. Hosp. Pharmacists, Elks. Democrat. Roman Catholic. Home: PO Box 147 Wagon Mound NM 87752-0147

ABLAD, BJORN ERIC BERTIL, manufacturing executive; b. Vasteras, Sweden, July 4, 1945; came to U.S., 1982; s. Bertil Eric Gunnar and Ellen Inga Lill Asta (Sigroth) A.; m. Siv Elisabeth Hallsmar, Aug. 13, 1976 (div. Apr. 1984); 1 child, Andreas; m. Judith Ann Rose, June 22, 1985; children: Eric, Rebecca. Zimmermanska skolan, Vasteras, Sweden, 1970; Student, U. Stockholm, 1971-72. Export mgr. Nord Transmission AB, Sala, Sweden, 1973-79; mng. dir. Kungsors Pressprodukter AB, Kugsor, Sweden, 1980-81; CEO BH/SALA Inc., Salt Lake City, 1982-85; pres. AROS, Inc., Salt Lake City, 1986—; sec., bd. dirs. BH/SALA, Inc., Salt Lake City, 1982-85, Hornell Speedglas, Inc., Twinsburg, Ohio, 1986-89, AROS, Inc., Salt Lake City, 1986—, Swedish/Am. C. of C., Salt Lake City, 1990—. Mem. YMCA, Vasteras, Sweden, 1960-82; player Swedish Nat. Basketball Team, Stockholm, 1972-75; mem. Swedish Heritage Soc., Salt Lake City, 1989—. Corp. Swedish Air Force, 1965-66. Named Hon. Tex. Citizen, 1963, Hon. Asst. Atty. Gen., State of Tex., 1963. Office: AROS Inc 883 S 200 E Salt Lake City UT 84111-4202

ABNER, EDDIE LEE, lawyer; b. Oran, Mo., Nov. 10, 1950; s. Edgar and Ruby Ellen (Wood) A.; m. Margaret Abner, July 2, 1980; children: Eric, Damian, Rebecca; stepchildren: Nicole, Desiree, Arlene Miranda. BA, Southeast Mo. State U., 1975; JD, Whitter Coll. Sch. Law, 1982. Real estate salesman Los Altos Realty, Hacienda Heights, Calif., 1976-80; pvt. practice law San Dimas, Calif., 1982—. Author: The Comin of the Crowned and Conquering Child, 1993, The Defense Reses, 1995. Served with USMC, 1968-72, Vietnam. Office: 163A Bonita Ave Ste B San Dimas CA 91773

ABO, RONALD KENT, architect; b. Rupert, Idaho, July 10, 1946; s. Isamu and Ameria (Hachiya) A.; children: Tamiko N., Reiko D. BArch, U. Colo., 1969. Lic. architect, Colo. Designer SLP & Ptnrs., Denver, 1968-71; dir. Community Design Ctr., Denver, 1971-72; assoc. Barker, Rinker, Seacat, Denver, 1972-76; pvt. practice Denver, 1976-80; pres. Abo Gude Architects, Denver, 1980-84, Ron Abo Architects, Denver, 1984-91, Abo Architects PC, Denver, 1991-94, Abo Copeland Architecture, 1995—; chmn. Minority Architects Com., Denver, 1985—; thesis advisor U. Denver. Prin. works include Morrison Horticulture Ctr., 1983 (W.O.O.D. Inc. citation 1983), Highland Square, 1982 (AIA citation 1983), Loft House Community Correctional Facility, Tropical Discovery Ctr. Denver Zoo, New Denver Internat. Airport Concourse Bldgs., Roxborough Elem. Sch. Active Denver Community Leadership Forum, 1986, Neighborhood Housing Service, 1988—, Colfax-on-the-Hill, 1988—, U. Colo. Alumni Bd., Denver Private Industry Coun. Recipient Design Excellence award W.O.O.D. Inc., Denver, 1982. Mem. AIA (bd. dirs., pres.-elect Denver chpt. 1990, pres. 1991). Democrat. Club: Colo. Aikido Assn. Office: Abo Copeland Architecture 1448 Pennsylvania St Denver CO 80203-2012

ABRAHAMS, SIDNEY CYRIL, physicist, crystallographer; b. London, May 28, 1924; arrived in U.S., 1948; s. Aaron Harry and Freda (Cohen) A.; m. Rhoda Banks, May 1, 1950; children: David Mark, Peter Brian, Jennifer Anne. BSc, U. Glasgow, Scotland, 1946; PhD, U. Glasgow, 1949, DSc, 1957; Fil. Dr. (hon.), U. Uppsala, Sweden, 1981. Rsch. fellow U. Minn., Mpls., 1949-50; mem. staff MIT, Cambridge, 1950-54; rsch. fellow U. Glasgow, 1954-57; mem. tech. staff Bell Labs., Murray Hill, N.J., 1957-82; disting. mem. tech. staff AT&T Bell Labs., Murray Hill, 1982-88; Humboldt sr. scientist Inst. Crystallography, U. Tübingen, Fed. Republic Germany, 1989-90; guest scientist, Brookhaven Nat. Lab., Upton, N.Y., 1957—; vis. prof., U. Bordeaux, France, 1979, 90; adj. prof. physics dept. So. Oreg. State Coll., 1990—. Mem. editorial bd., Rev. Sci. Instruments, 1963-65; co-editor, Anomalous Scattering, 1975; editor, World Directory of Crystallographers, 1977, Acta Crystallographica, 1978-87; book rev. editor, Ferroelectrics, 1975—. Recipient Sr. U.S. Scientist award, Alexander von Humboldt Found., 1989-90. Fellow AAAS, Am. Phys. Soc.; mem. Am. Crystallographic Assn. (pres. 1968, mng. editor 1965-90), Royal Soc. Chemistry, Am. Inst. Physics (chmn. pub. policy com. 1981-91), Internat. Union Crystallography (chmn. commn. on crystallographic apparatus 1972-75, commn. on jours. 1978-87, commn. on crystallographic nomenclature 1978—), Sigma Xi (founding pres. So. Oreg. State Coll., 1993-95). Home: 89 Mallard St Ashland OR 97520-7316 Office: So Oreg State Coll Physics Dept Ashland OR 97520

ABRAHAMSON, JAMES ALAN, transportation executive, retired military officer; b. Williston, N.D., May 19, 1933; s. Norval S. and Thelma B. (Helle) A.; m. Susan R. Lewis, Aug. 20, 1988; children: Kelly Anne, James A.; stepchildren: James W. Lewis, Jr., Jennifer Lewis, Christopher Lewis. BS in Aero. Engrng., MIT, 1955; MS in Aerospace Engrng., U. Okla., 1961. Commd. 2d lt. U.S. Air Force, 1955; advanced through grades to lt. gen. USAF, 1978; flight instr. U.S. Air Force, Bryan AFB, Tex., 1957-59; spacecraft project officer Vela nuclear detection saltellite program U.S. Air Force, Los Angeles AF Sta., 1961-64; figher pilot Tactical Air Command, 1964; astronaut USAF Manned Orbiting Lab., 1967-69; mem. staff Nat. Aeronautics and Space Coun. Exec. Office of Pres. of U.S., Washington, 1969-71; program dir. Maverick Program, 1971-73; comdr. 495th test wing U.S. Air Force, Wright Patterson AFB, Ohio, 1973-74; insp. gen. Air Force Systems Command, 1974-76; sys. program dir. multinat. F-16 program USAF, 1976-80; dep. chief of staff sys. AF Sys. Command, Andrews AFB, Md., 1980-81; NASA assoc. admistr. for space flight Washington, 1981-84; dir. Pres. Reagan's strategic def. initiative The Pentagon USAF, Washington, 1984-89; ret. USAF, 1989; pres. transp. sector, exec. v.p. for devel. Hughes Aircraft Co., L.A., 1989-92; chmn. bd. Oracle Corp., computer software co., Redwood Shores, Calif., 1992—. Decorated Def. D.S.M. with one oak leaf cluster, Air Force D.S.M., NASA D.S.M., Dept. Energy Exceptional Svc. medal, Norwegian Order of King Olaf, Netherlands Order of Orange, Belgian Order of King Leopold; recipient award Daedalian Weapon Sys. Mgmt. Assn., Aerospace Power award Air Force Assn., Von Karmen lectr. Astronautics AIAA, 1993, Goddard Space Flight trophy. Office: Oracle Corp PO Box 659525 500 Oracle Pkwy Redwood Shores CA 94065

ABRAM, DONALD EUGENE, federal magistrate judge; b. Des Moines, Feb. 8, 1935; s. Irwin and Freda Phyllis (Gibson) A.; m. Frances Jennette Cooley, Apr. 22, 1962; children: Karen Lynn, Susan Ann, Scott Alan, Diane Jennette. BS in Bus., U. Col., 1957, JD, 1963. Ptnr. Phelps, Fonda, Hays, Abram and Shaw (now Peterson & Fonda, PC), Pueblo, Colo., 1963-75; dist. judge Colo. 10th Jud. Dist., Pueblo, 1975-81; chief U.S. magistrate judge U.S. Dist. Ct. State of Colo., 1981—; lectr. law in criminal procedure U. Denver Sch. of Law, 1983-90; adj. prof. sociology, instr. bus. law U. So. Colo., Pueblo, 1977-81. Mng. editor, bd. dir. Colo. Law Review, 1961-63. Vice chmn. Pueblo County Rep. Party, 1973-75; city councilman Pueblo, 1970-73; pres. Pueblo city coun., 1972-73, Pueblo Goodwill Industries, 1965, Pueblo United Fund, 1968; chmn. consolidation planning com. Pueblo County Sch. Dists. 60, 70, 1968-70; mem. gov's. milit. affairs adv. com., 1975-78; mem. gov's. commn. children and families, 1978-80. Lt. (j.g.) USN, 1957-60, capt. Res. ret. Recipient Disting. Svc. award Colo. Jaycee, 1970, Disting. Citizen Svc. award, Pueblo Rotary, 1975. Mem. Fed. Magistrate Judges Assn. (pres. 1990-91), Pueblo C. of C.(bd. dirs. 1972, chmn. edn. com. 1970-71), Colo. Bar Assn. (1st v.p. 1975-76), Nat. Coun. U. S. Magistrates (dir., officer 1984-89), Juvenile Judges Assn. Colo. (chmn. 1979-80), Colo. Navy League (state pres. 1976-78). Lutheran. Office: US Dist Ct US Courthouse C-566 1929 Stout St Denver CO 80294-3576

ABRAM, JOHN CHARLES, energy consultant; b. Des Moines, Sept. 1, 1920; s. John C. and Mary (Jones) A.; m. Dorothy Jean Buettner, Dec. 28, 1946; children: James Morgan, Susan Diane. AA, Glendale Coll., 1940; BS in Engrng., UCLA, 1949; postgrad., U. Calif., Berkeley, 1949. With Pacific Lighting Service Co., 1959-69, v.p., 1969-71; with So. Calif. Gas Co., Los Angeles, 1951-57, 71-85, v.p., 1972-74, sr. v.p., 1974-81, vice chmn., 1980-81, chmn. bd., chief exec. officer, 1981-85; chief exec. officer AEA Internat. Ltd., Los Angeles, 1985—. Vice chmn. Calif. Mus. Sci. and Industry Found., Los Angeles, 1985-86; vice chmn. Econ. Devel. Corp. Los Angeles County, 1984-85, Cen. City Assn., 1983-85. Mem. Internat. Gas Union, Internat. Energy Economists, The Atlantic Council, U.S.-Japan Energy Conf., Pacific Coast Gas Assn. (bd. dirs. 1973-82, chmn. 1980-81), Am. Gas Assn. (bd. dirs. 1981-85, Disting. Service award 1984), Gas Research Inst. (bd. dirs. 1980-87, chmn. 1981-83), UCLA Alumni Assn., U. Calif. at Berkeley Alumni Assn., Australian Gas Assn., Japan Am. Soc., Asia Soc., Japanese Am. Cultural and Community Ctr. Republican. Congregationalist. Clubs: The Los Angeles, Calif.; Oakmont Country (Glendale, Calif.).

ABRAMOVITZ, MICHAEL JOHN, lawyer; b. N.Y.C., Feb. 7, 1939; s. Max and Anne (Causey) A.; m. Patricia Carson, 1959 (div. 1968); 1 child, Deborah Woodbury; m. Frances Koncilja, Nov. 12, 1972 (div. 1983); 1 child, Nicholas; m. Carol Lay, May 24, 1988; 1 child, Alexandra. AB, Harvard U., 1961; MA in Maths., U. Calif., 1967; postgrad., U. Calif., Berkeley; JD, U. Colo., 1972. Bar: Colo. 1972, U.S. Dist. Ct. Colo. 1972, U.S. Ct. Appeals (10th cir.) 1973, U.S. Tax Ct. 1973, U.S. Supreme Ct. 1975, U.S. Ct. Claims 1977. Law clk. to presiding justice Colo. Supreme Ct., Denver, 1972-73; ptnr. Drexler, Wald & Abramovitz, Denver, 1973-84, Berenbaum & Weinshienk, Denver, 1984-86, Abramovitz, Merriam & Shaw, Denver, 1987-94, Abramovitz & Merriam, Denver, 1994—. Mem. ABA (taxation sect., civil and criminal tax penalties com., litigation sect.), Colo. Bar Assn. Office: Abramovitz & Merriam 1625 Broadway Ste 770 Denver CO 80202-4707

ABRAMOVITZ, MOSES, economist, educator; b. Bklyn., Jan. 1, 1912; s. Nathan and Betty (Goldenberg) A.; m. Carrie Glasser, June 23, 1937; 1 son, Joel Nathan. A.B., Harvard U., 1932; Ph.D., Columbia U., 1939; Ph.D. (hon.), Uppsala U., Sweden, 1985, U. Ancona, Italy, 1992. Instr. Harvard U., 1936-38; mem. research staff Nat. Bur. Econ. Research, 1938-69; lectr. Columbia U., 1940-42, 46-48; prof. econs. Stanford U., 1948—, Coe prof. Am. econ. history, exec. head dept. econs., 1963-65, 71-74; vis. prof. U. Pa., 1955; prin. economist WPB, 1942, OSS, 1943-44; econ. adviser to U.S. rep. on Allied Commn. on Reparations, 1945-46; econ. adviser to sec.-gen. Orgn. for Econ. Coop. and Devel., 1962-63; vis. fellow All Souls Coll., Oxford, Eng., 1968. Author: Price Theory for a Changing Economy, 1939, Inventories and Business Cycles, 1950, The Growth of Public Employment in Great Britain, 1957, (with Vera Eliasberg) Thinking About Growth, 1989; also articles.; editor: Capital Formation and Economic Growth, 1955; mng. editor Jour. Econ. Lit., 1981-85. Served as lt. AUS, 1944-45. Recipient Nitti prize Accademia Nazionale Dei Lincei, Rome, 1990. Fellow Am. Acad. Arts and Scis., Am. Econ. Assn. (disting., pres. 1980), Am. Statis. Assn.; mem. Am. Econ. History Assn. (pres. 1991-92), Western Econ. Assn. (pres. 1988), Accademia Nazionale dei Lincei (fgn.), Phi Beta Kappa. Home: 762 Dolores St Stanford CA 94305-8428 Office: Stanford Univ Stanford CA 94305

ABRAMS, FREDRICK RALPH, physician, clinical ethicist; b. N.Y.C., June 18, 1928; s. David and Jane R. (Rein) A.; m. Alice Marilyn Engelhard, Nov. 25, 1949; children: Reid, Glenn, Hal. BA, Cornell U., 1950, MD, 1954. Diplomate Am. Bd. Ob-Gyn. Intern Letterman Army Hosp., San Francisco, 1954-55; pvt. practice gynecology Denver, 1962—; resident Fitzsimons Army Hosp., Denver, 1956-59; prof. U. Colo. Grad. Sch. Pub. Affairs, Denver, 1987—; dir. biomed. ethics Ctr. for Health Ethics and Policy, U. Colo., 1987-92; commr. Govs. Commn. on Life and the Law, State of Colo., 1991—; vis. prof. Iliff Sch. Theology; founder Ctr. for Applied Biomed. Ethics Rose Med. Ctr., Denver, 1982-87; assoc. med. dir. Colo. Found. for Med. Care, 1992—; Lectr. for pub. edn. in med. ethics; mem. Nat. Adv. Bd. on Ethics in Reproduction, 1995—. Contbr. chpts. to book and articles to profl. jours. Maj. U.S. Army, 1955-62. Grantee Robert Wood Johnson, 1988-89, Colo. Trust, 1987-90, Rose Found., 1982-87. Mem. Internat. Soc. for Advancement of Humanistic Studies in Gynecology (past pres.), Denver Med. Soc. (past v.p.), Colo. Med. Soc., Am. Coll. Ob-Gyn. (past chmn. ethics com.). Office: 2530 S Parker Rd Aurora CO 80014-1628

ABRAMS, HELAYNE JOAN, preschool educator; b. Chgo., Apr. 15, 1937; d. Isidore and Fanny (Weinberg) Kremen; divorced; children: Lisa, Leda Abrams Miller, Lenore Abrams DeSpain. BA in Elem. Edn. with distinction, U. N.Mex., 1975. Lic. tchr., N.Mex. Tchr., dir. Albuquerque Pre-Sch. Coop., 1966—; multi-cultural and anti-bias curriculum workshop presenter, N.Mex., 1988—. Author:: Learning the Rainbow: A Multi-Cultural, Anti-Bias Activity Book for Teachers, 1992. Founding mem., bd. dirs. Living Through Cancer, 1984-87; bd. dirs. Albuquerque Ctr. for Peace and Justice, 1989-90, developer children's peace mus., 1990. Recipient Peace award Albuquerque Ctr. for Peace and Justice, 1992; grantee Mary Ann Binford Found., 1989, 90. Mem. Nat. Assn. for Edn. Young Children for Edn. Young Children. Home: 4715 Grand Ave NE Albuquerque NM 87108-1232

ABRAMS, JANE ELDORA, artist; b. Eau Claire, Wis., Jan. 2, 1940; children: John, Joan. BS, U. Wis., Menomonie, 1962, MS, 1967; MFA, Ind. U., 1971. Regent's prof. U. N.Mex., Albuquerque, 1971-93, prof. emeritus, 1993—. One-woman show include Fine Arts Gallery, Ind. U., Bloomington, Ind., Nora Eccles Harrison Mus. of Art, Logan, Utah, 1989-90, Zimmerman/Saturn Gallery, Nashville, 1989, Marilyn Butler Fine Arts, Santa Fe, R.S. Levy Gallerys, Austin, 1988, Norman R. Eppink Gallery, Emporia (Kans.) State U., 1988, Kron/Reck Gallery, Albuquerque, 1987, Owings-Dewey Fine Art, Santa Fe, 1993, Charlotte Jackson Fine Art, Santa Fe, 1993, Robischon Gallery, Denver, 1993, Amarillo (Tex.) Mus. Art, 1995, Charlotte Jackson Fine Arts, 1995, and numerous others; exhibited in group shows at Albuquerque Mus., 1991, Robischon Gallery, Denver, 1989-90, Janus Gallery, Santa Fe, 1989, Lew Allen/Butler Gallery, N.Mex., Guadalajara, 1994, Mus. of N.Mex., Santa Fe, 1994, Ind. U. Art Mus, Bloomington, 1994. Grad. studies fellowship Ind. U., 1969, 70, rsch. fellowship, 1970; grantee Tamarind Inst., 1973, Roswell Mus. & Art Ctr., N.Mex., 1985-86, NEA, 1984, 94; recipient disting. alumni award Ind. U., 1991, U. Wis., 1992. Home and Studio: 7811 Guadalupe Trl NW Albuquerque NM 87107-6507 Office: U NMex Dept Art And History Albuquerque NM 87131

ABRAMS, MORRIS ALEC, book company executive; b. Johannesburg, South Africa, Feb. 11, 1951; came to U.S., 1991; s. Simon and Lisa Lottie (Bürkner) A.; m. Janet Marie Laird, Oct. 30, 1983; children: Tamara, Chava, Daphne. Student, Fulmer U., Eng., 1976-79. Cert. Brit. Horse Soc. instr. Gen. mgr. Hout Apple Stud, Eng., 1979-81; profl. rider, 1981-84; dir. Blue Knight Security, South Africa, 1986-91; nat.sales dir. Wonder Books, Escondido, Calif., 1991-94; pres. The Book People, Penasequites, Calif., 1994—. Served as maj. South African Reconaissance, 1970-75. Office: 13451 Sawtooth Rd San Diego CA 92129-2619

ABRAMS, NORMAN, law educator, university administrator; b. Chgo., July 7, 1933; s. Harry A. and Gertrude (Dick) A.; m. Toshka Alster, 1977; children: Marshall David, Julie, Hanna, Naomi. AB, U. Chgo., 1952, JD, 1955. Bar: Ill. 1956, U.S. Supreme Ct. 1967. Assoc. in law Columbia U., 1955-57; rsch. assoc. Harvard U., 1957-59; sec. Harvard-Brandeis Coop. Rsch. for Israel's Legal Devel., 1957-58, dir., 1959; mem. faculty law sch. UCLA, 1959—, prof. law, 1964—, assoc. dean law, 1989-91, vice chancellor acad. pers., 1991—, co-dir. Ctr. for internat. and strategic studies, 1982-83, chmn. steering com., 1985-87, 88-89; vis. prof. Hebrew U., 1969-70, Forchheimer vis. prof., 1986; vis. prof. Bar Ilan U., 1970-71, 78, U. So. Calif., 1972, 73, Stanford U., fall 1977, U. Calif. at Berkeley, fall 1977, Loyola U., Los Angeles, summers 1974, 75, 76, 79; spl. asst. to U.S. atty. gen., also prof.-in-residence criminal div. Dept. Justice, 1966-67; reporter for So. Calif. indigent accused persons study Am. Bar Found., 1963; cons. Gov. Calif. Commn. L.A. Riots, 1965, Pres.'s Commn. Law Enforcement and Adminstrn. Justice, 1966-67, Nat. Commn. on Reform of Fed. Criminal Laws, 1967-69, Rand Corp., 1968-74, Ctr. for Adminstrv. Justice, ABA, 1973-77, Nat. Adv. Commn. on Criminal Justice Stds., Organized Crime Task Force, 1976; spl. hearing officer conscientious objector cases Dept. Justice, 1967-68; vis. scholar Inst. for Advanced Studies, Hebrew U., summer, 1994. Author: (with others) Evidence, Cases and Materials, 7th edit., 1983, 8th edit., 1988, Federal Criminal Law and Its Enforcement, 1986, 2d edit. (with S. Beale), 1993; mem. editorial bd. Criminal Law Forum, 1990—. Chmn. Jewish Conciliation Bd., L.A., 1975-81; bd. dirs. Bet Tzedek, 1975-85, L.A. Hillel Coun., 1979-82; chmn. So. Calif. region Am. Profs. for Peace in Middle East, 1981-83; bd. dirs. met. region Jewish Fedn., 1982-88, v.p. 1982-83; pres. Westwood Kehillah Congregation, 1985. Mem. Soc. for Reform of Criminal Law (mem. exec. com. 1994—), Phi Beta Kappa. Office: UCLA 405 Hilgard Ave Los Angeles CA 90024-1301

ABRAMS, OSSIE EKMAN, fundraiser; b. Olofstrom, Blekinge, Sweden, Jan. 8, 1952; came to the U.S., 1972; d. Ossian B. and Margit A. (Adolfsson) Ekman; m. Howard L. Abrams, Nov. 17, 1973 (div. Sept. 1983); m. David B. Orser, Aug. 1992. Student, Lärarhögskolan, 1972, New Sch. for Social Rsch., 1975; BA (hon.), Rocky Mountain Coll., 1994. Dental asst., sec. Samuel Meyer DDS, N.Y.C., 1973-74; office mgr., adminstr. Irving Percss DDS, N.Y.C., 1974-81; chief adminstr. Allen Kozin DDS, N.Y.C., 1981-87; head devel. Rocky Mountain Coll., Billings, Mont., 1991-92; owner, operator Ranch, Park City, Mont.; bd. mem. Mental Health Found., Billings, 1991, 92, bd. pres., 1993, 94. Active The Met. Opera Gild, N.Y.C., N.Y.C. Ballet Guild, N.Y. Philharm. Soc.; supporter Billings Symphony, Billings Studio Theatre; mem. selection com. Order Chair, Coll. Bus., Mont. State U., Bozeman, 1988-90; fundraiser ann. campaign Yellowstone Art Ctr., Billings, 1989; fundraiser bus. dir. Rocky Mountain Coll., Billings, 1990; vol. Rocky Mountain Coll. Black Tie and Blue Jeans Ball, mem. auction com., 1990-93, chair auction com. 1994, 95; mem. Nat. Adv. Coun., 1993-95. Recipient Alumni Hall of Fame award Rocky Mountain Coll., 1993, Leadership award Mental Health Found., Billings, 1994. Home: 1420 Granite Ave Billings MT 59102-0716 Office: 10 Douglas Ct, London NW6 4PT, England

ABRAMS, REID ALLEN, surgeon, educator; b. San Antonio, July 26, 1955. BA in Biology, Lawrence U., 1977; MD, U. Colo., 1982. Diplomate Am. bd.Orthopaedic Surgery; lic. physician, Calif, Colo., Washington. Intern then resident in orthopedic surgery U. Colo. Health Scis. Ctr., Denver, 1982-87; fellow pediatric orthopedics Children's Hosp. and Health ctr., San Diego, 1987-88; gen. orthopedist Group Health Coop. Puget Sound, 1989-90; fellow hand and microvascular surgery Brigham and Women's Hosp., Boston, 1988-89; asst. prof. in residence, chief hand & microvascular surgery U. Calif. Med. Ctr., San Diego, 1990—. Contbr. numerous articles to profl. jours. Mem. Acad. Orthopaedic Soc., Am. Acad. Orthopaedic Surgeons, Am. Soc. Surgery of the Hand, Kiros Soc., Phi Sigma. Office: U Calif Med Ctr Orthopedic Surgery 200 W Arbor Dr San Diego CA 92103-1911

ABRAMS, ROBERT EDWARD, English educator; b. N.Y.C., May 9, 1943; s. George Justice and Pearl (Bilsky) A.; m. Ellen Prashner Azose, July 14, 1973 (div. Nov. 1979). BA, Dartmouth Coll., 1965; PhD, Ind. U., 1973. English prof. U. Wash., Seattle, 1973—; sec. Am. Lit., Philological Assn. Pacific Coast, 1983, presiding officer, 1984; adv. bd. Ind. Study, U. Wash., Seattle, 1991-94. Contbr. articles to profl. jours. Bd. dirs. Taylor-Lee Homeowners Assn., Seattle, 1991-92, pres., 1992-93; bd. dirs. Honest Ballot Assn., N.Y.C., 1979-85. Capt. U.S. Army, 1969-71. Grad. Study Rsch. Fund grantee U. Wash., 1984; John H. Edwards fellow, Ind. U., 1967-68, Univ. fellow, 1966-67. Mem. MLA. Home: 1250 Taylor Ave N Apt 401 Seattle WA 98109-3347 Office: Univ of Washington Dept of English Seattle WA 98195

ABRAMSON, ALBERT, television historian, consultant; b. Chgo., June 9, 1922; s. Joseph David and Minnie Lillian (Edelstein) A.; m. Arlene Betty Corin, Jan. 8, 1950; children: Jay Allen, Susan Marie. BA, U. So. Calif., 1950. Tchr. L.A. City Schs., 1950-52; TV engr. CBS-TV, Hollywood, Calif., 1952-87; hist. cons. RCA, Princeton, N.J., Ampex Mus., Redwood City, Calif., UCLA/ATAS TV Archives, L.A. Author: Electronic Motion Pictures, 1955, The History of Television, 1880-1941, 1987, Zworykin: Pioneer of Television, 1995—; contbr. articles to profl. jours. With U.S. Army Air Forces. Mem. IEEE, Royal TV Soc. London, Brit. Kinematagraph, Sound and TV Soc., LeComité d'histoire de la Télévision, ATAS, SMPTE. Democrat. Jewish. Home: 214 Garnet Ave Newport Beach CA 92662

ABRAVANEL, ALLAN RAY, lawyer; b. N.Y.C., Mar. 11, 1947; s. Leon and Sydelle (Berenson) A.; m. Susan Ava Paikin, Dec. 28, 1971; children: Karen, David. BA magna cum laude, Yale U., 1968; JD cum laude, Harvard U., 1971. Bar: N.Y. 1972, Oreg. 1976. Assoc. Paul, Weiss, Rifkind, Wharton & Garrison, N.Y.C., 1971-72, 74-76; fellow Internat. Legal Ctr., Lima, Peru, 1972-74; from assoc. to ptnr. Stoel, Rives, Boley, Fraser & Wyse, Portland, Oreg., 1976-83; ptnr. Perkins Coie, Portland, 1983—. Editor, pub. Abravanel Family Newsletter. Vice pres. Chamber Music N.W. Mem. ABA, Inter-Am. Bar Assn., Phi Beta Kappa. Office: Perkins Coie 1211 SW 5th Ave Portland OR 97204-3713

ABRUMS, JOHN DENISE, internist; b. Trinidad, Colo., Sept. 20, 1923; s. Horatio Ely and Clara (Apfel) A.; m. Annie Louise Manning, June 15, 1947; children: Louanne C. Abrums Sargent, John Ely. BA, U. Colo., 1944; MD, [illegible] Denver, 1947. Diplomate Am. Bd. Internal Medicine. Intern Wisc. Gen. Hosp., Madison, 1947-48; resident in internal medicine VA Hosp., Albuquerque, 1949-52, attending physician, 1956-80; mem. staff Presbyn. Hosp. Ctr., Albuquerque; cons. staff physician St. Joseph Hosp., Albuquerque, 1957-85; attending physician U. N.Mex. Hosp. (formerly Bernalillo County Med. Ctr.), Albuquerque, 1954-86; med. dir. Turquoise Lodge, Albuquerque; cons. physician A.T. & S.F. Meml. Hosp., Albuquerque, 1957-83; clin. assoc. in medicine U. N.Mex.; mem. N.Mex. Bd. of Med. Examiners. Bd. dirs. Blue Cross/Blue Shield, 1962-76. Brig. gen. M.C., U.S. Army, ret., N.Mex. Nat. Guard. Fellow ACP (life), AMA, Am. Soc. Internal Medicine (trustee 1976-82, pres. 1983-84), N.Mex. Soc. Internal Medicine (pres. 1962-64), N.Mex. Med. Soc. (pres. 1980-81), Nat. Acads. Practice (disting. practitioner), Albuquerque and Bernalillo County Med. Assn. (bd. govs. 1959-61, chmn. pub. rels. com. 1959-61), Am. Geriatric Soc., 1992—. Brig. gen. M.C., U.S. Army, ret. Republican. Episcopalian. Office: Med Dir Turquoise Lodge Albuquerque NM 87105

ABUL-HAJ, SULEIMAN KAHIL, pathologist; b. Palestine, Apr. 20, 1925; s. Sheik Khalil and S. Buteina (Oda) Abul-H.; B.S., U. Calif. at Berkeley, 1949; M.S., U. Calif. at San Francisco, 1951, M.D., 1955; m. Elizabeth Abood, Feb. 11, 1948; children—Charles, Alan, Cary; came to U.S., 1946, naturalized, 1955. Intern, Cook County Hosp., Chgo., 1955-56; resident U. Calif. Hosp., San Francisco, 1949, Brooke Gen. Hosp., 1957-59; chief clin. and anatomic pathology Walter Reed Army Hosp., Washington, 1959-62; assoc. prof. U. So. Calif. Sch. Medicine, Los Angeles, 1963—; sr. surg. pathologist Los Angeles County Gen. Hosp., 1963; dir. dept. pathology Community Meml. Hosp., Ventura, Calif., 1964-80, Gen. Hosp. Ventura County, 1966-74; dir. Pathology Service Med. Group, 1970—; cons. Calif. Tumor Tissue Registry, 1962—, Camarillo State Hosp., 1964-70, Tripler Gen. Hosp., Hawaii, 1963-67, Armed Forces Inst. Pathology, 1960—. Bd. dirs. Tri-Counties Blood Bank, Am. Cancer Soc. Served to maj., M.C., U.S. Army, 1956-62. Recipient Borden award Calif. Honor Soc., 1949; Achievement cert. Surgeon Gen. Army, 1962. Fellow Am. Soc. Clin. Pathologists, Coll. Am. Pathologists; mem. Internat. Coll. Surgeons, World Affairs Council, Jonathan Club. Contbr. articles to profl. jours. Research in cardiovascular disease, endocrine, renal, skin diseases, also cancer. Home and Office: 105 Encinal Way Ventura CA 93001-3317

ABU-MOSTAFA, AYMAN SAID, computer consultant; b. Giza, Egypt, June 1, 1953; came to U.S., 1978; s. Said S. Abu-Mstafa and Faiza A. Ibrahim. BME, Cairo U., 1976; MS in Mech. and Aerospace Engring., Okla. State U., 1980, PhD, 1984. Teaching asst. Cairo U., Giza, Egypt, 1978; teaching asst. Okla. State U., Stillwater, 1978-79, rsch. assoc., 1979-81; software engr. SEAM Internat. Corp., Palos Verdes, Calif., 1984-87; computing and networking cons. Calif. State U., Los Alamitos, 1987-92; sr. systems analyst Allied Signal Aerospace, Torrance, Calif., 1992-93; pres., CEO NeuroDollars, Inc., Huntington Beach, Calif., 1993—. Author papers, articles in field. Undergrad. fellow Ministry of Higher Edn., Cairo, 1971, 72, 76; NASA/Ames grantee, 1979-81. Mem. AIAA, IEEE, Assn. for Computing Machinery. Muslim. Home: 4740 Warner Ave Apt 201 Huntington Beach CA 92649-5028 Office: NeuroDollars Inc PO Box 2420 Huntington Beach CA 92647-0420

ABU-SAMRAH, SAMEER ABDALLAH, internist; b. Jerusalem, Mar. 13, 1953; came to U.S., 1973; s. Abdallah Tawfiq and Neamati Abdul-Jabbar (Salaymeh) A.; m. Cynthia Marie Trahms, Nov. 1, 1975. BS in Chemistry, So. Ill. U., 1979, MD, 1983. Intern in internal medicine L.A. County Hosp., 1983-84; resident in internal medicine Kaiser-Permanente Hosp., Santa Clara, Calif., 1984-86; internist FHP Sr. Ctr., Huntington Beach, Calif., 1986-87; vice chmn. dept. internal medicine FHP Hosp., Fountain Valley, Calif., 1987-88; chmn. dept. internal medicine FHP Hosp., 1988-90, assoc. med. dir., 1990-91, med. dir., 1991-92; internist FHP Garden Grove Med. Clinic, Fountain Valley, 1992—, 1992-94; med. dir. Sierra Health Svcs., Las Vegas, Nev., 1994—; asst. clin. prof. Sch. Medicine U. Nev., Las Vegas, 1994—. Mem. Am. Coll. Physician Execs. Home: 8980 W El Campo Grande Ave Las Vegas NV 89129-3347 Office: Sierra Health Svcs PO Box 15645 Las Vegas NV 89114-5645

ACEVEDO, ANGELIQUE MARIE, art educator; b. Houston, Dec. 11, 1953. Art cert. K-12, Metro. State Coll., Denver, 1987; vocat. edn. cert., U. N.Mex., 1982, MA, 1981; BFA, Va. Commonwealth U., 1975; doctoral studies in curriculum & instrn., U. Denver, 1992. Resource tchr. Profl. Arts Resource Team, Colo., 1988—; curriculum resource tchr. State Dept. Edn., Colo., 1988—; global exchange U. Denver, 1989-90; curriculum integration strategies resource tchr. Minn. Dept. Pub. Instrn., Stillwater, 1991; part time art and music methods classroom tchr. Metro. State Coll., Colo., 1991-92; artist and classroom curriculum developer Young Audiences, Colo., 1991—; tchr. researcher N.Y.U., 1991; classroom resource and tchr. trainer Pub. Edn. Coalition, Colo., 1991—; K-12 art instr. Jefferson County Sch. Dist., Colo., 1989—; cons. Talamasca Integrated Arts,Lakewood, Colo., Binney and Smith Crayola Corp., Colo. Coun. on Arts and Humanities Indiv. Artists Program, Artist in Residence Program and Young Audiences, NYU Tchr. Rschr. Program, Geraldine Dodge Found., Ednl. Concepts, Atlanta, 1994, Nat. Endowment for the Arts in Edn. Program, 1994; coun. mem. arts ednl. consensus project Nat. Assessment Ednl. Progress, 1993—; bd. dirs. Nat. Bd. Profl. Teaching Standards; mem. Coun. Chief State Sch. Officers. Author: Collage, Colo., 1992, A Multicultural Resource Guide, Colo., 1991-92. Mem. Nat. History Mus., Denver Art Mus., Denver Botanic Gardens; mem. urban arts com. City of Lakewood; bd. mem. arts coun. City of Arvada, Colo., 1994; mem. Arts Task Force Colo. Dept. Edn., 1994. Named Colo. Art Educator of Yr., 1991-92; nominated Colo. Educator of Yr., 1992, finalist Colo. Educator of Yr., 1993; recipient Disney Am. Tchr. Visual Arts award, 1992, Excellence in Edn. award for Colo., 1992. Mem. NEA, Nat. Art Edn. Assn., Art Student League Denver, Colo. Alliance for Arts in Edn., Art Edn. Equity Network, Profl. Arts Resource Team, Colo. Art Edn. Assn. (rep. coun. exec. bd. mem. 1994). Democrat. Roman Catholic. Home: 214 Wright St Apt 104 Lakewood CO 80228-1408 Office: Jefferson County Sch Dist 1829 Denver West Dr Bldg 27 Golden CO 80401-3146 also: Bear Creek Sr High Sch 3490 S Kipling Lakewood CO 80227

ACHABAL, DALE DOMINGO, business educator; b. Stockton, Calif., Jan. 15, 1946; s. John Donato and Martha Elizabeth (Hesner) A.; m. Carol T. Theis, Dec. 16, 1967; children: Jonathan, Stephen. BA, San Francisco State U., 1967, MA, 1970; PhD, U. Tex., 1975. Faculty U. Calif., Berkeley, 1973-75; asst. prof. Ohio State U., Columbus, 1975-80; assoc. prof. Santa Clara (Calif.) U., 1980-89; L.J. Skaggs Disting. prof. and dir. Retail Mgmt. Inst. Leavey Sch. Bus., Santa Clara U., 1989—; cons. in field to AT&T, IBM, NCR, Mervyn's, The Limited, Woolworth, Safeway. Contbr. articles to profl. jours. Bd. dirs. KTEH Pub. TV, San Jose, 1990—. 1st lt. USAF. NATO fellow, 1972. Mem. Am. Mktg. Assn. (chpt. pres. 1979), Nat. Retail Fedn. (bd. dirs. info. svcs. div. 1992—), Beta Gamma Sigma. Home: 17191 Buena Vista Ave Los Gatos CA 95030-2381 Office: Santa Clara Univ Leavey Sch of Bus Santa Clara CA 95030

ACHEN, MARK KENNEDY, city manager; b. Vancouver, Wash., Apr. 13, 1943; s. George Ben and Marjorie Beth (Pierson) A.; m. Mary Ann Uzzell, Aug. 14, 1971; children: Wyndi Marie, Kara Lynn. BA, U. Wash., 1967; MA, U. Mo., 1981. Asst. to city mgr. City of Ferguson, Mo., 1972-74; city adminstr. City of Mounds View, Minn., 1974-79; city mgr. City of Gladstone, Mo., 1979-84, City of Grand Junction, Colo., 1984—; cons. U.S. Nat. Fire Acad., Emmitsburg, Md., 1990-91, adj. faculty, 1991—. Gates Found. fellow Harvard U. Sr. Govt. Exec. Program, 1987. Mem. ASPA (Kansas City chpt. Adminstr. of Yr. 1983), Colo. City Mgmt. Assn. 9pres. 1988-89, bd. dirs. 1985-91), Internat. City Mgmt. Assn. (chmn. 1988, internat. conf. planning com., co-chmn. 1995, internat. conf. host com.), Rotary (pres. 1983-84, bd. dirs. 1989-90, 92-93, Paul Harris fellow 1991). Home: 3344 Northridge Dr Grand Junction CO 81506-1926 Office: City of Grand Junction 250 N 5th St Grand Junction CO 81501-2628

ACHESON, ALICE BREWEN, publicist; b. Indiana, Pa., July 26, 1936; d. Stewart F. and Anna M.J. (Mohr) Brewen; m. Donald H. Acheson, Dec. 12, 1970 (dec.); m. Edward B. Greub, Sept. 8, 1990. AB, Bucknell U., 1958; MA, CUNY, 1963. Tchr. English and Spanish, Mt. Vernon (N.Y.) High Sch., 1958-69; exec. sec., then exec. asst. Media Medica, Inc., N.Y.C., 1969-71; with McGraw Hill Book Co., N.Y.C., 1971-78, assoc. editor, 1971-76, publicity assoc., 1977-78; assoc. publicity dir. Simon & Schuster, N.Y.C., 1979-80, Crown Pubs., Inc., N.Y.C., 1980-81; ind. publicist, prin. Alice B. Acheson, N.Y.C., 1981-88, San Francisco, 1988—; mem. faculty Willamette Writers' Conf., 1981, Folio Pub. Week, 1983, 84, Face to Face Pub. Conf. and Expn., 1977, 79, 81, Howard U. Press Book Pub. Inst., 1984, NYU Pub. Inst., 1985, Nat. Writers Union seminar, 1985, Small Press Expo, 1987, 88, Pubs. Mktg. Assn., 1990-94, Tucson Book Pubs. Assn., 1991-92; mem. publishing bd. Aperture Found., 1987-89. Recipient Ptnr.-in-Edn. award N.Y.C. Bd. Edn., 1977, 78, award for outside svcs. advertising, promotion, publicity, Literary Market Place, 1993. Mem. NAFE, COSMEP (pub. conf. 1993-94), Pubs. Publicity Assn. (program com. 1979-83), No. Calif. Book Publicists Assn. (bd. dirs. 1989-92), Pubs. Mktg. Assn. (bd. dirs. 1991-92). Office: 3362 Laguna St San Francisco CA 94123-2208

ACHTEL, ROBERT ANDREW, pediatric cardiologist; b. Bklyn., May 5, 1941; s. Murray and Amelia (Ellian) A.; m. Erica Noel Woods, Mar. 10, 1963; children: Bergen Alison, Roland Hugh. BA, Adelphi U., 1963; MD, U. Cin., 1967. Diplomate Am. Bd. Pediatric Cardiology. Intern, Cin. Children's Hosp., 1967-68; resident in pediatrics Yale U., 1968-69, fellow in pediatric cardiology, 1969-71; clin. instr. pediatrics U. Calif.-Davis, 1972-73, clin. asst. prof., 1977-83; asst. prof. pediatrics, U. Ky., 1973-76; dir. pediatric ICU, Sutter Meml. Hosp., Sacramento, 1977-85, dir. pediatric Cardiology, 1982—, chmn. instl. rev. com., 1981-85; chmn. dept. pediatrics Mercy Hosp., Sacramento, 1981-83, vice chmn. pediatrics, 1983-85, 95—; dir. pediatric ICU, 1982-83; dir. Laurel Hills Devel. Ctr., 1985-89.; chmn. rsch com. Sutter Inst. for Med. Rsch., 1989—; trustee, mem. exec. com. Sutler Hosps. Found., vice chmn., 1992-93, CEO Access Care, 1994-95, med. dir. FastServe Med. Group, 1995; mem. tech. adv. com. pediat. cardiology State of Calif.; CEO AccessCare. Contbr. articles in cardiovascular research. Bd. dirs. Sutter Meml. Hosp. Found., 1986—; bd. dirs. Sutter Found., 1989, trustee, 1989—. Maj. M.C., USAF, 1971-73. Recipient grants from Heart Assn., U. Ky. Tobacco and Health Research Found. Mem. Am. Heart Assn. (dir. Sacramento chpt., mem. councils congenital heart disease and atherosclerosis and cardiovascular surgery), Am. Coll. Chest Physicians, Am. Acad Pediatrics, SW Pediatric Cardiology Soc., So. Soc. Pediatric Research. Office: Pediatric Cardiology Assocs 5609 J St Ste A Sacramento CA 95819-3948

ACKER, JOAN ELISE ROBINSON, sociology educator; b. Springfield, Ill., Mar. 18, 1924; d. Harold D. Robinson and Frieda (Steinman) Ellsworth; children: Michael, David, Steven. BA, Hunter Coll., 1946; MA, U. Chgo., 1948; PhD, U. Oreg., 1967. Med. social worker N.Y. Hosp., N.Y.C., 1948-56; instr. U. Calif., Berkeley, 1956-58; dir. Ctr. for the Sociol. Study of Women, U. Oreg., Eugene, 1973-81, Ctr. for the Study of Women in Soc., U. Oreg., Eugene, 1982-86; from asst. prof. to prof. U. Oreg., Eugene, 1966-80; rsch. prof. Swedish Ctr. for Working Life, Stockholm, 1987-89; disting. vis. prof. Ont. Inst. for Studies in Edn., Toronto, 1990; cons. Ont. Pay Equity Commn., Toronto, 1990, Equality Commn., Helsinki, Finland, 1988-89, Inst. for Social Sci. Rsch., Oslo, Norway, 1988-93. Author: Doing Comparable Worth, 1989; editor Econ. and Indsl. Democracy, 1982, 2d edit. 1993, Internat. Jour. Sociology, 1976; contbr. articles to profl. jours. Task force mem. Pay Equity, State of Oreg., Salem, 1983-85; chairperson Women's Studies Coun., U. Oreg., Eugene, 1979-81; bd. dirs. Nat. Coun. for Rsch. on Women, N.Y.C., 1983-86. Ford Found. fellow, 1965. Mem. Am. Sociol. Assn. (chair sex and gender sect. 1979-80, coun. 1992-95, Jessie Bernard award 1989, Career of Disting. Scholarship award 1993), Internat. Sociol. Assn., Pacific Sociol. Assn. (v.p. 1975), Sociologists for Women in Soc., Phi Beta Kappa. Office: U Oreg Dept Sociology Eugene OR 97403

ACKER, LOREN CALVIN, medical instrument company executive; b. Lamar, Colo., Mar. 3, 1934; s. John C. and Ada M. (Ecton) A.; m. Judy N. Willms, Sept. 17, 1955 (dec. Oct. 1968); children: Cheryl Acker Hoge, Keith B., Karen Acker Kime; m. Darla C. Copeland, July 24, 1976. BS in Mech. Engring., Fresno State Coll., 1956; Bus. and Mgmt. cert., U. Calif., Berkeley, 1961; MBA, U. Santa Clara, 1966. Flight test technician NASA, Edwards, Calif., 1954-56; engring. mgr. Westinghouse, Sunnyvale, Calif., 1956-69; assoc. dir. Kitt Peak Nat. Obs., Tucson, Ariz., 1969-73; chmn., CEO, founder Engring. & Rsch. Assocs., Inc., Tucson, 1973—; gen. ptnr. Winged Foot Assocs., Tucson, 1974—; dir., founder NYPA Inc., Tucson, 1988—. Patentee in field. Chmn. park and recreation City of Cupertino, Calif., 1968. Mem.Am. Assn. Blood Banks, Am. Soc. Apherises. Republican. Home: 4831 Winged Food Pl Tucson AZ 85718 Office: 500 N Tucson Blvd Tucson AZ 85716-4412

ACKERLEY, BARRY, professional basketball team executive, communications company executive. Student, U. Iowa, 1956. Exec. v.p. Advan, Inc.; owner Golden West Outdoor Advt., 1968-75; chmn., CEO Ackerley Comm., Inc., 1975—; owner, chmn. bd. dirs. Seattle SuperSonics, 1984—. Office: Seattle SuperSonics PO Box C-900911 190 Queen Anne Ave N Ste 200 Seattle WA 98109-9711 also: Ackerley Communications Inc 800 5th Ave Seattle WA 98104-3122*

ACKERLY, WENDY SAUNDERS, aeronautic engineer, systems analyst; b. Chgo., July 23, 1960; d. Robert S. Jr. and Linda Ackerly. BS in Atmospheric Sci., U. Calif., Davis, 1982; postgrad., U. Nev., Reno, 1985. Programmer U. Calif, Davis, 1982-83; cons. software Tesco, Sacramento, 1983; software engr. Bently Nev. Corp., Minden, Nev., 1984-85; mgr. computer scis. Jensen Electric Co., Reno, 1985-86; software engr. Jensen Electric Co., Cameron Park, Calif., 1986-89; sr. engr. Aerojet, Sacramento, 1989—; sec.-treas. Kerry King Constrn. Co., Inc., 1991—. Pres. Four Springs Homeowners Assn., 1993—. Mem. Nat. Space Soc., Am. Meteorol. Soc., Planetary Soc., U.S. Tennis Assn., Calif. Aggie Alumni Assn. Republican. Office: Aerojet PO Box 13222 Sacramento CA 95813-6000

ACKERMAN, GERALD MARTIN, art historian, consultant; b. Alameda, Calif., Aug. 21, 1928; s. Alois M. and Eva L. (Sadler) A. B.A., U. Calif.-Berkeley, 1952; postgrad., U. Munich, W.Ger., 1955-58; Ph.D., Princeton U., 1964. Instr. Bryn Mawr Coll., Pa., 1960-64; asst. prof. Stanford U., Calif., 1964-70; assoc. prof. dept. art Pomona Coll., Claremont, Calif., 1970-75, prof., 1975-89, chmn. dept. art, 1972-82; prof. emeritus, 1989—; Fulbright prof. U. Leningrad, 1980. Author: (plays) Family and Friends, 1979, The Surfer, 1981, The Life and Work of J.L. Gerome, 1986, British Orientalists, 1995, American Orientalists, 1994, also articles. Appleton eminent scholar Fla. State U., 1994. Democrat. Home: 360 S Mills Ave Claremont CA 91711-5331

ACKERMAN, H. DON, automotive dealership executive; b. Davenport, Iowa, Sept. 25, 1926; s. Harold George and Virginia (Stearnes) A.; m. Elizabeth Hall, May 5, 1983; children: H. Gary, Deborah Ackerman Lo Palo. BA, U. Calif., 1948. Sales mgr. Gaudin Motors, Salinas, Calif., 1951-54; salesman Harbor Lincoln Mercury, Long Beach, Calif., 1954-56; sales mgr. Gaudin Ford, Las Vegas, Nev., 1956-72; owner Gaudin Ford and Import Ctr., Las Vegas, Nev., 1972—. With USN, 1944-46. Mem. Las Vegas Country Club (dir. 1978-84). Republican. Presbyterian. Office: Gaudin Ford-Porsche 2121 E Sahara Ave Las Vegas NV 89104-4117

ACKERMAN, HELEN PAGE, librarian, educator; b. Evanston, Ill., June 30, 1912; d. John Bernard and Florence Page. B.A., Agnes Scott Coll., Decatur, Ga., 1933; B.L.S., U. N.C., 1940. Cataloger Columbia Theol. Sem., 1942-43; post librarian U.S. Army, Aberdeen Proving Ground, Md., 1943-45; asst. librarian Union Theol. Sem., Richmond, Va., 1945-49; reference librarian UCLA, 1949-54, asst. univ. librarian, 1954-65, assoc. univ. librarian, 1965-73, univ. librarian, 1973-77, prof. Sch. Info. and Library Sci., 1973-77, 82, 83; vis. prof. Sch. Librarianship, U. Calif., Berkeley, 1978, 80. Recipient Disting. Alumni award U. N.C., 1973; award of distinction in library sci. UCLA Alumnae Assn., 1977, Disting. Career Citation Assn. Coll. and Rsch. Librs., 1989. Mem. Am., Calif. library assns., AAUW (Status of Women award 1973), Council on Library Resources (bd. dirs. 1975-90). Home: 310 20th St Santa Monica CA 90402-2414

ACKERMAN, LINDA DIANE, manufacturing executive; b. Portland, Oreg., May 4, 1964; d. David Gilbert and Diane (Sause) A. BA in Econs., U. Wash., 1991. Office mgr. Hawaii Wood Preserving Co., Kahului, 1984-85, v.p., 1987-94, pres., 1994—; with inventory control dept. Monarch Bldg. Supply, Kahului, 1986-87. Adminstrv. asst. I Have A Dream Program, Kahului, 1990-91; mem. area com. Spl. Olympics Maui County. 1993; unified softball coach Spl. Olympics, 1994—. Mem. Am. Wood Preservers Assn., Chi Omega (pres. Phi chpt. 1985). Republican. Mem. Christian Ch. Home:

43 Nonohe Pl Paia HI 96779-9701 Office: Hawaii Wood Preserving Co 356 Hanakai St Kahului HI 96732-2407

ACKERMAN, ROBERT EDWIN, anthropology educator. BA, U. Mich., 1950, MA, 1951; PhD, U. Pa., 1961. Rsch. asst. U. Mus., U. Pa., 1957-59; fellow in anthropology Ea. Pa. Psychiat. Inst., Phila., 1959-61; instr. anthropology U. Del., 1960-61; from instr. to prof. anthropology Wash. State U., 1961—, acting chmn. dept. anthropology, 1971-72, editor report of investigations dept. anthropology, 1987-88, dir. Mus. Anthropology, 1987—; rschr. and lectr. in field. Contbr. articles to profl. jours. Fellow AAAS, Am. Anthropol. Assn., Arctic Inst. N.Am., Explorers Club; mem. Internat. Arctic Social Scis. Assn., Alaska Anthropol. Assn., Am. Quaternary Assn., Can. Archaeol. Assn., Pacific Sci. Assn., Soc. for Am. Archaeology, Sigma Xi. Office: Mus Anthropology Dept Anthropology Wash State Univ Pullman WA 99164-4910

ACKLES, JANICE VOGEL, fundraising executive, writer; b. Pasadena, Calif.; d. Roy George August and Genevieve Irene (Hunter) Vogel; m. David Thomas Ackles, Dec. 9, 1972; 1 child, George Arthur Vogel. BA in Art History, Calif. State U., L.A.; postgrad., U. So. Calif. Free-lance writer, 1972—; asst. editor Am. Jour. Physiology, L.A., 1980-84; dir. devel. rsch. World Vision, Monrovia, 1985-88; v.p. major gifts and rsch. Childrens Hosp., L.A., 1988-93; principal Ackles Communications, Tujunga, Calif., 1993—; dir. devel. Alzheimer's Assn., L.A., 1993-95, Classical Theatre Co., Glendale, Calif., 1995—. Contbr. articles to nat. mags. and newspapers. Vol. researcher L.A. County Mus. Art, 1973-75; mem. Assistance League So. Calif., L.A., East African Wildlife Soc., Mus. Contemporary Art, L.A., Greater L.A. Zoo Assn., Natural History Mus. Mem. Am. Prospect Rsch. Assn., Nat. Soc. Fund Raising Execs. (bd. dirs., cert.), Assn. for Hosp. Philanthropy, Ind. Writers So. Calif., Calif. Press Women, Inc. (bd. dirs.). Democrat.

ACKLEY, MARJORIE ROSE, health educator; b. Shanghai, China, Nov. 15, 1922; came to U.S., 1926; d. Millard Charles Ackley and Luella Alice (Williams) Scharffenberg; m. Donald Wilton Oswald, Sept. 24, 1942 (div. 1955); children: Donald Theodore Oswald, Jaclyn Rae Hoiland. AS, Grossmont Coll., 1977; BS in Allied Health Professions, Loma Linda U., 1987, MPH, 1988. RN, registered dietitian, fitness instr.; lic. M/V operator. Adminstrv. grant sec. Palo Alto (Calif.) Med. Research Found., 1962-67; devel. dir. San Francisco Eye and Ear Hosp., 1967-70; fin. planner Robert W. P. Holstrom Co., San Francisco, 1971-74; health educator San Francisco, 1972-74; registered nurse Groves Registry, San Francisco, 1977-88, Humana Hosp., Anchorage, 1983-85; owner, dir. Profl. Health Svcs., 1984-95; nurse Providence Hosp., Anchorage, 1983-85, 90-95; registered nurse MedPro Nurses Registry, San Diego, 1984-89; cardiac rehab. Providence Hosp., Anchorage, 1990-95; health educator Anchorage, 1983-95; med. coord. Canvasback Mission, Inc., Benecia, Calif., 1988-93; health educator, Sch. of Pub. Health, Loma Linda, Calif., 1988, Seventh-Day Adventist Ch., San Francisco, 1973, Health Expo, Yucaipa, Calif., 1988; health edn. lectr. 1990-93. Author of numerous articles in field. Vol. Health Expo, Alaska, 1988. Mem. Am. Dietetic Assn. (Eleanor Mitchell Meml. award 1986), Alaska Dietetic Assn., Seventh-Day Adventist Dietetic Assn., Am. Pub. Health Assn., Inst. for Advancement of Health. Republican. Seventh-Day Adventist. Home: 3225 Boniface Pky Anchorage AK 99504-3741

ACOBA, SIMEON RIVERA, JR., judge; b. Honolulu, Mar. 11, 1944; s. Simeon R. and Martina (Domingo) A. BA, U. Hawaii, 1966; JD, Northwestern U., 1969. Bar: Hawaii 1969, U.S. Dist. Ct. Hawaii, U.S. Ct. Appeals (9th cir.). Law clk. Hawaii Supreme Ct., Honolulu, 1969-70; housing officer U. Hawaii, Honolulu, 1970-71; dep. atty. gen., Honolulu, 1971-73; pvt. practice, Honolulu, 1973-80; judge 1st Cir. Ct., State of Hawaii, Honolulu, 1980-94; judge Intermediate Ct. of Appeals, State of Hawaii, 1994—; atty. on spl. contract Div. OSHA, Dept. Labor, Honolulu, 1975-77, Pub. Utilities Div., State of Hawaii, 1976-77, Campaign Spending Com., State of Hawaii, 1976; staff atty. Hawaii State Legislature, 1975. Bd. dirs. Hawaii Mental Health Assn., 1975-77, Nuuanu YMCA, 1975-78, Hawaii Youth at Risk, 1990-91; mem. Gov.'s Conf. on Yr. 2000, Honolulu, 1970, Citizens Com. on Adminstrn. of Justice, 1972, State Drug Abuse Commn., 1975-76, Com. to Consider the Adoption of ABA Model Rules of Profl. Conduct, 1989-91; subcom. chmn. Supreme Ct. Com. Pattern Jury Instrns., 1990-91; mem. Hawaii Supreme Ct. Ad Hoc Com. Jury Master List, 1991-92, Judicial Edn. Com., 1992-93, Hawaii State Bar Assn. Jud. Adminstrn. Com., 1992-94, Permanent Com. Rules of Penal Procedure and Cir. Ct. Rules, 1992—; instr. criminal law Hawaii Pacific U., 1992, 93, 94; 1st Cir. Ct. liaison Dept. Health Com. Sanity Panel Training Needs, 1992—; Recipient Liberty Bell award, 1964. Mem. ABA, Hawaii State Bar Assn. (dir. young lawyers sect. 1973, mem. com. Cert. of Psychologists and Psychiatrists, 1992—), Assn. Trial Lawyers Am. Office: Intermediate Ct of Appeals State of Hawaii PO Box 2560 Honolulu HI 96804-2560

ACOSTA, NELSON JOHN, civil engineer; b. Newark, N.J., July 8, 1947; s. Pedro Nelson and Bertha Maud (Williams) A.; m. Twyla Liasine Flaherty, June 19, 1970; children: Jeffrey Thomas, Stephen Patrick, Bryan Edward. BCE, Ga. Inst. Tech., 1969, MSCE, 1970. Registered profl. engr., Ill.; API cert. aboveground storage tank inspector. Design engr. Chgo. Bridge and Iron Co., Birmingham, Ala., 1970-73; sales estimator Chgo. Bridge and Iron Co., Oak Brook, Ill., 1973-74; contracting engr. Chgo. Bridge and Iron Co., Atlanta, 1975-79, CBI Constructors, Ltd., London, 1979-80, Arabian CBI Ltd., Al Khobar, Saudi Arabia, 1980-84, CBI Na-Con, Inc., Fontana, Calif., 1984-88; mgr. spl. projects and estimating HMT, Inc., Cerritos, Calif., 1989-94; mgr. engring. HMT Inspection & Engring. Svcs., Cerritos, 1994—. Recipient traineeship NSF, Atlanta, 1969. Mem. ASCE. Republican. Roman Catholic. Office: HMT Inc 1227 S Claudina St Anaheim CA 92805

ACOSTA-HESS, JOSEFINA ELIZABETH, Spanish language educator; b. Santiago, Dominican Republic, Apr. 10, 1951; came to U.S., 1975; d. José Ramón and Celeste (Pujol) Hess, June 30, 1968; children: Rachel, Karen. BA in Edn., U. Caolica Madre Maestra, Santiago, 1975; MA in Spanish, U. Calif., Irvine, 1981, PhD in Spanish, 1986. Tchg. asst. U. Calif., Irvine, 1979-84, lectr., 1986-88; instr. Irvine Valley Coll., 1985, Orange Coast Coll., Costa Mesa, Calif., 1985-88; assoc. prof. Calif. State U., Fullerton, 1988—. Author: (book) Galdo's y la novela de Adulterio, 1988; contbr. articles/poems to profl. jours. Recipient Humanities Rsch. award U. Calif., Irvine, 1984; faculty enhancement and instrnl. grantee, Calif. State U., Fullerton, 1989. Mem. MLA, Calif. Faculty Assn., Assn. Tchrs. of Spanish and Portuguese, South-Cen. Modern Lang. Assn. Home: 19432 Sierra Luna Rd Irvine CA 92715-3815 Office: Dept Fgn Langs and Lits Calif State Univ Fullerton Fullerton CA 92634

ACREE, MICHAEL COY, psychology educator; b. Terre Haute, Ind., May 6, 1946; s. Coy Ray and Roberta Ann (Shank) A.; m. Harriet Roberts O'Neal, Oct. 5, 1985 (div. Dec. 1986). BA, Oberlin Coll., 1968; MA, Clark U., 1973, PhD, 1978. Asst. prof. U. Nebr., Lincoln, 1978-79; rsch. psychologist Ctr. on Deafness U. Calif., San Francisco, 1980-85; asst. prof. Pacific Grad. Sch. Psychology, Palo Alto, Calif., 1985-90; assoc. prof. Calif. Inst. Integral Studies, San Francisco, 1991-95; sr. statistician Ctr. for AIDS Prevention Studies, U. Calif., San Francisco, 1994—. Grantee Nat. Inst. Handicapped Rsch. 1984, Chapman Rsch. Fund 1986. Home: 859 45th Ave San Francisco CA 94121-3223 Office: UCSF Ctr for AIDS Prevention Studies 74 Montgomery St Ste 600 San Francisco CA 94104-4601

ACTON, EDWARD MCINTOSH, medicinal chemist; b. Morgan Hill, Calif., May 30, 1930; s. John Edward and Margaret (McIntosh) A. BS, Stanford (Calif.) U., 1951; PhD, MIT, 1957. Chemist Merck & Co., Rahway, N.J., 1951-53; organic chemist SRI Internat., Menlo Park, Calif., 1957-75, program mgr., 1975-85; prof. medicinal chemistry U. Tex. M.D. Anderson Hosp. and Cancer Inst., Houston, 1985-87; dep. br. chief, expert Nat. Cancer Inst., Bethesda, Md., 1987-91; cons. Menlo Park, 1991—. Editorial bd. Cancer Chemotherapy and Pharmacology, 1981-87, Am. Cancer Soc., Adv. Com. on Clin. Invest II--Chemotherapy and Hematology, 1984-87, Nat. Cancer Inst., Devel. Therapeutics Contracts Rev. Com., 1983-86; contbr. numerous articles to profl. jours. Numerous grants Nat. Cancer Inst., 1976-87. Mem. AAAS, Am. Chem. Soc., Royal Soc. of Chemistry. Republican. Congregationalist. Home and Office: 281 Arlington Way Menlo Park CA 94025-2316

ACTON, WILLIAM JOHN, real estate appraiser and consultant; b. Jackson, Mich., Apr. 17, 1958; s. Richard David and Patricia Jean (Rifenberg) A. BA in Econs./Mgmt. and Polit. Sci., Albion (Mich.) Coll., 1980. Cert. gen. real estate appraiser, Ariz. Sr. appraiser cons. Greenberg Chin Cons., Tucson, 1984-87; chief appraiser Pima County Govt., Tucson, 1987-92; pres. Acton Valuation Group, Inc., Tucson, 1992—; Pima County rep. Govt. Chief Appraisers Inter-Agy. Coalition, Phoenix, 1988-93. Benefactor Boys and Girls Club, Tucson, 1993, 94, Jacobs YMCA, Tucson, 1994. Sustaining Paul Harris fellow Rotary Internat. Mem. Internat. Right of Way Assn., Met. Tucson C. of C., MAI Appraisal Inst., Rotary Club of Tucson (chmn. house com. 1992—, chmn. 4 way test com.), Encanto Canyon Homeowners Assn. (bd. dirs). Republican. Home: 7864 E Castle Valley Way Tucson AZ 85715-7042 Office: Acton Valuation Group Inc 6890 E Sunrise Dr #120-344 Tucson AZ 85715

ADA, ALMA FLOR, education educator, writer; b. Camagüey, Cuba, Jan. 3, 1938; came to U.S., 1970; d. Modesto Arturo Ada and Alma Lafuente; children: Rosalma, Alfonso, Miguel, Gabriel Zubizarreta. Diploma in Spanish studies, U. Complutence, Madrid, 1960; B of Humanities, U. Cath., Lima, Peru, 1963, PhD, 1965. Assoc. prof. Emory U., Atlanta, 1970-72; prof. Mercy Coll. Detroit, 1972-75; prof. Sch. Edn. U. San Francisco, 1976—. Author: (children's books) The Gold Coin (Christopher award 1991), My Name is María Isabel, 1993, The Unicorn of the West, 1994, Dear Peter Rabbit, 1994, Where the Flametrees Bloom, 1995. Recipient Ann. award L.A. Bilingual Dirs. Assn., 1993, Calif. State PTA Assn.; Fulbright scholar, 1966-68. Mem. Internat. Bd. Books for Young People, Nat. Assn. for Bilingual Edn., Calif. Assn. for Bilingual Edn. Home: 475 Connecticut San Francisco CA 94107 Office: U San Francisco Ignatian Heights San Francisco CA 94117

ADACHI, DEREK KASUMI, pharmacist, computer programmer; b. Seattle, Aug. 2, 1961; s. Seiichi and Yoko (Horita) A. BS in Pharmacy, U. Wash., 1985; MS in Pharmacology, Wash. State U., 1989; MS in Computer Sci., Pacific Luth. U., 1992. Registered pharmacist. Clin. pharmacist Puyallup Tribal Health Authority, Tacoma, Wash., 1985-87, 89-92; microcomputer cons. Pacific Luth. U., Tacoma, 1989-92; clin. pharmicist, health care systems analyst, mgr. pharmacy Caremark Inc., Redmond, Wash., 1992—. Contbr. articles to profl. jours. Mem. IEEE, Am. Pharm. Assn., Assn. for Computing Machinery, Wash. State Pharmacists Assn. Mem. United Ch. Christ. Home: 19223 34th Ave S Seatac WA 98188-5313 Office: Caremark 6645 185th Ave NE Ste 151 Redmond WA 98052-5038

ADAIR, OLIVIA VYNN, cardiologist; b. Mobile, Ala., Apr. 18, 1958; d. Howard Van Voorhes and Eunice Margarette (Tanner) A.; m. Mark Malyak, June 5, 1988; children: Lisa Allison, Matthew Adair. BS, U. Ala., 1978; MS, MA, U. South Ala., 1979; MD, Am. U. Caribbean Monteserrat, British West Indies, 1982. Diplomate Am. Bd. Cardiology; lic. physician, N.Y., Pa., Colo. Intern then resident SUNY Health scis. ctr., Bklyn., 1982-85, cardiology fellow, 1985-87; clin. instr. SUNY Health Sci. Ctr., Bklyn., 1985-87, instr. dept. medicine, 1987-91; dir. coronary care unit Kings County Hosp. Ctr., Bklyn., 1988; dir. non-invasive cariodlogy Denver Gen. Hosp., 1988—, dir. coronary care unit, 1991—, dir. pacemaker svc., 1993—; asst. prof. U. Colo. Health Sci. Ctr., Denver, 1991—, staff cardiologist, 1988—. Author, editor: Cardiology Secrets, 1994; contbr. articles to profl. jours. Grantee, NIH, 1988—, faculty U. Colo., 1992—, Berlin, Germany, 1992—, Denver Gen. Hosp., 1990—. Fellow ACP; mem. Am. Coll. Cardiology, Am. Fedn. Clin. Rsch., N.Y. Cardiol. Soc. Office: Denver Gen Hosp 777 Bannock St # 4000 Denver CO 80204-4507

ADAM, CORNEL See LENGYEL, CORNEL ADAM

ADAMS, ANN ELIZABETH, corporate communications executive, lawyer; b. Guthrie, Okla., Jan. 29, 1948; d. Jack P. and Billie E. (May) A. BA in Journalism, U. Okla., 1970, MA, 1971; JD, Oklahoma City U., 1984. Lic. atty. Supr. teleshopper advt. KOCO-TV, Oklahoma City, 1971-72; pub. info. officer Met. Libr. System, Oklahoma City, 1972-78; editor/writer Kerr-McGee Corp., Oklahoma City, 1978-79, assoc. editor, 1979-81, mgr. publs., 1981-84, mgr. corp. communications, 1984-88; asst. to chancellor Okla. State Regents for Higher Edn., Oklahoma City, 1988-90; dir. pub. rels. div. Jordan Assocs. Advt./Communications, Oklahoma City, 1990-93; dir. pub. rels. and advtg. The Dial Corp., Phoenix, 1993—. Mem. Myriad Gardens Conservatory, Oklahoma City, 1986-92, bd. dirs., 1986-88; pres. Friends of Met. Libr. System, Oklahoma City, 1990-92, bd. dirs., 1986-92; divsn. chmn. United Way Greater Oklahoma City, 1989; women's adv. bd. Bapt. Med. Ctr., 1990-93; trustee Met. Library System Endowment Trust, 1992-93; mem.mktg. com. Phoenix Zoo, 1993—; bd. dirs. Scottsdale Prevention Inst., 1995—; mem. Scottsdale Ctr. of the Arts, Desert Botanical Gardens, Phoenix Art Mus., Valley Leadership Alumni Assn. Recipient Paragon award Leadership Oklahoma City, 1986, 92, Outstanding Alumni award U. Okla. Sch. of Journalism and Mass Communication, 1993, Addy award Am. Advt. Fedn., 1984, Pub. Rels. award N.Am. Advtg. Agy. Network, 1992. Mem. Women in Communications, Inc. (pres. Oklahoma City chpt. 1987-88, chmn. nat. progress of women in communication com. 1989-90, chmn. nat. pub. rels. com. 1990-91), Publ. Rels. Soc. Am., Okla. Bar Assn., Friends and Alumni of U. Okla. Sch. Journalism and Mass Communication (pres. 1989-90), Leadership Oklahoma City Alumni Assn. Episcopalian. Home: 8012 E Via Campo Scottsdale AZ 85258-2833 Office: Dial Corp 1850 N Central Ave Phoenix AZ 85004-4527

ADAMS, ANN LOUISE, publisher; b. Palestine, Tex., Nov. 17, 1934; d. Henry George and Ola Monteel (Goodin) Beard; m. J.G. Price, Mar. 15, 1956 (div. 1973); m. Mark Adams, May 12, 1979. BA, U. Tex., Austin, 1957. Proofreader Austin (Tex.) Am.-Statesman, 1960-67; typesetter Tulsa World, 1967-68, San Antonio Express-Light, 1970-73, Austin Am.-Statesman, 1973-77, Albuquerque Jour., 1977-78, Everett (Wash.) Herald, 1978-80; editor U. Okla. Press, Norman, Okla., 1968-70; freelance editor Everett and Oak Harbor, Wash., 1981--; pub. Packrat Press, Oak Harbor, 1981--; pub. cons. Wash. Pub. Utility Dists. Assn., Seattle, 1987-88; news clk. Whidbey News-Times, 1989—. Editor: The Clay Pedestal (Wash. Gov.'s award), 1981, Public. and Private Letters of Franklin Jones, Sr. (4 vols.), 1982-89; author: Travels With A Donkey, 1982; contbr. articles to various publs. Mem. Com. of Corr., Pandorans. Home and Office: Packrat Press 4366 N Hamilton Dr Oak Harbor WA 98277-9549

ADAMS, ANN MARIE, parasitologist, researcher; b. Omaha, Apr. 23, 1958. BS, U. Nebr., 1979, MS, 1981; PhD, U. Washington, 1988. Teaching asst. U. Nebr., Lincoln, 1980-81; rsch. and teaching asst. U. Washington, 1982-88, rsch. technologist, 1985-89, fellow, 1988-89, auxiliary faculty, 1992—; rsch. parasitologist seafood products rsch. ctr. U.S. Food & Drug Adminstrn., Seattle, 1989—; acting supr. Microanalytical Lab., 1993; scientific coord. ORA, 1992; task force regulatory levels of parasites in seafood, CFSAN, 1991. Reviewer for numerous jours. in field; contbr. articles to profl. jours. Acting supr. Microanalytical Lab., 1993; scientific coord. ORA, 1992; task force regulatory levels of parasites in seafood, CFSAN, 1991. Recipient Cuckler fellowship, 1980, Rogick Meml. award, 1980, faculty scholarship Sch. of Pub. Health, 1985, Arctic Inst. Am. grant, 1986. Mem. Am. Microscopical Soc., Am. Soc. Parasitologists (priorities com. 1993, 1994), Helminthological Soc. Washington, Pacific Northwest Bird and Mammal Soc., Pacific Fisheries Technologists, Soc. Marine Mammalogy, Soc. Systematic Zoology, Wildlife Disease Assn., Sigma Xi. Office: US Food & Drug Adminstrn PO Box 3012 22201 23rd Dr SE Bothell WA 98041

ADAMS, BERNARD SCHRODER, retired college president; b. Lancaster, Pa., July 20, 1928; s. Martin Ray and Charlotte (Schroder) A.; m. Natalie Virginia Stout, June 2, 1951; children: Deborah Rowland, David Schroder. B.A., Princeton, 1950; M.A., Yale, 1951; Ph.D., U. Pitts., 1964; LL.D. (hon.), Lawrence U., 1967; cert., Inst. for Ednl. Mgmt., Harvard U., 1975. Asst. dir. admissions, instr. English Princeton, 1953-57; dir. admissions and student aid U. Pitts., 1957-60, spl. asst. to chancellor, 1960-64; dean students, lectr. English Oberlin (Ohio) Coll., 1964-66; pres. Ripon (Wis.) Coll., 1966-85, Ft. Lewis Coll., Colo., 1985-87; ednl. cons. pvt. practice, Colo. Springs, 1987-88; v.p. resources Goodwill Industries, Colorado Springs, Colo., 1988-94; dir. Wis. Power & Light Co., Newton Funds, 1970-85; cons., examiner Commn. on Instns. Higher Edn., North Cen. Assn. Colls. and Secondary Schs., 1972-87, exec. commr., 1981-86; bd. dirs. Four Corners Opera Assn., 1985-87, pres., 1986-87. Contbr. articles to profl. jours. Bd. dirs. Keep Colo. Springs Beautiful, 1990—, Colo. chpt. Nat. Assn. Fundraising Execs., 1990—, Tradition of Excellence Found., 1991—, Colo. Springs Symphony Vols., 1992—, Domestic Violence Prevention Ctr., 1995—. 1st lt. USAF, 1951-53. Woodrow Wilson fellow, 1951. Mem. Assoc. Colls. Midwest (bd. dirs. 1966-85, pres. 1973-75), Wis. Assn. Ind. Colls. and Univs. (bd. dirs. 1966-85, pres. 1969-71, 83-85). Home: 90 Ellsworth St Colorado Springs CO 80906-7954

ADAMS, CHARLES FRANCIS, advertising and real estate executive; b. Detroit, Sept. 26, 1927; s. James R. and Bertha C. (DeChant) A.; m. Helen R. Harrell, Nov. 12, 1949; children: Charles Francis, Amy Ann, James Randolph, Patricia Duncan. BA, U. Mich., 1948; postgrad., U. Calif., Berkeley, 1949. With D'Arcy-MacManus & Masius, Inc., 1947-80, exec. v.p., dir., 1970-76, pres., chief operating officer, 1976-80; pres. Adams Enterprises, 1971—; exec. v.p., dir. Washington Office, Am. Assn. Advt. Agys., 1980-84; chmn., chief exec. officer Wajim Corp., Detroit; past mem. steering com. Nat. Advt. Rev. Bd.; mem. mktg. com. U.S. Info. Agy.; pres. Internat. Visitors Ctr. of the Bay Area, 1988-89. Author: Common Sense in Advertising, 1965, Heroes of the Golden Gate, 1987, California of the Year 2000, 1992, The Magnificent Rogues, 1994. Past chmn. exec. com. Oakland U. Mem. Am. Assn. Advt. Agys. (dir., mem. govt. relations com.), Advt. Fedn. Am. (past dir.), Nat. Outdoor Advt. Bur. (past chmn.), Theta Chi, Alpha Delta Sigma (hon.). Republican. Roman Catholic. Clubs: Bloomfield Hills Country; Carmel Valley Ranch (Calif.); Nat. Golf Links Am. (Southampton, L.I.); Olympic, The Family (San Francisco). Home: 2240 Hyde St San Francisco CA 94109-1509 also: 25450 Loma Robles Dr Carmel CA 93923-8409 Office: 10 W Long Lake Rd Bloomfield Hills MI 48304-2765

ADAMS, CLINTON, artist, historian; b. Glendale, Calif., Dec. 11, 1918; s. Merritt Cooley and Effie (Mackenzie) A.; m. Mary Elizabeth Atchison, Jan. 9, 1943; 1 child, Michael Gerald. Ed.B., UCLA, 1940, M.A., 1942. Instr. art UCLA, 1946-48, asst. prof., 1948-54; prof. art, head dept. U. Ky.; also dir. Art Gallery, 1954-57; prof. art, head dept. U. Fla., 1957-61; dean Coll. Fine Arts U. N.Mex., Albuquerque, 1961-76, asso. provost, dean faculties, 1976-77; dir. Tamarind Inst., 1970-85; asso. dir. Tamarind Lithography Workshop, Los Angeles, 1960-61, program cons., 1961-70. Represented in permanent collections Bklyn. Mus., Art. Inst. Chgo., Australian Nat. Gallery, Grunwald Center Graphic Arts, Mus. Modern Art, Los Angeles County Art Mus., and others; author: (with Garo Antreasian) The Tamarind Book of Lithography: Art and Techniques, 1970, Fritz Scholder: Lithographs, 1975, American Lithographers, 1900-1960: The Artists and Their Printers, 1983, (with others) Lasting Impressions: Lithography As Art, 1988, Printmaking in New Mexico, 1880-1990, 1991, Crayonstone: The Life and Work of Bolton Brown, 1993; editor The Tamarind Papers, 1974-95; subject: bibliography Clinton Adams: Paintings and Watercolors 1945-87; exhbn. catalogue Albuquerque: University of New Mexico Art Mus., 1987; biography A Spectrum of Innovation: Color in American Printmaking, 1890-1990, 1990. Recipient Gov.'s award for outstanding contbns. to arts of N.Mex., 1985. Mem. NAD (academician), Coll. Art Assn. (program chmn. 1963), Nat. Coun. Fine Arts Deans (chmn. 1965-67), Mid-Am. Coll. Art Assn. (pres. 1973). Home: 1917 Morningside Dr NE Albuquerque NM 87110-4927

ADAMS, DUNCAN MACLEOD, writer, psychotherapist; b. Roanoke, Va., Aug. 5, 1954; s. William Duval and Nancy Ovid (Macleod) A.; m. Deborah Kaye Williams Kytchen, Aug. 23, 1974 (div. Nov. 1981); m. Cynthia Riechert Perkins, Nov. 19, 1992; 1 child, William Macleod; 1 stepchild, Aaron Farrington. BA, U. Va., 1976; MEd, James Madison U., 1982; MA in Journalism, Northeastern U., Boston, 1989. Lic. clin. profl. counselor. Counselor Patrick Henry C.C., Martinsville, Va., 1982-83; mental health tech. Rockingham Meml. Hosp., Harrisonburg, Va., 1983-85; milieu therapist Human Resource Inst., Brookline, Mass., 1985-86; psychotherapist The Clearview Ctr., Tyngsboro, Mass., 1986-88; reporter The Beacon, Acton, Mass., 1988-89; asst. editor The Somerville (Mass.) Jour., 1989-90; reporter The Mont. Std., Butte, 1990-92; free-lance writer Anaconda, Mont., 1992—; creative writing tchr. Copper Village Mus. and Arts Ctr., Anaconda, 1993, bd. sec., 1993—, Mont. Tech. Continuing Edn., Butte, 1993. Vol. counselor Martinsville Mental Health, 1982-83. Recipient 1st pl. best serious column Mont. Newspaper Assn., 1992, 1st pl. best spot news coverage, 1992; named Conservation Communicator of Yr. Mont. Wildlife Fedn., 1992. Mem. Am. Counseling Assn., Am. Mental Health Coun. Assn., Mont. Clin. Mental Health Coun. Assn. Democrat. Home: Echo Lake Rd PO Box 1384 Anaconda MT 59711 Office: PO Box 1384 Anaconda MT 59711

ADAMS, FRANK STEWART, family service agency director, pastor/chaplain; b. Ludlow, Mass., Mar. 16, 1944; s. Leon S. and Alice G. (Bell) A.; m. Suzan Y. Blocker, Apr. 17, 1993; children: Rochelle, Matthew, Ashlee. BS in Nuclear Engring., U. Mo., Rolla, 1962; MDiv, Weston Sch. Theology, Cambridge, Mass., 1980; M in Devel. Psychology, Jesuit Sch. Theology, Berkeley, Calif., 1982; PhD, Ohio State U., 1985. Quality assurance inspection engr. U.S. Indsl. Chem. Co., Tuscola, Ill., 1966-69; project quality assurance engr. Gilbert Assocs., Reading, Pa., 1969-71; quality control supt. Monsanto, Joliet, Ill., 1971; pastor, tchr. Mo. Prov. Edn. Inst., St. Louis, 1972-81, 85-90; grad. asst. Ohio State U., Columbus, 1982-85; supt. schs., pastor St. Francis X, Corozal, Belize, 1990-91; pvt. practice counselor Aurora, Colo., 1992; instr. Met. State Coll., Denver, 1992; area dir. Luth. Family Svcs., Ft. Collins, Colo., 1992—; engring. cons., Reading, 1969-72; domestic violence counselor, 1991-92; chaplain Hospice of Larimer County, Ft. Collins, 1993—. Author: Technical-Ethical Aspects of Nuclear Power Debate, 1979; monthly columnist Belize Diocesan Paper, 1991-92. Home: 3225 Killdeer Dr Fort Collins CO 80526-2831 Office: Lutheran Family Svcs 503 Remington St Fort Collins CO 80524-3022

ADAMS, FREDERICK MARSHALL, mathematical educator; b. Durham, N.C., Nov. 25, 1943; s. E. Clark and Frances Marshall A.; m. Sheila Anne Wloff, June 14, 1975 (div. Sept. 1982). Student, U. Fla., 1962-64; BSBA, U. Ariz., 1967; postgrad., San Jose State U., 1970. Labor negotiator Kaiser Inds., Lucerne Valley, Calif., 1967-70; educator math. East Side Union High Sch. Dist., San Jose, Calif., 1970—; travel agt. Ind. Travel Cons., San Jose, Calif., 1994—; mentor East Side Union High Sch., 1986, 90-93. Author: Math A, 1992. Mem. NEA (rep., del. 1991-92), Calif. Tchrs. Assn. (state rep. 1982-92), East Side Tchrs. Assn. (exec. bd. dirs. 1978-92, labor negotiator 1982-87). Home: 6944 Avenida Rotella San Jose CA 95139-1109 Office: Ind Travel Cons 1361 S Winchester Blvd Ste 109 San Jose CA 95128-4328

ADAMS, HEIDI-CHRISTA, counselor; b. Ludwigsburg, Germany, Oct. 5, 1953; came to U.S., 1956; d. Gustav and Anna Elisabeth (Pfeffer) Rieger; m. Daniel Mark Adams, Aug. 17, 1981; 1 child, Anngela Christina. BS in Edn., U. Wis., Whitewater, 1976; MS in Edn. Psychology, U. Wis., Milw., 1980. German, French, Spanish tchr. Oshkosh (Wis.) Middle Sch., 1976-77; German, French tchr. Wauwatosa (Wis.) H.S., 1977-80; counselor Valley Luth. H.S., Phoenix, 1981-84, Chandler (Ariz.) H.S., 1984-92, Mesa (Ariz.) C.C., 1992—; creator peervention program Mesa C.C., 1992—. Author: Peervention, 1994, Eliminating Self-Defeating Behaviors, 1994, Celebrate Multicultural Diversity Through Classroom Climate, 1991. Ariz. Dept. Edn. Consortium grantee Fund for the Improvement of Postsecondary End., 1994; recipient Educator award Ariz. Am. Legion Womens Aux., 1990, Mathew B. Juan award, 1989, Future Farmers Assn. award, 1990. Mem. Am. Counseling Assn., Am. Sch. Counselor Assn., Phi Kappa Phi. Office: Mesa CC 1833 W Southern Ave Mesa AZ 85202

ADAMS, JACK, film company executive, screenwriter, producer, educator; b. Lakehurst, N.J., Sept. 15, 1952; s. John Carey and Dorothy Jeanne (Conover) A.; m. Shirley Janulewicz, June 28, 1975; children: Carey Miller, Chanine Angelina, Mikael Walter, Jozef Conover. MusB in Music Edn., U. Del., 1974. Pres. Koala Studio, Valencia, Calif., 1977—; v.p. devel. Unifilms, Inc., North Hollywood, Calif., 1984—; instr. film, TV writing and script analysis Coll. of Canyons, Valencia, 1988—, L.A. City Coll., 1989—, EveryWoman's Village, Van Nuys, Calif., 1990—, Info. Exch., L.A., 1990—, Learning Tree U., Chatsworth, Calif., 1990—, U. Wis., Madison, 1991—, U. Hawaii, 1992—, USIA, Washington, 1991—, Info. Network, South Pasadena, Calif., 1990—, Moorpark Coll., 1991—, Oxnard Coll., 1991—, Northwestern U., Evanston, Ill., 1991—, Glendale (Calif.) Community Coll., 1991—; co-founder ScripTip, 1990, Classes Unlimited, 1992—, Johnson County Community Coll., Kansas City, 1993, Univ. Wis., Milwaukee, 1993, Irvine (Calif.) Valley Coll., 1992—, Shenandoah Valley Writer's Guild, Front

Royal, Va., 1993—, Rancho Santiago Coll., Santa Ana, Calif., 1993—, Orange Coast Coll., Costa Mesa, Calif., 1993—; script cons. Wis. Screenwriters Forum; mem. KNX Speakers Bur., CBS Radio, 1989—, Story Bd. Devel. Group, Paramount Studios, 1989—; pres. NBC Writers Workshop; mem. Larry Wilson Devel. Workshop, Paramount Studios, Le Group, Paramount Studios; founding mem., officer, bd. dirs. L.A. Filmmakers Workshop, 1989-91; founder Santa Clarita Scriptwriters Workshop, Writers Anonymous, 1988; pres. Entertainment Writers' Workshop, 1990, Adams Entertainment, 1993; ptnr. Flying Cow, 1994; mem. Ind. Feature Project West; presenter numerous seminars and workshops. Composer (film) Eat, 1980 (Filmex award 1981, best short film award Cinemagic mag. 1981); writer, co-creator sitcom pilot Lola, Universal Studios, 1991; writer, developer sitcom pilot Fat Farm; writer, producer, dir. sitcom pilot Box # 22; line producer sitcom pilots Zebra, It's Not My Fault; creator: Screenwriting Warriors: Basic Training, 1988; columnist: Creative Screenwriting Mag., 1994—; TV editor Freelance Screenwriters' Forum Newsletter; columnist ScreenWrite Now mag.; creator (audiotapes) Top 50 Script Marketing Tips, Get An Agent to Sell Your Script, Write To Get Past the Script Reader, Pitch Your Film and Television Projects. Mem. Indian Guides/Princesses Program, chief Apache tribe YMCA, 1990—, produce annuel haunted house fundraiser for Santa Clarita Family YMCA, 1992, participate in annual fundraising campaign, 1990, Am. Youth Soccor Orgn. AYSO, 1988. Mem. Am. Film Inst. (alumni assn. writers workshop), Scriptwriters Network (bd. advisors), Film Artists Network, Ind. Writers So. Calif. Scriptwriters Caucus, Assn. Info. Systems Profls. (bd. dirs. 1983), Freelance Screenwriter's Forum (founding), Comedy Writers Co-op (founding ABC), Wis. Screenwriters Forum (advisor 1989—). Home and Office: 22931 Sycamore Creek Dr Santa Clarita CA 91354-2050

ADAMS, JAMES FREDERICK, psychologist, educational administrator; b. Andong, Korea, Dec. 27, 1927; s. Benjamin Nyce and Phyllis Irene (Taylor) A.; m. Carol Ann Wagner, Jan. 17, 1980; children—James Edward, Dorothy Lee Adams Vanderhorst, Robert Benjamin. B.A. In Psychology, U. Calif.-Berkeley, 1950; Ed.M. in Counseling and Psychology, Temple U., 1951; Ph.D. in Exptl. Psychology, Wash. State U., 1959. Cert. psychologist, Wash., Pa.; lic. psychologist, Pa. Psychometrician Measurement and Research Ctr., Temple U., Phila., 1951-52; asst. prof. psychology Whitworth Coll., Spokane, Wash., 1952-55; teaching and research asst. State U. Wash., 1955-57; research assoc. Miami U., Oxford, Ohio, 1957-59; asst. prof. psychology Coll. Liberal Arts, Temple U., 1959-62, assoc. prof., 1962-66, prof., 1966-80, chmn. dept. counseling psychology, 1969-72; vis. prof. psychology Coll. Soc. Scis., U. P.R., Rio Piedras, 1963-64, Coll. Scis., Cath. U., Ponce, P.R., 1971-72; chmn. dept. counseling psychology Coll. Edn., Temple U., 1973-77, coordinator div. ednl. psychology, 1974-76; grad. dean, prof. psychology Grad. Coll., U. Nev., Las Vegas, 1980-85; acad. (sr.) v.p. Longwood Coll., Farmville, Va., 1985-86. Author: Problems in Counseling: A Case Study Approach, 1962, Instructors Manual for Understanding Adolescence, 1969; (exhbn. catalogue with J. D. Selig) Colonial Spanish Art of the Americas, 1976; (comml. pamphlet with C. L. Davis) The Use of the Vu-graph as an Instructional Aid, 1960; editor: Counseling and Guidance: A Summary View, 1965, Understanding Adolescence: Current Developments in Adolescent Psychology, 1968, 4th edit., 1980, Human Behavior in a Changing Society, 1973, Songs that had to be Sung (by B. N. Adams), 1979; contbr. chpts., articles, tests and book revs. to profl. publs. Served to cpl. USMC, 1945-46. Recipient Alexander Meiklejohn award AAUP, 1984; James McKean Cattell research fund grantee Miami U., Oxford, Ohio, 1958, Bolton fund research grantee Temple U., 1960, 62, faculty research grantee Temple U., 1961, 63, Commonwealth of Pa. research grantee Temple U., 1969, 70, 71, 72, summer research fellow Temple U., 1979; recipient scholarship U. Munich, 1955. Fellow Am. Psychol. Assn. (divs. 26, 17); mem. Eastern Psychol. Assn., Western Psychol. Assn., Interam. Soc. Psychology, Sigma Xi, Psi Chi. Home: 130 Palacio Rd Corrales NM 87048-9648

ADAMS, JAMES RUSSELL, semiconductor electronics company executive; b. North Platte, Nebr., Apr. 10, 1945; s. George Howard and Verle Margaret (Kinnan) A.; m. Judy Ann Killham, June 18, 1967; 1 child, Janelle. BSEE, U. Nebr., 1967, MSEE, 1969, PhD in Elec. Engring., 1974. Mem. tech. staff Sandia Nat. Labs., Albuquerque, 1969-79; mgr. product tech. devel. Inmos Corp., Colorado Springs, Colo., 1979-83, v.p. quality and reliability, 1983-85; v.p. R & D Triad Semiconductors, BV, Colorado Springs, 1985-86; dir. advanced tech. devel. Monolithic Memories, Inc., Santa Clara, Calif., 1986-87; mgr. tech. programs United Techs. Microelectronics, Colorado Springs, 1987-88, dir. strategic planning, 1988-93; v.p. engring. Intellectual Property Cons., Inc., Colorado Springs, 1993—. Contbr. 24 articles to profl. jours.; 4 patents in field. Recipient TOBIE award for Best R & D Achievement Electronics-UK, 1981. Mem. IEEE (sr., best paper award GOMAC conf. 1978), Electrochem. Soc., Sigma Xi, Eta Kappa Nu, Sigma Tau.

ADAMS, JEANNE CLARE, computer scientist; b. Utica, N.Y., June 15, 1921; d. Charles W. and Rose C. (Struve) Clare; children: Clare, Douglas, Samuel. BA, U. Mich., 1943; MA, U. Colo., 1979. With Nat. Ctr. for Atmospher Rsch., Boulder, Colo., 1960-82, various mgnt. positions, 1960-75; mgr. user svcs. and planning Nat. Ctr. for Atmospher Rsch., Boulder, 1975-82, mem. computational support group, 1985—; CYBER 205 project coord., mgr. sys. Inst. for Computational Studies, Colo. State U., 1982-84; chair and convenor Internat. Fortran Experts under ISO, 1977-85; chair fortran stds. com. X3J3 Am. NAt. Stds. Orgn., 1977-92. Author: Programmers Guide to Fortran 90, 1990, Fortran 90 Handbook, 1992, Fortran Top 90, 1994; mem. editorial bd. Computer Standards and Interfaces; contbr. numerous articles to profl. jours. Mem. Assn. for Computing Machinery, Am. Nat. Stds. Orgn., Internat. Stds. Orgn. Office: Nat Ctr Atmospheric Rsch PO Box 3000 Boulder CO 80309

ADAMS, JO-ANN MARIE, data processing consultant; b. L.A., May 27, 1949; d. Joseph John and Georgia S. (Wein) A.; AA, Pasadena City Coll., 1968; BA, Pomona Coll., 1970; MA, Calif. State U., L.A., 1971; MBA, Pacific Luth. U., 1983; cert. in Telecomm. and Info. Resource Mgmt., U. Hawaii, 1993; postgrad. Santa Clara U., 1993—. Secondary tchr. South Pasadena (Calif.) Unified Schs., 1970-71; appraiser Riverside County (Calif.) Assessor's Office, 1972-74; systems and procedures analyst Riverside County Data Processing Dept., 1974-76, supervising systems analyst, 1976-79; systems analyst computer Boeing Computer Svcs. Co., Seattle, 1979-81; sr. systems analyst Thurston County Central Svcs., Olympia, Wash., 1981-83, data processing systems mgr., 1983-84; data processing systems engr. IBM Corp., 1984-87; realtor-assoc., Dower Realty, 1987-92; corp. sales rep. UniGlobe Met. Travel, 1988-89; project mgr. Servco Pacific, 1989-90, Scott Software Systems, 1990-91; systems analyst Dept. Atty. Gen., 1991-93; cons. in field, 1993—; law clerk Law Offices Thomas R. Hagan, 1995—; instr. Riverside City Coll., 1977-79. Chairperson legis. task force Riverside/San Bernardino chpt. NOW, 1975-76, chpt. co-chairperson, 1978; mem. ethics com. Calif. NOW Inc., 1978; alt. del. Calif Dem. Caucus, 1978. Mem. NAFE, Pomona Coll. Alumni Assn. Home: 18415 Purdue Dr Saratoga CA 95070-4712

ADAMS, JOHN ANDREW, physicist, engineering company executive; b. Cin., Feb. 15, 1946; s. John Andrew and Joan Loretta (Rasfeld) A.; m. Sally Ann Howard, June 6, 1969; children: John Michael and Sarah Louise (twins). BS in Physics, U. San Diego, 1968; PhD in Physics, Ariz. State U., Tempe, 1978. Project mgr., staff sr. scientist IRT Corp., San Diego, 1978-81, mgr. logging svcs., 1981-84, mgr. tech. devel., 1984-86; co-founder, chief scientist Four Pi Systems, San Diego, 1986-94, chief scientist, dir. engring., 1991-94; chief scientist Athens Corp., Oceanside, Calif., 1994—. Patentee automated laminography, automated inspections. With USN, 1969-73. Recipient IR100 award R&D Mag., 1984. Mem. Inst. Interconnecting and Packaging Electronic Circuits.

ADAMS, JOHN M., library director; b. Chicago, Ill., June 10, 1950; s. Merlin J. and Esther (Bohn) A.; m. Nancy Ileen Coultas, June 12, 1970; 1 child, Arwen Lee. B.A. in English, U. Ill., 1972, M.L.S., 1973. Grad. asst. U. Ill. Libr., Urbana, 1972-73; libr.-reference Sherman Oaks Libr., L.A., 1973-75; libr. philosophy dept. L.A. Pub. Libr., 1975-77, head gen. reading svc., 1977-78; dir. Moline Pub. Libr., Ill., 1978-83, Tampa (Fla.)-Hillsborough County Pub. Libr. System, 1983-91; dir., county librarian Orange County (Calif.) Public Library System, 1991—; dir. Tampa Bay Libr. Con- [illegible] Santiago Libr. Sys., 1991—; mem. adv. com. on pub. libr. OCLC, 1992-95. Contbr. articles to profl. jours. Bd. dirs. Planned Parenthood of Tampa, 1984. Recipient Frontier award ALA Mag., 1981; named Outstanding Young Man, Moline Jaycees, 1983. Mem. ALA (J.C. Dana award 1982, 93), Calif. Libr. Assn., Calif. County Librs. Assn., Orange County C. of C. Office: Orange County Pub Libr 1501 E Saint Andrew Pl Santa Ana CA 92705-4930

ADAMS, JOHN PHILLIPS, JR., economics educator, forensic economics consultant; b. Dothan, Ala., June 29, 1920; s. John Phillips Sr. and Lucile (Brown) A.; m. Flavienne Marcelle David, Dec. 5, 1946; children: Gilles David, Sidney Michel. Student Ga. Sch. Tech., 1939-43, U. S.C., 1964-65; M.A., Claremont Grad. Sch., 1968, Ph.D., 1972. Commd. 2d lt. U.S. Army, 1943, advanced through grades to lt. col., 1963, ret., 1963; lectr. econs. Calif. State Poly. U., Pomona, 1968-70; prof. econs., Calif. Poly. State U., San Luis Obispo, 1970-90; prof. emeritus, 1990—; trustee Calif. Council on Econ. Edn., 1972-78; forensic econs. cons., San Luis Obispo, 1976—. Pres. Calif. Cen. Coast chpt. Mended Hearts, Inc., Arroyo Grande, 1983-84. Mem. Am. Econ. Assn., Am. Rehab. Econs. Assn. (exec. bd. dirs. 1992-94), Western Econ. Assn. Internat., Atlantic Econ. Soc., Western Soc. Scis. Assn., Nat. Assn. Forensic Economists (charter mem., West regional dir. 1986-87, v.p. 1988-92, pres. 1995—), Nat. Acad. Econ. Arbitrators (charter mem., bd. dirs. 1989—), Nat. Assn. Uniform Svcs. (life), Am. Acad. Econ. and Fin. Experts, Ret. Officers Assn. (life), White Sands Pioneer Group (life), Aircraft Owners and Pilots Assn., Omicron Delta Epsilon, Delta Sigma Pi, Alpha Tau Omega. Home: 2000 Wilding Ln San Luis Obispo CA 93401-3049 Office: Calif Poly State U Coll of Bus San Luis Obispo CA 93407

ADAMS, KEN R., marketing professional, historian; b. Carson City, Nev., Sept. 8, 1942; s. Maurice Adams and Gertrude Aloha (Wilson) Burke; m. Maria C. Saldavia, Mar. 15, 1971; 1 child, John Anthony. Prin. Ken Adams and Assoc., Sparks, Nev., 1990—; coord. gaming history series of the oral history program U. Nev., continuing edns. hotel gaming program adv. com., 1988, chmn., 1988. Co-author: Playing the Cards That Are Dealt, 1992, Always Bet on the Butcher, 1994; publ., assoc. editor: Nev. Gaming Almanac, 1991-94, Nev. Gaming Directory, 1993-94, Adams' Report. Chmn. mktg. com. Downtown Renovation Assn., 1994—; steering com., chmn. gaming com. Festival Reno, 1984-86. With U.S. Army, 1960-63. Mem. Nat. Speakers Assn., Speakers Bur. Gaming Industry Assn. Home and Office: Ken Adams and Assoc 5370 Point View Way Sparks NV 89431-1019

ADAMS, LILIANA OSSES, music performer, harpist; b. Poznan, Poland, May 16, 1939; came to U.S., 1978; d. Sylwester and Helena (Koswenda) O.; m. Edmund Pietryk, Sept. 4, 1965 (div. Aug. 1970); m. Bruce Meredith Adams, Feb. 3, 1978. MA, Music Acad. Poznan, Poland, 1971. Prin. harpist Philharm. Orch. of Szczecin, Poland, 1964-72, Imperial Opera and Ballet Orch., Tehran, Iran, 1972-78; pvt. music tchr. Riyadh, Saudi Arabia, 1979-81; soloist Austrian Radio, 1981-86; solo harpist, pvt. tchr. harp and piano Antioch, Calif., 1986—; music cons. Schs. and Librs., Calif., 1991—. Contbr. articles to profl. jours. Mem. Am. Fedn. of Musicians, Am. Harp Soc., Internat. Soc. of Harpers, U.K. Harp. Assn., Internat. Harp Ctr. (Switzerland). Home: PO Box 233 Antioch CA 94509-0023

ADAMS, LINDA ALCORN, telecommunications policy professional; b. L.A., Feb. 28, 1943; d. William Fort and Marilynne (Dalton) Alcorn; m. Judd Noah Adams, Sept. 26, 1964; 1 child, Julisa Danae. BA, UCLA, 1966; MA, Sangamon State U., Springfield, Ill., 1975. Adminstrv. asst. U. Calif. Santa Barbara Alumni Office, 1967-70; grad. student advisor UCLA Sch. Architecture and Urban Planning, 1970-72; program analyst Econ. and Fiscal Commn., Springfield, 1972-75; dir. program rev. and investigation Conn. Gen. Assembly, Hartford, 1975-79; dir. adminstrn. and fin. Nat. Conf. State Legislatures, Denver, 1979-83; govt. affairs dir. AT&T, Denver, 1983—; mem. exe. com. Nat. Conf. State Legislatures, Denver, 1977-79; bd. dirs. Wyo. Taxpayers Assn., Cheyenne, 1990—, Found. for State Legislatures, Denver, 1986—; pres. State Govt. Affairs Coun., Washington, 1992-93. Named to Outstanding young Women of Am., 1978. Mem. N.Am. Trail Ride Conf. (nat. championship 1988), Boulder County Horsemen's Assn. (bd. dirs.). Democrat. Home and Office: 179 Cordova Ct Boulder CO 80303-4906

ADAMS, LISA KAY, artist; b. Bristol, Pa., Aug. 3, 1955; d. Charles Joseph Jr. and Liese-Lotte (Leiss) Adams. Student, U. Heidelberg, West Germany, 1976; BA, Scripps Coll., Claremont, Calif., 1977; MFA, Claremont Grad. Sch., 1980. Exhibited in one-person shows at Newspace, L.A., 1989, 90, 92, 93, Daniel Maher Gallery, L.A., 1991, Century Gallery, Sylmar, Calif., 1992, William Turner Gallery, Venice, Calif., 1994, Coll. So. Nev., North Las Vegas, 1995; group shows include U. Calif., Irvine, Soho Ctr. for Visual Arts, N.Y.C., East Hawaii Cultural Ctr., Hilo, Santa Monica (Calif.) Art Complex, L.A. Mcpl. Art Gallery, Lanning Gallery, Houston, Dorothy Goldeen Gallery, Santa Monica, Calif., William Turner Gallery, Venice, Calif.; represented in permanent collections at Aratex, Burbank, Calif., Laguna Mus. of Art, Laguna Beach, Calif., Nippon Steel USA Inc., L.A.; also pvt. collections. Artist's rep. Laraba, L.A., 1994-95; bd. mem. Side St. Projects, 1994-95. Brody Arts Fund fellow, 1992. Mem. L.A. Contemporary Exhbns. Home and Office: 2118 E 7th Pl Los Angeles CA 90021-1762

ADAMS, LYNN DONELLE, pet sitting company executive; b. Wichita, Kans., Apr. 26, 1957; d. George Adams and Bonnie Jo (Lambert) Walker. BBA, U. Tex., 1978, MBA, 1980. Nat. acct. mgr. AT&T, Houston, 1981-82, systems mgr., 1983-84; regional sales support mgr. AT&T, San Francisco, 1985-86; strategy devel. mgr. mktg. AT&T, Basking Ridge, N.Y., 1987-88, exec. asst., 1989-90; product mgr. AT&T, Bedminster, N.Y., 1990-91; pres. Lynn Adams Communications Inc., Pacific Palisades, Calif., 1992-93, Feline Friends & Canine Companions, Pacific Palisades, Calif., 1994—. Mem. NAt. Assn. Profl. PEt Sitters, Nat. Assn. Info. Svcs., PAcific Palisades C of C., Malibu C. of C., Santa Monica C. of C. Office: Feline Friends & Canine Companions 17374 Sunset Blvd Ste 250 Pacific Palisades CA 90272

ADAMS, MARGARET BERNICE, retired museum official; b. Toronto, Ont., Can., Apr. 29, 1936; came to U.S., 1948, naturalized, 1952; d. Robert Russell and Kathleen Olive (Buffin) A.; m. Alberto Enrique Sánchez-Quiñonez, Nov. 30, 1956 (div. 1960). AA, Monterey Peninsula Coll., 1969; BA, San Jose State U., 1971; MA, U. Utah, 1972. Curator ethnic arts Civic Art Gallery, San Jose, 1971; staff asst. Utah Mus. Fine Arts, Salt Lake City, 1972; lectr./curator Coll. Seven, U. Calif., Santa Cruz, 1972-74; part-time educator Cabrillo Coll., Aptos, Calif., 1973, Monterey Peninsula Coll., 1973-84; dir. U.S. Army Mus., Presidio of Monterey, 1974-83; chief. mus. br. Ft. Ord Mil. Complex, 1983-88; Guest curator Am. Indian arts Monterey Peninsula Mus. Art, 1975-88. Author: Indian Tribes of North America and Chronology of World Events in Prehistoric Pueblo Times, 1975, Historic Old Monterey, 1976; cntbg. editor Indian Am., (exhibit catalogue) Writing on the Wall: WWII Patriotic Posters, 1987; contbr. articles to jours. Mem. native Am. adv. panel AAAS, Washington, 1972-78; mem. rev. and adv. com. Project Media, Nat. Indian Edn. Assn., Mpls., 1973-78; working mem. Program for Tng. Am. Indian Counsellors in Alcoholism Counselling and Rehab. Programs, 1972-74; mem. hist. adv. com. Montery County Bd. Suprs., 1987-89. Grad. fellow, dean's scholar U. Utah, 1972; dean's scholar Monterey (Calif.) Peninsula Coll., 1969, San Jose (Calif.) State U., 1971. Mem. Am. Anthrop. Assn., Am. Assn. Museums, Soc. for Applied Anthropology, Soc. Am. Archeology, Am. Ethnol. Soc., Nat., Calif., Indian edn. assns. Home: 1000 Pacific Grove Ln Apt 7 Pacific Grove CA 93950-3831

ADAMS, MARK, artist; b. Ft. Plain, N.Y., Oct. 27, 1925; s. Earl D. and Edith (Wohlgemuth) A.; m. Beth Van Hoesen, Sept. 12, 1953. Student, Syracuse U., 1943-46, Hans Hofmann Sch. Fine Arts, 1946, 48, Jean Lurcat, 1955. Instr. San Francisco Art Inst., 1961; panelist Internat. Symposium on Tapestry, San Francisco, 1976; disting. vis. prof. U. Calif. at Davis, 1978; painter in residence Am. Acad. in Rome, 1963. Book: Mark Adams, 1985; one-man shows include deYoung Mus., San Francisco, 1959, Portland (Oreg.) Mus., 1961, Calif. Palace of Legion of Honor, San Francisco, 1961, retrospective, 1970, San Francisco Mus. Modern Art, 1962, French & Co., N.Y.C., 1964, John Berggruen Gallery, San Francisco, 1978, 80, 82, 83, 85, 87, 90, 94, Graham Modern, N.Y.C., 1981, 84, Jane Haslem Salon, Washington, 1989, Palo Alto (Calif.) Cultural Ctr., 1990; exhibited in numerous group shows including Mus. Contemporary Crafts, N.Y.C., 1957, 58, 62, 65, Dallas Mus., 1958, Internat. Biennial of Tapestry, Lausanne, Switzerland, 1962, 65, St. Louis Art Mus., 1964, Norfolk Mus., 1966; represented in permanent collections San Francisco Mus. Modern Art, Dallas Mus. Fine Arts, Chase Manhattan Bank, N.Y.C., San Francisco Pub. Library, Legion of Honor Mus., San Francisco; maj. archtl. commns. include tapestries, Bank of Calif., San Francisco, Weyerhauser Co., Tacoma, Wash., Fairmont Hotel, Dallas, San Francisco Internat. Airport, Luth. Brotherhood, Mpls., stained glass, Temple Emanu-el, San Francisco, St. Thomas More Cath. Ch., San Francisco, St. Andrews Episcopal Ch., Saratoga, Calif. Office: care John Berggruen Gallery 228 Grant Ave San Francisco CA 94108-4612

ADAMS, MARY ELIZABETH, counselor, psychotherapist, writer; b. Washington, Iowa, Oct. 22, 1920; d. Arthur Ernest and Annabelle (Marshall) Atchison; m. Clinton Adams, Jan. 9, 1943; 1 child, Michael Gerald. BA, UCLA, 1943; MA, U. N.Mex., 1978. Cert. counselor, Nat. Bd. Cert. Counselors; lic. profl. clin. counselor N.Mex. Counseling and Therapy Practice Bd. Sec., adminstrv. asst. USAF, Colorado, N.Y., 1943-46; tchr. L.A. Pub. Schs., 1946-50; sec., bur. bus. econ. rsch. UCLA, 1951-53; asst. to dir. J. Paul Getty Mus., Malibu, Calif., 1954; news reporter Radio WLAP/UPress, Lexington, Ky., 1955-57; adminstrv. asst. mgmt. sci. rsch. UCLA, 1960-62; editor U. N.Mex. Press, Albuquerque, 1962-68, mng. editor N.Mex. Quarterly, 1965-68, acting dir., 1967; resource developer HELP, N.Mex., 1969-78; counselor/therapist med. sch. U. N.Mex., Albuquerque, 1978-88; pvt. practice Albuquerque, 1981—; cons. The Ford Found., Colo., N.Mex., Tex., 1977-82. Freelance editor, 1978—; contbr. articles to profl. jours., periodicals, books. Active Friends of Art, Albuquerque, 1962—; vol. counselor Cmty. Mental Health Ctrs., Albuquerque, 1978—; bd. dirs. Albuquerque Symphony, 1962-63, Friends of Dance, Albuquerque, 1990-95. Mem. Am. Counseling Assn., Nat. Cert. Clin. Mental Health Counselors Assn., N.Mex. Counseling Assn., N.Mex. Clin. Mental Health Counselors Assn. Democrat. Home: 1917 Morningside Dr NE Albuquerque NM 87110-4927

ADAMS, MICHAEL CHRISTOPHER, counselor; b. Dallas, Mar. 7, 1965; s. Lloyd Ray and Janet Faye (Kirby) A.; m. Melissa Ann Jones, May 24, 1986 (dec. June 1988). AS, Lon Morris Coll., 1985; BS, Southwestern U., 1987; MS, St. Mary's U., 1990. Lic. profl. counselor, Colo. Pastor United Meth. Ch., Tex., 1983-87; social worker Four Seasons, San Antonio, 1988-90; proprietor Life-Care Concepts, S. Tex., 1989-91; counselor PPMHC/First Choice/CFMT, Colorado Springs, 1991-95; cons., trainer Davison and Shipp, Colorado Springs, 1994; pvt. practice Monument, Colo., 1995—; researcher, Colorado Springs, 1994. Co-founder Mu Lambda Chi, Jacksonville, Tex., 1983; vol. Am. Cancer Soc., San Antonio, 1989; vol., coach Colorado Springs Parks & Recreation, 1993. Recipient Ministerial award Beulla-Alice Blackwell Awards, 1984, 85. Mem. Am. Counseling Assn., Am. Assn. Testing and Assessment. Office: M C Adams P O Box 1622 Monument CO 80132

ADAMS, PHILIP, lawyer; b. Los Angeles, July 18, 1905; s. Thaddeus Lafayette and Lena (Kelly) A.; m. Alice Rahman, 1933; children: Stephen, Judith, Deborah, Kate; m. Elaine Margaret Anderson, 1968. Student, Pomona Coll., 1924-27; JD, Hastings Coll. Law, U. Calif., 1938; LLD (hon.), Ch. Div. Sch. of Pacific, Berkeley, Calif., 1965. Bar: Calif. 1938. Purser Panama Mail S.S. Line, 1928-29; profl. investigator, 1930-38; individual practice law San Francisco, 1938—; atty. U.S. Govt., 1942-46; instr. domestic relations Golden Gate Law Sch., 1971-72. Author: Adoption Practice in California, 1956. Dir. Children's Protective Soc., 1939-44, United Cerebral Palsy Assn., San Francisco, 1952-72, Assn. Mental Health, 1952—, United Bay Area Crusade, 1955-61, United Community Fund, San Francisco,1957-62, San Francisco State Coll., 1964-69; trustee Ch. Divinity Sch. of Pacific, 1951-76; nat. v.p. Episcopal Evang. Fellowship, 1952-61; chancellor Episcopal Diocese Calif., 1960-67; dep. Episcopal Gen. Conv., 1946-70; trustee Grad. Theol. Union, Berkeley, 1959-66, pres. bd., 1963-66. Fellow Am. Acad. Matrimonial Lawyers (dir. No. Calif. chpt. 1968—), Acad. Calif. Adoption Lawyers (dir. 1988—); mem. ABA (chmn. com. on adoption, family law sect. 1959-60), Calif., San Francisco Bar Assn., Lawyers Club San Francisco (gov. 1956), San Francisco Symphony Assn., Chamber Soloists San Francisco (dir. 1985—), Soc. Genealogists (London). Clubs: Villa Taverna, Commonwealth. Home: 2170 Jackson St San Francisco CA 94115-1550 Office: 220 Montgomery St San Francisco CA 94104-3402

ADAMS, QUENTIN JOHN, construction engineering analyst. Student, Mich. State U., Ill. Inst. of Tech. Asst. to the project mgr. Bertrum Goldberg, AIA, Chgo., 1957-60; pres. Environmental Dynamics, Inc., Washington, 1960-73; project mgr. Blue Ridge Investment Trust, Alexandria, Va., 1974-75; cons. Washington, 1975-80; project mgr., coord./tech. integrator Robert Starkovich, AIA, Phoenix, 1980-84; cons. project mgr., coord./tech. integrator Energy Res., Inc., Phoenix, 1984-86; pres., prin. Earth Resources Tech. Svcs., Phoenix, 1986—; spkr. U. Ala., Tuscaloosa, 1995, among others. Contbr. articles to profl. publs. Mem. Am. Cogeneration Assn., Ocean Energy Coun., SunSat Energy Coun., Internat. Assn. for Hydrogen Energy, World Future Soc.

ADAMS, RICHARD, electro-mechanical engineer; b. Wichita, Kans., Nov. 15, 1944; s. M. Lewis and G. Juliette (Barton) A. Student in bus., Phoenix Coll.; student in electronics, Electronic Tech. Coll. Tech. rep. Unicopy Inc., Phoenix; electro-mech. engr. Savin Inc., Phoenix; owner Adams' Solarwerks, Phoenix, Adams' Tax Svc., Phoenix. Candidate Ariz. State Senate, 1988; state chair Dem. Rep. Party, Ariz. With USN, 1964-68, Vietnam. Mem. AAAS, Mental Health Assn., Smokers' Human Rights. Baptist. Home: 217 4th Ave W Buckeye AZ 85326-1007 Office: PO Box 56036 Phoenix AZ 85079-6036

ADAMS, ROBERT GRANVILLE, marketing professional; b. Indpls., July 2, 1927; s. Jack and Iris (Trippeer) A.; m. Marilyn Howe (div.); m. Ilona Molnar; children: Lynn, Victoria, Amy. BS, Ind. U., 1953. Capt. USAF, 1945-65; horse rancher Am. Quarter Horse Assn., Scottsdale, Ariz., 1965-88; wholesaler Nat. Home Furnishings Assn., Scottsdale, 1988—; pres. Adams Mktg., Inc., Scottsdale, 1980—. Mem. Desert Caballeros (Wickenburg, Ariz., bd. dirs.), Rancheros Visitadores, Santa Barbara Club (Calif.), Sigma Chi (life Loyal Sig). Home: 5817 E Crocus Dr Scottsdale AZ 85254-5551 Office: PO Box 14350 Scottsdale AZ 85267-4350

ADAMS, ROBERT MONROE, dermatologist, educator; b. Pasadena, Calif., May 4, 1926; s. Oscar D. and Mamie (Butler) A.; m. Lorene Tassi, Mar. 21, 1948; children: Cynthia, Gregory. AB with distinction, Stanford U., 1946, MD, 1950. Diplomate Am. Bd. Dermatology. Rotating intern San Francisco City and County Hosp., 1949-50; resident in internal medicine Tripler Army Hosp., Honolulu, 1950-52; pvt. practice in family medicine Stockton, Calif., 1952-64; dermatologist Palo Alto (Calif.) Med. Clinic, 1967-75; resident in dermatology Stanford (Calif.) U. Med. Ctr., 1964-67, fellow in dermatology, 1966-67, dir. Contact Dermatitis and Occupational Skin Disease Clinic, 1967—; from instr. to clin. prof. dermatology Stanford U., 1966-82, clin. prof. dermatology, 1982—; mem. staff Stanford U. Hosp., 1967—; pvt. practice in dermatology Menlo Park, Calif., 1975—; dir. or co-dir. various profl. courses and symposia; guest lectr. many sci. confs. and ednl. instns., most recently Skin and Cancer Found. Seminar, Sidney, Australia, 1992, Cypress Found., Carmel, Calif., 1994, U. Calif., San Francisco, L.A. and Davis, numerous occasions. Author: (textbooks) Occupational Contact Dermatitis, 1969, Occupational Skin Disease, 1983, 2nd edit., 1990; co-author: Color Text of Contact Dermatitis, 1992; editor: Occupational Medicine, State of the Art Reviews, 1986; contbr. 13 chpts. to books; founding editor Am. Jour. Contact Dermatitis, editor-in-chief, 1989-92, mem. editl. bd., 1992—; mem. editl. bd. Jour. Am. Acad. Dermatology, 1986—, Health Hazards of the Workplace Report, 1989; contbr. numerous articles and revs. to sci. jours. Recipient Jean Spencer Felton award for Excellence in Sci. Writing, 1983. Mem. AMA (mem. adv. panel on med. standards 1979-83), Am. Acad. Dermatology (mem. task force on contact dermatitis 1976-91, Gold award for Teaching 1981, bd. dirs. 1989-93), Calif. Med. Assn. (mem. adv. panel on occupational medicine 1975-83), We. Occupational Med. Assn. (pres. 1983-84), Am. Soc. for Contact Dermatitis (pres., founder 1989-91), Am. Conf. Govtl. Indsl. Hygienists, San Francisco Dermatology Soc. (pres. 1985-86), Soc. for Investigative Dermatology, Pacific Dermatol. Assn., Internat. Soc. for Tropical Dermatology, Santa Clara Med. Soc., Brit. Assn. Dermatologist (hon.), Mex. Acad. Dermatology (hon.), Chilean Soc. Dermatology (hon.), Venezuelan Soc. Dermatology (hon.), Chinese Contace Dermatitis Rsch. Group (hon.). Home: 555 Laurel

Ave Apt 108 San Mateo CA 94401-4157 Office: 1300 University Dr Ste 8 Menlo Park CA 94025

ADAMS, RUSSELL FRANCIS, computer company executive, consultant; b. San Diego, May 17, 1955; s. Robert E. Adams and Marjorie Lois (Reece) Omer; m. Rosa Lee Andrews, June 23, 1984. AAS, Nat. U., San Diego, 1983, BBA magna cum laude, 1990. Analyst Home Fed. Savs. & Loan, San Diego, 1979-83; analyst, programmer Nat. Steel and Shipbuilding, San Diego, 1983-85; cons. Am. Fin. Systems, Detroit, 1985; pres. Russell F. Adams, Inc., San Diego, 1986—; cons. Soc. Bank N.A., Cleve., 1985-87, 90-93, 94—, Australia and New Zealand Bank, 1993-94, IBM Employees Fed. Credit Union, Poukeepsie, N.Y., 1988-90, Automated Mgmt. Systems, Detroit, 1986—. Mem. Mercedes Benz Club Am., Internat. 190 SL Group. Republican. Home and Office: 405 W Washington St Ste 206 San Diego CA 92103-1932

ADAMS, SARAH VIRGINIA, family counselor; b. San Francisco, Oct. 23, 1955; d. Marco Tulio and Helen (Jorge) Zea; m. Glenn Richard Adams, Mar 22, 1980; children: Mark Vincent, Elena Giselle, Johnathan Richard. BA, Calif. State U., Long Beach, 1978, MS, 1980; postgrad., Fuller Theological Sem., Pasadena, 1990—. Lic. marriage, family, child counseling. Tutor math. and sci. Montebello, Calif., 1979-82; behavioral specialist Cross Cultural Psychol. Corp., L.A., 1979-80; psychol. asst. Legal Psychology, L.A., 1980-82, Eisner Psychol. Assocs., L.A., 1982-83; assoc. dir. Legal Psychodiagnosis and Forensic Psychology, L.A., 1982-83; adminstrv. dir. Diagnostic Clinic, Calif., 1983-85; dir. Diagnostic Clinic of West Covina, Calif., 1985-87; owner Adams Family Counseling Inc., Calif., 1987—; tchr. piano, Montebello, 1973-84; ins. agent Am. Mut. Life Ins., Des Moines, 1982-84. Fellow Am. Assn. Marriage and Family Therapists, Am. Psychol. Assn.; mem. NAFE, Calif. Assn. Marriage and Family Therapists, Calif. State Psychol. Assn., Calif. Soc. Indsl. Medicine and Surgery, Western Psychol. Assn., Psi Chi, Pi Delta Phi. Republican. Roman Catholic. Office: Adams Family Counseling Inc 260 S Glendora Ave # 101 West Covina CA 91790-3041

ADAMS, STEPHEN ROY, biochemist, researcher; b. Stockport, Cheshire, Eng., Dec. 16, 1959; came to U.S., 1984; s. Roy William and Jean Mary (Knapman) A.; m. Catherine Agnes Murrell, July 31, 1982; children: Katrina Louise, Christopher Stephen, Matthew Sean, Ryan Andrew. BSc with honors, U. London, 1981; PhD, Cambridge (Eng.) U., 1984. Postgrad. researcher U. Calif., Berkeley, 1984-88, asst. researcher, 1989-89; assoc. Howard Hughes Med. Inst., San Diego, 1989-91; asst. researcher U. Calif., San Diego, 1991-95, assoc. rschr., 1995—. Contbr. articles to profl. jours. Office: U Calif 9500 Gilman Dr La Jolla CA 92093-5003

ADAMS, TUCKER HART, economic research company executive; b. Prescott, Ark., Jan. 11, 1938; d. Hugh Ross and Mildred (Dunn) Hart; m. Daniel Williams Adams, Sept. 6, 1957; children: Virginia Schoenthaler, Carolyn, Catherine Adams-Gravley, Anne Green. BA in Math., Wellesley Coll., 1959; MA in Econs., U. Colo., 1977, PhD in Econs., 1979. V.p., chief economist United Banks of Colo., Denver, 1978-88; pres., chief exec. officer The Adams Group, Inc., Colorado Springs, Colo., 1988—; pres. Am. Russian Collaborative Enterprises, LLC, 1994—; bd. dirs. Mortgage Analysis Corp., Entech, Inc., Guaranty Nat. Corp., Ag Am., Tax Free Fund Colo., Rocky Mountain Equity Fund. Author: (newsletter) Today's Economy: A Colorado Viewpoint, 1989—. Bd. dirs. Colo. Health Facilities Authority, Denver, Nat. Honcy Bd., Longmont, Colo., 1987-90, Univ. Hosp., Denver, U. Colo. Found., Boulder. Pendleton scholar Wellesley Coll., 1955; grad. fellowship U. Colo., 1977. Mem. Colo. Womens Forum (pres. 1988). Republican. Presbyterian. Office: The Adams Group Inc 4822 Alteza Dr Ste 300 Colorado Springs CO 80917-4002

ADAMS, WARREN DALE, resource development and communications director; b. Twin Falls, Idaho, Dec. 11, 1949; s. Dale Lewis and Fern Louella (Ebersole) A.; m. Lucille Fern Bertram, June 20, 1970. BA in English, Coll. of Idaho, 1972. Reporter Idaho Press Tribune, Nampa, 1972-77, city editor, 1977-79; mng. editor Herald and News, Klamath Falls, Oreg., 1979-86; v.p. resource devel. and comm. United Way/Benton & Franklin Counties, Kennewick, Wash., 1986—; participant Nat. Acad. Voluntarism, Alexandra, Va., 1994-95, Stanford (Calif.) U., 1990, 94; trainer United Way Am., Alexandria, 1986-89; cons. Lake County Examiner, Lakeview, Oreg., 1984-85; advisor Dirs. of Vols. in Agys., Tri-Cities, Wash., 1986—. Vol. dep. sheriff Owyhee County Sheriff's Office, Murphy, Idaho, 1972-77; chair tourism com. Klamath Falls C. of C., 1984-85; vol. chair gen. campaign United Way of Klamath Basin, Klamath Falls, 1985; fundraising cons. Tri-City Corp. Coun. for arts, 1992-95; adminstrv. dir., co-founder Columbia River Music Festival, 1991; vol. fundraising cons. Goodwill Games Tri-Cities, 1990; fundraiser Tri-Cities Econ. Devel. Coun. Renaissance, 1989. Mem. Nat. Mgmt. Assn. (charter, sec. 1988, 92-93, pres. 1989, bd. dirs., Outstanding Chpt. award 1989), Columbia Basin Area Coun. (bd. dirs., pres. 1990—, Mgr. of yr. 1992), Wash. State U. (Tri-Cities br. campus curriculum com. 1988), Mid-Columbia Symphony Soc. (bd. dirs., sec. 1990-92), Kiwanis. Home: 5201 W 16th Ct Kennewick WA 99337-1734 Office: United Way Benton & Franklin Counties 401 N Young St Kennewick WA 99337

ADAMS, WILLIAM WESLEY, III, architect; b. Lexington, Ky., Dec. 18, 1961; s. William Wesley II and Cathryn (Inman) A.; m. Lesli Rachelle Lewis, July 15, 1989; 1 child, William Wesley IV. BArch, Howard U., 1986. Lic. architect, Calif. Architect Clas, Riggs, Owens & Ramos, Silver Spring, Md., 1986-88; prin. Kennard Design Group Architecture & Planning, L.A., 1988—; draftsman Washington pub. schs., 1984, NSF, Washington, 1985. Mem. AIA, Nat. Orgn. Minority Architects (nat. treas. 1992—, svc. award 1993). Home: 3823 Sutro Ave Los Angeles CA 90008-1924 Office: Kennard Design Group 3600 Wilshire Blvd Ste 1820 Los Angeles CA 90010-2622

ADAMSON, ARTHUR WILSON, chemistry educator; b. Shanghai, China, Aug. 15, 1919; s. Arthur Quintin and Ethel (Rhoda) A.; m. Virginia Louise Dillman, Mar. 24, 1942; children—Carol Ann, Janet Louise, Jean Elizabeth. B.S. with honors, U. Calif.-Berkeley, 1940; Ph.D. in Phys. Chemistry, U. Chgo., 1944; PhD (hon.), U. Ferrara, Italy, 1993. Research assoc. Manhattan Project, Oak Ridge, 1944-46; asst. prof. U. So. Calif., 1946-49, assoc. prof., 1949-53, prof., 1953-89, prof. emeritus, 1989—, chmn. dept. chemistry, 1972-75; Foster lectr. U. Buffalo, 1970; Venable lectr. U. N.C., 1975; Bikerman lectr. Case Western U., 1982; Reilly lectr. Notre Dame U., 1984. Author: Concepts of Inorganic Photochemistry, 1975, Understanding Physical Chemistry, 1980, Textbook of Physical Chemistry, 1986, Physical Chemistry of Surfaces, 1990; editor Langmuir Am. Chem. Soc., 1984-89; editor emeritus, 1990—; contbr. articles to profl. jours. Recipient Creative Scholarship and rsch. award U. So. Calif., 1971, Excellence in Teaching award, 1979, Raubenheimer award, 1984, Disting. Emeritus award, 1991; Alexander von Humboldt Sr. Scientist award, 1971, others. Fellow Am. Inst. Chemists (Gold medal 1994); mem. Am. Chem Soc. (councillor So. Calif. sect. 1964-80, chmn. 1964, Tolman award 1967, Kendall award 1979, Langmuir lectr. 1981, Disting. Svc. in Inorganic Chemistry award 1982, Chem. Edn. award 1984, Agnes Ann Green Disting Svc. award 1989, Harry and Carol Mosher award 1990, Arthur W. Adamson Award for Disting. Svc. in Advancement of Surface Chemistry established in his honor 1992), Palos Verdes Tennis Club. Republican. Office: U So Calif Dept of Chemistry U Park Los Angeles CA 90089-0744

ADAMSON, GEOFFREY DAVID, reproductive endocrinologist, surgeon; b. Ottawa, Ont., Can., Sept. 16, 1946; came to U.S., 1978, naturalized, 1986; s. Geoffrey Peter Adamson and Anne Marian Allan; m. Rosemary C. Oddie, Apr. 28, 1973; children: Stephanie, Rebecca, Eric. BSc with honors, Trinity Coll., Toronto, Can., 1969; MD, U. Toronto, 1973. Diplomate Am. Bd. Ob-Gyn., Am. Bd. Laser Surgery; cert. Bd. Reproductive Endocrinology. Resident in ob-gyn. Toronto Gen. Hosp., 1973-77, fellow in ob-gyn., 1977-78; fellow reproductive endocrinology Stanford (Calif.) U. Med. Ctr., 1978-80; practice medicine specializing in infertility Los Gatos, Calif., 1980-84; instr. Stanford U. Sch. Medicine, 1980-84; clin. asst. prof. Stanford U. Sch. Medicine, Stanford Univ., Calif., 1984-92; clin. assoc. prof. Stanford U. Sch. Medicine, 1992—; assoc. clin. prof. Sch. Medicine U. Calif., San Francisco, 1992—. Mem. editorial adv. bd. Can. Doctor mag., 1977-83; contbr. numerous articles to sci. jours. Ontario Ministry of Health fellow, 1977-78. Fellow ACS, Royal Coll. Surgeons Can., Am. Coll. Ob-Gyns.; mem. AAAS, AMA, Am. Soc. Reproductive Medicine, Soc. Reproductive Endocrinologists (charter), Soc. Reproductive Surgeons (charter, treas.), Soc. Assisted Reproductive Tech. (dir.), Pacific Coast Fertility Soc. (dir.), Soc. Gynecologic Surgeons, Pacific Coast Ob-Gyn. Soc., San Francisco Ob-Gyn. Soc., Bay Area Reproductive Endocrinologists Soc. (founding pres.), Am. Assn. Gynecol. Laparoscopists, Gynecol. Laser Soc., N.Y. Acad. Scis., Shufelt Gynecol. Soc., Peninsula Gynecol. Soc. (past pres.), Calif. Med. Assn., San Mateo County Med. Assn., Santa Clara County Med. Assn., Am. Fedn. Clin. Rsch., Nat. Resolve (bd. dirs.), Can. Assn. Interns and Residents (hon. life, pres. 1977-79, bd. dirs. 1974-79, rep. AMA resident physician sect. 1978-79, rep. Can. Med. Protective Assn. 1975-78, rep. Can. Med. Assn. 1975-78, Disting. Svc. award 1980), Profl. Assn. Interns and Residents Ont. (bd. dirs. 1973-76, v.p. 1974-75, pres. 1975-76), Royal Coll. Physicians and Surgeons Can. (com. exams. 1977-80), Ont. Med. Assn. (sec. interns and residents sect. 1973-74). Home: 16520 S Kennedy Rd Los Gatos CA 95032-6406 Office: 540 University Ave # 200 Palo Alto CA 94301-1912

ADAMSON, H. DOUGLAS, English language educator; b. Salt Lake City, Sept. 30, 1944; s. Jack Hale and Margaret (Boyle) A.; m. Alice Leeth, Dec. 29, 1969; children: Marie Donnell, Katherine Boyle. AB in English, U. Calif., Berkeley, 1967; cert., UCLA, 1970; MA in Linguistics, San Jose State U., 1972; PhD in Linguistics, Georgetown U., 1980. Asst. prof. George Mason U., Fairfax, Va., 1979-88; assoc. prof. U. Ariz., Tucson, 1988—, dir. grad. studies English dept., 1992-94, advisor PhD program in second lang. acquisition, 1994—. Author: Variation Theory and Second Language Acquisition, 1988, Academic Competence: Theory and Classroom Practice, 1993. Mid-career fellowship Mellon Found., 1988. Mem. Linguistics Soc. of Am., TESOL, Ariz. TESOL. Office: English Dept U Ariz Tucson AZ 85721

ADAMSON, JACK, communications executive; b. Lehi, Utah, Oct. 16, 1923; s. Glen R. and Ida V. (Halliday) A.; m. Norma Hicken, June 25, 1948; children—John Frederic, Susan Adamson Sundwall, David H., Amy A. Tingey, Andrew H. B.A., U. Utah, 1949. Ptnr. Sta. KWIC-Radio, Salt Lake City, 1964-68; sales mgr. Sta. KMBZ, Kansas City, Mo., 1968-72; v.p., gen. mgr. Sta. KIRO, Seattle, 1972-78; pres., gen. mgr. Sta. KBIG, Los Angeles, 1978-85, Sta. KOIT, San Francisco, 1978-85; sr. v.p. Bonneville Internat. Corp., Salt Lake City, 1985—, KSL div. BIC; pres. KSL Div. BIC. Bd. dirs. Pioneer Meml. Theatre. Served with USAAF, 1942-45. Republican. Mormon. Home: 1505 Devonshire Dr Salt Lake City UT 84108-2531 Office: Bonneville Internat Corp Broadcast House 5 Triad Ctr Ste 800 Salt Lake City UT 84180-1102

ADAMSON, ROBERT MICHAEL KNAGGS, wellness and conflict resolution specialist; b. Elkins, W.Va., Sept. 14, 1945; s. Howard Robert and Elizabeth Jane (Adamson) Knaggs; 1 child, Galen Dougal. BS, W.Va. U., 1967, MEd in Wellness Promotion, 1973, MEd in Counseling, 1974. Dir. The 7th Level, San Diego, 1982—; therapist Palomar/Pomerado Hosps., Escondido, Calif., 1991-93, therapist, counselor, 1988-90; counselor Palomar Coll., San Marcos, Calif., 1990—; dir. health edn. Meml. Gen. Hosp., Elkins, W.Va., 1982-84. Author: Serenity Principle, 1993, Secret of Transformation, 1994, How to Solve Your Problems by Not Facing Them, 1995. Office: The 7th Level 12194 Waverly Downs San Diego CA 92128

ADAPA, RAMBABU, electrical engineer; b. Adapavaripalem, Andhra Pradesh, India, Sept. 2, 1956; s. Kanakayya and Vanavalamma (Annisetti) A.; m. Indira Devi Samba, Oct. 30, 1983; 1 child, Priyanka Sai. BTech in Elec. Engring, Jawaharlal Nehru Tech. U., Andhra Pradesh, India, 1979; MTech in Elec. Engring., Indian Inst. Tech., Kanpur, India, 1981; PhD in Elec. Engring., U. Waterloo, Ont., Can., 1986. Registered profl. engr., Wis. Power sys. staff engr. Thomas A. Edison Tech. Ctr., McGraw-Edison Power Sys., Franksville, Wis., 1986-89; mgr. power sys. engring., power delivery group Electric Power Rsch. Inst., Palo Alto, Calif., 1989—. Mem. IEEE (sr., vice chmn. local Santa Clara Valley PES chpt. 1983-84, chmn. chpt. 1994-95, awards chmn. Pitts. sect., chmn. edn. com. Pitts. chpt., mem. numerous other coms.). Home: 3242 Alder Ave Fremont CA 94536-3502 Office: Electric Power Rsch Inst 3412 Hillview Ave Palo Alto CA 94304-1395

ADCOCK, MURIEL W., special education educator; b. Chgo.. BA, U. Calif. Sonoma State, Rohnert Park, 1979. Cert. spl. edn. tchr., Calif., Montessori spl. edn. tchr. Tchr. The Concordia Sch., Concord, Calif., 1980-85; tchr., cons. Tenderloin Community Children's Ctr., San Francisco, 1985-86; adminstr. Assn. Montessori Internat.-USA, San Francisco, 1988, tchr., advisor, 1989—; course asst. Montessori Spl. Edn. Inst., San Francisco, 1985-87, tchr. spl. edn., 1990, tchr. cons., 1991—, rschr. 1992—. Contbr. articles to profl. jour. Sec. Internat. Forum World Affairs Coun., San Francisco, 1990-95, program chair, 1993-95. Mem. ASCD, Coun. for Exceptional Children, Nat. Assn. Edn. Young Children, Am. Orthopsychiat. Assn., Am. Assn. Mental Retardation, Assn. Montessori Internat., N.Am. Montessori Tchrs. Assn., Assn. Childhood Edn. Internat., Smithsonian Assocs., N.Y. Acad. Scis., Nat. Geog. Soc., Menninger Found. Office: PO Box 424519 San Francisco CA 94142-4519

ADDAMS, ROBERT JEAN, business and financial consultant; b. Salt Lake City, Sept. 24, 1942; s. Harvey J. and Virginia (Dutson) A.; children: Ryan, Kelley, Amy, Michael. BS, U. Utah, 1968, MBA, 1969. Fin. analyst Western Airlines, Inc., Los Angeles, 1969-72, mgr. budgets and cost control, 1972-74, controller mktg. div., 1974-76, dir. budgets and cost control, 1976-80; v.p., gen. mgr. Ball Bros., Inc., Everette, Wash., and Anchorage, 1980-82; pres., cons. Addams & Assocs., Woodinville, Wash., 1982—. Author: Care and Handling of Wetsalted Cod Fish, 1984; also articles on budgeting and business plans to monthly newsletter. Scoutmaster, Explorer advisor Gt. Salt Lake and Los Angeles councils Boy Scouts Am., 1973-75; served 2-yr. mission for Ch. Jesus Christ Latter-day Saints, 1962-64. Served with U.S. Army, 1961-62. Named Outstanding Grad., Coll. Bus., 1968, Beehive Honor Soc., 1969. Mem. U. Utah Alumni Assn. (pres. So. Calif. chpt. 1976-80), U. Utah Coll. of Bus. Alumni (pres. So. Calif. group 1978-79), Alpha Kappa Psi. Republican. Home and Office: Addams & Assocs 14700 NE 171st St H-103 Woodinville WA 98072

ADDICOTT, WARREN OLIVER, retired geologist, educator; b. Fresno, Calif., Feb. 17, 1930; s. Irwin Oliver and Astrid (Jensen) A.; m. Suzanne Aubin, Oct. 2, 1976; m. Susanne Smith, Aug. 20, 1955 (div. 1974); children: Eric Oliver, Carol. BA cum laude, Pomona Coll., Calif., 1951; MA, Stanford U., Calif., 1952; PhD, U. Calif.-Berkeley, 1956. Teaching asst. U. Calif.-Berkeley, 1952-54; paleontologist Standard Oil Co. Calif., 1953; geologist Mobil Oil Co., 1954-62; research geologist U.S. Geol. Survey, Menlo Park, Calif., 1962-94; cons. prof. Stanford U., Calif., 1962-81; dep. chmn. Circum-Pacific Map Project, Menlo Park, Calif., 1979-82, gen. chmn., 1982-86, project advisor, 1986—; adj. prof. So. Oreg. State Coll., 1989—; bd. dirs. Circum-Pacific Coun. Energy and Mineral Resources, 1983-86. Contbr. articles to profl. jours. Fellow AAAS, Geol. Soc. Am., Calif. Acad. Scis.; mem. Paleontol. Soc. (pres. 1979-80), Am. Assn. Petroleum Geologists, Paleontol. Res. Instn. (bd. dirs. 1980-81). Unitarian. Home: 2260 Old Siskiyou Hwy Ashland OR 97520

ADDIE, HARVEY WOODWARD, retired secondary education educator, music director; b. Birmingham, Ala., June 14, 1930; s. LeRoy and Frances (Driscoll) A.; m. Gwendolyn Marie Mendes, June 5, 1955; children: Cynthia Marie Corra, Julie Ann Lorch, Mary Elizabeth Dunaway. MusB, Coll. Pacific, 1959; MusM, U. Pacific, 1970. Cert. life music tchr., Calif. Mgr. dept. S.H. Kress and Co., Santa Monica and Stockton, Calif., 1953-55; head produce, mgr. area Safeway Stores Inc., Lodi, Stockton, Calif., 1955-61; tchr. music Manteca (Calif.) Elem. Sch. Dist., 1959-61, San Joaquin County Sch. Music Office, Stockton, 1961-71; mgr. store Bill's Music Sales, Stockton, 1971-73; dir. music El Dorado High Sch., Placerville, Calif., 1973, Stockton Unified Sch. Dist., 1973-89; pres. San. Joaquin County Band Dirs. Assn., Stockton, 1984-86, Stagg High Sch. Faculty Assn., 1984-85. 1st. v.p. San Joaquin Concert Ballet Assn., Stockton, 1966; bd. dirs. Stockton opera Assn., 1968, Stockton Concert Band Assn., 1986-88. Served to cpl. U.S. Army, 1951-53, Korea. Mem. Assn. Jazz Edn., Calif. Music Educators Assn. (bd. dirs. 1983-87), Stockton Tchrs. Assn. (treas. 1986-89), Am. Fedn. Musicians (life mem., bd. dirs., sec.-treas. 1992—, pres. 1995—), Calif. Tchrs. Assn. (state coun. 1986-89), Noble Grand Fraternal Order of Odd Fellows (dist. dep. Grand Master Calif., trustee Saratoga Home 1994—). Democrat. Methodist. Home: 1426 W Euclid Ave Stockton CA 95204-2903 Office: Stockton Musicians' Assn 33 W Alpine Ave Stockton CA 95204-3607

ADDINGTON, RAYMOND JOSEPH, wholesale groceries company executive. Pres. Kelly Douglas & Co. Ltd., Vancouver, B.C., Can. Office: Kelly Douglas & Co Ltd, PO Box 2039, Vancouver, BC Canada V6B 3S1 also: Loblaw Cos Ltd, 22 St Clair Ave E, Toronto, ON Canada M4T 2S8

ADDIS, RICHARD BARTON, lawyer; b. Columbus, Ohio, Apr. 9, 1929; s. Wilbur Jennings and Leila Olive (Grant) A.; m. Marguerite C. Christjohn, Feb. 9, 1957; children: Jacqueline Carol, Barton David. BA, Ohio State U., 1954, JD, 1955. Bar: Ohio 1956, U.S. Dist. Ct. (no. dist.) Ohio 1957, N.Mex. 1963, U.S. Dist. Ct. N.Mex. 1963, Laguna Pueblo (N.Mex.) Tribal Ct. 1986. Pvt. practice, Canton, Ohio, 1956-63, Albuquerque, 1963—, Laguna Pueblo, Navajo Nation, 1986—. Counsel N.Mex. Cultural Arts Ctr. at Angel Fire, 1990. With USMC, 1946-48, 50-52. Mem. Ohio Bar Assn., N.Mex. Bar Assn., Am. Arbitration Assn. (arbitrator 1968—), Soc. Mining Engrs. Office: 5111 San Mateo Blvd NE Albuquerque NM 87109-2483

ADDIS, THOMAS HOMER, III, professional golfer; b. San Diego, Nov. 30, 1945; s. Thomas H. and Martha J. (Edwards) A.; student Foothill Jr. Coll., 1963, Grossmont Jr. Coll., 1965; degree in profl. golf mgmt. (hon.) Ferris State U.; m. Susan Tera Buckley, June 13, 1966; children: Thomas Homer IV, Bryan Michael. Head golf profl., mgr. Sun Valley Golf Course, La Mesa, Calif., 1966-67; head golf profl., dir. golf Singing Hills Country Club and Lodge, 1969—; pres. PGA of Am., 1994—; gen. chmn. Nat. Jr. Golf championship U.S. Golf Assn., 1973, 89; lectr.; owner Golf Cons. & Design, Rocky Mountain Chocolate Factory, Mammoth. Pres. Calif. State Open, 1980-84; chmn. Nat. Com. Liaison for Physically Challenged, 1984-88. Recipient Retailer award Golf Industry mag., 1985; named to Lady Aztec San Diego State U. Hall of Fame. Mem. PGA (pres. San Diego chpt. 1978-79; pres. sect. 1980-82, bd. dirs. sect. 1974-90, speaker, chmn. mem. svc. com. 1986-87, bd. dirs. San Diego sect. 1974-90, assn. coord. bus. schs. and seminars, named Profl. of Yr. So. Calif. sect. 1979, 89, Horton Smith award So. Calif. sect. 1980-81, 89, PGA Golf Profl. of Yr. 1989, Nat. Horton Smith award 1981, Resort Merchandiser of Yr., So. Calif. sect. 1978, 83, mem. nat. bd. control 1978-85, chmn. nat. bd. control 1991-92, membership com. 1978, 89-90, nat. edn. com. 1980-85, 89-90, nat. bd. dirs., 1986-88, rules com. 1986-90, championship com. 1986—, hon. life mem. So. Calif. sect. and San Diego PGA, sec. PGA Am. 1991, 92, v.p. PGA Am. 1993, 94, pres. 1994—), Nat. Golf Found. (Joe Graffis award, 1988) Nat. Amputee Golf Assn. (hon. mem.), San Diego Jr. Golf Assn. (dir.), Assn. Golf Educators, Golf Collector's Soc., Singing Hills Tennis Club, Rotary. Author articles. Office: Singing Hills Golf Course 3007 Dehesa Rd El Cajon CA 92019-2806

ADDISON, JOHN ROBERT, counselor; b. Northfield, Mass., Aug. 4, 1927; s. Warren Grant and Mildred Elizabeth (Vorce) A.; m. Emily Loveland Kirk, Jan. 3, 1953; children: Karen Louise, David Martin. BA, U. Mass., 1950; MA, U. Colo., 1963, postgrad., 1964-87. Tchr. Jeffco Pub. Schs., Arvada, Colo., 1956-64; counselor Jeffco Pub. Schs., Arvada Sr. High Sch., Arvada, Colo., 1964-91; admissions counselor Red Rocks C.C., Golden, Colo., 1991—; mem. Jeffco Area Vocat. Sch. Adv. Coun., 1990-91; mem. Cooperative Occupational Adv. Bd., 1976-91; mem. various adv. coms. Warren Occupational Tng. Ctr., 1970-91. Coach Arvada Soccer Assn., 1971-76; chmn., trustee Arvada Pub. Libr.; active charter rev. com. City of Arvada. With U.S. Army, 1945-47; lst lt. USAF, 1950-55. Decorated Air medal. Mem. NEA, Jefferson County Edn. Assn. (pres. salary com.), Jeffco Counselors Assn. (pres.), Colo. Edn. Assn., Colo. Guidance Counselors Assn. Home: 6066 Lewis Ct Arvada CO 80004-4928 Office: Red Rocks Cmty Coll 13300 W 6th Ave Lakewood CO 80401-5398

ADDY, JO ALISON PHEARS, economist; b. Ger., May 2, 1951; d. William Phears and Paula Hubbard; m. Tralance Obuama Addy, May 25, 1979; children: Mantse, Miishe, Dwetri, Naakai. BA, Smith Coll., 1973; MBA, Adelphi U., 1975; postgrad., Stanford U., 1975-78. Economic analyst Morgan Guaranty, N.Y.C., 1973-75; econ. cons. Nat. Planning Assn., Washington, 1976; economist Rand Corp., 1978; economist World Bank, Washington, 1979-80; asst. v.p., internat. economist Crocker Bank, San Francisco, 1980-85; asst. v.p., economist, money markets 1st RepublicBank, Dallas, 1985-87, prin. SEGI Internat., Dallas, 1987—; pres. Unimed Ventures, Inc., 1991—; lectr. in field. Docent Bowers Mus.; vice chmn. St. John's Sch. Adv Com. NSF fellow, 1976-79. Mem. Am. Econ. Assn. Office: 8 Palomino Trabuco Canyon CA 92679-4820

ADELMAN, IRMA GLICMAN, economics educator; b. Cernowitz, Rumania, Mar. 14, 1930; came to U.S., 1949, naturalized, 1955; d. Jacob Max and Raissa (Ettinger) Glicman; m. Frank L. Adelman, Aug. 16, 1950 (div. 1979); 1 son, Alexander. BS, U. Calif., Berkeley, 1950, MA, 1951, PhD, 1955. Teaching assoc. U. Calif., Berkeley, 1955-56; instr. U. Calif., 1956-57, lectr. with rank asst. prof., 1957-58; vis. asst. prof. Mills Coll., 1958-59; acting asst. prof. Stanford, 1959-61, asst. prof., 1961-62; assoc. prof. Johns Hopkins, Balt., 1962-65; prof. econs. Northwestern U., Evanston, Ill., 1966-72, U. Md., 1972-78; prof. econs. and agrl. econs. U. Calif. at Berkeley, 1979-94; prof. emeritus, 1994—; cons. divsn. indsl. devel. UN, 1962-63, AID U.S. Dept. State, Washington, 1963-72, World Bank, 1968—, ILD, Geneva, 1973—. Author: Theories of Economic Growth and Development, 1961, Institutions and Development Strategies: Selected Essays of Irma Adelman Volume I, 1994, Dynamics and Income Distribution: Selected Essays of Irma Adelman Volume II, 1994, Selected Essays (in Spanish), 1994, (with A. Pepelasis and L. Mears) Economic Development: Analysis and Case Studies, 1961, (with Eric Thorbecke) The Theory and Design of Economic Development, 1966, (with C.T. Morris) Society, Politics and Economic Development—A Quantitative Approach, 1967, Practical Approaches to Development Planning-Korea's Second Five Year Plan, 1969, (with C.T. Morris) Economic Development and Social Equity in Developing Countries, 1973, (with Sherman Robinson) Planning for Income Distribution, 1977-78, (with C. T. Morris) Comparative Patterns of Economic Growth, 1850-1914, 1987. Fellow Center Advanced Study Behavioral Scis., 1970-71. Fellow Am. Acad. Arts and Scis., Econometric Soc., Royal Soc. Encouragement Arts, Mfgs. & Commerce; mem. Am. Econ. Assn. (mem. exec. com., v.p. 1969-71). Office: Univ Calif Dept Agr & Natural Resources 207 Giannini Hall #3310 Berkeley CA 94720-3310

ADELMAN, JANET ANN, English literature educator; b. Mt. Kisco, Jan. 28, 1941; d. Emanuel and Ceil (Greenfeld) A.; m. Robert Osserman, July 21, 1976; children: Brian, Stephen. BA, Smith Coll., 1962; postgrad., Oxford (Eng.) U., 1962-63; MA, Yale U., 1968, PhD, 1968. Prof. English lit. U. Calif., Berkeley, 1968—. Author: The Common Liar: An Essay on Antony and Cleopatra, 1973, Suffocating Mothers: Fantasies of Maternal Origin in Shakespeare, Hamlet to The Tempest, 1992; editor: Twentieth Century Interpretations of King Lear, 1978. Fellow Am. Coun. Learned Socs., 1976-77, Guggenheim Found., 1981-82. Mem. MLA, Shakespeare Assn. Am. Office: U Calif Dept English Berkeley CA 94720

ADELMAN, JONATHAN REUBEN, political science educator, consultant; b. Washington, Oct. 30, 1948; s. Benjamin and Kitty (Sandler) A.; m. Dora Zhu, Aug. 12, 1988; 1 child, David Shanghai. BA, Columbia U., 1969, MA, 1972, M in Philosophy, 1974, PhD, 1976. Vis. asst. prof. Columbia U., N.Y.C., 1977; vis. asst. prof. U. Ala., Tuscaloosa, 1977-78; asst. prof. Grad. Sch. Internat. Studies U. Denver, 1978-85, assoc. prof., 1985-92, prof. polit. sci., 1992—; sr. rsch. analyst Sci. Applications, Inc., Denver, 1981-87; cons. 1988-89; Lady Davis vis. assoc. prof. Hebrew U. Jerusalem, 1986; vis. fellow Soviet Acad. Scis., 1989, 90, Chinese Inst. Contemporary Internat. Rels., Beijing, 1988, People's U., Beijing, 1990, 94; vis. prof. Beijing U., 1989, U. Haifa, Israel, 1990; vis. speaker Soviet Acad. Scis., 1990, Barcelona (Spain) U. and Complutense U., 1990, Cambridge U., England, 1991; vis. lectr. Japan, India, Hong Kong, Yugoslavia, Spain, 1990, 91, Germany, 1991, Bulgaria, 1991; vis. speaker Conf. for Study of European Ideas, Aalborg U., Denmark, 1992; vis. prof. People's U., Beijing, 1990, Janus Pannonius U., Pecs, Hungary, 1991. Author: The Revolutionary Armies, 1980, Revolution, Armies and War, 1986, Prelude to the Cold War: Tsarist, Soviet and U.S. Armies in Two World Wars, 1988, Tarrents of Spring: Soviet and Post Soviet Politics, 1994; co-author: The Dynamics of Soviet Foreign Policy, 1988; editor: Communist Armies in Politics, 1982, Terror and Communist Politics, 1984, Superpowers and Revolution, 1986; co-editor: Contemporary Soviet Military Affairs: The Legacy World War II, 1989; contbr. numerous articles in field to profl. jours. Charles Phelps Taft fellow U. Cin., 1976-77; Am. Philos. Soc. grantee, 1980. Mem. Am. Polit

vancement Slavic Studies. Democrat. Jewish. Office: U Denver Grad Sch Internat Studies Denver CO 80208

ADELMAN, WILLIAM JAMES (WILLIAM MYLAR), information systems analyst, musician, songwriter; b. Sacramento, Sept. 28, 1954; s. Gordon Phillip and Carol Ann (Popesco) A.; m. Judith Lynn Carerra, Aug. 21, 1983; children: Linda Marie, Lennon Michael. Student, Calif. State U., Sacramento, 1973, 80-81, Charles J.T. Schulte Sch. Performing Arts, Anaheim, Calif., 1976. Vol. Kibbutz Ein Harod, Gilboa, Israel, 1973-74; actor, theater technician, 1974-78, musician,, 1978-84; program technician Calif. Dept. Motor Vehicles, Sacramento, 1981-84, supr., 1984-86, info. systems analyst, 1986—, safety coord. emergency response team, 1988-92; space planner Calif. Div. EDP Svc., Sacramento, 1986—, systems adminstr. CAD Svcs., Sacramento, 1989—. Author, performer: (recs.) Folk Wave Music, 1979, One World, One People, 1987, Sweet Alibi, 1992, Let's Dance, 1993; lead singer William Mylar Band, 1992—. Umpire, coach Northridge Little League, Fair Oaks, Calif., 1991, 92. Recipient dir.'s quality svc. award Calif. Dept. Motor Vehicles, 1987, employee safety award Gov. of Calif., 1990. Mem. Intercap Graphics Users Soc., Inter Works-Hewlett-Packard Group. Jewish. Office: Calif DMV 2415 1st Ave Sacramento CA 95818-2606

ADELSMAN, (HARRIETTE) JEAN, newspaper editor; b. Indpls., Oct. 21, 1944; d. Joe and Beatrice Irene (Samuel) A. BS in Journalism, Northwestern U., 1966, MS in Journalism, 1967. Copy editor Chgo. Sun-Times, 1967-75, fin. news editor, 1975-77, entertainment editor, 1977-80, asst. mng. editor features, 1980-84; now mng. editor Daily Breeze, Torrance, Calif. Office: Daily Breeze 5215 Torrance Blvd Torrance CA 90503-4009

ADELSON, LEONARD JOSEPH, physician; b. N.Y.C., June 3, 1950; s. Arthur and Alice (Schorr) A.; m. Rose Ann Vasta, 1974 (div. 1982); m. Lorin Ann Schiff, Sept. 7, 1985; children: Aaron S., Matthew S. BA in Math. and Psychology, U. Pa., 1972; MD, Jefferson Med. Sch., 1977. Diplomate Am. Bd. Internal Medicine, Am. Bd. Critical Care, Am. Bd. Pulmonary Diseases. Intern internal medicine Med. Ctr. U. So. Calif., 1977-78, resident internal medicine Med. Ctr., 1978-80, pulmonary disease fellow Med. Ctr., 1981-83; pvt. practice Mid. Valley Pulmonary Med. Group, North Hollywood, Calif., 1983—; pulmonary cons., med. dir. respiratory therapy Sherman Oaks (Calif.) Hosp. and Health Ctr., 1983—, chief of staff, 1994—. Fellow Am. Coll. Chest Physicians; mem. AMA, Calif. Med. Assn., L.A. County Med. Assn. Home: 4811 Andasol Ave Encino CA 91316-3802 Office: 12626 Riverside Dr # 404 North Hollywood CA 91607

ADELSON, MERVYN LEE, entertainment and communication industry executive; b. Los Angeles, Oct. 23, 1929; s. Nathan and Pearl (Schwarzman) A.; m. Thea Nesis, May 10, 1986; children from previous marriage: Ellen, Gary, Andrew. Student, Menlo Park Jr. Coll. Pres. Markettown Supermarket and Builders Emporium, Las Vegas, 1953-63; mng. ptnr. Paradise Devel., Las Vegas, 1958—; pres. Realty Holdings, 1962—, La Costa, Inc., 1963-87; chmn. bd. dirs. Lorimar Inc., Culver City, Calif., 1969-86; chmn. bd. dirs., chief exec. officer Lorimar Telepictures Corp., Culver City, 1986-89; vice chmn. Warner Communications, 1989—; chmn. East-West Capital Assocs., Inc., 1989—; bd. dirs. Time-Warner Inc. Co-founder Nathan Adelson Hospice Found. Recipient Sherill Corwin Human Relations award Am. Jewish Com., 1987. Mem. Am. Film Inst. (trustee), Am. Mus. of Moving Images (trustee), Entertainment Industries Council (trustee), Acad. Motion Pictures Arts and Scis., Acad. TV Arts and Sciences, Nat. Acad. Cable Programming, Alliance for Capital Access (bd. dirs.), Com. Publicly Owned Cos. (bd. dirs.).

ADELSTEIN, ROBERT MILTON, social worker; b. Sioux City, Iowa, Dec. 8, 1934; s. Morris and Bertha (Greenburg) A.; m. Joanie Greintz, Aug. 26, 1956 (div. Nov., 1972); children: Deborah Kay Adelstein Morrison, Dana Jo Adelstein Schwartz, David Aaron; m. Sheila Greenberg, Sept. 18, 1986. BA, Met. State Coll., Denver, 1971; MSW, U. Denver, 1975. Lic. social worker II, Colo. Equipment mgr. Northwestern Engring. Co., Denver, 1957-69, corp. sec., 1969-91; pvt. practice psychiat. social work and family therapy Denver, 1975-. Trustee Allied Jewish Fedn., Denver, 1979-90; bd. dirs. Coun. Jewish Fedns., N.Y., 1988-89; v.p. Jewish Telegraph Agy., N.Y.C., 1981-93; nat. commr. B'nai B'rith Hillel, Washington, 1986-91; pres. Hillel Coun. Colo., 1987-89, trustee, 1989—. Mem. Acad. Cert. Social Workers, Am. Assn. Marriage and Family Therapists, Nat. Assn. Social Workers (diplomate in clin. social work, cert. IMAGO therapist). Republican. Office: 3601 S Clarkson St Ste 540 Englewood CO 80110-3949

ADENIRAN, DIXIE DARLENE, library administrator; b. L.A., May 26, 1943; d. Alfred and Madge (Clare) Harvey. BA, U. Calif., Santa Barbara, 1965; MA, Mich. State U., 1968; MLS, U. Mich., 1970. Libr. Free Libr. of Phila., 1970-72, Coll. Sci. and Tech., Port Harcourt, Nigeria, 1972-73; libr. Ventura (Calif.) County Libr. Svcs. Agy., 1974-79, libr. dir., 1979—. Pres. Ventura County Master Chorale and Opera Assn., 1985. Mem. ALA, Calif. Libr. Assn. (assembly 1994—), Calif. County Librs. Assn. (pres. 1988), Soroptimists (pres. Ventura club 1984). Home: 5548 Rainier St Ventura CA 93003-1135 Office: Ventura County Libr Svcs 4274 Telegraph Rd Ventura CA 93003-3706

ADESSA, ANTHONY THOMAS, violinist, music educator, conductor; b. Chgo., Sept. 14, 1951; s. Sylvester Louis and Dorothy (Rubin) A.; m. Lori Lynn Jantz, May 22, 1983. MusB, Ind. U., 1973, MusM, 1975, MusD, 1982. Asst. prof. music Ind.-Purdue U., Ft. Wayne, 1979-83, Southwestern U., Georgetown, Tex., 1983-89; assoc. prof. music, chmn. music dept. Wesleyan Coll., Macon, Ga., 1989-92; dir. advancement Macon Coll., 1993; assoc. prof. music, chmn. music dept. Holy Names Coll., 1993-94; participant Music in London, Southwestern U., summer 1987, Internat. Violin master class, Namur, Belgium, summer 1981, Internat. Chamber Music master class, Ernen, Switzerland, summer 1984; performer Siena (Italy) Music Festival, 1986; participant NEH faculty study tour to China and Thailand, 1988. Mem. AAUP, Coll. Music Soc., Nat. Soc. Fund Raising Execs., Music Educators Nat. Conf., Am. String Tchrs. Assn., Pi Kappa Lambda, Sigma Alpha Iota. Home: 320 20th Ave San Francisco CA 94121-2205

ADEYEMO, ADEDAPO, geologist; b. London, Jan. 20, 1962; arrived in Nigeria, 1967; s. Ayoade Adeyemo and Christianah (Agbaje) A. BSc in Geology with honors, U. Ibadan, Nigeria, 1983. Geologist Chevron Nigeria Ltd., Lagos, 1985-93, formation evaluation specialist exploration svcs., 1993—. Mem. Am. Assn. Petroleum Geologists, Soc. Profl. Well Log Analysts, Nigerian Assn. Petroleum Explorationists (gen. sec. 1992-94, 3d best paper award 1990, svc. award 1993, 94). Office: Chevron Overseas PI 6001 Bollinger Canyon Rd San Ramon CA 94583-2324

ADKINS, BEN FRANK, management and engineering consultant; b. West Liberty, Ky., Mar. 6, 1938; s. Stuart Kendall Adkins and Dorothy Elizabeth (Shaver) Indes; m. Judith Ann Williams, Mar. 14, 1959; children: Michelle Rene, Lori Lee. BS in Indsl. Engring., Ariz. State U., 1964; MBA, Western New Eng. Coll., Springfield, Mass., 1971; MS in Systems Mgmt., U. So. Calif., 1983. Registered profl. engr. Enlisted USAF, 1955, commd. 2d lt., 1964, advanced through grades to maj., 1975, ret., 1979; internal cons., mgr. State of Wash., Olympia, 1979-87; mgmt. and engring. cons. Olympia, 1987-88; sr. rsch. sci. Battelle Pacific N.W. Labs., Richland, Wash., 1988-89; mng. prin. Ben Adkins & Assocs., Olympia, 1989—. Decorated Bronze star USAF. Mem. Inst. Indsl. Engrs. (sr. mem., bd. dirs. Puget Sound chpt. 1984-86, asst. dir. and dir. govt. div. 1979-83, v.p. Washington chpt. 1969-76). Home: 6606 Miner Dr SW Olympia WA 98512-7257 Office: Ben Adkins & Assocs PO Box 7613 Olympia WA 98507-7613

ADKINS, JEANNE M., state legislator; b. North Platte, Nebr., May 2, 1949. BA, U. Nebr. Journalist; mem. Colo. Ho. of Reps., chairwoman judiciary com., vice-chairwoman legal svcs. com., mem. fin. com., regional air quality control coun., state edn. accountability commn. Founding sec. Douglas County Econ. Devel. Coun., bd. dirs., 1988. Fellow Vanderbilt U. Govt., Gates fellow JFK Sch. Govt. State/Local Program, Toll fellow. Mem. Am. Soc. Newspaper Editors, Soc. Profl. Journalists, Suburban Newspaper Assn. Republican. Baptist. Home: 6505 E Alcorn Ave Parker CO 80134-8003 also: 11086 Rodeo Cir Parker CO 80134-7344 Office: Office of State Senate State Capital Denver CO 80203

ADKINS, RONALD VERN, financial planner; b. Huntington, W.Va., Feb. 16, 1939; s. A. Hobert and Amelia (Eaton) A.; m. Sharon Kaye Estep, Mar. 20, 1965 (div. Sept. 1985); children: Darrett B., Jason E. BA, George Washington U., 1964; MA, Marshall U., 1965; doctoral studies, U. Denver, 1971-74; CFP, Coll. for Fin. Planning, 1993. History instr. Shenandoah Coll., Winchester, Va., 1965-67; history prof., honors dir. Huron (S.D.) Coll., 1967-72; dir. admissions ea. region U. Denver, 1973-75; dir. admissions and fin. aid. U. Puget Sound, Tacoma, 1975-77, dir. acad. advising, 1977-85; personal fin. planner Am. Express Fin. Svcs., Tacoma, 1987—. Democrat. Presbyterian. Office: Am Express Fin Svcs 4002 Tacoma Mall Blvd Tacoma WA 98409-7702

ADLER, CHARLES HOWARD, neurologist; b. N.Y.C., Mar. 6, 1958. BA summa cum laude, Temple U., 1980; MS, N.Y.U., 1984, PhD, 1986, MD, 1986. Intern NYU Manhattan VA Hosp., N.Y.C., 1986-87; resident Hosp. U. Pa., Phila., 1987-90; sr. assoc. cons. neurology Mayo Clinic, Scottsdale, Ariz., 1991-94, cons. neurology, 1994—; asst. prof. neurology Mayo Med. Sch., Scottsdale, Ariz., 1992—. Contbr. articles to profl. jours. Movement Disorders fellow, Phila., 1990-91; Pres.'s scholar, Temple U., 1980. Mem. AMA, Am. Acad. Neurology, Movement Disorders Soc. Office: Mayo Clinic 13400 E Shea Blvd Scottsdale AZ 85259-5499

ADLER, CHARLES SPENCER, psychiatrist; b. N.Y.C., Nov. 27, 1941; s. Benjamin H. and Anne (Greenfield) A.; m. Sheila Noel Morrissey, Oct. 8, 1966 (dec.); m. Peggy Dolan Bean, Feb. 23, 1991. BA, Cornell U., 1962; MD, Duke U., 1966. Diplomate Nat. Bd. Med. Examiners, Am. Bd. Psychiatry and Neurology. Intern Tucson Hosps. Med. Edn. Program, 1966-67; psychiat. resident U. Colo. Med. Sch., Denver, 1967-70; pvt. practice medicine specializing in psychiatry and psychosomatic medicine Denver, 1970—; chief divsn. psychiatry Rose Med. Ctr., 1982-87; co-founder Applied Biofeedback Inst., Denver, 1972-75; prof. pro tempore Cleve. Clinic, 1977; asst. clin. prof. psychiatry U. Colo. Med. Ctr., 1986—, chief of psychiatry and psychophysiology Colo. Neurology and Headache Ctr., 1988—; med. dir. Colo. Ctr. for Biobehavioral Health, Boulder, 1994—; bd. dirs. Acad. Cert. Neurotherapists. Author: (with Gene Stanford and Sheila M. Adler) We Are But a Moment's Sunlight, 1976, (with Sheila M. Adler and Russell Packard) Psychiatric Aspects of Headache, 1987; contbr. (with S. Adler) sect. biofeedback med. and health ann. Ency. Britannica, 1986; chpts. to books, articles to profl. jours.; mem. editorial bd. Cephalalgia: an Internat. Jour. of Headache, Headache Quar. Emeritus mem. Citizen's Adv Bd. Duke U. Ctr. Aging and Human Devel. Recipient Award of Recognition, Nat. Migraine Found., 1981; N.Y. State regents scholar, 1958-62. Fellow Am. Psychiat. Assn.; mem. AAAS (rep. of AAPB to med. sect. com.), Am. Assn. Study Headache, Internat. Headache Soc. (chmn. subcom. on classifying psychiat. headaches), Am. Acad. Psychoanalysis (sci. assoc.), Colo. Psychiat. Soc., Biofeedback Soc. Colo. (pres. 1977-78), Assn. for Applied Psychophysiology and Biofeedback (rep. to AAAS, chmn. ethics com. 1983-87, bd. dirs. 1990-93, Sheila M. Adler cert. honor 1988). Jewish. Office: 955 Eudora St Apt 1605 Denver CO 80220-4341

ADLER, ERWIN ELLERY, lawyer; b. Flint, Mich., July 22, 1941; s. Ben and Helen M. (Schwartz) A.; m. Stephanie Ruskin, June 8, 1967; children: Lauren, Michael, Jonathan. B.A., U. Mich., 1963, LL.M., 1967; J.D., Harvard U., 1966. Bar: Mich. 1966, Calif. 1967. Assoc. Pillsbury, Madison & Sutro, San Francisco, 1967-73; assoc. Lawler, Felix & Hall, L.A., 1973-76, ptnr., 1977-80; ptnr. Rogers & Wells, L.A., 1981-83, Richards, Watson & Gershon, L.A., 1983—. Bd. dirs. Hollywood Civic Opera Assn., 1975-76, Children's Scholarships Inc., 1979-80. Mem. ABA (vice chmn. appellate advocacy com. 1982-87), Calif. Bar Assn., Phi Beta Kappa, Phi Kappa Phi. Jewish. Office: Richards Watson & Gershon 333 S Hope St Bldg 38 Los Angeles CA 90071-1406

ADLER, EUGENE VICTOR, forensic toxicologist, consultant; b. Detroit, June 28, 1947; s. Leonard Eugene and Beatrice Doris (Goldfarb) A.; m. Patricia Ann Vangeloff, Sept. 7, 1969; children: Kimberly, Emily. BS in Chemistry with honors, Wayne State U., 1969. Diplomate Am. Bd. Forensic Toxicology. Analyst crime lab. Mich. Health Dept., Lansing, 1970-72; criminalist crime lab. Ariz. Dept. Pub. Safety, Phoenix, 1972—; cons., lectr. Dept. Transp., Washington, 1990—; lectr. various traffic safety confs., 1988—. Co-editor, co-founder: The DRE newsletter and jour., 1989-93. Mem. AAAS, Am. Acad. Forensic Scis., Internat. Assn. Forensic Toxicologists, Calif. Assn. Toxicologists, Camelback Toastmasters, U.S. Corr. Chess Team (player). Office: Ariz Dept Pub Safety Crime Lab PO Box 6638 2310 W Encanto Blvd Phoenix AZ 85009-1823

ADLER, LAUREL ANN, educational administrator, consultant; b. Cleve., Sept. 6, 1948; d. Clarence Linsley and Margaret Ann (Roberts) Wheeler; children: David, Anthony, Jennifer. BA, U. Calif.-Irvine, 1968; MA, UCLA, 1972; EdD, U. La Verne, 1980. Adult Edn. adminstr. Hacienda La Puente Unified Sch. Dist., 1972-79; dir. career and vocat. edn. El Monte Union High Sch. Dist., 1979-83; supt. East San Gabriel Valley Regional Occupational Ctr., West Covina, Calif., 1984—; instr. Calif. State U.-L.A., 1979-81; instr. UCLA, 1989—; cons. Trust Ty. Pacific Islands, 1979—, L.A. Community Colls, 1993—. Recipient Nat. Vol. Action award 1974; Calif. Consortium Ind. Study Recognition award of Outstanding Ednl. Program, 1983, Calif. Sch. Adminstrs. award, 1981, Woman Achievement award YWCA, 1991; named Citizen of Yr., La Puente C. of C., 1977, Outstanding Vocat. Educator, Hoffman Ednl. Systems, 1983. Mem. Assn. Calif. Sch. Adminstrs., Internat. Reading Assn., Assn. Supervision and Curriculum Devel., Calif. Consortium Ind. Study, Phi Delta Kappa. Author: A Self Evaluation Model for Micronesian Education Programs, 1987, Poor Readers, What Do They Really See on the Page?, 1987, Shedding Light on Reading Disabilities, 1989, How Students and Programs Benefit From Business/Education Partnerships, 1993; pub. Essential English for Micronesians, Beginning, 1980; Essential English for Micronesians, 1980; Reading Exercises for Micronesians, 1980; contbr. articles to profl. jours. Home: 3366 S Garden Terrace Ln La Puente CA 91745-6244 Office: E San Gabriel Valley Regional Occupational Ctr 1024 W Workman Ave West Covina CA 91790-1755

ADLER, LOUISE DECARL, bankruptcy judge; b. 1945. BA, Chatham Coll., Pitts.; JD, Loyola U., Chgo. Bar: Ill., 1970, Calif., 1972. Staff atty. Chgo. Title and Trust Co., 1970-71; practicing atty. San Diego, 1972-84; standing trustee in bankruptcy Bankruptcy Ct. for So. Dist. Calif., 1974-79; judge bankruptcy Bankruptcy Ct. for So. Dist. Calif., San Diego, 1984—. Mem. editorial bd. Calif. Bankruptcy Jour., 1991-92. Fellow Am. Coll. Bankruptcy; mem. San Diego County Bar Assn. (chair bus. law study sect. 1979, fed. ct. com. 1983-84), Lawyers Club of San Diego (bd. dirs. 1972-73, treas. 1972-75, sec. 1972-74, v.p. 1974-75), San Diego Bankruptcy Forum (bd. dirs. 1989-92), Nat. Conf. Bankruptcy Judges (bd. dirs. 1989-91, sec. 1992-93, v.p. 1993-94, pres. 1994-95). Office: US Bankruptcy Ct 325 W F St San Diego CA 92101-6017

ADLER, PETER, sociologist, educator; b. N.Y.C., Feb. 3, 1952; s. Jacob and Beatrice (Kaplan) A.; m. Patricia Ann Heller, Aug. 20, 1972; children: Jori, Brye. AB, Washington U., St. Louis, 1973; MA, U. Chgo., 1974; PhD, U. Calif., San Diego, 1980. Asst. prof. U. Tulsa, 1980-86; assoc. prof. Washington U., 1986-87; assoc. prof., chair sociology dept. U. Denver, 1987-93, prof. sociology, 1993—. Author: Momentum, 1981, Membership Roles in Field Research, 1987, Backboards and Blackboards, 1991; editor: (book) Constructions of Deviance, 1994, Jour. of Contemporary Ethnography, 1986—, Sociol. Studies of Child Devel., 1985-92. Mem. Am. Sociol. Assn. (chair sect. on children), Soc. for Study of Social Problems, Soc. for Study of Symbolic Interaction (v.p.), Midwest Sociol. Soc. Office: U Denver Dept Sociology Denver CO 80208

ADLER, RICHARD PAUL, computer company executive, writer; b. N.Y.C., Nov. 8, 1942; s. Alan and Pauline (Bloomgarden) A.; m. Elizabeth Walcott Fouratt Adler, Aug. 11, 1968; 1 child, Hilary Elizabeth Walcott Adler. AB, Harvard Coll., 1964; MA, U. Calif., Berkeley, 1968; MBA, McLaren Sch. Bus., 1992. Asst. dir. Aspen Inst., Palo Alto, Calif., 1972-76; sr. rsch. fellow Inst. for the Future, Menlo Park, Calif., 1979-90; sr. v.p. SeniorNet, San Francisco, 1990—; asst. prof. Oberlin (Ohio) Coll., 1969-72; bd. dirs. Interactive Svcs. Assn., Arlington, Va. (chair rsch. com. 1986-88). Co-author: The Electronic Box Office, 1974, The Effects of Television Advertising on Children, 1979, Teletext and Videotex in the United States, 1984, Electronic Banking-A Decision Makers Guide, 1988. Home: 425 Seale Ave Palo Alto CA 94301 Office: SeniorNet One Kearny St San Francisco CA 94108

ADLER, SHELLEY, business owner, poet, English educator; b. Detroit, Sept. 28, 1945; d. Calvin Jerome and Florence Jeanne (Cohen) Goodman; m. Norman T. Adler, 1968 (div. 1986); children: Shira Tamar, Tanya Aviv, Ari Chaim, Kiva Tal, Tahg Khorin; life ptnr. Susan B. Weinstein. BA in English, UCLA, 1966, MA in English, 1968; MS in Edn., U. Pa., 1972; MS in Counseling, Villanova U., 1983. Cert. secondary tchr., calif.; lic. barber, Pa., Calif. Tchr. English Carlmont High Sch., Belmont, Calif., 1986; counselor San Mateo (Calif.) Youth Devel. Bd., 1988-89; tchr. English Menlo Oaks Sch., East Palo Alto, Calif., 1990, Chabot Coll., Hayward, Calif., 1991; owner Home Haircuts, Millbrae, Calif., 1993. Author poems pub. in 4 Lyric Poets, 1968, Voices of Two Women, 1974, Seasons, 1980, Little Rages, 1985, Poems of a Pervert, 1995. Committeeman Narberth (Pa.) City, 1973-75; mem. task force Phila., 1984, 85. Sgt. U.S. Women's Army Res., 1973-75. Mem. NOW, NGLTF, Nat. Parks & Conservation Assn., Sha'ar Zahav, Temple Beth Jacob. Democrat. Jewish.

ADOLPH, MARY ROSENQUIST, financial executive; b. Springfield, Mass., Oct. 7, 1949; d. Jesse Woodson and Doris May (Marquette) Rosenquist; m. Earl Anthony Soares, Mar. 18, 1972 (div. 1982); m. Joseph Edward Adolph, Oct. 3, 1986. Student San Domenico Sch., 1966-68, Dominican Coll., San Rafael, 1967-69, Calif., San Francisco Conservatory of Music, 1968-70; A.A., Coll. of Marin, 1969. Asst. v.p. Western Travelers Life Ins. Co./Putnam Fin. Services, San Rafael, 1970-80; v.p. Unimarc, Ltd., Novato, Calif., 1980-83; v.p. mktg. Western States Monetary Planning Services, Inc., Newhall, Calif., 1983-88; asst. to pres. Fed. Inventory Wholesale, Inc., 1988-90; v.p. E.W. Richardson & Assocs. Inc., Newhall, Calif., 1991-94; dir. ops. Tri Telic Inc., Santa Rosa, Calif., 1994—. Prodr. Radio Talk Show Financial Information, 1994—. Mem. exec. com. San Marin Valley Homeowners Assn., 1979-81. Mem. Internat. Assn. Fin. Planners, Life Underwriters Assn. Democrat. Roman Catholic. Home: 1676 Guerneville Rd Santa Rosa CA 95403-4110 Office: Tri Telic Inc 555 5th St Ste 320 Santa Rosa CA 95401-6324

ADRANGI, BAHRAM, business educator; b. Tabriz, Iran, Jan. 8, 1953; s. Javad Adrangi and Roohangiz Ghalibofian. BS in Econs., U. Tehran, Iran, 1973; MBA, Western Ill. U., 1975; PhD in Econs., U. Oreg., 1982. Prof. bus. U. Portland, Oreg., 1982—; mem. coun. econ. advisors Metro, Portland, 1994—. Contbr. articles to profl. publs. Recipient Best Paper award Midwest Bus. Adminstrn. Assn., 1992, Transp. Rsch. Forum, 1987. Mem. Am. Econ. Assn., Western Econ. Assn., Atlantic Econ. Assn., Western Decision Sci. Assn., Western Regional Sci. Assn. Office: U Portland Sch Bus 5000 N Willamette Blvd Portland OR 97203-5743

AFFLECK, JULIE KARLEEN, accountant; b. Upland, Calif., Dec. 23, 1944; d. Karl W. and Juliette O. (Oppegaard) Hall; m. William J. Affleck, Aug. 29, 1964; children: Stephen, Tamara. BS in Bus., U. Colo., 1967; MBA, U. Denver, 1972. CPA, Colo. Cost acct. IBM, Boulder, Colo., 1967-71; audit supr. Ernst & Young, Denver, 1972-79, Rosemary E. Weiss & Co., Denver, 1979-80; ptnr. Affleck, Melaragno, Gilman & Co., Denver, 1980—; tchr. Colo. Soc. CPA's., U. Denver; dir., corp. sec. Better-Way Electric, Inc. Treas., bd. dirs. Bal Swan Children's Ctr. for Handicapped, Broomfield, Colo. Mem. Am. Inst. CPA's., Colo. Soc. CPA's., Am. Soc. Women Accts. (pres. chpt. 1980-81), Nat. Assn. Women Bus. Owners (treas., dir., pres. 1988-89). Republican. Lutheran. Home: 1270 Elmwood Ct Broomfield CO 80020-7609

AFSARI, KHOSROW, physician, consultant, internist; b. Babol, Mazandoran, Iran, Apr. 26, 1941; came to U.S., 1970; s. Abraham and Afsar (Shahgholi) A.; m. Susan Mahshid Abedi, June 21, 1970; children: Peter, Mary, Bobby, Michael. BA, U. Shiraz, Iran, 1963; MD, Shiraz Med. Sch., 1969. Diplomate Am. Bd. of Internal Medicine. Rotaing intern U. Hosp. of Shiraz Med. Sch., 1969-70; intern in internal medicine Balt. City Hosp., 1970-71; fellow dept. medicine and infectious disease Johns Hopkins Med. Sch. and Hosp., Balt., 1970-73; asst. resident Balt. City Hosp., 1971-72, sr. resident in medicine, 1972-73; sr. resident in medicine U. Ill., Chgo., 1973-74; mem. staff Abraham Lincoln Med. Sch. U. Hosp., 1974-75; pvt. practice Lombard, Ill., 1974-75; mem. staff Elmhurst (Ill.) Hosp., 1974-75; asst. prof. medicne U. of Shiraz Med. Sch., 1975-76; pvt. practice internal medicine, cons. infectious diseases San Pablo, Calif., 1977—; mem. staff, cons. Brookside Hosp., San Peublo, 1977, chmn. antibiotic com., mem. infectious control com., 1978—, chmn. dept. medicine, 1982-84, pres. med. staff, 1987, chmn. physician well-being com., 1991—; clin. asst. prof. medicine U. San Francisco, 1994; mem. staff, cons. infectious diseases Dr.'s Hosp. of Pinole, Calif., 1977—, mem. infectious disease control com., 1988—; chmn. physician well-being com. Brookside Corp., 1992—. Fellow ACP; mem. AMA, ACCMA, CMA. Home: 4052 Happy Valley Rd Lafayette CA 94549-2428 Office: 2089 Yale Rd # 21 San Pablo CA 94806

AGCAOILI, LAWRENCE E., systems analyst/programmer; b. Honolulu, June 1, 1964; s. Pacifico Malasig and Loraine (Balanay) A.; m. Lorna Gayle Chang, May 25, 1987; children: Leanna, Andrew. BS in Computer Sci., Chaminde U., Honlulu, 1987. Sr. programmer, analyst Chaney, Brooks & Co., Honolulu, 1987-94; pres. Advanced Computer Cons., Honolulu, 1994—; pres. Advanced Computer Consulting, Honolulu, 1980—. Mem. Data Processing Mgmt. Assn. (Edn. Spl. Interest Group), Hawaii PC Users Group, Hawaii Macintosh and Apple User's Soc. Office: Advanced Computer Consulting PO Box 17040 Honolulu HI 96817

AGEE, VICTORIA VALENTINE, librarian, freelance indexer; b. L.A., Sept. 21, 1947; d. Edward S. and Florence Armanella (Davie) Powers; m. Forrest Jack Agee, Feb. 17, 1973; children: Forrest Jack, Amber Valentine. AA, Mt. San Antonia Jr. Coll., 1967; BA, UCLA, 1969, MLS, 1970. Libr. asst. children's svcs. Pomona (Calif.) Pub. Libr., 1962-67; libr. asst. English reading room UCLA, 1968-70, cataloger engring. & math. scis. libr., 1970-71; chief tech. processing Nat. League Cities/U.S. Conf. Mayors, Washington, 1971-72; libr. Cable TV Info. Ctr., Washington, 1972-73; pub. svcs. libr./asst. libr. The Urban Inst., Washington, 1974-77; dir. Agee Indexing Svcs., Silver Spring, Md., 1979—, Albuquerque, N.Mex., 1993—; instr. USDA cours, 1994—. Mem. Am. Soc. Indexers (bd. dirs. D.C. chpt. 1987-89), N.Mex. Book Assn., Spl. Librs. Assn., Westerners, Beta Phi Mu. Democrat. Presbyn.

AGEE, WILLIAM J., transportation, engineering and construction company executive; b. Boise, Idaho, Jan. 5, 1938; s. Harold J. and Suzanne (McReynolds) A.; m. Mary Cunningham, June 5, 1982; children: Mary Alana, William N. AA, Boise Jr. Coll., 1958; BS with high honors, U. Idaho, 1960; MBA with distinction, Harvard U., 1963; DSc in Indsl. Mgmt. (hon.), Lawrence Inst. Tech., 1977, Nathaniel Hawthorne Coll., 1977; D.C.S., Eastern Mich. U., 1978; LLD (hon.), U. Detroit, 1980; DBA (hon.), Bryant Coll., 1980, Cleary Coll., 1980. Various positions Boise Cascade Corp., 1963-69, sr. v.p., CFO, 1969-72; exec. v.p., CFO Bendix Corp., Southfield, Mich., 1972-76, pres., 1976-79, COO, 1976-77, chmn. bd., 1977-83; chmn., CEO Semper Enterprises, Inc., Osterville, Mass., from 1983; chmn. bd., pres., CEO Morrison Knudsen Corp., Boise, 1988-95; bd. dirs. Key Corp.; chmn. data processing and office automation grace Commn., 1981-82; presdl. appointee U.S. Quadrennial Commn., 1988. Chmn. Gov.'s Higher Edn. Capital Investment Adv. Com., 1979; mem. adv. coun. Japan-U.S. Econ. Relations, 1982-84. Named Disting. Alumnus Boise State U. (formerly Boise Jr. Coll.), 1972; recipient Alumni Achievement Award Harvard U. Bus. Sch., 1977; named to U. Idaho Hall of Fame, 1978. Mem. AICPA, Idaho Soc. CPAs, Mich. Assn. CPAs, Coun. on Fgn. Rels., Brit-N.Am. Com., Conf. Bd., Bus. Roundtable, Harvard Bus. Sch. Assocs., Phi Kappa Phi, Arid Club Boise, Economic Club, Hillcrest Country Club, Oyster Harbors Club (Osterville, Mass.). Republican. Roman Catholic. Office: Morrison Knudsen Corp Morrison Knudsen Plz PO Box 73 Boise ID 83729*

AGER, STEPHANIE, public relations executive; b. Seattle, Apr. 28, 1946; d. Robert Lee and Jean (Purrington) Ager; B.A. in Art, U. Wash., 1969; m. Howard Lutz Kirz, Mar. 9, 1978. V.P., gen. mgr. Cole & Weber Pub. Relations subs. Ogilvy & Mather; pres. Ager & Assocs., advt. agy.; pres., chief exec. officer Ager/BP&N Pub. Relations, 1986—. Pres., Wash. Panhellenic, 1967-68; with Ager & Assocs. Pub. Rels., 1990—. Mem. Women in

Communications (v.p. fin. 1981), Pub. Relations Soc. Am. (Totem award 1980, 86), Kappa Kappa Gamma. Club: Seattle Tennis, Columbia Tower. Home: 705 Mcgilvra Blvd E Seattle WA 98112-5051 Office: Ager & Assocs 411 University St Fl 12 Seattle WA 98101-2507

AGERBEK, SVEN, mechanical engineer; b. Soerabaya, Dutch Indies, Aug. 2, 1926; came to U.S., 1958, naturalized, 1964; s. Niels Magnus and Else Heidam (Nielsen) Agerbek-Poulsen; m. Helen Hadsbjerg Gerup, May 30, 1963; 1 child, Jesper. MSME, Tech. U., Denmark, 1952; LLB, LaSalle Ext. U., 1967; postgrad., UCLA, 1969. Registered profl. engr., Calif., Ohio, Fla. With Danish Refrigeration Research Inst., Copenhagen, 1952; engr. B.P. Oil Co., Copenhagen, 1952-54; refrigeration insp. J. Lauritzen, Copenhagen, 1954-56; engr. Danish-Am. Gulf Oil Co., Copenhagen, 1956-58; instr. Ohio U., Athens, 1958-60; asst. prof. Calif. State Poly. U., San Luis Obispo, 1960-62; prin. engr., environment dept. Ralph M. Parsons Co., Los Angeles, 1962-73; engrng. supr. Bechtel Power Co., Norwalk, Calif., 1973-85; pres., owner Woodcraft Cabinets, Inc., Rancho Cordova, Calif., 1985-90; owner Acrebrook Cons., Fair Oaks, Calif., 1990—; exec. v.p. U.S.E., Inc., Incline Village, Nev., 1994—. Past mem. Luth. Ch. council, pres. Luth. Sch. bd. Served with Danish underground movement, World War II. Mem. ASHRAE (mem. tech. com., author Guide on Air Conditioning of Nuclear Power Plants), Danish Engrng. Soc. Home and Office: Acrebrook Consulting 5201 Vista Del Oro Way Fair Oaks CA 95628-4148 also: USE Inc Engrng Office 9244 Old State Hwy Newcastle CA 95658

AGNER, WAYNE RICHARD, journalist; b. Encino, Calif., Oct. 15, 1956; s. Edwin Carvel and Beverly Roberta (Jones) A. BS, Calif. State U., Fresno, 1982. Reporter Paradise (Calif.) Post, 1983, mng. editor, 1984-86; reporter Selma (Calif.) Enterprise, 1984; editor Manteca (Calif.) Bulletin, 1986-88; news editor Santa Maria (Calif.) Times, 1988-90, mng. editor, 1990—. Bd. dirs. Santa Maria Valley Jaycees, 1989—. Newspaper recipient gen. excellence award Calif. Newspaper Pubs. Assn., 1987, 94. Mem. Nat. Press Photographers Assn., Soc. Newspaper Design.

AGONIA, BARBARA ANN, emeritus English language educator, communications consultant; b. St. Louis, June 11, 1934; d. Robert Lewis and Suzanne (Carter) Klinefelter; m. Robert James Agonia, Mar. 25, 1972. Student, U. Exeter, Devon, Eng., 1954-55; BA, Hanover Coll., 1957; MA, U. Nev., Las Vegas, 1971; postgrad., U. Nev., Reno, 1983-84. Tchr. Carrollton (Ill.) Community Unit High Sch., 1955-56, 59-61, White Hall (Ill.) Community Unit High Sch., 1957-59; tchr., chmn. dept. English ROVA Community Unit High Sch., Oneida, Ill., 1961-69; prof. English Clark County Community Coll., North Las Vegas, Nev., 1971-89, chmn. dept., 1972-75, 87-89, dir. re-entry ctr., 1980-83; interim v.p. acad. affairs Clark County C.C., North Las Vegas, Nev., 1994-95; speaker in field, Ind., Ill., Nev., Eng., 1952—. Author poems. Vol. Opportunity Village, Las Vegas, Nev., 1985—; bd. dirs. Friends of Nev. Wilderness, Las Vegas, 1985—, Community Action Against Rape. Mem. Western Lit. Assn. (Golden award 1984), Shakespeare Assn. Am., Coll. Conf. Composition and Communication (exec. com.), Nev. State Edn. Assn. (exec. bd. 1975-79), League United Latin Am. Citizens (nat. parliamentarian 1978-82), Internat. Platform Assn., Soroptimist Internat. (parliamentarian Las Vegas 1984—, pres.-elect 1986-87, pres. 1987-88, Women Helping Women award 1983, Woman of Distinction 1986, dist. dir. 1994—), Order of Eastern Star (Worthy Matron 1960-61). Methodist. Home and Office: 3411 Frontier St Las Vegas NV 89102-8158

AGOSTON, MAX KARL, computer science educator; b. Stockerau, Austria, Mar. 25, 1941; s. George Anton Agoston and Grete (Mihokovic) Broadwell. BA, Reed Coll., 1962; MS, Yale U., 1964, PhD, 1967; MS in Computer Sci., Stanford U., 1977. Lectr. Wesleyan U., Middletown, Conn., 1966-67, asst. prof., 1967-75; lectr. San Jose (Calif.) State U., 1976-77, asst. prof., 1977-80, assoc. prof., 1980—; vis. lectr. Heidelberg U., Germany, 1970-71; vis. fellow U. Auckland, New Zealand, 1973-74. Author: Albebraic Topology: A First Course, 1976; contbr. articles to profl. jours. Mem. Assn. Computing Machinery, Am. Math. Soc., Computer Soc. IEEE, Spl. Interest Group in Computer Graphics of ACM. Office: San Jose State U Dept Math and Computer Sci San Jose CA 95192

AGRAS, WILLIAM STEWART, psychiatry educator; b. London, May 17, 1929; came to U.S., 1959; s. Harry and Isabel (Stewart) A.; m. Mary J. Jenkins, Jan. 7, 1955; children: Alison, Peter, Andrew, Catrin. MD, U. London, 1955; diploma in psychiatry, McGill U., Montreal, Que., Can., 1962. From instr. to prof. psychiatry U. Vt. & State Agrl. Coll., Burlington, 1962-69; prof., chmn. dept. U. Miss., University, 1969-73; prof. Stanford (Calif.) U., 1973—. Author: Behavior Therapy: Toward an Applied Clinical Science, 1979, Panic, 1985; editor Jour. Applied Behavioral Analysis, Annals Behavioral Medicine; contbr. numerous articles to profl. jours. Fellow Royal Coll. Physicians, Ctr. Advanced Study Behavioral Sci.; mem. Soc. Behavioral Medicine (pres. 1979), Assn. for Advancement Behavioral Therapy (pres. 1986). Home: 515 Gerona Rd Palo Alto CA 94305-8451

AGRESTI, JACK JOSEPH, construction company executive; b. San Francisco, 1937. Grad., San Jose State U., 1959. Pres., CEO Guy F. Atkinson Co., South San Francisco. Mem. Constrn. Industry Inst., Soc. Am. Mil. Engrs., Am. Arbitration Assn. Office: Guy F Atkinson Co 1001 Bayhill Dr Fl 2 San Bruno CA 94066-3013*

AGUIAR, WILLIAM, JR., music and dance critic; b. San Francisco, Feb. 8, 1933; s. William and Maria Theresa (von Heyden) A. Pvt. mus. studies with, Igor Stravinsky, Kempff and Igor Markevitch, Wilhelm Kempff, and Igor Markevitch. Music and dance critic Hokubei Mainichi, San Francisco, 1968—. Mem. Music Critic Assn., Press Club of San Francisco. Democrat. Roman Catholic.

AGUILAR, GALE RAMON, computer industry executive; b. Pitts., June 6, 1932; s. Henry Ramon and Jessie Bell (Pahel) A.; m. Alice Josephine Jackan; children: Karen, Robert Ramon, Barbara Annette. BA in Econs., Calif. State U., L.A., 1958. Sales rep. IBM, Phoenix and L.A., 1955-61; mktg. rep. IBM, L.A., 1961-67; mktg. exec. dir. IBM, N.Y.C., 1967-79; mktg. and devel. exec. dir. IBM, N.Y.C. and Calif., 1979-82; v.p. mktg. Prime Corp., Boston, 1982-88, Stardent Corp., Sunnyvale, Calif., 1988-89; exec. v.p. SF2-MTI SF2-MIT, Sunnyvale, 1989-92; pres. Aguilar & Assocs., Watsonville, Calif., 1992—. Inventor storage product, 1991. Committeeman Rep. Party, 1960-62. Sgt. U.S. Army, 1952-54. Home: 12225 Watsonville Rd Gilroy CA 95020-9471 Office: Aguilar & Assocs 12225 Watsonville Rd Gilroy CA 95020-9471

AGUILAR, RAUL ABRAHAM, adult school administrator; b. L.A., Feb. 12, 1954; s. Arturo Joseph and Angie (Sierra) A.; m. Ofelia G. Vasquez, 1990; children: Julio, Angie. BA in English, Calif. State U., L.A., 1979; MS in Edn., Mount St. Mary's Coll., 1985. Tchr. Met. High Sch. L.A.U.S.D., L.A., 1980-85; in-house dean W. Hollywood Opportunity Ctr., L.A., 1985-87; prin. John Hope High Sch. L.A.U.S.D., L.A., 1987-89, Highland Park High Sch. L.A.U.S.D., L.A., 1989-91; asst. prin. Pacoima Skills Ctr. L.A. Unified Sch. Dist., 1991-92; asst. prin. L.A. Community Adult Sch., 1992—; tchr., adv. Belmont Community Adult Sch., L.A., 1988-91; mem. adv. com. Mount St. Mary's Coll., L.A., 1987-90. Mem. Calif. Continuing Edn. Assn. (v.p. 1990-91, sec. 1989-90, Jerry Dean Medallion award 1984), Associated Adminstrs. L.A., Coun. Mex.-Am. Adminstrs., Calif. Assn. Regional Occupational Programs/Ctrs., Assn. Calif. Sch. Adminstrs., Aussi Toastmasters (cert. toastmaster 1989), The Cousteau Soc., Ctr. Marine Conservation. Democrat. Home: 810 S Chevy Chase Dr Glendale CA 91205-2538 Office: LA Community Adult Sch 4650 W Olympic Blvd Los Angeles CA 90019-1831

AGUILAR, ROBERT P., federal judge; b. Madera, Calif., Apr. 15, 1931. B.A., U. Calif., Berkeley, 1954; J.D., Hastings Coll. Law, San Francisco, 1958. Bar: Calif. 1960, U.S. Supreme Ct. 1966. Ptnr. Mezzetti and Aguilar, 1960-70, Aguilar and Aguilar, 1970-76, Aguilar & Edwards, San Jose, Calif., 1976-79; superior ct. judge Santa Clara County, 1979-80; judge U.S. Dist. Ct., No. Dist. Calif., San Francisco, 1980—; Mem. Regional Criminal Justice Planning Bd., from 1974; chmn. Santa Clara County (Calif.) Juvenile Justice Commn., 1975; mem. Santa Clara County Drug Abuse Task Force, 1974. Mem. Calif. Trial Lawyers Assn., Santa Clara County Criminal Trial Lawyers Assn., Am. Bar Assn., Calif. Bar Assn., Santa Clara County Bar Assn. (pres. 1972). Office: US Dist Ct 280 S 1st St San Jose CA 95113-3002*

AGUILAR-POSADA, GLADYS MARIA, counselor; b. Mérida, Mexico, Mar. 16, 1965; came to the U.S., 1968; d. Francisco Javier and Gladys Maria (Salazar) Aguilar; m. Ramon Jorge Posada, June 30, 1990; 1 child, Emmanuel. BS cum laude, Loyola Marymount U., 1987; MS, Calif. State U., 1990. Cert. in pupil personnel svcs. Youth min. St. Francis of Assisi Parish, L.A., 1987-88; sch. counselor Concern Counseling Svcs., Fullerton, Calif., 1988-89; sch. counselor, tchr. St. Lucy's Priory High Sch., Glendora, Calif., 1989-90; intern Cath. Psychol. Svcs. Cath. Charities of L.A., L.A., 1990-93; bilingual elem. sch. counselor L.A. Unified Sch. Dist., 1993—; behavioral therapist Inst. for Applied Behavioral Analysis, L.A., 1988-89; marriage, family and child counseling intern Brown & Assocs., Whittier, Calif., 1989-93. Eucharistic min., lector St. Francis of Assisi Cath. Ch., 1986-92. Mem. Calif. Assn. Marriage and Family Therapists, L.A. Sch. Counselors Assn., Psi Chi, Alpha Sigma Nu. Home: 836 Forest Hills Dr Covina CA 91724

AGUILERA, DONNA CONANT, psychologist, researcher; b. Kinmundy, Ill.; d. Charles E. and Daisy L. (Frost) Conant; m. George Limon Aguilera; children: Bruce Allen, Craig Steven. B.S., UCLA, 1963, M.S., 1965; Ph.D., U. So. Calif., 1974. Teaching asst. UCLA, 1965, grad. rsch. asst., 1965-66; prof. Calif. State U., L.A., 1966-81; cons. crisis intervention Didi Hirsch Community Mental Health Ctr., L.A., 1967-82; mem. Def. Adv. Com. Women in the Services, 1978-82; originator, project dir. Project Link Lab. U. Author: Crisis Intervention: Theory and Methodology, 1974, 7th edit., 1993 (pub. in 11 langs, braille and tapes), Review of Psychiatric Nursing, 1977, 7th edit., 1978, Crisis Intervention: Therapy for Psychological Emergencies, 1983; contbr. articles to profl. jours. Docent Huntington Libr. San Marino, Calif. 1991—. NIH fellow, 1972-75. Fellow Am. Acad. Nursing (sec. 1976-77, pres. 1977-78), Acad. Psychiat. Nurse Specialists, Internat. Acad. Eclectic Psychotherapists (pres. 1987-89); mem. Am. Nurses Assn., Faculty Women's Assn., Am. Psychol. Assn., Calif. Psychol. Assn., AAUP, Alpha Tau Delta, Sigma Theta Tau. Home: 3924 Dixie Canyon Ave Sherman Oaks CA 91423-4830 Office: 450 N Bedford Dr Ste 210 Beverly Hills CA 90210-4306

AGUIRRE, LINDA G., state legislator; b. Flagstaff, Ariz., July 12, 1951; m. John Aguirre; children: Eric, Stephanie. BA, Ariz. State U., 1978. Educator; mem. Ariz. Ho. of Reps., mem. banking and ins., human svcs. and transp. coms. Active Ariz. Sch. Bd., Nat. Sch. Bd., Nat. Hispanic Sch. Bd., Ariz. Citizens Edn. Mem. South Mountain C. of C. Democrat. Office: Ariz House of Reps State Capitol Phoenix AZ 85007

AGUIRRE-BATTY, MERCEDES, Spanish/English language and literature educator; b. Cd Juarez, Mex., Dec. 20, 1952; came to U.S., 1957; d. Alejandro M. and Mercedes (Péon) Aguirre; m. Hugh K. Batty, Mar. 17, 1979; 1 child, Henry B. BA, U. Tex., El Paso, 1974, MA, 1977. Instr. ESL Paso del Norte- Prep Sch., Cd Juarez, 1973-74; teaching asst. ESL and English U. Tex., El Paso, 1974-77; instr. ESL English Lang. Svcs., Bridgeport, Conn., 1977-80; instr. Spanish and English, coord. modern lang. Sheridan (Wyo.) Coll., 1980—; pres. faculty senate Shridan (Wyo.) Coll., 1989-90; adj. prof. Spanish, U. Autonoma Cd Juarez, 1975; adj. prof. Spanish and English, Sacred Heart U., Fairfield, Conn., 1977-80; spkr. in field. Bd. dirs. Wyo. Coun. for the Humanities, 1988-92; translator county and dist. cts., Sheridan. NEH fellow, 1991, 92; Wyo. State Dept. Edn. grantee, 1991. Mem. Wyo. Fgn. Lang. Tchrs. Assn. (pres. 1990-92), Am. Assn. Tchrs. Spanish and Portuguese (founder, 1st pres. Wyo. chpt. 1987-90), TESOL, Sigma Delta Mu (v.p. 1992—), Sigma Delta Pi (pres. 1974-75). Office: Sheridan Coll NWCCD 3059 Coffeen Ave Sheridan WY 82801-9133

AHERN, ARLEEN FLEMING, retired librarian; b. Mt. Harris, Colo., Oct. 15, 1922; d. John R. and Josephine (Vidmar) Fleming; m. George Irving Ahern Jr., June 14, 1944; 1 child, George Irving. BA, U. Utah, 1943; MA, U. Denver, 1962; postgrad. U. Colo., 1967. Library asst. Army Air Force Library, Salt Lake City, 1943-44; library asst. Colo. Women's Coll. Library (now U. Denver/CWC Campus), 1952-60, acquisitions librarian, 1960—, rep. Adult Edn. Council Denver, 1960-90, reference librarian Penrose Library, WEC librarian, assoc. prof. librarianship through 1987, U. Denver Penrose Libr.; prof. emeritus, U. Denver; retired. Committeewoman, Republican Com., Denver, 1958-59; vol., Opera Colo. Guild, Denver Lyric Opera, U. Denver Women's Libr. Assn., bd. dirs., 1992-93, Samaritan House Guild, Jeanne Jugan (Little Sisters Poor) Aux., Colo. Symphony Guild, Cinema Study Club Colo., Carson Brierly Dance Libr., bd. dirs. Mem. AAUP, ALA, Mountain Plains Library Assn., Colo. (1st v.p., pres. 1969-70, dir. 1971—), Library Assn., Altrusa Club of Denver (2d v.p. 1968-69, dir. 1971-74, 76, 78), Soc. Am. Archivists, Mountain Plains Adult Edn. Assn., Denver Botanic Gardens. Home: 746 Monaco Pky Denver CO 80220-6041

AHERN, GEOFFREY LAWRENCE, behavioral neurologist; b. N.Y.C., Feb. 20, 1954. BA, SUNY, Purchase, 1976; MS, Yale U., 1978, PhD in Psychology, 1981, MD, 1984. Med. intern Waterbury (Conn.) Hosp., 1984-85; resident in neurology Boston U., 1985-88; fellow in behavioral neurology Beth Israel Hosp., Boston, 1988-90; instr. neurology Harvard Med. Sch., Boston, 1988-90; asst. prof. neurology and psychology U. Ariz., Tucson, 1990—. Contbr. articles to profl. jours., chpts. to books. Mem. Am. Acad. Neurology. Office: Univ Med Ctr Dept Neurology 1501 N Campbell Ave Tucson AZ 85724

AHERNS, PAMELA BENGSON, state legislator; b. Portland, Oreg., Nov. 15, 1945; 1 child, Melissa Ann. Student, Ea. Wash. State U. Mem. Idaho Ho. of Reps., 1983—; with equipment rental bus. Active Boise State Found. Named to Hall of Fame, Idaho Rep. Party. Mem. Idaho Hosp. Assn. (dir. polit. activities), Idaho Rep. Women's Fedn. (pres. 1983—). Republican. Presbyterian. Home: 2854 S Swallowtail Ln Boise ID 83706-6138 Office: Dept of Administration State of Idaho 650 W State St Boise ID 83720

AHLEM, DIANA GRACE, systems analyst; b. Turlock, Calif., Sept. 12, 1952; d. Ralph Nathaniel Ahlem and Grace Diana (Labes) Torbonn; m. Charles James Schwartz, Jan. 28, 1984; 1 child. BA, Stanford U., 1974; MPH, U. Hawaii, 1977. Sys. analyst UCLA Extension, L.A., 1987. Mem. Stanford Assn. Democrat. Office: Demometrika 2302 Glencoe Ave Venice CA 90291-4041

AHLFELD, CHARLES EDWARD, nuclear industry executive; b. Peoria, Ill, Aug. 9, 1940; s. John Frederick and Kathryn Louise (Weisbruch) A.; m. Barbara Anne Slusher, Dec. 29, 1962; children: Judith Anne, Nancy Lynn, Sharon Leigh (dec.). BS, U. Fla., 1962; MS, Fla. State U., 1964, PhD, 1968. Grad. asst. Fla. State U., Tallahassee, 1962-67; research physicist E.I. du-Pont-Savannah River Lab., Aiken, S.C., 1967-75, staff physicist, 1975-78, research mgr., 1985-86; asst. chief supr. E.I. duPont-Savannah River Plant, Aiken, 1978-81, chief supr., 1981-84, asst. dept. supt., 1984-85, program mgr., 1987-89; dept. mgr. Westinghouse Savannah River Co., Aiken, 1989-93; head engrng. divsn. joint ctrl. team Internat. Theronuclaer Exptl. Reactor, La Jolla, Calif., 1993—. Patentee in field. Chmn. sch. bd. St. Mary's Sch., Aiken, 1977; active United Way, Aiken, 1982-85. Mem. Am. Nuclear Soc. (sect. chmn. 1983-84, Cert. of Governance 1984), Am. Phys. Soc. Roman Catholic. Home: 5720 Desert View Dr La Jolla CA 92037 Office: 11025 N Torrey Pines Rd La Jolla CA 92037-1030

AHLGREN, GIBSON-TAYLOR, real estate broker; b. Memphis, Sept. 7, 1940; s. Frank Richard and Nona Elizabeth (Alley) A. B.S., U. Md., 1967; J.D., Western State U., San Diego, 1978. Legis. clk. U.S. Senate, Washington, 1963-67, spl. asst., 1970-71; legis. rep. Associated Gen. Contractors, Washington, 1971-73, San Diego, 1973-74; campaign dir. Brown for Gov. Calif., 1974; mgmt. cons. Ahlgren, Peters & Assocs., La Jolla, Calif., 1975-77; v.p., dir. pub. affairs Gt. Am. First Savs. Bank, San Diego, 1977-84; polit. cons., 1984-85; real estate broker, 1986—. Served to lt. USN, 1967-70; Vietnam. Mem. Pi Kappa Alpha.

AHLSTROM, JOHN, computer infosystem engineer, educator; b. Jamestown, N.Y., July 1, 1942; s. Paul A. and Ruth M. (Conner) A.; m. Anne D. Pemberton, Dec. 15, 1964 (div. June 1976); m. Janice Tribe, June 17, 1982; 1 child, Elizabeth. BA in Internat. Relations, Am. U., Washington, 1964, MA in Internat. Relations, 1968. Founder, systems mgr. Data Resources Inc., Lexington, Mass., 1969-74; operating systems programmer Burroughs Corp., Goleta, Calif., 1974-76; computer micro architect Data Gen. Corp., Mass. and Calif., 1976-78; mgr. software devel. Olivetti Corp., Cupertino, Calif., 1978-79; founder CompuShop Inc., Dallas, 1976-85; mgr. systems architecture Bell-No. Research, Mountain View, Calif., 1979-82; founder, dir. systems engrng. DAVID Systems, Sunnyvale, Calif., 1982-86; adj. prof. computer sci. San Francisco State U., 1976-86, assoc. prof. computer sci., 1986-87; architect network systems Avant-Grade Computing, 1988-89, Boole & Babbage, San Jose, Calif., 1990-95; founder, mng. dir. YASCo L.L.C., Cupertino, Calif., 1995—. Inventor in field. Mem. Assn. Computing Machinery, Computer Soc. of IEEE (affiliate). Office: YASCo 22608 Poppy Dr Cupertino CA 95014

AHMED, IQBAL, psychiatrist, consultant; b. Tumkur, Karnataka, India, Aug. 23, 1951; came to U.S., 1976; s. Rahimuddin Ahmed and Arifa (Banu) Rahimuddin; m. Lisa Suzanne Rose, Oct. 9, 1983; children: Yasmin, Jihan. BS, MB, St. John's Med. Coll., Bangalore, India, 1975. Diplomate in gen. psychiatry and geriatric psychiatry Am. Bd. Psychiatry and Neurology. Intern St. Martha's Hosp., Bangalore, India, 1974-75; resident in psychiatry U. Nebr. Med. Ctr., Omaha, 1976-79; fellowship in consultation Boston U. Sch. Medicine, 1979-81; staff psychiatrist in consultation liaison psychiatry Boston City Hosp., 1981-87, staff psychiatrist, geriatric psychiatry, 1983-85, dir. geriatric neuropsychiatry unit, 1985-87, dir. geriatric psychiatry, 1988-92; assoc. dir. consultation liaison psychiatry New England Med. Ctr., Boston, 1989-92; asst. prof. psychiatry Sch. Medicine, Boston, U., 1981-87, Sch. Medicine Tufts U., Boston, 1987-92; dir. med. student edn. in psychiatry Boston City Hosp., 1981-87; chief spl. svcs. Hawaii State Hosp., 1992-94, pres. med. staff, 1994-95, chief geriatric psychiatry, 1994—; assoc. prof. John A. Burns Sch. Medicine, U. Hawaii, 1992—, faculty senate, 1994—. Contbr. articles to profl. jours. Mem. Mass. State Dem. Party Minority Caucus, Boston, 1983. Mem. AMA, Am. Psychiat. Assn., Am. Neuropsychiatry Assn., Royal Coll. Psychiatrists, Acad. Psychosomatic Medicine, Am. Acad. Geriatric Psychiatry. Democrat. Office: Hawaii State Hosp 45-710 Keaahala Rd Kaneohe HI 96744-3528

AHN, SAMUEL SEUNGHAE, vascular surgeon, researcher, consultant; b. Pusan, Korea, Feb. 9, 1954; came to U.S., 1959; s. Chai Ho and Sun Duk A.; m. Mi Ryu, Aug. 20, 1983; children: Justin, Alexander. BA in Biology, U. Tex., 1972-74; MD, U. Tex. Southwestern, 1974-78. Dimplomate Am. Bd. Surgery, Am. Bd. Med. Examiners; lic. Tex., Calif. Gen. surgery intern UCLA Med. Ctr., 1978-79, jr. resident gen. surgery, 1979-80, NIH rsch. fellow in surg. oncology, 1980-82, sr. resident gen. surgery, 1982-83, chief resident gen. surgery, 1983-84, clin. fellwo vascular surgery, 1984-85, rsch. fellow vascular surgery, 1985-86, attending surgeon, 1984—; asst. prof. surgery UCLA Med. Sch., 1986-93, assoc. clin. prof., 1994—; adj. asst. prof. surgery UCLA Med. Ctr., 1984-85; attending surgeon Sepulveda (Calif.) VA Med. Ctr., 1985-94; cons. surgeon UCLA Student Health Svcs., 1986—; surg. cons. Endovascular Equipment Cos., 1986-94; organizer facilities and programs in field; task force mem.; numerous com. appointments UCLA, 1985—; guest lectr. and researcher in field. Editor: (with W.S. Moore) Endovascular Surgery, 1989, 2d edit., 1992, (with J. Seeger) Endovascular Surgery for Peripheral Vascular Disease: Surgical Clinics of North America, 1992, (with D. Eton, K. Hodgson) Current Concepts in Endovascular Surgery, 1994; mem. editorial bd. Vascular Forum, 1993-94, Jour. Endovascular Surgery, 1994, Vascular Surgery, 1994; guest reviewer Jour. of Vascular Surgery, 1991-94, Postgraduate Vascular Surgery Jour., 1992-93, Surgery, 1992, Atherosclerosis and Thrombosis, 1992, Jour. of Am. Geriatrics Soc., 1992-93; abstractor Jour. of Vascular Surgery, 1994; contbr. chpts. books, articles to profl. jours. Mem. stroke coun. Am. Heart Assn., 1991—; vol. Korean Med. Missionary, 1969-88, Pub. Edn. of Cancer, 1980-83. East Tex. Chest Found. fellow East Tex. Chest Hosp., Tyler, 1976, Sigvaris award 1986; preceptee Am. Soc. Anestehsiologists, 1976; grantee E.R. Squibb and Sons. 1985-87, 85-86, Olympus Corp., 1985-86, UCLA Med. Aux., 1986, BioQuantum Tech., 1986-87, W.L. Gore and Assocs., 1986-87, 94, UCLA Sch. Medicine, 1986-87, NIH, 1987, 88, 93, Boston Scientific/Diasonics, 1989, Quadralogic Tech., Inc., 1990, Endo Vascular Instruments, Inc., 1993-94, Echocath and Acuson, 1993-94. Fellow Am. Coll. Surgeons; mem. AMA, Assn. Academic Surgery, Internat. Soc. Cardiovascular Surgery (N.Am. Chapter, rsch. fellow 1992, 93), So. Calif. Vascular Surg. Soc., Western Vascular Soc., Pacific Coast Surg. Assn., L.A. Surg. Soc., Acad. Surg. Rsch., Peripheral Vascular Surgery soc., Soc. Clin. Vascular Surgery, The Soc. for Vascular Surgery, Longmire Surg. Soc. Office: UCLA Med Ctr 100 Ucla Medical Plz Ste 510 Los Angeles CA 90024-6970

AHN, TINA MARIE, association executive; b. San Francisco, Sept. 8, 1959; d. Wilson and Hei Kyung (Hong) A. BA, San Francisco State U., 1982; MBA, U. San Francisco, 1994. Admissions supr. Calif. Acad. Scis., San Francisco, 1982-85, membership coord., 1985-87; mktg. assoc. Coun. on Edn., Walnut Creek, Calif., 1987-88; asst. dir. Western Network for Edn. in Health Adminstrn., Berkeley, Calif., 1989-91; dir. membership Neighbor to Neighbor, San Francisco, 1993-94; dir. devel. On Lake Inc., San Francisco, 1994—; bd. mem., treas. Neighbor to Neighbor Action Fund, San Francisco, 1993—. Vol. Tenderloin Neighborhood Devel., San Francisco, 1993-94, Bridge for Kids, San Francisco, 1992-93; mem. World Affairs Coun., San Francisco, 1994. Office: Neighbor to Neighbor 2601 Mission St Ste 400 San Francisco CA 94110-3111

AHRENS, ERICK KARL FREDERICK, computer software executive; b. Detroit, Feb. 22, 1949; s. Herman Frederick Ahrens and Evelyn (Metcalf) Finch; m. Dorothy Ann Swiercz, June 22, 1972. AA in Math., Coll. San Mateo, Calif., 1975; BS in Engrng. Math., U. Calif., Berkeley, Calif., 1980; MBA in Bus. Analysis, San Francisco State U., 1987. Applications analyst Victor Comptometer Corp., South San Francisco, Calif., 1975; R&D engr. Earl and Wright Consulting Engrs., San Francisco, 1976-83; v.p. product engrng. MDL Info. Systems, San Leandro, Calif., 1984-93; v.p. R&D UDI Software, Novato, Calif., 1994—. Contbr.to profl. jours. With USN, 1969-73, Vietnam. Mem. IEEE Computer Sc., Assn. Computing Machinery, Am. Chem. Soc., Marin Power Squadron (past comdr.), Corinthian Yacht Club (Tiburon, Calif.). Home: PO Box 20984 Castro Valley CA 94546-8984 Office: MDL Info Systems 14600 Catalina St San Leandro CA 94577-6608

AHURUONYE, HYACINTH CHIDI, accountant, consultant; b. Aba, Imo, Nigeria, Sept. 20, 1961; came to U.S., 1983; s. Silas A. and Evelyn Ahuruonye); m. Terri Anita Sharp, May 28, 1988; children: Derrick Chidi, Amara Jenay. BS in Acctg. with honors, Ala. A&M U., 1987. enrolled agt. Mng. prin. HCA Acctg. & Tax Svcs., San Francisco, 1987—; acct. R.H. Macys, Inc., San Francisco, 1990, staff acct. Den-Herder & Co., CPA's, San Francisco, 1989-91; tax preparer H&R Block, San Francisco, 1988; cons. in field, 1987—; mem Accreditation Coun. for Accountancy and Taxation, Inc. Co-prodr. Designer of the Yr. Awards, 1991—. Mem. Rep. Nat. Com., Washington, 1990—, San Francisco Refugee Com., Mayor's Employment 1000 Task Force, Ala. A&M Univ. Youth Motivation Task Force. Recipient Mayoral Proclamation, Disting. Alumni Citation of Yr. award, 1994. Mem. Nat. Soc. Pub. Accts., Nat. Asst. Enrolled Agts., Nat. Assn. Tax Practitioners, Nat. Assn. Black Accts., Am. Soc. Accts., Calif. Soc. Enrolled Agts. (treas. Golden Gate chpt.), Calif. Soc. Ind. Accts., Nat. Assn. Equal Opportunity Higher Edn., Ala. A&M U. Alumni Assn. (pres. San Francisco Bay Area chpt. 1991—), Alpha Phi Alpha (rec. sec.). Office: HCA Acctg & Tax Svcs 988 Market St Ste 603 San Francisco CA 94102-4007

AIELLO, ELIZABETH ANN, public relations liaison; b. Pitts., Apr. 10, 1922; d. Edward Aloysius and Sarah Marie (Short) Maroney; m. William Peter Aiello, June 4, 1946 (dec. Nov. 1989); children: David Robert, Beverly Ann Aiello Reecer. BA, Chatham Coll., 1943; MA, St. John's Coll., Santa Fe, N.Mex., 1969; postgrad., U. N.Mex., 1970—. Cert. tchr. elem./secondary English, history, social studies, govt., civics. Secondary instr. history Moon Twp. Schs., Coraopolis, Pa., 1943-44; secondary instr. English, Latin Blawnox (Pa.) Schs., 1944-49; elementary instr. upper primary Los Alamos (N.Mex.) Schs., 1949-59, secondary instr. advanced placement English/history, 1959-82; chair English dept. U. N.Mex., Los Alamos, 1982-90, head humanities div., 1986-90, dir. reentry program for women in sci., 1984-89, dir. reentry program for Native Am./Hispanic students, 1987-90; ednl. pub. rels. liaison Los Alamos Nat. Lab., 1984—; Great Books discussion groups coord. No. N.Mex., 1992—; adv. bd. N.Mex. Women in Sci., Santa Fe, 1980-84, Los Alamos Women in Sci., 1984-90; Fulbright teaching fellow U.S. Dept. Edn., Washington, 1971-72. Author: Perigrinations at [illegible]

1974, Consumation and Other Poems, 1984, New Hope for Dying Muse, 1986, Perceptions and Reality, 1991, Perceptions I-IV. Phoebe Brashear Soc. scholar, Pitts., 1939-43; Am. Hist. Soc.-NEH joint fellow, 1976, William Robertson Coe fellow, 1981; rsch. grantee AAUW, 1982, Carl Perkins grantee N.Mex. Dept. Vocat.-Tech. Edn., 1986-90; named Outstanding N.Mex. History Tchr., DAR, 1976, One of 80 Women to Watch in 80's, N.Mex. Women's Polit. Caucus, 1980; recipient N.Mex. Women at Work award Nat. Coun. Working Women and Minority Affairs, Washington, 1975, Gov.'s award Gov. N.Mex., N.Mex. Commn. Status of Women, 1986, 89. Mem. NEA, AAUW (dir. adv. bd. 1985-90, nat. adv. bd. 1985-89, June B. West fellow N.Mex. div. 1969, Grace Braker Wilson award 1990), Los Alamos Nat. Edn. Assn. (adv. bd., pres. 1975-80), Delta Kappa Gamma. Office: Los Alamos Nat Lab Box 1663 MS C330 Los Alamos NM 87545

AIKAWA, JERRY KAZUO, physician, educator; b. Stockton, Calif., Aug. 24, 1921; s. Genmatsu and Shizuko (Yamamoto) A.; m. Chitose Aihara, Sept. 20, 1944; 1 son, Ronald K. A.B., U. Calif., 1942; M.D., Wake Forest Coll., 1945. Intern, asst. resident N.C. Baptist Hosp., 1945-47; NRC fellow in med. scis. U. Calif. Med. Sch., 1947-48; NRC, AEC postdoctoral fellow in med. scis. Bowman Gray Sch. Medicine, 1948-50, instr. internal medicine, 1950-53, asst. prof., 1953; established investigator Am. Heart Assn., 1952-58; exec. officer lab. service Univ. Hosps., 1958-61, dir. lab. services, 1961-83, dir. allied health program, 1969—, assoc. dean allied health program, 1983—, pres. med. bd.; assoc. dean clin. affairs asst. prof. U. Colo. Sch. Medicine, 1953- 60, asso. prof. medicine, 1960-67, prof., 1967—, prof. biometrics, 1974—, assoc. dean clin. affairs, 1974—; Pres. Med. bd. Univ. Hosps. Fellow ACP, Am. Coll. Nutrition; mem. Western Soc. Clin. Research, So. Soc. Clin. Research, Soc. Exptl. Biology and Medicine, Am. Fedn. Clin. Research, AAAS, Central Soc. Clin. Research, AMA, Assn. Am. Med. Colls., Phi Beta Kappa, Sigma Xi, Alpha Omega Alpha. Home: 3233 Lake Albano Cir San Jose CA 95135-1467 Office: U Colo Sch Medicine 4200 E 9th Ave Denver CO 80220-3706

AIKEN, DOROTHY LOUISE, secondary education educator; b. Washington, Apr. 27, 1924; d. Willard Ross and Gertrude (Rucker) Snyder; m. William David Aiken, May 22, 1948 (dec. 1988); children: Katherine Aiken Schwartz, Mary Aiken Fishback, Sally Aiken Fitterer, Jerome. BS, George Washington U., 1946; postgrad., Wash. State U., 1946-47. Teaching fellow Wash. State U., Pullman, 1946-47; tchr. secondary sch. D.C. Schs., Washington, 1947-50; tchr. Sunnyside (Wash.) Sch. Dist. 201, 1962-80. Sec. vestry Holy Trinity Ch., 1968-70; staff Evergreen Girls State, 1972-81; Dem. precinct committeeman, Sunnyside, 1980-86; mem. com. Margaret Rayburn Legislator campaign, Grandview, Wash., 1990; vice chair Yakima Valley C.C., 1994-95, trustee; trustee Assn. Cmty. and Tech. Colls., mem. conf. com., 1992; co-producer Valley Mus. Comedy Co. Prodns., 1989-91; chmn. Hospice Light Up a Life, 1991; vol., program head ARC. Mem. Am. Legion Aux. (pres. 1974-76, meritorious svc. citation 1983, 88), Nouvella Federated Women's Club (2d v.p. 1984-86), Women's Golf Assn. (pres.). Episcopalian. Home: 1241 Sunset Pl Sunnyside WA 98944-1720

AIKENS, C(LYDE) MELVIN, anthropology educator, archaeologist; b. Ogden, Utah, July 13, 1938; s. Clyde Walter and Claudia Elena (Brown) A.; m. Alice Hiroko Endo, Mar. 23, 1963; children: Barton Hiroyuki, Quinn Yoshihisa. A.S., Weber Coll., 1958; B.A., U. Utah, 1960; M.A., U. Chgo., 1962, Ph.D., 1966. Curator U. Utah Mus. Anthropology, Salt Lake City, 1963-66; asst. prof. U. Nev.-Reno, 1966-68; asst. prof. U. Oreg., Eugene, 1968-72, assoc. prof., 1972-78, prof. anthropology, 1978—. Author: Fremont Relationships, 1966, Hogup Cave, 1970, Great Basin Archaeology, 1978, The Last 10,000 Years in Japan and Eastern North America, 1981, From Asia to America: The First Peopling of the New World, 1990, Archaeology of Oregon, 1993; co-author: Prehistory of Japan, 1982, Great Basin Numic Prehistory, 1986, Early Human Occupation in Far Western North America, 1988; editor: Archaeological Studies Willamette Valley, 1975; co-editor: Prehistoric Hunter-Gatherers in Japan, 1986, Pacific Northeast Asia in Prehistory, 1992, Archaeological Researches in the Northern Great Basin, 1994. NSF research grantee, 1970, 73, 78-80, 84; NSF Sci. Faculty fellow Kyoto U., Japan, 1971-72; Japan Found. research fellow Kyoto U., 1977-78, Tokyo U., 1986. Fellow Am. Anthrop. Assn., AAAS; mem. Soc. for Am. Archaeology. Home: 3470 Mcmillan St Eugene OR 97405-3317 Office: U Oreg Dept Anthropology Eugene OR 97403-1218

AILOR, KAREN TANA, magazine writer, proposal consultant; b. Seattle, June 1, 1943; d. Dale Ingram and Neva Gail (Houck) A. Student, U. Calif., Berkeley, 1961-63; BA in Journalism, U. Oreg., 1992. Copy editor Physical Review Letters, Brookhaven, N.Y., 1963-65; proposal writer TRW Def. Systems, L.A., 1965-73; mktg. support mgr. TRW Electronics, L.A., 1973-79; proposal cons. TRW, Hughes, Northrop, Logicon, and others, L.A., 1980—; contbg. writer Old Oreg. Mag., Eugene, 1991—. Mem. Phi Beta Kappa (award 1992), Kappa Tau Alpha (award 1991). Democrat. Home and Office: 125 Rosetta Ave Eugene OR 97404

AINSWORTH, HARRIET CRAWFORD, journalist, public relations consultant; b. Columbus, Ohio, Nov. 27, 1914; d. Harry Hoskins and Pansy Lucy (Graham) Crawford; m. J. Gordon Ainsworth, Oct. 6, 1945; children: J. Gordon Jr., Adeline Ainsworth Forrest. BA, Ohio Wesleyan U., 1934; postgrad., Columbia U. Sch. Journalism, 1934-35, Gonzaga U., 1940, Calif. Coll. Arts and Crafts, 1968; life adult edn.-C.C. tchg. credential, U. Calif., Berkeley, 1967. Reporter Portland Oregonian, 1936-37; ind. pub. rels. writer, 1937-42; fgn. corr. Oakland Tribune, Indpls. Star, Japan, China, The Philippines, 1946; pub. info. dir. Am. Cancer Soc., Contra Costa County, Calif., 1958-89; cons. Calif. divsn. Am. Cancer Soc., 1965-77; pres. Ainsworth-Powell Pub. Rels., 1965-77; v.p. Corp. Identity Assocs., Orinda, Calif., 1968-94, pres., 1994—; columnist (Sunbeams), feature writer Contra Costa Sun, Contra Costa Times, 1990—. Co-author: The Road Back, 1968; contbr. articles to profl. jours., newspaper columns. Mem. Citizen's Recreation Commn., dist. 6, Orinda, 1974-79; founder, pres. Orinda Found., 1975; chmn. spl. events Calif. Shakespeare Festival Amphitheater campaign, 1988-92. Lt. comdr. USNR, 1942-58. Named Orinda Citizen of Yr., 1976; recipient Plaque and Resolution Commendation Recreation Dist. 6, Orinda, 1979, Recognition award Plaque Pres. U.S. People-to-People Sports Com. Mem. San Francisco Pub. Rels. Round Table, Contra Costa Press Club, East Bay Women's Press Club (pres.), Orinda Country Club, Orindawoods Tennis Club, Orinda Tennis Club, Kappa Alpha Theta (co-founder Diablo Valley chpt.).

AIRD, ROBERT BURNS, neurologist, educator; b. Provo, Utah, Nov. 5, 1903; s. John William and Emily Dawn (McAuslan) A.; m. Ellinor Hill Collins, Oct. 5, 1935 (dec. 1992); children: Katharine (dec. 1992), Mary, John, Robert. BA, Cornell U., 1926; MD, Harvard Med. Sch., 1930. Diplomate Nat. Bd. Med. Examiners, Am. Bd. Psychiatry and Neurology. Intern Strong Meml. Hosp-U. Rochester (N.Y.) Sch. Medicine, 1930-31, resident, 1931-32; rsch. assoc. U. Calif., San Francisco, 1932-35, instr., 1935-39, from asst. to assoc. prof., 1939-49, prof. neurology, 1949-71, founder dept. neurology, 1947, emeritus prof., 1971—, established Electroencephalographic Lab., 1940, dir. Electroencephalographic Lab., 1940-71; trustee Deep Springs Coll., Inyo County, Calif., 1959-71, dir. coll., 1960-66, hon. trustee, 1971—; founder No. Calif. chpt. Multiple Sclerosis Soc.; mem. five coms. NIH, Washington, 1953-63; rep. of AMA on Residency Rev. Bd., 1967-73; lectr. in field, U.S. and 10 fgn. countries. Author: Foundations of Modern Neurology: A Century of Progress, 1993; sr. author: Management of Epilepsy, 1974, The Epilepsies--A Critical Review, 1984; author: (with others) Clinical Neurology, 1955, Textbooks of Medicine, 1959, 62; edit. bd. Internat. Jour. Electroencephalography and Clin. Neurophysiology, 1945-65, Jour. Nervous and Mental Disorders, 1952-67; contbr. more than 280 articles to profl. jours. Founding chmn. William G. Lennox Trust Fund, 1961-69. Comdr. Order of Hipolito Unanaae, Govt. of Peru, 1963; Fulbright scholar, 1957-58; recipient Royer Significant Contbns. to Advancement of Neurology award, 1969, Hope Chest award Nat. Multiple Sclerosis Soc., 1962, 72, 82; founder vis. professorship in neurology U. Calif., San Francisco, 1949, endowed and named in his honor, 1973, professorship established, 1991; bldg. named in his honor Deep Springs Coll., 1971, professorship, 1993;. Mem. AAAS, Am. Epilepsy Soc. (hon., pres. 1959-60, Lennox award 1970), Am. Electroencephalographic Soc. (charter mem., pres. 1953-54), Am. Neurol. Assn. (v.p. 1955, 69, 72, sr. mem.), Pan-Am. Med. Soc. (N.Am. v.p. 1966), Calif. Acad. Sci. (life), Calif. Acad. Medicine, San Francisco Neurol. Soc. (co-founder, pres. 1951-52), Am. Bd. Qualification in Electroencephalography (founding chair), Western Soc. Electroencephalography (founder, pres. 1947), Assn. Brit. Neurologists (hon.). Office: U Calif Dept Neurology M-794 PO Box 0114 San Francisco CA 94143-0001

AITCHISON, STEWART WAYNE, photojournalist; b. Chgo., Sept. 27, 1947; s. Lawrence Foster and Leona Rachel (Bogdansky) A.; m. Margaret Ann Kramer, Aug. 14, 1981; 1 child, Kate Lynne Kramer Aitchison. BS, No. Ariz. U., 1969. Rsch. biologist Mus. of No. Ariz., Flagstaff, 1967-78; freelance writer/photographer Flagstaff, 1968—; naturalist Lindblad Spl. Expdns., others, 1976—. Author/photographer: A Traveler's Guide to Monument Valley, 1993, Red Rock-Sacred Mountain, 1992, A Wilderness Called Grand Canyon, 1991, others; contbr. articles, photographs to numerous publs. Bd. dirs. Kokopeli Adventures in Learning, 1979-82. Mem. No. Ariz. Natural History Assn., The Author's Guild, Inc. Home and Office: 995 Tolani Trl Flagstaff AZ 86001-9613

AITKEN, ROBERT CAMPBELL, engineer; b. Vancouver, B.C., Can., Apr. 21, 1963; came to U.S., 1990; s. Robert and Mary Elizabeth A.; m. Denise Kathleen Maloney, Aug. 2, 1986; 1 child, Robert James. BS with hons., U. Victoria, B.C., Can., 1985, MS, 1986; PhD, McGill U., Montreal, Que., Can., 1990. Rsch. assoc. Alberta Rsch. Coun., Calgary, Alberta, Can., 1986-87; mem. tech. staff Hewlett-Packard Co., Palo Alto, Calif., 1990—; local arrangements chmn. Internat. Conf. on Computer-Aided Design, Santa Clara, 1995, tech. program com. mem., 1993-94; tech. program com. Custom Integrated Cirs. Conf., Santa Clara, 1995; panel and poster chmn. Test Synthesis Workshop, Santa Barbara, Calif., 1995. local arrangements chmn. Internat. Conf. on Computer-Aided Design, Santa Clara, 1995, tech. program com. mem., 1993-95; tech. program com. Custom Integrated Cirs. Conf., Santa Clara, 1995; panel and poster chmn. Test Synthesis Workshop, Santa Barbara, Calif., 1995. Recipient award for Best paper, Internat. Test Conf., Balt., 1992, hon. mention, 1991. Mem. IEEE. Office: Hewlett-Packard Co 1501 Page Mill Rd # Ms 6uk Palo Alto CA 94304-1126

AITKEN, STUART CAMPBELL, geography educator; b. Glasgow, Scotland, July 20, 1958; came to U.S., 1980; s. William Scott and Margaret Brodie (Fleming) A.; m. Peggy Ann Beninger, July 6. 1987; children: Ross, Catherine. BSc, Glasgow U., 1980; MA, Miami U., Oxford, Ohio, 1981; PhD, U. West Ont., London, Can., 1985. Prof. geography U. Ariz., Tucson, 1985-86; asst. prof. San Diego State U., 1986-89, assoc. prof., 1990-92, prof., 1993—; vis. faculty fellow U. Edinburgh, Scotland, 1993. Author, editor: Place, Power, Situation and Spectacle, 1994; author: Putting Children in Their Place, 1994. Creator/organizer Children's Geographies of San Diego Program, 1988-91. NSF grantee, 1990-94. Office: San Diego State Univ Dept Geography San Diego CA 92182-4493

AITYAN, SERGEY K., scientist, administrator; b. Baku, USSR, Dec. 21, 1947; came to U.S., 1992; s. Khachatur A. Aityan and Vera A. Osipova; m. Valentina E. Emelina, Sept. 21, 1982. MS in Math and Mechanics, Moscow State U., 1970, DSc in Math and Physics, 1987; PhD in Chemistry, USSR Acad. Scis., 1976. Staff rschr. Inst. Electrochemistry, USSR Acad. Sci., Moscow, 1971-83; lab head, dept. head Moscow Exptl. Computer Ctr., 1983-87; dept. head Moscow State Inst. Lack & Varnish Industry, 1987-89; prof. computer sci. Moscow Mining Inst., 1987-90; regional sci. dir. Soviet-USA Joint Venture LAIKS, Moscow-Riga, 1989-91; rsch. engr. Tex. A&M U., College Station, 1992-93; prin. architect Auto-trol Tech., Denver, 1993—; vis. prof. U. Regensburg, West Germany, 1990-91, U. Dortmund, West Germany, 1991-92; adj. prof. U. Houston, 1992-93; prof. U. Colo., Denver, 1994—. Mem. editl. bd. Internat. Jour. Neural, Parallel & Sci. Computations, 1992—; guest editor Spl. Issue of Neurocomputing, 1993—. Alexander von Humboldt Found. fellow, 1990-92. Mem. Interdisciplinary Neural Modeling Soc. (pres., organizer 1992—). Home: 15 Benthaven Boulder CO 80303

AJER, RANDOLF E., airport terminal executive; b. 1953. With Union Home Loans, L.A., 1974-80, Maytag Aircraft Corp., Colorado Springs, Colo., 1981—. Office: Maytag Aircraft Corp 3939 E San Miguel St Colorado Springs CO 80909-3409*

AKAKA, DANIEL KAHIKINA, senator; b. Honolulu, Sept. 11, 1924; s. Kahikina and Annie (Kahoa) A.; m. Mary Mildred Chong, May 22, 1948; children: Millannie, Daniel, Gerard, Alan, Nicholas. BEdn, U. Hawaii, 1952, MEdn, 1966. Tchr. schs. in Hawaii, 1953-60; vice prin., then prin. Ewa Beach Elem. Sch., Honolulu, 1960-64; prin. Pohakea Elem. Sch., 1964-65, Kaneohe Elem. Sch., 1965-68; program specialist Hawaii Compensatory Edn., 1978-79, from 1985; dir. Hawaii OEO, 1971-74; spl. asst. human resources Office Gov. Hawaii, 1975-76; mem. 95th-101st Congresses from 2d Dist., Hawaii, 1977-90; U.S. senator from Hawaii, 1990—; chmn. Hawaii Principals' Conf. Bd. dirs. Hanahauoli Sch.; mem. Act 4 Ednl. Adv. Council, Library Adv. Council.; Trustee Kawaiahao Congl. Ch. Served with U.S. Army, 1945-47. Mem. NEA, Musicians Assn. Hawaii. Democrat. Office: US Senate 720 Senate Hart Bldg Washington DC 20510*

AKBARIAN, SHAH-ROKH, management consultant; b. Abadan, Khuzestan, Iran, May 20, 1953; came to U.S., 1969; s. Ramezan and Mahin (Behbahani-Gaphazany) A.; m. Joni Louise Stump, Nov. 1, 1980; 1 child, Katayun Alexandra. BA, Westminster Coll., 1976, BS, 1977; M of Internat. Mgmt., Am. Grad. Sch. Internat. Mgmt., Glendale, Ariz., 1980; postgrad., U. Utah, 1993. Account exec. Bonneville Rsch., Salt Lake City, 1980-84; prin. Pendar Internat., Salt Lake City, 1984—; bd. dirs. Sports Am, Salt Lake City, 1980—. Pub., editor Commerce Internat. News; contbr. articles to profl. jours. Mem. adv. bd. U. Utah Internat. Ctr., 1992—, mem. chmn. bus. & industry com.; mem. adv. bd. Salt Lake County Cmty. and Econs. Devel., 1994—; exec. coun. Westminster Coll. Alumni Assn., 1993—, pres., 1995—, trustee, 1995—, mem. instnl. advancement com., 1994—; alumni ednl. counselor Am. Grad. Sch. Internat. Mgmt., 1994—; adv. bd. Salvation Army, 1982-84. Mem. Inst. Indsl. Engrs., Assn. MBA Execs., Salt Lake Area C. of C. (mem. export devel. com., mem. editl. bd. chamber newsletter, pub. rels. coord.).

AKELEY, KURT BARTON, computer graphics company executive, engineer; b. Wilmington, Del., June 8, 1958; s. David Francis and Marcy Claire (McCullough) A. BSEE, U. Del., 1980; MSEE, Stanford U., 1982. Mem. tech. staff, co-founder Silicon Graphics, Inc., Mountain View, Calif., 1982-87, prin. engr., 1987-89, chief engr., 1989-90, v.p., chief engr., 1990—; mem. Coll. Engring. Adv. Coun., U. Del., 1993—. Patentee, inventor in field; contbr. articles to profl. publs. Named Disting. Alumnus, Dept. Elec. Engring., Coll. Engring., U. Del., 1993. Mem. Assn. Computing Machinery. Home: 3360 Milton Ct Mountain View CA 94040-4500 Office: Silicon Graphics Inc 2011 N Shoreline Blvd Mountain View CA 94043-1321

AKELLA, JAGANNADHAM, geochemist, materials science investigator; b. Kakinada, Andhra, India, Sept. 13, 1937; came to U.S., 1965; s. Visweswara Rao and Balatripura Sundari (Gollakota) A.; m. Lalita-Vemparala, July 14, 1967; children: Anita Sundari, Sadhana Sri, Mamata Kumari. BS with honors, U. Coll. Andhra U., Vizag (A.P.), India, 1957; MS, Andhra U., 1958; PhD, Indian Inst. Tech., Kharagpur (W.B.), India, 1962. Cert. tchr., Calif. Univ. System. Sr. lectr. dept. geology Rajastan U., Udaipur, Raj, India, 1962-63; acad. exchange scholar U. Göttingen (Fed. Republic of Germany), 1963-65; rsch. assoc. UCLA, 1965-66, 67-71; fellow Geophys. Lab. Carnegie Instn., Washington, 1971-74; sr. resident rsch. assoc. NASA Johnson Space Ctr., Houston, 1974-77; sr. scientist Lawrence Livermore (Calif.) Nat. Lab. U. Calif., 1977—; petrology group leader Lawrence Livermore Nat. Lab. Earth Scis., Livermore, 1979-82; adj. prof. Calif. State U., Hayward, 1983, Chabo Coll. Valley Campus, Livermore, 1984; advisor high pressure rsch. UN Devel. Program, Nat. Geophys. Rsch. Inst. Hyderabad, India, 1986. Contbr. numerous articles to profl. jours. Treas. Hindu Community Cultural Ctr., Livermore, 1987-90, bd. dirs., 1990-93, pres., 1992-93. Named German Acad. Exchange scholar, 1963-65, sr. rsch. fellow NAS and NRC, 1974-77. Fellow Indian Mineral. Soc., Mineral. Soc. Am., Carnegie Instn. Geophys. Lab.; mem. Am. Geophys. Union. Democrat. Hindu. Home: 2667 Chateau Way Livermore CA 94550-5735 Office: U Calif Lawrence Livermore Nat Lab Livermore CA 94550

AKER, DIANNE LEE, academic administrator, consultant; b. Kankakee, Ill., July 5, 1941; d. Herald Wilson Stockton and Marjorie Rose (Martin) Walley; m. Paul Mundschenk, Aug. 26, 1965 (div. Mar. 1978); m. William Bryson Smith, Jul. 15, 1989. BS, S.W. Miss. State U., 1963; MA, Ohio U., 1973; PhD, Union Inst., 1977. Coord. supr. Frontier Dist. Mental Health Ctr., Marietta, Ohio, 1974-75; leader-in-residence Esalen Inst., 1975-78; dir. U.S. Internat. U., Nairobi, Kenya, 1979-84; v.p. internat. campuses U.S. Internat. U., Nairobi, 1985-86; dir. Orange County campus U.S. Internat. U., Irvine, Calif., 1986-90; producer/host KUSI TV, San Diego, 1985-91; dean of acad. affairs U. Humanistic Studies, Del Mar, Calif., 1991-93; columnist Women's Times, San Diego, 1991-94; pres. U. Humanistic Studies, San Diego, 1993—; cons. Governmental and NGO's, 1985—; vis. fellow Ctr. for Studies of Person, La Jolla, Calif., 1978-79; vis. lectr. various univs., U.S., Europe, Africa, 1975—; vis. scientist, Poland, 1979. Producer: Uganda -An African Phoenix, 1987; producer, host TV programs, 1985-91. Active County Human Rels. Media Com., San Diego, 1990-92. Recipient Women of Merit award Blade-Citizen Newspapers, 1994, Wonderwoman in Edn. award, Small Bus. Assn., 1990, Career Achievement award, Rancho Santiago Coll., 1988. Mem. AAUW, Assn. for Women in Devel., Nat. Acad. of TV Arts & Scis., The Women's Found. of Orange County (founding, adv. bd. 1986-91), Am. Women in radio & TV (adv. bd.), Carl Rogers Inst. for Peace (founding). Democrat. Office: Univ for Humanistic Studies 380 Stevens Ave Ste 210 Solana Beach CA 92075

AKINS, GEORGE CHARLES, accountant; b. Willits, Calif., Feb. 22, 1917; s. Guy Brookins and Eugenie (Swan) A.; A.A., Sacramento City Coll., 1941; m. Jane Babcock, Mar. 27, 1945. Accountant, auditor Calif. Bd. Equalization, Dept. Finance, Sacramento, 1940-44; controller-treas. DeVons Jewelers, Sacramento, 1944-73, v.p., controller, 1973-80, v.p., chief fin. officer, dir., 1980-84; individual accounting and tax practice, Sacramento, 1944—. Accountant, cons. Mercy Children's Hosp. Guild, Sacramento, 1957-77. Served with USAAF, 1942. Mem. Soc. Calif. Pioneers, Nat. Soc. Pub. Accountants, U.S. Navy League, Calif. Hist. Soc., Drake Navigators Guild, Internat. Platform Assn., Mendocino County Hist. Soc. (life), Sacramento County Hist. Soc. (life), Crocker Art Mus. (life). Republican. Roman Catholic. Clubs: Commonwealth of Calif., Comstock. Contbg. author: Portfolio of Accounting Systems for Small and Medium-Sized Business, 1968, rev., 1977. Home and Office: 96 S Humboldt St Willits CA 95490-3539

AKIYAMA, CAROL LYNN, motion picture industry executive; b. Chgo., Dec. 5, 1946; d. Makio M. Akiyama and Mary (Uyeda) Maruyama; m. Peter Richard Bierstedt, Aug. 23, 1980. BA magna cum laude, U. So. Calif., 1968, JD, 1971. Bar: Calif. Atty. NLRB, Los Angeles, 1971-75, ABC-TV, Hollywood, Calif., 1975-79, So. Calif. Edison, Rosemead, 1980-81; asst. gen. atty. CBS Inc., Los Angeles, 1981-82; sr. v.p. Alliance of Motion Picture and TV Producers, Sherman Oaks, Calif., 1982-88; ind. producer and writer TV and motion pictures Rancho Palos Verdes, 1988—. Mem. Los Angeles County Bar Assn. (chmn. labor law sect. 1981-82, exec. com. 1975-85), Phi Kappa Phi, Phi Beta Kappa.

AKLESTAD, GARY C., state legislator. Mem. Mont. Senate from 6th Dist. Home: PO Box 32 Galata MT 59444-0032

AKSOY, ERCUMENT GALIP, economics educator; b. Nigde, Turkey, Jan. 29, 1952; came to U.S., 1978; s. Semsettin and Nezahat (Tartanoglu) A.; m. Guven Asuman, Oct. 18, 1976; children: Can Aksoy, Sinan Aksoy. BS, Middle East T.U., Ankara, Turkey, 1976; MS, Ea. Mich. U., 1980; PhD, Mich. State U., 1988. Chief of fgn. exch. The Cen. Bank, Ankara, 1976-78; instr. U. Mich., Flint, 1985, GMI Engring. and Mgmt. Inst., Flint, 1986-87; instr. Calif. State U., Pomona, 1987-88; instr. Calif. State U., Fullerton, 1988-89, lectr., 1989—. Author: The Problem of Multiple Interpretation of Ricardo, 1991; contbr. articles to profl. jours. Mem. History of Econs. Soc., Am. Econs. Assn., Western Econs. Assn. Home: 2841 N Mountain Ave Claremont CA 91711-1550 Office: Calif State Fullerton Dept Econs Fullerton CA 93635

AKUBUILO, FRANCIS EKENECHUKWU, secondary school educator; b. Ebe-Udi, Enugu, Nigeria, Mar. 25, 1952; came to U.S., 1984; d. Robert O. and Regina N. (Agada) A.; m. Assumpta Ify Chinegwu, Aug. 22, 1987; children: Frank-Roberts, Olivia, Nneoma, Christopher-Daniel. AS, Fachhochschule, Stuttgart, Fed. Republic of Germany, 1983; MArch, Fachhochschule, Frankfurt, Fed. Republic of Germany, 1984; D in Bus., Pacific State U., 1985; M in Adminstrn., Nat. U., San Diego, 1989. BDB, Germany; cert. tchr. bus. & indsl. mgmt., basic edn., bus. edn., social sci., vocat. tng. Asst. archtl. engr. Albrecht Assocs., Stuttgart, 1978-83; asst. lectr. Fachhochschule, Frankfort, 1981-83; legal researcher Control Data, L.A., 1984; legal edn. researcher Am. Legal Systems, L.A., 1984-86; head para-lega litigation, supr. Chase, Rotchford, et. al., L.A., 1986—; instr. Coll. of Canyons, Valencia, Calif., 1990—; tchr. Calif. Youth Authority, Whittier, Calif., 1992—, Hacienda/ La Puente Sch., Whittier, Calif., 1992-93; cons. Udi Div. Schs., Udi-Enugu, Nigeria, 1981-83, Frank's Consulting Svcs., L.A., 1988—; dir., pres. Okuli Enterprises, L.A., 1991—; dir. Enugu Cultural Assn., L.A., 1992—. Mem. German Architects Engrs. Assn. Roman Catholic. Home: 7122 Bon Villa Cir La Palma CA 90623-1167

AKUTAGAWA, DONALD, psychologist, educator; b. Grace, Idaho, June 7, 1923; s. Fred T. and Shizue (Oyama) A.; children: Trina Bortko, Murray, Doran. MA, U. Chgo., 1951; PhD, U. Pitts., 1956. Group counselor Orthogenic Sch., U. Chgo., 1951-52; clin. psychologist Inst. Pa. Hosp., Phila., 1959-67; pvt. practice Phila., 1957—, Bellevue, Wash., 1968—; chief community services Eastside Community Mental Health Center, Bellevue, 1968-72; clin. prof. psychology U. Wash., Seattle, 1974-90. Served with AUS, 1944-46. Fellow Am. Orthopsychiat. Assn. Office: Family Treatment Ctr 10845 Main St Bellevue WA 98004-6323

ALAMEDA, RUSSELL RAYMOND, JR., radiologic technologist; b. San Jose, Calif., Oct. 13, 1945; s. Russell Raymond and Rose Margaret (Manzone) A.; m. Gayle Evileen Allison, Feb. 16, 1969 (div. 1975); children: Lynda Rae, Anthony David. Student San Jose City Coll., 1963-65. Served with U.S. Navy, 1966-75; x-ray technician VA Hosp., Palo Alto, Calif., 1975-78; office mgr., radiologic technologist, responsible safety officer, orthopedic surgery Mountain View (Calif.), 1978—; owner, operator Ren-Tech, San Jose, 1982-87; radiologic technologist San Jose (Calif.) Med. Clinic, 1982-93. Mem. DeFrank Community Ctr. Recipient Mallinckrodt Outstanding Achievement award Mallinckrodt Corp., 1971. Mem. DAV (life), ACLU, NOW, Am. Registry of Radiologic Technologists, United We Stand Am., BAYMEC, Lamda Legal Def., Calif. Soc. Radiologic Technologists, Am. Soc. Radiologic Technologist. Republican. Lutheran. Home: 165 Blossom Hill Rd # 76sp San Jose CA 95123 Office: Orthopedic Surgery 2500 Hospital Dr Bldg 7 Mountain View CA 94040-4115

ALANIZ, MIGUEL JOSÉ CASTAÑEDA, library director; b. L.A., Oct. 21, 1944; s. Francisco and Amalia (Castañeda) A.; m. Mercedes P., June 7, 1980. AA, Chabot C.C., 1972; BS in Child/Human Devel., Calif. State U., Hayward, 1974; MS in LS, Calif. State U., Fullerton, 1975; MS Pub. Admnstrn., Calif. State U., San Bernardino, 1988. Spanish svcs. libr. Alameda County Libr., Hayward, 1975-77; branch mgr. San Jose Pub. Libr., 1977-78, Santa Ana (Calif.) Pub. Libr., 1978-79; divsn. chief, tech. process San Bernardino (Calif.) County Libr., 1979-84; city libr. Azusa City (Calif.) Libr., 1984-92; libr. dir. Inglewood Pub. (Calif.) Libr., 1992—. With U.S. Army, 1965-71. Recipient Grad. Rsch. Fellow Clif. State U., 1974. Mem. ALA, Calif. Libr. Assn., Reforma. Office: City of Inglewood Public Library 101 W Manchester Blvd Inglewood CA 90301-1753

ALARCON, ARTHUR LAWRENCE, federal judge; b. L.A., Aug. 14, 1925; s. Lorenzo Marques and Margaret (Sais) A.; m. Sandra D. Paterson, Sept. 1, 1979; children—Jan Marie, Gregory, Lance. B.A. in Polit. Sci, U. So. Calif., 1949, J.D., 1951. Bar: Calif. 1952. Dep. dist. atty. L.A. County, 1952-61; exec. asst. to Gov. Pat Brown State of Calif., Sacramento, 1962-64, legal adv. to gov., 1961-62; judge L.A. Superior Ct., 1964-78; assoc. justice Calif. Ct. Appeals, L.A., 1978-79; judge U.S. Ct. Appeals for 9th Circuit, L.A., 1979—. Served with U.S. Army, 1943-46, ETO. Office: US Ct Appeals 9th Cir 312 N Spring St Los Angeles CA 90012-4701*

ALARCÓN, FRANCISCO XAVIER, poet, educator; b. L.A., Feb. 21, 1954; s. Jesús Pastor and Consuelo (Vargas) A. Student, East L.A. Coll., 1973-74; BA, Calif. State U., Long Beach, 1977; MA, Stanford U., 1979.

Rsch. asst. Mex.-Am. Studies, Calif. State U., Long Beach, 1976-77; summer youth counselor Horizons Unltd., San Francisco, 1981; program dir. Milagro Books, Oakland, Calif., 1981-82; translator Computer Curriculum Corp., Palo Alto, Calif., 1984; Spanish tchr. San Francisco U. High Sch., 1984; lectr. U. Calif., Santa Cruz, 1985-92, Davis, 1992—; pres. Aztlán Cultural/Centro Chicano de Escritores, Oakland, 1985—. Author: (poetry) Tattoos, 1985, Quake Poems, 1989, Body in Flames, 1990, Loma Prieta, 1990, Of Dark Love, 1992, Poemas Zurdos, 1992, Snake Poems, 1992, No Golden Gate for Us, 1993, (with others) Ya vas, carnal, 1985, Mundo 21, 1995; co-editor Chicanas y Chicanos en diálogo, 1989. Bd. dirs. La Raza/Galería Posada, Sacramento, 1993—, Familia Ctr., Santa Cruz, 1990-92, Mission Cultural Ctr., San Francisco, 1986—, San Francisco Poetry Ctr., 1988—. Recipient Am. Book award, 1993, PEN Oakland Josephine Miles Lit. award, 1993, Writer's fellowship Calif. Arts Coun., 1989-90, Fulbright fellowship, 1982-83, Dorothy Danforth Compton Dissertation fellowship Stanford U., 1983; recipient First Prize 10th Ann. Chicano Lit. prize U. Calif., 1984, Palabra Nueva 2d prize U. Calif., 1983. Mem. Nat. Poetry Assn. (bd. dirs.). Home: 1712 Albion Pl Davis CA 95616-1446 Office: U Calif Dept Spanish Davis CA 95616

ALARID, ALBERT JOSEPH, judge; b. Albuquerque, Sept. 4, 1948; s. Albert Joseph and Evelyn Sylvia (Torres) A. BA, U. N.Mex., 1970; JD, Georgetown U., 1973. Bar: N.Mex. 1973, U.S. Dist. Ct. N.Mex. 1973, U.S. Supreme Ct. 1977. Civil rights atty. U.S. Dept. Justice, Washington, 1973-74; legis. counsel to U.S. Senator Joseph Montoya, Washington, 1974-77; asst. atty. gen. Office of N.Mex. Atty. Gen., Santa Fe, 1977-80; judge. Met. Ct., Albuquerque, 1980-81; 2d Jud. Dist., Albuquerque, 1981-83, N.Mex. Ct. Appeals, Santa Fe, 1984—, chief judge, 1990-93; adj. prof. U. N.Mex. Sch. Pub. Adminstrn., Albuquerque, 1980-81; summer legal instr. U. NM, 1992, 94; chmn. Jud. Performance Evaluation Com., 1990—; mem. Supreme Ct. Commn. Fin. Cts., 1993—. Mem. Gov.'s Com. on Disting. Svc., Santa Fe, 1984; bd. dirs. N.Mex. Coun. on Crime and Delinquency, Albuquerque, 1983-84, Albuquerque Civic Light Opera, 1989-93; mem. adv. bd. N.Mex. Law Related Edn. Project. Mem. N.Mex. Jud. Conf. (chmn. 1983-84), U. N.Mex. Alumni (bd. dirs. 1981-84, mem. appellate and dist. ct. jud. nominating commns.), Delta Theta Phi. Democrat. Roman Catholic. Office: N Mex Ct of Appeals PO Box 2008 Santa Fe NM 87504-2008

ALAYETO, OFELIA LUISA, writer, researcher, educator; b. Havana, Cuba, July 24; came to U.S., 1960; d. Pedro O. and Ofelia Luisa (Martínez-Torres) A.; m. Allan W. Solomonow, Oct. 16, 1967; children: Gregory Igal, Seth Rafael. BA, CUNY, 1973, MPhil, 1980, PhD, 1983. Spl. asst. to exec. dir. Sierra Club, San Francisco, 1984-90, assoc. dir. rsch., 1990-93; lectr. U. San Francisco, 1987—, San Francisco, 1987—; rsch. analyst U. Calif., San Francisco, 1994—. Author: Sofia Casanova: Spanish Poet, Journalist and Writer, 1992; contbr. articles to profl. jours. Recipient Humanities award Richmond Coll./CUNY, 1973, Arleigh Williamson award, 1973. Mem. MLA, Am. Assn. Tchrs. Spanish and Portuguese, Sierra Club. Democrat. Roman Catholic. Office: Univ of San Francisco Presentation Campus 103 Ignatian Heights San Francisco CA 94117-1080

ALBA, FELIX, industrial computer systems company executive; b. Burgos, Spain, May 14, 1948; came to the U.S., 1983; s. Francisco Paula and Maria Salome (Juez) A.; m. Susana Agüero, Dec. 30, 1976; children: Araceli, Nicholas. MA in Elec. Engring., U. Nacional del Sur, Argentina, 1974. Adj. prof. U. Nacional San Juan, Argentina, 1974-77, assoc. prof., 1977-78, prof., 1978-83; postdoctoral fellow U. Utah, 1983, rsch. assoc., 1984-87; pres. Felix Alba Cons., Murray, Utah, 1987—. Patentee in field. Mem. AAAS, Instrument Soc. Am., Assn. for Computer Machinery, Soc. Mining Engrs., Indsl. Computer Soc., The Planetary Soc. Home and Office: 5760 Ridge Creek Rd Murray UT 84107-6617

ALBAND, LINDA ANN, small business owner; b. Portland, Oreg., Apr. 30, 1948; d. John and Jean (Whitlock) A. AAS in Computer Tech., North Seattle C.C., 1985; BA in Tech. & Profl. Writing summa cum laude, San Francisco State U., 1994. Mgr. REP Bookcenter and Press, Portland, Oreg., 1970-73; program mgr. microcomputer program North Seattle C.C., 1985-88; owner, operator Linda Alband Bookseller, San Francisco and Oakland, Calif., 1988—; personal asst., rschr. to author Randy Shilts, San Francisco, 1988-94; rsch. and devel. profl. Woman Vision, 1994—; cons. conduct Unberming CD-Rom, 1993-95. Editor, fact checker Conduct Unbecoming, 1990-94. Oreg. organizer, mem. nat. steering com. Vietnam Vets Against War, 1970-73; co-founder, bd. dirs. Bay Area Mil. Studies Group, San Francisco, 1974-80; video project developer, prodr. San Francisco Bay Area Book Festival, 1992—, Harvey Milk Archives, 1995—; prodr. Randy Shilts Pub. Meml., Glide Meml., San Francisco, 1994. Mem. Calif. Lawyers for Arts, San Francisco Bay Area Book Coun., San Francisco Cinematheque, Nat. Writers Union, Media Alliance, Film Arts Found., Bay Area Video Coalition. Home and Office: 4611 Eighteenth St #1 San Francisco CA 94114

ALBANESE, MARY DALENE, writer, educator, geologist; b. Syracuse, N.Y., Sept. 20, 1954; d. Earl E. and Eunice (Kolbe) Ross; m. Thomas Albanese, May 9, 1979; children: Yvonne Eunice, Amy Rosemarie. BA, SUNY, Stony Brook, 1977; MS, U. Alaska, 1980; D in metaphysical Sci., U. of Metaphysics L.A., Studio City, Calif., 1994. Cert. tchr. and geologist. Instr. U. Alaska, Fairbanks, 1979-87; geologist Alaska Div. Geol. and Geophys. Surveys, Fairbanks, 1980-87; instr. U. Alaska S.E., Juneau, 1994—. Author: To Romania, with Love, 1992, Startmother, 1995 (2d place award Inspirational Writers Alive! 1993), Tales for the Far Side: The Ins and Outs of Astral Projection; author, illustrator: (coloring book) Kira, A Alaskan Peregrine Falcon, 1994. Mem. Am. Inst. Profl. Geologists, Nat. Assn. Geology Tchrs., Alaska Women in Mining. Home: 3499 Meander Way Juneau AK 99801-9626

ALBANESE, THOMAS, minerals company executive; b. Akron, Ohio, Sept. 9, 1957; s. Paul F. Albanese and Rosemarie (Helm) Rovito; m. Mary D. Ross, June 14, 1979; children: Yvonne, Amy. BS in Mining Econs., U. Alaska, 1979, MS in Mining Engring., 1981. Engr. Resource Assocs. Alaska, Fairbanks, 1981-82; various positions to COO, Nerco Minerals Co., Portland, Oreg., 1993; pres. Pikes Peak, Portland, 1993; sr. v.p. Nerco, Inc., Portland, 1993; gen. mgr. Kenncott Gen. Co., Juneau, Alaska, 1993—; bd. dirs. Silver Inst./Silver Trust, N.Y.C., 1988-93. Bd. dirs. Glo Inst., Washington, 1988-93, Alaska Producers Coun., Juneau, 1993—; pres., chmn. Western States Pub. Lands, Pueblo, Colo., 1991-92. Home: 3499 Meander Way Juneau AK 99801-9626

ALBANO, ANDRES, JR., real estate developer, real estate broker; b. Honolulu, Apr. 16, 1941; s. Andres Pacis and Florence (Paglinawan) A.; m. Sandra Kam Mee Ymas, Nov. 29, 1961; children: Cheryl Ann, Denise Lynn. BEE, U. Hawaii, 1965, MBA, 1972. Engr. nuclear power USN, 1965-67; elec. engr. U.S. Aviation Adminstrn., Honolulu, 1967-69, Honolulu Bd. Water Supply, 1969-79; exec. v.p. MidPac Devel. Ltd., Honolulu, 1979-84; pres. Albano & Assocs., Honolulu, 1984—; prin. broker Gen. Growth Mgmt. of Hawaii, Inc., 1993—. Mem. NSPE, Hawaii Soc. Profl. Engrs. (pres. 1979-80), Devel. Assn. Hawaii (pres. 1992-93), Nat. Assn. Realtors, Hawaii Developers Coun. (pres. 1995-96), Rotary, Beta Gamma Sigma. Roman Catholic. Home: 748 Kokomo Pl Honolulu HI 96825-1603 Office: Albano & Assocs Inc 3322 Campbell Ave Honolulu HI 96815-3856

ALBERG, TOM AUSTIN, communications executive, lawyer; b. San Francisco, Feb. 12, 1940; s. Thomas A. and Miriam A. (Twitchell) A.; m. Mary Ann Johnke, June 8, 1963 (div. July 1989); children—Robert, Katherine, John; m. Judith Beck, Aug. 8, 1989; children: Carson, Jessica. AB, Harvard Coll., 1962; JD, Columbia U., 1965. Bar: N.Y. 1965, Wash. 1967. Assoc. Cravath, Swaine & Moore, N.Y.C., 1965-67; assoc. Perkins, Coie, Stone, Olsen & Williams, Seattle, 1967-71, ptnr., 1971-90, chmn. exec. com., 1986-90; exec. v.p. legal and corp. affairs, McCaw Cellular Comm. Inc., Kirkland, Wash., 1990—; bd. dirs., Commerce Bank, 1990—, Digital Sys. Internat., Inc., 1992-93; pres., COO, dir. Lin Broadcasting Inc., Kirkland, 1991—; active Voice Corp., 1994—, LIN-TV Corp., 1994—; lectr. on securities and fin. law. Editor Law Rev., Columbia U. contbr. articles to profl. jours. Mem. found. bd. Children's Hosp., 1992; pres. Seattle Legal Svcs., 1973-74, Intiman Theatre, Seattle, 1981-83, Pacific Sci. Ctr. Found., Seattle, 1982-84; co-chmn. Discovery Inst., 1991—, Seattle Commons, 1991—; trustee Children's Hosp. Found., 1992—, Pacific Sci. Ctr., 1994—, Univ. Puget Sound, 1994—, Sta. KING-FM, 1994—; bd. dirs. Seattle Commons, 1992—. Stone scholar Columbia U., 1963-65. Mem. ABA, Wash. State Bar Assn. (chmn. corp. sect. 1975-76, securities com. 1974-75), University, Club, Seattle Yacht Club. Office: McCaw Cellular Communications 5700 Carillon Pt Kirkland WA 98033-7356

ALBERS, ARDELL (BUD ALBERS), software development executive; b. Belleville, Ill., Jan. 14, 1964; s. Ardell O. and Marcella A. (Hummert) A.; m. Tiffany K. Hoffmann, Feb. 14, 1987; children: Danielle Nicole, Zachary Jacob. BS in Computer Sci., McKendree Coll., Lebanon, Ill., 1986. Data base adminstr. CyberTel Cellular Telephone, St. Louis, 1987-89; sr. info. tech. mgr. The Trane Co., St. Louis, 1989-92; dir. devel. and integration R&D Sys., Colorado Springs, Colo., 1992-95, v.p. devel. & svcs. UDS divsn., 1995—; speaker Show Case V, St. Louis; adv. Washington U., St. Louis. Home: 105 Starlint Ct Southlake TX 76092 Office: R&D Systems 5225 N Academy Blvd Colorado Springs CO 80918-4070

ALBERS, WILLIAM MARION, retail food distribution executive; b. St. Louis, Aug. 31, 1932; s. William Henry and Ruth (Marien) A.; m. Mary Ellen Albers, Mar. 8, 1951 (div. Dec. 1966); children: William, Ellen Kay, Beth Ann; m. Dorothy Helen Albers, Apr. 1, 1967; children: Michael, Ronald, Karyn. Student, U. Mo., St. Louis, 1950-52. With prodn. control Am. Fixtures and Mfg., St. Louis, 1951-52; terminal mgr. Consol. Forwarding, St. Louis, 1952-57; gen. foreman McDonnell Douglas Corp., St. Charles, Mo., 1957-70; v.p. Wetterau Inc., Hazelwood, Mo., 1970-84; sr. v.p. dist. Safeway Stores Inc., Oakland, Calif., 1984—; chmn. bd. dirs. trans Continental Leasing Co., Hazelwood; bd. dirs. Oakland Property Brokerage, Oakland. Patentee in field. Dir. civil def. City of Florissant, Mo., 1965-66; mem. council Messiah Luth. Ch., Danville, Calif., 1986. Mem. Am. Inst. Indsl. Engrs. (Merit award 1978), Soc. Logistics Engrs. (Merit award 1981). Clubs: Diablo (Calif.) Country. Home: 4471 Walnut Blvd Walnut Creek CA 94596-6131 Office: Safeway Stores Inc 201 4th St Oakland CA 94607-4311

ALBERTS, DAVID, artistic director, mime artist; b. Akron, Ohio, Nov. 14, 1946; married (div. 1972); 1 child, Morgan Elizabeth; married (div. 1992); children: Sarah Aimee, Samantha Kaitlin Wynne. BA in Music, Kent State U., 1972; MA in Theatre, West Va. U., 1978; PhD in Theatre, Bowling Green State U., 1989. Instr. Akron (Ohio) U., 1970-71, W.Va. U., 1978, Va. Commonwealth U., Richmond, 1979-81, Calif. State U., Turlock, Calif., 1981-83, Kent (Ohio) State U., 1986-87, Bowling Green (Ohio) State U., 1987-89; artistic dir. Theatre of the One Actor, San Diego, 1995—; mime artist in field. Author: Pantomime: Exercises and Elements, 1971, Talking About Mime, 1994 (San Diego Book award 1994), Rehearsal Managment for Directors, 1995, (play) Death By Arrangement, 1981; contbr. articles to profl. jours. Recipient Founders award Internat. Thespian Soc., 1972, Directing award Am. Coll. Theatre Festival, 1982. Mem. Internat. Mimes and Pantomimes, Assn. for Theatre in Higher Edn., Speech Comms. Assn.

ALBERTS, DAVID SAMUEL, physician, pharmacologist, educator; b. Milw., Dec. 30, 1939; m. Heather Alberts; children: Tim, Sabrina. BS, Trinity Coll., Hartford, Conn., 1962; MD, U. Va., 1966. Cert. physician, Ariz. Dir. clin. pharmacology Ariz. Cancer Ctr., Tucson, 1975—, prof. medicine and pharmacology, 1982—, dir. cancer prevention and control, 1988—, dep. dir., 1989—; external adv. U. Chgo. Cancer Ctr., 1993—, Tulane U. Cancer Ctr., New Orleans, 1993—, divsn. cancer prevention M.D. Anderson Cancer Ctr., Houston, 1994—, Norris Cotton Cancer Ctr., Hanover, 1995—; mem. bd. sci. counselors divsn. Cancer Prevention and Control, NCI-NIH, 1990-94; chmn. gynecologic cancer com. S.W. Oncology Group, 1977—; mem. monitoring and adv. panel Nat. Prostate Lung-Colon-Ovary Cancer Study, NCI-NIH, 1994—; chmn. cancer prevention com. Gynecologic Oncology Group, 1995—. Assoc. editor Cancer Rsch., 1989—, Cancer Chemother and Pharmacol., 1992—, Clin. Cancer Rsch., 1994—; contbr. articles to profl. jours.; inventor azamitosene and anthracene anti-cancer agts., tumorimeter, hypodermic needle with automatic retracting point. NIH grantee, 1975—. Mem. Am. Soc. for Clin. Pharmacology and Therapeutics, Am. Soc. Clin. Oncology, Am. Soc. Preventive Oncology, Am. Assn. for Cancer Rsch., Soc. Gynecologic Oncologists. Office: Ariz Cancer Ctr 1515 N Campbell Ave Tucson AZ 85724

ALBERTSON, DAVID, food products executive. V.p., treas. Ballantine Produce Co. Inc., Sanger, Calif., 1971—. Office: Ballantine Produce Co Inc 325 L St Sanger CA 93657-2122*

ALBIN, RANDY CLARK, record company executive; b. Pasadena, Calif., Sept. 25, 1957; s. Clark Eugene and Aileen Mary (Vrooman) A. AA, Foothill Coll., Los Altos Hills, Calif., 1983; student, Stanford U., 1984; BA, Menlo Coll., 1985. With Recreation Tennis, Inc., Stanford, Calif., 1986, Roberta's Personnel Agy., Palo Alto, Calif., 1988, Wollborg-Michelson Personnel, Palo Alto, Calif., 1988; pres., chief exec. officer Randall Record Co., Los Altos, Calif., 1988—. Mem. Foothill Coll. Alumni Assn. (bd. dirs. 1986—), Menlo Coll. Alumni Assn. (treas. 1988). Home and Office: PO Box 920 Los Altos CA 94023-0920

ALBINO, JUDITH E. N., university president; b. Jackson, Tenn.; m. Salvatore Albino; children: Austin, Adrian. BJ, U. Tex., 1967, PhD, 1973. Mem. faculty sch. dental medicine SUNY, Buffalo, 1972-90, assoc. provost, 1984-87, dean sch. arch. and planning, 1987-89, dean grad. sch., 1989-90; v.p. acad. affairs and rsch, dean system grad. sch. U. Colo., Boulder, 1990-91, pres., 1991—. Contbr. articles to profl. jours. Acad. Adminstrn. fellow Am. Coun. on Edn., 1983; grantee NIH. Fellow APA (treas., bd. dirs.); mem. Behavioral Scientists in Dental Rsch. (past pres.), Am. Assn. Dental Rsch. (bd. dirs.). Office: U Colo System Office of President Campus Box 128 Boulder CO 80309-0128*

ALBRECHT, ALBERT PEARSON, electronics engineer, consultant; b. Bakersfield, Calif., Aug. 23, 1920; s. Albert Waldo and Elva (Shuck) A.; m. Muriel Elizabeth Grenell, June 15, 1942 (dec. Apr. 1943); m. Edith J. Dorner, July 18, 1944. BSEE, Calif. Inst. Tech., 1942; MSEE, U. So. Calif., L.A., 1947. Registered profl. engr., Calif. Rsch. assoc. radiation lab. MIT, Cambridge, Mass., 1942-43; chief engr. Gilfillan Bros., L.A., 1943-58; v.p. Space Gen. Corp., El Monte, Calif., 1958-68; exec. v.p. Telluran Cons., Santa Monica, Calif., 1968-72; dir. systems evaluation Office of Asst. Sec. of Def. for Intelligence, Washington, 1972-76; assoc. adminstr. FAA, Washington, 1976-86; cons., prin. AP Albrecht-Cons., Alexandria, Va., 1986—; bd. dirs. Air Traffic Control Assn.; mem. exec. bd. RADIO Tech. Commn. for Aeronautics, Washington, 1980-86; mem. aeronautics adv. com. NASA, Washington, 1980-90. Co-author: Electronic Designers Handbook-Design Compendium, 1957, 2d edit., 1974. Fellow AIAA (adv. com. Aerospace Am. 1984—), IEEE (Engr. Mgr. of the Yr. 1989). Home and Office: 3224 Eagle Ridge Way Bellingham WA 98226-7821

ALBRECHT, JOIE, television and film producer, director, writer; b. Denver; d. Alfred Emil and Virginia Lee Albrecht; m. Scott N. Garen, Sept. 17, 1977 (div. Aug. 1987). Student, U. Colo., 1976-78, U. Calif., Bakersfield, 1979. V.p. Garen/Albrecht Prodns. Inc., Santa Monica, Calif., 1980-88; owner, pres. Albrecht & Assocs., Inc., Topanga, Calif., 1989—; guest lectr. Am. Film Inst., L.A., 1981, Women's Image Network, L.A., 1994; judge Emmy awards, L.A., 1985—; prodr., writer, dir. Scandals, pilot for ABC, Stephen J. Cannell Prodns.; writer CBS Comedy Bloopers, 1990. Author: Adam's Guide to Eve, 1994; prodr., dir. The Cliffwood Avenue Kids, Up Close, HBO, 1978; co-creator, developer, prodr. Sixty Years of Seduction, ABC spl., 1979; prodr. TV spl. Carole King: One to One, TV's Bloopers and Practical Jokes, NBC; developer, prodr., writer Television's Greatest Commercials, NBC spls., 1982; creator, prodr., writer, dir. Down and Out with Donald Duck, NBC, 1987; prodr., writer, co-dir. Mickey's 60th Birthday, NBC, 1988; also others. Recipient Belding bowl for outstanding contbn. to advt. Belding Awards, 1984, gold award for Smart Investing, N.Y. Film Festival, 1986, bronze award for outstanding achievement in film and TV music video category Cindy Awards, 1988; talent scholar U. Colo., 1974-76. Mem. AFTRA, ASCAP, SAG, Dirs. Guild Am. (women's com. 1991—), Writers Guild Am., Women in Film, Topanga Assn. for Scenic Cmty., Old Topanga Homeowners Assn. Democrat. Office: PO Box 8626 Calabasas CA 91372-8626

ALBRECHT, STERLING JEAN, university library director; b. Loa, Utah, June 22, 1937; s. John William and Clara (Russell) A.; m. Nancy Laureen Boley, June 15, 1961; children: Melanie, Craig, Brent, Todd. B.S. in Bus. Mgmt., U. Utah, 1962; M.L.S., Brigham Young U., 1971. Indsl. devel. agt. So. Pacific Co., San Francisco, 1962-66; gifts and exchange librarian Brigham Young U., Provo, Utah, 1966-70, humanities and arts librarian, 1970-72, assoc. univ. librarian, 1972-79, acting univ. librarian, 1979-80, univ. librarian, 1980—. Mem. Research Libraries Group (bd. dirs. 1979—), Utah Library Assn. (2nd v.p. 1974-75), ALA (council 1978-80), Assn. Research Libraries (bd. dirs. 1980-83), Utah Coll. Library Council (chmn. 1982-83, 88-89). Republican. Mem. Ch. of Jesus Christ of Latter-day Saints. Home: 424 S 850 E Orem UT 84058-6543 Office: Brigham Young Univ 3080 Hbll Provo UT 84602-1035

ALBRIGHT, LOIS, operetta company executive director; b. Elwood, Ind., May 17, 1904. Student, Chgo. Musical Coll., Berlin Conservatory (scholar), Vienna Conservatory. Concertmaster Nashville Symphony; 1st violinist Gary String Ensemble, 1935; condr. Opera in the Parks, Chgo., Harding U. Choir, South Music Festival, Chgo. Music Festival, Phoenix Symphonic Choir, Phoenix Opera Assn., 1948-53, Ariz. Music Drama Guild, 1954, others; tchr. voice Glendale Community Coll., Phoenix, 1964-72; chmn. music dept. Harding U., Ark., 1935-40; founder, artistic dir. Phoenix Opera Assn., Inc.; exec. dir. Phoenix Oratorio, Opera Singers; lectr. on Hopi lore throughout U.S. to museums, univs., high schs., others; pianist, first concert at age four; concerts in Midwest; soloist with mem. Chgo. Symphony Orch. Hall; tours throughout U.S.; violinist, concerts throughout Midwest; played many chamber music concerts throughout Midwest and East coast; mem. Chgo. Women's Symphony; compositions include Psalm 99, S.A.T.B. with soprano obbligato, Psalm 136, S.A.T.B. with piano, Isaiah 62, S.A.T.B. tenor, mezzo and soprano solos with piano, Revelation 22, S.A.T.B. soprano, tenor mezzo and soprano solos with piano, Psalm 45, soprano or tenor solo, with piano, others; coach Opera for Chgo. Opera Co.; tchr. voice Chgo., Los Angeles, Phoenix, N.Y.C.; founder, artistic dir. Phoenix Opera Assn., Inc.; exec. dir. Phoenix Oratorio/Opera Singers; founder, exec. dir., Viennese Operetta Co. of N.Y., Inc., N.Y.C., 1975—, pres., condr. at Sun Dial, Sun City, Ariz, 1990; pres. Viennese Operetta Co. Am., Inc., 1989—, condr. in Sun City, 1990; condr. all performances Lincoln Ctr., toured West Coast, 1982, East Coast, 1983. Author: Saul and the Medium, 1965; composed: Hopitu, folk opera, 1955; presented: Three Opuses, 1987; condr. six performances of Viennase Operetta Co., Phoenix, Sun City, Ariz., 1992, tchr. artist students Met. Opera, N.Y.C., N.Y. C. Opera, 1991-92. Recipient award Internat. Robert Stolz Soc. of Vienna. Mem. N.Y. Singing Tchrs. Assn. (rec. sec. 1959-60), Sun City Symphony Assn. (bd. dirs.). Home and Office: 13842 N 109th Ave Sun City AZ 85351-2585*

ALCANTARA, THEO, conductor; b. Cuenca, Castile, Spain, 1941; student Real Conservatorio de Musica, Madrid; grad. Akademie Mozarteum, Salzburg, Austria, 1964; m. Susan Alcantara; children: Rafael, Carlos. Conducting debut with Teatro de la Zarzuela, Madrid; condr. Frankfurt Opera Theatre Orch., 1964-66; dir. orchs. U. Mich., Ann Arbor, 1968-73; music dir., condr. Grand Rapids Symphony, 1973-78; music dir., prin. condr. Phoenix Symphony Orch., from 1978; music dir., condr. Music Acad. of West Summer Festival, Santa Barbara, Calif., 1981-85, prin. condr. Pitts. Opera, 1987—; artistic dir., prin. condr. Bilbao Symphony, Spain, 1993—; prin. guest condr. Nat. Orch. Spain, 1994—; guest condr. numerous orchs. including: world premier Christopher Columbus, Teatro Colon, Buenos Aires, Met. Opera, Pitts. Opera, Washington Opera, Am. Symphony, orchs. of Paris, Berlin, Madrid, Barcelona, Mexico City, Montevideo, New Orleans, Detroit, Pitts., Rochester (N.Y.) Philharm., Oreg. Symphony, Utah Symphony. Recipient Lili Lehman medal; silver medal Dimitri Mitropoulous Internat. Conducting Competition, 1966; Disting. Service award Mich. Found. for the Arts, 1977. Office: 7820 N 65th St Paradise Valley AZ 85253

ALCHALABI, NEAL KAMAL, manufacturing engineer; b. Ann Arbor, Mich., Feb. 21, 1952; s. Kamal T. and Bunny Lee (Mosgrave) A.; 1 child, Collin Thompson. Real estate salesperson Carpenters et al, Palmdale, Calif., 1980-84; mfg. engr. Seagate Tech., Scotts Valley, Calif., 1984—. Peace and freedom activist, 1966—; dir. Pastime Future Fact Mgmt., Inc., 1990—, Acad. of Awareness, 1968—. Home: PO Box 3063 Santa Cruz CA 95063-3063

ALCORN, MICHAEL SCOTT, food products executive; b. Bonne Terre, Mo., May 8, 1952; s. Denys Love and Nancy Ann (Theno) A.; m. Suzan Joy McCluen, June 23, 1974; 1 child, Spencer. BA, U. Calif., 1975. From mgr. to pres. Rainbo Ice Cream Jobbers Inc., Union City, Calif., 1974-89; pres. Golden Bear Distbn., Phoenix, 1989—. Served USAF, 1975-82. Office: RHLS Inc PO Box 388 Del Mar CA 92014-0388

ALDAG, RICHARD JEFFREY, composer, educator; b. N.Y.C., Aug. 8, 1955; s. Russell Thomas and Emily (Carro) A.; m. Maria Celi, July 2, 1977 (div.); m. Astrid Juárez, Dec. 30, 1989. B.A., Queens Coll., 1977, M.A., 1979; Ph.D., CUNY, 1990. Music events coordinator CUNY Grad. Ctr., N.Y.C., 1981-84; chmn. dept. theory Bklyn. Conservatory Music, Flushing, N.Y., 1981-92; exec. dir. Musica Poetica Publs., 1992—; adj. asst. prof. Fordham U., Bronx, 1984-92; bd. dirs. Am. New Music Consortium, N.Y.C., 1985-86, Access Chamber Ensemble, N.Y.C., 1987—; dir. Silicon Valley Youth Conservatory, 1994—; lectr. music San Jose (Calif.) State U., 1993—; vis. prof. composition Shanghai Conservatory of Music, 1993-94. Composer numerous vocal and instrumental works. CUNY fellow, 1980, 84. Mem. League of Composers/Internat. Soc. for Contemporary Music (bd. dirs. 1988-91), Internat. Alban Berg Soc. (sec.-treas. 1982-86), Roger Sessions Soc. (v.p. 1988—). Avocation: Mexican cooking.

ALDEN, SUSAN JANE, technical writing agency executive; b. Cleve., Mar. 17, 1952; d. Walter Everett and Irvina Mary (Knight) Watson; m. John Hansen Alden, Sept. 11, 1982; children: Jonathan Starbuck, Darcy Priscilla. BFA, Miami U., Oxford, Ohio, 1974. Textile designer Von Hamm Textiles, Inc., Honolulu, 1974-75; artist/designer Capricorn Graphics, Inc., Honolulu, 1975-80; tech. writer/cons. CFC, Inc., Dayton, Ohio, 1980-82; freelance writer/producer Northlight Comm., L.A., 1982-87; sr. mgr. tech. publ. dept. Fujitsu GTE Bus. Systems, Phoenix, 1987-89; owner, pres. The Alden Agy., Ventura, Calif., 1990—. Author software manuals. Recipient purchase award City of Honolulu, 1977. Mem. NAFE, Soc. Tech. Comm., Phoenix Art Mus. Republican. Methodist.

ALDERMAN, MINNIS AMELIA, psychologist, educator, small business owner; b. Douglas, Ga., Oct. 14, 1928; d. Louis Cleveland Sr. and Minnis Amelia (Wooten) A. AB in Music, Speech and Drama, Ga. State Coll., Milledgeville, 1949; MA in Supervision and Counseling Psychology, Murray State U., 1960; postgrad. Columbia Pacific U., 1987—. Tchr. music Lake County Sch. Dist., Umatilla, Fla., 1949-50; instr. vocal and instrumental music, dir. band, orch. and choral Fulton County Sch. Dist., Atlanta, 1950-54; instr. English, speech, debate, vocal and instrumental music, dir. drama, band, choral and orch. Elko County Sch. Dist., Wells, Nev., 1954-59; tchr. English and social studies Christian County Sch. Dist., Hopkinsville, Ky., 1960; instr. psychology, counselor critic prof. Murray (Ky.) State U., 1961-63, U. Nev., Reno, 1963-67; owner Minisizer Exercising Salon, Ely, Nev., 1969-71, Knit Knook, Ely, 1969—, Minimimeo, Ely, 1969—, Gift Gamut, Ely, 1977—; prof. dept. fine arts Wassuk Coll., Ely, 1986-91, assoc. dean, 1986-87, dean, 1987-90; counselor White Pine County Sch. Dist., Ely, 1960-68; dir. Child and Family Ctr., Ely Indian Tribe, 1988-93, Family and Community Ctr., Ely Shoshone Indian Tribe, 1988-93; adv. Ely Shoshone Tribal Youth Coun., 1990-93, Budge Stanton Meml. Scholarship, 1991-93, Budge Stanton Meml. Living Mus. and Cultural Ctr., 1991-93; fin. aid contracting officer Ely Shoshone Tribe, 1990-93; supr. testing Ednl. Testing Svc., Princeton, N.J., 1960-68, Am. Coll. Testing Program, Iowa, 1960-68, U. Nev., Reno, 1960-68; chmn. bd. White Pine Sch. Dist. Employees Fed. Credit Union, Ely, 1961-69; psychologist mental hygiene div. Nev. Pers., Ely, 1969-75, dept. employment security, 1975-80; sec.-treas. bd. dirs. Gt. Basin Enterprises, Ely, 1969-71; speaker at confs. Author various news articles, feature stories, pamphlets, handbooks and grants in field. Pvt. instr. piano, violin, voice and organ, Ely, 1981—; bd. dirs. band Sacred Heart Sch., Ely, 1982—; mem. Gov.'s Mental Health State Commn., 1963-65, Ely Shoshone Tribal Youth Camp, 1991-92, Elys Shoshone Tribal Unity Conf., 1991-92, Tribal Parenting Skills Coord., 1991; bd. dirs. White Pine County Sch.

Employees Fed. Credit Union, 1961-68, pres., 1963-68; 2d v.p. White Pine Community Concert Assn., 1965-67, pres., 1967, 85—, treas., 1975-79, dr. chmn., 1981-85; chmn. of bd., 1984; bd. dirs. White Pine chpt. ARC, 1978-82; mem. Nev. Hwy. Safety Leaders Bd., 1979-82; mem. Gov.'s Commn. on Status Women, 1968-74, Gov.'s Nevada State Juvenile Justice Adv. Commn., 1992-94, White Pine Overall Econ. Devel. Plan Coun., 1992-94; sec.-treas. White Pine Rehab. Tng. Ctr. for Retarded Persons, 1973-75; mem. Gov.'s Commn. on Hwy. Safety, 1979-81, Gov's. Juvenile Justice Program; sec.-treas. White Pine County Juvenile Problems Cabinet, 1994—; dir. Ret. Sr. Vol. Program, 1973-74; vice chmn. Gt. Basin Health Coun., 1973-75, Home Extension Adv. Bd., 1977-80; sec.-treas. Great Basin chpt. Nev. Employees Assn.; bd. dirs. United Way, 1970-76; vice chmn. White Pine Coun. on Alcoholism and Drug Abuse, 1975-76, chmn., 1976-77; grants author 3 yrs. Indian Child Welfare Act, originator Community Tng. Ctr. for Retarded People, 1972, Ret. Sr. Vol. Program, 1974, Nutrition Program for Sr. Citizens, 1974, Sr. Citizens Ctr., 1974, Home Repairs for Sr. Citizens, 1974, Sr. Citizens Home Assistance Program, 1977, Creative Crafters Assns., 1976, Inst. Current World Affairs, 1989, Victims of Crime, 1990-92; bd. dirs. Family coalition, 1990-92, Sacred Heart Parochial Sch., 1982—, dir. band, 1982—; candidate for diaconal ministry, 1982-93; dir. White Pine Community Choir, 1962—, Ely Meth. Ch. Choir, 1960-84; choir dir., organist Sacred Heart Ch., 1984—. Precinct reporter ABC News 1966; speaker U.S. Atty. Gen. Conf. Bringing Nev. Together; bd. dirs. White Pine Juvenile Cabinet, 1993—. Recipient Recognition rose Alpha Chi State Delta Kappa Gamma, 1994. Fellow Am. Coll. Musicians, Nat. Guild Piano Tchrs.; mem. NEA (life), UDC, n. Ind. Bus. (dist. chair 1971-85, nat. guardian coun. 1985—, state guardian coun. 1987—), AAUW (pres. Wells br. 1957-58, pres. White Pine br. 1965-66, 86-87, 89-91, 93—, bd. dirs. 1965-87, rep. edn. 1965-67, implementation chair 1967-69, area advisor 1969-73, 89-91), Nat. Fedn. Bus. and Profl. Women (1st v.p. Ely chpt. 1965-66, pres. Ely chpt. 1966-68, 74-76, 85—, bd. dirs. Nev. chpt. 1966—, 1st v.p. Nev. Fedn. 1970-71, pres. Nev. chpt. 1972-73, nat. bd. dirs. 1972-73), White Pine County Mental Health Assn. (pres. 1960-63, 78—), Mensa (supr. testing 1965—), Delta Kappa Gamma (br. pres. 1968-72, 94—, state bd. 1967—, chpt. parliamentarian 1974-78, state 1st v.p. 1967-69, state pres. 1969-71, nat. bd. 1969-71, state parliamentarian 1971-73), White Pine Knife and Fork Club (1st v.p. 1969-70, pres. 1970-71, bd. dirs. 1979—), Soc. Descendants of Knights of Most Noble Order of Garter, Nat. Soc. Magna Charta Dames. Home: 945 Ave H PO Box 150457 East Ely NV 89315-0457 Office: 1280 Avenue F East Ely NV 89301-2511

ALDOUS, DUANE LEO, pharmacist; b. Albuquerque, Nov. 2, 1930; s. Clarence Moroni and Sarah Eunice (Robinson) A.; m. Barbara K. Kekauoha, July 21, 1955; children: Keith, Valerie, Jeffrey, Melanie, Wade. BS in Pharmacy, U. N.Mex., 1953, PhD in Chemistry, 1961, postgrad., 1962. Registered pharmacist, N.Mex. Postdoctoral fellow U. N.Mex., Albuquerque, 1961-62; rsch. chemist E.I. duPont de Nemours & Co., Inc., Kinston, N.C., 1962-68; asst. prof. pharm. chemistry Xavier U. of La., New Orleans, 1968-71, assoc. prof., 1971-80, dean Coll. of Pharmacy, 1973-79; rsch. assoc. Nat. Ctr. for Health Svcs. Rsch., Silver Spring, Md., 1979-80; prof. pharm. chemistry Xavier U. of La., New Orleans, 1980-90; dir. Nu Skin Labs., Provo, Utah, 1990—. Contbr. to book: Pyridazines, 1972. Bishop LDS Ch., Metairie, La., 1978-87. With U.S. Army, 1953-56. Named Outstanding Educator Ciba-Geigy Pharm. Co., New Orleans, 1988. Mem. Soc. Cosmetic Chemists, Am. Chem. Soc., Sigma Xi. Office: Nu Skin Internat Inc 1 Nuskin Plz Provo UT 84601-8413

ALDRICH, DANIEL EUGENE, small business owner; b. Colony, Kans., May 26, 1954; s. Harold Eugene and Dorothy May (Connor) A.; m. Sandra May Lindsay, Aug. 16, 1972 (div. 1976); children: Latisha Ilean, Blain Dean, Paula L., Amber Dove; m. Donna L. Audet, Mar. 15, 1977 (div. Apr. 1979). AA, Big Bend C.C., 1979; student, Ea. Wash. U., 1981-83. With Bunker Hill Mines, Kellogg, Idaho, 1972-74; prin. Aldrich Inc., South Beach, Oreg., 1988—. Vol. Lincoln County Food Share, Newport, Oreg., 1988-90. With U.S. Army, 1974-76. Mem. ABATE of Oreg. Republican. Methodist. Home and Office: 11628 SE Birch St South Beach OR 97366-9766

ALDRICH, DAVID LAWRENCE, public relations executive; b. Lakehurst Naval Air Sta., N.J., Feb. 21, 1948; s. Clarence Edward and Sarah Stiles (Andrews) A.; m. Benita Susan Massler, Mar. 17, 1974. BA in Communications, Calif. State U.-Dominguez Hills, 1976. Pub. info. technician City of Carson (Calif.), 1973-77; pub. rels. dir./adminstrv. asst. Calif. Fed. Savs., L.A., 1977-78; v.p., group supr. Hill & Knowlton, L.A., 1978-81; v.p., mgr. Ayer Pub. Rels. western div. N.W. Ayer, L.A., 1981-84; pres. Aldrich and Assocs. Inc., L.A., 1984—; bd. dirs., exec. com. Drum Corps Internat. With USAF, 1968-72. Home: 25 15th Pl Unit 704 Long Beach CA 90802-6061 Office: Aldrich & Assocs 110 Pine Ave Ste 620 Long Beach CA 90802-4422

ALDRICH, MICHAEL RAY, organization executive; b. Vermillion, S.D., Feb. 7, 1942; s. Ray J. and Lucile W. (Hamm) A.; AB, Princeton, 1964; MA, U. S.D., 1965; PhD, SUNY, 1970; m. Michelle Cauble, Dec. 26, 1977. Fulbright tutor Govt. Arts and Commerce Coll., Indore, Madhya Pradesh, India, 1965-66; founder Lemar Internat., 1966-71; mem. faculty Sch. Critical Studies, Calif. Inst. Arts, Valencia, 1970-72; workshop leader Esalen Inst., San Francisco, 1972; co-founder AMORPHIA, Inc., The Cannabis Coop., Mill Valley, Calif., 1969-74; curator Fitz Hugh Ludlow Meml. Libr., San Francisco, 1974—. Freelance writer, photographer, lectr., cons. on drug rsch., and sociolegal reform specializing in drug laws and history to various colls., drug confs., publishers, svc. groups; cons. Commn. of Inquiry into Non-Med. Use of Drugs, Ottawa, Ont., 1973; rsch. aide, select com. on control marijuana Calif. Senate, 1974. Bd. dirs. Ethno-Pharmacology Soc., 1976-83. Calif. Marijuana Initiative, 1971-74; mem. nat. adv. bd. Nat. Orgn. for Reform of Marijuana Laws, 1976—; mem. Princeton working group Future of Drug Policy, 1990—; asst. dir. Nat. Inst. on Drug Abuse AIDS Project Menu Youth Environment Study, San Francisco, 1987-88; project adminstr. YES Tng. Ctr., 1989, program coord. Calif. AIDS Intervention Tng. Ctr., 1990—. Author: The Dope Chronicles 1850-1950, 1979, Coricancha, The Golden Enclosure, 1983; co-author: High Times Ency. of Recreational Drugs, 1978, Fiscal Costs of California Marijuana Law Enforcement, 1986, YES Tng. Manual, 1989, Methods of Estimating Needle Users at Risk for AIDS, 1990; editor: Marijuana Review, 1968-74, Ludlow Library Newsletter, 1974-81; contbg. author Cocaine Handbook, 1981, 2d edit., 1987; mem. editorial rev. bd. Jour. Psychoactive Drugs, 1981—, marijuana theme issue editor, 1988; research photographer Life mag., 1984; contbg. editor High Times, 1979-85; contbr. articles to profl. publs. Office: PO Box 640346 San Francisco CA 94164-0346

ALDRIDGE, DONALD O'NEAL, military officer; b. Solo, Mo., July 22, 1932. BA in History, U. Nebr.-Omaha, 1974; postgrad. Creighton U., 1975. Commd. 2d lt. U.S. Air Force, 1958, advanced through grades to lt. gen., 1988; asst. dir. plans U.S. Air Force, Washington, 1978-79; spl. asst. to dir. Joint Chiefs of Staff, Washington, 1979-80; dep. dir. Def. Mapping Agy., Washington, 1980-81; dep. U.S. rep. NATO Mil. Com., Brussels, Belgium, 1981-83; rep. Joint Chiefs of Staff, Geneva, Switzerland, 1983-86; comdr. 1st Strat. Aerospace div. Vandenberg AFB, Calif., 1986-88; vice-CINC Strategic Air Command, Offutt AFB, Nebr., 1988-91; mgmt. cons. Sacramento, Calif., 1991—. Office: Aldridge Assocs 159 Orange Blossom Cir Folsom CA 95630-8117

ALENIKOV, VLADIMIR, motion picture director and writer; b. Leningard, Russia, Aug. 7, 1948; came to U.S., 1990; s. Michael and Stella (Alenikova) Volkenshtein; 1 child, Philip; m. Tamara Karpovitch; 1 child, Anastassia. Student, Leningrad State U., 1965-67, Leningrad Inst. Theatre, 1967-69, Moscow State U., 1969-72. Tchr. Russian lit. and french, dep. prin. Secondary Sch. 2, Moscow, 1969-72; dir. Gorky Film Studios, Moscow, 1974-78, 88-89, Odessa Film Studio, 1982-84; dir. music Ekran TV Studio, Moscow, 1979-81, dir., 1985-87; dir., pres. Aquilon Co., Moscow, 1989—; dir., owner Destiny Films, L.A., 1992—; lectr. at film showsing; mem. 1st Soviet del. of cinematographers, Cyprus, Greece. Author: The White Page, 1972, The Mysteries of a Women's Heart, 1975, also articles, poems and short stories; Dir. and writer of feature films: The Garden, 1973, The Composer Comitas, 1974, The Room of Laughter, 1975, What a Mess, 1976, There Lived a Piano-Tuner, 1979, The Adventures of Petrov and Vasechkin, Ordinary and Extraordinary, 1982, The Hooligan, 1983, The Knight, 1983, Unique, 1986, Valuable Friends, 1987, The Drayman and the King, 1989, The Time of Darkness, 1991, The Awakening, 1991, Monique, 1993; Dir. and writer of stage plays: The Locals, 1976, The Adventures of d'Artagnan, 1986, (with David Wolcomb), Peace Child, 1985, The Hooligan is Coming, 1986, The Tale of the Warrior, 1987, The Tower, 1988, White Mercedes, 1992; Screen plays include: August Weather Forecast, 1984, A Night Story, 1985, To Kill and be Alive, 1990, The Incredible Adventures of Ricky Plim, 1992, Without Past, 1993, War of Princess, 1993. Pres. Russian-Am. Art Ctr., L.A., 1992—. Recipient 1st prize for best TV film 22d Internat. Festival Children and Youth Films Gijon Spain 1984, award for best film dir.'s debut Internat. Festival TV Films Montreux Switzerland 1979, Danube prize 8th Internat. Festival Childrens' TV Films Bratislava Czechoslovakia 1985, Grand Prix Soviet Nat. Festival Youth-83 1983, Grand Prix First Moscow Film Festival of Children's Scetches 1987, prize for funniest movie 10th Internat. Festival Children's Films Moscow 1987, AFI Film Internat. Festival award L.A. 1990, Jerusalem Film Festival award 1990, Toronto Festival of Festivals diploma 1990, Moscow Internat. Film Festival award 1991; also others. Mem. Russian Film Makers, Russian Guild Scriptwriters, Russian Guild Dir., Moscow Guild Diirs., L.A. Press Club. Jewish. Home and Office: 1308 9th St Apt 8 Santa Monica CA 90401-1861

ALEXANDER, GEORGE JONATHON, legal educator, former dean; b. Berlin, Germany, Mar. 8, 1931; s. Walter and Sylvia (Grill) A.; m. Katharine Violet Sziklai, Sept. 6, 1958; children: Susan Katina, George Jonathon II. AB with maj. honors, U. Pa., 1953, JD cum laude, 1969; LLM, Yale U., 1965, JSD, 1969. Bar: Ill. 1960, N.Y. 1961, Calif. 1974. Instr. law, Bigelow fellow U. Chgo., 1959-60; instr. internat. relations Naval Res. Officers Sch., Forrest Park, Ill., 1959-60; prof. law Syracuse U. Coll. Law, 1960-70, assoc. dean, 1968-69; prof. law U. Santa Clara (Calif.) Law Sch., 1970—, Disting. univ. prof., 1994—, pres.-elect faculty senate, 1995—, dean, 1970-85; dir. Inst. Internat. and Comparative Law, 1986—; vis. prof. law U. So. Calif., 1963; vis. scholar Stanford (Calif.) U. Law Sch., 1985-86, 92; cons. in field. Author: Civil Rights, U.S.A., Public Schools, 1963, Honesty and Competition, 1967, Jury Instructing on Medical Issues, 1966, Cases and Materials on Space Law, 1971, The Aged and the Need for Surrogate Management, 1972, Commercial Torts, 1973, 2d edit. 1988, U.S. Antitrust Laws, 1980, Writing A Living Will: Using a Durable Power of Attorney, 1988; author, editor: International Perspectives on Aging, 1992; also articles, chpts. in books, one film. Dir. Domestic and Internat. Bus. Problems Honors Clinic, Syracuse U., 1966-69, Regulations in Space Project, 1968-70; ednl. cons. Comptroller Gen. U.S., 1977—; mem. Nat. Sr. Citizens Law Ctr., 1983-89, pres., 1986-90; co-founder Am. Assn. Abolition Involuntary Mental Hospitalization, 1970, dir., 1970-83. With USN, 1953-56. U.S. Navy scholar U. Pa., 1949-52; Law Bds. scholar, 1956-59; Sterling fellow Yale, 1964-65; recipient Ralph E. Kharas Civil Liberties award, 1970, Owens award as Alumnus of Yr., 1984, Disting. prof. Santa Clara Univ. Faculty Senate, 1994-95. Mem. Calif. Bar Assn. (first chmn. com. legal problems of aging), Assn. Am. Law Schs., Soc. Am. Law Tchrs. (dir., pres. 1979), AAUP (chpt. pres. 1962), N.Y. Civil Liberties Union (chpt. pres. 1965, dir., v.p. 1966-70), Am. Acad. Polit. and Social Sci., Order of Coif, Justinian Honor Soc., Phi Alpha Delta (chpt. faculty adviser 1967-70). Home: 11600 Summit Wood Ct Los Altos CA 94022-4500 Office: U Santa Clara Santa Clara CA 95053

ALEXANDER, HENRY ALAN, academic administrator; b. Berkeley, Calif., Aug. 24, 1953; s. Ernest and Frances (Connelley) A.; m. Shelley Tornheim, Aug. 24, 1975; children: Aliza, Yonina, Yehuda. AB in Philosophy summa cum laude, UCLA, 1976; BA in Philosophies of Judaism, U. Judaism, 1977; MA in Judaic Studies, The Jewish Theol. Sem. Am., 1982; EdS in Evaluation Studies, Stanford U., 1982, PhD in Edn. and Humanities, 1985. Ordained rabbi, 1982. Instr. philosophy and edn. U. Judaism, L.A., 1983-85, asst. prof., 1985-88, assoc. prof. philosophy and edn., 1988—, from acad. coord. to dean Lee Coll., 1984—, dean acad. affairs, 1990—, v.p. acad. affairs, 1992—; program dir. Camp Young Judaea, St. Helena, Calif., summer 1973; ednl. activities coord. Hashachar/Young Judaea, L.A., 1972-74; dir. informal edn. Herzl High Sch., L.A., 1976-77; day camp dir. Encino, Calif., summer 1976; staff tng. coord. Camp Ramah in the Berkshires, summer 1981; dir. leadership devel. The Jewish Theol. Sem. Am., 1980-82; prof. edn. in residence, dir. Mador Leadership Tng. Program Camp Ramah in Calif., summers 1984, 85, prof. in residence, summers 1986, 87; vis. scholar The Hebrew U. of Jerusalem, 1982-83; vis. scholar, lectr. Sch. Edn. UCLA, 1989—; dir. Lee Coll. U. Judaism, 1986-89; editor: Religious Education, 1991—. Reviewer Jour. Curriculum Inquiry, 1989, The Jour. of Moral Edn., 1987-88; editor Religious Edn., 1991—; mem. editorial bd. Educational Theory; contbr. chpts. to books and articles to profl. jours. Rsch. cons. Commn. on Jewish Edn. in N.Am., 1989, Commn. Jewish Future Jewish Fedn. Coun., L.A., 1988-89; curriculum cons. Wexner Found. Project Stanford U., 1989; trustee Jewish Educators Assembly, 1989—; ednl. dir. Congregation Beth Sholom, San Francisco, 1978-80; chair leadership devel. program Temple Beth Am. L.A., 1986—; evaluation cons. Hollywood Temple Beth El, L.A., 1985, Bur. Jewish Edn., Sacramento, 1985. Scholar-in-residence Australian Inst. for Jewish Affairs Outlook Conf., 1991, Australian Union Jewish Students, 1992. Mem. ASCD, Am. Conf. Acad. Deans, Am. Ednl. Rsch. Assn., Am. Assn. Higher Edn., Am. Phils. Assn., Assn. Philosophy Education, Assn. Jewish Studies, Calif. Assn. Philosophy Edn. (pres. 1989-91), Farwestern Philosophy Edn. Soc., Moral Edn. Assn., Coalition for Advancement of Jewish Edn., Jewish Edn. Rsch. Network, Jewish Educators Assembly, Nat. Soc. for Study of Edn., Philosophy Edn. Soc. (program chair 1991—), Rabbinical Assembly. Office: U Judaism 15600 Mulholland Dr Los Angeles CA 90077-1519

ALEXANDER, JOHN CHARLES, editor, writer; b. Lincoln, Nebr., Jan. 25, 1915; s. John Merriam Alexander and Helen (Abbott) Boggs; m. Ruth Edna McLane, Aug. 20, 1955. Student, U. Nebr., 1933-37, Chouinard Art Inst./Ben Bard Playhouse Sch., L.A., 1937-38, Pasadena Playhouse, 1939-42, UCLA, 1945-47. Aircraft assembler N. Am. aviation, Inglewood, Calif., 1941-42; engring. writer Lockheed-Vega Aircraft, Burbank, Calif., 1942-45; prodn. mgr/actor Gryphon Playhouse, Laguna Beach, Calif., 1947-49; asst. producer/writer Young & Rubicam/ABC, Hollywood, Calif., 1949-51; editor-in-chief Grand Cen. Aircraft, Tucson, 1952-53; sr. writer/editor various cos., Calif., 1953-60; sr. editor/writer, sec. Sci. Guidance Rsch. Coun. Stanford Rsch. Inst., U.S. Army Combat Devel. Command, Menlo Park, Calif., 1962-66; editor-in-chief Litton Sci. Support Lab. USACDC, Fort Ord, Calif., 1966-70; editorial dir./sec. The Nelson Co., Film and Video Prodn., Tarzana, Calif., 1971—; editorial cons., dir. Human Resources Rsch. Office, George Washington U., The Presidio, Monterey, Calif., 1960-62; book editor The Dryden Press, Hinsdale, Ill., 1971-72; book editor/adaptor Gen. Learning Press, Silver Burdette Co., Morristown, N.J., 1972-74; contbg. editor West Coast Writers Conspiracy mag., Hollywood, Calif., 1975-77; contbg. editor/book reviewer Santa Ynez Valley Times, Solvang, Calif., 1976-77; participant Santa Barbara Writers Conf., Montecito, Calif., 1974, 75. Author: (TV plays) Michael Has Company for Coffee, 1948, House on the Hill, 1958, (radio drama) The Couple Next Door, 1951; co-author nine films for U.S. Dept. Justice: Under the Law, Parts I and II, 1973; co-author 10 films for Walt Disney Ednl. Media Co.: Lessons in Learning, Parts I and II, 1978-81; author: (with others) The American West Anthology, 1971; editorial cons. Strangers in Their Land: CBI Bombardier, 1939-45, 1990-92. Recipient award for short story, Writer's Digest, 1960, 61, Gold award, The Festival of the Americas, Houston Internat. Film Festival, 1977. Mem. Nat. Cowboy Hall of Fam, Nat. Geog. Soc., Nat. Soc. Lit. and Arts, Western Hist. Soc., Calif. Acad. Sci., Nat. Air and Space Mus., Smithsonian Instn., Woodrow Wilson Internat. Ctr. for Scholars, Aircraft Owners and Pilots Assn., Air Force Assn., Sigma Nu, Alpha Phi Omega. Home: 23123 Village 23 Camarillo CA 93012-7602

ALEXANDER, JOHN DAVID, JR., college administrator; b. Springfield, Tenn., Oct. 18, 1932; s. John David and Mary Agnes (McKinnon) A.; m. Catharine Coleman, Aug. 26, 1956; children: Catharine McKinnon, John David III, Julia Mary. BA, Southwestern at Memphis, 1953; student, Louisville Presbyn. Theol. Sem., 1953-54; DPhil (Rhodes Scholar), Oxford (Eng.) U., 1957; LLD, U. So. Calif., Occidental Coll., 1970, Centre Coll. of Ky., 1971, Pepperdine U., 1991, Albertson Coll. Idaho, 1992; LHD, Loyola Marymount U., 1983; LittD, Rhodes Coll., 1986; LLD, Pepperdine U., 1991, Albertson Coll. Idaho, 1992. Assoc. prof. San Francisco Theol. Sem., 1957-65; pres. Southwestern at Memphis, 1965-69; pres. Pomona Coll., Claremont, Calif., 1969-91, trustees prof., 1991; Am. sec. Rhodes Scholarship Trust, 1981—; mem. commn. liberal learning Assn. Am. Colls., 1966-69, mem. commn. instl. affairs, 1971-74; mem. commn. colls. So. Assn. Colls. and Schs., 1966-69; mem. Nat. Commn. Acad. Tenure, 1971-72; dir. Am. Coun. on Edn., 1981-84, Nat. Assn. Ind. Colls. and Univs.; bd. dirs. Gt. Western Fin. Corp., Children's Hosp. L.A.; trustee Tchrs. Inst. and Annuity Assn., 1970—, Woodrow Wilson Nat. Fellowship Found., 1978—, Seaver Inst., 1992—, Phi Beta Kappa Assocs., 1993—, Wenner-Gren Found. for Anthrop. Rsch., 1995—, Webb Schs. Calif., 1995—; bd. overseers Huntington Libr., 1991—. Mem. Soc. Bib. Lit., Soc. Religion in Higher Edn., Phi Beta Kappa Alumni in So. Calif. (pres. 1974-76), Century Club, Calif. Club, Bohemian Club, Phi Beta Kappa, Omicron Delta Kappa, Sigma Nu. Office: Pomona Coll Office Am Sec Rhodes Scholarship Trust 333 N College Way Claremont CA 91711-4429

ALEXANDER, KATHARINE VIOLET, lawyer; b. N.Y.C., Nov. 19, 1934; d. George Clifford and Violet (Jambor) Sziklai; m. George Jonathon Alexander, Sept. 6, 1958; children: Susan Katina, George J. II. Student, Smith Coll., Geneva, 1954-55; BA, Goucher Coll., 1956; JD, U. Pa., 1959; student specialized courses, U. Santa Clara, 1974-76. Bar: Calif. 1974, U.S. Dist. Ct. (no. dist.) Calif. 1974, U.S. Ct. Appeals (9th cir.) 1974; cert. criminal lawyer Calif. State Bar Bd. Legal Specialization. Research dir., adminstr. Am. Bar Found., Chgo., 1959-60; lectr. law San Jose (Calif.) State U., 1972-74; sr. atty. Santa Clara County, San Jose, 1974—. Editor: Mentally Disabled and the Law, 1961; contbg. author: The Aged and the Need for Surrogate Management, 1969-70, Jury Instructions on Medical Issues, 1965-67. Community rep. Office Econ. Opportunity Com., Syracuse, N.Y., 1969-70. Mem. AAUW, Food and Wine Inst., Calif. Bar Assn., Santa Clara County Bar Assn. (trustee 1981-82), Calif. Attys. for Criminal Justice (bd. govs. 1988-92), Calif. Pub. Def. Assn., Jr. League. Presbyterian. Home: 11600 Summit Wood Ct Los Altos Hls CA 94022-4500 Office: County Govt Ctr West Wing 70 W Hedding St San Jose CA 95110-1705

ALEXANDER, MARIE BAILEY, consulting editor, family economist; b. Chattanooga, Sept. 2, 1913; d. Claude Esmond and Elsie Blanche (Peterson) Bailey; m. Theron Alexander, Aug. 29, 1936; children: Thomas T., Mary E. BS, Maryville (Tenn.) Coll., 1935; postgrad., Fla. State U., 1950-51. Mktg. cons. Gas & Electric Co., Chattanooga, 1935; tchr. North High Sch., Chattanooga, 1935-36; cons. editor Iowa City, Iowa, 1957-65, Phila., 1966-86, Menlo Park, Calif., 1987—. Deacon, Valley Presbyn. Ch., Portola Valley, Calif., 1989-90. Mem. AAUW (co-chmn. internat. rels. sect. Menlo-Atherton br. 1987-89, chmn. 1989—, mem. lit. group 1986—, bd. dirs. 1987—), P.E.O. (del. regional bd. Calif. 1988-89, pres. chpt. E 1979-81). Democrat. Home: 50 Gresham Ln Atherton CA 94027-3918

ALEXANDER, MARY ELSIE, lawyer; b. Chgo., Nov. 16, 1947; d. Theron and Marie (Bailey) A.; m. Lyman Saunders Faulkner, Jr., Dec. 1, 1984; 1 child, Michelle. BA, U. Iowa, 1969; MPH, U. Calif.-Berkeley, 1975; JD, U. Santa Clara, 1982. Bar: Calif. 1982, U.S. Dist. Ct. (no. dist.) Calif. 1982, U.S. ct. Appeals (9th cir.) 1982. Rschr., U. Cin., 1969-74; dept. dir., sr. environ. health scientist Stanford Rsch. Inst., Menlo Park, Calif., 1975-80; cons. Alexander Assocs., Ambler, Pa., 1980-82; assoc. Caputo, Liccardo Rossi Sturges & McNeil, San Jose, Calif., 1982-84; assoc. Cartwright, Slobodin, Bokelman, et al, San Francisco, 1984-88, ptnr., 1988—. Com. mem. Cancer Soc., San Jose, 1983; elder Valley Presbyn. Ch., Portola Valley, 1987-90; active Am. Heart Assn., Santa Clara County. Named one of top 10 Trial Lawyers San Francisco Bay Area, San Francisco Chronicle, 1990. Nat. Inst. Occpational Safety and Health scholar U. Calif., Berkeley, 1975. Mem. ABA, Assn. Trial Lawyers Am. (state del.), Consumer Attys. Calif. (formerly Calif. Trial Lawyers Assn.) (PAC bd. 1989—, parliamentarian 1991, v.p. 1992, chair mem. com., editor Forum, pres. elect 1995), San Francisco Trial Lawyers Assn., Trial Lawyers for Pub. Justice, Calif. Women Lawyers, Am. Indsl. Hygiene Assn. (bd. dirs. 1979-81, treas. 1977-79), Nat. Assn. Advancement of Sci., Santa Clara Trial Lawyers Assn. (bd. dirs. 1983-84). Democrat. Office: Cartwright Bokelman Boronsky Moore Harris Alexander & Gruen 101 California St Fl 26 San Francisco CA 94111-5802

ALEXANDER, RICHARD, lawyer; b. Cleve., Sept. 26, 1944; m. Nancy L. Biebel, Mar. 16, 1968; children: Marshall, Meredith. BA, Ohio Wesleyan U., 1966; JD (Nat. Honor scholar), U. Chgo., 1969. Bar: Mich. 1969, U.S. Dist. Ct. (ea. and we. dists.) Mich. 1970, U.S. Dist. Ct. (so. dist.) Ind. 1970, Calif. 1971, U.S. Dist. Ct. (no. dist.) Calif. 1971, U.S. Ct. Appeals (9th cir.) 1971, U.S. Dist. Ct. (cen. dist.) Calif. 1972, U.S. Dist. Ct. (ea. dist.) Calif. 1973, U.S. Dist. Ct. D.C. 1980. Diplomate Nat. Bd. Trial Advocacy. Asst. prof. Grad. Sch. Bus., Mich. State U., 1969-71; assoc. Belli, Ashe, Ellison, Choulos & Lieff, San Francisco, 1971-72, Lieff, Alexander, Wilcox & Hill, San Francisco, 1972-74, Boccardo, Lull, Niland & Bell, San Francisco and San Jose, Calif., 1974-80; ptnr. Boccardo Law Firm, San Jose, 1980-87; Alexander & Bohn, San Jose, 1987-91; The Alexander Law Firm, San Jose, 1992—; v.p. State Bar Calif., 1987-88, bd. govs. 1985-88; mem. Santa Clara County Criminal Justice Adv. Bd., 1978-82, chmn., 1978-80; mem. Santa Clara County Jail Over-crowding Task Force, 1978-81; mem. Santa Clara County Pub. Defender Charter Amendment Task Force, 1980; judge pro tem Santa Clara County Superior Ct., 1976-83, 85-90 arbitrator, 1976—; co-chmn. Superior Ct. Arbitration Adminstrn. Com., 1979—; spl. master State Bar Calif., 1980—, lectr. continuing edn., 1975, 78, 81-89, bd. govs. 1985—, mem. com. profl. ethics, 1977-80; speaker legal seminars. Contbr. articles to profl. jours. Mem. Palo Alto (Calif.) Unified Sch. Dist. Task Force on Spl. Edn., 1975-79; vice chmn. sch. improvement program Palo Alto Unified Sch. Dist., 1977-78, mem. found. exploration com., 1984; mem. Santa Clara County Data Confidentiality Commn., 1976-78, chmn., 1977-78; mem. Santa Clara County Democratic Central Com., 1978-80; bd. dirs. Japanese Am. Environ. Conf., 1979-81. Recipient Santa Clara County Youth Commn. medal, 1980, Man of Yr. Women's Fund.; commendation for disting. service Mayor San Jose, 1982; Roscoe Pound fellow; named one of Outstanding Young Men of Am., Man of Yr. The Women's Found., 1989; recipient Pro Bono award Ctr. Occupl. Safety Health, 1993. Mem. San Francisco Bar Assn., Nat. Bd. Trial Advocacy (cert. civil adv. 1980, 85, 90), Nat. Bar Register of Preeminent Lawyers, Santa Clara County Bar Assn. (pres. 1984), Calif. Attys. for Criminal Justice (founding; treas. 1972-74, gov. 1972-75), Calif. Trial Lawyers Assn. (recognized trial lawyer 1980-89, bd. govs. 1989-94), Nat. Assn. Consumer Advocates (founding), Consumer Attys. Calif. (v.p. 1995), State Bar Calif. (bd. govs., 1985—, v.p. 1987—), Assn. Trial Lawyers Am., Sierra Club, NAACP, Stanford Alumni Assn., Alexander Graham Bell Assn. for Deaf, Nat. Trust Hist. Preservation, San Jose Mus. San Jose Symphony. Clubs: U. Chgo. Alumni, Silicon Valley Capital.

ALEXANDER, ROBB SMITH, JR., academic program director; b. Salt Lake City, Mar. 13, 1955; s. Robb Smith and Jane (Felt) A.; m. Cami Blau, Apr. 26, 1985; children: Nathan Spencer, Parker Thomas. BA, Weber State U., 1978. Ter. mgr. Burroughs Corp., Salt Lake City, 1978-81; dir. advt. and pub. rels. A&K Railroad Materials, Inc., Salt Lake City, 1981-84; asst. dir. devel. Weber State U., Ogden, Utah, 1984-92, dir. donor rels., 1992—. Recipient Outstanding Alumni award Weber State U., 1983. Mem. Utah Soc. Fund Raisers (bd. dirs. 1986-87), Coun. for Support and Advancement Edn., Ogden/Weber C. of C. (pub. rels. adv. com. 1990-92, chair 1993-94), Ogden Breakfast Exch. Club, Mt. Ogden Rotary Club. Office: Weber State U Devel Office Ogden UT 84408-1008

ALEXANDER-KING, PEARL COQUEECE, nurse; b. Drumright, Okla., Dec. 21, 1936; d. Alonzo Cottrol and Marjorie Opal (Price) Alexander; degree Long Beach City Coll., 1961; R.N., Assoc. Sci., 1971; B.S.N., Calif. State U.-Long Beach, 1983; cert. psychiat./mental health nurse, chem. dependency nurse specialist; m. Carl Dee King, Dec. 8, 1951; children: Carl Dee, Crystal, Michael (dec.), Marcus. Office nurse for gen. practitioner, Long Beach, Calif., 1961-66; nurse VA Hosp., Long Beach, 1966-69; nursing supr. outpatient alcoholism treatment and rehab. center Long Beach Gen. Hosp., 1971-78; dir. nursing Viewpark Community Hosp., Los Angeles, 1978-79; asst. nursing dir. Augustus F. Hawkins Psychiat. Facility, Los Angeles, 1981-84; mental health counselor Long Beach Mental Health Clinic, 1984—; dept. adminstr. chem. dependency svcs. addiction medicine dept. Kaiser Permanente Med. Ctr., Orange, Calif., 1984—; tchr. Long Beach City Coll., 1975. Rotary Club scholar, 1970-71; Cert. of Honor, Long Beach City Coll., 1971. Mem. Nat. Consortium Chem. Dependency Nurses Inc., Consolidated Assn. Nurses in Substance Abuse, Calif., Sigma Theta Tau (Iota Eta chpt.). Democrat. Baptist. Office: 4201 W Chapman Ave Orange CA 92668-1505

ALFARO, ARMANDO JOFFROY, plastic surgeon; b. Tucson, Sept. 18, 1950; s. Armando J. and Yolanda (Joffroy) A.; m. Jill Heinrich, May 21,

1983; children: Karina, Janella, Brittany, Briana. BS in Zoology, Ariz. State U., 1972; MD, U. Ariz., 1976. Cert. Am. Bd. Plastic Surgeons; diplomate Am. Bd. Plastic Surgeons, Am. Coll. Surgeons. Intern Emory U. Affiliated Hosps., Atlanta, 1976-77, resident gen. surgery, 1976-81; resident plastic surgery U. Rochester (N.Y.), 1981-83; pvt. practice plastic surgery Tucson, 1983—; assoc. prof. surgery Med. Sch. U. Ariz., Tucson, 1983—; chmn. plastic surgery Tucson Med. Ctr., St. Mary's Hosp., Tucson, St. Joseph's Hosp., Tucson. Mem. AMA, Plastic Surg. Ednl. Found., Tucson Hand Surg. Soc., Am. Soc. Plastic & Reconstructive Surgeons, Rocky Mountain Assn.-Plastic Surgeons, Pima County Med. Assn. Republican. Roman Catholic. Office: 2304 N Rosemont Blvd Tucson AZ 85712-2139

ALFARO, FELIX BENJAMIN, physician; b. Managua, Nicaragua, Oct. 22, 1939; came to U.S., 1945, naturalized, 1962; s. Agustin Jose and Amanda Julieta (Barillas) A.; student (State scholar) U. San Francisco, 1958-59, 61-62; M.D., Creighton U., 1967; m. Carmen Heide Meyer, Aug. 14, 1965; children—Felix Benjamin, Mark. Clk., Pacific Gas & Electric Co., San Francisco, 1960-61; intern St. Mary's Hosp., San Francisco, 1967; resident Scenic Gen. Hosp., Modesto, Calif., 1970; practice family medicine, Watsonville, Calif., 1971—; active staff Watsonville Community Hosp., 1971—. Served to capt., M.C., U.S. Army, 1968-69. Lic. physician, Nebr., La., Calif. Diplomate Am. Bd. Family Practice. Fellow Am. Acad. Family Practice; mem. AMA, Calif. Med. Assn., Santa Cruz County Med. Soc., 38th Parrallel Med. Soc. of Korea, Nat Rifle Assn., VFW. Republican. Roman Catholic. Office: 30 Brennan St Watsonville CA 95076-4303

ALFORD, JOAN FRANZ, entrepreneur; b. St. Louis, Sept. 16, 1940; d. Henry Reisch and Florence Mary (Shaughnessy) Franz; m. Charles Hebert Alford, Dec. 28, 1978; stepchildren: Terry, David, Paul. BS, St. Louis U., 1962; postgrad. Consortium of State U., Calif., 1975-77; MBA, Pepperdine U., 1987, postgrad., Fielding Inst., 1988-90. Head user svcs. Lawrence Berkeley Lab., Calif., 1977-78, head software support and devel. Computer Ctr., 1978-82, dep. head, 1980-81; regional site analyst mgr. Cray Rsch., Inc., Pleasanton, Calif., 1982-83; owner, pres. Innovative Leadership, Oakland, Calif., 1983-91; realtor, assoc. Mason-McDuffie Real Estate, Inc., 1991—; bd. dirs. East Bay Regional Data, Inc., Oakland Multiple Listing Svc., also treas., 1994—; co-chair computer user com. OAR, 1992-93, chair, 1993-94; bd. dirs. Oakland Assn. Realtors, 1995—. Contbr. articles to profl. jours. Bd. dirs., sec. Vol. Ctrs. of Alameda County, 1985, chair nominating com., 1990-91, pres. bd. dirs., 1991—; campaign mem. Marge Gibson for County Supr., Oakland, 1984; pres. bd. dirs. Vol. Ctrs. Alameda City, 1991-92; mem. Oakland Piedmont Rep. Orgn., Alameda County Apt. Owners Assn., 1982. Mem. Assn. Computing Machinery, Spl. Interest Group on Computer Pers. Rsch. (past chmn.), Nat. Assn. Realtors, Calif. Assn. Realtors, Oakland Assn. Realtors, Internat. Platform Assn., Small Owners for Fair Treatment. Republican. Clubs: Claremont Pool and Tennis, Lakeview, San Francisco Opera Guild. Avocations: swimming, skiing, opera, horseback riding, gardening. Home: 2605 Beaconsfield Pl Piedmont CA 94611-2501 Office: Mason McDuffie Real Estate Inc 342 Highland Ave Piedmont CA 94611-4042

ALFRIEND, KYLE TERRY, aerospace engineer; b. Macon, Ga., Aug. 17, 1940; s. Kyle Terry Sr. and Esther Alfriend; m. Bonnie Gray Chattin; children: Kyle, Kim. BS, Va. Poly. Inst. & State U., 1962; PhD, Stanford (Calif.) U., 1967, MS, 1964. Asst. prof. Cornell U., Ithaca, N.Y., 1967-74; head advanced systems br. Naval Rsch. Lab., Washington, 1974-85; dir. Washington br. Gen. Rsch. Corp., Vienna, Va., 1985-93; editor-in-chief AIAA Jour. Guidance, Control and Dynamics, 1992—; Navy TENCAP space chair prof. Naval Postgrad. Sch., Monterey, Calif., 1994—. Editor-in-chief AAS Jour. Astronaut. Scis., 1985-87; contbr. numerous articles to profl. jours. Fellow AIAA (chmn. Astrodynamics Tech. Com.), Am. Astronaut. Soc. (Dirk Brouwer award 1990).

ALGER, DAVID TOWNLEY, religious organization director; b. Warsaw, N.Y., June 4, 1945; s. Clifton and Dorothy (Townley) A.; m. Sarah Ileene Alger, Aug. 17, 1968; 1 child, Hannah Ileene. BA, Coll. of Wooster, 1967; MSW, U. Ill., Chgo., 1971; MDiv, McCormick Theol. Sem., Chgo., 1971. Ordained to ministry Presbyn. Ch. (U.S.A.), 1971. Assoc. pastor 1st Presbyn. Ch., Grand Forks, N.D., 1971-75; pastor Riverside Presbyn. Ch., Clinton, Iowa, 1975-79; exec. dir. Associated Ministries, Tacoma, 1980—; mem. Adv. Coun. on Ch. and Soc., United Presbyn. Ch. in U.S.A., 1976-82, mem. Coun. on Ch. and Race, 1981-82; chair mission strategy and evangelism com. Olympia (Wash.) Presbytery, 1982-88; accredited visitor World Coun. of Chs., 1983; del., planner Pacific Ecumenical Forum, Hilo, Hawaii, 1990. Mem. Clinton City Coun., 1978-80; pres. Tacoma Community House Bd., 1980-88; vice-chair Tacoma Housing Com., 1991—. Reicpient key ot city City of Clinton, 1979, St. Francis award Franciscan Found., 189, Disting. Citizen award Tacoma chpt. Rotary, 1989, Disting. Citizen award Mcpl. League Tacoma/Pierce County, 1992. Mem. Presbyn. Health, Edn. and Welfare Assn., Nat. Asn. Ecumenical Staff, Wash. Assn. Chs. (bd. dirs. 1980—, treas. 1991-95). Democrat. Home: 4510 N Defiance St Tacoma WA 98407 Office: Associated Ministries 1224 S I St Tacoma WA 98405-5021

ALHADEFF, DAVID ALBERT, economics educator; b. Seattle, Mar. 22, 1923; s. Albert David and Pearl (Taranto) A.; m. Charlotte Pechman, Aug. 1, 1948. B.A., U. Wash., 1944; M.A., Harvard U., 1948, Ph.D., 1950. Faculty U. Calif.-Berkeley, 1949-87, prof. bus. adminstrn., 1959-87, prof. emeritus, 1987—, assoc. dean Sch. Bus. Adminstrn., 1980-82, 85-86. Author: Monopoly and Competition in Banking, 1954, Competition and Controls in Banking, 1968, Microeconomics and Human Behavior, 1982; Contbr. articles to profl. jours., chpts. to books. Served with AUS, 1943-46. Recipient The Berkeley Citation U. Calif.-Berkeley, 1987. Mem. Am. Econ. Assn., Western Econ. Assn., Am. Fin. Assn. Home: 2101 Shoreline Dr Apt 456 Alameda CA 94501-6209 Office: Haas Sch Bus Berkeley CA 94720

ALI, S. SALIH, physicist, materials scientist; b. Mograt, Nile, Sudan, Aug. 6, 1954; came to U.S., 1979; s. Shamseldin Salih and Amna Musa; m. Kholoud G. Salih, July 30, 1981; children: Mohammed, Mustafa, Yasir. BS in Physics with hons., U. Khartoum, Sudan, 1978; MS in Physics, N.C. State U., 1982, PhD in Materials Sci. and Engring., 1986. Rsch. assoc. N.C. State U., Raleigh, 1985-87; materials scientist Gen. Instrument, Hicksville, N.Y., 1987-92; device devel. mgr. Motorola Semiconductor, Phoenix, 1992—. Patentee Controlling Speed of Power Devices, 1992, Multi Layer Epitaxy, 1994. Mem. Materials Rsch. Soc. (Von Hippel student award 1984), IEEE (assoc.), Electrochem. Soc., Alpha Sigma Mu. Home: 1100 W Myrna Ln Tempe AZ 85284-2830 Office: Motorola Semicondr Prod Sec Power Products Divsn D304 5005 E McDowell Rd Phoenix AZ 85008

ALINDER, MARY STREET, writer; b. Bowling Green, Ohio, Sept. 23, 1946; d. Scott Winfield and McDonna Matlock (Sitterle) Street; m. James Gilbert Alinder, Dec. 17, 1965; children: Jasmine, Jesse, Zachary. Student, U. Mich., 1964-65, U. N.Mex., 1966-68; BA, U. Nebr., 1976. Mgr. The Weston Gallery, Carmel, Calif., 1978-79; chief asst. Ansel Adams, Carmel, 1979-84; exec. editor, bus. mgr. The Ansel Adams Pub. Rights Trust, Carmel, 1984-88; freelance writer, lectr., curator, Gualala, Calif., 1989—; ptnr. The Alinder Gallery, Gualala, 1990—; selector and writer biographies Focal Press Ency., 3d edit., 1993; curator Ansel Adams: 80th Birthday Retrospective, Friends of Photography, Carmel, Acad. Sci., San Francisco, Denver Mus. Natural History; co-curator One With Beauty, M.H. deYoung Meml. Mus., 1987, Ansel Adams: American Artist, The Ansel Adams Ctr., San Francisco; lectr. Nat. Gallery Art, Barbican Ctr., M.H. deYoung Meml. Mus., Stanford U., L.A. County Mus., U. Mich. Author: Picturing Yosemite (Places), 1990, The Limits of Reality: Ansel Adams and Group f/64 (seeing straight), 1992; co-author: Ansel Adams: An Autobiography, 1985; co-editor: Ansel Adams: Letters and Images, 1988; contbr. articles to jours. and popular mags. Office: Alinder Gallery PO Box 1146 Gualala CA 95445-1146

ALISKY, MARVIN HOWARD, political science educator; b. Kansas City, Mo., Mar. 12, 1923; s. Joseph and Bess June (Capp) A.; m. Beverly Kay, June 10, 1955; children: Sander Michael, Joseph. BA, U. Tex., 1946, MA, 1947, PhD, 1953; cert., Instituto Tecnologico, Monterey, Mex., 1951. News corr. S.W. and Latin Am. NBC, 1947-49, news corr. Midwest, 1954-56; news corr. NBC and Christian Sci. Monitor, Latin Am., 1957-72; asst. prof. Ind. U., 1953-57; assoc. prof. journalism and polit. sci. Ariz. State U., Tempe, 1957-60; prof. polit. sci. Ariz. State U., 1960—, founding chmn. dept. mass communication (now Sch. Journalism and Telecommunications), 1957-65, founding dir. Ctr. Latin Am. Studies, 1965-72; vis. fellow Princeton U., 1963-64, Hoover Inst., Stanford, 1978; Fulbright prof. Cath. U., Lima, Peru, 1958, U. Nicaragua, 1960; researcher U.S.-Mex. Interparliamentary Conf., Baja, Calif., 1965, Latin Am. Inst., Chinese Acad. Social Scis., Beijing, 1986, European Inst. Def. and Strategic Studies, London, 1985, Politics Inst., Copenhagen, Denmark, 1987, U. So. Calif., 1982—; U.S. del. UNESCO Conf., Quito, Ecuador, 1960; dir. Gov.'s Ariz.-Mex. Commn., 1975—; U.S. State Dept. lectr., Costa Rica, Peru, Argentina, Chile, 1983, 88; bd. dirs. Goldwater Inst. Pub. Policy Rsch., 1989—. Author: Governors of Mexico, 1965, Uruguay: Contemporary Survey, 1969, The Foreign Press, 1964, 70, Who's Who in Mexican Government, 1969, Political Forces in Latin America, 1970, Government in Nuevo Leon, 1971, Government in Sonora, 1971, Peruvian Political Perspective, 1975, Historical Dictionary of Peru, 1979, Historical Dictionary of Mexico, 1981, Latin American Media: Guidance and Censorship, 1981, Global Journalism, 1983; co-author: Political Systems of Latin America, 1970, Political Parties of the Americas, 1982, Yucatan: A World Apart, 1980, (with J.E. Katz) Arms Production in Developing Nations, 1984, Mexico: Country in Crisis, 1986, (with Phil Rosen) International Handbook of Broadcasting Systems, 1988, Dictionary Latin American Political Leaders, 1988, (with W.C. Soderlund) Mass Media and the Caribbean, 1990; contbr. numerous articles to profl. jours. and mags. Bd. dirs. Phoenix Com. on Fgn. Res., 1975—, Ariz. Acad. Town Hall, 1981, Tempe Pub. Libr., 1974-80; mem. U.S. Bd. Fgn. Scholarships Fulbright Commn. Bd., 1984—, Acad. Coun. Goldwater Inst. of Pub. Policy, 1989—. Ensign USNR, 1944-45. NSF grantee, 1984, Ariz. State U. rsch. grantee, 1962, 65, 70, Southwestern Studies Ctr. rsch. grantee, 1983, Latin Am. Rsch. in China grantee, 1986, World Media Rsch. in Soviet Union grantee, 1989, rsch. grantee, London, 1992, 94, Edinburgh, 1994. Fellow Hispanic Soc. Am.; mem. Am. Polit. Sci. Assn., Western Polit. Sci. Assn., Latin Am. Studies Assn., Pacific Coast Coun. Latin Am. Studies (bd. dirs.), Inter-Am. Press Assn., Inter-Am. Broadcasters Assn. (rsch. assoc.), Assocs. Liga de Municipios de Sonora, Friends of Mex. Art, Southwestern Polit. Sci. Assn. (chmn. 1976-77), Nat. Assn. Scholars, Soc. Profl. Journalists (life), Tempe Rep. Men's Club, Knights of Sq. Roundtable, Sigma Delta Chi. Home: 44 W Palmdale Dr Tempe AZ 85282-2139 Office: Ariz State U Dept Polit Sci Tempe AZ 85287-2001

ALKANA, LINDA KELLY, history educator; b. Calgary, Alta., Can., Nov. 9, 1946; came to U.S., 1963; d. Bernard Joseph and Lorna Lucille (Sutherland) Kelly; m. Ronald Lee Alkana, Sept. 12, 1970; children: Alexander Philippe, Lorna Jane. BA, UCLA, 1969; MA, U. Calif., Irvine, 1975, PhD, 1985. Lectr. humanities U. Calif., Irvine, 1985-93; lectr. history Calif. State U., Long Beach, 1981—; affiliate scholar Ctr. for the Study of Women, L.A., 1987-89; lectr. in women, popular culture and peace, critical thinking. Assoc. editor The History Teacher, 1987—; contbr. articles to profl. jours. Mem. Am. Hist. Assn., Western Assn. of Women Historians. Office: Dept of History Calif State U Long Beach 1250 N Bellflower Blvd Long Beach CA 90840-0006

ALKANA, RONALD LEE, neuropsychopharmacologist, psychobiologist; b. L.A., Oct. 17, 1945; s. Sam Alkana and Madelyn Jane Davis; m. Linda Anne Kelly, Sept. 12, 1970; children; Alexander Philippe Kelly, Lorna Jane Kelly. Student, UCLA, 1963-66; PharmD, U. So. Calif., 1970; PhD, U. Calif., Irvine, 1975. Postdoctoral fellow Nat. Inst. Alcohol Abuse and Alcoholism, U. Calif., Irvine, 1974-76; resident asst. dir. div. neurochemistry, dept. psychiatry and human behavior U. Calif., Irvine, 1976; asst. prof. pharmacy (pharmacology) U. So. Calif., L.A., 1976-82, assoc. prof. pharmacy (pharmacology and toxicology), 1982-89, prof. molecular pharmacology and toxicology, 1989—. Editl. bd. Alcoholism: Clinical and Experimental Research, 1989-94, assoc. editor, 1994—; contbr. chpts. to books, articles to profl. jours. Recipient various scholarships and grants. Mem. AAAS, Soc. Neurosci., Am. Soc. Pharmacology and Exptl. Therapeutics, Internat. Soc. Biomed. Research on Alcoholism, Research Soc. Alcoholism, Internat. Brain Rsch. Organizational World Fedn. Neuroscientists, Western Pharmacology Soc., Sigma Xi, Phi Delta Chi. Office: Sch Pharmacy U So Calif Dept Molecular Pharmacolgy Toxicology 1985 Zonal Ave Los Angeles CA 90033-1058

ALL, WILLIAM HAMILTON, IV, military officer; b. Honolulu, Aug. 7, 1958; s. William Hamilton III and Mary Eleanor (Swain) A.; m. Teresa Ann Ysseldyke, Dec. 10, 1983; children: Maile Ann, Ryland Makena. BA in Econs., Emory U., 1982; MA in Strategic Planning, Naval Postgrad. Sch., 1992. Commd. ensign USN, 1983, advanced through grades to lt. comdr., 1993; naval aviator Patrol Squadron Four, USN, Honolulu, 1984-88; flight instr. Patrol Squadron Thirty One, USN, Mt. View, Calif., 1989-90; asst. air officer USS Nimitz, USN, Bremerton, Wash., 1993-95; dept. head Patrol Squadron Forty NAS, Whidbey Island, Wash., 1995—; mem.-at-large VP Internat., Halifax, Nova Scotia, 1990—. Mem. Chi Phi. Episcopalian. Home: 9640 Dishman Rd NW Bremerton WA 98312-9102 Office: Patrol Squadron Forty NAS Whidbey Island WA

ALLADA, VIVEKANAND, pediatric cardiologist, researcher; b. Peddapurum, India, Aug. 17, 1961; came to U.S., 1967; s. Sambasiva Rao and Jayalakshmi (Batchu) A.; m. Stacey Elizabeth Drant, Sept. 1, 1991; 1 child, Michael Anand. BS in Biomed. Scis., U. Mich., 1983, MD, 1986. Resident, pediatrics Children's Hosp. of L.A., 1986-89; pediatric cardiology fellow UCLA Sch. Medicine, 1989-92, clin. instr. pediatric cardiology, 1992—; cons. pediatric cardiology St. Bernadine Med. Ctr., San Bernardino, Calif., 1992—; researcher positron emission tomography, developmental cardiac physiology, UCLA Sch. Medicine, 1989—. Recipient Frances Donnally Winzer award Children's Hosp. L.A.-UCLA Sch. Medicine, 1987, Mead Johnson award Children's Hosp. L.A.-UCLA Sch. Medicine, 1989, NIH fellowship, 1990-92, Am. Heart Assn. Greater L.A. Affiliate fellowship, 1992—. Fellow Am. Acad. Pediatrics; mem. Am. Coll. Cardiology, Calif. Soc. Pediatric Cardiology. Office: Pediatric Cardiology UCLA Sch Medicine 10833 Le Conte Ave Los Angeles CA 90024

ALLAMANDOLA, LOUIS JOHN, low temperature chemist/astrophysicist; b. N.Y.C., Aug. 28, 1946; s. Louis John Allamandola and Santina (Nella) Nicoletti; m. Mary Ellen Scott, June 8, 1968; children: Monica, Patrick, David Kees, Anthony. BSc, St. Peter's Coll., Jersey City, 1968; PhD in Phys. Chemistry, U. Calif., Berkeley, 1974. Rsch. assoc. chem. dept. Oreg. State U., Corvallis, 1974-76; asst. prof. lab. astrophysics Leiden (the Netherlands) U., 1976-79, assoc. prof. lab. astrophysics, 1979-83; NRC sr. assoc. NASA Ames Rsch. Ctr., Mountain View, Calif., 1983—, lab. astrophysics group leader, 1985—; mem. adv. panels NASA, Washington, 1988—; co-chair IAU Symposium 135 on Interstellar Dust, Santa Clara; chmn. sci. meeting ESA-Comet project, Monterey, Calif., 1991. Editor: Interstellar Dust, 1989; contbr. over 120 articles to profl. jours., including Astrophysics Jour. and Jour. Chem. Phys. Recipient Nat. Medal for Exceptional Sci. Achievement, NASA, 1992, H. Julian Allen award NASA, 1987; NRC sr. fellow, 1983-85, NSF-Energy Related fellow, 1976. Mem. ACS, Am. Astron. Soc., Internat. Astron. Union (co-chmn. sci. meeting 1988), Friends of Berkeley Chemistry. Roman Catholic. Office: NASA Ames Rsch Ctr Ms 245 # 6 Mountain View CA 94035-1000

ALLAN, ROBERT MOFFAT, JR., corporate executive, educator; b. Detroit, Dec. 8, 1920; s. Robert M. and Jane (Christman) A.; m. Harriet Spicer, Nov. 28, 1942; children: Robert M. III, Scott, David, Marilee. B.S., Stanford U., 1941; postgrad. Stanford Grad. Sch. Bus., 1941-42; M.S., UCLA, 1943; postgrad. Loyola Law Sch., 1947-50. Economist research dept. Security First Nat. Bank, 1942; exec. Marine Ins., 1946-53; asst. to pres., work mgr. Zinsco Elec. Products, 1953-55, v.p., dir., 1956-59; asst. to pres. The Times-Mirror Corp., 1959-60, corp. v.p., 1961-64; pres., dir. Cyprus Mines Corp., 1964-67; pres. Litton Internat., 1967-69; pres. U.S. Naval Postgrad. Sch. Found., prof. internat. mgmt. 1969-85. Bd. dirs., advisor U.S. Naval Acad.; trustee Boys Republic, Pomona Grad. Sch., Claremont Grad. Sch., Del Monte Forest Homeowners; vis. prof. of internat. mgmt. grad. schs. of bus. MBA Stanford, Harvard, U. of Chgo., UCLA, USA and Internat. Inst. Fgn. Studies, Monterey. Capt. USAF, 1942-45. Recipient award Helms Athletic Found., 1947, 49, Navy Cross of Merit, 1976, Plaque of Merit USCG, 1990, Medal for Heroism, 1990; named Outstanding Businessman of Yr., L.A., Nat. Assn. Accts., 1966; elected to Sailing Hall of Fame, 1969; named Monterey Inst. Fgn. Studies trustee and sr. fellow, 1976. Mem. Mchts. and Mfrs. Assn. (dir.), Intercollegiate Yachting Assn. (regional dir. 1940-55), Phi Gamma Delta, Phi Delta Phi. Clubs: Newport Harbor Yacht (commodore 1962), Trans-Pacific Yacht, Carmel Valley Country. Home: 165 Del Mesa Carmel CA 93923

ALLARD, JAMES WILLARD, JR., philosophy educator; b. Lincoln, Nebr., Dec. 8, 1945; s. James Willard Sr. and Mary Irene (Dieterich) A.; m. Celia Anne Ahrens, Jan. 2, 1968 (div. May 1990); 1 child, Mary Dorinda; m. Mary Catherine Bushing, Sept. 22, 1994. BA, U. Mont., 1969, MA, 1970; PhD, Princeton U., 1976. Instr. philosophy Mont. State U., Bozeman, 1973-76, asst. prof., 1976-84, assoc. prof., 1984—. Co-editor F.H. Bradley: Writings on Logic and Metaphysics, 1994; contbr. chpt. to book and articles to profl. jours. Mem. Am. Philos. Assn., Bradley Soc. Office: Mont State U Dept History and Philosophy Bozeman MT 59717

ALLARD, ROBERT WAYNE, geneticist, educator; b. L.A., Sept. 3, 1919; s. Glenn A. and Alma A. (Roose) A.; m. Ann Catherine Wilson, June 16, 1944; children: Susan, Thomas, Jane, Gillian, Stacie. B.S., U. Calif., Davis, 1941; Ph.D., U. Wis., 1946. From asst. to assoc. prof. U. Calif., Davis, 1946—, prof. genetics, 1955—. Author books; contbr. articles to profl. jours. Served to lt. USNR. Recipient Crop Sci. award Am. Soc. Agronomy, 1964, DeKalb Disting. Career award Crop Sci. Soc. Am., 1983; Guggenheim fellow, 1954, 60; Fulbright fellow, 1955. Mem. Nat. Acad. Scis., Am. Acad. Arts and Scis., Am. Soc. Naturalists (pres. 1974-75), Genetics Soc. Am. (pres. 1983-84), Am. Genetics Assn. (pres. 1989), Phi Beta Kappa, Sigma Xi, Alpha Gamma Rho, Alpha Zeta. Democrat. Unitarian. Home: PO Box 185 Bodega Bay CA 94923-0185 Office: U Calif Davis 133 Hunt Davis CA 95616-2322

ALLARD, THURMAN J., electrical engineer; b. U.S. Canal Zone, Nov. 15, 1959; s. George W. and Martha Cynthia (Rapp) A.; m. Heather Lorelei Ingham, Aug. 12, 1983; children: Chase Kehr, Duncan G. BSEE, U. N.Mex., 1981; MSEE, Purdue U., 1982. With Sandia Nat. Labs., Albuquerque, 1977-80, mem. tech. staff, 1980—, dept. mgr., 1990—. Mem. IEEE. Republican. Home: 13617 Crested Butte Dr NE Albuquerque NM 87112-6623 Office: Sandia Nat Labs PO Box 5800 Albuquerque NM 87185

ALLARD, WAYNE A., congressman, veterinarian; b. Ft. Collins, Colo., Dec. 12, 1943; m. Joan Malcolm, Mar. 23, 1967; children: Cheryl, Christie. D.V.M., Colo. State U., 1968. Veterinarian, Allard Animal Hosp.; mem. Colo. State Senate, 1982-91, chmn. health, environment and instn. com., chmn. senate majority caucus; mem. 102nd-103rd Congresses from 4th dist., Colo., 1991—; mem. agrl. com., 1991-92, 93-94, mem. small bus. com., 1991-92, mem. interior and insular affairs com., 1991-92, mem. com. on coms., 1991-92, 93-94, mem. budget com., 1993-94, mem. natural resources com., 1993-94, mem. joint com. on reorganization of Congress, 1993-94, chmn. subcom. of agr. conservation, forest and water; health officer Loveland, Colo.; mem. regional adv. council on vet. medicine Western Interstate Commn. Higher Edn.; mem. Colo. Low-level Radioactive Waste Adv. Com. Chmn. United Way; active 4-H Found. Mem. Loveland C. of C., AVMA, Colo. Vet. Medicine Assn., Latimer County Vet. Medicine Assn. (past pres.), Bd. Vet. Practitioners (charter mem.), Am. Animal Hosp. Assn., Nat. Conf. State Legislatures (vice chmn. human resources com. 1987—, healthcare cost containment com.). Republican. Methodist. Home: 1203 Jennifer Dr Loveland CO 80537-8054 Office: US House of Reps Offices Of House Members Washington DC 20515*

ALLARDICE, LINDA MARIE, controller, financial executive; b. Pitts., Mar. 12, 1953; d. Martin Joseph and Marian Ruth (Altenhof) Stickley; m. Dwight W. Buben, Sept. 12, 1975 (div. Mar. 1982); children: Eric Michael, Andrew Brian, David J.; m. Jeremiah Daniel Allardice, Apr. 26, 1989. BSBA, U. Ariz., 1975. Various retail positions Globe Discount, 1971-76; auditor Bd. of Regents Audit Staff, Tucson, 1976-77; asst. to comptroller, bus. agt. Pima C.C., Tucson, 1981-82; comptroller La Frontera Ctr., Inc., Tucson, 1983—. Mem. Healthcare Fin. Mgrs. Assn. Democrat. Lutheran. Office: La Frontera Ctr Inc 502 W 29th St Tucson AZ 85713-3353

ALLAWAY, WILLIAM HARRIS, retired university official; b. Oak Park, Ill., Mar. 31, 1924; s. William Horsford and Helen Margaret (Harris) A.; m. Olivia Woodhull Foster, June 28, 1952; children: William Harris Jr., Ben Foster, Eve Olivia. BS, U. Ill., 1949; postgrad., U. Grenoble, France, 1950-51; MA, U. Ill., 1951; EdD, U. Denver, 1957. Traveling sec. World Student Svc. Fund, 1947-48; spl. asst. to chmn. U.S. Nat. Commn. for UNESCO, 1949; asst. to field dir. World U. Svc. attached to Internat. Refugee Orgn., Salzburg, Austria, 1951; field rep. Inst.of Internat. Edn., Chgo. and Denver, 1952-54; gen. sec. U. Kans. YMCA, 1954-57; asst. dean of men and dir. Wilbur Hall Stanford (Calif.) U., 1957-61; dir. edn. abroad program U. Calif., Santa Barbara, 1961-89, spl. asst. to chancellor, 1990-93; cons. and lectr. in field; mem. ednl. assoc. adv. com. Inst. Internat. Edn., 1984-87; mem. Pres.'s Coun. for Internat. Youth Exch., 1982-85; mem. U.S. Del. to conf. on ednl. exch. between U.S. and U.K., 1970, 1974. Co-chair Peace and Justice Com., Goleta Presbyn. Ch., chair steering com. PAX 2100; mem. Nuclear Age Peace Found., Santa Barbara, Internat. Peace Rsch. Assn., Yellow Springs, Ohio; mem. Coun. on Internat. Ednl. Exch., 1961—, chmn. bd. dirs. 1978-83; past bd. dirs., hon. trustee Am. Ctr. for Students and Artists, Paris; bd. advisors Hariri Found., 1987—; exec. sec. Internat. Com. for Study of Edn. Exch., 1970-95, exec. com. Inter-U. Centre Postgrad. Studies, Dubrovnik, 1988—. With USAAF, 1943-46. Hon. DHC, U. Sussex, Eng., 1992; PhD h.c. U. Bergen, Norway, 1990; DHC, U. Bordeaux, France, 1988; Hon. Dr. of U. of Stirling, Scotland, 1981; recipient Scroll of Appreciation Leningrad State U., 1989, Award for Svc. to Internat. Ednl. Exch. Council on Internat. Ednl. Exch., 1989, Silver medal U. Lund, Sweden, 1990, Alumni Achievement award Coll. Liberal Arts and Sci. Alumni Assn. U. Ill., 1990, Gold Medal of Honor of the Complutense U. of Madrid, Spain, 1991. Mem. NAFSA, Assn. Internat. Educators (hon. life mem.), Comparative and Internat. Edn. Soc., European Assn. for Internat. Edn. Soc., European Assn. for Internat. Edn., Internat. Assn. Univs. (dep. mem., adminstrv. bd. 1995—), La Cumbre Golf and Country Club. Democrat. Presbyterian. Home: 724 Calle De Los Amigos Santa Barbara CA 93105-4439

ALLBEE, CHARLES EUGENE, English language educator; b. Holly, Colo., Nov. 18, 1937; s. Claudius Evan and Cora Ellen (Gillispie) A.; m. Nancy Jo Aughenbaugh, Dec. 23, 1961; children: Brian Dean, Janet Lynn. BA, Adams State Coll., Alamosa, Colo., 1960, MA, 1961; ArtsD, U. N. Colo., Greeley, 1979. Instr. Adams State Coll., 1961-64, asst. prof., 1965-80, assoc. prof., 1980-84; prof. English Met. State Coll., Denver, 1984—; pres. Faculty Senate Met. State Coll., 1986-88. Mem. Nat. Council Tchrs. English, Conf. on Coll. Composition and Communication. Democrat. Home: 6824 Urban St Arvada CO 80004-2339

ALLBEE, SANDRA MOLL, real estate broker; b. Reading, Pa., July 15, 1947; d. Charles Lewars and Isabel May (Ackerman) Frederici; m. Thomas J. Allbee, Oct. 18, 1975 (div. 1987). Exec. sec. Hamburg (Pa.) State Sch. and Hosp., 1965-73; regional mgr. Am. Bus. Service Corp., Newport Beach, Calif., 1973-78; v.p. T.A.S.A., Inc., Long Beach, Calif., 1978-86; realtor Very Important Properties, Inc., Rolling Hills Estates, Calif., 1986-90, Re/Max Palos Verdes Realty, Rolling Hills Estates, Calif., 1990—. Bd. dirs., v.p. Nat. Coun. on Alcoholism, Torrance, Calif., 1987; pres. Rollingwood Homeowners Assn., Rolling Hills Estates, Calif., 1985-92. Mem. Palos Verdes Rep. Women's Club (bd. dirs. 1989-94). Office: Re/Max Palos Verdes Realty 4030 Palos Verdes Dr N Ste 104 Rolling Hills CA 90274

ALLDREDGE, RENDEL BURDETTE, volunteer, retired government official; b. Portland, Oreg., Jan. 2, 1920; s. Joseph Melvin and Elda (Vollentine) A.; m. Esther Amelia Needham, June 4, 1943 (div. Sept. 1946); m. Edna Blanche Swannell, June 25, 1949 (div. June 1977); 1 child, Marguerite Beryl. BS, U. Oreg., 1942; postgrad., Stanford U., 1946-49. Instr. in econs. Stanford U., Palo Alto, Calif., 1946-49; asst. prof. econs. Tex. Tech U., Lubbock, 1950-52; economist U.S. Office of Price Stabilization, Lubbock, Tex., 1951-52; economist U.S. Nat. Park Svc., Washington, 1952-53, chief statistician, 1956-66, policy officer, 1970-73; econ. advisor Govt. of Eritrea U.S. Internat. Coop. Adminstrn, Asmara, Ethiopia, 1954-56; mem. high commrs. cabinet program and budget Trust Terr. of Pacific Islands, Saipan, M.I., 1967-70; chief crude oil prodn. ERA U.S. Dept. Energy, Washington, 1973-80; pres., v.p., moderator Atkinson Meml. Ch., Oregon City, Oreg., 1984-93, 94—; pvt. practice cons., Oregon City, 1980-83. Capt. U.S. Army, 1944-46, PTo. Recipient Silver medal Dept. Interior, Washington, 1967,

Superior Achievement award Dept. Energy, Washington, 1980; named Hon. Sen., Congress Micronesia, 1969. Home and Office: 14114 S Livesay Rd Oregon City OR 97045-9013

ALLEMAN, GEORGIA CARMIN, medical technologist; b. Douglas, Wyo., Sept. 18, 1950; d. George Eastmen and Ruby Esther (Edson) Carmin; m. Mark Stephen Palmer, June 7, 1975 (div. Aug. 1984); children: Robynn, Justin, Brian; m. Darryl Duane Alleman, Nov. 1, 1985; stepchildren: Daron Alleman, Kristen Alleman, Karen Gabriel, David Alleman. BS, U. Wyo., 1973. Cert. med. technologist Am. Soc. Clin. Pathologists. Med. technologist West Anaheim Cmty. Hosp., Orange, Calif., 1973-75, Sweetwater Meml. Hosp., Rock Springs, Wyo., 1975-77, Ivinson Meml. Hosp., Laramie, Wyo., 1977-79, Med. Arts Assn., Laramie, 1979-81; pres., owner WyoMed Lab., Inc., Laramie, 1981—. Bd. dirs. Albany County United Way, Laramie, 1990-93; bd. dirs., team rep. Laramie Blizzard Soccer, 1993-94; sec., player agt., sponsorship dir. Laramie Youth Baseball, 1991-94; deaconess 1st Christian Ch., Laramie, 1992-93. Mem. Zonta Internat. Republican. Office: WyoMed Lab Inc 204 Mccollum Laramie WY 82070-5151

ALLEN, ARTHUR WILLIAM, pastor, educator; b. Eldora, Iowa, Apr. 6, 1914; s. William Alonzo and Ethel Pamelia (Doud) A.; m. Verna Marion Josephs, Jan. 24, 1942; children: Dorothy, Margaret, Robert, David. BTh, Northwestern Sem., 1941; DD, Bapt. Bible Coll., 1958; D in Lit., Pillsbury Bapt. Coll., 1983; ThM, Triune Bible Sem., 1986, ThD, 1987. Pastor Bapt. Chs., Baker, Dillon, Laurel, Mont., 1942-66; exec. sec. Minn. Bapt. Assn., Mpls., 1966-83; prof. Cen. Bapt. Sem., Mpls., 1966-75; editor North Star Bapt., Mpls., 1983-89; prof. Mtn. States Coll., Great Falls, Mont., 1983-89; tour leader Israel & Middle East, 1972-94. Pres. Castle Rock Baptist Camp, Bozeman, Mont., 1961-63; bd. dirs. Denver Bapt. Coll., 1960-66, San Francisco Bapt. Sem., 1960-66, Pillsbury Bapt. Coll., Owatonna, Minn., 1966-83. Republican. Home: 815 W 9th St Laurel MT 59044-1601 Office: First Bapt Ch 400 7th Ave Laurel MT 59044-2320

ALLEN, BONNIE LYNN, pension actuary; b. L.A., Oct. 2, 1957; d. David and Lucille M. (Scott) A. B.A. summa cum laude, UCLA, 1979. Math. tutor, L.A., 1971—; reader math. dept. UCLA, 1977-79; pension actuary Martin E. Segal Co., L.A., 1980-92. Author short stories and poetry. Active mentor program UCLA Alumni Assn., 1978-79, bd. dirs. Westside Bruins. Mem. Math. Assn. Am., Am. Math. Soc., L.A. Film Tchrs'. Assn., Acad. Sci. Fiction, Fantasy and Horror Films, UCLA Alumni Assn. (life), Westside Bruin Club (bd. dirs.), L.A. Actuarial Club, Phi Beta Kappa.

ALLEN, BRUCE JOHN, writer, activist; b. Buffalo, Apr. 16, 1960; s. John Edgar and Isabel Sarah (Nicholson) A.; m. Sarah Bragg Lindsey, Mar. 31, 1992. BA in English Lit. magna cum laude, U. Colo., 1985. Columnist Colo. Daily, Boulder, 1985; field mgr. Colo. Pub. Interest Rsch. Group, Boulder, 1985-86; editor Nat. Student News Svc., Boston, 1986-88; writer The New Paper, Providence, 1988-91; comms. dir. Save the Bay, Providence, 1990-92, Ctr. for Econ. Conversion, Mountain View, Calif., 1993—; pubis. cons. Calif. Abortion Rights Action League, San Francisco, 1993. Mem. Save El Dorado Mountain Campaign, Boulder, 1985; advisor People Against the CIA, Providence, 1989; co-founder Preserve the Presidio Campaign, San Francisco, 1994. Home: 995 Guerrero St # 2 San Francisco CA 94110-2225 Office: Ctr for Econ Conversion 222 View St Mountain View CA 94041-1344

ALLEN, CHARLES RICHARD, retired financial executive; b. Cleve., Mar. 10, 1926; s. Charles Ross and Jennie (Harmon) A.; m. Marion Elizabeth Taylor, Aug. 17, 1946; children: Kathleen Allen Templin, Jeanne Allen Duffy, Kenneth. Student, Occidental Coll., 1942-43; BS, UCLA, 1945. Acctg. supr. N.Am. Aviation, Inc., Los Angeles, 1946-55; div. controller TRW, Inc., Los Angeles, 1955-61, dir. fin., 1961-64; assoc. controller TRW, Inc., Cleve., 1964-66, controller, 1966-67, v.p., 1967-77, exec. v.p., 1977-86, chief fin. officer, 1967-86; advisor New Court Ptnrs., N.Y.C.; bd. dirs. Titan Corp., San Diego. Trustee Maritime Mus. San Diego; mem. San Diego World Affairs Coun. Served with USNR, 1943-46. Mem. Fin. Execs. Inst., Univ. Club, City Club of San Diego. Home: 1730 Avenida Del Mundo Coronado CA 92118-3021

ALLEN, CHUCK, football team executive. V.p. football ops. Seattle Seahawks. Office: Seattle Seahawks 11220 NE 53rd St Kirkland WA 98033-7505*

ALLEN, DAVID CHARLES, computer science educator; b. Syracuse, N.Y., Jan. 15, 1944; s. Charles Robert and Jane Loretta (Doolittle) A.; m. Mary Ann Stanke, June 15, 1968 (div. Mar. 1994); children: Meredith Rae, Amelia Kathrine, Carl James; m. Barbara Ann Riis, Mar. 14, 1994. B.Tech. Edn., Nat. U., San Diego, 1983, MA in Human Behavior, 1984. Dir. retail sales Nat. U. Alumni Assn., 1981-83; audiovisual technician Grossmont Union High Sch. Dist., La Mesa, Calif., 1983-84; spl. project instr. San Diego Community Coll., 1985-91; instr. computer tech. Coleman Coll., 1991—. Mem. Presdl. Task Force; mem. Congl. Adv. Com. on Vets. Benefits for congressmen 44th. With USN, 1961-81. Mem. DAV, VFW, Am. Legion, Vietnam Vets. Am., Fleet Reservation Assn., Nat. U. Student and Alumni Assn., Am. Tech. Edn. Assn., Beta Sigma Phi (hon.). Republican. Roman Catholic. Office: Coleman Coll Computer Applications and Networking 7380 Parkway Dr La Mesa CA 91942-1532

ALLEN, DAVID HARLOW, business educator, consultant; b. Lynn, Mass., May 26, 1930; s. Donald H. and Miriam Ellsworth (Harlow) A.; m. Roberta Arlene Miller, July 15, 1952; children: Donald Bruce, Richard Leroy, William David. BS in Gen. Edn., U. Nebr., Omaha, 1967; MBA, N.Mex. Highlands U., 1978. Cert. profl. logistician, cert. cost analyst. Commd. 2d lt. USAF, 1955, advanced through grades to lt. col., 1970; instr., planner, aircraft maintenance, staff, prodn. control officer, squadron comdr., wing asst. dep. comdr. maintenance SAC, 1948-74; dir. aircraft maintenance, dir. material Air Force Inspection and Safety Ctr., San Bernardino, Calif., 1969-72; dep. dir. logistics Air Force Test and Evaluation Ctr., Albuquerque, 1974-78; ret., 1978; sr. systems analyst, space systems project leader Arinc Rsch. Corp., 1978-84; airborne missile system dep. program mgr. for logistics, logistics project mgr. Ventura div. Northrop Corp., 1984-91; assoc. prof. Coll. Bus. and Mgmt. West Coast U., L.A., 1988—, asst. dean, 1988-90; mem. com. chmn. So. Calif. Logistics Conf. and Workshop, 1989, 91, 92, 93; v.p., mem. bd. govs. Logistics Edn. Found., 1993—; program chmn. 29th Internat. Logistics Conf. and Tech. Expn., 1994. Contbr. articles to profl. publs. Mem. state and nat. Rep. orgns., 1978—; mem. Ventura County-Santa Barbara County Planning Com. for Nat. Engring. Week., 1990—; v.p. bd. govs. Logistics Edn. Found., 1993—. Decorated Bronze Star. Mem. Nat. Contract Mgmt. Assn., Soc. Logistics Engrs. (chmn. chpt. 1988-90, Pres.'s Merit award 1994), Inst. Cost Analysis, Configuration and Data Mgmt. Assn. (chmn. fin. com. 1989), Am. Mgmt. Assn., Air Force Assn., Phi Kappa Phi. Home and Office: 428 Moondance St Thousand Oaks CA 91360-1209

ALLEN, DEBORAH COLLEEN, state legislator; b. Denver, Jan. 25, 1950; d. Anton Jr. and Esther Ochs; m. Bob Allen; 1 child, Dallas. Student, Aurora C.C. Jr. acct. Am. TV & Comm.; bus mgr. Deer Trail Pub. Schs., sch. bus driver; data entry clk. United Banking Svcs.; caretaker Evergreen Cemetery; owner, mgr. Custom Data Sys. Specialists, Aurora, 1979—; mem. Colo. Ho. of Reps., 1992—, mem. various coms., 1993—. Former sec., vice chmn., chmn. Arapahoe County Rep. Party; past pres. Aurora Rep. Forum; active Arapahoe County Chmn.'s Cir.; block capt. Am. Cancer Soc., Am. Arthritis Found. Recipient 5 Yr. Award as Leathercraft Instr., 4-H. Mem. Nat. Fedn. Rep. Women, Colo. Fedn. Rep. Women, South Metro C. of C., Colo. Rep. 250 Club, Arapahoe Rep. Men's Club. Republican. Home: 923 S Ouray St Aurora CO 80017-3152 Office: Colo House of Reps State Capitol Denver CO 80203

ALLEN, DENISE NEWBOLD, music educator; b. Salt Lake City, Apr. 25, 1963; d. Dennis Marlin and Deanna (Jeffery) Newbold; m. Gordon J. Allen, June 5, 1987; children: Bethany, Heidi. AAS in Music, Ricks Coll., 1983; BA in Music, Utah State U., 1986; MA in Musicology, George Washington U., Washington, 1992. Asst. class piano instr. Ricks Coll., Rexburg, Idaho, 1982-83; pvt. piano instr. Utah State U. Youth Conservatory, Logan, 1983-86; music critic/reporter Utah Statesman, Utah State U., Logan, 1986; adj. piano faculty/resident advisor Idyllwild (Calif.) Sch. Music and the Arts, 1986-87; grad. asst. George Washington U., Washington, 1987-89; pvt. piano instr. Calif., Wash., Utah, 1986—; instr. Kindermusik, Jordan, Utah, 1991—. Mem. Music Tchrs. Nat. Assn., Utah Music Tchrs. Assn. (treas. 1993-94), Am. Orff-Schulwerk Assn., Kindermusik Tchrs. Assn./Early Childhood Music Assn. (level 1 cert. 1993). Mem. LDS Ch.

ALLEN, DONALD VAIL, investment executive, author, concert pianist; b. South Bend, Ind., Aug. 1, 1928; s. Frank Eugene and Vera Irene (Vail) A.; m. Betty Dunn, Nov. 17, 1956. BA magna cum laude, UCLA, 1972, MA, 1973, D (hon.), 1973. Pres., chmn. bd. dirs. Cambridge Investment Corp.; music editor and critic Times-Herald, Washington; music critic L.A. Times; lectr. George Washington U., Am. U., Washington, Pasadena City Coll. Transl. works of Ezra Pound from Italian into English; author of papers on the musical motifs in the writings of James Joyce; mem. Steinway Roster of Concert Artists; specialist in works of Beethoven, Chopin, Debussy and Liszt; premiere performances of works of Paul Creston, Norman dello Joio, Ross Lee Finney, appearances in N.Y., L.A., Washington; represented by William Matthews Concert Agy., N.Y.C. Pres. Funds for Needy Children, 1974-76. Mem. Ctr. for Study Presidency, Am. Mgmt. Assn., Nat. Assn. Securities Dealers, Am. Guild Organists, Chamber Music Soc. Republican. Congregationalist. Home: QueensGate 2503 Russett Glen Escondido CA 92029-6650

ALLEN, DONALD WAYNE, accountant, educator; b. Billings, Mont., Apr. 9, 1936; s. D. Wayne and Olga Carmen (Ferguson) A.; m. Judith Marie Johnson, Dec. 28, 1959; children: Brian Kieth, Brendan Kirk. BS in Bus. Adminstrn., U. Denver, 1958. CPA, Mont., Wyo. Staff acct. Pan Am. Petroleum Corp., Casper, Wyo., 1958-61, Raab, Roush & Gaymon CPAs, Casper, 1961-64; office mgr. Sumatra Oil Corp., Billings, 1964-68; treas., dir. Oil Resources, Inc., Billings, 1968-73; ptnr. Smith, Birkeland, Mangis, Allen & Deming, Billings, 1973-78; pres. Allen & Nelson CPAs P.C., Billings, 1978-88, Donald W. Allen, CPA, P.C., Billings, 1988—; instr. Ea. Mont. Coll., Billings, 1983-85. Treas. Billings Jaycees, 1965; pres. Yellowstone Kiwanis, Billings, 1971; bd. dirs. J.K. Ralston Found., Billings, 1988-91, Billings Symphony Orch., 1990-92, treas., 1991-92. Mem. AICPA, Mon. Soc. CPAs (dir. 1968-71, instr., 1982-85, Outstanding Com. Chmn. 1984), Wyo. Soc. CPAs, Billings Rotary. Home: 3221 Country Club Cir Billings MT 59102-0609 Office: 490 N 31st Ste 206 Billings MT 59101-1256

ALLEN, DORIS, state legislator; b. Mo., May 26, 1936. Student, U. Wyo., Long Beach C.C., Golden West Coll. Lic. real estate agent. Spkr. Calif. State Assembly, 1982—, mem. various coms.; mem. Calif. Planning Coun. Mental Health Master Plan, 1990. Active Orange County Commn. Status Women, Met. Water Dist. Speakers' Bur., West Orange County Consortium Spl. Edn.; founder, dir. Orange County Bus-Bloc, 1978; mem. adv. bd. Casa de Bienvenidos; bd. dirs. Coastline C.C. Found., Huntington Beach Conf. and Visitors Bur.; trustee Huntington Beach Union High Sch., 1976-81, pres., 1980. Recipient Spl. Recognition, Calif. Assn. Work Experience Educators, 1987, Nat. Coalition Marine Conservation, 1987, 90, Soc. Preservation Bighorn Sheep, 1988, Calif. Spl. Edn. Local Planning Area Adminstrs., 1989, Order of Jassid, Sierra Pacific Flyfisher, 1988, Project Workability award State Dept. Edn., 1988, Conservation award Internat. Game Fish Assn., 1992; named Legislator of Yr., Sportsmen's Coun. Ctrl. Calif., 1986, Calif. Bus. Educators Assn., 1987, 91, Calif. Indsl. and Tech. Edn. Assn., Inc., 1989, Pacific region Nat. Coalition Marine Conservation, 1989, Pub. Ofcl. of Yr., Orange County chpt. Am. Soc. Pub. Adminstrn., 1987, Woman of Distinction, Westminster Soroptimist Internat., 1987, Personality of Yr., Hunting and Fishing News, 1989, Nat. Legislator of Yr., Am. Fishing Tackle Mfrs. Assn., 1991. Mem. Am. Bus. Women's Assn., Calif. Elected Women;s Assn. Edn. and Rsch., L.A. Rod and Reel Club (hon.). Office: 16052 Beach Blvd Ste 160 Huntington Beach CA 92647-3808

ALLEN, EDGAR BURNS, records management professional; b. L.A., Sept. 1, 1929; s. Harry James and Hela Ruth (Graham) A.; m. Eleanor Angela Gregory, July 24, 1960; children: Linda Marie, Lisa Ann. AA, L.A. City Coll., 1958; student, Calif. State U., L.A., 1958, 81; BS, UCLA, 1985. Supr. records ctr. L.A. Dept. Water and Power, 1958-67, records mgr., 1967-76; records mgmt. officer City of L.A., 1976-85; records mgmt. cons. L.A., 1985—; profl. creator records mgmt. systems, tax preparer, L.A., 1990—. Chmn. Leimert Pk. Community Assn., L.A., 1972-75. Mem. Assn. Records Mgrs. and Adminstrs. (bd. dirs. 1975-76), Soc. Calif. Archivists, All Yr. Figure Skating Club (bd. dirs. 1970-79). Democrat. Roman Catholic.

ALLEN, EDWARD RAYMOND, retired business educator, accountant; b. Indpls., Sept. 30, 1913; s. Edward L. and Emmeline (Rice) A.; BS in Commerce, Drake U., 1950, MA in Accounting, 1951; m. Norma D. M. Brennan, May 10, 1941. CPA, Idaho. Asst. prof. bus. adminstrn. Parsons Coll., Fairfield, Iowa, 1952-56; faculty Coll. of Idaho, Caldwell, 1956-93, prof. bus. adminstrn., 1956-73, head dept., 1962-70, chmn. dept., 1970-73, emeritus, 1973—, vis. lectr., 1973-74; practicing CPA, Caldwell, 1958-92; ret., 1992. Contbr. articles to profl. jours. Served to capt. AUS, 1942-46; lt. col. Res. ret. Decorated Bronze Star with 1 palm. Mem. AICPA, Idaho Soc. CPAs (dir., regional v.p. 1958-61, mem. standards of practice com. 1974-83, chmn. com. 1980-83, chmn. relations with ednl. instns. com. 1984-86, mem. 1993—), AAUP (past pres. Coll. of Idaho chpt.), Elks, Pi Kappa Phi. Home: PO Box 336 Caldwell ID 83606-0336

ALLEN, GARY KING, aerospace advance development engineer; b. Buffalo, June 27, 1944; s. Howard W. and Ethel M. (King) A.; m. Catherine Reardon, July 12, 1969; children: Matthew W., Sarah A. BSCE, Clarkson U., 1966; MBA with distinction, Nat. U., San Diego, 1977. Lead prin. engr. Boeing Co., Seattle, 1966-73, 90—; lead preliminary design engr. Rohr Industries, Chula Vista, Calif., 1974-78; advanced devel. specialist Rho Co., Bellevue, Wash., 1978-82; sr. specialist on assignment to Lockheed Corp., Burbank, Calif., 1982-83, on assignment to Boeing, Seattle, 1978-82, 84-89. Mem. nat. adv. bd. Am. Security Council, 1970-76. Recipient Pride in Excellence award Boeing Co., 1980, 86, 95. Mem. AIAA. Home: 702 Kirkland Way Apt 17 Kirkland WA 98033-3957 Office: The Boeing Co PO Box 3707 Seattle WA 98124-2207

ALLEN, HENRY WESLEY, biomedical researcher; b. Louisville, Oct. 16, 1927; s. John Turk and Irene Victoria (Slater) A.; m. Evelyn Chen, Dec. 29, 1968 (div. Dec. 1988); children: Lillian Chen, Rosaniline Chen, Dianne Chen. Student, U. Louisville, 1945-46, U. Chgo., 1946-47, U. So. Calif., 1960-61. Rschr. Loma Linda (Calif.) U., 1962-77, Am. Biologics, Chula Vista, Calif., 1977—. Author: International Protocols in Cancer Management, 1983, The Study of Reactive Oxygen Toxic Species and Their Metabolism, 1985, The Biochemistry of Live Cell Therapy, 1986; contbr. articles to Jour. of Theoretical Biology, Analytical Biochemistry, Nature, others. Office: Am Biologics 1180 Walnut Ave Chula Vista CA 91911-2622

ALLEN, HOWARD NORMAN, cardiologist, educator; b. Chgo., Nov. 19, 1936; s. Herman and Ida Gertrude (Weinstein) A.; children: Michael Daniel, Jeffrey Scott. BS, U. Ill., Chgo., 1958, MD, 1960. Diplomate Am. Bd. Internal Medicine, Am. Bd. Cardiovascular Disease, Nat. Bd. Med. Examiners. Intern Los Angeles County Gen. Hosp., L.A., 1960-61; resident in internal medicine Wadsworth VA Med. Ctr., L.A., 1961, 64-66; fellow in cardiology Cedars-Sinai Med. Ctr., L.A., 1966-67, dir. cardiac care unit Cedars of Lebanon Hosp. div., 1968-74, dir. Pacemaker Evaluation Ctr., 1968-89, dir. Cardiac Noninvasive Lab., 1972-88; Markus Found. fellow in cardiology St. George's Hosp., London, 1967-68; attending physician cardiology svc. Sepulveda (Calif.) VA Med. Ctr., 1972-86; pvt. practice Beverly Hills, Calif., 1988—; asst. prof. medicine UCLA, 1970-76, assoc. prof., 1976-84, adj. prof., 1984-88, clin. prof., 1988—; cons. Sutherland Learning Associates, Inc., L.A., 1970-75; cardiology cons. Occidental Life Ins. Co., L.A., 1972-86. Contbr. articles to med. jours., chpts. to books. Commr. L.A. County Emergency Med. Svcs., 1989-91. Capt. M.C., U.S. Army, 1962-63, Korea. Fellow NSF, 1958, NIH, 1966-67. Fellow ACP, Am. Coll. Cardiology; mem. Am. Heart Assn. (fellow coun. on clin. cardiology, pres. Greater L.A. affiliate 1987-88, bd. dirs. 1979-94; recipient Heart of Gold 1994), U. Ill. Alumni Assn. (life), Big Ten Club So. Calif. (bd. dirs. 1994—), Alpha Omega Alpha, Pi Kappa Epsilon. Office: 414 N Camden Dr Ste 1100 Beverly Hills CA 90210-4532

ALLEN, JACQUELYN MAY, school psychologist, consultant; b. L.A., Nov. 6, 1943; d. John Richard and Ida May (Townsend) Hinson; m. James William Allen, Dec. 19, 1970; children: Julene May, Jason William. BA, U. Redlands, 1965; MA, Berkeley Bapt. Div. Sch., 1969; MS, Calif. State U., Hayward, 1972; DEd, U. San Francisco, 1990. Lic. marriage and family counselor, Calif; nat. cert. counselor, nat. cert. sch. counselor. ESL tchr. U. Mexico, Mexico City, 1967; missionary Am. Bapt. Conv., El Salvador, Ctrl. Am., 1966-67; tchr. Foothill Intermediate Sch., Walnut Creek, Calif., 1968-72; marriage, family, child counselor Fremont Inst. Transactional Analysis, Fremont, Calif., 1977-78; career cons. Pvt. Sch. & Chronicle Guidance Project, Fremont, 1989-91; CEO, pres. Am. Sch. Counselor Assn., Alexandria, Va., 1993-94; cons. Allen Cons. Assocs., Fremont, 1985—; sch. psychologist, sch. counselor Fremont Unified Sch. Dist., 1972—; liaison counseling for high skills De Witt Wallace Reader's Digest, Manhattan, Kans., 1994-95; liaison for Am. Sch. Counseling Assn., Nat. Bus. Adv. Bd., Alexandria, Va., 1993-95; project coord. Ednl. Devel. Ctr. Grant on Comprehensive Health and HIV, AIDS Prevention, Boston, 1994-95; pres., negotiator Fremont Counseling and Psychologists Assn., 1972-73, 75-77, 90-91; mem. retirement and bilingual spl. edn. coms. Fremont Unified Sch. Dist., 1994-95. Editor: (compendium) Action-Oriented Desk Guide for Professional School Counselors, 1992. Treas. Antelope Hills Home Owners Assn., Fremont, 1984-85; leader troop 1382 Girl Scouts Am., Fremont, 1990-94. Named Outstanding Young Educator Fremont Jaycees, 1974. Mem. ACA (mem. governing coun., mem. exec. com. 1993-94), Am. Sch. Counselor Assn. (pres., CEO 1993-94, exec. and fin. com. 1992-95, grant 1990), Calif. Assn. Counseling and Devel. Edn. Found. (bd. dirs. 1991-95), Calif. Assn. Counseling and Devel. (pres. 1991-92), Calif. Career Devel. Assn. (conf. com. (grant 1990), Delta Kappa Gamma (rsch. chair 1988-92, scholarships 1988-89). Home: 705 Montana Vis Fremont CA 94539-6242

ALLEN, JANICE FAYE CLEMENT, nursing administrator; b. Norfolk, Nebr., Aug. 19, 1946; d. Allen Edward and Hilda Bernice (Stange) Reeves; m. Roger Allen Clement, Oct. 6, 1968 (dec. July 1974); m. August H. Allen, Sept. 17, 1988. RN, Meth. Sch. Nursing, Omaha, 1967; BS in Nursing, magna cum laude, Creighton U., 1978; MS in Nursing, U. Nebr., 1981; cert. in nursing adminstrn. With Meth. Hosp., 1967-68, 72-83, asst. head nurse, 1974-77, staff devel. nurse, 1977-81, dir. staff adminstrv. services, 1981-83; pub. health nurse Wichita-Sedgwick County Health Dept., Wichita, Kans., 1970-72; dir. nursing Meth. Med. Ctr., St. Joseph, Mo., 1983-84, Broadlawns Med. Ctr., Des Moines, 1984-93; dir. staff mgmt./infection control Ea. N.Mex. Med. Ctr., Roswell, 1993—; adj. clin. faculty nursing Drake U. Nursing, Des Moines, 1986-93, mem. adv. bd., 1984-93, Cen. Campus Practical Nursing, 1984-93; mem. adv. bd. Des Moines Area Community Coll. Dist., 1987—, Des Moines Area C.C. Nursing Bd., 1987-93, Grandview Coll., 1988-93; bd. dirs. Vis. Nurse Svcs., 1988-93. Mem. Am. Nurses Assn., Am. Orgn. Nurse Execs., N.Mex. Nurses Assn. (bd. dirs. 1995), Cen. Iowa Nursing Leadership Conf. (pres. 1985), Colloquium Nursing Leaders Cen. Iowa, Iowa League for Nursing (treas. 1987-89, pres. 1989), Iowa Orgn. Nurse Execs. (treas. 1987, sec. 1989, pres.-elect 1993), Assn. Infection Control and Epidemiology, Sigma Theta Tau (pres. Zeta Chi chpt. 1990-92). Democrat. Presbyterian. Avocations: flying, sewing, golf, walking, reading. Home: 3201 Allison Dr Roswell NM 88201-1011 Office: Ea NMex Med Ctr 405 W Country Club Rd Roswell NM 88201-5209

ALLEN, JEFFREY DOUGLAS, engineering manager; b. San Francisco, Nov. 17, 1954; s. Douglas D. and Marilyn Klea (Miles) A.; m. Leann Bair, May 7, 1977; children: Jacob, Louis, Anneliese, Miriam, Mark. BSME, Brigham Young U., 1979; MSME, Stanford U., 1984. R&D engr. Hewlett Packard Co., Boise, Idaho, 1979-84; R&D project mgr. Hewlett Packard Co., Greeley, Colo., 1984-86; R&D project mgr. Hewlett Packard Co., Boise, 1986-92, mfg. engring. mgr., 1992-93, R&D sect. mgr., 1993—. Patroller Nat. Ski Patrol, Boise, 1991—. Office: Hewlett Packard Co Disk Memory Divsn PO Box 39 Boise ID 83707

ALLEN, JEFFREY MICHAEL, lawyer; b. Chgo., Dec. 13, 1948; s. Albert A. and Miriam (Feldman) A.; m. Anne Marie Guaraglia, Aug. 9, 1975; children: Jason M., Sara M. BA in Polit. Sci. with great distinction, U. Calif., Berkeley, 1970, JD, 1973. Bar: Calif. 1973, U.S. Dist. Ct. (no. and so. dists.) Calif. 1973, U.S. Ct. Appeals (9th cir.) 1973, U.S. Dist. Ct. (ea. dist.) Calif. 1974, U.S. Dist. Ct. (cen. dist.) Calif. 1977, U.S. Dist. Ct. (so. dist.) Calif., U.S. Supreme Ct.; lic. real estate broker. Ptnr. Graves, Allen, Cornelius & Celestre and predecessor firms, Oakland, Calif., 1973—; teaching asst. dept. polit. sci. U. Calif., Berkeley, 1970-73; lectr. St. Mary's Coll., Moraga, Calif., 1976—; bd. dirs. Family Svcs. of the East Bay, 1987-92, 1st v.p., 1988, pres., 1988-91; mem. panel arbitrators Ala. County Superior Ct.; arbitrator comml. arbitration panel Am. Arbitration Assn. Mem. editorial bd. U. Calif. Law Rev., 1971-73, project editor, 1972-73; mem. Ecology Law Quar., 1971-72; contbr. articles to profl. jours. Treas. Hillcrest Elem. Sch. PTA, 1984-86, pres., 1986-88; past mem. GATE adv. com., strategic planning com. on fin. and budget, dist. budget adv. com., instructional strategy counsel Oakland Unified Sch. Dist., 1986-91; mem. Oakland Met. Forum, 1987-91, Oakland Strategic Planning Com., 1988-90; mem. adv. com. St. Mary's Coll. Paralegal Prog.; bd. dirs. Montera Sports Complex, 1988-89; bd. dirs. Jack London Youth Soccer League, 1988-94; commr. Bay Oaks Youth Soccer, 1988-94; asst. dist. commr. dist. 4 Calif. Youth Soccer Assn., 1990-92, also bd. dirs., pres. dist. 4 competitive league, 1990-93; sec., bd. dirs. Calif. Youth Soccer Assn., 1993—. Mem. ABA (chmn. real property com. gen. practice sect. 1987-91, mem. programs com. 1991-93, chmn. subcom. on use of computers in real estate trans. 1985-86, advocacy coord. 1993—, sect. coun. 1994), Alameda County Bar Assn. (past vice chmn. com. continuing edn.), Calif. Bar Assn., Calif. Scholarship Fedn., U.S. Soccer Fedn. (nat. C lic. coach and state referee, referee instr. and state referee assessor), Calif. North Referee Assn. (referee adminstr. dist. 4 1992—), Oakland C. of C., Rotary (bd. dirs. Oakland 1992-94). Office: Graves Allen et al 2101 Webster St Ste 1590 Oakland CA 94612-3037

ALLEN, JOHN DAVID, sales executive; b. Lima, Ohio, Jan. 12, 1957; s. Darrell and Margaret (Dumm) A.; m. Denice Hana Knezovich, May 28, 1983; children: Adrienne Yvonne, Alana Nadyne. BA in Internat. Affairs, Ohio U., 1979; M Internat. Mgmt., Am. Grad. Sch. Internat. Mgmt., Glendale, Ariz., 1981. Latin Am. dir. LeRoi div. Dresser Industries, Sidney, Ohio, 1981-82; v.p. sales & mktg. Wilden Pump & Engring., Grand Terrace, Calif., 1982—. Mem. Orthodox Ch. Home: 7185 Rock Spring Ln Highland CA 92346-5460 Office: Wilden Pump & Engring 22069 Van Buren St Grand Terrace CA 92313-5607

ALLEN, JOHN ELIOT, geology educator, writer; b. Seattle, Aug. 12, 1908; s. Eric William and Ida (Sally) (Elliott) A.; m. Margaret Lucy Moss, July 26, 1933; 1 dau., Margaret (Sally) (Mrs. Scott McNall). B.A., U. Oreg., 1931, M.A., 1932; Ph.D., U. Calif. at Berkeley, 1944. Ranger naturalist Crater Lake, 1935; field geologist Rustless Iron & Steel Corp., 1935-38; Geologist Oreg. Dept. Geology and Mineral Industries, 1938-47; assoc. prof. Pa. State Coll., 1947-49; head dept. geology N.Mex. Sch. Mines, 1949-52; sr. geologist N.Mex. Bur. Mines, 1952-56; head dept. geology Portland (Oreg.) State U., 1956-74, prof. emeritus, 1974—; prof. Whitman Coll., 1975; research geologist Nev. Bur. Mines, 1976, N.Mex. Bur. Mines, 1977; faculty U. Calif., Santa Barbara, summers 1952, 61, 65, U. Hawaii, summer 1966. Author: Magnificent Gateway, 1979, 2d edit., 1984, Cataclysms on the Columbia, 1987, 2d edit., 1991; columnist Time Travel, The Oregonian, 1983-87, Time Travel Scrapbook (1st 120 columns), 1985, (2d 100 columns), 1987. Bd. dirs. Oreg. Nature Conservancy, 1980-86, landmark and life mem., 1987. Hon. mem. Oreg. Mus. Sci. and Industry. Recipient Silver Beaver award Boy Scouts Am., 1955; SEATO prof. U. Peshawar, Pakistan, 1963-64. Mem. Geol. Soc. Am., Nat. Assn. Geology Tchrs. (pres. 1967), Am. Inst. Profl. Geologists (pres. Oreg. sect. 1973), Geol. Soc. Ore. Country, Phi Beta Kappa, Sigma Xi, Delta Upsilon.

ALLEN, JOHN JEFFREY BECK, psychology educator; b. Northampton, Mass., Aug. 10, 1961; s. Ronald Royce and JoAnne Elizabeth (Kuehl) A; m. Connie J. A. Beck. BS, U. Wis., 1986; MA, U. Minn., 1991, PhD, 1992. Lic. psychologist, Ariz. Instr. psychology U. Minn., Mpls., 1988-92; intern psychology VA Med. Ctr., Mpls., 1991-92; asst. prof. psychology U. Ariz., Tucson, 1992—. Contbr. articles to profl. jours. Acupuncture as a treatment for depression grantee NIH, 1993-95. Mem. APA, Am. Psychol. Soc., Soc. for Psychophysiol. Rsch., Internat. Neuropsychol. Soc., Cognitive Neurosci. Soc., Sigma Xi, Phi Beta Kappa, Phi Kappa Phi. Office: Dept Psychology Univ Ariz Tucson AZ 85721

ALLEN, JUDITH MARTHA, nursing administrator, career officer; b. Syracuse, N.Y., Feb. 4, 1942; d. Bernard J. and Genevieve R. (Greene) Arndt; m. Anthony S. Allen, Nov. 1984. Diploma, Champlain Valley Sch. Nursing, Plattsburg, N.Y., 1964; BSN, D'Youville Coll., 1974; postgrad., U. N.C., 1976; MS, U. San Francisco, 1984. Cert. cardiovascular nurse clinician; CPR instr. trainer; CCM. Head nurse CCU Millard Fillmore Hosp., Buffalo, 1974-80; commd. officer U.S. Army, 1976, advanced through grades to lt. col., 1986; chief surg. nursing Ireland Army Community Hosp., Ft. Knox, Ky., 1985-87, chief nursing edn. and staff devel., 1987-88; clin. coord. ICU, CCU, asst. chief spl. projects officer Letterman Army Med. Ctr., San Francisco, 1980-85, head nurse post operative cardiovascular/neurosurg. unit, 1988-89, asst. chief nursing edn., staff devel. svc., 1989-91, asst. chief evenings/nights, 1991-92, asst. quality improvement nurse, 1992, chief nursing adminstrn., days, med. surg. sect. chief, 1992-94; rev. coord. State Indsl. Ins. Sys. Universal Health Network, Sparks, Nev., 1994—; speaker in field. Contbr. articles to profl. jours. Lt. col. Nev. State NG. Mem. AACCN, Nev. State Nurses Assn. Home: PO Box 1026 Virginia City NV 89440-1026 Office: 2345 E Prater Way Sparks NV 89434-9600

ALLEN, JUDITH SYMA, art educator, artist; b. N.Y.C., Jan. 21, 1956. BA, Oberlin Coll., 1977; postgrad., Columbia U., 1978; MFA, Mills Coll., 1990. Lectr. photography Cornish Coll. of the Arts, Seattle, 1992—; lectr. photography San Francisco State U., 1991, 92, Acad. Art Coll., San Francisco, 1991, 92, Calif. State Summer Sch. for Arts, Oakland, 1990, 91. One-woman shows include Lloyd Gallery, Spokane, Wash., 1982, New Performance Gallery, San Francisco, 1982; exhibited in group shows at Ctr. on Contemporary Art, Seattle, 1994, 95, Fisher Gallery, Seattle, 1993, 94, 95, San Francisco Arts Commn. Gallery, 1991, Berkeley (Calif.) Art Ctr., 1991, Richmond (Calif.) Art Ctr., 1991, 86, San Francisco State U. Art Gallery, 1991, Intersection for Arts, San Francisco, 1990, 88, Bellevue (Wash.) Art Mus., 1994. Fellow Nat. Endowment for Arts, 1990-91; recipient Trefethen award Mills Coll., 1989, Betty Bowen Meml. Spl. Recognition award Seattle Art Mus., 1994. Mem. Soc. for Photographic Edn., Coll. Art Assn. Office: Cornish Coll of Arts 1501 10th Ave E Seattle WA 98102-4210

ALLEN, KURT LEONARD, poultry industry executive; b. El Paso, Tex., Jan. 17, 1963; s. Barry Leonard and Janet Kay (Soukup) A.; m. Sylvia Christina Allen, Sept. 24, 1988; children: Ryan Kurt, Alexandra, Christina. BA in Econs., U. Calif., Irvine, 1984. Sales engr. Murata Erie N.Am. Inc., Smyrna, Ga., 1984-88, Abbott Transistor Labs. Inc., L.A., 1988-90; v.p., gen. mgr. Illy Sunnyslope Farms Inc., Beaumont, Calif., 1990—; mem. Calif. Egg. Commn., Upland, 1994—; dir. Inland Empire Poultrymen Assn, Riverside, Calif., 1993—. Fellow Phi Delta Theta (men's alumni assn.). Republican. Home: 10930 Golden Hills Dr Yucaipa CA 92399

ALLEN, LEW, JR., laboratory executive, former air force officer; b. Miami, Fla., Sept. 30, 1925; s. Lew and Zella (Holman) A.; m. Barbara Frink Hatch, Aug. 19, 1949; children: Barbara Allen Miller, Lew III, Marjorie Allen Dauster, Christie Allen Jameson, James Allen. BS, U.S. Mil. Acad., 1946; MS, U. Ill., 1952, PhD in Physics, 1954. Commd. 2d lt. USAAF, 1946; advanced through grades to gen. USAF, 1977, ret., 1982; physicist test div. AEC, Los Alamos, N.Mex., 1954-57; sci. advisor Air Force Spl. Weapons Lab., Kirtland, N.Mex., 1957-61; with office of spl. tech. sec. of Def., Washington, 1961-65; from dir. spl. projects to dep. dir. adv. plans Air Force Space Program, 1965-72; dir. Nat. Security Agy., Ft. Meade, Md., 1973-77; comdr. Air Force Systems Command, 1977-78; vice chief of staff USAF, Washington, 1978, chief of staff, 1978-82; dir. Jet Propulsion Lab., Calif. Inst. Tech., Pasadena, Calif., 1982-90; chmn. bd. Draper Lab, Boston, 1991—. Decorated Def. D.S.M. with two clusters, Air Force D.S.M. with one cluster, Nat. Intelligence D.S.M., NASA D.S.M., Legion of Merit with two oak leaf clusters; recipient Robert H. Goddard Astronautics award Am. Inst. Aeronautics and Astronautics, 1995. Fellow Am. Phys. Soc.; mem. Am. Geophys. Union, Nat. Acad. Engring., Coun. on Fgn. Rels., Sigma Xi, Sunset Club (L.A.), Alfalfa Club (Washington). Republican. Episcopalian. Office: Draper Charles Stark Lab Inc 555 Technology Sq Cambridge MA 02139-3539

ALLEN, MERRILL JAMES, marine biologist; b. Brady, Tex., July 16, 1945; s. Clarence Francis and Sara Barbara (Finlay) A. BA, U. Calif., Santa Barbara, 1967; MA, UCLA, 1970; PhD, U. Calif., San Diego, 1982. Cert. jr. coll. tchr., Calif. Asst. environ. specialist So. Calif. Coastal Water Rsch. Project, El Segundo, 1971-77; postdoctoral assoc. Nat. Rsch. Coun., Seattle, 1982-84; oceanographer Nat. Marine Fisheries Svc., Seattle, 1984-86; sr. scientist MBC Applied Environ. Scis., Costa Mesa, Calif., 1986-93; prin. scientist So. Calif. Coastal Water Rsch. Project, Long Beach and Westminster, Calif., 1993—; tech. adv. com. Santa Monica Bay Restoration Project, Monterey Park, Calif., 1989—; steering com. So. Calif. Bight Pilot Project, 1993—; affiliate asst. prof. sch. fisheries U. Wash., Seattle, 1985-89. Mem. AAAS, Am. Inst. Fisheries Rsch. Biologists (dir. So. Calif. dist. 1991-93), Am. Fisheries Soc., Am. Soc. Ichthyologists and Herpetologists. Office: So Calif Coastal Water Rsch Project 7171 Fenwick Ln Westminster CA 92683-5218

ALLEN, MITCHELL JACK, publisher, archaeologist; b. Los Angeles, July 30, 1951; s. Aaron Archie and Rhoda Anita (Fox) A.; m. Laurie Ann Foier, Oct. 29, 1978 (div. 1986); m. Ariadne H. Prater, 1987; children: Alexis Rachel, Joshua Nicholas, Elena Berit. B.A. in History and Anthropology, U. Calif.-Santa Barbara, 1973; M.A. in Near East Studies, U. Mich., 1976. Editor Sage Publs., Beverly Hills, Calif., 1976-84, 85-95; field archaeologist Helmand Sistan Project, Sistan, Afghanistan, 1974-75; dancer Aman Folk Ensemble, Los Angeles, 1973-84, exec. dir. 1984-85; dir. Ashkelon Reg. Archaeological Survey, 1986-90; pub. Altamira Press, Walnut Creek, Calif., 1995—; lectr. in Archaeology Santa Clara U., 1995—. Author: (with Christine S. Smedley) Getting Your Book Published, 1993; editor mag. Folk Dance Scene, 1982-84. U. Mich. Rackham and Ford grantee, 1974-75. Mem. Am. Anthrop. Assn., Am. Sociol. Assn., Am. Schs. Oriental Research, Soc. Am. Archaeology, Folk Dance Fedn. Calif., Phi Beta Kappa.

ALLEN, NORM, entertainer, marketing entrepreneur; b. Naples, June 8, 1952; s. William Oscar and Barbara Gail (Horton) A.; m. Sandra Sharp Powell, Dec. 31, 1971 (div. Feb. 13, 1979); children: Lori Ann Fuller, Jeremy Doyle; m. Nancy Pagdett, Aug. 7, 1993. Student, Texarkana (Tex.) Coll., 1973-74, Southwestern U., 1974-76. Med. tech. Amigos de las Americas, Morazon, Guatemala, 1969, Peace Corps, India, 1971-72; with United Meth. Ministry, Tex., 1973-79; entertainer various cities, 1979—; pres., owner Calif. Customer Svcs., Glendale, 1991—; adv. Merchand Adv. Com., Glendale, 1991—. Music writer, 1971-94. Bd. mem. ARC, Glendale, 1994-95; charter pres. Glendale Galleria Kiwanis, 1994-95. With USMC, 1970. Republican. Methodist. Home: 1665 Arbor Dr Glendale CA 91202-1339 Office: Calif Customer Svcs 2123A Glendale Galleria Glendale CA 91210-2101

ALLEN, PAUL, computer executive, professional sports team owner. Student, Wash. State U. Co-founder Microsoft Corp., Redmond, Wash., 1975, exec. v.p., 1975-83; founder Asymetrix Corp., Bellevue, Wash., 1985—, Starwave Corp., Bellevue, Intervas Rsch., Palo Alto, Calif.; owner, chmn. bd. Portland (Oreg.) Trail Blazers, 1988—; bd. dirs. Egghead Discount Software, Microsoft Corp., Darwin Molecular, Inc.; owner, chmn., bd. dirs. Ticketmaster Holdings Group, L.A. Office: The Paul Allen Group Ste 530 110-110th Ave NE Bellevue WA 98004

ALLEN, REX WHITAKER, architect; b. San Francisco, Dec. 21, 1914; s. Lewis Whitaker and Maude Rex (Allen) A.; m. Elizabeth Johnson, Oct. 11, 1941 (div. 1949); children: Alexandra A. (Mrs. Daniel D. Fleckles), Frances Lambert (Mrs. Andrew Dunn); m. Ruth Batchelor, Apr. 1, 1949 (div. 1971); children: Mark B., Susan Moore (Mrs. Kofy Lechner); m. Bettie J. Crossfield, Nov. 6, 1971. A.B., Harvard U., 1936, M.Arch., 1939; student, Columbia U. Arch. Sch., 1936-37. With Research and Planning Assos., N.Y.C., 1939-42, Camloc Fastener Corp., N.Y.C., 1942-45, Isadore Rosenfield (architect), N.Y.C., 1945-48, Blanchard and Maher (architects), San Francisco, 1949-52; established pvt. practice San Francisco, 1953; pres. Rex Whitaker Allen & Assos., San Francisco, 1961-71, Archtl. Prodns., Inc., 1971-76; prin. Hugh Stubbins/Rex Allen Partnership, 1968, Rex Allen Partnership, 1971-76; pres. Rex Allen-Drever-Lechowski, Architects, 1976-85, Rex Allen/Mark Lechowski & Assocs., 1985-87; cons. architect, health facility planner, 1987—; mem. Calif. Bldg. Safety Bd., 1973-93. Author: (with Ilona von Karolyi) Hospital Planning Handbook, 1976; Contbr. articles to profl. jours.; prin. works include French Hosp, San Francisco, Mercy Hosp, Sacramento, Roseville (Calif.) Dist. Hosp, Highland Hosp, Oakland, St. Francis Hosp, San Francisco, Dominican Hosp, Santa Cruz, Alta Bates Hosp, Berkeley, Calif., Boston City Hosp, Out-Patient bldg. Woodland (Calif.) Meml. Hosp, Stanislaus Meml. Hosp, Modesto, Calif., Madera (Calif.) Community Hosp, Sacred Heart Hosp, Eugene, Oreg., St. Joseph Hosp, Mt. Clemens, Mich., Commonwealth Health Center, Saipan, Guam Meml. Hosp. and Nursing Facility. Chmn. Mill Valley Adv. Edn. Council, 1956. Fellow AIA (v.p. No. Calif. chpt. 1964, bd. dirs. Calif. council 1955-56, 1962-64, nat. pres. 1969-70); hon. fellow Royal Archtl. Inst. Can.; mem. Constrn. Specification Inst. (pres. San Francisco 1961), San Francisco Zool. Soc. bd. dirs. 1974-86, 1988—, chmn. design standards com. Assn. Western Hosps, chmn. arch. sect. 1957-58), Calif. Hosp. Assn., Am. Hosp. Assn., Internat. Hosp. Fedn., Am. Assn. Hosp. Planning (pres. 1971-72), Union Internat. des Architectes Public Health Work Group (dir. 1979-80), La Sociedad de Arquitectos Mexicanos (hon. mem.), Federación Panamericana de Asociaciones de Arquitectos (v.p. 1980-84), San Francisco Planning and Urban Renewal Assn., San Francisco Mus. Modern Art, Mus. Soc., San Francisco Symphony Found., Sierra Club. Club: Harvard (N.Y.C. and San Francisco). Home and Office: 1070 Siesta Way Sonoma CA 95476-4413

ALLEN, RICK (FREDERICK ALLEN KLYCINSKI), magician, advertising and publicity consultant; b. Detroit, Nov. 4, 1941; s. Chester Bruno and Johana Jean (Guzdzial) Klycinski; m. Marie DeLeon, Nov. 2, 1965 (div. Mar. 1985); children: John Paul, Marie Louise, Diane Lynn, Mark Frederick. AA, Pasadena Coll., 1961. Account exec. Knight Ridder Newspapers, Long Beach, Calif., 1966-68, advt. mgr., 1969-71; advt. mgr. Copley Newspapers, Torrance, Calif., 1972-73; cons. Scripps Newspapers, Napa, Calif., 1974-75; founder, owner, mgr. Creative Advt. Svc., Vallejo, Calif., 1976—; dir. mail advt. cons. Vallejo, 1980—; profl. magician for fund-raising orgns., 1976—. Author: Public Relations and Publicity for Entertainers, 1978; editor: Stick to the Cash Register, 1970; contbr. articles to various publs. Founder Anti-Grafitti Task Force. Named top fund raiser United Way, L.A., Long Beach, 1971; recipient awards for creative advt. Calif. Advt. Assn., Calif. Pubs. Assn., Am. Assn. Advt. Agys. Mem. Soc. Am. Magicians, Internat. Brotherhood Magicians, Pacific Coast Assn. Magicians, Lions. Home and Office: 122 Clearview Dr Vallejo CA 94591-7137

ALLEN, ROBERT EUGENE BARTON, lawyer; b. Bloomington, Ind., Mar. 16, 1940; s. Robert Eugene Barton and Berth R. A.; m. Cecelia Ward Dooley, Sept. 23, 1960 (div. 1971); children: Victoria, Elizabeth, Robert; m. Judith Elaine Hecht, May 27, 1979 (div. 1989). BS, Columbia U., 1962; LLB, Harvard U., 1965. Bar: Ariz. 1965, U.S. Dist. Ct. Ariz. 1965, U.S. Tax Ct., 1965, U.S. Supreme Ct. 1970, U.S. Ct. Customs and Patent Appeals 1971, U.S. Dist. Ct. D.C. 1972, U.S. Ct. Appeals (9th cir.) 1974, U.S. Ct. Appeals (10th, and D.C. cirs.) 1984, U.S. Dist. Ct. N.Mex., U.S. Dist. Ct. (no. dist.) Calif., U.S. Ct. Appeals (fed. cir.) 1992. Ptnr., dir. Brown & Bain, Phoenix, Tucson, Palo Alto (Calif.); spl. asst. atty. gen. pro tem Ariz. Ct. Appeals, atty. gen. pro-tem, 1978, 84, 92. Nat. pres. Young Dems. Clubs Am., 1971-73; mem. exec. com. Dem. Nat. Com., 1972-73; mem. Ariz. Gov.'s Kitchen Cabinet working on wide range of state projects; bd. dirs. Phoenix Bapt. Hosp. and Health Systems, Phoenix and Valley of the Sun Conv. and Visitors Bur., United Cerebral Palsy Ariz., 1984-89, Planned Parenthood of Cen. and No. Ariz., 1984-90; mem. Ariz. Aviation Futures Task Force; chmn. Ariz. Airport Devel. Criteria. Subcom.; mem. Apache Junction Airport Rev. Com.; Am. rep. exec. bd. Atlantic Alliance of Young Polit. Leaders, 1973-77, 1977-80; trustee Am. Counsel of Young Polit. Leaders, 1971-76, 1981-85, mem. Am. delegations to Germany, 1971, 72, 76, 79, USSR, 1971, 76, 88, France, 1974, 79, Belgium, 1974, 77, Can., 1974, Eng., 1975, 79, Norway, 1975, Denmark, 1976, Yugoslavia and Hungary, 1985; Am. observer European Parliamentary elections, Eng., France, Germany, Belgium, 1979, Moscow Congressional, Journalist delegation, 1989, NAFTA Trade Conf., Mexico City, 1993, Atlantic Assembly, Copenhagen, 1993; trustee Environ. Health Found., 1994, Friends of Walnut Canyon, 1994. Spkr. seminars and profl. assns.; contbr. articles on comml. litigation to profl. jours. Mem. ABA, Ariz. Bar Assn., Maricopa County Bar Assn., N. Mex. State Bar, D.C. Bar Assn., Am. Judicature Soc., Fed. Bar Assn., Am. Arbitration Assn., Phi Beta Kappa. Democrat. Episcopalian (lay reader). Club: Harvard (Phoenix). Office: Brown & Bain 2901 N Central Ave Ste 2000 Phoenix AZ 85012-2740

ALLEN, ROY VERL, life insurance company executive; b. Hyrum, Utah, Aug. 3, 1933; s. Winfrd A. and Sarah Ann (Nielsen) A.; m. Judith Green, Aug. 11, 1961; children: Ann Marie Allen Webb, Michael R., Blair J. BS, Utah State U., 1958. CLU, Chartered Fin. Cons. Mgr. employee benefits Thiokol Chem. Corp., Brigham City, Utah, 1959-61; employment interviewer Hercules, Salt Lake City, 1962-63; agy. mgr. Standard Ins. Co., Salt Lake City, 1963—. Maj. U.S. Army Res., 1962-79. Mem. CLUs (bd. mem. 1973-75), Estate Planning Coun. (bd. mem. 1979-81), Utah Gen. Agts. and Mgrs. (sec., v.p., pres. 1979-83), Utah Assn. Life Underwrtiers (pres. 1988-89), Exchange Club. Republican. Mormon. Home: 2526 Olympus Dr Salt Lake City UT 84124-2916 Office: Standard Ins Co 525 3rd Ave Salt Lake City UT 84103-2973

ALLEN, RUSSELL PLOWMAN, opera company executive; b. Washington, Dec. 30, 1951; s. Gale Wilson and Anne (Plowman) A. BA, Macalester Coll., 1974. Gen. mgr. Shreveport (La.) Symphony Orchestra, 1979-80; mgr. Houston Symphony Orchestra, 1980-84, San Antonio Symphony Orchestra, 1984-86; gen. mgr. Phoenix Symphony Orchestra, 1986-94, Va. Opera, Norfolk, 1994—; cons. N.Mex. Symphony Orchestra, Albuquerque, 1986, Chattanooga (Tenn.) Symphony Orchestra, 1986. Mem. grants rev. panel Ariz. commn. on Arts, Phoenix, 1987-90, Phoenix Arts Commn., 1987; program chmn. Phoenix Symphony Coun., 1986-94; mem. mktg. com. Downtown Phoenix Parternship Class XIII, Valley Leadership; mem. Heritage Sq. Adv. Bd., 1991-94. Mem. Am. Symphony Orchestra League, Phoenix City Club. Office: Va Opera PO Box 2580 Norfolk VA 23501-2580

ALLEN, SALLY ROTHFUS, editor; b. Pitts., Sept. 5, 1941; d. Elmer Arthur and Olive Corrine (Thompson) Rothfus; m. Arthur William Allen Jr., Dec. 27, 1964 (div. Oct. 1983); 1 child, Rebecca Rothfus Allen. BA, U. Mich., 1963; MBA, Golden Gate U., 1985. Writer, editor various newspapers, univs., 1964-69; with investment dept. investor rels. Homestead Savs., Burlingame, Calif., 1986-88; securities analyst Fisher Investments Inc., Woodside, Calif., 1988—; supervisory analyst, sr. editor rsch. dept. Robertson, Stephens & Co., San Francisco, 1993—. Mem. Nat. Investor Rels. Inst., San Francisco, 1987-88; mem. coun. Soc. for Encouragement Contemporary Art, San Francisco Mus. Modern Art, 1984-89; mem. Northern Calif. coun. Nat. Mus. for Women in the Arts, 1992—; bd. dirs. San Francisco Cinematheque, 1989-92. Mem. Security Analysts of San Francisco. Republican. Presbyterian. Office: 555 California St San Francisco CA 94104-1502

ALLEN, SAM RAYMOND, organization development specialist; b. Cody, Wyo., Oct. 6, 1953; s. Robert Sam and Jerrine (Cross) A.; m. Melinda Jo Daniels, Oct. 23, 1979; children: Eric Samuel, Andrew William. BS, U. Wyo., 1976, MBA, 1986; postgrad., George Washington U., 1977-79, Hastings Coll., Nebr., 1972-74. Accredited pub. rels. cert. Teller Bank of Va., Rosslyn, Va., 1978-79; legis. asst. U.S. Senate/Alan K. Simpson, Washington, 1979-81; bus. mgr. Coors Brewing Co., Golden, Colo., 1986-87; vol. prog. mgr. Coors Brewing Co., 1987-90, tng. mgr., 1990—. Editor V.I.C.E. Activity Guide newsletter, 1987-90. Bus. advisor Jr. Achievement, Denver, 1988-90; corp. mem. Assn. for Vol. Adminstrn., Boulder, 1987-90; elder Shepherd of the Hills Presbyn. Ch., 1986-89. Named Outstanding Corp. Coord., Adopt-A-School, Denver, 1987. Mem. ASTD, U. Wyo. Alumni Assn., Pub. Rels. Soc. Am., Rotary (community svc. dir. 1989), Alpha Kappa Psi. Republican. Presbyterian. Home: 11636 W 74th Way Arvada CO 80005-3274 Office: Coors Brewing Co 311 10th St Golden CO 80401-5811

ALLEN, STEPHANIE WEST, mediator; b. Modesto, Calif., Feb. 6, 1948; d. Charles Douglas Allen and Patricia Ann (West) King; m. Richard J. Bartlett, Aug. 13, 1977 (div. 1986). BS, U. Calif., Davis, 1970; JD, Santa Clara U., 1979. Bar: Calif. Dir. program integration vision resource ctr. SunRise Springs Resort, Santa Fe, 1987-88; dir. living ctr. Ctr. SunRise Springs Resort, Santa Fe, 1987-89; mgr. prof. svcs. Davis, Graham & Stubbs, Denver, 1989-93; adj. prof. Regis Coll., Denver, 1991, U. Colo., Denver, 1993; hon. instr. U. colo., 1994; lectr., writer and speaker in field. Author: Triversity Fantasy: Seven Keys to Unlock Prejudice, 1994; writer: (tng. forum) Lawyer Hiring and Training Report. Mem. Scribes. Republican. Episcopalian. Office: West Allen PO Box 300093 Denver CO 80203-0093

ALLEN, STEPHEN VALENTINE PATRICK WILLIAM, television comedian, author, pianist, songwriter; b. N.Y.C., Dec. 26, 1921; s. Carroll and Isabelle (Donohue) A.; m. Dorothy Goodman, Aug. 23, 1943; children: Stephen, Brian, David; m. Jayne Meadows, July 31, 1954; 1 child, William Christopher. Student journalism, Drake U., 1941, State Tchrs. Coll., Ariz., 1942. Radio announcer Sta. KOY, Phoenix, 1942, Stas. KFAC and KMTR, Los Angeles, 1944; comedian MBS, 1945; entertainer CBS, 1948-50; wrote narration and appeared in movie: Down Memory Lane; also appeared in motion pictures Warning Shot, The Benny Goodman Story, Amazon Women on the Moon, Great Balls of Fire, The Player, after 1950; appeared in Broadway play The Pink Elephant, 1953; creator, host Tonight Show, NBC, 1953-57; host TV shows Steve Allen Show, NBC, 1956-60, WBC syndicate, 1961-64, I've Got A Secret, 1964-67, Laughback, 1976-77, Meeting of Minds, 1977-81; composer over 5,000 songs including Picnic, Impossible, This Could Be The Start; author 43 books including Fourteen for Tonight, 1955, Bop Fables, 1955, The Funny Men, 1956, Wry on the Rocks, 1956, The Girls on the Tenth Floor, 1958, The Question Man, 1959, Mark It and Strike It; autobiography, 1960, Not All of Your Laughter, Not All of Your Tears, 1962; Letter to a Conservative, 1965, The Ground is Our Table, 1966, Bigger Than A Breadbox, 1967, A Flash of Swallows, 1969, The Wake, 1972, Princess Snip-Snip, 1973, Curses!, 1973, Schmock-Schmock!, 1975, What To Say When It Rains, 1974, Meeting of Minds, 1978, Chopped Up Chinese, 1978, Ripoff, 1979, Explaining China, 1980, Funny People, 1981, The Talk Show Murders, 1982, More Funny People, 1982 Beloved Son: A Story of the Jesus Cults, 1982, More Funny People, 1982, How To Make a Speech, 1986, How To Be Funny, 1987, Murder on the Glitter Box, 1989, (with Bill Adler Jr.) The Passionate Nonsmoker's Bill of the Rights, 1989, Dumbth: And 81 Ways to Make Americans Smarter, 1989, The Public Hating, 1990, Murder in Manhattan, 1990, Steve Allen and The Bible: Religion and Morality, 1990, Murder in Vegas, 1991, Hi-Ho, Steverino! My Adventures in the Wonderful Wacky World of TV, 1992, How to be Funny, 1992, The Murder Game, 1993, More Steve Allen on the Bible, Religion & Morality, Book Two, 1993, Make 'Em Laugh, 1993, Reflections, 1994, Murder on the Atlantic, 1995, The Man Who Turned Back the Clock and Other Short Stories, 1995. Recipient Grammy award for Gravy Waltz, 1964; named to TV Acad. Hall of Fame, 1986. Address: 15201 Burbank Blvd Van Nuys CA 91411-3532

ALLEN, THOMAS LAVERN, university development administrator; b. St. Louis, June 24, 1947; s. Ottis Lavern and Lillian Wanda A.; m. Sharon Marie Kuntzman, June 6, 1969; children: Nathaniel Thomas, Rebekah Sarah. BJ, U. Mo., 1969. Vol. tchr. U.S. Peace Corps, Bondoukou, Ivory Coast, 1969-71; editor Meramec Valley Transcript, Pacific, Mo., 1972-73; asst. dir. fund raising Midwestern Area Office ARC, St. Louis, 1973-77; dir. pub. relations, fin. devel. Epworth Children's Home, Webster Groves, Mo., 1977-83; v.p. Welch Assocs., St. Louis, 1983-85; dir. devel. St. Louis Mercantile Libr. Assn., 1985-86; devel. cons. Mt. W. Ctr. for Regional Studies, Logan, Utah, 1986-89; exec. dir. of devel. Utah State U., Logan, 1989—. Active Nat. Com. Planned Giving, Coun. Advancement and Support of Edn., Utah Planned Giving Roundtable. Named Ky. Col., Gov. Commonwealth of Ky., 1974; recipient Presdl. citation, Religious Pub. Rels. Coun., 1986. Mem. Nat. Soc. Fund Raising Execs. (cert. fund raising exec., nat. bd. dirs. 1984, 85, 1st v.p. St. Louis 1984, 85), Utah Soc. Fund Raisers (v.p. professionalism and edn. 1992-93), Am. Long Rifle Assn. (western partisan 1989-90). Methodist. Home: PO Box 138 Millville UT 84326-0138 Office: Utah State Univ Old Main # 101 Logan UT 84322-1420

ALLEN, TIMOTHY BURBANK, recreational company executive; b. Burlington, Vt., Feb. 12, 1956; s. George Wyman and Helen Louise (Hamilton) A.; m. Karen Ann Sprague, Sept. 28, 1991; children: Kristen Alison, Kyle Hamilton. Owner, operator Windsurf Del Valle, Livermore, Calif., 1980—; windsurfing instr. Internat. Windsurf Sailing Schs., Vt., 1978—. Appeared as clown on skis, juggler on skis for Spl. Olympics, ABC Sports, 1979-80; co-author: Family Windsurfing, 1983. Celebrity ski instr. Celebrity Pro-Am, Heavenly Valley Tahoe, 1979-80, 80-81. Company named Largest Windsurfing Sch. in the U.S.A., 1984. Mem. Profl. Ski Instrs. Am. (alpine ski inster 1978—), Am. Windsurf Industries Assn. (Sch. of Yr. 1990, bd. dirs. 1991-93).

ALLEN, VICKI LYNETTE, physical education educator; b. Denver, Oct. 27, 1952; d. Donald Joseph and Jacqueline (Jones) Roth; m. Robert Craig Allen, Aug. 14, 1976; children: Jeffrey, Gregory, Stacy. BA magna cum laude, Calif. State U., Northridge, 1974; MEd summa cum laude, U. Nev., Las Vegas, 1987. Cert. tchr., Nev. Tchr. phys. edn., jr. varsity basketball coach Beverly Hills (Calif.) Unified Sch. Dist., 1975-78; tchr. secondary phys. edn. Clark County Sch. Dist., Las Vegas, 1978-89, elementary tchr. phys. edn., 1989—, basketball coach, 1988-89; adj. instr. U. Nev., Las Vegas, 1993—; mem. phys. fitness task force Clark County Sch. Dist., 1990-91, integrated curriculum task force, 1992-93; mem. Nev. State Dept. Edn. com. to set stds. for phys. edn. tchr. licensure, 1993; presenter workshops, 1990-94. Author phys. fitness and multicultural games publs.; mem. editl. bd. Teaching Elem. Phys. Edn., 1995—. Coach Nev. State Youth Soccer Orgn., Las Vegas, 1988-91, Am. Youth Soccer Orgn., 1992; eucharistic min. St. Thomas More Cath. Ch., Las Vegas, 1991—; core leader for youth group, Las Vegas, 1994-95. Jr. League Nev. grantee, 1991. Mem. NEA, AAHPERD, Nev. Alliance Health, Phys. Edn., Recreation and Dance (membership chair 1993-94, v.p. elect. 1994-95), U.S. Phys. Edn. Assn., Phi Kappa Phi. Office: Whitney Elem Sch 5005 Keenan Ave Las Vegas NV 89122-7461

ALLEN, VICKY, business development technical specialist; b. Springfield, Pa., May 27, 1957; d. James Joseph and Ann Marie (Cifone) Cattafesta; m. James Francis DeLeone, Aug. 11, 1979 (div. 1982); m. Dennis Ronald Allen, June 30, 1990; 1 child, Amber. BBA in Computer Sci., Temple U., 1979. Quality assurance Burroughs Corp., Downingtown, Pa., 1977, software QA, 1978, systems analyst, 1979-81; program analyst Crocker Internal Systems, San Jose, Calif., 1981-83; sr. systems analyst Avantek, Inc., Santa Clara, Calif., 1983-84; bus. devel. tech. specialist Micro Focus, Palo Alto, Calif., 1984—; programmer cons. Fin. Group, Palo Alto, 1985-86. Active Sierra Club. Mem. Phi Sigma Sigma (sec. 1978-79). Democrat. Roman Catholic. Office: Micro Focus 2465 E Bayshore Rd Ste 400 Palo Alto CA 94303-3205

ALLEN, WILLIAM MERLE, university administrator, educator; b. San Luis Obispo, Calif., Oct. 9, 1939; s. Lloyd Marion and Berwyn Rose (Palmer) A.; m. Janet Laurentine Clayton, June 11, 1963; children: Barbara, Gregory. BA in Chemistry, La Sierra Coll., 1961; PhD in Organic Chemistry, U. Md., 1967. From instr. to asst. prof. chemistry Andrews U., Berrien Springs, Mich., 1966-68; from asst. prof. to assoc. prof. chemistry Loma Linda U., Riverside, Calif., 1968-84; sr. v.p. acad. adminstrn. So. Coll. Seventh Day Aventists, Collegedale, Tenn., 1984-87; dean grad. sch. Loma Linda U., 1987-88; dir. ctr. lifelong learning, world mus. natural history La Sierra U., Riverside, 1988—; chair chemistry dept. Loma Linda U., 1971-79, dir. divsn. natural sci., 1977-81; sec., trustee So. Coll. Seventh Day Adventists, 1984-87; bd. dirs. Inst. Global Leadership. Trustee Smyrna Hosp., Atlanta, 1986-87. Mem. Riverside C. of C., LaSierra Divsn. C. of C. (bd. dirs. 1991-93). Republican. Office: La Sierra U 4700 Pierce St Riverside CA 92515-8247

ALLENDER, NANCY G., corporate turnaround specialist, commercial print broker; b. Eugene, Oreg., May 30, 1957; d. Marvin Loren and Leslie Marie (Ramsey) A. BS in Adminstrn., Oreg. State U., 1979; postgrad., Ariz. State U., 1979, Rockhurst U., Kansas City, Mo., 1983. Asst. gen. mgr./player-coach Dallas Diamonds, Women's Basketball League, 1979-80; circulation asst. Dallas Cowboys, NFL, 1979-82; season ticket mgr., asst. mktg. dir. Kansas City (Mo.) Kings, NBA, 1982-84; sales mgr. Northwest Web, Eugene, Oreg., 1984-86; pres., owner NGA & Assocs., Portland, Oreg., 1986-90; turnaround workout cons. Hamstreet and Co., 1990—; asst. coach Women's Pro-Am Summer League, Garland, Tex., 1979-80; basketball coach NBA Summer/Winter Youth Prog., Kansas City, 1982-83. Big sister Y-Round Table Big Bro./Sister, Corvallis, 1975-79; track ofcl. Spl. Olympics, Tempe, Ariz., 1979; bd. vols. Scottish Rite Hosp. for Crippled Children, Dallas, 1981; coordinator Autistic Soc. for Children, Dallas, 1979-82;

Teens & Co. Theater Prodn., Planned Parenthood, 1995; participant animal assistance therapy Oreg. Humane Soc., 1995. Recipient Tex. Disting. Svcs. award, State of Tex., 1981. Mem. NAFE, NOW, Oreg. State U. Alumni Assn., Kappa Alpha Theta (Panhellenic del.), Sigma Chi, Delta Chi. Republican. Office: NGA & Associates PO Box 987 Lake Oswego OR 97034-0109

ALLERY, KENNETH EDWARD, air force officer; b. Holyoke, Mass., Mar. 3, 1925; s. Alfred Edward and Anne (Millen) A.; m. Constance DuFresne, June 22, 1946; children—Katherine Ann, Kenneth Scott, Bryan Keith, David Edward. B.A., Park Coll., 1965; M.S., George Washington U., 1969; grad., Air Command and Staff Coll., 1961, Nat. War Coll., 1969. Commd. 2d lt. U.S. Army Air Force, 1944; advanced through grades to brig. gen. U.S. Air Force, 1972; insp. with Insp. Gen. Team 17th Air Force; exec. officer, ops. officer 526th Fighter Interceptor Squadron, Ramstein Air Base, Germany, 1961; sr. Air Force adviser Oreg. Air N.G., Portland Internat. Airport, 1965-67; dir. ops. and tng. 1st Air Force, Stewart AFB, N.Y., 1967-68; mem. N.Am. br. Directorate Plans and Programs, Orgn. Joint Chiefs of Staff, 1969-71; asst. dep. chief of staff for plans Aerospace Def. Command, Ent AFB, Colo., 1971-72; asst. dep. chief of staff for plans N.Am. Air Def. Command/Continental Air Def. Command, 1972-73, asst. dep. chief of staff for ops., 1973-74; also dep. chief of staff for ops. Aerospace Def. Command; command insp. gen. NORAD/CONAD/ADC, 1974-76; ret.; asst. to v.p. Syscon Corp., Colorado Springs, 1976-85; bus. devel. mgr. Litton Computer Services, Colorado Springs, 1985—; bd. govs. Nat. Coll., Colorado Springs, 1993-94. Decorated D.S.M., D.F.C., Air medal with 4 oak leaf clusters, Meritorious Service medal with oak leaf cluster, Air Force Commendation medal. Home: 1320 Rangely Dr Colorado Springs CO 80921-2692 Office: Litton Computer Svcs 985 Space Center Dr Ste 204 Colorado Springs CO 80915-3638

ALLGOWER, EUGENE LEO, mathematics educator; b. Chgo., Aug. 11, 1935; s. Eugene and Martha (Kettner) A.; m. Solveig Allgower, Aug. 30, 1958; 1 child, Chris. BS in Math., Ill. Inst. Tech., 1957, MS in Math., 1959, PhD in Math., 1964. Prof. math. Colo. State U., Fort Collins, 1966—. Co-author: (with K. Georg) Numerical Continuation Mehods, 1990, Computational Solution of Nonlinear Systems, 1990; editor: (with H.O. Peitgen) Numerical Solution of Nonlinear Systems, 1981; (with K. Bohmer and M. Golubitsky) Bifurcation and Symmetry, 1992; (with K. Georg and R. Miranda) Exploiting Symmetry, 1993; contbg. writer to SIAM Rev. Alexander V. Humboldt Found. sr. fellowship, Bonn, Germany, 1988-89. Mem. Am. Math. Soc., Soc. for Indsl. and Applied Math. Office: Colo State Univ Dept Math Fort Collins CO 80523

ALLIN, ROBERT CAMERON, obstetrician and gynecologist; b. Evanston, Ill., Sept. 29, 1938; s. Frank Cameron and June Barber A.; m. Joann Elaine Spencer, Sept. 20, 1969; children: Blake Cameron, Kimberly June. BA, Northwestern, 1960, MD, 1964. Diplomate Am. Bd. of Obstetrics and Gynecology. Intern Highland Gen. Hosp., Oakland, Calif., 1964-65; resident Santa Clara Valley Med. Ctr., San Jose, Calif., 1967-70; med. staff Hawaii Permanente Med. Group, Honolulu, 1970-82; pvt. practice Honolulu, 1982—. Capt. USMC, 1965-67, Vietnam. Mem. Am. Coll. Obstetrics and Gynecology, Hawaii Med. Assn., Hawaii County Med. Assn. Republican. Club: Outrigger Canoe. Home: 1452 Kamole St Honolulu HI 96821-1422

ALLING, ABIGAIL KINGSLEY, scientist, biosphere system executive; b. N.Y.C., Oct. 12, 1959; d. Charles Booth and Abigail Parsons (McMaster) A.; 1 child, Christopher. Student sea semester, Boston U., 1977; grad. in organic chemistry with honors, Harvard U., 1979; grad. in zoology lab. with honors, Cambridge (Eng.) U., 1981; BA in Biology with honors, Middlebury Coll., 1982; MS in Environ. Studies with honors, Yale U., 1985; postgrad., George Mason U., 1991—, George Mason U. Project coord. Cetacean Seas Rsch., Lincoln, Mass., 1985, Oceanic Rsch. and Comm. Alliance, 1987; project dir., RV heraclitus, expedition chief Expedition to Circumnavigate S.Am., 1987-89; dir. marine sys. Space Biospheres Ventures, 1985-94, assoc. dir. R&D, 1991-94, dir. devel., 1992-94, asst. v.p. biospheric devel., 1993-94; pres., dir. Planetary Coral Reef Found., Belize, 1991—; exec. v.p., dir. Cyberspheres, Inc., 1994—; pres. Ocean Expeditions Inc., 1985-93; sci. chief, marine sys. mgr. Biosphere 2, 1991-93. Author: Life Under Glass, 1994; contbr. articles to sci. jours. Recipient Internat. Cetacean Soc. award, 1982; Thomas J. Watson fellow, 1981, N.Y. Explorers Club fellow, 1993-94. Home: 32038 Caminito Quieto Bonsall CA 92003-4305

ALLINGTON, KARBY KAY, dietitian; b. Champaign, Ill., May 22, 1961; d. Preston K. and Etta Mae (Courtney) Martin; m. Steven Proctor Allington, July 23, 1983; children: Kelsy Preston, Clifford John. BS in Nutrition, U. Tex., 1983. Registered dietitian. Clin. dietitian Harborview Med. Ctr., San Diego, 1983-86; nutritionist LaJolla (Calif.) Eating Disorders Clinic, 1986-87; cons. dietitian in pvt. practice, San Diego, 1986-91; spa dietitian La Costa (Calif.) Hotel and Spa, 1987-89; nutrition instr. San Diego Mesa Coll., 1990-91; cons. dietitian Ft. Collins, Colo., 1991—; hospice dietitian Hospice of Larimer County, Ft. Collins, 1994—. Author, contbg. editor Christian Parenting Today, 1993—. Home: 1536 Preston Trail Fort Collins CO 80525

ALLISON, ANDREW M., foundation administrator; b. Long Beach, Calif., May 21, 1949; s. Howard C. and Wilma A. (Franks) A.; m. Kathleen L. Anderson, May 28, 1971; children: Rebecca, Nathan, Joanna, Spencer, Jacob, Camilla. AA, Glendale (Ariz.) C.C., 1972; BA in History, Brigham Young U., 1974; PhD of Polit. Sci., Coral Ridge U., 1993. Cert. secondary tchr., Ariz., Utah. Adminstrv. staff, editor Brigham Young U., Provo, Utah, 1972-74; adminstrv. asst. LDS Ch., Salt Lake City, 1977-79; prin., tchr. LDS Seminaries, Ariz.,Utah, 1974-77, 79-80; assoc. editor, art dir. Bookcraft Publs., Salt Lake City, 1983-85; dir. rsch. and publs. Nat. Ctr. for Constl. Studies, Salt Lake City, 1980-83, 85-91; chmn., pres. Nat. Ctr. for Constl. Studies, West Jordan, Utah, 1991-95; product devel. editor Deseret Book Co., Salt Lake City, 1995—. Author: The Real Thomas Jefferson, 1982, The Real Benjamin Franklin, 1983, The Real George Washington, 1991; contbr. articles to profl. jours. Mem. Phi Kappa Phi.

ALLISON, LAIRD BURL, business educator; b. St. Marys, W.Va., Nov. 7, 1917; s. Joseph Alexander and Opal Marie (Robinson) A.; m. Katherine Louise Hunt, Nov. 25, 1943 (div. 1947); 1 child: William Lee; m. Genevieve Nora Elmore, Feb. 1, 1957 (dec. July 1994). BS in Personnel and Indsl. Relations magna cum laude, U. So. Calif., 1956; MBA, UCLA, 1958. Chief petty officer USN, 1936-51, PTO; asst. prof. to prof. mgmt. Calif. State U., L.A., 1956-83; asst. dean Calif. State U. Sch. Bus. and Econs., L.A., 1971-72, assoc. dean, 1973-83, emeritus prof. mgmt., 1983—; vis. asst. prof. mgmt. Calif. State U., Fullerton, 1970. Co-authored the Bachelors degree program in mgmt. sci. at Calif. State U., 1963. Mem. U.S. Naval Inst., Navy League U.S. Ford Found. fellow, 1960. Mem. Acad. Mgmt., Inst. Mgmt. Sci., Western Econs. Assn. Internat., World Future Soc., Am. Acad. Polit. Social Sci., Calif. State U. Assn. Emeriti Profs., Calif. State U. L.A. Emeriti Assn. (program v.p. 1986-87, v.p. adminstrn. 1987-88, pres. 1988-89, exec. com. 1990-91, treas. 1991—), Am. Assn. Individual Investors, Am. Assn. Ret. Persons, Ret. Pub. Employees Assn. Calif. (chpt. sec. 1984-88, v.p. 1989, pres. 1990-92), Am. Legion, Phi Kappa Phi, Beta Gamma Sigma, Alpha Kappa Psi. Home: 2176 E Bellbrook St Covina CA 91724-2346 Office: Calif State U Dept Mgmt 5151 State University Dr Los Angeles CA 90032-4221

ALLISON, LOYETTE E., construction company executive; b. Delano, Calif., July 7, 1946; d. Dempsey Willard and Billie Wanda (Fink) Bogard; m. Robert Lee, Nov. 30, 1963; children: Cindy Kay, Ann Rena. Photography student Northwestern U., 1963 student Pima Coll., 1979, U. Denver, 1983; AA in Gen. Edn. Pima Coll., 1995; postgrad. U. Ariz., 1995—. Sales mgr. K-Mart, Tucson, 1975-78; clk.-typist Fairfield Green Valley, Ariz., 1978-81; purchasing agt. Tobin Homes, Tucson, 1981-83; constrn. mgr. Fairfield La Cholla Hills, Tucson, 1983-86; v.p. ops. Fairfield Sunrise, 1986-91, Fairfield Pusch Ridge, 1989, Fairfield comml. divsn.; spkr. in field. Notary public State of Ariz; civic leader on behalf of women and community. Recipient Persuasive Comm. award Dept. Real Estate State of Ariz., 1989, Women on the Move Leadership award YMCA, Citizens for a Sound Economy award. Mem. Nat. Assn. Female Execs., Am. Bus. Inst. (2000 notable women). Baptist. Avocations: stock car racing; aerobics, modern dance. Home: 2151 W Felicia Pl Tucson AZ 85741-3101

ALLISON, LYNN DEE, university program administrator, consultant; b. Long Beach, Calif., July 22, 1948; d. Herbert Jesse and Jean Mavis (Ellis) Neff; m. Michael Joseph Allison, Dec. 16, 1967 (div. Oct. 1978); children: Leland Michael, William Joseph. AA, Long Beach (Calif.) City Coll., 1976; BA, Calif. State U., Long Beach, 1986, MPA, 1992. Adminstrv. asst. to gen. ptnr. Little & Gray, Inc., Irvine, Calif., 1978-82; bookkeeping cons. Trafalgar Tours West, Inc., Irvine, Calif., 1982-83; adminstrv. asst. Ctr. Multicultural/Multilingual Rsch. U. So. Calif., L.A., 1986; adminstrv. coord. for grad. nursing Calif. State U., Long Beach, 1985-87, adminstrv. asst. to the dean Sch. Bus. Adminstrn., 1987-89, acting faculty and staff coord. Sch. Bus. Adminstrn., 1989-92, fiscal officer Ocean Studies Inst., 1992—. Mem. ASPA, Golden Key Honor Soc., Phi Kappa Phi. Office: Calif State U Long Beach Ocean Studies Inst 820 S Seaside Ave San Pedro CA 90731-7330

ALLISON, TERRY LANE, librarian; b. Ft. Worth, Oct. 2, 1955; s. Franklin D. and Betty (Burnett) A. AB, U. Calif., Berkeley, 1977, M Libr. and Info. Sci., 1983; MA in Comparative Lit., U. Calif., San Diego, 1992, postgrad., 1993-95. Libr. asst. Gen. Libr. U. Calif., Berkeley, 1977-83; libr. I-II N.Y. Pub. Libr., Rsch. Librs., N.Y.C., 1983-86; asst. then assoc. libr. Ctrl. Libr. U. Calif.-San Diego, La Jolla, 1986-91; collections libr. Calif. State U., San Marcos, 1991—; statewide senator Acad. Senate-Calif. State U., Long Beach, 1994—. Contbr. to books: Gay and Lesbian Literature, 1994, Recruiting, Educating and Training Librarians for Collection Development, 1994. Mem. ALA (chair program planning com., gay and lesbian task force 1992-94), MLA, Popular Culture Assn. Democrat. Office: Calif State U Libr Svcs San Marcos CA 92096-0001

ALLISON, WILLIAM ROBERT, management consultant; b. Newport, Vt., Feb. 4, 1941; s. William Hugh and Eva Marie (Herbert) A.; m. Linda Kay Jarrett, Aug. 13, 1962 (div. Nov. 1974); children: Cherie Louise Allison Coughlin, William Robert Jr.; m. Joan Marie Lisowski, Aug. 4, 1979; 1 child, Donna Marie. BS in Bus. and Psychology, La Roche Coll., 1981. Foreman RCA Computer Systems, Palm Beach Gardens, Fla., 1965-67; mgr. tng. and adminstrn. RCA Computer Systems, Marlboro, Mass., 1967-72; dir. tng. Fruehauf Corp., Detroit, 1972-73; mgr. tng. and edn.automotive ops. Rockwell Internat., Troy, Mich., 1973-76, mgr. personnel adminstrn., 1977-79; mgr. mgmt. succession planning corp. Rockwell Internat., Pitts., 1979-81, dir. exec. resources, 1981-82, dir. orgn. planning, 1982-85; dir. mgmt. and orgn. planning Rockwell Internat., El Segundo, Calif., 1985-88, v.p. orgn. and human resources planning, 1988-91; mgmt. cons. William Allison & Assocs., Rancho Palos Verdes, Calif., 1991—, Blue Marble Ptnrs., Torrance, Calif., 1994—; corp. bd. advisors Nat. Coun. of La Raza, Washington, 1988-91; bd. advisors MESA, Berkeley, Calif., 1989-91; bd. dirs. Couns. Roundtable So. Calif., 1992—, chmn., 1995—. Served with USAF, 1961-65. Mem. N.Am. Coun. on Mgmt. and Orgn. (conf. bd.), Am. Soc. Human Resources Mgmt., Human Resources Planning Soc., Va. Country Club of Long Beach, Calif. (bd. dirs. 1991-93). Republican. Roman Catholic.

ALLMAN, CLESSON DALE, air force officer; b. Erie, Pa., Feb. 27, 1952; s. Frank C. and Josephine N. (Nye) A.; m. Laura L. Mathews Dec. 31, 1983 (div. 1992). Cert. hotel adminstr. Commd. 2d lt. USAF, 1974; advanced through grades to lt. col., 1991; ops. officer N.E. Commissary Complex, Air Force Commissary Svc., Hanscom AFB, Mass., 1979-80; strategic missile flight comdr. 742d Strategic Missile Squadron, Minot AFB, N.D., 1980-82; wing self-inspection program mgr. 91st Strategic Missile Wing, Minot AFB, 1982-84; food svc. officer 437th Svcs. Squadron, Charleston AFB, S.C., 1984-85; comdr. 43d Svcs. Squadron, Andersen AFB, Guam, 1985-87; dir. resource mgmt. Pacific region HQ Air Force Commissary Svc., Hickam AFB, Hawaii, 1987-89; exec. officer HQ Air Force Commissary Svc., Kelly AFB, Tex., 1989-91; subsistence dir. HQ U.S. Ctrl. Command Air Forces, Riyadh, Saudi Arabia, 1990-91; comdr. 3415th Morale, Welfare, Recreation and Svcs. Squadron, Lowry AFB, Colo., 1991-94; dir. product svcs and mktg. Def. Pers. Support Ctr. Pacific, Alameda, Calif., 1994-95; cmdr. Def. Pers. Support Ctr. Pacific, Alameda, 1995—. Decorated Bronze Star. Mem. VFW, Am. Legion, Air Force Assn., KQED. Presbyterian. Home: 18409 Carlwyn Dr Castro Valley CA 94546-2029 Office: Def Pers Support Ctr Pacific 620 Central Ave Alameda CA 94501-3874

ALLMAN, JOHN MORGAN, neurobiology educator; b. Columbus, Ohio, May 17, 1943. BA, U. Va., 1965; PhD, U. Chgo., 1970. Asst. prof. biology Calif. Inst. Tech., Pasadena, 1974-77, assoc. prof., 1977-84, prof., 1984, Hixon prof. psychobiology, 1989—. Grantee NIH, 1974—. Mem. Soc. for Neurosci. Office: # 216-76 Calif Inst Tech Pasadena CA 91125

ALLRED, EUGENE LYLE, physician, educator, small business owner; b. Glendale, Calif., Dec. 29, 1949; s. Linville H. and Earlene (Campbell) A.; m. Margaret C. Petersen, Sept. 2, 1973; children: Ryan, Jason, Kyle. BA summa cum laude, U. Calif., Santa Barbara, 1972; MD, U. So. Calif., L.A., 1976. Emergency physician Siskiyou Hosp., Yreka, Calif., 1979—; owner Adventure Whitewater, Ashland, Oreg., 1981—; dir. Mountain Med. Seminars, Ashland, 1982—. Lt. USPHS, 1976-78. Mem. Wilderness Med. Soc. (founder), Audubon Soc. (founder Marble Mountain chpt. 1982), Phi Beta Kappa. Republican. Home: 352 Terrace St Ashland OR 97520-3002 Office: Mountain Med Seminars PO Box 321 Yreka CA 96097-0321

ALLRED, RUEL ACORD, education educator; b. Spring City, Utah, Mar. 30, 1929; s. Reid Henderson and Anna Elizabeth (Acord) A.; m. Betty Brown Best, Sept. 3, 1954; children: Anita, Chad R., Lynette, Eileen, Brent B., Marie, Reid R. AA, Snow Jr. Coll., Ephraim, Utah, 1949; BS in Elem. Edn. with honors, Brigham Young U., 1954, MS in Pers. and Guidance with honors, 1958; EdD in Elem. Edn., U. Oreg., 1965. Elem. sch. tchr. Provo City (Utah) Sch. Dist., 1958-61; elem. tchr. lab. sch. Brigham Young U., Provo, 1961-62, writer curriculum materials lab. sch., 1962-63, prin. elem. lab. sch., 1963-64, clin. instr. elem. edn., 1965-66, asst. prof., 1966-68; assoc. prof., 1968-73; prof. Brigham Young U., Provo, Utah, 1963-94, prof. emeritus, 1994—; grad. coord. elem. edn., 1971-78; assoc. dean coll. edn. Brigham Young U., Provo, 1988-92; prof. emeritus, 1994; test adminstr. Provo City Sch. Dist., 1958; vis. prof. U. Mo., St. Louis, 1966, U. Ala., Anchorage, 1974, 76; cons. in field, 1967—. Author: Spelling: The Application of Research Findings, 1977, Spelling Trends, Content, and Methods, 1984, 2nd edit., 1987; co-author: The Sucher-Allred Reading Placement Inventory, 1972, 2nd edit., 1981, Continuous Progress in Spelling: An Individualized Spelling Program, 1972, 2nd edit., 1977, 3rd edit., 1982, Keys to Spelling Mastery: A Basal Spelling Program for Schools: Grades 1-8, 1984, Micrrospell: A Comprehensive Computer Spelling Program for Schools: Grades 2-8, 1984, AEC Spelling: A Spelling Program for the Home: Grades 2-8, 1984, The Computer and Education, 1984, 2nd edit., 1991, McGraw Hill Spelling Grades 1-8, 1990. Missionary Netherlands Mission LDS Ch., 1949-52; mission pres. Belgium Antwerp Mission LDS Ch., 1978-81; bd. dirs. Provo City Libr., 1984-89. Lt. USAF, 1955-57, Japan. Recipient Disting. Svc. award Brigham Young U. Alumni Assn., 1976, Karl G. Maeser Disting. Teaching award, 1977; Outstanding Alumnus award Snow Coll., 1988. Mem. Phi Kappa Phi. Mem. LDS Ch. Home: 1067 Grand Ave Provo UT 84604-3009

ALLSWANG, JOHN MYERS, computer science educator, historian; b. Chgo., Jan. 16, 1937; s. Eugene Allen and Katherine (Myers) A.; m. Suzanne Menzel, Dec. 19, 1964; children: Eden, Yael. BA, U. Ill., 1959; MA, U. Iowa, 1960; PhD, U. Pitts., 1967. Instr. No. Ill. U., Dekalb, 1965-66; asst. prof. No. Mich. U., Marquette, 1966-68; prof. Calif. State U., Los Angeles, 1968—, chair, 1992—; vis. prof. Hebrew U., Jerusalem, 1971-72, U. Leiden, The Netherlands, 1977-78. Author: California Initiatives and Referendums, 1912-1990, 1992, Bosses, Machines and Urban Voters, 1986, Physician's Guide to Computers, 1985, New Deal and American Politics, 1978, House for All Peoples, 1972. Dir. Calif. Direct Democracy Project. IBM fellow, 1968; recipient Merit award Calif. State U., Los Angeles, 1985, 86, 87, 88, 89. Mem. Orgn Am. Historians, Am. Hist. Assn. Democrat. Jewish. Home: 2438 La Condessa Dr Los Angeles CA 90049-1222 Office: Calif State U 5151 State University Dr Los Angeles CA 90032-4221

ALLUMBAUGH, BYRON, grocery company executive. Student, Long Beach, Calif., City Coll. Dir. meat ops. Ralph's Grocery Co., Compton, Calif., from 1958, v.p. store ops., 1967-69, exec. v.p., then pres.; chmn., CEO Ralph's Grocery Co., 1976—. Office: Ralph's Grocery Co 1100 W Artesia Blvd Compton CA 90220-5108*

ALMON, WILLIAM JOSEPH, data processing company executive; b. St. Louis, Nov. 22, 1932; s. Daniel Joseph and Louise Frances (Norder) A.; m. Susan Elizabeth Moore, June 11, 1955; children: William Joseph Jr., Rosemary, Jane, Philip, Patricia. BS, U.S. Mil. Acad., 1954; postgrad., Georgetown U., 1959-64. Commd. 2d lt. U.S. Army, 1954, advanced through grades to 1st lt.; resigned, 1958; salesman IBM, St. Louis, 1958-65; dir. IBM, Gaithersburg, Md., 1965-69; exec. asst. to pres. IBM, Armonk, N.Y., 1969-78; v.p. IBM, San Jose, Calif., 1978-89; pres., chief oper. officer Conner Peripherals, San Jose, 1989—; bd. govs. Electronics Industries Assn., Washington, 1991—. Bd. dirs. The Tech. Ctr., San Jose, 1990—. Republican. Roman Catholic. Home: 1031 The Old Dr Pebble Beach CA 93953-2508 Office: Conner Peripherals 3081 Zanker Rd San Jose CA 95134-2127

ALMOND, JOAN HARWOOD ELKINS, photographer; b. L.A., June 3, 1935; d. Benjamin and Jeanne (Yourell) Harwood; m. George W. Elkins Jr., June 12, 1954 (dec. 1969); children: George W. III, Tracy Ann Elkins Stoker, Timothy J., Chris H. Solo exhbns. include Saiyde Bronfman Ctr., Montreal, 1987, Tekeyan Cultural Ctr., Montreal, 1988, Manougian Cultural Ctr., Detroit, 1989, Soc. Contemporary Photography, Kansas City, 1992, Nile Gallery, Cairo, 1992, Schatten Gallery, Atlanta, 1993, Brooks Inst. Photography, Santa Barbara, Calif., 1994; group exhbns. include Internat. Design Ctr., Montreal, 1988, U. Judaism, L.A., 1990, Jacob Javits Conv. Ctr., N.Y., 1991; permanent pub. collections include Bernaissance Mus., Montreal, and other pvt. collections; photographer: (films) Killing of a Chinese Bookie, The Disappearence, Opening Night, Every Person is Guilty, The Burning Book, Ups and Downs, Captive Heart, The Dance Goes On; (theatre) Knives, Lovestreams; also featured in numerous articles. Studio: PO Box 954 Malibu CA 90265-0954

ALMORE-RANDLE, ALLIE LOUISE, special education educator; b. Jackson, Miss., Apr. 20; d. Thomas Carl and Theressa Ruth (Garrett) Almore; m. Olton Charles Randle, Sr., Aug. 3, 1974. BA, Tougaloo (Miss.) Coll., 1951; MS in Edn., U. So. Calif., L.A., 1971. Recreation leader Pasadena (Calif.) Dept. Recreation, 1954-56; demonstration tchr. Pasadena Unified Schs., 1956-63; cons. spl. edn. Temple City (Calif.) Sch. Dist., 1967; supr. tchr. edn. U. Calif., Riverside, 1971; tchr. spl. edn. Pasadena Unified Sch. Dist., 1955-70, dept. chair spl. edn. Pasadena High Sch., 1972—; also adminstrv. asst. Pasadena High Sch., 1993—; supr. Evelyn Frieden Ctr., U. So. Calif., L.A., 1970; mem. Coun. Exceptional Children, 1993—. Organizer Northwest Project, Camp Fire Girls, Pasadena, 1963; leader Big Sister Program, YWCA, Pasadena, 1966; organizer, dir. March on The Boys' Club, the Portrait of a Boy, 1966; pub. souvenir jours. Women's Missionary Soc., AME Ch., State of Wash. to Mo.; mem. NAACP, Ch. Women United, Afro-Am. Quilters L.A. Recipient Cert. of Merit, Pasadena City Coll., 1963, Outstanding Achievement award Nat. Coun. Negro Women, Pasadena, 1965, Earnest Thompson Seton award Campfire Girls, Pasadena, 1968, Spl. Recognition, Outstanding Community Svc. award The Tuesday Morning Club, 1967, Dedicated Svc. award AME Ch., 1983, Educator of Excellence award Rotary Club of Pasadena, 1993, Edn. award Altadena NAACP, 1994; named Tchr. of Yr., Pasadena Masonic Bodies, 1967, Woman of the Yr. for Community Svc. and Edn., Zeta Phi Beta, 1992; grad. fellow U. So. Calif., L.A., 1970. Mem. NAACP (bd. mem., chmn. ch. workers com. 1955-63, Fight for Freedom award West Coast region 1957, NAACP Edn. award Altadena, Calif. chpt. 1994), ASCD, Calif. Tchrs. Assn., Nat. Coun. Negro Women, Phi Delta Gamma (hospitality chair 1971—), Alpha Kappa Alpha (membership com.), Phi Delta Phi (founder, organizer 1961). Democrat. Mem. AME Ch. Home: 1710 La Cresta Dr Pasadena CA 91103-1261

ALONZO, R. GREGORY, professional speaker; b. San Bernadino, Calif., Apr. 9, 1954; s. Rudy and Remi (Vicente) A. BA, Pitzer Coll., Claremont, Calif., 1980. Dir. programs P.T. Bina, Jakarta, Indonesia, 1980-84; v.p. sales PacTel, Cypress, Calif., 1984-89; prof. sales trainer R. Gregory Alonzo Unltd., Brea, Calif., 1989—. Mem. Nat. Speakers Assn., Profl. Speakers Network, Internat. Platform Assn. Democrat. Roman Catholic. Office: R Gregory Alonzo Unltd 8502 E Chapman Ave Ste 184 Orange CA 92669

ALPERT, DEIRDRE WHITTLETON, state legislator; b. N.Y.C., Oct. 6, 1945; d. Harry Mark and Dorothy (Lehn) Whittleton; m. Michael Edward Alpert, Jan. 1, 1964; children: Lehn, Kristin, Alison. Student, Pomona Coll., 1963-65; LLD (hon.), Western Am. U., 1994. Mem. from 78th dist. Calif. State Assembly, Sacramento, 1990—; chairwoman Women's Legislators Caucus, Sacramento, 1993; active Calif. Tourism Commn., Sacramento, 1990—, Calif. Libr. Allocations Bd., Sacramento, 1993—. dist. rep., troop leader Girl Scouts Am., San Diego, 1977-83; spl. advocate Voices for Children, San Diego, 1982-90; mem. bd. Solana Beach (Calif.) Sch. Bd., 1983-90, also pres.; pres. beach and county guild United Cerebral Palsy, San Diego, 1986. Recipient Legis. award Calif. Regional Occupation Program, 1991-92, Am. Acad. Pediats., 1991-92, San Diego Psychol. Assn., 1993-94, Commitment to Children award Calif. Assn. for Edn. of Young Children, 1991-92, Legis. Commendation award Nat. Assn. for Yr.-Round Edn., 1991-92, State Commn. on Status of Women, 1993-94; named Friend of Yr., Children's PKU Network, 1991-92, Woman of Yr., Nat. Women's Polit. Caucus San Diego, 1991-92, Orgn. for Rehab. through Tng., 1993-94, Legislator of Yr., Am. Electronics Assn., 1991-92, 1993-94, Calif. Sch.-Age Consortium, 1993-94, Women of Distinction, Soroptimists Internat. of La Jolla, 1993-94, Assemblymember of Yr., Calif. Assn. Edn. Young Children, 1993-94. Mem. Charter 100 of San Diego, Calif. Elected Women's Assn. for Edn. and Rsch. (v.p. 1994—). Democrat. Mem. Congregation Ch. Office: 1350 Front St Ste 6013 San Diego CA 92101-3607

ALPINE, ANDREW ELLIOT, publisher; b. N.Y.C., Feb. 5, 1944; s. Mack and Mildred (Shanbron) A.; m. Lisa McCreery, May 16, 1982; 1 child, Galen Mark. BA, Bklyn. Coll., 1964; JD, MS of Internat. Affairs, Columbia U., 1968. Cons. IRM Inc., N.Y.C., 1970-73; economist Secretariat Office of UN, N.Y.C., 1971; dir. Briarpatch Network, San Francisco, 1973-80; pub. Common Ground, San Anselmo, Calif., 1974—, Splty Travel Index, San Anselmo, 1979—. Editor: Adventure Vacation Catalog, 1986. Vol. Ctr. for Attitudinal Healing, Tiburon, Calif., 1993. Home: 404 Oakcrest Rd San Anselmo CA 94960-1257 Office: Splty Travel Index/Common Ground 305 San Anselmo Ave San Anselmo CA 94960

ALSADI, AKEEL, economist, consultant, educator; b. Baghdad, Iraq, Apr. 23, 1936; came to U.S., 1966; s. Hany Saeed and Nouria Jasim (Altimimi) A.; m. Maria Rosillo Rodriguez Alvarez de Toledo, Feb. 18, 1973. BA in Bus. and Econs. with Honors, U. Baghdad, 1962; MA in Econs., U. Southern Calif., 1969, PhD in Econs., 1972. Asst. adminstr. Civil Svc. Commn., Baghdad, 1958-62; lectr., head stats. lab. Coll. Econs. U. Baghdad, 1962-67; lectr., econs. and stats. Univ. Coll., Baghdad, 1964-67; lectr. U. So. Calif., L.A., 1969-71; asst. prof. Calif. State U., San Diego, 1971; cons. pub. fin. devel. planning The World Bank-Mission to Malaysia, Washington, 1972-73; economist The World Bank, Washington, 1973-80; proj. dir., chief technical advisor Food & Agrl. Orgn. of UN, Islamabad, Pakistan, 1983-84; cons. economist pvt. practice, Monterey, Calif., 1980—; real estate broker; lectr. in field. Author: (textbook) Applications of Statistics, 1965; contbr. reports, articles and reviews to profl. jours. Mem. Am. Econs. Assn., Western Econs. Assn., Assn. for Comparative Econ. Studies, The 1818 Soc., U. So. Calif. Nation's Capital Alumni Assn., Omicron Delta Epsilon, Phi Beta Kappa. Home and Office: 984 Portola Dr Monterey CA 93940-5512

ALSAKER, ROBERT JOHN, information systems specialist; b. Los Angeles, June 15, 1945; s. Lauris Ronald and Hazel Mildred (Danz) A.; m. Cynthia Ann Gillesvog, Feb. 25, 1984; children: Troy R., Erik G., Karlee A. AA, Fullerton (Calif.) Jr. Coll., 1966; BS, Moorhead (Minn.) State Coll., 1970. Project mgr. Jet Propulsion Lab., Pasadena, Calif., 1970-80; mgr. mgmt. info. systems Kroy Inc., Scottsdale, Ariz., 1980-85; adminstr. City of Pasadena, 1985-86; mgr. tech. cons. U.S. West Info. Systems, Phoenix, 1986-88; v.p. MIS ACB Cos., Phoenix, 1988-95; dir. MIS Midwest Pub., Inc., Phoenix, 1995—. Served in U.S. Army, 1968-69, Vietnam. Republican. Lutheran. Office: 10844 N 23d Ave Phoenix AZ 85029

ALSCHULER, FRED H., lawyer; b. L.A., Nov. 18, 1949; s. Walter Woodrow and Selma L. (Morris) A.; m. Lidia E. Lozano, Jan. 13, 1985; children: Alexander Reagan, Rebecca Elizabeth, Vanessa Renee. BA in Philosophy summa cum laude, UCLA, 1971, JD, 1975. Bar: Calif. 1976. Assoc. Walter W. Alschuler, L.A., 1975-77; ptnr. Solish, Jordan & Weiner, L.A., 1977-78, Alschuler, Alschuler, Alschuler & Alschuler, L.A., 1979-93;

pvt. practice L.A., 1994—. Author: Discovery in Products Liability, 1987. Sec. Mt. Washington (Calif.) Coop., 1991-92. Mem. ABA, ATLA, Calif. Pub. Defenders Assn., Calif. Trial Lawyers Assn., Calif. Attys. for Criminal Justice, L.A. Trial Lawyers Assn., Phi Beta Kappa. Office: PO Box 41556 Los Angeles CA 90041-0556

ALSPACH, BRIAN ROGER, mathematics educator; b. Minot, N.D., May 29, 1938; s. Eugene Victor A. and Dolores Elaine (Barke) Kennedy; m. Linda Jo Nelson, June 14, 1978 (div.); children: Alina Rae, Mark Cameron; m. Katherine Anne Heinrich, Jan. 1, 1980. BA, U. Wash., 1961; MA, U. Calif., Santa Barbara, 1964, PhD, 1966. Asst. prof. Simon Fraser U., Burnaby, B.C., Can., 1966-73, assoc. prof., 1973-80, prof. math., 1980—; bd. editors Jour. Graph Theory, Discrete Math., Amsterdam, The Netherlands, Ars Combinatoria, Winnipeg, Man., Can., Can. Jour. Math. and Can. Math. Bull., Toronto, Ont., Can., 1989—. Editor: Algorithmic Aspects of Combinatorics, 1977, Cycles in Graphs, 1985; contbr. articles to profl. jours. Natural Scis. Engring Rsch. Coun. Can. grnatee, 1966—. Mem. Am. Math. Soc., Math. Assn. Am., Can. Math. Soc., Combinatorics Math. Soc. Australasia. Office: Simon Fraser U, Dept Math, Burnaby, BC Canada V5A 1S6

ALSTON, LELA, state senator; b. Phoenix, June 26, 1942; d. Virgil Lee and Frances Mae Koonse Mulkey; B.S., U. Ariz., 1967; M.S., Ariz. State U., 1971; children—Brenda Susan, Charles William. Tchr. high sch., 1968—; mem. Ariz. State Senate, 1977—. Named Disting. Citizen, U. Ariz. Alumni Assn., 1978. Mem. NEA, Ariz. Edn. Assn., Am. Home Econs. Assn., Ariz. Home Econs. Assn., Am. Vocat. Assn. Methodist. Office: Ariz State Sen State Capitol Phoenix AZ 85007-2812

ALSTROM, SVEN ERIK, architect; b. Emporia, Kans., July 27, 1951; s. William E. and Willa M. (Russell) A.; m. Lynn M. Mathews, June 22, 1974 (div. June 1983). B. Gen. Studies, U. Kans., 1975; student evening div. U. Denver Coll. Law, 1984. Registered architect, Calif., Colo., Kans., Mo., N.Mex.; cert. Nat. Council Archtl. Registration Bds. Architect, PGAV Architects, Kansas City, Mo., 1972-74, Horner Blessing, Kansas City, 1977-79, MSFS Architects, Kansas City, 1979-80, Marshall & Brown, Kansas City, 1980-81, Urban Design, Denver, 1981-82, Dominick Assocs., Denver, 1983-84; with C. Welton Anderson & Assocs., Aspen, Colo., 1989-90; pvt. practice Alstrom Group, Aspen, 1990—. Mem. AIA, Colo. AIA, Denver AIA, Am. Zone. Presbyterian. Home: PO Box 551 Aspen CO 81612-0551 Office: Alstrom Group 312 F Aspen Airport Business Ctr Aspen CO 81611

ALTER, EDWARD T., state treasurer; b. Glen Ridge, N.J., July 26, 1941; s. E. Irving and Norma (Fisher) A.; m. Patricia R. Olsen, 1975; children: Christina Lyn, Ashly Ann, Darci Lee. B.A., U. Utah., 1966; M.B.A., U. Utah, 1967. C.P.A., Calif., Utah. Sr. acct. Touche Ross & Co., Los Angeles, 1967-72; asst. treas. U. Utah, Salt Lake City, 1972-80; treas. State of Utah, Salt Lake City, 1981—; pres. Nat. Assn. State Treas., 1987-88. Bd. dirs. Utah Housing Fin. Agy., Utah State Retirement Bd., pres., 1984-93; mem. Utah State Rep. Ctrl. Com., 1981—, Anthony Com. on Pub. Fin., 1988-92. Sgt. USAR, 1958-66. Named to All-pro Govt. Team, City and State Mag., 1988; recipient Jesse M. Uhruh Award for Svc. to State Treas.', 1989. Mem. Am. Inst. CPAs, Nat. Assn. State Treas. (past sr. v.p., pres. 1987), Delta Sigma Pi, Delta Phi Kappa. Club: Utah Bond (pres. 1981-82). Office: State Capitol 215 State Capitol Building Salt Lake City UT 84114-1202

ALTER, GERALD L., real estate executive; b. Rensselaer, Ind., Aug. 24, 1910; s. Leslie and Lettie (Willis) A.; m. Margaret A. Davis, Sept. 15, 1939; children: Judith Ann (dec.), John Edward. Student Bus. Coll., 1927-28. Clk. and office mgr., 1929-35; bldg. contractor, 1936-45; with U.S. Army, 1945-46; real estate broker, 1946—; officer Torrance Police Res., 1948-63; pres. Alter Realty & Ins., Leads, Inc., investments, Alter Ins. Agy., Inc., REMCO Real Estate Mgmt. Co., Alter Devel. Co.; pres. Developers & Builders. Planning commr. City of Torrance, 1966-83, chmn. Torrance Planning Commn. 1982-83; water commr. City of Torrance, 1982-91, chmn. 1987-88; former bd. dirs. Harbor Area United Way. Mem. Torrance-Lomita-Carson Bd. Realtors (pres. 1978, v.p. 1980-81), Calif. Assn. Realtors (dir. 1978-81), Nat. Assn. Realtors, Torrance C. of C. (past dir.), Am. Legion, Rotary (recipient Torrance Rotary 36 yr. perfect attendance pin 1994). Republican. Clubs: OX-5 (pioneer airman). Home: 1337 Engracia Ave Torrance CA 90501-2603 Office: 2305 Torrance Blvd Torrance CA 90501-2520

ALTFELD, MERWIN RICHARD, artist, educator; b. Elyria, Ohio, Sept. 19, 1913; s. Otis Charles and Kate Gertrude (Klein) A.; m. Mildred Frances Kirschbaum, June 23, 1936; children—Linda Voorsanger, Pamela Malone. B.A., Case Western Res. U., 1934; postgrad. UCLA, 1966-68. Cert. tchr., Calif. One-man shows: Calif. State U., Sacramento, 1978, SUNY, Alfred, 1979, Nylander Mus., Caribou, Maine, 1979; Loyola U., New Orleans, 1980, Santa Monica Library (Calif.), 1983; Senior Eye, Long Beach, Calif. 1984; group shows include: San Diego Mus., 1963, Swedish Mus., Stockholm, 1972, Nat. Acad. Design, N.Y.C., 1972, Watercolor U.S.A., Springfield, Mo., 1973, 88, 90, 92, 95, Palm Desert Mus., Palm Springs, Calif., 1974, San Diego Internat., 1981, 84, 85, 93, 94; represented in permanent collections: Queen Mary ship, Long Beach, Calif., Brugger Collection, Los Angeles; gen. mgr. Ford's Drug Stores, Buffalo, 1940-47; owner Merwin R. Altfeld & Assocs., Los Angeles, 1948-86. Active Jewish Big Bros., Los Angeles, 1965-74; hon. mem. Long Beach (Calif.) Mus., 1986—; bd. dirs. Artists for Ednl. Action, Los Angeles, 1978-82. Recipient Am. Traditional awards, 1955; Santa Monica ann. award, 1964; Delmar ann. graphics award 1964; Westwood ann. award, 1963, Nat. Watercolor Soc. award, 1974, San Diego Internat. Silver award, 1994. Mem. Los Angeles Contemporary Art Gallery, (bd. dirs., pres. 1989, 90), Westwood Centre of Arts (pres. 1965), Hollywood Press Club, Hollywood Media Assn. Nat. Watercolor Soc. (pres. 1972). Home: 18426 Wakecrest Dr Malibu CA 90265-5621

ALTHEIMER, BRIAN P. See TUTASHINDA, ABD KARIM KWELI

ALTMAN, ADELE ROSENHAIN, radiologist; b. Tel Aviv, Israel, June 4, 1924; came to U.S., 1933, naturalized, 1939; d. Bruno and Salla (Silberzweig) Rosenhain; m. Emmett Altman, Sept. 3, 1944; children: Brian R., Alan L., Karen D. Diplomate Am. Bd. Radiology. Intern Queens Gen. Hosp., N.Y.C., 1949-51; resident Hosp. for Joint Diseases, N.Y.C., 1951-52, Roosevelt Hosp., N.Y.C., 1955-57; clin. instr. radiology Downstate Med. Ctr., SUNY, Bklyn., 1957-61; asst. prof. radiology N.Y. Med. Coll., N.Y.C., 1961-65, assoc. prof., 1965-68; assoc. prof. radiology U. Okla. Health Sci. Ctr., Oklahoma City, 1968-78; assoc. prof. dept. radiology U. N.Mex. Sch. Medicine, Albuquerque, 1978-85. Author: Radiology of the Respiratory System: A Basic Review, 1978; contbr. articles to profl. jours. Fellow Am. Coll. Angiology, N.Y. Acad. Medicine; mem. Am. Coll. Radiology, Am. Roentgen Ray Soc., Assn. Univ. Radiologists, Radiol. Soc. N.Am., B'nai B'rith Anti-Defamation League (bd. dirs. N.Mex. state bd.), Hadassah Club.

ALTMAN, DREW E., foundation executive; b. Boston, Mar. 21, 1951; s. George and Harriet A.; m. Pamela Koch; children: Daniel, Jessica. BA magna cum laude, Brandeis U., 1973; MA, Brown U., 1974; PhD in Polit. Sci., MIT, 1983. Postdoctoral fellow, rsch. assoc. Harvard U. Sch. Pub. Health, Boston, 1975-76, 78-80; prin. rsch. assoc. Codman Rsch. Group, Boston, 1976-80; spl. asst. office of adminstr. Health Care Fin. Adminstrn. Dept. HHS, Washington, 1979-81; v.p. Robert Wood Johnson Found., Princeton, N.J., 1981-86; commr. N.J. Dept. Human Svcs., Trenton, 1986-89; program dir. health and human svcs. The Pew Charitable Trusts, Phila., 1989-90; pres., CEO Henry J. Kaiser Family Found., Menlo Park, Calif., 1990—. Contbr. articles to profl. jours. Mem. Inst. of Medicine, Nat. Acad. of Soc. Ins., Assn. for Health Svcs. Rsch. Office: Henry J. Kaiser Found Quadrus 2400 Sand Hill Rd Menlo Park CA 94025-6941

ALTMAN, IRWIN, psychology educator; b. N.Y.C., July 16, 1930; s. Louis L. and Ethel (Schonberg) A.; m. Gloria Seckler, Jan. 2, 1953; children: David Gary, William Michael. BA, NYU, 1951; MA, U. Md., 1954, PhD, 1957. Asst. prof. psychology Am. U., Washington, 1957-58, sr. rsch. scientist, assoc. prof., 1960-62, adj. prof., 1962-69; rsch. scientist in human scis. Arlington, Va., 1958-60; rsch. psychologist Naval Med. Rsch. Inst., Bethesda, Md., 1962-69; adj. prof. U. Md., 1968-69; prof. U. Utah, Salt Lake City, 1969-79, chmn. dept. psychology, 1969-76, dean Coll. Social and Behavioral Scis., 1979-83, v.p. for acad. affairs, 1983-87, disting. prof., 1987—. Author: (with J.E. McGrath) Small Groups, 1966, (with D.A. Taylor) Social Penetration, 1973, Environment and Social Behavior, 1975, (with M.Chemers) Culture and Environment, 1980, (with J. Wohlwill) Human Behavior and Environment: Vol. I, 1976, Vol. II, 1977, Vol. III, 1978, Vol. IV, 1980, Vol. V, 1981, Vol. VI, 1983, Vol. VII, 1984, (with C. Werner) Vol. VIII, 1985, (with A. Wandersman) Vol. IX, 1987, (with E. Zube) Vol. X, 1989, (with K. Christensen) Vol. XI, 1990, (with S. Low) Vol. XII, 1992, (with A. Churchman) Women and the Environment, Vol., XIII, 1994, (with D. Stokols) Handbook of Environmental Psychology, Vols. I & II, 1987; mem. editorial bds.: Small Groups, 1970-79, Man-Environment Systems, 1969-73, Jour. Applied Social Psychology, 1973-85, Sociometry, 1973-76, Environment and Behavior, 1975, Jour. Personality and Social Psychology, 1974-83, Contemporary Psychology, 1975-86, Environ. Psychology and Nonverbal Behavior, Psychology, 1976-90, Am. Jour. Community Psychology, 1978-81, Population and Environment, 1979, Jour. Environ. Psychology, 1982, Computers and Human Behavior, 1985, Internat. Jour. Applied Social Psychology, 1984, Communication Monographs, 1992-95; assoc. editor Am. Jour. Community Psychology, 1988-92; co-editor Jour. of Eviron. Psychology, 1990—; contbr. articles to profl. jours. 1st lt. Adj. Gen. Corps, AUS, 1954-56. Mem. APA (pres. divsn. population and environment), AAAS, Soc. Exptl. Social Psychology, Soc. Psychol. Study of Social Issues, Soc. Personality and Social Psychology (pres.), Environ. Design Rsch. Assn., Am. Psychol. Soc.

ALTMAN, JACK, plant pathologist, educator. BS in Plant Pathology, Rutgers U., 1954, PhD, 1957. Grad. rsch. fellow Squibb Inst. Rutgers U., 1954-57; asst. prof., plant pathologist Colo. State U., 1957-63, assoc. prof., plant pathologist, 1963-70, prof., plant pathologist, 1970—; head symposium sect. on soil fumigation Internat. Congress Soil Disinfestation, Brussels, 1973; leader Plant Pathology Delegation, Peoples Rep. China, 1986, Internat. Plant Pathology Delegation, Sweden, Russia, Yugoslavia, Germany, 1989; head plant pathology lab. Dier Allah Expt. Sta., Jordan, 1987. Author, editor: Pesticide Interactions in Crop Production: Beneficial and Deleterious Effects, 1993; contbr. articles to sci. jours.; rsch. on interaction of pesticides in plant disease complexes. Recipient Sr. U.S. Scientist Alexander von Humboldt award Hannover Tech. U., 1977-78, 93; Peoples Rep. China and Nat. Acad. of Sci. Disting. Scholar Exch. program, 1981; Sr. Rural Agrl. fellow Res. Bank Australia, 1988. Mem. Am. Phytopathological Soc., Internat. Soc. Plant Pathology, Soc. Nematologists, Sigma Xi. Office: Colo State U Dept Plant Path Weed S Fort Collins CO 80523

ALTMAN, LEONARD CHARLES, physician; b. Fresno, Calif., Sept. 1, 1944; s. Martin and Ida (Sharnoff) A.; m. Gaylene M. Bouska, Dec. 26, 1970; children: Jonathan David, Matthew Charles, Katherine Ann. BA, U. Pa., 1965; MD, Harvard U., 1969. Diplomate Am. Bd. Internal Medicine, Am. Bd. Allergy and Immunology, Nat. Bd. Med. Examiners. Intern, resident U. Wash. Affiliated Hosps., Seattle, 1969-71; sr. rsch. assoc. NIDR/NIH, Bethesda, Md., 1971-74; chief med. resident Harborview Med. Ctr., Seattle, 1974-75, chief allergy divsn., 1979—; asst. prof. medicine U. Wash., Seattle, 1975-79, assoc. prof. medicine, 1979-85, clin. assoc. prof. medicine, 1985-88, clin. prof. medicine, affiliate prof. environ. health, 1988—; ptnr. N.W. Asthma and Allergy Ctr., Seattle, 1985—; reviewer Alaska Soc. Tech. Found. Editor: Clinical Allergy and Immunology, 1984, Autoimmune Diseases, 1993; mem. editl. bd. Infection and Immunity; contbr. articles to profl. jours. Lt. col. USPHS. Mem. ACP, Am. Acad. Allergy and Clin. Immunology, Am. Assn. Immunologists, Am. Fedn. for Clin. Rsch., Am. Soc. for Microbiology, Clin. Immunology Soc., Infectious Disease Soc. Am., King County Med. Soc. (environ. health com. chmn. 1987—), Western Soc. for Clin. Rsch., Wash. State Med. Assn., Wash. State Soc. of Allergy and Immunology (sci. program com. chmn., v.p., pres.), Reticuloendothelial Soc., Puget Sound Allery Soc. (pres. 1977), N.W. Allergy Forum (sci. program com. chmn.), Physicians Bur. King County (adv. com., rep. on allergy), Seattle Acad. Internal Medicine, Alpha Epsilon Delta, Alpha Omega Alpha. Office: NW Asthma & Allergy Ctr Ste 200 4540 Sand Point Way NE Seattle WA 98105

ALTMAN, SHELDON, veterinarian; b. Denver, May 15, 1937; s. Sam Bernard and Bessie (Radetsky) A.; BS in Biol. Sci., Colo. State U., 1959, DVM, 1961; m. Arlene Barbara Heller, Aug. 23, 1959; children: Susan Wendy, Howard William, Eden Debra. With Newmark Animal Hosp., 1961-62, Lockhart Animal Hosp., 1964; founder, operator Universal City Pet Clinic, North Hollywood, Calif, 1965-70, merged with M.S. Animal Hosps., Inc., Burbank, 1970-94, v.p., 1970-94; with Vet. Ctrs. Am., 1994—; dir. vet. rsch. and cons. acupuncture rsch. project, pain control unit UCLA, 1975-80; hon. prof. Chinese Medicine U. Oriental Studies, Sch. Chinese Medicine, Los Angeles; mem. faculty Internat. Vet. Acupuncture Soc. Ctr. for Chinese Medicine. Author: An Introduction to Acupuncture for Animals; mem. editorial adv. bd. Calif. Veterinarian, Internat. Jour. Chinese Medicine; contbr. articles on vet. acupuncture to vet. jours.; contbg. author Veterinary Internal Medicine, 4th edit., Problems in Veterinary Medicine, Veterinary Acupuncture. Bd. dirs. Emek Hebrew Acad. Served with AUS, 1962-64. Mem. AVMA (conv. speaker 1982, 87), So. Calif., Calif. (co-chmn. com. on alternative therapies) vet. med. assns., Am. Animal Hosp. Assn., Am. Veterinarians for Israel (chpt. pres. 1972-73), Assn. Orthodox Jewish Scientists, Internat. Vet. Acupuncture Soc. (dir.), Ctr. for Chinese Medicine, Internat. Congress Chinese Medicine, Acupuncture Rsch. Inst., Colo. State U. Alumni Assn., Nat. Assn. Vet. Acupuncture (dir. rsch. 1976), Phi Kappa Phi, Phi Zeta, Beta Beta Beta. Jewish (pres. congregation 70-71, dir. 1964—). Home: 5647 Wilkinson Ave North Hollywood CA 91607-1629 Office: 2723 W Olive Ave Burbank CA 91505-4532

ALTO, RONALD LOUIS, marketing professional; b. Boston, July 24, 1949; married with two children. AS in Aero./A&P with honors, Wentworth Inst., 1969; BS in Aero./Flight with honors, Ariz. State U., 1971; postgrad., U. S.C., 1973-81, Allied Signal Schooling, 1981—. Cert. scuba diver. Flight instr. Tech Aero Svc., Bedford, Mass., 1971; airport mgr. flight ops. Logan Internat. Airport, Mass. Port Authority, Boston, 1972-73; aero. engr. devel. test and evaluation engring. GE Co., Lynn, Mass., 1973-74; field program engr. GE Co., Mojave, Calif., 1974-78; fligh propulsion integration mgr. GE Co., L.A., 1976-78; DC-10/CF6-6K cert. program mgr. GE Co., Evendale, Ohio, 1978-80; mgr. N.Am. comml. engine sales GE Co., Evendale, 1980-81; mgr. F109 and derivative sales Garrett Turbine Engine Co., 1981-85; dir. light helicoptor turbine engine co. bus. devel., v.p. internat. sales Allied Signal Aerospace, Phoenix, 1985—. 2d lt. USAF, 1971-72. Mem. AIAA, Am. Defense Preparedness Assn., Aircraft Owners & Pilots Assn., Am. Helicopter Soc., Army Aviation Assn., Assn. of U.S. Army, Planetary Soc., Regional Airline Assn.-U.S., European Regional Airlines Assn., Asian Aviation, Am. Ag Aviation Assn., Alpha Eta Rho (co-founder Alpha Sigma chpt.). Home: 1649 W Kiowa Ave Mesa AZ 85202-6506

ALTSCHUL, DAVID EDWIN, record company executive, lawyer; b. N.Y.C., Apr. 8, 1947; s. Norbert and Grace (Aderer) A.; m. Margaret Berne, July 4, 1969; children: Jonathan, Jared, Eric, Emily. BA summa cum laude, Amherst Coll., 1969; JD, Yale U., 1974. Bar: Calif. 1974. Law clerk U.S. Dist. Ct. Conn., Hartford, 1974-75; assoc. Tuttle & Taylor, Los Angeles, 1975-76, Pryor, Cashman, Sherman & Flynn, Beverly Hills, Calif., 1976-77, Hardee, Barovick, Konecky & Braun, Beverly Hills, 1977-79; prin. Rosenfeld, Kassoy & Kraus, Beverly Hills, 1979-80; dir. bus. affairs Warner Bros. Records, Inc., Burbank, Calif., 1980-83, v.p. bus. and legal affairs, 1983-88, sr. v.p. bus. and legal affairs, 1988-93, gen. counsel and sr. v.p. bus. affairs, 1993-95, vice chmn., 1995—; bd. dirs. Rec. Industry Assn. Am. Bd. dirs. Los Encinos Sch., Encinos, Calif., 1986—, treas., 1986-87, pres., 1987-92; bd. dirs. People for the Am. Way, 1991—, bd. dirs. exec. com., 1993—; bd. dirs. San Fernando Valley Neighborhood Legal Svcs., Inc., 1989-90. Mem. Phi Beta Kappa. Democrat. Jewish. Office: Warner Bros Records Inc 3300 Warner Blvd Burbank CA 91505-4632

ALTSHILLER, ARTHUR LEONARD, secondary education educator; b. N.Y.C., Aug. 12, 1942; s. Samuel Martin and Betty Rose (Lepson) A.; m. Gloria Silvern, Nov. 23, 1970 (div. 1975); m. Carol Heiser, Aug. 16, 1980. BS in Physics, U. Okla., 1963; MS in Physics, Calif. State U., Northridge, 1971. Elec. engr. Garrett Corp., Torrance, Calif., 1963-64, Volt Tech. Corp., Phoenix, 1965; engr., physicist Aerojet Gen. Corp., Azusa, Calif., 1966-68; elec. engr. Magnavox Rsch. Labs., Torrance, 1968-69; sr. engr. Litton Guidance & Control, Canoga Park, Calif., 1969; physics tchr. L.A. Unified Sch. Dist./Van Nuys Math/Sci. Magnet High Sch., 1971—; math. instr. Valley Coll., Van Nuys, Calif., 1986—; part-time physics and chemistry tchr. West Coast Talmudical Sem., L.A., 1978-88; foster tchr. Seti Inst. and NASA Ames Rsch. Ctr., 1994; coach Van Nuys (Calif.) H.S. Nat. Championship Sci. Bowl Team, 1995. Mesa Club sponsor Math.-Engring. Sci. Achievement L.A. High Sch. and U. So. Calif., 1984-87. Recipient Cert. of Honor Westinghouse Sci. Talent Search, 1990. Mem. AAAS, Am. Assn. Physics Tchrs., Nat. Coun. Tchrs. Math., N.Y. Acad. Scis., Am. Meteorol. Soc., So. Calif. Striders, Santa Monica Astron. Soc., United Tchrs. L.A. Home: 6776 Vickiview Dr Canoga Park CA 91307-2751 Office: Van Nuys High Sch 6535 Cedros Ave Van Nuys CA 91411-1506

ALVAREZ, ROBERT SMYTH, editor, publisher; b. San Francisco, June 7, 1912; s. Walter Clement and Harriet (Smyth) A.; m. Janet Crosby, Nov. 4, 1935; children: David Crosby, Robert Smyth, Nancy (Mrs. Eric Wallace). AB, U. Chgo., 1934, PhD, 1939; BSLS, U. Ill., 1935. Dir. Brockton (Mass.) Public Library, 1941-43, Nashville Public Library, 1946-59, Berkeley (Calif.) Public Library, 1959-61, South San Francisco Public Library, 1966-80; Editor, pub. Libr. Adminstrs. Digest (formerly Adminstrs. Digest), 1965—, Bus. Info., 1969—, Supt.'s Digest, 1977-88; pres. Adminstrs. Digest Press, Foster City, Calif., 1987—; tchr. public library adminstrn. George Peabody Coll., Nashville, 1946-59; library cons., surveyor. Author: Qualifications of Public Library Directors in North Central States, 1943, Library Boss, 1987, Library Log, 1991; pub. Business Books Buying Guide, 1990—; contbr. articles to profl. jours. Chmn. Boy Scouts Am., North San Mateo County, 1973. Named Boss of Year Nashville Secs. Assn., 1958, Citizen of Year, South San Francisco, 1976. Mem. Sequoia Swimming and Tennis Club (organizer), Glendale Club (Nashville), Reliez Valley Country Club (Pleasant Hill, Calif.) (organizer), Calif. Golf Club (South San Francisco), Rotary (pres. South San Francisco 1979-80), Phi Gamma Delta. Episcopalian. Home: 719 San Miguel Ln Foster City CA 94404-3722 Office: PO Box 993 South San Francisco CA 94083

ALVARI, KIMBERLEE ANN, dietitian; b. Parsons, Kans., Jan. 10, 1960; d. Eric H. and Nancy Ann (Shumaker) Vollmer; m. Richard B. Alvari, May 24, 1986; children: Bryce, Danielle. AA with highest honors, Cabrillo Coll., Aptos, Calif., 1981; BS magna cum laude, Calif. Poly. U., 1984. Registered dietitian; cert. nutrition support dietitian. Nutrition cons. Saga Foods, Spokane, Wash., 1984-85; dietitian U. Calif., San Francisco, 1987-88, The OptiFast Program, Fremont, Calif., 1990-92, Home Health Plus, San Leandro, Calif., 1990-93, Washington Hosp., Fremont, 1988—; vol. Am. Heart Assn., Oakland, Calif., 1994; guest speaker Cable Channel 13, Fremont, 1988; cons. Bayhill Athletic Club, Milpitas, Calif., 1988. Author, editor: Nutritional Information for Persons with AIDS, 1988. Mem. Am. Dietetic Assn. (sports and cardiovascular practice group), Am. Soc. for Parenteral and Enteral Nutrition. Christian. Office: 2000 Mowry Ave Fremont CA 94538-1716

ALVES, CAROL ANN, administrative assistant; b. Salem, Oreg., July 10, 1947; d. Elver John and Virginia Alexina (French) Owings; m. James William Alves, July 21, 1989. Student, Inst. Applied Sci., 1972, Chemeketa C.C., 1982. Clk. typist Oreg. State Police Criminal Divsn., Salem, 1966-68; data entry operator Oreg. State Police Data Processing Divsn., Salem, 1968-70; fingerprint technician Oreg. State Police Bur. Criminal Identification, Salem, 1970-85, clerical specialist, 1985-89; recs. clk. San Bernardino (Calif.) County Sheriff, 1989; office asst. Hesperia (Calif.) City Clks. Office, 1989-93, Hesperia Animal Control, 1993-95; planning commn. sec., 1995—. Columnist: Yesterday's Tomorrows, 1992—, Lightsabre, 1992—. Vol. San Bernardino County Mus., Redlands, Calif., 1994; dir., southwest regional rep. Sci. Fiction Mus., 1991—. Mem. Coun. British Socs., Costumers Guild West, Jedi Knights (v.p. 1990-92). Office: Sci Fiction Mus PO Box 18091 Salem OR 97305

ALVI, KHISAL AHMED, chemist; b. Karachi, Pakistan, Mar. 15, 1958; came to U.S., 1989; s. Wisal Ahmed Alvi and Abida Begum; m. Tanvir Sultana, July 4, 1989; children: Rida, Rohail. BS with honors, U. Karachi, 1981, MS, 1983, PhD, 1987. Rsch. asst. U. Southhampton, Eng., 1988-89; postdoctoral rsch. fellow U. Calif., Santa Cruz, 1989-92; rsch. scientist PANLABS, Inc., Bothell, Wash., 1993—; presenter in field. Contbr. articles to profl. jours. Spl. predoctoral scholar U. Grant Commn. Pakistan, 1986, postdoctoral scholar U. Calif. Cancer Rsch. Coordinating Com., 1989. Mem. Am. Chem. Soc., Am. Soc. Pharmocognosy, Pakistan Chem. Soc. Office: PANLABS Inc 11804 N Creek Pky Bothell WA 98011

ALWAN, AMEEN, writing educator; b. Damascus, Syria, July 6, 1930; came to U.S., 1930; s. Muneer and Fausya (Zimberkji) A.; m. Georgia Joy Hueber (div. 1992); 1 child, Yasmine. Student, NYU; BA, Mexico City Coll., Mexico, 1957, postgrad. Writing tchr. through workshops, 1974—; poet-in-residence L.A. Ctr. Enriched Studies, 1980—. Contbr. poetry and transls. to numerous jours. With U.S. Army, 1952-54. Grantee Columbia U., 1975, L.A. Cultural Affairs Dept., 1993—; recipient Artist in Schs. award Calif. Arts Coun., 1980-81, 82-93. Home and Office: 992 N Madison Ave Pasadena CA 91104-3625

AMACK, LEWIS OWEN, lawyer; b. Evanston, Ill., July 26, 1951; s. Lester Gweynn and Lois Ilene (Trinrud) A. BA in Sociology, Northeastern Ill. U., 1973; MA in Sociology, U. Ill., 1977; MBA, Calif. State U., L.A., 1988; MA in Psychology, Calif. State U., 1993; JD, U. Wash., 1994. Teaching asst. Calif. State U., L.A., 1982-86; civil engr. City of L.A., 1986-87; chief auditor San Francisco VA Med. Ctr., 1987-88; fellow Rand Corp., Santa Monica, Calif., 1988-89; tech. cons. Intelligence Ware, L.A., 1990-91; cons. Santa Monica (Calif.) Hosp. Med. Ctr., 1992. Mem. Defenders of Wildlife, Cousteau Soc., Audubon Soc., World Wildlife Fund, Wilderness Soc., Sierra Club (outings leader 1984-90, chair conservation com. 1985-86), Environ. Law Soc. (chair 1993-94), Smithsonian Assocs. Home and Office: 11729 Riverside Dr Valley Village CA 91607

AMADO, HONEY KESSLER, lawyer; b. Bklyn., July 20, 1949; d. Bernard and Mildred Kessler; m. Ralph Albert Amado, Oct. 24, 1976; children: Jessica Reina, Micah Solomon, Gabrielle Beth. BA in Polit. Sci., Calif. State Coll., Long Beach, 1971; JD, Western State U., Fullerton, Calif., 1976. Bar: Calif. 1977, U.S. Dist. Ct. (ctrl. dist.) Calif. 1981, U.S. Ct. Appeals (9th cir.) 1981, U.S. Supreme Ct. 1994. Assoc. Law Offices of Jack M. Lasky, Beverly Hills, Calif., 1977-78; pvt. practice Beverly Hills, Calif., 1978—; lectr. in field. Contbr. articles to profl. jours. Mem. Com. Concerned Lawyers for Soviet Jewry, 1979-90; bd. dirs. Jewish Nat. Fund, L.A., 1990—, sec. L.A. region, bd. dirs. Sephardic Temple Tifereth Israel, 1991-94, Am. Jewish Congress, Jewish Feminist Ctr., 1992—; mem. Commn. on Soviet Jewry of Jewish Fedn. Coun. Greater L.A., 1977-83, chmn., 1979-81, commn. on edn., 1982-83, comty. rels. com., 1979-83. Mem. Calif. Women Lawyers (bd. govs. 1988-90, 1st v.p. 1989-90, jud. evaluations co-chair 1988-90), San Fernando Valley Bar Assn. (family law mediators and arbitrators planel 1983-94, judge pro-tem panel 1987-94), Beverly Hills Bar Assn. (family law mediators panel 1985-94), L.A. County Bar Assn. (family law sect., appellate cts. com. 1987—, chmn. subcom. to examine reorgn. Calif. Supreme Ct. 1990-94, judge pro tem panel 1985—, appellate jud. evaluations com. 1989—), Calif. State Bar. Democrat. Jewish. Office: 261 S Wetherly Dr Beverly Hills CA 90211-2515

AMADOR, TAMERA DIANE, nursing director; b. Pueblo, Colo., Dec. 27, 1958; d. Scott and Jessie Marie (Mirelez) Chadwick; m. Arthur Amador, Apr. 5, 1979 (div. Jan. 1983); 1 child, Sophia Lorraine. Diploma, L.A. County Sch. Nursing, 1985; BSN, Calif. State U., Long Beach, 1989; JD, Loyola Law Sch., 1994. RN; cert. pub. health nurse, Calif., respiratory therapist, emergency nurse, nurse administrator; Bar: Calif. 1994. From staff nurse to nurse dir. Dept. Emergency Medicine L.A. County and U. So. Calif. Med. Ctr., 1985—; legal extern L.A. City Atty's Office, 1994—; instr. Am. Heart Assn., 1991—; cons. Harrington, Foxx, Dubrow & Canter, L.A., 1992. 2d lt. USAR, 1987-95. Mem. Am. Assn. Nurse Attys., Emergency Nurses Assn. Republican. Office: LA County USC Med Ctr 1200 N State St Rm 1060 R Los Angeles CA 90033-4525

AMALFI, FREDERICK ANTHONY, limnologist; b. Rochester, N.Y., Feb. 8, 1950; s. Fred and Elizabeth Virginia (Biorde) A.; 1 child, James Anthony. BS in Biology, St. John Fisher Coll., Rochester, 1972; MS in Biology, U. Ariz., 1974; PhD in Botany, Ariz. State U., 1988. Sr. chemist

Pima County Wastewater Mgmt., Tucson, 1977-78; sr. pretreatment engr. Planning Rsch. Corp., Yuma, Ariz., 1979-81; lab. dir. North Am. Labs., Tempe, Ariz., 1981-82, Western Tech., Inc., Phoenix, 1982-84; teaching asst. Ariz. State U., Tempe, 1984-88; lab. dir. Aquatic Cons. & Testing, Inc., Tempe, 1988—; faculty assoc. Ariz. State U., Tempe, 1987-91; advisor Ariz. Lab. Adv. Com., 1992, tech. adv. State Ariz. Water Reuse Com. Contbr. articles to profl. jours. Soccer coach Tempe YMCA, 1978-88, cert. lake mgr. N. Am. Lake Mgmt. Soc. Recipient Award for Coll. Scientists ARCS Found., 1987; grantee Ariz. Water Resources Rsch. Ctr., 1991, Ariz. Disease Control, 1988. Mem. Water Environ. Fedn., Am. Water Wks. Assn., North Am. Lake Mgmt. Soc., Am. Water Resources Assn., Fla. Aquatic Lake Mgmt. Soc., Ariz.-Nev. Acad. Scis., Sigma Xi. Office: Aquatic Cons & Testing Inc # 106 1525 W University Dr Ste 106 Tempe AZ 85281-3280

AMAN, REINHOLD ALBERT, philologist, publisher; b. Fuerstenzell, Bavaria, Apr. 8, 1936; came to U.S., 1959, naturalized, 1963; s. Ludwig and Anna Margarete (Waindinger) A.; m. Shirley Ann Beischel, Apr. 9, 1960 (div. 1990); 1 child, Susan. Student, Chem. Engring. Inst., Augsburg, Germany, 1953-54; B.S. with high honors, U. Wis., 1965; Ph.D., U. Tex., 1968. Chem. engr. Munich and Frankfurt, Ger., 1954-57; petroleum chemist Shell Oil Co., Montreal, Que., Can., 1957-59; chem. analyst A. O. Smith Corp., Milw., 1959-62; prof. German U. Wis., Milw., 1968-74; editor, pub. Maledicta Jour., Maledicta Press Publs., Santa Rosa, Calif., 1976—; pres. Maledicta Press, Santa Rosa, 1976—; dir. Internat. Maledicta Archives, Santa Rosa, 1975—. Author: Der Kampf in Wolframs Parzival, 1968, Bayrisch-oesterreichisches Schimpfwoerterbuch, 1973, 86; gen. editor Mammoth Cod (Mark Twain), 1976, Dictionary of International Slurs (A. Roback), 1979, Graffiti (A. Read), 1977; editor Maledicta: The Internat. Jour. Verbal Aggression, 1977—, Maledicta Monitor, 1990—; contbr. articles to profl. jours. U. Wis. scholar, 1963-65; U. Wis. research grantee, 1973, 74; NDEA Title IV fellow, 1965-68. Mem. Internat. Maledicta Soc. (pres.), Am. Dialect Soc., Am. Name Soc., Dictionary Soc. N.Am. Home and Office: PO Box 14123 Santa Rosa CA 95402-6123

AMARI, KATHRYN JANE, elementary education educator; b. Sopris, Colo.; d. Thomas S. and Catherine (Ossola) Parker; m. Carl Leo Amari Sr., July 27, 1957; children: Jayne Amari Graham, Carl Leo Amari Jr. AA, Trinidad State Jr. Coll., 1951; BA, Western State Coll., 1954. Cert. tchr., Colo. Tchr. Valdez (Colo.) Elem. Sch., 1951-54, Trinidad (Colo.) Pub. Sch. Dist. #1, 1954-95; mem. lang. curriculum com., sch. improvement com. Contbr. articles to profl. mags. Mem. PTA, Trinidad, 1954-91. Mem. AAUW, Trinidad Edn. Assn. (sec. 1958-59), Colo. Edn. Assn. (rep. 1954-64), Trinidad State Jr. Coll. Alumni, Delta Kappa Gamma, Beta Sigma Phi. Democrat. Roman Catholic. Home: 307 S Spruce St Trinidad CO 81082-3536 Office: Park St Sch 612 Park St Trinidad CO 81082-2307

AMATO, CAROL JOY, writer, anthropologist; b. Portland, Oreg., Apr. 9, 1944; d. Sam Lawrence and Lena Dorothy (Dindia) A.; m. Neville Stanley Motts, Aug. 26, 1967 (div. 1978); children: Tracy, Damon. BA, U. Portland, 1966; MA, Calif. State U., 1986. Freelance writer, Westminster, Calif., 1969—; human factor cons. Design Sci. Corp., L.A., 1979-90; dir. software documentation Trans-Ed Communications, Westminster, 1980-84, pres. Advanced Profl. Software, Inc., Westminster, 1984-86, Systems Rsch. Analysis, Inc., Westminster, 1986-95, pres. Stargazer Pub. Co., Westminster, 1995—. Author: The Earth, 1992, Astronomy, 1992, The Human Body, 1992, Inventions, 1992, Inside Out: The Wonders of Modern Technologies Explained, 1992, 50 Nifty Science Fair Projects, 1993, The Super Science Project Book, 1994, The World's Easiest Guide to Using the APA, 1994; editor, Cultural Futuristics, 1975-80, numerous articles and short stories; participant in numerous radio and TV interviews. Sec. bd. dirs. Am. Space Meml. Found., L.A., 1986-87; bd. dirs. Orange County Acad. Decathalon, 1986-94. Mem. Ind. Writers of So. Calif. (bd. dirs. Orange County sect. 1986-93), Profl. Writers Orange County (bd. dirs. 1993—, pres. 1994—), Writers' Club of Whittier, Inc., Internat. Pen. Home: 10151 Heather Ct Westminster CA 92683-5754 Office: Stargazer Pub Co PO Box 2178 Westminster CA 92683

AMBERIADIS, KOSTAS G., electronics company executive; b. Serre, Greece, May 20, 1952; came to U.S., 1978; s. George and Athanasia (Sirpa) A; m. Dimitra Gousi, Feb. 24, 1990; 1 child, Athanasia. Diploma in Elec. Engring., U. Patras, Greece, 1975; MSc in Elec. Engring., Carleton U., Ottawa, Ont., Can., 1978; PhD in Elec. Engring., U. Minn., 1982. Rsch. asst. U. Minn., Mpls., 1978-83; mem. tech. staff David Sarnoff Rsch. Ctr., Princeton, N.J., 1983-86; staff engr. Siliconix Inc., Santa Clara, Calif., 1986-90; mgr. process integration LSI Logic, Milpitas, Calif., 1990-94; mgr. yield enhancement LSI Logic, Santa Clara, Calif., 1994—. Contbr. articles to profl. jours. and encys. Mem. IEEE (sr.), Greek Chamber of Engrs. Office: LSI Logic Inc 3115 Alfred St Santa Clara CA 95054-3305

AMBROSE, THOMAS CLEARY, communications executive; b. Kalispell, Mont., Mar. 6, 1932; s. William Patrick and Anne Marie (Cleary) A.; m. Joyce Leona Demco, Aug. 13, 1960; children: Thomas Neal, John Alan, Bridget Sharon. BA in Journalism, U. Mont., 1952. Editor Choteau (Mont.) Acantha, 1952; reporter Daily Chronicle, Spokane, Wash., 1954-57, bus. editor, 1957-64; rep., mgr. media rels. Weyerhaeuser Co., Tacoma, 1964-74, dir. external communications, 1974-91; prin. Ambrose & Assocs., Seattle and Sun Valley, 1991—. Author, editor: Where The Future Grows, 1989. Pres. Spokane Editorial Soc., 1963-64, Spokane Press Club, 1959-60; dir. Federal Way C. of C., 1968-71, Ketchum/Sun Valley Hist. Soc., 1995—. 1st lt. U.S. Army, 1952-54, Korea.

AMBROSIA, VINCENT GERARD, geographer and researcher; b. Chgo., July 19, 1956; s. Vincent Walter and June Marjorie (Morrissey) A.; m. Mary Ann Murray, Apr. 10, 1982; children: Rachael Louise, Caitlin Marjorie. BS, Carroll Coll., Waukesha, Wis., 1978; MS, U. Tenn., 1980. Rsch. scientist T.G.S. Tech., Moffett Field, Calif., 1980-89; remote sensing lab. scientist ATAC Inc., Moffett Field, 1989-92; rsch. scientist J.C.W.S., Inc., Moffett Field, 1992—; cons. VGA Cons., San Jose, 1989—. Mem. Assn. Am. Geographers (chmn. remote sensing com.), Nat. Coun. for Geog. Edn. (bd. dirs., mem. remote sensing com.), Gamma Theta Upsilon. Republican. Roman Catholic. Office: JCWS Inc MS 242-4 NASA Ames Rsch Ctr Moffett Field CA 94035

AMELIO, GILBERT FRANK, electronics company executive; b. N.Y.C., Mar. 1, 1943; s. Anthony and Elizabeth (DeAngelis) A.; m. Glenda Charlene Amelio; children: Anthony Todd, Tracy Elizabeth, Andrew Ryan; stepchildren: Brent Paul Chappell, Tina LaRae Chappell. B.S. in Physics, Ga. Inst. Tech., 1965, M.S. in Physics, 1967, Ph.D. in Physics, 1968. Tech. dir., cofounder Info. Sci., Atlanta, 1962-65; mem. tech. staff Bell Telephone Labs., Murray Hill, N.J., 1968-71; div. v.p., gen. mgr. Fairchild, Mountain View, Calif., 1971-83; pres. semiconductor products div. Rockwell Internat., Newport Beach, Calif., 1983-88; pres. communication systems Rockwell Internat., Dallas, 1988-91; pres., chief exec. officer Nat. Semicondr. Corp., Santa Clara, Calif., 1991—; mem. nat. adv. bd. Ga. Inst. Tech., Atlanta, 1981-87, Ga. Inst. Tech. Rsch. Inst., 1982-89; bd. dirs. SEMATECH Chiron Corp., Emeryville, Calif.; bd. dirs., chmn. Recticon, Pottstown, Pa., 1983-87. Patentee in field. Mem. chief exec. roundtable Univ. Calif., Irvine, 1985-89. Fellow IEEE (chmn. subcom. 1974-81, Masaru Ibuka consumer electronics award 1991); mem. Semiconductor Industry Assn. (bd. dirs. 1983—, vice chmn. 1992, chmn. 1994), Electronic Industries Assn. (bd. govs.), Nat. Assn. Mfrs. (bd. govs.), Bus. Higher Edn. Forum. Republican. Roman Catholic. Home: 13416 Middle Fork Ln Los Altos CA 94022-2420 Office: National Semiconductor Corp PO Box 58090 Santa Clara CA 95052-8090

AMEMIYA, TAKESHI, economist, statistician; b. Tokyo, Mar. 29, 1935; s. Kenji and Shizuko A.; m. Yoshiko Miyaki, May 5, 1969; children: Naoko, Kentaro. B.A., Internat. Christian U., 1958; M.A. in Econs., Am. U., 1961; Ph.D., Johns Hopkins U., 1964. Mem. faculty Stanford U., (Calif.), 1964-66, 68—, prof. econs., 1974-86, Edward Ames Edmonds prof. econs., 1986—; lectr. Inst. Econ. Research, Hitotsubashi U., Tokyo, 1966-68; cons. Author books and articles; mem. editl. bd. profl. jours. Recipient U.S. Sr. Scientist award Alexander von Humboldt Found., Fed. Republic Germany, 1988; Ford Found. fellow, 1963; Guggenheim fellow, 1975; NSF grantee; fellow Japan Soc. for Promotion of Sci., 1989. Fellow Econometric Soc., Am. Acad. Arts and Scis., Am. Statis. Assn.; mem. Internat. Statis. Inst., Am. Econ. Assn., Inst. Math. Stats., Phi Beta Kappa. Home: 923 Casanueva Pl Stanford CA 94305-1001 Office: Stanford Univ Dept of Econs Stanford CA 94305

AMEND, WILLIAM JOHN CONRAD, JR., physician, educator; b. Wilmington, Del., Sept. 17, 1941; s. William John Conrad and Catherine (Broad) A.; m. Constance Roberts, Feb. 3, 1962; children—William, Richard, Nicole, Mark. B.A., Amherst Coll., 1963; M.D., Cornell U., 1967. Diplomate Am. Bd. Internal Medicine. Asst. clin. prof. U. Calif. Med. Ctr., San Francisco, 1974-76; assoc. clin. prof. U. Calif. Med. Ctr., 1977-82, prof. clin. medicine and surgery, 1982—; physician Falmouth Med. Assocs., Mass. Contbr. articles to med. jours. Chmn. med. adv. com. No. Calif. Kidney Found., 1987-88; stewardship com. 1st Presbyn. Ch., Burlingame, Calif., 1983, 84, elder, 1982-85, 93—. Maj. U.S. Army, 1969-71. Simpson fellow, 1963; recipient Gift of Life award No. Calif. Kidney Found., 1994. Fellow ACP. Republican. Home: 2860 Summit Dr Burlingame CA 94010-6257 Office: U Calif Med Ctr 3D and Parnassus San Francisco CA 94143

AMER, KENNETH BENJAMIN, helicopter engineer; b. Bklyn., Mar. 23, 1924; s. Harry and Rose (Wolkow) Am; m. Hedie Ankle, Dec. 25, 1946; children: Harold, Les. B Aero. Engring., NYU, 1944; MS in Aero. Engring., MIT, 1947. Rsch. engr. NACA, Langley Field, Va., 1947-53; rsch. engr. Hughes Helicopters, L.A., 1953-60, mgr. tech. dept., 1960-85; chief scientist McDonnell Douglas Helicopter Co., L.A., 1985-86; helicopter cons. Rand Corp, Santa Monica, Calif., 1987—. Contbr. articles on helicopters to profl. jours.; patentee helicopter field. McDonnell Douglas Corp. engring. and rsch. fellow, 1986. Fellow Am. Helicopter Soc. (hon., Alexander Klemin award 1976). Home: 8025 Alverstone Ave Los Angeles CA 90045-1436

AMER, M(OHAMED) SAMIR, pharmacologist, researcher; b. Tanta, Egypt, Sept. 2, 1935; came to U.S., 1958; s. M.M. and Z.H. (Saad) A.; m. Laila E. El-Fatatry, June 21, 1958 (div. Sept., 1987); m. C. Marguerite Smith, Sept. 13, 1987; children: Amre S., Namay S., Mona S., Suzanne S. PhD in Pharmacology, U. Ill., Chgo, 1962; MS in Bus., Columbia U., 1980. Dir. biol. rsch. Bristol Myers Internat., N.Y.C., 1977-83; pres., prin. Sam Amer & Co., Inc., Santa Barbara, Calif., 1983—. Mem. Am. Soc. Pharm. Exptl. Therapy, Am. Soc. Biolog. Chemistry.

AMERMAN, JOHN W., toy company executive; b. 1932; married. BA, Dartmouth Coll., 1953, MBA, 1954. With Colgate-Palmolive Co., 1958-64, Warner-Lambert Co., 1965-80; v.p. Du Barry Cosmetics, 1971-72, v.p. internat. group, 1972-77, v.p. Am. Chicle div., 1977-79, pres. Am. Chicle div., 1979-80; pres. Mattel Internat., from 1980; chmn., CEO Mattel Inc., El Segundo, Calif., 1987—; also bd. dirs. Mattel Inc., Hawthorne, Calif.; bd. dirs. Unocal Corp. Served with U.S. Army, 1954-57. Office: Mattel Inc 333 Continental Blvd El Segundo CA 90245-5032*

AMES, LAWRENCE COFFIN, JR., investment counsellor; b. Oakland, Calif., July 27, 1925; s. Lawrence Coffin and Helen (Rodolph) A.; m. Beatrice Feer, Dec. 9, 1959 (div. 1971); children: Lawrence III, Catherine, Philip; m. Betty Mitchell, Aug. 1, 1973. BS, Stanford U., 1947. Investment counsellor Turrell & Dahl, San Francisco, 1962-68, Bank of Calif., San Francisco, 1968-71, Ames & Co., Piedmont, Calif., 1971—. Served to 1st lt. USAF, 1951-52. Club: Bohemian (San Francisco). Home and Office: PO Box 11277 Piedmont CA 94611-0277

AMES, MICHAEL MCCLEAN, university museum director, anthropology educator; b. Vancouver, B.C., Can, June 19, 1933; s. Ernest Oliver Francis and Elsie A.; children: Daniel J., Kristin Julia. BA with honors, U. B.C., 1956; PhD, Harvard U., 1961. Asst. prof. sociology McMaster U., Hamilton, Can., 1962-64; asst. prof. to full prof. of anthropology U. B.C., Vancouver, 1964—, dir. Mus. Anthropology, 1974—. Author: Museums, The Public and Anthropology, 1986, Cannibal Tours and Glass Boxes: The Anthropology of Museums, 1992; co-editor: Man-like Monsters on Trial, 1980; contbr. articles to profl. jours. Guggenheim fellow, 1970-71; Nat. Mus. Can. grantee, 1976—. Fellow Royal Soc. Can., Am. Anthrop. Soc., Can. Anthropology Soc., Soc. Applied Anthropology Can.; mem. Indian Sociol. Assn. Office: U BC Mus Anthropology, 6393 NW Marine Dr, Vancouver, BC Canada V6T 1Z2

AMES, NORMA HARRIET, wildlife consultant, writer; b. Buffalo, Aug. 17, 1920; d. Robert Martin and Flora Mary (Wiener) Knipple; m. Donald Fairbanks Ames, July 8, 1944 (div. 1956); 1 child, Karyn Roberta; m. Richard Allen Rasmussen, Dec. 20, 1991. BA, Smith Coll., 1942; postgrad., Wellesley Coll., 1942, U. Colo., 1964. Asst. chief game mgmt. N.Mex. Dept Game and Fish, Santa Fe, 1956-76, asst. chief pub. affairs, 1976-82; leader Mex. wolf recovery team U.S. Fish and Wildlife Service, 1979-91; wildlife cons. Santa Fe, 1982-87, Colville, Wash., 1988—; wolf breeder and researcher Rancho Ma'ii-tsoh, Santa Fe, 1971-87. Author: My Path Belated, 1970, Whisper in the Forest, 1971, (book revs.) Science Books and Films, 1970—; author/illustrator booklets, 1960-82; author/editor: New Mexico Wildlife Management, 1967 (conservation edn. award 1968);. Named Conservationist of Yr., Sta. KOB TV and Radio, Albuquerque, 1980; recipient Leopold Conservation award The Nature Conservancy, 1983. Mem. AAAS, The Nature Conservancy, Soc. for Conservation Biology, Defenders of Wildlife, Can. Nature Fedn., Nat. Wildlife Fedn., Am. Livestock Breeds Conservancy, Inland Empire Pub. Lands Coun., N.W. Rivers Coun., AK Wildlife Alliance, The Wildlife Soc. (cert.), Am. Soc. Mammologists, Sierra Club (lectr.), Nat. Audubon Soc. (lectr.), Phi Beta Kappa, Sigma Xi. Home and Office: Raven Spirit Ranch 2509 Aladdin Rd Colville WA 99114-9158

AMES, RICHARD GALYON, epidemiologist; b. Boston, June 2, 1935; s. Lawrence Marion and Willa Love (Galyon) A.; m. Sue Ann Roedell, June 19, 1971; 1 child, Andrea Elizabeth. BA, George Washington U., 1958; MA, Am. U., 1962; PhD, U. N.C., 1970; MPH, U. Calif., Berkeley, 1980. Instr. sociology U. So. Calif., L.A., 1965-67; asst. prof. sociology Syracuse (N.Y.) U., 1967-69; asst. prof. sociology Calif. State U., Hayward, 1969-71, assoc. prof., 1971-86, prof., 1986-87; epidemiologist, demographer NIOSH, Morgantown, W.Va., 1980-84; epidemiologist Calif. EPA, Berkeley, 1985—. Co-author: The Handicapped Children of Alamance County, 1965, Elementary Statistical Theory in Sociology, 1976; contbr. numerous articles to profl. jours. USPHS fed. trainee, Berkeley, 1979-80; So. Pacific Co., L.A., 1967, U.S. Forest Svc., Hayward, 1978-80. Mem. APHA. Home: 16872 Columbia Dr Castro Valley CA 94552-1614 Office: Calif EPA OEHHA 2151 Berkeley Way # 11 Berkeley CA 94704-1011

AMEY, RAE, television and video developer, producer; b. Shreveport, La., Sept. 26, 1947; d. Bruce Harold and Genevieve (Amey) Gentry; m. John E. Scarborough, Dec. 18, 1971 (div. Nov. 1979). Student, La. State U., 1968-70, U. Houston, 1972-74; BA in Liberal Arts, Antioch U., 1985; grad., U. So. Calif., 1988—. Freelance photographer Calif., 1973—; adminstrn. coord. Y.E.S. Inc., Sta. KCET-TV, L.A., 1980-83; freelande edtl. TV writer, cons. L.A., 1983-84; asst. to pres. prodn. So. Calif. Consortium, Cypress, 1984, project mgr., dir. devel., project dir. The Human Condition, 1985-87; v.p. devel. and outreach The California Channel, L.A., 1990-92, project dir., 1991, 92; pres. Video Nexus, L.A., 1987—. Editor TV guide book, 1985; photography exhbns. include: Contemporary Art Mus., Houston, 1973, Galveston (Tex.) Arts Ctr., 1975, Cameravision Gallery, L.A.,1980, Aloft, Pasadena, 1989. Co-founder Harbor Arts Alliance; mem., bd. dirs. African Am. Arts Coun.; founder, chair, bd. dirs. CIVICS: a video project for cmty. edn. and conversation, 1993—; advisor Congress on Racial Equality. Ellen Torgenson Shaw scholar Annenberg Sch. Communications, U. So. Calif., 1989. Mem. Women in Communications (bd. dirs., v.p. campus svcs. 1987-88, exec. v.p. 1988-89, bd. dirs. scholarship and edn. fund L.A. chpt.). Democrat. Home: 255 S Grand Ave Apt 2201 Los Angeles CA 90012-6017

AMICO, CHARLES WILLIAM, management consultant; b. Boston, May 6, 1942; s. William Charles and Marie Josephine (Nicholas) A. Assoc. in Engring., Franklin Inst., 1962; BS, Suffolk U., 1968. Jr. chem. technician Avco Corp., Lowell, Mass., 1963-64; advanced vacuum tech. technician Nat. Rsch. Corp., Newton, Mass., 1964-68; semicondr. engr. IBM, Essex Junction, Vt., 1968-72, semicondr. mfg. engring. mgr., 1972-76, mgmt. devel. cons., 1976-86; founder, pres., CEO Creative Directions, Inc., San Francisco, Burlington, Vt., 1982—; bd. dirs. Holiday Project, 1987-88. State chmn. Vt. Hugh O'Brian Youth Leadership Seminar; bd. dirs. Vt. Hugh O'Brian Youth Seminars, Inc., CEO, 1984-85; corp. pres. Hugh O'Brian Youth Found., No. Calif., 1994-95. Recipient Hugh O'Brian Outstanding State Chmn. in Nation award, 1984, 85. Office: Creative Directions Inc 2932 Pierce St San Francisco CA 94123-3825

AMIN, JAMILLAH MAARIJ (JOYCE MARIE JOSEPH), real estate agent, food technologist; b. Lake Charles, La., Jan. 11, 1947; d. Anthony Armo and Edna (LeMelle) Joseph; m. Yusuf D. Amin Sr., Aug. 31, 1968 (div. Dec. 1981); children: Laval Vallare, Yusuf, Ishmael, Harun, Caliph; m. Guy R. Grant, July 27, 1985. Student San Jose City Coll., 1965-67, San Jose State Coll., 1967-68, Calif. Poly. Inst., 1970-71; AA, Yuba Coll., 1970; BS, Calif. State U.-Fresno, 1973. Quality control technician Adolph Coors Co., Golden, Colo., 1979, food technologist, 1979-80; asst. mgr. food service Am. River Coll., Sacramento, 1982-83; food service mgr. U. Calif., Davis, 1983-84; pub. service dir. KMFO Broadcasting, Aptos, Calif., 1984-85; real estate agt. Cornish and Carey Realtors, Hollister, Calif., 1985-87; agt., property mgr. IFS Inc., Hollister, 1987-88; owner, broker Newcomer Real Estate, Hollister, 1988-94; broker J. Grant Fin., Gilroy, Calif., 1994—; instr. St Elizabeth Seton Sch. Diocese of San Jose, Palo Alto, Calif., 1994—. Vice-chmn. planning commn. City of Hollister, 1989-91, chmn., 1990-91. Recipient Outstanding Service award Sabin Sch., 1977; Outstanding Service award Gold Oak Sch., 1981. Mem. Inst. Food Technologists, San Benito County Bd. Realtors (sec. 1988), San Jose Real Estate Bd. Republican. Avocations: writing poetry; choir. Home: 7175 Orchard Dr Gilroy CA 95020-6306

AMINOFF, MICHAEL JEFFREY, medical educator; b. Little Paxton, Eng., May 24, 1941; came to U.S., 1974; s. A.S. and Helena (Cate) A.; m. Janette Dawn Williamson, July 22, 1976; children: Alexandra, Jonathan, Anthony. BS with hons., U. London, 1962, MB, BS, 1965, MD, 1973. Diplomate Am. Bd. Clin. Neurophysiology. Diplomate Am. Bd. Psychiatry and Neurology. Jr. staff mem. various London teaching hosps., 1965-69; registrar in applied electrophysiology Nat. Hosp., London, 1969-70, registrar and sr. registrar in neurology, 1971-76; registrar in neurology Middlesex Hosp., London, 1970-71; vis. asst. prof. neurology U. Calif., San Francisco, 1974-75, assoc. prof. neurology, 1976-82, prof. neurology, 1982—; dir. clin. neurophysiol. labs., movement disorders clinic, attending physician U. Calif., San Francisco, 1976—. Contbr. 135 scientific articles to profl. jours., author or editor of 12 med. books. Recipient Queen Square prize for rsch. Inst. of Neurology, London, 1973, Royer award U. Calif. San Francisco, 1991. Fellow Royal Coll. Physicians, Am. Acad. Neurology; mem. Am. Neurol. Assn., Am. EEG Soc. (pres. 1994-95), Am. Acad. Clin. Neurophysiology (pres. 1991-93). Office: U Calif San Francisco 505 Parnassus Ave # 0114 San Francisco CA 94122-2722

AMIOKA, WALLACE SHUZO, retired petroleum company executive; b. Honolulu, June 28, 1914; s. Tsurumatsu and Reye (Yoshimura) A.; B.A., U. Hawaii, 1966, M.B.A., 1968; m. Ellen Misao Honda, Aug. 9, 1942; children—Carol L. Amioka Price, Joanne M. Amioka Chikuma. With Shell Oil Co., 1931-77, fin. svcs. mgr., Honolulu, 1962-77; pub. affairs cons., Honolulu, 1977-87; gen. ptnr. Pub. Affairs Cons. Hawaii, 1988-94; ret., 1994; lectr. econs. U. Hawaii, 1969-79. Mem. Honolulu Police Commn., 1965-73, vice chmn., 1966, 68, chmn., 1971; U.S. civil adm. Ryuku Islands, 1950-52. Mem. City and County of Honolulu Charter Commn., 1981-82; bd. dirs. Honolulu Symphony Soc., 1968. Served with M.I., AUS, 1944-48. Mem. M.I. Service Vets. (pres. 1981-82), Hawaii C. of C. (chmn. edn. com. 1963-64, chmn. pub. health com. 1966-67), Hui 31 Club, Hui Aikane Club, Honolulu Police Old Timers Club, Phi Beta Kappa, Phi Kappa Phi. Home: 4844 Matsonia Dr Honolulu HI 96816-4014

AMIRKHANIAN, JOHN DAVID, geneticist, researcher, educator; b. Julfa-Isfahan, Iran, Nov. 10, 1927; came to U.S., 1979; s. Gregor D. and Astghik (Alexandrian) A.; m. Romelia Grigorian, Jan. 30, 1957; children: Varouj, Areg, Aspet. BSc in Biology, Tehran U., 1973; PhD in Genetics, King's Coll., U. London, 1977. Researcher on genetics of insect vectors of diseases Tehran U. Sch. Pub. Health, 1967-70; asst. prof. Sch. of Pub. Health Tehran U., 1977-79; rsch. scientist and assoc. Natural History Mus., L.A., 1980—; vis. prof. U. So. Calif., L.A., 1979-81; mem. faculty, sr. rsch. assoc. UCLA Sch. Medicine-King-Drew Med. Ctr., 1981-92; neonatal lung researcher, surfactant replacement models, mechanisms of lung surfactant damage by oxygen-derived species U. Calif., Davis, 1992—. Fellow Royal Micros. Soc. London, Linnean Soc. London; mem. AAAS, Inst. Biology, Genetics Soc. Eng., N.Y. Acad. Scis. Office: U Calif Sch of Medicine Divsn Neonatology TB 193 Davis CA 95616

AMME, ROBERT C., physics educator; b. Ames, Iowa, May 15, 1930; s. Lewis Earnest and Kathryn Pearl (Swartz) A.; m. Janice E. Fausch, June 23, 1951; children: Amy, David. BS in Physics, Iowa State U., 1953, MS in Physics, 1956, PhD in Physics, 1958. Grad. asst. Iowa State Engring. Experiment Sta., Ames, 1953-57; rsch. engr. Exxon Prodn. Rsch. Ctr., Houston, 1958-59; rsch. physicist Denver Rsch. Inst. U. Denver, 1959-65; asst. prof. physics dept. U. Denver, 1961-65, assoc. prof. physics dept., 1965-68, prof., sr. rsch. physicist, 1968—, chmn. physics dept., 1980-85; assoc. dean Coll. Arts & Scis. U. Denver, 1973-75, acting dean, 1975-76; dean, dir. acad. rsch. Grad. Sch. Arts & Scis. U. Denver, 1976-80. Author: Excited State in Chemical Physics, 1975; contbr. ency. of physics, 1975; contbr. numerous sci. paper to profl. jours. Mem. Govs. Task Force on Sci. Edn., 1983. Grantee NSF, USAF Office Sci. Rsch., U.S. Army Rsch. Office; internat. travel grantee NSF, NAS. Fellow Am. Phys. Soc.; mem. Soc. Automotive Engrs., Am. Assn. Physics Tchrs., Acoustical Soc. Am., Phi Beta Kappa, Sigma Xi (pres. Denver chpt. 1986-88), Pi Mu Epsilon, Sigma Pi Sigma. Office: U Denver Physics Dept Space Sci Denver CO 80208

AMMIRATI, MARIO, neurosurgeon; b. Naples, Italy, Nov. 22, 1953; came to U.S., 1980; s. Giuseppe and Bianca (D'Elia) A.; 1 child, Giuseppe. MD, U. Naples, 1977. Diplomate Am. Bd. Neurol. Surgery. Resident, neurosurgery U. Naples, 1977-80; resident, neurosurgery Northwestern U., Chgo., 1980-87; post-doctoral fellow Nordstadt Krankenhaus, Hanover, Germany, 1987-89; asst. prof. divsn. neurosurgery UCLA Med. Ctr., L.A., 1989-95; chief divsn. neurosurgery Olive View/UCLA Med. Ctr., L.A., 1989-95; assoc. prof., chief sect. neuro-oncology/skull base surgery U. Calif., Irvine, 1995—. Recipient Neurosurgery fellowship Alexander von Humboldt Found., Bonn, Germany, 1987-89. Fellow ACS. Home: 4324 Promenade Way Apt 316 Marina Dl Rey CA 90292-6289 Office: Dept Neurosurgery U Calif at Irvine Med Ctr Orange CA 92668-3298

AMOAKO, JAMES KWAKU, transportation services executive, financial analyst; b. Nkwatia, Ghana, Dec. 4, 1951; came to U.S., 1970; s. Kwame and Amma (Nyame) A.; m. Rose Tiokor; children: James Jr., Nicole, Jennifer. AS, Cosumnes River Coll., 1977; BS, Calif. State U., Sacramento, 1978; MBA, Golden Gate U., 1979; doct. cand., Walden U., 1994. Bank examiner Calif. State Banking Dept., San Francisco, 1979-80; fin. analyst Artec Internat. Corp., Mountain View, Calif., 1980-83; cost acct. Sun Microsystems, Mountain View, Calif., 1983-88; pres., CEO Alpha Transp. Corp., Phoenix, Ariz., 1988—. Recipient Svc. award Am. Field Svc., 1970. Home: 8826 W Encanto Blvd Phoenix AZ 85037-3619 Office: Alpha Transp Corp 4024 S 16th St Phoenix AZ 85040-1315

AMONSON, JOHANNE LESLIE, barrister, solicitor; b. Edmonton, Alta., Can., Mar. 28, 1949; d. Leslie Earl and Trudy Johanna (Fritz) A.; married, Mar. 6, 1981; 1 child: Matthew Charles Arthur. BA, U. Oreg., 1970; LLB, U. Alta., 1977. Bar: Alta. 1978. Assoc. Weeks Joyce, Edmonton, 1978-85; ptnr. Peterson Ross, Edmonton, 1985-89, McLennan Ross, Edmonton, 1989—; appointed Queen's Counsel Lt. Gov. of Alberta, 1992; appointee fed. jud. appointments com. Province of Alberta, 1991-93, appointed a fellow of the Am. Coll. of Estates and Trusts Coun., 1995; mem. Atty. Gen. Alberta Surrogate Rules Amendment Project; panel chmn. Legal Edn. Soc. Alberta; tchr., lectr. on legal edn. tchr. Bavarian Ministry of Edn., Germany, 1972-73; sessional lectr. U. Alberta Law Sch., 1987, 88. Exhbns. registrar Glenbow Mus. Calgary, 1973-74. Named to Dean's List, U. Ore., 1969-70, U. Alta. Law Rev., 1975-77; recipient of fgn. student scholarship, U. Ore., 1967-70. Fellow Am. Coll. Trust and Estate Counsel; mem. Law Soc. Alta. (mentor), Can. Bar Assn. (panelist, nat. coun. and provincial exec. com., coord. no. sects., past chair wills and trusts sect.), Edmonton Bar Assn., Internat. Commn. Jurists, Can. Tax Found. (surrogate rules com.). Conservative.

Lutheran. Office: McLennan Ross, POB 12040 12220 Stony Plain Rd, Edmonton, AB Canada T5J 3L2

AMOR, SIMEON, JR., photographer, historian; b. Lahaina, Hawaii, Apr. 24, 1924; s. Simeon and Victoria Amor. Grad. high sch., Hilo, Hawaii. Post commdr. Engrs. Post #22, Am. Legion, Honolulu, 1952-53; approp. acct. Hawaii Air Nat. Guard, Honolulu, 1953-64; prodn. control supr. Svc. Bur. Corp., Honolulu, 1964-73; prodn. control computer ops. Bank of Hawaii, Honolulu, 1973-86; owner, propreitor Image Engring., Honolulu, 1986—; historian VFW Dept. Hawaii, Honolulu, 1987-90, First Filipino Infantry Regiment Hawaii Connection; treas. DAV Dept. Hawaii, Honolulu. Cpl. U.S. Infantry, 1943-46, master sgt. USNG, 1952-64. Recipient Disting. Svc. award Nat. Disabled Am. Vet., 1992-94, OAHU Cup Disabled Am. Vet., 1992-94. Mem. Am. Photographer's Internat. Home: 1634 Kino St Honolulu HI 96819-2651 Office: Disabled Am Vets 2685 N Nimitz Hwy Honolulu HI 96819-2263

AMORY, THOMAS CARHART, management consultant; b. N.Y.C., Oct. 29, 1933; s. George Sullivan and Marion Renee (Carhart) A.; m. Elisabeth Andrews Jackson, June, 1956 (div. Mar. 1969); children: Renee Elizabeth, Caroline Carhart, Gillian Brookman; m. Carolyn Marie Pesnell, May 10, 1969 (div. Nov. 1987) ; m. Doris Ruth Mack, Mar. 18, 1989. A.B., Harvard U., 1956. Comml. mgr. N.Y. Telephone Co., N.Y.C., 1957-60; sales mgr. Royce Chem. Co., East Rutherford, N.J., 1960-62; asst. to chmn. Seatrain Lines, Inc., Edgewater, N.J., 1963-65; mgmt. cons. Booz Allen & Hamilton, N.Y.C., 1966-67; ptnr. William H. Clark Assocs., Inc., N.Y.C., 1967-75, pres., 1975-79, chmn., 1979-88; mgmt. cons. Montecito, Calif., 1989—. Trustee Mus. City, N.Y., 1971-92, Santa Barbara Mus. Art, 1990-95, Santa Barbara Chamber Orch., 1991—, United Boys' and Girls' Clubs of Santa Barbara County, 1995—. Mem. River Club, Santa Barbara Club, Birnam Wood Golf Club. Republican. Roman Catholic. Office: 1187 Coast Village Rd Ste 1-386 Santa Barbara CA 93108-2737

AMSTUTZ, HARLAN CABOT, orthopaedic surgeon; b. Santa Monica, Calif., July 17, 1931; m. Patricia Price, 1957; children: Julie, Mark, Catherine. BA, UCLA, 1953, MD, 1956. Cert. Calif., N.Y., Am. Bd. Orthopaedic Surgeons. Intern L.A. County Hosp., 1956-57; resident gen. surgery UCLA, 1957-58, resident hosp. spl. surgery-orthopaedics, 1958-61; fellow Royal Nat. Orthopaedic Hosp., London, 1963-64; assoc. scientist Hosp. for Spl. Surgery, N.Y.C., 1964-70, chief prosthetics, 1965-70, dir. bioengring., 1968-70; prof., chief orthopaedics UCLA Med. Ctr., L.A., 1970-89, prof., chief joint replacement, 1970-91, prof. emeritus, 1991—; med. dir. Joint Replacement Inst., L.A., 1991—; lectr. in bioengring. Poly. Inst. Bklyn., N.Y., 1967-70; chief orthopaedic surgery V.A. Wadsworth Med. Ctr., L.A., 1975-89; sci. advisor, mem. Orthomet, Mpls., 1993—. Author: Hip Arthroplasty, 1991; editl. bd. mem. Gaucher's Clin. Perspectives, 1993—, Hip Internat., 1993—, The Knee, 1993—; inventor in field. Capt. USAF, 1961-63. Fellow ACS; mem. Am. Acad. Orthopaedic Surgeons (chmn. com. on biomed. engring. 1978-81), Am. Orthopaedic Assn. (pres. 1992-93), Assn. Bone and Joint Surgeons (pres. 1984-85, Nicolas Andry award 1987), Orthopaedic Rsch. Soc. (pres. 1973), Internat. Hip Soc., The Hip Soc. (pres., exec. com. 1979-80, John Charnley award 1977, 84, 90, 94, Otto Aufranc award 1979), Phi Beta Kappa. Office: Joint Replacement Inst 3d Fl 2400 S Flower St Fl 3 Los Angeles CA 90007-2629

AMUNDSON, EVA DONALDA, civic worker; b. Langdon, N.D., Apr. 23, 1911; d. Elmer Fritjof and Alma Julia (Nelson) Hultin; m. Leif Amundson, Mar. 1, 1929 (dec. 1974); children: Constance, Eleanor, Ardis, Priscilla. Bd. dirs. Opportunity Workshop, Missoula, Mont., 1950—, Rockmont Group Homes, Missoula, 1976—, Bethany L'Arche (group home for girls), 1976—; sec. bd. dirs. Opportunity Industries, 1990-91, pres. 1991—; mem. Missoula Sr. Citizen's Ctr., 1980-82, 88—, pres., 1982-85, bd. dirs., 1988—; tchr. Norwegian cooking and baking, 1954-56, Norweigan Rosemaling, 1975-79; treas. Sacakawea Homemakers Club, 1979-81; mem. Am. Luth. Ch. Women St. Pauls' Lutheran Ch., 1951—; active Easter Seal Program, Heart Fund, March of Dimes, United Way, Campfire Girls; mem. adv. council Area Agy. on Aging, Missoula, 1984—. Recipient Outstanding Sr. award Missoula Jr. C. of C., 1984. Mem. Sons. of Norway (sec. 1989—), Orchard Homes Country Club (mem. art judging com.), Order of Eastern Star, Elks. Avocations: rosemaling, oil painting, poetry. Home: 324 Kensington Ave Missoula MT 59801-5726

AMUR-UMARJEE, SHASHI GURURAJ, neurobiologist, researcher; b. India, Mar. 14, 1955; came to U.S., 1981; d. Gururaj Shyamacharya and Shanta Gururaj Amur; m. Dheerendra Madhwarao Umarjee, Feb. 2, 1987; 1 chld, Sphoorti Dheerendra Umarjee. BSc, S. B. Coll., Aurangabad, Maharashtra, India, 1973; MSc, Marathwada U., Aurangabad, Maharashtra, India, 1975; PhD in Biochemistry, Indian Inst. Sci., Bangalore, India, 1981. Post-doctoral rschr. Temple U., Phila., 1981-84; pool officer Indian Inst. Sci., 1985-88; postgrad. rschr. UCLA, 1988-90, sr. rsch. assoc. I, 1991-92, sr. rsch. assoc. III, 1992—; sci. coord. UCLA, 1992—. Univ. Grant Commn. scholar, 1973, rsch. fellow, 1975-76; BRSG grantee NPI, UCLA, 1988-89. Mem. Am. Soc. Neurochemistry. Office: UCLA 760 Westwood Plz Los Angeles CA 90024-8300

AMYLON, MICHAEL DAVID, physician, educator; b. Providence, Apr. 30, 1950; s. Sidney Robert and Mary Elisabeth (Alexander) A. AB, Brown U., 1972; MD, Stanford U., 1976. Diplomate sub-bd. hematology/oncology Am. Bd. Pediatrics. Resident physician Stanford (Calif.) U. Hosp., 1976-79; post-doctoral scholar Stanford U., 1979-81, acting asst. prof., 1981-82, asst. prof. pediatrics, 1982-89, assoc. prof. pediatrics, 1989—; dir. marrow transplant svc. Children's Hosp. at Stanford, Palo Alto, Calif., 1986—; coord. nat. rsch. clin. trials in treatment pediatric leukemia and lymphoma Pediatric Oncology Group, St. Louis, Chgo., 1986—. Contbr. articles to profl. jours. Bd. dirs. Touchstone Support Network, Palo Alto, 1982—, Robert J. Sturhahn Found., Novato, Calif., 1986-93, Okizu Found., Novato, 1993—; med. dir. No. Calif. Oncology Camp, Nevada City, 1986—. Recipient For Those Who Care award Sta. KRON, 1990, "Ronnie" award, Ronald McDonald House, 1992-93. Mem. Am. Acad. Pediatrics, Am. Soc. Clin. Oncology, Am. Soc. Hematology, Am. Soc. Pediatric Hematology/Oncology, Am. Soc. Blood and Marrow Transplantation. Office: Packard Children's Hosp 725 Welch Rd Palo Alto CA 94304-1601

AN, HAEJUNG, food technology educator; b. Seoul, Republic of Korea, May 13, 1958; came to U.S., 1981; d. Sung-Ho Ahn and Seung-Ah Park; m. Thomas A. Seymour, June 18, 1986; 1 child, Jillian A. BS, Seoul Nat. U., 1981; MS, La. State U., 1984; PhD, U. Fla., 1989. Postdoctoral U. Fla., Gainesville, 1989-90; asst. prof. Oreg. State U., Astoria, 1991—. Contbr. articles to profl. jours. Grantee Oreg. State U., 1991-93, Sea, 1993-95, USDA, 1993. Mem. AAAS, Am. Inst. Fihsery Rsch. Biologists, Isnt. Food Technologists. Home: 2272 Manion Dr Warrenton OR 97146-9784 Office: Oreg State U Seafood Lab 250 36th St Astoria OR 97103-2403

ANAND, SURESH CHANDRA, physician; b. Mathura, India, Sept. 13, 1931; came to U.S., 1957, naturalized, 1971; s. Satchit and Sumaran (Bai) A. m. Wiltrud, Jan. 29, 1966; children: Miriam, Michael. MB, BS, King George's Coll., U. Lucknow (India), 1954; MS in Medicine, U. Colo., 1962. Diplomate Am. Bd. Allergy and Immunology. Fellow pulmonary diseases Nat. Jewish Hosp., Denver, 1957-58, resident in chest medicine, 1958-59, chief resident allergy-asthma, 1960-62; intern Mt. Sinai Hosp., Toronto, Ont., Can., 1962-63, resident in medicine, 1963-64, chief resident, 1964-65, demonstrator clin. technique, 1963-64, U. Toronto fellow in medicine, 1964-65; rsch. assoc. asthma-allergy Nat. Jewish Hosp., Denver, 1967-69; clin. instr. medicine U. Colo., Denver, 1967-69; internist Ft. Logan Mental Health Ctr., Denver, 1968-69; pres. Allergy Assocs. & Lab., Ltd., Phoenix, 1974—; mem. staff Phoenix Bapt. Hosp., chmn. med. records com., 1987; mem. staff St. Joseph's Hosp., St. Luke's Hosp., Human Hosp., John C. Lincoln Hosp., Good Samaritan Hosp., Phoenix Children's Hosp., Tempe St. Luke Hosp., Desert Samaritan Hosp., Mesa Luth. Hosp., Scottsdale Meml. Hosp., Phoenix Meml. Hosp., Chandler (Ariz.) Regional Hosp., Valley Luth. Hosp., Mesa, Ariz.; pres. NJH Fed. Credit Union, 1967-68. Contbr. articles to profl. jours. Mem. Camelback Hosp. Mental Health Ctr. Citizens Adv. Bd., Scottsdale, Ariz., 1974-80; mem. Phoenix Symphony Coun., 1973-90; mem. Ariz. Opera Co., Boyce Thmpson Southwestern Arboretum; mem. Ariz. Hist. Soc., Phoenix Arts. Mus., Smithsonian Inst. Fellow ACP, Am. Coll. Chest Physicians (critical care com.), Am. Acad. Allergy, Am. Assn. Cert. Allergists, Am. Coll. Allergy and Immunology (aerobiology com., internat. com., pub. edn. com.); mem. AAAS, AMA, Internat. Assn. Allergy and Clin. Immunology, Ariz. Med. Assn., Ariz. Allergy Soc. (v.p. 1988-90, pres. 1990-91), Maricopa County Med. Soc. (del. Ariz. Med. Assn.), West Coast Soc. Allergy and Immunology, Greater Phoenix Allergy Soc (v.p. 1984-86, pres. 1986-88, med. adv. team sports medicine Ariz. State U.), Phoenix Zoo, N.Y. Acad. Scis., World Med. Assn., Internat. Assn. Asthmology, Assn. Care of Asthma, Ariz. Thoracic Soc., Nat. Geographic Soc., Village Tennis Club, Ariz. Club, Ariz. Wild Life Assn. Office: 1006 E Guadalupe Rd Tempe AZ 85283-3044 also: 6553 E Baywood Ave Mesa AZ 85206-1752 also: 7331 E Osborn Dr Ste 350 Scottsdale AZ 85251-6422

ANASTOLE, DOROTHY JEAN, electronics company executive; b. Akron, Ohio, Mar. 26, 1932; d. Leonard L. and Helen (Sagedy) Dice; children: Kally, Dennis, Christopher. Student, De Anza Jr. Coll., Cupertino, Calif., 1969. Various secretarial positions in mfg., 1969-75; office mgr. Sci. Devices Co., Mountain View, Calif., 1975-76; exec. adminstrv. sec. corp. office Cezar Industries, Palo Alto, Calif., 1976-77; office and personnel mgr. AM Bruning Co., Mountain View, 1977-81; dir. employee relations Consol. Micrographics, Mountain View, 1981-83; personnel mgmt. cons., 1983-84; mgr. adminstrn./employee relations Mitsubishi Electronics Am., Inc., Sunnyvale, Calif., 1984-89, sr. mgr., 1989-91, corp. v.p., 1991—. Bd. dirs. Agnew State Hosp., San Jose, Calif., 1966-72, div. chmn. program mentally retarded, 1966-72, staff tutor, 1966-72; bd. dirs. Project Hired, Sunnyvale, 1991-93. Recipient Scv. award Agnew State Hosp., 1972. Office: Mitsubishi Electronics Am 1050 E Arques Ave Sunnyvale CA 94086-4601

ANAWALT, PATRICIA RIEFF, anthropologist; b. Ripon, Calif., Mar. 10, 1924; d. Edmund Lee and Anita Esto (Capps) Rieff; m. Richard Lee Anawalt, June 8, 1945; children: David, Katherine Anawalt Arnoldi, Harmon Fred. BA in Anthropology, UCLA, 1957, MA in Anthropology, 1971, PhD in Anthropology, 1975. Cons. curator costumes and textiles Mus. Cultural History UCLA, 1975-90, dir. Ctr. for Study Regional Dress, Fowler Mus. Cultural History, 1990—; trustee S.W. Mus., L.A., 1978-92; rsch. assoc. UCLA Inst. Archaeology, 1994—, San Diego Mus. of Man, 1981—; traveling lectr. Archaeol. Inst. Am., U.S., Can., 1975-86, 94-95, Pres.'s Lectureship, 1993-94, trustee, 1983—; cons. Nat. Geog. Soc., 1980-82, Denver Mus. Natural History, 1992-93; apptd. by U.S. Pres. to Cultural Property Adv. Com., Washington, 1984-93; fieldwork Guatemala, 1961, 70, 72, Spain, 1975, Sierra Norte de Puebla, Mex., 1983, 85, 88, 89, 91. Author: Indian Clothing Before Cortés: Mesoamerican Costumes from the Codices, 1981, paperback edit., 1990; co-author: The Codex Mendoza, 4 vols., 1992 (winner Archaeol. Inst. Am. 1994 James Wiseman Book award). Adv. com Textile Mus., Washington, 1983-87. Recipient NEH grant, J. Paul Getty Found. grant, Nat. Geog. Soc. grants, 1983, 85, 88, 89, 91, Guggenheim fellowship, 1988-89. Fellow Am. Anthrop. Assn., L.A. County Mus. Natural History; mem. Centre Internat. D'Etude Des Textiles Anciens, Am. Ethnol. Soc., Soc. Am. Archaeology, Soc. Women Geographers (Outstanding Achievement award 1993), Textile Soc. Am. (bd. dirs. 1992—, co-coord. 1994 biennial symposium), Pres.'s Patrons Cir. L.A. County Mus. Art, AIA So. Calif. Soc. (pres. 1986-89, v.p. 1983-86, sec. 1979-83), Archaeol. Inst. Am. (trustee 1983—). Office: Fowler Mus Cultural History Ctr Study of Regional Dress Los Angeles CA 90095-1549

ANCELL, JUDITH ANNE, gemologist, custom/specialty business owner; b. Coldwater, Mich., Feb. 20, 1943; d. Frederick Hall and Beatrice Marguerite (Cornell) Weeks; m. William Joseph Ancell, Oct. 1, 1961; children: William Joseph II, Brian Eugene, Mark Edward. Various certs., Gemol. Inst. Am., Santa Monica, Calif. Cert. gemologist, diamontologist wholesale. Owner Turquoise Mesa, 1974-79; salesperson various jewelry stores, 1979-85; owner Judith A. Ancell Fine Jewelry, Boise, Idaho, 1985—, Geneal. & Hist. BookSource, Boise, Idaho, 1992—. Vol. co-coordinator Cross Cultural Comm. for Fgn. Student Host Family Program, Mich. State U., 1969-72. Mem. Idaho Soc. Profl. Engrs. Aux. (pres. S.W. chpt. 1989), Am. Bus. Women's Assn., Idaho State Geneol. Soc. (bd. dirs. 1992-94), Huguenot Soc. State of Idaho (v.p. 1992-94). Office: PO Box 6443 Boise ID 83707-6443

ANCHIE, TOBY LEVINE, health facility administrator; b. New Haven, Conn., Jan. 21, 1944; d. Solomon and Mary (Karlins) Levine; children: Michael D. Anchie, Robert P. Anchie. BSN, U. of Conn., 1966; MA in Edn. magna cum laude, Nor. Ariz. U., 1984. RN Ariz., Conn. Coord. spl. projects, nurse coord., adult day hosp. Barrow Neurol. Inst. of St. Joseph's Hosp. and Med. Ctr., Phoenix, 1984-87, mgr., 1985-92; mgr. adminstrv. and support svcs., neuroscis. Barrow Neurol. Inst. of St. Joseph's Hosp. and Med. Ctr., 1992-94; mgr. clin. rsch., 1994—; cons.; presenter in field; mem. faculty U. Phoenix; adv. bd. mem. Myasthenia Gravis Assn.; mem. adv. coun. Office Disability Prevention Ariz. Dept. Health Svcs., mem. strategic planning com. Contbr. articles to profl. jours., chpts. Mem. NAFE, Assn. Rebah. Nurses, Am. Assn. Neurosci. Nurses (bd. dirs., pres.), World Fedn. Neurosci. Nurses, Nat. Fedn. Splty. Nursing Orgn. (chair membership com. 1993-95), Ariz. Assn. Neurosci. Nurses. Home: 3112 S Los Feliz Dr Tempe AZ 85282-2854

ANCOLI-ISRAEL, SONIA, psychologist, researcher; b. Tel Aviv, Israel, Dec. 25, 1951; came to U.S., 1955.; m. Andrew G. Israel; 2 children. BA, SUNY, Stony Brook, 1972; MA, Calif. State U., Long Beach, 1974; PhD, U. Calif., San Francisco, 1979. Lic. psychologist, Calif. Staff psychologist U. Calif. San Diego, La Jolla, 1979-84, asst. adj. prof., 1984-88, assoc. prof., 1988-94; prof., 1994—; assoc. dir. Sleep Disorders Ctr., VA Med. Ctr., San Diego, 1981-92, dir., 1992—. Contbr. numerous articles to profl. jours. Bd. mgrs. Jewish Cmty. Ctr., La Jolla, 1985-91; mem. exec. bd. Nat. Sleep Found. Recipient Robert E. Harris Meml. award, U. Calif. San Franicsco, 1978. Mem. AAAS, Sleep Rsch. Soc., Am. Sleep Disorders Assn., Gerontol. Soc. Am., Biofeedback Soc. Am., Soc. Psychophysiol. Rsch., N.Y. Acad. Sci.

ANCONA, GEORGE EPHRAIN, photographer, film producer, author; b. N.Y.C., Dec. 4, 1929; s. Ephraim Jose and Emma Graziana (Diaz) A.; m. Helga Von Sydow, July 20, 1968; children: Lisa, Gina, Tomas, Isabel, Marina, Pablo. Student, Academia de San Carlos, Mexico, 1949, Art Students League, 1950, Cooper Union Sch. Design, 1950. Art dir. Esquire Inc., N.Y.C., 1951-53, Seventeen mag., N.Y.C., 1953-54, Grey Advt. Agy., N.Y.C., 1954-58, Daniel & Charles Advt. Agy., N.Y.C., 1958-60; free lance photographer, film producer N.Y.C., 1960—; lectr. graphic design, photography Rockland Community Coll., 1973—, Parsons Sch. Design, 1974—, Sch. Visual Arts, 1978—. Author: Handtalk, 1974, Monsters on Wheels, 1974, What Do You Do?, 1976, I Feel, 1977, Growing Older, 1978, It's A Baby!, 1979, Dancing Is, 1981, Bananas, from Manolo to Margie, Team Work, 1983, Monster Movers, Sheepdog, Helping Out, Freighters, 1985, Handtalk Birthday, 1986 (N.Y. Times 10 Best Illustrated Children's Books of Yr.), Turtle Watch, 1987, The American Family Farm, 1989, Handtalk Zoo, 1989, Riverkeeper,1990, Harry's Helicopter, 1990, Handtalk School, 1991, The Aquarium Book, 1991, Man and Mustang, 1992, Pow Wow, 1992, My Camera, 1992, Pablo Remembers, 1993, The Piñatamaker, 1994, The Golden Lion Tamarin Comes Home, 1994, Fiesta U.S.A., 1995, Cutters, Carvers & the Cathedral, 1995, Sally's Submarine, 1995, Georgie, Then and Now, 1995, Earth Daughter, 1995; designer, photographer over 80 books. Address: RR 10 Box 94G Santa Fe NM 87501-9642

ANDARY, THOMAS JOSEPH, biochemist; b. Sault Sainte Marie, Mich., Oct. 8, 1942; s. Joseph Boula and Marion (Schwifetti) A. BS, No. Mich. U., 1966, MA, 1968; PhD, Wayne State U., 1974. Instr. biology No. Mich. U., Marquette, 1967-69; rsch. assoc. physiology Wayne State U., Detroit, 1973-76; sr. rsch. scientist, mgr. coagulation research Hyland Labs., Costa Mesa, Calif., 1976-83; dir. quality control Hyland Therapeutics, Glendale, Calif., 1983-90; dir. quality assurance and regulatory affairs Baxter/Hyland Div., Glendale, 1990-91; v.p. quality assurance and regulatory affairs, 1991—, responsible head, 1993—; lectr. in field. Mem. Parenteral Drug Assn. NDEA fellow, 1969-72. Mem. Am. Chem. Soc., N.Y. Acad. Sci., Internat. Assn. Biol. Standardization, Sigma Xi (Rsch. award 1973). Roman Catholic. Contbr. over 25 articles to profl. publs. Home: 531 N Canyon Blvd Monrovia CA 91016-1707 Office: 550 N Brand Blvd Glendale CA 91203-1900

ANDERBERG, ROY ANTHONY, journalist; b. Camden, N.J., Mar. 30, 1921; s. Arthur R. and Mary V. (McHugh) A.; m. Louise M. Brooks, Feb. 5, 1953; children: Roy, Mary. AA, Diablo Valley Coll., 1975. Enlisted USN, 1942, commd. officer, 1960, ret., 1970; waterfront columnist Pacific Daily News, Agana, Guam, 1966-67; pub. rels. officer Naval Forces, Mariana Islands, 1967; travel editor Contra Costa (Calif.) Times, 1968-69; entertainment and restaurant editor Concord (Calif.) Transcript, 1971-75; entertainment editor Contra Costa Advertiser, 1975-76; dining editor Rossmoor News, Walnut Creek, Calif., 1977-78; free-lance non-fiction journalist, 1976—. Recipient Best Feature Story award Guam Press Assoc., 1966. Mem. VFW, DAV, U.S. Power Squadron, Ret. Officers Assn., Am. Legion, U.S. Submarine Vets. WWII (state comdr., regional dir., nat. 2d v.p.), Naval Submarine League (XO), Martinez Yacht Club (charter), Rossmoor Yacht Club (commodore 1995), Toastmasters. Democrat. Home: 1840 Tice Creek Dr #2228 Walnut Creek CA 94595 Office: PO Box 52 Concord CA 94522-0052

ANDEREGG, RONALD HENRY, artist; b. Portland, Oreg., Mar. 22, 1939; s. Henry Herman and Isabel (Dimbat) A. Designer, artist Walt Disney Entertainment, Burbank, Calif., 1962; soldier, artist U.S. Army, Washington, 1963-64; comml. artist Richter/Mracky Advt. Agy., L.A., 1965-72, Anderegg/Thornton Design Studio, L.A., 1972-85; fine artist, painter, sculptor L.A., 1986—; creative art dir., graphic designer Max Factor Point of Purchase Displays and Catalogs, Hollywood, Calif., 1965-85. designer display for John F. Kennedy, 1963, Max Factor Mus., 1985. Home and Office: 8101 Laurelmont Dr Los Angeles CA 90046

ANDERS, WILLIAM ALISON, aerospace and defense manufacturing executive; b. Hong Kong, Oct. 17, 1933; s. Arthur Ferdinand and Muriel Florence (Adams) A.; m. Valerie Elizabeth Hoard, June 26, 1955; children: Alan Frank, Glen Thomas, Gayle Alison, Gregory Michael, Eric William, Diana Elizabeth. BS, U.S. Naval Acad., Annapolis, 1955; MS in Nuclear Engring., U.S. Inst. Tech., Wright-Patterson AFB, 1962. Commnd. 2d lt. U.S. Air Force, 1955, pilot, engr., 1955-69; astronaut NASA-Johnson Space Ctr., Houston, 1963-69, Apollo 8, 1st lunar flight, 1968; exec. sec. Nat. Aero. and Space Council, Washington, 1963-72; commr. AEC, Washington, 1973-74; chmn. Nuclear Regulatory Commn., Washington, 1975-76; U.S. Ambassador to Norway, 1976-77; v.p., gen. mgr. nuclear energy products div. Gen. Electric Co., 1977-80; v.p., gen. mgr. aircraft equipment div. Gen. Electric Co., DeWitt, N.Y., 1980-84; sr. exec., v.p. ops. Textron Inc., Providence, R.I., 1984-89; vice chmn. Gen. Dynamics, St. Louis, 1990-91; chmn., CEO Gen. Dynamics, 1991—; chmn. bd. dirs. N000, 1993—; pres. Apogee Group. Trustee Battell Meml. Inst. Maj. gen. USAFR, 1983-88. Decorated various mil. awards; recipient Wright, Collier, Goddard and Arnold flight awards; co-holder several world flight records. Mem. Soc. Exptl. Test Pilots , Nat. Acad. Engring., Tau Beta Pi. Office: Apogee Group PO Box 1630 Eastsound WA 98245

ANDERSEN, DORIS EVELYN, real estate broker; b. Christian County, Ky., Oct. 30, 1923; d. William Earl and Blanche Elma (Withers) Johnston; m. Roger Lewis Shirk, July 9, 1944 (div. 1946); 1 child, Vicki Lee Shirk Sanderson; m. DeLaire Andersen, July 6, 1946; children: Craig Bryant, Karen Rae, Kent DeLaire, Chris Jay, Mardi Lynn. Diploma, South Bend Coll. Commerce, 1942; diploma in banking, Notre Dame U., 1946; student, Ind. U., 1942-44. Tng. dir. Portland, Oreg., 1963-69; assoc. broker Stan Wiley, Inc., Portland, 1969-79; prin. Doris Andersen & Assocs., Portland, 1979-91; sales mgr. VanVleet & Assocs. Real Estate, Ashland, Oreg., 1991-93; real estate appraiser Andersen and Assocs., 1993—; co-owner ServiceMaster of the Cascades; tchr. media spokesperson courses; speaker at seminars; mem. Gov.'s Task Force Coun. on Housing, Salem, Oreg., 1985-86; mem. Oreg. Real Estate Bd., 1992—. Contbr. articles to profl. jours. Regional dir. Dale & Dorothy Carnegie Courses for Women Ind. Inst. Leadership Tng., 1954-56; gov.'s appointee Oreg. Real Estate Bd., 1992-94; mem. task force Oreg. Dept. Energy, Salem, 1984-85. Mem. Nat. Assn. Realtors (bd. dirs. 1983—, regional v.p. Northwest region 1988), Oreg. Assn. Realtors (dir. 1979—, pres. 1986—), Portland Bd. Realtors (pres. 1982), Women's Council Realtors (local pres. 1977, state pres. 1978, gov. nat. orgn. 1979), Internat. Platform Assn., Internat. Biog. Assn. Home: 2700 Pioneer Rd Medford OR 97501-9642 Office: PO Box 1546 Medford OR 97501-0116

ANDERSEN, ERNEST CHRISTOPHER, lawyer; b. Minden, Nebr., Sept. 10, 1909; s. Dines Peter and Marie (Jensen) A.; m. Audrey Etta Robertson, Sept. 10, 1954; 1 dau., Elaine Carolyn Andersen Smith; 1 stepson, Albert Henry Whitaker. JD, U. Denver, 1952, BS in Bus. Adminstrn., 1956. Bar: Colo. 1954, U.S. Supreme Ct. 1960; CPA, Colo. With U.S. Treasury Dept., Denver, 1935-39; accountant, Denver, 1939-41; with Civilian Prodn. Adminstrn., Denver, 1946-49; dep. state auditor Colo., 1949-51; with U.S. Commerce Dept., Denver, 1951-52; mgmt. cons., Denver, 1953-54; sole practice law, Denver, 1955-56, 69-75; asst. dir. GAO, Los Angeles, 1957-58, Denver, 1959, Washington, 1960-69, cons., 1969-75; sole practice law, Cedaredge, Colo., 1975-86; owner Cedar Crest Farm, 1983—, Stand Sure Press (later Christopher Pub. Co.), 1977—; mem. faculty U. Denver, 1948-56; mcpl. judge Cedaredge, 1977-86; exec. in residence Tulane U., spring 1973. Bd. dirs. Delta Montrose Electric Assn., 1976-84, Colo.-Ute Electric Assn., 1980-84. Served to lt. col. USAR, 1939-62. Recipient Meritorious Service award GAO, 1968. Republican. Presbyterian. Clubs: Masons, Shriners. Home: 1856 Rd 2375 Cedaredge CO 81413 Office: PO Box 747 Cedaredge CO 81413-0747

ANDERSEN, JAMES A., retired state supreme court justice; b. Auburn, Wash., Sept. 21, 1924; s. James A. and Margaret Cecelia (Norgaard) A.; m. Billiette B. Andersen; children: James Blair, Tia Louise. BA, U. Wash., 1949, JD, 1951. Bar: Wash. 1952, U.S. Dist. Ct. (we. dist.) Wash. 1957, U.S. Ct. Appeals 1957. Dep. pros. atty. King County, Seattle, 1953-57; assoc. Lycette, Diamond & Sylvester, Seattle, 1957-61; ptnr. Clinton, Andersen, Fleck & Glein, Seattle, 1961-75; judge Wash. State Ct. of Appeals, Seattle, 1975-84; justice Wash. State Supreme Ct., Olympia, 1984-92, chief justice, 1992-95; ret., 1995. Mem. Wash. State Ho. of Reps., 1958-67, Wash. State Senate, 1967-72. Served with U.S. Army, 1943-45, ETO. Decorated Purple Heart. Mem. ABA, Wash. State Bar Assn., Am. Judicature Soc. Home: 3008 98th NE Bellevue WA 98004

ANDERSEN, MICHAEL PAUL, government agency payroll manager; b. Denver, Oct. 13, 1946; s. Donald Paul and Betty Jean (Webber) A.; m. Carolyn Ann Antolini, Dec. 29, 1966; children: Andrew, Dawn. BS in Psychology, Colo. State U., Ft. Collins, 1968. Pers. specialist U.S. Army Ft. Carson, Colorado Springs, Colo., 1968-70, U.S. Civil Svc. Commn., Denver, 1970-71; area mgr. U.S. Civil Svc. Commn., Providence, 1972-73; adminstrv. officer Action Region 8, Denver, 1973-75; program mgr. Office of Pers. Mgmt., Denver, 1975-81; owner, mgr. Ski N Sport Ltd., Arvada, Colo., 1979-82; mgmt. cons. Denver Bur. Reclamation, 1981-82, program mgr., 1983—; aide White House Fellows, Denver and Washington, 1980-81; author/pub. Wagering to Win!, Mutual Press, Inc., Denver. Mem. Fed. Exec. Coun., Providence, 1972-73; cons. ARC, Denver, 1973-75, City of Denver Auditor's Office, 1989. Recipient Gubenatorial Citation Gov. of R.I., 1973. Mem. Devel. Plus Inc. (assoc.), Pres.'s Coun. Mgmt. Improvement (Excellence award 1990). Republican. Home: Mutual Press Inc PO Box 36094 Denver CO 80236-0094

ANDERSEN, NIELS HJORTH, chemistry educator, biophysics researcher, consultant; b. Copenhagen, Denmark, Oct. 9, 1943; came to U.S. 1949; s. Orla and Inger (Larsen) A.; m. Sidnee Lee (div. 1986); children: Marin Christine, Beth Arkady; m. Susan Howell, July 21, 1987. BA, U. Minn., 1963; PhD, Northwestern U., 1967. Rsch. assoc and fellow Harvard U., Cambridge, Mass., 1966-68; asst. prof. U. Wash., Seattle, 1968-72, assoc. prof., 1972-76, prof., 1976—; prin. scientist ALZA Corp., Palo Alto, Calif., 1970-75; cons. Genetic Systems, Seattle, 1984-86, Bristol-Myer Squibb, Princeton, N.J., 1984-95, Amylin Pharmaceutics, San Diego, 1992—. Contbr. articles to profl. jours. Pres. Friends of Northshore, Bothell, Wash., 1980-86. Recipient Teacher-Scholar award Dreyfus Found., 1974-79, Career Devel. award NIH, 1975-80. Mem. AAAS, Am. Chem. Soc., Protein Soc. Democrat. Office: U Wash Box 351700 Seattle WA 98195-1700

ANDERSON, ANNELISE GRAEBNER, economist; b. Oklahoma City, Nov. 19, 1938; d. Elmer and Dorothy (Zilisch) Graebner; m. Martin Anderson, Sept. 25, 1965. B.A., Wellesley Coll., 1960; M.A., Columbia U., 1965, Ph.D., 1974. Assoc. editor McKinsey and Co., Inc., 1963-65; researcher Nixon Campaign Staff, 1968-69; project mgr. Dept. Justice, 1970-

71; from asst. prof. bus. adminstrn. to assoc. prof. Calif. State U.-Hayward, 1975-80; sr. policy adviser Reagan Presdl. campaign and transition, Washington, 1980; assoc. dir. econs. and govt. Office Mgmt. and Budget, Washington, 1981-83; sr. rsch. fellow Hoover Instn., Stanford U., Calif., 1983—, assoc. dir., 1989-90; mem. Nat. Sci. Bd., 1985-90; Author: The Business of Organized Crime: A Cosa Nostra Family, 1979, Illegal Aliens and Employer Sanctions: Solving the Wrong Problem, 1986, The Ruble Problem: A Competitive Solution, 1992; co-editor: Thinking About America: The United States in the 1990's, 1988; contbr. articles to profl. jours., chpts. to books. Mem. bd. overseers Rand/UCLA Ctr. for Soviet Studies, L.A., 1987-91. Mem. Am. Econ. Assn., Western Econ. Assn., Beta Gamma Sigma. Office: Stanford U Hoover Institution Stanford CA 94305

ANDERSON, ARTHUR GEORGE, laboratory director, former computer company executive, consultant; b. Evanston, Ill., Nov. 22, 1926; s. Arthur G. and Margaret (Bree) A.; m. Eliza Chavez Heninger, 1975; children: Joseph S., Robin R., Jennifer M. B.S., U. San Francisco, 1947-49; M.S., Northwestern U., 1951; Ph.D., NYU, 1958. With IBM Corp., 1951-84, head numerous engring. and managerial positions, 1951-65; staff dir. corporate tech. com. IBM Corp., Armonk, N.Y., 1965-67; dir. research IBM Corp., Yorktown, N.Y., 1967-69; v.p., dir. research IBM Corp., Yorktown, 1969-70; dir. tech. assessment IBM Corp., 1971-72; pres. Gen. Products div. IBM Corp., San Jose, Calif., 1972-79, 82-83; v.p., group exec. Data Products group IBM Corp., White Plains, N.Y., 1979-81; ret., 1984—; dir. Compression Labs Inc., 1984—. Served with USNR, 1944-46. Fellow Am. Phys. Soc. (Pake award 1984), IEEE; mem. AAAS, Nat. Acad. Engring. Home: PO Box 1032 Prescott AZ 86302-1032

ANDERSON, ARTHUR LEE, gem cutter, writer; b. Washington, Nov. 28, 1952; s. Kenneth Arthur and Marjorie Ruth (Anderson) A.; m. Marion Mann, Oct. 18, 1981 (div. Nov. 1987); 1 child, Tanya Leah. Grad., Gemological Inst. Am., Santa Monica, Calif., 1986. Importer Washington, 1971-75; contractor New Orleans, 1976-80; deckhand Chotin Shipping Co., New Orleans, 1980-81; gem cutter, sculptor Speira Gems, Ashland, Oreg., 1984—; vol. speaker on gemstone-related topics, pub. schs., Ashland, 1990—. Contbr. tech. articles to Gems and Gemology, Lapidary Jour. Recipient 1st place for creative gem cut Am. Gem Trade Assn., 1992, 1st place for objet d'art, 1993, 2d place fancy gem cut, 1994, 3d place pairs and suites, 1994, others. Libertarian. Office: Speira Gems PO Box 849 Ashland OR 97526

ANDERSON, ARTHUR SALZNER, publishing company executive, marketing executive; b. Boise, Idaho, Jan. 17, 1923; s. Howard Ballantyne and Mildred Ina (Salzner) A.; m. Janice Virginia Jacobsen, June 21, 1948; children: Roger Bruce, Gregory Bryan, Julie Janice Olsen, Lane Jacobsen, Margaret Virginia Ence, Heidi Gail Eldredge, Steven Jacobsen. B.A., U. Utah, 1947. Sales promotion asst. Internat. Harvester Co., 1947-48, zone mgr., 1948-51; sr. v.p., dir., chmn. exec. com. Evans Communications, Inc., Salt Lake City, 1977-84, dir., chmn. exec. com., 1984-87, pres., 1984-87; chmn. bd. Panoram Prodns., 1977-82; pres. Deseret Book Co., 1975-80, dir., 1975-92; pres., chief exec. officer Anderson Mktg. Inc., Salt Lake City, 1987—. Author: By Example, 1961. Vice-pres. Salt Lake Area United Fund, 1977-80; mem. governing bd. Primary Children's Med. Ctr., 1975—, vice chmn., 1981-83, chmn., 1983-92; bd. dirs. Osmond Found., 1982-83. Served with AUS, 1943-46. Mem. Utah Advt. Fedn. (pres. 1967-68), Sales and Mktg. Execs. Utah (pres. 1965-66). Mem. LDS Ch. Home: 2242 Kensington Ave Salt Lake City UT 84108 Office: Anderson Mktg Inc Graystone Office Plz 1174 E 2700 S Ste 19 Salt Lake City UT 84106-2673

ANDERSON, AUSTIN GILMAN, economics research company consultant; b. Mpls.; s. Clifford Hawkins and Katharine (Irving) A.; m. Marilyn Wheeler, Mar. 17, 1968; children: Guy, Alisa, Michael, Emily. BS, Stanford U., 1964, MBA, 1966. Systems analyst Jet Propulsion Lab., Pasadena, Calif., 1966-68; assoc. Econs. Rsch. Assoc., L.A., 1968-72, sr. v.p., 1977-88, pres., chief exec. officer, 1988—; dir. rsch. Property Rsch. Corp., L.A., 1972-73; prin. Levander, Partridge & Anderson, Beverly Hills, Calif., 1973-77; instr. Grad. Sch. Mgmt. UCLA, 1989, extension, 1987; bd. dirs. Crown Iron Works Co., Mpls., 1983—; mem. bd. counselors Sch. Urban and Regional Planning U. So. Calif., L.A., 1984—; mem. bd. trustees Real Estate Investment Trust of Calif., 1994—. Mem. Urban Land Inst. Home: 328 17th St Manhattan Beach CA 90266-4636 Office: Econs Rsch Assocs 10990 Wilshire Blvd Ste 1600 Los Angeles CA 90024-3913

ANDERSON, BARBARA LOUISE, retired library director; b. San Diego, Jan. 5, 1933; d. Lorenzo and Louise (Morgan) A.; 1 child, Sean Allen. BS, San Diego State U., 1954; MLS, Kans. State Teachers Coll., 1955. Br. librarian L.A. Pub. Library, 1956-59; br. librarian, reference, young adult librarian San Diego Pub. Library, 1959-64; librarian U.S. Army, Europe, 1964-69; coordinator Serra Reference Project, Serra Regional Library System, San Diego, 1969-71; head readers services Riverside (Calif.) City and County Pub. Library, 1972-74; county librarian San Bernardino County (Calif.) Library, 1974-94; ret. 1994; del. White House Conf. on Libraries and Info. Services, 1979. Bd. dirs. Inland Empire Symphony, 1982-84, Riverside Mental Health Assn., 1975-79; mem. citizens adv. bd. San Bernardino YWCA, 1988-89. Mem. ALA, Calif. Library Assn., Black Caucus of Calif. Library Assn., Congress of Pub. Library Systems (pres. 1984), Calif. County Librarians Assn., Calif. Soc. Librarians (pres. 1974-75, mem. OCLC Users Council 1984-88), AAUW (pres. Riverside Br. 1976-77), NAACP, Bus. and Profl. Women San Bernardino. Democrat. Baptist. Contbr. articles to publs. in field. Office: San Bernardino County Libr 104 W 4th St San Bernardino CA 92401-1413

ANDERSON, BRADFORD WILLIAM, food company sales executive; b. Redlands, Calif., Feb. 17, 1956; s. B.W. and Helen Louise (Wisel) A.; m. Diane Elizabeth Hutt, Aug. 22, 1981; 1 child, David B. BS in Mgmt., U. Redlands, 1978; MBA in Mktg. Mgmt., Calif. State U., 1982. Cert. instr. in bus. edn., Calif. Store mgr. Fringer's Market, Redlands, Calif., 1978-80; ter. mgr. Carnation Co., Fullerton, Calif., 1980-82, sr. ter. mgr., trainer, 1982-84, dist. sales coord., 1984-85; nat. mgr. sales planning Carnation Co., L.A., 1985-91; nat. mgr. sales tech. Nestle Food Co., Glendale, Calif., 1991—; implementation coord. Carnation Co., L.A., 1984; nat. mgr. sales tech. Nestle Food Co., Glendale, Calif., 1991—; instr. Chaffey Coll., Alta Loma, Calif., 1984-87. Mem. Muckenthaler Cultural Ctr. and Theater, 1987—, Friends of Santa Ana Zoo, 1988, Diamond Bar Improvement Assn., Diamond Bar Ranch Festival, L.A. Zoo Friends and Support, 1990—, Diamond Bar Children's Ctr. Parent Aux.; trustee Diamond Bar Congl. Ch. Named one of Outstanding Young Men in Am., Jaycees, 1984; recipient P. Pat Patterson Meml. Award, Santa Fe Fed. Savs., 1978; Harris Meml. scholar Harris Dept. Stores, 1978. Mem. Am. Mgmt. Assn., Food Industry Sales Club, Alumni Assn. San Bernardino, Calif., Young Alumni Com. U. Redlands, Alpha Gamma Nu. Republican. Home: 24442 E Rosegate Pl Diamond Bar CA 91765-1465 Office: Nestlé Food Co 800 N Brand Blvd Glendale CA 91203-1244

ANDERSON, BRUCE CARL, orthopedic medicine physician; b. San Diego, Nov. 3, 1949; s. Earl Woodrow and Eva (Allison) A.; m. Sherry Poole, June 10, 1979 (div. June 1980); 1 child, Jennifer Elizabeth; m. Gwendolyn Joy, May 6, 1987; children: Jeremy, Ryan. BS in Chemistry, San Diego State U., 1972; MD, UCLA, 1976. Resident Providence Hosp., Portland, Oreg., 1976-79; physician Kaiser Sunnyside Hosp., Clackamas, Oreg., 1980—; orthopedic medicine dept. dir. Kaiser Sunnyside Hosp., Clackamas, 1986—. Author: Office Orthopedics for Primary Care, 1992, House Officer's Guide to Arthrocentesis and Soft Tissue Infection, 1994; contbr. articles to profl. jours.

ANDERSON, BRUCE MORGAN, computer scientist; b. Battle Creek, Mich., Oct. 8, 1941; s. James Albert and Beverly Jane (Morgan) A.; m. Jeannie Marie Highight, May 24, 1975; children: Ronald, Michael, Valerie, John, Carolyn. BEE, Northwestern U., 1964; MEE, Purdue U., 1966; PhD in Elec. Engring., Northwestern U., 1973. Rsch. engr. Zenith Radio Corp., Chgo., 1965-66; assoc. engr. Ill. Inst. Tech. Rsch. Inst., Chgo., 1966-68; sr. electronics engr. Rockwell Internat., Downers Grove, Ill., 1973-75; computer scientist Argonne (Ill.) Nat. Lab., 1975-77; mem. group tech. staff Tex. Instruments, Dallas, 1977-88; sr. scientist BBN Systems and Techs., Cambridge, Mass., 1988-90; systems engr. Lockheed Martin, Denver, 1990-94; sr. scientist CTA Inc., Englewood, Colo., Colo., 1994—; lectr. computer sci. U. Tex.-Arlington and Dallas; adj. prof. computer sci. N. Tex. State U.; vis. indsl. prof. So. Meth. U.; computer systems cons. Info. Internat., Culver City, Calif., HCM Graphic Systems, Gt. Neck, N.Y.; computer cons. depts. geography, transp., econs., sociology and computer sci. Northwestern U., also instr. computer sci.; expert witness for firm Burleson, Pate and Gibson. Contbr. articles to tech. jours. NASA fellow Northwestern U., 1973. Mem. IEEE Computer Soc. (chmn. Dallas 1984-85), Am. Assn. Artificial Intelligence, Assn. Computing Machinery (publs. chmn. 1986 fall joint computer conf. IEEE and Assn. Computing Machinery), Toastmasters Internat., Sigma Xi, Eta Kappa Nu, Theta Delta Chi. Home: 3473 E Euclid Ave Littleton CO 80121-3663 Office: CTA Inc Ste 200 5670 Greenwood Plaza Blvd Englewood CO 80111-2406

ANDERSON, BRUCE NILS, psychiatrist; b. L.A., May 26, 1939; s. Charles Landis and Elizabeth (Caviness) A.; m. Audrey A. Thompson, Dec. 30, 1962; children: Steven, Elizabeth, John. BA, Pacific Union Coll., 1960; MD, Loma Linda U., 1964; MS, Ohio State U., 1969. Diplomate Am. Bd. Psychiatry and Neurology. Intern, resident in medicine Stanford U. Hosps., Palo Alto, Calif., 1964-65; resident in psychiatry Harding Hosp., Worthington, Ohio, 1967-70; fellow in child psychiatry Ohio State U. Hosps., Columbus, 1969; pvt. practice, Hinsdale, Ill., 1970-78, Deer Park, Calif., 1978—; med. dir. mental health programs St. Helena Hosp., Deer Park, 1986—, chief staff, 1986. Chmn. Walter Utt Endowment Com., 1986—. Capt. M.C., U.S. Army, 1965-67. Mem. Am. Psychiat. Assn., Napa County Med. Soc., Am. Judo and Jujitsu Fedn. (black belt), Alpha Omega Alpha. Republican. Adventist. Office: Silverado Psychiat Ctr PO Box 508 Deer Park CA 94576-1508

ANDERSON, CARL E., newspaper reporter, editor, writer; b. Brighton, Colo., Feb. 14, 1932; s. Carl Gustus and Elizabeth Helen (Distel) A.; m. Gloria Jane Green, Aug. 21, 1954; children: Gregory, Stanley, Laurel. BA, Reed Coll., 1967. Freelance writer Oreg., 1954-88; mng. editor, news editor Headlight-Herald, Tillamook, Oreg., 1988—. Author: (poker book) Hold 'Em Poker for Winners, 1984. Pres. Woodstock Boosters, Portland, Oreg., 1955-69; precinct chair Dem. Party, Portland, 1956-59; hwy. adviser U.S. Pres.'s Adv. Cou., Portland, 1958. Served with U.S. Army, 1952-54, Korea. Decorated Commendation for Bravery. Home: PO Box 936 Pacific City OR 97135-0936

ANDERSON, CAROL RUTH, secondary school educator; b. Conewango, N.Y., Aug. 24, 1926; d. Maynard William and Hila Martha (Kent) Phillips; m. George Boyer, Mar. 27, 1948 (div. July 1967); children: Gregory, Gail, Martha; m. Donald Anderson, Jan. 13, 1978 (div. Jan. 1981). Assoc. BS, Jamestown (N.Y.) Community Coll., 1962; BEd, U. Buffalo, 1966; MS in Edn., SUNY, Fredonia, 1971; postgrad., Ariz. State U., 1980-81. Cert. secondary tchr., N.Y., Ariz. Sec. Jamestown Metal Corp., 1957-61; sec. to judge Cattaraugus County, Little Valley, N.Y., 1961-66; bus. educator Jamestown High Sch., 1966-82, Phoenix Union High Sch. Dist., 1982-88; ret., 1988. Rep. committeewoman Cattaraugus County, 1960-62. Mem. N.Y. State Ret. Tchr.'s Assn., U of Buffalo Alumni Assn., NEA, Jamestown High Sch. Tchrs. Club (sec., treas. 1967-82), Ariz. State Ret. Tchrs. Assn., Am. Legion, VFW, Women of Moose. Republican. Methodist.

ANDERSON, CHARLES MICHAEL, accountant; b. Londonderry, N. Ireland, England, July 15, 1944; came to U.S., 1946; s. Albert and Elizabeth (McDaid) A.; m. Terri Lynn Good, Oct. 6, 1981; children: Sean Michael, Kevin Patrick, Kelli Marie. BS, Northern Ill. U., 1966; MBA, U. Southern Calif., 1970. CPA. Staff acct. Price Waterhouse Co., Chgo., 1966-69; mgmt. cons. Price Waterhouse Co., L.A., 1970-72, pvt practice, Manahttan Beach, Calif., 1972-73; mgr. corp. budgets Great Southwest Corp., L.A., 1973-76; dir. internal audit Standard Brands Paint, Torrance, Calif., 1976-86; dir. control systems Standard Brands Paint, 1986-87; chief fin. officer One-Day Paint & Body, Torrance, 1988-89; ptnr. Anderson & Assocs., Manhattan Beach, 1989—. Contbr. articles to profl. jours. Chmn. city budget rev. com. Torrance Area C. of C., 1990-93; pres. Joie De Vive Homeowners Assn., Manhattan Beach, 1979-82, treas., 1985—; pres., chmn. Calif. Mus. Sci. & Industry, L.A., 1975-78; mem. Cath. Big Bros., Torrance, 1973-84 (Ten Yr. award 1984). Fellow AICPA, Calif. Soc. CPAs, Am. Inst. Profl. Bookkeepers; mem. Irish Network So. Calif., Le Tip Internat. (treas./sec. 1991—), Rotary (bd. dirs. 1989—). Democrat. Roman Catholic. Home: 1155 11th St Unit 1 Manhattan Beach CA 90266-6054

ANDERSON, CHARLES RAY, health science facility administrator; b. Big Spring, Tex., Mar. 4, 1943; s. William Madison and Lucille Irene (Plew) A.; m. Tommye Lela Whitehead, Dec. 22, 1967; children: Janice, Leah, Christopher, Clay, Timon. BA, Tex. Tech U., 1966; MEd, Eastern N.Mex. U., 1979. Asst. supt. N.Mex. Christian Children's Home, Portales, 1972—; exec. dir. Christian Child Placement Services div. N.Mex. Christian Children's Home, Portales, 1979—. Served to capt. USAF, 1966-70. Mem. N.Mex. Christian Child Care Assn. (pres. 1984-87), N.Mex. Alliance Adoption Svc. Providers (sec., treas. 1978, 86-88, pres. 1988-92), Am. Assn. Counseling and Devel. Office: NMex Christian Children's Home W Star Rt Box 48 1356 NM 236 Portales NM 88130

ANDERSON, CHARLES ROSS, civil engineer; b. N.Y.C., Oct. 4, 1937; s. Biard Eclare and Melva (Smith) A.; m. Susan Breinholt, Aug. 29, 1961; children: Loralee, Brian, Craig, Thomas, David. BSCE, U. Utah, 1961; MBA, Harvard U., 1963. Registered profl. engr.; cert. land surveyor. Owner, operator AAA Engring. and Drafting, Inc., Salt Lake City, 1960—; mem. acad. adv. com. U. Utah, 1990-91. Mayoral appointee Housing Devel. Com., Salt Lake City, 1981-86; bd. dirs., vice chmn., cons. Met. Water Dist., Salt Lake City, 1985—; bd. dirs., pres., v.p., sec. bd. Utah Mus. Natural History, Salt Lake City, 1980-92; asst. dist. commr. Sunrise Dist. Boy Scouts Am., Salt Lake City, 1985-86; fundraising coord. architects and engrs. United Fund; mem. Sunstone Nat. Adv. Bd., 1980-88; bd. dirs. Provo River Water Users Assn., 1986—. Fellow Am. Gen. Contractors, Salt Lake City, 1960; recipient Hamilton Watch award, 1961. Mem. ASCE, Am. Congress on Surveying and Mapping, U. Utah Alumni Assn. (bd. dirs. 1989-92), Harvard U. Bus. Sch. Club (pres. 1970-72), The Country Club, Bonneville Knife and Fork Club, Rotary (v.p. 1990-91, chmn. election com. 1980-81, vice chmn. and chmn. membership com. 1988-90), Pi Kappa Alpha (internat. pres. 1972-74, trustee endowment fund 1974-80, Outstanding Alumnus 1967, 72), Phi Eta Sigma, Chi Epsilon, Tau Beta Pi. Home: 2689 Comanche Dr Salt Lake City UT 84108-2846 Office: AAA Engring & Drafting Inc 1865 S Main St Salt Lake City UT 84115-2045

ANDERSON, CLIFFORD WARREN, marketing executive; b. San Diego, Mar. 15, 1946; s. Eugene Neu and Ruth Elizabeth (Troch) A.; m. Allison Diane White, Sept., 17, 1973; children: Erin Emily, Briana Elizabeth. BS in Psychology, Aurora Coll., 1968; MA in Psychology, San Diego State U., 1973. Founder San Diego Research Assn., 1972-73; sr. researcher Jagger-Pueschel & Assocs., San Diego, 1973-74, GMA Research, Portland, Oreg., 1974-79; pres. Griggs-Anderson Research, Portland, 1979—. Editor: New Scholar, 1969-73. Mem. Happy Valley Planning Commn. (Oreg.), 1981-82. Mem. Am. Mktg. Assn., Am. Advt. Fedn. Office: Griggs-Anderson Rsch 308 SW 1st Ave Portland OR 97204-3400*

ANDERSON, CLIFTON EINAR, editor, writer; b. Frederic, Wis., Dec. 17, 1923; s. Andrew John and Ida Louise (Johnson) A.; m. Phyllis Mary Nolan, Oct. 5, 1943; children: Kristine, Craig. BS, U. Wis., 1947; MA, U. Calif., Berkeley, 1954. News editor Chgo. Daily Drover's Jour., 1943-45; asst. editor The Progressive, Madison, Wis., 1946-47; dir. publs. Am. Press, Beirut, 1948-53; mgr. rural programs Houston C. of C., 1957-62; faculty Tex. A&M U., College Station, 1962-65; rsch. fellow U. Tex., Austin, 1965-68; faculty Southwestern Okla. U., Weatherford, 1968-72; extension editor U. Idaho, Moscow, 1972—; speaker John Macmurray Centennial Conf., Marquette U., 1991; speaker Nat. Conf. on Peacemaking and Conflict Resolution, 1993, moderator the UN at 50 seminar, 1995; moderator Korea Today and Tomorrow Symposium, Wash. State U., 1995. Editor: The Horse Interlude, 1976; author: (with others) Ways Out: The Book of Changes for Peace, 1988, The Future: Opportunity Not Destiny, 1989, The Years Ahead: Perils, Problems and Promises, 1993, Eating Agendas: Food and Nutrition as Social Problems, 1995; contbr. articles to profl. jours. and mags. Treas. Moscow Sister City Assn., 1986—; founding mem. Coalition for C.Am., Moscow, 1986; chmn. U. idaho Affirmative Action Com., 1990; mem. coun. on home and cmty. care Area Agy. on Aging, 1995; writer campaign staff Senator R.M. La Follette, Jr., Madison, Wis., 1946; on senatorial campaign staff of Hubert H. Humphrey, Mpls., 1948; chmn. Borah Found. for Outlawry of War, U. Idaho, 1986-87, chmn. Borah Symposium, 1986-87. Recipient rsch. award Fund for Adult Edn., 1954-55, U.S. Office Edn., 1965-68, 1st prize in newswriting competition Assn. Am. Agrl. Coll. Editors, 1976, merit award Agrl. Rels. Coun., 1995. Fellow Martin Inst. Peace Studies and Conflict Resolution; mem. World Future Soc. (speaker 6th gen. assembly 1989, 7th gen. assembly 1993), Agr., Food and Social Values Soc., Agrl. Communicators in Edn., Am. Acad. Religion, Profs. World Peace Acad., World Constn. and Parliament Assn., Nat. Assn. Mediation in Edn. Democrat. Home: 234 N Washington St Moscow ID 83843-2757 Office: U Idaho Agrl Communications Ctr Moscow ID 83844-2332

ANDERSON, DAN ROGERS, economist; b. Geneva, Ill., Dec. 12, 1951; s. John Rogers and Clara Idele (Brelsford) A.; m. Jane Frances Stricklin, June 15, 1974. BA in Math. and Econs., Blackburn U., 1974; MS in Econs., Ariz. State U., Tempe, 1976. Staff economist Ariz. Dept. Econ. Security, Phoenix, 1975-80, sr. economist, 1980-84, rsch. adminstr., 1984—; mem. fin. adv. com. State of Ariz.; mem. interagy. policy com. Ariz. Econ. Roundtable, now sec., 1994; cons. in field. Contbr. articles to profl. jours. Recipient U.S. Dept. Labor internship award, 1979; co-recipient Vladimir Chavrid award Interstate Conf. Employment Security Agys., 1991. Mem. Am. Econ. Assn., Phoenix Futures Forum, Western Regional Sci. Assn., Omicron Delta Epsilon. Office: Ariz Dept Econ Security Rsch Adminstrn-733A 1789 W Jefferson St Phoenix AZ 85007-3202

ANDERSON, DAVID, agricultural products executive. V.p. New Beginning Enterprises Inc., Salinis, Calif. Office: New Beginning Enterprises Inc 1355 Abbott St Salinas CA 93901-4566*

ANDERSON, DAVID BOWEN, lawyer; b. Seattle, Sept. 19, 1948; s. Gordon Browne and Elizabeth Josephine (Bowen) A.; m. Laura Ann Jorgensen, May 23, 1975; children: Elizabeth Christine, Christina Louise. BA with great distinction, Stanford U., 1970; JD, U. Mich., 1974; MBA, Western Wash. U., 1982. Bar: Wash. 1974, U.S. Dist. Ct. (we. dist.) Wash. 1974. Assoc. Bogle & Gates, Seattle, 1974-77; ptnr. Anderson & Connell, Bellingham, Wash., 1977—; arbitrator Whatcom County, Am. Arbitration Assn.; instr. Pacific N.W. Admiralty Law Inst., Seattle, 1983, Nat. Fishery Law Symposium, Seattle, 1984. Mem. adv. com. Bellingham Sch. Bd., 1981-82, Bellingham Vocat. Tech. Inst., 1986; mem. Bellingham Pub. Sch. Found. Bd., 1992, pres., 1992-93. Mem. ATLA, ABA, Wash. State Bar Assn. (spl. dist. counsel, rules of profl. practice com.), Whatcom County Bar Assn. (pres. 1986), Maritime Law Assn. U.S. (proctor), Wash. Athletic Club (Seattle), Bellingham Rotary Club, Bellingham Yacht Club, Bellingham Golf and Country Club, Phi Beta Kappa. Presbyterian. Home: 500 16th St Bellingham WA 98225-6315 Office: Anderson & Connell 1501 Eldridge Ave Bellingham WA 98225-2801

ANDERSON, DAVID ELLIOTT, aeronautical engineer; b. Portland, Oreg., Apr. 24, 1964; s. Richard Harold and Barbara Janet (Elliott) A. BS in Aero. and Astronautical Engring., MIT, 1986, MS, 1988. Rsch. asst. MIT Space Systems Lab., Cambridge, Mass., 1986-88; sr. engr./scientist McDonnell Douglas Space Systems Co., Huntington Beach, Calif., 1988—. Mem. Pacific Chorale, Orange County, Calif., 1988—. Mem. AIAA (sr., chmn. robotics tech. com.), Sigma Xi. Republican. Episcopalian. Office: McDonnell Douglas Space Sys 5301 Bolsa Ave Huntington Beach CA 92647-2048

ANDERSON, DAVID MATTHEW, computer programmer; b. Kennewick, Wash., Jan. 25, 1955; s. Samuel Kingdon Anderson and Beverly Jean Clarke. BA, Columbia Coll., 1977; MA, Columbia U., 1980, MPhil, 1981. Project analyst Integral Rsch. Inc., N.Y.C., 1981-84; instr. econs. Iowa State U., Ames, 1984-87; data analyst Cutter Labs Miles Inc, Berkeley, Calif., 1987-89; programmer The Learning Co., Fremont, Calif., 1990-93, Know Ware, Fremont, 1993—. Mem. steering com. Islanders, Lafayette, Calif., 1991—. Democrat. Home: 1940 7th Ave # 19 Oakland CA 94606 Office: Know Ware 2450 Peralta Blvd # 201 Fremont CA 94536

ANDERSON, DEE, government relations consultant; b. Fresno, Calif., Dec. 23, 1953; d. Calvin Carroll Coolidge and Gonvella (Parrish) A.; 1 child, Shakibria Shauntae. BA, U. Wash., 1978, MPA, 1987. Cert. secondary tchr., 1978. Adminstrv. asst. Head Start Program, Seattle, 1981-82; bus. tchr. Seattle and Renton, Wash., 1983-84; bus. edn. instr. Seattle Cen. Community Coll., 1984-86; grad. teaching asst. U. Wash., Seattle, 1985-87; program specialist Wash. State Office of Minority and Women's Bus. Enterprises, Olympia, 1987-89; exec. dir. Operational Emergency Ctr., Seattle, 1989-93; dir. Ctrl. Area Youth Assn., Seattle, 1993—; legis. asst. Seattle City Council, 1984. Dep. dir. Mondale-Ferraro Presdl. campaign, Seattle, 1984; mem. World Affairs Coun., Seattle; Seattle King County Pvt. Industry Coun., 1990—; U.S. del. Seattle Goodwill Games Women's Conf., 1990; USSR/U.S./G.B./Ireland/Japan Internat. Women's Forum in Soviet Union; mem. Dem. Nat. Com., 1992—; U.S. alt. del., White House Conf. on Small Bus., 1995. Mem. Nat. Women's Politic Caucus (honored as Wash. state woman leader 1989), Alpha Kappa Alpha. Democrat. Baptist.

ANDERSON, DONALD BERNARD, oil company executive; b. Chgo., Apr. 6, 1919; s. Hugo August and Hilda (Nelson) A.; m. Patricia Gaylord, 1945 (dec. 1978); m. Sarah Midgette, 1980. BS in Mech. Engring, Purdue U., 1942. Vice pres. Hondo Oil & Gas Co. (formerly Malco Refineries, Inc.), Roswell, N.Mex.; vice pres. Hondo Oil & Gas Co. and subs. corps., Roswell, N.Mex., 1946-63; pres. Anderson Oil Co., Roswell, 1963—; pres. Cotter Corp., 1966-70, chmn. bd., 1966-74; founder, pres. Anderson Drilling Co., Denver, 1974-77; chmn. bd. Anderson Drilling Co., 1977-85. Curator fine arts, mem. acquisitions com. Roswell Mus. and Art Center, 1949-56, trustee, 1956-85, pres. bd., 1960-85, 87—, trustee, pres. 1987-90; bd. dirs. Sch. Am. Rsch., Santa Fe, chmn. bd., 1985-88, bd. dirs. 1989—; bd. dirs. Jargon Soc., Penland, N.C.; regent Ea. N.Mex. U., 1966-72; commr. Smithsonian Instn., Nat. Mus. Am. Art, 1980-88. Lt. USNR, 1942-46. Office: PO Box 1 Roswell NM 88202-0001

ANDERSON, DONALD H., gas industry executive; b. 1948. Graduate, U. Colo., Boulder, 1970. Acct. Peat, Marwick, Mitchell Y Co., Denver, 1970-78, Western Crude Oil Inc., Denver, 1978-82; Lantern Petroleum Corp., Denver, 1983—. Office: Associated Natural Gas Corp 370 17th St Denver CO 80202-5656

ANDERSON, DONALD NORTON, JR., retired electrical engineer; b. Chgo., Aug. 15, 1928; s. Donald Norton and Helen Dorothy (Lehmann) A. BS, Purdue U., 1950, MS, 1952. With Hughes Aircraft Co., Culver City and El Segundo, Calif., 1952-84, sect. head, sr. project engr., 1960-65, tech. mgr. Apollo program, 1965-66, mgr. visible systems dept., 1966-69, 70-73, project mgr., 1969-70, mgr. space sensors lab., 1973-79, mgr. space electro-optical systems labs., 1979-80, mgr. space electro-optical systems labs., 1980-84, ret., 1984. Recipient Apollo Achievement award, 1970; Robert J. Collier Landsat award, 1974. Mem. Research Soc. Am., Nat. Speleological Soc., Am. Theatre Organ Soc., Sigma Xi (sec. Hughes Labs. br. 1974-75), Eta Kappa Nu, Sierra Club. Home: 1885 Craig's Store Rd Afton VA 22920-9634

ANDERSON, DOROTHY FISHER, social worker, psychotherapist; b. Funchal, Madeira, May 31, 1924; d. Lewis Mann Anker and Edna (Gilbert) Fisher (adoptive father David Henry Fisher); m. Theodore W. Anderson, July 8, 1950; children: Robert Lewis, Janet Anderson Yang, Jeanne Elizabeth. BA, Queens Coll., 1945; AM, U. Chgo., 1947. Diplomate Am. Bd. Examiners in Clin. Social Work; lic. clin. social worker, Calif.; registered cert. social worker, N.Y. Intern Cook County (Ill.) Bur. Pub. Welfare, Chgo., 1945-46, Ill. Neuropsychiat. Inst., Chgo., 1946; clin. caseworker, Neurol. Inst. Presbyn. Hosp., N.Y.C., 1947; therapist, Mental Hygiene Clinic VA, N.Y.C., 1947-50; therapist, Child Guidance Clinic Pub. Elem. Sch. 42, N.Y.C., 1950-53; social worker, counselor Cedarhurst (N.Y.) Family Service Agy., 1954-55; psychotherapist, counselor Family Service of the Midpeninsula, Palo Alto, Calif., 1971-73, 79-86, George Hexter, M.D., Inc., 1972-83; clin. social worker Tavistock Clinic, London, 1974-75, El Camino Hosp., Mountain View, Calif., 1979; pvt. practice clin. social work, 1978-92, ret., 1992; cons. Human Resource Services, Sunnyvale, Calif., 1981-86. Hannah G. Solomon scholar U. Chgo., 1945-46; Commonwealth fellow U. Chgo., 1946-47. Fellow Soc. Clin. Social Work (Continuing Edn. Recognition award 1980-83); mem. Nat. Assn. Social Workers (diplomate in clin. social work).

ANDERSON, EDWARD V., lawyer; b. San Francisco, Oct. 17, 1953; s. Virgil P and Edna Pauline (Pedersen) A.; m. Kathleen Helen Dunbar, Sept. 3, 1983; children: Elizabeth D., Hilary J. AB in Econs., Stanford U., 1975, JD, 1978. Bar: Calif. 1978. Assoc. Pillsbury Madison & Sutro, San Francisco, 1978—, ptnr., 1987-94; ptnr. Skjerven Morrill McPherson Franklin and Friel, San Jose, Calif., 1994—. Bd. editors Antitrust Law Development, 1983-86. Trustee Lick-Wilmerding High Sch., San Francisco, 1980—, pres. Mem. ABA, Calif. Bar Assn., San Francisco Bar Assn., Santa Clara Bar Assn. (counsel), City Club San Francisco, Stanford Golf Club, Phi Beta Kappa. Republican. Episcopal. Home: 45 Dorantes Ave San Francisco CA 94116-1430 Office: Skjerven Morrill et al # 700 25 Metro Dr San Jose CA 95110

ANDERSON, FORD A., II (DREW ANDERSON), foundation executive; b. June 8, 1968; m. Ann Arthur, June 8, 1968; 1 child, Megan Elizabeth. BA in History magna cum laude, Butler U., 1968; MA in Am. History, U. Wis., 1973, MA in Bus., 1976. Adminstrv. asst. The Kresge Found., Troy, Mich., 1976-80; program officer M.J. Murdock Charitable Trust, 1980-84, sr. program officer, 1985-88, exec. dir., 1988—. Former pres., mem. adv. bd. Ctr. Arts Adminstrn., U. Wis.-Madison; past pres., treas. Pacific N.W. Grantmakers Forum. Officer Engr. and Mil. Intelligence Specialists, U.S. Army, 1968-71, lt. col. res. Mem. Res. Officer Assn. (former v.p. Army Oreg. dept., former sec., pres. 1993-94). Office: MJ Murdock Charitable Trust PO Box 1618 Vancouver WA 98668-1618*

ANDERSON, GEOFFREY ROBERT, research manager; b. Eckville, Alta., Can., July 30, 1946; s. Milton Carson and Gladys Norma (Albrecht) A.; m. M. Lee, Oct. 10, 1971; children: Scott Jared, Matthew Jason. BS in Zoology, U. Calif., Long Beach, 1968; MS in Physiology, UCLA, 1969. Rsch. assoc. in immunology City of Hope, Duarte, Calif., 1970-72; rsch. assoc. in biomed. engring. U. So. Calif., L.A., 1972-73; biology instr. Mt. St. Mary's Coll., L.A., 1973-78; rsch. assoc. in biochemistry UCLA-Harbor Med. Ctr., Torrance, Calif., 1978-80; rsch. chemist Diagnostic Products Corp., L.A., 1980-81; rsch. sci., sr. sci. Beckman Instruments, Brea, Calif., 1981-86; rsch. program mgr. Hycor Biomedical Inc., Garden Grove, Calif., 1986—. Contbr. articles to profl. jours. Mem. Am. Chem. Soc., Am. Assn. Clin. Chemists, Am. Soc. Microbiology, Calif. Assn. Toxicologists, Clin. Ligand Assay Soc. Office: Hycor Biomedical Inc 7272 Chapman Ave Garden Grove CA 92641-2103

ANDERSON, GERALD VERNE, retired aerospace company executive; b. Long Beach, Calif., Oct. 25, 1931; s. Gordon Valentine and Aletha Marian (Parkins) A.; m. Judith B. Marx, May 14, 1992; children by previous marriage: Lori Jean Anderson Fronk, Gregory Verne, David Harman, Lynn Elaine Anderson Lee, Brian Earl, Michael Gordon. AA, Long Beach City Coll., 1952; BS, U. Calif., Berkeley, 1958. Registered profl. engr., Calif. Tech. specialist N. Am. Aviation Co., L.A., 1958-65; tech. specialist McDonnell Douglas Astronautics, Huntington Beach, Calif., 1965-84; mgr. McDonnell Douglas Astronautics, Huntington Beach, 1984-87; sr. mgr. McDonnell Douglas Aerospace, Huntington Beach, 1987-94; cons. Mitsubishi Heavy Industries, Nagoya, Japan, 1972-73, Aeritalia, Turin, Italy, 1975-76. Patentee, portable vacuum chamber, electron beam welding device. Mem. Westminster (Calif.) Planning Com., 1974, Huntington Beach Citizens Adv. Com., 1975, Westminster Bicentennial Com., 1976, L.A. Classical Ballet Guild, 1992—. Mem. Soc. Mfg. Engrs., Soc. Automotive Engrs., Aerospace Industries Assn., AIAA. Republican. Home: 3452 Falcon Ave Long Beach CA 90807-4814

ANDERSON, GLEN CLARK, judge; b. Glendale, Calif., Nov. 26, 1944; s. O. Kenneth and Rhoda S. (Putzig) A.; m. Diane L. Decker, Aug. 26, 1967 (div. 1978); 1 child, Kenneth Paul; m. Yvonne Iryne Owens, Jan. 2, 1983. BS, Colo. State U., 1967, MA, 1970; JD, Willamette U., 1974. Bar: Alaska 1974, U.S. Dist. Ct. Alaska 1976, U.S. Ct. Appeals (9th cir.) 1976. Tchr. Cheyenne (Wyo.) Pub. Schs., 1967-68, Richland (Wash.) Pub. Schs., 1968-71; law clk. to hon. justice Robert Erwin Alaska Supreme Ct., Anchorage, 1974-75; asst. dist. atty. Alaska Dept. of Law, Anchorage, 1975-77, asst. atty. gen., 1977-78; judge State of Alaska Dist. Ct., Anchorage, 1978-91, State of Alaska Superior Ct., Valdez, 1991—. Mem. ABA (jud. adminstrn. div.), Alaska Bar Assn. Methodist. Home: P O Box 1622 Medford OR 97501-0124 Office: Superior Ct PO Box 127 Valdez AK 99686-0127

ANDERSON, GORDON SUTHERLAND, periodontist; b. Chgo., Dec. 19, 1934; s. Donald Sutherland and Elsie Florence (Ferguson) A.; m. Marilynn LaVance Holm, Sept. 26, 1964; children: Lindsey Paige, Tracey Elisabeth. Student, Wheaton Coll., Ill., 1952-55; DDS, Northwestern U., Chgo., 1959; MSD, U. Wash., 1964. Pvt. practice peridontics San Mateo, Calif., 1964-82, Grants Pass, Oreg., 1983—; mayor City of Grants Pass, 1993—. Mem. Grants Pass City Coun., 1987-92, pres., 1989; pres. So. Oreg. Coun. Mayors, 1994. Lt. USN, 1959-61. Mem. We. Soc. Peridontology (sec. 1975-77), Am. Dental Assn., Oreg. Dental Assn., Am. Acad. Peridontology, Oreg. Soc. Peridontists, Rogue Valley Dental Soc., Rotary. Republican. Office: 1201E NE 7th St Grants Pass OR 97526-1423

ANDERSON, GRANT ALLEN, librarian; b. San Diego, Jan. 31, 1949; s. Grant Symons and Elizabeth (Allen) A.; m. Lucile Rollins Hurst, Feb. 2, 1978; children: Stewart, Shannon, Kimberly, Whitney. AB, San Diego State U., 1973; MLS, Brigham Young U., 1975. Ref. librarian hist. dept. Church of Jesus Christ of Latter Day Saints, Salt Lake City, 1976-77; supr., gen. ref. Church of Jesus Christ of Latter Day Saints, 1978-84, mgr. pub. svcs., 1984-86, mgr. library, 1987-88, dir. library divsn., 1989—, acting dir. spl. projects, 1993—. Mem. ALA, Utah Library Assn. Office: LDS Ch Hist Dept Ch Libr Archives 50 E North Temple Salt Lake City UT 84150-0002

ANDERSON, HAROLD PAUL, historian, archivist, bank executive; b. Darby, Pa., Oct. 4, 1946; s. Harold P. and Mary Ann A.; B.A., Villanova U., 1968; M.A., Ohio State U., 1969, Ph.D., 1978. Teaching and research fellow Stanford U., 1973-75; archives and library specialist Hoover Instn., Stanford, Calif., 1975-77; asst. archivist dept. history Wells Fargo Bank, N.A., San Francisco, 1977-79, pub. relations officer and corp. archivist dept. history, 1979, asst. v.p. and corp. archivist dept. history, 1979—, v.p. dept. history, 1984—; v.p. and divsn. mgr., corp. mktg. and adv., 1992—; v.p., divsn. mgr. Wells Fargo Brand Mgmt., 1994—; lectr. Stanford U., 1981; bd. dirs. Nat. Council on Pub. History, 1981-83. Mem. Am. Hist. Assn., Orgn. Am. Historians, Soc. Am. Archivists. Office: Wells Fargo Bank 420 Montgomery St San Francisco CA 94104-1205

ANDERSON, HENRY LEE NORMAN, academic administrator; b. Ogeechee, Ga., May 23, 1934; s. Lee and Louise Anderson; m. Agnes A. Fox, 1961; 3 children. BSEd, Cheyney U. Pa., 1957; EdD, UCLA, 1972; MAR, Yale U., 1973. Lic. marriage, family, child counsellor. Tchr. L.A. County Schs., 1961-66; instr., adminstr. L.A. Unified Schs. Dist., 1967-68; assoc. dir. dept. spl. edn. program UCLA, 1968-69; dir. Evaluations & Mgmt. Internat., Inc., 1971—. HELP, Inc; prin. Worldwide Trading Co.; v.p. Windsor U., L.A., 1973-75; chancellor, univ. pres. City U. L.A., 1974—; pres. Bakersfield Sch. Law, City U. Sch. Law; asst. prof. Grad. Sch. Edn., Loyola U. and Calif. State U., L.A., 1968-72; cons. in field; real estate developer; internat. commodities broker/cons. Author: You & Race: A Christian Reflects, 1960, No Use Cryn, 1961, Revolutionary Urban Teaching, 1973, Helping Hand: 8 Day Diet Diet Programs, 1986, Helping Hand: A Guide to Healthy Living, 1990, Wellness Guide Book (German edit.), 1992, The American Diet (Japanese edit.), 1994, Mood Poetry for Everyone, 1994, Anderson Small Books series: Fountain of Youth Discovered, What Vegetarians Should Know About Wellness, others; editor, publisher What If...? newsletter; hosts weekly talk radio and wellness TV series (1991 Renaissance award as best cable TV talk show); prodr. (TV show) Dr. Henry L.N. Anderson on Wellness Issues; lectr. in field. Founder, chancellor Martin Luther King Meml. Urban Core Multi-Versity; founder Young Internat. Entrepreneurs in Wellness, Organic Wellness Network, The H.O.L.I.S.T.I.C. Group, Youth Employment Svcs., Organic Wellness Crusade, Imahe Wellness Village. Mem. NAACP (life), Nat. Speakers' Assn., Wilshire C. of C., UCLA Alumni Assn., Cheyney Alumni Assn., Yale Club Soc. Calif., World Fedn., Million Dollar Club. Republican. Episcopalian. Address: PO Box 7219 Beverly Hills CA 90212-7219 Office: City Univ Los Angeles 3960 Wilshire Blvd Ste 501 Los Angeles CA 90010-3324

ANDERSON, HERSCHEL VINCENT, librarian; b. Charlotte, N.C., Mar. 14, 1932; s. Paul Kemper and Lillian (Johnson) A. B.A., Duke U., 1954; M.S., Columbia U., 1959. Library asst. Bklyn. Public Library, 1954-59; asst. bookmobile librarian King County Public Library, Seattle, 1959-62; asst. librarian Longview (Wash.) Public Library, 1962-63; librarian N.C. Mus. Art, Raleigh, 1963-64; audio-visual cons. N.C. State Library, Raleigh, 1964-68; dir. Sandhill Regional Library, Rockingham, N.C., 1968-70; asso. state librarian Tenn. State Library and Archives, Nashville, 1970-72; unit dir. Colo. State Library, Denver, 1972-73; state librarian S.D. State Library, Pierre, 1973-80; dir. Mesa (Ariz.) Public Library, 1980—; dir. Bibliographical Ctr. for Rsch., Denver, 1974-80, v.p. 1977; mem. Western Coun. St. Librs., 1975-80, v.p., 1978, pres., 1979; mem. Ariz. St. Libr., LSCA Adv. Coun., 1981-84, pres., 1982-83; Ariz. Libr. Devel. Coun., 1991-93; mem. libr. technician tng. adv. com. Mesa C.C., 1982-85, mem. commn. for excellence, 1993—; chmn. Serials On-Line in Ariz. Consortia, 1985-86. Jr. warden St. Mark's Episcopal Ch., Mesa, 1985-87, vestryman, 1987-90, 95—; del. ann. conv. Diocese of Ariz., 1989-92, 94—, mem. archives com., 1990—; mem., treas. Maricopa County Libr. Coun., 1991—, pres., 1983, 93; mem. Valley Citizens League, 1991—. With U.S. Army, 1955-57. Recipient Emeritus Honors Ariz. Library Friends, 1987. Mem. ALA, S.D. Libr. Assn. (hon. life, Libr. of Yr. award 1977), Mountain Plains Libr. Assn. (pres. 1974, bd. dirs. 1974-77, 86-87, Intellectual Freedom award 1979, Ariz. Libr. Assn. (exe. com. 1986-87), Chief Officers of State Libr. Agys. (bd. dirs. 1974-76), Kiwanis (bd. dirs. Mesa 1981-86, v.p. 1983, pres. 1985-86), Phi Kappa Psi. Office: Mesa Pub Libr 64 E 1st St Mesa AZ 85201-6768

ANDERSON, HOLLY GEIS, women's clinic executive, radio personality; b. Waukesha, Wis., Oct. 23, 1946; d. Henry H. and Hulda (Sebroff) Geis; m. Richard Kent Anderson, June 6, 1969. BA, Azusa Pacific U., 1970. CEO Oak Tree Antiques, San Gabriel, Calif., 1975-82; pres., founder, CEO Premenstrual Syndrome Treatment Clinic, Arcadia, Calif., 1982—, Hormonal Treatment Ctrs., Inc., Arcadia, 1992-94; lectr. radio and TV shows, L.A.; on-air radio personality Women's Clinic with Holly Anderson, 1990—. Author: What Every Woman Needs to Know About PMS (audio cassette), 1987, The PMS Treatment Program (video cassette), 1989, PMS Talk (audio cassette), 1989. Mem. NAFE, The Dalton Soc. Republican. Office: PMS Treatment Clinic 150 N Santa Anita Ave Ste 755 Arcadia CA 91006-3113

ANDERSON, IRIS ANITA, retired secondary education educator; b. Forks, Wash., Aug. 18, 1930; d. James Adolphus and Alma Elizabeth (Haase) Gilbreath; m. Donald Rene Anderson, 1951; children: Karen Christine, Susan Adele, Gayle Lynne, Brian Dale. BA in Teaching, U. Wash., 1969; MA in English, Seattle U., 1972. Cert. English tchr., adminstr., Calif. Tchr. Issaquah (Wash.) Sr. High Sch., 1969-77, L.A. Sr. High Sch., 1977-79. Nutrition vol. Santa Monica (Calif.) Hosp. Aux., Jules Stein Eye Inst., L.A.; mem. Desert Beautiful, Palm Springs Panhellenic; mem. Rancho Mirage Reps. W-Key activities scholar U. Wash. Mem. NEA, DAR (vice-regent Palm Springs, 1st vice-regent Cahuilla chpt.), AAUW, LWV, Wash. Speech Assn., Nat. Thespians, Bob Hope Cultural Ctr., Palm Springs Press Women, Coachella Valley Hist. Soc., Palm Desert Womens Club, Calif. Ret. Tchrs. Assn., CPA Wives Club, Desert Celebrities, Rancho Mirage Womens Club, Round Table West, World Affairs Coun. Republican.

ANDERSON, JACK JOE, communications and training consultant; b. Lipan, Tex., Oct. 22, 1928; s. William Amon and Tommie Lucille (Roberts) A.; B.A., San Jose State U., 1965, M.A., 1967; postgrad. in bus. adminstrn. Pepperdine U., Los Angeles; m. Maria I. Kamantauskas, Mar. 13, 1976; children: Mark, Douglas, Craig. Asst. mgr. edn. systems Lockheed Missiles & Space Co., Sunnyvale, Calif., 1966-69; v.p. Learning Achievement Corp., San Jose, Calif., 1969-74; mgr. instrnl. systems Ford Aerospace & Communications Corp., Pasadena, Calif., 1974-83; pres. Anderson & Assocs., Alta Loma, Calif., 1983—; cons. tng. programs and systems, 1969—. Served with USAF, 1946-66. Recipient Nat. award for tng. program design Indsl. TV Assn., 1974. Mem. Am. Mgmt. Assn., Am. Soc. Tng. and Devel. Contbr. tech. and gen. instrnl. materials in field. Office: Anderson & Assocs 9155 Carrari Ct Alta Loma CA 91737-1557

ANDERSON, JAMES THOMAS, telecommunications executive; b. Atlanta, Ga., Apr. 26, 1939; s. Leeman and Dorothy (Shippey) A.; m. Elizabeth McLean Black, Mar. 9, 1986; children: James T. Jr., Daniel B. BS summa cum laude, Davidson Coll., 1961; postgrad., U. Va., 1961-63. Various comptroller positions C&P Telephone, Washington, 1963-72; budget dir. AT&T, N.Y.C., 1972-75, dir. banking relations, 1976; v.p., comptroller Northwestern Bell, Omaha, 1977-82, v.p. regulatory affairs, 1982-84; v.p., treas. U.S. West, Inc., Englewood, Colo., 1984—. Treas. YMCA of Omaha-Council Bluffs, Omaha, 1977-82; pres. Jr. Achievement of Omaha, 1982-84. NSF fellow, 1961-63, Woodrow Wilson fellow, 1963. Mem. Fin. Execs. Inst., Colo. Assn. Commerce and Industry (bd. dirs. 1985—), Phi Beta Kappa. Republican. Presbyterian. Club: Metropolitan (Englewood). Office: US West Inc 7800 E Orchard Rd Englewood CO 80111-2533

ANDERSON, JANET ALM, librarian; b. Lafayette, Ind., Dec. 20, 1952; d. Charles Henry and Lenore Elaine Alm; m. Jay Allan Anderson, May 21, 1983. BS, Bemidji State U., 1975; MA in Folklore, Western Ky. U., 1981, MSLS in Libr. Sci., 1982; PhD in Recreation Resources Mgmt., Utah State U., 1994. Cert. elem. tchr., sch. libr. and media specialist. Storyteller, puppeteer North Country Arts Coun., Bemidji, Minn., 1975-76; head children's libr. Bemidji State U., 1976-77; mid. sch. libr. Custer County Sch. Dist., Miles City, Mont., 1977-79; tchr. of gifted and talented Custer County Sch. Dist., Miles City, 1979-80; folklore archivist Western Ky. U., Bowling Green, 1981-83; head children's and young adults' svcs. Bowling Green Pub. Libr., 1983-85; head of serials Utah State U., Logan, 1986-91, campus svcs. libr., 1991—, adj. asst. prof. forestry, 1995—, chmn. adv. bd. Women's Ctr., 1988-92; adj. instr. Miles Community Coll., 1978-80; cons. to various Am. outdoor museums; speaker Utah Endowment for the Humanities Speakers Bur., Salt Lake City, 1987-90. Author: Old Fred, 1972, A Taste of Kentucky, 1986 (Ky. State Book Fair award), Bounty, 1990; (with others) Advances in Serials Management, Vol. 3, 1989, Vendors and Library Acquisitions, 1991; contbr. to Ency. of Am. Popular Beliefs and Superstitions, articles on folklore, librarianship and museology to mags. and periodicals; delivered radio and TV presentations on folklore and librarianship. Co-founder and past pres. Rosebud chpt. Nat. Audubon Soc., Miles City, Mont., 1978-80; invited author Ky. State Book Fair, 1986, Utah Arts Festival, 1991; mem. Women and Gender Rsch. Inst., Friends of Brooks Free Libr. (life). Recipient Exhibit and Program Grant Nat. Endowment for the Arts, Bowling Green, Ky., 1984-85. Mem. ALA, Nat. Audubon Soc. (bd. trustees Bridgerland chpt. 1995—), Nat. Assn. Interpretation, John Muir Assn. (founder environ. ctr.), Utah Libr. Assn., Consortium of Utah Women in Higher Edn. (campus coord. 1989-91), Am. Folklore Soc., Utah Folklore Soc., Assn. Living Hist. Farms and Agrl. Mus., Visitor Studies Assn., Am. Assn. Mus., Assn. Coll. and Rsch. Librs., Old Main Soc., Xi Sigma Pi. Democrat. Lutheran. Home: 1090 S 400 E Providence UT 84332-9461 Office: Utah State U Merrill Libr Logan UT 84322-3000

ANDERSON, JANETTE BERYL, clergy member; b. Longview, Wash., June 27, 1953; d. Guy Orrin and Ruby Mae (Alexander) A.; m. James Melvin Butler, July 16, 1988. BA magna cum laude, U. Puget Sound, 1975; MDiv, Princeton Theol. Sem., 1978; Cert. Spiritual Dir., Seattle U. Grad. intern Trenton (N.J.) Ecumenical Area Ministries, 1978-79; assoc. pastor 1st United Meth. Ch., Seattle, 1979-80; pastor Capitol Hill United Meth. Ch., Seattle, 1980-84; founder, dir. Ctr. for Christian Feminist Ministries, Seattle, 1984-90; Protestant chaplain St. Cabrini Hosp., Seattle, 1986-89; marriage prep coord. campus Christian ministry U. Wash., Seattle, 1989-91; spiritual dir., cons. Wildernes Retreats, Seattle, 1992—; lectr. in field. Contbg. author: Womenpsalms, 1993. Mem. AAS com. Ch. Coun. Greater Seattle, 1981-82; mem. bd. of ch. and soc. PNW United Meth. Ch., Seattle, 1980-84, mem. comn. on status and role of women, 1990-91, mem. conf. bd. ordained ministry, Wash. and Idaho, 1992—; mem. religion dept. scholarship com. U. Puget Sound, Tacoma, Wash., 1993—. Recipient Town and Country award Capital Hill United Meth. Ch., 1982. Com. mem. Ch. Coun. Greater Seattle, 1981-82; bd. ch. and soc. PNW United Meth. Ch., Seattle, 1980-84, mem. commn. on status and role of women, 1990-91, mem. conf. bd. ordained ministry, Wash. and Idaho, 1992—; mem. religion dept. scholarship com. U. Puget Sound, Tacoma, Wash., 1993—; bd. dirs. Pastoral Therapy Assocs., Tacoma, Wash., 1995—. Methodist. Office: Woodland Park United Meth Ch 302 N 78th St Seattle WA 98103

ANDERSON, JEAN BLANCHE, fiction writer; b. St. Louis, Sept. 13, 1940; d. Clifford George and Blanche Jean (Pell) Schulze; m. Donald Wyckliffe Anderson; children: Thomas, Laura. AA, Harris Tchrs. Coll., 1960; student, U. Mo., 1965-66; BA, U. Alaska, 1977, MFA, 1980. Lectr. in English U. Alaska, Fairbanks, 1980-85, 88-89, vis. asst. prof., 1990-91; book reviewer Fairbanks Daily News-Miner, Heartland, Alaska, 1985-88; poet in the schs. Fairbanks Arts Assn., 1981-82; faculty mem. Midnight Sun Writers' Conf., Fairbanks, 1990, 91, 92. Author: In Extremis and Other Alaskan Stories, 1989; co-editor Inroads: Alaska's Twenty-Seven Fellowship Writers, 1988; contbr. short stories, poems and essays to periodicals. Fellowship Alaska State Coun. on Arts, 1982; recipient PEN Syndicated Fiction award PEN Am. Ctr., 1985. Mem. Poets and Writers Inc. Home: 509 Aquila St Fairbanks AK 99712-1320

ANDERSON, JOHN DAVID, architect; b. New Haven, Dec. 24, 1926; s. William Edward and Norma Vere (Carson) A.; m. Florence A. Van Dyke, Aug. 26, 1950; children—Robert Stewart, David Carson. A.B. cum laude, Harvard U., 1949, M.Arch., 1952. Draftsman John K. Monroe, Architect, Denver, 1952-54; draftsman, designer, assoc. Wheeler & Lewis, Architects, Denver, 1954-60; prin. John D. Anderson, Denver, 1960-64; ptnr. Anderson, Barker Rinker, Architects, Denver, 1965-69, A-B-R Partnership, Architects, Denver, 1970-75; prin., pres. Anderson Mason Dale P.C., Denver, 1975—; vis. lectr. U. Colo., U. N.Mex., U. Nebr., U. Cape Town, Colo. State U., Plymouth Polytech., Eng.; chmn. Denver Bldg. Dept. Bd. Appeals, 1974-75; chmn. Colo. Gov.'s Task Force on Removal of Archtl. Barriers, 1972-74; vice chmn. Colo. Bd. Non-Residential Energy Conservation Stds., 1978-80. Prin. works include: Community Coll. Denver, North campus, Westminster, 1977, Solar Energy Rsch. Inst., Golden, 1980 (award winning solar heated structures). Served with USNR, 1944-46. Fellow AIA (pres. Colo. chpt. 1967, Silver Medal, 1984, Firm of Yr. award 1986 Western Mountain region); mem. Colo. Soc. Architects (Architect of Yr. award 1987, pres. 1971), Internat. Solar Energy Soc., Council Ednl. Facility Planners (internat. chmn. energy com. 1980). Republican. Congregationalist. Home: 30262 Rainbow Hills Rd Golden CO 80401-8301 Office: Anderson Mason Dale PC 1615 17th St Denver CO 80202-1203

ANDERSON, JOLENE SLOVER, small business owner, publishing executive, consultant; b. Tulare, Calif.; James P. Sr., and Helen B. (Walters) Slover; m. Douglas R. Anderson, June 14, 1975; 1 child by previous marriage, Sabrina Jo. Student, Victor Valley Coll., Riverside City Coll. Model Connor Sch. Modeling, Fresno, Calif., 1955-65; actress M. Kosloff Studios, Hollywood, Calif., 1965; nat. sales mgr. Armed Services Publs., Hollywood, Calif., 1966-68; pres., dir. Sullivan Publs., Inc., Riverside, Calif., 1970-82; pres., chief exec. officer Heritage House Publs., Riverside, 1983-84; pres. Jolene S. Anderson Pub. Cons., Inc., Riverside, 1987—; bd. dirs. Riverside County Econ. Devel. Coun. Co-comdr. March AFB, Riverside Tourists and Conv.; mem. YWCA, City of Riverside Cultural Heritage Bd., Yr. 2000 Com., 1988, Riverside County Philharm. Bd., Temecula-Murrieta Econ. Devel. Corp. Named Woman of Achievement YWCA, 1989, Humanitarian of Yr. Rotary, 1990. Mem. Riverside Downtown Assn., Sun City/Menifee Valley C. of C., Greater Riverside C. of C., Temecula Valley C. of C., Temecula Valley Econ. Devel. Corp., Soroptimists (Riverside chpt.). Office: PO Box 800 Riverside CA 92502-0800

ANDERSON, JONPATRICK SCHUYLER, financial consultant, therapist, archivist; b. Chgo., July 20, 1951; s. Ralph Anderson and Helena Hilda (Robinson) Hardy; children: André, Mary, David. Attended, Cen. YMCA Cmty. Coll., Chgo., 1970, Lawrence Merrick Acad. Dramatic Arts, 1972-73, Cmty. Coll. Air Force, 1974, U. Md., 1975, Grossmont C.C., 1994; AA, L.A. Trade Tech. Coll., 1978; attended, Calif. State U., L.A., 1978-79; BA, UCLA, 1979; attended, San Diego Cmty. Coll. Dist., 1981, 89-92; postgrad., SUNY, Albany, 1983, Govs. State U., 1985, San Diego State U., 1982-83; MRE, PhD, Internat. Sem. (in coop. with Unification Theol. Sem. N.Y.), 1989, DMin, 1994. Clerical supr. VA, L.A., 1976-80; fin. adminstr. Antioch Primitive Bapt. Ch., L.A., 1979-80; pres., exec. dir. All-Around Prodns., L.A., 1980-83; assoc. minister St. Stephen Ch., San Diego, Calif., 1983-87; stadium mgr. San Diego Jack Murphy Stadium, 1985-87; mgr. Horton Plaza Shopping Ctr., San Diego, 1985-86; exec. dir. Christ-Immanuel Ministerial Assn., San Diego, 1983—; acting supr. psychiatry dept. VA Mental Health Clinic, San Diego, 1991—; intern in counseling and psychiatry U. Calif. San Diego Med. Ctr., 1992-93; supr. Enid Rockwell MD, 1992-93; pvt. investigator Merit Protective Svcs., L.A., 1972-74; adminstrv. asst. Dept. Def., 1981; cons. pvt. practice mgmt., cons. comptr., San Diego, 1981-82; cons. writer All-Around Music divsn. Broadcast Music, Inc., San Diego, 1980—; instr. San Diego Community Coll. Dist., 1984; libr. asst. San Diego State U., 1982-83; chaplain of the Day U. Calif., San Diego, 1984-85; archives technician Nat. Archives & Records Adminstrn., Laguna Niguel, Calif., 1988; ind. assoc. Pre-paid Legal Svcs., San Diego, 1994—. Mem. Am. Freedom Coalition, Washington, 1988, Causa, USA, Washington, 1985-87; mem. Internat. Coun. of Cmty. Chs. With USMC, Vietnam, 1968-70; with U.S. Army, 1975-76; with USAF, 1974, 80-82; 2d lt. USAR, 1979-80. Grammy nominee NARAS, 1980; recipient Personal award former Pres. Ronald Reagan, L.A., 1988, Letter of Commendation from Duncan Hunter, U.S. Rep., 52nd Dist., Calif., 1994. Mem. NAACP (life), NARAS, AFTRA, AGVA, Assn. MBA Execs. (Bus. award 1980), UCLA Alumni Assn. (life, interviewing com. adv. and scholarship program 1988—, bd. dirs. scholarship chmn. 1991—), Res. Officers Assn. of U.S. (life), UCLA Black Alumni Assn. (life, bd. dirs., scholarship chmn.), N.G. Assn. Calif. (life), U. Calif.-San Diego Med. Ctr. Aux. (life), Nat. Conf. Ministry to Armed Forces, VFW (life), DAV (life), AMVETS, Am. Legion, Ret. Officers Assn. U.S., Am. Assn. Religious Counselors. Democrat. Mem. Ch. of God. Office: Christ-Immanuel Ministries PO Box 1202 San Diego CA 92112-1202

ANDERSON, JUDITH ANNE, academic administrator; b. Little Falls, Minn., June 23, 1943; d. Thomas Martin and Elda Rose Ethel (Klapel) McDonnell; m. Gene Wesley Anderson, Aug. 12, 1961 (div. 1993); children: Jeffery Thomas, Gregory Carl, Joel Michael, Julie Ann. AA, Cambridge (Minn.) Anoka-Ramsey C.C., 1982; BA, Met. State U., St. Paul, 1987; MS, Cardinal Stritch Coll., Milw., 1990. Bookkeeper Peoples State Bank, Cambridge, 1971-77; bus. mgr. Cambridge Anoka-Ramsey C.C., 1979-90; ednl. coord. Barnes Bus. Coll., Denver, 1991-92, dir., 1992-94; cons. for low-income families U. Minn. Extension Dept., Isanti County, 1987-90. Treas. Govt. Maple Ridge Twp., Isanti County, Minn., 1978-91; chmn. United Charities Dr., Maple Ridge Twp., 1980-85, Jefferson County Ext. Adv. Bd., 1994—. Named State Vol. Gov. of Minn., 1987, 88, 89, 90. Mem. AAUW (Denver), Muskies Inc., Women for Fishing, Hunting and Wildlife, Lady Ducks, Nat. Outdoors Women, Phi Theta Kappa (Alpha Minn. chpt.). Republican. Mem. Covenant Ch. Home: 6836 S Everett Ct Littleton CO 80123-4023

ANDERSON, JUDSON TRUETT, psychiatrist; b. Durham, N.C., Oct. 23, 1933; s. Henry Brown and Grace Elizabeth (Ganzert) A.; m. Evelyn Marie Hunt, June 17, 1955; 1 child, David Brian. BS, Wake Forest Coll., 1955; MD, Bowman Gray Med. Sch., 1959. Diplomate Am. Bd. Psychiatry and Neurology. Intern Fitzsimmons Gen. Hosp., Denver, 1959-60; flight surgeon USAF, 1960-63; resident in psychiatry U. Colo., Denver, 1963-66; chief of psychiatry USAF Acad. Hosp., Colo., 1966-71; pvt. practice Colorado Springs, Colo., 1971-73; psychiatrist Psychiat. Assocs., P.C., Colorado Springs, 1973—; mem. staff Meml. Hosp., Colorado Springs, 1971—; mem. courtesy staff Penrose-St. Francis Health Care System, Colorado Springs, 1971—. Cedar Springs Psychiat. Ctr., Colorado Springs, 1971—; med. cons. Divsn. Vocat. Rehab., Colorado Springs, 1976—. Lt. col. USAF, 1959-71. Mem. Colo. Med. Soc., Colorado Springs Psychiat. Soc., El Paso County Med. Soc., Phi Beta Kappa. Baptist. Office: Psychiat Assocs PC 1155 Kelly Johnson Blvd Ste 111 Colorado Springs CO 80920-3957

ANDERSON, KARL RICHARD, aerospace engineer, consultant; b. Vinita, Okla., Sept. 27, 1917; s. Axel Richard and Hildred Audrey (Marshall) A.; B.S., Calif. Western U., 1964, M.A., 1966; Ph.D., U.S. Internat. U., 1970; m. Jane Shigeko Hiratsuka, June 20, 1953; 1 son, Karl Richard. Engr. personnel subsystems Atlas Missile Program, Gen. Dynamics, San Diego, 1960-63; design engr. Solar divsn. Internat. Harvester, San Diego, 1964-66, sr. design engr., 1967-69, project engr., 1970-74, product safety specialist, 1975-78;

aerospace engring. cons., 1979-86; cons. engring., 1979—; lectr. Am. Indian Sci. and Engring. Soc. Served to maj. USAF, 1936-60. Recipient Spl. Commendation award San Diego County Bd. Supervisors, 1985, Spl. Commendation award San Diego City Council, 1985, Spl. Commendation award City of San Diego, 1994, Grace "Peter" Sargent award San Diego City Natural Park, 1994. Registered profl. engr., Calif. Republican. Episcopalian. Home: 5886 Scripps St San Diego CA 92122-3212

ANDERSON, KATHERYN LUCILLE, language arts educator and author; b. Aberdeen, Md., Aug. 17, 1949; d. Boyd Frederick and Lucy Charlotte Anderson. BS in Edn., U. Md., 1973; MA in Spl. Edn., Adams State Coll., Alamosa, Colo., 1977; MA in Ednl. Tech., U. Colo., 1986. Lic. profl. tchr., Colo. Mental health paraprofl. Prince George's County Mental Health, Landover, Md., 1970-73; spl. edn. tchr. Fountain/Ft. Carson (Colo.) Sch. Dist., 1973-75; instr. mil. program Pikes Peak Cmty. Coll., Colorado Springs, Colo., 1977-78; spl. edn. tchr. Harrison Sch. Dist., Colorado Springs, 1978-88, tchr. lang. arts, 1988—, team leader lang. arts, 1989—, dept. chair, 1992—; lectr. in field. Author: English and American Culture, 1991, English and American Culture 6, 1993, English and American Culture 7, 1993, A Writing Companion, 1993; co-author: The Sound of the Apple IIe, 1986, The Shape of the Apple IIe, 1986. Chpt. II Ednl. Program Devel. grantee Harrison Sch. Dist., 1991, 92, 93. Mem. Colo. Assn. Middle Level Educators, Colo. Lang. Arts Soc., Nat. Coun. Tchrs. English, Nat. Women's History Project Network, Tenn. Walking Horse Assn. (rep., stock show and horse exposition 1993-94), Tenn. Walking Horse Breeders and Exhibitors Assn. Democrat. Office: Carmel Middle Sch 1740 Pepperwood Dr Colorado Springs CO 80910-1525

ANDERSON, KATHLEEN GAY, mediator, hearing officer, arbitrator, educator; b. Cin., July 27, 1950; d. Harold B. and Trudi L. (Chambers) Briggs; m. J.R. Carr, July 4, 1988; 1 child, Jesse J. Anderson. Student, U. Cin., 1971-72, Antioch Coll., 1973-74; cert., Nat. Jud. Coll., U. Nev., Reno, 1987, Inst. Applied Law, 1987, Acad. Family Mediators, 1991. Cert. Am. Arbitration Assn., Lemmon Mediation Inst., Acad. Family Medicators. Paralegal Lauer & Lauer, Santa Fe, 1976-79, Wilkinson, Cragun & Barker, Anchorage, 1981-82; employment law paralegal specialist Hughes, Thorsness, Gantz, Powell & Brundin, Anchorage, 1983-91; investigator, mediator Alaska State Commn. Human Rights, 1992-93; mediator, arbitrator, trainer The Arbitration and Mediation Group, Anchorage, 1987—; hearing officer Municipality of Anchorage, 1993—; State of Alaska, 1994—; mem. faculty Nat. Jud. Coll., U. Nev., Reno, 1988-89; adj. prof. U. Alaska, Anchorage, 1985—, Alaska Pacific U., 1990—, Chapman U., 1990; mem. Alaska Supreme Ct. Mediation Task Force, 1991; adv. com. Am. Arbitration Assn. for Alaska, 1994—; trainer mediation svcs. pvt. profit and nonprofit groups, pub. groups, U.S. mil., state and fed. govt. Author, editor: Professional Responsibility Handbook for Legal Assistants and Paralegals, 1986; contbr. articles to profl. jours. Lectr. Alaska Bar Assn., 1989—, NLRB, Anchorage, 1986, Alaska Assn. Bus. and Profl. Women, 1988—, Coun. on Edn. and Mgmt., 1993—, Small Bus. Devel. Coun., various employers and bus. groups. Mem. ABA (ethics com., alt. dispute resolution sect.), Soc. Profls. in Dispute Resolution, Nat. Assn. Mediation in Edn., Nat. Fedn. Paralegal Assn. (edn. task force coord. 1988-89, adminstrv. v.p. 1988-91), Conflict Resolution Ctr. Internat., Acad. Family Mediators (cert., practitioner mem.), Alaska Bar Assn. (employment, alt. dispute resolution, family law sects., Bus. and Profl. Women, Alaska Dispute Settlement Assn. (v.p. 1992-93, chair com. on credentialing and standards of practice). Home: PO Box 100098 Anchorage AK 99510-0098 Office: PO Box 240783 Anchorage AK 99524-0783

ANDERSON, KENNETH JEFFERY, family financial planner, accountant, lawyer; b. Daytona Beach, Fla., May 7, 1954; s. Kenneth E. and Petronella G. (Jeffer) A.; m. Susan Wagner, Aug. 19, 1978; children: Melissa, Kiersten. BSBA, Valparaiso U., 1976, JD, 1979. CPA, Ill. Prof. staff, mgr. Arthur Andersen & Co., Chgo., 1979-84; mgr. Arthur Andersen & Co., L.A., 1984-90, ptnr., 1990—, dir. individual tax fin. svcs., western region. Gov., treas. Idyllwild (Calif.) Sch. Music and the Arts, 1990; mem. Assocs. Bd. Chgo. Lung Assn., 1980-84; vol. Hospice of the North Shore, Winnetka, 1981. Mem. AICPA, Fla Bar Assn., Ill. Bar Assn., Ill. CPA Soc., Calif. CPA Soc. (apptd. to state com. on personal fin. planning), Soc. CPA-Fin. Planners (bd. dirs. 1987-89), Sports Lawyers Assn., Calif. Club. Republican. Home: 28 Cinch Rd Bell Canyon CA 91307-1003 Office: Arthur Andersen & Co 633 W 5th St Fl 32D Los Angeles CA 90071-2005

ANDERSON, LAWRENCE KEITH, electrical engineer; b. Toronto, Ont., Can., Oct. 2, 1935; came to U.S., 1957; s. Wallace Ray and Irene Margaret (Linn) A.; m. Katherine Florence Drechsler, Sept. 21, 1963; children—Susan Barbara, Robert Keith. B. in Engring. Physics, McGill U., 1957; PhDEE, Stanford U., 1962. With Bell Labs., 1961-85; dir. electronic components and Subsystems lab. Bell Labs., Allentown, Pa., 1981-85; v.p. component devel. Sandia Nat. Labs., Albuquerque, 1985-88; exec. dir. AT&T Bell Labs. Interconnection and Power Tech. Div., Parsippany, NJ, 1988-89; prof., dir. Alliance for Photonic Tech., Albuquerque, 1990-91; dir. Colo. Inst. Tech. Transfer and Implementation, U. Colo., Colorado Springs, 1991—. Fellow IEEE (pres. Electron Devices Soc. 1976-77, dir. 1979-80). Home: 2545 Karamy Ct Colorado Springs CO 80919-3572 Office: UCCS/CITTI PO Box 7150 Colorado Springs CO 80933-7150

ANDERSON, LEE ROGER, solar, environmental, recreation and site planner; b. Boone, Iowa, July 24, 1945; s. Carl Donald and Hazel Irene (Erickson) A.; m. Linda Jean Parker, May 28, 1966; children: Eric Lee, Tai Denise. BS in Landscape Architecture, Iowa State U., 1967, M in Landscape Architecture, 1968. Registered landscape architect, Calif. Dept. Consumer Affairs. Designer, draftsman H&F Builders, Ames, Iowa, 1966-68; landscape architect Simonds & Simonds, Pitts., 1968-70, Shasta-Trinity Nat. Forest, Redding, Calif., 1970-73, Klamath Nat. Forest, Yreka, Calif., 1973-81; prin. Designs for Living, Yreka, 1981-87, Solid Rock Prodns, 1983-86, Lee Roger Anderson, Environ. Cons., Planning and Design, 1986—; promoter contemporary Christian concerts, 1983-85; environ. and visual resource planner Celeron/All-Am. Pipeline Project, 1986-87; planner Eddy Meadow Resort, 1985, Mt. Shasta Ski Area, 1985-89, other nat. recreation area resorts; environ., recreation and visual resource planner, Grider Recovery Project Environ. Impact Statement, 1988; master planner, Gallatin Marina at Eagle Lake, Calif., 1987-88, Eagle Lake Ranger Sta., Susanville, Calif., 1991; Yreka Creek Greenway Project, 1988-90; Springhill Planned Unit Devel., Mt. Shasta, Calif.; Seven Up Pete Joint Venture Gold Mine, Lincoln, Mont., 1994; recreation & visual resource planner Kern River Hydroelectric Relicensing Project, 1989—; designer solar houses. Mem. Yreka City Planning Commn., 1976-80. Recipient award for design of children's playground Yreka Lions Club, 1976. Mem. Am. Soc. Landscape Architects (Nat. award for Highway 140 Viewshed Implementation Guide 1990), Tau Sigma Delta. Democrat. Author: (with others) Visual Absorption Capability, 1979, Visual Management Support Systems, 1979, Environmental Impact Report, Environmental Impact Statement Proposed Celeron All American and Getty Pipeline Projects, 1985, Pacific Pipeline Environmental Assessment, 1991-92, Forest Service Update for Visual Management System, 1991-92, Landscape Aesthetics: A Handbook for Scenery Management, 1991-93, Barklay Fire Salvage E.I.S., 1995. Office: Environ Consulting Planning & Design PO Box 1191 Mount Shasta CA 96067-1191

ANDERSON, LORRAINE PEARL, editor, writer; b. San Jose, Calif., July 3, 1952; d. Edward Eltwood Jr. and Audrey Beatrice (Haug) A. BA, U. Utah, 1975. Editorial asst. Lifetime Learning Publs., Belmont, Calif., 1979-80, prodn. editor, 1980-81; freelance writer and editor Palo Alto, Calif., 1981-90, Davis, Calif., 1990—. Editor: Sisters of the Earth: Women's Prose and Poetry About Nature, 1991; co-author: (with Rick Palkaric): Cooking With Sunshine: The Lazy Cook's Guide to Solar Cuisine, 1994. Mem. Assn. for Study of Lit. and Environment, Sierra Club (life). Mem. Green Party. Home and Office: 2431 Westernesse Rd Davis CA 95616-2900

ANDERSON, LOUISE STOUT, crime analyst; b. Wellsville, N.Y., Aug. 11, 1952; d. Carlton C. and Mary (Gasdik) Stout; m. Leonard M. Anderson, June 2, 1973. BA in German Lit., Polit. Sci., Mt. Holyoke Coll., 1974; MA in Polit. Sci., San Diego State U., 1977; MS Human Resources and Organizational Devel., 1993. Cert. C.C. tchr., Calif. Statistician Grossmont Coll., El Cajon, Calif., 1976-78; crime analyst San Diego Police Dept., 1978-80; crime analyst Career Criminal Apprehension Program, Marin County Sheriff's Office, San Rafael, Calif., 1980-83; crime analyst CCAP Unit, Sonoma County Sheriff's Office, Santa Rosa, Calif., 1983-85; mgr. mktg. svcs. Command Data Systems, Dublin, Calif., 1985-87, client svcs. mgr., 1988-92; contracts mgr. Tiburon Inc., 1992; mgr. field svcs. OCS Techs., 1992-94, v.p. nat. customers support, 1994—; cons. Search Group Inc. for Automated Crime Analysis. Contbr. articles in field. Owner Acacia Assocs., public safety cons. and training orgn. Mem. Antioch Police Commn.; alumna recruiter Mt. Holyoke Club No. Calif., 1981-86. Office: Acacia Assocs 1931 Acacia Ave Antioch CA 94509-2607

ANDERSON, MARGARET ALLYN, carpet showroom manager; b. Meeker, Okla., Aug. 1, 1922; d. Edgar Allen and Maggie May (Smith) Martin; m. Ralph Carlos Huffman, Dec. 23, 1939 (div. Dec. 1954); children: Ronald Carlos, Darrell Duane; m. Walter Monroe Anderson, June 4, 1956. Student, San Antonio Jr. Coll., 1950-51. Clk. stenographer Sinclair Oil Co., Tulsa, 1947-48; clk. stenographer to sec. U.S. Govt. Civil Svc., San Antonio, 1948-55, Wiesbaden, Germany, 1956, Denver, 1956-57, Boise, Idaho, 1957-64; co-owner, sec./treas. Anthane, Inc., Boise, Idaho, 1964-87; co-owner, showroom mgr., sec. Anthane, Inc., San Francisco, 1987-94. Mem. Am. Bus. Womens Assn. Democrat. Mem. Christian Ch. Home: Winter Gardens Pointe 8003 Winter Gardens Blvd # 208 El Cajon CA 92021

ANDERSON, MARILYN NELLE, elementary educator, librarian, counselor; b. Las Animas, Colo., May 5, 1942; d. Mason Hadley Moore and Alice Carrie (Dwyer) Coates; m. George Robert Anderson, Sept. 4, 1974; children: Lisa Lynn, Edward Alan, Justin Patrick. BEd magna cum laude, Adams State Coll., 1962, postgrad., 1965; MEd, Ariz. State U., 1967; postgrad., Idaho State U., 1971, 86, Columbia Pacific U., 1991—. Cert. elem. tchr., K-12 sch. counselor. Tchr. Wendell (Idaho) Sch. Dist. 232, 1962-66, Union-Endicott (N.Y.) Sch. Dist., 1967-68; counselor, librarian West Yuma (Colo.) Sch. Dist., 1968-69; elem. sch. counselor Am. Falls (Idaho) Sch. Dist. 381, 1969-73; project dir. Gooding County (Idaho) Sr. Citizens Orgn., 1974-75; tchr. Castleford (Idaho) Sch. Dist. 417, 1982-92; placement specialist, referral counselor Idaho Child Care Program S. Cen. Idaho Community Action Agy., Twin Falls, 1992—; mem. Castleford Schs. Merit Pay Devel. program, 1983-84, Accreditation Evaluation com., 1984-85, Math. Curriculum Devel. com., 1985-86. Leader Brownie Scouts, Endicott, 1967-68; chmn. fundraising com. Am. Falls Kindergarten, 1971-73; leader Gooding County 4-H Council, Wendell, 1983—. Recipient Leader's award Nat. 4-H Conservation Natural Resources Program, 1984. Mem. NEA, Nat. Assn. Edn. Young Children, Idaho Edn. Assn., Idaho Coun. Internat. Reading Assn., Magic Valley Reading Assn., Internat. Platform Assn., Idaho Coun. Tchrs. of English, Support Unltd. Providers and Parents. Republican. Baptist. Home: RR 1 Box 293 Wendell ID 83355-9801 Office: S Ctrl Idaho Community A Twin Falls ID 83301

ANDERSON, MARK ALEXANDER, lawyer; b. Santa Monica, Calif., Nov. 15, 1953; s. William Alexander and Christina (Murray) A.; m. Rosalie Louise Movius, Nov. 28, 1986; 1 child, Morgan Anderson Movius. AB, U. So. Calif., 1974; JD, Yale U., 1978. Bar: Calif. 1979, U.S. Dist. Ct. (no. dist.) Calif. 1979, U.S. Ct. Appeals (9th cir.) 1979, Oreg. 1982, U.S. Dist. Ct. Oreg. 1982, Wash. 1985, U.S. Dist. Ct. (we. dist.) Wash. 1986, U.S. Supreme Ct. 1989. Law clk. U.S. Ct. Appeals (9th cir.), San Francisco, 1978-79, U.S. Dist. Ct. Oreg., Portland, 1980-82; atty. Miller, Nash, Wiener, Hager & Carlsen, Portland, 1983-92; gen. counsel Dark Horse Comics, Inc., Milwaukie, Oreg., 1992—. Chair Raleigh Hills-Garden Home Citizen Participation Orgn., 1992-93. Mem. ABA, N.W. Lawyers and Artists (pres. 1988-90), State Bar Calif., Wash. State Bar Assn., Oreg. State Bar (chair antitrust, trade regulation and unfair bus. practices sect. 1991-92), U.S. Dist. Ct. Oreg. Hist. Soc., City Club of Portland (chair arts and culture standing com. 1990-92). Home: PO Box 8154 Portland OR 97207-8154 Office: Dark Horse Comics Inc 10956 SE Main St Milwaukie OR 97222-7644

ANDERSON, MARK EUGENE, specialized truck driver, safety inspector; b. Richland Center, Wis., Oct. 9, 1952; s. Harold Eugene and Laila Marie (Jacobson) A.; m. Marilyn Jones, June 22, 1972 (div. 1984); children: Michael, Kenneth, Thomas; m. Georgina Therese Scinta, Sept. 29, 1984. Grad., Mich. Ctr. for Design Driving, 1993, Mich. Ctr. Decision Driving. Enlisted U.S. Army, 1970, ret., 1977; mgr. Taco Bell, Farmington, N.Mex., 1977-78; truck driver Farmington Meat Processors, 1978-80, Nobel/Sysco, Albuquerque, 1980-89; specialized truck driver transuranic nuclear waste Dawn Enterprises Inc., Farmington, 1989—; truck driver, cert. safety inspector Comml. Vehicle Safety Alliance, Oreg., 1991; truck driver transp. safeguards div. U.S. Dept. Energy, Albuquerque, 1989. Mem. Mich. Truck Safety Commn., 1993. Named N.Mex. State Truck Driving Champion N.Mex. Motor Carriers, 1988, Grand Champion Truck Driving Championship, N.Mex. Motor Carriers, 1994. Home: 5201 Chuckwagon Trl NW Albuquerque NM 87120-2889 Office: Dawn Enterprises Inc PO Box 204 Farmington NM 87499-0204

ANDERSON, MARK ROBERT, data processing executive, biochemist; b. Oak Park, Ill., Aug. 11, 1951; s. Robert Hugo and Marilyn Pettee (Johnson) A.; m. Mary Jane Helsell, June 6, 1980; children: Berit Bracken, Evan Robert. BS, Stanford U., 1972; MS, Stanford U., Hopkins Marine Sta., 1973; postgrad., U. Brit. Columbia, Vancouver, 1973. Publisher Potlatch Press, Friday Harbor, Wash., 1974-77; assoc. prof. Western Wash. U., Bellingham, 1977, Harvard U., Boston, 1978; chief scientist Ocean Research & End. Soc., Boston, 1978; v.p. Moclips Cetological Soc., Friday Harbor, 1979-81; founder, dir. The Whale Mus., Friday Harbor, 1979-81; pres. The Oikos Co., Friday Harbor, 1980—, San Juan Software, Friday Harbor, 1983-84; pres., bd. dirs. Island Tech. Inc., Friday Harbor, 1984—; founder, pres. Tech. Alliance Ptnrs., 1989—; bd. dirs. Worldesign; bd. advisors HIT Lab., U. Wash., 1991—; founder Strategic News Svc., 1995—. Author: Nineteen Fathers, 1971, (software) The Agent's Advantage, 1983; producer TV film Survivors, 1980; editor, founder Jour. Cetus, 1981; discoverer Resonance Theory, 1981. Founder San Juan Musicians Guild, 1974-78, Anti-Spray Coalition, 1977. Mem. Wash. Software Assn. (bd. dirs. 1988-90, chair pres.'s group 1989—), Database Standards Com., Am. Electronics Assn.

ANDERSON, MARK T., business developer, entrepreneur, financier; b. Provo, Utah, Jan. 28, 1953; s. Billy Joe and Norma (Tucker) A.; m. Aleca Alleman, May 5, 1976; children: John Tucker, Amy, Megan. BS in Econs. and Fin., Brigham Young U., 1984. Lic. pvt. and comml. pilot; cert. SCUBA diver. Pres., dir. G.B. Mark T. Inc., Orem, Utah, 1975—, Mark Anderson & Assocs., Provo, 1979—, R&D Connections Inc., Salt Lake City, 1983-85; dir., exec. v.p. Kara Signature Chocolates Inc., Salt Lake City, 1985-88; mng. dir. Network Capital LTD., Salt Lake City, 1986—; pres. Mark Anderson Mgmt. Co., 1988—; mng. dir. Network Fin. Group Inc., Salt Lake City, 1992-93; exec. v.p. Viking Internat. Airlines, Inc. (DBA Eagle Airlines), Ft. Lauderdale, Fla., 1993—, Viking Internat. Airlines (doing bus. as Eagle Airlines), Atlanta, 1993-94; wxec. v.p. Viking Internat. Airlines (doing bus. as Eagle Airlines), Las Vegas, 1993-94. Trustee, gen. mgr. Furresa's Trust Salt Lake City and L.A. Recipient Eagle Scout award, Boy Scouts Am. Mem. Riverside Country Club, Ridge Athel Club, Elks. Republican. Mem. LDS Ch. Home: 4101 Timpview Dr Provo UT 84604-5130

ANDERSON, MARSHALL L., law enforcement administrator; b. Buffalo, Mar. 21, 1928; s. Floyd Raymond and Ella Minnie (LeRoy) A.; m. Dorothy McCarron, June 12, 1948 (div. Apr. 1961); children: Michael, Donna; m. Patricia Jane Watts, Apr. 8, 1974; children: Liane, Victoria. Cert. traffic policy adminstrn., Northwestern U. Traffic Inst., 1969; MBA, Pepperdine U., 1974; cert. managerial policy, U. So. Calif., 1978. Dep. chief police L.A. Police Dept., 1952-80; security mgr. L.A. Olympic Organizing Com., 1983-84; chief police Housing Authority City of L.A. Police Dept., 1987-89; cons. L.A., 1980—; v.p., sr. ptnr. Law Enforcement Cons. and Rsch. Inc., L.A., 1989—. Author numerous police manuals, 1956-80. Mem. adv. bd. Salvation Army, L.A., 1992—; mem. Police Adv. Coun., West L.A., 1994—. With USNR, 1945-46, PTO. Recipient Mgmt. Cert. Peace Officers Stds. and Tng., L.A., 1974. Mem. Am. Soc. Indsl. Security, Peace Office Assn. Los Angeles County, Calif. Peace Officers Assn. (various bds.), Rotary Internat. (dist. gov. 1994-95), Rotary Club of Westwood Village (pres. 1989-90, Rotarian of Yr. 1992). Republican. Presbyterian. Home: 12236 Dunoon Ln Los Angeles CA 90049-4002

ANDERSON, MICHAEL GEORGE, marketing and advertising executive; b. Boulder, Colo., Aug. 3, 1951; s. George Martin and Annette Elizabeth (Girmann) A.; m. Susan Elliott, Mar. 19, 1977; children: Gregory Michael, Richard Charles. BS in Aero. Engring., U. Colo., 1973, MBA in Fin., 1978. Design engr. Beech Aircraft, Boulder, 1976-78, liaison engr., 1978-79; mech. engr. Dieterich Standard, Boulder, 1979-80, mgr. engring. design, 1980-84, quality assurance mgr., 1984-87, mgr. advt., mktg. strategic planning and quality assurance, 1987-90, mgr. regional mktg., advt. mgr., 1990—. Author (computer software) Tektronix Header Program, 1982. Vice-pres. Luth. Ch. Coun., 1988-91; asst. scoutmaster Troop 161 Boys Scouts Am. Recipient NPT Stamp and Cert., ASME, Boulder, 1986. Mem. Instrument Soc. Am., Boulder Flycasters Club, U. Colo. Alumni Assn. (bd. dirs. 1985-87, v.p. bd. dirs. Boulder chpt. 1985-86), Buff Club (v.p., bd. dirs. 1985-87, pres. 1988-90), Moose. Republican. Home: 7400 Mount Meeker Rd Longmont CO 80503-7143 Office: Dieterich Standard PO Box 9000 Boulder CO 80301-9000

ANDERSON, MICHAEL KENNETH, marketing professional; b. Des Moines, Feb. 4, 1953; s. Gerald Vernon and Marianne (Blachley) A.; m. Elizabeth S. Cunningham, May 8, 1976; children: Sarah Elizabeth, Jennifer Suzanne. BSBA, Calif. State U., Sacramento, 1981. Mgr. mktg. and pub. rels. western divsn. Pargas Inc., Waldorf, Md., 1981-84; nat. mgr. advt./sales Amerigas Inc., Sacramento, 1984-87; pres. Anderson Solone Inc., Sacramento, 1987—. Office: Anderson Solone Inc 3100 Fite Cir Ste 101 Sacramento CA 95827-1805

ANDERSON, MICHAEL ROBERT, marketing representative; b. Mpls., Nov. 3, 1953; s. Arthur Robert Anderson and Patricia Roberta Carlson; divorced; children: Jenna Courtney, Evan Brendan. BSEE, U. Minn., 1976; MS in Sys. Mgmt., U. So. Calif., 1981. Microelectronics engr. Hughes Aircraft Co., Fullerton, Calif., 1977; mktg. rep. Hewlett Packard, Orange County, Calif., 1977-81; regional mgr. Group III Elec., Orange County, 1981-85; mktg. rep. Lisp Machines Inc., L.A., 1985-87, Sun Microsys., Inc., Orange, Calif., 1987-91; mktg.rep. Auspex Sys., Inc., Santa Clara, Calif., 1992—. Big Brother, Big Bros. Inc., Orange, Calif., 1979-81. Fellow AAAS, Am. Assn. Artificial Intelligence, Planetary Soc. Home: PO Box 5199 San Clemente CA 92674-5199 Office: Auspex 3601 N Aviation Blvd Manhattan Beach CA 90266-3706

ANDERSON, MITCHELL, chiropractor; b. L.A., Aug. 9, 1963; s. Charles Terry and Anita Louise (Rose) A.; m. Patricia Elaine Evora, June 10, 1989. AA, Cerritos Coll., 1983; BS, Cleveland Chiropractic Coll., L.A., 1985; D of Chiropractic, Cleveland Chiropractic Coll., 1987; sports cert., L.A. Chiropractic Coll., 1988. Cert. chiropractor Nat. Bd. Chiropractic Examiners; bd. eligible/Diplomate Am. Bd. Chiropractic Sports Physicians; lic. chiropractor, Calif., Hawaii. Massage therapist/owner Body Work by Mitch, Downey, Calif., 1983-87; chiropractor Anderson Chiropractic Ctr., Los Alamitos, Calif., 1987—; referal doctor/owner Anderson Worker's Referal Svc., Orange, Calif., 1991—; physician Rossmor Athletic Club, Seal Beach, Calif., 1987—, Bretheren Christian High Sch., Cypress, Calif., 1988—; team chiropractor Anaheim Bullfrogs, 1993—; pres. Calif. Chiropractic Coun. on Sports Injuries and Phys. Fitness; physician 1992 Olympic Games, Barcelona, Spain, Profl. Rodeo, 1992—. Mem. Am. Chiropractic Assn. (sports cert. 1989, coun. sports injuries 1988—), Fed. Internat. Chiropractic Sportive, Calif. Chiropractic Assn., Rotary, Masons (3 degree), Scottish Rite (32 degree). Republican. Baptist. Home: 5570 Camino De Bryant Yorba Linda CA 92687-4206 Office: Anderson Chiropractic Ctr 10671 Los Alamitos Blvd Los Alamitos CA 90720-2148

ANDERSON, NED, SR., Apache tribal chairman; b. Bylas, Ariz., Jan. 18, 1943; s. Paul and Maggie (Rope) A.; m. Delphina Hinton; children—Therese Kay, Linette Mae, Magdalene Gail, Ned, Sean. AA, Ea. Ariz. Coll., 1964, AAS in computer sci., 1989; BS, U. Ariz., 1967, JD, 1973. Field dir. Nat. Study Indian Edn., dept. anthropology U. Ariz., Tucson, 1968-70; tech. asst. Project Head Start, Ariz. State U., Tempe, 1970; ethnographer Smithsonian Instn., Washington, 1970-73; dir. Jojoba Project, Office of Arid Land Studies, U. Ariz. Tucson, 1973-76; with Jojoba devel. project San Carlos Apache Tribe, Ariz., 1976-78, tribal councilman, 1976-78, 93—, tribal chmn., 1978-86, gen. mgr. spl. housing projects, 1991—. Contbr. articles to profl.jours. Bd. dirs. Southwestern Indian Devel., Inc., 1971; mem. affirmative action com. City of Tucson, 1975-76; bd. dirs. Indian Enterprise Devel. Corp., 1976-78; mem. study panel NAS, 1975-77; pres. Inter-Tribal Coun. Ariz., 1979—; mem. supervisory bd. Ariz. Justice Planning Commn., 1978—, Indian adv. bd. Intergovtl. Personnel Program, 1978—; pres. bd. Ft. Thomas High Sch. Unified Dist., 1987—, clk. bd., 1989—; trustee Bacone Coll., 1986—; mem. adv. bd. Am. Indian Registry for Performing Arts, 1985—, San Carlos Fish and Game Commn., 1975—, chmn., 1976—; mem. exec. com. San Carlos Apache Tribal Coun., 1976-78, budget, fin. com., 1976—, constn. and ordinance com. 1976-78, chmn. law and order com., 1976-78; adv. bd. Gila Pueblo Community Coll. extension Ea. Ariz. Coll., 1979—; mem. sch. bd. Ft. Thomas High Sch. Unified Dist., 1977—, clk., 1987—, pres. sch. bd., 1992—; mem. County Govt. Study Commn. State Ariz., 1981-84; adv. bd. Indian Edn., Ariz. State U., Tempe, 1978—, U. Ariz., Tucson, 1978—; bd. dirs. San Carlos Lake Devel., 1994—, Western Apache Constrn. Co., 1994—; mem. reinvention mgmt. lab. workgroup Nat. Housing Improvement Program, 1995—. Recipient Outstanding Community Coll. Alumni award Ariz. Community Coll. Bd./Ea. Ariz. Coll., 1982, Outstanding Cooperation award U.S. Secret Svc., 1984, A.T. Anderson Meml. scholarship, 1989, Univ. Rels. award AT&T, 1989. Mem. Nat. Tribal Chmn.'s Assn. (bd. edn. 1978—, adv. bd. 1978—), Ariz. Acad., Globe C. of C., Phi Theta Kappa.

ANDERSON, NORMAN HENRY, psychology educator, researcher; b. Mpls., July 23, 1925. BS in Physics, U. Chgo., 1946, MS in Math., 1949; MS in Psychology, U. Wis., 1955, PhD in Psychology, 1956. Mathematician ERA/Sperry Rand, Arlington, Va., 1951-53; asst. prof. psychology UCLA, 1958-62, assoc. prof., 1962-65; prof. U. Calif.-San Diego, La Jolla, 1965—; vis. asst. prof. Yale U., New Haven, Conn., 1957-58, Ind. U., Bloomington, 1962-63; mem psychobiology panel NSF, 1963-65, mem. social psychology panel, 1973-75. Author: Foundations of Information Integration Theory, 1981, Methods of Information Integration Theory, 1982; editor, contbr.: Information Integration Theory, Vols. I-III, 1991; mem. editorial bd. Jour. Math. Psychology, 1964-73, Behavior Research Methods and Instrumentation, 1968-80; contbr. numerous articles to profl. jours. Served with U.S. Army, 1946-47. Recipient Socio-Psychol. prize AAAS, 1972; fellow Ctr. Advanced Study in Behavioral Scis., Stanford U., 1968-69. Mem. Soc. Exptl. Psychologists. Office: U Calif Psychology La Jolla CA 92093-0109

ANDERSON, OLIN DARRELL, molecular biologist; b. DeQuincy, La., Aug. 7, 1944; s. Frederick Ernest Anderson and Bess (Gearen) O'Neale; m. Carol Leland Reade, May 11, 1974. BA, U. Calif., Berkeley, 1971; PhD, Purdue U., 1977. Fellow Purdue U., West Lafayette, Ind., 1977-81, U. Calif., Berkeley, 1981-84; rsch. geneticist USDA, Albany, Calif., 1984-89, supervisory rsch. geneticist, 1989—; mem. wheat crop adv. com., Washington, 1990—, Internat. Tritrceae Mapping Initiative, Davis, Calif., 1991-94; coord. Wheat Computer Database project, Albany, 1990—. Contbr. articles to profl. jours. Mem. AAAS, Am. Soc. Plant Physiology, Internat. Soc. Plant Molecular Biologists. Office: USDA ARS We Regional Rsch Ctr 800 Buchanan St Berkeley CA 94710-1105

ANDERSON, PATRICK LEE, electrical/electronics engineer; b. Clarinda, Iowa, Mar. 17, 1959; s. Richard Lee and Gene Ann Anderson; m. Divina Guytingco, May 30, 1987; children: Christopher, Colin. BS in Psychology, Iowa State U., 1978, BS in Speech, 1978, MS in Elec./Computer Engring., 1988; MS in Speech Pathology and Audiology, U. Iowa, 1980. Speech pathologist Laconia (N.H.) State Sch., 1980-81, Southbury (Conn.) Tng. Sch., 1981-84; pvt. practice Woodbury, Conn., 1981-84; rsch. and tchg. asst. Iowa State U., Ames, 1985-88; rsch. engr. Boeing Comml. Airplane, Seattle, 1988—. Inventor in field. Block coord. Am. Cancer Soc., Redmond, Wash., 1994; sponsor Child Reach, Providence, R.I., 1994. Mem. IEEE Computer Soc., Iowa State Alumni Assn., Am. Speech and Hearing Assn., Phi Beta Kappa. Democrat. Roman Catholic. Home: 21602 NE 29th St Redmond WA 98053-6361

ANDERSON, PAUL NATHANIEL, oncologist, educator; b. Omaha, May 30, 1937; s. Nels Paul E. and Doris Marie (Chesnut) A.; BA, U. Colo., 1959, MD, 1963; m. Dee Ann Hipps, June 27, 1965; children: Mary Kathleen,

Anne Christen; Diplomate Am. Bd. internal Medicine, Am. Bd. Med. Mgmt. Intern Johns Hopkins Hosp., 1963-64, resident in internal medicine, 1964-65; rsch. asso., staff assoc. NIH, Bethesda, Md., 1965-70; fellow in oncology Johns Hopkins Hosp., 1970-72, asst. prof. medicine, oncology Johns Hopkins U. Sch. Medicine, 1972-76; attending physician Balt. City Hosps., Johns Hopkins Hosp., 1972-76; dir. dept. med. oncology Penrose Cancer Hosp., Colorado Springs, Colo., 1976-86; clin. asst. prof. dept. medicine U. Colo. Sch. Medicine, 1976-90, clin. assoc. prof., 1990—; dir. Penrose Cancer Hosp., 1979-86, chief dept. medicine, 1985-86; founding dir. Cancer Ctr. of Colorado Springs, 1986-95; dir. Rocky Mountain Cancer Ctr., Colorado Springs, 1995—; med. dir. So. Colo. Cancer Program, 1979-86; pres., chmn. bd. dirs. Preferred Physicians, Inc., 1986-92; mem. Colo. Found. for Med. Care Health Standards Com., 1985, sec., exec. com., 1990, bd. dirs., pres. 1992-93; mem., chmn. treatment com. Colo. Cancer Control and Rsch. Panel, 1980-83; prin. investigator Cancer Info. Svc. of Colo., 1981-87. Editor Advances in Cancer Control; editorial bd. Journal of Cancer Progam Management, 1987-92, Health Care Management Review, 1988—. Mem. Colo. Gov.'s Rocky Flats Employee Health Assessment Group, 1983-84; mem. Gov.'s Breast Cancer Control Commn. Colo., 1984-87; pres., founder Oncology Mgmt. Network, Inc., 1985-95; founder, bd. dirs. Timberline Med. Assocs., 1986-87; founder, dir. So. Colo. AIDS project 1986-91; mem. adv. bd. Colo. State Bd. Health Tumor Registry, 1984-87; chmn., bd. dirs. Preferred Physicians, Inc., 1986-92; bd. dirs. Share Devel. Co. of Colo. Share Health Plan of Colo., 1986-90, vice chmn., 1989-91; bd. dirs., chmn. Preferred Health Care, Inc., 1991-92; mem. health care standards com., trustee Colo. Found. for Med. Care (PRO); mem. nat. bd. med. dirs. Fox Chase Cancer Ctr. Network, Phila., 1987-89; mem. tech. expert panel Harvard Resource-Based Relative Value Scale Study for Hematology/Oncology, 1991-92; founding dir. Colo. Healthcare Improvement Found., 1994-95. Served with USPHS, 1965-70. Diplomate Am. Bd. Internal Medicine, Am. Bd. Med. Oncology. Mem. Am. Soc. Clin. Oncology (chmn. subcom. on oncology clin. practice standards, mem. clin. practice com., rep. to AMA 1991—, mem. healthcare svcs. rsch. com., chmn. clin. guidelines subcom. 1993—), Am. Assn. Cancer Rsch., Am. Assn. Cancer Insts. (liaison mem. bd. trustees 1980-92), Am. Coll. Physician Execs., Am. Hospice Assn., Am. Soc. Internal Medicine, Nat. Cancer Inst. (com. for community hosp. oncology program evaluation 1982-83), Colo. Soc. Internal Medicine, Assn. Community Cancer Ctrs. (chmn. membership com. 1980, chmn. clin. rsch. com. 1983-85, sec. 1983-84, pres.-elect 1984-85, pres. 1986-87, trustee 1981-88), AAAS, N.Y. Acad. Scis., Johns Hopkins Med. Soc., AMA (mem. practice parameters forum 1989—, adv. com. to HCFA on uniform clin. data set), Colo. Med. Soc., Am. Mgmt. Assn., Am. Assn. Profl. Cons., Am. Soc. for Quality Control, Am. Acad. Med. Dirs., Am. Coll. Physician Execs., El Paso County Med. Soc., Rocky Mountain Oncology Soc. (chmn. clin. practice com. 1989-94, pres.-elect 1990, pres. 1993-95), Acad. Hospice Physicians, Coalition for Cancer, Colo. Springs Clin. Club, Alpha Omega Alpha. Contbr. articles to med. jours. Office: Rocky Mountain Cancer Ctr 110 East Monroe St Ste 200 PO Box 7148 Colorado Springs CO 80933-7148 also: 32 Sanford Rd Colorado Springs CO 80906-4233

ANDERSON, PEGGY REES, accountant; b. Casper, Wyo., Sept. 8, 1958; d. John William and Pauline Marie (Harris) Rees; m. Steven R. Anderson, May 26, 1984 (div. Sept. 1990). BS in Acctg. with honors, U. Wyo., 1980. CPA. Audit staff to sr. Price Waterhouse, Denver, 1980-84; asst. contr. to contr. Am. Investments, Denver, 1984-88; cons. ADI Residential, Denver, 1988-89; contr., treas. Plante Properties, Inc., Denver, 1989-92; acctg. mgr. Woodward-Clyde Group, Inc., Denver, 1992—. Recipient diving scholarship U. Wyo., 1976-77, 77-78. Mem. Colo. Soc. CPAs. Roman Catholic. Office: Woodward-Clyde Group Inc 4582 S Ulster St Ste 600 Denver CO 80237-2635

ANDERSON, RACHAEL KELLER, library administrator; b. N.Y.C., Jan. 15, 1938; d. Harry and Sarah Keller; m. Alexander M. Goldstein (dec.); m. Paul J. Anderson; 1 child, Rebecca. A.B., Barnard Coll., 1959; M.S., Columbia U., 1960. Librarian CCNY, 1960-62; librarian Mt. Sinai Med. Ctr., N.Y.C., 1964-73, dir. library, 1973-79; dir. Health Scis Libr. Columbia U., N.Y.C., 1979-91, acting v.p., univ. libr., 1982; dir. Ariz. Health Scis. Libr., U. Ariz., Tucson, 1991—; bd. dirs. Med. Library Ctr. of N.Y., N.Y.C., 1983-91; mem. biomed. library rev. com. Nat. Library Medicine, Bethesda, Md., 1984-88, chmn., 1987-88; mem. bd. regents Nat. Libr. Medicine, 1990-94, chmn., 1993-94. Contbr. articles to profl. jours. Mem. Med. Library Assn. (bd. dirs. 1983-86), Assn. Acad. Health Scis. Library Dirs. (bd. dirs. 1983-86, pres. 1991-92). Office: Ariz Health Scis Libr 1501 N Campbell Ave Tucson AZ 85724-0001

ANDERSON, RAYMOND EUGENE, land revegetation company executive; b. Joliet, Ill., Aug. 22, 1927; s. Albert Robert and Ebba Evelyn (Nelson) A.; m. Nilene Washburn, 1955 (div.); children: Leslie Lynne, Terry Evelyn, Allison Rae. BS in Agr., Utah State U., 1951; BS in Fgn. Trade, Am. Inst. Fgn. Trade, 1957. Cowboy, ranch hand, 1948-54; range conservationist Bur. Land Mgmt., Phoenix, Ariz., 1954-56; Ariz. fieldman Western Livestock Jour., L.A. and Denver, 1957-61; ranch mgr. Sonora, Mex., 1962-64; livestock cons. Inter-Am. Devel. Bank, Caracas, Venezuela, 1965-66; livestock advisor fgn. aid program U. Ariz., Ceará, Brazil, 1967-71; livestock cons. Niger, Iran, Botswana, Kenya, Turkey, 1971-84; pres. Land Revegetation Internat., Tucson, 1982-86; developer specialization in dry land revegetation without irrigation, reversing desertification and climate change. Contbr. articles on desertification to profl. jours. including UN publs. Desertivication Control Bull. and CERES, also Agroforestry Today, World Farming, Rangelands Western Livestock Jour., Ariz. Daily Star. Served with USAAC, 1945-47. Mem. Am. Soc. for Range Mgmt. (author Rangelands). Home and Office: Land Revegetation Internat PO Box 12594 Tucson AZ 85732-2594

ANDERSON, RICHARD ALAN, mechanical engineer; b. N.Y.C., Mar. 7, 1933; s. Douglas Alexander and Alice Katrina (Wenning) A. BSME, CCNY, 1955. Engr. Raytheon Corp., Wayland, Mass., 1955-59, CDI, Needham, Mass., 1959-79, GE, Wilmington, Mass., 1979-92; sr. tech. staff specialist Kaiser Electronics, San Jose, Calif., 1992-95. Inventor LCD packaging, circuit interconnect to liquid crystal display. Home: 4356 Lakeshore Dr Santa Clara CA 95054-1333

ANDERSON, RICHARD ERNEST, energy and chemical research and development company executive, rancher; b. North Little Rock, Ark., Mar. 8, 1926; s. Victor Ernest and Lillian Josephine (Griffin) A.; m. Mary Ann Fitch, July 18, 1953; children: Vicki Lynn, Lucia Anita. BSCE, U. Ark., 1949; MSE, U. Mich., 1959. Registered profl. engr., Mich., Va., Tex., Mont. Commd. ensign USN, 1952, advanced through grades to capt., 1968, ret., 1974; v.p. Ocean Resources, Inc., Houston, 1974-77; mgr. maintenance and ops. Holmes & Narver, Inc., Orange, Calif., 1977-78; pres. No. Resources, Inc., Billings, Mont., 1978-81; v.p. Holmes & Narver, Inc., Orange, Calif., 1981-82; owner, operator Anderson Ranches, registered Arabian horses and comml. Murray Grey cows, Pony, Mont., 1982—; pres., dir. Carbon Resources Inc., Butte, Mont., 1983-88, Agri Resources, Inc., Butte, Mont., 1988—. Trustee Lake Barcroft-Virginia Watershed Improvement Dist., 1973-74; pres. Lake Barcroft-Virginia Recreation Center, Inc., 1972-73. With USAAF, 1944-45. Decorated Silver Star, Legion of Merit with Combat V (2), Navy Marine Corps medal, Bronze Star with Combat V, Meritorious Service medal, Purple Heart; Anderson Peninsula in Antarctica named in his honor. Mem. ASCE, Soc. Am. Mil. Engrs. (Morrell medal 1965). Republican. Methodist. Home: PO Box 266 Pony MT 59747-0266 Office: Agri Resources Inc 305 W Mercury St Butte MT 59701-1659

ANDERSON, RICHARD LEE, ophthalmologist, educator; b. Grinnell, Iowa, Feb. 24, 1945; s. James Lee and Priscilla Jane (McKibbin) A.; m. Karen Nettie Altemeier, Aug. 21, 1965 (div. 1990); m. Susan Annette Aho, July 31, 1992; children: Mark, Erin, Sadie. BA, Grinnell Coll., 1967; MD, U. Iowa, 1971. Diplomate Am. Bd. Ophthalmology. Resident in ophthalmology U. Iowa, Iowa City, 1971-74; resident in plastic surgery U. Calif., San Francisco, 1974-76; from asst. prof. to prof. ophthalmology U. Iowa, Iowa City, 1976-84; prof. ophthalmology U. Utah, Salt Lake City, 1984—, chief div. ophthalmic plastic surgery, 1986—. Author: Clinical Orbital Anatomy, 1983; assoc. editor Archives Ophthalmology, 1984-94, Ophthalmic Surgery, 1984—, Ophthalmic Plastic and Reconstructive Surgery, 1984—; contbr. more than 300 articles to profl. jours. Served to maj. U.S. Army N.G., 1971-76. Named to Best Drs. in Am., 1991,-94; named to Best 400 Drs. in Am., Good Housekeeping mag., 1991. Fellow ACS; mem. Am. Acad. Ophthalmology (Sr. Honor award 1994, Heed award 1990), Am. Soc. Ophthalmic Plastic and Reconstructive Surgery (v.p. 1984-85), Am. Acad. Facial Plastic and Reconstructive Surgery, Alpha Omega Alpha. Republican. Christian. Office: U Utah Dept Ophthalmology Moran Eye Ctr 50 N Medical Dr Salt Lake City UT 84132-0001

ANDERSON, ROBERT ERNEST, safety engineer, consultant; b. Heavener, Okla., July 30, 1926; s. Ernest L. and Dewey M. (Vaught) A., m. Eleanor Jeanne Mauzy, Sept. 15, 1948; children: Robert, Sarah, David, Hans. BS, Okla. State U., 1949, MS, 1950. Registered profl. engr., Calif.; cert. safety profl. Instr. Okla. State U. Agr. and Applied Sci., Stillwater, 1950-51, asst. prof., 1951-52; with Mine Safety Appliances Co., Beaumont, Tex., Gary, Ind., and Little Rock, 1952-63; mgr. safety products MSA Internat., Pitts., 1963-67; mgr. intermountain dist. MSA, Salt Lake City, 1967-87; pvt. practice safety engring. cons. Salt Lake City, 1987—; adj. asst. prof. safety engring. U. Utah., 1988—; cons. Indsl. Health Inc. With USNR, 1944-46. Mem. AIME, Am. Indsl. Hygiene Assn., Am. Soc. Safety Engrs. (v.p. region II 1986-87, Safety Profl. of Yr. Utah chpt. 1993), Masons. Democrat. Methodist. Home and Office: 3372 Pioneer St Salt Lake City UT 84109-3048

ANDERSON, ROBERT K., health care company executive; b. Brainerd, Minn., Oct. 20, 1935; s. Kenneth F. and Ida Anderson; m. Sydney M. Anderson, June 18, 1976; 1 child, Kimberly C.; children from previous marriage; Robert W., Richard K., Laura A. BEE, U. Minn., 1963. Co-founder, chief exec. officer, chmn. Valleylab, Inc., Boulder, Colo., 1969-86, chmn., 1986—; bd. dirs. Med. Devices, Inc., Pfizer Hosp. Products Group, Am. Med. Sys., Meritech, Inc., Camino Labs., Inc.; pres. Pfizer Health Care Ventures; chmn. bd. Contbr. articles to profl. jours.; patentee in field. Recipient Outstanding Achievement award U. Minn., 1992. Mem. IEEE, Health Industry Mfrs. Assn. (dir., mem. exec. com., treas. 1982-83), Assn. Advancement Med. Instrumentation (bd. dirs., corp. v.p. 1978-81), Young Pres.' Orgn. (edn. chmn. 1982, chpt. chmn. 1983, membership chmn. 1984), N.Y. Acad. Scis. Home: 7262 Old Post Rd Boulder CO 80301-3916 Office: Valleylab Inc 5920 Longbow Dr Boulder CO 80301-3202

ANDERSON, ROBERT ORVILLE, oil and gas company executive; b. Chgo., Apr. 13, 1917; s. Hugo A. and Hilda (Nelson) A.; m. Barbara Phelps, Aug. 25, 1939; children: Katherine, Julia, Maria, Robert Bruce, Barbara Burton, William Phelps, Beverley. B.A., U. Chgo., 1939. With Am. Mineral Spirits Co., Chgo., 1939-41; pres. Malco Refineries, Inc., Roswell, N.Mex., 1941-63; with Atlantic Richfield Co., Los Angeles, retired chmn. bd., chief exec. officer; chmn. Hondo Oil and Gas Co., Roswell; mem. Com. Econ. Devel., Washington. Hon. chmn. Aspen Inst.; chmn. emeritus Lovelace Med. Found.; trustee Calif. Inst. Tech., U. Chgo. Mem. Nat. Petroleum Council, Am. Petroleum Inst. Clubs: Century (N.Y.C.); California (Los Angeles); Pacific-Union (San Francisco). Office: Hondo Oil & Gas Co PO Box 2208 Roswell NM 88202-2208

ANDERSON, ROBERT WAYNE, oil company financial officer; b. Brigham, Utah, July 16, 1951; s. Everett Carl and Margaret (Hatch) A.; m. Brenda Bingham, Dec. 1, 1971; children: Carl Arch, Mary-Esther, Hollyanna, Rex, Kirk, Trent. BS, Utah State U., 1975. CPA, Utah. Auditor Haskins and Sells, Salt Lake City, 1975-79; dir. internal auditing Browning Co., Mountain Green, Utah, 1979-80; internal auditor Thiokol Corp., Brighmam, 1980-83; dir. internal auditing, chief fin. officer Flying J Inc., Brighmam, 1983—; fin. exec. Honeyville (Utah) Grain Inc. Baseball coach Little League, Corinne, Utah, 1983-85; scouting coordinator Boy Scouts Am., Corinne, 1986-87. Republican. Mormon. Office: Honeyville Grain Inc PO Box 678 Brigham City UT 84302-0678

ANDERSON, ROSCOE ODELL (DALE), retired personnel officer; b. Snowville, Utah, Aug. 15, 1913; s. Roscoe Joseph and Diantha Jane (Robbins) A.; m. Elizabeth Jeanne Neil, June 4, 1939; 1 child, Dale Neil. BS, U. Utah, 1937, MS, 1943; postgrad., Cornell U., 1965, U. San Francisco, 1972. Cert. tchr. and adminstr. in secondary edn. Employee relations officer Utah Gen. Depot, Ogden, 1943-48; dir. civilian personnel Sharpe Army Depot, Lathrop, Calif., 1948-52, Aberdeen Proving Ground U.S. Army, Aberdeen, Md., 1952-55; field rep. Office Civilian Personnel Dep. Chief Staff Personnel, San Francisco, 1955-60; chief employee mgmt. div. Office Civilian Personnel Dep. Chief Staff Personnel, Washington, 1960-66; dir. civilian personnel 6th U.S. Army, Presidio, San Francisco, 1966-73; zone IV coord. U.S. Dept. Defense, San Francisco, 1973-76; cons. Defense Supply Agy., GSA, 1977-80; nat. v.p. Soc. for personnel Adminstrn., 1962, charter mem., pres. No. Calif., 1967, charter mem., pres., Hartford County, Md., 1955; guest lectr. U. San Francisco, 1969; chmn. Fed. Personnel Coun./No. Calif., San Francisco, 1967-68. Mem. Marin coun. ARC, Marin County, Calif., 1975-80; sec. Ogden City Svc. Baseball League, 1944-47; chmn. fed. employee div. Community Chest Drive, San Joaquin County, Calif., 1952, dep. chmn., Aberdeen Proving Ground, 1955. Recipient Meritorious Civilian Svc. award Dept. Army, Sec. Def., 1966, Meritorious Civilian Svc. award with Bronze Laurel Leaf Cluster, Dept. Army, 1972, Meritorious Civil Svc. award Sec. of Def., 1972. Mem. Army Civilian Personnel Alumni Assn., Nat. Assn. Ret. Fed. Employees, Am. Assn. Ret. Persons, Wilderness Soc., Audubon Soc., Sierra Club, Utah Golf Assn., Crimson Club U. Utah, Coun. Fgn. Rels. Mormon.

ANDERSON, ROSS, columnist. Editorial writer The Seattle Times. Recipient Pulitzer Prize for nat. reporting, 1990. Office: The Seattle Times 1120 John St PO Box 70 Seattle WA 98111

ANDERSON, ROY A., finance company executive; b. Ripon, Calif., Dec. 15, 1920; s. Carl Gustav and Esther Marie (Johnson) A.; m. Betty Leona Boehme, 1948; 4 children. Grad. Humphrey's Sch. Bus., Stanford U. Mgr. factory acctg. Westinghouse Electric Corp., 1952-56; mgr. acctg. and fin., dir. mgmt. controls Lockheed Missiles and Space Co., 1956-65; dir. finance Lockheed Ga. Co., 1965-68; asst. treas. Lockheed Aircraft Corp. (now Lockheed Corp.), 1968-69, v.p., controller, 1969-71, sr. v.p. finance, 1971-75, vice chmn. bd. dirs., chief fin. adminstrv. officer, 1975-77, chair, CEO, 1977-85, dir., chair exec. com., cons., 1985-88, chair emeritus, 1989—; chair Weingart Found., 1994—. Office: Lockheed Corp 23d Flr 606 S Olive St Los Angeles CA 90014*

ANDERSON, ROYAL JOHN, advertising agency executive; b. Portland, Oreg., Sept. 12, 1914; s. John Alfred and Martha Marie (Jacobsen) A.; m. Leticia G. Anderson; children: Michael, Johnny, Dora Kay, Mark Roy, Stan Ray, Ruth Gay, Janelle A., Jennifer T., Joseph, Daisy, Dina; 1 adopted dau., Muoi-Muoi. BA, Albany Coll., 1939; postgrad., U. Oreg., 1939-41, Oreg. Inst. Tech., 1940-41. Corp. cons. Dupont Corp., Beverly Hills, Calif., 1967-68; editor-pub. Nev. State Dem., Carson City, 1967-68, Nev. State Pub. Observer, Carson City, 1967-68, Nev. State Congl. Assn., Carson City, 1962-78; pres. Allied-Western Produce Co., Yuma, Ariz., 1962-78, Nev. Dem. Corp., 1966-78, Western Restaurant Corp., 1978-81, Nev. State Sage Co., 1979—, Midway Advt. Co., 1979—, Environ. Research Corp., 1983—, Mid-City Advt. Agy., 1983—, Nat. Newspaper Found., 1969, 71-76, The Gt. North Banks Seafood Co., 1984—, Food Services Corp., 1985—, Sterling Cruise Lines, 1986—, No-Tow Mfg. Inc., 1986—, Manila Mortgage Co., 1991—; pres. Trident Toothpaste Mfg., 1992-93, chmn. bd., pres., 1993—; chmn bd. Press/Register Daily Newspapers, Foster Mortgage Co., 1983—. Inventor No-Tow, 1988 worldwide; designer prefabricated milk carton container, 1933, well water locating under-stream device, 1938, no-tow automotive product under fgn. mfrs. for world mfg. Bishop Ch. of Palms, Mexico; pres. Ch. of the Palms Found. Corp.; dep. registrar voters Washoe County, Nev., 1966; mem. Clark County Econ. Opportunity Bd., 1988-91; v.p. Trident Toothpaste Found., 1991-92, pres. 1990-93, chmn. bd. 1992-93. Recipient Heroism award for rescue, 1933; Research fellow, Alaska, 1936. Mem. Am. Hort. Soc., Nev. State C. of C. (pres.), Sparks C. of C. (pres. 1970-93), U.S. C. of C., Chatso Farm Assn. (pres. 1962-88), Smithsonian Assocs., N.Am. C. of C. Execs., Nat. Geog. Soc., Am. Newspaper Alliance (v.p. 1976), Millionare Club, Kiwanis, Elks, Lions. Address: 5600 E Sundance Ave Las Vegas NV 89110-3825 also: 5600 Sundance Ave Las Vegas NV 89110-3825

ANDERSON, STEPHEN HALE, federal judge; b. 1932; m. Shirlee G. Anderson. Student, Eastern Oreg. Coll. Edn., Brigham Young U.; LLB, U. Utah, 1960. Bar: Utah 1960, U.S. Claims Ct. 1963, U.S. Tax Ct. 1967, U.S. Ct. Appeals (10th cir.) 1970, U.S. Supreme Ct. 1971, U.S. Ct. Appeals (9th cir.) 1972, various U.S. Dist. Cts. Tchr. South High Sch., Salt Lake City, 1956-57; trial atty. tax div. U.S. Dept. Justice, 1960-64; ptnr. Ray, Quinney & Nebeker, 1964-85; judge U.S. Ct. Appeals (10th cir.), Salt Lake City, 1985—; spl. counsel Salt Lake County Grand Jury, 1975. Editor in chief Utah Law Rev. Cpl. U.S. Army, 1953-55. Mem. Utah State Bar (pres. 1983-84, various offices), Salt Lake County Bar Assn. (pres. 1977-78), Am. Bar Found., Salt Lake Area C. of C. (bd. govs. 1984), U. Utah Coll. Law Alumni Assn. (trustee 1979-83, pres. 1982-83), Order of Coif. Office: US Ct Appeals 4201 Fed Bldg 125 S State St Salt Lake City UT 84138-1102*

ANDERSON, STEVEN CLEMENT, biology educator; b. Grand Canyon, Ariz., Sept. 7, 1936; s. Howard Theodore and Lois Belle (Patterson) A.; m. Kay Allison Bratsch, June 29, 1960; 1 child, Malcolm Ross. BA, U. Calif., 1957; MA, San Francisco State U., 1962; PhD, Stanford U., 1966. From asst. to assoc. curator of herpetology Calif. Acad. Scis., San Francisco, 1963-70, research assoc., 1975—; prof. biology U. Pacific, Stockton, Calif., 1970—. Author: (with others) Handbook of Amphibians and Reptiles of the Middle East, 1992; cons. editor Ency. Iranica, 1978—; contbr. articles to sci. jours. Fellow Calif. Acad. Scis., Herpetologists' League; mem. Am. Soc. Ichthyologists and Herpetologists, Soc. Study of Amphibians and Reptiles, Sigma Xi. Office: U Pacific Dept Biology Stockton CA 95211

ANDERSON, SUSAN LYNNE, sales executive; b. Pitts., Dec. 21, 1964; d. James Edward and Marianne (Meininger) A. BSEE, Iowa State U., 1987. Tech. sales rep. Tex. Instruments Inc., San Jose, Calif., 1988-93, regional sales mgr., 1993—. Shelter vol. Family Living Ctr., Santa Clara, 1989-92; vol. Jr. Achievement. Mem. Soc. Women Engrs., Iowa State Alumni Club (officer). Democrat. Lutheran. Office: Tex Instruments Inc 2825 N 1st St Ste 200 San Jose CA 95134-2047

ANDERSON, THEODORE WILBUR, statistics educator; b. Mpls., June 5, 1918; s. Theodore Wilbur and Evelynn (Johnson) A.; m. Dorothy Fisher, July 8, 1950; children: Robert Lewis, Janet Lynn, Jeanne Elizabeth. BS with highest distinction, Northwestern U., 1939, DSc, 1989; MA, Princeton U., 1942, PhD, 1945; LittD, North Park Coll. and Theol. Sem., 1988. Asst. dept. math. Northwestern U., 1939-40; instr. math. Princeton U., 1941-43, rsch. assoc., 1943-45; rsch. assoc. Cowles Commn., U. Chgo., 1945-46; staff Columbia U., 1946-67, successively instr. math. stats., asst. prof., assoc. prof., 1946-56, prof., 1956-67, chmn. math. stats. dept., 1956-60, 64-65, acting chmn., 1950-51, 63; prof. stats. and econs. Stanford U., 1967-88, prof. stats. and econs. emeritus, 1988—; dir. project Office Naval Rsch., 1950-82; prin. investigator NSF project, 1969-92, Army Rsch. Office project, 1982-92; vis. prof. math U. Moscow, 1968; vis. prof. stats. U. Paris, 1968; vis. prof. econs. NYU, 1983-84; acad. visitor math. Imperial Coll. Sci. and Tech., U. London, 1967-68, London Sch. Econs. and Polit. Sci., 1974-75, U. So. Calif., 1989; C.G. Khatri Meml. lectr. Pa. State U., 1992; rsch. visitor Tokyo Inst. Tech., 1977; sabbaticant IBM Systems Rsch. Inst., 1984; rsch. assoc. Naval Postgrad. Sch., 1986-87; cons. RAND Corp., 1949-66; mem. com. on basic rsch. adv. Office Ordnance Rsch., Nat. Acad. Scis.-NRC, 1955-58; mem. panel on applied math. adv. Nat. Bur. Standards, 1964-65; chmn. com. on stats. NRC, 1961-63; mem. exec. com. Conf. Bd. Math. Scis., 1963-64; mem. com. on support rsch. in math. scis. Nat Acad. Scis., 1965-68; mem. com. Pres.'s Statis. Socs., 1962-64; sci. dir. NATO Advanced Study Inst. on Discriminant Analysis and Its Applications, 1972. Author: An Introduction to Multivariate Statistical Analysis, 1958, 2d edit., 1984, The Statistical Analysis of Time Series, 1971, (with Somesh Das Gupta and George P.H. Styan) A Bibliography of Multivariate Statistical Analysis, 1972, (with Stanley Sclove) Introductory Statistical Analysis, 1974, An Introduction to the Statistical Analysis of Data, 1978, 2d edit., 1986, (with Barry P. Eynon) MINITAB Guide to the Statistical Analysis of Data, 1986; editor: (with Krishna B. Athreya and Donald L. Iglehart) Probability, Statistics and Mathematics: Papers in Honor of Samuel Karlin, 1989, (with Kai Tai Fang) Statistical Inference in Elliptically Contoured and Related Distributions, 1990, (with K.T. Fang and I. Olkin) Multivariate Analysis and Its Applications, 1994; editor Anns. of Math. Stats., 1950-52; assoc. editor jour. Time Series Analysis, 1980-88; mem. adv. bd. Econometric Theory, 1985—, Jour. Multivariate Analysis, 1988—; mem. editl. bd. Psychometrika, 1954-72. Recipient R.A. Fisher award Pres.'s Statis Socs., 1985, Disting. Alumnus award North Park Coll. and Theol. Sem., 1987, Minnehaha Acad., 1992, Samuel S. Wilks Meml. medal Am. Statis. Assn., 1988, award of merit Northwestern U. Alumni Assn., 1989; named Wesley C. Mitchell Vis. Prof. Columbia U., 1983-84; Guggenheim fellow, 1947-48, fellow Center for Advanced Study in Behavioral Scis., 1957-58; vis. scholar, 1972-73, 80; Sherman Fairchild disting. scholar Calif. Inst. Tech., 1980; vis. dist. prof. Norwegian Coun. Sci. and Indsl. Rsch. at U. Oslo; Abraham Wald Meml. lectr., 1982; S.S. Wilks Meml. lectr. Princeton U., 1983; R.A. Fisher lectr. Am. Statis. Assn., 1985; P.C. Mahalanobis Meml. lectr., 1985; S.N. Roy Meml. lectr. Calcutta U., 1985; Allen T. Craig lectr. U. Iowa, 1991. Fellow AAAS (chmn. sect. U. 1990-91), Am. Statis. Assn. (v.p. 1971-73), Econometric Soc., Royal Statis. Soc., Inst. Math. Stats. (pres. 1963), Am. Acad. Arts and Scis.; mem. NAS, Am. Math. Soc., Indian, Internat. Statis. Insts., Statis. Soc. Can., Psychometric Soc. (coun. dirs.), Bernouilli Soc. for Math. Stats. and Probability, Norwegian Acad. Sci. and Letters (fgn.), Phi Beta Kappa. Home: 746 Santa Ynez St Palo Alto CA 94305-8441 Office: Stanford U Dept of Stats Sequoia Hall Stanford CA 94305-4

ANDERSON, THOMAS E., computer scientist, educator; b. Orlando, Fla., Aug. 28, 1961; s. John L. Anderson and Elizabeth D. Bond; m. Robin Briggs; 1 child, Alexandra. AB in Philosophy cum laude, Harvard U., 1983; MS in Computer Sci., U. Wash., 1989, PhD, 1991. Devel. engr., sr. devel. engr. GenRad Inc., 1983-87; rsch. asst. dept. computer sci. U. Wash., Seattle, 1987-91; asst. prof. Computer Sci. divsn. U. Calif., Berkeley, 1991—; cons. Digital Equipment Corp. Systems Rsch. Ctr., Palo Alto, Calif., 1991—, Xerox Corp. Palo Alto Rsch. Ctr., 1993—. Contbr. articles to profl. jours. IBM grad. fellow, 1989-91; NSF nat. young investigator, 1992; Alfred P. Sloan rsch. fellow, 1994; NSF Presdl. Faculty fellow, 1994. Office: U Calif Berkeley Computer Sci Div Berkeley CA 94720

ANDERSON, THOMAS LEIF, physician, researcher; b. New Orleans; s. Maurice John and Kitty Thordis (Thomstad) A.; m. Charlotte Ann Hull, Oct. 11, 1980; children: Laurel Emelia, Timothy Leif. BA, Denison U., 1971; MD, Yale U., 1975. Diplomate Am. Bd. Pschiatry and Neurology. Intern in medicine U. Fla. Hosps., Gainesville, 1975-76; resident Harbor-UCLA Med. Ctr., Torrance, 1976-79; fellow Barnes Hosp., St. Louis, 1979-80, staff physician, 1980—; mem. med. adv. com. L.A. County Muscular Dystrophy Assn., 1982—. Mem. Am. Acad. Neurology. Presbyterian. Office: Harbor-UCLA Med Ctr 1000 W Carson St Torrance CA 90502-2004

ANDERSON, WALTER TRUETT, author; b. Oakland, Calif., Feb. 27, 1933; s. Elbert William and Susan Alice (Martin) A.; m. Maurica Griffith Osborne, Feb. 10, 1968; 1 child, Daniel Griffith. BA in Polit. Sci., U. Calif., Berkeley, 1955; MA in Polit. Sci., Calif. State U., Northridge, 1967; PhD in Polit. Sci., U. So. Calif., L.A., 1972. Pvt. practice writer and lectr., 1965—; vis. lectr. Sch. Pub. Policy, U. Calif., Berkeley, 1988-89; fellow, faculty mem. Western Behavioral Scis. Inst., La Jolla, Calif., 1988-92; cons. Values and Lifestyles Program, SRI Internat., Menlo Park, Calif., 1991-92; v.p. Meridian Internat. Inst., San Francisco, 1992—. Author: Evaluating Democracy (with Joseph Allman), 1973, A Place of Power, 1976, Therapy and the Arts, 1977, Open Secrets, 1979, 80, 89, The Upstart Spring, 1983, 84, Rethinking Liberalism, 1983, To Govern Evolution, 1987, Reality Isn't What It Used To Be, 1990, 92, others; assoc. editor, columnist Pacific News Svc., San Francisco, 1982—; bd. editors: Jour. Humanistic Psychology, 1976—; editorial cons. Calif. Tomorrow, 1976-81; contbg. editor Human Behavior Mag., 1971-80. mem. adv. bd. Rollo May Ctr. for Humanistic Studies, San Francisco, 1987—, U. Calif. Biotech. Rsch. and Edn. Program, 1988—; mem. coun. Biofocus Found., Stockholm, 1988—; chair biotech. task force Sierra Club, San Francisco, 1988-92; bd. dirs. Bay Area Biosci. Ctr., Oakland, 1990—; bd. trustees Inst. for Sci. in Soc., Washington, 1991—; chair bd. trustees Saybrook Inst. and Grad. Sch., San Francisco, 1992-94. With U.S. Army, 1954-56. Mem. Assn. for Politics and the Life Scis., Internat. Soc. Polit. Psychology, World Future Soc., World Future Studies Fedn., Am. Inst. Biol. Scis., World Acad. Art and Sci. (pres. Am. divsn. 1993—). Office: Meridian Internat Inst Ste 2100 One Sansome St San Francisco CA 9410

ANDERSON, WILLIAM, retail company executive, business education educator; b. L.A., May 21, 1923; s. William Bert and Marie (Novotney) A.; m. Margaret Lillian Phillips, Aug. 16, 1951; children: Margaret Gwen, Deborah Kay, William Keven, Denise Marie. BA in Econs., UCLA, 1948, MEd, 1957. Cert. secondary tchr. (life), Calif. Tchr. bus. edn. Big Bear Lake (Calif.) High Sch., 1949-52, Ventura (Calif.) Unified Sch. Dist. Buena High Sch., 1952-89; chief exec. officer Day's Aircraft Inc., Santa Paula, Calif., 1967—; cons. micro computers Calif. State Dept. Edn., 1983-85; pres. "Dollars for Schollars", Ventura. Crew chief Olympic Games basketball stats., 1984, basketball stats. World Games for the Deaf, 1985, U.S. Olympic Festival, 1991; vol. Calif. Police Olympics, 1989. With USAAF, 1943-45, PTO. Mem. NEA (life), Calif. Bus. Edn. Assn. (pres. So. sect. 1959-60, state sec. 1960-61, hon. life 1991), Internat. Soc. Bus. Edn. (voting del. to Soc. Internat. Pour l'Enseignemer Comml., Western rep. 1988-89, apptd. historian 1991), Am. Aviation Hist. Soc., Calif. Assn. Work Experience Educators (life), Air Force Assn. (life), So. Calif. Badminton Assn. (past bd. dirs.), Phi Delta Kappa, Delta Pi Epsilon (hon. life). Democrat. Lutheran. Home: 334 Manzanita Ave Ventura CA 93001-2227 Office: Day's Aircraft Co Inc PO Box 511 Santa Paula CA 93061-0511

ANDERSON, WILLIAM SCOVIL, classics educator; b. Brookline, Mass., Sept. 16, 1927; s. Edgar Weston and Katrina (Brewster) A.; m. Lorna Candee Bassette, June 12, 1954 (dec. Dec. 1977); children: Judith, Blythe, Heather, Meredith, Keith; m. Deirdre Burt, May 28, 1983. B.A., Yale U., 1950, Ph.D., 1954; A.B., Cambridge U., (Eng.), 1952; M.A., Cambridge U., 1955. Prix de Rome fellow Am. Acad. in Rome, 1954-55; instr. classics Yale U., 1955-59; resident in Rome, Morse fellow, 1959-60; mem. faculty U. Calif., Berkeley, 1960—, prof. Latin and comparative lit., 1966—, prof. charge Intercollegiate Ctr. Classical Studies, 1967-68, chmn. classics, 1970-73; rsch. prof. U. Melbourne, 1984; Robson lectr. Victoria Coll., Toronto, 1987; Blegen rsch. prof. Vassar Coll., 1989-90, vice chair comparative lit., 1990-93; vis. disting. prof. Fla. State U., spring 1995. Author: The Art of the Aeneid, 1969, Ovid, Metamorphoses, Critical Text, 1977, Essays on Roman Satire, 1982, Barbarian Play: Plautus' Roman Comedy, 1993. Served with AUS, 1946-48, Korea. NEH sr. fellow, 1973-74. Mem. Am. Philol. Assn. (pres. 1977), Danforth Assocs., Soc. Religion. Episcopalian. Office: Univ Calif Dept Classics Berkeley CA 94720

ANDRADE, JOE RUSSELL, lumber company executive, artist; b. San Antonio, Oct. 17, 1947; s. Joe Nieto Andrade and Norma (Gonzales) Tindall; m. Kathleen Phillips, Oct. 2, 1993; 1 child, Noah Russell. MA, Calif. State U., Northridge, 1979. Pres. Pacific West Designs, Venice, Calif., 1979-83; v.p. Tradewest Hardwood Co., Rancho Dominguez, Calif., 1983-91; pres., gen. mgr. All City Milling Svcs. and Forestal Industries, Los Angeles, 1991—; fine artist Santa Monica, Calif., 1979—; v.p. KL Communications, 1992—. Proponent of post modernist art movement conjuctivism, 1994—; works exhibited at Armand Hammer Mus., Art Rental Gallery. Pres. Assn. Venice Artists, 1975. Cpl. USMC, 1968-70, Vietnam. Santa Monica City Coll. scholar, 1976. Mem. Mus. Contemporary Art, L.A. County Mus. Art. Democrat. Roman Catholic. Home: 236 S Westgate Ave Los Angeles CA 90049-4206 Office: All City Milling Svcs and Forestal Industries 115 E 58th St Los Angeles CA 90011-5313

ANDRAIN, CHARLES FRANKLIN, political science educator; b. Fortuna, Calif., Feb. 22, 1937; s. Milton D. and Alberta W. (Gatton) A. A.B., Whittier Coll., 1959; M.A., U. Calif.-Berkeley, 1961, Ph.D., 1964. Asst. prof. dept. polit. sci. San Diego State U., 1964-67, assoc. prof., 1967-70, prof., 1970—, chmn. dept., 1972-74; research assoc. Inst. Internat. Studies, U. Calif.-Berkeley, 1975-76, 78-79, 80-81, 82, 86. Author: Children and Civic Awareness, 1971; Political Life and Social Change, 2d edit., 1975; Politics and Economic Policy in Western Democracies, 1980; Foundations of Comparative Politics: A Policy Perspective, 1983, Social Policies in Western Industrial Societies, 1985, Political Change in the Third World, 1988, Comparative Political Systems, 1994, (with David E. Apter) Political Protest and Social Change, 1995. Woodrow Wilson Found. fellow, 1959-60; Nat. Def. Edn. Act fellow, 1960-63; Ford Found. fellow, 1968-69; NIMH fellow, 1971-72. Mem. Am. Polit. Sci. Assn., Am. Sociol. Assn., Internat. Soc. Polit. Psychology. Office: San Diego State U Dept Polit Sci San Diego CA 92182

ANDRASICK, JAMES STEPHEN, agribusiness company executive; b. Passaic, N.J., Mar. 27, 1944; s. Stephen Adam and Emily (Spolnik) A.; children: Christopher J., Gregory O. BS, USCG Acad., 1965; MS, MIT, 1971. Commd. ensign USCG, 1965, advanced through grades to lt., 1968; assigned to Vietnam, 1967-68; resigned, 1969; systems analyst Jamesbury Corp., 1970; mem. corp. fin. and product devel. staffs Ford Motor Co., 1971-74; mgr. corp. devel. IU Internat. Corp., Phila., 1974-78; v.p. planning, controller C. Brewer & Co., Ltd., Honolulu, 1978-81, sr. v.p. fin., chief fin. officer, 1981-83, exec. v.p., 1983-92, pres., 1992—; chmn. bd., mng. gen. ptnr. Mauna Loa Macadamia Ptnrs., 1986-88; chmn. bd. HCPC, Olokele Sugar Co., Hawaiian Sugar & Transp. Cooperative; chmn. Hawaiian Sugar Planters Assn., 1992-93; bd. dirs. Wailuku Agribusiness Co. Bd. dirs. Aloha United Way, Honolulu, 1983-89; treas., bd. dirs. ARC, Hawaii, 1983-94, chmn., 1989-90; bd. dirs. Hawaii Employers Coun., 1992—, chmn., 1995—; trustee UH Found., 1988-94, vice chmn., 1992-93, chmn., 1993-94; trustee Hawaii Maritime Ctr., 1993—; bd. dirs. Coast Guard Found., chmn. 1994. Home: 2140 Aha Niu Pl Honolulu HI 96821-1007 Office: C Brewer & Co Ltd 827 Fort Street Mall Honolulu HI 96813-4317

ANDRE, JAMES P., nuclear engineer; b. Kenmore, N.Y., May 7, 1959; s. Ambrose J. Jr. and Erma C. (Ellis) A.; m. Teresa A. McGarry, Nov. 10, 1984; children: Kristen L., Brian J. BS in Physics, Rensselaer Polytechnic Inst., 1981, MBA, 1988. Physicist U.S. Dept. Energy/Schenectady (N.Y.) Naval Reactors Office, 1981-92; sr. devel. engr. Battelle, Pacific Northwest Lab., Richland, Wash., 1992—; adj. faculty U.S. Dept. Energy Ctrl. Tng. Acad., Albuquerque, 1992—; mem. USDOE Material Control and Accountability Tng. Working Group, Albuquerque, 1992-94; material control and accountability rep. U.S. Dept. Energy/Material Control and Accountability Rep. Com., Washington, 1985-92. Bd. dirs. Three Rivers Children's Mus., Kennewick, Wash., 1993—, pres., 1994-95; tech. adv. Adult Literacy Program, Columbia Basin Coll., Pasco, Wash., 1993—. Mem. Inst. Nucl. Materials Mgmt., IEEE, Nat. Trust Hist. Preservation. Home: 8109 W Hood Ave Kennewick WA 99336-1618 Office: Battelle Pacific NW Lab PO Box 999 Richland WA 99352

ANDREOPOULOS, SPYROS GEORGE, writer; b. Athens, Greece, Feb. 12, 1929; came to U.S., 1953, naturalized, 1962; s. George S. and Anne (Levas) A.; m. Christiane Loesch Loriaux, June 6, 1958; 1 child, Sophie. AB, Wichita State U., 1957. Pub. info. specialist USIA, Salonica, Greece, 1951-53; asst. editorial page editor Wichita (Kans.) Beacon, 1955-59; asst. dir. info. svcs., editor The Menninger Quar., The Menninger Found., Topeka, 1959-63;; info. officer Stanford U. Med. Ctr., 1963-83; dir. comm., editor Stanford Medicine, 1983-93, dir. emeritus comm., editor emeritus, 1993—; editor Sun Valley Forum on Nat. Health, Inc. (Idaho), 1972-83, 85—. Co-author, editor: Medical Cure and Medical Care, 1972, Primary Care: Where Medicine Fails, 1974, National Health Insurance: Can We Learn from Canada? 1975, Heart Beat, 1978, Health Care for an Aging Society, 1989; contbr. articles to profl. jours. With Royal Hellenic Air Force, 1949-50. Mem. AAAS, Assn. Am. Med. Colls., Nat. Assn. Sci. Writers, Am. Med. Writers Assn., Am. Hosp. Assn., Am. Soc. Hosp. Mktg. and Pub. Rels., Coun. for Advancement and Support of Edn. Home: 1012 Vernier Pl Palo Alto CA 94305-1027

ANDRESEN, MARK NILS, electrical engineer; b. Patuxent River, Md., Mar. 21, 1957; s. Ronald N. and Nancy R. (Foster) A.; m. Silia M. Andrews, Nov. 6, 1982; children: Lauren, Jonathan, Jaqueline, Kimberly. BSEE, Va. Tech., 1980. Design engr. U.S. Army Corps Engrs., Norfolk, Va., 1977-79; R & D engr. Hewlett Packard, Cupertino, Calif., 1980-85; applications engr. Oneac Corp., Sunnyvale, Calif., 1985-86; pvt. practice cons. San Jose, Calif., 1989; tech. instr. Basic Measuring Instruments, Foster City, Calif., 1989-91, product mgr., 1991-92, sr. applications engr., power quality specialist, 1992-93; dir. of edn., 1993-94, pvt. practice, 1994—; presenter in field, 1989—. Mem. Calvary Cmty. Ch., San Jose, Calif., pastor staff, 1986-89; mem. Cupertino Foursqare Ch., 1991—, Springs of Life Fellowship, 1995—. Mem. IEEE (editor publ., chpt. chair), Assn. Energy Engrs., Nat. Fire Protection Agy. Republican. Home and Office: 10344 N [illegible] Cupertino CA 95014-2351

ANDRESS, CATHY, psychologist, educator; b. Akron, Ohio, June 17, 1960; d. Samuel Coe and Joan (Ferguson) A. BA, Randolph-Macon Woman's Coll., 1982; MA, So. Ill. U., Edwardsville, 1985; PsyD, Chgo. Sch. Profl. Psychology, 1991. Child and family therapist No. Wyo. Mental Health Ctr., Newcastle, 1988-89; sr. therapist Tri-City Community Mental Health Ctr., East Chicago, Ind., 1990; part-time instr. Oakton C.C., Des Plaines, Ill., 1989-91, adj. counselor, 1991; part-time instr. Northeastern Ill. Univ., Chgo., 1990-91; instr. psychology Big Bend C.C., Moses Lake, Wash., 1991—. Mem. NEA, Assn. for Humanistic Psychology, Assn. for Transpersonal Psychology, Wash. Edn. Assn. (mem. minority affairs commn. 1992—, mem. woman's caucus 1994—), Wash. State Psychol. Assn. Office: Big Bend CC 7662 Chanute St NE Moses Lake WA 98837-3293

ANDREW, JANE HAYES, non-profit organization executive; b. Phila., Jan. 1, 1947; d. David Powell and Vivian Muriel (Saeger) Hayes; m. Brian David Andrew, June 14, 1977; 1 child, Kevin Hayes. AB, Barnard Coll., 1968, grad., Harvard Arts Administrn. Instit., 1972; MBA, U. Wash., 1994. Mgr. theater Minor Latham Playhouse, Barnard Coll., N.Y.C., 1970-74; co. mgr. Houston Ballet, 1974-77, Ballet West, Salt Lake City, 1978-83; gen. mgr. Pacific N.W. Ballet, Seattle, 1983-87; organizer non-profit consortium nat. ballet cos. and nat. presenting orgns., 1987; pres., exec. dir. Ballet/America, 1988-91; ind. cons. arts mgmt., 1991-94; dir. Found. for Internat. Understanding Through Students, 1995—. panelist NEA Dance Program Presentors, 1987-88, 88-89, 89-90, Seattle Arts Commn. dance grants, 1989, 90; cons. Ariz. Arts Commn., Phoenix, 1985-86; com. mem. 25th Anniversary of World's Fair, Seattle, 1986-87; panelist NEA Local Programs, 1987. Editor (directory) Philadelphia Cultural Orgns., 1977. Bd. dirs. Good Shepherd Adv. Bd., Seattle, 1985-87. Recipient Dorothy D. Spivack award Barnard Coll., N.Y.C., 1972. Mem. Dance/USA (chmn. Mgrs. Coun. 1986). Home and Office: 7706 146th Ave NE Redmond WA 98052-4105

ANDREW, LUCIUS ARCHIBALD DAVID, III, corporate executive; b. Highland Park, Ill., Mar. 5, 1938; s. Lucius Archibald David Jr. and Victoria (Rollins) A.; m. Susan Ott, June 1, 1963 (div. 1973); children: Ashley W., L.A. David IV; m. Phoebe Haffner Kellogg, Dec. 21, 1974; children: Gaylord M., Charles H., Matthew K., Louise M. Kellogg. BS, U. Pa., 1962; MBA, NYU, 1965. Asst. treas. The Bank of N.Y., N.Y.C., 1962-68; instl. salesman Drexel, Harriman, Ripley, N.Y.C., 1968-70; v.p., br. mgr. Drexel, Firestone, Inc., Chgo., 1970-72; ptnr., br. mgr. Fahnestock & Co., Chgo., 1972-74; vice chmn. Viner's, Ltd., Sheffield, Eng., 1981-82; pres. N.E.A., Inc., 1975-85; chmn. exec. com. Cert. Mfg. Co., Shelton, Wash., 1975-85; bd. dirs. First Am. Bank, Chgo., 1965-91, chmn., 1982-91; dir. First Am. Bank Corp., 1985—, First Am. Data Corp., 1982—; chmn. FGI, Inc., Forest Grove, Oreg., 1985-86, Union St. Capital Corp., Seattle, Wash., 1986-87, Brudi Inc., Seattle, 1988-90, Emerald Automation, 1990—. Trustee Brooks Sch.; past trustee Seattle Repertory Theatre; bd. dirs. The Found. for Lifetime Advocacy and Guardian Svcs., Swedish Med. Ctr. Found. Mem. The Brook, Racquet and Tennis (N.Y.C.); Racquet (Chgo.); Rainier, University, Golf, Tennis, (Seattle). Home: The Highland Seattle WA 98177 Office: 200 First Ave West Ste 402 Seattle WA 98119

ANDREWS, GARTH E., public relations executive; b. Bakersfield, Calif., Mar. 5, 1943; s. Milton Dale and F. Janice (Schermerhorn) A.; m. Lennie May Husen, Dec. 22, 1964; children: Corinna, Heather. BA in Radio-TV, East Wash. U., Cheney, 1967. Accreditated pub. rels. Reporter, photographer King Broadcasting, Seattle, Spokane, Wash., 1967-68; reporter, anchorman, exec. producer KBOI/KBCI Radio/TV, Boise, Idaho, 1968-75; adminstrn. pub. info. Idaho Pub. Utilities Commn., Boise, 1975-78; sr. pub. rels. assoc. P. R. Mallory & Co. Inc., Indpls., 1978-79; communications rep. S.W. Gas Corp., Las Vegas, Nev., 1979-81, dir. pub. info., 1981-83; dir. communications S.W. Gas Corp., Tucson, Ariz., 1983-87; dir. communications S.W. Gas Corp., Phoenix, 1987-94, mgr. comm., 1994—. Mem. publicity steering com. Fiesta Bowl, Phoenix, 1987-88; publicity chmn. Fiesta Bowl Hot Air Balloon Classic, Phoenix, 1988-89; trustee Ariz. Mus. Sci. and Tech., Phoenix, 1987-94; mem. Pima County Energy Commn., Tucson, 1984-87. With USNR, 1962-64. Mem. Pub. Rels. Soc. Am. (pres. (Valley of the Sun chpt. 1993). Republican. Presbyterian. Office: SW Gas Corp 10851 N Black Canyon Hwy Phoenix AZ 85029-4755

ANDREWS, JOHN KNEELAND, youth worker; b. Winchester, Mass., May 29, 1920; s. George Angell and Frances (Kneeland) A.; m. Marianne Hutchinson, Mar. 21, 1943 (dec. July 1978); children: John. K. Jr., James H., Eleanor Andrews Keasey, Sally Andrews Griego; m. Mary Folds, Feb. 14, 1979. BA, Principia, Elsah, Ill., 1942. Mgr. Fennville (Mich.) Milling Co., 1945-48; asst. traffic mgr. Mich. Fruit Canners, Fennville, 1948-50; food broker Rosen Brokerage Co., St. Louis, 1950-53; alumni sec., asst. to treas. The Principia, St. Louis, 1953-55; exec. dir. Sky Valley Ranch, Inc., Buena Vista, Colo., 1955-60; chief exec. officer, chmn. bd. dirs. Adventure Unltd., Englewood, Colo., 1960-83; chmn. emeritus Adventure Unltd., Englewood, 1983—; sole practice youth worker Denver, 1983—. Lt. Submarine Svc., USNR, 1942-45, PTO. Decorated Silver Star. Mem. Briarwood Country Club (Sun City West, Ariz.), Cherry Hills Country Club (Englewood), Rotary (bd. dirs. Denver chpt. 1983-85). Republican. Christian Scientist. Home and Office: Unit 464 8505 E Temple Dr Denver CO 80237

ANDREWS, MARY ANN, nursing services director; b. Geneva, N.Y., Apr. 3, 1928; d. Joseph John and Catherine (Gillotte) Yannotti; m. Donald R. Andrews Sr., Mar. 28, 1947 (dec. 1989); children: Donald Jr., Michael J., Thomas C., Maryrose Arimoto. AA in Nursing, De Anza Coll., 1975; BA in Health Sci. Adminstrn., St. Mary's Coll., Morega, Calif., 1982; MPA in Health Sci. Adminstrn., U. San Francisco, 1988; Mgmt. Cert., San Jose State U., 1987. RN; cert. direct staff devel. Pharmacy Corp. Am. Asst. head nurse San Jose (Calif.) Health Ctr., 1975-82; shift supr. San Benito Hosp. Dist., Hollister, Calif., 1982-86, AMI Cmty. Hosp., Santa Cruz, Calif., 1986-88; dir. nursing svcs. Care West Enterprises Inc., Watsonville, Calif., 1988-91; dir. nursing Hillhaven Corp., San Jose, Calif., 1991-92, Guardian Corp., San Jose, Calif., 1992-93; with Horizons West, San Jose, Calif., 1994—. Roman Catholic. Home: 1406 Alma Ter San Jose CA 95125

ANDREWS, RALPH HERRICK, television producer; b. Chgo., Dec. 17, 1927; s. Henry Karl and Sylvia Angelica (Lorenzen Barth; m. Margaret Ann Belt, Feb. 5, 1951 (div. 1977); m. aleksandra Vaz vel Wezykowska, June 1, 1986; children: William, Herrick, Phyllis, Patrice, Peter, James, Jakub, Matthew. Announcer, disc jockey, salesman radio stas. WSAM and WKNX, Saginaw, Mich.; page NBC, Hollywood; with Don Fedderson Prodns., Ralph Edwards Prodns.; dir. live programming Desilu; prin. Ralph Andrews Prodns.; co-founder, bd. dirs. Entertainment Industries Coun. Producer: Divorce Hearing, By the Numbers, Zoom, Show Me, You Don't Say, I'll Bet, Wedding Party, The Family Game, It Takes Two, It's Your Bet, Liars Club, The Mickie Finn Show, Celebrity Sweepstakes, 50 Grand Slam, Lingo, (movies) Silent Treatment, Skyjacked; producer, host: Lie Detector. Cand. for Congress, 1972; nat. dir. edn. and tng. Rep. Nat. Com., Washington, 1972 (Presidential commendation). Republican. Roman Catholic. Home and Office: 5449 Paradise Valley Rd Hidden Hills CA 91302-2435

ANDREWS, RICHARD OTIS, museum director; b. L.A., Nov. 8, 1949; s. Robert and Theodora (Hammond) A.; m. Colleen Chartier, Jan. 3, 1976; 1 child, Bryce. BA, Occidental Coll., L.A., 1971; BFA, U. Wash., 1973, MFA, 1975. Project mgr. Art in Pub. Places, Seattle Arts Commn., 1978-80, coord., 1980-84; dir. visual arts program Nat. Endowment for Arts, Washington, D.C., 1985-87; dir. Henry Art Gallery, U. Wash., Seattle, 1987—; co-curator Art Into Life: Russian Constructivism 1914-1932; cons. pub. art program devel., 1982-84. Author: Insights/On Sites, 1984, James Turrell: Sensing Space, 1992; editor Artwork/Network, 1984; contbg. editor Going Public, 1988. Office: U Wash Henry Art Gallery Box 353070 Seattle WA 98195-3070

ANDREWS, RUSSELL JOSEPH, neurosurgeon, educator; b. Pitts.; s. Harold J. and Barbara (McCreight) A.; m. Yong Sim Park, Apr. 30, 1980; children: Adrienne, Alethea. BA, Dartmouth Coll., 1967, MD, 1978; EdD, Harvard U., 1974. Diplomate Am. Bd. Neurol. Surgery. Surg. intern Walter Reed Army Med. Ctr., Washington, 1978-79; flight surgeon U.S. Army, Natick, Mass., also South Korea, 1979-81; resident in neurosurgery Stanford U. Med. Ctr., 1981-86; asst. prof. U. Calif. Davis Med. Ctr., Sacramento, 1986-91; mem. staff VA Med. Staff, Martinez, Calif., 1986-91; asst. prof. Stanford U. Med. Ctr., 1992—; mem. staff VA Med. Ctr., Palo Alto, Calif., 1992—. Home: 22831 Mercedes Rd Cupertino CA 95014-3919

ANDRIANO-MOORE, RICHARD NORVEL GRAF, naval officer; b. Petaluma, Calif., May 25, 1932; s. Norvel Moore and Thelma Elizabeth (Cook) Koch-Andriano Atkins; m. Janice Lynn Hironaka, Jan. 10, 1976 (div. Feb. 1990); children: Erika Lynn, Stephen Albert. BA, San Jose State U., 1956; MBA, Pepperdine U., 1979; BA, U. Metaphysics, 1993. Commd. ens. USN, 1957, advanced through grades to comdr.; 1st lt., and gunnery officer U.S.S. Jefferson Count LST1068, 1957-60; 7th grade tchr. Oasis Sch., Riverside County, Calif., 1960-63; pers. and legal officer U.S.S. Maury AGS-16, 1963-65; commdg. officer Naval & Marine Corps reserve Training Cen, Port Arthur, Tex., 1965-68; ops. officer U.S.S. Muliphen LKA 64, 1968-69; ASW & surface program officer 11th Naval Dist., San Diego, 1970-74; commdg. officer Naval Reserve Cen., Hunters Point, Calif., 1974-75; comdr. officer Army, Navy & Marine Corps Reserve Ctr, San Bruno, Calif., 1975-79; dir. of adminstrn. Nat. Com. for Employer, Washington, 1979-82; comdr., recruiting coord. Regional 10 Western states, Alameda, Calif., 1982-84; chief of staff N.R. Readiness comdr., Treasure Island, Calif., 1984-85; sub. tchr., Shoreline Unified Sch. Dist., Tomales, Calif., 1985-92. Editor-in-chief: California Compatriot, 1976-80. Inspector Precinct Bd., Petaluma, Calif., 1987-90; scoutmaster Boy Scouts Am., 1981-82, dist. exec., 1992-94. Decorated Defense Meritorious Svc. medal Sec. of Def., Washington, 1982; recipient Ancestral Coat of Arms of the Counts of Andriano, Wappenrolle, Austria, 1985, Rome, Italy, 1994, Disting. Alumni award San Jose State U., 1991. Mem. The Augustan Soc. Inc. (v.p. 1990-94)., Calif. Soc. Sons of the Am. Revolution (state pres. 1986-87, Patriot medal 1985, San Francisco chpt. pres. 1976-77, Silver Good Citizenship medal 1978, Meritorious Svc. medal 1987), The Military Order of the Loyal Legion of the U.S. (Calif. comdr. 1982-88), The Naval Order of The U.S. Home: 197 Upland Dr Petaluma CA 94952-1037 Office: BSA Redwood Empire Coun 2240 Professional Dr Santa Rosa CA 95403-3005

ANDRIELLA, STEVEN L., information systems manager. BA, Syracuse U.; MS, SUNY, Buffalo. Asst. mgr. Saudi Arabian Army Air Def. Sch., Jeddah, Saudi Arabia, 1979-83; computer systems rep. Computer Ark, Lawrence, Kans., 1984-85; pub. systems rep. Computer Graphics Ctr., Palo Alto, Calif., 1986-87; human resources systems cons. VRC Consulting, Los Altos, Calif., 1987-88; sr. employee devel. specialist Bank of Am., San Francisco, 1988-92; cons. Automatic Data Processing, Concord, Calif., 1992-93, Bank of Am., San Francisco, 1993-94, Heublein Wines Group, San Mateo, Calif., 1994—. Active Little Hands Coop. Sch., Ganon Daycare Ctr. Mem. San Mateo C. of C. Home: 2406 Read Ave Belmont CA 94002-1516

ANDRING, RONALD PAUL, protective services official; b. Yakima, Wash., Apr. 17, 1953; s. Richard Joseph and JeRene Estelle (Krienke) A.; m. Margaret Anne Yount, Jan. 13, 1978; children: Margaret Ann, Ronald Paul Jr. BA in Criminal Justice, Ea. Wash. U., 1990, MPA, 1995. Enforcement officer Wash. State Patrol, Kennewick, 1975-78, Walla Walla (Wash.) Police Dept., 1978-79; correctional officer Wash. State Penitentiary, Walla Walla, 1979-89, adminstrv. asst., 1990-91, correctional sgt., 1991—; mem. regional adv. com. Dept. Corrections, Olympia, Wash., 1991-93, trainer, 1988-91. Contbr. articles to profl. jours. and mags. Organizer Jr. Achievement awards, Walla Walla, 1991-93, Kid's Classic Fun Run, Walla Walla, 1991-93; candidate 14th legis. dist. Dem. Cen. Com., Wash., 1972; vol. Friends and Families of Violent Crime Victims, 1989-92; chair publs. com. Blue Ridge PTA, 1989-91. Recipient Pub. Adminstrn. Honors Student award Ea. Wash. U., 1995. Mem. Am. Correctional Assn. (adv. com. 1991—, del. assembly 1994—), Wash. Correctional Assn. (exec. bd. 1989—, treas. 1994-95, Spl. Svc. award 1993), Western Correctional Assn., Am. Criminological Soc., Am. Platform Assn. (coord. 1995 mid-winter conf., coord. 125th Congress of Correction), Masons (master 1992-93), Scottish Rite. Congregationalist. Home: 502 W Chestnut St Walla Walla WA 99362-3963 Office: Washington State Penitentiary PO Box 520 Walla Walla WA 99362-0520

ANDRUS, CECIL DALE, academic administrator; b. Hood River, Oreg., Aug. 25, 1931; s. Hal Stephen and Dorothy (Johnson) A.; m. Carol Mae May, Aug. 27, 1949; children: Tana Lee, Tracy Sue, Kelly Kay. Student, Oreg. State U., 1948-49; LLD (hon.), Gonzaga U., U. Idaho, U. N.Mex., Coll. Idaho, Idaho State U., Whitman Coll. State gen. mgr. Paul Revere Life Ins. Co., 1969-70; gov. State of Idaho, 1971-77, 87-95; sec. of interior, 1977-81; dir. Albertson's, Inc., 1985-87, 95—, Coeur d'Alene Mines, 1995—; chmn. Andrus Ctr. for Pub. Policy, Boise (Idaho) State U., 1995—; mem. Idaho Senate, 1961-66, 69-70; mem. exec. com. Nat. Gov.'s Conf., 1971-72, chmn., 1976; chmn. Fedn. Rocky Mountain States, 1971-72. Chmn. bd. trustees Coll. of Idaho, 1985-89; bd. dirs. Sch. Forestry, Duke U. With USN, 1951-55. Recipient Disting. Citizen award Oreg. State U., 1980, Collier County Conservancy medal, 1979, Ansel Adams award Wilderness Soc., 1985, Audubon medal, 1985, Statesman of the Yr. award Idaho State U., 1990, Torch of Liberty award B'nai B'rith, 1991; named Conservationist of Yr. Nat. Wildlife Fedn., 1980, Idaho Wildlife Fedn., 1972, Man of Yr., VFW, 1959. Mem. VFW, Idaho Taxpayers Assn. (bd. dirs. 1964-66). Democrat. Office: Andrus Ctr for Pub Policy Boise State U 1910 University Dr Boise ID 83725

ANG, PAUL THIENCHAI, entrepreneur, international business consultant; b. Bangkok, July 4, 1937; came to U.S., 1982; s. Jer Tang and Noi Poh (Ear) A.; m. Agnes Lovett; children: Paul L., Paulette A. BCommerce, Melbourne Inst. Tech., Australia, 1959; student Advanced Mgmt. Program, Harvard U., 1980. Mktg. exec. Exxon, Thailand, 1960-63; comml. mgr. Thai Dairy Industry, 1963-65; div./dept. mgr. East Asiatic Co., Thailand, 1965-70; comml. mgr., regional chief exec. Imperial Chem. Industies, Thailand, 1971-72; pres., CEO Chem. Thailand Co. and Multi-Thai Co., 1973-81, PTA Internat. Inc., N.J., 1982-93, Success Pacific Corp., Calif., 1993—. Roman Catholic.

ANGEL, ARMANDO CARLOS, rheumatologist, internist; b. Las Vegas, N.Mex., Mar. 25, 1940; s. Edmundo Clemente and Pauline Teresa (Flores) Sanchez A.; m. Judith Lee Weedin, Aug. 5, 1961; children: Stephanie, Renee. BA, San Jose State U., 1963; MS, U. Ariz., 1970, PhD, 1971, M.D., 1977. Chemist Tracerlab, Inc., Richmond, Calif., 1963-67; prof. chemistry Pima Coll., Tucson, Ariz., 1971-74; intern U. N.Mex., Albuquerque, 1977-78, resident, 1978-80; resident VA Hosp., Lovelace Med. Ctr., Albuquerque, 1978-80; practice medicine specializing in internal medicine, Las Cruces, N.Mex., 1980-88; pvt. practice, El Paso, Tex., 1990—; dir. pain program Rio Vista Rehab. Hosp., 1992; cons. minority biomed. sci. project NIH, Washington, 1970-74, Ednl. Assocs., Tucson, 1971-74. Author: Llevve Tlaloc No. 2, 1973. Treas. Nat. Chicano Health Orgn., Los Angeles, 1974-75; v.p. Mexican-Am. Educators, Tucson, 1973-74; pres. N.Mex. affiliate Am. Diabetes Assn., Albuquerque, 1983-85. Fellow U. Ariz., 1988-90. Fellow Am. Coll. Rheumatology; mem. AMA, Tex. Med. Soc., El Paso County Medical Soc., Am. Diabetes Assn., ACP, Dona Ana County Med. Soc. (pres. 1983), Am. Coll. Rheumatology, Am. Assn. Internal Medicine, Alpha Chi Sigma.

ANGELE, ALFRED ROBERT, police labor union executive; b. N.Y.C., Dec. 9, 1940; s. Alfred Otto and Alma Margaret (Branda) A.; m. Barbara Ann Chavez, Sept. 30, 1961; children: Cynthia Lynn, Lynda Renee. AA, L.A. Valley Coll., 1968. Cert. tchr. community coll. police adminstrn. Patrolman Burbank (Calif.) Police Dept., 1963-67, detective, 1967-74, sgt., dept. self def. instr., 1974-78; gen. mgr. Calif. Orgn. Police and Sheriffs, Sacramento, 1978-89, exec. dir., 1989—; internat. sec./treas. Internat. Union Police Assns. AFL-CIO, Alexandria, Va., 1985-90; internat. sec./treas. emeritus Internat. Union Police Assns. AFL-CIO, Alexandria, 1990-92; Govt. appt. commr. on Peace Officer Standards/Tng., Sacramento, 1979-84; mem. AFL-CIO observer team sent to Nicaragua to monitor presdl. election, 1990, Police Adv. Coun. on Car Clubs, 1967-70; mem. exch. progrm with German Police Union, 1987. Contbr. articles to profl. jours. including USA Today. Mem. L.A. Host committee for nat. tour Bill of Rights, 1991. Recipient Mike Maggiora Meml. Humanitarian award Maggiora family, 1980, Commendations, Letters of Appreciation Burbank Bar Assn., Elks, Calif. Hwy. Patrol, Mayor's Drug and Alcohol Abuse Com., L.A. County Dist. Atty.'s Office, Houston Police Patrolmans Union, Calif. Dept. Corrections, Mayor of L.A., numerous others; named 1st Officer of the Month Jaycees, 1977. Mem. Burbank Police Officers Assn. (pres. 1976-81, named dir. of yr. 1972, commendation award), Internat. Union Police Assns. AFL-CIO (sec.-treas. 1985—, dir. 1981-85, named law enforcement editor of the yr. 1987), Calif. Narcotics Officers Assn., Calif. Orgn. Police/Sheriffs (gen. mgr. 1978—, sec. 1976-78, commendation award), Calif. Narcotics Info. Network. Democrat. Roman Catholic. Office: 175 E Olive Ave Ste 400 Burbank CA 91502-1821

ANGELL, KARLA MICHELLE, school counselor; b. Columbus, Ohio, July 4, 1963; d. Norman Dean and Patricia Jean (Kelly) A. BJ, U. Ariz., 1985; MEd, Coll. of Idaho, 1990. Lic. profl. counselor, Idaho; cert. K-12 sch. counselor, Idaho. Copy editor The Idaho Statesman, Boise, 1986-89; office mgr. Boise Care Unit, 1990-91; sch. counselor Boise Sch. Dist., 1991-92; sch. counselor McMillan Elem. Sch., Meridian Sch. Dist., Boise, 1992—; chem. dependency counselor Mercy Med. Ctr., Nampa, Idaho, 1991—; group facilitator, program coord. Touchstone Ctr., Boise, 1990-92; co-facilitator parent edn. classes Meridian Sch. Dist., 1993—, facilitator tobacco edn. classes, 1994—. Tchr. religious edn. St. Paul's Cath. Ch., Boise, 1987-89. Recipient 1st place for headline writing Idaho Press Club, 1987, 2d place for headline writing Pacific N.W. Excellence in Journalism Competition, 1987. Mem. ACA, Am. Sch. Counseling Assn., Idaho Counseling Assn., Idaho Sch. Counseling Assn., Phi Beta Kappa. Office: Meridian Sch Dist 911 N Meridian Rd Meridian ID 83642

ANGELO, CHRISTOPHER EDMOND, lawyer, consultant; b. L.A., Dec. 19, 1949; s. Edmond James and Shirley Ann (Richards) A.; m. Patrice Lonnette Brown, Apr. 26, 1980; 1 child, Alexander Bradshaw. BA, U. Calif., Riverside, 1972; JD, Loyola U., 1975. Bar: Calif. 1976, U.S. Dist. Ct. Calif. 1976. Trial atty. Spray, Gould & Bowers, L.A., 1976-78, Harrington, Foxx, Dubrow & Canter, L.A., 1978-83, Gage & Mazursky, Beverly Hills, Calif., 1983-85; trial atty., ptnr. Gage, Mazursky, Schwartz, Angelo & Kussman, Beverly Hills, Calif., 1986-88; trial atty., gen. ptnr. Mazursky, Schwartz & Angelo, L.A., 1988—; faculty lectr. Calif. Judges Assn., 1989; mem. Loyola Law Sch. Law Review, L.A., 1974-75. Author books and articles in field of tort and ins. bad faith liability. Cons. Bet Tzedak Legal Aid Found., L.A., 1992; counsel Christopher Sampson Non-Profit Found. for Catastrophically Injured, L.A., 1991, dir., founder. Recipient Highlander scholarship U. Calif., 1968-72. Mem. ABA, Italian Am. Lawyers Assn. (bd. govs. 1979-83), Calif. Trial Lawyers Assn. (lectr. 1983—, Cert. of Appreciation), Calif. Bar Assn., Consumer Attys. Assn. L.A. (lectr. 1983—, Cert. of Appreciation). Office: Mazursky Schwartz & Angelo 6th Fl 10877 Wilshire Blvd Fl 6 Los Angeles CA 90024-4341

ANGELOV, GEORGE ANGEL, pediatrician, anatomist, teratologist; b. Bulgaria, May 12, 1925; came to U.S., 1978; s. Angel Christov and Maria Angelov; m. Olga Valerie Minkova, Dec. 21, 1952; 1 child, Angel. MD, Sch. of Medicine, Sofia, Bulgaria, 1952. Pediatrician Distric Hosp., Bulgaria, 1952-53; asst. prof. Sch. of Medicine, Sofia, Bulgaria, 1953-64; prof. anatomy and anthropology Sch. of Biology, Sofia, Bulgaria, 1964-77; mgr. reproductive toxicology Lederle Labs., Pearl River, N.Y., 1979-89; cons. reproductive toxicology pvt. practice, Laguna Niguel, Calif., 1989—; assoc. dean Sch. of Biology, Sofia, 1970-72; vis. scientist Sch. of Medicine, Geneva, 1971, 74. Author: (textbook) Anatomy, 1970; mem. glossary com. Teratology Glossary, 1987-89; reviewer several sci. jours.; contbr. numerous sci. pubs. on anatomy, teratology, and growth and devel. of adolescents to profl. jours. Mem. Teratology Soc. USA, European Teratology Soc., Human Biology Coun. USA, Free Union of Univ. Profs. of Anatomy. East Orthodox.

ANGEVIN, ROBERT PERKINS BROWN, real estate development executive; b. Lake Forest, Ill., June 16, 1963; s. John Jay Angevin and Stella (Brown) Kenly. BA, Williams Coll., 1985; M Real Estate, U. So. Calif., 1992. Assoc. Continental Ill., Chgo., 1985-87; project mgr. JMB Realty Co., L.A., 1987-91; supervised loan specialist, supervised assets divsn. Bank of Calif., L.A., 1992—; bd. dirs. The Keystone-Garrett Corp., L.A. Founder, The Food Network, L.A.

ANGLESIO, FRANCO J., hotel executive; b. Turin, Italy, Sept. 14, 1943; s. Cesare and Alma (Cattaneo) A.; m. Mary C. Bartlett, Aug. 22, 1970; children: Marco P., Michael S. Gen. mgr. Chateau Laurier, Ottawa, Can., 1980-83, Hotel Vancouver, Can., 1983-86; v.p. ops. Coast Hotels & Resorts, Vancouver, 1986-91, exec. v.p., 1991-92, pres., 1992—; bd. dirs. Coast Hotels & Resorts Ltd., Vancouver, Okabe N.Am. Inc., Vancouver. Mem. Skal Club, Chaine des Rotisseurs. Roman Catholic. Home: 1278 Bracknell Pl, North Vancouver, BC Canada V7R1V5 Office: Coast Hotels & Resorts, 900-1090 W Georgia St, Vancouver, BC Canada V6E 3V7

ANGUIANO, LUPE, business executive; b. La Junta, Colo., Mar. 12, 1929; d. Jose and Rosario (Gonzalez) A. Student, Ventura (Calif.) Jr. Coll., 1948, Victory Noll Jr. Coll., Huntington, Ind., 1949-52, Marymount Coll., Palos Verdes, Calif., 1958-59, Calif. State U., L.A., 1965-67; M.A., Antioch-Putney-Yellow Springs, Ohio, 1978. S.W. regional dir. NAACP Legal Def. and Ednl. Fund, L.A., 1965-69; civil rights specialist HEW, Washington, 1969-73; S.W. regional dir. Nat. Coun. Cath. Bishops, Region X, San Antonio, 1973-77; pres. Nat. Women's Employment and Edn., Inc., L.A., 1979-91; pres., cons. Lupe Anguiano & Assocs., 1981—; cons. Tex. Dept. Human Resources, Dept. Labor, Women's Bur.; proposal reader U.S. Office Edn.-Women's Equity Act; mem. Tex. Adv. Coun. on Tech.-Vocat. Edn. Calif. del. White House Conf. on Status Mexican-Ams. in U.S., 1967; founding mem. policy coun. Nat. Women's Polit. Caucus, from 1971; Tex. and nat. del. Internat. Women's Year, 1976-77; chmn. Nat. Women's Polit. Caucus Welfare Reform Task Force, from 1977; co-chmn. Nat. Peace Acad. Campaign, 1977-81; founder, bd. dirs. Nat. Chicana Found., Inc., 1971-78; bd. dirs. Calif. Coun. Children and Youth, 1967, Rio Grande Fedn. Chicano Health Ctrs., S.W. Rural States, 1974-76, Women's Lobby, Washington, 1974-77, Rural Am. Women, Washington, from 1978, Small Bus. Coun. Greater San Antonio; mem. Pres.'s Coun. on Pvt. Sector Initiatives, 1983. Recipient Community award Coalition Mexican-Am. Orgns., 1967, Outstanding Svc. award Washington, 1968, Thanksgiving award Boys' Club, 1976, Outstanding Svc. award Tex. Women's Polit. Caucus, 1977, Liberty Bell award San Antonio Young Lawyers, 1981, Vista award for exceptional svc. to end poverty, 1980, Headliner award San Antonio Women in Communications, 1978, Woman of Yr. award Tex. Women's Polit. Caucus, 1978, Pres.'s Vol. Action award 1983, Leadership award Nat. Network Hispanic Women, 1989; named Outstanding Woman of Yr., L.A. County, 1972, Woman of the 80s Ms. mag., 1980; Nat. Pres.'s award Nat. Image, Inc., 1981, Wonder Woman Found. award, 1982, Pres.' Vol. Action award 1983, Adv. of Yr. San Antonio SBA, 1984; selected Am. 100 Most Important Women, Ladies Home Jour., 1988, 89; featured in CBS TV series An Am. Portrait, 1985, Leadership award Nat. Network Hispanic Women, 1989. Mem. Assn. Female Execs., Pres.'s Assn., Am. Mgmt. Assn. Republican. Roman Catholic. Author: (with others) U.S. Bilingual Education Act, 1967, Texas A.F.D.C. Employment and Education Act, 1977; manuals Women's Employment and Education Model Program.

ANJARD, RONALD PAUL, SR., business and industry executive, consultant, educator, technologist, importer; b. Chgo., July 31, 1935; s. Auguste L. and Florence M. (Byrne) A.; m. Marie B. Sampler; children: Ronald Paul Jr., Michael P., Michele M., John R. BS in Metall. Engring., Carnegie Mellon U., 1957; MS/MBA in Indsl. Adminstrn., Purdue U., 1968; AS in Supervision, Ind. U., 1973; BS, U. State of N.Y., 1978; PDE, U. Wis., 1976; BA in Humanities, USNY, 1979; PhD in Edn., Columbia Pacific U., 1981, PhD in Metall. Engring., 1982; postgrad., Ind. U. Law Sch., 1975, La. State U., 1978, U. Calif., 1978; MS in Computer Resource Mgmt., Webster U., 1992; postgrad., U. Calif. Berkeley, 1978, La State U., 1979. Metallurgist U.S. Steel Corp., Braddock, Pa., 1956-57; metall. engr. Crucible Steel Co., Pitts., 1957-58; process engr. Raytheon Mfg. Co., Newton, Mass., 1958-59; program mgmt. engr. Delco Electronics div. GM, Kokomo, Ind., 1959-81; div. quality mgr. AVX Materials Div. Delco Electronics div. GM, Kokomo, 1981-82, div. quality mgr., JMI Electronic Materials div., 1982-83; v.p. engring. AG Tech, 1983—; pres. Anjard Internat. Cons., 1983, 86—, Anjard Solder Paste Tech., 1983—, Anjard Solder and Mfg. Tech., 1987—; corp. dir. quality Kaypro Corp., 1983-87; pres. Anjard Imports, 1965-80, 92—; sr. bank officer Mission Viejo (Calif.) Nat. Bank, 1986-87; v.p. mktg. Alpha Cast Products, 1987-93; v.p. adminstrn. Triage Network, 1988-93; sr. exec. broker Futures Investment Firm, 1983; quality cons. Gen. Dynamics, Convair, 1987, 92; SPC coord. Gen. Dynamics Electronics Div., 1989-94; distbr. Vertical Computer System, 1987; free-lance writer, photographer, 1966—; retail salesman Nurseryland, 1987-88; instr. Ball State U., 1970-71, 75-76, Kokomo Apprentice Program, 1971-81, Ind. Vocat. Tech. Coll., 1978-81, U. Phoenix, 1983, U. So. Calif., 1985-90, U. La Verne, 1985-92, Ala. A&M U., 1983, Chapman Coll., 1983-92, Nat. U., 1982-83, San Diego Community Coll., 1984—, U. Calif. San Diego, 1986-92, Golden State U., 1986-92, U. La Jolla, San Diego Job Corps, Union of Experimental Colls. and Univs., 1987—, Karanovich Counseling Ctr., Cen. Tex. Coll., 1987-92, numerous others; thesis mentor Columbia Pacific U., 1981—. Rev. editor Solid State Tech., rev. edit. Microelectronics and Reliability, 1982—, Ceram, 1985—, IEEE Circuits and Devices, 1985-93; contbr. to tech. and non-tech. publs. Pres. Greater Kokomo Assn. Chs., 1972-74; chmn. Diocesan Pastoral Council, Diocese Layfayette, Ind., 1977-78, diocesan ecumenical officer, 1972-78, diocesan impact coordinator, 1972-81; mem. Ascension Council, 1984—; active Ind. Council Chs., 1971-81; mem. Tierra Santa Town Council, 1988-90; councilman Howard County Council, Ind., 1981; trustee Clay Twp., 1970-75; dir. 5th dist. Ind. Twp. Trustees Assn.; vice chmn. Ind. State U. Young Republicans; del. Rep. State Conv., 1970, 74, 78, 80, dep. registration officer, 1970, 72, 74, 76, 80; mem. Rep. Nat. Com., 1970-75, mem. San Diego Rep. Cen. Com.; resolutions chmn. Young Reps. Conv., 1969; state minority chmn., dir. Howard County Young Reps.; regional dir. Leadership Tng. Sch.; chmn. 5th Dist. Young Reps.; mem. San Diego Rep. Cen. Com., 1985—; mem. Ind. State Com. for Med. Assistance, Ind. Citizens Adv. Council on Alcoholism, Ind. Citizens Council on Addictions, Mayor's Human Rights Com.; active Meshingomesia council Boy Scouts Am.; chmn. Clay Twp. Bicentennial Com., 1974-76; mem. exec. com. Kokomo Bicentennial Com., 1974-76; govt. agys. chmn. Howard County Bicentennial Com., 1974-76; capt. capital fund drive Sangralea Valley Boys Home Campaign, 1968; mem. San Diego Rep. Cen. Com., 1985—; regional bd. dirs. Drug Abuse Council, Howard County; bd. dirs., membership chmn. Mental Health Assn.; lector Ascension, San Diego, 1984—, mem. council, 1985-91, also numerous other civic activities. Served to capt., Ordnance Corps U.S. Army, 1957-66. Recipient Ind. Mental Health citations, 1969, 70, Howard County Mental Health citations, 1969, 70, ep. Hard Charger award, 1970, Gen. Motors Community Service award, 1970, Jaycee Disting. Service award, 1970, Disting. Service award Ind. Young Reps., 1971, Layman of Year award K.C., 1971, Ind. Mental Health award, 1971-72, Heart Fund award, 1973, Ind. Gov.'s Vol. Action commendation, 1975, 78, award Greater Kokomo Council of Chs., 1975; named Outstanding Ind. Young Rep., 1970; fellow Harry S. Truman Library, 1974—. Mem. Internat. Soc. for Hybrid Microelectronics (Midwest regional dir., charter state pres., treas., v.p., publicity chmn., program chmn., others 1970), Semicondr. Materials Soc., Am. Soc. Quality Control (editor non-periodic publs., electronics div.), Am. Soc. Metals, Am. Bar Assn., ASTM (chmn. subcoms. 1963-68), AIME, Kokomo Engring. Soc., Internat. Platform Assn., Internat. Brick Collector's Assn. (pres., gov. bd. 1983-93), Am. Indian Assn., Ind. Chess Assn., Nat. Hist. Soc., Ind. Hist. Soc., Howard County Hist. Soc. (bd. dirs.), Tippecanoe County Hist. Assn., Found. Ill. Archeology, Epigraphic Soc., Nat., Fla., Clearwater Audubon socs., N.Am. Acad. Ecumenists, Soc. Investigation of Unexplained, Ancient Astronaut Soc., Internat. Assn. for Investigation Ancient Civilizations (internat. dir. 1980—), Internat. UFO Registry, Kokomo Fine Arts Assn., Nat. Wilderness Soc., Whitewater Valley R.R. Assn., Kokomo Mgmt. Club (auditor 1970), Am. Hort. Soc., Nat. Greentown Glass Assn., San Diego Hist. Soc., San Diego Archeol. Soc., Calif. Archeol. Soc., San Diego Zool. Soc., Soc. for Hist. Archaeology, Soc. for Calif. Archaeology, San Diego Cymbidium Soc., San Diego Orch. and Soc., Nat. Acad. Ecumenists, Internat. Order St. Luke the Physician, Sigma Xi, numerous other organizations. Clubs: Kokomo Photo Guild, Ind. Chess, Donora Sportsman, Sycamore Racquet, Kokomo Rose Soc., Kokomo Astronomy, Kokomo Poetry, Kokomo Swim, East County Rep., Orion. Home: PO Box 420950 San Diego CA 92142-0950

ANKRUM, JOAN WHEELER, art dealer; b. L.A., Jan. 8, 1913; d. Raymond Bert and Margaret Lucille (Ozier) Wheeler; m. Morris W. Ankrum, Aug. 15, 1935 (Dec. 1964); 1 child, David; m. William Challee, 1986 (dec. 1989). Diploma in Theater Arts, Pasadena Playhouse/Calif., State Theater Sch., 1933. Historian Art Dealers Assn. Calif., L.A., 1989—. Recipient award for cultural enrichment of L.A., City Coun., L.A., 1993. Office: Ankrum Gallery 327 N Orange Dr Los Angeles CA 90036-2613

ANN, KAREN, author, lecturer, concept design artist; b. Fresno, Calif.. BA in Sociology and Psychology, San Jose State U. Cert. polarity health educator, Calif. Child welfare specialist; coord., designer first Big Sister Program, San Jose, 1969; numerous vol. projects. Author: Searching the Seed, 1988, An Act of Love: Gourmet Vegetarian Feasts, 1992; workshop facilitator, author, concept-design artist and producer in bio-dramatic experimentation; appeared on TV and radio; keynote speaker and panelist at health forums such as Whole Life Expo, 1986, 89, 93. Mem. Friends of Carl Jung in Carmel, Calif. Home: PO Box 144 Davenport CA 95017

ANNERINO, JOHN JOSEPH, photojournalist, author; b. Chgo.; s. John Samuel and Ida Barbra (Schwan) A.;m. Alejandrina Delgado, Jan. 30, 1993. BA, Prescott Coll., 1975. Freelance photographer Gamma-Liaison, N.Y.C., 1983—. Photojournalist, author: High Risk Photography: The Adventure Behind the Image, 1991, Canyons of the Southwest, 1993, Wild Country of Mexico/La tierra salvaje de Mexico, 1994; author: Adventuring in Arizona, 1991, Running Wild: Through the Grand Canyon, 1992, Hiking the Grand Canyon, 1993. Home and Office: 2325 W Wagon Wheels Dr Tucson AZ 85745-1379

ANNON, JACK STAFFORD, forensic and criminal psychologist, detective; b. Chgo., Nov. 26, 1929; s. Stafford Dorcey and Marjorie Louise (Sites) A.; m. Leilehua Becker, 1955 (div. 1961); 1 child, Jeffrey; m. Arvillie Ann Reed, Sept. 16, 1962; children: Jason Kaipokea, Tyron Makua, Marselene Uanoe. BA in Psychology summa cum laude, U. Hawaii, 1966, MA in Counseling Psychology, 1968, PhD in Clin. Psychology, 1971. Diplomate Am. Bd. Forensic Psychology. Am. Bd. Med. Psychotherapists, Am. Bd. Sexology, Am. Bd. Forensic Examiners. In TV ops. and prodn., 1952-63; tng. and rsch. in psychology and counseling, 1966-68; counseling psychologist U. Hawaii, 1968-69; psychologist Merry-Go-Round Child Care Ctrs., Inc., Honolulu, 1968-81; clin. and forensic psychologist in pvt. practice Honolulu, 1971—; assoc. prof. clin. faculty dept. psychiatry John A Burns Sch. Medicine, U. Hawaii, Honolulu, 1979—; pvt. investigator Honolulu, 1983—. Contbr. numerous articles to profl. jours. Fellow APA, Am. Acad. Clin. Sexologists, Am. Assn. Marriage and Family Therapy, Am. Assn. State Psychology Bds., Am. Coll. Forensic Psychology, Internat. Coun. Sex Edn. and Parenthood, Behavior Therapy and Rsch. Soc.; mem. Acad. Forensic Psychology, Am. Fedn. Police, Am. Law Enforcement Officers Assn., Am. Police Acad., Am. Soc. Law and Medicine, Am. Soc. Trial Cons., Assn. for Applied Psychophysiology and Biofeedback, Assn. of Sexologists, Soc. Sci. Study Sex, World Assn. Detectives, Phi Beta Kappa, Sigma Xi, Phi Eta Sigma, Psi Chi, Phi Kappa Phi, Omicron Delta Kappa.

ANSAK, MARIE-LOUISE, health care executive; b. Berne, Switzerland, Aug. 10, 1928; came to U.S., 1954; d. Hugo and Emmy Studer. Student, U. Sorbonne, Paris, City of London Coll., U. Berne; diploma, Sch. Social Work, Zurich, Switzerland, 1954; MSW, Smith Coll., 1958. Case worker various social svc. orgns. in Switzerland and and Calif., 1954-62; program dir., casework dir. Internat. Inst. San Francisco, 1962-69; project developer and cons. Chinese Newcomers Svc. Ctr., San Francisco, 1969; staff devel. supr. dept. social svcs. San Francisco Gen. Hosp., 1970-71; exec. dir. On Lok Sr. Health Svcs., San Francisco, 1971-90, On Lok, Inc., San Francisco, 1990—; presenter in field at various profl. meetings and conferences; contbr. articles to profl. jours. Contbr. articles to profl. jours. Recipient Gustav O. Lienhard award Inst. Medicine of NAS, 1988. Mem. Am. Assn. Homes for Aging, Calif. Assn. Homes for Aging (Pub. Svc. award 1987). Office: On Lok Inc 1441 Powell St San Francisco CA 94133-3848

ANSAR, JASMIN, utilities executive. BA in Econs. and Math. with honors, U. Southhampton, Eng., 1975, MSc in Econometrics and Ecnos., 1976, PhD in Econs., 1984. Power contracts resource analyst Pacific Gas and Electric, San Francisco, 1988, sr. energy economist, 1988-90, dir. ops. rsch. gas supply, 1993—, mem. strategic planning dept., 1994—; vis. prof. econs. U. B.C., Vancouver, 1985-86; vis. prof. agrl. econs. Purdue U., West Lafayette, Ind., 1987-88; assoc. prof. econs. and econometrics City U., London, 1978-87; asst. prof. quantitative methods St. Mary's Coll., Moraga, Calif., 1990-91. Author: (with others) Working Below Capacity, 1988; contbr. articles to profl. jours. Office: Pacific Gas and Electric Co Gas Ops Planning 444 Market St Rm 5305 San Francisco CA 94111-5325

ANSEL, LEE, surgeon; b. Chgo., Jan. 9, 1947; s. Harvey and Dorothy Ansel. BS, No. Ill. U., 1968; MD, Loyola U., 1972. Intern St. Joseph's Hosp., Phoenix, 1972-73; resident in surgery Michael Reese Hosp., Chgo., 1973-74; resident in surgery Maricopa County Hosp., Phoenix, 1974-77, fellow, 1977-78; pvt. practice Phoenix, 1979—; mem. exec. com. St. Joseph's Hosp. Grad. Valley Leadership, Phoenix, 1982. Mem. ACS (past pres. Ariz. chpt. 1989), AMA, F.A.C.S., S.W. Surg. Congress, Soc. Clin. Vascular Surgeons,. Office: Ariz Vascular Surgeons 1144 E Mcdowell Rd Phoenix AZ 85006-2664

ANSELL, GEORGE STEPHEN, metallurgical engineering educator, academic administrator; b. Akron, Ohio, Apr. 1, 1934; s. Frederick Jesse and Fanny (Soletsky) A.; m. Marjorie Boris, Dec. 18, 1960; children: Frederick Stuart, Laura Ruth, Benjamin Jesse. B. in Metall. Engring., Rensselaer Poly. Inst., 1954, M. in Metall. Engring., 1955, PhD, 1960. Physical metallurgist USN Research Lab., Washington, 1957-58; mem. faculty Rensselaer Poly. Inst., Troy, N.Y., 1960-84, Robert W. Hunt prof., 1965-84, chmn. materials div., 1969-74, dean engring., 1974-84; pres. Colo. Sch. Mines, Golden, 1984—; bd. dirs. Norwest Bank, Cyprus Minerals Co., Norwest Colo., Cyprus Amax Minerals Co., OEA, Inc. Editor books; patentee in field; contbr. over 100 articles to profl. jours. Served with USN, 1955-58. Recipient Hardy Gold Medal AIME, 1961, Curtis W. McGraw award Am. Soc. Engring. Edn., 1971, Souzandrade Gold Medal of Univ. Merit Fed. U. Maranhao, 1986. Fellow Metall. Soc. (pres. 1986-87), Am. Soc. Metals (Alfred H. Geisler award 1964, Bradley Stoughton award 1968); mem. NSPE, Am. Soc. Engring. Edn. (Curtis W. McGraw award 1971), Sigma Xi, Tau Beta Pi, Phi Lambda Upsilon. Club: Denver. Office: Colo Sch of Mines Pres Office 1500 Illinois St Golden CO 80401-1887*

ANSFIELD, JOSEPH GILBERT, psychiatrist, educator; b. Milw., Jan. 7, 1932. BS, U. Wis., 1953; MD, Chgo. Med. Sch., 1958. Diplomate Nat. Bd. Med. Examiners. Gen. rotating intern Mt. Sinai Hosp., Milw., 1958-59; gen. practice medicine Chgo. and Morton Grove, Ill., 1961-63; psychiatry resident Northwestern U., Chgo., 1963-66, chief resident, 1964-65, clin. instr. dept. psychiatry, 1966-67; dir. Chgo. Suicide Prevention Ctr., 1966-67; pvt. practice adolescent and young adult psychiatry Chgo., 1966-67; asst. prof. psychiatry, cons. to dept. psychology U. Ariz., 1967-69; assoc. Stone Brandel Ctr., Chgo., 1969-70; asst. prof. psychiatry Chgo. Med. Sch., 1970-77; psychiat cons. Peace Corps., 1967-69; cons. Ariz. Ranch Sch. for Boys, 1967-69; organizer, cons. Tucson Suicide Prevention Ctr., 1968; mem. admissions com. Chgo. Med. Sch., U. Health Scis.; psichiat. cons. State Dept. Mental Health, 1971-77; mem. bd. govs. Fox River Hosp., Chgo., 1972-73; courtesy staff N.W. Cmty. Hosp., Arlington Hts., Ill., 1972-77; active staff mem. Alexian Bros. Med. Ctr., Elk Grove Village, Ill., 1973-76; cons. Mich. Dept. Corrections, 1978-80, 81—, chmn. dept. psychiatry. Author: The Adopted Child, 1971; (with others) Progress in Neurology and Psychiatry, 1964, 65, 66. Mem. Am. Psychiatry Assn., Am. Soc. Adolescent Psychiatry, Calif. Med. Assn., Ctrl. Calif. Psychiatry Soc., Kern County Med. Soc. Office: Kern Med Ctr Dpt Psychiatry 1830 Flower St Bakersfield CA 93305-4144

ANSHEL, JEFFREY ROBERT, optometrist; b. Chgo., Nov. 8, 1949; s. Bernard and Rochelle (Berger) A.; m. Elaine Denise Bussinger, June 3, 1990; children: Trisha, David, Casey. BS, Ill. Coll. Optometry, 1974, OD, 1975. Pvt. rpactice Mission Vision Ctr., Oceanside, Calif., 1990—; pres. Corporate Vision Consulting, La Costa, Calif., 1990—; vis. lectr. Santa Fe Coll. Natural Medicine, 1979-83. Author: Healthy Eyes, Better Vision, 1990. Lt. USN, 1975-77. Mem. Am. Optometry Assn., Am. Acad. Optometry, Coll. Optometrists in Vision Devel., Calif. Optometric Assn., Quid Pro Quo Bus. Club. Home: 2404 Sacada Cir # A Carlsbad CA 92009-8030 Office: Mission Vision Ctr 461 College Blvd Ste 1 Oceanside CA 92057-5439

ANSLEY, JULIA ETTE, elementary education educator, consultant, poet, writer; b. Malvern, Ark., Nov. 10, 1940; d. William Harold and Dorothy Mae (Hamm) Smith; m. Miles Ansley, Nov. 8, 1964 (div. June 1976); children: Felicia Dianne, Mark Damon. BA in Edn., Calif. State U., Long Beach, 1962; postgrad., UCLA Ext. Early childhood edn., life, Miller-Unruh reading specialist credentials, Calif. Elem. tchr. L.A. Unified Sch. Dist., 1962—; coord. Proficiency in English Program, L.A., 1991-93; mem., advisor P.E.P. instrnl. tchrs. network, 1993—, workshop presenter in field; also poetry presentations, L.A., 1989—; owner Poetry Expressions, L.A.; marketer poetry posters. Bd. dirs. New Frontier Dem. Club, L.A., 1990-93; mem. exec. bd. L.A. Panhellenic Coun., rec. sec., 1993-95. Honored by Teacher mag., 1990; recipient Spirit of Edn. award Sta. KNBC-TV, L.A., 1990; grantee L.A. Ednl. Partnership, 1985, 87, 89, 93. Mem. L.A. Alliance African-Am. Educators (exec. bd. 1991-95, parliamentarian 1992-95), Black Women's Forum, Black Am. Polit. Assn. (edn. co-chair 1993—), Sigma Gamma Rho. Mem. AME Ch. Home: 3739 S Gramercy Pl Los Angeles CA 90018 Office: Hillcrest Dr Sch 4041 Hillcrest Dr Los Angeles CA 90008-2902

ANSON, FRED COLVIG, chemistry educator; b. Los Angeles, Feb. 17, 1933; m. Roxana Anson; children: Alison, Eric. BS, Calif. Inst. Tech., 1954; MS, Harvard U., 1955, PhD, 1957. Instr. chemistry Calif. Inst. Tech., Pasadena, 1957-58, asst. prof., 1958-62, assoc. prof., 1962-68, prof. chemistry, 1968—, chmn. divsn. chemistry and chem. engring., 1984-94. Contbr. numerous articles to profl. jours. Fellow J.S. Guggenheim Found., U. Brussels, 1964, Alfred P. Sloan Found., 1965-69; scholar Fulbright-Hays Found., U. Florence, Italy, 1972, A. von Humboldt Found., Fritz Haber Inst., Berlin, 1984, 86, 94. Mem. AAAS, Nat. Acad. Sci., Am. Chem. Soc., Am. Electrochem. Soc., Internat. Soc. Electrochemistry, Soc. Electroanalytical Chemistry, Tau Beta Pi. Office: Calif Inst Tech Divsn Chemistry and Chem Engring MS 127-72 Pasadena CA 91125

ANTELMAN, BRUCE, information delivery company executive; b. Columbia, Mo., Nov. 2, 1957; s. Morton and Joan (Pauer) A. BS, Reed Coll., 1981; postgrad., Stanford U., 1982-85. Pres. Info. Express, Palo Alto, Calif., 1985—. Adminstr. Morton Antelman Scholarship, Palo Alto, 1990—. Mem. Nat. Fedn. Indexing and Abstracting, Am. Soc. Info. Dissemination Ctrs. Office: Info Express 3250 Ash St Palo Alto CA 94306-2239

ANTHONY, ELAINE MARGARET, real estate executive, interior designer; b. Mpls., Apr. 23, 1932; d. Jerome Pius and Adeline (Shea) Clarkin; m. Ronald Carl Anthony, Aug 28, 1954 (div. 1977); children: Richard, Lisa, Laura. Student, U. Minn., 1950-51; AA, Diablo Valley Coll., 1978; postgrad., San Jose (Calif.) State U., 1979, U. Calif., Berkeley, 1983-91. Agt., broker Sycamore Realty, Danville, Calif., 1972-75; broker, project sales mgr. Crocker Homes, Dublin, Calif., 1975-80; exec. v.p. BlackHawk Properties, Danville, 1980-82; broker, project sales mgr. Harold W. Smith Co., Walnut Creek, Calif., 1982-86; pres. Elaine Anthony & Assocs., Inc., San Francisco, 1986—. Mem. vol. coun. San Francisco Symphony, 1986. Mem. Bldg. Industry Assn. (Outstanding Sales Person of Yr. No. Calif. chtp. 1983), Nat. Assn. Home Builders, Inst. Residential Mktg., Commonwealth Club Calif., Calif. Assn. Realtors, San Mateo/Burlingame Bd. Realtors, Bellevue Athletic Club Alameda County. Republican. Roman Catholic. Home and Office: 1875 Grand View Dr Oakland CA 94618-2339

ANTHONY, HARRY ANTONIADES, city planner, architect, educator; b. Skyros, Greece, July 28, 1922; came to U.S., 1951, naturalized, 1954; s. Anthony G. and Maria G. (Ftoulis) Antoniades; m. Anne C. Skoufis, Sept. 23, 1950; children: Mary Anne Anthony Smith, Kathryn Harriet. B.Arch., Nat. Tech. U., Athens, Greece, 1945; student, Ecole Nat. Supérieure des Beaux Arts, Paris, France, 1945-46; M.City Planning, U. Paris, 1947; Docteur d'Université, Sorbonne, Paris, 1949; Ph.D. in Arch. and Urban Planning, Columbia, 1955. Architect-planner with Constantinos A. Doxiadis, Athens, 1943-45, LeCorbusier, Paris, 1946-47, ECA, Paris, 1949-51; city planner with Maurice E.H. Rotival, N.Y.C., 1951-52; chief planner Brown & Blauvelt, N.Y.C., 1952-54; city planner Skidmore, Owings & Merrill, N.Y.C., 1954-56; prin. planning cons. Brown Engrs. Internat., N.Y.C., 1956-60; prin. Brown & Anthony City Planners, Inc., N.Y.C., 1960-69; v.p. Doxiadis Assocs., Inc., Washington, 1971-72; mem. faculty Columbia U., 1953-72, from asst. to assoc. prof., 1956-63, prof. urban planning, 1963-72, dir. grad. div. urban planning Grad. Sch. Architecture and Planning, 1962-65; prof. urban planning Calif. State Poly. U., Pomona, 1972-83, prof. emeritus urban and regional planning, 1983—; chmn. dept. Calif. State Poly. U., 1972-76; vis. prof. urban design Tulane U., 1967-68; vis. lectr. U. Calif. at Berkeley, Stanford U., Dartmouth, San Diego State U., CUNY, U. Okla.,

Ohio U., Auburn U., Salk Inst. Biol. Studies, U.S. Internat. U.; vis. prof. urban studies and planning U. Calif., San Diego, 1980-82; scholar-in-residence U. B.C., Vancouver, 1978; planning, zoning, urban renewal and urban design cons. to several cities, U.S. and abroad; also cons. to UN, Am. Med. Bldg. Guild, corps. and pvt. firms, to govts. and univs.; planning commr., Leonia, N.J., 1958-64; master planner, cons. architect for Ss. Constantine and Helen Greek Orthodox ch. and village for the elderly, Cardiff-by-the-Sea, Calif., 1983-95. Author, co-author, contbr.: Four Great Makers of Modern Architecture: Gropius, Le Corbusier, Mies Van Der Rohe, Wright, Dictionary of American History, The Challenge of Squatter Settlements—With Special Reference to the Cities of Latin America, La Défense à Paris et le Quartier d'Affaires de Vancouver: Une Comparaison Urbaine, New Orleans Air Rights Study, Woodstock Growth Plan and Land Use Controls, others; several master plans, city and regional planning reports, urban design plans and programs, environ. impact reports, zoning ordinances, educational videocassettes on urban planning subjects.; Contbr. articles to profl. jours., mags., newspapers. Recipient Premier Grand Prix Internat. Exhbn. Housing and City Planning, Paris, 1947; William Kinne Fellows travelling fellow in planning N.Am., 1956, French Govt. fellow, 1945-47; research award Urban Center of Columbia U., 1969; named Outstanding Prof. Calif. State Poly. U., 1975. Mem. AIA (Arnold W. Brunner scholar 1958), Am. Inst. Cert. Planners, Am. Planning Assn. (Disting. Service award 1984), Order of Am. Hellenic Ednl. Progressive Assn., Land Econs. Soc. of Lambda Alpha (Richard T. Ely Disting. Educator award 1988). Home: 7665 Caminito Avola La Jolla CA 92037-3956

ANTHONY, JAMES PETER, plastic surgeon, educator; b. Queens, N.Y., Dec. 19, 1957; s. James Francis and Wilma Helen (Stadelman) A.; m. Christine Anita Evers, Aug. 12, 1979. BS, Stony Brook U., 1979, MD, 1983. Asst. prof. surgery U. Calif., San Francisco, 1990—. Contbr. articles to profl. jours. Office: U Calif San Francisco Divsn Plastic Surgery 350 Parnassus Ste 509 San Francisco CA 94143-2932

ANTHONY, KAY CARROLL, librarian; b. Taft, Calif., Mar. 9, 1937; d. Henry Martin and Kathryn Grace (Hall) Carroll; m. David B. Anthony, Oct. 12, 1958; children: Jonathan David, Andrew James. Student, West-Hills Coll., 1955-56. Ref. libr. Coalinga (Calif.) Libr. Dist., 1965-79, adult svcs. libr., 1979-89, dist. libr., 1989—. Bd. dirs., sec. Coalinga Youth Baseball, 1982-86; treas. Ctrl. Valley Rabbit and Cavy Breeders Assn., Handford, Calif., 1992—. Mem. ALA, Calif. Libr. Assn., Pub. Libr. Assn. Office: Coalinga Libr Dist 305 N 4th St Coalinga CA 93210-2817

ANTIOCO, JOHN F., convenience store chain executive. Pres., CEO The Circle K Corp., Phoenix, 1991—; COO Pearle Vision, Dallas, 1990; pres., COO Circle K Corp, Phoenix, Ariz., 1991—. Office: The Circle K Corporation Box 52084 Phoenix AZ 85072-2084*

ANTOCH, ZDENEK VINCENT, electrical engineering educator; b. Prague, Czechoslovakia, Oct. 16, 1943; came to U.S., 1950; s. Zdenek Antoch and Marta (Smidova) Frank; m. Maureen O. Shaw, June 24, 1968 (div.); 1 child, Anna Marie. BS, Portland State U., 1971, postgrad. in Engring., 1971-73, postgrad. in Physics, 1973-75, MS, 1989, postgrad., 1989—. Research asst. Portland (Oreg.) State U., 1972-75; electronics instr. Portland (Oreg.) Community Coll., 1975-80, 81—. Mem. IEEE, Am. Soc. Engring. Edn. Democrat. Office: Portland Community Coll 12000 SW 49th Ave Portland OR 97219-7197

ANTON, WILLIAM R., retired school system administrator, consutant. Supt. of schools Los Angeles Public Schools, 1991-92; exec. cons. Alhambra, Calif., 1992—. Office: 917 N Cordova Ave Alhambra CA 91801

ANTONE, STEVE, state legislator, farmer; b. Burley, Idaho, Nov. 17, 1921; s. Andrew and Margaret (Glover) A.; m. Helen McKevitt, June 15, 1950 (dec. May 27, 1975); 1 child, Steven K.; m. Diane Meacham, Sept. 16, 1977; 1 child, Jill. State rep., legislature State of Idaho, 1968-94. Named Statesman of Yr., Pi Sigma Alpha, 1986, Disting. Citizen, Idaho Statesman News, 1986, Friend of Agr., Idaho Farm Bur., 1992, Friend of Idaho Cities, Outstanding Rep. Legislator, State Rep. Party, 1994; recipient Boyd Martin award Assn. Idaho Cities, 1984. Republican. Methodist. Home: 1141 Link St Rupert ID 83350-1544

ANTONOFF, STEVEN ROSS, educational consultant, author; b. Waukon, Iowa, Dec. 14, 1945; s. Ben H. and Florence R. A. BS, Colo. State U., 1967; MA, U. Denver, 1970, PhD, 1979. Spl. asst. to dean U. Denver, 1970-71, dean student life, 1971-74, dean Ctr. for Prospective Students, 1974-75, exec. dir. admissions and student affairs, 1975-78, dean admissions and fin. aid, 1978-81, adj. prof. speech communication, 1979-88; dir., now pres. Antonoff Assocs., Inc.; active Secondary Sch. Admission Testing Bd., Princeton, N.J. Author: College Match, The Coll. Finder; contbr. chpts. and articles to profl. jours. Chmn. Mayor's Commn. on Arts, Denver, 1979-81; trustee Congregation Emanuel, 1977-82; chmn. bd. dirs. Hospice of Met. Denver, 1970-84; mem. Denver Commn. on Cultural Affairs, 1984-86; mem. scholarship com. Mile High Cablevision, 1982—; chmn. Cultural Affairs Task Force, City of Denver, 1988-89. Recipient Clara Barton award for meritorious vol. leadership ARC, 1992. Mem. ACA, Rocky Mountain Assn. Coll. Admissions Counselors, Am. Ednl. Rsch. Assn., New Eng. Assn. Coll. Admission Officers, Nat. Assn. Coll. Admissions Counselors, Ind. Ednl. Cons. Assn. (chmn. bd. 1992-94), Rotary Internat., Zeta Beta Tau (found. bd. dirs.). Office: 425 S Cherry St Ste 215 Denver CO 80222-1229

ANTREASIAN, GARO ZAREH, artist, lithographer, art educator; b. Indpls., Feb. 16, 1922; s. Zareh Minas and Takouhie (Daniell) A.; m. Jeanne Glascock, May 2, 1947; children: David Garo, Thomas Berj. BFA, Herron Sch. Art, 1948; DFA (hon.), Ind. U.-Purdue U. at Indpls., 1972. Instr. Herron Sch. Art, 1948-64; tech. dir. Tamarind Lithography Workshop, Los Angeles, 1960-61; prof. art U. N.Mex., 1964-87, chmn. dept. art, 1981-84; tech. dir. Tamarind Inst., U. N.Mex., 1970-72; vis. lectr., artist numerous univs.; Bd. dirs. Albuquerque Mus., 1980-90; printmaker emeritus Southern Graphics Coun., 1994. Prin. author: The Tamarind Book of Lithography: Art and Techniques, 1970; one-man shows include Malvina Miller Gallery, San Francisco, 1971, Marjorie Kauffman Gallery, Houston, 1975-79, 84, 86, U. Colo., Boulder, 1972, Calif. Coll. Arts & Crafts, Oakland, 1973, Miami U., Oxford, Ohio, 1973, Kans. State U., 1973, Atlanta Coll. Art, 1974, U. Ga., Athens, 1974, Alice Simsar Gallery, Ann Arbor, 1977-79, Elaine Horwich Gallery, Santa Fe, 1977-79, Mus. of N.Mex., Santa Fe, 1979, Robischon Gallery, Denver, 1984, 86, 90, Moss-Chumley Gallery, Dallas, 1987, Rettig-Martinez Gallery, Santa Fe, 1988, 91, 92, U. N.Mex. Art Mus., 1988, Albuquerque Mus., 1988, Louis Newman Gallery, L.A., 1989, Expositum Gallery, Mexico City, 1989, State U. Coll., Cortland, N.Y., 1991, Mus. Art, U. Ariz., Tucson, 1991, Indpls. Mus. Art, 1994, Ruschmon Gallery, Indpls., 1994, Mitchell Mus. Art, Vernon, Ill., 1995; exhibited group shows Phila. Print Club, 1960-63, Ind. Artists, 1947-63, White House, 1966, Nat. Lithographic Exhbn. Fla. State U., 1965, Library Congress, 1961-66, Bklyn. Mus., 1958-68, 76, U.S. Pavilion Venice Biennale, 1970, Internat. Biennial, Bradford, Eng., 1972-74, Internat. Biennial, Tokyo, 1972, City Mus. Hong Kong, 1972, Tamarind UCLA, 1985, Roswell Mus., 1989, Pace Gallery, 1990, Worcester (Mass.) Art Mus., 1990, Amon Carter Mus., Ft. Worth, 1990, Albuquerque Mus., 1991, 92, Art Mus. U. N.Mex., 1991, 92; represented in permanent collections: Bklyn. Mus., Guggenheim Mus., N.Y.C., Cin. Mus., Chgo. Art Inst., Ind. State Mus., Mus. Modern Art, N.Y.C., Library of Congress, Met. Mus., N.Y.C., also, Albuquerque, Boston, Indpls., Seattle, Phila., San Diego, Dallas, N.Mex., Worcester Art Museums, Los Angeles County Mus., Roswell Mus. and Art Ctr., murals, Ind. U., Butler U., Ind. State Office Bldg. Fulbright vis. lectr. U. São Paulo and Found. Armando Alvares Penteado, Brazil, 1985. Combat artist with USCGR, World War II, PTO. Recipient Distinguished Alumni award Herron Sch. Art, 1972, N.Mex. Annual Gov.'s award, 1987; Grantee Nat. Endowment for Arts, 1983. Fellow NAD; mem. World Print Coun. (bd. dirs. 1980-87), Nat. Print Coun. Am. (co-pres. 1980-82), Coll. Art Assn. Am. (bd. dirs. 1977-80). Home: 725-18 Tramway Vista Dr NE Albuquerque NM 87122

ANUTA, KARL FREDERICK, lawyer; b. Menominee, Mich., May 16, 1935; s. Michael J. and Marianne (Strelic) A.; m. Barbara L. Olds Anuta, June 23, 1956; children: Karl Gregory Anuta, Natasha Louise Anuta. BA, Macalester Coll., 1957; LLB, U. Colo. Sch. Law, 1960. Bar: U.S. Supreme Ct., U.S. Dist. Ct., U.S. Ct. Appeals (D.C. and 10th cirs.). Staff atty. Office of Regional Solicitor U.S. Dept. Interior, Denver, 1960-63; staff atty. Frontier Refining Co., Denver, 1963-67, gen. counsel, 1967-68; sr. atty. Husky Oil Co., Denver, 1968-79, chief regional atty., 1979-83, gen. counsel, 1983-84; counsel Duncan, Weinberg & Miller, Denver, 1985-87; atty. pvt. practice, Boulder, Colo., 1987—. Pres. Interfaith Coun. Boulder, 1964, Hist. Boulder, Inc., 1980; mem. City Boulder Landmarks Bd., 1981-91; v.p. Colo. Chautauqua Assn., 1982, Boulder Hist. Soc., 1992; chmn. Boulder Coun. Internat. Visitors, 1986-88; bd. dirs. Spl. Transit Sys. Boulder County, 1988—, pres. 1995; mem. County Hist. Preservation Adv. Bd., 1992—. Mem. ABA, Colo. Bar Assn. Republican. Presbyterian. Office: 1720 14th St PO Box 1001 Boulder CO 80306

APATOFF, MICHAEL JOHN, finance executive; b. Harvey, Ill., June 12, 1955; s. William and Frances (Brown) A. BA, Reed Coll., 1980. Chief legis. asst. to U.S. Congressman Al Ullman, Chmn. Ways and Means Com., Washington, 1978-80; spl. asst. to U.S. Congressman Tom Foley, Majority Whip, Washington, 1981-85; exec. v.p., COO Chgo. Merc. Exch., 1986-90; exec. v.p., COO, prin. RCM Capital Mgmt., San Francisco, 1991—. Mem. World Affairs Coun., Com. on Fgn. Affairs, Japan Am. Soc. Democrat. Home: 2400 Pacific Ave Apt 710 San Francisco CA 94115-1229 Office: RCM Capital Mgmt Four Embarcadero San Francisco CA 94111

APLON, ROGER LAURENCE, writer, poet; b. Chgo., July 28, 1937; s. Carl Bernard and Mildred (Schneider) A.; m. Judith Rubinstein, July 5, 1962 (div. Nov. 1967); 1 child, Jason Alexander; m. Ellen Virginia Perkins/Flippen, Mar. 26, 1992. BA, Roosevelt U., 1994. Author: (book of poetry) Stiletto, 1976, By Dawn's Early Light at 120 mph, 1983. Mem. PEN West, Acad. Am. Poets. Home: 2238 Oak Hill Dr Escondido CA 92027-3808

APODACA, RUDY SAMUEL, judge; b. Las Cruces, N.Mex., Aug. 8, 1939; s. Raymond and Elisa (Alvarez) A.; m. Bunny N. Gray, Nov. 1958 (div. 1963); m. Nancy R. Apodaca, Jan. 16, 1967; children: Cheryl Ann, Carla Renee, Cynthia Lynn, Rudy Samuel. BS, N.Mex. State U., 1961; JD, Georgetown U., 1964. Bar: N.Mex. 1964, U.S. Dist. Ct. N. Mex. 1965, U.S. Ct. Appeals (10th cir.) 1965, U.S. Supreme Ct. 1971. Pvt. practice Las Cruces, 1964-86; appellate judge N.Mex. Ct. Appeals, Santa Fe, 1987-94, elected chief judge, 1994—; real estate broker, Las Cruces, 1984-86; gen. counsel Citizens Bank Las Cruces, 1976-86. Author: The Waxen Image, 1977; author screenplay: A Rare Thing, 1987. Bd. regents N.Mex. State U., 1975-83; mem. Coord. Coun. for Higher Edn., Santa Fe, 1975-78; pres. Assocs. N.Mex. State U., Las Cruces, 1982-84; bd. dirs. Am. S.W. Theatre Co., Las Cruces, 1984-86. Capt. U.S. Army, 1964-66. Mem. Inst. Jud. Adminstrn., N.Mex. Bar Assn., Poets and Writers, Phi Kappa Phi, Am. Mensa, Intertel, Pen Ctr. USA West, Pen N.Mex. Democrat. Home: 829 Canterbury Arc Las Cruces NM 88005-3715 Office: NMex Ct Appeals 180 W Amador Ave Las Cruces NM 88001-1202

APPEL, JACOB J., information services technology executive; b. N.Y.C., Sept. 2, 1940; s. Gustav and Hilda A.; m. Anne M. Liuzzo, Feb. 1, 1962. BEE, Cooper Union, N.Y.C., 1961; MSEE, UCLA, 1963; ScD in Elec. Engring., Columbia U., 1970; Degree in Advanced Mgmt., Harvard U., 1992. Mem. tech. staff Hughes Aircraft, Culver City, Calif., 1961-65; with Bell Labs., various cities, N.J., 1965-83; asst. v.p. Bell Communications Rsch., various cities in N.J., 1984-86; asst. v.p. tech. planning Pacific Bell, San Ramon, Calif., 1986-88; v.p. tech. ops. Pacific Bell Info. Svcs., San Ramon, 1988—. Contbr. articles to profl. jours. Sci. adv. coun. Mills Coll., Oakland, Calif., 1986—. Hughes Aircraft fellow; doctoral fellowship Bell Labs. Mem. IEEE (chmn. COMSOC com. network ops. and mgmt.), IEEE Communications Soc., IEEE Computer Soc. Home: 1364 Virginia St Danville CA 94526-1243

APPELBAUM, BRUCE DAVID, physician; b. Lincroft, N.J., Apr. 24, 1957; s. John S. and Shirley B. (Wolfson) A. BS in pharmacy, Rutgers Coll., 1980; MS in pharmacology, Emory U., 1983, PhD in pharmacology, 1985; MD, Medical Coll. Ga., 1989. Diplomate Nat. Bd. Med. Examiners. Rsch. assoc. Emory U. Dept. Pharmacology, Atlanta, 1985; resident physician U. Calif. Dept. Psychiatry, Irvine, Calif., 1989-93; pvt. practice Pacifica Therapists, Huntington Beach, Calif., 1993—; cons. Avalon Med. Group, Garden Grove, Calif., 1990—; clin. assoc. U. Calif., Irvine, 1993—. Contbr. articles to profl. jours. Recipient Nat. Rsch. Svc. award Nat. Inst. Health, 1982 83, Ea. Student Rsch. Forum U. Miami Medical Sch., 1984, Nat. Student Rsch. Forum, 1987. Mem. AMA, Am. Psychiat. Assn., Orange County Psychiat. Soc., N.Y. Acad. Scis., Sigma Xi. Home: 18602 Creek Ln Huntington Beach CA 92648-1629 Office: 18811 Huntington St Ste 200 Huntington Beach CA 92648-6003

APPLE, DANIEL BRYCE, finance company executive, financial planner; b. Nevada City, Calif., June 30, 1951; s. Stanley Bryce and Bonnie Ruth (Kelley) A. BA, Chico (Calif.) State U., 1973. Engring. technician Clendenen & Assoc., Auburn, Calif., 1976-77; field engr. Pacific Gas & Electric Co., Sacramento, 1974-76, United Engrs. & Contractors, Richland, Wash., 1977-81; civil and structural engr. Bechtel Corp., Richland, 1981-84; rep. Fin. Network Investment Corp., Grass Valley, Calif., 1984-89, br. mgr., 1984—, prin., 1989—. Past. pres. Nevada County Arts Coun., 1993-94. Mem. Inst. Cert. Fin. Planners, Gold Country Estate Planning Coun. (chrter, past treas. Grass Valley chpt. 1989—). Republican. Office: Fin Network Investment Corp 350 Crown Point Cir Ste 200 Grass Valley CA 95945-9088

APPLE, JACQUELINE B. (JACKI APPLE), artist, writer, educator; b. N.Y.C.. Student, Syracuse U.; grad., Parsons Sch. Design. Curator exhbns. and performance Franklin Furnace, N.Y.C., 1977-80; prodr., host Sta. KPFK-FM, North Hollywood, Calif., 1982—; mem. faculty Art Ctr. Coll. Design, Pasadena, Calif., 1983—; mem. faculty adv. com. Art Ctr. Coll. Design, Pasadena, 1993. Contb. writer: L.A. Weekly, 1983-89; contbg. editor: Artweek, 1983-90, High Performance Mag., 1984—; writer, performer, dir., prodr.: (record) The Mexican Tapes, 1979-80, (performance/radio work) Voices in the Dark, 1989-90, (radio art work) Swan Lake, 1989; artist, prodr.: (installation and audio work) The Culture of Disappearance, 1991-95; author, designer: (book, installation) Trunk Pieces, 1975-78, (cd) Thank You for Flying American, 1994; author: Doing it Right in L.A., 1990. Recipient Vesta award Media Arts Women's Bldg., 1990; NEA visual artists fellow, 1979, 81; InterArts program grantee NEA, 1984-85, 91-92. Mem. Internat. Art Critics Assn., Nat. Writers Union, Coll. Art Assn. Home: 3827 Mentone Ave Culver City CA 90232-3108

APPLE, STEVEN ANTHONY, city official; b. Los Angeles, Dec. 27, 1954; s. Nick P. and Joanne (Wilkin) A.; m. Rebecca McCorkle, Aug. 9, 1980. BA in Anthropology, Ohio State U., 1977; M in City Planning, San Diego State U., 1983. Freelance environ. cons. San Diego, 1979-80; environ. planner MSA, Inc., San Diego, 1981-82; land use planner New Horizons Planning Cons., San Diego, 1982-84, County San Diego, 1984-86; dir. community devel. City of Solana Beach (Calif.), 1986—; guest lectr., San Diego State U. 1984. Environ. chmn. Torrey Pines Community Planning Group, Del Mar, Calif., 1985-89. Univ. scholar, San Diego State U., 1983. Mem. Am. Planning Assn., San Diego County Archeol. Soc. (libr. 1979-80), Eagle Scout Alumni Assn. (exec. com. San Diego 1985), Mensa. Office: City of Solana Beach 635 S Highway 101 Solana Beach CA 92075-2215

APPLEBERRY, WALTER THOMAS, aerospace engineering project executive; b. Wilmington, N.C., Mar. 8, 1926; s. William Pembroke and Carroll Ernesteen (Shingleton) A.; m. Mae Magdalene Bozeman, Feb. 21, 1953; children: Thomas Kent, Robert William, Rebecca Jean. BS in Mech. Engring., Calif. State U., Long Beach, 1974. Facilities engr. Douglas Aircraft, Long Beach, 1942-50; missionary Mormon Ch., Salt Lake City, 1950-53; supr. engring. test McDonnell Douglas, Huntington Beach, Calif., 1953-74; adv. engring. project mgr. Rockwell Internat., Downey, Calif., 1974-94. Patentee in field. Mem. Pi Tau Sigma. Republican. Mormon. Home: 3440 Val Verde Ave Long Beach CA 90808-3148

APPLEGATE, ARTHUR DAVID, computer software developer, consultant; b. Glendale, Calif., May 23, 1965; s. Howard Cornell Applegate and Mary Alice Keenan. BS in Computer Sci. with distinction, U. Sydney, Australia, 1985. Pres. Crystal Script, Sydney, 1983-85; sr. computer scientist Inference Corp., L.A., 1986-90; software engr. Wall Data Inc., Redmond, Wash., 1990-91; pres. Applegate Software, Redmond, Wash., 1991—. Author computer software FastData, 1991, OptiMem for Windows, 1991, SmartHeap, 1992, HeapAgent, 1994. Mem. Wash. Software Assn. (speaker 1992).

APREA, SHARON MARTIN, merchandiser; b. Portsmouth, Va., July 17, 1956; d. Addison Berkley and Nancy Carolyn (Kiser) M.; m. Marc Angelo Aprea, Dec. 24, 1985. AS in Bus. Adminstrn., Va. Intermont, 1976; BSBA, Va. Tech., 1978. Ill. regional sales rep. Broyhill Furniture, Lenoir, N.C., 1979-82; sales mgr., acct. rep. Economon & Assocs., Dallas, 1982-87; nat. sales dir. Cavendish Furnitures, Dallas, Ipswich, England, 1987-88; accessories buyer J.C. Penney, Portfolio, Dallas, 1988-90, Breuners, Pleasant Hill, Calif., 1991-92; with Schnadig Internat. Corp., Chgo., Calif., 1992—. Columnist profl. mag., 1990—. Campaign rep. Judge Superior Ct., Rep. party, Dallas, 1990. Mem. Ill. Home Furnishings Reps. Assn. (treas. 1980-82), Internat. Trade Club (com. leader 1985-88), Southwest Trade Commn. (assoc. mem. 1982-85), Cimarron Club (dir. programs 1986-87, 1st v.p. and social chmn. 1987-88, pres. 1988-90), 500, Inc. (organizing com. mem. 1988-90). Republican. Baptist. Home: 171 Tomlinson Dr Folsom CA 95630-7406

APTHEKER, BETTINA FAY, women's studies educator; b. Ft. Bragg, N.C., Sept. 2, 1944; d. Herbert and Fay P. Aptheker; m. Jack H. Kurzweil, Aug. 29, 1965 (div. Jan. 1979); children: Joshua, Jennifer; life ptnr., Kathleen C. Miller. BA, U. Calif., Berkeley, 1967; MA, San Jose State U., 1976; PhD, U. Calif., Santa Cruz, 1983. Lectr. San Jose State U., San Jose, Calif., 1976-79; adj. lectr. U. Calif., Santa Cruz, 1980-87, asst. prof., 1987-89, assoc. prof., 1989—. Author: The Morning Breaks: The Trial of Angela Davis, 1975, Woman's Legacy: Essays on Race, Class and Sex in American History, 1982, Tapestries of Life: Women's Work, Women's Consciousness and the Meaning of Daily Experience, 1989. Mem. Nat. Women's Studies Assn., Assn. Black Women Historians, Lesbian Alliance, Monterey Bay Zen Ctr. Jewish. Office: U Calif Kresge Coll Dept Womens Studies Santa Cruz CA 95064

APURON, ANTHONY SABLAN, archbishop; b. Agana, Guam, Nov. 1, 1945; s. Manuel Taijito and Ana Santos (Sablan) P. BA, St. Anthony Coll., 1969; MDiv, Maryknoll Sem., 1972, M Theology, 1973; MA in Liturgy, Notre Dame U., 1974. Ordained priest Roman Catholic ch., 1972, ordained bishop, 1984, installed archbishop, 1986. Chmn. Diocesan Liturgical Commn., Agana, 1974-86; vice chmn. Chamorro Lang. Commn., Agana, 1984-86; aux. bishop Archdiocese of Agana, 1984-85, archbishop, 1986—; chmn. Interfaith Vols. Caregivers, Agana, 1984—; mem. Civilian Adv. com., Agana, 1986—; pres. Cath. Bishops' Conf. of Pacific, 1990—; v.p. Cath. Bishops' Conf. of Aceania, 1990—. Author: A Structural Analysis of the Content of Myth in the Thought of Mircea Eliade, 1973. Chmn. Cath. Ednl. Radio. Named Most Outstanding Young Man, Jaycees of Guam, 1984. Office: Archbishop's Office Cuesta San Ramon Agana GU 96910*

ARABIA, FRANCISCO ALBERTO, cardiovascular and thoracic surgeon; b. San Juan, P.R., Sept. 5, 1957; s. Francisco A. and Lillian (Gonzalez) A.; m. Dorothy Patricia Burkle, Dec. 29, 1984; children: Christina, Francisco Jr. BS, Tulane U., 1979; MD, U. Pa., Phila., 1983. Diplomate Am. Bd. Surgery, Am. Bd. Thoracic Surgery; lic. physician, P.R., La., Md., Ariz. Intern gen. surgery Tulane U. Affiliated Hosps., New Orleans, 1983-84, resident, 1984-85, 87-89, chief resident gen. surgery, 1989-90; clin. assoc. surg. br. Nat. Heart and Lung Inst., NIH, Bethesda, Md., 1985-87; resident cardiothoracic surgery U. Ariz., Tucson, 1990-91, chief resident, 1991-92, asst. prof., 1993—; pvt. practice San Juan, P.R., 1992-93; cons. engr. St. Jude Med., St. Paul, 1979; instr. phys. diagnosis Tulane U. Sch. Medicine, New Orleans, 1988-90. Contbr. articles to profl. jours., chpts. to books. Am. Heart Assn. undergrad. rsch. grantee. Assoc. fellow ACS; mem. Soc. Thoracic Surgeons (candidate), Am. Coll. Cardiology, Am. Soc. Artificial Internal Organs, Andrew Morrow Soc. Cardiovascular Surgeons, Tau Beta Pi. Roman Catholic. Office: U Ariz Coll Medicine 1501 N Campbell Ave Rm 4402 Tucson AZ 85724-0001

ARABIAN, ARMAND, state supreme court justice; b. N.Y.C., Dec. 12, 1934; s. John and Aghavnie (Yalian) A.; m. Nancy Arabian, Aug. 26, 1962; children: Allison Ann, Robert Armand. BSBA, Boston U., 1956, JD, 1961; LLM, U. So. Calif., L.A., 1970; LLD (hon.), Southwestern Sch. Law, 1990, Pepperdine U., 1990, U. West L.A., 1994. Bar: Calif. 1962, U.S. Supreme Ct. 1966. Dep. dist. atty. L.A. County, 1962-63; pvt. practice law Van Nuys, Calif., 1963-72; judge Mcpl. Ct., L.A., 1972-73, Superior Ct., L.A., 1973-83; assoc. justice U.S. Ct. Appeals Calif., L.A., 1983-90, U.S. Supreme Ct. Calif., San Francisco, 1990—. 1st lt. U.S. Army, 1956-58. Recipient Stanley Litz Meml. award San Fernando Valley Bar Assn., 1986, Lifetime Achievement award San Fernando Valley Bar Assn., 1993/. Republican. Office: US Supreme Ct Calif 303 2nd St Ste 9 San Francisco CA 94107-1366

ARAGER, FRANCES, rehabilitation nurse; b. N.Y.C., Dec. 17, 1931; d. Simon and May Matisoff; m. William Arager, Oct. 10, 1953; children: Joy Diane, Jack Lester, Scott. AAN, Rockland C.C., 1973; BSN, Dominican Coll. Blauvelt, 1978. RN, Nev., Ill. Asst. charge nurse Summit Park Hosp., Pomona, N.Y., 1973-78; relief supr. Topanga Terr. Nursing Home, Northridge, Calif., 1983-84; staff nurse, charge nurse Univ. Med. Ctr., Las Vegas, Nev., 1984—, founder pet therapy program, 1988. Mem. Assn. Rehab. Nurses. (cert. rehab. RN). Home: 1004 Pagosa Way Las Vegas NV 89128 Office: Univ Med Ctr Rehab Unit 1800 W Charleston St Las Vegas NV 89102

ARAGON, MANNY M., state legislator. Mem. N.Mex. Senate from 14th Dist.

ARAKAKI, DUKE TSUYOSHI, computer engineer, consultant; b. Honolulu, Mar. 29, 1968; s. Harold Kembo Arakaki and Joyce Harumi (Uyeno) Nomura; m. Doris Jayne Tam, Sept. 11, 1993. BS, U. Pacific, 1991. Electronic tech. Varian Assocs., Palo Alto, Calif., 1989-91; software engr. EDP/Temps, San Bruno, Calif., 1991; computer engr. USAF, Norton AFB, Calif., 1991-93; software engr. Dapru Inc., Sacramento, Calif., 1993-94. Lt. USAF, 1991-93. Decorated Achievement medal USAF, 1993. Home: 5011 Laguna Woods Dr Elk Grove CA 95758-4156

ARAKAWA, MARY K., systems analyst; b. Inglewood, Calif., Dec. 23, 1961; d. Tadashi Tom and Mitsuko A. BS in Bus. Adminstrn., Calif. State U., Long Beach, 1985; MBA, U. Redlands, 1992. Installation cons. Profl. Hosp. Services div. Am. Med. Internat., Los Angeles, 1985-86; system and documentation analyst Info. Systems Group of Am. Med. Internat., Los Angeles, 1986-87; systems analyst mgmt. and info. systems Douglas Aircraft, Long Beach, Calif., 1987-88; sr. tech. trainer Douglas Aircraft, 1988-90; info. systems edn. analyst Long Beach Meml. Med. Ctr., 1990-93; systems analyst II info. svcs. CMSI, Inc., 1993-94; client svc. supr. CMSI, Inc., Integrated Network Svcs., 1994—. Mem. Los Angeles County Mus. Art., 1986—. Mem. Women in Mgmt., Women in Tech. Office: CMSI Inc 2801 Atlantic Ave Long Beach CA 90806-1737

ARAUZ, CARLOS GASPAR, city official; b. Havana, Cuba, Jan. 6, 1949; came to U.S., 1960, naturalized, 1974; s. Agnelio Alejandro and Mariana (Rodriguez) A.; BS, Loyola U., Los Angeles, 1970; MS, Ga. Inst. Tech., 1975, postgrad., 1975—. Bacteriologist, Emory U. Hosp., Atlanta, 1970-72; rsch. psychologist Atlanta Regional Commn., 1973-74; dir. personnel City of College Park (Ga.), 1974-75; indsl. psychology cons. Lockheed Ga. Co., Marietta, 1976; asst. dir. human resources City of Miami, 1976-81, spl. asst. to city mgr., 1981-82; bur. chief labor rels./personnel adminstrn. City of Orlando, Fla., 1982-85; dir. personnel and labor relations City of Corpus Christi, Tex., 1985-86; dir. personnel City of Phoenix, 1986—; cons. govt. and industry. Bd. dirs. Valle del Sol, Inc., Ariz. Govt. Tng. Svc. Mem. Internat. Personnel Mgmt. Assn. (young personnel profl. award N. Ga. 1975; pres. N. Ga. chpt. 1976, S. Fla. chpt. 1978, pres. So. region 1980-81, exec. coun. 1990-92, pres.-elect 1993, pres. 1994), Soc. Human Resource Mgmt., Metro Phoenix Human Resource Mgmt. Assn., Internat. City Mgmt. Assn., Nat. Pub. Employer Labor Rels. Assn., Rocky Mountain Pub. Employer Labor Rels. Assn. (pres. 1989-91), Sigma Xi. Roman Catholic. Club: Lake Arrowhead Yacht and Country. Office: City of Phoenix 135 N 2nd Ave Phoenix AZ 85003-2018

ARAZI, LORRI ROSENBERG, realtor; b. Bowling Green, Ohio, Apr. 5, 1958; d. Benjamin George and Peggy Lee (Hull) Rosenberg; m. Yaacov Kobi Arazi, June 22, 1986 (div. Dec. 1993). BA, U. Calif. Berkeley, 1979; postgrad., Antioch U., San Francisco, 1981-82; MA, San Francisco State U., 1994. Dist. mgr. ClothesFreak, Berkeley, 1977-79; asst. buyer Emporium Dept. Stores, San Francisco, 1980-82, asst. store mgr., 1983-84; dist. mgr. Maquette Leather Fashions, Tel Aviv, Israel, 1985-86; pers. mgr. Ross Stores, Walnut Creek, Calif., 1986-88; residential realtor Mason-McDuffie Real Estate, Berkeley, 1993—. Democrat. Jewish. Office: Mason-McDuffie Real Estate 1539 Shattuck Ave Berkeley CA 94709

ARBEGAST, DAVID ELWOOD, landscape architect; b. Arthur, Iowa, Aug. 19, 1924; s. William Andrew and Hazel (Hartong) A.; m. May E. Kitazawa, Aug. 16, 1952; children: Deborah, Lisa, Michael, Katherine. Student, Buena Vista Coll., Storm Lake, Iowa, 9146-47; BS, Iowa State U., 1950; MS, U. Calif., Berkeley, 1953. Registered landscape architect, Calif. Draftsman Litton and Whitney, Berkeley, 1951-52; assoc. landscape architect Geraldine Knight Scott-Landscape Architect, Berkeley, 1952-55, Osmundson and Staley, San Francisco, 1954-63, Osmundson and Assocs., San Francisco, 1963-68; ptnr. Arbegast & Newton, Berkelely, 1968-74; pres. Arbegast Newton & Griffith, Berkekely, 1974—; instr. dept. landscape architecture U. Calif., Berkeley, 1968-82. Designer ednl. part Prusch Park, San Jose, Calif., 1976. Oral commr. Dept. Consumer Affairs, State of Calif., 1984-86. Served to sgt. U.S. Army, 1942-45, BWI. Fellow Am. Soc. Landscape Architects (chmn. chpt. rev. bd. 1968). Home: 1330 Spruce St Berkeley CA 94709-1435 Office: Arbegast Newton & Griffith 1647 Hopkins St Berkeley CA 94707-2712

ARBET-ENGELS, VINCENT PAUL, electrical engineer, researcher; b. Scionzier, France, June 23, 1962; came to U.S., 1987; s. Gerard and Eenise (Sulzer) Engels; m. Claudine Marie-Louise Bréant, July 10, 1993; 1 child, Axel Jerome. BS, Swiss Fed. Inst. Tech., 1985, MS, 1986; MS, UCLA, 1989, PhD, 1993. Registered profl. engr., Calif. Rsch. officer French Nat. Def., Paris, 1986; process engr. E.M. Microelectronic Marin, Switzerland, 1987; grad. student researcher UCLA, 1988-93, rsch. engr., 1993—; cons. in phys.-optics, L.A., 1993. With French Armed Forces, 1986. Fellow Swiss Govt., 1987-88, UCLA, 1989-91; recipient monetary award Materials Rsch. Soc., 1989. Mem. AAAS, Am. Phys. Soc., Soc. Photo-Optical Inst. Engr. Office: U Calif 405 Hilgard Ave Los Angeles CA 90024-1301

ARBIB, MICHAEL ANTHONY, computer scientist, educator, neuroscientist, cybernetician; b. Eastbourne, U.K., May 28, 1940; came to U.S., 1961; s. John R. and Helen (Arbib) A.; m. Prue Hassell, Dec. 29, 1965; children: Phillipa Jane, Benjamin Giles. BSc with honors, U. Sydney, 1960; PhD in Math., MIT, 1963. Mem. faculty Stanford (Calif.) U., 1965-70, assoc. prof. elec. engring., 1969-70; adj. prof. psychology, prof. computer and info. sci. U. Mass., Amherst, 1970-86, chmn. dept. computer and info. sci., 1970-75; dir. Ctr. for Systems Neurosci., 1974-86, dir. Cognitive Sci. Program, 1980-82, dir. Lab. Perceptual Robotics, 1982-86; prof. biomed. engring., computer sci., elec. engring., neurobiology, physiology and psychology U. So. Calif., L.A., 1986—, dir. Ctr. for Neural Engring., 1987-94; dir. human brain project Ctr. for Neural Engring., 1994—; vis. prof. U. Western Australia, Perth, 1974, Technion, Israel, 1975, Washington U., St. Louis, 1976, U. Edinburgh, 1976-77, U. Calif., Irvine, 1980; vis. scientist Inst. Cybernetics, Barcelona, spring 1985, Cognitive Scis. Inst., U. Calif., San Diego, 1985-86; vis. lectr. U. New South Wales, Australia, 1962, 65, 68, Mont. State U., summers, 1963, 65, Imperial Coll. London, 1964; Gifford lectr. in natural theology U. Edinburgh, Scotland, 1983; John Douglas French lectr. Brain Rsch. Inst., UCLA, 1993; lectr. tours to U.S., USSR, Japan, Australia and China. Author: Brains, Machines and Mathematics, 1964, 2d. edit., 1987, Theories of Abstract Automata, 1969, The Metaphorical Brain, 1972, Computers and the Cybernetic Society, 1977, 2d edit., 1984, In Search of the Person, 1985, The Metaphorical Brain 2, 1989; (with others) Topics in Mathematical System Theory, 1969, System Theory, 1974, Discrete Mathematics, 1974, Conceptual Models of Neural Organization, 1974, Arrows, Structures and Functors, 1975, Design of Well-Structured and Correct Programs, 1978, A Basis for Theoretical Computer Science, 1981, A Programming Approach to Computability, 1982, Algebraic Approaches to Program Semantics, 1986, The Construction of Reality, 1986, From Schema Theory to Language, 1987, An Introduction to Formal Language Theory, 1988; editor: The Handbook of Brain Theory and Neural Networks, 1995, (with others) Algebraic Theory of Machines, Languages and Semigroups, 1968, Neural Models of Language Processes, 1982, Competition and Cooperation in Neural Nets, 1982, Adaptive Control of Ill-Defined Systems, 1983, Vision, Brain and Cooperative Computation, 1987, Dynamic Interactions in Neural Networks: Models and Data, 1988, Visuomotor Coordination: Amphibia, Comparisons, Models, and Robots, 1989, Natural and Artificial Parallel Computation, 1990, Visual Structures and Integrated Functions, 1991, Neuroscience: From Neural Networks to Artificial Intelligence, The Handbook of Brain Theory and NeuralrNetworks, 1995; contbr. articles to profl. jours. Mem. IEEE, AAAS, Soc. Neurosci. Office: U So Calif Ctr for Neural Engring Los Angeles CA 90089-2520

ARBIT, BERYL ELLEN, legal assistant; b. L.A., Aug. 16, 1949; d. Harry A. and Norma K. (Michelson) A. BA, UCLA, 1970. From legal asst. to sr. legal asst. O'Melveny & Myers, L.A., 1977—; guest lectr. atty. asst. tng. program UCLA, 1991. Mem. UCLA Atty. Asst. Alumni Assn. (bd. dirs. 1980-82), Alpha Omicron Pi (treas. West L.A. alumnae chpt. 1993—), Nu Lambda (corp. bd. pres. 1978-80, chpt. adv. 1976-78). Office: O'Melveny & Myers 400 S Hope St Los Angeles CA 90071-2801

ARBOGAST, GENEVIEVE L., interior designer; b. Belington, W.Va., Jan. 19, 1936; m. Norman R. Arbogast, June 11, 1955. AS in Interior Design with honors, Miami-Dade C.C., 1975. Facilities space planner-interior designer Bank Western, Denver, 1978-89; owner Ambience N.W., Everett, Wash. Prin. works include interior design for numerous bank brs., office bldg. for Shelter-Am., Inc. Mem. Am. Soc. Interior Designers (Seattle chpt.). Office: 12424 36th Ave SE Everett WA 98208-5671

ARCADI, JOHN ALBERT, urologist; b. Whittier, Calif., Oct. 23, 1924; s. Antonio and Josephine (Ramirez) A; m. Doris M. Bohanan, Apr. 11, 1951; children: Patrick, Michael, Judith, Timothy, Margaret, William, Catherine. BS cum laude, U. Notre Dame, 1947; MD, Johns Hopkins U., 1950. Diplomate Am. Bd. Urology. Intern The Johns Hopkins Hosp., Balt., 1950-51, resident, 1951-52, 53-55; instr. urology Johns Hopkins U., Balt., Md., 1953-55, U. So. Calif., Los Angeles, 1955-60; research assoc. Whittier (Calif.) Coll., 1957-70, research prof., 1970—; coord. prostate cancer rsch. Huntington Med. Rsch. Inst., Pasadena, Calif., 1993—; staff mem. urology sect. Presbyn. Hosp., Whittier, 1960—. Fellow AAAS, Am. Coll. Surgeons; mem. Endocrine Soc., Am. Urology Assn., Am. Soc. Cell Biology, Am. Micro Soc., Internat. Urol. Soc., Am. Assn. Clin. Anatomy, Am. Assn. Anatomists, Soc. for Basic Urologic Rsch., Soc for Invertebrate Pathology. Republican. Roman Catholic. Home: 6202 Washington Ave Whittier CA 90601-3640 Address: PO Box 9220 Whittier CA 90608-9220

ARCHER, DOUGLAS ROBERT, mayor, insurance services executive; b. Winnipeg, Man., Can., Mar. 23, 1948; s. Robert Clive and Annette Diane (Brabant) A.; m. Gloria Jean Knight, Feb. 28, 1976; children: James, Lindsey, Tracy. BA in Econs., U. Sask., Saskatoon, Can., 1970. Civil servant Govt. Sask., Regina, 1971-83; ptnr. Knight Archer Ins. Svcs., Regina, 1983—; mayor City of Regina, 1988—; chair City Coun., Regina Bd. Police Commrs., Wascana Centre Authority, Mayor's Bd. of Inquiry into Hunger in Regina. Mem. Regina Econ. Devel. Authority, Mayor's Task Force on Women, Sherwood-Regina Dist. Planning Commn.; chair Mayor's Task Force on Accessibility; past pres. Regina Open Door Soc., Sask. Fedn. Community Clinics. Mem. Fedn. Can. Municipalities (bd. dirs.), Regina Exhbn. Assn. Office: Office of Mayor, Queen Elizabeth II Ct PO Box 1790, Regina, SK Canada S4P 3C8*

ARCHER, JAMES ERNEST, sales professional; b. L.A., Feb. 25, 1949; s. Earl John and Marie Agnes (Friedrich) A.; m. Margaret C. Rhoads, Feb. 12, 1977; children: Robert, Christine. BSEE, Calif. State Poly., 1972. Sales profl. Culter-Hammer, Anaheim, Calif., 1972-77; sales profl. Gould Inc. Modicon Divsn., L.A., 1977-81, area mgr., 1981-85; regional mgr. Siemen Energy & Automix, Irvine, Calif., 1985-88; sales mgr. Siemen Energy & Automix, Irvine, 1988-89; major accounts mgr. AT&T Istel, Gardena, Calif., 1989—. Mem. IEEE, Instrumentation Soc. Am., Indsl. Computing Soc. Home: 1036 Via La Paz San Pedro CA 90732-2307 Office: AT&T Istel 1225 W 190th Ste 220 Gardena CA 90248

ARCHER, MARY JANE, state agency administrator; b. Oakland, Calif., Aug. 23, 1949; d. Doris Marlene (Howard) Wood; m. Bradley Eugene Archer; Nov. 10, 1984. BS in Acctg., Calif. State U., Hayward, 1971, MBA in Acctg., 1977. Auditor Calif. State Controller's Office, Sacramento, 1972-81, supr., 1981-84, asst. div. chief, divsn. tax adminstrn., 1984-90; acting div. chief, 1990—, bur. chief, divsn. acctg. and reporting. Tutor Sacramento Literacy Ctr. Mem. Calif. Assn. Mgmt., Assn. Govtl. Accountants. Republican. Office: Calif State Contr's Office Div Acctg & Reporting PO Box 942850 Ofc Sacramento CA 94250-0001

ARCHER, STEPHEN HUNT, economist, educator; b. Fargo, N.D., Nov. 30, 1928; s. Clifford Paul and Myrtle Mona (Blair) A.; m. Carol Rosa Mohr, Dec. 29, 1951 (div. Feb. 1971); children—Stephen Paul, Timothy William, David Conrad; m. Lana Jo Urban, Sept. 23, 1972. B.A., U. Minn., 1949, M.S., 1953, Ph.D., 1958; postdoctoral student (Ford Found. grantee), U. Calif. at Los Angeles, 1959-60. Mgr. trader J.M. Dain Co., Mpls., 1950; account exec. J.M. Dain Co., 1952-53; instr. econs. U. Minn., Mpls., 1954-56; asst. prof. fin. U. Wash., Seattle, 1956-60; assoc. prof. U. Wash., 1960-65, prof., 1965-73, chmn. dept. fin., bus. econs. and quantitative methods, 1966-70; dean Grad. Sch. Adminstrn. Willamette U., Salem, Oreg., 1973-76, 83-85; prof. Willamette U., 1976-79, Guy F. Atkinson prof., 1979—; Fulbright sr. lectr. Bocconi U., Milan, Italy, 1982; v.p. Hinton, Jones & Co., Inc. (investment brokers), Seattle, 1969-70; cons. Wash. Bankers Assn., 1971-72, Weyerhaeuser Co., 1971, Bus.-Econs. Adv. & Research Inc., 1969-77, State of Oreg., 1984, 86, 88, 91; vis. prof. Manchester Bus. Sch., Manchester, Eng., 1990-91. Author: Introduction to Mathematics for Business Analysis, 1960, Business Finance: Theory and Mgmt, 1966, revised edit., 1972, The Theory of Business Finance, 1967, 2d revised edit., 1983, Portfolio Analysis, 1971, revised edit., 1979, Introduction to Financial Management, 1979, revised edit., 1983, Cases and Readings in Corporate Finance, 1988; editor Jour. Fin. and Quantitative Analysis, 1966-70, Economic Perspectives, Economica Aziendale, Jour. Bus. and Entrepreneurship. Served with USNR, 1950-52. Mem. Fin. Mgmt. Assn. (pres. 1973-74), Western Fin. Assn., Am. Fin. Assn., Phi Beta Kappa. Home: PO Box 249 Neotsu OR 97364

ARCHIE, CAROL LOUISE, obstetrician and gynecologist, educator; b. Detroit, May 18, 1957; d. Frank and Mildred (Barmore) A.; m. Edward Louis Keenan III, Mar. 7, 1993. BA in History, U. Mich., 1979, postgrad. in Pub. Health Adminstrn., 1979-83; MD, Wayne State U., 1983. Diplomate Am. Bd. Ob-Gyn., Am. Bd. Maternal-Fetal Medicine. Resident ob-gyn. Wayne State U., Detroit, 1983-87; fellow in maternal fetal medicine UCLA, 1987-89, asst. prof. ob-gyn., 1987—; cons. Office Substance Abuse Prevention, Washington, 1989—, NIH, Bethesda, Md., 1990—, RAND, 1995—. Peer reviewer: (jour.) Obstetrics and Gynecology, 1989—; Author (book chpts. in) Drug Dependency in Pregnancy: Managing Withdrawal, 1992, Essentials of Obstetrics and Gynecology, 1991. Mem. internal rev. bd. Friends Med. Rsch., 1991—; bd. dirs. Matrix Inst. on Addictions, L.A., 1993—; bd. dirs., vice chair Calif. Advocates for Pregnant Women, 1993—; bd. dirs. Venice (Calif.) Free Clinic, 1994—. Clin. Tng. grantee UCLA, 1993—; recipient Faculty Devel. award Berlex Found., 1992. Fellow ACOG; mem. AMA, APHA, Soc. Perinatal Obstetricians, Royal Soc. of Medicine (Eng.), Assn. Profs. of Gynecology and Obstetrics. Office: Dept Ob-gyn UCLA Sch Medicine Rm 22-132 10833 Le Conte Ave Los Angeles CA 90024

ARCHULETTA, PATTI STOLKIN, performing arts association administrator; b. Chgo., Nov. 3, 1946; d. Walter Jerome and Billie Kay (Horn) Stolkin; m. Gilbert M. Archuletta, Dec. 28, 1982; 1 child, Michael J. BA in Spanish Lang. and Lit., De Pauw U., 1968. Flight attendent TWA, Chgo., 1968-70; TV co-host Oceanside (Calif.) Cablevision, 1970-71; TV reporter Theta Cable Calif., L.A., 1971-72; field dep. State Assemblyman Paul Priolo, L.A., 1973-75, L.A. City Councilman Joel Wachs, 1975-79; western regional dir. Nat. Found. Ileitis & Colitis, L.A., 1979-83; dir. govt. rels. Nat. Med. Enterprises, Santa Monica, Calif., 1983-87; So. Calif. Coord. Calif. Reps. for Choice, L.A., 1988-91; dir. Calif. Film Commn., Hollywood, Calif., 1992—. Mem. steering com. Calif. Reps. for Choice, L.A.; mem. exec. com. Pro-Wilson Women's Orgn. Office: Calif Film Commn 6922 Hollywood Blvd Ste 600 Los Angeles CA 90028-6126

ARCINIEGA, TOMAS ABEL, university president; b. El Paso, Tex., Aug. 5, 1937; s. Tomas Hilario and Judith G. (Zozaya) A.; m. M. Concha Ochotorena, Aug. 10, 1957; children: Wendy, Lisa, Judy, Laura. B.S., N. Mex. State U., 1960; M.A., U. N. Mex., 1966, Ph.D., 1970; postdoctoral, Inst. for Ednl. Mgmt., Harvard U., 1989. Asst. dean Grad. Sch. U. Tex.-El Paso, 1972-73; co-dir. Southwestern Schs. Study, U. Tex.-El Paso, 1970-73; dean Coll. Edn. San Diego State U., 1973-80; v.p. acad. affairs. Calif. State U., Fresno, 1980-83; pres. Calif. State U., Bakersfield, 1983—; prof. ednl. adminstrn. and supervision U. N.Mex., U. Tex.-El Paso, San Diego State U., Calif. State U., Fresno, Calif. State U., Bakersfield; cons. in edn. to state and fed. agys., instrns.; USAID advisor to Dominican Republic U.S. Dept. State, 1967-68; dep. chief party U. N.Mex. AID Project, Colombia, 1969-70. Author: Public Education's Response to the Mexican-American, 1971, Preparing Teachers of Mexican Americans: A Sociocultural and Political Issue, 1977; co-author: Chicanos and Native Americans: The Territorial Minorities, 1973; guest editor: Calif. Jour. Tchr. Edn., 1981; editor Commn. on Hispanic Underrepresentation Reports, Hispanic Underrepresentation: A Call for Reinvestment and Innovation, 1985, 88. Trustee emeritus Carnegie Corp. N.Y.; trustee Ednl. Testing Svc., Princeton, N.J., The Aspen Inst.; bd. dirs. Math., Engring., Sci. Achievement, Berkeley, Calif.; mem. bd. dirs. Air U., Nat. Hispanic Scholarship Fund; mem. Am. Coun. on Edn.; founding mem., trustee Tomas Rivera Policy Studies Ctr. Recipient Legis. commendation for higher edn. Calif. Legislature, 1975-78, Meritorious Service award Am. Assn. Colls. Tchr. Edn., 1978, Meritorious Svc. award League United L.Am. Citizens, 1983, Pioneer award Nat. Assn. Bilingual Edn., 1994; named to Top 100 Acad. Leaders in Higher Edn. Change Mag., 1978. Mem. Am. Ednl. Rsch. Assn. (editl. com. 1979-82), Assn. Mexican Am. Educators (various commendations), Am. Assn. Higher Edn. (instl. rep.), Western Coll. Assn. (past pres.). Democrat. Roman Catholic. Home: 2213 Sully Ct Bakersfield CA 93311-1560 Office: Calif State U 9001 Stockdale Hwy Bakersfield CA 93311-1022

ARDANTZ, HENRI, agricultural products executive; b. 1936. Student, Fresno State Coll. With Ferini & Ardantz, Santa Maria, Calif., 1958-63; ptnr. Betteravia Farms, Santa Maria, Calif., 1963—. Office: Betteravia Farms PO Box 5845 Santa Maria CA 93456-5845*

ARDEN, WAYNE RICHARD, automotive technology educator, consultant, systems analyst; b. Denver, Apr. 19, 1957; s. Michael and Ruth Victoria (Swanson) A. BA in Psychology, Computer Sci., U. Colo., 1980; MEd, Colo. State U., 1995. Cert. occupational edn. NIASE CMAT, Colo. Land surveyor Contract Surveyors Ltd., Denver, 1981-83; ptnr., mgr. Arden Performance Ent., Lakewood, Colo., 1983—; mem. staff field inspections mechanical & safety Mfrs. & Ins. Cos., 1990—. Vol. coord. Winter Spl. Olympics, Habitat For Humanity; mem. staff to promote cmty. recycling., Colo. Mem. Am. Welding Soc., Nat. Inst. for Automotive Svc. Excellence, Assn. for Computing Machinery, The Cousteau Soc. Office: W P C PO Box 1486 Golden CO 80402

ARDOLINO, FRANK RICHARD, English language educator; b. Bklyn., May 16, 1941; s. Fred Anthony and Helen (Stanganelli) A.; m. June Marie Stanaway, May 17, 1968. BS in Edn., St. John's U., 1962; MA in English, NYU, 1964; PhD in English, U. Calif., Riverside, 1977. Tchr. English Bd. Edn., N.Y.C., 1962-66, Glendora (Calif.) Unified Sch. Dist., 1966-68; prof. English U. Hawaii, Honolulu, 1977—. Author: Thomas Kyd's Mystery Play, 1985; contbr. articles to profl. jours. Mem. MLA, N.Am. Assn. Sports History, Soc. Am. Baseball Rsch., Sports Lit. Assn., Marlowe Soc. Am. Office: Univ Hawaii 1733 Donaghho Rd Honolulu HI 96822-2315

ARELLANES, AUDREY SPENCER, society administrator; b. Lance Creek, Wyo., Feb. 23, 1920; d. William Sidney and Edith Catherine (Hall) Spencer; m. Lane James Thomas III, Nov. 13, 1943 (div. 1946); m. Lester Glenn Arellanes, Sept. 28, 1946 (div. Oct. 1978); 1 child, Denetia Ynez. Student, UCLA, 1944. Sec. to claims mgr. Calif. Physicians Svc., L.A., 1946-54; asst. editor house organ and sec. to v.p. Calcor, Whittier, Calif., 1954-58; rsch. asst. biokinetics lab. Calif. Coll. Medicine, L.A., 1958-62; human resources employee benefits Avery Internat., Pasadena, Calif., 1963-85; ret.; pub. pvt. press Bookworm Press, Alhambra. Author: Bookplates: A Selective Annotated Bibliography of the Periodical Literature, 1971; editor: Bookplates in the News: 1970-85, 1985. Mem. Am. Soc. Bookplate Collectors & Designers (dir. 1970—, editor Year Book, Bookplates in the News quar.), Rounce and Coffin Club, The Book Collectors, Miniature Book Soc., Manuscript Soc. (nat. exec. sec. 1975-80, local treas., award of distinction 1980), Huntington Corral of Westerners Internat. (posse mem. 1980-86, trail boss 1984, registrar marks and brands 1982-83, keeper of chips 1985-86), Zamorano Club. Home and Office: Am Soc Bookplate Collectors and Designers 605 N Stoneman Ave Apt F Alhambra CA 91801-1406

ARENDS, JACK, journalist; b. Olympia, Wash., Nov. 30, 1956; s. John Henry and Carol Louise (Ellingson) A. BA, Wash. State U., 1979. Reporter intern St. Maries (Idaho) Gazette-Record, spring 1978; copyeditor intern Medford (Oreg.) Mail-Tribune, summer 1978; copyeditor Memphis Press-Scimitar, 1979-81, zone sect. editor, 1981-83; copyeditor Tacoma (Wash.) News-Tribune, 1984, The Jour. Am., Bellevue, Wash., 1984-89; editor The Ind., Port Orchard, Wash., 1991-93, Queen Anne/Magnolia News, Seattle, 1993—. Mem. Soc. Profl. Journalists. Office: Queen Anne/Magnolia News 225 W Galer St Seattle WA 98119-3331

ARENOWITZ, ALBERT HAROLD, psychiatrist; b. N.Y.C., Jan. 12, 1925; s. Louis Isaac and Lena Helen (Skovron) A.; m. Betty Jane Wiener, Oct. 11, 1953; children: Frederick Stuart, Diane Helen. BA with honors, U. Wis., 1948; MD, U. Va., 1951. Diplomate Am. Bd. Psychiatry, Am. Bd. Child Psychiatry. Intern Kings County Gen. Hosp., Bklyn., 1951-52; resident in psychiatry Bronx (N.Y.) VA Hosp., 1952-55; postdoctoral fellow Youth Guidance Ctr., Worcester, Mass., 1955-57; dir. Ctr. for Child Guidance, Phila., 1962-65, Hahnemann Med. Service Eastern State Sch. and Hosp., Trevose, Pa., 1965-68; dir., tng. dir. Child and Adolescent Psychiat. Clinic, Phila. Gen. Hosp., 1965-67; asst. clin. prof. psychiatry Jefferson Med. Coll., Phila., 1974-76; exec. dir. Child Guidance and Mental Health Clinics, Media, Pa., 1967-74; med. dir. Intercommunity Child Guidance Ctr., Whittier, Calif., 1976—; cons. Madison Pub. Schs., 1957-60, Dane County Child Guidance Ctr., Madison, 1957-62, Juvenile Ct., Madison, 1957-62; clin. asst. prof. child psychiatry Hahnemann Med. Coll., Phila., 1966-74; asst. clin. prof. psychiatry U. Wis., Madison, 1960-62, clin. asst. prof. psychiatry, behavioral scis. and family medicine U. So. Calif., L.A., 1976—; mem. med. staff Presbyn. Intercommunity Hosp., Whittier, 1976—. Pres. Whittier Area Coordinating Coun., 1978-80; chmn. ethics com. Presbyn. Intercommunity Hosp. Flight officer, navigator USAF, 1943-45. Decorated Air medal, POW medal. Fellow Am. Psychiat. Assn., Am. Acad. Child Psychiatry; mem. AAAS, Los Angeles County Med. Assn., So. Calif. Psychiat. Soc., So. Calif. Soc. Child Psychiatry, Phila. Soc. Adolescent Psychiatry (pres. 1967-68). Office: Intercommunity Child Guidance Ctr 8106 Broadway Ave Whittier CA 90606-3118

ARENSON, BARBARA LEVINE, special education educator; b. N.Y.C., Apr. 22, 1947; d. Abraham and Rebecca Levine; m. Paul Arenson, June 6, 1971; children: Adam, Aliza. BA in Sociology, U. Calif.-Berkeley, 1969; MA, San Francisco State U., 1970. Cert. elem., learning handicapped, severely handicapped tchr., adminstr., Calif. Spl. edn. tchr. Contra Costa County Pub. Schs., Alamo, Calif., 1970-72; spl. edn. diagnostic tchr. Children's Hosp., Boston, 1972-73; spl. edn. tchr. San Diego City Schs., 1973-76, spl. project tchr., 1976-78, resource tchr., 1978-82, mainstream project resource tchr., 1982-84, spl. edn. infant tchr., 1984—. Co-author: Hand in Hand--A Teacher's Guide to Preschool Mainstreaming, 1983. Mem. Assn. for Retarded Citizens, Phi Beta Kappa. Office: Alcott School 4680 Hidalgo Ave San Diego CA 92117-2503

ARENSTEIN, WALTER ALAN, environmental scientist; b. N.Y.C., Apr. 17, 1955; s. Fred and Evelyn (Eckhaus) A.; m. Gina Lilia Facca, June 6, 1993. BA in Human Ecology, Ramapo Coll. N.J., Mahwah, 1976; MA in Environ. and Urban Studies, CUNY, 1978; postgrad., U. Calif., Irvine. Cert. tchr. cmty. coll. ecology, Calif., biology and gen. sci., N.Y. Assoc. mem. profl. staff S.W. Regional Lab. for Ednl. Rsch. and devel., Orange County, Calif., 1979-80; mgr. L.A. Children's Mus., 1981-82; city coun. aide City of Irvine, 1983-86; instr. U. Calif., Irvine, 1985-87; cons. Rand Corp., Santa Monica, Calif., 1988; staff specialist South Coast Air Quality Mgmt. Dist., L.A., 1989-91; air pollution control officer Placer County Air Pollution Control Dist., Auburn, Calif., 1992-94; sr. scientist Midwest Rsch. Inst., Kansas City, Mo., 1994-95; pres. Writrac Cons., Chico, Calif., 1984—. Contbr. articles to profl. jours. Organizer, spkr. Earth Day Activities, N.Y., Calif., 1970-90; mem. Calif. Uniform Air Quality Tng. Task Force, 1989—. Recipient Cert. of Appreciation, Placer County Econ. Devel. Bd., 1993. Mem. AAAS, Assn. Environ. Profls., Calif. Air Pollution Control Officers Assn. (bd. dirs. 1993-94), Air and Waste Mgmt. Assn. (chair cmty. rels. com. 1993—).

ARENTZ, DICK, photographer; b. Detroit, May 19, 1935; s. Ewald and Hermina (Auner) A.; children: Paul, James, Pamela. DSc, U. Mich., 1959, MS, 1964. One-man shows include G. Ray Hawkins Gallery, L.A., 1987, Etherton Gallery, Tucson, 1987, U. Mo., St. Louis, 1988, Galerie Stockeregg, Zurich, 1989, Houston Ctr. for Photography, 1989, Huntington Mus. of Art, 1990, U. Ky., 1991, Phoenix Art Mus. Trienniel, 1990; represented in permanent collections Mus. Moderan Art, George Eastman House, Corcoran Gallery, Can. Ctr. for architecture, Amon Carter Mus. Western Art, Oakland Art Mus., Nat. Mus. Am. Art. Capt. USAF, 1959-61. Isaac W. Bernheim fellow, 1988; grantee NEA, 1990. Mem. Soc. Photographic Edn., Phi Kappa Phi. Home and Office: 1640 Spyglass Way Flagstaff AZ 86004-7382

ARGENBRIGHT, ED FRANK, school administrator; b. Cut Bank, Mont., Dec. 3, 1934; s. Frank Paul Argenbright and Cleo (Newman) Overstreet; m. Betty Jane Fuller, June 30, 1956; children: Mark E., Bret F. B.A., U. Mont., 1956, EdD, 1989; M.A., San Jose State Coll., 1964. Cert. tchr., adminstr., Mont. Tchr., coach Granite County High Sch., Philipsburg, Mont., 1956-57; tchr. Campbell Union Schs., Calif., 1960-66; tchr., prin., supt. Sch. Dist. # 1, Big Timber, Mont., 1966-80; co-owner McLeod Resort Corp., Mont., 1966-70; supt. pub. instrn. State of Mont., Helena, 1980-89; dir., regional liaison U.S. Dept. Edn., 1989-90, dir. recognition divsn., 1990-92; commr. polit. practices State of Mont., 1993—; dir. Northwest Edn. Lab., Portland, Oreg., 1980-88; mem. Mont. Land Bd., Tchr. Retirement Bd., Bd. Govs., Helena, 1980-88, Council Chief State Sch. Officers, Washington, 1980-88; mem., sec. Mont. Bd. Edn., Helena, 1980-88; nat. adv. council Statue of Liberty Ellis Island Found., N.Y.C., 1983-84. Mem. exec. com. Mont. Rep. Party, Helena, 1980-88; pres. Mont. Econ. Edn., Helena. Served to capt. USAF, 1957-60. Recipient Degree Hon. State Farmer Future Farmers Am., 1984, Sec. Regional award Dept. Edn., 1983; named to Basketball Hall Fame U. Mont., 1968. Mem. Sch. Adminstrs. Mont., Am. Assn. Sch. Adminstrs., Sigma Nu. Presbyterian. Lodges: Masons, (master 1976, Mont. Mason of Yr. 1988), Lions. Office: PO Box 202401 Helena MT 59620-2401

ARGENTERI, LETIZIA, history educator; b. Milano, Lombardy, Italy, May 2, 1950; came to U.S., 1974; d. Antonio and Giacomina (Milesi) A. Doctorate, U. Milano, 1973; PhD in History, UCLA, 1989. Teaching assoc. UCLA, 1983-85; editor The J. Paul Getty Ctr., Santa Monica, Calif., 1985-90; asst. prof. dept. history U. San Diego, Calif., 1991—; vis. prof. Bosphorus U., Istanbul, Turkey, 1980-81. Paul Harris fellow Rotary, Pavia, Italy, 1989; grantee Italian Embassy, Washington, 1986-88; nominated jr. fellowship Soc. of Fellows, Harvard U., 1988. Mem. Am. Hist. Assn., Am. Italian Hist. Assn., Friends of Teatro Alla Scala (Milano), Western Assn. Women Historians, Phi Beta Kappa (grantee 1985). Office: Univ San Diego Dept History Alcala Park San Diego CA 92110

ARGERIS, GEORGE JOHN, lawyer; b. Ten Sleep, Wyo., May 12, 1931; s. John Brown and Martha (Wilsonoff) A. BA, U. Colo., 1954; JD, U. Wyo., 1959. Bar: Wyo. 1959, U.S. Dist. Ct. Wyo. 1959, U.S. Supreme Ct. 1968. Asst. atty. gen. State of Wyo., Cheyenne, 1960-63; supervisory atty. Fgn. Claims Commn. U.S., Washington, 1963-68; dep. gen. counsel U.S. Info. Agy., Washington, 1972-74; ptnr. Guy, Williams, White & Argeris,

Cheyenne, 1974-94; of counsel Orr, Buchhammer & Kehl (was Guy, Williams, White & Argeris), 1994—. Assoc. editor U. Wyo. Law Rev., 1957-58. Mem. ABA, Assn. Def. Trial Lawyers, Wyo. Def. Lawyers Assn., Wyo. Trial Lawyers Assn., Omicron Delta Kappa, Chi Gamma Iota. Home: 3619 Carey Ave Cheyenne WY 82001-1227 Office: Orr Buchhammer & Kehl 1600 Van Lennen Ave Cheyenne WY 82001-4636

ARGUE, JOHN CLIFFORD, lawyer; b. Glendale, Calif., Jan. 25, 1932; s. J. Clifford and Catherine Emily (Clements) A.; m. Leah Elizabeth Moore, June 29, 1963; children: Elizabeth Anne, John Michael. AB in Commerce and Fin., Occidental Coll., 1953, LLD (hon.), 1987; LLB, U. So. Calif., 1956. Bar: Calif. 1957. Since practiced in Los Angeles; mem. firm Argue & Argue, 1958-59, Flint & MacKay, 1960-72; mem. firm Argue, Pearson, Harbison & Myers, 1972-94, of counsel, 1995—; bd. dirs. Avery Dennison, Calif. Mat Inc., Compensation Resource Group; mem. adv. bd. LAACO, Ltd., TCW/DW Mut. Funds, TCW Galileo Funds; chmn. Rose Hills Meml. Pk. Assn., Amateur Athletic Found., Criminal Justice Legal Found. Pres. So. Calif. Com. Olympic Games, 1972—; founding chmn. L.A. Olympic Organizing Com., 1978-79; trustee, vice chmn. Pomona Coll., U. So. Calif., Occidental Coll., Mus. Sci. and Industry, U.S. Olympic Tng. Ctr.; chmn. bd. Greater L.A. affiliate Am. Heart Assn., 1982, chmn. adv. bd., 1985—; chmn. Verdugo Hills Hosp., 1979, chmn. adv. bd., 1983—; pres. Town Hall of Calif., 1985, U. So. Calif. Assocs., 1988-93; chmn. PGA Championship, 1983, L.A. Sports Coun., 1988—, Magic Johnson's Golf Clasic, 1988-94; vice chmn., sec. L.A. 2000 Com., 1991 Olympic Sports Festival, 1993 Superbowl, bid com. 1994 Worldcup; chmn. adv. bd. 1995 PGA Championship; chmn. Rose Hills Meml. Park Assn. Mem. L.A. Bar Assn., Calif. Bar Assn., Southern Calif. Golf Assn. (pres. 1979), Calif. Golf Assn. (v.p. 1979), L.A. Area C. of C. (chmn. 1989), Chancery Club (pres. 1985-86), Calif. Club (pres. 1983-84), L.A. Athletic Club, Riviera Country Club, Oakmont Country Club (pres. 1972), L.A. Country Club, Flint Canyon Tennis Club, Calif. State Srs. Golf Assn., Rotary, Phi Delta Phi, Alpha Tau Omega. Home: 1314 Descanso Dr La Canada Flintridge CA 91011-3149 Office: 801 S Flower St Ste 5000 Los Angeles CA 90017-4607

ARIAS, JOE, agricultural products company executive. With subsidiaries of Valley Fresh Foods, Inc., 1966—; pres., chmn. bd. Valley Fresh Foods, Inc., Turlock, Calif., 1991—. Office: Valley Fresh Foods Inc 3600 E Linwood Ave Turlock CA 95380-9108*

ARIEFF, ALLEN IVES, physician; b. Chgo., Sept. 30, 1938. BS in Math. and Chemistry, U. Ill., 1960; MS in Physiology, Northwestern U., 1964, MD, 1964. Intern Phila. Gen. Hosp., 1964-65; resident SUNY, Bklyn., 1967-68; renal fellow U. Colo., Denver, 1968-69; rsch. and edn. assoc., clin. investigator Wadsworth VA Med. Ctr., L.A., 1970-74; asst. prof. medicine, rsch. scientist UCLA Med. Ctr., 1971-74; asst. prof. medicine, dir. hemodialysis U. Calif. VA Med. Ctr., San Francisco, 1975-76, assoc. prof. medicine, dir. nephrology sect., 1976-83, prof. medicine, chief clin. nephrology, 1983-86, prof. medicine, dir. rsch. & edn. geriatrics, 1986—; cons. and speaker in field. Author 6 books; contbr. 54 chpts. med. textbooks, over 300 articles to profl. jours. Fellow ACP; mem. Am. Soc. Nephrology, Am. Fedn. Clin. Rsch., Am. Diabetes Assn., Am. Physiol. Soc., Am. Soc. Neurochemistry, Am. Soc. Clin. Investigation, Am. Soc. Bone and Mineral Rsch., Assn. Am. Physicians, Western Assn. Physicians, Western Soc. Clin. Rsch., Internat. Soc. Nephrology, Soc. Neurosci. Office: VAMC/UCSF 4150 Clement St # 111G San Francisco CA 94121-1545

ARIELI, ADI, aerospace company executive; b. Bucharest, Romania, Apr. 15, 1947; came to U.S., 1978; s. David and Rebecca (Greenberg) A.; m. Mihaela Popescu, July 31, 1969; 1 child, Robert Philip. Diploma engring., Polytech Inst., 1970; MS, Technion, 1976; PhD, U. Calif., Davis, 1979. Supr. metals tech. Israel Aircraft Inds., Lod, 1971-78; rsch. assoc. U. Calif., Davis, 1978-80; sr. scientist Olin Corp., New Haven, Conn., 1980-81; mgr. Northrop Corp., Hawthorne, Calif., 1981—; mem. bd. advisors dept. mech., aero. and materials engring. U. Calif., Davis, 1989—, mem. mfg. engring. adv. bd., UCLA, 1986—. Contbr. scientific and tech. articles to profl. jours. Mem. SAE (chmn. aerospace mfg. activity 1990—, vice chmn. 1988-90), ASM (materials, synthesis and processing coms. 1987—), N.Y. Acad. Scis. Home: 120 S Fuller Ave Los Angeles CA 90036-2810 Office: Northrop Corp 1 Northrop Ave Hawthorne CA 90250-3236

ARISMENDI-PARDI, EDUARDO J., mathematics educator; b. Caracas, Venezuela, May 28, 1960; s. Edward Jesse Arismendi and Cecilia Pardi-Valero; m. Cheryl Annette Knutson, Dec. 20, 1980; 1 child, Mikhail Andrej Arismendi-Knutson. AA, Cerritos Coll., 1981; BS, Calif. State U., Long Beach, 1984; MS summa cum laude, West Coast U., 1991. Cert. community coll. tchr. math., computers, bus. and mgmt., Calif. Asst. engr. Rockwell Internat., Downey, Calif., 1980-82; math. instr. Our Lady of Victory High Sch., Van Nuys, Calif., 1982-83; math. tchr. asst. Calif. State U., Long Beach, 1983-86; math. tchr. La Salle High Sch., Pasadena, Calif., 1986-87; statistics tchr. asst. U. Calif., L.A., 1987-88; mgmt. scientist McDonnell Douglas Corp., Long Beach, 1988-91; math. instr. Orange Coast Coll., Costa Mesa, Calif., 1989-91; math. prof. Orange Coast Coll., Costa Mesa, 1991—; mgmt. scientist Scandinavian Airline System, Oslo, Norway, 1989, Am. Airlines, Tulsa, 1989-91, Sorin Biomedical, Inc., Irvine, Calif., 1992—; lectr. quantitative methods West Coast U., L.A., 1992—. Mem. Am. Math. Soc., Am. Statistical Soc., Math. Assn. Am., Am. Fedn. Tchrs., Ops. Rsch. Soc. Am., Faculty Assn. Calif. Community Colls. Democrat. Roman Catholic. Home: 9 Wildflower Pl Phillips Ranch Pomona CA 91766 Office: Orange Coast College PO Box 5005 2701 Fairview Rd Costa Mesa CA 92626-5561

ARISS, DAVID WILLIAM, SR., real estate developer; b. Toronto, Ont., Can., Nov. 29, 1939; s. William H. and Joyce Ethel (Oddy) A.; m. Lillie Ariss, Jan. 26, 1962 (div. 1989); m. Debra Ann Nocciolo, Nov. 17, 1990; children: Katherine Joyce, David William Jr., Dylan William. BA, Claremont Men's Coll., 1961. Lic. real estate broker. Real estate broker Coldwell Banker, Torrance, Calif., 1971-75; v.p. The Lusk Co., Irvine, Calif., 1975-77; pres. DAL Devel. Co., Corona, Calif., 1977-84; mng. dir. Calif. Commerce Ctr. at Ontario, Ontario, Calif., 1984—. Chair Inland Empire Econ. Coun., Ontario, Calif., 1991-92; pres. comml./indsl. coun. Baldy View chpt. Bldg. Industry Assn., San Bernardino County, Calif., 1987-88; pres., adv. com. Chaffey Coll., Ontario, 1989—; apptd. Calif. World Trade Commn., 1993, 95. Maj. USMC, 1961-70, Vietnam. Decorated Silver Star, Disting. Flying Cross, two Purple Hearts, numerous Air medals. Mem. Urban Land Inst., Nat. Assn. Fgn. Trade Zone, Nat. Assn. Indsl. and Office Parks. Republican. Office: Calif Commerce Ctr 3200 Inland Empire Blvd Ste 235 Ontario CA 91764-5513

ARISS, RUSHDI ALBERTO, marketing professional, systems engineer; b. L.A., May 11, 1967; s. Hassan René and Maria Helena (Rodriguez) A.; m. Kristi Jean Pfeil, June 13, 1992. BSEE, Calif. State U., Northridge, 1992. Instrnl. technician Calif. State U., Northridge, 1989-92; sys. engr. GTE Govt. Sys., Thousand Oaks, Calif., 1992—, mem. exec. steering com., 1994—; mktg. exec. RKA & Assocs., Winnetka, Calif., 1994—; reviewer Tech. Users Newsletter, 1994. With USNR, 1985—. Mem. IEEE, Internat. Network Assn. Republican. Roman Catholic.

ARITA, GEORGE SHIRO, biology educator; b. Honolulu, Oct. 9, 1940; s. Ichimatsu and Natsu (Kimoto) A.; m. Harriet Yooko Ide, Dec. 26, 1964; children: Laurie Reiko, Daren Shizuo. BA, U. Hawaii, 1962, MS, 1964; MS, U. B.C., Vancouver, 1967; postgrad., U. Calif., Santa Barbara, 1967-71. Cert. community coll. tchr., Calif. Prof. biology Ventura (Calif.) Coll., 1971—, curator fish collection, 1976—, head dept. biology, 1989—. Author: (with others, lab. manual) Basic Concepts in Biology, 1981, Study Guide to Accompany Biology: Today and Tomorrow, 2d edit., 1984; contbr. articles on ichthyology to profl. jours. Fushiminomiya Meml. scholar U. Hawaii, 1961-62, Fisheries Assn. B.C. scholar U. B.C., 1964-65; NSF grad. trainee U. Calif. Santa Barbara, 1969-71. Mem. AAAS, Am. Soc. Ichthyologists and Herpetologists, Western Soc. Naturalists, Sigma Xi. Home: 94 Howard Ave Oak View CA 93022-9524 Office: Ventura Coll Dept Biology Ventura CA 93003

ARKENBERG, JEROME STEPHEN, law and history researcher; b. Oak Park, Ill., June 20, 1958; s. Raymond John and Genevieve Catherine (Sejud) A. BA, Loyola U. Chgo., 1980, MA, 1988; JD, U. Ill., 1983; PhD, UCLA, 1990. Bar: Ill. 1983, U.S. Dist. Ct. (no. dist.) Ill. 1984, U.S. Ct. Appeals (7th cir.) 1984, U.S. Supreme Ct. 1985. Prin. Law Offices Jerome S. Arkenberg, Esq., Oak Park, 1983-86; rschr. Loyola U. Chgo., 1986-87; lectr. Calif. State U., L.A., 1992-93; rschr. Ctr. Medieval and Renaissance Studies, L.A., 1993-94, Huntington Libr., San Marino, Calif., 1992—. Contbr. articles to profl. jours. Fellow faculty Loyola U., Chgo., 1986, UCLA, 1987-91, Andrew Mellon Found., 1992, Ball Bros. Found., 1993; recipient Brit. Acad. Neil Ker award, 1994. Mem. ABA, Am. Soc. Legal History, Am. Hist. Assn., Medieval Acad. Am., Assn. Ancient Historians, Selden Soc. Office: Huntington Libr 1151 Oxford Rd San Marino CA 91108-1218

ARLEN, JENNIFER HALL, law educator; b. Berkeley, Calif., Jan. 7, 1959; d. Michael John and Ann (Warner) A.; m. Robert Lee Hotz, May 21, 1988; 1 child, Michael Arlen Hotz. BA, Harvard U., 1982; JD, NYU, 1986; PhD in Econs., NYU, 1992. Bar: N.Y. 1987, U.S. Ct. Appeals (11th cir.) 1987. Summer clk. U.S. Dist. Ct. (ea. dist.) N.Y., Bklyn., 1984; summer assoc. Davis Polk & Wardwell, N.Y.C., 1985; law clk. U.S. Cir. Judge, 11th cir., Savannah, Ga., 1986-87; asst. prof. law Emory U., Atlanta, 1987-91, assoc. prof. law, 1991-93; prof. law U. So. Calif., L.A., 1994—; vis. prof. law U. So. Calif., 1993. Olin fellow U. Calif. Sch. Law, Berkeley, 1991. Mem. ABA, Am. Assn. Law Schs. (chair remedies sect. 1994,mem. exec. com. 1990-91, chair torts sect. 1995, treas. 1991, sec. 1992-93, exec. com. bus. assns. sect. 1994-95), Am. Law and Econ. Assn. (bd. dirs. 1991-93), Am. Econ. Assn., Order of Coif. Democrat. Office: U So Calif Law Ctr Los Angeles CA 90089

ARMACOST, CATHY LOA, nutritionist, consultant; b. Seattle, July 2, 1957; d. James George and Virginia Loa (Angerer) Fuller; m. Ronald R. Armacost, Jan. 26, 1985. BA in political sci., Wash. State U., 1980; BS in nutrition, Whitworth Coll., 1989; MS in human nutrition, Wash. State U., 1994. Registered dietitian. Legs. advocate VISTA Vol., Pendleton, Oreg., 1980-81; adminstrn. asst. Area Agy. on Aging, Pendleton, Oreg., 1981-83; geriatric caseworker Elderly Svcs., Cmty. Mental Health, Spokane, Wash., 1983-85; food svc. mgr. Zip Trip Stores, Spokane, Wash., 1988-90; sports nutrition cons. Spokane, Wash., 1994—. Sec., founding mem. Liberty Lake Rep. Women, Liberty Lake, Wash., 1992. Mem. Am. Dietetic Assn., U.S. Rowing Assn., Pi Beta Phi. Episcopalian. Home: 1222 S Starr Ln Liberty Lake WA 99019-9530 Office: Zip Trip N 111 Greene St Spokane WA 99202

ARMALEH, SONIA HANNA, civil engineer, educator; b. Lattakia, Syria, Feb. 6, 1956; came to the U.S., 1982; d. Hanna and Helaneh Armaleh; m. Albert Moussa; children: Christine, Carmen. BS, U. Tishreen, 1978; MS, U. Ariz., 1986, PhD, 1990. Registered civil engr., Ariz. Civil engr. Alsahel Co., Lattakia, 1978-79; teaching asst. U. Tishreen, Lattakia, 1979-81; teaching asst. and assoc. U. Ariz., Tucson, 1983-90, asst. prof., 1990—. Jane Rider scholar U. Ariz., 1984-89. Mem. ASCE, Assn. Women Faculty, Sigma Xi. Office: U Ariz Tucson AZ 85721

ARMENTROUT, STEVEN ALEXANDER, oncologist; b. Morgantown, W.Va., Aug. 22, 1933; s. Walter W. and Dorothy (Gasch) A.; m. Johanna Ruszkay; children—Marc, Susan, Sandra, Nancy. A.B., U. Chgo., 1953, M.D., 1959. Intern U. Hosp., Cleve., 1959-60; resident in medicine, fellow Am. Cancer Soc. Western Res. U. Hosp., 1960-63; project dir. USPHS, 1963-65; asst. prof. Case Western Res. U. Med. Sch., 1965-71; mem. faculty U. Calif. Med. Sch., Irvine, 1971—; prof. medicine, chief divsn. hematology-oncology U. Calif. Med. Sch., 1978—, also dir. program in oncology.; pres. med. staff U. Calif.-Irvine Med. Ctr., 1983-85; researcher in multiple sclerosis. Mem. Am. Assn. Cancer Research, AAUP, ACP, Am. Cancer Soc. (chmn. bd. 1973, pres. Orange County chpt. 1985-86), AMA, Am. Soc. Clin. Oncology, Am. Soc. Hematology, Orange County Med. Assn., Am. Soc. Internal Medicine, Calif. Med. Assn., Cen. Soc. Clin. Research, Leukemia Soc. Am., Orange County Chief of Staff Council. Office: 101 City Blvd W Orange CA 92668-2901

ARMEY, DOUGLAS RICHARD, minister; b. Fresno, Calif., Oct. 23, 1948; s. Wilbur Rutter and Mildred (Broadbent) A.; m. Jennifer Louise Armey, Sept. 23, 1972; children: Laura Elizabeth, Andrew Douglas. AA, Fresno (Calif.) City Coll., 1969; BS summa cum laude, Calif. State U., Fresno, 1971; MA, Mennonite Brethren Sem., Fresno, 1976. Ordained to ministry, Ch. of Brethren, 1973. Intern pastor The Peoples Ch. of Fresno, 1972-73; founding chaplain Fresno County Juvenile Hall, 1973; pres. Precision Parts Distbrs., Inc., Fresno, 1973-80, Rutter Armey Engine Co., Inc., Bakersfield, Calif., 1980-88; sr. pastor Fresno Ch. of the Brethren, 1988—; radio broadcaster Fresno Fellowship of Christian Athletes/KIRV Radio, 1987—. Contbr. articles to profl. jours. and mags. Bd. dirs. Fresno Youth for Christ, 1985-87. With Calif. Air N.G., 1968-74. Mem. Nat. Assn. Evangelicals, Sigma Alpha Epsilon, Sunnyside Country Club. Republican. Ch. of the Brethren. Office: 3901 E Clinton Ave Fresno CA 93703-2517

ARMFIELD, W. W., retired agricultural products company executive. Pvt. practice Pacific Palisades, 1966-87; with Spokane (Wash.) Seed Co., 1987—, v.p.; retired. Office: Spokane Seed Co 6015 E Alki Ave Spokane WA 99212-1019*

ARMIJO, JACQULYN DORIS, interior designer; b. Gilmer, Tex., July 2, 1938; d. Jack King and Iris Adele (Cook) Smith; children—John, Christy, Mike; m. Chet Wigton. Student North Tex. State Coll., U. N.Mex. Profl. model, 1961-75; sec. State Farm Ins., Albuquerque, 1965-71; life ins. agt. Mountain States, Albuquerque, 1980; owner Interiors by Jacqulyn, Albuquerque, 1961—; cons., lectr. in field. Mem. Alby Little Theatre, Friends of Little Theatre, Symphony Women; fund raiser for Old Town Hist. Com., Arthritis Fund. Mem. Am. Soc. Interior Design (chmn. historic restoration Albuquerque), Internat. Soc. Interior Design, Internat. Platform Assn., Civil War Club (pres. local chpt.) Republican. Roman Catholic. Clubs: Albuquerque Jr. Women's, Los Amapolas Garden. Home and Office: 509 Chamiso Ln NW Albuquerque NM 87107-6601

ARMINANA, RUBEN, academic administrator, educator; b. Santa Clara, Cuba, May 15, 1947; came to U.S., 1961; s. Aurelio Ruben and Olga Petrona (Nart) A.; m. Marne Olson, June 6, 1954; children: Cesar A. Martino, Maria G. Arminana. AA, Hill Jr. Coll., 1966; BA, U. Tex., 1968, MA, 1970; PhD, U. New Orleans, 1983; postgrad. Inst. of Applied Behavioral Scis., Nat. Tng. Labs., 1971. Nat. assoc. dir. Phi Theta Kappa, Canton, Miss., 1968-69; dir. ops. and tng. Inter-Am. Ctr., Loyola U., New Orleans, 1969-71; administrv. analyst City of New Orleans, 1972, adminstrv. analyst and organizational devel. and tng. cons., 1972-78; anchor and reporter part time STA. WWL-TV, New Orleans, 1973-81; v.p. Commerce Internat. Corp., New Orleans, 1978-83; exec. asst. to sr. v.p. Tulane U., New Orleans, 1983-85, assoc. exec. v.p., 1985-87, v.p., asst. to pres., 1987-88; v.p. fin. and devel. Calif. State Poly U., Pomona, 1988-92; pres. Sonoma State U., 1992—; TV news cons., New Orleans, 1981-88; lectr. Internat. Trade Mart, New Orleans, 1983-89, U.S. Dept. Commerce, New Orleans. Co-author: Hemisphere West-El Futuro, 1968; co-editor: Colloquium on Central America-A Time for Understanding, Background Readings, 1985. Bd. dirs. Com. on Alcoholism and Substance Abuse, 1978-79, SER, Jobs for Progress, Inc., 1974-82, Citizens United for Responsive Broadcasting, Latin Am. Festival Com; dir., bd. advisors Sta. WDSU-TV, 1974-77; mem. Bus. Govt. Rsch., 1987-88, Coun. Advancment of Support to Edn.; mem. League of United Latin Am. Citizens, Mayor's Latin Am. Adv. Com., Citizens to Preserve the Charter, Met. Area Com., Mayor's Com. on Crime. Kiwanis scholar, 1966, Books scholar, 1966. Mem. Assn. U. Related Rsch. Prks., L.A. Higher Edn. Roundtable, Soc. Coll. and U. Planning, Nat. Assn. Coll. and U. Bus. Officers Cou., Am. Econ. Assn., Assn. of Evolutionary Econs., Am. Polit. Sci. Assn., AAUP, Western Coll. Assn. (pres. 1994-95), Latin Am. C. of C. (founding dir. New Orleans and River Region 1976-83), Cuban Profl. Club, Phi Theta Kappa, Omicron Delta Epsilon, Sigma Delta Pi, Delta Sigma Pi. Democrat. Roman Catholic. Avocation: mask collecting. Office: Sonoma State U 1801 E Cotati Ave Rohnert Park CA 94928-3613

ARMINTROUT, EDWARD GILBERT, human resources executive; b. Englewood, Colo., June 25, 1940; s. Gilbert Edgar and Lucy Henrietta (Grotz) A.; m. Jeanne Kathleen Vuich, Feb. 28, 1986; children: Julie Elizabeth, Lori Anne. BS, U. Colo., 1967. Mng. human resources Litton Industries Corp., Beverly Hills, Calif., 1967-69, Syntex Corp., Palo Alto, Calif., 1969-73; dir. human resources SYVA Co., Palo Alto, 1973-75; cons. human resources Denver, 1975-80; v.p. human resources Wells Fargo Bank, San Francisco, 1980-82, John Muir Med. Ctr., Walnut Creek, Calif., 1982-90; v.p. Drake Beam Morin, San Jose, Calif., 1990-93; cons. Drake Beam Morin, Denver, 1993—. Author: Guide to Effective Hiring, 1990. Cons. to sch. bd. Albany County Schs., Laramie, Wyo., 1994. Republican. Home and Office: 1661 Inca Dr Laramie WY 82070-5072

ARMITAGE, CARINTHIA URBANETTE, realtor; b. Honolulu, Aug. 27, 1954; d. Urban Edward and Salome Lilinoe (Needham) Kunewa; children: Marvel K.O., George K. III, Daven W.H.K., Keoni A.U., Chanelle B.K., Michelle C.W. AA in Liberal Arts, U. Hawaii, 1990, BA in Psychology, 1993, BA in Bus. Adminstrn., 1993, MSW, 1995. Tax preparer certs. H&R Block, Waianae, Hawaii, 1987-90; realtor assoc. Debra and Co., Aiea, Hawaii, 1986—; program dir. Ho'omau Ke Ola Day Treatment Program, 1994. Mem. Women in Transition, Leeward Coll., 1987—. Mem. NASW, Nat. Bd. Realtors, Honolulu Bd. Realtors. Home: 86-263 Alamihi St Waianae HI 96792-2910

ARMOUR, GEORGE PORTER, lawyer; b. Bryn Mawr, Pa., June 10, 1921; s. Charles Joseph and Florence (Eagle) A.; m. Isabel Blondet, Nov. 22, 1958; children: Luis O., Carlos O. B.A., Temple U., 1943, J.D., 1949. Bar: Pa. 1949, N.Y. 1969, Calif. 1975. Assoc. Bennett & Bricklin, Phila., 1949-59; atty. Atlantic Richfield Co., 1959-83, gen. atty., Phila., 1965-68, assoc. gen. counsel, Phila., N.Y.C., L.A., 1968-78, dep. gen. counsel, L.A., 1978-83; pvt. practice law, 1983—; chmn. Internat. and Comparative Law Ctr., Southwestern Legal Found., Dallas, 1980-82. Mem. Assocs. Calif. Inst. Tech., 1981—; mem. Soc. of Fellows Huntington Library and Art Gallery, San Marino, Calif., 1982—. Served with USAAF, 1943-46. Mem. ABA, Calif. Bar Assn., Calif. Club (L.A.), Valley Hunt Club (Pasadena). Republican. Episcopalian. Home and Office: 1621 Orlando Rd Pasadena CA 91106-4130

ARMSBY, ROBERT, architect. Ptnr. Skidmore, Owings & Merrill, San Francisco. Office: Anderson Debartolo Pan Inc 801 Montgomery St San Francisco CA 94133-5164

ARMSTRONG, ANDREW ROBERT, film director, producer; b. Farnham Common, Eng., Aug. 28, 1953; s. Robert Munro and Ann (Hendy) A.; m. Madeleine Jane King, Sept. 18, 1975 (div. 1983); children: Joanna Jane, James Robert. Student, Hich Wycombe Tech. Coll. Asst. dir. numerous films, 1973-88, action dir. numerous films, 1986—, producer, assoc. producer numerous films, 1987—; dir. Stunts, Inc. Internat., 1991—. 2d unit dir.: (films) Highlander, 1986, Rambo 3, 1988; producer: Nightbreed, 1989, Double Impact, 1990, Joshua Tree, 1992; stunt act coord.: (films) Homicide, 1990, Citizen Cohn, 1991, Hoffa, 1992, Flesh and Bone, 1992, The Firm, 1992, Stargate, 1993, Override, 1994. Mem. SAG, Dirs. Guild Am., Assn. Cinema and TV Technicians, Brit. Actors Equity Assn. Office: care Jeffrey Ross CPA Sherman and Ross Jode Profl Plz 193 Rte 9 S Manalapan NJ 07726

ARMSTRONG, ANNA DAWN, marketing professional, writer; b. San Francisco, Jan. 28, 1943. BBA, U. Portland, Oreg., 1964. Mktg. asst. Food Giant Markets, L.A., 1964-65; copywriter Young & Rubicam Advt., L.A., 1965-67; creative dir. Capitol Direct Mktg. Corp., Hollywood, Calif., 1967-70; ptnr. Harrison Assocs., L.A., 1970-73; mktg. officer Security Pacific Bank, L.A., 1973-76; creative cons. Dawn Armstrong, L.A., 1976-78; v.p., creative dir. Mktg. and Fin. Mgmt. Enterprises, Inc., Encino, Calif., 1978-81, Direct Mktg. Corp. Am., L.A., 1981-83; pres., creative dir. A Creative Group, Sebastopol and Lake Tahoe, Calif., 1983—; v.p. Mktg. Concepts and Mgmt., Lake Tahoe, Nev., 1991—; v.p., creative dir. Membership Clubs Internat., Century City, Calif., 1978-81, Direct Mktg. Internat., Australia, Can., France, U.K., 1981-83. Author: (7 book-series) Direct Marketing, 1988; contbr. articles to profl. jours. Exec. dir. South Lake Tahoe (Calif.) Humane Soc. and Lake Tahoe Humane Soc. (Nev.), 1991—; tutor State of Calif. Literacy Program, South Lake Tahoe, 1991—. Mem. Lake Tahoe Press Club (charter). Office: A Creative Group PO Box 612006 South Lake Tahoe CA 96152-2006

ARMSTRONG, BILLIE BERT, retired highway contractor; b. Roswell, N.Mex., Apr. 18, 1920; s. Gayle G. and Murphy (Shannon) A.; m. Betty-Ellen Wilcox, Aug. 16, 1941; children: Billie B. Jr., Judith C., Robert G., Riley A. Student, N.Mex. Mil. Inst., 1935-39, Washington & Lee U., 1939-41. Mng. ptnr. Armstrong & Armstrong Ltd., Roswell, 1950—, G.G. Armstrong & Son, Ltd., Roswell, 1950—; chmn. bd. dirs. Sunwest Nat. Bank, 1967-84; pres. Assoc. Gen. Contractors Am., Washington, 1966-67, Assoc. Contractors N.Mex., Santa Fe, 1952-53, 63. Pres. Conquistador Coun. Boy Scouts Am., Roswell, 1981-82, bd. regents N.Mex. Mil. Inst., Roswell, 1960-62. Major U.S. Army, 1942-45. Named Citizen of Yr. Realtors N.Mex., 1969, Roswell, 1968, Jaycees, 1964; recognized for svc. to mankind Sertoma, 1966. Mem. Masons, Shriners, Jesters. Methodist. Home: 2619 Coronado Dr Roswell NM 88201-3404 Office: Armstrong & Armstrong Ltd PO Box 1873 Roswell NM 88202-1873

ARMSTRONG, C. MICHAEL, computer business executive; b. Detroit, Oct. 18, 1938; s. Charles H. and Zora Jean (Brooks) A.; m. Anne Gossett, June 17, 1961; children: Linda, Julie, Kristy. B.S. in Bus. Econs, Miami U., Oxford, Ohio, 1961; grad., Dartmouth Inst., 1976. With IBM Corp., 1961-92, dir. systems mgmt. mktg. div., White Plains, N.Y., 1975-76, v.p. market ops. East, 1976-78, pres. data processing div., 1978-80, v.p., asst. group exec. plans and controls, data processing product group, 1980-83, v.p., group exec., 1983-84, sr. v.p., group exec., 1984—; also pres. IBM Corp., Europe, Paris, until 1988; pres., dir. gen. World Trade Europe/Middle East/Africa IBM Corp., 1987—, chmn. World Trade Corp., 1989—; chmn., CEO Hughes Aircraft Co., L.A., 1992—; bd. dirs. Travelers Corp., Hartford, Conn. Mem. bus. adv. coun. Miami U.; bd. dirs. Found. Devel. Polish Agr.; mem. Coun. on Fgn. Rels.; mem. nat. adv. com. Coll. Engring. U. Mich.; trustee Johns Hopkins U., Conf. Bd.; mem supervisory bd. Thyssen-Bornemisza Group. Office: Hughes Aircraft Co PO Box 800208 Los Angeles CA 90080*

ARMSTRONG, DALE P., plastic surgeon; b. Detroit, July 25, 1933; s. Clifford Earl and Lauretta Marie (Wilson) A.; m. Margaret Charlotte Goebel, June 16, 1956; children: Karen, Clifford, Douglas. BS, U. Mich., 1958, MD, 1958. Diplomate Am. Bd. Plastic Surgery. Intern U. Mich., Ann Arbor, 1958-59, resident gen. surgery, 1959-62; resident plastic surgery Duke U., 1962-65; pvt. practice plastic and reconstructive surgery Denver, 1965-66, Ventura, Calif., 1966—; presenter in field. contbr. articles to books and med. jours. chmn. United Way Ventura County Physician's Campaign, 1981-83, bd. trustees 1981-83; chief of staff Cmty. Meml. Hosp., 1984, bd. trustees 1984-85; clin. faculty mem. UCLA, 1985—; bd. dirs. Ventura Meml. Healthcare Found., chmn. svcs. assessment com., 1984—. Fellow ACS; mem. AMA, Am. Soc. Plastic and Reconstructive Surgeons, Am. Soc. Aesthetic Plastic Surgery, Calif. Med. Assn., Ventura County Med. Soc. (sec. 1972-73), L.A. Soc. Plastic Surgeons (pres. 1980-81), Soc. Clin. Aesthetic Surgery. Republican. Home: 1051 Rancho Vista Ln Santa Paula CA 93060 Office: 168 N Brent St Ste 403 Ventura CA 93003-2824

ARMSTRONG, DAVID MICHAEL, biology educator; b. Louisville, July 31, 1944; s. John D. and Elizabeth Ann (Horine) A.; children: John D., Laura C. BS, Colo. State U., 1966; MA in Teaching, Harvard U., 1967; PhD, U. Kans., 1971. From asst. prof. natural sci. to full prof. U. Colo., Boulder, 1971-93, prof. Environ., Population, and Organomic Biology, 1993—; sr. scientist Rocky Mountain Biol. Lab., Gothic, Colo., 1977, 79; resident naturalist Sylvan Dale Ranch, Loveland, Colo., 1984—; acting dir. Univ. Mus., 1987-88, dir., 1989-93; cons. ecologist. Author: Distribution of Mammals in Colorado, 1972, Rocky Mountain Mammals, 1975, 87, Mammals of the Canyon Country, 1982; co-author: Mammals of the Northern Great Plains, Mammals of the Plains States, Mammals of Colorado. Mem. non-game adv. council Colo. Div. Wildlife, 1972-76, Colo. Natural Areas Council, 1975-80. Mem. Am. Soc. Mammalogists (editor 1981-87), Southwestern Assn. Naturalists (editor 1976-80), Rocky Mountain Biol. Lab. (trustee 1979-83), The Nature Conservancy (Colo. chpt. trustee 1989—). Office: U Colo PO Box 334 Boulder CO 80309-0334

ARMSTRONG, F(REDRIC) MICHAEL, retired insurance company executive; b. Wichita, Kans., Dec. 20, 1942; s. Frederick Dale and Virginia Pauline A.; m. Patricia R. Latif, Dec. 13, 1976. BS in Elec. Engring., MIT, 1964; MBA, Stanford U., 1966. Mgr. capital appropriations Trans World

Airlines, N.Y.C., 1966-69; corp. planner Transam. Corp., San Francisco, 1969-70; v.p. Transam. Film Service, Salt Lake City, 1970-73, also bd. dir.; v.p. fin. Europe Transam. Airlines, Madrid, Spain, 1973-75, v.p. planning and info. svcs., Oakland, Calif., 1975-77; exec. v.p. fin. Budget Rent a Car Corp., Chgo., 1977-83, also bd. dir.; exec. v.p., chief adminstrv. officer Transam. Ins. Group, L.A., 1983-93, also bd. dir.; bd. dirs. Melia Internat. Hotels, Panama, The Canadian Surety Co., Ins. Value Added Network Service, River Thames Ins. Co., London, Fairmont Fin. Inc., Mason-McDuffie Ins. Svc., Inc., The Completion Bond Co. Mem. adv. coun. Pierce Coll.

ARMSTRONG, GENE LEE, systems engineering consultant, retired aerospace company executive; b. Clinton, Ill., Mar. 9, 1922; s. George Dewey and Ruby Imald (Dickerson) A. m. Lael Jeanne Baker, Apr. 3, 1946; children—Susan Lael, Roberta Lynn, Gene Lee. BS with high honors, U. Ill., 1948, MS, 1951. registered profl. engr., Calif. With Boeing Aircraft, 1948-50, 51-52; chief engr. astronautics div., corp. dir. Gen. Dynamics, 1954-65; chief engr. Def. Systems Group TRW, Redondo Beach, Calif., 1956-86; pvt. cons. systems engring. Def. Systems Group TRW, 1986—; Mem. NASA Research Adv. Com. on Control, Guidance & Navigation, 1959-62. Contbr. chpts. to books, articles to profl. publs. Served to 1st lt. USAAF, 1942-45. Decorated Air medal; recipient alumni awards U. Ill., 1965, 77;. Mem. Am. Math. Soc., AIAA, Nat. Mgmt. Assn., Am. Def. Preparedness Assn., Masons. Home: 5242 Bryant Cir Westminster CA 92683-1713 Office: Armstrong Sys Engring Co PO Box 86 Westminster CA 92684-0086

ARMSTRONG, GLENN GARNETT, artist, retired postal executive; b. Nashville, May 19, 1916; s. Garnett and Frances Elizabeth (Hawkins) A.; m. Mary Jule Zito, July 5, 1960; children: Barbara Lynn, Elizabeth Marie, Rebecca Ann, Glenn Garnett Jr. Student, U. N.Mex., 1934-36; studied art with Carl Von Hassler, 1946-48; student, U. Ga., 1960, Northwestern U., 1962. Clk. U.S. Postal Svc., Albuquerque, 1936-47, foreman, 1947-50, asst. supt. mails, 1950-55, dist. mgr., 1955-59; regional mgr. U.S. Postal Svc., Atlanta, 1959-71; real estate broker Atlanta, 1971-80; ind. artist Albuquerque, 1980—; chief nat. staffing survey team U.S. Postal Svc., Washington, 1966; speaker in field. One-man shows include Mus. N.Mex., Santa Fe, 1952, Botts Meml. Gallery, Albuquerque, 1953; oil paintings represented in Gov.'s Gallery, Santa Fe, 1993 and permanent collections, nationwide. Mem. City Planning Bd., Albuquerque, 1950. With U.S. Army, 1943-45, ETO. Mem. N.Mex. Art League, Albuquerque United Artists, Albuquerque Arts Alliance. Republican. Roman Catholic. Home and Office: 1501 Park Ave SW Albuquerque NM 87104-1023

ARMSTRONG, JOANNA, education educator; b. Vienna, Austria, Feb. 3, 1915; came to U.S., 1946; m. David B. Armstrong, Mar. 12, 1946 (dec. Feb. 1992). Diploma, Kindergarten Tchr. State Coll., Vienna, 1933, Sorbonne, 1935; MA, U. Utah, 1951; EdD, U. Houston, 1959. Caseworker, interpreter Czech Refugee Trust Fund, London, 1939-41; tchr. French Gt. Missenden, Bucks, 1941-43; sec., interpreter U.S. Army, England and France, 1943-46; instr. Coll. William and Mary, Williamsburg, Va., 1951-55, U. St. Thomas, Houston, 1957-59; chmn. langs. sect. South Tex. Coll., Houston, 1961-62; assoc. prof. fgn. langs. Tex. So. U., Houston, 1962-68, dir. NDEA Inst., 1964, 65; assoc. prof. sch. edn. tng. headstart tchrs. U. Tex., El Paso, 1968-71; cons. office Child Devel. HEW, Kansas City, Mo., 1973-75; ret., 1975; cons. Tex. Edn. Agy., Austin, 1965; sec. U.S. Forest Svc., Ely, Nev., 1948; dir. summer programs U. Bordeaux, Pau, U. Zaragoza. Author: (book) A European Excursion-From the Mediterranean to the Alps, 1967, Surprising Encounters, 1994; contbr. articles to profl. publs. Vol. Long Beach (Calif.) Symphony, 1978-81, Long Beach Opera, 1982-88, Long Beach Cambodian Scs., 1983-85; mem. Normandy Found. (participant 50th D-Day anniversary 1994). Decorated chevalier Ordre des Palmes Académiques; recipient award Heart Start, 1971, Pres. plaque Alliance Francaise El Paso, 1971, Commemorative medal of Freedom, Coun. of Normandy, France, 1994. Mem. Long Beach Women's Music Club (program chmn. 1986-88, mem. choral sect. 1989-94, 1st v.p. 1990-92, rec. sec., chmn. opera sect. 1993-94), U.S.-China People Friendship Assn. (sec. 1987—, rec. sec. 1992-93). Home: 120 Alamitos Ave Apt 34 Long Beach CA 90802-5330

ARMSTRONG, JOE EDWIN, energy management educator, consultant; b. Texarkana, Tex., July 23, 1927; s. Terry Milton and Clara Jepta (Parker) A.; m. Allene Wright, Dec. 1949; children: Keith, Donna, Shelly; m. Marilyn Duffy, Sept. 1975; m. Karen Francis Urke, Sept. 24, 1988. BSEE, U. Tex., 1952, MS in Comm. Engring., 1956, PhD in Elec. Engring., 1960; MA in Ancient History, San Jose State U., 1975. Lab. mgr. Sylvania EDL, Mountain View, Calif., 1960-64, ESL, Inc., Sunnyvale, Calif., 1964-66; cons. Nat. Security Agy., Washington, 1966-68; prof. engring. San Jose (Calif.) State U., 1968-75; rschr. energy policy SRI Internat., Menlo Park, Calif., 1975-81; lectr. Sonoma State U., Rohnert Park, Calif., 1981—; prin. Armstrong Assoc., Healdsburg, Calif., 1981—. Author: Strategies for Conducting Technology Assessment, 1979, Tales of a Fledgling Homestead, 1985, P.K. Preacher Kid Stories from Arkansas, 1993; editor newsletter Hard Row to Hoe, 1988—. Lt. comdr. USN, 1946-49, 56-58, Korea. Home: 239 East St Healdsburg CA 95448-4446

ARMSTRONG, JOHN A., food products executive; b. 1925. V.p. Fresh Internat. Corp., Salinas, Calif., 1973—; v.p., sec. Bruce Church Sys. Inc., Salinas, 1973—. Office: Bruce Church Inc 1020 Merrill St Salinas CA 93901-4409*

ARMSTRONG, LLOYD, JR., university official, physics educator; b. Austin, Tex., May 19, 1940; s. Lloyd and Beatrice (Jackson) A.; m. Judith Glantz, July 9, 1965; 1 son, Wade Matthew. B.S. in Physics, M.I.T., 1962; Ph.D. in Physics, U. Calif., Berkeley, 1966. Postdoctoral physicist Lawrence Berkeley (Calif.) Lab., 1965-66, cons., 1976; sr. physicist Westinghouse Research Labs., Pitts., 1967-68, cons., 1968-70; research asso. Johns Hopkins U., 1968-69, asst. prof. physics, 1969-73, assoc. prof., 1973-77, prof., 1977-93, chmn. dept. physics and astronomy, 1985-87, dean Sch. Arts and Scis., 1987-93; provost, sr. v.p. for acad. affairs U. So. Calif., L.A., 1993—, prof. physics, 1993—; assoc. rsch. scientist Nat. Ctr. Sci. Rsch., Orsay, France, 1972-73; vis. fellow Joint Inst. Lab. Astrophysics, Boulder, Colo., 1978-79; program officer NSF, 1981-93, mem. adv. com. for physics, 1985-87, mem. visitors com. physics divsn., 1991; chmn. com. atomic and molecular scis. NAS/NRC, 1985-88, mem. bd. physics and astronomy, 1989—; mem. adv. bd. Inst. for Theoretical Physics, Santa Barbara, 1992—, chmn., 1994-95, Inst. Theoretical Atomic and Molecular Physics, Cambridge, Mass., 1994—. Author: Theory of Hyperfine Structure of Free Atoms, 1971; contbr. articles to profl. jours. NSF grantee, 1972-90; Dept. Energy grantee, 1975-82. Fellow Am. Phys. Soc. Office: Office of Provost ADM 102-4019 Los Angeles CA 90089-4019

ARMSTRONG, ORVILLE, lawyer; b. Austin, Tex., Jan. 21, 1929; s. Orville Alexander and Velma Lucille (Reed) A.; m. Mary Dean Macfarlane. BBA, U. Tex., Austin, 1953; LLB, U. So. Calif., 1956. Bar: Calif., 1957, U.S. Ct. Appeals (9th cir.) 1958, U.S. Supreme Ct. 1980. Ptnr., Gray, Binkley & Pfaelzer, 1956-61, Pfaelzer, Robertson, Armstrong & Woodard, L.A., 1961-66, Armstrong & Lloyd, L.A., 1966-74, Macdonald, Halsted & Laybourne, L.A., 1975-88, Baker & McKenzie, 1988-90; judge Superior Ct. State of Calif., 1991-92, assoc. justice ct. appeal State of Calif., 1993—; lectr. Calif. Continuing Edn. of Bar. Served with USAF, 1946-49. Fellow ABA, Am. Coll. Trial Lawyers; mem. State Bar Calif. (gov. 1983-87, pres. 1986-87), L.A. County Bar Assn. (trustee 1971-72), Chancery Club (pres. 1988), Calif. Club. Baptist. Home: 2385 Coniston Pl San Marino CA 91108-2102 Office: 300 S Spring St Los Angeles CA 90013-1230

ARMSTRONG, PAUL BRADFORD, English educator, dean; b. Morristown, N.J., Oct. 31, 1949; s. James Harrison and Asta (Jensen) A.; m. Christina Meryl Buck, Jan. 2, 1971; children: Timothy Buck, Margaret Buck. AB in History and Lit. summa cum laude, Harvard U., 1971; AM in Modern Thought and Lit., Stanford U., 1974, PhD in Modern Thought and Lit., 1977. Asst. prof. English U. Va., Charlottesville, 1976-83; assoc. prof. English Ga. Inst. Tech., Atlanta, 1983-86; prof. English U. Oreg., Eugene, 1986—, head dept. English, 1986-91, assoc. dean Coll. Arts and Scis., 1994—; vis. prof. Free U. of Berlin, 1985-86, U. Copenhagen, fall 1994. Author: The Phenomenology of Henry James, 1983, The Challenge of Bewilderment: Understanding and Representation in James, Conrad, and Ford, 1987, Conflicting Readings: Variety and Validity in Interpretation, 1990; mem. editl. bd. Henry James Rev. Mem. exec. com. Assn. Depts. of English, 1990-93. Recipient prize in lit. criticism Twentieth Century Lit., 1985; Alexander von Humboldt Found. rsch. fellow U. Konstanz, Fed. Republic Germany, 1981-82. Mem. MLA (William Riley Parker prize 1983, rep. English Coalition Conf. 1987), Nat. Coun. Tchrs. English (commn. on lit. 1990-93), Tchrs. for a Dem. Culture, Soc. for Critical Exch., Joseph Conrad Soc., Phi Beta Kappa. Office: U Oreg Dept English Eugene OR 97403

ARMSTRONG, PETER BROWNELL, biologist; b. Syracuse, N.Y., Apr. 27, 1939; s. Philip Brownell and Marian Louise (Schmuck) A.; m. Margaret Tryon, Sept. 22, 1962; children: Katharine, Elisabeth, Philip. BS, U. Rochester, 1961; PhD, Johns Hopkins U., 1966. Asst. prof. Biology U. Calif., Davis, 1966-72, assoc. prof. Biology, 1972-80, prof. Biology, 1980—; sci. trustee Marine Biol. Lab., Woods Hole, Maine, 1986-90. Contbr. articles to profl. jours. Office: U Calif Dept Molecular and Cell Biology Davis CA 95616-8755

ARMSTRONG, R(OBERT) DEAN, entertainer; b. Serena, Ill., July 2, 1923; s. Francis Robert and Viola D. (Thompson) A.; m. Ardith Roberta Taylor, Jan. 10, 1943; 1 child, Larry Dean. Grad. high sch., Serena, Ill.; student, Joliet (Ill.) Conservatory of Music, 1942. Host Dean Armstrong Show Sta. KOLD-TV, Tucson, 1953-75; leader, owner Ariz. Dance Hands, Tucson, 1946—. Served with U.S. Mil., 1943-45, ETO, PTO. Recipient Jefferson award Am. Inst. for Pub. Svc., 1992; inducted into Tucson Area Music Assn. Hall of Fame, 1994. Mem. Tucson Musicians Assn. (meritorious svc. award 1981), VFW, Western Music Assn. (charter mem.), Profl. Western Music Assn. Democrat. Methodist. Lodges: Elks, Eagles. Home and Office: 4265 N Avenida Del Cazador Tucson AZ 85718-7005

ARMSTRONG, SAUNDRA BROWN, federal judge; b. Oakland, Calif., Mar. 23, 1947; d. Coolidge Logan and Pauline Marquette (Bearden) Brown; m. George Walter Armstrong, Apr. 18, 1982. B.A., Calif. State U.-Fresno, 1969; J.D., U. San Francisco, 1977. Bar: Calif. 1977, U.S. Supreme Ct. 1984. Policewoman Oakland Police Dept., 1970-77; prosecutor, dep. dist. atty. Alameda County Dist. Atty., Oakland, 1978-79, 80-82; staff atty. Calif. Legis. Assembly Com. on Criminal Justice, Sacramento, 1979-80; trial atty. Dept. Justice, Washington, 1982-83; vice chmn. U.S. Consumer Product Safety Commn., Washington, 1984-86; commr. U.S. Parole Commn., Washington, 1986-89; judge Alameda Superior Ct., 1989-91, U.S. Dist. Ct. (no. dist.) Calif., San Francisco, 1991—. Recipient commendation Calif. Assembly, 1980. Mem. Nat. Bar Assn., ABA, Calif. Bar Assn., Charles Houston Bar Assn., Black C. of C., Phi Alpha Delta. Democrat. Baptist. Office: US Dist Ct 450 Golden Gate Ave Rm 17-6618 PO Box 36060 San Francisco CA 94102*

ARMSTRONG, WALLACE DOWAN, JR., data processor; b. Los Angeles, Feb. 9, 1926; s. Wallace Dowan and Vina Edith (Kreinbring) A.; BS cum laude, U. So. Calif., 1951; postgrad. U. Oslo (Norway), 1955; 1 son, Erik Bentung. Supr. accounting Ramo Wooldridge Corp., 1955-60; mgr. programmers, systems analyst Aerospace Corp., El Segundo, Calif., 1960-80, mgr. bus. systems, 1980—. Mem. Common Cause, Handgun Control, Inc. With USMCR, 1944-46, 51. Mem. Data Processing Mgmt. Assn. Home: 25713 Crest Rd Torrance CA 90505-7022 Office: Aerospace Corp 2350 E El Segundo Blvd El Segundo CA 90245-4609

ARNAULT, RONALD J., petroleum company executive; b. 1943. BA, Amherst Coll., 1965; MBA, U. Pa., 1969. With Gen. Electric Co., 1965-66, Singer Co., 1966-67, Atlantic Richfield Co., Los Angeles, 1969—; analyst N.Y. office, 1969-70, asst. controller, 1970-72; mgr. integrated planning L.A. office, 1972-75, mgr. planning & control, 1975-77, v.p. planning div., 1977-80, sr. v.p., div. pres., 1980-84, exec. v.p., CFO, 1984-90; bd. dirs. ARCO, 1987—, CFO, 1992—; bd. dirs. ARCO Chem. Co. Office: Atlantic Richfield Co 515 S Flower St Los Angeles CA 90071-2201

ARNE, KENNETH GEORGE, mining executive, mineral consultant; b. Prairie City, Oreg., Feb. 5, 1942; s. John Ralph Arne and Mary Louise (Roland) Noud; m. Elizabeth Andre Spodnick, Mar. 23, 1968 (div. June 1992); children: Christopher L., Melissa A.; m. Nina A. Sablina, Aug. 31, 1994. BS in Engring., Mont. Tech., Butte, 1964; MBA, Stanford U., 1969. Registered profl. engr., Ariz., Colo. Petroleum engr. Amoco, Inc., Denver, 1964-67; dir. uranium mktg. Conoco, Inc., Stamford, Conn., 1969-79; 2d v.p. Continental Ill. Bank, Chgo., 1979-82; gen. mgr. Can-Am Corp., Tucson, 1982-88; fin. analyst Minorco, U.S.A. and affiliates, Denver, 1988-92; mineral cons. in pvt. practice Denver, 1992-93; mgr. ops. M.K. Gold Co., 1994—; v.p. commonwealth and British minerals Plc Taror Mine, Penjikent Region, Tajikistan; cons. Econ. Adv. Project, Republic of Georgia, 1992. Mem. AIME, Can. Inst. Mining and Metallurgy, Colo. Mining Assn. (bd. dirs. 1990-92), Denver Rep. Club, Rotary Club Evergreen, Theta Tau. Roman Catholic. Home: 1170 Crescent Ave Klamath Falls OR 97601-2516 Office: Sogdiana Townsite, Penjikent Tajikistan

ARNELL, WALTER JAMES WILLIAM, mechanical engineering educator, consultant; b. Farnborough, Eng., Jan. 9, 1924; came to U.S., 1953, naturalized, 1960; s. James Albert and Daisy (Payne) A.; m. Patricia Catherine Cannon, Nov. 12, 1955; children—Sean Paul, Victoria Clare, Sarah Michele Arnell. Aero. Engr., Royal Aircraft Establishment, 1946; BSc, U. London, 1953, PhD, 1967; MA, Occidental Coll., Los Angeles, 1956; MS, U. So. Calif., 1958. Lectr. Poly. and Northampton Coll. Advance Tech., London, 1948-53; instr. U. So. Calif., Los Angeles, 1954-59; asst. prof. mech. engring. Calif. State U., Long Beach, 1959-62, assoc. prof., 1962-66, prof., 1966-71, chmn. dept. mech. engring., 1964-65, acting chmn. div. engring., 1964-66, dean engring., 1967-69, researcher Ctr. Engring. Research; affiliate faculty dept. ocean engring. U. Hawaii, 1970-74; adj. prof. systems and insdl. engring. U. Ariz., 1981—; pres. Lenra Assocs. Ltd., 1973—; chmn., project mgr. Hawaii Environ. Simulation Lab., 1971-72. Contbr. articles to profl. jours. Trustee Rehab. Hosp. of the Pacific, 1975-78. Mem. Royal Aero. Soc., AIAA, IEEE Systems Man and Cybernetics Soc., AAUP, Am. Psychol. Assn., Soc. Engring., Psychology, Human Factors Soc., Ergonomics Soc., Psi Chi, Alpha Pi Mu, Tau Beta Pi, Phi Kappa Phi, Pi Tau Sigma. Home: 4491 E Ft Lowell Rd Tucson AZ 85712-1106

ARNESON, PATRICIA ANN, speech communication educator; b. Glencoe, Minn., Mar. 22, 1961; d. Richard Norman and Darlene Marie (Hanke) A. AA, St. Cloud State U., 1981, BA, 1983; MS, So. Ill. U., 1984; PhD, Ohio U., 1987. Teaching asst. So. Ill. U., Carbondale, 1983-84, Ohio U., Athens, 1984-87; asst. prof. speech comm. Bowling Green (Ohio) State U., 1987-90; asst. prof. speech comm. U. No. Colo., Greeley, 1990-93, assoc. prof., 1993—; cons. Colo. Air N.G., Greeley, 1994; speaker and trainer in field. Author book chpts.; contbr. articles to profl. jours. Vol. A Woman's Place, Greeley, 1991-93, Eldergarden, Greeley, 1994—. Recipient Pres.'s Spl. Recognition award U. No. Colo., 1993; named to Outstanding Young Women of Am., 1989. Mem. Speech Comm. Assn., We. States Comm. Assn. (sec., vice chair, chair comm. theory and rsch. div.), Colo. Speech Comm. Assn. (co-chair interpersonal, small group and orgnl. comm. interest group). Office: U No Colo Dept Speech Comm Greeley CO 80639

ARNEY, JAMES DOUGLAS, forestry biometrics consultant; b. Hoquiam, Wash., Dec. 9, 1941; s. James Dennis and Martha (Wylam) A.; m. Jo Ann Joyce Loehrke, Febr. 14, 1991; children: Michael, BettiJean. BS in Forest Mgmt., U. Mont., 1965; MS in Forest Mensuration, Oreg. State U., 1968, PhD in Forest Biometrics, 1971. Forest mensurationist U.S. Forest Svc. Expt. Sta., Portland, 1965-66; rsch. scientist Canadian Forestry Svc., Victoria, B.C., 1970-72; rsch. mgr. Weyerhaeuser Co., Centralia, Wash., 1973-80; mgr. forest dept. Reid, Collins & Assocs., Vancouver, B.C., 1980-81; rsch. forester Potlatch Corp., Lewiston, Idaho, 1982-84; forestry cons. Applied Biometrics, Spokane, Wash., 1985-88, Mason, Bruce & Girard, Inc., Portland, 1989-94, Forest Biometrics, Gresham, Oreg., 1995—. Mem. Soc. Am. Foresters, We. Forestry Assn. Home: 3486 SW Tegart Ave Gresham OR 97080 Office: Forest Biometrics 655 W Burnside Rd Gresham OR 97030

ARNITZ, RICK, artist; b. St. Louis, Dec. 4, 1949. BA, U. Calif., Berkeley, 1975, MA, 1980, MFA, 1982. One-man shows include Worth Rider Gallery, Berkeley, 1980, Pro Arts Gallery, Oakland, 1983, Union Gallery, San Jose, Calif., 1984, Stephen Wirtz Gallery, San Francisco, 1988, 91, 93, 94; San Francisco Mus. Modern Art, 1989, Univ. Art Mus., Santa Barbara, Calif., 1990, Plz. Gallery, San Francisco, 1993; exhibited in group shows at Richmond (Calif.) Art Ctr., 1980, 83, San Jose Inst. Contemporary Art, 1981, Berkeley Art Ctr., 1981, Univ. Art Mus., Berkeley, 1982, San Jose Inst. Contemporary Art, 1983, Pro Arts Gallery, 1985, 1078 Gallery, Chico, Calif., 1986, Berkeley Art Ctr., 1987, Nexus Gallery, Berkeley, 1988, Oakland Mus., 1990, David Beitzel Gallery, N.Y.C., 1990, Stephen Wirtz Gallery, 1991, 95, Elizabeth Leach Gallery, Portland, Oreg., 1991, Calif. Palace of Legion of Honor, San Francisco, 1991, Betsy Senior Contemporary Prints, N.Y.C., 1991, Susan Cummins Gallery, Mill Valley, Calif., 1992, Miller Block Gallery, Boston, 1992, Capp Street, San Francisco, 1994, others. Recipient Roslyn Schneider Eisner award U. Calif. Berkeley, 1980, First award Berkeley Art Ctr., 1981, Third award Calif. State Fair, 1981, Art Space Support grant, 1990, Nat. Endowment for the Arts award, 1992. Office: Stephen Wirtz Gallery 49 Geary St 3rd Fl San Francisco CA 94108-5707

ARNN, LARRY PAUL, foundation executive, editor; b. Borger, Tex., Oct. 8, 1952; s. Robert Paul and Georgia (Asberry) A.; m. Penelope Margaret Carus Houghton, Oct. 20, 1979; children: Katy, Henry, Alice. BA in Polit. Sci., Ark. State U., 1974; MA in Govt., Claremont (Calif.) U., 1976, PhD, 1985. Dir. rsch. Winston Churchill Biography, Oxford, Eng., 1977-80; treas. Claremont Inst., Montclair, Calif., 1980-85; pres. Claremont Inst., 1985—; editor Pub. Rsch., Syndicated, Montclair, 1980-85; pres. Pub. Rsch., Syndicated, 1985—; exec. dir. Aequus Inst., Montclair, 1985—; bd. dirs. North Cen. Life Ins. Co., chair various profl. panels; mem. Nat. Commn. on Regulatory Barriers to Affordable Housing, 1990—; lectr. on Winston Churchill. Editor The Claremont Letter, 1981-83; pub. Claremont Review of Books, 1985—; contbr. numerous articles to profl. jours. Mem. planning com. United Way, Upland, Calif., 1990. Fellow Earhart Found., 1978-80, Rotary Found. fellow, 1977-78, Alcoa Found. fellow, 1972-74, Ark. State U. fellow, 1971-72, Richard M. Weaver fellow Intercollegiate Studies Inst., 1975. Mem. Am. Polit. Sci. Assn., Winston S. Churchill Assn. U.S. (fellow 1977-80), Western Polit. Sci. Assn., Phila. Soc., Pi Sigma Alpha. Republican. Episcopal. Home: 1136 W Iowa Ct Claremont CA 91711-2419 Office: Claremont Inst 250 W 1st St Ste 330 Claremont CA 91711-4744

ARNOLD, JAMES RICHARD, chemist, educator; b. New Brunswick, N.J., May 5, 1923; s. Abraham Samuel and Julia (Jacobs) A.; m. Louise Clark, Oct. 11, 1952; children: Robert C., Theodore J., Kenneth C. A.B., Princeton U., 1943, M.A., 1945, Ph.D., 1946. Postdoctoral fellow Inst. Nuclear Studies, U. Chgo., 1946-47, mem. faculty, 1948-55; NRC fellow Harvard U., 1947-48; mem. faculty chemistry Princeton U., 1955-58; assoc. prof. chemistry U. Calif., San Diego, 1958-60; prof. U. Calif., 1960-92, Harold C. Urey prof., 1983-92, chmn. dept. chemistry, 1960-63; assoc. Manhattan Project, 1943-46; dir. Calif. Space Inst., 1980-89; prin. investigator Calif. Space Grant Consortium, 1989—; mem. various bds. NASA, 1959; mem. space sci. bd. NAS, 1970-74, mem. com. on sci. and pub. policy, 1970-77. Mem. editorial bd.: Ann. Rev. Nuclear Chemistry, 1972; asso. editor: Revs. Geophysics and Space Physics, 1972-75, Moon, 1972—; contbr. articles to profl. jours. Pres. Torrey Pines Elem. Sch. PTA, 1964-65; pres. La Jolla Democratic Club, 1965-66; mem. nat. council World Federalists-U.S.A., 1970-72. Recipient E.O. Lawrence medal AEC, 1968, Leonard medal Meteoritical Soc., 1976, Kuiper award Am. Astron. Soc., 1993; asteroid 2143 named Jimarnold in his honor, 1980; Guggenheim fellow, India, 1972-73. Mem. Nat. Acad. Sci., Am. Acad. Arts and Scis., Internat. Acad. Astronautics, Am. Chem. Soc., AAAS, Fedn. Am. Scientists, World Federalist Assn. Office: U Calif San Diego Dept Chemistry Code 0524 La Jolla CA 92093

ARNOLD, JAMES TRACY, physicist; b. Taiyuanfu, Shansi, China, Oct. 23, 1920; s. Roger David and Eleanor (Tracy) A.; m. Marna Craig, Aug. 17, 1957; children: Erica, Laura, David, Andrew. BA, Oberlin Coll., 1942; grad., USN Test Pilot Sch., 1946; PhD, Stanford U., 1954. Cert. jr. coll. tchr. Instr. Oberlin (Ohio) Coll., 1947-48; grad. asst. Stanford (Calif.) U., 1948-54, rsch. assoc., 1955-57; spl. asst. to dir. European Ctr. for Nuclear Rsch., Geneva, 1954-55; asst. prof. Oreg. State U., Corvallis, 1957-58; engr. Varian Assocs., Palo Alto, Calif., 1958-62, sr. scientist, 1962—. Author: Simplified Digital Automation With Microprocessors, 1976; contbr. articles to profl. jours. Active St. Andrews Sch. Bd., Saratoga, Calif., 1960-72. With USN, 1942-47, comdr. Res., 1950-72. Republican. Episcopalian. Office: Varian Assocs 3075 Hansen Way Palo Alto CA 94304-1025

ARNOLD, JANET NINA, health care consultant; b. Poughkeepsie, N.Y., Apr. 23, 1933; d. Paul Dudley and Pauline Katherine (Board) Bartram; AB, Vassar Coll., 1955; postgrad. Sch. Med. Tech., Albany Med. Center, 1955-56; MS, Vassar Coll., 1963; MHSM, Webster Coll., 1981; m. Robert William Arnold, Dec. 19, 1954; children: Paul Dudley, Janet Elizabeth. Research asst., med. technologist H. Aird Boswell, M.D., Troy, N.Y., 1956-59; teaching supr., adminstrv. cons. Vassar Bros. Hosp., Poughkeepsie, N.Y., 1959-69; adv. to med. lab., lectr. med. mycology Vassar Coll., Poughkeepsie, 1961-66; asst. adminstr., lab. mgr. Boulder (Colo.) Meml. Hosp., 1975-80; cons. hosp. planning Mercy Med. Center, Denver, 1981-82; clin. lab. dir./adminstr. Humana, 1982-85, cons. health care mgmt., 1982-85; with MRI, 1985—, ptnr., 1988; pres. Arnold and Assocs., 1992—; ptnr. InterExec (divsn. MRI), 1994—; acad./adminstrv. cons. U. Guam, Vassar Coll., Boulder Community Hosp., Humana Int., 1990—, others. Sec., bd. dirs. Sanitas Fed. Credit Union, 1977-78, pres., 1979-82; teaching fellow Vassar Coll., 1961-63, unrestricted fund chmn., 1989—. Contbr. NMC, 1988-92. NSF research fellow, 1960-62. Mem. Am. Acad. Microbiology, Soc. for Gen. Microbiology, Am. Soc. Med. Technologists, Colo. Public Health Assn., Med. Mycological Soc. of the Ams. Republican. Episcopalian. Asso. editor Am. Jour. Med. Tech., 1980-88; contbr. articles to profl. jours. Home: 4195 Chippewa Dr Boulder CO 80303-3610

ARNOLD, JEANNE ELOISE, anthropologist, educator; b. Cleve., July 9, 1955; d. Lawrence Fred and Marybelle Eloise (Culp) A. BA, U. Mich., 1976; MA, U. Calif., Santa Barbara, 1979, PhD, 1983. Prof. anthropology U. No. Iowa, Cedar Falls, 1984-88; assoc. dir. Inst. Archaeology UCLA, 1988—, prof. anthropology, 1988—; vis. instr. anthropology Rice U., Houston, 1981; vis. prof. anthropology Oreg. State U., Corvallis, 1983-84; sr. archaeologist Infotec Rsch., Inc., Sonora, Calif., 1986-87; cons. in field. Author 3 books; contbr. articles and revs. to over 40 profl. jours and over 35 chpts. to books. Rsch. grantee NSF, 1988-91, 95-98; Rsch. and Ednl. grantee U. Calif. at L.A. and Santa Barbara, 1977—. Mem. Am. Anthropol. Assn., Soc. Am. Archaeology, Soc. Calif. Archaeology, Inst. Archaeology (mem. editorial bd. 1988—), Sigma Xi, Phi Beta Kappa. Office: UCLA Dept Anthropology 405 Hilgard Ave Los Angeles CA 90095-1553

ARNOLD, JOAN DEAN, publisher; b. Marshall, Mo., Jan. 12, 1944; d. Alfred Douglas and Imogene Devonia (Simmons) Kidd; m. John Gerald Arnold (div.); children: John Douglas, Christopher Alan. Owner, mgr. Harbor Shopping Ctr., Harbor Landing, Mile Sq. Plaza and Garfield Plaza, Huntington Beach, Calif., 1975-83; designer, owner The Dream Factory, Huntington, 1974—; founder, owner Huntington Pacific Thrift and Loan, 1982—; owner, pub. Sandwich Island Pub Co. Ltd., Lahaina, Hawaii, 1984—; pub. The Best of Maui, 1989—; artist Sea Side Fine Art, Lahaina, Hawaii; developer, owner Double Gemini Corp., Huntington, 1978-83; chairwoman Sandwich Islands Pub. Co., Ltd., 1984—; mem bd. dirs. Lahainatown Action Com., 1990—, Kapalua Art Sch. Mem. archtl. com. Orangewood Home for Battered Children, Orange, Calif., 1980; dist. chmn. Maui County Reps.; bd. dirs. W. Maui Youth Ctr., Lahania, Lahania Salvation Army, Kapalua Art Sch. Mem. Nat. Oil and Acrylic Painter Soc., Am. Soc. Classical Realism, Hawaii Pub. Assn., Small Mag. Pub. Assn., Hawaii Visitors Assn., Maui C. of C. (bd. dirs.), Hotel Assn. Hawaii, Lahaina Art Soc. (bd. dirs), Soroptimists (bd. dirs.), Confrerie de la Chaine des Rotisseurs. Home: 31 Kai Pali Pl Lahaina HI 96761-1661 Office: PO Box 10669 Lahaina HI 96761-0669

ARNOLD, KENNETH JAMES, lawyer, publishing company executive; b. Brighton, Colo., Sept. 10, 1927; s. Kenneth Wilburt and Frances Irene (Lloyd) A. BA, U. Calif., Berkeley, 1949; JD, U. Calif., San Francisco, 1958. Bar: Calif. 1959. Pvt. practice law San Francisco, 1959-60, 63—, Sacramento, 1960-62; owner Law Book Svc. Co., San Francisco, 1969—; rsch. atty. Calif. Supreme Ct., Sacramento, 1960-62, Calif. Ct. Appeals for 1st Appelate Dist., San Francisco, 1958-60; asst. sr. editor-in-chief Matthew Bender & Co., San Francisco, 1963-81, staff author, 1981-87, sr. staff author,

1987-92; lectr. in field, 1972-81; cons. Calif. State Jud. Coun., 1970-75, Calif. Ctr. Jud. Edn. and Rsch., 1974—, Calif. Coll. Trial Judges, 1975, McGeorge Coll. Law, U. Pacific, 1975-80; mem. Calif. Legal Forms Com., 1971-73. Author: California Courts and Judges Handbook, 1968, 2d rev. edit., 1973, 3d rev. edit., 1979, 4th rev. edit., 1985, 5th rev. edit., 1988, 6th rev. edit., 1993, with supplements for all edits.; California Justice Court Manual, 1971 supplement, Commencing Civil Actions in California, 1975, and supplements; (with others) California Points and Authorities, 23 vols., 1964-92, California Forms of Pleadings and Practice, 55 vols., 1966-92, California Legal Forms, 25 vols., 1967-69, California Family Law Practice, 6 vols., 1977-78, California Civil Actions, 5 vols., 1982-92; other manuals and handbooks; feature writer Barclays Law Monthly, 1979-82; editor-in-chief Vector Mag., 1965-67. Bd. dirs. Soc. for Individual Rights, 1965-67, PRIDE Found., San Francisco, 1974-77. With U.S. Army, 1952-55. Mem. State Bar Calif., U. Calif. Hastings Alumni Assn., Calif. Supreme Ct. Hist. Soc., 9th Jud. Dist. Hist. Soc., VFW, Am. Legion. Home and Office: 369 Harvard St San Francisco CA 94134-1345

ARNOLD, MICHAEL JAMES, naval officer, aerospace engineer; b. Guatemala City, Guatemala, Jan. 8, 1946; s. James Elliott and Roberta Elaine (Anderson) A.; m. Michelle Lee Connelly, Feb. 1, 1969; children: Reenie Lee, Tige, Donovan. BS in Mech. Engring., U. Idaho, 1969; MS in Aero. Engring. with distinction, Naval Postgrad. Sch., 1978. Commd. ensign USN, 1969, advanced through grades to comdr., 1984; helicopter flight tng. Pensacola, Fla., 1969-70; pilot search and rescue Kingsville, Tex., 1970-72; pilot antisubmarine warfare (HS-4) San Diego, 1972-76; with USS Tarawa, San Diego, 1979-81, Antisubmarine Warefare Wing Pacific Fleet, San Diego, 1981-84, Naval Air Systems Command, Washington, 1984-88; dep. dir. Cruise Missiles Prog. Western Region, San Diego, 1988-91, dir., 1991-92; ret., 1992. Mem. Assn. Old Crows, Navy Helicopter Assn., Apple Programmers and Developers Assn. (ind.), Sigma Xi (assoc.). Roman Catholic.

ARNOLD, MICHAEL NEAL, real property appraiser, consultant; b. Madera, Calif., June 6, 1947; s. John Patrick and Patricia (Neal) A.; m. Suzanne Elizabeth Badal, Aug. 31, 1968; children: C. Matthew Neal Arnold, Nathaniel T. Badal Arnold, Andrew T. White Arnold, Thomas A. Badal Arnold. BA in Geography, U. Calif., Santa Barbara, 1974. Cert. appraiser. Assoc. R.W. Raymond & Co., Santa Barbara, 1974; appraiser Madera County Assessor Office, 1975; assoc. Pickthorne & Assocs., San Bruno, Calif., 1975-76; ptnr. Hammock, Arnold, Smith, Santa Barbara, 1976—; instr. Santa Barbara City Coll., 1980-85. Contbr. articles to profl. jours. Coach AYSO, Santa Barbara, 1978—; cub master Boy Scouts Am., Santa Barbara, 1985. Mem. Vieja Valley Site Coun., Santa Barbara Coun. Real Estate Appraisers (sec., speaker bur.), Appraisal Inst. (instr. 1990—, grader, com. chair, officer), Amateurs Club, Tennis Club of Santa Barbara, Santa Barbara Club, Santa Barbara City Coll. (adv. coun. mem.). Episcopalian. Home: 2325 Santa Barbara St Santa Barbara CA 93105-3547 Office: Hammock Arnold Smith & Co Spencer House 200 W Victoria St Santa Barbara CA 93101-3627

ARNOLD, ROBERT LLOYD, investment broker; b. Seattle, June 18, 1952; s. Vern Lloyd and Ruth Francis (Bruty) A. Student, Bellevue Coll., Wash., 1971-71; BS magna cum laude, U. Wash., 1975; MS, Yale U., 1977. Lic. fed. securities agt. Group leader U.S. Govt., Miramonte, Calif., 1977-78; economist U.S. Govt., Walla Walla, Wash., 1978-79; gen. mgr. Full Value Roofing, Bellevue, 1979-81; transp. mgr. N.W. Hydra-Line, Inc., Seattle, 1981-83; owner Fairfields, Seattle, 1982—; investment broker Waddell & Reed, Inc., Seattle, 1983—; coord. Charles Givens Found., Seattle, 1984-85, 88—; lectr. Community Sch., Seattle, 1984—; guest speaker Kiwanis, Puyallup, Wash., 1985; seminar leader Chgo. Title Ins. Co, Seattle, 1985—. Fund raiser ARC, Seattle, 1984-85; chmn. fin. com. Unity Ch. of Seattle, 1988-90. Grantee Bloedel Found., 1973-74, Bishop Soc. grantee, 1974-75; fellow Yale U., 1975-77. Mem. Rainier Club (reciprocity com. 1994—, young Rainers com. 1994—), Yale Alumni Assn., Seattle Delta Group (lifetime, chmn. 1985—), U. Wash. Alumni Assn., Xi Sigma Pi (treas. 1974-75). Republican.

ARNOLD, ROCKY RICHARD, business and marketing consultant; b. Iola, Kans., Dec. 27, 1948; s. Dick William Virgil and Betty Jean (Rhodes) A.; m. Nazmiye Ertan, Jan. 6, 1972 (div. Aug. 1987); 1 child, Sevgi Zübeyde; m. Moneca Holly, July 28, 1990. BSME, U. Mo., Rolla, 1970; MSME, MIT, 1972; MSCE, Stanford U., 1980, PhD in Civil Engring., 1983; MBA in Mktg., Coll. Notre Dame, 1993. Registered profl. engr., Calif. Asst. structures engr. United Tech. Corp., Sunnyvale, Calif., 1972-73, sr. engr., 1978-81; staff engr. Acurex Corp., Mountain View, Calif., 1973-75; sr. engring. specialist Ford Aero. & Communications Corp., Palo Alto, Calif., 1981-83; cons. engr. Anamet Labs., Inc., Hayward, Calif., 1975-78, mgr. new bus., 1983-94; pres. Paragon Solutions, Inc., San Mateo, Calif., 1994—. Contbr. articles to profl. jours. Served to capt. USAR, 1970-78. Assoc. fellow AIAA; mem. ASME, Am. Mktg. Assn., Am. Helicopter Soc., Soc. for Advancement of Materials and Processes in Engring., Sigma Xi, Kappa Mu Epsilon, Phi Kappa Phi, Pi Tau Sigma. Republican. Baptist. Office: Paragon Solutions Inc 1 Waters Park Dr Ste 231 San Mateo CA 94403-1137

ARNOLD, RONALD HENRI, nonprofit organization executive, consultant; b. Houston, Aug. 8, 1937; s. John Andrew and Carrie Virginia (Henri) A.; m. Phoebe Anne Trogdon, Oct. 12, 1963 (dec. Feb. 1974); 1 child, Andrea; m. Janet Ann Parkhurst, Aug. 8, 1974; stepchildren: Andrea Wright, Rosalyn Wright. Tech. publ. Boeing Co., Seattle, 1961-71; cons. Northwoods Studio, Bellevue, Wash., 1971—; exec. v.p. Ctr. for Def. of Free Enterprise, Bellevue, 1984—; advisor Nat. Fed. Lands Conf., 1988-92. Author: James Watt and the Environment, 1981, Ecology Wars, 1987, The Grand Prairie Years, 1987, (with Alan Gottlieb) Trashing the Economy, 1993; editor: Stealing The National Parks, 1987; contbg. editor Logging Mgmt. mag., 1978-81, Western Conservation Jour., 1974-81. Recipient Editorial Achievement award Am. Bus. Press, 1981. Mem. AFTRA, Forest History Soc. Republican. Home: 12605 NE 2nd St Bellevue WA 98005-3206

ARNOLD, SHEILA, former state legislator; b. N.Y.C., Jan. 15, 1929; d. Michael and Eileen (Lynch) Keddy; coll. courses; m. George Longan Arnold, Nov. 12, 1960; 1 child, Peter; 1 child by previous marriage, Michael C. Young; stepchildren: Drew, George Longan, Joe. Mem. Wyo. Ho. of Reps., 1978-93, vice chmn. Laramie Regional Airport Bd. Former mem., sec. Wyo. Land Use Adv. Coms.; past pres. Dem. Women's Club, Laramie; past chmn. Albany County Dem. Party; past mem. Dem. State Com.; mem. adv. bd. Wyo. Home Health Care; former mem. Nat. Conf. State Legislatures Com. on Fiscal Affairs and Oversight Com. Recipient Spl. Recognition award from Developmentally Disabled Citizens of Wyo., 1985. Mem. Laramie Area C. of C. (pres. 1982; Top Hand award 1977), LWV (Laramie bd. dirs. 1993-94), Internat. Platform Assn., Faculty Women's Club (past pres.), VFW Ladies Aux. (pres. Post 2221), Zonta, Laramie Women's Club.

ARNOTT, ROBERT DOUGLAS, investment company executive; b. Chgo., June 29, 1954; s. Robert James Arnott and Catherine (Bonnell) Cameron; m. Roberta Faith Baker, Oct. 28, 1979; 1 child, Robert Lindsay. BA, U. Calif., Santa Barbara, 1977. V.p. Boston Co., 1977-84; pres., chief exec. officer TSA Capital Mgmt., L.A., 1984-87; v.p., strategist Salomon Bros. Inc., N.Y.C., 1987-88; pres., CEO First Quadrant Corp., Morristown, N.J., Pasadena, Calif., and London, 1988—; mem. chmn.'s adv. coun. Chgo. Bd. Options Exch., 1989—; bd. dirs. Internat. Faculty in Fin.; mem. product adv. bd. Chgo. Mercantile Exch., 1990. Editor: Asset Allocation, 1988, Active Asset Allocation, 1992; mem. editorial bd. Jour. of Investing, 1990—, Jour. Portfolio Mgmt., 1984—; contbr. articles to profl. jours. and chpts. to books. Mem. Fin. Analysts Fedn., Inst. Internat. Rsch. (adv. bd. 1990—), Assn. for Investment Mgmt. and Rsch., Inst. Quantitative Rsch. in Fin., Toronto Stock and Futures Exch. (adv. coun. 1992—). Office: 1st Quadrant Corp PO Box 7183 Pasadena CA 91109-7183

ARNQUIST, JEANETTE GREEN, charitable foundation administrator; b. Muskogee, Okla., June 11, 1944; d. Jess Edwin and Violet (Bisoni) Green; m. Clifford Warren Arnquist, Sept. 26, 1970; children: Catherine Ann, Paula Jeanette, Steven Clifford. BA, La. Poly. U., 1966; MA, Ariz. State U., 1968. Asst. mgr. Fashion Fabrics, L.A., 1972-73; substitute tchr. Hemet (Calif.) Unified Sch. Dist., 1980-84; tchr. Aquinas H.S., San Bernardino, Calif., 1984; instr. Mt. San Jacinto C.C., San Jacinto, Calif., 1984-89; coord. children and family coun. Cath. Charities, Colton, Calif., 1991—; pres. bd. dirs. Valley Restart Shelter, Hemet, 1989—; bd. dirs. Calif. Homeless and Housing Coalition, Sacramento. Mem. Cath. Social Action Dirs. of Calif., Roundtable. Office: Cath Charities 150 E Olive St Colton CA 92324-2758

ARNST, ALBERT, editor, forester; b. Portland, Oreg., July 9, 1909; s. David and Alwina (Lorenz) A. BS in Forestry, Oreg. State U., 1931; m. Della Coleen Irwin, May 1, 1939; children: Audrey Karen, Robert Craig, Rosemary. Forester, Forest Svc., U.S. Dept. Agr., Portland, Oreg., 1931-35, Medford, Oreg., 1935-36, Lakeview, Oreg., 1937, pub. info. officer, Washington, 1962-75; with Soil Conservation Svcs., Dayton, Spokane and Sedro-Woolley, (all in Wash.), 1937-45, Corvallis and Portland, Oreg., 1941-43; sales rep Skagit Steel & Iron Works, Sedro-Woolley, 1945-46; pub. info. rep. Weyerhaeuer Co., Tacoma, 1946-52; editor Timberman mag., Portland, 1952-53; editor Miller Freeman Publs., Portland, 1954-62; mng. editor Western Conservation Jour., Portland, 1975-82. Contbr. articles on forestry to profl. jours. Fellow Soc. Am. Foresters; mem. Soil Conservation Soc. Am. (charter), Oreg. Logging Conf. (hon. life), Oreg. Soc. Am. Foresters (Lifetime Achievement award 1989), Internat. Assn. Bus. Communicators (Rodney Adair Meml. award 1978, pres. 1962, 71, 79, named Communicator of Yr. 1966 nat. Pres.'s award 1983), Foggy Bottom Club (Washington) (pres. 1971), Lions. Democrat. Home: 3102 SE Holgate Rm C-201 Portland OR 97202

ARO, GLENN SCOTT, environmental and safety executive; b. Balt., Jan. 18, 1948; s. Raymond Charles Sr. and Elizabeth Virginia (Chopra) A.; m. Marlene Rose Lefler, Jan. 8, 1972 (div. June 1987); children: Vincent Wade, Marlene Irene; m. Rosie Ann Lucero, Nov. 22, 1994. BS in Mech. Engring., Gen. Motors Inst., Flint, Mich., 1972; MBA in Fin., Wayne State U., 1980. Registered environmental assessor, Calif. From engr. to supr. GM, Detroit, Balt., L.A., 1966-84; environ. specialist New United Motor, Fremont, Calif., 1984-86; environ. engring. mgr. Def. Systems FMC Corp., San Jose, Calif., 1986-89; cons./exec. sales rep. Gaia Systems, Menlo Park, Calif., 1990; corp. environ. & safety mgr. Ampex Corp., Redwood City, Calif., 1990-92; gen. ops. mgr. Hughes Environ. Systems, El Segundo, Calif., 1992—; lectr. colls. and seminars Environ. Regulatory Issues, 1988—. Author: Developing a National Environmental Policy in a Global Market, 1989; contbd. articles to profl. jours. Panel mem. Toxics Awareness Project, San Francisco, 1989—; com. mem. Environ. Working Group, Sacramento, 1986-88. Mem. Peninsula Indsl. & Bus. Assn. (bd. dirs., v.p. 1988-91). Republican. Roman Catholic. Home: 241 Palos Verdes Dr W Apt 203 Palos Verdes Estates CA 90274

ARONOWITZ, JOEL ALAN, plastic and reconstructive surgeon; b. Memphis, Dec. 5, 1956. MD, Baylor Coll. Medicine, 1982. Attending plastic surgeon Cedars Sinai Med. Ctr., 1987—. Office: 8635 W 3rd St Ste 1170W Los Angeles CA 90048-6101

ARONS, ARNOLD BORIS, physicist, educator; b. Lincoln, Nebr., Nov. 23, 1916; s. Solomon and Esther (Rosen) A.; m. Jean M. Rendall, Aug. 17, 1942; children: Marion, Janet, Kenneth, Paul. ME, Stevens Inst. Tech., 1937, MS, 1940; PhD, Harvard U., 1943; MA (hon.), Amherst (Mass.) Coll., 1953; DE (hon.), Stevens Inst. Tech., 1982. Rsch. scientist Woods Hole (Mass.) Oceanographic Inst., 1942-68; from asst. to assoc. prof. Stevens Inst. Tech., Hoboken, N.J., 1946-52; prof. physics Amherst Coll., 1952-68; prof. physics U. Wash., Seattle, 1968-82, prof. emeritus, 1982—; cons. in field, 1946-65; mem. Commn. on Coll. Physics, 1962-68. Author: A Guide to Introductory Physics Teaching, 1990; contbr. articles to profl. jours. Guggenheim Found. fellow, 1957-58, NSF fellow, 1962-63. Fellow AAAS, Am. Phys. Soc.; mem. Am. Assn. Physics Tchrs. (pres. 1966-67, Oersted medal 1972), Am. Geophys. Union, Nat. Sci. Tchrs. Assn. Home: 10313 Lake Shore Blvd NE Seattle WA 98125-8160 Office: Dept Physics U Wash Box 351560 Seattle WA 98195

ARORA, SANJEEV, gastroenterology educator; b. India, Sept. 26, 1956; came to U.S., 1980; s. Ramrakha and Sudarshan (Chopra) A.; m. Madhu Ahuja, July 21, 1956; children: Anita, Sarah. Grad., Maharajah's Coll., Jaipur, India, 1974; MB, BS, Armed Forces Med. Coll., Pune, India, 1978. Diplomate Am. Bd. Internal Medicine, Am. Bd. Gastroenterology. Intern Army Hosp., Delhi, India, 1978-80; resident in medicine Safdurjung Hosp., New Delhi, 1980-81, Sisters of Charity Hosp., SUNY, Buffalo, 1982-85; resident in surgery Maimonides Med. Ctr., Bklyn., 1981-82; fellow in gastroenterology New Eng. Med. Ctr., Boston, 1985-87, staff physician, 1987-93; asst. prof. medicine Tufts U. Sch. Medicine, Boston, 1987-93, assoc. prof., 1993; assoc. prof. medicine, sect. chief U. N.Mex., Albuquerque, 1993—; staff gastroenterologist U. N.Mex. Hosp., 1993—; numerous lectures in field. Contbr. articles and abstracts to med. jours., chpts. to books. Fellow Am. Coll. Gastroenterology; mem. ACP, AAAS, Am. Gastroenterology Assn. Office: U NMex Dept Medicine 2211 Lomas Blvd NE # 5 Albuquerque NM 87106-2745

ARRANAGA, THOMAS JOHN, physicist, video company executive; b. L.A., Oct. 6, 1949; s. Bernard and Theresa (Jimenez) A. BA in Physics, U. Calif., Irvine, 1976. Student engr. Hughes Aircraft Co., Malibu, Calif., 1972-76; scientist Teledyne Brown, Costa Mesa, Calif., 1977-80, SAI, Irvine, 1981-82; pres. Terror Tech. Inc., Laguna Hills, Calif., 1981-85; v.p. Migent Inc., Lake Tahoe, Nev., 1986, Opus, Inc., Irvine, 1987—. Recipient Genius award Mensa, N.Y.C., 1981. Roman Catholic. Home: PO Box 7831 Newport Beach CA 92658-7831

ARREOLA, DANIEL DAVID, geography educator; b. Santa Monica, Calif., May 20, 1950; s. Salvador Arreola and Beatrice (Diaz) Chamberlain; m. Patricia Marie Becerra, Aug. 1, 1980. BA, UCLA, 1972; MA, Calif. State U., 1975; PhD, UCLA, 1980. Vis. asst. prof. Tex. A&M U., College Station, 1980; asst. prof. U. Ariz., Tucson, 1980-83; from asst. to assoc. prof. Tex. A&M U., College Station, 1983-90; assoc. prof. Ariz. State U., Tempe, 1990-94, prof., 1994—. Author: The Mexican Border Cities, 1993; mem. editl. bd. The Profl. Geographer, 1986-90; editl. adv. bd. Geog. Rev., 1993—; contbr. articles to profl. jours. Fellow Am. Geog. Soc.; mem. Assn. Borderland Scholars, Conf. Latin Am. Geographers, Assn. Am. Geographers, Assn. Pacific Coast Geographers. Office: Ariz State Univ Dept Geography Box 870104 Tempe AZ 85287

ARRIETA, OLIVIA, humanities educator; b. Morenci, Ariz., Oct. 4, 1948; d. Gilberto B. and Aurora (Lopez) A. BA, U. Ariz., 1970, MA, 1972, PhD, 1984. Staff anthropologist U.S.-Mex. Environ. Control Project, Tucson, 1971-73; rsch. asst. Bur. Ethnic Rsch. U. Ariz., Tucson, 1973-74; rsch. evaluator Tucson Unified Sch. Dist., 1983-89; asst. rsch. social scientist Mex. Am. studies U. Ariz., 1988-89; vis. rsch. scholar S.W. Hispanic Rsch. Inst. U. N.Mex., Albuquerque, 1989-90; vis. faculty Mex. Am. studies U. Ariz., Tucson, 1990-91; rsch. assoc. Family and Consumer Resource Family and Consumer Resources, Tucson, 1991-92; adj. faculty U. Ariz., Tucson, 1991-92; asst. prof. Ctr for Studies of Ethnicity and Race U. Colo., Boulder, 1992-94. Author: (monograph) Tribal Management Procedures-Ak Chin Reservation, 1975. Precinct rep. Dem. Party, Tucson, 1983; mem. Mujeres Activas en Letras y Cambio Social, Davis, Calif., 1988-94; ofcl. historian Sociedad Nuevo Mexican ada Mutua Proteccion, Albuquerque, 1990-94; mem. Pueblo for La Paz, Tucson, 1991-94. Postdoctoral fellow Ford Found., 1991, Rockefeller Found., 1989. Mem. Am. Anthropol. Assn., Soc. for Applied Anthropology, Nat. Assn. for Chicano Studies. Home: PO Box 793 Morenci AZ 85540-0793 Office: Pascua Yaqui Tribe CSERA 4747 W Calle Vicam Tucson AZ 85746

ARRINGTON, HARRIET ANN, historian, biographer, writer; b. Salt Lake City, June 22, 1924; d. Lyman Merrill and Myrtle (Swainston) Horne; m. Frederick C. Sorensen, Dec. 22, 1943 (div. Dec. 1954); children: Annette S. Rogers, Frederick Christian, Heidi S. Swinton; m. Gordon B. Moody, July 26, 1958 (div. Aug. 1963); 1 child, Stephen Horne; m. Leonard James Arrington, Nov. 19, 1983. BS in Edn., U. Utah, 1957. Cert. tchr., Utah, Ga. Supr. surg. secs. Latter-day Sts. Hosp., Salt Lake City, 1954-58; tchr. Salt Lake City Schs., 1954-57, Glynn County Schs., Brunswick, Ga., 1958-59; from med. sec. to office mgr. Dr. Horne, Salt Lake City, 1962-83; tchr. Carden Sch., Salt Lake City, 1973-74, women's history rschr., tchr.; mem. Utah Women's Legis. Coun.; co-establisher Arrington Archives, Utah State U. Author: Heritage of Faith, 1988; contbr. articles to profl. jours. and confs. Dist. chmn. Utah Rep. Com., 1972-76; mem. art com. Salt Lake City Bd. Edn.; chmn. art exhibit Utah Women's Conf., 1986-87; active LDS Women's Relief Soc.; chmn. Utah Women Artists' Exhbn., AAUW, Utah divsn., 1986-87. Recipient Vol. Action award Utah Women Artists' Exhbn., 1987, resolution of appreciation Utah Arts Coun., 1989. Mem. AAUW (Utah state cultural refinement chmn., cert. of appreciation 1988), DAR (Utah Am. history chmn., Friends of Humanities, Arts, Scis. & Social Sci. award 1995), Old Main Soc. Utah State U., Chi Omega (past pres. alumni chpt.). Home and Office: 2236 S 2200 E Salt Lake City UT 84109-1135

ARROW, KENNETH JOSEPH, economist, educator; b. N.Y.C., Aug. 23, 1921; s. Harry I. and Lillian (Greenberg) A.; m. Selma Schweitzer, Aug. 31, 1947; children: David Michael, Andrew. BS in Social Sci., CCNY, 1940; MA, Columbia U., 1941, PhD, 1951, DSc (hon.), 1973; LLD (hon.), U. Chgo., 1967, CUNY, 1972, Hebrew U. Jerusalem, 1975, U. Pa., 1976, Washington U., St. Louis, 1989; D. Social and Econ. Scis. (hon.), U. Vienna, Austria, 1971; LLD (hon.), Ben-Gurion U. of the Negev, 1992; D. Social Scis. (hon.), Yale, 1974; D (hon.), Université René Descartes, Paris, 1974, U. Aix-Marseille III, 1985, U. Cattolica del Sacro Cuore, Milan, Italy, 1994, U. Uppsala, 1995; Dr.Pol., U. Helsinki, 1976; MA (hon.), Harvard U., 1968; DLitt, Cambridge U., Eng., 1985. Research assoc. Cowles Commn. for Research in Econs., 1947-49; asst. prof. econs. U. Chgo., 1948-49; acting asst. prof. econs. and stats. Stanford, 1949-50, assoc. prof., 1950-53, prof. econs., statistics and ops. research, 1953-68; prof. econs. Harvard, 1968-74, James Bryant Conant univ. prof., 1974-79; exec. head dept. econs. Stanford U., 1954-56, acting exec. head dept., 1962-63, Joan Kenney prof. econs. and prof. ops. research, 1979-91, prof. emeritus, 1991—; economist Coun. Econ. Advisers, U.S. Govt., 1962; cons. RAND Corp. Author: Social Choice and Individual Values, 1951, Essays in the Theory of Risk Bearing, 1971, The Limits of Organization, 1974, Collected Papers, Vols. I-VI, 1983-85; co-author: Mathematical Studies in Inventory and Production, 1958, Studies in Linear and Nonlinear Programming, 1958, Time Series Analysis of Interindustry Demands, 1959, Public Investment, The Rate of Return and Optimal Fiscal Policy, 1971, General Competitive Analysis, 1971, Studies in Resource Allocation Processes, 1977, Social Choice and Multicriterion Decision Making, 1985. Served as capt. AUS, 1942-46. Social Sci. Research fellow, 1952; fellow Center for Advanced Study in the Behavioral Scis., 1956-57; fellow Churchill Coll., Cambridge, Eng., 1963-64, 70, 73, 86; Guggenheim fellow, 1972-73; Recipient John Bates Clark medal Am. Econ. Assn., 1957; Alfred Nobel Meml. prize in econ. scis., 1972, von Neumann prize, 1986. Fellow AAAS (chmn. sect. K. 1983), Am. Acad. Arts and Scis. (v.p. 1979-81, 91-93), Econometric Soc. (v.p. 1955, pres. 1956), Am. Statis. Assn., Inst. Math. Stats., Am. Econ. Assn. (exec. com. 1967-69, pres. 1973), Internat. Soc. Inventory Rsch. (pres. 1983-90); mem. NAS (mem. coun. 1990-93), Internat. Econs. Assn. (pres. 1983-86), Am. Philos. Soc., Inst. Mgmt. Scis. (pres. 1963, chmn. coun. 1964), Finnish Acad. Scis. (fgn. hon.), Brit. Acad. (corr.), Western Econ. Assn. (pres. 1980-81), Soc. Social Choice and Welfare (pres. 1991-93), Pontifical Acad. Social Scis. Office: Stanford U Dept Econs Stanford CA 94305-6072

ARSHAM, GARY, medical educator; b. Cleve., 1941; s. Sanford Ronald and Florence A.; m. Diana Silver, 1971. AB cum laude, Harvard U., 1963; MD, Case-Western Res. U., 1967; PhD, U. Ill., 1971. Fellow in med. edn. U. Ill., Chgo., 1968-71; asst. then assoc. dean curriculum devel., asst. prof. medicine and health scis. communication SUNY, 1971-72; assoc. prof., prof. health professions edn. U. of Pacific, San Francisco, 1972-79; chmn. Council on Edn. Pacific Med. Ctr., San Francisco, 1976-81; v.p. Arsham Cons., Inc., San Francisco, 1981—; adminstr. Pacific Vision Found., 1977-84, dir. edn., 1983—; mem. nat. adv. bd. John Muir Hosp. Med. Film Festival, 1981—; mem. task force on interdisciplinary edn. Nat. Joint Practice Commn., 1973-74; bd. dirs. U.S.-China Ednl. Inst., 1980—, sec., 1986-88, treas., 1993—; chair, CEO Nat. Accreditation Commn. for Schs. and Colls. of Acupuncture and Oriental Medicine, 1993—. Co-author: Diabetes: A Guide To Living Well, 1989, 2d edit. 1992; chief editor Family Medicine Reports, San Francisco, 1983. Fellow ACP; mem. Am. Assn. Individual Investors (chpt. bd. dirs. 1984-88), Am. Ednl. Rsch. Assn., Assn. Am. Med. Colls., Assn. Study Med. Edn., Assn. Hosp. Med. Edn. (past exec. com., sec.-treas.), Am. Diabetes Assn. (chpt. bd. dirs. 1984—, pres. 1990-91, v.p. Calif. 1992-93, pres.-elect 1993-94, pres. 1994-95, nat. bd. dirs. 1995—), Am. Assn. Diabetes Educators (assoc. editor 1985-92, bd. dirs. 1994—), Calif. Med. Assn., San Francisco Med. Soc., Harvard Club San Francisco (bd. dirs., past pres.), Lane Med. Soc., Tech. Security Analysts Assn. Office: Arsham Cons Inc PO Box 15608 San Francisco CA 94115-0608

ARTEAGA, ALFRED, English educator; b. L.A., May 2, 1950; s. Alfredo Lopez-Arteaga and Lillian (Frias) Arteaga; m. Paula Maria Contreras, Dec. 27, 1972 (div. 1995); children: Marisol, Xóchitl, Mireya. AB, U. Calif., Santa Cruz, 1972, PhD, 1987; MFA, Columbia U., 1974. Asst. prof. English, U. Houston, 1987-90, U. Calif., Berkeley, 1990—; mem. editl. adv. bd. Smithsonian Instn. Press, N.Y.C., 1994-96. Author: Cantos, 1991; editor: An Other Tongue, 1994. Chancellor's fellow U. Calif., Berkeley, 1989-90, Gaspar de Portolà fellow, Barcelona, Spain, 1991, fellow Rockefeller Found., 1993-94, Poetry fellow NEA, 1995. Mem. Raza Unida Party. Office: U Calif English Dept 322 Wheeler Berkeley CA 94720-1030

ARTERS, LINDA BROMLEY, public relations consultant, writer; b. Phila., Dec. 18, 1951; d. Edward Pollard and Rosalyn Irene (Bromley) A. BA, Thiel Coll., 1973. Cert. emergency med. tech., Ariz. Dir. customer rels. Artmann Devel. Corp. Inc., Media, Pa., 1973-74; with S.E. Nat. Bank, Malvern, Pa., 1974-78, coord. pub. rels., 1976-78; pvt. practice pub. rels. consultant Media, 1978-84, Phoenix, 1984-88; mgr. community rels. City of Tempe, Ariz., 1988-; lectr. in field; past mem. pvt. industry coun. County Del (Pa.) Comprehensive Emplyment Tng. Act Program. free lance writer for local, regional and nat. mags. and newspapers. Past chmn. Emergency Dept. Vols. Chandler Regional Hosp.; past bd. dirs. South Chester County Advanced Life Support, Inc., United Cerebral Palsy of Del County; former mem. Phila Indoor Tennis Corp., 1977-82; mem. East Valley steering com. Ariz. Humane Soc.; past mem. Critical Incident Stress Debriefing Team Phoenix Fire Dept.; past coord. CISD program City of Tempe. Mem. PRSA (past mem. eligibiilty com. Phoenix chpt., mem. counselors group), Stress Mgmt. Nat. Network (chmn. S.W. region critical incident). Republican. Presbyterian. Office: 1303 W Lisa Ln Tempe AZ 85284

ARTHUR, ALAN ROBERT, ink manufacturing company executive; b. Darlington, Wis., May 13, 1962; s. Robert Samuel and Dorothy Mae (Seffrood) A.; m. Phyllis Elizabeth Schmitt, May 23, 1987; 1 child, Caitlin Anne. BS in Mech. Engring., U. Wis., 1985. Engring. asst. Kippcast Corp., Madison, Wis., 1983-85; engr. Hewlett Packard, Corvallis, Oreg., 1985-92, sr. mem. tech. staff, 1992-93, project mgr., 1993—. Inventor printhead having memory element. Mem. ASME. Republican. Lutheran.

ARTHUR, PAUL KEITH, electronic engineer; b. Kansas City, Mo., Jan. 14, 1931; s. Walter B. and Frieda J. (Burckhardt) A.; m. Joy N. Lim, Apr. 26, 1958; children: Gregory V., Lia F. Student Ohio No. U., 1947, Taylor U., Upland, Ind., 1948-49; BSEE, Purdue U., 1956; postgrad. N.Mex. State U., 1957-78. Registered profl. engr., N.Mex.; cert. army acquisition profl.; cert. Naval engring. duty officer. With White Sands Missile Range, N.Mex., 1956—, electronic engr. field engring. group missile flight surveillance office, 1956-60, chief field engring. group, 1960-62, project engr. Pershing weapon system Army Missile Test and Evaluation Directorate, 1962-74, chief high altitude air def. projects br., 1974-82, chief air def. materiel test div., 1982-91, dep. dir. Materiel Test Directorate, 1991—, spec. asst. to WSMR comdr. for Space Programs, 1994—; mem. N.Mex. Spaceport Commn., Southwest Regional Space Task Force, Metro Planning Orgn.; past pres. missile range pioneer group; bd. dirs. Dagupan Electric Corp. of the Philippines. Chmn. adminstrv. bd. Meth. Ch. Served with USN, 1949-53, USNR, 1954-87, rear adm. and, sr. engring. duty officer, 1984-87. Decorated Legion of Merit, Meritorious Svc. medal, Navy Achievement medal, Mil. Order St. Barbara, others. Mem. Am. Def. Preparedness Assn. (past pres.), AIAA (past vice chmn.), Assn. Old Crows, Naval Res. Assn., Res. Officers Assn. (pres. 1983-85), United Vets. Council (chmn. 1984-85), Am. Soc. Naval Engrs., Naval Inst., Navy League, Surface Navy Assn., Assn. U.S. Army, U.S. Field Arty. Assn., Purdue Alumni Assn. (past pres.), N.Mex. State U. Alumni Assn., Mesilla Valley Track Club, Bujutsukan Acad. Martial Arts. Author numerous plans and reports on weapon systems test and evaluation and topics in naval engring. Home: 2050 San Acacio St Las Cruces NM 88001-1570 Office: STEWS-MTD White Sands Missile Range NM 88002

ARTHUR, WILLIAM LYNN, environmental advocate; b. Spokane, Wash., May 22, 1954; s. Robert Cyril and Mabel Mildred (Collison) A.; m. Debora Lee Donovan, Feb. 2, 1975; children: Kathleen, Jonathan. BA in Econs., Wash. State U., 1976, postgrad., 1982-83. Rsch. asst. Wash. State U., 1976-77; project mgr. Ctr. Environ. Understanding, Cheney, Wash., 1977-78; program dir. Wash. Energy Extension Svc., Spokane, 1978-79; econs. instr. Spokane Falls Community Coll., 1977-81; economist, cons. Biosystems Analysis Inc., Spokane, 1983; assoc. N.W. rep. Sierra Club, Seattle, 1983-87, N.W. rep., 1987-91, N.W. regional dir., 1992—; chmn. bd. N.W. Conservation Act Coalition, Seattle, 1982-83, bd. dirs., 1988—; adv. com. N.W. Renewable Resources Ctr., Seattle, 1987-91, bd. dirs., 1992—; cons. energy workshops N.W. Regional Found., Spokane, 1982; mem. exec. com. Save Our Wild Salmon Coalition, 1991—; mem. adv. com. Inland Empire Pub. Lands Coun., 1990—. Chmn., mem. city commn. Environ. Quality Commn., Pullman, Wash., 1976-77; bd. dirs. Ryegrass Sch., Spokane, 1978-81; conservation rep. Internat. Mountain Caribou Tech. Com., 1978-81; bd. dirs. Wash. Citizens for Recycling, Seattle, 1980-82; chair Washington State Environmentalists for Clinton/Gore Com., 1992; environ. rep. Northwest Forest Conf. convened and chaired by Pres. Clinton, Apr. 2, 1993; mem. steering com. on the No Initiative 164 Coalition, 1995. Office: Sierra Club NW Office 1516 Melrose Ave Seattle WA 98122-3608

ARTRU, ALAN ARTHUR, anesthesiologist, educator; b. Oakland, Calif., Apr. 30, 1949; s. Frank George and Evelyn Dolores (Markstrom) A.; m. Linda Marie Mason, Aug. 18, 1973; children: Rebecca, Naomi, Aaron, Alana. BA in Psychology and Biology, U. Calif., Santa Cruz, 1971; MD, Med. Coll. Wis., 1975. Resident U. Calif., San Francisco, 1975-78; assoc. cons. in anesthesiology Mayo Cliic, Rochester, Minn., 1978-80; asst. prof. U. Wash., Seattle, 1980-84, assoc. prof., 1984-89, prof., 1989—; head rsch. dept. anesthesiology U. Wash., 1992—; cons. in field; reviewer Collaboration in Basic Sci. and Engring. Nat. Rsch. Coun. NIH, Bethesda, Md., 1993. Contbr. chpts. to books; mem. editorial bd. Jour. Neurosurg. Anesthesiology, 1987—. Del. Wash. State Rep. Conv., Bellingham, 1994; head adult edn. com. St. Madeline Sophie Ch., Bellevue, Wash., 1986. Mem. Soc. Neurosurg. Anesthesiology and Critical Care (past pres. 1993-94), Am. Soc. Anesthesiologists, Internat. Soc. Cerebral Blood Flow and Metabolism, Internat. Anesthesia Rsch. Soc., Am. Heart Assn., Am. Assn. Lab. Animal Sci. Roman Catholic. Home: 6308 129th Pl SE Bellevue WA 98006-4045 Office: U Wash Med Sch Dept Anesthesiology 1959 Pacific Box 356540 Seattle WA 98195-6540

ARVESCHOUG, STEVEN NEIL, communications executive, state representative; b. Maui, Hawaii, Dec. 19, 1958; s. Neil Gary and Vera Mae (Helm) A.; m. Christine Janice Gutcheck, June 5, 1982. BS, Mont. Coll. Mineral Sci. and Tech., 1982. Sales rep. Sunbrook Broadcasting/KQUY, Butte, Mont., 1982-83; sales mgr. Sunbrook Broadcasting/KCEZ, Butte, Mont., 1984-85, Sunbrook Broadcasting/KCSJ, Pueblo, Colo., 1984-86; gen. sales mgr. Sunbrook Broadcasting/KCSJ/KUSN, Pueblo, Colo., 1986-87, gen. mgr., 1987-88; licenced agt. N.Y. Life Ins. Co., Butte, Mont., 1983-84; pres., gen. mgr. Martec Broadcasting, Pueblo, 1988—; lectr. and speaker in field. Senate intern U.S. Senator Max Baucus, Butte, 1981; treas. Bob Boyd for County Treas., Pueblo, 1986; del. State Rep. Conv., Colo., 1986, 88; State Rep. Dist. 44, Pueblo, 1988—. Mem. Colo. Broadcasters Assn., Pueblo C. of C. (bd. dirs. 1987, Leadership Pueblo award 1987), Kiwanis Club (bd. dirs. 1985-88), Pachyderms (bd. dirs. 1986-88). Baptist. Home: 4 Gunsmith Ct Pueblo CO 81008-1907

ARVIZU, DAN ELIAB, mechanical engineer; b. Douglas, Ariz., Aug. 23, 1950; s. Walter and Ella (Rodriguez) A.; m. Patricia Ann Brady, Feb. 23, 1980; children: Joshua, Angela, Elizabeth, Kayley, Tecia. BSME, New Mexico State U., 1973; MSME, Stanford U., 1974, PhD in Mech. Engring., 1981. Mfg. engring. asst. Texas Instruments, Dallas, 1969-72; mem. tech. staff Bell Telephone Labs., Denver, 1973-77; mem. solar thermal tech. staff Sandia Nat. Labs., Albuquerque, 1977-81, mem. solar photovoltaic tech. staff, 1981-86, supr. photovoltaic cell rsch., 1986-88, mgr. tech. transfer, 1988-91, dir. tech. transfer, 1991-93; dir. adv. energy tech. Sandia Nat. Labs., 1993—; mem. tech. transfer steering com. Nat. Ctr. for Mfg. Scis., Ann Arbor, Mich., 1992; mem. tech. transfer mgrs. adv. bd. Nat. Tech. Transfer Ctr., Wheeling, W.Va., 1992—; mem. commercialization adv. bd. Solar II power plant, Barstow, Calif., 1993—. Contbr. articles to profl. jours. Named Disting. Engring. Alumnus N.Mex. State U., 1988, Ingeniero Eminente, 1990; named Rising Star in Sci. Albuquerque Tribune newspaper, 1989. Mem. ASME (solar standards com. 1981-83, nat. lab. tech. transfer com. 1990-93), IEEE, IEEE Electronic Device Soc. (adminstrv. com. 1986-91), Tech. Transfer Soc. Office: Sandia Nat Labs Adv Energy Tech Ctr 6200 PO Box 5800 # 6200 Albuquerque NM 87185

ARZUBE, JUAN ALFREDO, bishop; b. Guayaquil, Ecuador, June 1, 1918; came to U.S., 1944, naturalized, 1961; s. Juan Bautista and Maria (Jaramillo) A. B.S. in Civil Engring, Rensselaer Poly. Inst., 1942; B.A., St. John's Sem., 1954. Ordained priest Roman Catholic Ch., 1954; asso. pastor St. Agnes Ch., Los Angeles, Resurrection Ch., Los Angeles, Ascension Ch., Los Angeles, Our Lady of Guadalupe Ch., El Monte, Calif.; aux. bishop, vicar gen. Diocese L.A., Los Angeles, 1971-93; episcopal vicar for Spanish speaking Los Angeles, 1973—; mem. nat. bishops coms. Ad Hoc Com. for Spanish Speaking; chmn. Com. for Latin Am. Recipient Humanitarian award Mexican Am. Opportunity Found., 1978, John Anson Ford award Los Angeles County Commn. Human Relations, 1979. Home: 3149 E Sunset Hill Dr West Covina CA 91791-2242 Office: San Gabriel Region 16009 Cypress Ave Irwindale CA 91706-2122

ASANO, HISAKO, fine arts educator; b. Osaka City, Japan, Jan. 5, 1944; came to the U.S., 1960; d. Denzo and Matsuko Asano; m. Michael B. Gould, Feb. 12, 1972 (div. 1981). BFA, U. So. Calif., 1966, MFA, 1971. Educator U. So. Calif., L.A., 1970—; educator Loyola Marymount U., L.A., 1971-72, L.A. County High Sch., 1986, South Bay Adult Sch., Manhattan Beach, Calif., 1977-88, L.A. County Mus. Art, 1989, Palos Verdes (Calif.) Art Ctr., 1989-90, Torrance (Calif.) Art Ctr., 1990—, So. Coast Botanic Garden, Rolling Hills, Calif., 1987—, L.A. Harbor Coll., 1976—. Exhibited works in numerous shows including U. So. Calif., 1971, Malone Gallery, L.A., 1975, L.A. Mus., 1974-75, So. Coast Botanic Garden, 1989. Mem. Printmaking Soc., Women Archtl. League, L.A. Jr. Chamber Com., Friends of Fine Arts. Home: 27838 Palos Verdes Dr E Rancho Palos CA 90275-5151 Office: U So Calif University Park Los Angeles CA 90089-0292

ASBURY, JUDITH SMITH, public relations professional; b. Pasadena, Calif., Oct. 12, 1954; d. Josiah Edward Smith and Eleanor Evelyn Bingham; m. Griffith Evan Williams, July 17, 1977 (div. June 1990); children: Kathryn Elizabeth Williams, Florence Judith Williams; m. Greg Alan Asbury, Aug. 3, 1991; 1 stepchild, Dirk Asbury. BA in East Asian Studies and Mgmt., U. Redlands, 1976. Spl. events coord. So. Calif. chpt. Nat. Multiple Sclerosis Soc., Glendale, 1977-79; publicist Coll. Continuing Edn., U. So. Calif., L.A., 1979-80, dir. pub. rels., 1980-82; owner Judy Williams Pub. Rels., Altadena, Calif., 1982-85; account supr. Fisher & Assocs., Sherman Oaks, Calif., 1985-87; owner Smith Williams Mktg. Comm., Pasadena, 1987—; pres. Smith Asbury Inc. Recipient 75th Alumni award U. Redlands, 1982, award Internat. Assn. Business Comm., L.A., 1991. Mem. Pub. Rels. Soc. Am. (accredited pub. rels. profl., 2 merit awards 1990), Publicity Club L.A. (treas., Merit award 1990, Pro award 1991), Rotary Club Pasadena (Environ. award 1991, merit award 1993, prism award 1994, pro award 1994). Presbyterian. Home: 2440 Glen Canyon Rd Altadena CA 91001-3548 Office: Smith Asbury Inc 527 S Lake Ave Ste 102 Pasadena CA 91101-3529

ASBURY, TIMOTHY EDWARD, editor; b. Bloomington, Ill., July 12, 1949; s. Earl E. and Sally (Carstens) A.; m. Nancy Lynne Coleman, Aug. 26, 1972; children: Jill, Katie, John. BS, U. Colo., 1972. Reporter Estes Park (Colo.) Trail-Gazette, 1972-79, editor, 1979—. Recipient Bausch & Lomb Sci. award Las Animas High Sch., 1967. Mem. Internat. Soc. Weekly Newspaper Editors, Nat. Press Photographers Assn., Colo. Press Assn. (open recs. com. 1989—). Home: PO Box 83 Estes Park CO 80517-0083 Office: Estes Park Trail-Gazette PO Box 1707 Estes Park CO 80517-1707

ASCENSÃO, JOÃO LUIS AFONSO, physician, researcher; b. Maputo, Mozambique, July 6, 1948; came to U.S., 1974; s. João F. A. and Maria (Almeida) A.; m. Vivian Pereyra, June 27, 1993; 1 child, João Andre. MD, U. Lisbon Sch. Medicine, 1972, PhD, 1989. Resident U. Hosp. St. Mary, Lisbon, Portugal, 1972-74; immunology fellow Meml. Sloan-Kettering Cancer Ctr., N.Y.C., 1974-76; internal medicine resident U. Minn. Hosps., Mpls., 1977-78, hematology oncology fellow, 1979-81, instr., 1981-82, asst. prof., 1982-84; assoc. prof., assoc. dir. BMT program N.Y. Med. Coll., Valhalla, 1984-89; assoc. prof., assoc. dir. EMT program U. Conn. Health Sci. Ctr., Farmington, 1989-92; prof. medicine, pathology, microbiology and immunology U. Nev. Sch. Medicine, Reno, 1992—; adv. bd. mem. Calif. Cancer Ctr., Modesto, 1992—; bd. mem. Nev. Am. Cancer Soc., Reno, 1992—. Editor: Regulation of Erythropoiesis, 1987, Molecular Biology of Hemopoiesis, 1988, Molecular Biology of Erythropoiesis, 1989. Portugal Sci. Found. fellow Ministry of Edn., Lisbon, 1974-75, Charles H. Revson Found. fellow N.Y.C., 1984-86; recipient Yount Investigator award NIH, Nev., 1991-94. Fellow ACP; mem. Am. Soc. Hematology, Am. Soc. Clin. Oncology, Am. Assn. Cancer Rsch., Internat. Soc. Experimental Hematology, European Soc. Med. Oncology, Clin. Immunology Soc. Office: Univ Nev Sch Medicine 1000 Locust St Reno NV 89520-0102

ASCHAFFENBURG, WALTER EUGENE, composer, music educator; b. Essen, Germany, May 20, 1927; came to U.S., 1938, naturalized, 1944; s. William Arthur and Margarete (Herz) A.; m. Nancy Dandridge Cooper, Aug. 14, 1951 (div.); children: Ruth Margareta, Katherine Elizabeth; m. Rayna Klatzkin Barroll, Aug. 5, 1987. Diploma, Hartford Sch. Music, 1945; BA, Oberlin Coll., 1951; MA, Eastman Sch. Music, 1952. Prof. composition and music theory, former chmn. composition dept. Oberlin (Ohio) Coll. Conservatory of Music, prof. emeritus, 1987—, also former chmn. dept. music theory., 1952-87. Composer: Ozymandias-Symphonic Reflections for Orch., 1952, cello Sonata, 1953, Sonata for Solo Violin, 1954, Piano Sonatina, 1954, String Quartet, 1955, Bartleby-opera, 1962, Elegy for Strings, 1961, Three Dances for Orch., 1966, Three Shakespeare Sonnets, 1967, Quintet for Winds, 1967, Proem for Brass and Percussion, 1969, Duo for Violin and Cello, 1971, Conversations-Six Pieces for Piano, 1973, Libertatem Appellant for Tenor, Baritone and Orch., 1976, Carrousel—24 Pieces for Piano, 1980, Concertino for Violin, Ten Winds and Contrabass, 1982, Laughing Time for Mixed Chorus, 1983, Concerto for Oboe and Orch., 1985, From South Mountain for Brass Quintet, 1988, Coalescence for Oboe and Cello, 1989, Sonata for the Fortepiano or Pianoforte, 1990, Parings for Clarinet and Piano, 1993. Served with AUS, 1945-47. Recipient award Fromm Music Found., 1953; Nat. Inst. Arts and Letters award, 1966; Cleve. arts prize, 1980; Guggenheim fellow, 1955-56, 73-74. Mem. ASCAP, Soc. Composers, Am. Music Ctr., Soc. Music Theory. Home: 4639 E Monte Way Phoenix AZ 85044-7517

ASCHENBRENNER, FRANK ALOYSIOUS, former diversified manufacturing company executive; b. Ellis, Kans., June 26, 1924; s. Philip A. and Rose E. Aschenbrenner; m. Gertrude Wilhelmina DeBie, Nov. 15, 1946; children: Richard David, Robert Wayne, Mary Lynne. BS with high honors, Kans. State U., 1950; PhD in Physics, M.I.T., 1954. Mgr. physics and math. Gen. Electric, Cin., 1958-61; asst. dir. space div. Rockwell Internat., Downey, Calif., 1961-69; corp. dir. tech. Rockwell Internat., Pitts., 1969-71; v.p., gen. mgr. div. yarn machinery Rockwell Internat., Charlotte, N.C., 1971-75; pres. COR, Inc., Charlotte, 1975-77; v.p. research and devel. and engring. Ball Corp., Muncie, Ind., 1977-86; pvt. bus. cons. Poway, Calif., 1986—; chmn. bd. RAMZ Corp., Dunkirk, Ind., 1985—; nat. bd. advisors Rose-Hulman Inst., Terre Haute, Ind., 1984—, U. Tenn. Space Inst., Tullahoma, 1982—. Served with USN, 1943-47. Mem. AIAA, Am. Phys. Soc., Naval Res. Assn., San Diego Venture Group. Home and Office: 14258 Palisades Dr Poway CA 92064-6443

ASH, LAWRENCE ROBERT, public health educator, administrator; b. Holyoke, Mass., Mar. 5, 1933; s. Lawrence Clifton and Alice (Sartini) A.; m. Luana Lee Smith, Aug. 4 1960; 1 child, Leigh I. BS in Zoology, U. Mass., 1954, MA in Zoology, 1956; PhD in Parasitology, Tulane U., 1960. Asst. parasitologist U. Hawaii, Honolulu, 1960-61; instr. Tulane U., New Orleans, 1961-65; med. parasitologist South Pacific Commn., Noumea, New Caledonia, 1965-67; asst. prof. pub. health UCLA Sch. Pub. Health, 1967-71, assoc. prof., 1971-75, prof., 1975-94, chmn. dept., assoc. dean, 1979-84, prof. emeritus, 1994—; mem. panel U.S. Panel on Parasitic Diseases, U.S.-Japan Program, Washington, 1972-78, chmn., 1978-84; cons. Naval Med. Rsch. Unit # 2, Taipei, Republic of China, Mainla, 1970-80. Sr. author: Atlas of Human Parasitiology, 1980, 3d rev. edit., 1990, Parasites: A guide to Laboratory Procedures and Identification, 1987; co-author: Parasites in Human Tissues, 1995. NIH grantee, 1970-84. Fellow Royal Soc. Tropical Medicine and Hygiene; mem. Am. Soc. Tropical Medicine and Hygiene (councilor 1974-77), Am. Soc. Parasitologists (councilor 1972-75, 88-92, v.p. 1982-83). Home: 10400 Northvale Rd Los Angeles CA 90064-4332 Office: UCLA Sch Pub Health Los Angeles CA 90024

ASH, WALTER BRINKER, lawyer; b. Wichita, Kans., June 8, 1932; s. Walter Bonsall and Gladys Elvira (Brinker) A.; m. Fern Ostrom, Sept. 16, 1986; children: Paul B., Allison L., Carolyn A. BA, U. Kans., 1955, BL, 1957. Bar: Kans. 1957, Colo. 1959. Personal asst. to Solicitor Gen. U.S. Dept. Justice, Washington, 1957-58, trial atty., 1958-59; assoc. Davis, Graham & Stubbs, Denver, 1959-63, ptnr., 1964-82; ptnr. Wade Ash Woods Hill & Guthery P.C., Denver, 1982-91, Wade Ash Woods & Hill P.C., Denver, 1991-93, Wade Ash Woods Hill & Farley, P.C., Denver, 1993—. Fellow Am. Coll. Trust and Estate Counsel; mem. ABA, Colo. Bar Assn., Denver Bar Assn., Internat. Acad. Estate and Trust Law. Home: 6814 N Trailway Cir Parker CO 80134-6200 Office: Wade Ash Woods Hill & Farley 360 S Monroe St Ste 400 Denver CO 80209-3709

ASHBY, DARREL LEROY, history educator; b. Grand Junction, Colo., Nov. 19, 1938; s. Samuel Franklin and Mildred May (Hooker) A.; m. Mary Elizabeth Gross, July 3, 1958; children: Steven Eugene, Eric Lee (dec.). AA, Mesa Jr. Coll., Grand Junction, Colo., 1958; BA, Adams State Coll., 1960; MA, U. Wyoming, 1961; PhD, U. Md., 1966. Asst. prof. history U. Bridgeport, Conn., 1966-70, Ill. State U., Normal, 1970-72; assoc. prof. history Wash. State U., Pullman, 1972-76, prof. history, 1976-94, Claudius and Mary Johnson prof. history, 1994—. Author: The Spearless Leader, 1972, Saving the Waifs, 1984, William Jennings Bryan, 1987; co-author (with Rod Gramer) Fighting the Odds, 1994. Named Prof. of Yr., State of Wash., Coun. for Advancement & Support of Edn., 1990, 93. Mem. Orgn. of Am. Historians, Am. Studies Assn., Western History Assn. Home: NE 1280 Hillside Cir Pullman WA 99163 Office: Wash State Univ Dept History Pullman WA 99164

ASHBY, EDWARD HOWARD, publisher; b. Harrisburg, Pa., Mar. 24, 1935; s. William Mack Ashby and Jane Elizabeth (Coomer) Pue; m. Susan T. Koyama, Jan. 29, 1991; children: Joann Linda, Michael Richard, Charles Wesley, Paul Fitzgerald. BA, U. Md., 1965; MS, U. So. Calif., L.A., 1971. State editor Meridian Star, Miss., 1971-74; pub. Rifle Citizen-Telegram, Colo., 1974-77; reporter Gazette-Telegraph, Colorado Springs, 1977-79; editor and pub. Military Times, Colorado Springs, 1979-84; dir. publs. Assn. Operating Room Nurses, Denver, 1984-85; pub. Sr. Spotlite, Denver, 1986—. Contbr. articles to profl. jours. Recipient Essay award Freedoms Found., Valley Forge, Pa., 1964, 72, Feature Writing award Colo. Press Assn., Denver, 1978. Mem. Toastmasters (area gov. 1968-94). Office: Era Ken Rice Assoc 5771 Wadsworth Byp Arvada CO 80002-2538

ASHBY, NORMA RAE BEATTY, journalist, beauty consultant, Mont., Dec. 27, 1935; d. Raymond Wesley Beatty and Ella Mae (Lamb) Beatty Watson Mehmke; m. Shirley Carter Ashby, Sept. 5, 1964; children: Ann, Tony. BA, U. Mont., Missoula, 1957. Reporter, Helena Ind. Record, 1953-56; picture dept. Life mag., N.Y.C., 1957-58; picture researcher MD Med. Newsmag., N.Y.C., 1959-61; producer, hostess TV Show Today in Mont., Sta. KRTV, Great Falls, 1962-85; editor Noon News, Sta. KRTV, 1985-88, beauty cons. Mary Kay Cosmetics, Inc., 1988—; freelance journalist, 1988—. Author: What Is A Montanan?, 1971, Montana Woman, 1977, Montanans, 1982, scriptwriter: Last Chance Gulch, 1964, Gentle Giants, 1969, Our Latchstring is Out, 1979, Paris Gibson, 1983, Martha, Pioneer Woman, 1984, Great Falls Centennial, 1984, First Ladies of Montana, 1986, Anuka, Montana's Island Home, 1986, North American Indian Days, 1987, Missiles of October, 1987, (co-author) Symbols of Montana, 1989. Mem. First Presbyn. Ch.; co-chmn. Cascade County Bicentennial Com., Great Falls, 1974-76; founder, chmn. C.M. Russell Auction, Great Falls, 1979; bd. dirs. Mont. Physicians Service, Helena, 1980-87; co-chmn. Great Falls Centennial Com., 1982-84; Festivals chmn. Cascade Coounty 89ers, 1987-89; coord. Mont. Statewide BellRinging Project, 1989; chair Mont. Jefferson awards; pres. Cascade County Mental Health Assn., 1980-82; elder First Presbyn. Ch.; bd. dirs. Cascade County Hist. Soc., 1987-91, Mental Health Assn. Mont., also editor; coord. Mont. Statehood Centennial Bell Award, 1990—. Co-host Children's Miracle Network Telethon, 1989-94. Recipient TV Program of Yr. award Greater Mont. Found. 1982-88, Communication and Leadership award Mont. Toastmasters Internat., 1983, Preservation award Cascade County Hist. Soc., 1994; named Tribune Most Influential Woman in Great Falls, 1984, hon. mem. Blackfeet Tribe Blackfeet Reservation, Browning, Mont., 1981, Mont. TV Broadcaster Yr., 1985. Mem. Women in Communications (founder, pres. Great Falls, Mont. chpt. 1988-90), Great Falls Advt. Fedn. (dir., Silver medal 1980, Scriver Bronze medal 1993), AWRT (founder, pres. Mt. Big Sky chpt. 1967, recipient cert. of commendation 1982). Club: PEO, Broadcast Pioneers.

ASHCRAFT, CHARLES OLIN, business educator; b. Kiowa, Kans., June 22, 1936; s. Olin N. and Esther Pauline (Young) A.; m. Letha May Bray, June 2, 1963; children: Farrah Elaine, Kyle Bray. BBA, Phillips U., 1958, MEd, 1965; postgrad., Air War Coll., 1977; diploma, Command & Gen. Staff Coll., 1975. Cert. tchr., Alaska. Tchr. Anchorage High Sch., 1958-61, East Anchorage (Alaska) High Sch., 1961-65; sch. adminstr. Ursa Maj. Elem. Sch., Ft. Richardson, Alaska, 1965-68, Arcturus Jr. High Sch., Ft. Richardson, 1965-73; instr. Anchorage Community Coll., 1959-73; instr. Bartlett High Sch., Anchorage, 1973-90, rifle coach, 1980-90; mem. adj. faculty Command & Gen. Staff Coll., Ft. Leavenworth, Kans., 1990—. Mem. Rep. Dist. 16, Anchorage, 1986-90; scoutmaster Western Alaska coun. Boy Scouts Am., 1976-80; post advisor Explorer Scout Post, Anchorage, 1980-91. Col. USAR, 1958-91. Recipient Silver Beaver award Western Alaska Boy Scouts Am., 1984; named to U.S. Army Inf. Officer Candidate Sch. Hall of Fame, 1991. Mem. NEA (life), NRA (life), Nat. Guard Assn. of U.S. (life), Res. Officers Assn. (life), Mil. Order of World Wars (life), F&AM Glacier Lodge, Pioneers for Ala. Igloo, Al Aska Shrine Temple, Scottish Rite, Orient of Alaska, Cert. Residential Specialists. Republican. Methodist.

ASHDOWN, FRANKLIN DONALD, physician, composer; b. Logan, Utah, May 2, 1942; s. Donald and Theresa Marie (Hill) A. BA, Tex. Tech. U., 1963; MD, U. Tex., 1967. Chief of med. Holloman Air Force Base, New Mexico, 1971-73; chief of staff Gerald Champion Mem. Hosp., Alamogordo, N.M., 1976, 91, 92; pres. Otero County Concerts Assn., Alamogordo, 1985-94, Otero County Med. Soc., Alamogordo, 1986; cons. New Mexico Sch. for Visually Handicapped, Alamogordo, 1973-76. Composer of more than 30 published and recorded works. Bd. dirs. Otero County Mental Health Assn., Alamogordo, 1973-77, Flickinger Found. for Performing Arts, 1995; bd. trustees Gerald Champion Meml. Hosp., 1992. Mem. Gerald Champion Mem. Hosp., N.M. Med. Soc., Am. Soc. Internal Med., ASCAP. Republican. Home: 1435 Rockwood Alamogordo NM 88310-3920 Office: 1301 Cuba Ave Alamogordo NM 88310-5727

ASHER, JAMES EDWARD, forestry consultant, engineer, arborist, forensic expert; b. L.A., July 22, 1931; s. John Edward and Dorothy (Ingraham) A.; m. Marilyn Lee Struebing, Dec. 28, 1953; children: Lynne Marie, Laure Ann. Student Pasadena City Coll., 1949-50; BS, Oreg. State U., 1954. Certs. continuing forestry edn. Soc. of Am. Foresters. With U.S. Forest Svc., San Bernardino (Calif.) Nat. Forest, summers 1950-53, forester, 1956-57; prin. James E. Asher, ACF, Cons. Forester, 1957—; capt., bn. chief, asst. chief, fire prevention officer Crest Forest Fire Protection Dist., Crestline, Calif., 1960-69, chief, 1969-71; forester Big Bear div. Golden State Bldg. Products, Redlands, 1972, timber mgr., 1972-74; mem. profl. foresters exam. com. Calif. Bd. Forestry, 1978-90, vice chmn., 1982-90; mem. Calif. Forest Pest Control Coun.; mem. Forest Adv. Com., 1982—; chmn. Profl. Foresters Ad Hoc Task Force, 1983-90. Vol. firewarden State of Calif., 1967—; mem. adv. com. Range Mgmt. Program, 1986-90; chmn. Tree Conservation Subcom., First Dist. Suprs. Ad Hoc Com. on Soil Erosion and Sediment Control, County of San Bernardino, 1984—; forensic expert witness. With AUS, 1954-56. Recipient Certificate of Merit Nat. Fire Protection Assn., San Bernardino Mountains Assn.; Resolution of Commendation, County Bd. Suprs.; Forester of Year award So. Calif. sect. Soc. Am. Foresters, 1977; others. Registered profl. forester, registered profl. engr., Calif.; lic. pest control advisor, pest control applicator, Calif. Mem. Internat. Soc. Arboriculture (cert. arborist 1988—), So. Calif. Assn. Foresters and Fire Wardens, Soc. Am. Foresters (cert., chmn. licensing and ethics com. So. Calif. sect., chmn. So. Calif. 1983), Assn. Cons. Foresters, Internat. Soc. Arboriculture, Calif. Urban Forests Coun., Calif. Agrl. Prodn. Cons. Assn., Pesticide Applicators Profl. Assn., Masons, Tau Kappa Epsilon. Presbyterian. Author: (with others) A Technical Guide for Community and Urban Forestry in Washington, Oregon and California. Contbr. 72 articles to profl. jours.; presenter in field. Office: PO Box 2326 Lake Arrowhead CA 92352-2326

ASHER, JAMES JOHN, psychology educator; b. Detroit, Aug. 10, 1929; s. James Joseph and Antoinette Marie (Abdo) Asher; m. Virginia Lee Gardner, Apr. 20, 1954; children: Jeffrey John Asher, Melissa Marie Smith. BA, U. N.Mex., 1951; MA, U. Houston, 1955, PhD, 1957; postdoctoral, various univs. Instr. dept. psychology U. Houston, 1956-57; asst. prof. dept. psychology San Jose (Calif.) State U., 1957-60, assoc. prof., 1961-65, prof., 1965—, assoc. dean sch. of social scis., 1976-78; lectr. in psychology U. Calif., Berkeley, 1960-61, U. Santa Clara, Calif., 1964, Monterey Peninsula Coll., 1964; vis. lectr. NYU, 1966, 67 summer, UCLA, 1971, U. Calif., Santa Barbara, 1971. Author: Learning Another Language Through Actions, 4th edit., Brainswitching, 1988, The Super School of the 21st Century, 1995; contbr. numerous articles to profl. jours. With U.S. Army, 1951-54. Rsch. grantee U.S. Office of Edn., Office of Naval Rsch., Office of Postal Rsch. and Engring., Dept. of Def., Def. Lang. Inst., State of Calif. Mem. Am. Psychol. Assn., Western Psychol. Assn., Am. Speech-Lang. Hearing Assn. (editl. bd. 1994). Home: PO Box 1102 Los Gatos CA 95031-1102

ASHFORD, EVELYN, track and field athlete; m. Ray Washington; 1 child, Rana. Student, UCLA. Track and field athlete, 1976—. Competed in 1976 Olympics; winner 2 Gold medals, 1984 Olympics (Women's 100 Meters, Women's 4x100-Meter); winner Gold medal, 1988 Olympics (Women's 4x100-Meter); recipient Flo Hyman award Women's Sport Found., 1989; winner Gold medal, 1992 Olympics, Barcelona, Spain (4x100-Meter). Address: 818 N Plantation Ln Walnut CA 91789-1282*

ASHLAND, CALVIN KOLLE, federal judge; b. Mason City, Iowa, Feb. 22, 1933; m. Ilse Doerr, 1957. BS, Iowa State U., 1957; JD, George Washington U., 1963. Bar: Calif. 1973, D.C. 1964, Md. 1968. Credit mgr. GE, Laurel, Md., 1957-67; atty. Law firm of David S. Rubenstein, Bethesda, Md., 1967-72, Sulmeyer Kupetz Baumann and Rothman, L.A., 1972-76; judge U.S. Bankruptcy Ct., L.A., 1976—, 9th Cir. Bankruptcy Appellate Panel, L.A., 1982—; chief bankruptcy judge Cen. Dist. Calif., 1991—; treas. Fin. Lawyers Conf., L.A., 1987—. With U.S. Army, 1954-56. Fellow Am. Coll. Bankruptcy; mem. ABA, L.A. County Bar Assn., Comm. Law League, Am. Bankruptcy Inst. Office: US Bankruptcy Ct 255 E Temple St # 1634 Los Angeles CA 90012-3334*

ASHLEY, MARK JAMES, speech pathologist, health facility administrator; b. Ogdenburg, N.Y., Aug. 9, 1956; s. Cecil Erwin and Mary (Bernier) A.; m. Susan Marie Hess, Sept. 12, 1975; children: Matthew James, Nicholas Anthony, Benjamin Daniel. BS in Speech Pathology, SUNY, Geneseo, 1977; MS in Speech Pathology, So. Ill. U., 1978. Lic. speech pathologist, Calif., Fla., Tex. Rehab. asst. Ctr. for Comprehensive Services, Carbondale, Ill., 1977-78; clin. supr. Speech Pathology, Inc., Bakersfield, Calif., 1979-80; co-dir. Ctr. for Neuro Skills, Bakersfield, 1980—; lectr. numerous assns., agys., 1978—; instr. U. Calif., Santa Barbara, 1980; adj. prof. So. Ill. U., Dept. Communication Disorders and Scis., Carbondale, 1985. Author: (with Krych, Persel and Persel) Working with Behavior Disorders: Strategies for Traumatic Brain Injury Rehabilitation, 1995; (with Krych) Traumatic Brain Injury Rehabilitation, 1995. Bd. dirs. Kern County (Calif.) chpt. Am. Cancer Soc., 1980-82, service com. mem. 1979-82; cons. Bakersfield Assn. Retarded Citizens, 1981. Regents scholar State N.Y., 1974-77; recipient Disting. Alumni of Yr. Dept. Comm. Scis. and Disorders So. Ill. U., Carbondale, 1995. Mem. Am. Speech Lang. Hearing Assn. (cert.), Calif. Speech and Hearing Assn., Nat. Rehab. Assn., Nat. Rehab. Counselors, Nat. Rehab. Adminstrn. Assn., Nat. Assn. Ind. Living, Am. Congress Phys.

Medicine and Rehab. (chmn. subcom. post-acute care and rehab. standards with head injury task force), Nat. Head Injury Found., Traumatic Head Injury Profl. Assn. Calif., Internat. Assn. Laryngectomies (founder Kern County chpt. 1980-81). Home: 1901 Haggin Oaks Dr Bakersfield CA 93311-1529 Office: Ctr for Neuro Skills 2658 Mount Vernon Ave Bakersfield CA 93306-2924

ASHLEY, ROSALIND MINOR, writer; b. Chgo., Oct. 10, 1923; d. Jack and Frances (Wasser) Minor; m. Charles Ashley, Mar. 1, 1941; children: Stephen David, Richard Arthur. Grad., Moser Bus. Coll., Chgo., 1940; BS in Edn., Northwestern U., 1963; postgrad., Nat. Coll. Edn., 1968. Sec. Platt Luggage, Inc., 1944; Chgo. producer, performer Story Book Ladies WEAW, Evanston, Ill., 1954-55; elem. tchr. Sch. Dist. No. 65, Evanston, 1962-63, Sch. Dist. No. 39, Wilmette, Ill., 1964-70; assoc. editor Scott, Foresman & Co., Inc., Glenview, Ill., 1970-72; weekly humor columnist Citizen, Del Mar Citizen and La Costan, Solana Beach, Calif., 1986-87; freelance writer San Diego edit. L.A. Times and Citizen, 1987—; cons. Carlsbad (Calif.) Unified Sch., 1986-87. Author: Successful Techniques for Teaching Elementary Language Arts, 1970, paperback edit., 1981, Activities for Motivating and Teaching Bright Children, 1973, Simplified Teaching Techniques and Materials for Flexible Group Instruction, 1976, Portfolio of Daily Classroom Activities with Model Lesson Plans, 1979; editor: Language and How to Use It, 1970; contbr. articles to profl. and popular publs. Vol. Recs. for Blind, Chgo.; publicity chmn. Rancho Santa Fe (Calif.) Community Concerts Assn., 1986-88; play judge Assoc. Community Theatres. Recipient grand prize for poetry Sta. KFAC-FM, L.A., 1984. Mem. AAUW, Welcome Wagon Club. Democrat. Jewish. Home: 11521 Eastridge Pl San Diego CA 92131-3549

ASHLEY, SHARON ANITA, pediatric anesthesiologist; b. Goulds, Fla., Dec. 28, 1948; d. John H. Ashley and Johnnie Mae (Everett) Ashley-Mitchell; m. Clifford K. Sessions, Sept. 1977 (div. 1985); children: Cecili, Nicole, Erika. BA, Lincoln U., 1970; postgrad., Pomona Coll., 1971; MD, Hahnemann Med. Sch., Phila., 1976. Diplomate Am. Bd. Pain Mgmt., Am. Bd. Anesthesiologists. Intern pediatrics Martin Luther King Hosp., L.A., 1976-77, resident pediatrics, 1977-78, resident anesthesiology, 1978-81, mem. staff, 1981—. Named Outstanding Tchr. of Yr., King Drew Med. Ctr., Dept. Anesthesia, 1989, Outstanding Faculty of Yr., 1991. Mem. Am. Soc. Anesthesiologists, Calif. Med. Assn., L.A. County Med. Soc., Soc. Regional Anesthesia, Soc. Pediatric Anesthesia. Democrat. Baptist. Office: Martin Luther King Hosp 12021 Wilmington Ave Los Angeles CA 90059-3019

ASHMEAD, ALLEZ MORRILL, speech-hearing-language pathologist, orofacial myologist, consultant; b. Provo, Utah, Dec. 18, 1916; d. Laban Rupert and Zella May (Miller) M.; m. Harvey H. Ashmead, 1940; children: Harve DeWayne, Sheryl Mae Harames, Zeltha Janeel Henderson, Emma Allez Broadfoot. BS, Utah State U., 1938; MS summa cum laude, U. Utah, 1952, PhD summa cum laude, 1970; postgrad., Idaho State U., Oreg. State Coll., U. Denver, U. Utah, Brigham Young U., Utah State U., U. Washington, U. No. Colo. Cert. secondary edn., remedial reading, spl. edn., learning disabilities; cert. ASHA clin. competence speech pathology and audiology; profl. cert. in orofacial myology. Tchr. pub. schs. Utah, Idaho, 1938-43; speech and hearing pathologist Bushnell Hosp., Brigham City, Utah, 1943-45; sr. speech correctionist Utah State Dept. Health, Salt Lake City, 1945-52; dir. speech and hearing dept. Davis County Sch. Dist., Farmington, Utah, 1952-65; clin., field supr. U. Utah, Salt Lake City, 1965-70, 75-78; speech pathologist Box Elder Sch. Dist., Brigham City, 1970-75, 78-84; teaching specialist Brigham Young U., Provo, 1970-73; speech pathologist Primary Children's Med. Ctr., Salt Lake City, 1975-77; pvt. practice speech pathology and orofacial myology, 1970-88; del. USSR Profl. Speech Pathology seminar, 1984, 86; participant numerous internat. seminars. Author: Physical Facilities for Handicapped Children, 1957, A Guide for Training Public School Speech and Hearing Clinicians, 1965, A Guide for Public School Speech Hearing Programs, 1959, Impact of Orofacial Myofunctional Treatment on Orthodontic Correction, 1982, Meeting Needs of Handicapped Children, 1975, Relationship of Trace Minerals to Disease, 1972, Macro and Trace Minerals in Human Metabolism, 1971, Electromotive Potential Differences Between Stutterers and Non-stutterers, 1970, Learning Disability, An Educational Adventure, 1969, New Horizons in Special Education, 1969, Developing Speech and Language in the Exceptional Child, 1961, Parent Teacher Guidance in Primary Stuttering, 1951, numerous others; contbr. research articles to profl. jours. Student Placement chair Am. Field Service, Kaysville, Utah, 1962-66; ednl. del. Women's State Legis. Council, Salt Lake City, 1958-70; chairwoman fund raising Utah Symphony Orch., Salt Lake City, 1970-71; sec., treas. Utah chpt. U.S. Council for Exceptional Children, 1958-62, membership com. chair, 1962-66, program com. chair, 1966-68. Recipient Scholarship award for Higher Edn. U. Utah, Salt Lake City, 1969; Delta Kappa Gamma scholar, 1968; rsch. grantee Utah Dept. Edn., 1962. Mem. NEA, Utah Ednl. Assn., Am. Speech, Lang. Hearing Assn. (life, continuing edn. com. 1985, Ace award for Continuing Edn. 1984), Western Speech Assn., Internat. Assn. Orofacial Myology (life, bd. examiners, Sci. Contribution award 1982), Utah Speech, Hearing and Lang. Assn. (life, sec., treas. 1956-60), AAUW (Utah state bd. chair status of women 1959-62, Kaysville br. 1957-60, bd. dirs. Kaysville-Davis br. 1987-92, chair internat. rels. 1987-91, chair cultural interests Kaysville-Davis br. 1991-92), Delta Kappa Gamma (state scholarship award 1968, del. Woman's State Legis. Coun. 1958-70, profl. affairs chair 1963-67, tchr. of yr. award 1978), AAUW (bd. dirs. internat. rels. Kaysvile-Davis br., 1988-91), Sigma Alpha Eta, Theta Alpha Phi, Psi Chi, Zeta Phi Eta, Phi Kappa Phi. Republican. Mormon. Lodges: Daus. Utah Pioneers (parlimentarian Kaysville chpt. 1980-92, historian 1975-80, lesson leader 1992—), Soroptimist Internat. (charter mem. 1954, bd. dirs. 1954-56, pres. Davis County chpt. 1965-69, treas. 1956-54, Rocky Mountain regional bd. dirs. 1965-70, community service award 1968, pub. service award 1970). Home: 719 E Center St Kaysville UT 84037-2138

ASHTON, RICK JAMES, librarian; b. Middletown, Ohio, Sept. 18, 1945; s. Ralph James and Lydia Marie (Thornbery) A.; m. Marcia K. Zuroweste, Dec. 23, 1966; children: Jonathan Paul, David Andrew. AB, Harvard U., 1967; MA, Northwestern U., 1969, PhD, 1973; MA, U. Chgo., 1976. Instr., asst. prof. history Northwestern U., Evanston, Ill., 1972-74; curator local and family history Newberry Library, Chgo., 1974-77; asst. dir. Allen County Pub. Library, Ft. Wayne, Ind., 1977-80, dir., 1980-85; city librarian Denver Pub. Library, 1985—; mem. Ind. Coop. Libr. Svcs. Authority, 1980-85, pres., 1984-85; cons. NEH, Nat. Ctr. Edn. Stats., Northwestern U. Office Estate Planning; mentor Snowbird Leadership Inst., 1995—. Author: The Life of Henry Ruiter, 1742-1819, 1974, The Genealogy Beginner's Manual: A New Edition, 1977, Stuntz, Fuller, Kennard and Cheadle Ancestors, 1987 (with others) Trends in Urban Library Management, 1989. Bd. dirs. Cmty. Coordinated Child Care, Evanston, 1972-74, Three Rivers Montessori Sch., Ft. Wayne, 1977-80; bd. dirs., sec. Allen County-Ft. Wayne Hist. Soc., 1977-83; conscientious objector. Recipient Nat. Merit scholar, 1963-67, Old City Hall Hist. Service award, 1985; NDEA fellow, 1967-69; Woodrow Wilson fellow, 1971-72. Mem. ALA, Colo. Libr. Assn., Colo. Alliance Rsch. Librs. (pres. 1987-88, sec. 1939-95, chmn. 1995—). Home: 2974 S Verbena Way Denver CO 80231-4219 Office: Denver Pub Libr 10 14th Avenue Pky Denver CO 80204-2749*

ASHTON-COOMBS, TAMARAH M., learning disabilities specialist, consultant; b. Toledo, Dec. 5, 1961; d. Harold Leroy and Patricia Marie (Casto) Ashton; m. John G. Coombs, Feb. 11, 1989; 1 child, Rebecca Marie. MusB, Western Mich. U., 1984; MS, San Diego State U., 1988, MA, 1990, postgrad., 1990. Cert. tchr., Calif. Tchr. spl. edn., counselor Lincoln High Sch., San Diego, 1988-89; learning disabilities specialist San Diego State U., 1989-90, instr. dept. of spl. edn., 1992—; pvt. practice ednl. cons., San Diego, 1990—; rsch. asst. doctoral program edn. San Diego State U., 1990-93. Mem. Assn. Ednl. Therapists (profl.), Coun. for Exceptional Children (profl.), Phi Kappa Phi, Pi Lambda Theta (sec. 1990-92, v.p. 1992-93, pres. 1993-94). Home and Office: 4689 49th St San Diego CA 92115-3240

ASHWORTH, ALAN A., human resources professional; b. Wichita, Kans., Sept. 23, 1929; s. Arthur Albert and Oma Marie (Swindell) A.; m. Rose Elaine Edwards, Aug. 22, 1953; children: Randall M. Durant, Jay A. Ashworth, Dan A. Ashworth, Candace J. Hulse. Student, Wichita State U., 1956, 62-63, Cornell U., 1975. Owner, mgr. Dairy Queen franchise, Augusta, Kans., 1950-53; illustrator, planner depts. mfg., engring. Boeing Corp., Wichita and Seattle, 1952-59; supr. various factory, flight line and field assignments Boeing Corp., Wichita, Phila., Seattle, 1959-65; tech. assist team mgr. mfg. and human resource depts. Boeing Corp., Seattle, 1965-77, Spain, 1975-76; dir. human resources fabrication div. Boeing Corp., Seattle and Macon, Ga., 1978-85; dir. human resources Boeing Support Svcs., Seattle, 1985—; Boeing Corp. rep. Presdl. Com. for Employment of People With Disabilities, Washington, 1989—, Puget Sound Transit Com., Seattle, 1989—. Adult leader Boy Scouts Am., Kirkland, Wash., 1965-70; officer, coach Little League Baseball, Kirkland, 1965-71; mem. citizen adv. com. Lake Washington Sch. Dist., Kirkland, 1967-70. With U.S. Army, 1954-56. Home: 11507 Holmes Point Dr NE Kirkland WA 98034-3446 Office: Boeing Support Svcs Div MS 3W-EW PO Box 3707 Seattle WA 98124

ASHWORTH, WAYNE OLIVER, school system administrator; b. Exeter, Calif., Apr. 26, 1942; s. Oliver Eugene and Clara Elva (Getman) A.; m. Beverly Ann Kleinjan, Jan. 1, 1966; children: William Blair, Barton Oliver Wayne. BBA, U. Oreg., 1965; MEd, Oreg. State U., 1969; LLD, Pacific States U., L.A., 1977. Notary pub., Calif. V.p. fin. Pacific Christian Coll., Fullerton, Calif., 1973-79; dir. bus. devel. Whittier (Calif.) Christian Schs., 1980—. Pres. Oreg. Bus. Edn. Assn., 1972-73, Oreg. Gov's. Coun. on the Improvement of Instruction, 1973. Mem. Christian Mgmt. Assn., Calif. Christian Estate Planners, Nat. Notary Assn. Office: Whittier Christian Schs 6548 Newlin Ave Whittier CA 90601-4009

ASKELID, BERTIL RUNE, computer scientist; b. Bromölla, Sweden, June 11, 1952; came to U.S., 1988; s. Rune G. and Suzanne (Sterner) A.; m. Anja Ruben, May 21, 1982; children: Andreas, Rebecca, Nicolas. MS in Engring. Physics, Lund (Sweden) Inst. Tech., 1979. Mem. tech. staff Ericsson Telecom, Stockholm, 1980-88, U.S. West Advanced Techs., Denver, 1988-90, Ericsson Bus. Syss., Cypress, Calif., 1991—. Office: Ericsson Bus Systems 5757 Plaza Dr Cypress CA 90630

ASKIN, JERALD MARK, podiatrist; b. Detroit, Feb. 16, 1949; s. Davis and Sarah Askin; m. Bonni R. Fish, Feb. 10, 1980; children: Josh, Amy, Jeff. BS, U. Mich., 1971; DPM, Calif. Coll. Podiatric Medicin, 1975. Diplomate Am. Bd. Podiatric Surgery. Preceptor Earl Kaplan DPM Kern Hosp., Warren, Mich., 1975-76; pvt. practice Paramount, Calif., 1977—. Fellow Am. Coll. Foot Surgeons. Home: 25701 Dillon Rd Laguna Hills CA 92653-5871

ASKIN, LEON, artistic director, actor, producer, writer; b. Vienna, Austria, Sept. 18, 1907; came to U.S., 1940, naturalized, 1943; s. Samuel and Malvine (Susman) Aschkenasy; m. Annelies Ehrlich, Apr. 12, 1955; 1 child, Irene Hartzell. Grad., New Sch. for Dramatic Arts (now Reinhardt Seminar), Vienna, 1927; postgrad., Columbia U., 1951. Actor Dumont Playhouse, Dusseldorf, Fed. Republic of Germany, 1927-33; dir. cabaret, writer, actor Paris, 1933-35; dir. 1st Legion, Linz, Austria, 1935; artistic dir. lit. and polit. cabaret ABC, Vienna, 1935-38; scriptwriter films Paris, 1938-40; artistic dir. Washington Civic Theatre, 1940-42; tchr. modern play analysis Am. Theater Wing, 1946-47; dir. Dramatic Workshop, N.Y.C., 1947-48; hon. life dir., chmn. various coms. Actors Equity Libr. Theatre, 1947-52; founder Actors Equity Community Theatre, 1948; lectr. theater UCLA, U. So. Calif., Riverside, 1988, 89, 91, 92, The Denver Ctr. Performing Arts Conservatory, 1985, Goethe's Faust prodn. UCLA, 1992, U. Calif., Santa Barbara, 1992; lectr., mem. panel polit. discussions on cabaret in Austria and on Piscator U. So. Calif., UCLA, 1987-88. Dir. Troilus and Cressida (Most Outstanding Prodn. 1941), The Applecart, American Way; staged: Faust for Goethe Festival, N.Y.C., 1948-49; dir., actor: (broadway play) The Merchant of Venice, 1952; appeared in motion pictures including The Robe (with Richard Burton), 1953, One, Two, Three (with James Cagney), 1962, Do Not Disturb, 1966, Guns for San Sebastian, 1967, Hammersmith is Out, Going Ape, 1980, Horror Star, 1981, Airplane II, 1982; starring roles in films including First Strike, 1984, Savage Island, 1984, Summer Jobs, 1984, Stiffs, 1985, Deshima, 1986; starred as Gen. Burkhalter in TV series Hogan's Heroes, 1966-71, Martin Luther and Karl Marx in Steve Allen's TV series Meeting of Minds; dir.: (plays) St. Joan (George Bernard Shaw), 1954, Julius Caesar (Shakespeare), 1964, The Egg (Felicien Marceau) (Outstanding Prodn. of 1975 The Reporter), 1975, Fever in the Brain (Marvin Aron), 1980; co-starred with Gloria Shanson and Jose Ferrer 20th Century on Broadway, with Jack Lemmon in Idiots Delight, 1971 L.A. Ahmanson Theatre; played Othello on stage in Berlin and Hamburg, Fed. Republic of Germany, 1957 (acclaimed as greatest German Othello of 20th Century); contbr. articles to Los Angeles Times, Der Morgen, Vienna, Die Furche, Vienna, also essays to U. Hamburg Arbeitastelle fur Exilliteratur; author: Quietude and Quest, 1989. With U.S. Army, 1942-46; editor in chief The Orientation Digest Air Tech. Svc. Command (15 citations). Decorated Medal of Honor, City of Vienna, 1983, Austrian Cross of Honour, 1988. Mem. AFTRA, ANTA (nat. bd.), Actors Equity (dir. West Coast adv. com. 1952-55), Screen Actors Guild (dir. 1973), Am. Film Inst., Acad. Motion Picture Arts and Scis. (mem. com. for selecting best fgn. lang. film), Acad. TV Arts and Scis., Am. Nat. Theatre and Acad. West (chmn. bd. 1976-78, pres. 1979-82, pres. emeritus 1983—, organized and presented Nat. Artist award to Fred Astaire, Henry Fonda, Helen Hayes, Bob Hope, Jimmy Stewart and Roger Stevens), Equity Library (hon. lifetime bd. dirs.).

ASKIN, RICHARD HENRY, JR., entertainment company executive; b. Flushing, N.Y., Feb. 11, 1947; s. Richard H. and Anne Margaret A.; children: Jennifer Leigh, Michael Richard. BA in Econs., Rutgers Coll., 1969; MA in Comm., U. Tex., 1971; MBA in Fin., Fordham U., 1976. Sales rep. Proctor & Gamble Distbg. Co., Jericho, N.Y., 1969; account exec. CableRep, Inc., N.Y.C., 1973-74, WNBC-TV Nat. Broadcasting Co., N.Y.C., 1974-75, NBC-TV, NBC, N.Y.C., 1975-76, sales mgr. KNBC-TV, Los Angeles, 1976-79, dir. sales, 1979-85; v.p. domestic sales Fries Distbn. Co., Los Angeles, 1985-86, sr. v.p. distbn., 1986-87; pres. TV, The Samuel Goldwyn Co., L.A., 1987—; pres. The Breckford Group, Inc. Served to 1st lt. Adj. Gen. Corps, U.S. Army, 1971-73. Decorated Army Commendation medal; Alcoa fellow, 1969-70. Mem. Hollywood Radio and TV Soc., Advt. Industry Emergency Fund (pres., bd. dirs.), Acad. of TV, Arts and Scis., Sierra Club, Alpha Rho Alumni Assn., Chi Psi. Republican. Home: 1520 Aldercreek Pl Westlake Vlg CA 91362-4211 Office: Samuel Goldwyn Co 10203 Santa Monica Blvd Los Angeles CA 90067-6405

ASKREN, MISHA, physician; b. Holton, Kans., Jan. 27, 1952; s. Melvin Earl Askren and Bonita Marie (Cornelssen) Askren Anderson; m. Ruth Ellen Moskovitz, Sept. 9, 1979; children: Hana Leora, Ariella, Shoshana Clara. BA in Chemistry and Zoology, Pomona Coll., Clarement, Calif., 1974; MD, U. Calif., Davis, 1978. Diplmomate Am. Bd. Family Physicians. Intern in family practice Kaiser Found., L.A., 1978-79, resident in family practice, 1979-81; pvt. practice L.A., 1981-93; physician FHP, Inc., Cerritos, Calif., 1993—. Fellow Am. Acad. Family Practice. Office: FPH Inc 29050 S Western Ave San Pedro CA 90732

ASMONAS, VLADAS, career officer, retired; b. Marijampole, Lithuania, Oct. 23, 1910; came to U.S., 1961; s. Jonas and Elizabeth (Galeckas) A.; m. Ona Kacergius, Mar. 29, 1937; children: Arvydas, Lina. Grad. gymnasium, Marijampole, 1930; grad. mil. coll., Lithuania, 1932. Commd. 2d lt. Lithuanian army, 1932, infantry platoon comdr., 1932-36, infantry co. comdr., 1938-40, retired, 1976; sport instruction, nursing sick people. Contbr. articles to profl. jours. Mem. AAAS, N.Y. Acad. Scis. Home: 986 Jasmine Dr Salt Lake City UT 84123-3341

ASPERIN, MILAGROS R., career counselor, educator, journalist; b. Ponce, P.R., July 5, 1947; d. Jose Rios Cabrera and Providenica Orza Torres; m. Primitivo Asperin, May 12, 1968; children: Vivian Milagros and Lilian Mercedes (twins), Vilma Raquel. BSS in English/Spanish Edn., Cath. U. P.R., Ponce, 1968, MEd in Guidance Counseling, 1972, MEd in Adminstrn./Supervision, 1984. Cert. c.c. counselor, Calif.; nat. cert. career counselor. Freshmen counselor Cath. U. P.R., 1979; h.s. career counselor Prep. Sch. Academia C.R., Ponce, 1981-83; asst. prin. Colegio S.J. Tadeo, Ponce, 1985; acad./career counselor Orange Coast Coll., Costa Mesa, Calif., 1989, Long Beach (Calif.) C.C., 1989-91; counselor ESL Inst. Rancho Santiago Coll., Santa Ana, Calif., 1990-93; ABE instr. ESL Cypress (Calif.) Coll., 1994—; career counselor in pvt. practice, Garden Grove, Calif., 1993—; freelance journalist El Panamericano News, Santa Ana, 1993—, Orange County News, Garden Grove, 1991—, La Perla Del Sur, Ponce, 1983-86. Author: Guide for Principals on Counselor Supervision, 1985. Seminar presenter City of Garden Grove, 1993—, City of Stanton, Calif., 1994—; vol. Republican Party, Garden Grove. Recipient scholarships and awards. Mem. ACA, Am. Coll. Counselors Assn. Roman Catholic.

ASQUITH, RONALD H., petroleum corporate executive; b. 1932. BS, Bradley U., 1953; MA, Bradley U., Mass., 1958; PhD, Purdue U., 1960. V.p. Hooker Chem. Corp., Houston, Tex., 1979—, Empl. Rins.; exec. v.p. Human Resources, Occidental Petroleum Corp., 1979—. USAF, 1954-56; USAFR, Dow. Chem. Europe., 1970-79. Office: Occidental Petroleum Corp 10889 Wilshire Blvd Los Angeles CA 90024-4201

ASTLE, RICHARD SHARP, computer programmer, poet; b. Lexington, Ky., May 19, 1943; s. Melvin Jensen and Alice (Sharp) A.; m. Ruth Sallein, May 18, 1966; divorced; 1 child, Jennifer; m. Leslie Brooke Neilson, July 19, 1981 (dec. Mar. 1986); m. Sarai Austin, Apr. 30, 1995. BS in Math., Stanford U., 1964; MA in Creative Writing, San Francisco State U., 1968; PhD in English Lit., U. Calif., San Diego, 1977. English lectr. UCLA, 1976-77, San Diego State U., 1977-82; lit. lectr. U. Calif., San Diego, 1977-82; programmer Centaurus, Inc., San Diego, 1982-83; sr. engr. Practor Care, Inc., San Diego, 1984—. Contbr. articles and fiction to profl. jours. Mem. Assn. of Computing Machinery, Forth Interest Group. Home: 20120 Date Ln Escondido CA 92029 Office: 4115 Sorrento Valley Blvd San Diego CA 92121-1406

ASTURIAS, JOSEPH LOUIS, priest, foundation administrator; b. Guatemala, May 18, 1908; came to U.S., 1910; s. Manuel Francisco and Rosa (Coblentz) A. Student, St. Thomas Coll., 1927-30; BA, BD, St. Albert's Sem., 1939. Parish priest Dominican Order, Seattle, 1930-35, San Francisco, 1935-40; missionary Dominican Order, Western U.S., 1940-58, Alaska, 1958-63, Mex., 1963-70; dir. Dominican Mission Found., San Francisco, 1971—. Author monthly bull. Missionaries in Action, 1979—. Home: 2390 Bush St San Francisco CA 94115-3124 Office: Dominican Mission Found 2506 Pine St San Francisco CA 94115-2610

ATAIE, ATA JENNATI, oil products marketing executive; b. Mashad, Iran, Mar. 15, 1934; s. Hamid Jennati and Mohtaram (Momeni) A.; came to U.S., 1957, naturalized, 1969; B.S. in agr., Fresno (Calif.) State U., 1964; B.A. in Econs., San Francisco State U., 1966; m. Judith Garrett Bush, Oct. 7, 1961; children—Ata Jennati, Andrew J. Mktg. exec. Shell Oil Co., Oakland, Calif., 1966-75; pres. A.J. Ataie & Cos., Danville, Calif., 1975—; Am. Value Inc., 1976—. Served as 2d lt. Iranian Army, 1953. Mem. Nat. Petroleum Retailers Assn. Democrat.

ATCHESON, SUE HART, business educator; b. Dubuque, Iowa, Apr. 12; d. Oscar Raymond and Anna (Cook) Hart; m. Walter Clark Atcheson (div.); children: Christine A. Hischar, Moffet Zoe, Claye Williams. BBA, Mich. State U.; MBA, Calif. State Poly. U., Pomona, 1973. Cert. tchr. and adminstr. Instr. Mt. San Antonio Coll., Walnut, Calif., 1968-90; bd. dirs. faculty assn. Mt. San Antonio Coll.; mem. acad. senate Mt. San Antonio Coll.; originator vol. income tax assistance Mt. San Antonio Coll.; speaker in field. Author: Fractions and Equations on Your Own, 1975. Speaker Howard Ruff Nat. Conv., San Diego, 1983, Mike DeFalco Numismatics Seminar, Claremont, Calif., 1986; charter mem. Internat. Commn. on Monetary and Econ. Reform; panelist infrastructure funding reform, Freeport, Ill., 1989. Mem. Community Concert Assn. of Inland Empire (bd. dirs.), Scripps Coll. Fine Arts Found.

ATCHISON, OLIVER CROMWELL, retired accountant; b. Berkeley, Calif., Jan. 19, 1918; s. Frederick Charles and Lillie Louise (Chapman) A. Student, Am. Inst. Banking, San Francisco, 1936-38. Asst. cashier Bank Am. NT&SA, San Francisco, Oakland, Calif., 1936-41; sr. warehouse acct. Alltrans Express USA Inc., San Francisco, 1953-82; ret., 1982. Editor The Dispatcher, 1984— (silver award 1985, 86, bronze award 1986, 87). With USNR, 1941-45. Recipient silver medal Chgo. Philatelic Soc., 1989. Fellow Am. Topical Assn. (treas., editor Casey Jones R.R. unit 1984—), Am. Philatelic Soc. Office: Am Topical Assn Casey Jones RR Unit PO Box 31631 San Francisco CA 94131-0631

ATCHLEY, ROBBIE RENE, farmer; b. Portales, N.Mex., Apr. 14, 1963; d. Robert Lee and Edith Irene (Davis) Jones; m. Robert Burdean Atchley, July 26, 1986 (div. 1994); m. Greg Kendal Smith, Nov. 26, 1994 (div. 1995). BS, N.Mex. State U., 1985. With ins. mktg. dept. Bob Jones State Farm, Corrales, N.Mex., 1986-90; farmer Clovis, N.Mex., 1990—. Mem. Altrusa (treas., bd. dirs. Clovis chpt. 1993—), Cattle Capital Cowbelles. Republican. Methodist. Home and Office: 1898 Sr 311 Clovis NM 88101-1249

ATENCIO, J(OSEPH) ANDREW, computer systems official, computer designer; b. Canon City, Colo., May 26, 1965; s. Joseph Andrew Atencio and Carol Lynn (Gordon) Pross; m. Kimberly Ann Maritz, Aug. 8, 1992. AS in Applied Techs., Phoenix Inst. Tech., 1988. Cert. AUTOCAD technician. Designer, drafter Fine Line Designs, Tempe, Ariz., 1987-89; tchr. Phoenix Inst. Tech., 1989-90; computer aided designer, computer system mgr. PRC Environ. Mgmt., Inc., Denver, 1990-91; mgr. computer systems RUST Environment and Infrastructure (formerly SEC Donohue), Englewood, Colo., 1991-92, regional info. systems mgr., 1992—; computer aided drafter Greeley & Hansen Engrs., Phoenix, 1988-90; owner, designer, cons. Midnight Wind Design Svcs., Phoenix and Denver, 1990—. Mem. Am. Design Drafting Assn. Democrat. Office: SEC Donohue 6143 S Willow Dr Ste 200 Englewood CO 80111-5123

ATHORP, ANN LESLIE, mental health services professional; b. Sheboygan, Wis., Nov. 21, 1967; d. Robert Wesley and Kathleen Ann (Schueffner) A. BA in Psychology, Grinnell Coll., 1990; MS in Counseling Psychology, Utah State U., 1994, postgrad. Mental health specialist Cmty.-Family Partnership, Logan, Utah, 1991—; intern in enrollment mgmt. and student life Drake U., 1990; psychologist-in-tng. Utah State U., 1991—, interdisciplinary trainee 1992—, lectr./teaching asst., 1993. Troop leader, adult trainer, assn. del. Girl Scouts of the U.S.A., Grinnell, Iowa and Logan, Utah, 1986—; student rep. to grad. faculty Dept. Psychology Utah State U., Logan, 1992-94. Recipient Pres's. fellow Utah State U., 1990, Pamela G. Cheney scholar, 1991. Mem. APA, ACA, Phi Beta Kappa. Home: PO Box 3572 Logan UT 84323-3572 Office: Community-Family Partnership Ctr for Persons with Disabilities Utah State U Logan UT 84322-6825

ATKIN, ARLO KAY, systems analyst, consultant; b. Bakersfield, Calif., July 5, 1956; s. Levi Kay and Beverly Jean (Kinghorn) A.; m. Myrna Jarvis, Nov. 17, 1978 (div. Jan. 1991); children: Tyson, Cameron, Bryce, Austin, Taylor; m. Shyla Stevens, Oct. 26, 1991; 1 child, Steven. BA, Brigham Young U., 1980; MPA, Ariz. State U., 1990. Customer svc. rep. D. H. I., Provo, Utah, 1978-80; asst. mgr. Area Processing Ctrs., Provo, 1980-82, mgr., 1982-84; asst. dir. St. Luke's Hosp., Phoenix, 1984-86; sr. analyst Ariz. State U., Tempe, 1986-90; sr. cons. Bus. Info. Tech., Concord, Calif., 1990-91; owner, operator Comstar Computers, Ventura, Calif., 1991-95; pres. Ventura Cstar, Inc., 1995—. Bishop Ch. of Jesus LDS, Chandler, Ariz., 1986-89; v.p. Boy Scouts Am., Phoenix, 1988-89; acting dir. Ariz. State U., 1989. Mem. Human Resource Systems Profls. Republican. Office: Comstar Computers 4255-6 E Main St Ventura CA 93003

ATKIN, RUTH, social worker; b. Urbana, Ill., Jan. 30, 1958; d. J. Myron and Ann (Spiegel) A. BA cum laude, Brandeis U., 1979; MSW, Yeshiva U., 1982. Program coord. Jewish Community Ctr. Greater Boston, Boston, Brookline, Mass., 1980-81; community worker Elizabeth Peabody House, Somerville, Mass., 1981-82; day camp dir. Albert L. Schultz Jewish Community Ctr., Palo Alto, Calif., 1983; caseworker Jewish Home for Aged, San Francisco, 1984; program coord. Berkeley (Calif.)/Richmond Jewish Community Ctr., 1984-85; vol. dir. Jewish Family Svc. of Greater East Bay, Oakland, Calif., 1985-87; dir. in-home svcs. registry Bay Area Community Svcs., Oakland, 1986-88; sr. info. and referral coord. Contra Costa County Office on Aging, Martinez, Calif., 1988-92; outpatient social worker VA No. Calif. System Clinics, 1992—; bd. dirs. Support Svcs. Srs. of Alameda County, Hayward, Calif., 1985-89; bd. dirs., v.p. Pacific Ctr., Berkeley, 1991-92; bd. dirs. West County Sr. Svcs. Network, 1989-93. Editor: (periodicals) Genesis 2, 1979-82; co-founder, editor: Jewish Women's Newsletter, 1985-89, BRIDGES, 1989—. Recipient Steve Berman Social Action award Congregation Ahavat Shalom, 1987. Mem. NASW. Jewish. Office: VA Outpatient Clinic 150 Muir Rd Martinez CA 94553-4612

ATKINS, STUART (PRATT), German language and literature educator; b. Balt., Mar. 8, 1914; s. (George) Robert and Huldah M. (Pratt) A.; m. Lillian E. Reed, June 7, 1946; 1 son, Stuart Reed. A.B. summa cum laude, Yale U., 1935, Ph.D., 1938; A.M. (hon.), Harvard U., 1948. Instr. Dartmouth Coll., 1938-41, Harvard U., 1941-43, Princeton U., 1946; asst. prof. German Harvard U., 1946-48, assoc. prof., 1948-56, prof., 1956-65, chmn. dept. Germanic langs. and lits., 1952-57, 60-65; prof. German U. Calif., Santa Barbara, 1965-84, 88, 90, prof. emeritus, 1984, faculty rsch. lectr., 1973; Guggenheim fellow, 1955, 68; vis. prof. U. Goettingen, Germany, 1962; guest prof. Ripon Coll., 1964; Jasper-Jacob-Stahl lectr. Bowdoin Coll., 1972. Author: The Testament of WErther, 1949, Goethe's Faust: A Literary Analysis, 1958, The Age of Goethe, 1969, Essays on Goethe, 1995; editor, author revision: Bayard Taylor's Faust, trans., 1962, Goethe's Faust, Part I, bilingual edit., 1963, Heine: Werke, Bd. I, 1973, Bd II, 1977, Goethe: Torquato Tasso, 1977; translator, editor: Goethe: Faust I and II, 1984, 94; also articles; editor: German Quar., 1952-57, Harvard Germanic Studies, 1960-65; mem. editl. bds. Series in German Literature, Pa. State U., Sociocriticism and Literature; contbr. articles to profl. jours. Mem. Cambridge (Mass.) Aux. Police, 1942-44. With USAAF, 1943-46. Decorated Bronze Star, Criox de Guerre; recipient gold medal Goethe Institut, 1968, Wiemar Goethe Soc., 1995, Friedrich Gundolf prize German Acad. Lang. and Lit., 1984. Mem. MLA (pres. 1972), Am. Acad. Arts and Scis., Goethe Soc. N.Am., Heinrich Heine Gesellschaft, Faust Gesellschaft, N.Am. Heine Soc., Modern Humanities Rsch. Assn., Am. Assn. Tchrs. German (hon., exec. coun. 1966-68), Philol. Assn. Pacific Coast, Goethe Gesellschaft, U. Calif. Santa Barbara Emeriti Assn. (bd. dirs. 1989-95), Phi Beta Kappa. Home: 300 Hot Springs Rd Montecito CA 93108-2038

ATKINS, WILLIAM THEODORE, community volunteer, retired insurance executive; b. Lebanon, Pa., May 14, 1918; s. William Theodore and Edna Marie (Phillips) A.; m. Katherine Melinda Shank, Apr. 25, 1942 (dec. June 1973); children: Karen J. Birdsall, Judith Ann Karman, William T., Sarah J. Ramsey; m. Elena Garcia Ramsey, Sept. 29, 1974. BS in Commerce, Ctrl. YMCA Coll., 1945; JD, DePaul U., 1949. Bar: Ill. 1950, Calif. 1960. Surety claim adjuster Continental Casualty Co., Chgo., 1940-52; mgr. surety claims Mfrs. Casualty/Pacific Nat. Fire Ins. Cos., Phila. and San Francisco, 1952-59; with United Pacific/Reliance Ins. Cos./United Pacific Life Ins., Tacoma, Wash., 1959-81, v.p., assoc. counsel, 1981; v.p. Reliance Ins. Co., Tacoma, 1975-81; ret., 1981. Pres. Pacific Claim Execs. Assn., 1966-67; chmn. N.W. adv. coun. Nat. Assn. Ins. Adjusters, 1965-67; trustee, 1st pres. United Meth. Found. of N.W., 1966-69; chmn. fin. com. Lihue, Hawaii United Ch., 1982-86, 89—, moderator, 1987-88; bd. dirs. Kauai (Hawaii) Concert Assn., 1982—, pres., 1983-85, treas., 1986—; bd. dirs. Hawaii Assn. Music Socs., Honolulu, 1983-90, treas., 1985-87, pres., 1987-89; sec. Na Lima Kokua, Kauai, 1987-91, treas., 1991—; bd. dirs. Hawaii United Meth. Union, Honolulu, 1993—, fin. com., 1994—; treas. Kauai Interfaith Coun., 1994—; trustee Waioli Corp.-Grove Farm Homestead Mus., Hanalei Mission House Mus., Lihue, 1985—, mem. fin. com., 1985-90, mem. pers. com. 1986-90, mem. exec. com., 1987-90, pres., 1990—; treas. Kauai Interfaith Iniki Recovery Effort, Lihue, 1992—. Mem. ABA (vice chmn. fidelity and surety com. 1969-81), State Bar Calif., Kauai Orchid Soc. (treas. 1994). Republican. Methodist. Home: 5867 Haaheo Pl Kapaa HI 96746-9646

ATKINSON, DANIEL EDWARD, biochemist, educator; b. Pawnee City, Nebr., Apr. 8, 1921; s. Max and Amy (Neiswanger) A.; m. Elsie Ann Hemmingson, 1948; children: Kristine Ruth, Owen Rolf, Joyce Elaine, Ellen Lee, David Eric. B.Sc., U. Nebr., 1942, D.Sc., 1975; Ph.D., Iowa State U., 1949. Rsch. fellow Calif. Inst. Tech., 1949-50; assoc. scientist Argonne Nat. Lab., 1950-52; mem. faculty UCLA, 1952-91, prof. chemistry, 1962-81, prof. biochemistry, 1981-91, prof. emeritus, 1991—; vis. prof. MIT, 1966-67, U. B.C., 1975. Author: Cellular Energy Metabolism and Its Regulation, 1977; co-author: Dynamic Models in Biochemistry, 1987, Dynamic Models in Chemistry, 1990; assoc. editor: Jour. Biol. Chemistry, 1972-77; contbr. articles to profl. jours. Served with USNR, 1943-46. Guggenheim fellow, 1966-67. Mem. Am. Soc. for Biochemistry and Molecular Biology, Am. Chem. Soc. (chmn. div. biol. chemistry 1978), Am. Soc. Microbiology, Am. Physiol. Soc. Home: 3123 Malcolm Ave Los Angeles CA 90034-3406

ATKINSON, DONALD D., SR., real estate broker; b. Hutchinson, Kans., Aug. 22, 1933; s. Theodore Sherman and Florence Marie (Morris) A.; m. Barbara Clara, Apr. 22, 1954; children: Sheryl Lynn, Donald D., Jr., Richard Lee. AA, Chaffey Jr. Coll., Alta Loma, Calif., 1965-71; BABA, San Bernadino State U., 1973-79. Telegrapher Santa Fe Railroad, San Bernardino, Calif., 1951-52; maintenance supr. Kaiser Steel Corp., Fontana, Calif., 1952-80; real estate salesman Acacia Realty, Fontana, 1980-82, Am. Pacific, Colton, Calif., 1982-83; ins. sales office mgr. State Farm Ins., Fontana, 1983-87; real estate sales office mgr. 5th Ave. Realty, Fontana, 1987-88; real estate sales office mgr. A&B Realty, Fontana, 1988-92, real estate broker, 1992—. Control and regulate trash, taxis, tow trucks, Bur. Franchise, City of Fontana, 1982-88. Sgt. U.S. Army, 1953, Korea. Mem. Nat. Assn. Realtors Property Mgmt. (founding), Bus. Devel. Assn., Realty Investment Assn. Calif., San Bernardino Valley Bd. Realtors. Republican. Office: A&B Realty 8675 Nuevo Ave Fontana CA 92335-3827

ATKINSON, JOHN CHRISTOPHER, magazine editor, critic, writer; b. Hitchin, Eng., June 12, 1948; came to U.S., 1987; s. Harry Archer and Jacqueline Ellen (Elliott) A.; m. Maree Froy, Dec. 12, 1970 (div. 1981); m. Pamela Margaret Edwards, June 19, 1982 (div. 1987); 1 child, Heather Louise; m. Laura Jean LoVecchio, Nov. 28, 1987; children; Henry Joseph, Emily Claire. BSc in Chemistry and Physics, U. London, 1972; grad. cert. in edn., 1974. Sci. officer Warren Spring Lab., Stevenage, Eng., 1969-72; freelance bass guitarist, London, 1972-76; news editor Hi-Fi News and Record Rev. mag., Croydon, Surrey, Eng., 1976-78, dep. editor, 1978-82, editor, 1982-86; internat. editor Stereophile UK Ltd., London, 1986-87; editor Stereophile mag., Santa Fe, 1987—. Prodn. compact discs Hi-Fi News Test Disc, 1985, Poem (flute/piano music), 1989, Stereophile Test Disc, 1990, Intermezzo (Brahms piano music), 1991, Stereophile Test CD2, 1992, Concert (piano recital), 1994, Stereophile Test CD 3, 1995, Sonata (Liszt piano music), 1995; contbr. numerous articles and revs. of hi-fidelity components to music mags. Office: 208 Delgado St Santa Fe NM 87501-2728

ATKINSON, RICHARD CHATHAM, academic administrator, cognitive psychologist, educator; b. Oak Park, Ill., Mar. 19, 1929; s. Herbert and Margaret (Feuerbach) A.; m. Rita Loyd, Aug. 20, 1952; 1 dau., Lynn Loyd. Ph.B., U. Chgo., 1948; Ph.D., Ind. U., 1955. Lectr. applied math. and stats. Stanford (Calif.) U., 1956-57, assoc. prof. psychology, 1961-64, prof. psychology, 1964-80; asst. prof. psychology UCLA, 1957-61; dep. dir. NSF, 1975-76, acting dir., 1976, dir., 1976-80; chancellor, prof. cognitive sci. U. Calif., San Diego, 1980—. Author: (with Atkinson, Smith and Bem) Introduction to Psychology, 11th edit., 1993, Computer Assisted Instruction, 1969, An Introduction to Mathematical Learning Theory, 1965, Studies in Mathematical Psychology, 1964, Contemporary Developments in Mathematical Psychology, 1974, Mind and Behavior, 1980, Stevens' Handbook of Experimental Psychology, 1988. Served with AUS, 1954-56. Guggenheim fellow, 1967; fellow Ctr. for Advanced Study in Behavioral Scis., 1963; recipient Distinguished Research award Social Sci. Research Council, 1962. Fellow APA (pres. exptl. div. 1974, Disting. Sci. Contbn. award 1977, Thorndike award 1980), AAAS (pres. 1989-90), Am. Psychol. Soc. (William James fellow 1985), Am. Acad. Arts and Scis.; mem. Soc. Exptl. Psychologists, Nat. Acad. Scis., Am. Philos. Soc., Nat. Acad. Edn., Inst. of Medicine, Psychonomic Soc., Cognitive Sci. Soc., Cosmos Club (Washington), Explorer's Club (N.Y.C.). Home: 9630 La Jolla Farms Rd La Jolla CA 92037-1131 Office: U Calif at San Diego Office of Chancellor La Jolla CA 92093*

ATKINSON, RICK MILTON, manufacturing executive; b. Boise, Idaho, Feb. 4, 1959; s. Robert Milton and Hope Caroline (Bowen) A.; m. Michelle Marie Kinzer, Apr. 18, 1987; children: Alexis Michelle, Oliver Warren. BBA, Boise State U., 1981. CPA, Idaho. Systems cons. mgmt. info. Arthur Andersen and Co., Denver, 1981-82; controller Aluma-Glass Ind., Inc., Nampa, Idaho, 1982-86, v.p. info., 1986-93, pres., 1993—, also bd. dirs. Com. mem. Fundsy Civic Auction, Boise, 1990. Mem. Bronco Athletic Assn. (bd. dirs. 1986-87). Republican. Roman Catholic. Office: Aluma Glass Ind Inc 16265 Star Rd Nampa ID 83687-8415

ATKINSON, ROLAND MOORE, psychiatrist; b. San Jose, Calif., Feb. 19, 1936; s. Roland Moore and Mayme June (Scales) A.; (div. 1969); children: Barry David, Julia Lynn, Michael Ian, Daniel Paul. BA in Biology, Stanford U., 1957, MD, 1961; postgrad. in Geriatric Psychiatry, U. London, Eng., 1987. Intern UCLA, 1961-62; resident UCLA Neuropsychiatric Inst., L.A., 1962-65; asst. chief Psychiatry U.S.P.H.S. Hosp., S.I., N.Y., 1965-67; mem. faculty in Psychiatry UCLA, 1967-70, U. Calif., Irvine, 1970-76; assoc. prof. Psychiatry Oreg. Health Scis. U., Portland, 1976-84, prof. Psychiatry, 1984—; staff mem. VA Med. Ctr., Portland, 1976—, chief of svc., 1980-94, acting chmn.psychiatry dept., 1994-95; rschr. Clin. Studies of Alcoholism and Aging, 1982—; dir. Geriatric Psychiatry Fellowship, 1990-95. Editor (book) Alcohol and Drug Abuse in Old Age, 1984; contbr. articles to profl. jours. Mem. Oreg. Gov.'s Adv. Com. on Alcohol and Drug Problems, 1978-85; cons. Samaritan Pastoral Counseling Ctr., Portland, 1985-92. Fellow Am. Psychiat. Assn.; mem. Am. Assn. for Geriatric Psychiatry, Gerontologic Soc. Am., Am. Geriatrics Soc., Internat. Psychogeriatric Assn., Oreg. Psychiatry Assn. Democrat.

ATKINSON, SHERIDAN EARLE, lawyer; b. Oakland, Calif., Feb. 14, 1945; s. Arthur Sheridan and Esther Louise (Johnson) A.; m. Margie Ann Lehtin, Aug. 13, 1966. 1 son, Ian Sheridan. BS, U. Calif.-Berkeley, 1966, MBA, 1971; JD, U. San Francisco, 1969. Bar: Calif. 1970. Prin. Atkinson & Assocs., fin. and mgmt. cons., corp. and bus. valuations, San Francisco, 1968—; assoc. Charles O. Morgan, Jr., San Francisco, 1972-76; pvt. practice, San Francisco Bay Area,1976—. With USAR, 1970-76. Mem. Calif. Bar Assn. Republican.

ATLAS, JAY DAVID, philosopher, consultant, linguist; b. Houston, Tex., Feb. 1, 1945; s. Jacob Henry and Babette Fancile (Friedman) A. AB summa cum laude, Amherst (Mass.) Coll., 1966; PhD, Princeton (N.J.) U., 1976. Mem. common rm. Wolfson Coll., Oxford, Eng., 1978, 80; vis. fellow Princeton U., 1979; rsch. assoc. Inst. for Advanced Study, Princeton, 1982-84; vis. lectr. U. Hong Kong, 1986; vis. assoc. prof. UCLA, 1988, vis. prof., 1989-95; prof. Pomona Coll., Claremont, Calif., 1989—; sr. assoc. Jurecon, Inc., L.A.; lectr. 2d European Summer Sch. in Logic, Lang. and Info., 1990; examiner U. Edinburgh, Scotland, 1993, U. Groningen, The Netherlands, 1991, 93, 94, vis. prof., 1995. Author: Philosphy Without Ambiguity, 1989; contbr. to PC Laptop Computer Mag., 1994, articles to profl. jours. Mem. Am. Philos. Assn., Linguistic Soc. Am. Office: Pomona Coll 551 N College Ave Claremont CA 91711

ATTIG, JOHN CLARE, secondary education educator, consultant; b. Chgo., Apr. 2, 1936; s. Clare McKinley and Elsie Bertha (Nagel) A.; m. Harriet Jane Rinehart, June 13, 1959; children: Laura, Victoria. BA, DePauw U., 1958; MA, U. Chgo., 1961. Cert. tchr., Calif. Social studies tchr. Lyons Twp. H.S., LaGrange, Ill., 1961-65, Henry Gunn H.S., Palo Alto, Calif., 1965-72, 78—; univ. faculty assoc. Simon Fraser U., Burnaby, Canada, 1972-73; social studies tchr. Jordan Jr. H.S., Palo Alto, 1973-75, Cubberley Sr. H.S., Palo Alto, 1975-78; lectr., demonstrator simulation games for classes in history and govt. various univs. and sch. dists. in U.S. and Canada. Contbr. numerous articles to profl. jours.; author numerous simulation games. With USAR, 1958-64. NEH fellow, 1983, 87, 89, Tchr. fellow St. Andrews U., Scotland, 1993. Mem. NEH (project dir. Masterworks Seminar 1991), Western History Assn., Ednl. Excellence Network. Methodist. Office: Henry Gunn Sr HS 780 Arastradero Rd Palo Alto CA 94306

ATTOE, WAYNE OSBORNE, architecture educator, author, designer; b. Madison, Wis., Dec. 28, 1940; s. Osborne James and Charlotte (Brakken) A. AB, Cornell U., 1963; BArch, U. Calif., Berkeley, 1967; PhD, Union Inst., 1975. Teaching assoc. Franconia (N.H.) Coll., 1967-68; asst. prof. Ohio U., Athens, 1968-69; assoc. prof. U. Wis., Milw., 1969-78; cons. Attoe Assocs., Berkeley, 1978-84; adj. prof. U. Tex., Austin, 1984-89; prof. architecture La. State U., Baton Rouge, 1989-93, coord. grad. architecture, 1989-93; prin. Attoe Assocs., Rsch., Pub., Design, 1990—. Author: Architecture and Critical Imagination, 1978, Skylines, 1981, (with others) American Urban Architecture, 1989; editor: Transit, Land Use, Urban Form, 1988, Architecture of Ricardo Legorreta, 1990. Fellow Inst. for Urban Design, Nat. Trust.

ATUTIS, BERNARD P., manufacturing company executive; b. Phoenix, Jan. 24, 1933; m. Ursula Igna Weiss, May 22, 1954; children: Diana, Bernard E., Robert A., Bernardine E., Mark A. Student, Cornell U., 1966-77, SUNY, Binghamton, 1972; grad., Ariz. State U., 1994. Sr. programmer IBM, White Plains, N.Y., 1955-72; with Control Data, Mpls., 1977-79; assoc. programmer Karsten Mfg. Corp., Phoenix, 1979-81, CAD/CAM sales staff, 1982-85, project coord., 1985-92, prin. engr. GPS vehicle tracking, 1992—; grad. asst. Dale Carnegie Tng./Sales, Binghamton, 1961-69; cropland rschr. Agr. Ext. Svc., Binghamton, 1960-80; soil water chmn. U.S. Dept. Agr./ASC, Little Falls, N.Y., 1954; mem. Coun. Agriculture Sci. and Tech., 1994. Contbr. articles to profl. jours. Instl. rep. Boy Scouts Am., Binghamton, 1955-60; active 4-H Club, Ithaca, 1961-72. With USAF, 1950-54. Mem. Coun. for Agrl. Sci. and Tech., Am. Legion, Moon Valley Golf Course. Republican. Roman Catholic. Home: 4109 W Banff Ln Phoenix AZ 85023-4531 Office: Karsten Mfg Corp 2201 W Desert Cove Ave Phoenix AZ 85029-4912

ATWATER, STEPHEN DENNIS, professional football player; b. Chicago, Oct. 28, 1966. BS in Bus. Adminstrn., U. Ark., 1989. Safety Denver Broncos, 1989—. Named to Sporting News NFL All-Pro team, 1992, Pro-Bowl, 1990-93. Office: Denver Broncos 13655 Broncos Pky Englewood CO 80112-4150*

ATWOOD, KELLY PALMER, insurance agency executive; b. Portland, Oreg., Jan. 7, 1946; s. Baird Ewing and Lelia Claire (Donham) McNeese A.; m. Regina Louise Hamilton, July 30, 1983; children: Derek, Lynn, Jason, Beri, Courtney. Student, U. Oreg., 1964-66, Chemeketa Community Coll., 1976-78. Pres., chief exec. officer Group Ins. Mktg., Inc., Salem, Oreg., 1970-85, Contractors Ins. Svcs. Inc., Lake Oswego, Oreg., 1985—; also bd. dirs. Metro Ins. Agy., Inc., Lake Oswego, Oreg. Contbr. articles on ins. to profl. jours. Former mem. Reagan Task Force, Washington, 1985-86, Denny Smith Task Force on Crime, Salem, 1988. Served with USN, 1967-69. Named Sr. Agt. of Yr. Salem Life Underwriters Assn., 1980, 81. Mem. Nat. Assn. Life Underwriters, Nat. Assn. Home Builders, Oreg. State Home Builders Assn., Home Builders Assn. Met. Portland (bd. dirs. 1985—). Republican. Home: 3300 River Woods Pl Lake Oswego OR 97034-5115 Office: Contractors Ins Svcs Inc PO Box 2267 Lake Oswego OR 97035-0071

ATWOOD, MARY SANFORD, writer; b. Mt. Pleasant, Mich., Jan. 27, 1935; d. Burton Jay and Lillian Belle (Sampson) Sanford; B.S., U. Miami, 1957; m. John C. Atwood, III, Mar. 23, 1957. Author: A Taste of India, 1969. Mem. San Francisco/N. Peninsula Opera Action, Hillsborough-Burlingame Newcomers, Suicide Prevention and Crisis Center, DeYoung Art Mus., Internat. Hospitality Center, Peninsula Symphony, San Francisco Art Mus., World Affairs Council, Mills Hosp. Assos. Mem. AAUW, Suicide Prevention Aux. Republican. Club: St. Francis Yacht. Office: 40 Knightwood Ln Hillsborough CA 94010-6132

ATWOOD, ROBERT BRUCE, publisher; b. Chgo., Mar. 31, 1907; s. Burton H. and Mary Beach (Stevenson) A.; m. Evangeline Rasmuson, Apr. 2, 1932; children: Marilyn A. Odom, Sara Elaine. A.B., Clark U., 1929; Litt.D. (hon.), Alaska Meth. U., 1967; D.Journalism (hon.), U. Alaska, 1979. Reporter Worcester (Mass.) Telegram, 1926-29, 34-35, Ill. State Jour., Springfield, 1929-34; pres. and pub. Anchorage Times, 1935-89, pub. emeritus, 1989-92; dir. Alaska Sales and Svc., Inc., Anchorage, 1991—. Author pamphlets, articles, editorials pub. in various jours. Chmn. Alaska Statehood Com., 1949-59; hon. Norwegian consul at Anchorage, 1960-86; mem. civilian affairs bd. Alaskan Air Command, 1962—, now chmn.; bd. dirs. Commonwealth North; founder Atwood Found. Decorated knight of first rank Order of St. Olaf, 1976; Alaska commr. to Expo '88, Australia. Mem. Am. Soc. Newspaper Editors, Am. Polar Soc. (bd. govs.), C. of C. (pres. 1944, 48), Soc. Profl. Journalists. Republican. Presbyterian. Clubs: Explorers, Nat. Press. Lodges: Sons of Norway, Rotary, Elks, Masons, Pioneers of Alaska. Home and Office: 2000 Atwood Dr Anchorage AK 99517-1333

AU, BERTHA LIN TAI CHANG, school librarian, educator; b. Honolulu, Nov. 23, 1938; d. Louis Francis Ah Chong and Dorothy Ah Ngun Won Chang; m. Frederick Hung Fo Au, July 8, 1961; children: Celia Ann Tower, Matthew Alan, Beth Amity, Mitchell Avery. BEd, U. Hawaii, 1960; MEd/LS, U. Nev., Las Vegas, 1983. Tchr. St. Ann's Sch., Kaneohe, Hawaii, 1960-61; lang. tutor to Japanese children Corvallis, Oreg., 1961-62; asst. to libr. Oreg. State U. Libr., Corvallis, 1962-63; tchr. 7th and 8th grades St. Mary's Cath. Sch., Corvallis, 1963-64; tchr. kindergarten Washington Elem. Sch., Corvallis, 1964-65; tchr. music St. Viator's Cath. Sch., Las Vegas, 1973-74, libr., 1974-82; libr. Gordon McCaw Elem. Sch., Henderson, Nev., 1982-84, Jim Bridger Mid. Sch., North Las Vegas, Nev., 1984—, Clark County Sch. Libr. Assn., Nev., 1982—; Mem. adv. coms. Clark County Sch. Dist., Las Vegas, 1989-90, vol. Rev. of Asian Materials for Elem. Sch., 1983. Curriculum writer A Cultural Celebration K-12, 1991. Mem. NEA (sec. women's caucus 1994-96, Asian liaison officer 1991-93), Nev. State Edn. Assn. (chair minority affairs com. 1992-96), Cath. Daus. Am. (charter mem., treas. 1981-83), Clark County Classroom Tchrs. Assn. (chair minority afairs com. 1991-92). Home: 3763 Randa Ct Las Vegas NV 89104-4911 Office: Jim Bridger Mid Sch 2505 N Bruce St North Las Vegas NV 89030

AUER, BENEDICT LEROY, education educator, college official, priest; b. Chgo., Nov. 4, 1939; s. William F. and Marcelline D. (Boudreau) A. BS in Humanities, Loyola U., Chgo., 1962; MA in History, Creighton U., 1964; MDiv, St. Meinrad Sch. Theology, Ind., 1980; HHD (hon.), London Inst. for Applied Rsch., 1991; D in Ministry, San Francisco Theol. Sem., 1993. Joined Order St. Benedict, 1976, Roman Cath. Ch., ordained priest, 1980. Teaching fellow and scholar Creighton U., Omaha, 1963-64; instr. history Marymount Coll., Salina, Kans., 1964-65; chmn. English dept. Jr. Mil. Acad., Chgo., 1965-67; chmn. humanities Univ. Sch. Milw., 1967-71; tchr. history and English, St. Viator High Sch., Arlington Heights, Ill., 1972-76; chmn. English dept., assoc. coll. counselor, dir. admissions Marmion Mil. Acad., Aurora, Ill., 1980-88; dir. campus ministry St. Martin's Coll., Lacey, Wash., 1988-94, asst. prof. edn., 1991—; various pastoral assignments Diocese of Rockford, Ill., 1980-88; assoc. pastor St. Joseph Parish, Aurora, 1981-88; textbook editor social studies div. Laidlaw Bros., Ill., 1971-72. Author: (poetry) Touching Fingers with God, 1986, Priestless People, 1990, From Chicago to Canterbury: A Poetic Pilgrimage, 1991, Godspeak: Thirteen Characters in Search of an Author, 1991; contbr. articles to profl. jours., poetry to numerous mags. Recipient Poem of Yr. award Jubilee Press, 1987; scholar St. Meinrad Sch. Theology, 1977-80. Mem. Internat. Parliament for Peace and Safety, Acad. Midi, Pi Gamma Mu, Phi Alpha Theta. Home: St Martin's Abbey Lacey WA 98503 Office: St Martin's Coll 5300 Pacific Ave SE Lacey WA 98503-7500

AUERBACH, BRYAN NEIL, pediatrician; b. Chgo., May 6, 1946; s. Max R. and Jennie (Helman) A.; m. Angela Grace Anzalone, Apr. 14, 1973; children: Kimberly, Suzanne, David. BS, U. Mich., 1968; MD, U. Ill., Chgo., 1972. Diplomate Am. Bd. Pediatrics, Nat. Bd. Med. Examiners. Intern, resident pediatrics U. Ariz. Med. Ctr., 1972-75; pvt. practice, South Lake Tahoe, Calif., 1975-81, Tucson, 1981—. Fellow Am. Acad. Pediatrics. Office: 5335 E Erickson Dr Tucson AZ 85712-2826

AUERBACK, SANDRA JEAN, social worker; b. San Francisco, Feb. 21, 1946; d. Alfred and Molly Loy (Friedman) A. BA, U. Calif., Berkeley, 1967; MSW, Hunter Sch. Social Work, 1972. Diplomate clin. social work. Clin. social worker Jewish Family Services, Bklyn., 1972-73; clin. social worker Jewish Family Services, Hackensack, N.J., 1973-78; pvt. practice psychotherapy San Francisco, 1978—; dir. intake adult day care Jewish Home for the Aged, San Francisco, 1979-91. Mem. NASW (cert., bd. dirs. Bay Area Referral Svc. 1983-87, chmn. referral svc. 1984-87, state practice com. 1987-91, regional treas. 1989-91, rep. to Calif. Coun. Psychiatry, Psychology, Social Work and Nursing, 1987—, chmn. 1989, 93, v.p. cmty. svcs. 1991-93, chair Calif. polit. action com. 1993—), Am. Group Psychotherapy Assn., Mental Health Assn. San Francisco (trustee 1987—). Home: 1100 Gough St Apt 8C San Francisco CA 94109-6638 Office: 450 Sutter St San Francisco CA 94108-4206

AUESTAD, AMY EILEEN, freelance writer, poet; b. Seattle, Feb. 16, 1960; d. Gerald Arthur and Mae Charlotta (Johnson) Florence; m. Gregory Dwayne Gesell, July 16, 1983 (div. Jan. 1985); m. Craig Alan Auestad, Apr. 26, 1986; 1 child, Rachle Marie. BA, U. Wash., 1982. Supr. Time-Life Librs., Seattle, 1979-82; exec. asst. Wash. State Med. Assn., Seattle, 1982-86, cons., 1986-87; program adminstr. Wash. Physicians Health Program, Seattle, 1987-89; asst. adminstr. Wash. State Assn. Water and Wastewater Dists., Seattle, 1989-90; sr. sec. to chmn. emeritus-acting dir. dept. anesthesiology U. Wash., Seattle, 1990—; freelance writer, author, Bellevue, Wash., 1985—. Author: (with F.J. Fox) Geriatric Emergency Clincial Pharmacology, vol. 8, 1990; (mus. plays) (with A.J. Klockars) Gideon, 1992, Mama, There's A Muggle under My Bed, 1993. Vol. sr. high youth group Univ. Congl. United Ch. of Christ, Seattle, 1988—, organizer, moderator faith and ethics, faith and med. ethics, faith and bus. ethics, faith and criminal justice sys. series, 1993. Mem. Woodland Park Zoo, Crohn's and Colitis Found. Am., Pacific Sci. Ctr. Home: 9827 NE 27th St Bellevue WA 98004-1848

AUFDERHAAR, SUSAN, data processing executive; b. Celina, Ohio, Feb. 14, 1951; d. Norman Robert and Eleanor Belle (Shook) Aufderhaar; 1 child, Laura Michelle. B.G.S., U. Nebr., Omaha, 1978; cert. MIT, 1980; M.B.A., Webster U., 1985. Programmer/systems analyst Dept. Def. USAF, 1969-75; sr. programmer, analyst, mgr. quality assurance Majers Market Rsch., 1978-79; staff mgr. bus. systems Northwestern Bell Tel. Co., Omaha, 1979-82; mgr. area consultative staff AT&T Info. Systems, 1982-83; sr. dir. mktg. Datapoint Corp., 1983-85; sr. exec. data processing cons., mgr. exec. cons. services Boeing Computer Services, Seattle, 1985—; mgr. infosystems NASA, Houston; mgr. commercial airplanes support infosystems; owner Misty Ridge Kennel. Mem. NAFE, Assn. Computing Machinery (past sec.), Data Processing Mgrs. Assn. (exec. bd., sec.), Am. Mgmt. Assn., Smithsonian Instn., Cousteau Soc., Women Data Processing, Sweet Adelines (Lakeside chpt.), Gordon Setter Club of Am., World Wide Dream Builders, Nat. Honor Soc., Eastern Star. Republican. Mem. United Ch. of Christ. Office: The Boeing Co PO Box 24346 Seattle WA 98124-0346

AUGERBRIGHT, PAMELA JEAN, entrepreneur; b. San Pedro, Calif., Oct. 24, 1944; d. Thurman and Ernestine (Smith) Thomas; m. Theodore Alfred Augerbright, Feb. 3, 1963; 1 child, Theodore Alfred II. Student, Long Beach City Coll., 1978—. Owner Cake Decorating by PJ, Long Beach, Calif., 1964-78; statis. clk./sec. Douglas Aircraft Co., Long Beach, 1977-80; owner Pam's Bridal Experience, Long Beach, 1978—; buyer/sec. Hughes Aircraft Co., El Segundo, Calif., 1981-85. Author: I Remember Mom Bet, 1992. Sec. to pastor St. John Bapt. Ch., Long Beach, 1990—. Home and Office: 866 W 33rd Way Long Beach CA 90806-1257

AUGUSTYN, DAMIAN HENRY, gastroenterologist; b. Seattle, Jan. 11, 1952; m. Caroline Craig; 2 children. BS in Biol. Scis. with honors, Stanford U., 1974; MD, Harvard Med. Sch., 1978. Diplomate Am. Bd. Internal Medicine, Am. Bd. Gastroenterology. Intern U. Colo. Med. Ctr., Denver, 1978-79, resident in internal medicine, 1979-80; sr. resident in internal medicine U. Calif. Med. Ctr., San Francisco, 1980-81, gasteroenterology fellow, 1981-83, from clin. instr. to asst. clin. prof. medicine, 1983-91, assoc. clin. prof. medicine, 1991—; pvt. practice San Francisco, 1994—; staff Calif. Pacific Med. Ctr., San Francisco, 1983—, chmn. gastroenterology fellowship selection com., 1987—, chmn., divsn. gastroenterology and hepatology, 1994—, chmn. gastroenterology fellowship rev. com., 1987—, U. Calif., San Fracnsico, 1983—, St. Marys Hosp. and Med. Ctr., 1983—; bd. dirs., pres. Patient Assistance Found. Office Patient Svcs., Calif. Pacific Med. Ctr., 1986-93, pres., 1994—; mem. bd. med. advisors Blue Cross Calif., Woodland Hills; cons. physician Inflammatory Bowel Disease Ctr., 1992—; mng. ptnr. Pacific Internal Medicine Assoc., San Francisco, 1985—. Mem. ACP, Am. Gastroenterological Assn. (fin. com. mem. 1987-90, 93—), Am. Soc. Gastrointestinal Endoscopy (stds. practice com. mem. 1993—, No. Calif. rep. to coun. regional endoscopic soc.), Calif. Med. Assn. (del. representing gastroenterology in Calif. 1992-93), San Francisco Med. Soc., No. Calif. Soc. for

Clinical Gastroenterology (bd. dirs. 1987-94, pres. 1992-93), Calif. Fedn. Digestive Disease Soc. (bd. dirs. 1989—, pres. 1991-93). Office: Calif Pacific Profl Bldg 2100 Webster St Ste 423 San Francisco CA 94115-2380

AULT, PHILLIP HALLIDAY, author, editor; b. Maywood, Ill., Apr. 26, 1914; s. Frank W. and Bernda (Halliday) A.; m. Karoline Byberg, June 5, 1943 (dec. Jan. 1990); children: Frank, Ingrid, Bruce; m. Jane Born, May 1, 1993. AB, DePauw U., 1935. Reporter LaGrange (Ill.) Citizen, 1935-37; corr. editor UPI, Chgo., N.Y.C., Iceland, Norht Africa, London, 1938-48; bur. chief UPI, London, 1944-45; asst. mng. editor, dir. editorial page Times-Mirror Co., L.A., 1948; editorial page editor L.A. Mirror-News, 1948-57; exec. editor Associated Desert Newspapers, 1958-68; assoc. editor South Bend (Ind.) Tribune, 1968-79, cons. editor, 1979—. Author: This Is the Desert, 1959, News Around the Clock, 1960, How to Live in California, 1961, Home Book of Western Humor, 1967, Wonders of the Mosquito World, 1970, These Are The Great Lakes, 1972, Wires West, 1974, All Aboard, 1976, By the Seat of Their Pants, 1978, Whistles Round the Bend, 1982; co-author: Springboard to Berlin, 1943, Reporting and Writing the News, 1983, Introduction to Mass Communications, 1960, Public Relations: Strategies and Tactics, 1986; editor: Santa Maria Historical Photo Album, 1987. Mem. Am. Soc. Newspaper Editors, Assn. Edn. in Journalism, Western Writers Am. (Spur award 1977), Sigma Nu. Home: 21408 N 157th Dr Sun City West AZ 85375-6626

AURAND, CHARLES HENRY, JR., music educator; b. Battle Creek, Mich., Sept. 6, 1932; s. Charles Henry and Elisabeth Dirk (Hoekstra) A.; m. Donna Mae Erb, June 19, 1954; children: Janice, Cheryl, Sandra, Charles III, William. MusB, Mich. State U., 1954, MusM, 1958; PhD, U. Mich., 1971. Cert. tchr., Mich., Ohio. Asst. prof. music Hiram Coll., Ohio, 1958-60; dean, prof. music Youngstown State U., 1960-73; dean No. Ariz. U., Flagstaff, 1973-88, prof. music, 1988-94, prof. emeritus, 1994—; chmn. Ariz. Alliance for Arts Edn., 1974-77; solo clarinetist Flagstaff Symphony; solo, chamber music and orch. musician, 1973-86; fine arts cons. Miami U. of Ohio, 1982. Author: Selected Solos, Methods, 1963. Elder Presbyterian Ch., 1965; chmn. Boy Scouts Am., Coconino dist., 1974-78; bd. dirs. Ariz. Com. Arts for the Handicapped, 1982-88, Flagstaff Symphony Orch., 1973-85, Flagstaff Festival of Arts, 1973-89; bd. dirs. Sedona Chamber Mus. Soc., 1989—; conf. dir. Internat. Clarinet Soc., 1991. Served to 1st lt. USAF, 1955-57. Recipient award of merit Boy Scouts Am., 1977; cert. appreciation John F. Kennedy Ctr. Performing Arts, 1985. Mem. Am. Assn. Higher Edn., Ariz. Humanities Assn., Music Educators Nat. Conf., State Adminstrs. of Music Schs. (chmn. 1971-73), Internat. Clarinet Soc./ClariNetwork Internat. (conf. dir. 1991). Republican. Presbyterian. Lodge: Kiwanis (pres. 1984-85). Home: 140 Fairway Oaks Ln Sedona AZ 86351-8835 Office: No Ariz U Box 6040 Flagstaff AZ 86011

AURILIA, ANTONIO, physicist, educator; b. Napoli, Italy, May 14, 1942; came to U.S., 1986, naturalized, 1993; s. Clemente and Assunta (Ligesto) A.; m. Elizabeth Christine Adams, Dec. 1, 1972; children: Darius Matthew, Alexandra Rebecca. Laurea in Physics, U. Naples, Italy, 1966; PhD in Physics, U. Wis., Milw., 1970. Postdoctoral fellow dept. physics U. Alta., Edmonton, 1970-72; rsch. assoc. dept. physics Syracuse (N.Y.) U., 1972-74; rsch. scientist Internat. Ctr. Theoretical Physics, Trieste, Italy, 1974-75, Nat. Inst. Nuclear Physics, Trieste, 1975-86; prof. dept. physics Calif. State Poly. U., Pomona, 1986—. Mem. Am. Phys. Soc., Am. Assn. Physics Tchrs., N.Y. Acad. Sci., Sigma Xi. Democrat. Roman Catholic. Office: Calif State U Dept Physics 3801 W Temple Ave Pomona CA 91768-2557

AURNER, ROBERT RAY, author, corporate executive; b. Adel, Iowa, Aug. 20, 1898; s. Clarence Ray and Nellie (Slayton) A.; m. Kathryn Dayton, June 16, 1921; 1 son, Robert Ray II. B.A. summa cum laude, U. Iowa, 1919, M.A., 1920, Ph.D., 1922. Dir. customer relations, new bus. The State Bank, Madison, Wis., 1925-28; research dir. Walker Co., 1925-30; established Aurner and Assocs., Cons. to Mgmt., bus. adminstrn., market distbn. and human relations, pres., chmn., chief exec. officer, 1938—, pres., 1988—; v.p., dir. Pacific Futures, Inc., 1962—; dir., chmn. bus adv. com. VNA Corp., 1959-62; fin. cons., dir. Carmel Savs. & Loan Assn., Calif., 1960-71; lectr. NBC Station WTMJ, 1929-30; state commr. Wis. Library Certification Bd., 1931-38; pres. Am. Bus. Communication Assn., 1939 40; mem. faculty, adminstrv. staff U. Wis., 1925-48, ranking research prof. bus. adminstrn., chmn. adminstrn. and mgmt. div., mem. univ. lectr. bur., 1930-48; vis. prof. bus. mgmt. U. Pitts., 1934, 36, 39; vis. research prof. Rare Book Rm., Huntington Library, San Marino, Calif., 1941; adminstrv. cons. Internat. Cellucotton Products Co., Chgo., 1947-52; cons., dir. Communications Div., Fox River Paper Corp., Appleton, Wis., 1947-60; v.p., gen. cons., dir. Scott, Inc., Milw. and Carmel, 1949—; cons. U.S. Naval Postgrad. Sch., Mgmt. Sch. Div., Dept. Navy, Dept. Def., 1957—, Jahn & Ollier Corp., Morris, Schenker, Roth, Inc., First Nat. Bank, Chgo., Library Research Service, New Haven, Nat. Assn. Real Estate Bds., N.Y.C., Allis-Chalmers Corp., Milw.; ltd. partner Salinas-Peninsula Investment Co., 1963-72; cons. Wis. Div. Vital Statistics, 1930-48; Dean Coll. of Commerce, Biarritz Am. U., France, U.S. Army Univ. Center No. 2, ETO, 1945-46; attached U.S. Army, USFET, I. and E. Div., Field Grade, rank of col., 1945-46; spl. lectr. Netherlands Sch. Econs., Rotterdam, 1945; U.S. State Dept. rep. Dutch-Am. Conf., The Hague, Holland, 1945; mem. nat. adv. com. Conf. Am. Small Business Orgns., 1947—; Dir. SAE Corp., Evanston, Ill., 1943-53, pres., chmn. bd., chief exec. officer, 1951-53, Eminent Supreme Archon; mem. nat. adv. counsel Atlantic Union, Inc., 1949—. Author: Specialized Field Approach, 1963, Language Control for Business, 1965, Success Factors in Executive Development, 1967, Effective English for Colleges, 6th edit., 1980, Effective English for Business Communication, 8th edit., 1982, Effective Communication in Business with Management Emphasis, 8th edit., 1988; contbg. editor: Am. Ency. Social Scis.; co-author, contbg. editor, American Business Practice (4 vols.). Trustee Levere Meml. Found., Chgo., 1943-53, pres., chmn. bd., chief exec. officer, 1951-53; chmn. bd., pres., chief exec. officer Carmel Found., Calif., 1981-85, v.p., 1977-81, dir., past chmn. fin. com., past chmn. meml. policy com. mem. internal trusteeship com., exec. com., 1954-83; mem. bd. investment mgmt. Hazeltine Fund Calif., 1963-83; adv. gov., bd. dirs. Monterey Fund Edn., 1965—; dir., chmn. com. endowments York Sch., 1966-69; bd. dirs. Wis. div. AAA, 1936-47. Recipient Disting. Service award with gold medal Sigma Alpha Epsilon, 1967; Championship Gold Medal award N.O.L. Big Ten Univ. Debate Competition, 1919. Fellow Assn. Bus. Communication (hon.); mem. Am. Mktg. Assn., Nat. Assn. Mktg. (v.p. 1931), Smithsonian Instn. Nat. Assos., Wis. Acad. Scis., Arts and Letters, State Hist. Soc. Iowa, Phi Beta Kappa, Delta Sigma Rho, Alpha Kappa Psi (vice chmn. com. profl. programs, exec. group 1955—), Sigma Alpha Epsilon (supreme council 1943-53, nat. pres. 1951-53). Clubs: Continental (Chgo.); Highlands (Monterey Peninsula), Decemvir (Monterey Peninsula), Convivium (Monterey Peninsula); Statesman's (Los Angeles); The Group (Pebble Beach, Calif.). Home: San Antonio and Inspiration Aves PO Box 3434 Carmel By Sea CA 93921-3434 Office: PO Box 3434 Carmel CA 93921-3434 also: Bristlecone Trading and Devel Corp 908 Long Beach Blvd Surf City NJ 08008-5300

AUSFAHL, WILLIAM FRIEND, household products company executive; b. San Francisco, Apr. 20, 1940; s. Robert Hugh and Doris Jane (Friend) A.; m. Trudy Lynn Wierman, June 23, 1962; children: Thomas, Andrew, Matthew. A.B. in Econs., U. Calif., Berkeley, 1961; M.B.A., Stanford U., 1963. Asst. to dean Stanford U. Grad. Sch. Bus., 1963-64; with Cutter Labs., Inc., 1964-82; treas., dir. fin. Cutter Labs., Inc., Emeryville, Calif., 1973-77; v.p. fin., mem. ops. com. Cutter Labs., Inc., 1977-82; sr. v.p. fin., mem. ops. com. Miles Labs., Elkhart, Ind., 1979-82; group v.p., chief fin. officer, dir. Clorox Co., Oakland, Calif., 1982—. Bd. dirs. Merritt-Peralta Inst., Merritt-Peralta Found. Mem. Fin. Execs. Inst. Republican. Office: Clorox Co 1221 Broadway Oakland CA 94612-1837

AUST, STEVEN DOUGLAS, biochemistry, biotechnology and toxicology educator; b. South Bend, Wash., Mar. 11, 1938; s. Emil and Helen Mae (Crawford) A.; m. Nancy Lee Haworth, June 5, 1960 (dec.); children: Teresa, Brian; m. Ann Elizabeth Lacy, Feb. 4, 1972. BS in Agr., Wash. State U., 1960, MS in Nutrition, 1962; PhD in Dairy Sci., U. Ill., 1965. Postdoctoral fellow dept. toxicology Karolinska Inst., Stockholm, 1966; N.Z. facial eczema sr. postdoctoral fellow Ruakura Agrl. Research Ctr., Hamilton, 1975-76; mem. faculty dept. biochemistry Mich. State U., East Lansing, 1967-87, prof., 1977-87, assoc. dir. Ctr. for Environ. Toxicology, 1980-85, dir. Ctr. for the Study of Active Oxygen, 1985-87; dir. biotech. ctr. Utah State U., Logan, 1987-91, prof. chem. biochemistry, 1987—; dir. basic rsch. and tng. program Super Fund Nat. Inst. Environ. Health Scis., 1988—; mem. toxicology study sect. NIH, 1979-83; mem. environ. measurements com., mem. sci. adv. bd. EPA, 1980-83; mem. toxicology data bank, mem. peer rev. com. Nat. Libr. Medicine, 1983-85; mem. Mich. Toxic Substance Control Commn., 1979-82, chmn., 1981-82; exec. v.p. rsch. Intech One-Eighty Corp., North Logan, Utah, 1993—. Contbr. articles to profl. jours. Recipient Nat. Rsch. Svc. award NIH, USPHS, 1966, Dupont Sci. and Engring. award, 1988; NRC facial eczema fellow Ruakuna Agrl. Rsch. Ctr., Hamilton, New Zealand, 1975. Fellow Acad. Toxicology Scis., Oxygen Soc.; mem. Am. Soc. Biol. Chemists, Am. Soc. Pharmacology and Exptl. Therapeutics, Soc. Toxicology, Am. Soc. Photobiology, Am. Soc. Microbiology. Office: Utah State U Biotech Ctr Logan UT 84322-4705

AUSTEN, HALLIE IGLEHART, author; b. N.Y.C., Nov. 4, 1947; d. Francis Nash and Harriet Austen (Stokes) Iglehart. AB, Brown U., 1969; student, Union Grad. Sch., Columbus, Ohio, 1983-86. instr. Nat. Women's Studies Assn. Rutgers U., Camden, N.J., 1984, Graduate Theol. Union, Berkeley, Calif., 1984; lectr. UN Non-Govtl. Orgns, Women's Conf., Copenhagen, 1980, U. Calif., Santa Cruz, Calif., 1978, Berkeley, Calif., 1975-76, 86, 88, Feminist Therapy Ctr. Conf., Malibu, Calif., 1980, Heartwood Coll., Santa Cruz. 1981, Ancient Ways Festival, Harbin, Calif. 1984, Welcome Home Conf., San Francisco State U., 1985, Long Beach Woman spirit, 1988, John F. Kennedy U., Orinda, Calif., 1988, The Spotted Fawn Gallery, Pt. Reyes, 1988. Mem. Museum of Modern Art, San Francisco, 1978, Glyptotek Museum, Copenhagen, 1980, Damon Studio, N.Y.C., 1980, Cerridwen Salon, N.Y.C., 1980, Esalen Inst., Big Sur, Calif., 1981, U. Calif., L.A., 1985; dir., instr. Women In Spiritual Edn., Berkeley, Point Reyes, Calif., 1975—; instr. Nat. Women's Studies Assn. Rutgers U., Camden, N.J., 1984; lectr. U. Calif., Berkeley, 1975-76, 86, 88, Santa Cruz, 1978, Feminist Therapy Ctr. Conf., Malibu, Calif., 1980, UN Non-Govtl. Orgns. Women's Conf., Copenhagen, 1980, San Jose State U., 1980, Heartwood Coll., Santa Cruz, 1981, Interface Ctr., Boston, 1984, San Francisco State U., 1985, Women's Alliance, Nevada City, Calif., 1985-86, Long Beach Womanspirit, 1988, U. Calif., 1988, John F. Kennedy U., Orinda, Calif., 1988, Calif. Sch. of Herbal Studies, Guerneville, Calif., 1978-80, 83-84, 87-88, Oasis Ctr., Chgo., 1992. Appeared in Take Back the Night, 1978, Presence of the Goddess (Balcorman Films), 1985; author: Womanspirit: A Guide to Women's Wisdom, 1983, The Heart of the Goddess: Art, Myth and Meditations of the World's Sacred Feminine, 1990, Quest: A Feminist Quarterly, 1977; contbr. numerous articles to books, newspapers and mags. Counselor San Francisco Women's Switchboard, 1973-74; instr. Am. Friends Svcs. Com., San Francisco, 1974; workshop leader Nat. Conf. on Violence Against Women, San Francisco, 1977; mem. Nat. Caucus of Women and the Arts, San Francisco, 1982, San Francisco Art Inst., 1982, Nat. Film Bd. of Can., 1985. Mem. San Francisco Women's Found. (assoc. 1983—), Point Reyes Dzog Chen, San Francisco Sonar, Druid Heights Artists Retreat (v.p. 1988—). Democrat. Office: Women In Spiritual Edn PO Box 697 Point Reyes Station CA 94956-0697

AUSTEN, SHELLI, actress; b. Tulsa, Sept. 8, 1954; m. Fred Chris Sorenson, Dec. 31, 1984 (div. Oct. 1988); 1 child, Kristen Amara. BA, U. Calif., Santa Barbara, 1974. With various improvisational acting troupes, 1974-80; news dir. Sta. KMVI, Maui, Hawaii, 1980-83; v.p. Bill Baker Advt., Honolulu, 1983-85; advt. dir. Ground Swell Mag., Haleiwa, 1985-87; prodr., reporter, anchor Sta. KHVH, Honolulu, 1987-92; dir. adv. Beachcomber Mag., 1992-93; disc jockey Sta. KGY, Olympia, Wash., 1994—; reporter Alameda (Calif.) Times Star, 1994—; media cons. Rep. Party of Hawaii, Honolulu, 1987—; actress Starlight Theatre, Pasadena Playhouse, Altarina Playhouse. Contbr. articles to profl. jours. Media coord. Merimed found., Honolulu, 1988; del. Rep. Party, Honolulu, 1989, mem. presdl. task force, Honolulu, 1989-90. Episcopalian. Home: 849 Cedar St Alameda CA 94501-5215

AUSTERER-WILLIAMS, ELEONORE, art gallery owner, director; b. Vienna, Austria, Nov. 19, 1944; came to U.S., 1982.; d. Maximilian Julius and Maria Magdalena (Mitsche) Austerer; m. Mark R. Williams. BA in Liberal Arts, Hochschule, 1962; postgrad., U. Geneva, 1962-66. Translator in German, French, Spanish, English UN, Geneva, 1968-71; real estate agent Edificio Marino S.A., Marbella, Spain, 1971-73; dir., owner Chelsea Market, Art & Antiques, Marbella, 1973-81; art cons. Eleonore Austerer Fine Art, San Mateo, Calif., 1982-87; dir., owner Eleonore Austerer Gallery, San Francisco, 1987—. Co-author/editor: Catalogue Raisonnee "A Retrospective" of the works by artist Roberto Lauro, 1992. Mem. Mus. Modern Art, San Francisco, 1981, San Francisco Visitors & Convention Bur., 1988. Office: Eleonore Austerer Gallery 540 Sutter St San Francisco CA 94102-1102

AUSTIN, HARRIET BUCHANAN, physiologist; b. Woodbury, N.J., Aug. 8, 1957; d. Mike Edward and Dorris (Myrick) Buchanan; m. Brice Wesley Thomas, May 17, 1980; children: John, Matt. BS in Biology, Vanderbilt U., 1979; MA in Biology, U. Colo., 1985, PhD in Biology, 1988. Rsch. assoc. U. Colo., Boulder, 1993—; asst. prof. Widener U., Chester, Pa., 1988-89, U. Wyo., Laramie, 1989-93. Author: (with others) Contributions in Herpetology, 1992; contbr. articles to profl. jours. Grantee NSF, 1992, NIH, 1992. Mem. AAAS, Sigma Xi. Office: U Colo Biology Dept Campus Box 334 Boulder CO 80309

AUSTIN, JOHN NORMAN, classics educator; b. Anshun, Kweichow, China, May 20, 1937; s. John Alfred and Lillian Maud (Reeks) A. B.A., U. Toronto, Ont. Can., 1958; M.A., U. Calif.-Berkeley, 1959, Ph.D., 1965. Vis. lectr. Yale U., New Haven, 1971; asst. prof., then assoc. prof. UCLA, 1966-76; Aurelio prof. Greek Boston U., 1976-78; prof. classics U. Mass., Amherst, 1978-80; prof. classics U. Ariz., Tucson, 1980—, acting dean humanities, 1987-88, head, dept. classics, 1995—. Author: Archery at the Dark of the Moon, 1975, Meaning and Being in Myth, 1990, Helen of Troy and Her Shameless Phantom, 1994; editor: (with others) The Works of John Dryden, vol. III; sr. editor Calif. Studies Classical Antiquity, vols. VI and VII. Jr. fellow Ctr. for Hellenic Studies, 1968-69, J.S. Guggenheim Found. fellow, 1974-75. Mem. Am. Philol. Assn. (bd. dirs. 1983-86). Episcopalian. Home: 2939 E 3rd St Tucson AZ 85716-4122 Office: U Ariz Dept Of Classics Tucson AZ 85721

AUTH, ROBERT RALPH, art educator; b. Bloomington, Ill., Oct. 27, 1926; s. Phillip C. and Frances E. A. BFA, Ill. Wesleyan U., 1953; MFA, Wash. State U., 1963. Art tchr. Burley, Idaho, 1959, Boise (Idaho) Ind. Sch. Dist., 1960-81; art supr. Boise Ind. Sch. Dist., Boise, ID, 1981-87. Author: ID State Humanities Curriculum Guide, 1985; creator historic prints, paintings, sculptures. Cmty. svc. adv. Boise's Jr. League; mem. Allied Arts Coun.; bd. dirs., Boise Gallery of Art, Boise Edn. Assn., Alliance for Arts in Edn. Recipient Allied Arts Coun. Artist of the Year award, 1972, Nat. Art Edn. award, 1979, Ind. Hist. Soc. Hon. Curator of Military Hist. award, 1983, Gov. of Ind. medal for Excellence in the Arts, 1988, The Ind. Statesman's Distinguished Citizen award, 1988, Phi Delta Kappa Friend of Edn. award, 1989. Roman Catholic. Home: PO Box 91 Yellow Pine ID 83677-0091

AUTOLITANO, ASTRID, consumer products executive; b. Havana, Cuba, Aug. 25, 1938; came to U.S., 1966; d. Manuel and Efigenia (Giquel) Rodriguez; m. Dominick Autolitano, July 23, 1977; children: Astrid Martinez, Manuel Martinez. Student, U. Havana, 1962-64, El Camino Coll., Torrance, Calif., 1968-71, UCLA, Westwood, 1973-75, Columbia U., 1983. Multi-lingual sec. Mattel Toys, Hawthorne, Calif., 1966-69, coord. internat. sales, 1969-73, mgr. Pan Am. sales, 1973-78, dir. export sales and licensees, 1978-83, v.p. Latin Am., 1983-89; sr. v.p. Latin Am. Mattel Toys, El Segundo, Calif., 1989—. Office: Mattel Toys 333 Continental Blvd El Segundo CA 90245-5032

AUTRY, GENE (ORVON GENE AUTRY), actor, entertainer, broadcasting executive, baseball team executive; b. Tioga, Tex., Sept. 29, 1907; s. Delbert and Elnora (Ozmont) A.; m. Ina Mae Spivey, Apr. 1, 1932; m. Jacqueline Ellam, 1981. Grad., Tioga (Tex.) High Sch., 1925. R.R. telegraph operator Sapulpa, Okla., 1925; owner, chmn. bd. Calif. Angels; pres. Flying A Prodns.; owner KSCA-FM, L.A., Golden West Broadcasters; chmn. bd. Autry Mus. of Western Heritage, L.A.; pres. several music and publ. cos. Made first phonograph record of cowboy songs, 1929; radio artist Sta. WLS, Chgo., 1930-34; motion picture actor, 1934-53, including In Old Santa Fe; starred in 88 musical Western feature pictures, 91 half-hour TV pictures 1950-55; has written or co-written over 200 songs including That Silver-Haired Daddy of Mine, 1931(1st gold record given to anyone), You're the Only Star in My Blue Heaven, 1938, Dust, 1938, Tears On My Pillow, 1941, Be Honest With Me, 1941, Tweedle O'Twill, 1942, Here Comes Santa Claus, 1948; host Melody Ranch Theater Nashville Network, 1987, 88. With USAAF, 1942-45. Recipient: D.W. Griffith award, 1991. Mem. Internat. Footprinters. Clubs: Masons (33 degree), Shriners, Elks. Office: 4383 Colfax Ave Studio City CA 91604-2837

AVAKIAN, JAMES LAWRENCE, engineering executive; b. L.A., Feb. 14, 1957; s. James Haig and Alice Louise Avakian; m. Alice Arzoumanian. Degree in electronics engring., Calif. Poly., 1986. Pres. Computer Tech., Inc., San Luis Obispo, Calif., 1985-86; devel. engr. Hughes Aircraft Co., El Segundo, Calif., 1986-87; pres. Optical Automation, Inc., Tarzana, Calif., 1987—, owner, 1994—. Inventor in field. Mem. IEEE, Internat. Solid State Circuits Conf., Digital Signal Processing Exposition, Visual Hardware Descriptive Lang. Internat., Optical Lab. Assn., Optical Mfr. Assn. Democrat.

AVAKOFF, JOSEPH CARNEGIE, medical and legal consultant; b. Fairbanks, Alaska, July 15, 1936; s. Harry B. and Margaret (Adams) A.; m. Teddy I. Law, May 7, 1966; children: Caroline, Joey, John. AA, U. Calif., Berkeley, 1956, AB, 1957; MD, U. Calif., San Francisco, 1961; JD, Santa Clara U., 1985. Bar: Calif. 1987; diplomate Am. Bd. Surgery, Am. Bd. Plastic Surgery. Physicist U.S. Naval Radiol. Def. Lab., San Francisco, 1957, 59; intern So. Pacific Gen. Hosp., San Francisco, 1961-62; resident in surgery Kaiser Found. Hosp., San Francisco, 1962-66; resident in plastic surgery U. Tex. Sch. Medicine, San Antonio, 1970-72; pvt. practice specializing in surgery Sacramento, 1966-70; pvt. practice specializing in plastic surgery Los Gatos and San Jose, Calif., 1972-94; cons. to med. and legal professions, 1994—; clin. instr. surgery Sch. Medicine U. Calif., Davis, 1967-70; chief dept. surgery Mission Oaks Hosp., Los Gatos, 1988-90, chief div. plastic surgery Good Samaritan Hosp., San Jose, 1989-91; presenter numerous med. orgns. Contbr. numerous articles to med. jours. Mem. San Jose Adv. Commn. on Health, 1975-82; bd. govs. San Jose YMCA, 1977-80. Mem. AMA, Calif. Med. Assn., Santa Clara County Bar Assn., Santa Clara County Med. Assn., Union Am. Physicians and Dentists, Phi Beta Kappa, Phi Eta Sigma. Republican. Presbyterian. Home: 6832 Rockview Ct San Jose CA 95120-5607

AVALLE-ARCE, JUAN BAUTISTA, language educator; b. Buenos Aires, Argentina, May 13, 1927; came to U.S., 1948; s. Juan B. and Maria Martina Avalle-Arce; m. Constance Marginot, Aug. 20, 1953 (dec. 1969); children: Juan Bautista, Maria Martina, Alejandro Alcantara; m. Diane Janet Pamp, Aug. 30, 1969; children: Maria la Real Alejandra, Fadrique Martin Manuel. AB, Harvard U., 1951, MA, 1952, PhD, 1955; LittD (hon.), U. Castilla-La Mancha, Spain. Tutor, Harvard U., 1953-55; asst. prof., then assoc. prof. Spanish, Ohio State U., 1955-62; prof. Spanish, Smith Coll., Northampton, Mass., 1962-66, Sophia Smith prof. Hispanic studies, 1966-69; William Rand Kenan, Jr. prof. Spanish, U. N.C., Chapel Hill, 1969-85; prof. Spanish U. Calif., Santa Barbara, 1985—, chmn. dept. Spanish and Portuguese, 1991-95, dir. Summer Inst. Hispanic Langs. and Culture, 1991—, José Miguel de Barandiarán prof. Basque studies, 1993—; vis. scholar Univ. Ctr. Ga., 1972, lectr., 1961—, Univ. Ctr. Va., 1976; vis. prof. U. Salamanca, 1982, 84, 86, 88, U. Málagá, 1987, 90, 91, U. della Tuscia (Italy), 1988, Sophia U. (Japan), 1988, Kyoto U. Fgn. Affairs, 1988, U. Cuyo, U. Buenos Aires, 1989, Alcalá de Henares, 1995; vis. Hillyer Prof. Humanities U. Nev., Reno, 1995; Ph.D. program evaluator N.Y. State Bd. Regents; cons. Coun. Grad. Schs. in U.S.; reader Nat. Humanities Ctr., Govt. Found. for 5th Centennial of Discovery of Am., Spain; cultural corr. Radio Nacional de España; official guest Euskadiko Erradio, Spain, 1988-89. Author: Conocimiento y vida en Cervantes, 1959, La novela pastoril española, 1959, 2d enlarged edit., 1974, La Galatea de Cervantes, 2 vols., 1961, 2d rev. edit., 1987, Gonzalo Fernández de Oviedo, 1962, 2d edit., 1989, El Inca Garcilaso en sus Comentarios, 1961, Deslindes cervantinos, 1961, Three Exemplary Novels, 1964, Bernal Francès y su Romance, 1966, El Persiles de Cervantes, 1969, Los entremeses de Cervantes, 1969, Don Juan Valera y Morsamor, 1970, El cronista Pedro de Escavias Una vida del Siglo XV, 1972, Suma cervantina, 1973, Narradores hispoamericanos de hoy, 1973, Las Memorias de Gonzalo Fernández de Oviedo, 2 vols., 1974, El Peregrino en su patria de Lope de Vega, 1973, Nuevos deslindes cervantinos, 1974, Temas hispánicos medievales, 1975, Don Quijote como forma de vida, 1976, Dintorno de una época dorada, 1978, Cervantes, Don Quixote, annotated critical edit., 2 vols., 1978, rev. and enlarged edit., 1995, Cervantes, Novelas ejemplares, annotated edit., 3 vols., 1982, Lope de Vega, Las hazañas del Segundo David, 1984; La Galatea de Cervantes: 400 Años Despuès, 1985, Garci Rodriguez de Montalvo: Amadís de Gaula, 2 vols., 1985, Amadís de Gaula: El primitivo y el de Montalvo, 1991, Lecturas, 1987, Gonzalo Fernández de Oviedo, Batallas y quinquagenas, 1989, Garci Rodriguez de Montalvo Amadis de Gaula, 2 vols., 1991, Cancionero del Almirante don Fadrique Euriquez, 1993, Enciclopedia Cervantina, 1995. Trustee Teutonic Order of the Levant, Marqués de la Lealtad. Recipient Bonsoms medal Spain, 1961; Guggenheim fellow, 1961; grantee Am. Council Learned Socs., 1965, 68; grantee NEH, 1968, 1978-80; grantee Am. Philos. Soc., 1961, 67; recipient Susan Anthony Potter Lit. prize, 1951; Centro Gallego Lit. prize, 1947; Diploma of Merit, Università delle Arti, Italy; named Grand Companion, Société Internationale de la Noblesse Héréditaire. Sr. fellow Southeastern Inst. Medieval and Renaissance Studies; hon. fellow Soc. Spanish and Spanish Am. Studies; fellow Colegio Mayor Arzobispo D. Alonso de Fonseca of U. Salamanca; mem. Acad. Lit. Studies, Am. Acad. Rsch. Historians Medieval Spain, Academia Argentina de Letras, Anglo Am. Basque Studies Soc., Cervantes Soc. Am. (pres. 1979—), Ctr. for Medieval and Renaissance Studies, UCLA (assoc.), Soc. de Bibliofilos Espanoles, Modern Humanities Research Assn., South Atlantic Modern Lang. Assn., Assn. Internac. de Hispanistas, Modern Lang. Assn., Renaissance Soc. Am. (nat. del. to exec. coun. 1971), Real Sociedad Vascongada de Amigos del País, Centro de Estudios Jacobeos, Inst. d'Etudes Medievales, Inst. de Lit. Iberoamericana, Hispanic Soc. Am., Acad. Lit. Studies (charter), Mediaeval Acad. Am., Real Academia de Buenas Letras de Barcelona, Instituto Internacional de Literatura Iberoamericana, Sovereign Mil. Teutonic Order of the Levant (bailiff, knight grand cross, Grand Prior, Grand Priory of the U.S.), Harvard Club. Clubs: Triangle Hunt (Durham) (gentleman Whipper-in); U. N.C. Polo, Combined Training Events Assn. Office: U Calif 4323 Phelps Hall Santa Barbara CA 93106

AVERETT, ROBERT LEE, information systems professional, educator; b. Richfield, Utah, Dec. 4, 1952; s. Robert Elmo and Patsy (Meyer) A.; m. Alice Greenhalgh, Mar. 23, 1972; children: Nathan Christopher, Rachel Leah, Christian Alexander, Jeduthan William. BA, Brigham Young U., 1975, MLS, 1976; MA, Ball State U., 1979; D of Pub. Adminstrn., George Mason U., 1991. Cert. computer profl.; cert. secondary tchr., counselor, Utah. Commd. 2d lt. U.S. Army, 1976, advanced through grades to lt. col., 1993; chief adminstrv. svcs. Army Tng. Ctr., Ft. Jackson, S.C., 1979-82; chief personnel info. system dept. Mil. Personnel Ctr., Alexandria, Va., 1982-84; info. systems project mgr. Orgn. of Joint Chiefs of Staff, The Pentagon, 1984-85; mgmt. info. systems officer Hqrs. Dept. of Army, The Pentagon, 1985-87; comdr. 201st Signal Co., Seoul, Republic of Korea, 1987-89, Mil. Entrance Process Sta., Amarillo, Tex., 1989-92; asst. prof. mil. sci. Brigham Young U., Provo, Utah, 1992-93; chair, prof. mil. sci. U. Utah, Salt Lake City, 1993—; program dir. Armed Forces Comms.-Electronics Assn., Seoul, 1987-89; cons., adj. Amarillo Coll., 1989-92, Limestone Coll., 1979-82. Leader Boy Scouts Am., Nat. Capitol Coun., Alexandria, 1982-87, Golden Spread Coun., Amarillo, 1987-98. Recipient Meritorious Svc. award N.G. Bur., 1987, Armed Forces Comm-Elec Assn., 1989. Mem. ASPA. Home: 466 E 2780 N Provo UT 84604-5919 Office: Univ Utah Dept Military Science Salt Lake City UT 84112

AVERY, ELAINE ELVIRA, life insurance representative, retired; b. Belden, N.D., Aug. 10, 1924; d. Oscar Lofgren and Ina (Niemi) Karni; m. William H. Avery, Aug. 20, 1950; children: Ned, Jon, Mark. BS, U. Minn., 1946; MS, U. Wyo., 1962. Secondary tchr., Cook, Minn., 1946-47, Douglas, Wyo., 1947-50; instr. Sheridan (Wyo.) Coll., 1957-67, dean women, 1959-65, chmn. social studies div., 1964-66; dietitian Meml. Hosp., Sheridan, 1967-76; rep. N.Y. Life Ins. Co., Sheridan, 1976-94, retired, 1994. Vice chmn. Wyo. Commn. on Status of Women, 1967-74; chmn. adminstrv. bd. Meth. Ch., Sheridan, 1985, lay leader, 1986; membership chmn. Community Concert Assn., Sheridan, 1989—; mem. Vols. Am., Sheridan, 1991—. Mem. Million

Dollar Round Table, AAUW (pres. 1965-67), P.E.O., Daus. of Nile, Phi Upsilon Omicron (sec.). Republican.

AVERY, JULIA MAY, speech pathologist, organizational volunteer; b. Holly, Colo., May 2, 1917; d. Willard Smith and Bertha Eudora (Knuckey) A. AA, Colo. Women's Coll., 1936; BA, U. Colo., 1939; postgrad., UCLA, 1942, U. Calif., 1944; MA in Speech Pathology, U. Colo., 1960. Cert. life tchr. and speech pathologist, Colo. Tchr. 4th-8th grades Mt. Harris (Colo.) Pub. Schs., 1939-41; tchr. 2d grade, spl. edn., speech pathology Pueblo (Colo.) Pub. Schs., 1941-77, spl. edn. tchr. physically handicapped, 1946-54; speech pathologist Pueblo, 1954—. Co-author: DiBur Speech Therapy Card Games (32 sets), 1959. Mem. adv. bd. Area Agy. on Aging; active United Way, Retarded Citizens Assn., bd. dirs. YWCA, also past pres.; past pres., sec. Greehorn Valley Arts Coun., 1994-95. Named Tchr. of Yr., Star Jour., 1971, Chieftain, 1949-50; recipient Community Svc. award Optimists, 1985, 86, 87, numerous others. Mem. AARP (Colo. state legis. com. 1984-88, program dir. Community Housing Info. Sr. Svcs. 1991-93, health advocacy svc. local coord. 1993-94), NEA (life), DAR (past pres. local chpt.), Colo. Gerontol. Soc. (bd. dirs. 1989-95), United Srs. of Colo. (pres. 1989, Colo. sr. lobby, area rep., lobbyist), Am. Speech and Hearing Assn. (past local pres.), Colo. Speech and Hearing Assn., Southeastern Colo. Hist. Soc. (pres. 1990-95), Colo. Archeol. Soc. (past state pres.), League Club Bus. and Profl. Women (pres. 1991-95), Terr. Daus. Colo., Pueblo Beautiful Assn. (pres. 1994-95). Republican. Episcopalian. Home: 725 W Grant Ave Pueblo CO 81004-1414

AVERY, KEITH WILLETTE, artist, educator; b. Lansing, Mich., Dec. 3, 1921; s. Norton Louis and Ruby Mae (Willette) A.; m. Carol Joyce Haddan, Oct. 10, 1946; children: Carleton Louis, David Keith, Jane Ellen Avery Gray. BS, N.Mex. State U., 1955, LittD, 1986. Cert. secondary edn. tchr., N.Mex., Ariz., Mich. Horse trainer and exhibitor A.B. Johnson Chevrolet Co., Grand Rapids, Mich., 1946-47; ranch foreman and horse trainer Lazy U Ranch, Bartlesville, Okla., 1949-50, Mill Iron Lazy 3 Ranch, Carrizozo, N.Mex., 1950-51; artist N.Mex. State U., Las Cruces, 1951-55; instr. and calf roping coach Judson Sch., Scottsdale, Ariz., 1955-59; instr. Lowell (Mich.) High Sch., 1961-74; artist horseman Springer, Roswell, N.Mex., 1974—; dir. alumni rels. N.Mex. State U., Las Cruces, 1959-60. Author: Ridden Hard and Put Up Wet, 1990, Campfire Echoes, 1994. With U.S. Air Force, 1942-46. Recipient Champion Working Stock Horse Nat. Horse Show Assn., Chgo., 1946, Gold, Silver, and Bronze medals Phippen Invitational Art Show, Prescott, Ariz., 1978, Stetson Hat award Tex. Cowboy Artists Gold Medal Exhibit, San Angelo, Tex., 1983, Best of Show Painting award Southwest Regional Art Show Roswell, 1982; rep. N.Mex. Cowboy Poetry Gathering Nat. Endowment for the Arts, Elko, Nev., 1986. Republican. Methodist. Home: 2809 S Graves Rd Roswell NM 88201-9024

AVERY, ROGER MICHAEL, engineering executive; b. Belfast, Northern Ireland, Sept. 19, 1944; came to U.S., 1977; s. Norman Stead and Ivy Joan (Capel) A.; m. Rose Marie McGilly, July 14, 1973; children: Simon, Jonathan, Peter. BSc in Engring., U. London, 1966. Registered profl. engr., Md., N.Y., Ill., Mo., N.J., Ont.; chartered engr., U.K.; European engr. 1st, 2nd and 3rd engr. Ctrl. Electricity Generating Bd., London, 1962-74; sr. engr. Balfour Beatty Engring., Sidcup, Kent, Eng., 1974-77; prin. engr. Electrack, Inc. subs. Balfour Beatty, Hyattsville, Md., 1977-80, sr. staff engr., 1980-82; chief engr. power system Electrack Can. subs. Balfour Beatty, Toronto, Ont., 1982-85; dir. signal engring. N.Y.C. Transit Authority, 1985-88; mgr. systems LS Transit Systems, Bloomfield, N.J., 1988-93; mgr. systems integration Bay Area Rapid Transit Dist., Oakland, Calif., 1993—. Troop chmn. Somers Troop 1, Boy Scouts Am., Amawalk, N.Y., 1987-92. Mem. IEEE (sr.; exec. com. land transp. divsn. 1988-94, chmn. 1992), Am. Rwy. Engring. Assn. (mem. com. 33 electrification 1979—), Assn. Am. R.R.s Comm. and Signal Divsn. (mem. com. F-2 spl. applications 1982). Office: Bay Area Rapid Transit Dist 1000 Broadway Ste 626 Oakland CA 94607-4039

AVIEL, JO ANN B. FAGOT, political science educator; b. Mpls., May 15, 1942; d. Joseph B. and Joyce B. (Cawley) Fagot; m. S. David Aviel; children: Rebecca, Sara. BA, Lone Mt. Coll., 1964; MA, Fletcher Sch. Law and Diplomacy, 1965, MALD, 1966, PhD, 1971. Asst. prof. social studies U. Costa Rica, San Jose, 1966-68; asst. prof. polit. sci. Humboldt State U., Arcata, Calif., 1968-70; prof. internat. rels. dept. San Francisco State U., 1970—; bd. advisors Internat. Pub. Policy Inst. in N.Y.; vis. fellow Leonard Davis Inst. for Internat. Rels. Hebrew U., Jerusalem, 1975; vis. prof. Diplomatic Acad. Peru, 1984. Author: Resource Shortages and World Politics, 1979; reviewer Western Polit. Quarterly, The Jour. of Developing Areas, Westview Press; contbr. articles to profl. jours. Mem. Am. Polit. Sci. Assn., Western Polit. Sci. Assn., N. Calif. Polit. Sci. Assn., Women's Caucus for Polit. Sci. (nat. pres. 1973-74), Internat. Studies Assn., Latin Am. Studies Assn., Pacific Coast Coun. for Latin Am. Studies (mem. pres.' adv. coun., bd. govs.), U.N. Assn. San Francisco (bd. dirs.), World Affairs Coun. No. Calif. (guest lectr.). Home: 868 Overlook Ct San Mateo CA 94403-3860 Office: San Francisco State U Dept Internat Rels 1600 Holloway Ave San Francisco CA 94132-1722

AVOLIO, WENDY FREEDMAN, speech and language pathologist; b. Phila., Feb. 24, 1953; d. Harold Stanley and Phyllis Maxine (Broodno) Freedman; m. Michael Howard Strauss, Aug. 31, 1975 (div. 1981); children: Nicole Erin, Mallary Blair; m. Mark Richard Avolio, Mar. 24, 1985. BS, Bradley U., 1973; MA, No. Ill. U., 1975. Speech-lang. pathologist Bartlett (Ill.) Sch. Dist., 1975-76, Proviso Area for Exceptional Children, Maywood, Ill., 1976-77, Cen. Reading and Speech Clinic, Mt. Prospect, Ill., 1977-78, Tucson Unified Sch. Dist., 1978-79, Handmaker Jewish Geriatric Ctr., Tucson, 1981; mgr. speech-lang. therapy program Dept. Econ. Security/Div. Devel. Disabilities, Tucson, 1981-86, So. Ariz. Spl. Edn. Coop., Vail, 1986-92, Amphitheater Sch. Dist., 1992-95; therapeak Life Care Ctr.-Tucson, 1993—; cons. speech-lang. Parent Support Group, Tucson, 1981-87, Ariz. Adv. Com. For Deaf-Blind, Tucson, 1983-87; lang. cons. Community Outreach Program for Deaf, Tucson, 1983. Active youth and children com. Jewish Comty. Ctr., Tucson, 1986-88, Tucson Classics, 1989-94; bd. dirs. Tucson Residence Found., 1993—. Mem. Am. Speech Lang. and Hearing Assn. (cert.), Ariz. Speech and Lang. Assn. Home and Office: 3532 N Fiesta Del Sol Tucson AZ 85715-2013

AVRIL, JACK JOSEPH, ceramic engineer, forensic scientist; b. Tacoma, Wash., Jan. 17, 1932; s. Charles Walter (Jack) and Madge Lorena (Hall) A.; m. Janice A. Hardison, Aug. 23, 1958; children: Susan, Michael, Margaret. BS in Ceramic Engring., U. Wash., 1959. Registereed profl. engr., Calif. Sr. scientist, owner Ind. Forensics, Inc., Tacoma, Wash., 1980—. Active in 28th Dist. Dem. Orgn., Lakewood, Wash., 1980—; bd. dirs. YMCA Tacoma, 1984-92, Lakewood United, 1988—. Mem. Internat. Assn. Arson Investigators (cert. fire investigator, 1st v.p. Wash. chpt. 1991-92, pres. 1992-93), Nat. Assn. Fire Investigators (cert. fire and explosion investigators, cert. fire investigator instr.), Nat. Fire Protection Assn. Baptist. Office: Ind Forensics Inc PO Box 97192 Tacoma WA 98497-0192

AVRIN, DAVID LAWRENCE, public relations executive, legislative liason, vocalist; b. San Gabriel, Calif., Oct. 9, 1963; s. Philip Avrin and Barbara (Tell) A. BA in Journalism and Mass Comms., U. No. Colo., 1987; post grad. study in pub. rels. mgmt., Colo. State U., 1991—. Copywriter, producer KYOU Radio, Greeley, Colo., 1987; account exec., copywriter Up the Creek Newspaper, Greeley, 1987-89, copywriter , conceptmedia advt., pub. rels., 1989; spokesman Denver City Health Dept. and Denver Gen. Hosp., 1989-92; spokesman, media rels. dir. The Children's Hosp., Denver, 1992-93, legis. liaison, 1993-95; pres. The Capitol Group, Denver, 1995—; mgr., performer The Diners, male a cappella siinging group; part time profl. announcer, spokesman. Recipient Eugenia Rawls scholarship, Univ. departmental music scholarship. Mem. Pub. Rels. Soc. Am. (accredited pub. rels. profl., mem. health acad.), Colo. Healthcare Comms. (bd. dirs.), Am. Soc. for Healthcare Pub. Rels. and Mktg., Colo. Child Advocacy and Safety Coalition, Mortar Board. Home: PO Box 24886 Denver CO 80224-0886 Office: The Capitol Group 515 E 2d Ave Denver CO 80203

AWBREY, MARY STUART, interior designer; b. Boston, Jan. 20, 1934; d. Alexander Craig and Frances Guy (Davis) Veasey; m. William Wade Awbrey, Feb. 4, 1956; children: Frances Blair, John Craig, Mary Elisabeth. AA in Design with high honors, Canada Coll., Redwood City, Calif., 1979. Cert. interior designer, Calif. Design asst. Glenna B. Cook Interiors, Hillsborough, Calif., 1979; prin. designer Stuart's Interiors, Atherton, Calif., 1980—. Vignette designer Nativity Antique Show, 1990; designer rms. Peninsula Symphony Showhouse, 1987, others. Docent Octagon House, 1988-94; participant various house tour coms. Lucille Salter Packard Found. facilitator, 1992-93. Mem. ASID (profl.; adv. bd. Student Career Forum 1991-93, participant in showhouses), Jr. League of Palo Alto (various coms.), Nat. Soc. Colonial Dames Am. (membership com.), Nat. Trust for Historic Preservation. Republican. Episcopalian.

AXELROD, DANIEL ISAAC, geology and botany educator; b. Bklyn., July 16, 1910; s. Morris and Augusta (Gallup) A.; m. Nancy Robinson, June 3, 1939 (div. Sept. 1965); 1 son, James Peter; m. Marilyn Gayler, Apr. 6, 1985. A.B., U. Calif. at Berkeley, 1933, M.A., 1936, Ph.D., 1938. Asst. prof. UCLA, 1946-48, assoc. prof., 1948-52, prof. geology, 1952—, prof. geology and botany, 1962—; prof. botany U. Calif. at Davis, 1968—. Decorated Bronze Star; recipient N.Y. Bot. Garden award Bot. Soc., 1972, Hayden Meml. Geol. award Phila. Acad. Natural Scis., 1979, Fellows medal Calif. Acad. Scis., 1980, Internat. medal Palaeobot. Soc., 1985, medal Paleontology Soc. Am., 1990; Guggenheim fellow, 1952-53; NRC fellow U.S. Nat. Mus., 1939-41, Bot. Soc. of Amer. Merit award, 1993. Fellow AAAS; mem. Am. Acad. Arts and Scis., Geol. Soc. Am., Paleontol. Soc. (medal 1990), Soc. for Study Evolution. Home: 2305 Goldberry Ln Davis CA 95616-2961 Office: Univ Calif Dept Botany Davis CA 95616

AXELROD, STEPHEN LEE, physician; b. Detroit, June 23, 1951; s. Reuben and Selma Josia (Kazanoff) A.; m. Paula Evans, May 24, 1986. BS, U. Mich., 1972; MD, Wayne State U., 1977. Diplomate Am. Bd. Emergency Medicine. Intern Presbyn.-Denver Med. Ctr., 1977-78; emergency physician Emergency Cons. Inc., Petoskey, Mich., 1978-80, Colo. Emergency Med. Assocs., Thornton, 1980-87; physician, med. dir. Med. Ctrs. Colo., Denver, 1980-89; med. dir. Coors Brewing Co., Denver, 1990—; pres. The Axelrod Group-Healthcare Cons., Denver, 1992—; clin. instr. Okla. Coll. Medicine and Surgery, Tulsa, 1982-87; chmn. credential com. Humana Hosp., Thornton, 1984-88; mem. editorial adv. bd. Medictr. Mgmt. jour., 1985-87. Mgmt. jour., 1985-87; editorial adv. bd. Medicenter Mgmt. jour., 1986-89. Physician Family Builders by Adoption- Fun Run, Denver, 1985-86, Community Home Health Care-Greek Marathon, Seattle, 1984; physician advisor Broomfield (Colo.) Vol. Ambulance Svc., 1980-83; corp. sponsor fin. com. Allied Jewish Fedn., Denver, 1987. Fellow Am. Coll. Emergency Physicians; mem. Colo. Med. Soc., Nat. Assn. Ambulatory Care (bd. dirs. 1984-86, cert. of recognition 1985), Am. Coll. Physician Execs., Am. Coll. Occupational Medicine. Home: 45 S Dexter St Denver CO 80222-1050 Office: Med First Inc 1200 17th St Ste 1950 Denver CO 80202-5835

AXELSON, JOSEPH ALLEN, professional athletics executive, publisher; b. Peoria, Dec. 25, 1927; s. Joseph Victor Axelson and Florence (Ealen) Massey; m. Malcolm Rae Smith, Oct. 7, 1950 (dec.); children: David Allen, Mark Stephen, Linda Rae. B.S., Northwestern U., 1949. Sports info. dir. Ga. So. U., Statesboro, 1957-60, Nat. Assn. Intercollegiate Athletics, Kansas City, Mo., 1961-62; tournament dir. Bowling Proprs. Assn. Am., Park Ridge, Ill., 1963-64; asst. exec. sec. Nat. Assn. Intercollegiate Athletics, Kansas City, Mo., 1964-68; exec. v.p., gen. mgr. Cin. Royals Profl. Basketball Team, Cin., 1969-72; mgr. Cin. Gardens, 1970-72; pres., gen. mgr. Kansas City Kings Profl. Basketball Team, Kansas City, Mo., 1972-79, 82-85; pres., gen. mgr. Sacramento Kings Profl. Basketball Team, 1985-88, exec. v.p., 1988-90; pres. Arco Arena, Sacramento, 1985-88; exec. v.p. Sacramento Sports Assn., Arco Sports Complex, 1988-90, Profl. Team Publs., Inc., Stamford, Conn., 1991-92; pub. Between The Vines Newsletter, 1993—; exec. v.p. ops. NBA, N.Y.C., 1979-82, chmn. competition and rules com., 1975-79; trustee Naismith Basketball Hall of Fame; co-host The Sports Page, Sta. KFMB-AM, San Diego, 1994—. Author: Basketball Basics, 1987. Mem. Emil Verban Meml. Soc., Washington. Capt. Signal Corps. AUS, 1949-54. Named Nat. Basketball Exec. of Yr. The Sporting News, St. Louis, 1973; recipient Annual Dirs. award Downtown, Inc., Kansas City, Mo., 1979, Nat. Assn. Intercollegiate Athletics Frank Cramer Nat. Svc. award, 1983, Man of Yr. award Sacramento (Calif.) C. of C., 1986; named to Ga. So. U. Sports Hall of Fame, 1990. Mem. Am. Philatelic Soc., Phi Kappa Psi. Republican. Presbyterian. Office: 1112 1st St Ste 410 Coronado CA 92118-1407

AXON, DONALD CARLTON, architect; b. Haddonfield, N.J., Feb. 27, 1931; s. William Russell Sr. and Gertrude L. (Ellis) A.; m. Rosemary Smith, Sept. 1952 (div. Oct. 1967); children: Donald R., James K., Marianne Axon Flannery, Darren H., William R. II; m. Janice Jacobs, Mar. 16, 1968; stepchildren: Jonathan Lee, Elise Marie. BArch, Pratt Inst., 1954; MS in Arch., Columbia U., 1966. Registered architect, N.Y., Pa., Calif. Designer, drafter Keith Hibner, Assoc., Hicksville, N.Y., 1954-56; designer Charles Wood, Riverhead, N.Y., 1956-59; architect, prin Donald C. Axon, Assoc., Wantaugh, N.Y., 1959; ptnr. Bailey-Axon & Assoc., Long Beach, N.Y., 1960-66; project mgr. Caudill Rowlett Scott, Houston, 1966-69; in-house architect Kaiser Permanente Hosp., L.A., 1969-75; dir. med. facilities Daniel Mann Johnson Mendenhall, L.A., 1975-78, Lyon Assocs., L.A., 1979-80; pres. Donald C. Axon, FAIA, Inc., L.A., 1980—; tchr. bldg. sci. program U. So. Calif., 1978-82; lectr. in field; profl. advisor dept. architecture U. Tex., 1968-69; advisor to chmn. Sch. Architecture Rice U., Houston, 1968-69; profl. dir. Future Architect Am., 1965-66. Mem. Crestwood Hills Assn., bd. dirs. 1971-75, pres., 1973-75, archtl. rev. com., 1987—; bd. dirs. Brentwood Community Fedn., 1973-75, v.p., 1974-75. Recipient L.A. Beautiful award KPH Norwalk Hosp. Fellow AIA (Calif. regional bd. dirs. 1987-89, mem. nat. com. on architecture for health 1975—, mem. various subcoms., chair steering com. 1980, liaison 1991—, bd. dirs. L.A. chpt. 1983-84, pres. 1986, chair com. on architecture for health 1974, chair health facilities com. Calif. coun. 1975, Disting. Svc. citation 1992), Archtl. Found. L.A. (founding, v.p. 1985-89, pres. 1989-90), Internat. Conf. Bldg. Ofcls., Am. Hosp. Assn., Forum for Health Care Planning (bd. dirs. 1982—, pres. 1993-94), Royal Soc. Health, Health Facilities Inst. Office: 823 Hanley Ave Los Angeles CA 90049-1913

AYALA, FRANCISCO JOSÉ, geneticist, educator; b. Madrid, Mar. 12, 1934; came to U.S., 1961, naturalized, 1971; s. Francisco and Soledad (Pereda) A.; m. Hana Lostakova, Mar. 8, 1985; children by previous marriage: Francisco José, Carlos Alberto. BS, Universidad de Madrid, 1954, D. honoris causa, 1986; MA, Columbia U., 1963, Ph.D., 1964; D. honoris causa, Universidad de León (Spain), 1982, Universidad de Barcelona, Spain, 1986, U. Athens, Greece, 1991. Research assoc. Rockefeller U., 1964-65; asst. prof. Providence Coll., 1965-67, Rockefeller U., 1967-71; assoc. prof. to prof. genetics U. Calif., Davis, 1971-87; disting. prof. biology U. Calif., Irvine, 1987-89; Donald Bren prof. of Biol. scis., 1989—; bd. dirs. basic biology NRC, 1982-91, chmn., 1984-91, mem. commn. on life scis., 1982-91; mem. nat. adv. coun. Nat. Inst. Gen. Med. Scis.; mem. exec. com. EPA, 1979-80; mem. adv. com. directorate sci. and engring. edn. NSF, 1989-91; mem. nat. adv. coun. for human genome rsch. NIH, 1990-93; mem. Pres. com. advisors sci. and tech., 1994—. Author: Population and Evolutionary Genetics, 1982, Modern Genetics, 1980, 2d edit., 1984, Evolving: the Theory and Processes of Organic Evolution, 1979, Evolution, 1977, Molecular Evolution, 1976, Studies in the Philosophy of Biology, 1974. Recipient medal Coll. de France, 1979, Mendel medal Czech Republic Acad. Scis., 1994; Guggenheim fellow, Fulbright fellow. Fellow AAAS (Scientific Freedom and Responsibility award 1987, bd. dirs. 1989-93. pres.-elect 1993-94, pres. 1994—), chmn. com. on health of sci. enterprise 1991—, mem. nat. coun. for sci. and edn. for phase II, project 2061 1990—); mem. NAS (sect. population biology evolution and ecology chmn. 1983-86, councillor 1986-89, bd. dirs. Nat. Acads. Corp. 1990—), Am. Acad. Arts & Scis., Am. Soc. Naturalists (sec. 1973-76), Genetics Soc. Am., Am. Genetic Assn. (hon. life mem., Wilhelmine E. Key award), Ecology Soc. Am., Am. Philos. Soc., Soc. Study Evolution (pres. 1979-80), Royal Acad. Scis. Spain (fgn. mem.), Russian Acad. Sci. (fgn. mem.), Russian Acad. Natural Scis. (fgn. mem.). Home: 2 Locke Ct Irvine CA 92715-4034 Office: U Calif Dept Ecology and Evolutionary Biology Irvine CA 92717

AYALA, JOHN, librarian, dean; b. Long Beach, Calif., Aug. 28, 1943; s. Francisco and Angelina (Rodriguez) A.; m. Patricia Marie Dozier, July 11, 1987; children: Juan, Sara. BA in History, Calif. State U., Long Beach, 1970, MPA, 1981; MLS, Immaculate Heart Coll., L.A., 1971. Library paraprofl. Long Beach Pub. Library, 1963-70; librarian L.A. County Pub. Libr., 1971-72; librarian Long Beach City Coll., 1972-90, assoc. prof., 1972-90, pres. acad. senate, 1985-87; dean, Learning Resources Fullerton (Calif.) Coll., 1990—; chmn. Los Angeles County Com. to Recruit Mexican-Am. Librs., 173-74; mem. acad. senate Calif. Cmty. Colls., 1985-90. Editor Calif. Librarian, 1971. Served with USAF, 1966-68, Vietnam. U.S. Office Edn. fellow for library sci., 1970-71. Mem. ALA (com. mem. 1971-85), Calif. Libr. Assn., REFORMA Nat. Assn. to Promote Spanish Speaking Libr. Svc. (founding mem., v.p., pres. 1973-76). Democrat. Roman Catholic. Office: Fullerton College Library 321 E Chapman Ave Fullerton CA 92632-2011

AYBAR, CHARLES ANTON, aviation executive; b. N.Y.C., Sept. 27, 1956; s. Louis Adolf and Elisabeth A. (Schwarz) A.; m. Deborah Ann Benson, May 1, 1988; 1 child, Heidi Brita. AS in aeronautics, Embry-Riddle Aero. U., 1987; BS in Aviation Mgmt., Pacific-Western U., 1988, MBA in Mktg., 1988, PhD in Mgmt., 1993. Lic. airline transport pilot; cert. FAA flight instr. and aircraft dispatcher. Mdse. mgr. Korvettes, Inc., N.Y.C., 1976-79; gen. mgr. Family Games Ctr., Inc., Bklyn., 1979-81; pres. N.Am. Sch., Inc., Bklyn., 1979-81; exec. dir. of acad. Laces, Inc., New Hyde Park, N.Y., 1981-85; pilot Air Sedona (Ariz.) Airlines, Inc., 1986-88; v.p. Ruidoso (N.Mex.) Airlines, Inc., 1988; pres. S&S Aircraft, Inc., Plant City, Fla., 1989-91; dir. flight ops. Plant City Airport, Inc., 1991-92; chief flight instr. airline prep. program Scottsdale (Ariz.) Aeromech, Inc., 1992-94; cons. Westwind Aviation, 1994—; written test examiner FAA, Orlando, Fla., 1989—, accident prevention counselor, 1991—; cons. Laces, Inc., 1981-84, Hillsborough Aviation Authority, Tampa, Fla., 1989—, CBS TV Network, 1979-80; prodr., host TV show series Flightline, Aviation Today in Ariz., 1994-95. Inventor children's toothpaste; performer, choreographer CBS-TV Spls., Soap Factory, 1979-82; contbr. articles to periodicals. Recruiter USAF-CAP, Prescott, Ariz., 1987. Recipient A.C.E. award FAA. Mem. Tampa Bay Super Bowl Task Force, Assn. Ind. Airmen, Roller Skating Rink Operators Assn., U.S. Amateur Confederation Roller Skating. Home: Box 152 4839 E Greenway Rd Scottsdale AZ 85254

AYER, CAROL ANNE, librarian; b. Olympia, Wash., Sept. 6, 1953; d. Harold Stevens and Leoni (Bleston) A. BS, Portland State U., 1975; M of Librarianship, U. Wash., 1977. Libr. USDA Forest Svc., Juneau, Alaska, 1980-87, Washington, 1987; tech. info. officer USDA Forest Svc., Ogden, Utah, 1987—. Mem, bd. dirs. Pinto Horse Assn. Am., Ft. Worth, Tex., 1990—; sec., bd. dirs. Utah Arabian Horse Club, 1994—. Mem. Am. Libr. Assn., Spl. Librs. Assn., Utah Libr. Assn. (sec. spl. libr. sect. 1990-94). Democrat. Unitarian-Universalist. Office: USDA Forest Svc Intermountain Rsch Sta 324 25th St Ogden UT 84401-2310

AYER, DAVID CLAY, architect; b. Salt Lake City, Dec. 26, 1952; s. John Lowell and Ethel (Schumann) A.; m. Colleen J. Dorsey, May 8, 1982; children: Kaitlin Ashley, Austin Michael. BS with honors, U. Utah, 1976, MArch, 1979. Registered architect, Utah, Hawaii. Project architect EDA, Salt Lake City, 1978-80, project mgr., assoc., 1981-83; project mgr. IMH Architects, Salt Lake City, 1980-81; dir. architecture DMJM-Utah, Salt Lake City, 1983-88; prin. STA Ltd., Honolulu, 1988-92; divsn. mgr. DMJM-Hawaii, Honolulu, 1992—; bd. dirs. Assist, Inc., Salt Lake City, 1986. Recipient 1st place award City and County of Honolulu, 1991. Mem. AIA (chair com. 1981-94, bd. dirs. 1986, Merit award 1991), Nat. Assn. Indsl. and Office Parks, Urban Land Inst., Rotary. Office: DMJM Hawaii 1099 Alakea St Ste 1230 Honolulu HI 96813-4500

AYERS, EVERETTE LEE, highway patrol director; b. Bowling Green, Va., Dec. 20, 1940; s. Everette L. and Hauzie (Rouse) A.; m. Donna Rae Rose, Aug. 24, 1961; children: Jeff, Shelley. Student, Laramie County Community Coll., 1976-77. Patrolman Wyo. Hwy. Patrol, Wheatland, 1964-72; sgt. Wyo. Hwy. Patrol, Rawlins, 1972-76; sgt. Wyo. Hwy. Patrol, Laramie, 1976-78, lt., 1978-81; maj. Wyo. Hwy. Patrol, Cheyenne, 1982-85, col., 1985—. Served with USAF, 1959-63. Mem. Peace Officer's Standards Tng. Commn., Internat. Assn. Chiefs of Police, Am. Assn. Motor Vehicle Adminstrs., Wyo. Hwy. Patrol Assn. Methodist. Lodge: Odd Fellows. Office: Wyo Hwy Patrol 5300 Bishop Blvd PO Box 1708 Cheyenne WY 82002-9019

AYERS, RENDALL PAUL, public relations consultant; b. Wichita Falls, Tex., Aug. 25, 1937; s. Richard Kelly and Gertrude Christine (Paul) A.; m. Sara Lee Hoffman, Aug. 27, 1960; children: Sydney Lynn, Reed A. BA in Journalism, U. Colo., 1961. Asst. bur. chief AP, Helena, Mont., 1960-61; asst. city editor Denver Post, 1962-67; dist. mgr. Ins. Info. Inst., Denver, 1968-69; pub. relations mgr. Denver div. Safeway Stores, Inc., 1970-74; pres. William Kostka & Assocs., Denver, 1975-80; prin. Rendall Ayers Pub. Relations, Denver, 1980-87; ptnr. Ayers, Grimm, Starzel & Assocs., Denver, 1985-87; chmn., Darcy Communications, Inc., Denver, 1988—; lectr. in field. Bd. dirs. Men's Assistance Ctr., 1970-82, pres., 1974-76; bd. dirs. Colo. Heart Assn., 1970—, pres., 1977-78, chmn. Colo. Heart Fund campaign, 1971-73; v.p. Hope for the Children, 1987-88; bd. dirs. Goodwill Industries Denver, 1970-84, v.p. 1981-84; bd. dirs. Colo. Retail Council, 1972-74, Kempe Nat. Ctr. for Prevention and Treatment Child Abuse, 1984-87; dir. Colo. chpt. Am. Parkinson Disease Assn., 1993—. Recipient award Outstanding Reporting, Denver Newspaper Guild, 1966; Outstanding Vol. award Colo. Heart Assn., 1973. Fellow Pub. Rels. Soc. Am. (accredited, pres. Colo. chpt. 1978, mem. Counselors Acad.), Sigma Delta Chi, Alpha Delta Sigma. Republican. Unitarian. Clubs: Press, Lakewood Country, Meadow Creek Racquet (Denver). Office: 1800 Platte St Denver CO 80202-1036

AYERS, STEPHEN M., lawyer; b. Oakland, Calif., Oct. 7, 1946; s. John Martin Ayers and Marica Crosby (McLean) Ogle; m. Mary Frances Petrin, Dec. 7, 1979; children: Douglas, David. BS, U. Idaho, 1969, JD, 1974. Bar: Idaho 1974, U.S. Dist. Ct. Idaho 1974. Law clerk to Hon. Fred M. Taylor U.S. Dist. Ct., Boise, Idaho, 1974-76; pvt. practice Coeur d'Alene, Idaho, 1976—; magistrate judge U.S. Dist. Ct., Coeur d'Alene, 1977-92. Bd. dirs. Idaho Spl. Olympics, Boise, 1988-91, legal com., 1991—; trustee Cooper Charitable Found., Coeur d'Alene, 1990—. 1st lt. U.S. Army, 1968-70. Mem. Idaho Bar Assn., First Dist. Bar Assn. Office: 1424 E Sherman Ave Coeur D Alene ID 83814-4045

AYLER, MAYNARD FRANKLIN, mining engineer; b. Tacoma, Wash., Oct. 15, 1922; s. Thomas Frank and Edith Agusta (Sivear) A.; m. Marjory Annabelle Loyd, Aug. 25, 1945; children: Corliss Ann, David Franklin. Engr. of Mining, Colo. Sch. Mines, Golden, 1945; MS, Colo. Sch. Mines, 1963. Registered profl. engr., Colo. Geologist U.S. Bur. Reclamation, Denver, 1945-47; petroleum geologist Calif. Co., Denver, 1947-52; mining engr. Bur. of Mines, Denver, 1961-64, 66-77; faculty Colo. Sch. Mines, Golden, 1958-63; chief Libyan Geol. Survey, Tripoli, 1964-66; faculty U. Md. Overseas, Tripoli, 1965-66; mining cons. Golden, 1952—; pres. Oil Mining Corp., Golden, 1986—, Oil Mining Group Ltd., Seattle, 1993—. Patentee in field. Playing mem. Jefferson Symphony, Golden, 1956-75, Denver Concert Band, 1975—, Rocky Mountain Symphony, Denver, 1988—; playing mem., bd. dirs. Brico Symphony, Denver, 1958-85; founder, playing mem. Mostly Strauss Orch., Denver, 1980—. Mem. Am. Def. preparedness Assn. (dir. 1982—).

AYLESWORTH, JOHN RICHARD, software professional; b. Manhattan, N.Y., July 9, 1962; s. John Banzley and Nancy Lee (Eberle) A.; m. Natalie Jane Herrebrugh, June 20, 1987. AA in Bus., Santa Monica Coll., 1987. Asst. mgr. tech. support Arrays, Inc./Continental Software, L.A., 1984-86; prod. support engr. C.ITOH Electronics, Irvine, Calif., 1986-88; supr., software support Ashton-Tate Corp., Torrance, Calif., 1988-91; product group mgr. Borland Internat., Scotts Valley, Calif., 1991-94; acting mgr./pro technical support Novell, Inc., San Jose, Calif., 1994; supr. tech. support Lotus Devel. Copr., Montain View, Calif., 1995—. Officer Civil Air Patrol, USAF Aux., 1983—. Democrat. Lutheran. Home: 1324 S Winchester Blvd Apt 72 San Jose CA 95128-4323

AYLOUSH, CYNTHIA MARIE, personnel director; b. Jackson, Mich., July 2, 1950; d. Leonard Edward and Violet Caroline (Kroeger) Ullrich; m. Abbott Selim Ayloush, June 21, 1980; children: Sasha Christine, Nadia Marie, Ramsey Abbott. AA, Fullerton Coll., 1970; diploma in fashion mdse., Brooks Coll., 1975; BS, Pepperdine U., 1980. Receptionist, Hydraflow, Commerce, Calif., 1968-74, pers. mgr., Cerritos, Calif., 1979—, treas., 1979—, corp. sec., 1985—, exec. v.p., CFO, 1995—; with sales dept. Robinson's, Cerritos, Calif., 1974-75, dept. mgr., 1975-79. Mem. Am. Soc. Pers. Adminstrs., Pers. Indsl. Rels. Assn., Mchts. and Mfrs. Assn., Cerritos

C. of C. (bd. dir. 1983-89). Republican. Roman Catholic. Clubs: Soroptimist (sec. 1979—, pres. 1993-94), Damas de Caridad (sec. 1992-93), Century, Pepperdine U. Office: Hydraflow 13259 166th St Cerritos CA 90703-2203

AYLWARD, J. PATRICK, lawyer; b. Walla Walla, Wash., Aug. 20, 1951; s. James F. and Mary Jane (Little) A.; m. Peggy D. Deobald, Feb. 13, 1982; children: Alana Nicole, Sean Patrick. BA, Stanford U., 1973; JD, U. Wash., 1976. Bar: Wash. 1976, U.S. Dist. Ct. (ea. dist.) Wash. 1980, U.S. Tax Ct. 1984, U.S. Ct. Appeals (9th cir.) 1984, U.S. Dist. Ct. (we. dist.) 1987. Assoc. Hughes, Jeffers and Danielson, Wenatchee, Wash., 1976-81; prin. Jeffers, Danielson, Sonn and Aylward, P.S., Wenatchee, 1981—; mem. Ltd. Practice Bd., Olympia, Wash., 1985-90; tchr., panel mem. Continuing Edn. Seminars for Attys. and Ltd. Practice Officers, 1981—. Vol. Wash. State Centennial Games, Wenatchee, 1989. Mem. ABA (real property, probate and trust sect.), Wash. State Bar Assn. (exec. com. real property, probate and trust sect. 1991-93, legis. com. 1988—, chair legis. com. 1994—), Chelan-Couglas County Bar Assn. (pres. 1990-91, v.p. 1988-90, past sec., participant legal aid and edn. programs 1976—), Aircraft Owners and Pilots Assn., Exch. Club. Office: Jeffers Danielson Sonn & Aylward PS 317 N Mission St Wenatchee WA 98801-2005

AYNESMITH, LAWRENCE, publishing executive; b. Owensboro, Ky., May 29, 1954. Editl. asst. Indiana U., Bloomington, 1982-83, teaching asst., 1984-85; CEO White Cliffs Media, Tempe, Ariz., 1985-95, Aynderson Press, Tempe, Ariz., 1994-95. Editor trade and scholarly books; contbr. poetry, reviews, and essays to lit. jours. Recipient Editor of Outstanding Acad. Book Choice, 1990, Sigrid Starke Lit. award Purdue U., 1975; grantee Valparaiso U., 1977. Mem. Assn. Am. Pubs., Nat. Assn. Ind. Record Dealers. Office: PO Box 433 Tempe AZ 85280

AYRAUD, PAUL FRANK, engineer; b. Phoenix, Sept. 27, 1955; s. Frank Edward and Coral John Presnell (West) A.; m. Charla-Judine Brown, May 21, 1988; 1 child, Alexandra Clarissa. AASEET, Phoenix Coll., 1980. Electronic technician Theta Com Divsn. Texscan, Phoenix, 1981-83; electronic technician I Motorola, GEG, Inc., Chandler, Ariz., 1984-85, electronic technician II, 1985-91; final test technician ASM Am., Inc., Phoenix, 1991-94, svc. engr., 1994—, sec. Quest com., 1992-94. Singer Phoenix Boys Choir, 1968-69. Mem. Phi Theta Kappa (v.p. Phoenix chpt. 1980). Republican. Lutheran. Home: 2623 E Oakleaf Dr Tempe AZ 85281-5070 Office: ASM Am Inc 3411 E Harbour Dr Phoenix AZ 85034

AYRES, JANICE RUTH, social service executive; b. Idaho Falls, Idaho, Jan. 23, 1930; d. Low Ray and Frances Mae (Salem) Mason; m. Thomas Woodrow Ayres, Nov. 27, 1953 (dec. 1966); 1 child, Thomas Woodrow Jr. (dec.). MBA, U. So. Calif., 1952, M in Mass Comms., 1953. Asst. mktg. dir. Disneyland, Inc., Anaheim, Calif., 1954-59; gen. mgr. Tamasha Town & Country Club, Anaheim, Calif., 1959-65; dir. mktg. Am. Heart Assn., Santa Ana, Calif., 1966-69; state exec. dir. Nev. Assn. Mental Health, Las Vegas, 1969-71; exec. dir. Clark Co. Easter Seal Treatment Ctr., Las Vegas, 1971-73; mktg. dir., fin devel. officer So. Nev. Drug Abuse Coun., Las Vegas, 1973-74; exec. dir. Nev. Assn. Retarded Citizens, Las Vegas, 1974-75; assoc., cons. Don Luke & Assocs., Phoenix, 1976-77; program dir. Inter-Tribal Coun. Nev., Reno, 1977-79; exec. dir. Ret. Sr. Vol. Program, Carson City, Nev., 1979—; conductor workshops in field. Mem. bd. suprs. Carson City, Nev., 1992—; commr. Carson City Parks and Recreation, 1993—; mem. obligation bond. com., legis. chair Carson City; mem. N.W. Assn. for Transit Svcs.; bd. dirs. Nev. Dept. Transp., 1993; mem. V&TRR Commn., 1993, vice-chmn., chmn. pub. rels. com., bd. dirs. Hist. V&TRR Bd., chmn. PR Cmty./V&RR Commn., vice chmn. Carson City Gen. Obligation Bond Commn, Nev. Home Health Assn; mem. No. Corp. for Nat. and Cmty. Svc. by Gov., 1994; appointed liaison Carson City Sr. Citizens Bd., 1995. Named Woman of Distinction, Soroptimist Club, 1988, Outstanding Dir. of Excellence, Gov. State of Nev., 1989, Outstanding Dir., Vol. Action Ctr., J.C. Penney Co.; named to Western Fairs Assn. Hall of Fame for outstanding contbns. to the fair industry, 1995. Mem. AAUW, Am. Mgmt. Assn. (bd. dirs.), Am. Mktg. Assn., Internat. Platform Assn., Nat. Pub. Rels. Soc. Am. (chpt. pres.), Women Radio & TV, Nat. Soc. Fund Raising Execs., Nev. Fair & Rodeo Assn. (pres.), Nev. Assn. Transit Svcs. (bd. dirs., legis. chmn). Home: 1624 Karin Dr Carson City NV 89706-2626 Office: Ret Sr Vol Program 801 N Division St Carson City NV 89703-3925

AZZOPARDI, MARC ANTOINE, astrophysicist, scientist; b. Philippeville, Algeria, Oct. 28, 1940; s. Antoine Philippe and Marie Madeleine (Grech) A.; divorced; children: Pauline, Mathilde, Marceau; m. Alexandra L. Giorla, June 30, 1994; children: Anne-Sophie, Mary. Lic. es sci., Alger and Marseilles U., Algeria, 1963; DSc, Toulouse U., France, 1981. Astronomy aide U. Toulouse, 1964-81, adj. astronomer, 1981-83; sci. assoc. European South Obs., Garching, Fed. Republic of Germany, 1983-87; mem. sci. adv. coun. Can.-France-Hawaii Telescope Co., 1984-87;, 1990-91; astronomer 2nd class U. Marseilles, France, 1987-92, astronomer 1st class, 1992—; vis. scholar U. Tex., Austin, 1982-83; mem. sci. adv. coun. Can.-France-Hawaii Telescope Co., 1984-87, vis. scientist, 1994—; chmn. user's com. European South Obs., Garching, 1990-91, guest prof., 1992-93. Contbr. articles to profl. jours. Recipient NSF-Ctr. Nat. Sci. Rsch. award, 1982-83. Mem. Soc. French Specialists in Astronomy, Am. Astron. Soc., European Astron. Soc. Roman Catholic. Home: Paakea St 68-1793 Waikoloa HI 96738 Office: Can-France Hawaii Telescope PO Box 1597 Kamuela HI 96743-1597

BAACK, BRET ROLYN, plastic surgeon; b. Albuquerque, July 27, 1958; s. Rolyn Ernest and Karen Lee (Engelbert) B.; m. Elena Lisa Sandoval, Feb. 14, 1987; children: Amy, David. BS in Chemistry, U. N.Mex., 1979, BA in Biology, 1979, MD, 1983. Diplomate Am. Bd. Plastic Surgery. Asst. prof. U. N.Mex., 1990—. Fellow ACS; mem. Am Soc. Plastic and Reconstructive Surgeons (socioecon. com. 1993—), Alpha Omega Alpha, Phi Beta Kappa. Luth. Office: Univ Hosp Dept Surg 2211 Lomas Blvd NE Albuquerque NM 87131

BAAS, JACQUELYNN, art historian, museum administrator; b. Grand Rapids, Mich., Feb. 14, 1948. BA in History of Art, Mich. State U.; Ph.D. in History of Art, U. Mich. Registrar U. Mich. Mus. Art, Ann Arbor, 1974-78, asst. dir., 1978-82; editor Bull. Museums of Art and Archaeology, U. Mich., 1976-82; chief curator Hood Mus. Art, Dartmouth Coll., Hanover, N.H., 1982-84, dir., 1985-89; dir. Univ. Art Mus. and Pacific Film Archive, Berkeley, Calif., 1989—. Contbr. articles to jours. and catalogues. NEH fellow, 1972-73; Nat. Endowment Arts fellow, 1973-74, 87-88. Mem. Coll. Art Assn. Am., Print Council Am., Am. Assn. Museums, Assn. Art Mus. Dirs.. Office: Univ Art Mus and Pacific Film Archive 2625 Durant Ave Berkeley CA 94704-1710

BABAYANS, EMIL, financial planner; b. Tehran, Iran, Nov. 9, 1951; came to U.S., 1969; s. Hacob and Jenik (Khatchatourian) B.; m. Annie Ashjian. B.S., U. So. Calif., 1974, M.S., 1976; Cert. fin. planner; chartered life underwriter, fin. cons. Pres. Babtech Internat., Inc., Sherman Oaks, Calif., 1975-85; sr. ptnr. Emil Babayans & Assocs., Woodland Hills, Calif., 1985—. Mem. Am. Mgmt. Assn., Nat. Assn. Life Underwriters, Inst. Cert. Fin. Planners, Internat. Assn. Fin. Planners, Am. Soc. CLU and Chartered Fin. Cons., Million Dollar Round Table. Armenian Orthodox. Office: 21700 Oxnard St Ste 1100 Woodland Hills CA 91367-3668

BABB, ALVIN CHARLES, beverage company executive; b. Rising City, Nebr., Sept. 25, 1932; s. Lorren William and Merna Janet (Ruth) B.; m. Patricia Ann Schworer, Feb. 14, 1951; children: Mike, Terri, Cae, Al. Student, Kearney State Coll., 1950-51, U. Denver, 1963-64, U. Colo., 1957-60. Warehouse mgr. Adolph Coors Co., Golden, Colo., 1964-71, packaging warehouse v.p., 1971-75, packaging/shipping/utility v.p., 1976-78, sr. v.p. brewery ops., 1978-82, group v.p., 1982-83, group v.p. container ops., exec. v.p., plant mgr., 1983—. Author: Quality in Vertically Integrated Brewery, 1983, Beer Packaging: The Human Element, 1982, Management Commitment of Hearing Conservation, 1976, Scheduling-Packaging to Shipping by Computer, 1970. Eucharistic minister St. Joseph's Ch., Golden, 1976-82, pres. parish council, 1970; mem. City Charter Commn., Golden, 1960. Named Jaycees Boss of Yr., 1971; recipient Disting. Service Jaycees, 1968. Mem. Master Brewery Assn. Am., Master Brewer Rev. Bd., Golden C. of C. (dir. 1968-71). Republican. Roman Catholic. Club: Lions (pres.) (1976-77). Home: 16106 W 32nd Ave Golden CO 80401-1215 Office: Adolf Coors Co 17755 W 32nd Ave Golden CO 80401-1217

BABCOCK, DALE ARLAN, school psychologist, counselor; b. Albert Lea, Minn., Oct. 6, 1940; s. Terrance Babcock and Lorraine (Stieler) B.; m. Karen D. Wholrabe, Mar. 28, 1968; children: Jacqueline, Juliet. BS, Mankato State Coll., 1964; MS, Bemidji State Coll., 1968. Cert. sch. psychologist, Idaho; lic. profl. counselor, Idaho. Tchr. McIntosh (Minn.) Pub. Schs., 1964-65; tchr. Menahga (Minn.) Pub. Schs., 1965-68, sch. counselor, 1968-75; sch. psychologist Meridian (Idaho) Pub. Schs., 1975—; pvt. practice Meridian, 1984—; presenter workshops on depression, self-esteem, parenting, marriage, Boise, 1989—; hotline cons. Reachout, Boise, 1989—. Co-author: I Don't Know Who You Are Anymore, 1992. Mem. ACA, Nat. Bd. Cert. Counselors, Am. Mental Health Counselors Assn., Nat. Assn. Sch. Psychologists, Idaho Soc. Individual Psychology. Office: Inst for Counseling 939 E 1st Meridian ID 83642

BABCOCK, JO WARREN, artist, educator; b. St. Louis, Feb. 24, 1954; s. Boyd Leon and Shirley Lynn (Hamm) B.; m. Diane DeVoto, Aug. 20, 1973 (div. June 1975). Student, UCLA, 1975; BFA, San Francisco Art Inst., 1976, MFA, 1979. Color printer Rolling Stone mag., San Francisco, 1976, Outside mag., San Francisco, 1977; cameraman 1st Calaif. Press, San Francisco, 1977-80; electrician Bros. Electric, San Francisco, 1984-89; assoc. prof. San Francisco Art Inst., 1989—; exhibit designer Levi Strauss & Co., 1989—. One-man shows include Marcuse Pfeiffer Gallery, N.Y.C., 1988, Artspace, San Francisco, 1989; exhibited in group shows at Sao Paulo (Brazil) Bienale, San Francisco Moma, 1989, Friends of Photography Gallery, Carmel, 1976, 100 Years of Landscape Art in the Bay Area, M.H. de Young Mus., San Francisco, 1995, Bay Area Landscapes, Yerba Buens Ctr. for the Arts, San Francisco, 1995; represented in permanent collections at San Francisco Mus. Modern Art, Bklyn. Mus., Newport Harbor Art Mus., Lightwork, Syracuse, N.Y., La Biblioteque, Avignon, France, San Francisco Pub. Libr., San Francisco Arts Commn., George Eastman House, Rochester, N.Y., Nat. Collection, Smithsonian Instn., others. Grantee City of Oakland, 1985, N.Y. State Coun. on Arts, 1988, Nat. Endowment for Arts, 1989-94. Mem. South of Market Boys, Primitive Hunting Soc. Home: 378 San Jose Ave Apt B San Francisco CA 94110 Studio: 42 Leese St San Francisco CA 94110-5826

BABCOCK, JOHN WALTER, engineering executive; b. Denver, Nov. 11, 1946; s. Lee Edmond and Evelyn Brigit (Powers) B.; m. Linda Kay Harris, Aug. 12, 1972; children: Sarah Kathryn, Ryan Lee, Brigit Elizabeth. BSME, Colo. U., 1969. Exec. v.p. Mountain Concrete Mfg., Eagle, Colo., 1973-76; pres. Natural Devel. Corp., Eagle, 1976-78; project mgr. Amcor, Ogden, Utah, 1979-81; pres. Stresswall Internat., Ft. Collins, Colo., 1982-92, Earth Structures, Inc., Ft. Collins, 1992—. Patentee retaining wall, sound wall. Office: Transwall PO Box 3733 Ogden UT 84409-1733

BABCOCK, LEWIS THORNTON, federal judge; b. 1943. BA cum laude, U. Denver, 1965, JD, 1968; LLM, U. Va., 1968. Ptnr. Mitchell and Babcock, Rocky Ford, Colo., 1968-76; atty. City Las Animas, Colo., 1969-74, City Rocky Ford, 1970-76; asst. dist. atty. 11th Jud. Cir., La Junta, Colo., 1973-76, dist. judge, 1978-83; judge Colo. Ct. Appeals, 1983-88, U.S. Dist. Ct. Colo., Denver, 1988—; escrow and loan closing agt. FHA, Rocky Ford, 1973-76. Bd. dirs. Colo. Rural Legal Svcs. Inc., 1974-76. With Colo. N.G., 1968-74. Named to Order St. Ives. Mem. ABA, Colo. Bar Assn., Denver Bar Assn., Colo. Bar Found., North Ind. Dist. Bar Assn. Office: US Dist Ct 1929 Stout St Rm 246C Denver CO 80294-2900*

BABCOCK, RODNEY LEE, manufacturing manager; b. Alameda, Calif.; s. Donald Howard and Margaret Edith (Hoover) B.; m. Catherine Frances Bailey, June 18, 1977; children: Grace Catherine, Emily Rose. Student, Columbia Jr. Coll., 1973-74, San Joaquin Delta Coll., 1983-84; cert. in mgmt./supervision, Calif. Poly. State U., 1989; student, U. Calif., Santa Barbara, 1991, 92. Firefighter Calif. Dept. Forestry, Murphys; machinist Cloud Co., Arnold, Calif., 1977-86; constrn. project mgr. J.M. Perry Corp., Stockton, Calif., 1986-87; sales and installations profl. Masterworks Doors and Windows, Stockton, 1987; acct. mgr., cost estimator Louis Trotter Constrn., Livermore, Calif., 1988; ops. mgr. Cloud Co., San Luis Obispo, Calif., 1988-93; chem. mech. planarization mfg. mgr. R. Howard Strasbaugh, Inc., San Luis Obispo, 1993—; prin., owner Stellar Solutions, San Luis Obispo, 1990-94; team bldg. cons. J. M. Perry Corp., Palo Alto, Calif., 1990-94. Mem. Am. Soc. Metals, Am. Prodn. and Inventory Control Soc., Nat. Ski Patrol (avalanche advisor 1978-88, 10 Yr. Svc. award 1988). Home: 1687 Southwood Dr San Luis Obispo CA 93401-6029

BABCOCK, ROSEMARY ANN DOUGLAS, animal behavior researcher, biomedical librarian, naturalist; b. Wenatchee, Wash., Mar. 12, 1940; d. Donald Stephens and Myrle Alice (Miller) Douglas; m. Michael Jamieson Babcock, Aug. 18, 1963. BA magna cum laude, Lewis and Clark Coll., 1962; postgrad., Ind. U., 1965-71, San Francisco State U., 1985-92. Rsch. asst. Agrl. Rsch. Svc., USDA, Aberdeen, Idaho; tchr. music various pub. schs., Cleve., Ohio, 1962-67, Coos Bay and Parkrose, Oreg., 1962-67; teaching asst., assoc. instr. Ind. U., Bloomington, 1968-71; vis. faculty Chgo. Mus. Coll. of Roosevelt U., 1974; lectr. fine arts (music) Loyola U. Chgo., 1972-77; reader, rsch. asst., editor disability rsch. ctrs. San Francisco State U., U. Calif.-Davis, 1985-92; info. pers. Stanford (Calif.) U. Data Ctr., 1986-90; naturalist City of Palo Alto (Calif.), 1989—; libr., info. specialist Linus Pauling Inst. Sci. and Medicine, Palo Alto, 1990—; animal behavior researcher Chelonian Connection, Mountain View, Calif., 1979—; pvt. cons., editor, music tchr. Copy editor The Vivarium, 1991-92; contbr. articles to profl. jours. NEH fellow Summer Seminar for Coll. Tchrs., 1977. Mem. Animal Behavior Soc., Soc. for Study Amphibians and Reptiles, Bay Area Amphibian and Reptile Soc. (bd. dirs.-at-large, corr. sec.), Nature Sounds Soc., Pi Kappa Lambda (hon., sec. pro tem, chmn. scholarship benefit). Home: 2511 Alvin St Mountain View CA 94043-2707 Office: Linus Pauling Inst Sci & Medicine 440 Page Mill Rd Palo Alto CA 94306-2025

BABCOCK, WALTER CHRISTIAN, JR., membrane company executive; b. Oakland, Calif., Oct. 20, 1947; s. Walter Christian and Beatrice Alice (Sommerfield) B.; m. Jacqueline Ann Mills, Dec. 30, 1971; children: Jennifer Suzanne, Rebecca Christine. BS, U. Calif., San Diego, 1969; MS, U. Oreg., 1970, PhD, 1976. V.p. Rsch. Cons. and Design, La Jolla, Calif., 1970-71; rsch. chemist Bend (Oreg.) Rsch. Inc., 1976-81, dir. separations div., 1981-86, v.p., 1983-87, pres., 1987—, chief oper. officer, 1987-89, chief exec. officer, 1989—, pres.; bd. dirs. Consep Membranes, Bend. Contbr. articles to profl. jours. Bd. dirs. St. Charles med. Ctr., Bend, 1986. Mem. Am. Chem. Soc., N.Am. Membrane Soc., Oreg. Biotech. Assn. (bd. dirs. 1990-91). Republican. Office: Bend Rsch Inc 64550 Research Rd Bend OR 97701-8583*

BABICH, ALAN FRANCIS, computer scientist; b. Sewickley, Pa., Nov. 21, 1943; s. John and Hedwig Joanna (Bitautos) B. BS in Physics, Carnegie Inst. Tech., 1965; MSEE, Carnegie Mellon U., 1966; PhD in Elec. Engring., Carnegie-Mellon U., 1972. Sr. programmer Burroughs Corp., Mission Viejo, Calif., 1971-75, mgmt. systems analyst, 1975, project leader, 1975-79; architect large systems Basic Four Corp., Tustin, Calif., 1979-83; system architect File Net Corp., Costa Mesa, Calif., 1983—. Mem. Capt. Hook and the Sky Pirates sport Parachuting team, Elsinore, Calif., 1974-76. Recipient awards in parachuting accuracy competitions, 1967-72, including 1st Pl. award, Tucumseh, Mich., 1970; named to Parachuting Hall Fame, 1976. Mem. IEEE, Assn. Computing Machinery, Mensa, Sigma Xi. Home: 27341 Osuna Mission Viejo CA 92691-1015 Office: FileNet Corp 3565 Harbor Blvd Costa Mesa CA 92626-1405

BABIKIAN, GEORGE H., petroleum products company executive. BS, Syracuse U., 1953. With Atlantic Refining Co., 1954-69, sales supr., 1957-67, regional mgr., 1967-69; with Atlantic Richfield Co. (now ARCO), 1969—, mgr. sales devel., 1969-70, gen. mgr. Rocky Mountain Plains area, 1970-72, retail mgr. East Coast, 1972-74, retail sales mgr., 1974-76, v.p. retail mktg., 1976-77, v.p. wholesale mktg., 1977-78, sr. v.p., 1978—; now pres. ARCO Products Co. With USN, 1946-48, 51-53. Office: ARCO Products Co 1055 W 7th St Los Angeles CA 90017-2577

BABINEC, GEHL P., convenience store company executive. BSBA, Xavier U., 1964; JD, U. Cin., 1967. Bar: Ohio 1967, U.S. Dist. Ctl. (so. dist.) Ohio 1969. Sr. v.p., gen. counsel Circle K Stores Inc., Phoenix, 1986—. Capt. U.S. Army, 1967-69. Mem. ABA, Corps. Commn. Office: Circle K Stores Inc PO Box 52084 Phoenix AZ 85072-2084

BABU, UMA MAHESH, health/medical products executive; b. Mysore, Karnataka, India, Mar. 29, 1947; came to U.S., 1963; s. Chinnaswamy and Rajalakshmi (Kusuma) Setty; m. Vimala Govindaraj, Nov. 16, 1975; 1 child, Ravi K. BS, U. Mysore, India, 1968; PhD, U. Nebr., 1974. Postdoctoral fellow U. Manitoba, Winnipeg, Manitoba, Can., 1974-77; postdoctoral fellow Thomas Jefferson U., Phila., 1977-78, rsch. assoc. prof., 1978-84, adj. asst. prof., 1984—; sr. scientist Pittman-Moore, Washington Crossing, N.J., 1984-86; prin. scientist Ortho Pharm. Corp., Raritan, N.J., 1986-88; asst. dir. Immunobiology Rsch. Inst., Annandale, N.J., 1988-92; dir. Empyrean Diagnostics, Inc., Mountain View, Calif., 1993—. Named to Exch. program Am. Field Svc., 1963; named Regent's scholar U. Nebr., 1969. Mem. Triveni-Kannada Assn. (cultural sec. 1982-83), Telugu Assn. North Am. Hindu. Home: 4452 Pomponi St Union City CA 94587-2589 Office: Empyrean Diagnostics Inc 2761 Marine Way Mountain View CA 94043-1127

BABULA, WILLIAM, university dean; b. Stamford, Conn., May 19, 1943; s. Benny F. and Lottie (Zajkowski) B.; m. Karen L. Gemi, June 19, 1965; children: Jared, Joelle. BA, Rutgers U., 1965; MA, U. Calif., Berkeley, 1967, PhD, 1969. Asst. prof. English U. Miami, Coral Gables, Fla., 1969-75; assoc. prof. U. Miami, Coral Gables, 1975-77, prof., 1977-81, chmn. dept. Eng., 1976-81; dean of arts and humanities Sonoma State U., Rohnert Park, Calif., 1981—. Author: Shakespeare and the Tragicomic Archetype, 1975, Shakespeare in Production, 1935-79, 1981; (short stories) Motorcycle, 1982, Quarterback Sneak, 1983, The First Edsel, 1983, Ransom, 1983, The Last Jogger in Virginia, 1983, The Orthodontist and the Rock Star, 1984, Greenearth, 1984, Football and Other Seasons, The Great American Basketball Shoot, 1984, Ms. Skywriter, Inc., 1987; (plays) The Fragging of Lt. Jones (1st prize Gualala Arts Competition, 1983), Creatures (1st prize Jacksonville U. competition 1987), The Winter of Mrs. Levy (Odyssey Stage Co., New Play Series 1988), Nat. Playwright's Showcase, 1988, Theatre Americana, 1990 (James Ellis award), Basketball Jones, Black Rep of Berkeley, 1988, West Coast Ensemble, Festival of One Acts, 1992, Mark Twain Masquers, 9th Ann. Festival One Act Plays, 1994 (2d Place award), The Last Roundup, 1991 (Odyssey Stage Co.); (novels) The Bombing of Berkeley and Other Pranks (1st prize 24th Ann. Deep South Writers' Conf. 1984), St. John's Baptism, 1988, According to St. John, 1989, St. John and the Seven Veils, 1991, St. John's Bestiary, 1994; contbr. articles to profl. pubs. and short stories to lit. mags. Mem. Dramatists Guild, Assoc. Writing Programs, Mystery Writers Am., Phi Beta Kappa. Office: Sonoma State U Sch Arts and Humanities Rohnert Park CA 94928

BACA, JOSEPH FRANCIS, state supreme court chief justice; b. Albuquerque, Oct. 1, 1936; s. Amado and Inez (Pino) B.; m. Dorothy Lee Burrow, June 28, 1969; children: Jolynn, Andrea, Anna Marie. BA in Edn., U. N.Mex., 1960; JD, George Washington U., 1964; LLM, U. Va., 1992. Asst. dist. atty. 1st Jud. Dist., Santa Fe, 1965-66; pvt. practice Albuquerque, 1966-72; dist. judge 2d Jud. Dist., Albuquerque, 1972-88; justice N.Mex. Supreme Ct., Santa Fe, 1989—; spl. asst. to atty. gen. Office of N.Mex. Atty. Gen., Albuquerque, 1966-71. Dem. precinct chmn., albuquerque, 1968; del. N.Mex. Constl. Conv., Santa Fe, 1969; bd. dirs. State Justice Inst., 1994—. Recipient Judge of Yr. award Peoples Commn. for Criminal Justice, 1989, Quincentennial Commemoration Achievement award La Hispanidad Com., 1992, Luchando por la Justicia award Mex. Am. Law Students Assn. U. N.Mex. Law Sch., 1993; J. William Fulbright Disting. Pub. Svc. award George Washington U. Alumni Assn., 1994, Recognition and Achievement award Commn. on Opportunities for Minorities in the Profession, 1992, others. Mem. ABA, Hispanic Nat. Bar Assn., N.Mex. Bar Assn., Albuquerque Bar Assn., Santa Fe Bar Assn., Alumni Assn. (pres. 1980-81), Kiwanis (pres. Albuquerque chpt. 1984-85), KC (dep. grand knight 1968). Roman Catholic. Office: Supreme Ct NMex PO Box 848 Santa Fe NM 87504-0848

BACA, SHERRY ANN, secondary school educator; b. Huron, S.D., Jan. 11, 1950; d. Myron Marion Moberg and Emily Ann (Matkovich) Baxter; m. Ed R. Baca, Oct. 14, 1972; children: Jamie Marie, Jennifer Lea. BS in Edn., No. Az. U., 1971, M.A. T. in Math., 1972, cert. secondary sch. principle, 1982. Cert. secondary sch. math. tchr., secondary sch. prin., supr. Math. tchr. Prescott (Ariz.) Jr. High, 1972-75; adj. math. tchr. Yavapai Coll., Prescott, 1975-84; math. tchr. grades 7-9 and dept. chmn. Granite Mt. Jr. High, Prescott, 1976-88; math. coord. Prescott Unified Schs., 1979—; math. tchr. grades 9-12 Prescott High Sch., 1988—; adj. math. instr. Prescott Coll., 1980—, No. Ariz. U., 1988—; dir. math. sect. N. Ctrl. Ariz. Consortium, 1992—; presenter and lectr. at many ednl. workshops and confs. Editor (monthly sci./ math. newsletter) Prescott Unified Schs., 1979—; contbr. articles to profl. pubs. Recipient Quality Edn. Program award, Ariz. Dept. Edn., 1981, Gov.'s citation for excellene in math. teaching, 1984, Presidential award for excellence in math. teaching, 1984,, Disting. Alumni award No. Ariz. U., 1989, State Farm Good Neighbor award, 1992, Outstanding Women in Edn. award, Delta Kappa Gamma, 1992, 93; featured in mags. and on TV; named U.S. West Tchr. of Yr. for Ariz., 1993; recipient Tandy Tech. Scholar award for excellence in math. teaching, 1995. Mem. Nat. Coun. Tchrs. of Math., Nat. Coun. Suprs. of Math., Coun. Presidential Awardees in Math. (co-historian 1989—), Ariz. Assn. Tchrs. of Math. (sec. 1984-87, v.p. 1989-91, newsletter editor 1991-95, pres. 1995—), Ariz. Sci. Tchrs. Assn., Ariz. Alliance for Math. Sci. and Tech. Edn. (bd. dirs. 1986-88, adv. bd. 1988—, continued svc. award 1991), Ariz. Math. Coalition (adv. bd. 1990—), Ariz. Math. Network (regional dir. 1989-91), Sch. Sci. and Math. Assn., Phi Delta Kappa (many offices), Alpha Delta Kappa. Office: Prescott High Sch 1050 Ruth St Prescott AZ 86301-1730

BACH, MARTIN WAYNE, stockbroker, owner antique clock stores; b. Milw., Mar. 30, 1940; s. Jack Baer and Rose (Weiss) B.; m. Roberta Sklar, Aug. 19, 1962; children: David Louis, Emily Elizabeth. BA, U. Wis., 1963. Stockbroker J. Barth & Co., Oakland, Calif., 1966-72, v.p., 1970-72; sr. v.p., stockbroker Dean Witter & Co., Oakland, 1972—; founder The TimePeace, Carmel, Calif., 1972-83, San Francisco, 1975-83, La Jolla, 1977-83; instr. fin. San Leandro, Lafayette and Hayward (Calif.) Adult Sch., 1970—. Chmn. bd. dirs. Diablo Light Opera Co., 1985-87; bd. dirs. East Bay Hosp., 1985-90. lst lt. U.S. Army, 1963-65. Mem. Calif. Thoroughbred Breeders Assn., Calif. Thoroughbred Assn., Nat. Assn. Clock and Watch Collectors, Am. Horse Coun., East Bay Brokers Club, Moraga Country Club, Dean Witter Chairmen's Club, B'nai B'rith. Home: 4431 Deer Ridge Rd Danville CA 94506 Office: 1 Kaiser Plz Ste 1950 Oakland CA 94612-3610

BACH, MURIEL DUNKLEMAN, author, actress; b. Chgo., May 14, 1918; d. Gabriel and Deborah (Warshauer) Dunkleman; m. Joseph Wolfson, June 16, 1940 (div. Apr. 1962); 1 child, Susan; m. Ira J. Bach, Apr. 14, 1963 (dec. Mar. 6, 1985); stepchildren: Caroline Bach Marandos, John Lawrence; m. Josef Diamond, May 18, 1986. Student Carleton Coll., 1935-37; BS, Northwestern U., 1939. Researcher original manuscripts for One-Woman Theatre, also costume designer, writer, set designer; actress TV commls., indsl. films, radio commls.; photog. model; tchr. platform speaking techniques to corp. execs. Active sr. citizens groups, youth groups. Recipient Career Achievement award Chgo. Area Profl. Pan Hellenic Assn., 1971, Women of Achievement award Women in Comm., Inc., 1991. Mem. Screen Actors Guild, AFTRA, Arts Club, Wash. Athletic Club, Seattle Tennis Club, Rainiers Club, Zeta Phi Eta. Author: (plays) Two Lives, 1958, ... because of Her!, 1963, Madame, Your Influence is Showing, 1969, MS ... Haven't We Met Before?, 1973, Lady, You're Rocking the Boat!, 1976, Freud Never Said It Was Easy, 1978, Of All the Nerve, 1982, Talk on Aging, The Older You Get, the longer You Live, vignettes for theatre.

BACHENHEIMER, BETH ADAIR, artist, educator; b. L.A., Aug. 20, 1948; d. Kur Joseph and Barbara May (Mirkin) B. Student, Chouinard Art Inst., 1967, U. Guadalajara, Mex., 1969; BA, Calif. Inst. Arts, 1972; postgrad., Vt. Coll., 1994—. Tchr. L.A. Unified Sch. Dist., 1987—; with Met. H.S., 1993-94; chair art and spl. edn. dept. Duke Ellington H.S., 1995; artist in residence Irvine Art Ctr., 1993; presenter, lectr. workshops and seminars in field. One women shows include 11 E. Ashland Gallery, Phoenix, 1988, L.A. Arts Festival, 1990, El Camino Coll., Torrance, Calif., 1990, Centro Colombo Americano, Bogota Colombia, Medellin Colombia, 1991, Musco de Arte Moderno/Cámara de Comercio, Bucaramanga, Colombia, 1991, Museo Arqueológico La Merced, Cali, Colombia, 1991, Brand Art Libr., Glendale, Calif., 1991, Art Store, West Los Angeles, Calif., 1991, Museo de Moderne Arte, CartegeÑa, Colombia, 1992, Museo Bolivariano de Arte Contempo, Santa Marta, Colombia, 1992, El Area Cultural del Banco de la República,

Cucuta, Colombia, 1993, Midnight Spl., Santa Monica, Calif., 1993, Post-Columbian Antiques, Venice, Calif., 1994; group shows include Calif. State U., LA., 1971, Otis Parsons Sch. Design, L.A., 1980, L.A.C.E. Gallery, L.A., 1981, 84, Long Beach (Calif.) Mus. Art, 1983, 88, 89, 90, Mesa Coll., San Diego, 1986, 4 Zero 9 Gallery, Venice, 1987, Irvine (Calif.) Art Ctr., 1987, 93, L.A. Art Coun., 1988, Artworks, L.A., 1988, Downey (Calif.) Mus. Art, 1989, City Hall, L.A., 1990, Sumner Sch., Washington, 1991, Space Gallery, Hollywood, Calif., 1992, Da Vinci Gallery, L.A., 1993, Megaboom Gallery, Hollywood, 1993, Orange County Ctr. for Contemporary Arts, Santa Ana, Calif., 1994, Barnsdall Mcpl. Art Gallery, L.A., 1994, Bronx Mus. Art, N.Y.C., 1995; represented in permanent collections Art Resource Ctr., Laguna Beach, Calif., Mitsui Corp., L.A., Museo de Arte Moderna de Medellin, Colombia, numerous pvt. collections; author: Power of Feminist Art, Other Vision; Other Guests. Grantee Calif. Art Coun./Nat. Endowment Arts, 1992, L.A. Cultural Affairs Dept., J.P. Getty Found., 1992, Irvine Art Ctr., 1993, L.A. Cultural Affairs Dept., 1993-94, L.A. Arts Recovery Program, 1992. Home: 1419 S Bentley Ave # 103 Los Angeles CA 90025

BACHER, ROSALIE WRIDE, educational administrator; b. L.A., May 25, 1925; d. Homer M. and Reine (Rogers) Wride; m. Archie O. Bacher, Jr., Mar. 30, 1963. AB, Occidental Coll., 1947, MA, 1949. Tchr. English, Latin, history David Starr Jordan High Sch., Long Beach, Calif., 1949-55, counselor, 1955-65; counselor Lakewood (Calif.) Sr. High Sch., Long Beach, 1965-66; rsch. asst., counselor Poly. High Sch., Long Beach, 1966-67; counselor, office occupational preparation, vocat. guidance sect. Long Beach Unified School Dist., Long Beach, 1967-68; vice prin. Washington Jr. High Sch., Long Beach, 1968-70; asst. prin. Lakewood Sr. High Sch., Long Beach, spring 1970; vice prin. Marshall Jr. High Sch., Long Beach, 1981-87, 1981-87; vice prin. Lindbergh Jr. High Sch., Long Beach, 1987—; counselor Millikan High Sch., Calif., 1988—, Hill Jr. High Sch., Calif., 1988-89; ret. Hill Jr. High Sch., 1989; chmn. vocat. guidance steering com. Long Beach Unified Sch. Dist., 1963—. V.p. Palos Verdes Woman's Club, 1993—, philanthropy com., garden tour chmn.; docent coun. sec. Palos Verdes Art Ctr., 1991—; leader TOPS CA 471, 1992-93. Mem. AAUW, Long Beach Pers. and Guidance Assn. (dir. 1958-60), Long Beach Sch. Counselors Assn. (sec. high sch. segment 1963-64), Phi Beta Kappa, Delta Kappa Gamma (pres., area dir. Delta Psi chpt., Calif. profl. affairs com. chmn. 1972-74), Phi Delta Gamma (pres. chpt. 1977-78, 87-90, nat. chmn. bylaws com. 1980-91, 87-90, nat. conv. com. 1987-88, nat. nominating com. 1989), Pi Lambda Theta (pres. chpt. 1974-76, v.p. So. Calif. coun. 1974-76, sec. 1991), Phi Delta Kappa (sec. Long Beach chpt. 1977-80). Home: 265 Rocky Point Rd Palos Verdes Estates CA 90274 also: 17721 Misty Ln Huntington Beach CA 92649-4915

BACHTEL, ANN ELIZABETH, educational consultant, researcher, educator; b. Winnipeg, Man., Can., Dec. 12, 1928; d. John Wills and Margaret Agnes (Gray) Macleod; m. Richard Earl Bachtel, Dec. 19, 1947 (dec.); children: Margaret Ann, John Macleod, Bradley Wills; m. Louis Philip Nash, June 30, 1978 (div. 1987). AB, Occidental Coll., 1947; MA, Calif. State U.-L.A., 1976; PhD, U. So. Calif., 1988. Cert. life tchr., adminstr., Calif. Elem. tchr. pub. and pvt. schs. in Calif., 1947-50, 64-77; dir. Emergency Sch. Aid Act program, spl. projects, spl. arts State of Calif., 1977-80; leader, mem. program rev. team Calif. State Dept. Edn., 1981-85; cons. Pasadena Unified Sch. Dist., 1981-86; teaching asst., adj. prof. U. So. Calif.; cons. sch. dists., state depts. internat. edn.; presenter workshops/seminars; mem. legis. task forces. Chmn. resource allocation com. City of Pasadena, 1982-90, Pasadena-Mishima (Japan) Sister Cities Internat. Com., 1983-87; asst. chair Pasadena-Jarvenpaa, Finland, 1990-92, chair, 1992-95; mem. L.A. World Affairs Coun., Bonita Unified Sch. Dist. Curriculum Coun., 1990-93, Dist. Task Force Fine Arts, 1990-93, Dist. Task Force Tech., 1990-93, Dist. Handwriting Task Force, 1993; active Pasadena Hist. Soc., Pasadena Philharm. Com., Women's Com. Pasadena Symphony Assn.; deacon Pasadena Presbyn. Ch., 1989-92. Emergency Sch. Aid Act grantee, 1977-81. Named to Hall of Fame Bonita Unified Sch. Dist., 1990-91. Mem. World Coun. Gifted and Talented Children, Internat. Soc. Edn. Through Art, Nat. Art Educators Assn. (dels. assembly 1988-92), Clan MacLeod Soc. (bd. dirs. So. Calif. chpt.), Phi Delta Kappa, Kappa Delta Pi, Pi Lambda Theta (Ella Victoria Dobbs Nat. Rsch. award 1989, pres. L.A chpt. 1991-95, nat. rsch. awards com. 1989-91, chair 1991-95, co-pres. region V 1993-95, Outstanding Pi Lambda Thetan in region V 1993-95), Assistance League of Pasadena. Contbr. articles to publs.; writer/editor: Arts for the Gifted and Talented, 1981; author Nat. Directory of Programs for Artistically Gifted and Talented Students, K-12.

BACHUS, BENSON FLOYD, mechanical engineer, consultant; b. LeRoy, Kans., Aug. 10, 1917; s. Perry Claude and Eva Pearl (Benson) B.; m. Ruth Elizabeth Beck, May 31, 1942; children: Carol Jean Schueler, Bruce Floyd, Linda Ruth Gadway. Degree, Hemphill Diesel Sch., Chgo., 1937; student, Sterling Coll., 1937-39; BSME, Kans. State U., 1942; postgrad., Ohio State U., 1961, Stevens Inst., 1964; MBA, Creighton U., 1967. Registered profl. engr., Ariz., Ill., Nebr. Researcher, mech. engr. Naval Ordnance Rsch. Lab., Washington, 1942-43; jr. product engr. Western Electric Co., Inc., Chgo. and Eau Claire, Wis., 1944-46; sr. devel. engr. Western Electric Co., Inc., Chgo., 1946-56; devel. engr. Western Electric Co., Inc., Omaha, 1960-66; product engr. mgr. Century Electronics and Instruments, Inc., Tulsa, Okla., 1956-60; sr. staff engr. Western Electric Co. div. AT&T Techs., Phoenix, 1966-85; cons. in field, 1985-93; cons. in field, Phoenix, 1985—; chmn. energy conservation AT&T Techs., Inc., 1973-85; advisor to student engrs. Ariz. State U., 1967-87. Patentee in field (9). Trustee, Village of Westchester (Ill.), 1949-53; sec.-treas. Westchester Broadview Water Commn., 1949-53; Sunday Sch. supr. Westchester Community Ch., 1949-56; vol. campaign worker, precinct committeeman Phoenix Rep. Party, 1986—. Named Westchester Family of Yr., Westchester Community Ch., 1952; recipient Centennial medal Am. Soc. Engrs., 1979. Fellow ASME (state legis. coord. 1985-86, 88-93, treas. Ariz. sect. 1971-72, sec. 1972-73, vice chmn. 1973-74, chmn. 1974-75, 50-Yr. Membership award, President's Dedicated Svc., Devotion, Leadership, Performance award 1992, Dedicated Svc. award 1993); mem. TAPPI, NSPE (Engr. of Yr. award 1979), Soc. Profl. Engrs. (editor mag. 1972-86), Ariz. Coun. Engring. and Sci. Assn., Am. Security Coun., Soc. Plastics Engrs., Weoma Sci. Club (pres. 1963-66), Tel. Pioneers Am., Order of Engrs., Elks, Airstream Wally Byam Caravan Club Internat. Trailer Club, 1986. Home and Office: 5229 N 43d St Phoenix AZ 85018

BACIGALUPA, ANDREA, art gallery owner, writer, artist; b. Balt., May 26, 1923; s. Andrew Leo and Maria Laura (Merolla) B.; m. Ellen Wilcox Williams, Oct. 9, 1952; children: Gian Andrea, Pier Francesca, Ruan Saire, Chiara Domenica, Daria Concessa. BFA, Md. Inst. of Fine Arts, 1950; postgrad., Accademia di Belli Arti, Florence, Italy, 1950-51. Owner The Studio of Gian Andrea, Santa Fe, 1954—; cons. on interior sacred art and ch. design Diocese of Amarillo, Tex., 1974—, St. Thomas More Ch., Manhattan, Kans., 1987-90, Our Lady of the Rosary Ch., Albuquerque, 1990-92, Shrine of St. Therese, Pueblo, colo. Author: Journal of Itinerant Artist, 1977, Good and Perfect Gift, 1978, Song of Guadalupana, 1979, Franco and Pirata, 1985 (column) The Santa Fe Reporter, 1989-92; feature reporting, contbr. The Santa Fe New Mexican, 1993-94; bronze sculptures exhibited Santa Fe City Hall, San Francisco, 1980, Santa Maria del Lauro, Meta di Sorrento, Italy, 1993. Sgt. U.S. Army, 1943-46, ETO. Recipient 1st Prize City of Santa Fe, 1980. Mem. AIA (1st Prize 1975). Roman Catholic.

BACIU, MICHAEL, photographer; b. Bucharest, Romania, Mar. 17, 1955; came to U.S., 1983; s. Clement Baciu and Sultanica (Chirulescu) Niculescu-Baciu; m. Doina Sherban, Aug. 18, 1980. Student, U. Bucharest, 1974-79, UCLA, Santa Cruz, 1984-90. One-man shows including Bella Gallery, Santa Monica, Calif., 1993; exhibited in groups shows at Miami Internat. Show, 1991, ArtFest, Corona del Mar, Calif., 1991. Home and Office: 5271 Newcastle Ave 3 Encino CA 91316-3005

BACKLUND, MICHAEL ANDERS, clinical psychologist, priest; b. San Bernardino, Calif., Mar. 13, 1951; s. James William and Dorothy Mae (Anderson) B. BA, U. San Diego, 1973, MS, 1975; MDiv, St. Patrick's Sem., Menlo Park, Calif., 1979; PhD, Pacific Grad. Sch. Psychology, Palo Alto, Calif., 1990. Lic. psychologist, Calif.; ordained Episcopal priest. Vicar Christ Ch., Calumet, Mich., 1980-82; asst. rector All Saint's Ch., Palo Alto, Calif., 1982-84; assoc. priest Grace Cathedral, San Francisco, 1984-89; psychotherapist Seattle, 1989-91; clin. psychologist San Francisco, 1990—; assoc. priest Trinity Ch., San Francisco, 1991—; clin. psychologist Calif. Dept. of Corrections, Vacaville and San Quentin, Calif., 1991-93, San Francisco, 1993—. Author: Faith and AIDS, 1990. Episcopal Ch. Found. fellow, 1985. Mem. APA, Calif. Psychol. Assn. Democrat. Office: 3241 Sacramento St San Francisco CA 94115-2047

BACKUS, JOHN, computer scientist; b. Phila., Dec. 3, 1924; m. Una Stannard, 1968; children: Karen, Paula. BS, Columbia U., 1949, AM, 1950; D.Univ. (hon.), U. York, Eng., 1985; DSc (hon.), U. Ariz., 1988; Docteur honoris causa, Université de Nancy 1, France, 1989; DSc (hon.), U. Ind., 1992. Programmer IBM, N.Y.C., 1950-53, mgr. programming rsch., 1954-59; staff mem. IBM T.J. Watson Rsch. Ctr., Yorktown Heights, N.Y., 1959-63; IBM fellow IBM Rsch., Yorktown Heights and San Jose, Calif., 1963-91; mgr. functional programming IBM Almaden Rsch. Ctr., San Jose, 1980-91; cons., 1991—. Mgr. Incest Info. Bay Area, 1992—. With AUS, 1943-46. Recipient W. Wallace McDowell award IEEE, 1967; Nat. medal of Sci., 1975; Harold Pender award Moore Sch. Elec. Engring., U. Pa., 1983; Achievement award Indsl. Research Inst., Inc., 1983. Fellow Am. Acad. Arts and Scis.; mem. NAS, NAE (Charles Stark Draper prize 1993), Assn. Computing Machinery (Turing award 1977). Home: 91 St Germain Ave San Francisco CA 94114-2129

BACKUS, VARDA PELLER, psychiatrist; b. Tel Aviv, Aug. 5, 1931; came to U.S., 1950; d. Moshe Peller; m. Leo Ganz, June 18, 1956 (div. Dec. 1976); children: Eric David, Karen Jennifer; m. George Edward, Jan. 18, 1977. Intern, Michael Reese Hosp., Chgo., 1957-58; resident in psychiatry, Mass. Mental Health Ctr., Boston, 1958-60; psychoanalytic tng., Boston Psychoanalytic Soc., 1960-62; BS cum laude, CCNY, 1953; MD, U. Chgo., 1957. Bd. cert. psychiatry and neurology. Pvt. practice psychiatrist Riverside, Calif., 1963-65, N.W. Clinic of Psychiatry and Neurology, Seattle, 1966; psychiatrist ct. and corrections unit Psychiat. Mental Health Cons. Svc., San Mateo County, San Mateo, Calif., 1967-69; psychiatrist for med. students Stanford (Calif.) U., 1968-69, psychiatrist Cowell Student Health Svc., 1969-77, clin. coord. Student Health Svc., 1974-77; psychiatrist Scripps Clinic Med. Group, La Jolla, Calif., 1977—; Editorial bd.: Jour. Hosp. and Cmty. Psychiatry, 1977-89, Am. Psychiat. Press, Inc., 1985-88. Editorial bd.: Jour. Hosp. and Cmty. Psychiatry, 1977-89, APPI Press, 1985-88. Bd. mem. La Jolla (Calif.) Chamber Music Soc. Recipient Appreciation for Excellent Tchg. award U. Calif., San Diego, 1985-86, Am. Coll. Psychiatrists, 1993—. Fellow APA (life, constl. membership com. 1984-87); mem. San Diego Soc. for Psychiat. Physicians (chair membership com. 1978-79, chair peer rev. com. 1980-82, chair com. on women 1982-84, chair ethics com. 1993—), San Diego Soc. for Adolecent Psychiatry (chairperson 1985), Sigma Alpha. Office: Scripps Clinic Med Group 10666 N Torrey Pines Rd La Jolla CA 92037-1027

BACON, LEONARD ANTHONY, accounting educator; b. Santa Fe, June 10, 1931; s. Manuel R. and Maria (Chavez) Baca; m. Patricia Balzaretti; children—Bernadine M., Jerry A., Tiffany A. B.E., U. Nebr.-Omaha, 1965; M.B.A., U. of the Americas, Mexico City, 1969; Ph.D., U. Miss., 1971. CPA; cert. mgmt. acct., internal auditor. Commd. 2d lt. U.S. Army, 1951, advanced through grades to maj., 1964, served fin. and acctg. officer mainly Korea, Vietnam; ret., 1966; asst. prof. Delta State U., Cleveland, Miss., 1971-76; assoc. prof. West Tex. State U., Canyon, 1976-79; prof. acctg. Calif. State U., Bakersfield, 1979—; cons. Kershen Co. (now Atlantic Richfield Oil Co.), Canyon, 1979-80. Contbr. articles to profl. jours. U.S., Mex., Can., papers to profl. confs. Leader Delta area Boy Scouts Am., Cleveland, 1971-76; dir. United Campus Ministry, Canyon, 1976-79; min. Kern Youth Facility, Bakersfield, 1983—, Christians in Commerce, 1990—. Paratrooper Brazilian Army, 1955. Mem. Am. Acctg. Assn., Am. Inst. CPA's, Am. Assn. Spanish Speaking CPA's, Inst. Mgmt. Accts. (pres. Bakersfield chpt. 1981-82, Most Valuable Mem. award 1981), Am. Mgmt. Assn., Inst. Mgmt. Acctg., Calif. Faculty Assn., Acad. Internat. Bus., Inst. Internal Auditors, Inst. Cost Estimators and Analysts, Alpha Kappa Psi (Dedicated Service award 1979), Omicron Delta Epsilon, Beta Gamma Sigma. Clubs: Jockey (Rio de Janeiro). Lodges: Lions (v.p. Cleveland 1971-73), Kiwanis (v.p. 1974-79, A Whale of a Guy award, Cleveland 1975, Plaque of Appreciation, 1992-93). Office: Calif State U 9001 Stockdale Hwy Bakersfield CA 93311-1099

BACON, PAUL CALDWELL, training system company executive, aviation consultant, engineering test pilot; b. Camp Lejeune, N.C., Oct. 8, 1945; s. Franklin Camp and Marjorie Edna (Caldwell) B.; m. Carol Wetherell, June 7, 1967 (div. Oct. 1974); 1 child, Paul Caldwell Bacon Jr.; m. Martha Jean Court, Feb. 2, 1986; 1 child, Catherine Caldwell Bacon. BS in Aerospace Engring., U.S. Naval Acad., 1967; MS in Aerospace Engring., U.S. Air Force Test Pilot Sch., 1976; MS in Systems Mgmt., U. So. Calif., 1979. Commd. 2nd lt. USMC, 1967, advanced through grades to maj., 1978, ret., 1980; advanced through grades to lt. col. USMCR, 1980—; fighter pilot, maintenance mgr. USMC, Beaufort, S.C., 1969-70, Danang, Republic of Vietnam, 1970-71, Kaneohe, Hawaii, 1971-73; advanced flight instr. USMC, Meridian, Miss., 1973-75; exptl. test pilot 1st F18 USMC, Patuxent River, Md., 1977-80; engring. test pilot United Airlines, Denver, 1980-84; test pilot 1st DC-8 hands-off landing maneuver, 1980; FAA airling transport rating, DC-8 and B 737, 1980; project mgr. phase II approved DC-8 flight simulator FAA, 1982, project mgr. phase II approved B-737 flight simulator, 1983; dir. systems implementation United Airlines Svcs. Corp., Lakewood, Colo., 1984-86; dir. product assurance, chief pilot United Airlines Svcs. Corp., Lakewood, 1986-90; mgr., tng. systems mktg. Hughes Aircraft Co., Manhattan Beach, Calif., 1990-91; program mgr. tng. systems Rockwell Internat., L.A., 1991—; dir. internat. flight test team Deutsche Aerospace, Manching, Germany, 1993-94; team leader Rockwell J. Pats Flight Evaluation Team, 1994; cons. Nat. Traffic Safety Bd., FAA, NASA, USAF, Australian Aviation Agy., Time-Life Books, aircraft simulator mfrs., 1980—; info. officer U.S. Naval Acad., Denver. Decorated Air medal. Mem. Soc. Exptl. Text Pilots, Nat. Mgmt. Assn., U. So. Calif. Alumni Assn., U.S. Naval Acad. Alumni Assn., Hornet 100 Club. Republican. Presbyterian. Home: 4407 W Lansing Pl Broken Arrow OK 74012 Office: Rockwell Internat NAm Aircraft 2600 Westminster Ave Seal Beach CA 90740-5600

BACON, VICKY LEE, lighting services executive; b. Oregon City, Oreg., Mar. 25, 1950; d. Herbert Kenneth and Lorean Betty (Boltz) Rushford; m. Dennis M. Bacon, Aug. 7, 1971; 1 child, Randene Tess. Student, Portland Community Coll., 1974-75, Mt. Hood Community Coll., 1976, Portland State Coll., 1979. With All Electric Constrn., Milwaukie, Oreg., 1968-70, Lighting Maintenance Co., Portland, Oreg., 1970-78; svc. mgr. GTE Sylvania Lighting Svcs., Portland, 1978-80, br. mgr., 1980-83; div. mgr. Christenson Electric Co. Inc., Portland, 1983-90, v.p. mktg. and lighting svcs., 1990-91, v.p. svc. ops. and mktg., 1991—. Mem. Illuminating Engring. Soc., Nat. Assn. Lighting Maintenance Contractors. Office: Christenson Electric Co Inc 111 SW Columbia St Ste 480 Portland OR 97201-5838

BACON, WALLACE ALGER, speech communications educator, author; b. Bad Axe, Mich., Jan. 27, 1914; s. Russell Alger and Mana (Wallace) B. A.B., Albion Coll., 1935, Litt. D., 1967; A.M., U. Mich., 1936, Ph.D., 1940; LL.D., Emerson Coll., 1975. Instr. English U. Mich., 1941-47; chmn. dept. interpretation Northwestern U., Evanston, Ill., 1947-79; asst. prof. English and speech Northwestern U., 1947-50, assoc. prof. English and speech, 1950-55, prof. speech, 1955-80, prof. emeritus, 1980—; Fulbright lectr., Philippines, 1961-62, Fulbright-Hays lectr., 1964-65; vis. prof. U. Calif.-Berkeley, U. Wash., Nihon U., Tokyo, U. N.C., Chapel Hill, N.Mex. State U., U. Philippines, Santo Tomas U., Philippines; mem. adv. bd. Inst. for Readers Theatre, 1974-85; mem. adv. bd. Harwood Found. of U. N.Mex., 1982-91, pres., 1984-87, 90-91, v.p. 1988-89. Author: verse play Savonarola, 1950 (Bishop Sheil award 1946), William Warner's Syrinx, 1950, (with Robert S. Breen) Literature as Experience, 1959, Literature for Interpretation, 1961, (with N. Crame-Rogers and C. V. Fonacier) Spoken English, 1962, (with C.V. Fonacier) The Art of Oral Interpretation, 1965; The Art of Interpretation, 1966, 3d edit., 1979, Oral Interpretation and the Teaching of Literature in Secondary Schools, 1974, also articles, poetry, monographs.; editor: Festschrift for Isabel Crouch: Essays on the Theory, Practice and Criticism of Performance, 1988; assoc. editor: Performance of Literature in Historical Perspectives, 1983; editor Text and Performance Quar., 1989-91, assoc. editor, 1992—; assoc. editor Quar. Jour. Speech, 1957-59, 63-65, 75-77, Speech Monographs, 1966-71; adv. editor Lit. in Performance, 1980-82, assoc. editor, 1983-88. Served with AUS, 1942-46. Decorated Legion of Merit; Alfred Lloyd postdoctoral fellow U. Mich., 1940-41; Rockefeller fellow, 1948-49; Ford Found. fellow, 1954-55; recipient Hopwood Major Writing Drama award U. Mich., 1936; spl. citation U. Philippines, 1965, 70; spl. commendation Ednl. Found. Philippines, 1965; Disting. Alumnus award Albion Coll., 1986. Mem. Speech Communication Assn. (Golden Anniversary Prize Fund award 1965, 74, disting. service award 1983, awards com. 1967, 85, 2d v.p. 1975, 1st v.p. 1976, pres. 1977), Western States Communication Assn., Malone Soc., AAUP, Phi Beta Kappa, Delta Sigma Rho, Theta Alpha Phi, Zeta Phi Eta. Home: PO Box 2257 Taos NM 87571-2257

BACON, WILLIAM FRANCIS, tribal judge; b. Omaha, Apr. 28, 1956; s. Gilbert A. and Arlene (Hewett) B. BA, Northwestern U., Evanston, Ill., 1978; JD, U. Idaho, 1981. Bar: Idaho 1981, U.S. Dist. Ct. Idaho 1981, Shoshone Bannock Tribal Bar 1983, U.S. Claims Ct. 1988, U.S. Ct. Appeals (9th cir.) 1989. Assoc. Racine, Olson, Nye, Cooper & Budge, Pocatello, Idaho, 1981-85; ptnr. Johnson, Olson, Bacon, Chartered, Pocatello, 1985-90; atty. Bannock County Prosecutor, 1990-92; tribal judge Shoshone-Bannock Tribe, Pocatello, 1993—; pres. S.E. Idaho Claims Assn., Pocatello, 1985-86; mem. congl. action com. Nat. Assn. for Home Health, 1992—. Fellow Med. Ctr. Found.; mem. Assn. Trial Lawyers Am. (Acutane subcom.), Nat. Coll. Advocacy, Def. Rsch. Inst., Idaho Def. Coun., Pocatello C. of C., State of Idaho Jaycees, Pocatello Jaycees. Home: 1600 Arlington Dr Pocatello ID 83204-5012

BADER, STEPHEN LEIGH, communications executive; b. Louisville, May 28, 1942; s. Ralph Edward and Phyllis Del (Lucas) B.; m. Julie Ann Groot, Dec. 1960 (div. 1980); children: Barbara Ann, Natalie Lucas. Student, U. Louisville. Salesman Eve Printing Co., Louisville, 1964-66; v.p. R.L. White Co., Louisville, 1966-80; owner Lucas Investments, Louisville, 1975-83; territorial mgr. TMC Long Distance(TM), 1983-85; pres. TMC of San Diego, 1985—; bd. dirs. Clark-Bader, Inc., Louisville; vis. lectr. U. Calif., San Diego, 1985; chief exec. officer, pres. TMC Long Distance (TM); v.p. Access Communications Group; pres. Escondido Telephone, 1990—. Mem. San Diego Employers Assn., Calif. Assn. Long Distance Tel. Cos. (bd. dirs.), Alternative Carrier Telecommunication Assn., San Diego C. of C. Office: TMC Long Distance (TM) 3965 5th Ave Ste 400 San Diego CA 92103-3107

BADGER, SANDRA RAE, health and physical education educator; b. Pueblo, Colo., Nov. 2, 1946; d. William Harvey and Iva Alberta (Belveal) Allenbach; m. Graeme B. Badger, Oct. 9, 1972; 1 child, Jack Edward. BA in Phys. Edn., U. So. Colo., Pueblo, 1969; MA in Arts and Humanities, Colo. Coll., 1979; postgrad., Adams State U., Alamosa, Colo., 1980-91. Cert. tchr., secondary endorsement in health and phys. edn., Colo. Head women's swimming coach Mitchell High Sch., Doherty High Sch., Colorado Springs, Colo., 1969-90; head dept. Health Edn. Doherty High Sch., 1979—; trainer student asst. program CARE, Colorado Springs, 1983—; trainer drug edn. U.S. Swim Olympic Tng. Ctr., Colorado Springs, 1988-89; trainer in track and field, Colorado Springs, 1989, 91; cons. Assocs. in Recovery Therapy, 1989—; speaker in field. Author, editor: Student Assistant Training Manual, 1983-95. Bd. dirs. ARC, Colorado Springs, 1990—, sec., 1991—, mem. health and safety com., 1990-95; mem. comprehensive health adv. com. Dept. Edn., State of Colo., Denver, 1991. Recipient Svc. award ARC, 1985, Coach of Yr. award Gazette Telegraph, 1979, 84, CARE award State of Colo., 1988, others; Gamesfield grantee, 1985; Nat. Coun. on Alcoholism grantee, 1990. Mem. NEA, Colorado Springs Edn. Assn. Office: Doherty High Sch 4515 Barnes Rd Colorado Springs CO 80917-1519

BADGETT, ANN WILSON, mental health nurse, rehabilitation nurse; b. Ft. Knox, Ky., Mar. 22, 1961; d. Robert H. and Christina (Berg) B. BA in Behavioral Sci., Midland Luth. Coll., 1984; ADN, U. Albuquerque, 1985; MA in Counseling Svcs., Webster U., 1987; postgrad., Chapman Coll. RN, N.Mex., Calif.; cert. rehab. nurse. Charge nurse adolescent unit Vista Sandia Psychiat. Hosp., Albuquerque; per diem staff nurse Heights Psychiat. Hosp., Albuquerque; brain injury unit coord. St. Joseph's Rehab. Hosp., Albuquerque, acting dir. nursing, admissions coord./ nurse liaison; nurse mgr. rehab. Stanford U. Hosp., Calif.; nurse mgr., dir. nursing for subacute unit So. Ariz. Rehab. Hosp., Tucson; instr. Mandt System for Managing Aggressive/Non-Aggressive People. Vol. safety edn. Heads Up Program, South Bay Assn. Rehab. Nurses (pres. elect). Capt. Nurse Corps USAFR. Mem. Assn. Rehab. Nurses (sec. Saguaro chpt. 1995).

BADGLEY, JOHN ROY, architect; b. Huntington, W. Va., July 10, 1922; s. Roy Joseph and Fannie Myrtle (Limbaugh) B.; m. Janice Atwell, July 10, 1975; 1 son, Adam; children by previous marriage: Dan, Lisa, Holly, Marcus, Michael. AB, Occidental Coll., 1943; MArch, Harvard, 1949; postgrad., Centro Internazionale, Vincenza, Italy, 1959. Pvt. practice, San Luis Obispo, Calif., 1952-65; chief architect, planner Crocker Land Co., San Francisco, 1965-80; v.p. Cushman & Wakefield Inc., San Francisco, 1980-84; pvt. practice, San Rafael, Calif., 1984—; tchr. Calif. State U. at San Luis Obispo, 1952-65; bd. dirs. Ft. Mason Ctr., Angel Island Assn. Served with USCGR, 1942-46. Mem. AIA, Am. Arbitration Assn., Golden Gate Wine Soc. Home and Office: 1356 Idylberry Rd San Rafael CA 94903-1074

BADGLEY, JUDETH BIRDWELL, motivational learning consultant; b. Cheyenne, Wyo., Dec. 29, 1954; d. Weldon James and Patricia (Finnerty) Birdwell; m. Michael Benedict Badgley, Oct. 7, 1983; children: Sara Pat, Brian, Mark. BA in Edn., U. Mont., 1979; MA in Edn. Adminstrn., No. Ariz. U., 1986. Tchr. Crane Sch. Dist., Yuma, Ariz., 1979-86; adminstrv. intern Crane Sch. Dist., 1986-87; owner/cons. Success Express, Yuma, 1986—; prin. summer sch. Crane Sch. Dist., 1989; guest lectr. in field; instr. No. Ariz. U., Flagstaff, 1989—. Author: Teaching with Style, 1990, I'm Positive: Building Self-Esteem, 1987, It's About Time, 1989, Discipline with Dignity and Self Respect, 1990, Handling the Gulf War Crisis on the Homefront, 1991, S.T.E.P.S. Toward Success, 1992. Chmn. City of Yuma Task Force, 1990—; chmn. com. Unted Way, Yuma, 1988-90; mem. Friends of the Ballet, 1986—; coord. Girl Scouts U.S., Yuma, 1979-91. Mem. Assn. Supervision and Curriculum Devel., Nat. Staff Devel. Coun., Ariz. Sch. Adminstrs. Roman Catholic. Home: 1239 S 40th Dr Yuma AZ 85364-4079

BADSTUEBNER, HANS ALEXANDER, electric company executive; b. Berlin, Feb. 26, 1916; came to U.S. 1960; s. Alexander and Emilie (Luechters) B.; m. Vera Ott, Jan. 9, 1939; 1 son, Stefan . Grad. E.E., Berlin, 1938, PhD, 1972. Asst. to gen. mgr. research, devel. depts. Telefunken G.M.B.H., Leubus and Berlin, 1942-45; con. efficiency engring. Berlin, 1945-52; owner Elba Electric Co., Burnaby, B.C., Can., 1952-60; v.p. prodn. engring. R.M. Hadley Co., Inc., L.A., 1960-64; sr. v.p. engring. Baum Electric Co., Inc., Garden Grove, Calif., 1964—; owner Hansera Co., Fullerton, Calif., 1969—; cons. Foster-Mathews Electric Co., 1981—. Inventor in various fields. Mem. Soc. Plastic Engrs., Am. Mensa Selection Agy., Triple Nine Soc., Cincinnatus High IQ Soc., Minerva High IQ Soc., Masons, Shriners. Home: 17222 Fern Ridge Rd SE Stayton OR 97383-9318

BADZEY, PETER GYULA GUSZTAV, aerospace engineer; b. L.A., Apr. 9, 1966; s. Eugene Sandor Jr. and Dora Amalia (Szabo) B. BS in Aerospace Engring., Calif. State Polytechnic U., 1989. Assoc. engr. scientist McDonnell Douglas Aerospace, Huntington Beach, Calif., 1989-90, engr. scientist, 1990—. Comm. dir. Corpus Christi Fellowship, 1993-94, meeting planning dir., 1994-95. Mem. AIAA (Nat. Student Design Competition 1st pl. award 1989), Sigma Gamma Tau. Republican. Roman Catholic. Office: McDonnell Douglas Aerospace 5301 Bolsa Ave Huntington Beach CA 92647

BAENA, JULIO, Spanish language and literature educator; b. Madrid, Sept. 15, 1955; came to U.S., 1980; s. Domingo and Albina (Martinez) B.; m. Obdulia Castro, Aug. 2, 1980; 1 child, Diego. Licenciado en Letras summa cum laude, U. Catolica Andres Bello, Caracas, Venezuela, 1980; MS in Spanish, Georgetown U., 1982, PhD in Spanish Lit., 1986. Lectr. Georgetown U., Washington, 1983-86; vis. asst. prof. St. Lawrence U., Canton, N.Y., 1986-87; asst. prof. Spanish U. Wyo., Laramie, 1987-89, U. Colo., Boulder, 1989—. Author: El Poemario de Fray Luis de Leon, 1989; contbr. articles to profl. jours. Mem. MLA, Am. Assn. Tchrs. Spanish and Portuguese, Cervantes Soc. Am., Assn. Comediantes. Home: 450 S Michigan Ave Lafayette CO 80026-2242 Office: U Colo Dept Spanish and Portuguese Campus Box 278 Boulder CO 80309-0278

BAER, D(AVID) RICHARD, film archive administrator; b. Oakland, Calif., Jan. 18, 1946; s. Oliver Albrecht and Beatrice Faye (Shrager) B. BS in Bus.

Adminstrn., UCLA, 1967. Founder, pres. Hollywood Film Archive, 1972—. Author: The Film Buff's Bible of Motion Pictures, 1915-72, 1972, The Film Buff's Checklist of Motion Pictures, 1912-1979, 1979; editor Film Superlist series; reprint editor Harrison's Reports and Film Reviews, 1919-1962. Mem. Am. Political Item Collectors. Office: Hollywood Film Archive 8344 Melrose Ave West Hollywood CA 90069-5496

BAER, WILLIAM BRUCE, ophthalmologist; b. Louisville, Sept. 30, 1938; s. Louis and Miriam (Wile) B.; m. Joan Anita Teckler, Apr. 26, 1966 (dec. Oct. 1968); m. Sydney Ann Anker, Dec. 26, 1976; children: Allison, Louis. BSEE, MIT, 1960; BA, U. Louisville, 1961, MS in Pathology, MD cum laude, 1965. Diplomate Am. Bd. Ophthalmology. Intern, then resident SUNY Upstate Med. Ctr., Syracuse, 1965-67; resident in ophthalmology U. Oreg., Portland, 1969-72; pvt. practice, Portland, 1972—. Capt. USAF, 1967-69. Fellow Am. Acad. Ophthalmology; mem. AMA, Oreg. Med. Assn., Oreg. Acad. Ophthalmology, Multnomah County Med. Soc. (trustee 1988-90), Multnomah Athletic Club, Oswego Lake Country Club. Jewish. Office: 1130 NW 22nd Ave Portland OR 97210-2900

BAERWALD, SUSAN GRAD, television broadcasting company executive producer; b. Long Branch, N.J., June 18, 1944; d. Bernard John and Marian (Newfield) Grad; m. Paul Baerwald, July 1, 1969; children: Joshua, Samuel. Degre des Arts and Lettres, Sorbonne, Paris, 1965; BA, Sarah Lawrence Coll., 1966. Script analyst United Artists, L.A., 1978-80; v.p. devel. Gordon/Eisner Prodns., L.A., 1980-81; mgr. mini-series and novels for TV, NBC, Burbank, Calif., 1981-82, dir. mini-series and novels for TV, 1982, v.p. mini-series and novels for TV, 1982-89; exec. producer NBC Prodns., 1989—. Producer TV mini-series: Blind Faith, 1990, Lucky Chances (Jackie Collins), 1990, One Spl. Victory, 1991, Cruel Doubt, 1993, A Time to Heal, 1994. Bd. dirs. The Paper Bag Players, N.Y.C., 1974—; vol. L.A.Children's Mus., 1978—; mem. awards com. Scott Newman Found., 1982-84. Recipient Vol. Incentive award NBC, 1983. Mem. ATAS (bd. govs. 1993—), Am. Film Inst., Hollywood Radio and TV Soc.

BAESEL, STUART OLIVER, architect; b. Charlotte, N.C., Feb. 5, 1925; s. Edward Franklin and Rose (Engel) B.; m. Betsey London Cordon, Nov. 23, 1949; children—Stuart Oliver, Betsey London, Cordon Telfair. Student, U. N.C., 1940-42, Ecole des Beaux Arts, Fountainbleau, France, 1948; B.Arch., N.C. State U., 1950; M.Arch., Cranbrook Acad. Art, 1951. Architect A.G. Odell, Jr. & Assocs., Charlotte, 1951-55; architect-designer Skidmore, Owings, Merrill, N.Y.C., 1955-59, LBC & W Assocs., Columbia, S.C., 1959-65; dir. design J.N. Pease Assocs., Charlotte, 1965-72; mem. faculty Architecture Sch. Calif. State U., Pomona, 1972-74; prin. Stuart Baesel, Architect, Design Group, La Jolla, Calif., 1972—; dir., sec. treas. Design World, Inc., Charlotte, 1968-72; dir., pres. Space Planning Assocs., Charlotte, 1966-72. Editor: Rev. Architecture, Columbia, S.C., 1962-65. Cons. Charlotte Planning Bd., 1954. Served with USAAF, 1943-46, PTO. Recipient various profl. awards, including Honor award S.C. chpt. AIA, 1964, 65, 66, N.C. chpt. AIA, 1956, 66, 68, 69, 70, 72. Fellow AIA (bd. dirs. N.C.); mem. N.Y. Archtl. League, Phi Delta Theta. Episcopalian. Club: La Jolla Beach and Tennis. Home: 303 Coast Blvd Apt 1 La Jolla CA 92037-4630 Office: PO Box 1237 La Jolla CA 92038-1237 also: Les Flots Bleus, 06230 Villefranche Sur Mer France

BAGARRY, ALEXANDER ANTHONY, III, quality assurance professional; b. McAllen, Tex., Nov. 10, 1949; s. Edward Louis and Billie Jean (Hajee) B.; m. Susan Lynn King, Sept. 21, 1988; 1 child, Alexander Anthony IV. Degree Level II inspector, USN Tng. Sch., San Diego, 1973; degree Level III examiner, Bettis Atomic Power Lab., West Mifflin, Pa., 1976. Cert. inspector Am. Petroleum Inst., 1993. Dimensional inspector Solar Turbines Internat., San Diego, 1979-81; nuclear power plant inspector Ametek-Straza Corp., El Cajon, Calif., 1981-82; chief inspector Astro-Cast Corp., Cucamonga, Calif., 1982-83; quality control mgr. Hemet Casting Co., Cucamonga, 1983-87, Vard Newport Co., Santa Ana, Calif., 1987-89; dir. quality control M.M.P. Quality Inspections, Inc., Long Beach, Calif., 1989—; Level III cons. in field, 1989—. with USN, 1971-79. Mem. Am. Soc. for Non-Destructive Testing, Am. Welding Soc., Pacific Energy Assn. Republican. Roman Catholic. Home: 4201 W 5th St Apt 109 Santa Ana CA 92703-3284 Office: MMP Quality Inspections Inc 1875 Coronado Ave Signal Hill CA 90804-1245

BAGDIKIAN, BEN HAIG, journalist, emeritus university educator; b. Marash, Turkey, Jan. 30, 1920; came to U.S., 1920, naturalized, 1926; s. Aram Theodore and Daisy (Uvezian) B.; m. Elizabeth Ogasapian, Oct. 2, 1942 (div. 1972); children: Christopher Ben, Frederick Haig; m. Betty L. Medsger, 1973 (div.); m. Marlene Griffith, 1983. A.B., Clark U., 1941, LittD, 1963; LHD, Brown U., 1961, U. R.I., 1992. Reporter Springfield (Mass.) Morning Union, 1941-42; assoc. editor Periodical House, Inc., N.Y.C., 1946; successively reporter, fgn. corr., chief Washington corr. Providence Jour., 1947-62; contbg. editor Sat. Eve. Post, 1963-67; project dir. study of future U.S. news media Rand Corp., 1967-69; asst. mng. editor for nat. news Washington Post, 1970-71, asst. mng. editor, 1971-72; nat. corr. Columbia Journalism Review, 1972-74; prof. Grad. Sch. Journalism, U. Calif., Berkeley, 1976-90, prof. emeritus, 1990—, dean, 1985-88. Author: In the Midst of Plenty: The Poor in America, 1964, The Information Machines: Their Impact on Men and the Media, 1971, The Shame of the Prisons, 1972, The Effete Conspiracy, 1972, Caged: Eight Prisoners and Their Keepers, 1976, The Media Monopoly, 1983, rev. edit., 1987, 3d edit., 1990, 4th edit., 1992; also pamphlets; contbr.: The Kennedy Circle, 1961; editor: Man's Contracting World in an Expanding Universe, 1959; bd. editors: Jour. Investigative Reporters and Editors, 1980-88. Mem. steering com. Nat. Prison Project, 1974-82; trustee Clark U., 1964-76; bd. dirs. Nat. Capital Area Civil Liberties Union, 1964-66, Com. to Protect Journalists, 1981-88, Data Ctr., Oakland, Calif., 1990—; pres. Lowell Mellett Fund for Free an Responsible Press, 1965-76; acad. adv. bd. Nat. Citizens Com. for Broadcasting, 1978—. Recipient George Foster Peabody award, 1951, Sidney Hillman Found. award, 1956, Most Perceptive Critic citation Am. Soc. Journalism Administrs., 1978, career achievement award Soc. Profl. Jours.; named to R.I. Journalism Hall of Fame, 1992; fellow Ogden Reid Found., 1956, Guggenheim fellow, 1961-62. Mem. ACLU. Home: 25 Stonewall Rd Berkeley CA 94705-1414

BAGLEY, CONSTANCE ELIZABETH, lawyer, educator; b. Tucson, Dec. 18, 1952; d. Robert Porter Smith and Joanne Snow-Smith. AB in Polit. Sci. with distinction, with honors, Stanford U., 1974; JD magna cum laude, Harvard U., 1977. Bar: Calif. 1978, N.Y. 1978. Tchg. fellow Harvard U., 1975-77; assoc. Webster & Sheffield, N.Y.C., 1977-78, Heller, Ehrman, White & McAuliffe, San Francisco, 1978-79; assoc. McCutchen, Doyle, Brown & Enersen, San Francisco, 1979-84, ptnr., 1984-90; lectr. bus. law Stanford (Calif.) U., 1988-90, lectr. mgmt., 1990-91, lectr. law and mgmt., 1991-95, sr. lectr. law and mgmt., 1995—; also lectr. Stanford Exec. Program; lectr. exec. program for growing cos. Stanford U.; bd. dirs. Alegre Enterprises, Inc.; mem. corp. practice series adv. bd. Bur. Nat. Affairs, 1984—; mem. faculty adv. bd. Stanford Jour. Law, Bus. and Fin., 1994—; lectr., mem. planning com. Calif. Continuing Edn. of Bar, L.A. and San Francisco, 1983, 85-87; lectr. So. Area Conf., Silverado, 1988, Young Pres. Orgn. Internat. U. for Pres., Hong Kong, 1988. Author: Mergers, Acquisitions and Tender Offers, 1983, Proxy Contests and Corporate Control, 1990, Managers and the Legal Environment: Strategies for the 21st Century, 1991, 2d edit., 1995; co-author: Negotiated Acquisitions, 1992, Cutting Edge Cases in the Legal Environment of Business, 1993. Vestry mem. Trinity Episcopal Ch., San Francisco, 1984-85; vol. Moffit Hosp. U. Calif., San Francisco, 1983-84. Mem. ABA, Acad. Legal Studies in Bus., Stanford Faculty Club (bd. dirs.), Phi Beta Kappa. Republican. Office: Stanford U Grad Sch Bus Stanford CA 94305-5015

BAGLEY, FENTON LLOYD, mechanical engineer; b. Van Wert, Ohio, Sept. 29, 1934; s. Fenton Lloyd and Mildred Ida (Ries) B.; m. Jessie Marie Barnett, June 2, 1956; children: Fenton Dean, Enora Marie, Joan Lea. BSME, Purdue U., 1956; MSME, MIT, 1960; postgrad., Carnegie Mellon U., 1965-68. Teaching asst. MIT, Cambridge, 1957-58; project engr. Rodman Lab., Watertown, Mass., 1958-60; rsch. engr. PPG Glass Rsch. Ctr., Pitts., 1960-65; tchr. Steel Valley Tech. Sch., West Mifflin, Pa., 1965-66; assoc. prof. Allegheny C.C., Pitts., 1966-73; project engr. Snap-Tite, Inc., Union City, Pa., 1973-78; design cons. Am. Sterilizer, Erie, Pa., 1978; design engr. Reed Mfg. Co., Erie, 1979-81; ptnr. Fenton Bagley, Holman, N.Mex., 1981—; contbr. to 4th Internat. Congress on Reology. Capt. USAR, 1956-70. Home and Office: Rural Box 1 Holman NM 87723-9801

BAGLEY, JOHN NEFF, social worker, consultant; b. Murray, Utah, Apr. 21, 1944; s. Ben and Marie (Pearson) B.; m. Meggin Catmull, Nov. 18, 1981. BS, U. Utah, 1966, MSW, 1973. Lic. clin. social worker, marriage and family counselor, Utah. Sch. social worker Salt Lake City Bd. of Edn., 1973-74; psychiat. social worker Holy Cross Hosp., Salt Lake City, 1974-76; alcohol and drug counselor County of Salt Lake, 1976-78; dir. Salt Lake City Recovery Ctr., 1978-79; clin. social worker Richfield (Utah) Dept. Social Svcs., 1982—; mem. grad. faculty social work U. Utah, 1975-93, 86-93, Human Affairs, Ltd., Richfield, 1987-93, Gunnison (Utah) Hosp., 1988-93, U.S. Behavior Health, 1995—, Sorenson's Ranch Sch., Koosharem, Utah, 1990-93; with Employee Assistance Program Utah Power and Light Co., Richfield, 1986-94, Bur. Land Mgmt., Richfield, 1986-94, Dept. of Corrections, Gunnison, Utah, 1984—. Capt. USAF, 1967-71, Vietnam. Home: 1109 N 2450 W Monroe UT 84754-3447 Office: Richfield Dept Social Svcs 500 N 201 E Richfield UT 84701

BAGNULL, GARY LYNN, accountant; b. Jefferson City, Mo., June 24, 1956; s. Paul Edward and Irma Marie (Mueller) B.; m. Julie Anne Brown, May 12, 1990. Student, Mesa C.C., San Diego, 1974-76; BS in Bus. Admnistrn. and Mgmt., U. Phoenix, San Diego, 1993-95. Warehouseman Navy Exch., San Diego, 1974-76; drafting aide Archtl. div. County of San Diego, 1976-77; account clk. Probation Dept., County of San Diego, 1978-80; night auditor Best Western Inn, Jefferson City, 1981-82; night auditor Sheraton Harbor Island Hotel, San Diego, 1983-85, income auditor, 1986-87, project contr., 1990-91; chief acct. Sheraton San Diego Hotel & Marina (formerly Sheraton Harbor Island Hotel), San Diego, 1988—.

BAGSHAW, BRADLEY HOLMES, lawyer; b. Salem, Mass., Mar. 26, 1953; s. James Holmes and Hope (Bradley) B.; m. Suzanne LuBien, Aug. 23, 1975. AB summa cum laude, Bowdoin Coll., 1975; JD cum laude, Harvard U., 1981. Bar: Wash. 1981, U.S. Dist. Ct. (we. dist.) Wash. 1981, U.S. Dist. Ct. (ea. dist.) Wash. 1989, U.S. Ct. Appeals (9th cir.) 1989. Assoc. Helsell, Fetterman, Martin, Todd & Hokanson, Seattle, 1981-88, ptnr., 1988—; mng. ptnr. Helsell Fetterman Martin Todd, Seattle, 1991—. Home: 6240 27th Ave NE Seattle WA 98115-7114 Office: Helsell Fetterman Martin Todd & Hokanson 1325 4th Ave Seattle WA 98101

BAGWELL, STEVEN KENT, newspaper editor; b. Kokomo, Ind., Mar. 22, 1948; s. Chester A. and Lois Alberta (Gordon) B.; m. Dolly Jean Demase, June 10, 1974; children: Stephanie, Bryan. BA in History, Stanford U., 1970; MA in Journalism, U. Oreg., 1973. Sportswriter Coos Bay (Oreg.) World, 1971-72; reporter, photographer Springfield (Oreg.) News, 1972-73, The Daily Astorian, Astoria, Oreg., 1973-76; reporter, copy editor, asst. city editor, assoc. city editor, mem. editl. bd. The Oreg. Statesman and Salem (Oreg.) Statesman-Jour., 1976-86; city editor, editl. page editor The Idaho Statesman, Boise, 1986-91; mng. editor The Bull., Bend, Oreg., 1991—. Mem. Atty. Gen.'s Victim's Rights Task Force, Boise, 1989-90. Recipient over 30 state, regional, and national awards for photography, newswriting, investigative reporting, pub. svc., editl. writing, among others. Mem. Soc. Profl. Journalists, Pacific N.W. Newspaper Assn., Oreg. Newspaper Assn., State Bar/Press/Broadcasters Coun., AP Mng. Editors, Oreg. Assoc. Press Editors (pres. 1994-95). Office: The Bulletin 1526 NW Hill St Bend OR 97701

BAHMA, JERRY, agricultural products company executive; b. 1949. Graduate, U. Minn., 1971. Various mgmt. positions Land O Lakes, St. Paul, 1977-83, dir. administrn., 1980-89; dist. mgr. Swiss Valley Farms, Iowa and Ill., 1978-80; CFO Superior Farming Co., Bakersfield, Calif., 1989-91; with Diamond Walnut Growers, Inc., Stockton, Calif., 1991—. Office: Diamond Walnut Growers Inc 1050 Diamond St Stockton CA 95205-7020*

BAHR, DIANA MEYERS, humanities educator; b. Long Beach, Calif., Sept. 14, 1930; d. Omar Nelson Wood and Ruth Lulu (Harscher) Crossman; m. Ian Henry Meyers, June 25, 1950 (dec. Mar. 1973); children: Gary, Timothy, Christopher; m. Ehrhard Carl Bahr, Nov. 21, 1973. PhD in Am. Indian Studies, UCLA, 1990. Founder, dir. Northrop U. Lang. Inst., Inglewood, Calif., 1976-84; lectr. S.W. Mus., L.A., 1990—, UCLA, 1990 ; cons. A&E TV Series Mysteries of the Bible, L.A., 1994, TV Series Am. Indian Issues, L.A., 1991—. Author: From Mission to Metropolis: Cupeno Indian Women in Los Angeles, 1993. Vol. lectr. Fowler Mus. Cultural History, UCLA, 1986—, Calif. Coast Walk, Sebastopal, Calif., 1994. Mem. Oral History Assn., Calif. Hist. Soc., Ethnic Arts Coun. L.A. Home: 2364 Nalin Dr Los Angeles CA 90077-1806 Office: Coun for Ednl Devel UCLA 80 Powell Los Angeles CA 90024

BAHR, HOWARD MINER, sociologist, educator; b. Provo, Utah, Feb. 21, 1938; s. A. Francis and Louie Jean (Miner) B.; m. Rosemary Frances Smith, Aug. 28, 1961 (div. 1985); children: Bonnie Louise, Howard McKay, Rowena Ruth, Tanya Lavonne, Christopher J., Laura L., Stephen S., Rachel M.; m. Kathleen Slaugh, May 1, 1986; children: Alden Keith, Jonathan Andrew. B.A. with honors, Brigham Young U., 1962; M.A. in Sociology, U. Tex., 1964, Ph.D., 1965. Research asso. Columbia U., N.Y.C., 1965-68; vis. lectr., summer 1968; lectr. in sociology N.Y. U., 1967-68, Bklyn. Coll., City U. N.Y., 1967; asso. prof. sociology Wash. State U., Pullman, 1968-73; prof. Wash. State U., 1972-73, chmn. dept. rural sociology, 1971-73; prof. sociology Brigham Young U., Provo, Utah, 1973—; dir. Family Research Inst., 1977-83; fellow David M. Kennedy, 1992; vis. prof. sociology U. Va., 1976-77, 84-85. Author: Skid Row: An Introduction to Disaffiliation, 1973, Old Men Drunk and Sober, 1974, Women Alone: The Disaffiliation of Urban Females, 1976, American Ethnicity, 1979, Sunshine Widows: Adapting to Sudden Bereavement, 1980, Middletown Families, 1982, All Faithful People: Change and Continuity in Middletown's Religion, 1983, Life in Large Families, 1983, Divorce and Remarriage: Problems, Adaptations and Adjustments, 1983, Social Science Research Methods, 1984, Recent Social Trends in the United States 1960-90, 1991; contbr. articles to profl. jours.; asso. editor: Rural Sociology, 1978-83, Jour. Marriage and the Family, 1978-83. NIMH grantee, 1968-70, 71-73; NSF grantee, 1971-72, 76-80. Mem. Soc. Applied Anthropology, Rural Sociol. Assn., Nat. Coun. Family Rels. Mem. LDS Ch. Office: Dept Sociology 842 SWKT Brigham Young U Provo UT 84602

BAIK, HYO WHI, automotive import company executive; b. Kae Sung, Republic of Korea, Sept. 6, 1942; came to U.S., 1987; s. Sun Kyung and Soo (Park) B.; m. Young Jin Chang, Dec. 9, 1969; children: Sung Hak, Ji Yun. BA, Korea U., Seoul, 1968. Mng. dir. Hyundai Engring. and Constrn. Co., Republic of Korea, throughout Asia, 1968-85, Hyundai Motor Co., 1985-87; pres., chief exec. officer Hyundai Motor Am., Garden Grove, Calif., 1987—. Office: Hyundai Motor Am PO Box 20850 Santa Ana CA 92728-0850

BAILEY, BRENDA MARIE, accountant; b. Chgo., June 21, 1940; d. Walter E. and Dorothy Virginia (Seyl) B.; m. Norman R. Hill, Nov. 30, 1985 (dec. Nov. 1993); 1 stepchild, Andrea M. Hill. BS, So. Ill. U., 1966. CPA, Calif. U.S. govt. gen. svcs. adminstrn. auditor U.S. Navy, Barstow, Calif., 1966-69; staff acct. Stanford Bruns & Co., San Diego, 1969-74; pvt. practice La Mesa, Calif., 1974-91; ptnr. Bailey & Dana CPAs, La Mesa, 1991—; cons. to dirs. Santa Fe Rlwy. Hist. Soc., L.A., 1988—; treas. Pacific S.W. Rlwy. Mus., San Diego, 1979-86, San Diego Rlwy. Mus. of Balboa Park, 1981—. Mem. planning com., treas. Santa Fe Ry. Hist. Soc. ann. conv., 1986, 94; mem. planning and adminstrv. com. Nat. Model R.R. Assn. (Pacific S.W. divsn.) Conv., 1994. Mem. AICPAs, Calif. Soc. CPAs, La Mesa C. of C., Am. Soc. Women Accts. (bd. dirs. 1975-77, pub. editor 1976-77). Republican. Presbyterian. Home: 1931 Aspen Ln El Cajon CA 92019-4178 Office: 4817 Palm Ave # 3 La Mesa CA 91941-3840

BAILEY, BRIAN DENNIS, management consultant, author, publisher; b. Tacoma, June 10, 1952; s. Hugh Charles and Elsie Denise (Hinds) B.; BBA, Pacific Luth. U., Tacoma, 1975; MBA, City U. Seattle, 1982; PhD in Bus. Adminstrn., Century U., Beverly Hills, Calif., 1985. Prin. B.D. Bailey Svcs., Tacoma, 1975—; pres. and chief exec. officer Baico Industries Inc., Tacoma, 1975—; adj. instr. City U., Seattle, 1986—. With USAF, 1971-73, with res. 1973-77. Mem. Full Gospel Businessmen's Fellowship Internat., World Bible Way Fellowship, Inc., Christian Writers Guild, Grange of Washington State. Office: Baico Industries Inc PO Box 44757 Tacoma WA 98444-0757

BAILEY, CHARLES-JAMES NICE, linguistics educator; b. Middlesborough, Ky., May 2, 1926; s. Charles Wise and Mary Elizabeth (Nice) B. AB in Classical Philology with highest honors, Harvard Coll., 1950, MTh, 1955; DMin, Vanderbilt U., 1963; AM, U. Chgo., 1966, PhD, 1969. Mem. faculty dept. linguistics U. Hawaii, Manoa, 1968-71, Georgetown U., 1971-73; prof. Technische U. Berlin, 1974-91, univ. prof. emeritus, 1991—; vis. prof. U. Mich., Ann Arbor, 1973, U. Witwatersrand, Johannesburg, 1976, U. Brunei, Darussalam, 1990; Forcheimer prof. U. Jerusalem, 1986; proprietor Orchid Land Publs.; hon. col. Staff Gov. of Ky. Fellow Netherlands Inst. Advanced Study (life), Internat. Soc. Phonetic Scis.; mem. European Acad. Arts, Scis. and Humanities (corr.), Linguistic Soc. Am., Soc. Linguistica Europaea, Am. Dialect Soc., Internat. Palm Soc. Home: PO Box 1416 16-650 Orchid Land Dr Keaau HI 96749-1416

BAILEY, CLAYTON GEORGE, artist, educator; b. Antigo, Wis., Mar. 9, 1939; s. Clayton Pence and Mary (Pence) B.; m. Betty Graveen, Oct. 11, 1958; children: Kurt Douglas, Robin Lynn, George Gladstone. BS, U. Wis., 1961, MS, 1962. Asst. prof. U. Wis.-Whitewater, 1963-67; with ceramic dept. U. S.D., 1967-68; prof. Calif. State U.-Hayward, 1968—, chmn. dept. art, 1980-83. Exhibited in shows Mus. Contemporary Crafts, N.Y.C., Everson Mus. Art, Syracuse, Addison Gallery Am. Art, Andover, Mass., Milw. Art Ctr., Walker Art Ctr., Mpls., Art Inst. Chgo., San Francisco Art Inst., Richmond Art Mus., Renwick Gallery, Wash., Joseph Chowning Gallery, San Francisco, Natural History Mus., San Diego, U. Ariz. Mus. Art, Tucson, Am. Crafts Mus., Palm Springs Desert Mus. (Calif.), Triton Mus., Santa Clara, Calif., Ctr. George Pompidou, Paris, others; represented in permanent collections U. Wis., Addison Gallery Am. Art, Brooks Meml. Gallery U. Okla., State U. Iowa, Milw. Art Ctr., Hokkoku Shinbun, Korinbo, Japan, Sacramento State Univ., Johnson Found., Racine, Wis., Laguna Art Museum, L.A. County Art Mus., Metromedia Collection, USIA, San Francisco Mus. Art., Mus. Contemporary Crafts, N.Y.C., Mus. Contemporary Art, Honolulu, L.A. County Mus., Redding (Calif.) Mus., Mills Coll., Oakland, Calif., USIA, Crocker Gallery, Sacramento, Oakland Mus., Asahi Shimbun, Japan, Karlstadt, Germany, others; founder, curator and ceramic sculptor Kaolithic curiosities Wonders of the World Mus., Port Costa, Calif.; patentee in field. Louis Comfort Tiffany Found. grantee, 1963; Am. Craftsmen's Council grantee, 1963; recipient George Gladstone award, 1970; Piltdown Found. grantee, 1972; Nobel Prize nominee in physics, 1976; NEA grantee, 1979, 90; Nat. Council for Edn. in Ceramic Arts fellow, 1982. Home: PO Box 69 Port Costa CA 94569-0069

BAILEY, EXINE MARGARET ANDERSON, soprano, educator; b. Cottonwood, Minn., Jan. 4, 1922; d. Joseph Leonard and Exine Pearl (Robertson) Anderson; m. Arthur Albert Bailey, May 5, 1956. B.S., U. Minn., 1944; M.A., Columbia U., 1945; profl. diploma, 1951. Instr. Columbia U., 1947-51; faculty U. Oreg., Eugene, 1951—, prof. voice, 1966-87, coordinator voice instrn., 1969-87, prof. emeritus, 1987—; faculty dir. Salzburg, Austria, summer 1968, Europe, summer 1976; vis prof., head vocal instrn. Columbia U., summers 1952, 59; condr. master classes for singers, developer summer program study for high sch. solo singers, U. Oreg. Sch. Music, 1988—. Profl. singer, N.Y.C.; appearances with NBC, ABC symphonies; solo artist appearing with Portland and Eugene (Oreg.) Symphonies, other groups in Wash., Calif., Mont., Idaho, also in concert; contbr. articles, book revs. to various mags. Del. fine arts program to Ea. Europe, People to People Internat. Mission to Russia for 1990. Recipient Young Artist award N.Y.C. Singing Tchrs., 1945, Music Fedn. Club (N.Y.C.) hon. award, 1951; Kathryn Long scholar Met. Opera, 1945. Mem. Nat. Assn. Tchrs. Singing (lt. gov. 1968-72), Oreg. Music Tchrs. Assn (pres. 1974-76), Music Tchrs. Nat. Assn. (nat. voice chmn. high sch. activities 1970-74, nat. chmn. voice 1973-75, 81-85, NW chmn. collegiate activities and artists competition 1978-80, editorial com. Am. Music Tchr. jour. 1987-89), AAUP, Internat. Platform Assn., Kappa Delta Pi, Sigma Alpha Iota, Pi Kappa Lambda. Home: 17 Westbrook Way Eugene OR 97405-2074 Office: U Oreg Sch Music Eugene OR 97403

BAILEY, FRANK RONALD, government executive, technology educator; b. Grafton, N.D., Oct. 12, 1942; s. Frank Fischer Bailey and Dorothy Evelyn Lykken Lowe; m. Kaylen Gale Snell, Apr. 29, 1967; children: Larisa Ann, Erika Lyn. BS, Iowa State U., 1964, MS, 1967, PhD in Aerospace Engring. and Mechanics, 1970; student, von Karman Inst., Brussels, 1969. Rsch. scientist NASA Ames Rsch. Ctr., Moffett Field, Calif., 1970-79, chief NAS processing system br., 1979-82, chief NAS study office, 1982-83, mgr. NAS projects office, 1983-86, chief NAS systems div., 1986-90, dir. aerophysics, 1990-94; cons. prof. Stanford (Calif.) U., 1994—; mem. adv. coun. RCI, Ltd., Mpls., 1994. Bd. dirs. Orchards, Sunnyvale, Calif., 1978; treas. Election Reform Initiative Com., Sunnyvale, 1976; mem. City Charter Revision Com., Sunnyvale, 1974. Recipient Laurels award Aviation Week and Space Tech. Mag., 1986, Outstanding Ledership medal NASA, 1986, Presdl. Meritorious Exec. award U.S. Govt., 1993. Fellow AIAA (Disting. lectr. 1986-87); mem. IEEE Computer Soc. Home: 775 Steuben Dr Sunnyvale CA 94087-2247

BAILEY, HOWLAND HASKELL, physicist, consultant; b. Boston, Apr. 5, 1912; s. William Henry and Edith Stone (Haskell) B.; m. Anne Margaret Becchetti, Aug. 30, 1941; children: Bernadine Oberst, Barbara Ruth Kernochan. AB, Haverford Coll., 1932; student, Duke U., 1932-34; PhD, Calif. Inst. Tech., 1941. Tchr. Am. Coll., Tarsus, Turkey, 1934-36; grad. asst. Calif. Inst. Tech., Pasadena, 1936-40; asst. prof. U. Wyo., Laramie, 1940-41, U. Okla., Norman, 1941-43; staff mem., group leader Radiation Lab. MIT, Cambridge, 1943-45; mem. tech. staff Bell Telephone Labs., Whippany, N.J., 1945-53; mem. tech. staff, group leader Rand Corp., Santa Monica, Calif., 1953-87, cons., 1987-91; cons. Sci. Applications, Inc., La Jolla, Calif., 1977-81, Northrop Corp., Anahaeim, Calif., 1978-80, Pacific Sierra Rsch., Santa Monica, 1983. Contbr. articles to profl. jours. Mem. several Air Force Sci. Adv. Bd. Coms. Fellow Explorers Club; mem. Sierra Club (chpt. treas. 1980-82), Phi Beta Kappa. Home: 28791 Via Los Arboles San Juan Capistrano CA 92675-5510

BAILEY, JOHN ARTHUR, management consultant; b. Bryan, Tex., July 6, 1918; s. Arthur Chester and Laura Elizabeth (Brogdon) B.; m. Barbara Jane Elliott, Jan. 6, 1946; children: Louise B. Duback, John Elliott. BS in Mech. Engring., Tex. A & M U., 1939; M in Govt. Adminstrn. cum laude, U. Pa., 1949, PhD in Polit. Sci., 1966. Registered profl. engr., Pa. Engr. Pepsi-Cola Co., L.I., N.Y., 1946-48; mgr. Edgeworth (Pa.) Borough, 1949-53; dep. mng. dir. City of Phila., Pa., 1953-61; exec. dir. Passenger Svc. Improvement Corp., Phila., 1961-64; dep. gen. mgr. S.E. Pa. Transp. Authority, Phila., 1964-67; dir., prof. Transp. Ctr., Northwestern U., Evanston, Ill., 1967-75; v.p. Murphy Engring., Chgo., 1975-76; ptnr. L. T. Klauder & Assoc., Phila., 1976-81; pres. Transp. Sys. Assocs., Inc., Santa Fe, 1983—; pres., chmn. Soc. for Advancement of Mgmt., Phila., 1953-55, Met. Planning Coun., Chgo., 1969-73; mem. rapid transit com. Transp. Rsch. Bd., Washington, 1984-90. Mem., chmn. Santa Fe County Transp. Devel. Dist., 1993—; mem., sec. Park Plazas Cmty. Svcs. Assn., Santa Fe, 1993—; mem. N.Mex. First; mem. com. on rail transit sys. Transp. Rsch. Bd., Washgnton, 1992—. Fels scholar, Phila., 1948-49. Mem. Am. Pub. Works Assn. (life), Am. Soc. for Polit. & Social Scis., Cosmos Club (Washington), Tau Beta Pi. Democrat. Unitarian.

BAILEY, JOSELYN ELIZABETH, physician; b. Pine Bluff, Ark.; d. Joseph Alexander and Angeline Elaine (Davis) B.; B.Music, Manhattanville Coll., 1952; M.Music Edn., Manhattan Sch. Music, 1954; M.D., Howard U., 1971. Straight med. intern Huntington Meml. Hosp., Pasadena, Calif., 1971-72, resident, 1972-74; fell in nephrology Wadsworth VA Hosp., Los Angeles, 1975-77; practice medicine specializing in internal medicine and nephrology, Torrance, Calif.; assoc. staff Torrance Meml., South Bay; active Little Company of Mary hosps.; attending staff Harbor Gen. Hosp.; clin. faculty Dept. Medicine, UCLA; active staff Bay Harbor Hosp., trustee, 1982—.

BAILEY, KATHERINE CHRISTINE, artist, writer; b. Glendale, Calif., Dec. 1, 1952; d. Carl Leonard and Anna Alice (Dzamka) Abrahamson; m. David Francis Bailey, Sept. 27, 1975. BA, Calif. State U., L.A., 1974, MA, 1975; PhD, U. N.Mex., 1982. Exhbns. include Miniature Painters Sculptors

& Gravers Soc., Washington, Oil Pastel Assn., N.Y.C., Mont. Miniature Art Soc. Internat., many others; author: (novel) Brush With Death; also numerous short stories. Recipient hon. mention in mixed media category Nat. Western Small Painting Show, Bosque Art Gallery, N.Mex., 1985, 2d pl. award in pastels, 1986, Cert. of Merit award 4th Ann. Holiday Exhbn. of Oil Pastel Assn., 1994; tuition fellow U. N.Mex., 1977; Alpha Gamma Sigma scholar, 1972. Mem. Oil Pastel Assn., Nat. Mus. Women in Arts, Mont. Miniature Art Soc., Laramie Art Guild, N.W. Pastel Soc., Phi Kappa Phi, Alpha Gamma Sigma. Home and Studio: PO Box 301 Daggett CA 92327-0301

BAILEY, MARSHA ANN, association executive; b. Muskegon, Mich., Oct. 26, 1950; d. Howard Charles and Shirley Eileen (Wiersma) B.; m. Francis Joseph Borden III, Sept. 8, 1973 (div. 1978); m. William Lawton Rader Anderson, May 3, 1986; children: (twins) Samuel Lawton Bailey Anderson, Maxwell Channing Bailey Anderson. BA (with honors), Mich. State U., 1972; MA, U. Calif., Santa Barbara, 1984. Regional advt. dir. MacElhenny, Levy & Co., Santa Barbara, 1978-80; publicist Berkus Group Archs., Santa Barbara, 1980-81; cmty. edn. dir. Rape Crisis Ctr., Santa Barbara, 1983-88; exec. dir., founder Women's Econ. Ventures, 1988—; faculty mem. Santa Barbara (Calif.) City Coll., 1989-90; bd. dirs. Fund for Santa Barbara, Calif., 1990—, Pvt. Industry Coun., Santa Barbara, 1993—; adv. bd. Santa Barbara (Calif.) City Coll. Small Bus. Assistance Ctr., 1992—. Named Woman of Distinction, Soroptimists Internat., Goleta, Calif., 1994. Democrat. Office: Womens Econ Ventures 1136 E Montecito St Santa Barbara CA 93103-2635

BAILEY, MICHAEL JOHN, computer scientist; b. Phila., Oct. 16, 1953; s. Theodore Warren and Anne (Pomeroy) B. BS in Mech. Engring., Purdue U., 1975, MS in Mech. Engring., 1976, PhD, 1979. Mem. tech. staff Sandia Nat. Labs., Albuquerque, 1979-81; prof. mech. engring. Purdue U., West Lafayette, Ind., 1981-85; dir. advanced devel. Megatek Corp., San Diego, 1985-89; mgr. sci. visualization San Diego Supercomputer Ctr., 1989—; assoc. prof. applied mechanics and engring. scis. U. Calif., San Diego; freelance cons. in field, 1981—. Recipient Ralph Teetor Teaching award Soc. Automotive Engrs., 1983. Mem. Assn. Computing Machinery, Spl. Interest Group on Computer Graphics (chmn. course 1984-85, 87-88, 94, exec. com. 1986-90, conf. co-chair 1991), ASME. Office: San Diego Supercomputer Ctr PO Box 85608 San Diego CA 92186-5608

BAILEY, PHILIP SIGMON, JR., university official, chemistry educator; b. Charlottesville, Va., Mar. 17, 1943; s. Philip Sigmon Bailey and Marie Jeanette (Schultz) Hatch; m. Christina Anne Wahl; children: Karl, Jennifer, Kristen, Michael, Nhu Y Tran. Student, Am. U., Cairo, 1961; BS in Chemistry, U. Tex., 1964; PhD, Purdue U., 1969. Asst. prof. chemistry Calif. Poly. State U., San Luis Obispo, 1969-73, prof., assoc. dean, 1973-83, prof. chemistry, dean Coll. Sci. and Math., 1983-89, v.p. acad. affairs, sr. v.p., 1989-90, dean, 1990—. Author: (lab texts) Experimental Chemistry for Contemporary Times, 1975, Organic Chemistry, 1978, (textbook) Organic Chemistry, 1978, 5th edit., 1995. Mem. Am. Chem. Soc., Alpha Chi Sigma. Home: 1628 Royal Way San Luis Obispo CA 93405-6334 Office: Calif Poly State U Coll Sci And Math San Luis Obispo CA 93407

BAILEY, ROBERT C., opera company executive; b. Metropolis, Ill., Dec. 28, 1936; m. Sally McDermott, July 13, 1958. BA in Speech, U. Ill., 1958, MA in English, 1960; BM in Applied Voice, Eastman Sch. Music, 1965; MM in Applied Voice, New Eng. Conservatory Music, 1969. Music producer Nat. Pub. Radio, Washington, 1971-73, dir. cultural programming, 1973-75; mgr. Western Opera Theater, San Francisco, 1975-79; instr. arts mgmt. Golden Gate U., San Francisco, 1977-82; cons. arts mgmt., San Francisco, 1980-82; gen. dir. Portland Opera Assn., Oreg., 1982—; dir. Oreg. Advocates Arts, Portland, 1982—; cons. On-Site Program Nat. Endowment Arts, Washington, 1982—; judge Met. Opera Auditions, 1977—. Mem. Bohemian Club (San Francisco), City Club (Portland), Arlington Club, Rotary. Office: Portland Opera Assn Inc 1515 SW Morrison Portland OR 97205-1899

BAILEY, STEPHEN FAIRCHILD, museum director and curator, ornithologist; b. Stamford, Conn., Feb. 7, 1948; s. Edwin Montgomery and Frances (Sherman) B.; m. Karen Lynn Burtness Bailey, Aug. 18, 1971 (div. July 1987); divorced. BA in Biology magna cum laude, Beloit Coll., 1971; PhD in Zoology, U. Calif., Berkeley, 1978. Museum dir. and curator Pacific Grove Mus. of Natural Hist., Calif., 1992—; collections mgr. for ornithology and mammalogy Calif. Acad. Scis., San Francisco, 1984-92; biological cons., 1979-92; adj. prof. biology San Francisco State U., 1986—; teaching Albany Adult Sch., Calif., 1979-85. Co-author Atlas of the Breeding Birds of Monterey County, 1993; co-author, photographer Audubon Society Master Guide to Birding 3 vols., 1983; regional editor American Birds jour.; contrb. articles to profl. jours. Rsch. fellowship Christensen Rsch. Inst., Papua New Guinea, 1989. Mem. Am. Birding Assn. (elected), Ecological Soc. Am. (life), Am. Ornithologists Union, Cooper Ornithological Soc. (life), Pacific Seabird Group, Soc. Preservation of Natural Hist. Collections, Phi Eta Sigma, Phi Beta Kappa. Home: 830 Sunset Dr Apt J Pacific Grove CA 93950 Office: Pacific Grove Museum Natural History 165 Forest Ave Pacific Grove CA 93950-2612

BAILLY, JULIE ANN, manufacturing engineer; b. Pittsfield, Mass., Sept. 3, 1969; d. Richard August and Barbara Louise (Gillett) B. BS in Mfg. Engring., Worcester Polytech. Inst., 1992. Quality assurance trainee Pratt & Whitney Aircraft, East Hartford, Conn., 1992; mfg. engr. Ragsdale Machinery Ops. Alcoa Packaging Machinery, Englewood, Colo., 1993—. Mem. Am. Soc. Quality Control, Am. Welding Soc., Soc. Mfg. Engrs., Soc. Women Engrs. Office: Alcoa Packaging Machinery 4535 S Santa Fe Dr Englewood CO 80110-5531

BAILY, EVERETT MINNICH, electrical engineer; b. Twin Falls, Idaho, June 9, 1938; s. Charles Levi Baily and Helen Louise (Minnich) Wall; m. Donna Rae Larson, Sept. 8, 1961; children: Susan Gayle, Brian Charles. BSEE, U. Idaho, 1961, MSEE, 1964; PhD, Stanford U., 1968. Asst. prof. U. Idaho, Moscow, 1965-71; assoc. prof. U. Idaho, 1971-74, prof., 1974; prodn. engr. Hewlett Packard Co., Boise, Idaho, 1974-75; devel. engr. Hewlett Packard Co., 1975-81, reliability engr., 1981-83, reliability engring. mgr., 1983-86, prodn. engring. mgr., 1986-89, sr. mfg. engr., 1990—; cons. researcher U. Idaho Rsch. Found., Moscow, 1971-73. Patentee in field. Recipient Dow Outstanding Young Faculty award, Am. Assn. Engring. Edn. Pacific Northwest sect, 1970. Mem. IEEE (Boise sect. chmn. 1979, numerous com. offices), Model A Ford Club Am., Lions. Home: 12080 Chinden Blvd Boise ID 83714-1035 Office: Hewlett Packard Co 11311 Chinden Blvd # 514 Boise ID 83714-1021

BAIN, JAMES WILLIAM, lawyer; b. Suffern, N.Y., Dec. 19, 1949; s. William James and Agnes (Hoey) B.; m. Colleen K., Mar. 23, 1974; children: Rebecca, Meghan. BA, U. Conn., 1972; JD, U. Fla., 1976. Bar: Fla. 1977, U.S. Dist. Ct. (ea. dist.) Tenn. 1980, Tenn. 1984, U.S. Ct. Appeals (11th cir.) 1984, U.S. Ct. Appeals (D.C. cir.) 1984, Colo. 1986, U.S. Dist. Ctl Colo 1986, U.S. Ct. Appeals (10th cir.) 1988. Atty. trial Tenn. Valley Authority, Knoxville, 1977-85; atty. dir. Roath & Brega, P.C., Denver, 1985-89, Brega & Winters, P.C., Denver, 1989—; instr. U. Fla., Gainesville, 1976, U. Colo., Boulder, 1987-90; seminar chmn. Inst. for Advanced Legal Study, Denver, 1987. Contbr. articles to profl. jours. Recipient Civil Litigation Writing award for 1986-87, Denver Colo. Bar Assn., 1987. Mem. ATLA, Colo. Bar Assn., Fla. Bar Assn., Am. Judicature Soc., Am. Arbitration Assn. (arbitrator 1986). Office: Brega & Winters PC 1700 Lincoln St Ste 2222 Denver CO 80203-4522

BAIN, WILLIAM JAMES, JR., architect; b. Seattle, June 26, 1930; s. William James and Mildred Worline (Clark) B.; m. Nancy Sanford Hill, Sept. 21, 1957; children: David Hunter, Stephen Fraser (dec.), Mark Sanford, John Worthington. BArch, Cornell U., 1953. Ptnr NBBJ (formerly Naramore, Bain, Brady & Johanson), Seattle; lectr. U. Wash., Seattle, mem. affiliate program steering com. Coll. Architecture and Urban Planning, 1969-71; lectr. Wash. State U.; organizer founding bd. dirs. Pacific N.W. Bank. Prin. works include office bldgs., hotels, retail bldgs., civic bldgs. and various research facilities. Bd. dirs. Corp. Coun. for Arts, 1989—, Arboretum Found., 1971-74; bd. dirs. Downtown Seattle Assn., 1980—, 1st vice chmn., 1990-91, chmn., 1991-92; bd. dirs. Seattle Symphony Orch., 1974-87, pres., 1977-79; mem. coun. Cornell U., 1987-91, 94—. With C.E., U.S. Army, 1953-55. Recipient Cert. of Achievement Port of Whittier, Alaska, 1955, Disting. Alumnus award Lakeside Sch., 1985. Fellow AIA (pres. Seattle chpt. 1969, chmn. N.W. regional student profl. fund 1971, pres. Wash. coun. 1974, co-commn. Seattle centennial yr.), N.W. Regional Round. (pres. 1975); mem. Seattle C. of C. (bd. dirs. 1980-83), Urban Land Inst., N.W. Real Estate Inst., N.W. Forum, Am. Arbitration Assn. (comml. panel 1975—), L'Ogive Soc., Rotary (bd. dirs. 1970-72, svc. found. bd. 1976-80), Lambda Alpha, Phi Delta Theta. Episcopalian. Clubs: Rainier, Wash. Athletic, Tennis (Seattle); University, Columbia Tower (founding bd. dirs.). Home: 2033 1st Ave Seattle WA 98121-2132 Office: NBBJ 111 S Jackson St Seattle WA 98104-2820

BAINTON, DOROTHY FORD, pathology educator, researcher; b. Magnolia, Miss., June 18, 1933; d. Aubrey Ratcliff and Leta (Brumfield) Ford; m. Cedric R. Bainton, Nov. 28, 1959; children: Roland J., Bruce G., James H. BS, Millsaps Coll., 1955; MD, Tulane U. Sch. of Medicine, 1958; MS, U. Calif., San Francisco, 1966. Postdoctoral rsch. fellow U. Calif., San Francisco, 1963-66, postdoctoral rsch. pathologist, 1966-69, asst. prof. pathology, 1969-75, assoc. prof., 1975-81, prof. pathology, 1981—, chair pathology, 1987-94, vice chancellor acad. affairs, 1994—; mem. Inst. of Medicine, NAS, 1990—. NIH grantee, 1978—. Mem. AAAS, Am. Soc. for Cell Biology, Am. Soc. Hematology, Am. Soc. Histochemists and Cytochemists, Am. Assn. of Pathologists. Democrat. Mem. Soc. of Friends. Office: Office of Acad Affairs U Calif San Francisco Med Scis Bldg Rm 115 San Francisco CA 94143-0400

BAIRD, ALAN C., screenwriter; b. Waterville, Maine, Jan. 5, 1951; s. Chester A. and Beverly E. (Gilbert) B. BA, Mich. State U., 1973. Pres. Souterrain Teeshirts, Nice, France, 1977-78; page NBC, N.Y.C., 1979-80; producer, dir. Random Prodns., Hollywood, Calif., 1981; writer, producer Preview STV, N.Y.C., 1982-83, Sta. KCOP-TV, Hollywood, 1983-84; writer Vidiom Prodns., Hollywood, 1985—. Author: ATS Operations, 1976, Writes of Passage, 1992; prodr. TV script Live at the Palomino, 1981; writer TV scripts Night Court, 1986, 20/60, 1986, Golden Girls, 1986, Family Ties, 1986, Max Headroom, 1987, Dave's World, 1993, movie scripts Trading Up, 1988, Merlinsky, 1989, Eleven Thousand Virgins, 1994. Crisis counselor San Francisco Suicide Prevention, 1975; prodn. asst. March of Dimes Telethon, Hollywood, 1985; escort, host, vol. Verdugo Hills Hosp., 1994—. Recipient Harvard Book prize Harvard U., Cambridge, Mass., 1969.

BAIRD, LOURDES G., federal judge; b. 1935. BA with highest honors, UCLA, 1973, JD with honors, 1976. Asst. U.S. atty. U.S. Dist. Ct. (ctrl. dist.) Calif., L.A., 1977-83, U.S. atty., 1990-92; ptnr. Baird & Quadros, 1983-84, Baird, Munger & Myers, 1984-86; judge East L.A. Mcpl. Ct., 1986-87; adj. prof. law Loyola U., L.A., 1986-90; judge L.A. Mcpl. Ct., 1987-88, L.A. Superior Ct., 1988-90; U.S. atty. ctrl. dist. Calif., 1990-92; judge U.S. Dist. Ct. (ctrl. dist.) Calif., L.A., 1992—; faculty civil RICO program Practicing Law Inst., San Francisco, 1984-85, western regional program Nat. Inst. Trial Advocacy, Berkeley, Calif., 1987-88; adj. prof. trial advocacy Loyola U., L.A., 1987-90. Recipient Silver Achievement award for the professions YWCA, 1994; named Woman of Promise, Hispanic Womens' Coun., 1991, Alumnus of Yr., UCLA Sch. Law, 1991. Mem. Mexican-Am. Bar Assn., Calif. Women Lawyers, Hispanic Nat. Bar Assn., UCLA Sch. Law alumni Assn. (pres. 1984). Office: US Dist Ct Ctrl Dist Calif Edward R. Roybal Bldg 255 E Temple St Ste 770 Los Angeles CA 90012-3334*

BAIRD, MELLON CAMPBELL, JR., electronics industry executive; b. Corsicana, Tex., Feb. 24, 1931; s. Mellon Campbell and Katherine (Wasson) B.; m. Mary Beth Norman, Dec. 27, 1956. BBA, North Tex. State U., 1957, MBA, 1961. Adminstrv. asst. VARO Inc., Garland, Tex., 1957-59; western region mgr. VARO Inc., Los Angeles, 1959-61; dir. mktg. VARO Inc., Santa Barbara, Calif., 1961-63; exec. v.p., pres. F&M Systems Co., Dallas, 1963-74; pres., bd. dirs. fed. systems group Sanders Assocs. Inc., Nashua, N.H., 1974-81; pres. def. and electronics group Eaton Corp., Cleve., 1981-86; pres., chief oper. officer, bd. dirs. Tracor Inc., Austin, 1986-87, pres., chief exec. officer, 1988-89; pres., chief exec. officer, chmn. bd. dirs. Delfin Systems, Sunnyvale, Calif., 1990—; bd. dirs. Software Spectrum Inc., Dallas, EDO Corp., College Point, N.Y. Served with USN, 1951-55. Mem. Nat. Security Indsl. Assn. (trustee 1974—), Navy League U.S. (life), Armed Forces Communications & Electronics Assn., Assn. Old Crows (life, tech. symposium chmn. 1987), Security Affairs Support Assn. (bd. dirs. 1988-91), Tex. Assn. Taxpayers (bd. dirs. 1988-91). Home: 4204 Green Cliffs Rd Austin TX 78746-1241 Office: Delfin Systems 3000 Patrick Henry Dr Santa Clara CA 95054-1814

BAJCZYK, WILLIAM RICHARD, secondary education educator; b. Milw., June 2, 1960; s. Richard John and Marion Julia (Waletzko) B. BA, Creighton U., 1982; MA, Georgetown U., 1985. Cert. tchr., Alaska. Editor Nat. Assn. Civilian Conservation Corps., Falls Church, Va., 1982-84; substitute house parent A Place For Us, Balt., 1984-85; domestic violence counselor MEN, Inc., Juneau, Alaska, 1985-87; English tchr. Bering Strait Sch. Dist., Gambell, Alaska, 1988-89; bookstore clk. Webster's Book Store, Milw., 1989-90; English tchr. Lower Kuskokwino Sch. Dist., Napaskiak, Alaska, 1990—. Home: PO Box 6106 Napaskiak AK 99559-6106

BAKEMAN, CAROL ANN, administrative services manager, singer; b. San Francisco, Oct. 27, 1934; d. Lars Hartvig and Gwendolyne Beatrice (Zimmer) Bergh; student UCLA, 1954-62; m. Delbert Clifton Bakeman, May 16, 1959; children: Laurie Ann, Deborah Ann. Singer, Roger Wagner Chorale, 1954-92, L.A. Master Chorale, 1964-86, The Wagner Ensemble, 1991—; libr. Hughes Aircraft Co., Culver City, Calif., 1954-61; head econs. libr. Planning Rsch. Corp., L.A., 1961-63; corporate libr. Econ. Cons., Inc., L.A., 1963-68; head econs. libr. Daniel, Mann, Johnson & Mendenhall, archs. and engrs., L.A., 1969-71, corporate libr., 1971-77, mgr. info. svcs., 1978-81, mgr. info. and office svcs., 1981-83, mgr. adminstrv. svcs., 1983—; pres., Creative Libr. Sys., L.A., 1974-83; libr. cons. ArchiSystems, div. SUMMA Corp., L.A., 1972-81, Property Rehab. Corp., Bell Gardens, Calif., 1974-75, VTN Corp., Irvine, Calif., 1974, William Pereira & Assos., 1975; mem. office systems and bus. edn. adv. bd. Calif. State U. Northridge, 1992—. Mem. Assistance League, So. Calif., 1956-86, mem. nat. auxilaries com. 1968-72, 75-78, mem. nat. by laws com. 1970-75, mem. asso. bd. dirs., 1966-76. Mem. AFTRA, SAG, Am. Guild Musical Artists, Adminstrv. Mgmt. Soc. (v.p. Los Angeles chpt. 1984-86, pres. 1986-88, internat. conf. chmn. 1988-89, internat. bd. dirs. 1988-90, internat. v.p. mgmt. edn. 1990-92), Los Angeles Master Chorale Assn. (bd. dirs. 1978-83), L.A. Bus. Travel Assn. (bd. dirs. 1995—), Nat. Bus. Travel Assn. (nat. convention seminar com. 1994—).

BAKER, ALLISON PAIGE, former wholesale distribution executive, photographer, musician, educator; b. Bend, Oreg., Aug. 21, 1950; s. Franklin Lyle and Juanita (Martin) B.; m. Andrea Lea Premazzi, Aug. 13, 1982 (div. Mar. 1992). BA in Edn. and Music, Ctrl. Wash. U., 1978; postgrad., U. Portland, 1978-82. Cert. tchr., Wash. Comml. fisherman, Oreg., Wash., and Alaska, 1968-83, profl. musician and sound engr., Wash. and Oreg., 1971-84; part-time tchr., grad. asst. U. Portland, 1978-84; prof. music Mt. Hood C.C., Gresham, Oreg., 1978-84; membership and mktg. mgr. Costco Wholesale, Alaska, 1984-86; mgr. membership and adminstrn. Costco Wholesale, Clackamas, Oreg., 1986-88, supervising field engr. computer sys. N.W. region, 1988-93; receiving and front end mgr. Costco Wholesale, Tualatin, Oreg., 1993—. Bd. dirs. Oreg. Repertory Singers, Portland, 1994—, singer, 1st tenor, 1980-83, 93—; mem. Mazamas, 1993—. Named Outstanding Musician Nat. Assn. Jazz Educators, 1974. Democrat. Home: 6305 SE 89th Ave Portland OR 97266-5341 Office: Costco Wholesale Corp 18120 Lower Silver Boones Fry Rd Tigard OR 97224

BAKER, ALTON FLETCHER, III, newspaper editor, publishing executive; b. Eugene, Oreg., May 2, 1950; s. Alton Fletcher II and Genevieve (Mertzke) B.; m. Wendy Walker, Jan. 27, 1979; children: Benjamin A., Lindsay A. BA in Comms., Washington State U., 1972. Reporter Associated Press, Des Moines, 1972-79; asst. city editor The Register-Guard, Eugene, 1979-80, city editor, 1980-82, mng. editor, 1982-86, editor, 1986-87, editor, publisher, 1987—; pres. Guard Publishing Co., Eugene, 1987—; pres. Cmty. Newspapers, Inc., Portland. Dir. YMCA, Eugene, 1989, United Way of Lane County, Eugene, 1985-94, Eugene Festival Musical Theatre, 1990-94. Office: Guard Publishing Co 975 High St Eugene OR 97440

BAKER, BONNIE ANN, real estate broker; b. Rock Springs, Wyo., Apr. 5, 1946; d. Clarence Heber and Vivian Doan Sargent; m. Joel Cheney Baker, Feb. 7, 1969; children—Michelle Leigh, Joelle Doan. A.A., Western Wyo. Coll., 1971; B.F.A., U. Wyo., 1984. Lic. broker Wyo.; CRS. Mem. public relations staff Janss Corp., Rock Spring, Wyo., 1980-81; salesman Sweetwater Realty, Green River, 1982-85; broker, owner Twin Pines Realty, Green River, 1985—; bd. dirs. Pioneer Nat. Title Co. Trustee, Western Wyo. Coll., 1977-84; mem. Dem. Precinct Com., Green River, 1977-88, 89; pres. Sweetwater County Dem. Women's Club, 1989-90; trustee Castle Rock Hosp. Spl. Dist., 1981-84, City of Green River Tourism Com., 1988-90, Centennial Com., 1989-90, Flaming Gorge Days Com., 1990-91, pres., 1992, co-chmn. Parade. Recipient Wyo. Diana award ESA, 1989. Mem. Sweetwater County Bd. Realtors (chmn. com. 1983—, v.p. 1993, pres. 1994), Green River C. of C. (bd. dirs. 1986-91, pres. 1989-90), Rotary (co-chmn. Mother's day flowers Green River club 1990-91). Avocations: reading, painting, sculpture-lost wax. Home: 184 S 5th West St Green River WY 82935-4138 Office: Twin Pines Realty 489 W Flaming Gorge Way Green River WY 82935-4108

BAKER, BRIDGET DOWNEY, newspaper executive; b. Eugene, Oreg., Sept. 14, 1955; d. Edwin Moody and Patricia (Petersen) B.; m. Guy Dominique Wood, June 30, 1977 (div. Oct. 1981); m. Rayburn Keith Kincaid, June 27, 1987; stepchildren: Benjamin, Jacob. BA in English, French and Theatre, Lewis and Clark Coll., 1977; MA in Journalism, U. Oreg., 1985. Circulation dist. supr. The Register-Guard, Eugene, 1978-80, pub. relations coordinator, 1980-83, promotion dir., 1983-86, mktg. dir., 1986-88; corp. pub. rels. dir., 1989—; bd. dirs. Guard Pub. Co., Eugene. Bd. dirs. Wilani Coun. Camp Fire, 1982-88, pres. bd. dirs., 1986-88; bd. dirs. Lane County United Way, 1982-88, community info. com. chairperson, 1982-84; chair planning com., 1987-88; bd. dirs. Eugene Opera, 1988-91, pres. bd. dirs., 1990-91. Recipient 1st pl. advt. award Editor and Pub. Mag., N.Y.C., 1984, also 1st pl. TV promotion, 1st pl. newspaper rsch. award, 1988, Best Mktg. Idea/Campaign award Oreg. Newspaper Pub. Assn., 1984, 85; named Woman of Yr., Lane County Coun. of Orgns., 1994. Mem. Internat. Mktg. Assn. (bd. dirs. Western region 1986-88, 8 1st pl. Best in the West awards 1983-91), Pub. Rels. Soc. Am. (pres. Greater Oreg. chpt. 1995—, Spotlight award 1986), Eugene C. of C. (bd. dirs. 1989-92), U. Oreg. Alumni Assn. (bd. dirs. 1990-93), Lane Cmty. Coll. Foun. bd. dirs., 1995—, Town Club bd dirs., 1995—; Downtown Athletic Club, Eugene Yacht Club, Zonta Internat. (pres. Eugene club 1994—). Republican. Office: Guard Pub Co 1065 High St Ste 1 Eugene OR 97401-3254

BAKER, BRUCE FREDERICK, health services association administrator; b. Seattle, Sept. 23, 1930; s. Frederick Edward and Edel (Peterson) B.; m. Joyce Marie Norwick, Jan. 24, 1951; children: Jeffry, David, Bryan. BA, U. Wash., 1954. Assoc. Cappy Ricks and Assocs., Seattle, 1954-56; v.p. Ayer/Baker, Seattle, 1956-69; NW mgr. Boyden Assocs., Seattle, 1969-71; v.p. Pacific First Fed. Savs. Bank, Tacoma, 1971-74; sr. v.p. Wash. Mut. Savs. Bank, Seattle, 1974-81; pres. Donworth Taylor Assocs., Seattle, 1981-83; pres., chief exec. officer First Mut. Bank, Bellevue, Wash., 1983-92, also bd. dirs., 1983-92; chpt. dir. March of Dimes, Seattle, 1992—. Contbr. articles to profl. jours. Trustee Seattle Found., 1983-92, Mus. History and Industry, 1991; pres. chief Seattle coun. Boy Scouts Am., 1981-82. Mem. Japan-Am. Soc. Wash. (v.p. 1988, dir. 1986—), Bellevue C. of C. (chmn. 1989-90), Rotary, Rainier Club. Mem. Congregational Ch. Office: March of Dimes 1904 3rd Ave Seattle WA 98101-1126

BAKER, C. B., retired day care director, organizer, communicator; b. Ft. Wayne, Ind.; d. James Edwin Sr. and Susie Mae (Nutter) Doelling; m. Gerald R. Baker, June, 1962 (div. 1966); 1 child, Erin Lee; m. Jeffrey E. Baker, June, 1967 (div. 1972); 1 child, Shannon Rae; m. Gilbert Erbisch, 1985. Student, Internat. Bus. Coll., Ft. Wayne, 1961. Expeditor Wayne Fabricating, Ft. Wayne, 1971; county adminstr. Champaign (Ill.) County Bd., 1974-76; sec. WICD-TV, Champaign, 1976-77; ops. chmn. 40 Plus of Colo., Inc., Denver, 1983, v.p., 1984-85, pres., 1985-86; asst. dir. St. Anne's Extended Day Program, Denver, 1986-88, ret., 1988. Editor The Village Voice newsletter, Savoy, Ill., 1974. Chmn. Winfield Village Swimming Pool Com., Savoy, 1975; dir. Mich. Sugar Festival, 1991. Mem. Am. Bus. Women's Assn.

BAKER, CHARLES DEWITT, research and development company executive; b. Dayton, Ohio, Jan. 5, 1932; s. Donald James and Lillian Mae (Pund) B.; m. June Thordis Tandberg, June 25, 1954; children: Charles, Robert, Thomas, Michael. AA in Electrical Engring., Long Beach City Coll., 1953; Boston U., 1954, Pacific Coast U., 1963, U. Utah, 1980. Registered profl. mfg. engr., Calif. Chemist Shell Oil, Torrance, Calif., 1957-60; materials and process engr. Northrop Corp., Hawthorne, Calif., 1960-63; packaging engr. Jet Propulsion Lab., Pasadena, Calif., 1963-71; med. design engr. Utah Biomed. Test Lab., Salt Lake City, 1971-78, sect. mgr., 1978-83; v.p. Tech. Rsch. Assocs., Salt Lake City, 1983-88, pres., 1988—; pres. Thordis Corp., 1980—. Contbr. articles to profl jours.; 20 patents in field. Com. mem. Heart and Lung Inst. Community Adv. Com., spl. study sect rev. NIH, Tech. Transfer Forum, U. Utah, 1984. Recipient Cost Reduction award NASA, 1969, New Tech. award, 1969, 71, 75. Mem. ASME, Soc. Mfg. Engrs., Utah Mfg. Assn., Acad. of Tech., Entrepreneurs and Innovators. Republican. Office: Tech Rsch Assocs 2257 S 1100 E Salt Lake City UT 84106-2379

BAKER, CHUCK, journalist, author; b. Chgo., Jan. 19; s. S.M. and Helen B.; m. Linda F. Guiffreda, Jan. 2, 1982; children: Tyrone, Nicholas. AA, L.A. City Coll., 1972; BL, LaSalle U., 1978; student, Calif. State U., 1983. Editor So. Calif. Indsl. News, L.A., 1982-83; pub. rels. dir. Kaye Pub. Rels., Granada Hills, Calif., 1983-87; freelance journalist L.A., 1987-89; real estate editor Review-Jour., Las Vegas, 1989-94; instr. Con. Ed. U. Nevada, 1990—, Learning Annex, Calif.; dir. Interstate 15 Pub. Co., Las Vegas, 1994. Author: (book) The Rockin' Fifties, 1973, How Virtually Anybody Can Buy Real Estate, 1994; writer, prodr. (video) Basic Real Estate Investing, 1988 (Best Ednl. Video award Film Tchrs. Assn. 1989). vice chmn. Historic Preservation Com., Las Vegas, 1993-94. With U.S. Army, 1964-66. Recipient Purple Heart U.S. Army, 1965, Best Real Estate Section award Classified Ad Execs., 1987. Mem. Nat. Assn. Real Estate Editors (dir.), Disabled Am. Vets. Calif. (dept. commdr. 1988-89), Disabled Am. Vets. Nev., Soc. Am. Bus. Editors. Baptist. Office: 8635 W Sahara Ave # 440 Las Vegas NV 89117-5858

BAKER, DANIAL EDWIN, director, consultant, pharmacy educator; b. Whitefish, Mont., May 25, 1955; s. Arby E. and Cathy Lee (Yarroll) B.; m. Patricia Samuelson, Aug. 28, 1976; 1 child, Kristin Nicole. B in Pharmacy, Wash. State U., 1978; PharmD, U. Minn., 1980. Lic. pharmacist, Wash. Instr. in pharmacology for respiratory therapist St. Paul Tech. Vocat. Inst., 1980; asst. prof. U. Okla., 1980-83; asst. prof. Wash. State U., Spokane, 1983-88, dir. Drug Info. Ctr., 1983—, assoc. prof., 1988-95; prof. Wash. State U., 1995—; dir. clin. pharmacy programs, interim chmn. pharmacy dept.; mem. drug formulatory adv. com. divsn. med. assistance Wash. Dept. Social and Health Svcs., Olympia, 1990, chmn., 1990-92; mem. cons. panel The UpJohn Co., Kalamazoo, 1990-93; mem. adv. panel on drug info. sci. U.S. Pharmacopeial Conv., Inc., Rockville, Md., 1990—; mem. Inst. for Safe Medication Practices, Inc., Huntinton Valley, Pa., 1990—, Inst. Rev. Bd., Spokane, 1992—, Wash. State U., 1993—; mem. adv. bd. Syntex Area Adv. Bd., Denver, 1994—. Mem. Nat. Ski Patrol, 1994—. Recipient Pharmacist Achievement award Merck Sharps & Dohme, 1993; Named one of Outstanding Young Men of Am., 1982, 83. Fellow Am. Soc. Cons. Pharmacists, Am. Soc. Hosp. Pharmacists; mem. Am. Assn. Colls. Pharmacy, Am. Coll. Clin. Pharmacy, Am. Diabetes Assn., Am. Pharm. Assn., Am. Soc. Cons. Pharmacists, Am. Soc. Hosp. Pharmacists, Wash. Pharmacists Assn. (senator 1991—, continuing edn. com. 1988—, award com. 1989—, co-chairperson undergrad. affairs com. 1990-92, del. Quinquinnel conv. 1987—, Pharmacist of Yr. award 1992), Wash. Soc. Hosp. Pharmacists (coun. edn. and manpower 1989-92, chmn. 1990-92, bd. dirs. 1989-93, pres. Spokane chpt. 1992-93), Wash. Pharmacy Coun., Drug Info. Assn. Republican. Office: Wash State U 601 W 1st Ave Spokane WA 99204-0317

BAKER, DEBORAH ANN, business owner; b. Washington, May 12, 1956; d. Richard John and Shirley Ann (Jackson) Dunagan; m. Don Steven Baker, June 20, 1980; children: Adam Ross, Jason Richard, Natalie Rae. Grad. High Sch., Novato, Calif. Buyer, dept. mgr. Carithers. Dept. Store, Novato, Calif., 1975-77; mgr. books Baker Installations, Denver, 1977-79; mgr. Fashion Carpets, Englewood, Colo., 1979-83; owner, operator Baker Interiors, Inc., Englewood, 1983—, pres., 1991—. Office: Baker Interiors Inc 209 W Littleton Blvd Littleton CO 80120-2331

BAKER, DON ROBERT, chemist; b. Salt Lake City, Apr. 6, 1933; s. Ralph H. and Ruth Eve (Thalmann) B.; m. Shirley May Nelson, Nov. 20, 1954 (dec. 1993); children: Robert, David, George, Barbara; m. Shirlee Ann Call, Sept. 17, 1994. AA, Sacramento City Coll., 1953; AB, Calif. State U., Sacramento, 1955; PhD, U. Calif., Berkeley, 1959. Sr. rsch. chemist Stauffer Chem. Co., Richmond, Calif., 1958-72, rsch. assoc., 1970-74, supr., 1974-85; sr. rsch. assoc. ICI Ams. Inc. Zeneca Ag Products, Richmond, 1985—. Editor Calif. Chemists Alert, 1986—, Synthesis and Chemistry of Agrochems., 1987, 90, 92, 95; contbr. articles to profl. jours.; patentee in field. Mem. Am. Chem. Soc. (chmn. Calif. sect. 1973, councilor 1971—, chmn. nat. divsn. profl. rels. 1980, coordinating com. Calif. sects. 1970—, chmn. agrochems. divsn. 1995, Walter Petersen award 1991), Plant Growth Regulator Soc. (vice chmn. agrochem. divsn. 1993, Fellow award 1992), Orchid Soc. Calif. (pres. 1979-80), Oakland Family History Ctr. (libr. 1967—). Republican. Mormon. Home: 15 Muth Dr Orinda CA 94563-2805 Office: Zeneca Ag Products 1200 S 47th St Richmond CA 94804-4610

BAKER, DUSTY (JOHNNIE B. BAKER, JR.), professional baseball team manager; b. Riverside, Calif., June 15, 1949. Student, Am. River Coll. Player Atlanta Braves, 1968-75, L.A. Dodgers, 1976-83, San Francisco Giants, 1984, Oakland A's, 1985-86; coach San Francisco Giants, 1988-92, mgr., 1993—; mem. Nat. League All-Star Team, 1981-82. Recipient Silver Slugger award, 1980-81, Gold Glove, 1981; named to Sporting News All-Star Team, 1980. Office: San Francisco Giants Candlestick Park San Francisco CA 94124*

BAKER, EDWIN MOODY, retired newspaper publisher; b. Cleve., Dec. 20, 1923; s. Alton Fletcher and Mildred Elizabeth (Moody) B.; m. Patricia Petersen, 1954 (dec. 1983); children: Bridget Baker Kincaid, Amanda Baker Barber, Jonathan; m. Marie Kottkamp Randall, 1984; children: Steven, Mark, Bruce Randall. B.S. in Bus. Adminstrn., U. Oreg., 1948. With Eugene (Oreg.) Register-Guard, 1948-88, successively advt. mgr., bus. mgr., gen. mgr., pub., pres., chmn. bd. Guard Pub. Co.; pres. Community Newspapers, Inc., Beaverton, Oreg., v.p. N.W. Web. Mem. exec. bd. Oreg. Trail Council, Boy Scouts Am., 1953—, pres. 1960-61, chmn. Region XI Area I (Northwest) 1971, pres., 1972, mem. nat. exec. bd., 1971-72, nat. adv. council, 1972-82; trustee U. Oreg. Found., 1975-90, Lane Community Coll.; bd. dirs. Oreg. Community Found., 1982-90; Oreg. Hist. Soc., 1988-92; trustee Eugene Arts Found., 1980-85; pres. Oreg. Pacific Econ. Devel. Corp., 1984-85; 2d v.p. Eugene Springfield Met. Ptnrship.; mem., chmn. Sister City com., 1986-88. Served with AUS, World War II. Decorated Bronze Star, Purple Heart; recipient Silver Beaver award, Boy Scouts Am., 1962, Silver Antelope, 1965, Pioneer award U. Oreg., 1982, Disting. Eagle Scout, 1982, Awbrey Watzig award Lewis and Clark Coll., 1988; named Eugene First Citizen, 1983. Mem. Am. Newspaper Pubs. Assn. (research inst. lab. com. 1978-79), Oreg. Newspaper Pubs. Assn. (dir. 1982-90, pres. 1988-89), U. Oreg. Pres. Assocs., Nat. Assn. Fund Raising Execs. (vol. 1994 Oreg. chpt., Fund Raiser of Yr. 1993), Rotary, Eugene Country Club. Home: 2121 Kimberly Cir Eugene OR 97405-5821 Office: Guard Pub Co PO Box 10188-2188 975 High St Eugene OR 97401-3204

BAKER, EDWIN STUART, retired computer consultant; b. Ottumwa, Iowa, Feb. 14, 1944; s. Edwin Moore and Geraldine Vivian (Irby) B; m. Wilma Jeanne Parker, 1968 (div. 1970). Student, Whitman Coll., 1962-64; BS, Oreg. State U., 1978. Programmer agrl. engring. dept. Oreg. State U., Corvallis, 1977-78, rsch. asst., 1979-83, sr. rsch. asst., 1984-89; measurement standards specialist Oreg. Dept. Agr., Salem, 1990-93; cons. in field. Mem. IEEE, Assn for Computing Machinery, Am. Legion, DAV, NRA, Nat. Intercollegiate Rodeo Assn., 59ers Svc. Club. Home: PO Box 68 Fairview OR 97024-0068 Office: Oreg Dept Agr Measurements Standards Divsn Salem OR 97310

BAKER, FRED GREENTREE, hydrogeologist; b. Chgo., July 26, 1950; s. Con James and Ethel M. (Skowbo) B.; m. Judith Ann Krill, 1972 (div. 1974); m. Hannah F. Pavlik, Apr. 26, 1976. BS in Geology, U. Wis., 1972, MS in Soil Sci., 1975; MS in Civil Engring., U. Colo., Boulder, 1981, PhD in Geology, 1985. Registered geologist, Calif.; registered profl. engr., Colo.; cert. engring. geologist, Calif. Rsch. specialist Wis. Geol. and Natural History Survey, Madison, 1973-76; rsch. assoc. dept. civil engring. Colo. State U., Fort Collins, 1977-78; hydrologist U.S. EPA, Denver, 1979-81; engring. geologist Charles C. Bowman Assocs., Inc., Boulder, Colo., 1982-85; sr. hydrogeologist Dames & Moore, Sacramento, 1985-88; dir. ops. On-Site Technologies, Inc., Sacramento, 1989; mgr. hydrogeologic svcs. Woodward-Clyde Cons., Denver, 1989-90; cons. engr., hydrogeologist Ebasco Environmental, Lakewood, Colo., 1990-91; pres. Baker Consultants, Inc., Golden, Colo., 1991—. Contbr. articles to profl. jours. Mem. ASCE, ASTM, Am. Geophys. Union, Soil Sci. Soc. Am., Am. Assn. Petroleum Geologists, Assn. Ground Water Scientists and Engrs., Sigma Xi. Office: Baker Cons Inc 2801 Youngfield St Ste 310 Golden CO 80401

BAKER, GLADYS ELIZABETH, retired microbiologist, educator; b. Iowa City, Iowa, July 22, 1908; d. Richard Philip and Katherine (Riedelbauch) B. BA, U. Iowa, 1930, MS, 1932; PhD, Washington U., St. Louis, 1935. Biology instr. Hunter Coll., N.Y.C., 1936-40; instr., then asst. prof. Vassar Coll., Poughkeepsie, N.Y., 1940-45; assoc. prof., then prof., chmn. dept. plant scis. Vassar Coll., Poughkeepsie, 1945-61; prof. botany U. Hawaii, Honolulu, 1961-73; acting chmn. botany dept., U. Hawaii, 1965. Illustrator: The Myxomycetes, 1934; contbr. articles on mycology to profl., sci. jours. Recipient 3 research grants NSF, 1952-60, others. Fellow AAAS; mem. Mycol. Soc. Am., British Mycol. Soc., Med. Mycol. Soc. of the Ams. (charter). Episcopalian. Home: 158 Sierra Winds 17300 N 88th Ave Peoria AZ 85382-3533

BAKER, HAROLD DEAN, foreign language educator and researcher; b. Attleboro, Mass., Nov. 23, 1954; s. Harold Dean and Helen Frances (Ballou) B.; m. Deborah Janet Petch, June 1976 (div. 1983); m. Marianna Olegovna Zhutovskaia, Aug. 24, 1987; 1 child, Anna Helen. BA in English, Hobart Coll., 1976; MA in Comparative Lit., Brown U., 1985, PhD in Comparative Lit., 1988. Tchr. French and English Providence (R.I.) Country Day, 1976-80; tchr. English U. Dijon, France, 1983-84; assoc. dir. Coop. Russian Lang. Program Coun. for Internat. Edn. Exch., Leningrad, Russia, 1985-86; vis. instr. English Gustavus Adolphus Coll., St. Peter, Minn., 1987-88; vis. asst. prof. Russian Oberlin (Ohio) Coll., 1988-89; asst. prof. Russian U. Calif., Irvine, 1989—. Contbr. articles to profl. jours. Mem. MLA, Am. Assn. Tchrs. Slavic. Democrat. Episcopalian. Home: 59 Whitman Ct Irvine CA 92715-4063 Office: Russian/156HH Univ Calif Irvine Irvine CA 92717

BAKER, HERBERT GEORGE, botany educator; b. Brighton, Eng., Feb. 23, 1920; came to U.S., 1957; s. Herbert Reginald and Alice (Bambridge) B.; m. Irene Williams, Apr. 4, 1945; 1 dau., Ruth Elaine. B.S., U. London, 1941, Ph.D., 1945. Research chemist, asst. plant physiologist Hosa Research Labs., Sunbury-on-Thames, Eng., 1940-45; lectr. botany U. Leeds, Eng., 1945-54; research fellow Carnegie Instn., Washington, 1948-49; prof. botany U. Coll. Ghana, 1954-57; faculty U. Calif., Berkeley, 1957—, assoc. prof. botany, 1957-60, prof., 1960-90, prof. integrative biology emeritus, 1990—, dir. bot. garden, 1957-69. Author: Plants and Civilization, 1965, 70, 78 (translated into Spanish and Japanese); editor: (with G. L. Stebbins) Genetics of Colonizing Species, 1965; series editor: Bot. Monographs, 1971-84; contbr. articles to sci. jours. Fellow Assn. Tropical Biology, AAAS (past pres. Pacific div.); mem. Am. Acad. Arts and Sci., Am. Philos. Soc., Am. Inst. Biol. Sci., Brit. Ecol. Soc. (hon. mem.), Soc. Econ. Botany (Disting. mem. award), Internat. Assn. Botanic Gardens (past v.p.), Ecol. Soc. Am., Soc. for Study Evolution (past pres.), Bot. Soc. Am. (past pres.), Sigma Xi. Home: 635 Creston Rd Berkeley CA 94708-1239

BAKER, JANITA LOU, musician, luthier; b. Santa Monica, Calif., June 12, 1952; d. Lewis Edward and Marybelle (Lohrman) Forein; m. Robert Nicholas Baker, Aug. 31, 1973. BA, U. Calif., Riverside, 1971. Self-employed musician San Luis Obispo, Calif., 1973—; self-employed luthier Santa Margarita, Calif., 1977—. Author: The Dulcimer: A Manual for Schools, 1978; author, rec. artist Fingerpicking Dulcimer, 1982; rec. artist Pasttime with Good Company, 1983, Solace, 1993. Mem. adv. bd. Gt. Plains Folk Festival, Chgo., 1993—. Recipient Cert. of Appreciation, Calif. State Assembly, 1984. Mem. Calif. Traditional Music Soc. (adb. bd. 1986—). Home and Office: Blue Lion Musical Instruments 4665 Parkhill Rd Santa Margarita CA 93453-9650

BAKER, JOSEPH RODERICK, III, aviculturist; b. Middletown, Ohio, Sept. 26, 1947; s. Joseph Roderick and Lois Patricia (Barnhart) B. BS in Math., Rensselaer Poly. Tech., 1969. Systems rep. Burroughs Corp., Honolulu, 1973-80; mgr. data processing Kenault Inc., Honolulu, 1980-81; v.p. Software Solutions Inc., Honolulu, 1982-83; br. mgr. DataPhase Corp., Honolulu, 1983-88; pres. Birds of Paradise, Kurtistown, Hawaii, 1987—. Lt. (j.g.) USN, 1969-73. Mem. Am. Fedn. Aviculture, Nat. Cockatoo Soc., Macaw Soc. Am., Eclectus Soc., Am. Contract Bridge League, Pionus Breeders Assn., Amazona Soc.

BAKER, KATHLEEN ANN, student services counselor; b. Seattle, Oct. 6, 1935; d. Clifford A. and Inez E. (Clark) Duncan; m. David G. Baker, June 11, 1955; children: Mark Allen, Susan Baker Abyad. BS in Home Econs., UCLA, 1958, postgrad., 1959; MA in Human Devel., Pacific Oaks Coll., 1976. Calif. Community Coll. Teaching Credentials; cert. nursery sch. and presch. educator, community coll. supr. Teaching asst. UCLA, 1958-59; coll. instr. Fullerton (Calif.) Coll., 1959-61, 73-83; dir. Placentia (Calif.) Coop Nursery Sch., 1970-72; coll. counselor Fullerton Coll., 1983-85, dir. sch. and coll. rels., 1985-92, counselor, articulations officer, 1992—; pres. Pacific Oaks Coll. Alumni Assn., Pasadena, Calif., 1987-88, Faculty Senate, Fullerton Coll., 1981-82; del. Calif. C.C. Gt. Tchrs. Conf., Santa Barbara, 1982, Asilomar (Calif.) Leadership Skills Seminar, 1986. Editor: Fullerton College Guide to Majors, 1985—. Charter pres. AAUW, Placentia, Yorba Linda, Calif., 1967; trustee Yorba Linda Elem. Sch. Dist., 1973-76; mem. Orange County Child Care Task Force, Santa Ana, Calif., 1983. Named one of Outstanding Young Woman of Am., 1968, Outstanding Home Econs. for Rsch. and Leadership, 1977; recipient Cert. of Achievement, No. Orange County YWCA, 1986, Cert. of Appreciation, Calif. Articulation Number System, 1989. Mem. Nat. Assn. Women Deans, Adminstrs. & Counselors, Assn. of Psychol. Type, South Counties Women in Edn., UCLA and Pacific Oaks Coll. Alumni Assns., Calif. Tchrs. Assn., Calif. Community Coll. Counselors Assn., Am. Assn. Collegiate Registrars and Admissions Officers. Presbyterian. Office: Fullerton Coll 321 E Chapman Ave Fullerton CA 92632-2011

BAKER, KENT ALFRED, television news director; b. Sioux City, Iowa, Mar. 22, 1948; s. Carl Edmund Baker and Miriam M. (Hawthorn) Baker Nye. Student, Iowa State U., 1966-70. Editor Iowa State Daily, 1969-70; mem. U.S. Peace Corps., 1971-72; editor The Glidden (Iowa) Graphic, 1973-75; bureau chief The Waterloo (Iowa) Courier, Iowa, 1975; state editor The Des Moines Register, 1976-77; news dir. Sta. WQAD-TV, Moline, Ill., 1978; Sunday editor The Des Moines Sunday Register, 1979; news dir. Sta. KHON-TV, Honolulu, 1980—; chmn. Hawaii Freedom of Info. Coun., 1992. Mem. hist. Hawaii Assn., Honolulu. Recipient news writing awards Iowa Press Assn., 1973-74. Mem. Radio and TV News Dirs. Assn. (state coord.), Bishop Mus. Assn., East-West Ctr. Assn., Hoover Libr. Assn., Iowa State U. Alumni Assn. (state bd. dirs.). Home: PO Box 23015 Honolulu HI 96823-3015 Office: Sta KHON-TV 1170 Auahi St Honolulu HI 96814-4917

BAKER, LARRY CURTIS, minister; b. L.A., Sept. 19, 1945; s. Charles Leonard and Genevee (Becker) B.; m. Mary Callicoat, Oct. 23, 1964; children: Christopher Daniel, Sarah Morgan. BA, Hardin-Simmons U., 1970; MDiv, Golden Gate Sem., 1975; PhD, Internat. Seminary, 1994. Ordained to ministry So. Bapt. Conv., 1969. Pastor First Bapt. Ch., Maryneal, Tex., 1968-69, Cen. Bapt. Ch., Stamford, Tex., 1969-71, DeAnza Bapt. Ch., Cupertino, Calif., 1971-73; pub. rels. assoc. Golden Gate Bapt. Sem., Mill Valley, Calif., 1973-75; pastor First So. Bapt. Ch., Lodi, Calif., 1975-77, Ventura, Calif., 1977-81; v.p. communications Golden Gate Sem., Mill Valley, 1981-83; pastor Bethel Bapt. Ch., Concord, Calif., 1983—. Editor newspaper the HSU Brand, 1968-70; asst. pubr. newspaper Stamford Am., 1970-71. With USAF, 1963-67. Republican. Office: Bethel Bapt Ch 3578 Clayton Rd Concord CA 94519-2448

BAKER, LILLIAN L., author, historian, artist, lecturer; b. Yonkers, N.Y., Dec. 12, 1921; m. Roscoe A. Baker; children: Wanda Georgia, George Riley. Student, El Camino (Calif.) Coll., 1952, UCLA, 1968, 77. Continuity writer Sta. WINS, N.Y.C., 1945-46; columnist, free-lance writer, reviewer Gardena (Calif.) Valley News, 1964-76; free-lance writer, editor Gardena, 1971—; lectr. in field; founder, editor Internat. Club for Collectors of Hatpins and Hatpin Holders, monthly newsletter Points, ann. Pictorial Jour., 1977—, conv. and seminar coord., 1979, 82, 84, 87, 90, 92. Author: Collector's Encyclopedia of Hatpins and Hatpin Holders, 1976, third printing, 1993, 100 Years of Collectible Jewelry 1850-1950, 1978, rev. edit., 1986, 88, 89, 91, 92, 94, Art Nouveau and Art Deco Jewelry, 1980, rev. edit. 1985, 87, 88, 90, 91, The Concentration Camp Conspiracy: A Second Pearl Harbor, 1981 (Scholarship Category award of Merit, Conf. of Calif. Hist. Socs. 1983), Hatpins and Hatpin Holders: An Illustrated Value Guide, 1983, rev. edit. 1988, 90, 91, 94, Creative and Collectible Miniatures, 1984, rev., 1991, Fifty Years of Collectible Fashion Jewelry: 1925-1975, 1986, rev. edit., 1988, rev., 1991, 94, Dishonoring America: The Collective Guilt of American Japanese, 1988, American and Japanese Relocation in World War II: Fact Fiction and Fallacy, 1989 (Pulitzer prize nomination, George Washington Honor medal Freedom Found., 1991), rev. edit., 1991, The Japanning of America: Redress and Reparations Demands by Japanese-Americans, 1991, 20th Century Fashionable Plastic Jewelry, 1992, revised 1994, The Common Doom, 1992, Dishonoring America: The Falsification of World War II History, 1995; established The Lillian Baker Collection Hoover Archives, 1989; author poetry; contbg. author Vol. VII Time-Life Encyclopedia of Collectibles, 1979; numerous radio and TV appearances. Co-founder Ams. for Hist. Accuracy, 1972, Com. for Equality for All Draftees, 1973; chair S. Bay election campaign S.I. Hayakawa, for U.S. Senator from Calif., 1976; witness U.S. Commn. Wartime Relocation, 1981, U.S. Senate Judiciary Com., 1983, U.S. Ho. Reps. Judiciary Com., 1986, U.S. Ho. Reps. Subcommittee on Appropriations, 1989; guest artist U.S. Olympics, 1984. Recipient award Freedoms Found., 1971, George Washington Honor medal, 1989, Ann. award Conf. Calif. Hist. Socs., 1983, monetary award Hoover Instn. Stanford (Calif.) U., 1985, award Pro-Am. Orgn., 1987, Golden Poet award Internat. Poets Soc., 1989, Editor's Choice award for outstanding achievement in poetry Nat. Libr. Poetry, 1994. Fellow Internat. Biog. Assn. (life); mem. Nat. League Am. Pen Women, Nat. Writers Network, Nat. Writers Club, Soc. Jewelry Historians U.S.A. (charter), Art Studenets League N.Y. (life), Nat. Historic Soc. (founding), Nat. Trust Historic Preservation (founding), Ams. for Hist. Accuracy (co-founder), WWII Nat. Commemorative Assn. (adv. bd. 1993-95), other orgns. Home and Office: 15237 Chanera Ave Gardena CA 90249-4042

BAKER, MARJORIE NEUMAN, information broker; b. Bakersfield, Calif., Nov. 28, 1939; d. Herbert Henry and Margaret Emma (Woodham) Neuman; children from previous marriage: Brian E. Nelson, Bradley R. Nelson; m. James Lawrence Baker, Nov. 28, 1986. BA, UCLA, 1961, MLS, 1962. Reference libr. L.A. Pub. Libr., 1972-86; dep. dir. rsch. Rsch. on Demand, Berkeley, Calif., 1987-92, pres. Info. First, Alameda, Calif., 1992—. Mem. Spl. Librs. Assn., Assn. Ind. Info. Profls.

BAKER, MARK W., psychologist; b. Kansas City, Mo., June 26, 1953; s. Charles Kelly and Patricia Diane (Walker) B. BA, U. Kans., 1976; MDiv, Fuller Theol. Seminary, Pasadena, Calif., 1982; PhD, Fuller Grad. Sch. Psychology, 1984. Min. Campus Christians, Lawrence, Kans., 1976-78; psychol. asst. The LaVie Ctr., Pasadena, Calif., 1980-84, dir., 1992—; marriage, family and child counselor Pasadena, Thousand Oaks, 1984-89; pvt. practice in clin. psychologist Pasadena, Brentwood, 1986—; exec. dir. The LaVie Ctr., 1993—; gen. ptnr. Mark W. Baker, PhD, Ltd., Pasadena, 1992—. Contbr. articles to profl. jours. Mem. Am. Psychol. Assn., Am. Assn. of Marriage and Family Therapists, Pasadena Area Psychol. Assn., Calif. State Psychol. Assn. Office: La Vie Ctr 26400 La Alameda # 202 Mission Viejo CA 92691-6318

BAKER, RICHARD EARL, business management educator; b. Inglewood, Calif., Sept. 22, 1928; s. Glyn Maynard and Ruth Elizabeth (Norton) B.; m. Dorotha Jean Mayo; children: Mary K. Walton, Thomas P., Kimberlee S. Tillman, Scott R. BS, U. So. Calif., L.A., 1951, MBA, 1956; postgrad., U. Calif., Berkeley, 1958-60. Various mgmt. positions AT&T Co., 1952-76; cons. Graves & Campbell, L.A., 1974-79; prof. U. LaVerne (Calif.), 1976-79, Calif. State Poly. U., Pomona, 1976-80; cons. Kingman, Ariz., 1980—; instr. Mohave Community Coll., Kingman, 1980—; bd. dirs. Profession Sales Gen. Motors Dealership, Kingman, 1987; adj. prof. Prescott (Ariz.) Coll., 1982—; sr. cons. Roberts & Heck Assocs., L.A., 1974-78; cons. Svc. Corps of Retired Execs. SBA, 1980—. Editor: Stress/Assertiveness, 1981; contbr. articles to profl. jours. Foster parent Foster Parent Assn., L.A., 1965-78; counselor Teenage Drug Rehab., L.A. 1970-78; coun. commr. Boy Scouts Am., L.A., 1975, scoutmaster, 1965-74; coord. Vocat. Adv. Coun., 1980-90. Lt. comdr. USN, 1945-48, PTO, 1950-52. Mem. Kingman C. of C., Kiwanis, Beta Gamma Sigma. Republican. Home: 4909 Scotty Dr Kingman AZ 86401-1077 Office: Mohave Community Coll 1971 Jagerson Ave Kingman AZ 86401-1238

BAKER, RICHARD W., structural and architectural engineer; b. Glendale, Calif., Aug. 16, 1945; s. Elwood V. and Eleanor J. (Vickers) B.; m. Judith K. Fields, July 5, 1969; children: Carrie A., Brian R. AA, Pasadena City Coll., 1965; BS in Archtl. Engring., Calif. State Poly. Coll., San Luis Obispo, 1968. Naval architect Long Beach (Calif.) Naval Shipyard, 1968-69; stress engr. Lockheed Aero. Systems Co., Burbank, Calif., 1969-73, 75-87, Rockwell Internat., Downey, Calif., 1974; group engr. Lockheed Advanced Devel. Co., Burbank, Calif., 1987-89, project structures engr., 1989-90; dep. chief engr. Lockheed Advanced Devel. Co., Burbank, 1991-93; dir. engring. Lockheed Martin Skunk Works, Palmdale, Calif., 1994—; archtl. cons., Cerritos, Calif., 1972-. Editor: Aircraft Stress Analysis, 1987. Mgr. Frontier Little League, Cerritos, 1985-92; coach City of Cerritos Parks & Recreation Dept., 1982-87. Mem. AIAA. Republican. Methodist. Home: 23038 Parkview Dr Santa Clarita CA 91321-3600 Office: Lockheed Martin Skunk Works Dept 25-01 Bl 608 Plant 10 1011 Lockheed Way Palmdale CA 93599-2501

BAKER, ROSALYN, state legislator; b. El Campo, Tex., Sept. 20, 1946; m. Vaughn Baker. BA, Southwest Tex. State U., 1968; MA, U. Southwestern La., 1969. Lobbyist, asst. dir. Govt. Rels. Nat. Edn. Assn., Washington, 1969-80; owner, retail sporting goods store Maui, Hawaii, 1980-87; legis. aide to Hon. Karen Honita Hawaii Ho. of Reps., Honolulu, 1987, mem., 1989—; majority leader; vice chairwoman transp. com.; mem. fin., labor, pub. employment and intergovtl. rels., and internat. affairs coms.; co-chair rules com. Hawaii State Dem. Conv., 1990. Del.-at-large Dem. Nat. Conv., 1984; mem. exec. com. Maui County Dem. Com., 1986-88; vice chmn. Maui Svc. Area Bd. on Mental Health and Substance Abuse; active Am. Cancer Soc., Work Day Vol., Soroptimist Internat. Democrat. Home: PO Box 10394 Lahaina HI 96761-0394 Office: Hawaii Ho of Reps State Capitol Honolulu HI 96813

BAKER, SUSAN LEIGH, manufacturing company executive; b. Inglewood, Calif., Sept. 24, 1962; d. Richard Leigh and Betty Ann (Payne) B. BS, U. Calif., Irvine, 1990. Computer operator Screening Systems, Inc., Laguna Hills, Calif., 1980-85, systems analyst, 1985-87, acctg. supr., 1987, fin. mgr., 1987-90, corp. sec., 1989—, v.p. fin., 1991—. Republican. Office: Screening Systems Inc 7 Argonaut Aliso Viejo CA 92656-1423

BAKER, VICTOR RICHARD, geology researcher, educator, planetary sciences researcher; b. Waterbury, Conn., Feb. 19, 1945; s. Victor A. Baker and Doris Elizabeth (Day) MacGregor; m. Pauline Marie Heaton, June 10, 1967; children: Trent Heaton, Theodore William. BS, Rensselaer Poly. Inst., 1967; PhD, U. Colo., 1971. Geophysicist U.S. Geol. Survey, Denver, 1967-71; asst. prof. geology U. Tex., Austin, 1971-76, assoc. prof., 1976-81; prof. U. Ariz., Tucson, 1981—, Regents' prof., 1988—; cons. Lunar and Planetary Inst., Houston, 1983-86, Slat River Project, Phoenix, 1984-87, Argonne (Ill.) Nat. Lab., 1983-93, Sandia (N.Mex.) Nat. Labs., 1991-92, U.S. Bur. of Reclamation, 1994—; com. mem. NRC, Washington, 1978—, NASA, 1978—; vis. fellow Nat. Inst. Hydrology, Roorkee, India, 1987-88, Deccan Coll., Pune, India, 1987-88, U. Adelaide, Australia, 1988, Udall Ctr. for Studies in Pub. Policy, Tucson, 1994-95. Author: The Channels of Mars, 1982, co-author: Surficial Geology, 1981; editor: Catastrophic Flooding, 1981, co-editor: The Channeled Scabland, 1978, Flood Geomorphology, 1988. Served to capt. U.S. Army, 1971-72. Fulbright sr. research fellow, 1979-80, vis. fellow Australian Nat. U., Canberra, 1979-80; research grantee NASA, 1975—, NSF, 1977—. Fellow AAAS (chmn. geol., geography sect. 1992-93, councilor 1992-93), Geol. Soc. Am. (chmn. planetary geology divsn. 1986, Quaternary geology and geomorphology divsn. 1987, councilor 1990-93); mem. Internat. Assn. of Geomorphologists (treas. 1993—), Am. Geophys. Union, Am. Quaternary Assn., Nat. Assn. Geology Tchrs., Soc. Sedimentary Geologists, Polish Acad. Scis. (fgn. mem.), Sigma Xi. Office: U Ariz Dept Geoscis Tucson AZ 85721

BAKER, WARREN J(OSEPH), university president; b. Fitchburg, Mass., Sept. 5, 1938; s. Preston A. and Grace F. (Jarvis) B.; m. Carol Ann Fitzsimons, Apr. 28, 1962; children: Carrie Ann, Kristin Robin, Christopher, Brian. B.S., U. Notre Dame, 1960, M.S., 1962; Ph.D., U. N.Mex., 1966. Research assoc., lectr. E. H. Wang Civil Engring. Research Facility, U. N.Mex., 1962-66; assoc. prof. civil engring. U. Detroit, 1966-71, prof., 1972-79, Chrysler prof., dean engring., 1973-78, acad. v.p., 1976-79; NSF faculty fellow M.I.T., 1971-72; pres. Calif. Poly. State U., San Luis Obispo, 1979—; mem. Bd. Internat. Food and Agrl. Devel., 1968-80; mem. Nat. Sci. Bd., 1985-94,Calif. Bus. Higher Edn. Forum, 1993—; founding mem. Calif. Coun. on Sci. and Tech., 1989—; trustee Amigos of E.A.R.T.H. Coll., 1991—; bd. dirs. John Wiley & Sons, Inc.; bd. regents The Am. Architectural Found., 1995—; co-chair Joint Policy Coun. on Agr. and Higher Edn., 1995—. Contbr. articles to profl. jours. Mem. Detroit Mayor's Mgmt. Adv. Com., 1975-76; mem. engring. adv. bd. U. Calif., Berkeley, 1984—; bd. dirs. Calif. Coun. for Environ. and Econ. Balance, 1980-85; trustee Nat. Coop. Edn. Assn.; chmn. bd. dirs. Civil Engring. Rsch. Found., 1989-91, bd. dirs., 1991-94. Fellow Engring. Soc. Detroit; mem. ASCE (chmn. geotech. div. com. on reliability 1976-78, civil engring. edn. and rsch. policy com. 1985-89), NSPE (pres. Detroit chpt. 1976-77), Am. Soc. Engring. Edn., Am. Assn. State Colls. and Univs. (bd. dirs. 1982-84). Office: Calif Polytech State U Office of Pres San Luis Obispo CA 93407

BAKER, WILLIAM BLAKE, dermatologist, dermatopathologist; b. Eastman, Ga., Mar. 14, 1928; s. Shirley Adolphus and Elva Elaine (Bell) B.; m. Velma Nadine Metzger, Mar. 17, 1951 (div. 1978); children: Carol Elaine, Jennifer Susan, Theodore Emerson, Elizabeth Ann, Mark William; m. Erna Elisabeth Langer, Feb. 10, 1979 (div. Dec. 30, 1994). BS in Physics, Yale U., 1949; MD, U. Wash., 1953. Diplomate Am. Bd. Dermatology, sub-bd. dermatopathology. Spl. tng. in dermatology U. Mich., Ann Arbor, 1953-60; chief of dermatology Group Health Corp., Seattle, 1960-61; sr. clin. instr. U. Wash., Seattle, 1961-64, asst. clin. prof., 1964-68, assoc. clin. prof., 1968-72, clin. prof., 1972—, dir. clin. tng./dermatology residency, 1964-90; chief dermatology Harborview-King County Med. Ctr., Seattle, 1964-88; pvt. practice dermatology Minor & James Group, Seattle, 1960—, pres. bd. dirs., 1982-84; bd. dirs. Seattle Psoriasis Treatment Ctr., 1976-95, sec., 1986-95. Precinct committeeman Rep. Party, Seattle, 1965-66, Mercer Island, 1968-69. Served to lt. comdr. USN, 1954-57, Korea, Japan. Nat. Merit scholar, 1945. Fellow Am. Acad. Dermatology, Am. Soc. Dermatopathology, Am. Soc. Dermatologic Surgery; mem. Seattle Dermatologic Soc. (pres. 1962-72), Puget Sound Dermatopathology Soc. (pres. 1976-84), King County Med. Soc. Episcopalian. Office: Minor & James Med 515 Minor Ave Seattle WA 98104-2138

BAKER, WILLIAM P. (BILL BAKER), congressman; b. Oakland, Calif., June 14, 1940; m. Joanne Atack; children: Todd, Mary, Billy, Robby. Grad. in Bus. and Indsl. Mgmt., San Jose State Coll. Budget analyst State Dept. Fin., Calif.; assemblyman 15th dist. State of Calif., 1980-93; mem. 103rd Congress from 10th Calif. dist., 1993—; vice chmn. budget writing Ways and Means Com., 1984-91. Exec. v.p. Contra Costa Taxpayers Assn.; active Contra Costa County Farm Bur. With USCG, 1958-65. Republican. Office: House of Representatives Washington DC 20515

BAKER HOLLIDAY, KAREN, hotel executive; b. Hollywood, Calif., Mar. 21, 1948; d. Frank A. Kelly Jr. and Dee A. (McWhorter) Kelly Archer; m. Kenneth J. Holliday, June 21, 1969 (div. Mar. 1978); 1 child, Tiffany Ann; m. Toby Evans Baker, June 8, 1980 (separated Sept. 1984). Student pub. schs., Woodland Hills, Calif. Mgr., Zane Grey Hotel, Avalon, Calif., 1969—, owner, 1975—; owner Catalina Custom Baskets, 1989-91, Two's Co. of Avalon, 1991—. Chairperson Vehicle Rev. Bd., Avalon, 1982—; chairperson accomodations com. Avalon C. of C. Republican. Club: Catalina Racquet (sec. 1972-80, pres. 1985-87) (Avalon). Avocations: tennis; swimming; water skiing; needlework. Home: 199 Chimes Tower Rd Avalon CA 90704 Office: Zane Grey Pueblo Hotel PO Box 216 Avalon CA 90704-0216

BAKER-LIEVANOS, NINA GILLSON, jewelry store executive; b. Boston, Dec. 19, 1950; d. Rev. John Robert and Patricia (Gillson) Baker; m. Jorge Alberto Lievanos, June 6, 1981; children: Jeremy John Baker, Wendy Mara Baker, Raoul Salvador Baker-Lievanos. Student, Mills Coll., 1969-70; grad. course in diamond grading, Gemology Inst. Am., 1983; student in diamondtology designation, Diamond Coun. Am., 1986—. Cert. store mgr., Jewelers Cert. Coun., Jewelers Am. Artist, tchr. Claremont, Calif., 1973-78; escrow officer Bank of Am., Claremont, 1978-81; retail salesman William Pitt Jewelers, Puente Hills, Montclair, Calif., 1981-83, asst. mgr., 1983; mgr. William Pitt Jewelers, Puente Hills, Santa Maria, Calif., 1983-91, corp. sales trainer, 1988-89; sales and design specialist Merksamer Jewelers, Santa Maria, 1991; mgr. Merksamer Jewelers, San Luis Obispo, Calif., 1991-92, Santa Maria, Calif., 1992-94; diamond specialist cons. Merksamer Jewelers, Santa Maria, 1994—. Artist tapestry hanging Laguna Beach Mus. Art, 1974. Mem. Cen. Coast Pla. Adv. Bd., 1992. Recipient Cert. Merit Art Bank Am., 1968. Mem. NAFE, Internat. Platform Assn., Speaker's Bur., Santa Maria C. of C., Compassion Internat. Republican. Roman Catholic. Office: Merksamer Jewelers 141 Santa Maria Town Ctr Santa Maria CA 93454

BAKHIET, NOUNA, microbiologist, researcher; b. Khartoum, Sudan, Apr. 9, 1956; d. Mukhtar and Amna Bakhiet. BS in Microbiology, U. Iowa, 1981, MS in Microbiology, 1984, PhD in Microbiology, 1990. Rsch. asst. Min. of Health, Tripoli, 1977-78; teaching and rsch. asst. U. of Al Fatah, Tripoli, 1978-80; grad. teaching asst. U. Iowa, Iowa City, 1984-90, microbiology tutor, 1982-90; postdoctoral researcher U. Calif., Davis, 1990-91; rsch. assoc. Loma Linda U., 1991-94; postdoctoral rsch. assoc. LaJolla (Calif.) Cancer Rsch. Found., 1994—. Contbr. articles to profl. jours. U. Iowa Grad. Student Scholar, 1981-84. Mem. Am. Soc. Microbiology, Sigma Xi. Office: La Jolla Cancer Rsch Found Alumni Hall Cancer Rsch Ctr La Jolla CA 92037

BAKKEN, GORDON MORRIS, law educator; b. Madison, Wis., Jan. 10, 1943; s. Elwood S. and Evelyn A. H. (Anderson) B.; m. Erika Reinhardt, Mar. 24, 1943; children: Angela E., Jeffrey E. B.S., U. Wis., 1966, M.S., 1967, Ph.D., 1970, J.D., 1973. Asst., then assoc. prof. history Calif. State U.-Fullerton, 1969-74, dir. faculty affairs, 1974-86, prof. history, 1974—; cons. Calif. Sch. Employees Assn., 1976-78; cons. Calif. Bar Commn. Hist. Law., 1985—; mem. mgmt. task force on acad. grievance procedures Calif. State Univ. and Colls. Systems, 1975; mem. Calif. Jud. Coun. Com. Trial Ct. Records Mgmt., 1992—. Placentia Jusa referee coordinator, 1983. Russell Sage resident fellow law, 1971-72; Am. Council Learned Socs. grantee-in-aid, 1979-80; Am. Bar Found. fellow in legal history, 1979-80, 84-85. Mem. Orgn. Am. Historians, Am. Soc. Legal History, Law and Soc. Assn., Western History Assn., Calif. Supreme Ct. Hist. Soc. (v.p.). Democrat. Lutheran. Author 5 books on Am. legal history; contbr. articles to profl. jours. Office: Calif State U 800 N State College Blvd Fullerton CA 92631-3547

BAKKER, JAN, English language educator; b. N.Y.C., Jan. 27, 1936; s. Albertus Haaie and Elise Anna Wilhelmina B. BA, U. Va., 1958, MA, 1961; PhD, U. Tenn., 1975. Instr. Clemson (S.C.) U., 1960-62, Memphis (Tenn.) State U., 1962-63; instr., tchg. asst. U. Tenn., Knoxville, 1963-67, 72-77; asst. prof. Armstrong State Coll., Savannah, Ga., 1967-68; lectr. U. Md., 1968-72; prof. English Utah State U., Logan, 1977—; sr. Fulbright prof. Gadjah Mada U., Yogyakarta, Indonesia, 1980-81, Heidelberg (Germany) U., summer 1991. Author: Pastoral in Antebellum Southern Romance, 1989; cons. editor: Children's Literature, 1973—; contbr. articles to profl. jours. Capt. USAR, 1959-75. NEA Scholarship grantee U. Tenn., Knoxville, 1965-67. Mem. MLA, Am. Lit. Assn., Soc. for the Study So. Lit., Am. Studies Assn., Children's Lit. Assn., York Rite Freemasonry, Harmony Lodge F & A.M., Jefferson Soc., Theta Delta Chi. Home: 167 E 100 N Apt E Logan UT 84321 Office: Dept English Utah State Univ Logan UT 84322-3200

BAKKO, ORVILLE EDWIN, retired health care executive, consultant; b. Kenyon, Minn., Oct. 10, 1919; s. Marcus and Caroline (Leding) B.; m. Norma Evelyn Cronquist, Sept. 25, 1951; children: Sandra Karen, Kristi Camille. BA, St. Olaf Coll., Northfield, Minn., 1941; M. in Hosp. Adminstrn., Northwestern U., 1948. Adminstrv. intern, resident U. Iowa Hosps., 1947-49; adminstrv. asst. Kadlec Hosp., Richland, Wash., 1949-50, asst. adminstr., then adminstr., 1950-56; asst. supt. Arroyo Del Valle Sanatorium, Livermore, Calif., 1956-60, Highland Hosp., Oakland, Calif., 1958-60; adminstr. Fairmont Hosp., San Leandro, Calif., 1960-82; vis. scholar Agder Coll., Kristiansand, Norway, 1983-84. Author: The Administrative Internship—What Can the Field Contribute to the Program?, 1948, Administration of Group Clinics, 1949, Employee Safety Program, 1970, Survey of Medical Rehabilitation in Norway, 1984. Mem. Alameda County Work Safety Com., 1959-72; mem. med. svcs. adv. com. Chabot Coll., San Leandro, 1962-72; mem. dis. svcs. adv. com. area 1 Regional Med. Program, 1970-72; 2d v.p., bd. dirs. Wash. State Hosp. Assn., 1954-55; pres. Southeast Wash. Hosp. Coun., 1953-54; chmn. Tri-City Hosp. Coun., 1954-56; trustee Commn. on Accreditation Rehab. facilities, 1974-76; mem. Internat. Hosp. Fedn., 1982-88. Capt. Med. Adminstrv. Corps, AUS, 1942-46, NATOUSA. Decorated officer Ordre du Nichan-Iftikhar (Tunisia). Fellow Am. Coll. Healthcare Execs. (life); mem. Am. Hosp. Assn. (life; governing coun. rehab. and chronic disease hosp. sect. 1972-77, chmn. 1976), Calif. Hosp. Assn. (mem. com. on continuing care and rehab. 1967-70), Assn. Western Hosps., Health Care Execs. No. Calif., East Bay Hosp. Conf. (exec. com. 1971-72), Commonwealth Club of Calif., Richland Toastmasters Club (officer 1949-56), Rotary (charter). Mem. Emmanuel Faith Comm. Ch. Home: 11887 Caminito Corriente San Diego CA 92128-4552

BAKUS, GERALD JOSEPH, biology educator; b. Thorp, Wis., Dec. 5, 1934; s. Joseph John and Marie Loretta (Kalkstein) B.; m. Grace Elaine Munsey, Dec. 26, 1953; children: Melanie Ann, Paul Gerald. BA in Biology, Calif. State U., L.A., 1955; MA in Zoology, U. Mont., 1957; PhD, U. Wash., 1962. Asst. prof. biology Calif. State U., Northridge, 1961-62; asst. prof. U. So. Calif., L.A., 1962-67, assoc. prof., 1967-85, prof., 1986—; staff officer Nat. Acad. Sci., Washington, 1969-70; chief biologist Tetra Tech Inc., Pasadena, 1976-79. Author: The Spanish Guitar, 1977, Computers and Programs for Beginners, 1984, Quantitative Ecology and Marine Biology, 1990, Coral Reef Ecosystems, 1994. Fulbright fellow, 1987. Fellow Great Barrier Reef Com. Australia, AAAS; mem. Internat. Soc. Chem. Ecology, Pacific Sci. Assn., Western Soc. Naturalists. Office: U So Calif Dept Biological Sciences Los Angeles CA 90089-0371

BALCH, GLENN MCCLAIN, JR., academic administrator, minister, author; b. Shattuck, Okla., Nov. 1, 1937; s. Glenn McClain and Marjorie (Daily) B.; student Panhandle State U., 1958-60, So. Meth. U., summers 1962-64; BA, S.W. State U. Okla., 1962; B.D., Phillips U., 1965; MA, Chapman Coll., 1973, MA in Edn., 1975, M.A. in Psychology, 1975; PhD, U.S. Internat. U., 1978; postgrad. Claremont Grad. Sch., 1968-70, U. Okla., 1965-66; m. Diana Gale Seeley, Oct. 15, 1970; children: Bryan, Gayle, Wesley, Johnny. Ordained to ministry Meth. Ch., 1962; sr. minister First Meth. Ch., Eakly, Okla., 1960-63, First Meth. Ch., Calumet, Okla., 1963-65, Goodrich Meml. Ch., Norman, Okla., 1965-66, First Meth. Ch., Barstow, Calif., 1966-70; asst. dean Chapman Coll., Orange, Calif., 1970-76; v.p. Pacific Christian Coll., Fullerton, Calif., 1976-79; pres. Newport U., Newport Beach, Calif., 1979-82; sr. pastor Brea United Meth. Ch., 1978-89; pres., CEO So. Calif. Inst., 1988-95; pres. Westmar U., Le Mars, Iowa, 1995—; edn. cons. USAF, 1974-75; mental health cons. U.S. Army, 1969. Mem. Community Adv. Bd. Minority Problems; Mayor's rep. to County Dependency Prevention Commn.; mem. Brea Econ. Devel. Com.; bd. dirs. Found. Internat. Community Assistance, Brea Found. With USMC, 1956-57. Recipient Eastern Star Religious Tng. award, 1963, 64; named Man of Year, Jr. C. of C., Barstow, 1969; Broadhurst fellow, 1963-65. Mem. Calif. Assn. Marriage and Family Therapists, Am. Assn. Marriage and Family Therapist, Rotary (pres. 1969-70, 83-84, dist. gov. 1987-88, 88-89), Masons, Shriners, Elks. Home: 935 4th Ave SE Le Mars IA 51031 Office: Westmar Univ 1002 3rd Ave SE Le Mars IA 51031

BALCOM, ORVILLE, engineer; b. Inglewood, Calif., Apr. 20, 1937; s. Orville R. and Rose Mae (Argo) B.; B.S. in Math., Calif. State U., Long Beach, 1958, postgrad., 1958-59; postgrad. UCLA, 1959-62; m. Gloria Stadtmiller, July 23, 1971; children—Cynthia, Steven. Engr., AiResearch Mfg. Co., 1959-62, 64-65; chief engr. Meditron, El Monte, Calif., 1962-64; chief engr. Astro Metrics, Burbank, Calif., 1965-67; chief engr., gen. mgr. Varadyne Power Systems, Van Nuys, Calif., 1968-71; owner, chief engr. Brown Dog Engring., Lomita, Calif., 1971—. Mem. IEEE Computer Group, Independent Computer Cons. Assn. Patentee in field. Club: Torrance Athletic. Home: 24521 Walnut St Lomita CA 90717-1260 Office: PO Box 427 Lomita CA 90717-0427

BALDOCK, BOBBY RAY, federal judge; b. Rocky, Okla., Jan. 24, 1936; s. W. Jay and S. Golden (Farrell) B.; m. Mary Jane (Spunky) Holt, June 2, 1956; children: Robert Jennings, Christopher Guy. Grad., N.Mex. Mil. Inst., 1956; JD, U. Ariz., 1960. Bar: Ariz. 1960, N.Mex. 1961, U.S. Dist. Ct. N.Mex., 1965. Ptnr. Sanders, Bruin & Baldock, Roswell, N.Mex., 1960-83; adj. prof. Eastern N.Mex. U., 1962-81; judge U.S. Dist. Ct. N.Mex., Albuquerque, 1983-86, U.S. Ct. Appeals (10th cir.), 1986—. Mem. N.Mex. Bar Assn., Chaves County Bar Assn., Ariz. Bar Assn., Phi Alpha Delta. Office: US Ct Appeals PO Box 2388 Roswell NM 88202-2388*

BALDON, CLEO, interior designer; b. Leavenworth, Wash., June 1, 1927; d. Ernest Elsworth and Esther Jane (Hannan) Chute; m. Lewis Smith Baldon, Nov. 20, 1948 (div. July 1961); 1 child, Dirk; m. Ib Jørgen Melchior, Jan. 18, 1964; 1 stepson, Leif Melchior. BS, Woodbury Coll., 1948. Ptnr. Interior Designs Ltd., Los Angeles, 1948-50; freelance illustrator Los Angeles, 1952-54; prin. Cleo Baldon & Assocs., Los Angeles and Venice, Calif., 1954—; ptnr. Galper/Baldon Assocs., Venice, 1970—. Author: Steps and Stairways; contbr. articles to profl. jours.; patentee in field. Recipient City Beautification awards L.A., 1974-77, 80, 83, 85-90, 92, Beverly Hills, 1982, Calif. Landscape Contbr., 1975, 79, Pacifica award Resources Coun., CAlif., 1979. Home: 8228 Marmont Ln West Hollywood CA 90069-1624 Office: Galper/Baldon Assocs 723 Ocean Front Walk Venice CA 90291-3270

BALDRIDGE, THAD CLIFTON WALKER, psychotherapist, consultant; b. Oklahoma City, Okla., Oct. 8, 1939; s. Thad Spires and Winifred Ernestine (Glass) B.; m. Jeanne Ellen Gallagher, Aug. 15, 1958 (div. 1962); children: Dorothy Joyce, Thad Matthew, Deborah Jeanne, Kenneth Michael; m. Ruth Marie Mendus, May 15, 1978 (div.); children: Summer Earthsong, Fletcher. BS summa cum laude, Mo. Valley Coll., 1991; M of Counseling, U. Phoenix, Tucson, 1993. Cert. profl. counselor, Ariz., cert. substance abuse counselor, Ariz.; nat. bd. cert. clin. hypnotherapist, counselor. Resident house dir. Mo. Valley Coll., Marshall, Mo., 1989-91; chemical dependency counselor La Frontera Ctr., Inc, Tucson, 1991-93, Gateway, Inc., Tucson, 1991-93; human svcs. specialist Ariz. Dept Econ. Security, Tucson, 1993-94; psychotherapist Ariz. Dept. Health Svcs., Tucson, 1994-95; cons. Pathways of Casa Grande, Tucson, 1994-95; psychotherapist Coronado Behavioral Healthcare, Inc., Sierra Vista, Ariz., 1995—, Eastern Mont. Mental Health Ctr., Glasgow, 1995; allied staff (cons.) Santa Cruz Family Counseling and Guidance, Nogales, Ariz., Francis Mahon Deaconess Hosp., Glasgow. Mem. nat. disaster mental health svcs. team ARC. Mem. ACA, Nat. Assn. Alcoholism and Drug Abuse Counselors. Republican. Mem. Unitarian Ch.

BALDWIN, BETTY JO, computer specialist; b. Fresno, Calif., May 28, 1925; d. Charles Monroe and Irma Blanche (Law) Inks; m. Barrett Stone Baldwin Jr.; two daughters. AB, U. Calif., Berkeley, 1945. With NASA Ames Rsch. Ctr., Moffett Field, Calif., 1951-53, math tech. 14' Wind Tunnel, 1954-55, math analyst 14' Wind Tunnel, 1956-63, supr. math analyst Structural Dynamics, 1963-68, supervisory computer programmer Structural Dynamics, 1968-71, computer programmer Theoretical Studies, 1971-82, adminstrv. specialist Astrophys. Experiments, 1982-85, computer specialist, resource mgr. Astrophysics br., 1985—; v.p. B&B Baldwin Farms, Bakersfield, Calif., 1978—. Mem. IEEE, Assn. for Computing Machinery, Am. Geophys. Union, Am. Bus. Womens Assn. (pres., v.p. 1967, one of Top 10 Women of Yr. 1971). Presbyterian. Office: NASA Ames Rsch Ctr Mail Stop 245-6 Moffett Field CA 94035-1000

BALDWIN, C. ANDREW, JR., retired science educator; b. Chgo., May 18, 1927; s. C. Andrew Sr. and Lillian (Evans) B.; m. Claire Awkerman, July 10, 1954; children: Debbie, Judi. BA in Zoology, U. Tex., 1951; MA in Theology, Berkeley Bapt. Sem. of West, 1956, MDiv, 1961; postgrad., numerous colls., univs. Cert. elem. tchr., Calif., secondary tchr., Calif., Tex., edn. adminstr., Calif. Sci. tchr. Brazosport Ind. Sch. Dist., Freeport, Tex., 1951-53; sustitute tchr. Chgo. Pub. Sch., 1953-54; child care and substitute tchr. Berkeley (Calif.) Pub. Sch., 1954-56; tchr. 7th and 8th grades Redwood City (Calif.) Elem. Sch., 1956-60; swimpool mgr. San Mateo County Parks/Recreation, 1957-64; biology, 6th grade/jr. high sci. tchr., coord. field biology Palo Alto (Calif.) Unified Sch. Dist., 1960-93; vice prin. Franklin-McKinley Sch. Dist., San Jose, Calif., 1970-71; Biology, 1-12th grade substitute Salem and Woodburn, Oreg. schs., Salem and Woodburn, Oreg., 1993—; founder, dir. pvt. summer ecology and field biology camp program-Summer Sci. Safaris, 1972-76; coord. sci. fairs Wilbur Jr. H.S. & Stanford Middle Sch. Contbr. articles to publs. Active YMCA, Chgo. Boys Club and Cath. Youth Orgn., summers 1945-56; elected trustee Redwood City Sch. Dist. Bd. Edn., 1961-69, pres. com. against racism Sequoia Union H.S., Dist., various others; candidate U.S. Congress, 1967; pres. Sequoia YMCA's Men's Club, Redwood City, 1967-69, Lorelei Homeowners Assn., Menlo Park, Calif., 1959-60; elder Trinity Presbyn. Ch., San Carlos, Calif., mem. choir, various coms., 1st Presbyn. Ch., San Mateo, rep. to No. Calif. Presbyn. United Mission Advance; staff assoc. Carlmont Meth. Ch.; vol. asst. min. Woodside Meth. Ch.; v.p. Hoover Elem. Sch. PTA, 1959-60; merit nadge counselor Boy Scouts Am.; elected Sequoia Unified Sch. Dist. Bd.; vol. guide Salem (Oreg.) Mission Mill. Grantee Chevron Corp., 1985; named Outstanding Citizen, Redwood City YMCA, 1968, Realtors, South San Mateo County, 1967; recipient Oak Leaf and Life Membership award Calif. PTA, 1959, 5 and 10 yr. Vol. pin ARC, Vol. pin Chgo. Boys' Club; nominated for Presdl. award for excellence in teaching, 1992. Mem. AAAS, NEA Calif. Tchrs. Assn., Palo Alto Edn. Assn. (sch. rep., salary com.), Christian Educators Assn. Internat., Astron. Soc. Pacific, Earth Sci. Tchrs. Assn., Calif. Sci. Tchrs. Assn., Nat. Sci. Tchrs. Assn. (12th dist. dir. 1984-86, lcoal leader 1993—), Oreg. Sci. Tchrs. Assn., Nat. Assn. Biology Tchrs., Phi Kappa Tau, Alpha Phi Omega, Phi Delta Kappa.

BALDWIN, CATHY L., occupational health nurse, consultant; b. Ft. Worth, Sept. 28, 1955; d. Jack L. and Alva (Pearce) LeMond; m. Dan L. Baldwin, Aug. 23, 1979; children: Andrew, Matthew, John. BSN, U. Tex., Arlington, 1983; MS, U. LaVerne, 1993. RN, Tex., Calif.; cert. occupational health nurse, occupational health hearing conservationist. Occupational health nurse Motorola, Inc., Ft. Worth, 1985-88, Koch Refinery, Corpus Christi, 1988, Wynn's Climate Systems, Ft. Worth, 1988-90, Kaiser Permanente/So. Calif., Woodland Hills, 1990; occupl. health svc. line mgr. Kaiser Permanente-Occupl. Health, Woodland Hills, Calif., 1994-95; occupational health nurse Kaiser Permanente Regional Lab., North Hollywood, Calif., 1995—; svc. line mgr., occpl. health svc. Kaiser Permanente Occpl. Health Svc., Woodland Hills, Calif., 1995—; preceptor UCLA Sch. Occupational Health, 1992—. Author health/wellness articles for employer publs; designer, developer employer occupational health programs. Mentor, speaker Youth Motivation Task Force, Kaiser/Los Angeles County, 1990—. Mem. ANA, Am. Assn. Occupational Health Nurses, So. Calif. Occupational Health Nurses Assn., Kaiser Permanente Women in Mgmt., Kaiser Permanente Regional Occupational Health Coords. (co-chmn. So. Calif. region 1992). Republican. Roman Catholic. Home: 841 Wiladonda Dr La Canada Flintridge CA 91011-2528 Office: Kaiser Permanente Occpl Health Svc 5601 DeSoto Ave Woodland Hills CA 91365

BALDWIN, CHARLENE MARIE, librarian; b. San Francisco, Jan. 12, 1946; d. Gale Warren and Lois (Ward) Hudkins; children: Christopher Ward, Anne Haynes, Sarah Isabella. BA, Calif. State U., Sacramento, 1970; MA, U. Chgo., 1973. Librarian Calif. Inst. Tech., Munger Library, Pasadena, 1974-75, Tetra Tech., Inc., Pasadena, 1976-81; chief reference librarian Lockheed-Calif. Co., Burbank, 1981-82; librarian Sci.-Engring. Library U. Ariz., Tucson, 1984-88, tng. cons. Office of Arid Lands Studies, 1986-87; head map libr. U. Ariz., 1988-94; divsn. head sci. librs. U. Calif., Riverside, 1994—; free-lance info. specialist, Nigeria, 1975-76; field cons. sponsored devel. project U.S. Agy. Internat. Devel., Niamey, Niger, 1986; adj. libr. Office of Arid Lands Studies, U. Ariz., 1986-94. Co-author: Yoruba of Southwestern Nigeria, 1976. Vice pres., founding mem. Friends of Calif. Inst. Tech. Librs.; founding mem. Internat. Librarianship Round Table, 1988, Transbarder Libr. Forum, 1989—; vol. U.S. Peace Corps Govt. Nigeria, Western State, 1966-68. Mem. Ariz. State Libr. Assn., Spl. Librs. Assn. (pres. Ariz. chpt. 1988-89, bd. dirs. 1991-93, 94—), Ariz. Online User Group (chmn. 1985-86). Office: Univ Calif Rivera Libr PO Box 5900 Riverside CA 92517-5900

BALDWIN, EWART MERLIN, geologist, educator; b. Pomeroy, Wash., May 17, 1915; s. Charles Milton and Augusta Elizabeth (Sears) B.; m. Margaret Ethel Maxwell, Oct. 2, 1942; children—Donald Maxwell, Neil Alan. B.S., Wash. State U., 1938, M.S., 1939; Ph.D., Cornell U., 1943. Cert. profl. geologist. Geologist, Oreg. Dept. Geology and Mining Industry, Portland, 1943-47; asst. prof. geology U. Oreg., Eugene, 1947-50, assoc. prof., 1950-59, prof., 1959-80; Arnold vis. prof. Whitman Coll., Walla Walla, Wash., 1981; Fulbright prof. U. Dacca, East Pakistan, 1959-60; prof. emeritus U. Oreg., Eugene, 1980—. Author: Geology of Oregon, 1959, 64, 76, 81. Contbr. articles to profl. jours. Mem. Geol. Soc. Am. (v.p. cordilleran sect. 1961), Am. Assn. Petroleum Geologists, Paleontol. Soc. (cordilleran sect. chmn.), Am. Inst. Profl. Geologists, N.W. Sci. Soc. (life). Club: Civitan (pres.) (Eugene). Home: 1020 E 18th Ave Apt 3 Eugene OR 97403-1313 Office: Dept Geology U Oreg Eugene OR 97403

BALDWIN, LARELL HARDISON, insurance company executive; b. Hanford, Calif., May 12, 1940; s. Leo H. and Bernice (Gash) B.; m. Kathleen L. Hardison, June 23, 1979; children: Jennifer Lin, Leslie Kari, Richard Allen, Michael Maxwell, Brenn Alexandria. Student Pasadena Coll., 1958-61; grad. Alexander Hamilton Inst. Bus., 1967. V.p. mortgage lending div. Standard Life & Accident Ins. Co. of Okla., Phoenix, 1961-64; sales mgr. Peterson Baby Products Inc., Burbank, Calif., 1964-67; v.p. sales Rotorway Aircraft Corp., Tempe, Ariz., 1967-69; pres. Trans World Arts Inc., San Jose, Calif., 1969-75, Baldwin Assocs. Devel. Corp., Santa Cruz, Calif., 1975-80; ptnr., v.p. Assurance Distbg. Co. Ltd., Santa Ana, Calif., 1979-82; pres. Baldwin Assurance Mktg. Corp., 1982-90; pres. Heritage Assurance Mktg., 1990—; nat. cons. ins. cos., author, lectr. Author in field. Office: Baldwin Assurance Mktg Corp PO Box 66972 Scotts Valley CA 95067-6972

BALDWIN, RICHARD EUGENE, real estate executive; b. Sona Bota, Belgian Congo, July 25, 1940; came to U.S., 1942.; s. Russell Eugene and Jesse Adele Baldwin; m. Margaret Alice Kearns, Aug. 11, 1962; 1 child, Robert Lanoue. BA, Northwestern U., 1962; MA, U. Calif., Berkeley, 1964, PhD, 1967. Asst. prof. English U. Wash., Seattle, 1967-74; sales assoc. Windermere Real Estate, Seattle, 1974-77; broker, pres. Windermere Real Estate/Capitol Hill, Inc., 1977—; v.p. Windermere-Wall St., 1983—. Editor: Neighborhood Coun. Newsletter, Seattle, 1977-81; contbr. articles to profl. jours. Chmn. steering com. Pike/Pine Project, 1989—. Mem. Seattle-King County Bd. Realtors, Capitol Hill C. of C. (pres. 1985-87). Office: Windermere Real Estate 1112 19th Ave E Seattle WA 98112-3505

BALENTINE, JOHN L., county official; b. Hollywood, Calif., Apr. 14, 1948; s. John L. and Roberta Ella (Wyatt) B.; m. Eva A. Grimm, Sept. 20, 1975 (div. Feb. 8, 1992). AA, L.A. Valley Coll., Van Nuys, Calif., 1968; BA, San Fernando Valley State Coll, Northridge, Calif., 1970. Cert. purchasing mgr. Nat. Assn. Purchasing Mgmt. Spl. asst. to Mayor City of L.A., 1967-75; CEO, ptnr. Total Travel Internat., Nashville, 1975-78; program evaluator II Comptroller Office, State of Tenn., Nashville, 1978-80; asst. chief security Onslow Hotel/Casino, Reno, Nev., 1980-85; sr. buyer State of Nev., Carson City, 1986-92; purchasing and contract adminstr. Washoe County, Reno, 1992—. Contbr. articles to profl. jours. Dir. No. Nev. Consortium of Coop. Purchasing, Reno, 1986—, Washoe County Detention Facility Industries, Reno, 1992—; res. dep. sheriff Washoe County Sheriff's Office, Reno, 1982-85. Recipient Meritorious Citation, Gov. of Nev., 1991, Cert. of Merit, Human Rels. Commn., City of L.A., 1971, Cert. of Appreciation, Mayor of L.A., 1971, Youth Adv. Coun. of L.A., 1969. Mem. Nat. Assn. Purchasing Mgmt. (cert., No. Nev. chpt. pres. 1989—), Nat. Purchasing Inst., Nat. Inst. Govt. Purchasing, Nat. St. Rod Assn. Jehovah's Witnesses. Home: PO Box 143 Sparks NV 89432-0143 Office: Washoe County Purchasing PO Box 11130 Reno NV 89520-0027

BALESH, JAMES R., lawyer; b. L.A., Dec. 17, 1967; s. Ronald James and Stella Ann B. BA, U. Notre Dame, 1989; JD, Santa Clara U., 1993. Field dep. L.A. (Calif.) City Councilman Michael Woo, 1990; law clk. L.A. (Calif.) City Attys. Office, 1991, Law Office of Carlos Lloreda, L.A., 1992; pvt. practice lawyer L.A., 1994—; ABA rep. Santa Clara (Calif.) U., 1992-93. Editor Santa Clara (Calif.) Computer and High Tech Jour., 1992-93. Recipient Cmty. Svc. award Santa Clara U., 1993. Mem. State Bar Calif., Phi Alpha Delta (vice chair Santa Clara chpt. 1992-93). Roman Catholic. Home: 2250 N Catalina St Los Angeles CA 90027

BALESTRERO, DAN CHARLES, voice teacher, TV producer; b. July 5, 1949. MA, Brigham Young U.; studies with Ray Arbizy; tng. at Robert Redford's Sundance, Ctr. for the Arts. Pvt. voice tchr. Chgo., 1987—; guest master coach San Francisco Opera Adler Fellows, 1985-89; vocal cons. to artistic dir. Chgo. Opera Theatre, 1992—; vocal and theatrical workshop leader. Singer, dir. and actor in more than 50 prodns. in opera, music theater, TV and film. Home: 11740 Wilshire Blvd # A1607 Los Angeles CA 90025-6536

BALINT, JOSEPH PHILIP, medical products executive; b. Passaic, N.J., Mar. 24, 1948; s. Joseph and Margaret (Birish) B. BA, Rutgers U., 1970, PhD, 1977. Cert. med. technologist, Am. Soc. Clin. Pathology. Med. technologist N.J. Coll. Medicine and Dentistry, Newark, 1970-72; grad. student Rutgers U., New Brunswick, N.J., 1972-77; rsch. fellow Rsch. Inst. of Scripps Clinic, La Jolla, Calif., 1977-80; rsch. assoc. Baylor Coll. Medicine, Houston, 1980-82, rsch. instr., 1982; cons. Imré Corp., Seattle, 1982-83, rsch. dir., 1983-89, v.p. product devel., 1989-92, dir. device devel., 1993, v.p. R & D, 1994—. Contbr. articles profl. jours., patentee in field. Recipient N.J. State scholarship, 1966-70, NIH rsch. grants, 1983, 84, Nat. Cancer Inst. grant, 1984. Office: Imré Corp 401 Queen Anne Ave N Seattle WA 98109-4517

BALL, BERT, foundation executive, arts consultant; b. Bronxville, N.Y., May 16, 1952; s. Herbert Morton and Joan Florence (Cameron) B. BA, Lehigh U., 1976; MFA, UCLA, 1994. Mng. dir. Arts and Commerce Found., N.Y.C., L.A., 1981-91; dir. City of L.A. Clutural Affairs Dept. Materials for the Arts, L.A., 1991-93; exec. dir. L.A. Shares, L.A., 1993—; bd. dirs. Dorland Mountain Arts Colony, L.A., Griffith Park Resource Bd., L.A. Recipient Calmax award State of Calif., 1992, Cert. of Recognition award L.A. Unified Sch. Dist., Cert. of Appreciation award L.A. City Coun., Environ. Pride award L.A. Mag., 1994. Office: L A Shares 3224 Riverside Dr Los Angeles CA 90027-1415

BALL, DONALD EDMON, architect; b. Evansville, Ind., July 18, 1942; s. Harvey and Myrl (Norris) B. BA in Design, So. Ill. U., 1967. Registered architect Ariz., Calif., Colo.; cert. Nat. Coun. Archtl. Registration Bd. With design dept. Leo A. Daly Co., Architects and Engrs., Omaha, 1968; project mgr. Buetow & Assocs., St. Paul, 1969-70; ptnr. Comprehensive Design, Mpls., 1971-73; with Caudill Assocs., Aspen, Colo., 1973-76, Hagman Yaw, Ltd., Aspen, 1977; project mgr. Hauter Assocs., Aspen, 1978; pres. Jacobs, Ball & Assocs., Architects, Aspen and Denver, 1978-85; project mgr. Moshe Safdie & Assocs., Boston, 1985-87; dir. design Dwayne Lewis Architects, Inc., Phoenix, 1987-88; prin. Donald Ball and Assocs., Scottsdale, Ariz., 1988—. Mem. Aspen Bldg. Insp. Selection Com., 1982, Pitkin County Housing Authority Bd., Aspen, 1984. Mem. AIA (chmn. Colo. West chpt., documents com.), Ariz. Soc. Architects (profl. practice com.). Home: 7869 E Horseshoe Ln Scottsdale AZ 85250-4786 Office: 7201 E Camelback Rd Ste 325 Scottsdale AZ 85251-3318

BALL, JAMES HERINGTON, lawyer; b. Kansas City, Mo., Sept. 20, 1942; s. James T. Jr. and Betty Sue (Herington) B.; m. Wendy Anne Wolfe, Dec. 28, 1964; children: James H. Jr., Steven Scott. AB, U. Mo., 1964; JD cum laude, St. Louis U., 1973. Bar: Mo. 1973. Asst. gen. counsel Anheuser-Busch, Inc., St. Louis, 1973-76; v.p., gen. counsel, sec. Stouffer Corp., Solon, Ohio, 1976-83; sr. v.p., gen. counsel Nestle Enterprises, Inc., Solon, 1983-91; gen. counsel, sr. v.p., bd. dirs. Nestle USA, Inc., Glendale, Calif., 1991—. Editor-in-chief St. Louis U. Law Jour., 1972-73. Bd. dirs. Alliance for Children's Rights, L.A., 1992—. Served to lt. comdr. USN, 1964-70, Vietnam. Mem. Mo. Bar Assn. Office: Nestle USA Inc 800 N Brand Blvd Glendale CA 91203-1244

BALL, JAMES WILLIAM, check cashing company executive; b. Tacoma, June 23, 1942; s. Montgomery McKinley and Ann Marie Ball; m. Patricia Miller, July 29, 1977; children: Katherine Kendall, Molly Elizabeth. Student, St. Martin's Coll., Lacy, Wash., 1960-61, San Jose City Coll., 1966-68; BA, San Jose State U., 1970, MA, 1971; postgrad., U. Calif., Irvine, 1971-72. Store mgr. Food Villa Inc., San Jose, Calif., 1972-76; asst. mgr. Ralph's Inc., San Jose, 1976-78; pres., owner Ball Liquors Inc., San Jose, 1978-88; pres. Fast Cash Inc., San Jose, 1984—. Mem. Calif. Check Cashers Assn. (v.p. 1988—). Office: Fast Cash Inc 4110 Monterey Hwy San Jose CA 95111-3626

BALL, LAWRENCE, retired physicial scientist; b. Albion, N.Y., Aug. 10, 1933; s. Harold Witheral and Gladys (Gibbs) B.; m. Caroline Moran, June 21, 1957; children: Daniel Lawrence, Logan Edward, Stacey Laura Ball Lucero, Ryan Laird (dec.). Diploma, Williston Acad., 1952; BSME, Antioch Coll., 1957; MSc in Elec. Engring., Ohio State U., 1962. Engring. aid Wright Air Devel. Ctr., Dayton, Ohio, 1957-60; engr. Deco Electronics Inc., Boulder, Colo., 1962-66; sr. engr. Westinghouse Rsch. Labs., Boulder, 1966-73, Westinghouse Ocean Rsch. Lab., Annapolis, Md., 1973-74; program mgr. div. geothermal energy U.S. Dept. Energy, Washington, 1974-79; lab. dir. U.S. Dept. Energy, Grand Junction, Colo., 1979-93; ret., 1993; pres. Liberty Cons. Co., Grand Junction, 1984—. Co-inventor coal mine communications; contbr. articles to profl. jours. Mem. various vol. fire depts., 1954-79; mem., sr. patroller Nat. Ski Patrol System, Md., Colo., 1973-92; bd. dirs. Colo. Head Injury Found., chpt. pres., 1989-91. Named Profl. Govt. Employee of Yr., Western Colo. Fed. Exec. Assn., 1991. Mem. Soc. Exploration Geophysicists, Toastmasters Internat. (area gov. 1991-92, divsn. gov. 1992-93, Toastmaster of Yr. We. Colo. 1990, DTM & ATM-S 1994), West Slope Wheelman (charter bd. dirs. 1992-93), We. Colo. Amateur Radio Club (pres. 1994-96), Amateur Radio Emergency Svcs. (emergency coord. 1995—).

BALL, ROBERT EDWIN, engineering educator; b. Indpls., Aug. 2, 1935; s. Robert Raymond and Marjory May (McComb) B.; m. Rana Niola Applegate, Sept. 2, 1956; children: Robert Edwin Jr., Susan Marie Ball Culcasi. BSCE, Northwestern U., 1958, MSCE, 1959, PhD, 1962. Disting. prof. dept. aeronautics and astronautics Naval Postgrad. Sch., Monterey, Calif., 1967—. Author: The Fundamentals of Aircraft Combat Survivability Analysis and Design, 1985. Fellow AIAA (chmn. survivability tech. com. 1989-92). Home: 642 Toyon Dr Monterey CA 93940-4225

BALL, ROBERT JEROME, classics educator; b. N.Y.C., Nov. 4, 1941; s. William and Pauline Ball. BA, Queens Coll., 1962; MA, Tufts U., 1963; PhD, Columbia U., 1971. Asst. prof. classics U. Hawaii, Honolulu, 1971-76, assoc. prof., 1976-83, prof., 1983—. Author: Tibullus The Elegist: A Critical Survey, 1983, Reading Classical Latin: The Second Year, 1990; editor: The Classical Papers of Gilbert Highet, 1983; co-editor: Alfred Burns' Biography, From Austria to Hawaii: Odyssey of a Classicist, 1994. Recipient Excellence in Teaching award U. Hawaii, 1979; Presdl. scholar U. Hawaii, 1985. Mem. Am. Philol. Assn. (Excellence in Teaching award 1981). Office: U Hawaii at Manoa Dept European Langs Li Honolulu HI 96822

BALL, RULON WAYNE, toxicologist. BS in Health Sci., Brigham Young U., 1977, MHEd, 1978; MPH in Environ. Health, Loma Linda (Calif.) U., 1986; PhD in Toxicology, Utah State U., 1989. Diplomate Am. Bd. Toxicology. Mgr. subchronic/chronic toxicology Utah Biomed. Test Lab., Salt Lake City, 1990-92, assoc. dir. toxicology, 1992—. Contbr. articles to profl. jours. Mem. Am. Assn. for Lab. Animal Sci. (Utah br.), Am. Coll. Toxicology, Soc. of Toxicology, Phi Kappa Phi, Delta Omega. Home: 8634 Buena Vista Dr Sandy UT 84094-1826 Office: Utah Biomed Test Lab 520 Wakara Way Salt Lake City UT 84108-1213

BALL, WILLIAM PAUL, physicist, engineer; b. San Diego, Nov. 16, 1913; s. John and Mary (Kajla) B.; m. Edith Lucile March, June 28, 1941 (dec. 1976); children: Lura Irene Ball Raplee, Roy Ernest. AB, UCLA, 1940; PhD, U. Calif., Berkeley, 1952. Registered profl. engr. Calif. Projectionist, sound technician studios and theatres in Los Angeles, 1932-41; tchr. high sch. Montebello, Calif., 1941-42; instr. math. and physics Santa Ana (Calif.) Army Air Base, 1942-43; physicist U. Calif. Radiation Lab., Berkeley and Livermore, 1943-58; mem. tech. staff Ramo-Wooldridge Corp., Los Angeles, 1958-59; sr. scientist Hughes Aircraft Co., Culver City, Calif., 1959-64; sr. staff engr. TRW-Def. Systems Group, Redondo Beach, Calif., 1964-83, Hughes Aircraft Co., 1983-86; cons. Redondo Beach, 1986—. Contbr. articles to profl. jours.; patentee in field. Bd. dirs. So. Dist. Los Angeles chpt. ARC, 1979-86. Recipient Manhattan Project award for contbn. to 1st atomic bomb, 1945. Mem. AAAS, Am. Phys. Soc., Am. Nuclear Soc., N.Y. Acad. Scis., Torrance (Calif.) Area C. of C. (bd. dirs. 1978-84), Sigma Xi. Home and Office: 209 Via El Toro Redondo Beach CA 90277-6561

BALLANCE, LISA TAYLOR, marine ecologist; b. Los Alamos, N.Mex., June 6, 1959; d. Harry Earl and Vilma (Taylor) B. BA, U. Calif., San Diego, 1981; MS, Moss Landing Marine Labs., 1987; PhD, UCLA, 1993. Fisheries biologist S.W. Fisheries Sci. Ctr., La Jolla, Calif., 1988-93; marine ecologist S.W. Fisheries Sci. Ctr., La Jolla, 1993—; vis. asst. prof. Sch. Field Studies, Beverly, Mass., 1985, 86, 87, U. Oreg., Charleston, 1989, 90, 91, 92, 94, Northeastern U., 1993. Contbr. articles to peer-reviewed jours. on seabird ecology. Recipient Nat. Rsch. Coun. postdoctoral rsch. award, 1993-94, Nat. Marine Fisheries Grad. Rsch. award, 1988-93; grantee Packard Found., 1983, Am. Mus. Natural History, 1983, Am. cetacean Soc., 1984, UCLA, 1991. Mem. Am. Ornithologists' Union (Jocelyn Van Tyne award 1991), Assn. Women in Sci., Brit. Ornithologists' Union, Ecol. Soc. Am., Soc. Marine Mammalogy. Office: SW Fisheries Sci Ctr 8604 La Jolla Shores Dr La Jolla CA 92037-1508

BALLANTINE, MORLEY COWLES (MRS. ARTHUR ATWOOD BALLANTINE), newspaper editor; b. Des Moines, May 21, 1925; d. John and Elizabeth (Bates) Cowles; m. Arthur Atwood Ballantine, July 26, 1947 (dec. 1975); children—Richard, Elizabeth Ballantine Leavitt, William, Helen Ballantine Healy. A.B., Ft. Lewis Coll., 1975; L.H.D. (hon.), Simpson Coll., Indianola, Iowa, 1980. Pub. Durango (Colo.) Herald, 1952-83, editor, pub., 1975-83, editor, chmn. bd., 1983—; dir. 1st Nat. Bank, Durango, 1976—, Des Moines Register & Tribune, 1977-85, Cowles Media Co., 1982-86. Mem. Colo. Land Use Commn., 1975-81, Supreme Ct. Nominating Commn., 1984-90; mem. Colo. Forum, 1985—, Blueprint for Colo., 1985-92; pres. S.W. Colo. Mental Health Ctr., 1964-65, Four Corners Opera Assn., 1983-86; bd. dirs. Colo. Nat. Hist. Preservation Act, 1968-78; trustee Choate/Rosemary Hall, Wallingford, Conn., 1973-81, Simpson Coll., Indianola, Iowa, 1981—, U. Denver, 1984—, Fountain Valley Sch., Colorado Springs, 1976-89; mem. exec. com. Ft. Lewis Coll. Found., 1991—. Recipient 1st place award for editorial writing Nat. Fedn. Press Women, 1955, Outstanding Alumna award Rosemary Hall, Greenwich, Conn., 1969, Outstanding Journalism award U. Colo. Sch. Journalism, 1967, Distinguished Service award Ft. Lewis Coll., Durango, 1970; named to Colo. Community Journalism Hall of Fame, 1987; named Citizen of Yr. Durango Area Chamber Resort Assn., 1990. Mem. Nat. Soc. Colonial Dames, Colo. Press Assn. (bd. dirs. 1978-79), Colo. AP Assn. (chmn. 1966-67), Federated Women's Club Durango, Mill Reef Club (Antigua, W.I.) (bd. govs. 1985-91). Episcopalian. Address: care Herald PO Drawer A Durango CO 81302

BALLANTYNE, JAMES HENRY, IV, investor, developer; b. Boise, Idaho, Jan. 8, 1932; s. James Henry III and Meta Christina (Houmann) B.; m. Mary Rand, June 12, 1954; children: Janet Marie, John Irving, Helen Kristina, Michael Joseph, Mary Elizabeth. BS, U. Idaho, 1954; student, Gonzaga Coll. at Boise, 1977-78, Boise State U., 1967—. Lic. real estate broker, Idaho. Owner farms and ranch, Idaho and Oreg., 1956—; owner, broker Ballantyne Land Co., Boise, 1963-89; ptnr. Succor Creek Oil Co., Boise, 1975-80; owner Ice Rink, Inc., Boise, 1975-87, investment/devel. co., Boise, 1963—; mem. adv. bd. dept. geology Boise State U., 1988—; mem. fin. bd. Diocese of Boise, Cath. Ch., 1985-89. Artist, working in India ink; author: (poetry) Cold Drill, 1984. Bd. dirs. Head Start, Ada County, Idaho, 1991—, Ada County 4-H Endowment, 1989—; mem. adv. bd. Nazareth Retreat Ctr., Boise, 1978—; pres. Ecumenical Chs. in Idaho, 1980-85. Lt. USNR, 1954-56, Korea. Named Citizen of Yr., Grange, Maple Grove, Boise, 1988; recipient various awards. Mem. Agrarian Club (pres.), Wranglers, Friday Fried Poets, Kiwanis Internat. (gov. 1994-95, Disting. lt. gov. 1991), Alpha [illegible] Home: 10250 Whispering Cliffs Dr Boise ID 83704-1907

BALLANTYNE, MICHAEL ALAN, legislator; b. Toronto, Ontario, Can., Feb. 27, 1945; s. Earnest Alan and Barbara Joyce (Stevens) B.; m. Penny Leanne Aumond, Aug. 2, 1987; Children: Erin, Alexandra, Nicholas. Attended, Carleton U., Ottawa, Ontario, 1966. With Giant Yellowknife Mines, 1976-79; alderman City of Yellowknife, 1976-79. Alderman City of Yellowknife. 1979, mayor 1980-83; elected MLA Yellowknife North, 1983, 87, 91, chmn. finance com. 1983-85, mem. special com. on housing; cabinet appointee, minister of housing 1985-87, minister of justice 1985-87; cabinet re-appointee, minister of justice 1987-91, minister of finance 1987-91, chair treasury bd. 1987-91, chair legislation and house planning com. 1987-91, govt. house leader 1987-91, minister responsible for pub. utilities bd. 1989-91, Aboriginal langs. 1989-90, chair of special com. on constitutional reform 1989-91; elected speaker legislative assembly of the NWT 1991—, chair mgmt. svcs. bd. 1991—. Office: Speaker/Legislative Assembly, PO Box 1320, Yellowknife, NT Canada X1A 2L9

BALLANTYNE, REGINALD MALCOLM, III, healthcare executive; b. Columbus, Ga., Oct. 2, 1943; s. Reginald Malcolm and Constance Aimee (Martin) B.; m. Cynthia Sue Truair, Mar. 28, 1987; 1 child, Steven Truair. BS, Coll. Holy Cross, 1965; MBA, Cornell U., 1967. Adminstrv. resident Glen Cove (N.Y.) Community Hosp., 1966; asst. adminstr. St. Luke's Hosp. Med. Ctr., Phoenix, 1970-73; adminstr. Meml. Hosp., Phoenix, 1973-74; exec. v.p., adminstr. Meml. Hosp. Phoenix, 1974-76, pres. Phoenix Meml. Hosp., 1976-84; pres. PMH Health Resources, Inc., Phoenix, 1984—; bd. dirs. Preferred Health Network, Ariz. Voluntary Hosp. Fedn., Ariz. Healthcare Alliance, Premier Healthcare; pres. Phoenix Regional Hosp. Coun.; chmn. Florence Crittendon Svcs. Ariz.; preceptor Cornell U., Ariz. State U.; speaker in field. Edit. adv. bd. Bus. Jour.; contbr. articles to profl. jours. Health Care Cost Containment and Regulation com. Ariz. Legis. Coun.; Hosps. svc. agys. unit chmn. Phoenix-Scottsdale United Way Campaign; emergency med. svcs. coun. Ariz. Dept. Health Svcs.; Ariz. Statewide Health Coord. Coun.; chmn. Ariz.Affordable Health Care Found., Valley Emergency Med. Svcs., Ariz. Emergency Med. Svcs., Phoenix Revitalization Corp.; adv. bd. Sun Angel Found., Jr. League Phoenix; pres. Hosp. Shared Svcs. Ariz.; bd. dirs., exec. com. Mountain States Shared Svcs. Corp.; bd. dirs. Community Orgn. Drug Abuse Control, Ariz. Vol. Hosp. Assn., chmn. sr. mgmt. group, mem. planning com., Ariz. C. of C., Phoenix Community Alliance, Phoenix Civic Plz. Bldg. Corp., Ariz. Coalition for Tomorrow, Phoenix C. of C., Citizens Com. Better Health; chmn. anti-crime com. Greater Phoenix Leadership. Health svcs. officer, pub. health advisor Commn. Corps USPHS, 1967-70. Recipient N.Y. State Scholar Incentive award Cornell U.; Alfred P. Sloan scholar, fellow Cornell U. Fellow Am. Coll. Healthcare Execs. (ad hoc com. role hosp. CEO); mem. APHA (Commd. Officers Assn.), Am. Hosp. Assn. (bd. trustees, ho. dels., bd. dirs. ins. resource inc., spkr., various coms.), Joint Commn. Accreditation Healthcare Orgn. (bd. commrs.), Am. Acad. Med. Adminstrs. (state chmn.), Am. Soc. Law and Medicine, Assn. Western Hosps. (ho. dels., nominating com.), Ariz. Hosp. Assn. (bd. chmn., chmn. various couns.), Ariz. Coop. Purchasing Assn. (bd. chmn.), Ariz. Pub. Health Assn., Comprehensive Health Planning Coun. Maricopa County (steering com.), Soc. Pub. Health Edn., Phoenix Sunrise Rotary Club (pres.). Roman Catholic. Home: 3266 E Valley Vista Ln Paradise Valley AZ 85253-3738 Office: PMH Health Resources Inc PO Box 21207 Phoenix AZ 85036-1207

BALLARD, JACK STOKES, strategic systems educator; b. Gravette, Ark., July 23, 1928; s. Freeman Stokes and Chloe Katherine (Clarry) B.; m. Arleda Anne Greenwood, Feb. 21, 1954; children: Kenneth Stokes, Donald Steven, Cheryl Anne. BSE, U. Ark., 1950; MA, U. So. Calif., 1953; PhD, UCLA, 1974. Cert. secondary tchr. Commd. 2d lt. USAF, 1954, advanced through grades to lt. col., 1974, ret., 1980; tchr. Coalinga & Whittier (Calif.) High Schs., 1951-54; tng. and pers. officer USAF, Travis AFB, Calif., Alaska, 1954-59; asso. prof. air sci. Occidental Coll., L.A., 1959-64; asst. prof. history USAF Acad., Colorado Springs, Colo., 1964-69; sr. tng advisor Korean Air Force Tng. Wing, Taejon, 1969-70; air force historian Office of Air Force History, Washington, 1970-74; chief plans and requirement div. Lowry Tech. Tng. Ctr., Denver, 1974-80; chief strategic systems tng. Martin Marietta Corp., Denver, 1980-92; instr. history, U. Alaska, Anchorage, 1958-59, U. Md., Taejon, 1969-70; adj. instr. history U. Colo., Colorado Springs, 1977-83, U. Colo., Denver, 1983-87. Author: Development and Employment of Fixed Wing Gunships, 1982, Shock of Peace, 1983; contbg. author USAF in S.E. Asia, 1977; contbr. articles to profl. jours. Pres. Occidental Coll. Faculty Club, 1962-63; chmn. Adv. Coun. Sch. Improvement, Littleton, Colo., 1984-89; sec. Large Sch. Dist. Accountability Coun., Denver, 1988-89; elected sch. bd. dirs. Littleton Pub. Schs., 1991; sec. Mile High chpt. Air Force Assn., 1988; 1st v.p. Littleton Lions Club, 1995—. Recipient Commendation medal USAF, Washington, 1970, Meritorious Svc. medal, Lowry AFB, 1974. Mem. Orgn. Am. Historians, Western History Assn., Air Force Hist. Found., Am. Def. Preparedness Assn., Colo. Hist. Soc. Republican. Methodist. Home: 7820 S Franklin Way Littleton CO 80122-3116

BALLARD, JAMES KENNETH, association executive, horticulture executive; b. Custer, S.D., May 15, 1920; s. Peter Albert and Mabelle Alice (Severns) B.; m. Marian Jane Walker, June 30, 1944 (dec. Sept. 1980); children: Gary Kenneth, Kathleen Marie; m. Stella Schoenfelt, Oct. 24, 1984. BS in Horticulture, Colo. State U., 1946; MS in Horticulture, Wash. State U., 1952; D in Horticulture, U. Chihuahua, Mexico, 1972. Rsch. aide Wash. State U., Prosser, 1945-52; AG ext. agt. Chelan County, Wenatchee, Wash., 1952-62, Yakima County, Yakima, Wash., 1962-80; horticulture advisor Carlton Nursery, Dayton, Oreg., 1980-87, Pacific N.W. Fruit Tester's Assn., Selah, Wash., 1987—; horticulture advisor U.S. AID to Pakistan, 1978, U.S. World Bank, Xian, China, 1988, Pacific N.W. Fruit Tester's Assn., Japan, China, 1990, Australia, 1992. Lt. U.S. Infantry, 1945-46. Home: 1101 W Orchard Ave Selah WA 98942-1271

BALLARD, LORREN LEE, fire protection official; b. Denver, May 8, 1939; s. David Crockett and Dorothy (Canter) B.; m. Barbara Ballard, Feb. 15, 1961 (div. 1967); children: Lorren Jr., Christopher; m. Donna Mae Veenstra, Dec. 30, 1988; 1 child, Erika Rasmussen. BS, Regis Coll., 1987. From firefighter to divsn. chief City of Denver, 1963-89; fire chief City of Billings, Mont., 1989—; active Comm. Ctr. Adv. Bd., Billings, 1989—. Chmn. Local Emergency Planning Com., Billings, 1989—; v.p. adv. bd. Salvation Army, 1989—; chmn. adv. bd. Critical Incident Stress Debriefing Team, 1989—. Office: Billings Fire Dept 2305 8th Ave N Billings MT 59101

BALLENTINE, LEE KENNEY, publishing company executive; b. Teaneck, N.J., Sept. 4, 1954; s. George Kenney and Veda Avis Maxine (Havens) B.; m. Jennifer Ursula Marie Moore, Aug. 20, 1983; 1 child, Philip Alden Emerson. Student, Harvey Mudd Coll., 1972-73; BS in Computer Sci., SUNY, Albany, 1976; postgrad., U. Colo., 1976-77, U. Calif., Berkeley, 1977-78. Software engr. Osborne & Assocs. Pubs., Berkeley, 1978-80, Triad Systems Corp., Sunnyvale, Calif., 1981-84; group leader, operating systems and communications Daisy Systems Corp., Sunnyvale, 1984-85; software applications engr. mgr. Fairchild Clipper Div., Palo Alto, Calif., 1985-87; cons. numerous electronic and pub. industry clients, 1987-88; pres. Ocean View Tech. Publs., Mountain View, Calif., 1989-91, Profl. Book Ctr., Denver, 1991—; pub. Ocean View Books, Denver, 1986—; seminar presenter Willamette Writer's Conf., Portland, Oreg., 1990, Rocky Mountain Book Festival, 1993, Rocky Mountain Book Publishers, 1993, Denver Book Mall, 1994, Talleres Cover Book Store, 1993, 94, Boulot Pub. Libr., 1995; cons. Prentice-Hall Pub. Co., Englewood Cliffs, N.J., 1989-90, Amdahl Corp., Sunnyvale, 1988-90; mem. New Eng. Book Show, 1991. Author: Directional Information, 1981, Basements in the Music Box, 1986, Dream Protocols, 1992, Phase Language, 1995; editor: Poly: New Speculative Writing, 1989; pub. Phi Beta Kappa newsletter, San Francisco, 1987-89. Presenter Mount View Pub. Libr., 1990. Recipient Ednl. Explorations award Reader's Digest, 1975, Outstanding Scholarly Book award Am. Pub. Assn., 1995; Nat. Merit scholar, 1972. Mem. Am. Book Producers Assn., Sci. Fiction Writers of Am., Sci. Fiction Poetry Assn., USR Group Unix Profl. Assn., Book Builder's West (cert. of merit), The Am. Booksellers Assn., Small Press Book Ctr., Poeisis (advisory bd. 1993). Office: Profl Book Ctr PO Box 102650 Denver CO 80250-2650

BALLINGER, CHARLES EDWIN, educational association administrator; b. West Mansfield, Ohio, June 3, 1935; s. William E. and Mildred Arlene (Jester) B.; m. Venita Dee Riggs, June 12, 1982. BA, De Pauw U., 1957; MA, Ohio State U., 1958, PhD, 1971. Tchr. pub. schs., Ohio, 1958-62, Ohio State U. Lab. Sch., Columbus, 1962-63; asst. supt. North Canton (Ohio) City Schs., 1964-67; cons. Franklin County Schs., Columbus, 1967-70, Ohio Dept. Edn., Columbus, 1970-71; coord. San Diego County Office Edn., San Diego, 1971—; exec. dir. Nat. Assn. for Yr.-Round Edn., San Diego, 1980—. Contbr. numerous articles to profl. jours. Home: 4891 Jellett St San Diego CA 92110-2226 Office: Nat Assn for Yr-Round Edn P O Box 711386 San Diego CA 92171-1386

BALLINGER, CHARLES KENNETH, information specialist; b. Johnstown, Pa., July 28, 1950; s. Delores Jean (Cool) B.; m. Deb C. Delger, Sept. 14, 1985. Programmer analyst Cowles Pub. Co., Spokane, Wash., 1975-78; systems analyst Old Nat. Bank, Spokane, 1978-82; software engr. ISC System, Spokane, 1982; micro computer analyst Acme Bus. Computers, Spokane, 1982-85; info. ctr. analyst Wash. Water Power Co., Spokane, 1985-92; office automation analyst EDS Corp., Spokane, 1992—; cons. IDP Co., Spokane, 1978—. Contbr. articles to profl. jours. Served with Signal Corps, U.S. Army, 1968-71. Mem. IEEE (assoc.), Spokane Health Users Group (pres. 1979-83). Home: 3810 S Havana St Spokane WA 99223-6006 Office: EDS-I/S Wash Water Power Co 1411 E Mission Ave Spokane WA 99202-2617

BALLOT, MICHAEL HARVEY, business administration educator, consultant; b. N.Y.C., Jan. 8, 1940; s. Max and Claire (Bayer) B.; m. Nancy Diann Christiansen, Feb. 23, 1963; children: Michele Ann Dodge, David Andrew, Edward Carter. BME, Cornell U., 1962; MBA, U. Santa Clara, 1964; MA in Econs., Stanford U., 1968, PhD in Bus. and Econs., 1973. Mfg. engr. Lockheed Missiles & Space Co., Sunnyvale, Calif., 1962-64, Beckman Instruments, Palo Alto, Calif., 1964-65; asst. prof. econs. Chico (Calif.) State Coll., 1968-71; asst. prof. bus. adminstrn. Univ. of Pacific, Stockton, Calif., 1971-74, assoc. prof., 1974-79, prof., 1979—; cons., spkr. in field; arbitrator BBB, Stockton, Calif., 1975—. Author: Decision-Making Models in P/OM, 1986, Labor Management Relations in a Changing Environment, 1992. Cons. U.S. Dept. Transp., 1973, Stockton State Hosp., 1974, Stockton Econ. Devel. Agy., 1971, 85-86. Mem. Decision Scis. Inst., Am. Econs. Assn., Soc. for Computer Simulation, Am. Acad. Polit. and Social Sci., Prodn. and Ops. Mgmt. Assn., Indsl. Rels. Rsch. Assn., Beta Gamma Sigma. Home: 5149 Gadwall Cir Stockton CA 95207-5331 Office: U of the Pacific Eberhardt Sch Bus Stockton CA 95211

BALLOU, NATHAN ELMER, chemist; b. Rochester, Minn., Sept. 28, 1919; s. Sidney Vaughan and Josephine (Elmer) B.; m. Elaine Louise Chapman, Dec. 28, 1973; children: Robert K., Douglas P. BS, Duluth State Tchrs. Coll., 1941; MS, U. Ill., 1942; PhD, U. Chgo., 1947. Rsch. scientist Manhattan Project, Oak Ridge, Tenn., 1942-46; rsch. assoc. U. Calif., Berkeley, 1947-48; head nuclear chemistry br. Naval Radiol. Def. Lab., San Francisco, 1948-69; chief chemistry dept. Belgian Nuclear Energie Ctr., Mol, 1959-61; mgr. analytical and nuclear rsch. sect. Battelle-Northwest, Richland, Wash., 1969-87; scientist Battelle-Northwest, Richland, 1987—. Contbr. numerous articles to profl. jours. Fellow NAS, 1946-47; recipient Superior Svc. award USN, 1966. Mem. NAS (subcom. Radiochemistry chmn. 1962-66, Nat. Rsch. Coun., fellow 1946-47), Am. Chem. Soc. (treas. Nuclear Chemistry and Tech. divsn. 1969—, Nuclear Sci. com. 1962-66). Office: Battelle-Northwest PO Box 999 Richland WA 99352-0999

BALOIAN, EDWARD, food products executive; b. 1921. With Charles Baloian Co., Fresno, Calif., 1946-86; v.p. Balo Packing Co., Inc., Fresno, 1978—; chmn. bd. dirs. Baloian Packing Co., Fresno, 1985—. Office: Baloian Packing Co 324 N Fruit Ave Fresno CA 93706-1420*

BALOIAN, TIMOTHY, food products executive; b. 1952; s. Edward Baloian. Pres. Balo Packing Co., Fresno, 1978—, Baloian Packing Co., Fresno, 1985—. Office: Baloian Packing Co Inc 324 N Fruit Ave Fresno CA 93706-1420*

BALTAKE, JOE, film critic; b. Camden, N.J., Sept. 16; s. Joseph John and Rose Clara (Bearint) B.; m. Susan Shapiro Hale. BA, Rutgers U., 1967. Film critic Gannett Newspapers (suburban), 1969, Phila. Daily News, 1970-86; movie editor Inside Phila., 1986—; film critic The Sacramento Bee, 1987—; leader criticism workshop Phila. Writer's Conf., 1977-79; film critic. Contbg. editor: Screen World, 1973-87 ; author: The Films of Jack Lemmon, 1977, updated, 1986; contbr. articles to Films in Rev., 1969—, broadcast criticism for Prism Cable TV, 1985; cons. Jack Lemmon: American Film Institute Life Achievement Award, 1987, Jack Lemmon: A Life in the Movies, 1990. Recipient Motion Picture Preview Group award for criticism, 1986, citation Phila. Mag., 1985. Mem. Nat. Soc. Film Critics. Office: Sacramento Bee 2100 Q St Sacramento CA 95816-6816

BALUNI, ALICE, electronics company executive; b. Cairo, Dec. 10, 1945; came to U.S., 1975; s. Arthur Z. and Angele Baluni. M Physics of Semicondrs., Moscow State U., 1969; M Engring. Mgmt., Santa Clara U., 1981. Lectr. solid state physics Yerevan (Armenia) State U., 1969-75; engring. supr. Intel Co., Santa Clara, Calif., 1975-81; sr. design engr. Synertek Co., Santa Clara, 1981-82; product engring. mgr. Syngnetics Co., Sunnyvale, Calif., 1982-85; v.p. reliability and quality assurance Zilog Co., Campbell, Calif., 1985—. Mem. IEEE, Am. Soc. for Quality Control. Republican. Office: Zilog Co 210 Hacienda Ave Campbell CA 95008

BALZA, JOHN JOSEPH, research and development manager; b. Green Bay, Wis., Jan. 31, 1949; s. G. Tony and Grace M. (Angst) B.; m. Mary Margaret Grosche, July 17, 1976; children: Laura Marie, Mary Elizabeth. BS in Elec. Engring., Ill. Inst. Tech., 1971; MS in Elec. Engring., U. Wis., 1972; MBA, Colo. State U., 1985. Engr. Hewlett Packard Co., Loveland, Colo., 1972-76; project mgr. Hewlett Packard Co., Fort Collins, Colo., 1976-83; R&D section mgr. Hewlett Packard Co., Fort Collins, 1983-89, R&D lab. mgr., 1989-93; quality mgr., 1993—. Democrat. Roman Catholic. Home: 713 Hinsdale Dr Fort Collins CO 80526-3917

BALZER, ANTHONY JAMES, academy director; b. San Francisco, Dec. 24, 1945; s. Jospeh Francis and Ingerlise Merete (Molich) B.; m. Dianne Marie Simionato, Oct. 12, 1968; children; Christina Marie, Sanda Luisa, Eric Anthony. BA, San Francisco State U., 1968; MPA, Golden Gate U., 1974, PhD in Pub. Adminstrn., 1982. Cert. secondary tchr., Calif. With San Francisco Police Dept., 1968—; dir. San Francisco Police Acad., 1968—; adj. prof. Golden Gate U., San Francisco, 1982—, St. Mary's Coll., Moraga, 1993—; dir. security San Francisco Gen. Hosp., 1982, 84. Mem. Am. Soc. Pub. Adminstrn., Internat. Polic Assn., UN Assn. San Francisco, San Francisco Polic Officers Assn. Republican. Roman Catholic. Office: San Francisco Police Acad 350 Amber Dr San Francisco CA 94131-1630

BANAS, EMIL MIKE, physicist, educator; b. East Chicago, Ind., Dec. 5, 1921; s. John J. and Rose M. (Valcicak) B.; m. Margaret Fagyas, Oct. 9, 1948; children: Mary K., Barbara A. Student, Ill. Benedictine Coll., 1940-43; BA (U.S. Rubber fellow), U. Notre Dame, 1954, PhD, 1955. Instr. math. and physics Ill. Benedictine Coll., Lisle, 1946-48, adj. faculty mem., 1971-82, trustee, 1959-61; with Civil Svc., State of Ind., Hammond, 1948-50; lectr. physics Purdue U., Hammond, 1955-60; staff rsch. physicist Amoco Corp., Naperville, Ill., 1955-82; cons., 1983—. Served with USNR, 1943-46. Mem. Ill. Benedictine Coll. Alumni Assn. (Alumnus of Yr., 1965, pres. 1959-60), U. Notre Dame Alumni Assn. (sec. grad. physics alumni), Sigma Pi Sigma. Roman Catholic. Clubs: Soc. of Procopians. Contbr. articles to sci. jours. Home: SE 1426 Fancy-Free Dr Pullman WA 99163

BANAUGH, ROBERT PETER, computer science educator; b. L.A., Oct. 27, 1922; s. Rudolph Otto and Elizabeth (Mantz) B.; m. Catherine Haun, July 6, 1946; children: Elizabeth Anne, Catherine Marie, Robert George, Mary Louise, Laura Jean, Marjorie Theresa, John Gerard, Peter Andrew. AA, Pasadena Jr. Coll., 1942; BA, U. Calif., Berkeley, 1943, MA, 1952, PhD, 1962. Secondary sch. tchr. Richmond (Calif.) Jr. High Sch., 1947-50; instr. math. U. Calif., Berkeley, 1949-72, vis. prof., 1975-76; prof. computer sci. U. Mont., Missoula, 1964-75, 76—; vis. prof. U. Wollongong, Australia, 1985; physicist Boeing Aircraft, Seattle, 1966-72; applied mechanics scientist Appled Theory, Los Angeles, 1968-75; computer scientist U.S. Forest Service, Missoula, 1968-71, engr., 1972—. Contbr. numerous articles to profl. jours. Served to 1st lt. USAAF, 1943-45. Home: 9401

Upper Miller Creek Rd Missoula MT 59803 Office: U Mont Dept Computer Sci Missoula MT 59812

BANCEL, MARILYN, fund raising management consultant; b. Glen Ridge, N.J., June 15, 1947; d. Paul and Joan Marie (Spangler) B.; m. Rik Myslewski, Nov. 20, 1983; children: Carolyn, Roxanne. BA in English with distinction, Ind. U., 1969. Cert. fund raising exec. Ptnr. The Sultan's Shirt Tail, Gemlik, Turkey, 1969-72; prodn. mgr. High Country Co., San Francisco, 1973-74; pub. Bay Arts Rev., Berkeley, Calif., 1976-79; dir. devel. Oakland (Calif.) Symphony Orch., 1979-81; assoc. dir. devel. Exploratorium, San Francisco, 1981-86, dir. devel., 1986-91; prin. Fund Devel. Counsel, San Francisco, 1991-93; v.p. The Oram Group, Inc., San Francisco, 1993—; mem. fin. com. Synergy Sch., San Francisco, 1992—, co-chair endowment com., 1993—; adj. faculty U. San Francisco, 1993—. Fellow U. Strasberg, France, 1968. Mem. Nat. Soc. Fund Raising Execs. (bd. mem. Golden Gate chpt.), Devel. Execs. Roundtable, Phi Beta Kappa. Democrat. Office: The Oram Group 44 Page St Ste 604C San Francisco CA 94102-5986

BANDT, PAUL DOUGLAS, physician; b. Milbank, S.D., June 22, 1938; s. Lester Herman and Edna Louella (Sogn) B.; m. Mary King, Aug. 26, 1962 (div. Feb. 1974); children: Douglas, Peggy; m. Inara Irene Von Rostas, Apr. 1, 1974; 1 child, Jennifer. BS in Edn. with distinction, U. Minn., 1960, BS in Medicine, 1966, D in Medicine, 1966. Diplomate Am. Bd. Diagnostic Radiology, Am. Bd. Nuclear Medicine. Intern U.S. Pub. Health Svc., San Francisco, 1966-68; physician U.S. Pub. Health Svc., Las Vegas, 1968-69; resident Stanford U., Palo Alto, Calif., 1969-72; physician Desert Radiologists, Las Vegas, 1972—; vice chief med. staff Desert Springs Hosp., Las Vegas; immediate past chief of staff U. Med. Ctr. So. Nev., Las Vegas. Contbr. articles on diagnostic radiology to profl. jours. With USPHS, 1966-69. Mem. AMA, Am. Coll. Radiology, Am. Coll. Nuclear Medicine, Clark Med. Soc. Office: Desert Radiologists 2020 Palomino Ln Las Vegas NV 89106-4812

BANGHAM, ROBERT ARTHUR, orthotist; b. San Antonio, Sept. 12, 1942; s. Robert Dave and Marguerite C. (Wyckoff) B. Student, Northwestern U., 1965, 71, 76, NYU, 1969, Washtenaw C.C., Ann Arbor, Mich., 1971; misc. courses in field, various hosps., and med. orgns. Cert. orthotist; ordained to ministry Jehovah's Witness Ch., 1957. Orthotic resident J. R. Reets, Ann Arbor, Mich., 1960-65; orthotist Dreher-Jouett, Inc., Chgo., 1965-68; cert. orthotist U. Mich., 1968-75, Wright & Filipis, Inc., Alpena, Mich., 1975-78; mgr., orthotist Hittenbergers, Concord, Calif., 1978-81, 88-90; mgr., cert. orthotist x, Oakland, Calif., 1981-90, Hittenbergers, Concord, Oakland, 1988-90; mktg. mgr. western region Nat. Orthotic Labs., Winter Haven, Fla., 1990; CEO Mobile Orthotic & Prosthetic Assocs., Antioch, Calif., 1990-94, Oakland, Calif., 1995—; orthotics cons. Benchmark Med. Group, 1992—; cons. Health Careers Profl. Assn., Calif. State Dept. Edn., 1992—; presenter papers in field to profl. assns., hosps., govtl. bodies. Contbr. articles to profl. jours. Fellow Am. Back Soc. (internat. profl. rels. com., co-chair orthotics divsn., vice chair orthotics com., AAOP liaison rep. to ABS), Am. Acad. Neurological and Orthopedic Surgeons (head dept. orthotics); mem. Am. Prosthetic Assn., Am. Acad. Orthotics and Prosthetists (nat. dir. 1988-91, pres. Calif. chpt. 1986-87, chpt. dir. 1989-91, sci. com. chmn., societies com., charter chmn. Spinal Orthotics Soc. 1991, 92, sec. lower extremity orthotics soc., bd. dirs. No. Calif. chpt., past pres. No. Calif. chpt., rep. Calif. coalition Allied Health Profls. No. Calif. chpt., co-chmn. sci. edn. com. No. Calif. chpt.), Am. Orthotics and Prosthetics Assn. (bd. dirs., chair NSF program), Internat. Soc. Orthotists and Prosthetists, Calif. Coalition Allied Health Professions (pres. 1989-90). Home and Office: Mobile O & P Assocs PO Box 19600 Oakland CA 94619-0600

BANGS, CATE (CATHRYN MARGARET BANGS), film production designer, interior designer; b. Tacoma, Mar. 16, 1951; d. Henry Horan and Belva Virginia (Grandstaff) B.; m. Steve Bangs, Nov. 1, 1986. Student, Hammersmith Coll Art and Bldg., London, 1971; BA cum laude, Pitzer Coll., 1973; MFA, NYU, 1978. Owner Flying Pencil Design, Hollywood Hills, Calif., 1981—. Prodn. designer: Lucky Day, 1990, (TV series) My So Called Life, 1994, (TV series and pilot) Fudge-a-Mania, 1994. Bd. dirs. Hollywood Heights Assn., 1985-87, Cahuenga Pass Property Owners Assn.,1990; 1st v.p. Friends of the Highland-Camrose Bungalow Village, 1985—. Recipient Dramalogue Critics award, 1983. Mem. Soc. Motion Picture and TV Art Dirs., Set Designers and Model Makers (cert., exec. bd. 1980—, v.p. 1989-91, pres. 1991—), United Scenic Artists. Democrat. Buddhist. Home: Angel Haven 3180 Oakshire Dr Hollywood CA 90068-1743 Office: 3208 Cahuenga Blvd W # 121 Los Angeles CA 90068-1369

BANGS, JOHN WESLEY, III, law enforcement administrator; b. Phila., Dec. 26, 1941; s. John Wesley Jr. and Sarah Emily (Morcom) B.; m. Donna Louise McClanahan, June 1, 1963; children: Louis M., Terry M., John W. IV. AA summa cum laude, E. Los Angeles Coll., 1976. Calif. Commn. on Peace Officer Standards and Training: Basic, Intermediate, Advanced, Supervisory, Mgmt. Police officer Los Angeles Police Dept., 1964-70, sgt., 1970-74, lt., 1974-84; chief spl. officer I L.A. Dept. Airports Police, 1988—; lectr. U. So. Calif., 1978-79. Author: Narcotics Overview, 1983, Psychological Evaluation for Police Candidates, 1969. Cub master Cub Scouts Am., Ontario, Calif., 1968; scout master Boy Scouts Am., Ontario, 1971; explorer leader Explorer Scouts Am., Los Angeles, 1976; mem. Greater Los Angeles Scouting Council, 1976. Sgt. U.S. Army, 1959-62. Mem. Calif. Peace Officers Assn., Calif. Narcotics Officers, Los Angeles Police Protective League, Los Angeles Police Relief Assn., Lions Internat. Republican. Episcopalian. Office: Los Angeles Airport Police 1 World Way Los Angeles CA 90045-5803

BANGSUND, EDWARD LEE, aerospace company executive; b. Two Harbors, Minn., July 16, 1935; s. Ilo Henry and Hildur Margaret (Holter) B.; m. Caryl Ann Billingsley, Oct. 10, 1956; children: Julie Ann, Trina Lee, John Kirk, Edward Eric. BME, U. Wash., 1959. With Boeing Co., 1956-71; engr. Apollo program Boeing Co., Cape Kennedy, Fla., 1967-69, Houston, 1969-71; mgr. space vehicle design Space Systems div. Boeing Aerospace, Seattle, 1971-76, mgr. Inertial Upper Stage Futures, 1976-85, mgr. space transp., 1985-87, dir. strategic planning, 1987-90, dir. space mktg., 1990-95; pres., CEO BCA Enterprises, 1995—. Contbr. articles to profl. publs.; patentee in field. Pres. Springbrook Parents Adv. Com., 1972-75; chmn. Citizens Budget Rev. Com., 1973-75, 76-78, Citizens Facility Planning Com., 1977-78, Citizens for Kent (Wash.) Schs. Levy, 1974, 76; bd. dirs. Kent Youth Ctr., 1980-83; pres. Kent Sch. Bd., 1978-84. Named to Apollo-Saturn Roll of Honor, NASA, 1969; recipient Golden Acorn award Wash. Congress PTA, 1977, Vol. of Yr. award Kent Sch. Dist., 1977, 78. Fellow AIAA (assoc., mem. space systems tech. com. 1985-87, dep. dir. region VI 1986-89, chmn. space transp. tech. com. 1987-90, pub. policy com. 1989-94); mem. Internat. Acad. Astronautics, Internat. Astronautical Fedn. (chmn. space transp. exec. com. 1991-94), Nat. Space Found., Aerospace Industries Assn. (mem. space com. 1987-94, chmn. 1990-94), Space Bus. Roundtable (pres. Seattle chpt., bd. dirs. 1988-95), Boeing Mgmt. Assn. (vice chmn. 1990-91, chmn. 1993-94). Republican. Lutheran. Home and Office: 9441 S 202d St Kent WA 98031-1421

BANISTER, JAMES HENRY, JR., manufacturing company executive, consultant; b. Springfield, Mo., June 18, 1930; s. James Henry and Frances Kellond (Williams) B.; m. Sara Lee Cinegran, Mar. 27, 1933; children: Jeffrey, James, Mark, Robert, Douglas. SB in Mgmt., MIT, 1951. Mgr. contract adminstrn. SRI Internat., Menlo Park, Calif., 1953-64; contracts mgr. Physics Internat., San Leandro, Calif., 1964-67, v.p. adminstrn., 1967-70; pres. Cintra, Inc., Sunnyvale, Calif., 1970-71; sr. v.p. fin. and adminstrn. Physics Internat., San Leandro, 1972-87; pres. MSI, Chantilly, Va., 1987-89; cons. in mgmt. Alamo, Calif., 1989-93; pres. Kinetic Ceramics Inc., Hayward, Calif., 1993—; bd. dirs. JMAR Industries, San Diego, Pacific Precision Labs., Chatsworth, Calif. 1st lt. USAF, 1951-53. Republican. Home: 721 Fair Oaks Dr Alamo CA 94507-1457 Office: Kinetic Ceramics 26242 Industrial Blvd Hayward CA 94545-2922

BANK, MILTON HAROLD, II, aviation safety and aeronautical engineering educator; b. Brockton, Mass., Aug. 11, 1935; s. Milton Harold and Fern Elaine (Richey) B.; m. Linda Hollis, Apr. 12, 1958; children—Baynes W., Milton H. B.S., U.S. Naval Acad., 1957; B.S. in Aero. Engring., Naval Postgrad. Sch., 1964; Aero. Engr., Stanford U., 1967; M.S., Ga. Tech., 1970, Ph.D., 1971. Registered profl. engr., Calif. Commd. ensign U.S. Navy, 1957, advanced through grades to lt. comdr., 1965; ret. 1968; assoc. prof. aviation safety and aero. engring. Naval Postgrad. Sch., Monterey, Calif., 1971—; cons. automobile accident reconstructionist. Decorated Air Medal with gold stars (2). Mem. AIAA, Soc. Automotive Engrs., U.S. Fencing Coaches Assn., Soc. Exptl. Stress Analysis, Internat. Assn. Accident Reconstrn. Specialists. Presbyterian. Office: Naval Postgrad Sch Code # 034 Bt Monterey CA 93943

BANKOFF, PETER ROSNER, anesthesiologist; b. Michigan City, Ind., Apr. 18, 1951; s. Milton Lewis and Sylvia (Rosner) B.; m. Mary Patrice Norman, Aug. 18, 1974; children: Amy Elizabeth, Michael Jacob, Benjamin Eric. MusB cum laude, Ind. U., 1974, BA in Chemistry, 1977, MD, 1981. Diplomate Am. Bd. Anesthesiology. Intern Good Samaritan Hosp., Phoenix, 1981-82; resident Maricopa Med. Ctr., Phoenix, 1982-84; anesthesiologist Cigna Healthplan of Ariz., Phoenix, 1984-85, Med. Ctr. Anesthesiologists, Phoenix, 1985-92, Park Ctrl. Anesthesiologists, Phoenix, 1992—; mem. anesthesia com. Good Samaritan Regional Med. Ctr., Phoenix, 1988-92, Phoenix Children's Hosp., Phoenix, 1990, 92, 94. Founding mem. Physicians for Phoenix (Ariz.) Symphony, 1988—; com. precinctman Rep. Party, Phoenix, 1994; bd. dirs. Intgrochem (Mich.) Ctr. for the Arts Alumni Orgn., 1995-96. Mem. AMA, Am. Soc. Anesthesiologists, Internat. Anesthesia Rsch. Soc., Soc. for Ambulatory Anesthesia. Home: 5201 E Mountain View Rd Paradise Valley AZ 85253

BANKS, CHERRY ANN MCGEE, education educator; b. Benton Harbor, Mich., Oct. 11, 1945; d. Kelly and Geneva (Smith) McGee; m. James A. Banks, Feb. 15, 1969; children: Angela Marie, Patricia Ann. BS, Mich. State U., 1968; MA, Seattle U., 1977, EdD, 1991. Tchr. Benton Harbor Pub. Sch., 1968; staff assoc. Citizens Edn. Ctr. N.W., Seattle, 1984-85; edn. specialist Seattle Pub. Schs., Seattle, 1985-87; pres. Edn. Material and Svcs. Ctr., Edmonds, Wash., 1987—; asst. prof. edn. U. Wash., Bothell, 1992—; cons. Jackson (Miss.) Pub. Schs., 1988, Seattle Pub. Schs., 1988-90, Little Rock Pub. Schs., 1989, Scott Foreman Pub. Co., Glenview, Ill., 1992—; vis. asst. prof. Seattle U., 1991-92. Co-author: March Toward Freedom, 1978; co-editor: Multicultural Education: Issues and Perspectives, 1989, rev. edit., 1993; assoc. editor Handbook of Rsch. on Multicultural Edn.; contbr. chpts. to books. Mem. Jack and Jill Am., Seattle, 1978-94, First AME Headstart Bd., Seattle, 1981-83; trustee Shoreline C.C., Seattle, 1983—; bd. dirs. King County Campfire, Seattle, 1985-88. Recipient Outstanding Commitment and Leadership of C.C. award Western Region Nat. Coun. on Black Am. Affairs, 1989. Mem. ASCD, Nat. Coun. for Social Studies Programs Com. (vice chairperson Carter G. Woodson Book award com. 1991-92, chair person 1992-93, mem. nominating com.), Am. Rsch. Assn., Phi Delta Kappa (founding, Seattle U. chpt.). Office: U Wash Edn Program 22011 26th Ave SE Bothell WA 98021-4900

BANKS, ERNEST (ERNIE BANKS), moving company executive, retired professional baseball player; b. Dallas, Jan. 31, 1931; s. Eddie B.; m. Eloyee Ector, Apr. 6, 1953. Student, Northwestern U. Baseball player Kansas City Monarchs (Negro Am. League), 1950-51, 53; baseball player Chgo. Cubs, 1953-71, mgr. group sales, to 1982; with New World Van Lines, Garden Grove, Calif., 1984—; formerly co-owner, v.p. Bob Nelson-Ernie Banks Ford, Inc., Chgo.; with Associated Films Promotions, L.A., 1982-84. Author: (with Jim Enright) Mr. Cub. Past mem. bd. Chgo. Transit Authority; active Boy Scouts Am., YMCA. Served with AUS, 1951-53, Europe. Named most valuable player Nat. League, 1958, 59; recipient awards from Fans, 1969, awards from Press Club, 1969, awards from Jr. C. of C., 1971; inducted into Tex. Sports Hall Fame, 1971, Baseball Hall of Fame, 1977; mem. Nat. League All-Star Team, 1957-70; hold major league record for most career grand slam home runs. Office: New World Van Lines 14322 Commerce Dr Garden Grove CA 92643-4946*

BANKS, JAMES ALBERT, educational research director, educator; b. Marianna, Ark., Sept. 24, 1941; s. Matthew and Lula (Holt) B.; m. Cherry Ann McGee, Feb. 15, 1969; children: Angela Marie, Patricia Ann. A.A., Chgo. City Coll., 1963; B.E., Chgo. State U., 1964; M.A. (NDEA fellow 1966-69), Mich. State U., 1967, Ph.D., 1969; LHD, Bank St. Coll. Edn., 1993. Tchr. elementary sch. Joliet, Ill., 1965, Francis W. Parker Sch., Chgo., 1965-66; asst. prof. edn. U. Wash., Seattle, 1969-71; assoc. prof. U. Wash., 1971-73, prof., 1973—, chmn. curriculum and instrn., 1982-87; dir. Ctr. for Multicultural Edn., 1991—; vis. prof. edn. U. Mich., 1975, Monash U., Australia, 1985, U. Warwick, Eng., 1988, U. Minn., 1991; vis. lectr. U. Southampton, Eng., 1989, Harry F. and Alva K. Ganders disting. lectr. Syracuse U., 1989; disting. scholar lectr. Kent State U., 1978, U. Ariz., 1979, Ind. U., 1983; vis. scholar Brit. Acad., 1983; com. examiners Ednl. Testing Svc., 1974-77; nat. adv. coun. on ethnic heritage studies, U.S. Office Edn., 1975-78; com. on fed. role in ednl. rsch. NAS, 1991-92, mem. com. on developing a rsch. agenda on edn. of ltd. proficient and bilingual students, 1995—. Author: Teaching Strategies for Ethnic Studies, 1975, 5th edit., 1991, Teaching Strategies for the Social Studies, 1973, 4th edit., 1990, Teaching the Black Experience, 1970, Multiethnic Education: Practices and Promises, 1977, An Introduction to Multicultural Education, 1994, (with Cherry Ann Banks) March Toward Freedom: A History of Black Americans, 1970, 2d edit., 1974rev. 2nd edit., 1978, Multiethnic Education: Theory and Practice, 1981, 3rd edit., 1994, (with others) Curriculum Guidlines for Multicultural Education, 1976, rev. edit., 1992, We Americans: Our History and People, 2 vols., 1982; contbg. author Internat. Ency. of Edn., 1985, Handbook of Research on Teacher Education, 1990, Handbook of Research on Social Studies Teaching and Learning, 1991, Encyclopedia of Ednl. Rsch., 1992, Handbook of Research on the Education of Young Children, 1993, Review of Research in Education, vol. 19, 1993; editor: Black Self Concept, 1972, Teaching Ethnic Studies: Concepts and Strategies, 1973, (with William W. Joyce) Teaching Social Studies to Culturally Different Children, 1971, Teaching the Language Arts to Culturally Different Children, 1971, Education in the 80's: Multiethnic Education, 1981, (with James Lynch) Multicultural Education in Western Societies, 1986, (with C. Banks) Multicultural Education: Issues and Perspectives, 1989, 2d edit., 1993, Handbook of Research on Multicultural Education, 1995; editorial bd. Jour. of Tch. Edn., 1985-89, Coun. Interracial Books for Children Bull., 1982-92, Urban Edn., 1991—; contbr. articles to profl. jours. Recipient Outstanding Young Man award Wash. State Jaycees, 1975, Outstanding Service in Edn. award Seattle U. Black Student Union, 1985; Spencer fellow Nat. Acad. Edn., 1973-76; Kellogg fellow, 1980-83; Rockefeller Found. fellow, 1980. Mem. ASCD (bd dirs. 1976-79, Disting. lectr. 1986, Disting. scholar, lectr. 1994), Nat. Coun. Social Studies (bd. dirs. 1973-74, 80-85, pres. 1982), Internat. Assn. Intercultural Edn. (editl. bd.), Social Sci. Edn. Consortium (bd. dirs. 1976-79), Am. Ednl. Rsch. Assn. (Disting. scholar/rschr. on minority edn. 1986, Rsch. Review award 1994, com. on role and status of minorities in edn. rsch. 1992-94, mem. publs. com. 1995—), Phi Delta Kappa, Phi Kappa Phi, Golden Kay Nat. Honor Soc. Office: U Wash 110 Miller Hall Box 353600 Seattle WA 98195-3600

BANKSTON, MARY GAY, retired gas industry executive; b. Lakeland, Fla., Nov. 27, 1952; d. Rex Lane and Frances (Williams) Gay; m. Clyde Perry Bankston, June 15, 1974. BA in Econs., Agnes Scott Coll., 1974. Asst. v.p. Citizens and So. Nat. Bank, Atlanta, 1974-79; v.p., area mgr. Lloyds Bank Calif., L.A., 1979-85; sr. v.p., dir. mktg. and planning First Interstate Bank of Calif., L.A., 1985-91; v.p. planning So. Calif. Gas Co., L.A., 1991-94. Democrat.

BANNER, BOB, television producer, director; b. Ennis, Tex., Aug. 15, 1921; s. Robert James and Viola (Culbertson) B.; m. Alice Jane Baird, Jan. 14, 1946; children—Baird Allen, Robert James, Charles Moore. B.B.A., So. Meth. U., 1943; M.A., Northwestern U., 1948. Pres. Bob Banner Assocs.; vis. prof. So. Meth. U. Dir. Garroway-at-Large, NBC-TV; producer, dir. Fred Waring Show, CBS-TV; dir. Omnibus; TV producer, pres., Bob Banner Assos.; TV shows include (series) The Uptown Comedy Club, It's Showtime at the Apollo, Garroway At Large, Fred Waring Show, Don Ho, Omnibus, Jr. Almost Anything Goes, Almost Anything Goes, Candid Camera, Carol Burnett Show, Garry Moore Show, Dinah Shore Chevy Show, Kraft Summer Music Hall, Solid Gold, Star Search, It's Showtime at the Apollo, The Uptown Comedy Club; (spls.) Perry Como Holiday Spls., Carnegie Hall Salutes Jack Benny, Julie & Carol at Carnegie Hall, Ford Motor Co.'s 75th Ann., Am. West of John Ford, A Spl. Sesame St. Christmas; spls. starring Bob Hope, Julie Andrews, Andy Williams; (movies) My Sweet Charlie, My Husband is Missing, Warning Shot, Journey from Darkness, The Darker Side of Terror, If Things were Different, Yes Virginia There Is A Santa Claus, 1991, Crash Landing, 1992, With Murder In Mind, 1992, The Sea Wolf, 1993. Recipient 15 Emmy awards, 11 Christopher awards, 3 Peabody awards. Mem. Acad. of TV Arts and Scis. Presbyn. Office: Bob Banner Assocs 1875 Century Park E Ste 2250 Los Angeles CA 90067-2523

BANSAK, STEPHEN A., JR., investment banker, financial consultant; b. Bridgeport, Conn., Sept. 19, 1939; s. Stephen A. and Genevieve Bansak; m. Susan Jean Dizon, July 20, 1984; children: Cynthia A., Thomas S., Stephen A. III, Kirk C. BS, Yale U., 1961; MBA, U. Pa., 1968. With Kidder, Peabody & Co., Inc., N.Y.C., 1968-89, v.p., 1971-75, co-mgr. dept. corp. fin., 1975-84; vice chmn. Kidder, Peabody Internat., 1984—; bd. dirs. Kidder Peabody P.R., KP Realty Advisers; sr. cons. Concord Capital Mgmt. Internat., 1990—, Bentley Assocs., 1990-92; vice chmn. Myers, Craig, Vallone, Francois, Inc., 1992-93; sr. advisor Norcross Securities, Inc., Universal Tech. Inst., Buenavenjura Filamor Echauz (Manila), Universal Tech. Inst.; vis. lectr. Wharton Grad. Sch., U. Pa., 1989; bd. dirs. Motay Electronics, Inc., Nephrogenix, Inc., Fibrin, Inc., Square Industries, Inc., The Finisterre Fund, Inc. Past trustee, v.p. Rumson (N.J.) Country Day Sch. 1t. USN, 1962-66, Vietnam. Mem. Securities Industry Assn. (chmn. corp. fin. com., rule 415 com.), Am. Stock Exchange (official), Philippine-Am. C. of C. (exec. com.), U.S.-Asia Inst. (past bd. dirs.), India House (past pres. Broad St. club), Navesink Country Club, Yale Club (N.Y.C.), Troon Golf and Country Club (Ariz.). Office: Missouri Falls Bldg 645 E Missouri Ave Phoenix AZ 85012-1369

BANUELOS, BETTY LOU, rehabilitation nurse; b. Vandergrift, Pa., Nov. 28, 1930; d. Archibald and Bella Irene (George) McKinney; m. Raul, Nov. 1, 1986; children: Patrice, Michael. Diploma, U. Pitts., 1951; cert., Loma Linda U., 1960. RN, Calif.; cert. chem. dependency nurse. Cons. occupational health svcs. Bd. Registered Nurses, 1984—; lectr., cons. in field. Recipient Scholarship U. Pitts. Mem. Dirs. of Nursing, Calif. Assn. Nurses in Substance Abuse. Home and Office: 15 Oak Spring Ln Laguna Beach CA 92656-2980

BAÑUELOS, ROBERT ALEXANDER, insurance company executive; b. L.A., Nov. 3, 1940; s. Robert G. and Juliette P Bañuelos; m. Mary Helen Fuentes, May 27, 1961; children: Laura, Mark, Steven, Cathryn. BSBA, Pacific Christian Coll., 1976. With Transamerica Occidental Life Ins., L.A., 1960-91, claims examiner, 1960-65, supr., asst. mgr. group life and disability claims, 1965-72, dept. mgr., consumer credit benefits officer, 1972-80, dept. mgr., group health benefits officer, 1980-82, subdivsn. mgr., asst. v.p. group health benefits, 1982-84, divsn. mgr., asst. v.p. group health benefits, 1984-85, divsn. mgr., 2d v.p. credit ins. adminstrn., 1985-91; asst. v.p. credit ins. claims Balboa Life and Casualty, Irvine, Calif., 1991—; Participant seminars and courses in field. Lt. col. USAR, 1959-90; with Calif. Army N.G. Mem. Orange County Claims Assn. (exec. com. 1992, pres. 1994), L.A. Life and Accident Claims Assn. (pres. 1990), Western Claims Conf. (chmn. conf. 1984, 86, 94, chmn. exec. com. 1987-90, exec. com. 1991—), Internat. Claims Assn. (assoc. life and health claims, group claims and program coms., now West Coast Rep. to Regional Claims Assn., mem. nominating com.), HIAA (Transamerica Occidental Rep., also assignments to HIAA Calif. State Coun.), Los Angeles County Med. Assn. (peer rev. mtgs.). Office: Balboa Life and Casualty 17770 Cartwright Rd Irvine CA 92714-5850

BAO, JOSEPH YUE-SE, orthopaedist, microsurgeon, educator; b. Shanghai, China, Feb. 20, 1937; s. George Zheng-En and Margaret Zhi-De (Wang) B.; m. Delia Way, Mar. 30, 1963; children: Alice, Angela. MD, Shanghai First Med. Coll., 1958. Intern affiliated hosps. Shanghai First. Med. Coll.; resident Shanghai Sixth People's Hosp., orthopaedist, 1958-78, orthopaedist-in-charge, 1978-79, vice chief orthopaedist, 1979-84; rsch. assoc. orthopaedic hosp. U. So. Calif., L.A., 1985-90, 94—, vis. clin. assoc. prof. dept. orthopaedics, 1986-89; coord. microvascular svcs. Orthopaedic Hosp., L.A., 1989-91; clin. assoc. prof. dept. orthopaedics U. So. Calif., L.A., 1989—; attending physician Los Angeles County and U. So. Calif. Med. Ctr., L.A., 1986, 90—; cons. Rancho Los Amigos Med. Ctr., Downey, Calif., 1986. Contbr. articles to profl. jours., chpts. to books. Mem. Internat. Microsurgical Soc., Am. Soc. for Reconstructive Microsurgery, Orthopaedic Rsch. Soc. Home: 17436 Terry Lyn Ln Cerritos CA 90703-8522 Office: LA County Med Ctr Dept Orthopaedics 1200 N State St Los Angeles CA 90033-4526

BARAB, MARVIN, financial consultant; b. Wilmington, Del., July 16, 1927; s. Jacob and Minnie (Press) B.; m. Gertrude Klein, June 13, 1951; children: Jordan, Neal, Caryn. BS with distinction, Ind. U., 1947, MBA, 1951. Dir. mktg. Edward Weiss & Co., Chgo., 1951-56; dir. bus. rsch. Parker Pen Co., Janesville, Wis., 1956-59; dir. mktg. rsch. packaging and graphics Mattel Inc., Hawthorne, Calif., 1959-65; pres. Barcam Pub. Co., Rolling Hills Estates, Calif., 1959-70, Rajo Publs., Rolling Hills Estates, 1967-70, So. Calif. Coll. Med. & Dental Careers, Anaheim, 1970-81, Barbrook, Inc., Rolling Hills Estates, 1981—; cons. Marvin Barab & Assocs., Rolling Hills Estates, Calif., 1981—. Editor: Rand McNally Camping Guide, 1967-70; contbr. articles to various publs., 1982-87. Treas. Harbor Free Clinic, 1990-92; bd. dirs. So. Bay Contemporary Art Mus., 1993-94, sec., 1994. Mem. Nat. Assn. Trade and Tech. Schs. (hon. life, sec. 1977-79, pres. 1979-81, bd. dirs.), Calif. Assn. Paramed. Schs. (pres. 1973-77). Office: Barbrook Inc 904 Silver Spur Rd Ste 110 Palos Verdes Peninsula CA 90274-3800

BARAD, JILL ELIKANN, toy company executive; b. N.Y.C., May 23, 1951; d. Lawrence Stanley and Corinne (Schuman) Elikann; m. Thomas Kenneth Barad, Jan., 28, 1979; children: Alexander David, Justin Harris. BA English and Psychology, Queens Coll., 1973. Asst. prod. mgr. mktg. Coty Cosmetics, N.Y.C., 1976-77, prod. mgr. mktg., 1977; account exec. Wells Rich Greene Advt. Agy., L.A., 1978-79; product mgr. mktg. Mattel Toys, Inc., L.A., 1981-82, dir. mktg., 1982-83, v.p. mktg., 1983-85, sr. v.p. mktg., 1985-86, sr. v.p. product devel., from 1986, exec. v.p. product design and devel., exec. v.p. mktg. and worldwide product devel., 1988-89; pres. girls and activity toys div. Mattel Toys, Inc. (name now Mattel Inc.), L.A., 1989—; pres., bd. dirs. Mattel USA, El Segundo, Calif., 1990—; pres., COO Mattel, Inc., El Segundo, Calif., 1992—; bd. dirs. Arco Toys, Reebok Internat., Bank of Am. Bd. dirs. Town Hall of Calif.; trustee Queens Coll.; chair exec. adv. bd. Children Affected by AIDS Found. Mem. Am. Film Inst. (charter). Office: Mattel Inc 333 Continental Blvd El Segundo CA 90245-5032*

BARATZ, DAVID MICHAEL, physician; b. Chgo., Mar. 16, 1959; s. Robert Alan and Joan (Atkins) B.; m. Sharon Jacobs, Jan. 30, 1988. BA in Psychology, U. Denver, 1981; MD, U. Ariz., 1985. Diplomate Am. Bd. Internal Medicine, Am. Bd. Sleep Medicine. Resident in internal medicine U. Calif., Irvine, 1985-88; fellow in pulmonary medicine Cedars-Sinai Med. Ctr., L.A., 1988-91; pvt. practice Phoenix, 1991—; asst. dir. sleep disorders ctr. Good Samaritan Med. Ctr., Phoenix, 1991—. Fellow Am. Coll. Chest Physicians, ACP, Am. Sleep Disorders Assn. Office: Pulmonary Assocs 1112 E McDowall Rd Phoenix AZ 85006

BARBAKOW, JEFFREY, health facility administrator; b. 1944. BS, San Jose U.; MBA, U. So. Calif. With Merrill Lynch Capital Mkts. and several additional affiliates, 1972-88, MGM/UA Communications Inc., 1988-91, Donaldson, Lufkin & Jenrette Securities Corp., 1991; dir. Nat. Med. Enterprises, 1990—, chmn. bd., CEO, 1993—. Office: Nat Med Enterprises Inc PO Box 4070 Santa Monica CA 90411-4070

BARBAS, JEFFREY LAWRENCE, finance company executive; b. Detroit, Oct. 22, 1947; s. Sidney and Betty (Rosenberg) B.; m. Lynne Goodstein, Feb. 15, 1974 (div. Mar. 1990); children: Sean, Christopher. BA in Journalism, Calif. State U., Northridge, 1973. Dist. mgr. CIT Group, L.A., 1974-79; v.p., mgr. Cmty. Bank, L.A., 1979-85; v.p., gen. mgr. Mazak Corp., Gardena, Calif., 1985-91; pres. C D Financing, Inc., La Mirada, Calif., 1991—; bd. dirs. Finex, Inc., L.A.; cons. Impact Cad/Cam, Glendale, Calif.,

Fine CNC Sys., La Mirada. Author: (poem) Poem for the Living, 1991; author Fin. Forum, 1984—. Comdr. Club L.A. Rescue Mission; medallion mem. Orange (Calif.) County Rescue Mission. With mil. intelligence U.S. Army, 1965-69, Vietnam. Home: 5752 Anthony Ave Garden Grove CA 92645-2612 Office: C D Financing Inc 16820 Valley View Ave La Mirada CA 90638-5825

BARBEE, JOE ED, lawyer; b. Pharr, Tex., Feb. 27, 1934; s. Archie Allen and Concha (Leal) B.; m. Yolanda Margaret Atonna, Feb. 17, 1962; children—Cynthia M., Adam A., Walter J. BSEE, U. Ariz., 1961; JD, Western New Eng. Coll., 1973. Bar: Mass. 1973, U.S. Patent Office 1973, U.S. Ct. Appeals (fed. cir.) 1982. Engr. Gen. Electric Co., Pittsfield, Mass., 1961-73; patent atty. Fort Wayne, Ind., 1973-75, Magnavox, Fort Wayne, 1975-76, Motorola, Inc., Phoenix, 1976—. Sgt. U.S. Army, 1953-56. Recipient Outstanding Performance award U.S. Civil Svc., 1960. Mem. ABA, Am. Patent Law Assn., Am. Intellectual Property Law Assn. Republican. Methodist. Home: 7611 N Mockingbird Ln Paradise Vly AZ 85253-3126 Office: Motorola Inc 8220 E Roosevelt St # B3 Scottsdale AZ 85257-3804

BARBER, CLARENCE LYLE, economics educator; b. Wolseley, Sask., Can., May 5, 1917; s. Richard Edward and Lulu Pearl (Lyons) B.; m. Barbara Anne Patchet, May 10, 1947; children—Paul Edward, Richard Stephen, David Stuart, Alan Gordon. BA, U. Sask., 1939; MA, Clark U., 1941; postgrad., U. Minn., 1941-43, PhD, 1952; LLD (hon.), U. Guelph, 1988. With Stats. Can., 1945-48; mem. faculty McMaster U., 1948-49, U. Man., Winnipeg, Can., 1949-85; prof. econs. U. Man., 1956-85, disting. prof., 1982-85, emeritus, 1985—, head dept., 1963-72; vis. prof. Queen's U., 1954-55, McGill U., 1964-65; Commr. Royal Commn. on Farm Machinery, 1966-71; spl. adviser on nat. income Phillipines Govt., 1959-60; commr. for study welfare policy in Man., 1972; mem. Nat. Commn. on Inflation, 1979, Royal Commn. Econ. Union and Devel. Prospects for Can., 1982-85. Author: Inventories and the Business Cycle, 1958, The Theory of Fiscal Policy as Applied to a Province, 1966, (with others) Inflation and Unemployment: The Canadian Experience, 1980, Controlling Inflation: Learning from Experience in Canada, Europe and Japan, 1982, False Promises: The Failure of Conservative Economics, 1993. Served with RCAF, 1943-45. Named Officer in Order of Can., 1987; Can. Coun. Profl. Leave fellow, 1970-71. Fellow Royal Soc. Can.; mem. Canadian Assn. U. Tchrs. (pres. 1958-59), Canadian Econ. Assn. (pres. 1971-72), Am. Econ. Assn., Royal Econ. Soc., Social Sci. Research Council Can. (mem. exec. 1972-73), U. Victoria Faculty Club. Home: 766 Richmond Ave, Victoria, BC Canada V8S 3Z1

BARBER, ELIZABETH JANE WAYLAND, archeology and linguistics educator, researcher; b. Pasadena, Calif., Dec. 2, 1940; d. James Harold and Virginia Jane Wayland; m. Paul Thomas Barber, June 14, 1965. BA, Bryn Mawr (Pa.) Coll., 1962; PhD, Yale U., 1968. Rsch. assoc. Princeton (N.J.) U., 1968-69; asst. to assoc. to full prof. Occidental Coll., L.A., 1970—. Author: Archaeological Decipherment, 1974, Prehistoric Textiles, 1991, Women's Work- The First 20,000 Years, 1994. Grantee Am. Coun. Learned Soc., 1977, Edn. grant NEH, 1972-74, 1993; fellow John Simon Guggenheim Meml. Found., 1979-80. Mem. Linguistic Soc. Am., Archeol. Inst. Am., Textile Soc. Am. Office: Occidental Coll 1600 Campus Rd Los Angeles CA 90041-3384

BARBER, JOHN WILLIAM MCKENZIE, private investor; b. New Haven, Apr. 7, 1959; s. William Joseph and Sheila Mary (Marr) B.; m. Nicola Rosemary St. John, June 10, 1995. BA, Yale U., 1980. Analyst Morgan Stanley & Co., Inc., N.Y.C., 1980-83; assoc. Morgan Stanley Internat., London, 1983-84, Sydney, Australia, 1984-85; chmn. Ind. Devel. Resources Corp., N.Y.C., 1986-87; v.p. WSGP Ptnrs. L.P., L.A., 1987-92; bd. dirs. Camden Fruit Corp., L.A. Mem. Andover-Abbot Assn. So. Calif., Yale Alumni Fund (class agt. 1980—), My Friend's Place (bd. dirs.). Democrat. Presbyterian. Home: 930 20th St Apt 6 Santa Monica CA 90403-3351 Office: Camden Fruit Corp 2716 Ocean Park Blvd Ste 3088 Santa Monica CA 90405-5208

BARBER, MICHAEL J., cardiologist, educator; b. Gary, Ind., Feb. 3, 1954; s. Joseph W. and Patricia (Remsburg) B.; m. Virginia Berry, Mar. 27, 1993. AB, Wabash Coll., 1976; PhD, Loyola U., Chgo., 1980; MD, Ind. U., Indpls., 1984. Intern U. Va., Charlottesville, 1984-85, resident, 1985-87, asst. prof. of medicine, 1990-93; cardiology fellow Duke U., Durham, N.C., 1987-90; cardiologist Colo. Springs (Colo.) Cardiologists, 1993—; presenter in field. Contbr. sci. papers to profl. publs., chpts. to book Clinical Electrophysiology. Recipient Nat. Rsch. Svc. award NIH, 1989. Mem. Am. Coll. Cardiology (Young Investigator award 1982, scholar 1987), Am. Physiol. Soc., Biophys. Soc., Am. Heart Assn. (mem. basic-sci. coun.). Office: Colo Springs Cardiologists 25 E Jackson St Ste 301 Colorado Springs CO 80907-6854

BARBER, PATRICIA LOUISE, clinical specialist; b. St. Paul, Jan. 11, 1953; d. James Bernard and Margaret Mary (Neagle) B. BSN, U. Minn., 1975; cert. nurse practitioner, U. Ill., 1978. RN, Colo., Ill., Minn. Staff nurse U. Minn., Mpls., 1974-75; transplant coord. U. Ill., Chgo., 1978-90; nurse practitioner emergency rm. Denver Presbyn., 1990-92; nurse practitioner in-patient svc. cardiovascular Denver Presbyn. St. Luke's Med. Ctr., 1992-95, nurse practitioner nephrology, 1995—; cons. in field, Chgo., 1983—. Editor: Resource Manual for Transplant Coordinators, 1982. Cochmn. S/A Patient Svcs. Com., 1983-90. Mem. N.Am. Transplant Coords. Orgn. (co-chmn. 1979-90, Honors 1983), Am. Diabetes Assn. (speakers bur. 1982—), Nat. Kidney Found. (bd. dirs. 1983-90). Office: Denver Presbyn St Lukes Med Ctr 1719 E 19th Ave Denver CO 80218-1235

BARBER, STEVEN ALDEN, telecommunications analyst; b. Norfolk, Va., Feb. 1, 1961; s. James Alden and Beverly (Kingsbury) B.; m. Cristina Annette Howard, June 15, 1985. Student in broadcast mgmt., U. So. Calif., 1979-84. Sales rep. SBS Skyline, L.A., 1984-86; field sales rep. U.S. Telecom., Newport Beach, Calif., 1986-87; mktg./sales mgr. MMZ Graphics, L.A., 1987; sales support mgr. ITT Comm., L.A., 1987-88; regional sales mgr. Am. Teleshare, L.A., 1988-89; acct. rels. mgr. LDDS Comm., Newport Beach, 1989-94; regional tech. cons. LDDS Comm., L.A., 1994—. Author/editor: A Learner's Permit to the Info Superhighway, 1995; contbr. fiction to various newspapers. Vol. friends of Long Beach Libr., 1993—, Smithsonian West com., 1993. Mem. U.S. Naval Inst., Writers' Bloc of L.A. Democrat. Office: LDDS World Com Inc Ste 208 1451 Quail St Newport Beach CA 92660

BARBERA, HENRY RAYMOND, sociology educator; b. N.Y.C., Dec. 21, 1929. PhD, Columbia U., 1971. Prof. City Coll., N.Y.C., 1971-82, U. Calif., Irvine, 1983—. Author: Rich Nations and Poor in Peace and War, 1973, The First Absolute State, 1994, Hope and Discontent, 1995; co-editor newsletter Sicilia Parra, 1980—. Mem. Am. Socio. Assn., Am. Polit. Sci. Assn., Patrons of Italian Culture (pres. 1992—). Home: 24975 Acacia Ln Laguna Hills CA 92653-4909

BARBERA, SHARON GAIL, banker; b. Derby, Conn., Oct. 18, 1947. BA, U. West Fla., 1969; MBA, Ariz. State U., 1979. Cert. sr. escrow officer. Escrow officer First Am. Title, Phoenix, 1979-83, br. mgr., 1983-84; sr. comml. escrow officer Transam. Title, Phoenix, 1984-87, br. mgr., 1987-92; pres. GailShay Worldwide Inc, Scotts Dale, Ariz., 1992—; mktg. cons. Dance Inst., Scottsdale, Ariz., 1978-79. Mem. Cen. Ariz. Escrow Assn. (pres. 1984-85, chmn. bd. 1985-86), Ariz. State Escrow Assn. (pres. 1986-87), Ariz. Mortgage Bankers Assn., Scottsdale Bd. Realtors.

BARBERS, RICHARD GEORGE, physician, educator; b. Calasiao, The Philippines, Jan. 12, 1949; came to U.S., 1960; s. Jess Victor and Mary (Fernandez) B.; m. Stephanie Gertrude Weck, June 4, 1994. BS, Loyola Coll., Balt., 1971; MD, Georgetown U., 1975. Intern internal medicine Med. Ctr. U. So. Calif., L.A., 1975-76, assoc. prof. clin. medicine, 1990—; resident internal medicine Cedars-Sinai Med. Ctr., L.A., 1976-78; postdoctoral fellow clin. immunology and allergy Med. Ctr. UCLA, 1979-81, postdoctoral fellow pulmonary disease Med. Ctr., 1981-82, adj. asst. prof. Sch. Medicine, 1982-87; asst. prof. Med. Sch. U. Mass., Worcester, 1987-90; dir. UCLA Asthma & Immunology Lung Disease Ctr., 1982-87, U. So. Calif. Bronchoscopy Svcs., 1990—, Asthma and Allergy Ctr., 1994—; co-dir. U. So. Calif. Lung Transplant Program, 1992—. Contbr. articles to med. jours. and books. Fellow ACP, Am. Coll. Chest Physicians, Am. Acad. Allergy and Immunology; mem. Am. Thoracic Soc., Am. Fedn. Clin. Rsch., Internat. Heart and Lung Transplant Soc., Nat. Tri-Beta Hon. Soc. Roman Catholic. Office: USC Sch Med GH 11-900 2025 Zonal Ave Los Angeles CA 90033

BARBEY, PETER DIENER, bookseller; b. Boston, May 10, 1957; s. Edwin Quier and Ruth Virginia (Diener) B.; m. Pamela Jane Terry, Dec. 29, 1981; 1 child, Matthew Terry. BA, U. Ariz., 1980; MBA, Ariz. State U., 1982. Analyst, ops. div. Merabank, Phoenix, 1983-84, asst. to the exec. v.p. for mktg., 1985-86; asst. v.p. Chase Manhattan, Scottsdale, Ariz., 1987; pres. Houle Books, Scottsdale, 1987—; mem. adv. bd. Phoenix Coll. Creative Writing Program, 1994, U. Ariz. Press, 1993—. Bd. dirs. Ariz. Humanities Coun., 1991—, sec., 1994; bd. dirs. Ariz. Ctr. for the Book, Phoenix, 1992—, Friends of the Phoenix Pub. Libr., 1992—; bd. dirs. Ctr. Dance Ensemble, Phoenix, 1991—, pres., 1994; precinct committeeman Dist. 24, Paradise Valley, Ariz., 1994—. Mem. Borgata Mchts. Assn. (bd. dirs. 1993-94, pres. 1994), Uptown Plz. Mchts. Assn. (pres. 1991-93). Republican. Episcopalian. Home: 5031 E Desert Jewel Dr Paradise Vly AZ 85253-3051 Office: Houle Books 6166 N Scottsdale Rd Scottsdale AZ 85253-5438

BARBIERI, DAVID ARTHUR, company executive; b. Denver, Oct. 16, 1930; s. Alfred J. and Edna M. (Rowland) B.; m. Beatrice Beck, Apr. 23, 1953 (div.); children: Scott, Kurt; m. Karen Kai, Aug. 18, 1988; 1 child, Christopher. Student, U. Mo., 1948, Keio U., Tokyo, 1950, Coll. of San Mateo, 1952. Sales mgr. Lever Bros Co., N.Y.C., 1959-64; v.p. Sarvis Web Co., Tenafly, N.J., 1964-72, Security Market Group, Honolulu, 1972-75; pres. DABAR Co., Inc., Honolulu, 1975—; cons. Dryers of Hawaii, Honolulu, 1976-79, Contact Distbn., Honolulu, 1978-83. Author: Working with Brokers, 1962. Pres. United Cerebral Palsy Hawaii, 1985, 89. Staff sgt. USAF, 1948-51, Korea. Mem. Am. Logistic Assn. (v.p., bd. dirs. 1977), Sales and Mktg. Execs. (membership chair 1976), Assn. Apt. Owners (pres., bd. dirs. 1984), Oahu Country Club (2d v.p., bd. dirs. 1992, pres. 1994-95). Republican. Roman Catholic. Office: Dabar Co Inc PO Box 10176 Honolulu HI 96816-0176

BARBOSA-CÁNOVAS, GUSTAVO VÍCTOR, food engineering educator; b. Minas, Lavalleja, Uruguay, Nov. 1, 1949; came to U.S., 1980; s. Walter V. and Elida (Cánovas-Marmo) Barbosa-Trias; m. Ana M. Rodriguez Vivaldi, July 21, 1981; children: Juan Manuel, Gabriela Maria, Jorge Antonio. BS in Mech. Engring., U. Uruguay, Montevideo, 1977; MS in Food Engring., U. Mass., 1982, PhD in Food Engring., 1985. Registered profl. engr., Uruguay. H.S. physics lab. asst. Inst. Batlle y Ordoñez and Inst. Zorrilla, Montevideo, 1973-78; instr. Sch. Engring U. Uruguay, Montevideo, 1974-77, asst. prof. mech. engring. dept., 1978-80; mech. engr. Uruguayan Brewery, Montevideo, 1977-78, Uruguay River Dam Project, Buenos Aires, 1978-80; rsch. asst. food engring. dept. U. Mass., Amherst, 1980-85; asst. prof. chem. engring. dept. Sch. Engring. U. P.R., Mayagüez, 1985-90; asst. prof. biol. systems engring. Wash. State U., Pullman, 1990-94, assoc. prof., 1994—; vis. prof. food and chem. engring. dept. U. Las Americas, Puebla, Mexico, 1991—; rsch. assoc. Basic Scis. Devel. Program, UN, 1992—; vis. prof. food sci. and tech. dept. U. Chihuahua, Mexico, 1993—, U. Lleida, Spain, 1994; advisor Uruguayan Inst. Standardization, 1985; cons. prodn. divsn. Starkist Caribe, Mayagüez, 1987, H.J. Heinz, Alimentos Heinz de Venezuela, Valencia, 1989; cons. tech. divsn. Caribik-Sun, Mayagüez, 1989-90, Campbell Soup, Casera foods divsn., Barceloneta, P.R., 1990. Editor: Dehydration of Foods, 1993, Food Rheology, 1994; book reviewer: Rheological Methods in Food Processing Engineering, 1992; editl. bd. Fluid/Particle Separation Jour., 1988—, Spanish Coun. Fodd Sci. and Tech., 1991—, BIOTAM, U. Autñnoma de Tamaulipas, Mexico, 1993—, Jour. of Food Engring.; editor: Food Science and Technology Internat.; contbr. articles to profl. jours. Pres. Uruguayan Movement for Welfare, Montevideo, 1970. Recipient Govt. Israel Scholarship, Ministry Fgn. Affairs, 1980, Fulbright Scholarship U. Mass., Amherst, 1980-82, U. Mass. Fellowship, 1982-85, Scholarly Productivity award NSF, 1988, 89, U. Lerida (Spain) Fellowship, 1994; named Hon. Prof. U. Uruguay, 1993, Disting. Internat. Prof. Govt. Catalunya, Spain, 1994. Mem. ASME, AIChE, AAAS, Inst. Food Technologists, Am. Soc. Agrl. Engrs., Am. Soc. Engring. Edn., Food Process Engring. Inst., Uruguayan Soc. Engrs., Am. Filtration Soc., Controlled Release Soc., Caribbean Food Crops Soc., Puerto Rican Assn. for Food Sci. and Tech., Sigma Xi, Gamma Sigma Delta. Home: SE 1260 Earthtone Ct Pullman WA 99163 Office: Wash State U Dept Biol Systems Engr Pullman WA 99164-6120

BARBOUR, ALTON BRADFORD, human communication studies educator; b. San Diego, Oct. 13, 1933; s. Ancel Baxter and Mary Jane (Fay) B.; m. Betty Sue Burch, Aug. 19, 1961 (div. 1991); children: Elizabeth, Christopher, Damon, Meagan. BA, U. No. Colo., 1956; MA, U. Denver, 1961, PhD, 1968; postdoctoral, Moreno Inst., 1976. Diplomate Am. Bd. Psychotherapy. Lectr. Colo. Sch. Mines, Golden, 1964-65; instr. U. Denver, 1965-68; asst. prof. human comm. studies U. Denver, Denver, 1968-71, assoc. prof., 1971-77, prof., 1977—, chairperson dept. human comm. studies, 1980—; vis. lectr. Swiss Inst. for Group Psychotherapy, Switzerland, 1992, Chinese U. of Hong Kong. Co-author (books) Interpersonal Communication: Teaching Resources, 1972, Louder Than Words: Nonverbal Communication, 1974, Assessing Functional Communication, 1978; contbr. articles to profl. jours. With USN, 1956-58. Fellow Am. Soc. for Group Psychotherapy and Psychodrama, Am. Bd. of Med. Psychotherapists, Internat. Acad. of Behavioral Medicine, Counselling and Psychotherapy; mem. Am. Bd. Examiners in Group Psychotherapy (sec. 1983-93). Home: 1195 S Vine St Denver CO 80210-1830 Office: U Denver Human Communications Studies Denver CO 80208

BARBUT, EROL, mathematics educator; b. Istanbul, Turkey, July 30, 1940; came to U.S. 1959; s. Mark and Margit (Herrman) B.; m. Ann Wilby, Apr. 23, 1963 (div. Aug. 1980); children: Eric, Sylvia; m. Alice Pope, Aug. 8, 1981; 1 child, Sarah. BA, U. Calif., Berkeley, 1963, MA, 1965; PhD, U. Calif., Riverside, 1967. Asst. prof., then assoc. prof. math. U. Idaho, Moscow, 1967-87, prof., 1988—, chmn. dept., 1994—. Contbr. articles to profl. jours. Mem. Math. Assn. Am., Am. Math. Soc. Office: U Idaho Dept Math Moscow ID 83843

BARCA, GEORGE GINO, winery executive, financial investor; b. Sacramento, Jan. 28, 1937; s. Joseph and Annie (Muschetto) B.; m. Maria Sclafani, Nov. 19, 1960; children—Anna, Joseph, Gina and Nina (twins). A.A., Grant Jr. Coll.; student LaSalle U., 1963. With United Vintners, U.S.A., San Francisco, 1960-80; pres., gen. mgr. Barcamerica U.S.A., Sacramento, 1963—; pres., gen. mgr. Barca Wine Cellars, Calif. Wine Cellars, U.S.A., Calif. Grape Growers, U.S.A., Calif. Vintage Wines, U.S.A., Am. Vintners, U.S.A.; cons. in field. Named Best Producer of Sales, United Vintners, U.S.A. Mem. Calif. Farm Bur., Met. C. of C., Better Bus. Bur., Roman Catholic. Club: KC. Developer wine trademarks.

BARCA, KATHLEEN, marketing executive; b. Burbank, Calif., July 26, 1946; d. Frank Allan and Blanch Irene (Griffith) Barnes; m. Gerald Albino Barca, Dec. 8, 1967 (dec. May 1993); children: Patrick Gerald, Stacia Kathleen. Student, Pierce Coll., 1964; B in Bus., Hancock Coll., 1984. Teller Security Pacific Bank, Pasadena, Calif., 1968-69, Bank Am., Santa Maria, Calif., 1972-74; operator Gen. Telephone Co., Santa Maria, Calif., 1974-83, supr. operator, 1983-84; account exec. Sta. KRQK/KLLB Radio, Lompoc, Calif., 1984-85; owner Advt. Unltd., Orcutt, Calif., 1986-88; regional mgr. A.L. Williams Mktg. Co., Los Alamos, Calif., 1988-89; supr. Matol Botanical Internat., 1989-91; account exec. Santa Maria Times, 1989—. Author: numerous local TV and radio commercials, print advt. Activist Citizens Against Dumps in Residential Environments, Polit. Action Com., Orcutt and Santa Maria; chmn. Community Action Com., Santa Maria, Workshop EPA, Calif. Div., Dept. Health Svcs. State of Calif.; vice coord. Toughlove, Santa Maria, 1988-89; parent coord., mem. steering com. ASAP and Friends, 1988-89. Mem. NAFE, Womens Network-Santa Maria, Ctrl. Coast Ad (recipient numerous awards), Santa Maria C. of C. (amb. representing Santa Maria Times 1990-94, asst. chief amb. 1993-94). Democrat. Home: 357 Saratoga Ave Grover Beach CA 93433

BARCLAY, JOHN ALLEN, lawyer; b. L.A., Feb. 14, 1951; s. George H. and Shirley Iris (Handler) B. AA, L.A. Valley Coll., 1970; BA, U. Southern Calif., 1972, JD, 1975. Bar: Calif. 1975, U.S. Dist. Ct. (cen., ea., and no. dists.) Calif. 1976, U.S. Ct. Appeals (9th cir.) 1976, U.S. Tax Ct. 1976. Assoc. Karno & Fisher, Encino, Calif., 1975-78; prin. Barclay & Brestoff, Encino, 1978-80, Barclay & Moskatel, Beverly Hills, Calif., 1980-82, Barclay Law Corp., Newport Beach, Calif., 1982—; instr. U. Calif.-Irvine, 1985-87, UCLA, 1982-85, L.A. Valley Coll., Van Nuys, 1980-82. Author: Exchanging in the '80's, 1986, Accumulating Wealth, 1987, Insurance for Environmental Claims Against Bankruptcy Estates, 1992, (with others) Deducting Your Down Payment, 1984; contbr. articles to profl. jours. Mem. ABA, Legion Lex (bd. dirs. Orange County chpt. 1987—, pres. 1992), Newport Harbor C. of C., Masons (master Hollywood chpt. 1982). Jewish. Office: Barclay Law Corp 5000 Birch St # 2900 Newport Beach CA 92660

BARCLAY, STEVEN CALDER, lawyer; b. Phoenix, Ariz., Jan. 17, 1956; s. Leslie Calder and Ruth (Lindke) B.; m. Janice Marie Reno, Sept. 25, 1982; 1 child, Jordan Nicole. BA magna cum laude, Oral Roberts U., 1977; JD cum laude, Notre Dame U., 1980. Bar: Ariz. 1980, U.S. Dist. Ct. Ariz. 1980, U.S. Ct. Appeals (9th cir.) 1980. Assoc. Snell & Wilmer, Phoenix, 1980-83; corp. counsel S.W. divsn. Cigna Healthplans, Inc., Phoenix, 1983-85; ptnr. Barclay & Reece, Phoenix, 1985-87; sole practice Phoenix, 1987-90; shareholder, pres. Barclay & Goering, P.C., Phoenix, 1990—. Mem. editl. bd. Today's Health Care Mag., 1994—. Mem. ABA, State Bar Ariz., Ariz. Assn. Managed Care Plans (counsel, lobbyist 1987—), Ariz. Assn. Health Care Lawyers, Pub. Affairs Profls. Ariz. (dir.), Maricopa County Bar Assn. Republican. Office: Barclay & Goering PC 1001 N Central Ste 600 Phoenix AZ 85004

BARDACH, SHELDON GILBERT, lawyer; b. Holyoke, Mass., Sept. 4, 1937; s. Arthur Everett and Ruth (Goodstein) B.; m. Martha Robson, June 7, 1970; 1 child, Noah Arthur. AB, Bklyn. Coll., 1958; JD, UCLA, 1961. Bar: Calif. 1962. Pvt. practice Beverly Hills, Calif., 1962-67, Century City, Calif., 1967-85; sr. mem. Law Offices Sheldon G. Bardach, L.A.; bd. dirs. Mambo Films, Inc.; arbitrator L.A. Superior Ct., 1979—; gen. counsel Century Artists, Ltd.; mem. nat. and internat. panels arbitrators Am. Arbitration Assn. Bd. editors Law in Transition Quar., 1967; contbr. articles to profl. jours. Bd. govs. Studio Watts Workshop, 1963-71; founder, bd. dirs. UCLA Sch. Law, 1968. Recipient Lubin award Sch. Law UCLA, 1961, Bancroft-Whitney award UCLA Sch. Law, , 1961. Mem. ABA, Calif. Bar Assn., Beverly Hills Bar Assn. (bd. govs. varristers 1964-69), Am. Arbitration Assn., UCLA Law Sch. Alumni Assn. (bd. dirs. 1991-94), L.A. County Bar Assn., Assn. Trial Lawyers Am., Comml. Law League Am., Vikings of Scandia, Zeta Beta Tau, Phi Alpha Delta. Democrat. Jewish. Office: 12100 Wilshire Blvd Los Angeles CA 90025-4109

BARDAS, SANDRA LEIGH, pharmacist. BA magna cum laude, Wheaton Coll., Norton, Mass., 1972; BS in Pharmacy, Mass. Coll. Pharmacy, Boston, 1975. Pharmacy resident Mass. Gen. Hosp., Boston, 1976-77, staff pharmacist, 1977-78; clin. pharmacist Stanford (Calif.) U. Hosp., 1979—. Office: Stanford Univ Hosp Dept Of Pharmacy Ho # 301 Stanford CA 94305

BARDEN, TIMOTHY JOHN, insurance executive; b. Providence, R.I., June 26, 1959; s. James John and Leona Marie (Camire) B.; m. LeiLani Ann Escobar, Apr. 25, 1987 (div. Sept. 1989); children: Jason James, Alyssa Nicole. BA, U. R.I., 1981; MPA, Calif. State U., 1984. Sr. underwriter Transamerica Occidental, L.A., 1982-87; asst. v.p. underwriting U.S. Benefits, Costa Mesa, Calif., 1987—. Home: 3941 S Bristol St # 188 Santa Ana CA 92704-7400 Office: US Benefits 650 Town Center Dr Ste 1600 Costa Mesa CA 92626-1925

BARDHAN, KALPANA, translator, writer; b. Calcutta, India, Jan. 4, 1940; came to U.S., 1976; d. Debendra N. Bose and Renuka Ray; m. Pranab K. Bardhan, Jan. 26, 1962; 1 child, Titash. BA, Presidency Coll., Calcutta, 1958; MA in Econs., Calcutta U., 1960; PhD in Econs., Cambridge U., Eng., 1968. Lectr. econs. Bethune Coll., Calcutta, 1961-62; sr. fellow Agro-econ. Rsch. Ctr., Delhi, India, 1969-70; dep. dir. Indian Coun. Social Sci. Rsch., Delhi, 1972-75; lectr. econs. dept. U. Calif., Berkeley, 1976-86; cons. World Bank, Washington, 1976, Asian Devel. Bank, Manila, 1989-90; cons. Project on Women and Work U.N.U., Tokyo, 1986-87; rsch. assoc. Ctr. for South Asia Studies U. Calif., Berkeley, 1989-93. Editor, translator, introduction writer: Of Women, Outcasts, Peasants and Rebels, 1990, A River Called Titash, 1993; translator lit. from Bengali to English, Berkeley, 1987—. Home: 1266 Grizzly Peak Blvd Berkeley CA 94708-2128

BARELA, BERTHA CICCI, retired elementary education educator, artist; b. McKeesport, Pa., June 13, 1913; d. James and Julia (Kolesar) Faix; m. John Slebodnik, June 23, 1934 (dec. 1967); children: Dolores S. Garvis, James, John, Judith Greene, Jane Minda, William, Cyrilla Lombardi, Rosemary Lewis, Martha Williams; m. Amerigo Cicci, May 25, 1974 (dec. 1975); m. Abran Barela, Dec. 8, 1984 (div. Nov. 1992). BA, Seton Hill Coll., 1970. Elem. tchr. Blessed Sacrament Sch., Greensburg, Pa., 1967-74; ind. artist, clown Phoenix, 1985—; guest art tchr. various schs., 1980—; Westmoreland (Pa.) County Coun. Girl Scout Leader; internat. del. St. Louis. Formerly news and mag. writer; numerous commissioned art works. Dep. registrar Maricopa County, Phoenix, 1983-86, election bd. worker, 1980—; Dem. committeewoman, election worker, Pa., 1960-73, Phoenix, 1980—. Mem. Sunnyslope Recreation Ctr. Home: 841 E Cinnabar Ave Phoenix AZ 85020-1732

BARENIS, PAT PEASTER, wholesale distribution company executive; b. Greenville, Miss., Sept. 7, 1951; d. Thomas Benjamin and Min (Young) Peaster; m. Uldis Atis Barenis, Nov. 13, 1975; children: Karl Alexander, Nicholas Benjamin. Mem. sales staff Nationwide Programming Co., Memphis, 1972-73; mktg. mgr. Nationwide Programming Co., Louisville, 1973-74; piano tchr. Deer Creek Acad., Arcola, Miss., 1977-80; pres., owner, chief exec. officer Barenis & Assocs., Vancouver, Wash., 1985—; cons. Security Products Group, Vancouver, 1987—; CEO T.B. Peaster, Inc., 1993. Bd. dirs. West Coast Life Safety and Communications, Inc., 1991-93; tutor coord. hosts program Felida Elem. Sch., Vancouver, 1985-91; mem. bd. exec. PTA, 1987-91. Mem. Salmon Creek Soccer Club (exec. bd. 1990-91), Lakeshore Athletic Club. Republican. Office: Barenis & Assocs 11703 NW 18th Ave Vancouver WA 98685-3725

BARFORD, LEE ALTON, computer scientist; b. Cheltenham, Pa., Oct. 14, 1961; s. Robert Alton and Frances Huber (Munz) B. AB summa cum laude, Temple U., 1982; MS, Cornell U., 1985, PhD, 1987. Cert. flight instr., FAA. Programmer TNR, Inc., Willow Grove, Pa., 1979-80; dir. software devel. Positioning Devices, Inc., Willow Grove, 1980-83; tech. staff mem. Hewlett-Packard Labs., Palo Alto, Calif., 1987—. Contbr. articles to profl. jours. Patentee in field. Search and rescue pilot CAP, Palo Alto, 1987—, chief check pilot, 1992—; active Accident Prevention Coun., FAA. Mem. IEEE, Palo Alto Flying Club (instr.), Phi Beta Kappa. Office: Hewlett-Packard Labs 1501 Page Mill Rd M/S 4AD Palo Alto CA 94303-0889

BARGER, JAMES DANIEL, physician; b. Bismarck, N.C., May 17, 1917; s. Michael Thomas and Mayte (Donohue) B.; m. Susie Belle Helm, 1945 (dec. 1951); m. Josephine Steiner, 1952 (dec. 1971); m. Jane Ray Regan, Apr. 21, 1980 (dec. Feb. 1991); children: James Daniel, Mary Susan, Michael Thomas, Mary Elizabeth. Student, St. Mary's Coll., Winona, Minn., 1934-35; A.B., U. N.D., 1939, B.S., 1939; M.D., U. Pa., 1941; M.S. in Pathology, U. Minn., 1949. Diplomate Am. Bd. Pathology; registered quality engr., Calif. Intern. Milw. County Hosp., Wauwatosa, Wis., 1941-42; fellow in pathology Mayo Found., Rochester, Minn., 1941-49; pathologist Pima County Hosp., Tucson, 1949-50, Maricopa County Hosp., Phoenix, 1950-51; chmn. dept. pathology Good Samaritan Hosp., 1951-63; assoc. pathologist Sunrise Hosp., Las Vegas, Nev., 1964-69, chief pathology dept., 1969-81, sr. pathologist, 1981—; former med. dir. S.W. Blood Bank, Blood Services, Ariz., Blood Services Nev.; treas. Commn. for Lab. Assessment, 1988; emeritus clin. prof. pathology U. Nev. Sch. Medicine, 1988. Served to maj. AUS, 1942-46. Recipient Sioux award U. N.D. Alumni Assn., 1975; recipient disting. physician award NSMA, 1983; ASCP-CAP Disting. Service award, 1985. Mem. AAAS, AMA, Am. Assn. Pathologists, Am. Assn. Clin. Chemists, Am. Assn. History Medicine, Coll. Am. Pathologists (gov. 1966-72, sec.-treas. 1971-79, v.p. 1979-81, pres. 1980-81, historian 1988—, Pathologist of Yr. 1977), Nev. Soc. Pathologists (AMA del. 1990), Am. Assn. Blood Banks, Am. Soc. Quality Control (sr. mem.), Am. Mgmt. Assn., Soc. Advancement Mgmt., Am. Soc. Clin. Pathologists, Am. Cancer Soc. (nat. dir. 1974-80), Nat. Acad. Practice Medicine (dist. practitioner 1984—, del. AMA Ho. Dels. 1989—), others. Lodge: Knights of St. Lazarus (comdr.

1983). Home: 1307 Canosa Ave Las Vegas NV 89104-3132 Office: 3196 S Maryland Pky #405 Las Vegas NV 89109-2306

BARGHINI, SANDRA JEAN, curator; b. San Francisco, Dec. 3, 1951; d. Emo and Alice Barghini. BA, William Smith, 1974; MA, U. Ariz., 1976. Cons. museum Mission San Luis Obispo, San Luis Obispo, Calif., 1977-78; curator collections Chesapeake Bay Maritime Museum, St. Michaels, Md., 1979-84; curator Hearst Castle, San Simeon, Calif., 1984—; guest curator San Francisco Fall Antiques show, 1994; lectr. L.A. County Mus. of Art, McFadden Ward House, 1994. Editorial cons. (book) America's Hidden Corners, 1983; project dir. (exhibits) History News, 1984, William R. Hearst, 1988. Fellow NEH, 1989. Mem. Am. Assn. Museums (panelist 1993 meeting), Archaeological Inst. Am. Office: Hearst San Simeon State Hist Monument 750 Hearst Castle Rd San Simeon CA 93452-9740

BARHAM, PATTE (MRS. HARRIS PETER BOYNE), publisher, author, columnist; b. L.A.; d. Frank Barham and Princess Jessica Meskhi Gleboff; student U. So. Calif., U. Ariz.; LittD, Trinity So. Bible Coll.; hon. doctorate, Cambridge, Eng., D Internat. Arts, Sci. and Cable TV. War corr., Korea; syndicated columnist; acting sec. of state, State of Calif., 1980-81; Life mem. AAU, former v.p. pub. rels.; active House Ear Inst.; internat. com. L.A. Philharmonic. Author: Pin up Poems; Rasputin: The Man Behind the Myth, 1977; Peasant to Palace: Rasputin's Cookbook, 1990; Marilyn: The Last Take, 1992. Decorated dame Sovereign Order of Alfred the Great, Grand Cross, Patron of Honor; Campagnon de la Couronne d'Epines, Ancienne Abbaye-Principaute de San Luigi. Mem. DAR, Outrigger Canoe, Waikiki Yacht (Hawaii); Wilshire Country, Ebell, Balboa Bay; Met. (N.Y.C.); Delta Gamma.

BARHAM, STEVEN WALTER, state official; b. Ogden, Utah, Apr. 18, 1953; s. Henry Garfield and Betty Jane (Chester) B.; m. Leona Ellen Shepherd, Nov. 19, 1982; 1 stepchild, Lisa Chappell. BS, Oreg. Coll. Edn., 1974; MBA, Portland (Oreg.) State U., 1981. Spl. projects aide Ea. Oreg. Hosp., Pendleton, 1975-77; asst. supr. adminstrv. services, bus. mgr. Callahan Ctr., Wilsonville, Oreg., 1978-80; bus. mgr. Bd. Nursing, Portland, 1981-85; exec. dir. Oreg. Racing Commn., Portland, 1985—; vice chmn. security com. Assn. of Racing Commrs. Internat., Lexington, Ky., 1986-87.

BARHAM, WARREN SANDUSKY, horticulturist; b. Prescott, Ark., Feb. 15, 1919; s. Clint A. and Hannah Jane (Sandusky) B.; m. Margaret Alice Kyle, Dec. 27, 1940; children: Barbara E., Juanita S., Margaret Ann, Robert W. BS in Agr., U. Ark., 1941; PhD, Cornell U., 1950. Grad. asst. in plant breeding Cornell U., Ithaca, N.Y., 1942-45; assoc. prof. horticulture N.C. State U., Raleigh, 1949-58; dir. raw material R & D Basic Vegetable Products, Inc., Vacaville, Calif., 1958-76; prof., head dept. hort. sci. Tex. A&M U., College Station, 1976-82; v.p. Castle & Cook Technoculture, Watsonville, Calif., 1982-84; dir. watermelon R & D Tom Castle Seed Co., Morgan Hill, Calif., 1984-86; pres. Barham Seeds Inc., Gilroy, Calif., 1987—; cons. Basic Vegetable Products, Inc., Vacaville, 1976-78, U.S. AID, Central Am., 1977, Egypt and U.S., 1980-82, Gentry Foods & Gilroy Foods, 1978—, Fed. Republic Germany Govt., Ethiopia, 1984; industry rep. adv. com. Onion Rsch. Program USDA, 1960-70. Contbr. articles to profl. jours. Bd. dirs., pres. Vacaville Sch. Bd., 1964-74. Sgt. USAF, 1942-45, ETO. Fellow Am. Soc. Hort. Sci. (pres. 1982, bd. dirs. 1979-83); mem. Sons in Retirement (v.p. 1993, pres. 1994), Rotary Inernat. (bd. dirs. 1964). Home and Office: 7401 Crawford Dr Gilroy CA 95020-5421

BARISH, JONAS ALEXANDER, English language educator; b. N.Y.C., Mar. 22, 1922; s. Philip H. and Mollie (Schaffer) B.; m. Mildred Ann Seaquist, July 26, 1964; children—Judith Rose, Rachel Alexandra. B.A., Harvard U., 1942, M.A., 1947, Ph.D., 1952. Instr. English Yale U., New Haven, 1953-54; asst. prof. English U. Calif., Berkeley, 1954-60, assoc. prof. English, 1960-66, prof. English, 1966-91, prof. English emeritus, 1991—. Author: Ben Jonson and the Language of Prose Comedy, 1960, The Antitheatrical Prejudice (Barnard Hewitt award for outstanding research in theater history 1982), 1981. Served with Signal Corps, U.S. Army, 1944-46. Fulbright research fellow, Paris, 1952-53, 61-62; Am. Council Learned Socs. fellow, 1961-62; NEH fellow, 1973-74, 86-87. Fellow Am. Acad. Arts and Scis., MLA, Malone Soc., Internat. Shakespeare Assn.; mem. Shakespeare Assn. Am. (trustee 1982-87, pres. 1984-85). Democrat. Jewish. Home: 107 Tamalpais Rd Berkeley CA 94708-1948 Office: U Calif Dept English Berkeley CA 94720

BARKAN, PHILIP, mechanical engineer; b. Boston, Mar. 29, 1925; s. Philip and Blanche (Seifert) B.; m. Hinda Brody, Sept. 5, 1948 (dec. Aug. 1979); children—Ruth, David; m. Susan Albro Sheehan, July 28, 1991. B.S.M.E., Tufts U., 1946; M.S.M.E., U. Mich., 1948; Ph.D. in Mech. Engring, Pa. State U., 1953. Asst. prof. engring. research Pa. State U., 1948-51; sect. mgr. applied physics and mech. engring. Gen. Electric Co., Phila., 1953-77; prof. mech. engring. Stanford U., 1977-93, emeritus prof., 1993—; vis. prof. Israel Inst. Tech., Haifa, 1971-72; cons. electric power industry, 1977—, concurrent engring., 1986—; bd. dirs. Xerox Inst. for Design Excellence, 1993. Contbr. numerous articles to profl. publs. Pres. bd. trustees Middletown (Pa.) Free Library, 1959-61; chmn. bd. trustees Sch. in Rose Valley, 1967-68; Democratic candidate for Middletown Twp. Supr., 1959, 61, 63; pres. Middletown Dem. Club, 1960. Served with USN, 1943-46. Recipient 1st Charles P. Steinmetz medal and award Gen. Electric Co., 1973; Electric Power Research Inst. grantee, 1979. Fellow IEEE; mem. ASME, Nat. Acad. Engring., Soc. Mfg. Engrs., Am. Soc. Engring. Educators, Sigma Xi. Office: Stanford U Dept Mech Engring Design Divsn Stanford CA 94305

BARKER, ALAN FREUND, internist; b. St. Louis, Aug. 27, 1944; s. Irven M. and Gladys (Freund) B.; m. Julieann Brixner; children: Sara, David. BA, Carleton Coll., 1966; MD, U. Mo., 1970. Internship internal medicine U. Wash. Affiliated Hosps., Seattle, 1970-71, residency internal medicine, 1971-73; chief med. resident internal medicine U. Wash. Affiliated Hosps., USPH Hosp., Seattle, 1973-74; fellow pulmonary medicine U. Calif., San Diego, 1974-76; asst. prof. medicine Oreg. Health Scis. U., Portland, 1976-82, assoc. prof. medicine Divsn. Pulmonary & Critical Care, 1982—; med. dir., cons Respiratory Therapy Program, Mt. Hood C.C., 1978—, chair adv. com., 1992—; cons. Multnomah County Tuberculosis Clinic, 1981—. Contbr. articles to profl. jours. and chpts. to books. Mem. Gov.'s Commn. for Pub. Health Policy, 1984-85; bd. dirs. Univ. Med. Assocs., 1980-85, pres., 1983-85; mem. Med. Bd. Univ. Hosp., 1984-87, exec. coun., 1984-85. Grantee NIH, 1989-94, Genentech, 1993-94, Miles, 1993-94. Fellow Am. Coll. Chest Physicians; mem. Am. Thoracic Soc., Oreg. Thoracic Soc. (pres. 1982-83). Office: Oreg Health Scis U Pulmonary/Critical Care Portland OR 97201

BARKER, DOUGLAS P., food products executive; b. 1935. With Sunkist Growers, Van Nuys, Calif., 1961-78, Sun World Internat. Inc., Bakersfield, Calif., 1978-81, 84—, Blue Anchor, Sacramento, Calif., 1981-84. Office: Sun World Internat Inc 5544 Cal Ave Ste 280 Bakersfield CA 93309*

BARKER, JOHN A., research scientist; b. Corrigin, Australia, Mar. 24, 1925; came to U.S., 1969; s. Thomas Louis and Dorothy Erica (Janes) B.; m. Avril Hope Johnston, Apr. 18, 1950; children: Jonathan, David, Katie. BS, U. Melbourne, 1944, BA, 1945, DSc, 1958; DSc (hon.), Latrobe U., Australia, 1992. Rsch. staff mem. IBM Almaden Rsch. Ctr., San Jose, Calif., 1969—; prof. applied math and physics U. Waterloo, Ontario, Can., 1968-69; rsch. scientist Divsn. of Indsl. Chemistry and Phys. Chemistry/CSIRO, Melbourne, 1950-68. Editorial bd. Jour. of Statistical Physics, 1975-78; assoc. editor: Jour. Computational Physics, 1979-82, Jour. of Chem. Physics, 1981-83; author: Lattice Theories of the Liquid State, 1963; contbr. articles to profl. publs. Fellow of Australian Acad. Sci., Royal Soc. London. Office: IBM Alameda Rsch Ctr K43802 650 Harry Rd San Jose CA 95120-6001

BARKER, JOSEPH CORY, computer scientist, educator; b. Provo, Utah, Oct. 28, 1957; s. Joseph Keith and Lucille Dorothy (Van Alfen) B.; m. Colette Maureen Montgomery, Feb. 13, 1981; children: Joseph Brandon, Brooke Marie, Benjamin Michael, Rebekah Mary. BS, Brigham Young U., 1982, PhD, 1994. Software/hardware engr. Tektronix, Inc., Wilsonville, Oreg., 1983, 85-86; software engr. Logicon, Inc., Clearfield, Utah, 1983-85, Nichols Rsch. Corp., Orem, Utah, 1986-87, 90-92, Microcosm, Inc., Beaverton, Oreg., 1987-89; asst. prof. computer sci. Brigham Young U.-Hawaii, Laie, 1994—. Air Force Office Sci. Rsch. grad. fellow, 1991. Mem. Assn. for Computing Machinery. Mormon. Home: 55-446 Moana St Laie HI 96762-1122 Office: Brigham Young U Laie HI 96762

BARKER, MITCHELL FREDERICK, former government public relations official; b. Tulsa, June 29, 1948; s. Albert B. and Dorothy L. (Bashe) B. B. Univ. Studies, U. N.Mex., 1976; now postgrad. News dir. Sta. KBRR-AM, Leadville, Colo., 1976-77, Sta. KAFE-AM-FM, Santa Fe, 1977; pub. affairs asst. U.S. Army Engr. Dist., Albuquerque, 1978-79; seminar asst. VA InterWest Regional Med. Edn. Ctr., Salt Lake City, 1979-80; tech. writer Robins AFB, Ga., 1980-81; pub. affairs specialist U.S. Army Engr. Dist., Walla Walla, Wash., 1981-82; pub. affairs officer Fitzsimons Army Med. Ctr., Aurora, Colo., 1982-84. Served with U.S. Army, 1969-73. Recipient Keith L. Ware award for radio prodn. Dept. of Army, 1972. Mem. Pub. Relations Soc. Am., Colo. Soc. Hosp. Pub. Relations, Aurora C. of C. (mil. affairs com.). Unitarian.

BARKER, NANCIE LYNNE, engineer; b. Berkeley, Calif., Apr. 25, 1942; d. Paul Thomas Marsh and Roberta Mildred (Wiggins) Brubaker; m. Loy Lee Barker, July 27, 1963; 1 child, Cindy Elizabeth. AS in Tool Design magna cum laude, De Anza Coll., 1979. Quality mgr. KRAS-West Corp., San Jose, Calif., 1979-82; quality engring. mgr. Siliconix, Santa Clara, Calif., 1982-87, package devel. engr., 1987-89, sr. engr. purchasing dept., 1989-91, mgr. supplier quality programs, 1991—; leader task force Semicondr. Equipment Materials Inst., Mountain View, Calif., 1989-91, co-chairperson packaging com., 1993—. Leader Camp Fire Girls, Cupertino, Calif., 1970-80; instr. in first aid ARC, San Jose and Los Gatos, Calif., 1970-84. Mem. Am. Soc. Metals, Internat. Soc. Hybrid Mfg., Microelectronic Packaging and Processing Engrs., Am. Soc. for Quality Control. Office: Siliconix 2201 Laurelwood Rd Santa Clara CA 95054-1516

BARKER, PETER KEEFE, investment banker; b. Chgo., Nov. 16, 1948; s. Norman and Sue (Keefe) B.; m. Robin Baily, June 20, 1970; children—Kelly, Todd, Ryan. Student, Colgate U., 1966-68, Claremont-McKenna Coll., 1968-69; M.B.A., U. Chgo., 1971. Assoc. Goldman, Sachs & Co., N.Y.C., 1971-74, v.p., 1974-77; v.p. Goldman, Sachs & Co., Los Angeles, 1977-82, ptnr., 1982—. Bd. dirs. Los Angeles Met. YMCA, 1981-85; fellow Claremont Grad. Sch., Calif., 1984-85; trustee Poly. Sch., Pasadena, Calif., 1984-85, Chandler Sch., Pasadena, 1982-85.

BARKER, ROBERT WILLIAM, television personality; b. Darrington, Wash., Dec. 12; s. Byron John and Matilda Kent (Tarleton) B.; m. Dorothy Jo Gideon, Jan. 12, 1945 (dec. Oct. 1981). BA in Econs. summa cum laude, Drury Coll., 1947. Master of ceremonies: Truth or Consequences, Hollywood, Calif., 1957-75, Price is Right, 1972—, Miss Universe Beauty Pageant, 1966-87, Miss U.S.A. Beauty Pageant, 1966-87, Pillsbury Bake-Off, 1969-85, Bob Barker Fun and Games Show, 1978—; host: Rose Parade, CBS, 1969-88. Served to lt. (j.g.) USNR, 1943-45. Recipient Emmy award for Best Daytime TV Host, 1981-82, 82-83, 86-87, 87-88, 89-90, 90-91, 93-94; Best Game Show Host, 1991-92. Mem. AGVA, AFTRA, Screen Actors Guild. Office: 5750 Wilshire Blvd Ste 475W Los Angeles CA 90036-3697

BARKER, WILEY FRANKLIN, surgeon, educator; b. Santa Fe, Oct. 16, 1919; s. Charles Burton and Bertha (Steed) B.; m. Nancy Ann Kerber, June 8, 1943; children: Robert Lawrence, Jonathan Steed, Christina Lee. B.S., Harvard, 1941, M.D., 1944. Intern, then resident Peter Bent Brigham Hosp., Boston, 1944-46; Arthur Tracy Cabot fellow Harvard Med. Sch., 1948-49; asst. chief surg. service, then chief surg. sect. Wadsworth VA Hosp., Los Angeles, 1951-54; attending physician Wadsworth VA Hosp., 1951—; mem. faculty U. Calif. at Los Angeles Med. Sch., 1954—, prof. surgery, 1964-86, prof. emeritus, 1986—, chief div. gen. surgery, 1955-77; cons. Sepulveda VA Hosp., 1966-78, chief of staff, 1978-83; Mem. com. trauma NRC, 1964-68. Author: Surgical Treatment of Peripheral Vascular Disease, 1962, Peripheral Arterial Disease, 1966, 2d edit., 1976, Clio Chirugica: The Arteries, vols. I and II, 1992, , also papers, chpts. in books. Served as lt. (j.g.) M.C. USNR, 1946-47. Harvard Nat. scholar, 1937-44. Fellow ACS (2d v.p. 1986-87); mem. Am. Surg. Assn., Am. Bd. Surgery (diplomate, bd. dirs. 1964-70), Soc. Clin. Surgery (pres. 1972-74), Soc. Univ. Surgeons, Soc. Vascular Surgery (pres. 1972-73), Internat. Cardiovascular Soc. (v.p. N.Am. chpt. 1964-65, pres. 1979-80), So. Surg. Assn., Pacific Coast Surg. Assn. (pres. 1982-83), Pan Pacific Surg. Assn. (pres. 1986-88), Am., Calif., Los Angeles County med. assns., Phi Beta Kappa, Sigma Xi, Alpha Omega Alpha. Republican. Episcopalian. Mailing Address: 13216 Dobbins Pl Los Angeles CA 90049 Office: Dept Surgery Univ Calif Sch Medicine Los Angeles CA 90024

BARKLEY, CHARLES WADE, professional basketball player; b. Leeds, Ala., Feb. 20, 1963. Student, Auburn U., 1981-84. mem. U.S. Olympic Basketball Team, 1992. With Phila. 76ers, 1984-92, Phoenix Suns, 1992—; mem. U.S. Olympic team, 1992. Author: (with Roy S. Johnson) Outrageous! The Fine Life and Flagrant Good Times of Basketball's Irresistible Force, 1992; film appearances include: Forget Paris, 1995. Recipient NBA All-Star Game Most Valuable Player award, 1991, Schick Pivotal Player award, 1986-88, NBA Most Valuable Player Award, 1993, IMB award, 1986-88; named to NBA All-Star team, 1988-93. Office: Phoenix Suns 201 E Jefferson St Phoenix AZ 85004-2412*

BARKLEY, THIERRY VINCENT, lawyer; b. Paris, Mar. 21, 1955; s. Jacques and Michéline Marié (Rossi) B.; came to U.S., 1967, naturalized, 1974; m. Mary Ellen Gamble, June 18, 1983; children: Richard A., Robert V., Marriah E., Christopher R. BA in Polit. Sci., UCLA, 1976; JD, Calif. Western Sch. Law, San Diego, 1979. Bar: Nev. 1980, U.S. Dist. Ct. Nev. 1982, U.S. Supreme Ct. 1986. Intern, Calif. Ct. Appeals 4th Circuit, San Diego, 1978-79; law clk. Nev. Dist. Ct., 7th Jud. Dist., Ely, 1979-81; assoc. firm C.E. Horton, Ely, 1982-83; asst. city atty. Ely, 1982-83; assoc. firm Barker, Gillock & Perry, Reno, 1983-87, Perry & Spann, 1987-89, ptnr., 1990—. Editor Internat. Law Jour., 1979. Mem. Internat. Moot Ct. Team, 1978; recipient Dean's award Calif. Western Sch. Law, 1979. Mem. Rep. Presdl. Task Force, 1990. Mem. Nev. Bar Assn., Washoe Bar Assn., U.S. Jaycees (past pres. White Pine, Nev.). Republican. Roman Catholic. Lodge: Elks (past treas. Ely club). Office: Perry & Spann 6130 Plumas St Reno NV 89509-6060

BARKLEY, WILLIAM DONALD, museum executive director; b. New Westminster, B.C., Can., Apr. 4, 1941; s. Donald MacMillan and Ethel Margaret (Mines) B.; m. Helen Gayle Alanson, Aug. 29, 1964; children: Warren Vincent, Colleen Michelle. BS, U. B.C., 1964, MA, 1971. Cert. tchr. Can. Tchr. Salmon Arm (B.C.) Sr. Secondary Sch., 1965-68; wildlife biologist Wye Marsh Wildlife Ctr., Midland, Ont., Can., 1968-72; chief interpretation Can. Wildlife Svc., Ottawa, Ont., 1972-77; asst. dir. B.C. Provincial Mus., Victoria, 1977-84; dir. Royal B.C. Mus., Victoria, 1984—; advisor cultural resource mgmt. program U. Victoria, 1985—; lectr. univs. Contbr. articles to Nat. History Interpretation mag., 1965—. Bd. dirs. Tourism Victoria, 1985—. Recipient Disting. Svc. award Interpretation Can., Ottawa, 1983. Mem. Can. Mus. Assn. (pres. 1987-89), B.C. Mus. Assn., Internat. Coun. of Mus.-Can., Can. Pks. and Wilderness Soc., Can. Nature Fedn., Victoria A.M. Tourism Svcs. Assn. (treas.), Union Club. Mem. United Ch. Can. Office: Royal BC Mus, 675 Belleville St, Victoria, BC Canada V8V 1X4

BARLEY, LEONARD VAUGHN, physician; b. San Antonio, Mar. 21, 1946; s. Leonard V. Sr. and Peggy (Stalnecker) B.; m. Linda M. Malo, Dec. 23, 1967; 1 child, Isaac E. BS, U. Houston, 1969; MA, U. Tex., San Antonio, 1973. Resident in psychiatry Letterman Army Med. Ctr., San Francisco, 1973-76; chief outpatient svcs. Brooke Army Med. Ctr., San Antonio, 1976-78; med. dir. West Ctrl. Mental Health, Carson City, Colo., 1979-82; pvt. practice Colorado Springs, Colo., 1978—; med. dir. Eating Disorders, Colorado Springs, Colo., 1992—; chmn. MedLogic Global Corp., Colorado Springs, Colo., 1992—; med. dir. Cedar Springs, Colorado Springs, Colo., 1994—. Patentee in field. Chmn. Victim Compensation Bd., Colorado Springs, 1986-88. Maj. U.S. Army, 1973-88. Fellow Am. Psychiat. Assn.; mem. Colo. Psychiat. Assn. (trustee 1986-88), Colorado Springs Psychiat. Soc. (pres. 1986). Office: 2135 Southgate Rd Colorado Springs CO 80906-2605

BARLOW, HAVEN J., state legislator, realtor; b. Clearfield, Utah, Jan. 4, 1922; s. Jesse and Asdora (Beck) B.; m. Bonnie Rae Ellison, Nov. 23, 1944; children: Jesselie Anderson, Heidi Harris, Rachel, Haven J., Stewart E., Duncan. BS, Utah State U., 1944, postgrad. U. Utah Law Sch., Harvard U. Sch. Bus. Mem. Utah Ho. of Reps., 1953-57, senator Utah State Senate, 1957-94; pres. Barlow Ins., Inc. 1950—; bd. dirs. 1st Nat. Bank of Layton. Past pres. Lake Bonniville council Boy Scouts Am.; bd. dirs., former trustee Utah State Symphony; mem. Davis County Pvt. Industry council. Served to lt. (j.g.) USN, 1942-44; PTO, ETO. Recipient Disting. Service award Utah State U., 1986, Humanitarian award Utah Vocat. Assn., Light of Learning award State Bd. Edn., Silver Beaver award Boy Scouts Am., Disting. Svc. award Weber State U., 1988, Profl. Achievement award Utah State U., Disting. Svc. award Utah Symphony Orch. Republican. Mormon. Home: 552 Elm St Layton UT 84041-4308

BARLOW, WILLIAM PUSEY, JR., accountant; b. Oakland, Calif., Feb. 11, 1934; s. William P. and Muriel (Block) B.; student Calif. Inst. Tech., 1952-54. AB in Econs., U. Calif.-Berkeley, 1956. CPA, Calif. Acct. Barlow, Davis & Wood, San Francisco, 1960-72, ptnr., 1964-72; ptnr., J.K. Lasser & Co., 1972-77, Touche Ross & Co., San Francisco, 1977-78; self employed acct., 1978-89; ptnr. Barlow & Hughan, 1990—. Co-author: Collectible Books: Some New Paths, 1979, The Grolier Club, 1884-1984, 1984; editor: Book Catalogues: Their Varieties and Uses, 2d edit., 1986; contbr. articles to profl. jours. Fellow Gleeson Libr. Assocs., 1969, pres., 1971-74; mem. Coun. Friends Bancroft Libr., 1971—, chmn., 1974-79; bd. dirs. Oakland Ballet, 1982—, pres. 1986-89, chmn. 1995—. Recipient Sir Thomas More medal Gleeson Libr. Assocs., 1989; named to Water Ski Hall of Fame, 1993. Mem. Am. Water Ski Assn. (bd. dirs., regional chmn. 1959-63, pres. 1963-66, chmn. bd. 1966-69, 77-79, hon. v.p. 1969—), Internat. Water Ski Fedn. (exec. bd. 1961-71, 75-78), Bibliog. Soc. Am. (coun. 1986—, pres. 1992—), Grolier Club (N.Y.C.), Roxburghe Club (San Francisco), Book of Calif. Club (bd. dirs. 1963-76, pres. 1968-69, treas. 1971-83). Home: 1474 Hampel St Oakland CA 94602-1346 Office: 449 15th St Oakland CA 94612-2821

BARMAN, ROBERT JOHN, home electronics company executive; b. Glendale, Calif.; s. Robert Grant and Geraldine (Howe) B.; m. Jean Ann Crane, June 19, 1965; children: John Robert, Jeffrey Wynn. BS in Mktg., Calif. State U., L.A., 1965. Sales coord. Teledyne Packard Bell, L.A., 1965-67; dist. mgr. Teledyne Packard Bell, Fresno, L.A., 1968-71; regional sales mgr. Teledyne Packard Bell, Boston, 1971-73; major accounts sales mgr. Quasar Co., L.A., 1973-75, regional sales mgr., 1975-76, sales mgr., 1976-77, zone mgr., 1985—; v.p., br. mgr. Quasar Co., Seattle, 1977-84; gen. mgr. Matsushita, L.A., 1985-95; mem. mgmt. com. Matsushita Elec. Corp. of Am. West, Quasar Co., Chgo., mem. distbg. coun.; mgr. spl. markets Panaconic Co. West. Bd. dirs. Irvine (Calif.) Aquatics Swim Team, Bellevue (Wash.) Athletic Club Swim Team. Office: Panasonic Co West 6550 Katella Ave Cypress CA 90630

BARMANN, BERNARD CHARLES, SR., lawyer; b. Maryville, Mo., Aug. 5, 1932; s. Charles Anselm and Veronica Rose (Fisher) B.; m. Beatrice Margaret Murphy, Sept. 27, 1965; children: Bernard Charles Jr., Brigit. PhD, Stanford U., 1966; JD, U. San Diego, 1974; MPA, Calif. State U., Bakersfield. Bar: Calif. 1974, U.S. Dist. Ct. (so. dist.) Calif. 1974, U.S. Dist. Ct. (ea. dist.) Calif. 1978, U.S. Ct. Appeals (9th cir.) 1984, U.S. Supreme Ct. Asst. prof. Ohio State U., Columbus, 1966-69, U. Toronto, Ont., Can., 1969-71; dep. county counsel Kern County, Bakersfield, Calif., 1974-85; county counsel Kern County, Bakersfield, 1985—; adj. prof. Calif. State U., Bakersfield, 1986—. Editor: The Bottom Line, 1991-93, contbr. articles to profl. jours. Mem. exec. bd. So. Sierra coun. Boy Scouts Am., Bakersfield, 1986—; bd. dirs. Kern County Acad. Decathlon, Bakersfield, 1988—. Danforth Found. fellow, 1963-65; grantee Fulbright Found., 1963-65. Mem. Calif. Bar Assn. (law practice mgmt. sect. exec. com.), County Counsel Assn. Calif. (bd. dirs. 1990—, chair 1993-94), Rotary. Office: Kern County Office of County Counsel 1115 Truxtun Ave Bakersfield CA 93301-4617

BARNA, ARPAD ALEX, electrical engineering consultant; b. Budapest, Hungary, Apr. 3, 1933; came to U.S., 1957; s. Sandor and Erzsebet (Markus) B. Diploma of Elec. Engring., Tech. U. Budapest, 1956; Degree of Engr., Stanford U., 1966, PhD in Elec. Engring., 1968; BA in Lit., U. Calif., Santa Cruz, 1986. Part-time grad. asst. Poly. U. Budapest, 1954-56; with Ctrl. Rsch. Inst. for Physics, Hungarian Acad. Scis., Budapest, 1957, Calif. Inst. Tech., Pasadena, 1957-61, Ransom Systems, San Pedro, Calif., 1961, U. Chgo., 1961-63, Stanford Linear Accelerator Ctr., 1963-69; assoc. prof. elec. engring. U. Hawaii, Honolulu, 1969-72; with Hewlett-Packard Labs., Palo Alto, Calif., 1972-83; pvt. elec. engring. cons. Capitola, Calif., 1966—; cons. Harshaw Chem. Co., Cleve., 1966-69, Cintra, Inc., Mountain View, Calif., 1969, Avantek, Inc., Santa Clara, 1969-72, W.W. Hansen Labs. of Physics, Stanford U., 1972-83, Audio Devel., Inc., Palo Alto, 1977, Monolithic Microsystems, Inc., Santa Cruz, Calif., 1982-84, SiScan Corp., Campbell, Calif., 1982-86, IMEC, Berkeley, Calif., 1990—; mem. faculty Calif. State U., Sacramento, 1972, UCLA, 1977, 81, Stanford U., 1981, U. Calif., Santa Cruz, 1984, 87. Reviewer IEEE Jour. Solid State Circuits, IEEE Transactions on Info. Theory, Jour. Optical Soc. Am., IEEE Electron Devices Letters, IEEE Proceedings, Jour. Applied Physics; contbr. articles to profl. jours.; author: High Speed Pulse Circuits, 1970, Operational Amplifiers, 1971, 2d edit. 1989, High Speed Pulse and Digital Techniques, 1980, VHSIC Technologies and Tradeoffs, 1981; co-author: Integrated Circuits in Digital Electronics, 1973, 2d edit. 1987, others. Mem. IEEE (sr.). Jewish. Home and Office: 750 Bay Ave Apt 305 Capitola CA 95010-2741

BARNARD, ANNETTE WILLIAMSON, elementary school educator; b. Phoenix, Nov. 29, 1948; d. Water Albert and Geraldine Williamson; m. Richard W. Heinrich, Sept. 1969 (div.); 1 child, Jennifer Anne; m. Charles Jay Barnard, June 6, 1981. AA, Mesa C.C., 1979; BA in Spl. Edn., Elem. Edn., Ariz. State U., 1981, postgrad., 1989; No. Ariz. U., 1995—. Cert. tchr., Ariz. Tchr. spl. edn. Tempe (Ariz.) Sch. Dist., 1981-83, tchr. Indian community, 1983-84; tchr. elem. sch. Kyrene Sch. Dist., Tempe, 1984-86, 90—; sch. dist. mentor coord., 1994—; tchr. Chandler (Ariz.) Sch. Dist., 1986-89; chair profl. stds. and cert. com. Ariz. Bd. Edn., Phoenix, 1990-94; chair facilitator Kyrene Legis. Action Community, 1991-94; mentor Kyrene Sch. dist., 1990—; commencement spkr. Ariz. State U., 1981; design. team. mem. Quality Cert. Employee Appraisal System; speaker in field. Contbg. author: Environmental Education Compendium for Energy Resources, 1991, System of Personnel Development, 1989. Bd. dirs. Ariz. State Rep. Caucus, Phoenix, 1990-93, precinct committeewoman, Tempe, 1990-92. Recipient Profl. Leadership award Kiwanis Club Am., Tempe, 1984; nominee to talent bank Coun. on Women's Edn. Programs U.S. Dept. Edn., 1982; named Tchr. of Yr., local newspaper, 1993. Mem. ASCD, Kyrene Edn. Assn. (chair legis. com. 1990-94), Kappa Delta Pi, Phi Kappa Phi, Phi Theta Kappa, Pi Lambda Theta. Home: 3221 W Jasper Dr Chandler AZ 85226-1421

BARNARD, DALE LYNN, microbiologist; b. Ogden, Utah, July 13, 1951; s. Wayne Taylor and Lottie Elaine (Child) B.; m. Vickie Lynn Wilde, Aug. 14, 1974; children: Nikolas, Joseph, Melissa, David, Thomas. BS in Microbiology, Chemistry, Weber State Coll., 1977; MS in Microbiology, Idaho State U., 1979; PhD in Microbiology, Biochemistry, Brigham Young U., 1987; postgrad., Utah State U., 1988. Teaching asst. dept. microbiology & chemistry Idaho State U., Pocatello, 1979; instr., rsch. asst. dept. microbiology Brigham Young U., Provo, Utah, 1979-87; lab. tech. Utah state health dept. Brigham Young U., Utah County Mosquito Abatement Dist., Provo, 1983; instr. Snow Coll., 1983; rsch. asst. prof. dept. animal, dairy & vet. scis. Utah State U., Logan, 1988—; chmn. Associated Students Brigham Youn gU. Rsch. Fund, 1983-81; presenter in field. Contbr. articles to profl. jours. Asst. scoutmaster Boy Scouts Am., Nibley, Utah, 1989-90, 90-92, chartered orgn. rep., 1992-93, explorer post leader, 1993-94; mem. Up with Down's Syndrome Soc. Postdoctoral fellow Dept. Animal, Dairy & Vet. Scis., Utah State U., 1987-88. Mem. Internat. Soc. Antiviral Rsch., Am. Soc. Microbiology (sec. Intermountain br. 1990-91), Am. Soc. Virology, Sigma Xi. Mem. LDS Ch. Office: Utah State U Dept ADVS Inst Antiviral Rsch Logan UT 84322-5600

BARNARD, ROLLIN DWIGHT, retired financial executive; b. Denver, Apr. 14, 1922; s. George Cooper and Emma (Riggs) B.; m. Patricia Reynolds Bierkamp, Sept. 15, 1943; children: Michael Dana, Rebecca Susan (Mrs. Paul C. Wulfestieg), Laurie Beth (Mrs. Kenneth J. Kostelecky). B.A., Pomona

Coll., 1943. Clk. Morey Merc. Co., Denver, 1937-40; ptnr George C. Barnard & Co. (gen. real estate and ins.), Denver, 1946-47; v.p. Foster & Barnard, Inc., 1947-53; instr. Denver U., 1949-53; dir. real estate U.S. P.O. Dept., Washington, 1953-55, dep. asst. postmaster gen., bur. facilities, 1955-59, asst. postmaster gen., 1959-61; pres., dir. Midland Fed. Savs. & Loan Assn., Denver, 1962-84; vice chmn. Bank Western Fed. Savs. Bank, 1984-87; vice chmn., pres. Western Capital Investment Corp., 1985-87. Mayor City of Greenwood Village, Colo., 1989-93, chmn. Planning and Zoning Commn., 1969-73, mem. coun., 1975-77; pres. Denver Area coun. Boy Scouts Am., 1970-71, mem. exec. bd., 1962-73; mem. adv. bd. Denver Area coun. Boy Scouts Am., 1973—; bd. dirs. Downtown Denver Improvement Assn., pres., 1965; bd. dirs. Bethesda Found., Inc., 1973-82, Children's Hosp., 1979-84, treas., 1983-84; bd. dirs. Children's Health Corp., Inc., 1982-93; trustee Mile High United Fund, 1969-72, Denver Symphony Assn., 1973-74; bd. dirs. Colo. Coun. Econ. Edn., 1971-80, chmn. 1971-76; trustee, v.p., treas. Morris Animal Found., 1969-81, pres., chmn. 1974-78, trustee emeritus, 1981—; trustee Denver Zool. Found., 1994—; mem. acquisitions com. Friends Found. Denver Pub. Libr., 1994—. Nominated One of Ten Outstanding Young Men in Am., U.S. Jaycees, 1955, 57; recipient Disting. Svc. award Postmaster Gen. U.S., 1960; Silver Beaver award Boy Scouts Am., 1969; named Outstanding Citizen of Yr., Sertoma, 1982, Colo. Citizen of Yr., Colo. Assn. Realtors, 1982, Citizen of West, Nat. Western Stockshow, 1994. Mem. Greater Denver C. of C. (pres. 1966-67), U.S. League Savs. Instns. (bd. dirs. 1972-77, vice chmn. 1979-80, chmn. 1980-81, mem. nat. legis. com., exec. com. 1974-77), Savs. League Colo. (exec. com. 1969-73, pres. 1971-72), Colo. Assn. Commerce and Industry (dir. 1971-76), Fellowship Christian Athletes (Denver area dir. 1963-76), Western Stock Show Assn. (dir. 1971—, exec. com. 1982-94, 1st v.p. 1985-94), Mountain and Plains Appaloosa Horse Club (pres. 1970-71), Roundup Riders of the Rockies (bd. dirs. 1979—, treas. 1980-87, v.p. 1987-89, pres.-elect 1989-91, pres. 1991-93). Republican. Presbyterian. Home: 3151 E Long Rd Littleton CO 80121-1716

BARNARD, WILLIAM CALVERT, retired news service executive; b. Corpus Christi, Tex., Feb. 25, 1914; s. W.C. and Eleanor (Erb) B.; m. Julia Lacy Salter, Mar. 25, 1961; children: William Cornell, Diana Eugenia. Student, Tex. Coll. Arts and Industries, Kingsville, 1933-35. Reporter-columnist Corpus Christi Caller-Times, 1935-40; feature editor San Antonio Express-News, 1941-42; writer, state editor AP, Dallas Bur., 1942-50; AP war corr. Korean War, Far East news editor, 1953-54; bur. chief AP, Dallas, 1954-62; gen. exec. AP, N.Y.C., 1962-71; gen. exec. for ten Western states AP, San Francisco, 1971-81; gen. exec. for 24 Western states AP, 1981-85. Recipient Journalism Forum award for coverage Korean War So. Meth. U., 1954. Presbyterian. Home: 3395 Melendy Dr San Carlos CA 94070-3463

BARNARD, WILLIAM MARION, psychiatrist; b. Mt. Pleasant, Tex., Dec. 17, 1949; s. Marion Jaggers and Med (Cody) B. BA, Yale U., 1972; MD, Baylor U., 1976. Diplomate Am. Bd. Psychiatry and Neurology. Resident NYU/Bellevue Med. Ctr., 1976-79; fellow L.I. Jewish/Hillside Med. Ctr., 1979-80; chief, liaison, consultation psychiatrist Queens (N.Y.) Med. Ctr., 1980-83; liaison, consultation psychiatrist Mt. Sinai Med. Ctr., N.Y.C., 1983-84; clin. asst. prof. adminstrn. NYU Med. Sch., N.Y.C., 1984-87; emergency psychiatrist VA Med. Ctr., N.Y.C., 1985-87; pvt. practice Pasadena, Calif., 1987—; chief psychiat. svc. Las Encinas Hosp., Pasadena, 1989, chief staff, 1990, med. dir. gen. adult. psychiat. svc., 1990-92, asst. med. dir., 1992; med. dir. CPC Alhambra Hosp., Rosemead, Calif., 1992—. Chmn. mental health com. All Saints AIDS Svc. Ctr., Pasadena, 1990-94, bd. dirs. , 1991-94; bd. dirs. Pasadena Symphony, 1989—, Whiffenpoof Alumni, New Haven, 1991—. Wilson scholar Yale U., 1973. Mem. Am. Psychiat. Assn., NYU-Bellevue Psychiat. Assn., Am. Soc. Addiction Medicine, Amateur Comedy Club, Met. Opera Club, Yale Club N.Y.C. Republican. Episcopalian.

BARNEA, URI N., music director, conductor, composer, violinist; b. Petah-Tikvah, Israel, May 29, 1943; came to U.S., 1971; s. Shimon and Miriam Burstein; m. Lizbeth A. Lund, Dec. 15, 1977; 2 children. Teaching cert., Oranim Music Inst., Israel, 1966; postgrad. Hebrew U., Israel, 1969-71; MusB, Rubin Acad. Music, Israel, 1971; MA, U. Minn., 1974, PhD, 1977. Mus. dir. Jewish Cmty. Ctr., Mpls. 1971-73; condr. Youval Chamber Orch., Mpls., 1971-73; asst. condr. U. Minn. Orchs., Mpls., 1972-77; music dir., condr. Unitarian Soc., Mpls., 1973-78, Kenwood Chamber Orch., Mpls., 1974-78, Knox-Galesburg Symphony, 1978-83, Billings Symphony Soc., Mont., 1984—; asst. prof. Knox Coll., Galesburg, Ill., 1978-83; violinist, violist Yellowstone Chamber players, Billings, 1984—; violist Tri-City Symphony, Quad-Cities, Ill., Iowa, 1983-84; condr. Cedar Arts Forum String Camp, Cedar Falls, Iowa, 1981, 82; European conducting debut, London, Eng., Neuchatel and Fribourg, Switzerland, 1986. Can. conducting debut No. Music Festival, North Bay Ont., 1989; Violin Concerto, 1990; Russian conducting debut Symphony Orch. Kuzbass, Kemerovo, 1993; recordings include: W. Piston's Flute and Clarinet Concertos, Mario Lombardo's Oboe Concerto, two compact discs of Am. music; composer of numerous compositions including String Quartet (1st prize Aspen Composition Competition 1976), Sonata for Flute and Piano, 1975 (Diploma of Distinction 26th Viotti Internat. Competition, Italy 1975), Ruth, a ballet, 1974 (1st prize Oberhoffer Composition Contest 1976), Active in music adv. panel Ill. Arts Coun., 1980-83; v.p. Cmty. Concert Assn., Galesburg, 1980-83; bd. dirs. Knox Coll. Credit Union, Galesburg, 1982-83, Sta. KEMC Pub. Radio, Billings, 1984—, Fox Theater Corp., Billings, 1984-86. Recipient Friend of Arts title Sigma Alpha Iota, 1982; Ill. Arts Coun. grantee, 1979; Hebrew U. Jerusalem scholar, 1972-74, Hebrew U. and Rubin Acad. Mus. scholar, 1969, 70; Individual Artist fellow Mont. Arts Coun., 1986. Mem. NEA (music adv. panel 1990—), ASCAP, Minn. Composers Forum, Conductors Guild, Am. String Tchrs. Assn. Office: Billings Symphony Soc PO Box 7055 Billings MT 59103-7055

BARNERT, CYRIL, III, psychiatrist; b. Jan. 7, 1942; s. Cyril Barnert Jr. and Janet Claire (Watnik) Nisselson; m. Margo Diana MacDonald, Feb. 5, 1966 (div. June 1976); children: Steven, David; m. Susan Maya Barnert, June 11, 1977; 1 child, Elizabeth. Student, U. Mich., 1959-61; BA, Johns Hopkins U., 1963, MD, 1966. Diplomate Am. Bd. Psychiatry and Neurology. Resident in psychiatry UCLA Neuropsychiatric Inst., 1967-70, fellow in legal psychiatry, 1970-71; staff psychiatrist Resthaven Cmty. Mental Health Ctr., L.A., 1970-71; program chief Vietnam Vets. inpatient unit VA Med. Ctr., Brentwood, Calif., 1974-77; unit chief inpatient svc. unit IV VA Med. Ctr., Brentwood, 1974-77; chief evaluation/admissions unit Brentwood Divsn. West L.A. VA Med. Ctr., 1981-84, assoc. chief of psychiatry for inpatient svcs., 1985-88, acting quality assurance officer, 1986, acting chief psychiat. svc., 1987-88, assoc. chief of staff for ambulatory care, 1988-93, deputy chief of staff for mental health, 1993—; assoc. clin. prof. dept. psychiatry UCLA, 1986—, vice chmn., 1993—; rsch. clk. Nat. Inst. Neurologic Diseases and Blindness, San Juan, P.R., 1965; presenter UCLA Neuropsychiat. Inst. Colloquium, 1971, Brentwood Med. Staff Conf., 1975, 79, 82, 85, Met. State Hosp., 1987; cons. psychiatrist Terminal Island (Calif.) Fed. Correctional Instn., 1970-71; examiner Am. Bd. Psychiatry and Neurology, 1980-82, 91, 93; supr. psychiat. residents and psychology interns, Ctr. for Legal Psychiatry, Santa Monica, Calif., 1981-84; cons. Calif. Bd. Prison Terms, 1988—, IntraCorp Med. Rev. Svcs., 1989-92, Managed Health Network, 1990—, Calif. Psychol. Health Plan, 1991-93;. Contbr. articles to profl. jours. Maj. USAF, 1971-73. Mem. Am. Psychiat. Assn., Soc. USAF Psychiatrists, So. Calif. Psychiat. Soc. (peer rev. com. 1988-90), Assn. Brentwood Clin. Psychiatrists (pres. 1976-77), Nat. Assn. VA Psychiatrists (Brentwood divsn. rep. 1984-87, Dist. XII dir. 1987—). Office: West Los Angeles VA Med Ctr Los Angeles CA 90073

BARNES, CLIFFORD V., artist; b. Bell, Calif., June 19, 1940; s. Kenneth F. and Veda I. (Meacham) B.; m. Betty V. Marhad, Mar. 29, 1969. BFA, Art Ctr. Sch. Design, L.A., 1962. Archtl. illustrator ITT Gilphilin & L.W. Davidson, L.A., 1963-69; owner Cliff Barnes Art Gallery, Lake Arrowhead, Calif., 1969—; curator art exhibits San Bernardino County Mus., Redlands, Calif., 1987-89; juror Fine Arts Inst., Redlands, 1983-85; judge Anaheim Conv. Wildlife and West Show, 1995. Recipient gold medal in watercolor Festival of Western Art, San Dimas, Calif., 1990-93, in drawing, 1990-93, 95, Art in Parks excellence award Nat. Parks Assn., Grand Tetons, Wyo., 1993. Mem. Watercolor West (bd. dirs.), Am. Indian & Cowboy Artists (past pres., bd. dirs. 1990-95, Eagle Feather award 1989, 91, 93). Home and [illegible] PO Box 741 Lake Arrowhead CA 92352-0741

BARNES, CLOYD RAY, sculptor, retired engineer; b. Hartford, Ark., July 18, 1934; s. Cloyd Hiram and Esta Elizabeth (McCafferty) B.; m. Wanda Jean Carlton, Oct. 17, 1954; children: Mark E., Stephanie Barnes Veasman. BS in Physics, Tulsa U., 1968. Mem. tech. staff N.Am. Rockwell, Tulsa, 1964-68; sr. aerosystems engr. Gen. Dynamics, Alamogordo, N.Mex., 1968-72; mgr. project engrng. Dynalectron Corp., Alamogordo, 1972-77; mgr. ops. dept. Dynalectron Corp., Alamagordo, 1977-80, tech. dir. radar backscatter divsn., 1980-84, tech. dir., site mgr., 1984-86; mgr. radio frequency test ops. Martin Marietta Denver Aerospace, 1986-89, dept. staff engr., 1989-91; represented by numerous galleries, including Fenn Galleries, Santa Fe, N.Mex., Knox Galleries, Vail and Beaver Creek, Colo., Fine Art at Cherry Creek, Denver, Visual Individualists United, Bklyn., Paint Horse Gallery, Breckenridge, Colo., Greenhouse Gallery, San Antonio; interim instr. Denver Art Students League, 1994. Exhibited in group shows at Southeastern Wildlife Expo, Charleston, S.C., Nat. Acad. Design, N.Y.C., Audubon Show, N.Y.C., Am. Artists Profl. League, N.Y.C., (Helen G. Oehler award), 1991, Nat. Wildlife Show, Kansas City, 1993 (Best of Show), Cantigny Park, Chgo., BCCFA Show, Clifton, Tex. (Best of Show award), Western Regional Show, Cheyenne, Wyo., N.Am. Sculpture Exhibit, Golden, Colo., Rough Rider Art Show, Williston, N.D., 1993 (Grand Prize 1993), Ho. Reps. Office Bldg.-Rotunda, Washington, 1994, Am. Artists Profl. League, 1994 (Leila G. Sawyer award), VIU, 1995 (Grumbacher Silver Medallion award). Mem. IEEE, Rocky Mountain Elk Found. (assoc.), Allied Artists Am. (assoc.), Knickerbocker Artists (assoc.). Home and Studio: 7425 S Milwaukee Way Littleton CO 80122-1951

BARNES, ELIZABETH J., operating room nurse; b. Middletown, N.Y., Nov. 10, 1964; d. Ronald S. and Linda E. (Richardson) B. AA, Fla. Community Coll., Jacksonville, 1987, AS, 1989. RN, Fla., cert. in perioperative nursing. Physician's asst. Jacksonville; oper. rm. nurse Univ. Med. Ctr., Jacksonville, 1990-91; traveling nurse Humana Hosp. Brandon, Fla., 1991, Shady Grove Adventist Hosp., Rockville, Md., 1991, Dorchester Gen. Hosp., Cambridge, Md., 1991, So. Hills Med. Ctr., Nashville, 1992, St. Luke's, Phoenix, Ariz., 1992; with Kaiser Permanente Med. Ctr., Honolulu, 1993—. Mem. Fla. Nurses Assn. (nominating com.), Assn. Oper. Rm. Nurses.

BARNES, GERALD R., bishop; b. Phoenix, Ariz., June 22, 1945. Grad., St. Leonard Sem., Dayton, Ohio; student, Assumption-St. John's Sem., San Antonio. Ordained priest Roman Cath. Ch., 1975, titular bishop of Monte Fiascone. Aux. bishop San Bernardino, Calif., 1992—. Office: Chancery Office 1450 N D St San Bernardino CA 92405-4739*

BARNES, JOANNA, author, actress; b. Boston, Nov. 15, 1934; d. John Pindar and Alice Weston (Mutch) B. BA, Smith Coll., 1956. Actress appearing in motion pictures: Auntie Mame, 1958, B.S. I Love You, 1971, Spartacus, 1963, The Parent Trap, 1966, The War Wagon, 1971; TV appearances include What's My Line, The Tonight Show with Johnny Carson, Merv Griffin Show, Trials of O'Brien, Dateline: Hollywood, Murder She Wrote; book reviewer L. A. Times, syndicated columnist Chgo. Tribune, N.Y. News Syndicate, 1963-65; author: Starting from Scratch, 1968, The Deceivers, 1970, Who Is Carla Hart, 1973, Pastora, 1980, Silverwood, 1985. Mem. Phi Beta Kappa.

BARNES, MICHAEL KEITH, transit marketing executive; b. N.Y.C., Apr. 22, 1942; s. Arthur M. and Roberta (Keith) B.; m. Ann M. Thomas, Feb. 11, 1967; children: Thomas, David. BA, U. Iowa, 1965, MA, 1969. Writer, editor, broadcaster Stas. KXIC and WSUI, Iowa City, Iowa, 1964-67; sr. publicist/account exec. Gen. Elec. Co., Chgo., 1970-73; news bureau mgr. So. Calif. Rapid Transit Dist., L.A., 1973-81; mktg. mgr. Orange County Transit Dist., Garden Grove, Calif., 1981-83; publ. and video programming mgr. So. Calif. Rapid Transit Dist., L.A., 1983-93; pub. info. mgr. Los Angeles County Met. Transp. Authority, L.A., 1993—; instr. reporting U. So. Calif., 1975-78. Active AFS, 1990-94. With U.S. Army, 1967-69. Recipient 1st Pl award Am. Pub. Transit Assn., 1992. Republican. Office: LA Co Met Transp Authority Dept 2630 PO Box 194 Los Angeles CA 90053-0194

BARNES, PETER FRANCIS, physician, researcher, medical educator; b. Kowloon, Hong Kong, Apr. 22, 1956; came to U.S., 1974; s. Robert Joseph and Sylvia Maria (Remedios) B.; m. Susan Alison Barrows, July 12, 1980; children: Jason, Amanda. BS in Biology, Stanford U., 1977; MD, U. So. Calif., 1981. Diplomate Am. Bd. Internal Medicine, Am. Bd. Infectious Diseases. Intern U. So. Calif. Med. Ctr., L.A., 1981-82, resident, 1982-84, chief resident, 1984-85; asst. prof. clin. medicine U. So. Calif., L.A., 1985-88, asst. prof. medicine, 1989-92, assoc. prof. medicine, 1992—. Contbr. articles to profl. jours. Infectious Diseases fellowship U. So. Calif. Med. Ctr., 1992-94. Mem. Am. thoracic Soc. (program com. 1990—, long-range planning com. 1990—), Am .Soc. for Microbiology, Western Soc. for clin. Investigation, Am. Assn. Immunologists, Internat. Union Against Tuberculosis, Alpha Omega Alpha. Office: U So Calif Sch Medicine HMR 904 2025 Zonal Ave Los Angeles CA 90033

BARNES, RAMONA, state legislator; b. Pikeville, Tenn., July 7, 1938; d. Ellison Wheeler; m. Larry Barnes, 1960; children: Randall, Michael, Michelle. Attended, Mich. State Coll., Waipahu C.C., Hawaii. Pres. Arctic Rsch. Cons. Internat.; mem. Alaska Ho. of Reps., 1978—; majority leader, spkr. pro tem, 1983-84; minority whip, 1991-92; minority leader, 1992; former chmn. judiciary com.; former mem. numerous coms. Mem. sch. bd. City of Elmendorf, Alaska, 1973-76; mem. adv. sch. bd. City of Anchorage, Alaska, 1975-76, now precinct committeewoman; del. Alaska Rep. State Conv., 1976, 78. Recipient Appreciation award Alaska Peace Ofcl. Assn., 1982, Appreciation cert. Anchorage Cmty. Mental Health Svcs., 1983-85, Am. Outstanding Legislator award Am. Exch. Coun., 1984; named Legislator of Yr., Alaska Sportsmen's Coun. and Nat. Wildlife Fedn., 1980, 81. Mem. Anchorage Rep. Women's Club, Nat. Fedn. Rep. Women, Navy League, Bus. and Profl. Women's Club, Am. Legis. Exch. Coun., Nat. Order Women Legislators. Mem. Ch. of Christ. Home: 2230 Paxson Dr Anchorage AK 99504-3412 also: PO Box 3382 Anchorage AK 99510-0001 Office: Alaska Ho of Reps 716 W 4th Ave Ste 600 Anchorage AK 99501-2133 also: PO Box 103382 Anchorage AK 99510-3382

BARNES, RAYMOND EDWARD, fire department official; b. Denver, Colo., May 1, 1950; s. Carroll E. and Margaret A. (Minckler) B.; m. Katherine Michele Sanchez, Jan. 3, 1970; 1 child, Tamara Adrienne. BS in Aerospace Tech., Bus., Edn., Met. State Coll., 1971; postgrad., Red Rocks C.C., 1974-75, U. No. Colo., 1976; grad. exec. fire officer program, Nat. Fire Acad., 1990; MPA, U. Colo., 1991. With City of Aurora (Colo.) Fire Dept., 1971—, paramedic and rescue technician, 1976-79, lt., 1979-82, capt., 1982-85, battalion chief, suppression, 1985-87, dir. tng., 1987-91, fire chief, 1991—; adj. instr. Nat. Fire Acad., Md., 1987—; co-dir. Rocky Mountain Fire Acad.; metro co-chair Region VIII Tng. Resources and Data Exch. Active Aurora Gang Task Force; past committeeman, del. to county, state polit. assemblies;. Mem. Internat. Assn. Fire Chiefs, Internat. Assn. Metro Fire Chiefs, Internat. Soc. Fire Svc. Instrs., Internat. Assn. Firefighters (occupational safety and health com.), Soc. Nat. Fire Acad. Instrs., Soc. Exec. Fire Officers, Fire Dept. Safety Officers Orgn., State Fire Chiefs, Denver Metro Fire Chiefs, Aurora C. of C. (bd. dirs. leadership forum), Homeowners Assn. (past pres. bd. dirs.). Home: 3966 S Sable Cir Aurora CO 80014-5176 Office: City of Aurora Fire Dept 1470 S Havana St Aurora CO 80012-4014

BARNES, STEPHEN PAUL, financial planner; b. Corsicana, Tex., July 30, 1957; s. Paul Gordon and Barbara Jewell (Hawkins) B.; m. Tina Marie Dacus, Dec. 20, 1980 (div. 1985); m. Kathie Jo Beck, Feb. 20, 1988; 1 child, Stephanie Kathryn. BS, Grand Canyon U., 1982. Cert. fin. planner. Sales rep. Phil Bramsen Distbrs., Mesa, Ariz., 1978-81, credit mgr., 1981-82; registered rep. John Hancock Fin. Svcs., Phoenix, 1983-86; mktg. mgmt. assoc. John Hancock Fin. Svcs., Boston, 1986-87; sales mgr. John Hancock Fin. Svcs., Phoenix, 1987-90; fin. planner Barnes Investment Adv., Phoenix, 1990—; dir. Desert Schs. Fed. Credit Union, 1990—, vice-chmn. bd., 1994, chmn. bd., 1995. Pub. address announcer home basketball games Grand Canyon Coll., 1977—; dir. United Way capital dr. Western region John Hancock Fin. Svcs., 1988, 89; com. chair capital dr. John C. Lincoln Day Care Ctr., Phoenix, 1987. Mem. Inst. Cert. Fin. Planners (past pres., dir. Phoenix soc.), Assn. for Investment Mmgt. and Rsch., Phoenix Soc. of Fin. Analysts, Ariz. Assn. of Inst. of Cert. Fin. Planners (chmn. 1993—). Republican. Methodist. Home: 7516 N 22nd St Phoenix AZ 85020-4705 Office: Barnes Investment Adv 5225 N Central Ave Ste 208 Phoenix AZ 85012 also: PO Box 32413 Phoenix AZ 85064-2413

BARNES, WILLIAM ANDERSON, real estate investment manager; b. Cin., Mar. 11, 1944; s. Frederick Walter and Catherine Gardner (Bowden) B.; m. Sara Winkler, Dec. 13, 1980; children: Tucker, Charlie, Hanne. BA, Yale U., 1966; MBA, Harvard U., 1970; postgrad. in Internat. Econs., Inst. D'Etudes Politiques, Paris, 1993. Adminstrv. asst. to pres. Boise Cascade Corp., Palo Alto, Calif., 1970-71; project gen. mgr. Boise Cascade Corp., Incline Village, Nev., 1971-73; sr. devel. dir. The Rouse Co., Columbia, Md., 1973-76; exec. dir. Pa. Ave. Devel. Corp., Washington, 1977-82; mng. dir. Edward Plant Co., San Francisco, 1982-87; pres. Broadacre Pacific Corp., San Francisco, 1987-92, Barnes and Co., San Francisco, 1992—; guest lectr. Harvard Bus. Sch., Cambridge, Mass.; faculty mem. Profl. Devel. Seminar; panelist Urban Land Inst.; lectr. Smithsonian Instn., U. San Francisco, mem. adv. coun. Trustee Navy Meml. Found., Brichard Properties Trust, S.H. Children's Svcs., Inc., Columbia Interfaith Housing Corp., 1974-76; mem. U.S./USSR Trade Mission, 1975, Bay Area Coun. Housing Action Task Force, 1983-85, Mill Valley City Gen. Plan Com.; treas. Yale U. Class of 1966. U.S. White House fellow, Washington, 1976, German Marshall Fund fellow, 1979; recipient Presdl. Design award, 1988. Office: Barnes and Co 1 Embarcadero Ctr Ste 860 San Francisco CA 94111-3629

BARNES, WILLIE R., lawyer; b. Dallas, Dec. 9, 1931; M. Barbara Ann Bailey; children: Michael, Sandra, Traci, Wendi, Brandi. BA, UCLA, 1953, JD, 1959. Bar: Calif. 1960, U.S. Dist. Ct. (cen. dist.) Calif. 1960. Various atty. positions Calif. Dept. of Corps., L.A., 1960-70, asst. commr. of corps., 1970-75, commr. of corps., 1975-79; ptnr., chmn. corp. dept. Manatt, Phelps, Rothenberg & Phillips, L.A., 1979-88; ptnr. Wyman, Bautzer, Kuchel & Silbert, L.A., 1989-91, Katten Muchin Zavis & Weitzman, L.A., 1991-92, Musick, Peeler & Garrett, L.A., 1992—; chmn. svc. plan com. Knox-Keene Health Care, 1976-79; mem. securities regulatory reform com. State of Calif., 1979-81; mem. shareholders rights and securities transactions Calif. Senate Commn. on Corp. Governances, 1986—; chmn. Leveraged Real Estate Task Force, Inst. Cert. Planners, 1985-86; gen. counsel UCLA Alumni Assn., 1982-86. Co-mng. editor: Calif. Bus. Law Reporter, 1982-83. With U.S. Army , 1954-56. Named Law Alumnus of Year UCLA, 1976; recipient Resolution of Commendation Calif. Senate, 1979, Calif. Assembly, 1979. Mem. ABA (fed. regulation of securities and state regulation of securities coms., franchise forum, futures regulation com.), State Bar Calif. (bus. law sect. 1979, exec. com. 1983-86, vice chmn. 1985-86, com. on corps. 1982-83, ad hoc com. on corp. governance and takeovers 1986-88), Beverly Bar Assn. (corp. and comml. law sect.) Century City Bar Assn., L.A. Bar Assn., M.W. Securities Commrs. Assn., N.Am. Securities Assn., Ind. Commn. on L.A. Police Dept. Democrat. Office: Musick Peeler & Garrett One Wilshire Blvd Ste 2000 Los Angeles CA 90017

BARNES-ROBERTS, PHILIP IRWIN, engineer; b. L.A., Jan. 19, 1945; s. Charles Herman and Romania Vera (Pratt) Roberts; m. Kathy Ashby, June 2, 1966 (div. 1974); children: Romania Valerie Roberts Fowler, Kristi Ann Roberts; m. Donna Lynn Barnes, June 30, 1984. Student, Palomar Coll., 1962-63, U. Utah, 1966-68; AA, Orange Coast Coll., 1976; student, Calif. State U., L.A., 1986—. Lic. FCC Gen. Radiotelephone. Gyro-optic mechanic Philco-Ford Aeronutronics, Newport Beach, Calif., 1972-74; rsch. assoc. Hughes Aircraft, Newport Beach, 1974-80; systems engr. Anderson Jacobson I.O.S., Anaheim, Calif., 1980-83; sr. hardware engr. Honeywell Ericsson Devel. Co., Anaheim, 1983-85; engrng. assoc. Jet Propulsion Lab., Pasadena, Calif., 1985-93; devel. engr. Loral E.O.S., Pasadena, 1993-95. Sgt. USMC, 1964-72. Mem. Assn. Computing Machinery, Forth Interest Group, Nat. Space Soc. Libertarian.

BARNETT, DAVID HUGHES, software engineer, network engineer; b. Rockville Centre, N.Y., Oct. 9, 1947; s. Paul Wilson Jr. and Patricia (Hughes) B.; m. Rosemary Friday, July 9, 1979 (div. 1983). BA, Drew U., 1970. Program analyst So. Nev. Drug Abuse Coun., Las Vegas, 1974-75; project supr. Treatment Alternatives to Street Crime, Las Vegas, 1975-78; sr. project assoc. Helix Group, Berkeley, Calif., 1978-81; cons. Pacific Inst. for Rsch. and Evaluation, Berkeley, 1979-80; rsch. tech. Sonoma State U., Rolmert Park, Calif , 1981-82; system mgr. Database Minicomputers, San Francisco, 1982-84; cons. sys. programmer Wells Fargo Bank, San Francisco, 1984-89; messaging architect Kaiser Permanente, Walnut Creek, Calif., 1989—. Contbr. articles to profl. jours. Mem. Am. Soc. for Quality Control (cert. quality engr.).

BARNETT, ERNA JUSTINE, nonprofit organization administrator; b. N.Y.C., Nov. 12, 1945; d. Arvom Barnett and Ella Moewes. BA, U. Colo., 1983. Dir. pub. rels. Seattle Opera Assn., 1964-73; program mgr. Seattle Arts Commn., 1973; gen. coord., CEO Bumbershoot Arts Festival, Seattle, 1973-74; mgr. pub. rels. Centrum Found., Pt. Townsend, Wash., 1974-75; fin. adminstr. Wash. Commn. for Humanities, Seattle, 1986-91; exec. dir. Comty. Ctr. for Performing Arts, Eugene, Oreg., 1991-92; fin. adminstr. Child Care Support Svcs., Portland, Oreg., 1992-93; fin. cons. Oreg. Coun. for Humanities, Portland, 1992—; mktg. cons. Providence Med. Ctr., Portland, 1993—; mgmt. cons. Specialized Housing, Inc., Portland, 1993-94. Contbr. poetry to anthologies, articles to mags. Dir. New City Theater, Seattle, 1991; mem. devel. com. Women's Found. of Oreg., Portland, 1994; grant writer, vol. Friends of Trees, Portland, 1992. Recipient Spl. Achievement award Wash. Press Women, 1972. Mem. Am. Soc. Women Accts. (bd. dirs. 1991), Women in Comms., Inc., Willamette Valley Devel. Officers. Office: PO Box 82606 Portland OR 97282-0606

BARNETT, JEANIE MAUREEN, writer, editor; b. Chgo., Feb. 11, 1958; d. Earl D. and Laura E. (Parkhurst) B. BA, U. Ill., 1980. Writer Pioneer Press/North Shore Mag., Wilmette, Ill., 1980-82; Peace Corps vol. U.S. Peace Corps, Ghana, West Africa, 1982-84; univ. instr. U. Redlands, Calif., 1988-89; editorial coord. L.A. Herald Examiner, 1988-89; exec. editor Minority Bus. Entrepreneur, L.A., 1985—; co-founder, editor Women's Bus. Exclusive, L.A., 1993—. Author: (book) Let's Visit Ghana, 1988; contbr. numerous articles to mags. Mem. Calif. Coun. to Promote Bus. Ownership by Women, Calif., 1993—. Mem. Nat. Assn. Women Bus. Owners. Democrat. Office: Minority Bus Entrepreneur Women's Bus Exclusive 3528 Torrance Blvd Ste 101 Torrance CA 90503-4826

BARNEY, KLINE PORTER, JR., engineering company executive, consultant; b. Dec. 16, 1934; s. Kline Porter and Doris (Nielsen) B.; m. Cheryl Kathleen Taylor, June 14, 1957; children: Peter, Suzanne, Cathleen, Patrick, Andrew. BS, U. Utah, 1957; MPA, San Diego State U , 1971. Registered profl. engr., 14 states. Asst. engr. Fallbrook (Calif.) Pub. Utility Dist., 1960-63; pres. Engrng. Sci., Inc., Arcadia, Calif., 1963-85, Parsons Mcpl. Svcs., Inc., Pasadena, Calif., 1985-89; sr. v.p. Parsons Engrng. Sci., Inc., Pasadena, 1989—; presenter on field of privatization, 1983—; environ. cons. Contbr. articles to profl. jours. Mem. exec. bd. San Gabriel coun. Boy Scouts Am., 1981—. Capt. USMC, 1957-60. Mem. ASCE, NSPE, Am. Acad. Environ. Engrs. (diplomate), Am. Pub. Works Assn., Am. Waterworks Assn., Water Environ. Fedn., Cons. Engrs. Assn. Calif., Assn. Calif. Water Agys. (assoc.), L.A. C. of C. (water resources com.), Nat. Water Resources Assn., Watereuse, Tau Beta Pi, Chi Epsilon, Phi Eta Sigma. Republican. Mem. LDS Ch. Home: PO Box 660997 Arcadia CA 91066-0997 Office: Parsons Engrng Sci Inc 100 W Walnut St Pasadena CA 91124-0001

BARNHART, BEVERLY HOMYAK, management consultant; b. Denver, Colo., Oct. 6, 1929; d. John Henry and Adeline Esther (Gray) Homyak; m. Robert W. Barnhart, 1951 (div. 1983); children: Barbara, Bonnie, Betsy, Bruce, Becky. BA, U. No. Colo., 1951; MS, Mt. State U., 1977. Tchr. Jefferson Ct. Sch., Colo., 1951-54, Greeley (Colo.) Schs., 1954-55, Golden Pre Sch., Colo., 1969-71; dir. Retired Sr. Vol. Program, Bozeman, Mont.; pvt. cons. Bozeman, Mont., 1988—; mem. Mont. State House. Contbr. articles to prof. mags. Sec. Gallatin County Democrats, Bozeman, 1987—, Gallatin County Assoc. Vol. Adminstrs., 1987-89, Aide two state Senators, 1989; bd. dirs. Career Transitions, 1989-91. Named Women of the Yr., Bozeman BPW, 1987, Mont. BPW, 1988. Mem. AARP (women's initiative spokesperson Mont.), Retired Sr. Vol. Dirs., Nat. Assn. Vol. Adminstrs., Rotary Internat. Democrat. Catholic. Office: Mt State Senate State Capitol Helena MT 59620-0001

BARNHURST, CHRISTINE LOUISE, broadcast executive; b. Salt Lake City, Sept. 3, 1949; d. Joseph Samuel and Luana Jean (Jackson) B. BS, U. Utah, 1971. From account exec. to mktg. specialist Bonneville Internat. Corp. KSL TV, Salt Lake City, 1972-84; mgr. corp. media funding U. Utah, Salt Lake City, 1985-86; dir. advt. Larry H. Miller Group, Salt Lake City, 1986-89; dir. mktg. and promotion Sta. KXIV TV Am. TV of Utah, Salt Lake City, 1989-92; gen. sales, mktg. and promotion mgr. Sta. KJZZ TV Larry H. Miller Comms., Salt Lake City, 1993—; freelance producer of corp. sales and tng. videos. Bd. dirs., telethon producer March of Dimes; bd. dirs. YWCA; bd. dirs. relief soc. LDS Ch. Recipient Nat. Print Ad award Athena, 1990, Walt Disney Top Mktg. and Promotion award, 1992, INTV Indy award, 1991, BPME Gold/Silver/Bronze awards, 1989-93, Telly awards, 1992, 93, Gold/Silver/Bronze Addy award Utah Advt. Fedn., Emmy award, 1992, 94, March of Dimes Recognition Svc. award, 1982. Mem. Am. Mktg. Assn.

BARNUM, WILLIAM LAIRD, periodontist; b. Medford, Oreg., Nov. 12, 1916; s. William Henry and Jessie Amelia (Eifert) B.; m. Amy B. Elliott, June 20, 1937; children: William Laird, Robert Elliott. D.M.D., U. Oreg., 1940; postgrad. in Periodontics, Coll. Physicians and Surgeons, San Francisco, 1946. Gen. practice dentistry Portland, Oreg., 1940-45; practice specializing in periodontics Portland, 1945-64, Medford, 1964-80; mem. dental staff Rogue Valley Meml. Hosp., 1964-79; dir. Dental Health Program, Portland Pub. Schs., 1946-64; instr. periodontics and dental hygiene U. Oreg. Dental Sch., Portland, 1945-60. Editor alumni publ. The Caementum, 1947-49. Pres. Adminstrs. and Suprs. Assn. for Portland Pub. Schs., 1958-59; chmn. health div. Portland Community Council, 1961-62. Fellow Internat. Coll. Dentists, Am. Coll. Dentists; mem. ADA (chmn. coun. on dental journalism 1952-56), Am. Soc. Dentistry for Children (pres. Oreg. unit 1952-53), Oreg. Dental Soc. (editor Oreg. Dental Jour. 1949-53), So. Oreg. Dental Soc. (pres. 1969-70), Am. Dental Interfraternity Coun. (pres. 1971-72, exec. sec. 1989-92), So. Oreg. Hist. Soc. (trustee 1985-87), Xi Psi Phi (supreme pres. 1965-67, supreme sec.-treas. 1970-91, editor Quar. 1953-58), Masons. Republican. Unitarian. Home: 245 Yale Dr Medford OR 97504-9736 Office: 832 E Main St # 13 Medford OR 97504-7153

BARON, CHARLOTTE FOEHNER, publishing executive; b. Hugoton, Kans., Aug. 7, 1941; d. John Garland and Marjorie Corinne (Parsons) Persinger; m. Olin Harold Foehner, Jr., Sept. 9, 1962 (dec. May 1983); children: Brett Olin, Kristen Kathleen; m. Robert Charles Baron, Nov. 29, 1986. BS in Med. Tech., U. Colo., Boulder, 1965; MPA, U. Colo., Denver, 1980. Registered med. technologist. Rsch. asst. virology U. Colo., Denver, 1965-66; med. technologist So. Nev. Meml. Hosp., Las Vegas, 1966, AMC Cancer Rsch. Ctr., Denver, 1975-78; computer systems analyst Fitzsimons Army Med. Ctr., Denver, 1981-82, Pentagon, Army Chief of Staff, Washington, 1982-83; computer specialist Bur. Reclamation, Denver, 1983-85; chief fin. and adminstrn. Fulcrum Pub., Inc., Golden, Colo., 1985—; treas., dir. Oxion, Inc., Hugoton, Kans., 1990—, Yale Heights Homeowners, Denver, 1992—; presdl. mgmt. intern Office Pers. Mgmt., Washington, 1980. Author: The Widows Handbook, A Guide for Living, 1988; writer, presenter articles, speeches women's groups, fin., banks, fin. seminars, 1988-92. Mem. Denver Pub. Libr. Friends, 1991-94, Denver Natural History Mus., Denver, 1992-94. Mem. Am. Soc. Pub. Adminstrn., Pi Alpha Alpha. Republican. Methodist. Home: 6969 W Yale Ave Apt 62 Denver CO 80227-3585 Office: Fulcrum Pub Inc 350 Indiana St Ste 350 Golden CO 80401-5093

BARON, MELVIN FARRELL, pharmacy educator; b. L.A., July 29, 1932; s. Leo Ben and Sadie (Bauchman) B.; m. Lorrane Ross, Dec. 20, 1953; children: Lynn Baron Friedman, Ross David. PharmD, U. So. Calif., 1957, MPA, 1973. Lic. pharmacist, Calif. Pres. Shield Health Care Ctrs., Van Nuys, Calif., 1957-83; v.p. Shield Health Care Ctrs., Inc. (C.R. Bard, Inc. subsidiary), 1983-86; pres. Merit Coll., 1988-92, PharmCom., L.A., 1990—; asst. prof. clin. pharmacy U. So. Calif., L.A., 1991—, asst. dean pharm. care programs, 1995—; adj. asst. prof. U. Without Walls, Shaw U., Raleigh, N.C., 1973; project dir. Hayne Found. Drug Rsch. Ctr. U. So. Calif., L.A., 1973; assoc. dir. Calif. Alcoholism Found., 1973-75; adj. asst. prof. clin. pharmacy Sch. of Pharmacy U. So. Calif., L.A., 1981-91; cons. Topanga Terr. Convalescent Hosp., 1970-80, Calif. Labor Mgmt. Plan for alcoholism programs and coords., 1974, Office of Alcoholism, State of Calif., Nat. In-Home Health Svc., 1975, Continuity of Life Team, 1975, others. Adv. bd. Pharmacist Newsletter, 1980—. Chmn. Friends of Operation Bootstrap, 1967-77; svc. chmn. tng. coord. Am. Cancer Soc., San Fernando Valley, Calif., 1980; mem. adv. bd. L.A. VNA, 1982; bd. dirs. pres. QSAD, 1987-88; pres. bd. Everywoman's Village, 1988-89; bd. dirs. Life Svcs., 1988—; pres. bd. counselors, U. So. Calif., 1988-92, mem. Calif. State Bd. Pharmacy Com. on Student/Preceptor Manual, 1991-93. Named Disting. Alumnus of Yr., U. So. Calif., Sch. of Pharmacy Alumni Assn., 1979, U. So. Calif. Torchbearer, 1990-91, hon. mem. Phi Lambda Sigma, L.A., 1994. Mem. Am. Pharm. Assn., Calif. Pharmacist Assn., Am. Soc. Pub. Adminstrn., Am. Assn. Colls. of Pharmacy, Phi Kappa Phi, Rho Chi. Home: 323 San Vicente Santa Monica CA 90402-1629 Office: U So Calif 1985 Zonal Ave Los Angeles CA 90033-1058

BARON, ROBERT CHARLES, publishing executive; b. L.A., Jan. 26, 1934; s. Leo Francis and Marietta (Schulze) B.; m. Faye Helen Rogers, Jan. 28, 1961 (div. 1984); m. Charlotte Rose Persinger, Nov. 29, 1986; stepchildren: Brett, Kristen. BS in Physics, St. Joseph's Coll., 1956. Registered profl. engr., Mass. Engr. RCA, Camden, N.J., 1955-57, Computer Control Co., Framingham, Mass., 1959-61; program mgr. Mariner II and IV space computers Computer Control Co., Framingham, 1961-65, engrng. mgr., 1965-69; worldwide systems mgr. Honeywell Minicomputer, Framingham, 1970-71; founder, pres., CEO Prime Computer, Framingham, 1971-75; pvt. practice Boston, 1976-83; founder and pres. Fulcrum Pub., Golden, Colo., 1984—; bd. dirs. Prime Computer, Framingham, Mass., Alling-Lander, Cheshire, Conn., Oxion, Hugoton, Kans., Fulcrum Pub., Golden Colo. Author: Digital Logic and Computer Operations, 1966, Micropower Electronics, 1970, America in the Twentieth Century, 1995; editor: The Garden and Farm Books of Thomas Jefferson, 1987, Soul of America: Documenting Our Past, 1492-1974, 1989, Colorado Rockies: The Inaugural Season, 1993. Trustee Lincoln Filene Ctr., Tufts U., Medford, Mass., 1982-84; vice chmn. bd. dirs., Mass. Audubon Soc., Lincoln, 1980-85; bd. dirs. Rocky Mountain Women's Inst., Denver, 1987-90; pres., bd. dirs. Denver Pub. Libr. Friends Found., 1989—. Mem. Am. Antiquarian Soc. (bd. dirs., chmn. 1993—), Internat. Wilderness Leadership Found. (bd. dirs. 1990—, chmn. 1994—), Thoreau Soc., Mass. Hist. Soc., Western History Assn., Erolier Club. Office: Fulcrum Pub 350 Indiana St Ste 350 Golden CO 80401-5093

BARR, CARLOS HARVEY, lawyer; b. Greeley, Colo., Oct. 12, 1936; s. Charles Allen B. and Zelma Arvilla (Sechler) Turner; m. Martha Lucia Sanchez-Morales, May 10, 1985. BA in Polit. Sci., U. Wash., 1959, MA in Polit. Sci., 1967; JD, George Wash. U., 1971. Bar: Wash. 1971, U.S. Dist. Ct. (ea. dist.) Wash. 1972, U.S. Dist. Ct. (we. dist.) Wash. 1979, U.S. Ct. Appeals (9th cir.) 1973, U.S. Supreme Ct. 1981, U.S. Tax Ct. 1985. Mgmt. intern U.S. Dept of Army, Ft. Lewis, Wash., 1960; joined Fgn. Svc., Dept. State, 1960, officer, 1960-61; vice consul U.S. Consulate Gen., Monterrey, Mexico, 1961-64; consular officer, third sec. Am. Embassy, Khartoum, Sudan, 1964-66; analyst Latin Am. Bur., Washington, 1967-68; personnel officer Washington, 1968-70, consular affairs officer, 1970-71, resigned; dir. legal svcs. Community Action Com. OEO, Pasco, Wash., 1971-72; lawyer Spokane (Wash.) County Legal Svc., 1972-73; pvt. practice Kennewick, Wash., 1973-75, Richland, Wash., 1975—; Spanish-English ct. interpreter State of Wash., 1990—. Mem. ABA, ATLA, Wash. Bar Assn., Wash. Trial Lawyers Assn., Fed. Bar Assn., Hispanic Bar Assn. Wash., Inter-Am. Bar Assn., Hispanic Nat. Bar Assn., Acad. Polit. Sci., Toastmasters Internat., Monterey, N.L. Lodge. Office: 1207 George Washington Way Richland WA 99352-3446

BARR, JOHN TILMAN, IV, research and development executive; b. Newport, Ark., June 27, 1948; s. John Tilman III and Dorothy Lee (Cook) B.; m. Barbara Jane Hastreiter, Mar. 20, 1971; children: Jennifer Rebecca, Kathleen Marie. BSEE, Ga. Inst. Tech., 1971; MSEE, Stanford U., 1974, MS Engring. Mgmt., 1982. With Hewlett Packard, Palo Alto, Santa Rosa, Calif., 1971-81; R & D project mgr. Hewlett Packard, Santa Rosa, Calif., 1981-88, R & D program mgr., 1988-92, R & D sect. mgr., 1992—. Contbr. tech. articles, to profl. jours.; patentee in field. Active Gen. Plan Adv. Com., Santa Rosa, 1989. Mem. IEEE (sr., svc. award Redwood Subsect. 1985), Automatic RF Techniques Group (pres. 1987-89, chair 28th Conf. 1986, 36th Conf. 1990, Svc. award 1986, Best Paper award 1990, Disting. Svc. award 1990). Office: Hewlett Packard 1400 Fountain Grove Pky Santa Rosa CA 95403-1738

BARR, SCOTT, state legislator. Mem. Wash. State Senate from 7th Dist. Office: RR 1 Box 130 Edwall WA 99008-9739

BARRAS, BOBBI ANN, psychologist, educator, consultant; b. Piqua, Ohio, Mar. 7, 1938; d. Howard and Anna B. (Elzea) Mabbitt; children: Deborah Seifert, Tony, Brian. BS, Long Beach (Calif.) State U., 1980. Model Florence Smales, Santa Ana, Calif., 1968-76; salesperson, bookkeeper Pacific Mfg. Engring. Co., Los Alamitos, Calif., 1972-74; program coord. Quaker Gardens, Stanton, Calif., 1968-72; tchr. Garden Grove (Calif.) Unified Sch. Dist., 1972—; prof. psychology Coastline Coll., Fountain Valley, Calif., 1976—; cons. in pvt. practice, Westminster, Calif., 1976—. Sr. advisor 4 documentaries To Hear, PBS, 1981. Mem. NAFE. Republican. Home: 9941 Westhaven Cir Westminster CA 92683-7552 Office: Coastline CC 11460 Warner Ave Fountain Valley CA 92708

BARRETT, BRUCE RICHARD, physics educator; b. Kansas City, Kans., Aug. 19, 1939; s. Buford Russell and Miriam Aileen (Adams) B.; m. Gail Louise Geiger, Sept. 3, 1961 (div. Aug. 1969); m. Joan Frances Livermore, May 21, 1979. BS, U. Kans., 1961; postgrad., Swiss Poly., Zurich, 1961-62; MS, Stanford U., 1964, PhD, 1967. Research fellow Weizmann Inst. Sci., Rehovot, Israel, 1967-68; postdoctoral research fellow, research assoc. U. Pitts., 1968-70; asst. prof. physics U. Ariz., Tucson, 1970-72, assoc. prof., 1972-76, prof., 1976—, assoc. chmn. dept., 1977-83, mem. faculty senate, 1979-83, 88-90, 91—; program dir. theoretical physics NSF, 1985-87; chmn. dir. theoretical physics NSF, 1985-87; chmn. adv. com. Internat. Scholars, Tucsn, 1985—; chmn. rsch. policy com. U. Ariz. Faculty Senate, 1993-94, 95-96. Woodrow Wilson fellow, 1961-62; NSF fellow, 1962-66; Weizmann Inst. fellow, 1967-68; Andrew Mellon fellow, 1968-69; Alfred P. Sloan Found. research fellow, 1972-74; Alexander von Humboldt fellow, 1976-77; NSF grantee, 1971-85, 87—; Netherlands F.O.M. research fellow Groningen, 1980; recipient sr. U.S. scientist award (Humboldt prize) Alexander von Humboldt Found., 1983-85. Fellow Am. Phys. Soc. (mem. publs. com. 1983-86, mem. program com. 1993-94, divsn. nuclear physics), Phi Beta Kappa (pres. Alpha Ariz. chpt. 1992), Sigma Xi, Sigma Pi Sigma, Omicron Delta Kappa, Beta Theta Pi. Office: U Ariz Dept Physics Bldg 81 Tucson AZ 85721

BARRETT, CRAIG R., computer company executive; b. 1939. Assoc. prof. Stanford U., 1965-74; with Intel Corp., 1974—, v.p. components tech. and mfg. group, sr. v.p., gen. mgr. components tech. and mfg. group, exec. v.p., mgr. components tech., now exec. v.p., COO, dir. Office: Intel Corp 2200 Mission College Blvd Santa Clara CA 95052*

BARRETT, DONALD JOHN, library administrator; b. St. Paul, Sept. 30, 1927; s. Lawrence John and Pauline Catherine (Huth) B.; m. June Lorraine Medalen, Jan. 27, 1962; 1 child, Barbara Sue. BS, Coll. St. Thomas, 1950; MA, U. Minn., 1954. Reference librarian Coll. St. Thomas Library, St. Paul, 1950-54; librarian Electronic Supply Office, Great Lakes, Ill., 1954-55; reference librarian USAF Acad. Library, Denver, 1955-58; chief pub. svcs. div. USAF Acad. Library, Colorado Springs, 1959-69, asst. dir. pub. svcs., 1969—; library bldg. cons., 1975—. Contbr. articles to profl. jours. With U.S. Army, 1946-47. Mem. ALA, Assn. Coll. and Rsch. Librs., Colo. Libr. Assn. (Lifetime Achievement award 1990), Libr. Adminstrn. and Mgmt. Assn., Air Force Assn. Roman Catholic. Home: 2624 Flintridge Dr Colorado Springs CO 80918-4425 Office: U S A F Acad Libr U S A F Academy CO 80840

BARRETT, DOROTHY, performing arts administrator; b. L.A., Feb. 28, 1917; d. Lester Arnold and Kathryn (Halverson) Silvera; m. Robert A.H. Cochrane, May 20, 1949 (div. Feb. 1965); 1 stepchild, Michele Cochrane. Student, LA C.C., 1937-38. Adminstrv. dir. Am. Nat. Acad. of Performing Arts, 1964—; founder, dir. Acad. Children's Workshop, 1964—; produced, choreographed 30 Christmas shows, 1964—; tchr. of dance Barrett Sch. of the Arts, North Hollywood, 1948, Am. Nat. Acad., Studio City, 1964—, tchr. of acting, 1964—; tchr. of speech UCLA Extension, West Hollywood, 1972. Actress: (motion pictures) Connecticut Yankee in King Arthurs Court, 1947, California, 1947, Samson and Delilah, 1948, Monsieur Beaucaire, 1945, The Imperfect Lady, 1947, Perils of Pauline, 1945, The Stork Club, 1945, Mildred Pierce, 1945, A Bell for Adano, 1945, Weekend at the Waldorf, 1945, Hot Money, 1944, Juke Box Soundies, 1942, Frisco Sal, Wizard of Oz, 1939, Gone With the Wind, 1939, Earl Carroll's Vanities, 1939, The Great Waltz, 1938, Miss Culver City, 1937; (Broadway stage productions) Buddy De Sylva's Louisiana Purchase, 1940, Billy Rose's Diamond Horseshoe, 1943, George Abbott's Beat the Band, 1942, others; (TV) co-star KTLA's Secrets of Gourmet, 1946; author: (poetry) Between the Bookends, 1942, The Tolucan, The Legal Journal, 1959, Valley Green Sheet & Van Nuys News; contbr. articles to jours. Active Am. Women's Vol. Svc., 1942. Recipient award ARC, 1943, Humanitarian award City of L.A., 1994. Office: Am Nat Acad Performing Arts 10944 Ventura Blvd Studio City CA 91604-3340

BARRETT, ELEANOR EDIE, lawyer, mediator; b. N.Y.C., Feb. 20, 1945; d. Leslie Charles and Margie Eloise (Crawford) Edie; m. Alan Kliner, July 31, 1966 (div. 1975). BA in Sociology and French, Dickinson Coll., Carlisle, Pa., 1967; JD cum laude, Whittier Coll., 1978. Bar: Calif. 1978. Caseworker N.Y.C. Dept. Social Svcs., 1968-69; supr., caseworker Los Angeles County Dept. Pub. Social Svcs., L.A., 1969-73, appeals worker, 1973-78; dep. dist. atty. Los Angeles County Dist. Atty.'s Office, L.A., 1978—; mediation cochair Lawyers for Human Rights, L.A., 1991-93. Co-chair adv. coun. Lesbian/Gay Cmty. Mediation Project, 1993—; mem. City of West Hollywood's Gay and Lesbian Issues Task Force, 1989. Recipient Angel Amidst award City of West Hollywood, 1993, Wiley W. Manual award for pro bono legal svcs. State Bar Calif., 1992, commendation for vol. legal svcs., 1983. Mem. NOW (legal coord. 1981-83, Hollywood pres. 1984-85, 88-90), L.A. County Bar Assn. (bd. dirs. Dispute Resolution Svcs. 1993—), Women Lawyers of L.A., League of Women Prosecutors. Democrat. Office: Los Angeles County Dist Atty's Office 849 S Broadway Fl 11 Los Angeles CA 90014

BARRETT, JAMES EMMETT, federal judge; b. Lusk, Wyo., Apr. 8, 1922; s. Frank A. and Alice C. (Donoghue) B.; m. Carmel Ann Martinez, Oct. 8, 1949; children: Ann Catherine Barrett Sandahl, Richard James, John Donoghue. Student, U. Wyo., 1940-42, LLB, 1949; student, St. Catherine's Coll., Oxford, Eng., 1945, Cath. U. Am., 1946. Bar: Wyo. 1949. Mem. firm Barrett and Barrett, Lusk, 1949-67; atty. gen. State of Wyo., 1967-71; judge U.S. Circuit Ct. Appeals (10th cir.), 1971—; county and pros. atty. Niobrara County, Wyo., 1951-62; atty. Town of Lusk, 1952-54, Niobrara Sch. Dist., 1950-64. Active Boy Scouts Am.; sec.-treas. Niobrara County Republican Central Com.; trustee St. Joseph's Children's Home, Torrington, Wyo., 1971-85. Served as cpl. AUS, 1942-45, ETO. Recipient Distinguished Alumni award U. Wyo., 1973. Mem. VFW, Am. Legion, Order of Coif (hon. mem. Wyo. Coll. Law/U. Wyo. chpt.). Office: US Ct Appeals PO Box 1288 Cheyenne WY 82003-1288

BARRETT, LARRY LEON, housing and dining services administrator; b. Taft, Calif., July 5, 1940; m. Jean Orrison, Nov. 17, 1989. BS in Phys. Sci., Calif. State Poly., San Luis Obispo, 1964. Supr. trainee U. Calif., Santa Barbara, 1964-65, unit mgr., 1965-69, food svc. dir., 1969-72; dir. housing and dining svc. U. Calif., San Diego, 1972—. Contbr. articles to profl. jours. Recipient Food Svc. Operator of Yr. Silver Plate award Internat. Food Mfrs. Assn., 1981. Mem. Nat. Assn. of Coll. and Univ. Food Svc. (treas. 1979, pres. 1979-81, Theodore Minah Disting. Svc. 1990). Office: U Calif # 0090 La Jolla CA 92093

BARRETT, LENORE HARDY, state legislator, mining and investment consultant; b. Newkirk, Okla., June 16, 1934; d. Floyd Jack and Minnie Bell (O'Dell) Hardy; m. Robert Michael Barrett, 1964; 1 child, Michael Hardy. BS, Okla. Bapt. U., 1956. State legislator Ho. of Reps., Boise, Idaho, 1993—. Active Idaho Farm Bureau Political Action Com., 1990-92; dir. Salmon River Electric Coop., Inc., Challis; police commr. Challis City Coun., 1984-89; mem. Assn. Idaho Cities Legis. Com., 2 yrs.; state committeewoman Custer County Rep. Ctrl. Com., Challis, 1982—. Mem. Nat. Inholder's Assn., Idaho Rep. Party, Ctrl. Idaho Mining Assn. (sec.), Custer County Farm Bureau, Grassroots for Multiple Use, Blue Ribbon Coalition, Order of Eastern Star (Grand Organist award Grand Chpt. Idaho 1985-86). Baptist. Home: PO Box 347 143 W Pleasant Challis ID 83226 Office: Idaho Ho of Reps State Captiol Boise ID 83720

BARRETT, PEIGIN CATHERINE, marine mammal center executive; b. New Haven, Conn., July 19, 1942; d. James Daniel and Margaret Mary (Macauley) B. BA, Coll. of New Rochelle, 1964; MPA, Golden Gate U., 1981. Asst. curator, dir. Explorers Hall, Nat. Geog. Soc., Washington, 1965-68; art instr. D.C. Pub. Schs., 1968-70; author, creative cons. Harcourt, Brace Pubs., San Francisco, N.Y.C., 1971-81; exec. dir., CEO Marine Mammal Ctr., Sausalito, Calif., 1982—; mem. Marine Fisheries Adv. Com., Washington, 1989—, chair protected resource subcom., 1991—, vice chair steering com., 1993—; art chmn. Washington Nat. Zoo, 1966-67; judge Saltonstall-Kennedy Industry Review Panel for Nat. Oceanic and Atmospheric Adminstrn./Nat. Marine Fisheries Svc., 1987; cooperator Gill Net Monitoring Program with Calif. Dept. Fish and Game, 1986-88; mem. environ. consultation review panel Marin Community Found., 1988; mem. steering com. Marin Environ. Alliance, 1988-90. Creator Children's Art Scholarship Fund, Washington, 1968. Recipient Daisy award San Francisco Bay Girl Scouts Coun. 1993, Gold medal 17th Internat. Film and TV Festival N.Y., Silver award, 18th Internat. Film and TV Festival N.Y., Silver Screen award U.S. Indsl. Film Festival, Cindy award 17th Ann. Cindy Awards, Bronze award 19th Ann. Internat. Film and TV Festival, Cert. of Merit, 12 Ann. Internat. Film Festival. Office: Marine Mammal Ctr Marin Headlands Sausalito CA 94965

BARRETT, REGINALD HAUGHTON, biology educator, wildlife management educator; b. San Francisco, June 11, 1942; s. Paul Hutchison and Mary Lambert (Hodgkin) B.; m. Katharine Lawrence Ditmars, July 15, 1967; children: Wade Lawrence, Heather Elizabeth. BS in Game Mgmt., Humboldt State U., 1965; MS in Wildlife Mgmt., U. Mich., 1966; PhD in Zoology, U. Calif., Berkeley, 1971. Rsch. biologist U. Calif., Berkeley, 1970-71, acting asst. prof., 1971-72; rsch. scientist div. wildlife rsch. Commonwealth Scientific and Indsl. Rsch. Orgn., Darwin, Australia, 1972-75; from asst. prof. to prof. U. Calif., Berkeley, 1975—; dir. Sagehen Creek Field Sta., Truckee, Calif., 1985—. Author: (with others) Report on the Use of Fire in National Parks and Reserves, 1977, Research and Management of Wild Hog Populations, Proceedings of a Symposium, 1977, Sitka Deer Symposium, 1979, Symposium on Ecology and Management of Barbary Sheep, 1980, Handbook of Census Methods for Birds and Mammals, 1981, Wildlife 2000: Modeling Habitat Relationships of Terrestrial Vertebrates, 1986, Translocation of Wild Animals, 1988, Wildlife 2001: Populations, 1992; contbr. articles, abstracts, reports to profl. jours. Recipient Outstanding Profl. Achievement award Humboldt State U. Alumni Assn., 1986, Bruce R. Dodd award, 1965, Howard M. Wight award, 1966; Undergrad. scholar Nat. Wildlife Fedn., 1964, NSF grad. fellow, 1965-70; Union found. Wildlife Rsch. grantee, 1968-70. Mem. The Wildlife Soc. (pres. Bay Area chpt. 1978-79, cert. wildlife biologist, R.F. Dasmann Profl. of Yr. award western sect. 1989), Am. Soc. Mammalogists (life), Soc. for Range Mgmt. (life), Ecol. Soc. Am. (cert. sr. ecologist), Soc. Am. Foresters, Australian Mammal Soc., Am. Inst. Biol. Scis., AAAS, Calif. Acad. Scis., Internat. Union for the Conservation of Nature (life), Calif. Bot. Soc., Orgn. Wildlife Planners, Sigma Xi, Xi Sigma Pi. Episcopalian. Office: U Calif 145 Mulford Hall Berkeley CA 94720

BARRETT, WILLIAM OWEN, academic administrator; b. Hartford, Conn., Sept. 1, 1945; s. Fredric Deyoe and Elsie (Owen) B.; m. Diane Wyman Hamilton, Feb. 22, 1969; 1 child, Alexander Owen. BFA in Indsl. Design, R.I. Sch. of Design, 1967; MA in Edn., NYU, 1978. Asst. dir. admissions Parsons Sch. of Design, N.Y.C., 1970-73, dir. admissions, 1973-78, dean of students, 1978-80, asst. dean, 1980-81; dean Corcoran Sch. of Art, Washington, 1981-87; pres. San Francisco Art Inst., 1987-94; exec. dir. Assn. Ind. Colls. Art and Design, San Francisco, 1994—. Mem. design panel D.C. Commn. on Arts and Humanities, 1987; mem. adv. com. San Francisco High Sch. of the Arts, 1988-91; With U.S. Army, 1967-70, Korea. Mem. Nat. Assn. Schs. Art and Design (life mem., treas. 1986-89, v.p. 1989-90, pres. 1990-93, fellowship 1994), Nat. Coun. Arts Adminstrs. (treas. 1983-86), Alliance Ind. Colls. Art (v.p. 1989-91), Assn. Ind. Coll. Art and Design (bd. dirs. 1991-94). Democrat. Office: Assn Ind Colls Art & Design 3957 22nd St San Francisco CA 94114-3205

BARRETTA-KEYSER, JOLIE, professional athletics coach, author; b. Phila., Aug. 17, 1954; d. Philip Francis and Norma Roberta (Podoszek) Barretta; m. Joel D. Keyser; children: Evan Barrett, Kyra Lani. Student, U. Calif., Long Beach, 1972-76, U. Florence, Italy, 1974-75. Tchr. gymnastics Los Angeles City Sch. Dist., 1973-77, judge, 1976-82; coach, choregrapher Kips Gymnastic Club, Long Beach, Calif., 1976-78, So. Calif. Acrobatics Team, Huntington Beach, Calif., 1979-81, UCLA, 1980-82; pres. West Coast Waves Rhythmic Gymnastics, Rolling Hills Estates, Calif., 1980—; mem. coaching staff U.S. Nat. Rhythmic Gymnastics Team, 1983—; coach Centro Olimpico Nazionale Italia, Rome, 1974-76; lectr. dance, phys. edn. Calif. State U., Dominguez Hills, Carson, 1981-92; French lang. mistress of ceremonies rhythmic gymnastics event U.S. Olympic Games, L.A., 1984; invited observer Inst. Phys. Culture, Bejing, 1985, Bulgarian Gymnastics Fedn., Sophia, 1982-90; meet dir. state and regional championships, L.A. County, 1984, '86; internat. lectr. body alignment; pres. Rhythymic Gymnasts Devel. Program, 1984—; developer RIGOR (Rhythmic Gymnastics Outreach) for U.S.A. recreation programs; mem. rhythmic gymnastics adv. com. & bd. Internat. Spl. Olympics, 1990—. Author: Body Alignment, 1985; columnist Internat. Gymnast Mag., 1987-90. Tour leader Acad. Tours Inc. U.S./Bulgaria Friendship Through Sports Ann. Tour, N.Y. and Bulgaria, 1987. Recipient recognition plaque U.S. Womens Sports Awards Banquet, 1984-89. Mem. U.S. Rhythmic Gymnastics Coaches Assn. (pres. 1984—), U.S. Gymnastics Fedn. (bd. dirs. 1985—, nat. team coach 1984—, mem. del., coach internat. competitions U.S., Mex., Hungary, Bulgaria, Belgium, Can. 1984—, choreographer age group devel. compulsory div. 1987, staff Olympic Tng. Ctr. 1984—), Inst. Noetic Scis., Internat. Spl. Olympics (adv. bd. rhythmic gymnastics). Republican. Office: West Coast Waves 11661 San Vicente Blvd Ste 609 Los Angeles CA 90049-5114

BARRETT-CONNOR, ELIZABETH LOUISE, epidemiologist, educator; b. Evanston, Ill., Apr. 8, 1935; m. James D. Connor. BA, Mt. Holyoke Coll., 1956; MD, Cornell U., 1960. Diplomate Am. Bd. Internal Medicine, Nat. Bd. Med. Examiners. Instr. medicine U. Miami, Fla., 1965-68, asst. prof. medicine, 1968-70; asst. prof. community and family medicine U. Calif., San Diego, 1970-74, assoc. prof. community and family medicine, 1974-81, prof. community and family medicine, 1981—, acting chair dept. community and family medicine, 1981-82, chmn. dept. family and preventative medicine, 1982—; vis. prof. Royal Soc. Medicine, London, 1989; mem. hosp. infection control com. VA Med. Ctr., San Diego, 1971—. Contbr. articles to profl. jours. NIH grantee, 1970-89, 78-80, 91-95, Janssen Pharm., 1976-78, Am. Heart Assn. grantee, 1980-81. Mem. Am. Heart Assn. (chmn. budget com. coun. on epidemiology 1987-88, chmn. coun. on epidemiology 1988-89), Am. Pub. Health Assn. (chmn. epidemiology sect. 1989—), Assn. Tchrs. Preventive Medicine (bd. dirs. 1987—), Inst. Medicine. Office: U Calif # 0628 La Jolla CA 92093

BARRIE, LITA, editor, publisher, art critic, cultural theorist; b. Auckland, New Zealand, Oct. 3, 1955; came to U.S., 1990; d. William Glen and Lallah Lillian (McNamara) B.; m. Michael Saito, Oct. 31, 1990. BA, Victoria U., Wellington, New Zealand, 1976, BA with honors/first class, 1978, MA, 1980. Lic. securities, series 22, life ins. With Centre Continuing Edn., Wellington, 1986-88; weekly art columnist New Zealand Nat. Bus. Rev., Wellington, 1987-90; instr. philosophy Rio Hondo Coll., Whittier, Calif., 1991-92; contbg. editor Artweek Mag., L.A., 1990-94; L.A. corr. Artspace mag., 1992-93; vis. critic art dept. Claremont (Calif.) Grad. Sch., 1993—; editor, pub. Vernacular mag., L.A., 1994—; curator L.A. Art Festival, 1990; pub. spkr. New Zealand Art Educators Conf., Auckland, 1992, Travel Abroad, L.A. Art critic: (exhbn. catalogs) Barbara Kruger, 1988, Walters, Bambury, Gimblett, 1992, Shared Techlines, 1993, Andrew Drummond; contbg. essayist Action, Realities, Transformations, 1994. Grantee Queen Elizabeth II Arts Coun. New Zealand, 1985, 87, 92. Mem. Assn. Internat.

Des Critiques D'Art (art critic). Home and Office: 5630 W 6th St Los Angeles CA 90036-3839

BARRIOS, ALFRED ANGEL, psychologist; b. N.Y.C., Oct. 1, 1933; s. Arthur Domingo and Carmen Maria (Vidal) B. BS, Calif. Inst. Tech., 1955; PhD, UCLA, 1969. Chem. engr. Mobil Oil Co., Torrance, Calif., 1955-57; instr. psychology East L.A. Coll., 1969-72, UCLA, 1972-73, Southwest Coll., L.A., 1973-74, Santa Monica (Calif.) Coll., 1975; psychologist Self-Programmed Control Ctr., L.A., 1972—, pres., 1975—. Author: Towards Greater Freedom and Happiness, 1978, The Stress Test, 1984, The Habit Buster, 1987; inventor Stress Control Biofeedback Card. Office: SPC Ctr 11949 Jefferson Blvd Ste 104 Culver City CA 90230-6336

BARRITT, CLAY FRANKLIN, psychiatrist, educator; b. Marion, Kans., May 31, 1925; s. Clay Franklin and Temple Nadine (White) B.; children: Theresa Jean Ferguson, Christopher Franklin Barritt, Timothy Paul Barritt. Student, Stanford U.; grad., Washington U., 1944, MD, 1948. Diplomat Am. Bd. Psychiatry and Neurology; lic. Calif., Mo., Md., D.C., Pa. Jr. resident psychiatry Henry Phipps Psychiatric Clinic Johns Hopkins Hosp., Balt., 1949-50, sr. resident, 1951-52; sr. resident Letterman Army Hosp., San Francisco, 1952-53, Chestnut Lodge Sanitarium, Rockville, Md., 1954-56; psychoanalyst Washington Psychoanalytic Inst., 1954-65; pvt. practice Rockville, Md., 1955-62, Kensington, Md., 1962-64, Washington, 1964-67, Bethesda, Md., 1967-70, Chevy Chase, Md., 1970-74, Santa Monica, Calif., 1978-86, Calabasas, Calif., 1986-87, Woodland Hills, Calif., 1987-90, Pacific Palisades, Calif., 1990-93; ret., 1993; chief acute psychotic adolescent inpatient unit, med. program cons. adolsescent treatment ctr. Camarillo (Calif.) State Hosp., 1974-77, chief acute psychotic adult inpatient unit, med. program cons., 1977-81, chief male geriatric psychotic admission unit, 1981-83; psychiatric cons. Brentwood VA Hosp., 1983-85, chief crisis-oriented psychiatric evaluation svc., 1985-86, staff psychiatrist evaluations and admissions svcs, 1986-88; asst. clin. prof. UCLA, 1983—, instr., 1983-88; rsch. prof. psychiatry, cons. counseling svcs. Gallaudet Coll. for Deaf, Washington, 1963-66; mem. teaching faculty Camarillo State Hosp., 1977-83, chief of staff, pres. med. staff, 1978-79, mem. various coms.; cons. Parkwood Cmty. Hosp. and Valley Park Med. Ctr., Canoga Park, Calif., 1981-85, Humana Hosp., West Hills, Calif., 1985-89, Pathways Valley Presbyn. Hosp., Van Nuys, Calif., 1985-86; active med. staff A Touch of Care, L.A., 1989-90; mem. med. exec. com. Life Plus CCH and TCA Hosps., 1989-90; chmn. med. records com. Life Plus Treatment Ctr., 1989-90, mem. active staff, 1988-91; mem. pharmacy and therapeutics com. Coldwater Canyon Hosp., 1988-89; vice-chief of staff Ingleside Hosp., 1993, chmn. quality assurance med. records and risk mgmt. com., 1993, med. dir. John Bradshaw Ctr., 1990-93, hon. mem. med. staff, 1993. Writer and presenter in field. With AUS, 1943-46; capt. Regular Army Med. Corps, 1950-54; psychiatrist third inf. divsn., 1950-51, Korea. Mem. Am. Psychiatric Assn. (life), So. Calif. Psychiatric Soc. Republican. Home: 1539 Michael Ln Pacific Palisades CA 90272-2022

BARRON, TIANA LUISA, educator; b. Omaha, Mar. 26, 1952; d. James Patrick Barron and Maria Isabel (Pasos) McAdoo; m. Jerry Peter Mastora (div.); children: Peter Uriah Mastora, Travis Burnell Thom, Taylor Morgan Lewis. Pres., founder S.A.V.E., Sherman Oaks, Calif., 1987—; producer, writer, dir. S.A.V.E., L.A., 1992—. Author: Mommy Was I Adopted, 1992. Adv. bd. The Family Hispanic Ins., L.A., 1990; vol., counselor San Fernando Valley Juvenile Hall, Slymar, Calif., 1990, Sojourn. Recipient Honor for S.A.V.E. Day George Bush, George Deukmejian, Mayor Bradley, Bd. Suprs., L.A., 1989. Home and Office: 4375 Ventura Canyon Ave # 1 Sherman Oaks CA 91601-5105

BARROW, THOMAS FRANCIS, artist, educator; b. Kansas City, Mo., Sept. 24, 1938; s. Luther Hopkins and Cleo Naomi (Francis) B.; m. Laurie Anderson, Nov. 30, 1974; children—Melissa, Timothy, Andrew. B.F.A., Kansas City Art Inst., 1963; M.S., Ill. Inst. Tech., 1965. With George Eastman House, Rochester, N.Y., 1966-72; asst. dir. George Eastman House, 1971-72; assoc. dir. Art Mus., U. N. Mex., Albuquerque, 1973-76; assoc. prof. U. N.Mex., 1976-81, prof., 1981—, Presdl. prof., 1985-90. Author: A Letter with Some Thoughts on Photography's Future, 1970, The Art of Photography, 1971, 600 Faces by Beaton, 1970; sr. editor: Reading into Photography, 1982, contbr. to Brit. Ency. Am. Art, 1973, A Hundred Years of Photographic History: Essays in Honor of Beaumont Newhall, 1975, Experimental Vistion, 1994; foreward the Valiant Knights of Daguerre, 1978; one-man shows include Light Gallery, N.Y.C., 1974-76, 79, 82, Amarillo Art Ctr., 1990, Andrew Smith Gallery, Santa Fe, 1992; exhibited in group shows including Nat. Gallery Can., 1970, Pace Gallery, N.Y.C., 1973, Hudson River Mus., Yonkers, N.Y., 1973, Internat. Mus. Photography, Rochester, 1975, Seattle Art Mus., 1976, Mus. Fine Arts, Houston, 1977, Retrospective exhbn. Los Angeles County Mus. Art, 1987—; represented in permanent collections Nat. Gallery Can., Mus. Modern Art, Getty Ctr. for Arts and Humanities. Nat. Endowment for Arts fellow, 1971, 78. Office: U NMex Dept Art Albuquerque NM 87131

BARROWS, ROBERT GUY, scriptwriter; b. Ft. Collins, Colo., Feb. 9, 1926; s. Barney M. and Marian Louise (Walker) B.; div.; children: Bret, Larry, David, Daniel, Josh, Grace; m. Georgia Jerilyn Harvey, June 30, 1989. BA, U. Colo., 1950; MA, UCLA, 1954. Freelance writer NBC-TV, CBS-TV, ABC-TV, MGM, 20th Century Fox, Universal, Paramount, Columbia, Warner Bros., various ind. TV and film prodn. cos.; faculty mem., theater, TV and film NYU, 1957-62, Am. Acad., N.Y.C., 1960-62, UCLA, 1964-70, Art Ctr., Pasadena, Calif., 1980-82; mem. faculty, theater, TV and film Loyola Marymount U., Los Angeles, 1981-82. Writer, producer, dir.: (films) I Dream of Blood, Danger Has Two Faces; writer: (TV episodes) Bonanza, Ben Casey, Combat, Destry, Daniel Boone, The Bold Ones, The Big Valley, Empire, The Fugitive, The Green Hornet, Felony Squad, Ironside, Kraft Suspense Theater, The Man Who Never Was, Mission: Impossible, Run for Your Life, Wild, Wild West, The Virginian. Served to master sgt. U.S. Army, 1943-46. Recipient Samuel Goldwyn Creative Writing award. Mem. Writers Guild Am.

BARRY, BONNIE B., trade association executive; b. Pocatello, Idaho, July 17, 1940; d. Kyle and Lael Corrine (Smith) Bettilyon; 1 child, Robyn Matthies Randall. Student, Mills Coll., 1958-59; BA, U. Utah, 1962; cert., ITCA, 1976. CCIM. Spl. svcs. mgr. Sperry Rand Missile Div., Salt Lake City, 1962-64; mgr. travel dept. Utah Motor Club, Salt Lake City, 1965-67; owner Aggie Travel Svc., Davis, Calif., 1968-77, also bd. dirs.; founding ptnr. SECRET Travel Svc., Maui, Hawaii, 1979—; exec. v.p. Assn. Retail Travel Agts., 1979—; pres., CEO Bettilyon Investment Co., Salt Lake City, 1990—; tng. dir. ednl. work-study programs for mem. travel agys., U.S. and Can.; mem. faculty U. Calif. Extension, Davis, 1974-77. Mem. Nat. Travel Agts. (adv. bd. to Pan Am. World Airways 1973-77), Assn. Retail Travel Agts. (nat. bd. dirs. 1974-78), Giants Travel Coop. (v.p. Western chpt. 1972-74), Am. Assn. Retail Travel Agts., Soroptimists. Republican. Morman. Home: 3 Nail Driver Ct # 1388 Park City UT 84060-6707 Office: Bettilyon Investment Co 333 2nd Ave # D Salt Lake City UT 84103-2626

BARRY, DAVID N., III, utility executive. AB, Stanford U., 1948; JD, U. So. Calif., 1951. Bar: Calif. 1951. Assoc. gen. counsel So. Calif. Edison, Rosemead, 1981-89, v.p., gen. counsel, 1989—. Office: SCE Corp 2244 Walnut Grove Ave Rosemead CA 91770-3714

BARRY, EDWARD LOUIS, lawyer; b. Greenville, Mich., Mar. 20, 1951; s. Edward H. and Gertrude (Hamper) B.; divorced; children: Jane, Laura, Anne Marie. BA with high honors, Mich. State U., 1975; postgrad. U. So. Calif., 1977, Oxford U., 1975; JD, Ariz. State U., 1979. Bar: Ariz. 1979, U.S. Dist. Ct. Ariz. 1979. Sole practice law, Phoenix, 1979—. Recipient Am. Jurisprudence award, 1977. Mem. Assn. Trial Lawyers Am. Office: 1010 E Jefferson St Phoenix AZ 85034-2222

BARRY, JAMES MICHAEL, property management company executive; b. Fontana, Calif., Dec. 22, 1956; s. Walter and Georgia Elizabeth (Spaeth) B.; m. Melanie Lee; 1 child, Krista Marie. BA in Econs., U. Colo., 1979. Sales rep. Proctor & Gamble, Denver, 1979-81; sales rep. Becton Dickinson, Orangeburg, N.Y., 1981-84; dist. mgr., new dealer devel. Control-O-Fax, Denver, 1984-85; dist. br. mgr. Norrell Health Care, Denver, 1985-87; prin., owner Innovative Mgmt. Svcs., Inc., Denver, 1987—; owner Info Port, Inc., 1993-95; ptnr. Resnova Software, Inc., Huntington Beach, Calif., 1994—. Treas. Delta Upsilon Corp. Colo., Boulder, 1980-87; pres. Chestnut Homeowners Assn., Littleton, Colo., 1984-87, 94-95; bd. dirs. S.W. Mental Health Svcs., Denver, 1988-90; chmn. Rep. State Sen. Dist., Denver, 1987-92, Rep. State Rep. Dist., Denver, 1987-92, Rep State Rep Dist., Adams County, 1994—. Mem. Community Assn. Inst. Republican. Roman Catholic. Home: 4732 W 69th Ave Westminster CO 80030-5706 Office: Resnova Software 5011 Argosy Dr #13 Huntington Beach CA 92649

BARRY, JAMES PAUL, consulting arborist, educator; b. Pasadena, Calif., Jan. 1, 1953; s. Donald J. and Jeanne S. (Wells) B. BS, Calif. State Poly. U., 1976; MS, Colo. State U., 1983. Cert. tchr., Calif. Prodn. mgr. Alta Loma (Calif.) Nursery, 1973-75; field rep. Wilbur-Ellis Co., Commerce, Calif., 1976-77; merchandise supr. K-Mart, Monrovia, Calif., 1977-78; field supt. Easyscape Co., San Jose, Calif., 1978-79; disturbed lands coord. Colo. State U., Ft. Collins, Colo., 1980-83; pvt. practice soil cons. Arcadia, Calif., 1984-85; instr. Mt. San Antonio Coll., Walnut, Calif., 1985, Calif. State Poly. U., Pomona, 1985-91, U. Calif., Irvine, 1990—; pres. Barry Tree Care & Mobile Soil Labs., Fullerton, Calif., 1986-92, Barry Environ. Consulting, Orange, Calif., 1992—; instr. arborculture Fullerton (Calif.) Coll., 1993—. Contbr. articles to profl. publs. Mem. Soc. Ecol. Restoration, Am. Soc. Surface Mining Reclamation, Soil and Water Conservation Assn., Am. Soc. Landscape Architects (affiliate), Alpha Zeta (life), Gamma Sigma Delta (life). Office: Barry Environ Consulting 4705 E Chapman Ave Orange CA 92669-4112

BARRY, RICK (RICHARD FRANCIS DENNIS BARRY, III), sportscaster, retired professional basketball player, marketing professional; b. Elizabeth, N.J., Mar. 28, 1944; s. Richard Francis and Alpha Monique (Stephanovich) B.; m. Pamela Hale, June 1965 (div.); children: Richard Francis IV, Jon Alan, Brent Robert, Drew William, Shannon Leigh; m. Pamela Stenesen, Sept. 1981 (div.); m. Lynn Norenberg, Aug. 1991; 1 child, Canyon Shane. Student, U. Miami, 1961-65. Basketball player San Francisco Warriors, NBA, 1965-67, Oakland Oaks, Am. Basketball Assn., 1967-69, Washington, Am. Basketball Assn., 1969-70, Virginia Squires, 1970, N.Y. Nets, Am. Basketball Assn., 1970-72, Golden State Warriors, NBA, 1972-78, Houston Rockets, NBA, 1978-80; sports broadcaster, basketball analyst CBS Sports, 1974-81; NBA color analyst Turner Sports, 1984-91; dir. mktg. Profl. Logistics Mgmt. Inc., Lafayette, Calif., 1994—. Mem. Am. Basketball Assn. All-Star Team, 1968-72, NBA All-Star Team, 1966-67, 73-78, NBA Championship Team, 1975; named Rookie of Yr., NBA, 1966, Most Valuable Player All Star Game, 1966, Most Valuable Player Championship Series, 1975; inducted into Basketball Hall of Fame, 1986. *

BARRY, STEVE, sculptor, educator; b. Jersey City, June 22, 1956; s. Thomas Daniel and Lorraine (Lowery) B. BFA, Sch. Visual Arts, N.Y.C., 1980; MFA, Hunter Coll., N.Y.C., 1984. Adj. lectr. Hunter Coll., 1984-89; assoc. prof. U. N.Mex., Albuquerque, 1989—. Exhbns. include Bklyn. Army Terminal, N.Y.C., 1983, City Gallery, N.Y.C., 1986, 90, Storefront for Art and Architecture, 1988, Artists Space, N.Y.C., 1989, Santa Barbara Art Mus., 1990, Kohler Arts Ctr., Sheboygan, Wis., 1991, Hirshhorn Mus., Washington, 1990, Fla. State U., 1992, Contemporary Art Mus., Houston, 1992, CAFE Gallery, Albuquerque, 1993, Charolette Jackson, Santa Fe, 1993, Ctr. for Contemporary Arts, Santa Fe, 1994, U. Wyo. Art Mus., 1995. Grantee Clocktower Nat. Studio, 1985, NEA, 1986, 88, 90, N.Y. State Coun. for the Arts, 1987, N.Y. Found. for the Arts, 1988; recipient AVA award, 1990. Home: PO Box 1046 Corrales NM 87048 Office: U NMex Dept Art and Art History Albuquerque NM 87131-1401

BARS, ITZHAK, physics educator, researcher, consultant; b. Izmir, Turkey, Aug. 31, 1943; came to U.S., 1967; s. Albert Shemoel and Claire (Benshoam) Barsimantov; m. Paulette P. Navaro, Aug. 22, 1967 (div. 1993); m. Annie S. Rosenschein, Oct. 1993; children: Julie, Jamie. BS in Physics, Robert Coll., 1967; MPhil in Physics, Yale U., 1969, PhD in Physics, 1971. Asst. rsch. physicist U. Calif., Berkeley, 1971-73; asst. prof. Stanford (Calif.) U., 1973-75; asst. prof. Yale U., New Haven, 1975-79, assoc. prof., 1979-83; prof. U. So. Calif., L.A., 1983—; vis. asst. prof. Harvard U., Cambridge, Mass., 1978; mem. Inst. for Advanced Study, Princeton, N.J., 1979, 90. Editor: (book) Symmetries in Particle Physics, 1984; contbr. articles to profl. jours. Fulbright scholar Robert Coll., 1964-67; Gibbs fellow Yale U., 1967-69, grad. fellow IBM, 1969-71; A.P. Sloan Found. fellow, 1976-80; recipient 1st award Gravity Rsch. Found., 1988; named Outstanding Jr. Investigator U.S. Dept. Energy, 1983. Fellow Am. Phys. Soc., N.Y. Acad. Scis. Democrat. Jewish. Home: 1827 El Vista Cir Arcadia CA 91006-1662

BARSAN, RICHARD EMIL, oral and maxillofacial surgeon; b. Selma, Ala., Dec. 18, 1945; s. Emil and Letitia (Dobrin) B.; m. Sandra Sherrick, June 22, 1974; children: Kelly Lynn, Robert Scott. BS in Chem. Engring., U. Cin., 1968; DDS, Ohio State U., 1979. Diplomate Am. Bd. Oral and Maxillofacial Surgeons. Chem. engr. various cos., 1968-76; resident VA Hosp., Sepulveda, Calif., 1979-80; resident in oral and maxillofacial surgery La. State U., New Orleans, 1980-84; pvt. practice, La Jolla and El Centro, Calif., 1985—. Chrysler scholar U. Cin., 1964. Fellow Am. Assn. Oral and Maxillofacial Surgeons; mem. ADA, Calif. Dental Assn., San Diego County Dental Soc. (bd. dirs. 1988-92), San Diego County Oral Surgeons (pres. 1990), So. Calif. Soc. Oral and Maxillofacial Surgeons, Imperial Valley Dental Soc. (pres. 1993—), Paul Revere Study Club (pres. 1988), Toastmasters (pres. La Jolla chpt. 1988), Omicron Kappa Upsilon. Republican. Home: 3211 Via Marin La Jolla CA 92037-2937 Office: 4320 Genesee Ave Ste 101 San Diego CA 92117-4900 also: 1745 S Imperial Ave #107 El Centro CA 92243

BARSCH, WULF ERICH, artist, educator; b. Reudnitz, Bohemia, Aug. 27, 1943; came to U.S., 1967; s. Erich and Maria Klaubert; m. Sandra Proter; children: Kelee, Garn, James, Aram, Joseph. Studied drawing, Studienatelier K. Kaschak, Hamburg, Fed. Republic of Germany, 1961-62; studied design, Staatliche Hochschule fur Bildende Kunste, Hamburg, Germany, 1962-63; BFA, Werkkunstschule, Hannover, Germany, 1968; MA in Printmaking, Brigham Young U., 1971, MFA in Painting, 1972. Tchr. German Lang. Tng. Mission, 1970-71; tchr. D.L.I. Inst., Monterey, Calif., 1971, Utah Tech. Coll., Provo, Utah, 1972; prof. dept. art Brigham Young U., Provo, Utah, 1972—; adminstr. asst. Brigham Young U. One-man shows include Galerie des Volksheims, Hamburg, 1966, Galerie Werkkunstschule, Hannover, 1969, Salt Lake City Ctr., 1971, 80, Am. Acad., Rome, 1976, Harris Fine Arts Ctr., Provo, 1976, 84, Kimball Art Ctr., Park City, Utah, 1979, Utah Mus. Art, Salt Lake City, 1984, Scottsdale (Ariz.) Ctr. for Arts, 1985, Oklahoma Ctr. for Arts, Oklahoma City, 1985, Mus. Ch. History and Art, Salt Lake City, 1985-86, Gremillion Fine Art, Houston, 1986, Mack Gilman Galleries, Chgo., 1986, Amarillo (Tex.) Ctr. for Arts., 1986, Gremillion & Co. Fine Arts, Atlanta, 1987, 88, 91, Dolores Chase Fine Arts, Salt Lake City, 1987, 89, 91, River Ctr. Gallery, Memphis, 1988, NO HO Gallery, Stamfort, Conn., 1988, Van der Voort Fine Art, Houston, 1988, Ricks Coll., Rexburg, Idaho, 1988, Art Space, Atlanta, 1989, Liza Kurtz Gallery, Memphis, 1989, Trinity Gallery, Atlanta, 1989, 91, 93, Strecker Gallery, Manhattan, Kans., 1991, Elaine Horwitcz Galleries, Scottsdale, 1991, Sylvia Schmidt Gallery, New Orleans, 1991, 1 Tego Arcaner Dei Gremillion & Co. Fine Arts, Houston, 1993; exhibited in group shows at Mus. Art, Monterey, Calif., 1973, Bringham Young U, Provo, Utah, 1973, 74, 75, 76, 77, 78, 79, 80, 81, 82, 84, 86, 87, Mus. Modern Art, San Francisco, 1974, 76, 83, Am. Acad. Rome, 1975, Am. Acad. Rome, N.Y.C., 1975, Springville Mus. Art, 1977, 78, 80, Centennial Arts Ctr., Surrey, B.C., Can., 1977, Fine Arts Mus., Anchorage, 1977, Smithsonian Inst. traveling show, Washington, 1977-78, 80-82, U. Art Gallery SUNY, Albany, 1978, Salt Lake Art Ctr., Salt Lake City, 1979, 80, 92, Brusberg Gallerie, Hanover, 1979, Mus. Art, Salt Lake City, 1980, Madras (Oreg.) Art Gallery, 1980, Siskiyous Art Gallery, Weed, Calif., 1980, Utah Mus. Art, Salt Lake City, 1981, 83, 86, Mus. Art, Denver, 1982, Mus. Art, Long Beach, Calif., 1983, Bklyn. Mus., 1983, Mus. Art, Albuquerque, 1983, Mus. Ch. History and Art, Salt Lake City, 1984, 86, 91, Dolores Chase Fine Arts, 1985, 86, Marilyn Butler Fine Arts, Scottsdale, Ariz., 1985, Colorado Springs Fine Art Ctr., 1986, Gremillion & Co. Fine Arts, Inc., Houston, 1987, Nora Eccles Harrison Mus. Art, Logan, Utah, 1988, Prairie Lee Gallery, Chgo., 1988, Utah Arts Festival, 1989, Zoe Machs Gallery, Salt Lake City, 1990, MacGillman-Gruen Galleries, Chgo., 1991, Frederic Weissman Collection, Japan, 1991, Dixie Coll., St. George, Utah, 1991, Bharan Internat. Biennial Prints, India, 1991, and more. Recipient CCAC Spl. Edition Purchase award alternate San Francisco Mus. Modern Art, 1973, Rome prize in painting, Am. Acad. Rome, 1975-76, award Springville Mus. Art, 1980, Snowbird Inst. award in art, 1980, Printmaking award Western States Art Found., 1980, Merit award Sch. Art, Terme, Italy, 1981, Visual Arts Nomination award, 1982, World Culture award Centro Studie Ricerecke Belle Nazioni, Italy, 1983, Western States Painting award, 1983, Gold medal nomination Accademia Italia, Parma, Italy, 1980, 85, Karl G. Maeser Rsch. and Creative Arts award Karl G. Maeser Found., 1985, Purchase award Springville Mus. Arts, 1986, Purchase award Cliff Lodge Inaugural Exhbn., 1987, Utah Works on Paper award, 1989. Home: PO Box 1359 Boulder UT 84716-1359 Office: Brigham Young Univ C502 Hfac Provo UT 84602-1026

BARSDATE, MARY KATHRYN, educator; b. Windber, Pa., Apr. 28, 1933; d. Stephen and Kathryn (Shuster) Haschak; m. Robert John Barsdate, June 9, 1959; children: Lory Ann, Kelly Joan. BA, Allegheny Coll., 1955, MA, 1960. Cert. tchr., Pa. Tchr. pub. schs., Pa., 1955-62; sec. dept. linguistics U. Alaska, Fairbanks, 1966, lectr., 1966-67; instr. Ednl. Complex, Ft. Wainwright, Alaska, 1987-92; critic tchr. U. Pitts.,1960-62; tutor, Fairbanks, 1968—; ind. editor, Fairbanks, 1977—. Chmn. Alaska Gov.'s State Adv. Coun. on Librs., 1989-91; mem. Fairbanks North Star Borough Libr. Commn., 1983-94, vice chmn., 1985-88, chmn., 1983-85; bd. dirs. Arts Alaska, Inc., Anchorage, 1983—, mem. exec. com., 1985—; bd. dirs. adv. coun. Sta. KUAC-TV-FM Pub. Broadcasting, Fairbanks, 1982-88, chmn., 1984-88; founder Fairbanks Montessori Assn., 1966-71; coord. Alaska State High Sch. Debate-Forensics Tournaments, 1984; trustee, sec.-treas. Libr. Found., Noel Wien Pub. Libr., Fairbanks, 1979—; sec. Weeks Field Park Assn., 1990-92. Recipient Gov.'s Award for Arts, 1986. Mem. Nat. Assn. Pub. TV Stas. (lay rep. bd. dels. 1984-88), Alaska State Coun. Arts (v.p. 1981-83), Assn. Alaska Sch. Bds. (v.p. 1977-78), Literacy Coun. Alaska (bd. dirs. 1978-86), Fairbanks Arts Assn. (sec. 1970-79), Phi Beta Kappa. Republican. Carpatho-Russian Orthodox. Home and Office: PO Box 80174 Fairbanks AK 99708-0174

BARSIS, EDWIN HOWARD, physicist; b. N.Y.C., June 28, 1940; s. Morris J. and Rose Barsis; children: James, Benjamin. BEP, Cornell U., 1963, MS, 1965, PhD, 1967. Mem. tech. staff Sandia Nat. Labs., Livermore, Calif., 1967-69; supr. applied physics Sandia Nat. Labs., Livermore, 1969-75, supr. advanced weapons div., 1975-77; mgr. electronic subsystems dept. Sandia Nat. Labs., Albuquerque, 1977-86, dir. computer scis. and math., 1986—, dir. engring. scis., 1989—; chmn. bd. dirs. Urologics, Inc., Albuquerque, 1984—. Contbr. articles to profl. jours. Capt. C.E., U.S. Army, 1967-69. Mem. Am. Phys. Soc. Home: 1538 Catron Ave SE Albuquerque NM 87123-4259 Office: Sandia Nat Labs PO Box 5800 Albuquerque NM 87185

BARSKY, MARTIN, editor, publisher; b. Phila., Jan. 26, 1927; s. Philip and Mollie (Cohen) B.; children: Larry, Steve, Laura. Grad. high sch., Phila. Advt. mgr. Kiddie City Stores, Phila., 1954; mgr., prodr. various radio and TV stas., Pa., Mont., Calif., 1955-70; founder, editor, pub. So. Calif. Retailer, L.A., 1971-81; owner, editor, pub. Retailer News, Anaheim, Calif., 1981-88; pres., pub. Video Software Dealer News, L.A., 1984-86, Rental Dealer News, Orange, Calif., 1987-90; founder, editor, pub. Buying Group News mag. and Retailing News newspaper, Anaheim, 1990—. Prodr. Folk Music Theatre, 1967; contbr. articles to profl. jours. Bd. dirs. City of Hope Consumer Electronics, L.A., 1987-88, pres., 1985-86. Sgt. USAAF, 1943-45. Recipient Cert. of Appreciation, Am. Legion, 1968, Outstanding Contbns. award Associated Vol. Buyers, 1977, United Stores Inc., 1980. Mem. Soc. Profl. Journalists, Electronics Reps. Republican. Jewish. Home: 13490 Prospector Ct Victorville CA 92392-8849 Office: Retailing News 14962 Bear Valley Rd Ste 288 Victorville CA 92392-9236

BART, PETER BENTON, newspaper editor, film producer, novelist; b. N.Y.C., July 24, 1932; m. Leslie Cox; children: Colby, Dilys. BA, Swarthmore Coll., 1954; MA, London Sch. Econs., 1956. Staff reporter The Wall Street Jour., N.Y.C., 1956-57, The N.Y. Times, N.Y.C., 1957-67; v.p. Paramount Pictures, Los Angeles, 1967-74; pres. Bart Palevsky Prodn., L.A., 1974-77, Lorimar Film Co., Los Angeles, 1977-82; sr. v.p., film producer Metro Goldwyn Mayer/United Artists, L.A., 1982-85; v.p., editorial dir. Variety and Daily Variety, L.A., 1989—. Author: Destinies, 1980, Thy Kingdom Come, 1983, Fade Out: The Calamitous Final Days of MGM, 1990; prodr.: (films) Fun with Dick and Jane, Islands in the Stream, Youngblood. Office: Variety 5700 Wilshire Blvd Ste 120 Los Angeles CA 90036-3659

BARTEL, ARTHUR GABRIEL, educational administrator, city official; b. San Francisco, Oct. 20, 1934; s. Irving Peter and Elian Leah (Barker) B.; m. Dottie Lu Smith, Dec. 14, 1963 (dec. Apr. 1972); children: Brian Blake, Scott Michael; m. Suzane M. Loftis, Feb. 14, 1989. Student, San Jose State Coll., 1952-54; BS, U. Calif., Berkeley, 1957; postgrad., U. So. Calif., 1968-70; MA, Pepperdine U., 1973, Calif. State U., Fresno, 1995. Cert. FAA air traffic controller, 1957-77, naval flight officer, 1965; lic. standard tchr., life standard svc., life cmty. coll. life chief coll. adminstrv. officer, life cmty. coll. supr., life comty. coll. instr., spl. edn. svcs. credential, Calif. Enlisted USMC, 1954, commd. 2d lt., 1957, advanced through grades to maj., 1967; comdg. officer VMFA-314 Fighter-Attack Squadron USMC, El Toro, Calif., 1970-72; ret. USMC, 1977; gen. mgr. Nieuport 17 Restaurant, Santa Ana, Calif., 1977-78; pres., chief exec. officer High Flight Inc., Hanford, San Diego, Calif., 1978-81; teaching vice prin. Armona (Calif.) Union Elem. Sch., 1982-84, tchr. sci. and lang. arts., 1981-84; curriculum cons. Kings County Office Edn., Hanford, 1984-86; program specialist Kings County Supt. Schs., Hanford, 1986-91; prin. Kings County Cmty. Sch., Hanford, 1994—; councilman City of Hanford, 1986-90, mayor, 1988-90; mem. adv. bd. San Joaquin Valley Writing Project, 1984-86, 92—. Vice chmn. Hanford Planning Commn., 1982-86; vice chmn. bd. trustees Sacred Heart Hosp., 1987-93; bd. dirs. Navy League, 1992—. Decorated Air medal, Vietnam Cross of Gallantry; fellow internat. writing project U. Calif., Irvine, 1985. Mem. Assn. Calif. Sch. Adminstrs., Calif. Soc. Program Specialists, Hanford C. of C., DAV (life), Ret. Officers Assn., Navy League (v.p. 1993-95), Delta Upsilon (life). Office: Kings County Office Edn Kings Govt Ctr Hanford CA 93230

BARTELINK, DIRK JAN, physicist, engineer; b. Heumen, The Netherlands, Oct. 28, 1933; came to U.S., 1958; s. Dirk Leonard and Johanna Judith (Jannink) B.; m. Donna Maurie Merifield, Mar. 2, 1957; children: Debbie Bartelink Jones, John Dirk. BSc, U. Western Ont., London, 1956; MS, Stanford U., 1959, PhD, 1962. Mem. tech. staff AT&T Labs., Murray Hill, N.J., 1961-66, supr., 1966-73; prin. scientist, area mgr. Xerox, Palo Alto, Calif., 1973-82; dept. mgr. Hewlett-Packard Labs., Palo Alto, Calif., 1982—; with Semiconductor Rsch. Corp., Research Triangle Park, N.C., 1995—; vis. scientist Stanford U., 1981-82; mem. strategic adv. bd. SEMATECH, Austin, Tex., 1989—; mem. nat. tech. roadmap Semiconductor Industry Assn., San Jose, 1992, 94; chmn. symposium on Ultra Large Scale Integration Tech., 1990-91. Mem. IEEE (sr.). Office: Hewlett-Packard Labs 3500 Deer Creek Rd Palo Alto CA 94304-1317

BARTER BOWLUS, NADINE CHRISTENA, biology educator; b. Seattle, May 25, 1948. BS in Liberal Arts, Regents Coll., U. State N.Y., Albany, 1989; MA in Biology, San Jose (Calif.) State U., 1992. Grad. asst. San Jose State U., 1989-93, lectr. biology, 1993—; instr. biology San Jose City Coll., 1993—, West Valley C.C., Saratoga, Calif., 1993—. Co-author: Using Macintosh, Tools for Biologists, 2d edit., 1994. Mem. Ecol. Soc. Am. (sec. We. chpt. 1990-94), Nat. Assn. Biology Tchrs., Am. Inst. Biol. Scis., Soc. for Conservation Biology (sec. No. Calif. chpt. 1994).

BARTH, DAVID VICTOR, computer systems designer, consultant; b. Tulsa, Sept. 23, 1942; s. Vincent David and Norma (Bell) B. BS summa cum laude, Met. State Coll., Denver, 1977; MS, U. Colo., 1982; PhD, Kennedy-Western U., 1995. Programming mgr. Am. Nat. Bank, Denver, 1967-72; cons. Colo. Farm Bur. Ins. Corp., Denver, 1972; systems analyst Mid-Continent Computer Services, Denver, 1972-73; programming mgr. Bayly Corp., Denver, 1973-75; project leader Cobe Labs. Inc., Denver, 1976-84; part-time tchr. Met. State Coll., 1982-83; systems analyst Affiliated Banks Service Co., Denver, 1985-87; real estate broker Van Schaack & Co., Denver, 1985; tech. supr. Affiliated Banks Svc. Co., Denver, 1987-89; software engr. Computer Data Systems, Inc., Aurora, Colo., 1990-91, 1994—; sr. computer systems designer Martin Marietta Corp., Golden, Colo., 1991-92; owner, operator Computer Shop, Lakewood, Colo., 1992-93; cons. Ross Co., Denver, 1993-95; sr. software engr. Computer Data Systems, Inc., Aurora,

Colo., 1994—; freelance flight instr., 1977—. Vol. Am. Red Cross, 1987—; Served with USN, 1961-66. Mem. Soc. for Info. Mgmt. (editor newsletter 1983), Exptl. Aircraft Assn. (editor newsletter chpt. 660, 1989-91), Aircraft Owners and Pilots Assn., Flying Circus Skating Club. Republican. Home: 509 S Cody St Lakewood CO 80226-3047

BARTH, UTA, artist, educator; b. Berlin, Jan. 29, 1958. BA, U. Calif., Davis, 1982; MFA, UCLA, 1985. From asst. prof. to assoc. prof. art dept. U. Calif., Riverside, 1990—. One-woman shows include Howard Yezersky Gallery, Boston, 1990, Rochester (N.Y.) Inst. Tech., 1993, Calif. Mus. Photography, Riverside, 1993, Wooster Gardens, N.Y.C., 1994, Santa Monica Mus. Art, 1995, Huntington Beach Art Ctr., 1995; group shows include Tom Solomon's Garage, L.A., 1994, Long Beach (Calif.) Mus. Art, 1994, Mus. De Beyerd, Netherlands, 1994, Los Angeles County Mus. Art, 1994, Haines Gallery, San Franicsco, 1994, San Bernardino County Mus., 1994, The New Mus., N.Y.C., 1995, Mus. Modern Art, N.Y.C., 1995. NEA grantee, 1990-91, 94-95; Art Matters Inc. grantee, 1992-93, 95. Home and Office: 245 Ruth Ave Venice CA 90291-2711

BARTLETT, ALBERT ALLEN, retired physics educator; b. Shanghai, China, Mar. 21, 1923; s. Willard William and Marguerite (Allen) B.; m. Eleanor Frances Roberts, Aug. 24, 1946; children—Carol Louise, Jane Elizabeth, Lois Jeanne, Nancy Marie. Student, Otterbein Coll., 1940-42; B.A., Colgate U., 1944; M.A., Harvard U., 1948, Ph.D., 1951. Research asst. Los Alamos Sci. Lab., 1944-46; faculty U. Colo., Boulder, 1950—; prof. physics U. Colo., 1962-88, chmn. faculty council, 1969-71, prof. emeritus, 1988—; faculty Harvard U. Summer Sch., 1952, 53, 55, 56; vis. research worker Nobel Inst. Physics, Stockholm, Sweden, 1963-64; lectr. on arithmetic, population and energy. Contbr. articles to profl. jours. Mem. Boulder City Parks and Recreation Adv. Bd., 1967-72, vice chmn., 1969, 70, chmn., 1971. Recipient Thomas Jefferson award U. Colo., 1972, Robert L. Stearns award, 1974, service award Girl Scouts Am., 1974, Univ. Gold medal, 1978, Plan Boulder County Ann. award, 1990. Fellow AAAS, Am. Phys. Soc.; mem. Am. Assn. Physics Tchrs. (recipient Disting. Service citation 1970, Robert A. Millikan award 1981, pres. 1978, Melba Newell Phillips award 1990), Phi Beta Kappa, Sigma Xi, Alpha Tau Omega. Clubs: Colo. Mountain, Rocky Mountain Railroad. Home: 2935 19th St Boulder CO 80304-2719

BARTLETT, DAVID CARSON, state legislator; b. New London, Conn., Feb. 2, 1944; s. Neil Riley and Susan Marion (Carson) B.; m. Barbara Hunting, July 14, 1973 (div. 1974); m. Janice Anne Wezelman, Feb. 11, 1979; children: Daniel Wezelman, Elizabeth Anne. Student, Wesleyan U., Middletown, Conn., 1962-64; BA, U. Ariz., 1966, MA, 1970; JD, Georgetown U., 1976. Teaching asst. U. Ariz., Tucson, 1967-69; program analyst U.S. Dept. Labor, Washington, 1970-76; assoc. Snell & Wilmer, Tucson, 1976-77; pvt. practice Tucson, 1976-79; assoc. Davis, Eppstein & Hall, Tucson, 1979-85; mem. Ariz. Ho. of Reps., Tucson, 1983-88, Ariz. State Senate, 1989-92; chief counsel for civil rights Ariz. Atty. Gen.'s Office, Tucson, 1993—. Democrat. Home: 3236 E Via Palos Verdes Tucson AZ 85716-5854 Office: Ariz Attorney Gen 400 W Congress Ste 215 Tucson AZ 85701

BARTLETT, NEIL, chemist, educator; b. Newcastle-upon-Tyne, Eng., Sept. 15, 1932; s. Norman and Ann Willins (Vock) B.; m. Christina Isabel Cross, Dec. 26, 1957; children: Jeremy John, Jane Ann, Christopher, Robin. B.Sc., Kings Coll., U. Durham, Eng., 1954; Ph.D. in Inorganic Chemistry, Kings Coll., U. Durham, 1957; D.Sc. (hon.), U. Waterloo, Can., 1968, Colby Coll., 1972, U. Newcastle-upon-Tyne, 1981, McMaster U., Can., 1992; D.Univ. (hon.), U. Bordeaux, France, 1976, U. Ljubljana, Slovenia, 1989, U. Nantes, France, 1990; LLD, Simon Fraser U., Can., 1993. Lectr. chemistry U. B.C., Vancouver, Can., 1958-63; prof. U. B.C., 1963-66; prof. chemistry Princeton U., N.J., 1966-69, U. Calif., Berkeley, 1969—; mem. adv. bd. on inorganic reactions and methods Verlag Chemie, 1978—; mem. adv. panel Nat. Measurement Lab., Nat. Bur. Stds., 1974-80; E.W.R. Steacie Meml. fellow NRC, Can., 1964-66; Miller vis. prof. U. Calif., Berkeley, 1967-68; 20th G.N. Lewis Meml. lectr., 1973; William Lloyd Evans Meml. lectr. Ohio State U., 1966; A.D. Little lectr. Northeastern U., 1969; Phi Beta Upsilon lectr. U. Nebr., 1975; Henry Werner lectr. U. Kans., 1977; Jeremy Musher Meml. lectr., Israel, 1980, Randolph T. Major Meml. lectr. U. Conn., 1985, J.C. Karcher lectr. U. Okla., 1988; Brotherton vis. prof. U. Leeds, Eng., 1981; Erskine vis. lectr. U. Canterbury, New Zealand, 1983; Wilsmore fellow Melbourne U., Australia, 1983; vis. fellow All Souls Coll., Oxford U., 1984; Miller prof. U. Calif.-Berkeley, 1986-87; George H. Cady lectr. U. Wash., Seattle, 1994; Leermakers lectr. Wesleyan U., 1995. Bd. editors Inorganic Chemistry, 1967-79, Jour. Fluorine Chemistry, 1971-80, Synthetic Metals, Revue Chimie Minerale; mem. adv. bd. McGraw-Hill Ency. Sci. and Tech. Recipient Rsch. Corp. award; E.W.R. Steacie prize, 1965; Elliott Cresson medal Franklin Inst., 1968; Kirkwood medal Yale U. and Am. Chem. Soc. (New Haven sect.), 1969; Dannie-Heinemann prize The Gottingen acad. 1971; Robert A. Welch award in chemistry, 1987; Alexander von Humboldt Found. award, 1977; medal Jozef Stefan Inst., Slovenia, 1980; Moissan medal, 1986; Prix Moissan, Paris, 1988; fellow Alfred P. Sloan Found., 1964-66; Bonner Chemiepries, Bonn, 1991; Berkeley citation, 1993. Fellow Royal Soc., Am. Acad. Arts and Scis., Royal Inst. Chemistry, Chem. Inst. Can. (1st Noranda lectr. 1963); mem. NAS (fgn. assoc.), Leopoldina Acad. (Halle, Salle), Akademie der Wissenschaften in Gottingen, Associé Etranger, Académie des Sciences, Institut de France, Am. Chem. Soc. (chmn. divs. fluorine chemistry 1972, inorganic chemistry 1977, award in inorganic chemistry 1970, W.H. Nichols award N.Y. sect. 1983, Pauling medal of Pacific N.W. sects. 1989, Disting. Svc. award 1989, award for Creative Work in Flourine Chemistry 1992), Phi Lambda Upsilon (hon.). Home: 6 Oak Dr Orinda CA 94563-3912 Office: U Calif Dept Chemistry Berkeley CA 94720

BARTLETT, STEVEN THADE, aerospace engineer; b. Glendale, Calif., Sept. 13, 1962; s. Ronald Thade Bartlett and Frances Mae (Bailey) Arrington. BS in Physics, Calif. State U., Long Beach, 1985, MS in Aerospace Engring., 1993. Retail salesman Tandy Corp., Beverly Hills, Calif., 1982-85; aerospace systems engr. McDonnell Douglas Corp., Huntington Beach, Calif., 1986—. Fellow Space Studies Inst.; mem. AIAA (sr.), Nat. Space Soc., Orgn. for the Advancement of Space Industrialization and Settlement (v.p.), Aricraft Owners and Pilots Assn., L.A. Sci. Fantasy Soc., World Future Soc., Pacific Rocket Soc., Nature Conservancy, Challenger Ctr., Habitat for Humanity. Libertarian. Office: McDonnell Douglas Space Co 5301 Bolsa Ave Huntington Beach CA 92647-2048

BARTLETT, SUE, state legislator; b. Billings, Mont., July 4, 1947; m. Gene Fenderson. BA, Wash. U. Clk., recorder Lewis and Clark County, 1983-91; asst. sec. Mont. Senate, 1991-92, mem.; tech. writer. Democrat. Home: 416 N Beattie St Helena MT 59601-3701

BARTLETT, THOMAS ALVA, educational administrator; b. Salem, Oreg., Aug. 20, 1930; s. Cleave Wines and Alma (Hanson) B.; m. Mary Louise Bixby, Mar. 20, 1954; children: Thomas Glenn, Richard A., Paul H. Student, Willamette U., 1947-49, DCL (hon.), 1986; A.B., Stanford U., 1951, Ph.D., 1959; M.A. (Rhodes scholar), Oxford U., 1953; L.H.D. (hon.), Colgate U., 1977, Mich. State U., 1978, Union Coll., 1979; D.C.L. (hon.), Pusan Nat. U., Korea, 1985, U. Ala., 1983. Mem. U.S. Permanent Mission to UN, 1956-63; advisor Gen. Assembly Dels., 1956-63; pres. Am. U., Cairo, 1963-69, Colgate U., Hamilton, N.Y., 1969-77, Assn. Am. Univs., Washington, 1977-82; chancellor U. Ala. System, 1982-89, Oreg. State System of Higher Edn., Eugene, 1989-94; ret.; mem. UAR-U.S. Ednl. Exch. Commn., 1966-69; mem. Task Force on Financing Higher Edn. in N.Y. State (Keppel Commn.), 1972-73; chmn. Commn. Ind. Colls. and Univs. N.Y., 1974-76; bd. dirs. Nat. Assn. Ind. Colls. and Univs., 1975-76; trustee Univs. Field Staff Internat., 1985-87; mem. NASA Comml. Space Adv. Com., 1988-90. Mem. nat. bd. examining Chaplains Episcopal Ch., 1978-91; trustee Gen. Theol. Sem., 1977-82, Am. U. in Cairo, 1978—, U.S.-Japan Found., 1988—. Mem. Coun. Fgn. Rels., Cosmos Club (Washington), Phi Beta Kappa. Home: 1209 SW 6th Ave # 904 Portland OR 97204-1089

BARTLETT, THOMAS HENRY, chemist; b. Great Falls, Mont., Jan. 1, 1931; s. Thomas Henry and Sophia (Stenseth) B.; m. Alice Kay Lee, Dec. 29, 1959 (div. Feb. 1962); one child, Brady; m. Iris Elaine Cooper, Aug. 25, 1967; children: Karleen, Elaine. BS, Coll. Great Falls, 1952; postgrad., U. Wash., 1953, LaSalle Extension U., 1958-63. Chemist Anaconda Co., Great Falls, 1954-57, Am. Chrome Co., Nye, Mont., 1957-61; chief chemist Western Nuclear Inc., Jeffery City, Wyo., 1962-67; gen. mgr. Chem. and Geol. Labs., Casper, Wyo., 1967-76; pres., chief exec. officer WAMCO Lab. Inc., Casper, 1977—. Chmn., pres. Winter Meml. Presbyn. Ch., Casper, 1982—. Mem. ASTM. Lodge: Elks. Home: 3301 E 12th St Casper WY 82609-3033 Office: WAMCO Lab Inc PO Box 2953 Casper WY 82602-2953

BARTLEY, OPELENE, actress, consultant; b. Chouteau, Okla., June 27, 1924; d. Leroy and Drucilla (Moore) Johnson; m. Paul Udell Bartley, Aug. 31, 1946 (dec. Feb. 1990). AA, L.A. Community Coll., 1985; stuent, U. So. Calif., L.A., 1986-87; student, Buffalo State Coll., 1962-63. Ordained to ministry, 1980. Dist. rep. Primerica Fin. Svcs. Walker Internat., Culver City, Calif., 1989—. Actress appeared in (TV series) including White Shadow, Hill Street Blues, General Hosp., Redd Foxx, The Judge, L.A. Law, Amen, Superior Ct., (films) Let's Do It Again, Emergency Room, Falcon & The Snowman, Once Bitten, What's Hot, What's Not, The Blob, Let it Ride, (spl.) Roots II-Second Generation, (on stage) Raisin In the Sun, Happy Endings, Contribution, The Great White Hope, Black Girl, Something Cool, (comml.) Lee Jeans. Fundraiser Hunger & Homeless Coalition, 1987, 88, 90; donator Women Shelters Abused, Tenn., 1990—; owner Emotional People & Retardees, Detroit, 1968-72; bd. dirs. Jefferson Haven Forster Homes, Detroit, 1967. Recipient Community Svc. award L.A. Voter Edn. Project, 1977, Proclamation, City of L.A., 1987, Community Svc. award Sta. KTLA. Democrat. Home: PO Box 43723 Los Angeles CA 90043-0723 Office: Bartley and Assoc Unltd PO Box 43723 Los Angeles CA 90043-0723 also: 5839 Green Valley Cir Ste 200 Culver City CA 90230

BARTLING, JUDD QUENTON, research corporation executive; b. Muncie, Ind., July 24, 1936; s. Hubert George and Hildagarde (Good) B.; m. Madeline Levesque, June 9, 1973 (div. 1989); stepchildren—Mary Johnson, Michael Johnson. BA, U. Calif., 1960, PhD, 1969; MS, Purdue U., 1964. Research asst. U. Calif., Riverside, 1965-69; cons. Dept. Def. Rsch., Azak Corp., Chatsworth, Calif., 1969-71, pres., 1971—. Served with U.S. Army, 1960-62. NSF grantee U. Fla., 1969. Research in bus., solid state physics, signal processing, quantum electronics, electromagnetics and radar.

BARTON, ANN ELIZABETH, financial executive; b. Long Lake, Mich., Sept. 8, 1923; d. John and Inez Mabel (Morse) Seaton; m. H. Kenneth Barton, Apr. 3, 1948; children: Michael, John, Nancy. Student Mt. San Antonio Coll., 1969-71, Adrian Coll., 1943, Citrus Coll., 1967, Golden Gate U., 1976, Coll. Fin. Planning, 1980-82. CFP. Tax cons., real estate broker, Claremont, Calif., 1967-72, Newport Beach, Calif., 1972-74; v.p., officer Putney, Barton, Assocs., Inc., Walnut Creek, Calif., 1975-94; bd. dir. Fin. Svc. Corp. Cert. fin. planner. Mem. Internat. Assn. Fin. Planners (registered investment advisor), Calif. Soc. Enrolled Agts., Nat. Assn. Enrolled Agts., Nat. Soc. Public Accts., Inst. CFP. Office: Putney Barton Assocs Inc 1243 Alpine Rd Ste 219 Walnut Creek CA 94596-4431

BARTON, DAVID M., electronics engineer, consultant; b. Portland, Oreg., Jan. 23, 1939; s. Delwin Walter and Lillian (Strom) B.; m. Laura Schuette, June 1, 1962 (div. 1980); children: Kenneth Randall, Wesley Keith; m. Susan MIchelle Smith, Mar. 30, 1983. BA in Physics, Linfield Coll., 1961. Design engr. Field Emission Corp., McMinnville, Oreg., 1961-62, Tektronix, Inc, Beaverton, Oreg., 1962-64; sr. engr. Monsanto Co., St. Louis, 1964-66; mem. tech. staff Fairchild Instrumentation Div., Mountain View, Calif., 1966-69, Develco, Inc., Mountain View, 1969-72; sr. mem. tech. staff Litronix, Inc., Cupertino, Calif., 1972-76; product mktg. mgr. Litronix, Inc., Cupertino, 1976-80; sr. mem. tech. staff Victor Techs., Scotts Valley, Calif., 1980-84; engr. pvt. practice San Jose, Calif., 1984—; dir., bus. cons., Personal Tng. Systems, San Jose, 1986-91. Mem. Amateur Radio News Svc. (editor newsletter), No. Calif. DX Club. Republican. Home and Office: 14842 Nelson Way San Jose CA 95124

BARTON, LARRY LUMIR, mircobiology educator, consultant; b. West Point, Nebr., May 13, 1940; s. Lumir and Sophia Tresa (Ahrndt) B.; m. Sandra L. Reiners, Aug. 21, 1968; children: Brian, Gregory. BS in biology and chem., U. Nebr., 1962, MS in microbiology, 1966, PhD in microbiology, 1969. Rsch. assoc. dept. biochemistry U. Ga., Athens, 1969-71; asst. prof. dept. pathobiology Johns Hopkins U., Balt., 1971-72; asst. prof. dept. biology U. N.Mex., Albuquerque, 1972—; vis. scientist life sci. div. Los Alamos Nat. Lab., Los Alamos, 1988; dir. microbiology div. Northwestern N.Mex. Sci. and Engring. Sci. Fair; editorial bd. Biology of Metals, 1988-91, Biometals, 1991—; editor-in-chief Anaerobes: Academic Press Jour. 1994—. Author numerous book chpts.; editor numerous books; contbr. articles to profl. jours. Jt. appointment Am. Leprosy Assn., Washington, 1971-72. Mem. Am. Soc. Microbiology (pres. 1987-89), Sigma Xi (treas. 1991-93, v.p. 1993-94). Office: U N Mex Dept Biology Albuquerque NM 87131

BARTSCH, WILLIAM HENRY, development economist, author; b. Washington, Jan. 18, 1933; s. Henry G. and Elsa Margit (Nilsson) B.; m. Lila Sepehri, Aug. 5, 1965; children: Shadi, Blake. BA in Econs., Washington and Lee U., 1955; MA in Fgn. Affairs, U. Va., 1959; PhD in Devel. Econs., U. London, 1970. Asst. program officer U.S. AID, Kingston, Jamaica, 1963; research economist Internat. Labour Office, Geneva, 1969-73, manpower planning advisor, Suva, Fiji, 1973-75, Jakarta, Indonesia, 1975-78, interregional advisor, Geneva, 1978-81, sr. liaison officer, Washington, 1982-89, sr. economist, Geneva, 1989-92; cons. human resource planning; writer mil. history, 1993—. Author: Problems of Employment Creation In Iran, 1970, The Economy of Iran, 1940-70, 1971, Employment and Technology Choice in Asian Agriculture, 1977, Doomed at the Start, 1992. Contbr. articles to profl. jours. Fulbright fellow, 1956-57; Helen Lee Wessel fellow, 1955-56. Mem. Am. Econ. Assn., Am. Com. for History of 2d World War, Am. Aviation Hist. Soc., Soc. Mil. History, U.S. Naval Inst., Phi Beta Kappa. Democrat. Episcopalian. Avocations: tennis, swimming, traveling.

BARUCH, RUTH-MARION EVELYN, photographer, writer; b. Berlin, Ger., June 15, 1922; d. Max and Bertha (Zweigenhaft) Baruch; m. Pirkle Jones, 1949. BA in Creative Writing, U. Mo., 1944, BJ, 1944; MFA in Photography, Ohio U., 1946; postgrad., Calif. Sch. Fine Arts, San Francisco, 1946-47. Grad. asst. Ohio U., 1944-46; tchr. workshops Home Studio, Mill Valley, Calif., 1969-71; guest artist San Francisco Art Inst., 1970, 85. Works in permanent collections at San Francisco Mus. Art, Oakland Mus. Art, Polaroid Corp., Cambridge, Mass., George Eastman House, Rochester, N.Y., Ctr. for Creative Photography (Ansel Adams Collection), U. Ariz., Tucson, Ariz. State U., Temple; author: The Vanguard: A Photographic Essay on the Black Panthers, 1970; included in Photography in the Twentieth Century, 1967, Photographers Ency. Internat., book and exhbn.: Family of Man, 1954; one person shows at San Francisco Mus. Modern Art, 1966, Carmel Photography Ctr., 1967, M.H. DeYoung Meml. Mus., San Francisco, 1968, Amon Carter Mus. Western Art, Ft. Worth, 1968, Focus Gallery, San Francisco, 1976, San Francisco Mus. Modern Art Rental Gallery, 1980; group shows include Mus. Modern Art, N.Y.C., 1954, Kongresshalla, Berlin, 1957, George Eastman House, 1960, DeCordova Mus., Lincoln, Mass., 1967, Focus Gallery, San Francisco, 1976, 80, Friends of Photography, Carmel, 1984, Monterey Peninsula Mus. Art, 1986, Ariz. State U., 1987. Home and Office: 663 Lovell Ave Mill Valley CA 94941-1086

BARUSCH, LAWRENCE ROOS, lawyer; b. Oakland, Calif., Aug. 23, 1949; s. Maurice Radston and Phyllis (Rose) B.; m. Susan Amanda Smith, Aug. 7, 1983; children: Nathaniel M., Ariana G. BA summa cum laude, Harvard U., 1971, JD cum laude, 1975. Bar: Calif. 1975. Assoc. Cotton, Seligman & Ray, San Francisco, 1975-77; gen. counsel Jones & Guerrero Co., Inc., Agana, Guam, 1977-82; ptnr. Klemm, Blair & Barusch, P.C., Agana, Guam, 1982-85; assoc. Davis, Graham & Stubbs, Salt Lake City, 1986-87; counsel Parsons, Behl & Latimer, Salt Lake City, 1987-89, shareholder, 1989—; counsel Guam Tax Code Commn., 1990-94; mem. com. U.S. activities on foreigners and tax treaties, tax sect. ABA, 1994—. Contbr. articles to Guam Bar Jour. and Tax Notes. Sheldon fellow Harvard U., 1971. Mem. Guam Bar Assn. (pres. 1982-84), No. Marianas Bar Assn., Utah Bar Assn. (chmn. tax sect. 1994-95), Calif. Bar Assn., Phi Beta Kappa. Office: Parsons Behle & Latimer 201 S Main St Ste 1800 Salt Lake City UT 84111-2218

BARUT, ASIM ORHAN, physicist, educator; b. Malatya, Turkey, June 24, 1926; came to U.S., 1953, naturalized, 1962; m. Pierrette Helene Gervaz, July 2, 1954. Diploma, Swiss Fed. Inst. Tech., 1949, DSc, 1952, D (hon.), 1982, 87. Mem. faculty U. Chgo., 1953-54, Reed Coll., Portland, Oreg., 1954-55, U. Montreal, Que., Can., 1955-56, Syracuse (N.Y.) U., 1956-61, U. Calif., Berkeley, 1961-62; prof. physics U. Colo., Boulder, 1962—, rsch. lectr., 1982; lectr. ednl. instns., various countries. Editor, mem. editorial bd. Found. of Physics, Reports in Math. Physics, Hadronic Jour., Annales Fondat L. de Broglie, Com. Theoretical Physics. Mem. staff Internat. Ctr. for Theoretical Physics, Trieste, Italy, 1964-65, 68-69, 72-73, 86-87; bd. dirs. NATO Advanced Study Insts., 1966, 67, 70, 72, 77, 83, 84, 89, 94. Recipient Alexander von Humboldt award, 1974-75, 76, 85, Medal of Sci., Turkey, 1982, Rsch. Lectureship award, 1983; faculty rsch. fellow, 1968, 72, 78, 85; Erskine fellow U. Canterbury, New Zealand, 1970. Fellow Am. Phys. Soc. Home: 760 12th St Boulder CO 80302-7519 Office: U Colo at Boulder Dept Physics Box 390 Boulder CO 80309

BARVILLE, REBECCA PENELOPE, elementary school educator; b. Tulare, Calif., Nov. 7, 1936; m. David Leopold Barville, June 8, 1958; children: Mark, Becky, Curtis. BA, Simpson Coll., San Francisco, 1958; MA summa cum laude, Fresno State U., 1974. Cert. reading specialist, edn. adminstr., elem. tchr., Calif. Social worker Tulare County Welfare Dept., Porterville, Calif., 1961-63, San Bernadino Welfare, Ontario, Calif., 1963-65; tchr., reading specialist Pleasant View Sch., Porterville, 1969—; instr. Porterville Coll., 1993. Pres. PTA, Lindsay, Calif., 1966-67. Fellow Delta Kappa Gamma; mem. AAUW (bd. dirs. 1974-83), Calif. Reading Assn. (sec. 1974), Pleasant View Educators Assn. (past pres., sec. 1985—). Republican. Presbyterian. Club: P.E.O. (v.p. 1986-87).

BARZ, RICHARD L., microbiologist; b. Rockford, Ill., Mar. 22, 1955; s. William Edward Barz and Rosemary Alice (Easton) Scott; m. Nancy Ellen Kozakewich, May 14, 1976 (div. Nov. 1985); m. Susan Jane Hennefent, May 12, 1989; children: Megan, Richard L. Jr. BS in Microbiology, Colo. State U., 1975. Microbiologist Leprino Foods, Denver, 1975-76, rsch. technician, 1976-78, mgr. quality assurance, 1978-82, dir. quality assurance, researcher, 1982-86, v.p., 1986—. Mem. Am. Dairy Assn. Home: 5368 E Mineral Cir Littleton CO 80122-4009 Office: Leprino Foods 1830 W 38th Ave Denver CO 80211-2225

BASCH, REVA, information services company executive; b. Chgo., Aug. 1, 1947; d. Victor Hugo and Hertha (Levi) B.; m. Jerrald C. Shifman, Apr. 17, 1982. Student, U. Pitts., 1965-66, BA in English Lit. summa cum laude, 1969, MLS, U. Calif., Berkeley, 1971. Head libr. Cogswell Coll., San Francisco, 1971-72; tech. info. specialist Gilbert Assocs. Inc., Reading, Pa., 1973-79; tech. libr. NuTech, San Jose, Calif., 1980-81; rsch. assoc. Info. on Demand, Berkeley, Calif., 1981-82, asst. dir. rsch., 1982-83, dir. rsch., 1983-86, v.p., dir. rsch., 1985-86; software designer Mead Data Ctrl., Personal Computer Sys. Group, Menlo Park, Calif., 1986-88; pres. Aubergine Info. Svcs., Berkeley, 1986—. Author: Secrets of The Super Searches, 1993, Electronic Information Delivery: Ensuring Quality and Value, 1995; contbg. editor The Info. Advisor; contbr. articles to profl. jours. Recipient award for best paper UMI/Data Courier, 1990, Online Champion award Dun & Bradstreet. Mem. Assn. of Ind. Info. Profl.(pres.1991-92), Spl. Librs. Assn. , Assn. Info. and Dissemination Ctrs., Info. Bay Area, So. Calif. Online Users Group. Office: Aubergine Info Svcs 1945 San Antonio Ave Berkeley CA 94707-1649

BASCONCILLO, LINDY, insurance and financial services company executive; b. Honolulu, Dec. 11, 1943; s. Catalino M. and Primitiva (Barientos) B.; children: Lisa M., Rod Alan. BA, Pacific Union Coll., 1965; MA, Azusa Pacific U., 1979. Chartered life underwriter, chartered fin. cons. Tchr., vice prin. Santa Monica (Calif.) Jr. Acad., 1965-68; tchr., coach Temple City (Calif.) Unified Sch. Dist., 1968-79; sales agent N.Y. Life Ins. Co., Eugene, Oreg., 1980-81, tng. mgr., 1981-87; sales mgr. MONY Fin. Svcs., Eugene, 1987-88; sr. mktg. cons. Prudential Ins. and Fin. Svcs., Woodland Hills, Calif., 1988-89; sales mgr. Prudential Ins. and Fin. Svcs., Sacramento, 1989-91; bus., estate, retirement specialist John Deere Life Ins. Co., Calif. and Nev., 1991-94; dist. sales mgr. Mut. of Omaha, 1991—; mng. dir. Eute Consulting, Lincoln, Calif., 1994-95; brokerage dir. Nat. Life of Vt., 1995—; bus. cons. Jr. Achievement, Eugene, 1986; pres.-elect Eugene Life Underwriters Assn., 1988, v.p., 1987; chairperson Life Underwriter Tng. Coun., 1987, moderator, 1984-86. Mem. coun. for minority edn. U. Oreg., Eugene, 1986-88; mem. Lane County Tng. and Devel. Com., Eugene, 1985-87. Mem. Sacramento Chpt. CLU's, Sacramento Life Underwriters Assn. Home: 1812 5th St Lincoln CA 95648-2328 Office: 2868 Prospect Park Dr Ste 145 Rancho Cordova CA 95670-6020

BASHARDOOST, FRED, structural engineer; b. Tehran, Iran, June 7, 1963; came to U.S., 1978; BS in Civil Engring., U. Calif., Irvine, 1984, MS in Structural Engring., 1985. Registered civil engr., Calif. Rsch. and devel. engr. Elektra Power Industries, Irvine, Calif., 1984-85; assoc. structural engr. Sargent & Lundy Engrs., Chgo., 1985-87, Ralph M. Parsons, Pasadena, Calif., 1987-88, Fluor/Daniel, Irvine, 1988; consulting structural engr. California Steel Industries, Fontana, Calif., 1991—; owner Technic of Kaveh Engring., Anaheim, Calif., 1992—. Home: 1108 S Country Glen Way Anaheim CA 92808-2604 Office: Technic of Kaveh Engring 751 S Weir Canyon Rd Anaheim CA 92808-1962

BASICHIS, GORDON ALLEN, author, screenwriter; b. Phila., Aug. 23, 1947; s. Martin and Ruth (Gordon) B.; m. Marcia Hammond; 1 child, Casey James. BS, Temple U., 1969. Reporter Phila. Bull., 1969; writer, reporter Santa Fe News, 1971-72; with advt., pub. relations Jay Bernstein Pub. Relations, Los Angeles, 1978-80; screenwriter various studios, networks, Los Angeles, 1978-83, Metro Goldwyn Mayer Feature Films, Culver City, Calif., 1982-83; ind. writer, 1983—; pres. Moonlight, Inc., Los Angeles, 1982—; research cons. various pubs. Author: Beautiful Bad Girl: The Vicki Morgan Story, 1985, (novel) Constant Travelers, 1978; producer, dir. (video documentary) Jerry: One Man's Triumph, 1980; co-prodr. (TV series) Frank and Jesse; screenwriter (feature film) Return of the Jersey Devil, 1988, Crash, 1994. Mem. Dem. Nat. Com. Mem. Writers Guild Am. West, Am. Film Inst., Simon Wiesenthal Inst., Nat. Rifle Assn., Statue of Liberty/Ellis Island Found. Office: PO Box 1511 Beverly Hills CA 90213-1511

BASILE, PAUL LOUIS, JR., lawyer; b. Oakland, Calif., Dec. 27, 1945; s. Paul Louis and Roma Florence (Paris) B.; m. Linda Lou Paige, June 20, 1970; m. 2d Diane Chierichetti, Sept. 2, 1977. BA, Occidental Coll., 1968; postgrad., U. Wash., 1969; JD, UCLA, 1971. Bar: Calif. 1972, U.S. Dist. Ct. (cen. dist.) Calif. 1972, U.S. Dist. Ct. (no. dist.) Calif. 1985, U.S. Ct. Appeals (9th cir.) 1972, U.S. Tax Ct. 1977, U.S. Ct. Claims. 1978, U.S. Customs Ct. 1979, U.S. Ct. Customs and Patent Appeals 1979, U.S. Ct. Internat. Trade 1981, U.S. Supreme Ct. 1977; cert. specialist in taxation law Bd. of Legal Specialization, State Bar of Calif. Assoc. Parker, Milliken, Kohlmeier, Clark & O'Hara, L.A., 1971-72; corp. counsel TFI Cos., Inc., Irvine, Calif., 1972-73; pvt. practice L.A., 1973-80, 90—; memb. Basile & Siener, L.A., 1980-86, Clark & Trevithick, L.A., 1986-90; ptnr. Wolf, Rifkin & Shapiro, L.A., 1990, of counsel, 1990-92; gen. counsel J.W. Brown, Inc., L.A., 1980—, asst. sec., 1984-92; sec., gen. counsel Souriau, Inc., Valencia, Calif., 1981-90; v.p., sec., dir., gen. counsel Pvt. Fin. Assocs., L.A., 1983-94. Trustee, sec. Nat. Repertory Theatre Found., 1975-94, mem. exec. com., 1976-94, chmn. bd. dirs., 1991-94; mem. fin. com., bd. dirs. Calif. Music Theatre, 1988-92; bd. dirs. March of Dimes Birth Defects Found., Los Angeles County, 1982-87, mem. exec. com., 1983-86, sec., 1985-86; dist. fin. chmn. L.A. Area coun. Boy Scouts Am., 1982-83; trustee Occidental Coll., L.A., 1989-94; active L.A. Olympic Organizing Com., Ketchum Downtown YMCA, Vols. Am. L.A., others. Mem. ABA (taxation sect., corp. tax com. 1994, vice chmn. closely held bus. com. 1992-94, chair, 1994—, chmn. subcom. on continuing legal edn. 1990-94, chmn. subcom. on estate planning 1992, bus. law sect., real property sect., probate and trust law sect., spl. problems of bus. owners com., estate planning and drafting, pre-death planning issues com.), State Bar Calif. (taxation law adv. commn. 1994—, vice-chmn. 1995—, bus. law sect., nonprofit and unicorporated orgns. com. 1989-92, taxation sect., estate planning, trust and probate sect.), L.A. County Bar Assn. (taxation sect., com. on closely-held and pass-through entities, bus. and corps. law sect., sole practitioner section exec. com. 1995—), Beverly Hills Bar Assn. (probate, trust & estate planning section, taxation section, law practice mgmt. section), Can. Calif. C. of C. (dir. 1980-89, 2d v.p. 1983-84, 1st v.p. 1984-85, pres. 1985-87), L.A.-Vancouver Sister City Assn. (dir., exec. com. 1987-92, treas. 1987-89, pres. 1989-92), French-Am. C. of C. (councilor 1979-84, v.p. 1980, 82-84), L.A. Area C. of C. (dir. 1980-81), Occidental Coll. Alumni Assn.

(pres. 1979-80, v.p. 1978-79, alumni bd. govs. 1977-81, chmn. annual fund campaign 1990-91), Grand People (bd. dirs. 1985-92, chmn. bd. 1986-92), Rotary Club of L.A. (dir. 1994—, sergeant-at-arms 1986-87, chmn. gateway com. 1993-94, chmn. world cmty. svc. com. 1991-93, chmn. vols. Am. of L.A. com. 1988-90, chmn. golf com. 1986-87, vice-chmn. pres. com. 1985-86), Rotary Internat. (chmn. club extension com. 1995—, cmty. svc. dir. 1993-95, chmn. gift of life com. 1992-93), Small Bus. Coun. of Am., Inc. (legal adv. bd. 1989—), The Group, Inc. Democrat. Baptist. Home: 3937 Beverly Glen Blvd Sherman Oaks CA 91423-4404 Office: 11400 W Olympic Blvd Ste 9 Los Angeles CA 90064-1557

BASILIO, ELEANOR VASCO, electronics and aerospace engineer; b. Manila, Philippines, Feb. 6, 1961; d. Sergio Rivera and Suerte (Ocampo) Vasco; m. Ralph Ramos Basilio, July 1, 1989. BA, UCLA, 1983; BS, Calif. State U., 1988; Engring. Mgmt. Cert., Calif. Inst. Tech.-Indsl. Rels. Ctr., 1989. Electronics engr. Jet Propulsion Lab./Calif. Inst. Tech., Pasadena, 1987-89; spacecraft systems engr. Jet Propulsion Lab./Calif. Inst. Tech., 1989-94, leader tech. group, 1994—. Calif. state scholar, 1978-82; recipient Award for Community Svc., County of L.A., 1978, achievement award NASA Guidance & Control Group, 1991, NASA group achievement award, 1992, 93. Mem. IEEE, Soc. Women Engrs., Engr. Honor Soc., Eta Kappa Nu. Roman Catholic. Home: 2055 Nordic Ave Chino Hills CA 91709-4769 Office: Jet Propulsion Lab 4800 Oak Grove Dr Pasadena CA 91109-8001

BASINGER, RICHARD LEE, lawyer; b. Canton, Ohio, Nov. 24, 1941; s. Eldon R. and Alice M. (Bartholomew) B.; m. Rita Evelyn Gover, May 14, 1965; children: David A., Darron M. BA in Edn., Ariz. State U., 1963; postgrad. Macalester Coll., 1968-69; JD, U. Ariz., 1973. Bar: Ariz. 1973, U.S. Dist. Ct. Ariz. 1973, U.S. Tax Ct. 1977, U.S. Ct. Appeals (6th cir.) 1975, U.S. Ct. Appeals (9th cir.) 1976, U.S. Supreme Ct. 1977. Assoc. law offices, Phoenix, 1973-74; sole practice, Scottsdale, Ariz. 1974-75; pres. Basinger & Assocs., P.C., Scottsdale, 1975—, also bd. dirs. Contbr. articles to profl. jours. Bd. dirs. Masters Trail Ventures, Scottsdale, 1984-85, Here's Life, Ariz., Scottsdale, 1976—; precinct committeeman Republican Party, Phoenix, 1983—; bd. dir. Ariz. Coll. of the Bible, 1992-93. NSF grantee, 1968-69. Mem. ABA, Ariz. Bar Assn., Maricopa County Bar Assn., Ariz. State Horseman's Assn. (bd. dirs. 1984-86, 1st v.p. 1986), Scottsdale Bar Assn., Western Saddle Club (bd. dirs. 1983-86, pres. 1985-86), Scottsdale Saddle Club, Saguaro Saddle Club. Baptist. Office: Basinger & Assocs PC 5010 E Shea Blvd Scottsdale AZ 85254

BASLER, RICHARD ALAN, biomedical instruments manufacturer; b. San Francisco, Sept. 12, 1939; s. Henry Edwin and Margaret Henrietta (Cooper) B.; m. Carol Audrey Foster, Aug. 4, 1962; children: Rodney Giles, Eric Richard. BA, U. Calif., Berkeley, 1960; MBA, U. Phoenix, Irvine, Calif., 1983. Indsl. engr., prodn. supr. Standard Register, Oakland and Corcoran, Calif., 1967-72; knitting supt. Duplan Knits West, Carson, Calif., 1972-75; prodn. supr. Am. Edwards Labs., Irvine, 1976-78, chief indsl. engr., 1978-80, supr. mfg. engring., 1980-86, with engring. systems devel., 1986-87; mgr. quality assurance/quality control Cardiovascular Devices Inc., 1987-88; dir. quality assurance/quality control Applied Vascular Devices Inc., 1988-90, dir. compliance, 1990-94; dir. compliance Micro Therapeutics, Inc., 1994—; owner Internat. Numismatics, Irvine, 1974—. Editor Calif. Engr. mag., 1959; contbr. articles to mags. Bd. dirs. UNCAP, Inc., L.A., 1980-82; pres. Colonnade of History, 1990—. Lt. USN, 1960-67, Vietnam., with res. 1967-81. Recipient Kenneth Brainard Meml. Literary award, George Bennett Meml. Literary award. Mem. Am. Soc. Quality Control, U.S. Kerry Blue Terrier Club (gov. 1983-85), Gt. Western Terrier (bd. dirs. 1979-92). Republican. Office: Micro Therapeutics, Inc 27412-BLaguna Hills Dr Aliso Viejo CA 92656

BASNIGHT, ARVIN ODELL, public administrator, aviation consultant; b. Manteo, N.C., Sept. 14, 1915; s. Thomas Allen and Mary Meekins Basnight; m. Marjorie Jane Gauthier, Dec. 6, 1942; children: Mary Ann Basnight Wolf, William Gaylord, Michael André. Student in Mech. Engring., N.C. State U., 1932-35; student in Pub. Adminstrn., Am. Univ., 1936-42. Park ranger U.S. Nat. Parks, Kitty Hawk, N.C. and Mesa Verde, Colo., 1938-40; pers. adminstr. CAA, Washington, 1940-42; fin., budget accounts FAA, Washington, 1945-62; adminstr. Washington, Atlanta, L.A., 1962-74; bd. dir., chmn. bd. Palos Verdes (Calif.) Nat. Bank, 1982-92; aviation cons., L.A., 1974-92. Co-chmn. Salute to Doolittle Raiders, Santa Monica, Calif., 1991; pres. Palos Verdes Breakfast Club, 1990. Maj. USAF, 1942-45. Decorated D.F.C.; recipient Disting. Svc. medal U.S. Fed. Aviation, 1966. Mem. Nat. Aeros. Assn. (Honor award 1991), Aero Club So. Calif. (pres., bd. dirs. 1974-92). Home: 1536 Paseo Del Mar Palos Verdes Estates CA 90274-1852

BASS, AUDREY, commodities trader; b. 1946. With Berger & Plate Co., San Francisco, 1966-74, Berger & Co., San Francisco, 1974-88; asst. sec., treas. Berdex Internat. Inc., San Francisco, 1988—. Office: Berdex International Inc 1050 Sansome St Ste 300 San Francisco CA 94111-1325*

BASS, CHARLES MORRIS, financial and systems consultant; b. Miami, Fla., Sept. 21, 1949; s. Benjamin and Ellen Lucille (Williams) B; children: Cheryl Ellen, Benjamin Charles. BA, U. Md., 1972; MS, Am. Coll., 1982. CLU; chartered fin. cons. Group rep. Monumental Life Ins. Co., 1972-73; agt. Equitable Life Ins. Co., N.Y., 1973-76; ptnr. Bass, Bridge and Assocs., Columbia, Md., 1976-81; pres. Multi-Fin Svc., Inc., Balt., 1981-83; gen. mgr. Mfrs. Fin. Group, Denver, 1983-85; ptnr. Regency Econometrics Group, Denver, 1985—; speaker in field. Chmn. United Way Howard County, 1977-78; mem. Econ. Devel. Adv. Coun. Howard County, 1979-83. Served with USAF, 1968-71. Mem. Million Dollar Round Table, Nat. Assn. Life Underwriters, Am. Soc. C.L.U.s, Gen. Agts. and Mgrs. Assn., Columbia Life Underwriters Assn. (pres. 1982), Estate Planning Coun., Howard County C. of C., Howard County Bus. Club, Columbia Bus. Exchange. Methodist. Home and Office: 5690 W Coal Mine Ave Littleton CO 80123

BASS, DAVID JASON, manufacturing engineer; b. Denver, July 8, 1954; s. Grover Terrell and Laura Annie (Whiting) B.; m. Debra Jean Meyer, Aug. 10, 1974; children: Jenell, Kevin, Kristyn, Staci. AS in Drafting Tech., Ea. Ariz. Coll., 1974; BS in Tech. Mgmt., Regis U., 1988. Cert. prodn. and inventory mgmt. Am. Prodn. and Inventory Control Soc. Electro-mech. designer govt. electronics group Motorola, Inc., Scottsdale, Ariz., 1974-79; mech. designer Motorola, Inc., Tempe, Ariz., 1979-80; mech. and tooling engr. Kustom Electronics, Chanute, Kans., 1980-81, liaison engr., 1981-82, mgr. mfg. engring., 1982-84; sr. design engr. Martin Marietta Co., Denver, 1984-87, sr. mfg. engr., 1987; supr. mfg. engring. Allied Signal, Prescott, Ariz., 1987-93, total quality mgmt. coord., 1993-94; 9000 coord. Internat. Stds. Orgn., Prescott, Ariz., 1994—. Mem. curriculum adv. com. Ea. Ariz. Coll., Thatcher, 1976-80; treas. Prescott Area Christian Schs. Assn., Inc., 1993—. Mem. Soc. Mfg. Engrs., Am. Prodn. and Inventory Control Soc. Republican. Home: 2090 Dineh Dr Prescott AZ 86301-3911 Office: Allied Signal 6400 Wilkinson Dr Prescott AZ 86301-6164

BASS, DAVID LOREN, artist; b. Conway, Ark., July 19, 1943; s. Deward Clark Bass and Gillian Henrietta (Oliver) Bass Carter. BS in Edn., Ark. State Tchrs., Coll., 1965; student Aspen Sch. Contemporary Art, summer 1964; MFA, U. N.C.-Greensboro, 1975; postgrad. U. N.C., Chapel Hill, summer 1974. Tchr. 7th-8th grades Met. Schs. Nashville and Davidson County, Tenn., 1965-67; tchr. 7th-12th grades U.S. Def. Dept., Kenitra, Morocco, 1967-73; artist, Greensboro, N.C., 1975-92, Santa Fe, 1992—; artist-in-residence Washington and Lee U., Lexington, Va., 1976; curator Peter Agostini sculpture exhbn. DuPont Art Gallery, Lexington, 1976; cons. Waterworks Gallery, Salisbury, N.C., 1983; dir. United Arts Council, Greensboro, 1978-80, Ctr. for Creative Arts, Greensboro, 1978-80, Green Hill Ctr. for N.C. Art, Greensboro, 1977-80, 83—. One-man shows include: Theater Art Gallery, High Point, N.C., 1977, 82, 90, Asheville Art Mus., 1980, Recent Works, 1985, St. John's Mus. Art, Wilmington, N.C., 1989; group shows include: Miss. Mus. Art, Jackson, 1980, Biennial Exhbn. Piedmont Painting, Mint Mus., Charlotte, N.C., 1983, Equitable Gallery, N.Y.C., 1994, Springfield (Mo.) Mus. Art, 1993, Hickory (N.C.) Mus. Art, 1994. Bd. dirs. O. Henry Festival, Greensboro, 1985. Fellow Corp. Yaddo, Saratoga Springs, N.Y., 1978, 81, 84. Ossabaw Island Project, Ga., 1979, Va. Ctr. for Creative Arts, Sweetbriar, 1978. Mem. Greenhill Ctr. for N.C. Art, Southeastern Ctr. for Contemporary Art, Weatherspoon Art Gallery, Artists' Choice Mus., N.C. Arts Soc. (adv. council 1981-83). Home: 319 Villeros St Santa Fe NM 87501-1424

BASS, HAROLD NEAL, pediatrician, medical geneticist; b. Chgo., Apr. 14, 1939; s. Louis A. and Minnie (Schachter) B.; m. Phyllis Appell, June 25, 1961; children: Laura Renee, Alana Suzanne. Student, U. Ill., 1956-59; MS in Pharmacology, U. Chgo., 1963, MD, 1963. Diplomate Am. Bd. Pediatrics, Am. Bd. Med. Genetics, Nat. Bd. Med. Examiners. Intern Children's Meml. Hosp., Chgo., 1963-64; resident Children's Meml. Hosp., 1964-65, chief resident, 1965-66, fellow in med. genetics, 1965-66; chief pediatrics and profl. svcs. Norton AFB Hosp., Calif., 1966-68; attending pediatrician/med. geneticist Kaiser Permanente Med. Ctr., Panorama City, Calif., 1968—; dir. med. genetics prog. Kaiser Permanente Med. Care Program So. Calif., 1987—; clin. prof. pediatrics UCLA Med. Sch., 1970—; pres. med. staff Kaiser Permanente Med. Ctr., 1989. Contbr. articles to profl. jours. Mem. transp. commn. San Fernando Valley, City of L.A., 1973-78. Capt. M.C., USAF, 1966-68. Fellow Am. Coll. Human Genetics, Western Soc. Pediatric Rsch., L.A. Pediatrics Soc., San Fernando Valley Interfaith Coun., Pacific S.W. Regional Genetics Network, Handgun Control, ACLU, Amnesty Internat., Am. Soc. Human Genetics. Democrat. Jewish. Home: 11922 Dunnicliffe Ct Northridge CA 91326-1324 Office: Kaiser Permanente Med Ctr 13652 Cantara St Panorama City CA 91402-5423

BASS, MARTHA POSTLETHWAITE, high school principal; b. Wichita, Kans., Dec. 6, 1942; d. John Emmett and Norma Louise (Lanning) Postlethwaite; m. Elmer Lee Bass, July 22, 1981; step children: Sheryl, Terry. BA in Edn., U. N.Mex., 1964, MA, 1966. Endl. lic. adminstr., supt., English tchr., drama speech tchr., counselor. Asst. dean women, instr. Hanover (Ind.) Coll., 1966-68; asst. dean women U. N.Mex., Alburquerque, 1968-69; elem. counselor Alburquerque Pub. Schs., 1969-74, guidance coord., 1974-77, high sch. asst. prin., 1977-87; high sch. prin. Del Norte High Sch. Alburquerque Pub. Schs., 1987—; bd. dirs. Albuquerque Child Guidance Ctr.; pres., cons. Acad. Ednl. Leadership, Alburquerque, 1986-90. Title VII Fed. grantee Child Encouragement Project, Alburquerque, 1977; named Woman on the Move YWCA, Alburquerque, 1990. Mem. Nat. Assn. Secondary Sch. Prins., Albuquerque Assn. Secondary Sch. Prins. (past. bd. mem., treas., 1986-87), Rotary Club of Albuquerque (RYLA chair, 1990—). Office: Del Norte High Sch 5323 Montgomery Blvd NE Albuquerque NM 87109-1302

BASSETT, BARBARA WIES, editor, publisher; b. Dec. 5, 1939; m. Norman W. Bassett. BA, U. Conn., 1961; student, New Sch. for Social Rsch., 1961-62. Product devel. Fearn Soya, Melrose Park, Ill., 1973-75; product devel. Modern Products, Milw., 1973-75; editor, pub. Bestways Mag., Carson City, Nev., 1977-89; pub. The Healthy Gourmet Newsletter, 1989-91, Fine Wine-Good Food Newsletter, 1991—; publicity dir. Nev. Artists Assn., 1994-95; owner Gualala (Calif.) Galleries, 1989-90; owner, operator cooking sch. Greensboro N.C. 1969-73. Author: Natural Cooking, 1968, Wok and Tempura, 1969, Japanese Home Cooking, 1970, The Wok, 1971, Super Soy, 1973, The Health Gourmet, 1981, International Healthy Gourmet, 1982; one-woman show paintings Dolphin Gallery, Gualala, Calif., 1990, River Gallery, Reno, 1994; 2-women show 1992, 94, Dolphin Gallery, Calif., 1994, solo exhbn. Nev. Artists Assn. Gallery, 1993, 95; restaurant critic Reno Gazette jour., 1995—. Mem. Nat. League Am. Penwomen, Inst. Food Technologists, Pastel Soc. of the West Coast, Inst. Am. Culinary Profls.

BASSETT, CAROL ANN, magazine, video, and radio documentary writer, producer, journalism educator; b. Langley AFB, Va., Mar. 2, 1953; d. William Brainard and Genevieve (Rivaldo) B. BA summa cum laude in Humanities, Ariz. State U., 1977; MA in Journalism, U. Ariz., 1982. Freelance writer Tucson, 1980—; ptnr. Desert West News, Tucson, 1985-90; Contbr. numerous articles to nat. and internat. mags. including N.Y. Times. Editor Tucson Weekly, 1989-90; contbr. numerous articles to nat. and internat. mags. and newspapers. Recipient 2d Place Gen. Reporting award Ariz. Press Club, 1987, Gold medal for best environ. documentary Houston Internat. Film Festival, 1990, 1st Place Gen. Reporting award Ariz. Press Club, 1992, Silver Medal for Energy Issues documentary, Houston Internat. Film Festival, 1992; co-recipient Alfred I. duPont Columbia award, 1984-85, First Place award Investigative Reporting, 1986, 1st Place Polit. Reporting, 1989, First Amendment Journalism award, 1986; grantee Fund for Investigative Journalism, 1985, 87, Corp. for Pub. Broadcasting, 1988, Oxfam Am., 1991.

BASSETT, EDWARD POWERS, university official; b. Boston, Feb. 27, 1929; s. Fraser W. and Fanny (Powers) B.; m. Karen Elizabeth Jack, Dec. 21, 1954; children: Sarah Jack Bassett Williams, Laura Powers. AB, Washington and Lee U., 1951, LLD, 1984; MA, U. Mich., 1955; PhD, U. Iowa, 1967. Ct. reporter Louisville Courier-Jour., 1955-56; asst. editor Falmouth (Mass.) Enterprise, 1956-57; city editor Anderson (Ind.) Herald, 1957-58; editorial writer Longview (Wash.) Daily News, 1958-60; instr., pub. U. Iowa, 1960-67; asst. prof. journalism U. Mich., 1967-70, acting chmn. dept. journalism, 1969-70; dean Sch. Journalism U. Kans., 1970-74, assoc. vice chancellor acad. affairs, 1974-75; dir. Sch. Journalism U. So. Calif., 1975-80; editor Statesman-Jour., Salem, Oreg., 1980-84; dean Medill Sch. Journalism Northwestern U., Evanston, Ill., 1984-89; McKenzie scholar, dir. Sch. Communications U. Wash., Seattle, 1989—; adj. prof. Can. studies U. Wash., 1992—. Recipient citation for reporting Am. Polit. Sci. Assn., 1960. Mem. Assn. Edn. in Journalism and Mass Comm. (pres. 1975-76), Am. Assn. Schs. and Depts. Journalism (pres. 1974-75, Freedom Forum Adminstr. medal 1993), Soc. Profl. Journalists. Office: Univ of Washington Sch of Communications Box 353740 Seattle WA 98195-3740

BASSETT, H(ENRY) GORDON, petroleum company executive; b. Newton, Mass., Nov. 12, 1924; s. Harry and Phyllis Mildred (Proctor) B.; m. Marion Mae Griffiths, July 11, 1949; children—Alan, Beverly, James. B.Sc., McGill U., 1949, M.Sc., 1950; A.M., Princeton U., 1952, Ph.D., 1952. Registered profl. geologist, Can. Div. stratigrapher Shell Can. Ltd., Calgary and Edmonton, Alta., Can., 1952-72, head stratigraphic services, Houston, 1972-80; mgr. geologic tech. Sohio Petroleum Co., San Francisco, 1980-85; cons. geologist, 1986—. Served with RCAF, 1943-45. Recipient Pres.'s Gold medal Can. Inst. Mining and Metallurgy, 1950. Fellow Geol. Assn. Can.; mem. Am. Assn. Petroleum Geologists, Can. Assn. Petroleum Geologists, Edmonton Geol. Soc. (pres. 1966). Republican. Home: 3320 Las Huertas Rd Lafayette CA 94549-5109

BASSETT, JOHN WALDEN, JR., lawyer; b. Roswell, N.Mex., Mar. 21, 1938; s. John Walden Sr. and Evelyn (Thompson) B.; m. Patricia Lubben, May 22, 1965; children: John Walden III, Loren Patricia. AB in Econs., Stanford U., 1960; LLB with honors, U. Tex., 1964. Bar: Tex. 1964, N.Mex. 1964. Assoc. Atwood & Malone, Roswell, 1964-66; White House fellow, spl. asst. to U.S. atty. gen., Washington, 1966-67; ptnr. Atwood, Malone, Mann & Turner and predecessors, P.A., Roswell, 1967-95, Bassett & Copple, 1995—; bd. dir. A.H. Belo Corp., Dallas. Assoc. editor: U. Tex. Law Review, 1962; mem. N.Mex. State Bd. of Edn., 1987-91. Pres., chmn. bd. United Way of Chaves County, N.Mex., 1973; bd. dirs. Ednl. Achievement Found., Roswell, 1992—. 1st lt. U.S. Army, 1961-68. Mem. ABA, Tex. Bar Assn., N.Mex. Bar Assn., Chaves County Bar Assn., Order of Coif, Rotary (pres. 1976, Roswell), N.Mex. Amigos, Phi Delta Phi. Republican. Episcopalian. Home: 5060 Bright Sky Rd Roswell NM 88201 Office: Bassett & Copple 400 N Pennsylvania Ave Ste 1110 Roswell NM 88201

BASSETTI, FRED FORDE, architect; b. Seattle, Jan. 31, 1917; s. Frederick Michael and Sophie Marie (Forde) B.; m. Mary Wilson, June 30, 1944 (div. 1969); children: Ann, Catherine, Margaret; m. Moira Feeney, June 29, 1971 (div. 1985); children: Megan, Michael; m. Gwenyth Piper Caldwell, Dec. 20, 1989; stepchildren: Megan, Ben, Piper, Sam. BArch, U. Wash., 1942; MArch, Harvard U., 1946. Registered architect, Alaska, Idaho, Mont., Oreg., Wash. Draftsman Paul Thiry, Seattle, 1944, Alvar Aalto, Cambridge, Mass., 1946; designer Naramore, Bain, Brady & Johanson, Seattle, 1946; prin. Bassetti & Morse, Seattle, 1947-62, Fred Bassetti & Co., Seattle, 1962-81, Bassetti, Norton, Metler, Seattle, 1981-85, Bassetti, Norton, Metler, Rekevics, Seattle, 1985-94, Bassetti Architects, Seattle, 1994—; bd. dirs. Discuren Found., Seattle. Prin. works include Coll. Engring. Bldgs., U. Wash., 1970, Fed. Office Bldg., Seattle, 1975, U.S. Embassy, Lisbon, Portugal, 1984, PACCAR Tech Ctr., Mt. Vernon, Wash., 1985, AT&T Gateway Tower, Seattle, 1990; patentee in field. Mem. Seattle Design Com., 1976-78, Seattle Landmarks Bd., 1978-79. Named Best Local Architect, Seattle Weekly poll, 1988. Fellow AIA (pres. Seattle chpt. 1967, 57 nat. or regional awards, 1951-91, Seattle chpt. medal 1988); mem. Nat. Acad. Design (assoc.), Allied Arts of Seattle and King County (pres. 1970-72). Office: Bassetti Architects 1011 Western Ave Seattle WA 98104-1040

BASSIST, DONALD HERBERT, academic administrator; b. Dallas, Oct. 28, 1923; s. Ellis and Adele (Gutz) B.; m. Norma Dale Andersen, Oct. 14, 1950; children: Matthew Perry, Bradford Beaumont. AB, Harvard U., 1948; MBA, Portland State U., 1975; grad., U.S. Army command and Gen. Staff Coll., 1967. Pres. Bassist Coll., Portland, Oreg., 1963—; chmn. ednl. adv. bd. pvt. vocat. schs., Salem, Oreg., 1972-78; active Oreg. Ednl. Coordinating Coun., 1970-73. Writer, dir. (film) Fashion: The Career of Challenge, 1969 (N.Y. Internat. Bronze award). Lt. A.C., U.S. Army, 1943-46. Mem. Nat. Assn. Scholars, Japanese Garden Soc. (bd. dirs. 1988-93), Portland Advt. Fedn. (bd. dirs. 1969-72).

BASTIAANSE, GERARD C., lawyer; b. Holyoke, Mass., Oct. 21, 1935; s. Gerard C. and Margaret (Lally) B.; m. Paula E. Paliska, June 1, 1963; children: Elizabeth, Gerard. BSBA, Boston U., 1960; JD, U. Va., 1964. Bar: Mass. 1964, Calif. 1970. Assoc. Nutter, McClennen & Fish, Boston, 1964-65; counsel Campbell Soup Co., Camden, N.J., 1965-67; gen. counsel A&W Internat. (United Fruit Co.), Santa Monica, Calif., 1968-70; ptnr. Kindel & Anderson, Los Angeles, 1970—. Mem. ABA, Calif. Bar Assn., Mass. Bar Assn., Japan Am. Soc., Asia Soc., World Trade Ctr. Assn. Clubs: California (Los Angeles); Big Canyon Country (Newport Beach, Calif.). Home: 2 San Sebastian Newport Beach CA 92660-6828 Office: Kindel & Anderson 5 Park Plz Ste 1000 Irvine CA 92714-8528

BASU, ASOKE ARIEL, sociologist, educator; b. Calcutta, India, Apr. 28, 1938; came to U.S., 1958; s. Sri Sudhir and Srimati Ila (Dutta) B.; m. Mollie Saine Pope, Nov. 13, 1944; 1 child, Melissa. BA in Sociology, W.Va. U., 1961; MA in Sociology, Okla. U., 1963, PhD in Polit. Sci., 1966. Asst. prof.sociology U. So. Calif., Los Angeles, 1966-68; prof. Calif. State U., Hayward, 1968—; research assoc., Ctr. for S. Asian Studies U. Calif., Berkeley, 1978-79; spl. asst. to the dean Sch. of Arts, Letters and Social Scis. Calif. State U., Hayward; rsch. assoc. dept. sociology U. Calif., Berkeley, 1992—; chair dept. sociology Calif. State U., Hayward, 1992-95; vis. scholar Harvard U., Boston, 1973, Hoover Inst., Stanford, Calif., 1981-83. Author: Elementary Statistical Theory in Society, 1976, Culture, Politics and Critical Academics, 1981; co-author: Poverty in America: The Welfare Dilemma, 1981; contbr. articles to profl. jours. Named Outstanding Immigrant Internat. Inst. of the East Bay, 1972; recipient Scholarly Pub. award, Calif. State U., Northridge, 1981; Sr. Fulbright lectureship Council Internat. Exchange of Scholars, 1984-85; Sr. Smithsonian Research fellow Am. Inst. Indian Studies, 1985, Adminstrv. fellow Calif. State U. Chancellor's Office, 1987-88; Fulbright grantee U.S. Dept. Edn., 1988—. Fellow AAAS; nen. Indian Sociol. Assn. (life), Internat. Soc. Assn. (pres. research com. sociology edn.), Pacific Soc. Assn. (chmn. com. status of minorities inthe profession). Home: 2378 Woolsey St Berkeley CA 94705 Office: Calif State U Dept Sociology Hayward CA 94542

BASU, HIRAK SUBHRA, biophysicist, researcher; b. Calcutta, India, Mar. 12, 1954; came to U.S., 1984; s. Parimal Chandra and Karuna Basu; m. Aparajita Sarkar, Jan. 2, 1988; 1 child, Kurchi. B in Chemistry, Calcutta (India) U., 1974, M in Biochemistry, 1976; PhD in Biochemistry, Indian Inst. Sci., Bangalore, India, 1985. Rsch. assoc. Indian Isnt. Sci., Bangalore, India, 1983-84; vis. postdoctoral fellow U. Calif., San Francisco, 1985-87, vis. asst. rsch. biochemist, 1987-89, asst. rsch. biophysicist neurol. surgery, 1989-94; asst. prof. dept. human oncology U. Wis., Madison, 1994—; lectr. in field. Ad hoc reviewer jours.; contbr. articles to profl. jours. Faculty fellow U. Calif., 1990—; grantee Govt. of India, 1971-74, Nat. Cancer Inst., 1990-94, REAC Simon Fund, 1991-92. Mem. Am. Assn. Cancer Rsch., Am. Biophys. Soc.

BATCHELOR, JAMES KENT, lawyer; b. Long Beach, Calif., Oct. 4, 1934; s. Jack Morrell and Edith Marie (Ottinger) B.; m. Jeanette Lou Dyer, Mar. 27, 1959; children: John, Suzanne; m. Susan Mary Leonard, Dec. 4, 1976. AA, Sacramento City Coll., 1954; BA, Long Beach State Coll., 1956; JD, Hastings Coll. Law, U. Calif., 1959. Bar: Calif. 1960, U.S. Dist. Ct. (cen. dist.) Calif. 1960, U.S. Supreme Ct. 1968; cert. family law specialist Calif. Bd. Legal Specialization. Dep. dist. atty., Orange County, Calif., 1960-62; assoc. Miller, Nisson, Kogler & Wenke, Santa Ana, Calif., 1962-64; ptnr. Batchelor, Cohen & Oster, Santa Ana, 1964-67, Kurilich, Ballard, Batchelor, Fullerton, Calif., 1967-72; pres. James K. Batchelor, Inc., Santa Ana, 1972—; tchr. paralegal sect. Santa Ana City Coll.; judge pro-tem Superior Ct., 1974—; lectr. family law Calif. Continuing Edn. of Bar, 1973—. Contbr. articles to profl. jours. Fellow Am. Acad. Matrimonial Lawyers (pres. So. Calif. chpt. 1989-90); mem. ABA, Calif. State Bar (placque chmn. family law sect. 1975-76, advisor 1976-78), Orange County Barristers (founder, pres., placque 1963), Calif. State Barristers (placque 1965, v.p.), Orange County Bar Assn. (placque sec. 1977, pres. family law sect. 1968-71, best lawyers in Am. 1989-90, 91-92, 93-94, 95—). Republican. Methodist. Office: 765 The City Dr S Ste 270 Orange CA 92668-4942

BATCHELOR, KAREN LEE, English language educator; b. Oregon City, Oreg., June 17, 1948; d. Jewel Elaine Durham; m. Luis Armando, Mar. 17, 1978 (div. Aug. 1988); children: Virginia, Travis. BA in English, San Francisco State U., 1971, MA in English, 1980. Vol. U.S. Peace Corps, Andong, South Korea, 1972-74; tchr. English as second lang. City Coll. San Francisco, 1975—; tchr. trainer U. Calif., Berkeley, 1986—; acad. specialist USIA, 1991—; speaker in field. Co-author: (textbooks) Discovering English, 1981, In Plain English, 1985, More Plain English, 1986, The Writing Challenge, 1990; contbr. articles to profl. jorus. Mem. Tchrs. English to Speakers of Other Langs., Calif. Tchrs. English to Speakers of Other Langs. Office: City Coll San Francisco 50 Phelan Box L 168 San Francisco CA 94112

BATDORF, KURT RICHARD, editor; b. Tacoma, Wash., Jan. 26, 1963; s. Richard Lewallen Batdorf and Annette Elizabeth (Nordine) Doud. BA, Evergreen State Coll., 1986. Editor, prodn. mgr. Skagit River Post, Burlington, Wash., 1985-86, Courier-Times, Sedro-Woolley, Wash., 1986-88; mng. editor Monroe (Wash.) Monitor, 1988-91; editor North Snohomish Weekly, Arlington, Wash., 1991-95; copy editor Whidbey Press, Oak Harbor, Wash., 1995—. Blood donor Puget Sound Blood Bank, Everett, Wash., 1988—; mem. precinct com. Island County Dems., Coupeville, Wash., 1992; strategic plan rev. com. Stanwood (Wash.) Sch. Dist., 1994. Mem. Wash. Newspaper Pub. Assn. (Best Comprehensive News award 1989, Spot News Photography award 1989, Best Editl. award 1993, mem. better newspaper contest com. 1994), Soc. Profl. Journalists (Best Spot News award 1991, Best Headlines award 1993, Editl. writing awards 1992, 93, 94). Office: PO Box 10 Oak Harbor WA 98277

BATEMAN, DAVID ALFRED, lawyer; b. Pitts., Jan. 28, 1946; s. Alfred V. and Ruth G. (Howe) B.; m. Trudy A. Heath, Mar. 13, 1948; children: Devin C., Mark C. A.B. in Geology, U. Calif.-Riverside, 1966; J.D., U. San Diego, 1969; LL.M., Georgetown U., 1978. Bar: Calif. 1970, U.S. Dist. Ct. (so. dist.) Calif. 1970, U.S. Ct. Mil. Appeals 1972, Wash. 1973, U.S. Dist. Ct. (we. dist.) Wash. 1973, U.S. Supreme Ct. 1974, D.C. 1976, U.S. Dist. Ct. D.C. 1977, U.S. Ct. Claims 1979, U.S. Ct. Appeals (9th cir.) 1981. Assoc. Daubney, Banche, Patterson and Nares, Oceanside, Calif., 1969-72; asst. atty. gen. State of Wash., Olympia, 1977-81; ptnr. Bateman & Woodring, Olympia, 1981-85, Woodring, Bateman & Westbrook, 1985-89, Hanemann & Bateman, 1989-92, Hanemann, Bateman & Jones, 1992—; instr. Am. Inst. Banking, San Diego, 1972, U. Puget Sound, Olympia campus, spring, 1979. Served to capt. JAGC, USAF, 1972-77; col. JAGC, USAFR, 1977—. Mem. ABA (internat. law and environ. law sect.), Am. Soc. Internat. Law (environ. law sect.), Wash. State Bar Assn. Roman Catholic. Club: Rotary (past chmn. internat. services com.).

BATEMAN, GEORGE W., computer systems consultant; b. Milw., May 30, 1946; s. George W. and Violet B. (Kaltenbrun) B.; m. Toni E. McLean, Nov. 30, 1986. BA, U. Wis., 1969. Systems programmer RCA, 1969-72, U. Pa., Phila., 1972-73, Siemens, Munich, 1973-76; computer cons. Sperry Corp., London, 1976-86, Tandem Computers, Cupertino, Calif., 1987—. Office: Tandem Computers 18922 Forge Dr Cupertino CA 95014-0701

BATEMAN, JANE BRONWYN, ophthalmology educator; b. Rochester, Minn., Aug. 17, 1948; d. Gordon and Olive Bateman; m. Douglas Hershey. Chair dept. ophthalmology U. Colo., Denver. Office: U Colo Box B204 4200 E 9th Ave Denver CO 80262

BATEMAN, ROBERT EARL, II, technology management consultant; b. Spokane, Wash., Apr. 4, 1958; s. Robert Earl and DeNai (McMullin) B.; m. Candace Elaine Harper, Dec. 17, 1979; children: Ronni, Robert August, Wilson Arthur, Kalli, Talya, Cecy. BS, Brigham Young U., 1981; M in Bus., Am. U., 1982; postgrad., U. Utah, 1993—. Staff intern Senate Banking Com., Washington, 1982; svc. mgr. Ken Garff Imports, Salt Lake City, 1982-85; adminstrv. officer U.S. State Dept., Washington, 1985-86; adminstrv. officer Am. Embassy, Riyadh, Saudi Arabia, 1986-88, San Jose, Costa Rica, 1988-90; pres. Integrated Systems Tech., Alpine, Utah, 1990—; dir. of internat. ops. Promodel Corp., Orem, Utah, 1993—; guest lectr. at univs. in U.S. and abroad; cons. Lascasiana S.A., San Luis Potosi, Mex., 1991, Geneva Steel Corp., Provo, Utah, 1991-93, Technistar, Longmont, Colo., 1992, IOMEGA, Ogden, 1992, Nat. Productivity Corp., Malaysia, 1993—; speaker in field. Contbr. articles to profl. jours. Scout leader Boy Scout Am., Alpine, 1990—; mem. City Coun., Alpine, 1994—. Mem. Internat. Assn. Mgmt. Tech., Internat. Assn. for Impact Assessment, World Devel. Coun., Inst. Indsl. Engrs. LDS. Office: Integrated Systems Tech 755 W 800 S Alpine UT 84004-1514

BATES, CHARLES EMERSON, library administrator; b. Los Angeles, Dec. 1, 1946; s. Willard Emerson Bates and Erica (Schmidt) Bates Beckwith; m. Mary Joan Genz, Aug. 7, 1971; children—Christopher, Noah, Colin. BA, Valparaiso U., 1968; MEd, Loyola U., Chgo., 1970; MLS, Rosary Coll., 1973. Head of reference Decatur Pub. Libr., Ill., 1973-74; cons. Rolling Prairie Libr. System, Decatur, 1974-76; asst. dir. Fond du Lac Pub. Libr., Wis., 1976-81; dir. Pueblo Libr. Dist., Colo., 1981—. Bd. dirs. Pueblo United Way, 1982-86, Sangre de Cristo Arts and Conf. Ctr., Pueblo, 1990—; pres. bd. dirs. Rosemount Victorian House Mus., Pueblo, 1984—. Mem. ALA, Colo. Libr. Assn., Ark. Valley Libr. System (pres. 1984-85, 89-90), Rotary (pres. bd. dirs. 1981—). Lutheran. Office: Pueblo Libr Dist McClelland Libr 100 E Abriendo Ave Pueblo CO 81004-4232

BATES, CHARLES WALTER, human resources executive, lawyer, educator; b. Detroit, June 28, 1953; s. E. Frederick and Virginia Marion (Nunneley) B. BA in Psychology and Econs. cum laude, Mich. State U., 1975, M in Labor and Indsl. Rels., 1977; postgrad. DePaul U., 1979-80; JD William Mitchell Coll. Law, 1984. Bar: Wash. 1990, U.S. Dist. Ct. (we. dist.) Washington, 1992; cert. sr. profl. in human resources. Vista vol., paralegal, Ventura County Legal Aid Assn. (now Channel Counties Legal Aid Assn.), Calif., 1975-76; job analyst Gen. Mills, Inc., Mpls., 1977-78, plant pers. asst. II, Chgo., 1978-80, asst. plant pers. mgr., Chgo., 1980-81, pers. mgr. consumer foods mktg., Mpls., 1981-82; pers. mgr. consumer foods mktg. divs. Saluto Pizza, Mpls., 1982-84; human resources mgr. Western div., Godfather's Pizza, Inc., Costa Mesa, Calif., 1984-85, human resources mgr. Western U.S., Can., Bellevue, Washington, 1985-91; dir. human resources. Royal Seafoods, Inc., Seattle, 1991-92, dir. human resources and employee rels. counsel, 1992-95, dir. human resources and coun., 1995—; instr. employee and labor rels., Lake Wash. Tech. Coll., 1992—. Contbr. articles and commentary to Bellevue Jour.-Am., Seattle Times, Seattle Post-Intelligencer; mem. editorial adv. bd. Recruitment Today mag., 1990-91. Candidate for lt. gov., 1982, Minn.; asst. scoutmaster Boy Scouts Am., 1971—, asst. advisor-activities Order of Arrow, 1989-92 (recipient Vigil Honor 1990); elected Sammamish Community Coun., Bellevue, 1989, councilman, 1990-93; mem. E. Bellevue Transp. Study Adv. Group, 1989-92. Rep. precinct com. officer, 1990-94, 48th Legis. Dist. Republican Candidate Search Com, 1992; del. state conv. Wash. State Rep. Party, 1992, 94. Recipient Scouter's Tng. award Boy Scouts Am., 1979, Dist. award of merit, 1991, Nat. Vantage Recruiting award, 1990. Mem. ABA (labor and employment law), Nat. Eagle Scout Assn., N.W. Human Resources Mgmt. Assn. (Seattle chpt.), Soc. for Human Resources Mgmt, Wash. State Bar Assn., Fed. Bar Assn. (labor law, labor rels.), King County Bar Assn. (labor law, maritime and fisheries law), Mich. State U. Alumni Assn., William Mitchell Coll. Law Alumni Assn. Home: 232 168th Ave NE Bellevue WA 98008-4522 Office: Royal Seafoods Inc PO Box 19032 Seattle WA 98109-1032

BATES, DWIGHT LEE, mechanical engineer; b. Miles City, Mont., Aug. 19, 1943; s. Edmond Russell and Verna Elizabeth (Johnson) B.; m. Diane Marie Seppi, Aug. 19, 1967. BSME, U. Wyo., 1966; MBA in Mktg., Seattle U., 1971. Registered profl. engr., Wash. Rsch. engr. comml. airplane div. Boeing Co., Seattle, 1966-70; product devel. engr. internat. mktg. div. Warn Industries, Seattle, 1972-73, 1972-73; prin. engr. Heath Tecna, Kent, Wash., 1973-74; mech. design engr. Puget sound naval shipyard U.S. Dept. Def., Bremerton, Wash., 1974-78; supervisory indsl. engr. Supship Seattle, 1978-85; sr. specialist engr. Comml. Airplane div. Boeing Co., Seattle, 1985—; cons. in field. Contbr. publs. in field. Pres. Melrose E. Condo Assn., Seattle, 1978-81; bus. adv. coun. Resource Ctr. for Handicapped. With USCG Aux. Recipient 2 letters of appreciation and 2 letters of commendation U.S. Dept. Def., award Am. Mktg. Assn., 1973; honored as grad. with successful career U. Wyo. Coll. Engring., 1993. Mem. Resource Ctr. for Handicapped Bus. Adv. Coun. (7 letters of commendation, Mus. Flight award, Seattle Block Capt. award), AIAA (pres. Laramie, Wyo. chpt. 1966), NSPE, Wash. State Profl. Engrs. Soc., Wash. State Power Squadron, Am. Inst. Indsl. Engrs., Seattle U. MBA Assn.. Democrat. Lutheran. Home: 1912 E Mcgraw St Seattle WA 98112-2629 Office: Boeing Co PO Box 707 Seattle WA 98111-0707

BATES, GEORGE E., oil industry executive; b. 1943. BS, U. Hawaii, 1967, MBA, 1981. With Gasco, Inc., Honolulu, 1967-91. Office: B H P Petro Americas Hawaii Inc 733 Bishop St Honolulu HI 96813-4022

BATES, GEORGE EDMONDS, bishop; b. Binghampton, N.Y., Aug. 11, 1933; m. Sue Onstott; children: Richard Howard, Katherine Bates Schey. BA in Sociology and English, Dartmouth Coll., 1955; MDiv, Episcopal Theol. Sem., 1958. ordained deacon, The Episcopal Ch., 1958, priest, 1959. Parish priest Ithaca and Syracuse, N.Y.; rector Ch. of the Redeemer, Pendleton, Oreg., 1970-83, St. Mark's-on-the-Mesa, Albuquerque, 1983-86; consecrated bishop Diocese of Utah, 1986. Chmn. bd. dirs. St. Mark's Hosp.; bd. dirs. Westminster Coll., Rowland Hall-St. Mark's Sch.; mem. Gov.'s Task Force on Health Care Costs, Utah Econ. Devel. Office: Diocese of Utah 231 E 1st S Salt Lake City UT 84111-1604*

BATES, JAMES ROBERT, newspaper editor; b. Great Bend, Kans., Dec. 12, 1954; s. Robert Lane and Phyllis Fern (Koltermann) B.; m. Jennifer Petkus, Nov. 7, 1986. BS, U. Kans., 1977; postgrad., U. Colo., 1979-80. Copy editor Springfield (Mo.) Daily News, 1977-78; reporter Colo. Springs (Colo.) Sun, 1978-79, news editor, 1980-86; copy editor, asst. news editor Denver Post, 1986-87, news editor, 1987-89, exec. news editor, 1989—. Recipient design and editing awards Colo. Press Assn., Colo. AP, 1986—. Mem. Soc. Newspaper Design. Office: The Denver Post 1560 Broadway Denver CO 80202-5133

BATES, KENNETH NORRIS, scientist; b. Dallas, June 15, 1949; s. Kenneth L. Bates and Lesta J. (Norris) Burt; m. Carmen Lorz, June 14, 1981; children: Kevin, Cassandra. BS, U. Tex., 1972; MS, Stanford (Calif.) U., 1975, PhD, 1982. Project mgr. Hewlett Packard, Palo Alto, Calif., 1979-82; prin. engr. Advanced Tech. Labs., Bothell, Wash., 1982-85; founder, v.p. engring. Ariel Electronics, Sunnyvale, Calif., 1985-89; sr. scientist KLA Instruments Corp., Springfield, Oreg., 1989-91; pres. Applied Concepts, Eugene, Oreg., 1991—. Contbr. articles on materials, signal processing, acoustics and ednl. aids to profl. jours.; inventor solar collector device. Mem. AAAS, IEEE, AIUM, Internat. Soc. for Optical Engring. Office: Applied Concepts 575 Stonegate St Eugene OR 97401-5819

BATES, STANLEY FRANCIS, public administrator; b. Walla Walla, Wash., Oct. 28, 1947; s. Edward Mark and Fern Christina (Kiichle) B.; m. Elaine Gail Smack, Feb. 3, 1973 (div. June 1989); children: Sandra Lynn, Amber Leigh; m. Sandra Lou May Strand, Dec. 7, 1991; children: Sonja Kirsten Strand, Andrea May Strand. BS in Pub. Adminstrn., U. Ariz., 1978. Program coord. Alternatives to Incarceration, Tucson, Ariz., 1975-77; counselor Ariz. Dept. Corrections, Florence, 1977-79; correctional program supr. Ariz. Dept. Corrections, Phoenix, 1979-80, reception ctr. adminstr., 1980-81, asst. warden, 1981-82, warden, state prison complex, 1982-88, asst. dir. adminstrv. svcs., 1988—; vice chmn. Venture Team, Phoenix, 1989—; reviewer of grant proposals Project Head Start, Washington, 1990—. Ssgt. USAF, 1967-74, Japan. Recipient Dean Hibbs scholarship U. Ariz., Tucson, 1976, Joint Svc. Commendation medal USAF. Mem. Am. Correctional Assn., Ariz. Probation Parole and Correctional Assn., Am. Pub. Safety Comm. Assn., Am. Legion, Ariz. Gnome Club (pres. 1992—), Desert Gnome Club (v.p. 1991-92). Office: Ariz Dept Corrections 1601 W Jefferson St # 232 Phoenix AZ 85007-3002

BATKI, STEVEN L., health facility administrator, educator, physician; b. Budapest, Hungary, Jan. 5, 1949; came to U.S., 1957; children: Maya, Eden. BA, Columbia U., 1970; MD, SUNY, Syracuse, 1979. Diplomate Am. Bd. Psychiatry and Neurology. Med. dir. substance abuse svcs. San Francisco Gen. Hosp., 1983—; clin. prof. psychiatry Sch. of Medicine U. Calif., San Francisco, 1989—; bd. dirs. Walden House, San Francisco. Contbr. articles to profl. jours. Office: San Francisco Gen Hosp Substance Abuse Svcs 1001 Potrero Ave ward 93 San Francisco CA 94110-3518

BATLIN, ROBERT ALFRED, editor; b. San Francisco, Aug. 24, 1930; S. Philip Alfred and Lavenia Mary (Barnes) B.; m. Diane Elise Giblin, July 4, 1956; children—Lisa, Philippa. B.A., Stanford U., 1952, M.A., 1954. Reporter San Bruno Herald, 1952-53; copy editor, then dept. editor San Francisco News, 1956-59; dept. editor San Francisco News-Call Bull., 1959-65; feature editor San Francisco Examiner, 1965-74, arts editor, 1974-85, asst. style editor, 1985—. Served with AUS, 1954-56. Mem. Soc. of Profl. Journalists. Home: 91 Fairway Dr Daly City CA 94015-1215 Office: 110 5th St San Francisco CA 94103-2918

BATSON, DARRELL LYNN, librarian, consultant; b. Las Vegas, Nev., Nov. 24, 1951; s. George Burnell and Olive Emily (Lang) B.; m. Laurel Jean Bushman, May 21, 1974; children—Gary Burnell, Eric Louis, Jeremy Lynn, Lacey Jean, Katrina Lauren, Genevieve Lee. A.S., Dixie Jr. Coll., 1971; B.A., Brigham Young U., 1975, M.L.S., 1976. Reference librarian Elko Library, Nev., 1977-78; outreach librarian Clark County Library, Las Vegas, 1978-80, adminstr., 1980-94, dir., 1994—; cons., 1982. Mem. ALA, Mountain Plain Library Assn., Nev. Library Assn. Republican. Mem. Ch. of Jesus Christ of Latter-day Saints. Office: Las Vegas Clark County Libr Dist 833 Las Vegas Blvd N Las Vegas NV 89101-2030

BATSON, RAYMOND MILNER, retired cartographer; b. Lincoln, Nebr., July 8, 1931; s. Avery A. and Margaret Elizabeth (Milner) B.; m. Rhoda May Meier, Aug. 31, 1955; children: Beverly Ann Batson White, Frederick Avery, Thomas Raymond. Student, U. Colo., 1953-57, BA, 1962. Field engr., photogrammetrist U.S. Geol. Survey, Denver, 1957-63; rsch. cartographer U.S. Geol. Survey, Flagstaff, Ariz., 1963-94, chief planetary cartography, 1963-92; ret., 1994; mem. planetary cartography working group NASA, Washington, 1978-94, mem. planetary geol. and geophys. working group, 1982-92, expert mem. U.S./USSR joint working group for planetary data exch., 1988-92. Author, editor: Planetary Mapping, 1990. Staff sgt. USAF, 1951-52. Fellow Am. Soc. for Photogrammetry; mem. Am. Soc. Photogrammetry (chmn. extraterrestrial sci. com. 1981-88), Astron. Soc. of the Pacific (hon.), Internat. Soc. PHotogrammetry (chmn. working group 3 com. IV 1982-85), Internat. Astron. Union (working group for planetary system nomenclature com. 16, 1991-94).

BATT, PHILIP E., governor; b. Wilder, Idaho, Mar. 4, 1927; m. Jacque Batt, 1948; children: Bill, Rebecca, Leslie. Attended, U. Idaho, 1944-48. Elected mem. Idaho State Legislature, 1965; lt. gov. State of Idaho, 1978-82, now gov. First pres. Idaho Food Producers; co-chmn. Wilder United Charity Auction; mem. Idaho Potato Growers Commn.; mem. bd. dirs. Wilder Farm Labor Com.; mem. bd. trustees Coll. Idaho; past pres. Idaho Hop Growers Assn., Hop Growers of Am., Homedale PTA. Office: Office of the Gov PO Box 83720 Boise ID 83720-0002*

BATTENBURG, JOHN DOUGLAS, English educator, consultant; b. Inglewood, Calif., Aug. 30, 1961; s. Joseph Richard Battenburg and Mary Estelle (Antisdel) Durkin; m. Lisa Ann Pate, Mar. 25, 1992; children: Andrew Justin, Adam Daniel, Alexandra Hope. Diploma French studies, Seminaire du Salève, Collonges-sous Salève, France, 1980; BA in English, Andrews U., 1982; MA in Linguistics, Ohio U., 1984; PhD in English, Purdue U., 1989. Grad. instr. Ohio U., Athens, 1982-84, Purdue U., West Lafayette, Ind., 1984-89; instr. English Lang. and Multicultural Inst., Dayton, Ohio, 1984; asst. prof. English, Calif. Poly. State U., San Luis Obispo, 1989—, assoc. prof., 1989—, coord. linguistics minor, 1994—, linguistics project dir. Egyptian peace fellowship program, 1993-94; English lang. cons. Coll. of Agrl., Costa Rica, 1992-93; faculty advisor cmty.-based tchr. preparation program Hancock Coll., 1993. Author: Monolingual Learners' Dictionaries: A User-Oriented Study, 1991; contbr. articles, book revs. and essays to profl. publs. Recipient Excellence in Tchg. award Purdue U., 1988, David Ross dissertation fellow Purdue U., 1988; grantee Calif. Poly. State U., 1990. Mem. MLA, TESOL, Linguistic Soc. Am., Dictionary Soc. N.Am., Calif. TESOL, Am. Assn. Applied Linguists. Office: Calif Poly State U English Dept San Luis Obispo CA 93407

BATTIN, JAMES FRANKLIN, judge, former congressman; b. Wichita, Kans., Feb. 13, 1925; m. Barbara Choate; children: Loyce Battin Peterson, Patricia Battin Pfeiffer, James Franklin. J.D., George Washington U., 1951. Bar: D.C., Mont. Practice in Washington, 1951-52; now in Billings; past dep. county atty.; past sec.-counsel City-County Planning Bd.; past asst. city atty. Billings; then city atty.; mem. Mont. Ho. of Reps., 1958-59; mem. 87th-91st Congresses from 2d Mont. dist., Mont.; resigned when apptd. U.S. dist. judge Mont., 1969; chief judge U.S. Dist. Ct. Mont., Billings, 1978-90, sr. judge, 1990—. Served with USNR, World War II. Mem. Am. Legion, DeMolay Legion of Honor. Presbyterian. Club: Mason (Shriner). Office: US Dist Ct 5319 Fed Bldg 316 N 26th St Ste 1476 Billings MT 59101-1362

BATTIN, MARGARET PABST, philosophy educator; b. New Orleans, Nov. 29, 1940; d. William Richard Jr. and Margaret Hayes (Richards) Pabst; m. Blake Norris Battin, Apr. 11, 1964 (div. 1976); children: Michael Wood, Sara Richards; m. Roger Brooke Hopkins, Jan. 1, 1986. Student, U. Munich, 1961-62; BA in Philosophy with honors magna cum laude, Bryn Mawr Coll., 1963; MFA in Fiction Writing, U. Calif., Irvine, 1973, PhD in Philosophy, 1976. Asst. prof. U. Utah, Salt Lake City, 1977-81, assoc. prof., 1981-88, prof., 1988—; philosopher in residence VA Med. Ctr., Salt Lake City, 1981; adj. prof. divsn. med. ethics U. Utah Sch. Medicine, 1990—. Author: Ethical Issues in Suicide, 1982, 94, Ethics in the Sanctuary: Examining the Practices of Organized Religion, 1990, The Least Worst Death: Essays in Bioethics on the End of Life, 1994; co-author: (with A. Silvers, R. Moore, J. Fisher) Puzzles About Art: An Aesthetics Casebook, 1989, (P. Windt, P. Appleby, L. Francis, B. Landesman) Ethical Issues in the Professions, 1989; co-editor: (David Mayo) Suicide: The Philosophical Issues, 1980, 81, (Michael Rudick) John Donne's Biathanatos, 1982, (T. Smeeding, L. Francis, B. Landesman) Should Medical Care be Rationed by Age?, 1987, (Robert Huefner) Changing to National Health Care: The Ethical Issues, 1992; cons. or adv. editor: Sucide and Life Threatening Behavior, Jour. Aesthetic Edn., 1987-89, Jour. Pharm. Care in Pain and Symptom Mgmt., Profl. Ethics: A Multidisciplinary Jour., 1993—; contbr. to profl. jours.; contbr. short stories to mags. Recipient Short Stories 1st prize Utah Arts Coun., 1981, David P. Gardner award U. Utah, 1984, Ramona W. Cannon award U. Utah, 1988; Woodrow Wilson hon. fellow, 1963-64, NEH, 1977-78, 86, David P. Gardner Faculty fellow U. Utah, 1980, Faculty fellow U. Utah, 1988; named to Spinoza Chair U. Amsterdam Academic Med. Ctr., The Netherlands, 1993. Mem. Am. Philos. Assn. (pacific divsn. program com. 1985-88, program chair, 1987, com. on philosophy and medicine, 1987-90), Am. Soc. for Aesthetics (trustee, 1985-88, pacific divsn pres. 1985-86), Am. Assn. Suicidology (bd. dirs. 1986-89, chair ethics com. 1992-95), Soc. Scientific Study of Religion, Am. Soc. Law and Medicine, Soc. for Health and Human Values, European Soc. for Philosophy of Medicine and Health Care, Am. Assn. Bioethics (bd. dirs. 1993—), Am. Coun. of Learned Societies, Phi Kappa Phi. Office: U Utah Dept Philosophy 340 Orson Spencer Hall Salt Lake City UT 84112-1103

BATTISTELLI, JOSEPH JOHN, electronics executive; b. Bridgeport, Conn., Oct. 22, 1930; s. Joseph John and Maria (Brunetti) B.; m. Helen Josephine Thompson, Apr. 5, 1961; children: Jay Dominick, Randall Victor. BSEE, U. Conn., 1958; MSEE, U. Ariz., 1960. Registered electrical engr., Ariz., Ohio. V.p. Electro Tech. analysis Corp., Tucson, 1960-68; rsch. engr. Ohio U., Athens, 1968-72; sr. engr. Hughes Aircraft Co., Culver City, Calif., 1972-74; dir. engring. Lockheed Aircraft Co., Ont., Calif., 1974-80; dir. Riyadh area Litton Industries, Beverly Hills, Calif., 1980-91; v.p. Orion Ltd., Reston, Va., 1991—; cons. FAA, Washington, 1962-72, U.S. Army Electronics Command, Ft. Monmouth, N.J., 1962-74, Lochkeed Aircraft Co., Ont., 1980—. Contbr. articles to profl. jours. With U.S. Army, 1952-54. Mem. IEEE, Sigma Xi, Tau Beta Pi, Eta Kappa Nu, Phi Kappa Phi. Office: Orion Ltd 6855 E Dorado Blvd Tucson AZ 85715-4840

BATTISTI, DAVID STEPHEN, atmospheric sciences educator; b. Ithaca, N.Y., May 19, 1956; s. Frank Leon and Charlotte (Tayntor) B.; m. Lynn Alison McMurdie, Sept. 14, 1985; children: Eric Michael, Adrian Thomas. BS in Physics, U. Mass., 1978; MS in Oceanography, U. Washington, Seattle, 1981; PhD in Atmospheric Scis., 1988. Rsch. assoc. JISAO, Seattle, 1988; asst. prof. Dept. Meteorology U. Wis., Madison, 1989-90, Dept. Atmospheric Scis. U. Washington, Seattle, 1990-94; assoc. prof. Dept. Atmospheric Scis. U. Wash., Seattle, 1995—. Contbr. numerous articles to profl. jours. Mem. Am. Meteorol. Soc., Am. Geophys. Union Panels of Nat. Rsch. Coun. for NAS. Office: U Wash 351640 Dept Atmospheric Scis Seattle WA 98195

BATTISTI, PAUL ORESTE, county supervisor; b. Herkimer, N.Y., Mar. 16, 1922; s. Oreste and Ida (Fiore) B.; m. Constance Muth Drais, May 18, 1985; children—Paul J., Cathy (Mrs. D. Capage), Deborah, Thomas, Daniel, Melora, Stephen. Student, Cornell U., Ithaca, N.Y., 1947-48, U. Neb., 1951-52. With VA, 1946-75; dir. VA Hosp., Martinez, Calif., 1969-73; western region dir. San Francisco, 1973-75; adminstr. State Vets. Home Calif., 1976-86; supr. County of Napa, 1989—; chmn., chief exec. officer Medam., Inc.; dir. Med. Am. Corp.; mem. Contra Costa County Comprehensive Health Planning, Health Facilities Task Force; chmn. adv. com. East Bay Med. Program.; bd. dirs. East Bay Hosp. Conf. Bd. dirs. Easter Seals Contra Costa County. With AUS, 1942-46. Fellow Am. Coll. Hosp. Adminstrs.; mem. Hosp. Conf. No. Calif. (pres.), Nat. Assn. State Vets. Homes (pres.), Rotary (Napa). Home: Silverado Country Club 117 Milliken Creek Dr Napa CA 94558-1240 Office: County Bd of Suprs County of Napa 1195 3rd St Napa CA 94559-3035

BATTLE, THOMAS HOWARD, human resources executive; b. Denver, Nov. 7, 1950; s. Louis and Zular (Bumpers) B.; m. Ella Louise Maye, Feb. 12, 1977; children: Kellie, Bryan. BBA, Loyola Marymount U., 1972; MBA, Pepperdine U., 1980. Compensation adminstr. Mattel Toy Co., Hawthorne, Calif., 1975-78; supr. compensation/benefits The Gillette Co., Santa Monica, Calif., 1978-80, supr. employment and affirmative action, 1980-82; territory sales rep. The Gillette Co., L.A., 1982-84; mgr. employment and tng. The Gillette Co., Santa Monica, 1984-86, mgr. employment tng., security and employee rels., 1986-89, div. mgr. human resources, 1989—. Pres. Neighborhood Block Club, Gardena, Calif., 1988. With U.S. Army, 1972-74. Decorated Army Commendation medal. Mem. Soc. for Human Resource Mgmt. Democrat. Methodist. Home: 14912 Van Buren Ave Gardena CA 90247-3041 Office: The Gillette Co 1681 26th St Santa Monica CA 90404-4016

BATTS, MICHAEL STANLEY, German language educator; b. Mitcham, Eng., Aug. 2, 1929; s. Stanley George and Alixe Kathleen (Watson) B.; m. Misao Yoshida, Mar. 19, 1959; 1 dau., Anna. BA, U. London, 1952, BA with honors, 1953, LittD, 1973; PhD, U. Freiburg, Germany, 1957; M.L.S., U. Toronto, 1974. Mem. faculty U. Mainz, Germany, 1953-54, U. Basel, Switzerland, 1954-56, U. Wurzburg, Germany, 1956-58; instr. German U. Calif., Berkeley, 1958-60; mem. faculty dept. German U. B.C., Can., 1960-91; prof. U. B.C., 1967-91, head dept., 1968-80. Author: Die Form der Aventiuren im Nibelunenlied, 1961, Bruder Hansens Marienlieder, 1964, Studien zu Bruder Hansens Marienliedern, 1964, Das Hohe Mittelalter, 1969, Das Nibelungenlied-Synoptische Ausgabe, 1971, Gottfried von Strasburg, 1971, A Checklist of German Literature, 1945-75, 1977, The Bibliography of German Literature: An Historical and Critical Survey, 1978, A History of Histories of German Literature, 1985-1914, 1993; editor: Seminar, 1970-80. Served with Brit. Army, 1947-49. Alexander von Humboldt fellow, 1964-65, 83; Can. Council sr. fellow, 1964-65, 71-72; Killam fellow, 1981-82. Fellow Royal Soc. Can.; mem. Canadian Assn. Univ. Tchrs. German (pres. 1982-84), Modern Humanities Rsch. Assn., Alcuin Soc. (exec. v.p. 1972-79, pres. 1979-80), Internat. Assn. for Germanic Studies (pres. 1990-95). Office: U Brit Columbia, German Dept, Vancouver, BC Canada V6T 1Z1

BATTY, HUGH KENWORTHY, physician; b. Kansas City, Kans.; s. James Jacob and Genevieve Adeline (Johnston) B.; m. Mercedes Aguirre, Mar. 17, 1979; 1 child, Henry Briton. BS in Zoology, U. Wash., 1970; PhD in Anatomy, U. Utah, 1974; MD, Ciudad Juárez, Mex., 1977. Intern, asst. resident St. Vincent's Med. Ctr., Bridgeport, Conn., 1977-78, resident, 1978-79, chief resident, 1979-80; pvt. practice Sheridan, Wyo., 1981—; chmn. dept. medicine Meml. Hosp. Sheridan, 1989-91, chmn. intensive care unit, 1995. Contbr. articles to profl. jours. Eleanor Roosevelt Cancer Rsch. Found. grantee, 1972. Mem. ACP, Wyo. Med. Soc., Sheridan County Med. Soc. Office: 1260 W 5th St Sheridan WY 82801-2702

BATY, ROGER MENDENHALL, anthropology educator; b. Helena, Mont., Oct. 2, 1937; s. Harvey Franklin and Emma Lou (Neffner) B.; m. Phebe Nelson, June 14, 1966; children: Iliniza Mary, Jonathan Harvey, Marquerite Louise. BA cum laude, U. Mont., 1958; BA, MA, U. Oxford, 1964; PhD, Stanford U., 1970. Dir. intercultural dimension U. Redlands, Calif., 1969-79; dir. Armacost Libr. U. Redlands, 1979-83, prof. anthropology, 1983—; Farquhar prof. Am. Southwest, 1989—. Author: Re-educating Teachers for Cultural Awareness, 1972, Faustino Pena - Potter of Tzintzuntzan, 1978. Commr., dist. chmn. Boy Scouts Am., Redlands, 1979-89. Rhodes scholar, 1958. Fellow Am. Anthropology Assn.; mem. Am. Geol. Soc., Archaeol. Survey Assn. So. Calif. (pres. 1991-94). Episcopal. Office: Dept Sociology/Anthropology U Redlands 1200 E Colton Ave Redlands CA 92373

BATZDORF, ULRICH, neurosurgeon, educator; b. Breslau, Germany, July 22, 1928; came to U.S., 1940; s. Erwin Erich and Lotte Marie (Ollendorff) B.; m. Ellen Kirstein Batzdorf, Dec. 17, 1962; children: Nicholas, Mark, Caroline. BS cum laude in Chemistry, CCNY, 1948; MS in Biochemistry and Physiology, Rutgers U., 1950; MD, N.Y. Med. Coll., 1955. Diplomate Am. Bd. Neurosurgery. Intern U.S. Naval Hosp., Newport, R.I., 1955-56; asst. resident in Surgery U. Md. Hosp., Balt., 1958-60; trainee in neuropathology Nat. Inst. for Neurol. Diseases and Blindness, San Francisco, 1961-62; asst. resident Wadsworth VA Hosp., L.A., 1962-63; resident in neurol. surgery UCLA Ctr. for Health Scis., L.A., 1963-65, sr. resident in neurosurgery, 1965, from asst. to assoc. attending physician, 1968-79, attending physician, 1979—; attending physician Wadsworth VA Hosp., L.A., 1967—; asst. instr. Biochemistry N.Y. Med. Coll., N.Y.C., 1950-53; asst. prof. in residence dept. surgery/neurosurgery UCLA Ctr. for Health Scis., L.A., 1966-68, asst. prof., 1968-71, assoc. prof., 1971-79, prof., 1979—; cons. physician St. John's Hosp. and Health Ctr., Santa Monica, Calif., 1993—; lectr. in field; med. staff Olive View-UCLA Med. Ctr, 1993—. Ad hoc reviewer Clin. Orthopaedics and Related Rsch., 1968—; mem. editl. bd.: Neurosurgery, 1992—; contbr. articles to profl. jours., chpts. to books. Rsch. grantee 1967-78. Mem. ACS, AAAS, AMA, Am. Assn. for Neurol. Surgeons (chmn. Bylaws com. 1976-77), Am. Assn. Cancer Rsch., Assn. Acad. Surgery, Bay Surg. Soc. (bd. dirs. 1987), Brain Rsch. Inst., Calif. Assn. Neurol. Surgeons (bd. dirs. 1982—, 2d v.p. 1987, 1st v.p. 1989, pres. 1991), Calif. Med. Assn., Congress of Neurol. Surgeons, Jonsson Comprehensive Cancer Ctr., L.A. Soc. Neurol. Sci., So. Calif. Neurosurg. Soc. (pres. 1979-80), Tissue Culture Assn., Internat. Assn. Study of Pain, Sigma Xi, Alpha Omega Alpha. Office: UCLA Med Ctr Box 956901 Los Angeles CA 90095-6901

BAUCH, THOMAS JAY, lawyer, apparel company executive; b. Indpls., May 24, 1943; s. Thomas and Violet (Smith) B.; m. Ellen L. Burstein, Oct. 31, 1982; children: Chelsea Sara, Elizabeth Tree. BS with honors, U. Wis., 1964, JD with highest honors, 1966. Bar: Ill. 1966, Calif. 1978. Assoc. Lord, Bissell & Brook, Chgo., 1966-72; lawyer, asst. sec. Marcor-Montgomery Ward, Chgo., 1973-75; spl. asst. to solicitor Dept. Labor, Washington, 1975-77; dep. gen. counsel Levi Strauss & Co., San Francisco,

1977-81, sr. v.p., gen. counsel, 1981—; mem. U. Wis. Law Review, Madison, 1964-66. Bd. dirs. Urban Sch., San Francisco, 1986-91; bd. visitors U. Wis. Law Sch., 1991—. Mem. Am. Assn. Corp. Counsel (bd. dirs. 1984-87), Bay Area Gen. Counsel Assn. (chmn. 1994), Univ. Club, Villa Taverna Club, Order of Coif. Office: Levi Strauss & Co 1155 Battery St San Francisco CA 94111-1230

BAUCUS, MAX S., senator; b. Helena, Mont., Dec. 11, 1941; s. John and Jean (Sheriff) B.; m. Wanda Minge, Apr. 23, 1983. BA, Stanford U., 1964, LLB, 1967. Bar: D.C. 1969, Mont. 1972. Staff atty. CAB, Washington, 1967-68; lawyer SEC, Washington, 1968-71; legal asst. to chmn. SEC, 1970-71; sole practice Missoula, Mont., 1971-74; mem. Mont. Ho. of Reps., 1973-74; mem. 94th-95th congresses from 1st Dist. Mont., 1975-79, mem. com. appropriations; U.S. senator from Mont., 1979—, ranking minority mem., mem. environ. and pub. works com., mem. fin. subcom. on internat. trade, mem. medicare, long-term care and health ins., mem. agrl./nutrition and forestry coms., mem. intelligence/joint com. on taxation, mem. Senate Dem. steering and coordination com. Office: US Senate 511 Hart Senate Bldg Washington DC 20510-2602

BAUDER, SISTER MARIANNA, hospital administrator; b. Leavenworth, Kans., Sept. 13, 1943; d. Elmer Leon and Gertrude Hartnett (Zeugin) B. BS in Chemistry & Biology, St. Mary Coll., Leavenworth, Kans., 1970; MS in Adminstrn., U. Notre Dame, 1980. Registered med. technologist. Staff med. technologist St. Mary Hosp. Med. Ctr., Grand Junction, Colo., 1971-75, supr. lab., 1975-79; asst. adminstr. St. Francis Hosp., Topeka, 1981-85; pres., chief exec. officer St. Mary Hosp. and Med. Ctr., Grand Junction, 1985-89; pres., CEO St. Joseph Hosp., Denver, 1990—. Bd. dirs. St. Vincent's Hosp. & Health Ctr., Billings, Mont., 1989—, Samaritan Inst. Bd., 1990-93; Mile High United Way, 1992—, Denver U. Adv. Coun. on Healthcare Programs, 1991—, St. Vincent Home for Emotionaly Disturbed Children Devel. Coun., 1992—, Denver Civic Ventures Bd., 1991-93, Mountain States Employers Coun. Bd., 1994; Denver Metro C. of C. bd., 1995—; Colo. Hosp. Assn. Bd., 1994—; regent of Regis U., 1994—. Recipient First Class Leadership award Greater Topeka C. of C., 1984. Fellow Am. Coll. Heathcare Execs.; mem. Rotary Internat. Democrat. Roman Catholic. Office: St Joseph Hosp 1835 Franklin St Denver CO 80218-1126

BAUER, A(UGUST) ROBERT, JR., surgeon, educator; b. Phila., Dec. 23, 1928; s. A(ugust) Robert and Jessie Martha-Maynard (Monie) B.; BS, U. Mich., 1949, MS, 1950, MD, 1954; M Med. Sci.-Surgery, Ohio State U., 1960; m. Charmaine Louise Studer, June 28, 1957; children: Robert, John, William, Anne, Charles, James. Intern Walter Reed Army Med. Ctr., 1954-55; resident in surgery Univ. Hosp., Ohio State U., Columbus, also instr., 1957-61; pvt. practice medicine, specializing in surgery, Mt. Pleasant, Mich., 1962-74; chief surgery Ctrl. Mich. Community Hosp., Mt. Pleasant, 1964-65, vice chief of staff, 1967, chief of staff, 1968; clin. faculty Mich. State Med. Sch., East Lansing, 1974; mem. staff St. Mark's Hosp., Salt Lake City, 1974-91; pvt. practice surgery, Salt Lake City, 1974-91; clin. instr. surgery U. Utah, 1975-91. Trustee Rowland Hall, St. Mark's Sch., Salt Lake City, 1978-84; mem. Utah Health Planning Coun., 1979-81. Served with M.C., U.S. Army, 1954-57. Diplomate Am. Bd. Surgery. Fellow ACS, Southwestern Surg. Congress; mem. AMA, Salt Lake County Med. Soc., Utah Med. Assn. (various coms.), Utah Soc. Certified Surgeons, Salt Lake Surg. Soc., Pan Am. Med. Assn. (affiliate), AAAS (affiliate), Sigma Phi Epsilon, Phi Rho Sigma. Episcopalian. Club: Zollinger. Contbr. articles to profl. publs., researcher surg. immunology. Office: PO Box 17533 Salt Lake City UT 84117-0533

BAUER, BARBARA LOIS, county official; b. Salt Lake City, Aug. 29, 1957; d. Richard Leuking and Lois Darlene Saathoff. BBA, Boise State U., 1981; MBA, U. Idaho, 1986. Advt. cons. Boise (Idaho) State U., 1980; house dir. Kappa Alpha Theta, Moscow, Idaho, 1981-83; mgr. Saga Corp., Boise, 1983-84; fin. and investment dep. Ada County, Boise, 1985-86, treas., 1986—. Trustee, pension bd. Evang. Luth. Ch. Am., Mpls., 1991—, treas., mem. exec. com., mem. synod coun., Eastern Wash./Idaho Synod, 1986—; mktg. v.p. Jr. League of Boise, 1989, mem. exec. com., 1989, bd. dirs., 1988-90; bd. dirs. Luth. Social Svcs. of Idaho, 1990—; mem. Ada County Task Force on Teen Pregnancy, 1988-89; pres. Ada County Rep. Women, 1987; active March of Dimes, 1990-91; mem. disbursement panel United Way of Ada County, 1989—; officer Ada County Rep. Cen. Com., 1976-82, 85-88, 1992—. Mem. Nat. Assn. County Treas.' and Fin. Officers (continuing edn. rev. com. 1989), Idaho Assn. County Treas.' (legis. com. 1986-87, chmn. forms com. 1987-88, chmn. edn. com. 1989-91), Govt. Fin. Officers Assn. Home: 4991 Bitterbrush Dr Boise ID 83703-3805 Office: Ada County Treas PO Box 2868 Boise ID 83701-2868

BAUER, BERNARD OSWALD, geography educator; b. Salmon Arm, B.C., Can., Feb. 7, 1957; s. Joseph and Gerda (Frisch) B. BSc. with honors, U. Toronto (Can.), 1980, MSc., 1982; PhD, Johns Hopkins U., 1988. Instr. U. Toronto, 1985-86; asst. prof. U. So. Calif., L.A., 1987-93; assoc. prof. U. So. Calif., 1993—; prin. GeoCan Cons., Toronto, 1985—. Author: (reference bibliography) Council of Planning Librarians, 1981, (lab. manual) Laboratory Exercises in Physical Geography, 1990; contbr. articles to profl. jours. Recipient J. Warren Nystrom award Assn. Am. Geographers, 1989, Hydrolab award Internat. Assn. for Great Lakes Rsch., 1986, Presdl. Young Investigator award Nat. Sci. Found., 1991; Postgrad. scholar Nat. Scis. and Engring. Coun., Ottawa, Can., 1981-85. Mem. Assn. Am. Geographers (bd. dirs. coastal and marine geography specialty group 1990-92, vice chair 1992-93, chair 1993-95). Office: U So Calif 3620 S Vermont Ave Los Angeles CA 90007-3944

BAUER, CECILE RUTH, grant coordinator; b. Kenmore, N.Y., Apr. 20, 1936; d. Cecil James and Mary Elva (Black) Ramier; m. David P. Bauer Sr., Nov. 22, 1952; children: David Jr., Mary, Russell, Barbara, Jean, Rose, Jason, Thomas, Michael, James. Student, Rosary Hill, 1970, Am. River, 1988. Assoc. West End Hotel, Hamburg, N.Y., 1962-64, Howard Johnson's, Athol Springs, N.Y., 1964-67, Holiday Inn, Hamburg, 1968-86; agent Pierce & Cash, Hamburg, 1970-74; transp. trainer Eden (N.Y.) Ctrl. Schs., 1979-86; grant coord. St. Gleaners Inc., North Highlands, Calif., 1988—; computer trainer Sr. Gleaners inc., North Highlands, 1990—. Author: Mona/L.U., 1987, Escape to Sun city, 1994; contbg. author: Angels Get No Respect, 1987. Maj. founder The Basic Baby Needs program Sr. Gleaners, 1990—; eucharist min. St. Lawrence Ch., North Highlands, 1986—, leader scripture studies, 1987-94. Grantee Sr. Gleaners Inc. Mem. Nat. Writers Orgn. (profl. mem.), Saturday Morning Writers (co-leader 1988—). Office: Sr Gleaners Inc 3185 Longview Dr North Highlands CA 95660-5714

BAUER, CHARLES EDWARD, microelectronics consultant; b. Astoria, Oreg., May 11, 1950; s. Leo Leu and Evelyn Marie (Fordyce) B.; m. Katherine Blanche Harrison, July 31, 1976; children: Scott Charles, Christopher Harrison. BS in Materials Sci. Engring., Stanford U., 1972; MS in Metallurgical Engring., Ohio State U., 1975; PhD in Materials Sci. Engring., Oreg. Grad. Inst., 1980; MBA in Mktg. and Internat. Bus., Portland U., 1988. Materials scientist, engr. III Tektronix Inc., Beaverton, Oreg., 1978-80, engring. mgr. I, 1980-84, engring. mgr. II, 1984-86, IC packaging ops. mgr., 1986-89; dir. rsch. & tech. MicroLithics Corp., Golden, Colo., 1989-90; mng. dir. Tech Lead Corp., Evergreen, Colo., 1990—; judge Milton S. Kivor Awards, Anaheim, Calif., 1993—; advisor Elec. Packaging and Prodn. Mag., Des Plaines, Ill., 1993—. Contbr. articles to profl. jours.; patentee/inventor in field. Pres. Nat. Plains Youth Soccer Assn., North Plaine, Oreg., 1986-87; founder Evergreen Enterprises Exch., 1994—; asst. chair, chair Washington (Oreg.) City Citizens Adv. Bd., 1982-84. Ohio State Student fellow, 1973-75. Fellow ISHM Microelectronic Soc. (nat. tech. v.p. 1988-90, dir. ednl. found. 1988-90); mem. IEEE, ASM Internat. (fellow 1972), Colo. Advanced Tech. Inst. (adv. bd. 1991—), Surface Mount Tech. Assn. (pres. Rocky Mountain chpt. 1994), Semicondr. Equipment and Materials Internat. (advisor 1993—), Hiwan Golf Club. Roman Catholic.

BAUER, ELIZABETH KELLEY (MRS. FREDERICK WILLIAM BAUER), consulting energy economist; b. Berkeley, Calif., Aug. 7, 1920; d. Leslie Constant and Elizabeth Jeanette (Worley) Kelley; A.B., U. Calif. at Berkeley, 1941, M.A., 1943; Ph.D. (fellow), Columbia U., 1947; m. Frederick William Bauer, July 5, 1944; children: Elizabeth Katherine Bauer Keenan, Frederick Nicholas. Instr. U.S. history and studies Barnard Coll., N.Y.C., 1944-45; lectr. history U. Calif. at Berkeley, 1949-50, 56-57; rsch. asst. Giannini Found., 1946-49, asst. rsch. agrl. economist, 1957-60; exec. sec. Internat. Conf. on Agrl. and Coop. Credit, U. Calif. at Berkeley, 1952-53, exec. sec. South Asia Project, 1955-56; registrar Holy Names Coll., Oakland, Calif., 1971-72; rsch. assoc. Brookings Instn. and Nat. Acad. Pub. Adminstrn., Washington, 1973; fgn. affairs officer Internat. Energy Affairs, Fed. Energy Adminstrn. Washington, 1974-77; fgn. affairs officer Office of Current Reporting, Internat. Affairs, Dept. Energy, Washington, 1977-81; dir. policy analysis and evaluation Nat. Coal Assn., Washington, 1981-83. Mem. Calif. Com. to Revise the Tchrs. Credential, 1961; trustee Grad. Theol. Union, Berkeley, 1972-74; bd. dirs. St. Paul's Towers and Episcopal Homes Found, Oakland, 1971-72. Recipient Superior Achievement award Dept. Energy, 1980; U. Calif. Alumni citation, 1983, 93. Mem. AAUW (Calif. chmn. for higher edn. 1960-62), Prytanean Honor Soc., AAAS, P.E.O., Mortar Bd., Phi Beta Kappa, Pi Lambda Theta, Sigma Kappa Alpha, Phi Alpha Theta, Pi Sigma Alpha. Democrat. Episcopalian. Author: Commentaries on the Constitution, 1790-1860, 1952; (with Murray R. Benedict) Farm Surpluses: U.S Burden or World Asset?, 1960; (with Florence Noyce Wertz) The Graduate Theological Union, 1970. Co-author, editor: The Role of Foreign Governments in the Energy Industries, 1977. Home: 708 Montclair Dr Santa Rosa CA 95409-2822

BAUER, ERWIN ADAM, photographer; b. Cin., Apr. 22, 1919; s. Adam John and Louise (Volz) B.; m. Doris Parker, 1940 (div.); children: Parker, Robert; m. Grace Margaret (Peggy) Reid, 1972; stepchildren: Stephen Politi, Paul Politi, Charles Politi. Student, U. Cin., 1935-38. Field asst. U.S. Army Corps of Engrs., 1939-41; outdoors columnist Ironton Tribune, Ohio, 1939-41, 1947-48; state game warden Lawrence County, Ohio, 1948; editor Ohio Conservation Bull., to 1955; editor at large Outdoor Life Mag., 1973—. Author of twenty-five books including Bass in America, 1951, Bass Fisherman's Bible, 1959, Saltwater Fisherman's Bible, 1962, Duck Hunter's Bible, 1965, Treasury of Big Game Animals, 1972, Cross-Country Skier's Bible, 1972, Cross-Country Skiing and Snowshoeing, 1973, Photographing the West, 1981, Deer in Their World, 1983, Wildlife Adventures with a Camera, 1984, Bear in Their World, 1985, Predators of North America, 1987, Wild Alaska, 1988, Yellowstone, 1993, Whitetails, Wild Dogs of North America, 1994, Antlers, Baja to Barrow, 1995; contbr. numerous articles to profl. jours. Capt. U.S. Army, 1942-46, 51-53. Decorated Croisx de Guerre, Free French, five Battle Stars and Purple Heart; recipient six gold and silver awards Soc. Am. Travel Writers, 1991, 92, award BBC Gas, 1991. Democrat. Home and Office: Wildstock PO Box 987 Livingston MT 59047-0987

BAUER, HENRY LELAND, lawyer; b. Portland, Oreg., June 7, 1928; s. Henry and Emma L. (Peterson) B.; m. Doris Jane Philbrick, Sept. 11, 1952 (dec.); children: Henry Stephen, Thomas Leland. BS in Bus., Oreg. State U., 1950; JD, U. Oreg., 1953. Bar: Oreg. 1953, U.S. Dist. Ct. Oreg., 1956; U.S. Ct. Appeals (9th cir.), 1960. Mem. Bauer & Bauer, Portland, Oreg., 1955-70, Bauer, Murphy, Bayless & Fundingsland, and successor firms, Portland, 1970-75; prin. Henry L. Bauer & Assocs. P.C., Portland. Past mem. adv. council Oreg. State U. Coll. Bus.; past bd. dirs., vice chmn. St. Vincent Hosp. and Med. Ctr.; mem., past pres. council of trustees St. Vincent Med. Found.; lifetime trustee Kappa Sigma Emdowment Fund; bd. dirs., past pres. Nat. Interfrat. Conf.; past pres. Columbia Pacific council Boy Scouts Am., mem. nat. com.; past pres. Portland Civic Theatre; bd. visitors U. Oreg. Sch. Law, 1979-83; trustee Oreg. State U. Found. 1st lt. USAF, 1953-55. Recipient Silver Antelope award Boy Scouts Am.; named Disting. Alumnus, Oreg. State U., 1994. Mem. ABA, Oreg. Bar Assn., Multnomah County Bar Assn., Am. Judicature Soc., Oreg. State U. Alumni Assn. (bd. dirs.), Delta Theta Phi, Kappa Sigma (past nat. pres.). Republican. Presbyterian. Clubs: Multnomah Athletic, Arlington, Masons, Rotary. Office: 25-3 NW 23rd Ave Portland OR 97210-3517

BAUER, HERBERT, physician; b. Vienna, Austria, Jan. 21, 1910; came to U.S., 1940; s. Fritz and Irma (Lindenfeld) B.; m. Hanna Goldsmith, 1939; children: Timothy, Christopher. MD, U. Vienna, Austria, 1936; MPH, U. Calif., Berkeley, 1948. Chief county physician San Luis Obispo County, San Luis Obispo, Calif., 1942-47; med. dir. Sacramento Health Dept., 1948-52; pub. and mental health dir. Yolo County, Calif., 1952-72; clin. prof. U. Calif., Davis, Calif., 1972-92. Recipient Liberty Bell award Bar Assn. Woodland, Calif., 1955, Peace and Justice award City of Davis, Calif., 1991. Mem. AMA, APHA, Am. Psychiat. Assn., Am. Acad. Child Psychiatry, Am. Acad. Psychiatry and Law, Calif. Med. Assn. Democrat. Unitarian. Home and Office: 831 Oeste Dr Davis CA 95616-1856

BAUER, JAY S., architect. AB, Washington U., 1970, MArch, 1972. Fellow AIA. Office: Bauer and Wiley 2507 W Coast Hwy Ste 202 Newport Beach CA 92663-4722

BAUER, JEFFREY ERVIN, aerospace engineer; b. Cin., Mar. 25, 1963; s. Ervin Leonard and Linda (Latcha) B.; m. Deborah Jean Moll, May 20, 1989. BS in Aero. & Astro. Engring., Purdue U., 1986, MS, 1988. Co-op student NASA Ames-Dryden, Edwards AFB, Calif., 1982-86; engr. PRC, Edwards, 1987-89; ERAST program chief engr. NASA Dryden, Edwards AFB, 1989—. Mem. Ptnrs. Citizen Task Force, Lancaster, Calif., 1992-93; mem. edn. com. City of Lancaster, 1993—. Sr. mem. AIAA (chmn. Antelope Valley sect. 1994—). Office: NASA Dryden FRC PO Box 273 Edwards CA 93523-0273

BAUER, JEROME LEO, JR., chemical engineer; b. Pitts., Oct. 12, 1938; s. Jerome L. and Anna Mae (Tucker) B.; children from previous marriage: children: Lori, Trish, Jeff. BSChemE, U. Dayton, 1960; MSChemE, Pa. State U., 1963; postgrad., Ohio State U., 1969. Registered profl. engr., Ohio. Asst. prof. chem. engring. U. Dayton, Ohio, 1963-67; mgr. advanced composites dept. Ferro Corp., Cleve., 1967-72; engring. material and process specifications mgr. Lockheed Missiles & Space Co., Inc., Sunnyvale, Calif., 1972-74; gen. dynamics design specialist Convair Div., San Diego, 1974-76, project devel. engr., 1976-77; dir. research Furane div. M&T Chems. Inc., Glendale, Calif., 1980-82; mem. tech. staff Jet Propulsion Lab., Calif. Inst. Tech., Pasadena, Calif., 1977-80, 82-90; mem. tech. staff mfg. engring. The Aerospace Corp., El Segundo, Calif., 1990—. Editor: Materials Sciences for Future, 1986, Moving Foreward With 50 Years of Leadership in Advanced Materials, 1994; contbr. articles to profl. jours. Jr. warden St. Luke Episcopal Ch., La Crescenta, Calif., 1980, sr. warden 1981. Mem. Am. Inst. Chem. Engrs. (founder, chmn. Dayton sect. 1964-66, spl. projects chmn. Cleve. sect. 1968-69), Soc. Advancement of Material Process Engring. (membership chmn. no. Calif. sect. 1973-74, sec. San Diego sect. 1974-75, vice chmn. 1975-76, chmn. 1976, chmn. Los Angeles sect. 1977, nat. treas. 1978-82, gen. chmn. 31st internat. symposium exhibition, Las Vegas, Nev., 1986, Meritiorious Achievement award 1983, internat. v.p. 1987-89, internat. pres. 1989-90), Internat. Electronics Packaging Soc. (pres. Los Angeles chpt. 1982), Phi Lambda Upsilon, Delta Sigma Epsilon. Republican. Home: PO Box 3298 El Segundo CA 90245-8398 Office: The Aerospace Corp 2350 E El Segundo Blvd El Segundo CA 90245-4609

BAUER, JUDY MARIE, minister; b. South Bend, Ind., Aug. 24, 1947; d. Ernest Camiel and Marjorie Ann (Williams) Derho; m. Gary Dwane Bauer, Apr. 28, 1966; children: Christine Ann, Steven Dwane. Ordained to ministry Christian Ch., 1979. Sec. adminstrv. asst. Bethel Christian Ctr., Riverside, Calif., 1975-79; founder, pres. Kingdom Advancement Ministry, San Diego, 1979—, trainer, mgr. cons., Tex., Ariz., Calif., Oreg., Washington, Ala., Okla., Idaho and Republic of South Africa, Guam, Egypt, The Philippines, Australia, Can., Mozambique, Malarwie, Mex., Zimbabwe, Guatemala, Israel, Scotland, Ireland, Japan, Eng., Zambia, Botheswana, Holland, 1979—; pres. Witty Outerwear Distbrs. Internat., Inc., 1993—; founder, co-pastor Bernardo Christian Ctr., San Diego, 1981-91; evangelism dir. Bethel Christian Ctr., 1978-81, undershepherd minister, 1975-79, adult tchr., 1973-81; pres., founder Bethel Christian Ctr. of Rancho Bernardo, Calif., 1991—; condr. leadership tng. clinics, internat. speaker, lectr. in field. Author syllabus, booklet, tng. material packets. Pres., founder Bethel Christian Ctr. of Rancho Bernardo, 1991—, Bernardo Christian Ctr., San Diego, 1981-91. Mem. Internat. Conv. Faith Ministries, Inc. (area bd. dirs. 1983-88).

BAUER, LOUIS EDWARD, retail bookstore executive, educator; b. Chgo., Mar. 11, 1937; s. Hermann Martin and Louise Eva (Winckler) B.; m. Inez Marie Gugel, Aug. 26, 1961; children: Erik Nathan, Ethan Joel, Elizabeth Marie, Elena Louise. Student, Valparaiso U., 1955-56; BS, No. State U., Aberdeen, S.D., 1961; MEd, Idaho State U., Pocatello, 1969. Asst. dir. student union No. State U., 1961-62; program dir. student union Idaho State U., 1962-67, dir. student union, 1967-69; dir. union and recreation U. Calif., Davis, 1969-74; dir. Stony Brook Union SUNY, Stony Brook, 1974-77; mng. dir. student union San Francisco State U., 1977-79; dir. aux. svcs. No. State U., 1979-87; pres., gen. mgr. Portland (Oreg.) State Bookstore, 1987—; adj. instr. Faculty of Bus., No. State U., 1979-87; maj. prof. Accelerated Degree program Concordia U., Portland, 1990—. Bd. dirs. Luth. Campus Coun., Portland, 1989-95. Mem. Optimists Internat. (lt. gov. 1985-86), Viking Athletic Club (bd. dirs. 1994—), City Club Portland. Democrat. Lutheran. Home: 11845 NW Vaughan Ct Portland OR 97229-4859 Office: Portland State U Bookstore 1880 SW 6th Ave Portland OR 97201-5204

BAUER, MICHAEL, newspaper editor. Food and home editor San Francisco Chronicle. Office: San Francisco Chronicle 901 Mission St San Francisco CA 94103-2905

BAUER, RALPH LEROY, business executive; b. Evansville, Ind., Dec. 19, 1925; s. John George and Elfrieda Louise (Gresser) Huber; m. Margaret Ellen Masters, Sept. 11, 1948 (div. 1975); children: Clinton L., Warren L., Brian E., Scott A.; m. Anna Mae Cooke, Nov. 9, 1984. BSEE, U. Evansville, 1950; postgrad., U. Calif., Riverside, 1956-58, UCLA, 1960, 65, U. Mich., 1969. Ordnance engr. Internat. Harvester Co., Evansville, Ind., 1950-54; test & product design Naval Ordnance Lab., Silver Springs, Md., 1954-55; test engr. Naval Ordnance Lab., Carona, Calif., 1955-57, br. head, 1957-61, div. head, 1961-70; div. head Naval Weapons Ctr., China Lake, Calif., 1970-82, assoc. dept. head, 1982-83; pres. RB Assocs. Inc., Lake Arrowhead, Calif., 1983-95; cons. to major aerospace firms in missile guidance/fuzing and electronic counter-countermeasures. Inventor in field. Elder, local sec. Presbyn. Ch., U.S.A., 1994-96. With U.S. Army Air Corps, 1944-46, radar operator-VH Bomb Group. Mem. IEEE (life mem., sect. chmn. 1968, sect. vice chmn. 1967, sect. sec.-treas. 1966), Am. Def. Preparedness Assn., Assn. Old Crows. Home: 987 LeMont Way Lake Arrowhead CA 92352 Office: RB Assocs Inc PO Box 2172 Lake Arrowhead CA 92352-2172

BAUER, RANDY MARK, management training firm executive; b. Cleve., Sept. 2, 1946; s. Ralph I. and Gloria P. Bauer; B.S. summa cum laude, Ohio State U., 1968; M.B.A., Kent State U., 1971; m. Sue Dellva, July 4, 1975; children—Sherri, Kevin. Mgmt. auditor Peat Marwick Mitchell & Co., Cleve., 1971-72; mgmt. devel. specialist GAO, Denver, 1972-80; adj. prof. mgmt. Columbia Coll., Denver, 1979—; pres. Leadership Tng. Assos., Denver, 1979—; condr. exec. devel. workshops U. Colo., Denver, 1979—. Recipient Best in 1976 award GAO. Mem. Am. Soc. for Tng. and Devel., Beta Gamma Sigma. Address: 10462 E Prentice Ave Englewood CO 80111-6200

BAUER, RICHARD PATRICK, electrical engineer; b. Connellsville, Pa., Nov. 29, 1965; s. Walter Stanley Bauer and Margaret June (Mihaly) Emerick; m. Teresa Carol Sokol, July 6, 1991. AAS in Instr. Tech., C.C. of the Air Force, Denver, 1991, AAS in Aircraft Armament Systems, 1992; BSEE, U. Colo., Denver, 1993. Armament system specialist USAF, Lakenheath, Eng., 1986-88; instr. electronics USAF, Denver, 1988-94; mem. tech. staff Hughes Aircraft, Aurora, Colo., 1994—. Mem. IEEE, Assn. Computing Machinery, Power Engring. Soc., Order of Engr. Home: 7670 Jared Way Littleton CO 80125-8974 Office: Hughes Aircraft 16800 E Centretech Pky Aurora CO 80011-9046

BAUER, STEVEN MICHAEL, cost containment engineer; b. Hemet, Calif., Nov. 8, 1949; s. Donald Richard and Jeanne Patricia (Lamont) B.; m. Myung-Hee Min, Sept. 10, 1983; children: Claudia Margaret, Monica Anne. BA in Physics, Calif. State U., San Bernardino, 1971, BS in Physics, 1984, cert. in acctg., 1980, cert. in computer programming, 1986; postgrad., U. Calif., 1974, Calif. State U., 1982-87; cert. in counseling skills, U. Calif. extension, 1991., cert. in alcohol and other drug studies, 1992. Registered engr. in tng., Calif., 1976. Asst. nuclear engr. So. Calif. Edison Co., Rosemead, 1973-76, assoc. nuclear engr., 1976-88, cost containment engr., 1988—; cons. rsch. dept. Jerry L. Pettis Meml. Vets. Hosp., 1978-79, Calif. State U., San Bernardino, 1983-84; cons. planning San Bernardino County, 1975-76; cons. alumni rels. Calif. State U., San. Bernardino, 1989-90. Supporter St. Labre Indian Sch., 1984, Asian Relief Fund, 1985—, So. Poverty Law Ctr., Amnesty Internat., Freedom Writer, 1988; mem. Greenpeace, Wilderness Soc., Internat. Platform Assn.; supporter United Negro Coll. Fund., 1985, vol., 1988; vol. counselor San Bernardino Girl's Juvenile Hall, ARC, 1990—; fellow Casa Colina Hosp.; mem. L.A. County Mus. Art; campaign vol. Congressment George E. Brown, 1966; block capt. Neighborhood Watch Assn., sec., 1991-92, v.p., 1992-93, pres., 1994—; chpt. sec. Sierra Club, 1992. Mem. Am. Nuclear Soc. (assoc.), Calif. State U. San Bernardino Alumni Assn. (sec. bd. 1979-80, rep. food com. 1980-82), Nat. Assn. Accts., Astron. Soc. Pacific, Assn. Computing Machinery (assoc.), Ams. for Energy Independence (bd. dirs. 1990—), K.C. (sec., recorder 1989, community dir., Outstanding Svcs. award 1989), Toastmasters, Numismatic Assn. So. Calif., UCLA Alumni (life), Calif. State U. Fullerton Computer Club, Sierra Club (sec. San Gorgonio chpt. 1992). Home and Office: 131 Monroe Ct San Bernardino CA 92408-4137

BAUGH, ROBERT H., construction executive; b. 1926. BS in Civil Engring., U. Wash., 1950. Engr. Peter Kiewit & Sons Inc., Seattle, 1950-55, John H. Sellen Constrn. Co., Seattle, 1950-55; officer Baugh Constrn. Co. Inc., Seattle, 1955—. Office: Baugh Enterprises Inc 900 Poplar Pl S Seattle WA 98144-2830*

BAUGHN, ALFRED FAIRHURST, lawyer; b. Florence, Ariz., May 1, 1912; s. Otis James and Mary Holman (Fairhurst) B.; m. Barbara Hobbs, June 17, 1935; children: Brent F., Barbara E. AB, U. So. Calif., 1935, JD, 1938. Bar: Calif. 1938, U.S. Dist. Ct. (so. dist.) Calif. 1939, U.S. Ct. Appeals (9th cir.) 1945, U.S. Dist. Ct. Ariz. 1948, Ariz. 1959, U.S. Supreme Ct. 1967. With Title Guarantee & Trust, L.A., 1937-41; corp. counsel Pacific Western Oil Co., 1942-43; pvt. practice law, L.A. and Hollywood, Calif., 1943-56; head Ariz. atty. Signal/Garrett Co., 1956-77, ret., 1977; pvt. practice law, Ariz. and Calif., 1977—; Ariz. Assn. Industries spl. atty. utility rate hearings Ariz. Corp. Commn., 1977-80; bd. dirs. EPI-HAB, Inc., 1974-90. Adopted by Hopi Indian Chief Seletstewa and Squaw (2d Mesa), 1967; Pres. scholar U. So. Calif., 1931-35. Mem. Ariz. Bar Assn., Calif. Bar Assn., L.A. Philanthropic Found. (life), Skull and Scales (U. So. Calif.), Phi Alpha Delta (chpt. pres. 1938), Kappa Sigma (pres. L.A. alumni 1945, pres. Phoenix Alumni 1960). Republican. Mem. Christian Ch. Clubs: Hollywood Exch. (pres. 1947); Kiwanis (Phoenix pres. club 1965); Kachina Klub (organizer, charter v.p. 1974), Hon. Order Ky. Cols. (pres. Phoenix chpt. 1980—), Phoenix Teocali of Order Quetzalcoatl (pres. 1984), Ariz. Bola Tie Soc., Masons (Master 1953), Shriners (Potentate 1971), Jesters (head Phoenix Ct. 1969), Internat. Gorillas (chief 1971—).

BAUGHN, WILLIAM HUBERT, former business educator and academic administrator; b. Marshall County, Ala., Aug. 27, 1918; s. J.W. and Beatrice (Jackson) B.; m. Mary Madiera Morris, Feb. 20, 1945; children: Charles Madiera, William Marsteller. BS, U. Ala., 1940; MA, U. Va, 1941, PhD, 1948. Instr. U. Va., 1942-43, asst. prof., 1946-48; assoc. prof., then prof. econs. and bus. adminstrn. La. State U., 1948-56; prof. U. Tex., 1956-62, chmn. fin. dept., 1958-60, assoc. dean Coll. Bus. Adminstrn., 1959-62; assoc. dir. Sch. Banking of South, 1952-66; dean Coll. Bus. and Pub. Adminstrn. U. Mo., 1962-64; dean Coll. Bus. and Adminstrn. U. Colo., 1964-84, pres., 1985, acting chancellor, 1986-87; pres. U. Colo. System, Boulder, 1990-91; pres. Am. Assembly Collegiate Schs. Bus., 1973-74; chmn. Big Eight Athletic Conf., 1970-71, 78-79, 86-87; dir. Stonier Grad. Sch. of Banking, Rutgers U., 1966-86; mem. council Nat. Collegiate Athletic Assn., 1983-86. Author: (with E.W. Walker) Financial Planning and Policy, 1961; editor: (with C.E. Walker) The Bankers' Handbook, 1966, (with C.E. Walker and T.I. Storrs) 3d rev. edit., 1988, (with D. R. Mandich) The International Banking Handbook, 1983. Served to 1st lt. USAAF, World War II; lt. col. Res. Home: 555 Baseline Rd Boulder CO 80302-7421 Office: U Colo System Boulder CO 80309

BAULE, JOHN ALVIN, museum director, consultant; b. Dubuque, Iowa, July 20, 1948; s. Kenneth Edward and Edith (Stiles) B. BA in Math. and Physics summa cum laude, U. Dubuque, 1970; postgrad., Loras Coll., Dubuque, 1972-75, Coll. of St. Thomas, St. Paul, 1990; MA in History of Mus. Studies, SUNY, Oneonta, 1979. Dir. St. Lawrence County Hist. Assn.,

Canton, N.Y., 1976-86, Hennepin County Hist. Soc., Mpls., 1986-90; assoc. dir. Hist. Soc. Western Pa., Pitts., 1990-92; dir. Yakima (Wash.) Valley Mus., 1992—; interpretive cons. Minn. Hist. Soc., Hennepin History Mus. and City of Mpls., 1992; mus. aid panelist N.Y. State Coun. on Arts, N.Y.C., 1983-86; grant reviewer Inst. Mus. Svcs., Washington, 1988-91; mem. long-range planning com. Am. Swedish Inst., Mpls., 1988-90; mem. St. Anthony Falls Heritage Bd., Mpls., 1988-90; founding chmn. Preservation Adv. Bd., Canton, 1978-82; trustee, mem. exec. com., workshop leader, speaker, sec. corp. Regional Conf. Hist. Agys., Manlius, N.Y., 1978-84; also others. Contbr. articles to profl. publs. Coord. 50th Anniversary Exhbn., Mpls. Aquatennial Assn., 1989; performer, treas. Grasse River Cmty. Theater, Canton, 1977-86; mem. citizens adv. group West River Parkway Task Force, Mpls., 1988-89; pres. Rivermill Townhomes Assn., 1987-90; chmn. entertainment div. 4th of July Cmty. Celebration Com., 1993—. Recipient North Country citation St. Lawrence U., Canton, 1986, pub. commendation Hennepin County Bd. Commrs., 1990; fellow Bush Found., 1990. Mem. Am. Assn. for State and Local History, Am. Assn. Mus., Mid-Atlantic Mus. Conf., Midwest Mus. Conf., Wash. Assn. Mus., Rotary. Home: 1800 River Rd Apt 18 Yakima WA 98902-6209 Office: Yakima Valley Mus 2105 Tieton Dr Yakima WA 98902-3766

BAUM, CARL EDWARD, electromagnetic theorist; b. Binghamton, N.Y., Feb. 6, 1940; s. George Theodore and Evelyn Monica (Bliven) B. BS with honors, Calif. Inst. Tech., 1962, MS, 1963, PhD, 1969. Commd. 2d lt. USAF, 1962; advanced through grades to capt., 1967, resigned, 1971; project officer Phillips Lab. (formerly Air Force Weapons Lab.), Kirtland AFB, N.Mex., 1963-71, sr. scientist for electromagnetics, 1971—; pres. SUMMA Found.; U.S. del. to gen. assembly Internat. Union Radio Sci., Lima, Peru, 1975, Helsinki, Finland, 1978, Washington, 1981, Florence, Italy, 1984, Tel Aviv, 1987, Prague, Czechoslovakia, 1990, Kyoto, Japan, 1993; mem. Commn. B U.S. Nat. Com., 1975—, Commn. E, 1982—, Commn. A, 1990—. Author: (with others) Transient Electromagnetic Fields, 1976, Electromagnetic Scattering, 1978, Acoustic, Electromagnetic and Elastic Wave Scattering, 1980, Fast Electrical and Optical Measurements, 1986, EMP Interaction: Principles, Techniques and Reference Data, 1986, Lightning Electromagnetics, 1990, Modern Radio Science, 1990, Recent Advances in Electromagnetic Theory, 1990, Direct and Inverse Methods in Radar Polarimetry, 1992, Review of Radio Science, 1990-92, Elektromagnetische Vertraglichkeit, 1994; co-author: (with A.P. Stone) Transient Lens Synthesis: Differential Geometry in Electromagnetic Theory, 1991; co-editor: (with H.N. Kritikos) Electromagnetic Symmetry, 1995; contbr. articles to profl. jours. Recipient award Honeywell Corp., 1962, R & D award USAF, 1970, Harold Brown award Air Force Systems Command, 1990; Electromagnetic pulse fellow. Fellow IEEE (Harry Diamond Meml. award, 1987, Richard R. Stoddart award, 1984); mem. Electromagnetics Soc. (pres. 1983-85), Electromagnetics Acad., Sigma Xi, Tau Beta Pi. Roman Catholic. Home: 5116 Eastern Ave SE Apt D Albuquerque NM 87108-5618 Office: Phillips Lab/WSR Kirtland AFB NM 87117

BAUM, KENNETH FRANCIS, medical educator, physician; b. Dyersville, Iowa, Jan. 25, 1950; s. F. Gerald and Clarabelle (Loes) B.; m. Patti Jo Threen, June 17, 1978; children: Alexander, Christina. BS, St. John's U., Collegeville, Minn., 1972; MS, U. N.D., 1975, MB, 1977; MD, U. Pa., 1979. Diplomate Nat. Bd. Med. Examiners, Am. Bd. Internal Medicine (infectious diseases). Intern U. Wis. Hosps., Madison, 1979-80, resident in internal medicine, 1980-82; fellow in infectious diseases U. Colo. Health Scis. Ctr., Denver, 1984-87, instr. divsn. infectious diseases, dept. medicine, 1987-89, asst. prof. divsn. infectious diseases, dept. medicine, 1989—, dir. Sexually Transmitted Diseases Clinic, 1991-92; med. dir. Exclusive Healthcare Colo., 1995—; clin. investigator MRC Sickle Cell Unit, U. W.I., Kingston, Jamaica, 1982-83; staff Riverside Hosp., Wisconsin Rapids, Wis., 1984, Univ. Hosp., Denver, 1987—, Denver VA Med. Ctr., 1989—; med. dir. Exclusive Healthcare of Colo., 1995—; prin. investigator Ctr. for Disease Control Hantavirus Treatment Task Force, State of Colo. Contbr. articles to profl. jours. Nat. Found. for Infectious Diseases and Eli Lilly Corp. fellowship, 1986-87. Mem. Infectious Disease Soc. Am., Soc. Protozoology, Am. Soc. Microbiology. Office: Univ of Colo HSC Divsn Infectious Diseases 4200 E 9th Ave # B168 Denver CO 80220-3706

BAUM, KERRY ROBERT, retired military officer; b. LaGrande, Oreg., May 25, 1939; s. Guy Hiatt B. and Niola (Anderson) Jones; m. Lynda Sue Christian, Dec. 18, 1964; children: Kerry Jr., Tatia D., Christian H., Buffy Jo, Patrick H., Britta Sue, Natalie A. BA in History, Brigham Young U., 1967; MBA in Mktg., Murray State U., 1978; postgrad., Webster Coll., St. Louis, 1979-80. Commd. 2d lt. U.S. Army, 1957, advanced through grades to col., 1990, ret., 1991; mgr. emergency preparedness Brigham Young U., 1993—; U.S. rep. to Major NATO Comdrs. Alert Conf., 1987-90; joint staff rep LIVE OAK, 1986-90. Author, editor: NATO Alert Procedures for Joint Staff, 1988, Transfer of U.S. Forces to NATO Command, 1990, Focal Point Procedures Manual, 1989. Bishop Mormon Ch., Hopkinsville, Ky., 1974-78, councilor, bishopric, Newport, R.I., 1985-86. Decorated Bronze Star, Army Commendation medal, Air Force Commendation medal, Defense Superior Service Medal. Mem. Res. Officer Assn., Ret. Officers Assn. Home: 10938 N 5870 W American Fork UT 84003-9487

BAUM, PHYLLIS GARDNER, travel management consultant; b. Ashtabula, Ohio, Dec. 13, 1930; d. Charles Edward Schneider and Stella Elizabeth (Schaefer) Gardner; m. Kenneth Walter Baum, Oct. 21, 1948 (div. July 1971); children: Deidre Adair, Cynthia Gail; m. Dennis Carl Marquardt, Sept. 22, 1979 (dec. 1991). Grad. high sch., Cleve. Am. Soc. Travel Agents. Travel cons. Fredo Travel Svc., Ashland, Ohio, 1960-66; sales mgr. Travelmart, Willoughby, Ohio, 1966-68; br. mgr. Travelmart, Mentor, Ohio, 1966-68, Diners Fugazy Travel, Sun City, Ariz., 1968-69; travel cons. Jarrett's Travel Svc., Phoenix, 1969-72; sr. cons. Loyal Travel, Phoenix, 1972-74; co-mgr. Phil Carr Travel, Sun City, 1974-77; tour ops. mgr. ASL Travel, Phoenix, 1978-79; owner, mgr. Travel Temporaries, Glendale, Ariz., 1979—; cons. and lectr. in field. Adv. bd. mem. Small Bus. Devel. Ctr., Phoenix, 1986—. Mem. Pacific Asia Travel Assn. Ariz. (bd. dirs. 1986—), Ariz. Women in Travel, NAFE, Altrusa. Republican. Home and Office: Travel Temporaries 10249 N 45th Ave Glendale AZ 85302-1901

BAUM, THOMAS HENLE, writer, director, producer; b. N.Y.C., June 1, 1940; s. Otto Sigmund and Margaret Whitney (Moore) B.; m. Carol Nina Friedland, sept. 1, 1963; children: Will, Fred. BA, Harvard U., 1962. Copywriter NBC Advt. Dept., 1964-67; speechwriter NBC, 1967-68; writer, editor, producer, dir. Writer-dir. TVL series including The Hitchhiker, Nightmare Cafe; writer-dir. TV movies including In the Line of Duty: Taxman, Witness to the Execution, Drop Dead Gorgeous; features include The Manhattan Project, The Sender, Carny, Simon, Hugo the Hippo; after sch. spls. including P.J. and the President's Son, The Horrible Honchos, The Amazing Cosmic Awareness of Duffy Moon; writer: (novels) It Looks Alive to Me!, Carny, Hugo the Hipo, Counterparts.

BAUMAN, EARL WILLIAM, accountant, government official; b. Arcadia, Nebr., Jan. 30, 1916; s. William A. and Gracia M. (Jones) B.; m. Margaret E. Blackman, Oct. 21, 1940 (dec. 1984); children: Carol Ann Bauman Ammerman. Earl William Jr.; m. Jessie C. Morgan, Dec. 23, 1990. BS with honors, U. Wyo., 1938; postgrad. Northwestern U., 1938-39. Acct., Haselmire, Cordle & Co., Casper, Wyo., 1939-42; asst. dir. fin. VA, Chgo., 1946-49, chief acctg. group VA, Washington, 1949-52, supr. systems acctg. GAO, Washington, 1952-55; supervising auditor GAO, Washington, 1955-58; dir. finance, asst. dir. Directorate Acctg. and Fin. Policy, Office Asst. Sec. Def., Washington, 1958-63; tech. asst. to comdr. AF Acctg. and Fin. Ctr., Denver, 1963-73; mem. investigations staff Ho. of Reps. Appropriations Com., 1953-54; prof. acctg. Benjamin Franklin U., 1960-63; mem. exec. council Army Finance, 1963-64; dir. Real Estate Investment Corp., 1962-64; sr. ptnr. EMB Enterprises, 1973—; chmn. Acctg. Careers Council Colo., 1969-71. Chmn. Aurora Citizens Adv. Budget Com., 1975-76; chmn. fin. and taxation com. Denver Met. Study, 1976-78. Served with AUS, 1942-46; col. Res., now ret. CPA. Mem. AICPA, Wyo. Assn. CPAs, Fed. Govt. Accts. Assn. (nat. v.p. 1972-73, pres. Denver 1973-74), Army Finance Assn., Am. Soc. Mil. Comptrollers, Denver Am. Soc. Mil. Comptrollers (pres. 1968-69), Citizens Band Radio Assn. (pres. 1963), Nat. Assn. Ret. Fed. Employees (Aurora 1072 pres. 1986-87), Alpha Kappa Psi, Beta Alpha Psi, Phi Kappa Phi. Club: Columbine Sertoma (pres. 1975-76). Avocations: photography, tennis, collector cars. Home: 536 Newark Ct Aurora CO 80010-4728

BAUMAN, JOSEPH MATTHEW, journalist, author; b. Phila., Apr. 10, 1946; s. Joseph Matthew and Mary Elberta (Stone) B.; m. Cory Jeanne Wilcox, Jan. 7, 1971; 1 child, Sky Joseph Cornelius Bauman. Student, U. Utah, 1965-68, U. Md., 1969-70. Tchr. Trust Territory of Pacific, Ebeye, Marshall Islands, 1966; tchr. Head Start U.S. Cmty. Action Project, Snow Hill, Md., 1967; reporter WBOC-TV, Salisbury, Md., 1968-69; reporter/photographer Beachcomber, Ocean City, Md., 1969, Delmarva News, Selbyville, Del., 1970; editor Beachcomber, Ocean City, 1971; gen. reporter Deseret News, Salt Lake City, 1971-73, environ. specialist, 1973-93, sci./med. reporter, 1993—. Author: Stone House Lands, 1987; editor: The Iron House, 1990. Recipient numerous journalism awards including 1st place personal cols. Utah-Idaho-Spokane AP Assn., 1982, 2d place spot news, 1986, 1st place spot news, 1989, 2d place in ongoing coverage, 1991, 1st place cols. Soc. Profl. Journalists, Utah Headliners chpt., 1984, 2d place, 1988, 1st place series/spl. projects, 1994, 1st place news writing Rocky Mountain Collegiate Press Assn., 1968, 2d place cols., 1968. Mem. Mensa. Office: Deseret News 30 E 100 S Salt Lake City UT 84111-1902

BAUMAN, MARTIN HAROLD, psychiatrist, therapist; b. N.Y.C., Oct. 14, 1936. Pre-med. student, U. Fla., 1952-54, Tulane U., 1955-56, U. Tenn., 1956-67; MD, Northwestern U., 1957-59. Diplomate Am. Bd. Psychiatry and Neurology; lic. Calif., Wis., Vt., N.H. Rotating gen. intern L.A. County Hosp., 1959-60; psychiatric resident U. Wis. Med. Sch., Madison, 1964-67; clin. asst. prof. Dartmouth Coll. Med. Sch., Hanover, N.H., 1967-70; psychiatrist, outpatient, family and couple therapy Sonoma County Mental Health Svcs., Santa Rosa, Calif., 1970-72; pvt. practice Santa Rosa, 1972—; psychiatrist Sonoma State U. Student Health Ctr. and Counseling Svc., Rohnert Park, Calif., 1970—; asst. clin. prof. family and community medicine U. Calif., San Francisco, 1976-82, assoc. clin. prof. family and cmty. medicine, 1982—, assoc. clin. prof. psychiatry, 1982—; co-dir. family therapy program Langley Porter Neuropsychiat. Inst., San Francisco, 1982—; supr. of residents Mendocino State Hosp., Talmage, Claif., 1970-71; psychiatric dir. Social Advocates for Youth, Santa Rosa, 1971-80; assoc. prof. counseling dept., Sonoma State U., 1971—; med. dir. Cherry St. House, Santa Rosa, 1974-81; cons. Dept. Vocat. Rehab, Calif., 1974—, Sonoma County Mental Health Assn., 1976—, Occidental (Calif.) County Health Ctr., 1982—; bd. dirs. Santa Rosa R. House, Family Svc. Agy. Sonoma County; psychiatric supr. U. Calif., San Francisco, 1972—; family practice residency supr. Community Hosp., Santa Rosa, 1972—, lectr. in field. Lectr. in field; contbr. articles to profl. jours. Bd. dirs. Sonoma County Big Brothers, 1977-78; psychiatric work group North Bay Health Systems Agy., 1980-81. Mem. Am. Psychiat. Assn., Am. Acad. Psychotherapists, Am. Assn. Tchrs. of Family Medicine, Am. Family Therapist Acad. (charter), Am. Orthopsychiat. Assn., No. Calif. Psychiat. Assn., Redwood Empire Psychiat. Soc. (sec.-treas. 1976-77, pres. 1978-79, acting pres. 1982—). Office: Waterfall Towers #300 B 2455 Bennett Valley Rd Santa Rosa CA 95404-5663

BAUMAN, WALTER JOSEPH, telecommunication company executive; b. Berlin, Nov. 1, 1946; s. William Louis and Lois Lanora (Sickels) B.; m. Sharon Sue Hatfield, July, 1965 (div. Mar. 1977); children: Leslie Lynn, Julie Ann, Christopher Michael, Brian Anthony. BS in Edn., Mo. Western U., 1970. Tchr. H.S. history Bishop LeBland H.S., St. Joseph, Mo., 1970-76, Sch. Dist. Kansas City, Mo., 1978-81, Metro State Coll., Denver, 1983-84; project coord., field engr. Coaxial Analysts, Denver, 1986-92; pres., owner Infotechs, Colorado Springs, Colo., 1992—. Roman Catholic. Home: 2878 Maverick Dr Colorado Springs CO 80918-1636

BAUMAN, WILLIAM WINTER, financial company executive; b. Washington, July 30, 1961; s. Walter Winter Bauman and Helen Charles (Murrell) Smith; m. Elizabeth Anne Mitchell. BS in Fin. magna cum laude, Ariz. State U., 1983, MBA, 1985. Treasury analyst Greyhound Capital Corp., Phoenix, 1983-84; investment analyst Greyhound Capital Mgmt. Corp., Phoenix, 1984-86; dir. investment analysis Venture Capital Mgmt. Corp., Phoenix, 1986-88; mgr. acquisitions Bell Atlantic Systems Leasing, Internat., Phoenix, 1988-89, portfolio sales manager, 1989-90; gen. mgr. JLC Fin., Phoenix, 1990—. Republican. Presbyterian. Home: 5330 E Calle Del Norte Phoenix AZ 85018-4449 Office: JLC Fin 7878 N 16th St Phoenix AZ 85020-4449

BAUMANN, FREDERICK, management consultant; b. Los Angeles, Nov. 26, 1930; s. Christian Frederick and Marie (Tiemann) B.; m. Flora Jane Sick, May 5, 1962; children: David, Chris, Hilary. B.S., UCLA, 1952; Ph.D., U. Wis., 1956. Rsch. chemist Chevron Rsch. Corp., Richmond, Calif., 1956-65; tech. group leader Varian Instrument Group, Walnut Creek, Calif., 1965-70, rsch. and engring. mgr., 1970-80, mng. dir., Melbourne, Australia, 1980-81, tech. dir., Palo Alto, Calif., 1981-82, mgr. lab. data systems, Walnut Creek, 1983-89, mgr. tech. and strategic planning, 1989-91; cons., 1991—; mem. adv. bd. Analytical Chemistry, Washington, 1972-75; instr. U. Calif.-Berkeley, 1968-74. Contbr. articles to profl. jours. Mem. Am. Chem. Soc., Sigma Xi, Alpha Chi Sigma. Home and Office: 166 Rudgear Dr Walnut Creek CA 94596-6316

BAUMANN, THEODORE ROBERT, aerospace engineer, consultant, army officer; b. Bklyn., May 13, 1932; s. Emil Joseph and Sophie (Reiblein) B.; m. Patricia Louise Drake, Dec. 16, 1967; children: Veronica Ann, Robert Theodore, Joseph Edmund. B in Aerospace Engring., Poly. U., Bklyn., 1954; MS in Aerospace Engring., U. So. Calif., L.A., 1962; grad., US Army C&GS Coll., 1970, Indsl. Coll. of Armed Forces, 1970, US Army War Coll., 1979, Air War Coll., 1982. Structures engr. Glenn L. Martin Co., Balt., 1954-55; structural loads engr. N.Am. Rockwell, L.A., 1958-67; dynamics engr. TRW Systems Group, Redondo Beach, Calif., 1967-71, systems engr., 1971-75, project engr., 1975-84, sr. project engr., 1984-92; cons. SAAB-Scania Aerospace Div., Linkoping, Sweden, 1981-82; asst. dir. Dir. Weapons Systems, U.S. Army, Washington, 1981-85, staff officer Missile & Air Def. System div., 1975-81. Contbr. articles to Machine Design, tech. publs., tech. symposia. Asst. scoutmaster Boy Scouts Am., Downey, Calif., 1985-93; instr. Venice Judo Boys Club, 1966-86. Served from 2d lt. U.S. Army to col. USAR, 1954-88. Decorated Legion of Merit. Mem. AIAA; mem. Soc. Am. Mil. Engrs (life), Am. Legion, Res. Officers Assn. (life), U.S. Judo Fedn., Nat. Rifle Assn. Republican. Roman Catholic. Office: Theodore R Baumann & Assoc 7732 Brunache St Downey CA 90242-2206

BAUMGARTNER, ANTON EDWARD, automotive sales professional; b. N.Y.C., May 18, 1948; s. Hans and Carmen Maria (Figueroa) B.; m. Brenda Lee Lemmon, May 24, 1969 (div. 1990); 1 child, Anton Nicholaus; m. Virginia Thiele, 1992; 1 child, Bree Alexandra. BS, Woodbury U., 1970. Sales mgr. Maywood Bell Ford, Bell, Calif., 1966-69, O.R. Haan, Inc., Santa Ana, Calif., 1969-72; pres. Parkinson Volkswagen, Placentia, Calif., 1972-77; exec. v.p. United Moped, Fountain Valley, Calif., 1975-82; pres. Automobili Intermeccanica, Fountain Valley, 1975-82; gen. mgr. Bishop (Calif.) Volkswagen-Bishop Motors, 1982-85, Beach Imports-Irvine Imports, Newport Beach, Calif., 1985-88; chmn. bd. Stan and Ollie Ins. Co., Santa Ana, Calif., 1989—; exec. v.p. Asterism, Inc., 1992—; mem. faculty, Automotive World Congress, Detroit, 1980. Contbr. articles to weekly serial publs. Mem. Coachbuilders Assn. N.Am. (sec. 1975-78). Office: Asterism Inc 1000 N Kraemer Pl Anaheim CA 92806-2610

BAUMRIND, DIANA, research psychologist; b. N.Y.C., Aug. 23, 1927. A.B., Hunter Coll., 1948; M.A., U. Calif., Berkeley, 1951, Ph.D., 1955. Cert. and lic. psychologist, Calif. Project dir. psychology dept. U. Calif., Berkeley, 1955-58; project dir. Inst. of Human Devel., 1960—, also rsch. psychologist and prin. investigator family socialization and devel. competence project; lectr. and cons. in field; referee for rsch. proposals Grant Found., NIH, 1970—, NSF, 1970—. Contbr. numerous articles to profl. jours. and books; author 2 monographs; mem. editorial bd. Devel. Psychology, 1986-90. Recipient Rsch. Scientist award, NIMH; grantee NIMH, 1955-58, 60-66, Nat. Inst. Child Health and Human Devel., 1967-74, MacArthur Found., Grant Found., 1967-92. Fellow Am. Psychol. Assn., Am. Psychol. Soc. (G. Stanley Hall award 1988); mem. Soc. Research in Child Devel. Office: U Calif Inst of Human Devel 1203 Tolman Hall Berkeley CA 94720

BAUSANO, DONNA ANN, marketing professional; b. Calument, Mich., Oct. 7, 1950; d. Edward Anton and Marion Elizabeth (LaRochelle) Swetich; m. Michael Dennis Bausano, Dec. 21, 1970. BS, No. Mich. U., 1974. Chartered life underwriter. Ins. agt. Equitable Life Ins, Waterbury, Conn., 1974, Mfrs. Life Ins., Findlay, Ohio and Fresno, Calif., 1975-80; brokerage dir. Conn. Mutual Life, Fresno, 1980-91; mktg. dir. Rudy E. Facciani Co., Ins. Mktg. Inc., Fresno, 1991—; instr. Life Underwriter Tng. Coun., Fresno, 1986, 89. Bd. dirs. Saint Agnes Hosp. Found., Fresno, 1986-88; fundraiser Celebrity Waiters Lunch, Fresno, 1986-88; steering com. Women's Network, Fresno, 1986; chmn. Guard-A-Kid Fundraiser, Fresno, 1987. Mem. Fresno chpt. CLU (all offices), Fresno Life Underwriters Assn. (pres. 1987-88, Mem. of Yr. 1986). Republican. Roman Catholic. Office: Rudy E Facciani Ins Mktg 7045 N Fruit Ave Fresno CA 93711-0761

BAUSTIAN, ROBERT FREDERICK, conductor; b. Storm Lake, Iowa, June 4, 1921; s. Alfred A. and Grace E. (Martin) B. MusB, Eastman Sch. Music, 1942, MusM, 1948; postgrad., Zurich (Switzerland) Conservatory., 1948-49. Coach, condr. Zurich Opera, 1949-53; 2d condr. Hessian State Opera, Wiesbaden, Fed. Republic of Germany, 1953-57; prof. orch. U. Kans., Lawrence, 1957-66; prof. conducting Oberlin (Ohio) Coll. Conservatory, 1966-83; condr., coach Merola Program, San Francisco, 1983-87; condr., mus. administr. Santa Fe Opera, 1957-78; adj. Met. Opera auditions, Tex., 1975—; bd. dirs. Santa Fe Opera, 1984-90, Santa Fe Symphony, 1985-93. Guest condr. Ariz. Opera, N.Y.C. Opera, orchs. of Atlanta, Kansas City, Akron, also Spain, France, Yugoslavia. Served with AUS, 1942-46, ETO. Decorated Bronze Star. Mem. Am. Symphony Orch. League, Nat. Opera Assn., Pi Kappa Lambda. Republican. Home and Office: 424 Abeyta St Santa Fe NM 87501-2806

BAUTISTA, ANTHONY HERNANDEZ, biomedical company executive; b. Palo Alto, Calif., Sept. 19, 1955; s. Anthony Hernandez and Velma Rose (Morinan) B.; m. Jill Davis, June 17, 1978; children: Evan Thomas, Laura Anne. AA in Electronic Tech., Coll. of San Mateo, 1976; BSEE, San Jose (Calif.) State U., 1994. Elec. engr. Hewlett Packard, Palo Alto, Calif., 1976-86; engring. mgr. Molecular Devices Corp., Menlo Park, Calif., 1986-91; ops. dir. LJL Biosystems, Inc., Sunnyvale, Calif., 1991—. Mem. Toastmasters (adminstrv. v.p. 1990), Tau Beta Pi.

BAUTISTA, MICHAEL PHILLIP, school system administrator; b. Merced, Calif., June 15, 1952; s. Ynacio and Frances (Garcia) B.; m. Peggy Joyce Watkins, May 26, 1976; children: Michael P., Lisa M. B Music Edn., Emporia State U., 1974, MA, 1975; PhD, Tex. Tech U., 1981; adminstrv. cert., Okla. State U., 1986. Cert. adminstr., Colo., Supt., secondary prin., Okla., bldg. adminstr., Kans. Instr. U. Nebr., Lincoln, 1977-79; asst. prof. U. Tulsa, 1979-82; dir., adminstr. Jenks Pub. Schs., Tulsa, 1983-92; coord., adminstr. Denver Sch. of the Arts, Denver Pub. Schs., 1991—; part-time instr. Tex. Tech U., Lubbock, 1975-77, Tulsa Jr. Coll., 1982-83; theatrical cons. MPB Assocs., Tulsa, 1983-91. Author: Ten Years of Stage Design at the Met (1966-1976); theatrical designer for various stage prodns. Bd. dirs. Carson-Brierly Dance Libr., Denver, 1992—, Friends of Chamber Music, Denver, 1992—; mem. steering com. Harwelden Inst., Tulsa, 1983-91; active Boy Scouts Am.; mem. Mayor's subcom. Arts Edn.; mem. exec. bd. Colo. Arts Assn. for Edn. Recipient Svc. award St. Bernhards Parish, 1990, Amoco award for set design Am. Coll. Theatre Festival, 1989, Documentary citation Kansas City, Mo. Star, 1970. Mem. ASCD, U.S. Inst. Theatre Tech. Roman Catholic. Home: 4802 W 34th Ave Denver CO 80212-1819 Office: Denver Sch Arts 3240 Humboldt St Denver CO 80205-3934

BAWDEN, MURRAY G., construction executive. With Fletcher Challenge Ltd., Auckland, N.Z., 1960—; now pres. Fletcher Pacific Cons. Co., Honolulu, 1985—. Office: Fletcher Pacific Cons Co Ocean View Ct 707 Richards St Ste 400 Honolulu HI 96813-4623*

BAXTER, CAROL CAIRNS, computer scientist; b. Oakland, Calif., Dec. 24, 1940; d. Walter V. and Helen Cairns; m. William F. Baxter, Mar. 27, 1987; 1 child, Bernard Treanor. AB, Stanford U., 1962; MA, U. Calif., Berkeley, 1966, EdD, 1969. Systems engr. Internat. Bus. Machines, Oakland, Calif., 1962-64; rsch. specialist U. Calif., Berkeley, 1969-71; rsch. dir. Ctr. for Advanced Study, Stanford, Calif., 1972-81; dir. computer rsch. Am. Enterprise Inst., Washington, 1981-83; rsch. dir. Ctr. for Advanced Study, Stanford, Calif., 1983-93.

BAXTER, DUBY YVONNE, government official; b. El Campo, Tex., July 21, 1953; d. Ray Eugene and Hazel Evelyn (Roades) Allenson; m. Loran Richard Baxter, April 7, 1979. Student, Alvin Jr. Coll., 1971, Tex. Tech U., 1972; cert. legal sec., Alaska Bus. Coll., 1974; student, Alaska Pacific U., 1981, Anchorage Community Coll., 1981-85, U. Santa Clara, 1982-83; BBA in Mgmt. cum laude, U. Alaska, Anchorage, 1985. Sr. office assoc., legal sec. Municipality of Anchorage, 1975-78; exec. sec. Security Nat. Bank, Anchorage, 1978-80, Alaska Renewable Resources Corp., Anchorage, 1980-82; pers. mgmt. specialist Dept. of Army, Ft. Richardson, Alaska, 1986-87; pers. mgmt. specialist, position classification specialist 10th Mtn. Div. (Light) Civilian Pers. Office, Ft. Drum, N.Y., 1987-89; pers. mgmt. specialist Civilian Pers. Office Alaska Dist. U.S. Army C.E., Anchorage, 1989-90; position classification specialist Civilian Pers. Office, 6th Inf. Divsn. (Light)-USA Garrison, Ft. Richardson, Alaska, 1990-91, 11th AF Cen. Civilian Personnel Office, Elmendorf AFB, Alaska, 1991-93, U.S. Army C.E., Anchorage, 1994—; small bus. owner, 1994—; by-laws com. mem. spl. emphasis program Fed. Women's Program, Ft. Richardson, 1986-87; instr. Prevention of Sexual Harassment, Ft. Richardson, 1986-87. Contbr. Alaska Repertoire Theater, Anchorage, 1982-87; leader Awana Christian Youth Orgn., Anchorage, 1985-87; ch. treas. Watertown (N.Y.) Bible Brethren Ch., 1988-89; mission bd. mem. Anchorage Grace Brethren Ch., 1991-92. Mem. NAFE, Classification and Compensation Soc., Missions Bd., U. Alaska Alumni Assn., Bernese Mountain Dog Club, Safari Club Internat., N.Am. Hunting Club, Concerned Women for Am. Office: USACE CENPA-HR PO Box 898 Anchorage AK 99506-0898

BAXTER, MARVIN RAY, state supreme court judge; b. Fowler, Calif., Jan. 9, 1940; m. Jane Pippert, June 22, 1963; children: Laura, Brent. BA in Econs., Calif. State U., 1962; JD, U. Calif.-Hasting Coll. Law, 1966. Bar: Calif. 1966. Dep. dist. atty. Fresno County, Calif., 1967-68; assoc. Andrews, Andrews, Thaxter & Jones, 1968-70, ptnr., 1971-82; prin. advisor to gov. Office of Gov., 1983-88; assoc. justice Calif. Ct. Appeal (5th dist.), 1988—. Mem. Fresno County Bar Assn. (bd. dirs. 1977-82, pres. 1981), Calif. Young Lawyers Assn. (bd. gov. 1973-76, sec.-treas. 1974-75), Fresno County Young Lawyers Assn. (pres. 1973-74), Fresno County Legal Svcs., Inc. (bd. dirs. 1973-74), U. Calif. Alumni Assn. (pres. 1970-71), Alumni Trust Coun. (pres. 1970-75). Office: Jud Coun of Calif Adminstrv Office Cts 303 2nd St San Francisco CA 94107-1366*

BAXTER, PAT ANN, accountant, educator; b. Oct. 17, 1929; d. Homer H. and Ada Irene (Dowell) Layman; m. Cecil William Baxter Jr., June 6, 1951; children: Cecil William, Michael Kent, Patrick Alan. BA, Kans. Wesleyan U., 1951; MA, U. Tex., 1970. Instr. Belleville (Kans.) High Sch., 1951-54; substitute instr. area high schs., Nevada, Mo., 1954-63; instr. Manpower Devel. & Tng., Nevada, Mo., 1963-64; chief acct. Multi-Svc. Ctr., Bothell, Wash., 1977-80. Com. chair Bothell United Meth. Ch., 1985-89, vice-chair women, 1988-89; mem. King County Libr. Bd., 1986-88. Mem. AAUW. Democrat. Home: 18726 56th Ave NE Seattle WA 98155-4430

BAXTER, WILLIAM FRANCIS, lawyer, educator; b. N.Y.C., July 13, 1929; s. William F. and Ruth C. B.; children—William Francis, Marcia, Stuart Carlton; m. Carol Cairns Treanor, Mar. 27, 1987. AB, Stanford U., 1951, JD, 1956. Bar: Calif. 1956, U.S. Supreme Ct. 1960, D.C. 1983. Asst. prof. law Stanford U., 1956-58, prof. law, 1960—; mem. firm Covington & Burling, Washington, 1958-60; asst. atty. gen. of U.S., Antitrust Div. Washington, 1981-83; of counsel Shearman & Sterling, N.Y.C., 1984—; cons. various intervals to Am. Petroleum Inst., Brookings Instn., Citcorp, Exxon Corp., Fairchild Corp., Fed. Res. Bd., Hoffman-LaRoche, Jet Propulsion Labs., Levi Strauss, Marcor, Nat. Retail Mchts. Assn., Northrup, Siemans Inc., Turner Broadcasting, Visa, Varian Assocs.; cons., project dir. FAA Study on Legal and Econ. Aspects of Aircraft Noise, 1966-68; vis. prof. Yale U. Law Sch., 1964-65; fellow Ctr. for Advanced Study in Behavioral Scis., 1972-73; mem. Pres.'s Task Force on Comm. Policy, 1968, Pres.'s Task Force on Antitrust Policy, 1968. Author: People or Penguins, An Optimum Level of Pollution, 1974; (with others) Retail Banking in Electronic Age: The Law and Economics of Electronic Funds Transfer, 1977; contbr. numerous articles to profl. jours. Served with USN, 1951-54. Mem. Am. Econ. Assn. Office: Stanford U Sch Law Stanford CA 94305

BAYDA, EDWARD DMYTRO, judge; b. Alvena, Sask, Can., Sept. 9, 1931; s. Dmytro Andrew and Mary (Bilinski) B.; m. Marie-Thérèse Yvonne Gagné, May 28, 1953; children: Paula, Christopher, Margot, Marie-Therésè, Sheila, Kathryn. BA, U. Sask., 1951, LLB cum laude, 1953; LLD (hon.), 1989. Bar: Sask. 1954. Barrister, solicitor Regina, Sask., 1953-72; sr. ptnr. Bayda, Halvorson, Scheibel & Thompson, 1966-72; justice Ct. Queen's Bench for Sask., Regina, 1972-74, Ct. Appeal for Sask., Regina, 1974-81; chief justice Sask., Regina, 1981—. Mem. Assiniboia Club (past bd. dirs.). Roman Catholic. Home: 3000 Albert St, Regina, SK Canada S4S 3N7 Office: Ct Appeal Sask Courthouse, 2425 Victoria Ave, Regina, SK Canada S4P 3V7

BAYLESS, RAYMOND, artist; b. Oakland, Calif., 1920. Author 6 books on parapsychology; contbr. articles to profl. jours., publs.; represented in permanent collections including U.S. Dept. Air Force, U.S. dept. Navy, U.S. Dept. State, Art in Embassies Program, Nat. Air and Space Mus., Internat. Aerospace Hall of Fame, Kern Oil and Refining Co., Long Beach, Bank of Am., L.A., Weingart Found., L.A.; exhibits include Air Force Art Collection, Pentagon, Washington, Navy Mus., Washington Ship Yard. Address: 11348 Cashmere St Los Angeles CA 90049-3426

BAYLEY, CHRISTOPHER T., international investment banking executive; b. Seattle, May 25, 1938; s. Emery P. and Dorothy (Dunn) B.; m. Cynthia Conroy, May 31, 1972; children—Elizabeth, Kathryn. AB magna cum laude, Harvard U., 1960, JD, 1966. Bar: Wash. 1967. Dep. atty. gen., chief consumer protection and antitrust div. Atty. Gens. Office, Seattle, 1969-70; pros. atty. King County, Seattle, 1971-79; of counsel Perkins Coie, Seattle, 1979-80, ptnr., 1980-82; sr. v.p. law Burlington Resources (formerly Burlington Northern Inc.), Seattle, 1983-86, corp. affairs, 1986-93; pres., CEO Glacier Park Co., Seattle, 1985-93; chmn. New Pacific Partners, Seattle, 1993—; bd. dirs. Interpoint Corp., The Commerce Bank. Past. chmn. Seattle Found.; bd. dirs. Seattle Internat. Music Festival; past mem. bd. overseers Harvard Coll.; trustee Bush Sch., Discovery Inst.; past mem. bd. govs. The Nature Conservancy. Served with USN, 1960-63, capt. Res. ret., 1985. Mem. University Club, Seattle Tennis Club, Knickerbocker Club (N.Y.C.). Home: 3702 E Prospect St Seattle WA 98112-4442 Office: New Pacific Ptnrs 1411 4th Ave Ste 1430 Seattle WA 98101-2216

BAYLOR, DON EDWARD, professional baseball manager; b. Austin, Tex., June 28, 1949; s. George Edward and Lillian Joyce B.; m. Rebecca Giles, Dec. 12, 1987; 1 child by previous marriage, Don Edward. Student, Miami-Dade Jr. Coll., Miami, Fla., Blinn Jr. Coll., Brenham, Tex. With Balt. Orioles, 1970-76, Oakland Athletics, 1976, 88, California Angels, 1976-82, N.Y. Yankees, 1983-86, Boston Red Sox, 1986-87, Minnesota Twins, 1987; mem. World Series Championship Team, 1987; mgr. Colorado Rockies, Denver, CO, 1992—; Set new career record for hit by pitches; hit safely in 12 consecutive Am. League Championship Series games. Chmn. nat. sports Cystic Fibrosis Found. Recipient Designated Hitter of Yr. award, 1985, 86, Roberto Clemente award, 1985; named Am. League's Most Valuable Player, 1979, Sporting News Player of Yr., 1979; player All-Star Game, 1979. Office: Colorado Rockies 2001 Blake St Denver CO 80205-2010 Office: Major League Baseball Players Assn 805 3rd Ave New York NY 10022-7513

BAYLOR, ELGIN GAY, professional basketball team executive; b. Washington, Sept. 16, 1934; m. Elaine; 1 dau., Krystle. Ed., Coll. Idaho, Seattle U. Profl. basketball player Los Angeles (formerly Minneapolis) Lakers, 1958-72; asst. coach New Orleans Jazz, NBA, 1974-76, coach, 1976-79; exec. v.p., gen. mgr. Los Angeles Clippers, 1986—, v.p. basketaballops. Most Valuable Player, NCAA Tournament, 1958; mem. NBA All-Star Team, 1959-65, 67-70; Rookie of the Yr., NBA, 1959; co-Most Valuable Player, NBA All-Star Game, 1959; named to NBA 35th Anniversary All-Time Team, 1980. Office: Los Angeles Clippers 3939 S Figueroa St Los Angeles CA 90037-1200*

BAYNE, KIM MIKLOFSKY, marketing communications and public relations professional, consultant, author. BA in Music, Colo. Coll.; MA in Computer Resources Mgmt., Webster U. Mktg. communications mgr., mktg. & sales rep. Info. Storage Inc., Colorado Springs, 1985; various positions Laser Magnetic Storage Internat. Co., Colorado Springs, 1986-91; mktg. communications/pub. rels. assoc. Origin Systems, Inc., Colorado Springs, 1991; mktg. communications mgr. Array Microsystems, Inc., Colorado Springs, 1991-93; mktg. communication/pub. rels. specialist, freelance writer Colorado Springs, 1981-93; pres. wolfBayne Communications, Colorado Springs, 1993—; bd. dirs. Colo. Springs Software Roundtable; founder, owner HTMARCOM online Internet High-Tech. Mktg. Comm. Forum, 1994—. Contbr. articles to profl. jours.; speaker in field. Bd. dirs. Keep Colo. Springs Beautiful, Inc., 1993-94. Recipient Excellence award for print ad campaign Bus. Communicators and Mktg. Assn. L.A., 1991, Award of Excellence, Award of Achievement Soc. for Tech. Communication, 1991, numerous awards Toastmasters Internat. Mem. Colo. MARCOM Network (pres. 1993, chairperson Silcon Mountain symposium 1992). Office: wolfBayne Communications PO Box 50287 Colorado Springs CO 80949-0287

BAYS, ERIC, bishop; b. Portage La Prairie, Manitoba, Can., Aug. 10, 1932; s. Percy Clarence and Hilda (Harper) B.; m. Patricia Ann Earle, Dec. 28, 1967; children: Jonathan Edmund, Rebecca Jane. BS, U. Man., Winnipeg, Can., 1955; BA, U. Sask., Saskatoon, Can., 1959; L in Theology, U. Emmanuel Coll., Saskatoon, 1959, DD (hon.), 1987; M in Ministry, Christian Theol. Sem., Indpls., 1974. Ordained to ministry Anglican Ch., 1959. Asst. curate All Saints' Anglican Ch., Winnipeg, 1959-61; lectr. Emmanuel Coll., Saskatoon, 1961-62; mission priest Diocese Caledonia, B.C., 1962-64; novice in religion Community of the Resurrection, Mirfield, Eng., 1964-65; vicar St. Saviour's with St. Catherine Parish, Winnipeg, 1965-67; rector All Saints' Parish, Winnipeg, 1968-76; prof. Coll. Emmanuel/St. Chad, Saskatoon, 1976-81; vice-prin. Coll. of Emmanuel/St. Chad, Saskatoon, 1981-86; bishop Diocese Qu'Appelle, Regina, Sask., 1986—. With RCAF, 1955-59. Office: Diocese of Qu'Appelle, 1501 College Ave, Regina, SK Canada S4P 1B8

BEACH, ARTHUR O'NEAL, lawyer; b. Albuquerque, Feb. 8, 1945; s. William Pearce and Vivian Lucille (Kronig) B.; BBA, U. N.Mex., 1967, JD, 1970; m. Alex Clark Doyle, Sept. 12, 1970; 1 son, Eric Kronig. Bar: N.Mex. 1970. Assoc. Smith & Ransom, Albuquerque, 1970-74; assoc. Keleher & McLeod, Albuquerque, 1974-75, ptnr., 1976-78, shareholder Keleher & McLeod, P.A., Albuquerque, 1978—; teaching asst. U. N. Mex., 1970. Bd. editors Natural Resources Jour., 1968-70. Mem. ABA, State Bar N.Mex. (unauthorized practice of law com., adv. opinions com., med.-legal panel, legal-dental-osteo.-podiatry com., jud. selection com., specialization bd.), Albuquerque Bar Assn. (dir. 1978-82). Democrat. Mem. Christian Sci. Ch. Home: 2015 Dietz Pl NW Albuquerque NM 87107-3240 Office: Keleher & McLeod PA PO Drawer AA Albuquerque NM 87103

BEACH, LEE ROY, psychologist, educator; b. Gallup, N.Mex., Feb. 29, 1936; s. Dearl and Lucile Ruth (Krumtum) B.; m. Barbara Ann Heinrich, Nov. 13, 1971. B.A., Ind. U., 1957; M.A., U. Colo., 1959, Ph.D., 1961. Aviation psychologist U.S. Sch. Aviation Medicine, Pensacola, Fla., 1961-63; human factors officer Office of Naval Research, Washington, 1963-64; postdoctoral research U. Mich., Ann Arbor, 1964-66; faculty dept. psychology U. Wash., Seattle, 1966-89; faculty mgmt. & policy, psychology U. Ariz., Tucson, 1990—, McClelland chair mgmt. & policy, 1989—. Contbr. articles to profl. jours. Recipient Feldman rsch. award, 1981, Disting. Tchr. award U. Wash., 1986, Prof. of Yr. award State of Wash., 1989, nat. teaching award Coun. for Advancement and Support Edn., 1989; fellow NIMH, 1964-66. Fellow Am. Psychol. Soc.; mem. Soc. for Orgnl. Behavior. Office: Coll Bus and Pub Adminstrn Univ Arizona Tucson AZ 85721

BEACH, ROGER C., oil company executive; b. Lincoln, Nebr., Dec. 5, 1936; s. Melvin C. and L. Mayme (Hoham) B.; m. Elaine M. Wilson, Oct. 1954 (div. 1972); children: Kristi, Mark, Anne; m. Karen Lynn Ogden, July 27, 1974. BS, Colo. Sch. Mines, 1961. Registered profl. petroleum refining engr., Calif. With Unocal Corp., L.A., 1961—; mgr. spl. projects Unocal Corp., Los Angeles, 1976-77, dir. planning, 1977-80, v.p. crude supply, 1980-86, pres. refining and mktg., 1986-92, corp. sr. v.p., 1987-1992, pres., 1992-94, CEO, 1994—, now pres. and COO. Vice chmn. bd. trustees Nat. 4-H Coun. Mem. Am. Petroleum Inst. (bd. dirs.), Nat. Petroleum Refiner's Assn., Pres.'s Interchange Exec. Alumni Assn. Office: Unocal Corp PO Box 7600 1201 W 5th St Los Angeles CA 90051*

BEACH, WILLIAM BROWN, psychiatrist, educator; b. Scranton, Pa., Mar. 22, 1921; s. William Brown and Florence Mae (Sluman) B.; m. J. Mona Boyden. BS in Pharmacy, Wash. State U., 1943; MD, U. Chgo., 1947. Diplomate Am. Bd. Psychiatry and Neurology. Intern Highland Alameda County Hosp., Oakland, Calif., 1947-48; psychiatric resident Ea. State Hops., Medical Lake, Wash., 1949-50, Inst. of Living, Hartford, Conn., 1950-51, 52-53; fellow in child psychiatry Langley Porter Neuropsychiat. U. Calif. Sch. Medicine, San Francisco, 1953-55; asst. dir. outpatient dept. Calif. Dept. Mental Hygiene, San Francisco, 1955-57, chief of child psychiatry Berkeley State Mental Hygiene, 1957, regional chief No. Calif. Cmty. Svcs. Divsn., 1957-61, chief bur. mental retardation and children's svcs., 1961-65, dep. dir. cmty. mental health, 1965-71; dep. sec. for mental health and med. programs Pa. Dept. Pub. Welfare, 1971-74; group leader White House Conf. on Children and Youth, Washington, 1960; chmn. Calif. Statewide Conf. on Children and Youth; surveyor, cons. NIMH, HCFA on medicare reimbursement program, 1974-86; intermittent physician surveyor Hosp. Accreditation Svcs., Joint Commn. on Accreditation of Healthcare Orgns., 1987—; participant, cons. Child Psychiatry Residency Tng. Program, Children's Hosp. and Med. Ctr., U. Wash., Dept. Psychiatry and Behavioral Scis., 1989—; vice chmn., chmn. Atlantic States Conf. Contbr. articles to profl. jours. Trustee Vt. Hosp. Assn., 1974-88, Windham Coll., Putney, Vt.; mem. Vt. State Bd. of Health, 1975-88; mem., bd. dirs. Vt. Profl. Rev. Orgn., 1986-88; chmn. Vt. State Mental Health Adv. Coun., 1976-79. Capt. USAF, 1951-52. Fellow Am. Acad. Child Psychiatry (life), Am. Psychiat. Assn. (life, program com. Inst. on Hosp. and Cmty. Psychiatry 1981-86, chmn. 1986), Am. Coll. Mental Health Adminstrs. (founding), Am. Coll. Psychiatrists (long-range planning and policy com. 1986-89, task force on psychiat. edn.); mem. King County Med. Soc., Wash. State Med. Assn.

BEAGLE, JOHN GORDON, real estate broker; b. Spokane, Wash., Dec. 31, 1943; s. Gordon Avril and Sylvia Alberta (Dobbs) B.; m. Shihoko Ledo, Nov. 14, 1964; children: James, Steven, Kevin, Melanie. BS, Mont. State U., 1970; GRI, Realtors Inst., Helena, Mont. Cert. real estate broker. Instr. Kalispell (Mont.) High Sch., 1970-71; gen. mgr. Equity Coop. Assn., Harlem, Mont., 1971-76; owner, operator Howards Pizza, Livingston, Mont., 1976-79; broker, owner ERA Beagle Properties, Sidney, Mont., 1979—. Mem. City Coun. City of Harlem, 1975. With USN, 1963-67. Mem. Mont. Assn. Realtors (v.p. ea. dist. 1982-84), Gateway Bd. Realtors (pres. 1987-88), Kiwanis, Lions. Republican. Mem. Ch. of Christ. Home: Holly & North Dr Sidney MT 59270 Office: ERA Beagle Properties 120 2d Ave SW Sidney MT 59270

BEAIRD, STEVEN EDWARD, fundraising professional; b. Rockford, Ill., June 1, 1955; s. Edward Louis and Jeanette Josephine (Renk) B.; m. Linda Teresa Moreno, May 6, 1988. BA in Comms., U. Wash., 1977; MBA in Mgmt., Marylhurst Coll., Portland, Oreg., 1993. Asst. dir. pub. rels. St. Peter Hosp., Olympia, Wash., 1978-80; devel. dir. Cath. Diocese of Spokane, 1980-84, Cath. Diocese of Tucson, 1984-89; v.p. devel. and pub. rels. Jesuit High Sch., Portland, 1989—. Past bd. dirs. Nat. Cath. Stewardship Coun.; mem. St. Cecilia Parish, Beaverton, Oreg.; bd. dirs. Giving in Oreg. Coun. Mem. N.W. Planned Giving Roundtable, Jesuit Secondary Edn. Assn. Advancement and Alumni Dirs. (nat. chair), Willamette Valley Devel. Officers (bd. dirs.), City Club of Portland, Alpha Delta Phi. Roman Catholic. Office: Jesuit High Sch 9000 SW Beaverton Hwy Portland OR 97225

BEAKE, JOHN, professional football team executive; m. Marcia Beake; children: Jerilyn, Chip, Christopher. Grad., Trenton (N.J.) State Coll.; M degree, Pa. State U. Asst. coach Pa. State U., 1961-62, Kansas City Chiefs, NFL, 1968-74, New Orleans Saints, NFL, 1976-77; offensive coordinator Colo. State U., 1974-76; dir. profl. personnel Denver Broncos, NFL, 1979-83, dir. football ops., 1983-84, asst. gen. mgr., 1984-85, gen. mgr., 1985—. Office: Denver Broncos 13655 Broncos Pky Englewood CO 80112-4150*

BEALL, BURTCH W., JR., architect; b. Columbus, Ohio, Sept. 27, 1925; s. Burtch W. and Etta (Beheler) B.; m. Susan Jane Hunter, June 6, 1949; children: Brent Hunter, Brook Waite. Student, John Carroll U., 1943; BArch, Ohio State U., 1949. Draftsman Brooks & Coddington, Architects, Columbus, 1949-51, William J. Monroe, Architects, Salt Lake City, 1951-53, Lorenzo Young, Architect, Salt Lake City, 1953-54; prin. Burtch W. Beall, Jr., Architect, Salt Lake City, 1954—; vis. lectr. Westminster Coll., 1955; adj. prof. U. Utah, 1955-85, 92-95; treas. Nat. Coun. Archtl. Registration Bds., 1982-84. Restoration architect Salt Lake City and County Bldg; contbr. projects to: A Pictorial History of Architecture in America, America Restored, This Before Architecture. Trustee Utah Found. for Arch., 1985, pres., 1987-91; mem. Utah State Bd. Fine Arts, 1987-95, chmn., 1991-92; chmn. Utah State Capitol Adv. Com., 1986-90, Western States Art Fedn., Bd. trustees, 1991-94; mem. exec. residence com. State of Utah, 1991-95; mem. Utah: A Guide to the State Found. With USN, 1943-45. Recipient several merit and honor awards; Found. fellow Utah Heritage Found., 1985. Fellow AIA; mem. Sigma Alpha Epsilon. Methodist. Club: Masons. Home: 4644 Brookwood Cir Salt Lake City UT 84117-4908 Office: Burtch W Beall Jr Architect 2188 Highland Dr Salt Lake City UT 84106-2837

BEALL, DENNIS RAY, artist, educator; b. Chickasha, Okla., Mar. 13, 1929; s. Roy A. and Lois O. (Phillips) B.; 1 son, Garm. Musician,, Okla. City U., 1950-52; B.A., San Francisco State U., 1953, M.A., 1958. Registrar Oakland (Calif.) Art Mus., 1958; curator Achenbach Found. for Graphic Arts, Calif. Palace of the Legion of Honor, San Francisco, 1958-1965; asst. prof. art San Francisco State U., 1965-69, assoc. prof., 1969-76, prof. art, 1976-92; prof. emeritus, 1992—. Numerous one-man shows of prints, 1957—, including: Award Exhbn. of San Francisco Art Commn., Calif. Coll. Arts and Crafts, 1978, San Francisco U. Art Gallery, 1978, Los Robles Galleries, Palo Alto, Calif.; numerous group shows, 1960—, including, Mills Coll. Art Gallery, Oakland, Calif., Univ. Gallery of Calif. State U., Hayward, 1979, Marshall-Meyers Gallery, 1979, 80, Marin Civic Center Art Galleries, San Rafael, Calif., 1980, San Francisco Mus. Modern Art, 1985; touring exhibit U. Mont., 1987-91; represented in numerous permanent collections including, Library of Congress, Washington, Mus. Modern Art, N.Y.C., Nat. Library of Medicine, Washington, Phila. Mus., U.S. embassy collections, Tokyo, London and other major cities, Victoria and Albert Mus., London, Achenbach Found. for Graphic Arts, Calif. Palace of Legion of Honor, San Francisco, Oakland Art Mus., Phila. Free Library, Roanoke (Va.) Art Center, various colls. and univs. in U.S. Served with USN, 1947-50, PTO. Office: San Francisco State Univ Art Dept 1600 Holloway Ave San Francisco CA 94132-1722

BEALL, DONALD RAY, multi-industry high-technology company executive; b. Beaumont, Calif., Nov. 29, 1938; s. Ray C. and Margaret (Murray) B. BS, San Jose State Coll., 1960; MBA, U. Pitts., 1961; postgrad., UCLA; D of Engring. (hon.), GMI Engring. and Mgmt. Inst., 1994, Milw. Sch. Engring., 1994. With Ford Motor Co., 1961-68; fin. mgmt. positions Newport Beach, Calif., 1961-66; mgr. corp. fin. planning and contracts Phila., 1966-67; controller Palo Alto, Calif., 1967-68; exec. dir. corp. fin. planning N.Am. Rockwell, El Segundo, Calif., 1968-69, exec. v.p. electronics group, 1969-71; exec. v.p. Collins Radio Co., Dallas, 1971-74; pres. Collins Radio Group, Rockwell Internat. Corp., Dallas, 1974-76; corp. v.p., pres. Electronic Ops., Dallas, 1976-77; exec. v.p. Rockwell Internat. Corp., Dallas, 1977-79; pres., chief operating officer Rockwell Internat. Corp., Pitts., 1979-88; chmn. bd., chief exec. officer Rockwell Internat. Corp., Seal Beach, Calif., 1988—; mem. bd. overseers and Grad. Sch. of Mgmt.; bd. visitors U. Calif., Irvine, 1988—; trustee Calif. Inst. Tech.; bd. dirs. Procter & Gamble Co., Amoco Corp., Times-Mirror Corp., L.A. World Affairs Coun.; mem. Bus. Higher Edn. Forum, Bus. Coun., Bus. Roundtable, SRI Adv. Coun., Coun. on Competitiveness. Recipient Exemplary Leadership in Mgmt. award John E. Anderson Sch. Mgmt., UCLA, 1991, Excellence in Tech. award Gartner Group, 1991, Spirit of Achievement award Jr. Achievement of So. Calif., 1993, Fleet Adm. Chester W. Nimitz award Navy League, 1995. Fellow AIAA, Soc. Mfg. Engrs.; mem. Navy League U.S., Young Pres.'s Orgn., Sigma Alpha Epsilon, Beta Gamma Sigma. Office: Rockwell Internat Corp PO Box 4250 2201 Seal Beach Rd Seal Beach CA 90740-8250

BEAM, WILLIAM WASHINGTON, III, data coordinator; b. L.A., Jan. 21, 1960; s. William Washington and Ada Frances (Towler) B. BS, UCLA, 1982; MA, U. Wash., 1985. Paralegal Arco, L.A., 1985-88, programmer, 1988-90, data coord., 1990-94, network adminstr., 1994—. Mem. Am. Econ. Assn. Office: Arco 515 S Flower St Ste 4661 Los Angeles CA 90071-2201

BEAN, DONNA RAE, healthcare facility executive; b. Wichita, Kans., Dec. 31, 1950; d. Roy E. and Esther E. (Young) B. BS, Azusa (Calif.) Pacific U., 1972; MT, San Bernardino (Calif.) Hosp., 1974; MBA, Boise (Idaho) State U., 1984. Med. technologist Caldwell (Idaho) Health Ctr., 1975-77, supr. lab., 1978-80, clinic mgr., 1980-81; systems mgr. Payette (Idaho) Health Care, 1982-85; dir. material svcs./PI Holy Rosary Med. Ctr., Ontario, Calif., 1985—; lab. cons. State of Idaho, Boise, 1985—; systems cons. in field. Boise State U. scholar, 1982, 83, Whittenberger Found. scholar, 1983-84. Mem. Am. Soc. Clin. Pathologists, Healthcare Material Mgmt. Soc., NAFE. Republican. Methodist. Office: Holy Rosary Med Ctr 351 SW 9th St Ontario OR 97914-2639

BEAN, JAMES WOOLSON, JR., bank executive; b. Pasadena, Calif., Aug. 11, 1947; s. James Woolson and Mildred (Hand) B.; m. Linda Badi Bean, Oct. 18, 1978 (div. Dec. 1988); children: Linda Marie, Christina Suzanne. BA in Econs., Pomona Coll., 1969; MBA in Fin., Harvard U., 1971; PhD, Claremont U., 1994. CPA, Calif. Sr. mgr. Price Waterhouse, N.Y.C., 1971-84; div. contr. 1st Interstate Bank, L.A., 1984-85; chief auditor Glendale (Calif.) Fed. Bank, 1985—. Mem. com. Tournament of Roses, Pasadena. Mem. Fin. Execs. Inst., Fin. Mgrs. Soc. (pres. 1989-90), La Canada Country Club. Republican. Presbyterian. Home: 715 Lakewood Pl Pasadena CA 91106-3923 Office: Glendale Fed Bank 401 N Brand Blvd Glendale CA 91203-2307

BEAR, GREGORY DALE, writer, illustrator; b. San Diego, Aug. 20, 1951; s. Dale Franklin and Wilma (Merriman) B.; m. Christina Marie Nielsen, Jan. 11, 1975 (div. 1981); m. Astrid May Anderson, June 18, 1983; children: Erik William, Alexandra. AB in English, San Diego State U., 1973. Tech. writer, host Reuben H. Fleet Space Theater, 1973; freelance writer, 1975—. Author: Hegira, 1979, Psychlone, 1979, Beyond Heaven's River, 1980, Strength of Stones, 1981, The Wind From a Burning Woman, 1983, The Infinity Concerto, 1984, Blood Music, 1985, Eon, 1985, The Serpent Mage, 1986, The Forge of God, 1987, Eternity, 1988, Tangents, 1989, Heads, 1990, Queen of Angels, 1990, Anvil of Stars, 1992, Moving Mars, 1993 (Nebula award 1994), Song of Earth and Power, 1993, Legacy, 1995; short stories: Blood Music (Hugo and Nebula awards), 1983, Hardfought (Nebula award), 1993, Tangents (Hugo and Nebula awards), 1987; editor: New Legends, 1995. Cons. Citizen's Adv. Council on Nat. Space Policy, Tarzana, Calif., 1983-84. Mem. Sci. Fiction Writers of Am. (editor Forum 1983-84, chmn. grievance com. 1985-86, v.p. 1987, pres. 1988-90). Home: 506 Lakeview Rd Lynnwood WA 98037-2141

BEARDS, JULIE ANN, medical/surgical nurse, consultant; b. Hampton, Iowa, May 22, 1955; d. Carl Henry and O. Ramona (Murley) Neumann; m. William M. Beards, July 11, 1988. Diploma in Nursing, Allen Sch. Nursing, Waterloo, Iowa, 1976; BSN, U. Iowa, 1982. Staff nurse/head nurse/supr. VA Hosp., Iowa City, Iowa, 1977-81; head nurse Ptnrs. Health Maint. Orgn., Tucson, 1982-83; adminstr./supr. Hillhaven Hosp. Home Care, Tucson, 1983-84; utilization review coord. Univ., Physicians, Inc., Tucson, 1984-87; nurse supr. Catalina In Home Care, Inc., Tucson, 1987; quality assurance analyst Univ. Med. Ctr., Tucson, 1987-88; health educator/staff nurse N.Y. Telephone Portamedic, White Plains, N.Y., 1988-89; dir. nursing/cons. Tucson Care Givers, Inc., 1988-90; dir. quality mgmt. Charter Hosp., Tucson, 1990-91; quality mgmt. specialist, float nurse VA Hosp., Tucson, 1991—; health educator NYNEX/Hager-Wiley Fitness Concepts, Inc., White Plains, 1988-89; health care cons. Tucson Care Givers, Inc., 1988—. Vol. ARC Crisis Ctr./Free Med. Clinic, Iowa City, 1977-82; chmn. Home Health Agencies/Tucson, 1984; healthcare rep. Leads Club, Tucson, 1989—. Mem. Ariz. Assn. Quality Assurance Profls. (editorial bd. newsletter 1991—), Nat. Assn. Quality Assurance Profls., Nurses Orgn. of Vets. Hosps. Home: 10201 N 44th Dr Apt 2115 Glendale AZ 85302-2018 Office: Vets Med Ctr 3601 S 6th Ave Tucson AZ 85723-0001

BEARLEY, WILLIAM LEON, consulting company executive; b. Hays, Kans., June 6, 1938; s. William L. and Wilma M. (Sechrist) B.; BS, U. Wyo., 1969, MEd, 1964; EdD, U. La Verne, 1983; M.H.R.D., Univ. Assos. Grad. Sch. Human Resource Devel., 1980; also grad. Lab. Edn. Intern Program; m. Diane Lee Kiser, Dec. 15, 1967. Tchr. math. Baldwin Park Unified Sch. Dist., Baldwin Park, Calif., 1961-64, chmn. dept. math, 1962-64; chmn. math. dept. Citrus Coll., Azusa, Calif., 1965-69, chmn. data processing dept., 1969-80, dir. computing and info. systems, 1972-80; pres. Computer Info. Assocs., Inc., Pasadena, Calif., 1980-82; prof. Edn. Mgmt., U. LaVerne, 1982—; v.p. Organizational Universe Systems, Valley Ctr., Calif., 1985—; cons., trainer info. resource mgmt., 1981—. Mem. Data Processing Mgmt. Assn. (cert.), Am. Soc. Tng. and Devel., Orgn. Devel. Network, Assn. Computing Machinery, Assn. Systems Mgmt. (cert.), Phi Delta Kappa. Author/co-author computer software, books and articles in field. Home: 18825 Santee Lane Valley Center CA 92082-4023 Office: U La Verne 1950 3rd St La Verne CA 91750-4401

BEARMAN, SCOTT IRVIN, internist, educator; b. Coral Gables, Fla., Nov. 16, 1954; s. Julius Edwin and Martha (Ebstein) B.; m. Theresa Ann Skalabrin, Mar. 17, 1990; children: Samuel Asher, Anna Gabriel. BS, Tufts U., 1976, MD, 1981. Diplomate Am. Bd. Internal Medicine. Intern in Medicine U. Wash., Seattle, 1981-82, resident in Medicine, 1982-84, fellow in Med. Oncology Fred Hutchinson Cancer Rsch. Ctr., 1984-87, assoc. clin. rsch. Fred Hutchinson Cancer Rsch. Ctr., 1987-91; clin. dir. Bone Marrow Transplant program Health Scis. Ctr. U. Colo., Denver, 1991—, assoc. prof. Medicine, 1991—, co-dir. Clin. Investigations Core Cancer Ctr., 1992—, prin. investigator S.W. Oncology Group, 1992—. Reviewer: (jours.) Blood, Bone Marrow Transplantation, Am. Jour. Hematology, Clin. Cancer Rsch., Jour. AMA, Experimental Hematology, Annals of Internal Medicine. Mem. ACP, Am. Fedn. Clin. Rsch., Am. Soc. Hematology, Am. Soc. Clin. Oncology, Am. Soc. Blood and Marrow Transplantation, Phi Beta Kappa. Office: U Colo Health Sci Ctr PO Box B 190 4200 E 9th Ave Denver CO 80220-3706

BEARNSON, LISA DOWNS, editor-in-chief; b. Yankton, S.D., Jan. 26, 1964; d. Robert Henry and Clarine Elizabeth (Kiehl) Downs; m. Steven R. Bearnson, Nov. 25, 1989; children: Steven Kade, Collin Downs. BA, Brigham Young U., 1988. Customer support rep. WordPerfect Corp., Orem, Utah, 1988-89; asst. editor WordPerfect Mag., Orem, 1989-90; sr. editor Wordperfect Mag., Orem, 1990-91, editor-in-chief, 1992—. Republican. Ch. Jesus Christ Latter Day Saints. Office: WordPerfect Mag 270 W Center St Orem UT 84057

BEARSON, JOHN MICHAEL, utility company executive; b. Fargo, N.D., Sept. 8, 1951; s. John Martin and Helen (Durkin) B.; div. 1972; 1 child, Amy Lynn. AA, Ft. Steilcoom C.C., 1975. Field investigator Tacoma City Light. Served in U.S. Army, 1971-73. Democrat. Roman Catholic. Home: 4210 222d St E Spanaway WA 98387-6815 Office: Tacoma City Light 3604 35th St S PO Box 11007 Tacoma WA 98411-0007

BEARWALD, JEAN HAYNES, company executive; b. San Francisco, Aug. 31, 1924; d. Joseph Robert and Edna Haynes (Goudey) Bearwald; m. William Henry Sherburn, Apr. 12, 1969 (dec. 1970); 1 child by previous marriage, David Richard Cross. BA, Stephens Coll., Columbia, Mo., 1945. Adminstrv. asst. Bearwald & Assocs., Sacramento, 1966-78; acct. Truck Parts Co., Sand City, Calif., 1979-80; pres., chief exec. officer Bearwald and Assocs., Fresno, Calif., 1980-89, Las Vegas, N.Mex., 1989-91; owner Traditions D'Elegance, Santa Fe, 1991—; program dir. hosp. and institution State of Calif. Ann. Conf., Carmel, 1980-82. Chmn. Sunset Serenade Gala, Santa Fe Opera Guild, 1993-94. Republican. Episcopalian. Home and Office: 941 Calle Mejia Apt 1604 Santa Fe NM 87501-1470

BEASLEY, BRUCE MILLER, sculptor; b. L.A., May 20, 1939; s. Robert Seth and Bernice (Palmer) B.; m. Laurence Leaute, May 21, 1973; children: Julian Bernard, Celia Beranice. Student, Dartmouth Coll., 1957-59; B.A., U. Calif. at Berkeley, 1962. bd. dirs. Internat. Sculpture Ctr., Washington.

Sculptor in metal and plastic; solo exhbns. Everett Ellin Gallery, L.A., Kornblee Gallery, N.Y.C., Hansen-Fuller Gallery, San Francisco, David Stuart Gallery, L.A., Andre Emmerich Gallery, N.Y.C., De Young Mus., San Francisco, Santa Barbara Mus. Art, Fine Arts Gallery, San Diego, Sonoma State U., Rhonert Park, Calif., Hooks-Epstein Gallery, Houston, Oakland (Calif.) Mus., Fresno (Calif.) Art Mus., John Natsoulas Gallery, Davis, Calif., Galerie Scheffel, Bad Homburg, Germany, Galerie Utermann, Dortmund, Germany, Kunsthalle Mannheim, Germany, Galerie Rudolfinum, Prague, Czech Republic, Galerie Marie-Louise Wirth, Zurich, Switzerland, Yorkshire Sculpture Park, Eng.; exhibited in group shows Mus. Modern Art, N.Y.C., Guggenheim Mus., N.Y.C., Albright Knox Gallery, Buffalo, LaJolla (Calif.) Art Mus., Musée d'Art Moderne, Paris, San Francisco Mus. Art, Krannert Art Mus. at U. Ill., Jewish Mus., N.Y.C., Luxembourg Gardens, Paris, Calif. Palace of Legion of Honor, De Young Mus., Middleheim (Fed. Republic of Germany) Sculpture Park, Yorkshire (Eng.) Sculpture Park, Santa Barbara Art Mus., others; represented in permanent collections Mus. Modern Art, Guggenheim Mus., Musée d'Art Moderne, Paris, L.A. County Art Mus., Univ. Art Mus., Berkeley, Oakland (Calif.) Mus., Wichita (Kans.) Art Mus., San Francisco Art Commn., Santa Barbara Art Mus., Dartmouth Coll., U. Nebr.-Lincoln, Kunsthalle Mannheim, Germany, Fine Arts Mus., San Francisco, Xantus Janos Mus., Gyor, Hungary; major sculpture commns. include State of Calif., 1967, Oakland Mus., 1972, City of San Francisco, 1976, U.S. govt., 1976, City of Eugene, Oreg., 1974, City of Salinas, Calif., 1977, Miami Internat. Airport, Fla., 1978, San Francisco Internat. Airport, 1981, Stanford U., 1982, City of Anchorage, Alaska, L.A. Olympic Stadium, 1984, Gateway Ctr., Walnut Creek, Calif., 1991, Fed. Home Loan Bank, San Francisco, 1992, Fresno (Calif.) Art Mus., 1994. Recipient Andre Malraux purchase award Biennale de Paris, 1961. Mem. Nat. Mus. Am. Art, Crocker Art Mus., Internat. Sculpture Ctr. (bd. dirs.). Home: 322 Lewis St Oakland CA 94607-1236

BEASLEY, GREGORY DEAN, electrical engineer; b. Washington, Ind., Aug. 14, 1968; s. Owen Kermit and Annette Yvonne (Walker) B. BSEE, Purdue U., 1991. EIT. Coop. engr. GM, Flint, Mich., 1987-90. With USN, 1990—. Mem. IEEE, U.S. Naval Inst. Republican. Roman Catholic. Home: 4927 Brighton Ave San Diego CA 92107

BEASLEY, JAMES MERCER, travel environmentalist, consultant; b. Chgo., May 2, 1923; s. Charles Mercer Beasley and Katherine Audrey (Browne) Beasley Parker. Founder, pres. El Gato Theatres, various locations, 1937-68; pres. Beasley Cons., San Francisco, San Diego, 1968-76; chmn. Travel Coun. of the World, Inc., San Diego, 1976—. Author numerous and varied publs. Catalyst candidate for Pres. U.S., San Diego, 1970-76, 86; mem. adv. bd. Calif. Water Resources Bd., Sacramento, 1974-76. With USN, 1942-44, PTO. Recipient Life Achievement award Travel Coun. of the World, 1994.

BEASON, JAMES DOUGLAS, military officer, physicist, writer, educator; b. Alexandria, La., Dec. 3, 1953; s. James Larry and Martha Grace (McCluney) B.; m. Cynthia Marie Olsen, Jan. 20, 1979; children: Amanda Grace, Tamara Jo. Student, La. Tech. U., 1972-73; BS in Physics and Math., U.S. Air Force Acad., 1977; MS in Physics, U. N.Mex., 1980, PhD in Physics, 1983; student, Def. U., Ft. McNair, Washington, 1995—. Commd. 2d lt. USAF, 1977, advanced through grades to lt. col., 1991; computational physicist USAF Weapons Lab. USAF, Kirtland AFB, N.Mex., 1977-79, sect. chief nuclear effects, 1979-80; asst. prof. physics USAF Acad. USAF, Colorado Springs, Colo., 1983-86; chief plasma physics USAF, Kirtland AFB, N.Mex., 1986-88, chief advanced concepts, 1988-90, deputy dir. Advanced Weapons and Survivability Philips Lab., 1991; sr. policy analyst White House Office Sci. and Tech. Policy, Washington, 1991-93; assoc. prof. physics USAF Acad., Colorado Springs, Colo., 1993-94, dir. faculty rsch., 1994-95; rsch. advisor NRC; cons. Lawrence Livermore (Calif.) Nat. Lab., 1985, Ames Rsch. Ctr., NASA, Sunnyvale, Calif., 1985, cons. White House, 1993—; mem. Stafford Commn., Synthesis Group for Nat. Space Exploration Initiative, Fed. Coord. Coun. for Sci., Engring. and Tech. Working Group, 1991-93; adj. Nat. Space Coun., Office of V.P. of U.S., 1992-93; exec. sec. White House TOPAZ Rev. Com., 1994-95. Author: Reture to Honor, 1989, Assault on Alpha Base, 1990, Lifeline, 1990, Strike Eagle, 1991, The Trinity Paradox, 1991, Assemblers of Infinity, 1993, Virtural Destruction, 1996, Ill Wind, 1995. Bd. dirs. Albuquerque Bible Coll., 1987-88. Decorated Def. Superior Svc. medal with oak leaf cluster; finalist NEBULA award Sci. Fiction Writers Am. Best Novel of Yr., 1994. Mem. Am. Phys. Soc., Sci. Fiction Writers Am., Air Force Assn., Air Force Acad. Assn. of Grads. Presbyterian. Office: ICAF Nat Def U Sci Office Ft McNair Washington DC 80840

BEATHARD, BOBBY, professional football team executive; b. Zanesville, Ohio, Jan. 24, 1937; m. Christine Beathard; children: Kurt, Jeff, Casey, James. Student, Calif. Poly. Inst. Scout Kansas City Chiefs, Am. Football League, 1963-68, Atlanta Falcons, NFL, 1968-72; dir. player personnel Miami Dolphins, NFL, 1972-78; gen. mgr. Washington Redskins, NFL, 1978-89, San Diego Chargers, NFL, 1990—. Office: San Diego Chargers Jack Murphy Stadium PO Box 609609 San Diego CA 92160-9609*

BEATTIE, GEORGE CHAPIN, orthopaedic surgeon; b. Bowling Green, Ohio, Sept. 24, 1919; s. George Wilson and Mary Turner (Chapin) B.; m. Nancy U. Fant, Mar. 1, 1947; children: Michael, Suzanne, Eric. BA, Bowling Green U., 1939; MD, U. Chgo., 1943. Diplomate Am. Bd. Orthopaedic Surgery. Commd. lt. (j.g.) MC USN, 1943, advanced through grades to lt. comdr., 1951; med. officer, intern U.S. Naval Hosp., Great Lakes, Ill., 1943-44; resident, fellow in orthopaedic surgery Lahey Clinic, Boston, 1944; ward med. officer orthopaedic services Naval Hosp., Guam, 1944-46; sr. med. officer USN, Manus Island, Papua New Guinea, 1946; resident tng. in orthopaedic surgery U.S. Naval Hosp. St. Albans, N.Y.C., 1947-48; resident in orthopaedic surgery Children's Hosp., Boston, 1949; asst. chief orthopaedic surgery U.S. Naval Hosp. Oak Knoll, Oakland, Calif., 1950-52; comdg. officer med. co. 1st Marine Div. Med. Bn., Republic of Korea, 1952-53; chief orthopaedic service Dept. Phys. Medicine and Navy Amputee Ctr. U.S. Naval Hosp., Phila., 1954; resigned USN, 1954; practice medicine specializing in orthopaedic surgery San Francisco, 1954—; co-chmn. handicapping conditions com. Health Action Study San Mateo County, 1965; 1st chmn. orthopaedic sect. surg. dept. Peninsula Hosp. and Med. Ctr., Burlingame, Calif., 1967, chmn. rehab. service, 1967-71, chmn. phys. therapy and rehab. com., 1956—, vice chmn. orthopaedic dept., 1973-76, chmn., 1977-79; med. dir. research and rehab. ctr. San Mateo (Calif.) County Soc. Crippled Children and Adults, 1958-63; mem. exec. com. Harold D. Chope Community Hosp., San Mateo, 1971-76, chief, co-chmn. orthopaedic sect., 1971-76; chief orthopaedic surg. sect. Mills Meml. Hosp., San Mateo, 1976-78; others. Contbr. articles to profl. jours. Active Indian Guides, 1972-77; pres. Calif. Easter Seal Soc., 1969-71. Decorated Bronze Star. Fellow Am. Acad. Orthopaedic Surgeons (exhibit com. 1979-86); mem. AMA (Billings Bronze medal 1954), Western Orthopaedic Assn. (pres., bd. dirs. 1986), Leroy Abbott Orthopaedic Soc. U. Calif. San Francisco (assoc. clin. prof.), Alpha Omega Alpha. Office: 1828 El Camino Real Ste 606 Burlingame CA 94010-3120

BEAUDET, ROBERT ARTHUR, chemistry educator; b. Woonsocket, R.I., Aug. 18, 1935; s. Ralph Edgar and Blanche L. (Pelchat) B.; m. Julia Marie Hughes, Sept. 14, 1957; children: Susan, Donna, Debra, Stephanie, Michelle, David, Nicole. BS, Worchester Poly. Inst., 1957; MA, Harvard U., 1960, PhD, 1962. Asst. prof. chemistry U. So. Calif., Los Angeles, 1963-66, assoc. prof., 1966-72, prof., 1972—. Served to lt. U.S. Army, 1961-63. Fellow NSF, 1957-61, A.P. Sloan Found., 1966-67, Humboldt, Cologne, Germany, 1974-75. Mem. Am. Chem. Soc., Am. Phys. Soc. Roman Catholic. Home: 887 Vallombrosa Dr Pasadena CA 91107-5642

BEAUMONT, MONA, artist; b. Paris; d. Jacques Hippolyte and Elsie M. (Didisheim) Marx. m. William G. Beaumont; children: Garrett, Kevin. Postgrad., Harvard U., Fogg Mus., Cambridge, Mass. One-woman shows include Galeria Proteo, Mexico City, Gumps Gallery, San Francisco, Palace of Legion of Honor, San Francisco, L'Armitiere Gallery, Rouen, France, Hoover Gallery, San Francisco, San Francisco Mus. Modern Art, Galeria Van der Voort, San Francisco, William Sawyer Gallery, San Francisco, Palo Alto (Calif.) Cultural Ctr., Galerie Alexandre Monnet, Brussels, Honolulu Acad. Arts; group shows include San Francisco Mus. Modern Art, San Francisco Art Inst., DeYoung Meml. Mus., San Francisco, Grey Found. Tour of Asia, Bell Telephone Invitational, Chgo., Richmond Art Ctr., L.A. County Mus. Art, Galerie Zodiaque, Geneva, Galerie Le Manoir, La Chaux de Fonds, Switzerland, William Sawyer Meml. Exhibit, San Francisco, others; represented in permanent collections Oakland (Calif.) Mus. Art, City and County of San Francisco, Hoover Found., San Francisco, Grey Found., Washington, Bulart Found., San Francisco; also numerous pvt. collections. Mem. Soc. for Encouragement of Contemporary Art, Bay Area Graphic Art Coun., San Francisco Art Inst., San Francisco Mus. Modern Art, Capp Street Project, others. Recipient ann. painting award Jack London Square, 2 ann. awards San Francisco Women Artists, One-man Show award San Francisco Art Festival; purchase award Grey Found., San Francisco Women Artists (2), San Francisco Art Festival; included in Printworld Internat., Internat. Art Diary, Am. Artists, N.Y. Art Rev., Calif. Art Rev., Art in San Francisco Bay Area. Address: 1087 Upper Happy Valley Rd Lafayette CA 94549-2805

BEAUVAIS, EDWARD R., airline executive; b. 1936. BS, Regis Coll., 1958. With Frontier Airlines, 1960-63; asst. v.p. Airwest Inc., Phoenix, 1963-70; chief exec. officer, prin. Beauvais Roberts and Kurth, 1970-81; with Am. West Airlines, Inc., 1981—; now chmn., chief exec. officer. Office: Am W Airlines Inc 4000 E Sky Harbor Blvd Phoenix AZ 85034-3802

BEAVER, WILLIAM LAWRENCE, retired scientist, educator, consultant; b. Yucalpa, Calif., Oct. 9, 1920; s. Ivon Rosco and Velma (White) B.; m. May Merit Beaver, Oct. 21, 1944; children: Judith Elizabeth, Robert Alan. BS, U. Calif., Berkeley, 1944, PhD, 1951. Sr. scientist Varian Assocs., Palo Alto, Calif., 1951-66, mgr. microwave tube rsch., 1957-61, mgr. applied math., 1965-66; rsch. fellow in physiology sch. medicine Stanford (Calif.) U., 1966-67; sr. scientist Varian Assocs., Palo Alto, Calif., 1967-74; adj. prof. Stanford (Calif.) U., 1974-78; cons. Varian Assocs., Palo Alto, Calif., 1974-78, Medical Graphics Corp., St. Paul, 1982-85, UCLA Sch. Medicine, 1968—. Contbr. articles to profl. jours. With U.S. Army, 1944-46, ETO. Mem. Am. Physiol. Soc., IEEE (sr. life mem.), Sigma Xi. Home: P O Box 390157 Mountain View CA 94039

BEAVERS, LYNNE, real estate broker, importer company executive; b. Donaldsonville, La., Jan. 9, 1946; d. A. L. and Ena May (Esneault) B.; m. William J. Prickett, Nov. 11, 1978 (dec. July 1985). BS in Home Econs., U. Tex., Austin, 1968. Buyer Neiman Marcus, Dallas, 1968-78; real estate broker Lynne Beavers and Assocs., L.A., 1978—; pres., owner BPA Collectables Inc., L.A., 1985—; pres. L.A. (Calif.)-LDS Feliz-Silverlake Real Estate Brokers Assn., 1983-84; dir. L.A. (Calif.) Assn. Realtors, 1987-94. Auction chmn. Pacific Asia Mus., Pasadena, Calif., 1993, 94. Mem. HK Trade Assn., LA-Guangzhon Soc., KKM Alumnae Assn. (reference chmn. 1978-81). Democrat. Home: 2017 N Kenmore Ave Los Angeles CA 90027-1813 Office: BPA Collectables Inc Lynne Beavers & Assocs 1315 W Pico Blvd Los Angeles CA 90015-2421

BEBOUT, ELI DANIEL, oil executive; b. Rawlings, Wyo., Oct. 14, 1946; s. Hugh and Dessie Bebout; m. Lorraine J. Tavares; children: Jordan, Jentry, Reagen, Taggert. BEE, U. Wyo., 1969. With U.S. Energy Co., Riverton, Wyo., 1972-75; field engr. Am. Bechtel Corp., Green River, Wyo., 1975-76; pres. NUPEC Resources, Inc., Riverton, 1976-83, Smith-Collins Pharm. Inc., Riverton, 1976-83; cons. Nucor Drilling, Inc., Riverton, 1984-87, v.p., 1987—. Mem. Wyo. Ho. of Reps.; mem. appropriations com. Mgmt. Coun. Republican. Office: Nucor Drilling PO Box 112 Riverton WY 82501-0112

BECERRA, XAVIER, congressman, lawyer; b. Sacramento, Jan. 26, 1958; s. Manuel and Maria Teresa B.; m. Carolina Reyes, 1987. AB, Stanford U., 1980, JD, 1984. Atty., 1984—; dir. dist. office State Senator Art Torres, L.A.; dep. atty. gen. dept. justice, Calif., 1987-90; assemblyman, 59th dist. State of Calif., 1990-93; mem. 103rd Congress from 30th Calif. dist., 1993—; mem. com. econ. & ednl. opportunity com. judiciary; majority whip-at-large; mem. Congl. Hispanic Caucus. Mem. Mexican-Am. Bar Assn., Calif. Bar Assn., Assn. Calif. State Attys. and Adminstrv. Law Judges. Democrat. Office: House of Representatives 1119 Longworth Bldg Washington DC 20515-0530*

BECHER, STUART LORENZ, writer, planetarium show producer; b. Harvey, Ill., May 16, 1949; s. Raymond Edwin and Margurite Elsie (Lorenzen) B.; m. Debra Balbach. BS, U. Ill., Chgo., 1980. Engring. technician Grayhill Electronics, La Grange, Ill., 1977-81; in quality control Knowles Electronics, Franklin park, Ill., 1981-85; R&D technician Sorensen Rsch., Salt Lake City, 1986-87; designer technician Hansen Planetraium, Salt Lake City, 1987—; lectr. in field. Author: (children's show scripts) A Perfect Place for Penguins, 1989, SCIPPI, The Magic Telescope, 1991, (show script) The Endless Horizon, 1992, (book) The Endless Horizon, 1993; writer, dir., prodr. Riders in the Sky, 1995, The Doorway to Doom, 1995. Vol. Pioneer Trails State Park, Salt Lake City, 1991—; served to sgt. USAF, 1967-72, Viet Nam. Office: Hansen Planetraium 15 S State St Salt Lake City UT 84111-1518

BECHTEL, PETER JOHN, biology educator; b. Mpls., Apr. 9, 1943; s. Martin John and Audrey (Jensen) B.; m. Edith Jane Rietfors, 1964; children: Christian, Matthew. BS, Parsons Coll., 1966; PhD, Mich. State U., 1971. Chemist Quaker Oats Co., Chgo., 1966-67; biologist Agrl. Research Service, USDA, Bettsville, Md., 1970-71; research fellow U. Calif., Davis, 1971-75; research expert NIH NCI Mol. Biol., Bethesda, Md., 1976-77; asst. prof. biology Iowa State U., Ames, 1977-80; assoc. prof. U. Ill., Urbana, 1980-86, prof. biology, 1986-90; prof., dept. head food sci. and human nutrition Colo. State U., Ft. Collins, 1990—; vis. prof. dept. med. genetics Med. Nobel Inst. Kavolinska Inst., Stockholm, 1988-89. Editor: Muscle as Food, 1986. Fellow USPHS, Muscular Dystrophy Assn. Am. Mem. Am. Inst. Nutrition, Inst. Food Technologist, Am. Meat Sci. Assn., Am. Soc. Animal Sci. Home: 5607 Hummel Ln Fort Collins CO 80525-9453 Office: Dept Food Sci Human Nutrition 205 Gifford Blvd Colorado State University CO 80523

BECHTEL, STEPHEN DAVISON, JR., engineering company executive; b. Oakland, Calif., May 10, 1925; s. Stephen Davison and Laura (Peart) B.; m. Elizabeth Mead Hogan, June 5, 1946; 5 children. Student, U. Colo., 1943-44; BS, Purdue U., 1946, D. in Engring. (hon.), 1972; MBA, Stanford U., 1948; DSc (hon.), U. Colo., 1981. Registered profl. engr., N.Y., Mich., Alaska, Calif., Md., Hawaii, Ohio, D.C., Va., Ill. Engring. and mgmt. positions Bechtel Corp., San Francisco, 1941-60, pres., 1960-73, chmn. of cos. in Bechtel group, 1973-80; chmn. Bechtel Group, Inc., 1980-90, chmn. emeritus, 1990—; bd. dirs. Remington Arms, former chmn., mem. bus. coun., emeritus life councillor, past chmn. conf. bd.; chmn. emeritus Fremont Group, Inc., Sequoia Ventures, Inc., 1995—. Trustee, mem., past chmn. bldg. and grounds com. Calif. Inst. Tech.; mem. pres.'s coun. Purdue U.; adv. coun. Inst. Internat. Studies, bd. visitors, former charter mem., adv. coun. Stanford U. Grad. Sch. Bus. With USMC, 1943-46. Decorated officer French Legion of Honor; recipient Disting. Alumnus award Purdue U., 1964, U. Colo., 1978, Ernest C. Arbuckle Disting. Alumnus award Stanford Grad. Sch. Bus., 1974, Disting. Engring. Alumnus award 1979; named Man of Yr. Engring. News-Record, 1974, Outstanding Achievement in Constrn. award Moles, 1977, Chmn.'s award Am. Assn. Engring. Soc., 1982, Washington award Western Soc. Engrs., 1985, Nat. Medal Tech. from Pres. Bush, 1991, Golden Beaver award 1992, Herbert Hoover medal 1980. Fellow ASCE (Engring. Mgmt. award 1979, Pres. award 1985), AAAS, Instn. Chem. Engrs. (U.K., hon.); mem. AIME, NSPE (hon. chmn. Nat. Engrs. Week 1990), Nat. Acad. Engring. (past chmn.), Calif. Acad. Scis. (hon. trustee), Am. Soc. French Legion Honor (bd. dirs., Disting. Achievement medal 1994), Am. Acad. Arts and Scis., Royal Acad. Engring. (U.K., fgn. mem.), Pacific Union Club, Bohemian Club, San Francisco Golf Club, Claremont Country Club, Cypress Point Club, Met. Club (Washington), St. Francis Yacht Club, Bear River Club (Utah), Wild Goose Club (Calif.), Chi Epsilon, Tau Beta Pi. Office: Bechtel Group Inc PO Box 193965 San Francisco CA 94119

BECHTELHEIMER, ROBERT RUSSELL, retired career naval officer; b. Camden, Ark., May 13, 1932; s. Jesse Cletus and Margie (Launius) B.; m. Dottie Logan, Nov. 5, 1966; children: Russ, David, Lisa, John. BS, South Ark. U., 1954. Cert. internal auditor. Commd. ensign USN, 1954, advanced through grades to capt., 1975, ret., 1982; dir. West region Naval Audit Svc., San Diego, 1982-89; chief fin. officer Rockwell Fed. Credit Union, Downey, Calif., 1989-90; pres. RFCU Svcs., Inc., Downey, 1990-91, Rockwell Fed. Credit Union, Downey, 1991-95. Mem. Kiwanis (sec. 1988-89, v.p. 1989-90, pres. 1990-91). Methodist.

BECHTLE, ROBERT ALAN, artist, educator; b. San Francisco, May 14, 1932; m. Nancy Elizabeth Dalton, 1963 (div. 1982); children: Max Robert, Anne Elizabeth; m. Whitney Chadwick, 1982. B.A., Calif. Coll. Arts and Crafts, Oakland, 1954, M.F.A., 1958; postgrad., U. Calif.-Berkeley, 1960-61. Graphic designer Kaiser Industries, Oakland, 1956-59; instr. Calif. Coll. Arts and Crafts, 1957-61, assoc. prof. to prof.; lectr. U. Calif.-Berkeley, 1965-66; vis. artist U. Calif.-Davis, 1966-68; assoc. prof. San Francisco State U., 1968-76, prof., 1976—. One-man shows Mus. of Art, San Francisco, 1959, 64, Berkeley Gallery, 1965, Richmond Art Ctr. (Calif.), 1965, U. Calif.-Davis, 1967, O.K. Harris Gallery, N.Y.C., 1971, 74, 76, 81, 84, 87, 92, Berggruen Gallery, San Francisco, 1972, E.B. Crocker Art Gallery, Sacramento, 1972, Univ. Art Mus., U. Calif.-Berkeley, 1979, Daniel Weinberg Gallery, Santa Monica, 1991, Gallery Paul Anglim, San Francisco, 1991, San Francisco Mus. Modern Art, 1991; exhibited in group shows San Francisco Art Inst., 1966, Whitney Mus. N.Y.C., 1967, Milw. Art Ctr., 1969, Mus. Contemporary Art, Chgo., 1971, Serpentine Gallery, London, 1973, Toledo Mus. Art, 1975, San Francisco Mus. Modern Art, 1976, Pushkin Fine Arts Mus., Moscow, 1978, Pa. Acad. Fine Arts, Phila., 1981, San Antonio Mus. Art, 1981, Pa. Acad. Fine Arts, Phila, 1981, Calif. Palace of Legion of Honor, San Francisco, 1983, Mus. Contemporary Art, L.A., 1984, San Francisco Mus. Modern Art, 1985, Univ. Art Mus., U. Calif., Berkeley, 1987; represented in permanent collections Achenbach Found. for Graphic Arts, San Francisco, Chase Manhattan Bank, N.Y.C., E.B. Crocker Art Gallery, Sacramento, Gibbes Art Gallery, S.C., High Mus. Art, Atlanta, Hunter Art Mus., Chattanooga, Library of Congress, Washington, Lowe Art Mus.-U. Miami, Coral Gables, Fla., Mills Coll., Oakland, Mus. Modern Art, N.Y.C., Met. Mus., N.Y.C., Neue Gal der Stadt Aachen, West Germany, Oakland Mus., San Francisco Mus. Modern Art, Univ. Art Mus.-U. Calif-Berkeley, Fine Arts Mus. of San Diego, Rose Art Mus., Brandeis U., Waltham, Mass., U. Nebr.-Lincoln, Whitney Mus., N.Y.C., Guggenheim Mus., N.Y.C., Nat. Academician, Nat. Acad. Design, 1993. Served with U.S. Army, 1954-56. Recipient James D. Phelan award, 1965; named Nat. Academician, Nat. Acad. Design, 1993; Nat. Endowment for Arts grantee, 1977, 83, 89, Guggenheim grantee, 1986. Office: San Francisco State U Dept Art San Francisco CA 94132

BECK, COLLEEN MARGUERITE, archaeologist; b. San Jose, Calif., Feb. 21, 1951; d. William Robert and Willa Rose (Moore) Beck; m. William Keith Kolb; children: William Logan Kolb, Alexa Rose Kolb. BA, U. Calif., Berkeley, 1973, MA, 1974, PhD, 1979. Dir. Agy. for Conservation Archaeology, Eastern N.Mex. U., Portales, 1980-83, asst. prof., 1983-84; rsch. assoc. Lowie Mus. Anthropology, Berkeley, 1985-89; asst. rsch. prof. Desert Rsch. Inst., Las Vegas, 1990-92, dep. dir. quaternary scis. ctr., 1992—; postdoctoral fellow Carnegie Mus. Natural History, Pitts., 1979-80; mem. N.Mex. Hist. Preservatio Adv. Bd., Santa Fe, 1981-86; mem. San Joaquin County Historic Records Commn., Stockton, Calif., 1986-89. Author: Ancient Roads on the North Coast of Peru, 1979; editor: Views of the Jornada Mogollon, 1984; author articles. Mem. tech. adv. bd. Las Vegas Sch. Dsit., 1994. NSF fellow, 197-76; Tinker Found. grantee, 1974-77. Fellow Am. Anthropology Assn. (life); mem. Soc. for Am. Archaeology, Nev. Archaeology Assn. (bd. dirs. 1993—, pres. 1995—), Archaeo-Nev. Soc., Nat. Trust for Hist. Preservation, Inst. Andean Studies (life), Nev. State Mus. Hist. Soc. Office: Desert Rsch Inst 755 E Flamingo Rd Las Vegas NV 89119-7363

BECK, DORIS OLSON, library media director; b. Kingsville, Tex., June 4, 1930; d. Thomas Leon and Estelle (Fosselman) Olson; m. John Roland Beck, Feb. 9, 1951; children: Elizabeth Joan, Thomas Roland, Patricia Lind, John William. BS in Chemistry, Tex. A & I Coll., 1949, BSChemE, 1950; MLS, Wayne State U., 1975. Cert. secondary educator with libr. endorsement, Ariz. Chemist Patterson's Lab., Harlingen, Tex., 1950-51; asst. libr. Tex. A & I Coll., Kingsville, Tex., 1951; chemist U.S. Geol. Svc., Stillwater, Okla., 1951-53; bookkeeper, nurse's aide McKenzie Co. Hosp., Watford City, N.D., 1953-54; math. tchr. Prescott Jr. High, Corpus Christi, Tex., 1954; chemist U.S. Geol. Svc., Columbus, Ohio, 1957-58; math. tchr. Christiansberg (Va.) High Sch., 1967-69; sci. tchr. East Jr. High Sch., Farmington, Mich., 1969-70; sci./math. tchr. Jane Addams Jr. High Sch., Royal Oak, Mich., 1970-78; math support Oakland Vocat. Sch., Royal Oak, 1978-79; head libr. S.W. Bapt. Coll., Pontiac, Mich., 1977-79; libr. media dir. Humboldt (Ariz.) Jr. High, 1979-87, Bradshaw Mt. Jr. High, Dewey, Ariz., 1987—; site based com. Bradshaw Mt. Jr. High Sch., Dewey, Ariz., 1992—. Mem. Ariz. Libr. Assn., Ariz. Ednl. Media Assn., Delta Kappa Gamma, Alpha Delta Kappa. Republican. Baptist. Home: 3829 Valorie PO Box 25824 Prescott Valley AZ 86312 Office: Bradshaw Mt Jr High Sch Humboldt Unified Sch Dist Dewey AZ 86327

BECK, GORDON EUGENE, art history educator, consultant; b. Goshen, Ind., Mar. 23, 1929; s. Ralph Lea and Lydia Elizabeth (Greenlee) B.; m. Elizabeth Alice Arnholt, Mar. 22, 1951; children: Anne Elizabeth, Susan Elizabeth, Stephen Lea, John Lyons. BA, Bowling Green State U., 1951; MA, Western Res. U., 1952; PhD, U. Ill., 1964; postdoctoral student, Cini Found., Venice, Italy, 1979. Asst. instr. U. Ill., Urbana, 1954-56; instr. Bowling Green (Ohio) State U., 1956-57; instr., dir. univ. theatre U. Kans., Lawrence, 1957-65; asst. prof., dir. univ. theatre Cornell U., Ithaca, N.Y., 1965-71; prof. art history Evergreen State Coll., Olympia, Wash., 1971-94, prof. emeritus art history and archaeology, 1994—; cons. European travel, Euro-Files, Olympia; dir. U. Kans. Theatre, 1957-65, Cornell U. Cinema, 1965-70, Mus. and Monuments Program, Olympia, 1975—. Editor, Players Mag., 1961-67; contbr. articles to Theatre Ann., 1964-69, Ency. World Drama, 1969; producer feature film, Branches, 1970. Cpl. M.C., U.S. Army, 1952-54. Mem. Coll. Art Assn., Mediaeval Acad. Am., Am. Soc. Aesthetics. Democrat. Home: 2406 18th Ave NW Olympia WA 98502-4119 Office: Evergreen State Coll 3313 Library Bldg Olympia WA 98505

BECK, JEROME JOSEPH, health care administrator, biomedical technologist; b. Mesa, Ariz., Nov. 7, 1957; s. Robert Leon and Marie Margaret (Curry) B.; m. Catherine Elizabeth Williams, June 27, 1981; 1 child, John Robert. BSBA, U. Phoenix, 1989. Cert. hemodialysis technologist Bd. of Nephrology Examiners Nursing & Tech. Dialysis unit housekeeper Good Samaritan Hosp., Phoenix, 1976-78, dialysis equipment technician, 1978-81, dialysis sr. equipment technician, 1981-83, coord. tech. staff devel., 1983-88, mgr. dialysis tech. svcs., 1988-89; dir. tech. svcs. East Valley Dialysis Svcs., Mesa, 1989-91, program dir., 1991-93; ops. mgr. Renalwest L.C. (formerly East Valley Dialysis Svcs.), Mesa, 1993—; bd. dirs. Bd. Nephrology Examiners, Madison, Wis., 1990—; mem. renal disease and detoxification com. Assn. for the Advancement of Med. Instrumentation, 1989—; mem. technicians com. ESRD Network VI, Albuquerque, 1984-85; nephrology conf. lectr. nationwide. Contbr. articles to profl. jours. Mem. Nat. Assn. Nephrology Technologists (bd. dirs., western v.p. 1989-91, Torchbearer award 1994). Republican. Office: Renalwest LC 1750 S Mesa Dr Ste 110 Mesa AZ 85210-6226

BECK, JOHN CHRISTEN, sociologist, educator, businessman; b. Provo, Utah, Dec. 7, 1959; s. Jay Vern and Allida Faye (Ellison) B.; m. Martha Nibley, June 21, 1983; children: Katherine, Adam, Elizabeth. BA, Harvard U., 1983, MA, 1988, PhD, 1989. Pub. The Asian Century Bus. Report, Provo, 1991—; prof. Am. Grad. Sch. of Internat. Mgmt., Glendale, Ariz., 1994—; sr. strategic advisor Royal Govt. of Cambodia, 1994—. Author: Breaking the Cycle of Compulsive Behavior, 1990, The Change of a Lifetime, 1994; contbr. articles to profl. jours. Harvard Bus. Sch. grantee, 1988, fellow, 1984-89; recipient Hoopes Rsch. prize Harvard U., 1983; Rotary scholar, 1983-84. Office: Asian Bus Info PO Box 4 Provo UT 84603-0004

BECK, JOHN ROLAND, environmental consultant; b. Las Vegas, N.Mex., Feb. 26, 1929; s. Roland L. and Betty L. (Shrock) B.; m. Doris A. Olson, Feb. 9, 1951; children: Elizabeth J., Thomas R., Patricia L., John William. BS, Okla. A. & M. U., 1950; MS, Okla. State U., 1957; postgrad., U. Tex., 1954, George Washington U., 1965. Registered sanitarian, Ohio, Ariz.; cert. wildlife biologist. Wildlife researcher King Ranch, Kingsville, Tex., 1950-51; faculty Inst. Human Physiology U. Tenn., Martin, 1954-55; rsch. biologist FWS, USDI, Grangeville, Idaho, 1955-57; ctr. dir. Job Corps, OEO, Indiahoma, Okla., 1965-67; supr. animal control biology FWS, USDI, 1953-69; operating v.p. Bio-Svc. Corp., Troy, Mich., 1969-78; pres. BECS

Ltd., Prescott, Ariz., 1981-85; spl. asst. USDA - APHIS, Washington, 1986-87; prin. cons. Biol. Environ. Cons. Svc. Inc., Phoenix, 1978-93; faculty assoc. Ariz. State U., Tempe, 1980-89; expert witness in bus. evaluations, 1979-94; expert witness in pesticide litigations, 1989-94; participant fin. seminars, 1980-85. Sr. author: Managing Service for Success, 1987, 2d edit., 1991; columnist mo. column on pest control in 2 mags., 1980-88; contbr. articles to profl. jours. Capt. USAR, 1950-62. Fellow Royal Soc. Health, N.Y. Explorers Soc.; mem. ASTM, Wildlife soc., Sigma Xi. Republican. Baptist.

BECK, JONATHAN P., French language educator; b. Mpls., Aug. 28, 1947; s. Joseph H. and Sophia Belle (Shapero) B.; m. Sharon McInerney, June 20, 1970 (div. Mar. 1980); 1 child, Jonathan Matthew; m. Ann K. Farmer, Jan. 9, 1992; children: Nicholas William, Galen Joseph. BA, Columbia U., 1970; MA, Harvard U., 1971, PhD, 1974. Asst. prof. Emory U., Atlanta, 1974-80; assoc. prof. U. Ariz., Tucson, 1983-86, prof. French, 1987—, dept. head French and Italian, 1985-90; vis. assoc. prof. Stanford (Calif.) U., 1980. Author: Le Concil de Basle, 1979, Theatre et propagande, 1986; mem. editl. bd. Romance Philology, 1989—; contbr. articles to profl. jours. Grantee Am. Coun. Learned Socs., 1977, 86; Guggenheim fellow John Simon Guggenheim Meml. Found., 1982. Home: 1138 High Ct Berkeley CA 94708 Office: U Ariz Dept French Tucson AZ 85721

BECK, KENNETH EUGENE, English as a second language educator; b. Modesto, Calif., Jan. 27, 1945; s. Curtis E. and Helen A. (Kiernan) B.; life ptnr. Andrew C. Wong. MA in Linguistics, U. Calif, Berkeley, 1968; MA in Teaching English as Fgn. Lang., Calif. State U., San Francisco, 19973. Instr. ESL San Francisco C.C. Dist., 1971—; rschr. in field of Am. ind. lang. Co-author: It's Up To You, Language Skills and Strategies for Getting a Job, 1980; involved in materials devel. Mem. TESOL. Home: 26 Brighton Ave San Francisco CA 94112-2316

BECK, RODNEY ROY, professional baseball player; b. Burbank, Calif., Aug. 3, 1968. With Oakland (Calif.) Athletics, 1986-88; pitcher San Francisco Giants, 1988—; mem. Nat. League All-Star Team, 1993, 94. Office: San Francisco Giants Candlestick Park San Francisco CA 94124*

BECK, THOMAS EDWIN, business owner, furniture maker; b. Stockton, Calif., Dec. 31, 1946; s. Harold Marquis and Verna (Johnson) B.; m. Ellen Marie Hill, June 1, 1973; 1 child, Alexander Hill-Beck. Student, San Francisco City Coll., 1964-66, U. Calif., Berkeley, 1966-67, Coll. of the Desert, 1984-85, Calif. Poly. State U., 1985. Carpenter U.B.C. of Am., Portland, Oreg., 1972—; cabinetmaker apprentice Drago Dimitri/Furniture, Calgary, Alta., Can., 1976; owner, operator Thomas Beck Fine Furniture, Morongo Valley, Calif., 1981—; cons. San Bernadino County Regional Employment. Conscientious objector, Vietnam War. Recipient Best of Show award Bellevue Art Mus., 1990; Design in Wood award Calif. Expo., 1993. Home and Office: 52355 Altadena Dr Morongo Valley CA 92256-9671

BECK, TIMOTHY DANIEL, human resources specialist, consultant; b. Santa Monica, Calif., Mar. 21, 1953; s. James Daniel and Bettye June (Cisler) B.; m. Marcia Ann Smith, Jan. 16, 1977; children: Tracy Beth and Erica Brandy (twins), Jenna Michelle. AA, El Camino Community Coll., 1974; BA, Calif. State U., Northridge, 1979. Registered health underwriter, registered employee benefits cons. Candidate cert. employee benefit specialist, group claims supr. Prudential Ins. Co. Am., L.A., 1973-79; employee benefits cons. Olanie, Hurst & Hemrich, L.A., 1979-81; v.p. policyholder svc. dept. Health Maintenance Life Ins. Co., Fountain Valley, Calif., 1981; v.p. Robert E. French Ins. Svcs., Inc., Huntington Beach, Calif., 1981-85; v.p., mng. cons. employee benefits Warren, McVeigh & Griffin, Inc., Newport Beach, Calif., 1985-91; mng. cons. employee benefits A. Foster Higgins and Co., Inc., 1991—; mem. Kaiser Permanente Orange County Consumer Coun., 1987—; mem. pub. edn. com. Calif. Health Decision, 1988—; mem. bus. and health adv. panel Am. Health Pub.; speaker to confs. and profl. socs. Creator, contbg. editor Employee Benefits Mgmt. Letter, 1985-91; contbr. articles to profl. publs. Mem. Internat. Found. Employee Benefits, Nat. Assn. Health Underwriters, Calif. Assn. Health Underwriters, Employee Benefit Planning Assn. So. Calif. (bd. dirs. 1992-93), So. Calif. Assn. Benefit Plan Adminstrs., Orange County Assn. Health Underwriters (founder, 1st v.p. 1987-88), Orange County Employee Benefit Coun., Calif. State U. Northridge Alumni Assn.

BECKER, ANNE MARGARET, neonatal nurse; b. San Rafael, Calif., Sept. 4, 1953; d. Robert E. and Helen (Grondorf) Spitzer; m. Michael Becker, Nov. 21, 1973; children: Miriam, Davina. Diploma, St. Luke's Sch. Nursing, San Francisco, 1974; AS, San Francisco Community Coll., 1974; BS, U. Calif., San Francisco, 1984, MS, 1986. RN, Calif.; cert. high-risk perinatal nurse ANCC. Staff nurse II Children's Hosp. Med. Ctr., Oakland, Calif., 1974-86; outreach educator Children's Hosp., San Francisco, 1986; staff nurse Med. Personnel Pool, San Francisco, 1986-87; staff nurse II-IV Stanford (Calif.) U. Hosp., 1987-91; staff nurse IV Lucile Salter Packard Children's Hosp., Stanford, Palo Alto, Calif., 1991—, acting clin. nurse specialist, 1993—. Mem. editorial bd. Neonatal Network jour., Petaluma, Calif., 1987—; peer reviewer Jour. Am. Acad. Nurse Practitioners, Pitts., 1990-92; author (poetry) Waiting, 1989. Vol. Quention Kopp for State Senator Campaign, South San Francisco, 1990; pres. local chpt. PTA, South San Francisco, 1987. Mem. ANA (exec. com. coun. on maternal-child nursing 1993-94, exec. com. mem. coun. for acute care nursing practice 1994-95), ANCC (perinatal nurse test devel. com. 1989-92, bd. on cert. for maternal-child nursing 1989-91), Calif. Nurses Assn. (chair nursing practice commn. 1991-93, commr. 1991-94, co-founder, vice chair coun. on children and families 1991-94), Nat. Assn. Neonatal Nurses, U. Calif. San Francisco Nursing Alumni Assn. (editorial cons. grad. nursing students 1991-92). Republican. Episcopalian. Home: 612 Stonegate Dr South San Francisco CA 94080-1564

BECKER, BRUCE DOUGLAS, mechanical engineer; b. Tacoma, Mar. 19, 1959; s. Walter A. and Mary Jane (Barr) B.; m. Jamie M. Russell, Sept. 10, 1988; 1 child, Catherine Anne. BSME, Wash. State U., 1981. Registered profl. engr., Oreg. Design engr. Hyster Corp., Portland, Oreg., 1981-85; devel. engr. Precision Castparts Corp., Portland, 1985-95; design engr. Autostack Corp., Portland, 1995—. Eagle scout Boy Scouts Am., Pullman, Wash., 1975; citizen amb. People to People Internat., People's Republic of China, 1985; mem. Milw. Presbyn. Ch., 1993—. Mem. ASME (assoc.), NSPE. Home: 9323 SE 29th Ave Milwaukie OR 97222-6401 Office: Autostack 4350 NW Front Ave Portland OR 97210-1422

BECKER, ELEEN MARIE, secondary education educator; b. Seattle, Aug. 23, 1949; d. Glenn O.N. and Marjorie Eleen (Hays) Riedasch; m. Richard Lee Northcutt, Aug. 12, 1972 (dec. Jan. 1984); children: Brian Lee, Sara Eleen; m. Larry Lee Becker, May 19, 1990. BA in History, Wash. State U., 1972; MA in Teaching, Whitworth Coll., 1985. Cert. tchr. Wash. Substitute tchr. Spokane (Wash.) Sch. Dist. 81, 1979-84; tchr. talented and gifted in history and English Mead Sch. Dist. 354, Spokane, Wash., 1984—; chmn. Mead Vocabulary Com., 1989-91, co-adv. Northwood Jr. High Sch. Writing Club, Spokane, 1988-90, mem. Secondary Lang. Arts Curriculum, Spokane, 1985-92, edn. svc. dist. 101 mini-grant com., 1986-94, Mead essential learnings com., 1991-92, Mead writing assessment com., 1991—, mem. exec. com. Learning Across Curriculum, Spokane, 1987-90, co-adv. State History Day Northwood Jr. High Sch., 1987-91; presenter Nat. Sci. Conf., 1989, student-tchr. seminar Washington State U., 1991-93; varsity coach girls golf team Mead High Sch., 1993—. Mem. Parent Adv. Coun. Woodridge Elem. Sch., Spokane, 1987-88, asst. dir. Wash. Jr. Golf Assn., Spokane, 1988—, v.p. Ascension Luth. Ch. Women, Spokane, 1981-82, asst. supt. Sunday Sch., 1982-84. Mem. Nat. Coun. Tchrs. English, Nat. Coun. Social Studies, Internat. Order Rainbow Girls (adv. bd. pres. 1978-80), Secondary Social Studies Com., Order Ea. Star. Home: 10017 N Larchwood St Spokane WA 99208-9480

BECKER, JULIETTE, psychologist, marriage and family therapist; b. L.A., Sept. 22, 1938; d. Louis Joseph and Elissa Cecelia (Bevacqua) Cevola; m. Richard Charles Sprenger, Aug. 13, 1960 (div. Dec. 1984); children: Lisa Anne, Stephen Louis, Gina Marie, Paul Joseph, Gretchen Lynette; m. Vance Benjiman Becker, Nov. 7, 1986. BA in Psychology, Calif. State U., Fullerton, 1983; M in Marriage and Family Therapy, U.S. Internat. U., 1985; PhD in Clin. Psychology, William Lyon U., 1988. Therapist Villa Park (Calif.) Psychol. Svcs., 1985-88, psychologist, 1988—. Mem. APA, Am. Assn. Marriage, Family and Child Therapists, Calif. Assn. Marriage, Family and Child Therapists. Office: Villa Park Psychol Svcs 17871 Santiago Blvd Ste 206 Orange CA 92667-4131

BECKER, PATRICIA WINIFRED, hotel and casino company executive. BS, U. Nev., Reno; JD, Calif. Western Sch. Law. Bar: Calif. 1976, Nev. 1976. Sr. v.p., gen. counsel Harrah's, Reno, Nev.

BECKER, ROBERT DEAN, academic administrator, educator, author, consultant; b. Sutton, Nebr., Dec. 15, 1936; s. E.A. McNulty and Leona (Peters) Becker; m. V. Joliece McClendon, Dec. 14, 1986. BA, U. Colo., Colorado Springs, 1967; MA, U. Colo., 1969, PhD, 1972. Internal auditor Calif. Fed. Savs. and Loan, L.A., 1960-61; comptr. Security Savs. and Loan, Colorado Springs, 1961-65; instr. history Midwestern State U., Wichita Falls, Tex., 1970-74, asst. prof., 1974-78, assoc. prof., 1978-85; prof. gen. studies, history Western State Coll., Gunnison, Colo., 1988-95, coord. core II and gen. studies, 1988-91, dean core and gen. studies, 1991-94, dean acad. programs, 1994-95; dean Sch. Arts and Scis. Clayton State Coll., Morrow, Ga., 1995—. Author: Pathways to the Present, 1979; editor, contbr.: Out of the Tempest, 1977; contbr. articles to profl. jours. NEH grantee, 1983; NDEA Title IV fellow, 1969-70; named Hardin Prof., Hardin Found., 1980. Mem. ASCD, Am. Assn. for Higher Edn., Assn. for Gen. and Liberal Studies, Am. Coun. Acad. Deans, Inst. for Humane Studies, Phi Alpha Theta. Office: Sch Arts and Scis Clayton State Coll Morrow GA 30260

BECKER, STEPHEN ARNOLD, museum director; b. Redwood City, Calif., Aug. 24, 1951; s. Leo H. and May B. (Goldberg) B.; m. Beverly Nichols-Fredotovich, July 31, 1977; 1 child, Joseph Nikola. Asst. curator mus. Ind. U., Bloomington, 1973-77, lectr. folklore dept., 1975-77; historian Sacramento History Ctr., 1977-78; dir. history divsn. County Pks. Dept., Riverside, Calif., 1979-85; asst. dir. Mus. Internat. Folk Art, Santa Fe, 1985-89; dir. Mus. Indian Arts and Culture/Lab. Anthropology, Santa Fe, 1989-95; exec. dir. Turtle Bay Park and Mus., Redding, Calif., 1995—. Mem. Am. Assn. Museums, Am. Folklore Soc. Office: Turtle Bay Park and Mus PO Box 494516 Redding CA 96049

BECKER-KLICKER, MARGARET CHAN, library director; b. Tronoh, Perak, West Malaysia; came to U.S., 1972; d. Chan Heong and Ng Tai; m. Millage W. Becker, Oct. 10, 1972 (dec. Sept. 1984); m. Alfred Klicker, June 19, 1991. Degree in bus., Bus. Inst., Ipoh, West Malaysia. Cert. libr., N.Mex. Sec. dist. and land office Malaysian Govt., Batu Gajah, 1963-72; health and social coord. Migrant Coun., Burley, Idaho, 1977-78; clk. Deming (N.Mex.) Pub. Libr., 1979-87, asst. dir., 1987-92, acting dir., 1992, dir., 1993—. Mem. N.Mex. Libr. Assn. Home: PO Box 745 Deming NM 88031-0745 Office: Deming Pub Libr 301 S Tin St Deming NM 88030-3646

BECKMAN, JAMES WALLACE BIM, economist, marketing executive; b. Mpls., May 2, 1936; s. Wallace Gerald and Mary Louise (Frissell) B. BA, Princeton U., 1958; PhD, U. Calif., 1973. Pvt. practice econ. cons., Berkeley, Calif. 1962-67; cons. Calif. State Assembly, Sacramento, 1967-68; pvt. practice market rsch. and econs. cons., Laguna Beach, Calif., 1969-77; cons. Calif. State Gov.'s Office, Sacramento 1977-80; pvt. practice real estate cons., L.A. 1980-83; v.p. mktg. Gold-Well Investments, Inc., L.A. 1982-83; pres. Beckman Analytics Internat., econ. cons. to bus. and govt., L.A. and Lake Arrowhead, Calif., 1983—, East European/Middle East Bus. and Govt., 1992—; adj. prof. Calif. State U. Sch. Bus., San Bernardino, 1989—, U. Redlands, 1992—; cons. E European, environmental issues. Contbr. articles on regional & internat. econ. devel. & social change to profl. jours. Maj. USMC 1958-67. NIMH fellow 1971-72. Fellow Soc. Applied Anthropology; mem. Am. Econs. Assn., Am. Statis. Assn., Am. Mktg. Assn. (officer), Nat. Assn. Bus. Economists (officer). Democrat. Presbyterian. Home: PO Box 1753 Lake Arrowhead CA 92352-1753

BECKMAN, KENNETH OREN, film and video specialist, researcher; b. Detroit, Nov. 26, 1948; s. Aron J. Beckman; m. Sally Tuttle, Sept. 9, 1963; children: Oren Rigel, Sienna Grace. BA in Theater, Mich. State U., 1970; MA in Film, San Francisco State U., 1982. Freelance producer, 1969-74; tech. dir. Center for Contemporary Music, Oakland, Calif., 1974-76; producer Optic Nerve, San Francisco, 1976-78; dir. video lab. Xerox/Parc, Palo Alto, Calif., 1978-86; founding ptnr. SIRIUS Communications Group, La Honda, Calif., 1984-90; sr. communications mgr., mgr. video lab. Systems Rsch. Ctr. Digital Equipment Corp., Palo Alto, 1986—; founder Foton Factory, La Honda, 1991; cons. Apple Computer, Multi-Media Group, Oceanic Inst. Dir. video art including A Man With an Idea, Reach Out, 1986, Clean Machine, 1987, Song of the Street of the Singing Chicken, 1982 (1st place award Santa Cruz Video Festival 1982, Am. Film Inst. Nat. Winner 1982); patentee in field. Recipient Hometown USA Video Festival award, Denver, 1984. Fellow Photon Factory (dir. 1984-87, Wave/Particle award 1986); mem. Music Video Dirs. Guild (dir. 1985-87, Deep Purple Music TV award 1985), Soc. Motion Picture TV Engrs. Office: Foton Factory PO Box 251 La Honda CA 94020-0251

BECKMANN, JANE MILUNA, acoustical company executive, consultant; b. Ostrava, Slezko, Czechoslovakia, Nov. 27, 1935; came to U.S., 1969; d. František Mašín and Miloslava (Pospíšilová) Mašínová; m. Raoul Beckmann; 1 child, Denisa Ann Rafalowski. BS in Structural Engring., Archtl. Tech. U. Prague, Czechoslovakia, 1955, MS in Structural Engring., 1958; postgrad. sch. cert., Electro-Engring. Tech. U. Prague, Czechoslovakia, 1962. Engr. Bldg. Isolation Inst., Prague, 1958-62, mgr., 1962-66; rsch. engr. Inst. Prefabricated Bldgs., Prague, 1966-68; acoustical cons. Bolt Beranek and Newman Inc., L.A., 1969-87; prin., treas. Acoustical Analysis Assocs. Inc., Canoga Park, Calif., 1987—. Mem. Acoustical Soc. Am. Republican. Roman Catholic. Office: Acoustical Analysis Assocs Inc 22148 Sherman Way Ste 206 Canoga Park CA 91303-1145

BECKMANN, JON MICHAEL, publisher; b. N.Y.C., Oct. 24, 1936; s. John L. and Grace (Hazelton) B.; m. Barbara Ann Efting, June 26, 1965. BA, U. Pa., 1958; MA, NYU, 1961. Sr. editor Prentice-Hall Inc., Englewood Cliffs, N.J., 1964-68; v.p., editor Barre Pubs., Mass., 1970-73; pub. Sierra Club Books, San Francisco, 1973-94; pres. Beckmann Assocs. and Millennium Press, Sonoma, Calif., 1994—. Contbr. articles, book revs., poetry to pubs. Mem. Book Club of Calif. Office: Beckmann Assocs & Millennium Press 18185 7th St E Sonoma CA 95476-4701

BECKMANN, ROBERT OWEN, artist; b. Phila., Mar. 20, 1942; s. John Harry and Hazel (Bowers) B.; m. Pauline Kay Hahn, Sept. 29, 1984. BA, Coll. of Wooster, Ohio, 1964; MA, U. Iowa, 1966, MFA, 1967. Instr. art U. South Ala., Mobile, 1967-68, No. Ill. U., Dekalb, 1968-71; artist Beckmann Studio, Denver, 1971-77; project dir. cmty. murals project City of Las Vegas, Nev., 1977-79; pres. Wallternatives, Inc., Las Vegas, 1979-92; artist Beckmann Studio, Las Vegas, 1992—; artist-in-residence Artrain, NEA, Mich. Arts Coun., Fedn. Rocky Mountain States, 1973, NEA, Idaho State U., Pocatello, 1974-75, Nev. State Coun. on Arts, Carson City, 1976, Las Vegas, 1977. One man shows include Ferrari Gallery, Las Vegas, 1989, The Body of a House Nev. Mus. Art, Reno, 1993, U. Nev., Las Vegas, 1993, HERE Art, N.Y.C., 1994, Coll. Charleston, S.C., 1995, pARTs Gallery, Mpls., 1995; group shows include Monumental Propaganda World Fin. Ctr., N.Y.C., 1993, Inst. Contemporary Art, Moscow, 1993, Internat. Gallery at Smithsonian, Washington, 1995, Dunlop Gallery Regina Pub. Libr., Saskatchewan, Can., 1995, Contemporary Art Mus., Tallinn, Estonia, 1995, Lubiljana, Slovenia, 1995. Commr. Las Vegas Arts Commn., 1994—. Recipient Laura Slobe Meml. prize Chgo. Art Inst., 1971; Western States Arts Found. fellow, 1976, Nev. State Coun. on the Arts fellow, 1990.

BECKNER, ARDIS STERN, nutrition specialist, educator; b. Gillett, Wis., Jan. 15, 1935; d. Herman G. and Marie Adam (Kopitzke) Stern; m. William G. Beckner, Dec. 24, 1961 (div.); children: Robert M., Cheryl S.; m. Lloyd M. Eggebrecht, Jan. 1992. AA in Elem. Edn., Andrews U., 1955, BS in Nutrition, 1959; MS in Nutrition, Loma Linda U., 1963. Registered dietition, Calif.; cert. diabetes educator, lactation educator, Calif. Elem. sch. tchr. Am. Tchrs. Assn., Gobles, Mich., 1956-58; jr. h.s. home econ. tchr. Am. Tchrs. Assn., Berrien Springs, Mich., 1958-59; home econ. fellow Andrews U., Berrien Springs, 1959-60; clin. dietition White Meml. Hosp., L.A., 1961-64; metabolic genetic dietition L.A. Children's Hosp., 1964-67, Loma Linda (Calif.) U. Hosp., 1969-76; clin. dietetics and metabolic nutritionist Kaiser Permanente Med. Group, Fontana, Calif., 1976—; part-time instr. nutrition and dietetics Loma Linda (Calif.) U., 1963—, Mt. San Jacinto Coll., Gillman Hot Springs, Cali.f, 1967-69; cons. in field. Editor: SDA Diet Manual, 1964, Diabetes Manual, 1989; author chpt. to book. Leader, counselor pathfinder clubs Seventh Day Adventist Ch., Loma Linda, 1974-84; instr. handicapped Calif. Handicapped Sports and Recreation Assn., Big Bear, 1989—, vol. instr. Bear Mountain Handicapped Ski Sch.; vol., mem. publs., news and info. com. Nat. Forest Svc., 1992—. Recipient Spkrs. award Foster Parents Assn. Inland Execs., 1990, Everyday Heros award San Bernardino (Calif.) Sun, 1993, Vol. Svc. award Nat. Forest Svc., 1994; named Outstanding Program Dir., Pathfinder Clubs So. Calif., 1977, 78, 79. Mem. Am. Dietetic Assn. (prin. investigator), Am. Assn. Diabetes Educators. Home: 1465 Padua Ave Redlands CA 92374-3866 Office: Kaiser Permanente Med Group 9985 Sierra Ave Fontana CA 92335-6720

BECKS, RONALD ARTHUR, film producer; b. N.Y.C., July 9, 1953; s. Wellington and Vivian (Newkirk) B. Student, York Coll., 1969-71; cert. for prodrs., Cintel Corp., 1974-75; cert., Ch. Religious Sc., 1975-77; D of Religious Communication (hon.), Temple Faith, 1974. Owner, pres., chmn. Ronald A. Becks Internat. Theatre Soc., N.Y.C., 1978-90; v.p. Miracle Prodns., N.Y.C., 1978-90; pres. Magic Circle Players, Australia and Hong Kong, Sodeko Films, Australia and Hong Kong; mktg. dir. V.R.B. Enterprises, Australia and Hong Kong, Multi-Media Svcs., Australia and Hong Kong; pres. Noduki Films, Australia and Hong Kong, 1990, Face Affair, Beverly Hills, Calif., 1991, Film Gods Prodns., Beverly Hills, 1991—; founder, pres. STN TV Network, 1994; v.p. BBH Cosmetics Labs., Beverly Hills, 1994; adv. coun. Internat. Biog. Ctr. Author: The 3rd Testament, 1990, Legend of Billy Blue, 1988, Black Diamond, 1989, Come and Get It, 1991, Say a Little Prayer, 1991, Stagecoach Mary, 1993, Gigi and the Bogey-Man, 1993; prodr.: You Bring Out the Best in Me, 1984 (top 40 song); inventor phone device. Dep. chmn. UN Assn., 1979, dep. amb., 1979, chmn. Song Quest, 1979; entertainment coord. Keep Australia Beautiful, 1980; prodr. children's show Consulate of Peru, 1979; prodr. and host I Love New York, N.Y.C., 1978. Mem. Prodrs. and Dirs. Guild, Prodrs. Assn., PEN Internat., NAACP, Internat. Platform Assn., Rainbow Coalition, Writers Guild, Journalists Club. Home and Office: 505 S Beverly Dr Ste 364 Beverly Hills CA 90212-4542

BECKSTEAD, DOUGLAS STEPHEN, cultural resources professional; b. Salt Lake City, Sept. 24, 1958; s. Rodney Andrew and Raye Mary (Golatz) B.; m. Carol Rae DeMille, June 25, 1984; children: Jeremiah Grafton, Rebekkah Rae Golatz Beckstead. BA, U. Utah, 1985, MA, 1992. Archivist Utah State Archives, Salt Lake City, U. Utah Archives, Salt Lake City; tchng. asst. U. Utah, Salt Lake City, 1985-87, tchng. fellow, 1987-89; historian U.S. Bur. of Reclamation, Salt Lake City, 1989-90, Nat. Park Svc., Anchorage, 1990-94; chief div. cultural resources Nat. Park Svc., Fairbanks, Alaska, 1994—; firearms instr. Nat. Park Svc., Anchorage, 1992—; dir. Dog Mushers Mus., Fairbanks, 1994—. Contbr. articles to profl. jours., publs. Mem. Utah State Hist. Soc., Am. Soc. Legal History, Alaska Hist. Soc., Alaska Sled Dog and Racing Assn., Alaska K-9 Weight Pull Assn., Orgn. of Am. Historians, Phi Alpha Theta (chpt. pres. 1986-87). Democrat. Office: Nat Park Svc PO Box 75187 Fairbanks AK 99707-5187

BECK-VON-PECCOZ, STEPHEN GEORGE WOLFGANG, artist; b. Munich, Oct. 18, 1933; came to U.S., 1937; s. Wolfgang Anna Marie and Martha Jeanette (Morse) Beck-von-P.; m. Dorothy Ann Freytag, June 16, 1956 (div. 1971); m. Michele Marie Perry, Feb. 8, 1972; children: Stephen Jr., David, Kenneth, Lisa. BEE, Cornell U., 1956; MA in Art, Calif. State U., San Diego, 1974. Electronic engr. Stromberg Carlson Co., San Diego, 1958-60; project mgr. Control Data Corp., San Diego, 1960-65, Digital Devel. Corp., San Diego, 1965-66; project engr. Stromberg Datagraphix, Inc., San Diego, 1966-69; project mgr. Digital Sci. Corp., San Diego, 1969-71; artist San Diego, 1974—; cons. elec. engring., San Diego, 1974-78. Served to 2d lt. USAF, 1956-58. Mem. Artists Equity Assn., Internat. Sculpture Ctr., Kappa Alpha Soc. Home and Studio: 636 Nardito Ln Solana Beach CA 92075-2306

BECKWITH, CHARLES ALLAN, healthcare administrator, consultant; b. L.A., Feb. 15, 1940; s. Harry Spencer and Mary Dorothy (Riley) B.; m. Roberta Louise Sommerdorf, Nov. 27, 1963 (dec. Jan. 1966); m. Susan Ann Robinson, Aug. 24, 1969; 1 child, Mary Aileen. BS in Psychology, Loyola-Marymount U., 1962; cert., George Washington U., 1989; M of Profl. Studies: Hosp. and Health Svcs. Adminstrn., Cornell U., 1976. Cert. facilitator Toward Excellence Exec. Action Process program, cert. trainer Suprs. in the Toward Excellence Frontline Leadership Process program. Adminstr. Grover M. Hermann divsn. Cmty. Gen. Hosp. Sullivan County, Callicoon, N.Y., 1976-77; assoc. dir. Cmty. Gen. Hosp. Sullivan County, Harris, N.Y., 1977-78; adminstr. for ambulatory care USPHS Hosp., Balt., 1978-81; program cons. Office Ambulatory Care Bur. Med. Svcs., Hyattsville, Md., 1981; adminstr. area contract health svcs., program/internal auditor Albuquerque Area Indian Health Svc., 1981-84, internal auditor Office of Area Dir., 1984; sr. internal auditor Calif. Area Indian Health Svc., Sacramento, 1984-89, spl. adminstrv. asst., 1989—; mem. health svcs. adminstrn. adv. bd. Sch. Pub. Adminstrn., U. So. Calif., 1988-93; adminstrv. residency preceptor for M. of Healthcare Adminstrn. students Sacramento campus U. So. Calif., 1992-94; presenter profl. papers ann. meeting USPHS Profl. Assn., Scottsdale, Ariz., 1988, 93; mem. Sloan Program Hosp. and Health Svcs. Adminstrn., Grad. Sch. Bus. and Pub. Adminstrn., Cornell U., 1976; presenter in field. Contbr. articles to profl. publs. Alumni admissions interviewer Johnson Grad. Sch. Mgmt., Cornell U., 1985—; co-master of ceremony duties for commemorative awards Indian Health Svcs. Honor Awards Ceremony, Rockville, Md., 1989, 91. Capt. USPHS, 1978—. Decorated Bronze Star medal; recipient Calif. Area Dir.'s award for Managerial Excellence for leadership in advancement of healthcare adminstrn., 1994, award of appreciation Combined Fed. Campaign Coord., 1993, award for Area Office with Best Overall Performance, U.S. Savs. Bond Campaign Coord., 1994, PHS Outstanding Svc. medal, 2 PHS Commendation medals, PHS Citation and Unit Citation. Fellow Am. Coll. Healthcare Execs. (membership examiner); mem. Commd. Officers Assn. Roman Catholic. Office: CA Area Indian Health Ser 1825 Bell St Ste 200 Sacramento CA 95825-1020

BEDERKA, STEPHEN EDWARD, management consultant; b. N.Y.C., July 6, 1930; s. Stephen and Emilia Rose (Toth) B.; m. Ann Sabina Canor, Nov. 29, 1952; children: Celeste Ann, Valerie Ann Bederka Collins. BS in Physics, St. Bernadine of Siena, 1952; postgrad., Stanford U., 1968. Radar design engr. GE, Utica, N.Y., 1952-55; communications system engr. Lockheed Missiles and Space Co., Sunnyvale, Calif., 1955-66, system engring. mgr., 1966-74, program mgr., 1974-91; founder, mgmt. and bus. cons. Toth Co., Los Gatos, Calif., 1991—; counselor Svc. Corps Ret. Execs., 1992—. Contbr. articles to profl. jours. and mags. Mem. IEEE (past officer San Francisco chpt.). Home and Office: 15286 Via Palomino Los Gatos CA 95030-2238

BEDFORD, AMY ALDRICH, public relations executive, corporation secretary; b. Pendleton, Oreg., July 13, 1912; d. Edwin Burton and Elsie (Conklin) Aldrich; m. J.M. Bedford (wid.); 1 child, Jacqueline Bedford Brown. BS, Oreg. State U., 1933. Mgr. comml. dept. East Oregonian, Pendleton, 1950-75, mgr. pub. rels., 1975—; corp. sec. East Oregonian Pub. Co., Pendleton, 1950—. Bd. dirs. Oreg. Status of Women Com., 1972-75, Oreg. Law Enforcement Commn., 1975-82, Arts Coun. Pendleton. Recipient Pendleton First Citizen award C. of C., 1962, Gov.'s award for the Arts, 1988. Mem. Women in Communications, Oreg. Press Women, AAUW (pres. 1956-58, grantee 1965), LWV, Pendleton River Parkway Found., World Affairs Coun. Oreg., Altrusa. Home: PO Box 1456 Pendleton OR 97801-0365 Office: East Oregonian Pub Co PO Box 1089 Pendleton OR 97801-1089

BEDROSIAN, JAMES KENNETH, food products executive; b. 1944. V.p., sec. Sunshine Raisin Corp., Fowler, Calif. Office: Sunshine Raisin Corp 626 S 5th St Fowler CA 93625-9745*

BEEBE, JOHN HOWARD (JACK BEEBE), economist, banker; b. Hackensack, N.J., May 11, 1942. BA, Williams Coll., 1964; MS in Indsl. Engring., U. Tex., 1966; MA in Econs., Stanford U., 1970, PhD in Econs., 1972.

Asst. prof. bus. Calif. Polytech. State U., San Luis Obispo, Calif., 1966-68; economist FRS Assocs., Menlo Park, Calif., 1972-76; vis. lectr. Stanford (Calif.) Grad. Sch. Bus., 1979-82, 86; from economist to v.p. Fed. Reserve Bank San Francisco, 1976-86, sr. v.p., dir. rsch., 1987—; Bd. dirs. 1990 Inst., Burlingame, Calif. 1993—. Co-author: (book) Television Economics, 1974; contbr. numerous articles to profl. jours. Asst. scoutmaster Boy Scouts of Am., Menlo Park, Calif., 1984-88. Mem. Am. Econs. Assn. Office: Fed Res Bank San Francisco 101 Market St San Francisco CA 94105-1530

BEEBE, MARY LIVINGSTONE, curator; b. Portland, Oreg., Nov. 5, 1940; d. Robert and Alice Beebe. B.A., Bryn Mawr Coll., 1962; postgrad. Sorbonne, U. Paris, 1962-63. Curatorial asst. Fogg Art Mus., Harvard U., Cambridge, Mass., 1966-68; Apprentice Portland Art Mus., 1963-64, Boston Mus. Art, 1964-65; exec. dir. Portland Ctr. for Visual Arts, 1973-81; dir. Stuart collection U. Calif.-San Diego, La Jolla, 1981—; cons. in field. Mem. art steering com. Portland Devel. Commn., 1977-80; bd. dirs. Henry Gallery, U. Wash., Seattle, 1977-80; project cons. Nat. Research Ctr. for Arts, N.Y.C., 1978-79; bd. dirs. Art Mus. Assn. San Francisco, 1978-84; bd. dirs., trustee Art Matters Inc., 1985—; trustee Russell Found., 1982-94; hon. mem. bd. dirs. Portland Ctr. for Visual Arts, 1984-91; mem. arts adv. bd. Centre City Devel. Corp., San Diego, 1982-94; arts adv. bd. Port of San Diego; panel mem., cons. Nat. Endowment Arts; juror numerous art shows and exhbns. Nat. Endowment Arts fellow, 1979. Recipient Allied Professions award AIA, 1992. Contbr. articles to profl. jours. Office: The Stuart Collection U Calif San Diego 9500 Gilman Dr La Jolla CA 92093-5003

BEEBE, SANDRA E., retired English language educator, artist, writer; b. March AFB, Calif., Nov. 10, 1934; d. Eugene H. and Margaret (Fox) B.; m. Donald C. Thompson. AB in English and Speech, UCLA, 1956; MA in Secondary Edn., Calif. State U., Long Beach, 1957. Tchr. English, Garden Grove (Calif.) High Sch., 1957-93, attendance supr., 1976-83, ret., 1993. Contbr. articles to English Jour., chpts. to books; exhbns. include AWS, NWS, Okla. Watercolor Soc., Watercolor West, San Diego Internat., La. Watercolor Soc., San Diego Art Inst., Knickerbocker Artists N.Y., Montana WCS, Midwest Watercolor Soc., Butler Inst. Am. Art, Youngstown, Ohio, Kings Art Ctr., Audubon Artists N.Y.; cover artist Exploring Painting, 1990, title page Understanding Watercolor, American Artist, 1991. Named one of the Top Ten Watercolorists The Artists Mag., 1994. Mem. Am. Watercolor Soc., Nat. Watercolor Soc., Midwest Watercolor Soc., Watercolor West, Nat. Arts Club, Knickerbocker Artists N.Y., Audubon Artists N.Y., West Coast Watercolor Soc., Rocky Mountain Nat. Watermedia Honor Soc., Jr. League Long Beach, Kappa Kappa Gamma. Republican. Home: 7241 Marina Pacifica Dr S Long Beach CA 90803-3899 Studio: B-Q Gallery 3920 E 4th St Long Beach CA 90814-1656 also: 239 Mira Mar Ave Long Beach CA 90803-6153 also: JJ Brookings Gallery 669 S Mission San Francisco CA

BEEDLE, JOSEPH MICHAEL, SR., bank executive, financial consultant; b. Ellensburg, Wash., Jan. 24, 1952; s. Homer Roy and Elaine Violet (Dupuis) B.; m. Barbara Lolita Cavitt, Aug. 12, 1972; children: Marie Teresa, Joseph Michael Jr. BBA, U. Alaska, 1975; grad., U. Wash., 1985. Gov.'s intern State of Alaska, Juneau, 1972; mgmt. trainee Nat. Bank of Alaska, Fairbanks, 1974-75; planning/acctg. officer Nat. Bank of Alaska, Anchorage, 1975-77; asst. v.p. Nat. Bank of Alaska, Kenai and Anchorage, 1977-80; v.p. 1st Bank Ketchikan, Alaska, 1980-85; exec. v.p., sr. leader Key Bank, Anchorage, 1985-93; prin., owner, cons. Beedle and Assoc. Consulting, Anchorage, 1993—; pres., CEO Goldbelt Inc., 1994—; sr. rep. Robert Morris Assocs., Anchorage and Fairbanks, 1985-93; mem. Key Corp. Nat. Credit Com., Albany, N.Y., 1992-93. Bd. dirs., treas. Ketchikan Conv. and Vis. Bur., 1981-82; found. bd. trustees U. Alaska, 1993—; mem. exec. com., treas. United Way Anchorage, 1992—, Cath. Social Svcs., Anchorage, 1992—; mem. exec. com., past chair Jr. Achievement Alaska, Anchorage, 1989—; bd. dirs. World Trade Ctr. Alaska, Anchorage, 1992—. Recipient Joel Weigert award U. Alaska, 1975. Mem. Small Bus. Devel. Ctr. (chair bd. dirs. 1992—), Ketchikan C. of C. (pres. 1982-89), KC (recorder 1992—). Republican. Roman Catholic. Home: PO Box 32959 Juneau AK 99803-2959

BEEGLE, EARL DENNIS, family physician; b. Ashland, Ohio, July 24, 1944; s. Ray Benjamin and Alice Mae (Imhoff) B.; m. Isabel Sloan-Kerr Adamson, Sept. 3, 1964; children: Ryan Benjamin, Kevin Ian. BA, Manchester Coll., 1967; MS, Purdue U., 1970; MB BChir, MD, BAO, Queen's U., Belfast, No. Ireland, 1978. Diplomate Am. Bd. Family Practice. Life scis. tchr. Elkhart (Ind.) Schs., 1967-72; house officer Nat. Health Svc. of U.K., No. Ireland and U.K., 1978-79; resident in family practice Med. Coll. Ohio, Toledo, 1979-81, chief resident, 1981-82; pvt. practice Everett, Wash., 1982-93; med. dir. Providence Primary Care Network, Everett, 1993—; med. dir. Planned Parenthood, Everett, 1983-86; chmn. utilization Providence Hosp., Everett, 1987-90; chmn. quality assurance Combined Med. Staff, Everett, 1991-92; chmn. family practice dept. Providence-Gen. Med. Ctr., Everett, 1993-94; dir. Sisters of Providence Health Plans, Seattle, 1993—. Active Friends of the Somme, No. Ireland, 1991—. NSF fellow, 1967-70. Fellow Am. Acad. Family Practice; mem. Irish and Am. Pediatric Soc., Snohomish County Med. Soc., Associated Physicians of Snohomish County (bd. dirs.), Internat. Soc. Travel Medicine. Office: Providence Claremont Clinic 5007 Claremont Way Everett WA 98203-3321

BEEKMAN, WILLIAM ARTHUR, technical executive; b. Turlock, Calif., Mar. 4, 1936; m. Marjory Anne Brown, Sept. 4, 1959; children: Brett William, Bryan Stanley. BS in agrl. engr., Calif. Poly. Tech., 1960. Registered engr., Calif. Application engr. Fairbanks Morse, Fresno, Calif., 1960-63, mgr. svc. ctr., 1963-67; application engr. Floway Pumps, Fresno, Calif., 1967-70, chief engr., 1970-76, v.p. engring., 1977-80, v.p. R&D, 1980-84, tech. dir., 1984—; com. chmn. Hydraulic Inst., 1976-82, com. chmn. test code, 1982-91, com. mem. API 610, 1982-84, com. mem. intake design Hydraulic Inst., 1994—. Bd. dirs. Cen. of Irrightion Tech., Fresno, 1983-88. Recipient Pump Symposium award Tex. A&M, 1988, 90. Republican. Lutheran. Home: 7791 E Carmen Ave Fresno CA 93727-9789 Office: Floway Pumps 2494 S Railroad Ave Fresno CA 93706-5109

BEEKS, GRAYDON FISHER, JR., musicology educator; b. Long Beach, Calif., Oct. 15, 1948; s. Graydon Fisher and Mary Eugene (Swift) B.; m. Serena Elizabeth, July 16, 1978. BA, Pomona Coll., 1969; MA, U. Calif., Berkeley, 1971, PhD, 1981. Editorial asst. Grove's Dictionary, London, 1974-76; dir. music St. Clements Ch., Berkeley, 1976-78; assoc. U. Calif., Berkeley, 1977-78; instr. Vassar Coll., Poughkeepsie, N.Y., 1978-80; vis. instr. Kenyon Coll., Gambier, Ohio, 1980-81; lectr., libr. Pomona Coll., Claremont, Calif., 1983-89, dir. music programming, assoc. prof., 1989—; dir. music St. Ambrose Ch., Claremont, 1986-90. Mem. editl. bd. Hallische Händel Ausgabe; contbr. article to profl. jours. Alfred Hertz fellow U. Calif., Berkeley, 1973-74; grantee Am. Council Learned Socs., 1985, NEH, 1989. Mem. Am. Musicol. Soc., Music Libr. Assoc., Coll. Band Dirs. Nat. Assn., Am. Handel Soc. Democrat. Home: 283 E Green St Claremont CA 91711-5027 Office: Pomona Coll Music Dept 340 N College Ave Claremont CA 91711

BEENE, M. MELANIE, arts management consultant; b. Athens, Tenn., Mar. 13, 1948; d. Jones C. and Margaret F. (Nankivell) B. BA, Vanderbilt U., 1970, MA in Asian Art History, 1976; JD, U. Tenn., Knoxville, 1977. Bar: Calif. Pub. info. specialist Brevard (N.C.) Music Ctr., summer 1977; assoc. devel. dir. San Francisco Symphony, 1977-78; assoc. dir. Calif. Assn. for the Am. Conservatory Theater, San Francisco, 1978-79; dir. mgmt. assistance program Nat. Alliance of Media Arts Orgns., 1984-88; cons. to non-profit orgns., 1979—; cons. to the advancement program Nat. Endowment for the Arts, Washington, 1983-90, 94—, mng. cons. for the advancement program, 1990-94; workshop facilitator, panel mem.; mem. faculty, arts adminstrn. program U. Calif., San Francisco Extension, 1981; also tchr. law and art history courses. Author: (with F. Johnson and P. Mitchell) Autopsy of an Orchestra, (with J.Grenzeback) Arts Manager/s Toolbox-Financial Management, 1991. Bd. dirs. Paul Dresher Ensemble; mem. bd. advisors Inst. Non-Profit Mgmt., U. San Francisco; mem. nat. adv. com. Asian CineVision; bd. dirs. Headlands Ctr. for Arts, 1984, Legal Svcs. for Children, 1984; vol. counselor Planned Parenthood, 1982-83; treas. San Francisco Arts Advocates, 1978-79. Mem. State Bar Calif. Office: Melanie Beene & Assocs 221 Brookside Dr San Anselmo CA 94960-1418

BEER, FRANCIS ANTHONY, political science educator; b. N.Y.C., Feb. 5, 1939; s. William Joseph and Anne (Benedikt) B.; m. Diana Darnall, June 12, 1965; children: Omar, Marie, Jeremy. AB cum laude, Harvard U., 1960; MA, U. Calif., Berkeley, 1963, PhD, 1967. Asst. prof. dept. govt. U. Tex., Austin, 1967-70, assoc. prof. dept. govt., 1970-75; prof. dept. polit. sci. U. Colo., Boulder, 1975—. Author: Integration and Disintegration in NATO: Processes of Alliance Cohesion and Prospects for Atlantic Community, 1969, Peace Against War: The Ecology of International Violence, 1981; editor Alliances: Latent War Communities in the Contemporary World, 1970; (with Ted. R. Gurr) Conflict, Violence, Peace: An International Series of Books, 1990-93; asst. editor Jour. Politics, 1968-71; contbr. articles to profl. jours. Lt. USNR, 1960-62. Fulbright fellow, 1965-66, 71, Mershon fellow, 1966-67, NEH fellow, 1990; grantee Earhart Found., 1972, Inst. World Order, 1974-77. Mem. Am. Polit. Sci. Assn., Internat. Studies. Assn. Office: U Colo Polit Sci Dept Campus Box 333 Boulder CO 80309

BEER, JOSEPH ERNEST, telecommunications manager; b. Pasadena, Calif., June 5, 1959; s. Joseph Andrew and Pauline Sylvia (Micciche) B.; m. Amy Shun-Fong Wu, Oct. 13, 1984. BS in Internat. Bus., Calif. State U., L.A., 1982; MBA in Info. Tech. Mgmt., U. So. Calif., 1987. Asst. engr. ARCO-Electronics & Telecommunications, L.A., 1979-83, sr. coord., 1983-84, project engr., 1984-85, sr. project engr., 1985-87; sr. mgr. Ernst & Young, L.A., 1987-91; dir. telecommunications and network svcs. South Coast Air Quality Mgmt. Dist., L.A., 1991-94; mgr. info, tech. svcs. Tosco Northwest Co., Seattle, 1994—. Recipient scholarship, Ebell Found., L.A., 1981, Bank Am. scholarship, Bank Am. Found., 1981. Mem. Soc. Telecommunications Consultants, Project Mgmt. Inst. Republican. Home: 24012 SE 37th St Issaquah WA 98027 Office: Tosco Northwest 601 Union St Ste 2521 Seattle WA 98101

BEERS, ALVIN LAFRANCE, JR., physician; b. Great Bend, Kans., Dec. 4, 1946; s. Alvin LaFrance Sr. and Mildred Pauline (Roper) B.; m. Lucile Florence Henke, Feb. 16, 1974 (div. Feb. 1982); children: Stephen LaFrance, Jeffrey Charles; m. Laura Ann Haupenthal, June 1, 1985. BA in Biochemistry, Kans. U., 1968, MD, 1972. Med. intern/resident St. Louis U., 1972-75; clin./rsch. fellow dept. hematology/oncology U. Wis., Madison, 1975-77; rsch. assoc. fellow Columbia U., N.Y.C., 1977-78; chief oncology AMC Cancer Rsch. Ctr., Lakewood, Colo., 1978-81; pvt. practice hematology/oncology Kaiser-Permanente, Denver, 1981—. Mem. ACP, Am. Soc. Clin. Oncology. Democrat. Office: Kaiser Permanente 2005 Franklin St Denver CO 80205-5401

BEERS, ROBERT CHARLES, metallurgical engineer, separations consultant; b. Chgo., Mar. 27, 1942; s. Robert Tindall and Florence Elizabeth (Parvin) B.; m. Virginia O'Dell Rupe, Jan. 27, 1978. BS in Metall. Engring., Mont. Coll. Mineral Sci.-Tech., 1966, MS in Mineral Dressing, 1968; postgrad., Colo. Sch. Mines, 1968; PhD in Engring., Calif. Coast U., 1992. Registered profl. engr., Colo., Mont., N.Mex., Calif., Ariz. Rsch. engr. Hazen Rsch. Inc., Golden, Colo., 1968-69; project engr. Rsch. Inst., Colo. Sch. Mines, Golden, 1969-72; sr. project engr. Mont. Tech. Found. Mineral Rsch. Ctr., Butte, 1972-74; sr. processing engr. Nord Resources Corp., Albuquerque, 1974-76; rsch. and project engr. Occidental Rsch. Corp., Irvine, Calif., 1976-79; prin. engr. Holmes & Narver, Inc., Orange, Calif., 1979-82, Bechtel, Inc., San Francisco, 1982—; separations cons. U.S. Borax, Sask., Can., 1969, Johnson & Johnson, N.J., 1970-72, Brush Wellman Inc., Ohio, 1982-87, COMINCO Ltd., B.C., Can., 1984-86. Patentee method for embrittling cellulosic fraction of mcpl. solid waste. Inland Steel fellow, 1968. Mem. AIME, N.Y. Acad. Scis., Can. Inst. Mining and Metallurgy, Nat. Soc. Profl. Engrs., AAAS, Order of Engrs. Congregationalist. Office: Bechtel Inc PO Box 193965 San Francisco CA 94119-3965

BEESON, DIANE KAY, language educator; b. Boulder, Colo., Sept. 3, 1949; d. Donald Russell and Dorothy Maxine (Patton) B. Tchr., Lindenwood Coll., 1972; MA, Middlebury Coll., 1974; T.O.E.F.L., Fundacion Ponce de Leon, Madrid, 1985; postgrad., NYU, 1980. Tchr. several indsl. cos., Madrid, 1973-76; tchr. trainer Burroughs, Madrid, 1979-82; mem. faculty U. Calif./U. Madrid, 1982-84, English Acad., 1984-86, Linguactr. Acad., 1986-89, Assn. Cultural Hispano, 1989-90; mem. faculty info. sci. dept. U. Del./U. Madrid, 1989-90; prof. lang. translation U. Cluny, Madrid, 1991-93; tchr. adult bus. English Brit. Consulate, Madrid, 1995—; tchr., cons. Coopers & Lybrand, 1994—; dir. English classes Grupo Anaya Pub., 1984-91; chmn. lang. dept. Conway Day Sch., St. Charles, Mo., 1971-73; co. translator Laboratorios Andromaco, Madrid, 1984-88, Santillana Pub. Co., Madrid, 1986-88. Contbr. articles and poems to profl. publs.; author textbooks, 1986-88. U. Mex. scholar, 1970. Mem. AAUW, MLA, Nat. League Am. Pen Women, Am. Assn. Tchrs. Spanish and Portuguese. Home: 1615 S La Canada Green Valley AZ 85614

BEESON, MONTEL EILEEN, human services administrator, gerontologist; b. El Dorado, Ark., Dec. 22, 1939; d. Waymon Willett and Myrtle May (Roach) B. BS in Recreation, Calif. State U., Hayward, 1963; MA in Edn. and Human Devel., Holy Names Coll., Oakland, Calif., 1979. Lic. nursing home adminstr.; cert. community coll. instr.; cert. gerontology. Dist. exec. Ariz. Cactus-Pine Girl Scouts Coun., Phoenix, 1963-66, dist. exec. San Francisco Bay coun., Oakland, Calif., 1966-68, bus. mgr., 1968-71, exec. dir. Shabonee coun., Moline, Ill., 1971-73, Tongass-Alaska coun., Ketchikan, 1973-74, Muir Trail coun., Modesto, Calif., 1974-78; asst. adminstr. Beulah Home, Inc., Oakland, 1980-86; elder care cons., 1986—; exec. dir. Community Adult Day Health Svcs., Oakland, 1987-88; adminstr. Greenhills Retirement Ctr. Millbrae, Calif., 1988—. Mem. Am. Coll. Health Care Adminstrs., Am. Soc. on Aging. Avocations: cross-country skiing, history, travel, reading, music. Home: 3393 Kiwanis St Oakland CA 94602-4005

BEESTON, JOSEPH MACK, metallurgist; b. Fillmore, Utah, Aug. 12, 1918; s. Joseph W. and Florence (Swallow) B.; m. Blanche Weight, Dec. 20, 1946; children: Miriam, Jolynn. BChEng, U. Utah, 1949; postgrad., Oreg. State U., 1949-50; PhD in Metall. Engring., U. Utah, 1953. Asst. prof. Wash. State U., Pullman, 1953-58; sr. metallurgist Phillips Pet Atomic Energy Div., Idaho Falls, Idaho, 1958-61, leader irr. material group, 1961-64; chief materials rsch. sect. Idaho Nuclear, Idaho Falls, 1964-71; chief irradiation material engring. Aerojet Gen., Idaho Falls, 1971-78; sci. specialist EG&G Idaho Inc., Idaho Falls, 1978-85; cons. metallurgist Garrison, Utah, 1985—. Contbr. over 100 articles to profl. jours. With USAF, 1941-45. Mem. ASTM (com. nuclear tech. and applications), Am. Soc. Metals. Home and Office: 625 Circle Dr Garrison UT 84728

BEETHAM, STANLEY WILLIAMS, international management consultant; b. Montpelier, Idaho, Nov. 2, 1933; s. Harry Stanley and Mary (Williams) B.; m. Barbara Burnham, June 20, 1987; 1 child, Lara Mary. BA, Wesleyan U., 1956; MA, U. Amsterdam, The Netherlands, 1957; postgrad., Harvard U., 1958-59, U. Wash., 1959-60. Internat. market mgr. U.S. Rubber/Uniroyal, N.Y.C., 1960-63; corp. mktg. cons. GE, N.Y.C., 1963-65; assoc. dir. Benton & Bowles, Inc., N.Y.C., 1965-67; dir. corp. planning Esmark, Chgo., 1967-72, Consol. Packaging Co., Chgo., 1972-74; sr. cons. Booz Allen Hamilton/Hay Assocs., N.Y.C. and Phila., 1975-80; sr. v.p. U.S. Tobacco Co., Greenwich, Conn., 1981-87; pres. S.W. Beetham & Co., Seattle, 1987—. Contbr. articles in field. Candidate for U.S. Congress from 13th Ill. Dist., 1972, 74; chmn. roundtable Westchester (Conn.) Planning Forum. Fulbright scholar, 1956, Marshall scholar, 1957; Woodrow Wilson fellow, 1958. Mem. N.Am. Soc. Corp. Planning, Nat. Assn. Bus. Economists, Coun. for Urban Econ. Devel., Internat. Soc. for Planing and Strategic Mgmt., Rainier Club, Phi Beta Kappa. Office: 202 W Olympic Pl Apt 301 Seattle WA 98119-3783

BEEVERS, HARRY, biologist; b. Shildon, Eng., Jan. 10, 1924; came to U.S., 1950, naturalized, 1958; s. Norman and Olive (Ayre) B.; m. Jean Sykes, Nov. 19, 1949; 1 child, Michael. BSc, U. Durham, Eng., 1945, PhD, 1947; DSc, U. Newcastle-on-Tyne, 1974, Purdue U., 1972, Nagoya U., 1986. Research fellow Oxford U., Eng., 1946-50; asst. to prof. Purdue U., West Lafayette, Ind., 1950-69; prof. biology U. Calif., Santa Cruz, 1969-90, prof. emeritus, 1990—; fellow Crown Coll. U. Calif., Santa Cruz, 1969—. Author: Respiratory Metabolism in Plants, 1961; contbr. articles to profl. jours. Recipient von Humboldt Sr. Scientist award, 1987. Mem. NAS, Am. Soc. Plant Physiologists (Stephen Hales award 1970, pres. 1960), Am. Soc. Biol. Chemists, Am. Acad. Arts and Scis., Accademia Nazionale dei Lincei, Deutsche Botanische Gesselschaft (hon.), Academia Europaea (fgn.). Home: 46 S Circle Dr Santa Cruz CA 95060-1816 Office: U Calif Santa Cruz Dept Biology Santa Cruz CA 95064

BEEZER, ROBERT ARNOLD, mathematics educator; b. Seattle, Sept. 4, 1958; s. Robert Renaut and Hazlehurst Plant (Smith) B.; m. Patricia Ina Dorsey, Aug. 2, 1986; children: David Ross, Robert Patrick. BS, Santa Clara U., 1978; MS, U. Ill., 1982, PhD, 1984. Asst. prof. U. Puget Sound, Tacoma, 1984-90, assoc. prof., 1990—. Contbr. articles to profl. jours. Martin Nelson Jr. Sabbatical fellow, 1988. Fellow Inst. Combinatorics and its Applications; mem. Am. Math. Soc., Math. Assn. Am., Coun. Undergraduate Rsch., Seattle Tennis Club, Phi Eta Sigma. Office: Univ Puget Sound Math Dept 1500 N Warner St Tacoma WA 98416-0001

BEEZER, ROBERT RENAUT, federal judge; b. Seattle, July 21, 1928; s. Arnold Roswell and Josephine (May) B.; m. Hazlehurst Plant Smith, June 15, 1957; children: Robert Arnold, John Leighton, Mary Allison. Student, U. Wash., 1946-48, 51; BA, U. Va., 1951, LLB, 1956. Bar: Wash. 1956, U.S. Supreme Ct. 1968. Ptnr. Schweppe, Krug, Tausend & Beezer, P.S., Seattle, 1956-84; judge U.S. Ct. Appeals (9th cir.), Seattle, 1984—; alt. mem. Wash. Jud. Qualifications Commn., Olympia, 1981-84. 1st lt. USMCR, 1951-53. Fellow Am. Coll. Trust and Estate Counsel, Am. Bar Found.; mem. ABA, Seattle-King County Bar Assn. (pres. 1975-76), Wash. Bar Assn. (bd. govs. 1980-83). Clubs: Rainier, Tennis (Seattle). Office: US Ct Appeals 802 US Courthouse 1010 5th Ave Seattle WA 98104-1130

BEGAM, ROBERT GEORGE, lawyer; b. N.Y.C., Apr. 5, 1928; s. George and Hilda M. (Hirt) B.; m. Helen C. Clark, July 24, 1949; children—Richard, Lorinda, Michael. B.A., Yale U., 1949, LL.B., 1952. Bar: N.Y. bar 1952, Ariz. bar 1956, U.S. Dist. Ct. Ariz. 1957, U.S. Ct. Appeals (9th cir.) 1958, U.S Supreme Ct. 1973. Assoc. firm Cravath, Swaine & Moore, N.Y.C., 1952-54; spl. counsel State of Ariz., Colorado River Litigation in U.S. Supreme Ct., 1956-58; pres. Begam, Lewis Marks & Wolfe, P.A., Phoenix. Author: Fireball, 1987. Pres. Ariz. Repertory Theater, 1960-66, trustee Atla Roscoe Pound Found.; bd. dirs. Phoenix Theater Ctr., 1955-60, 87—, Boys Clubs of Met. Phoenix; bd. govs. Welzmann Inst. Sci., Rehovot, Israel. Fellow Internat. Soc. Barristers; mem. Assn. Trial Lawyers Am. (pres. 1976-77, chmn. polit. action com. 1979-86), Western Trial Lawyers Assn. (pres. 1970), Am. Bd. Trial Advocates, State Bar Ariz. (cert. specialist in injury and wrongful death litigation). Clubs: Yale (N.Y.C.), Desert Highlands Country (Scottsdale, Ariz.), Pinetop Country (Pinetop, Ariz.), Wig and Pen (London). Office: Begam Lewis Marks and Wolfe 111 W Monroe St Ste 1400 Phoenix AZ 85003-1735

BEGAY, JEFFERSON LEE, general contracting company executive; b. Kayenta, Ariz., May 22, 1943; s. Harold Navajo and Stella Rose (Begay) Drake; m. Judith Ann Begay, Nov. 23, 1966 (div. Oct. 1983); children: Allison Marie, Tanabah Zahnie; m. Ella C. Jackson, Sep. 1, 1990. AA in Engring. Scis., Phoenix Coll., 1971; BS in Constrn., Ariz. State U., 1974. Community planner and developer Navajo Tribe, 1974-76, 83-84; estimator, field engr. Kitchell Contractors, Inc., 1976-77; instr. constn. contracting and materialslab. No. Ariz. U., 1978; in charge tech. assistance and tng. programs Indian Devel. Dist. Ariz., 1978-79; field supr. structural steel design, constrn. and inspection M.M. Sundt Constrn. Co., 1979-80; with Hemley Lee Assocs., 1980; project engr. Terra Grande Constructors, Inc., 1980-82, Chanen Constrn. Co., 1982-83; project engr., estimator Fisher Contracting Co., 1981-82; pres. Amerind Constrn., Inc., Tempe, 1983-84, Amerind Devel., Inc., Tempe, Ariz., 1985—; spl. asst. to Navajo tribal chmn. Peterson Zah, Navajo-Hopi-Indian land dispute. Past bd. dirs. Utah Navajo Devel. Coun.; mem. Gov.'s Commn. on Ariz. Environ., 1974-76; mem. fin. com. Jenny Norton for State Rep., Tempe, 1986; mem. NCCJ, 1988—; mem. VFW, Vietnam, 1967-68; mem. adv. coun. Rough Rock Community Sch., 1991—; bd. dirs. Urban Coalition West, Phoenix, 1987-89, NCCJ, 1988—. Sgt. U.S. Army, 1966-68, Vietnam. Vinnell Found. scholar, 1972-73, Kitchell Corp. scholar, 1973-74. Mem. Am. Soc. Profl. Estimators, Am. Inst. Constructors, Ariz. State U. Alumni Assn. (pres. 1989-90). Republican. Office: Amerind Constrn Inc 1820 W Drake St Tempe AZ 85283

BEGGS, HARRY MARK, lawyer; b. Los Angeles, Nov. 15, 1941; s. John Edgar and Agnes (Kentro) B.; m. Sandra Lynne Mikal, May 25, 1963; children: Brendan, Sean, Corey, Michael. Student, Ariz. State U., 1959-61, Phoenix Coll., 1961; LL.B., U. Ariz., 1964. Bar: Ariz. 1964, U.S. Dist. Ct. Ariz. 1964, U.S. Ct. Appeals (9th cir.) 1973; U.S. Supreme Ct. 1991. Assoc. Carson Messinger, Elliott, Laughlin & Ragan P.L.L.C., Phoenix, 1964-69; ptnr. Carson Messinger, Elliott, Laughlin & Ragan, Phoenix, 1969-93, mem., 1994—. Mem. editorial bd. Ariz. Law Rev. 1963-64; contbr. articles to profl. jours. Recipient award for highest grade on state bar exam. Atty. Gen. Ariz., 1964; Fegtly Moot Ct. award, 1963, 64; Abner S. Lipscomb scholar U. Ariz. Law Sch., 1963. Fellow Ariz. Bar Found. (founder); mem. State Bar Ariz., Ariz. Acad., Maricopa County Bar Assn., Plaza Club. Office: PO Box 33907 Phoenix AZ 85067-3907

BEHLMER, RUDY H., JR., director, writer, film educator; b. San Francisco, Oct. 13, 1926; s. Rudy H. and Helen Mae (McDonough) B.; 1 child by previous marriage, Curt; m. Stacey Endres, Oct. 1992. Student, Pasadena Playhouse Coll., 1946-49, Los Angeles City Coll., 1949-50. Dir. Sta. KLAC-TV, Hollywood, Calif., 1952-56; network TV dir. ABC-TV, Hollywood, 1956-57; TV comml. producer-dir., exec. Grant Advt., Hollywood, 1957-60; exec. producer-dir. Sta. KCOP-TV, Hollywood, 1960-63; v.p., TV comml. producer-dir. Hollywood office Leo Burnett USA, 1963-84; lectr. film Art Ctr. Coll. of Design, Pasadena, Calif., 1967-92, Calif. State U., Northridge, 1984-92, UCLA, 1988. Author: Memo from David O. Selznick, 1972, (with Tony Thomas) Hollywood's Hollywood, 1975, America's Favorite Movies-Behind the Scenes, 1982, Inside Warner Bros., 1985, Behind the Scenes: The Making of..., 1990, Memo From Darryl F. Zanuck, 1993; co-author: The Films of Errol Flynn, 1969; text on warner Bros. Fifty Years of Film Music, 1973; editor: The Adventures of Robin Hood, 1979, The Sea Hawk, 1982 (Wis./Warner Bros. screenplay series); contbr. articles on film history; writer and narrator for laserdiscs and video documentaries. Served with AC, USNR, 1944-46. Mem. Dirs. Guild Am.

BEHNEY, CHARLES AUGUSTUS, JR., veterinarian; b. Bryn Mawr, Pa., Nov. 30, 1929; s. Charles Augustus and Victoria Parks (Wythe) B.; B.S., U. Wyo., D.V.M., Colo. State U., 1961; m. Judith Ann Boggs, May 26, 1979; children—Charles Augustus III, Keenan F. Owner, Cochise Animal Hosp., Bisbee, Ariz., 1961—; veterinarian, dir. S.W. Traildust Zoo, Bisbee, 1966—; owner Kazam Arabians, Bisbee, 1969—; asso. prof. Cochise Coll. Chmn., Comprehensive Health Planning, Cochise County, Ariz., 1968. Mem. Am. Vet. Med. Assn., Soc. for Breeding Soundness, Internat. Platform Assn. Republican. Episcopalian. Rotarian, Elk. Patentee ultrasound device and eye cover for treating infections, apparatus to alter equine leg conformation, external vein clamp, equine sanitation instrument; developer ear implant instrumentation system. Home and Office: PO Box 4337 Bisbee AZ 85603-4337

BEHRENBRUCH, WILLIAM DAVID, filmmaker, educator; b. South Bend, Ind., July 23, 1946; s. Willard Herman and Mildred Kathleen (Steele) B.; m. Ingrid M. Neuschwander, Aug. 16, 1969 (div. 1975). Student, Ind. U., 1970-71; BA, Brooks Inst., 1974. Editor Rex Fleming Prodns., Santa Barbara, Calif., 1974-76, Golden Coast Films, Santa Barbara, 1976; pres. Visual Systems, Santa Barbara, 1976—; adj. instr. Brooks Inst., Santa Barbara, 1978—. Graphic designer (motion picture) Sweat, 1986; designer optical effects and titles Death Spa, 1986, War, 1986, Private Road, 1987, Blue Movies, 1987, Prime Suspect, 1988, Never Cry Devil, 1988, Ghosts Can't Do It, 1989, The Night Visitor, 1989, The Treasure, 1990, Grim Prairie Tales, 1990. Served to sgt. USAF, 1966-70. Mem. Soc. Motion Picture and TV Engrs., Assn. Ind. Video and Film Producers, Aircraft Owners and Pilots Assn. Club: Santa Barbara Flying. Office: Visual Systems 22 Anacapa St Santa Barbara CA 93101-1802

BEHREND, DONALD FRASER, university administrator; b. Manchester, Conn., Aug. 30, 1931; s. Sherwood Martin and Margaret (Fraser) B.; m. Joan Belcher, Nov. 9, 1957; children: Andrew Fraser, Eric Hemingway, David William. BS with honors and distinction, U. Conn., 1958, MS, 1960; PhD in Forest Zoology, SUNY, Syracuse, 1966. Forest game mgmt. specialist Ohio Dept. Natural Resources, Athens, 1960; res. asst. Coll. Forestry, SUNY, Newcomb, 1960-63, res. assoc., 1963-67; dir. Adirondack ecol. ctr. Coll. Environ. Science and Forestry, SUNY, Newcomb, 1968-73; acting dean grad. studies Syracuse, 1973-74; asst. v.p. research programs, exec. dir. Inst. Environ. Program Affairs, 1974-79, v.p. acad. affairs, prof., 1979-85, prof. emeritus, 1987—; asst. prof. wildlife mgmt. U. Maine, Orono, 1967-68; provost, v.p. acad. affairs U. Alaska Statewide System, Fairbanks, 1985-87, exec. v.p., provost, 1988; chancellor U. Alaska, Anchorage, 1988-94, chancellor emeritus, 1994—; mem. patent policy bd. SUNY, 1983-85, chmn. Res. Found. com. acad. res. devel., 1984-85; chmn. 6-Yr. planning com. U. Alaska, 1985-86; bd. dirs. Commonwealth North, 1991-92; mem. selection com. Harry S. Truman Scholarship Found.; mem. Pres.'s Commn., NCAA, 1992-95; chmn. spl. com. on student athlete welfare access and equity, 1993-95. Contbr. numerous articles and papers to profl. jours. Mem. Newcomb Planning Bd., 1967-69; mem., pres. Bd. Edn. Newcomb Cent. Sch., 1967-73; chmn. governing bd. N.Y. Sea Grant Inst., 1984-85; trustee U. Ala. Found., 1990-94. Served with USN, 1950-54. Mem. Wildlife Soc., Soc. Am. Foresters, AAAS, Phi Kappa Phi (hon.), Sigma Xi, Gamma Sigma Delta, Sigma Lambda Alpha (hon.). Lodges: Rotary (bd. dirs. Fairbanks club 1985-86), Lions (bd. dirs. Newcomb club 1966-67). Home: # 403 333 M St Apt 403 Anchorage AK 99501-1902

BEHRENS, BARBARA BLAUTH, healthcare administrator; b. Bklyn., Apr. 20, 1937; d. Robert James and Theresa (Enriquez) Blauth; m. Herbert Harry Behrens, Mar. 21, 1959 (div. July 1986); children: Christopher Charles, Catherine Ann. RN grad., Bellevue Sch. Nursing, N.Y.C., 1957; BA with distinction, U. of Redlands, 1976, MA in Mgmt. Human Resources with distinction, 1979. RN, Hawaii, Calif., N.Y.; cert. advanced cardiac life support, basic cardiac life support instr./trainer, cert. emergency nurse, mobile intensive care nurse. Staff nurse med.-surg. and critical care depts. U. Calif., Moffett Hosp., San Francisco; with Bellevue Hosp., N.Y.C.; relief nurse all units Stanford (Calif.) Univ. Hosp., 1962-69, staff nurse IV, acting insvc. instr., 1972-76, ednl. coord., 1976-78, clin. nursing coord., 1978-82, asst. dir. dept. emergency svcs., 1982-86; dir. critical care and emergency svcs. Queen's Med. Ctr., Honolulu, 1986-89; exec. dir. Queen's Heart Inst., 1989—. Mem. ACCA, Am. Coll. Cardiovascular Adminstrs. (state dir. Hawaii chpt.), Am. Acad. Med. Adminstrs. (state dir. Hawaii chpt.), Am. Heart Assn. (Hawaii ACLS faculty, bd. dirs. exec. com. Hawaii affiliate), Am. Orgn. Nurse Execs. (chair nominating com., legis. com.), Emergency Nurses Assn, Nat. League of Nursing (bd. dir. Hawaii affiliate). Home: 1030 Aoloa Pl # 304A Kailua HI 96734 Office: Queens Med Ctr Heart Inst 1301 Punchbowl St Honolulu HI 96813-2413

BEHRENS, BEREL LYN, physician, academic administrator; b. New South Wales, Australia, 1940. MB, BS, Sydney (Australia) U., 1964. Cert. pediatrics, allergy and immunology. Pediatric pulmonary intern Royal Prince Alfred Hosp., Australia, 1964; resident Loma Linda (Calif.) U. Med. Ctr., 1966-68; with Henrietta Egleston Hosp. for Children, Atlanta, 1968-69, T.C. Thompson Children's Hosp., Chattanooga, 1969-70; instr. pediatrics Loma Linda U., 1970-72, with dept. pediatrics, 1972—, dean Sch. Medicine, 1986-91, pres., 1990—. Office: Loma Linda U Office of the President Loma Linda CA 92350

BEHRENS, LAURENCE, educator, writer; b. Manchester, Eng., June 14, 1942; came to U.S., 1953; s. Cyril and Freda (Minkin) B.; m. Bonnie Michiko Arai, Sept. 22, 1965; 1 child, Michael Arai. AB, Brandeis U., 1964; MFA, Columbia U., 1966; MA, UCLA, 1972, PhD, 1974. Lectr. U. Calif., Irvine, 1974-75; asst. prof. American U., Washington, 1975-82; lectr. U. Calif., Santa Barbara, 1985—. Co-author: Writing and Reading Across the Curriculum, 1982, 5th edit., 1994, Writing Papers in College, 1986, Reading for College Writers, 1987, Theme and Variations: The Impact of Great Ideas, 1988, The American Experience: A Sourcebook for Critical Thinking and Writing, 1992, Allyn & Bacon Handbook, 1992, 2d edit., 1994; contbr. articles to profl. jours. Staff sgt. USAF, 1965-69. Mem. Nat. Coun. Tchrs. English, Am. Fedn. Tchrs. Democrat. Jewish. Office: Univ Calif Writing Program Santa Barbara CA 93106

BEHRING, KENNETH E., professional sports team owner; b. Freeport, Ill., June 13, 1928; s. Elmer and Mae (Priewe) B.; m. Patricia Riffle, Oct. 16, 1949; children: Michael, Thomas, David, Jeffrey, Scott. Student, U. Wis., 1947. Owner Behring Motors, Monroe, Wis., 1953-56, Behring Corp., Ft. Lauderdale, Fla., 1956-72; owner Blackhawk Corp., Danville, Calif., 1972—, also chmn. bd. dirs.; owner Seattle Seahawks, NFL, 1988—; Calif. land developer; mem. policy adv. bd. real estate and urban econs. U. Calif., Berkeley.; chmn. bd. dirs. Behring-Hofmann Ednl. Inst., Inc. U. Calif. Trustee U. Calif., Berkeley; regent St. Mary's Coll., Moraga, Calif., Holy Name Coll., Oakland, Calif.; hon. trustee Mt. Diablo Hosp. Found., Concord, Calif.; hon. chmn. Seattle Art Mus., Am. Cancer Soc., Muscular Dystrophy, Silverado Concours. Named Man of Yr. Boys Town Italy, Entrepreneur of Yr. INC mag. Mem. Am. Acad. Achievement (honoree 1989), Assn. Wash. Bus., Seattle Master Builders Assn., Blackhawk Club, Vintage Club, Seattle Yacht Club, Wash. Athletic Club. Office: Blackhawk Corp PO Box 807 Danville CA 94526-0807 also: Seattle Seahawks 11220 NE 53rd St Kirkland WA 98033-7505*

BEHRMANN, JOAN GAIL, newspaper editor; b. N.Y.C.; d. Jerome and Jeannette (Silverman) Metzner; m. Larry Jinks, Oct. 2, 1960 (div. 1970); children: Laura Jinks Kastigar, Daniel Carlton; m. Nicolas Lee Behrmann, Dec. 21, 1972. BA, Queens Coll., 1956; MS, Columbia U., 1958. Reporter Charlotte (N.C.) Observer, 1958-60, Miami (Fla.) Herald, 1960-64, Miami News, 1965-66; asst. prof. Miami Dade C.C., 1968-72; assoc. prof. Boston U., 1975-78; Sunday editor The Saragotan, Saratoga Springs, N.Y., 1979-80; editor Gannett Westchester, Westchester County, N.Y., 1981-83; page one editor, entertainment editor USA Today, Rosslyn, Va., 1983-87; exec. editor The Desert Sun, Palm Springs, Calif., 1987—. Co-author: Questioning Media Ethics, 1978. Bd. dirs. Coll. of the Desert Found., Palm Desert, 1993—, Jewish Family Svcs., Palm Springs, 1994—, Palm Springs Opera Guild, 1989-91; founder Every Women's Coun., Glens Falls, N.Y., 1978-80. Recipient Athena award Palm Springs C. of C., 1991. Mem. Assn. Press Mng. Editors Orgn. (bd. dirs. 1991—, com. chair), Am. Soc. Newspaper Editors, Women in Comms., Inc., Calif. Press Women. Office: Desert Sun 750 N Gene Autry Trl Palm Springs CA 92262-5463

BEICHMAN, ARNOLD, political scientist, educator, writer; b. N.Y.C., May 17, 1913; s. Solomon and Mary Beichman; mm. Doris Modry (div. 1946); m. Carroll Aikins, Oct. 9, 1950; children: Charles, Janine, John, Anthony (dec.). BA in Polit. Sci., Columbia U., MA in Polit. Sci., PhD in Polit. Sci., 1973. Assoc. prof., polit. scientist U. Mass., 1970-78; assoc. prof. polit. sci. U. B.C., 1974-75, U. Calgary, Alta., Can.; 1977; adj. prof. polit. sci. Georgetown U.; mem. editorial adv. bd., columnist Washington Times; vis. scholar Hoover Instn., 1982—, rsch. fellow, 1988—. Author: The "Other" State Department, 1969, Nine Lies About America, 1972, Herman Wouk: The Novelist as Social Historian, 1986, (with others) Yuri Andropov: New Challenge to the West, 1983, The Long Pretense: Soviet Treaty Diplomacy from Lenin to Gorbachev, 1991, Anti-American Myths: Their Causes and Consequences, 1993; contbr. numerous articles to profl. jours. Founding mem. Consortium for the Study of Intelligence, Washington. Home: PO Box 37, Naramata, BC Canada V0H 1N0 Office: Hoover Instn Stanford U Stanford CA 94305

BEILENSON, ANTHONY CHARLES, congressman; b. New Rochelle, N.Y., Oct. 26, 1932; s. Peter and Edna (Rudolph) B.; m. Dolores Martin, June 20, 1959; children: Peter, Dayna, Adam. B.A., Harvard Coll., 1954; LL.B., Harvard U., 1957. Bar: Calif. 1957. Mem. Calif. Assembly from 59th Dist., 1963-66, Calif. Senate from 22d Dist., 1967-76, 95th-103rd Congresses from 23rd (now 24th) Calif. Dist., 1977—; ranking minority mem. subcom. on Rules & Orgn. of Ho. Democrat. Office: Ho of Reps 2465 Rayburn Bldg Washington DC 20515-0005

BEIRNE, DANIELLE ULULANI, state legislator; m. David Haili Keawe; 4 children. AA, Windward C.C., 1988; BA, U. Hawaii, 1988, postgrad., 1988-92. Rep. dist. 46 State of Hawaii; with Outrigger Hotels; mem. bd. dirs. Hui Na'auao; v.p. Kahana 'Ohana Unity Coun. Mem. Ko'olauloa Hawaiian Civic Club (v.p.), Ka'a'awa, Kahana, Punaiu'u, Hauula, Laie, Kahalu'u & Ko'olauloa Cmty. Assns. Democrat. Home: PO Box 653 Kaneohe HI 96744-0653 Office: Hawaii House Reps State House Honolulu HI 96813

BEJAR, EZRA, pharmacologist, biology educator; b. Mexico City, Sept. 2, 1958; came to the U.S., 1987; s. Ezra and Marisabel (Ocampo) B.; m. M. Veronica Angeles, Dec. 29, 1982; children: Ezra A., Paula C. BS, Autonomous Met. U., Mexico City, 1981, MSc, 1985; PHD, U. of the Pacific, 1991. Assoc. scientist Mexican Med. Inst., Mexico City, 1985-87; rsch. scientist Rsch. Inst. Pharm. Scis., U. Miss., Oxford, 1991-92; lab. dir. Rees-Stealy Rsch. Found., San Diego, 1993—; adj. prof. San Diego (Calif.) State U., 1993—; peer reviewer Jour. Nat. Products, 1993—. Contbr. articles to profl. jours. Rsch. grantee Sharp Found., San Diego, 1994, Calif. Metabolic Rsch. Found., San Diego, 1994; Rsch. scholar Med. Mexican Inst., 1982-85; scholar Nat. Coun. for Sci. and Tech. of Mexico, 1983-85, 87-90. Mem. Am. Soc. Pharmacognosy (Travel award 1989), Southeastern Pharmacology Soc., Soc. for the Advancement Chicanos and Native Ams. in Sci. Home: 5702 Baltimore Dr Apt 265 La Mesa CA 91942-1667 Office: 2001 4th Ave San Diego CA 92101-2303

BEKAVAC, NANCY YAVOR, academic administrator, lawyer; b. Pitts., Aug. 28, 1947; d. Anthony Joseph and Elvira (Yavor) B. BA, Swarthmore Coll., 1969; JD, Yale U., 1973. Bar: Calif. 1974, U.S. Dist. Ct. (cen. dist.) 1974, (no. dist.) Calif. 1975, (so. dist.) Calif. 1976, U.S. Ct. Appeals (9th cir.) 1975, (8th cir.) 1981, U.S. Supreme Ct. 1979. Law clk. at large U.S. Ct. Appeals (D.C. cir.), Washington, 1973-74; assoc. Munger, Tolles & Rickershauser, L.A., 1974-79, ptnr., 1980-85; exec. dir. Thomas J. Watson Found., Providence, 1985-87, cons., 1987-88; counselor to pres. Dartmouth Coll., Hanover, N.H., 1988-90; pres. Scripps Coll., Claremont, Calif., 1990—; adj. prof. law UCLA Law Sch., 1982-83. Bd. mgrs. Swarthmore Coll., 1984-88, 90—; trustee Wenner-Gren Found. for Anthrop. Rsch., 1987—. Recipient Human Rights award L.A. County Commn. on Civil Rights, 1984; Woodrow Wilson fellow, Thomas J. Watson fellow, 1969. Mem. L.A. County Bar Assn. (trustee 1980-84, chair com. on individual rights and responsibilities 1984-85), Assn. Bus. Trial Lawyers (lectr. 1985). Office: Scripps Coll Office of President 1030 Columbus Claremont CA 91711-3948*

BEKEY, GEORGE ALBERT, computer scientist, educator, engineer; b. Bratislava, Czechoslovakia, June 19, 1928; came to U.S., 1945, naturalized, 1956; s. Andrew and Elizabeth B.; m. Shirley White, June 10, 1951; children: Ronald Steven, Michelle Elaine. B.S. with honors, U. Calif., Berkeley, 1950; M.S., UCLA, 1952, Ph.D., 1962. Research engr. UCLA, 1950-54; mgr. computer center Beckman Instruments, Los Angeles and Berkeley, 1955-58; mem. sr. staff, dir. computer center TRW Systems Group, Redondo Beach, Calif., 1958-62; mem. faculty U. So. Calif., Los Angeles, 1962—, prof. elec. and biomed. engring. and computer sci., 1968-82, chmn. dept. elec. engring. systems, 1978-86; dir. Robotics Lab., chmn. computer sci. dept. U. So. Calif., L.A., 1984-89, dir. Ctr. for Mfg. and Automation Research, 1987-94; chair computer sci. Gordon Marshall, 1990—; cons. to govt. agys. and indsl. orgns. Author: (with W.J. Karplus) Hybrid Computation, 1968, (with K. Goldberg) Robotics and Neural Networks, 1994; editor 4 books; mem. editorial bd. 3 profl. jours.; founding editor IEEE Trans. Robotics and Automation; editor Autonomous Robots; contbr. over 180 articles to profl. jours.; patentee in field. Served with U.S. Army, 1954-56. Recipient Disting. Faculty award, 1977, Sch. Engring. and Service award U. So. Calif., 1990. Fellow AAAS, IEEE, Am. Inst. Med. and Biol. Engring.; mem. NAE, Am. Assn. for Artificial Intelligence, Assn. for Computing Machinery, Soc. for Computer Simulation, Neural Network Soc., Biomed. Engring. Soc., World Affairs Coun., Sigma Xi, Tau Beta Pi, Eta Kappa Nu. Office: U So Calif Dept Computer Sci Los Angeles CA 90089-0781

BEKEY, SHIRLEY WHITE, psychotherapist; b. L.A.; d. Lawrence Francis and Alice (King) White; m. George Albert Bekey, June 10, 1951; children: Ronald S., Michelle E. BA in Psychology, Occidental Coll., L.A., 1949; MSW in Psychiat. Social Work, UCLA, 1954; PhD in Edn. Psychology, U. So. Calif., 1980. Lic. clin. social worker, Calif.; cert. in pupil pers., parent-child edn. Caseworker outpatient svcs. Calif. State Dept. Mental Health, Montebello; caseworker Lowman Sch. for Handicapped, L.A. Unified Sch. Dist., North Hollywood, Calif., 1971-72; psychotherapist Hofmann Psychiat. Clinic, Glendale (Calif.) Adventist Hosp., 1973-75; pvt. practice psychotherapy Encino, Calif., 1980—; speaker nat. radio, TV expert on children's emotional problems. Mem. World Affairs Coun., L.A., 1960—. Fellow Soc. for Clin. Social Work; mem. NASW, APA, Am. Ednl. Rsch. Assn., Nat. Assn. Gifted Children, Assn. Transpersonal Psychology, Inst. Noetic Scis., Assn. Ednl. Therapists, Soc. Calif. Soc. Clin. Hypnosis, Analytical Psychology Club L.A., Nat. Assn. Poetry Therapy, Calif. Assn. Gifted. Democrat. Office: 18075 Ventura Blvd Encino CA 91316-3517

BEKIR, NAGWA ESMAT, electrical engineer, educator, consultant; b. Cairo, Dec. 31, 1944; came to U.S., 1972; s. Mohammed Ragab Shalaby and Kamla (Abdel Megeed) Mahmood; m. Esmat Chibl, Sept. 23, 1971; children: Ahmad C., Badr E. BSEE, Cairo U., Egypt, 1966; MSEE, U. So. Calif., 1975, PhD in EE, 1978. Rsch. and hardware engr. Egyptian Indsl. Rsch. Inst., Cairo, 1966-69; quality control engr. Nat. Egyptian Co. for TV and Electronics, Cairo, 1969-72; mem. tech. staff Axiomatics, L.A., 1978, Hughes Aircraft Co., Canoga Park, Calif., 1978-80; assoc. prof. elec. and computer engring. dept. Calif. State U., Northridge, 1980-83, prof., 1984—; tech. staff ITT Gilfillan, Van Nuys, Calif., 1984; sr. staff engr. Hughes Aircraft Co., Canoga Park, Calif., 1985; cons. Aircraft divsn. Northrop Co., El Segundo, Calif., 1987; cons. Budlong & Assocs., Inc., Agoura Hills, Calif., 1992-93. Contbr. articles to profl. jours. Recipient Meritorious Performance and Profl. Promise award Calif. State U., Northridge, 1989, Outstanding Faculty awards Sch. of Engring. and Computer Sci., 1990. Mem. IEEE (sr.), Health and Tennis Corp. Am., Eta Kappa Nu, Tau Beta Pi. Office: Calif State U 18111 Nordhoff St Northridge CA 91330-0001

BELCHER, DONALD DAVID, manufacturing company executive; b. Kansas City, Mo., Nov. 29, 1938; s. Donald Duy and Elizabeth Jane (Martin) B.; m. M. Marie Langguth, Dec. 29, 1962; children: Devon, Eric, Kristin. B.A., Dartmouth Coll., 1960; M.B.A., Stanford U., 1964. Mktg. mgr. Pillsbury Co., Mpls., 1964-70; pres. Troutdale Ranch, Gravios Mills., Inc., Mo., 1970—; also dir. Troutdale Ranch, Gravois Mills., Inc., Mo., 1970—; gen. mgr. various divs. Avery Internat., Azusa, Calif., 1972-77; group v.p. Fasson Europe, Lieden, Holland, 1977-82; group v.p. consumer group Fasson Europe, Pasadena, Calif., 1982—. Served to capt. U.S. Army, 1960-62. Home: 273 Monte Pl Arcadia CA 91006-1541

BELCHER, JENNIFER MARION, state legislator, management consultant; b. Beckley, W.Va., Jan. 4, 1944; d. Grover Emerson and Virginia Dare (Phillips) Marion. Student, Bethany Coll., 1962-63; program for sr. execs., Harvard U., 1986. Adminstrv. sec. Planning and Community Affairs Agy. State of Wash., 1967-72; spl. asst. Office of Gov., Olympia, Wash., 1973-79; owner, pres. Mgmt. Dynamics, 1980—; mem. Wash. Ho. of Reps., Olympia, 1982—. Bd. dirs. United Way Thurston County, Olympia, 1976—; pres. Wash. State's Women's Polit. Caucus, 1979. Mem. Wash. State Employees Credit Union (bd. dirs. 1976-82), Wash. Bus. and Profl. Women's Club. Democrat. Home: 323 Maple Park Ave SE Olympia WA 98501-2360 Office: Wash State Ho Reps 406 House Ofc Bldg Olympia WA 98504

BELCHER, WILLIAM WALTER, JR., electronics company executive; b. Sayre, Pa., Oct. 22, 1943; s. William Walter Sr. and Mildred Rae (Smith) B.; m. Carole Jean Drake, June 12, 1965; children: Jon Christian, Katryna Dora. BE, Mansfield (Pa.) State Coll., 1964. Cert. tchr., Pa. Tchr. Galeton (Pa.) Pub. Schs., 1964-65, Susquehanna Valley Cen. Schs., Conklin, N.Y., 1965-66; quality engr. GE, Binghamton, N.Y., 1966-74, mgr. quality engring., 1974-75; mgr. reliability and quality assurance GE, Erie, Pa., 1975-79; mgr. x-ray tube mfg. GE, Milw., 1979-85; mgr. mfg. GE, Syracuse, N.Y., 1985-87; v.p. ops. NavCom Def. Electronics, Inc., El Monte, Calif., 1988-93; owner C.B. Productions, San Dimas, Calif., 1993—. Mem. adv. coun. Calif. State Poly. Inst., Pomona, Calif., 1988—, ind. adv. coun. El Monte Adult Edn.; chmn. com. Boy Scouts Am., Erie, 1978, Waukesha, Wis., 1983-85; mem. adminstrv. coun. Salem Meth. Ch., Waukesha, 1981; elder First Presbyn. Ch., Waukesha, 1985; mem. fin. com. United Meth. Ch., Glendora. Recipient Nat. Dir.'s award for outstanding achievement in labor rels. U.S. Dept. Labor, 1991. Mem. Armed Forces Communications and Electronics Assn. Republican. Home: 774 Bradford Ave Pomona CA 91767-4606 Office: 609 E Calle Santa Barbara San Dimas CA 91773-3949

BELEC, MARGUERITE ELIZABETH, naval officer; b. Newark, Aug. 24, 1952; d. Marvin Benson and Betty Mae (Job) Emmons; m. James Medric Belec, Nov. 10, 1984; children: Renee Medric, Aaron Amadeus Fiqiri, AnnaLisa Danielle Fiquirete. BS in Consumer Scis., U. Wis., 1974; MA in Ednl. Adminstrn., San Diego State U., 1989; MA in Nat. Security/Strategic Studies, Naval War Coll., Newport, R.I., 1993. Commd. ensign U.S. Navy, 1982, advanced through grades to lt. comdr., 1992; comdr. Seattle Mil. Entrance Processing Sta., 1994—. Decorated Navy Commendation medal, Navy Achievement medal. Office: Mil Entrance Processing Sta 2801 3rd Ave Seattle WA 98121-1242

BELILLE, RONALD, safety and security coordinator; b. Portland, Nov. 22, 1947; s. Frank and Geraldine (Kron) B. AA in Law Enforcement, Portland Community Coll., 1970; student, Fed. Law Enforcement Tng. Ctr., Glynco, Ga., 1978; BS in Adminstrn. Justice, Portland State U., 1979; AA in Occupational Safety and Health, Mt. Hood Community Coll., 1985; grad., Police Reserve Acad., Oregon City, Oreg., 1985; grad. Intermediate Security Acad., Clackamas Community Coll., 1987; AA in Mgmt. and Supervisory Devel., Portland Community Coll., 1988; postgrad., Portland State U., 1985. Cert. emergency med. technician 1. Correctional officer State Penitentiary, Salem, Oreg., 1972; fed. protective officer Fed. Protective Svcs., Portland, 1978; safety/security officer Precision Castparts, Portland, 1979-83, security coordinator, 1983-93; CPR instr., first aid instr., portable fire extinguishers instr. Precision Castparts, 1983-85; chmn. steering com. Intermediate Security Acad. Clackamas Community Coll., 1987; project coord.City of Portland Office of the City Auditor, 1993, project asst. City of Portland Office of the Mayor, 1994. Vol. asst. counselor Multiple County Adult Probation/Parole, Portland, Oreg., 1975; vol. asst. recognizance Officer Multiple County Ct., Oreg., 1982; mem. police and law enforcement task force Citizen's Crime Commn., 1989-93); vice chair Citizens Bur. Adv. Coordinating Com. City of Portland; mem. Portland bur. adv. com. Portland Police Bureau; bd. dirs. Ryles Med. Ctr. Evaluation and Treatment. With USAF, 1966-68. Mem. Am. Soc. for Indsl. Security (chmn. legis. com. 1989-90, treas. 1990-91), Am. Soc. Safety Engrs., Nat. Assn. Chiefs Police, Portland Police Athletic Assn., Masons, Elks, Phi Theta Kappa. Home: 1238 SE 47th Ave Portland OR 97215-2512

BELJAN, JOHN RICHARD, university administrator, medical educator; b. Detroit, May 26, 1930; s. Joseph and Margaret Anne (Brozovich) B.; m. Bernadette Marie Marenda, Feb. 2, 1952; children: Ann Marie, John Richard, Paul Eric. B.S., U. Mich., 1951, M.D., 1954. Diplomate: Am. Bd. Surgery. Intern U. Mich., Ann Arbor, 1954-55, resident in gen. surgery, 1955-59; dir. med. services Stuart div. Atlas Chem. Industries, Pasadena, Calif., 1965-66; from asst. prof. to assoc. prof. surgery U. Calif. Med. Sch., Davis, 1966-74, from asst. prof. to assoc. prof. engring., 1968-74, from asst. dean to assoc. dean, 1971-74; prof. surgery, prof. biol. engring. Wright State U., Dayton, Ohio, 1974-83, dean Sch. Medicine, 1974-81, vice provost, 1974-78, v.p. health affairs, 1978-81, provost, sr. v.p., 1981-83; prof. arts and scis., assoc. v.p. med. affairs Cen. State U., Wilberforce, Ohio, 1976-83; provost, v.p. acad. affairs, dean Sch. Medicine Hahnemann U., Phila., 1983-85, prof. surgery and biomed. engring., 1983-86, spl. adviser to pres., 1985-86; v.p. acad. affairs Calif. State U., Long Beach, 1986-89, prof. anat., physiology and biomed. engring., 1986-91, provost, 1989-91; pres. Northrop U., L.A., 1989-93, pres. emeritus, 1993—; trustee Cox Heart Inst., 1975-77, Drew Health Ctr., 1977-78, Wright State U. Found., 1975-83, CSULB Found., 1986-89, 49er Athletic Found., 1986-89; trustee, regional v.p. Engring. and Sci. Inst. Hall of Fame, 1983—; bd. dirs. Miami Valley Health Sys. Agy., 1975-82, UCI Ctr. for Health Edn., 1987-90, Long Beach Rsch. Found., 1989-94; cons. in field. Author articles, revs., chpts. in books. Served with M.C. USAF, 1955-65. Decorated Commendation medal; Braun fellow, 1949; grantee USPHS, NASA, 1968—. Fellow A.C.S.; mem. Los Angeles County Med. Assn., Mich. Alumni Club (Dayton, Outstanding Alumnus award 1976), Oakwood Fur Club, Fin and Feather Club, Phi Beta Delta, Phi Beta Kappa, Alpha Omega Alpha, Phi Eta Sigma, Phi Kappa Phi, Alpha Kappa Kappa. Home and Office: 6490 E Saddle Dr Long Beach CA 90815-4740

BELK, JOHN BLANTON, educational and cultural organization executive; b. Orlando, Fla., Feb. 4, 1925; s. John Blanton and Jennie (Wannamaker) B.; m. Elizabeth Jane Wilkes, Dec. 11, 1954; children: Virginia Elizabeth, Katherine Wilkes. Student, Davidson Coll., 1943, U. N.C., 1943-45. With Moral Re-Armament (numerous locations), 1950-68, exec. dir., 1966-68; founder, chmn. bd., pres. Up With People, Tucson, 1968-91, chmn. exec. com., 1991—. Bd. dirs. Internat. Fund Sports Disabled, Arnhem, Netherlands; mem. Gov.'s Ariz.-Mexico Commn. Lt. (j.g.) USNR, 1943-45. Decorated officer Order Vasco Nunez de Balboa (Panama); officer Order of Leopold (Belgium). Mem. Zeta Psi. Clubs: Mountain Oyster; Guaymas Yacht (Mexico). Home: 2920 E Cerrada Los Palitos Tucson AZ 85718-4222 Office: Up With People 7070 N Oracle Rd Ste 260 Tucson AZ 85704-4339

BELL, ALAN, lawyer, environmental health activist; b. N.Y.C., Aug. 13, 1954; s. Julius and Vivian B.; 1 child, Ashlee. BBA magna cum laude, U. Miami, 1976, JD, 1979. Bar: Fla. 1979, U.S. Dist. Ct. (so. dist.) Fla. 1980. Cert. legal intern felony and juvenile divs. Dade County State Atty. Office, Miami, Fla., 1978-79; asst. state atty. Broward County, Ft. Lauderdale, Fla., 1980-86; corp. counsel and atty. The Travelers Insur. Co., Ft. Lauderdale, Fla., 1986-89; lawyer pvt. practice, 1989-91; co-chmn., founder Environ. Health Found., Tucson, Ariz., 1992—. Chief justice Student Supreme Ct., U. Miami, 1976. Mem. Omicron Delta Kappa (hon., pres.). Home: 4161 N Camino del Celador Tucson AZ 85718

BELL, ALAN, publishing company executive; b. L.A., Mar. 14, 1945. BA in Sociology, UCLA, 1969; postgrad., NYU, 1972-73; BS in Bus., SUNY, 1985; postgrad., Calif. State U., L.A., 1991. Psychiat. social worker dept. forensic psychiatry NYU Med. Ctr., Bellevue Hosp. Prison Ward, 1969-71; exec. asst. to vice chancellor adminstrv. affairs CUNY, 1971-72; pres. Intertypographics, N.Y.C., 1973-79; product mgr. Graphic Products, Inc., L.A., 1986-89; prodn. mgr. Ili-Speed Advt. Typography, Inc., L.A., 1979-89; film critic L.A. Sentinel, 1985-94; pres. Blk Pub. Co., Inc., L.A., 1988—; film reviewer Motion Picture Assn. Am., 1986—. Appt. to Coun. on Intergroup Rels., 1979. Recipient Martin Luther King. Jr. grant, 1973, 73-74, N.Y. State Scholar Incentive award, 1972-74, Francis Emory Fitch Meml. award Printing Industries of Met. N.Y., 1975. Home: 5903 S Corning Ave Los Angeles CA 90056-1403

BELL, BRIAN MAYES, lawyer; b. Columbus, Tex., Aug. 21, 1940; s. Robert Harvey and Edith Virginia (Kimball) B.; m. Karen Ann Roof, May 25, 1962 (div. 1973); m. Charlotte Jean Starks, Dec. 28, 1973 (div. 1980); m. Sue Ann Curry, July 25, 1980; children: Robin L., Susan L., Michael K., Miles A. Franz, Alex F. Franz. BS, So. Meth. U., 1962; JD, U. Denver, 1968. Bar: Colo. 1969, U.S. Dist. Ct. Colo. 1969, U.S. Ct. Appeals (10th cir.) 1969. Assoc. Rovira, DeMuth & Eiberger, Denver, 1968-72; atty., asst. sec. Mountain Bell Tele. Co., Denver, 1972-83; sr. corp. counsel, asst. sec. U.S. West, Inc., Englewood, Colo., 1983-93; adj. prof. U. Colo., Denver, 1974-83. Mem. ABA, Am. Soc. Corp. Secs. (bd. dirs. 1990-93, pres. Colo. chpt. 1988-89), Am. Corp. Counsel Assn. (bd. dirs. Colo. chpt. 1989-95), Met. Club, Valley Country Club. Republican. Presbyterian. Home: 3233 Country Club Pkwy Castle Rock CO 80104

BELL, CHARLES VESTER, college administrator; b. Starkville, Miss., Mar. 19, 1934; s. Homer Vester and Hattie Pearl (Hester) B.; m. Margaret

Lenore Reynolds, Dec. 21, 1954; children: Charles Michael, Carey Scott, David Randolph. BSEE, Miss. State U., 1956; MSEE, Stanford U., 1957, PhD, 1960. Registered profl. engr., Washington, Calif. Sect. head Hughes Aircraft Co., Fullerton, Calif., 1962-72; asst. prof. physics Walla Walla Coll., College Place, Wash., 1960-62, assoc. prof. physics, 1972-74, dean engring., 1974-84; acad. v.p. Pacific Union Coll., Angwin, Calif., 1984—; cons. Bendix Research Labs., Southfield, Mich., 1960-62. Contbr. microwave electronics articles to profl. jours. First oboist Walla Walla Symphony, 1972-84. Mem. IEEE (sr.), Am. Soc. Engring. Edn., Internat. Double Reed Soc., Sigma Xi. Seventh-day Adventist. Lodge: Rotary. Home: 175 Edgewood Pl Angwin CA 94508-9750 Office: Pacific Union Coll One Angwin Ave Angwin CA 94508

BELL, CHESTER GORDON, computer engineering company executive; b. Kirksville, Mo., Aug. 19, 1934; s. Roy Chester and Lola Dolph (Gordon) B.; m. Gwendolyn Kay Druyor, Jan. 3, 1959; children: Brigham Roy, Laura Louise. BSEE, MIT, 1956, MSEE, 1957; DEng (hon.), Worcester Poly. Inst., 1993. Engr. Speech Communication Lab., MIT, Cambridge, 1959-60; mgr. computer design Digital Equipment Corp., Maynard, Mass., 1960-66, v.p. engring., 1972-83; prof. computer sci. Carnegie-Mellon U., 1966-72; vice chmn. Encore Computer Corp., Marlboro, Mass., 1983-86; asst. dir. NSF, Washington, 1986-87; v.p. R & D Stardent Computer, Sunnyvale, Calif., 1987-89; cons. The Bell-Mason Group, 1989—; bd. dirs. Ambit Design, Cirrus Logic, The Bell-Mason Group, Univ. Video Comm.; bd. dirs., trustee Computer Mus., 1982—. Author: (with Newell) Computer Structures, 1971, (with Grason, Newell) Designing Computers and Digital Systems, 1972, (with Mudge, McNamara) Computer Engineering, 1978, (with Siewiorek, Newell) Computer Structures, 1982, (with McNamara) High Tech Ventures, 1991. Recipient 6th Mellon Inst. award, 1972, Nat. Medal Tech., U.S. Dept. Commerce Tech. Adminstrn., 1991, award for greatest econ. contbn. to region Am. Electronics Assn., 1993, MCI Smithsonian award for Innovation, 1995. Fellow IEEE (McDowell award 1975, Eckert-Mauchly award 1982, von Neumann medal 1992), AAAS, Am. Acad. Arts and Scis., Assn. for Computing Machinery; mem. NAE, Eta Kappa Nu. Home and Office: 450 Old Oak Ct Los Altos CA 94022-2634

BELL, DANIEL CARROLL, realtor, ranch and land manager; b. Chgo., July 17, 1940; s. Daniel Gregory and Inez Margarite (Carroll) B.; m. Elaine Paula Rhody, Feb. 1, 1960; children: Tana Lou, Daniel Arden, Andrea Jane. Student, Colo. State U., 1958-62, Reisch Coll. Auctioneering, Mason City, Iowa, 1983. Mgr. ptnr. Three Bell Ranch, Ft. Collins, Colo., 1958-69; sales rep. Pacific Vegetable Oil Co., San Francisco, 1969-70; mng. dir. Paveocor A.G. subs. PVO Internat., Rotterdam, Netherlands, 1970-71; nat. sales mgr. PVO Internat., San Francisco, 1971-72; v.p. commodity trading San Pablo Mfg. Co. subs. PVO Internat., Manila, Philippines, 1972-74; v.p. Rothschild Brokerage Co., San Francisco, 1975-76; owner, prin. Feed, Etc., Harbor, Oreg., 1976-79; commodity specialist Shearson Loeb Rhodes, Medford, Oreg., 1979-80; exec. v.p., gen. mgr. Superior Credit Assocs., Inc., Medford, 1981-86; mng. ptnr. Three Bell Land Co., Pierce, Colo., 1986—; ptnr. Legacy Transp. Co., 1986-93; co-owner Bell & Assocs., 1993—; gen. mgr. Greenfield Village RV Resort Assn., 1995—; photography judge, 1989—; ptnr. Bell & Assocs., 1993—; gen mgr. RV Resort Assn., 1995—. Mem. Medford (Oreg.) Planning Coun., 1981-84, Medford Sister Cities Commn., 1984; treas. Jackson County Rep. Cen. Com., Medford, 1982-84; arbitrator Better Bus. Bur., Medford and Ft. Collins, Colo., 1984-89; candidate Oreg. Ho. Reps., 1984; mem. Mesa (Ariz.) Human Svcs. Adv. Bd. With USAR, 1958-63, Colo. Air N.G., 1963-65. Mem. Nat. Assn. Realtors, Ariz. Assn. Realtors, Mesa, Chandler, Tempe Assn. Realtors, Profl. Photographers Am., Am. Legion, Elks. Republican. Presbyterian. Office: 111 S Greenfield Mesa AZ 85206

BELL, DENISE LOUISE, newspaper reporter, photographer, librarian; b. Washington, Nov. 27, 1967; d. Richard Keith Bell and Kay Lorraine (Sutherland) Reynolds. Student, Inst. Adventiste du Salare, Collonges, France, 1988; BA in French, Loma Linda U., 1990. Yearbook editor Loma Linda U., La Sierra, Calif., 1989-90; desk technician Loma Linda U., Loma Linda, Calif., 1990-92; staff writer Inland Empire Cmty. Newspapers, Colton, Calif., 1990-91; city editor Inland Empire Cmty. Newspapers, San Bernardino, Calif., 1991-94; asst. circ. supr. Del Webb Meml. Libr. Loma Linda (Calif.) U., 1994—. Asst. leader Girl Scouts U.S., Walla Walla, Wash., 1986; co-leader Girl Scouts Switzerland, Geneva, 1987, Girl Scouts U.S., Loma Linda, 1988-93. Mem. Toastmasters. Home: 10944 Evans St Loma Linda CA 92354-2760

BELL, DONALD WILLIAM, experimental psychologist; b. Los Angeles, Apr. 28, 1936; s. Samuel Chamblis and Betty M. (Welz) B. BA, U. So. Calif., 1959, MA, 1963, PhD, 1966. Research assoc. Subcom. on Noise Research Ctr., Los Angeles, 1962-66; postdoctoral fellow Stanford (Calif.) U., 1966-68; research psychologist SRI Internat., Menlo Park, Calif., 1968-76, sr. research psychologist, 1976-82, program mgr., 1982-83, dir. speech research program, 1983-89; dir., sensory sci. and tech. ctr., 1989-93; pres. Digital Voice Corp., 1982—. Contbr. articles to profl. jours. Mem. planning commn. Town of Portola Valley, Calif. Mem. IEEE, Acoustical Soc. Am., Psychonomic Soc., Am. Voice I/O Soc. (dir.). Republican. Home and Office: 15 Peak Ln Portola Valley CA 94028

BELL, DOUGLAS SCOTT, internist; b. Toledo, May 20, 1963; s. Kenneth Charles and Barbara Jean (Freed) B. BA in Biochemistry, Case Western Res. U., 1985; MD with honors, Harvard U., 1990. Intern Mt. Auburn Hosp., Cambridge, Mass., 1990-91; rsch. fellow in med. informatics Harvard Med. Sch., Boston, 1991-94; resident in internal medicine Stanford (Calif.) U. Hosp., 1994—. Contbr. articles to profl. jours. Rsch. scholar Howard Hughes Med. Inst., 1988-89. Mem. ACP (assoc.), NAAS, Am. Med. Informatics Assn., Soc. for Med. Decision Making, Assn. for Computing Machinery, N.Y. Acad. Scis.

BELL, HELEN LAVIN, artist; b. Allentown, Pa.; d. Thomas Joseph and Anna Helen (Miko) Lavin; m. Paul Edward Bell, June 10, 1950; children: Celine Butler, Sharon Neiman, Paul Jr., Christine Schlacter. Student, Western Md. Coll., 1945-47, Md. Inst. Art, 1947-48, Telfair Acad. Arts, 1958-59, U. Calif., Riverside, 1970-71, 80-81. Asst. art dir. Davison's, Atlanta, 1950-51. One-woman shows include Riverside (Calif.) Art Mus., 1980, Mind's Eye Gallery, Riverside, 1983, Rizzoli Internat., Costa Mesa, Calif., 1987, Zola Fine Art, Beverly Hills, Calif., 1990, others; group shows include City of Riverside, Calif., 1975, Riverside County Mus., Beaumont, Calif., 1976, 90, Nat. Orange Show, San Bernardino, Calif., 1976, 89, Calif. Poly. U., Pomona, 1987, Calif. Small Works, Santa Rosa, 1992, 93, others. Event chair Nat. Charity League, Riverside, Calif., 1979-83; trustee Riverside Art Mus., 1979-82. Merit scholar Telfair Acad. Arts and Scis., Savannah, Ga., 1958. Mem. Redlands Art Assn. (trustee 1985-87, 91-95, sec.), Art Alliance (pres. 1979-80, com. chairs 1978, 81, 82), Nat. Assn. Women Artists, Inc. Republican. Roman Catholic. Office: Valerie Miller Fine Arts 73100 El Paseo Palm Desert CA 92260-4263

BELL, JUDY KAY, disaster survival planning company executive; b. Burbank, Calif., July 8, 1947; d. Robert Francis and Geraldine (Wutschel) Ball; m. George L. Sellers, Aug. 24, 1969 (div. 1975); 1 child, Thomas R.; m. Kenneth G. Bell, Apr. 16, 1988. BA in English, Calif. State U., Northridge, 1967; MBA in Mgmt., Golden Gate U., 1980. Cert. emergency planner Nat. Coordinating Coun. Emergency Mgmt. Div. mgr. Pacific Bell, various cities, Calif., 1965-88; pres. Disaster Survival Planning, Inc., Port Hueneme, Calif., 1988—; spkr. bus. and govt. seminars. Author: Disaster Survival Planning: A Practical Guide for Businesses, 1991; contbr. articles to profl. jours. Mem. Am. Soc. Profl. Emergency Planners, Bus. and Industry Coun. for Emergency Planning and Preparedness (bd. dirs. 1991-92, treas. 1991-92), So. Calif. Emergency Svc. Assn. Republican. Home and Office: Disaster Survival Planning Inc 669 Pacific Cove Dr Port Hueneme CA 93041-2171

BELL, LARRY STUART, artist; b. Chgo., Dec. 6, 1939; s. Hyman David and Rebecca Ann (Kriegmont) B.; three children. Student, Chouinard Art Inst., L.A., 1957-59. One man exhbns. include Stedelijk Mus., Amsterdam, 1967, Pasadena (Calif.) Art Mus., 1972, Oakland (Calif.) Mus., 1973, Ft. Worth Art Mus., 1975, Santa Barbara (Calif.) Mus. Art, 1976, Washington U., St. Louis, 1976, Art Mus. So. Tex., Corpus Christi, 1976, Erica Williams, Anne Johnson Gallery, Seattle, 1978, Hayden Gallery, MIT, Cambridge, Mass., 1977, Hudson River Mus., Yonkers, N.Y., 1981, Newport Harbor Art Mus., 1982, Marian Goodman Gallery, N.Y.C., 1982, Ruth S. Schaffner Gallery, Santa Barbara, Calif., Arco Ctr. Visual Arts, L.A., 1983, Unicorn Gallery, Aspen, Colo., 1983, Butler Inst. Am. Art, Youngstown, Ohio, 1984, Leigh Yawkey Woodson Art Mus., Wausau, Wis., 1984, Colorado Springs, Colo. Fine Arts Ctr., 1987, Cleve. Ctr. for Contemporary Art, Ohio, 1987, Mus. Contemporary Art, L.A., 1987, Am. Acad. and Inst. Arts and Letters, N.Y.C., 1987, Boise (Idaho) Gallery Art, 1987, Gilbert Brownstone Gallery, Paris, 1987, Braunstein/Quay Gallery, San Francisco, 1987, 89, Fine Arts Gallery, N.Mex. State Fairgrounds, 1987, Laguna Art Mus., Laguna Beach, Calif., 1987, High Mus. Art, Atlanta, 1988, Sena Galleries West, Santa Fe, 1989, Kiyo Higashi Gallery, L.A., 1989, 90, 94, Musee D'Art Contemporain, Lyon, France, 1989, Contemporary Art Ctr., Kansas City, Mo., 1989, San Antonio Art Inst., 1990, New Gallery, Houston, 1990, Braunstein/Quay Gallery, San Francisco, 1990, Galerie Rolf Ricke, Koln, Fed. Republic Germany, 1990, Galerie Montenay, Paris, 1990, The Works Gallery, L.A., 1990, Galerie Kammer, Hamburg, Germany, 1990, Tony Shafrazi Gallery, N.Y.C., 1991, Tucson Mus. Art, 1991, New Gallery, Houston, 1991, Janus Gallery, Santa Fe, 1992, Kiyo Higashi Gallery, L.A., 1992, 93, New Gallery, Houston, 1992, Tampa Mus. Art, 1992, Kiyo Higashi Gallery, L.A., 1993, 94, New Directions Gallery, Taos, N.M., 1993, Dartmouth St. Gallery, Albuquerque, 1994, Braunstein/Quay Gallery, San Francisco, 1994, Leedy/Voulkos Gallery, Kansas City, 1994, Kiyo Higashi Gallery, L.A., 1994, U. Wyo. Art Mus., Laramie, 1995, Denver Art Mus., 1995, Indigo Gallery, Boca Raton, Fla., 1995; group exhbns. include Mus. Modern Art, N.Y.C., 1965, 79, Jewish Mus., N.Y.C., 1966, Whitney Mus. Am. Art, 1966, Guggenheim Mus., N.Y.C., 1967, Tate Gallery, London, 1970, Hayward Gallery, London, 1971, Detroit Inst. Arts, 1973, Nat. Collections Fine Arts, 1975, San Francisco Mus. Modern Art, 1976, Museo de Arte Contemporaneo de Caracas, Venezuela, 1978, Aspen Ctr. for Visual Arts, 1980, Fruit Market Gallery, Edinburgh, Scotland, 1980, Albuquerque Mus., 1980, Art Inst. Chgo., 1982, Santa Barbara Art Mus., 1984, The Rufino Tamayo Mus., Mexico City, 1985, Colorado Springs Fine Art Ctr., 1986, Mus. Comtemporary Art, 1986, AAAL, 1986, Ariz. State U., Tempe, 1987, Phoenix Art Mus., 1987, Braunstein/Quay Gallery, 1987, The Works Gallery, Long Beach, 1987, Davis/McClain Gallery, Houston, 1987, Basel (Switzerland) Art Fair, 1989, Galerie Joan Prats, Barcelona, Spain, 1989, Musee d'Art Contemporain, Lyon, 1989, Harcus Gallery, Boston, 1989, Colorado Springs Gallery Contemporary Art, 1990, Mus. Contemporary Art, L.A., 1990, Musee de Grenoble, France, 1990, L.A. County Mus. Art, 1991, U. So. Calif. Fisher Gallery, L.A., 1991, Espace Lyonnais d'Art Contemporain, France, 1991, Galerie Montenay, Paris, 1991, Galerie Rolf Ricke, Köln, Germany, 1991, Arolsen, Germany, 1992, Leedy/Voulkos Gallery, Kansas City, Mo., 1993, Musee du Palais du Luxembourg, Paris, 1993, Denver Art Mus., 1993, New Gallery, Houston, 1993, Whitney Mus. Am. Art, N.Y.C., 1993, Conn., 1994, Parrish Art Mus., Southampton, N.Y., 1994, Kiyo Higashi Gallery, L.A., 1994; represented in permanent collections including Nat. Collection Fine Arts, Musee de Art Contemporaine, Lyon, France, Mus. of Fine Arts, Santa Fe, N.Mex., Whitney Mus. Am. Art, N.Y.C., 1994, Laguna Gloria Mus., Austen, 1994, H & W Bechtler Gallery, Charlotte, 1994, Calif. Crafts Mus., San Francisco, 1994, Parrish Art Mus., Southampton, 1994, Tate Gallery, London, Gallery New South Wales, Australia, Albright-Knox Gallery, Buffalo, Art Inst. Chgo., Denver Art Mus., Dallas Mus. Fine Arts, Guggenheim Mus., Houston, L.A. County Mus., Victoria and Albert Mus., London, San Antonio Mus. Art, The Menil Collection, Houston, Mpls. Inst. Arts, Mus. Ludwig, Koln, Albuquerque Mus., Mpls. Inst. Arts, others; instr. sculpture, U. South Fla., Tampa, U. Calif., Berkeley, Irvine, 1970-73, So. Calif. Inst. of Architecture, 1988, Taos (N.Mex.) Inst. of Art, 1989-94. Copley Found. grantee, 1962; Guggenheim Found. fellow, 1970; Nat. Endowment Arts grantee, 1975; recipient Gov.'s award for excellence in visual arts, N.Mex., 1990. Office: PO Box 4101 Taos NM 87571-9998

BELL, LEE PHILLIP, television personality, television producer; b. Chgo.; d. James A. and Helen (Novak) P.; m. William Joseph Bell, Oct. 23, 1954; children: William J., Bradley, Lauralee. B.S. in Microbiology, Northwestern U., 1950. With CBS-TV, Chgo., 1952-86; pres. Bell-Phillip TV Prodns., 1985—; bd. dirs. William Wrigley, Jr. Co., Chgo. Bank Commerce, Phillips Flowers Inc. TV and radio shows include Lee Phillip Show, Chgo., from 1952, Lady and Tiger Show WBBM Radio, from 1962, WBBM TV from 1964; hostess Noon Break, numerous TV Spls. including Forgotten Children, The Rape of Paulette (nat. Emmy award, duPont Columbia award); Children and Divorce (Chgo. Emmmy award) co-creator: (with William Bell) The Young and the Restless CBS-TV daytime drama, 1973 (Emmy award); co-creator, exec. producer The Bold and the Beautiful, 1987—. Bd. dirs. United Cerebral Palsy, Chgo. Unlimited, Northwestern U. Hosp., Chgo. Heart Assn., Nat. Com. Prevention of Child Abuse, Mental Health Assn., Children's Home and Aid Soc., Salvation Army (L.A. bd. dirs.), Family Focus; mem. Chgo. Maternity Ctr.; life mem. Northwestern U. Bd. Trustees. Recipient 16 Chgo. Emmys; Top Favorite Female award TV Guide mag., 1956, Outstanding Woman of Radio and TV award McCall's mag., 1957-58, 65, bd. govs. award Chgo. chpt. Nat. Acad. TV Arts and Scis., 1977, William Booth award for community svc. Salvation Army, 1990; named Person of Yr. Broadcast Advt. Club, Chgo., 1980. Mem. Am. Women Radio and TV (Golden Mike award 1968, Broadcaster of Yr. 1993), Acad. TV Arts and Scis. (bd. dirs.), Chgo. chpt. Acad. TV Arts and Scis., Women's Athletic Club of Chgo., Comml. Club, Delta Delta Delta. Office: CBS-TV City 7800 Beverly Blvd Los Angeles CA 90036-2165

BELL, LEO S., retired physician; b. Newark, Nov. 7, 1913; s. Alexander M. and Marie (Saxon) B.; AB, Syracuse U., 1934; MD, 1938; m. Edith Lewis, July 3, 1938; children: Jewyl Linn, David Alden. Intern, N.Y.C. Hosp., 1938, Bklyn. Hosp., 1939-40; resident in pediatrics Sea View Hosp., N.Y.C., 1940-41, N.Y.C. Hosp., 1941-42; practice medicine specializing in pediatrics, San Mateo, Calif., 1946-86; mem. staff Mills Meml. Hosp., San Mateo, Peninsula Hosp. & Med. Ctr., Burlingame, Children's Hosp., San Francisco; assoc. clin. prof. pediatrics U. Calif. Med Sch., San Francisco, prof. emeritus Stanford Med. Sch., Palo Alto; mem. curriculum & ednl. affairs comm. U. San Francisco Med. Sch., adminstv. coun.; med. columnist San Mateo Times. Bd. dirs. Mills Hosp. Found., San Mateo, U. Calif. San Francisco Hosp., San Mateo County Heart Assn., Hillsborough Schs. Found. (Calif.), 1980-83. Capt. as flight surgeon USAAF, 1942-46. Recipient bronze and silver medals Am. Heart Assn. Diplomate Am. Bd. Pediatrics. Fellow Am. Acad. Pediatrics, Am. Pub. Health Assn.; mem. Clin. Faculty Assn. (pres.), Calif. Fedn. Pediatric Socs. (pres.), Am. Fedn. Pediatric Socs. (pres.), Calif. Med. Assn., Am. Pub. Health Assn., Air Force Assn., AMA (alt. del. to ho. of dels.), Calif. Med. Assn. (ho. of dels.), San Mateo County Med. Assn., Internat. Snuff Bottle Soc., Hong Kong Snuff Bottle Soc., San Francisco Gem and Mineral Soc., World Affairs Coun. San Francisco, U. San Francisco Med. Sch. Clin. Faculty Assn. (coun., pres.), Peninsula Golf and Country Club, Commonwealth Club. Contbr. articles to profl. jours. Home: 220 Roblar Ave Burlingame CA 94010-6846 Office: PO Box 1877 San Mateo CA 94401-0946

BELL, MAXINE TOOLSON, state legislator, librarian; b. Logan, Utah, Aug. 6, 1931; d. John Max and Norma (Watson) Toolson; m. H. Jack Bell, Oct. 26, 1949; children: Randy J. (dec.), Jeff M., Scott Alan (dec.). Assocs. in Libr. Sci., Coll. So. Idaho; CSI, Idaho State U., 1975. Librarian Sch. Dist. 261, Jerome, Idaho, 1975-88; mem. Idaho Ho. of Reps., 1988-. Bd. dirs. Idaho Farm Bur., 1976-77; rep. western states Am. Farm Bur. Women, 1990-93, vice chmn., 1993—; vice chmn. Am. Farm Bur., 1992—; mem. Jerome County Rep. PRecinct Com., 1980-88. Home: 194 S 300 E Jerome ID 83338-6532

BELL, MICHAEL STEVEN, art curator; b. Joplin, Mo., July 4, 1946; s. Vernon L. and Alpha Marie (Russell) B.; children—Shannon, Ororah, Justin, Mercury. B.F.A. (scholar), Calif. Inst. Arts, 1970; M.F.A., U. Ky., 1972. Teaching asst. Calif. Inst. Art, 1970-71, U. Ky., 1971-72; designer Amorphia, Inc., Mill Valley, Calif., 1972; asst. dir. reprodns. dept. Vorpal Gallery, San Francisco, Calif., 1973-74; curatorial asst. Oakland (Calif.) Mus., 1975-76, registrar, 1976-80; dir. Midland (Mich.) Art Council, 1980-81; art curator San Francisco Mus. Modern Art, 1981-84; asst. dir. San Francisco Arts Commn., 1984-87, curator, visual art access, 1987—. Exhibited in group shows including: Evansville (Ind.) Mus. Art and Sci., 1971, San Francisco Mus. Modern Art, 1978; contbr. poems and articles to various publs. Served with USAF, 1963-67. Mem. Art Mus. Assn., Am. Assn. Mus., Internat. Council Museums. Episcopalian. Office: Visual Art Access PO Box 2880 Santa Fe NM 87504-2880

BELL, RICHARD G., lawyer; b. Billings, Mont., Sept. 16, 1947; s. George A.W. and Mary Helen (Sharp) B.; m. Linda Carol Riggs, June 21, 1969; children: Stephen, Geoffrey. AB, Stanford U., 1969; JD, U. Calif., San Francisco, 1972. Bar: Calif.; U.S. Supreme Ct., 1990; U.S. Ct. Appeals Calif. (9th cir.) 1973; U.S. Dist. Ct. Calif. (no. dist., 1972, cen. dist., 1976). Assoc. Finch, Sauers, Player & King, Palo Alto, Calif., 1972-76; ptnr. Finch, Sauers, Player & Bell, Palo Alto, 1976-83; gen. counsel Watkins-Johnson Co., Palo Alto, 1983-90; v.p., gen. counsel Watkins-Johnson Co., 1990—. Bd. dirs. Family Svc. Assn., Palo Alto, 1981-87; trustee Mountain View Los Altos Union H.S. Dist., 1990—; pres. bd. Los Altos Conservatory Theater, 1991-95. Mem. ABA, Calif. Bar Assn., Santa Clara County Bar Assn., Peninsula Assn. Gen. Counsel, Am Corp. Counsel Assn., Palo Alto Area Bar Assn. Republican. Episcopalian. Office: Watkins-Johnson Co 3333 Hillview Ave Palo Alto CA 94304-1204

BELL, WAYNE STEVEN, lawyer; b. L.A., June 24, 1954; s. Joseph and Jane Barbara (Barsook) B.; m. M. Susan Modzelewski, Apr. 1, 1989. BA magna cum laude, UCLA, 1976; JD, Loyola U., L.A., 1979; Advanced Mgmt. Program, Rutgers U., 1992. Bar: Calif. 1980, U.S. Dist. Ct. (cen. dist.) 1981, U.S. Tax Ct. 1981, U.S. Ct. Appeals (9th cir.) 1981, U.S. Dist. Ct. (so. and no. dists.) Calif. 1983, U.S. Supreme Ct. 1984, D.C. 1986; lic. real estate broker, Calif. Intern office of gov. State of Calif., Sacramento, summer 1976; assoc. Levinson, Rowen, Miller, Jacobs & Kabrins, L.A., 1980-82; sr. assoc. Montgomery, Gascou, Gemmill & Thornton, L.A., 1982-84; counsel, project developer Thomas Safran & Assocs., L.A., 1984-85; of counsel Greenspan, Glasser & Medina, Santa Monica, Calif., 1984-86; assoc. gen. counsel Am. Diversified Cos., Costa Mesa, Calif., 1985-88; legal cons. Project Atty., L.A., 1988-89; sr. counsel Ralphs Grocery Co., L.A., 1989—; judge pro tem Mcpl. Ct. South Bay Jud. Dist., 1987, L.A. Superior Ct., 1991, 94, settlement officer L.A. Mcpl. Ct., Settlement Officer Program, 1990-92; spl. master State Bar Calif., 1991-92. Chief note and comment editor Loyola U. Law Rev., 1978-79; contbr. articles to profl. jours. and gen. pubs. Vol. atty. Westside Legal Services, Santa Monica, 1982-87; legal ombudsman Olympics Ombudsman program L.A. County Bar Assn., 1984; gov. appointed mem. Calif. adv. council Legal Services Corp., 1982-88, Autism Soc. Am., Amnesty Internat.; contbg. mem. Dem. Nat. Com., So. Poverty Law Ctr.; charter mem. presdl. task force Ams. for Change; bd. dirs. Am. Theatre Arts, Hollywood, Calif., 1983-84; pres., mem. exec. com., bd. dirs. Programs for the Developmentally Handicapped, Inc., L.A., 1987-92; chmn. bd. appeals handicapped accommodations City of Manhattan Beach, 1986-88; bd. dirs. The Foodbank of So. Calif., 1991-94, sec., 1993; mem. tech. adv. panel Legal Corps. L.A., 1994—. Mem. Calif. Bar Assn. (legal svcs. sect. standing com. legal problems of aging 1983-86, chmn. legis. subcom. 1984-86, conf. dels. alternate 1987), D.C. Bar Assn. (real estate sect. com. on comml. real estate), L.A. County Bar Assn., Legal Assistance Assn. Calif. (bd. dirs., mem. exec. com., legis. strategy com. 1984-86), Loyola Law Sch. (advocate). Democrat. Office: Ralphs Grocery Co PO Box 54143 Los Angeles CA 90054-0143

BELLAH, ROBERT NEELLY, sociologist, educator; b. Altus, Okla., Feb. 23, 1927; s. Luther Hutton and Lillian Lucille (Neelly); m. Melanie Hyman, Aug. 17, 1949; children: Jennifer, Harriet. B.A., Harvard U., 1950, Ph.D., 1955. Research assoc. Inst. Islamic Studies, McGill U., Montreal, Can., 1955-57; with Harvard U., Cambridge, Mass., 1957-67; prof. Harvard U., 1966-67; Elliott prof. sociology U. Calif., Berkeley, 1967—. Author: Tokugawa Religion, 1957, Beyond Belief, 1970, The Broken Covenant, 1975 (Sorokin award Am. Sociol. Assn. 1976), (with Charles Y. Glock) The New Religious Consciousness, 1976, (with Phillip E. Hammond) Varieties of Civil Religion, 1980, (with others) Habits of the Heart, 1985, (with others) The Good Society, 1991. Served with U.S. Army, 1945-46. Fulbright fellow, 1960-61; recipient Harbison award Danforth Found., 1971. Mem. Am. Acad. Arts and Scis., Am. Sociol. Assn., Am. Acad. Religion. Episcopalian. Office: U Calif Dept Sociology Berkeley CA 94720

BELLAMY, JOHN CARY, civil engineer, meteorologist; b. Cheyenne, Wyo., Apr. 18, 1915; s. Benjamin Charles and Alice Elizabeth (Cary) B.; m. Josephine Marie Johnston, Sept. 21, 1940; children: John Cary, Agnes Louise, Charles Fulton, William Delaney, Mary Elizabeth. BCE, U. Wyo., 1936; PhM, U. Wis., 1938; PhD in Meteorology, Chgo. U., 1947. Registered profl. engr., Wyo. Ptnr. Bellamy & Sons Engrs., Lamont, Wyo., 1938-42; asst. prof. U. Chgo., 1942-47; assoc. dir. Cook Rsch. Labs., Chgo., 1947-60; dir. NRRI U. Wyo., Laramie, 1960-73; prof. civil engring. U. Wyo., 1973-81; prin. Bellamy & Sons Engrs., Laramie, 1981—; dir. Inst. Tropical Meteorology, U. P.R., 1943-44; spl. cons. U.S. Army Air Corps, Washington, 1944-45; mem. Western Interstate Nuclear Bd., Denver, 1964-75. Contbr. articles to profl. jours.; contbr. to books; patentee in field. Recipient Losey award, Inst. Aero. Sci., 1944, Medal of Freedom, Pres. U.S.A., 1946, Thurlow award Inst. Navigation, 1946. Fellow Am. Meteorol. Soc. (dir. 1948-52); mem. Wyo. Engring. Soc., Am. Geophys. Union, Inst. Navigation (pres. 1962), Nat. Soc. Profl. Engrs. (chpt. pres. 1976), Lions (chpt. pres. 1981, 84). Home and Office: 2308 Holliday Dr Laramie WY 82070-4847

BELLAMY, WILLIAM TRACEY, pathology educator; b. Norfolk, Va., June 29, 1954; s. Wilbur Gore and Joyce Kathyleen (Smith) B.; m. Karen Lea Marine, July 3, 1982. BA in Biology, U. Va., 1976; BS in Pharmacy summa cum laude, Va. Commonwealth U., 1984; PhD summa cum laude, U. Ariz., 1988. Asst. dir. rsch. dept. plastic surgery rsch. U. Va. Med. Ctr., Charlottesville, 1976-81; pharmacy intern Comp-U-Dose Pharmacy, Richmond, Va., 1982-83; staff pharmacist King's Daus. Children's Hosp., Norfolk, 1984; postdoctoral fellow dept. molecular biology Ariz. Cancer Ctr., U. Ariz., Tucson, 1988-90, rsch. assoc. cancer pharmacology program, 1989-91, rsch. asst. prof. dept. internal medicine, 1990-91; dir. core molecular pathology lab. dept. pathology Ariz. Health Sci. Ctr., U. Ariz., Tucson, 1991—, asst. prof. pathology dept. pathology, 1991—; adj. asst. prof. pharmacology and toxicology U. Ariz., Tucson, 1993—; presenter in field. Reviewer: (jours.) Cancer Rsch., Biochem. Pharmacology, Lab. Investigation, Jour. Cancer Rsch. and Clin. Oncology, Brit. Jour. Cancer, Toxicology and Applied Pharmacology, Cancer Chemotherapy and Pharmacology; contbr. chpts. to books and articles to profl. jours. Named A.D. Williams Summer Rsch. fellow Med. Coll. Va., 1982, Daniel T. Watts Disting. Predoctoral fellow Sch. Basic Scis., Med. Coll. Va., 1984, Am. Found. for Pharm. Edn. fellow, 1985-86, Sterling-Winthrop Pharmacology and Toxicology fellow Am. Found. for Pharm. Edn., 1986-88; recipient A.D. Williams Scholarship award Med. Coll. Va., 1982, 83; grantee Am. Cancer Soc., 1989-90, U. Ariz., 1990, Friend's of the Ariz. Cancer Ctr., 1990-91, 92-93, U. Ariz. Sch. Medicine, 1992, NIH, 1992—. Mem. AAAS, Am. Assn. Colls. Pharmacy, Am. Assn. for Cancer Rsch., Am. Soc. Clin. Pathologists, Rho Chi, Am. Soc. Investigative Pathologists, Phi Kappa Phi. Office: U Ariz Health Sci Ctr Dept Pathology 1501 N Campbell Ave Tucson AZ 85724-0001

BELLER, GERALD STEPHEN, magician, former insurance company executive; b. Phila., Aug. 6, 1935; s. Nathan and Adelaide B. (Goldfarb) B.; m. Nancy R. Nelson, June 8, 1968; children: Fay A., Mark S., Royce W., Merrilee A., Marie A., Frank A. CLU, Am. Coll., Bryn Mawr, Pa., 1972. Spl. agt. Prudential Ins. Co., San Bernardino, Calif., 1959-62, div. mgr., 1962-66; agy. supr. Aetna Life & Casualty, L.A., 1966-69, gen. agt., 1969-77; rsch. analyst Investigative Svcs. Bur. San Bernadino County Sheriff's Dept., 1991-95; capt. specialized svcs. bur. San Bernardino County (Calif.) Sheriff's Dept.; mem. Magician Magic Castle, Hollywood, Calif. mem. sheriff's coun. San Bernardino County Sheriff's Dept., Apple Valley sheriff's adv. bd. Served with USAF, 1953-57. Recipient Man of Year award, 1961; Manpower Builders award, 1966-69; Agy. Builders award, 1970-72; Pres.'s Trophy award, 1973-74. Mem. Life Underwriters Assn. L.A., Am. Soc. CLUs, Golden Key Soc., Internat. Exec. Svc. Corps. (vol.), Acad. Magical Arts, Internat. Brotherhood of Magicians (Outstanding Magic Lectr. of Yr. 1989-90, Aldini Meml. award 1990), Soc. Am. Magicians. Home: 20625 Tonawanda Rd Apple Valley CA 92307-5736

BELLES, DONALD ARNOLD, pastoral therapist, mental health counselor; b. Sayre, Pa., Mar. 7, 1948; s. William and Alice (Arnold) B.; m. Linda Scheel, July 9, 1981. BA, St. Martin's U., 1973; MDiv, Fuller Theol. Sem., 1977; PhD, Calif. Grad. Sch. Theology, 1981; MBA, City U. Bellevue, 1994. Lic. amateur radio operator; ordained to ministry Worldwide Congl. Fellowship, 1989; cert. c.c. tchr., Calif., mental health counselor, Wash., profl. stage hypnotist. Chaplain Vols. of Am., L.A., 1976-78; therapist Greater life

Found., Seattle, 1979-81; industrial engr. commercial airplane divsn. Boeing, 1979-80, program planner aerospace divsn., 1980-86, sr., lead program planner electronics divsn., 1986-89, systems analyst, contract tech. mgr., software engring. practices process analyst, total quality improvement project mgr., 1989—; therapist, dir. clinic Creative Therapies, Seattle, 1982-83; clin. dir. Applied Hypnosis, Tacoma, 1984-87; dir. Active Therapy Assoc., Tacoma, 1988-89; dean of students Coll. Therapeutic Hypnosis, Puyallup, Wash., 1989-93; cons. theological issues, abduction rsch., psychic phenomena, paranormal events; adult edn. instr. Tacoma Community Coll., 1987-88, Pierce Coll., 1990-92; mem. U.S. Acad. Team to CIS, U. St. Petersburg, Russia, 1994; presenter, lectr. in field; instr. Olympia Diocese Sch. of Theology, 1995. Contbr. articles to profl. jours.; producer videos in field. Exec. dir. Nat. Assn. to Prevent and Eliminate Child Abuse, Tacoma, 1987-89. Maj. U.S. Army, 1969-75, USAR, 1975—. Fellow Am. Assn. Profl. Hypnotherapists; mem. Nat. Assn. Clergy Hypnotherapists (bd. dirs. 1987-88, editor jour. 1987), Internat. Med. Dental Hypnotherapy Assn., Wash. State Head Injury Found.

BELLEVILLE, PHILIP FREDERICK, lawyer; b. Flint, Mich., Apr. 24, 1934; s. Frederick Charles and Sarah (Adelaine) B.; m. Geraldean Bickford, Sept. 2, 1953; children—Stacy L., Philip Frederick II, Jeffrey A. BA in Econs. with high distinction and honors, U. Mich., 1956, J.D., 1960. Bar: Calif. 1961. Assoc. Latham & Watkins, LA., 1960-68; ptnr. Latham & Watkins, L.A. and Newport Beach, Calif., 1968-73; ptnr., chmn. litigation dept. Latham & Watkins, L.A. and Newport Beach, 1973-80; ptnr. Latham & Watkins, L.A., Newport Beach, San Diego, Washington, 1980—, Chgo., 1983—, N.Y.C., 1985—, London, 1990—, Moscow, 1992—. Asst. editor Mich. Law Rev., Ann Arbor, 1959-60. Past mem. So. Calif. steering com. NAACP Legal Def. Fund, Inc., L.A.; mem. cmty. adv. bd. San Pedro Peninsula Hosp., Calif., 1980-88. James B. Angell scholar U. Mich., 1955-56. Mem. ABA (antitrust and trade regulation and bus. law sects.), L.A. County Bar Assn. (bus. trial lawyers sect.), Assn. Bus. Trial Lawyers, Order of Coif, Jack Kramer Tennis Club (Rolling Hills Estates, Calif.), Portuguese Bend (Calif.) Club, Palos Verdes (Calif.) Golf Club, Phi Beta Kappa, Phi Kappa Phi, Alpha Kappa Psi. Republican. Office: Latham & Watkins 633 W 5th St Ste 4000 Los Angeles CA 90071-2005

BELLINO, PETER VINCENT, JR., marketing manager; b. N.Y.C., Mar. 31, 1935; s. Peter Vincent and Valerie Anna Bellino; m. Anna Kukulka, June 16, 1956; children: Victor Peter, Valerie Eve, Victoria Marie. BBA, CCNY, 1956. Sales engr. Mergenthaler Linotype, N.Y.C., 1956-63; mktg. mgr. Motorola Inc., Scottsdale, Ariz., 1963—. Served to 1st lt. U.S. Army, 1953-62. Mem. Am. Def. Preparedness Assn. (sect. chmn. 1991-93, v.p. Ariz. chpt. 1990—), Assn. U.S. Army (bd. govs. Ariz. chpt. 1985). Home: 8432 E Gary Rd Scottsdale AZ 85260-6620 Office: Motorola Inc 8220 E Roosevelt St Scottsdale AZ 85257-3804

BELLIS, CARROLL JOSEPH, surgeon; b. Shreveport, La.; s. Joseph and Rose (Bloome) B.; m. Mildred Darmody, Dec. 26, 1939; children: Joseph, David. BS, U. Minn., 1930, MS in Physiology, 1932, PhD in Physiology, 1934, MD, 1936, PhD in Surgery, 1941. Diplomate Am. Bd. Surgery. Resident surgery U. Minn. Hosps., 1937-41; pvt. practice surgery Long Beach, Calif., 1945—; mem. staff St. Mary's Med. Ctr., Long Beach; cons. surgery Long Beach Gen. Hosp.; prof., chmn. dept. surgery Calif. Coll. Medicine, 1962—; surgical cons. to Surgeon-Gen., U.S. Army. Author: Fundamentals of Human Physiology, 1935, A Critique of Reason, 1938, Lectures in Medical Physiology; contbr. numerous articles in field of surgery, physiology to profl. jours. Served to col. M.C. AUS, 1941-46. Recipient Charles Lyman Green prize in physiology, 1934, prize Mpls. Surg. Soc., 1938, ann. award Mississippi Valley Med. Soc., 1955; Alice Shevlin fellow U. Minn., 1932. Fellow ACS, Royal Soc. Medicine, Internat. Coll. Surgeons, Am. Coll. Gastroenterology, Am. Med. Writers Assn., Internat. Coll. Angiology (sci. council), Gerontol. Soc., Am. Soc. Abdominal Surgeons, Nat. Cancer Inst., Phlebology Soc. Am., Internat. Acad. Proctology, Peripheral Vascular Soc. Am. (founding); mem. AAAS, Am. Assn. Study Neoplastic Diseases, Mississippi Valley Med. Soc., N.Y. Acad. Scis., Hollywood Acad. Medicine, Am. Geriatrics Soc., Irish Med. Assn., Am. Assn. History Medicine, Pan Pacific Surgical Assn., Indsl. Med. Assn., L.A. Musicians Union (hon.), Pan Am. Med. Assn. (diplomate), Internat. Bd. Surgery (cert.), Internat. Bd. Proctology (cert.), Wisdom Soc. (wisdom award of honor), Sigma Xi, Phi Beta Kappa, Alpha Omega Alpha. Office: 904 Silver Spur Rd Ste 804 Rolling Hills Estates CA 90274

BELLIS, DAVID JAMES, public administration educator; b. Nashville, May 1, 1944; s. Carroll Joseph and Helen Louise (Jett) B.; m. Ann Seagreaves, Dec. 23, 1972; 1 child, James. BS, UCLA; MA, U. So. Calif., 1969, PhD, 1977. Dir. narcotics prevention project Los Angeles, 1970-72; dir. West End drug abuse control Ontario, Calif., 1972-75; cons. Project Heavy, Los Angeles, 1975-78; dir. econs. Telacu, Los Angeles, 1978-80; asst. dir. Youth Gang Services, Los Angeles, 1980-81; councilman City of Signal Hill, Calif., 1980-86, mayor, 1983-84; assoc. prof. pub. adminstrn. Calif. State U., San Bernardino, 1985-89, prof. pub. adminstrn., 1989—; cons. San Bernardino County Sheriff's Dept., 1993—, San Bernadino Police Dept., 1993—, U.S. Dept. State, 1992—. Author: Heroin and Politicians, 1983. Home: PO Box 1064 Cedar Glen CA 92321-1064 Office: Calif State U 5500 University Pky San Bernardino CA 92407-2318

BELLISARIO, DONALD P., television director; b. Charleroi, Pa., Aug. 8, 1935; s. Albert and Dana (Lapcevic) B.; 7 children. TV dir., writer, prodr. series Black Sheep Squadron (also known as Baa Baa Black Sheep), 1977-78; writer, exec. prodr. series Quincy, M.E., 1978; dir., supervising prodr. co-author series Battlestar Galactica, 1978-79; creator (with Glen A. Larson), dir., writer, exec. prodr. series Magnum, P.I., 1980-88 (Emmy award nomination outstanding drama series 1981, 82, Edgar Allen Poe award Mystery Writers Am. best tv series episode China Doll 1981); exec. prodr. (with Stephen J. Cannell), writer series Stone, 1980; creator, exec. prodr., writer Tales of the Gold Monkey, 1982-83; creator, dir., exec. prodr., writer series Quantum Leap, 1989-93 (Emmy award nominations outstanding drama series 1989, 90, Writers Guild Am. award nomination best tv episode 1991), Tequila and Bonetti (also known as Tequila and Boner), 1992; TV pilots: Magnum, P.I., 1980, Tales of the Gold Monkey, 1982, Airwolf, 1983, Quantum Leap, 1989, Tequila and Bonetti, 1992; TV movies: creator, dir., exec. prodr. Three on a Match, 1987; screenwriter, dir., exec. prodr. film Last Rites, 1988; TV series writer Kojak, 1973, Airwolf, 1984. Roman Catholic. Office: Broder Kurland Webb Uffner 9242 Beverly Blvd Ste 200 Beverly Hills CA 90210-3710

BELLONI, ROBERT CLINTON, federal judge; b. Riverton, Oreg., Apr. 4, 1919; s. John Edward and Della (Clinton) B.; children: James L., Susan K. BA, U. Oreg., 1941, LLB, 1951. Bar: Oreg. 1951. Practiced in Coquille, Oreg., 1951-52, Myrtle Point, Oreg., 1952-57; judge Oreg. Circuit Ct., Coos and Curry Counties, Coquille, 1957-67; U.S. dist. judge Dist. Oreg., 1967—, chief judge, 1971-76. Councilman, Myrtle Point, 1953-57, mayor, 1957; chmn. Coos County Democratic Central Com., 1957; Hon. trustee Boys and Girls Aid Soc. Oreg., 1960. Served to 1st lt. AUS, 1942-46. Robert C. Belloni Boys Forest Ranch dedicated in his honor Coos County Bd. Commrs., 1969. Mem. ABA, Oreg. Bar Assn., Am. Judicature Soc., Oreg. Juvenile Ct. Judges Assn. (pres. 1963), Circuit Ct. Judges Assn. Oreg. (pres. 1966), 9th Circuit Dist. Judges Assn. (pres. 1980-81), Sigma Alpha Epsilon, Delta Theta Phi. Episcopalian. Office: US Dist Ct 708 US Courthouse 620 SW Main St Portland OR 97205-3037

BELLOWS, ROBERT ALVIN, research physiologist; b. Bozeman, Mont., Aug. 22, 1934; s. Alvin O. and Lucy E. (Norman) B.; m. Laura Mae Pasha, Dec. 27, 1957; children: Donna Kay, William, Norman, David. BS, Mont. State U., 1956, MS, 1958; PhD, U. Wis., 1962. Registered profl. animal scientist. Rsch. physiologist U.S. Dept. Agr.-Agrl. Rsch. Svc., Miles City, Mont., 1962-67, rsch. physiologist, investigations leader, 1967-71, rsch. physiology supr., 1971-79, rsch. leader, 1979-84, rsch. physiologist, 1984—; reviewer, cons. State Expt. Stas., U.S. Dept. Agr.-Agrl. Rsch. Svc., Can., Mexico, Egypt, Soviet Union, Kazakhstan, Kyrgyzstan, Nat. Cattleman's Assn., Angus, Hereford, Charolais and Simmental Breed Assn., 1971—. Mem. Am. Soc. Animal Sci. (western dir. 1967, sec., pres. elect, pres. western sect. 1989-91, disting. svc. award 1983, animal mgmt. award 1993), Soc. for Study of Reprodn., Coun. Agrl. Sci. and Tech., Alpha Zeta. Office: US Dept Agr Agrl Rsch Svc Livestock & Range Rsch Lab Rt 1 Box 2021 Miles City MT 59301

BELLOWS, WILLIAM, public relations executive. Editor, reporter Harte-Hanks Newspapers, 1977-78, Ottaway Newspapers, N.Y., 1978-80; comms. specialist IBM, 1980-84; v.p. gen. mgr. Bean PR, 1984-86, Miller Comms., 1986-88; ptnr. Copithorne & Bellows PR, San Francisco, 1988—. Office: Copithorne & Bellows 131 Steuart St Ste 220 San Francisco CA 94105-1230

BELLRINGER, STEPHEN TERRENCE, gas company executive; b. Birmingham, Eng., July 5, 1946; married. B of Commerce, U. Windsor, 1968, MBA, 1969. Pres. Union Gas Ltd., 1968-93; pres., CEO Trans Mountain Pipeline Co., Ltd., 1993—; dir. Vancouver Bd. Trade. Chmn. bd. govs. U. Windsor. Mem. Can. Gas Assn. (past chmn.), Ont. Gas Assn. (past chmn.). Office: Vancouver Bd Trade, 1333 W Broadway Ste 900, Vancouver, BC Canada V6H 4C2

BELLUOMINI, FRANK STEPHEN, accountant; b. Healdsburg, Calif., May 19, 1934; s. Francesco and Rose (Giorgi) B.; m. Alta Anita Gifford, Sept. 16, 1967; 1 child, Wendy Ann. AA, Santa Rosa Jr. Coll., 1954; BA with honors, San Jose State U., 1956. CPA, Calif. Staff acct. Hood, Gire & Co., CPA's, San Jose, Calif., 1955-60, ptnr., 1960-66; ptnr. Touche Ross & Co., CPA's, San Jose, 1967-89, ptnr.-in-charge San Jose office, 1971-85, sr. ptnr. San Jose office, 1985-89; ptnr. Deloitte & Touche, San Jose, 1989-95. Bd. dirs. Santa Clara Valley chpt. ARC, 1993—, chmn. 1995—; mem. adv. bd. Salvation Army, San Jose, 1979-85, San Jose Children's Coun., 1982-89; mem. citizens adv. coun. The Crippled Children's Soc. of Santa Clara County, 1989-94, bd. dirs., 1995—; trustee Santa Clara County (Calif.) United Way, 1979-95, v.p. planning and allocations, 1981-83, vice chmn., 1985-87, chmn. 1987-89; bd. dirs. San Jose Mus. Art, 1984-86; mem. Presentation High Sch. Devel. Bd., 1989-92; mem. dean's adv. coun. San Jose State U. Bus. Sch., 1990-95, mem. adv. bd. The Acad. of Fin., 1992-94. Named Disting. Alumnus, San Jose State U. Sch. Bus., 1978. Mem. Santa Clara County Estate Planning Council (pres. 1979-80), Calif. Soc. CPA's (pres. chpt. 1968-69, state v.p. 1976-77), Am. Inst. CPA's (chmn. state and local govt. com. 1976-79), San Jose State Alumni Assn. (treas. 1960-61, dir. 1961-62, exec. com. 1961-62), San Jose State Acctg. Round Table (bd. dirs., treas. 1982-87, 92—, pres. 1994-95), Beta Alpha Psi (San Jose State U. Outstanding Alumnus award 1986). Roman Catholic. Clubs: San Jose Rotary (dir. 1979-81, trustee and treas. San Jose Rotary Endowment 1976-83), Silicon Valley Capital. Office: 60 S Market St San Jose CA 95113

BELLUS, RONALD JOSEPH, marketing and communications executive; b. Travis AFB, Calif., Feb. 25, 1951; s. Vincent Joseph and Katherine Veronica (Giudice) B.; m. Beth Ann Johnson, June 26, 1976 (div.); children: Veronica Lee, Joseph Vincent, Kenneth James; m. Gina Jean Prom, Aug. 9, 1990; children: Anthony Taylor, Andrew Taylor. BA in Communications, Brigham Young U., 1977. Lic. FCC radio telephone operator, 1979. Sports dir. Sta. KGUY-AM, Palm Desert, Calif., 1979; news, sports dir. Sta. KBLQ-AM/FM, Logan, Utah, 1979-80; gen. sales mgr. Sta. KSTM-FM/KVVA-AM, Phoenix, 1980-84, Sta. KLFF-AM/KMZK-FM, Phoenix, 1984-85; media cons. Mediacorp Planning & Buying, Phoenix, 1985-86; press sec. Gov. of Ariz., Phoenix, 1986-87; asst. dir. Ariz. Office of Tourism, Phoenix, 1987-88; media cons. Bellus Media, Phoenix, 1988—; ptnr. Desertwest Media Group, Inc., Phoenix, 1988—; v.p. Nat. Restaurant Group, Inc., Phoenix, 1990-91; media cons. Mecham for Gov. com., Glendale, Ariz., 1986; host cable TV show Arizona-Now and Then, Dimension Cable, 1990—; v.p. Infosystems, Tempe, 1991-94, Green Valley Health Group, Phoenix, 1992—; co-founder Cinema Concepts Found., Scottsdale, 1994—, Bronze Memorres Ltd., Phoenix, 1994—. Author: Mecham: Silence Cannot Be Misquoted, 1988, Ariz. Tourism Travel Planner, 1988. Comm. mem. Phoenix Boys Choir, 1988; precinct committeeman Rep. State Com., Phoenix, 1987-89, del., 1988; candidate for state senate, Phoenix, 1988; bd. dirs. Cinema Concepts Found., 1994—; mem. Gilbert Anti-Gang Task Force, 1994—, Gilbert Action Inter-Faith Network, 1994—. Named one of Outstanding Young Men Am., 1987. Mem. Phoenix Press Box Assn. (treas. 1984-85, exec. dir. 1985-86). Ch. of Latter Day Saints. Office: 7150 E Camelback Rd Ste 300 Scottsdale AZ 85251

BELMONT, LARRY MILLER, health association executive; b. Reno, Apr. 13, 1936; s. Miller Lawrence and Madeline (Echante) B.; m. Laureen Metzger, Aug. 14, 1966; children: Miller Lawrence, Rebecca Madeline, Amie Echante, Bradley August. BA in Psychology, U. Nev., 1962; MPH, U. Mich., 1968; cert. in environ. mgmt., U. So. Calif., 1978; M in Pub. Adminstrn., U. Idaho, 1979. Rep. on loan to city health depts. USPHS, Los Angeles and Long Beach, 1962-63; advisor pub. health on loan to Alaska dept. health and welfare USPHS, Anchorage, 1963-64, Juneau and Anchorage, 1964-67; dep. dir. Wash./Alaska Regional Med. Program, Spokane, Wash., 1968-71; dir. Panhandle Health Dist., Coeur d'Alene, Idaho, 1971—; mem. adj. faculty Whitworth Coll., Spokane; presenter papers nat., region, state confs., 1981-82; testifier congl. coms., Washington, 1973, 76, state legis. com., Idaho, 1972-82. Chmn. nominating com. Kootenai Econ. Devel. Council, Idaho, 1985, bd. dirs. 1981-86; mem. adv. com. Kootenai County Council Alcoholism, 1979-80; regional coordinator Gov.'s Com. Vol. Services, Idaho, 1979-80; chmn. Montessori Adv. Bd., Idaho, 1975-79; chmn. personnel com. North Idaho Hospice, 1985-88, bd. dirs. 1985-88; bd. dirs. North Idaho Spl. Services Agy., 1972-76; bd. dirs., vice chmn. Pub. Employees Credit Union, 1990—; bd. dirs. United Way of Kootemai County, Inc., 1990-91; mem. steering com. APEX/PH, 1987-91; active numerous other organizations. USPHS trainee U. Mich., 1967-68, EPA trainee U. So. Calif., 1978. Mem. Am. Pub. Health Assn., Nat. Assn. Home Health Agys. (chmn. legis. com. 1979-81, bd. dirs. 1978-81), Nat. Assn. County Health Ofcls. (bd. dirs. 1986-88, registry com. 1990), Idaho Pub. Health Assn. (bd. dirs., treas. 1973-77), Idaho Conf. Dist. Health Dirs. (vice-chmn. and chmn. 1993-95), Idaho Forest Owners Assn., Kootenai County Environ. Alliance, Washington Pub. Health Assn., Idaho Conservation League, Ducks Ultd. Democrat.

BELNAP, NORMA LEE MADSEN, musician; b. Tremonton, Utah, Dec. 2, 1927; d. Doyle Franklin and Cleo (Crawforth) Madsen; m. H. Austin Belnap, Jan. 19, 1980; 7 stepchildren. Student, Brigham Young U., summer 1947, San Francisco Conservatory of Music, summer 1949; B.S., U. Utah, 1951; postgrad., Aspen Inst. Music, 1953, Music Acad. of West, Santa Barbara, Calif., 1962. Sec.-treas., dir., mem. faculty Treasure Mountain Festival of Arts, 1965, 66; mem. nat. adv. com. Nat. Black Music Colloquium and Competition, 1951-93; instr., 1965, adj. asst. prof. music, 1969-73, adj. assoc. prof., 1973-77, adj. prof., 1977-93; exec. v.p. LOZO Pub. Co., 1991-94. Violinist, Utah Symphony, 1944-93, ret. 1993; asst. concert master Utah Symphony, 1977-93, mem., Utah Opera Theatre Orch., 1951-54, Utah Ballet Theatre Orch., 1953-93; assoc. concertmaster Southwest Symphony St. George, Utah, 1994—, Melody Maids, 4 violins and piano, 1943-49; active in chamber music circles, 1946-81, concert mistress, U. Utah Symphony, 1947-58, prin. violist, 1958-62, soloist, Utah Artist Series, 1964, mem., Treasure Mountain String Quartet, Park City, Utah, 1964, 65, 66; appeared as violin soloist, U. Utah Symphony and Ballet Theatre Orch., 1954, 56, 57, 82; 2d violinist (affiliated with Young Audiences, Inc.) Utah String Quartet, 1958-68; Quartet-in-residence U. Utah, 1968-81, Idaho State U., 1967; with Bach Festival Orch., Carmel, Calif., 1963, 69, Sunriver Festival Orch., summer 1988, Utah-ASTA Faculty Quartet, 1970-79, tour of Europe with Utah Symphony, 1966, 77, 81, 86, S. and Cen. Am., 1971, Brit. Isles, 1975, Hawaii, 1979, concertizing throughout Western states, frequent festival adjudicator; numerous solo recitals. Recipient Tchr. Recognition award Music Tchrs. Nat. Assn., 1971, 72, 73. Mem. Music Educators Nat. Conf., Utah String Tchrs. Assn. (state membership chmn. 1969-73), Utah Music Tchrs. Assn. (state cert. bd. 1968-94), Utah Fedn. Music Clubs (1st v.p.), Am. String Tchrs. Assn. (dir. Utah nat. string conf. ann. 1970-79), Mortar Bd., Mu Phi Epsilon (founder, 1st pres. U. Utah chpt. 1950, compiler Mu Phi Epsilon Composers and Their Works 1956, nat. v.p., music adv., province gov. 1954-58, chpt. honoree for 30 yrs. of dedicated svc. 1981, chpt. honoree for 50 yrs. as mem. with Utah Symphony, honoree for 43 yrs of svc. 1994), Alpha Lambda Delta, Phi Kappa Phi, Alpha Xi. Delta, Lambda Delta Sigma. Mem. LDS Ch. Home: 1854 S 430 West Cir Saint George UT 84770-8737

BELOVANOFF, OLGA, retired health care facility administrator; b. Buchanan, Sask., Can., July 1, 1932; d. Frederick Alexander and Dora (Konkin) B. Grad. high sch., Kamsack, Sask., Can. From clk. to adminstrv. officer Sask. Health Dept. Cancer Clinic, Saskatoon, 1951-78; bus. mgr. Sask. Cancer Found. Saskatoon Clinic, 1979-90. Dir. Sask. Br. Can. Tenpin Fedn., Inc. Home: 420 3d Ave N, Saskatoon, SK Canada S7K 2J3

BELPORT, STANLEY CURTIS, computer professional; b. Tucson, Ariz., June 7, 1949; s. Samuel Abraham and Dortha Jean (Luttrell) B.; m. Mary Sue Huddle, Aug. 10, 1991. BA in Radio and TV, U. Ariz., 1974, postgrad., 1975-79. Applications architect & developer, project leader Data Systems Ariz., Tucson, 1980-84; cons. CER Corp., Las Vegas, 1984-87, SAI Corp., Las Vegas, 1987-89, Computer Task Group, Las Vegas, 1989-94, Belpart Consulting Inc., Las Vegas, 1994—. Producer, writer local PBS TV shows, 1973-74. Active Cato Inst., Washington, 1993—, Drug Policy Found., Washington. Cpl. USMC, 1969-71. Mem. Assn. for Computing Machinery, MicroSoft Developer Network, Sisity Raidus. Office: 6740 Coley Ave Las Vegas NV 89102

BELSHAW, JANINE, research and development executive; b. 1953. BSBA, San Jose State U., 1978. Various positions Advanced Electronics Design, Sunnyvale, Calif., 1978-82; sec., treas., contr. Olivetti Advanced Tech. Ctr., Cupertino, Calif., 1982—. Office: Olivetti Advanced Tech Ctr 20300 Stevens Creek Blvd Cupertino CA 95014-2240*

BELT, AUDREY E(VON), social worker, consultant; b. New Orleans, June 23, 1948. BS in Social Work and Psychology, Grambling State U., 1970; MSW in Adminstrn. and Policy, U. Mich., 1972. Adult probation officer City/County San Francisco Hall of Justice, 1973-74; child welfare worker dept. social svcs. City/County San Francisco, 1974-79; rsch. and planning specialist City of Ann Arbor (Mich.) Model Cities Interdisciplinary Agy; cons. San Francisco; cons. in field. Grambling State U. scholar, 1966-70, U. Mich. scholar, 1971-72. Mem. ABA, NASW (edn. task force), Am. Orthopsychiat. Assn., Am. Humane Soc. (exec. asst. dir., sec. exec. bd.), Child Welfare League Am., N.Y. Acad. Scis., Smithsonian Rsch. Instn., Alpha Kappa Delta. Democrat. Roman Catholic. Home and Office: PO Box 424288 610 Polk St San Francisco CA 94142-4288

BELTRAMO, MICHAEL NORMAN, management consultant; b. L.A., Feb. 9, 1942; s. Blase and Violette (Murphy) B.; m. Susan Annette Lawton, Dec. 24, 1969 (div. 1980); m. Jane Sinden Spiegel, Apr. 21, 1984; children: Helen Weedon, Anna Sinden, Emily Murphy. AB, UCLA, 1964; MPA, U. So. Calif., 1967; PhD, Rand Grad. Inst., Santa Monica, Calif., 1983. Cert. cost estimator/analyst. Mem. tech. staff The RAND Corp., Santa Monica, 1969-75; dep. mgr. Sci. Applications Internat. Corp., L.A., 1975-80; pres. Beltramo and Assocs., L.A., 1980—. Author: LA County Economic Adjustment Strategy for Defense Reduction; contbr. articles to profl. publs. Named Ky. Col. Commonwealth of Ky., 1973. Mem. Soc. Cost Estimating and Analysis (cert., bd. dirs. 1987-88). Republican. Methodist. Home and Office: 13039 Sky Valley Rd Los Angeles CA 90049-1037

BELTRÁN, ANTHONY NATALICIO, military non-commissioned officer, deacon; b. Flagstaff, Ariz., Aug. 17, 1938; s. Natalicio Torres and Mary Mercedes (Sandoval) B.; m. Patricia Emily Cañez, Nov. 18, 1962; children: Geralyn P., Bernadette M., Albert A., Catherine M., Elizabeth R., Michael J., Theresa R., Christopher M. AA, Phoenix Jr. Coll., 1971, C.C. of Air Force, 1992; grad., Def. Equal Oppty. Mgmt. Inst., 1991. Gen. clk. Blue Cross Blue Shield, Phoenix, 1958-61; enlisted Air N.G., advanced through ranks to chief master sgt.; unit clk. Ariz. Air N.G., Phoenix, 1961, personnel technician, 1962-65, adminstrv. supr., 1965-81, support services supr., 1981-88, equal employment specialist, 1988—. Bd. dirs. Friendly House, Phoenix, 1982-86, mem. aux. bd., 1989—; mem. Alma de la Gente, Phoenix, 1982-92, Chiefs Police Community Adv. Group, Phoenix, 1984-85, Mayor's Task Force on Juvenile Crime, Phoenix, 1979-81; pres. IMAGE de Phoenix, 1985-87. Staff sgt. USAF, 1961-62. Recipient Community Service award Phoenix C. of C., 1982. Mem. Fed. Exec. Assn. (sec., treas. Phoenix chpt. 1985-86, 1st v.p. 1987, pres. 1987-88, Community Svc. award 1986), Ariz. Hispanic Employment Program Mgrs. (treas. 1980-81, v.p. 1981-82, pres. 1982-84, named Outstanding Mem. of Yr. 1981, 83), Enlisted Assn. N.G. Ariz. (pres. Copperhead chpt. 1987-90), Non-Commd. Officers Acad. Grad. Assn. (chpt. 46 v.p. 1992-94). Democrat. Home: 4109 W Monte Vista Rd Phoenix AZ 85009-2005 Office: NG Ariz Hdqrs Human Resource Mgmt Office 5636 E Mcdowell Rd Phoenix AZ 85008-3455

BELZBERG, HOWARD, critical care physician, educator; b. Bronx, N.Y., Apr. 11, 1951. BA in Psychology, U. Calif., L.A., 1974; MD, Autonomus U., Guadalajara, Mex., 1978, Albert Einstein Coll. Medicine, SUNY, Bronx, N.Y., 1979. Diplomate Am. Bd. Internal Medicine, Am. Bd. Critical Care Medicine; cert. instr. advanced cardiac life support, advanced trauma life support. Residency in internal medicine Kern Med. Ctr., UCLA, Bakersfield, Calif., 1979-82; fellowship in critical care medicine U. Md. Shock Trauma Ctr., MIEMSS, Balt., 1982-83; attending intensivist Shock Trauma Ctr., Md. Inst. for Emergency Med. Svcs. Sys., Balt., 1982-92; sr. intensivist Neuro Trauma Ctr., Balt., 1986-92; asst. prof. medicine U. Md., Balt., 1987-92; asst. prof. surgery U. So. Calif., L.A., 1993—; assoc. dir. surgical intensive care unit L.A. County and Univ. So. Calif. Med. Ctr., L.A., 1993—; chair UMMS Pharmacy and Therapeutics Com., 1985-92, Monitoring and Data Transmission Com., 1990-92; med. dir. Md. Inst. for Emergency Med. Svcs. Sys. Computer Ctr., 1990-92; mem. L.A. County and U. So. Calif. Pharmacy and Therapeutics Com., 1993—, L.A. County Violence Prevention Coalition, 1993—; mem. adv. com. L.A. County Trauma Hosp., 1993—; rep. for L.A. County and U. So. Calif. Trauma Divsn. to Tech. Reinvestment Project, 1993—. Contbr. to profl. jours. Fellow Coll. Chest Physicians, Coll. Critical Care Medicine (task force on tech. assessment 1993—); mem. Am. Trauma Soc., Pan Am. Trauma Soc., Soc. for Computer Clin. Data Mgmt. Sys. Office: LAC & USC Med Ctr Dept Surgery 1200 N State St Rm 9900 Los Angeles CA 90033-4525

BELZBERG, SAMUEL, real estate investment professional; b. Calgary, Alta., Can., June 26, 1928; s. Abraham and Hinda (Fishman) B.; m. Frances Cooper; children: Cheryl Rae, Marc David, Wendy Jay, Lisa. B.Comm., U. Alta., Edmonton, 1948. Pres. Bel-Fran Investments, Ltd., Vancouver, B.C., Can., 1968—, Balfour Holdings, Inc., 1992—; pres. First City Fin. Corp. Ltd., Vancouver, 1970-83, 86-91, chmn., 1983-91; bd. dirs. Franklin Supply Co., Ltd., D. Grant MacDonald Capital Corp., Westminster Capital, Inc. Home: 3711 Alexandra St, Vancouver, BC Canada V6J 4C3 Office: 1177 W Hastings St Ste 2000, Vancouver, BC Canada V6E 2K3

BENACH, SHARON ANN, physician assistant; b. New Orleans, Aug. 28, 1944; d. Wilbur G. and Freda Helen (Klaas) Cherry; m. Richard Benach, Dec. 6, 1969 (div. Oct. 1976); children: Craig, Rachel. Degree, St. Louis U., 1978. Physician asst. VA Hosp., St. Louis, 1982-84, Maricopa County Health Svcs., Phoenix, 1984—. Served with USPHS, 1978-82. Recipient Outstanding Performance award HHS. Mem. Maricopa Faculty Assn. (div. internal medicine), Mensa. Jewish. Home: 5726 N 10th St No 5 Phoenix AZ 85014-2273

BENALLY, COURAGE CLAH, elementary education educator; b. Pinon, Ariz., Sept. 10, 1951; s. Clah and Lena (Nez) B.; m. Pat Birdsbill, Aug. 15, 1972 (div. Dec. 1980); children: Steven, Alicia Rae, Loverty, Brandon; m. R. Marina Sabbas, Aug. 25, 1986; children: Amanda, Terrance, Keezhone. BA in Kinesiology, U. Wash., 1984; cert., We. Wash. U., 1986. Cert. tchr. Jeweler Marlens Gem, Bellingham, Wash., 1986-88; tchr. Seattle Sch. Dist. # 1, 1990—. Composer and dancer Native Am. Culture. Roadman Native Am. Ch., 1993—. Home: 6551 5th Ave NE Seattle WA 98115-6418 Office: Indian Heritage Sch 1330 N 90th St Seattle WA 98103-4016

BEN-ASHER, M. DAVID, physician; b. Newark, June 18, 1931; s. Samuel Irving and Dora Ruth (Kagan)B.; m. Bryna S. Zeller, Nov. 22, 1956. BA, Syracuse U., 1952; postgrad., U. Buffalo Sch. Med., 1956. Intern E.J. Meyer Mem. Hosp., Buffalo, N.Y., 1956-57; resident Jersey City Med. Ctr., 1957-58; asst. chief med. service U.S. Army Hosp., Ft. McPherson, Ga., 1958-60; resident Madigan Mem. Hosp., Tacoma, Wash., 1960-62; chief gen. med. service Walson Army Hosp., Ft. Dix, N.Y., 1962-64; attending staff St. Mary's Hosp., Tucson, Ariz., 1964—; pvt. practice Tucson, 1964—; mem. Ariz. State Bd. Med. Examiners, 1978-88. Bd. dirs. Tucson Symphony, 1971-73; mem. Ariz. State Bd. Med. Examiners, 1978-88 (joint bd. for regulation of physicians' assts. 1990—); bd. trustees United Synagogue Am., 1981-87, nat. adv. bd., 1987-91. Mem. Pima County Med. Soc. (bd. dirs. 1971-77, pres. 1976), Ariz. Med. Assn., AMA, ACP. Democrat. Home: 3401 N Tanuri Dr Tucson AZ 85715-6735 Office: So Ariz Med Specialists 4711 N 1st Ave Tucson AZ 85718-5610

BENBOW, RICHARD ADDISON, psychological counselor; b. Las Vegas, Dec. 27, 1949; s. Jules Coleman and Bonnie Ray B. BBA, U. Nev. 1972, MS in Counseling, 1974; AAS in Bus. Mgmt. and Real Estate, Clark County Community Coll., 1980; PhD in Clin. Psychology, U. Humanistic Studies, 1986. Cert. tchr., Nev.; cert. clin. mental health counselor, secondary sch. counselor, Nev., substance abuse counselor, Nev., substance abuse program adminstr., Nev.; nat. cert. counselor. Jud. svcs. officer Mcpl. Ct. City of Las Vegas, 1983-88, pretrial program coord., 1988—; inmate classification technician Detention and Correctional Svcs., 1982-83; stress mgmt. cons. Mem. Biofeedback Soc. Am., Assn. Humanistic Psychology, Nat. Assn. Psychotherapists, Am. Counseling Assn., Am. Mental Health Counselors Assn., Am. Acad. Crisis Interveners, Jr. C. of C., U.S. Jaycees (presdl. award of honor 1978-79), Delta Sigma Phi. Democrat. Christian Scientist. Office: Mcpl Ct Jud Svcs City of Las Vegas 400 Stewart Ave Las Vegas NV 89101-2942

BENCHIMOL, ALBERTO, cardiologist, author; b. Belem, Para, Brazil, Apr. 26, 1932; s. Isaac I. and Nina (Siqueira) B.; came to U.S., 1957, naturalized, 1964; B.S., State Coll., Rio de Janeiro, Brazil, 1950; M.D., U. Brazil, 1956; m. Helena Lourdes Levy, Apr. 14, 1962; children—Nelson, Alex. Intern, U. Brazil Med. Center, Rio de Janeiro, 1956-57, resident in medicine, 1957; fellow in medicine U. Kans. Med. Center, Kansas City, 1958-60, Scripps Clinic, La Jolla, Calif., 1960-61; practice medicine specializing in cardiology, La Jolla, now Phoenix; research assoc. Inst. Cardiopulmonary Diseases, Scripps Clinic and Research Found., La Jolla, 1961-63, assoc., 1963-66; dir. Inst. Cardiovascular Diseases, Good Samaritan Med. Center, Phoenix, 1966-82; vis. prof. U. Brazil, 1966, Desert Hosp., Palm Springs, Calif., 1971; tutor U. Mo. Sch. Medicine, Kansas City, 1974-77, lectr., 1978-81; prof. in residence U. Oreg., Portland, 1975; vis. prof. Nagasaki U., Japan, 1970, Letterman Gen. Hosp., San Francisco, 1972. Haskell fellow in cardiology, 1957-59. Fellow ACP, Am. Coll. Cardiology, Am. Coll. Chest Physicians, Am. Coll. Angiology; mem. Am., Ariz. heart assns., Am. Physiol. Soc., Western Soc. Clin. Research, AMA, Biol. and Med. Scis. Research Club San Diego, Am. Fedn. Clin. Research. Author: Atlas of Vectorcardiography, 1971; Atlas of Phonocardiography, 1971; Vectorcardiography, 1973; Non-Invasive Diagnostic Techniques in Cardiology, 1977, 2d edit., 1981; Noninvasive Techniques in Cardiology for the Nurse and Technician, 1978; contbr. articles on cardiology and cardiography to profl. jours., chpts. to med. books; editorial bd. Am. Heart Jour., 1968-76, Am. Jour. Cardiology, 1969-76, Catheterization and Cardiovascular Diagnosis, 1974—, Chest, 1974; producer films on cardiography, 1962, 66. Home: 195 E Desert Park Ln Phoenix AZ 85020-4030

BENDER, BETTY WION, librarian; b. Mt. Ayer, Iowa, Feb. 26, 1925; d. John F. and Sadie A. (Guess) Wion; m. Robert F. Bender, Aug. 24, 1946. B.S., N.Tex. State U., Denton, 1946; M.A., U. Denver, 1957. Asst. cataloger N. Tex. State U. Library, 1946-49; from cataloger to head acquisitions So. Meth. U., Dallas, 1949-56; reference asst. Ind. State Library, Indpls., 1951-52; librarian Ark. State Coll., 1958-59, Eastern Wash. Hist. Soc., Spokane, 1960-67; reference librarian, then head circulation dept. Spokane (Wash.) Public Library, 1968-73, library dir., 1973-88; vis. instr. U. Denver, summers 1957-60, 63, fall 1959; instr. Whitworth Coll., Spokane, 1962-64; mem. Gov. Wash. Regional Conf. Libraries, 1968, Wash. Statewide Library Devel. Council, 1970-71. Bd. dirs. N.W. Regional Found., 1973-75, Inland Empire Goodwill Industries, 1975-77, Wash. State Library Commn., 1979-87, Future Spokane, 1983-88, vice chmn., 1986-87, pres., 1987-88. Recipient YWCA Outstanding Achievement award in Govt., 1985. Mem. ALA (mem. library adminstrn. and mgmt. assn. com. on orgn. 1982-83, chmn. nominating com. 1983-85, v.p./pres.-elect. 1985-86, pres. 1986-87), Pacific N.W. Library Assn. (chmn. circulation div. 1972-75, conv. chmn. 1977), Wash. Library Assn. (v.p./pres.-elect 1975-77, pres. 1977-78), AAUW (pres. Spokane br. 1969-71, rec. sec. Wash. br. 1971-73, fellowship named in honor 1972), Spokane and Inland Empire Librarians (dir. 1967-68), Am. Soc. Pub. Adminstrn. Republican. Lutheran. Club: Zonta (pres. Spokane chpt. 1976-77, dist. conf. treas. 1972). Home: E221 Rockwood Blvd # 504 Spokane WA 99202

BENDER, COLEMAN COALPORT, company executive; b. Coalport, Pa., Mar. 30, 1921; s. Harry and Annie Bender; m. Pauline Evelyn, Apr. 12, 1948; children: Sue Ann, David. BA, Pa. State U., 1946, MA, 1947; PhD, U. Ill., 1955; AM (hon.), Emerson Coll., 1961. Instr. Pa. State U., State College, 1946-48, U. Ill., Champaign, 1948-50, USAF, Chanute, Ill., 1950-51; prof., chmn. Emerson Coll., Boston, 1951-69, dir. edn1. rsch., 1969-71, dir. orgn. rsch., 1969-82; prof. Am. Coll. of Greece, Athens, 1980-81; asst. prof. U. Hawaii, Honolulu, 1982-88; pres. C.C. Bender and Assocs., Honolulu, 1988—; cons. Aloha Airlines, Honolulu, 1982-87, Hawaii Electric, Honolulu, 1983-90, Dole Pineapple, Honolulu, 1983-90, U. Pa. Med. Sch., Phila., 1975-90. Author: Speaking is a Practical, 1968, Speech Communications, 1976, Words in Context, 1970. Staff sgt. USAF, 1942-46, PTO. McAllister scholar Pa. State U., State College, 1939; fellow in speech U. Ill., Champaign, 1950. Mem. Eastern Speech Assn. (exec. sect. 1965-68), Soc. for Inst. Tech. (v.p. 1967-69), Mass. Speech Assn. (pres. 1962-64, Speaker of Yr. 1970). Home: 3138 Waialae Ave Apt 436 Honolulu HI 96816-1547 Office: U Hawaii Manoa Campus Honolulu HI 96822

BENDER, FRANK NORCROSS, warehouse executive; b. Reno, Oct. 5, 1920; s. Edwin Samuel and Adele Cutts (Norcross) B.; m. Barbara Syble Weston, Dec. 6, 1944 (div. July 1977); children: Chris Norcross, Leslee; m. Terry Axtell Rooney, July 10, 1977. U. Calif., Berkeley, 1943. Ptnr. Bender Warehouse Co., Reno, 1946-60, pres., 1960-88, CEO, 1988—. Pres. Greater Reno C. of C., 1959-61; mem., bd. dirs. Nev. State Dept. Econ. Devel., Carson City, Nev., 1964-77; chmn. bd. Am. Warehouse Assn., Chgo., 1981-82; pres., founder U. Nev. Ctr. for Logistics, Reno, 1988. Lt. USNR, 1943-46. Named Reno Civic Leader of Yr., Reno C. of C., 1970, Nev. Ambassador, 1986; recipient Pres.'s medal U. Nev., 1990; named to Bus. Leader's Hall of Fame, Jr. Achievement, 1991. Mem. Prospectors Club (dir. 1969-70), Rotary Club of Reno (pres. 1969-70), Nev. Area Coun. Boy Scouts of Am. (v.p. 1971), Jr. Achievement (dir. 1970s), Nev. Roundtable Coun. of Logistics Mgmt. (pres. 1990-91). Republican. Episcopalian. Office: Bender Warehouse Co 345 Parr Circle PO Box 11430 Reno NV 89510

BENDER, GARY NEDROW, television sportscaster; b. Norton, Kans., Sept. 1, 1940; s. Herbert Leo and Helen Dolores (Nedrow) B.; m. Linda Wright, Aug. 4, 1963; children: Trey, Brett. B.A., Wichita State U., 1962; M.A., U. Kans., 1964. Sportcaster WIBW-TV, Topeka, Kans., 1966-68, U. Kans. Network, Lawrence, 1968-70, WKOW-TV, Madison, Wis., 1970-75, KMOX TV-Radio, St. Louis, 1975-80, CBS Network, N.Y.C., 1975-87, ABC-TV Sports, N.Y.C., 1987-92; sportscaster Turner Sports-TNT, Atlanta, 1992—. Bd. dirs. Fellowship Christian Athletes, Kansas City, Mo., 1981-89; com. mem. Fiesta Fowl, Phoenix, 1982—. Named State Sportscaster of Yr. Nat. Assn. Sportscasters and Writers, 1973, 74; recipient Emmy for best live telecast Radio-TV Sports Com., 1982. Mem. Pen and Mike Club (pres. 1973-74). Republican. Lodge: Rotary.

BENDER, GRAHAM I., forest products executive; b. Radisson, Saskatchewan, Can., Nov. 26, 1939; s. Elmer Ivan and Jeanetta (McMillan) B.; m. Marion Christine Jackson, Oct. 20, 1962; children: Joyce Elizabeth, John Barton, Marnie Jo. BCE, U. Saskatchewan, 1961; MBA, McGill U., 1967; AMP, Harvard U., 1984. Engring. economist Can. Nat. Rys., Montreal, 1961-66, mktg. officer, 1967-68; distbn. MacMillan Bloedel Ltd., Vancouver, B.C., 1968-70, asst. chartering mgr., 1970-71, mgr. trans. rsch., 1971-73, gen. mgr. trans., 1973-75, v.p. Can. transp. Co., 1975-78, v.p. trans., pres. Can. Trans. Co., 1978-81; gen. mgr. Harmac Pulp MacMillan Bloedel Ltd., Nanimo, B.C., 1981-87, gen. mgr. Powell River div., 1987-89; pres. Caribo Pulp & Paper Co., 1989—; sr. v.p. Pulp, Weldwood of Can. Ltd., 1989-92; pres., COO Weldwood of Can. Ltd., Vancouver, 1992—, pres., CEO, 1993—, also bd. dirs.; bd. dirs. Canfor-Weldwood Distbn. Ltd., Seaboard Lumber/Shipping Co. Ltd., Can. Pulp & Paper Assn., Coun. Forest Industries; bd. trustees Forest Alliance of B.C.; bd. govs., exec. com. Bus. Coun. B.C. Bd. dirs. United Way, Nanaimo, 1983-86, pres., 1985-86; bd. dirs. Shakespeare Players, 1982-86. Mem. Can. Pulp and Paper Assn. (bd. dirs.), Coun. Forest Industries (bd. dirs.), Vancouver Club. Home: 5350 Westhaven Wynd, West Vancouver, BC Canada V7W 3E8 Office: Weldwood Can Ltd, 1055 W Hastings St PO Box 2179, Vancouver, BC Canada V6B 3V8

BENDER, RALPH JAY, educator; b. Long Beach, Calif., Nov. 17, 1943; s. Jay E. and Gladys Allah (Cook) B.; m. Sandra Lee Genthner Bender, Nov. 18, 1978; children: Valerie Sue Bender Felli, Lisa Allah Bender Hall. BA in Biblical Studies, Grace Bible Inst., 1978; MA in Biblical Studies, Grace Grad. Sch. Theology, 1980; PhD in New and Old Testaments, Calif. Grad. Sch. Theology, 1992. Cert. sci., math., bible tchr., Calif. Tchr., sci. dept. chair. Brethren Christian Jr. and Sr. H. S., Cypress, Calif., 1987—; theology educator Internat. Biblical Christian Coll., Fullerton, Calif., 1993—; lt. cnl. U.S.A.R., 1966—; chmn. Christian Edn. Bd., Carson, Calif. Commdr. Carson (Calif.) Bible Ch. AWANA, 1993—. Recipient leadership excellence award Calif. Assn. Sci. Specialists, 1992. Mem. Assn. Supervision and Curriculum Devel., Nat. Sci. Tchrs. Assn., Smithsonian Nat. Assn. Republican. Protestant. Office: Brethren Christian Jr/Sr H S 5172 Orange Ave Cypress CA 90630

BENDING, DAVID ALEXANDER GLEN, mining executive, geoscientist; b. Chicoutimi, Quebec, Can., Dec. 12, 1954; came to U.S., 1962; s. Glen Charles Bending and Beatress Elizabeth (Long) Wilkinson; m. Ginette Lilianne Bourdeau, May 10, 1986; children: Michael David, Katherine Marie. BSc in Geology, U. Oreg., 1976; MSc iin Geology, U. Toronto, Can., 1979. Mine and exploration geologist GRC Exploration Co., Metaline Falls, Wash., 1976-77; field party chief geologist Rio Tinto Can. Exploration, Vancouver, 1978-79; project geologist Tex. Gulf Exploration, Vancouver, 1979-82; rsch. assoc., cons. U. Toronto, 1982-84; exploration geologist, mgr. Homestake Mining Co., 1985-93; v.p. no. S.Am. Homestake Mining Co., Reno, 1993—; pres. D. Bending & Assoc., Ltd., Toronto, 1982-85; v.p. Homestake Venezuela, Puerto Ordaz, 1993—, Minera Rio Carichapo, Puerto Ordaz, 1993—, Minera Rio Marwani, Puerto Ordaz, 1993—. Fellow Soc. Econ. Geologists, Geol. Assn. Can.; mem. Can. Inst. Mining. Republican.

BENEDETTI, THOMAS JOSEPH, obstetrician-gynecologist, educator; b. Tacoma, June 15, 1947; s. Aldo Joseph and Norma Loraine (Gagliardi) B.; m. Jacqueline K. Benedetti, June 10, 1973; children: Allison, Michelle, Daniel. BA with honors, Stanford U., 1969; MD, U. Wash., 1973. Diplomate Am. Bd. Ob-Gyn, Am. Bd. Maternal-Fetal Medicine. Intern U. Pitts., 1974; resident in ob-gyn L.A. County, U. So. Calif. Med. Ctr., 1974-77, fellow maternal/fetal medicine, clin. instr., 1977-79; asst. prof. dept. ob-gyn U. Wash. Med. Ctr., Seattle, 1979-83, assoc. prof., 1983-87, prof., 1987—, dir. perinatal medicine, 1983—. Contbr. articles to profl. jours.; author abstracts, other med. publs. Fellow Am. Coll. Obstetricians and Gynecologists (Best Paper award 1978, Excellence in Med. Rsch. award 1980); mem. AMA, Wash. State Med. Soc., Soc. Perinatal Obstetrics, Am. Coll. Ob-Gyn. Office: U Wash McDLenter Obgyn RH 20 1959 NE Pacific St Seattle WA 98195-0004

BENEDICT, BURTON, retired museum director, anthropology educator; b. Balt., May 20, 1923; s. Burton Eli Oppenheim and Helen Blanche (Deiches) B.; m. Marion MacColl Steuber, Sept. 23, 1950; children: Helen, Barbara MacVean. AB cum laude, Harvard U., 1949; PhD, U. London, 1954. Sr. rsch. fellow Inst. Islamic Studies, McGill U., Montreal, Que., Can., 1954-55; sociol. rsch. officer Colonial Office, London and Mauritius, 1955-58; sr. lectr. social anthropology London Sch. Econs., 1958-68; prof. anthropology U. Calif., Berkeley, 1968-91, prof. emeritus, 1991—, chmn. dept., 1970-71, dean social scis., 1971-74, dir. Hearst Mus. Anthropology, 1989-94; dir. emeritus Hearst Mus. Anthropology, 1994—; dir. U. Calif. Study Ctr. for U.K. and Ireland, London, 1986-88. Author: Indians in a Plural Society, 1961; author and editor: Problems of Smaller Territories, 1967, (with M. Benedict) Men, Women & Money in Seychelles, 1982, The Anthropology of World's Fairs, 1983; contbr. numerous articles to profl. jours. Sgt. USAF, 1942-46. Recipient Western Heritage award Nat. Cowboy Hall of Fame, 1984; rsch. fellow Colonial Office, 1955-58, 60, U. Calif., Berkeley, 1974-75; grantee NEH, 1981-83. Fellow Royal Anthrop. Inst. (mem. coun. 1962-65, 67-68, 86-89), Am. Anthrop. Assn.; mem. Assn. Social Anthropologists of Brit. Commonwealth, Athenaeum Club (London). Office: U Calif Berkeley Dept Anthropology Berkeley CA 94720

BENES, ANDREW CHARLES, professional baseball player; b. Evansville, Ind., Aug. 20, 1967. Student, U. Evansville. With San Diego Padres, 1988—; mem. U.S. Olympic Baseball Team, 1988, Nat. League All-Star Team, 1993. Named Sporting News Rookie Pitcher of Yr., 1989. Office: San Diego Padres PO Box 2000 San Diego CA 92112-2000*

BENEŠ, NORMAN STANLEY, meteorologist; b. Detroit, July 1, 1921; s. Stanley and Cecelia (Sereneck) B.; m. Elinor Simson, May 5, 1945 (div. Feb. 1972); children: Gregory, Heather, Michelle, Francine; m. Celia Sereneck, Mar. 3, 1972. BS, U. Wash., 1949; postgrad., U. Calif., Davis, 1963, U. Mich., 1966. Chief meteorologist Hawthorne Sch. of Aero., Moultrie, Ga., 1951-55; meteorologist U.S. Weather Bur., Phoenix, 1955-57, 59-60; meteorologist in charge NSF, Hallett, Antarctica, 1958; sta. sci. leader NSF, Byrd, Antarctica, 1960-61; meteorologist Nat. Weather Service, Sacramento, Calif., 1962-84; mem. Exec. Com. Range Benes Peak, Antarctica. Contbr. articles to profl. jours. Pres. local chpt. PTA, 1965. With USN, 1943-46, PTO. Mem. AAAS, Am. Meteorol. Soc., Am. Geophys. Union, Nat. Weather Assn., Masons. Home: 3311 Holiday Ln Placerville CA 95667-9076

BENET, THOMAS CARR, journalist; b. Paris, France, Sept. 28, 1926; s. Stephen Vincent and Rosemary (Carr) B.; m. Joan Gregory, Aug. 27, 1952; children: Rebecca Benet Sawyer, Alice. B.A., Yale U., 1949. Reporter San Francisco Chronicle, 1950-60, asst. city editor, 1968-78, editorial writer, 1978-88, chief editorial writer, 1988-94. Served with AUS, 1945-47. Recipient Christophers award Christophers Orgn., 1954. Mem. San Francisco Com. on Fgn. Relations Club: Century Assn. Office: San Francisco Chronicle 901 Mission St San Francisco CA 94103-2905

BENFIELD, ARTHUR MERRILL, social sciences educator; b. Gary, Ind., Nov. 6, 1944; s. Leslie Merrill and Bernice Neva (Sowards) B.; m. Susan Lea Reynolds, July 31, 1970; children: Zachary Merrill, Jacob Arthur, Elizabeth Ann. BA, Western N.Mex. U., 1969; MA, Western State Coll., 1973. Tchr. social studies Cen. H.S. Dist. 60, Pueblo, Colo., 1969-79, Roncalli Mid. Sch., Pueblo, 1980-82; tchr., chmn. dept. social sci. South H.S. Dist. 60, Pueblo, 1982—; bd. dirs. Ctr. for Teaching and Learning, U. So. Colo., Pueblo. Author: Economics Today and Tomorrow, 1994. Coach Pueblo Soccer and Sport Assn., 1983-88, Odyssey of the Mind, Pueblo elem., mid. and h.s., 1987—. Mem. Nat. Coun. for Social Studies, Nat. Trust for Hist. Preservation, Colo. Hist. Soc., Pi Gamma Mu, Phi Alpha Theta, Blue Key. Home: 29 Sepulveda Dr Pueblo CO 81005-2923 Office: South H S 1801 Hollywood Dr Pueblo CO 81005-2511

BENGELSDORF, IRVING SWEM, science writer, consultant; b. Chgo., Oct. 23, 1922; s. Jacob and Frieda (Wiener) B.; m. Beverly Devorah Knapp, June 12, 1949; children: Ruth, Lea, Judith. BS in Chemistry with highest honors, U. Ill., 1943; student, Cornell U.; MS, U. Chgo., 1948, PhD, 1951. Mem. chemistry faculty UCLA, 1952-54; rsch. chemist Gen. Electric Rsch. Lab., Schenectady, N.Y., 1954-59; rsch. group leader Texaco-U.S. Rubber Rsch. Ctr., Parsippany, N.J., 1959-60; sr. scientist U.S. Borax Rsch. Corp., Anaheim, Calif., 1960-63; sci. editor L.A. Times, 1963-70; dir. sci. communication Calif. Inst. Tech., Pasadena, 1971-80; contbg. sci. columnist L.A. Herald-Examiner, 1978-86; tech. writer, specialist Jet Propulsion Lab., Calif. Inst. Tech., Pasadena, 1980-88; contb. sci. columnist Oceanside (Calif.) Blade-Citizen, 1992—; cons. Jet Propulsion Lab., 1988—; Disting. vis. prof. U. So. Calif., L.A., 1971-90; tchr. TV course in Russian lang. Gen. Electric Rsch. Lab., Schenectady, 1958; cons. NASA, 1979. Author: Spaceship Earth: People and Pollution, 1969; co-author: Biology: A Unique Science, 1978; contbr. chpts. to books, articles to profl. jours.; patentee in field. Participant 19th Pugwash Conf. on Sci. and World Affairs, Sochi, USSR, 1969; mem. cabinet U. Chgo. Alumni Cabinet, 1968-71; mem. U. Calif. Water Resources Ctr. Adv. Coun., Riverside, 1973—; mem. Mayor Bradley's Energy Policy Com., L.A., 1974. With USN, 1944-46. Recipient Claude Bernard Sci. Journalism award Nat. Soc. for Med. Rsch., 1968, Bicentennial Humanitarian award City of L.A., 1981. Mem. AAAS (Westinghouse Writing award 1967, 69), Am. Chem. Soc. (James T. Grady award 1967), Nat. Assn. Sci. Writers, U. Chgo. Alumni Club L.A. (Disting. Alumnus award 1975), Soc. for Tech. Communication (hon.), Sigma Xi. Home and Office: 3778 Via Las Villas Oceanside CA 92056-7258

BENGHIAT, JACQUES, computer science engineer, consultant; b. Apr. 23, 1955; s. Samuel and Celine (Gholam) B. BS, Imperial Coll., London, 1976; MS, U. Manchester, Eng., 1978, PhD, 1981. Engr. Marconi Space and Def., Eng., 1977, 78, OSM Computer Corp., Mountain View, Calif., 1982-84; v.p. engring. Synergistic Computers, Milpitas, Calif., 1988-91; engr., prin. Syscon Consulting, Cupertino, Calif., 1984—; pres. Northport Techs., Fremont, Calif., 1989—, Centerpointe Techs., Cupertino, 1990—, Syscon Devel. Corp., Cupertino, 1991—. Office: Syscon Devel Corp 22330 Homestead Rd Apt 201 Cupertino CA 95014-0133

BENGTSON, BETTY GRIMES, library administrator; b. Milledgeville, Ga., June 22, 1940; d. Lodrick Livingston and Nancy Rachel (Clack) G.; m. Peter Yeager Bengtson, Aug. 4, 1962; 1 child, David Eric. BA, Duke U., 1962; MLS, Cath. U., 1967; M Gen. Adminstrn., U. Md., 1986. Asst. catalog libr. Macalester Coll. Libr., St. Paul, 1967-68; cataloger Notre Dame Coll. Libr., Belmont, Calif., 1968-72; cataloger Georgetown U. Libr., Washington, 1972-74, asst. acquisitions libr., 1974-75, head cataloging dept., 1975-82; assoc. dir. tech. svcs. U. Tenn. Libr., Knoxville, 1982-88; assoc. dir. bibliog. control U. Wash. Libr., Seattle, 1988-90; dir. librs. U. Wash., Seattle, 1990—. Editor: Classification of Library Materials, 1990. Mem. ALA, Assn. for Coll. and Rsch. Librs., Libr. and Info. Tech. Assn. (bd. dirs. 1994—), Commn. Preservation and Access (bd. dirs. 1993—), Online Computer Libr. Ctr. Users Coun. (pres. 1990-91), Wash. Libr. Assn., Seminars on Acad. Computing (bd. dirs. 1993—). Office: U Wash Allen Libr FM-25 Seattle WA 98195

BENHAM, JAMES MASON, mutual fund executive; b. Joliet, Ill., Nov. 24, 1935; s. Charles Orville and Helen Florence (Mason) B.; m. Maribeth Ann Naughton, Sept. 27, 1962; children—James Anthony, William Charles, Timothy Joseph. B.A., Mich. State U., 1959, M.A., 1961. Asst. bank examiner Fed. Res. Bank San Francisco, 1961-63; account exec. Merrill Lynch, Pierce, Fenner & Smith, San Jose, Calif., 1963-71; pres., chmn. bd. Benham Capital Mgmt. Group, Mountain View, Calif., 1974—, also pres., chmn. bd.; lectr. in field. Mem. No. Load Mut. Fund Assn. (gov. 1974—), Investment Co. Inst. (bd. govs. 1988—). Office: Benham Capital Mgmt Group 1665 Charleston Rd Mountain View CA 94043-1211

BENI, GERARDO, electrical and computer engineering educator, robotics scientist; b. Florence, Italy, Feb. 21, 1946; came to U.S., 1970; s. Edoardo and Tina (Bazzanti) B.; m. Susan Hackwood, May 24, 1986; children: Catherine Elizabeth, Juliet Beatrice. Laurea in Physics, U. Firenze, Florence, Italy, 1970; PhD in Physics, UCLA, 1974. Research scientist AT&T Bell Labs., Murray Hill, N.J., 1974-77; research scientist AT&T Bell Labs., Holmdel, N.J., 1977-82, disting. mem. tech. staff, 1982-84; prof. elec. and computer engring. U. Calif., Santa Barbara, 1984-91, dir. Ctr. for Robotic Systems in Microelectronics, 1985-91; prof. elec. engring., dir. distbn. robotic system lab. U. Calif., Riverside, 1991—. Founder, editor: Jours. Robotic Systems, 1983 (Jour. of Yr. award 1984); editor: Recent Advances in Robotics, 1985, Vacuum Mechatronics, 1990; contbr. more than 130 articles to tech. jours.; 16 patents in field. Fellow Am. Physics Soc. Office: U Calif-Riverside Coll Engring Riverside CA 92521

BENIGER, JAMES RALPH, communications educator, writer; b. Sheboygan, Wis., Dec. 16, 1946; s. Ralph Joseph and Charlotte Emma (Nitsch) B.; m. Kay Diane Ferdinandsen, Dec. 7, 1984. BA magna cum laude, Harvard U., 1969; MA in Sociology, U. Calif., Berkeley, 1973, MS in Statistics, 1974, PhD in Sociology, 1978. Lectr. U. Calif., Berkeley, 1976-77; instr. Princeton U., N.J., 1977-79; asst. prof. Princeton U., 1979-85; assoc. prof. Annenberg Sch. of Communications U. So. Calif., L.A., 1985—; editorial bd. Pub. Opinion Quar., Ann Arbor, Mich., 1982-87; bd. overseers Gen. Social Survey, U. Chgo., 1984-87; adv. coun. U.S. Congress Office of Tech. Assessment, 1991; assoc. editor Communication Rsch., L.A., 1988—. Author: Trafficking in Drug Users, 1983, The Control Revolution, 1986 (Assn. of Am. Pubs. award 1987, N.Y. Times Book Rev., Notable Paperback award 1989). Named Samuel Lazero Meml. Lectr. Inst. for Sci. Info., Phila., 1988, Disting. Guest Contbr. Keio U., Tokyo, 1988; John Randolph Haynes and Dora Haynes Found. grantee, 1994—. Mem. aAAS, Am. Assn. Pub. Opinion Rsch. (sec., treas. 1988-90, chair 50th Anniversary Conf. 1994—), Am. Sociol. Assn. (program chmn. 1987-88), Internat. Comm. Assn., Am. Statis. Assn. Home: 1204 Elm Ave Manhattan Beach CA 90266-5116 Office: U So Calif Sch of Communications Los Angeles CA 90089-0281

BENIRSCHKE, KURT, pathologist, educator; b. Glueckstadt, Germany, May 26, 1924; came to U.S., 1949, naturalized, 1955; s. Fritz Franz and Marie (Luebcke) B.; m. Marion Elizabeth Waldhausen, May 17, 1952; children: Stephen Kurt, Rolf Joachim, Ingrid Marie. Student, U. Hamburg, Germany, 1942, 45-48, U. Berlin, Germany, 1943, U. Wuerzburg, Germany, 1943-44; M.D., U. Hamburg, 1948. Resident Teaneck, N.J., 1950-51, Peter Bent Brigham Hosp., Boston, 1951-52, Boston Lying-in-Hosp., 1952-53, Free Hosp. for Women, Boston, 1953, Children's Hosp., Boston, 1953; pathologist Boston Lying-in-Hosp., 1955-60; teaching fellow, assoc. Med. Sch. Harvard, 1954-60; prof. pathology, chmn. dept. pathology Med. Sch. Dartmouth, Hanover, N.H., 1960-70; prof. reproductive medicine and pathology U. Calif. at San Diego, 1970-94; chmn. dept. pathology U. Calif. at San Diego (Sch. Med.), La Jolla, 1976-79; ret. U. Calif. at San Diego, 1994; dir. research San Diego Zoo, 1975-86, trustee, 1986—; cons. NIH, 1957-70. Served with German Army, 1942-45. Mem. Am. Soc. Pathology, Internat. Acad. Pathology, Am. Coll. Pathology, Teratol. Soc., Am. Soc. Zool. Veterinarians. Home: 8457 Prestwick Dr La Jolla CA 92037-2023 Office: U Calif at San Diego San Diego CA 92013-8321

BENJAMIN, KARL STANLEY, artist, educator; b. Chgo., Dec. 29, 1925; s. Eustace Lincoln and Marie (Klamsteiner) B.; m. Beverly Jean Paschke, Jan. 29, 1949; children: Beth Marie, Kris Ellen, Bruce Lincoln. Student, Northwestern U., 1943, 46; BA, U. Redlands, 1949; MA, Claremont Grad. Sch., 1960. With dept. arts Pomona Coll., Claremont, Calif., 1979—, Loren Barton Babcock Miller prof., artist-in residence, 1978-94; prof. art Claremont Grad. Sch. Traveling exhbns. include New Talent, Am. Fedn. Arts, 1959, 4 Abstract Classicists, Los Angeles and San Francisco museums, 1959-61, West Coast Hard Edge, Inst. Contemporary Arts, London, Eng., 1960, Purist Painting, Am. Fedn. Arts, 1960-61, Geometric Abstractions in Am, Whitney Mus., 1962, Paintings of the Pacific, U.S., Japan and Australia, 1961-63, Artists Environment, West Coast, Amon Carter Mus., Houston, 1962-63, Denver annual, 1965, Survey of Contemporary Art, Speed Mus., Louisville, 1965, The Colorists, San Francisco Mus., 1965, Art Across Am, Mead Corp., 1965-67, The Responsive Eye, Mus. Modern Art, 1965-66, 30th Biennial Exhbn. Am. Painting, Corcoran Gallery, 1967, 35th Biennial Exhbn. Am. Painting, 1977, Painting and Sculpture in California: The Modern Era, San Francisco Mus. Modern Art, 1976-77, Smithsonian Nat. Collection Fine Arts, Washington, 1976-77, Los Angeles Hard Edge: The Fifties and Seventies, Los Angeles County Mus. Art, 1977, Corcoran Gallery, Washington, Cheney Cowles Mus., Spokane, 1980, Calif. State U., Bakersfield, 1982, Henry Gallery, U. Wash., 1982, U. Calif., Santa Barbara, 1984, L.A. Mcpl. Art Galleries, Barnsdall Park, 1986, Turning the Tide: Early Los Angeles Modernists, Santa Barbara Mus. Art, Oakland Mus., others, 1989-91; rep. permanent collections, Whitney Mus., L.A. County Mus. Art, San Francisco Mus. Art, Santa Barbara (Calif.) Mus. Art, Pasadena (Calif.) Art Mus., Long Beach (Calif.) Mus. Art, La Jolla (Calif.) Mus. Art, Fine Arts Gallery San Diego, U. Redlands, Mus. Modern Art, Israel, Pomona Coll., Scripps Coll., Univ. Mus., Berkeley, Calif., Wadsworth Atheneum, Nat. Collection Fine Arts, Seattle Mus. Modern Art, Newport Harbor Mus., U. N.Mex. Mus. Art, Wash. State U., L.A. Mus. Contemporary Art; retrospective exhbn. covering yrs. 1955-87 Calif State U. at Northridge, 1989, retrospective exhbn. 1979-94, Pomona Coll., 1994. Served with USNR, 1943-46. Visual Arts grantee NEA, 1983, 89. Address: 675 W 8th St Claremont CA 91711-4213 Office: Pomona Coll Dept Arts 333 N College Way Claremont CA 91711-4429

BENJAMIN, LORNA SMITH, psychologist; b. Rochester, N.Y., Jan. 7, 1934; d. Lloyd Albert and Esther (Tack) Smith; children: Laureen,

Linda. A.B., Oberlin Coll., 1955; Ph.D., U. Wis., 1960. NIMH fellow dept. psychiatry U. Wis., 1958-62, clin. psychology intern, 1960-64, asst. prof., 1966-71, assoc. prof., 1971-77, prof. psychiatry, 1977-88; prof. psychology U. Utah, 1988—; research asso. Wis. Psychol. Inst., Madison, 1962-66. Contbr. articles to profl. jours. Mem. Am. Psychol. Assn., Soc. Psychotherapy Research, Phi Beta Kappa. Office: U Utah Dept Psychology Salt Lake City UT 84112

BENKERT, JOSEPH PHILIP, JR., lawyer; b. Phila., Apr. 16, 1958; s. Joseph Philip Sr. and Caroline Beatrice (Whitehouse) B.; m. Mary Russell Doherty, Oct. 22, 1988. BS cum laude, James Madison U., 1979; MS, JD cum laude, Syracuse U., 1981. Bar: D.C. 1982, Colo. 1987, U.S. Ct. Appeals (fed. cir.) 1983, U.S. Ct. Appeals (D.C. cir.) 1984. Assoc. Liberman, Sanchez & Bentley, Washington, 1982-84, Dutton, Kappes & Overman/McFadden, Evans & Sill, Washington, 1984-86, Gardner, Carton & Douglas, Washington and Denver, 1986-90; Holme, Roberts and Owen, 1990-92; assoc. Hopper and Kanouff, Denver, 1992—; sr. fellow, bd. advisors Inst. Info. Law and Policy, Ctr. for the New West, 1994—; spkr. in field. Mem. ABA, D.C. Bar Assn., Colo. Bar Assn., Denver Bar Assn., Denver C. of C., Fed. Commn. Bar Assn., Rocky Mountain Home Bused and Bus. Assn. (founder, bd. dirs. 1995—, Outstanding Friend of Home Based Bus. award 1994). Office: Hopper and Kanouff 1610 Wynkoop St Ste 200 Denver CO 80202-1135

BENNETT, BARBARA ESTHER, controller; b. Norfolk, Nebr., Nov. 24, 1953. AA, Northeastern Nebr. Community Coll., Norfolk, Nebr., 1973; student, U. Nebr., 1980, U. Colo., Denver, 1985. Bookkeeper McIntosh, Inc., Norfolk, 1971-77; credit, office mgr. Goodyear Service Stores Inc., Norfolk, 1977-81; pvt. practice acct. Norfolk, 1971-81; base adminstr. Evergreen Helicoptors Inc., Greeley, Colo., 1981-82; pvt. practice acctg. and tax service Denver, 1984—; acctg. supr, asst. controller Saltzgitter Machinery, Inc., Louviers, Colo., Saltzgitter, Fed. Republic Germany., 1982-85; corp. controller Satter, Inc., Denver, 1985—. Past Sunday sch. tchr., past chmn. bd. fin. Redeemer Luth. Ch. Mem. Am. Soc. Women Accts., Am. Legion Aux., Phi Theta Kappa, Phi Beta Lambda. Republican. Home: 963 S Patton Ct PO Box 19070 Denver CO 80219-0070 Office: Satter Distbg Co Inc 4100 Dahlia St Denver CO 80216-4406

BENNETT, BRENDA G., secondary school counselor, mathematics educator; b. Portland, Oreg., July 17, 1940; d. Edwin E. and Mable Maru (Wilhelm) Osgood; m. Steven L. Bennett, June 18, 1961; children: Sheryl Born, Laura Navarro, Katherine. BA in Math., Portland State U., 1962, MS in Counseling, 1976. Registered counselor, Wash.; lic. counselor, Oreg.; cert. advanced math. tchg., Oreg. Lab. asst. U. Oreg. Med. Sch., Portland, 1961-64; math. and science tchr. Franklin H.S., Portland, 1973-74; math. tchr. Grant H.S., Portland, 1974-79, counselor, 1979—; counselor Counseling Ctr. Vancouver, Wash., 1984-93; math. instr. Portland C.C., 1987—.

BENNETT, BRIAN O'LEARY, utilities executive; b. Bklyn., Dec. 5, 1955; s. Robert Joseph and Barbara Ashton (Michael) B. BA in Econs., George Washington U., 1982; JD, Southwestern U., 1982. Legis. caseworker U.S. Sen. James L. Buckley, Washington, 1973-77; legis. asst. U.S. Congressman Bob Dornan, D.C., 1977-78; dist. field rep. Congressman Bob Dornan, L.A., 1978-83; dir. comm. Calif. Dept. Housing & Community Devel., Sacramento, 1983-84; chief of staff U.S. Congressman R.K. Dornan, Washington, 1985-89; reg. affairs mgr. So. Calif. Edison Co., Santa Ana, 1989-94; corp. mgr. mcpl. rels. So. Calif. Edison Co., Rosemead, Calif., 1994-95; exec. dir. corp. pub. affairs So. Calif. Edison Co., Rosemead, Calif., 1995—. Contbr. articles to L.A. Times. Active organizing com. Calif. Bush for U.S. Pres., 1986-88; Calif. del. selection com., 1988, 92; campaign mgr. Dornan for U.S. Congress, 1984, 86, 88; mem. ctrl. com. Calif. State Rep. Party, mem. platform com., 1988, vice chair proxies and credentials com., 1993-94; del. Rep. Nat. Conv., 1988, 92; mem. Orange County Pro-Life PAC; mem. Orange County Forum World Affairs Coun., Orange County Urban League, Orange County Task Force on Air Quality, Orange County Pub. Affairs Assn., Orange County Forum, Orange County Boy Scout Coun. Roman Catholic. Office: So Calif Edison Rm 417 2244 Walnut Grove Ave Rosemead CA 91770

BENNETT, BRIAN RICHARD, investment broker; b. Sweet Home, Oreg., May 21, 1950; s. Clinton J. and Hilda (Ditchfield) B.; m. Joy Denise Gendron, June 23, 1973; children: Brian Richard Jr., Drew Edward. BA, Drake U., Des Moines, 1971. Account exec. E.F. Hutton & Co., Colorado Springs, Colo., 1976-78, Dean Witter Reynolds, Colorado Springs, 1978-79; account exec. Boettcher & Co., Colorado Springs, 1979-82, spl. ptnr., 1982-87; sr. v.p. sales Boettcher & Co., Inc., Colorado Springs, 1987-91; v.p. D.E. Frey & Co., Inc., Colorado Springs, 1991; pres. Bennett & Rawlings Fin. Group LLC, dba D.E. Frey & Co., Inc., Colorado Springs, 1994—. Pres. bd. Consumer Credit Counseling Svc. Pikes Peak region, Colorado Springs, 1987—. Mem. East Colorado Springs Rotary (pres. 1990-91), Rotary Internat. (Paul Harris fellow 1989). Republican. Episcopalian. Home: 17 Sequoyah Rd Colorado Springs CO 80906-4300 Office: D E Frey & Co Inc 102 S Tejon St Ste 820 Colorado Springs CO 80903-2239

BENNETT, CARL MCGHIE, engineering company executive, consultant, army reserve and national guard officer; b. Salt Lake City, Sept. 11, 1933; s. M. Woodruff and Sybil L. (McGhie) B.; m. Ardel Krantz, Aug. 10, 1954; children: Carlene, Matt, Brent, Dale, Hugh, Caren, Teri. BS, U. Utah, 1956; postgrad., U.S. Army Engr. Sch., 1964; M, Command and Gen. Staff Coll., 1974; postgrad., Indsl. Coll. Armed Forces, 1976. Commd. 2d. lt. ROTC U.S. Army, 1953; treas. and office mgr. Hercules Inc. and Data Source Corp., Salt Lake City and Los Angeles, 1963-70; controller Boise Cascade, Los Angeles, 1970-72; corp. controller Griffin Devel. Co., Los Angeles, 1972-75; controller Dart Industries, Dart Resorts, Los Angeles, 1975-78; chief fin. officer Ford, Bacon & Davis, Salt Lake City, 1978-87; pres. B & Assocs., 1987-92; cons. in field, 1992—. Rep. County Del., 1992-94. Lt. col. USAR, 1953-79, col. Utah N.G., 1985-93, AUS, 1993—. Recipient Meritorious Service medal Pres. of the U.S., 1979. Mem. Controllers Council, Nat. Assn. Accts. (v.p., bd. dirs. 1979-85), Inst. Mgmt. Accts. Office: 8425 South 20th East C-5 Sandy UT 84093

BENNETT, CHARLES LEON, vocational and graphic arts educator; b. Salem, Oreg., Feb. 5, 1951; s. Theodore John and Cora Larena (Rowland) B.; m. Cynthia Alice Hostman, June 12, 1976 (div.); m. Lynn Marie Toland, Aug. 12, 1977 (div.); children: Mizzy Marie, Charles David; m. Christina M. Crawford, Dec. 19, 1987 (div.). AS in Vocat. Tchr. Edn., Clackamas C.C., 1977; AS in Gen. Studies, Linn Benton C.C., 1979; BS in Gen. Studies, Ea. Oreg. State Coll., 1994. Tchr. printing Tongue Point Job Corps, Astoria, Oreg., 1979-80; tchr., dept. chmn. Portland (Oreg.) pub. schs., 1980—; owner, mgr. printing and pub. co., Portland, 1981-87. With AUS, 1970-72. Mem. NRA, Oreg. Vocat. Trade-Tech. Assn. (dept. chmn., pres. graphic arts div., Indsl. Educator of Year 1981-82), Oreg. Vocat. Assn. (Vocat. Tchr. of Yr. 1982-83), Graphic Arts Tech. Found., In-Plant Printing Mgmt. Assn., Internat. Graphic Arts Edn. Assn. (v.p. N.W. region VI), Oreg. Assn. Manpower Spl. Needs Personnel, Oreg. Indsl. Arts Assn., Internat. Platform Assn. Nat. Assn. Quick Printers, Am. Vocat. Assn., Pacific Printing & Imaging Assn., Inplant Printing Mgmt. Assn., Portland Club Lithographers and Printing House Craftsmen. Republican. Home: 20295 S Unger Rd Beavercreek OR 97004-9758 Office: 8020 NE Tillamook St Portland OR 97213-6655

BENNETT, CHARLES TURNER, social welfare administrator; b. Egypt, Ark., June 17, 1932; s. Charley Clower and Lois LaJoy (Turner) B.; m. Ella Jane Fye, July 6, 1962; children: Rebeca Joy, Lisa Anne. Grad., Moody Bible Inst., Chgo., 1953; student, UCLA, 1970; MA, Fuller Theol. Seminary, Pasadena, Calif., 1972, Claremont (Calif.) Grad. Sch., 1983. Bush pilot Mission Aviation, Mexico, Mexico, 1955-68; dir. research Mission Aviation Fellowship, Fullerton, Calif., 1968-72; pres., chief exec. officer Mission Aviation Fellowship, Redlands, Calif., 1973-85; exec. dir. Presby. Ctr. for Mission Studies, Fullerton, 1972-73; exec. v.p. Food for the Hungry Internat., Geneva, Switzerland, 1985-88, Scottsdale, Ariz., 1988-91; pres. Ptnrs. Internat., San Jose, Calif., 1992—; bd. chmn. Air Serv. Internat. Redlands; bd. dirs. Evang. Fgn. Missions Assn., Washington, 1976-82; founder Redlands Aviation Corp., 1980; adv. bd. Presbyn. Ctr. for Mission Studies, 1983—. Author: Tinder in Tabasco, 1968, Pantano Ardiente, 1989, (with others) From Nairobi to Berkeley, 1967, God, Man and Church Growth, 1973. Chmn. world service Redlands Rotary Club., 1982-85. Named Alumnus of Yr. Fuller Theol. Seminary, 1985. Democrat. Home: 2395 Delaward-Sp 161 Santa Cruz CA 95060-5726 Office: Ptnrs Internat 2302 Zanker Rd San Jose CA 95131

BENNETT, CONNIE SUE, food products executive, real estate investor; b. Richland Center, Wis., Oct. 4, 1955; d. Robert Eugene And Lillian Theresa (Crusan) Cottrill; m. James A. Bennett III, Oct. 22, 1977 (div. Jan. 1989). Grad. high sch., Ithaca, Wis. Owner, chef A Taste Of Heaven Restaurant, Anchorage, 1978-80, Saucy Sisters Catering, Anchorage, 1980-86; pres. Good Taste Inc., Anchorage, 1986—, Sable Properties, 1990—, Flamingo Properties, 1989—. Mem. adv. bd. Hugh O'Brian Found., 1987-89. Named Small Bus. Person of Yr. State of Alaska, 1987, U.S. Western Region, 1987. Mem. Internat. Assn. Cooking Profl., Am. Inst. Wine and Food, James Beard Found., Inflight Food Svc. Assn. Office: PO Box 202530 Anchorage AK 99520-2530

BENNETT, EUGENE PEART, artist; b. Central Point, Oreg., Dec. 20, 1921; s. Edward Carl and Mable Ann (Peart) B. Student, U. Oreg., 1940-43, Park Coll., 1943; student evening classes, DePaul U., 1949-50; BA in Art Edn., Art Inst. Chgo., 1951; student evening classes, U. Chgo., 1951-53; MA in Art Edn., Art Inst. Chgo., 1954; student, Florence, Italy, 1954-55. Tchr. Eugene Bennett Summer Art Classes, Medford, Oreg., 1948-53; tchr. jr. sch. Art Inst. Chgo., 1950-51; tchr. New Trier Twp. H. S., Winnetka, Ill, 1951-54, Abbott Labs., N. Chgo., 1951-53, Katharine Lord's Studio, Evanston, Ill., 1952-53; tchr. life drawing Art Inst. Chgo., 1953-54; tchr. 414 Art Workshop, Chgo., 1953-54, 1955-58; tchr. New Trier Twp. H. S., Winnetka, Ill., 1955-58; co-dir. 414 Art Workshop Gallery, Chgo., 1956-58; pvt. classes Medford and Jacksonville, Oreg., 1959-69; bd. dirs., founder Rogue Valley Art Assn., Medford, Oreg., 1959—, pres. 1959-60. One man shows include Portland (Oreg.) Art Mus., 1950, 60, Mus. of Art U. Oreg., Eugene, 1969, 82, So. Oreg. Hist. Soc., Jacksonville, 1983, Schneider Mus. Art So. Oreg. State Coll., Ashland, 1994; group shows include Mcpl. Art Gallery, Jackson, Miss., 1948, Portland Art Mus., 1950, Bklyn. Mus., 1951, Mus. Modern Art, N.Y.C., 1953, Art Inst. Chgo., 1954, 56, Madison Square Garden, 1958, San Francisco Mus. Art, 1961, Meml. Union Art Galleries Oreg. State U., Corvallis, 1963, Alba, Italy, 1963, State Capital Mus., Olympia, Wash., 1964, Oreg. Arts. Commn., 1986, Expo 86, Seattle, 1986, Galleria State Capitol, Salem, Oreg., 1991; represented in pub. collections Mus. Modern Art, Mus. Art. U. Oreg., Haseltine Collection of N.W. Art, Coos Art Mus., Schneider Mus. Art, Bundy Art Mus., Miss. Art Mus., Pacific Power; prin. work includes Oreg. Pavillion, Seattle Worlds Fair, 1962; executed two groups of wood sculpture U.S. Nat. Bank of Oreg., Eugene, 1961, bas relief, wood screens Salishan Lodge, Gleneden, Oreg. Bd. dirs. So. Oreg. Hist. Soc., Medford, 1969-73; chmn. Jacksonville (Oreg.) Historic Preservation Commn., 1968-70; mem. Jacksonville (Oreg.) Planning Commn., Oreg. Arts Commn. With USN, 1943-46. Recipient Pauline Palmer prize Art Inst. Chgo, 1956, Renaissance prize, 1957, award of merit Am. Assn. Mus., 1984; honrable mention Oreg. Centennial Exhibn., 1959. Mem. So. Oreg. Soc. of Artists (hon. life), Sch. of Art Inst. Chgo. (alumni), Oreg. Advs. for Arts, Schneider Mus. Art. Home: P O Box 328 355 S Oregon St Jacksonville OR 97530

BENNETT, FRED LAWRENCE, engineering educator; b. Troy, N.Y., Apr. 4, 1939; s. Fred A. and Dorothy (Lee) B.; m. Margaret Ann Musgrave, Aug. 25, 1962; children: Matthew Lawrence, Andrew Lee. BCE, Rensselaer Poly. Inst., 1961; MS, Cornell U., 1963, PhD, 1965. Registered profl. engr., Alaska, Pa., N.H. Planning and scheduling engr. United Engrs. & Cons. Inc., Phila., 1965-68; assoc. prof. engring. mgmt. U. Alaska, Fairbanks, 1968-74, prof. engring. mgmt., 1974—, asst. to chancellor, 1977-79, vice chancellor acad. affairs, 1979-82, acting v.p. for acad. affairs, 1982-83, head dept. engring. and sci. mgmt., 1969-80, 83—; owner F. Lawrence Bennett, P.E., Engring. and Mgmt. Cons., 1969—; vis. prof. engring. Luleå, Sweden, 1992. Author: Critical Path Precedence Networks, 1977, (with others) Construction in Cold Regions, 1991; contbr. papers and articles on engring. mgmt. and cold regions constrn. to profl. publs. Mem. coun. exec. bd. Boy Scouts Am., Fairbanks, 1982-92. Fellow ASCE; mem. NSPE, Am. Soc. Engring. Edn., Am. Soc. Engring. Mgmt., Project Mgmt. Inst., Soc. Logistics Engrs., Sigma Xi, Phi Kappa Phi, Tau Beta Pi, Chi Epsilon. Home: PO Box 83009 Fairbanks AK 99708-3009 Office: U Alaska PO Box 755900 Fairbanks AK 99775-5900

BENNETT, JACQUELINE BEEKMAN, school psychologist; b. Santa Paula, Calif., Sept. 4, 1946; d. Jack Edward and Margaret Blanche (MacPherson) Beekman.; m. Thomas LeRoy Bennett Jr., Aug. 5, 1972; children: Shannon, Brian, Laurie. BA, U. Calif., Davis, 1968; MS, Colo. State U., 1975, PhD, 1984. Histologist Sch. Veterinary Medicine, Davis, 1969-71; sch. psychologist Poudre Sch. Dist. R-1, Ft. Collins, Colo., 1983—. Mem. augment panel Colo. State Grievance Bd., 1988—; nominating chmn. United Presbyn. Women, Timnath, Colo., 1982, pres., 1986; mem. Women and the Ch. com. Boulder Presbytery, Colo., 1985-86; elder Timnath Presbyn. Ch., 1985—. Mem. Colo. Soc. Sch. Psychologists (cert.), Nat. Assn. Sch. Psychologists (cert.), NEA, Am. Psychol. Assn., Ft. Collins Parents of Twins (pres. 1977-78), Sigma Xi, Phi Kappa Phi. Democrat. Club: Squaredusters (Ft. Collins) (v.p. 1977-78). Home: 213 Camino Real Fort Collins CO 80524-8907 Office: Poudre Sch Dist R-1 2407 La Porte Ave Fort Collins CO 80521-2211

BENNETT, JAMES CHESTER, computer consultant, real estate developer; b. Chico, Calif., May 14, 1932; s. George Clerk and Georgia Mae (James) B.; m. Grace M. Schutrum, Feb. 14, 1955 (div. 1967); children: Ronald, Becky Ann, Todd Bryant. BA in Bus., Calif. State U., Long Beach, 1965. Sgt. USAF, 1947-62; customer engr. IBM, L.A., 1962-70; mgr. computer systems Continental Airlines, L.A., 1970-82; instr. ITT Tech. Inst., Buena Park, Calif., 1982-84; dir. Ramasat Comm., LTD, Bangkok, Thailand, 1984-89; instr. ITT Tech. Inst., San Diego, 1989-90; pres. The Systems Group, Inc., Ramona, Calif., 1990—. Home: PO Box 789 209 Tenth St Ramona CA 92065-0789

BENNETT, JAMES P., construction executive; b. 1936. Pres. J.A. Jones Co. SA, Tenn., 1959-78, Rogers Cons., Nashville, 1978-87; with PCL Enterprises Inc., Denver, 1987—, now pres. Office: PCL Enterprises Inc 2000 S Colorado Blvd Ste 4000 Denver CO 80222-7911*

BENNETT, KENNETH R., oil company executive, school board executive; b. Tucson, Aug. 1, 1959; s. Archie Roy and Donna Lucille (Bulechek) B.; m. Jeanne Tenney Bennett, Mar. 13, 1982; children: Ryan, Dana, Clifton. BS, Ariz. State U., 1984. Ceo Bennett's Oil Co., 1984—; mem. Ariz. State Bd. Edn., Phoenix, 1992— (v.p.), Ariz. State Bd. for Charter Schs., Phoenix, 1994—, Governor's Task Force Edn. Reform, Phoenix, 1991-92. Mayor Pro Tempore City of Prescott (Ariz.), 1988; councilman City of Prescott (Ariz.), 1985-89; scoutmaster Boy Scouts of Am., 1993—. Republican. LDS. Home: 1826 Oaklawn Prescott AZ 86301 Office: Bennett Oil Co 810 E Sheldon Prescott AZ 86301

BENNETT, LAWRENCE ALLEN, psychologist, criminal justice researcher; b. Selma, Calif., Jan. 4, 1923; s. Allen Walter and Eva Eleanor (Hall) B.; m. Beth J. Thompson, Aug. 14, 1948; 1 son, Glenn Livingston; 1 child, Yvonne Irene Solis. B.A., Fresno State Coll., 1949; M.A., Claremont Grad. Sch., 1954, Ph.D., 1968. Supervising psychologist Calif. med. facility Calif. Dept. Corrections, Vacaville, 1955-60, departmental supr. clin. psychology, Sacramento, 1960-67, chief of research, Sacramento, 1967-76; dir. Center for Study of Crime, Delinquency and Corrections, So. Ill. U., Carbondale, 1976-79; dir. Office of Program Evaluation, 1979-84; dir. Crime Prevention and Enforcement Div. Nat. Inst. of Justice, Washington, 1985-86; dir. Adjudication and Corrections Div., 1987-88; criminal justice cons., Sacramento, 1988—; practice clin. psychology, Sacramento, 1988—; mem. part-time faculty U. Calif., Davis, U. Calif., Berkeley, 1959-76, Calif. State U., Sacramento, 1988—; mem. bd. Calif. Crime Technol. Research Found., 1970-75; mem. Calif. State Interdepartmental Coordinating Council, 1967-76, chmn., 1970; bd. dirs. Am. Justice Inst., Sacramento, 1970-79, 88—, v.p., 1989-90, pres., 1991—; mem. juvenile adv. bd. State of Ill., 1977-79; commr. Calif. Blue Ribbon Commn. on Inmate Population Mgmt., 1988-90. Served with U.S. Army, 1942-45, 49-50. Decorated Bronze Star with oak leaf cluster. Mem. Acad. of Criminal Justice Scis., Am. Psychol. Assn., Am. Soc. Criminology, Am. Correctional Assn. (mem. rsch. coun. 1992—), Evaluation Research Soc., Assn. for Correctional Rsch. and Info. Mgmt. (pres. 1989-90). Unitarian. Author: (with Thomas S. Rosenbaum and Wayne R. McCollough) Counseling in Correctional Environments, 1978; contbr. articles in field to profl. jours. Home: 1129 Rivara Cir Sacramento CA 95864-3720 Office: Am Justice Inst 2717 Cottage Way Ste 15 Sacramento CA 95825-1222

BENNETT, LESLIE ROBERT, radiological sciences educator, researcher; b. Denver, Feb. 13, 1918; s. Lester and Margaret E. (Gleason) B.; m. Vera Collier, Dec. 17, 1949; children: Robert Joe, Ann Bennett-Rogers, John C., Andrew C. BA, U. Calif., Berkeley, 1940; MD, U. Rochester, 1943; hon. degree, U. Uruguay, 1982. Asst. prof. radiol. scis. UCLA, 1949-54, assoc. prof., 1954-60, prof., 1960-87, prof. emeritus, 1987—; cons. HHS, L.A., 1952—, VA, L.A., 1968—. Contbr. over 100 articles on nuclear medicine and cancer radiobiology to profl. publs. Lt. USN, 1944-46. Mem. AAAS, AMA, Am. Roentgen Ray Soc., Radiation Rsch. Soc., Soc. Nuclear Medicine, Radiol. Soc. N. Am., Mexican Soc. Nuclear Medicine (hon.) Cath. U. Faculty of Medicine of Chile.

BENNETT, LEWIS TILTON, JR., advertising and communications company executive, actor; b. Manchester, N.H, Jan. 14, 1940; s. Lewis Tilton and Elizabeth (Goodwin) B. BBA, Babson Inst., 1961; BA in Film, San Francisco State U., 1965. Pres. Bennett, Inc., San Francisco, 1967—, Luxembourg, 1967—; v.p. Europe United Films, Luxembourg, 1968—. actor in films: Petulia, Guess Who's Coming to Dinner, Bullitt, Zabriski Point, Strawberry Statement, Harold and Maude, Magnum Force, Towering Inferno, Time After Time, Over My Dead Body, Casualties of War, Final Analysis, Jagged Edge, Dead Pool, Presidio, also TV commls.; tchr. San Francisco Film Clinic, 1968-71, 74—; stand-in for film actor Steve McQueen, Richard Gere, Michael Douglas, Anthony Hopkins, Jack Warden in TV series Crazy Like A Fox; also photographer. Mem. San Francisco Symphony Found., 1967—; del. sponsor San Francisco Internat. Film Festival, 1967, 68, 69. Mem. SAR, SAG, Screen Extras Guild (adv. bd. 1986—). Clubs: Olympic, Lakeside Country, Carmel Beach, Commonwealth, West Coast Yacht, Racket, University, Europe United. Home (summer): 20 rue des Roses, Luxembourg Luxembourg Office: 1348 Sacramento St San Francisco CA 94109-4263

BENNETT, PAUL GROVER, agribusiness executive; b. Ancon, C.Z., Panama, Sept. 1, 1940; s. Arden Lamont and Mercedes (Reluz) B.; m. Diane Huarte, Dec. 17, 1967; children: Courtney, Kimberly, Christopher, Michael. BA, Northwestern U., 1962; MBA, Stanford U., 1968. Fin. analyst, research supt. Standard Fruit Co., Limon, Costa Rica, 1968-70, research dir., La Ceiba, Honduras, 1970-72, asst. gen. mgr., Guayaquil, Ecuador, 1972-73; v.p., regional controller Castle & Cooke Foods, San Francisco, 1973-74, v.p., gen. mgr., Davao, Philippines, 1974-76, v.p., gen. mgr., Medellin, Colombia, 1977-78; v.p., gen. mgr. Mauna Loa Macadamia Nut Corp., Hilo, Hawaii, 1978-81, pres., 1981-83; group v.p. diversified services Internat. Air Service Co. Ltd., Foster City, Calif., 1983-86; pres. Hawaiian Holiday Macadamia Nut Co., Honolulu, 1986-89; sr. ptnr. Agricon Hawaii, Honolulu, 1989-91; pres., CEO Calif. Ammonia Co., Stockton, Calif., 1991-93, Naturipe Berry Growers, Watsonville, Calif.; dir. Agrl. Coun. of Calif.; alt. dir. Calif. Strawberry Commn. Served to lt. comdr. USN, 1962-66. Mem. Stanco, Stanford Alumni Assn., Phi Gamma Delta. Republican. Office: 305 Industrial Rd Watsonville CA 95076-5118*

BENNETT, PAUL LESTER, producer, manager; b. Jamaica, N.Y., Mar. 25, 1946; s. Frank and Frances (Katz) B. BA in Speech, Theater, L.I. U., 1970. Mgr. dir., producer New Artef Players, L.A., 1976-78, Actors Workshop & Repertory Co., West Palm Beach, Fla., 1982-83, Hippodrome State Theatre, Gainesville, Fla., 1983-84, East Coast Arts, New Rochelle, N.Y., 1986-87; mng. dir. Dupree Dance Acad., L.A., 1978-82; mng. dir., assoc. producer Two-Head Video Prodns., Gainesville, 1984-86; dir. mktg. Hesperia (Calif.) Incorporation Com., 1987-88; dir. promotions Comic Relief, L.A., 1988-95; pres. Ain't Too Proud To Beg Prodns., L.A., 1992-94, PB Mgmt., L.A., 1994—; producer Laugh For Life, L.A., 1989, 90, 92; mng. cons. Fla. Theatre, Gainesville, 1985; mem. Gainesville Cultural Affairs Adv. Bd., 1985; mem. bd. dirs. Family Assistance Program, 1995—. Recipient Addy award, Golden Images award, Fla. Pub. Rels. Assn., 1984. Democrat. Jewish.

BENNETT, ROBERT F., senator; b. Salt Lake City, Utah, 1933; s. Wallace F. Bennett; m. Joyce McKay; 6 children. BS, U. of Utah, 1957. Various staff positions U.S Ho. of Reps., U.S. Senate, Washington; CEO Franklin Quest, Salt Lake City, 1984-90; U.S. senator from Utah, 1993—; chmn. Health Care Task Force Senate GOP; mem. banking, housing, urban affairs com., appropriations com., joint economic com., small bus. com.; lobbyist various orgns., Washington; head Dept. Transp's. Congl. Liaison. Author: Gaining Control. Chmn. Education Strategic Planning Commn. Utah State Bd. Edn. (mem. Edn. Strategic Planning Com.). Recipient Light of Learning award for Outstanding Contbns. to Utah edn., 1989; named Entrepreneur of Yr. for Rocky Mtn. region INC. magazine, 1989. Republican. Office: US Senate Office Of Senate Mems Washington DC 20510

BENNETT, RONALD THOMAS, photojournalist; b. Portland, Oreg., Nov. 6, 1944; s. E.E. Al and Donna Mae (Thomas) B.; m. Joan M. Wildman, Sept. 3, 1993; children: R. Thomas, Gardina W. Student, Portland State U., 1964-67; student in photojournalism, U. Wash., 1965; student pre-law and bus. mgmt, Multnomah Coll., Portland, 1963-64. Lab. technician, photographer Sta. KATU-TV, Portland, 1963-65; staff photographer Oreg. Jour., Portland, 1965-68, UPI Newspictures, L.A., 1968-70; staff photojournalist UPI at White House, 1970-88; sr. photo editor The San Diego Union, 1988-89; owner, CEO Capital TV, La Jolla, Calif., 1989—; tchr. photojournalism Portland State U., 1967; mem. standing com. U.S. Senate Press Photgraphers Gallery, 1980-89, sec., treas. Photographer: Assassination, 1968; one-man show Lake Oswego, Oreg., 1979; group exhbns. Libr. of Congress, 1971-89. Mem. coun. Town of La Jolla, Calif., active Associated Volume Buyers, chmn. Brown Goods. Recipient 1st prize World Press Photo Assn., 1969, Calif. Press Photographers, 1968, 69, Gold Seal competition, 1968, 69; nominated for Pulitzer prize, 1968, 76, 77, 78. Mem. White House News Photographers (bd. dirs. photo exhbn. com. 1974-78, 1st prize 1976, 77, 78, 80, 84, 86, 87), Nat. Headliner Club (1st prize 1969, 78), Nat. Press Photographers Assn. (1st prize 1972), Rotary (staff photographer La Jolla chpt., Achievement award Am. Project 1992, 93). Baptist. Home: 12907 La Tortola San Diego CA 92129-3057

BENNETT, WILLIAM PERRY, lawyer; b. Inglewood, Calif., Aug. 28, 1938; s. George William and Lenora (Perry) B.; m. Linda L. Schneider, Aug. 19, 1961; children: Greg, Mark, Carin. BA, Calif. State U., Long Beach; MA in Specialized Ministry magna cum laude, Grace Theol. Sem.; JD, U. So. Calif.; DMin. magna cum laude, Reformed Theol. Sem. Lic. real estate broker; cert. real estate investment specialist, real estate mgmt. specialist, family law specialist; life time teaching credential specialized subject; bar: Calif. 1965, U.S. Ct. Appeals (9th cir.) 1965, U.S. Supreme Ct. 1993. Ptnr. Powars, Tretheway & Bennett Law Corp., 1965-78; sr. ptnr. William P. Bennett Law Corp., 1978-95; sr. real estate atty. Wise, Wiezorek, Timmons & Wise, 1991-94; owner, broker Century 21 Pacific Coast Realty, 1979-88, Pacific Coast Properties, Long Beach, 1988—; assoc. prof. bus. and real estate law Calif. State U., Long Beach, 1965-86; gen. counsel Campus Crusade for Christ, 1991-93; alumni pres., univ. adv. bd. Calif. State U., Long Beach; real estate arbitrator Am. Arbitration Assn. Panel, 1965—, L.A. County Superior Ct. Arbitrator/Pro Tem Judge, Christian Conciliation Svc., L.A. and Orange Counties; bus. adv. bd. Long Beach City Coll.; legal adv. Internat. Christian Leadership U.; spl. counsel numerous chs. and religious orgns. including Chs. Uniting in Global Mission, Crystal Cathedral Ministries, Calvary Chapel, Founsa Intern; adj. prof. of law Simon Green Leaf U. Bd. dirs., leagl advisor Long Beach Area March of Dimes, 1973-90; exec. dir. Legal Ministry Campus Crusade for Christ, dir. property mgmt. Campus Crusade, exec. mgmt. team Arrowhead Springs Conf Ctr. Mem. Long Beach Bar Assn. (bd. govs. 1970-76), Long Beach Area C. of C. (bd. dirs. 1985-86, Bus. Person of Yr. award 1987), Seal Beach C. of C. (pres. 1985-86, 89-90), Kiwanis Internat. (pres., lt. gov., Kiwanian of Yr.), Century 21 Orange County Brokers Coun. (pres. 1984), So. Calif. Investment Soc. (pres. 1988). Republican. Home: PO Box 2460 Seal Beach CA 90740-1460

BENNEWITT, LOI DENE, personnel director; b. Thermopolis, Wyo., Sept. 19, 1946; d. Lloyd Henry and Doratha Edith (Kimber) Groseclose; m. Robert L. Williams, Sept. 10, 1965 (div. Nov. 1985); m. Richard Bennewitt,

Nov. 5, 1989; 1 child, Kendra Kathleen Williams. BA cum laude, U. Wyo., 1974. Various pers. positions Job Svc. of Wyo., Laramie, 1975-79, U. Wyo., Laramie, 1979-87; dir. pers. Ariz. Western Coll., Yuma, 1987—. Contbr. articles to profl. jours. Office: Ariz Western Coll PO Box 929 Yuma AZ 85366-0929

BENNEY, GHISLAINE FRANÇOISE, religious organization executive; b. Montreal, Que., Can., Mar. 8, 1944; came to U.S., 1973; d. Henri Rosaire and Andréa Annonciade (Côté) Trudeau; m. John J. Spires, Aug. 28, 1966 (dec. Oct. 1969); m. Charles Henry Benney, May 24, 1975. BA, Notre Dame de la Trinité, Montreal, 1962. Sales mgr. Ontario and Western Provinces Lancôme Can., Toronto, Ont., Can., 1970-72; tng. mgr. Estée Lauder Can., Toronto, 1972-73; dir. tng. and mgmt. devel. Estée Lauder Internat., N.Y.C., 1973-77; asst. v.p tng. and mgmt. devel. Citibank, N.Y.C., 1977-81, v.p. human resources, 1981-84, v.p. mktg., 1984; dir. support svcs. divsn. Ethiopia World Vision Internat., Arcadia, Calif., 1984-86; mission vol. Presbyn. Ch. U.S.A., N.Y.C., 1986-91; dir. comm. Mission Aviation Fellowship, Redlands, Calif., 1991—. Editor-in-chief LifeLink, 1991—; editor, contbg. author: Giving Wings to the Gospel, 1995. Mem. Mayor Ed Koch's N.Y.C. Sr. Employment Adv. Coun., N.Y.C. Dept. Aging, 1981. Recipient Outstanding Use of Graphic Arts in Effective Comm. award Strathmore, 1992. Mem. ASTD (chmn. sales tng. divsn. 1979-81), Am. Mgmt. Assn., 1974-84. Republican. Baptist. Office: Mission Aviation Fellowship Box 3202 1849 Wabash Redlands CA 92373

BENNINGTON, LESLIE ORVILLE, JR., insurance agent; b. Sedalia, Mo., Dec. 29, 1946; s. Leslie Orville Sr. and Eunice May Marguerite (Cole) B.; m. Susan Frances Grotha, June 1, 1968; children: Leslie O. III, Jeremy Lawrence. BSME, U. Mo., Rolla, 1968; postgrad., U. Tenn. Space Inst., 1969; ChFC, Am. Coll., 1988. CLU; chartered fin. cons.; registered profl. engr., Wash., Wyo. Design engr. Arnold Research Orgn., Tullahoma, Tenn., 1968-70; engr. Pacific Power & Light, Glenrock, Wyo., 1973-75; agt., asst. gen. agt. Am. Nat. Ins. Co., Casper, Wyo., 1975-85; gen. agt. Ins. Sales, Glenrock, 1985—; pres. Cen.Wyo. Estate Planning Coun., Casper, 1985-86. Mem. Glenrock Vol. Fire Dept., 1973—, asst. chief, 1982, pres., 1993—; pres., v.p. Converse County Recreation Bd., Douglas, Wyo., 1980-90; judge dist. high sch. speech contests, Glenrock; bd. dirs. Converse County Sch. Dist. 2, 1976; bd. dirs. Greater Glenrock Recreation Dist., 1990—, pres., 1992-94; guide Helluva Hunt for physically disabled hunters, 1986—, bd. dirs., 1991—; bd. dirs. Nat. Bow Hunt, Glenrock, 1994—. Mem. Nat. Assn. Life Underwriters (Nat. Quality award, Health Ins. Quality award, Nat. Sales Achievement award), Cen. Wyo. Life Underwriters (pres. 1978-80), Wyo. Life Underwriters Assn. (chmn. membership com. 1985-87, nat. com. 1982-87, v.p. 1986-87, bd. dirs. 1980-90, Ins. Agt. of Yr., 1980, pres. 1988-89), West Cen. Wyo. CLUs (pres. 1986-88), Million Dollar Round Table, Nat. Pony Express Assn. (pres. Ea. Wyo. div. 1985—, v.p. Wyo. div. 1989—), KC (grand knight, faithful navigator). Republican. Roman Catholic. Home: 6 Shannon Dr Glenrock WY 82637 Office: PO Box 2049 1260 Hwy 20-26-87 Glenrock WY 82637-9509

BENNION, JOHN STRADLING, engineering educator, consultant; b. Salt Lake City, Sept. 19, 1954; s. Mervyn S. Jr. and LaRee (Stradling) B. BS in Chemistry, U. Utah, 1987, BSChemE, 1987, MS in Nuclear Engring., 1990, PhD in Nuclear Engring., 1994. Registered profl. engr., Utah, Idaho, radiation protection technologist Nat. Registry of Radiation Protection Technologists; lic. sr. reactor operator U.S. Nuclear Regulatory Commn. Carpenter various cos. Utah, 1974-86; sr. reactor engr. U. Utah Nuclear Engring. Lab., Salt Lake City, 1987-93; instr. mech. engring. dept. U. Utah, Salt Lake City, 1992—; asst. prof. Coll. Engring. Idaho State U., Pocatello, 1995—; mem. reactor safety com. U. Utah, Salt Lake City, 1987-93. Author tech. papers and reports. Mem. AAAS, ASME, NSPE, IEEE, Am. Chem. Soc., Am. Soc. Engring. Edn., Nuclear and Plasma Scis. Soc. of the IEEE, Am. Nuclear Soc. (student br. pres. 1988-90), Am. Soc. Quality Control, Health Physics Soc. (sec./treas. Great Salt Lake chpt. 1993-94, 94-95), Internat. Soc. Radiation Physics, Utah Acad. Arts & Scis., Phi Kappa Phi, Alpha Nu Sigma, Pi Tau Sigma, Tau Beta Pi, Sigma Xi. Republican. Mem. LDS Church. Office: Idaho State U Coll of Engring Campus Box 8060 Pocatello ID 83209

BENNION, JOHN WARREN, urban education educator; b. Salt Lake City, Nov. 25; s. M. Lynn and Katherine Bennion; m. Sylvia Lustig; children: Philip, Stanford, David, Bryan, Grant, Andrew. BS in Philosophy, English, U. Utah, 1961, MA in Edn. Adminstrn., 1962; PhD in Edn. Adminstrn., Ohio State U., 1966. Tchr. Granite High Sch., Salt Lake City, 1961-63; asst. instr. Ohio State U., Columbus, 1963-64, adminstrv. asst., 1965-66; adminstrv. intern Parma (Ohio) Sch. Dist., 1964-65; asst. supt. Elgin (Ill.) Pub. Schs., 1966-68; asst. prof. edn. adminstrn. Ind. U., Bloomington, 1968-69; supt. Brighton Cen. Schs., Rochester, N.Y., 1969-79, Bloomington (Minn.) Pub. Schs., 1979-80, Provo (Utah) Sch. Dist., 1980-85, Salt Lake City Schs., 1985-94; prof. urban edn., dir. Utah Edn. Consortium U. Utah, Salt Lake City, 1994—. Recipient Nat. Superintendent of the Yr. award, Utah, Am. Assn. of School Administrators, 1992. Mem. Assn. Supervision and Curriculum Devel., Assn. Early Childhood Edn., Am. Assn. Sch. Adminstrs., Phi Delta Kappa, Rotary. Home: 1837 Harvard Ave Salt Lake City UT 84108-1804 Office: Univ Utah Grad Sch of Edn 225 Milton Bennion Hall Salt Lake City UT 84112-1169

BENNIS, WARREN GAMELIEL, business administration educator, author, consultant; b. N.Y.C., Mar. 8, 1925; s. Philip and Rachel (Landau) B.; m. Clurie Williams, Mar. 30, 1962 (div. 1983); children: Katharine, John Leslie, Will Martin; m. Mary Jane O'Donnell, Mar. 8, 1988 (div. 1991); m. Grace Gabe, Nov. 29, 1992. A.B., Antioch Coll., 1951; hon. cert. econs., London Sch. Econs., 1952; Ph.D., MIT, 1955; LL.D. (hon.), Xavier U., Cin., 1972, George Washington U., 1977; L.H.D. (hon.), Hebrew Union Coll., 1974, Kans. State U., 1979; D.Sc. (hon.), U. Louisville, 1977, Pacific Grad. Sch. Psychology, 1987, Gov.'s State U., 1991; LHD (hon.), Doan Coll., 1993. Diplomate Am. Bd. Profl. Psychology. Asst. prof. psychology MIT, Cambridge, 1953-56, prof., 1959-67; asst. prof. psychology and bus. Boston U., 1956-59; prof. Sloan Sch. Mgmt., 1959-67; provost SUNY-Buffalo, 1967-68, v.p. acad. devel., 1968-71; pres. U. Cin., 1971-77; U.S. prof. corps. and soc. Centre d'Etudes Industrielles, Geneva, Switzerland, 1978-79; exec.-in-residence Pepperdine U., 1978-79; George Miller Disting. prof.-in-residence U. Ill., Champaign-Urbana, 1978; Disting. prof. Bus. Adminstrn. Sch. Bus., U. So. Calif., L.A., 1980-88; univ. prof. U. So. Calif., L.A., 1988—; vis. lectr. Harvard U., 1958-59, Indian Mgmt. Inst., Calcutta; vis. prof. U. Lausanne (Switzerland), 1961-62, INSEAD, France, 1983; bd. dirs. The Foothill Group. Author: Planning of Change, 4th edit., 1985, Interpersonal Dynamics, 1963, 3d and 4th edits., 1975, Personal and Organizational Change, 1965, Changing Organizations, 1966, repub. in paperback as Beyond Bureaucracy, 1974, The Temporary Society, 1968, Organization Development, 1969, American Bureaucracy, 1970, Management of Change and Conflict, 1972, The Leaning Ivory Tower, 1973, The Unconscious Conspiracy: Why Leaders Can't Lead, 1976, Essays in Interpersonal Dynamics, 1979; (with B. Nanus): Leaders, 1985, On Becoming a Leader, 1989, (with I. Mitroff) The Unreality Industry, 1989, Why Leaders Can't Lead, 1989, Leaders on Leadership, 1992, An Invented Life: Reflections on Leadership and Change, 1993, Beyond Bureaucracy, 1993, (with J. Goldsmith) Learning to Lead, 1994; cons. editor Jour. Higher Edn., Jour. Occupational Behavior, Ency. of Econs. and Bus., Calif. Mgmt. Rev., Mgmt. Series Jossey-Bass Pubs. Mem. Pres.' White House Task Force on Sci. Policy, 1969-70; mem. FAA study task force U.S. Dept. Transp., 1975; mem. adv. com. N.Y. State Joint Legis. Com. Higher Edn., 1970-71; mem. Ohio Gov.'s Bus. and Employment Council, 1972-74; mem. panel on alt. approaches to grad. edn. Council Grad. Schs. and Grad. Record-Exam Bd., 1971-73; chmn. Nat. Adv. Commn. on Higher Edn. for Police Officers, 1976-78; adv. bd. NIH, 1978-84; trustee Colo. Rocky Mountains Sch., 1978-82; bd. dirs. Am. Leadership Forum, 1984-89, Foothill Group; mem. vis. com. for humanities MIT, 1975-81; trustee Antioch Coll., Salk Inst., Claremont U. Ctr. Capt. AUS, World War II. Decorated Bronze Star, Purple Heart; recipient Dow Jones award, 1987, McKinsey Fedn. award, 1967, 68. Mem. Am. Acad. Arts and Scis. (co-chmn. policy coun. 1969-71), Am. Soc. Pub. Adminstrn. (nat. coun.), Am. Mgmt. Assn. (dr. 1974-77), U.S. C. of C. (adv. group scholars). Office: U So Calif Sch Bus University Park Los Angeles CA 90089-1421

BENO, CAROLYN ELIZABETH, pharmacist, marketing professional; b. Council Bluffs, Iowa, Sept. 2, 1953; d. Adolph Frank Jr. and Gertrude Marie Sophia (Spetman) B. BA, U. Nebr., 1975, BS in Pharmacy, 1976; MS, U. Iowa, 1978; postgrad., U. S.C., 1980—. Pharmacy intern Walgreens Gateway, Lincoln, Nebr., 1974-75; pharmacist Hushaw Drug Co., Council Bluffs, Iowa, 1976-77; grad. asst. U. Iowa, Iowa City, 1977-78; asst. prof. pharmacy Temple U., Phila., 1978-80; pharmacist Kroger and Springwood Lake Pharmacies, Columbia, S.C., 1982-84; sr. analyst U.S. pharm. and nutrition group Bristol Myers, Evansville, Ind., 1985-89; mgr. client svcs. Hosp. Data Svcs./Walsh Am., Scottsdale, Ariz., 1989-92; dir. data integrity Walsh Am./PMSI, Phoenix, Ariz., 1992-94; mgmt. cons. analytic svcs. Alsh Am./PMSI, Phoenix, Ariz., 1994—; chmn. drug edn. com. coll. pharmacy U. Nebr., Lincoln, 1973-74; vol. cons. Chem. Dependency Agy. S. W. Iowa, Council Bluffs, 1975-77; vol. pharmacist Iowa City (Iowa) Free Med. Clinic, 1977-78. Contbr. articles to profl. jours. Mem. Am. Pharm. Assn., Health Care Businesswomen's Assn., Alpha Mu Alpha, Kappa Epsilon (co-advisor 1983-84), Phi Lambda Sigma. Republican. Lutheran. Home: 5309 E Wallace Ave Scottsdale AZ 85254-1119 Office: Walsh Am 2394 E Camelback Rd Phoenix AZ 85016-3429

BENREY, JEFF MICHAEL, marketing professional; b. Istanbul, Turkey, Sept. 8, 1962; came to the U.S., 1980; s. Michael and Denise Liliana (Farhi) B. BS in Engring. cum laude, Princeton U., 1984; MBA, UCLA, 1989. R&D engr. Imagen Corp., Santa Clara, Calif., 1984-87; project mgr. Sun Microsystems, Mountain View, Calif., summer 1988; product mktg. mgr. Apple Computer Inc., Cupertino, Calif., 1990-93; v.p. mktg. Ductus Inc., Mountain View, 1993-95; creative products mgr. Silicon Studio, Inc. (subsidiary of Silicon Graphics), 1995—. Mem. Tau Beta Pi, Beta Gamma Sigma. Office: Silicon Graphics 2011 N Shoreline Blvd Mountain View CA 94043

BENSCH, KLAUS GEORGE, pathology educator; b. Miedar, Germany, Sept. 1, 1928; (married); 3 children. M.D., U. Erlangen, Germany, 1953. Diplomate: Am. Bd. Pathology. Intern U. Hosps. of Erlangen, 1953-54; resident in anat. pathology U. Tex. and; M.D. Anderson Hosp., Houston, 1954-56, Yale, 1956-57; instr. pathology Yale Med. Sch., 1958-61, asst. prof., 1961-64, assoc. prof., 1964-68; prof. pathology Stanford Med. Sch., 1968—, acting chmn. dept. pathology, 1984-85, chmn. dept. pathology, 1985—. Mem. Am. Assn. Pathology and Bacteriology. Office: Stanford U Med Sch Dept Pathology 300 Pasteur Dr Stanford CA 94305

BENSICK, CAROL MARIE, English literature educator. BA summa cum laude, Wellesley Coll., 1977; MA, Cornell U., 1980, PhD, 1982. Asst. prof. U. Denver, 1982-85; asst. prof. U. Ore., 1985-88, assoc. prof., 1988—; asst. prof. U. Calif., Riverside, 1988—; vis. asst. prof. UCLA, 1988, 89, 91, 92, Cornell U., 1983, 84, 86; planning com. Am. Lit. Pacific Northwest Renaissance Conf., 1988; asst. dir. grad. studies U. Denver, 1984-85; adj. faculty dept. religious studies U. Ore., post-tenure review com. dept. religious studies, cons. history dept. search in colonial Am. History, participating faculty honors coll., ctr. for humanities, dept. comparative lit., faculty mem. philosophy club, search coms. English Dept., 1985-86, 86-87, curriculum, qualifying exam., creative writing and computer coms., participant student advising, judge creative writing contests, 1987, 88; mem. com. on courses U. Calif., Riverside, faculty mem. honors program, adj. faculty mem. dept. religious studies, dept. women's studies, guest lectr., mem. undergrad. coun., chair search com. in Black Am. Lit., English Dept., interviewing mem. search com. Am. Lit. to 1900, mem. grad. com., panel on feminism and pedagogy, undergrad. com., com. nonsalaried appointments, chair grad. prize essay com., mem. writing courses com.; chair panel early Am. lit. Rocky Mount. Modern Lang. Assn., 1989-90; reader Vanderbilt U. Press, 1989, Northeastern U. Press, 1993, numerous profl. jours. Author: La Nouvelle Beatrice: Renaissance and Romance in Nouvelle "Rapaccini's Daughter," 1985; contbr. chpts. to books, articles and reviews to profl. jours. Mem. MLA, AAUW, Am. Philosoph. Assn., Am. Lit. Assn., Nat. Women's Studies Assn., Nathaniel Hawthorne Soc., Soc. for Early Americanists, Soc. Women in Philosophy, Soc. for the Study of Women Philosophers, Soc. for Advancement of Am. Philosophy, Assn. for Advancement of Philosophy and Psychiatry, Nat. Coun. for Rsch. on Women. Office: U Calif Dept English Riverside CA 92521

BENSINGER, LENORE COOPER, theater director; b. Washington, Sept. 10, 1943; d. J.D. and R.Z. (Zeidner) Cooper; m. Richard E. Bensinger, Dec. 14, 1968; children: Kenneth, Gregory. AB, Am. U., 1965; MA, Washington U., 1977; MFA, U. Wash., 1991. Legis. asst. U.S. Congress, Washington, 1962-68; policy analyst NIH Bethesda, Washington, 1968-70; policy planner U.S. Dept. Health and Human Svcs., Washington, 1970-73; intern Edison Theater, Wash. U., St. Louis, 1973-77; artistic intern Columbus Theater, San Francisco, 1977-78; dir. Rain City Theater, Seattle, 1988—; cons. Annex Theater, Seattle, 1988—. Author over 20 plays. Chmn. Dramaturge League N.W. Recipient King County Playwriting award King County Arts Commn., 1986, Seattle Arts award Seattle Arts Commn., 1987, Wash. State fellowship Wash. State Arts Commn., 1989. Office: Rain City Studio Theater 5263 17th Ave NE Seattle WA 98105-3407

BENSON, DAVID BERNARD, computer science educator; b. Seattle, Nov. 18, 1940; s. Allan I. and Martha (White) B.; BS in Engring., Calif. Inst. Tech., 1962, MSEE, 1963, PhD (NASA fellow), 1967; m. Nancy Elaine Dollahite, Sept. 17, 1962 (div. Aug. 1986); children: Megan, Bjorn, Nils, Amy, Kjell, Ingri. Rsch. engr. N. Am. Rockwell, Downey, Calif., 1963-64; asst. prof. U. N.C., Chapel Hill, 1967-70; vis. assoc. prof. U. Colo., Boulder, 1976-77; asst. prof. Wash. State U., Pullman, 1970-72, assoc. prof., 1972-79, prof. computer sci., 1979—; vis. computer scientist U. Edinburgh, Scotland, 1983, U. Sydney, Australia, 1990; pres. BENTEC, 1985-89. Contbr. over 30 articles to profl. jours. Precinct chmn. 72d Precinct, Whitman County, Wash., 1978-82; Whitman County Dem. Conv. del., 1972, 76. NSF grantee, 1969-89. Mem. Assn. Computing Machinery, Am. Math. Soc., AAAS, AAUP, Sigma Xi. Mem. Soc. of Friends. Home: 725 NE Illinois St Pullman WA 99163-3920 Office: Wash State U Sch Elec Engring & Computer Sci Pullman WA 99164-2752

BENSON, DEE VANCE, federal judge; b. Salt Lake City, Aug. 25, 1948; s. Gilbert and Beryl Butler (Despain) B.; m. Patricia Brown; children: Angela, Natalie, Lucas, Katherine. BA, Brigham Young U., 1973, JD, 1976. Bar: Utah 1976, U.S. Dist. Ct. Utah 1976, U.S. Ct. Appeals (10th cir.) 1976, U.S. Supreme Ct. 1984, U.S. Ct. Appeals (5th cir.) 1988. Ptnr. Snow, Christensen & Martineau, Salt Lake City, 1976-84; legal counsel Senate Judiciary Com., Washington, 1984-86; chief of staff Senator Orrin Hatch's Office, Washington, 1986-88; assoc. dep. atty. gen. U.S. Dept. Justice, Washington, 1988; U.S. atty. U.S. Dept. Justice, Salt Lake City, 1989-91; judge U.S. Dist. Ct., Salt Lake, 1991—; legal counsel Iran-Contra Congl. Investigating Com., Washington, 1987. Contbg. author univ. law rev. Mem. ABA, Utah State Bar (com. on cts. and judges), Salt Lake County Bar Assn., Phi Alpha Delta. Mem. LDS Ch. Office: US Dist Ct 350 S Main St Salt Lake City UT 84101-2106*

BENSON, EDGAR CHARLES, JR., retired pilot; b. Highland Park, Ill., Apr. 3, 1931; s. Edgar Charles and Adaline Verna (Olson) B.; m. Martha Lynn Pagitt, Nov. 23, 1956; children: Edgar Charles III, Sonja Lee, William Daniel. Student, Kendall Coll., 1948-50, Lake Forest Coll., 1951, U. Ala., 1953. Commd. 2d lt. USAF, Dover, Del., 1954; advanced through grades to lt. col. USAF, 1971; pilot/aircraft comdr./instr. USAF, Dover, 1955-62; instr., pilot examiner USAF, Oklahoma City, 1962-65; spl. air missions pilot USAF, Andrews AFB, Md., 1965-70; air/combat rescue pilot USAF, Camrah Bay, Vietnam, 1970-71; advisor, instr. USAF, Marietta/Savannah, Ga., 1972-75; ret. USAF, 1975; instr., pilot examiner Flight Safety, Internat., Savannah, 1975-78; pilot Davis Oil Co., Denver, 1978-86; chief pilot Davis Oil Co., L.A., 1986-94; ret., 1994. Decorated Air Force Commendation medal, Disting. Flying Cross, Air medal with six oak leaf clusters. Mem. Aero Club of Soc. Calif., AOPA, Retired Officers Assn., Nat. Aero Club of U.S. Methodist. Home: 8875 S Wild Iris Run Highlnds Rnch CO 80126-2677 Office: Davis Oil Co 6201 W Imperial Hwy Los Angeles CA 90045-6323

BENSON, FRANCIS M., production coordinator, radio producer; b. Bklyn., Oct. 7, 1958; s. Francis Gerald Benson and Grace Angela (Superty) Brothers; divorced; children: Megan Kristine, Lindsey Nicole. Student, Palmdale High Sch., Calif. Cert. Airframe & Powerplant Mechanic, Calif. Structure mechanic B Lockheed Aircraft Co., Palmdale, Calif., 1979-80, final assembly mechanic, 1980-83, structure mechanic B, 1985-86, mfg. supr., 1986-87; structure mechanic B Rockwell Internat., Palmdale, Calif., 1983-85, hydraulic checkout mechanic, 1985; structure mechanic A Northrop B-2 Division, Palmdale, Calif., 1987-88, mfg. supr., 1988, mfg. planner, 1988-89, mfg. engr., 1989-92; program coord., prodr. Capital Cities/ABC, 1992-94, prodn. coord./prodr., 1994—; union steward Internat. Assn. Machinists & Aerospace, Palmdale Calif. Republican. Roman Catholic. Home: 6526 Ocean Crest Dr # A-110 Rancho Palos Verdes CA 90274 Office: 3321 S La Cienega Blvd Los Angeles CA 90016

BENSON, JAMES BERNARD, JR., clinical hypnotherapist; b. Phila., May 8, 1930; s. James Bernard Benson and Elizabeth (Smeaton) Caswell; m. Hiroko Nakamura, Apr. 14, 1955. LLD (hon.), Nat. Law Enforcement Acad., 1968; BA in Police Sci., Pacific Coll., 1976; PhD (hon.), St. John's U., Springfield, La., 1988. Cert. behavioral therapist, Calif. Chief criminal investigator U.S. Marine Corps, 1947-66; corp. officer Bank of Am., L.A., 1966-85; pvt. practice Anaheim, Calif., 1985-93; instr. police sci. St. John's U., Springfield, La. Editor: (poetry) Devotion in Blue, 1973, Lawman's Lament, 1974; contbr. articles to police mags. Fellow Am. Assn. Profl. Hypnotherapists; mem. Nat. Soc. Clin. Hypnotherapists. Republican. Home and Office: 1400 S Sunkist St Ste 199 Anaheim CA 92806-5624

BENSON, JOAN ELLEN, dietetics educator, researcher; b. San Francisco, Aug. 26, 1954; d. Lloyd F. and Joan A. (Sullivan) B.; m. Dwight T. Hibdon, July 13, 1977. BS with honors, U. Calif., Berkeley, 1977, registered dietician, 1978; MS, U. Utah, 1987. Cert. dietitian, Utah. Clin. dietitian Contra Costa County Med. Svcs., Martinez, Calif., 1978-85; nutrition cons. Cardiovascular Genetics, Salt Lake City, 1987-90; adj. instr. dietectics U. Utah, Salt Lake City, 1987—, rsch. assoc. Sch. Medicine, 1991—; nutrition cons. Ctr. for Sports Medicine, St. Francis Hosp., San Francisco, 1984-87; vis. rsch. assoc. Inst. Rsch., Eidgenössische Sportschule, Magglingen, Switzerland, spring 1987; nutrition cons. Optifast progrAm LDS Hosp., Salt Lake City, 1988-90; book reviewer Benjamin Cummings Pub. Co., Redwood City, Calif., 1989—, Mosby-Yearbook Pubs., St. Louis, 1990-91. Author: Coaches Guide to Nutrition, 1990; contbr. articles to profl. publs., chpts. to books; creator 15 part TV series Sci. Founds. of Human Nutrition, KULC, 1995. Com. chmn. Am. Heart Assn., Salt Lake City, 1991-92. Calif. State scholar, 1975-77, Phoebe Hearst scholar, 1975-77; Spikes biomed. rsch. grantee U. Utah, 1986. Mem. Am. Dietetic Assn., Utah Dietetic Assn., Sports and Cardiovascular Nutritionists (state rep. 1990-91), Nat. Off-Road Biking Assn. (Utah Vet Mountain bike champion 1990, 92), Phi Kappa Phi. Democrat. Roman Catholic. Home: 4716 Silver Meadows Dr Park City UT 84060-5939 Office: U Utah Family-Preventive Medicine 50 N Medical Dr Salt Lake City UT 84132

BENSON, KAREN A., nursing educator; b. Havre, Mont., Sept. 10, 1946; d. William Duncan and Norma Evelyn (Erickson) Ross; children: Alice, Evan, David, Marc. BSN, Mont. State U., 1968; MS in Biology, Wash. State U., 1978, PhD in Vet. Sci., 1983; MS in Nursing, Oreg. Health Scis. U., 1986. Lectr. Seattle U. Contbr. articles to profl. publs. Dr. Lynn A. George scholar; Sigma Xi rsch. grantee. Mem. ANA, Wash. State Nurses Assn., Am. Holistic Nurses Assn., Sigma Theta Tau, Phi Kappa Phi. Home: 17103 25th Ave NE Seattle WA 98155-6124

BENSON, KEITH RODNEY, science educator; b. Portland, Oreg., July 22, 1948; s. Norman Harold and Nancy Ellen (Cochran) B. BA, Whitworth Coll., 1970; MA, Oreg. State U., 1973, PhD, 1979. Asst. prof. Pacific Luth. U., Tacoma, Wash., 1979-81; asst. prof. U. Wash., Seattle, 1981-88, assoc. prof., 1988-94, prof., 1994—. Editor: Development of American Biology, 1988, Expansion and American Biology, 1991. Recipient Sr. Scholar award NSF, 1987, Forschungsschwerpunkt, Berlin, 1994. Mem. Am. Soc. Zoologists (divsn. chair 1985—), History of Sci. Soc. (exec. sec. 1993—), Columbia History of Sci. Group (dir. 1982—). Home: 7024 16th Ave NE Seattle WA 98115-5735 Office: U Wash SB-20 Dept Med History & Ethics Seattle WA 98195

BENSON, SHARON STOVALL, primary school educator; b. Clovis, N.Mex., Apr. 18, 1946; d. Travis and Anna Gene (Crump) Stovall; m. Merle John Benson, Aug. 21, 1966; children: Brenda Kay, Linda Carol. BS, U. N.Mex., 1968, MA, 1980. Cert. tchr., N.Mex. Kindergarten aide Albuquerque Pub. Schs., 1976-78; tchr. LaMesa Little Sch., Albuquerque, 1987-88, Congl. Presch., Albuquerque, 1991—; parent rep. South Atlantic Regional Resource Ctr., Plantation, Fla., 1986-87; sec. bd. Albuquerque Spl. Presch., 1975. Trained evaluator Assn. Retarded Citizens, Albuquerque, 1988—. Mem. Parents Reaching Out, Assn. Retarded Citizens, N.Mex. Assn. Edn. Young Children, Pi Lambda Theta. Methodist. Home: 7409 Carriveau Ave NE Albuquerque NM 87110-1490

BENSON, SIDNEY WILLIAM, chemistry researcher; b. N.Y.C., Sept. 26, 1918; m. Anna Bruni, 1986; 2 children. A.B., Columbia Coll., 1938; A.M., Harvard U., 1941, Ph.D., 1941; Docteur Honoris Causa, U. Nancy, France, 1989. Rsch. asst. Gen. Electric Co., 1940; rsch. fellow Harvard U., 1941-42; instr. chemistry CCNY, 1942-43; group leader Manhattan Project Kellex Corp., 1943; asst. prof. U. So. Calif., 1943-48, assoc. prof., 1948-51, prof. chemistry, 1951-64, 1976-89, Disting. prof. emeritus, 1989—, dir. chem. physics program, 1962-63; dir. dept. kinetics and thermochemistry Stanford Rsch. Inst., 1963-76; sci. dir. Hydrocarbon Rsch. Inst. U. So. Calif., 1977-90, sci. dir. emeritus, 1991—; rsch. assoc. dept. chemistry and chem. engring. Calif. Inst. Tech., 1957-58; vis. prof. UCLA, 1959, U. Ill., 1959; hon. Glidden lectr. Purdue U., 1961; vis. prof. chemistry Stanford U., 1966-70, 71, 73; mem. adv. panel phys. chemistry Nat. Bur. Standards, 1969-72, chmn., 1970-71; hon. vis. prof. U. Utah, 1971; vis. prof. U. Paris VII and XI, 1971-72, U. St. Andrews, Scotland, 1973, U. Lausanne, Switzerland, 1979; Frank Gucker lectr. U. Ind., 1984—; Brotherton prof. in phys. chemistry U. Leeds, 1984; cons. G.N. Lewis; lectr. U. Calif., Berkeley, 1989, scientific adv. coun. Amaler medicales de Nancy, 1993—. Author: Foundations of Chemical Kinetics, 1960, Thermochemical Kinetics, 1968, 2d edit., 1976, Critical Survey of the Data of the Kinetics of Gas Phase Unimolecular Reactions, 1970, Atoms, Molecules, and Chemical Reactions, 1970, Chemical Calculations, 3d edit., 1971; founder, editor-in-chief Internat. Jour. Chem. Kinetics, 1967-83; mem. editorial adv. bd. Combustion Sci. and Tech., 1973—; mem. editorial bd. Oxidation Communications, 1978—, Revs. of Chem. Intermediates, 1979-87; mem. Hydrocarbon Letters, 1980-81; mem. editorial bd. Jour. Phys. Chemistry, 1981-85; mem. scientific adv. coun. Annales Medicales de Nancy, 1993—. Recipient Polanyi medal Royal Soc. Eng., 1986; faculty rsch. award U. So. Calif., 1984, Presdl. medal, 1986; Guggenheim fellow, 1950-51, Fulbright fellow, France, 1950-51, fellow NSF, 1957-58, 71-72. Fellow AAAS, Am. Phys. Soc.; mem. NAS, Am. Chem. Soc. (Tolman medal 1977, Hydrocarbon Chem. award 1977, Langmuir award 1986, Orange County award 1986), Faraday Soc., Indian Acad. Sci., Phi Beta Kappa, Sigma Xi, Pi Mu Epsilon, Phi Lambda Upsilon, Phi Kappa Phi. Home: 1110 N Bundy Dr Los Angeles CA 90049-1513 Office: U So Calif University Pk MC-1661 Los Angeles CA 90089

BENSON, STEPHEN R., editorial cartoonist. BA in Polit. Sci. cum laude, Brigham Young U., 1979. With Senate Rep. Policy Com., 1979-80; cartoonist The Ariz. Republic, Phoenix, 1980-90, 91—, The Morning-News Tribune, Tacoma, Wash., 1990-91. Author: Fencin' with Benson, 1984, Evanly Days, 1988, Back at the Barb-B-Cue, 1991, Where Do You Draw the Line?, 1992. Recipient Nat. Headliner award, 1984, 1st Place Best of the West, 1991, 92, 93, Pulitzer Prize finalist editorial cartooning, 1984, 89, 92, 94, Pulitzer Prize for editorial cartooning, 1993. Office: The Arizona Republic 20 E Van Buren St Phoenix AZ 85004-2226

BENTHEM, JACK J., electrical engineer; b. Niehove, Groningen, Holland, Sept. 28, 1964; came to U.S., 1980; s. Jan and Syke Aaltje (Kielstra) B.; m. Kelly Rae Stepp, Jan. 29, 1994. BSEE, Dordt Coll., 1986; MSEE, U. N.Mex., 1989. Elec. engr. electronic warfare U.S. Army, Albuquerque, 1989—. Mem. IEEE. Republican. Home: 2916 Montclaire Dr NE Albuquerque NM 87110-2922

BENTLEY, KENTON EARL, aerospace scientist, researcher; b. Detroit, June 1, 1927; s. Kenneth and Marion Isabel (Tillman) B.; m. Elizabeth Montrose, Apr. 18, 1953. B.S. in Chemistry, U. Mich., 1950; Ph.D. in Analytical Chemistry, U. N.M., 1959. Research phys. chemist Consol. Electrodynamics Corp., Pasadena, Calif., 1956-57; research scientist

Lockheed Calif. Co., Burbank, 1962-63; scientist, task leader Jet Propulsion Lab., Calif. Inst. Tech., Pasadena, 1963-65; head electrochemistry group Hughes Aircraft Co., Culver City, Calif., 1965-67; dir. sci. and applications br., dir. Iran earth resources programs Lockheed Electronics Co., Inc., Houston, 1967-88; mgr. life scis. flight payload integration program Lockheed Engring. & Scis., Co., Moffett Field, Calif., 1988-94; pres. Kiva Enterprises, Sparks, Nev., 1994—; Vis. prof. chemistry Highlands (N.M.) U., 1959; asst. prof. chemistry Am. U. Beirut, Lebanon, 1959-61. Contbr. numerous articles to profl. jours. Served with USNR, 1945-46. Los Alamos research fellow, 1954-56. Mem. Am. Chem. Soc., AAAS (life), AAUP, Am. Astronautical Soc. (sr.; dir. 1969-73), Nat. Mgmt. Assn., Sigma Xi (life), Alpha Chi Sigma. Home: 1245 Baring Blvd Ste 153 Sparks NV 89434-8669

BENTLEY, WILLIAM ARTHUR, engineer, electro-optical consultant; b. Jan. 21, 1931; s. Garth Ashley and Helen (Dieterle) B.; m. Erika Bernadette Seuthe, Nov. 17, 1956; children: David Garth, Barbara Elizabeth. BS in Physics, Northwestern U., 1952; MS in Systems Engring., Calif. State U., Fullerton, 1972. Engr. N. Am. Aircraft, Downey, Calif., 1956-69; chief engr. Fairchild Optical, El Segundo, Calif., 1969-72; sr. staff engr. Advanced Controls, Irvine, Calif., 1975-80; prin. Instrument Design Cons., Santa Ana, Calif., 1978—; mgr. mfg. research and devel. Xerox Electro-Optical, Pomona, Calif., 1980-83; cons. Kasper Industries, Sunnyvale, Calif., 1977-78, Lincoln Laser Co., Phoenix, 1983—, Coopervision, Irvine, 1984-88, Baxter, 1988-90, Indsl. Dynamics Co., 1990—, Polyscan Corp., Tucson, 1992—, Pacific Optical, 1995—. Patentee in field including 1st automatic optical PWB inspector. Mem. Soc. Photo-optical Instrumentation Engrs., Optical Soc. Am., Mensa. Democrat. Home: 170 The Masters Cir Costa Mesa CA 92627-4640 Office: Instrument Design Cons PO Box 2203 Santa Ana CA 92707-0203

BENTLY, DONALD EMERY, electrical engineer; b. Cleve., Oct. 18, 1924; s. Oliver E. Bently and Mary Evelyn (Conway) B.; m. Susan Lorraine Pumphrey, Sept. 1961 (div. Sept. 1982); 1 child, Christopher Paul. BSEE with distinction, U. Iowa, 1949, MSEE, 1950; DS (hon.), U. Nev., 1987. Registered profl. engr., Calif., Nev. Pres. Bently Nev. Corp., Minden, 1961-85, chief exec. officer, 1985—; chief exec. officer Bently Rotor Dynamics and Research Corp., Minden, 1985—; also chmn. bd. dirs. Bently Nev. Corp., Minden; chief exec. officer Gibson Tool Co., Carson City, Nev., 1978—; bd. dirs. Sierra Pacific Resources, 1982-83. Contbr. articles to profl. jours.; developer electronic instruments for the observation of rotating machinery, and the algorithm for rotor fluid-induced instability; inventor in field. Trustee Inst. World Politics. With USN, 1943-46, PTO. Named Inventor or Yr., State of Nev. Invention and Tech. Coun., 1983; recipient first Decade award Vibration Inst. Mem. ASME (industry adv. bd.), Am. Petroleum Inst., St. Petersburg (Russian Fedn.) Acad. Engring., Sigma Xi, Eta Kappa Nu, Tau Beta Pi, Sigma Alpha Epsilon. Episcopalian. Office: Bently Nev Corp PO Box 157 Minden NV 89423-0157

BENTON, FLETCHER, sculptor; b. Jackson, Ohio, 1931. BFA, Miami U., Oxford, Ohio, 1956, DFA (hon.), 1993; DFA (hon.), Rio Grande U., 1994. Mem. faculty Calif. Coll. Arts and Crafts, 1959, San Francisco Art Inst., 1964-67; asst. prof. art Calif. State U., San Jose, 1967-81; prof. Calif. State U., 1981-86. One-man shows include, San Francisco Mus. Modern Art, 1965, Albright-Knox Mus., Buffalo, 1970, Galeria Bonino, N.Y.C., 1969, Galerie Francoise Mayer, Brussels, San Francisco Mus. Modern Art, 1970, London Arts Gallery, Detroit, 1970, Galeria Bonino, Buenos Aires, Estudio Actual, Caracas, Venezuela, 1970, Landry-Bonino Gallery, N.Y.C., 1972, Phoenix Mus. Art, 1973, Galeria Bonino, Rio de Janiero, 1973, Calif. State U.-Berkeley, 1973, Neuberger Mus., N.Y., 1974, Hirshhorn Mus., 1974, Phila. Art Alliance, 1974, Elvehejem Mus. Art, Wis., 1976, San Francisco Modern Mus. Art, 1976, Huntsville Mus. Modern Art, Ala., 1977, Alrich Mus. Contemporary Art, Conn., John Berggruen Gallery, San Francisco, 1978, 84, 89, Am. Acad. and Inst. Arts and Letters, N.Y.C., 1979, Chgo. Arts Club, 1979, Milw. Art Ctr., 1980, Suermondt-Ludwig Mus., Asschen, Fed. Republic Germany, Klingspor Mus., Offenbach, Fed. Republic Germany, 1981, Kunsthandling Brigitte Haasner, Wiesbaden, Fed. Republic Germany, 1987, 92, Sung Dem Fine Arts, Seoul, Korea, 1991, Dorothy Goldeen Gallery, Santa Monica, Calif., 1988, 93, Gallerie Simone Sterne, New Orleans, 1990, 93, Riva Yares Gallery, Scottsdale, 1991, Miami U., Oxford, 1993; group shows include San Francisco Art Inst., 1964, San Francisco Modern Mus. Art, 1964, Calif. Pal. of Legion of Honor, 1964, Whitney Mus. Am. Art, N.Y.C., 1966, 68, Los Angeles County Mus., 1967, Phila. Art Mus., 1967, Walker Art Ctr., Mpls., 1968, Art Inst. Chgo., 1968, Internat. Mus. Fine Arts, Osaka, Japan, 1970, Hayward Gallery, London, 1970, Stanford (Calif.) Mus., 1971, Am. Acad. and Inst. Arts and Letters, N.Y.C., 1981, Amerika Haus, Frankfurt, 1981, Whitney Mus. Am. Art, N.Y.C., 1981, Oakland Mus., 1982, John Berggruen Gallery, 1983, Olympic Arts Festival, Los Angeles, France, Fed. Republic Germany, Eng., Norway, 1984, John Berggruen Gallery, 1985, 89, 92, Chapman Coll. (Calif.), 1985, The Adrich Mus. Contemporary Art, Conn., 1985, Centro de Arte Moderna, Lisbon, Portugal, 1986, Kleinewefers, Krefeld, Fed. Repbulic Germany, 1987, Kundsthandlung Brigitte Haasner, Wiesbaden, Fed. Republic Germany, 1987, 88, Dorothy Goldeen Gallery, Santa Monica, Calif., 1988, Andre Emmerich Gallery, 1991, 92, Rio Grande (Ohio) U., 1994, others; major collections Euroclear Hdqs. Brussels, Belgium, 1993, Modernesstadt Cologne, 1993, Gothaer, Cologne, Top Gallant, 1994, Pauling, N.Y., 1994; subject of book, Fletcher Benton by Paul Karlstrom and Edward Lucie-Smith, 1990. Served with USN, 1949-50. Recipient Disting. Svc. award to arts Am. Acad. and Inst. Arts and Letters, 1979, Career award Ohioana Libr. Assn., 1994; Pres.'s Scholar award San Jose State U., 1980. *

BENTON, HOMER GRABILL, business educator, consultant; b. Altoona, Pa., Oct. 11, 1926; s. Homer Soyster and Mary Elizabeth (Grabill) B.; m. Blanche Carolyn Saxe, Aug. 1947; children: Homer David, Stephen Richard, John Paul, Deborah Kay. BA, Wheaton Coll., 1947; ThM, Calif. Theol. Sem., 1955; MBA, Syracuse Grad. Sch. Mgmt., 1970; JD, Western State U., 1985. Ordained to ministry Ind. Chs. of Am., 1949. Pastor local chs., N.Y. and Calif., 1948-55; commd. lt. U.S. Army, 1955, advanced through grades to col., 1974; prof. U.S. Army Svc. Sch., 1970-74; comptr. U.S. Army European Hdqrs., 1974-77, dir. bookstore ops., 1974-77; part-time prof. Emory-Riddle U., Europe, 1976-77, ret., 1979; prof. Biola U., La Mirada, Calif., 1979-84; prof., chair bus. dept. Pacific Christian Coll., Fullerton, Calif., 1985-94, prof. emeritus, 1994—; cons. various profit and non-profit corps., Anaheim, Calif, 1988—, various small bus. corps., Anaheim, 1986—; newscaster Sta. KROP-AM, Brawley, Calif., 1951-53; book reviewer Voice Mag., Chgo., 1953-57; pres. So. Calif. Ind. Chs., L.A., 1956-59. Co-author: Pacific Coast Railways, 1960; editor So. Calif. Regional News, 1953-57, Brethren Genealogist, 1994—; contbr. articles to profl. jours. Pres. Mission to Migrants, L.A., 1953-59; bd. dirs. Hosp. Chaplain's Assn., L.A., 1953-55, Am. Ice, Inc., Long Beach, Calif., 1982-85; trustee Christian Heritage Coll., El Cajon, Calif., 1983-85. Decorated Army Commendation medal, Meritorious Merit medal; recipient Freedom Found. awards, 1967, 70; named Chaplain of Yr., Ind. Chs., 1974. Mem. Railway and Locomotive Hist. Soc. (editorial bd. 1962-70), Johannes Schwalm Hist. Assn., Christian Bus. Faculty Assn., Western Coll. and Univ. Faculty Assn., Lancaster Mennonite Hist. Soc., Christian Mgmt. Assn., Western Pa. Gen. and Hist. Soc. Home: 12482 Madera St Victorville CA 92392-6746 Office: Pacific Christian Coll 2500 E Nutwood Ave Fullerton CA 92631

BENYO, RICHARD STEPHEN, magazine editor, writer; b. Palmerton, Pa., Apr. 20, 1946; s. Andrew Joseph and Dorothy Rita (Herman) B.; m. Jill Wapensky, Apr. 29, 1972 (div. 1979); m. Rhonda Provost, Nov. 16, 1985. BA in English Lit., Bloomsburg (Pa.) State U., 1968. Mng. editor Times-News, Lehighton, Pa., 1968-72; editor Stock Car Racing mag., Alexandria, Va., 1972-77; sr. editor Stock Car Racing mag., 1977—; exec. editor Runner's World mag., Mountain View, Calif., 1977-84; editl. dir. Skier's mag. and Fit mag., Mountain View, 1980-84; editorial dir. Anderson World Books, Mountain View, 1980-84, Strength Tng. for Beauty mag., 1983-84; editor Corp. Fitness Report, Mountain View, 1980-84, Nat. Health & Fitness Report, 1982-84, Runner's World Quar., 1982-84; v.p. J.R. Anderson Enterprizes, Inc., 1982-84; pres., pub. Specific Publs., Inc., 1983—; fitness columnist San Francisco Chronicle, 1985-91; columnist Sports Care and Fitness, 1988-90; editor Silver Sport Mag., Los Gatos, Calif., 1993—; program dir. PTVC-TV, Palmerton, Pa., 1969-72. Author: The Grand National Stars, 1975, The Book of Richard Petty, 1976, Superspeedway, 1977, Return to Running, 1978; (with Rhonda Provost) The Indoor Exercise Book, 1980, Advanced Indoor Exercise Book, 1981, Feeling Fit in Your 40's, 1987; (with Kym Herrin) Sexercise, 1981; Masters of the Marathon, 1983; (with Elaine LaLanne) Fitness After 50, 1986, Dynastride!, 1988, Fitness After 50 Workout, 1989, Eating Right for a New You, 1992, Total Juicing, 1992; The Exercise Fix, 1989, The Death Valley 300, 1991, Making the Marathon Your Event, 1992; editor: The Complete Woman Runner, 1978, Running for Everybody, 1981. Mem. racing panel of experts Union 76; bd. dirs. Napa Valley Marathon; mem. The Athletic Congress, Pacific Assn. Ultramarathoning Grand Prix Com.; bd. dirs. E Clampus Vitus. Recipient 1st pl. award local column Pa. Newspaper Pubs. Assn., 1972; named Young Alumnus of Yr., Bloomsburg U., 1985. Mem. Am. Auto Racing Writers and Broadcasters Assn. (1st place award for tech. writing), Internat. Motor Press Assn., Athletic Congress, U.S. Ski Writers Assn., N.Y. Road Runners Club, Nat. Sportscasters and Sportswriters Assn., Track and Field Writers of Am., Internat. Sports Press Assn., Commonwealth Club (San Francisco). Democrat. Home and Office: 7050 Guisti Rd Forestville CA 95436-9637

BENZER, SEYMOUR, neurosciences educator; b. N.Y.C., Oct. 15, 1921; s. Mayer and Eva (Naidorf) B.; m. Dorothy Vlosky, Jan. 10, 1942 (dec. 1978); children: Barbara Ann Benzer Freidin, Martha Jane Benzer Goldberg; m. Carol A. Miller, May 11, 1980; 1 child, Alexander Robin. B.A., Bklyn. Coll., 1942; M.S., Purdue U., 1943, Ph.D., 1947, D.Sc. (hon.), 1968; D.Sc., Columbia U., 1974, Yale U., 1977, Brandeis U., 1978, CUNY, 1978, U. Paris, 1983, Rockefeller U., N.Y.C., 1993. Mem. faculty Purdue U., 1945-67, prof. biophysics, 1958-61, Stuart distinguished prof. biology, 1961-67; prof. biology Calif. Inst. Tech., 1967-75, Boswell prof. neurosci., 1975—; biophysicist Oak Ridge Nat. Lab., 1948-49; vis. asso. Calif. Inst. Tech., Pasadena, 1965-67. Contbr. articles to profl. jours. Rsch. fellow Calif. Inst. Tech., 1949-51; Fulbright rsch. fellow Pasteur Inst., Paris, 1951-52; sr. NSF postdoctoral fellow Cambridge, Eng., 1957-58; recipient Award of Honor Bklyn. Coll., 1956, Sigma Xi rsch. award Purdue U., 1957, Ricketts award U. Chgo., 1961, Gold medal N.Y. City Coll. Chemistry Alumni Assn., 1962, Gairdner award of merit, 1964, McCoy award Purdue U., 1965, Lasker award, 1971, T. Duckett Jones award, 1975, Prix Leopold Mayer French Acad. Scis., 1975, Louisa Gross Horwitz award, 1976, Harvey award Israel, 1977, Warren Triennial prize Mass. Gen. Hosp., 1977, Dickson award, 1978, Rosenstiel award, 1986, T.H. Morgan medal Genetics Soc. Am., 1986, Karl Spencer Lashley award, 1988, Gerard award Soc. Neurosci., 1989, Helmerich award, 1990, Wolf Found. Prize (in medicine), Israel, 1991, Bristol-Myers Squibb Neurosci. award, 1992, Crafoord prize Royal Swedish Acad. Scis., 1993, Mendel award Brit. Genetical Soc., 1994, Alberto Feltrinelli prize Accademia dei Lincei, Italy, 1994. Fellow Indian Acad. Scis. (hon.); mem. Nat. Acad. Scis., Am. Acad. Arts and Scis., Am. Philos. Soc. (Lashley award 1988), Harvey Soc., N.Y. Acad. Scis., AAAS, Royal Soc. London (fgn. mem.). Home: 2075 Robin Rd San Marino CA 91108-2831

BENZING, DAVID WARREN, semiconductor equipment company executive; b. Perth Amboy, N.J., Feb. 11, 1953; s. Walter Charles and Ruth E. (McBride) B.; m. Pamela Jean Drummond, Dec. 28, 1972 (div. 1982); 1 child, Thor A.; m. Cathleen Lynn Hays, Sept. 12, 1985 (div. 1988); 1 child, Allison G. BSChemE, U. Calif., Berkeley, 1974; PhD in Chem. Engring., Princeton U., 1978. Sr. engr. Signetics Corp., Sunnyvale, Calif., 1978-81, Applied Materials, Inc., Santa Clara, Calif., 1981-82; dir. research and devel. Anelva Corp., San Jose, Calif., 1982-84; pres., founder Benzing Techs., Inc., Santa Clara, 1984—; v.p., gen. mgr. Direction Inc., Sunnyvale, 1994—; lectr. Sci. and Tech. Inst., Mt. View, Calif., 1981-83; cons. Ube Industries, Ltd., Tokyo, 1984-87, Plasma Sys. Corp., Tokyo, 1993—. Contbr. articles to profl. jours.; patentee in field. Mem. Electrochem. Soc., Thin Film Soc., Semiconductor Equipment and Materials Inst. Republican. Office: Benzing Techs Inc 1203 Foxworthy Ave San Jose CA 95118-1212

BENZLER, BRUCE C., healthcare executive; b. 1941. With Guide Dogs for the Blind, 1963—, exec. dir., 1988. Office: Guide Dogs for the Blinds PO Box 151200 San Rafael CA 94915-1200*

BERARDINI, JACQUELINE HERNANDEZ, lawyer; b. Pueblo, Colo., Sept. 16, 1949; d. Basilio Hernandez and Lorenza (Huerta) Zamarripa; stepfather, John E. Zamarripa; m. Jose A. Soliz, Aug. 1971 (div. 1977); 1 child, Christopher A.; m. Brian J. Berardini, Oct. 17, 1981; 1 child, Michael J. BA in Psychology, U. Colo., 1971; MA in Counseling, U. No. Colo., 1973; JD, U. Denver, 1980. Bar: Colo. 1980, U.S. Dist. Ct. Colo. 1980, U.S. Ct. Appeals (10th cir.) 1990, U.S. Supreme Ct. 1991. Sr. rehab. counselor divsn. rehab. Colo. Dept. Social Svc., 1974-77; assoc. Jeffrey A. Springer, P.C., 1980-85; dep. atty. gen. CERCLA Litigation sect., Office Colo. Atty. Gen., 1985-91; dir. environ. integration group Office of Environment, Colo. Dept. Pub. Health & Environment, Denver, 1991—. Contbr. articles to profl. jours. Trustee Thorne Ecol. Inst.; Colo. rep. to Western Gov.'s Assn. regarding transp. of radioactive materials and opening of waste isolation pilot plant in N.Mex., to Nat. Gov.'s Assn. regarding implementation of Fed. Facilities Compliance Act; apptd. Superfund Reauth. Subcom. of Nat. Adv. Com. on Environ. Policy and Tech., U.S. EPA; apptd. Pueblo Army Depot Chem. Demilitarization Citizen Rev. Com.; alt. mem. high-level radioactive waste com. Western Interstate Energy Bd.; presenter in field. Mem. Colo. Bar Assn., Denver Bar Assn., Colo. Hispanic Bar Assn., Colo. Hispanic League.

BERCKEFELDT, JANET ANN, zoological park administrator, consultant; b. Oakland, Calif., June 8, 1945; d. Herbert Louis, Jr. and Margaret Manita (Baldwin) Wildenradt; m. David Law Throndson, Dec. 21, 1968 (div. June 1972), Denis Ray Berckefeldt, Dec. 29, 1984 (div. 1989). BA, U. Redlands, Calif., 1967; MPA, U. So. Calif., 1978. Supr. Div. Labor Law Enforcement, State of Calif., San Francisco, 1968; asst. to v.p. Computer Time-Sharing Corp., Palo Alto, Calif., 1968-69; bus. mgr. Family Service Agy. of San Mateo County, Burlingame, Calif., 1969-77; program adminstr. Alameda County Tng. and Employment Bd., Hayward, Calif., 1978; v.p. Shelton Fin. Services, Encino, Calif., 1979-81; CFO, assoc. exec. dir. Constl. Rights Found., Los Angeles, 1981-87; v.p. fin. and adminstrn., Greater L.A. Zoo Assn., 1987-92; exec. dir. Friends of the Washington Park Zoo, Portland, Oreg., 1992—; cons. in field. Congl. intern U.S. Congress, Washington, 1966; treas. Puppeteers Am., Inc., 1983—; bd. trustees Pittock Mansion Soc., Artists Repertory Theatre; chmn. United Way Track Leadership Com. Mem. Am. Assn. Zool. Parks and Aquariums, Nat. Soc. Fund Raising Execs., Am. Assn. of Mus. Democrat. Presbyterian. Avocations: scuba diving, cross-country skiing. Office: Friends of Washington Park Zoo 4001 SW Canyon Rd Portland OR 97221-2705

BERDJIS, FAZLOLLAH, physicist; b. Soley, Kurdistan, Iraq, Feb. 4, 1943; came to U.S., 1982; s. Muzaffar and Monireh Berdjis; divorced; children: Vahid, Monireh. Vordiplom in Physics, Univ. Munich, 1967, diplom in Physics, 1972, D in Physics, 1978. Sci. co-worker Max-Planck Inst., Germany, 1978-82; asst. prof. physics U. Ill., Chgo., 1982-85; prof. physics and maths. Orange Coast Coll., Costa Mesa, Calif., 1990—; vis. physicist, UCLA, 1985-90; mem. faculty U. Phoenix, 1990—; conducted seminars U. Munich, 1979, 80; reviewer Math. Revs. Contbr. articles to profl. jours. Mem. Internat. Assn. Math. Physicists, Am. Math. Soc., Am. Phys. Soc., UN Assn., Assn. for Baha'i Studies. Office: Orange Coast Coll PO Box 5005 2701 Fairview Rd Costa Mesa CA 92628

BERESFORD, THOMAS PATRICK, psychiatry educator, alcoholism researcher; b. Danville, Ill., Mar. 16, 1946; s. Thomas Edmund and Susan Elizabeth (Gonguar) B.; m. Carol Ahmann, Aug. 22, 1970; children: Thomas Edward, Henry Francis, Charles Edmund. BA, Stanford U., 1969; MD, U. Colo., 1973. Diplomate Am. Bd. Psychiatry and Neurology. Resident, chief resident Cambridge Hosp.-Harvard Med. Sch., Cambridge, Mass., 1973-76; jr. assoc. in medicine Peter B. Brigham Hosp., Boston, 1976-78; clin. instr. Stanford (Ca.) U. Sch. Medicine, 1978-80; asst. prof. psychiatry Med. Coll. Wis., Milw., 1980-82; assoc. prof. psychiatry U. Tenn. Sch. Medicine, Memphis, 1982-86; assoc. prof., prof. psychiatry U. Mich. Med. Sch., Ann Arbor, 1986-92; prof. psychiatry U. Colo. Sch. Medicine, Denver, 1992—; chief psychiatry VA Med. Ctr., Memphis, 1982-86; assoc. chair psychiatry U. Mich., 1986-88, sci. dir., Alcohol Rsch. Ctr., 1988-91; mem. numerous profl. coms.; presenter, cons. in field. Author: (poetry) The Pharos, 1979, Annals of Internal Medicine, 1981, (poetry) A Father's Handbook, 1982, Front Range, 1984, Handbook of Psychiatric Diagnosis Procedures, vol. I, 1984, editor vol. II, 1985; author: Liver Transplantation and the Alcoholic Patient, 1994; editor: Alcohol and Aging, 1995; mem. editl. bd. Psychiat. Medicine, 1981-92, Psychosomatics, 1982—; asst. editor, co-author numerous titles, contbr. numerous articles to profl. jours. Recipient Emanuel Friedman award U. Colo., 1972, Henry Russel award U. Mich., 1988; rsch. grantee Nat. Inst. Alcohol Abuse and Alcoholism, 1986, ctr. grantee, 1988, tng. grantee, 1990, Dept. Vets. Affairs Tng. grantee, 1995. Fellow Acad. Psychosomatic Medicine, Am. Psychiat. Assn., Mass. Psychiat. Soc., No. Calif. Psychiat. Soc., Wis. Psychiat. Assn., Tenn. Psychiat. Assn., Mich. Psychiat. Assn., Acad. Psychosomatic Medicine (Best Poster award 1991, Disting. Svc. award 1994), Soc. Biol. Psychiatry, Rsch. Soc. on Alcoholism. Home: 6410 S Olathe St Aurora CO 80016-1034 Office: U Colo VA Med Ctr 1055 Clermont St Denver CO 80220

BERETTA, GIORDANO BRUNO, computer scientist, researcher; b. Brugg, Aargau, Switzerland, Apr. 14, 1951; came to U.S., 1984; PhD, ETH, Zurich, Switzerland, 1984. Mem. rsch. staff Xerox Palo Alto (Calif.) Rsch. Ctr., 1984-90; charter mem., sr. scientist Canon Info. Systems, Palo Alto, 1990-93; mem. tech. staff Hewlett-Packard Labs., 1994—. Contbr. articles to profl. jours.; patentee digital color reprodn. Mem. The Internat. Soc. for Optical Engring., Inter-Soc. Color Coun. Office: Hewlett-Packard Labs 1501 Page Mill Rd Palo Alto CA 94304-1126

BEREZNAY, FRANK M., information systems specialist; b. Inglewood, Calif., Mar. 22, 1948; s. Francis Regis and Dorothy Louise (Brown) B.; m. Shana Jean Sweeney, July 9, 1977; 1 child, Catherine Louise. BA in Bus. Adminstrn., Calif. State U., Fullerton, 1975, BA in Econs., 1975; postgrad., UCLA, 1975-77. Project mgr. Rand Info. Systems, San Francisco, 1977-80; systems programme, mgr. systems mgmt. Santa Fe Internat., Orange and Alhambra, Calif., 1980-86; mgr. tech. svcs. Bergen Brunswig, Orange, 1986; data ctr. mgr. Automobile Club of So. Calif., Costa Mesa, 1986—; presenter, speaker in field; developer tech. tng. programs. Mem. editorial rev. bd. Enterprise Systems Jour. With USN, 1967-71. Mem. Computer Measurement Group (mem. editorial bd. for procs. 1988-92, chmn. program com. nat. conf. 1994, program chmn. So. Calif. region 1988-91, pres. So. Calif. region 1991-94, nat. treas. 1994—, Legent Resource Mgr. of Yr. award 1993). Home: 528 S Cardiff St Anaheim CA 92806-4334 Office: Automobile Club of So Calif 3333 Fairview Rd Costa Mesa CA 92626-1610

BERG, DAVE, television producer, writer; b. Hollywood, Calif., June 1, 1948; s. David Bernard and Beverly May (Sparks) B.; m. Mary Khourie, Sept. 24, 1983; children: Melissa, David. BA in Polit. Sci., Northwestern U., 1970; MS in Journalism, Kans. State U., 1974. Writer, producer Sta. KCUR-FM, Kansas City, Mo., 1971-73; anchor, reporter Sta. WFRV-TV, Green Bay, Wis., 1974-76; assignment mgr., anchor Sta. KTIV-TV, Sioux City, Iowa, 1976-78; assignment mgr., reporter Sta. KETV-TV, Omaha, 1978-80; exec. producer Sta. KOVR-TV, Sacramento, 1980-82; writer, producer NBC News-Burbank, 1982-89; bur. chief L.A. CNBC (cable div. NBC), Ft. Lee, N.J., 1989-92; segment producer The Tonight Show With Jay Leno, Burbank, Calif, 1992—; instr. writing TV news Coll. of Canyons, Valencia, Calif., 1991-93. Songwriter: (country songs) Gonna Walk, 1990, Can't Make Up My Heart, 1990. Liturgist, adult Sunday sch. tchr. United Meth. Ch., Valencia. NIMH fellow, 1973-74. Republican. Office: The Tonight Show 3000 W Alameda Ave # 2190 Burbank CA 91523-0001

BERG, KEVIN ALLAN, management consultant, retail executive; b. Harvey, Ill., Oct. 8, 1960; s. Mandel M. and Phyllis S. Berg; m. Melinda G. Berg, Aug. 16, 1981 (div. Dec. 10, 1987; children: Joshua Marcus, Jeremy Michael. BS in Math. and Computer Sci., No. Ill. U., 1982; postgrad., U. Ill., 1978-79. Cert. project mgmt. cons. Bring-up engr. Amdahl Corp., Sunnyvale, Calif., 1987-91; project mgr. Amdahl Corp., Fremont, Calif., 1991-93; project mgmt. cons. Berg Cons., Union City, Calif., 1993—; owner/author Child-Tech Books and Toys, Union City, 1992—; cons. in field. Author: (children's poetry book) Jibberish and Rhyme, 1993 (Book of the Yr. 1994); contbr. articles to profl. jours. Founder Union City-Yes, sec., 1993-94. Sol Savit scholar, 1979. Mem. Am. Soc. Quality Control, Union City Lions (bd. dirs. 1994, Blind Ctr. rep.). Democrat. Office: Child-Tech Books and Toys PO Box 2614 Union City CA 94587-7614

BERG, PAUL, biochemist, educator; b. N.Y.C., June 30, 1926; s. Harry and Sarah (Brodsky) B.; m. Mildred Levy, Sept. 13, 1947; 1 son, John. BS, Pa. State U., 1948; PhD (NIH fellow 1950-52), Western Res. U., 1952; DSc (hon.), U. Rochester, 1978, Yale U., 1978, Wash. U., St. Louis, 1986, Oreg. State U., 1989, Pa. State U., 1995. Postdoctoral fellow Copenhagen (Denmark) U., 1952-53; postdoctoral fellow sch. medicine Washington U., St. Louis, 1953-54; Am. Cancer Soc. scholar cancer research dept. microbiology sch. medicine Washington U., 1954-57, from asst. to assoc. prof. microbiology sch. medicine, 1955-59; prof. biochemistry sch. medicine Stanford U., 1959—, Sam, Lulu and Jack Willson prof. biochemistry sch. medicine, 1970-94; Robert W. Cahill prof. cancer rsch., 1994—; chmn. dept. sch. medicine Stanford U., 1969-74; dir. Stanford U. Beckman Ctr. for Molecular and Genetic Medicine, 1985—, Affymetrix, 1993—, Nat. Found. Biomed. Rsch., 1994—; non-resident fellow Salk Inst., 1973-83; adv. bd. NIH, NSF, MIT; vis. com. dept. biochemistry and molecular biology Harvard U.; bd. sci. advisors Jane Coffin Childs Found. Med. Rsch., 1970-80; chmn. sci. adv. com. Whitehead Inst., 1984-90; bd. sci. adv. DNAX Rsch. Inst., 1981—; internat. adv. bd. Basel Inst. Immunology; chmn. nat. adv. com. Human Genome Project, 1990-92. Contbr. profl. jours.; Editor: Biochem. and Biophys. Research Communications, 1959-68; editorial bd.: Molecular Biology, 1966-69. Trustee Rockefeller U., 1990-92. Served to lt. (j.g.) USNR, 1943-46. Recipient Eli Lilly prize biochemistry, 1959; V.D. Mattia award Roche Inst. Molecular Biology, 1972; Henry J. Kaiser award for excellence in teaching, 1969, 72; Disting. Alumnus award Pa. State U., 1972; Sarasota Med. awards for achievement and excellence, 1979; Gairdner Found. annual award, 1980; Lasker Found. award, 1980; Nobel award in chemistry, 1980; N.Y. Acad. Sci. award, 1980; Sci. Freedom and Responsibility award AAAS, 1982; Nat. Medal of Sci., 1983; named Calif. Scientist of Yr. Calif. Museum Sci. and Industry, 1963; numerous disting. lectureships including Harvey lectr., 1972, Lynen lectr., 1977, Priestly lectrs. Pa. State U., 1978, Dreyfus Disting. lectrs. Northwestern U., 1979, Lawrence Livermore Dir.'s Disting. lectr., 1983, Linus Pauling lectr., 1993. Fellow AAAS; mem. NAS, Inst. Medicine, Am. Acad. Arts and Scis., Am. Soc. Biol. Chemists (pres. 1974-75), Am. Soc. Cell Biology (chmn. pub. policy com. 1994—), Am. Soc. Microbiology, Am. Philos. Soc., Internat. Soc. Molecular Biology, Japan Biochem. Soc. (elected fgn. mem. 1978), French Acad. Sci. (elected fgn. mem. 1981), Royal Soc. (elected fgn. mem. 1992). Office: Stanford Sch Medicine Beckman Ctr B-062 Stanford CA 94305-5425*

BERG, ROBERT ALLEN, pediatrician, educator; b. Detroit, Dec. 12, 1949; s. Aaron and Mildred (Schuff) B.; m. Catherine Locke, May 8, 1982 (dec. Mar. 1994); children: David, Carolyn. BS, U. Mich., 1971; MD, U. Calif., San Francisco, 1975. Pediatric intern U. Calif., San Francisco, 1975-76, pediatric resident, 1976-77; chief resident dept. pediatrics Good Samaritan Hosp., Phoenix and San Francisco, 1977-78; dir. pediatric clinic and emergency rm. Maricopa Med. Ctr., Phoenix, 1978-84, dir. pediatric ICU, 1984-88; dir. pediatric ICU Tucson (Ariz.) Med. Ctr., 1989-91, U. Med. Ctr., Tucson, 1988—; asst. prof., clin. lectr. U. Ariz. Coll. Medicine, Tucson, 1983-88, clin. asst. prof., 1988-92, clin. assoc. prof., 1992-94, assoc. prof. with tenure, 1994—; pres.-elect Phoenix Pediat. Soc., 1987-88; nat. faculty pediat. advanced life support Am. Heart Assn.-Ariz. Affiliate, 1990-94, rsch. com., 1991-94, pediat. subcom. mem. emergency cardiac care, 1994, chmn. pediat. advanced life support task force, 1994, neonatology liaison emergency cardiac care, 1994; vis. prof. U. Hawaii, Okinawa, Japan, 1991. Contbr. articles to profl. jours. Med. dir. Pilot Parents, Phoenix, 1979-88; chmn. Child Care Safety Seat Task Force, Ariz., 1983; bd. dirs. Congregation Chaverim, Tucson, 1993-94; med./exec. com. U. Med. Ctr., Tucson, 1994. Rsch. grantee Ariz. Disease Control Rsch. Commn., 1994—. Fellow Am. Acad. Pediat., Am. Coll. Critical Care Medicine, Soc. Critical Care Medicine (chmn. clin. practice guidelines com. 1994—). Office: Univ Ariz Health Scis Ctr 1501 N Campbell Ave Tucson AZ 85724-0001

BERG, SUSAN ELAINE, nursing educator; b. St. Louis, June 21, 1946; d. John Albert and Winnifred (Fitzpatrick) Berg; m. Duane Isetti, Feb. 14, 1972 (div. 1977); 1 child, Derek Duane. BSN, U. San Francisco, 1968; MSN magna cum laude, U. Calif., San Francisco, 1971; Pediatric Nurse Practitioner, U. Calif., Davis, 1977; EdD magna cum laude, U. San Francisco, 1990. Lic. PNP, psychiat. mental health nurse practitioner, Oreg. Staff nurse U. Calif. Med. Ctr., San Francisco, 1968-69; pub. health nurse Alameda County Pub. Health Dept., Oakland, Calif., 1969-70; faculty

Modesto (Calif.) Jr. Coll., 1973-74; staff devel. instr. St. Joseph's Hosp., Stockton, Calif., 1974-77; pediatric nurse practitioner San Francisco Gen. Hosp., 1977-78; faculty Contra Costa Coll., San Pablo, Calif., 1978-80; faculty nursing Sonoma State U., Rohnert Park, Calif., 1980-83, 91-92, Santa Rose Jr. Coll., 1983-91; pediatric nurse practitioner in pvt. practice Santa Rosa, Calif., summers 1987-92; faculty nursing Dominican Coll., San Rafael, Calif., 1992-93; nursing faculty Rogue C.C., Grants Pass, Oreg., 1993-94; psychiat. mental health nurse practitioner Oreg., 1994-95, pediatric nurse practitioner, 1994-95. Adv. bd. River Child Care, Head Start, Santa Rosa. Mem. APA, NAPNAP, CNR. Democrat. Home: 4777 Glenn Echo Way Central Point OR 97502-9707

BERGÉ, CAROL, author; b. N.Y.C., 1928; d. Albert and Molly Peppis; m. Jack Bergé, June 1955; 1 child, Peter. Asst. to pres. Pendray Public Relations, N.Y.C., 1955; disting. prof. lit. Thomas Jefferson Coll., Allendale, Mich., 1975-76; instr. adult degree program Goddard Coll. at Asilomar, 1976; tchr. fiction and poetry U. Calif. Extension Program, Berkeley, 1976-77; assoc. prof. U. So. Miss., Hattiesburg, 1977-78; vis. prof. Honors Ctr. and English dept. U. N.Mex., 1978-79, 87; vis. lectr. Wright State U., 1979, SUNY, Albany, 1980-81; tchr. Poets and Writers, Poets in the Schs. (N.Y. State Council on Arts), 1970-72, Poets in the Schs. (Conn. Commn. Arts); proprietor Blue Gate Gallery of Art and Antiques, 1988-95. Author: (fiction) The Unfolding, 1969, A Couple Called Moebius, 1972, Acts of Love: An American Novel, 1973 (N.Y. State Coun. on Arts CAPS award 1974), Timepieces, 1977, The Doppler Effect, 1979, Fierce Meltronome, 1981, Secrets, Gossip and Slander, 1984, Zebras or Contour Lines, 1991; (poetry) The Vulnerable Island, 1964, Poems Made of Skin, 1968, The Chambers, 1969, Circles, as in the Eye, 1969, An American Romance, 1969, From a Soft Angle: Poems About Women, 1972, The Inexpected, 1976, Rituals and Gargoyles, 1976, A Song, A Chant, 1978, Alba Genesis, 1979, Alba Nemesis, 1979; editor: Center Mag., 1970-84, pub., 1991—; editor Miss. Rev., 1977-78, Subterraneans, 1975-76, Paper Branches, 1987, Light Years: Th eNYC Coffeehouse Poets of the 1960's, 1995; contbg. editor Woodstock Rev., 1977-81, Shearsman mag., 1980-82, S.W. Profile, 1981; editor, pub. CENTER Press, 1991-93; pub. Medicine Journeys (Carl Ginsburg), Coastal Lives (Miriam Sagan), 1991; co-pub. Zebras (Carol Berge). Nat. Endowment Arts fellow, 1979-80. Mem. Authors' League, Poets and Writers, MacDowell Fellows Assn., Nat. Press Women. Home: 562 Onate Pl Santa Fe NM 87501-3674

BERGEL, PETER ROBIN, editor; b. Bishop, Calif., Apr. 27, 1944; s. Kurt and Alice Rose (Berger) B.; m. Parry Pierce; 1 child, Shanti Pierce. BA in Physics, Reed Coll., 1965. Mem. process devel. staff Precision Castparts, Portland, Oreg., 1965-66; rsch. apparatus operator Atomic Energy Commn., Berkeley, Calif., 1966-70; mem. staff Energy Conservation Orgn., Eugene, Oreg., 1975-76; legis. intern Oreg. Legislature, Salem, 1979, legis. asst., 1981; dir. Citizens Allied for Responsible Energy, Salem, 1979-81; co-dir. Citizen Action for Lasting Security, Salem, 1981-86; nat. staff person Am. Peace Test, Salem, Las Vegas, 1986-88; editor Oreg. PeaceWorker, Salem, 1988—; columnist Stateman Jour. Newspaper, 1994—; editor Civilian Based Defense, 1995—; founding bd. dirs. McKenzie River Gathering, Eugene, 1975-78; bd. dirs. polit. action com. Oreg. PeaceWorks; pres. bd. Ctr. for Energy Rsch. Founder, participant Dr. Atomic's Medicine Show, Salem, Eugene, 1974—; founder Ch. of Ithilien, Willamina, Oreg., 1969-72; co-founder Am. Peace Test, 1985, Peace Tng. Inst., Salem, 1993; co-chmn. COPRED Nat. Conf., 1995. Recipient Human Rights award City of Salem, 1985, Award of Distinction Oreg. Mag., 1985. Democrat. Taoist. Office: Ctr for Energy Rsch 333 State St Salem OR 97301-3533

BERGEN, CHRISTOPHER BROOKE, opera company administrator, translator, editor; b. L.A., Jan. 11, 1949; s. Edward Grinnell Bergen and Alvina Ellen (Temple) Stevens; m. Tessa Jennifer von Grunebaum, May 7, 1972. BA, UCLA, 1971; MA, Yale U., 1977. Conf. officer IAEA, Vienna, Austria, 1973-75, data analyst, 1979-81; import mgr. COBEC Trading Corp., N.Y.C., 1978-79; assoc. Geissler Engring. Co., Oakland, Calif., 1982-83; dir. Yale Cons. Assocs., San Francisco, 1983-84; editor INPUT, Mountain View, Calif., 1984; adminstr. surtitles San Francisco Opera, 1985—. Editor profl. jours.; translator operatic texts for projection during performances at San Francisco Opera, Met. Opera, Lyric Opera of Chgo., many other opera cos., symphonies and conservatories in U.S., abroad. Mem. Dolphin Swimming and Boating Club of San Francisco, Amnesty Internat., Sierra Club. Democrat. Home: 1450 Greenwich St # 604 San Francisco CA 94109-1466 Office: San Francisco Opera War Meml Opera House San Francisco CA 94102

BERGEN, POLLY, actress; b. Knoxville, Tenn.; d. William and Lucy (Lawhorn) Burgin; m. Freddie Fields, Feb. 13, 1956 (div. 1976); children: Kathy, Pamela, Peter. Pres. Polly Bergen Cosmetics, Polly Bergen Jewelry, Polly Bergen Shoes. Author: Fashion and Charm, 1960, Polly's Principles, 1974, I'd Love To, But What'll I Wear, 1977; author, producer for TV: Leave of Absence, 1994; Broadway plays include Champagne Complex, John Murray Andersons' Almanac, First Impression, Plaza Suite, Love Letters; films include Cape Fear, Move Over Darling, Kisses for My President, At War with the Army, The Stooge, That's My Boy, The Caretakers, A Guide for the Married Man, Making Mr. Right, Cry-Baby, 1990, Dr. Jekyll and Ms. Hyde, When We Were Colored, 1994; performed in one woman shows in Las Vegas and Reno, Nev.; albums: Bergen Sings Morgan, The Party's Over, All Alone By the Telephone, Polly and Her Pop, The Four Seasons of Love, Annie Get Your Gun and Do Re Mi, My Heart Sings, Act One Sing Too; numerous TV appearances including star of The Polly Bergen Show, NBC-TV; other TV appearances include The Helen Morgan Story, 1957 (Emmy award as best actress), To Tell the Truth, Death Cruise, Murder on Flight 502, How to Pick Up Girls!, Born Beautiful; (co-star) TV series Baby Talk; miniseries include The Winds of War (Emmy nomination), 79 Park Ave, War and Remembrance, 1988 (Emmy nomination); starring in TV series Baby Talk, 1991-92; writer, prodr. NBC movie Leave of Absence, 1994. Bd. dirs. Martha Graham Dance Center; hon. canister campaign chairperson Cancer Care, Inc., Nat. Cancer Found.; founder Nat. Bus. Coun. for ERA; mem. Planned Prenthood Fedn., Am. Bd. Advocates; nat. adv. com. NARAL, Hollywood Women's Polit. Com.; bd. dirs. Calif. Abortion Rights Action League, Show Coalition. Recipient Fame award Top Ten in TV, 1957-58, Troupers award Sterling Publs., 1957, Editors and Critics award Radio and TV Daily, 1958, Outstanding Working Woman award Downtown St. Louis, Inc., Golden Plate award Am. Acad. Achievement, 1969, Outstanding Mother's award Nat. Mothers' Day Com., 1984, Best Achievement in New Jewelry Design, 1986, Cancer Care award, 1989, Woman of Achievement award LWV, 1990, Extraordinary Achievement award Nat. Women's Law Ctr., 1991; Polly Bergen Cardio-Pulmonary Rsch. Lab., Children's Rsch. Inst. and Hosp., Denver dedicated, 1970. Mem. AFTRA, AGVA, SAG, Actors Equity, AGVA, AFTRA, Show Coalition (bd. dirs.), Soc. Singers (bd. dirs.), Calif. Abortion Rights Action League (bd. dirs., Freedom of Choice award 1992). Office: care Jan McCormack 11342 Dona Lisa Dr Studio City CA 91604-4315

BERGEN, VIRGINIA LOUISE, principal, language arts educator; b. St. Louis, Apr. 5, 1945; d. Roland Daniel Paton and Gladys (Crawford) Gibson; m. Robert Elwood Bergen, July 11, 1964; children: Robert Brandon, Jennifer Lynn. BA, So. Ill. U., 1971, MS, 1973, EdS, 1975; Ednl. Adminstrn. Cert., U. Oreg., 1981. Cert. K-12 Ed. Ad., K-9 tchr., K-12 spl. edn., speech corr., reading specialist, Colo., Oreg., Ill, Mo., N.Mex. Speech therapist Dist. #175, Belleville, Ill., 1971-73; K-12 clin. tchr. Collinsville (Ill.) Unit #10, 1973-74, jr. high sch. LD tchr., 1974-78; edn. resource cons. Douglas Edn. Svc. Dist., Roseburg, Oreg., 1978-80; child devel. specialist Roseburg Dist. #4, 1980-82; asst. prin. Mesa County Valley Dist. #51, Grand Junction, Colo., 1982-85, prin., 1985—; vis. lectr. So. Ill. U., 1976-78; instr. Met. State Coll., Denver, 1989-91; lectr. Mesa State Coll., Grand Junction, 1991-92; in-svc. provider Mesa County Valley Sch. Dist. #51, 1982—, mem. standards and assessment steering com.; founding mem. governance bd. Basil T. Knight Staff Devel. Ctr., Dist. #51, Grand Junction, 1986-89. Mem. Colo. Assn. Sch. Execs., Phi Delta Kappa. Office: Fruitvale Elem Sch 585 30 Rd Grand Junction CO 81504-5658

BERGER, BONNIE G., sport psychologist, educator; b. Champaign, Ill., May 20, 1941; d. Bernard G. and Mildred W. Berger; 1 son, Stephen Casher. BS, Wittenberg U., 1962; MA, Columbia U., 1965, EdD, 1972. Tchr., George Rogers Clark Jr. High Sch., Springfield, Ohio, 1962-64; supr. phys. edn. Agnes Russell Elem. Sch., N.Y.C., 1964-65; asst. prof. SUNY, Geneseo, 1965-66; asst. prof. Dalhousie U., Halifax, N.S., Can., 1969-71; asst. prof. Bklyn. Coll., 1971-77, assoc. prof., 1978-81, prof., 1982-93, dir. Sport Psychology Lab., master degree program in psychosocial aspects of physical activity; dep. chair dept. phys. edn. Bklyn. Coll., 1989-93; prof., assoc. dean coll. health scis., sch. physical edn. U. Wyo., Laramie, 1993—; cons. sport psychology. Fellow Assn. for the Advancement of Applied Sport Psychology (exec. bd.), Am. Acad. Kinesiology and Phys. Edn.; mem. Am. Psychol. Assn., AAHPERD, Internat. Soc. Sports Psychology, N.Am. Soc. Psychology Sport and Phys. Activity, Can. Soc. Psychomotor Learning and Sport Psychology. Author: Free Weights for Women, 1984; contbr. articles to profl. jours., chpts. to books. Home: 1673 Apache Dr Laramie WY 82070-6967 Office: U Wyo Phys Edn & Health Edn Corbett Bldg Laramie WY 82070

BERGER, DALE EDMUND, psychologist, educator; b. Perham, Minn., Feb. 21, 1943; s. Albert D. and Evelyn E. (Pausch) B.; m. Peggy Marie Seaver, Dec. 16, 1978; children: Laura, Eric. BS in Math., U. Minn., 1964; MA in Psychology, UCLA, 1966, PhD, 1970. Math. tchr. Torrance (Calif.) Unified Sch. Dist., 1964-65; asst. prof. Claremont (Calif.) Grad. Sch., 1970-77, assoc. prof., 1977-83, prof., 1983—, chair grad. faculty in psychology, 1989—, dir. Ctr. for Orgnl. and Behavioral Scis., 1993—. Author, editor: Applications of Cognitive Psychology, 1987; contbr. articles to profl. jours. Mem. Phi Beta Kappa. Office: Claremont Grad Sch 123 E 8th St Claremont CA 91711-3955

BERGER, DAN LEE, newspaper wine columnist; b. Bklyn., Aug. 28, 1941; s. Joseph and Frances (Sarver) B.; m. D. J. Freeman, Nov. 28, 1976; children: Marc, Adam, Joel. BA, Calif. State U., L.A., 1967. Reporter AP, L.A., 1967-77; reporter, editor NFL Properties, L.A., 1977; reporter, columnist San Diego Union, 1978-86; editor, columnist Santa Rosa (Calif.) Press-Dem., 1986-88; columnist, reporter L.A. Times, 1988—. Author: Basketball: The Sports Playbook, 1975, San Diego: Where Tomorrow Begins, 1985, (with Richard Paul Hinkle) Beyond the Grapes: Napa, 1991, (with Richard Paul Hinkle) Beyond the Grapes: Sonoma, 1991. Recipient Father Junipero Serra award Calif. Wine Patrons, 1989; named Wine Writer of Yr. Wines and Vines mag., 1988. Jewish. Office: Los Angeles Times Times Mirror Sq Los Angeles CA 90012

BERGER, HOWARD MARTIN, industrial and service company executive; b. Jamestown, N.Y., Aug. 31, 1927; s. Frederick S. and Millicant (Petschau) B.; m. Barbara Diane Lubin, June 25, 1950; children: Teri Anne, Patricia Jeanne, Lisa Diane. BSE in Aeros. and Math., U. Mich., 1948; MS, Calif. Inst. Tech., 1949, PhD, 1954. Program dir. Inst. for Def. Analyses, Arlington, Va., 1961-66; dir. strategic forces div. Dept. Def., Arlington, 1966-69; mgr. strategic analysis Xerox Corp., Rochester, N.Y., 1969-75; sr. project mgr. Rand Corp., Santa Monica, Calif., 1975-76; asst. v.p. Sci. Applications Inc., El Segundo, Calif., 1976-77; pres. HMB Assocs., Palos Verdes, Calif., 1977-78; v.p. Analytical Assessments Corp., Marina del Rey, Calif., 1978-80, Logistics Tech. Internat., Torrance, Calif., 1980-81; pres., chmn. bd. Robotix Corp., Torrance, 1981—; bd. dirs., CFO Keats Manhattan, Inc., Torrance, 1980-94, Justin-Time Svcs., Inc., Torrance, 1980-93. Contbr. articles to profl. jours. With AUS, 1946-47. Recipient numerous scholarships and fellowships. Mem. Computer and Automated Systems Assn. of Soc. Mfg. Engrs. (sr., chmn. Greater L.A. chpt. 1987-88). Republican. Home: 2108 Via Fernandez Palos Verdes Peninsula CA 90274-2039 Office: Robotix Corp 3525 Lomita Blvd Ste 101 Torrance CA 90505-5016

BERGER, JAY VARI, executive recruiter, import company executive; b. San Francisco, Aug. 31, 1944; s. Jack Vari and Ruth (Wasserman) B.; m. Margareta Ahlberg, June 14, 1969; children: Karin Britta Margareta, John Vari Sten. BS, U. So. Calif., 1966, MS, 1967, PhD, 1971. Assoc. dean admissions U. So. Calif., L.A., 1969-76, dir. admissions, 1976-82, asst. v.p. devel., 1982-86; prin. ptnr. Morris & Berger, Pasadena, Calif., 1986—; chmn. bd. Berger & Berger Internat., Pasadena, 1976—. Author: (juvenile) Willie the Worm, 1986; columnist Venture Connections, 1988. Pres. bd. dirs. The Sycamores, Pasadena, 1985-94, Foothill Friends of Music, 1989-92; bd. dirs. Covenant House Calif.; pres., trustee Chandler Sch., Pasadena, 1987-89; trustee Flintridge Preparatory Sch., 1992—. Mem. Calif. Exec. Recruiters Assn., Calif. Assn. Ind. Schs. (bd. trustees 1988-91), Annandale Golf Club, Valley Hunt Club, Rotary (bd. dirs. Pasadena chpt. 1988-92). Home: 412 Oaklawn Ave South Pasadena CA 91030-1833 Office: Morris & Berger Cons Exec Search 201 S Lake Ave Ste 700 Pasadena CA 91101-3015

BERGER, JOHN MILTON, state agency administrator; b. Marysville, Ohio, June 24, 1943; s. John Howard and Betty Louise (Mossbarger) B.; m. Joy Lynne Ansley, Dec. 29, 1969. BSBA, Franklin U., 1971; postgrad., Ohio State U., 1972. Cert. hazard control mgr., assoc. Ins. Inst. Am. risk mgmt. designation. Claims adjuster State Compensation Ins. Fund, Denver, 1974-78, loss control cons., 1978-84; adminstrv. officer Indsl. Commn., Denver, 1984-86; self-ins. adminstrn. Colo. Div. Labor, Denver, 1986-91; ins. compliance mgr. div. workers' compensation Colo. Dept. Labor and Employment, Denver, 1991—; mem. legis. com. Colo. Div. Ins., Denver, 1989-91; mem. self-ins. subcom. of Internat. Assn. Indsl. Accident Bds. and Commns. Author: Workers' Compensation Loss Prevention and Loss Control Manual, 1990; contbr. article to profl. jour. With USN, 1961-64. Recognized for Outstanding Svc. to State Govt., 1986. Mem. Colo. Self-Insurers Assn. Republican. Home: 675 Dudley St Lakewood CO 80215-5406

BERGER, LELAND ROGER, lawyer; b. N.Y.C., Feb. 3, 1956; s. Albert and Audrey Sybil (Ellenbogen) B.; m. Lisa M. Burk, Feb. 15, 1987; 1 child, Robert Samson. Student, Am. U., 1977; BA, Dickinson Coll., 1978; JD, Lewis & Clark Coll., 1982. Bar: Oreg. 1983, U.S. Dist. Ct. Oreg. 1983, U.S. Ct. Appeals (9th cir.) 1990. Pvt. practice Portland, Oreg., 1983-84; assoc. Rieke, Geil & Savage, P.C., Portland, 1984-94; pvt. practice Portland, 1995—. Mem. Oreg. Bar Assn. (ad hoc com. to study multi-state bar exam. 1983-84, uniform criminal jury instrn. com. 1989-90, sec. 1990-91, criminal law sect.), Multnomah County Bar Assn. (corrections com. 1987), Oreg. Young Attys. Assn. (bd. dirs. 1983-84), Nat. Lawyers Guild (co-chair criminal justice com. Portland chpt. 1983-84), Oreg. Criminal Def. Lawyers Assn., Nat. Criminal Def. Lawyers Assn. Democrat. Jewish. Home: 2817 NE 12th Ave Portland OR 97212-3219 Office: Ste 3 950 Lloyd Center Portland OR 97232

BERGER, NEWELL JAMES, JR., security professional; b. Pitts., Oct. 26, 1926; s. Newell James and Marjorie Ikler (Herndon) B.; m. Darlene Ingram, Sept. 6, 1950 (dec. Nov. 1990). BS, Mich. State U., 1958; grad., U.S. Army Command and Gen. Staff Coll., 1963, U.S. Army War Coll., 1972; MA, Webster U., 1993. Enlisted man U.S. Army, 1944, advanced through grades to staff sgt., 1948, commd. 2d lt., 1948, advanced through grades to col., 1970; chief corrections hdqrs. U.S. Army, Washington, 1970-72, dir. security Office Surgeon Gen., 1972-73; dir. security Health Svcs. Command U.S. Army, Ft. Sam Houston, Tex., 1973-78; ret. U.S. Army, 1978; security cons. Phoenix and San Diego, 1979-84; chief plant security Teledyne Ryan Aero. Co., San Diego, 1985-86; chief of security GDE Systems, Inc., San Diego, 1986—. Decorated Legion of Merit with two oak leaf clusters. Mem. Internat. Assn. Chiefs Police, Am. Soc. for Indsl. Security (cert. protection profl.). Republican. Episcopalian. Home: 11872 Caminito Corriente San Diego CA 92128 Office: GDE Systems Inc PO Box 1198 Poway CA 92074-1198

BERGER, PAUL ERIC, artist, photographer; b. The Dalles, Oreg., Jan. 20, 1948; s. Charles Glen and Virginia (Nunez) B. B.A., UCLA, 1970; M.F.A., SUNY-Buffalo, 1973. Vis. lectr. U. Ill., 1974-78; prof. art U. Wash.-Seattle, 1978—. Exhibited one-man shows, photographs, Art Inst. Chgo., 1975, Light Gallery, N.Y.C., 1977, Seattle Art Mus., 1980, Light Gallery, N.Y.C., 1982, Univ. Art Mus., Santa Barbara, Calif., 1984, Cliff Michel Gallery, 1989, Seattle Art Mus., 1990, Fuel Gallery, 1993. NEA Photographer's fellow, 1979, NEA Visual Artist's fellow, 1986; recipient Artist's Commn., Wash. State Arts Commn., 1990. Mem. Soc. Photographic Edn. Office: U Wash Sch Art Box 353440 Seattle WA 98195

BERGER, ROBERT SYDNEY, paper company executive; b. N.Y.C., Feb. 13, 1917; s. Matthew M. and Deborah Jeanette (Newblatt) B.; m. Nancy Mock, Sept. 23, 1952; children: Jill DeJong Gross, Kathy DeJong Albert. BA, U. Pa., 1936; MA, Columbia U., 1939; JD, Harvard U., 1939. Bar: N.Y. Assoc. office A.L. Pomerantz, N.Y.C., 1939-41; v.p. McKenna & Phelps Inc., N.Y.C., 1946-47; chmn. bd. Rittenhouse Paper Co., Chgo., Los Angeles, 1948—. Mem. bd. edn. Highland Park, Ill., 1960-66. Served to capt. USN, 1941-46, 51-53, USNR, 1954-77. Club: Regency (Los Angeles). Home: 10375 Wilshire Blvd Los Angeles CA 90024-4728 Office: Rittenhouse Paper Co 2440 E 38th St Los Angeles CA 90058-1708

BERGESON, JOHN HENNING, denominational executive, theological educator; b. Ashland, Wis., May 10, 1919; s. Henning John and Lydia Roberta (Johnson) B.; m. Gladys Victoria Peterson, June 10, 1944; children: John Joel, Jane Ellen, Ruth Ann, Peter Lowell, Daniel Roger. BA, U. N.D., Grand Forks, 1943; BD, Bethel Theol. Sem., St. Paul, Minn., 1944; DD, Western Bapt. Sem., Portland, Oreg., 1983. Ordination by Baptist Gen. Conf. Pastor Alma Baptist Ch., Argyle, Minn., 1941-43, Eagle Point Baptist Ch., Stepen, Minn., 1941-43, Opstead Baptist Ch., Isle, Minn., 1944-53; exec. min. Platte Valley Baptist Conf., Gothenburg, Nebr., 1953-56, Rocky Mountain Baptist Conf., Denver, 1956-59; missions dir. Minn. Baptist Conf., St. Paul, Minn., 1959-70; exec. min. Columbia Baptist Conf., Seattle, 1970-85, British Columbia Bapt. Conf., Surrey, BC, Can., 1985-87; dir. of field edn. Bethel Theol. Sem., San Diego, 1987-92. Author: Churches Everywhere, 1978, Fourth Quarter, 1989. Named Moderator, Baptist Gen. Conf. Annual Meeting, Wheaton, Ill., 1973. Baptist. Home: 720 N 193rd Pl Seattle WA 98133-3942

BERGESON, SCOTT, retail executive; b. Logan, Utah, Feb. 7, 1938; s. Harold E. and Reba M. (Butler) B.; m. Elaine Ann Johnson, Sept. 7, 1962; children: Eric S., Todd K., Paula A., Jill E., Amy K., Sean M. B.S., Brigham Young U., Provo, Utah, 1962, M.B.A., 1965. With Skaggs Cos., Inc., 1972-79, corp. sec., 1977-79; v.p., sec. Am. Stores Co., Salt Lake City, 1979-81; pres., chief exec. officer subs. co. Am. Stores Mgmt. Systems Co., 1981-83; exec. v.p. Am. Stores Co., 1983-86; chmn. bd., chief exec. officer Osco Drug , Inc., Oak Brook, Ill., 1987-88; sr. v.p. Am. Stores Co., Salt Lake City, 1989—. Democrat. Mem. LDS Church. Office: Am Stores Co PO Box 27447 Salt Lake City UT 84127-0447

BERGFORS, JUDITH LYN, photographer; b. Clare, Mich., July 19, 1943; d. John Charles and Doris Elizabeth Marotzke; children: Michael Carl, Audrey Lyn. Jr. high sch. tchr. Rancho Santa Fe (Calif.) Sch., 1972-74; photographer, writer Aardvark Photographic, Carmel, Calif., 1992—; pub. Winston Publs., Carmel, 1973—; seamstress Wardrobe Magic, Carmel, 1970—; legal sec., Detroit, 1960-64. Author, photographer: Call It Universe, 1992. Mem. Kiwanis (pres. 1993, lt. gov. 1995—). Office: Aardvark Photographic PO Box 1536 Carmel CA 93921-1536

BERGGRUEN, JOHN HENRY, art gallery executive; b. San Francisco, June 18, 1943; s. Heinz and Lillian Z. B. Pres., owner John Berggruen Gallery, San Francisco. Office: John Berggruen Gallery 228 Grant Ave San Francisco CA 94108-4612

BERGH, DAVID MORGAN, entrepreneur; b. Boise, Idaho, Aug. 8, 1947; s. Rolfe Roald and Margaret Rose (Morgan) B.; m. Jan R. Seda, May 17, 1975; children: Hillary Lauren, Benjamin Morgan, Salle Alberta. BS in Mgmt., U. Idaho, 1972. Chpt. cons., then dir. expansion, asst. exec. dir. Kappa Sigma Internat. Fraternity, Charlottesville, Va., 1972-75; propr. Morgan's Exchange, Boise, 1975-79, Strato Lanes, Mountain Home, Idaho, 1979—; concessionaire various recreational concerns, Alaska and Idaho; supr. com. P.F. Credit Union. Chmn. Cen. Dist. Health, Idaho, 1983—; pres. Mountain Home Mil. Affairs Com., 1985—; sec., treas. Silver City Hist. Soc. Mem. Nat. Restaurant and Beverage Assn., Kappa Sigma (dist. pres. 1975—), Elks. Republican. Roman Catholic. Home and Office: PO Box 9 Mountain Home ID 83647-0009

BERGHOLZ, RICHARD CADY, political writer; b. Corvallis, Oreg., Apr. 13, 1917; s. William Orville and Mabel (Cady) B.; m. Elizabeth True Jamison, Feb. 22, 1941; children: Barbara Bergholz Stacy, Richard J., Elizabeth S.J. BA, U. Wash., 1938. Reporter Ventura (Calif.) Star-Free Press, 1938-41, AP, 1941-44; war corr. New Guinea, Philippines, China, Manchuria, 1944-46; reporter Glendale (Calif.) News-Press, 1946-47; polit. editor San Diego Evening Tribune, 1947-54, L.A. Mirror, 1954-62; polit. writer L.A. Times, 1962-83. Bd. dirs. Calif. First Amendment Coalition. Mem. Soc. Profl. Journalists, Pi Kappa Alpha. Home: 929 Crestview Dr Pasadena CA 91107-1950

BERGIN, ALLEN ERIC, clinical psychologist, educator; b. Spokane, Wash., Aug. 4, 1934; s. Bernard F. and Vivian Selma (Kullberg) B.; m. Marian Shafer, June 4, 1955; children: David, Sue, Cyndy, Kathy, Eric, Ben, Patrick, Daniel, Michael. BS, Brigham Young U., 1956, MS, 1957; PhD, Stanford U., 1960. Diplomate Am. Bd. Profl. Psychology. Postdoctoral fellow U. Wis., Madison, 1960-61; prof. psychology and edn. Tchrs. Coll., Columbia U., N.Y.C., 1961-72; prof. psychology Brigham Young U., Provo, Utah, 1972—, dir. Values Inst., 1976-78, dir. clin. psychology, 1989-93; sr. rsch. fellow Nat. Inst. Health Care Rsch., 1992—; assessment officer Peace Corps, Washington, 1961-66; cons. NIMH, Rockville, Md., 1969-75, 90. Co-author: Changing Frontiers in Psychotherapy, 1972; co-editor: Handbook of Psychotherapy, 1971, 4th edit., 1994 (citation classic 1979). Bishop LDS Ch., Emerson, N.J., 1970-72, Provo, 1981-84, stake pres., 1992-95; mem. steering com. Utah Gov.'s Conf. on Families, Salt Lake City, 1979-80. Recipient Biggs-Pine award AACD, 1986, Maeser rsch. award Brigham Young U. Alumni Assn., 1986. Fellow Am. Psychol. Assn. (Disting. Contbn. to Knowledge award 1989, William James award div. 36, 1990); mem. Soc. for Psychotherapy Integration (adv. bd.), Soc. for Sci. Study Religion, Soc. for Psychotherapy Rsch. (pres. 1974-75), Assn. Mormon Counselors (pres. 1979-80). Republican. Office: Brigham Young U 285 Tlrb Provo UT 84602-1052

BERGMAN, ARIEH, gynecologist; b. Feldafing, Germany, Aug. 5, 1947; came to U.S., 1982; s. Samuel and Sara (Passerman) B.; m. Irith Eshicol, July 2, 1973; children: Michal, Jonathan, Yova. MD, Sackler Sch. Medicine, Tel Aviv, 1975. Diplomate Am. Bd. Ob-Gyn. Resident in ob-gyn. Tel Aviv U. Med. Ctr., 1975-81; fellow in gynecol. urology UCLA, Torrance, 1982; asst. prof. gynecology UCLA, 1984-85; assoc. prof. gynecology Sch. Medicine U. So. Calif., L.A., 1989-92, prof. gynecology, 1992—. Assoc. editor: Year Book of Ob-Gyn., 1992—; assoc. editor Internat. Urogynecol., 1992—. Home: 349 S Swall Dr Beverly Hills CA 90211-3611 Office: U So Calif Gynecol Group 5400 Balboa Blvd Ste 220 Encino CA 91316-1529

BERGMAN, ELLEN MARIE, state legislator; b. Lincoln, Nebr., Mar. 19, 1942; d. Ralph Celestine and Barbara Ellen (McGinley) Roach; m. Paul Albert Berman, Nov. 9, 1963; children: Barry, Patrick, Bradley, Christopher. Grad. parochial high sch., Beatrice, Nebr. Hairdresser various shops, Lincoln, 1961-65; checker Henry's Market, Scottsbluff, Nebr., 1974-76; sales clk. J.C. Penney Co., Miles City, Mont., 1977-81; prosthesis technician Home Health Spltys., Miles City, 1990—; mem. Mont. Ho. of Reps., Helena, 1992-93. Reporter Family Issues Forum, Miles City, 1988—; vol. local nursing home and retirement home; vol. reach to recovery Am. Cancer Soc. Republican. Mem. Assembly of God. Home: 1019 S Strevell Ave Miles City MT 59301-4917

BERGMAN, EMILY ANNE, librarian; b. Tulsa, July 24, 1953; d. Arthur L. and Jean Lucy (Anson) B.; m. Mark Andrew Allen, June 20, 1982; children: Philip Isaac Allen, Brian Anson Allen. BA, Goucher Coll., 1975; MLS, U. Tex.-Austin, 1976; student Wroxton Coll., Banbury, Eng., 1974. Research librarian Tracy-Locke Advt., Dallas, 1977-78; cataloger Dallas Pub. Library, 1978-80, head spl. collections, 1980-81; info. specialist, Dallas, 1978-81; asst. library dir. Calif. Sch. Profl. Psychology, Los Angeles, 1981-90; catalog libr. Gene Autry Western Heritage Mus., L.A., 1990-92, head libr., 1992—. Mem. ALA (coms.), Spl. Library Assn., So. Calif. Spl. Library Assn., Calif. Acad. and Research Libraries, Libr. Instruction Round Table (vice treas., 1992-93, treas. 1993-94), Mental Health Librarians (v.p., pres.-elect 1987-88, pres. 1988-89). Democrat. Jewish. Home: 1001 Geneva St Glendale CA 91207-1709 Office: Autry Mus Western Heritage 4700 Western Heritage Way Los Angeles CA 90027-1462

BERGMAN, TERRIE, psychic consultant; b. Phila., Mar. 4, 1942; d. Harry Bernard and Berthe Rose (Simons) Goldberg; m. Clifford Coulston, May 4, 1960 (div. 1967); 1 child, Lori Coulston; m. Joel David Bergman, Dec. 22, 1979. B Metaphys. Sci., D Metaphys. Counseling, U. Metaphysics, 1994. Ordained to metaphys. ministry, 1994. Indsl. trainer, vocat. evaluator, mktg. mgr. Atlantic County Opportunity Ctr. for Handicapped, Atlantic City, N.J., 1971-74; job developer, vocat. evaluator, counselor Narcotics Addicts Rehab. Orgn., Atlantic City, 1974-75; psychic cons. Atlantic City & Las Vegas, 1973—; seminar facilitator on death and dying Las Vegas, 1990—; 1st, 2d, and 3d degree Reiki healer, Atlantic City and Las Vegas, 1984—. Appeared on TV programs, including People Are Talking, Hour Mag., others, 1974—; contbr. articles to mags. and newspapers. Vol. Nathan Adelson Hospice, 1989-94. Named 1 of 83 People to Watch, Atlantic City Mag., 1983; recipient Dynamics of Leadership cert. of achievement Human Factors, Inc., 1981, 82, 86. Mem. Network of Exec. Women in Hospitality. Home and Office: 208 Desert View St Las Vegas NV 89107-2355

BERGMANN, FREDRICK LOUIS, English language educator, theater historian; b. Tecumseh, Kans., Sept. 27, 1916; s. Curt and Minna (Herrmann) B.; m. Jean Marshall, July 6, 1941; children: Juliann, John Fredrick. A.B., Washburn Coll., 1937; M.A., State Coll. Wash., 1939; postgrad., Columbia, 1941; Ph.D., George Washington U., 1953. Asst. Washburn Coll., 1939-40; instr. English DePauw U., 1940-43, asst. prof., 1943-46, assoc. prof., 1946-54, prof., 1954-82, prof. emeritus, 1982—, head dept. English, 1956-78, dir. Conf. Am. Studies, 1956-78, James Whitcomb Riley prof. English lit., 1969-83, also chmn. internat. edn. com. Author: (with R.W. Pence) Writing Craftsmanship, 1956, Paragraph Rhetoric, 1967, Sentence Rhetoric, 1969, Essays: Method, Content, Conscience, 1970, Essays 2, 1975, (with H.W. Pedicord) The Plays of David Garrick, 7 vols, 1979-82; contbr. articles to profl. jours. Founder Greencastle Summer Theater, 1962; pres. English dept. chmn. Gt. Lakes Colls. Assn., 1968-69. Fellow Folger Shakespeare Library, 1951; fellow Grad. Council George Washington U. Mem. Ind. Coll. English Assn. (pres. 1956, 63), MLA, Am. Soc. 18th Century Studies, Societe francaise d'Etude du XVIIe Siecle, Johnson Soc. of Central Region, Am. English-Speaking Union, Sigma Delta Chi (Leather Medal award for greatest service to DePauw U. 1962), Delta Chi. Episcopalian. Home: 9823 W Taro Ln Peoria AZ 85382-2689

BERGMANN, MICHAEL DEAN, financial services company executive; b. St. Paul, Feb. 7, 1944; s. Edmund Karl and Karolyn Edna (Moyer) B.; m. Alma Jean Fleck, Sept. 9, 1967; children: Nathan, Kelley. BS magna cum laude, U. Minn., 1966; MS, Stanford U., 1969, PhD, 1970. Group mgr. Irwin Mgmt. Co., Columbus, Ind., 1970-72; cons. coord. Shearson, Hayden Stone, Beverly Hills, Calif., 1972-76; sr. exec. v.p. Asset Mgmt. Group, Denver, 1976—. Author: Expectations, Inflation and the Term Structure of Interest Rates, 1970. McCarthy fellow Stanford U., 1967. Mem. Am. Econ. Assn., Am. Fin. Assn., Nat. Assn. Bus. Econs., Phi Beta Kappa. Home: 5200 Lakeshore Dr Bow Mar CO 80123-1540 Office: Asset Mgmt Group # 500 N 6312 S Fiddlers Green Cir Englewood CO 80111-4943

BERGRUN, NORMAN RILEY, aerospace executive; b. Green Camp, Ohio, Aug. 4, 1921; s. Theodore and Naomi Ruth (Stemm) B.; m. Claire Michaelson, May 23, 1943; children: Clark, Jay, Joan. BSME, Cornell U., 1943; LLB, LaSalle U. Ext., 1955; DSc, World U., 1983. Registered profl. mech. engr. Thermodynamicist Douglas Aircraft Co., El Segundo, Calif., 1943-44; rsch. scientist NACA Ames Rsch. Lab., Mt. View, Calif., 1944-56; mgr. analysis Lockheed Missile & Space Co., Sunnyvale, Calif., 1956-67, staff scientist, 1967-69; dir. mgmt. systems Nielsen Engring. and Rsch., Mt. View, 1969-71; CEO, scientist Bergrun Rsch. and Engring., Los Altos, Calif., 1971—; advisor to bd. NSPE Edn. Found., Sacramento, Calif., 1985-92. Author: Ringmakers of Saturn, 1986, Tomorrow's Technology Today, 1972; photographer including The Sir Francis Drake Collection, 1990; contbr. more than 80 articles and reports to profl. jours. Incorporator Aurora Singers Found., Palo Alto, Calif., 1989. Chief USN, 1944-46. Named Man of Yr., Am. Biog. Assn.; recipient Archimedes award, 1988, Cert. of Appreciation, Eglin AFB, 1961. Assoc. fellow AIAA (sr. judge 7th and 8th Grade Essay Contest, Bay Area, Calif., 1992, 93, chair comm. sub-com.1992—); mem. NSPE Edn. Found. (Engr. of Yr., CEO 1985-86, Appreciation award 1986), Profl. Engrs. Soc. (pres. 1988-89, Integrity award 1989), L'Academie Europeene (speaker 1987). Office: Bergrun Rsch and Engring 26865 Saint Francis Rd Los Altos CA 94022-1910

BERK, GAIL ANDREA, lawyer, property manager; b. Chgo., Apr. 24, 1948; d. Benjamin and Rena (Srole) Burstyn; m. Glenn Harold Berk, Sept. 8, 1968; children: Casie Lynn, Jenni Rose. BA, Calif. State Coll., L.A., 1969; JD, U. West L.A., 1982. Bar: Calif. 1983; cert. tchr. (life.). Property mgr. Malibu, Calif., 1969-94; tchr. L.A., 1971-72, atty., 1983—; owner Nannie Employment Agy., Pacific Palisades, Calif., 1985-89. Co-author series 9 children's books. Home and Office: 146 Manzanita St Ashland OR 97520-2617

BERKE, GERALD SPENCER, surgeon; b. L.A., Jan. 8, 1950. BS, U. So. Calif., 1973, MD, 1978. Diplomate Nat. Bd. Med. Examiners, Am. Bd. Otolaryngologists. Resident in surgery Los Angeles County/U. So. Calif. Gen. Hosp., 1978-79; resident in surgery UCLA, 1979-80, resident in otolaryngology, 1980-84, assoc. prof. surgery, 1984-93, acting chief divsn. head and neck surgery, 1991, chief divsn. head and neck surgery, 1992—, prof. surgery, 1993—; chief otolaryngology sect. VA Wadsworth Med. Ctr., L.A., 1984-91; ad hoc reviewer NIH/NIDCD RFA Ctrs. of Excellence grants, 1993; imaging cons. Bruel & Kjaer Electronics. Editl. cons. Jour. Speech and Hearing, Laryngoscope, Head and Neck Surgery; editl. bd. Jour. of Voice; contbr. articles to profl. jours., chpts. to books. Fellow ACS (moderator 1993); mem. Triological Soc. (1st place residency rsch. award middle sect. 1994, Shirley Baron award Western sect. 1994), Am. Laryngol. Assn. (Award for Rsch. 1990, 94), Am. Rhinological Soc., Am. Acad. Otolaryngology, Head and Neck Surgery. Office: UCLA Sch Medicine Divsn Head and Neck 10833 Le Conte Ave Los Angeles CA 90024

BERKE, JUDIE, publisher, editor; b. Mpls., Apr. 15, 1938; d. Maurice M. and Sue (Supak) Kleyman; student U. Minn., 1956-60, Mpls. Sch. Art, 1945-59. Free lance illustrator and designer, 1959—; pres. Berke-Wood, Inc., N.Y.C., 1971-80, Manhattan Rainbow & Lollipop Co. subs. Berke-Wood, Inc., 1971-80; pres. Get Your Act Together, club act staging, N.Y.C., 1971-80; pres. Coordinator Pubs.,Inc., 1982-87; pres., chief exec. officer, Health Market Communications, 1987—; pres. Pub. and Media Services, Burbank, 1987—; pub., editor Continuing Care Coordinator, Health Watch mags.; pres. Continuing Care Coordinator Convs. and Seminars; pres. Rainbow and Lillipop Prodns., 1994—; cons. to film and ednl. cos.; guest lectr. various colls. and univs. in Calif. and N.Y., 1973—; cons., designer Healthy Lifestyles mag.; writer, illustrator, dir. numerous ednl. filmstrips, 1972—, latest being Focus on Professions, 1974, Focus on the Performing Arts, 1974, Focus on the Creative Arts, 1974, Workstyles, 1976, Wonderworm, 1976, Supernut, 1977; author, illustrator film Fat Black Mack (San Francisco Ednl. Film Festival award, part of permanent collection Mus. Modern Art, N.Y.C.), 1970; designer posters and brochures for various entertainment groups, 1963—; composer numerous songs, latest being Time is Relative, 1976, Love Will Live On in My Mind, 1976, My Blue Walk, 1976, You Make Me a Baby, 1982, Let's Go Around Once More, 1983, Anytime Anyplace Anywhere, 1987, Bittersweet, 1987, Sometimes It Pays, 1987, Gimme Back My Money Blues, Everybody Wants Me But the One I Love, Skin to Skin, It's Your Turn to Sing the Blues, Deny Till You Die, Men Just Call It Woman Talk, Poor Me, Women's Work is Never Done, 1993; composer/author off-Broadway musical Street Corner Time, 1978; producer: The Real Estate TV Shows 1988-89; contbr. children's short stories to various publs., also articles. Trustee The Happy Spot Sch., N.Y.C., 1972-75. Mem. Nat. Fedn. Bus. and Profl. Women, NAFE, Am. Acad. Polit. and Social Sci., Women in Animation.

BERKES, HOWARD, radio news reporter; b. Phila., Jan. 29, 1954; s. Milton and Ethel (Weintraub) B.; m. Wanda Gayle Heesch, May 22, 1985. Student, Temple U., 1971, Lane Community Coll., Eugene, Oreg., 1979, 80. Newscaster, reporter sta.-KLCC, Eugene, Oreg., 1979-80; ind. reporter, producer Eugene, Oreg., 1980; contract reporter Nat. Pub. Radio, Salt Lake City, 1981-82, staff reporter, 1982—; tng. cons. Nat. Pub. Radio, Washington, 1982, Alaska Pub. Radio, Anchorage, 1984; reporter 1984 Summer Olympic Games; tng. cons. Nat. Radio News Workshops, Alaska Pub. Radio, 1986-92, Toucan Prodns. Workshops, 1986-87; reporter Shuttle Launch Decision, 1986; cons., editor Mont. Humanities Com., Missoula, 1982-87; mem. guest faculty Poynter Inst., 1992, 93. Reporter, co-producer radio documentary, Delta, 1981 (Cindy award 1982). Recipient Cindy award, 1985, Champion-Tuck award for econ. reporting, 1986, Nat. Broadcasting award Nat. Assn. Sci. Writers, 1986, Sci. Journalism award AAAS, 1986, Maj. Armstrong award Armstrong Meml. Rsch. Found., Columbia U., 1987, award of excellence Aviation and Space Writers Writers Assn., 1989, Robert F. Kennedy Journalism award, 1992, Clarion award, 1992, Nat. Psychol. award APA, 1992, Ohio State award, 1993. Mem. Soc. Profl. Journalists (Nat. Radio Reporting award 1984). Home: 1565 Garfield Ave Salt Lake City UT 84105-3808 Office: Nat Pub Radio PO Box 52-6284 Salt Lake City UT 84152-6284

BERKHEMER-CREDAIRE, BETSY, public relations executive; b. Washington, Jan. 31, 1947; d. Robert Walter and Claire (Myers) Berkhemer; m. Criston Credaire, Mar. 23, 1985. B.S. in History, UCLA, 1968. Reporter Ventura (Calif.) Star Free Press, 1965-68; editor Gardena (Calif.) Valley News, 1968-70; writer Sta. KTTV Metromedia News, Los Angeles, 1970-71; publicist Disney Studios, NBC, Burbank, Calif., 1971-73; pres., owner Berkhemer & Kline Inc., Pub. Rels., Los Angeles, 1973-88; pres. Berkhemer, Kline, Golin, Harris Communications, 1988-93, exec. v.p. western region bus. devel., 1993—. Chmn. bd. dirs. March of Dimes So. Calif., Alliance Bus. for Childcare Devel., L.A. Edn. Ptnrship. Mem. UCLA Alumni Assn. (chmn. bd. dirs.). Office: Berkhemer Kline Golin/Harris One Bunker Hill 601 W 5th St Fl 4 Los Angeles CA 90071-2004

BERKICH, JOHN, city manager; b. Johnstown, Pa., Jan. 21, 1948; s. Nicholas and Ann B.; m. Jamie Mae Jeffries, May 20, 1974 (div. Aug. 2, 1976); m. Angela Marie, June 11, 1978; children: Michael, Garret, Ryan. BA, Elmhurst Coll., 1971; MBA, Golden Gate U., 1986. Cert. mgmt. acct. Cost acctg. supr. Western Elec. Co., Chgo., 1967-76; systems analyst supr. Wickes Corp., Wheeling, Ill., 1976-79; controller, data processing mgr. Frontier Enterprises, Carson City, Nev., 1979-83; audit divsn. mgr. Pub. Svc. Commn., Carson City, Nev., 1983-90; city mgr. City of Carson City, 1990—; cons. in field; coll. instr. Western Nev. C.C., Carson City, 1987-90. Recipient Disting. Svc. award No. Nev. Devel. Authority, 1992, Appreciation award U. Nev. Coop. Ext., 1993, Feed the Hungry award Friends in Svc. Helping, 1993. Mem. Internat. City Mgrs. Assn., Nat. Acctg. Assn., Am. Acctg. Assn., Inst. Mgmt. Accts., Rotary Club (Carson City). Republican. Methodist. Office: City of Carson City 2621 Northgate Ln Ste 2 Carson City NV 89706-1619

BERKLAND, JAMES OMER, geologist; b. Glendale, Calif., July 31, 1930; s. Joseph Omer and Gertrude Madelyn (Thompson) B. m. Janice Lark Keirstead, Dec. 19, 1966; children: Krista Lynn, Jay Olin. AA, Santa Rosa Jr. Coll., 1951; AB, U. Calif., Berkeley, 1958; MS, San Jose State U., 1964; postgrad., U. Calif., Davis, 1969-72. Rgistered geologist, Calif.; cert. engring. geologist, Calif. With U.S. Geol. Survey, 1958-64; engring. geologist U.S. Bur. Reclamation, 1964-69, cons. geologist, 1969-72; asst. prof. Appalachian State U., Boone, N.C., 1972-73; county geologist Santa Clara County, San Jose, Calif., 1973-94; ret., 1994; mem. geotech. adv. com. San Jose State U., 1973-75, adj. prof., 1975-76, lectr. Gen. Edn. Conf., Sci. and Tech. Soc., 1985-89, coord. com. Calif. Conv., 1978; mem. evening faculty San Jose City Coll.; mem. West Valley Legis. Com., 1979-90; lectr. ann. deposit receipt seminar San Jose Real Estate Bd., 1980-85; discoverer in field; featured spkr. Keynote Speakers, Inc. Contbr. to numerous articles to profl. jours.; originator seismic window theory for earthquake prediction, 1974; numerous TV and radio appearances including PBA, Frontline, Evening Mag., People are Talking, 48 Hours, Sightings, You Bet Your Life, Science Faction, Science Fiction Cable, Two on the Town, CNN News, WGN, KIRO, KSL, KIEV, KGO, KCBS, KNYV, KOA, Two at Noon, weekly interview show on Sta. KPFA-FM Radio, The Other Side, Northwest Afternoon, Town Meeting, Ron Owens Schow, Laura Lee Show; articles on work featured in OMNI, STERN, Wall Street Jour., Bergen's Tidende, San Francisco Examiner, San Francisco Chronicle, L.A. Times, Nat. Geographic, Am. Health, The Astrology Encyclopedia, others; pub. newsletter SYZYGY; co-founder Quakeline. Treas. Creekside/Park Place Homeowners Group; v.p. West Coast Aquatics, Creekside/Park Place Swim Team; mem. various city and county adv. bds.; mem. Ctr. for Study Early Man, East Valley YMCA, legis. com. West Valley, 1980—, Route 85 Task Force, Earthquake Watch, 1979-82, New Weather Observer; mem. Found. for the Study of Cycles, invited lectr. monthly and ann. meeting. Fellow Geol. Soc. Am. (abstract rev. com. 1977-78); mem. AARP, AAAS, Assn. Engring. Geologists (past vice chmn. San Francisco sect.), Seismol. Soc. Am., Chapparral Poets, Sierra Club, Santa Clara County Engrs. & Architects Assn. (v.p., 1st Disting mem. award 1987), Mining Lamp, Citizens and Scientists Concerned About Damage to Environment, San Jose Hist. Mus. Assn., Western Coun. Engrs., Internat. Platform Assn., Nat. Jogging Assn., Nat. Geog. Soc., Calif. State Employees Assn., Calif. State Firemen's Assn., Youth Sci. Inst. Peninsula Geol. Soc. (past treas.), Earthquake Engring. Rsch. Inst., Saber Soc. (co-founder, past pres., Spl. plaque award 1978), Bay Area Reviewing Geologists Assn., Time Rsch. Inst., Sons of Norway, Lions Club (charter, 1st v.p. 1986-87, pres. 1987-88, chmn. pub. rels. dist. 4C-6 1987-88, fellow Melvin Jones Found., newsletter editor 1984-88, sec. 1988-89, bd. dirs. 1989-90, zone chmn. 1991-92, dir. Western Lions Ear Found. 1991—, trustee Student Speaker Found. 1990-92, student speaker contest dist. chmn., 1990-91, chmn. bulletin contest 1988-90, A.J. Robinson Found., Lion's Eye Found., Student Speaker Found., Dist. Gov's. Appreciation award 1988, 91, 100% Pres. award, King of Clubs Lions 1988, Fred W. Smith Found. 1991, Ear of the Lion Found., Harry J. Aslan fellow 1989, Dwight E. Stanford fellow 1992, Bequest Club, Student Speaker Found., life mem. Lions Blind Ctr. San Jose 1994, Club Lion of Yr. award 1991-92, 93-94), Sierra Club, Sigma Xi. Democrat. Home: 14927 E Hills Dr San Jose CA 95127-2536

BERKLEY, JAMES DONALD, clergyman; b. Yakima, Wash., May 19, 1950; s. Donald William and Erma Ercile (Van Meter) B.; m. Deborah Milam, Aug. 18, 1974; children: Peter James, Mary Milam. BS, U. Wash., 1972; MDiv, Fuller Theol. Seminary, 1975, D Ministry, 1980. Intern First Presbyn. Ch., Yakima, Wash., 1971-73, Bel Air Presbyn. Ch., L.A., 1973-75; asst. pastor Community Presbyn Ch., Ventura, Calif., 1975-78; sr. pastor Dixon (Calif.) Community Ch., 1978-85; sr. assoc. editor Leadership jour. Christianity Today Inc., Carol Stream, Ill., 1985-90, editor Your Church, 1990-94; sr. assoc. pastor First Presbyn. Ch., Bellevue, Wash., 1994—. Author: Making the Most of Mistakes, 1987, Called into Crisis, 1988; gen. editor: Preaching to Convince, 1986, Leadership Handbooks of Practical Theology, Vol. I, 1992, Vols. II and III, 1994. Recipient 1st place award interview Evangelical Press Assn., 1991, 92. Republican. Home: 304 128th Ave NE Bellevue WA 98005 Office: First Presbyn Ch 1717 Bellevue Way NE Bellevue WA 98004

BERKLEY, ROBERT JOHN, federal agency professional; b. Albion, Mich., Oct. 2, 1933; s. Paul Clifford and Ina Muriel (Burroughs) B.; m. Sharon Irene Haynes, Sept. 9, 1955 (div. 1965); children: Thomas Alan, Richard Jon, Luann Michele; m. Jacquelyn Jane (Lewis) Ballou, Jan. 14, 1966. AA, Jackson (Mich.) Jr. Coll., 1953; BS in Police Adminstrn., Calif. State U., L.A., 1962. Police officer City of Claremont, Calif., 1959-62, 63-66; investigator U.S. Civil Svc. Commn., Washington and L.A., 1962-63, 66-72; spl. agt. FAA, Seattle, 1972—, office mgr., 1973—. Local chmn. Selective Svc. Bd., Wash., 1981—. Sgt. USMC, 1953-56, Korea. Mem. SAR (chpt. pres. 1989-90, state sec. 1989-91, state pres. 1992, Patriots medal 1990, Law Enforcement medal 1991, 92), Am. Legion, Eastern Star (patron 1989-90), Masons (master 1984, life), Scottish Rite, Shriners. Home: 4403 192d Pl SE Issaquah WA 98027-9708 Office: FAA SEA-CASFO 1601 Lind Ave SW Rm 230 Renton WA 98055-4056

BERKLEY, STEPHEN MARK, computer peripherals manufacturing company executive; b. N.J., 1944; s. Irving S. and Goldie A. Berkley; student London Sch. Econs., 1964-65; BA in Econs., Colgate U., 1966; MBA, Harvard U., 1968; children: David, Michael.Mgmt. cons. Boston Cons. Group, 1968, 71-73; mgr. strategic planning Potlatch Corp., 1973-77; v.p. bus. devel. Qume Corp. subs. ITT, Hayward, Calif., 1977-80, v.p., gen. mgr. memory products div., 1980-81; v.p. mktg. Quantum Corp., Milpitas, Calif., 1981-83, chmn., CEO, 1987-92, chmn., 1992-93; chmn., CEO Coactive Computing Corp., 1993-94; pres. Plus Devel. Corp. (Quantum subs.), 1983-87, chmn., CEO, 1987-92; pres., The Rosewood Found.; bd. dirs. Quantum Corp., Edify Corp., Coactive Computing Corp.; instr. bus. and econs. E. Carolina U., 1969-71. Served to lt. USNR, 1968-71. Mem. Corp. Planners Assn. (dir.), Harvard Bus. Sch. Club No. Calif., Phi Beta Kappa. Office: Quantum Corp 500 Mccarthy Blvd Milpitas CA 95035-7908

BERKMAN, SUSAN C. JOSEPHS, association executive; b. L.A., Apr. 17, 1953; d. Fred and Alice Hodes Josephs; m. Donald W. Berkman Jr., Aug. 10, 1974; 1 child, Daniel. BA, U. Calif., Irvine, 1974; MA, UCLA, 1977, Calif. State U., Los Angeles, 1988. Cert. adult edn. tchr. Specialist personnel mgmt. U.S. Civil Svc. Commn., Washington, 1974-75; teaching asst. UCLA, 1976-77; rsch. editor Regensteiner Press, Sherman Oaks, Calif., 1977; dir. music Braille Inst., L.A., 1978-82, asst. dir. student tng., 1982-87, dir. spl. projects, 1987-89, dir. bus. svcs., 1989-91; instr. Coll. of the Desert, Rancho Mirage, Calif., 1991—; exec. dir. Sr. and Disabled Citizens Coalition, 1992—. Author: Teaching Music to the Blind, 1980, Teaching Music to the Visually Handicapped, 1982; (ednl. program) Just Like Me, 1983. Mem. Hermosa Beach (Calif.) Coordinating Coun., 1986; bd. dirs. Community Family Guidance Clinic, Cerritos, Calif., 1987-91. Travel grantee, UCLA, 1977. Calif. State scholar, 1970-73, William S. Schwartz Meml. scholar, 1974. Mem. AAUW, Assn. for Edn. and Rehab. of the Blind and Visually Impaired (v.p. so. Calif. chpt. 1987-88, pres. 1988-91), Calif. Transcribers and Educators of the Blind and Visually Impaired, Soroptimist Internat., Kappa Delta Pi, Phi Kappa Phi. Baha'i. Home and Office: 43621 Vanda Cir Palm Desert CA 92260-2651

BERKUS, DAVID WILLIAM, venture capitalist; b. Los Angeles, Mar. 23, 1941; s. Harry Jay and Clara S. (Widess) B.; m. Kathleen McGuire, Aug. 6, 1966; children: Eric, Matthew, Amy. BA, Occidental Coll., 1962. Pres. Custom Fidelity Inc., Hollywood, Calif., 1958-74, Berkus Compusystems Inc., Los Angeles, 1974-81; pres., chief exec. officer Computerized Lodging Systems Inc. and subs., Los Angeles, 1981-93; pres. Berkus Tech. Ventures, venture capital, L.A., 1993—. Author: Better Than Money, 1994; author software Hotel Compusystem, 1979; creator 1st artificial intelligence-based yield mgmt. sys., 1987. Chmn. bd. Boy Scouts Am., San Gabriel Valley, 1986, v.p. area IV, 1993-94, pres. 1995—. Lt. USNR, 1963-72. Recipient Dist. award of merit Boy Scouts Am., 1986, INC. mag. 500 award, 1986, Silver Beaver award Boy Scouts Am., 1988. Mem. Am. Hotel-Motel Assn., Audio Engring. Soc. (chmn. Los Angeles sect. 1973-74). Office: 1430 Glencoe Dr Arcadia CA 91006-1909

BERLAK, HAROLD, writer, educator, consultant; b. Cambridge, Mass., July 31, 1932; s. William and Dora Berlak; m. Ann Carol Abramson, Sept. 23, 1962; children: Mariam, Rachel, Lev. BA, Boston U., 1954; AMT, Harvard U., 1956, EdD, 1963. Cert. secondary tchr., Mass. Tchr. social studies Wenham (Mass.) Schs., 1957-59; tchr. social studies Concord (Mass.) Pub. Schs., 1959-63, supr., 1962-63; asst. prof. U. Calif., Santa Barbara, 1963-64; prof. Wash. U., St. Louis, Mo., 1964-92; freelance writer, consultant Oakland, Calif., 1992-94; co-dir. Wash. U. Social Studies project, St. Louis, 1965-74; dir. Met. St. Louis Social Studies Ctr., St. Louis, 1965-75. Author: People, Choices, Decisions, 19785, Diplemmas of Schooling, 1982; author, editor: Democracy, Pluralism, and Social Studies, 1968, Toward New Science of Educational Testing and Measurement, 1992; bd. editors Havard Edn. Rev., 1961-62. Organizer, sec. Dem. Schs. Network, 1982-86. With U.S. Army, 1954-56. Home and Office: 1127 Wellington St Oakland CA 94602

BERLAND, KAREN INA, psychologist; b. N.Y.C., Nov. 14, 1947; d. Max and Lillian (Graf) B. BA in Psychology, SUNY, Buffalo, 1969; MEd in Ednl. Psychology, U. Ill., 1971; D. Psychology, U. Denver, 1984. Cert. sch. psychologist, clin. psychologist. Sch. psychologist City Sch. Dist. Rochester (N.Y.), 1971-73, Denver Pub. Sch., 1973—; psychology intern Vets. Hosp., West Haven, Conn., 1983-84; psychologist Aurora (Colo.) Community Mental Health Ctr., 1985-92; expert witness Denver County Ct. Mem. APA, Colo. Soc. Sch. Psychologists (pres. 1986-87, Leadership award 1987), Colo. Psychol. Assn. (fin. com., treas.), Colo. Women's Psychologists, Nat. Assn. Sch. Psychologists (Western Regional dir. and Colo. rep. 1976-83), Assn. for Advancement of Behavior Therapy, Mensa. Democrat. Jewish. Home: 1171 Forest St Denver CO 80220-4450

BERMAN, ARTHUR MALCOLM, newspaper editor; b. N.Y.C., Aug. 16, 1935; s. Jack Abraham and Pearl Sarah (Sann) B.; m. Elaine Ruth Kreiner, Sept. 22, 1956; children—Arthur Michael, Tonia Jean, Daniel Adlai. B.A., Antioch Coll., 1957. Reporter Daily News and Sun, Springfield, Ohio, 1957-59; reporter Star News, Pasadena, Calif., 1959-60, Mirror News, Los Angeles, 1960-61; reporter Los Angeles Times, 1962-69, asst. met. editor, 1970-77, suburban editor, 1978-82, View editor, 1983-87, asst. nat. editor, 1987-91, asst. Calendar editor, 1992—. Co-recipient Pulitzer Prize, 1966; Pulitzer Gold Medal, 1969, Best Local News Story award Greater Los Angeles Press Club, 1961, 64, 65, 67. Office: Los Angeles Times Times Mirror Sq Los Angeles CA 90012

BERMAN, DAVID ROBERT, political scientist, educator; b. Belvidere, Ill., June 11, 1939; s. Barney R. and Frances M. (Hughes) B.; m. Susan Landes, July 19, 1942; 1 child, Wendy E. BA, Rockford Coll., 1961; MA, Am. U., 1963, PhD in Govt., 1968. Lectr. Am. U., Washington, 1962-64; rschr. Am. Law div. Legis. Reference Svc. Libr. of Congress, also Dem. Nat. Com., Washington, 1962-64; rsch. assoc. Nat. League of Cities, Washington, 1964-66; acting dir. Inst. Pub. Adminstrn. Ariz. State U., Tempe, 1966-67, asst. dir. Inst. Pub. Adminstrn., 1966-69, asst. prof. polit. sci., 1966-72, assoc. prof., 1973-80, prof., 1981—. Contbr. numerous articles to profl. jours. Bd. dirs. Ariz. Consumers Coun., 1970-79; bd. dirs., pres. S.W. Assn. Housing Coops. Grantee Ariz. State U., NEH, Dept. of Justice, others. Mem. AAUP. Am. Acad. Polit. Sci., Am. Polit. Sci. Assn., Am. Soc. for Pub. Adminstrn., Ariz. Soc. for Pub. Adminstrn. (sec. and pres. 1970-71, bd. dirs. 1966-72), Midwestern Polit. Sci Assn., Nat. Civic League, Social Sci. History Assn., S.W. Social Sci. Assn., So. Polit. Sci. Assn., Acad. Polit. Sci., Textbook authors Assn., We. Polit. Sci. Assn., We. Social Sci. Assn. Home: 1619 E Del Rio Dr Tempe AZ 85282-2748 Office: Ariz State U Dept Polit Sci Tempe AZ 85287

BERMAN, HOWARD LAWRENCE, congressman; b. L.A., Apr. 15, 1941; s. Joseph M. and Eleanor (Schapiro) B.; m. Janis Berman, 1979; children: Brinley Ann, Lindsey Rose. BA, UCLA, 1962, LLB, 1965. Bar: Calif. 1966. Vol. VISTA, Balt., San Francisco, 1966-67; assoc. Levy, Van Bourg & Hackler, L.A., 1967-72; mem. Calif. State Assembly from 43d dist., 1972-82 (majority leader), 98th-104th Congresses from 26th Calif. dist.; adminstrv. law and gov. rels. subcom. 98th-103rd Congresses from 26th Calif. dist.; fresman rep. steering and policy com., 1983, mem. judiciary com., internat. law, immigration and refugees, intellectual property and jud. adminstrn., mem. internat. rels. subcom., ranking mem. Asia and Pacific, internat. ops. Pres. Calif. Fedn. Young Democrats, 1967-69 (budget com.); mem. adv. bd. Jewish Fund for Justice, Valley Internat. Trade Assn. Office: US Ho of Reps Rm 2231 Rayburn House Office Bldg Washington DC 20515*

BERMAN, MORRIS, historian, author; b. Rochester, N.Y., Aug. 3, 1944; s. Harry and Libbie Berman. BA, Cornell U., 1966; PhD, Johns Hopkins U., 1971. Asst. prof. Rutgers U., New Brunswick, N.J., 1970-75, Concordia U., Montreal, Que., 1980-82; Lansdowne professorship U. Victoria, B.C., 1982-88; free-lance writer, 1988—; vis. prof. Seattle U., 1990, Evergreen State Coll., Olympia, Wash., 1991, U. Kassel, Germany, 1991-92; Amy Freeman Lee chair in humanities Incarnate Word Coll., San Antonio, 1993, Garrey Carruthers chair in honors U. N.Mex., 1994-95. Author: Social Change and Scientific Organization, 1978, The Reenchantment of the World, 1981, Coming to Our Senses, 1989. Recipient Gov.'s Writers award Wash. State, Olympia, 1990, Rolla May Ctr. grant Rollo May Ctr., San Francisco, 1992. Mem. Am. Hist. Assn., Am. Anthropol. Assn. Democrat. Jewish. Home: 8015 Greenwood Ave N 305 Seattle WA 98103

BERMAN, MYLES LEE, lawyer; b. Chgo., July 11, 1954; s. Jordan and Eunice (Berg) B.; m. Mitra Moghimi, Dec. 19, 1981; children: Elizabeth, Calvin. BA, U. Ill., 1976; JD, Chgo. Kent Coll. of Law, 1979. Bar: Ill. 1980, Calif. 1987, U.S. Dist. Ct. (no. dist.) Ill. 1980, U.S. Dist. Ct. (cen. dist.) Calif. 1988, U.S. Supreme Ct. 1992. Asst. state's atty. Cook County State's Atty.'s Office, Chgo., 1980-82; pvt. practice law offices of Myles L. Berman, Chgo., 1982-91, L.A., 1988—; traffic ct. judge pro tem adminstr. Beverly Hills Mcpl. Ct., 1991—, Culver Mcpl. Ct., 1992—; probation monitor State Bar of Calif., 1992—. Editor: Century City Lawyer. Mem. ABA, Santa

Monica Bar Assn., L.A. County Bar Assn., Calif. Attys. for Criminal Justice, Nat. Assn. Criminal Def. Lawyers, Beverly Hills Bar Assn., Century City Bar Assn. (chmn. criminal law sect. 1989—, bd. govs. 1991—, Outstanding Svc. award Criminal Law Sect. 1990, 93, 94, spl. recognition 1994, treas. 1994, sec. 1995), Criminal Cts. Bar Assn. Office: 19255 W Sunset Blvd Ste 720 Los Angeles CA 90069-3304 also: 4630 Campus Dr # 200 Newport Beach CA 92660 also: 100 E Thousand Oaks Blvd # 259 Thousand Oaks CA 91360

BERMAN, SANFORD SOLOMON, motion picture sound designer, composer, arranger, artist; b. Long Branch, N.J., Nov. 14, 1951; s. Jerome Sidney and Marion (Solomon) B. BFA, Phila. Coll. Art, 1974. Freelance sound designer, record prodr./arranger, musician/composer. Sound designer, supr. (features) Wings of Courage, Bad Girls, Tombstone, Striking Distance Aladdin (Golden Reel winner, FX Editl., Oscar nomination), Love Field, Unlawful Entry, J.F.K. (FX Editl., Brit. Acad. award, Golden Reel nominee), Hot Shots!, Back to the Future (The Ride), Revenge (Golden Reel nominee), Immediate Family, Oliver & Company (Golden Reel winner), The Princess Bride (Golden Reel nominee), The Seventh Sign (Golden Reel nominee), da, Big Bad John, Going Under Cover, Mac & Me, Weeds, Jaws III, Cloak & Dagger, The Stone Boy, Wolfen, Strange Invaders, That Championship Season, The Sword & The Sorcerer, History of the World Part I, Miss Lonelyhearts, Ten to Midnight, The House on Sorority Row, Evilspeak, Q, Summerspell, Suburbia, Roar, Sweet Sixteen, The Fatal Game, Radioactive Dreams, The Glory of Khan, (short subjects) A Hard Rain, Ballet Robotique (Oscar nomination), The Wizard of Change, The Quest, A Trip to Tomorrow, Bird & The Robot, The Water Engine, Lean Machine, Wind Tunnel, Environmental Effects, New Magic, The Collector, Niagara, Lets Go!, Tour of the Universe, Runaway Train, Zargon, Deep Water Rescue, Rollercoaster, Monte Carlo Race, Alpine Highway, Toyota, Chevrolet, Jet Helicopter, Call from Space; creator comic effects Eat It (Grammy nomination), Like a Surgeon (Grammy nomination), New Duck (Grammy nomination); prodr., arranger, keyboardist Secret Smiles; composer (feature film scores) Screamers, Cataclysm, (comms.) Toyota, 1986, Celica, 1986; appeared with Bruce Springsteen, Steel, Hall & Oates, Chuck Berry, Dwayne Eddy, Jr. Walker & The All-Stars, others. Mem. ACLU, So. Calif., 1985—, People for the Am. Way, So. Calif., 1985—, Am. Jewish Congress, 1982—. Recipient Brit. Acad. award Brit. Acad. of Film and TV Arts, Gt. Britain, 1992. Mem. Motion Picture Sound Editors (pres. 1992—, Golden Reel award 1988, 92), Acad. of Motion Picture Arts and Scis., Nat. Acad. Recording Arts and Scis., Am. Soc. Music Arrangers and Composers, Motion Picture Editors Guild. Democrat.

BERMAN, SAUL JAY, strategic consultant; b. Phila., Jan. 1, 1946; s. Sherwood and Leona (Habelson) B.; m. S. Jann Gillen, June 6, 1980; 1 child, Ashley Scott. BS in Econs., U. Pa., 1967; MBA, Columbia U., 1969, PhD, 1973. Asst. prof. U. So. Calif., L.A., 1972-77; divisional v.p. Broadway Dept. Stores, L.A., 1977-82; case leader Boston Consulting Group, L.A., 1982-86; mng. ptnr. Price Waterhouse Strategic Change Group, 1986—; active Internat. Planning Forum, 1986—. Bd. dirs. Love is Feeding Everyone, L.A., 1988-89; mem. L.A. County Beach Commn., 1978-80, Planning Forum, L.A., 1987—, Town Hall, L.A., 1987—. Mem. U. Pa. Alumni Club (bd. dirs. 1986-88, So. Calif. assoc. alumni trustee 1990—), Columbia Bus. Sch. Club of So. Calif. (bd. dirs. 1992—). Office: Price Waterhouse 1880 Century Park E Fl 16 Los Angeles CA 90067-1600

BERMAN-BARRETT, SARA JANE, lawyer, educator; b. New Britain, Conn., Mar. 8, 1964; m. David K. Barrett. BA, U. Calif., Santa Barbara, 1986; JD, UCLA, 1989. Bar: Calif. 1989, U.S. Dist. Ct. (ctrl. dist.) Calif. 1990, U.S. Ct. Appeals (9th cir.) Calif. 1990. Assoc. Danning, Gill, Gould, Diamond & Spector, L.A., 1989-91; exec. dir., founder Performance Test Rev., L.A., 1991-94; legal cons. Nat. Ctr. Preventive Law, Denver, 1992—; adj. prof. law BarPassers, Santa Monica, Calif., 1994—. Co-author: Represent Yourself in Court: How to Prepare and Try a Winning Case, 1993. Office: PO Box 959 Redondo Beach CA 90277-0959

BERMINGHAM, RICHARD P., restaurant and food products company executive; b. Glen Ridge, N.J., Apr. 24, 1939. Student, U. Colo. With Arthur Andersen & Co., 1962-67; v.p., sec. fin. Collins Foods Internat., Los Angeles, 1967-73, v.p., sec., gen. mgr. Collins Food Service div., 1973-81, pres., chief operating officer, 1981-86, chief exec. officer, 1987—. Office: Collins Foods Internat Inc PO Box 92092 Los Angeles CA 90009-2092

BERNAL, HARRIET JEAN DANIELS, real estate salesperson; b. Cin., Sept. 28, 1931; d. Ernest Richard and Amy Lillian (Jeffries) Daniels; m. Gil Bernal, July 9, 1950; children: Gil Jr., Lisa, Nicholas, Colette, Michelle. AA in Theatre Arts, Los Angeles City Coll., 1949-62; student, Kimballs Real Estate Sch., Burbank, Calif., 1974; AA in Humanities, Glendale Coll., 1982; BA in Polit. Sci. Pre-Law, Calif. State U., Los Angeles, 1987. Lic. real estate agt. Dancer, entertainer Greek Theatre, Los Angeles, 1949-50; travel, reservation agt. Iver's Dept. Store, Los Angeles, 1970-73, editor, dept. store news letters, 1972-73; sec. to area supt. and social chmn. Los Angeles Bd. Edn., 1973-74; exec. sec. CBS-TV City, Los Angeles, 1974; real estate salesperson, relocation mgr. Century 21 Realty, Los Angeles, Pasadena, Calif., San Marino, Calif., 1974-86; real estate salesperson Coldwell Banker Residential, Pasadena, Calif., 1986-89, Glendale, Calif., 1989-91; real estate salesperson John Douglas Co., Pasadena, Calif., 1991-93; real estate sales, leasing agt., loan cons. Bill Davis & Assoc., South Pasadena, Calif., 1993—. Contbr. articles on sch. sci. ctrs., schs. in Russia, and schs. for the handicapped for local sch. paper, Ann. awards. Pres. San Pascual Elem. Sch. PTA, L.A., 1969-70, hon. life mem., 1970—; first soprano Consortium Angeli, 1991-92; fundraiser various groups to elect Mayor Tom Bradley, L.A.; wedding hostess Pasadena (Calif.) Ch. of Angels, 1980-88, also lic. lay minister. Mem. Pasadena Bd. Realtors (local govt. com., polit. affairs com.), Met. Player Guild. Democrat. Episcopalian. Home: 1075 Rutland Ave Los Angeles CA 90042-1536 Office: Bill Davis & Assocs 301 Pasadena Ave South Pasadena CA 91030-2904

BERNARD, ALEXANDER, airport police official; b. L.A., Apr. 23, 1952; s. Louis and Hannah (Bergman) B.; m. Diana LoRee Winstead, Dec. 17, 1976; children: Michael Alexander, Andrew Alexander. AA magna cum laude, Los Angeles Valley Coll., 1976; BS summa cum laude, Calif. State U., L.A., 1989. Parking meter collector L.A. City Clk.'s Office, 1973-79; police officer L.A. Airport, 1979-95; sgt. Police Svcs. Divsn. L.A. Airport, Ontario, Calif., 1995—. Contbr. articles to profl. jours. Active Boy Scouts Am. Mem. NRA (life), Internat. Police Assn. (life), Indsl. Rels. Rsch. Assn. Calif. Peace Officers Assn., L.A. County Peace Officers Assn, Peace Officers Rsch. Assn. Calif. (chpt. pres. 1982-84, 85-87, state bd. dirs. 1984-85, 88—, ethnic rels. com. 1993-94), L.A. Airport Peace Officers Assn. (pres. 1981-89, 94-95, bd. dirs. 1992-94), Airport Supervisory Police Officers' Assn. L.A., Calif. Rifle and Pistol Assn. (life), Golden Key (life), Phi Kappa Phi (life). Democrat. Mem. Assemblies of God Ch. Office: Police Svcs Divsn Ontario Internat Airport 1070 S Vineyard Ave Ontario CA 91761

BERNARD, JAMES WILLIAM, chemical distribution company executive; b. Brainerd, Minn., June 25, 1937; s. Paul Raymond and Maybelle Gertrude (Fynskov) B.; m. Maureen Day, Sept. 6, 1958; children: David, Kenneth, Kathleen. BS, U. Oreg., 1960. Trainee Univar Corp., San Francisco, 1960-61; resident mgr. Univar Corp., Honolulu, 1961-65; sales mgr. Univar Corp., San Francisco, 1965-67; v.p. Univar Corp., Phoenix, 1967-71; v.p. Univar Corp., San Francisco, 1971-74, corp. v.p., 1974-82; sr. v.p. Univar Corp., Seattle, 1982-83, exec. v.p., 1983-86, pres., CEP, 1986—; also bd. dirs. Univar Corp. (now Univar Van Waters & Rogers), Seattle; bd. dirs. VMR Corp., Bellevue, Wash., U.S. Bank of Washington. Bd. dirs. Jr. Achievement Greater Puget Sound, The Nature Conservancy Wash. chpt., Wash. Roundtable. Mem. Am. Chem. Soc., Chem. Mfgs. Assn. (bd. dirs.), Seattle C. of C., Columbia Tower Club, Rainier (Seattle) Club. Republican. Office: Univar Corp 6100 Carillon Pt Kirkland WA 98033-7357*

BERNARD, THELMA RENE, property management professional; b. Phila.; d. Michael John and Louise Thelma (Hoffman) Campione; m. Gene Bernard (div.). Sec. Penn. Mut. Life Ins. Co., Phila., Suffolk Franklin Savs. Bank, Boston, Holmes and Narver, Inc., Las Vegas; constrn. site office mgr. Miles R. Nay, Inc., Las Vegas; adminstrv. asst to pres. N.W.S. Constrn. Corp., Inc., Las Vegas, 1982-86, corp. sec., 1982-86; gen. mgr., corp. sec. D.A.P., Inc. property mgmt. com, Las Vegas, pres., 1991—. Author: Blue Marsh, 1972, Winds of Wakefield, 1972, Moonshadow Mansion, 1973, 2d edit., 1976, Spanish transl., 1974, German transl., 1977; contbr. articles to Doll Reader, Internat. Doll World, other mags.; past editor Cactus Courier; editor, pub. The Hoyer Enthusiastic Ladies Mail Assn., 1980-90, Friendly Tymes, 1991—; writer song lyrics. Mem. Nat. League Am. Pen Women (v.p. Red Rock Canyon br. 1986-88), Original Paper Doll Artists Guild, Am. Rose Soc., Heritage Rose Soc., Bookmark Collector Club. Office: PO Box 14002 Las Vegas NV 89114-4002

BERNARDI, GIACOMO, biology educator; b. Strasbourg, France, Aug. 28, 1963; came to U.S., 1991; s. Giorgio and Gabriella (Riva) B. BS in Biochemistry, U. Paris, 1985, MSc in Molecular Biology, 1986, PhD in Molecular Biology, 1989. Post doctoral Stanford U., Pacific Grove, Calif., 1991-94; asst. prof. biology U. Calif, Santa Cruz, Calif., 1994—. Contbr. to profl. jours. Mem. Molecular Evolution, Molecular Biology and Evolution, Am. Soc. Ichthyology. Home: 820 Trabing Rd Watsonville CA 95076 Office: U Calif Dept Biology Santa Cruz CA 95064

BERNARDI, MARIO, conductor; b. Kirkland Lake, Ont., Can., Aug. 20, 1930; s. Leone and Rina (Onisto) B.; m. Mona Kelly, May 12, 1962; 1 d., Julia. Ed., Coll. Piox, Treviso, Italy, Benedetto Marcello Conservatory, Venice, Italy, Mozarteum, Salzburg, Austria, Royal Conservatory, Toronto. Began career as pianist Italy; music dir. Sadler's Wells Opera Co., 1967-69; music dir., condr. Nat. Arts Centre, Ottawa, Ont., 1969-82; music dir. Calgary Philharm. Orch., 1984-93; prin. condr. CBC Vancouver Orch., 1982—; guest condr. with San Francisco Opera, Royal Opera House at Covent Garden, Vancouver Opera, Canadian Opera Co., Met. Opera, Chgo. Symphony, Washington Opera, Houston Symphony Orch.; prin. condr. with CBC, Vancouver Orch. Decorated companion Order of Can. Club: Savage. Office: Columbia Artists Mgmt ATT Judie Janowski 165 W 57th St New York NY 10019-2201

BERNDT, NORBERT, biochemist; b. Dusseldorf, Germany, Dec. 22, 1953; came to U.S., 1989; s. Franz and Irma (Rockstroh) B.; m. Ingrid Bahner, Nov. 24, 1989. MS, Heinrich Heine U., Düsseldorf, 1982; PhD, Heinrich Heine U., Dusseldorf, 1986. Postdoctoral rsch. asst. U. Dundee, Scotland, 1986-89; asst. prof. U. So. Calif., L.A., 1990—; cons. Upstate Biotechnology, Inc., Lake Placid, N.Y., 1993—. Contbr. articles to profl. jours. Rsch. grantee Tobacco-Related Disease Rsch. Program, Berkeley, Calif., 1993, NIH, Bethesda, 1993. Mem. AAAS, Am. Soc. Cell Biology. Office: Childrens Hosp LA 4650 W Sunset Blvd Los Angeles CA 90027-6016

BERNHOFT, FRANKLIN OTTO, psychotherapist, psychologist. BA in English, N.D. State U., 1966; MA in Counseling Psychology, U. N.D., 1970; MA in English, Calif. State U., 1978; PhD in Counseling Psychology, Brigham Young U., 1985. Cert. therapist, hypnotherapist, counselor, secondary tchr.; lic. marriage, family and child counselor, ednl. psychologist. Instr. Chapman Coll., Brigham Young U., U. N.D., U.S. I.U.; staff trainer Sacramento (Calif.) County Office Edn., 1977-82; therapist Lodi and Stockton, Calif., 1985—; therapist, family fitness trainer, master trainer systematic helping skills, devel. capable people trainer U. Pacific Behavioral Medicine Clinic; co-founder prevention/intervention project, Sacto County, 1977; presenter in field. Contbr. articles to profl. jours. Lt. U.S. Army, 1968-69. H.H. Kirk R. Askanase scholar; cert. achievement Ft. Carson; decorated Bronze star, combat med. badge Nat. Def. Svc. Vietnam. Mem. Am. Assn. Counseling and Devel., Children with Attention Deficit Disorders, Nat. Assn. Sch. Psychologists, Assn. Mormon Counselors and Psychotherapists, Calif. Assn. Marriage and Family Therapists,Sacramento Area Sch. Psychologists Assn., Calif. Continuation Edn. Assn. (past treas.), Calif. Assn. Lic. Edn. Psychologists, Mensa, Blue Key, Phi Eta Sigma. Office: Creative Therapy 310 W Lockeford St Lodi CA 95240-2033

BERNI, BETTY CATHERINE, actuary; b. Chgo., Feb. 2, 1942; d. James Gino and Helen M. (Gronkiewicz) B. BS, No. Ill. U., 1964, MS, 1968; postgrad., U. Ariz., 1968-70. Tchr. Proviso Twp. High Sch., Maywood, Ill., 1964-68; instr. U. Ariz., Tucson, 1969; actuarial asst. Wyatt Co. (now Watson Wyatt Worldwide), Washington, 1970, actuary, cons., San Francisco, 1970-80, actuary and mgr., Honolulu, 1980—. Fellow Soc. Actuaries (bd. dirs. 1993—), Conf. Consulting Actuaries; mem. Am. Acad. Actuaries, Am. Math. Soc., San Francisco Actuarial Club (pres. 1979), Rotary. Roman Catholic. Home: 3551 Waakaua St Honolulu HI 96822-1184 Office: Watson Wyatt Worldwide 737 Bishop St Ste 2340 Honolulu HI 96813-3214

BERNIER, MICHAEL SCOTT, graphic/sportswear designer, artist; b. Sierra Madre, Calif., Nov. 25, 1965; s. Gerard Donald and Janyce Sue (Cunningham) B. BFA, Calif. State U., Fullerton, 1988. Artist Am. Mktg. Works, Gardena, Calif., 1988-89; designer Chauvin Internat., L.A., 1989; owner, designer Eye Level Design, Sunset Beach, L.A., 1990—; creator lines of clothing Sub Culture, L.A., 1989, Back Country Clothing, 1994, Stare Back Designs, 1994—. Oil painter, 1992—. Office: Eye Level Designs 3811 Lyceum Ave Los Angeles CA 90066

BERNOCO, DOMENICO, immunogeneticist, educator; b. Cherasco, Cuneo, Italy, Apr. 6, 1935; s. Giuseppe and Lucia (Merlo) D.; m. Marietta Magdelene von Diepow, July 20, 1972. DVM, U. Torino, Italy, 1959; lic. vet. medicine, Rome, 1961; Libera Docenza, Ministry Pub. Instrn., Rome, 1971. Asst. prof. med. genetics U. Torino, 1961-70; mem. staff Basel (Switzerland) Inst. Immunology, 1970-76; assoc. rsch. immunologist dept. surgery UCLA, 1977-81; assoc. prof. vet. medicine reproduction U. Calif., Davis, 1981-94, prof. emeritus, 1994—. Contbr. 105 articles to profl. jours. Fellow Italian Nat. Coun. Rsch., 1962-63, Italian Ministry for Pub. Instrn., 1963-64, fellow for fgn. countries NATO, 1967-68. Mem. Am. Assn. Immunologists, Internat. Soc. Animal Genetics, Am. Soc. Histocompatibility and Immunogenetics. Home: 1002 Deodara Ct Davis CA 95616-5037 Office: Dept Population Health and Reproduction U Calif Sch Vet Medicine Davis CA 95616-8743

BERNS, PHILIP ALLAN, lawyer; b. N.Y.C., Mar. 18, 1933; s. Milton Benjamin and Rose (Aberman) Bernstein; m. Jane Klaw, June 7, 1959; children: David, Peter, Jay. BS in Marine Transp., N.Y. State Maritime Coll., 1955; LLB, Bklyn. Law Sch., 1960. Bar: N.Y. 1960, Calif. 1990, U.S. Ct. Appeals (2d cir.) 1962, U.S. Ct. Appeals (9th cir.) 1982. Admiralty atty. admiralty sect. U.S. Dept. Justice, N.Y.C., 1960-71, asst. atty. in charge admiralty sect., 1971-77; atty. in charge torts br. U.S. Dept. Justice, San Francisco, 1977—; adj. prof. McGeorge Law Sch., Sacramento, 1978-88; bd. dirs. Pacific Admiralty Seminar, San Francisco. Assoc. editor Am. Maritime Cases, 1978—. Chmn. exec. com. S.I. (N.Y.) Community Bds., 1969-70, 1st vice chmn. no. 3 bd., 1975-77, treas. no. 3 bd., 1973-74; chmn. 122d Precinct, Community Counsel, S.I., 1968-71; pres. Walnut Creek (Calif.) Little League, 1984-85, v.p. 1978-83; pres. Chestnut Hill Civic Assn., S.I., 1968-74, Congregation B'nai Jeshurun, S.I., 1973-76, v.p., 1971-73; cub pack leader Boy Scouts Am., S.I., 1969-70; bd. dirs. Mid-Island Little League, S.I., 1972-77, Jewish Community Ctr., S.I., 1976, Little League Dist. 4, Contra Costa (Calif.) County, 1984-90. Lt. USN, 1955-57. Named United Jewish Appeal Man of Yr., Congregation B'Nai Jeshurun, 1976. Mem. ABA (admiralty and maritime law com. 1991-94), Maritime Law Assn. U.S. (exec. com. 1991-94, vice chmn. practice and rules com. 1976-91, chmn. govt. liaison com. 1994—). Home: 3506 Sugarberry Ln Walnut Creek CA 94598-1746 Office: US Dept Justice Torts Br PO Box 36028 450 Golden Gate Ave San Francisco CA 94102-3400

BERNSTEIN, ARTHUR HAROLD, venture capital executive; b. N.Y.C., June 8, 1925; s. Charles and Eva (Aronson) B.; m. Barbara R. Ettinger, June 24, 1951; children: Jeffrey R., Diane. B of Chem. Engring., Cornell U., 1947, JD, 1950. Bar: N.Y. 1950, Fla. 1956, U.S. Supreme Ct. 1962, Calif. 1972. Staff atty. N.Y. Cen. R.R. Co., N.Y.C., 1950-55; gen. counsel Ryder System, Inc., Miami, 1955-58, v.p., treas., 1958-65; sr. assoc. Lazard Freres & Co., N.Y.C., 1966-68; v.p. Norton Simon, Inc., Los Angeles, 1968-70; sr. v.p. Max Factor & Co., Los Angeles, 1970-77; mgr. gen. ptnr. Calif. Capital Investors, Ltd., L.A., 1980-93; pres. Bancorp Capital Group Inc., Bancorp Venture Capital Inc., L.A., 1988—, also bd. dirs.; bd. dirs. Ryder System, Inc., Miami, Sierra Trust Funds, Sierra Variable Annuity Trust Funds. Bd. dirs. Phillips Grad. Inst., North Hollywood. With USN, 1943-46, PTO. Mem. ABA, Fla. Bar Assn., State Bar Calif. Jewish.

BERNSTEIN, ELLIOT ROY, chemistry educator; b. N.Y.C., Apr. 14, 1941; s. Leonard H. Bernstein and Geraldine (Roman) Goldberg; m. Barbara Wyman, Dec. 19, 1965; children—Jephta, Rebecca. A.B., Princeton U., 1963; Ph.D., Calif. Inst. Tech., 1967. Postdoctoral fellow U. Chgo., 1967-69; asst. prof. Princeton U., N.J., 1969-75; assoc. prof. Colo. State U., Ft. Collins, 1975-80, prof. chemistry, 1980—; cons. Los Alamos Nat. Lab., 1975-83, Philip Morris, 1984—, Du Pont Corp., 1985—. Contbr. articles to profl. jours. NSF fellow, 1961-62; Woodrow Wilson fellow, 1963-64. Fellow Am. Phys. Soc.; mem. AAAS, Am. Chem. Soc., Sigma Xi. Office: Colo State U Dept Chemistry Condensed Matter Scis Lab Fort Collins CO 80523

BERNSTEIN, GERALD WILLIAM, management consultant, researcher; b. Boston, Nov. 25, 1947; s. Alan Irwin and Anne (Fine) B.; m. Kathleen Ann Chaikin, Jan. 12, 1985. BS in Aero. Engring., Rensselaer Poly. Inst., 1969; MS in Engring., Stanford U., 1978. Transp. engr., dept. transp. State of N.Y., Albany, 1969-70; transp. planner Kennebec Regional Planning Com., Winslow, Me., 1974-77; dir. transp. dept. SRI Internat., Menlo Park, Calif., 1979-95; v.p. BACK Mgmt. Svcs., San Francisco, 1995—; session chmn. aviation workshop NSF, 1985, 91; profl. conf. chmn.; bd. dirs. Glob-Tran Corp., 1993—. Contbr. articles to profl. jours. Chmn. transp. com. Glenn Park Neighborhood Assn., San Francisco, 1982-85; dir. Balboa Terrace Neighborhood Assn., San Francisco, 1986-88; trustee Congregation Beth Israel-Judea, 1991-93. With U.S. Army, 1970-72. Recipient Cert. Appreciation City of Waterville, Maine, 1977. Mem. Am. Inst. Aeronautics and Astronautics (sr. mem.), Transp. Research Bd. of Nat. Research Council. Democrat. Jewish. Club: Toastmasters (Menlo Park, pres. 1986). Office: BACK Mgmt Svcs San Francisco CA 94127

BERNSTEIN, ROBERT DAVID, design engineer; b. Manchester, Conn., Nov. 25, 1958; s. Emil Oscar and Eleanor Rose (Mordell) B. Student, U. Calif., Berkeley, 1977-78; BS in Physics, MIT, 1980; MS in Sci. Instrumentation, U. Calif., Santa Barbara, 1984. Summer asst. Nat. Mus. Natural History, Washington, 1972-76; geodetic aide, programmer U.S. Geodetic Survey, Rockville, Md., 1976-77; rsch. asst. High Voltage Rsch. Lab., Cambridge, Mass., 1979; sr. technician CalDetect, Richmond, Calif., 1980-82; rsch. asst. U. Calif. Santa Barbara Instrumentation Lab., 1982-84; devel. engr. Nicomp Instruments, Goleta, Calif., 1984-86; sr. design engr. Digital Instruments, Santa Barbara, 1986—; bd. dirs. Amrita Corp., Menlo Park, Calif. Events coord. Ctrl. Am. Response Network, Goleta, 1984—; v.p. Santa Barbara Bicycle Coalition, 1992—; organizer Californians for Health Security, Santa Barbara, 1994. Mem. IEEE, ACLU, Sierra Club, Amnesty Internat., Am. Inst. Physics, MIT Alumni Assn. Democrat. Secular Humanist. Home: 448 Mills Way Apt B Goleta CA 93117-4047 Office: Digital Instruments 520 E Montecito St Santa Barbara CA 93103-3252

BERNSTEIN, SANDRA MARIE, county official; b. Brown City, Mich., Dec. 12, 1946; d. Raymond John and Margaret Helen (Hadrich) Tompsett; 1 child, Tammy Lynn; m. Charles Marc Bernstein, Dec. 30, 1988. AS, Ferris State U., 1983, BS, 1984; MBA, Calif. Coast U., 1992, PhD in Mgmt., 1995. Lic. registered social worker. Protective svcs. worker State of Mich., Stanton, 1984-88, facility mgr., 1987-88; North County coord. San Diego Svc. Ctr. for the Blind, 1988; protective svcs. worker County of San Diego, Calif., 1988-89; program specialist County of San Diego, 1989-90, contract analyst, 1990-91, budget, fiscal and chargeback mgr., 1991—; com. chair San Diego Commn. on Children and Youth, 1989-92. Exec. bd. County Employees Charitable Orgn., San Diego, 1993-94. Mem. San Diego Folk Heritage (bd. dirs. 1989-90). Office: County of San Diego 1600 Pacific Hwy San Diego CA 92101-2429

BERNSTEIN, SOL, cardiologist, educator; b. West New York, N.J., Feb. 3, 1927; s. Morris Irving and Rose (Leibowitz) B.; m. Suzi Maris Sommer, Sept. 15, 1963; 1 son, Paul. AB in Bacteriology, U. Southern Calif., 1952, MD, 1956. Diplomate Am. Bd. Internal Medicine. Intern Los Angeles County Hosp., 1956-57, resident, 1957-60; practice medicine specializing in cardiology L.A., 1960—; staff physician dept. medicine Los Angeles County Hosp. U. So. Calif. Med. Center, L.A., 1960—, chief cardiology clinics, 1964, asst. dir. dept. medicine, 1965-72; chief profl. services Gen. Hosp., 1972-74; med. dir. Los Angeles County-U So. Calif. Med. Center, L.A., 1974-94; med. dir. central region Los Angeles County, 1974-78; dir. Dept. Health Services, Los Angeles County, 1978; assoc. dean Sch. Medicine, U. So. Calif., L.A., 1986-94, assoc. prof., 1968—; cons. Crippled Childrens Svc. Calif., 1965—. Contbr. articles on cardiac surgery, cardiology, diabetes and health care planning to med. jours. Served with AUS, 1946-47, 52-53. Fellow A.C.P., Am. Coll. Cardiology; mem. Am. Acad. Phys. Execs., Am. Fedn. Clin. Research, N.Y. Acad. Sci., Los Angeles, Am. heart assns., Los Angeles Soc. Internal Medicine, Los Angeles Acad. Medicine, Sigma Xi, Phi Beta Phi, Phi Eta Sigma, Alpha Omega Alpha. Home: 4966 Ambrose Ave Los Angeles CA 90027-1756 Office: 1200 N State St Los Angeles CA 90033-4525

BERNSTEIN, STEVE MILLER, market research specialist; b. Boston, Apr. 30, 1958; s. Louis Marshall and Lillian Rose (Miller) B. BA in Econs. with honors, U. Calif., Berkeley, 1981; MS in Ops. Rsch., Stanford U., 1983. Sys. adminstr. Hewlett Packard Co., Palo Alto, Calif., 1983-85; sr. fin. analyst Hewlett Packard Co., 1985-86, mkt. rsch. mgr., 1986-89; market rsch. mgr. Consol. Freightways Inc., Menlo Park, Calif., 1989-91; market rsch. mgr. Apple Computer, Cupertino, Calif., 1991-93, global customer rsch. mgr., 1993—; adj. instr. mktg. rsch. U. Calif. Ext., Berkeley, 1993—. Contbr. articles to profl. jours. Commr. Cupertino Bicycle Adv. Com., 1992. Mem. Computer Mkt. Analysts Group. Democrat. Jewish.

BERNUCCI, LEOPOLDO MARCOS, educator; b. Jundiai, Brazil, Nov. 18, 1952; came to the U.S., 1978; s. Flavio and Mirthes (Garcia Lopes) B.; m. Blanche Rachelle Trerice, June 4, 1983; children: Alexandre, Paul, Marcel. BA, U. Sao Paulo, Brazil, 1977; MA, U. Mich., 1981, PhD, 1986. Asst. prof. Yale U., New Haven, 1986-91; assoc. prof. U. Colo., Boulder, 1991—. Author: Historia de un malentendido, 1989. Mem. MLA (regional del., exec. com.). Office: Univ Colo Campus Box 278 Boulder CO 80309

BERON, ALBERTO, mathematics educator, consultant, lecturer; b. Barranco, Lima, Peru, Nov. 26, 1940; came to U.S., 1962; s. Volf and Rosa (Ulfe) B.; m. Rachel K. Leggett, Dec. 19, 1981; children: Karina, Kristina. AA, L.A. City Coll., 1965; BS, Calif. State U., 1968; MA, Calif. State U., L.A., 1971. Math. specialist L.A. City Schs., 1968-71; prof. math. Moorpark (Calif.) Coll., 1971—; lectr. Calif. State U., Northridge, 1980—. Author: Mathematics Explained, 1980. Mem. Nat. Coun. Tchrs. Math., Calif. Math. Coun. Office: Moorpark Coll 7075 Campus Rd Moorpark CA 93021-1600

BERRIAN, JAMES EDWIN, biology teacher; b. Pasadena, Calif., Jan. 4, 1951; s. James Henry and Bette Jo (Durant) B.; m. Robyn M. Garcia, Nov. 11, 1989; 1 child, Nathaniel James. AA in Zoology with honors, Southwestern Coll., 1976; BS in Zoology, San Diego State U., 1978, postgrad., 1979-83; cert. tchr., Nat. U., San Diego, 1984. Sr. vet. technician Chula Vista (Calif.) Vet. Clinic, 1978-79; agrl. technician aide San Diego County Dept. Agr., 1980-81; curatorial asst., rsch. asst., field assoc. in herpetology San Diego Natural History Mus., 1981-83, 93; sci. tchr. Emerald Jr. H.S., El Cajon, Calif., 1984, Montgomery Mid. Sch., El Cajon, 1984-85, Bonita Vista High Sch., Chula Vista, 1985-92; sci. tchr. El Cajon Valley H.S., 1993—, chair dept. sci.; presenter workshops, seminars in field. Contbr. articles to profl. publs. Initiator schoolwide/cmty. paper recycling and water conservation projects; guest speaker to various cmty. groups. With USN, 1970-74. Mem. Nat. Ctr. for Sci. Edn., Soc. Vertebrate Paleontology, Am. Arachnological Soc., Nature Conservancy, U.S. Naval Inst. Home: 4325 1/2 Cleveland Ave San Diego CA 92103-2414

BERRY, CAROL A., insurance executive; b. Walla Walla, Wash., Sept. 8, 1950; d. Alan R. and Elizabeth A. (Davenport) B. BA, Wash. State U., 1972. Asst. mgr. L.A. reg. claims CIGNA, Santa Monica, Calif.; reg. adminstr. Equicor, Sherman Oaks, Calif.; dir. system for managed care Blue Cross of Calif., Woodland Hills, Calif.; dir. field account svcs. Managed Health Network, L.A.; dir. VertiHealth Adminstrv. Svcs., Burbank, Calif.; lectr. in field. Mem. Pres.'s Commn. on Status of Women. Mem. NAFE, Assn. Info. Mgrs. Healthcare Industry, HFMA, Wash. State U. Alumni Assn. Home: 6155 Lockhurst Dr Woodland Hills CA 91367-1203

BERRY, CHARLES EUGENE (CHUCK BERRY), state legislator; b. Pitts., Kans., July 1, 1950; s. Paul A. and Margaret F. (Fortune) B.; m. Maria Garcia, June 18, 1988; children: Anne, Martha, James. BA magna cum laude, U. Colo., 1972, JD, 1975. Bar: Colo., 1975. Dep. dist. atty. 4th Judicial Dist. Colo., 1975-77; asst. county atty. El Paso County, Colo., 1978-80, county atty., 1981-84; mem. Colo. Ho. Reps., 1985—, asst. majority leader, 1986-90, speaker of house, 1991—; mem. tax. policy study com. 1985-86, legis. coun., 1987-90, joint review com. on econ. devel., 1988, commn. on uniform state laws, commn. on bicentannial of U.S. constitution; chair interim com. on criminal justice, 1989. Chmn., vice chmn., treas. El Paso County Young Reps.; chmn. 21st Dist. Rep. Ctrl. Com. Mem. Colo. Bar. Assn., El Paso County Bar Assn. (treas. 1979), Colo. County Attys. Assn. (exec. com. 1981-83, treas. 1982-83), El Paso County Men's Club. Republican. Roman Catholic. Home: 314 Pine Ave Colorado Springs CO 80906-3263 Office: Colo Gen Assembly 200 E Colfax Ave Denver CO 80203-1716

BERRY, CHARLES RICHARD, lawyer; b. Louisville, Apr. 19, 1948; s. Charles Russell and Lillie Juanita (Crady) B.; m. Joan Phyllis Rosenberg, Aug. 29, 1970; children: Kevin Charles, Ryan Andrew. BA, Northwestern U., 1970, JD, 1973. Bar: Ariz. 1973, U.S. Dist. Ct. Ariz. 1973, U.S. Ct. Appeals (9th cir.) 1983. Assoc. Snell & Wilmer, Phoenix, 1973-77; ptnr. Tilker, Burke & Berry, Scottsdale, Ariz., 1978-80, Norton, Berry, French & Perkins, P.C. and predecessor firm Norton, Burke, Berry & French, P.C., Phoenix, 1980-86; dir. Fennemore Craig, Phoenix, 1986-90; ptnr. Titus, Brueckner & Berry, Scottsdale, 1991. Mem. Unitarian Ch. Lodge: Rotary. Home: 6148 E Mountain View Rd Scottsdale AZ 85253-1807 Office: Titus Brueckner & Berry 7373 N Scottsdale Rd Ste B252 Scottsdale AZ 85253-3550

BERRY, EDWIN X., physicist; b. San Francisco, June 20, 1935; s. Edwin Flower and Frances Alice (Foley) B.; m. Carole Dianne Wallace, Sept. 4, 1957 (div. 1972); children: Kim Andrew, Jay Scott, Ingrid Minette; m. Valerie S. Burge, Oct. 27, 1973. BSEE, Calif. Inst. Tech., 1957; MA in Physics, Dartmouth Coll., 1960; PhD in Physics, U. Nev., 1965. Rsch. assoc. Desert Rsch. Inst., Reno, Nev., 1965-72; program mgr. NSF, Washington, 1972-74, Burlingame, Calif., 1974-76; pres. Atmospheric Rsch. & Tech., Inc., Sacramento, 1976-86, Edwin X. Berry & Assocs., Sacramento, 1987—, ThinkNet Internat., Sacramento, 1994—; cons. Naval Weapons Ctr., China Lake, Calif. 1965-72, Zond Systems, Tehachapi, Calif., 1981—, Calif. Energy Comn., 1979-84, Westinghouse, 1988—. Contbr. articles to profl. publs.; patentee in field. Recipient People's Choice award Windows World Open, 1993; Gold medal Can. Olympic-Tng. Sailing Regatta, Kingston, 1974, U.S. Nat. Champion, Austin, 1975. Mem. Am. Meteorol. Soc. (cert. con. meteorologist). Republican. Office: Edwin X Berry & Assoc 6040 Verner Ave Sacramento CA 95841-2032

BERRY, JOHN CHARLES, clinical psychologist, educational administrator; b. Modesto, Calif., Nov. 29, 1938; s. John Wesley and Dorothy Evelyn (Harris) B.; A.B., Stanford, 1960; postgrad. Trinity Coll., Dublin, Ireland, 1960-61; Ph.D., Columbia, 1967; m. Arlene Ellen Sossin, Oct. 7, 1978; children—Elise, John Jordan, Kaitlyn. Research assoc. Judge Baker Guidance Center, Boston, 1965-66; psychology assn. Napa State Hosp., Imola, Calif., 1966-67, staff psychologist, 1967-75, program asst., 1975-76; program dir. Met. State Hosp., Norwalk, Calif., 1976-77; asst. supt. Empire Union Sch. Dist., Modesto, Calif., 1977-93, dep. supt., 1993—. Mem. Am. Psychol. Assn., Assn. Calif. Sch. Adminstrs., Sigma Xi. Contbg. author: Life History Research in Psychopathology, 1970. Home: 920 Eastridge Dr Modesto CA 95355-4672 Office: Empire Union Sch Dist 116 N Mcclure Rd Modesto CA 95357-1329

BERRY, KEN, publishing company executive; b. Tacoma, Hawaii, Apr. 2, 1943; s. Franklin Earl Berry and Elizabeth Deibel Berry Boyer; m. Karen Sayuri Yamada, July 22, 1991; children: Sheela Leilani, Shane Alika. BA in Journalism, BA in Art, U. Mont., 1970. Sports writer Daily Missoulian, Missoula, Mont., 1968-70; from editor to advt. mgr. West Hawaii Today, Kona, 1970-75; gen. mgr. Byerly Publ., Virginia Beach, 1975-76; pub. RFD Publ., Kaneohe, Hawaii, 1976—. With Spl. Forces, U.S. Army, 1967-69. Recipient Media of Yr. award Sales and Mktg. Execs., Honolulu, 1985, Disting. Alumni hon. mention Alumni Assn. U. Mont., 1991. Mem. Hawaii Pub. Assn. (pres. 1987), Masons, Shriners, Jesters, Kiwanis (promotion dir. Kona 1974-75). Home: PO Box 1498 Kaneohe HI 96744-1498 Office: RFD Publ 45-525 Luluku Rd Kaneohe HI 96744-1945

BERRY, KENNETH J., sociology educator. Prof. dept. sociology Colo. State U. Recipient Banner I. Miller award Am. Meteorol. Assn., 1994. Office: Colorado St Univ Dept Sociology Fort Collins CO 80523

BERRY, ROBERT WORTH, lawyer, educator, retired army officer; b. Ryderwood, Wash., Mar. 2, 1926; s. John Franklin and Anita Louise (Worth) B. B.A. in Polit. Sci., Wash. State U., 1950; J.D., Harvard U., 1955; M.A., John Jay Coll. Criminal Justice, 1981. Bar: D.C. 1956, U.S. Dist. Ct. (D.C.) 1956, U.S. Ct. of Appeals (D.C. cir.) 1957, U.S. Ct. Mil. Appeals 1957, Pa. 1961, U.S. Dist. Ct. (ea. dist.) Pa. 1961, U.S. Dist. Ct. (ctrl. dist.) Calif. 1967, U.S. Supreme Ct. 1961, Calif. 1967, U.S. Ct. Claims 1975. Research assoc. Harvard U., 1955-56; atty. Office Gen. Counsel U.S. Dept. Def., Washington, 1956-60; staff counsel Philco Ford Co., Phila., 1960-63; dir. Washington office Litton Industries, 1967-71; gen. counsel U.S. Dept. Army, Washington, 1971-74, civilian aide to sec. army, 1975-77; col. U.S. Army, 1978-87; prof., head dept. law U.S. Mil. Acad., West Point, N.Y., 1978-86; retired brigadier gen. U.S. Mil. Acad., 1987; mil. asst. to asst. sec. of army, Manpower and Res. Affairs Dept. of Army, 1986-87; asst. gen. counsel pub. affairs Litton Industries, Beverly Hills, Calif., 1963-67; chair Coun. of Def. Space Industries Assns., 1968; resident ptnr. Quarles and Brady, Washington, 1974-78; dir., corp. sec., treas., gen. counsel G.A. Wright, Inc., Denver, 1987-92, dir., 1987—; pvt. practice law Fort Bragg, Calif., 1993—. Served with U.S. Army, 1944-46, 51-53, Korea. Decorated Bronze Star, Legion of Merit, Disting. Service Medal; recipient Disting. Civilian Service medal U.S. Dept. Army, 1973, 74, Outstanding Civilian Service medal, 1977. Mem. Fed. Bar Assn., Army-Navy Club, Army-Navy Country Club, Phi Beta Kappa, Phi Kappa Phi, Sigma Delta Chi, Lambda Chi Alpha. Methodist.

BERRY, THOMAS CLAYTON, marketing professional, consultant; b. Roswell, N.Mex., May 23, 1948; s. Homer C. and Betty J. (Cronic) B.; m. Bonnie L. Shamas, May 30, 1969; children: Lisa C., Joshua E. AA, N.Mex. Mil. Inst., 1969; Assoc. course in real estate, 1984, NASD DPP rep. and prin. courses, 1983. Farmer Berry Farms, Dexter, N.Mex., 1969-72; sec., dir. Victor & Assoc., Phoenix, 1972-74; dir., foreman Berry Land & Cattle, Dexter, 1974-82; v.p., dir. Trinity Investment Corp., Roswell, 1982-83; pres., dir. Jordache Investments, Roswell, 1982-83; v.p., dir. Diamond Braich Realtors, Roswell, 1982-83; v.p., dir. Tierra Fin. Group, Roswell, 1985-86, pres., dir., 1986-88; v.p., dir. Tierra Capital Corp., Roswell, 1984-86, pres., dir., 1986-88; pres., dir. Tierra Energy Corp., Roswell, 1987-88; pres. Petroleum Mktg. Cons., Roswell, 1989—. Chmn. bd. dirs. Christian Profl. Counseling Svcs., Inc., 1992—; deacon North Phoenix Bapt. Ch., 1973-74; bd. dirs. First Assembly of God Ch., Roswell, youth group sponsor, 1978-86; coach Roswell Youth Soccer, 1978-80. Named one of Outstanding Men of Am., 1982. Mem. Nat. Assn. Securities Dealers, Roswell Realtor Assn., N.Mex. Realtor Assn. Republican. Mem. Christ's Ch. Home and Office: Petroleum Mktg Cons Inc 2010 Brazos St Roswell NM 88201-3374

BERRYMAN, DONALD CARROLL, cattle rancher; b. Cedarvale, N.Mex., Aug. 28, 1934; s. Benjamin Carroll and Jodie Lou (Harrel) B.; m. Sharron Lou Luster, May 31, 1968; children: Penny Jo, Robert Todd. Student, Portales U., 1952-54. Reg. bull producer. Co-owner, operator Berryman Ranch, Cebolla, N.Mex., 1954-56, owner, operator, 1960—; mem. Range Improvement Task Force, N.Mex. State U., 1988—; bd. dirs. Sunwest Bank, Espanola, N.Mex. Bd. dirs. Soil Conservation Agy., Chama, N.Mex., 1969-88. With U.S. Army, 1957-59. Recipient Excellence in Grazing award Soc. Range Mgmt., 1978. Republican. Office: Berryman Angus Ranch PO Box 188 Cebolla NM 87518-0188

BERSHON, LAWRENCE CHOLLETT, advertising executive; b. Toledo, July 21, 1933; s. Albert Louis and Miriam (Chollett) B.; m. Dorrine Bloom, June 3, 1962; children: Eric, Nicole. BA, Princeton U., 1955. Media buyer Benton & Bowles, N.Y.C., 1955-56, 57-59; media supr. McCann Erickson, N.Y.C., 1959-62; sr. account exec. Ted Bates, N.Y.C., 1962-65; v.p., account supr. Grey Advt., N.Y.C., 1965-67; mgr. product advt. Atlantic Richfield/Sinclair Oil, N.Y.C., L.A., 1967-74; dir. corp. advt. and pub. affairs ARCO, L.A., 1975-91; advt. and mktg. cons. Bershon Comm., L.A., 1992-94; dir. pub. affairs Kresser/Craig Advt., Santa Monica, Calif., 1992—. Bus. adv. bd. Am. Youth Symphony, L.A., 1991-94, Young Musicians Found., L.A., 1991-94, KCET (PBS), L.A., 1991-94; bd. dirs. Youth Job Awareness, L.A., 1992-93. Mem. Am. Advt. Fedn. (dir., sec. 1985-90, Silver medal award 1990), Western States advt. Agy. Assn., Advt. Industry Emerging Fund (dir. 1992-94), Advt. Club L.A. (pres. 1980-81), Hollywood Radio-TV Soc. (dir. 1986-90). Republican. Jewish. Home: 1646 Comstock Ave Los Angeles CA 90024-5321 Office: Kresser Craig Advt 2501 Colorado Ave Santa Monica CA 90404-3550

BERT, CAROL LOIS, educational assistant; b. Bakersfield, Calif., Oct. 15, 1938; d. Edwin Vernon and Shirley Helen (Craig) Phelps; m. John Davison Bert, Sept. 26, 1964; children: Mary Ellen, John Edwin, Craig Eric, Douglas Ethan. BS in Nursing, U. Colo., 1960. Med. surg. nurse U.S. Army, Washington, 1960-62, Ascom City, Korea, 1962-63, San Antonio, 1963, Albuquerque, 1964-65; ednl. asst. Jefferson County Schs., Arvada, Colo., 1979—. Sec. Parent, Tchr., Student Assn. Arvada West High Sch., 1987-88. Club: Colo. Quilting Coun. (1st v.p. 1988, 89, inducted into Hall of Fame, 1992). Avocations: reading, quilting, camping, fishing, tennis. Home: 5844 Oak St Arvada CO 80004-4739 Office: Allendale Elem Sch 5900 Oak St Arvada CO 80004-4741

BERTACCHI, GLORIA, health company executive; b. Sacramento, Calif., May 1, 1953; d. Jerome and Phyllis (Herr) B.; m. Larry Freeman, Apr. 4, 1987. Student, U. Santa Clara, 1971-73; D in Pharmacy, U. Pacific, 1978. Lic. pharmacist, Calif., Nev. Pres. Nat. Med. Seminars, Inc., Roseville, Calif., 1979—, Nat. Med. Staffing, Inc., Roseville, 1979—; guest spkr. on TV shows St. KOVR-Good Morning Calif., Sacramento, 1984, Sta. KXTV-CBS Affiliate, Sacramento, 1989, Sta. KJEO-Morning Edit., CBS Affiliate, Fresno, Calif., 1989, Geraldo Rivera Show, NBC, 1990, News Talk TV and WJNO Cable News; appeared on radio Sta. KSMF, Sacramento, 1990, Sta. KZAP, Sacramento, 1989, Sta. KXL-ABC/NBC, Ventura, Calif., 1989, Sta. WHO, Des Moines, 1989, Sta. WTOP, Washington, 1991, Sta. WFTL, Ft. Lauderdale, Fla., 1993-95, Sta. WAFL/WYUF, Phila., 1993, 94, 95, WBZT, South Fla., 1995, WOOD, 1995, WHYN, 1995, WBZT, 1995. Author: Drugs of Abuse, 1986, 89, AIDS: A Medical Review, 1984, 89, Overview of Antibiotics, 1987, 94, Obesity, Destiny or Choice, 1985, 89, Contraceptive Methods and Management, 1988, Osteoporosis: Prevention and Treatment, 1988, Drug Abuse in the Sports World, 1987, Drugs, Sex, and Aging, 1987, 89, Cocaine: Facts and Fantasy, 1987, 89, International Diseases: Prevention and Treatment, 1988, Prenatal Care, 1988, 89, Sexually Transmitted Diseases, 1988, Athletes and Drugs, 1988, Diet Secrets for Weight Control, 1988, Birth Control Choices, 1989, AIDS, Sex and Protection, 1989, Pregnancy Care, 1989, AIDS and HIV in Women and Children, 1994, Psychiatric Update: Violence, Abuse, Depression and Suicide, 1994, Medical Emergency Drugs, 1994, Hantavirus Mystery, 1994. Bd. dirs. Carmichael (Calif.) Park Bd., 1988. Office: Nat Med Staffing Inc PO Box 2699 Roseville CA 95746-2699

BERTAIN, G(EORGE) JOSEPH, JR., lawyer; b. Scotia, Calif., Mar. 9, 1929; s. George Joseph and Ellen Veronica (Canty) B.; m. Bernardine Joy Galli, May 11, 1957; 1 child, Joseph F. AB, St. Mary's Coll. Calif., 1951; JD, Cath. U. Am., 1955. Bar: Calif. 1957. Assoc. Hon. Joseph L. Alioto, San Francisco, 1955-57, 59-65; asst. U.S. Atty. No. Dist. Calif., 1957-59; pvt. practice of law San Francisco, 1966—. Editor-in-Chief, Law Rev. Cath. U. Am. (vol. 5), 1954-55. Mem. bd. regents St. Mary's Coll. Calif., 1980—; chmn. San Francisco Lawyers Com. for Ronald Reagan, 1966-78, San Francisco lawyers com. for elections of Gov./U.S. Pres. Ronald Reagan, 1966, 70, 80, 84; spl. confidential advisor to Gov. Reagan on jud. selection, San Francisco, 1967-74; chmn. San Francisco Lawyers for Better Govt., 1978—; confidential advisor to Senator Hayakawa on judicial selection, 1981-82, to Gov. Deukmejian, 1983-90, to Gov. Wilson, 1991-92. Recipient De La Salle medal St. Mary's Coll. Calif., 1951, Signum Fidei award, 1976. Mem. ABA, Calif. Bar Assn., Fed. Bar Assn. (del. to 9th cir. jud. conf. 1967-76), St. Thomas More Soc. San Francisco, U.S. Supreme Ct. Hist. Soc., Assn. Former U.S. Attys and Asst. U.S. Attys. No. Calif. (past pres.), Commonwealth Club, Wester Assn., Knights of Malta, KC. Republican. Roman Catholic. Office: 22 Battery St Ste 1100 San Francisco CA 94111-5525

BERTAPELLE, ALLEN LOUIS, flight test engineer; b. Greeley, Colo., Apr. 8, 1970; s. Anthony Louis and Connie Belle (Sayre) B.; m. Karen Louise Rogowski, May 29, 1993. BS in Elec. Engring., U. Colo., 1992. EIT, Colo. Commd. 1st lt. USAF, 1992; flight test engr. 4950th Test Wing USAF, Wright-Patterson AFB, 1992-94; flight test engr. 418th Flight Test Squadron USAF, Edwards AFB, Calif., 1994—. Decorated Air Force Commendation medal, 1994. Mem. Co. Grade Officers Coun., U. Colo. Alumni Assn. Home: 30 Glasgow Cir Edwards CA 93523-1714

BERTEA, HYLA HOLMES, real estate investor; b. L.A., June 14, 1940; d. George Dawson Holmes and Beth (Bay) Maher; m. Richard Bertea, Mar. 15, 1964; children: Baret Bertea Walker, Alex, Blake, Bay. BS, U. So. Calif., 1962. Tchr. L.A. City Schs., 1962-65; realtor Dalebout Assn., Newport Beach, Calif., 1988-90, Grubb & Ellis, Newport Beach, 1990—; bd. dirs. Pacific Enterprises, L.A.; founding presiding ptnr. Women's Investments.,. Co-commr. gymnastics L.A. Olympic Organizing Com., 1981-84; bd. dirs., co-chair U. So. Calif. Planning and Devel., Orange County; trustee Lewis and Clark Coll., Portland, Oreg.; commr. Calif. Horse Racing Bd. Recipient City of L.A. Commendation award U.S. Olympics, 1984. Republican. Presbyterian. Office: 23 Corporate Plaza Dr Newport Beach CA 92660-7911

BERTHELSDORF, SIEGFRIED, psychiatrist; b. Shannon County, Mo., June 16, 1911; s. Richard and Amalia (Morschenko) von Berthelsdorf; m. Mildred Friederich, May 13, 1945; children: Richard, Victor, Dianne. BA, U. Oreg., 1934, MA, MD, 1939. Lic. psychiatrist, psychoanalyst. Intern U.S. Marine Hosp., Staten Island, N.Y., 1939-40; psychiat. intern Bellevue Hosp., N.Y.C., 1940-41; psychiat. resident N.Y. State Psychiat. Hosp., N.Y.C., 1941-42; research assoc. Columbia U. Coll. Physicians and Surgeons, N.Y.C., 1942-43; asst. physician Presbyn. Hosp. and Vanderbilt Clinic, N.Y.C., 1942-51; supervising psychiatrist Manhattan (N.Y.) State Hosp., 1946-50; asst. adolescent psychiatrist Mt. Zion Hosp., N.Y.C., 1950-52; psychiat. cons. MacLaren Sch. for Boys, Woodburn, Oreg., 1952-84, Portland (Oreg.) Pub. Schs., 1952-67; clin. prof. U. Oreg. Health Scis. Ctr., 1956—; tng. and supervising analyst Seattle Psychoanalytic Inst., 1970—. Author: Treatment of Drug Addiction in Psychoanalytic Study of the Child, Vol. 31, 1976, Ambivalence Towards Women in Chinese Characters and Its Implication for Feminism, American Imago, 1988, (with others) Psychiatrists Look at Aging, 1992. Bd. dirs., v.p. Portland Opera Assn., 1960-64, Portland Musical Co., 1987-92; bd. dirs., pres. Portland Chamber Orch., 1964-70, 92-94. Maj. USAF, 1943-46. Recipient Henry Waldo Coe award U. Oreg. Med. Sch., Portland, 1939, citation Parry Ctr. for Children, Portland, 1970. Fellow Am. Psychiat. Assn. (life), Am. Geriatrics Soc. (founding fellow); mem. Am. Psychoanalytic Assn. (life), Portland Psychiatrists in Pvt. Practice (charter, pres. 1958), Mental Health Assn. (bd. dirs., chmn. med. adv. com. 1952-60), Multnomah County Med. Soc. (pres.'s citation 1979), Oreg. Psychoanalytic Found. (founding mem.), Am. Rhododendron Soc. (bd. dirs., v.p. Portland chpt. 1956-58, Bronze medal and citation 1974), Am. Rhododendron Species Found. (bd. dirs. 1960-75), Phi Beta Kappa, Sigma Xi, Phi Sigma. Home and Office: 1125 SW St Clair Ave Portland OR 97205-1127

BERTHOLF, NEILSON ALLAN, JR., aviation executive; b. Morristown, N.J., Jan. 6, 1933; s. Neilson Allan Sr. and Marion Edna (Tiger) B.; m. Geraldine Henrietta Crabtree, Aug. 6, 1955; children: Mark Allan, Karen Jo. BS in Bus. Mgmt., Fairleigh Dickinson U., Rutherford, N.J., 1960, MBA, 1966. Flight dispatcher Lockheed Aircraft Svc., Inc., Atlantic City, N.J., 1958-59; chief airport ops. and safety Fed. Aviation Agy., Atlantic City, 1959-64; airport ops. mgr. City of Kansas City, Mo., 1965-67, asst. dir. aviation, 1967-79; airport dir. County of Milw., 1979-82; aviation dir. City of Phoenix, 1982—. V.p. programs Boy Scouts Am., Phoenix, 1983—; com. mem. Fiesta Bowl Com., Phoenix, 1983—. With USN, 1951-55. Mem. Am. Assn. Airport Execs. (accredited; bd. dirs. S.W. chpt. 1988—), Airport Operators Coun. Internat. (official rep.; bd. dirs. 1981-84), Ariz. Airport Assn. (pres. 1983-84). Home: 3804 E Briarwood Ter Phoenix AZ 85044-7956 Office: Phoenix Aviation Dept 3300 E Sky Harbor Blvd Phoenix AZ 85034-4401*

BERTIN, JOHN JOSEPH, aeronautical engineer, educator, researcher; b. Milw., Oct. 13, 1938; s. Andrea and Yolanda G. (Pasquali) B.; m. Ruth Easterbrook; children: Thomas Alexander, Randolph Scott, Elizabeth Anne, Michael Robert. BA, Rice Inst., Houston, 1960; MS, Rice U., 1962, PhD, 1966. Aerospace technologist NASA Johnson Space Ctr., Houston, 1962-66; prof. U. Tex., Austin, 1966-89; program mgr. for space initiative MTS, Sandia Nat. Labs., Albuquerque, 1989-94; vis. prof. USAF Acad., Colorado Springs, Colo., 1988-89, prof. aero. engring., 1994—; cons. McGinnis, Lochridge & Kilgore, Austin, 1978-83, Sandia Nat. Labs., Albuquerque, 1980-89, BPD Difesa e Spazio, Rome, 1980-82, NASA, 1994—; detailed to Office of Space, U.S. Dept. Energy Hdqs., 1991-92; dir. Ctr. Excellence for Hypersonic Tng. and Rsch., 1985-89; mem. sci. adv. bd. USAF, 1989-93, mem. adv. group Flight Dynamics Labs., 1989-93. Author: Engineering Fluid Mechanics, 1987, Hypersonic Aerothermodynamics, 1994; co-author: Aerodynamics for Engineers, 1989; editor: Hypersonics, 1989, Advances in Hypersonics, 1992. Pres. Western Hills Little League, Austin, 1975; mem. arts subcom. NASA, 1987-91. Recipient Gen. Dynamics tchg. award U. Tex. Coll. Engring., 1978, Tex. Exec. tchg. award Ex-Students Assn. U. Tex., 1982, faculty award Tau Beta Pi, 1986, award for meritorious civilian svc. Dept. Air Force, 1993. Fellow AIAA (dir. region IV 1983-86, Disting. Lectr.).

BERTIN, MICHAEL STEPHEN, computer analyst, retired naval officer; b. Barksdale AFB, La., July 11, 1951. BS in Math., MS in Computer Sci., Rensselaer Poly. Inst., 1973. Commd. ensign USN, 1973, advanced through grades to comdr., 1988; pilot Attack Squadron 192, Lemoore, Calif., 1975-78; computer systems analyst Staff Comdr. in Chief Pacific, Honolulu, Hawaii, 1978-81; catapult and arresting gear officer USS Coral Sea (CV-43), 1982-83; dept. head Strike Fighter Squadron 195, Lemoore, Calif. & Atsugi, Japan, 1984-87; systems engr. Space and Naval Warfare Sys. Command, Washington, 1988-90; head rsch., devel., test & evaluation dept. Naval Weapons Evaluation Facility, Albuquerque, 1990-92; project mgr. Naval Tng. Systems Ctr., Orlando, 1992-94; ret., 1994; sr. analyst Sci. Applications Internat. Corp., Albuquerque, 1995—; instr. in computer sci. Roosevelt U. Extension, Honolulu, 1980-81, Chapman Coll. Extension, Lemoore, 1984. Asst. scoutmaster Boy Scouts Am., Troy, N.Y., 1969. Office: 2301 Yale Blvd SE Albuquerque NM 87106

BERTMAN, ROGER BRUCE, marketing executive; b. Portland, Oreg., Apr. 29, 1944; s. Arwid W. and Edna L. (Jackson) B.; m. Julie Pershin, Aug. 29, 1965; children: Jason M., Justin R. BA in Math., Portland State U., 1966; MS in Math. and Computer Sci., Stevens Inst. Tech., 1969. Mem. tech. staff Bell Labs., Holmdel, N.J., 1966-75; staff engr. AT&T Long Lines, N.Y.C., 1975-78; software support mgr. AT&T Long Lines, San Francisco, 1978-81; nat. account mgr. AT&T Long Lines, Boise, Idaho, 1981-84; dir. mktg. Rolm Corp., Santa Clara, Calif., 1984-89; v.p. mktg. Ungermann-Bass, Santa Clara, 1989-92; v.p., gen. mgr. mktg. VeriFone, Inc., Redwood City, Calif., 1992—. Home: 1250 Estate Dr Los Altos CA 94024-6100 Office: VeriFone Inc 3 Lagoon Dr Redwood City CA 94065-1565

BERTOLDO, JOSEPH RAMON, lawyer; b. Safford, Ariz., Nov. 24, 1950; s. Joe M. Bertoldo and Virginia (Burrell) Simmons. BS, U. Ariz., 1973, JD, 1976. Bar: Ariz. 1977, U.S. Dist. Ct. Ariz. 1977, U.S. Ct. Appeals (9th cir.) 1980, U.S. Supreme Ct. 1980. Asst. city atty. City of Flagstaff (Ariz.), 1977-81, city atty., 1981--. Bd. dirs. IMPACT, victim-witness advocacy group, Flagstaff, 1986; active Flagstaff unit Am. Cancer Soc. Mem. Ariz. Bar Assn., Coconino County Bar Assn. (v.p. 1989, pres. 1990), Ariz. City Attys. Assn., Nat. Inst. Mcpl. Law Officers (Ariz. state chair 1991-94, regional v.p. 1994), Phi Delta Phi. Democrat. Roman Catholic. Home: 4030 Spring Meadows Cir Flagstaff AZ 86004-9206 Office: City of Flagstaff 211 W Aspen Ave Flagstaff AZ 86001-5399

BERTONE, C. M. (BERT BERTONE), management consultant; b. Jersey City, July 12, 1930; s. Anthony Dominic and Dellora (Silvestri) B.; m. Stacey Ann Mueller, July 24, 1976; children: Kathleen, Victoria, Jenifer, Dana, Christopher, Amanda. BS, Seton Hall U., 1955; PhD, L.A. U., North Hollywood, Calif., 1972. Sr. social scientist The Rand Corp., Santa Monica, Calif., 1955-60; rsch. psychologist FAA, Pomona, N.J., 1960-62; sr. human factors engr. Lockheed Missile & Space Co., Sunnyvale, Calif., 1962-64; sr. scientist Bunker Ramo Corp., Canoga Park, Calif., 1964-72; pres. Bertone & Assocs., Calabasas, Calif., 1972-76; chief human factors engr. Sikorsky Aircraft, Stratford, Conn., 1976-86; mem. tech. staff McDonnell Douglas Helicopter Co., Mesa, Ariz., 1986-90; pres. The Phoenix Cons. Group, Fountain Hills, Ariz., 1990—; presenter 45 profl. meetings. Author: Soviet Psychology, 1968; contbr. 50 articles to profl. jours. Trustee Fountain Hills (Ariz.) Unified Rd. Dist., 1987-90. 1st sgt. USNG, 1947-57. Mem. Am. Assn. Profl. Hypnotists. Home: RR 1 Box 62A Mcalester OK 74501-9801

BERTRAM, CHRISTOPHER D., artificial intelligence researcher; b. Colorado Springs, Colo., Nov. 17, 1963; s. David Frederick and Carmen B. AS in Math., Merritt Coll., 1990, AA in Social and Behavioral Sci., 1990; AS, Am. River Coll., 1994. Numistic die finisher Treasury Dept., San Francisco, 1991-94; with TYN Rsch., Berkeley, Calif., 1994—. Editor/pub.: Bay Area Rock Mag., 1989-92; inventor passive prosthetic bionic light interpreter. With USN, 1985-90. Mem. IEEE, Assn. Computing Machinery. Office: TYN Rsch 48 Shattuck Sq # 163 Berkeley CA 94704-1119

BERTRAM, JACK RENARD, information systems specialist; b. Lincoln, Nebr., Nov. 20, 1943; s. John Lewis and Emma Louise (Doerr) B.; m. Ingrid Frieda Reschke, Feb. 14, 1975; children: Deborah Geniene, Kenneth Brian. BS, Stanford U., 1966, MA, 1971; MS, Santa Clara U., 1988. Scientific programming specialist Lockheed Missles & Space Co., Sunnyvale, Calif., 1980-92; pres. Hansatech Internat., Redwood City, Calif., 1993—. Mem. AIAA, IEEE Computer Soc., Am. Assn. for Artificial Intelligence, Am. Astronautical Soc., Assn. for Computing Machinery, Computer Profls. for Social Responsibility, Inst. Cert. Profl. Mgrs. (cert. mgr.), Space Studies Inst. Democrat. Home: 1580 Alameda De Las Pulgas Redwood City CA 94061 Office: Hansatech Internat PO Box 554 Redwood City CA 94064-0554

BERTRAM, MANYA M., lawyer; b. Denver; d. Samuel and Ruby (Feiner) Boran; m. Barry Bertram, June 19, 1938; children: H. Neal, Carel. JD magna cum laude, Southwestern U., 1962. Ptnr. Most and Bertram, L.A., 1963-83; of counsel Levin, Ballin, Plotkin, Zimring & Goffin, North Hollywood, Calif., 1983-92, Janice Fogg, 1993—. Former trustee Southwestern U. Sch. Law Alumni; former bd. advisors Whittier Coll. of Law, L.A., Beverly Coll. Law; former commr. Calif. Commn. on Aging, Sacramento, 1977-82; bd. dirs. Jewish Family Svc., L.A. Mem. ABA, Calif. State Bar Assn., L.A. County Bar Assn., Federacion Internac. de Abagados, Iota Tau Tau, B'nai B'rith (life mem.), Hadassah (life mem.).

BERTRAM, PHYLLIS ANN, lawyer, communications executive; b. Long Beach, Calif., July 30, 1954; d. William J. and Ruth A. Bertram; AA, Long Beach City Coll., 1975, BS in Acctg., U. So. Calif., 1977; MBA, Calif. State U., Long Beach, 1978; JD, Western State U., 1982. Bar: Calif. 1982, U.S. Ct. Appeals (9th cir.), U.S. Dist. Ct. Instr., lifeguard City of Long Beach, Calif., 1972-78; sports ofcl. swimming, softball, volleyball, and basketball, 1972—; asst. commr. Met. Conf. Community and Jr. Colls., Long Beach, 1978-84; instr. seamanship, fire sci. and bus. adminstrn. Long Beach City Coll., 1977—; mgmt. cons., 1978—; mgr. Pacific Bell, 1983—, Spl. Access Tariffs, Interconnection/Collocation Tariffs, Individual Case Basis Tariffs; guest lectr. sports officiating camps and tng. sessions. Instr. CPR, water safety, small craft, first aid ARC, 1972—; mem. Rep. Nat. Com. Recipient resolutions Calif. Senate and Assembly, Long Beach City Council; numerous service awards ARC; Ednl. research grantee, City of Long Beach, 1972. Mem. U. So. Calif. Alumni Assn., U. So. Calif. Commerce Assocs., Assn. of MBA Execs., Bay Area Career Women, Inc. (corp. sec., bd. dirs.), So. Calif. Volleyball Ofcls. Assn., Nat. Assn. Sports Ofcls., So. Calif. Basketball Ofcls. Assn., Women's Basketball Ofcls. Assn., Women's Swim Ofcls. Assn. (pres.), So. Calif. Softball Umpires Assn., State Bar Calif., ABA, Fed. Bar Assn. Los Angeles, Internat. Platform Assn., Town Hall Calif., Commonwealth Club of Calif., Los Angeles County Bar Assn., Calif. State U. at Long Beach Alumni

Assn., U. So. Calif. Alumni Assn., Delta Theta Phi. Republican. Club: Seal Beach Yacht. Office: 140 New Montgomery St Ste 2503 San Francisco CA 94105-3705

BERTRAND, KEITH JAY, electrical engineer; b. Newton, Kans., Dec. 16, 1963; s. Helmut and Helen Alice (Voth) B. BSEE, MIT, 1985. Hoser Sub Zero Systems Corp., Toronto, Ont., Can., 1985-86; engr. Delta Rsch. Group, Mountain View, Calif., 1986-87; staff engr. Ampex Corp., Redwood City, Calif., 1987—. Patentee in field. Mem. IEEE, Sons of the Chaco (pres.-elect 1994). Home: 214 Hamilton Ave Mountain View CA 94043-4207 Office: Ampex Corp 401 Broadway Redwood City CA 94063

BERUEFFY, ROBERT RYAN, retired chemist; b. Fort Worth, Tex., Mar. 16, 1914; s. Max and Wilhelmine (Goerte) B.; m. Edna Margaret Nelson, Feb. 21, 1948. BA, U. Colo., 1940; MA, Colo. Coll., 1944; PhD in Chemistry, St. Thomas U., 1948; PhD in Physiology, U. Nebr., 1956. Chemist U.S. Bur. of Stds., Washington, 1944-45, U.S. Dept. of Interior, Ketchikan, Alaska, 1945-47; head dept. chemistry Hartwick Coll., Oneanta, N.Y., 1949-52; prof. chemistry Omaha U., 1952-56; scientific dir. Lanpar Pharms., Dallas, 1956-57; pres. Bioassay Lab., Dallas and Seattle, 1957-87; cons. Swedish Hosp., Seattle, 1967-72; assoc. Nat. Rsch. Coun., Washington, 1956—; Patentee in field. Served in U.S. Navy, 1941-43. Fulbright prof., 1952. Mem. Phi Beta Kappa. Presbyterian. Home: 4861 Beach Dr SW Seattle WA 98116-4342

BERWICK, ANDREW STRUTHERS, JR., real estate executive; b. San Francisco, Dec. 24, 1933; s. Andrew Struthers and Janet (Miller) B.; m. Phyllis Elaine Pearson, Sept. 2, 1956; children: Jeanne E. , Andrew S. III. BBA, U. Oreg., 1955. Pres. Berwick-Pacific Corp., Burlingame, Calif., 1965—; Bd. dirs. Robert Half Internat.; chmn. emeritus Calif. Jockey Club. Bd. dirs. San Francisco Boys and Girls Clubs, pres. 1971-74, chmn. 1974-78; chmn. San Francisco Boys and Girls Club Endowment Trust Fund, 1976-89; pres. Crystal Springs Uplands Sch., Hillsborough, Calif., 1971-79, trustee 1976-86; regent U. Pacific, 1983-85; coucilman Town of Hillsborough, 1979-88, mayor, 1986-88; bd. govs. San Francisco Symphony, 1992—; bd. dirs. 1985-93, Mills-Peninsula Health System, chmn. 1985-87; founding chmn. Calif. Healthcare System 1986-93. Officer USAF, 1956-59. Named Vol. of Yr., San Mateo County, Citizen of Yr., HIllsborough, 1987. Mem. Hillsborough Racquet Club, Burlingame Country Club, The Pacific Union Club, San Francisco. Home: 419 Hillsborough Blvd Hillsborough CA 94010-6640 Office: Berwick-Pacific Corp. 840 Hinckley Rd Ste 201 Burlingame CA 94010-1509

BESEN, JANE PHYLLIS TRIPTOW, retired civic worker; b. Chgo., Aug. 6, 1921; d. Richard Herman and Rose (Krips) Triptow; student Northwestern U., 1946-47, East Los Angeles Coll., 1967-68; B.A. in English, Calif. State U., Los Angeles, 1978, postgrad. in English; m. Irving Besen, Mar. 25, 1951 (div. 1978); children—Glenn, Allen. Exec. sec. Chgo. Ordnance Dist., War Dept., 1941-46, Aubrey, Moore & Wallace, Advt. Agy., Chgo., 1946; exec. sec. sales office McGraw-Hill Pub. Co., Chgo., 1947-51; exec. sec. Security Pacific Nat. Bank, Los Angeles, 1978-90. Publicity chmn. Am Field Service, 1967-68; sec. Citizens Com for Good Govt., 1961; capt. United Crusade, Monterey Park, Calif., 1967—; publicity chmn. Monterey Park Art Assn., 1966-67, coor. sec., 1968, dir., 1965—, past pres., dir. newsletter, 1970—; chmn. Monterey Park Arts and Culture Com.; dir. in charge Bruggemeyer Library Shows, 1973-74; dep. registrar voters Calif. State U., Los Angeles, 1971-74; 3d v.p. in charge publicity Community Concerts Monterey Park; v.p. United Dem. Club of Monterey Park, 1988—, pres. 1995—. Recipient Top award Alhambra Open Show, 1972. Mem. Nat. League Am. Pen Women (rec. sec., treas. 1961-65), LWV (sec. Alhambra chpt. 1971-73, pres. chpt. 1973-74, action chmn., publicity chmn. 1977-78, hospitality chmn. 1980—), Residents Assn. Monterey Park. Club: Northwestern U. Alumni So. Calif. (corr. sec. 1979-80). Home: 1540 S Arriba Dr Monterey Park CA 91754-2350

BESHLIAN, LISA, interior designer; b. Beirut, Lebanon, Oct. 14, 1956; came to U.S., 1984; d. Antranig and Nelly (Ajemian) B. Student, Academie Des Beaux Arts, Beirut, 1977-81; Cert. in Interior Design, UCLA, 1990. Cons. Lisa Beshlian DEcoration, Beirut, 1982-87; asst. designer E.L.K. Assocs., L.A., 1991-93; prin., owner L.A.B. Interiors, L.A., 1993—; cons. Calif. State Univs. ADA Program, L.A., 1992; mem. design bd. Ronald McDonald Expansion Project, L.A., 1992-94; mem. programming com. ECO-EXPO Seminars, L.A., 1991. Mem. Young Women's Cir./United Armenian Congl. Ch., 1987—. Mem. Am. Soc. Interior Designers. Home and Office: 5400 Yarmouth Ave Apt 135 Encino CA 91316-2314

BESHUR, JACQUELINE E., pet training consultant, writer; b. Portland, Oreg., May 8, 1948; d. Charles Daniel and Mildred (Domreis) Beshears. BA, UCLA, 1970; MBA, Claremont Grad. Sch., 1980; postgrad., City U., Seattle, 1989-90. Dir. and founder L.A. Ctr. for Photog. Studies, 1972-76; precious gem distbr. Douglas Group Holdings, Australia, 1976-78; small bus. owner BeSure Cleaning, 1981-90; animal trainer, exotic livestock farmer, 1990—; mem. Inland Empire Pub. Lands Coun. Author: Good Intentions Are Not Good Enough, 1992. Dir. County Citizens Against Incineration, 1987—, Ames Lake Protection Com., 1989—. Mem. Bridges for Peace, Nature Conservancy, Wash. Wilderness Coalition, Issaquah Alps Club, Inland Empire Pub. Lands Coun. Republican. Fundamentalist. Office: BeSure Tng PO Box 225 Carnation WA 98014-0225

BESNETTE, FRANCIS HENRY (FRANK BESNETTE), state official, educator; b. N.Y.C., Jan. 6, 1939; s. Ulys Antoine and Evelyn Marie (Coullier) B.; m. Linda Sue Curton, Mar. 16, 1962; children: Carrie Anna, David Keith. BBA, Tex. Western Coll., 1962; MBA, Denver U., 1963; PhD in Bus. Adminstrn., Ariz. State U., 1970. Instr. bus. S.E. Mo. State Coll., Cape Girardeau, 1963-65; asst. prof. bus. No. Ariz. U., Flagstaff, 1967-69, assoc. dean, assoc. prof., 1969-73, prof., dean Coll. Bus. Adminstrn., 1973-80, v.p. adminstrn. and fin., 1980-88, exec. v.p., 1988-91; exec. dir. Ariz. Bd. Regents, Phoenix, 1992—; intern Office of Senator John McCain U.S. Senate, Washington, 1989. Contbr. articles to profl. jours. Bd. dirs. Flagstaff Health Mgmt. Corp., 1972-88; trustee Mus. No. Ariz., Flagstaff, 1984-89; founding dir. Flagstaff Leadership Program, 1990. Named Citizen of Yr. Ariz. Daily Sun, 1980. Mem. Flagstaff C. of C. (bd. dirs.). Republican. Methodist. Office: Ariz Bd Regents 2020 N Central Ave Ste 230 Phoenix AZ 85004-4503

BESS, HENRY DAVID, dean; b. New Haven, Conn., Apr. 15, 1939; s. Henry Alver and Ina Ozeal (Green) B.; m. Linda Lois Lyday, June 17, 1967; children: Tammy Loika, Cindy Loika. BS, U.S. Merchant Marine Acad., 1961; MBA, UCLA, 1964, PhD, 1967. Asst. prof., asst. dean of students U. Hawaii, Honolulu, 1967-70, assoc. prof., asst. dean of students, 1970-73, prof., assoc. dean coll. bus. adminstrn., 1974-80, prof., dean coll. bus. adminstrn., 1980—; vis. assoc. prof. U.S. Merchant Marine Acad., Kings Point, N.Y., 1973-74; vis. faculty Oreg. State U., 1992-93' vis. scholar UCLA, 1974; 2d officer Hawaiian Tug and Barge Co., Honolulu, 1961-63. Author: Marine Transportation, 1976, (with others) U.S. Maritime Policy: History and Prospects, 1981; contbr. articles to profl. jours. Bd. dirs. Hawaii Coun. Econ. Edn., Honolulu, 1982-89, Boy Scouts Am., Honolulu, 1984—, Japan-Am. Inst. Mgmt. Sci., Honolulu, 1988—, ARC, Honolulu, 1989—; trustee Grad. Mgmt. Admission Coun., 1992—. Lt. (j.g.) USN, 1961-68. Mem. Am. Assn. Univ. Adminstrs., Am. Assn. Higher Edn., C. of C. Hawaii, Hawaii Soc. Corp. Planners (bd. dirs. 1984-90), Am. Econ. Assn. (transp. and pub. utilities group), Rotary, Beta Gamma Sigma. Office: U Hawaii Coll Bus Adminstrn 2404 Maile Way Honolulu HI 96822-2223

BESSE, ROBERT GALE, food technologist; b. Calgary, Alta., Can., Feb. 11, 1923 (parents Am. citizens); s. Rene A. and Doria (Bray) B.; student N.Mex. State Tchrs. Coll., 1941-42; B.S., Oreg. State Coll., 1948; m. Mary A. McKay, Sept. 11, 1948; children—Rene A., Madeleine E., Leon J., Alan G., Michele M., Marc P., Angelique C. Supt., also in quality control Alderman Farms Frozen Foods, Dayton, Oreg., 1948-50, plant supt., 1950-54; chief food technologist Kuner Empson Co., Brighton, Colo., 1954-60; food technologist Northwest Packing Co., Portland, Oreg., 1960-62; food technologist research and devel. Nat. Can Corp., San Francisco, 1962-67, mgr. Pacific Area tech. research service, 1967-70; mgr. tech. services Western Can Co., 1970-86 ; customer tech. services Continental Can Co., 1986-88; cons. to food and can industries, RGB Cons., 1988—; dir. Material Metrics. Pres. St. Gregory's Theatre Guild; vol. hunting safety instr. Calif. Fish and Game Dept., 1972—. Served with Signal Corps, AUS, 1942-45. Mem. Soc. Plastic Engrs., Pacific Fish Tech. (pres.), Inst. Food Technologists (emeritus, sec.-treas. Rocky Mountain sect.; exec. com. Oreg. sect.), Confraternity of Christian Doctrine Cath. (pres.), N.W. Canners and Packers, Packaging Inst. (profl. mem.), Nat. Canners Assn. (mem. Western lab. adv. com.), No. Calif. Metal Decorating Assn. (pres.), Western Packaging Assn.; Soc. Mfg. Engrs. Club: Elks. Home and Office: 264 Portola Dr San Mateo CA 94403-2327

BESSER, HOWARD, information systems analyst; b. Chgo., July 17, 1952. BA, U. Calif., Berkeley, 1976, MLS, 1977, PhD, 1988. Rsch. asst. Afro-Am. studies dept. U. Calif., Berkeley, 1976-77, libr. asst. cooperative svcs., 1977-78, media/computer specialist sch. edn., 1977-86, info. systems mgr. univ. art mus., 1977-87, rsch. specialist inst. for study social change, 1982-89, image database specialist, 1986-89; asst. prof. sch. libr. and info. sci. U. Pitts., 1989-92; info. systems analyst Ctr. Canadien d'Architecture, Montreal, 1992-94; vis. prof. Sch. Info. and Libr. Studies, U. Mich., 1994—; computer cons. Getty Trust, 1993—, Met. Mus. Art, N.Y., 1993, Mus. Civilization, Ottawa, Can., 1993, Indira Ghandi Nat. Ctr. for Arts, 1990, Image Understanding Sys., Calif., 1987, Mus. Mgmt. Inst., Calif., 1986, Reel Rsch., Calif., 1979-81, others. Contbr. articles to profl. jours. Mem. Am. Assn. Mus., Internat. Stds. Orgn., Coalition for Networked Info., Clearinghouse for Mus. Info. (bd. dirs.), Computer Profls. for Social Responsibility, Am. Soc. for Info. Sci., ALA, Mus. Computer Network. Office: U Mich Sch Info & Libr Studies Ann Arbor MI 48109-1092

BEST, BARBARA, personal manager; b. San Diego, Dec. 2, 1921; d. Charles Lewis and Leila Harrison (Sanders) B. BA in Journalism, U. So. Calif., Los Angeles, 1943. Unit publicist 20th Century Fox Co., Los Angeles, 1943-50; reporter San Diego Jour., 1950; asst. to publicity dir. Stanley Kramer Co., Los Angeles, 1950-53; 0wner, mgr. Barbara Best & Assocs., Los Angeles, 1953-66; ptnr. Freeman and Best Pub. Rels., Los Angeles, 1967-75; owner, pres. Barbara Best, Inc., Pub. Relations, Los Angeles, 1975-87; personal mgr. Barbara Best Mgmt., Los Angeles, 1987—; exec. v.p. Maribar Prodns., Hollywood, Calif., 1986-. Co-founder, exec. dir. Vikki Carr Scholarship Found., Hollywood, 1971-82; pres. Publicists Fed. Credit Union, Hollywood, 1976-85. Mem. Hollywood Womens Press Club (past pres., bd. dirs.), Women in Film. Democrat. Episcopalian. Office: Barbara Best Mgmt 14159 Riverside Dr Sherman Oaks CA 91423-2362

BEST, MARY LANI, program coordinator; b. Hilo, Hawaii, June 3, 1944; d. Stanley Clark and Emma Holokahiki (Martinson) Brooks; m. Leningrad Elarionoff, Aug. 14, 1965 (div. 1981); children: Kimberly Kehaunani, Grad Ikaika; m. Gary Dean Best, Dec. 7, 1984. BA, U. Hawaii, Hilo, 1988; MS, Creighton U., 1991. Substitute tchr. Hilo High Sch., 1990; counselor secondary alternative program Westside High Sch., Omaha, 1991; coord. Ctr. for Gifted & Talented Native Hawaiian Children U. Hawaii, Hilo, 1991—. Contbr.: (book) Sociology of Hawaii, 1992; co-editor: Glimpses of Hawaiian Daily Life and Culture, 1994. Active Hale O Na Alii, Hilo, 1988—. Mem. AACD. Republican. Home: # 304 84 Pukihae St Hilo HI 96720 Office: U Hawaii 200 W Kawili St Hilo HI 96720-4075

BEST, ROGER NORMAN, real estate investment manager; b. L.A., Apr. 16, 1949; s. Norman Frank and Muriel Noreen (Atkinson) B.; m. Sheri Lyn Kruyer, Oct. 16, 1982. BA, U. Wash., 1971. Lic. Real Estate Broker, Calif., 1985. Musician, entertainer, 1963-69; pres. Best Enterprises, L.A., 1969—; head electronic media svcs. Cedars-Sinai Med. Ctr., L.A., 1971-73; pres. Tazio Prodns., L.A., 1973-76; v.p. Video Disco & Assocs., L.A., 1975-76, DSL Constrn. Corp., L.A., 1977-85; v.p., chief operating officer Scott Properties, Inc., L.A., 1978-85; pres., chief exec. Tazio Properties, Inc., L.A., 1980—. Inventor correctable typewriter ribbon; creator original music videos concept with Visual Music, 1974; featured columnist Apt. Age Mag., L.A., 1989—. Mem. Van Nuys Airport Adv. Coun., 1987-94. Citation of Appreciation, City of L.A., 1988, 89, 94. Office: Tazio Properties Inc 3580 Wilshire Blvd Fl 17 Los Angeles CA 90010-2501

BETANCOURT, HECTOR MAINHARD, psychology scientist, educator; b. Chile, Sept. 1, 1949; came to U.S. 1979; s. Hector and Eleonora (Mainhard) B.; m. Bernardita Sahli; children: Paul, Daniel. BA, Cath. U., Santiago, Chile, 1976; MA, UCLA, 1981, PhD in Psychology, 1983. From asst. prof. to assoc. prof. psychology Cath. U., Santiago, Chile, 1977-79, 83-85; from assoc. prof. to prof. of psychology Loma Linda U., Riverside, Calif., 1985-93, chmn., 1990-93; chmn., prof. psychology Grad. Sch. Loma Linda (Calif.) U., 1993—. Editor Interam. Psychologist, 1982-86; mem. editorial bd. Jour. Community Psychology, 1986-89, Spanish Jour. Social Psychology, 1986—, Conflict and Peace, 1993—; contbr. articles to profl. jours. Recipient Rotary Found. award for Internat. Understanding, Rotary Internat., 1976-77; Fulbright fellow, UCLA, 1979-80. Mem. APA (exec. com. and chmn. task force on ethnicity, div. 48 peace psychology 1994-95), Internat. Soc. Polit. Psychology, Internat. Soc. Cross-Cultural Psychology (exec. com. 1984-86), Interam. Soc. Psychology (sec.-gen. 1983-87), Soc. for Psychol. Study Social Issues, Soc. Personality and Social Psychology. Office: Loma Linda U Dept Psychology Grad S Loma Linda CA 92350

BETANCOURT, NELLIE, physician; b. San Juan, May 13, 1951; d. Ricardo and Nellie (Jimenez) B.; m. Alejandro Salicrup, July 1971 (div. Sept. 1988); children: Alejandro Salicrup, Ricardo Salicrup, Jose Enrique Salicrup; m. Rene Torres, Aug. 16, 1990. BA in Art/English Lit. magna cum laude, U. P.R., 1972, BS in Chemistry magna cum laude, 1975, MD, 1985; postgrad., Med. Coll. Wis., 1993—. Diplomate Am. Bd. Internal Medicine; cert. physician, Calif., P.R., Ga., qualified med. examiner. Intern, resident in internal medicine VA Hosp., Rio Piedras, P.R., 1985-88; pvt. practice internal medicine Ashford Meml. Hosp., San Juan, 1988-90; staff physician occupational medicine Howell Indsl. Clinic, Atlanta, 1990-91; dir. Hanover Network Indsl. Clinic, City of Industry, Calif., 1992-93; assoc. dir. indsl. medicine Friendly Hills HealthCare Network, La Habra, Calif., 1993—; mem. quality assurance com. The Travelers Ins. Co.-ConservCo, 1994—; bd. dirs. EarthBond, Inc., 1992—. Mem. AMA, ACP, Orange County Med. Assn., Am. Coll. Occupational and Environ. Medicine, Alpha Omega Alpha. Office: 18575 Gale Ave La Puente CA 91748

BETITA, KENNETH SIMON, academic counselor; b. San Luis Obispo, Calif., Oct. 20, 1963; s. Mauricio and Josefina (Balandres) B. BA in Bus. Econ., U. Calif., Riverside, 1985; MA in Counseling and Guidance, Calif. Poly. State U., San Luis Obispo, 1990; MA in Reading and Devel., U. Calif., Santa Barbara, 1994. Claim examiner Liberty Mutual Ins., San Jose, Calif., 1985-87; acad. counselor U. Calif., Santa Barbara, 1987—; coord., counselor transfer svcs. Santa Barbara C.C.; cons. East/West Partnership, Santa Barbara, 1992-94. Advisor Kapatirang Filipino, Santa Barbara, 1988-94, Asian Student Coalition, Santa Barbara, 1988-94. Recipient Calif. State U.-Hayward doctoral incentive, 1992. Mem. ACAD, Assn. Asian Studies, Filipino Educator Assn., Filipino Cmty. of San Luis Obispo. Home: 1163 Newport Ave Grover Beach CA 93433-1715

BETTELHEIM, ANN ELISE, nonprofit organization executive; b. Berkeley, Calif., Nov. 16, 1945; d. Albert Sweet and Elizabeth (Eldridge) B.; m. Michael Dennis Ongerth, May 24, 1968 (div. Nov. 1981); children: Stephen, Ann Michelle, Sharon. BA in History, U. Calif., Berkeley, 1967, cert. in bus. data processing, 1984; MBA in Computer Info. Sys., Hayward State U., 1991. Mgr. Tau House, Berkeley, 1989-94; owner Small Bus. Mgmt. Svcs., Berkeley, 1992—; cons. Westwind Dance Co., Oakland, Calif., 1993—, Oakland (Calif.) Ballet, 1994. Auditor fundraising publicity site coun. PTA, Bay Side Sch. Dist., Richmond, Calif., 1982-92; merit badge counselor, pres. mother's club Boy Scouts Am., Mt. Diablo Coun., 1988-91. Mem. NAFE, Nat. Soc. Pub. Accts. (assoc.), Assn. Fraternal Advisors, Alpha Epsilon Phi (advisor nat. house corp. chair nat. standards). Home: 30 Rincon Rd Kensington CA 94707-1026 Office: Small Bus Mgmt Svcs Ste 194 PO Box 1974 Berkeley CA 94701

BETTIN, JANENE EDNA, real estate broker; b. Schaller, Iowa, Nov. 11, 1943; d. Robert A. and Edna (Harris) Bath; m. Thomas L. Bettin, June 20, 1964; 1 child, Christopher. Student U. No. Iowa, 1961; BS, Tex. A&I U., 1965. Grad. Realtors Inst.; cert. residential specialist, residential brokerage mgr. Tchr. high sch., Corpus Christi, Tex., 1965-70; tchr. Village Acad., Mt. Lebanon, Pa., 1973-76; broker, assoc. Re/Max Metro Properties, Inc., Denver, 1977-86; broker, br. mgr. Perry & Butler, Littleton, Colo., 1986-89; broker Van Schaack Residential Realty, Inc., 1989; broker, owner Prime Properties, Englewood, Colo., 1989-94, Moore & Co., Denver, 1994—. Chmn. Blood Bank, South Suburban Bd. Realtors, 1980, chmn. Schs. Com., 1980; pres. South Suburban Bd. Realtors, 1985-86. Bd. dirs., officer Bristol Cove Homeowners Assn., Littleton, Colo., 1983; officer, treas. Arapahoe Youth League-Warriors, 1981. Mem. Realtors Nat. Mktg. Inst., Womens Coun. Realtors (pres. 1982-83), Colo. Assn. Realtors (instr. 1981—, dir. 1984, v.p. 1987), Cert. Residential Specialists (pres. Colo. chpt. 1984, nat. instr. 1985-86), Cert. Residential Brokerage Mgrs. (instr. 1986-92), Omega Tau Rho. Republican. Methodist. Club: Mt. Lebanon Newcomers (pres. 1973-74). Home: 7540 S Cove Cir Littleton CO 80122-3332

BETTIS, JOHN GREGORY, songwriter; b. Long Beach, Calif., Oct. 24, 1946; s. Wayne Douglas and Nellie Jane (House) B. Songwriter, music pub. Warner/Chappel Music, 1976-82; songwriter, pub. John Bettis Music, Santa Monica, Calif., 1982-94; songwriter, music pub. Triste Music, 1994—. Lyricist: (songs) Yesterday Once More, 1973 (Gold Record), Top of the World, 1974 (Gold Record), Heartland, Can You Stop the Rain, 1991, (Grammy nominee 1991), Promise Me You'll Remember, 1990 (acad. awards nominee 1991), One Moment In Time, 1988 (Emmie 1989), Crazy for You, 1985 (Gold Record), Slow Hand, 1981 (Gold Record), Human Nature, 1983 (Grammy cert.-Album of Yr. 1984); lyricist songs for movies including Say Anything, Star Trek V, Cocktail, Nothing in Common, Godfather Part III; lyricist TV theme songs. Recipient Top TV Series award for Growing Pains, ASCAP, 1986, for Just the Ten of Us, ASCAP, 1987, for Empty Nest, ASCAP, 1990, 24 Gold Records, Rec. Industry Assn. Am., 1970-90, 7 Platinum Records, Rec. Industry Assn. Am., 1970-90, 32 Performance awards ASCAP, 1970-90, Dir-Svengali, Lunch Musicals for Stage. Mem. ASCAP (bd. rev. 1982—), Nat. Acad. Songwriters (bd. dirs. 1980-94, chmn. bd. dirs. 1983-85). Office: John Bettis Music PO Box 668 Sunset Beach CA 90742-0668

BETTISON, CYNTHIA ANN, museum director, archaeologist; b. St. Louis, Sept. 8, 1958; d. William Leslie and Barbara Ann (Yunker) B. BA in Anthropology and Biology, Pitzer Coll., 1980; MA in Anthropology, Eastern N.Mex. Univ., 1983; PhD in Anthropology, U. Calif., Santa Barbara, 1996. Asst. curator, Dept. Anthropology Univ. Calif., Santa Barbara, 1988-89, curator, Dept. Anthropology, 1990-91; dir. Western N.Mex. Univ. Mus., Silver City, N.Mex., 1991—; co-dir. WNMU Archaeol. Field Sch., 1992, 94, 95; lectr. Western N.Mex. Univ., 1992—; assoc. Anthropology Univ. Calif., 1987-88, computer lab asst. dept. sociology, 1987-91, rsch. asst., 1988, statis. cons., 1987-88; various archaeol. positions, 1981—. Contbr. articles to profl. jours. Recipient Conservation Assessment Program grant, 1994-95, NEH, 1994; Gila Nat. Forest grantee, 1992, 94, 95, Mimbres Region Art Coun. Mimi grantee, 1992, Silver City Lodger's Tax Bd. grantee, Andrew Isabell Meml. Fund grantee Dept. Anthropology Univ. Calif., 1990, SIMSE Summer Inst. grantee, 1995. Mem. Am. Assn. Mus., Am. Anthrop. Assn., Am. Soc. Conservation Archaeol. N.Mex. Mus. Assn., Soc. for Am. Archaeology, Archaeol. Soc. N.Mex., N.Mex. Archaeol. Coun. (sec. 1993-94), Coun. Mus. Anthropology (sec. 1992-94), Mountain Plains Mus. Assn., Grant County Archaeol. Soc., Univ. Women's Club, Univ. Club, Optimist Club (sec. Silver City chpt.), Phi Kappa Phi. Office: Western NM Univ Mus 1000 W College Ave Silver City NM 88061-4158

BETTS, BARBARA LANG (MRS. BERT A. BETTS), lawyer, rancher, realtor; b. Anaheim, Calif., Apr. 28, 1926; d. W. Harold and Helen (Thompson) Lang. BA magna cum laude, Stanford U., 1948; LLB, Balboa U., 1951; m. Roby F. Hayes, July 22, 1948 (dec.); children: John Chauncey IV, Frederick Prescott, Roby Francis II; m. Bert A. Betts, July 11, 1962; 1 child, Bruce Harold; stepchildren: Bert Alan, Randy W., Sally Betts Joynt, Terry Betts Marsteller, Linda Betts Hansen, LeAnn Betts Wilson. Bar: Calif. 1952, U.S. Supreme Ct. 1978; pvt. practice law, Oceanside, Calif., 1952-68, San Diego, 1960—, Sacramento, 1962—; ptnr. Roby F. Hayes & Barbara Lang Hayes, 1952-60; city atty., Carlsbad, Calif., 1959-63; v.p. Isle & Oceans Marinas, Inc., 1970-80, W. H. Lang Corp., 1964-69; sec. Internat. Prodn. Assos., 1968—, Margaret M. McCabe, M.D., Inc., 1977-88 . Chmn. Traveler's Aid, 1952-53; pres. Oceanside-Carlsbad Jr. Chambrettes, 1955-56; vice chmn. Carlsbad Planning Commn., 1959; mem. San Diego Planning Congress, 1959; v.p. Oceanside Diamond Jubilee Com., 1958. Candidate Calif. State Legislature, 77th Dist., 1954; mem. Calif. Dem. State Central Com., 1958-66; co-chmn. 28th Congl. Dist., Dem. State Central Com., 1960-62; alt. del. Dem. Nat. Conv., 1960; co-sponsor All Am. B-24 Liberator Collings Found. Named to Fullerton Union High Sch. Wall of Fame, 1986. Mem. Am. Judicature Soc., Nat. Inst. Mcpl. Officers, ABA, Calif. Bar Assn., San Diego County Bar Assn., Oceanside C. of C. (sec. 1957, v.p. 1958, dir. 1953-54, 57-59), AAUW (legis. com. 1958-59); local pres. 1959-60; asst. state legis. chmn. 1958-59), Heritage League (2d div. 8th Air Force), No. San Diego County Assn. Cs. of C. (sec.-treas.), Bus. and Profl. Women's Club (So. dist. legislation chmn. 1958-59), DAR (regent Oceanside chpt. 1960-61), San Diego C. of C., San Diego Hist. Soc., Fullerton Jr. Assistance League, Calif. Scholarship Fedn., Loyola Guild of Jesuit High Sch., Phi Beta Kappa. Clubs: Soroptimist Internat. (pres. Oceanside-Carlsbad 1958-59, sec. pub. affairs San Diego, Imperial Counties 1954; pres. of pres.'s council San Diego and Imperial counties and Mexico 1958-59), Barristers, Stanford (Sacramento), Stanford Mothers, Heritage League (2nd air divsn. USAAF). Author: (with Bert A. Betts) A Citizen Answers. Home: 441 Sandburg Dr Sacramento CA 95819-2559 Office: Betts Ranch PO Box 306 Elverta CA 95626-0306 also: 1830 Avenida del Mundo #1608 Coronado CA 92118

BETTS, BARBARA STOKE, artist, educator; b. Arlington, Mass., Apr. 19, 1924; d. Stuart and Barbara Lillian (Johnstone) Stoke; m. James William Betts, July 28, 1951; 1 child, Barbara Susan (dec.). BA, Mt. Holyoke Coll., 1946; MA, Columbia U., 1948. Cert. tchr., N.Y., Calif., Hawaii. Art tchr. Walton (N.Y.) Union Schs., 1947-48, Presidio Hill Sch., San Francisco, 1949-51; free-lance artist San Francisco, 1951; art tchr. Honolulu Acad. Arts, summer 1952, 59, 63, 85, spring 61, 64; libr. aide art rm. Libr. of Hawaii, Honolulu, 1959; art tchr. Hanahauoli Sch., Honolulu, 1961-62, Hawaii State Dept. Edn., Honolulu, 1958-59, 64-84; owner Ho'olaule'a Designs, Honolulu, 1973—. Illustrator: Cathedral Cooks, 1964, In Due Season, 1986; exhibited in Hawaii Pavilion Expo '90, Osaka, Japan, State Found. of Culture and Arts, group shows since 1964; represented in Arts of Paradise Gallery, Waikiki, 1990—; traveling exhibns. include Pacific Prints, 1991, Printmaking East/West, 1993-95, Hawaii/Wis. Watercolor Show, 1993-94. Mem. Hawaii Watercolor Soc. (newsletter editor 1986-90), Nat. League Am. Pen Women (art chmn. 1990-92, sec. 1992-94), Honolulu Printmakers (dir. 1986, 87), Assn. Hawaii Artists. Republican. Episcopalian. Home: 1520 Ward Ave Apt 203 Honolulu HI 96822-3550

BETTS, BERT A., former state treasurer, accountant; b. San Diego, Aug. 16, 1923; s. Bert A. and Alma (Jorgenson) B.; m. Barbara Lang; children: Terry Lou, Linda Sue, Sara Ellen, Bert Alan, Randy Wayne, LeAnn, John Chauncey, Frederick P., Roby F., Bruce H. BBA, Calif. Western U., 1950. CPA, Calif. Accountant John R. Gillette, 1946-48; ptnr. Gillette & Betts, 1949-50; pvt. accounting practice, 1951-54; ptnr. Betts & Munden, Lemon Grove, Calif., 1954-57; sr. ptnr. Bert A. Betts & Co., 1958-59; treas. State of Calif., 1959-67; prin. Bert A. Betts & Assos., 1967-77; chief exec. officer Internat. Prodn. Assos., 1970-87; dir. Lifetime Communities Inc.; gen. partner Sacramento Met. Airport Properties 4, Ltd., 1970—. Mem. Lemon Grove Sch. Bd., 1954-57; Calif. chmn. Max Baer Heart Fund; state employees chmn. Am. Cancer Soc., 1962-64, bd. dirs. county br., 1963-69, Sacramento County campaign chmn., mem. exec. com., 1965, pres. Sacramento chpt., 1967-68; sponsor All Am. B-24. Served as 1st lt. USAAF, 1942-45. Decorated D.F.C., Air medal with four clusters; recipient Louisville award Municipal Finance Officers Assn. U.S. and Can., 1963; honored by Calif. Municipal Treas.'s Assn., 1964. Mem. Nat. Assn. State Auditors, Comptrs. and Treas.'s, Mcpl. Forum N.Y., Calif. Soc. CPAs, San Diego Squadron Air Force Assn. (past vice comdr.), Am. Legion, 2d Air Div. Assn., 8th Air Force Hist. Soc., VFW, Confederate Air Force (col.), Native Sons Golden West, Internat. B-24 Liberator Club, Foresters, Lemon Grove Masonic Lodge, Sigma Phi Epsilon, Beta Alpha Psi (hon.), Alpha Kappa Psi (hon.). Presbyn. Clubs: Eagles; Men's (Lemon Grove) (pres.), Lions (Lemon Grove) (treas.); Commonwealth. Home: 441 Sandburg Dr Sacramento CA 95819-2559 also: Betts Ranch East Levee Rd Elverta CA 95626

BETTS, JAMES WILLIAM, JR., financial analyst, consultant; b. Montclair, N.J., Oct. 11, 1923; s. James William and Cora Anna (Banta) B.; m.

Barbara Stoke, July 28, 1951; 1 child, Barbara Susan (dec.). BA, Rutgers U., 1946; MA, U. Hawaii, 1957. With Dun & Bradstreet, Inc., 1946-86, svc. cons., 1963-64, reporting and svc. mgr., 1964-65, sr. fin. analyst, Honolulu, 1965-86; owner Portfolio Cons. of Hawaii, 1979—; cons. Saybrook Point Investments, Old Saybrook, Conn., 1979—. Contbr. articles to mag. Served with AUS, 1943. Mem. Am. Econ. Assn., Western Econ. Assn., Atlantic Econ. Soc. Republican. Episcopalian. Office: Portfolio Cons Hawaii 126 Queen St Ste 222 Honolulu HI 96813-4411

BETTS, ROBERT BUDD, JR., dude ranch owner; b. Mt. Kisco, N.Y., Apr. 1, 1956; s. Robert Budd and Emile Louise (Woehrle) B.; m. Emily Hancock, Dec. 29, 1984; children: Lindsay, Robert. BA in Am. Studies, U. Wyo., 1979. Wrangler, guide Triangle X Ranch, Jackson Hole, Wyo., 1971-79; analyst James H. Marshall, Inc., N.Y.C., 1980-81; producer William Esty Advt., N.Y.C., 1979; dude rancher, outfitter Absaroka Ranch, DuBois, Wyo., 1981—; state ho. rep. dist. 22 Wyo. Ho. of Reps., 1992—. Bd. dirs. Wyo. Futures Project, 1985-86, Wyo. Community Foun., 1989-90. Mem. Lions. Republican. Home and Office: PO Box 929 Dubois WY 82513-0929

BETZ, RICHARD, agricultural products executive; b. 1943. Sec.- treas. Royal Pak Produce Inc., Hermiston, Oreg., 1968-74; with Bud-Rich Potato Inc., Hermiston, 1974—, now pres./treas. With U.S. Army, 1964-68. Office: Bud-Rich Potato Inc Butter Creek Hwy Hermiston OR 97838*

BETZ-ZALL, JONATHAN RICHARD, librarian; b. Boston, June 28, 1950; s. Paul M. and Elisabeth (Weisz) Zall; m. Rose E. Betz, Oct. 5, 1973; children: Marissa, David. BA, Swarthmore Coll., 1972; M of Librarianship, U. Wash., 1976. Head libr. Aircraft Tech. Pubs., San Francisco, 1976-77; libr. San Francisco Pub. Libr., 1977-78, Upper Merion Twp. Libr., King of Prussia, Pa., 1978-79, Free Libr. Phila., 1979-85, Sno-Isle Regional Libr. Sys., Marysville, Wash., 1985—. Contbr. book revs. and articles to libr. jours. Co-chmn. Greenwood Family Sing!, 1987—. Mem. Wash. Libr. Assn. (interest group rep. 1994-95, chmn. social responsibilites round table 1988-91, 93-94), N.W. Internat. Cmtys. Assn. (bd. dirs.). Office: Edmonds Libr 650 Main St Edmonds WA 98020-3056

BEVERETT, ANDREW JACKSON, marketing executive; b. Midland City, Ala., Feb. 21, 1917; s. Andrew J. and Ella Levonia (Adams) B.; m. Martha Sophia Landgrebe, May 26, 1951; children: Andrew Jackson III, James Edmund, Faye A. BS, Samford U., 1940; MBA, Harvard U., 1942. Various exec. positions in corporate planning and mgmt. United Air Lines, Chgo., 1946-66; dir. aviation econs., sr. mktg. and econ. cons. Mgmt. and Econs. Research, Inc., Palo Alto, Calif., 1966-71; sr. economist Stanford Research Inst., Menlo Park, 1971-72; pres. Edy's on the Peninsula stores, 1973-78; real estate broker, fin. and tax cons., Saratoga and San Jose, Calif., 1979—. Ensign to lt. USNR, 1942-46. Mem. Nat. Assn. Enrolled Agts., Nat. Assn. Realtors, Pi Gamma Mu, Phi Kappa Phi. Home: 6325 Whaley Dr San Jose CA 95135-1447

BEVERSDORF, ANNE ELIZABETH, educational marketing consultant, small business owner; b. Houston, Tex., Aug. 14, 1949; d. S. Thomas and Norma (Beeson) B. BA, U. Tex., 1972; MLS, Ind. U., 1974. Founding librarian Social Studies Devel. Ctr. Ind. U., Bloomington, 1975-79, info. specialist Vocat. Edn. Services, 1982-83, info. dissemination specialist Devel. Tng. Ctr., 1983; librarian Agy. for Instructional TV, Bloomington, 1980-82; info. specialist Ind. Clearinghouse for Computer Edn., Indpls., 1983-86; Calif. mktg. rep. Minn. Ednl. Computing Corp., San Marcos, Calif., 1986-88; pres., chief exec. officer Beversdorf Assocs., Ltd., Vista, Calif., 1988—; conf. planner Ind. Council for the Social Studies, Bloomington, 1976-79; cons. Procter & Gamble Ednl. Services, Cin., 1981-85, Brazil Office of Tech. Edn., Rio de Janeiro, Porto Alegre, 1986; instr. Ind. U., Indpls., 1986; mem. faculty San Diego State U., 1988-91. Editor computer newsletter; contbr. over 30 articles to profl. jours. Mem. NCGR, AFA, Computer Using Educators, Computers and Social Edn., Women in Sales. Home: 1119 Anza Ave Vista CA 92084-4517 Office: Beversdorf Assocs 956 Vale Terrace Dr Ste 212 Suite 204E Vista CA 92084

BEYERS, WILLIAM BJORN, geography educator; b. Seattle, Mar. 24, 1940; s. William Abraham and Esther Jakobia (Svendsen) B.; m. Margaret Lyn Rice, July 28, 1968. B.A., U. Wash., 1962, Ph.D., 1967. Asst. prof. geography U. Wash., Seattle, 1968-74, assoc. prof., 1974-82, prof., 1982—, chmn. dept. geography, 1991-95. Mem. Assn. Am. Geographers, Regional Sci. Assn., Am. Econ. Assn., Western Regional Sci. Assn. Home: 7159 Beach Dr SW Seattle WA 98136-2077 Office: U Wash Dept Geography DP 10 Seattle WA 98195

BEYERSDORF, MARGUERITE MULLOY, elementary education educator; b. Terry, Mont., Apr. 20, 1922; d. John William and Laura Agnes (Mahar) Mulloy; m. Curtis Alexander Beyersdorf, 1946; 1 child, Mary Jo Wright. Kindergarten-Primary Cert., Coll. St. Catherine, St. Paul, 1942; PhB, Marquette U., 1945; postgrad., Gonzaga U., Spokane, Wash., 1957-62, Ea. Wash. State U., 1977-79. Tchr. grade 3 Sacred Heart Sch., Oelwein, Iowa, 1942-43; tchr. grades 1 and 2 Jr. Mil. Acad., Chgo., 1943-44; tchr. history, English Fairfield (Wash.) High Sch., 1945-46; substitute tchr. Riverside High Sch., 1957; tchr. Mead (Wash.) Sch. Dist., 1958-75; owner/mgr. First Ave. Parking Lot, Spokane, Wash., 1957—. Vol. Spokane N.W. Communities Found., 1982—; active United Way Spokane, 1950, ARC, Am. Cancer Soc., Multiple Sclerosis Soc., others; vol. coord. Dominican Outreach Found. to Domicile Single Parent Families; canteen vol. Spokane Blood Bank, 1981—; vol. Miryam's House of Transition, 1989—. Recipient Vol. of Yr. Golden Rule award J.C. Penney Co., 1993; grantee NSF, Whitworth Coll., 1967. Mem. NEA, APGA, AAUW (bd. dirs. Spokane br., chmn. scholarship com.), Wash. Edn. Assn.-Retired (del. rep. assembly, mem. comm. com 1993—, chmn. comm. commn. 1993—), Mead Edn. Assn. (sec., exec. bd., former bldg. rep., mem. curriculum com.).

BEYLKIN, GREGORY, mathematician; b. St. Petersburg, USSR, Mar. 16, 1953; came to U.S., 1980; naturalized citizen, 1985; s. Jacob and Raya (Pripshtein) B.; m. Helen Simontov, 1974; children: Michael, Daniel. Diploma in Math., U. St. Petersburg, Leningrad, 1975; PhD in Math., NYU, 1982. Assoc. rsch. sci. NYU, 1982-83; mem. profl. staff Schlumberger-Doll Research, Ridgefield, Conn., 1983-91; prof. program in applied math. U. Colo., Boulder, 1991—. Contbr. articles to profl. jours. Mem. Am. Math. Soc., Soc. for Indsl. and Applied Math., Soc. Exptl. Geophysicists. Home: 3897 Promontory Ct Boulder CO 80304 Office: Program in Applied Math Univ Colo at Boulder University Of Colorado CO 80309-0526

BEYMER, DALE ALLEN, machine shop manager; b. Van Nuys, Calif., July 31, 1957; s. Lawerence Elmos and Patricia Anne (Bryce) B.; m. Anna Louise Beverage, June 3, 1984. Foreman Ronlo Engring. Ltd., Camarillo, Calif., 1975-79; gen. mgr. prodn. Alonian Enterprises Inc., Newbury Park, Calif., 1979-87; v.p. ops. J.M. Precision Inc., Chatsworth, Calif., 1987-88; mgr. machine shop Crane Co. Hydro-Aire Divsn., Burbank, Calif., 1988—; owner, pres. Dycal Systems, Newbury Park, 1982-92. Patentee torque limiting vise handle, 1985. Recipient Geometric Dimensioning and Tolerancing award Tech. Cons., Inc., 1993. Mem. Assn. for Integrated Mfg. Tech. Home: 11 E Avenida De Las Flores Thousand Oaks CA 91360-3104 Office: Crane Co Hydro-Aire Divsn PO Box 7722 Burbank CA 91510-7722

BEZANSON, RONALD SCOTT, JR., clergyman, army chaplain; b. Laconia, N.H., Oct. 28, 1936; s. Ronald Scott and Avis Maria (Preble) B.; m. Mary Joan Arthur, June 28, 1958; children: Deborah K. Rebecca K., Timothy S., Angela L. BA, Aurora (Ill.) Coll., 1958, BTh, 1959; MDiv, Evangel. Theol. Sem., Naperville, Ill., 1962; MBA, U. Tex., Austin, 1975. Ordained to ministry, Advent Christian Ch., 1962. Commd. 1st lt. U.S. Army, 1962, advanced through grades to col., 1982; chaplain, chief adminstrn. and mgmt. U.S. Army, Vietnam, 1970; staff chaplain Army Air Def. Command U.S. Army, Colorado Springs, Colo., 1971-73; instr. Chaplain Sch. U.S. Army, Ft. Wadsworth, N.Y., 1974-77; dep. chaplain materiel command U.S. Army, Alexandria, Va., 1977-81; chaplain 2d inf. div. U.S. Army, Camp Casey, Korea, 1981-82; dir. adminstrn., office chief chaplain, Pentagon U.S. Army, Washington, 1982-85; command chaplain hdqrs. Western command U.S. Army, Ft. Shafter, Hawaii, 1985-89; chief dept. of ministry and pastoral care Tripler Army Med. Ctr., Hawaii, 1989-92; pastor Ft. DeRussy Chapel, Honolulu, 1985-92; chaplain, coord. The Queen's Med. Ctr., Honolulu, 1992-93; interim pastor Christ Ch. Uniting Disciples & Presbyns., Kailua, Hawaii, 1994-95; treas. 1st United Presbyn. Ch., Woodbridge, Va., 1982-85; bd. dirs. Dept. Army Coun. Chaplain Cols., Washington, 1982-89. Pub., Westcom Chaplain newsletter, 1985-89; columnist, Hawaii Army Weekly, 1988-92. Mem. steering com., Gov.'s and Mayor's Prayer Breakfast, Honolulu, 1986-89. Decorated 2 Legions of Merit, 3 Bronze Star medals, 9 Air Medals. Mem. Mil Chaplains Assn., Officers Club, Army Golf Assn. Republican. Home: 46-381 Kumoo Loop Kaneohe HI 96744-3532 Office: Christ Ch Kailua HI 96734

BEZER, DAVID LEON, real estate appraiser; b. Phila., Nov. 25, 1943; s. Samuel and Frances (Rees) B.; m. Ellen Berkowitz, July 2, 1967; children: Daniel, Adam, Samara, John. Student, NYU, 1962-63, Temple U., 1969-70. Real estate salesman Magnus Internat. Inc., Camden, N.J., 1964-65; right of way agt. St. Davids, Pa., 1965-66; chief real estate appraiser Mfrs. Appraisal Co., Phila., 1966-70; exec. v.p. Enterprise Appraisal, Devon, Pa., 1971-75; pres. David L. Bezer & Co. Inc., Phila., 1975-86; v.p., treas. Valuation Network, Inc., N.Y.C., 1982-83, pres., 1983-84; pres. Valuation Network Inc. of So. Calif., San Diego, 1985-86; owner VNI Rainbow Appraisal Service, San Diego, 1986—. Mem. Am. Inst. Real Estate Appraisers, Am. Soc. Appraisers. Democrat. Jewish. Home: 2144 Belloc Ct San Diego CA 92109-1418 Office: VNI Rainbow Appraisal Service 2124 Garnet Ave San Diego CA 92109-3607

BHADURI, RAHUL SANKAR, metallurgical engineer; b. Calcutta, India, Aug. 23, 1956; came to U.S., 1981; s. Ajit and Sujita (Bhattacharjee) B.; m. Debjani Purkayastha, Jan. 4, 1985. BS in Metall. Engring., Jadavpur U., Calcutta, India, 1979; MS in Metall. Engring., U. Nev., 1987. Reg. profl. engr., Nev. Sales engr. Greaves-Foseco Ltd., Bombay, India, 1980; rsch., teaching asst. U. Nev., Reno, 1981-84; assayer, metallurgist Angst Inc., Gold Bar Mine, Beatty, Nev., 1987-88, metall. engr., 1988-89; metallurgist Atlas Gold-Gold Bar Mine, Eureka, Nev., 1990-92; metall. engr. Gold Fields Ops. Co.-Chimney Creek, Golconda, Nev., 1992-93, Santa Fe Pacific Gold-Twin Creeks Mine, Golconda, Nev., 1993—. Contbr. papers to profl. publs. Mem. Am. Inst. Mining, Metall. & Petroleum Engrs., Soc. Mineral Analysts, Toastmasters Internat. Office: Santa Fe Pacific Gold Twin Creeks Mine PO Box 492 Winnemucca NV 89446

BHAGWAN, SUDHIR, computer industry and research executive, consultant; b. Lahore, West Pakistan, Aug. 9, 1942; came to U.S., 1963; s. Vishan and Lakshmi Devi (Arora) B.; m. Sarita Bahl, Oct. 25, 1969; children: Sonia, Sunil. BSEE, Punjab Engring. Coll., Chandigarh, India, 1963; MSEE, Stanford U., 1964; MBA with honors, Golden Gate U., 1977. Engr. Gaylor Products, North Hollywood, Calif., 1964-68, Burroughs Corp., Pasadena, Calif., 1968-70; engring. mgr. Burroughs Corp., Santa Barbara, Calif., 1970-78; engring. mgr. Intel Corp., Hillsboro, Oreg., 1978-81, chmn. strategic planning, 1981-82, gen. mgr., 1983-88; pres., exec. dir., bd. dirs. Oreg. Advanced Computing Inst., Beaverton, 1988-90; strategic bus. mgr. INTEL Corp., Hillsboro, Oreg., 1990-92, gen. mgr. bus. multimedia products, 1992-93, bus. area mgr., 1993—; spkr. to high tech. industry, Oreg., 1988—; mem. organizing com. Distributed Memory Computing Conf., 1989-90, gen. chmn., 1990-91; chmn. computer tech. adv. bd. Oreg. Mus. Sci. and Industry, 1991-93; bd. dirs. II-Tracker Inc. Cons. Oreg. Econ. Devel. Dept., 1988-91; bd. dirs. St. Mary's Acad., Portland,, 1989-92. Mem. Am. Electronics Assn. (higher edn. com. Oreg. chpt. 1989-90, exec. com. 1990). Home: 13940 NW Harvest Ln Portland OR 97229-3653 Office: INTEL Corp 5200 NE Elam Young Pky Hillsboro OR 97124-6463

BHALLA, DEEPAK KUMAR, cell biologist, toxicologist, educator; b. Kasauli, India, Aug. 31, 1946; s. Khazan Chand and Shyama Bhalla; 1 child, Neel. BS, Punjab U., India, 1968, MS, 1969; PhD, Howard U., Washington, 1976. Postdoctoral fellow Harvard U., Boston, 1976-79; asst. rsch. cell biologist U. Calif., San Francisco, 1979-82; asst. prof. U. Calif., Irvine, 1982-86, assoc. prof., 1986—; speaker in field. Contbr. articles and revs. to profl. jours. NIH grantee, 1985-88, 88—, Calif. Air Resources Bd. grantee, 1990—. Mem. AAAS, Am. Thoracic Soc., Am. Soc. Cell Biology, Soc. Toxicology. Office: U Calif Community Environ Medi Irvine CA 92717

BHANU, BIR, computer information scientist, educator, director university program; b. Etah, India, Jan. 8, 1951; came to U.S., 1975; naturalized, 1987.; s. Rameshwar Dayal and Omwati Devi; m. Archana Bhanu Bhatnagar, Dec. 21, 1982; children: Shiv Bir, Ish Bir. BS with honors, Inst. Tech., Banaras Hindu U., Varanasi, India, 1972; M in Engring. with distinction, Birla Inst. Tech. and Sci., Pilani, India, 1974; SM and EE, MIT, 1977; PhD Image Processing Inst., U. So. Calif., 1981; MBA, U. Calif., Irvine, 1984; diploma in German, B.H.U., India, 1971. Lectr. in elec. engring. Birla Inst. Tech. and Sci., Pilani, 1974-75; acad. assoc. IBM Research Lab., San Jose, Calif., 1978; research fellow INRIA, Rocquencourt, France, 1980-81; engring. specialist Ford Aerospace and Communications Corp., Newport Beach, Calif., 1981-84; asst./assoc. prof. and dir. grad. admissions, dept. computer sci. U. Utah, Salt Lake City, 1984-87; staff scientist, Honeywell fellow, sr. Honeywell fellow Honeywell Systems and Rsch. Ctr., Mpls., 1986-91; prof. electrical engring., computer sci., program leader electrical engring. U. Calif., Riverside, 1991-94; dir. Visualization and Intelligent Systems Lab, U. Calif., Riverside, 1991—; cons. U. Calif., Irvine, 1983-84, Evolving Tech. Inst., San Diego, 1983-85, Bonneville Sci. Co., Salt Lake City, 1985-86, TRW, L.A., 1991—; pres. Internat. Student Assn. U. So. Calif., 1978-79; prin. investigator grants from ARPA, NSF, NASA, AFOSR, ARO, Rockwell, Ford, others. Co-author: Qualitative Motion Understanding, Kluwer, 1992, Genetic Learning for Adaptive Image Segmentation, Kluwer, 1994, Computational Learning for Adaptive Computer Vision, 1995; assoc. editor Jour. Math. Imaging and Vision, Pattern Recognition Jour., Internat. Jour. Machine Vision Applications; guest editor, co-editor IEEE Computer, 1987, Jour. Robotic Systems, 1992, Internat. Jour. Machine Vision and Applications, 1994, IEEE Transactions on Pattern Analysis and Machine Intelligence, 1994, IEEE Transactions on Robotics and Automation, 1994, IEEE Transactions on Image Processing, 1977; 5 patents in field; contbr. over 150 reviewed publications on subject of image processing, computer vision, artificial intelligence, machine learning and robotics. Recipient Outstanding Paper award Pattern Recognition Soc., 1990, Honeywell Motec and Alpha team awards, 1989, Project award Outstanding contbn. IBM Corp., 1978. Mem. IEEE (sr., gen. chair workshop applications computer vision 1992, program chair ARPA Image Understanding Workshop 1994, gen. chmn. IEEE conf. on computer vision and pattern recognition 1996), Assn. Computing Machinery, Soc. Photo-Optical and Instrumentation Engrs., Pattern Recognition Soc., Sigma Xi. Home: 6733 Canyon Hill Dr Riverside CA 92506-5672 Office: U Calif Coll Engring Riverside CA 92521

BHATIA, PETER K., editor, journalist; b. Pullman, Wash., May 22, 1953; s. Vishnu N. and Ursula Jean (Dawson) B.; m. Elizabeth M. Dahl, Sept. 27, 1981; children: Megan Jean, Jay Peter. BA, Stanford U., 1975. Polit. reporter, asst. news editor Spokesman Rev., Spokane, Wash., 1975-77; news editor Dallas Times Herald, 1980-81; asst. news editor San Francisco Examiner, 1977-80, news editor, 1981-85, dep. mng. editor/news, 1985-87; mng. editor Dallas Times Herald, 1987-88; editor York Dispatch, York, Pa., 1988-89; mng. editor The Sacramento Bee, 1989-93; exec. editor The Fresno Bee, 1993; mng. editor The Oregonian, Portland, 1993—; Pulitzer Prize juror, 1992-93. Editor-in-charge San Francisco Examiner's coverage of The Philippines and fall of Marcos, 1986-87 (Pulitzer Prize for spot news photography 1987). Sacramento Bee newspaper a recipient of 2 Pulitzer prizes for pub. svc. and beat reporting, 1992. Mem. Stanford U. Alumni Assn., Am. Soc. Newspaper Editors, AP Mng. Editors (bd. dirs. 1991), Asian Am. Journalists Assn., Nat. Assn. Minority Media Execs., Sigma Delta Chi, Theta Delta Chi. Office: The Oregonian 1320 SW Broadway Portland OR 97201

BHAYANI, KIRAN LILACHAND, environmental engineer, programs manager; b. Bhavnagar, Gujarat, India, Dec. 2, 1944; came to U.S., 1968, naturalized; s. Lilachand Premchand and Rasila (Chhotalal Shah) B.; m. Chandra Vasantlal Gandhi, June 24, 1971; children: Nikhil K., Mihir K. BEng with honors, U. Bombay, India, 1965, MEng, 1968; MS, U. R.I., 1970. Diplomate Am. Acad. Environ. Engrs.; registered profl. engr., Va., Ga., Utah. San. engr. Greeley & Hansen, N.Y.C., 1971-72, Hayes, Seay, Mattern & Mattern, Roanoke, Va., 1972-77; environ. engr. Hussey, Gay & Bell, Inc., Savannah, Ga., 1977-80; engring. mgr., Utah Div. Water Quality, Dept. Environ. Quality, Salt Lake City, 1980—; tech. transfer and sludge mgmt. coord., 1982—; mem. fair employment com. Dept. Health, Salt Lake City, 1982-90, adv. 1991-93, chmn., 1988-89, cons., 1989-91; mem. Utah Engrs. Coun., 1989—, vice-chmn., 1992-93, chmn. 1993-94, awards chmn., 1994-95; chmn. Engr's. Week, 1992; v.p. Gujarati Samaj of Utah, 1992-93. Reviewer (practice manual) Financing Sewer Projects, 1984; design of Municipal Wastewater Treatment Plants, 1990-91. Fellow ASCE (profl. coordination com. 1981-88, reviewer Jour. Environ. Engring. Div., Proceedings ASCE 1988—); mem. NSPE, Am. Acad. Environ. Engrs. (state chmn. 1988—), Am. Water Works Assn., Internat. Assn. Water Quality, Water and Environ. Fedn. (internat. com. 1984, mem. tech. rev. com. for manual of practice, 1990-95), MATHCOUNTS (chmn. 1985-88, bd. govs. 1988—, regional coord. 1988-95). Office: Utah Div Water Quality 288 N 1460 W Salt Lake City UT 84116-3100

BIAGI, SHIRLEY ANNE, journalism educator; b. San Francisco, June 21, 1944; d. Herbert Hamilton Rickey and Gerbina Mary (Biagi) Rickey; m. Victor J. Biondi, May 2, 1964; children: Paul and Tom (twins), David. BA, Calif. State U., Sacramento, 1967, MA, 1975. Prof. Calif. State U., Sacramento, 1975—, chmn. dept., 1987-92. Author: How to Write and Sell Magazine Articles, 1981, 2d rev. edit., 1989, Interviews That Work, 1986, 2d rev. edit., 1992, Media/Impact, 1988, 3d rev. edit., 1995, Media/Reader, 1990, 3d rev. edit., 1995. Recipient teaching award Poynter Inst., 1983; Danforth fellow, 1981-86. Mem. Assn. for Edn. in Journalism and Mass Comm. (exec. bd. 1990-94), Am. Journalism History Assn. (bd. dirs. 1994—). Office: Calif State Univ 6000 J St Sacramento CA 95819-2605

BIALOSKY, MARSHALL HOWARD, composer; b. Oct. 30, 1923. Student, Converse Coll., 1942-43, 46, Colo. Coll., 1948; MusB cum laude, Syracuse U., 1949; MusM, Northwestern U., 1950. Asst. prof. music Milton (Wis.) Coll., 1950-54; asst. conductor Milton Coll. Band, 1954; asst. prof. humanities and music U. Chgo., 1956-61; assoc. prof. music and humanities, conductor chorale SUNY, Stony Brook, 1961-64; prof., chmn. dept. fine arts Calif. State U., Dominguez Hills, 1964-77, founding chmn. dept. music, 1977-78, prof. dept. music, 1978-86, prof. emeritus dept. music, 1986—; mem. Calif. State Coll. Employee Assn. Statewide Acad. Coun., 1968-71; mem. Calif. State Coll. Internat. Program Acad. Coun. and Exec. Com., 1967-73; bd. dirs. Monday Evening Concerts, L.A., 1966-77; dir. Saturday Conservatory Music, L.A. chpt., 1967-71; coord. humanities M.A. program Calif. State U., Dominguez Hills; composer-in-residence Chamber Music Conf. and Composer's Forum of the East, Bennington Coll., 1989. Performer various cities, radio stas. and schs. Composer piano music including An Album for the Young, Five Western Scenes, mixed chorus including American Names, A Sight in Camp in the Daybreak Gray and Dim, Women's Chorus including American Poets Suite, At Last, Vocal Music including Two Songs to Poems of Howard Nemerov, folk songs, spirituals, Christmas music, music for wind instruments, string instruments, brass instruments, guitar and percussion instruments. Contbr. articles to jours. Fulbright award, 1954-56; Wurlitzer Found. grantee, 1979, N.Y.C. Meet-the-Composer grantee, 1984, 86; recipient Career Achievement award Profl. Fraternity Assn. Am., 1980. Mem. ASCAP (creative grant award 1976—), Coll. Music Soc., Am. Soc. Univ. Composers (nat. chmn. 1974-77), Nat. Assn. Composers U.S.A. (pres. 1978—), Soc. Composers Inc., Am. Assn. Choral Conductor. Office: Nat Assoc Composer USA PO Box 49652 Los Angeles CA 90049-0652

BIANCHI, RICHARD, food products executive; b. 1947. With Bianchi Land Co., Merced, Calif., 1968—, v.p., 1971—, now v.p., sec. Office: Bianchi Land Co 1975 W Olive Ave Merced CA 95348-1206*

BIANCO, JAMES A., research and development executive; b. 1956. BS cum laude with honors, NYU, 1979; MD, Mt. Sinai Sch. of Medicine, 1983. Intern, then resident Mt. Sinai Med. Ctr., N.Y.C., 1983-87; fellow in oncology U. Wash., Seattle, 1987-91, asst. prof. medicine, 1991-92; dir. bone marrow transplant program VA Med. Ctr., Seattle, 1990-92; asst. mem. Fred Hutchinson Cancer Rsch. Ctr., Seattle, 1991-92; pres., CEO Cell Therapeutics, Inc., Seattle, 1992—. Mem. Alpha Omega Alpha. Office: Cell Therapeutics Inc 201 Elliott Ave W Fl 4 Seattle WA 98119-4230*

BIANCO, NICOLE ANN, data processing executive; b. Allentown, Pa., Sept. 30, 1949; d. Welch Collerige and Ruth Ellen (Sacher) Everman; m. William Joseph Bianco, Aug. 19, 1971. Cert., Pa. State U., 1967. Programmer RCA, Moorestown, N.J., 1967-69, Trenton (N.J.) Trust Co, 1969-71, Food Fair, Inc., Phila., 1971-73; data processing officer Provident Nat. Bank, Phila., 1973-77; grant coordinator Burlington County Coll., Pemberton, N.J., 1977-79; asst. v.p. Valley Nat. Bank, Phoenix, 1979-85; cons. in field Phoenix, 1985-87; dir. tech. services Trak-Tech, Inc., Phoenix, 1987-89; mgr. corp. mgmt. infosystems Motorola, Inc., Scottsdale, Ariz., 1989—; educator/tchr. Computer Systems Devel., Phoenix, 1985-87; adv. editor John Wiley & Sons, Inc., 1986--. Author: (textbooks) Introduction to Data Base, 1985, Data Communications, 1985, Advanced Project Management, 1986; author and devel.: (software) Parolee Tracking System, 1987. Mem. Profl. Software Programmers Assn. Home: 863 W Happfield Dr Arlington Heights IL 60004-7141 Office: Motorola Inc 1299 E Algonquin Rd Schaumburg IL 60196-4040

BIBEL, BARBARA MITA, librarian; b. N.Y.C., Oct. 30, 1945; d. Seeling Isaac and Lillian (Serebreny) Chaikin; m. David J. Bibel, 1970 (div. 1977); 1 child, Sara. BA summa cum laude in French, UCLA, 1967; MA in Romance Lang., Johns Hopkins U., 1970; MLS, U. Calif., Berkeley, 1971. Cert. tchr., Calif. Libr. Fitz Hugh Ludlow Meml. Libr., San Francisco, Calif., 1972-75; reference libr. Info. Unlimited, Berkeley, 1977-79; indsl. safety trainer Chevron U.S.A., Richmond, Calif., 1980-82; asst. unit head humanities grad. svc. Gen. Libr. U. Calif., Berkeley, 1983-87; reference libr. IIsci, bus., sociology dept. Oakland (Calif.) Pub. Libr., 1986—; book reviewer Booklist, Chgo., 1988—, Libr. Jour., N.Y.C., 1989—, Am. Ref. Books Ann., Englewood, Colo., 1993—, R.R. Bowker, 1994; translator Berkeley Sci. Translation, 1977-79; instr. health edn. Vista Coll., Berkeley, 1977-81; reference libr. Bay Area Libr. Info. System, 1984-91, Berkeley Pub. Libr., 1984—; libr. Congregation Beth El., Berkeley, 1985-86; instr. sch. libr. and info. studies U. Calif., Berkeley, 1984-87; contbr. Encyclopedias, Dictionaries, Atlases for the 1990's. Editor: Reference Sources for Small and Medium-Sized Libraries, 6th edit., 1995. asst. coord. safety svcs. ARC, Berkeley, 1977-79. John Hopkins U. fellow, 1967-70; Calif. State U. scholar, 1963-67, UCLA Alumni scholar, 1963-67. Mem. ALA (editorial bd. Reference Books Bulletin), ACLU, Calif. Libr. Assn., Nat. Assn. Emergency Med. Technicians, Phi Beta Kappa. Office: Oakland Pub Libr 125 14th St Oakland CA 94612-4310

BIBLE, FRANCES LILLIAN, mezzo-soprano, educator; b. Sackets Harbor, N.Y.; d. Arthur and Lillian (Cooke) B. Student, Juilliard Sch. Music, 1939-47. Artist-in-residence Shepherd Sch. of Music Rice U., Houston, 1975-91. Appeared throughout U.S., Australia, Europe including Vienna Staatsoper, Karlsruhe Staatsoper, Dublin Opera Co., N.Y.C. Opera, NBC-TV Opera, San Francisco Opera, Glyndebourne Opera, San Antonio Opera Festival, New Orleans Opera, Houston Grand Opera, Miami Opera, Dallas Opera; appeared in concert with major symphonies. Named Woman of the Yr. in Opera, Mademoiselle Mag., 1950. Mem. Am. Guild Mus. Artists (past 3d v.p., bd. dirs. 1989-91), Sigma Alpha Iota (hon.), Beta Sigma Pi (hon.). Republican. Episcopalian. Home: 2377 Thata Way Hemet CA 92544-7009

BICE, SCOTT HAAS, lawyer, educator; b. Los Angeles, Mar. 19, 1943; s. Fred Haas and Virginia M. (Scott) B.; m. Barbara Franks, Dec. 21, 1968. B.S., U. So. Calif., 1965, J.D., 1968. Bar: Calif. bar 1971. Law clk. to Chief Justice Earl Warren, 1968-69; successively asst. prof., assoc. prof., prof. law., Carl Mason Franklin prof. U. So. Calif., Los Angeles, 1969—; assoc. dean U. So. Calif., 1971-74, dean, 1980—; vis. prof. polit. sci. Calif. Inst. Tech., 1977; vis. prof. U. Va., 1978-79; bd.dirs. Western Mut. Ins. Co., Residence Mut. Ins. Co., Imagine Films Entertainment Co., Jenny Craig, Inc. Mem. editl. adv. bd. Calif. Lawyer, 1989-93; contbr. articles to law jours. Bd. dirs. L.A. Family Housing Corp., 1989-93, Stone Soup Child Care Programs, 1988—. Affiliated scholar Am. Bar Found., 1972-74. Fellow Am. Bar Found.; mem. Am. Law Inst., Calif. Bar, Los Angeles County Bar Assn., Am. Judicature Soc., Calif. Club, Chancery Club, Calif. Yacht Club. Home: 787 S San Rafael Ave Pasadena CA 91105-2326 Office: U So Calif Law Ctr Univ Park Los Angeles CA 90026

BICK, ISRAEL, collectables and memorabilia company executive; b. Bronx, N.Y., Nov. 3, 1937; s. Benjamin and Sylvia (Berger) B.; m. Ida Hirsch, Feb. 8, 1970 (div. 1980); children: Benjamina, Mayer. BA, Yeshiva U., 1959. Founder, owner, CEO Bick Internat., Van Nuys, Calif., 1952—; cons. numerous charitable orgns.; appraiser for state, city, banks, and estates. Chmn. stamp and coin divsn. United Jewish Fund L.A. With U.S. Army, 1961-63. Named Soldier of Yr., U.S. Army, 1962; recipient plaque U.S. Postal Svc. Mem. Internat. Stamp Collectors Soc. (exec. dir.). Office: PO Box 854 Van Nuys CA 91408-0854

BICKEL, PETER JOHN, statistician, educator; b. Bucharest, Romania, Sept. 21, 1940; came to U.S., 1957, naturalized, 1964; s. Eliezer and P. Madeleine (Moscovici) B.; m. Nancy Kramer, Mar. 2, 1964; children: Amanda, Stephen. AB, U. Calif., Berkeley, 1960, MA, 1961, PhD, 1963; PhD (hon.), Hebrew U. Jerusalem, 1988. Asst. prof. stats. U. Calif., Berkeley, 1964-67, assoc. prof., 1967-70, prof., 1970—, chmn. dept. stats., 1976-79, dean phys. scis., 1980-86, chmn. dept. stats., 1993—; vis. lectr. math. Imperial Coll., London, 1965-66; fellow J. S. Guggenheim Meml. Found., 1970-71; NATO sr. sci. fellow, 1974. Author: (with K. Doksum) Mathematical Statistics, 1976, (with C. Klaassen, Y. Ritov and J. Wellner) Efficient and Adaptive Estimation in Semiparametric Models, 1993; assoc. editor Annals of Math. Stats., 1968-76, 86-93; contbr. articles to profl. jours. Fellow Inst. Math. Stats. (pres. 1980), Am. Statis. Assn., AAAS; mem. Royal Statis. Soc., Internat. Statis. Inst., Nat. Acad. Sci., Am. Acad. Arts Scis., Bernoulli Soc. (pres. 1990). Office: U Calif Dept Stats Evans Hall Berkeley CA 94720

BICKERSTAFF, BERNARD TYRONE, SR., professional basketball team executive; b. Benham, Ky., Nov. 2, 1943; m. Eugenia King; children: Tim, Robin, Cydni, Bernard, John. Grad., U. San Diego. Former head coach U. San Diego; then asst. coach Washington Bullets, Nat. Basketball Assn., Landover, Md.; head coach Seattle SuperSonics, 1985-90, v.p. ops., 1990; gen. mgr. Denver Nuggests, 1990—, also exec. v.p. Office: care Denver Nuggets 1635 Clay St Denver CO 80204-1799*

BICKFORD, PETER RICHARD, computer programmer; b. Pitts., June 27, 1967; s. Paul Bernard and Mary Edith (Davis) Deignan; m. Carolyn Johanna Bickford, Aug. 22, 1992. BA in Philosophy, U. Wis., 1992. Freelance programmer Wis./Minn., 1980-87; human interface champion Apple Computer, Inc., Cupertino, Calif., 1988—; prin. Human Computing, Sunnyvale, Calif., 1992—. Programmer (software) Comic Base, 1992. Office: Apple Computer Inc M/S 35-G 1 Infinite Loop Cupertino CA 95014-2083

BICKNELL, SUSAN MARCIA HERR, ecology educator; b. Indpls., July 30, 1949; d. George Aloysious and Marcia Louise (Edwards) Herr; m. Donald Wayne Bicknell, Jan. 30, 1971; 1 child, Jeffrey Joseph. AB in English, Ind. U., 1971; M in Forestry Sci., Yale U., 1975, PhD in Forest Ecology, 1978. From asst. prof. to prof. forestry Calif. State U.-Humboldt, Arcata, 1978—, chmn. dept. forestry, 1983-86; dean of grad. studies and rsch. Humboldt State Univ., Arcata, 1990—. Proceedings editor: Symposium, 1983-87; contbr. articles to profl. jours. Bd. dirs. Redwood Region Conservation Council, Santa Rosa, Calif., 1983-87, Humboldt State U. Found., 1987—. Grantee McIntire-Stennis-Fed., 1979-80, Inst. Ecosystem Studies, 1985-86, Calif. Air Resources Bd., Calif. Dept. Parks and Recreations, 1985-92. Mem. Soc. Am. Foresters, Ecol. Soc. Am. (cert. sr. ecologist). Office: Humboldt State U Office Rsch and Grad Studies Arcata CA 95521

BIDDLE, DONALD RAY, aerospace company executive; b. Alton, Mo., June 30, 1936; s. Ernest Everet and Dortha Marie (McGuire) B.; m. Nancy Ann Dunham, Mar. 13, 1955; children: Jeanne Kay Biddle Bednash, Mitchell Lee, Charles Alan. Student El Dorado (Kans.) Jr. Coll., 1953-55, Pratt (Kans.) Jr. Coll., 1955-56; BSME, Washington U., St. Louis, 1961; postgrad. computer sci. Pa. State U. Extension, 1963; cert. bus. mgmt. Alexander Hamilton Inst., 1958. Design group engr. Emerson Elec. Mfg., St. Louis, 1957-61; design specialist Boeing Vertol, Springfield, Pa., 1962; cons. engr. Ewing Tech. Design, Phila., 1962-66; chief engr. rotary wing Gates Learjet, Wichita, Kans., 1967-70; dir. engring./R & D BP Chems., Inc. Advanced Materials Div., Stockton, Calif., 1971-93; prin. Biddle & Assocs., Consulting Engrs., Stockton, 1993—. Guest lectr. on manrated structures various univs. and tech. socs. Cons. engr. Scoutmaster, counselor, instl. rep. Boy Scouts Am., St. Ann, Mo., 1958-61; mem. Springfield Sch. Bd., 1964. Mem. ASME, ASTM, AIAA, Am. Helicopter Soc. (sec.-treas. Wichita chpt. 1969), Am. Mgmt. Assn., Exptl. Pilots Assn., Soc. for Advancement of Metals and Process Engring. Republican. Methodist (trustee, chmn. 1974-76, 84-86, staff parish 1987—). Patentee landing gear designs, inflatable rescue system, glass retention systems, adjustable jack system, cold weather start fluorescent lamp, paper honeycomb core post-process systems. Home: 1140 Stanton Way Stockton CA 95207 Office: Biddle & Assocs 1140 Stanton Way Stockton CA 95207

BIDWILL, WILLIAM V., professional football executive; s. Charles W. and Violet Bidwill; m. Nancy Bidwill; children: William Jr., Michael, Patrick, Timothy, Nicole. Grad., Georgetown U. Co-owner St. Louis Cardinals Football Team (now known as Phoenix Cardinals), 1962-72, owner, 1972—, also chmn., 1972—; pres. St. Louis Cardinals Football Team (now known as Phoenix Cardinals), Phoenix, Ariz. Office: Ariz Cardinals P O Box 888 Phoenix AZ 85001-0888*

BIEBER-ROBERTS, PEGGY EILENE, communications educator, journalist; b. Mobridge, S.D., Jan. 8, 1943; d. John J. and Lenora (Schlepp) B. BS, No. State U., Aberdeen, S.D., 1966; MA, U. Wyo., 1984; PhD, U. Wash., 1990. Vol. Peace Corps, Turkey, 1966-68; tchr. secondary pub. schs., Idaho, 1968-69, Pine Ridge (S.D.) Reservation, 1969-71; legis. reporter various weekly newspapers, Wyo., 1980-82; owner, pub. Capitol Times mag., Cheyenne, Wyo., 1982-84; lectr. pub. rels. and advt. U. Wash., Seattle, 1988-90; rsch. analyst Elway Rsch./Jay Rockey Co., Seattle, 1989-90; asst. prof. mass media U. Wyo., Laramie, 1990—; indexer McGraw/Hill, Bedford Books, also others, 1988—. Author, editor hist. almanacs for various states, 1984-87; contbr. articles to profl. jours., chpts. to books. Publicity chmn. Laramie County Dem. Com., Cheyenne, 1982. Recipient 1st place award for feature writing, co-1st place award for editorials Wyo. Press Assn., 1982; Stout fellow U. Wash., 1990. Mem. Turkish Studies Assn., Internat. Assn. Mass Comm. Rsch., Assn. Ednl. Journalism and Mass Comm., Internat. Comm. Assn., Mid East Studies Assn. Office: U Wyo Dept Comm and Mass Media Laramie WY 82071

BIEDERMAN, DONALD ELLIS, lawyer; b. N.Y.C., Aug. 23, 1934; s. William and Sophye (Groll) B.; m. Marna M. Leerburger, Dec. 22, 1962; children: Charles Jefferson, Melissa Anne. AB, Cornell U., 1955; JD, Harvard U., 1958; LLM in Taxation, NYU, 1970. Bar: N.Y. 1959, U.S. Dist. Ct. (so. dist.) N.Y. 1967, Calif. 1977. Assoc. Hale, Russell & Stentzel, N.Y.C., 1962-66; asst. corp. counsel City of N.Y., 1966-68; assoc. Delson & Gordon, N.Y.C., 1968-69; ptnr. Roe, Carman, Clerke, Berkman & Berkman, Jamaica, N.Y., 1969-72; gen. atty. CBS Records, N.Y.C., 1972-76; sr. v.p. legal affairs and adminstrn. ABC Records, L.A., 1977-79; ptnr. Mitchell, Silberberg & Knupp, L.A., 1979-83; exec. v.p., gen. counsel bus. affairs Warner/Chappell Music Inc. (formerly Warner Bros. Music), L.A., 1983—; adj. prof. Sch. Law Southwestern U., L.A., 1982—, Pepperdine U., Malibu, Calif., 1985-87, Loyola Marymount U., L.A., 1992; lectr. Anderson Sch. Mgmt. UCLA, 1993. Editor: Legal and Business Problems of the Music Industry, 1980; co-author: Law and Busines of the Entertainment Industries, 1987, 2nd edit., 1991, 3d edit., 1995. Bd. dirs. Calif. Chamber Symphony Soc., L.A., 1981-92; dir. Entertainment Law Inst. U. So. Calif., 1993—. 1st lt. U.S. Army, 1959. Recipient Hon. Gold Record, Recording Industry Assn. Am., 1974, Trendsetter award Billboard mag., 1976. Mem. N.Y. Bar Assn., Calif. Bar Assn., Riviera Country Club, Cornell Club. Democrat. Jewish. Home: 2406 Pesquera Dr Los Angeles CA 90049-1225 Office: Warner/Chappell Music Inc 10585 Santa Monica Blvd Los Angeles CA 90025-4921

BIELBY, WILLIAM THOMAS, sociologist educator; b. Chgo., Sept. 17, 1947; s. Warren Munro and Sulvia (Bloom) B.; m. Denise Del Vento, June 7, 1969. BSEE, U. Ill., 1970, MA in Social Scis., 1972; PhD of Sociology, U. Wis., 1976. Prof. sociology U. Calif., Santa Barbara, 1977—; vis. prof. UCLA, 1985; statis. cons. Writers Guild of Am. W., West Hollywood, Calif., 1986—; expert witness discrimination litigation Fed. and State Cts., Calif., 1991—. Contbr. articles to profl. jours. Fellow Ctr. for Advanced Study in Behavioral Scis., 1983-84; recipient Reubin Hill award for Theory and Rsch. Nat. Coun. on Family Rels., 1993, Excellence in Feminist Studies award Popular Culture Assn., 1986. Mem. Am. Sociol. Assn. (sec.-treas. Methodology sect. 1984-88), Am. Econs. Assn., Am. Statis. Assn., Sociol. Rsch. Assn. Office: Univ Calif Dept Sociology Santa Barbara CA 93106

BIELE, HUGH IRVING, lawyer; b. Bridgeport, Conn., July 28, 1942; s. Ray James and Blanche (McClellan) B.; m. Pamela Althea Johnson, Aug. 21, 1965 (div.); children: Jonathan Christopher, Melissa Lynne. BA, St. Lawrence U., Canton, N.Y., 1965; JD, U. Utah, 1968. Bar: Utah 1968, U.S. Dist. Ct. Utah 1968, Calif. 1972, U.S. Dist. Ct. Calif. 1972, U.S. Ct. Appeals (9th and 10th cirs.). Instr. San Francisco Law Sch., 1971-73; atty. United Calif. Bank, San Francisco, 1971-74; v.p., sr. counsel First Interstate Bank, L.A., 1974-81; ptnr. Biele & Stuehrmann, L.A., 1981-83; sr. ptnr. Biele, Stuehrmann & Lapinski, L.A., 1983-84; founding ptnr. Biele & Lapinski, L.A., 1985-89; ptnr. Barton, Klugman & Detting, L.A., 1989-91, Grace, Skocypec, Cosgrove & Schirm, L.A., 1992—; bd. govs. Fin. Lawyer Conf., L.A., 1976—, pres. 1984-85. Author screenplay: Corporate Cancer, 1989, Hedge of Thorns, 1990. Bd. dirs. Community Counseling Svc., L.A., 1989—, pres., 1993—; bd. dirs., v.p., sec. Project New Hope, Inc., L.A., 1990-92; commr. Episc. Diocese AIDS Ministry, L.A., 1988-93; chmn. Vols. in Parole, L.A., 1979-80, 89-90. Maj. U.S. Army, 1968-70. Decorated Bronze Star with oak leaf cluster, Army Commendation medal. Mem. ABA, Fed. Bar Assn., L.A. County Bar Assn. (internat. sect. exec. com. 1978—, chmn. 1981-82, exec. com. comml. law and bankruptcy sect. 1986—, chair 1992-93), Calif. State Bar (fin. inst. com.), Internat. Bankers Assn. Calif., St. Lawrence U. Alumni Assn. (pres. 1979-91). Republican. Episcopalian. Home: 3016 Hollycrest Dr Los Angeles CA 90068-1802 Office: Grace Skocypec Cosgrove & Schirm 5700 Wilshire Blvd Ste 300N Los Angeles CA 90036-3659

BIER, JESSE, literature educator; b. Hoboken, N.J., July 18, 1925; s. Benjamin Arthur and Lenore (Greenberg) B.; m. Laure Victoria Darsa, July 21, 1950; children: Ethan, Leslie, Lilian. BA, Bucknell U., 1949; MA, Princeton U., 1952, PhD, 1956. From instr. to prof. lit. U. Mont., Missoula, 1955-90; Fulbright prof. U. Lyon and Clermont-Ferrand, France, 1957-58; vis. lectr. Bucknell U., Lewisburg, Pa., 1965-66; vis. prof. San Diego State Coll., 1971; chair in Am. lit. Université de Lausanne, Switzerland, 1971-72; vis. lectr. Sorbonne, 1995; cons. editor Bucknell U. Press, 1975-77; cons. Swiss Univ. System, Switzerland, 1978, U. Ottowa, Can., 1983. Author: The Rise and Fall of American Humour: Criticism, History, 1968, 81, Resistant Essays, 1993, criticism; novels: Trial at Bannock: 1963-64, A Hole in the Lead Apron, 1964, Year of the Cougar, 1976. Cpl. U.S. Army, 1943-45, ETO. Decorated Purple Heart. Home: 5850 Wildcat Rd Missoula MT 59802

BIERBAUM, JANITH MARIE, artist; b. Evanston, Ill., Jan. 14, 1927; d. Gerald Percy and Lillian (Sullivan) Turnbull; m. J. Armin Bierbaum, Apr. 17, 1948; children: Steve, Todd, Chad, Peter, Mark. BA, Northwestern U., 1948; student, Mpls. Art Inst., 1964; postgrad., St. Paul Art Inst., 1969-70. Rsch. asst. AMA, Chgo., 1948-49; tchr. Chgo. high schs., 1949-51; freelance artist Larkspur, Colo., 1951—. Exhibited in group shows at Foot Hills Art Ctr., 1985, 86, 87, Palmer Lake (Colo.) Art Assn., 1986-87, 88-89, Gov.'s Mansion, Bismarck, N.D., 1960; oil painting appeared in 1989 Women in Art Nat. calendar pub. by AAUW. Recipient 1st Place Purchase award U. Minn., Mpls., 1966, Coors Classic award Coors Beer, Golden, Colo., 1987. Mem. Colo. Artist Assn. Republican. Home and Office: 7787 S Perry Park Blvd Larkspur CO 80118-9005

BIERMAN, CHARLES WARREN, physician, educator; b. Ada, Ohio, May 27, 1924; s. Linn Carl and Margery (Warren) B.; m. Joan Wingate, May 15, 1952; children: Margot Ellen, Karen Linn, Charlotte Joane, Barbara Anne. MD, Harvard U., 1947. Diplomate Am. Bd. Pediat., Am. Bd. Allergy and Immunology (bd. dirs. 1971-77). Intern Lankenau Hosp., Phila., 1947-48; resident in pediat. Bellevue Hosp., N.Y.C., 1948-49; resident in pediatrics N.Y. Hosp., N.Y.C., 1949-50; fellow in neonatology N.Y. Hosp., 1950, Hosp. Enfants Malades, Paris, 1953-54; resident in allergy U. Wash., Seattle, 1965-67; pvt. practice specializing in pediat. and adult allergy Seattle, 1967—; mem. staffs Children's Hosp. and Med. Ctr., Univ. Hosp., Harborview Hosp.; instr. pediatrics Cornell Med. Sch., 1949-50; clin. instr. pediatrics U. Wash., Seattle, 1958-59, clin. asst. prof., 1959-62, clin. assoc. prof., 1962-70, clin. prof., 1970—, chief div. allergy dept. pediatrics, 1967—; hon. rsch. fellow dept. pharmacology, hon. cons. respiratory disease Univ. Coll. London, 1978-79; cons. Wash. State Dept. Social and Health Svcs., 1979-87; gov. Am. Bd. Allergy and Immunology, 1970-78, mem., vice chmn. residency rev. com., 1982-90; vis. prof. pediatrics United Med. Dental Schs., Guy's Hosp., London, 1989. Editor: (with D.S. Pearlman) Allergic Diseases of Infancy, Childhood and Adolescence, 1980, Allergic Diseases from Infancy to Adulthood, 1988, (with D.S. Pearlman, G.G. Shapiro and W. Busse) Allergy Asthma and Immunology, 1995; mem. editl. bd. Pediat., 1972-76, Pediat. in Review, 1977-82, Clin. Revs. in Allergy, 1981-87, Jour. Asthma, Annals of Allergy in Pediat. Allergy; contbr. articles to med. jours. With USN, 1944-46, 50-51, U.S. Army, 1951-52. Fellow Am. Acad. Allergy (exec. com. 1980-83), Am. Acad. Pediatrics (chmn. allergy sect. 1974-76); mem. AMA, Wash. State Med. Assn. (ho. of dels.), Wash. State Pediatrics Assn., Wash. State Allergy Soc., Puget Sound Allergy Soc., Seattle Pediatric Soc., Am. Pediatric Soc., Western Soc. for Pediatric Rsch., Brit. Soc. for Allergy and Clin. Immunology. Episcopalian. Home: 4524 E Laurel Dr NE Seattle WA 98105-3839 Office: 4540 Sand Point Way NE Seattle WA 98105-3941

BIERMAN, HOWARD RICHARD, physician; b. Newark, Jan. 27, 1915; m. Doris Simmons, May 16, 1946; children: Barry, Tracey, Dana. BS in Medicine, Washington U. St. Louis, 1939, MD, 1939. Intern Barnes Hosp., 1938-39, resident and fellow in hematology, 1939-41; prin. clin. investigator Nat. Cancer Inst., NIH, Bethesda, Md., 1946-53; chief clin. sect. lab. experimental oncology & medicine U. Calif., San Francisco, 1947-53; dir. hosp. for tumors and allied diseases City of Hope Med. Hosp., Duarte, Calif., 1953-59; chmn. dept. medicine City of Hope Med. Hosp., Durate, Calif., 1954-59, med. and scientific dir., 1955-59; dir. Bierman Med. Group, Inc., 1959—; scientific dir. Inst. for Cancer and Blood Rsch., Beverly Hills, Calif., 1959—; sr. attending physician L.A. County Gen. Hosp., 1959-68, sr. attending physician emeritus, 1968—; attending physician Cedars of Lebanon Hosp. and Mt. Sinai Hosp., L.A., 1959-76, Cedars-Sinai Med. Ctr., L.A., 1967—; attending physician, cons. Century City Hosp., Midway Hosp., 1976—; cons. hematology-oncology White Meml. Hosp., 1959—; vis. prof. Bangkok Sanitarium and Hosp., 1960, 63. Editor: Leukopoiesis and Disease, 1964, Am. Lectrs. Series in Tumors, 1970-72; author of 5 books; contbr. over 250 articles to profl. jours.; patentee in field. Comdr. USN, 1941-47, USNR, 1947-65. Fellow AAAS, Am. Coll. Physicians, Am. Coll. Angiology, Internat. Soc. Internal Medicine, N.Y. Acad. Scis.; mem. AMA, Am. Soc. Internal Medicine, Am. Soc. Clin. Oncology, Am. Soc. Pharmacology and Experimental Therapeutics, Am. Assn. Cancer Rsch., Am. Soc. Hematology, Am. Soc. Clin. Investigators, Am. Fedn. Clin. Rsch., Calif. Med. Assn., So. Calif. Acad. Clin. Oncology, Los Angeles County Med. Assn., Internat. Assn. Study Lung Cancer, Internat. Union Cancer, Internat. Soc. Preventive Oncology, Internat. Soc. Experimental Hematology, Western Pharmacology Soc., Western Soc. Clin. Rsch., Cell Kinetics Soc., Alpha Omega Alpha (Mo. chpt.).

BIERSTEDT, PETER RICHARD, lawyer, entertainment industry consultant; b. Rhinebeck, N.Y., Jan. 2, 1943; s. Robert Henry and Betty (MacIver) B.; m. Carol Lynn Akiyama, Aug. 23, 1980. AB, Columbia U., 1965, JD cum laude, 1969; cert., U. Sorbonne, Paris, 1966. Bar: N.Y. 1969, U.S. Supreme Ct. 1973, Calif. 1977. Atty. with firms in N.Y.C., 1969-74; pvt. practice cons. legal and entertainment industry, 1971, 75-76, 88—; with Avco Embassy Pictures Corp., L.A., 1977-83; v.p., gen. counsel Avco Embassy Pictures Corp., 1978-80, sr. v.p., 1980-83, dir., 1981-83; gen. counsel New World Entertainment (formerly New World Pictures), L.A., 1984-87, exec. v.p., 1985-87, sr. exec. v.p. Office of Chmn., 1987-88, also bd. dirs.; pres. subs. New World Prodns. and New World Advt. New World Pictures, 1985-88; guest lectr. U. Calif., Riverside, 1976-77, U. So. Calif., 1986, 91, UCLA, 1987; bd. dirs. New World Pictures (Australia), Ltd., FilmDallas Pictures, Inc., Cinedco, Inc. Exec. prodr. (home video series) The Comic Book Greats. Mem. Motion Picture Assn. Am. (dir. 1980-83), Acad. Motion Picture Arts and Scis. (exec. br.), N.Y. State Bar Assn., L.A. County Bar Assn., ACLU. Democrat. Home and Office: 6201 Quebec Dr Los Angeles CA 90068-2219

BIEVER, ANGELA MARY, finance company executive, information transaction processing executive; b. Lloydminster, Sask., Can., Aug. 19, 1953; came to U.S., 1977; d. Vernon Adam and Lila Mae (Enzenauer) B. B in Commerce with honors, Queen's U., Kingston, Ont., Can., 1975; MBA, Harvard U., 1979. Chartered acct., 1977. Auditor Peat, Marwick, Mitchell & Co., Toronto and Ottawa, Ont., 1975-77; cons. McKinsey & Co., N.Y.C., 1979-82; gen. mgr. ofcl. Olympic souvenir program Sports Illustrated subs. Time Inc., N.Y.C., 1983-84; dir. fin. and planning Books Group div. Time Inc., N.Y.C., 1984-87; v.p. mktg. Time-Life Home Video div. Time Inc., N.Y.C., 1986-87; v.p. corp. strategic planning Am. Express Co., N.Y.C., 1987-91; sr. v.p. fin. and planning First Data Corp. (formerly Am. Express Info. Svcs. Corp.), N.Y.C., 1991-92, sr. v.p., chief adminstrv. officer, 1992-93; pres. Anasazi Inc. subsidiary First Data Corp., Phoenix, Colo., 1993-94; exec. v.p. Integrated Svcs. divsn. First Data Corp., Englewood, Colo., 1995—; bd. advisors Search Alternatives Inc., Princeton, N.J., 1987-89. Mem. Century Club Harvard Bus. Sch., 1978. Office: First Data Corp 6200 S Quebec St 430 Englewood CO 80111-4750

BIGGS, STUART EDWARD, computer software engineer; b. Chico, Calif., Jan. 23, 1960; s. Marion Edward Biggs and Betty Louise (Pippitt) Harris. BSEE, Stanford U., 1982, MSEE, 1983. Software developer Sydis, San Jose, Calif., 1984-85; software engr. 3Com, San Jose, 1985-91, Synoptics, Santa Clara, Calif., 1991-92; sr. software engr. Cisco Sys., Santa Clara, 1992—; consulting engr. S.K. Comm., Mountain View, Calif., 1988—. Home: 141 Bradwell Ct San Jose CA 95138-1603

BIGGS, THOMAS WYLIE, chemical executive; b. Seattle, Oct. 28, 1950; s. Ray Wylie and Mildred Virginia (Ramsey) B.; m. Marcia Jean Holts, Aug. 4, 1973; children: Jennifer Tamar, Jordan Wylie. BA, U. Wash., 1972. Chemistry tchr. Samammish High Sch, Bellevue, Wash., 1972-74; sales rep. Litton Industries, Seattle, Wash., 1974-75; sales rep. Van Waters & Rogers (subs. Univar), Kent, Wash., 1975-80, area chem. mgr., 1988-90, br. mgr., 1990-94, field sales mgr., 1980-85; sales mgr. Van Waters & Rogers (subs. Univar), South Bend, Ind., 1985-86; mgr. chem. dept. Van Waters & Rogers (subs. Univar), Indpls., 1986-88; nat. raw materials mgr. Van Waters & Rogers, Kirkland, Wash., 1995—. 1st lt. USAR, 1973-80. Mem. Chgo. Drug and Chem. Assn., N.W. Paint and Coating Assn., Nat. Petroleum Refiners Assn. Office: Van Waters and Rogers 6100 Carillon Pt Kirkland WA 98033-7357

BIKLE, DANIEL DAVID, research physician; b. Harrisburg, Pa., Apr. 25, 1944; s. Charles Augustus and Sarah Elizabeth (Yaukey) B.; m. Mary Elizabeth Wanner, June 20, 1965; children: Christine, Hilary. BA, Harvard U., 1965; MD, U. Pa., 1969, PhD, 1974. Diplomate Am. Bd. Internal Medicine; cert. Nat. Bd. Med. Examiners. Research intern Letterman Army Inst. Research, San Francisco, 1974-79; asst. prof. medicine U. Calif., San Francisco, 1979-86, assoc. prof. medicine, 1986-91, prof. medicine, 1991—, prof. dermatology, 1993—; co-dir. spl. diagnostic and treatment unit VA Med. Ctr., San Francisco, 1986-91; prof. medicine, 1991—, prof. dermatology, 1993—. Editor: Assay of Calcium Regulating Hormones, 1984, Hormonal Regulation of Bone Mineral Homeostasis, 1995; contbr. articles to profl. jours., chpts. to books. Served to col. USAR, 1974—. Research grantee NIH, 1979—, NASA, 1979—, VA, 1979—. Fellow ACP; mem. Endocrine Soc. (mem. editl. bd. 1984—), Am. Soc. Clin. Investigation, Am. Soc. Clin. Nutrition, Am. Fedn. Clin. Rsch., Assocs of Am. Physicians. Republican. Mem. Christian Ch. Clubs: Commonwealth of Calif., Harvard (San Francisco). Office: VA Med Ctr 4150 Clement St San Francisco CA 94121-1545

BILBRAY, BRAIN P., congressman; b. San Diego, Calif.; m. Karen; 5 children. Supr.ctrl. and so. coastal regions San Diego County, Calif.; mem. 104th Congress from 49th Calif. dist., 1994—. Mem. San Diego County Air Pollution Control Bd., State Air Resources Bd., San Diego County Internat. Trade Com., Calif. Coastal Com., San Diego Bay Water Quality Panel, San Diego Coun. Literacy. Office: US House Reps 315 Cannon House Office Bldg Washington DC 20515-0549*

BILBRAY, JAMES HUBERT, former congressman, lawyer, consultant; b. Las Vegas, May 19, 1938; s. James A. and Ann E. (Miller) B.; m. Michaelene Mercer, Jan. 1960; children: Bridget, Kevin, Erin, Shannon. Student, Brigham Young U., 1957-58, U. Nev., Las Vegas, 1958-60; BA, Am. U., 1962; JD, Washington Coll. Law, 1964. Bar: Nev. 1965. Staff mem. Senator Howard Cannon U.S. Senate, 1960-64; dep. dist. atty. Clark County, Nev., 1965-68; mem. Lovell, Bilbray & Potter, Las Vegas, 1969-87; mem. Nev. Senate, 1980-86, chmn. taxation com., 1983-86, chmn. interim com. on pub. broadcasting, 1983; 100th-103d U.S. Congresses from 1st Nev. dist.; mem. 100th-103rd Congresses from 1st Nev. dist., 1987-95; mem. fgn. affairs com., 1987-88, mem. house armed svs. com., subcom. procurement, mil. contracts, sea power, mem. small bus. com., chmn. procurement, taxation and tourism subcom., 1989-95; ptnr. Alcalde & Fay, Arlington, Va., 1995—; mem. Spl. Panel on NATO and North Atlantic Alliance, fgn. affairs com., select com. on hunger, 1987-88, select com. on aging, 1988-93, subcoms. Africa, trade exports and tourism, select com. on intelligence, 1993-95; alt. mcpl. judge City of Las Vegas, 1987-89; del. North Atlantic Alliance, 1989-95. Bd. regents U. Nev. Sys., 1968-72; mem. Nat. Coun. State Govts. Commn. on Arts and Historic Preservation; mem. bd. visitors USAF Acad., 1991-93. Named Outstanding Alumnus U. Nev., Las Vegas, 1979, Man of Yr. Am. Diabetes Assn., 1989, Man of Yr. Haddassah (Nev.), 1990. Mem. Nev. State Bar Assn., Clark county Bar Assn., U. Nev.-Las Vegas Alumni Assn. (pres. 1964-69, Humanitarian of Yr. 1984), Phi Alpha Delta, Sigma Chi, KC. Democrat. Roman Catholic. Lodges: Elks, Rotary. Office: 1745 E Sahara 460 Las Vegas NV 89109

BILBY, RICHARD MANSFIELD, federal judge; b. Tucson, May 29, 1931; s. Ralph Willard and Marguerite (Mansfield) B.; m. Ann Louise Borchert, July 6, 1957; children: Claire Louise, Ellen M. Moore. B.S., U. Ariz., 1955; J.D., U. Mich., 1958. Bar: Ariz. 1959. Since practiced in Tucson; law clk. to Chief Judge Chambers, 9th Circuit Ct. Appeals, San Francisco, 1958-59; mem. firm Bilby, Thompson, Shoenhair & Warnock, 1959-79, partner, 1967-79; judge U.S. Dist. Ct., Dist. Ariz., Tucson, 1979—; chief judge U.S. Dist. Ct., Dist. Ariz., 1984-90; conscientious objector hearing officer Dept. Justice, 1959-62; chmn. Pima County Med.-Legal panel, 1968-70; Mem. Tucson Charter Revision Com., 1965-70. Chmn. United Fund Profl. Div., 1968; chmn. Spl. Gift Div., 1970, St. Joseph Hosp. Devel. Fund Drive, 1970; Republican state chmn. Vols. for Eisenhower, 1956; Rep. county chmn., Pima County, Ariz., 1972-74; Past pres. Tucson Conquistadores; bd. dirs. St. Josephs Hosp., 1969-77, chmn., 1972-75. Served with AUS, 1952-54. Fellow Am. Coll. Trial Lawyers; mem. Ariz. Acad., Town Hall (dir. 1976-79). Office: US Dist Ct US Courthouse Rm 426 44 E Broadway Blvd Tucson AZ 85701-1711*

BILECKI, RONALD ALLAN, financial planner; b. Cin., July 15, 1942; s. Allan Frederick and Ruth H. (Parker) B.; m. Judy A. Newberry, Jan. 25, 1964; children: Sherry D. Pavan, Sean P. BA in Chemistry, Calif. State U., 1968. Cert. fin. planner; registered investment adviser. Ins. agt. N.Y. Life Ins., Covina, Calif., 1973-75; asst. mgr. N.Y. Life Ins., Los Angeles, 1975-79; pvt. practice Rosemead, Calif., 1979-81; pres. Fin. Designs Corp., San Gabriel, Calif., 1981—; fin. planning cons. So. Calif. Edison, Rosemead, 1986—, So. Calif. Gas Co., 1991—, Capital Cities/ABC, 1991—. Mem. Gideons, Covina, 1987. Mem. Internat. Assn. Fin. Planning, Registry Fin. Planning Practitioners. Republican. Office: Fin Designs Corp 7220 Rosemead Blvd Ste 206 San Gabriel CA 91775-1316

BILEZIKJIAN, EDWARD ANDREW, architect; b. Los Angeles, Mar. 29, 1950; s. Andrew and Alice (Dardarian) B. BSArch, U. So. Calif., 1973, MArch, 1977. Registered architect, Calif. Project mgr. RMA Archtl. Group, Inc., Costa Mesa, Calif., 1977-78; dir. architecture Donald De Mars Assocs., Inc., Van Nuys, Calif., 1978-85; prin. architect EAB Architects, Sepulveda, Calif., 1985-87, Laguna Hills, Calif., 1988—; architect, planner III Trammell Crow Co., Irvine, Calif., 1986-88; prin. architect Fluor Daniel, Inc., Irvine, Calif., 1989—. Chmn. parish coun. Armenian Apostolic Ch. Newport Beach, 1988-91, 94-95. Mem. AIA, Triple-X Fraternity of Calif.

(corresponding sec. 1984-85), Nat. Coun. Archtl. Registration Bds. (cert.). Democrat. Mem. Armenian Apostolic Ch.

BILLINGS, PATRICIA ANN COLLINS, nurse practitioner; b. San Diego, Jan. 31, 1946; d. Normon Clyde and Mary Asunda (Fantoni) Collins; m. George M. Whitehead, June 12, 1966 (div. Mar. 1975); children: Garrett Grafton Rayne, Sharna Raynel, Adrianna Megan, Autumn Leigh; m. Russell F. Billings II, Aug. 19, 1989. BS in Nursing, Loma Linda (Calif.) U., 1967, MPH, 1971; cert. Pediatric Nurse Practitioner, U. Calif, San Diego, 1979. RN, Calif., Idaho; cert. nurse practitioner, Idaho, Calif. Pub. health nurse San Bernadino County, Calif., 1967-72, San Diego County, 1974; sch. nurse, pediatric nurse practitioner Vista (Calif.) Unified Sch. Dist., 1974-85; pediatric nurse practitioner Sharp Rees-Stealy Med. Group, San Diego, 1985-94; pediatric nurse practitioners Pediatric Ctr., Twin Falls, Idaho, 1994—. Contbg. editor Pediatric Nursing, 1994—. mem. Pres.'s Coun., San Diego, 1984-85; bd. dirs. Idahoans Concerned With Adolescent Pregnancy, 1995—. Recipient USPHS scholarship, 1971. Fellow Nat. Assn. Pediatric Nurse Practitioners (cert. chmn. 1987-93); mem. Am. Acad. Pediats. (mem. Idaho chpt.), San Diego Assn. Pediatric Nurse Practitioners (legis. chair 1993-94, editor pedits. nursing assessment 1995—, 1993 Pediatric Nurse Practitioner of Yr.). Republican. Office: Pediatric Ctr 388 Martin St Twin Falls ID 83301-4544

BILLINGS, THOMAS NEAL, computer and publishing executive, management consultant; b. Milw., Mar. 2, 1931; s. Neal and Gladys Victoria (Lockard) B.; m. Barta Hope Chipman, June 12, 1954 (div. 1967); children: Bridget Ann, Bruce Neal; m. Marie Louise Farrell, Mar. 27, 1982. AB with honors, Harvard U., 1952, MBA, 1954. V.p. fin. and adminstrn. and technol. innovation Copley Newspapers Inc., La Jolla, Calif., 1957-70; group v.p., dir. tech. Harte-Hanks Comm. Inc., San Antonio, 1970-73; exec. v.p. United Media, Inc., Phoenix, 1973-75; asst. to pres., dir. corp. mgmt. systems Ramada Inns, Inc., Phoenix, 1975-76; exec. dir. NRA, Washington, 1976-77; pres. Ideation Inc., N.Y.C., 1977-81; chmn. Bergen-Billings Inc., N.Y.C., 1977-80; pres. The Assn. Svc. Corp., San Francisco, 1978-91; pres. Recorder Printing and Pub. Co. Inc., San Francisco, 1980-82; v.p. adminstrn. Victor Techs. Inc., Scotts Valley, Calif., 1982-84; mng. dir. Saga-Wilcox Computers Ltd., Wrexham, Wales, 1984-85; chmn. Thomas Billings & Assocs., Inc., Reno, 1978—, Intercontinental Travel Svc. Inc., Reno, 1983-88, Oberon Optical Character Recognition, Ltd., Hemel-Hemstead, Eng., 1985-86; bd. dirs. 5M Corp., San Francisco, Intercontinental Rsch. Coun., London, Corp. Comm. Coun., Alameda; dir., CEO Insignia Software Solutions group, High Wycombe, Eng., Cupertino, Calif., 1986-89; chmn. Intercontinental News Svc. Inc., London and Alameda, Calif., 1989—; v.p. Cromer Equipment Co., Oakland, Calif., 1991-94; chmn. Newton Group of Cos., Las Vegas, 1993—, Info. Integrity Internat., Inc., Las Vegas, London, 1994—; bd. dirs. Digital Broadcasting Corp., Mountain View, Calif., Lenny's Restaurants Inc., Wichita, Kans., Tymyndr Corp., Dover, Del., Zzyzzyx Corp., Reno, Harrod's Hotel & Casino Corp., Las Vegas, Pandemonium Pictures, Inc., San Mateo, Calif., Bonanza Corp., Virginia City, Nev., Quillmill Ltd., London, Better Betting Systems, Inc., Alameda, Calif., Video Stream, Inc., Cupertino, Calif.; speaker and seminar leader; co-inventor Strok Savr Software, 1994. Bd. dirs. Nat. Allergy Found., 1973—, The Wilderness Fund, 1978—, San Diego Civic Light Opera Assn., 1965-69; chief exec. San Diego 200th Anniversary Expn., 1969; founder, exec. dir. Am. Majority Party, 1993—. Served with U.S. Army, 1955-57. Recipient Walter F. Carley Meml. award, 1966, 69. Fellow U.K. Inst. Dirs.; mem. Am. Newspaper Pubs. Assn., Inst. Execs. Inc. (dir.), Inst. Newspaper Fin. Officers, Sigma Delta Chi. Clubs: West Side Tennis, LaJolla Country; Washington Athletic; San Francisco Press; Harvard (N.Y.C.); Elks. Author: Creative Controllership, 1978, Our Credibility Crisis, 1983, Non-Euclidean Theology, 1987, Ruminations on Meta Mentality, 1990, Fixing our Broken System, 1992; editor: The Vice Presidents' Letter, 1978-92; pub. The Microcomputer Letter, 1982-94, Synthetic Hardware Update, 1987-93, Windows on Tomorrow Magazine, 1994—; editor: Intercontinental News Svc., London and Alameda, Calif., 1985—. Office: PO Drawer I Alameda CA 94501-0262

BILLINGSLEY, WILLIAM SCOTT, accountant, controller; b. Clearfield, Pa., Mar. 20, 1963; s. William Allen and Janice Marilyn (Bridges) B.; m. Donna Dolphin, June 17, 1989. BS in Acctg., Pa. State U., 1985. CPA, Calif. Cost acct. IBM Corp., Poughkeepsie, N.Y., 1984; staff acct. Arthur Young, Pitts., 1985-88; sr. acct. Ernst & Young, San Diego, 1988-89; contr., acct. Cinema Air Jet Ctr., Inc., Carlsbad, Calif., 1989—. Mem. AICPAs, Pa. Inst. CPAs, Calif. Soc. CPAs. Republican. Presbyterian. Home: 3014 Segovia Ct Carlsbad CA 92009-8352 Office: Cinema Air Jet Ctr Inc 2056 Palomar Airport Rd Carlsbad CA 92008-4812

BILLITER, WILLIAM OVERTON, JR., journalist; b. Cin., Sept. 3, 1934; s. William Overton and Laura Louise (Dorsey) B.; m. Maureen Ann Flanagan, June 22, 1962; children—Suzanne, Stephen, Mary, Patrick. B.A., U. Ky., 1956; M.S., U. Louisville, 1970. Reporter New Orleans Times-Picayune, 1959-61; instr. Ohio State U., 1961-62; legis. asst. U.S. Rep. F. Edward Hebert of La., 1962-65; reporter, polit. editor Louisville Courier-Jour., 1965-74; editorial writer, columnist Louisville Times, 1974-77, city editor, 1977-78; reporter Los Angeles Times, 1978—. Served with USAF, 1956-59. Mem. Soc. Profl. Journalists, AAUP. Democrat. Roman Catholic. Home: 9522 Telhan Dr Huntington Beach CA 92646-3622 Office: Los Angeles Times Orange County Office Costa Mesa CA 92626

BILOTTA, JAMES LOUIS, small business owner; b. Tokyo, Dec. 14, 1950; s. Frank Joseph and Elizabeth Fay (Bodway) B.; m. Cynthia Marie Gross, Jan, 6, 1973 (div. June 1978); m. Debbie Ann Schaefer, Dec. 27, 1985; 1 child, Danile James. Diploma in Acctg. and Mgmt., U. Pa., 1980. V.p. Fidelity Bank, Phila., 1977-84; sr. v.p., chief fin. officer Cen. Savs. and Loan Assn., San Diego, Calif., 1984-85, Westwood Savs. and Loan Assn., L.A., 1985-90, Inland Savs. and Loan Assn., Hemet, Calif., 1990-92; bus. owner Premier Pacific, Inc., San Diego, 1992—. Bd. dirs. Phila. Concerned About Housing, 1983-84. Mem. San Diego Balloon Assn. (v.p. 1992-94). Republican. Office: Premier Pacific Inc PO Box 8737 Rancho Santa Fe CA 92067

BILOW, STEVEN CRAIG, computer systems specialist; b. L.A., July 10, 1960; s. Norman and Selma (Rifkin) B.; m. Patricia S. Crabb, Nov. 5, 1989. BFA in Music Composition, Calif. Inst. of the Arts, 1982; cert. logic design/theory, U. So. Calif., 1983; postgrad., Portland State U., 1990—. Cert. tchr. of movement expression, L.A., 1985. Mfg. engr. Hughes Aircraft EDSG, El Segundo, Calif., 1981-85; project engr. electro-optical test systems Hughes Aircraft EDSG, El Segundo, 1985-86; sr. systems analyst Tektronix, Info Display Group, Woodland Hills, Calif., 1986-88; software engr., math. surface representation Interactive Techs. div. Tektronix, Wilsonville, Oreg., 1988-91; sr. tech. support specialist Unix and X Window systems Interactive Techs. div. Tektronix, Wilsonville, Oreg., 1991—; cons. in music composition and ethnomusicology Structured Perceptions Music, L.A., 1980-85; cons. in graphics SCBA Software, Lake Oswego, Calif., 1987—; mem. ACM Spl. Interest Group in Computer Graphics, 1988—; keynote spkr. NASA Window System 94, 1994. Composer various electro-acoustic instrumental and choral works, 1978 83; author (theater piece) Indra's Net, 1987; author, editor: (book) Designing For Producibility, 1980 Use Cases, Objects and X, 1993, Managers Guide to the Universal Distributed Desktop, 1995; book rev. editor Jour. of Object Oriented Programming, 1991—; contbr. articles, columns and book revs. to profl. jours. Mem. Human/Dolphin Found., Malibu, Calif., 1977, Self-Realization Fellowship, L.A., 1985. Recipient Technical Excellence award, Tektronix, Inc., Wilsonville, 1988, 94. Mem. Object Oriented Programming Sys., Langs., and Applications (exec. com. 1992, 93, 94, 95, sponsor workshop on object-oriented software metrics 1993, 94), IEEE (tech. com. on computer graphics 1985—, tech. com. on super computer applications 1988), Assn. Computing Machinery, Am. Musicol. Soc., Oreg. Master Gardner Assn., Am. Rose Soc. Democrat. Office: Tektronix Interactive Tech PO Box 1000 Wilsonville OR 97070-1000

BIMBER, BRUCE ALLEN, political science educator; b. Warren, Pa., Oct. 26, 1961; s. Gail E. and Joyce Kathleen B.; m. Laura L. Mancuso. BSEE, Stanford U., 1983; PhD, MIT, 1992. Mktg. engr. Hewlett-Packard Co., Palo Alto, Calif., 1983-86; assoc. pol. scientist Critical Techs. Inst., RAND Corp., Washington, 1992-93; asst. prof. polit. sci. U. Calif., Santa Barbara, 1993—; cons. NAS, Washington, Nat. Rsch. Coun., Washington, Carnegie Corp., N.Y.C., Critical Techs. Inst., Washington, ISyS Forum, Palo Alto, Calif. Contbr. articles to profl. jours. Rsch. fellow Brookings Inst., 1990-91. Mem. Tau Beta Pi. Home: 946 W Campus Ln Goleta CA 93117-4345 Office: U Calif Dept Polit Sci Santa Barbara CA 93106

BINDER, GORDON M., health and medical products executive; b. St. Louis, 1935. Degree in elec. engring., Purdue U., 1957; MBA, Harvard U., 1962. Formerly with Litton Industries, 1962-64; various fin. mgmt. positions Ford Motor Co., 1964-69; CFO Sys. Devel. Corp., 1971-81; v.p., CFO Amgen, Thousand Oaks, Calif., 1982-88, CEO, 1988—, chmn. bd., 1990—. Baker scholar Harvard U. Office: Amgen 1840 De Havilland Dr Thousand Oaks CA 91320-1701

BINDER, JAMES KAUFFMAN, computer consultant; b. Reading, Pa., Nov. 20, 1920; s. Paul Burdette and Edna (Kauffman) B.; B.A., Lehigh U., 1941; M.A., Johns Hopkins U., 1952; profl. cert. in systems mgmt. U. Calif.-San Diego, 1976; A.S. in Data Processing, San Diego Evening Coll., 1979, A.A. in Fgn. Lang., 1979; A.A. in Spanish, Mira Costa Coll., Oceanside, Calif., 1981. Instr. English, Notre Dame U., South Bend, Ind., 1948-49; prof. English, Athens (Greece) Coll., 1950-51; CARE rep., Greece, 1951-52; reporter, staff writer Athens News, 1952-53; dir. lang. tng. World Council Chs. Refugee Service, Athens, 1953-54; co-editor Am. Overseas Guide, N.Y., West Berlin, 1957-58; lectr. English, U. Md. Overseas Program, European and Far East divs., 1958-66; successively supr. Cen. Info. Ctr., supt. documents, sr. systems analyst GA Techs., Inc., La Jolla, Calif., 1968-85. Recipient Williams Prize, Lehigh U., 1939, 41; Johns Hopkins U. Grad. Sch. Pres. scholar, 1945-48. Roman Catholic. Clubs: Tudor and Stuart, Automobile of So. Calif. Author: The Correct Comedy, 1951; contbg. translator Modern Scandinavian Poetry, 1948; editor: (with Erwin H. Tiebe) American Overseas Guide, 1958.

BINDER, MARC DAVID, physiology educator; b. Brookline, Mass., June 8, 1949; m. Karin Kalff; 2 children. AB, Columbia U., 1971; MS, U. So. Calif., 1972, PhD, 1974. Rsch./teaching asst. biol. scis. and biomed. engring. U. So. Calif., 1972-74; rsch. cons. Ocean Sci. and Engring., Inc., Long Beach, Calif., 1972-73; rsch. assoc. Pacific Med. Ctr., San Francisco, 1974-75; instr. U. Calif. Extension, Davis, 1975; rsch. assoc. in physiology U. Ariz., Tucson, 1975-78; asst. prof. dept. physiology and biophysics U. Washington, Seattle, 1978-81, assoc. prof., 1981-86, prof., 1986—; vis. asst. prof. dept. physiology U. Ariz., 1978-81; vis. assoc. prof. dept. physiology and biophysics Harvard U., 1982-83; adj. prof. dept. oral biology U. Washington, 1990—. Editorial assoc.: Courts, Health Sci. and the Law, Brain and Behavioral Scis.; manuscript reviewer: Sci., Jour. Neurophysiology, Experimental Brain Rsch., Neurosci. Letters, Experimental Neurology, Jour. Neurosci., Muscle & Nerve, Jour. Applied Physiology, IEEE Transactions in Biomed. Engring.; contbr. articles to profl. jours. Recipient Tchr.-Investigator Devel. award Nat. Inst. Neurol. Diseases and Stroke, 1978-83, Neurosci. Teaching award U. Ariz., 1980, Jacob Javits Neurosci. Investigator award, 1992; fellow Arthur Vining Davis Found., 1972, Postdoctoral fellow Nat. Eye Inst., 1975, Muscular Dystrophy Assn., 1975, 76, Regents fellow U. Calif., 1975, Chancellor's fellow U. Calif., Davis, 1975; Biele grantee for grad. rsch., 1972, Internat. travel grantee Nat. Rsch. Coun., 1977. Mem. Internat. Brain Rsch. Orgn., Internat. Soc. Myochemistry, AAAS, Soc. Neurosci., Sigma Xi. Home: 15930 41st Ave NE Seattle WA 98155-6739 Office: U Wash Sch Medicine Dept Physiology & Biophys SJ-40 Seattle WA 98195

BINEGAR, GWENDOLYN ANN, social worker; b. Phoenix, Sept. 23, 1924; d. Glenn Marvin and Mary Lenore (Cartwright) Redington; B.S. in Sociology, Iowa State U., 1948; M. Social Svc., Bryn Mawr Coll., 1967; m. Lewis Albert Binegar, Nov. 2, 1951; children: Glen Albert, Birne Thomas, William Lewis, Alan Martin. Psychiat. social worker Child Study Inst., Bryn Mawr (Pa.) Coll., 1967-71; supervising counselor San Gabriel Valley Regional Ctr., Pomona, 1975-78, program mgr. six L.A. County Regional Ctrs' High Risk Infant Projects, 1978-79; chief case mgmt. svcs. San Diego Regional Ctr., 1981—, assoc. dir., 1988-91, cons., 1992—; v.p. Golden Years, Inc., Valley Ctr., Calif., 1987—. Lic. clin. social worker. Fellow Soc. Cert. Social Workers; mem. Am. Acad. Certified Social Workers, Am. Assn. on Mental Deficiency, Nat. Assn. Social Workers. Republican. Presbyterian. Home: 28809 Lilac Rd Valley Center CA 92082-5426

BINGAMAN, JEFF, senator; b. El Paso, Tex., Oct. 3, 1943; s. Jesse and Beth (Ball) B.; m. Anne Kovacovich, Sept. 13, 1968. BA in Govt., Harvard U., 1965; JD, Stanford U., 1968. Bar: N.Mex. 1968. Asst. atty. gen., 1969; atty. Stephenson, Campbell & Olmsted, 1971-72; ptnr. Campbell, Bingaman & Black, Santa Fe, 1972-78; former atty. gen. State of N.Mex.; now U.S. senator from N.Mex., mem. armed svcs. com., mem. joint econ. com., mem. Senate Dem. steering and coordination com., mem. Senate Den. tech. and comm. com., ranking minority mem., mem. energy and natural resources subcom. of energy prodn. and regulation. U.S. Army 1968-74. Democrat. Methodist. Home: PO Box 5775 Santa Fe NM 87502-5775 Office: US Senate 703 Hart Senate Bldg Washington DC 20510*

BINGHAM, CHARLES W., wood products company executive; b. Myrtle Point, Oreg., 1933. Grad., Harvard U., 1955, JD, 1960. Now exec. v.p. Weyerhaeuser Co.; bd. dirs. Puget Sound Power & Light Co. Mem. Nat. Forest Products Assn. (bd. govs.). Office: Weyerhaeuser Co 33663 Weyerhaeuser Way S Auburn WA 98001-9646

BINGHAM, EDWIN RALPH, history educator; b. Denver, Jan. 21, 1920; s. Guy Edwin and Helen (Hinckley) B.; m. Helen Hopkins, 1943 (div. 1951); children: Susan Kimball, Linda Christine; m. Virginia Wright, Aug. 24, 1952; children: Sheila Jeanne, Sara Lisa. BA, Occidental Coll., 1941, MA, 1942; PhD, UCLA, 1951. Instr. history U. Oreg., Eugene, 1949-51, asst. prof., 1952-57, assoc. prof., 1958-64, prof., 1965-84, prof. emeritus, 1982—; Fulbright lectr. Mysore U., India, 1977-78; lectr. U. Shandong, Jinan, Peoples' Republic of China, 1985. Author: Charles F. Lummis, Editor of the Southwest, 1955, Oregon!, 1978; contbr. articles to profl. jours. Mem. Oreg. Geog. Names Bd., Portland, 1965-88. 1st lt. USAAF, 1942-46. Grantee Ford Found., Yale U., 1954-55. Mem. Am. Hist. Assn. (pres. Pacific coast br. 1985-86), Oreg. Hist. Soc. Democrat. Home: 697 Crest Dr Eugene OR 97405-2793 Office: U Oreg Dept History Eugene OR 97403

BINGHAM, PARIS EDWARD, JR., electrical engineer, computer consultant; b. Aurora, Colo., Sept. 26, 1957; s. Paris Edward and Shirley Ann (Blehm) B.; m. Laurie Sue Piersol, May 9, 1981 (div. Sept. 1987); m. Helen Naef, Aug. 7, 1993. BS in Elec. Engring. and Computer Sci., U. Colo., 1979. Mem. tech. staff Western Electric Co., Aurora, 1979-81, system engr., 1981; mem. electronic tech. staff Hughes Aircraft Co., Aurora, 1981-83, staff engr., 1983-86, sr. staff engr., 1986-93, scientist, engr., 1993-94; area systems support engr. 4 Sun Microsystems, Inc., Englewood, Colo., 1994—; cons. RJM Assocs., Huntington, N.Y., 1987-91; cons. Aurora, 1988—. Mem. IEEE, Assn. for Computing Machinery. Republican. Presbyterian. Office: Sun Microsystems Inc 5251 Dtc Pky Ste 500 Englewood CO 80111-2734

BINKIEWICZ, ANNA I.S., pediatrician; b. Lwów, Poland, Apr. 14, 1938; came to U.S., 1957; d. Carl W. and Anna W. (Wysocka) Zisch; m. Longin W. Binkiewicz, Aug. 17, 1964 (dec. Dec. 1992). BA, Clark U. Womens Coll., 1961; MD, Tufts U., 1965. Diplomate Am. Bd. Pediat., Am. Bd. Pediat. Endocrinology. Intern Boston Floating Hosp., 1965-66, resident in pediat., 1966-68, fellow in emotional and social aspects in pediat., 1968-69, fellow in pediat. endocrinology, 1969-71; asst. in endocrinology New Eng. Med. Ctr., Boston, 1971-77, from coord. student edn. in pediat. to staff pediatrician, 1978-86; from instr. to assoc. prof. pediat. Tufts U. Sch. Medicine, Boston, 1971-86, prof. clin. pediat., 1986—; chief sect. gen. pediat. U. Ariz. Health Scis. Ctr., Tucson, 1986—; ednl. com. dept. pediat. U. Ariz. Coll. Medicine, 1988—, co-founder, child advocate group dept. pediat., 1987—; asst. endocrinologist New Eng. Med. Ctr., Boston, 1977-86, chief div. gen. pediat., 1978-86; coord. student edn. in pediatrics Tufts U. Sch. Medicine, Boston, 1980-86; acting med. dir. U. Affiliated Programs, 1991-93; lectr. in field. Contbr. articles to profl. jours. Active Govs. Task Force for Prevention Child Abuse in Ariz., 1989, Ariz. Coun. for Mothers and Children, 1989—. Recipient grants in field, 1994—, 1993—. Mem. Ambulatory Pediat. Assn., Am. Acad. Pediat., Am. Diabetes Assn., Pediat. Endocrine Soc., Nat. Com. for Prevention Child Abuse, Soc. for Prevention Child Abuse and Neglect, Am. Profl. Soc. on Abuse of Children, Ariz. Acad. Pediat. (steering com. mem. ann. conf. 1990), Boston Floating Alumni Assn. Office: Univ Ariz Health Sci Ctr 1501 N Campbell Ave Tucson AZ 85724-0001

BINKLEY, CLARK SHEPARD, forestry educator, consultant; b. Salt Lake City, Dec. 1, 1949; s. Otto Francis and Emily (Shepard) B.; m. Nadine Marie Bonda, July 1, 1972; children—Clayton Bonda, Emily Elizabeth, Alex Francis. A.B. cum laude in Applied Math., Harvard U., 1971, S.M. in Engring., 1975; Ph.D. in Forestry and Environ. Studies, Yale U., 1979. Dir. environ. quality div. Urban Systems Research and Engring., Inc., Cambridge, Mass., 1971-75; mem. faculty Yale U., New Haven, 1978—, assoc. prof. forestry, 1982-85; prof. forestry, organization/mgmt., 1985-90; dean faculty of forestry, U. B.C., Vancouver, 1990—; bd. dirs. West Fraser Timbers, Pacific Forest Products, Nelson Forests (NZ) Joint Venture, Ecotrust Inc, Forintek Canada Corp., Forest Engring. Rsch. Inst. Can.; cons. to govt. and industry; adviser to various govt. panels; mem. Marcus Wellenburg Prize Com. Contbr. articles in field to profl. jours. Mem. Soc. Am. Foresters, AAAS, Sigma Xi. Office: Faculty of Forestry, U British Columbia, Vancouver, BC Canada V6T 1Z4

BINKLEY, JOAN VIVIAN (JODY BINKLEY), artist, educator, gallery owner; b. Hanford, Calif., July 8, 1933; d. Albert Henry Lohse and Alice (Day) Romdall; m. Henry Alson Binkley, Sept. 20, 1958; children: Cameron, Brock, Clayton. Student, Colo. State U., 1951-53; studied with, Frederick Van Twente, Mary Ann Lohman, Larry Webster, Delbert Gish, Leslie B. Demille. Owner, instr. Studio West Galleries, Wheatridge, Colo., 1973-80; owner Studio West Galleries, Littleton, Colo., 1975-80; owner, instr. Country Lane Art Gallery, Lakewood, Colo., 1983-85, Lakewood Arts Studio Gallery, 1988—; workshop instr. Wheatridge Art Club, 1987, 89, 91. Exhbns. include Denver Career League Spring Benefit, 1989, 90, 91, 92, also Studio West Galleries, Wheatride and Littleton, Emily Ingram Galleries, Steamboat, Colo., 1984-92, Santa Fe Impressions, Littleton, 1987—, Gallery of Western Art, 1987—, Parade of Homes, 1988-89. Mem. Colo. Artist Assn., Lakewood Arts Coun., Foothills Art Ctr. Home: 12588 W 1st Pl Lakewood CO 80228-5004 Studio: Lakewood Arts Studio 85 S Union Blvd Lakewood CO 80228-2207

BINNIE, NANCY CATHERINE, nurse, educator; b. Sioux Falls, S.D., Jan. 28, 1937; d. Edward Grant and Jessie May (Martini) Larkin; m. Charles H. Binnie. Diploma, St. Joseph's Hosp. Sch. Nursing, Phoenix, 1965; BS in Nursing, Ariz. State U., 1970, MA, 1974. Intensive care charge nurse Scottsdale (Ariz.) Meml. Hosp., 1968-70, coordinator critical care, 1970-71; coordinator critical care John C. Lincoln Hosp., Phoenix, 1971-73; prof. nursing GateWay Community Coll., Phoenix, 1974—; coord. part-time evening nursing programs Gateway Community Coll., 1984—, interim dir. nursing, 1989, 91. Mem. Orgn. Advancement of Assoc. Degree Nursing. Office: Gateway C C 104 N 40th St Phoenix AZ 85034-1704

BIRCHARD, JAMES THOMAS, sanitation engineer, poet; b. Spencer, Nebr., Apr. 11, 1954; s. George Thomas and Frances Louise (Ripplinger) B.; 1 child, Austin James (dec.). Grad., high sch., 1972. Portrait photographer Photo-Pros West, Beaverton, Oreg., 1979-81; CEO, gen. mgr. T.J. Enterprises, Inc.-Landscaping, Hermiston, Oreg., 1983-85; salesman, sales mgr. Reid Bros. Circus, Coos Bay, Oreg., 1985-88; sanitation engr. Eastern Oreg. Correctional Inst., Pendleton, 1990—. Author: (poetry) Presures Upon Us, 1990, Fight for the Right, 1992. Served with USN, 1972-73. Recipient Editors Choice award Nat. Libr. of Poetry, 1993, 94. Roman Catholic. Home: 2500 Westgate Pendleton OR 97801-9613

BIRD, LESLEY ANN, computer engineer; b. Rome, N.Y., Nov. 10, 1963; d. Richard Andrew and Suzanne (Van Auken) B. BSEE, U. of the Pacific, Stockton, Calif., 1986; MSEE, U. Calif., Santa Barbara, 1990. Student engr. IBM Corp., San Jose, Calif., 1984-85; electronic design engr. Delco Electronics, Goleta, Calif., 1986-90; computer engr. Apple Computer, Cupertino, Calif., 1990—. Scholarship Soc. Women Engrs., 1984. Mem. IEEE, Eta Kappa Mu. Home: 2061 Foxhall Loop San Jose CA 95125-5984 Office: Apple Computer 20705 Valley Green Dr Cupertino CA 95014-1703

BIRD, ROBERT KENTON, journalist, educator; b. Kellogg, Idaho, Feb. 10, 1954; s. Robert Leizear and Amy Nell (Legg) B. BA in Journalism, U. Idaho, 1976; MEd, Univ. Coll., Cardiff, Wales, 1980; postgrad., Wash. State U., 1992—. Reporter Idahonian, Moscow, Idaho, 1975-77, acting mng. editor, 1979-80, asst. mng. editor, 1981-82, mng. editor, 1982-85, editor editl. page, 1985-92; editing intern Washington Post, 1977; news editor Lewiston (Idaho) Morning Tribune, 1980-81; asst. mng. editor Daily News, Pullman, Wash., 1981-82, mng. editor, 1982-85, editor editl. page, 1985-92; lectr. U. Idaho, Moscow, 1979, 91—; teaching asst. Wash. State U., Pullman, 1993—; cons. Cen. Idaho Star-News, McCall, 1981; commentator N.W. Pub. TV, Pullman, 1986-88. Mem. Moscow Comty. Theatre, 1976—, officer, 1982-86; mem. Moscow Comty. Band, 1984—, Malcolm Kerr Scholarship Com., Moscow, 1986-89, Moscow Centennial Commn., 1987; mem. Washington Idaho Symphony Bd., 1990—; vestryman St. Mark's Episcopal Ch., Moscow, 1988, sr. warden, 1991; mem. City of Moscow Bicycle Path Adv. Com., 1993—. Rotary Found. journalism fellow, 1978, Am. Polit. Sci. Assn. Congl. fellow, 1988-89. Office: Wash State U Dept History Pullman WA 99164-4030

BIRD, THOMAS D., neurologist; b. Newark, N.Y., Aug. 3, 1942; s. Donald and Virginia (Johnson) B.; m. Rosaline Merrill, July 1, 1967; children: Jeffrey, Caroline. BA, Dartmouth Coll., 1964; MD, Cornell U., 1968. Diplomate Am. Bd. Psychiatry and Neurology. Intern U. Wash. Med. Sch., Seattle, 1968-69, resident in neurology, 1969-70, 72-74; chief neurology VA Med. Ctr., Seattle, 1985—; prof. medicine U. Wash. Med. Sch., Seattle, 1988—; Editl. bd. Acta Neurologica Scandinavica, Annals of Neurology, European Neurology; contbr. more than 100 articles to profl. jours. Lt. comdr. USN, 1970-72. Grantee NIH, VA, Am. Health Assn. Found. Mem. AAAS, Am. Soc. Human Genetics, Am. Neurol. Assn., Am. Acad. Neurology (Wartenburg prize 1992). Office: VA Med Ctr Dept Neurology 1660 E Columbia St Seattle WA 98122-4635

BIRDNOW, BRIAN EVERETT, history educator, essayist, critic, reporter; b. St. Louis, Aug. 7, 1962; s. James Louis and Janet Claire (Kennedy) B. BA, St. Louis U., 1984, MA, 1987. Dir. St. Louis Univ. Shuttle, 1985-87; sales rep. R.J. Reynolds, Inc., St. Louis, 1987-88; instr. St. Louis C.C., 1988-90; instr. history Ctrl. Tex. Coll., San Diego, Calif., 1990—. Author critical revs. Intermission mag., 1990-92. Hon. city atty. Bellefontaine Neighbors (Mo.) City Coun., 1979; election judge St. Louis County Bd. Elections, 1988-89; mem. St. Louis County Rep. Com., 1990-92; mem. Heritage Found., 1992-93. Mem. Smithsonian Instn., Phi Alpha Theta. Roman Catholic. Home: 1218 Yukon Dr Saint Louis MO 63137-1141

BIRD-PORTO, PATRICIA ANNE, personnel director; b. N.Y.C., June 16, 1952; d. Jacques Robert and Muriel (Cooper) Bird; m. Joseph Porto, May 5, 1984, 1 child, Jennifer Ashley. BA, U. So. Calif., 1975; cert. in legal assistantship, U. Calif., Irvine, 1987. Cert. in transp. demand mgmt. Orange County Transit Dist., 1988. Mgr. Bullock's Westwood, West L.A., 1976-78; mgr. ops. Lane Bryant, L.A., 1978-79; supr. employment, dir. personnel May Co. Dept. Stores, 1979-81; adminstr. personnel, dir. benefits Zoetrope Studios, Hollywood, Calif., 1981-82; personnel and ops. analyst Auntie Barbara's, Beverly Hills, Calif., 1982-86; dir. personnel Baylylop, Santa Ana, Calif., 1986-88; pres. Creative Pers. Assocs., 1986-89; owner Flowerman Corona, Del Mar, Calif., 1985—; U.S. dir. human resources UIS, Inc. Co-chair Pro-Wilson Orange County. Home: 7 Stardust Irvine CA 92715-3769 Office: PO Box 9663 Newport Beach CA 92658-9663

BIRDSALL, BRIAN, food products executive; b. 1956. Grad., Wash. State U., 1979. With Pannell Kerr Foster Acctg., Wenatchee, Wash., 1979-88; pres., treas. Chief Wenatchee, 1988—. Office: Chief Wenatchee 1705 N Miller St Wenatchee WA 98801-1585*

BIRKBY, WALTER HUDSON, physical anthropologist, curator; b. Gordon, Nebr., Feb. 28, 1931; s. Walter Levy and Margery Hazel (Moss) B.; m. Carmen Sue Gates, Aug. 18, 1955; children: Jeffrey Moss, Julianne. BA, U. Kans., 1961, MA, 1963; PhD, U. Ariz., 1973. Diplomate Am. Bd. Forensic Anthropology (pres. 1985-87, exec. com. 1980-87). Med. and X-ray technician Graham County (Kans.) Hosp., Hill City, 1955-58; phys. anthropologist Ariz. State Mus., Tucson, 1968-85; lectr. anthropology U. Ariz., Tucson, 1981-90, adj. rsch. prof. anthropology, 1990—; curator phys. anthropology Ariz. State Mus., Tucson, 1985—; forensic anthropologist Pima County Med. Examiner's Office, Tucson, 1981—, Recovery of Victims of Alfred G. Packer party (1874), Lake City, Colo., 1989; dental cons. USAF Hosp., Davis Monthan AFB, Tucson, 1984—; human osteologist U. Ariz.-Republic of Cyprus Archaeol. Expdn., 1984-87, Lugnano in Teverina (Italy) Expdn., 1990-91; dir. dept. anthropology masters program in forensic anthropology, 1984—; cons. to Chief Armed Svcs. Graves Registration Office U.S. Army, 1987-93; mem. disaster mortuary team Nat. Disaster Med. Sys., 1994—. Mem. editorial bd. (jour.) Cryptozoology, 1982—; bd. editors Am. Jour. Forensic Medicine and Pathology, 1992—; co-author video tng. film Identification of Human Remains, 1980; contbr. articles to profl. jours. Served as sgt. USMCR, 1951-52, Korea. NIH fellow U. Ariz., 1966-68; recipient Achievement medal for Meritorious Svc., Pima County Sheriff's Dept., 1992. Fellow Am. Acad. Forensic Scis. (exec. com. 1978-81, T. Dale Stewart award in anthropology 1991); mem. Am. Assn. Phys. Anthropologists, Calif. Assn. Criminalists, Ariz. Identification Coun. of the Internat. Assn. for Identification, Ariz. Homicide Investigators Assn., Internat. Assn. Human Biologists, Sigma Xi (pres. local chpt. 1984-85). Republican. Home: 7349 E 18th St Tucson AZ 85710-4904 Office: U Ariz Ariz State Mus Human Identification Lab Tucson AZ 85721

BIRKENBACH, ADAM STEPHEN, engineer; b. Grant Twp., Mich., Jan. 26, 1937; s. Adam Christopher and Mary (Askey) B.; m. Fern Ellen Fox, Dec. 14, 1956 (div. June 1974); children: Stephanie, Jennifer; m. Angela Rivera, July 22, 1982; children: Frank, Michael Salvador. AA in Engring., E. L.A. Coll., 1960; BSEE, Calif. State U., L.A., 1962; MPA, Calif. State U., Long Beach, 1987. Jr. engr. IMC Magnetics, Maywood, Calif., 1960-62; assoc. elec. engr. Dept. of Water and Power, L.A., 1962-68; chief elec. engr. Port of L.A., San Pedro, Calif., 1968-79, chief of design, 1979-85, asst. chief harbor engr., 1985-95; chief harbor engr. Port of L.A., 1995—; port facilities cons. Asia/Am., Monterey Park, Calif., 1992-94, elec. engring. cons., San Pedro, 1968—. Contbg. author: (books) American National Standard Practice for Industrial Lighting, 1967, rev. edit. 1994, IESNA Lighting Handbook, 1980, rev. edit. 1994. Res. commdr. L.A. Sheriff Dept., Los Angeles County, 1968-94; pres. Penninsula Pointe Homeowners Assn., Rancho Palos Verdes, Calif., 1992-94; mem. Empty Saddle Club, Palos Verdes Estates, Calif., 1983-94. With USN, 1954-58, Asia, Korea. Mem. Illuminating Engring. Soc. of N.Am. (chmn. various coms. 1965-94), Permanent Internat. Assn. of Navigation Congress, Am. Soc. Civil Engrs., Propeller Club of U.S. (com. chmn. 1980-94), Soc. Port Engrs., Elks. Republican. Home: PO Box 532 San Pedro CA 90733-0532 Office: Worldport LA PO Box 151 San Pedro CA 90733

BIRKENKAMP, DEAN FREDERICK, editor, publishing executive; b. Litchfield, Ill., May 5, 1956; s. Arnold R. and Virginia Johanna (Droste) B. BA in Anthropology, U. Ill., 1978, MA in Libr. Sci., 1979; cert., Pub. Inst. U. Denver, 1979. Rsch. assoc. law libr. U. Ill., Urbana, 1978-79; editorial asst. Westview Press, Boulder, Colo., 1979-81, mng. editor, 1981-85, exec. editor, v.p., 1985-89, v.p., group dir. editorial acquisitions, 1989—. Mem. Am. Sociol. Assn. (mem. 1978—), Am. Anthrop. Assn. Office: Westview Press Inc 5500 Central Ave Boulder CO 80301-2847

BIRKINBINE, JOHN, II, philatelist; b. Chestnut Hill, Pa., Mar. 29, 1930; s. Olaf Weimer and Gertrude Marie (Tyson) B.; m. Ausencia Barrera Elen, Dec. 19, 1969; children: John III, Bayani Royd. Chmn., chief exec. officer Am. Philatelic Brokerages, Tucson, 1946—; chmn. bd. dirs. Ariz. Philatelic Rangers, Tucson, 1987—; bd. dirs. Confederate Stamp Alliance, 1987-88; bd. dirs. Postal History Found., 1991—. Chmn. bd. 1869 Pictorial Rsch. Assn., 1969, bd. dirs., 1970-76, chmn. Baha'i Faith Adminstrv. Body, Pima County, Ariz., 1977-81, 83-91; sheriff, chmn. Santa Catalina Corral of Westerners Internat., Tucson, 1986. Recipient Large Gold and Spl. award Spanish Soc. Internat., San Juan, P.R., 1982, New Zealand Soc. Internat., Aukland, 1990, Large Internat. Gold award Australian Soc. Internat., Melbourne. 1984, Swedish Soc. Internat., Stockholm, 1986, Internat. Gold award U.S. Soc. Internat., Chgo., 1986, Bulgarian Soc. Internat., Sofia, 1989. Mem. Am. Philatelic Soc. (U.S. Champion of Champions 1985), U.S. Philatelic Classics Soc., Am. Philatelic Congress (McCoy award 1969), Scandinavian Collectors Club, Collectors Club of N.Y., Western Cover Soc., Canal Zone Study Group,. Office: Am Philatelic Brokerages PO Box 36657 Tucson AZ 85740-6657 Address: PO Box 36657 Tucson AZ 85740-6657

BIRMAN, LINDA LEE, elementary education educator; b. Bellingham, Wash., Sept. 2, 1950; d. Ronald L. and Shirley Lee (Smith) Kindlund; m. Steven D. Birman, May 28, 1988; children: Stacy, Michele, Cameron, Colin. BA in Edn., We. Wash. State Coll., 1973; MA in Edn., We. Wash. U., 1978. Cert. elem. and secondary tchr., Wash. Tchr. 2d grade Bellingham, Wash., 1973—; affiliated teaching faculty We. Wash. U., Bellingham, 1992; subject advisory com. Washington State Student Learning Commn. Mem. NEA, ASCD, Learning Disabilities Assn. Wash.

BIRMINGHAM, RICHARD JOSEPH, lawyer; b. Seattle, Feb. 26, 1953; s. Joseph E. and Anita (Loomis) B. BA cum laude, Wash. State U., 1975; JD, U. Puget Sound, 1978; LLM in Taxation, Boston U., 1980. Bar: Wash. 1978, Oreg. 1981, U.S. Dist. Ct. (we. dist.) Wash. 1978, U.S. Tax Ct. 1981. Ptnr. Davis Wright Tremaine, Seattle, 1982-93; shareholder Birmingham Thorson & Barnett, P.C., Seattle, 1993—; mem. King County Bar Employee Benefit Com., Seattle, 1986, U.S. Treasury ad hoc com. employee benefits, 1988—. Contbg. editor: Compensation and Benefits Mgmt., 1985—; contbr. articles to profl. jours. Mem. ABA (employee benefits and exec. compensation com. 1982—), Wash. State Bar Assn. (speaker 1984-86, tax sect. 1982—), Oreg. State Bar Assn. (tax sect. 1982—), Western Pension Conf. (speaker 1986), Seattle Pension Round table. Democrat. Home: 505 Belmont Ave E Apt 204 Seattle WA 98102-4862 Office: Birmingham Thorson Barnett 3315 Two Union Square 601 Union St Seattle WA 98101-2327

BIRN, RAYMOND FRANCIS, historian, educator; b. N.Y.C., May 10, 1935; s. Saul Albert and Celia (Markman) B.; m. Randi Ingebrigtsen, July 18, 1960 (div. 1987); children—Eric Stephen, Laila Marie. B.A., NYU, 1956; M.A., U. Ill., 1957, Ph.D., 1961. Mem. faculty U. Oreg., Eugene, 1961—; assoc. prof. U. Oreg., 1966-72, prof. history, 1972—, head dept., 1971-78; vis. prof. École des Hautes Études en Sciences sociales, Paris, 1992. Author: Pierre Rousseau and the Philosophes of Bouillon, 1964, Crisis, Absolutism, Revolution: Europe, 1648-1789/91, 1977, revised edit., 1992; adv. editor Eighteenth-Century Studies, 1974-85, French Hist. Studies, 1977-80; editor: The Printed Word in the Eighteenth Century, 1984; contbr. articles to profl. jours. Mem. adv. screening com. Council for Internat. Exchange of Persons (Fulbright program), 1974-76. Served with AUS, 1959-60. Fulbright rsch. fellow to France, 1968-69; Nat. Endowment for Humanities sr. fellow, 1976-77, 87-88; Ctr. for History of Freedom fellow, 1992. Mem. Am. Hist. Assn., Soc. French Hist. Studies, Am. Soc. 18th Century Studies. Office: U Oreg Dept History Eugene OR 97403

BIRNBAUM, STEVAN ALLEN, investment company executive; b. L.A., Apr. 21, 1943; s. Eugene David and Bessie (Holtzman) B.; m. Barbara Patricia Ostroff, June 29, 1971 (div. Aug. 1991); children: Marc, Jill. BS in Engring., UCLA, 1965; MBA, Harvard U., 1967. Dir. advanced programs Whittaker Corp., L.A., 1967-69; v.p. Hohenberg & Assocs., Beverly Hills, Calif., 1969-74; dir. adminstrv. mgmt. Dames & Moore, L.A., 1974-77; prin. Xerox Venture Capital, L.A., 1977-81; venture capitalist, L.A., 1981-83; ptnr. Oxford Ptnrs., Santa Monica, Calif., 1983—; pres. Oxcal Venture Corp., Santa Monica, 1981—; founder, bd. dirs. Brentwood Savs. Bank, 1982; bd. dirs. Cogensys, La Jolla, Calif., Wangdat, Irvine, Calif., Quintar Corp., Torrance, Calif. Republican. Jewish.

BIROC, SANDRA LYN, biology educator, biologist; b. Los Angeles, Dec. 14, 1947; d. Robert Biroc and Doris Lynell (Haven) Rast; m. Daniel Bernard Unger, Mar. 27, 1982; children: Elizabeth Kaye, Douglas Gustav. BA in Biology, Calif. State U., Northridge, 1970; PhD in Biology, Johns Hopkins U., 1975. Postdoctoral fellow U. Calif., Davis, 1975-78; instr. Calif. State U., Sacramento, 1978-80; lab. coordinator, asst. prof. biology U. Colo., Boulder, 1980-90; founding mem., staff scientist Khepri Pharms., San Francisco, 1991—. Author: Developmental Biology, 1986. Dem. del., Colo., 1988. Mem. AAAS, Boulder Internat. Folk Dancers (pres. 1985-90), Masons (state rep. 1965-66), Assn. Women in Sci. Office: Khepri Pharmaceuticals Inc 260 Littlefield Ave South San Francisco CA 94080-6902

BIRRELL, G. WILLIAM (BILL BIRRELL), special effects executive; b. Port Chester, N.Y., Feb. 3, 1961; s. George Andrew and Lelia Carter (Panill) B.; m. Susan Buchanan Lierle, June 10, 1989; children: Caleigh, Emma, Grace. BA in Drama, Colo. Coll., 1983; MBA, U. Va., 1988. Mgmt. assoc. Sony Pictures Entertainment, L.A. and N.Y.C., 1988-90; dir. spl. projects Sony Pictures Entertainment, L.A., 1990-92; sr. v.p., exec. producer Sony Pictures Imageworks, L.A., 1992—.

BIRREN, JEFFREY EMMETT, lawyer; b. Chgo., Jan. 28, 1951; s. James E. and Elizabeth Ann (Solomon) B. AB, U. So. Calif., 1974, MA, 1980; JD, Southwestern U., Los Angeles, 1985. Bar: Calif. 1985, U.S. Dist. Ct. (so. dist.) Calif. 1985, U.S. Dist. Ct. (no., ea. and cen. dists.) Calif. 1986, U.S. Ct. Appeals (9th cir.) 1986. Asst. dir. mini coll. U. So. Calif., L.A., 1970-79, instr., 1979; with legal staff L.A. Raiders, 1980-85, gen. counsel, 1985—; adj. prof. Southwestern U. Sch. Law. Mem. Assn. Trial Lawyers Am., Los Angeles County Bar Assn. Unitarian. Office: LA Raiders 332 Center St El Segundo CA 90245-4047

BISBEE, DIANE PARKS, guidance counselor; b. Omaha, Nebr., May 24, 1945; d. Edward C. and Virginia M. (VanLuchene) Parks; m. Allan C. Bisbee, Sept. 16, 1967; children: Matthew, Cristin, Michael, Mark. BA in Sociology, Creighton U., 1967; MA in Counseling, U. Nev., 1986. Cert. sch. counselor, Nev. Youth counselor Tahoe Human Svcs., S. Lake Tahoe, Calif., 1988; high sch. guidance counselor Douglas County Sch. Dist., Zephyr Cove, Nev., 1988—; sch. rep. Tahoe Prevention Network, S. Lake Tahoe, 1991-92; faculty mem. Whittell H.S. Adv. Com., Zephyr Cove, 1992-94. Mem. Douglas County Drug Task Force, Minden, Nev., 1990-92. Mem. Am. Counseling Assn., Nev. Sch. Counselor Assn. Home: PO Box 615 Zephyr Cove NV 89448-0615

BISHOP, B. H., textile manufacturing executive. Office: Pendleton Woolen Mills Inc 220 NW Broadway Portland OR 97209-3509

BISHOP, BETTY JOSEPHINE, financial consultant; b. Seattle, Wash., Feb. 27, 1947; d. Arthur Joseph and Julia Teresa (Azzolina) Lovett; children: Deborah, Scott. BS, Wash. State U., 1969; postgrad., Ohio State U., 1983; JD, Santa Barbara Coll. of Law, 1994. Tchr. Seattle Sch. Dist., 1973-75; appraiser Pacific First Fed., Tacoma, 1977-78, asst. v.p., mgr., secondary market ops., 1978-82; regional exec. United Guaranty, Westlake Village, Calif., 1982-83; sr. v.p. comml. secondary mktg. FCA Am. Mortgage Corp./Am. Savs., Santa Monica, Calif., 1983-85; v.p., mgr. secondary market ops. County Savs. Bank, Santa Barbara, Calif., 1985-88; pres., fin. cons. SMC Fin. Svcs., Montecito, Calif., 1988—; mem. conf. subcom., sec. mktg. com. Calif. Savs. and Loan League, L.A., 1985-88; document subcom., sec. mktg. subcom. U.S. Savs. and Loan League, Chgo., 1987-88; expert witness secondary mktg. and mortgage banking. Contbr. articles to profl. jours. Fund drive chmn. Easter Seal Soc., Olympia, 1972. Mem. L.A. Trial Lawyers Assn., Santa Barbara Bar Assn., Santa Barbara Assocs., Conejo Ski Club (past woman of yr.), Santa Barbara Ski Club (past pres., past L.A. coun. rep.). Republican. Roman Catholic.

BISHOP, C. DIANE, state agency administrator, educator; b. Elmhurst, Ill., Nov. 23, 1943; d. Louis William and Constance Oleta (Mears) B. BS in Maths., U. Ariz., 1965, MS in Maths., MEd in Secondary Edn., 1972. Lic. secondary educator. Tchr. math. Tucson Unified Sch. Dist., 1966-86, mem. curriculum council, 1985-86, mem. maths. curriculum task teams, 1983-86; state supt. of pub. instrn. State of Ariz., 1987-95, gov. policy advisor for edn., 1995—; mem. assoc. faculty Pima C.C., Tucson, 1974-84; adj. lectr. U. Ariz., 1983, 85; mem. math. scis. edn. bd. NRC, 1987-90, mem. new standards project governing bd., 1991; dir. adv. bd. sci. and engring. ednl. panel, NSF; mem. adv. bd. for arts edn. Nat. Endowment for Arts. Active Ariz. State Bd. Edn., 1984-95, chmn. quality edn. commn., 1986-87, chmn. tchr. crt. subcom., 1984-95, mem. outcomes based edn. adv. com., 1986-87, liaison bd. dirs. essential skills subcom., 1985-87, gifted edn. com. liaison, 1985-87; mem. Ariz. State Bd. Regents, 1987-95, mem. com. on preparing for U. Ariz., 1983, mem. high sch. task force, 1984-85; mem. bd. Ariz. State Community Coll., 1987-95; mem. Ariz. Joint Legis. Com. on Revenues and Expenditures, 1989, Ariz. Joint Legis. Com. on Goals for Ednl. Excellence, 1987-89, Gov.'s Task Force on Ednl. Reform, 1991, Ariz. Bd. Regents Commn. on Higher Edn., 1992. Woodrow Wilson fellow Princeton U., summer 1984; recipient Presdl. Award for Excellence in Teaching of Maths., 1983, Ariz. Citation of Merit, 1984, Maths. Teaching award Nat. Sci. Research Soc., 1984, Distinction in Edn. award Flinn Found., 1986; named Maths. Tchr. of Yr. Ariz. Council of Engring. and Sci. Assns., 1984. Mem. AAUW, NEA, Nat. Coun. Tchrs. Math., Coun. Chief State Sch. Officers, Women Execs. in State Govt. (bd. dirs. 1993), Ariz. Assn. Tchrs. Math., Women Maths. Edn., Math. Assn. Am., Ednl. Commn. of the States (steering com.), Nat. Endowment Arts (adv. bd. for arts edn.), Nat. Forum Excellence Edn., Nat. Honors Workshop, Phi Delta Kappa. Democrat. Episcopalian. Office: Ariz Dept Edn 1700 W Washington Phoenix AZ 85007-3209

BISHOP, C. M., JR., textile company executive. Pres., Pendleton Woolen Mills Inc., Portland, Oreg. Office: Pendleton Woolen Mills Inc 220 NW Broadway Portland OR 97209-3509

BISHOP, CAROL WARD, dean; b. Sewickley, Pa., July 10, 1936; d. Earl Dawson and Wilma Henrietta (Obenour) Ward; m. Jack Lynn Bishop, Mar. 29, 1958; children: Lori Diane Bishop Dagg, Jeffrey Lynn. BS in Home Econs. and Journalism, Kans. State U., 1958; MS in Nutrition, Va. Poly. Inst., 1961. Registered dietitian. Asst. editor Household Mag., Topeka, 1958-59; rsch. instr. Va. Poly. Inst., Blackburg, 1964-67; instr. nutrition Modesto (Calif.) Jr. Coll., 1967-70; instr. nutrition Solano Coll., Suisun City, Calif., 1970-78, divsn. chair fine arts, 1978-90, dean fine and applied arts, 1990—; grant writer Tech-Prep State Presch., Fed. Block Grant, Child Devel. Consortium, Fed. Food Program, Foster Parent, Ind. Living, Nutrition Edn. Tng., Child Devel. Renovation and Repair; chair Tech. Prep. Adv. Com. Mem. Am. Dietetic Assn., Calif. Dietetic Assn., Diablo Valley Dietetic Assn., Danas Women's Club (bridge chmn.), Phi Kappa Phi, Delta Sigma Gamma. Home: PO Box 267 Bethel Island CA 94511-0267 Office: Solano Coll 4000 Suisun Valley Rd Suisun City CA 94585-4017

BISHOP, CAROLYN BENKERT, public relations counselor; b. Monroe, Wis., Aug. 28, 1939; d. Arthur C. and Delphine (Heston) Benkert; m. Lloyd F. Bishop, June 15, 1963. BS, U. Wis., 1961; grad., Tobe-Coburn Sch., N.Y.C., 1962. Merchandising editor Co-Ed Mag., N.Y.C., 1962-63; advt. copywriter Woodward & Lothrop, Washington, 1963-65; home furnishings editor Co-Ed Mag., N.Y.C., 1965-68; editor Budget Decorating Mag., N.Y.C., 1968-69; home furnishings editor Family Cir. Mag., N.Y.C., 1969-75; v.p., pub., editorial dir. Scholastic, Inc., N.Y.C., 1975-80; owner Mesa Store Home Furnishings Co., Aspen, Colo., 1980-83; dir. pub. rels. Snowmass Resort Assn., Snowmass Village, Colo., 1983-86; pres. Bishop & Bishop Mktg. Communications, Aspen, 1986—; mem. media rels. com. Colo. Tourism Bd., Denver, 1987-90. Author: 25 Decorating Ideas Under $100, 1969; editor: Family Circle Special Home Decorating Guide, 1973. Bd. dirs. Aspen Camp Sch. for the Deaf, 1987-90. Recipient Dallas Market Editorial award Dallas Market Ctr., 1973, Dorothy Dawe award Chgo. Furniture Market, 1973, Guardian of Freedom award, Anti-Defamation League Appeal, 1974. Mem. Rocky Mountain Pub. Rels. Group (chmn. 1991-93), Pub. Rels. Soc. Am. (accredited, small firms co-chair counselors acad. 1992-93), Aspen Writers' Found. (bd. dirs. 1991-93), Tobe-Coburn Alumni Assn., U. Wis. Alumni Assn. Democrat. Office: Bishop & Bishop Mktg Comms PO Box 300 1511-13th Ave Monroe WI 53566

BISHOP, GEORGE CAMERON, therapist; b. Toronto, Aug. 31, 1954; came to the U.S., 1983; s. Samuel Shaver Bishop and Jacqueline Marie-Blanche (Bergeron) Cleary; m. Violanta Marguerita Schabauer, Apr. 1972 (div. Jan. 1980); 1 child, Tanya Elizabeth Belinda; m. Pamela Suzanne Glahn, Dec. 28, 1985; 1 child, Isabel Lyn Bergeron. Agrl. technician, Kemptville (Ont.) Coll., 1980; B in Ednl. Psychology, Prescott Coll., 1985; M in Counseling Psychology, No. Ariz. U., 1988; M in Handwriting Analysis, Internat. Graphoanalysis, 1991. Cert. sr. addictions counselor Colo. State Dept. Health. Tchr. Primavera Elem., Prescott, Ariz., 1983-84, Prescott (Ariz.) Secondary, 1984-85; mental health worker Coconino Cmty. Clinic, Flagstaff, Ariz., 1985-87; counselor No. Ariz. U., Flagstaff, 1987-88; therapist Co-Dependency Recovery Ctr., Denver, 1988-89, New Beginnings, Denver, 1988-89, Larico Youth Homes, Ft. Collins, Colo., 1990-92; forensic examiner Investigative Solutions, Ft. Collins, 1993—; therapist Solutions, Ft. Collins, 1989—; presenter, trainer Mind-Body Wellness Seminars and Staff Devel., 1994—. Chmn. Centennial Loans Com., Kemptville, 1978-80; victims and witness advisor Victims and Witness Colonino, Flagstaff, 1987-88; facilitator Native Ams. Bear Lodge Tiosaype, Denver, 1990—; facilitator gang mems. getting out Gang Resistance in Power, Ft. Collins, 1993-94. Recipient Contbr. to Counselor Edn. and Devel., Nat. Disting. Svc. Registry, 1989-90; named Family Counselor of Yr., Am. Media, Ft. Collins, 1993-94; named Wellness Counselor of Yr., Am. Media Consumer Bus. Review, 1994-95. Mem. Am. Bd. Forensic Examiners (bd. cert.), Internat. Graphoanalysis Soc., Nat. Assn. Document Examiners, Am. Assn. for Counselor Devel., Nat. Bd. Clin. Hypnotherapists (cert. clin. hypnotherapist), Pow Wow Com., Ft. Collins. Office: Solutions 1020 Country Club Rd Fort Collins CO 80524

BISHOP, JAMES ALLEN, wood products consultant; b. Bend, Oreg., Jan. 28, 1950; s. Leo Allen and Alice May (Nelson) B.; m. Ramona June Morris, Sept. 21, 1974; children: Cheryl, Tracee. BS, MS, Stanford U., 1973. Prodn. scheduler Brooks-Scanlon, Inc., Redmond, Oreg., 1974-80; real estate salesman United Properties, Redmond, 1980-82; mgr. quality assurance Contact Lumber, Prineville, Oreg., 1982-85; plant mgr. Contact Lumber, Hines, Oreg., 1985-91; wood products cons. Bishop Engring., Burns, Oreg., 1991—; chmn. bd. dirs. Harney County Fed. Credit Union, Burns, 1987-91; treas. The Oreg. Consortium (Job Tng. Partnership Act), Albany, 1990. Mem. Harney County Planning Commn., 1986-89. Scholar Bend Found., 1968-72. Mem. Harney County C. of C. (bd. dirs. 1985-89, Boss of Yr. award 1987, Man of Yr. award 1988, Lumberman of Yr. award 1989). Democrat. Presbyterian. Home: PO Box 428 Burns OR 97720-0428

BISHOP, JEFF, airport terminal executive; b. 1958. BBA, U. Wyo., 1983. Acct. McGladrey, Hendrickson and Pullen, Casper, Wyo., 1983-87; with Casper Air Svc., 1987—. Office: Casper Air Svc 300 Airport Rd Casper WY 82604*

BISHOP, JOHN MICHAEL, biomedical research scientist, educator; b. York, Pa., Feb. 22, 1936; married 1959; 2 children. AB, Gettysburg Coll., 1957; MD, Harvard U., 1962; DSc (hon.), Gettysburg Coll., 1983. Intern in internal medicine Mass. Gen. Hosp., Boston, 1962-63, resident, 1963-64; rsch. assoc. virology NIH, Washington, 1964-66, sr. investigator, 1966-68; from asst. prof. to assoc. prof. U. Calif. Med. Ctr., San Francisco, 1968-72, prof. microbiology and immunology, 1972—, prof. biochemistry and biophysics, 1982—; dir. G.W. Hooper Rsch. Found., 1981—. Recipient Nobel prize in physiology or medicine, 1989, Biomed. Rsch. award Am. Assn. Med. Colls., 1981, Albert Lasker Basic Med. Rsch. award, 1981, Armand Hammer Cancer award, 1984, GM Found. Cancer Rsch. award, 1984, Gairdner Found. Internat. award, Can., 1984, Medal of Honor, Am. Cancer Soc., 1984; NIH grantee, 1968—. Fellow Salk Inst. (trustee 1991—); mem. NAS, Inst. Medicine. Office: U Calif Medical Ctr Dept Microbiology Box 0552 San Francisco CA 94143-0552*

BISHOP, LEO KENNETH, clergyman, educator; b. Britton, Okla., Oct. 11, 1911; s. Luther and Edith (Scovill) B.; m. Pauline T. Shamburg, Sept. 15, 1935; 1 dau., Linda Paulette. A.B., Phillips U., 1932; L.H.D., 1958; M.A., Columbia U., 1944; M.B.A., U. Chgo., 1957; Litt.D., Kansas City Coll. Osteopathy and Surgery, 1964. Ordained to ministry Christian Ch., 1932; asso. minister Univ. Place Ch., Oklahoma City, 1932-35; minister First Ch., Paducah, Ky., 1935-41, Central Ch., Des Moines, 1941-45; dir. St. Louis office NCCJ, 1945-48; v.p., dir. central div. NCCJ, Chgo., 1949-63; dir. pub. affairs People-to-People, Kansas City, Mo., 1963-66; v.p. Chgo. Coll. Osteopathy, 1966-72; pres. Bishop Enterprises, Colorado Springs, Colo., 1972—; also lectr. Contbr. religious and ednl. jours.; Developed: radio series Storm Warning; TV series The Other Guy, 1954. Cons. Community Social Planning Council, Mayor's Race Relations Com., YMCA, St. Louis; Am. del. Conf. World Brotherhood, Paris, 1950; bd. dirs. Am. Heritage Found. Recipient Paducah Jr. C. of C. Most Useful Citizen award, 1937, Distinguished Service award Dore Miller Found., 1958, Freedom Found. of Valley Forge award, 1961; named Chicagoan of Year, 1960. Clubs: Rotary, Union League, Winter Night. Home: 107 W Cheyenne Rd Colorado Springs CO 80906-2550 Office: PO Box 843 Colorado Springs CO 80901-0843

BISHOP, LOUISE MARIE, English language educator; b. Paterson, N.J., Feb. 3, 1954; d. Charles Hudson and Louise (Coleman) B.; m. James Whitby Earl, Mar. 19, 1982; children: Catherine Elizabeth Earl, Edward Charles Earl. BA in English, Fairleigh Dickinson U., 1978; MA in English, Fordham U., 1981, PhD in English, 1984. Tchg. fellow dept. English Fordham U., Bronx, N.Y., 1979-83; asst. dean Grad. Bus. Sch. Fordham U., N.Y.C., 1983-85, assoc. dean Grad. Bus. Sch., 1985-87; instr. dept. English U. Oreg., Eugene, 1987-93, sr. instr. dept. English, 1993—. Author: (chpt.) The Work of Work, 1994; curator manuscript exhibit, 1994. Bd. dirs. Friends of Libr., Knight Libr., U. Oreg., 1992—; mem. Fortnightly Club, Eugene, 1993—; lectr. Oreg. Coun. for Humanities, 1989, 91; chair child care and family support com. U. Oreg., 1992—. Mem. Am. Mgmt. Assn. (instr. 1981-83). Home: 1820 Olive St Eugene OR 97401 Office: Univ Oreg Dept English Eugene OR 97403-1286

BISHOP, MARGARET, retired educator, writer; b. Urbana, Ill., July 4, 1920; d. Charles Maxwell and Prudence Emily (Pratt) McConn; m. Edwin Samuel Bishop, Aug. 22, 1942; children—Peter Boehler, Margaret. B.A., Barnard Coll., N.Y.C., 1943. Reporter, wire editor York Gazette and Daily, York, Pa., 1942-45; remedial reading tutor, Queens, N.Y., 1958-68; in-house writer Appleton-Century-Crofts, N.Y.C., 1964-70, McGraw-Hill, N.Y.C., 1971-74; reading specialist Fortune Soc., N.Y.C., 1976-85. Author: The ABC's and All Their Tricks, 1986, Ode on Reason and Faith, 1981, (workbooks) Phonics with Write and See, 1968, also articles. Exec. sec. NAACP, York, 1943-48; mem. LWV, York, 1946-50, Reading Reform Found., N.Y.C., 1958—; pres. N.Y. met. chpt., 1981-85. Mem. Mayor's Profl. Exchange, Adult Basic Edn. Providers. Democrat. Humanist. Avocations: hiking; camping; backpacking.

BISHOP, ROBERT CHARLES, architect, metals and minerals company executive; b. Butte, Mont., June 6, 1929; s. Lester Farragut and Helen Katherine (Bauman) B.; m. B. Jean Rausch, June 29, 1957; children: Desta Fawn Bishop O'Connor, Valerie Dawn. BS in Gen. Engring., Mont. State U., 1958, BArch., 1960. Assoc. architect various firms, Mont., 1960-64; owner, architect R.C. Bishop & Assocs., Butte, Great Falls and Missoula, Mont., 1965-69; owner, chief exec. officer Val-Desta 4M, Butte, 1980—, Val-Desta Mines and Minerals, Louisville, Ky., 1985—; prin. Archtl. Assocs., 1969—; chief exec. officer, pres. Cove-Lock Log Home Mfrs., Inc., Butte, 1968-72, Busy Beaver Enterprises, Great Falls, 1968-72, New Horizon Homes, Missoula, 1968-72; asst. contracts adminstr. Davy-McKee Constrn. Engrs., Butte, 1982-83. Developer 9 major and 2 minor algorithms for mineral prospecting, valid for over 100 areas in Mont. and Idaho; discoverer 100 to 300 million tons of high grade bull quarts and rock crystal, copper and molybdenum, potential world class deposits; co-patentee in field. Advisor, Kiwanis, Jaycees, Nat. Res., 1960-72, Am. Legion, 1976. With U.S. Army, 1953-55. Named One of 2,000 Men of Achievement Melrose Press, 1970, 73. Mem. Internat. Platform Assn., Nat. Hist. Soc. (founding assoc. 1971), Elk Bow Hunting Club (bugle tchr. 1970-84), Butte Mulitlist Club (real estate tchr. 1978-84), Nat. Coun. Archtl. Registeration Bds. (registered architect seismic design 1965—). Presbyterian. Home and Office: 1008 W Galena St Butte MT 59701-1420

BISHOP, RODNEY PHILIP, physician; b. London, Mar. 22, 1932; came to U.S., 1993; s. Reginald Henry and Eileen Gertrude (Hill) B.; m. Ann Frances Margaret Swindale, July 17, 1965; children: James, Sarah, Amy. BA in Natural Sci., Cambridge (Eng.) U., 1955, MA in Natural Sci., 1959; MD, London Royal Coll., Eng., 1960; D in Pub. Adminstrn., Pacific Western U., 1988. Diplomate English Med. Bd., Can. Med. Bd. Intern Salvation Army Hosp., Winnipeg, Can., 1960-61; srug. tng. Salvation Army Hosp., Nagercoil, South India, 1962-64; maternity tng. Maternity Hosp., Aberdeen, Scotland, 1964-65; pvt. practice Bedforshire, Eng., 1960-73, New Westminster, B.C., Can., 1974—; med. dir. Queens Park Extended Care

Hosp., New Westminster, 1977-86; pres., rsch. Rodney Bishop Mgmt. Co., Inc., 1980—. Readership and youth group leader Episcopalian Ch., London, 1956-73. Lt. British Army, 1950-55. Mem. AMA, Brit. Med. Assn., Can. Med. Assn., N.Y. Acad. Sci. Episcopalian. Home: 4177 Patos Dr Ferndale WA 98248 Office: 604 625 5th Ave, New Westminster, BC Canada V3M 1X4

BISHOP, TILMAN MALCOLM, state senator, retired college administrator; b. Colorado Springs, Jan. 1, 1933; B.A., M.A., U. No. Colo.; m. Pat Bishop, 1951; 1 son, Barry Alan. Retired adminstr., dir. student services Mesa State Coll., Grand Junction, Colo.; mem., pres. pro tem Colo. Senate. World series com. Nat. Jr. Coll. Baseball. Served with U.S. Army. Mem. Am. Sch. Counselors Assn., Nat. Assn. for Counseling and Devel., Colo. Assn. for Counseling and Devel. Republican. Methodist. Lodges: Elks, Lions. Avocations: fishing, small game hunting. Office: State Capitol Bldg Denver CO 80203 Home: 2697 G Rd Grand Junction CO 81506-8367

BISHOP, VIRGINIA WAKEMAN, retired librarian and humanities educator; b. Portland, Oreg., Dec. 28, 1927; d. Andrew Virgil and Letha Evangeline (Ward) Wakeman; m. Clarence Edmund Bishop, Aug. 23, 1953; children: Jean Marie Bishop Johnson, Marilyn Joyce. BA, Bapt. Missionary Tng. Sch., Chgo., 1949, Linfield Coll., McMinnville, Oreg., 1952; MEd, Linfield Coll., McMinnville, Oreg., 1953; MA in Librarianship, U. Wash., 1968. Ch. worker Univ. Bapt. Ch., Seattle, 1954-56, 59-61, pre-sch. tchr. parent coop presch., 1965-66; libr. N.W. Coll., Kirkland, Wash., 1968-69; undergrad. libr. U. Wash., Seattle, 1970; libr., instr. Seattle Cen. Community Coll., 1970-91. Leader Totem coun. Girl Scouts U.S., 1962-65; pres. Wedgwood Sch. PTA, Seattle, 1964-65; chair 46th Dist. Dem. Orgn., Seattle, 1972-73; candidate Wash. State Legislature, Seattle, 1974, 80; bd. dirs. Univ. Bapt. Children's Ctr., 1989—, chair, 1990-95; vol. Ptnrs. in Pub. Edn., 1992—. Recipient Golden Acorn award Wedgwood Elem. Sch., 1966. Mem. LWV of Seattle (2d v.p. 1994—), U. Wash. Grad. Sch. Libr. and Info. Sci. Alumni Assn. (1st v.p. 1986-87, pres. 1987-88). Baptist. Home: 3032 NE 87th St Seattle WA 98115-3529

BISSELL, BETTY DICKSON, retired stockbroker; b. Salina, Kans., Sept. 9, 1932; d. Henry Shields and Alta May Dickson; m. Buford Lyle Bissell, Jr., Nov. 1, 1952; 1 child, Bradford Dickson. Student, U. Kans., 1949-52; cert. fin. planner, Coll. Fin. Planning, 1976. With Dean Witter Reynolds Inc., Menlo Park, Calif., 1975—, asst. br. mgr., 1978-82, asso. v.p. investments, 1980-82, 1st v.p. investments, 1982-86, sr. v.p. investments, 1986-94; ret., 1994; cons. in field. Pres. Jr. League San Jose (Calif.), 1963-64. Mem. Internat. Assn. Fin. Planners, Internat. Bd. Cert. Fin. Planners, Peninsula Stock and Bond Club, Pi Beta Phi, Commonwealth Club Calif., Summit League Club (Saratoga-Los Gatos), Jr. League Club (San Jose, Calif.). Republican. Episcopalian. Office: 1010 El Camino Real Ste 200 Menlo Park CA 94025-4306

BISSONETTE, JOHN ALFRED, research scientist; b. Colchester, Vt., July 9, 1941; s. Kenneth Joseph and Diane Marie (Gamache) B.; m. Mary Elizabeth Poe, Oct. 1, 1966; children: Nicole Elizabeth, Gabriel Jared. BA, U. Vt., 1964; MFS, Yale U., 1970; PhD, U. Mich., 1976. Vertebrate zoologist Ariz. State U., Tempe, 1975-77; asst. unit leader Okla. State U., Stillwater, 1977-81; asst. unit leader, act. leader U. Maine, Orono, 1981-85; leader Utah coop. fish & wildlife res. unit Utah State U., Logan, 1985—; mem., chmn. bd. govs. SNR-U. Mich., Ann Arbor, 1985-91; mem., bd. dirs. Natural Res. Coun. Maine, Augusta; bd. scientists Chihuahuan Desert Res. Inst., Alpine, Tex., 1987—; bd. dirs. N.Am. Loon Fund, N.H.; mem. Utah Nat. Resources Coordinating Coun., 1995—. Home: 1960 N 1380 E Logan UT 84541 Office: Utah State U Nat Biol Survey Coll Natural Resources Logan UT 84522-5290

BISTLINE, STEPHEN, retired state supreme court justice; b. Pocatello, Idaho, Mar. 12, 1921; s. Ray D. and Martha (Faber) B.; m. Sharon Mooney; children: Patrick, Claire, Susan, Shelley, Diana, Paul, Leslie, Arthur. LL.B., U. Idaho, 1949. Bar: Idaho 1949. Pvt. practice law Sandpoint, Idaho, 1950-76; justice Idaho Supreme Ct., Boise, 1976-94. Served with USN, 1941-45.

BITTENBENDER, BRAD JAMES, environmental safety and industrial hygiene manager; b. Kalamazoo, Dec. 4, 1948; s. Don J. and Thelma Lu (Bacon) B.; m. Patricia Stahl Hubbell, June, 1992. BS, Western Mich. U., 1972; Cert. Hazardous Material Mgmt., U. Calif., Irvine, 1987; Cert. Environ. Auditing, Calif. State U., Long Beach, 1992. Cert. safety profl. of the Ams.; cert. hazardous materials mgr. Supr. mfg. Am. Cyanamid, Kalamazoo, 1973-77; supr. mfg. Productol Chem. div. Ferro Corp., Santa Fe Springs, Calif., 1977-79, environ. adminstr., 1979-80; sr. environ. engr. Ferro Corp., Los Angeles, 1980-87, mgr. environ. safety and indsl. hygiene dept., 1988-91; mgr. environ. safety and indsl. hygiene dept. Structural Polymer Systems, Inc., Montedison, Calif., 1991—; bd. dirs., mem. adv. bd. safety and health extension program U. Calif. Irvine, 1985—. Bd. dirs. adv. com. hazardous materials Community Right to Know, Culver City, Calif., 1987—; mem. Calif. Mus. Found., L.A., 1985—, Mus. Contemporary Art, L.A., 1985—; founding sponsor Challenger Ctr. Mem. Am. Inst. Chem. Engrs., Nat. Assn. Environ. Mgmt., Acad. Cert. Hazardous Materials Mgrs., Suppliers of Advanced Composites Materials Assn. (mem. environ. health and safety com. 1989-92), Am. Indsl. Hygiene Assn., Am. Soc. Safety Engrs., Nat. Fire Protection Assn., Beta Beta Beta. Republican. Presbyterian. Office: Structural Polymer Systems Inc 5915 Rodeo Rd Los Angeles CA 90016-4312

BITTERMAN, MELVIN LEE, real estate developer; b. Yankton, S.D., Dec. 9, 1938; s. Edward Phillip and Amanda Bertha (Moke) B.; m. Constance Winfried Mann, Nov. 7, 1970; 1 child, Janet Amanda. BA, N. Tex. State U., 1967. Librarian City of Glendale, Calif., 1967-71; sales rep. Allstate Ins. Co., Glendale, 1971-86; property mgr./developer Glendale, 1986—. With U.S. Army, 1961-64. Mem. Rotary (sec. 1985), Alpha Beta Alpha. Republican. Roman Catholic. Address: 1400 Beaudry Blvd Glendale CA 91208-1708

BITTERMAN, MORTON EDWARD, psychologist, educator; b. N.Y.C., Jan. 19, 1921; s. Harry Michael and Stella (Weiss) B.; m. Mary Gayle Foley, June 26, 1967; children—Sarah Fleming, Joan, Ann. B.A., NYU, 1941; M.A., Columbia U., 1942; Ph.D., Cornell U., 1945. Asst. prof. Cornell U., Ithaca, N.Y., 1945-50; assoc. prof. U. Tex., Austin, 1950-55; mem. Inst. for Advanced Study, Princeton, N.J., 1955-57; prof. Bryn Mawr Coll., Pa., 1957-70, U. Hawaii, Honolulu, 1970—; dir. Békésy Lab. Neurobiology, Honolulu, 1991—. Author: (with others) Animal Learning, 1979; editor: Evolution of Brain and Behavior in Vertebrates, 1976; co-editor: Am. Jour. Psychology, 1955-73; cons. editor Jour. Animal Learning and Behavior, 1973-76, 85-88, Jour. Comparative Psychology, 1988-92. Recipient Humboldt prize Alexander von Humboldt Found., Bonn, W.Ger., 1981; Fulbright grantee; grantee NSF, Office Naval Research, NIMH, Air Force Office Sci. Research, Deutsche Forschungsgemeinschaft. Fellow Soc. Exptl. Psychologists, Am. Psychol. Assn., AAAS; mem. Psychonomic Soc. Home: 229 Kaalawai Pl Honolulu HI 96816-4435 Office: Univ Hawaii Bekesy Lab of Neurobiology 1993 E West Rd Honolulu HI 96822-2321

BITTERS, CONRAD LEE, biological sciences educator; b. Waco, Tex., Jan. 2, 1946; s. E. Conrad and Margaret Lee (Miles) B.; m. Karen Kay, May 1, 1970; children: Rebecca, Brian. BA, Calif. State U., Fresno, 1969. Life Credential, Biol./Phys. Sciences, Calif. Biology/zoology tchr. Clovis (Calif.) High Sch., 1970—, science dept. chmn., 1973-80, biology coordinator, 1980—; founder, sponsor Clovis (Calif.) High Ecology club, 1970—, Clovis High Fgn. Studies Club, 1978-87, 92-95; jr. div. judge Cen. Valley Sci. Fair, Fresno, Calif., 1975—; vertebrate advisory com. Cen. Valley Sci. Fair, 1978—; coach-sr. div. Cen. Valley Sci. Fair, Fresno, 1972—; dist. rep. Jr. Sci. and Humanities Symposium, Berkeley, Calif., 1974—; Calif. Ednl. Initiatives Fund Grant Dir., 1986. Recipient Faculty award Eastman Kodak Co., 1980, Nat. Jr. Sci. and Humanities Symposium, 1985, 93, 94, Merit award Rotary Club Fresno, 1985, 88, 93-94, Faculty Commendation Lawrence Hall of Sci., 1985, 87, 94, John D. Isaacs Scholarship Com., 1985, Outstanding Sci. Tchrs. Fresno County Dow Chem. Co., 1986, Presdl. award in sci. teaching Calif. State Dept. Edn., 1986, Faculty Commendation Calif. Sci. Fair, 1988, commendation Internat. Sci. Engring. Fair, 1982, 93-94, Commendation for Dept. Energy award, 1993. Mem. Nat. Sci. Teachers' Assn. Republican. Church of Jesus Christ of Latter Day Saints. Home: 2695 Armstrong Ave Clovis CA 93611-4167 Office: Clovis High Sch 1055 Fowler Ave Clovis CA 93611-2062

BITTLINGMAYER, GEORGE, educator; b. Heidelberg, Germany, May 29, 1951; came to U.S., 1957; s. Jakob and Theresia (Bleber) B.; m. Elizabeth Ann Nunn, Aug. 22, 1981; children: Adam, Stefan, Eric. BA, Lehigh U., 1975; AM, U. Chgo., 1977, PhD, 1981. Asst. prof. U. Mich., Ann Arbor, 1980-85; vis. economist Fed. Trade Commission, Washington, 1983-84; vis. assoc. prof. Washington U., St. Louis, Mo., 1984-85; rsch. fellow Sci. Cen. Berlin, 1986—; assoc. prof. U. Calif., Davis, 1988—; vis. prof. John M. Olin Found. U. Chgo., 1992. Contbr. articles to profl. jours. Mem. Am. Econ. Assn., Am. Fin. Assn., Western Econ. Assn. (nominating com. 1993). Office: U Calif Grad Sch Mgmt Davis CA 95616

BIVINS, SUSAN STEINBACH, systems engineer; b. Chgo., June 5, 1941; d. Joseph Bernard and Eleanor Celeste (Mathes) S.; BS, Northwestern U., 1963; postgrad. U. Colo., 1964, U. Ill., 1965, UCLA, 1971; m. James Herbert Bivins, June 7, 1980. With IBM, 1967-94, support mgr. East, White Plains, N.Y., 1977-78, systems support mgr., western region, L.A., 1978-81, br. market support mgr., 1981-84, mgr. IBM ops. and support L.A. Summer Olympics, 1984; mgr. IBM office supporting devel. FAA air traffic control system for 1990's, 1984-88, mgr. complex systems mktg., 1988-89, acct. devel. mgr. aerospace engring. and mfg., 1989-91, mgr. cons. and outsourcing indsl. sector trading area, 1991-92, cons. orgn. task forces, 1992-93; project exec. IBM Integrated Sys. Solutions Corp., 1993-94; exec. dir. BDM Tech., Inc., 1995—; pres. Jastech, 1986—. Vol. tchr. computer sci. Calif. Mentally Gifted Minor Programs; vol. L.A. Youth Motivation Task Force; dir. pub. rels. Lake of the Ozarks Jazz Festival, 1993-95; bd. dirs. Greater Lake Area Arts Coun., 1993-95. Mem. Systems Engring. Symposium, Pi Lambda Theta. Developed program to retrieve data via terminal and direct it to any appropriate hardcopy device, 1973. Office: BDM Tech Inc 1999 Broadway Ste 2000 Denver CO 80202-5720

BJORHOVDE, PATRICIA ORDONEZ, university development director; b. Summit, N.J., May 20, 1944; d. Carlos Midence and Beatrice Ellery (Graves) Ordonez; m. Reidar Bjorhovde, Oct. 30, 1972; children: Ian Douglas, Heather Leah Bebee. MusB, Bucknell U., 1966; postgrad., U. Alberta, Edmonton, Can., 1978-80; diploma in arts mgmt., Banff Ctr. Sch. Mgmt., Banff, Alberta, Can., 1981. Cert. fund raising exec. Mid. sch. music tchr. Mt. Laurel (N.J.) Bd. Edn., 1966-67; elem. tchr. Somerville (N.J.) Bd. Edn., 1967-72; ednl. evaluator Saal Lesser Assocs., Mt. Vernon, N.Y., 1974-76; music officer Alberta Culture, Edmonton, Can., 1979-81; gen. mgr. Ariz. Touring Orch., Tucson, 1982; dir. devel. Tucson Symphony Orch., 1982-87; mng. dir. Dance Alloy, Pitts., 1987-91; dir. ann. support Pitts. Symphony Soc., 1991-92; dir. devel., fine arts U. Ariz., Tucson, 1992—; cons. various arts orgn., Ariz., Pa., 1981—; adj. asst. prof. Carnegie Mellon U., Pitts., 1992; art grant panelist Ariz. Commn. on the Arts, Phoenix, 1986, 87, 93, 95, Tucson Pima Arts Coun., 1993-95; co-chair mgrs. coun. Dance USA, Washington, 1990-91. Bd. dirs. Cultural Alliance of Tucson, 1981-85, Catalina Foothills Sch. Found., Tucson, 1983-85, Cultural Alliance of Pa., Harrisburg, 1988-92, Friends of Carnegie Music Libr., Pitts., 1990-91, Ariz. Friends of Chamber Music, Tucson, 1994—. Mem. Nat. Soc. Fund Raising Execs. (So. Ariz. chpt. bd. dirs., co-chair state conf. 1984, v.p. 1986, pres. 1987, treas. 1994, pres. 1995, Western Pa. chpt. bd. dirs., asst. treas. 1990, 91, 92). Democrat. Office: Univ Ariz Fine Arts Adminstrn Music Bldg Rm 111 Tucson AZ 85721

BJORK, ROBERT DAVID, JR., lawyer; b. Evanston, Ill., Sept. 29, 1946; s. Robert David and Lenore Evelyn (Loderhose) B.; m. Linda Louise Reese, Mar. 27, 1971; children: Heidi Lynne, Gretchen Anne. BBA, U. Wis., 1968; JD, Tulane U., 1974. Bar: La. 1974, U.S. Dist. Ct. (ea. dist.) La. 1974, U.S. Ct. Appeals (5th cir.) 1974, U.S. Dist. Ct. (mid. dist.) 1975, U.S. Supreme Ct. 1977, U.S. Dist. Ct. (we. dist.) 1978, U.S. Ct. Appeals (11th cir.) 1981, Calif. 1983, U.S. Dist. Ct. (no. dist.) Calif. 1983, U.S. Dist. Ct. (ea. dist.) Calif. 1984. Ptnr. Adams & Reese, New Orleans, 1974-83; assoc. Crosby, Heafey, Roach & May, Oakland, Calif., 1983-85; ptnr. Bjork, Lawrence, Poeschl & Kohn, Oakland, 1985—; instr. paralegal studies Tulane U., New Orleans, 1979-82. Mem. Tulane U. Law Rev., 1973-74; editor Med. Malpractice newsletter, 1983—. Bd. dirs. Piedmont (Calif.) Coun. Camp Fire, 1984-92, pres., 1987-89; treas. Couhig Congl. Com., New Orleans, 1980-82. Lt. USNR, 1968-71. Mem. ABA, Calif. Bar Assn., La. Bar Assn. (chmn. young lawyers sect. 1982-83), Am. Soc. Law and Medicine. Home: 1909 Oakland Ave Piedmont CA 94611-3725 Office: Bjork Lawrence Poeschl & Kohn 483 9th St Oakland CA 94607-4047

BJORKLUND, JANET VINSEN, speech pathologist; b. Seattle, July 31, 1947; d. Vernon Edward and Virginia Lea (Rogers) B.; m. Dan Robert Young, Dec. 04, 1971; children: Emery Allen, Alanna Vinsen, Marisa Rogers. Student, U. Vienna, Austria, 1966-67; BA, Pacific U., 1969; student, U. Wash., 1970-71; MA, San Francisco State U., 1977. Cert. clin. speech pathologist, audiologist. Speech pathologist, audiological cons. USN Hosp., Rota, Spain, 1972-75; traineeship in audiology VA Hosp., San Francisco, 1976; speech pathologist San Lorenzo (Calif.) Unified Schs., 1975-77, 78-81; dir. speech pathology St. Lukes Speech and Hearing Clinic, San Francisco, 1977-78; audiologist X.O. Barrios, M.D., San Francisco, 1977-81; cons. Visually Impaired Infant Program, Seattle, 1981-82; speech pathologist Everett (Wash.) Schs., 1982-94; speech-lang. pathologist Sultan (Wash.) Schs., 1995—; supr. pediat. programs speech pathology Group Health Coop. Puget Sound, Seattle, 1994; cons. Madison House, Kirkland, Wash., 1983-88, NW Devel. Therapists, Everett, 1985-87, Providence Hosp. Childrens Ctr., Everett, 1985-93, Pacific Hearing and Speech, 1988-93. Author: (with others) Screening for Bilingual Preschoolers, 1977, (TV script), Clinical Services in San Francisco, 1978, Developing Better Communication Skills, 1982. Coord. presch. Christian edn. Kirkland Congl. Ch., 1983-85; organizer Residents Against Speeding Drivers, Madison Park, Seattle, 1985-87; chmn. staff devel. com. Everett Schs., 1988-89; rep. Barrier Resolution Project, 1989-89; mem. Strategic Planning Com., 1989-93. Mem. Am. Speech-Lang. and Hearing Assn., Wash. Speech and Hearing Assn. (regional rep. 1985-86, chair licensure task force 1986-88, rep. Birth to Six Project 1988-91, pres. 1993), Pub. Edn. Adv. Com. (rep. 1995), Phi Lambda Omicron (pres. Pacific U. chpt. 1968). Congregationalist.

BJORKLUND, KATHARINE BROWNE, librarian; b. Los Alamos, N.Mex., Feb. 17, 1952; d. Philip Lincoln and Margaret (Powell) Browne; m. Eric Alan Bjorklund, June 30, 1973. BA, U. N.Mex., 1974; MLS, U. Wis., 1978. Info. desk staffer Meml. Library, U. Wis., Madison, 1976-78; circulation desk clk. Mesa Pub. Library, Los Alamos, 1978-79, circulation chief, 1979-80, head adult services div., 1980-86, head adult services sect., 1986-88, head reference and info. div., 1988-93, head reference sect., 1993—. Mem. ALA, N.Mex. Library Assn. Presbyterian. Office: Mesa Pub Libr 2400 Central Ave Los Alamos NM 87544-4014

BJORKMAN, DAVID JESS, gastroenterologist, educator; b. Salt Lake City, Oct. 28, 1952; s. Jesse Harold and Violet Maureen (Neese) B.; m. Kaye Hansen, Aug. 20, 1975; children: D. James, Michael. BA, U. Utah, 1976, MD, 1980. Diplomate Am. Bd. Internal Medicine, Am. Bd. Gastroenterology. Intern Brigham and Womens Hosp., Harvard U. Med. Sch., 1980-81, resident in internal medicine, 1981-83; clin. fellow, rsch. fellow Harvard U. Med. Sch., Boston, 1983-85; instr. medicine U. Utah Sch. Medicine, Salt Lake City, 1985-88, asst. prof. medicine, 1988-92, assoc. prof. medicine, 1992—; dir. endoscopy U. Utah Med. Ctr., 1992—; sce. rev. com. Nat. Cancer Inst., Bethesda, Md., 1991. Contbr. articles to profl. jours. Fellow ACP, Am. Coll. Gastroenterology; mem. Utah State Med. Assn. (legis com. 1990—), Am. Soc. Laser Medicine and Surgery, Phi Beta Kappa, Alpha Omega Alpha (bd. dirs. 1979-82). Office: Univ Med Ctr 50 N Medical Dr Salt Lake City UT 84132-0001

BJORKMAN, OLLE ERIK, plant biologist, educator; b. Jonkoping, Sweden, July 29, 1933; came to U.S., 1964; s. Erik Gustaf and Dagmar Kristina (Svensson) B.; m. Monika Birgit Waldinger, Sept. 24, 1955; children: Thomas N.E., Per G.O. MS, U. Stockholm, 1957; PhD, U. Uppsala, 1960; DSc, U. Uppsala, Sweden, 1968. Asst. scientist dept. genetics and plant breeding U. Uppsala, 1956-61; rsch. fellow Swedish Natural Sci. Rsch. Coun., 1961-63; postdoctoral fellow Carnegie Instn. Wash., Stanford, Calif., 1964-65, mem. staff, 1966—; assoc. prof. biology by courtesy Stanford (Calif.) U., 1967-77, prof. biology by courtesy, 1977—; vis. fellow Australian Nat. U., Canberra, 1971-72, 78; advisor to pres. Desert Rsch. Inst., Nev., 1980-81; vis. sci. Australian Inst. Marine Sci., 1983; sci. advisor Kettering Found., 1976-77; mem. panel world food and nutrition study NRC, 1976; com. carbon dioxide effects Dept. Energy, 1977-82; competitive grants panel Dept. Agr., 1978; numerous other coms. and panels. Co-author: Experimental Studies of the Nature of Species V, 1971, Physiological Processes in Plant Ecology, 1980; mem. editorial bd. Planta, 1993—; contbr. articles to profl. publs. Recipient Linneus prize Royal Swedish Physiographic Soc., 1977. Fellow Am. Acad. Arts and Scis., AAAS; mem. NAS, Am. Soc. Plant Physiologists (Stephen Hales award 1986), Australian Acad. Sci. (Selby award 1987), Royal Swedish Acad. Scis., Australian Soc. Plant Physiologists. Home: 3040 Greer Rd Palo Alto CA 94303-4007 Office: Carnegie Inst Dept Plant Biology 290 Panama St Stanford CA 94305-4101

BJORNSSON, KEVIN SCOTT, manufacturing executive, writer; b. Fargo, N.D., Sept. 8, 1950; s. Magnus Alvin Bjornsson and Irene Elizabeth Horbeck. BA in Psychology, Concordia Coll., Moorhead, Minn., 1973; postgrad., Armstrong Bus. Coll., Berkeley, Calif., 1975-76. Evening mgr. Models Unltd., Mpls., 1976-80; owner Hydro-Tech, Seattle, 1981—; cons. various greenhouses/. Contbr. articles to profl. jours. Mem. various coms. Libertarian Party; moderator Liberty Club TV Program, Seattle, 1993—. Office: HydroTech 821 N 40th St Seattle WA 98103-7805

BLACHER, JOAN HELEN, psychotherapist, educator; b. L.A., Aug. 10, 1928; d. Albert Scribner and Isabel (Marriott) Oakholt; m. Norman Blacher, July 27, 1973; stepchildren: Eric, Steven, Mark. BA, U. Calif., Berkeley, 1950; MEd, U. So. Calif., 1971, PhD, 1981. Lic. ednl. psychologist, Calif.; lic. marriage, family and child counselor, Calif. Elem. tchr. L.A. Unified Sch. Dist., 1962-71, sch. psychologist, 1971-72, 73-74; sch. psychologist Pasadena (Calif.) Unified Sch. Dist., 1972-73; sch. psychologist Ventura (Calif.) County Supt. Schs., 1974-79, prin., 1979-86; assoc. prof. sch. edn., head counseling and guidance program Calif. Luth. U., Thousand Oaks, 1987—; pvt. practice, Ventura, 1984—. Bd. dirs. Coalition Against Household Violence, Ventura, 1984-85. Mem. APA, Am. Counselors Assn., Am. Ednl. Rsch. Assn., Calif. Assn. Counselors, Educators, Supervisors (pres.), Calif. Assn. Marriage & Family Therapists, Calif. Assn. Counseling Devel., Phi Delta Kappa. Republican.

BLACK, ALICE ANN, neonatal and pediatrics nurse educator; b. Paris, Tex., Mar. 2, 1955; d. James M. and Jimmie Lorayne (Reeves) Black; m. James Everett Ghiron, Sept. 1983 (div. 1985); 1 child, Chad Darek; m. Enoch Callaway Brabant, May 23, 1987; 1 child, Kristen Leigh. ADN, Paris Jr. Coll., 1975; BSN, U. Tex., Arlington, 1980; MSN, U. San Francisco, 1990. Clin. nurse McCuistion Regional Med. Ctr., Paris, 1975-77, Children's Med. Ctr., Dallas, 1977-82, U. Calif., San Francisco, 1982-90; neonatal/pediatric educator coord. Community Hosp., Santa Rosa, Calif., 1990—; affiliated faculty Am. Heart Assn. PALS, Santa Rosa, 1992. Mem. Drug Alcohol Abuse Coun., Santa Rosa, 1990—. Mem. Nat. Assn. Neonatal Nurses, Sigma Theta Tau. Democrat. Methodist. Home: 5952 Yerba Buena Rd Santa Rosa CA 95409-3960 Office: Community Hosp 3325 Chanate Rd Santa Rosa CA 95404-1707

BLACK, BARBARA CROWDER, educational consultant; b. Woodbine, Iowa, Feb. 11, 1922; d. John Hershel and Elsie May (Jenkins) Crowder; m. (Estel) Eugene Black, Sept. 1, 1944; 1 child, (Estel) Eugene Jr. (dec. 1993). AB, N.Mex. Western U., 1946; teaching credential, UCLA, 1964; cert. in reading, math., Calif. State U., 1969, 72; postgrad., Sacramento State U., 1977-89. Cert. tchr., Calif. Tchr. Chavez County Schs., Roswell, N.Mex., 1942-44; tchr. ESL 6th St. Elem. Sch., Silver City, N. Mex., 1946-47; girls athletic coach Silver City Jr. High Sch., Silver City, N. Mex., 1946-47; tchr. Lovington (N.Mex.) Pub. Schs., 1950-51, Long Beach (Calif.) Unified Sch. Dist., 1951-58, Santa Maria (Calif.) Elem. Sch. Dist., 1958-59; tchr. spl. edn. Bellflower (Calif.) Unified Sch. Dist., 1959-67; instr. Sacramento Unified Sch. Dist., 1968-79; co-owner, v.p. El Paso Southwestern R.R. Ednl. Consultants, Sacramento, 1985—; demonstration tchr. Long Beach Unified Sch. Dist., 1952-59; master tchr. to student tchrs. Calif. State U., Long Beach, 1954-59, Sacramento, 1972-73; supr. tchr. aides Sacramento Unified Sch. Dist., 1969-79; co-editor revision of math. testing materials, 1977; English instr. Jian Ping Mid. Sch., Shanghai, China, 1992; pvt. tutor in computers, math. and reading elem. sch. children, 1994—; seminar coord. China New Renaissance Soc, U. Calif., Sacramento. Co-author tchr. manuals in sci. and arithmetic, tchrs. guide for social studies; cons., editor: Barking at Shadows (Gene Black, Jr.), 1994, Effing the Ineffible (Gene Black, Jr.), 1995. Elder Westminster Presbyn. Ch., Sacramento, 1973—; docent Calif. State R.R. Mus., Sacramento, 1980—; vol. Jed Smith Sch. Computer Class, Sacramento, 1989, Habitat for Humanity, 1994. Grantee Sacramento County Office Edn., 1969, Calif. Dept. Edn., 1972-73; recipient cert. spl. commendation Calif. Dept. Parks, 1988. Mem. NAFE, ASCD, Calif. Tchrs. Assn., Calif. Ret. Tchrs. Assn., Sacramento State Parks Docent Assn. (membership chair 1981-87, Outstanding Svc. award 1983, 86, 87, 89), Sigma Tau Delta (pres. 1944-46).

BLACK, CARLIN J., industrial marketing consultant; b. Toledo, Ohio, July 10, 1940; s. Charles T. and Dorothy Edna (Stokely) B.; m. Virginia Ann Hess, June 30, 1963 (div. Jan. 1991); children: Carlin Steven, Kevin James; m. Shu-Ju Yoh, Sept. 18, 1993. BS in Chemistry, Stanford U., 1962, MBA, 1966. Chemist Aerojet Gen. Corp., Folsom, Calif., 1962-64; venture mgr. E.I. duPont de Nemours & Co., Wilmington, Del., 1966-71; flight svc. adminstrv. mgr. Pan Am. World Airways, N.Y.C., 1971-74, dir. capital budgets, 1974-76; orgn. analyst Interaction Analysts-Cons., N.Y.C., 1976-81; market devel. mgr. Allied Fibers & Plastics, Morristown, N.J., 1981-84; indsl. mktg. cons. CIMDI, N.Y.C., 1984-90, Carmichael, Calif., 1990—. Developer scientist inventions acrylic film mfg., 1975, wear resistant moldings, 1985. Bd. dirs. N.Y. Choral Soc., N.Y.C., 1985-88. Unitarian. Office: 2519 Mardell Way Mountain View CA 94043-2715

BLACK, CRAIG CALL, retired museum administrator; b. Peking, China, May 28, 1932; s. Arthur and Mary (Nichols) B.; children—Christopher Arthur, Lorna Varn; m. Mary Elizabeth King, Jan. 4, 1986. A.B., Amherst Coll., 1954; M.A. (Simpson fellow), Johns Hopkins U., 1957; Ph.D. (NIH fellow), Harvard U., 1962. Geologist Okla. Geol. Survey, summer 1956; asst. curator Carnegie Inst., Pitts., 1960-62; curator Carnegie Inst., 1962-70; prof. biology U. Kans., 1970-72; dir. Mus. of Tex. Tech. U., Lubbock, 1970-75, Carnegie Inst., 1975-82, L.A. Mus. Natural History, 1982-94; co-leader John F. Kennedy U. Western Mus. Conf. Seminar, 1983; faculty Am. Law Inst.-ABA Course of Study in Legal Problems of Mus. Adminstrn., 1980, 82; co-dir. Mus. Mgmt. Inst., U. Calif., Berkeley, summers, 1979, 80; adj. prof. U. Mus. and dept. geology U. Colo., 1965, Dept. of Marine Scis. U. So. Calif., 1987—; adj. prof. biology U. N.Mex., 1994—; assoc. com. on evolution UCLA, 1987—. Contbr. articles to profl. jours. Presdl. appointee Nat. Mus. Svc. Bd., 1982-85, NSF, 1985-90, Bd. Environment for the Americas, 1991—; mem. Bd. of U.S./Mexico Found. for Sci., 1994—; rev. panel Inst. of Mus. Svcs., Washington, 1978-79, policy panel, 1978-80. Simpson fellow, 1954-55; Kellog fellow, 1956-59; predoctoral fellow NIH, 1959-60. Fellow AAAS; mem. Am. Assn. Mus. (pres. 1980-82, mem. commn. on mus. for a new century 1982-84, mem. coun. 1977—), Explorers Club, Cosmos Club (Washington), Calif. Club (L.A.).

BLACK, EILEEN MARY, elementary school educator; b. Bklyn., Sept. 20, 1944; d. Marvin Mize and Anne Joan (Salvia) B. Student, Grossmont Coll., El Cajon, Calif., 1964; BA, San Diego State U., 1967; postgrad., U. Calif., San Diego, Syracuse U. Cert. tchr., Calif. Tchr. La Mesa (Calif.)-Spring Valley Sch. Dist., 1967—. NDEA grantee Syracuse U., 1968; recipient 25 Yrs. Svc. award La Mesa-Spring Valley Sch. Dist., 1992. Mem. Calif. Tchrs. Assn., Calif. Young Reps. Roman Catholic. Home: 9320 Earl St Apt 15 La Mesa CA 91942-3846 Office: Northmont Elem Sch 9405 Gregory St La Mesa CA 91942-3811

BLACK, ERIC, conductor; b. Washington, June 12, 1958; s. Ralph and Eva (Landsberger) B. MusB, BA, Oberlin Coll., 1981. Asst. condr. Prince William (Va.) Symphony Orch., 1983-85, Bedford (Pa.) Springs Festival, 1985-87, Arlington (Va.) Symphony, 1987-89; dir. music Mesa (Ariz.) Symphony Orch., 1989—. Mem. Am. Symphony Orch. League (profl. affiliate), Assn. Calif. Symphony Orchs. Office: Mesa Symphony Orch PO Box 1308 Mesa AZ 85211-1308

BLACK, FRANKLIN OWEN, physician, researcher; b. St. Louis, Aug. 8, 1937; s. Frank and Kathleen Ruth (Scowden) B.; m. Jorita Jenkins, Mar. 30, 1961; children: Owen Brent, Christopher Brian, Jeremy Benjamin. BA in Chemistry and Math., S.E. Mo. State U., Cape Girardeau, 1955; MD, U. Mo., 1963. Diplomate Am. bd. Otolaryngology. Assoc. prof. dept. otolaryngology Dept. Otolaryngology Eye and Ear Hosp. U. Pitts., 1974-82; vice chmn. dept. Eye and Ear Hosp., Pitts., 1976-81; mem. grad. faculty U. Pitts., 1977-82; mem. med. staff Children's Hosp., Pitts., 1980-82; clin. prof. Dept. Otolaryngology, Seattle, 1985-88; sr. scientist Neurol. Scis. Inst., Portland, 1982—; chief divsn. neuro-otology rsch. Good Samaritan Hosp., Portland, 1982—; dir. neuro-otologic rsch. Robert S. Dow Neurol. Scis. Inst., Portland, 1990—; chmn. NASA, 1982-84; adv. bd. U. Space Rsch. Assn., 1982—; mem. hearing rsch. study NIH, 1983-86. Author: Congenital Deafness, 1971; editor: Vestibular and Visual Control on Posture and Locomotor Equilibrium, 1985; co-inventor apparatus and method for Determining role of vestibular function in balance control. Bd. dirs. Am. Otology Svc. Rsch. Endowment Fund, N.Y.C., 1990-91. Lt. comdr. M.C., USNR, 1969-71, Vietnam. Mem. ACS, AMA, Am. Otological Soc., Barany Soc., Am. Neurotology Soc., Am. Acad. Otol-Head and Neck Surgery. Episcopalian. Home: 12496 NW Hartford St Portland OR 97229-3778 Office: Robert S Dow Neurol Scis Inst 1040 NW 22nd Ave Portland OR 97210

BLACK, KAREN L., not-for-profit administrator, social worker, advocate; b. Moscow, Idaho, June 5, 1950. BA in Social Work, Ea. Wash. U., 1990, MA in Social Work, 1992, MA in Pub. Adminstrn., 1993. Community organizer N.Y. Tenant Assn., N.Y.C., 1972-80; word processing supr. KTI Miller, Irvine, Calif., 1980-85, Assn. Retarded Citizens, Spokane, Wash., 1986-87; cons., founder Cheney Coop. Gardens, Cheney, Wash., 1990—; cons., adminstr. Cheney Outreach, Cheney, Wash., 1991-92. Recipient Community Svc. award Seattle Jaycees, 1992. Mem. Nat. Assn. Social Workers, Am. Soc. Pub. Adminstrs., Assn. Community Organizers and Social Adminstrs.

BLACK, KATHIE M., science educator; b. Albuquerque, Oct. 3, 1956; d. Donald Blaine and Phyllis Ann (Cross) U.; m. Lenny E. Black, May 19, 1979; children: Jeremy J., Joseph L., Kyle E. BSED in Secondary Sci. Edn., U. N. Mex., 1990, MA in Tech. Edn., 1992; PhD in Sci. Edn., U. N.Mex., 1993. Cert. secondary tchr., M.Mex. Tchr., instr. Profl. Ski Instrs. Am.-Rocky Mountain Dvsn., Albuquerque, 1975-92; instr. U. N.Mex., Albuquerque, 1991, 93, asst. prof. dept. social and natural scis.; asst. prof. U. Victoria, B.C., Can., 1993—; instr. Albuquerque Child Birth Assn., Albuquerque, 1980-84; tchr. Albuquerque Pub. Schs., 1988-91. Am. Bus. Women's Assn. scholar, 1988. Mem. AAAS, ASCD, Nat. Assn. Rsch. in Sci. Tchg. (rschr.'s com.), Nat. Sci. Tchrs. Assn., Can. Sci. Tchrs. Assn.

BLACK, MAUREEN, realty company executive; b. Manchester, Eng., Feb. 4, 1937; came to U.S., 1957, naturalized, 1962; d. William Henry and Kathleen Mary (Cleaver) Jackson; grad. Felt and Tarrant Comptometer Sch., Eng., 1953; student Alamogordo br. N.Mex. State U., 1959-60, 62-63; m. Charles J. Dugan, Nov. 1979; 1 dau., Karen Elizabeth Black. Office mgr., personnel dir. J.C. Penney Co., Alamogordo, 1958-66; exec. sec. to project mgr. Re-entry System div. Gen. Electric Co., Holloman AFB, 1967-68; soc. editor, columnist Alamogordo Daily News, 1968-73; regional corr. El Paso (Tex.) Times, 1968-75; free lance writer and photographer; script writer Film Unit 505, Alamogordo, 1971; realtor asso. Shyne Realty, Alamogordo, 1975-77, West Source Realtors, 1977-80; owner, broker Hyde Park West Realty Co., 1980—. Pres., Alamogordo Music Theatre, 1971-72. Mem. planning com. tourism, recreation, convs. Gov. of N.Mex., 1965; mem. N.Mex. State Film Commn., 1973-74; life mem. Aux. of Zia Sch. for Handicapped Children, pres. Aux., 1975-76, 80-82; mem. Zia Sch. Bd., 1988-89, v.p., 1991-92; pres. Zia Found., 1988-89, 91-92, v.p. Zia Found. 1994—. Recipient service award Nat. Found., March of Dimes, 1971; Americanism medal DAR, 1972; named Career Woman of Yr., Alamogordo chpt. Am. Bus. Women's Assn., 1971. Mem. Alamogordo C. of C. (chmn. convs. and motion picture com. 1965—), Nat. Assn. Realtors, Realtors Assn. N.Mex., Internat. Realtors Assn. Alamogordo Bd. Realtors (chmn. public relations com., v.p. 1981-82, pres. 1983-84), N.Mex. Opera Guild. Home: 1206 Desert Eve Dr Alamogordo NM 88310-5503 Office: PO Box 2021 Alamogordo NM 88311-2021

BLACK, NOEL ANTHONY, television and film director; b. Chgo., June 30, 1937; s. Samuel Abraham and Susan (Quan) B.; m. Catherine Elizabeth Cownie, June 1, 1988; children: Marco Eugene, Nicole Alexandra, Carmen Elizabeth, Catherine Ellen. BA, UCLA, 1959, MA, 1964. Ind. fil, TV dir., 1966—; asst. prof. grad. program Inst. Film and TV, Tisch Sch. of Arts, NYU, 1992-93. Dir. (TV films) Trilogy: The American Boy, 1967 (Outstanding Young Dir. award Monte Carlo Internat. Festival of TV, Silver Dove award Internat. Cath. Soc. for Radio and TV), I'm a Fool, 1977, Mulligan's Stew, 1977, The Golden Honeymoon, 1979, The Electric Grandmother, 1981 (George Foster Peabody award 1982), The Other Victim, 1981, Prime Suspect, 1981, Happy Endings, 1982, Quarterback Princess, 1983, Deadly Intentions, 1985, Promises to Keep, 1985, A Time to Triumph, 1985, My Two Loves, 1986, Conspiracy of Love, 1987, The Town Bully, 1988, The Hollow Boy, 1991, (short films) Skaterdater, 1966 (Grand Prix award Cannes XX Film Festival, Grand Prix Tech. Cannes XX Internat. Film Festival, awards Cork Film Festival, Silver medal Moscow Internat. Film Festival, others), Riverboy, 1967 (Lion of St. Mark award Venice Internat. Film Festival, 1st prize Vancouver Internat. Film Festival), (feature films) Pretty Poison, 1968, Mirrors, 1974, A Man, a Woman and a Bank, 1978; screenwriter Mischief, 1984.. Mem. Writers Guild Am., Dirs. Guild Am., Acad. Motion Picture Arts and Scis., Acad. TV Arts and Scis. Office: Starfish Prodns 126 Wadsworth Ave Santa Monica CA 90405-3510

BLACK, PETE, state legislator, educator; b. Ansbach, Germany, Sept. 16, 1946; came to U.S., 1948; s. Howard and Kadi (Fietz) B.; m. Ronda Williams, July 12, 1970; 1 child, Darin. BS, Idaho State U., 1975; postgrad., 1991—. Cert. elem. tchr. Tchr. Pocatello (Idaho) Sch. Dist., 1975—; mem. Idaho Ho. Reps., Boise, 1983—, asst. minority leader, 1987—, mem. edn. tech. coun.; mem. edn. tech. coun.; mem. adv. coun. chpt. II ESEA. Bd. dirs. Arts for Idaho. With USNR, 1964. Mem. NEA, Idaho Edn. Assn., Idaho Libr. Assn. Democrat. Home: 2249 Cassia St Pocatello ID 83201-2059 Office: Idaho Ho Reps Statehouse Mail Boise ID 83720

BLACK, ROBERT CLIFFORD, III, history educator; b. N.Y.C., Feb. 11, 1914; s. Robert Clifford and Beatrice (Cluett) B.; B.A., Williams Coll., 1937; M.A., U. Denver, 1947; Ph.D., Columbia U., 1951; m. Regina Ann Maleham, Sept. 5, 1939; children: Maleham C., R. Clifford, Beatrice (Mrs. Rolland W. Hoverstock), John N., Peter N., James A. Instr. history Rensselear Poly. Inst., Troy, N.Y., 1945-48; instr. history Trinity Coll., Hartford, Conn., 1950-52, assoc. prof., 1952-66; prof. history Colo. Women's Coll., Denver, 1965-79, emeritus, 1979—; lectr. in field. Dist. committeeman West Hartford Republican Com., 1954-66; bd. dirs. Hist. Denver Inc., 1974-76. Served to capt. AUS, 1942-45. Recipient Merit award Am. Assn. State and Local History, 1970. Mem. Am., Can., Conn., Colo. hist. assns., Assn. Am. Historians, Colo. Hist. Soc. (dir. 1969-88), Friends of Denver Pub. Library, Alpha Delta Phi., Pi Gamma Mu. Episcopalian. Clubs: Denver Country, Denver, Williams. Author: The Railroads of The Confederacy, 1952, The Younger John Winthrop, 1966, Island in the Rockies, 1969, Railroad Pathfinder, 1988. Home: Sky Valley Ranch PO Box 488 Tabernash CO 80478-0488

BLACK, SUZANNE ALEXANDRA, clinical psychologist, researcher; b. N.Y.C., May 6, 1958; d. Lawrence E. and Aline R. (Amsellem) B. BA in Psychology, Clark U., 1980; MA in Gen. Psychology, Yeshiva U., 1984, PsyD in Clin. Psychology, 1987; cert. in psychoanalytical psychotherapy, Inst. Contemporary Psychoanalysis, 1992-93. Lic. psychologist, Calif., 1989. Rsch. assoc. Inst. for Study of Exceptional Children Roosevelt Hosp. Ctr., 1980-82; rsch. cons. Sch. Pub. Health Columbia U., N.Y.C., 1982-83; clin. psychology extern Albert Einstein Coll. of Medicine Bronx Psychiat. Ctr., 1983-84; clin. psychology extern Jewish Bd. Family and Children's Svcs., N.Y.C., 1984-85; clin. pcychology, neuropsychol. extern NYU Med. Ctr./Bellevue Hosp., N.Y.C., 1985-86; pre-doctoral clin. psychology/neuropsychology intern Rusk Inst. Rehabilitation NYU Med. Ctr., N.Y.C., 1986-87; post-doctoral clin. psychology fellow in psychiat. emergency room and adult in-patient psychiatry Harbor/UCLA Med. Ctr., Torrance, 1987-89; inpatient and outpatient pvt. practice clin. psychology and neuropsychology Torrance, 1989-93; rsch. assoc. depts. neurology and psychiatry Harbor/UCLA Med. Ctr., 1987-93; dir. clin. svc. Adult Inpatient Psychiat. unit Suncrest Hosp. of South Bay, Torrance, Calif., 1992; inpatient and outpatient pvt. practice in psychology pvt. practice, San Francisco & Kentfield, Calif., 1993—; co-founder, co-therapist Marin Group Psychotherapy Assocs.; vice chair, divsn. of Psychology Main Gen. Hosp., 1994—; mem. group pvt. practice Behavioral Medicine Assocs., Marin County, 1993—; clin. asst. prof. psychology Fuller Grad. Sch. Psychology, Pasadena, Calif., 1987-88; clin. supr. psychiat. residents and psychology externs Harbor/UCLA Med. Ctr., 1987-89; lectr. in field; crisis specialist psychiat. emergency svc. Marin County Dept. Health and Human Svcs. Exec. producer teen talk show TeenVision TV, Viacom Cable TV, Main Channel 31, 1994. Vol. cert. in disaster mental health Bay Area chpt. ARC. NIMH grantee, 1986-87. Mem. APA, Calif. Psychol. Assn., Marin County Psychol. Assn., (chair ethics com.), San Francisco Psychol. Assn., Mental Health Assn. of Marin (bd. dirs., co-pres.). Office: Ste 100-5 1030 Sir Francis Drake Blvd Kentfield CA 94904-1400 also: 3354 Sacramento St Ste C San Francisco CA 94118

BLACK, WILFORD REX, JR., state senator; b. Salt Lake City, Jan. 31, 1920; s. Wilford Rex and Elsie Isabell (King) B.; m. Helen Shirley Frazer; children: Susan, Janet, Cindy, Joy, Peggy, Vanna, Gayle, Rex. Student schools in Utah. Locomotive engr. Rio Grande R.R., 1941-81; mem. Utah Senate, 1972—, speaker Third House, 1975-76, majority whip, 1977-78, minority leader, 1981-90; chmn., vice chmn. United Transp. Union, 1972-78; sec. Utah State Legis. Bd., United Transp. Chmn. bd. Rail Operators Credit Union, 1958-87; mission pres. Rose Park Stake Mormon Ch., high priest group leader Rose Park 9th Ward, 1980-83, mem. Rose Park Stake High Council, 1957-63. Served with U.S. Army, 1942-45. Recipient various awards r.r and legis. activities. Democrat. Office: 826 N 1300 W Salt Lake City UT 84116-3877

BLACKBURN, CHARLES EDWARD, company executive; b. Detroit, June 19, 1939; s. Wallace Manders and Elva Jean (Beetham) B.; m. Judith Ann Brady, June 30, 1979. BS, Baldwin-Wallace Coll., 1961; MBA, Pepperdine U., 1990. Assoc. rsch. chemist Parke-Davis and Co., Ann Arbor, Mich., 1963-71; mgr. Mallinckrodt Chem. Works, St. Louis, 1971-74; sr. product mgr. Packard Instrument Co., Downers Grove, Ill., 1974-77; product mktg. mgr. Beckman Instruments, Fullerton, Calif., 1977-80; gen. sales mgr. Wahl Instruments, Culver City, Calif., 1980-84; v.p. Signet Sci. Co., El Monte, Calif., 1984-91; chmn., CEO "C" Enterprises, San Marcos, Calif., 1991—. Contbr. articles to profl. jours. Mem. Rotary Internat. (sec. 1983, pres. 1984). Office: "C" Enterprises 540 S Pacific St San Marcos CA 92069-4056

BLACKBURN, DANIEL M., correspondent; b. Xenia, Ohio, Nov. 6, 1938; s. A. D. and Helen M. B.; m. Sue Ellen Heiny, June 20, 1959 (div. 1972); children: Laura Jeanne, Lynne Danielle; m. Mariko Fukuda, Sept. 6, 1986; children: Dylan Daniel, Fukuda Blackburn. BA, Purdue U., 1961. Reporter Sta. WBBM-TV, Chgo., 1963-64; reporter, writer Sta. WNEW, N.Y.C., 1964-65; bur. chief, corr. Metromedia News, Washington, 1965-70; dep. dir. pub. affairs The Peace Corps, Washington, 1970-71; reporter, news anchor Sta. KNX-TV, L.A., 1971-75; corr. NBC News, Burbank, Calif., 1975-88, Cable News Network, L.A., 1988—; chmn. The Friday Group, L.A., 1974—; mem. Nat. Adv. Com. on High Sch. Journalism, Washington, 1975; co-chmn. Robert F. Kennedy Journalism Awards, Washington, 1968-71; guest lectr. Western Journalism Conf., L.A., 1976. Author: Zen and the Cross Country Skier, 1975; contbr. articles to profl. jours. Recipient Golden Mike award So. Calif. Broadcasters, 1975, Grand award Los Angeles Press Club, 1975, Calif. State award Calif. Exposition, Sacramento, 1974. Mem. AFTRA, Writers Guild, Sierra Club. Home: 3219 Altura Ave Apt 3 La Crescenta CA 91214-3391

BLACKBURN, JOHN LEWIS, consulting engineer; b. Kansas City, Mo., Oct. 2, 1913; s. John Ealy and Lela (Garnett) B.; m. Margaret Bailey, Sept. 12, 1943; children: Susan T., Joan Blackburn Krist, Margot A. Blackburn Jahns. BSEE with high honors, U. Ill., 1935. With Westinghouse Electric Corp., Newark, 1936-78, cons. engr., 1969-78; pvt. practice cons., Bothell, Wash., 1979—; adj. prof. Poly. Inst. N.Y., 1949-65, Poly. Inst. N.J., Newark, 1958-71; spl. lectr. IEEE Ednl. Activities, 1952—; affiliate prof. U. Wash., 1988; instr. North Seattle Community Coll., 1988—. Author, editor: Applied Protective Relaying, 1978; author: Protective Relaying Principles and Application, 1987, Symmetrical Components for Power Systems Engineering, 1993. Trustee, treas. Millington Bapt. Ch., N.J., 1952-69. Recipient Order of Merit award Westinghouse Electric Corp., 1971, Attwood Assocs. award U.S. Nat. Com. Internat. Conf. for Large High Voltage Electric Systems, 1986. Fellow IEEE (chmn. publ. dept. Power Engring. Soc. 1972-76, sec., 1977-79, chmn. power system relaying com. 1969-70, Disting. Service award 1978, Outstanding Service award IEEE ednl. bd. 1979, Centennial medal 1984); mem. China Stamp Soc. Inc. (pres. 1979—), Am. Soc. Polar Philatelists (bd. dirs., treas. 1967—), Sigma Xi, Tau Beta Pi, Eta Kappa Nu, Phi Kappa Phi. Home: 21816 8th Pl W Bothell WA 98021-8153

BLACKBURN, MICHAEL PHILIP, lawyer; b. East St. Louis, Ill., June 7, 1945; s. Thomas Doyle and Erma Jeanette (Macke) B.; m. Phyllis Ann Macke, Feb. 10, 1972 (div. 1983). BA, So. Ill. U., 1967; JD, Western State U., Fullerton, Calif., 1982. Bar: Calif. 1983, U.S. Ct. Appeals (9th cir.) 1984, U.S. Dist. Ct. (cen. dist.) Calif. 1984, U.S. Tax Ct. 1984, U.S. Supreme Ct. 1992, U.S. Dist. Ct. (no. dist.) Calif. 1992, U.S. Dist. Ct. (ea. dist.) Calif. 1993. Lawyer pvt. practice, Long Beach, Calif., 1983-85; house counsel TransAmerica, Torrance, Calif., 1985-88; assoc. Mercer & Zinder, Orange, Calif., 1988-91; ptnr. Mercer & Zinder, Orange, 1991; mgr. bay area office Mercer & Zinder, Walnut Creek, Calif., 1991—, v.p. bd. dirs., 1994—. Dem. candidate U.S. House Reps., 42nd Congl. Dist., 1986. Capt. USAF, 1967-72. Recipient scholarship So. Ill. Univ., 1963. Roman Catholic. Office: Mercer & Zinder 2121 N California Blvd Walnut Creek CA 94596-3572

BLACKFIELD, CECILIA MALIK, civic volunteer, educator; b. Oakland, Calif., Jan. 18, 1915; d. Benjamin Malik and Mollie Saak; m. William Blackfield, Dec. 25, 1941; children: Leland Gregory, Pamela Esther, Karen Ann. BA, U. Calif., Berkeley, 1936; MEdn., San Francisco State Tchrs. Coll., 1937. cert. elem. tchr. Calif. (lifetime). Tchr. Albany (Calif.) Sch. Dist., 1938-43; rep. NEA, Alameda County, Calif., 1938-43. Pres. Calif. Tchrs. Assn., Alameda County, Calif., 1939; mem. (charter) Territorial Hosp. Aux., Kauikeolani Children's Hosp. (bd. dirs.); bd. dirs. Hastings Law Sch. Found., San Francisco, Calif., McCoy Pavilion Park, Honolulu, Hi., Daughters of the Nile, Honolulu, Temple Emmanuel; mem. Mayor's Citizen Advisory Com. for Diamond Head, Wakiki, Honolulu, Mayor's Adv. Com. for Community & Urban Renewal, Beautification Com., League of Women Voters; chmn. Hawaii Cancer Fund Crusade and many more; mem. master planning com. Vision for Waikiki 2020; mem. Preservation Rev. Com. Hist. Hawaii. Named Woman of the Year for Nat. Brotherhood Week, Honolulu, 1972. Mem. Nat. Assn. Home Builders (pres. Hawaii chpt. women's aux.), Outdoor Circle (pres.), Friends of Foster Gardens, Washington Palace State Capitol, Hadassah (past pres. Oakland chpt.), Women's Com. Brandeis U. (life mem.). Home: 901 Kealaolu Ave Honolulu HI 96816-5416

BLACKMAN, DAVID IRA, health science administrator; b. L.A., Mar. 12, 1951; s. Soli and Erika Louise (Ullmann) B. BS, U. So. Calif., 1975; MS, U. LaVerne, 1986. Cert. tchr., Calif. Fin. specialist U. Calif. Med. Ctr., San Francisco, 1975-79; adminstrn. specialist U. Calif. Med. Ctr., Irvine, 1979-80; adminstr. Kaiser Found. Health Plan, L.A., 1980—; COO Tower Health, Long Beach, Calif., 1993—; cons. health care DIB Group, Glendale, Calif., 1980—. Recipient Gold Achievement award United Way Campaigns, Los Angeles, 1984. Mem. Am. Guild Patient Acct. Mgrs., Health Care Fin. Mgmt. Assocs., Am. Mgmt. Assn., Am. Hosp. Assn., Nat. Right to Work Found., Assn. Western Hosps., Lake Mirage Country Club. Republican. Home: 5375 Crescent Dr Yorba Linda CA 92687-2725 Office: Tower Health 6th Fl 249 E Ocean Blvd Fl 6 Long Beach CA 90802-4806

BLACKMAN, DAVID LEE, research scientist; b. Chgo., Jan. 4, 1948; s. Sol and Carol Edith (Rothman) B. BS in Maths., U. Ariz., 1973; student, Laney Coll., Oakland, Calif., 1977-79; MS in Chemistry, San Francisco State U., 1983. Lic. technician. Rsch. cons. Detox Assn., San Bernadino, Calif., 1973-74; peer counselor Laney Coll., 1977-79; lectr. San Francisco State U., 1979-83; staff rsch. assoc. U. Calif., Berkeley, 1984—; speaker PEW Found., N.Y., 1989. Author: Flourescent Spectroscopy..., 1983; contbr. articles to profl. jours. Mem. adv. bd. P.P. Land Conservancy, Berkeley, 1984-86; bd. dirs. Cmty. Svcs. United, Berkeley, 1985-86; vol. No. Alameda ARES/RACES, Berkeley, 1992—. NSF grantee, 1989, 91. Mem. AAAS, Am. Assn. Physics Tchrs., Am. Chemistry Soc., Am. Radio Relay League, Co-op Am., Sierra Club, N.Y. Acad. Sci., Golden Gate Nat. Pk. Assn., Mensa. Democrat. Jewish. Home: 2633 Benvenue Ave Apt 5 Berkeley CA 94704-3437

BLACKNER, BOYD ATKINS, architect; b. Salt Lake City, Aug. 29, 1933; s. Lester Armond and Anna (McDonald) B.; m. Elizabeth Ann Castleton, June 4, 1955; children: Catherine Blackner Philpot, David, Elizabeth, Genevieve Blackner Tayler. B.Arch., U. Utah, 1956, B.F.A., 1956. Registered architect, Fla., Utah, Wyo. Asst. landscape architect Nat. Park Service, Mt. Rainier, Wash., 1956; job capt. Cannon, Smith & Gustavson, Salt Lake City, 1957, Hellmuth, Obata & Kassabaum, St. Louis, 1958-59, Caudill, Rowlett & Scott, Houston, 1959-60; project architect Victor A. Lundy, Sarasota, Fla., N.Y.C., 1960-63; pvt. practice architecture Salt Lake City, 1963—; lectr. Salt Lake C.C., 1994; mem. adv. coun., vis. juror, critic Grad. Sch. Architecture, U. Utah, 1983-94; grad. program dept. landscape architecture and environ. planning Utah State U., 1977-92; mem. region 8 adv. panel archtl. and engring. svcs. GSA, 1977-78. Mem. editorial adv. bd.: Symposia mag, 1977-83; contbr. articles to mags. Vice chmn. Utah Advanced Gift Heart Fund drive, 1964; co-chmn archtl. div. United Fund drive, 1964; mem. Salt Lake City City Walls Com., 1976-77, Salt Lake City Council for Arts, 1977-78, Utah Gov.'s Adv. Com. Low Income Housing, Utah Rev. Panel Emergency Energy Conservation Programs; adv. bd. Utah Citizens for Arts, Utah Soc. Autistic Children; mem. dinner exec. com. Nat. Jewish Hosp., Nat. Asthma Ctr., Denver, 1983; bd. dirs. Utah State Div. History, Utah State Hist. Soc., 1989—; mem. Gov.'s Strategic Initiatives for History Task Force, 1991. Recipient Danforth Honor award, 1951, also numerous AIA awards including regional design awards for U. Utah Library Fountain, 1970, Westminster Coll. Fountain Plaza, 1972, Nat. award for Kearns/Daynes/Alley Annex, 1978, Western Mountain Region Hist. award of merit for Daynes/Kearns/Alley Annex, 1977, Am. Assn. Sch. Adminstrs. Exhibit award for Wilson Elementary Sch. Green River, Wyo., 1974, Award merit Producers' Council, Inc., 1978, award Nat. Lincoln Arc Welding Found., 1978, Urban Design award 3d Ann. Program, 1979, award of honor We. Mountain Region for HUD Low Income Housing Project, Salt Lake City Housing Authority, 1988, ACI award for Seven Canyon's Fountain, Liberty Park, Salt Lake City, 1994, others. Fellow AIA (bd. dirs. Utah chpt. 1968, 7l, sec. 1972-73, chmn. regional conf. 1974, pres. 1975-76; chmn. jury for Wyo. chpt. design awards program 1974, regional rep. to housing com., nat. honor award jury 1979, recorder nat. conv. 1982, speaker West Mountain region conf. 1991); mem. Salt Lake Area C. of C. (v.p. 1980-8l, chmn. bd. 1982-83), U. Utah Alumni Assn. (bd. dirs. 1987-90), Salt Lake Swim and Tennis Club, Alta Club (bd. dirs. 1985-89, sec. 1991-92, pres. 1994—), Rotary (treas. Salt Lake City club 1976-77, pres. 1979-80, v.p. 1987, pres. found. 1990-92). Home: 1460 Military Way Salt Lake City UT 84103-4455 Office: Boyd A Blackner & Assocs 136 S Main St Salt Lake City UT 84101-1601

BLACKSTOCK, JOSEPH ROBINSON, newspaper editor; b. L.A., Dec. 8, 1947; s. Joseph Richard McCall and Doris Louise (Robinson) B.; m. Nancy Ruth Frederiksen, Feb. 9, 1974; children: Miriam, Susan, Cynthia, Catherine. BA, Calif. State U., L.A., 1970, MA, 1977. Sports writer Monterey Park Californian, 1986-72; sports and news writer, mng. editor San Gabriel Valley Tribune, West Covina, Calif., 1972-89; exec. editor Pasadena (Calif.) Star-News, 1989-93; copy editor Riverside (Calif.) Press-Enterprise, 1993—. With USAR, 1970-78.

BLACKWELL, CHARLES CURTIS, writer, visual artist; b. San Francisco, Aug. 11, 1950; s. Curtis H. and Gertrude Lizzie (Tinsley) B.; divorced. Student, Sacramento City Coll., 1968-70, American River Coll., Sacramento, 1972-74; BA in Sociology, Calif. State U., Chico, 1975; postgrad., Calif. State Sacramento U., 1975-76. Artist County of Sacramento and Calif. State U., Sacramento, 1977-78; tchr./counselor, art instr. Washington Therapeutic Arts for Handicapped, 1984; organizer in arts, performer Employment Support Ctr., Washington, 1987-90; art isntr./counselor D.C. Child Family Svcs., Washington, 1989; resident playwright Calif. Original Theatre, Sacramento, 1993—; writer instr. workshop William James Assn. Arts in Prison, Santa Cruz, Calif., 1992-94; organizer cultural arts The Cane Leaves Sway, Sacramento, 1994, The Bulu Project, Washington, 1987-88. Author: (plays) I's the Color of Mississippi Mud, 1985, I'm a Boxer, 1989, also poems. Mem. Nat. Conf. Artists, Z.I.C.A. Home: PO Box 417730 Sacramento CA 95841-7730

BLACKWELL, ELIZABETH KUHLMANN, physician; b. Paterson, N.J., Nov. 18, 1948; d. Rudolf and Ann (Pfaffmann) Kuhlmann; m. David Howarth Blackwell, July 22, 1977; children: Ann-Marie, Elise, Elizabeth, David. BS, Upsala U., 1970; MD, Thomas Jefferson U., 1974. Emergency dept. physician Ariz. Emergency Physicians, Inc., Mesa, 1976-77; urgent care ctr. physician, gen. med. clinic physician Brigham Young U. Health Ctr., Provo, Utah, 1977—, nurse practitioner program preceptor, 1989-90, eating disorders med. cons., 1990-91; lectr. Brigham Young U., Provo, 1994. Speaker on health issues to local community groups, Utah County, 1977—; unit commr., den leader Utah Nat. Parks coun. Boy Scouts Am., 1992—; mem. ad-hoc planning com. Highland City. Recipient Physician Recognition award AMA, 1992-95. Mem. Am. Coll. Emergency Physicians (mem. sect. on pediatric emergencies, 1992-94). LDS. Office: Brigham Young U MacDonald Health Ctr Provo UT 84602

BLACKWELL, GARLAND WAYNE, retired military officer; b. Roxboro, N.C., July 8, 1956; s. Garland and Mattie (Wright) B.; m. Joan Lelia Christensen, Mar. 12, 1984 (div. 1988); m. Sandra Luz Garcia, Feb. 9, 1991; children: Brandi Alexis, Garland Wayne Jr. BSBA, U. N.C., 1978; MBA, N.Mex. Highlands U., 1982; postgrad., Willamette U., 1995. CPA, cert. internal auditor. Commd. 2d lt. USAF, 1979, advanced through grades to major, 1990; dep. acctg. and fin. officer 1606 Air Base Wing USAF, Kirtland AFB, N.Mex., 1979-82; staff auditor Air Force Audit Agy., Vandenberg AFB, Calif., 1982-83, Torrejon AB, Spain, 1983-85; audit office chief Air Force Audit Agy., Castle AFB, Calif., 1985-89; audit mgr. Air Force Audit Agy., Norton AFB, Calif., 1989-92; comptroller 432 Fighter Wing USAF, Misawa AB, Japan, 1992-94. Active Caring By Sharing Maranatha Community Ch., L.A., 1989-92; bd. dirs. project alpha March of Dimes, San Bernadino, Calif., 1990-91. Decorated Commendation medal (3), Meritorious Svc. medal (2), Nat. Defense medal; named one of Outstanding Young Men Am., 1984, 86, 89, Most Eligible Bachelor Ebony Mag., 1989. Mem. Nat. Soc. Tax Profls., Inst. Internal Auditors, Am. Soc. Mil. Comptrollers (chpt. v.p. 1986-88), Nat. Black Masters in Bus. Adminstrn. Assn. (life), Air Force Assn., Tuskegee Airmen, Inc., Alpha Phi Alpha (life, chpt. v.p. 1981-82). Home: 2396 Church St NE Salem OR 97303

BLACKWELL, SAMUEL EUGENE, state legislator; b. Superior, Wyo., Aug. 31, 1930; s. Thomas Eugene and Panzey Fay (Dazey) B.; m. Beverly Joan Nottingham, Jan. 10, 1953; children: Michael, Nyla, Holly. Grad., high sch. Operator Halliburton Co., Rock Spring, Wyo., 1956-65, FMC of Wyo., Green River, 1965-92; mem. Wyo. Legislature, Cheyenne, 1982—. Served to cpl. U.S. Army, 1949-52, Korea. Mem. Elks, Am. Legion. Democrat. Home: 610 Donalynn Dr Rock Springs WY 82901-7309

BLADE, MELINDA KIM, educator, researcher, archaeologist; b. San Diego, Jan. 12, 1952; d. George A. and Arline A. M. (MacLeod) B. BA, U. San Diego, 1974, MA in Teaching, 1975, MA, 1975, EdD, 1986. Cert. secondary tchr., Calif.; cert. community coll. instr., Calif.; registered profl. historian, Calif. Instr. Coronado Unified Sch. Dist., Calif., 1975-76; head coach women's basketball U. San Diego, 1976-78; instr. Acad. of Our Lady of Peace, San Diego, 1976—, chmn. social studies dept., 1993—, counselor, 1984-92, co-dir. student activities, 1984-87, coord. advanced placement program, 1986-95, dir. athletics, 1990; mem. archaeol. excavation team U. San Diego, 1975—, hist. researcher, 1975—; lectr., 1981—. Author hist. reports and research papers. Editor U. San Diego pubs. Vol. Am. Diabetes Assn., San Diego, 1975—; coord. McDonald's Diabetes Bike-a-thon, San Diego, 1977, 78; bd. dirs. U. San Diego Sch. Edn. Mem. Nat. Council Social Studies, Calif. Council Social Studies, Soc. Bibl. Archeology, Assn. Supervision and Curriculum Devel., Assn. Scientists and Scholars Internat. for Shroud of Turin, Medieval Acad. Am., Medieval Assn. Pacific, Am. Hist. Assn., Western Assn. Women Historians, Renaissance Soc. Am., San Diego

Hist. Soc., Phi Alpha Theta (sec.-treas. 1975-77), Phi Delta Kappa. Office: Acad Our Lady of Peace 4860 Oregon St San Diego CA 92116-1340

BLAINE, DOROTHEA CONSTANCE RAGETTÉ, lawyer; b. N.Y.C., Sept. 23, 1930; d. Robert Raymond and Dorothea Ottilie Ragetté; BA, Barnard Coll., 1952; MA, Calif. State U., 1968; EdD, UCLA, 1978; JD, Western State U., 1981; postgrad. in taxation Golden Gate U. Bar: Calif. 1982, U.S. Dist. Ct. (ea., so. and cen. dists.) Calif., 1982. Mem. tech. staff Planning Rsch. Corp., L.A., 1964-67; assoc. scientist Holy Cross Hosp., Mission Hills, Calif., 1967-70; career devel. officer and affirmative action officer County of Orange, Santa Ana, Calif., 1970-74, sr. adminstrv. analyst, budget and program coord., 1974-78; spl. projects asst. CAO/Spl. Programs Office, 1978-80, sr. adminstrv. analyst, 1980-83; pvt. practice, 1982—; instr. Am. Coll. Law, Brea, Calif., 1987; judge pro tem Orange County Mcpl. Ct., 1988—. Bd. dirs. Deerfield Community Assn., 1975-78, Orange YMCA, 1975-77. Mem. ABA, ACLU, Trial Lawyers Am., Calif. Trial Lawyers Assn., Orange County Trial Lawyers Assn., Calif. Women Lawyers, Nat. Women's Polit. Caucus, Calif. Bar Assn., Orange County Bar Assn. (Orange County del. to Calif. State Bar Conv. 1985-94, bd. dirs. Orange County lawyers referral svc. 1988-92), Delta Theta Phi, Phi Delta Kappa.

BLAIR, CRAIG JOHN, utilities executive; b. Hackensack, N.J., June 14, 1943; s. Harold Irving B.; m. Susan Elizabeth Judd (div. Aug. 1978); children: Shannon Sue, Stacey Ann; m. Jane Masles; 1 child, Ryan Edward. BA, Franklin (Ind.) Coll., 1965. Mfg. mgmt. trainee GE, Evandale, Ohio, Ft. Wayne, Ind., 1967-69; buyer, pers. administr. Control Data, Roseville, Minn., 1969-71; v.p. pers. G.D. Searle Co., Skokie, Ill., 1987-82; dir. pers. ops. worldwide G.D. Searle Co., Skokie, 1971-82; v.p. pers. No. States Power Co., Mpls., 1982-84, v.p. electric utility, 1984-88, sr. v.p. electric utility, 1988-91, exec. v.p. power supply, 1991—. Bd. dirs Viking Coun. Boy Scouts Am., Mpls., 1985—, Better Bus. Bur., St. Paul, 1987—, Met. Econ. Devl. Assn., Mpls., 1989—, Minn. Coun. for Quality, Mpls., 1991—. Mem. Rolling Green Country Club (Hamel, Minn., golf com. 1988-89), Rotary. Republican. Presbyterian. Office: Northern States Power Co. 414 Nicollet Mall Minneapolis MN 55401-1927

BLAIR, FREDERICK DAVID, interior designer; b. Denver, June 15, 1946; s. Frederick Edward and Margaret (Whitely) B. BA, U. Colo., 1969; postgrad. in French, U. Denver, 1981-82. Interior designer The Denver, 1969-76, store mgr., 1976-80; v.p. Hartley House Interiors, Ltd., Denver, 1980-83; pvt. practice interior design Denver, 1983—; com. mem. Ice House Design Ctr., Denver, 1985-86, Design Directory Western Region, Denver, 1986; edn. com. for ASID Nat. Conf., Denver, 1991. Designs shown in various mags. Mem. Rep. Nat. Com.; bd. dirs. One Day, orgn. for children with AIDS, Very Spl. Arts, 1993; mem. steering com. Supporters of Children, 1994. Mem. Am. Soc. Interior Designers (co-chmn. com. profl. registration 1986, edn. com. nat. conf. 1991, bd. dirs. Colo. chpt. 1990—), Denver Art Mus., Nat. Trust Historic Preservation, Historic Denver, Inc. Christian Scientist.

BLAIR, KATHIE LYNN, social services worker; b. Oakland, Calif., Sept. 29, 1951; d. Robert Leon Webb and Patricia Jean (Taylor) Peterson; m. Terry Wayne Blair, Dec. 29, 1970 (div. 1972); 1 child, Anthony Wayne. Eligibility worker Dept. Social Services, San Jose, Calif., 1974-76; adult and family services worker State of Oreg., Portland, 1977-90; guest speaker welfare advocacy groups, Portland, 1987. Translator: Diary of Fannie Burkhart, 1991; contbr. articles to profl. jours. Mem. Nat. Geog. Soc., A Brotherhood Against Totalitarian Enactments, Oreg. State Pub. Interest Rsch. Group, Clan Chattan Assn., Portland Highland Games Assn., Harley Owners Group, Ladies of Harley. Democrat.

BLAIR, STEWART D., small business owner; b. Scotland, 1950. MA in Econs. and Polit. Sci., U. Glasgow, Scotland. With Chase Manhattan Bank, London, N.Y.C., from 1972; sr. v.p. tele-comm. Chase Manhattan Bank, Denver; CEO United Artists Entertainment Co.; chmn., CEO United Artists Theatre Cir., Englewood; also bd. dirs. United Artists Theatre Cir. Mem. Found. Motion Pictures Pioneers. Office: United Artists 9110 E Nichols Ave Englewood CO 80112-3450

BLAIRE, STEPHEN E., bishop; b. L.A., Dec. 22, 1942. Grad., St. John's Sem., Camarillo, Calif. Ordained priest Roman Cath. Ch., 1967, titular bishop of Lamzella. Aux. bishop L.A., 1990—. Office: Chancery Office 1531 W 9th St Los Angeles CA 90015-1112*

BLAISDELL, DONALD CHARLES, artist, educator; b. Syracuse, N.Y., Oct. 26, 1942; s. Irl Hazard and Francis Augusta (Redmond) B.; m. Karen Dale Thomas, Jan. 10, 1971; 1 child, Augustine Francis. Student, Pratt Inst., Bklyn., 1961-63, Syracuse U., 1963-65; BA, Calif. State U., Long Beach, 1974, MA, 1975. Prof. art Calif. State U., Long Beach, 1975, Santa Monica (Calif.) Coll., 1975-91, UCLA, 1980-91; art dir. Blaisdell Atelier, L.A., 1991—. Home: 5117 Tendilla Ave Woodland Hills CA 91364-1828

BLAKE, BAMBI REVA, international fine artist; b. Douglaston, N.Y., Sept. 26, 1955; d. Martin and Eva Mae (Patterson) B.; 1 child, Star Ray. BFA, Sch. Visual Arts, 1977. Founder Star Light Studios, Internat., N.Y., S.C., 1985-89; art dir. Bernstein Film Prodn., Hollywood, Calif., 1990-92; founder Spirit Dancer Fine Art, N.Mex., 1990-94; founder Spirit Dancer Fine Art, Boulder, Colo., 1993-94, internat. fine artist, 1970—. Author: Prince Star Ray Flys to Earth on his Magic Carpet of Birds, 1984, (screenplay) The Forbidden Galaxy, 1984; producer, dir. (movie) A Touch of Class, 1989, (video) Bambi Blake in Action, 1989; prin. works included in numerous collections including The Rhodes Collection Met. Mus. Art, N.Y.C. Active Childrite Art Auction, Taos, N.Mex., 1991, 92, 94, Santa Fe Opera Art Auction, 1992, Taos Valley Sch. Art Auction, 1994. Recipient Phillip Frankel Meml. award Art Chmns. Assn., 1973, Art award Master Eagle Family, 1973; scholar Sch. Art League, 1973. Mem. Mem. Santa Fe Art Alliance, Santa Fe Coun. for Arts, Longmont Artist Guild (1st place blue ribbon for sculpture 1994), Catron County Fair, Catron County Art Guild, Delaware Valley Arts & Alliance. Office: Spirit Dancer Fine Art PO Box 20036 Boulder CO 80308-3036

BLAKE, GILBERT EASTON, air conditioning company executive; b. Glendale, Calif., June 7, 1953; s. Easton and Barbara Lee (Hunt) B.; m. Joye Trottier, June 5, 1975; children: Kristopher, Xela, Kamaron, Joseph, Alexander, Andrew. Student, Brigham Young U., 1974-75. Owner, pres. Blake Roofing, Salt Lake City, 1976-77; pres. Conjoy Inc., Salt Lake City, 1977-85, Conjoy Enterprises, Inc., Salt Lake City, 1985—; v.p., bd. dirs. Associated Funding Inc., Salt Lake City; pres. Finest Gas Fireplaces and Logs, Salt Lake City. Councilman Taylorsville-Bennion Community Coun., 1989-90; scoutmaster Salt Lake Coun. Boy Scouts Am., 1982-84; judge concourse d'Elegance Car Show, U. Utah, 1983—, Auto Expo Car Show, 1985—. Mem. Rocky Mountain Gas Assn. Republican. Mormon. Office: Conjoy Enterprises Inc 3820 W 5400 S Salt Lake City UT 84118-3549

BLAKE, LAURA, architect; b. Berkeley, Calif., Dec. 26, 1959; d. Igor Robert and Elizabeth (Denton) B. BA in Art History, Brown U., 1982; MArch, UCLA, 1985. Architect The Ratcliff Architects, Berkeley, 1986-90, IDG Architects, Oakland, Calif., 1990-92, ELS Architects, Berkeley, 1992—. Organizer charity ball Spinsters San Francisco, 1988, sec., 1988-89, mem. adv. bd., 1989-92; mem. San Francisco Jr. League. Recipient Alpha Rho Chi bronze medal, 1985. Mem. AIA. Republican. Episcopalian. Office: ELS Architects 2040 Addison St Berkeley CA 94704-1104

BLAKE, WILLIAM BENJAMIN, management and financial consultant; b. Indpls., Aug. 6, 1934; s. William Arthur and Helen B. (Wheelen) B.; divorced; children: Karen Ann Foss, William A., Pamela J. BS, Ind. U., 1961, MS, 1968; grad., Command and Gen. Staff Coll., Ft. Leavenworth, Kans., 1973, Indsl. Coll. Armed Forces, Washington, 1982. Commd. 2d lt. U.S. Army, 1961; advanced through grades to col., 1982; Dep. Asst. Sec. Army Rsch., Devel. and Acquisition Washington, 1981-85; ret., 1985; project mgr. Texas Instruments, Dallas, 1985-86, mktg. mgr., 1986; v.p. mktg. Optic Electronics Corp., Dallas, 1986-88; internat. cons. George S. May Co., Chgo., 1988-89; pres. B & D Mgmt. Cons., Inc., Scottsdale, Ariz., 1989—; bd. dirs. Specimen Specialists, Inc., Labor Unltd, Extraordinary Lighting Svcs., Inc., B and D Mgmt. Cons., Inc. Decorated Bronze Star with Valor Svc., 1969, DFC, 1969, Legion of Merit, 1985. Mem. Army Navy Club. Republican. Home: 815 N 82d St Ste G1 Scottsdale AZ 85257-3853

BLAKELEY, JAMES EDWARD, III, interior designer; b. L.A., June 15, 1945; s. James Edward and Mary Ann (Carlise) B. BS, Woodbury U., 1964. Prin. Blakeley Bazeley Ltd., Beverly Hills, Calif., 1982—. Adv. bd. Venice (Calif.) Family Clinic, Valley Coll., Van Nuys, Calif. Dorothy Peterson Edn. grantee, 1994. Mem. Am. Soc. Interior Designers (L.A. chpt. pres. 1993-94), Designers Lighting Forum (bd. dirs. 1990-92). Office: Blakeley Bazeley Ltd PO Box 5173 Beverly Hills CA 90209-5173

BLAKELEY, LINDA, writer, producer, psychologist; b. Bklyn., July 26, 1941; d. Charles and Blanche (Josephson) Berkow; m. Dec. 17, 1961 (div. 1983); children: Stacey, Scott. BA, UCLA, 1964; MA, Calif. State U., Northridge, 1977; PhD, Calif. Grad. Inst., 1985. Founder, dir. Parents Sharing Custody, Beverly Hills, Calif., 1984-87; pvt. practice specializing in treatment of eating disorders Beverly Hills, 1984—; trainer Calif. Assn. Marriage and Family Therapists, 1988, 89; producer, host Positive Self Images interview/talk show. Author: ABC's of Stress Management, 1989, Do It with Love-Positive Parenting After Divorce, 1988, Success Strategies, 1992, Audio Tape. Mem. adv. bd. Nat. Coun. Alcoholism and Drug Abuse, 1991-92. Mem. Calif. Psychol. Assn. (state bd. dirs. media com. 1989-92, chair-elect media divsn.), Calif. Assn. Marriage and Family Therapists (chmn. ethics com. L.A. chpt.), Beverly Hills C. of C. (pres. women's network 1989-90, chmn. health care com. 1989), Women in Film, Nat. Assn. Anorexia, Bulimia Assn. Disorders. Office: 420 S Beverly Dr Ste 100 Beverly Hills CA 90212-4410

BLAKELY, DAVID ALBERT, county supervisor; b. Cali, Colombia, Oct. 8, 1950; s. Everett E. Blakely and Margaret Ann Spence; m. Naomi Gross, Mar. 29, 1980; children: Daniel Ryan, Colin Palmer. BS in Social Scis., Calif. Poly. Inst., 1973, secondary teaching credential, 1974. Tchr. Atascadero (Calif.) Unified Schs., 1975-89; county supr. County of San Luis Obispo, Calif., 1989—; adj. prof. Calif. Poly. Inst., San Luis Obispo, 1978-86. Area coord. Spl. Olympics, San Luis Obispo, 1980-81; chmn. Santa Margarita (Calif.) Adv. Coun., 1975-89, Friday Night Live, San Luis Obispo, 1990—; dir. Econ. Opportunity Commn., San Luis Obispo, 1989-94, San Luis Obispo Coun. Govts., 1989—. Mem. Calif. State Assn. Counties, Local Govt. Commn., Santa Margarita Moose. Home: PO Box 909 Santa Margarita CA 93453-0909 Office: San Luis Obispo Bd Suprs Rm 370 Government Center San Luis Obispo CA 93453

BLAKELY, EDWARD JAMES, economics educator; b. San Bernardino, Calif., Apr. 21, 1938; s. Edward Blakely and Josephine Elizabeth (Carter) Proctor; m. Maaike C. Vander Sleesen, July 1, 1971; children: Pieta C., Brette D. BA, U. Calif., Riverside, 1960; MA, U. Calif., Berkeley, 1964; MBA, Pasadena Nazerene Coll., 1967; EdD in Edn. and Mgmt., UCLA, 1971. Mgr. Pacific Telephone Co., Pasadena, Calif., 1960-65; exec. dir. Western Community Action Tng., Los Angeles, 1965-69; spl. asst. U.S. Dept. State, Washington, 1969-71; asst. chancellor, assoc. prof. U. Pitts., 1971-74; assoc. dean and prof. applied econs. and behavioral scis. U. Calif., Davis, 1974-77; asst. v.p. U. Calif., Berkeley, 1977-85, prof., chmn. dept. city and regional planning, 1985—; expert advisor Orgn. Econ. Cooperation and Devel., asst. to Mayor Elihu Harris, City of Oakland. Author: Rural Communities in Advanced Industrial Society, Community Development Research, Taking Local Development Initiative, Planning Local Economic Development SAGE, 1988, Separate Societies: Poverty and Inequality in U.S. Cities (Paul Davidoff award 1993), 1992. Chmn. fin. com. Pvt. Industry Council of Oakland (Calif.), 1978-85; vice chmn. Ecole Bilingue Sch., Berkeley, 1982-85, chmn., 1988—; chmn. bd. Royce Sch., Oakland, Calif., 1988—; sec., treas. Econ. Devel. Corp., Oakland, 1983; expert advisor Orgn. Econ. Corp. and Devel., Paris, 1986. Served to 1st lt. USAF, 1961-63. Recipient San Francisco Found. award, 1991, Paul Davidoff award, 1993; Guggenheim fellow, 1995-96, fellow Urban Studies Australian Inst. Urban St., 1985, German Acad. Exch., 1984; Fulbright St. scholar Internat. Exch. of Scholars, 1986; named to Athlete Hall of Fame, U. Calif. Riverside Alumni Press, 1992, 125th Anniversary Prof. U. Calif. at Riverside Berkeley Campus, 1992. Fellow Australian Inst. Urban Studies; mem. Community Devel. Soc. (bd. dirs. 1980-84, Service award 1983, Disting. Svc. award 1990), Calif. Local Econ. Devel. (mem. standing com. 1980-81), Am. Planning Assn. (mem. accreditation com.), Am. Assn. Collegiate Schs. of Planning, Nat. Assn. State and Land Grant Colls. (mem. exec. com. 1987), Phi Delta Kappa, Lambda Alpha. Club: Rueful Order. Home: 855 Old Mill Rd San Marino CA 91108-1741 Office: Univ of So Calif Sch Urban Regional Planning Los Angeles CA 90089-0042

BLAKEMORE, PAUL HENRY, JR., retired publishing executive; b. Des Moines, Mar. 7, 1925; s. Paul Henry and Mabel (Evstace) B.; m. Barbara Jane Spargur, Oct. 24, 1952; children: Paul H. III, John E. BSBA, Northwestern U., 1950. Regional dir. First Fin. Group, Brookline, Mass., 1955-62; sr. v.p. TV/Radio Age, N.Y.C., 1963-87, cons., 1987—. Capt. USMC, 1943-47. Mem. Lions. Republican. Home: PO Box 4024 Malibu CA 90264-4024

BLAKENEY, ALLAN EMRYS, Canadian government official, lawyer; b. Bridgewater, N.S., Can., Sept. 7, 1925; s. John Cline and Bertha (Davies) B.; m. Mary Elizabeth Schwartz, 1950 (dec. 1957); m. Anne Louise Gorham, May 1959; children: Barbara, Hugh, David, Margaret. BA, Dalhousie U., 1945, LLB, 1947, LLD (hon.); BA (Rhodes scholar), Oxford U., 1949, MA, 1955; DCL (hon.), Mount Allison U.; LLD (hon.), York U., Toronto, U. Western Ont., London, 1991, U. Regina, 1993, U. Sask., 1995. Bar: N.S. 1950, Sask. 1951. Queen's counsel, 1961; sec. to govt. fin. office Govt. Sask., 1950-55; chmn. Sask. Securities Commn., 1955-58; ptnr. Davidson, Davidson & Blakeney, Regina, Sask., 1958-60, Griffin, Blakeney, Beke, Koskie & Lueck, Regina, 1964-70; premier of Sask., 1971-82; Mem. Sask. Legislature, 1960-88; Officer of the Order of Can., 1992; leader of the opposition Sask. Legislature, 1970-71, 88-87; prof. Osgoode Hall Law Sch., York U., 1988-90, U. Sask., 1990-92; minister of edn., Sask., 1960-61, provincial treas., 1961-62, minister pub. health, 1962-64; mem. Royal Commn. on Aborginal Peoples, 1991-93. Home: 1752 Prince of Wales Ave, Saskatoon, SK Canada S7K 3E5 Office: U Saskatchewan, Coll Law, Saskatoon, SK Canada S7N 0W0

BLAKEY, SCOTT CHALONER, journalist, writer; b. Nashua, N.H., Nov. 19, 1936; s. Elmer F. and Mildred Livingstone (Chaloner) B.; m. Lone Erting, July 18, 1970 (div.); 1 child, Nicholas Scott; m. Caroline M. Scarborough, June 28, 1985; children: Alexandra Scarborough, Susannah Chaloner. BA, U. N.H., 1960. Reporter, photographer Nashua (N.H.) Telegraph, 1960-62, polit. reporter, 1963-64; legis. asst. Congressman James C. Cleveland, Washington, 1963; mng. editor Concord (N.H.) Monitor, 1964-68; urban affairs corr. San Francisco Chronicle, 1968-70, reporter, asst. city editor, 1979-84, TV corr., 1985-87; corr., asst. news dir. KQED-TV, San Francisco, 1970-74; free-lance writer San Francisco, 1974-79; news editor KRON-TV (NBC), San Francisco, 1987-89; nationally syndicated columnist KidVid L.A. Times Syndicate, 1990—; sr. news rep. div. corp. communications Pacific Gas & Electric Co., San Francisco, 1991—. Writer, field producer TV documentary 2251 Days, 1973 (2 Emmy awards 1974); author (books) San Francisco, 1976, Prisoner at War, 1978, Kid Vid, 1995; contbr. articles to profl. jours. Recipient Best Polit. Writing award New Eng. AP News Editors Assn., 1965, Dupont Columbia award, 1974. Mem. Authors Guild, Am. Air Mail Soc., Audubon Soc. Democrat. Home: 1801 Turk St Apt 17 San Francisco CA 94115-4429 Office: Pacific Gas & Electric 77 Beale St Ste 2935A San Francisco CA 94105-1814

BLALOCK, ANN BONAR, special policy analyst, evaluation researcher; b. Parkersburg, W.Va., Apr. 16, 1928; d. Harry and Fay (Conley) Bonar; m. Hubert Blalock, Jr., 1951; children: Susan Blalock Lyon, Kathleen Blalock McCarrell, James W. AB, Oberlin Coll., 1950; MA, U. N.C., 1954; MSW, U. Wash., 1978. Pvt. cons. Admiralty Inlet Consulting, Olympia, Wash. Editor Evaluation Forum, Evaluating Social Programs; co-author: Introduction to Social Research. Mem. State Assn. Social Workers, Nat. Assn. Social Labor (past pres. Wash. chpt.). Home: PO Box 409 Hansville WA 98340-0409

BLANCHARD, CHARLES ALAN, lawyer, former state senator; b. San Diego, Apr. 14, 1959; s. David Dean and Janet (Laxson) B. BS, Lewis & Clark Coll., 1981; M of Pub. Policy, Harvard U., 1985, JD, 1985. Bar: Ariz. 1987, U.S. Dist. Ct. Ariz. 1988, U.S. Ct. Appeals (D.C. cir.) 1988, U.S. Ct. Appeals (9th cir.) 1988. Law clk. to judge Harry T. Edwards Washington, 1985-86; law clk. to justice Sandra Day O'Connor U.S. Supreme Ct., Washington, 1986-87; assoc. ind. counsel Ind. Counsel James McKay, Washington, 1987-88; atty. Brown & Bain, P.A., Phoenix, 1988—; state senator State of Ariz., Phoenix, 1991-95; chmn. Senate Judiciary Com., Phoenix, 1991-93; Dem. candidate U.S. Congress, 1994. Contbr. articles to profl. jours. Bd. dirs. Florence (Ariz.) Immigrant and Refugee Rights Projects, 1990—, Homeless Legal Assistance Project, Phoenix, 1992—, Tempe Cmty. Action Agy., 1994—, Luth. Vol. Corps., Washington, 1986-88; state committeeman Ariz. Dem. Party, Phoenix, 1991—; chmn. Ariz. Dem. Leadership Coun., Inc., 1992—. Recipient Disting. Svc. award Ariz. Atty. Gen., 1992; Toll fellowship Coun. of State Govts., 1991; named Disting. Young Alumni Lewis and Clark Coll., 1987. Home: 315 W Cambridge Ave Phoenix AZ 85003-1004 Office: Brown & Bain PA 2901 N Central Ave Phoenix AZ 85012

BLANCHARD, WILLIAM HENRY, psychologist; b. St. Paul, Mar. 25, 1922; s. Charles Edgar and Ethel Rachael (Gurney) B.; m. Martha Ida Lang, Aug. 11, 1947; children: Gregory Marcus, Mary Lisa. Diploma in Sci. Mason City Jr. Coll., 1942; BS in Chemistry, Iowa State U., 1944; PhD in Psychology, U. So. Calif., 1954. Lic. clin. psychologist, Calif. Shift chemist B.F. Goodrich Chem. Co., Port Neches, Tex., 1946-47; court psychologist L.A. County Gen. Hosp., 1954-55; psychologist, dir. rsch. So. Reception Ctr. and Clinic, Calif. Youth Authority, Norwalk, 1955-58; social scientist Rand Corp., 1958-60, System Devel. Corp., 1960-70; mem. faculty Calif. State U.-Northridge, L.A., 1970; assoc. prof. UCLA, 1971; faculty group leader urban semester U. So. Calif., L.A., 1971-75; sr. rsch. assoc. Office of Chancellor, Calif. State U., L.A., 1975-76; sr. rsch. fellow Planning Analysis and Rsch. Inst., Santa Monica, Calif., 1976—; pvt. practice psychologist, Calif., 1976—; clin. assoc. dept. psychology U. So. Calif., 1956-58. Author: Rousseau and the Spirit of Revolt, 1967; Aggression American Style, 1978; Revolutionary Morality, 1984. Contbr. articles to profl. jours. Mem. com. on mental health West Area Welfare Planning Council, L.A., 1960-61; bd. dirs. L.A. County Psychol. Assn., 1969; commr. Bd. Med. Examiners, Psychology Exam. Com., State of Calif., 1969; v.p. Parents and Friends of Mentally Ill Children, 1968—, pres., 1966-68, trustee, 1968—. Mem. APA, AAAS, Internat. Soc. Polit. Psychology. Home: 4307 Rosario Rd Woodland Hills CA 91364-5546

BLANCHE, JOE ADVINCULA, aerospace engineer, consultant, educator; b. Rizal, Santa, Ilocos Sur, Philippines, Sept. 11, 1954; came to U.S. 1976; s. Emilio Peralta and Concepcion (Advincula) B.; m. Albine Selerio Lansangan, Oct. 9, 1982; children: Emmanuel Joseph, Earl Jordan. Cert. in mil. sci., U. Philippines, 1973; BS in Math., Adamson U., Manila, 1976; postgrad., Calif. State U., Long Beach, 1982-85; AAS in Avionics Systems Tech., Community Coll. Air Force, Maxwell AFB, Ala., 1990; cert. in mgmt., Cen. Tex. Coll., 1990; PhD in Mgmt., Pacific Western U., 1993; MA in Orgnl. Mgmt., U. Phoenix, 1995. Lic. real estate broker, Calif.; registered tax preparer, Calif.; notary pub., Calif. Assoc. engr./scientist McDonnell Douglas Corp., Long Beach, Calif., 1981-84; engr./scientist McDonnell Douglas Corp., 1984-86, engr./scientist specialist, 1987-88, sr. engr./scientist, 1988-94; lead aerospace engr. Sikorsky Aircraft-UTC, Stratford, Conn., 1986-87; founder, pres. J. & A. Blanche Ventures', Inc., Corona Hills, Calif., 1990—; avionics maint. inspector USAF, 1983-86, 87—. With USAF, 1976-80. Bur. Forestry grantee and scholar U. Philippines, 1971-73, USVA scholar Calif. State U., 1982-85. Mem. AIAA (sr. mem.), Nat. Notary Assn., NRA, So. Calif. Profl. Engrs. Assn., Corona-Norco Bd. Realtors, Internat. Soc. Allied Weight Engrs. (sr. mem.), Santanians USA Inc. (bd. dirs. 1984-87, pres. 1994-96), Marinduque Assn. So. Calif., Fil-Am. Assn. Corona (auditor 1993-94, bd. dirs. 1995-96). Republican. Roman Catholic. Home: 2179 Tehachapi Dr Corona CA 91719-1138 Office: J & A Blanche Ventures Inc Ste #111-333 420 McKinley St Corona Hills CA 90846-0003

BLANCHETTE, JEANNE ELLENE MAXANT, artist, educator, performer; b. Chgo., Sept. 25, 1944; d. William H. and L. Barbara (Martin) Maxant; m. Yasuo Shimizu, Apr. 28, 1969 (div. 1973); m. William B. Blanchet, Aug. 21, 1981 (dec. May 1993). BA summa cum laude, Northwestern U., 1966; MFA, Tokyo U., 1971; MA, Ariz. State U., 1978; postgrad., Ill. State U., 1979-80; PhD, Greenwich U., 1991. Instr. Tsuda U., Kodaira, Japan, 1970-71; free-lance visual, performing artist various cities, U.S., 1973—; artist in residence YMCA of the Rockies, Estes Park, Colo., 1976-81 summers; prof. fine arts Rio Salado Coll., Surprise, Ariz., 1976-91; lectr. Ariz. State U. West, Sun City, 1985-93; lectr., evaluator several arts couns. including Ariz. Humanities Coun., 1993; Prescott Melodrama ragtime pianist, 1993, 94; artist with Performing Arts for Youth, 1994—. Selected for regional, state, nat. juried art shows, 1975—, mus. and gallery one-woman shows of computer art, 1988—; author: Original Songs and Verse of the Old (And New) West, 1987, A Song in My Heart, 1988, Reflections, 1989, The Mummy Story, 1990; contbr. articles to newspapers, profl. jours. Founding mem. Del Webb Hosp. Woodrow Wilson fellow, 1966; ADA B.C. Welsh scholar, 1980; recipient numerous art, music awards, 1970—, major computer art awards in regional, nat., and internat. shows, 1990—. Mem. Nat. League Am. Pen Women (sec. chpt. 1987, v.p. 1988, pres. 1990-92), Ariz. Press Women (numerous awards in original graphics and writing 1980s, 90s), Nat. Fedn. Press Women, Northwestern U.'s John Evans Club, Henry W. Rogers Soc., P.E.O., Phi Beta Kappa.

BLAND, DOROTHY ANN, construction executive, real estate agent; b. Black Township, Pa., Jan. 12, 1945; d. Homer Charles and Edith Birdie (Hampe) Colflesh; m. Jonathan Lee Sharp, Sept. 28, 1963 (dec. Dec. 31, 1979); children: Deborah, Todd, Wade; m. Brian C. Bland, Nov. 2, 1985; stepchildren: Paulette, Kelli. Lic. Real Estate Agent, Utah. Beauty coll. recruiter, sec. Continental Coll. of Beauty, Salt Lake City, 1968-72; exec. sec. Vaughn Hansen Assoc., Salt Lake City, 1973-82; v.p., co-owner Bland Bros., Inc., West Jordan, Utah, 1985—; co-owner Blands Sand & Gravel, Utah, 1990—; real estate agent Preferred Properties, Salt Lake City, 1982-90, Mansell, Salt Lake City, 1990—. Office: Bland Brothers Inc 8630 S Redwood Rd West Jordan UT 84088

BLAND, JANEESE MYRA, editor; b. Evanston, Ill., Feb. 20, 1960; d. James Milton and Jeanette Malisa (Bryant) B. BA, U. Ark., 1980. Cert. tchr., Ark., Ill. Tutor counselor U. Ark., Pine Bluff, 1979; tchr. Pine Bluff High Sch., 1980, Chgo. Bd. Edn., 1981-84; editor, author, columnist, creator Beautiful Images Hollywood (Calif.) Gazette Newspaper, 1985—; VIP organizer People's Choice Awards, Beverly Hills, 1984—; exec. prodr. stas. Chgo. Access Corp., Century Cable Comms., L.A., BH-TV, Beverly Hills; hostess The Janeese Bland Show. Proof editor: Nursing Rsch. Jour., 1989. Polit. vol. Rep. Party, Santa Monica, 1988—; vol. organizer Windfeather, Inc., Beverly Hills, 1983—, United Negro Coll. Fund, L.A., 1984—, Sickle Cell Disease Rsch. Found., L.A., 1985—; pres., founder June Maria Bland Scholarship Found. Recipient Image award Fred Hampton Scholarship Found., 1983. Republican. Baptist. Office: Sta BH-TV PO Box 16472 Beverly Hills CA 90209-1472

BLAND-SCHRICKER, LAUREL LE MIEUX, human resources executive, consultant; b. Spokane, Wash., Feb. 23, 1926; d. Alfred Theodore Le Mieux and Bernice Catherine (Lawrence) Alburty; m. Curtis Allen Bland, July 22, 1944 (div. June 1972); children: Laurel Kathleen Bland Eisinger, Daniel Matthew; m. Frank Hubert Schricker, Mar. 30, 1976. AA, Anchorage Community Coll., 1966; vis. student, Hebrew U., Jerusalem, 1968; BE cum laude, U. Alaska, 1968, MA, 1969; PhD, U. N.Mex., 1974. Tech. asst. Alaska Human Rights Commn., Anchorage, 1967; liaison 2d jud. dist. Alaska Legal Svcs., Nome, 1968; founder, CEO Human Environ. Resources Svcs., Inc., Alaska, 1969-78; instr. edn. and history of Alaska Natives Alaska Meth. Univ., Anchorage, 1969-73; asst. prof. U. Alaska, Fairbanks, 1974; prof. cross cultural edn. Sheldon Jackson Coll., Sitka, Ak., 1975; chief exec. officer Human Environ. Resources Svcs., Inc., Kennewick, Wash., 1976—; project dir. spl hist. and cultural inventory Imuruk Basin, Ak., 1969-73; founder Oquilluk Legacy Collection, U. Alaska-Fairbanks Archives, 1970; cons. manpower devel. and cultural heritage documentation and preservation various state and fed. agys., others.; primary contbr. to the Oquilluk Legacy Collection, 1970—; advisor, cons. to mem. groups Bering Straits Native Corp., 1971—. Author: Northern Eskimos of Alaska, 1972, (with William Oquilluk) People of Kauwerak, 1973, 2d edit., 1980, Alaska Native Population and Manpower, 1978, Careless Boy, 1980; contbr. articles on edn. and anthropology to profl. jours., 1969—. Appointee gov. adv. com. Office

Minority and Women's Bus. Enterprises, Olympia, Wash., 1985-90; mem. apportionment panel United Way, Benton and Franklin Counties, Wash., 1988; participant seminar Future of Alaska, Brookings Inst., 1969. Teaching fellow Alaska Dept. Edn., 1968, 69. Roman Catholic. Home and Office: 1921 W 17th Ave Kennewick WA 99337-3432

BLANEY, LOREN FRANCIS, JR., software engineer; b. Los Alamos, N.Mex., Oct. 22, 1948; s. Loren Francis and Elizabeth Caldwell (Jones) B.; m. Monique Gene Didero, Nov. 12, 1988. BS in Physics, So. Colo. State Coll., 1970; BS in Elec. Engring., Colo. State. U., 1973. Registered profl. engr., Colo. Assoc engr. Viking mission to Mars Martin Marietta, Denver, 1974-75, engr., 1976-78; software engr. jet propulsion lab. Viking lander simulation team NASA, Pasadena, Calif., 1975-76; software cons. Nederland, Colo., 1979—. Software developer and creator. Mem. Assn. Computing Machinery. Home and Office: Magnolia Star Rt Nederland CO 80466

BLANEY, SUZANNE AVERY, artist; b. Washington, Nov. 12, 1931; d. Edward Frederick Avery and Marba Jean (Woolhiser) Randlemon; m. William Deshields Winder, June 12, 1950 (div. Feb. 1966); 1 child, Dale Beverly; m. Floyd Earl Blaney, June 1966. Student, U. Miami, 1949-50, Fredden Goldberg Art Acad., San Francisco, 1970-73, Calif. Sch. Arts and Crafts, 1981-82. Exec. sec. Bechtel Corp., San Francisco, 1953-58, J.C. Penney Regional Office, San Francisco, 1960-64, Parsons-Brinckerhoff-Tudor-Bechtel, San Francisco, 1964-66; realtor Coldwell Banker, Walnut Creek, Calif., 1980-81; profl. artist, 1981—; lectr. on pastels, 1991—. Solo shows include Artist Alley, San Francisco, 1971, San Francisco Coop. Gallery, 1973, New Masters Gallery, Walnut Creek, Calif., 1974, Beecher Room Gallery, Calif., 1991, 94, Tuttle Masion Gallery, Alburn, Calif., 1991, Old Ch. Gallery, Meadow Vista, Calif., 1991, Graphic Designs Gallery, Old Town Alburn, Calif., 1993, Placer County Civic Arts League, Auburn, 1994; group shows include Las Juntas Artists, Pleasant Hill, Calif. 1988 (2d place award), 88 (hon. mention), Scaramento Fine Arts Ctr., 1989, 90, 92, 93, 94, League of Carmichael Artists Exhibition, 1993, AAUW Annual Exhibition, 1993, Pastel Soc. of the West Coast Exhibition, 1988, 89, 90, 91, 92, 93, 94, Placer Arts League Exhibition, 1991 (hon. mention), 93, 94; represented in permanent collections throughout U.S. and Europe. Recipient awards for oil and pastel paintings. Fellow Royal Soc. Arts (London); mem. Pastel Soc. West Coast (signature mem., pres. 1989-91, bd. dirs. 1988—, mem. adv. bd. 1991—, editor quar. newsletter 1991—), Nat. Mus. Women in Arts, Placer Arts League, Soc. Western Artists, ArtCetera. Home and Studio: 1250 Grizzly Flat Ct Auburn CA 95603-5835

BLANKENSHIP, DALE CLIFFORD, electrical engineer; b. Dayton, Ohio, Apr. 22, 1957; s. George Willard and Dordeen Harriet (Holland) B.; m. Patricia Mae Dory, Aug. 14, 1982; children: Dory Leigh, Timothy Paul. BSEE, Ariz. State U., 1981. Hardware engr. Phoenix Digital Corp., 1981-83; sr. engr. Lee Data Corp., Scottsdale, Ariz., 1983-87, Motorola Inc., Tempe, Ariz., 1987—.

BLANKFORT, LOWELL ARNOLD, newspaper publisher; b. N.Y.C., Apr. 29, 1926; s. Herbert and Gertrude (Butler) B.; m. April Pemberton; 1 child, Jonathan. BA in History and Polit. Sci., Rutgers U., 1946. Reporter, copy editor L.I. (N.Y.) Star-Jour., 1947-49; columnist London Daily Mail, Paris, 1949-50; copy editor The Stars & Stripes, Darmstadt, Germany, 1950-51, Wall St. Jour., N.Y.C., 1951; bus., labor editor Cowles Mags., N.Y.C., 1951-53; pub. Pacifica (Calif.) Tribune, 1954-59; free-lance writer, Europe, Asia, 1959-61; co-pub., editor Chula Vista (Calif.) Star-News, 1961-78; co-owner Paradise (Calif.) Post, 1977—, Monte Vista (Colo.) Jour., Ctr. (Colo.) Post-Dispatch, Del Norte (Colo.) Prospector, 1978-93, Plainview (Minn.) News, St. Charles (Minn.) Press, Lewiston (Minn.) Jour., 1980—, Summit (Colo.) Sentinel, New Richmond (Wis.) News, 1981-87, Yuba City Valley Herald, Calif., 1982-85, TV Views, Monterey, Calif., 1982-87, Summit County Jour., Colo., 1982-87, Alpine (Calif.) Sun, 1987-93. Columnist, contbr. articles on fgn. affairs to newspapers. Mem. Calif. Dem. Cen. Com., 1963. Named Outstanding Layman of Yr. Sweetwater Edn. Assn., 1966, Citizen of Yr. City of Chula Vista, 1976, Headliner of Yr. San Diego Press Club, 1980. Mem. ACLU (pres. San Diego chpt. 1970-71), Calif. Newspaper Pubs. Assn., World Affairs Council San Diego (dir.), Ctr. Internat. Policy (bd. dirs. 1991—), Internat. Ctr. Devel. Policy (nat. bd. 1985-90), UN Assn. (pres. San Diego chpt. 1991-93, nat. coun. 1992—), World Federalist Assn. (nat. bd., pres. San Diego chpt. 1984-86), Soc. Profl. Journalists, East Meets West Found. (nat. exec. bd. 1992—), Inst. of the Ams. (assoc. 1989—, mem. internat. coun. 1994—). Home: Old Orchard Ln Bonita CA 91902 Office: 315 4th Ave Ste S Chula Vista CA 91910-3816

BLANTON, JOHN ARTHUR, architect; b. Houston, Jan. 1, 1928; s. Arthur Alva and Caroline (Jeter) B.; m. Marietta Louise Newton, Apr. 10, 1954 (dec. 1976); children: Jill Blanton Lewis, Lynette Blanton Rowe, Elena Diane. BA, Rice U., 1948, BS in Architecture, 1949. With Richard J. Neutra, Los Angeles, 1950-64; pvt. practice architecture, Manhattan Beach, Calif., 1964—; lectr. UCLA Extension, 1967-76, 85, Harbor Coll., Los Angeles, 1970-72. Archtl. columnist Easy Reader, 1994. Mem. Capital Improvements Com., Manhattan Beach, 1966, city commr. Bd. Bldg. Code Appeals; chmn. Zoning Adjustment Bd., 1990; active Planning Commn., 1993. Served with Signal Corps, U.S. Army, 1951-53. Recipient Best House of Year award C. of C., 1969, 70, 71, 83, Preservation of Natural Site award, 1974, design award, 1975, 84. Mem. AIA (contbr. book revs. to jour. 1972-76, recipient Red Cedar Shingle/AIA nat. merit award 1979). Designed nine bldgs. included in L.A.: An Architectual Guide; works featured in L'architettura mag., 1988; design philosophy included in American Architects (Les Krantz), 1989. Office: John Blanton AIA Architect 1456 12th St # 4 Manhattan Beach CA 90266-6113

BLASDALE, ALLAN WALTER, organist, choirmaster, pianist; b. Berkeley, Calif., July 5, 1953; s. Herbert Halsey and Jean Bevans (Coolbaugh) B. BA in Music, U. Calif., Berkeley, 1976; postgrad., Ch. Div. Sch. of Pacific, 1980. Organist Centennial Presbyn. Ch., Oakland, Calif., 1971-72; organist, choirmaster North Congl. Ch., Berkeley, 1972-83; organist Ch. Div. Sch. of Pacific, Berkeley, 1978-80; dir. music Ch. of Advent of Christ the King, San Francisco, 1983-87, Holy Innocents Ch., San Francisco, 1987-88; min. music First Congl. Ch., San Francisco, 1988-91, St. Stephen's Episcopal Ch., Orinda, Calif., 1991-92; dir. music Pilgrim Congl. Ch., Walnut Creek, Calif., 1976-92, Calvary United Meth. Ch., San Francisco, 1993—; with Nat. Park Svc., San Francisco, 1993—; ranger Alcatraz Island, Golden Gate Nat. Recreation Area, San Francisco, 1994—; concert organist, 1972—. Mem. Am. Guild Organists, Nat. Parks and Conservation Assn., Nat. Space Soc., Nat. Trust for Historic Preservation, Yosemite Assn., Planetary Soc., Calif. History Soc., Assn. Nat. Park Rangers. Democrat. Home: 1400 Mcallister St Apt 17 San Francisco CA 94115-4541

BLASE, NANCY GROSS, librarian; b. New Rochelle, N.Y.; d. Albert Philip and Elsie Wise (May) Gross; m. Barrie Wayne Blase, June 19, 1966 (div.); 1 child, Eric Wayne. BA in Biology, Marietta (Ohio) Coll., 1964; MLS, U. Ill., 1965. Info. scientist brain info. svc. Biomed. Libr., UCLA, 1965-66; libr. Health Sci. Libr., U. Wash., Seattle, 1966-68, Medlars search analyst, 1970-72, coord. Medline, 1972-79, head Natural Scis. Libr., 1979—; mem. libr. adv. com. Elizabeth C. Miller Libr., Ctr. for Urban Horticulture, Seattle, 1986—. Contbr. articles to profl. jours. NSF fellow interdept. tng. program for sci. info. specialists U. Ill., 1964-65. Mem. Am. Soc. for Info. Sci. (pres. personal computer spl. interest group 1993-94, rsch. grantee Pacific N.W. chpt. 1984-85), Geosci. Info. Soc., Coun. Bot. and Hort. Librs. (bylaws com. 1992—), Internat. Tng. in Comm. (pres. Pacific N.W. region 1994-95), Phi Beta Kappa (pres. Wash. Alpha chpt. 1993-94). Office: U Wash FM-25 Natural Scis Libr Seattle WA 98195

BLASGEN, SHARON WALTHER, lawyer; b. Bremerton, Wash., Apr. 12, 1942; d. William Edwin and Helen (Sobiegray) Walther; m. Michael William Blasgen, Sept. 10, 1965; children: Alexandra Helen, Nicholas William McKenna. BA, Scripps Coll., Claremont, Calif., 1964; JD, U. Calif., Berkeley, 1967. Bar: Calif. 1969, N.Y. 1970, D.C. 1983, U.S. Ct. Appeals (9th cir.), U.S. Dist. Ct. (no. and so. dists.) Calif., U.S. Dist. Ct. (so. dist.) N.Y. Law clk. Calif. Ct. Appeal, San Francisco, 1967-69; atty. IBM Corp., Armonk, N.Y., 1969-72; counsel, asst. sec. IBM World Trade Corp., N.Y.C., 1972-74; area counsel IBM Corp., San Jose, Calif., 1974-79; regional counsel IBM Corp., Washington, 1979-83; div. counsel IBM Corp., White Plains, N.Y., 1983-86, asst. group counsel, 1986-88; assoc. gen. counsel IBM Corp., Somers, N.Y., 1988-93; gen. coun. SSD, San Jose, Calif., 1993—; vol. atty. Westchester Legal Aid Soc., White Plains, 1971—; bd. dirs. Calif. Employment Law Coun. Bd. dirs. Boy Scouts of Westchester/Putnam, White Plains, 1989-91. Elected to YWCA Internat. Acad. Women Achievers, 1993. Mem. Penninsula Area Gen. Counsel's Orgn. Home: 17418 Paseo Carmelo Los Gatos CA 95032-6467 Office: 5600 Cottle Rd San Jose CA 95123-3696

BLASOR-BERNHARDT, DONNA JO, screenwriter, poet, author, photographer; b. Pittsburg, Kans., May 8, 1944; d. Donald Archie and Bessie Beryl (Tatham) Blasor; m. Richard Wayne Bernhardt, Oct. 29, 1964 (dec. Feb. 1987); children: Erik Wayne, Katherine Elizabeth. Student, U. Alaska, Anchorage, 1963-64. Reporter, poet Mukluk News Paper, Tok, Alaska, 1977—; interior, coord., technical advisor Alaska Nitty Gritty Dirty Band Alcan Caravan, 1992—; interior coord. Up With People Internat. Show, 1992, 94; interior Alaska coord. and tech. advisor Nitty Gritty Dirt Band Alcan Caravan TV spl., 1992. Author: (books) A Tent in Tok, 1980, More...A Tent in Tok, 1982, Friends of the Tent in Tok, 1987, (short story) K'hann De G'hann, 1989 (1st pl. adult writing 1989), (book) Beyond the Tent in Tok, 1990, The Tent, 1991, Before the Tent in Tok, 1992, Love and the Tent in Tok, 1994, Going to the End of the World, 1992, (audio tape mus. drama) Gettysburg, Fields of Love and Honor, 1993; writer featured story (TV) Paul Harvey's News and Commentary, 1978; featured writer Alaska's S.W. Regional Newsletter, Juneau, 1985, Sta. WAMU Pub. Radio, 1990; featured profile writer Fairbanks (Alaska) Northland News, 1985; featured guest Senator Frank Murkowski's Show, 1988, CBS TV Night Watch, 1989, Tok River Fire Exhibit Dedication, 1992, Channel 11-TV News, Anchorage, 1992, KTVA-TV Norma Goodman Show, Anchorage, 1992, 10th Ann. show Highway Daze, 1992; featured profiles in various publs.; contbr. articles, short stories and poetry pub. in Anchorage Times, Anchorage News, Haiku Highlights, Copper River Jour., Delta News, Mukluk News, Fairbanks Northland News, State of Alaska Newsletter, Divsn. of Forestry, Country mag., Fireweed Jour., Bell's Alaska/Yukon Travel Guide, Alaska Mag., The S.C. Observer, Seattle Times, Santa Monica Daily Breeze, Ark. Dem. Gazette, Chgo. Daily News, Angoon Yearbook, Gettysburg Times, RV Today. Named winner of Alaska State Diving Championship, 1958-62, Poet Laureate, 1990, Internat. Woman of Yr., Internat. Biol. Ctr., 1991-92, Poet Laureate of the Alaska Hwy., 1994; recipient 1st pl. Tok River Fire Writing Competition, 1990, 1st pl. Tok River Wildfire Photo Competition, 1990. Named Poet Laureate of the Alaska Highway, 1990, 1994; winners of Alaska State Diving Championship, 1958-62, Internat. Biological Ctr. Internat. Woman of Yr., 1991-92; recipient 1st pl. Tok River Fire Writing Competition, 1990, 1st pl. Tok River Wildfire Photo Competition, 1990. Office: A Tent in Tok Winter Cabin Prodns PO Box 110 Tok AK 99780-0110

BLATCHFORD, EDGAR PLEASANT, editor, publisher; b. Alaska, Nov. 24, 1950; s. Ernest and Lena Lois (Pleasant) B. BA in Social Sci., Alaska Meth. U., 1973; JD, U. Wash., 1976; MS in Journalism, Columbia U., 1988. Chmn. bd. Chugach Alaska Corp., Anchorage, 1979-83, 83-85, 89-91; editor, pub. The Seward (Alaska) Phoenix Log, 1984-91, Alaska Newspapers, Inc., 1989-91; commr. Alaska Dept. Community and Regional Affairs, Juneau, Alaska, 1991-94; vis. asst. prof. Coll. Rural Alaska, U. Alaska, Fairbanks, 1995—; bd. dirs. Alaska Bond Bank Authority, Alaska Housing Fin. Corp., Alaska Indsl. Devel. and Export Authority, Alaska Job Tng. Coun.; chmn. State Rural Devel. Coun. Mem. Nat. Coun. UN Assn., N.Y.C., 1994; trustee Alaska Pacific U., Anchorage, 1985—. Mem. Alaska Press Club, Alaska Newspaper Assn., Alaska Press Women. Home: PO Box 1344 Seward AK 99664-1344

BLATT, MELANIE JUDITH, small business owner, broker; b. Phila., Sept. 29, 1946; d. Jack and Rose (Ginsburg) Weinberger; children: Marnie, Keath, Lindsay. BA, Antioch U., 1980; MA, U. Phoenix, 1989. Cert. human service worker. Social worker Dept. Pub. Welfare Pa., Doylestown, 1977-80; mgr. customer service Qualidine Inc., Lansdale, Pa., 1980-81; sales rep. Sharp Products, Tempe, Ariz., 1982-83, Hobart Corp., Tempe, 1984-92; pres. Merit Enterprises, Fountain Hills, Ariz., 1992—. Bd. dirs. Bucks County Jewish Family Service, Bucks City, 1982. Mem. Retail Grocers Assn. Ariz., U. Phoenix Alumni Network (bd. dirs.). Home: 14637 N Winston Ln Fountain Hills AZ 85268-2338 Office: Merit Enterprises 16605 E Palisades Blvd Ste 124 Fountain Hills AZ 85268

BLATT, MORTON BERNARD, medical illustrator; b. Chgo., Jan. 9, 1923; s. Arthur E. and Hazel B. Student Central YMCA Coll., 1940-42, U. Ill., 1943-46. Tchr., Ray-Vogue Art Schs., Chgo., 1946-51; med. illustrator VA Center, Wood, Wis., 1951-57, Swedish Covenant Hosp., Chgo., 1957-76; med. illustrator Laidlaw Bros., River Forest, Ill., 1956-59; cons., artist health textbooks, 1956-59; illustrator Standard Edn. Soc., Chgo., 1960; art editor Covenant Home Altar, 1972-83, Covenant Companion, 1958-82. Served with USAAF, 1943-44. Mem. Art Inst. Chgo. Club: Chgo. Press. Illustrator: Atlas and Demonstration Technique of the Central Nervous System, also numerous med. jours.; illustrator, designer Covenant Hymnal, books, record jackets. Address: PO Box 489 Mill Valley CA 94942-0489

BLATTNER, MEERA MCCUAIG, computer science educator; b. Chgo., Aug. 14, 1930; d. William D. McCuaig and Nina (Spertus) Klevs; m. Minao Kamegai, June 22 1985; children: Douglas, Robert, William. BA, U. Chgo., 1952; MS, U. So. Calif., 1966; PhD, UCLA, 1973 . Rsch. fellow in computer sci. Harvard U., 1973-74; asst. prof. Rice U., 1974-80; assoc. prof. applied sci. U. Calif. at Davis, Livermore, 1980-91, prof. applied sci., 1991—; adj. prof. U. Tex., Houston, 1977—; vis. prof. U. Paris, 1980; program dir. theoretical computer sci. NSF, Washington, 1979-80. Co-editor: (with R. Dannenberg) Multimedia Interface Design, 1992. NSF grantee, 1977-81, 93—. Mem. Soc. Women Engrs., Assn. Computing Machinery, IEEE Computer Soc. Contbr. articles to profl. jours. Office: U Calif Davis/Livermore Dept Applied Sci Livermore CA 94550

BLAWIE, JAMES LOUIS, law educator; b. Newark, Mar. 26, 1928; s. Louis Paul and Cecelia Ruth (Grish) B.; m. Marilyn June Beyerle, May 30, 1952; children: Elias J., Cecelia R., Christiana L. BA, U. Conn., 1950; AM, Boston U., 1951, PhD, 1959; JD, U. Chgo., 1955. Bar: Conn. 1956, Calif. 1965, U.S. Dist. Ct. (no. dist.) Calif. 1965, U.S. Ct. Appeals (9th cir.) 1967, U.S. Supreme Ct. 1968. Instr. polit. sci. Mich. State U., East Lansing, 1955; assoc. prof. U. Akron, Ohio, 1956-57, Kent State U., 1956-57; asst. prof. bus. law U. Calif., Berkeley, 1958-60; assoc. prof. law Santa Clara U., Calif., 1960-63, prof. law, 1963—; vis. prof. polit. sci. Calif. State U., Hayward, 1966-67; adminstrv. law judge U.S. Equal Employment Opportunity Commn., Washington, 1982-85; complaints examiner U.S. Equal Employment Opportunity Agy., Office Equal Employment Opportunity; cons. in field. Author: (handbook) The Michigan Township Board, 1957; contbr. articles to profl. jours. Mem. Citizen's Adv. Com. on Capital Improvements, 1962-65; bd. dirs. Washington Hosp., 1964-68. Maj. U.S. Army, 1963-74. Boston U. Faculty fellow, 1951-53; U. Chgo. Law Sch. scholar, 1953-55; grantee Mich. State U. grantee, 1955-56, Helsinki Govt. Ministry Edn. grantee, 1980-81. Mem. ABA, Fairfield County Bar Assn., Mensa. Republican. Home: 41752 Marigold Dr Fremont CA 94539-4779 also: PO Box 1102 Fremont CA 94538-0110 Office: Santa Clara U Sch Law Santa Clara CA 95053

BLAYLOCK, CHET, state legislator; Mem. Mont. State Senate, 43d Dist., Helena. Home: 502 3rd Ave Laurel MT 59044-2441

BLEIBERG, LEON WILLIAM, surgical podiatrist; b. Bklyn., June 9, 1932; s. Paul Pincus and Helen (Epstein) B.; m. Beth Daigle, June 7, 1970; children: Kristina Noel, Kelley Lynn, Kimberly Ann, Paul Joseph. Student, L.A. City Coll., 1950-51, U. So. Calif., 1951, Case Western Res. U., 1951-53; DSc with honors, Temple U., 1955; PhD, U. Beverly Hills, 1970. Served rotating internship various hosps., Phila., 1954-55; resident various hosps., Montebello, L.A., 1956-58; surg. podiatrist So. Calif. Podiatry Group, Westchester (Calif.), L.A., 1956-75; health care economist, researcher Drs. Home Health Care Svcs., 1976—; podiatric cons. U. So. Calif. Athletic Dept., Morningside and Inglewood (Calif.) High Schs., Internet Corp., Royal Naval Assn., Long Beach, Calif. Naval Sta.; lectr. in field; healthcare affiliate Internat. div. CARE/ASIA, 1987; pres. Medica, Totalcare, Cine-Medics Corp., and World-Wide Health Care Svcs.; exec. dir. Internat. Health Trust, developer Health Banking Program; adminstr. Orthotic Concepts, 1993. Producer (films) The Gun Hawk, 1963, Terrified, Day of the Nightmare; contbr. articles to profl. jours. Hon. Sheriff Westchester 1962-64; commd. mem. Rep. Senatorial Inner Circle, 1984-86; co-chmn. health reform com. United We Stand Am., Thousand Oaks, Calif.; mem. exec. coun. State of Calif., United We Stand Am.; active 1st Security and Safety, Westlake Village, Calif., 1993—; lt. comdr. med. svcs. corps Brit.-Am. Sea Cadet Corps, 1984—; track coach Westlake High Sch., Westlake Village. With USN, 1955-56. Recipient Medal of Merit, U.S. Presdl. Task Force. Mem. Philippine Hosp. Assn. (Cert. of Appreciation 1964, trophy for Outstanding Svc. 1979), Calif. Podiatry Assn. (hon.), Am. Podiatric Med. Assn. (hon.), Acad. TV Arts and Scis., Royal Soc. Health (Eng.), Western Foot Surgery Assn., Am. Coll. Foot Surgeons, Am. Coll. Podiatric Sports Medicine, Internat. Coll. Preventive Medicine, Hollywood Comedy Club, Sts. and Sinners Club, Westchester C. of C., Hals Und Beinbruch Ski Club, Beach Cities Ski Club, Orange County Stamp Club, Las Virgenes Track Club, Masons, Shriners.

BLEMKER, MARGARET RUTH, educator, world mission executive; b. New Bremen, Ohio, Apr. 2, 1915; d. Rudolf William and Lillian (Kohl) B. BA, Heidelberg Coll., Tiffin, Ohio, 1936, LHD (hon.), 1958; MEd, Syracuse U., 1942. Tchr. North Canton (Ohio) High Sch., 1936-39, Timken Voc. High Sch., Canton, 1939-40, Amerikan Kiz Koleji, Izmir, Turkey, 1945-48; dir. residences Univ. Hosps., Cleve., 1942-45; Near East exec. United Ch. Bd. for World Ministries, Boston, N.Y.C., 1949-80. Mem. AAUW, LWV. Democrat. Mem. United Church of Christ.

BLESSING-MOORE, JOANN CATHERINE, physician; b. Tacoma, Wash., Sept. 21, 1946; d. Harold R. and Mildred (Benson) Blessing; m. Robert Chester Moore; 1 child, Ahna. BA in Chemistry, Syracuse U., 1968; MD, SUNY, Syracuse, 1972. Diplomate Am. Bd. Pediatrics, Am. Bd. Allergy Immunology, Am. Bd. Pediatric Pulmonology. Pediatric intern, then resident Stanford U. Sch. Medicine, Palo Alto, Calif., 1972-75, allergy pulmonology fellow, 1975-77; co-dir. pediatric allergy pulmonology dept. Stanford U. Children's Hosp., Palo Alto, Calif., 1977-84; clin. asst. prof. dept. pediatrics Stanford U. Sch. Medicine, Palo Alto, Calif., 1977-84, co-dir. pediatric pulmonology lab., 1977-84; clin. asst. prof. dept. immunology Stanford U. Hosp., 1984—; allergist Palo Alto Med. Clinic, 1984-90; pvt. practice allergy immunology-pediatric-pulmonary Palo Alto, Calif., 1990—; dir. ednl. program for children with asthma Camp Wheeze, Palo Alto, 1975—; cons. FDA, 1992—; cons. in field. Author handbooks, camp program manuals; co-editor jour. supplements; mem. edit. bd. Allergy jours.; contbr. articles to sci. publs. Fellow Am. Acad. Allergy Immunology (various offices 1980—, Task Force devel. parameters of care in allergy, 1989—), Am. Coll. Chest Physicians (com. mem. 1980—), Am. Acad. Pediatrics (mem. com. 1980—), Am. Coll. Allergy Immunology; mem. Am. Thoracic Soc., Am. Lung Assn., No. Calif. Allergy Found. (bd. dirs., pres.), Peninsula Women's Assn., Santa Clara and San Mateo County Med. Soc., Chi Omega. Republican. Presbyterian. Office: 770 Welch Rd Ste 232 Palo Alto CA 94304-1513 also: 100 S Ellsworth # 309 San Mateo CA 94402-1516 also: Stanford Univ Hosp Dept Immunology Palo Alto CA 94304

BLEVINS, BRUCE ALLYN, electrical engineer; b. Los Alamos, N.Mex., Jan. 7, 1951; s. David Jesse and Janice (Hazard) B.; m. Geri T. Murphy, Jan. 24, 1978; children: Joanie, Jessi. BS in Mathematics, N.Mex. Inst. Mining & Tech., 1972, MS in Physics, 1975; PhD. in Elec. Engring., N.Mex. State U., 1978. Rsch. assoc. N.Mex. Solar Energy Inst., Las Cruces, 1978-79; sr. engr. Physical Sci. Lab., Las Cruces, 1980-83, 85-88; adj. prof. N.Mex. State U., Las Cruces, 1980-83; instrumentation engr. N.Mex. Inst. Mining & Tech., Socorro, 1983-85; dir. rsch. and devel. Xytec Group, US Enertek, Farmington, N.Mex., 1983-88; owner Tesota Products, 1989—; sr. scientist Amparo Corp., Santa Fe, 1989-92; sr. engr. GTE, La Cruces, 1992—. Contbr. articles to profl. jours. Mem. IEEE. Democrat. Home: 4110 Tesota Dr Las Cruces NM 88011-7647 Office: GTE PO Box 235 Las Cruces NM 88004

BLEVINS, BRYAN O'DONNELL, management consultant, dentist; b. Baytown, Tex., July 19, 1939; s. Arthur Buster and Ollie (Norris) B.; m. Doris Vaughn, Feb. 15, 1964, (div. July 1989); children: Bryan O. Jr., Jaime D'Lea; m. Sandra Talley, Oct. 28, 1989; 1 stepchild, Talley Sullivan. BS, Northeast U., 1961; DDS, Baylor College of Denistry, 1965. Pvt. practice, 1965—; ptnr. Blevins, Rose Dental Group, 1965—; comml. real estate developer Oakhill Investors, Blevco Resources, 1967—; owner, gen. mgr. Gulf Coast Beverage, Tex., 1977-82; chief exec. officer and pres. Blevco Energy, Fairway Royalty, 1981—; lic. owner-operator casino properties Deadwood, S.D., 1989—; gen. ptnr. Full House Gaming Ltd. Casino Mgmt.; CEO, pres., vice chmn. Dion Entertainment, 1993-94. Mem. E. Tex. Producers and Royalty Assn. (v.p.), Stephen F. Austin State U. Alumni Assn. (pres., pres. alumni found.), Am. Affiliated Cons.

BLEVINS, SANDRA KAYE, director senior citizens facility; b. Alamosa, Colo., Nov. 15, 1943; d. Bernarr DePriest and Theda Louise (Nance) Earheart; m. Kenneth Daniel Kothe, June 24, 1961 (div. 1966); children: Kelly Douglas Kothe (dec.), Kendra Denise Bartee; m. Bill J. Blevins, Nov. 5, 1970; children: Jennifer Kay Blevins Jones, Rebecca Gail Blevins. Student, Barnes Sch. of Commerce, 1961-62. Asst. dir. Alamosa Sr. Citizens, Alamosa, 1979-85; personal property clk. Alamosa County Assessors, Alamosa, 1985-88; activity dir. San Luis Care Ctr., Alamosa, 1988-91; dir. Alamosa Sr. Citizens, Alamosa, 1991—; ombudsman 6 nursing homes, 1 asst. living State of Colo., various counties, 1992—; mem. adv. bd. San Luis Care Ctr., Alamosa, 1990—; mem. adult protection team Alamosa County Dept. Social Svcs., Alamosa, 1992—. Mem. Colo. Activity Profl. Assn. (past pres. S.W. chpt.), Alamosa County Nursing Assn., (pres. 1992—), Am. Legion Aux. (sec., chaplain). Democrat. Baptist. Home: 719 Graf Dr Alamosa CO 81101-2031 Office: Alamosa Sr Citizens Inc 509 First PO Box 1007 Alamosa CO 81101

BLEVINS, WILLARD AHART, electrical engineer; b. Jonben, W.Va., Nov. 20, 1949; s. Oakley Cameron and Peggy Jane (Agee) B.; m. Nancy Phyllis Bailey, June 26, 1971; children: Maria Dawn, Teresa Lynn. AA in Elec. Tech. with honors, N.D. State Sch. Sci., 1974; BSEE with honors, Ariz. State U., 1988. Technician Sperry Flight Systems, Phoenix, 1974-88; engr. Sperry/Honeywell, Phoenix, 1988—. Patentee out of lock detector. With USAF, 1968-72. Named Parent of Yr., Phoenix Children's Chorus, 1985. Home: 15810 N 47th Ln Glendale AZ 85306-2602 Office: Honeywell PO Box 21111-w33C Phoenix AZ 85036

BLIESNER, JAMES DOUGLAS, municipal/county official, consultant; b. Milw., Mar. 19, 1945; s. Milton Carl and Dorothy (St. George) B.; m. Phyllis Jean Byrd, June 15, 1966 (div. 1985); children: Tris, Cara. BA in Philosophy, Ea. Nazarene Coll., 1968; MA in Social Ethics, Andover Newton Theol. Sch., 1973; postgrad., Boston U., 1969-70; student, N.Y. Studio Sch./Delordoua, Mus. Sch., Milw. Tech. Art Sch. Exec. dir. San Diego Youth and Community Svcs., 1974-78; cons., analyst San Diego Housing Commn., 1979-84; dir. San Diego City-County Reinvestment Task Force, 1984—; bd. dirs. Calif. Community Reinvestment Corp.; vice chmn. Calif. Reinvestment Com., 1989—; founder, chmn. City Heights Community Devel. Corp., San Diego, 1980-89; fin. com. chairperson Mid-City Revitalization Com., San Diego, 1988. Author monographs, 1979; exhbns. include San Diego Arts Inst., Soc. Western Artists, Santa Barbara Contemporay Arts Forum, Calif. Coun. for Humanities; films exhibited in Centro Cultural, Tijuana, Mexico, Venice, Paris, Jerusalem, Mexico, Eng., China exhbns. Coun. appointee City of San Diego Com. on Reapportionment, 1990, Com. on Growth and Devel., San Diego, 1989; gov. appointee Gov.'s Office of Neighborhoods, Calif., 1987; mem. City Heights Redevel. Project Com., San Diego, 1992. Recipient Award of Honor, Am. Planning Assn., 1987, Spl. Project award, 1987, Merit award, 1989; named Citizen of Yr. Mid-City C. of C., 1986, award Calif. Coun. Humanities. Mem. Urban Land Inst. Methodist. Home: 4106 Manzanita Dr San Diego CA 92105-4508 Office: City County Reinvestment Task Force 1600 Pacific Hwy # A6 San Diego CA 92101-2429

BLINDER, JANET, art dealer; b. L.A., Sept. 21, 1953; d. Joseph and Margaret (Nadel) Weiss; m. Martin S. Blinder, Dec. 10, 1983. Founder Nationwide Baby Shops, Santa Monica, Calif., 1976-82; adminstr. Martin Lawrence Ltd. Editions, Van Nuys, Calif., 1982-90; art dealer L.A., 1990—. Mem. benefit com. AIDS Project L.A., 1988, prin. sponsor ann. fundraiser, 1990; mem. benefit com. Art Against AIDS, L.A., 1989; patron, sponsor Maryvale Orphanage, Rosemead, Calif., 1984—. Recipient Commendation for Philanthropic Efforts City of L.A. Mayor Tom Bradley, 1988. Mem. Mus. Modern Art, Whitney Mus. Am. Art, Guggenheim Mus., Palm Springs Mus. Art, Mus. of Contemporary Art (founder).

BLINDER, MARTIN S., business consultant, art dealer; b. Bklyn., Nov. 18, 1946; s. Meyer and Lillian (Stein) B.; m. Janet Weiss, Dec. 10, 1983. BBA, Adelphi U., 1968. Account exec. Bruns, Nordeman & Co., N.Y.C., 1968-69; v.p. Blinder, Robinson & Co., Westbury, N.Y., 1969-73; treas. BHB Prodns., L.A., 1973-76; pres. Martin Lawrence Ltd. Edits., Van Nuys, Calif., 1976-94, chmn., 1986-94, bd. dirs., 1994—; pres., dir. Corp. Art Inc., Visual Artists Mgmt. Corp., Art Consultants Inc.; lectr. bus. symposia. Contbr. articles to mags. and newspapers; appeared on TV and radio. Mem. Dem. Nat. Com.; mem. benefit com. AIDS project, L.A., 1988; bd. dirs. Very Spl. Arts, 1989—, chmn. visual arts Internat. Very Spl. Arts Festival, 1989; patron Guggenheim Mus., N.Y.C., Mus. Modern Art, N.Y.C., L.A. County Mus. Art, L.A. Mus. Contemporary Art (hon. founder), Whitney Mus. Am. Art, Palm Springs Mus. Art, Hirschhorn Mus., Washington, Skirball Mus., L.A., Diabetes Found. of City of Hope, B'nai B'rith Anti-Defamation League, Very Spl. Arts, Scottsdale Ctr. for the Arts; mem. Citizens for Common Sense; bd. dirs., pres. Rsch. Found. for Crohns Disease; mem. benefit com. Art Against AIDS, 1989; co-chair artists com. for Don't Bungle the Jungle Companions of Arts and Nature, 1989; prin. sponsor, ann. fundraiser AIDS Project, L.A., 1990. Read into Congl. Record, 1981, 83, 86, 88, 91; recipient resolution of commendation L.A. City Coun., 1983, State of Calif. resolution for contbn. to arts in Calif., 1983, Merit award Republic Haiti for contbn. to arts, 1985, U.S. Senate commendation, 1983, County of L.A. Bd. Suprs. resolution for Contbn. to arts in So. Calif., 1983, Gov. of R.I. resolution for contbns. to arts, 1985, commendation County of Los Angeles-Supr. Ed Edelman, 1991, commendation for contbns. to the arts and the healing arts City of L.A., 1991, commendation for contbns. to arts and philanthropy Mayor David Dinkins, N.Y.C., 1992; Nov. 18, 1985 declared Martin S. Blinder Day in L.A. in his honor by Mayor Tom Bradley. Mem. Fine Art Pub.'s Assn. (bd. dirs. 1990-94), Med. Art Assn. at UCLA. Office: MSB Fine Art 7000 E Shea Blvd # 1390 Scottsdale AZ 85254

BLISH, EUGENE SYLVESTER, trade association administrator; b. Denver, Oct. 9, 1912; s. George Joseph and Lillian Lenox (O'Neill) B.; m. Susan M. Monti, Feb. 21, 1950; children: Eugene A., Mary, Susan Blish Clarke, Julia Blish Gordon. BSC, U. Notre Dame, 1934. Advt. dir. Colo. Milling and Elevator Co., Denver, 1934-45; advt. and mktg. cons., Denver, 1945-57; asst. exec. dir. Am. Sheep Producers Council, Denver, 1957-74; merchandising rep. Nat. Potato Bd., Denver, 1974-87. Mem. alumni bd. dirs. U. Notre Dame, 1947-49. Mem. Soc. Mayflower Desc., Barnstable Hist. Soc. (Mass.). Clubs: Denver Athletic, Mt. Vernon Country, Denver Notre Dame. Home and Office: 1370 Madison St Denver CO 80206-2613

BLISS, EDWIN CROSBY, business executive, consultant; b. Salt Lake City, Feb. 15, 1923; s. Edwin S. and Naomi (Crosby) B.; m. Mary Elizabeth Miller, Jan. 21, 1956; children: Rebecca, William, Roger, Kevin. BS, U. Utah, 1949, MS, 1958. Cert. speaking profl. Reporter Salt Lake Tribune, Salt Lake City, 1947-48; Sunday mag. editor Deseret News, Salt Lake City, 1948-52; asst. dir. pub. relations U. Utah, Salt Lake City, 1952-54; Sunday mag. editor Columbus (Ohio) Dispatch, 1954-55; exec. asst. Senator Wallace F. Bennett, Washington, 1955-63; pub. affairs dir. Nat. Assn. Mfrs., Washington, 1963-77; cons. Edwin C. Bliss and Assocs., Kingsburg, Calif., 1973—. Author: Getting Things Done, 1976, Doing It Now, 1983. Contbr. articles to profl. jours. Served to lt. col. U.S. Army, 1944-46. Mem. Nat. Assn. Parliamentarians, Am. Inst. Parliamentarians (adv. council 1984—). Home and Office: Edwin C Bliss & Assocs 1550 Kamm Ave #119 Kingsburg CA 93631-1144

BLITZ, IRA ALLEN, obstetrician-gynecologist; b. Bklyn., July 4, 1944; s. Julius and Sylvia (Weprinsky) B.; m. Virginia Louise Johnson, June 9, 1974; children: Matthew, Daniel. BA, UCLA, 1966, MD, 1970. Intern UCLA Affiliated Hosps., 1970-71; resident Cedars-Sinai Med. Ctr., L.A., 1974-77; staff gynecologist Kaiser-Permanente, L.A., 1978-86, San Gabriel Valley, Calif., 1986—. Exec. v.p. Temple Shaarei Tikvah, Arcadia, Calif., 1987-91; ritual chmn. Congregation Shaarei Torah, Arcadia, 1994—. Fellow ACOG; mem. Am. Fertility Soc., L.A. Ob.-Gyn. Soc. Office: Kaiser-Permanente 1011 Baldwin Park Blvd Baldwin Park CA 91706-5806

BLITZ-WEISZ, SALLY, speech pathologist; b. Buffalo, Nov. 9, 1954; d. Isaac and Paula (Goldstein) Blitz; m. Andrew Weisz, Dec. 16, 1984; 1 child, Naomi Ariel Weisz. BA in Speech Pathology, Audiology, SUNY, Buffalo, 1976, MA in Speech Pathology, 1978; MS Sch Counseling, pupil pers credential, U. LaVerne, 1991. Lic. speech/lang. pathologist, Calif. Speech, lang. pathologist Lang. Devel. Program, Tonawanda, N.Y., 1978-82, Bailey and Drown Assocs., La Habra, Calif., 1982-83; speech, lang. specialist, cons. Pasadena (Calif.) Unified Schs., 1983—. Active Anti-Defamation League, San Fernando Valley, 1985-86; mem. 2d Generation Holocaust Survivors, Los Angeles, 1986—. Recipient Excellence in Studies award Temple Shaarey Zedek, Buffalo, 1968. Mem. Am. Speech-Lang.-Hearing Assn. Democrat. Club: Jewish Young Adults. Lodge: B'nai Brith. Home: 11671 Amigo Ave Northridge CA 91326-1849 Office: Pasadena Unified Sch Dist 351 S Hudson Ave Pasadena CA 91101-3507

BLIX, GLEN GARRY, preventive care educator; b. Central Butte, Can., Apr. 8, 1944; came to U.S., 1968; s. Rolf and Grace (Quigley) B.; m. Lorna Watts, Nov. 1963 (div. 1972); m. Arlene Jean Parrish; 1 child, Barton. BA, LaSierra U., 1970; MPH, Loma Linda U., 1984, DPH, 1987. Plant mgr. Loma Linda Foods, Mt. Vernon, Ohio, 1973-83; v.p. mfg. Loma Linda Foods, Riverside, Calif., 1983-86, v.p. rsch. and devel., 1986-87; dir. Loma Linda (Calif.) U., 1987-88, asst. prof. sch. pub. health, 1988—; cons. Nutrition, Riverside, 1988—, Worthington (Ohio) Foods, 1990—. Supr. LaLoma Credit Union, Loma Linda, 1988—. Mem. Sch. Pub. Health Alumni Assn. (pres. 1990-91), Delta Omega. Home: 690 N Temescal St Corona CA 91719-1123 Office: Loma Linda U Sch Of Public Health Loma Linda CA 92350

BLIZINSKY, MARLIN JOEL, lawyer; b. St. Paul, Dec. 16, 1947; s. Irwin M. and Jeannie (Weisberg) B.; m. Ellen E. Bert, Sept. 24, 1979; 1 child, Katherine D. BA, U. Minn., 1969; AM, U. Chgo., 1974; JD, U. Puget Sound Sch. Law, 1985. Bar: Wash. 1985. With King County Real Property Div., Seattle, 1986-90; mgr. King County Office Cable Comms., Seattle, 1990—; adj. prof. law Albers Sch. Bus., 1993—. Office: King County Office Cable Comms 700 5th Ave 23d Flr Seattle WA 98104

BLOCH, ERNEST, II, foundation administrator; b. Portland, Oreg., Nov. 15, 1938; s. Ivan and Mariana (Trotel) B.; m. Laurie M. Munro, Mar. 5, 1993; children by previous marriage: Peter Ernest, Suzanne M. Bloch-St. Clair. BS, Portland State U., 1961. Pricing mgr. Western Airlines, L.A., 1961-74; dir. pricing Tex. Internat., Houston, 1974-76; pres. Bus. Exch., Houston, 1976-79; v.p. Air Oreg., Portland, 1979-80; dir. corp. comms. NERCO, Portland, 1981-91; exec. dir. Pacific Corp. Found., Portland, 1991—. Treas. Chamber Music N.W. Portland, 1993—; citizen adviser St. Vincent Med. Hosp., Portland, 1992—; mem. adv. com. Oreg. Grad. Inst., Hillsboro, 1992—; advisor Portland Art Mus, 1995; mem. bus. mktg. com. Oreg. Symphony; staff, chair bd. dirs. 1998 World Masters Games. Mem. City Club of Portland, Grant Makers of Oreg. and S.W. Wash. (pres. 1993-94). Democrat. Jewish. Office: Pacific Corp Found 700 NE Multnomah 1600 Portland OR 97232

BLOCH, JULIA CHANG, bank executive, former government official; b. Chefoo, Peoples Republic of China, Mar. 2, 1942; came to U.S., 1951, naturalized, 1962; d. Fu-yun and Eva (Yeh) Chang; m. Stuart Marshall Bloch, Dec. 21, 1968. BA, U. Calif., Berkeley, 1964; MA, Harvard U., 1967, postgrad. in mgmt., 1987; DHL (hon.), Northeastern U., Boston, 1986. Vol. Peace Corps, Sabah, Malaysia, 1964-66, tng. officer East Asia and Pacific region, Washington, 1967-68, evaluation officer, 1968-70; mem. minority staff U.S. Senate Select Com. on Nutrition and Human Needs, Washington, 1971-76, chief minority counsel, 1976-77; dep. dir. Office of African Affairs, U.S. Internat. Comm. Agy., Washington, 1977-80; fellow Inst. Politics, Harvard U., Cambridge, Mass., 1980-81; asst. adminstr. Bur. for Food for Peace and Voluntary Assistance, AID, Washington, 1981-87, asst. adminstr. Bur. for Asia and Near East, 1987-88; assoc. U.S.-Japan Rels. Program, Ctr. for Internat. Affairs, Harvard U., Cambridge, Mass., 1988-89; ambassador to Kingdom of Nepal, 1989-93; group exec., v.p. Bank Am., San Francisco, 1993—; dir. Am. West Airlines, 1994—; trustee Eisenhower Exchange Fellowship, 1995—; U.S. Senate rep. World Conf. on Internat. Women's Yr., Mex., 1975; advisor U.S. Del. to Food and Agr. Orgn. Conf., Rome, 1975; rep. Am. Council Young Polit. Leaders, Peoples Republic China, 1977; charter mem. Sr. Exec. Svc., 1979; head U.S. del. Biennial Session World Food Programme, Rome, 1981-86, Devel. Assistance Com. Meeting on Non-Govtl. Orgns., Paris, 1985, Intergovtl. Group on Indonesia, The Hague, The Netherlands, 1987, World Bank Consultative Group Meeting, Paris, 1987, mem. exec. women in govt., 1988-93, mem. coun. fgn. rels., 1991—; mem. com. to visit art mus. Harvard U., 1989—; mem. U.S. Nat. Com. for Pacific Econ. Cooperation, 1984—; mem. adv. bd. Women's Campaign Fund, 1976-78, trustee, bus. leadership circle, 1994—; exec. bd. mem. Internat. Ctr. for Rsch. on Women, 1974-81; mem. presdl. adv. coun. Peace Corps, 1988-89; mem. Am. Himalayan Found. Bd., 1994, Am. Refugee Com. Bd., 1993—. Author: A U.S.-Japan Aid Alliance, 1991; co-author: Chinese Home Cooking, 1986; mem. Nat. Presdl. Debate Forum, 1987-92; mem. nat. adv. coun. Experiment in Internat. Living, 1981-83; commr. Asian Art Mus., San Francisco, 1994. Recipient Hubert Humphrey award for internat. svc., 1979, Humanitarian Svc. award AID, 1987, Leader for Peace award Peace Corps, 1987, Asian Am. Leadership award, 1989; named Outstanding Woman of Color, Nat. Inst. for Women of Color, 1982, Woman of Distinction, Nat. Conf. for Coll. Women Student Leaders and Women of Achievement, 1987, Woman of Yr. Orgn. Chinese Am. Women, 1987, Disting. Pub. Svc. award Nat. Assn. Profl. Asian Pacific Am. Women, 1989; Ford Found. Study fellow for internat. devel. Harvard U., 1966, Paul Harris award Rotary, 1992, Award of Honor Narcotic Enforcement Assn., 1992. Mem. Orgn. Chinese Am. Women (founder, chair 1977—, bd. dirs., Woman of Yr. 1987), Asia Soc. (pres. coun. 1989, trustee 1994), Prytannean Honor Soc., Coun. Fgn. Rels., Mortar Bd. Republican. Avocations: ceramics, gourmet cooking, collecting art. Office: Bank Am Corp Rels 8139 555 California St Ste 4730 San Francisco CA 94104-1502

BLOCK, MICHAEL KENT, economics and law educator, public policy association executive, former government official, consultant; b. N.Y.C., Apr. 2, 1942; s. Philip and Roslyn (Klein) B.; m. Carole Arline Polansky, Aug. 30, 1964; children: Robert Justin, Tamara Nicole. A.B., Stanford U., 1964, A.M., 1969, Ph.D., 1972. Research analyst Bank of Am., San Francisco, 1965-66; research assoc. Planning Assocs., San Francisco, 1966-67; asst. prof. econs. U. Santa Clara, 1969-72; asst. prof. econs. dept. ops. research and adminstrv. sci. Naval Postgrad. Sch., Monterey, Calif., 1972-74, assoc. prof., 1974-76; research fellow Hoover Instn., Stanford U., 1975-76, sr. research fellow, 1976-87; dir. Center for Econometric Studies of Justice System, 1977-81; ptnr. Block & Nold, Cons., Palo Alto, Calif., 1980-81; assoc. prof. mgmt., econs. and law U. Ariz., Tucson, 1982-85, prof. econs. and law, 1989—; mem. U.S. Sentencing Commn., Washington, 1985-89; exec. v.p. Cybernomics, Tucson, 1991—; pres. Goldwater Inst. for Pub. Policy, Phoenix, Ariz., 1992—; mem. Ariz. Residential Utility Consumer Bd., 1995—, chmn. Ariz. Constl. Defense Coun., 1994—; seminar dir. Econ. Devel. Inst./World Bank, 1992—; cons. in field. Author: (with H.G. Demmert) Workbook and Programmed Guide to Economics, 1974, 77, 80, (with James M. Clabault) A Legal and Economic Analysis of Criminal Antitrust Indictments:, 1955-80; contbr. articles to profl. publs. NSF fellow, 1965; Stanford U. fellow. Mem. Am. Econ. Assn., Phi Beta Kappa. Home: 2550 E Calle Los Altos Tucson AZ 85718-2062 Office: U Ariz Dept Econs Tucson AZ 85721

BLOCK, ROBERT JACKSON, investment banker; b. Seattle, Oct. 20, 1922; s. Max Harry and Esther Ida (Parker) B.; m. Dorothy Wolens, Aug. 11, 1946 (dec.); children: Jonathan, Adam, Daniel, Kenan, Susanna, Mary Judith; m. Mary Lou Moats, Dec. 26, 1972; children: Melinda Mulvaney, Newton Moats, Christina Moats, Tamara Moats. Student Stanford U., 1940-42, U. Wash., 1942-43. Asst. to pres. Block Shoe Stores, Inc., Seattle, 1946-56, pres., 1956-58; pres. Columbia-Cascade Securities Corp., Seattle, 1958-77; pres. Nat. Securities Corp., Seattle, 1977-80, chmn., chief exec. officer, 1980-85, founding dir., chmn. bd., 1985—; founding dir. North West Bank (merged with Old Nat. Bank); cons. Area Redevel. Adminstrn., 1961-62; exec. reservist policy secretariat Nat. Def. Exec. Res.; GSA, 1968—. Named to Seattle Ctr. Legion of Honor Seattle Ctr. Adv. Commn. & Seattle Ctr. Found., 1987. Pres. Block Found., Inc., Allied Arts Found.; former chmn. Puget Sound chpt. Nat. Found. March of Dimes; mem. nat. exec. council Am. Jewish Com.; former mem. Seattle Bd. Park Commrs.; chmn., dir. Cornish Inst., 1980-82; former trustee Pilchuck Sch., Stanwood, Wash.; bd. dirs. Seattle Pub. Library Found.; chmn. King County (Wash.) USO Com., 1950-52; chmn. Civic Ctr. Com., Seattle, 1954; co-chmn. Metro Campaign Com., Seattle, 1958, alt. del. Democratic Nat. Conv., 1956; King County co-chmn. Vols. for Stevenson, 1956; elected King County Freeholder, 1967. Mem. Wash. State Bar Assn. (fee arbitration panel, vis. cons.), College Club (Seattle), Rainier Club. Home: 1617 E Boston Ter Seattle WA 98112-2831 Office: Nat Securities Corp 1001 4th Ave Ste 2200 Seattle WA 98154-1101

BLODGETT, ELSIE GRACE, association executive; b. Eldorado Springs, Mo., Aug. 2, 1921; d. Charles Ishmal and Naoma Florence (Worthington) Robison; m. Charles Davis Blodgett, Nov. 8, 1940; children: Carolyn Doyel, Charleen Bier, Lyndon Blodgett, Daryl (dec.). Student Warrensburg (Mo.) State Tchrs. Coll., 1939-40; BA, Fresno (Calif.) State Coll., 1953. Tchr. schs. in Mo. and Calif., 1940-42, 47-72; owner, mgr. rental units, 1965—; exec. dir. San Joaquin County (Calif.) Rental Property Assn., Stockton, 1970-81; prin. Delta Rental Property Owners and Assocs., 1981-82; propr. Crystal Springs Health World, Inc., Stockton, 1980-86; bd. dirs. Stockton Better Bus. Bur. Active local PTA, Girl Scouts U.S., Boy Scouts Am.; bd. dirs. Stockton Goodwill Industries; active Vols. in Police Svc., 1993; capt. Delaware Alpine Neighborhood Watch, 1994—. Named (with husband) Mr. and Mrs. Apt. Owner of San Joaquin County, 1977. Mem. Nat. Apt. Assn. (state treas. women's div. 1977-79), Calif. Ret. Tchrs. Assn. Republican. Methodist. Lodge: Stockton Zonta. Home and Office: 2285 W Mendocino Ave Stockton CA 95204-4005

BLODGETT, FORREST CLINTON, economics educator; b. Oregon City, Oreg., Oct. 6, 1927; s. Clinton Alexander and Mabel (Wells) B.; m. Beverley Janice Buchholz, Dec. 21, 1946; children: Cherine (Mrs. Jon R. Klein), Candis Melis, Clinton George. BS, U. Omaha, 1961; MA, U. Mo., 1969; PhD, Portland State U., 1979. Joined C.E. U.S. Army, 1946, commd. 2d lt., 1946, advanced through grades to lt. col., 1965, ret., 1968; engring. assignments U.S. Army, Japan, 1947-49, U.K., 1950-53, Korea, 1955-56, Alaska, 1958-60, Vietnam, 1963; staff engr. 2d Army Air Def. Region U.S. Army, Richards-Gebaur AFB, Mo., 1964-66; base engr. Def. Atomic Support Agy., Sandia Base, N.Mex., 1966-68; bus. mgr., trustee, asst. prof. econs. Linfield Coll., McMinnville, Oreg., 1968-73, assoc. prof., 1973-83, prof., 1983-90, emeritus prof. econs., 1990—; pres. Blodgett Enterprises, Inc., 1983-85; founder, dir. Valley Community Bank, 1980-86, vice chmn. bd. dirs., 1985-86. Commr., Housing Authority of Yamhill County (Oreg.), chmn., 1980-83; mem. Yamhill County Econ. Devel. Com., 1978-83; bd. dirs. Yamhill County Found., 1983-91. Decorated Army Commendation medal with oak leaf cluster; recipient Joint Service Commendation medal Dept. of Def. Mem. Soc. Am. Mil. Engrs. (pres. Albuquerque post 1968), Am. Econ. Assn., Western Econ. Assn. Internat., Nat. Ret. Officers Assn., Res. Officers Assn. (pres. Marion chpt. 1976), SAR (pres. Oreg. soc. 1985-86, v.p. gen. Nat. Soc. 1991-93), Urban Affairs Assn., Pi Sigma Epsilon, Pi Gamma Mu, Omicron Delta Epsilon (Pacific NW regional dir. 1978-88), Rotary (pres. McMinnville club 1983-84). Republican. Episcopalian. Office: Linfield Coll Mcminnville OR 97128

BLOEDE, VICTOR CARL, lawyer, academic executive; b. Woodwardville, Md., July 17, 1917; s. Carl Schon and Eleanor (Eck) B.; m. Ellen Louise Miller, May 9, 1947; children—Karl Abbott, Pamela Elena. A.B., Dartmouth Coll., 1940; J.D. cum laude, U. Balt., 1950; LL.M. in Pub. Law, Georgetown U., 1967. Bar: Md. 1950, Fed. Hawaii 1958, U.S. Supreme Ct. 1971. Pvt. practice Balt., 1950-64; mem. Goldman & Bloede, Balt., 1959-64; counsel Seven-Up Bottling Co., Balt., 1958-64; dep. atty. gen. Pacific Trust Ter., Honolulu, 1952-53; asst. solicitor for ters. Office of Solicitor, U.S. Dept. Interior, Washington, 1953-54; atty. U.S. Justice, Honolulu, 1955-58; assoc. gen. counsel Dept. Navy, Washington, 1960-61, 63-64; spl. legal cons. Md. Legislature, Legis. Council, 1963-64, 66-67; assoc. prof. U. Hawaii, 1961-63, dir. property mgmt., 1964-67; house counsel, dir. contracts and grants U. Hawaii System, 1967-82; house counsel U. Hawaii Research Corp., 1970-82; legal counsel Law of Sea Inst., 1978-82; legal cons. Rsch. Corp. and grad. rsch. divsn. U. Hawaii, 1982—; spl. counsel to Holifield Congl. Commn. on Govt. Procurement, 1970-73. Author: Hawaii Legislative Manual, 1962, Maori Affairs, New Zealand, 1964, Oceanographic Research Vessel Operations, and Liabilities, 1972, Hawaiian Archipelago, Legal Effects of a 200 Mile Territorial Sea, 1973, Copyright-Guidelines to the 1976 Act, 1977, Forms Manual, Inventions: Policy, Law and Procedure, 1982; writer, contbr. Coll. Law Digest and other publs. on legislation and pub. law. Mem. Gov.'s Task Force Hawaii and The Sea, 1969, Citizens Housing Com. Balt., 1952-64; bd. govs. Balt. Cmty. YMCA, 1954-64; bd. dirs. U. Hawaii Press, 1964-66, Coll. Housing Found., 1968-80; appointed to internat. rev. commn. Canada-France Hawaii Telescope Corp., 1973-82, chmn., 1973, 82; co-founder, incorporator First Unitarian Ch. Honolulu. Served to lt. comdr. USNR, 1942-45, PTO. Grantee ocean law studies NSF and NOAA, 1970-80. Mem. ABA, Balt. Bar Assn., Fed. Bar Assn., Am. Soc. Internat. Law, Nat. Assn. Univ. Attys. (founder & 1st chmn. patents & copyrights sect. 1974-76). Home: 635 Onaha St Honolulu HI 96816-4918

BLOEM, KENNETH D., healthcare facility executive; b. East Grand Rapids, Mich., Apr. 5, 1946; s. Gerald Wesley and Nancy (Debruyn) B.; m. Royce K. Ragland, July 27, 1974; children: Bronwen, Callie. BA in Lit., Calvin Coll., 1968; MSPH, Harvard U., 1977. Assoc. dir., program dir. Health Policy Inst. Boston U. Med. Ctr., 1981-86, assoc. acad. v.p. health affairs, 1981-86; exec. v.p., COO U. Chgo. Hosps., 1986-89; pres., CEO Stanford (Calif.) U. Hosp., 1989—. USPHS fellow Harvard Sch. Pub. Health, 1975-76; named to Order Bifurcated Needle, WHO, 1980. Office: Stanford U Hosp 300 Pasteur Dr Palo Alto CA 94304-2203

BLOMQUIST, CARL ARTHUR, medical trust company executive, insurance executive; b. L.A., Feb. 2, 1947; s. Carl Arthur and Delphine Marie (Forcier) B.; m. Diane Leslie Nunez, May 5, 1973 (div. Dec. 1979); 1 child, Kristin; m. Patricia Marie Johnson, Feb. 3, 1984 (div. Dec. 1988). BS, U. San Diego, 1969; MPH, UCLA, 1973. Auditor Naval Area Audit Svc., San Diego, 1969-71; trainee USPHS, Washhington, 1971; asst. adminstr. Northridge (Calif.) Hosp., 1973-76; asst. adminstr. fin. and facilities St. Vincent Med. Ctr., L.A., 1976-77; asst. v.p. 1st Interstate Mortgage, Pasadena, Calif., 1977-79; chief exec. officer Coop. Am. Physicians/Mut. Protection Trust, L.A., 1979-94; spl. dep. Calif. ins. commr. Exec. Life Ins. Co., L.A., 1991-94, acting CEO, 1991-92; prin. Carl A. Blomquist Cons., Playa Del Rey, Calif., 1994—. Mem. Calif. Health Facilities Financing Authority, Sacramento, 1981—; co-chmn. Adv. Commn. on Malpractice Ins., Calif. Senate, Sacramento, 1984-92, mem. Commn. on Cost Containment in State Govt., 1984—; bd. dirs. Chaminade Coll. Prep. Sch., West Hills, Calif., 1988. Journalism grantee Helms Found., 1965. Mem. Am. Soc. Assn. Execs., Am. Coll. Healthcare Execs., Am. Hosp. Assn., President's Assn. of Am. Mgmt. Assn., Hosp. Coun. So. Calif., UCLA Health Care Mgmt. Alumni Assn. (bd. dirs. 1987—). Republican. Roman Catholic. Office: Carl A Blomquist Cons 6641 Vista Del Mar Playa Del Rey CA 90293

BLOOM, JOHN W., counselor, educator; b. Cleve., Mar. 15, 1945; s. William Warren and Audrey (Rebscher) B.; m. Susan Beth Staley, Apr. 6, 1968; children: Kristi Ann, Lori Beth. BA, Miami U. Ohio, 1967, MEd, 1967; PhD, Purdue U., 1973. Cert. profl. counselor, Ariz. English tchr. Mad-River Jr. H.S., Dayton, Ohio, 1967-69; counselor Spinning Hills Jr. H.S., Dayton, Ohio, 1969-70, Stebbins H.S., Dayton, Ohio, 1970-71; counselor Placement Ctr. Purdue U., West Lafayette, Ind., 1972-73; counselor Hershey Elem. Sch., Lafayette, Ind., 1972-73, Lindbergh H.S., St. Louis, 1973-76; counselor educator Ctrl. Mich. U., Mt. Pleasant, 1976, Iowa State U., Ames, 1976-77, No. Ariz. U., Flagstaff, 1977—; chair, bd. dirs. Nat. Bd. for Cert. Counselors, Greensboro, N.C., 1995—; 1st chair counseling Ariz. Bd. Behavioral Health Examiners, Phoenix, 1989. Editor Ariz. Counseling Jou., 1988-89, 91-92. Recipient Outstanding Rsch. award Am. Assn. State Counseling Bds., 1991-92, Profl. Svc. award Ariz. Counselors Assn., 1991. Mem. Am. Counseling Assn., Assn. for Counselor Edn. and Supervision, Am. Sch. Counselors Assn. (bd. dirs. 1989-91), Kiwanis (disting. pres. 1992-93). Methodist. Office: No Ariz U Box 5774 CEE Flagstaff AZ 86011-5774

BLOOM, ROSE ELLEN GIEHL, engineer; b. Des Moines, Mar. 20, 1951; d. Francis Richard and Geraldine Eunice (Dietrich) Giehl; m. James William Bloom, May 18, 1974; children: Brian (dec.), Emily, Catherine. BS, Iowa State U., 1972; MS, U. Mich., 1976. Lic. NRC sr. reactor operator. Rsch. technician GM Rsch. Labs, Warren, Mich., 1973-74; reactor operator Ford Nuclear Reactor, Ann Arbor, Mich., 1974-76; assoc. engr. Westinghouse, Pitts., 1976-77; tng. engr. Commonwealth Edison, Chgo., 1980-81; assoc. scientist Stone & Webster Engring., Boston, 1981-82; computer specialist Kankakee (Ill.) C.C., 1983-84; cons. El Sobrante, Calif., 1985—. Bd. dirs. Birthright, El Sobrante, Calif., 1987-94. Mem. St. Anne's #78 Young Ladies Inst., Soc. Physics Students (pres. Ames, Iowa chpt. 1969, v.p. 1970). Republican. Roman Catholic. Home: 3663 May Rd El Sobrante CA 94803-2019

BLOOM, STEPHEN MICHAEL, lawyer, judge; b. San Francisco, June 10, 1948; s. Alan I. and Wilma (Morgan) B.; m. Rebecca J. Nelson, June 19, 1976; children: Benjamin Jacob, Molly Marie, John Robert. Student, Dartmouth Coll., 1966-68; BA in English, Stanford U., 1970; student, Calif. State U., Sacramento, 1973-74; JD, Willamette Coll. Law, 1977. Bar: Oreg. 1977, U.S. Dist. Ct. Oreg. 1979. Adminstrv. asst. Calif. Dept. Edn., Sacramento, 1973-74; atty. Joyce & Harding, Corvallis, Oreg., 1977-78; dep. dist. atty. Umatilla County, Pendleton, Oreg., 1978-79; atty. Morrison & Reynolds, Hermiston, Oreg., 1979-81, Kottkamp & O'Rourke, Pendleton, 1981—; appointed U.S. magistrate, 1988. Bd. dirs. Edn. Svc. Dist., Pendleton, 1982-89. Lt. (j.g.) USN, 1970-72. Mem. ABA, Oreg. Bar Assn., Rotary (pres. 1990-91, bd. dirs. 1991). Office: US Dist Ct PO Box 490 Pendleton OR 97801-0490 also: Kottkamp & O'Rourke 331 SE 2nd St Pendleton OR 97801-2224

BLOOMBECKER, JAY JOSEPH, computer crime consultant; b. N.Y.C., Dec. 18, 1944; s. William Samuel and Dorothy (Freeman) Becker; m. Linda Bloom, Sept. 20, 1980. BA cum laude, CCNY, 1965; JD, Harvard U., 1968. Bar: Calif. 1970, U.S. Cir. Ct. (9th cir.) 1987. Dep. dist. atty. L.A. Dist. Atty.'s Office, 1970-80; dir. Nat. Ctr. for Computer Crime Data, Santa Cruz, Calif., 1980—; nat. lectr. Assn. for Computing Machinery, N.Y., 1983-88. Mem. editorial bd. Computer Law Strategist, N.Y., 1985—; editor: Computer Crime Law Reporter, 1985, Introduction to Computer Crime, 1986, Computer Crime, Computer Security, Computer Ethics, 1986. Active men's caucus Los Angeles Commn. on Assaults Against Women. Mem. ABA (computer crime com.), Internat. Fedn. for Info. Processing (chmn.), Working Group on Computer Law (chmn.). Office: 1222 17th Ave Santa Cruz CA 95062-3019

BLOOMER, WILLIAM ERNEST, thoracic and cardiovascular surgeon, educator; b. Denver, Dec. 20, 1916; s. Charles Ernest and Jane Winifred (French) B.; m. Cornelia Huntington Day, Oct. 29, 1959; children: Lianne French, William Ernest, Robert Day, Charles Campbell. BS, Stanford U., 1938; MD, Yale U., 1942. Diplomate Am. Bd. Surgery, Bd. Thoracic Surgery; lic. Calif., Conn., Washington. Intern in surg. svc. Stanford (Calif.) U. Hosp., 1942-43; fellow in thoracic surgery Yale U. Sch. Med., 1946-47; asst. resident in surgery New Haven (Conn.) Hosp., 1947-48, resident in thoracic surgery, 1949-50, assoc. resident in gen. surgery, 1950-51; vol. fellow dept. surgery Lahey Clinic, Boston, 1951; chief resident in surgery New Haven (Conn.) Hosp., 1952; fellow, rsch. asst. in cardiovasc. surgery Yale U. Sch. Med., 1952, instr. surgery, 1953-54, asst. prof. surgery, 1954-59; clin. asst. prof. surgery U. So. Calif., 1959-61; assoc. prof. in residence UCLA, 1961-66; chief thoracic and cardiovasc. surgery L.A. County Harbor Gen. Hosp., 1961-66; assoc. clin. prof. surgery UCLA Sch. Medicine, 1961—; ptnr. pvt. practice cardiac thoracic and vascular surgery St. Vincent's Hosp., L.A., 1959-60; ptnr. pvt. practice thoracic and cardiovasc. surgery Hosp. of Good Samaritan, L.A., 1960-61; ptnr. pvt. practice Long Beach, Calif., 1966-69; pvt. practice thoracic and cardiovasc. surgery Long Beach, 1969—; mem. courtesy staff Long Beach Cmty. Hosp., St. Mary Med. Ctr. Long Beach, Downey Cmty. Hosp., Hosp. of the Good Samaritan L.A., dir. pro tem hyperbaric rsch. and therapy unit, 1966-67; mem. attending staff Harbor Gen. hosp., Torrance, Calif.; mem. provisional courtesy staff Drs. Hosp. of Lakewood; mem. hon. staff UCLA Med. Ctr. Thoracic and Cariovasc. Surgery; active hon. staff Long Beach meml. Med. Ctr., chief thoracic and cariovasc. surgery sect., 1978-81, 84-85; travelling fellow Rockefeller Found. visit med. schs., S. Am., 1958. Contbr. numerous articles to profl. jours.

Served to maj. U.S. Army Med. Corps., 1943-46, ETO. Mem. AMA, ACS, Am. Coll. Cardiology, Internat. Cardiovasc. Soc., Am. Assn. Thoracic Surgery, Am. Coll. Chest Physicians, Am. Thoracic Soc., Calif. Med. Assn., Soc. Thoracic Surgeons, Soc. Vascular Surgery, New Eng. Surg. Soc., L.A. Acad. Medicine, L.A.. County Med. Assn., L.A. Surg. Soc., Long Beach Surg. Soc., Sigma Xi. Office: 2530 Atlantic Ave Ste A Long Beach CA 90806-2741

BLOOMFIELD, MASSE, publishing executive, writer; b. Franklin, N.H., Aug. 20, 1923; s. Harry and Ida Minnie (Steinberg) B.; m. Fay Koenigsberg, Feb. 21, 1954; children: Beth A., Ellen J., Dina A. BS, U. N.H., 1948; MLS, Carnerie Inst. of Tech., Pitts., 1951. Libr. USDA libr., Washington, 1951-53, U.S. Naval Ordnance Test Sta., China Lake, Calif., 1953-56, Atomics Internat., Canoga Park, Calif., 1956-62; head tech. libr. Hughes Aircraft Co., El Segundo, Calif., 1962-85; pres. Masefield Books, Canoga Park, Calif., 1991—. Author: How to Use a Library, 1991, Mankind in Transition, 1993; contbr. over 100 book revs. to profl. jours., over 30 articles to profl. jours. Lt. Col. USAF, 1943-45, ETO. Recipient Disting. Flying Cross, Air medal with 6 clusters USAF, 1945. Mem. World Future Soc., Nat. Space Soc., The Planetary Soc. Office: Masefield Books 7210 Jordan Ave Ste B-54 Canoga Park CA 91303-1223

BLOOMFIELD, SUZANNE, artist; b. Cleve., June 23, 1934. BSED, Ohio U., 1955; MEd, U. Ariz. 1975. Exhibited in group shows at Cleve. Mus. Art, 1950, U. Ariz., 1968, 72, No. Ariz. U., 1968, Walker Art Inst., N.Y.C., 1976, Ford Found., 1976, Fordham U., 1976, New Sch. Social Rsch., 1976, Ariz. Invitational, Flagstaff, 1980, Ohio U., 1981, U. S.D., 1981, U. Innsbruck, Austria, 1982, Iowa State U., 1983, Idaho State U., 1984, Grove Gallery U. Calif. San Diego, 1985, SUNY, Alfred, 1986, UN World Conf. on Women, Nairobi, Kenya, 1987, Pa. State U., 1987, U. Portland, 1987, Nat. Assn. Women Artists, N.Y.C., 1988, San Francisco Women Artists Gallery, 1990, Nat. Mus. Women in the Arts, Washington, 1990, City of Tucson, 1992-94, Ariz. State Capitol, 1994, Jain Marunouchi Gallery, N.Y.C., 1995; executed mural U. Ariz. Dept. Counseling & Guidance, 1975. Office: Suzanne Bloomfield Gallery 1830 E Broadway Blvd Tucson AZ 85719

BLOOMQUIST, RODNEY GORDON, geologist; b. Aberdeen, Wash., Feb. 3, 1943; s. Verner A. and Margaret E. (Olson) B.; m. Linda L. Lee, Dec. 19, 1964 (div. July 1968); m. Bente Brisson Jørgensen, Aug. 4, 1977; 1 child, Kira Brisson. BS in Geology, Portland State U., 1966; MS in Geology, U. Stockholm, 1970, PhD in Geochemistry, 1977. Rschr. U. Stockholm, 1974-77; asst. prof. Oreg. Inst. Tech., Klamath Falls, 1978-80; geologist Wash. State Energy Office, Olympia, 1980—; vis. prof. Internat. Sch. Geothermics, Pisa, Italy, 1990—; cons. U.S. Dept. Energy, Washington, 1990, Govt. of Can., 1984, Aesa-Stal Geoenergy, Lund, Sweden, 1985-86, City and County of San Francisco, 1988-89, Lake County, Calif., 1992, San Francisco State U., 1993. Author: Regulatory Guide to Geothermics, 1991; mem. editl. bd. Geothermics, 1985-88; also numerous books and articles. Smitts fellow, Sweden, 1974, Royal Rsch. fellow, Sweden, 1975-77; rsch. grantee U. Stockholm, 1975-77. Mem. Geothermal Resources Coun. (bd. dirs. 1985-92, pres. 1989, pres. Pacific N.W. sect. 1982-85), Internat. Dist. Heating and Cooling Assn. (western sect. bd. dirs. 1990—), Internat. Dist. Energy Assn. (bd. dirs. 1994—), N.Am. Dist. Heating and Cooling Inst. (bd. dirs. 1986-88), Am. Blade Smith Soc. (bd. dirs. 1989—). Democrat. Lutheran. Office: Wash State Energy Office 925 Plum St SE Olympia WA 98501-1529

BLOUIN, SCOTT E., engineering company executive; b. 1943. BS, MS, MIT, 1966. Rsch. engr. USA CRREL, Hanover, N.H., 1971-79; with CSI Inc., South Royalton, Vt., 1979-80, Applied Rsch. Assoc. Inc., Albuquerque, 1980—. With USAF, 1967-71. Office: Applied Rsch Assoc Inc 4300 San Mateo Blvd NE Albuquerque NM 87110*

BLOUKE, MILTON BAKER, lawyer; b. Chgo., Jan. 18, 1946; s. Pierre and Jessie (Scott) B.; m. Christine Hunt, Nov. 25, 1971; children: Scott M., Katie M. BS, U. Wash., 1970; JD, Lewis and Clark Law Sch., 1974; LLM in Taxation, Boston U., 1978. Bar: Oreg. 1974, U.S. Tax Ct. Atty. Dist. Counsel IRS, Boston, 1974-78, San Francisco, 1978-82; staff atty. Regional Counsel IRS, San Francisco, 1982-84; atty. Dist. Counsel IRS, San Jose, Calif., 1984-86; asst. dist. counsel Dist. Counsel IRS, San Jose, 1986-88, Seattle, 1988-91; atty. Dist. Counsel IRS, Las Vegas, Nev., 1991—. 1st lt. U.S. Army, 1966-69. Mem. ABA, Oreg. Bar Assn. Home: 2026 Grafton Ave Henderson NV 89014-0625 Office: Dist Counsel IRS 4750 W Oakey Blvd Las Vegas NV 89102-1500

BLOW, JOHN NEEDHAM, social services educator; b. Whitby, Ont., Can., Nov. 30, 1905; came to U.S., 1952; s. Ezekiel Richard and Edith May (Correll) B.; m. Emma Jane White, June 6, 1942; children: Carol Anne, Brenda Jane, Mary Roberta, Elizabeth Diane. BA, McMaster U., 1939; MSW, U. Toronto, Ont., 1948. Cert. elem. tchr., Toronto, community colls. instr., Calif. Exec. sec. Community Welfare Planning Council Ont., Toronto, 1948-52; exec. v.p. Motel Corp., Las Vegas, Nev., 1952-54; exec. dir. Nev. div. Am. Cancer Soc., 1954-56, assoc. exec. dir. Los Angeles County br., 1956-70; program assoc. Am. Heart Assn., Los Angeles, 1970-74; project dir., coordinator sr. community service employment program Orange County, Calif., 1974-75; instr. community service programs for adults North Orange County Community Coll. Dist. and Coastline Coll., 1976-79, Mira Costa and Palomar Community Colls., 1979-85. Author: (poems) New Frontiers, 1984. Vol. Arthritis Found.; asst. commr. tng. Boy Scouts Can., Ottawa, 1934-41; Chaplain Tri-City Coun. Navy League. Wing comdr. RCAF, 1941-46. Recipient Commendation for Outstanding Svc. to Srs., Orange County Sr. Citizens Coun., 1977, Gold award Orange County United Way, 1977, Golden Poet award, 1991, World of Poetry, 1989, 90. Mem. Nat. Assn. Social Workers, Acad. Cert. Social Workers, San Luis Rey Officers Club, Valley Sr. Ctr., North County Concert Assn., So. Calif. McMaster U. Alumni Assn. (past pres., inducted Alumni Gallery 1986), Can. Soc. Los Angeles (charter, past pres.), U. Toronto Alumni Assn. (exec. com., past pres. So. Calif. br.). Presbyterian. Lodge: Elks. Home: 3725 Sesame Way Oceanside CA 92057-8328

BLOYD, STEPHEN ROY, environmental manager, educator; b. Alameda, Calif., Aug. 17, 1953; s. William Allen and Alice Louella (Scott) B. Grad. high sch., Reedley, Calif., 1971. Cert. environ. mgr., Nev.; registered hazardous substances specialist. Reagent tech. Tenneco Corp., Gold Hill, Nev., 1982; environ. tech. Pierson Environ. Drilling, Modesto, Calif., 1982-84; pres. Bloyd and Assocs., Dayton, Nev., 1986—. Author: Hazardous Waste Site Operations for General Site Workers, 1992; editor: (newsletter) Pumper, 1991. Firefighter Dayton Vol. Fire Dept., 1975, capt., 1976-78, chief, 1978-83, tng. officer, 1984—; asst. prof. Dodd/Beals Fire Protection Tng. Acad. U. Nev., Reno, 1990—; instr. chemistry hazardous materials Nat. Fire Acad., Emmitsburg, Md., 1989—; mem. bylaw com. Dayton Regional Adv. Coun., 1989. Named Firefighter of Yr., City of Dayton, 1992. Mem. NFA, Nat. Environ. Tng. Assn., Nat. Environ. Health Assn., Nev. State Firemen's Assn. (1st v.p., 1992-93, 2d v.p. 1991-92, pres. 1993-94, chmn. hazardous materials com. 1987-93, mem. legis. com. 1991, byloaws com. 1986), Nev. Fire Chief's Assn., War on Regional Mismgmt. (pres. 1991-92), Citizen Alert, Internat. Platform Assn. Libertarian. Office: PO Box 113 Silver City NV 89428-0113

BLUE, JAMES GUTHRIE, veterinarian; b. Flora, Ind., Oct. 22, 1920; s. Van C. and Florence A. (Guthrie) B. AB, Wabash Coll., 1943; postgrad., Northwestern U., 1943; DVM, Ohio State U., 1950; AA in Labor Negotiation/Rels., L.A. Trade Tech. Coll., 1989. Pvt. practice cons., 1950-80; field vet. City of L.A., 1980—, acting chief vets., 1992, chief vets., 1992-95; rsch. project cons. Calif. State U., Northridge, 1980-87; pro med. svcs. sec.- negotiator AFSCME, L.A., 1983-95. Lt. comdr. USN, 1943-46. Mem. Am. Vet. Med. Assn., San Diego Vet. Med. Assn., So. Ariz. Vet. Med. Assn., Calif. Vet. Med. Assn. (environ. and pub. health ecology com. 1986-95, state ethics com. 1986-95, wellness com. 1990-95), So. Calif. Vet. Med. Assn. (coun. mem., polit. action com., continuing edn. com. 1980-95). Democrat. Episcopalian. Home: 6116 Fulton Ave Apt 103 Van Nuys CA 91401-3127

BLUECHEL, ALAN, state senator, wood structural components manufacturing company executive; b. Edmonton, Alta., Can., Aug. 28, 1924; s. Joseph Harold and Edith (Daly) B.; m. Aylene Loughnan, Nov. 2, 1958; children: Gordon, Turner; m. Jeanne Ehrlichman, Aug. 8, 1981. BApSc in Elec. Engring., BA, U. B.C.; postgrad. U. Wash.; diploma Harvard U., 1988. Vice pres. Loctwall Corp., Kirkland, Wash., 1948-64, pres., 1964—; pres. Crystal Mtn. Inn Co., developer condominiums, restaurants, hotels, swimming pools, 1968-80; mem. Wash. State Ho. of Reps., 1966-74; mem. Wash. Senate, 1974-95, pres. pro tem, 1988-89, vice-chmn. rules com. 1988-89, Rep. whip, 1979-81, 83—, majority whip, 1981-83, mem. ways and means, 1974-95, pres. Pacific Northwest Econ. Region, 1989—, Toll fellow, 1992, bd. dirs. Wash. State Inst. Pub. Policy, 1988-95, v.p. pro-tem 1990-92, rep. pres. protem 1993-95; mem. exec. com. Western Legis. Conf., 1988—, speaker various confs., convs., orgns. Mem. Wash. State Land Planning Commn., 1969-73, Wash. State Women's Coun., 1976, Spl. Com. on Office State Actuary, 1983; bd. dirs. Westrends, 1989-95; chmn. Wash. State Winter Recreation Commn., 1983-94, Wash. State Commn. on Environ. Policy, 1983; mem. arts, tourism and cultural affairs com. Nat. Conf. of State Legis., 1976-1987; mem. Juanita Citizens Devel. Coun., 1975-79, King County Conservation Com., 1967-69, King County Flood Control Adv. Bd., 1968-70, Com. To Save Sch. Trust Lands, 1975-84, Edwards Park Adv. Bd., 1977-79, Seattle Symphony Phonathon Fundraisers, 1980, 81, Gov.'s Coun. on Child Abuse and Neglect, 1983, Wash. State Expo '86 Commn., 1985-87; mem. conservation com. King County Environ. Devel. Commn., 1969-74; mem. internat. com. Coun. State Govts., 1993—, numerous other civic orgns. Recipient Outstanding Svc. award Lake Washington PTSA Coun., 1982, Mountaineers Club, Sun Valley Ski Club, Forelaufer Ski Club.

BLUESTONE, STUART MICHAEL, lawyer; b. Pitts., Oct. 17, 1946; s. Max L. and Charlotte G. (Goldfarb) B.; m. Judith E. Naumburg, May 24, 1987; children: Tahlia Jane, Darren Michael. BA, Trinity Coll., 1968; MPA, Harvard U., 1988; JD, Georgetown U., 1972. Bar: D.C. 1973, Pa. 1975, U.S. Supreme Ct. 1978, N.Mex. 1984. Assoc. Berlin, Roisman & Kessler, Washington, 1972-74; advisor, litigator Fed. Energy Adminstrn., Washington, 1974-76; assoc. Miller & Chevalier, Washington, 1978-83, asst. mng. ptnr., 1983-84; dir. consumer protection divsn. N.Mex. Atty. Gen.'s Office, Santa Fe, 1984-87; chief counsel judiciary com. N.Mex. Ho. of Reps., Santa Fe, 1987; dep. dir. N.Mex. Legis. Coun. Svc., Santa Fe, 1988—. Mem. N.Mex. Bar Assn. (chmn. bd. pub. law sect. 1992-93), Pi Gamma Mu, Phi Psi. Jewish. Office: Legis Coun Svc 311 State Capitol Santa Fe NM 87501

BLUM, ARTHUR MARVIN, academic administrator; b. Bklyn., Aug. 29, 1934; s. Albert R. and Lucy (Tax) Weiss; m. Joanne L. Finkelor, June 14, 1959; children: Sherry R., Laurie J., Katie J. BA in Psychology, U. Pa., 1956; MS in Speech Pathology, U. Pitts., 1958. Lic. speech pathologist, Calif. Grad. asst. dept. speech and theatre arts U. Pitts., 1956-58, clin. supr., instr. dept. speech and theatre arts, 1958-59; assoc. prof. psychology Point Park Coll., 1960-73; sec. of coll., dir. admissions Point Park Coll., Pitts., 1960-65, exec. v.p., sec. of coll., 1965-67, pres., 1967-73; gen. mgr., CEO San Francisco Ballet Assn., 1973-74; cons. Development, 1975-77; pres. San Francisco Sch. of Arts, San Anselmo, Calif., 1976-78; pres., bd. dirs. Marin Civic Ballet Assn., San Rafael, Calif., 1976-77; pres. New England Summer Programs in Arts, Pittsfield, Mass., 1978-83; speech pathologist, pvt. cons. San Anselmo, Calif., 1983-84; v.p. Columbia Pacific U., San Rafael, Calif., 1984—; lectr. Berkshire C.C., Pittsfield, 1979-80, San Francisco State U., 1983-84; cons. Bur. Measurement and Guidance, Carnegie Mellon U., 1959; assoc. dir. Camp Cascade, Eagle Bay, N.Y., 1956-59; pres. New Eng. Summer Programs in the Arts; chmn. bd. dirs., CEO Pitts. Playhouse; cons. on ednl. facility and theatre design Gismondi and Arnold, Architects, White Plains, N.Y.; cons., mem. evalaution teams Mid. State Assn. Colls. and Univs.; author/participant assembly on univ. goals and governance AAAS. V.p. Am. Wind Symphony Orch., 1968-73; past mem. sponsoring com. Allegheny Conf. on Cmty. Devel.; past bd. dirs. Waterways Wind Orch. of N.Y., C. of C. of Greater Pitts., Mt. Lebanon Civic League, Pa. Jr. Acad. Sci., Pitts. Chamber Music Soc., Pitts. Coun. on Higher Edn., Pitts. Symphony Soc.; incorporator, pres. bd. trustees San Francisco Sch. of Arts; active Marin Civic Ballet Assn. Mem. NEA, Am. Cleft Palate Assn., Am. Speech and Hearing Assn., Am. Acad. Polit. and Social Scis., Calif. Speech and Hearing Assn., Pa. Acad. Sci., Pa. Speech and Hearing Assn., Speech Assn. Am., Urban League Pitts., World Affairs Coun. Pitts., Young Pres.'s Orgn., Pa. Sports Hall of Fame, Scottish Rite. Home: 1090 Butterfield Rd San Anselmo CA 94960-1148 Office: Columbia Pacific U 1415 3rd St San Rafael CA 94901-2860

BLUM, DEBORAH, reporter. Sr. writer The Sacramento (Calif.) Bee; sci. writer in residence U. Wis., Madison, 1993. Author: The Monkey Wars, 1994. Recipient Pulitzer Prize for beat reporting, 1992. Mem. Nat. Assn. Sci. Writers (bd. dirs.), Sigma Xi. Office: Sacramento Bee PO Box 15779 Sacramento CA 95852-0779

BLUM, FRED ANDREW, electronics company executive; b. Austin, Tex., Nov. 30, 1939; s. Freddie A. and Margaret E. (Stark) B.; children: Craig Houston, Karisa Laine; m. Diane F. Harbert, June 11, 1988. BS in Physics, U. Tex., 1962; MS in Physics, Calif. Inst. Tech., 1963, PhD, 1968. Rsch. scientist Gen. Dynamics, Ft. Worth, 1963-64; mem. tech. staff Hughes Rsch. Labs., Malibu, Calif., 1966-68, Lincoln Lab., MIT, Lexington, 1968-73; program mgr. Cen. Rsch. Labs., Tex. Instruments, Dallas, 1973-75; dir. solid state electronics Rockwell Internat., Thousand Oaks, Calif., 1975-79; v.p. Microelectronics R & D Ctr. Rockwell Internat., Anaheim, Calif., 1979-81; pres. GigaBit Logic, Newbury Park, Calif., 1981-86; chief exec. officer Sequel, Westlake Village, Calif., 1986—. Mem. editorial bd. Fiber Optics and Integrated Optics, 1977-83; contbr. numerous articles on solid state electronics to sci. jours. Chmn. local adv. coun. Am. Cancer Soc., 1980-81. NSF fellow, Howard Hughes fellow. Fellow IEEE; mem. AAAS, Am. Phys. Soc., Am. Mgmt. Assn., Phi Beta Kappa, Sigma Xi. Office: Sequel 5655 Lindero Canyon Rd Ste 404 Westlake Village CA 91362

BLUM, JOAN KURLEY, fund raising executive; b. Palm Beach, Fla., July 27, 1926; d. Nenad Daniel and Eva (Milos) Kurley; m. Robert C. Blum, Apr. 15, 1967; children: Christopher Alexander, Martha Jane, Louisa Joan. BA, U. Wash., 1948. Cert. fund raising exec. U.S. dir. Inst. Mediterranean Studies, Berkeley, Calif., 1962-65; devel. officer U. Calif. at Berkeley, 1965-67; pres. Blum Assocs., Fund-Raising Cons., San Anselmo, Calif., 1967-92, The Blums of San Francisco, 1992—; mem. faculty U. Calif. Extension, Inst. Fund Raising, SW Inst. Fund-Raising U. Tex., U. San Francisco, U.K. Vol. Movement Group, London, Australasian Inst. Fund Raising. Contbr. numerous articles to profl. jours. Recipient Golden Addy award Am. Advt. Fedn.; Silver Mailbox award Direct Mail Mktg. Assn., Best Ann. Giving Time-Life award, others. Mem. Nat. Soc. Fund-Raising Execs. (dir.), Nat. Assn. of Hosp. Devel., Women Emerging., Rotary. Office: 202 Evergreen Dr Kentfield CA 94904-2708 also: PO Box 141, Hornsby Sydney Australia

BLUM, JOANNE LEE, development executive, educator; b. Pitts., Aug. 30, 1932; d. L. Herbert and Dorothy Ruth (Cimberg) Finkelhor; m. Arthur Marvin Blum, June 14, 1959; children—Sherry Ruth, Laurie Jill, Katie Jo. Student U. Chgo., 1947-49, Chatham Coll., Pitts., 1949-51; B.A., Brandeis U., 1953; M.Ed., Harvard U., 1954; postgrad. U. Pitts., 1963-65. Cert. fundraising exec. Tchr., Mt. Diablo Unifed Sch. Dist., Walnut Creek, Calif., 1954-55; asst. dir. Fgn. Policy Assn. Pitts. (now World Affairs Council Pitts.), 1955-57, assoc. dir., 1957-61, assoc. producer Focus on World Affairs, 1959-61; pres. Pitts. Internat. Travel, 1961-62; founder, chmn. dept. edn. Point Park Coll., Pitts., 1962-69, dir. preschool Lab. Program, 1964-69, dir. intermediate level Lab. Sch., 1972-73; co-founder, dean San Francisco Sch. Arts, San Anselmo, Calif., 1976-78; co-owner, dir. Camps Wahconah and Potomac and New Eng. Summer Programs in the Arts, Pittsfield, Mass., 1978-82; devel. and membership coordinator World Affairs Council of No. Calif., San Francisco, 1983-85; pvt. practice devel. cons., Calif., 1986-89; dir. devel. Project SEED, Berkeley, Calif., 1989—; cons. The Lighthouse for the Blind and Visually Impaired, San Francisco, Goodwill Industries Devel. Office, Internat. Visitors Ctr., 1985, Devel. Médecins du Monde, Paris; cofounder Pitts. Area Preschool Assn., 1965; lectr. Headstart program Carnegie-Mellon U., Pitts., 1965. Founding dir. Pitts. Ballet Theatre, 1965; cons. arts program for handicapped children Renaissance Ctr. for Arts, Mt. Lebanon, Pa., 1967. Mem. ASCD, Am. Edn. Rsch. Assn., Edn. Excellence Network, Nat. Soc. Fund Raising Execs. (sec. 1987), Devel. Execs. Roundtable (v.p. 1988, pres. 1989), Rotary. Jewish.

BLUM, JOHN ALAN, urologist, educator; b. Bklyn., Feb. 2, 1933; s. Louis J. and Pauline (Kushner) B.; m. Debra Merlin Ackerman, June 30, 1957; children: Louis Jeffrey, Alfred Merlin, Jacqueline. AB, Dartmouth, 1954; MD, NYU, 1958; MS, U. Minn., 1965. Diplomate Am. Bd. Urology. Intern, U. Minn. Hosp., Mpls., 1958-59, resident, 1959-64; practice medicine, specializing in urology, Chgo., 1964-66, Mpls., 1966-67, San Diego, 1969—; chmn. dept. urology Mt. Sinai Hosp., Chgo., 1965-66; asst. prof. urology U. Minn., Mpls., 1967; assoc. clin. prof. urology U. Calif., San Diego, 1969—; chief of staff Hillside Hosp., San Diego, 1989-92; chmn. dept. surgery, div. urology Mercy Hosp., San Diego, 1991-93; mem. staff Scripps Hosp., La Jolla, Calif., 1969—; adj. assoc. prof. uro-pathology Uniform Svcs. U. of Health Sci., Behtesda, Md., 1988—. Bd. dirs. Vietnam Vet. Leadership Program. Capt. USNR, 1967-93, Vietnam, ret. 1993. Fellow ACS; mem. Am., Calif. med. assns., Am. Urol. Assn., San Diego Urol. Soc. (pres. 1991-93), San Diego Surg. Soc. (pres. 1977), Phi Beta Kappa, Sigma Xi, Alpha Omega Alpha, San Diego Yacht Club. Research in devel. of silicone rubber for urinary tract. Home: 890 Cornish Dr San Diego CA 92107-4247 Office: 4060 4th Ave Ste 310 San Diego CA 92103-2120

BLUM, MANUEL, computer science educator; b. Caracas, Venezuela, Apr. 26, 1938; s. Bernardo and Ernestine (Horowitz) B.; m. Lenore Epstein, July 30, 1961; 1 child, Avrim. B.S. in Elec. Engring, MIT, 1959, M.S., 1961, Ph.D. in Math., 1964. Research asst. to research assoc. Research Lab. Electronics, MIT, 1960-65; asst. prof. dept. math. MIT, 1966-68; vis. asst. prof. to prof. dept. elec. engring. and computer scis. U. Calif.-Berkeley, 1968—, chmn. for computer sci., 1977-80, faculty rsch. lectr., 1995. Contbr. articles to profl. jours. Sloan Found. fellow, 1972-73. Fellow AAAS, IEEE, Am. Acad. Arts and Scis.; mem. Assn. for Computing Machinery, Sigma Xi (Monie A. Ferst award 1991). Home: 700 Euclid Ave Berkeley CA 94708-1334 Office: U Calif 583 Evans Hall Berkeley CA 94720

BLUMBERG, JOHN PHILIP, lawyer; b. Mpls., Dec. 6, 1949. BA cum laude, Calif. State U., Long Beach, 1972; JD, Western State U., Fullerton, Calif., 1976. Bar: Calif. 1976, U.S. Dist. Ct. (cen. dist.) Calif. 1978, U.S. Ct. Appeals (9th cir.); cert. civil trial specialist Nat. Bd. Trial Advocacy. Pvt. practice, L.A., Long Beach and Orange County, Calif., 1976—; dir. Dispute Resolution Ctr., Long Beach, 1993—; judge pro tem Long Beach-L.A. Mcpl. Ctr., 1979-92; arbitrator Los Angeles County and Orange County Superior Cts., civil litigation settlement officer; del. Calif. State Bar Conf., 1985-90; pres. Legal Aid Found., Long Beach, 1986-87, 92-93, also bd. dirs.; lectr. various profl. and edn. groups; mem. faculty Hastings Ctr. for Trial Advocacy, 1988-89. Assoc. editor Western State U. Law Review, 1975-76; contbr. articles to profl. jours. Mem. SAG, Assn. Trial Lawyers Am., Calif. Trial Lawyers Assn., Long Beach Bar Assn. (bd. govs., arbitrator atty.-client disputes, mem. legis. and legal aid coms., faculty trial advocacy clinic), Am. Bd. Trial Advs., Los Angeles County Bar Assn., L.A. Trial Lawyers Assn., Am. Arbitration Assn., Orange County Bar Assn., Calif. State Bar (chmn. com. on rules and procedures of ct. 1992-93). Office: 444 W Ocean Blvd Ste 1600 Long Beach CA 90802-4524

BLUMBERG, NATHAN(IEL) BERNARD, journalist, educator, writer and publisher; b. Denver, Apr. 8, 1922; s. Abraham Moses and Jeannette Blumberg; m. Lynne Stout, June 1946 (div. Feb. 1970); children: Janet Leslie, Jenifer Lyn, Josephine Laura; m. Barbara Farquhar, July 1973. B.A., U. Colo., 1947, M.A., 1948; D.Phil. (Rhodes scholar), Oxford (Eng.) U., 1950. Reporter Denver Post, 1947-48; assoc. editor Lincoln (Nebr.) Star, 1950-53; asst. to editor Ashland (Nebr.) Gazette, 1954-55; asst. city editor Washington Post and Times Herald, 1956; from asst. prof. to assoc. prof. journalism U. Nebr., 1950-55; asso. prof. journalism Mich. State U., 1955-56; dean, prof. Sch. Journalism, U. Mont., 1956-68, prof. journalism, 1968-78, prof. emeritus, 1978—; pub. Wood FIRE Ashes Press, 1981—; vis. prof. Pa. State U., 1964, Northwestern U., 1966-67, U. Calif., Berkeley, 1970; Dept. State specialist in Thailand, 1961, in Trinidad, Guyana, Surinam and Jamaica, 1964. Author: One-Party Press?, 1954; The Afternoon of March 30: A Contemporary Historical Novel, 1984, also articles in mags. and jours.; co-editor: A Century of Montana Journalism, 1971; editor: The Mansfield Lectures in International Relations, Vols. I and II, 1979; founder: Mont. Journalism Rev, 1958—; editor, pub. Treasure State Rev., 1991—. Served with arty. U.S. Army, 1943-46. Decorated Bronze Star medal. Mem. Assn. Am. Rhodes Scholars, Brasenose Soc., Kappa Tau Alpha (nat. pres. 1969-70). Home: PO Box 99 Bigfork MT 59911

BLUMBERG, ROBERT LEE, manufacturing executive; b. Bklyn., Apr. 1, 1942; s. William T. and Hazel Blumberg; m. Joyce T. Yavner, Mar. 29, 1969; children: Matthew Y., Michael L. BS, MIT, 1964, MS, 1965; MBA, Harvard U., 1967. Assoc. J.H. Whitney & Co., N.Y.C., 1970-72; ptnr. Idanta Ptnrs., N.Y.C. and San Diego, 1972-80; pres., chief exec. Spectragraphics Corp., San Diego, 1981—; mem. vis. com. MIT Mech. Engring. Dept., Cambridge, 1986-92; regional chmn. MIT Ednl. Coun., San Diego, 1978-88; chmn. MIT Enterprise Forum San Diego, 1989-92, 94—, bd. dirs. 1990—; trustee Francis W. Parker Sch., 1984-89; bd. dirs. Pacific Comm. Sci., Inc., San Diego, 1987-93. Served to lt. U.S. Army, 1967-69. Republican. Jewish. Office: Spectragraphics Corp 9707 Waples St San Diego CA 92121-2954

BLUME, JAMES BERYL, financial advisor; b. N.Y.C., Apr. 9, 1941; s. Philip Franklin Blume and Mary Kirschman Asch; m. Kathryn Weil Frank, Jan. 20, 1984; 1 child, Zachary Thomas Philip. BA, Williams Coll., Williamstown, Mass., 1963; MBA, Harvard U., Boston, 1966; M. Psychology, The Wright Inst., Berkeley, Calif., 1983, PhD in Philosophy, 1986. Security analyst Faulkner, Dawkins & Sullivan, N.Y.C., 1966-68; sr. v.p. Faulkner, Dawkins & Sullivan Securities, Inc., N.Y.C., 1968-73; ptnr. Omega Properties, N.Y.C., 1973-74; exec.v.p. Arthur M. Fischer, Inc., N.Y.C., 1974-77; psychotherapist in pvt. practice Berkeley, 1985-91, fin. cons., 1987—; pres. James B. Blume, Inc., fin. counsel and mgmt., Berkeley, 1993—; bd. dirs. RHL/Golden State Pub. San Francisco, 1991-92. Bd. dirs. ACLU No. Calif., San Francisco, 1988-94, treas., 1993-94; bd. dirs. East Bay Clinic for Psychotherapy, Oakland, Calif., 1981-85, Marin Psychotherapy Inst., Mill Valley, Calif., 1986-87; trustee The Wright Inst., 1981-85. Mem. Berkeley Tennis Club, Williams Club (bd. govs. 1968-72). Democrat. Jewish. Office: 1708 Shattuck Ave Berkeley CA 94709-1700

BLUMENKRANZ, MARK SCOTT, surgeon, researcher, educator; b. N.Y.C., Oct. 23, 1950; s. Edward and Helene (Cymberg) B.; m. Recia Kott, June 10, 1975. AB, Brown U., 1972, MD, 1975, MMS, 1976; postgrad., Stanford U., 1975-79, U. Miami, 1979-80. Intern, resident Stanford (Calif.) U. Med. Ctr., 1975-79; fellow Bascom Palmer Eye Inst. U. Miami, Fla., 1979-80; asst. prof. Bascom Palmer Eye Inst., Miami, 1980-85; assoc. prof. Wayne State U., Detroit, 1985-92; clin. prof. Stanford U., 1992—, dir. of retina, 1992—; chmn. sci. adv. bd. Escalon Ophthalmics, 1990—; assoc. examiner Am. Bd. Ophthalmology; bd. dirs. OIS, Midlabs. Mem. editl. bd. Ophthalmology, Retina, Vitreoretinal Tech., Graefes Archives; contbr. chpts. to books and articles to profl. jours.; inventor ophthalmic devices. Recipient Visual Scis. medal in Visual Scis. Rosenthal Found., 1990, Heed award Heed Found., 1988, Manpower award Rsch. to Prevent Blindness. Mem. Am. Acad. Ophthalmology (mem. preferred practice com., others), Macula Soc. (chmn. rsch. com. 1986-90), Assn. Rsch. in Vision and Ophthalmology (chmn. retina sect. 1987-90), Retina Soc. (mem. membership com.), Maimonodes Soc. (mem. exec. com.). Office: Dept Ophthalmology Boswell A-157 Stanford CA 94305 Also: 1225 Crane St Menlo Park CA 94025

BLUMENTHAL, RICHARD CARY, construction executive, consultant; b. Bklyn., Dec. 18, 1951; s. Mervin Harold and Barbara June (Engelson) B.; m. Ginnilyn Hawkins; children: Aaron Joseph, Meredith Taylor. BS, U. N.H., 1974. Planner RECON Assocs., Hamilton, Mont., 1976-77; project mgr. Grizzly Mfg., Hamilton, 1977-78; profl. carpenter Ed Brown Constrn., Bainbridge Island, Wash., 1978-79; pres. Richard Blumenthal Constrn., Inc., Bainbridge Island, 1979—; instr. Bainbridge Island Community Sch., 1993—. Mem. pk. bd. coun. City of Winslow, 1989-90; bd. dirs. Bainbridge Island Pub. Libr., 1992—; mem. Land Use Profls. Forum, 1992—; mem. advisory com. Bainbridge Band Park & Rec. Gymnastics Com., 1993—. Mem. Ind. Bus. Assn., C. of C. Home: 330 Nicholson Pl NW Bainbridge Island WA 98110-1702

BLUMER, HARRY MAYNARD, architect; b. Stillwater, Okla., Aug. 27, 1930; s. Harry H. and Nona A. (Ftizpatrick) B.; m. C. Sue Linebaugh, Sept. 2, 1952; children: Eric W., Laura B., Martha L. BArch, Okla. State U., 1953; BS in Bus., Ariz. State U., 1976. Designer, draftsman Norman Byrd Architect, Oklahoma City, Okla., 1952, Overend & Boucher Architects, Wichita, Kans., 1953-54; archtl. designer, draftsman Louis G. Hesselden

Architect, Albuquerque, 1956; project designer, planner, constrn. & contract adminstr. Flatow, Moore, Bryan & Fairburn Architects, Albuquerque, 1956-61; regional architect U.S. Forest Svc., Albuquerque, 1961-62; v.p. prodn. Guirey, Srnka, Arnold & Sprinkle, Phoenix, 1962-82, Guirey, Srnka, Arnold & Sprinkle Architects, Phoenix, 1962-82; cons., architect pvt. practice, Paradise Valley, Ariz., 1982—; lectr. architecture Ariz. State U., Tempe, 1968-69; speaker in field. Contbr. articles to profl. publs. Bd. dirs., camping com., camp master plan design Maricopa County Coun. Campfire Girls, 1962-69; pres. N.Mex. Cactus and Succulent Soc., 1959-60; sec. Advancement Mgmt., Phoenix, 1972-73, dir., 1971-72; bd. govs. Amateur Athletic Union U.S., 1972-75, chmn. nat. conv. registration com., 1975; v.p. Ariz. Assn. Bd. MGrs., 1972-73, pres., 1973; treas. Pop Warner Football Assn., 1975; pres. parents club Scottsdale YMCA Judo Club, 1970-80. 1st lt. U.S. Army, 1954-56. Recipient Edn. Commendation award Constrn. Specifications Inst., 1980. Fellow AIA, Constrn. Specification Inst.; mem. ASTM. Office: 8517 N 49th St Paradise Valley AZ 85253-2002

BLUMHARDT, JON HOWARD, college administrator; b. Ft. Benning, Ga., Oct. 3, 1951; s. Howard Jerome and Joan (Tisdal) B.; m. Lisette Susan Vinet, Jan. 26, 1973; children: Matthew, Malia, Mark. BA in History, U. Hawaii, 1973, MA in Sociology, 1978, MEd, 1979; EdS, U Va., 1984. Media specialist U.S. Army JAG Sch., Charlottesville, Va., 1980-85; adminstr. officer OPM Fed. Exec. Inst., Charlottesville, 1985-86; chief resources mgmt. IRS Honolulu Dist., 1986-87; dir. Ednl. Media Svcs. Honolulu Community Coll., 1987—. Mem. Nat. Space Soc., German Benevolent Soc. (Honolulu), 4th degree Knights of Clumbus Coun. 6307, Am. Legion, U. Va. Alumni Assn. (life). Named one of Outstanding Young Men in Am., 1989, Eagle Scout, 1965; recipient Mahalo award Mayor of Honolulu, 1978, Cert. of Merit Aloha Coun. Boy Scouts Am., 1978, Scoutmaster award of Merit Nat. Eagle Scout Assn., 1990. Mem. DAV (life). Republican. Roman Catholic. Home: 1140 Lauloa St Kailua HI 96734-4065 Office: Honolulu Community Coll 874 Dillingham Blvd Honolulu HI 96817-4505

BLUMM, MICHAEL CHARLES, law educator; b. Detroit, Mar. 3, 1950; s. Charles F. and Margaret E. (Wilson) B. BA, Williams Coll., Williamstown, Mass., 1972; JD, George Washington U., Washington, D.C., 1976, LLM, 1979. Bar: Pa. 1976, D.C. 1977. Atty. Ctr. for Natural Areas, Washington, 1976-77, EPA, Washington, 1977-78; teaching fellow Nat. Resources Law Inst., Portland, Oreg., 1978-79; prof. of law Lewis and Clark Law Sch., Portland, 1979—; investigator Oreg. State Sea Grant Program, Corvallis, 1979-90; adv. com. mem. Northwest Power Planning Coun., Portland, 1981-83; bd. dirs. Northwest Water Policy Project, 1994—. Editor: (legal newsletter) Anadromous Fish Law Memo, 1979-90; contbr. articles to numerous profl. jours. Office: Lewis and Clark Law Sch 10015 SW Terwilliger Blvd Portland OR 97219-7768

BLUMMER, KATHLEEN ANN, counselor; b. Iowa Falls, Iowa, Apr. 17, 1945; d. Arthur G. and Julia C. (Ericson) Thorsbakken; m. Terry L. Blummer, Feb. 13, 1971 (dec. 1980); 1 child, Emily Erica. AA, Ellsworth Coll., Iowa Falls, 1965; BA, U. Iowa, 1967; postgrad., Northeastern Ill. U., 1969-70, U. N.Mex., 1980—; MA, Western N.Mex. U., 1973. Asst. buyer Marshall Field & Co., Chgo., 1967-68; social worker Cook County Dept. Pub. Aid, Chgo., 1968-69; tchr. Chgo. Pub. Schs., 1968-69; student fin. aid counselor Western N.Mex. U., Silver City, 1971-72; family social worker, counselor Southwestern N.Mex. Svcs. to Handicapped Children and Adults, Silver City, 1972-74; career edn. program specialist Galluo McKinley County (N.Mex.) Schs., 1974-76; dir. summer sch. Loving (N.Mex.) Mcpl. Schs., 1977; counselor, dept. chmn. Carlsbad (N.Mex.) Pub. Schs., 1977-82; counselor Albuquerque Pub. Schs., 1982—. Mem. AAUW (topic chmn. Carlsbad chpt., v.p. Albuquerque chpt.), N.Mex. Personnel and Guidance Assn., Theos Club, Highpoint Swim and Racquet Club (Albuquerque), Elks. Democrat. Lutheran.

BLUNT, ROBERT MATTESON, pyrotechnics and ordnance researcher emeritus; b. Denver, Oct. 21, 1916; s. Laurence Calvin and Ruth Esther (Howe) B.; m. June Correan Romelle Buros, Sept. 9, 1939; children: Tona Louise, Robert Matteson, Peter Howe, Stephen Thomas, John Eric. Student, MIT, 1935-38; BSc, U. Denver, 1947, MSc, 1958. Registered profl. engr., Colo. Rsch. engr. Douglas Leigh Inc., N.Y.C., 1939; sr. ballistic engr. Denver Ordnance Plant, 1941-43; rsch. physicist Remington Arms Co., Bridgeport, Conn., 1943-46; rsch. physicist Labs. for Applied Mechanics U. Denver, Denver Rsch. Inst., 1948-80, sr. rsch. fellow, 1980-87; sr. rsch. fellow emeritus U. Denver Rsch. Inst. Labs. for Applied Mechanics, 1987—; founder, gen. chmn. Internat. Pyrotechnic Seminars, Denver, 1968-78, chmn. emeritus, 1980—. Mem. Internat. Pyrotechnics Soc. (founder, pres. 1980-84, life mem. 1984—), Masons, Sigma Xi, (pres. U. Denver chpt. 1975), Pi Delta Theta, Sigma Pi Sigma. Home: 2495 S Quebec St Apt 17 Denver CO 80231-6067

BOADO, RUBEN JOSE, biochemist; b. Buenos Aires, Argentina, Feb. 8, 1955; came to U.S., 1985; s. Osvaldo Ruben and Lucia B.; m. Adriana Graciela Swiecicki, Jan. 11, 1980; children: Augusto Ruben, Lucrecia Adriana. MS, U. Buenos Aires, 1979, Diploma in Biochemistry, 1980, PhD, 1982. Rsch. fellow endocrinology Nat. Coun. Scientific Rsch., Buenos Aires, 1979-81, postdoctoral rsch. fellow in endocrinology, 1981-83, established investigator, 1983-89; internat. fellow UCLA Sch. Medicine, 1985-88, asst. rsch. endocrinologist, 1988-91, asst. prof. medicine, 1991—. Author numerous scientific publs. Recipient Best Scientific Paper award Internat. Assn. Radiopharmacology, Chgo., 1981, Cross-Town Endocrine Soc., L.A., 1988. Mem. AAAS, European Neurosci. Assn., Argentine Soc. Clin. Rsch., Am. Thyroid Assn. (travel award 1987), Endocrine Soc. (travel award 1984), Brain Rsch. Inst., Soc. Neurosci. Office: UCLA Dept Medicine/Endocrin Rsch Labs C-Lot Rm 104 Los Angeles CA 90024-1682

BOAL, DEAN, retired arts center administrator, educator; b. Longmont, Colo., Oct. 20, 1931; s. Elmer C. and L. Mildred (Snodgrass) B.; m. Ellen Christine TeSelle, Aug. 23, 1957; children: Brett, Jed. B.Music, B.Music Edn., U. Colo., 1953; M.Music, Ind. U., 1956; D. Musical Arts, U. Colo., 1959. Mem. faculty Hastings (Nebr.) Coll., 1958-60; head piano dept. Bradley U., Peoria, Ill., 1960-66; dean, pianist Peabody Conservatory, Balt., 1966-70; prof. piano, chair music SUNY, Fredonia, 1970-73; pres. St. Louis Conservatory, 1973-76; dir. radio sta. KWMU, St. Louis, 1976-78; v.p., gen. mgr. Sta. WETA-FM, Washington, 1978-83; dir. arts and performance programs Nat. Pub. Radio, Washington, 1982-89; pres. Interlochen (Mich.) Ctr. for the Arts, 1989-95; pres. emeritus, 1995—. Author: Concepts and Skills for the Piano, Book I, 1969, Book II, 1970; contbr. articles to profl. jours. Mem. adv. bd. U. Colo. Coll. Music, 1987—; trustee Alma Coll. Served with U.S. Army, 1953-55. Woodrow Wilson teaching fellow, 1983-89; recipient Disting. Alumnus award in Profl. Music Univ. Colo., 1987. Mem. Eastern Public Radio Network (chmn. 1979-82), Coll. Music Soc., Pi Kappa Lambda, Mu Phi Epsilon, Phi Mu Alpha. Presbyterian.

BOARDMAN, DAVID, newspaper editor; m. Barbara Winslow; children: Emily, Madeline. BS in Journalism, Northwestern U., 1979; M in Comm., U. Wash., 1983. Copy editor Football Weekly, Chgo., 1977-79; reporter Anacortes (Wash.) American, 1979-80, Skagit Valley Herald, Mt. Vernon, Wash., 1980-81; reporter, copy editor The News Tribune, Tacoma, 1981-83; copy editor The Seattle Times, 1983, editor, reporter, 1984, nat. editor, 1984-86, local news editor, 1986-87, asst. city editor, 1987-90, regional editor, 1990—; vis. faculty Poynter Inst. Media Studies, St. Petersburg, Fla.; panelist nat. conv. Investigative Reporters and Editors, Portland, Oreg., 1992, N.Y.C., 1993; speaker Oreg. Newspaper Pub. Assn., 1992. Recipient Goldsmith Prize in Investigative Reporting JFK Sch. Govt. Harvard U., 1993, Worth Bingham prize, 1993, Investigative Reporters and Editors award, 1993, AP Mng. Editors Pub. Svc. award, 1992, 1st place nat. reporting Pulitzer Prize, 1990; named finalist Pulitzer Prize for Pub. Svc., 1993. Office: The Seattle Times PO Box 70 1120 John St Seattle WA 98111

BOAT, RONALD ALLEN, business executive; b. Dayton, Ohio, Nov. 16, 1947; s. Robert Mallory and Elvetta June (Smith) B. Student, Naval Acad./Army Sch. Music, Norfolk, Va., 1968-69, Ariz. State U., 1966-68. Pres. Prodn. Svcs., Phoenix, 1968—, Greek Specialties Corp., Phoenix, 1980-94; v.p. Am. Baby Boomers, San Diego, 1984-93; co-founder, v.p. Internat. Food Network, San Diego, 1985-90; founder, pres. AMC Food Svcs. Corp., 1991—; pres. The Natural Light Co., 1994—; ind. prodr. Intel, Honeywell, Best Western, Sperry, Phoenix, 1985—; mem. Lund Team Real Estate Adv. Bd., 1991—; bd. dirs. Lund Real Estate Corp., 1990—. Mem. Lund Team Real Estate Adv. Bd., 1991—. With U.S. Army, 1968-71. With U.S. Army, 1968-71. Named Outstanding sales rep. Club Am., Dallas, 1972-73, Top Distbr. Club Am., Dallas, 1973; recipient Top Restaurant award Am. Heart Assn., Phoenix, 1988, Best of Phoenix restaurant award, 1991. Mem. Am. Radio Relay League, Internat. Platform Assn., Phi Mu Alpha Sinfonia. Republican. Office: P S A 14628 N 48th Way Scottsdale AZ 85254-2203

BOATNER, JAMES WILLIAM, trial court administrator; b. Randolph County, Ark., Nov. 4, 1936; s. John H. and Birdie L. (Brooks) B.; m. Phyllis K. Scott, Dec. 30, 1955; children: Debra K., James R., John Scott. BSBA, Ark. State U., 1967; MPA, City U., Bellevue, Wash., 1990, MBA, 1991. Data processing technician IBM/Univac, 1959-65; programmer mgr. Neiman Marcus, Dallas, 1967-69; data processing mgr. Crown Zellerbach Corp., Portland, Oreg., 1969-75; profl. photographer Boatner's Portrait Studio, McMinnville, Oreg., 1975-78; real estate salesman Shasta Real Estate, Klamath Falls, Oreg., 1978-80; systems coord. Oreg. Jud. Dept., Portland, 1980-84; info. analyst Oreg. Jud. Dept., Salem, 1984-89; dir. exec. svcs. Oreg. Jud. Dept., Portland, 1989-91; trial ct. adminstr. Oreg. Jud. Dept., Albany/Corvallis, 1991—; mem. Juvenile Svcs. Commn., Linn County, Albany, 1993—, Linn/Benton (Oreg.) Mediation Commn., 1991—, Linn County Criminal Justice Coun., 1993—, Willamette Criminal Justice Coun., Corvallis, Oreg., 1993—. Mem. Young Reps., Jonesboro, Ark., 1966-67, Kiwanis, McMinville, 1975-78, C. of C., McMinnville, 1975-78. Served with USAF, 1955-59. Mem. Oreg. Assn. Ct. Adminstrs. Mem. Ch. of Christ. Office: Oreg Jud Dept PO Box 1749 Albany OR 97321-0491

BOATWRIGHT, DANIEL E., state legislator; m. Teresa Boatwright; children: Dan, David, Donald. AB, JD, U. Calif.-Berkeley. Former mayor City of Concord, Calif., mem. city council, 1966-72; city atty. City of Brentwood, Calif., 1965-72; former dist. atty. Contra Costa County, Calif.; sole practice, Concord, from 1970; former mem. Calif. State Assembly, Sacramento; mem. Calif State Senate, Sacramento, 1980—, chmn. bus. and professions com., select com. on state procurement and expenditure practices, mem. joint commn. on prison constrn. and ops., mem. coms. on appropriations, elections and reapportionment, revenue and taxation, fin., investment and internat. trade, transp.. Active community sporting and charitable orgns. Served with U.S. Army, Korea. Office: 3086 State Capital Sacramento CA 95814

BOAZ, DONIELLA CHAVES, psychotherapist, consultant; b. Grand Junction, Colo., Apr. 8, 1934; d. Leon T. and Marian (Fonder) Hutton; m. Richard Boas, Apr. 7, 1956 (div. 1983); children: Roxanne, Annika, Becca; m. Jack J. Chaves, Mar. 11, 1995. Cert. pastoral ministry Seattle U., 1978; cert. clin. pastoral edn. Va. Mason Hosp., 1979; BA, Antioch West, 1980; postgrad. Lan Ting Inst. cross-cultural studies PROC, 1986, 92, 94, C.G. Jung Inst., Zurich, 1986, 87, 89. Cert. neuro-linguistic programmer, 1983. Owner Donalee's Studio of Dance, Kirkland, Wash., 1952-63; adminstrv. asst. Ch. of Redeemer, Kenmore, Wash., 1974-76; counselor Eastside Mental Health, Bothell, Wash., 1976-79; psychotherapist, Seattle, 1979—; owner, cons. Optimum Options, Seattle, 1979—; founder DISCOVERIES Seminars, various other govt., bus., non-profit orgns., nat. and internat. trainer, cons.; mem. adj. faculty Seattle U., Northwest Coll. Holistic Studies and Huston Sch. Theology, 1980-87; mem. Wash. State Dept. Health Adv. Com. for Cert. Mental Health Counselors, 1994—. Author: Embrace Your Child-Self: Change Your Life, 1993. V.p. Episcopal Ch. standing com. on stewardship, 1979-81; active in local politics, 1968-80; mem. Clin. Pastoral Edn. Mem. Seattle Counselors Assn. (pres.). Avocations: philosophy, carpentry, bridge, entertaining, traveling. Office: Lane's End Pub Co Grosvenor House 500 Wall St Apt 309 Seattle WA 98121-1534

BOBB, PETER MICHAEL, health infection control technician; b. Appleton, Wis., Aug. 9, 1956; s. Franklin Conrad Bobb and Margaret Mary (Van Wie) Caporaso. BS, U. Iowa, 1991; postgrad., Purdue U., 1993, Utah State U., 1994. Cert. Nat. Inst. for Cert. of Sterile Processing and Distbn. Pers., cert. Registered Ctrl. Svc. Technician, cert. Sterile Processing and Distbn. Technician. Lab. technician in microbiology U. Iowa Hosp., Iowa City, 1981-84; v.p. computer programs Van Wie Enterprises, Galena, Ill., 1984; ctrl. svc. technician U. Iowa Hosp., Iowa City, 1985-91, St. Joseph Hosp., Tacoma, Wash., 1992—; owner Evergreen Infection Control, Tacoma, 1994—; sec. quality assurance com. St. Joseph Hosp., Tacoma, 1994—. Editor: Central Service Technical Manual, 1994. Mem. 43d Gov.'s Indsl. Safety and Health Conf., Wash., 1993—; mem. Health Care Panel, 1994—. Mem. AAAS, Am. Soc. Health Ctrl. Svc. Pers., Wash. State Ctrl. Svc. Assn., Internat. Assn. Healthcare Ctrl. Svc. Material Mgmt. (cert.). Office: Pete Bobb Enterprises 4214 N Huson St Tacoma WA 98407-4314

BOBERG, DOROTHY KURTH, author; b. Lincoln, Nebr., Mar. 17, 1930; d. Herman R. and Regina E. Kurth; m. John Elliott Boberg, Sept. 17, 1951; 1 child, Mark Craig. BA, U. Nebr., 1951; postgrad., Calif. State U., Northridge, 1959-62, U. So. Calif., 1981. Libr. Nebr. Legis. Coun., Lincoln, 1952; child welfare worker L.A. County, 1953-57, 67-68; rsch. assoc. Nuclear Facilities/Radiation Monitoring in Calif. Another Mother for Peace, Beverly Hills, Calif., 1975; exec. v.p. So. Calif. divsn. UN Assn., L.A., 1977-78. Author: Evolution and Reason Beyond Darwin, 1993; editor Nebraska Blue Book. Resolutions chair L.A. County Dem. Cen. Com.; chair UN Internat. Solar Exhibition, L.A., 1978, Mayor's Lifeline Com., Earthquake Prediction Task Force; pres. Northridge Civic Assn., 1971-73. Recipient Achievement award Nebr. Sec. State, 1993, Admiral, Nebr. Navy/Gov. State Nebr., 1993. Mem. AAAS, Soc. Study Evolution, AAUW (pres. San Fernando Valley Br. 1966-67), Phi Beta Kappa, Psi Chi, Alpha Kappa Delta. Home: 10912 Nestle Ave Northridge CA 91326-2849

BOBKOSKI, CARL F., research and development executive; b. 1954. Treas. Marion Labs., Kansas City, Mo.; pres., gen. mgr. Nordic Labs. (subs. of Marion Labs.), Montreal, Que., Can.; CEO, pres. Inc., Prairie View, Ill., 1988-91; exec. v.p. Gensia, Inc., San Diego, 1991—. Office: Gensia Inc 9360 Towne Centre Dr San Diego CA 92121-3030*

BOBRICK, STEVEN AARON, property manager; b. Denver, Apr. 11, 1950; s. Samual Michael and Selma Gertrude (Birnbaum) B.; m. Maria Diane Boltz, Oct. 5, 1980. Attended, U. Colo., 1968-72. Registered apt. mgr. Owner Bobrick Constrn., Denver, 1969-72; with Bell Mtn. Sports, Aspen, Colo., 1972-75; mgr. Compass Imports, Denver, 1975-80, Aurora (Colo.) Bullion Exch., 1980-81; contr. Bobrick Constrn., Aurora, 1981-85; appraiser Aurora, 1985-89; property mgr. Aurora Community Mental Health, Aurora, 1989—; active real estate and constrn. Aurora, 1989—. Co-author: Are You Paying Too Much in Property Taxes, 1990. Coun. mem. City of Aurora, 1981-89; chmn. Explore Commercial Opportunities, Aurora, 1986-89, bd. dirs.; bd. dirs. Adam County Econ. Devel. Commn., Northglenn, Colo., 1985-89; vice chair Aurora Urban Renewal Authority, 1982-89; chmn. Aurora Enterprise Zone Found., 1991—; bd. dirs. Aurora Community Med. Clinic, 1987-88. Office: Aurora Cmty Mental Health 10782 E Alameda Ave Aurora CO 80012

BOBROW, SUSAN LUKIN, lawyer; b. Cleve., Jan. 18, 1941; d. Adolph and Yetta (Babkow) Lukin; m. Michael L. Bobrow, Jan. 28, 1962 (div. Nov. 1975); children: Elizabeth Bobrow Pressler, Erica, David; m. Martin J. Bochower, Nov. 28, 1985 (div. Dec. 1987). Student, Antioch Coll., Yellow Springs, Ohio, 1958-61; BA, Antioch Coll., L.A., 1975; JD, Southwestern U., L.A., 1979. Bar: Calif., 1980. Atty. Law Offices of Susan Bobrow, Beverly Hills, Calif., 1983-88; assoc. Schulman & Miller, Beverly Hills, 1988-89; staff counsel Fair Polit. Practices Commn., Sacramento, Calif., 1990—; mem. panel for paternity defense L.A. Superior Ct., 1984. Bd. dirs. San Fernando Valley Friends of Homeless Women and Children, North Hollywood, Calif., 1985-88; mem. adv. bd. Project Home, Sacramento Interfaith Svc. Coun., 1990-91; v.p. cmty. affairs B'nai Israel Sisterhood, Sacramento, 1991-93. Recipient commendation Bd. Govs. State Bar of Calif., 1984. Mem. Inst. Noetic Scis. (steering coun. Sacramento Inst. Noetic Scis. 1994), Sacramento County Bar Assn. (com. on profl. responsibility 1993-94, alt. del. to state bar conv. 1991). Democrat. Office: Fair Polit Practices Commn 428 J St Ste 800 Sacramento CA 95814-2330

BOBRY, HOWARD HALE, electronics industry executive; b. Rochester, N.Y., Feb. 29, 1948; s. Gerald and Rose (Wolfson) B.; m. Valerie J. Jarosz, May 20, 1984. BSEE, Case Western Res. U., 1971; MBA, Baldwin Wallace Coll., 1980. Registered profl. engr. Project engr. Western Res. Electronics, Twinsburg, Ohio, 1970-72; cons. engr. Cleve., 1972-75; project engr. Lorain (Ohio) Products Corp., 1975-77; engring.mgr. Lortec Power Systems, North Ridgeville, Ohio, 1977-83; pres. H.H. Bobry & Co., Shaker Heights, Ohio, 1983-87, Mill Creek, Wash., 1983-87; pres. Albar Inc., Lynnwood, Wash., 1987-94, Custom Components, Inc., Edmonds, Wash., 1994—. Patentee in field (9 in electronics); contbr. articles to profl. jours. Mem. IEEE, NSPE, Nature Conservancy, Mensa. Office: Custom Components Inc 144 Railroad Ave Ste 226 Edmonds WA 98020-4100

BOCCIA, JUDY ELAINE, home health agency executive, consultant; b. San Diego, Aug. 29, 1955; d. Robert Garrett and Jerry Athalee (Carruth) Stacy; 1 child, Jennifer Lynn. BSN, Calif. State U., San Diego, 1978. RN, Calif.; lic. pub. health nurse, Calif. Staff nurse Univ. Hosp., U. Calif., San Diego, 1978-80, 81-82, Moffitt Hosp., San Francisco, 1980-81, Humana Huntington, Huntington Beach, Calif., 1982-84; intravenous and hospice vis. nurse Town & Country Nursing, Garden Grove, Calif., 1984-85; vis. nurse Vis. Nurse Assn., Orange, Calif., 1985-86; v.p. Doctors and Nurse Med. Mgmt., Newport Beach, Calif., 1986-89; dir. nursing HMSS, So. Calif., 1989-90; pres. Premier Care, Irvine, 1990-91, Homelife Nursing & Staffbuilders, Lake Forest, Calif., 1991—; cons., Calif., 1987—; pres. Homelife Nursing-Staff Builders, O.C., 1991—; AIDS educator; presenter in field. Mem. Oncology Nursing Soc., Intravenous Nurse Soc. Democrat. Methodist. Home: 28232 Festivo Mission Viejo CA 92692-2617 Office: Homelife Nursing Inc 23832 Rockfield Blvd Ste 280 Lake Forest CA 92630-2820

BOCHIN, HAL WILLIAM, speech communication educator; b. Cleve., Feb. 23, 1942; s. Harold Washington and Miriam Rita (Sherer) B.; m. Janet Suzanne Schindler, June 7, 1975; 1 child, Christopher. BA, John Carroll U., 1964; MA, U. Wis., 1967; PhD, Ind. U., 1970. Asst. prof. Calif. State U., Fresno, 1969-74, assoc. prof., 1974-78, prof., 1978—. Author: Richard Nixon: Rhetorical Strategist, 1990; co-author: Hiram Johnson: Political Revivalist, 1995, Hiram Johnson: A Bio-Bibliography, 1988, (with others) The Inaugural Addresses of 20th Century American Presidents, 1993, U.S. Presidents as Orators, 1995. Mem. Speech Communication Assn. Roman Catholic. Home: 2776 W San Ramon Ave Fresno CA 93711-2752 Office: Calif State U Dept Speech Communication Fresno CA 93740

BOCK, RUSSELL SAMUEL, author; b. Spokane, Wash., Nov. 24, 1905; s. Alva and Elizabeth (Mellinger) B.; m. Suzanne Ray, Feb. 26, 1970; children: Beverly A. Bock Wunderlich, James Russell. B.B.A., U. Wash., 1929. Part-time instr. U. So. Calif., UCLA, 1942-50; with Ernst & Ernst, CPAs, Los Angeles, 1938, ptnr., 1951-69; cons. Ernst & Young, 1969—. Author: Guidebook to California Taxes, annually, 1950—, Taxes of Hawaii, annually, 1964—; also numerous articles. Dir., treas. Cmty. TV So. Calif., 1964-74; dir., v.p. treas., So. Calif. Symphony-Hollywood Bowl Assn., 1964-70; trustee Internat. Ctr. for Ednl. Devel., 1969-72, Claremont Men's Coll., 1964-70; bd. dirs. Cmty. Arts Music Assn., 1974-76, 78-84, Santa Barbara Symphony Assn., 1976-78, Santa Barbara Boys and Girls Club, 1980-93, UCSB Affiliates, 1983-85, Direct Relief Internat., 1995—. Mem. Am. Inst. C.P.A.s (council 1953-57, trial bd. 1955-58, v.p. 1959-60), Calif. Soc. C.P.A.s (past pres.), Los Angeles C. of C. (dir. 1957-65, v.p. 1963), Sigma Phi Epsilon, Beta Alpha Psi, Beta Gamma Sigma. Clubs: Birnam Wood Golf, Santa Barbara Yacht. Office: 300 Hot Springs Rd Apt 190 Santa Barbara CA 93108-2069

BOCK, S. ALLAN, physician, educator; b. Balt., Apr. 28, 1946; s. Sam and Charlotte Bock; m. Judith Lloyd, Oct. 19, 1985; children: Sam, Lea. AB, Washington U., 1968; MD, U. Md., 1972. Diplomate Am. Bd. Pediatrics, Am. Bd. Allergy and Immunology; lic. physician, Colo. Intern U. Md. Hosp., Balt., 1972-73; resident in pediatrics U. Colo. Med. Ctr., Denver, 1973-74; asst. prof. pediatrics U. Colo. Med. Ctr., Boulder; fellow in pediatric allergy and immunology Nat. Jewish Hosp. and Rsch. Ctr., Denver, 1974-76; assoc. clin. prof. pediatrics U. Colo. Health Scis. Ctr., Boulder, 1982-90, clin. prof. pediatrics, 1990—; sr. staff physician Nat. Jewish Ctr. Immunology and Respiratory Medicine, 1976—; pediatric allergist Dept. Health and Hosps., 1976-84. Contbr. numerous articles to profl. jours. Recipient Jacob E. Finesinger prize for excellence in psychiatry, 1972. Fellow Am. Acad. Allergy and Immunology, Am. Acad. Pediatrics; mem. Alpha Omega Alpha. Office: Boulder Valley Asthma Allergy 3950 Broadway St Boulder CO 80304-1104

BOCZKIEWICZ, ROBERT EUGENE, freelance journalist; b. Galatia, Ill.. BJ, U. Mo., postgrad.; postgrad., U. Rochester. Bur. chief St. Louis Globe-Democrat, 1969-79; city editor Clarion-Ledger, Jackson, Miss., 1980; acting asst. city editor L.A. Herald-Examiner, 1980; freelance reporter Reuters Wire Svc., Denver Post, Kansas City Star, Pueblo Chieftan, The Oklahoman, Religion News Svc., 1987—; vis. instr. reporting U. Mo. Sch. Journalism, 1977; leader, panelist univ. and press inst. seminars; stringer N.Y. Times and other nat., regional and local news orgns., 1964—. Recipient Washington Journalism Ctr. grad. fellowship, 1967, 1st pl. feature story award Ill. AP, 1968; named to Nev. Fellows in Bus. Journalism U. Nev., Reno, 1994. Mem. Soc. Profl. Journalists (local officer, nat. conv. del., St. Louis chpt. excellence in news reporting award 1973), Religion Newswriters Assn. Office: PO Box 18669 Denver CO 80218-0669

BODDIE, LEWIS FRANKLIN, obstetrics-gynecology educator; b. Forsyth, Ga., Apr. 4, 1913; s. William F. and Luetta T. (Sams) B.; m. Marian Bernice Claytor, Dec. 27, 1941; children: Roberta Boddie Miles, Lewis Jr., Bernice B. Jackson, Pamela, Kenneth, Fredda, Margaret. BA, Morehouse Coll., 1933; MD, Meharry Med. Sch., 1938. Diplomate Am. Bd. Ob-Gyn (proctor parti exam Los Angeles area 1955-63). Intern Homer-Phillips Hosp., St. Louis, 1938-39, resident in ob-gyn, 1939-42; mem. attending staff Grace Hosp., Detroit, 1944-48, Parkside Hosp., Detroit, 1944-48, Los Angeles County Gen. Hosp., 1952-79; sr. mem. attending staff Queen of Angels Hosp., Los Angeles, 1964-91, chmn. dept. ob-gyn, 1968-70; asst. clin. prof. U. So. Calif. Sch. Medicine, L.A., 1953-79, prof. emeritus, 1979—; assoc. clin. prof. U. Calif., Irvine, 1956-81. vice chmn. bd. mgrs. 28th St. YMCA, Los Angeles 1960-75; steward African Meth. Episc. Ch., Los Angeles, 1949—. Fellow ACS (life), Am. Coll. Ob-Gyn (life), Los Angeles Ob-Gyn Soc. (life): mem. Los Angeles United Way (priorities and allocations coms., 1985—, standards com. 1987—, new admission com. 1988—), Children's Home Soc. (bd. dirs. 1952-89, , trustee 1989—, v.p. 1963-68, pres. 1968-70), Child Welfare League Am. (bd. dirs. 1969-76). Republican.

BODENSIECK, ERNEST JUSTUS, mechanical engineer; b. Dubuque, Iowa, June 1, 1923; s. Julius Henry and Elma (Sommer) B.; BSME, Iowa State U., 1943; m. Margery Elenore Sande, Sept. 9, 1943; children: Elizabeth Bodensieck Eley, Stephen. Project engr. TRW Inc., Cleve., 1943-57; supr. rocket turbomachinery Rocketydyne div. Rockwell Internat., Canoga Park, Calif., 1957-60, supr. nuclear turbomachinery Rocketydyne div., 1964-70; advance gear engr. Gen. Electric Co., Lynn, 1960-64; asst. mgr. engine components Aerojet Nuclear Systems Co., Sacramento, 1970-71; gear and bearing cons. AiResearch div. Garrett Corp., Phoenix, 1971-81; transmission cons. Bodensieck Engring. Co., Scottsdale, Ariz., 1981—. Registered profl. engr., Ariz. Mem. ASME, AIAA, Soc. Automotive Engrs. (various coms.), Aircraft Industries Assn. (various coms.), Am. Gear Mfrs. Assn. (mem. aerospace, gear rating and enclosed epicyclic coms.), Nat. Soc. Profl. Engrs., Pi Tau Sigma. Lutheran. Patentee in field. Home: 7133 N Via De Alegria Scottsdale AZ 85258-3812

BODEY, BELA, immuno-morphologist; b. Sofia, Bulgaria, Jan. 18, 1949; came to U.S., 1985, naturalized, 1994; s. Joseph and Rossitza (Derebeeva) B.; m. Victoria Psenko, Aug. 29, 1979; children: Bela Jr., Vivian. MD, Med. Acad., Sofia, 1973; PhD in Immuno-Biology, Inst. Morphology, Bulgarian Acad. Sci., Sofia, 1977. Lic. physician, exptl. pathologist, embryologist, immuno-morphologist. Asst. prof. Semmelweis Med. U., Budapest, 1977-80; prof. Inst. Hematology, Budapest, 1980-83; rsch. assoc. Tufts U., Boston, 1985; rsch. fellow immuno-pathology Mass. Gen. Hosp./Harvard U., Boston, 1986; rsch. fellow Childrens Hosp. L.A., 1987-90, rsch. scientist, 1991-92; asst. prof. rsch. pathology, Sch. of Medicine Univ. Southern Calif., 1992—; vis. prof. Alexander von Humboldt Found., Ulm, Fed. Republic Germany, 1984. Mem. Am. Assn. Cancer Rsch., Am. and Can. Acad. Pathology, French Soc. Cell Biology, French Soc. Electronmicroscopy, Internat. Soc. Exptl. Hematology, N.Y. Acad. Scis., Masons. Roman Catholic.

Home: 15745 Saticoy St Van Nuys CA 91406-3155 Office: U So Calif Sch Medicine 2011 Zonal Ave Los Angeles CA 90033-1034

BODILY, DAVID MARTIN, chemist, educator; b. Logan, Utah, Dec. 16, 1933; s. Levi Delbert and Norma (Christenson) B.; m. Beth Alene Judy, Aug. 28, 1958; children—Robert David, Rebecca Marie, Timothy Andrew, Christopher Mark. Student, Utah State U., 1952-54; B.A., Brigham Young U., 1959, M.A., 1960; Ph.D., Cornell U., 1964. Postdoctoral fellow Northwestern U., Evanston, Ill., 1964-65; asst. prof. chemistry U. Ariz., Tucson, 1965-67; asst. prof. fuels engring. U. Utah, Salt Lake City, 1967-70, assoc. prof., 1970-77, prof., 1977-92, prof. chem. and fuels engring., 1992—, chmn. dept. mining and fuels engring., 1976-83, assoc. dean Coll. Mines and Mineral Industries, 1983-89. Contbr. articles to profl. jours. Mem. Am. Chem. Soc. (chmn. Salt Lake sect. 1975). Mem. LDS Ch. Home: 2651 Cecil Dr Salt Lake City UT 84124-2905 Office: U Utah 3290 Meb Salt Lake City UT 84112-1180

BODILY, GERALD P., career counselor, consultant; b. Preston, Idaho, Apr. 13, 1913; s. Wilford and Albena (Peterson) B.; m. Nancy Katherine Prim, Dec. 26, 1939; children: Gerald P. Jr., Richard W., Margaret Nan, William Waite. BS in Psychology, Brigham Young U., 1939; MS in Career Counseling, Calif. State U., 1986. Supr. occupational analysis U.S. Dept. Labor, Washington, 1940-44; supr. job analysis Fairchild Engine & Aircraft Co., Hagerstown, Md., 1944-47; counselor career Byron Harless & Assocs., Tampa, Fla., 1947-53; specialist wage and salary aerospace firms L.A., 1953-57; pvt. practice Orange County, Calif., 1957-64; counselor State of Calif., 1964-80; presenter seminars, nat. and state convs., counseling assocs., 1987-91. Author: Job Evaluation Plan for Factory Occupations, 1955; co-author: PC Verbal Capacity Sampler (test), 1951. past pres. Calif. State U. Sr. Citizens Students, 1984-86. Mem. AACD (govt. rels. com.), Nat. Career Devel. Assn., Assn. Adult Devel. and Aging (govt. rels. com.), Calif. Assn. Adult Devel. and Aging (founding pres.), Calif. Assn. Counseling and Devel. (exec. coun.), Calif. Career Devel. Assn., Calif. Employment Counselors Assn. (editor, sec.- treas.). Home and Office: 7671 Hunter Way Stanton CA 90680-1512

BODIN, ARTHUR M., clinical psychologist; b. N.Y.C., July 11, 1932; s. Harry S. and Rose B.; m. Miriam Irene, June 25, 1961; children: Douglas Adam, Laura June. BA in Zoology, Swarthmore Coll., 1954; MA in Edn., NYU, 1957; PhD in Psychology, SUNY, Buffalo, 1966. Lic. psychologist, Calif.; lic. marriage, family & child counselor, Calif.; diplomate in clin. psychology Am. Bd. Profl. Psychology; diplomate in forensic psychology Am. Bd. Profl. Psychology. Sr. rsch. fellow Mental Rsch. Inst., Palo Alto, Calif., 1965—; ind. practice clin. psychology Palo Alto, 1967—; bd. dirs. Silicon Valley Ind. Practice Assn., Santa Clara County, Calif., Mental Rsch. Inst., Palo Alto. Editor: (newsletter) Calif. State Psychologist, 1973-74, (bulletins) Bull. Am. Acad. Forensic Psychologists, 1980-83, State Psychol. Assoc. Affairs, 1990-91; contbr. numerous chpts. to books, articles to profl. jours. Mem. early childhood edn. com. Palo Alto Unified Sch. Dist., Palo Alto, 1970. Elected Disting. Practitioner in Psychology, Nat. Acads. of Practice, 1993; recipient Disting. Achievement in New Directions in Family Therapy award Am. Family Therapy Assn., 1981. Fellow APA (coun. of reps. 1979-81, 83-85, 91, 93, Karl F. Heiser Presdl. award 1993, pres. divsn. family psychology 1988, pres. divsn. of state psychol. assn. affairs 1993, Family Psychologist of Yr. award 1990), Acad. Clin. Psychology, Profl. Acad. Custody Evaluators, Am. Orthopsychiat. Assn.; mem. Calif. Psychol. Assn. (pres. 1976, Disting. Svc. award 1978). Office: Mental Research Institute 555 Middlefield Rd Palo Alto CA 94301-2124

BODINSON, HOLT, conservationist; b. East Orange, N.J., Nov. 14, 1941; s. Earl Herdien and Hermoine (Holt) B. BA, Harvard, 1963; m. Ilse Marie Maier, Feb. 29, 1970. Sr. asso. Am. Conservation Assn., Inc., N.Y.C., 1966-70; dir. Office of Policy Analysis, N.Y. State Dept. Environ. Conservation, Albany, 1970-71, dir. div. ednl. services, 1971-77; dir. Ariz.-Sonora Desert Mus., 1977-78; exec. dir. Safari Club Internat./Safari Club Internat. Conservation Fund, Tucson, 1980-89; conservation dir. Safari Club Internat., Tucson, 1991-94, dir. wildlife and govtl. affairs, 1994—; committeeman, Montgomery Twp. Conservation Commn., 1967-70; sec. N.Am. del. Conseil Internat. de la Chasse et de la Conservation du Gibier, 1988—; gen. sec. World Hunting and Conservation Congress, 1988; dir. Internat. Wildlife Mus., 1991—; nat. sec. United Conservation Alliance, 1994—. Served with arty. AUS, 1964-66. Mem. Stony Brook-Millstone Watershed Assn. (dir.), Safari Club Internat. (dir. Ariz. chpt.), N.Y. Outdoor Edn. Assn. (dir.), Outdoor Writers Assn. of Am., N.Y. State Rifle and Pistol Assn. (dir.). Episcopalian. Club: Harvard of So. Ariz. (pres.). Author: (with Clepper and others) Leaders in American Conservation, 1971. Contbg. editor Jour. Environmental Edn., 1968-94; dir. Conservationist mag. 1971-77, N.Y. State Environment newspaper, 1971-74. Home: 4525 N Hacienda Del Sol Tucson AZ 85718-6619 Office: 4800 W Gates Pass Rd Tucson AZ 85745-9600

BODKIN, HENRY GRATTAN, JR., lawyer; b. L.A., Dec. 8, 1921; s. Henry Grattan and Ruth May (Wallis) B.; m. Mary Louise Davis, June 28, 1943; children: Maureen L. Dixon, Sheila L. McCarthy, Timothy Grattan. B.S. cum laude, Loyola U., Los Angeles, 1943, J.D., 1948. Bar: Calif. 1948. Pvt. practice Los Angeles, 1948-51, 53—; ptnr. Bodkin, McCarthy, Sargent & Smith (predecessor firms), L.A., 1948-51, 53—. Mem. L.A. Bd. Water and Power Commrs., 1972-74, pres., 1973-74; regent Marymount Coll., 1962-67; trustee Loyola-Marymount U., 1967-91, vice chmn., 1985-86. With USNR, 1943-45, 51-53. Fellow Am. Coll. Trial Lawyers; mem. Calif. State Bar (mem. exec. com. conf. of dels. 1968-70, vice chmn. 1969-70), California Club, Riviera Tennis Club, Tuna Club, Chancery Club (pres. 1990-91), Phi Delta Phi. Republican. Roman Catholic. Home: 956 Linda Flora Dr Los Angeles CA 90049-1631 Office: Bodkin McCarthy Sargent & Smith 707 Wilshire Blvd Fl 51 Los Angeles CA 90017-3501

BOEDER, THOMAS L., lawyer; b. St. Cloud, Minn., Jan. 10, 1944; s. Oscar Morris and Eleanor (Gile) B.; m. Carol-Leigh Coombs, Apr. 6, 1968. BA, Yale U., 1965, LLB, 1968. Bar: Wash. 1970, U.S. Dist. Ct. (we. dist.) Wash. 1970, U.S. Dist. Ct. (ea. dist.) Wash. 1972, U.S. Ct. Appeals (9th cir.) 1970, U.S. Supreme Ct. 1974, U.S. Ct. Appeals (D.C. cir.) 1975. Litigation atty. Wash. State Atty. Gen., Seattle, 1970-72, antitrust div. head, 1972-76, chief, consumer protection and antitrust, 1976-78, also sr. asst. atty. gen. and criminal enforcement, 1979-81; ptnr. Perkins Coie, Seattle, 1981—. Served with U.S. Army, 1968-70, Vietnam. Mem. ABA (antitrust sect.), Wash. State Bar Assn. (antitrust sect.). Lutheran. Office: Perkins Coie 1201 3rd Ave Fl 40 Seattle WA 98101-3000

BOEHM, FELIX HANS, physicist, educator; b. Basel, Switzerland, June 9, 1924; came to U.S., 1952, naturalized, 1964; s. Hans G. and Marquerite (Philippi) B.; m. Ruth Sommerhalder, Nov. 26, 1956; children: Marcus F., Claude N. M.S., Inst. Tech., Zurich, 1948, Ph.D., 1951. Research assoc. Inst. Tech., Zurich, Switzerland, 1949-52; Boese fellow Columbia U., 1952-53; faculty Calif. Inst. Tech., Pasadena, 1953—, prof. physics, 1961—, William L. Valentine prof., 1985-94, William L. Valentine prof. emeritus, 1995—; Sloan fellow, 1962-64; NSF Sen. fellow Niels Bohr Inst., Copenhagen, 1965-66; Sloan fellow Cern, Geneva, 1971-72, Laue-Langevin Inst., 1980. Recipient Humboldt award, 1980, 84, Bonner prize, 1995. Fellow Am. Phys. Soc. (Tom W. Bonner prize in nuclear physics 1995); mem. Nat. Acad. Scis. Home: 2510 N Altadena Dr Altadena CA 91001-2836 Office: Calif Inst Tech Mail Code 161 33 Pasadena CA 91125

BOEHM, PAUL EUGENE, pharmacist; b. Bismarck, N.D., Sept. 4, 1937; m. Judith Ann Boehm; children: Noelle, Scott, Kevin. BS, N.D. State U., 1959, MS, 1972. Commd. 2d lt. USAF, 1959, advanced through grades to capt., 1964; maj. USAFR, 1974-90, ret., 1990; asst. chief pharmacy svc. Bismarck Med. Ctr., 1959-60; asst. chief pharmacy sci. USAF Med. Ctr., Lackland AFB/San Antonio, Tex., 1960-63; chief pharmcy svc. USAF Med. Ctr., Wiesbaden, Germany, 1963-66, Wright Patterson/Dayton, Ohio, 1966-68; asst. chief pharmacy svc. VA Med. Ctr., Fargo, N.D., 1968-70, chief pharmacy svc., 1968-70; asst. chief pharmacy svc. VA Med. Ctr., Palo Alto, Calif., 1974-77, chief pharmacy svc., 1977—; pharmacy cons. to USAF Surgeon Gen., Wiesbaden, 1963-66; mem. USAF Inspector Gen. Team, Dayton, 1966-68. Coach children's soccer team Am. Soccer Assn., Cupertino, Calif., 1983-89, children's basketball team, YMCA, Cupertino, 1983-89, children's baseball team, Cupertino, 1987-89. Capt. USAF, 1960-68, Europe. Mem. N.D. Hosp. Pharmacists Assn. (v.p. 1969-70), N.D. Pharm. Assn., Am. Soc. Hosp. Pharmacists, Am. Pharm. Assn., Calif. Soc. Hosp. Pharmacists, Calif. Pharm. Assn., Quatra County Hosp. Pharmacists Assn.

BOEHM, ROBERT FOTY, mechanical engineer, educator, researcher; b. Portland, Oreg., Jan. 16, 1940; s. Charles Frederick and Lufteria (Christie) B.; m. Marcia Kay Pettibone, June 10, 1961; children—Deborah, Robert Christopher. B.S. in Mech. Engring., Wash. State U., Pullman, 1962, M.S., 1964; Ph.D., U. Calif., Berkeley, 1968. Registered profl. engr., Calif. With Gen. Electric Co., San Jose, Calif., 1964-66; mem. faculty U. Utah, Salt Lake City, 1968-90, prof. mech. engring., 1976-90, chmn. dept., 1981-84; Nat. Sandia Labs., Albuquerque, 1984-85; prof., chmn. dept. U. Nev., Las Vegas, 1990—, univ. sys. sr. liaison to Dept. Energy, 1994-95; mem. Utah Solar Adv. Com., Utah Energy Conservation and Devel. Coun., 1980-88; sr. univ. tech. liaison to U.S. Dept. Edn., 1994-95. Author: Design Analysis of Thermal Systems, 1987; editor: Direct Contact Heat Exchange, 1988; tech. editor Jour. Solar Energy Engring.; contbr. articles to profl. jours. Named Utah Engring. Educator of Yr., Utah Engrs. Coun., 1988, Disting. Tchr., U. Utah, 1989; recipient UNLV Barrick Sr. Rsch. award, 1994. Fellow ASME; mem. ASHRAE, Am. Soc. for Engring. Edn., Internat. Solar Energy Soc., Corvair Soc. Am., Vintage Chevrolet Club Am., Sigma Xi. Home: 4999 Mesa View Dr Las Vegas NV 89120-1216 Office: U Nev Mech Engring Dept Box 454027 Las Vegas NV 89154-4027

BOEKELHEIDE, VIRGIL CARL, chemistry educator; b. Cheslea, S.D., July 28, 1919; s. Charles F. and Eleonor (Toennies) B.; m. Caroline Barrett, Apr. 7, 1924; children: Karl, Anne, Erich. AB magna cum laude, U. Minn., Mpls., 1939, PhD, 1943. Instr. U. Ill., Urbana, 1943-46; asst. prof. to prof. U. Rochester, 1946-60; prof. dept. chemistry U. Oreg., Eugene, 1960—. Contbr. articles to profl. jours. Recipient Disting. Achievement award U. Minn., 1967; recipient Alexander von Humboldt award W.Ger. Govt., 1974, 82, Centenary Lectureship Royal Soc. G.B., 1983, Coover award Iowa State U., 1981; Disting. scholar designate U.S.-China Acad. Sci., 1981; Fulbright Disting. prof. Yugoslavia, 1972. Mem. NAS, Pharm. Soc. Japan (hon.). Home: 2017 Elk Ave Eugene OR 97403-1788 Office: U Oreg Dept Chemistry Eugene OR 97403

BOEREM, RONALD MERLE, educator; b. Munich, May 3, 1948; came to U.S., 1949; s. Richard D. and Helen I. (Schmid) B. AA, Chaffey C.C., 1968; BA, U. Calif., Riverside, 1970, MA, 1973. Tchr. Upland (Calif.)-Ontario Reading Svc., 1973-75, Arcadia Reading Clinic Pomona (Calif.), 1975-77; cartoonist Danney Ball Prodns., Hemet, Calif., 1977-79; tchr. Citrus Coll., Covina, Calif., 1989-90, Mt. San Antonio Coll., Walnut, Calif., 1975—; panelist H.P. Lovecraft Centennial Conf., Providence, R.I., 1990. Columnist/cartoonist: Newspaper Syndicate, 1977-79; contbr. articles to profl. jours. Home: 1041 W La Deney Dr Ontario CA 91762-1231 Office: Mt San Antonio Coll 1100 N Grand Ave Walnut CA 91789-1341

BOERSMA, LAWRENCE ALLAN, animal welfare administrator; b. London, Ontario, Can., Apr. 24, 1932; s. Harry Albert and Valerie Kathryn (DeCordova) B.; m. Nancy Noble Jones, Aug. 16, 1952 (div. 1962) children: Juliana Jaye, Dirk John; m. June Elaine Schiefer McKim, Nov. 22, 1962; children: Kenneth Thomas McKim, Mark Rennie McKim. BA, U. Nebr., 1953, MS, 1955; PhD, Sussex U., 1972. Journalism tchr. Tech. High Sch., Omaha, Nebr., 1953-55; dir. pub. rels., chair journalism dept. Adams State Coll., Alamosa, Colo., 1955-59; advt. sales analyst, advt. salesman Better Homes and Gardens, Des Moines, N.Y.C., 1959-63; advt. account exec. This Week Mag., N.Y.C., 1963-66; eastern sales dir., mktg. dir. Ladies' Home Jour., N.Y.C., 1966-75; v.p. assoc. pub., v.p. pub. Saturday Evening Post and The Country Gentleman, N.Y.C., 1975; v.p., dir. mktg. and advt. sales Photo World Mag., N.Y.C., 1975-77; advt. mgr. LaJolla (Calif.) Light, 1977-80; owner, photographer Allan/The Animal Photographers, San Diego, 1980—; pres., CEO The Photographic Inst. Internat., 1982-86; dir. comty. rels. San Diego Humane Soc./Soc. for Prevention Cruelty to Animals, 1985-94; assoc. exec. dir. The Ctr. for Humane Edn. for So. Calif., 1994—; adj. asst. prof. Grad. Sch. Bus., Pace U., N.Y.C., 1964-65; adj. instr. N.Y. Inst. of Advt., 1974-77; adj. prof. Sch. Bus. Mesa Coll., San Diego, 1981-84, City Coll., San Diego, 1982-86; adj. prof. Coll. Bus. Adminstrn. U. LaVerne, San Diego, 1985; pres., CEO United Animal Welfare Found., San Diego, 1992-94; bd. dirs. Escondido Humane Soc. Found., 1994—; chmn., CEO Internat. Dolphin Project, 1995—. Contbr. and photographer articles to mags. Spokesperson Coalition for Pet Population Control, San Diego, 1990, 93, Com. Against Proposition C-Pound Animals for Med. Rsch., San Diego, 1990, spay-Neuter Action Project, 1991, mem. steering com., 1991, bd. dirs., 1992-93; mem. evaluation subcom. County of San Diego Dept. Animal Control Adv. Com.; founder, chair Feral Cat Coalition of San Diego County, 1992-93; vol. in pub. info. San Diego/Imperial Counties chpt. ARC, 1993—; mem. pub. info. officers San Diego County Emergency Svcs. Orgns., 1993—. Fellow Royal Photographic Soc. of Great Britain, Profl. Photographers of Calif.; mem. PRSA (chmn. So. Tier, N.Y. chpt. 1972), Al Bahr Shrine (pres. 1988, Businessmen's Club), Shriners, Masons, Soc. Animal Welfare Adminstrs., Nat. Soc. Fund Raising Execs. (bd. dirs. 1988-89, treas. San Diego chpt. 1990-91, mem. nat. faculty, 1992-93). Republican. Presbyterian. Home: 3503 Argonne St San Diego CA 92117-1009

BOERSMA, P. DEE, ecologist, researcher, educator; b. Mt. Pleasant, Mich., Nov. 1, 1946; d. Henry W. and Vivian (Anspach) B. BS, Ctrl. Mich. U., 1969; PhD, Ohio State U., 1974. Asst. prof. Inst. Environ. Studies, U. Wash., Seattle, 1974-80, assoc. prof., 1980-88, prof. environ. studies, 1988-93, prof. zoology, 1988—, adj. prof. women's studies, 1993—, assoc. dir., 1987-93, acting dir., 1990-91; mem. sci. adv. com. for outer continental shelf Environ. Studies Program, Dept. Interior, 1980-83; prin. investigator Magellanic Penguin Project, N.Y. Zool. Soc., 1982—; Evans vis. fellow U. Otago, New Zealand, 1995. Contbr. articles to profl. jours. Mem. adv. U.S. del. to UN Status Women Commn., N.Y.C., 1973, UN World Population Conf., Romania, 1974; mem. Gov. Lowry's Task Force on Wildlife, 1993; sci. adv. EcoBios, 1985-95; bd. dirs. Zero Population Growth, 1975-82, Washington Environ. Coun., 1994—, Washington Nature Conservancy, 1995—; mem. scholar diplomatic program Dept. of State, 1977. Recipient Outstanding Alumni award Cen. Mich. U., 1978, Matrix award Women in Comm., 1983; named to Kellogg Nat. Leadership Program, 1982-85; recipient Top 10 Outsiders of Yr. award Outside Mag., 1987, Outstanding Centennial Alumni award Ctrl. Mich. U., 1993. Fellow Am. Ornithol. Union (regional rep. Pacific seabird group 1981-85); mem. AAAS, Ecol. Soc. Am., Wilson Ornithol. Soc., Cooper Ornithol. Soc., Soc. Am. Naturalists, Soc. for Conservation Biology (bd. govs. 1991-94, pres. elect 1995—). Club: Gopher Brokers (Seattle) (pres. 1982-83). Office: U Wash Dept Zoology Box 351800 Seattle WA 98195-1800

BOESE, SANDRA JEAN, publishing executive; b. Ely, Minn., July 31, 1940; d. John Frank and Millie Jean (Prebeg) Simonick; m. Lee Robert Boese Sr., June 15, 1963; children: Lee Robert Jr., Joy Karin. BA in Speech and Elem. Edn., Marquette U., 1962. Elem. tchr., 1962-67; pub., editor Classroom Connections, Inc., Merced and Sacramento, 1988—, also chmn. bd.; pres. Calif. State Bd. Edn., Sacramento, 1984-86; exec. dir. Teen Talk Radio Show, 1994—. Trustee Merced City Sch. Dist., 1975-83; commr. Calif. Post-Secondary Edn. Commn., Sacramento, 1983; bd. dirs. Far-West Lab., San Francisco, 1984, The Achievement Coun., San Francisco, 1985. Recipient Commendation of Exemplary Svc. award Calif. State Senate, 1983, Cert. of Appreciation, Calif. State Dept. Edn., 1983; named Woman of Distinction Soroptimist Internat., 1987. Mem. AAUW (Woman of Distintion 1986), Calif. Sch. Bds. Assn. (bd. dirs. del. assembly, 1978-81, chmn. conf. 1979-80, founder chmn. polit. action com. 1982-83, Outstanding Svc. award 1982, Spl. Recognition 1986), Merced City C. of C. (pres. 1985-86, Athena award 1988), Nat. Assn. State Bds. Edn. (bd. dirs. 1984-86), Assn. Marquette U. Women (Mary Neville Bielefeld award 1986). Republican. Roman Catholic. Office: Classroom Connections Inc 2824 Park Ave Ste C Merced CA 95348-3375

BOGARD-REYNOLDS, CHRISTINE ELIZABETH, financial services executive; b. Aberdeen, Md., Apr. 15, 1954; d. Charles Francis and Donna June (Mosbaugh) Bogard; divorced; 1 child, Zachary Kagan; m. Cary Polevoy. Student, U. Colo., 1972-73. Adminstrv. asst. Lange Co., Broomfield, Colo., 1973-74; field sales and svc. rep. Bowman Products Div., Denver, 1974-75; cashier Regency Inn, Denver, 1975-76; gen. mgr., sec.-treas., Edison Agy. Inc., Denver, 1976-81; gen. mgr. Edison Press, Inc., Englewood, Colo., 1979-80, 81; advt. dir. Blinder, Robinson & Co., Englewood, 1981-89; v.p., sec.-treas. CBF Market Svcs. (named change to Comvest Corp.), Inc., 1989-91; owner Document Prep., Englewood, Colo., 1991—; former corp. sec. Child Care Ctrs. North Am., Inc., 1984. Home: 6866 S Sycamore St Littleton CO 80120 Office: Document Prep 7310 S Alton Way Englewood CO 80112-2317

BOGART, FRANK JEFFREY, system/product planning engineer; b. Johnson City, Tenn., May 17, 1942; s. Frank Lavon and Mary Stein (Hattan) B.; m. JoAnne Ruth Hodgson, Aug. 1, 1964; children: Christopher Alan, Timothy Andrew. BS, U. R.I., 1963; MS, Rutgers U., 1965; postgrad., U. Colo., 1970-74. Disting. mem. tech. staff AT&T Bell Labs., Holmdel, N.J., 1963-65, 68-69; mem. tech. staff AT&T Bell Labs., Denver, 1969—; participant Career Awareness Program, AT&T, Denver, 1985—. Patentee in field. Various positions Boy Scouts Am., 1951—; treas. 1st Congl. Ch., United Ch. of Christ, 1994—. Served to capt. U.S. Army, 1965-67, Vietnam. Decorated Bronze Star; recipient God and Svc. award United Ch. of Christ, 1990, Silver Beaver award Boy Scouts Am., 1976, Disting. Commr. award Boy Scouts Am., 1991. Mem. Telephone Pioneers Am. Home: 4796 Devonshire St Boulder CO 80301-4137 Office: AT&T Bell Labs 11900 Pecos St Denver CO 80234-2703

BOGART, WANDA LEE, interior designer; b. Ashville, N.C., Feb. 26, 1939; d. Bob West and Virginia Elizbeth (Worley) McLemore-Snyder; m. Sterling X. Bogart, Feb. 12, 1962; children: Kevin Sterling, Kathleen Elizabeth. BA, San Jose (Calif.) State U., 1961. Cert. interior designer. Tchr. Redondo Beach (Calif.) Sch. Dist., 1962-65; free-lance interior designer Ladera, Calif., 1970-75; designer MG Interior Design, Orange, Calif., 1975-80; prin., pres. Wanda Bogart Interior Design Inc., Orange, 1980—. Contbr. articles to profl. jours. Named one of Top 20 Interior Designers in So. Calif. Ranch and Coast Mag., 1987. Mem. Internat. Interior Design Assn. (profl. mem., cert.), Am. Soc. Interior Design (cert.), Orange C. of C. Office: Wanda Bogart Interior Design Inc 1440 E Chapman Ave Orange CA 92666-2229

BOGATAY, TODD CUNNINGHAM, architect; b. Columbus, Ohio, Mar. 1, 1937; s. Paul Josef and Henrietta Beecher (Cunningham) B. AB cum laude, Harvard U., 1959, MArch, 1962. Lic. architectural, Ariz., Mass. Designer, draftsman William Lescaze FAIA, N.Y.C., 1962-63, 65-66, Antonin Raymond FAIA, Tokyo, 1963-65; designer, planner San Juan, 1966; designer I.M. Pei and Ptnrs., N.Y.C., 1967, Richard Meier, FAIA, N.Y.C., 1967-69; prin. Bogatay, Architect, N.Y.C., 1970-71, Boston, 1972-80, Bisbee, Ariz., 1981—; instr. Pratt Inst., Bklyn., 1969-70, Boston Archtl. Ctr., 1973-76. Designer Residence for Chief of State of Cambodia, 1962; arch. American Plywood Assn., 1970 (Design award). Recipient Heritage Fund Grant Ariz. State Parks, Bisbee, 1993. Mem. Nat. Coun. of Archtl. Registration Bds. Office: Bogatay Archs PO Box Z 6 Naco Rd Bisbee AZ 85603-0209

BOGDAN, CAROLYN LOUETTA, financial specialist; b. Wilkes-Barre, Pa., Apr. 15, 1941; d. Walter Cecil and Ethna Louetta (Kendig) Carpenter; m. James Thomas Bogdan, May 5, 1961; 1 child, Thomas James. Grad. high sch., Kingston, Pa. Head bookkeeper Forty Ft. (Pa.) State Bank, 1959-63, U.S. Nat. Bank, Long Beach, Calif., 1963-65; office mgr. United Parts Exchange, Long Beach, 1976-81; contract adminstr. Johnson Controls, Inc., Rancho Dominguez, Calif., 1981-88, credit coord., 1989—; co-owner, acct. Bogdan Elec. R & D, Lakewood, Calif., 1981—. Mem. Radio Amateur Civil Emergency Svc., Los Angeles County Sheriff Dept., 1974—, records keeper, 1988-93, radio comms. officer, 1994—. Mem. NAFE, Nat. Notary Assn., Am. Inst. Profl. Bookkeepers, Tournament of Roses Radio Amateurs (pin chmn. 1975—), Calif. State Sheriff's Assn. (assoc.). Republican. Home: 3713 Capetown St Lakewood CA 90712-1437 Office: Johnson Controls Inc 19118 S Reyes Ave Compton CA 90221-5810

BOGDAN, JAMES THOMAS, secondary education educator, electronics researcher and developer; b. Kingston, Pa., Aug. 14, 1938; s. Fabian and Edna A. (Spray) B.; m. Carolyn Louetta Carpenter, May 5, 1961; 1 child, Thomas James. BS in Edn., Wilkes U., Wilkes-Barre, Pa., 1960. Cert. chemistry and physics tchr., Calif. Tchr. Forty Fort (Pa.) Sch. Dist., 1960-63; tchr., chmn. sci. dept. L.A. Unified Sch. Dist., 1963—; owner, mgr. Bogdan Electronic Rsch. & Devel., Lakewood, Calif., 1978—; cons. Lunar Electronics, San Diego, 1978-83, T.E. Systems, L.A., 1988-89. Author, pub. The VHF Reporter newsletter, 1967-76. Tng. officer Los Angeles County Disaster Comm., 1968-91, UHF and microwave sys. staff officer, 1991-94, dep. chief comm. officer, 1994—; pin chmn. Tournament of Roses Comm. Group, Pasadena, Calif., 1985—. Mem. IEEE. Republican. Office: PO Box 62 Lakewood CA 90714-0062

BOGDANOFF, DAVID WELLS, aerospace research engineer; b. Summit, N.J., Feb. 25, 1941; s. David and Mary Joyce (Wells) B.; m. Sue Ellen Porter, Dec. 26, 1974. BME, McGill U., Montreal, Que.; PhD in Aerospace Engring., Princeton U., 1968. Postdoctoral fellow Plasma Physics Lab., Princeton (N.J.) U., 1968-69, Jet Propulsion Lab., Pasadena, Calif., 1969-71; research engr. UCLA, 1972; research engr. physics dept. U. So. Calif., Los Angeles, 1973-75; research engr. U. Wash., Seattle, 1976-88; sr. research sci. NASA Ames Research Ctr., Moffett Field, Calif., 1988—. Contbr. articles to profl. jours. Mem. AIAA, Sigma Xi. Democrat. Home: 572 E Arbor Ave Sunnyvale CA 94086-3767 Office: NASA AMES Research Ctr Mail Stop 230-2 Moffett Field CA 94035-1000

BOGGESS, TYREE M, technical writer; b. Portsmouth, N.H., Aug. 28, 1955; d. Ross Cafaro and Nancy Gladys (Utz) Balasky; m. Randolph Cowan Boggess; m. Frederick J. Overholt Jr., Sept. 16, 1989 (div.). AS in Occupational Elecs., United Elecs. Inst., 1981. Ins. rater USAA Ins., Tampa, Fla., 1981; elec. tech. Collins Avionics, Melbourne, Fla., 1981-82, Carson, Calif., 1982; tech. writer Raytheon Svc. Corp., San Diego, 1982-84; elec. tech. Teledyne Ryan Elecs., San Diego, 1984-85, tech. writer, 1985-88, engr. liaison, 1988-89; mktg. Geotel-Telemet, Hauppauge, N.Y., 1989-90; tech. writer Prespective Computer Analysis, Coronado, Calif., 1993-95; tech. writer, desktop pub. Internat. Technoprint, Inc., 1995—; CEC calligraphy instr. San Diego State U. Author: The Tale of the Three Lost Souls, 1991, The Diary of Dr. Samuel Colvin Cowan, Jr. 1899-1927, 1994; contbg. reporter TRE Newsletter, San Diego, 1985-89. Vol. Courthouse Children's Waiting Rm., San Diego, 1992-93; vol., data base mgr. Gerry Brummitt for City Coun., Coronado, 1992; coord. March of Dimes, San Diego, 1986; bd. dirs. Coronado Beach Hist. Mus., 1992, United Meth. Women, Coronado, 1993—, New Entra Casa, San Diego; tchr. St. Paul's Unitarian Meth. Ch., Coronado, 1992-93. Mem. Nat. Mgmt. Assn. (membership dir. 1986-87, dir. publicity and awards 1987, decorations chair 1987), Recreational Assn. (dir. trips and tours 1987-89), Teledyne Ryan Elec., Women's Internat. Ctr., Nat. and San Diego Geneal. Socs. Home: 811 I Ave Coronado CA 92118-2447

BOGGESS-GALLEGOS, FRANCES, management consultant; b. Baton Rouge, La., Mar. 8, 1963; d. Thomas Shelton and Lindley Jones (Cheatham) Boggess; m. Andrés Alvaro Gallegos, May 30, 1992; 1 child, Lindley Loraine. BA in Tech. Journalism, Colo. State U., 1988; MPA, U. Colo., Denver, 1992. Ind. cons. Denver, 1990-91; exec. dir. Sacramento Entrepreneurship Acad., 1991-93; pres. The Challenge Course Learning Co., Sacramento, 1992—. Vol. various Dem. polit. campaigns, Colo., 1986-91. Recipient Meyer J. Nathan Civic Svc. award 1988. Mem. ASTD (pub. rels. dir. 1992—), Assn. for Experiential Edn., Colo. State U. Alumni Assn. (bd. dirs. 1991—), Toastmasters. Democrat. Roman Catholic. Office: The Challenge Course Learning Co 352 Wagon Wheel Dr Phoenix AZ 85021

BOGGS, CARL ELWOOD, JR., political scientist, writer; b. Long Beach, Calif., July 22, 1937; s. Carl Elwood and Harriet M. (Watts) B.; m. Ann Incaviglia, Nov. 20, 1961 (div. 1970). BA, U. Calif., Berkeley, 1963, MA, 1965, PhD, 1970. Prof. Wash. U., St. Louis, 1970-77, U. Calif., Irvine, 1977-78, UCLA, 1978-81, U. So. Calif., L.A., 1981-84, Capleton U., Ottawa, Can., 1984-85, Nat. U., L.A., 1986—. Author: The Two Revolutions, 1984, Gramsci's Marxism, 1976, The Impasse of European Communism, 1982, Social Movements and Political Power, 1986, Intellectuals and the Crisis of Modernity, 1993; contbg. writer L.A. Weekly/Village View, 1989—; mem. editorial bd. Theory and Soc., 1977—, Socialist Rev., 1971—, Humanities in Soc., 1981-83, Radical Am., 1977—, Democracy and Socialism, 1989—. Mem. Peace and Freedom Party, Calif., 1968; L.A. coord. Green's, 1988-91; radio programmer Sta. KPFK, L.A., 1981—. Ford Found. fellow, 1967, teaching award fellow Wash. U., 1972, Dean's Coun. award Carleton U.,

1985. Home: 1251 Wellesley Ave # 103 Los Angeles CA 90025-1196 Office: Nat U 9920 S La Cienega Blvd Inglewood CA 90301-4423

BOGGS, SAM, JR., geology educator; b. Kings Creek, Ky., July 26, 1928; s. Sam and Lucinda (Caudill) B.; m. Sumiko Sasaki, Nov. 18, 1952; children: Barbara Sue, Steve R., Cindy L. BS in Geology, U. Ky., 1956; PhD, U. Colo., 1964. Registered geologist. Petroleum exploration geologist Phillips Petroleum Co., Colo., N.Mex., Utah, 1956-61; rsch. geologist Esso Prodn. Rsch. Co., Houston, 1964-65; mem. faculty Dept. Geol. Scis. U. Oreg., Eugene, 1965—, prof. geology, head dept. geology, 1974-80; rsch. geologist U.S. Geol Survey, Oreg., intermittent summers, 1966-81; vis. prof. geology Inst. Geology, Nat. Taiwan U., 1972-73; vis. rsch. prof. Ocean Rsch. Inst., U. Tokyo, 1981—; scientist-in-residence Argonne (Ill.) Nat. Lab., 1982; participant in ocean drilling program Leg 127, Japan Sea, 1989. Author: Principles of Sedimentology and Stratigraphy, 1987, 2nd edit., 1995, Petrology of Sedimentary Rocks, 1992; contbr. articles to profl. jours. With U.S. Army, 1949-52. NSF fellow, summer 1962, 63; NSF grantee U.S. China Coop. Sci. program, 1972-73; U. Tokyo rsch. awardee, 1981-82. Fellow Geol. Soc. Am. (Oreg.); mem. Am. Assn. Petroleum Geologists, Soc. Sedimentary Geology. Office: Univ Oreg Dept Geol Scis Eugene OR 97403

BOGGS, STEPHEN TAYLOR, cultural anthropologist, researcher, consultant; b. Chgo., July 13, 1924; s. Judge and Jeannette Francina (Neligh) B.; m. Joan Whitehorn, Feb. 15, 1929; children: Christofer H., Ellen E., Andrew K. AB summa cum laude, Harvard Coll., 1947; PhD, Washington U., St. Louis, 1954. Acting asst. prof. sociology Stanford (Calif.) U., 1953-56; social anthropologist NIMH, Bethesda, Md., 1957-60; exec. sec. Am. Anthrop. Assn., Washington, 1961-66; prof. anthropology U. Hawaii, Honolulu, 1966-83; emeritus U. Hawaii, Manoa, 1984—; expert witness on Hawaiian culture; rschr., cons. KEEP, Kamahameha Schs., Honolulu, 1971-73, Bishop Mus. Nanakuli Community Study, Hawaii, 1966-68, various native Hawaii groups. Author: Speaking, Relating, and Learning: A Study of Hawaiian Children at Home and at School, 1985; contbr. articles to profl. jours. Mem. Low Income Housing Coalition, Honolulu, 1989-94; vol. Amnesty Internat. Nederland, Colo., 1990—. With U.S. Army, 1943-46. Recipient Shaw fellowship Harvard Coll., 1947-48, Social Sci. Rsch. Coun. fellow, 1951-52. Fellow Am. Anthrop. Assn. Roman Catholic. Home: # 1922 46 033 Allanela Pl Kaneohe HI 96744-3707

BOGGS, STEVEN EUGENE, lawyer; b. Santa Monica, Calif., Apr. 28, 1947; s. Eugene W. and Annie (Happe) B. BA in Econ., U. Calif., Santa Barbara, 1969; D of Chiropractic summa cum laude, Cleveland Chiropractic, L.A., 1974; PhD in Fin. Planning, Columbia Pacific U., 1986; JD in Law, U. So. Calif., 1990. Bar: Calif. 1990, U.S. Dist. Ct. (cen. dist.) Calif. 1990, Hawaii 1991, U.S. Ct. Appeals (9th cir.); CFP; lic. real estate salesman, Hawaii; lic. chiropractor Hawaii, Calif.; lic. radiography X-ray supr. and operator. Faculty mem. Cleveland Chiropractic Coll., 1972-74; pres. clinic dir. Hawaii Chiropratic Clinic, Inc., Aiea, 1974-87; pvt. practice Honolulu, 1991—; cons. in field; seminar presenter 1990—. Contbr. articles to profl. jours. Recipient Cert. Appreciation State of Hawaii, 1981-84. Fellow Internat. Coll. of Chiropractic; mem. ABA, Am. Trial Lawyers Assn., Am. Trial Lawyers Assn. of Hawaii, Am. Chriopractic Assn., Hawaii State Chiropractic Assn. (pres. 1978, 85, 86, v.p. 1977, sec. 1979-84, treas. 1976, other coms., Valuable Svc. award 1984, Cert. Appreciation 1986, Cert. Achievement 1986, Chiropractor of Yr. 1986, Outstanding Achievement award 1991). Democrat. Office: 804 Fort Street Mall Honolulu HI 96813-4318

BOGUSKY, ALF, museum director; b. Lethbridge, Alta., Can., Mar. 16, 1947. BFA, U. Lethbridge, 1975. Dir., curator So. Alta. Art Gallery, Lethbridge, 1979-85; dir. Art Gallery of Windsor, Ont., 1985-92; exec. dir. Edmonton Art Gallery, Alberta, Can., 1992—. Author/curator numerous exhbn. catalogues. Mem. Can. Art Mus. Dirs. Orgn. (sec. 1987—, v.p.), Can. Mus. Assn., Assn. Cultural Execs., Ont. Assn. Art Galleries (chmn. govt. rels. com. 1989-92). Office: Edmonton Art Gallery, 2-Sir Winston Churchill Sq, Edmonton, AB Canada T5J 2C1

BOHANNAN, PAUL JAMES, anthropologist, writer, former university administrator; b. Lincoln, Nebr., Mar. 5, 1920; s. Hillory and Hazel (Truex) B.; m. Laura Marie Smith, May 15, 1943 (div. 1975); 1 child, Denis Michael; m. Adelyse D'Arcy, Feb. 28, 1981. B.A., U. Ariz., 1947; B.Sc., Oxford U., Eng., 1949, Ph.D., 1951. Lectr. social anthropology Oxford (Eng.) U., 1951-56; asst. prof. anthropology Princeton (N.J.) U., 1956-59; prof. Northwestern U., Evanston, Ill., 1959-75, U. Calif., Santa Barbara, 1976-82; prof., dean social scis. and communications U. So. Calif., Los Angeles, 1982-87, prof. emeritus, 1987—. Author: Justice and Judgement, 1957, Africa and Africans, 1964, Divorce and After, 1970, We, the Alien, 1991, How Culture Works, 1995. Served to capt. U.S. Army, 1941-45. Decorated Legion of Merit. Mem. Am. Anthrop. Assn. (pres. 1979-80), Am. Ethnol. Soc. (dir. 1963-66), African Studies Assn. (pres. 1963-64), Social Sci. Research Council (dir. 1962-64).

BOHANNON-KAPLAN, MARGARET ANNE, publisher, lawyer; b. Oakland, Calif., July 6, 1937; d. Thomas Morris and Ruth Frances (Davenport) Bohannon; m. Melvin Jordan Kaplan, Feb. 2, 1961; children: Mark Geoffrey, Craig Andrew, Stephen Joseph, David Benjamin, Jonathan Michael. Student Smith Coll., 1955-56, U. Cin., 1956; B.A. in Philosophy, U. Calif.-Berkeley, 1960; LL.B., LaSalle Extension U., 1982, Coll. Fin. Planning, 1985. Bar: Calif. 1982. Engaged in property mgmt., real estate investment Kaplan Real Estate, Berkeley and San Francisco, 1961-77; investment exec. Wellington Fin. Group, San Francisco, 1977—; cons. fin. planning and law, San Francisco and Carmel, Calif., 1982—; pres. Wellington Publs., Carmel, 1983—, Exec. Advt., Carmel, 1983—. Author: (pseudonym Helen P. Rogers), Everyone's Guide to Financial Planning, 1984, Social Security: An Idea Whose Time Has Passed, 1985, The American Deficit: Fulfillment of a Prophecy?, 1988, The Election Process, 1988, The Deficit: 12 Steps to Ease the Crisis, 1988, (series) Taking A Stand On, 1991, Alternatives, 1992; editor: Taking A Stand (series), 1991, What Role if Any, Should Government's Role be Regarding Child Care in the United States?, 1991, What if Any, Should Governments Role Be Regarding Halth Care in the United States, 1992, What Role Does, And What Role Should Media Play in Choosing Our Candidates for National Office?, 1993, Doesn't Anyone Care About the Children, 1994, Responsibility: Who Has It and Who Doesn't and What That Means to The Nation, 1994, White Hats: People Who Try To Make A Difference, 1994. Co-founder The Harry Singer Found., Carmel, Calif., 1988; ind. candidate for U.S. Senate, 1992. Mem. ABA, Calif. Bar Assn., Calif. Real Estate Assn., Inst. Cert. Fin. Planners, Estate Planning Council, The Federalist Soc. Club: Commonwealth (San Francisco). Office: PO Box 223159 Carmel CA 93922-3159

BOHANSKE, ROBERT THOMAS, psychologist; b. Amsterdam, N.Y., June 22, 1953; s. Thomas A. and Nadine K. (Grayson) B.; m. Jacquie C. Scholar, Apr. 20, 1980; children: Michael S., Jason A. BS, Ariz. State U., 1975; MS, U. So. Calif., 1977; PhD, U. Ariz., 1983. Lic. psychologist, Ariz., Calif. Resident Inst. Behavioral Medicine, Phoenix, 1982-83, postdoctoral fellow, 1983-84, asst. dir. out-patient services, 1985-87; chief psychologist Behavioral Health Inst. Mesa (Ariz.) Luth. Hosp., 1987-88; chief psychologist, clin. dir neurobehavioral program Meridian Pt. Rehab. Hosp., Scottsdale, Ariz., 1988-91; pvt. practice rehab. neuropsychology Mesa and Scottsdale, Ariz., 1991—; pres. MARC Behavioral Health Svcs., 1990—, Behavioral Edn. Inst., Mesa, 1992—. Mem. APA, Ariz. Psychol. Assn., Am. Congress of Rehab. Medicine. Jewish. Home: 5045 E Redfield Rd Scottsdale AZ 85254-2847 Office: 2058 S Dobson Rd Ste 3 Mesa AZ 85202-6455

BOHLIN, CAROL FRY, mathematics educator; b. Charlotte, N.C., Feb. 15, 1958; d. P. Allen and Carolyn J. (Sigmon) Fry.; married. BA, U. N.C., 1980, M of Human Devel. and Learning, 1982; PhD in Math. Edn. and Cognitive Neurosci., Ohio State U., 1987. Tchr. math. Quail Hollow Jr. High Sch., Charlotte, 1980-83; grad. teaching asst. Ohio State U., Columbus, 1983-87, asst. prof., 1987-88; asst. prof. math. edn. Ind. U., Bloomington, 1988-90; asst. prof. math. edn. Calif. State U., Fresno, 1990-93, assoc. prof., 1993—; dir. San Joaquin Valley Math. Project, Fresno, 1990—; cons. Fresno County Office Edn., 1990—. Editor: A Problem a Day for Primary People, 1990; also articles. Lowry Harding fellow Ohio State U., 1984; Calif. Jaycees Outstanding Young Educator award, 1992. Mem. ASCD, APA, Am. Ednl. Rsch. Assn., Sch. Sci. and Math. Assn. (fin. com. 1990-92, conf. com. 1993—, chair ann. conf. 1994), Nat. Coun. Tchrs. Math. (life), Calif. Math. Coun. (cons. 1990—, v.p./conf. chair 1994—), Math. Assn. Am., Am. Coun. for Learning Disabilities, Am. Psychol. Soc. (charter), Internat. Soc. Tech. in Edn., Internat. Group Psychology Math. Edn., N.Am. Group for Psychology Math. Edn. (conf. com. 1993), Internat. Orgn. Women and Math. Edn., Learning Disabilities Assn., Ohio Coun. Tchrs. Math., Phi Beta Kappa. Republican. Lutheran. Office: Calif State U Sch Edn and Human Devel 5005 N Maple Ave Fresno CA 93740-8025

BOHMAN, VERLE RUDOLPH, animal nutritionist; b. Peterson, Utah, Dec. 29, 1924; s. Victor Rudolph and Nancy A. (Fernelius) B.; m. Renee Jorgensen, June 22, 1945; children: Margaret Louise, Verle Duane, Jolene Renee, Van Reid, Gregory Nathan. BS, Utah State U., 1949, MS, 1951; PhD, Cornell U., 1952. Prof., researcher U. Nev., Reno, 1952-86; cons. Vet. Rsch. and Devel., Truckee, Calif., 1986—. Editor-in-chief: Jour. Animal Sci., 1970-72, sec. editor, 1968-70. With USN, 1944-46, PTO. Mem. Am. Soc. Animal Sci. (pres. 1974-75, pres. elect 1973-74). Mormon. Home and Office: 3924 W 3900 N Morgan UT 84050-9699

BOHN, DENNIS ALLEN, electrical engineer, consultant, writer; b. San Fernando, Calif., Oct. 5, 1942; s. Raymond Virgil and Iris Elouise (Johnson) B.; 1 child, Kira Michelle; m. Patricia Tolle, Aug. 12, 1986. BSEE with honors, U. Calif., Berkeley, 1972, MSEE with honors, 1974. Engring. technician Gen. Electric Co., San Leandro, Calif., 1964-72; research and devel. engr. Hewlett-Packard Co., Santa Clara, Calif., 1973; application engr. Nat. Semicondr. Corp., Santa Clara, 1974-76; engring. mgr. Phase Linear Corp., Lynnwood, Wash., 1976-82; v.p. research and devel., ptnr. Rane Corp., Mukilteo, Wash., 1982—; founder Toleco Systems, Kingston, Wash., 1980. Suicide and crisis ctr. vol., Berkeley, 1972-74, Santa Clara, 1974-76. Served with USAF, 1960-64. Recipient Am. Spirit Honor medal USAF, 1961; Math. Achievement award Chem. Rubber Co., 1962-63. Editor: We Are Not Just Daffodils, 1975; contbr. poetry to Reason mag.; tech. editor Audio Handbook, 1976; contbr. articles to tech. jours.; columnist Polyphony mag., 1981-83; 2 patents in field. Mem. IEEE, Audio Engring. Soc., Tau Beta Pi. Office: Rane Corp 10802 47th Ave W Mukilteo WA 98275-5000

BOHN, EDWARD M., research and development executive; b. 1942. PhD in Nuclear Engring., U. Ill., 1968; MBA, U. Chgo., 1976. With Argonne Nat. Labs., Lemont, Ill., 1968-79, TRW, 1979-90; pres. Quest Integrated, Kent, Wash., 1990—. Office: Quest Integrated 21414 68th Ave S Kent WA 98032-2416*

BOHN, PAUL BRADLEY, psychiatrist; b. Santa Monica, Calif., Apr. 11, 1957; m. Pamela Honey Summit, Nov. 17, 1990. BA in Pharmacology, U. Calif., Santa Barbara, 1980; MD, U. Calif., Irvine, 1984. Diplomate Am. Bd. Psychiatry and Neurology. Psychiat. resident UCLA, 1984-88, assoc. dir. anxiety disorders clinic, 1989—, dir. social anxiety clinic, 1993—; fellow U. So. Calif., L.A., 1988-89; cons. in psychiatry Didi Hirsch Community Mental Health Ctr., Venice, Calif., 1986-88; substance abuse group co-leader Main St. Counseling Svcs., Venice, 1987-88; v.p. Pacific Psychopharmacology Rsch. Inst., Santa Monica, 1990—; pvt. practice psychiatry Santa Monica, 1988—; asst. clin. prof. UCLA, 1990—; candidate L.A. Psychoanalytic Inst., 1988—. Chm. polio com., Rotary Club, Santa Monica, 1992. Grantee Ciba-Geigy, Santa Monica, 1992. Mem. Am. Psychiat. Assn., So. Calif. Psychiat. Assn., Anxiety Disorders Assn. of Am., Obsessive Compulsive Found.. Office: 2730 Wilshire Blvd Ste 325 Santa Monica CA 90403-4747

BOHNE, CORAL L., public relations specialist; b. Anchorage, Alaska, June 2, 1958; d. Dwight Dean and Jacqueline Marie (Day) Robinson; m. Scott Allen Bohne, Aug. 27, 1983; children: Tavis Lee, Nicole Marie. BBA, Pacific Luth. U., 1980; MBA, Alaska Pacific U., 1991. Front desk mgr. Sheffield Anchorage/Travelodge, Alaska, 1980-81; adminstrv. asst. to v.p. marketing Sheffield Hotels/Westmark, Anchorage, 1981-86; owner Adminstrv. Assistance, Anchorage, 1986-88; adminstrv. asst. to pres. Alaska Pacific U., Anchorage, 1988-91; asst. v.p. pub. rels. Key Bank of Alaska, Anchorage, 1991—. Comm. chair March of Dimes Walk Am., 1993-95; organizer Key Bank Alaska Neighbors Make the Difference, 1993-95; coord. com. United Way Day of Caring, 1994; vol. com. Kids Vote, 1993-94; dinner of champions com. Multiple Sclerosis Soc. Alaska, 1994-95. Mem. Am. Mktg. Assn. (treas. 1991-95, AMI award 1993), Pub. Rels. Soc. (Aurora award 1992, Excellence award 1993-94). Lutheran. Home: 13931 Venus Way Anchorage AK 99515 Office: Key Bank Alaska 101 W Benson Blvd Anchorage AK 99503

BOHRER, RICHARD WILLIAM, religious writer, editor, educator; b. N.Y.C., June 17, 1926; s. Jacob William and Elsie Marie (Wahlstad) B.; m. Elizabeth Anne Spencer, July 8, 1955; children: Joel Stephen, Janice Joy Bohrer Pruitt. BA, Westmont Coll., 1947; MSc, U. So. Calif., L.A., 1956; MA, Calif. State U., Long Beach, 1962. Tchr. grades 3, 4, 5 Haile Selassie I Elem. Sch., Gondar, Ethiopia, 1947-50, tchr. grades 9, 10, 11 Alhambra (Calif.) High Sch., 1954-55; tchr. grade 6 Maple Ave. Sch., Fullerton, Calif., 1955-56; tchr. grades 9, 10, 11 Orange (Calif.) High Sch., 1956-63; news editor Anaheim (Calif.) Gazette, 1961-62; prof., dir. journalism Multnomah Sch. of the Bible, Portland, Oreg., 1963-79; broker Dick Bohrer Realty Inc., Portland, 1968-81; sr. editor, mng. editor Moody Monthly mag., Chgo., 1979-83; pub. Glory Press, 1981—; prof. Liberty U., Lynchburg, Va., 1983-89, 91-94; asst. prof., head mag. sequence Ball State U., Muncie, Ind., 1989-90; dir. Maranatha Writers Conf., Muskegon, Mich., 1980-89. Author: Easy English, 1977, Edit, Yourself and Sell, 1980, They Called Him Shifta, 1981, 21 Ways to Write Stories for Christian Kids, 1980, 2d edit., 1982, John Newton, 1983, Bill Borden, 1984, How to Write What You Think, 1985, How to Write Features Like a Pro, 1986, Be an Editor Yourself, 1987, J. Edgar Beanpole: Football Detective, 1991, J. Edgar Beanpole: Volleyball Spy, 1991, J. Edgar Beanpole: Soccer Sleuth, 1991, J. Edgar Beanpole: Night Watcher, 1991, No Frills Editing Skills, 1993, John G. Mitchell: Lion of God, 1994; editor: The Battle for Your Faith by Willard M. Aldrich, The Schemer and the Dreamer by Luis Palau, Down to Earth by John Lawrence, Parables by the Sea by Pamela Reeve, An Everlasting Love by John G. Mitchell, Plague in Our Midst by Gregg Albers, MD, Right With God by John G. Mitchell, What Do You Say When.... by Nellie Pickard, Counseling the Terminally Ill by Gregg Albers, MD, The Self-Study of Liberty University, Maranatha, Our Lord, Come! by Renald Showers; acting editor Moral Majority Report, 1983-85, copy editor, 1985-88. Recipient Pres.'s Svc. award Liberty U., 1985, Tchr. of Yr. award, 1987, 89. Mem. Soc. Profl. Journalists. Republican. Mem. Clackamas Bible Ch. Home: PO Box 624 West Linn OR 97068-0624

BOHRNSTEDT, GEORGE WILLIAM, educational researcher; b. Arcadia, Wis., Sept. 9, 1938; s. Russell Gail and Agnes (Brecht) B.; m. Josephine Orlanda, Aug. 11, 1962 (div. 1973); children—Elizabeth (dec.), Brian, Matthew; m. Jennifer Lou Cain, Sept. 28, 1980; 1 child, Kassandra. Student, Winona State Coll., 1956-58; B.S., U. Wis., 1960, M.A., 1963, Ph.D., 1966. Research assoc. U. Wis., Madison, 1966-69; assoc. prof. Mpls., 1969-73, chmn. dept. sociology, 1970-73; prof. Ind. U., Bloomington, 1973-88, chmn. dept. sociology, 1982-86, dir. Inst. Social Research, 1974-79; sr. v.p., dir. Am. Inst. for Rsch., Palo Alto, Calif., 1988—. Author: (with others) Statistics for Social Data Analysis, 3d edit., 1994; Basic Social Statistics, 1991; editor: Sociological Methodology, 1970; editor Sociol. Methods and Rsch., 1971-79, 84-87, Social Psychology Quar., 1980-82. Served to U.S. Army, 1962. Fellow NSF, 1963, NIMH, 1964-66, Ctr. for Advanced Studies in Behavioral Scis., 1986-87; Found. for Child Devel. Belding scholar, 1976-77. Mem. Am. Sociol. Assn., Psychometric Soc., Am. Statis. Assn., Soc. Exptl. Social Psychologists. Office: Am Insts Rsch Behavioral Scis John C Flanagan Rsch Ctr PO Box 1113 Palo Alto CA 94302-1113

BOISSE, JOSEPH ADONIAS, library administrator; b. Marlboro, Mass., June 20, 1937; s. Anthony J. and Blanche Marie (Demers) B. BA, Stonehill Coll., 1963; MA, Brown U., 1965; MLS, Simmons Coll., 1967; EdD, Temple U., 1986. Regional librarian Va. Dept. Libraries, Montpelier, 1967-68, dep. state librarian, 1971-73; asst. library dir. Lawrence U., Appleton, Wis., 1968-71; dir. libraries U. Wis.-Parkside, Kenosha, 1973-79, Temple U., Phila., 1979-83; univ. librarian U. Calif., Santa Barbara, 1983—; bd. govs. Rsch. Librs. Group, Stanford, Calif., 1981-93; dir. Ctr. for Rsch. Librs., Chgo., 1983-89. Contbr. numerous articles to profl jours. Hon. mem. Found. of The Nat. Libr. Romania. Recipient Disting. Svc. award Wis. Library Assn., 1978, Disting. Svc. award U. Richmond, 1989. mem. ALA, Assn. Coll. and Rsch. Librs. (v.p. 1987-88, pres. 1988-89, Acad./Rsch. Libr. of Yr. 1995), Internat. Fedn. Libr. Assns. Home: 911 W Campus Ln Santa Barbara CA 93117-4339 Office: U Calif Univ Libr Santa Barbara CA 93106

BOLDEN, ROSAMOND, state official; b. Beggs, Okla., May 5, 1938; d. Benjamin James and Mary Crosby; m. James Alan Bolden, Jan. 27, 1963 (dec. Dec. 1973); 1 child, Stacie Lenore. B.S., U. Calif.-Berkeley, 1961, MA 1971. Employment counselor to office mgr. Calif. Dept. Employment, Sacramento, 1965-75; asst. civil rights officer Calif. Dept. Health, Sacramento, 1976-77; chief Office Bldg. and Grounds, Calif. Dept. Gen. Services, Sacramento, 1977—; chmn. merit award bd. dept. personnel adminstrn., State of Calif. Sacramento, 1979-84; mem. women's adv. bd. Calif. Personnel Bd., Sacramento, 1980-84. Bd. dirs. Tierra Del Oro coun. Girl Scouts U.S., Sacramento, 1984, Sacramento Urban League, 1986-89, sec., 1991-92; mem. citizen rev. bd., chmn. admission/allocation subcom. United Way, Sacramento, 1984; founding mem. Sacramento Black Women's Network, 1981; mem. adv. bd. Sutter Sr. Care, 1994—; active NAACP. Recipient award of appreciation United Calif. State Employee Campaign, 1980; cert. of appreciation Nat. Assn. Retarded Citizens, 1981 United Way, 1984; named Outstanding Pub. Adminstr., Am. Soc. for Pub. Adminstrs., 1989. Mem. Bldg. Owners and Mgrs. Assn. (founder Sacramento chpt. 1985, co-founder Calif. chpt. 1986, mem. govt. bldg. com., chairwoman bldg. ops. div. 1987-91, Pacific southwest regional v.p. 1991-92, sec., treas.-elect 1992-95), Black Advocates in State Svc., Alpha Kappa Alpha. Home: PO Box 22457 Sacramento CA 95822-0457 Office: State of Calif 1304 O St # 300 Sacramento CA 95814-5906

BOLDREY, EDWIN EASTLAND, retinal surgeon, educator; b. San Francisco, Dec. 8, 1941; s. Edwin Barkley and Helen Burns (Eastland) B.; m. Catherine Rose Oliphant, Oct. 20, 1973; children: Jennifer Elizabeth, Melissa Jeanne. BA with honors, De Pauw U., 1963; MD, Northwestern U., Chgo., 1967. Diplomate Am. Bd. Ophthalmology. Rotating intern U. Wash., Seattle, 1967-68; resident in gen. surgery U. Minn., Mpls., 1968-69; resident in ophthalmology U. Calif., San Francisco, 1971-74; Heed Found. fellow in retinal and vitreous surgery Washington U., St. Louis, 1974-75; mem. staff dept. ophthalmology Palo Alto (Calif.) Med. Clinic, 1975-91; dept. chmn., 1989-91; pvt. practice, San Jose, Mountain View, Calif., 1991—; clin. instr. Stanford (Calif.) U. Med. Sch., 1975-79, asst. clin. prof., 1979-87, assoc. clin. prof., 1987—; cons. VA Hosp., Palo Alto, Calif., 1976—; vice chmn. dept. ophthalmology Good Samaritan Hosp., San Jose, 1993-95, chmn., 1995—. Contbr. articles to med. jours., chpt. to book. Lt. comdr. M.C., USNR, 1969-71. Recipient Asbury award dept. ophthalmology U. Calif., San Francisco, 1973. Fellow ACS, Am. Acad. Ophthalmology (honor award 1989); mem. AMA, Retina Soc., Vitreous Soc. (charter), Peninsula Eye Soc. (pres. 1987-88), Western Retina StudyClub (charter, exec. sec.-treas. 1983-95), Cordes Eye Soc. (pres. 1995—), also others. Office: Retina Vitreous Assocs Inc 2512 Samaritan Ct Ste A San Jose CA 95124-4002

BOLDYREV, PETER MATVEEVICH, Russian language and culture educator, writer; b. Leningrad/St. Petersburg, USSR, Dec. 12, 1936; came to U.S., 1977; MA equivalent in History of Philosophy, Leningrad State U., 1975. Tchr. Russian lang. and culture Def. Lang. Inst., Monterey, Calif., 1981—. Author: Introduction to Soviet Period of Russian History, 1992, Russia's Lessons, 1993; mem. editorial bd. quar. mag. Contemporary, Toronto, 1979-80; author articles and essays. Founding mem. exec. bd. Russia Without Colonies, N.Y.C., 1977-80. Mem. Internat. PEN Club, Am. Philos. Assn. Home: PO Box 1362 Marina CA 93933-1362

BOLEN, MICHAEL D., construction executive; b. 1949. BS in Gen. Engring., USAF Acad., 1970; MA, U. No. Colo. Supt. Kitchell Contractors, Inc., Phoenix, 1973-81; with McCarthy Western Cons. Co. Office: Mc Carthy Western Constrs Inc 302 N 1st Ave Ste 500 Phoenix AZ 85003-1566*

BOLEN, TERRY LEE, optometrist; b. Newark, Ohio, Sept. 16, 1945; s. Robert Howard and Mildred Irene (Hoover) B.; BS, Ohio U., 1968; postgrad. Youngstown State U., 1973; O.D., Ohio State U., 1978; m. Debbie Elaine Thompson, Mar. 23, 1985. Quality control inspector ITT Grinnell Corp., Warren, Ohio, 1973, jr. quality control engr., 1974; pvt. practice optometry, El Paso, Tex., 1978-80, Dallas, 1980-81, Waco, Tex., 1981-85, Hewitt, Tex., 1983-89; comdr. U.S. Pub. Health Svc., 1989—; bd. dirs. Am. Optometric Found., 1975-77; nat. pres. Am. Optometric Student Assn., 1977-78; pres. El Paso Optometric Soc., 1980. Vol. visual examiner, Juarez, Mex., 1979—; chmn. Westside Recreation Ctr. Adv. Com., El Paso, 1979, Lions Internat. Sight Conservation and Work With the Blind Chmn. award, 1989 . Served to lt. USN, 1969-72; capt. USAIRNG, 1987-89. Recipient pub. svc. award, City of El Paso, 1980. Mem. Am. Optometric Assn., Tex. Optometric Assn., Assn. Mil. Surgeons of U.S. (life, USPHS HSO liaison 1990—, edn. coord. optometry section, 1992), Res. Officers Assn. (sec. chpt. # 1 Nev. 1994-95), Navy Res. Officers Assn. (sr. v.p. Nev., 1995—), Ret. Officers Assn. (sec. Reno chpt. 1994-95, sr. v.p. for Navy, state of Nev. dept. 1995—), Optometric Assn. (clin. assoc. Optometric Extension Program Found. 1978-89), Heart of Tex. Optometric Soc. (sec.-treas. 1984-85, pres.-elect 1986, pres. 1987), North Tex. Optometric Soc., USPHS (pres. No. Nev. chpt. Commd. Officers Assn. 1989-91), Epsilon Psi Epsilon (pres., 1977-78), Lions (3rd v.p. Coronado El Paso, svc. award, 1978, 79, Hewitt pres. 1985, v.p. W.Tex. Lions Eye Bank, 1980, 2d v.p. Cen. Tex. Lions Eye Bank, 1988, Hewitt Lion of Yr. 1987). Republican. Mem. Christian Ch. (Disciples of Christ). Home: 750 E Stillwater Ave Trlr 173 Fallon NV 89406-4063

BOLIN, RICHARD LUDDINGTON, industrial development consultant; b. Burlington, Vt., May 13, 1923; s. Axel Birger and Eva Madora (Luddington) B.; m. Jeanne Marie Brown, Dec. 18, 1948; children: Richard Luddington, Jr., Douglas, Judith, Barbara, Elizabeth. BS in Chem. Engring., Tex. A&M U., 1947; MS in Chem. Engring., MIT, 1950. Jr. rsch. engr. Humble Oil & Refining Co., Baytown, Tex., 1947-49; staff mem. Arthur D. Little, Inc., Cambridge, Mass., 1950-56, Caribbean office mgr. San Juan, 1957-61, gen. mgr., Mex., 1961-72; pres. Internat. Parks, Inc., Flagstaff, Ariz., 1973-94, chmn., 1995—; bd. dirs. Parque Indsl. de Nogales, Nogales, Sonora, Mex., The Flagstaff Inst.; dir. secretariat World Export Processing Zones Assn., 1985—; mem. adv. bd. Lowell Obs., Flagstaff, 1993-94. With U.S. Army, 1942-46. Mem. Univ. Club of Mex. Office: PO Box 986 Flagstaff AZ 86002

BOLIN, VERNON SPENCER, microbiologist, consultant; b. Parma, Idaho, July 9, 1913; s. Thadeus Howard Bolin and Jennie Bell Harm; m. Helen Epling, Jan. 5, 1948 (div. 1964); children: Rex, Janet, Mark; m. Barbara Sue Chase, Aug. 1965; children: Vladimir, Erik. BS, U. Wash., 1942; MS, U. Minn. 1949. Teaching asst. U. Minn.-Mpls., 1943-45; rsch. assoc. U. Utah, Salt Lake City, 1945-50, fellow in surgery, 1950-52; rsch. virologist Jensen-Salsbery Labs., Inc., Kansas City, Mo., 1952-57; rsch. assoc. Wistar Inst. U. Pa., 1957-58; rsch. virologist USPHS, 1958-61; founder Bolin Labs., , Phoenix, 1959—, also bd. dirs. Contbr. articles to profl. jours. Served with U.S. Army, 1931-33. Mem. N.Y. Acad. Scis., Phi Mu Chi. Home: 302 W Wahalla Ln Phoenix AZ 85027-4417

BOLIN, VLADIMIR DUSTIN, chemist; b. Inglewood, Calif., Feb. 25, 1965; s. Vernon Spencer and Barbara Sue (Chase) B.; m. Elizabeth Lynne Boswood, May 18, 1985; children: Ragnar Spencer, Roark Morgan. BS, U. Ariz., 1987. Chemist, microbiologist Bolin Labs., Inc., Phoenix, 1987-93; bd. dirs., pres. Aerotech Labs., Inc., Phoenix, 1993—, pres., 1993—; pres. Kalmar Labs., Inc., Pheonix, 1993—, also bd. dirs.; bd. dirs., pres. Kalmar Labs., Inc., Phoenix. Mem. ASTM, AAAS, Am. Water Works Assn. (pres.), Assn. Official Analytical Chemists, Am. Soc. Microbiolgoy, Am. Chem. Soc., N.Y. Acad. Scis. Home: 20201 N 17th Dr Phoenix AZ 85027-3537 Office: Bolin Labs Inc 2020 W Lone Cactus Dr Phoenix AZ 85027-2624

BOLING, JUDY ATWOOD, civic worker; b. Madras, India, June 19, 1921 (parents Am. citizens); d. Carroll Eugene and Marion Frances (Ayrer) Atwood; m. Jack Leroy Boling, Apr. 8, 1941 (dec. July 1988); children: Joseph Edward, Jean Ann, James Michael, John Charles. AA, San Antonio Jr. Coll., 1940; student Rogue Community Coll., Grants Pass, Oreg., 1978-79, So. Oreg. State Coll., Ashland, 1982—. Contbr. articles to profl. jours. First aid instr. ARC, various locations, 1940-65, chmn. vols., Calif., 1961-62, Eng., 1964-65; den mother cub scouts Boy Scouts Am., Monterey, Calif., 1951-52; active Girl Scouts U.S., 1953—, coun. pres., Winema (Oreg.) Coun., 1971-73, 79-82, historian, 1990—, del. to nat. coun., 1966, 72, 81, cons. for nat. pubs., 1971, 79; Sunday sch. tchr. Base Chapel, Pyote, Tex., 1949-51, choir dir., 1951; Sunday sch. adminstr. Base Chapel, Morocco, 1954-55; Sunday sch. tchr. Hermon Free Meth. Ch., L.A., 1956-57; active United Way campaign, 1967-84, Childrens Festival, 1974-88; former liaison with local people in Japanese-Am., Franco-Am., Anglo-Am. orgns.; mem., patron Rogue Craftsmen Bd., Grants Pass, 1972-85, sec., 1972-78, v.p., 1978-85; bd. dirs. Rogue Valley Opera Assn., 1978-85, sponsor/mem., 1978—; bd. dirs. Community Concert, 1979-88, 92—, mem. Grants Pass Friends of the Symphony, 1989— (bd. dirs. 1992—); vol. RSVP, 1982—; historian Josephine County Rep. Women, 1982-86, treas., 1986-94, sec., 1994—; elected Rep. precinct committeeperson, 1991—; sustaining mem. Sta. KSYS pub. TV; mem. Sta. KSOR pub. radio; frequent pub. speaker. Recipient Thanks badge Girl Scouts U.S., 1957, 60, 73, Girl Scouts Japan, 1959, U.K. Girl Guides, 1982; others; cert. of appreciation USAF, 1959, City of Hagi, City of Fukuoka (Japan), Gov. of Fukuoka Prefecture; 2 citations Internat. Book Project; Oreg. Vol. award Sen. Packwood, 1983; Community Woman of Year award Bus. and Profl. Women, 1984. Mem. Josephine County Hist. Soc. (bd. dirs. 1991—), So. Oreg. Resources Alliance, Am. Host Found., Friends of Libr., Grants Pass Art Mus., Knife and Fork Club (bd. dirs. 1994—). Address: 3016 Jumpoff Joe Creek Rd Grants Pass OR 97526-8778

BOLITHO, LOUISE GREER, educational administrator, consultant; b. Wenatchee, Wash., Aug. 13, 1927; d. Lon Glenn and Edna Gertrude (Dunlap) Greer; m. Douglas Stuart, June 17, 1950 (div. Dec. 1975); children: Rebecca Louise, Brian Douglas. BA, Wash. State U., 1949. With Stanford (Calif.) U., 1967-91, adminstrv. asst. physics labs., 1974-77, mgr. ctr. for research in internat. studies, 1977-84, law sch. fin. and adminstrv. services dir., 1984-86; computer cons., Palo Alto, Calif., 1984—; acting mgr. Inst. for Internat. Studies, 1987-88, fin. analyst, 1988-91. Mem. Peninsula vols., Menlo Park, Calif., 1986-94; budget com. chmn., bd. dirs. Mid-Peninsula Support Network, Mountain View, Calif., 1984-86; chairperson active older adults com. YMCA; pres. 410 Sheridan Ave. Homeowners Assn., 1989-93, treas., 1993—. Mem. AAUW (bd. dirs. 1987-88). Home and Office: 410 Sheridan Ave Apt 445 Palo Alto CA 94306-2020

BOLLER, JOHN HALL, JR., minister; b. N.Y.C., Sept. 4, 1949; s. John Hall Sr. and Claudia (Pinza) B.; m. Lillian Wong, June 1, 1974; children: Alisha Carole, Jenna Kaitlin. BS, Calif. State U., Long Beach, 1970; M of Christian Theology, San Francisco Theol. Sem., San Anselmo, Calif., 1972, M of Divinity, 1973; MS, Calif. State U., San Diego, 1978. Youth minister Chinese Congl. Ch., San Francisco, 1970-73; campus pastor U. Calif., Irvine, 1973-74; asst. pastor St. Mark's Presbyn. Ch., Newport Beach, Calif., 1973-74; assoc. pastor Coll. Park Presbyn. Ch., San Diego, 1974-79; pastor Northminster Presbyn. Ch., San Diego, 1979—; marriage, family and child counselor, San Diego, 1986—. Chmn. Dropout Prevention Roundtable, San Diego, 1987-89; moderator Presbytery of San Diego, 1988. Mem. Calif. Assn. Marriage and Family Therapists, Assn. Presbyn. Ch. Educators, Witherspoon Soc. Democrat. Club: San Diego Train. Office: Northminster Presbyn Ch 4324 Clairemont Mesa Blvd San Diego CA 92117-1945

BOLLES, CHARLES AVERY, librarian; b. Pine Island, Minn., Aug. 10, 1940; s. Arthur Marston and Clarice Ione (Figy) B.; B.A., U. Minn., 1962, M.A. in Library Sci., 1963, M.A. in Am. Studies, 1969, Ph.D. in Library Sci., 1975; m. Marjorie Elaine Hancock, May 17, 1964; children: Jason Brice, Justin Brian. Catalog and serials librarian U. Iowa, Iowa City, 1964-67; asst. prof. Emporia (Kans.) State U., 1970-76; dir. library devel. div. Kans. State Library, 1976-78; dir. Sch. Library Sci., Emporia State U., 1978-80; state librarian State of Idaho, Boise, 1980—. Mem. ALA, Chief Officers State Libraries Agys., Western Council State Libraries (chmn. 1985-86), Pacific N.W. Library Assn. (pres. 1990-91), Idaho Library Assn. Office: Idaho State Libr 325 W State St Boise ID 83702-6055

BOLLES, DONALD SCOTT, lawyer; b. Buffalo, Dec. 17, 1936; s. Theodore H. and Marie (Heth) B.; m. Jean Waytulonis Oct. 24, 1963 (dec. May 1983); children: Scott, Matthew; m. Geraldine Novinger, Feb. 14, 1988. BA, Alfred U., 1960; JD cum laude, U. San Diego, 1970. Bar: Calif. 1971, U.S. Dist. Ct. (so. and no. dists.) Calif. 1971. Ptnr. Hutton, Foley, Anderson & Bolles Inc., King City, Calif., 1971—. Editor lead articles San Diego Law Rev., 1969-70. Trustee Mee Meml. Hosp., King City, 1974-78, chmn., 1978-80; chmn. King City Recreation Commn., 1974-77; candidate mcpl. ct. judge primary and gen. election, Monterey County, Calif., 1986; sec., founding mem. bd. dirs. Project Teen Ctr. Inc.; bd. dirs. Sun St. Ctrs., Monterey Coll. Law, 1995—. Served to capt. U.S. Army, 1961-67, Vietnam. Mem. Monterey County Bar Assn. (exec. com. 1985-86). Republican. Club: Toastmasters (King City) (pres. 1972-74). Lodge: Lions (pres. 1975-76, sec. 1984-86 King City club). Office: Hutton Foley Anderson & Bolles Inc 510 Broadway St King City CA 93930-3201

BOLOCOFSKY, DAVID N., psychology educator, lawyer; b. Hartford, Conn., Sept. 29, 1947; s. Samuel and Olga Bolocofsky. BA, Clark U., 1969; MS, Nova U., 1974, PhD, 1975; JD, U. Denver, 1988. Bar: Colo. 1988; cert. sch. psychologist, Colo., Fla., cert. counselor, Fla. Tchr. high sch. Univ. Sch., Ft. Lauderdale, Fla., 1972-73; ednl. coord. Living and Learning Ctr., Ft. Lauderdale, 1972-75; asst. prof. U. No. Colo., Greeley, 1975-79, assoc. prof., 1979-90, dir. sch. psychology program, 1979-82; assoc. Robert T. Hinds Jr. & Assocs., Littleton, Colo., 1988-93; hearing officer State of Colo., 1991—; pres. David N. Bolocofsky, P.C., Denver, 1993—; psychol. cons. Clin. Assocs., Englewood, Colo., 1978—. Author: Enhancing Personal Adjustment, 1986, (chpts. in books) Children and Obesity, 1987, Obtaining and Utilizing a Custody Evaluation, 1989; contbr. numerous articles to profl. jours. Mem. ABA (family law sect.), Douglas-Elbert Bar Assn., Arapahoe Bar Assn., 1st Jud. Dist. Bar Assn., Nat. Assn. Sch. Psychologists (ethics com. 1988-91), Colo. Soc. Sch. Psychologists (bd. dirs. 1978—, treas. 1993—), Interdisciplinary Commn. on Child Custody (pro bono com. 1988—), Colo. Bar Assn. (family law sect., sec. juvenile law sect. 1990-92), Nat. Assn. Counsel for Children, Colo. Soc. Behavioral Analysis Therapy (treas. 1990—). Home: 9848 E Maplewood Cir Englewood CO 80111-5401 Office: 5353 W Dartmouth Ave Ste 500 Denver CO 80227-5517

BOLTON, LEON LESLIE, plastic surgeon; b. Memphis, Sept. 4, 1954. BA summa cum laude, U. Tenn., 1976; MD, U. Tenn., Memphis, 1980. Diplomate Am. Bd. Surgery, Am. Bd. Plastic Surgery. Resident in gen. surgery Emory U. Hosps., Atlanta, 1980-83, U. Ky. Hosps., Lexington, 1983-85; resident in plastic and reconstructive surgery U. So. Calif., L.A., 1985-87; pvt. practice Aesthetic Surgery Ctr., Long Beach, Calif., 1987—; clin. instr. surgery U. So. Calif., L.A., 1987—; spkr. in field. Contbr. articles to profl. jours. Fellow ACS; mem. AMA, AAAASF (chair oper. com. 1995—), Am. Soc. Plastic and Reconstructive Surgeons, Am. Soc. Aesthetic Plastic Surgery, Calif. Soc. Plastic Surgeons, Lipoplasty Soc. N.Am., L.A. County Med. Assn., Calif. Med. Assn., Phi Beta Kappa, Phi Kappa Phi, Alpha Omega Alpha. Office: Aesthetic Surgery Ctr # 150 4300 Long Beach Blvd Long Beach CA 90807-2011

BOLTON, MARTHA O., writer; b. Searcy, Ark., Sept. 1, 1951; d. Lonnie Leon and Eunice Dolores Ferren; m. Russell Norman Bolton, Apr. 17, 1970; children: Russell Norman II, Matthew David, Anthony Shane. Grad. high sch., Reseda, Calif. Freelance writer for various comedians, 1975-86; newspaper columnist Simi Valley Enterprise, Simi, Calif., 1979-87; staff writer Bob Hope, 1986—. Author: A Funny Thing Happened to Me on My Way Through the Bible, 1985, A View From the Pew, 1986, What's Growing Under Your Bed?, 1986, Tangled in the Tinsel, 1987, So, How'd I Get to be in Charge of the Program?, 1988, Humorous Monologues, 1989, Let My People Laugh, 1989, If Mr. Clean Calls Tell Him I'm Not In, 1989, Journey to the Center of the Stage, 1990, If You Can't Stand the Smoke, Get Out of My Kitchen, 1990, Home, Home on the Stage, 1991, TV Jokes and Riddles, 1991, These Truths Were Made For Walking, 1992, When the Meatloaf Explodes It's Done, 1993, Childhood Is A Stage, 1993, Honey, It's Time to Weed the Carpets Again, 1994, Walk A Mile in His Truths, 1994, The Cafeteria Lady on the Loose, 1994, On The Loose, 1994, If the Pasta Wiggles, Don't Eat It, 1995, Bethlehem's Big Night, 1995. Pres. Vista Elem. Sch. PTA, Simi, 1980-81. Recipient Emmy award nomination for outstanding achievement in music and lyrics NATAS, 1988, Internat. Angel award, 1990-91; named Pen Woman of Yr., 1995. Mem. Nat. League of Am. Pen Women (br. pres. 1984-86, Woman of Achievement award Simi Valley br. 1984), Writers Guild Am. West (award nomination 1994), ASCAP, Soc. Children's Book Writers, Acad. T.V. Arts and Scis. Office: PO Box 1212 Simi Valley CA 93062-1212

BOLTON, ROBERT FLOYD, construction executive; b. Dunlap, Iowa, Oct. 18, 1942; s. Russel J. And Mary Jane (Lacey) B.; m. Mary Louise Hartman, May 15, 1988. Lic. contractor. Sole practice farming Dunlap, Iowa, 1967-72; supr. Phillips Constrn. Co., Cottonwood, Ariz., 1972-84; contractor Bolton Bldg. and Devel. Co., Sedona, Ariz., 1984—; cons. in field. With U.S. Army, 1964-66. Mem. Nat. Assn. Home Builders, Am. Soc. Home Inspectors, C. of C., VFW, Meth. Mens Fellowship Club. Republican. Methodist. Home: 90 Evening Glow Pl Sedona AZ 86351-7912 Office: Bolton Bldg & Devel Co PO Box 754 Sedona AZ 86339-0754

BOLTZ, MARLYS PETERSON, nurse administrator; b. Blomford, Minn., Nov. 25, 1936; d. John B. and Gladys L. (Peterson) Peterson; m. Thomas J. Boltz, May 29, 1958; children; Gregg Alan, Brett Allison. Diploma, Swedish Hosp. Sch. Nursing, Mpls., 1957; BSN, Calif. State U., Sacramento, 1978; M Health Systems Leadership, U. San Francisco, 1986. RN, Calif. Staff nurse ICU VA Med. Ctr., Martinez, Calif., 1970-78, head nurse med. svc., 1978-79, head nurse ICU, 1979-84, nursing supr., 1984—; head nurse VA No. Calif. System of Clinics, Martinez, 1992—. Mem. AACN (cert., pres. Contra Costa chpt. 1991—). Republican. Baptist. Home: 663 Odin Dr Pleasant Hill CA 94523-1726 Office: 150 Muir Rd Martinez CA 94553-4612

BOLZ, CHRISTOPHER WILLIAM, family physician; b. Portland, Oreg., June 12, 1954; s. Reamer Augustus and Margaret Elizabeth (Krom) B.; m. Martha Ellen Luzzi, July 29, 1977; children: Megan Elizabeth, Jeremy Christopher. BS in Zoology with honors, U. Wyo., 1976; MD, Creighton U., 1980. Diplomate Am. Bd. Family Practicd. Resident in family practice U. Calif., Irvine, 1980-82, chief resident, 1982-83; pvt. practice, Laramie, Wyo., 1983-89, Cottage Grove, Oreg., 1989—; chief staff Cottage Grove Hosp., 1994—; med. dir. Albany County Cmty. Med. Fund, Laramie, 1984-89, High Country Home Health Care, Laramie, 1985-89, Bethesda Care Ctr., Laramie, 1984-89; chief medicine Ivinson Meml. Hosp., Laramie, 1986-87; mem. adj. clin. faculty U. Wyo. Sch. Pharmacy, Laramie, 1988-89; clin. inst. dept. family medicine Oreg. Health Scis. U., Portland, 1992—. Pres., bd. dirs. Crisis Pregnancy Ctr., Laramie, 1988-89; bd. dirs. Cottage Grove Cmty. Tennis Assn., 1993—. Mem. Lane County Med. Soc. Office: 1345 Birch Ave Cottage Grove OR 97424-1416

BONAFEDE, R. PETER, rheumatologist; b. Cape Town, South Africa, Aug. 12, 1950; came to U.S., 1986; m. Rosario Jones, Deb. 15, 1981; children: Sebastian, Caroline. MB, Ch. B, U. Cape Town, S. Africa, 1974; MD, U. Cape Town, 1979. Diplomate Am. Bd. Internal Medicine, Am. Bd. Rheumatology; lic. Brit. Med. Coun., S. Africa Med. Coun., Wash., Oreg. Intern ob/gyn. and surgery Groote Schuur Hosp., Captetown, South Africa, 1975-76; resident internal medicine Groote Schuur Hosp., Captetown, 1982-86; fellow in rheumatology Oreg. Health Scis. U., Portland, 1986-89; dir. Arthritis Ctr. Providence Hosp. and Med. Ctr., Portland, 1989-92; med. dir. Arthritis Ctr. Providence Hosp. & Med. Ctr., Portland, 1992—; clin. asst. prof. medicine divsn. arthritis, rheumatic diseases Oreg. Health Scis. U., Portland, 1989—; med. officer S. Africa nat. svc., 1976-77, internal medicine Addington Hosp., Durban, S. Africa, 1978; rsch. fellow human genetics U. Cape Town, 1976-78; emergency physician Groote Schuur Hosp., Capetown, 1979; tutor in internal medicine, U. Cape Town, 1983-86; attending physician Somerset Hosp., Cape Town, 1986; mem. planninc com. of ctrs. for bone and joint care, Providence Hosp. Ctr., 1989—; chmn. edn. com. Providence Ctrs. for Bone and Joint Care, 1993—. Contbr. articles and abstracts to profl. jours. Bd. dirs. Oreg. chpt. Arthritis Found., 1990—, med. and sci. com., 1990—, chmn. 1992-94. Recipient Univ. scholarship S. African Coll., 1969; named hon. pres. S. African Univs. Judo Assn., 1975, 76. Fellow ACP, Am.Coll. Rheumatology; mem. AMA, Multnomah County Med. Soc., S. African Arthritis and Rheumatism Assn. Home: 10560 SW 161st Ct Beaverton OR 97007-8171 Office: Providence Arthritis Ctr 5050 NE Hoyt St Ste 155 Portland OR 97213-2956

BOND, AUDREY MAE, real estate broker; b. New Orleans, June 17, 1932; d. Melvin and Ann Thomas (Freeman) Respert; m. Robert M. Bond, Aug. 16, 1975; children: Betty Lee, Deborah Huggins. AA, Oxnard (Calif.) Coll., 1977. Lic. real estate broker, Calif. Benefit authorizer Dept. HEW, San Francisco, 1955-75; pvt. practice realty, 1977-88; owner/broker A. Bond Realty, Oxnard, Calif., 1988—. Bd. dirs. Luth. Sem., 1992—; sec.-treas. Channel Islands confs. Evang. Luth. Ch. in Am., 1989—; chmn. fellowship com. Our Redeemer Luth. Ch., Oxnard; mem. Ventura County Bd. Suprs.; alt. mem. Assessment Appeals Bd. No. 1, 1994-95. Mem. Profl. Coll. Women's Orgn. (v.p.), Nat. Assn. Ret. Fed. Employees (1st v.p.), Calif. Bd. Realtors, Nat. Bd. Realtors, Oxnard Harbor Bd. Realtors (trustee 1992, chmn. membership com. award 1990), African Am. C. of C. Tri Counties (treas. 1994—), Zonta Internat., Zi Tau (pres. parliamentarian 1995-96). Home: 3420 Taffrail Ln Oxnard CA 93035-1684

BOND, GREGORY BUCK, construction company executive; b. Stromsburg, Nebr., Jan. 23, 1951; s. Floyd O. and Janet A. (Nelson) B.; m. Earlene Eldredge, Feb. 18, 1972; children: Scott Allen, Michelle René. Student, Ariz. State U., 1969-72. Estimator M.M. Sundt Constrn. Co., Phoenix, 1972-79, project engr., 1979-80; chief estimator M.M. Sundt Constrn. Co., Phoenix and Houston, 1980-82, Del Webb Constrn. Svcs., Dallas, 1982-84, Swinerton & Walberg, L.A., 1984-85; estimating mgr. J. A. Jones Constrn. Co., L.A., 1985—. Home: 1933 E Enrose St Mesa AZ 85203-5820

BOND, MICHAEL WAYNE, industrial gas company executive; b. Kingsport, Tenn., Mar. 21, 1950; s. James Harold and Luevinia (Hale) B.; m. Sherry Ramona Brainard, Dec. 29, 1973; children: Heather Michelle, Brienanna Nicole, James Jacob Wesley, Zachary William. Student, East Tenn. State U., Johnson City, 1971-74, Regis U., Denver. Distbn. mgr. Air Products & Chems. Inc., Kingsport, 1976-84; distbn. mgr. Air Products & Chems. Inc., Denver, 1984-86, plant mgr., 1986-88; terminal mgr. Air Products & Chems. Inc., Parkersburg, W.Va., 1988-91; regional transp. mgr. Air Products & Chems. Inc., Aurora, Colo., 1991-92, regional ops. mgr., 1992—; owner, pres. mktg./cons. co. Denver Universal, Westminster, Colo., 1994—. Colo. judge Odyssey of the Mind, 1994—. Office: Air Products & Chems Inc 12200 E Iliff Ave Ste 200 Aurora CO 80014-5375

BOND, RICHARD RANDOLPH, college administrator, legislator; b. Lost Creek, W.Va., Dec. 1, 1927; s. Harley Donovan and Marcella Randolph B.; m. Reva Stearns, Apr. 20, 1946; children: David, Philip, Josette, Michael. BS, Salem Coll., 1948, LHD (hon.), 1979; MS, W.Va. U., 1949; PhD, U. Wis., 1955; postdoctoral studies, U. Mich., 1958-59. Various teaching and fellowship positions, 1949-59; dean of faculty Elmira (N.Y.) Coll., 1959-63; dean coll. of Liberal Arts U. Liberia, Monrovia, 1963-64; chief of party Cornell U. Project in Liberia, Monrovia, 1964-66; v.p. acad. affairs Ill. State U., Normal, 1966-71; pres. U. No. Colo., Greeley, 1971-81, pres. emeritus, prof. zoology, 1981-89; state rep. Colo. Gen. Assembly, Denver, 1984-90; interim pres. Front Range Community Coll., Westminster, Colo., 1991; pres. Morgan Community Coll., Ft. Morgan, Colo., 1991—; founder Nat. Student Exch., 1st No. Savs. and Loan; cons., examiner North Ctrl. Accrediting Assn., 1969-82. Author: Colorado Postsecondary Options Act., 1988; contbr. articles to profl. jours. Bd. dirs., chmn. Sunrise Community Health Ctr.; founding mem. Dream Team on Dropout Prevention; Dem. candidate for Col. 4th Congl. Dist., 1990; co-founder Colo. chpt. Dem. Leadership Coun., 1991—; co-chmn. Clinton Campaign, Colo., 1992; trustee Teikyo Loretto Heights U. With U.S. Army, 1945-47. Recipient Legislator of Yr. award DAV, 1988, Colo. Acad. Pediatrics, 1989; Mental Health award, 1990, Polit. Educator of Yr. award, Colo. Edn. Assn., 1991; fellow NSF, 1953-54, Am. Physiol. Soc., 1958, Carnegie Found., 1958-59. Mem. Am. Ornithologists Union, Am. Assn. Colls. and Univs. (bd. dirs. 1979-81), Colo. Assn. Colls. and Univs. (chmn. 1979-81), Rotary (bd. dirs. local chpt.), Sigma Xi. Democrat. Presbyterian. Home: 38 Paynter Pl Fort Morgan CO 80701-9258

BOND, THOMAS MOORE, JR., labor mediation and arbitration executive; b. Louisville, Dec. 17, 1930; s. Thomas Moore and Louise Elleanor (Jones) B.; m. Kathryn Keith, Apr. 10, 1950 (dec.); children: Gilbert, Louise, Lela; m. Ethel Ayako Kuramitsu, Aug. 15, 1965; children: Richard, Jane, Julian Horace. BS in Econs., Ind. U., 1953. Bus. agt, organizer Hosp. Workers, San Francisco, 1961-65; internat. rep. organizer Svc. Employees' AFL-CIO, Louisville, 1965-70; exec. dir. Union Am. Physicians, San Francisco, 1973-78; owner Thomas Moore Bond Group, Berkeley, Calif., 1979—; pvt. practice labor mediator and arbitrator, mgmt., labor cons., Berkeley, 1981—. Editor: The Negro Conservative, 1981. Bd. dirs. adv. com. for paralegal tng. Merritt Coll., Oakland, Calif., 1983; mem. labor commn. City of Berkeley, 1986-88, 91. 1st lt. inf., U.S. Army, 1946-50. Mem Indsl. Rels. Rsch. Assn., Soc. Fed. Labor Rels. Profls., Inst. Advanced Law Study. Republican. Congregationalist. Office: Thomas Moore Bond Group 2123 1/2 5th St Berkeley CA 94710-2208

BOND, VINCENT EARL, public relations executive; b. Bethesda, Md., May 16, 1947; s. Norman Earl and Shirley Sybilla (Cavalier) B.; m. Betty Louise Huestis, Feb. 4, 1971; 1 child, Carolyn Anita. BA, Calif. State U., 1968; MBA, Nat. U., 1984. Supr. pub. info. Tucson Gen. Hosp, 1975; pub. info. officer Ariz. Dept. Transp., Phoenix, 1975-77; pub. affairs officer IRS, Phoenix, 1977-80; dir. communications Children's Hosp., San Diego, 1980-88; pub. affairs officer USN, San Diego, 1989-91, U.S. Customs Svcs., March AFB, Calif., 1991—. Mem. communications coun. March of Dimes, San Diego, 1990—. Capt. USAF, 1969-74. Recipient Excellence awards for best employee newsletter Ariz. Newspaper Assn., 1975, 76, Merit award for best mag. IABC, 1981, Excellence awards for best TV spot announcement and best print advertisement, 1986, Merit award for best print advertisement, 1986, Golden Advocate award So. Calif. Soc. for Hosp. Pub. Rels, 1982, Cert. of Excellence for best ann. report Am. Inst. Graphic Arts, 1983. Mem. Pub. Rels. Soc. Am. (publicity chmn. 1990-91, dir. at large 1990-91, profl. accreditation 1984). Democrat. Home: 2070 Basswood Ave Carlsbad CA 92008-1110 Office: USCS Aviations Ops Ctr West PO Box 6363 March AFB CA 92518-0363

BOND, WENDELL ANSON, petroleum geologist, oil company executive; b. Columbus, Ohio, Mar. 13, 1947; s. Ralph Hurd and Virginia (Barker) B.; m. Laurel J. Etkin, Apr. 25, 1987; children: Ryan, Erin, Sydney. BS in Geology, Capital U., 1969; MS in Geology, U. Colo., 1973. Registered profl. geologist, Wyo. Project geologist Intrasearch, Inc., Denver, 1973-74; corp. geologist Bond Exploration Co., Denver, 1974-76; project geologist Webb Resources, Inc., Denver, 1976-80; distr. geologist Sohio Petroleum Co., Denver, 1980-81; chief geologist Bird Oil Corp., Denver, 1981-82; pvt. practice cons. petroleum geologist Denver, 1982-84; chief geologist Samuel Gary Jr. and Assocs., Denver, 1984-88; pres. Bond Petroleum Corp., Boulder, 1988—, Wendell A. Bond, Inc., Boulder, 1989—; bd. mem. Denver (Colo.) Earth Resources Libr. Mem. Am. Assn. Petroleum Geologists, Denver Internat. Petroleum Soc., Rocky Mountain Assn. Geologists. Home and Office: Bond Petroleum Corp 1137 Barberry Ct Boulder CO 80303

BONDI, BERT ROGER, accountant, financial planner; b. Portland, Oreg., Oct. 2, 1945; s. Gene L. and Elizabeth (Poynter) B.; m. Kimberley Kay Higgins, June 18, 1988; children: Nicholas Stone, Christopher Poynter. BBA, U. Notre Dame, 1967. CPA, Colo., Calif., Wyo. Sr. tax acct. Price Waterhouse, Los Angeles, 1970-73; ptnr. Valentine Adducci & Bondi, Denver, 1973-76; sr. ptnr. Bondi & Co., Englewood, Colo., 1977—; dir. Citizens Bank. Bd. govs. Met. State Coll. Found.; bd. dirs. Am. Cancer Soc. Denver; mem. adv. bd. Jr. League of Denver. Served with U.S. Army, 1968-70. Mem. C. of C., Community Assns. Inst., Govt. Fin. Officers Assn., Home Builders Assn., Am. Inst. CPAs, Colo. Soc. CPAs, Wyo. Soc. CPAs., Rotary (Denver), Notre Dame Club, Metropolitan Club (Denver), Castle Pines Country Club. Roman Catholic. Home: 49 Glenalla Pl Castle Rock CO 80104-9026 Office: Bondi & Co 44 Inverness Dr E Bldg B Englewood CO 80112-5410

BONDS, BARRY LAMAR, professional baseball player; b. Riverside, Calif., July 24, 1964; s. Bobby B. Student, Ariz. State U. With Pitts. Pirates, 1985-92, San Francisco Giants, 1992—. Named Most Valuable Player Baseball Writers' Assn. Am., 1990, 1992, 1993, Maj. League Player Yr. Sporting News, 1990, Nat. League Player Yr. Sporting News, 1990, 91, mem. Sporting News Coll. All-Am. team, 1985, mem. All-Star team, 1990, 1992-94; recipient Gold Glove award, 1990-93, Silver Slugger award, 1990-94. Office: San Francisco Giants Candlestick Park San Francisco CA 94124*

BONDURANT, DAVID WILLIAM, marketing professional; b. Kirksville, Mo., June 8, 1948; s. William George and Leila Ruth (Mulford) B.; m. Judy Helen Rindahl, Mar. 17, 1973; children: Matthew David, Erik William. BSEE, U. Mo., Rolla, 1971; BS in Physics, Northeast Mo. State Coll., 1971. Registered profl. engr., Minn. Assoc. design engr. Control Data Corp., Arden Hills, Minn., 1971-72; sr. design engr. Sperry-Univac, Eagan, Minn., 1972-75; project engr. Robertshaw Controls Co., Richmond, Va., 1975-76; prin. design engr. Sperry-Univac, Eagan, 1976-80; mgr., systems applications Honywell Solid State, Electronics Div., Plymouth, Minn., 1980-84; com. bus. devel. mgr. Honywell Solid State, Electronics Div., Colorado Springs, Colo., 1984-88; dir. new bus. devel. Ramtron Corp., Colorado Springs, 1988-95; dir. mktg. Enhanced Memory Systems, Colorado Springs, 1995—; ind. cons. Technomics Cons., Chgo., 1987. Contbr. articles to profl. jours. Mem. IEEE (pres., v.p., sec. 1977-79), Twin Cities Computer Soc., Country Club of Colo., Tau Beta Pi, Eta Kappa Nu, Phi Kappa Phi. Republican. Lutheran. Home: 4025 Becket Dr Colorado Springs CO 80906-7681 Office: Ramtron Corp 1850 Ramtron Dr Colorado Springs CO 80921-3620

BONE, ROBERT WILLIAM, writer, photojournalist; b. Gary, Ind., Sept. 15, 1932; s. Robert Ordway and Georgia Juanita (Clapp) B.; m. Sara Ann Cameron, Aug. 14, 1965; children: Christina Ann, David Robert. BS in Journalism, Bowling Green State U., 1954. Editor, tng. literature The Armor Sch., Ft. Knox, Ky., 1954-56; reporter, photographer Middletown (N.Y.) Daily Record, 1956-59, San Juan (Puerto Rico) Star, 1959-60; news editor Popular Photography Mag., N.Y.C., 1960-62; editor-in-chief Brazilian Bus. Mag., Rio de Janeiro, 1962-63; picture editor Time-Life Books, N.Y.C., 1963-68; sr. writer Fielding's Travel Guide to Europe, Mallorca, Spain, 1968-71; staff writer Honolulu Advertiser, 1971-84; free-lancer Honolulu, 1984—; stringer Time-Life News Svc., 1981-86. Author: Maverick Guide to Hawaii, 1977, Maverick Guide to Australia, 1979, Maverick Guide to New Zealand, 1981, Fielding's Alaska and the Yukon, 1989; travel editor Honolulu mag., 1985-88, R.S.V.P. mag., 1988-89; contbg. editor Recommend mag., 1986—. 1st lt., U.S. Army, 1954-56. Named to Journalism Hall Fame Bowling Green State U., 1990. Mem. Soc. Am. Travel Writers (editor The Travel Writer), Am. Soc. Mag. Photographers. Democrat. Home and Office: 1053 Lunaai St Kailua HI 96734-4633

BONFIELD, ANDREW JOSEPH, tax practitioner; b. London, Jan. 26, 1924; s. George William and Elizabeth Agnes B.; came to U.S., 1946, naturalized, 1954; m. Eleanor Ackerman, Oct. 16, 1955; children: Bruce Ian, Sandra Karen. Gen. mgr. Am. Cushion Co., Los Angeles, 1948-50, Monson Calif. Co., Redwood City, 1951-58; mfrs. mktg. rep., San Francisco, 1958-62; tax practitioner, bus. cons., Redwood City, San Jose, Los Gatos, Calif., 1963—. Past treas., dir. Northwood Park Improvement Assn.; mem. exec. bd. Santa Clara County council Boy Scouts Am., 1971—, past council pres., mem. Nat. council; mem. Santa Clara County Parks and Recreation Commn., 1975-81, 82-86; mem. County Assessment Appeals Bd., 1978-86; mem. Hawaii Bd. Taxation Review, 1992—. Served with Brit. Royal Navy, 1940-46. Decorated King George VI Silver Badge; recipient Silver Beaver award, Vigil honor award Boy Scouts Am.; enrolled to practice before IRS. Mem. Nat. Soc. Public Accts., Nat. Assn. Enrolled Agts., Calif. Soc. Enrolled Agts., Hawaii Assn. Pub. Accts., Hawaii Soc. Enrolled Agrs., Royal Can. Legion (past state parliamentarian, past state 1st vice comdr.). Club: Rotary (pres. San Jose E. 1977-78, pres. Kihei-Wailea 1993-94). Home: 760 S Kihei Rd Apt 215 Kihei HI 96753-7517

BONGE, NICHOLAS JAY, JR., biological engineering company executive; b. Harve de Grace, Md., Aug. 3, 1954; s. Nicholas Joseph Bonge and Marie Irene (Cile) Andree; m. Lisa Marie Thompson, Aug. 3, 1991. BSME, U. Colo., 1976; postgrad., So. Calif. Inst. Architecture, 1990-91. Rsch. assoc. Colo. Sch. Mines, Golden, 1976-80; chief engr. Vac Tec Systems, Boulder, Colo., 1980-83; chief engr. systems Innotech Group, Simi Valley, Calif., 1983-86; pres. Biol. Engring., Inc., Ventura, Calif., 1986—; bd. dirs. LMT Mktg., Inc., Ventura; guest speaker conf. on water jet tech., Golden, Colo., 1977-80. Patentee in field; contbr. articles to profl. jours. Recipient Rsch. grant U.S. Dept. Energy, 1977, U.S. Bur. Mines, 1978, U.S. office of Surface

Mining, 1978, Dept. Army, 1980, South African Chamber of Mines, 1978. Mem. Am. Vacuum Soc. (guest speaker 1986—), Pet Industry Distbrs. Assn., Am. Pet Products Mfrs. Assn., Western World Pet Suppliers Assn. Office: Biol Engring Inc 2476 Palma Dr Ventura CA 93003-5760

BONHAM, CHARLIE LEONARD, college official; b. Richmond, Calif., Sept. 26, 1939; s. Leonard Shelby and Lavern Luella (McKay) B.; m. Pamela Ann Prahl, Feb. 23, 1963; children: Stephen Shelby, Karen Elizebeth, Tracy Michelle. BS in Marine Engring., Calif. Maritime Acad., 1960; BA in Internat. Rels., Navy Postgrad. Sch., Monterey, Calif., 1970. Lic. engr. U.S. Mcht. Marine. 3d asst. engr. Mil. Sea Transport Svc., San Francisco, 1960; commd. ensign USN, 1961, advanced through grades to capt., 1982, comdr. 4 USN ships; ret., 1989; v.p. external affairs Calif. Maritime Acad., Vallejo, 1989—, pres. Calmaritime Acad. Found., 1990—. Mem. Propeller Club U.S. (pres. San Francisco 1989-91). Republican. Office: Calif Maritime Acad 200 Maritime Academy Dr Vallejo CA 94590-8181

BONHAM, GEORGE WOLFGANG, magazine editor, writer, foundation executive; b. Free City of Danzig, Aug. 12, 1924; came to U.S., 1938, naturalized, 1943; s. Walter C. and Kate M. (Selbiger) B.; m. Sandra Timmermann; children by previous marriage: Mary Faith, Mark David. B.A., Ohio State U., 1943; M.A., Oxford U., 1947; postgrad., Columbia U., 1948-49, D.H.L. (hon.), 1975, LL.D. (hon.), 1977, DHL (hon.), 1986. Cultural info. Supreme Comdr. Allied Forces, Tokyo, N.Y.C., 1949-51, West German Govt., N.Y.C., Washington, 1951-53; account exec. public affairs firms Selvage, Lee & Chase and Communication Counsellors, N.Y.C., 1953-62; v.p. for sci. and edn. Howard Chase Assos., N.Y.C., 1963-66; pres. Sci. and Univ. Affairs; public affairs cons. to univs. Sci. and Univ. Affairs, N.Y.C., 1966—; editor in chief, pub. Change mag., 1969-81; exec. dir. Council of Learning, New Rochelle, 1977-84; sr. fellow Aspen Inst., N.Y.C., 1979-84; v.p. programs Palo Alto Med. Found., Calif., 1984-86; cons. Henry J. Kaiser Family Found., Menlo Park, Calif., 1986-87; dir. The Found. Project, 1989—. Editor: Inside Academe, 1972, On Learning and Change, 1973, Colleges and Money, 1975, The Future of Foundations, 1978, In the Public Interest, 1978, The Communications Revolution and the Education of Americans, 1980; Contbr. articles to nat. mags. Trustee various nonprofit orgns.; chmn. Citizens Com. Internat. Edn.; bd. dirs. Tech. in Edn. Task Force. Served with 44th Div. M.I., AUS, 1943-45. Home: 371 Cypress Point Rd Half Moon Bay CA 94019-2242

BONHAM, HAROLD FLORIAN, research geologist; b. L.A., Sept. 1, 1928; s. Harold Florian and Viola Violet (Clopine) B.; m. Sally Mae Reimer, Sept. 6, 1952; children: Cynthia Jean Kimball, Douglas Craig, Gary Stephen. AA in Physics, U. Calif. Berkeley, 1951; BA in Geology, UCLA, 1954; MS in Geology, U. Nev., 1963. Geologist So. Pacific Co., 1955-61; mining geologist Nev. Bur. Mines and Geology, Reno, 1963-93, acting dir., state geologist, 1993-95; cons. UN, Can., Australia, Peoples Republic of China, 1980-90; cons. in field. Contbr. articles to profl. jour. V.p. Palomino Valley Gen. Improvement Dist., Nev., 1986-88. With USN, 1946-49, PTO. Fellow Geol. Soc. Am., Soc. Econ. Geologist, Assn. Exploration Geochemists (councillor 1988—); mem. Geol. Soc. Nev. Republican. Home: 2100 Right Hand Canyon Rd Reno NV 89510-9300 Office: Nev Bur Mines & Geology Mill St Stop 18 Reno NV 89501

BONHAM, J. LEE, special education educator, consultant; b. Springfield, Mo., Apr. 7, 1927; s. Griffith Kinchloe and Mildred Esther (Cook) B.; m. Jennifer Irene Hacker; children: Heidi Ingred, Nandy Lindell, James John, Irene Eleanore. BA, U. N.Mex., 1953; MA in Edn., Chapman Coll., 1963; EdS in Vocat. Edn., U. Wyo., 1980. Cert. profl. edn. specialist, Wyo. Instr. Western Wyo. Coll., Rock Springs, 1965-67; fellow U. N.Mex., Albuquerque, 1967-68; chmn. sociology dept. Sch. of the Ozarks, Point Lookout, Mo., 1968-70; field engr. Bechtel Engring., Rock Springs, 1972-75; tchr. spl. edn. Anamas (N.Mex.) Schs., 1978-79, Jeffrey City (Wyo.) Schs., 1979-80; cons. Forestry Svc., Medicine Bow, Wyo., 1989-90, Am. Assn. Ret. Persons, Rock Springs, 1992—. With U.S. Army, 1945-46. Urban Inst. fellow George Williams Coll., Chgo., 1968; African Inst. fellow Northwestern U., Chgo., 1969. Fellow Am. Mus. Natural History, Smithsonian Instn.; mem. NEA, Wyo. Assn. Profl. Archaeologists, Elks. Democrat. Home: 419 Soulsby St Rock Springs WY 82901-5256

BONINE, LARRY STANLEY, transportation executive, engineer; b. Chattanooga, July 7, 1941; s. J.B. and Mildred (Sturdivant) B.; m. Rosemary Thornton, June 26, 1968; children: Michael, Kelly, Suzy. BCE, Tenn. Tech. U., 1964; MCE, U. Mo., 1970. Registered profl. engr., Tenn., Fla. Commd. 2nd lt. U.S. Army, 1964, advanced through ranks to col., 1990; dist. engr. U.S. Army, Little Rock; comdr. Facilities Command U.S. Army, Seoul, Korea, 1985-87; dist. engr. U.S. Army, Mobile, Ala., 1987-90; v.p. Wisdom Assocs., Inc., Stuart, Fla., 1990-91; area constrn. mgr., partnering champion Ctrl. Artery Tunnel Project, Boston, 1991-93; dir. Ariz. Dept. Transp., Phoenix, 1993—. Contbr. articles to profl. jours. Home: 5880 E Onyx Ave Scottsdale AZ 85253 Office: Ariz Dept Transp 206 S 17th Ave Phoenix AZ 85007-3213

BONINO, ANTHONY, air transportation executive; b. 1953. BS in Bus. Fin., U. San Francisco, 1975. V.p. Three Way Corp., Sunnyvale, Calif., 1974-84; pres. MCN Enterprises, Inc., South San Francisco, 1984—. Office: MCN Enterprises Inc 270 Lawrence Ave South San Francisco CA 94080*

BONNELL, VICTORIA EILEEN, sociologist; b. N.Y.C., June 15, 1942; d. Samuel S. and Frances (Nassau) B.; m. Gregory Freidin, May 4, 1971. B.A. Brandeis U., 1964; M.A., Harvard U., 1966, Ph.D., 1975. Lectr. politics U. Calif.-Santa Cruz, 1972-73, 74-76; asst. prof. sociology U. Calif.-Berkeley, 1976-82, assoc. prof., 1982-91, prof., 1991—; chair Berkeley Ctr. for Slavic and East European Studies, U. Calif.-Berkeley, 1994—. Recipient Heldt prize in Slavic women's studies, 1991; AAUW fellow, 1979; Regents faculty fellow, 1978; Fulbright Hays faculty fellow, 1977; Internat. Research and Exchanges Bd. fellow, 1977, 88; Stanford U. Hoover Instn. nat. fellow, 1973-74; Guggenheim fellow, 1985; fellow Ctr. for Advanced Study in Behavioral Scis., 1986-87; Pres.' Rsch. fellow in humanities, 1991-92; grantee Am. Philos. Soc., 1979, Am. Council Learned Socs., 1976, 90-91. Mem. Am. Sociol. Assn., Am. Assn. Advancement Slavic Studies. Am. Hist. Assn. Author: Roots of Rebellion: Workers' Politics and Organizations in St. Petersburg and Moscow, 1900-1914, 1983; editor: The Russian Worker: Life and Labor under the Tsarist Regime, 1983, (with Ann Cooper and Gregory Freidin) Russia at the Barricades: Eyewitness Accounts of the August 1991 Coup, 1994; contbr. articles to profl. jours.

BONNEY, JOHN DENNIS, oil company executive; b. Blackpool, Eng., Dec. 22, 1930; s. John P. and Isabel (Evans) B.; four children from previous marriage; m. Elizabeth Shore-Wilson, Aug. 1986; two children. B.A., Hertford Coll., Oxford U., Eng., 1954, M.A., 1959; LL.M., U. Calif., Berkeley, 1956. Oil adviser Middle East, 1959-60; fgn. ops. adviser, asst. mgr., then mgr. Chevron Corp. (formerly Standard Oil Co. of Calif.), San Francisco, 1960-72, v.p., from 1972, vice chmn., 1987—, also dir.; bd. dirs. Am. Petroleum Inst. Clubs: Commonwealth; World Trade (San Francisco); Oxford and Cambridge (London). Office: Chevron Corp PO Box 7137 San Francisco CA 94120*

BONNY, BLAINE MILAN, retired accountant; b. Midvale, Utah, Oct. 5, 1909; s. Frederick Fritz and Amelia (Poulson) B.; m. Helen Matilda Bolognese, Nov. 3, 1938 (dec. Nov. 18, 1988); 1 child, Brent G. Grad. West high sch., Salt Lake City. Corp. acct. Utah Pr. and Lt. Co., Salt Lake City, 1929-74; ret., 1974—. Patentee in field, 11 copyrights. Mem. Rep. N.H. Com., 1992. Mem. ASCAP, Copper Golf Club, Mason-Acacia Lodge #17, U.S. English, Inc. Home: 847 S 7th E Salt Lake City UT 84102-3505

BONSER, QUENTIN, surgeon; b. Sedro Wooley, Wash., Nov. 1, 1920; s. George Wayne and Kathleen Imogene (Lynch) B.; BA in Zoology, UCLA, 1943; MD, U. Calif., San Francisco, 1947; m. Loellen Rocca, Oct. 20, 1945; children: Wayne, Gordon, Carol, Patricia (Mrs. Martin Sanford). Intern U. Calif. Hosp., San Francisco, 1947-49, resident gen. surgery, 1949-56; practice gen. surgery, Placerville, Calif., 1956—; ret.; surgeon King Faisal Splty. Hosp., Saudi Arabia, Sept.-Oct., 1984; vis. prof. surgery U. Calif., San Francisco, 1968. Capt. M.C., USAF, 1950-51. Vol. physician, tchr. surgery Vietnam, 1971, 72, 73. Diplomate Am. Bd. Surgery. Fellow A.C.S.; mem. H.C. Naffziger Surg. Soc. (pres. 1974-75). Home: 2590 Northridge Dr Placerville CA 95667-3416

BOOCHEVER, ROBERT, federal judge; b. N.Y.C., Oct. 2, 1917; s. Louis C. and Miriam (Cohen) B.; m. Lois Colleen Maddox, Apr. 22, 1943; children: Barbara K., Linda Lou, Ann Paula, Miriam Deon. AB, Cornell U., 1939, JD, 1941; HD (hon.), U. Alaska, 1981. Bar: N.Y. 1944, Alaska 1947. Asst. U.S. atty. Juneau, 1946-47; partner firm Faulkner, Banfield, Boochever & Doogan, Juneau, 1947-72; asso. justice Alaska Supreme Ct., 1972-75, 78-80, chief justice, 1975-78; judge U.S. Ct. Appeals (9th cir.), 1980—; chmn. Ninth Cir. Libr. Com., 1995—, Alaska Jud. Coun., 1975-78; mem. appellate judges seminar NYU Sch. Law, 1975; mem. Conf. Chief Justices, 1975-79, vice chmn., 1978-79; mem. adv. bd. Nat. Bank of Alaska, 1968-72; guest spkr. Southwestern Law Sch. Disting. Lecture Series, 1992. Chmn. Juneau chpt. ARC, 1949-51, Juneau Planning Commn., 1956-61; mem. Alaska Devel. Bd., 1949-52, Alaska Jud. Qualification Commn., 1972-75; mem. adv. bd. Juneau-Douglas Community Coll. Served to capt. inf. AUS, 1941-45. Named Juneau Man of Year, Rotary, 1974; recipient Disting. Alumnus award Cornell U., 1989. Fellow Am. Coll. Trial Attys.; mem. ABA, Alaska Bar Assn. (pres. 1961-62), Juneau Bar Assn. (pres. 1971-72), Am. Judicature Soc. (dir. 1970-74), Am. Law Inst., Juneau C. of C. (pres. 1952, 55), Alaskans United (chmn. 1972). Clubs: Marine Meml., Cornell Club of L.A., Altadena Town and Country. Office: US Ct Appeals PO Box 91510 125 S Grand Ave Pasadena CA 91105-1652

BOOKKEY, GERALD C., agricultural products executive; b. 1925. With C.A. Swanson & Sons, Seattle, 1952-56; prin. Jumbo Corp., Seattle, 1952-78, 1956—. Office: Nat Food Corp 16740 Aurora Ave N Seattle WA 98133-5311*

BOOKMAN, MARK ANDREW, business educator, consultant; b. June 12, 1948; s. Milford Norman and Barbara Doris (Goffman) B.; m. Dena Sara Goldberg Bookman; children: Aron, Noah. BA in History, UCLA, 1970; JD, 1973. Pres. Srpoul Hall Residents Assn., U. Calif., L.A., 1968-69; adminstrv. v.p. Undergrad. Student Assn. U. Calif., L.A., 1969-70; asst. to dean Campus Programs and Activities U. Calif., L.A., 1970-71, pres. Grad. Student Assn., 1971-72, rsch. asst., 1972-73; dir. U. Calif., San Diego, 1973-76; gen. mgr. Calif. State U., 1976-84; asst. v.p. Student Affairs U. Houston, 1984-88; cons., author, pres. Edn. and Non-Profit Consulting, Inc., 1986—; vis. scholar Inst. for Higher Edn. Law and Governance U. Houston, 1989-90; prof. bus. U. Judaism, 1990—; Bar: Calif., 1973. Contbr. numerous articles to profl. jours. Pres., pres. Congregation Beth Israel, 1978, 1983-84; moderator Chico Unified Sch. Dist., 1982-84; trustee Chico Women's Crisis Fund, 1983-84; youth soccer coach. Recipient Outstanding Svc. to UCLA cert., Chancellor Young, 1973; named Honor Sr., 1970. Mem. Citizens Adv. Com. North Shore Adult Sch., Calif. Bar Assn., UCLA Alumni Assn.,. Home: 5438 Micaela Dr Agoura Hills CA 91301-4060 Office: University of Judaism 15600 Mulholland Dr Los Angeles CA 90077-1519

BOONE, BIRTHE SCHNOHR, nurse practitioner; b. Denmark, Jan. 7, 1945; came to U.S., 1980; d. Otto Johannes and Inger Sofie (Schnohr) Kristensen; m. Erik Højstrup Christensen, June 24, 1963 (div. 1968); 1 child, Peter Højstrup; m. Earle Marion Boone, Oct. 16, 1979. BSN, Calif. State U., L.A., 1986; MSN, Calif. State U., Long Beach, 1989. RN, Calif.; cert. adult nurse practitioner, gerontological nurse practitioner. Supr. Danish Nat. Svc. for Mentally Retarded, Copenhagen, 1968-77; dir. Mental Health Soc. for Developmentally Disabled Children, Amman, Jordan, 1977-79; staff nurse neurology Los Angeles County-U. So. Calif. Med. Ctr., 1984-85; staff nurse Torrance (Calif.) Meml. Hosp. Med. Ctr., 1985-87; clin. educator Kaiser Permanente Med. Ctr., L.A., 1987-88; nurse practitioner VA Med. Ctr., Long Beach, 1988-91, Phoenix, 1991—; adj. prof. Calif. State U., Long BEach, 1990-91; clin. preceptor U. Ariz., Tucson, 1993-94. Mem. Sigma Theta Tau. Office: VA Med Ctr 650 E Indian School Rd Phoenix AZ 85012-1839

BOONE, EARLE MARION, business executive; b. Panama City, Fla., Apr. 25, 1934; s. Earle Alpha and Lucy Marian (Jerkins) B.; m. Birthe Schnohr Kristensen Boone, Oct. 16, 1979; children: Tina Boone Broderick, Darlene Boone Moseley, Earle Marion Jr. BS in Aviation Mgmt., So. Ill. U., 1977; MS in Pub. Adminstrn., Calif. State U., 1983. Lic. airline transport pilot. USAF pilot, 1954-75; corp. pilot pvt. practice, 1975-78, aviation mgmt. cons., 1978-80; mktg. dir. Northrop Corp., Hawthorne, Calif., 1980-92; v.p. mktg. Cognitive Neurometrics, Scottsdale, Ariz., 1992-95; pres., CEO Cognitive Neurometrics Inc., Scottsdale, Ariz., 1995—; SR-71 pilot 9th Strat Recon Wing, Beale AFB, Calif., 1966-68; F4-E combat fighter pilot 388 Tactical Fighter Wing, Thailand, 1970-71; mktg. dir. Northrop Corp., Hawthorne, 1980-92; v.p. mktg. cognitive Neurometrics Inc., Scottsdale, Ariz., 1992—. lt. col. USAF, 1954-75, Vietnam. Recipient The Disting. Flying Cross, The Air medal, Bronze Star medal, Meritorious Svc. medal, Sec. Air Force, Vietnam, 1970-71,. Mem. Ret. Officers Assn., Order of Daedalians, Sierra Club, Phi Alpha Alpha. Republican. Home: 8607 E Lariat Ln Scottsdale AZ 85255-1456 Office: Cognitive Neurometrics Inc Scottsdale AZ 85255

BOONE, JEFFREY LYNN, internist; b. Wichita, Kans., Aug. 1, 1951; s. Stewart and Joyce (Henkle) B.; m. Colette Marie Felgate, May 20, 1978; children: Tyler, Parker, Hunter, Mackenzie. BS, Southwestern Coll., 1973; MS, Kans. State U., 1975; MD, U. Iowa, 1983. Diplomate Am. Bd. Internal Medicine. Intern, resident in internal medicine Good Samaritan Hosp. and Med. Ctr., Portland, Oreg., 1983-86; phys. fitness specialist YMCA, Des Moines, 1974-79; assoc. med. dir., then med. dir. Nat. Ctr. Preventive and Stress Medicine, Phoenix, 1986-87; med. dir. Inst. Stress Medicine, Denver, 1987-90; dir. preventive medicine Swedish Med. Ctr., Englewood, Colo., 1990—; asst. clin. prof. medicine U. Colo., Denver, 1990—; dir. and founder Preventive and Stress Medicine Ctr., 1992—. Contbg. author: Stress and Hypertension, 1991; guest editor: Primary Care: Clinics in Office Practice-Hypertension, 1991. Recipient award for innovations in disease prevention and health promotion HHS, 1986. Mem. Rotary Internat. Home: 1550 Crestridge Dr Littleton CO 80121-1315 Office: Preventive/Stress Medicine Ctr 8200 E Belleview # 390 Englewood CO 80111

BOONE, LOIS RUTH, legislator; b. Vancouver, B.C., Can., Apr. 26, 1947; d. George Charles Bearne and Ruth (Lindberg) Chudley; ; children: Sonia, Tanis. Tchr.'s cert., Simon Fraser U., 1969. Tchr. Sch. Dist. 57, Prince George, B.C., 1969-71, Sch. Dist. 27, Williams Lake, B.C., 1971-72; office mgr. Prince George YM-YWCA, 1972-73; case aide worker Vancouver YWCA, 1973-74; adminstrv. asst. Gov. B.C., Prince George, 1978-86; mem. legis. assembly Gov. B.C., Victoria, 1986—, min. govt. svcs., 1991-93, mem. I.C.B.C. Bd., 1994—. Trustee Sch. Dist. 57, Prince George, 1981-85. Mem. New Democratic Party. Office: New Democrat Gov Caucus, Rm 276M E Annex Parliament Bldgs, Victoria, BC Canada V8V 1X4

BOONE, NORMAN MCKIEGHAN, financial planner; b. Inglewood, Calif., June 4, 1947; s. Elton D. and Barbara (Lombard) B.; m. Elisa A. Boone, May 31, 1982; children: Andrew, Anaelisa. BA in Polit. Sci., Stanford U., 1969; MBA, Harvard Bus. Sch., 1977. Cert. Fin. Planner, Registry Fin. Planner. Vol. VISTA, Price, Utah, 1969-71; asst. v.p. Wells Fargo Bank, San Francisco, 1977-80; CFO Henderson Group, Oakland, Calif., 1980-82; v.p. fin. adminstrn. D'Arcy, McManus, Masius, San Francisco, 1982-84; v.p. Hibernia Bank, San Francisco, 1984-87; fin. planner Associated Securities, San Francisco, 1987—. Contbr. articles to profl. jours. Lt. U.S. Army, 1972-75. Mem. Internat. Assn. for Fin. Planning, Rotary Club, Estate Planning Coun. Office: Boone Assocs One Post St # 2750 San Francisco CA 94104-5231

BOOTH, JOHN LOUIS, service executive; b. Danville, Va., May 15, 1933; s. William Irvine and Melba (Harvey) B.; m. Ann Fennell, May 23, 1959; children: Mark, Robin. BA, U. Richmond, 1958; ThM, Dallas Theol. Sem., 1962, ThD, 1965, PhD, 1993; postgrad., Ariz. State U., 1972, 79. Pastor Skyway Bible Ch., Seattle, 1964-66, Mount Prospect (Ill.) Bible Ch., 1966-71, Camelback Bible Ch., Paradise Valley, Ariz., 1971-78; counselor Camelback Counseling Ctr., Phoenix, 1978-79; dir. Paradise Valley Counseling, Inc., Phoenix, 1980—; chmn. bd. Paradise Valley Counseling, Inc., 1980—; chmn. bd. Paradise Valley Counseling Found., Inc., Phoenix, 1982—; adj. prof. Grand Canyon U., 1981—, Southwestern Coll., Phoenix, 1979—, Talbott Theol. Sem. Phoenix Ext., 1983-85; seminar speaker frequent engagements, 1965—. Author: Understanding Today's Problems, 1980, Marriage by the Master Plan, 1980, Equipping for Effective Marriage, 1983, 95, (tape series) Starting Over, 1982, Enjoying All God Intended, 1988, 95. Precinct committeeman Rep. Party, Phoenix, 1983-84, 87-88, 90-91; chaplain Ariz. State Senate, Phoenix, 1973. Mem. Am. Psychol. Soc., Christian Assn. for Psychol. Studies, Am. Assn. Christian Counselors. Baptist. Office: Paradise Valley Counseling Inc 10210 N 32nd St Ste 211 Phoenix AZ 85028-3848

BOOTH, JOHN NICHOLLS, minister, magician, writer, photographer; b. Meadville, Pa., Aug. 7, 1912; s. Sydney Scott and Margaret (Nicholls) B.; m. Edith Kriger, Oct. 1, 1941 (dec. Sept. 1982); 1 child, Barbara Anne Booth Christie. BA, McMaster U., 1934; MDiv, Meadville Theol. Sch., 1942; LittD, New Eng. Sch. Law, 1950. Ordained to ministry Unitarian Ch., 1942. Profl. magician, 1934-40; min. Unitarian Ch., Evanston, Ill., 1942-48, 1st Ch., Belmont, Mass., 1949-57, 2d Ch., Boston, 1958-64, Unitarian Ch., Long Beach, Calif., 1964-71; interim pastor N.Y.C., Gainesville, (Fla.), Detroit, 1971-73; celebrity platform lectr., performer on conjuring, 1942-58; ministerial adviser to liberal students MIT, 1958-63; mem. books selection com. Gen. Theol. Library, Boston, 1960-63. Author: Super Magical Miracles, 1930, Magical Mentalism, 1931, Forging Ahead in Magic, 1939, Marvels of Mystery, 1941, The Quest for Preaching Power, 1942, Fabulous Destinations, 1950, Story of the Second Church in Boston, 1959, The John Booth Classics, 1975, Booths in History, 1982, Psychic Paradoxes, 1984, Wonders of Magic, 1986, Dramatic Magic, 1988, Creative World of Conjuring, 1990, Conjurians' Discoveries, 1992, The Fine Art of Hocus Pocus, 1995; contbr. articles to mags. and newspapers; photographer full length feature travel documentary films for TV, lecture platforms made in India, Africa, S.Am., Indonesia, South Seas, Himalayas; presented first color travelogue on TV in U.S. over NBC in N.Y.C., 1949; panel mem. radio program Churchmen Weigh The News, Boston, 1951-52; spl. corr. in Asia for Chgo. Sun-Times, 1948-49; by-line writer Boston Globe, 1952-62; producer motion picture Heart of Africa, 1954; photographer films Golden Kingdoms of the Orient, 1957, Treasures of the Amazon, Ecuador and Peru, 1960, Adventurous Britain, 1962, South Seas Saga in Tahiti, Australia and New Guinea, summer 1966, The Amazing America of Will Rogers, 1970, Spotlight on Spain, 1975. Co-founder Japan Free Religious Assn., Tokyo, 1948; co-founder Mass. Meml. Soc., 1962, dir., 1962-64; organizer Meml. Soc. Alachua County (Fla.), 1972; pres. Long Beach Mental Health Assn., 1964-66; adv. coun. Fair Housing Found. Decorated officer Ouissam Alaouite Cherifien, King of Morocco; selected for cinematographers' former Wall of Fame Town Hall, N.Y.C., 1967; recipient Star of Magic award N.Y.C., 1971, H. Adrian Smith literary award, 1985, 89, John Nevil Maskelyne prize London Magic Circle, 1987, Milbourne Christopher award, 1994; Acad. Magical Arts Literary fellow, 1977, Lifetime Achievement fellow, 1990. Mem. Unitarian-Universalist Mins. Assn. (past dir.), Am. Unitarian Assn. (past com. chmn.), Unitarian Mins. Pacific S.W. Assn. (v.p.), Clergy Counseling Svc. So. Calif., Soc. Am. Magicians (inducted into Hall of Fame 1983), Magic Castle Hollywood, Internat. Motion Picture and Lectrs. Assn., L.A. Adventurers Club (pres. 1983). Home and Office: 12032 Montecito Rd Los Alamitos CA 90720-4511

BOOTH, STEPHEN WALTER, English language educator; b. N.Y.C., Apr. 20, 1933; s. Frank and Ruth Joan (Friedman) B.; m. Susan Patek, June 20, 1959; children: Jason Michael, Mary. AB, Harvard U., 1955, PhD, 1964; BA, Cambridge (Eng.) U., 1957; LHD, Georgetown U., 1991. Asst. prof. U. Calif., Berkeley, 1962-69, assoc. prof., 1969-74, prof., 1974—. Author: An Essay on Shakespeare's Sonnets, 1969, paperback, 1972, The Book Called Holinshed's Chronicles, 1969, Shakespeare's Sonnets, Edited with Analytic Commentary, 1977, rev. edit., 1978, paperback, 1979, King Lear, Macbeth, Indefinition and Tragedy, 1983, (pamphlet) Liking Julius Caesar, 1991; mem. editorial bd. S.E.L., 1978—, Assays, 1979—, Mississippi Studies in English, 1979—, Shakespeare Quar., 1981—. Guggenheim Found. fellow, 1970-71; recipient Marshall scholarship British govt., Cambridge, 1955-57. Mem. MLA (James Russell Lowell prize 1978). Democrat. Episcopalian. Home: 98 The Uplands Berkeley CA 94705-2815 Office: Univ of Calif Dept English 322 Wheeler Hall Berkeley CA 94720-1030

BOOTHE, DYAS POWER, JR., emeritus finance company executive; b. Berkeley, Calif., Dec. 23, 1910; s. Dyas Power and Margaret (Stewart) B.; m. Margaret Kempenich, June 28, 1933 (div. 1966); children: Margaret Joanne (Mrs. Charles E. Turkington), Barry Power; m. Catherine Causey, 1967; 1 dau., Catherine Elizabeth Lifto. A.B., Stanford, 1931. Pres. Boothe Fruit Co., Modesto, Calif., 1946-59; co-founder and pres. U.S. Leasing Corp., 1952-55; pres. Boothe Leasing Corp., San Francisco, 1954-67; chmn., chief exec. officer Boothe Fin. Corp., Armco-Boothe Corp., to 1972; chmn., chief exec. officer GATX-Boothe Corp., 1967-81, chmn. emeritus; also domestic and fgn. subs. Courier Terminal Systems Inc., Phoenix, 1971-78, chmn. bd., dir., 1971-78; pres., chief exec. officer, trustee IDS Realty Trust, 1976-80; chmn., chief exec. officer IDS Mortgage Corp., 1976-80, pres., chief exec. officer Boothe Holdings, 1981—; dir. BEI Electronics, Inc., 1983-93, McMahon Fin. Svcs., Inc., 1981-88; chmn. Vacu Dry Co., 1983-95. Trustee Pacific Inst. Pub. Policy Rsch., 1977-94, Schs. of Sacred Heart, San Francisco, 1984-88; regent St. Mary's Coll., Moraga, Calif., 1985-91; adv. bd. Ctr. for Econ. Policy Rsch., Stanford U., 1988—. Comdr. USNR, 1942-46, PTO. Mem. Delta Tau Delta. Clubs: World Trade, Bankers (San Francisco). Home and Office: 33 San Carlos Ave Sausalito CA 94965-2015

BOOZE, THOMAS FRANKLIN, toxicologist; b. Denver, Mar. 4, 1955; s. Ralph Walker and Ann (McNatt) B.; m. Patricia Jude Bullock, Aug. 8, 1981; children: Heather N., Ian T. BS, U. Calif., Davis, 1978; MS, Kans. State U., 1981, PhD, 1985. Registered environ assessor, Calif. Asst. instr. Kans. State U., Manhattan, 1979-85; sr. consulting toxicologist Chevron Corp., Sacramento, 1985-92; sr. toxicologist Radian Corp., Sacramento, 1992—; cons. in field, Manhattan, Kans., 1981-83. contbr. articles to profl. jours. Vol. Amigos de las Americas, Marin County, Calif., 1973, Hospice Care, Manhattan, 1985. Mem. N.Y. Acad. Sci., Soc. Toxicology, Soc. for Risk Analysis, Sigma Xi. Home: 8338 Titian Ridge Ct Antelope CA 95843-5627 Office: Radian Corp 10389 Old Placerville Rd Sacramento CA 95827-2506

BORCHARDT, MARILYN, development administrator; b. Clintonville, Wis., Aug. 13, 1944; d. Millard E. and Rena (Schneiderwent) Gerbig; m. Glenn Borchardt, June 12, 1965; children: Nina, Natalie. BS, U. Wis., 1966; MS, Oreg. State U., 1969. Exec. dir. JACKIE, San Francisco, 1974-84; devel. dir. Lighthouse for the Blind, San Francisco, 1985-86; dep. dir. Inst. for Food and Devel. Policy, Oakland, Calif., 1986—; bd. dirs. Alameda County Community Food Bank, Oakland; founding dir. San Francisco Environ. Film Festival, 1993—. Mem. Devel. Execs. Roundtable. Office: Inst for Food and Devel Policy 398 60th St Oakland CA 94618

BORDELON, SCOTT LEE, computer systems engineer; b. Fullerton, Calif., May 23, 1967; s. Sidney Augusten and Carolyn Ann (Dobsky) B. BSEE, U. Calif., 1989, MS in Computer Engring., 1990. Registered profl. engr., Calif. Designer analog circuits Western Instrument Corp., Ventura, Calif., 1988; software engr. Rockwell Internat., Irvine, Calif., 1989; computer architecture rschr. UCSB Computer Architecture Lab., Goleta, Calif., 1988-90; systems design engr. Amdahl Corp., Sunnyvale, Calif., 1990-93; internat. applications engr. CrossCheck Tech. Corp., San Jose, Calif., 1993—; networks cons. U. Calif., Santa Barbara, 1990-91; expert in field integrated circuit test methodologies. Inventor in field. Vol. homeless shelter Cmty. Found. Santa Clara, Calif., 1991-92; vol. Second Harvest Food Bank, 1993-94. Mem. IEEE, Assn. Computing Machinery, Eta Kappa Nu. Unitarian. Office: CrossCheck Tech Corp 2833 Junction Ave Ste 100 San Jose CA 95134-1920

BORDNER, GREGORY WILSON, environmental engineer; b. Buffalo, Aug. 16, 1959; s. Raymond Gordon and Nancy Lee (Immegart) B.; m. Margaret Patricia Toon, June 14, 1981; children: Eric Lawrence, Heather Rae. BS in Chem. Engring., Calif. State Poly. U., 1982; MS in Systems Mgmt., U. So. Calif., 1987. Commd. 2nd lt. USAF, 1983, advanced through grades to capt., 1987; engr., mgr. various air launched missile, anti-satellite and strategic def. initiative projects Air Force Rocket Propulsion Lab., Edwards AFB, Calif., 1983-86; asst. mgr. space transp. Air Force Astronautics Lab., Edwards AFB, 1986-87; chief small intercontinental ballistic missiles ordnance firing system br. Hdqrs. Ballistic Missile Orgn., San Bernardino, Calif., 1987-90; sr. plant environ. engr. Filtrol Corp./Akzo Chems. Inc., L.A., 1991-92; water/soils project engr. TABC, Inc., Long Beach, Calif., 1992—. Author: (manual) Pyrotechnic Transfer Line Evaluation, 1984, (with others) Rocket Motor Heat Transfer, 1984. Mem. AIChE, Am. Water Works Assn. Home: 10841 Ring Ave Alta Loma CA 91737-4429

BOREL, JAMES DAVID, anesthesiologist; b. Chgo., Nov. 15, 1951; s. James Albert and Nancy Ann (Sieverson) B. BS, U. Wis., 1973; MD, Med. Coll. of Wis., 1977. Diplomate Am. Bd. Anesthesiology, Nat. Bd. Med. Examiners, Am. Coll. Anesthesiologists. Research asst. McArdle Lab. for Cancer Research, Madison, Wis., 1972-73, Stanford U. and VA Hosp., Palo Alto, 1976-77; intern. The Cambridge (Mass.) Hosp., 1977-78; clin. fellow in medicine Harvard Med. Sch., Boston, 1977-78, clin. fellow in anesthesia, 1978-80, clin. instr. in anaesthesia, 1980; resident in anesthesiology Peter Bent Brigham Hosp., Boston, 1978-80; anesthesiologist Mt. Auburn Hosp., Cambridge, 1980; fellow in anesthesiology Ariz. Health Scis. Ctr., Tucson, 1980-81; research assoc. U. Ariz. Coll. Medicine, Tucson, 1980-81, assoc. in anesthesiology, 1981—; active staff Mesa (Ariz.) Luth. Hosp., 1981—; courtesy staff Scottsdale (Ariz.) Meml. Hosp., 1982—; vis. anaesthetist St. Joseph's Hosp., Kingston, Jamaica, 1980. Contbr. numerous articles to profl. jours. Mem. AMA, AAAS, Ariz. Anesthesia Alumni Assn., Ariz. Soc. Anesthesiologists, Am. Soc. Regional Anesthesia, Can. Anesthetists' Soc., Internat. Anesthesia Rsch. Soc., Am. Soc. Anesthesiologists. Office: Valley Anesthesia Cons 2950 N 7th St Phoenix AZ 85014-5404

BOREN, KENNETH RAY, endocrinologist; b. Evansville, Ind., Dec. 31, 1945; s. Doyle Clifford and Jeannette (Koerner) B.; m. Rebecca Lane Wallace, Aug. 25, 1967; children: Jennifer, James, Michael, Peter, Nicklas, Benjamin. BS, Ariz. State U., 1967; MD, Ind. U., Indpls., 1972; MA, Ind. U., Bloomington, 1974. Diplomate Am. Bd. Endocrinology, Am. Bd. Nephrology, Am. Bd. Internal Medicine. Intern in pathology Ind. U. Sch. Medicine, Indpls., 1972; intern in medicine Ind. U. Sch. Medicine, 1972-73, resident in medicine, 1975-77, fellow in endocrinology, 1977-79, fellow nephrology, 1979-80, instr., 1980; physician East Valley Nephrology, Mesa, Ariz., 1980—; chief medicine Mesa Luth Hosp., 1987-89, chief staff, 1990-91. Bd. dirs. Ariz. Kidney Found., Phoenix, 1984—, pres. 1993-94. Lt. USN, 1973-75. Fellow ACP; mem. AMA, Maricopa County Med. Assn., Ariz. Med. Assn., Am. Soc. Nephrology, Internat. Soc. Nephrology, Am. Diabetes Assn. Republican. Latter Day Saints. Home: 4222 E Mclellan Rd Ste 10 Mesa AZ 85205-3119 Office: East Valley Nephrology East Valley Nephrology 560 W Brown # 3006 Mesa AZ 85201-3221

BORESI, ARTHUR PETER, author, educator; b. Toluca, Ill.; s. John Peter and Eva (Grotti) B.; m. Clara Jean Gordon, Dec. 28, 1946; children: Jennifer Ann Boresi Hill, Annette Boresi Pueschel, Nancy Jean Boresi Broderick. Student, Kenyon Coll., 1943-44; BSEE, U. Ill., 1948, MS in Mechanics, 1949, PhD in Mechanics, 1953. Research engr. N. Am. Aviation, 1950; materials engr. Nat. Bur. Standards, 1951; mem. faculty U. Ill., Urbana, 1953—, prof. theoretical and applied mechanics and nuclear engrng., 1959-79; prof. emeritus U. Ill. at Urbana, Urbana, 1979; Disting. vis. prof. Clarkson Coll. Tech., Potsdam, N.Y., 1968-69; NAVSEA research prof. Naval Postgrad. Sch., Monterey, Calif., 1978-79; prof. civil engrng. U. Wyo., Laramie, 1979-95, head, 1980-94, prof. emeritus, 1995—; vis. prof. Naval Postgrad. Sch., Monterey, Calif., 1986-87.; cons. in field. Author: Engineering Mechanics, 1959, Elasticity in Engineering Mechanics, 3d edit., 1987, Advanced Mechanics of Materials, 5th edit., 1993, Approximate Solution Methods in Engineering Mechanics, 1991; also articles. Served with USAAF, 1943-44; Served with AUS, 1944-46. Fellow ASME, ASCE; mem. Am. Soc. Engrng. Edn. (Archie Higdon Disting. Educator award 1993), Am. Acad. Mechanics (founding, treas.), Soc. Exptl. Mechanics, Sigma Xi. Office: U Wyo Box 3295 Univ Station Laramie WY 82071

BORG, AXEL EDWIN, librarian, educator; b. Frankfurt/Main, Hesse, Germany, Sept. 22, 1953; naturalized citizen, 1961; s. Lavern Gerald and Jane Scott (Wood) B.; m. Myra Lynn Kitchens, Dec. 17, 1988; 1 child, Laura Jane. BA in History, Pomona Coll., 1976; MLS, U. Calif., Berkeley, 1984. Libr. Natural Resources Libr. U. Calif., Berkeley, 1984-86; reference libr. Sci. Libr. U. Calif., Santa Cruz, 1986-88; wine bibliographer Shields Libr. U. Calif., Davis, 1988—; vis. lectr. Libr. Sch., U. Calif., Berkeley, 1987-89, 92; instr. Sacramento City Coll., 1991—. Capt. U.S. Army, 1976-83. Mem. Calif. Hist. Soc., Book Club Calif., Sacramento Book Collectors Club, Sci. and Engrng. Acad. Librs. Democrat. Methodist. Office: U Calif Shields Libr Davis CA 95616

BORGES, CARLOS FREITAS, computational mathematician; b. Seattle, Oct. 23, 1961; s. Carlos Rego and Margaret (Freitas) B.; m. Katherine Albright, Apr. 23, 1994. BS in Computer Sci., U. Calif., Davis, 1984, MS in Applied Math., 1986, PhD in Applied Math., 1990. Mem. tech. staff GTE Govt. Sys., Mountain View, Calif., 1986-90; prof. math. Naval Postgrad. Sch., Monterey, Calif., 1991—; vis. rschr. Ctr. for Image Processing and Integrated Computing, Davis, 1992—. Contbr. articles to profl. jours. Earle C. Anthony fellowship U. Calif., 1989-90. Mem. IEEE, Assn. for Computing Machinery, Optical Soc. of Am., Soc. for Indsl. and Applied Math., Phi Beta Kappa, Pi Mu Epsilon. Republican. Office: Naval Postgrad Sch Code Ma/Bc Monterey CA 93943

BORGES, CARLOS REGO, topology educator; b. Lomba da Fazenda, Azores, Portugal, Feb. 17, 1939; came to U.S., 1956; s. José Jacinto Rego and Maria do Nascimento (Borges) Borges; married; children: Mary Lou Freitas, Carlos F., Michael F. BS, Humboldt State Coll., 1960; MS, U. Wash., 1962, PhD, 1964. Asst. prof. U. Nev., Reno, 1964-65; asst. prof. U. Calif., Davis, 1965-68, assoc. prof., 1968-72, prof., 1972—. Contbr. articles to profl. jours. Republican. Roman Catholic. Office: U Calif Davis CA 95616

BORGES, STEPHANY PATRICIA, English language educator; b. Oakland, Calif., June 12, 1948; d. Harold Borges and Elsie (Hansen) Marron; m. Howard Bruce Waitzkin, Mar. 13, 1983; children: Sofia Borges Waitzkin, Daren Borges. MA, Sonoma State U., 1980; MFA in Fiction, U. Calif., Irvine, 1985, PhD, 1990. Tchg. assoc. U. Calif., Irvine, 1983-90; vis. asst. prof. Harvey Mudd Coll., Claremont, Calif., 1990-91; tchg. assoc. Irvine (Calif.) Valley Coll., 1991-94; English tchr. Cornelia Connelly Sch., Anaheim, Calif., 1994—; pvt. practice writer and tchr., Santa Ana, Calif., 1993—. Author: Rebels and Old Maids, 1990; author short stories. Recipient Best Essay awards Friends of the Libr., Corona del Mar, Calif., 1983, 85. Fellow MLA, Coll. English Assn., D.H. Lawrence Soc. Home: 2108 N Greenleaf Santa Ana CA 92706 Office: Cornelia Connelly Sch 2323 W Broadway Anaheim CA 92804-2306

BORGES, WILLIAM, III, environmental analyst; b. Long Beach, Calif., Nov. 21, 1948; s. William Borges Jr. and Dorothy Mae (Raymond) Morris; m. Rosalind Denise Marye, Nov. 23, 1968; children: William IV, Blake Austin. BA in Geography, Calif. State U., Sonoma, 1973. Environ. planner Mendocino County Planning Dept., Ukiah, Calif., 1976; project mgr. Engrng. Sci., Inc., Berkeley, Calif., 1976-79, Santa Clara County Planning Dept., San Jose, Calif., 1979-81, Internat. Tech. Corp., San Jose, 1985-88; mgr. sales ops. Adac Labs., Milpitas, Calif., 1983-85; prin. WT Environ. Cons., Phoenix, 1988-91; project mgr. Dynamac Corp., Newport Beach, Calif., 1991-93; prin. environ. scientist Midwest Rsch. Inst., Scottsdale, Ariz., 1993—. Contbr. photographs to various mags. Coord. pub. rels. Stellar Acad. for Dyslexics, Fremont, Calif., 1988. With M.I., U.S. Army, 1967-70. Mem. Am. Mensa. Office: Midwest Rsch Inst 11109 N 129th Way Scottsdale AZ 85259-4406

BORGESON, BET, artist; b. Mpls., Feb. 12, 1940; d. Claire Vernon and Adelaide Pauline (Zwiefel) Chamberland; m. Edwin George Borgeson, Jan. 21, 1920; children: Richard Raphael Sands, Scott Eric Sands. BS, Portland State U., 1978. Exhibited works in numerous one-woman shows including Maveety Gallery, Salishan, Oreg., 1991, 89, Lawrence Gallery, Portland, Oreg., 1984, 83; author: The Colored Pencil, 1993, 1983, Colored Pencil Fast Techniques, 1988, Color Drawing Workshop, 1984. Home: 3977 SW Condor Ave Portland OR 97201-4103

BORJAS, GEORGE J(ESUS), economics educator; b. Havana, Cuba, Oct. 15, 1950; came to U.S., 1962; s. Juan V. Borjas and Edita F. Diaz; m. Jane Maureen Walsh, Nov. 11, 1989; children: Sarah Jane Irene, Timothy Jorge, Rebecca Kathryn. BS, St. Peter's Coll., Jersey City, 1971; MA, M in Philosophy, PhD, Columbia U., 1975. Asst. prof. Queens Coll., Flushing, N.Y., 1975-77; research assoc. Nat. Bur. Econ. Research, Cambridge, Mass., 1983—; prof. econs. U. Calif., Santa Barbara, 1978-90, San Diego, 1990—; cons. Unicon Rsch. Corp., Santa Monica, Calif., 1982—; econs. adv. panel NSF, 1988-90; mem. Gov.'s Coun. of Econ. Advisers, 1993—. Author: Wage Policy in the Federal Bureaucracy, 1980, International Differences in the Labor Market Performance of Immigrants, 1988, Friends or Strangers: The Impact of Immigrants on the U.S. Economy, 1990, Labor Economics, 1995; editor: Hispanics in the United States, 1985, Immigration and the Work Force: Economic Consequences for the United States and Source Areas, 1992; mem. editl. bd. Quar. Jour. Econs., 1992—, Internat. Migration Rev., 1992—; contbr. articles to profl. jours. Fellow Columbia U. Alumni Fund, 1973, NIMH, U. Chgo., 1977; grantee Rockefeller Found., 1983-85, Sloan Found., 1986-93, NSF, 1986—, Russell Sage Found., 1991-93; vis. scholar Harvard U., 1988-89. Mem. NAS (panel 1984-85, 95—), Am. Econ. Assn. Roman Catholic. Home: 14820 Caminito Lorren Del Mar CA 92014-4157 Office: U Calif Dept Econs La Jolla CA 92093

BORN, JAMES THOMAS, private investigator; b. Chgo., Oct. 4, 1946; s. James Joseph and Helen Marjory (Christensen) B.; m. Becky Sue Southard, Aug. 18, 1973; children: Monica Marie, Heather Linnea, Mark Daniel. AA, L.A. Pierce Coll., 1973; student, L.A. City Coll., 1972, Calif. State U., Northridge, 1973, Thomas A. Edison State Coll., 1989-90. Lic. pvt. investigator, Nev., Calif.; lic. firearms instr., Nev.; notary pub., Nev. Distbn. clk. U.S. Post Office Dept., Canoga Park, Calif., 1968-71; police sgt. U.S. Postal Police Force, L.A., 1971-72; spl. agt. City of L.A., 1971-73; police officer Dunsmuir (Calif.) Police Dept., 1973-74, Capitola (Calif.) Police Dept., 1974-77; investigator Tomlin and Assocs., Monterey, Calif., 1977-78; supr. U.S. Postal Svc., Capitola, 1978-87; pvt. investigator Calif. Investigative Svcs., L.A., 1978—, Nev. Investigative Svcs., Henderson, 1989—; capt. Mineral County Sheriff's Dept., 1991-94, chief detective bur.; regional mgr. for western U.S., SIRCHIE Fingerprint Labs. Inc., 1991—; dir. Security Police Acad., Edn. Dynamics Inst., Las Vegas, Nev., 1990-91; dir. security curriculum Inst. Bus. and Tech. Mgmt., Chgo., 1989-90; coord. security br. Am. Computer Inst., Las Vegas, 1989; dir., chmn. bd. dirs. Am. Inst. for Profl. Devel., Henderson, 1990—; chief investigator Nev. Bd. Vet. Med. Examiners, 1993—; cons. Bibb County Coroner's Office, Macon, Ga., 1993; also others. Author: Security Officer Training Program, 1989, Law Enforcement Officer Training Program, 1992. With USNR, 1963-67, Vietnam; mem. USAR, 1963-86; maj. Nev. N.G. Res., 1992—. Recipient valor commendation City of Dunsmuir, Law Enforcement Commendation medal Nat. Soc. of Sons of the Am. Revolution, 1993, also numerous letters of appreciation and commendation from law enforcement orgns., 35 mil. decorations including 3 presdl. awards. Mem. Internat. Assn. for Identification, Am. Soc. for Law Enforcement Trainers, Internat. Soc. Stress Analysts, Am. Soc. Criminology, Internat. Soc. Pvt. Investigators. Republican. Baptist. Office: Nev Investigative Svcs PO Box 91434 Henderson NV 89009-1434

BORN, ROBERT HEYWOOD, consulting civil engineer; b. L.A., Nov. 7, 1925; s. Robert Bogle and Mignon Mary (Heywood) B.; m. Marilyn Alice Simpson, Aug. 15, 1947; 1 child, Stefanie Born. Student, Stanford U., 1943; BE, U. So. Calif., 1949, MSCE, 1956. Registered civil engineer Calif., Ariz., Nev., Utah, Tenn., Guam; registered agriculture engr. Calif. Assoc. hydraulic engr. Calif. Dept. of Water Resources, L.A., 1949-58; chief engr., county hydraulic engr. County Flood Control/Water Conservation Dist., San Luis Obispo, Calif., 1958-70; dir., exec. v.p., regional mgr. Camp, Dresser & McKee, Inc., Pasadena, Calif., 1970-78; v.p., regional mgr. Born, Barrett & Assoc./Barrett Cons. Group, Newport Beach, Calif., 1978-86, Memphis, 1978-86; prin. Robert H. Born Cons. Engrs., Memphis, 1986—, Irvine, Laguna Niguel, Calif., 1986—. Chmn. World Affairs Coun., San Luis Obispo, 1965. 1st lt. U.S. Army, 1943-47. Decorated Bronze star medal, 1944. Fellow ASCE (life); mem. Am. Water Works Assn. (com. chmn.), U.S. Com. on Large Dams, Am. Pub. Works Assn. (cert. outstanding pub. works achievement 1969), Floodplain Mgmt. Assn. Calif. Democrat. Presbyterian. Home: 15 Anacapri Laguna Niguel CA 92677-8630 Office: Robert H Born Cons Engrs 15 Anacapri Laguna Niguel CA 92677-8630

BORNELL, CECIL JEAN, computer graphics designer, small business owner; b. Alliance, Ohio, Oct. 31, 1929; d. William Cecil and Ethel Elizabeth (Borton) Headrick; m. Donald Gustave Bornell; 1 child, Gaynet Lee. BS, Ill. State U., 1951; postgrad., Tchrs. Coll., Columbia U., 1952, U. Ill., 1955-56; MA, UCLA, 1967. Art supv. Bement (Ill.) Union Sch. Dist., 1951-53; art tchr. North Hollywood H.S., L.A., 1955-56, Sequoia Jr. H.S., L.A., 1957-62, Hale Jr. H.S., L.A., 1963-65, Samoana H.S., Am. Samoa, 1971-72, Westmont Coll., Montecito, Calif., 1974-75; art instr. L.A. Pierce Coll., 1965-69; environ. designer Montecito, Calif., 1975-80, Santa Ynez, Calif., 1980-84; graphics designer MII, Santa Ynez, 1985—; feature artist Channel 7 TV, L.A., 1963; mem. art jury Litton Sys., L.A., 1969. Author: Sense Perception, Basis for Education, 1967; co-author: Body Friendly, 1989, Tap Dancing-The Body's Beat, 1990; editor, designer: What is Man?, 1969. Rsch. asst. Earthwatch, 1982—; mem. com. Friends of Ethnic Arts, 1983—. Mem. Am. Craft Coun., Ctr. Sci. in Public Interest. Home: 3901 Long Valley Rd Santa Ynez CA 93460-9588 Office: MII Internat 3901 Long Valley Rd Santa Ynez CA 93460-9588

BORNEMAN, JOHN PAUL, pharmaceutical executive; b. Darby, Pa., Oct. 18, 1958; s. John A. III and Ann (Conway) B.; m. Anne Marie Albert, July 18, 1980; 1 child, Elizabeth Anne. BS in Chemistry, St. Joseph's U., Phila., 1980, MS in Chemistry, 1983, MBA in Fin., 1986. V.p. Boiron-Borneman Inc., Norwood, Pa., 1980-86; dir. mktg. Standard Homeopathic Co., L.A., 1986-89, v.p., 1989—; chmn. FDA liaison com. Am. Homeopathic Pharm. Assn., 1986—. Editor Homeopathic Pharmacopoeia U.S., 1983—; columnist Resonance mag., 1986—; contbr. articles to homeopathic jours. Bd. dirs. Internat. Found. for Homeopathy, 1986-92, Nat. Ctr. for Homeopathy, 1987—. Mem. Am. Chem. Soc., Am. Pharm. Assn., Sigma Xi. Office: Standard Homeopathic Co Box 61067 210 W 131st St Los Angeles CA 90061

BORNSTEIN, ELI, artist, sculptor; b. Milw., Dec. 28, 1922; dual citizen, U.S. and Can.; m. Christina Bornstein; children: Sarah, Thea. BS, U. Wis., 1945, MS, 1954; student, Art Inst. Chgo., U. Chgo., 1943, Academie Montmartre of Fernand Leger, Paris, 1951, Academie Julian, 1952; DLitt, U. Sask., Can., 1990. Tchr. drawing, painting and sculpture Milw. Art Inst., 1943-47; tchr. design U. Wis., 1949; tchr. drawing, painting, sculpture, design and graphics U. Sask., Can., 1950-90; prof. U. Sask., 1963-90, prof. emeritus, 1990—, head art dept., 1963-71. Painted in France, 1951-52, Italy, 1957, Holland, 1958; exhibited widely, 1943—; retrospective exhbn. (works 1943-64), Mendel Art Gallery, Saskatoon, 1965, one man shows, Kazimir Gallery, Chgo., 1965, 67, Saskatoon Pub. Library, 1975, Can. Cultural Center, Paris, 1976, Glenbow-Alta. Inst. Art, Calgary, 1976, Mendel Art Gallery, Saskatoon, 1982, York U. Gallery, Toronto, 1983, Confedn. Ctr. Art Gallery, Charlottetown, P.E.I., 1983, Owens Art Gallery, Mt. Allison U., Sackville, N.B., 1984, Fine Arts Gallery, U. Wis.-Milw., 1984; represented in numerous pvt. collections; executed marble sculpture now in permanent collection, Walker Art Center, Mpls., 1947, aluminum constrn. for Sask. Tchrs. Fedn. Bldg., 1956, structurist relief in painted wood and aluminum for, Arts and Scis. Bldg., U. Sask., 1958, structurist relief in enamelled steel for, Internat. Air Terminal, Winnipeg, Man., Can., 1962, four-part constructed relief for, Wascana Pl., Wascana Ctr. Authority, Regina, Sask., 1983; also structurist reliefs exhibited, Mus. Contemporary Art, Chgo., Herron Mus. Art, Indpls., Cranbrook Acad. Art Galleries, Mich., High Mus., Atlanta, Can. House, Cultural Centre Gallery, London, 1983, Can. Cultural Ctr., Paris, 1983, Brussels, 1983, Milw. Art Mus., 1984, Bonn, 1985; model of aluminium construction, 1956 and model version of structurist relief in 5 parts, 1962, now in collection, Nat. Gallery, Ottawa, Ont., others in numerous collections.; Co-editor: periodical Structure, 1958; founder, editor: ann. publ. The Structurist, 1960—; Contbr. articles, principally on Structurist art to various publs. Recipient Allied Arts medal Royal Archtl. Inst. Can., 1968; honorable mention for 3 structurist reliefs 2d Biennial Internat. Art Exhbn., Colombia, S.Am., 1970. Address: Rural Route 5, Saskatoon, SK Canada S7K 3J8 Office: U Sask, Box 378 RPO U, Saskatoon, SK Canada S7N 4JB

BORNY, WALTER MICHAEL, lawyer, financial planner, general securities representative, real estate investment consultant; b. Bklyn., June 23, 1948; s. Walter S. and Dolores (Kaplon) B. Student, Clemson U., 1965-66; AA magna cum laude, County Coll. Morris, Randolph, N.J., 1973; BA magna cum laude, Rutgers U., 1975, JD, 1979. Bar: N.J. 1979; lic. gen. securities rep., real estate agt., life ins. agt., notary pub., Calif. Legal counsel, 2d v.p. Chase Manhattan Bank, Englewood Cliffs, N.J., 1981-83; legal counsel CIS Equipment Leasing Corp., San Francisco, 1983-84; pvt. practice law San Francisco, 1984-85, Borny & Assocs., Foster City, Calif., 1985—. Active March of Dimes Campaign for Healthier Babies, Make A Wish Found., San Francisco Child Abuse Found. Sgt. U.S. Army Security Agy., Vietnam, 1968-69. Decorated Vietnam medal, Vietnamese Cross of Gallantry with Palm; Rutgers Honors Program sr. fellow. Mem. ABA, N.J. State Bar Assn., Nat. Assn. Securities Dealers (cert. gen. securities rep.), Phi Beta Kappa, Phi Alpha Theta. Home: 120 Montgomery St Ste 900 San Francisco CA 94104-4312 Office: Equitable Fin Group 120 Montgomery St Ste 900 San Francisco CA 94104-4312

BOROSKIN, ALAN, counselor, psychotherapist; b. Bklyn., Apr. 13, 1942; m. Judith Rostagno, Dec. 30, 1979; children: Aaron, Gina. BA, Calif. State U., Fullerton, 1967, MA, 1969, postgrad., 1977-79. Lic. psychotherapist, Calif. Rsch. asst. Fairview State Hosp., Costa Mesa, Calif., 1968-72; project dir. dept. psychiatry and mental retardation UCLA, 1972-77; dir. psychol. svcs. Ctr. for Dynamic Therapy, Westminster, Calif., 1977-79; sr. cons. Corp. Dynamics, Inc., Santa Ana, Calif., 1979-81; owner, dir. Alan Boroskin, M.A., Inc., Santa Ana, 1981—; owner, dir. ABA Evaluation Ctr., Santa Ana, 1982—; speaker Nat. Advt. Coun. Devel. Disabilities, Washington, 1974, 75, Pres.'s Com. on Mental Retardation, Utah, 1975. Contbr. articles to profl. jours. Mem. Nat. Rehab. Assn., Vocat. Evaluation and Work Adjustment Assn., So. Calif. Rehab. Exch. (1st v.p. 1990, pres. 1991, 92), Calif. Assn. Marriage and Family Therapists. Democrat. Jewish. Office: 1833 E 17th St Ste 227 Santa Ana CA 92701-2914

BOROVANSKY, VLADIMIR THEODORE, librarian; b. Prague, Czechoslovakia, May 25, 1931; came to U.S., 1968; s. Ladislav and Karla (Uttlova) B.; m. Dagmar Korbelova, July 12, 1961; children: Dominika, Herbert. Cert., Czechoslavic Acad., Prague, 1946-49, 56-57; Grad. Libr., Charles U., Prague, 1965, PhD, 1990. Lab. mgr. Rsch. Inst. Ferrous Metal, Prague, 1955-65, asst. dir. info. ctr., 1965-67; sci. reference head Ariz. State U., Tempe, 1968-78; reference dept. head U. Petroleum and Minerals, Dhahran, Saudi Arabia, 1978-79; reference dept. head Ariz. State U., Tempe, 1979-82, Noble sci. libr. head, 1982—; vis. prof. Charles U., spring and fall, 1991; Fulbright lectr. to Czechoslovakia, 1991. Contbr. articles to profl. jours.; editor Meteoritics, 1971-87. Academic Specialist grantee Charles U., 1993, IREX Travel grantee, 1994. Mem. Am. Soc. Eng. Edn. (Engring. Library div.), Am. Soc. for Metals, Czechoslovakia Soc. Arts and Sci., Internat. Assn. of Tech. U. Libraries. Republican. Roman Catholic. Home: 7026 N 14th St Phoenix AZ 85020-5409 Office: Ariz State U Noble Sci and Engring Libr Tempe AZ 85287-1006

BOROVSKI, CONRAD, German and French literature and language educator; b. Prettin, Germany, Dec. 4, 1930; came to U.S. 1952; s. Jozef Lorenc and Anna (Truszis) B.; m. Catherine Angele Perrot, Apr. 10, 1962; 1 child, Julia Madeleine. BA, U. Calif., Berkeley, 1957, MA, 1958; PhD, U. Strasbourg, France, 1960. Asst. prof. German and French San Jose State U., 1962-72, assoc. prof., 1972-84, prof., 1984-94. Author: Active German Idioms, 1972, 2d edit. 1978. With U.S. Army, 1952-54, Korea. Decorated Bronze Star medal. Mem. Am. Assn. Tchrs. German No. Calif. (pres. 1983-85), Am. Assn. Tchrs. French No. Calif. (fellow). Office: San Jose State U One Washington Sq San Jose CA 95192

BORREGO, JESUS GARCIA, engineer; b. El Paso, Tex., Nov. 12, 1953; s. Jesus F. and Maria Luisa (Garcia) B.; m. Maria Magdalena Ornelas, Dec. 18, 1972; children: Maria M., Cristina, Jesus Jr. BSEE, Calif. State U., Fullerton, 1984; BS in Computer Sci., Calif. State U., Dominguez Hills, 1987; MS in Computer Sci., Loyola Marymount, L.A., 1992. Cert. tchr., Calif. Enlisted USMC, 1972-83; mem. tech. staff Logicon, Inc., San Pedro, Calif., 1983-87; tech. lead Advanced Tech., Inc., El Segundo, Calif., 1987-88; staff engr. Hughes Aircraft, El Segundo, Calif., 1988-89; sr. prin. engr. Arinc Rsch. Corp., Fountain Valley, Calif., 1989-94; mgr. Arinc, Colorado Springs, Colo., 1994—; prof. Regis U., Colorado Springs, 1995—, Webster U., Colorado Springs, 1995—; adj. faculty El Camino Coll., Torrance, Calif., 1989-94; cons. JMB Cons., Gardena, Calif., 1988-94. Contbr. articles to profl. jours. With USMC Res., 1983-92. Mem. IEEE, IEEE Computer Soc., Assn. for Computer Machinery. Republican. Roman Catholic. Office: Arinc 1925 Aerotech Dr Ste 212 Colorado Springs CO 80916-4219

BORSCH, FREDERICK HOUK, bishop; b. Chgo., Sept. 13, 1935; s. Reuben A. and Pearl Irene (Houk) B.; m. Barbara Edgeley Sampson, June 25, 1960; children: Benjamin, Matthew, Stuart. AB, Princeton U., 1957; MA, Oxford U., 1959; STB, Gen. Theol. Sem., 1960; PhD, U. Birmingham, 1966; DD (hon.), Seabury Western Theol. Sem., 1978, Gen. Theol. Sem., 1988; STD (hon.), Ch. Div. Sch. of Pacific, 1981, Berk Div. Sch. Yale U., 1983. Ordained priest Episcopal Ch., 1960; curate Grace Episcopal Ch., Oak Park, Ill., 1960-63; tutor Queen's Coll., Birmingham, Eng., 1963-66; asst. prof. N.T. Seabury Western Theol. Sem., Evanston, Ill., 1966-69, assoc. prof. N.T., 1969-71; prof. N.T. Gen. Theol. Sem., N.Y.C., 1971-72; pres., dean Berk Div. Sch. Yale U., Berkeley, Calif., 1972-81; dean of chapel, prof. religion Princeton U., 1981-88; bishop Episc. Diocese, L.A., 1988—; rep. Faith and Order Commn., Nat. Coun. Chs., 1975-81; mem. exec. coun. Episc. Ch., 1981-88, Anglican Cons. Coun., 1984-88; chair bd. of govs. Trinity Press Internat., 1989—. Author: The Son of May in Myth and History, 1967, The Christian and Gnostic Son of Man, 1970, God's Parable, 1976, Introducing the Lessons of the Church Year, 1978, Coming Together in the Spirit, 1980, Power in Weakness, 1983, Jesus: The Human Life of God, 1987, Many Things in Parables, 1988, Christian Discipleship and Sexuality, 1993; editor: Anglicanism and the Bible, 1984, The Bible's Authority in Today's Church, 1993. Keasbey scholar, 1957-59. Fellow Soc. Arts, Religion and Contemporary Culture; mem. Am. Acad. Religion, Soc. Bibl. Lit., Studiorum Novi Testamenti Societas, Phi Beta Kappa. Home: 2930 Corda Ln Los Angeles CA 90049-1105 Office: Episcopal Diocese of LA PO Box 2164 Los Angeles CA 90051-0164

BORSON, DANIEL BENJAMIN, physiology educator, inventor, researcher; b. Berkeley, Calif., Mar. 24, 1946; s. Harry J. and Josephine F. (Esterly) B.; m. Margaret Ann Rheinschmidt, May 22, 1974; children: Alexander Nathan, Galen Michael. BA, San Francisco State Coll., 1969; MA, U. Calif., Riverside, 1973; PhD, U. Calif., San Francisco, 1982; JD, U. San Francisco, 1995. Lic. comml. pilot, flight instr. FAA. Musician Composer's Forum, Berkeley, San Francisco, 1961-70; flight instr. Buchanan Flying Club, Concord, Oakland, Calif., 1973-77, pres., 1975-77; lectr. dept. physiology U. Calif., San Francisco, 1984-92, asst. rsch. physiologist Cardiovascular Rsch. Inst., 1988-92; lectr. physiologist U. San Francisco, 1992-95; vis. scientist Genentech Inc., South San Francisco, Calif., 1990-92. Contbr. articles, rev. chpts. and abstracts to profl. jours., legal periodicals and law rev. Fellow NIH, 1976-84, grantee, 1988-93; fellow Cystic Fibrosis Found., 1985, grantee, 1989-91; fellow Parker B. Francis Found., 1985-87; grantee Am. Lung Assn., 1985-87. Mem. ABA, Am. Physiol. Soc. (editl. bd. Am. Jour. Physiology 1990-92), Am. Soc. Cell Biology, Am. Intellectual Property Law Assn., San Francisco Patent and Trademark Law Assn., Bay Flute Club (pres. 1978). Home: 146 San Aleso Ave San Francisco CA 94127-2531

BORSON, ROBERT OLIVER, communication executive, consultant; b. Tyler, Minn., Oct. 5, 1938; s. Albert Oliver and Hazel Inga (Esping) B.; m. Elizabeth Jean Erickson, June 26, 1960 (div. Dec. 1976); children: Nathan Scott, Niklas Erik; m. Susan Arlene Haynes, June 15, 1984. BA, Concordia Coll., Moorhead, Minn., 1960. Writer, editor of employee publications Kemper Ins., Chgo., 1960-64; assoc. editor of VIP mag. HMH Publishing Co., Chgo., 1964-65; asst. editor of Sweden Now mag. Industria Press, Stockholm, 1965-68; foreign corr. Madrid, 1968-70; editor Pacific Bus. mag. Calif. C. of C., Sacramento, 1970-72; sr. communications officer BankAmerica Corp., San Francisco, 1972-79, chief speechwriter, 1979-82; prin. Borson Communications, Napa, Calif., 1982—; bd. dirs. Napa County Landmarks, Inc. Contbr. articles profl. jours. Mem. Napa County Landmarks, Inc., Napa Valley Opera House Assn.

BORTELL, LINDA LEE, psychotherapist, educator; b. Harrisburg, Pa., Jan. 25, 1963; d. Joseph Thomas and Ruth Janet (Mengel) B. BA, Ind. U. Pa., 1985; MA, Fairleigh Dickinson U., Morristown, N.J., 1987; PsyD in Psychology, Calif. Sch. Profl. Psychology, 1993. Charge person, psychiat. emergency team Kimball Med. Ctr., Lakewood, N.J., 1988-89; counselor

Chabad Rehab., Culver City, Calif., 1989-92; hotline counselor Open Quest Inst., Pasadena, Calif., 1990-91; intern The Switzer Ctr., Torrance, Calif., 1991-92; program coord., instr. Santa Anita Family Svc., Monrovia, Calif., 1991—; intern The Wright Inst., L.A., 1992-93; hotline counselor Child Help USA, Hollywood, Calif., 1991—; postdoctoral assoc. The Wright Inst., L.A.., 1993-94; registered psychol. asst. Santa Anita Family Svc., Monrovia, Calif., 1994—; mem. adj. faculty Calif. Sch. Profl. Psychology, Alhambra, 1994—. Author: What About Me, 1993. Recipient Psychology scholarship, Lucille Walker scholarship, Outstanding Doctoral Project Calif. Sch. Profl. Psychology, Alhambra, Calif., 1992, 93. Mem. APA, Calif. State Psychol. Assn., Pasadena Area Psychol. Assn., Div. 39 Psychoanalysis. Office: 1961 W Huntington Dr Ste 202 Alhambra CA 91801-1222

BORTON, GEORGE ROBERT, airline captain; b. Wichita Falls, Tex., Mar. 22, 1922; s. George Neat and Travis Lee (Jones) B.; m. Anne Louise Bowling, Feb. 5, 1944 (dec.); children: Trudie T., Robert B., Bruce M. AA, Hardin Coll., Wichita Falls, 1940. Cert. airline transport pilot, FAA flight examiner. Flight sch. operator Vallejo (Calif.) Sky Harbor, 1947-48; capt. S.W. Airways, San Francisco, 1948-55; check capt. Pacific Airlines, San Francisco, 1955-68, Hughes Air West, San Francisco, 1968-71; capt. N.W. Airlines, Mpls., 1971-82, ret., 1982. Col. USAF, 1943-73, ret. Decorated Air medal. Mem. Airline Pilots Assn., Res. Officers Assn., Air Force Assn., Horseless Carriage Club, Model T of Am. Club (San Jose, Calif.). Republican. Home: 325 Denio Ave Gilroy CA 95020-9203

BORUCHOWITZ, STEPHEN ALAN, health policy analyst; b. Plainfield, N.J., Sept. 24, 1952; s. Robert and Earla Louise (Sloat) B.; m. Linda Susan Grant, Sept. 16, 1989; 1 child, Grant Stephen. BA in Internat. Affairs, George Washington U., Washington, 1974; MA in Sci., Tech. and Pub. Policy, George Washington U., 1981. Food prog. specialist U.S. Food & Nutrition Svc., Washington, 1978-81; internat. affairs specialist Office International Cooperation & Devel., Washington, 1981-87; legis. analyst Wash. State Senate, Olympia, 1986-89; project dir. Wash. 2000 Project, Olympia, 1989-92; health svcs. adminstr. Wash. Dept. Health, Olympia, 1992—; mem. Pew Commn. task force on regulation of health professions, 1994-95. Editor newsletter: Project Update, 1990-92. Study team mem. Gov.'s Efficiency Commn., 1990-91; com. mem. Coun. of State Govts. Strategic Planning Subcom., Lexington, Ky., 1990-92; chmn. Montclair Divsn. IV Neighborhood Assn., 1989-92, Shadywood Homeowner's Assn., 1992-94; bd. dirs. Classical Music Supporters, Seattle, 1987-89. Recipient Superior Performance award, U.S. Dept. Agr., 1986. Mem. World Future Soc., Internat. Health Futures Network. Office: Wash Dept Health PO Box 47851 Olympia WA 98504-7851

BOS, JOHN ARTHUR, aircraft manufacturing executive; b. Holland, Mich., Nov. 6, 1933; s. John Arthur and Annabelle (Castelli) B.; m. Eileen Tempest, Feb. 15, 1974; children: John, James, William, Tiffany. BS in Acctg., Calif. State Coll., Long Beach, 1971. Officer 1st Nat. Bank, Holland, Mich., 1954-61; dir. bus. mgmt. McDonnell Douglas, Long Beach, 1962—. Mem. Inst. Mgmt. Accts. (cert. mgmt. acct. 1979), Nat. Assn. Accts. Office: McDonnell Douglas Aircraft Co 3855 N Lakewood Blvd Long Beach CA 90846-0003

BOSKIN, MICHAEL JAY, economist, government official, university educator, consultant; b. N.Y.C., Sept. 23, 1945; s. Irving and Jean B.; m. Chris Dornin, Oct. 20, 1981. AB with highest honors, U. Calif., Berkeley, 1967, MA in Econs., 1968, PhD in Econs., 1971. Asst. prof. Stanford (Calif.) U., 1970-75, assoc. prof., 1976-78, prof., 1978—, dir. Ctr. for Econ. Policy Rsch., 1986-89, Wohlford prof. econs., 1987-89; chmn. Pres.'s Coun. Econ. Advisors, The White House, Washington, 1989-93; Friedman Prof. Econs. Stanford (Calif.) U., 1993—; pres. Boskin & Co., Menlo Park, Calif., 1993—; vis. prof. Harvard U., Cambridge, Mass., 1977-78; disting. faculty fellow Yale U., 1993; scholar Am. Enterprise Inst.; rsch. assoc. Nat. Bur. Econ. Rsch., 1976—; mem. several corp. bds. dirs. Author: Too Many Promises: The Uncertain Future of Social Security, 1986, Reagan and the Economy: Successes, Failures Unfinished Agenda, 1987; contbr. articles to profl. jours., popular media. Mem. several philanthropic bds. dirs. Faculty Rsch. fellow Mellon Found., 1973; recipient Outstanding Rsch. award Nat. Assn. Bus. Economists, 1987. Fellow Nat. Assn. Bus. Econs. (Presdl. medal Italian Republic). Office: Stanford U 213 Hhmb Stanford CA 94305-6010

BOSKOVICH, GEORGE, JR., food products executive; b. 1946. With Boskovich Farms. Office: Boskovich Farms Inc 711 Diaz Ave Oxnard CA 93030-7247*

BOSSERT, PHILIP JOSEPH, information systems executive; b. Indpls., Feb. 23, 1944; s. Alfred Joseph and Phyllis Jean (Cashen) B.; m. Jane Elisabeth Shade, June 29, 1968 (div. Dec. 1990); m. ChaoYing Deng, May 22, 1992; 1 child, Lian Brittni. BA in Econs., Rockhurst Coll., 1968; cert. in Philosophy, U. Freiburg, Fed. Republic Ger., 1970; MA in Philosophy, Washington U., St. Louis, 1972, PhD in Philosophy, 1973. Asst. prof. philosophy Hawaii Loa Coll., Honolulu, 1973-76, pres., 1978-86; dir. Hawaii com. for the humanities Nat. Endowment for the Humanities, Honolulu, 1976-77; dir. long range planning Chaminade U., Honolulu, 1977-78; pres. Strategic Info. Solutions, Honolulu, 1986—; mgr. strategic info. systems GTE Hawaiian Telephone, Honolulu, 1987-91; asst. supt. info. & telecom. svcs. Hawaii State Dept. Edn., 1991-94; cons. Ssangyong Bus. Group, Seoul, Korea, 1987-90, Nat. Assn. Colls. Univs. and Bus. Officers, Washington, 1980-90. Author: Strategic Planning and Budgeting, 1989; author, editor numerous books on philosophy; contbr. articles to profl. jours. Sgt. U.S. Army, 1962-65. Fulbright-Hays fellow, 1968-70, Woodrow Wilson fellow, 1972-73, Nat. Endowment for Humanities fellow, 1976. Mem. Data Processing Mgmt. Assn., Pacific Telecom. Coun., Honolulu Com. on Fgn. Relations, Honolulu Rotary Club. Office: Strategic Info Solutions Inc PO Box 37849 Honolulu HI 96837-0849

BOSTON, MARCIA ANN, elementary school educator; b. Akron, Ohio, Jan. 19, 1938; d. Mark Emmett and Mary Elizabeth (McMuldren) Henery; m. Roger Eugene Boston, Aug. 18, 1963; children: Mark Eugene, Craig Henery. BA, Grand Canyon U., 1960. Cert. elem. tchr., Ariz. Tchr. Glendale (Ariz.) Dist., 1960-64; sub. tchr. Itazuke (Japan) Air Base Sch., fall 1964, Washoe County, Reno, Nev., 1965-66, Albany (Oreg.) Sch. Dist., 1968-69; sub. tchr. Wash. Dist., Phoenix, 1970-71, tchr., 1972—; mentor tchr. Orangewood Project, Albany State U. West, 1992-95. Recipient St. Cecilia award for choir, 1990. Mem. NEA, ASCD, Ariz. Edn. Assn., Washington Dist. Edn. Assn., S.W. Marine Educators Assn., Order Ea. Star (organist Sunnyslope chpt. 47, 1962, 77, 78, 79, 81, 82), Glendale Mothers Club (pres. 1981), Order of Demolay (state pres. 1983-84), Delta Kappa Gamma. Republican. Episcopalian. Office: Orangewood Sch 7337 N 19th Ave Phoenix AZ 85021-7915

BOSTWICK, ANGELINA CELESTE, technical writer; b. Longview, Wash., Nov. 6, 1969; d. Jonathan Wesley and Jenetta Ellen (Gray) Gain; m. Richard Brian Scott Bostwick, June 5, 1992. BA, San Jose State U., 1992. Adminstrv. asst. Biomed. Monitoring Systems, Campbell, Calif., 1987-90; layout editor The Writing Life, San Jose, Calif., 1991; prodn. mgr. Access Mag., San Jose, 1991; tech. writer AG Assocs., Sunnyvale, Calif., 1991-93, PLI, Fremont, Calif., 1993-94; sr. tech. writer Harvis Corp., San Carlos, Calif., 1994—; freelance writing and desktop pub., San Jose, 1987—. Counselor Los Gatos (Calif.) Christian Ch., 1988-90; voting inspector Santa Clara County, San Jose, 1990, Saratoga, Calif., 1992; poll clk. Alameda County, Fremont, Calif., 1992. Mem. Soc. for Tech. Communication, Reps. United Vol. Team.

BOSTWICK BALDO, TRACY DEE, counselor, educator; b. Marion, Ind., Oct. 21, 1964; d. John Dee and Peggy Jean (Wooldridge) Pormen; m. David Robert Bostwick, Aug. 9, 1986 (div. Apr. 1993); m. Anthony John Baldo, Oct. 17, 1994. BS in Supervision, Purdue U., 1986, MS in Counseling and Pers., 1989, PhD in Profl. Counseling, 1990. Nat. cert. counselor; lic. profl. counselor. Staff supr. Baskin Robbins Ice Cream, Marion, 1981-83, West Lafayette, Ind., 1984-86; line supr. GM, Muncie, Ind., 1985; mgr. TCBY Yogurt, Lafayette, Ind., 1986-87; counselor dean of students office Purdue U., West Lafayette, 1987-88, instr., 1987-90; counselor educator U. No. Colo., Greeley, 1991—; pvt. practice Counseling Clinic, Greeley, 1994—. Mem. ACA, Assn. Counselor Edn. and Supervision, Colo. Counseling Assn., Rocky Mountain Counselor Edn. and Supervision, Colo. Coll. Counseling Assn. (pres., mem. exec. bd. 1993-94). Home: 1906 20th St Greeley CO 80631-6804 Office: Univ No Colo McKee 248 PPSY Greeley CO 80639

BOSWELL, WINTHROP PALMER, writer; b. Bklyn., Dec. 17, 1922; d. Carleton Humphries and Winthrop (Bushnell) Palmer; BA, Smith Coll., 1943; postgrad. U. S.C., 1956-58; MA, San Francisco State Coll., 1969; m. James Orr Boswell, Oct. 26, 1946; children: James Lowell, Rosalind Palmer, John Winthrop. Rsch. asst. G-2 Spl. Br., U.S. Army, 1943-46; rsch. asst. Hoover Instn., Stanford, Calif., 1976; docent Filoli, 1979-80; books include The Roots of Irish Monasticism, 1970; Irish Wizards in the Woods of Ethiopia, 1971; The Snake in the Grove, 1972; The Killing of the Snake King in Abyssinia, 1973; Hisperica Famina or The Garden of God, 1974; Bruce and the Question of Geomancy at Axum: The Evidence from the Norman Bayeux Tapestry, 1986, Abyssinian Elements in the Life of Saint Patrick, 1991. Mem. Soc. History of Discoveries, Peninsula Country Club (San Mateo, Calif.), Francisca Club (San Francisco).

BOSWORTH, BRUCE LEIGHTON, school administrator, educator, consultant; b. Buffalo, Mar. 22, 1942; s. John Wayman and Alice Elizabeth Rodgers; children: David, Timothy, Paul. BA, U. Denver, 1964; MA, U. No. Colo., 1970; EdD, Walden U., 1984. Elem. tchr. Littleton (Colo.) Pub. Schs., 1964-67, 70-81; bldg. prin. East Smoky Sch. Div. 54, Valleyview, Alta., Can., 1967-70; pres., tchr. Chatfield Sch., Littleton, 1981—; adoption cons. hard-to-place children; edn1. cons. spl. needs children. St. Andrew Presbyn. Ch. (USA). Mem. ASCD, Council Exceptional Children, Masons, Shriners, York Rite. Home and Office: 3500 S Lowell Blvd # 316 Sheridan CO 80236

BOSWORTH, THOMAS LAWRENCE, architect, educator; b. Oberlin, Ohio, June 15, 1930; s. Edward Franklin and Imogene (Rose) B.; m. Abigail Lumbard, Nov. 6, 1954 (div. Nov. 1974); children: Thomas Edward, Nathaniel David; m. Elaine R. Pedigo, Nov. 23, 1974. B.A., Oberlin Coll., 1952, M.A., 1954; postgrad., Princeton U., 1952-53, Harvard U., 1956-57; M.Arch., Yale U., 1960. Draftsman Gordon McMaster AIA, Cheshire, Conn., summer 1957-58; resident planner Tunnard & Harris Planning Cons., Newport, R.I., summer 1959; designer, field supr. Eero Saarinen & Assocs., Birmingham, Mich., 1960-61, Hamden, Conn., 1961-64; individual practice architecture Providence, 1964-68, Seattle, 1968—; asst. instr. architecture Yale U., 1962-65, vis. lectr., 1965-66; asst. prof. R.I. Sch. Design, 1964-66, asso. prof., head dept., 1966-68; prof. architecture U. Wash., Seattle, 1968—, chmn. dept., 1968-72; chief architecture Peace Corps Tng. Program, Tunisia, Brown U., summers 1965-66; archtl. cons., individual practice Seattle, 1972—; dir. multidisciplinary program U. Wash., Rome, Italy, 1984-86; vis. lectr. Kobe U., Japan, Oct. 1982, Nov. 1990, Apr. 1993, May 1995; bd. dirs. N.W. Inst. for Arch. and Urban Studies, Italy, 1983-90, pres., 1983-85; mem. Seattle Model Cities Land Use Rev. Bd., 1969-70, Tech. Com. Site Selection Wash. Multi-Purpose Stadium, 1970; chmn. King County (Wash.) Environ. Devel. Commn., 1970-74; mem. Medina Planning Commn., 1972-74; chmn. King County Policy Devel. Commn., 1974-77; mem. steering adv. com. King County Stadium, 1972-74, others. Dir. Pilchuck Sch., Seattle, 1977-80, trustee, 1980-91, adv. coun., 1993-96. With U.S. Army, 1954-56. Winchester Traveling fellow Greece, 1960; assoc. fellow Ezra Stiles Coll. Yale U.; mid-career fellow in arch. Am. Acad. in Rome, 1980-81, vis. scholar, Spring 1988. Fellow AIA; mem. AAUP, Archtl. Inst. Japan, Soc. Archtl. Historians, Rainier Club, Monday Club, Tau Sigma Delta. Home: 4532 E Laurel Dr NE Seattle WA 98105-3839 Office: U Wash Dept Architecture JO-20 Seattle WA 98195

BOTELHO, BRUCE MANUEL, state official, mayor; b. Juneau, Alaska, Oct. 6, 1948; s. Emmett Manuel and Harriet Iowa (Tieszen) B.; m. Guadalupe Alvarez Breton, Sept. 23, 1988; 1 child, Alejandro Manuel. Student, U. Heidelberg, Federal Republic of Germany, 1970; BA, Willamette U., 1971, JD, 1976. Bar: Alaska 1976, U.S. Ct. Appeals (9th cir.), U.S. Supreme Ct. Asst. atty. gen. State of Alaska, Juneau, 1976-83, 1987—, dep. commr., acting commr. Dept. of Revenue, 1983-86; mayor City, Borough of Juneau, 1988-91, dep. atty. gen., 1991-94, atty. gen., 1994—. Editor: Willamette Law Jour., 1975-76; contbr. articles profl. jours. Assembly mem. City, Borough of Juneau, 1983-86; pres. Juneau Human Rights Commn., 1978-80; pres. SE Alaska Area Coun. Boy Scouts Am., 1991—; bd. dirs. Found. for Social Innovations, Alaska, 1990-93. Democrat. Methodist. Home: 401 F St Douglas AK 99824-5353 Office: Alaska Dept Law PO Box K Juneau AK 99811

BOTELLO, TROY JAMES, arts administrator, counselor; b. Long Beach, Calif., Sept. 2, 1953; s. Arthur P. and Jayme Alta (McBride) B. AA in Spl. Edn., Cerritos Coll., 1979; BA in Music Therapy, Calif. State U., Long Beach, 1984; cert. in arts adminstrn., U. So. Calif., Orange County, 1988; MA in Adminstrn., Calif. Polytech. Inst., Pomona, 1992. Cert. tchr., Calif. Asst. music dir. St. John Bosco High Sch., Bellflower, Calif., 1969-72; music dir. Bellflower Unified Schs., 1971-74; tchr. severely handicapped L.A. County Office of Edn., 1974-88; vocat. rehab. counselor Tesseler Counseling Group, Anaheim, Calif., 1988-91; dir. edn. Orange County Performing Arts Ctr., Costa Mesa, Calif., 1991—; exec. dir., co-founder Project: Arts in Motion, Bellflower, 1983—; edn1. cons. Edn. Div. Music Ctr., L.A., 1986—; vice chmn. La Mirada (Calif.) Community Concerts, 1976-79; v.p. grants Master Symphony Orch., Norwalk, Calif. Chairperson La Mirada Hist. Com., 1977-78; rep. Edn. Adv. Com., L.A., 1981; exec. prod., bd. dirs. Imagination Celebration of Orange County, 1991—; pres. Anaheim Cultural Arts Found., 1993-95; state pres., bd. dirs Very Special Arts Calif., 1992—. Mem. Assn. for Music Therapy Profls., So. Calif. Band and Field Judges, Profl. Arts Mgmt. Inst., Calif. Assn. Rehab. Profls., Am. Assn. Orff Schwelrk, Young Composers of Am., Alumni of Drum Corps Internat. Home: 14216 Neargrove Rd La Mirada CA 90638-3854 Office: Orange County Performing Arts Ctr 600 Town Center Dr Costa Mesa CA 92626-1916

BOTHWELL, DORR, JR., artist; b. San Francisco, May 3, 1902; d. John Stuart and Florence Isabel (Hodgson) B. Student, Calif. Sch. Fine Arts, Rudolph Schaeffer Sch. Design, U. Oreg. Painter Tau, Manu'a, Am. Samoa, 1928-29, France, 1930-31, 49-51, 89, Eng., 1960-61, 89, West Africa and North Africa, 1966-67, Indonesia, 1974, People's Republic China, 1982, Japan, 1985, Mex., 1987; instr. Calif. Sch. Fine Arts, San Francisco, 1945-58, San Francisco Art Inst., 1959-60, Rudolph Schaeffer Sch. Design, 1960-61, Mendocino (Calif.) Art Ctr., 1962-93, San Francisco Art Inst., 1961; instr. Sonoma State Coll., summer 1964, U. Calif. Ext., Mendocino Art Ctr., 1965-71, 90; faculty Ansel Adams Yosemite Workshop, 1964-77, Victor (Colo.) Sch. Photography, 1979. Exhibitor, West Coast exhbns., 1927—, 3d biennial São Paulo, Brazil, Pitts. Internat., 1952, 55, Art: U.S.A., 1958, Bklyn. Mus., 1976, Mendocino (Calif.) Art Ctr., 1992; one-man shows include De Young Meml. Mus., San Francisco, 1957, 63; retrospective exhbn. Bay Window Gallery, Mendocino, 1985, Spl. Anniversary exhbn. 1986-87, Tobey Moss Gallery, L.A., 1989, 91, 93, Bothwell Studio, Mendocino, Calif., 1989, Mendocino Art Ctr., 1992, Gallery Mendocino, 1994-95; travelling exhbn. Oakland (Calif.) Mus., 1995, UCLA Mus., Westwood, 1995, Logan (Utah) Art Mus., 1995; works in permanent collection, San Diego Gallery Fine Art, Crocker Gallery, Sacramento, San Francisco Mus. Art, Whitney Mus. Am. Art, Bklyn. Mus., Mus. Modern Art, Fogg Mus., Met. Museum, Victoria and Albert Museum, London, Brit. Mus., London, Bibliothèque Nationale, Paris, France, Worcester (Mass.) Art Mus., Cleve. Mus. Art, Boston Mus. Art, Oakland (Calif.) Mus., DeYoung Mus., San Francisco, L.A. County Mus., 1994; author: Notan: The Principle of Dark-Light Design, 1968, 2d edit., 1976, Danish edit., 1977, 3d edit., 1991. Recipient 1st prize, 4th ann. exhbn. San Francisco Soc. Women Artists, 1929; Pres.'s purchase prize, 1941; Leisser-Farnham award 7th ann. exhbn. San Diego Art Guild, 1932; hon. mention 7th ann. exhbn. So. Calif. Artists, 1933; spl. prize 9th ann. exhbn., 1937; Artists Fund prize ann. exhbn. drawings and prints San Francisco Art Assn., 1943; hon. mention 2d spring ann. Calif. Palace Legion of Honor, San Francisco, 1947; purchase prize 2d nat. print ann. Bklyn. Mus., 1948; 1st prize 9th ann. Nat. Serigraph Soc., N.Y.C., 1948. Home: 925 N Plaza Dr SP93 Apache Junction AZ 85220 also: HC1 Box 1055 Joshua Tree CA 92252 Office: Tobey Moss Gallery 7321 Beverly Blvd Los Angeles CA 90036-2503

BOTIMER, ALLEN RAY, retired surgeon, retirement center owner; b. Columbus, Miss., Jan. 30, 1930; s. Clare E. and Christel J. (Kalar) B.; m. Dorris LaJean, Aug. 17, 1950; children: Larry Alan, Gary David. BS, Walla Walla Coll., 1951; MD, Loma Linda U., 1955. Diplomate Am. Bd. Surgery. Intern U.S. Naval Hosp., San Diego, 1955-56, surg. resident, 1955-60; resident in surgery U.S. Naval Hosp., Guam, 1960-62; asst. chief surgery U.S. Naval Hosp., Bremerton, Wash., 1962-64; chief surgery Ballard Community Hosp., Seattle, 1970, chief of staff, 1972, chief surgery, 1986-87; pvt. practice Seattle, 1964-87; ret., 1987; ptnr. Heritage Retirement Ctr., Nampa, Idaho, 1972-82, owner, 1982—. Lt. comdr. USN, 1955-64. Fellow ACS, Seattle Surg. Soc.; mem. Wash. State Med. Soc., King County Med. Soc. Home and Office: 1319 Torrey Ln Nampa ID 83686

BOTSAI, ELMER EUGENE, architect, educator, former university dean; b. St. Louis, Feb. 1, 1928; s. Paul and Ita May (Cole) B.; m. Patricia L. Keegan, Aug. 28, 1955; children: Donald Rolf, Kurt Gregory.; m. Sharon K. Kaiser, Dec. 5, 1981; 1 dau., Kiana Michelle. AA, Sacramento Jr. Coll., 1950; A.B., U. Calif.-Berkeley, 1954. Registered architect, Hawaii, Calif. Draftsman, then asst. to architect So. Pacific Co., San Francisco, 1953-57; designer J.H. Ferguson Co., San Francisco, 1955; project architect Anshen & Allen Architects, San Francisco, 1957-63; prin. Botsai, Overstreet & Rosenberg, Architects and Planners, San Francisco, 1963-79, Elmer E. Botsai FAIA, Honolulu, 1979—; chmn. dept. architecture U. Hawaii, Manoa, 1976-80, prof., 1976—, dean Sch. Architecture, 1980-90, prof., 1990—; lectr. U. Calif., Berkeley, 1976, dir. Nat. Archtl. Accrediting Bd., 1972-73, 79; adminstrv. and tech. cons. Wood Bldg. Rsch. Ctr., U. Calif., 1985-90, mem. profl. preparation project com. at U. Mich., Ann Arbor, 1986-87; co-author water infiltration seminar series for Bldg. Owners and Mgrs. Rsch. Ctr., 1986-87; chief investigator effects of Guatemalan earthquake for NSF and AIA, Washington, 1976; steering com. on structural failures Nat. Bur. Standards, 1982-84; chmn., dir. gen. svcs. Adv. Com. State of Calif. Co-author: Architects and Earthquake, Research Needs, 1976, ATC Seismic Standards for National Bur. of Standards, 1976, Architects and Earthquakes: A Primer, 1977, Seismic Design, 1978, Wood-Detailing for Performance, 1990, Wood as a Building Material, 2d edit., 1991; contbr. articles and reports to profl. jours.; prin. works include expansion of Nuclear Weapons Tng. Facility at Lemoore Naval Air Sta., Calif., LASH Terminal Port Facility Archtl. Phase, San Francisco, Incline Village (Nev.) Country Club, 1365 Columbus Ave. Bldg., San Francisco, modernization Stanford Ct. Hotel, San Francisco; monument area constrn. several Calif. cenceteries. With U.S. Army, 1946-48. Recipient Cert. Honor Fedn. Archtl. Colls. Mex. Republic, 1984; NSF grantee for investigative workshop project, San Diego, 1974-80. Fellow AIA (bd. dirs., 1966-71, treas. No. Calif. chpt. 1968-69, pres. 1971, nat. v.p., 1975-76, nat. pres. 1978, pres. Hawaii 1985); hon. fellow Royal Can. Inst. Architects, N.Z. Inst. Architects, Royal Australian Inst. Architects, La Societed de Arquitectos Mexicano; mem. Archtl. Secs. Assn. (hon.), Forest Products Rsch. Soc., Soc. Wood Sci. and Tech., Internat. Conf. Bldg. Ofcls., Nat. Fire Protection Assn., Am. Arbitration Assn. Home: 321 Wailupe Cir Honolulu HI 96821-1524 Office: 2560 Campus Rd # 2B Honolulu HI 96822-2217

BOTTEL, HELEN ALFEA, columnist, writer; b. Beaumont, Calif.; d. Alpheus Russell and Mary Ellen (Alexander) Brigden; m. Robert E. Bottel; children: Robert Dennis, Rodger M., R. Kathryn Bottel Bernhardt, Suzanne V. Bottel Peppers. A.A., Riverside Coll. Calif.; student, Oreg. State U., 1958-59, So. Oreg. Coll., 1959. Writer, editor Illinois Valley News, Cave Junction, Oreg., 1950-56; writer Grants Pass (Oreg.) Courier, Portland Oregonian, Medford (Oreg.) Mail Tribune, 1952-58; daily columnist Helen Help Us King Features Syndicate, N.Y.C., 1958-83; daily columnist (with Sue Bottel) Generation Rap King Features Syndicate, N.Y.C.; mem. adv. bd. Internat. Affairs Inst., N.Y.C. and Tokyo, 1986—; freelance mag. writer, author, lectr., 1956—; columnist King Features Syndicate, 1969-83. Author: To Teens with Love, 1969, Helen Help Us, 1970, Parents Survival Kit, 1979; contbg. editor, columnist Real World mag., 1978-84; weekly columnist Yomiuri Shimbun, Tokyo, 1982-90; thrice weekly columnist Sacramento Union, 1986-88; newspaper and mag. columnist Look Who's Aging (with dau. Kathy Bernhardt), 1992—; contbr. nonfiction to books and nat. mags. Staff mem. ACT Handicapped Children Games, Sacramento, 1986—; bd. dirs. Illinois Valley Med. Center, 1958-62, Childrens Center, Sacramento, 1969, Family Support Programs, Sacramento, 1991—; mem. Grants Pass br. Oreg. Juvenile Adv. Com., 1960-62, Students League Against Narcotics Temptation, 1968-70; charter patron Cosumnes River Coll., Sacramento, 1972—; mem. nat. adv. bd. Nat. Anorexic Aid Soc., 1977—; mem. Nat. Spina Bifida Assn.; scholarship com. judge Exec. Women Internat., 1985. Recipient Women's Svc. Cup Riverside Coll., citation for aid to U.s. servicemen in Vietnam Gov. Ga., 1967, Disting. Merit citation NCCJ, 1970, 1st place award for books Calif. Press Women, 1970, Sacramento Regional Arts Coun. Lit. Achievement award, 1974, Alumna of Yr. award Riverside Coll., 1987, Gold and Silver medals Calif. Sr. Games (tennis), 1990-91. Mem. Am. Soc. Journalists and Authors, Internat. Affairs Inst. Presbyterian. Clubs: Calif. Writers, Southgate Tennis. Home: 2060 56th Ave Sacramento CA 95822-4112

BOTTI, RICHARD CHARLES, association executive; b. Brockton, Mass., May 1, 1939; s. Alfred Benecchi and Elizabeth Savini; stepson Ernest Botti; student Pierce Jr. Coll., 1959, Orange Coast Coll., 1964; m. Gwen Botti; children—Randolph K., Douglas S., Richard II. Pres., Legis. Info. Services Hawaii, Inc., Honolulu, 1971—; exec. dir., profl. lobbyist Hawaii Food Industry Assn., Honolulu, Hawaii Automotive & Retail Gasoline Dealers Assn., Inc., Honolulu, Hawaii Bus. League, Retail Liquor Dealers Assn. Hawaii, Liquor Dispensers of Hawaii, Hawaii Pubs. Assn., Automotive Body and Painting Assn.; gen. mgr. Hawaii Fashion Industry Assn. Mem. Food Industry Assn. Execs., Am. Soc. Assn. Execs., Aloha Soc. Assn. Execs. (dir. Hawaii Foodbank). Address: Legis Info Services 677 Ala Moana Blvd Ste 815 Honolulu HI 96813-5416

BOTTJER, DAVID JOHN, earth sciences educator; b. N.Y.C., Oct. 3, 1951; s. John Henry and Marilyn (Winter) B.; m. Sarah Ranney Wright, July 26, 1973. BS, Haverford Coll., 1973; MA, SUNY, Binghamton, 1976; PhD, Ind. U., 1978. NRC postdoctoral rsch. assoc. U.S. Geol. Survey, Washington, 1978-79; asst. prof. dept. geol. scis. U. So. Calif., L.A., 1979-85, assoc. prof. dept. geol. scis., 1985-91, prof. dept. earth scis., 1991—; rsch. assoc. L.A. County Mus. Natural History, 1979—, U. Calif., 1991—; vis. scientist Field Mus. Natural History, Chgo., 1986; guest prof. Swiss Fed. Inst. Tech., Zurich, 1993. Editor Palaios, 1989—; assoc. editor Cretaceous Rsch., 1988-91; mem. editl. bd. Geology, 1984-89, 95—, Hist. Biology, 1988-93; co-editor Columbia U. Press Critical Moments in Paleobiology and Earth History (book series), 1990—; chmn. Columbia U. Press Adv. Com. for Paleontology, 1990—. Fellow Geol. Soc. Am., Geol. Soc. London; mem. AAAS, Paleontol. Soc., Soc. Sediment Geology, Internat. Paleontology Assn. Office: U So Calif Dept Earth Scis Los Angeles CA 90089-0740

BOTWINICK, MICHAEL, museum director; b. N.Y.C., Nov. 14, 1943; s. Joseph and Helen (Shlisky) B.; m. Harriet Maltzer, Aug. 14, 1965; children: Jonathan Seth, Daniel Judah. B.A., Rutgers Coll., 1964; M.A., Columbia U., 1967. Instr. Columbia U., N.Y.C., 1968-69, CCNY, CUNY, 1969; asst. curator medieval art Cloisters Met. Mus. Art, N.Y.C., 1969; asso. curator medieval art Cloisters Met. Mus. Art, 1970, asst. curator-in-chief, 1971—; asst. dir. art Phila. Mus. Art, 1971-74; dir. Bklyn. Mus., 1974-83, Corcoran Gallery Art, 1983-87; sr. v.p. Knoedler-Modarco, S.A., N.Y.C., 1987-88; pres. Fine Arts Group, Chgo., 1989-91; dir. Newport Harbor Art Mus., Newport Beach, Calif., 1991—; pres. Cultural Instns. Group, 1975-76; mem. N.Y.C. Adv. Commn. Cultural Affairs, 1975-76, N.Y.C. Urban Design Coun., 1975; mem. adv. bd. WNET, N.Y.C., 1979-83; mem. Nat. Conservation Adv. Coun., 1979-80, exec. com. U.S. Com.-Internat. Coun. Mus., 1982-87, Yale U. Coun. Com. on the Art Gallery, 1983-88, Internat. Rsch. and Exch. Bd., fine arts com. German Dem. Republic, 1984-87, fine arts com. U.S. State Dept. Arts in Embassies Program, 1986-88; arts adminstrn. adv. com. U. Calif.-Irvine, 1993—. Mem. Assn. Art Mus. Dirs., Am. Assn. Museums, Coll. Art Assn., Steppenwolf Theater Co., Chgo. (bd. dirs. 1990-91). Office: Newport Harbor Art Mus 850 San Clemente Dr Newport Beach CA 92660-6301

BOTZLER, RICHARD GEORGE, wildlife educator; b. Detroit, Jan. 27, 1942; s. Otto and Elfriede (Nolte) B.; m. Sally Jo Nelson, Oct. 5, 1942; children: Emilisa, Tin, Dorothy, Sarah, Thomas. BS, Wayne State U., 1963; M of Wildlife Mgmt., U. Mich., 1967, PhD, 1970. Asst. prof. wildlife Humboldt State U., Arcata, Calif., 1970-74, assoc. prof., 1974-79, prof., 1979—; chair wildlife dept. Humboldt State U., 1977-80. Editor: Environmental Ethics: Divergence and Convergence, 1993; contbr. articles to profl. jours. Co-founder Humboldt County Coun. on Adoptable Children, 1971—. Recipient Outstanding Prof. for Calif. State U. System, 1992. Mem. Wildlife Disease Assn. (coun. mem. 1991—, asst. editor jour. of wildlife disease 1990-91, editor 1991—), Fulbright Assn. (life, fellow 1981-82), The Wildlife Soc., Soc. Conservation Biology, Soc. Vector Ecology. Office: Humboldt State U Dept Wildlife Humboldt State U Arcata CA 95521

BOUCHARD, PAUL EUGENE, artist; b. Providence, Sept. 26, 1946; s. Marcel Paul and Anna Theresa (Dullea) B.; m. Ann Marie, Nov. 18, 1971 (div. 1976); 1 child Michael Paul. BFA, Calif. State U., Long Beach, 1978. bd. dir, Angeles Gate Cultural Ctr., San Pedro, Calif., 1983-85. Exhibited group shows at Coos Art Mus., Coos Bay, Oreg., 1989, Vietnam Vet.'s Art Exhibit, 1988, St. Andrew's Priory, Valyermo, Calif., Riverside (Calif.) Art Mus., Rental Gallery, 1987, Sixth Street Gallery, San Pedro, Calif., Aquarius Gallery, Cambria, Calif., 1986, Rental Gallery, L.A. County Mus. of Art, 1985, Rental Gallery, Oakland Mus., 1984, Grants Pass Mus. of Art, 1991, Eastern Wash. U., 1992, Dept. Vets. Affairs Hdqs., Sidney, Australia, 1992-93, Australian Nat. Gallery, Brisbane City Hall Gallery, others. Recipient Contribution to the Arts, City of Torrance, Calif., 1985; grantee Franklin Furnace, N.Y.C., 1989-90, Artist Space, N.Y.C., 1989-90. Home: 33140 Baldwin Blvd Lake Elsinore CA 92530-5954

BOUGHTON, LESLEY D., library director; b. New Haven, Conn., Jan. 21, 1945; d. Robert and Marjorie (Anderson) D.; m. Charles E. Boughton, Sept. 5, 1964 (dec. 1991); children: Michael, James, Gregg. AB, Conn. Coll., 1971; MLS, So. Conn. State U., 1978. Dir. Platte County Library, Wheatland, Wyo., 1980-88, Carbon County Library, Rawlins, Wyo., 1988-93, Natrona County Pub. Library, Casper, Wyo., 1993—; mem. Gov's. Telecommunications Coun., Wyo., 1994—. Mem. ALA (chpt. councilor 1988, 91), Wyo. Library Assn. (pres. 1985, Disting. Svc. award 1991). Office: Natrona County Pub Libr 307 E 2nd St Casper WY 82601-2505

BOUKIDIS, CONSTANTINE MICHAEL, lawyer; b. Burbank, Calif., Nov. 16, 1959; s. Michael A. and Frances (Mavros) B.; m. Eugenia Demetra Rodinos, May 17, 1987; children: Michael Constantine, Frances Anastasia, Katherine Elizabeth. BA in Econs., Northwestern U., 1981; JD, Loyola Law Sch., L.A., 1984. Bar: Calif. 1985, U.S. Dist. Ct. (cen. dist.) Calif. 1985, U.S. Ct. Appeals (9th cir.), 1985. Investigator Harney & Moore, L.A., 1980-82; assoc. Law Offices of David M. Harney, L.A., 1985-92; pvt. practice, 1992—. Treas., chmn. cathedral planning com. St. Sophia Cathedral Orthodox Cmty. L.A., 1989, pres. cmty., 1994-95. Mem. ABA, Assn. Trial Lawyers Am., Calif. Trial Lawyers Assn., L.A. County Bar Assn., Glendale (Calif.) Bar Assn., Phi Kappa Sigma (trea. 1980-81). Democrat. Home: 1641 Country Club Dr Glendale CA 91208-2038 Office: Law Offices of Boukidis Ste 101 144 N Glendale Ave Glendale CA 91206-4903

BOULDIN, DANNY LEE, electrical engineer; b. Fyffe, Ala., Oct. 31, 1953; s. Virgil Dee and Johnnie Mag (Gibson) B.; m. Brenda Gale Wooten, Apr. 13, 1974; children: Kelly, Stacey. BSEE, Auburn U., 1978; MSEE, Fla. Inst. Tech., 1983. Sr. engr. Harris Corp., Ft. Walton Beach, Fla., 1978-80, Martin Marietta Aerospace Div., Orlando, Fla., 1980-83, ITT Corp., Roanoke, Va., 1983-85; engr./scientist Hewlett Packard Corp., Palo Alto, Calif., 1985—. Republican. Home: 2767 Gaspar Ct Palo Alto CA 94306-2557 Office: Hewlett Packard Corp 370 W Trimble Rd San Jose CA 95131-1008

BOULOS, PAUL FARES, civil and environmental engineer; b. Beirut, June 28, 1963; came to U.S., 1983; s. Fares and Marie-Rose (Abou Hadid) B. BS, Beirut U., 1985; BSCE, U. Ky., 1985, MSCE, 1986, PhD, 1989. Asst. prof. U. Ky., Lexington, 1990-91; dir. water distbn. tech. Montgomery Watson, Pasadena, Calif., 1991—; internat. hydraulic expert Consorcio Nitogoi, Cali, Colombia, 1988-90; cons. in field. Author: Comprehensive Network Analyzer, 1990; contbr. articles to profl. jours. Grantee NSF, 1987, Am. Water Works Rsch. Found., 1992. Mem. ASCE (treas. 1992), Am. Water Works Assn., Sigma Xi, Tau Beta Pi, Chi Epsilon (U.S. delegation to NATO Advanced Study Inst. 1993). Office: Montgomery Watson 301 N Lake Ave Ste 600 Pasadena CA 91101-4108

BOULTON, LYNDIE MCHENRY, professional society administrator; b. Corvallis, Oreg.; d. W.B. Jim and Lillian (Hosken) McHenry; m. Roger Boulton. BA in Anthropology, U. Calif., Santa Barbara, 1974. Ops. mgr. C. Brent Scott & Assocs., Sacramento, 1979-81; exec. dir. Am. Soc. Enology and Viticulture, Davis, Calif., 1981—. Mem. Nat. Assn. Expn. Mgrs., Am. Soc. Assn. Execs. Office: Am Soc Enology & Viticulture PO Box 1855 Davis CA 95617-1855

BOULWARE, RICHARD STARK, airport administrator; b. Chgo., Aug. 28, 1935; s. John Stark and Ellen Bradley (Bowlin) B.; m. Sylvia Grace Panaro, Sept. 17, 1960 (div. Jan. 1980); children: Susan Bradley, Robert Stark; M. Janice Gilliland Wells, Oct. 1, 1992. BFA, Art Ctr. Coll., 1967. Photographer Hughes Aircraft, Los Angeles, 1960-61; chief photographer U. Iowa, Iowa City, 1962-67; dir. audio/visual media TransWorld Airlines, N.Y.C., 1968-70; owner, mgr. RBA Prodns., Denver, 1970-80; dir. photography Colo. Inst. Art, Denver, 1980-84; dep. dir. aviation Stapleton Internat. Airport and Denver Internat. Airport, Denver, 1984—, Denver Internat. Airport, 1984—. Served with USN, 1954-58. Recipient Golden Eagle award CINE, 1976, award Bus. and Profl. Advt. Assn., Alfie award Denver Advt. Fedn., Christensen Meml. award Iowa Press Photographers Assn., award Art Dirs. Club Denver; named Nat. Photographer of Yr. U. Profl. Photographers Assn. Am., 1967. Mem. Pub. Relations Soc. Am. (award Colo. chpt.), Colo. Broadcasters Assn. Colo.Press Assn., Am. Assn. Airport Execs., Art Dirs Club Denver (v.p.). Home: 9112E E Amherst Dr Denver CO 80231-4006 Office: Denver Internat Airport Airport Office Bldg 8500 Pena Blvd Denver CO 80249-6357

BOUREKIS, JAMES GEORGE, dentist; b. Warren, Ohio, Mar. 30, 1930; s. George and Maria B.; m. Katherine Barbas, Sept. 2, 1956; children: Maria Theresa, George James. DDS, Northwestern U., 1954. Pvt. practice, Warren, 1957-59, Spokane, Wash., 1960—; bd. dirs. Modern Electric Water Co., Spokane. Capt. USAF, 1954-56. Mem. ADA, Wash. State Dental Assn., Spokane Dist. Dental Soc., Rotary. Office: 20 S Pines Rd Spokane WA 99206-5314

BOURKE, LYLE JAMES, electronics company executive, small business owner; b. San Diego, May 28, 1963; s. Robert Victor and Virginia (Blackburn) B. Cert. in electronics, Southwestern Coll., San Diego, 1984; cert. in microelectronics, Burr Brown, Miramar, Calif., 1985; student, NACS, Scranton, Pa., 1988; AA in Econs., Cuyamaca Coll., 1991, postgrad., 1991-92; student, Wendelstedt Umpire Sch., 1992-93. Counselor Dept. Parks and Recreation City of Imperial Beach, Calif., 1979-80; warehouse worker Seafood Cannery, Cordova, Alaska, 1981, Nat. Beef Packing, Liberal, Kans., 1983; night mgr. Southland Corp., San Diego, 1983-85; tech. developer Unisys Corp., San Diego, 1985-92; process enhancement technician Ben & Jerry's Homemade, Inc., Springfield, Vt., 1994—; founder Sparrells Ltd., 1992; instr. Harmonium Enrichment Program, 1993. Editor (handbook) College Policies, 1991; contbr. Cleanrooms mag., 1992; inventor Jacuzzi pillow. Vol. United Way, San Diego, 1987—; donor Imperial Beach Boys and Girls Club, 1988-93, Cal Farley's Boys Ranch, 1985-93, Assn. Handicapped Artists, 1988—, San Diego Jr. Theatre, 1992, Cabrillo Elem. Sch. Found., 1992. Named Most Valuable Player Mex. Amateur Baseball League, San Diego-Tijuana, 1990. Mem. Am. Assn. Ret. Persons, Am. Mgmt. Assn. (charter), Prognosticators Club. Democrat. Office: Unisys 8011 Fairview Ave La Mesa CA 91941-6416

BOURQUE, LINDA ANNE BROOKOVER, public health educator; b. Indpls., Aug. 25, 1941; d. Wilbur Bone and Edna Mae (Eberhart) Brookover; m. Don Philippe Bourque, June 3, 1966 (div. Nov. 1974). BA, Ind. U., 1963; MA, Duke U., 1964, PhD, 1968. Postdoctoral researcher Duke U., Durham, N.C., 1968-69; asst. prof. sociology Calif. State U., Los Angeles, 1969-72; asst. prof. to assoc. prof. pub. health UCLA, 1972-86, prof. pub. health, 1986—, acting assoc. dir. Inst. for Social Sci. Research, 1981-82, vice chair dept. community health scis., 1991-94. Author: Defining Rape, 1989, (with Virginia Clark) Processing Data: The Survey Example, 1992, (with Eve Fielder) How to Conduct Self-Administered and Mail Surveys, 1995; contbr. articles to profl. jours. Violoncellist with Santa Monica (Calif.) Symphony Orch., 1978—, Los Angeles Doctors' Symphony, 1981—. Mem. AAAS, Am. Sociol. Assn. (mem. med. sociology sect. council 1975-78, co-chmn. com. freedom research and teaching, 1975-78, cert. recognition 1980), Pacific Sociol. Assn. (co-chmn. program com. 1982, v.p. 1983), Am. Pub. Health Assn. (mem. standing com. on status of women 1974-76), Sociologists for Women in Society, Am. Assn. Pub. Opinion Rsch., Assn. Rsch. in Vision and Ophthalmology, Delta Omega, Phi Alpha Theta. Office: UCLA Sch Pub Health 10833 Le Conte Ave Los Angeles CA 90024-1772

BOURRET, MARJORIE ANN, educational advocate, consultant; b. Denver, Sept. 9, 1925; d. Walter Brewster and Grace Helen (Thompson) Leaf; m. Raymond Roland Bourret, May 28, 1955; children: Robert B., Ronald P. BSEE, BS in Engring. Physics, U. Colo., 1947. Cons. for child advocacy and interagy. coordination San Benito-Santa Cruz Spl. Edn. Local Plan Agy., Aptos, Calif., 1991; project coord. for Linkup to Learning Valley Resource Ctr., Ben Lomond, Calif., 1992—. Contbg. author: Board/Superintendent Roles, Responsibilities and relationships, 1980; prin. author: Citizens Guide to Scotts Valley, 1984; also articles. Trustee, pres. Scotts Valley (Calif.) Union Sch. Dist., 1970-81, mem. bond oversight com., 1995—; mem., chmn. policy devel. com. San Benito-Santa Cruz Spl. Edn. Coord. Agy., 1980-81; cons. on code sect. 7579, 1990; mem. Calif. Adv. Commn. on Spl. Edn., Sacramento, 1984-89, chmn. legis. com., 1984, chmn. policy rev. com., 1987-89; mem. chmn. Hazardous Materials Adv. Commn., Santa Cruz, 1984-87; organizer, bd. dirs. Friends Long Marine Lab., U. Calif., Santa Cruz, 1979-84; bd. dirs. Group Home Soc., Santa Cruz, 1984-86; others. Recipient Disting. Engring. Alumna award Coll. Engring. & Applied Sci. U. Colo., 1994. Mem. Nat. Sch. Bds. Assn. (fed. rels. network 1977-81), Calif. Sch. Bds. Assn. (bd. dirs., com. chmn. 1977-81, mem. del. assembly 1974-81), LWV (pres. Santa Cruz County chpt. 1967-69). Home: 1160 Whispering Pines Dr Scotts Valley CA 95066-4627

BOUSQUET, JOHN FREDERICK, security firm executive, desktop publishing executive, locksmith; b. Washington, Nov. 19, 1948; s. Kenneth Joseph and Margaret Isabel (Sherrin) B. BSBA, Lehigh U., 1971; student, DeAnza Coll. Cert. master locksmith. Staff asst. to gen. mgr. bank svcs. Yale Lock Co. Eaton Corp., Rye, N.Y., 1971; sales, installation, repairs alarms and electronic access controls Telcoa, Greenwich, Conn., 1971-73; from salesman to asst. mgr. Radio Shack, Stamford, Conn., 1973-74; sales rep. Electrolux, Stamford, 1974-75; pvt. practice locksmith contractor South San Francisco, 1975-85; locksmith NASA/Ames Rsch. Ctr. Smith Engring. & Contracting Svcs., Oakland, Calif., 1985-86, Bamsi Inc., Titusville, Fla., 1986-89, Quad S Co., Moffett Field, Calif., 1989-94, Security USA, Oakland, Calif., 1994—; prin. JFB Desktop Pub., South San Francisco; pres., CEO Computer Security Products, Inc., Am. Video Prodns., Inc.; dir. City Lock & Intercom., Inc., San Francisco, 1985-88; cons. NASA, Moffett Field, 1985—; spl. cons. Alcatraz Lock Renovation Project; asst. editor NASA Security Awareness Bulletin, 1988; guest lectr. adminstrn. justice dept. DeAnza Coll., 1991, 93, 95. Mem. Associated Locksmiths Am., Calif. Locksmiths Assn. (Man of Yr. award San Francisco Bay Area chpt. 1983, cert. appreciation 1984), Door Hardware Inst., Nat. Classification Mgmt. Soc., Comm. Security Assn., Phi Theta Kappa (palimentarian Alpha Sigma Alpha chpt. 1992-93). Republican. Episcopalian. Home: 112 Eucalyptus Ave South San Francisco CA 94080-2447 Office: Security USA Co NASA Ames Rsch Ctr MS: N253-1 Moffett Field CA 94035-1000

BOUTILIER, NANCY W., writer, secondary English educator; b. Worcester, Mass., Feb. 6, 1961; d. Richard James and Janet (Kallgren) B. AB, Harvard/Radcliffe, 1984; MA, Bread Loaf Sch. of English, 1990. Tchr. Phillips Acad., Andover, Mass., 1984-90, San Francisco U. High Sch., 1991—; columnist Bay Area Reporter, 1991—. Author: According to Her Contours, 1992; contbr. articles to profl. jours. Co-founder Phillips Acad. Gay/Straight Alliance, 1988, Bay Area Ind. Sch. Gay and Lesbian Caucus, 1992. Recipient Outstanding Columnist Cable Car award, 1992, 94. Office: San Francisco U HS 3065 Jackson St San Francisco CA 94115

BOUTONNET, EDWARD, food products executive; b. 1938. V.p. Boutonnet Farms, Inc., Castroville, Calif.; sec. Kleen Globe,Inc., Castroville, Calif., 1972—; with Calif. Artichoke, Castroville, Calif., 1982—. Office: Calif Artichoke 11500 Del Monte Ave Castroville CA 95012-3155*

BOUVIER, MARSHALL ANDRE, lawyer; b. Jacksonville, Fla., Sept. 30, 1923; s. Marshall and Helen Marion B.; m. Zepha Windle, July 11, 1938; children: Michael A., Debra Bouvier Williams, Mark A., Marshall André III, Suzanne, John A. (dec.), Wendy Bouvier Clark, Jennifer Lynn. AB, Emory U., LLB, 1949. Bar: Ga. 1948, Nev. 1960. Commd. USN, 1949; naval aviator, judge advocate; ret., 1959; atty. State of Nevada, 1959-60; pvt. practice, Reno, 1960-82, 88—; dist. atty. County of Storey, Nev., 1982-88, spl. cons. to Nev.Dist. Atty., 1991—, Storey County Dist. Atty., 1991—; cons. on corp. securites problems. Mem. Judge Advocates Assn., Am. Bd. Hypnotherapy, Ancient and Honorable Order Quiet Birdmen, Rotary, E Clampus Vitus, Phi Delta Phi, Sigma Chi.

BOVEY, TERRY ROBINSON, insurance executive; b. Oregon, Ill., May 13, 1948; s. John Franklin and Frances (Robinson) B.; m. Diana Carmen Rodriguez, Aug. 29, 1970 (div. 1980); 1 child, Joshua; m. Kathy Jo Johnston, Sept. 14, 1985; children: Courtney, Taylor. Student, Ariz. Western Coll., 1966-68, Grand Canyon Coll., 1968-69; BBA, U. Ariz., 1972. Salesman All-Am. Dist. Co., Yuma, Ariz., 1972-76; dist. asst. mgr. Equitable Life Ins., Yuma, 1976-81; gen. sales mgr. Ins. Counselors, Yuma, 1981-83; mng. gen. agt. First Capital Life Ins. Co., Ariz., Calif., Nev., N.C., 1983-90; master gen. agt. Comml. Union Life Ins. Co., Tucson, 1990—; regional commnr. Ariz. Interscholastic Assn., Yuma, 1972-88, Umpire Supt. A.C.C.A.C., 1993—. mem. Century Club, Boy's Club of Yuma. Mem. Million Dollar Round Table, Nat. Assn. Life Underwriters (numerous sales achievement awards, Nat. Quality awards), Life Underwriters Polit. Action Com., Tucson City Assn. Republican. Presbyterian.

BOWDICH, CARY ANN, college administrator; b. Albuquerque, Feb. 25, 1953; d. Herbert Earl and Marian Rose (Dyce) B.; m. John Mark Almon (div. 1988). BA, U. N.Mex., 1977; MS, Purdue U., 1983. Conf. coord. Purdue-Continuing Edn., West Lafayette, Ind., 1979-82; asst. dir. ann. support Purdue Devel. Office, West Lafayette, 1984-87; program specialist U. Wis. Stout, Menomonie, 1983; dir. instl. svcs. Coun. for Advancement and Support of Edn., Washington, 1987-89; dir. ednl. resources Assn. Governing Bds. of Univs. and Colls., Washington, 1989-90; dir. devel. Internat. Tennis Hall of Fame, N.Y.C., 1990-93, St. John's Coll., Santa Fe, 1993—; Speaker and cons. in field. Bd. dirs. YMCA, Lafayette, Ind., 1984-87, program dir., 1980-83, founder devel. edn. program, 1979; bd. dirs. Lafayette Handicapped Sports Assn., 1984-87; vol. ETA Metro. Coun.; pres. bd. Sante Fe Symphony & Chorus, 1993—; co-founder Sante Fe Youth Symphony; bd. dirs. KNME-TV, Santa Fe., 1994; prodr. Huck Finn Co. Democrat. Lutheran. Office: St John's Coll 1160 Camino Cruz Blanca Santa Fe NM 87501

BOWE, ROGER LEE, small business owner; b. Pueblo, Colo., Aug. 30, 1954; s. William Roy and Ruth Ann (Penn) B.; 1 child, Patrick William; m. Wendy C. Kempf, June 5, 1981. Grad. high sch., Denver. Mechanic Crest Motors, Denver, 1970-74; svc. mgr. Grand Prix Imports, Denver, 1974-76; line tech. Kerlin & Son, Denver, 1976-80; owner, operator Wheels of Fortune, Inc., Littleton, Colo., 1981—. Past mem. Vat. Fedn. Ind. Bus., 1988. Mem. Z Car Club Colo. (tech. advisor), Better Bus. Bur. Office: Wheels of Fortune Inc 2659 1/2 W Main St Littleton CO 80120-1914

BOWEN, CHRISTINE LYN, computerized healthcare billing company executive; b. Troy, N.Y., July 23, 1952; d. Joseph William and Evelyn Ann (Webster) Sneden; m. Alan Leslie Deyo, May 20, 1974 (div. Dec. 1977); 1 child, Jason Alan Deyo; m. Robert Charles Bowen, Sept. 12, 1981 (div. Feb. 1991). B in Applied Social Sci., SUNY-Binghamton, 1979. Office mgr. Maine Med. Group, N.Y., 1977-78; med. edn. coord. Binghamton Gen. Hosp., 1978-82; systems op. mgr. Med. Office Systems of So. Tier, Inc., Binghamton, 1983-85, chief oper. officer, systems ops. mgr., med. edn. coord., med. office mgr., 1985—; account rep. 3M Health Info. Systems, So. Calif. and Hawaii, 1985; past owner, operator tanning co.; owner, pres. CSB Assocs., 1986—; cons. N.Y. and Pa. Editor Erudition Digest newsletter, 1982. Mentor B-R-I-D-G-E, Binghamton, 1981-84; active Port Dickinson Community Assn., Binghamton, 1984—; co-chairperson disaster svc., bd. dirs. Broome County chpt. ARC, 1984-90. 1st lt. U.S. Army, 1970-73. Mem. NAQAP, AHIMA, Women's Network, MOSST User Group (bd. dirs. 1983-87), Altrusa (local treas. 1982-83). Avocations: cross-country skiing, antique hunting, camping, swimming, golfing. Home and Office: 354 Arno Way Pacific Palisades CA 90272-3347

BOWEN, CLOTILDE DENT, retired army officer, psychiatrist; b. Chgo., Mar. 20, 1923; d. William Marion Dent and Clotilde (Tynes) D.; m. William N. Bowen, Dec. 29, 1945 (dec.). B.A., Ohio State U., 1943, M.D., 1947. Intern, Harlem Hosp., N.Y.C., 1947-48; resident and fellow in pulmonary diseases, Triboro Hosp., Jamaica, L.I., N.Y., 1948-50; resident in psychiatry VA Hosp., Albany, N.Y., 1959-62; pvt. practice, N.Y.C. 1950-55; chief pulmonary disease clinic, N.Y.C. 1950-55; asst. chief pulmonary disease svc., Valley Forge Army Hosp., Pa., 1956-59; chief psychiatry VA Hosp., Roseburg, Oreg., 1962-66, acting chief of staff, 1964-66; asst. chief neurology and psychiatry Tripler Gen. Hosp., Hawaii, 1966-68; psychiatr. cons. and dir. Rev. Br., Office Civil Health and Med. Program, Uniform Svcs., 1968-70; commd. capt. U.S. Army, 1955, advanced through ranks to col., 1968; neuropsychiat. cons. U.S. Army Vietnam, 1970-71; chief dept. psychiatry Fitzsimons Army Med. Ctr., 1971-74; chief dept. psychiatry. Tripler Army Med. Ctr., 1974-75; comdr. Hawley Army Clinic, Ft. Benjamin, Harrison, Ind., 1977-78, chief dept. primary care and community medicine, 1978-83, chief psychiat. consultation svc., Fitzsimons Army Med. Ctr., 1983-85; chief psychiatry svc. med./regional office ctr. VA, Cheyenne, Wyo., 1987-90; staff psychiatrist Denver VA Satellite Clinic, Colorado Springs, Colo., 1990—; surveyor, Joint Commn. on Accreditation Healthcare Orgns., 1985-92; assoc. prof. psychiatry U. Colo. Med. Center, Denver, 1970-83. Decorated Legion of Merit, several other medals; recipient Colo. Disabled Am. Vets. award, 1994-95. Fellow Am. Psychiat. Assn. (life), Acad. Psychosomatic Medicine; mem. AMA, Nat. Med. Assn., Menninger Found. (charter). Home: 1020 Tari Dr Colorado Springs CO 80921-2257

BOWEN, DOUGLAS GLENN, electrical engineer, educator, consultant; b. Spanish Fork, Utah, May 6, 1951; s. William Morgan and Ferne (Davis) B.; m. Jarleen Ottesen, Dec. 28, 1972; children: Erica Anne, Emily Elizabeth, David, Summer. BS in Elec. Engring., MS in Elec. Engring., U. Wyo., 1975; MBA, Brigham Young U., 1993. Enlisted USAF, 1972, advanced through grades to capt., 1977; engr. USAF, El Segundo, Calif., 1975-81; resigned USAF, 1981; prin. engr. Martin Marietta, Littleton, Colo., 1981-83; sr. engr. Sperry Corp., Salt Lake City, 1983-85; from staff engr. to chief engr. Unisys Corp., Salt Lake City, 1985-94; tech. dir. Loral Corp., Salt Lake City, 1995—; dir. DWD Enterprises, Inc., 1994; instr. Weber Coll., Ogden, Utah, 1987-88, U. Northrup, Inglewood, Calif., 1976-78; cons. USAF, Office of Sec. Air Force and Def. Support Projects Office, Pentagon, Washington, 1988—; mem. Utah Ctr. for Excellence Steering Com.; mem. curriculum adv. com. U. Utah, 1994—. Patentee in field. Bd. dirs. Spanish Fork Utility Bd., 1986—, Utah Mcpl. Power Assn., Provo, 1990, DWD Enterprises, 1994, Utah Ctr. for Excellence, 1995. Mem. Am. Legion, Old Crows, Air Force Assn. (v.p. 1988-89), Tau Beta Phi.

BOWEN, HARRY ERNEST, management consultant; b. Elmira, N.Y., Jan. 31, 1941; s. Ernest William and Julia Cora (Forker) B.; m. Sandra Marie Fullerton, June 15, 1962; children: Harry Ernest Jr., Vicki Lynn Bowen Briggs, Nicholas Russel. AS in Gen. Studies, Mt. Wachusetts, Gardner, Mass., 1975; student, Ind. Inst. Tech., Ft. Wayne, 1984—. Enlisted U.S. Army, 1961; student Manual Morse Operator Sch. U.S. Army, Ft. Devens, Mass., 1961-62; sr. repairman U.S. Army, Sinope, Turkey, 1970-71; mem. maintenance office Intelligence and Security Command U.S. Army, Arlington Hall, Va., 1961-83; ret., 1983; assoc. dir. Martin & Stern, Inc., Chantilly, Va., 1983-89; program mgr. Paragon Sys., Inc., Centreville, Va., 1989-91; program mgr., mem. mgmt. staff Telos Fed. Sys., Sierra Vista, Ariz., 1991—; advisor Bowen Assoc., Sierra Vista, 1992—; ptnr. T and L Sys., Sierra Vista, 1991-94; advisor Bowen Assocs., Sierra Vista, 1992—. Mem. Soc. Logistics Engrs. (chairperson 1991-94, Sr. Membership award 1993), Kiwanis (sec. 1994—). Republican. Home: 1950 E Cottonwood Dr Sierra Vista AZ 85635-6318 Office: Telos Fed Sys 555 E Wilcox Dr Ste H Sierra Vista AZ 85635-2547

BOWEN, JIMMIE CARL, vocational education educator; b. Palmdale, Calif., Dec. 27, 1955; s. Charles Richard and Majorie Elizabeth (Cole) B.; m. Marsha Corrine Nuckolls, Apr. 30, 1978; 1 child, Allison Tiffany. AA, Antelope Valley Coll., Lancaster, Calif., 1988; AS, Antelope Valley Coll., 1989; Diploma Computerized Acctg., Ameritech Colls., Inc., Van Nuys, Calif., 1988, Diploma in Word Processing, 1988. 1st asst. mgr. Thrifty Corp.-Thrifty Drug and Discount, Lancaster, Calif., 1974-88; software cons. Calif. Freeware, Palmdale, 1989-90, Barbara's Choice Software, Lancaster, 1991—; computer/software instr. A-1 Computer Sch., Lancaster, 1992—; hardware/software cons. Bowen's Computer Cons., Palmdale, 1991—; bus. edn./computer instr. Ameritech Colls., Inc., Van Nuys, 1988-93; hardware/software instr. and cons. ABC Computer Learning Ctrs., Lancaster and Van Nuys, Calif., 1992-94, Computer Sci. Corp., Edwards AFB, 1994—. Contbr. articles to profl. jours. Mem. Nat. Assn. Desktop Pubrs., Antelope Valley Microcomputer Users Group, L.A. Amiga Users Group, Antelope Valley Commodore Users Group (pres., newsletter editor 1990—). Home: 38739 5th St E Apt 1 Palmdale CA 93550-3774

BOWEN, PETER GEOFFREY, real estate investment advisor, writer; b. Iowa City, Iowa, July 10, 1939; s. Howard Rothmann and Lois Berntine (Schilling) B.; m. Shirley Johns Carlson, Sept. 14, 1968 (div. 1991); children: Douglas Howard, Leslie Johns. BA in Govt. and Econs., Lawrence Coll., 1960; postgrad. U. Wis., 1960-61, U. Denver. cert. expert real estate witness, Denver Dist. Ct., 1987. Dir. devel. Mobile Home Communities, Denver, 1969-71; v.p. Perry & Butler, Denver, 1972-73; exec. v.p., dir. Little & Co., Denver, 1973; pres. Builders Agy. Ltd., Denver, 1974-75; pres. The Investment Mgmt. Group Ltd., Denver, 1975-87; independent investor, writer, Vail, Colo., 1987—; gen. ptnr. 8 real estate ltd. ptnrships.; bus. faculty mem. Colo. Mt. Coll.; lectr. on real estate syndications and entrepreneurships. Contbr. articles to profl. pubs. Mem. Colo. Coun. Econ. Devel., 1964-68; vice-chmn. Greenwood Village (Colo.) Planning and Zoning Commn., 1983-85; mem. Vail Planning and Environ. Commn., 1992-93; dir. Vail Alliance for Environ. Edn. 1993—; elected mem. City Council Greenwood Village, 1985-86, also mayor pro tem, 1985-86; trustee Vail Mountain Sch. Found., 1987-88; bd. dirs. Colo. Plan for Apportionment, 1966; speaker Forward Metro Denver, 1966-67. Mem. Rotary Club (bd. dirs. Vail chpt., named Rotarian of Yr. 1991-92), Lawrence U. Alumni Assn. (bd. dirs. 1966-72, 82-86). Home: 5047 Main Gore Dr Vail CO 81657-5440

BOWEN, RICHARD LEE, academic administrator, political science educator; b. Avoca, Iowa, Aug. 31, 1933; s. Howard L. and Donna (Milburn) B.; m. Connie Smith Bowen, 1976; children: James, Robert, Elizabeth, Christopher; children by previous marriage—Catherine, David, Thomas. B.A., Augustana Coll., 1957; M.A., Harvard, 1959, Ph.D., 1967. Fgn. service officer State Dept., 1959-60; research asst. to U.S. Senator Francis Case, 1960-62; legis. asst. to U.S. Senator Karl Mundt, 1962-65; minority cons. sub-com. exec. reorgn. U.S. Senate, 1966-67; asst. to pres., assoc. prof. polit. sci. U. S.D., Vermillion, 1967-69, pres., 1969-76; pres. Dakota State Coll., Madison, 1973-76; commr. higher edn. Bd. Regents State S.D., Pierre, 1976-80; Disting prof. polit. sci. U. S.D., 1980-85; pres. Idaho State U., Pocatello, 1985—. Served with USN, 1951-54. Recipient Outstanding Alumnus award Augustana Coll., 1970; Woodrow Wilson fellow, 1957, Congl. Staff fellow, 1965; Fulbright scholar, 1957. Office: Idaho State U Office of Pres Campus Box 8310 Pocatello ID 83209-0009

BOWEN, THOMAS EDWIN, cardiothoracic surgeon, retired army officer; b. Lackawanna, N.Y., Dec. 16, 1934; m. Margaret Marie Harrington, 1959; children: Matthew, Mark, James, John, Thaddeus, Mary Cristine. BS, St. Bonaventure U., 1961; MD, Marquette U., 1965; diploma, U.S. Army War Coll., 1985. Diplomate Am. Bd. Surgery, Am. Bd. Thoracic Surgery, Nat. Bd. Med. Examiners. Commd. 2d lt. U.S. Army, 1961, advanced through grades to brig. gen., 1988; intern Tripler Army Gen. Hosp., Honolulu, 1965-66, resident in gen. surgery, 1966-70; resident in gen. surgery Vietnam, 1970-71; resident in thoracic surgery Walter Reed Army Gen. Hosp., Washington, 1971-73; dep. dir. Profl. Svcs. Directorate Office of Surgeon Gen., Washington, 1985-87; comdr., surgeon 121st Evacuation Hosp., 1987-88; assoc. prof. dept. surgery Sch. Medicine Uniformed Svcs. U. of Health Scis., Bethesda, Md., 1981—; commanding gen. Fitzsimons Army Med. Ctr., Aurora, Colo., 1988-93; assoc. clin. prof. dept. surgery U. Colo. Sch.

Medicine, Denver, 1989—; assoc. prof. surgery U. So. Fla. Sch. Med.; chief of staff James A. Haley VA Med. Ctr., Tampa, Fla., 1994—. Contbr. articles to profl. publs. Chmn. Combined Fed. Campaign, Denver, 1990. Decorated D.S.M., Legion of Merit with three oak leaf clusters, Bronze Star, Alfredo Lezcano Gomez medal for Svc. to Republic of Panama; recipient Raymond Franklin Metcalf award, 1971. Mem. Assn. Mil. Surgeons, Am. Coll. Surgeons, Soc. Thoracic Surgeons, Denver C. of C., Aurora C. of C., Rotary. Roman Catholic. Office: James A Haley VA Med Ctr Tampa FL 33612

BOWEN-FORBES, JORGE COURTNEY, artist, author, poet; b. Queenstown, Guyana, May 16, 1937; came to U.S., 1966; s. Walter and Margarita V. (Forbes) Bowen. BA, Queens Coll., Eve Leary, Guyana, 1969; MFA, Chelsea (Eng.) Sch. Design, 1972. Comml. artist Guyana Litographic, Georgetown; art dir. Corbin Advt. Agy., Bridgetown, Barbados; tech. advisor Ministry of Info. and Culture, Georgetown; nat. juror Nat. Arts Club, N.Y.C., 1985, Nat. Soc. Painters in Casein and Acrylic. Major exhbns. include Expo 67, Can., Nat. Acad. Design, N.Y., Frye Mus., El Paso (Tex.) Mus., Wichita (Kans.) Centennial, Caribbean Festival of the Arts, Newark Mus.; 10 one-man exhbns. worldwide; works in collections including Nat. and Colgrain Collections, Guyana, El Paso Mus. Art, Kindercare Internat., Leon Loards Gallery, The McCreery Cummings Fine Art Collection, Bomani Gallery, San Francisco; poetry and articles pub. various jours. Recipient Silver medal of honor Allied Artists of N.Y., 1978, Gold medal of honor, 1975. Mem. Nat. Watercolor Soc. (signature mem.), Nat. Soc. Painters in Casein and Acrylics, Audubon Artists, Knickerbocker Artists (Gold Medal of Honor 1977, 79), Am. Watercolor Soc. (signature mem., High Winds medal 1984). Home and Office: PO Box 1821 Oakland CA 94604-1821

BOWER, ALLAN MAXWELL, lawyer; b. Oak Park, Ill., May 21, 1936; s. David Robert and Frances Emily (Maxwell) B.; m. Deborah Ann Rottmayer, Dec. 28, 1959. BS, State U. Iowa, 1962; JD, U. Miami, Fla., 1968. Bar: Calif. 1969, U.S. Supreme Ct. 1979. Civil trial practice L.A., 1969—; ptnr. Lane Powell Spears Lubersky, L.A., 1990—. Contbr. articles to profl. publs. Mem. ABA, L.A. Bar Assn., Lawyer-Pilots Bar Assn., Am. Judicature Soc., Am. Trial Lawyers Assn., Am. Arbitration Assn. (nat. panel arbitrators), Alpha Tau Omega. Republican. Presbyterian. Home: 2411 Century Hill Los Angeles CA 90067 Office: Lane Powell Spears Lubersky 333 S Hope St Ste 2400 Los Angeles CA 90071-3033

BOWER, DONALD EDWARD, author; b. Lockport, N.Y., July 19, 1920. BA, U. Nebr., 1942. D.E. Bower & Co., Inc., Denver, 1945-60; editor, pub. Arapahoe Tribune, 1960-62; editor Adams County Almanac, Adams County Dispatch, Jefferson County Herald, 1962-65; freelance staff Writer Fawcett Publs., 1962-64, lit. cons., 1962-67; editor, pub. Buyer's Showcase mag. and FURN Club News 1965-66; exec. editor Colo. mag., 1966-69; editor-in-chief, v.p., dir. Am. West Pub. Co., editor Am. West mag., 1970-74; pres. Colo. Authors League, 1975-76; dir. Nat. Writers Club, Denver, 1974-86; dir. Assoc. Bus. Writers Am., 1978-86, also pres. Assn. Hdqrs., 1978-86; editorial dir. Nat. Writers Press, 1982-86; lit. agent Don Bower Lit. Agy., 1991—. Author: Roaming the American West, 1970; Ghost Towns and Back Roads, 1972; intro. to The Magnificent Rockies, 1972; Fred Rosenstock: A Legend in Books and Art, 1976; The Professional Writers' Guide, 1984, rev. edition, 1990;Ten Keys to Writing Success, 1987, Sex and Espionage, 1990; also 4 paperback detective novels, 1960-64; editor: Living Water, Living Earth, 1971; Anasazi: Ancient People of the Rock, 1973; The Great Southwest, 1972; Edge of a Continent, 1970; The Mighty Sierra, 1972; The Magnificent Rockies, 1972; The Great Northwest, 1973; Gold and Silver in the West, 1973; Steinbeck Country, 1973; contbr. Western Writers Handbook, 1988, articles to mags. Mem. Authors Guild Am., Western Writers Assn. Am., Friends of Denver Pub. Libr., Sigma Delta Chi. Office: 3082 S Wheeling Way Apt 209 Aurora CO 80014-5611

BOWER, PAUL GEORGE, lawyer; b. Chgo., Apr. 21, 1933; s. Chester L. and Retha (Dausmann) B.; m. Elreen L. Thurlow, June 23, 1962; children: Stephanie, Julienne, Aimee. B.A., Rice U., 1955; postgrad., Calif. Inst. Tech., 1959-60; LL.B., Stanford U., 1963. Bar: Calif. 1964, U.S. Supreme Ct. 1969. Assoc. Gibson, Dunn & Grutcher, Los Angeles, 1963-67, ptnr., 1970—. Asst. dir. Nat. Adv. Com. Civil Disorder, 1967-68; spl. asst. to dep. atty. gen. U.S. Dept. Justice, 1968-69, consumer counsel, 1969; bd. dirs. Legal Aid Found.; trustee Sierra Club Legal Def. Fund, 1982—; mem. legal svcs. Trust Fund Commn., 1990-93, chair, 1993-94; dep. gen. counsel Webster Commn., 1992. With U.S. Army, 1956-59. Mem. Calif. Bar Assn., L.A. County Bar Assn., Beverly Hills Bar Assn., Order of Coif. Democrat. Office: Gibson Dunn & Crutcher 2029 Century Park E Los Angeles CA 90067-2901 also: Gibson Dunn & Crutcher 333 S Grand Ave Los Angeles CA 90071-1504

BOWER, RICHARD JAMES, minister; b. Somerville, N.J., June 9, 1939; s. Oneil A. and Mildred R. (Goss) B.; m. Helen Ann Cheek, Dec. 29, 1962 (div. 1985); 1 child, Christopher Scott. Student, Sorbonne, Paris, 1959-60; B.A., Wesleyan U., 1961; M.Div., Drew U., Madison, N.J., 1965; student, Oxford U., Eng., 1983. Ordained to ministry, Congregational Christian Ch., 1965. Minister Community Congl. Ch., Kewaunee, Wis., 1965-67; sr. minister Congl. Ch., Bound Brook, N.J., 1967-78, Congl. Ch. of the Chimes, Sherman Oaks, Calif., 1978—; mem. exec. com., dir. Nat. Assn. Congl. Christian Chs., 1973-77, chmn., 1976-77,asst. moderator, 1981-82, moderator, 1982-83, exec. search com., 1990-91, nominating com., 1991-93, chmn., 1992-93; mem. World Christian Rels. Commn., 1993—. Appeared on TV programs; contbr. poetry and articles to periodicals. Organizer, pres. Am. Field Service, Kewaunee, 1966-67; dir. Children's Bur., Los Angeles, 1981-88; bd. fellows Hollywood Congl. Ctr., 1979-82; bd. dirs. Heritage Playhouse, 1986—. Mem. Cal-West Assn. (dir., moderator 1986-87). Republican. Lodge: Bound Brook Rotary (pres. 1975-76). Home: 365 W Alameda Ave # 302 Burbank CA 91506-3339 Office: Congl Ch Chimes 14115 Magnolia Blvd Sherman Oaks CA 91423-1118

BOWER, WILLIAM DAVID, credit bureau firm executive; b. Atlanta, Jan. 22, 1964; s. Angus Bruce and Ellen (Everitt) B.; m. Sabrina Thai, June 20, 1984. BA in History, UCLA, 1988. Ptnr. Secret Svc. Limousine, Valencia, Calif., 1982-85; broker Prudential-Bache, Encino, Calif., 1985-87; pres., chief exec. officer Contemporary Info. Corp., Valencia, 1987—. Author: History of Darwin Days, 1985, Consumer's Guide to Credit, 1986. Nat. Rep. pollster, West L.A., 1985. Maj. U.S. Army Res., 1982—. Recipient Academic Scholarship U.S. Army, 1982. Mem. Valencia Ind. Assn. Santa Clarita C. of C., Santa Clarita Bruins (v.p. 1990—, pres. 1992—), UCLA Alumni San Juaquin, Sigma Chi. Lutheran. Office: Contemporary Info Corp Ste 110 25061 Avenue Stanford Santa Clarita CA 91355-3443

BOWERMAN, CHARLES LEO, oil company executive; b. Crawfordsville, Ind., Dec. 16, 1939; s. Thomas Edward and Hazel (Melvin) B.; m. Coralea Weir, June 12, 1960; children—Cynthia, Cristina, Candace. A.B., Wabash Coll., 1961. Jr. job analyst Phillips Petroleum, Bartlesville, Okla., 1961-62, sales trainee, 1962-64, various mktg. dept. positions, 1964-84, v.p. mktg., 1984-88; sr. v.p. petroleum products Phillips Petroleum, Bartlesville, 1988—. Mem. exec. bd. Cherokee Area council Boy Scouts Am.; trustee Boys Club of Bartlesville. Mem. Am. Petroleum Inst. (former chmn. gen. com. mktg.), Okla.-Kans. Oil and Gas Assn. (bd. dirs. 1985—), Hillcrest Country Club, Masons, Royal Order Jesters. Republican. Office: Phillips Petroleum Co 6A1 Phillips Bldg Bartlesville OK 74004

BOWERS, BOBBY EUGENE, metal products executive, small business owner; b. Bokosh, Okla., Apr. 12, 1933; s. Elmer Lefayet and Elizabeth (Hamilton) B.; m. Barbara Jean Baker, Feb. 2, 1952; children: Rory Eugene, Denise Lynn. Grad., Gemological Inst. Am., 1981, Revere Acad., 1985; postgrad., Trenton Sch. Jewelry Arts, 1985. Co-owner The Borrego Goldsmith, Borrego Springs, Calif., 1979-94, B.O.S. Recording Studio, Borrego Springs, 1985-94; ret., 1994; lectr. gem mines of the world El Der Hostle, San Diego, 1992, Grossmont Coll., San Diego, 1992. Designer numerous signed works of fine jewelry. Mem. Masons. Home: 1470 Rango Way Borrego Springs CA 92004

BOWERS, JACK (JOHN BURTON BOWERS, JR.), artist, graphics and digital color executive; b. Big Spring, Tex., Feb. 4, 1947; s. John Burton Bowers and Nola Mae Penny (Cuthberson) Reynolds; m. Victoria Barret Fuller, July 2, 1977 (div. 1982); m. Carol Ann Carbone, Oct. 11, 1985 (div. 1991); 1 child, Carly Elizabeth. Student, N. Tex. State U., 1965-66; MFA, San Francisco Art Inst., 1984. Lic. real estate agt., Tex. Agy. sales mgr. The Penn Mutual Life Ins. Co., Dallas, 1967-74; mng. gen. ptnr. Bowers Enterprises, San Francisco, 1975—; nat. mgr. corp. real estate Werner Erhard & Assocs., San Francisco, 1986-89; dir. client svcs. Rapid, San Francisco, 1993-95, Pacific Digital Image, San Francisco, 1995—; Artist in residency, Moffet County High Sch., Craig, Colo., 1981. Represented in shows at Vallauris, France, 1988, N.Y.U., 1988, Boulder (Colo.) Art Ctr., 1987, Chgo. Internat. Art. Expo, Navy Pier, 1987, Dorothy Weiss Gallery, San Francisco, 1987, Berkeley (Calif.) Exhibition '87, 1st Internat. Ceramics Show, Aichi-ken Chusho Kigyo Ctr., Mino, Japan, 1986, Pro Arts Annual Exhibition, Pro Arts Galleries, Oakland, Calif., 1985, San Francisco Fine Arts Show, 1983, Aspen (Colo.) Mus. Art, Arvada Ctr. for the Arts, 1980, El Paso (Tex.) Mus. Fine Art, 1977, and numerous others; works include Space Case, Black Box, First Blond, Red and Black Box, Sally's Cenotaph, 2 Dozen Roaring Valleys, and numerous others; works reviewed in numerous mags. including The San Francisco Mag., 1988, San Francisco Chronicle, 1987, Oakland Tribune, 1987, Rocky Mtn. News, 1981, Westword, 1981, Art Space, 1981. Named Best of Show, Redding (Calif.) Mus., 1987, U. Ark., 1987, Aspen Mus. Art, 1980; recipient Honorable Mention, Mino, Japan, 1986, Purchase award, State of Colo., 1980, 81, Aspen Mall Competition, 1978, Juror's award, Aspen Mus. Art, 1979. Mem. Art Inst. Alumni Assn. (pres. 1994—).

BOWERS, JOHN CHARLES, computer company executive; b. Pasadena, Calif., July 21, 1947; s. Charles Aubrey and Janet Noreen (Ewart) B.; m. Ann Marlene Haider, Nov. 21, 1970. BSEE, Calif. State U., Long Beach, 1980; MSEE, U. So. Calif., 1983, PhDEE, 1988. Elec. engr. Aerojet Gen., Azusa, Calif., 1969-79; sys. engr. TRW, Redondo Beach, Calif., 1979-84; supr. sys. engring. Aerojet Electro Sys., Azusa, 1984-88; mng. data sys. Gen. Corp Aerojet, Azusa, 1988-93, product dir. engring., 1993—; v.p. Computing Experience Corp., Laguna Niguel, Calif., 1992—; cons. Calif. State Poly. U., Pomona, 1986—; industry rep. Aerospace Industries Assn., 1992—. Chpt. pres. Young Reps., Alta Loma, Calif., 1993. Mem. IEEE, Calif. State U. Long Beach Alumni (pres. assoc.), L.A. Phil. Assn., Ceritos Performing Arts Assn., Assn. for Computing Machinery. Republican. Episcopalian.

BOWERS, ZELLA ZANE, real estate broker; b. Liberal, Kans., May 24, 1929; d. Rex and Esther (Neff) Powelson; m. James Clarence Bowers, Aug. 12, 1949; (div. 1977); 1 child: Dara Zane. BA, Colo. Coll., 1951. Cert. real estate brokerage mgr. Sec. Bowers Ins. Agy., Colorado Springs, Colo., 1955-59, Cen. Colo. Claims Svc., Colorado Springs, 1959-63; pres. Premium Budgeting Co., Colorado Springs, 1962-67; pres., owner Monument Valley Realty, Inc., Colorado Springs, 1981-89; mng. broker The Buick Co. Buyer's Market; broker Haley Realty, Inc., Colorado Springs, 1990—; pres. Realtor Svcs. Corp., 1989. Hon. trustee The Palmer Found., Colorado Springs, 1980—, pres., 1983-84; trustee Pikes Peak United Way, 1988-91; pres. Vis. Nurse Assn., Colorado Springs, 1966-67, 74; dir. Colo. League Nurses, Denver, 1968; steering com. The Kennedy Ctr. Imagination Celebration, Colorado Springs, 1989-93, chmn., 1990-92; sec. Care & Share, Colorado Springs, 1984; chmn. McAllister House Mus., Colorado Springs, 1973-74; docent chmn. Colorado Springs Fine Arts Ctr., 1969-70; mem. historic preservation bd. City of Colorado Springs, 1989-94, chmn. 1989-92, mem. Compreshnsive Plan Task Force City of Colo., 1990-91; charter rev. commn. City of Colorado Springs, 1991-92; commr. Colo. Springs City Planning, 1995—; pres. Friends of the Libr., 1971-72; pres. Woman's Edn. Soc. Colo. Coll., 1974-77; civil adminstrv. staff asst. Air Def. Filter Ctr., 1956-57, ground observer, 1956, others. Recipient Women's Trade Fair Recognition award, 1987. Mem. Nat. Assn. Realtors, Colo. Assn. Realtors (dir. 1987-91, v.p. S.E. dist. 1992, trustee edn. found. 1988-92, dir. housing opportunity found. 1991-93, Disting. Svc. award 1991, Polit. Svc. award 1992), Colorado Springs Bd. Realtors (pres. 1987-88, named Realtor of Yr. 1989), Pikes Peak Assn. Realtors, Children of the Am. Revolution (pres. 1956-57), Gamma Phi Beta. Avocations: genealogy, travel. Home: 128 W Rockrimmon Blvd # 104 Colorado Springs CO 80919-1876 Office: Haley Realty Inc 109 E Fontanero St Colorado Springs CO 80907-7452

BOWES, A. WENDELL, minister, religion educator; b. San Francisco, Nov. 6, 1945; s. Alpin P. and Betty J. (Smith) B.; m. Virginia H. Miller, June 17, 1967; children: Heidi, Shelley. BA, Northwest Nazarene Coll., Nampa, Idaho, 1967; MDiv, Nazarene Theol. Seminary, Kans. City, Mo., 1970; ThM, Princeton Theol. Seminary, 1971; PhD, Dropsie Coll., Merion, Pa., 1987. Ordained, 1973. Pastor Ch. of Nazarene, Port Elizabeth, N.J., 1971-74, Bristol, Pa., 1975-78, Selinsgrove, Pa., 1979-82; prof. religion Northwest Nazarene Coll., 1982—, head dept. religion, coord. grad. studies in religion, 1986—. Named one of Outstanding Young Men Am., 1978. Mem. Soc. Bibl. Lit., Am. Schs. Oriental Rsch., Nat. Assn. Profs. Hebrew. Home: 932 W Locust Ln Nampa ID 83686-8231 Office: Northwest Nazarene Coll Nampa ID 83686

BOWES, FLORENCE (MRS. WILLIAM DAVID BOWES), writer; b. Salt Lake City, Nov. 19, 1925; d. John Albreckt Elias and Alma Wilhelmina (Jonasson) Norborg; student U. Utah, 1941-42, Columbia, 1945-46, N.Y. U., 1954-55; grad. N.Y. TV Workshop, 1950; m. Samuel Ellis Levine, July 15, 1944 (dec. July 1953); m. William David Bowes, Mar. 15, 1958 (dec. 1976); 1 son, Alan Richard. Actress, writer Hearst Radio Network, WINS, N.Y.C., 1944-45; personnel and adminstrv. exec. Mut. Broadcasting System, N.Y.C., 1946-49, free-lance editor, writer, 1948-49; freelance writer NBC and ABC, 1949-53; script editor, writer Robert A. Monroe Prodns., N.Y.C., Hollywood, Calif., 1953-56; script and comml. dir. KUTV-TV, Salt Lake City, 1956-58; spl. editor, writer pub. relations dept. U. Utah, Salt Lake City, 1966-68, editor, writer U. Utah Rev., 1968-75; author: Web of Solitude, 1979; The MacOrvan Curse, 1980; Interlude in Venice, 1981; Beauchamp, 1983. Mem. Beta Sigma Phi. Home: 338 K St Salt Lake City UT 84103-3562

BOWIE, HERBERT HUGHES, JR., magazine editor; b. Washington, May 5, 1951; s. Herbert Hughes, Doris Elnora (Brown) B.; m. Pauline Marie Hendrickson, Sept. 13, 1980; 1 child, Stephen Lee. BA in English, U. Mich., 1973. Editor People Forever, Scottsdale, Ariz., 1989—. Editor: Together Forever: An Invitation to Physical Immortality, 1990, (mag.) Forever Alive, 1989—. Office: People Forever PO Box 12305 Scottsdale AZ 85267-2305

BOWIE, PETER WENTWORTH, lawyer, educator; b. Alexandria, Va., Sept. 27, 1942; s. Beverley Munford and Louise Wentworth (Boynton) B.; m. Sarah Virginia Haught, Mar. 25, 1967; children—Heather, Gavin. B.A., Wake Forest Coll., 1964; J.D. magna cum laude, U. San Diego, 1971. Bar: Calif. 1972, D.C. 1972, U.S. Ct. Appeals D.C. Cir. 1972, U.S. Dist. Ct. D.C. 1972, U.S. Dist. Ct. Md. 1973, U.S. Ct. Appeals (9th cir.) 1974, U.S. Dist. Ct. (so. dist.) Calif. 1974, U.S. Supreme Ct. 1980. Trial atty. honors program Dept. Justice, Washington, 1971-74; asst. U.S. atty. U.S. Atty.'s Office, San Diego, 1974, asst. chief civil div., 1974-82, chief asst. U.S. atty., 1982-88; lawyer rep. 9th Circuit Ct. Appeals Jud. Conf., 1977-78, 84-87; judge U.S. Bankruptcy Ct., San Diego, 1988—. lectr. at law Calif. Western Sch. Law, 1979-83; exec. com. mem. 9th Cir. Judicial Conf., 1991-94. Bd. dirs. Presidio Little League, San Diego, 1984; coach, 1983-84. Served to lt. USN, 1964-68; Vietnam. Mem. State Bar Calif. (hearing referee ct. 1982-86, mem. review dept. 1986-90), Fed. Bar Assn. (pres. San Diego chpt. 1981-83), San Diego County Bar Assn. (chmn. fed. ct. com. 1978-80, 83-85), Assn. Bus. Trial Lawyers (bd. gov.), San. Diego Bankruptcy Forum (bd. dirs.), Phi Delta Phi. Republican. Unitarian. Home: 2205 La Callecita San Diego CA 92103-1112 Office: US Bankruptcy Court 325 W F St San Diego CA 92101

BOWKER, GARY ADES, development executive; b. Tacoma, Wash., Dec. 14, 1935; s. Edwin G. and Mary (Ades) B.; m. Carolyn Grace Branda, Dec. 26, 1958; children: Gwen, Elizabeth, Griffin. BD, San Francisco Theol. Sem., 1965, DMin, 1976; MS, L.I. U., 1975; MA, Pacific Luth. U., 1978. Ordained to ministry Presbyn. Ch., 1965. Assoc. pastor La Crescenta (Calif.) Presbyn. Ch., 1965-66; pastor Millwood Presbyn. Ch., Spokane, Wash., 1988-93; dir. development Whitworth Coll., Spokane, 1993—; commr. Gen. Assembly Presbyn. Ch. U.S.A., Orlando, Fla., 1993, chair com. on ch. policy, 1993; chair ops. com. Presbytery Inland N.W., Spokane, 1988-93; commr. Synod of Alaska-N.W., Sitka, 1991. Pres. PTA, Nurnberg, Germany, 1973; bd. trustees Hospice of Spokane; chair human growth and development adv. coun. Sch. Dist. 81, Spokane, 1988-94. Col. U.S. Army, 1966-88. Decorated Legion of Merit, Bronze star. Mem. Direct Mktg. Assn. (pres. Green Bluff chpt. 1993), Rotary, Spokane Club, Pres. Club Wash. State U. Home: 8814 E Greenbluff Rd Colbert WA 99005-9506 Office: Whitworth Coll 300 W Hawthorne Rd Spokane WA 99251-2515

BOWLEN, PATRICK DENNIS, holding company executive, lawyer, professional sports team executive; b. Prairie du Chien, Wis., Feb. 18, 1944; s. Paul Dennis and Arvella (Woods) B. B.B.A., U. Okla., 1966, J.D., 1968. Bar: Alta. 1969. Read law Saucier, Jones, Calgary, Alta., Can., assoc., 1969-70; asst. to pres. Regent Drilling Ltd., 1970-71; pres. Batoni-Bowlen Enterprises Ltd., 1971-79, Bowlen Holdings Ltd., Edmonton, Alta., Can., 1979—; pres., chief exec. officer, owner Denver Broncos, 1984—. Mem. Law Soc. Alta., Can. Bar Assn., Young Presidents Orgn. Roman Catholic. Clubs: Mayfair Golf and Country; Edmonton Petroleum; Outrigger Canoe (Honolulu). Office: Denver Broncos 13655 Broncos Pky Denver CO 80216 also: Denver Broncos 13665 E Davies Pl Englewood CO 80112-4004*

BOWLER, LARRY DEAN, state legislator; b. Sacramento, Calif., July 30, 1939; s. Maurice Lyle Bowler and Helen Lynette (St. Louis) Gilbert; m. Mary Frances Crowson, Sept. 3, 1960 (div. Feb. 1973); children: Monica, Darren; m. Melva Beatrice Hill, June 22, 1973; 1 child, Kimberly. AA, Sacramento City Coll.; BA, U. San Francisco. Instr. Los Rios C.C., Sacramento; dep. sheriff Sacramento Sheriff's Office, 1962-93; mem. Calif. State Legis., 1993—. Mem. River City Reps., Sacramento, 1993—; mem. state adv. bd. on drug problems Gov. of Calif. Mem. No. Calif. Detention and Corrections Assn. (pres.). Office: 10370 Old Placerville Rd Sacramento CA 95827-2520

BOWLIN, GREGORY LEE, marketing professional; b. Denver, June 1, 1955; s. Robert Lee and Beryl Audrey (Carter) B.; m. Rebecca Ann Richardson, July 29, 1978; children: Paul Matthew, John Michael. AA, Columbia Coll., 1983; BS in Tech. Mgmt. magna cum laude, Regis Coll., 1987. Pvt. pilot's lic., FAA. Flight info. drafter Jeppesen Sanderson, Inc., Englewood, Colo., 1973-77; flight info. compiler Jeppesen Sanderson, Inc., Englewood, 1977-80, airline tech. acct. exec., 1980-83, mgr. air carrier mktg./sales/svc., 1983-88, dir. ops. info. svcs., 1988-90, dir. chart svcs. mktg., 1990-91, dir. airline svcs., 1991-94, dir. mktg., sales and svc., 1990—, v.p. flight info. svcs. mktg., 1995—. Pres., treas. Highpoint Neighborhood Partnership, Aurora, Colo., 1988—. Mem. Am. Mktg. Assn. (exec. mem.), Aircraft Owners and Pilots Assn. Republican. Baptist. Office: Jeppesen Sanderson Inc 55 Inverness Dr E Englewood CO 80112-5412

BOWLIN, MICHAEL RAY, oil company executive; b. Amarillo, Tex., Feb. 20, 1943; m. Martha Ann Rowland; 1 child, John Charles. BBA, North Tex. State U., 1965, MBA, 1967. Scheduler prodn. and transp. A. Brant Co., Ft. Worth, 1965-66; mktg. rep. R.J. Reynolds Tobacco Bo., 1967-68; personnel generalist Atlantic Richfield Co., Dallas, 1969-71; coll. relations rep. Atlantic Richfield Co., Los Angeles, 1971-72, mgr. internal profl. placement, 1973, mgr. corp. recruiting and placement, 1973-75, mgr. behavioral sci. services, 1975, sr. v.p. ARCO resources adminstrn., 1985, sr. v.p. ARCO internat. oil and gas acquisitions, 1987, sr. v.p., 1987—; employee relations mgr. Atlantic Richfield Co., Alaska, 1975-77; v.p. employee relations Anaconda Copper Co. (div. Atlantic Richfield Co.), Denver, 1977-81; v.p. employee relations ARCO Oil & Gas (div. Atlantic Richfield Co.), Dallas, 1981-82, v.p. fin. planning and control, 1982-84; sr. v.p. Atlantic Richfield Co., 1985-92; pres. ARCO Coal Co., 1985-87, ARCO Internat. Oil & Gas Co., 1987-92; CEO Atlantic Richfield Co., 1994—; pres., COO ARCO Internat. Oil & Gas Co., 1993, 1993, pres., CEO, 1994-95, chmn., CEO, 1995—. Office: Atlantic Richfield Co 515 S Flower St Los Angeles CA 90071-2201

BOWLING, LANCE CHRISTOPHER, record producer, publisher; b. San Pedro, Calif., May 17, 1948; s. Dan Parker and Sylvia Lois (Van Devander) B. BA in Polit. Sci. and History, Pepperdine U., 1966-70, M in Pub. Adminstrn., 1973. Owner, founder Cambria Master Recordings, Palos Verdes, Calif., 1972—. Editor: Joseph Wagner: A Retrospective of Composer-Conductor 1900-74, 1976, Hazards Pavilion, Jour of Soc for Preservation of South Calif. Mus. Heritage, 1985—; author: Eugene Hemmer: Composer-Pianist, 1983; producer over 90 classical records including works by Charles W. Cadman, Madeleine Dring, Mary Carr Moore, John Crown, Ed Bland, Florence Price, Elinor Remick Warren, Miklos Rozsa, Erich W. Korngold, Max Steiner, Ernst Gold, William Grant Still, Arthur Lange, also classical music radio station documentaries. Active allocation com. Region V, United Way, L.A., 1978-85; bd. dirs. Soc. for the Preservation of Film Music, Hollywood, Calif., New World Ctr. for Arts, L.A., L.A. Ballet. Recipient Golden Rose award Pi Iota chpt. Phi Beta, 1988. Mem. ASCAP, Assn. Recorded Sound Collections, Music Libr. Assn., Soc. for the Preservation of Film Music, Sonneck Soc. Episcopalian. Clubs: Variety Arts (Los Angeles); Mus. Arts (Long Beach). Home: 2625 Colt Rd Palos Verdes Peninsula CA 90275-6578 Office: Cambria Records and Pub 1659 W 7th St San Pedro CA 90732-3421

BOWLT, JOHN ELLIS, Slavic language educator; b. London, Dec. 6, 1943; s. Percy John and Dorothy Mary (Ellis) B.; m. Nicoletta Misler, 1981. BA, U. Birmingham, 1965, MA, 1966; PhD, U. St. Andrews, 1971. Prof. Slavic lang. U. Tex., Austin, 1971-88, U. So. Calif., L.A., 1988—; vis. prof. U. Kans., Lawrence, 1970-71, Wellesley Coll., 1980, U. Otago, New Zealand, 1982, Hebrew U., Jerusalem, 1985; guest curator Dallas Mus. Fine Arts, Dallas, 1980. Author: Russian Avamt-Garde, 1976, Silver Age, 1980, catalog Journey into Non-Objectivity, 1982; co-author: Pavel Filonov, 1986, Russian Art in Thyssen-Bornemisza Collection, 1993. Fellow Brit. Coun. Moscow U., 1966-68, Nat. Humanities Inst. Yale U., 1977-78, Internat. Rsch. and Exchange Bd., 1986, 88, 91, 94; recipient awards Am. Coun. Learned Socs., Paris, 1981, Rome, 1986, Wolfson Found., Miami, Borchard Found., France, 1995. Mem. Am. Assn. Advancement of Slavic Studies. Office: U So Calif PO Box 4353 Los Angeles CA 90089-0001

BOWMAN, BRIAN, airport services terminal; b. 1937. With Ryan Herco Products Corp., Burbank, Calif.; with Burbank Glendale Pasadena, Burbank, Calif., 1986—, v.p., 1990—, now pres. Office: Burbank Glendale Pasadena 2627 N Hollywood Way Burbank CA 91505-1076*

BOWMAN, BRICE, artist, educator; b. Kansas City, Mo., June 10, 1951. BA in Art, Calif. State U., San Francisco, 1978; MA in Art, Calif. State U., Sacramento, 1982. Prof. Napa (Calif.) Coll., 1983-85; prof. Chabot Coll., Livermore, Calif., 1985, U. Calif., Davis, 1985; lectr. on art Bay Area TV Consortium, San Jose, Calif., 1986; prof. Coll. of Marin, Kentfield, Calif., 1989, Solano Coll., Suisun City, Calif., 1984—, U. Calif., Davis, 1993-94; lectr. on art Walnut Creek, Calif. Civic Arts, 1984—; instr. on art Mendocino, Calif. Art Ctr., 1992. Works include 193 oil paintings, more than 1200 water colors, more than 900 drawings. Recipient Jurors Choice award San Francisco Mus. Modern Art, 1986, 2d pl. award, 1987.

BOWMAN, BRUCE, art educator, writer, artist; b. Dayton, Ohio, Nov. 23, 1938; s. Murray Edgar Bowman and Mildred May (Moler) Elleman; m. Julie Ann Gosselin, 1970 (div. 1980); 1 child, Carrie Lynn. AA, San Diego City Coll., 1962; BA, Calif. State U.-Los Angeles, 1964, MA, 1968. Tchr. art North Hollywood Adult Sch., Calif., 1966-68; instr. art Cypress Coll., Calif., 1976-78, West Los Angeles Coll., 1969—; tchr. art Los Angeles City Schs., 1966—; seminar leader So. Calif., 1986—. Author: Shaped Canvas, 1976; Toothpick Sculpture and Ice Cream Stick Art, 1976; Ideas: How to Get Them, 1985, (cassette tape) Develop Winning Willpower, 1986, Waikiki, 1988. Contbr. articles to profl. jours. One-man shows include Calif. State U.-Los Angeles, 1968, Pepperdine U., Malibu, Calif., 1978; exhibited in group shows McKenzie Gallery, Los Angeles, 1968, Trebor Gallery, Los Angeles, 1970, Cypress Coll., Calif., 1977, Design Recycled Gallery, Fullerton, Calif., 1977, Pierce Coll., Woodland Hills, Calif., 1978, Leopold/Gold Gallery, Santa Monica, Calif., 1980. Served with USN, 1957-61. Home: 28322 Rey De Copas Ln Malibu CA 90265-4463

BOWMAN, GARY MARTIN, social worker; b. Chatham, Ont., Can., July 13, 1943; came to U.S., 1960; s. John Martin and Hilda Ruth (Shaw) B.; m. Gwendolyn Yit-Wah Lee, July 3, 1970 (div. Dec. 1982); m. Jacqueline Custis Miller Lien, Mar. 17, 1984; 1 child, Alexander Stewart Bauman-Bowman. BA, Graceland Coll., 1965; MSW, U. Hawaii, 1972. Pub. social service worker Linn County Dept. Social Svcs., Cedar Rapids, Iowa, 1965-

67; dir. Joint Services Recreation Assn. for Handicapped, Honolulu, 1967-69, 71-72; social group worker Adolescent Unit Hawaii State Hosp., Kaneohe, 1970-73, 81-83; coordinator adolescent mental health svcs. St. Joseph's Hosp. Health Ctr., Syracuse, N.Y., 1973-74; community services coordinator Elmcrest Children's Svcs., Syracuse, 1974-75; psychiat. social worker Santa Rosa County Mental Health ctr., Milton, Fla., 1975-80, St. Francis Hosp. Health Care, Honolulu, 1980-81, Los Angeles County Coastal Community Mental Health Ctr., Carson, Calif., 1984-86, West-Cen. Family Mental Health Svcs., Los Angeles, 1986—; pvt. practice cons., therapy and tng. Burbank, 1986—; adj. faculty mem. U. Syracuse, Western Fla. U. at Pensacola, U. Hawaii, 1976-83; trainer crisis mgmt. Syracuse Police Dept., 1974; presentor Hawaii-Pacific Gerontology Conf., 1981, Happy Valley Singles Camp, Santa Cruz, Calif., 1984, Stas. KRLA-AM, KBZT-FM Separation/Divorce Trauma, Pasadena, Calif., 1986, Parenting By Men Cable TV, 1988, Buckhorn Women's Camp on Grief and Reconnection, Idlewild, Calif., 1988, Erie Beach Camp Families, Ont., Can., 1989, Nurturing Adolescent Nonconformists to Help Group, Van Nuys, Calif., 1989, Parents Without Ptnrs., Glendale, Calif., 1991, St. Luke's Hosp., Pasadena, 1991; examiner Consumer Svcs. for Licensing Social Workers, State of Calif., 1995—. Author: Joys, Fears, Tears, 1968; editor (newsletter) The Javelin, 1967-69; co-producer, dir. an interfaith gospel, country, western and contemporary music concert Spring Info Action - Reach Out for Excellence, Burbank, Calif., 1991; contbr. articles and poems to mags. Bd. dirs., program chmn. Summer Action Vol. Youth Program, Honolulu, 1972-73, 80-83; pres. Friends of Libr. Santa Rosa County, Milton, 1979-80; founder singles separated divorced support group Reorganized Ch. Jesus Latter-day Saints, Burbank, Calif., 1985-92; founder Camp In Search Of, 1978-80; coord. Concert for Dr. Sharma-Candidate for Inglewood City Coun., 1993. Named Citizen for Day Sta. KGU, Honolulu, 1972; recipient Unheralded Humanitarianism, Dist. 1 Mental Health Bd., 1980. Mem. NASW (diplomate clin. social work, cert., steering con. region H&I Calif. 1983—, alt. dir. region H Calif. 1984-85, chmn. licensing com. 1979-80, mem. program and continuing edn. coms. 1980-83, Loyal and Dedicated Leadership award 1980), Kiwanis (co-dir. Surrender Outreach Sports program 1991 Burbank club), Optimist (youth ctr. dir. Hiawatha, Iowa club 1966-67). Home: 4433 Sinova St Los Angeles CA 90032-1452

BOWMAN, JEAN LOUISE, lawyer, civic worker; b. Albuquerque, Apr. 3, 1938; d. David Livingstone and Charlotte Louise (Smith) McArthur; student U. N.Mex., 1956-57, U. Pa., 1957-58, Rocky Mountain Coll., 1972-74; B.A. in Polit. Sci. with high honors, U. Mont., 1982, J.D., 1985; children—Carolyn Louise, Joan Emily, Amy Elizabeth, Eric Daniel. Dir. Christian edn. St. Luke's Episcopal Ch., 1979-80; law clk. to assoc. justice Mont. Supreme Ct., 1985-87; exec. v.p. St. Peter's Community Hospital Found., 1987-91; exec. dir. Harrison Hosp. Found., Bremerton, Wash., 1991-93, St. Patrick Hosp. and Health Found., 1993—, Missoula Symphony Bd., 1993—; dir. 1st Bank West. Bd. trustees Rocky Mountain Coll., 1972-80; bd. dirs. Billings (Mont.) Area C. of C., 1977-80; mem. City-County Air Pollution Control Bd., 1969-74, chmn., 1970-71; del. Mont. State Constnl. Conv., 1971-72, sec. conv., 1971-72; chmn. County Local Govt. Study Commn., 1973-76; mem. Billings Sch. Dist. Long Range Planning Com., 1978-79; former pres. Billings LWV, dir., 1987-91, pres. Helena LWV, 2d v.p. Mont. LWV; former pres. Silver Run Ski Club. Named one of Billings' most influential citizens, Billings Gazette, 1977; Bertha Morton Scholar, 1982. Rotary. Republican. Home: 1911 E Broadway St Missoula MT 59802-4901

BOWMAN, JEFFREY R., protective services official; b. Akron, Ohio, Apr. 24, 1952; s. Roger Heath and Ruth Ann (Corrigan) B.; divorced; children: Katie, Andrew, Brian. BS in Orgnl. Behavior, U. San Francisco, 1986. Firefighter Anaheim (Calif.) Fire Dept., 1973-75, paramedic, 1975-79, capt., 1979-83, battalion chief, 1983-85, div. chief, 1985-86, fire chief, 1986—. Pres. bd. dirs. Anaheim Boys and Girls Club, 1988—; chmn. fundraising Boy Scouts Am., Anaheim, 1988. Mem. Internat. Assn. Fire Chiefs, Calif. Fire Chiefs Assn. Office: Anaheim Fire Dept PO Box 3222 500 E Broadway Anaheim CA 92805-4099*

BOWMAN, JON ROBERT, editor, film critic; b. Spokane, Wash., Nov. 9, 1954; s. Donald Ken and Carolyn Joyce (Crutchfield) B.; m. Geraldine Maria Jaramillo, Jan. 27, 1979 (div. Dec. 1985); m. Amy Farida Siswayanti, May 23, 1992. BA, U. N.Mex., 1976. Reporter, arts editor, news editor N.Mex. Daily Lobo, Albuquerque, 1972-76; film critic Albuquerque Jour., 1974-76; reporter Alamogordo (N.Mex.) Daily News, 1976; sci. writer, editor Los Alamos (N.Mex.) Monitor, 1976-81; reporter, arts editor New Mexican, Santa Fe, 1981-86, film critic, 1987—; editor New Mexico Mag., Santa Fe, 1986—; guest lectr. U. N.Mex., Coll. Santa Fe, 1976—. Author: (with others) Explore New Mexico, 1988, A New Mexico Scrapbook, 1990, Day Trip Discoveries: Selected New Mexico Excursions, 1993; contbr. articles to mags. and newspapers; author salutes for Greer Garson, James Coburn, and John Huston for festivals honoring them. Vol. tchr. Albuquerque pub. schs., 1972-76; organizer film festivals Albuquerque and Santa Fe. 1972-91, benefits including Ctr. for Contemporary Arts, Santa Fe. Recipient Sci. Writing award AP, 1978, citation AP, 1979, others. Mem. Regional Pub. Assn., City and Regional Mag. Assn. Home: 335 W Manhattan Ave Santa Fe NM 87501 Office: NMex Mag Lew Wallace Bldg 495 Old Santa Fe Trl Santa Fe NM 87503

BOWMAN, LARRY WAYNE, investigator, English and criminal justice educator; b. Mansfield, Ohio, Feb. 8, 1952; s. Ted L. Bowman and Mary Lou (Devore) Dessenberg. B in Criminal Justice, U. Md., 1978, M in Criminal Justice, 1980; MBA, So. Inst. Tech., 1987, MA English Lit., 1994. Lic. pvt. investigator. Pvt. investigator Ohio and Mont., 1974—; English and criminal justice prof. Yeung Jin Coll., Taegu, South Korea, 1994—; security cons., 1974-92; drug awareness educator, 1974-92. Mast. USAF, 1970-74, with Res. ret., 1992. Named Outstanding Young Man of Am., 1988. Mem. VFW (life), NRA, Air Force Security Police Assn., Am. C. of C. (Korea), Am. Legion, Lions, Optimist, Elks. Democrat. Presbyterian. Home: PO Box 6193 Great Falls MT 59406-6193 Office: Yeung Jin Coll, 218 Boklyun Dong Puk-gu, Taegu 702-020, Republic of Korea

BOWMAN, MICHAEL O., interior designer; b. Bluffton, Ind., Mar. 24, 1946; s. Daniel B. and Hilda M. (Steffen) B.; m. Rachel Valencia Bowman, Mar. 20, 1971; children: Catharine M. Bowman-French, Rachel Anne. Student, Parson's, Paris, 1979. Designer/mgr. Saxton's Inc., Tacoma, Wash., 1968-81, owner, 1981-91; owner Michael Bowman Interiors, Seattle, 1989-91; designer/mgr. Greenbaum's Home Furnishing, Bellevue, Wash., 1992-93, Westbay Interiors, Gig Harbor, Wash., 1994—. With U.S. Army, 1965-68. Recipient Design for Better Living award Am. Wood Coun., 1990. Mem. Am. Soc. Interior Designers (cert., bd. dirs. 1994—), Rotary, Elks, Tacoma C. of C. (mem. Pres.'s Club 1989-90). Roman Catholic. Office: Westbay Interiors Gig Harbor WA 98335

BOWMAN, ROBERT WILLIAM, minister; b. San Francisco, Mar. 10, 1947; s. Harold Emmet and Jeanne Suzanne (Klinger) B. BS, U. of State of N.Y., Albany, 1970; ThB, Geneva Theol., 1972; MCEd, Reformed Theol. Sem., 1980, MEd, 1985; STD, Geneva Theol. Sem., 1990. Ordained to ministry Episcopal Ch., 1971, Presbyn. Ch., 1982; cert. tchr. elem. and secondary; cert. adminstr. Rector St. Andrew's Episcopal Ch., Savannah, Ga., 1971-78, St. Paul's Episcopal Ch., Jackson, Miss., 1978-80; supply min. Holy Trinity Episcopal, Jacksonville, Fla., 1973-78, Ch. of the Nativity, Memphis, 1981-82; asst. pastor Orangewood Presbyn., Orlando, Fla., 1983-87; headmaster Orangewood Christian Sch., Orlando, 1983-87; asst. headmaster Northlake Christian Sch., Covington, La., 1980-82; assoc. pastor Ind. Presbyn. Ch., Savannah, Ga., 1987-92; trustee Covenant Coll., Lookout Mountain, Ga., 1986-90, 91-92; founder, bd. v.p. The Westminster Sch., Savannah, 1989-93; head Bridgemont Middle Sch., San Francisco, 1993—. Named Citizen of Day City of Savannah, 1977. Mem. Am. Assn. Tchr. French, Assn. Christian Sch. Adminstrs., Nat. Middle Sch. Assn., Nat. Assn. Secondary Sch. Prins., No. Calif. Presbytery PCA. Republican.

BOWNE, MARTHA HOKE, magazine editor, consultant; b. Greeley, Colo., June 9, 1931; d. George Edwin and Krin (English) Hoke; children: Gretchen, William, Kay, Judith. BA, U. Mich., 1952; postgrad., Syracuse U., 1965. Tchr. Wayne (Mich.) Pub. Schs., 1953-54, East Syracuse and Minoa Cen. Schs., Minoa, N.Y., 1965-68; store mgr. Fabric Barn, Fayetteville, N.Y., 1969-77; store owner Fabric Fair, Oneida, N.Y., 1978-80; producer, owner Quilting by the Sound, Port Townsend, Wash., 1987—, Quilting by the Lake, Cazenovia, N.Y., 1981—; organizer symposium Am. Quilters Soc.; founder, pres. Quilter's Quest Video Prodns., 1994. Contbr. articles to profl. jours. Mem., pres. Minoa Library, 1960-75; mem. Onondaga County Library, Syracuse, 1968-71. Mem. Nat. Quilting Assn., Am. Quilters Soc. (editor Am. Quilter mag. 1985—), New Eng. Quilt Mus. Home: 12 Brook Bay Rd Mercer Island WA 98040-4622

BOWSHER, ARTHUR LEROY, geologist, researcher, petroleum company executive; b. Wapakoneta, Ohio, Apr. 29, 1917; s. Dallas and Sally Loraine (Fox) B.; m. Lanorah Jane Higgins, Oct. 17, 1943 (div. Dec. 1965); m. Ruth E. Webber, Aug. 29, 1967; children: Sally Jane Drake, Arthur L. Jr., Anne Lorraine Atkinson, Dale C. BS in Petroleum Engring., U. Tulsa, 1941; postgrad., U. Kans., 1941-42, 46-47. Cert. geologist. Assoc. curator U.S. Nat. Mus., Washington, 1947-52; geologist U.S. Geol. Survey, Fairbanks, Alaska, 1952-57; chief exploration strategist U.S. Geol. Survey, Menlo Park, Calif., 1978-81; explorationist Arco and Sinclair Oil and Gas Co., Tulsa, Dallas, 1957-70; staff geologist Arabian Am. Oil Co., Dhahran, Saudi Arabia, 1970-78; sr. geologist Yates Petroleum Corp., Artesia, N.Mex., 1981-86, cons., 1986—; instr. U. Tulsa, 1938-41; instr. and geologist U. Kans., Lawrence, 1941-42, 46-47. Contbr. articles to profl. jours. Served to capt. U.S. Army C.E. Mem. Am. Assn. Petroleum Geologists (emeritus), Roswell Geol. Soc., Paleontologic Soc. Republican. Methodist. Home and Office: 2707 Gaye Dr Roswell NM 88201-3428

BOWYER, JANE BAKER, science educator; b. Dayton, Ohio, Mar. 16, 1934; d. Homer Kenneth and Helen Elizabeth (Brown) Baker; m. Charles Stuart Bowyer, Feb. 27, 1957; children: William Stuart, Robert Baker, Elizabeth Ann. BA, Miami U., Oxford, Ohio, 1956; MA, U. Calif., Berkeley, 1972, PhD, 1974. Abbie Valley prof. Mills Coll., Oakland, Calif., 1985—, head dept. edn., 1985—; cons. Lawrence Hall Sci., U. Calif., Berkeley, 1975—, Nat. Assn. Ednl. Progress, 1975-78, Utah State Bd. Edn., 1985-86; mem. Calif. Round Table's Math/Sci. Task Force, 1983-85; dir. ednl. research Industry Initiatives in Sci. and Math Edn., 1985-86, bd. dirs., 1985—; dir. Mills Coll./Oakland Unified Sch. Dist. Partnership, 1985—; dir. midcareer math. and sci. tchr. R&D, NSF, 1987—, prin. investigator and dir. systemic reform program, 1994—, Leadership Inst. Teaching Elem. Sci., Mills and Oakland, Calif., 1994—. Author: Science and Society, 1984, Science and Society Activity Book, 1984; contbr. articles to profl. jours. Bd. dirs. Oakland Sci. and Art Sch., 1979-82, Eric Erickson Sch., San Francisco, 1983-85; prin. investigator Projects in Sci. Edn.; cons. UNESCO, Paris Div. Sci. Edn., 1989-90, 93. Fulbright Research fellow, Germany, 1982-83. Mem. AAAS, Nat. Assn. Research in Sci. Teaching (mem. editorial bd. 1980-82, bd. dirs. 1985-88, Outstanding Paper award, 1979, 81), Am. Ednl. Research Orgn., Mortar Bd. Home: 147 Overhill Rd Orinda CA 94563-3110

BOWYER, JOAN ELIZABETH, medical technologist, realtor; b. Ellensburg, Wash., July 11, 1944; d. Chester Joseph and Rita Geneva (Newell) Howarth; 1 child, Suzanne Elise. BA, Ft. Wright Coll. of Holy Names, 1966; grad., Real Estate Sch. Oreg., 1982. Lic. med. technologist. Med. technologist Lab. of Clin. Medicine, Seattle, 1967-69, Sacred Heart Gen. Hosp., Eugene, Oreg., 1969-73, 74-76, McKenzie Willamette Hosp., Springfield, Oreg., 1976-77, Mid-Columbia Hosp., The Dalles, Oreg., 1977-82; realtor Red Carpet/Rick Hall Realty, Hillsboro, Oreg., 1982-85, Century 21 Columbia Realty, Portland, 1985—; med. technologist ARC, Portland, 1982-89, Corning Nicholas Inst. formerly Physicians Med. Lab., 1989-95, East Moreland Hosp., 1995—. Co-editor: The Dalles Gen. Hosp. Newspaper, 1980-82. Pres. Wasco County Edn. Service Dist. Parents Group, The Dalles, 1978-82; founder, pres. Mid-Columbia Parents of Deaf, 1978-82; parental spokesperson Spl. Edn. Adv. Com., Salem, Oreg., 1980-82; activist parent for deaf/hearing impaired, 1977—. Mem. Med. Technologists of Am. Soc. Pathologists, Nat. Assn. Realtors, NAFE, Century 21 Investment Soc., Million Dollar Club. Democrat. Avocations: photography, dancing, hiking, travel. Home: 704 SE 38th Ave Portland OR 97214-3206 Office: Century 21 Columbia 2208 SE 182nd Ave Portland OR 97233-5608

BOXER, ALAN LEE, accountant; b. Denver, Sept. 9, 1935; s. Ben B. and Minnette (Goldman) B.; m. Gayle, Dec. 21, 1958; children: Michael E., Jodi S., Richard S. BSBA in Acctg., U. Denver, 1956. CPA, Colo. Audit mgr. Touche, Ross & Co. CPAs, Denver, 1956-60, Ballin, Milstein & Feinstein CPAs, Denver, 1960-61; prin. Alan L. Boxer, CPA, Denver, 1961-69; v.p and treas. Pawley Co., Denver, 1969-78; pres. Sci-Pro Inc., Denver, 1978-82; regional mgr. A.T.V. Systems, Inc., Denver, 1982-83; prin. The Enterprise Group, Denver, 1983-86; shareholder, pres. Allerdice, Baroch, Boxer & Co., CPAs, Denver, 1986-87; prin. Alan L. Boxer, CPA, Denver, 1987—. Bd. dirs. Anti-Defamation League, Denver, 1986-90, BMH Congregation, Denver, 1986—, treas. 1990-93, v.p. 1993—. Mem. Am. Inst. CPAs, Colo. Soc. CPAs, Bnai Brith #171 (pres. 1982, trustee 1983-89). Democrat. Jewish.

BOXER, BARBARA, senator; b. Bklyn., Nov. 11, 1940; d. Ira and Sophie (Silvershein) Levy; m. Stewart Boxer, 1962; children: Doug, Nicole. BA in Econ., Bklyn. Coll., 1962. Stockbroker, econ. rschr. N.Y. Securities Firm, N.Y.C., 1962-65; journalist, assoc. editor Pacific Sun, 1972-74; congl. aide to rep. 5th Congl. Dist. San Francisco, 1974-76; mem. Marin County Bd. Suprs., San Rafael, Calif., 1976-82; mem. 98th-102d Congresses from 6th Calif. dist., mem. armed services com., select com. children, youth and families; majority whip at large, co-chair Mil. Reform Caucus, chair subcom. on govt. activities and transp. of house govt. ops. com., 1990-93, U.S. senator from Calif., 1993—, mem. banking, housing and urban affairs com., mem. budget com., mem. environ. and pub. works com. Pres. Marin County Bd. Suprs., 1980-81; mem. Bay Area Air Quality Mgmt. Bd., San Francisco, 1977-82, pres., 1979-81; bd. dirs. Golden Gate Bridge Hwy. and Transport Dist., San Francisco, 1978-82; founding mem. Marin Nat. Women's Polit. Caucus; pres. Dem. New Mems. Caucus, 1983. Recipient Open Govt. award Common Cause, 1980, Rep. of Yr. award Nat. Multiple Sclerosis Soc., 1990, Margaret Sanger award Planned Parenthood, 1990, Women of Achievement award Anti-defamation League, 1990. Jewish. Office: US Senate 112 Hart Senate Office Bldg Washington DC 20510-0505*

BOXER, JEROME HARVEY, computer and management consultant, vintner; b. Chgo., Nov. 27, 1930; s. Ben Avrum and Edith (Lyman) B.; AA magna cum laude, East L.A. Coll., 1952; m. Sandra Schaffner, June 17, 1980; children by previous marriage: Michael, Jodi. AB with honors, Calif. State U., L.A., 1954. CPA, Calif; cert. systems profl. Lab. instr. Calif. State U., L.A., 1953-54; staff acct. Dolman, Freeman & Buchalter, L.A., 1955-57; sr. acct. Neiman, Sanger, Miller & Beress, L.A., 1957-63; ptnr. firm Glynn and Boxer, CPAs, L.A., 1964-68; v.p., sec. Glynn, Boxer & Phillips Inc., CPA's, L.A.and Glendale, 1968-90, pvt. practice cons., 1990—; owner Oak Valley Vineyard; pres. Echo Data Svcs., Inc., 1978-90; instr. data processing L.A. City Adult Schs.; tchr. lectr., cons. wines and wine-tasting; instr. photography. Mem. ops. bd. Everywoman's Village; bd. dirs., v.p. So. Calif. Jewish Hist. Soc., v.p. Jewish Hist. Soc. of the Ctrl. Coast; co-founder Open Space Theatre; former officer Ethel Josephine Scantland Found.; past post adviser Explorer Scouts, Boy Scouts Am., also Eagle Scout. Recipient Youth Service award Mid-Valley YMCA, 1972-73; Mem. Am. Inst. CPAs, Calif. Soc. CPAs, Assn. for Systems Mgmt., Data Processing Mgmt. Assn., Am. Fedn. Musicians, Am. Jewish Hist. Soc., Friends of Photography, L.A. Photog. Ctr., Acad. Model Aeros., Nat. Model Railroad Assn., Maltese Falcons Home Brewing Soc., San Fernando Valley Silent Flyers, San Fernando Valley Radio Control Flyers, Associated Students Calif. State U., Los Angeles (hon. life), Acad. Magical Arts, Internal Brotherhood of Magicians, Soc. Preservation of Variety Arts, Am. Wine Soc., Knights of the Vine, Soc. Wine Educators, Napa Valley Wine Libr. Alumni Assn., L.A.-Bordeaux Sister City Affiliation, Soc. Bacchus Am., Paso Robles Dem. Club (pres. 1993), Ctrl. Coast Winegrowers Assn., Wines and Steins, Cellarmasters, Paso Robles Vintners and Growers Assn., German Shepherd Dog Club Am., German Shepherd Dog Club Los Angeles County, Blue Key, Alpha Phi Omega. Clubs: Verdugo, Exchange, Kiwanis (pres. Sunset-Echo Park 1968), Braemar Country, Pacific Mariners Yacht, S.Coast Corinthian Yacht (former dir., officer), B'nai B'rith. Cons., contbr. Wine World Mag., 1974-82. Home and Office: 1660 Circle B Rd Paso Robles CA 93446-9595

BOXER, LESTER, lawyer; b. N.Y.C., Oct. 19, 1935; s. Samuel and Anna Lena (Samovar) B.; m. Frances Barenfeld, Sept. 17, 1961; children: Kimberly Brett, Allison Joy. AA, UCLA, 1955, BS, 1957; JD, U. So. Calif., 1961. Bar: Calif. 1962; U.S. Dist. Ct. (cen. dist.) Calif. 1962. Assoc. Bautzer & Grant, Beverly Hills, Calif., 1961-63; pvt. practice Beverly Hills, 1963-65, 69—; ptnr. Boxer & Stoll, Beverly Hills, 1965-69; pvt. practice, 1969—. Mem. Calif. Bar Assn., L.A. County Bar Assn., Beverly Hills Bar Assn., Friars Club. Office: 1875 Century Park E Ste 2000 Los Angeles CA 90067-2521

BOYAJIAN, TIMOTHY EDWARD, public health officer, educator, consultant; b. Fresno, Calif., Feb. 22, 1949; s. Ernest Adam and Marge (Medzian) B.; m. Tassanee Bootdeesri, Apr. 23, 1987. BS in Biology, U. Calif., Irvine, 1975; M of Pub. Health, UCLA, 1978. Registered environ. health specialist, Calif. Rsch. asst. UCLA, 1978-81; lectr. Chapman U., 29 Palms, Calif., 1982-84, 88-89; refugee relief vol. Cath. Relief Svcs., Surin, Thailand, 1985-86; lectr. Nat. Univ., L.A., 1989-91; environ. health specialist Riverside County Health Svcs. Agy., Palm Springs, Calif., 1991—; cons. parasitologist S. Pacific Commn., L.A., 1979; pub. health cons. several vets. groups, L.A., 1981-84, Assn. S.E. Asian Nations, Bangkok, Thailand, 1988. Veterans rights activist, Vietnam Vet. Groups, L.A., 1981-84. With USMC, Vietnam, 1969-71. Recipient U.S. Pub. Health Traineeship, U.S. Govt., L.A., 1977-81. Mem. VFW, Calif. Environ. Health Assn.. Home: PO Box 740 Palm Springs CA 92263-0740

BOYARSKI, ADAM MICHAEL, physicist; b. North Bank, Alberta, Can., Apr. 14, 1935; came to U.S., 1963; s. Albert and Mary (Roskiewich) B.; m. Lorretta Sramek, June 1, 1968; children: Lisa A., Mike A. BA in Sci., U. Toronto, 1958; PhD, M.I.T., 1962. Rsch. assoc. M.I.T., Cambridge, 1962-63; staff physicist Stanford (Calif.) Linear Accelerator Ctr., 1963—; cons. in field. Author: (software) HANDYPAK, A Histogram and Display Package, 1980; contbr. articles to scientific jours. Coach Little League Baseball, Los Altos, Calif., 1980-83, Am. Youth Soccer Orgn., Los Altos, 1979-81. Mem. Am. Phys. Soc. Office: SLAC 2575 Sand Hill Rd Menlo Park CA 94025-7015

BOYARSKY, BENJAMIN WILLIAM, journalist; b. Berkeley, Calif., Oct. 21, 1934; s. Herman and Naomi (Heimy) B.; m. Nancy Elaine Belling, July 21, 1956; children: Robin Ann, Jennifer Lynn. AB, U. Calif., Berkeley, 1956. Copy boy, reporter Oakland (Calif.) Tribune, 1953-60; reporter, editor AP, San Francisco, 1960, Sacramento, 1960-70; polit. writer L.A. Times, 1970-75; nat. polit. writer L.A. Times, Washington, 1975-76; writer met. staff L.A. Times, 1976-78, chief city-county bur., 1978-89, columnist, 1989—. Author: The Rise of Ronald Reagan: Backroom Politics, 1974, (with wife) Ronald Reagan: His Life and Rise to the Presidency, 1981. Office: LA Times Times Mirror Sq Los Angeles CA 90012-3816

BOYCE, ALLAN R., human resources executive; b. Chgo., Aug. 27, 1943; s. John Allan and Ruth (Palmer) B.; m. Sally Ely, June 28, 1969; children—Laura, Jennifer. B.A., Dartmouth Coll., 1965; M.B.A., Stanford U., 1969. With Burlington No. R.R., St. Paul, 1969-81; asst. v.p. exec. dept. Burlington No. R.R., 1976-81; v.p. pub. affairs Burlington No., Inc., Seattle, 1981-84; sr. v.p. human resources Burlington No., Inc., 1984-88; sr. v.p. human resources, adminstrn. Burlington Resources, 1989—. Bd. dirs. Mcpl. League, Seattle, 1981—. Served to lt. USNR, 1965-67. Office: Burlington No Inc 777 Main St Fort Worth TX 76102

BOYCE, ANDREA ZYGMUNT, nurse; b. Miami, Fla., Sept. 17, 1956; d. Joseph A. and Eleanor F. (Haduck) Zygmunt; m. Brian W. Boyce, Apr. 27, 1985. BS in Nursing, Our Lady of Angels Coll., 1978. RN, Pa., Calif., Utah; cert. ACLS, BCLS, NRP, PALS. Staff nurse, then asst. head nurse pediatric intensive care St. Christopher's Hosp. Children, Phila., 1978-84; head nurse neonatal ICU, pediatrics Osteo. Med. Ctr., Phila., 1985-88, staff nurse pediatrics, emergency rm., 1988-90; staff nurse emergency rm. Doctors Hosp. of Montclair, 1990; mobile intensive care nurse emergency dept. Ontario (Calif.) Community Hosp., 1992-94; staff nurse pediatric intensive care Primary Childrens Med. Ctr., Salt Lake City, 1994—. Home: 1888 Foxmoor Pl Sandy UT 84092-5212

BOYCE, JAMES WARD, JR., association director, retired military officer; b. Childress, Tex., Dec. 17, 1936; s. James Ward and Minta (Smart) B.; m. Mary Ray Graves, June 24, 1961; children: Beverly Susan, Mary Elizabeth. BS in Mech. Engring., Texas A&M, 1960; MS in Guidance and Counseling, Ball State U., 1973. Commd. 2d lt. USAF, 1960, advanced through grades to col., 1981, navigator F-101B, RF-4C, 1960-74, staff officer, 1974-75; comdt. command NCO Acad. USAF, Bergstrom AFB, Tex., 1975-78, staff officer, 1978-80; comdr. gunnery range USAF, Gila Bend, Ariz., 1980-81; comdr. Cannon AFB USAF, Clovis, N.Mex., 1981-83; comdr. Zaragoza (Spain) Air Base USAF, 1983-86; dir. nuclear weapons test Def. Nuclear Agy. USAF, Albuquerque, 1986-87; comdr. March AFB USAF, Moreno Valley, Calif., 1987; ret. USAF, 1988; exec. dir. Am. Fighter Aces Assn., Mesa, Ariz., 1988—. Author: Training Aircraft of the Air Force, 1964; editor Am. Fighter Aces Assn. Bull., 1988—. Elder 1st Presbyn. Ch., Mesa, 1991-93. Decorated DFC, Air medal, Meritorious Svc. medal. Mem. VFW, Air Force Assn., Am. Fighter Aces Assn. (hon.), Am. Aviation Hist. Soc. Republican. Home: 1845 E Hale St Mesa AZ 85203-3916 Office: Am Fighter Aces Assn 4636 E Fighter Aces Dr Mesa AZ 85215-2502

BOYCE, KER, electrophysiologist, cardiologist; b. Augusta, Ga., Mar. 30, 1961; s. Andrew Summers and Monique Dechezelle (Davis) B. BS with high honors, Ga. Inst. Tech., 1979; MD, Emory U., 1983. Internship Emory U., Atlanta, 1983-84, resident in internal medicine, 1983-86; commd. ens. USN, 1979, advanced through grades to comdr., 1994; force med. officer U.S. Naval Support Force Antarctica, 1987-89; cardiology fellow Naval Hosp., San Diego, 1989-92; staff cardiology Naval Med. Ctr., San Diego, 1992-93, cardiology divsn. head, 1993—; electropsychology fellow U. Calif. San Diego Med. Ctr., 1991-92. Contbr. articles to profl. jours. Fellow ACP, Am. Coll. Cardiology; mem. Undersea and Hyperbasic Med. Soc., Aerospace Medicine Assn., Am. Heart Assn., Am. Soc. Circumpolar Health. Republican. Episcopalian. Office: Naval Med Ctr Cardiology Div San Diego CA 92134

BOYCE, MARY ELIZABETH, management educator, consultant; b. Chattanooga, Mar. 20, 1956; d. Everett Robert and Faith (Sandford) B. BA in Human Svcs., U. Tenn., 1978; MA in Social Sci., Azusa Pacific U., 1982; PhD in Human and Orgn. Systems, Fielding Inst., Santa Barbara, Calif., 1990. Pers. asst. Internat. Students, Inc., Colorado Springs, Colo., 1978--80, field worker, 1980-82, staff devel. specialist, 1985-86; internat. student coord. Azusa (Calif.) Pacific U., 1980-82; dir. counseling Calif. Luth. U., Thousand Oaks, 1982-85; assoc. dir. residence life Chapman Coll., Orange, Calif., 1986-88; mem. adj. faculty dept. mgmt. and bus. Whitehead Ctr., U. Redlands, Calif., 1988-90, asst. prof., 1990—; cons. on orgn. devel. Mem. NOW, Orgn. Behavior Teaching Soc., Acad. Mgmt., Western Acad. Mgmt., OD Network. Democrat. Office: U Redlands Whitehead Ctr 1200 E Colton Ave Redlands CA 92374-3755

BOYD, EDWARD HASCAL, retired military officer; b. Kevil, Ky., Sept. 4, 1934; s. Lloyd E. and D. Irene (Steinbeck) B.; m. D. Ann Creecy, Jan. 13, 1956 (dec. Mar. 1970); children: Lawrence H., Debra A.; m. Margaret Lorene Hogan, Nov. 7, 1970; 1 child, Laura Irene. AA, Phoenix Coll., 1954; BS, Ariz. State U., 1956, MBA, 1972. Cert. secondary tchr., Ariz. Commd. 2d lt. USMC, 1956, advanced through ranks to col., 1980, exec. officer Marine Detachment USS Helena, 1959-60; assigned Marine Corps Recruit Depot, San Diego, 1961-63; instr. ops. and intelligence Landing Force Tng. Command USMC, 1963-65, mem. 1st Bn. 4th Marines, 1966-67, instr. Amphibious Warfare Sch., 1967-70, Hdqrs. USMC, 1973-76; assigned to Devel. Ctr. Marine Corps Devel. and Edn. Command, 1977-80; comdr. Hdqrs. Bn., Camp Pendleton, Calif., 1981-84; ret. USMC, 1984; substitute tchr. Mesa (Ariz.) Unified Sch. Dist., 1984-86. Mem. Marine Corps Assn., Ret. Officers Assn., SAR, Alta Mesa Country Club, Delta Pi Epsilon, Alpha Tau Omega. Home: 5851 E Elmwood St Mesa AZ 85205-5833

BOYD, HARRY DALTON, lawyer, former insurance company executive; b. Huntington Park, Calif., June 13, 1923; s. Randall and Thelma L. (Lewis) B.; m. Margaret Jeanine Gamewell, June 13, 1948; children—Leslie Boyd Cotton, Wayne, Lynn Boyd Denby, Evan, Lance. LL.B., U. So. Calif., 1949, LL.M., 1960; Asso. in Mgmt., Ins. Inst. Am., 1972. Bar: Calif. bar 1950. Pvt. practice Los Angeles; assoc. Harvey & Viereck, Los Angeles, 1952-55; assoc. gen. counsel, corp. sec. Farmers Ins. Group, Los Angeles, 1955-77;

group v.p., gen. counsel Swett & Crawford Group, Los Angeles, 1977-83; gen. counsel, dir. Harbor Ins. Co., 1983-89; Calif. counsel Continental Ins. Co., 1987-89; of counsel Fidler & Bell, Burbank, Calif., 1990-93, Richard E. Garcia, Atty. at Law, L.A., 1994—; bd. dirs. FIG Fed. Credit Union, 1958-61, pres., 1960-61; mem. Sherman Oaks Property Owners Assn., 1967—, pres., 1969, 72; mem. Western Ins. Info. Svc., Spkrs. Bur., 1971-77; bd. dirs. Buffalo Reins. Co., 1983-87; expert witness in ins. litigation, 1990—. Mem. adv. council Chandler Elementary Sch., 1970-73; mem. adv. council Milliken Jr. High Sch., 1973-74. Served with USAAF, 1943-46. Mem. Calif. Ins. Guarantee Assn. (bd. govs. 1972-77), Los Angeles County Bar Assn. (chmn. exec. com. corp. law depts. sect. 1971-72), Reins. Assn. Am. (legal com. 1979-81), Nat. Assn. Ind. Insurers (chmn. surplus lines com. 1980-82), Calif. Assn. Ins. Cos. (exec. com. 1979-83), Wilshire C. of C. (bd. dirs. 1971-79, pres. 1975), Nat. Assn. Ins. Commrs. (industry adv. com. on reins. regulation 1983-90), Am. Arbitration Assn. (arbitrator). Republican. Lutheran (pres. council 1964-65). Home: 13711 Weddington St Van Nuys CA 91401-5825 Office: Richard E Garcia Atty Law 3700 Wilshire Blvd Los Angeles CA 90010-2901

BOYD, JOHN GARTH, manufacturing production and operations consultant; b. Greeley, Colo., Sept. 17, 1942; s. Jack Gardner and Madelyn Ilene (Bucher) B.; m. Cherie Kay Graves, Mar. 16, 1962 (div. June 1982); children: Jeffrey G., Daryl I., Peggy N.; m. Ellen Lea Meyers, Aug. 8, 1987; 1 child, Ian T. BA, U. No. Colo., 1963; MA, Colo. State U., 1965; MS, U. Colo., 1972. Teaching asst. Colo. State U., Ft. Collins, 1964-65; instr. No. Ariz. U., Flagstaff, 1965-67; teaching asst. U. Colo., Boulder, 1967-72; systems rep. Burroughs Corp., Englewood, Colo., 1972-76; mgr. Touche Ross & Co., Denver, 1977-84; chief fin. officer, chief operating officer Catalina Controls Corp., Longmont, Colo., 1984-86; ptnr. High Plains Ptnrship., Boulder, 1987—; adminstr. Martin Marietta Astronautics Group, Denver, 1988-92, honorarium instr. Grad. Sch. Bus. Adminstrn., U. Colo.-Denver, 1991—; instr. U. Denver, U. Coll., 1992—, Coll. Enging. and Applied Sci., U. Colo.-Boulder, 1995. Scoutmaster Boy Scouts Am., Boulder, 1969-72, troop scoutmaster, Denver, 1972-75; loaned exec. Colo. Gov.'s Mgmt. and Efficiency Study, 1982; chair house dist. 26 Jefferson County Dem. Party, 1994—. NASA fellow, 1968. Mem. Am. Soc. Quality Control, Am. Prodn. and Inventory Control Soc. (treas. Denver 1983-84, pres. 1984-85, Gold award 1985). Avocations: hiking, mountain climbing, fishing, cross-country skiing. Office: High Plains Ptnrship 9381 W Louisiana Ave Lakewood CO 80232-5178

BOYD, JOHN WILLARD, engineer, educator; b. Danville, Va., Aug. 19, 1925; s. John Willard and Marie Lee (Perry) B.; m. Winifred Marie Graham, June 4, 1950; children: Eric, Donna, John, Julie, Carol. BS in Aerospace Engring., Va. Poly. Inst., 1946; MS in Aerospace Engring., Stanford (Calif.) U., 1956, MBA, 1966. Aeronautical researcher Ames Rsch. Ctr., Moffett Field, Calif., 1947-61, tech. asst. dir. aerospace, 1961-63, tech. asst. dir. astronautics, 1963-65, rsch. asst. to the dir., 1966-70, dep. dir. aerospace and flight systems, 1970-78; assoc. dir. Ames Rsch. Ctr./NASA, Moffett Field, 1980-83; dep. dir. Dryden Flight Rsch. Ctr./NASA, Edwards AFB, Calif., 1979-80; assoc. adminstr. for mgmt. NASA Hdqrs., Washington, 1983-84; exec. and rsch. asst. to the chancellor U. of Tex. System, Austin, 1985-93; exec. dir. Ames Aerospace Encounter, San Jose State U. Found., 1993—; asst. dir. Hertz Found., Livermore, Calif., 1978—; mem. com. of 100 Va. Tech. Inst., Blacksburg, 1982—; pres. Stanford-Sloan Bd. Stanford-Sloan Program, 1985-87; mem. Pres. Reagan's Coun. of Mgmt. Improvement, Washington, 1984-85; mem. faculty U. Tex., Austin, 1990-92, El Paso, 1990-92, U. Tex. Pan Am, 1991-93. Co-author: Paper-Manned Exploration of the Solar System, 1991. Vice-chmn. Boy Scouts Am., Palo Alto, Calif., 1982-87. Recipient Army Comdrs. medal U.S. Army, 1985, Presdl. Rank of Disting. Exec. Pres. Office, 1985, Presdl. Rank of Meritorious, 1983. Fellow Am. Astron. Soc.; mem. AIAA, Pi Tau Sigma (v.p. 1946), Tau Beta Pi (v.p. 1945-46). Home: 14131 Shadow Oaks Way Saratoga CA 95070-5560

BOYD, LEONA POTTER, retired social worker; b. Creekside, Pa., Aug. 31, 1907; d. Joseph M. and Belle (McHenry) Johnston. Grad. Ind. (Pa.) State Normal Sch., 1927, student Las Vegas Normal U., N.Mex., 1933, Carnegie Inst. Tech. Sch. Social Work, 1945, U. Pitts. Sch. Social Work, 1956-57; m. Edgar D. Potter, July 16, 1932 (div.); m. Harold Lee Boyd, Oct. 1972. Tchr. Creekside (Pa.) Pub. Schs., 1927-30, Papago Indian Reservation, Sells, Ariz., 1931-33; caseworker, supr. Indiana County (Pa.) Bd. Assistance, 1934-54, exec. dir., 1954-68, ret. Bd. dirs. Indiana County Tourist Promotion, hon. life mem.; former bd. dirs. Indiana County United Fund, Salvation Army, Indiana County Guidance Ctr., Armstrong-Indiana Mental Health Bd.; cons. assoc. Community Rsch. Assocs., Inc.; mem. Counseling Ctr. Aux., Lake Havasu City, Ariz., 1978-80; former mem. Western Welcome Club, Lake Havasu City, Sierra Vista Hosp. Aux., Truth or Consequences, N.Mex. Recipient Jr. C. of C. Disting. Svc. award, Indiana, Pa., 1966, Bus. and Profl. Women's Club award, Indiana, 1965. Mem. Am. Assn. Ret. Persons, Daus. Am. Colonists, Common Cause (Nat., Washington and Ariz.). Lutheran. Home: 444 S Higley Rd Apt 219 Mesa AZ 85206-2186

BOYD, MALCOLM, minister, religious author; b. Buffalo, June 8, 1923; s. Melville and Beatrice (Lowrie) B. B.A., U. Ariz., 1944; B.D., Ch. Div. Sch. Pacific, 1954; postgrad., Oxford (Eng.) U., 1955; S.T.M., Union Theol. Sem., N.Y.C., 1956; DD (hon.), Ch. Div. Sch. of Pacific, 1995. Ordained to ministry Episcopal Ch., 1955. V.p., gen. mgr. Pickford, Rogers & Boyd, 1949-51; rector in Indpls., 1957-59; chaplain Colo. State U., 1959-61, Wayne State U., 1961-65; nat. field rep. Episcopal Soc. Cultural and Racial Unity, 1965-68; resident fellow Calhoun Coll., Yale U., 1968-71, assoc. fellow, 1971—; writer-priest in residence St. Augustine-by-the Sea Episcopal Ch., 1982-93; chaplain to commn. on AIDS Ministries of Episcopal Diocese of L.A., 1993—; lectr. World Council Chs., Switzerland, 1955, 64; columnist Pitts. Courier, 1962-65; resident guest Mishkenot Sha'ananim, Jerusalem, 1974; chaplain AIDS Commn. Episcopal Diocese L.A., 1989—. Host: TV spl. Sex in the Seventies, CBS-TV, Los Angeles, 1975; author: Crisis in Communication, 1957, Are You Running with Me, Jesus?, 1965, rev. 25th anniversary edit., 1990, Free to Live, Free to Die, 1967, Book of Days, 1968, As I Live and Breathe: Stages of an Autobiography, 1969, Human Like Me, Jesus, 1971, The Lover, 1972, When in the Course of Human Events, 1973, The Runner, 1974, The Alleluia Affair, 1975, Christian, 1975, Am I Running with You, God?, 1977, Take Off the Masks, 1978, rev. edit. 1993, Look Back in Joy, 1981, rev. edit., 1990, Half Laughing, Half Crying, 1986, Gay Priest: An Inner Journey, 1986, Edges, Boundaries and Connections, 1992, Rich with Years, 1993; plays Boy, 1961, Study in Color, 1962, The Community, 1964, others; editor: On the Battle Lines, 1964, The Underground Church, 1968, Amazing Grace: Stories of Gay and Lesbian Faith, 1991; book reviewer: Los Angeles Times.; contbr. articles to numerous mags. including Newsday, Parade, Modern Maturity, also newspapers. Active voter registration, Miss., Ala., 1963, 64; mem. Los Angeles City/County AIDS Task Force. Malcolm Boyd Collection and Archives established Boston U., 1973; Recipient Integrity Internat. award, 1978; Union Am. Hebrew Congregations award, 1980. Mem. Nat. Council Chs. (film awards com. 1965), P.E.N. (pres. Los Angeles chpt. 1984-87), Am. Center, Authors Guild, Integrity, Nat. Gay Task Force, Clergy and Laity Concerned (nat. bd.), NAACP, Amnesty Internat., Episc. Peace Fellowship, Fellowship of Reconciliation (nat. com.). Office: 1227 4th St Santa Monica CA 90401-1303

BOYD, MARC ADAM, real estate company executive; b. Seattle, July 29, 1960; s. William Goldstein and June Roslyn (Bender) B. BA in Econs., U. Wash., 1990. Salesman Bon Marche, Seattle, 1976-79; mktg. specialist Better Bus. Bur., Seattle, 1979-85; property mgr. Boyd Real Estate Investments, Mercer Island, Wash., 1985-90; v.p., treas., owner Boyd Real Estate Investments, Inc., Mercer Island, Wash., 1990—, Boyd Mortgage Security Co., 1994—; mortgage securities broker dealer, pres. Boyd Real Estate Devel., 1994—; exec. v.p., bd.d irs. Awareness Project, Inc., 1995—. Arbitrator Better Bus. Bur., Seattle, 1986—. Office: Boyd Real Estate Investments Inc 3645 Wallingford Ave Seattle WA 98103

BOYD, ROBERT JAMISON, construction equipment company executive; b. Morgantown, W.Va., Nov. 7, 1930; s. Carl Van Gilder and Opal Pauline (Jamison) B.; m. Mary Ann Gillespie, Aug. 15, 1959; children: Lynne Lee, Megan Ann. BSBA, W.Va. U., 1952; MBA, Stanford U., 1960. Exec. asst., analyst Calaveras div. Flintkote Co., San Francisco, 1960-64, dir. planning and adminstrn., 1964-67, controller, 1967-72; cons., controller Van Vorst Industries, Pasadena, Calif., 1972-73; treas. Burke Co., San Mateo, Calif., 1973-74, v.p. fin. and adminstrn., 1974-80, exec. v.p., chief operating officer, 1980—, also bd. dirs. Served to capt. USAF, 1952-58, col. Res. ret. Mem. Associated Gen. Contractors Calif. (bd. dirs. heavy constrn. 1984—), Nat. ASsn. Credit Mgmt. (bd. dirs. 1966-68). Republican. Episcopalian. Office: Burke Co 2655 Campus Dr San Mateo CA 94403-2519

BOYD, WILLIAM HARLAND, historian; b. Boise, Idaho, Jan. 7, 1912; s. Harland D. and Cordelia (Crumley) B.; AB, U. Calif.-Berkeley, 1935, MA, 1936, PhD, 1942; m. Mary Kathryn Drake, June 25, 1939; children: Barbara A. Boyd Voltmer, William Harland, Kathryn L. Boyd Nemeyer. Tchr. Fall River High Sch., McArthur, Calif., 1937-38, Watsonville (Calif.) High Sch., 1941-42, San Mateo (Calif.) High Sch., 1942-44; prof. history Bakersfield Coll., 1946-73, chmn. social sci. dept., 1967-73. Pres., Kern County Hist. Soc., 1950-52; adv. com. Kern County Mus., 1955-60; chmn. Fort Tejon Restoration Com. Bakersfield, 1952-55, sec., 1955-60; mem. Kern County Hist. Records Commn., 1977—, Bakersfield Hist. Preservation Commn., 1984-87. Recipient Merit award Kern County Bd. Trade, 1960; commendation Kern County Bd. Suprs., 1952, 76, 78. Mem. Calif. Tchrs. Assn., Am. Hist. Assn., Phi Alpha Theta. Republican. Baptist. Author: Land of Havilah, 1952, (with G.J. Rogers) San Joaquin Vignettes, 1955, (with others) Spanish Trailblazers in the South San Joaquin, 1957, A Centennial Bibliography on the History Kern County, California, 1966, A California Middle Border, 1972, A Climb Through History, 1973, Bakersfield's First Bapt. Church, 1975, Kern Country Wayfarers, 1977, Kern County Tall Tales, 1980, The Shasta Route, 1981, Stagecoach Heyday in the San Joaquin Valley, 1983, Bakersfield's First Baptist Church A Centennial History, 1989. Contbr. to Ency. Brit. Home: 1301 New Stine Rd Apt 216 Bakersfield CA 93309-3501

BOYDSTON, JAMES CHRISTOPHER, composer; b. Denver, July 21, 1947; s. James Virgal and Mary June (Wiseman) B.; m. Ann Louise Bryant, Aug. 20, 1975. BA in Philosophy, U. Tex., 1971. Lutenist and guitarist Collegium Musicum, U. Tex., Austin, 1968-70; tchr. classical guitar Extension div. The New Eng. Conservatory of Music, Boston, 1972-73. Arranger music: S. Joplins, "The Entertainer," 1976; arranger/composer/performer cassette recording: Wedding Music for Classical Guitar, 1988; inventor classical guitar bridge-saddle, 1990; author original poetry included in: The World of Poetry Anthology, 1991. Home: 4433 Driftwood Pl Boulder CO 80301-3104

BOYER, CARL, III, secondary education educator, city official; b. Phila., Pa., Sept. 22, 1937; s. Carl Boyer Jr. and Elizabeth Campbell Timm; m. Ada Christine Kruse, July 28, 1962. Student, U. Edinburgh, Scotland, 1956-57; BA, Trinity U., 1959; MEd in Secondary Edn., U. Cin., 1959; postgrad., Calif. State U., Northridge, 1964-72. Tchr. Edgewood High Sch., San Antonio, Tex., 1959-60; libr. U. Cin., Cincinnati, Ohio, 1960-61; tchr. Eighth Avenue Elem. Sch., Dayton, Ky., 1961-62, Amelia High Sch., Amelia, Ohio, 1962-63; instr. Kennedy San Fernando Comm. Adult Sch., San Fernando, Calif., 1964-74, Mission Coll., San Fernando, 1971; tchr. San Fernando High Sch., San Fernando, Calif., 1963—; faculty chmn. San Fernando High Sch., dept. chmn.; cons. Sofia (Bulgaria) City Coun., 1991. Author, compiler 10 books on genealogy and family history; contbr. articles to profl. jours. Councilman City of Santa Clarita, Calif., 1987—, mayor pro tem, 1989-90, 94, mayor, 1990-91; mem. Nat. League Cities Internat. Mcpl. Consortium, 1992—; mem. revenue and taxation com. League Calif. Cities, 1992—; sec. Calif. Contract Cities Assn., 1992-93; trustee Santa Clarita C.C. Dist., 1973-81, pres., 1979-81; bd. dirs. Castaic Lake Water Agy., 1982-84, Newhall-Saugus-Valencia Fedn. Homeowners Assn., 1969-70, 71-72; pres. Del Prado Condominium Assn., Inc., Newhall, Calif.; exec. v.p. Canyon County Formation Com.; chmn. Santa Clarita City Formation Com., 1987; pres. Santa Clarita Valley Internat. Program, 1991—; treas. Healing the Children Calif., 1994—. Mem. United Tchrs. L.A., New Eng. Hist. Geneal. Soc. Republican. Methodist. Home: PO Box 220333 Santa Clarita CA 91322-0333 Office: Santa Clarita City Hall 23920 Valencia Blvd Ste 300 Santa Clarita CA 91355-2175

BOYER, FORD SYLVESTER, relationship consultant; b. Cadet, Mo., Jan. 12, 1934; s. Wilford Robert and Mary Elizabeth (DeClue) B.; m. Juelle-Ann Rupkalvis, May 2, 1970. BA in Psychology, USAF Inst., 1957; DD, Am. Bible Inst., Kansas City, Mo., 1977; MA, John F. Kennedy U., 1994. Cert. alcohol specialist. Adminstr. Getz Bros., San Francisco, 1969-73; supr. word processing U.S. Leasing Corp., San Francisco, 1977-82, dir. tng. and applications-word processing, 1982-84; computer cons Petaluma, Calif., 1984-87; massage therapist Petaluma, 1985-87; pvt. practice hypnotherapy Alameda, Calif., 1987—; cons. for chem. dependency Alameda, 1987—. Contbr. articles to profl. publs.; writer, pub.: (newsletter) Starfire, 1988—. With USAF, 1953-57, Korea. Mem. Am Coun. Hypnotist Examiners, Nat. Assn. Alcohol and Drug Abuse Counselors, Calif. Assn. Alcohol and Drug Abuse Counselors, Calif. Assn. Alcohol Recovery Homes. Home and Office: Spiritual Comm Sys 3327 Cook Ln Alameda CA 94502-6939

BOYER, LAURA MERCEDES, librarian; b. Madison, Ind., Aug. 3, 1934; d. Clyde C. and Dorcas H. (Willyard) Boyer. A.B., George Washington U., 1956; A.M., U. Denver, 1959; M.L.S., George Peabody U., 1961. Pub. sch. tchr., Kankakee, Ill., 1957-58; asst. circulation librarian U. Kans., Lawrence, 1961-63; asst. reference librarian U. of Pacific Library, Stockton, Calif., 1963-65, head reference dept., 1965-84, coordinator reference services, 1984-86; reference librarian Calif. State U.-Stanislaus, Turlock, 1987-90, ref. coord., 1990—. Author: The Older Generation of Southeast Asian Refugees: An Annoteted Bibliography, 1991; compiler of Play Anthologies Union List, 1976; contbr. articles to profl. jours. Mem. Am. Soc. Info. Sci., ALA, Calif. Library Assn., AAUP, Nat. Assn. for Edn. and Advancement of Cambodian, Laotian and Vietnamese Ams., DAR, Daughters of Am. Colonists, Phi Beta Kappa, Kappa Delta Pi, Beta Phi Mu. Republican. Episcopalian. Home: 3123 Wooded Way Jeffersonville IN 47130-5937

BOYER, NANCY GAIL, language educator; b. Martinez, Calif., July 15, 1950; d. John Marcus and Esther (Mabey) B. BA in Spanish, Oreg. State U., 1972; MA in Tchr. ESL, Brigham Young U., 1976. ESL instr. Briam Inst./Am. Cultural Ctr., Madrid, 1972-73, Ch. Coll. of Western Samoa, Pesega, 1977-78; ESL instr. Brigham Young U., Laie, Hawaii, 1979-80, Provo, Utah, 1980-83; ESL instr. Ark. State U., Jonesboro, 1983-84, Kuwait U., 1984-90, Pasadena (Calif.) City Coll., 1990-91, Golden West Coll., Huntington Beach, Calif., 1991—. Mem. TESOL, Calif. TESOL. Republican. Mem. LDS Ch. Office: Golden West Coll 15744 Golden West St Huntington Beach CA 92647

BOYER, STEVEN EUGENE, educator, researcher, petroleum geologist; b. Williamsport, Pa., Apr. 6, 1950; s. Earl H. and Winifred (Wert) B.; m. Susan Marie Teil, Mar. 17, 1984. BS in Geology, Bucknell U., 1972; PhD in Geology, Johns Hopkins U., 1978. Geologist ARCO Exploration Co., Denver, 1978-80; sr. geologist Amoco Prodn. Co., Denver, 1980-81; research geologist Anschutz Corp., Denver, 1981-82; sr. geologist Sohio Petroleum Co., Denver, 1982-85; sr. research geologist Standard Oil Prodn. Co., Dallas, 1985-87; research assoc., prof. U. Wash., Seattle, 1987—; numerous guest lectures U.S. Geol. Survey, Reston, Va., Johns Hopkins U., Balt., U. Colo., Denver, Internat. Geol. Confs. Served to capt. USAR. Fellow Geol. Soc. Am. (tech. rev. com. 1982 meeting); mem. Am. Geophys. Union, Am. Assn. Petroleum Geologists. Lutheran. Office: U Washington Dept Geological Scis Seattle WA 98195

BOYKIN, JAMES LESTER, aerospace engineer, consultant; b. Clarendon, Tex., Jan. 6, 1928; s. Garland Lester and Lucy Edna (Matthews) B.; m. Dulcie Mildred Ligon, Sept. 2, 1958; children: Tracy Lynette, Leslie Dee, James Russell, Robin Elisa. BSME, N.Mex. State U., 1951, BSEE, 1959. Comml. pilot rating. With Hughes Aircraft Co., 1951-54; fighter pilot U. S. Air Force, 1954-58; flight test engr., test ops. supr. N.Am. Aviation div. Rockwell Internat., L.A., 1959-63, Las Cruces, N.Mex., 1963-69; test ops. supr. LTV (Ling Temco Vaught), Las Cruces, 1969-71, Dynalectron Corp., Las Cruces, 1971-74; with Rockwell Internat., Las Cruces, 1974-85, ops. supr., 1978-85, project engr., 1981, sr. project engr., 1981-85; cons.; charter flying, instr., 1985—. Capt. USAF, 1946-48, 54-58; with USAFR, 1969. (ret.). Mem. Nat. Rifle Assn. (life), Air Force Assn., Res. Officers Assn., Lions (pres. 1975-76). Republican. Methodist. Home: 2390 Rosedale Dr Las Cruces NM 88005-1448

BOYLAN, MERLE NELSON, librarian; b. Youngstown, Ohio, Feb. 24, 1925; s. Merle Nelson and Alma Joy (Kepple) B. B.A., Youngstown U., 1950; M.L.S., Carnegie-Mellon U., 1956; postgrad., U. Ariz., 1950-51, Ind. U., 1952. Librarian Pub. Health Library U. Calif., Berkeley, 1956-58; sci. librarian U. Ariz., Tucson, 1958-59; engring. librarian Gen. Dynamics/Convair, San Diego, 1959-61, Gen. Dynamics/Astronautics, 1961-62; assoc. librarian Lawrence Radiation Lab., U. Calif., Livermore, 1962-64; library mgr. Lawrence Radiation Lab., U. Calif., 1964-67; chief librarian NASA Ames Research Center, Moffett Field, Calif., 1968-69; asso. dir. libraries U. Mass., Amherst, 1969-70; dir. libraries, Univ. librarian U. Mass., 1970-72; dir. libraries U. Tex., Austin, 1973-77; dir. libraries U. Wash., Seattle, 1977-89, dir. emeritus, 1989—, prof. Sch. Librarianship, 1982-89; exec. bd. Amigos Bibliographic Council, 1974-77; mem. fin. com., governance com., user's council, computer service council Wash. Library Network, 1978—; del. Gov.'s Conf. Libraries and Info. Services, 1979; sec. Texas State Bd. Library Examiners, 1974-77; mem. bibliographic networking and resource sharing advisory group Southwestern Library Interstate Coop. Endeavor, 1975-77; sec., chmn. exec. bd. Pacific N.W. Bibliographic Center, 1977-83; mem. com. centralzed acquisitions of library materials for internat. studies Center for Research Libraries.; del. OCLC Users Council, 1981-86. Sec. bd. trustees Littlefield Fund for So. History, 1974-77, Fred Meyer Charitable Trust; mem. adv. bd. Library and Info. Resources for Northwest, 1984-87. Mem. ALA, Assn. Coll. and Research Libraries (legis. com. 1977-81), Assn. Research Libraries (bibliographic control com. 1979-83), Spl. Libraries Assn., Am. Soc. Info. Sci., Beta Phi Mu. Home: 1354 Bellefield Park Ln Bellevue WA 98004-6854 Office: Univ of Wash Libraries Suzzallo Library Seattle WA 98195

BOYLAN, RICHARD JOHN, psychologist, researcher, educator; b. Hollywood, Calif., Oct. 15, 1939; s. John Alfred and Rowena Margaret (Devine) B.; m. Charnette Marie Blackburn, Oct. 26, 1968 (div. June 1984); children: Christopher J., Jennifer April, Stephanie August; m. Judith Lee Keast, Nov. 21, 1987; stepchildren: Darren Andrew, Matthew Grant. BA, St. John's Coll., 1961; MEd, Fordham U., 1966; MSW, U. Calif., Berkeley, 1971; PhD in Psychology, U. Calif., Davis, 1984. Lic. psychologist, Calif.; lic. clin. social worker, Calif.; lic. marriage, family and child counselor, Calif. Assoc. pastor Cath. Diocese of Fresno, 1965-68; asst. dir. Berkeley (Calif.) Free Ch., 1970-71; psychiat. social worker Marin Mental Health Dept., San Rafael, Calif., 1971-77; dir. Calaveras Mental Health Dept., San Andreas, Calif., 1977-85; prof., coord. Nat. U., Sacramento, 1985-86; instr. Calif. State U., Sacramento, 1985-90, U. Calif., Davis, 1984-88; dir. U.S. Behavioral Health, Sacramento, 1988-89; pvt. practice psychotherapy, Sacramento, 1974—. Bd. dirs. Marin Mcpl. Water Dist., 1975-77; cons. Calif. State Legis., Sacramento, 1979-80; chmn. Calaveras County Bd. Edn., Angels Camp, Calif., 1981-84. Recipient Geriatric Medicine Acad. award NIH, 1984, Experiment Station grant USDA, Calif., 1983. Mem. APA, Sacramento Valley Psychol. Assn. (past pres.), Sacramento Soc. Profl. Psychologists (past pres.), Nat. Resources Def. Coun., Acad. Clin. Close-Encounter Therapists (founder, sec.-treas.). Democrat. Office: 2826 O St Sacramento CA 95816-6400

BOYLE, BARBARA DORMAN, motion picture company executive; b. N.Y.C., Aug. 11, 1935; d. William and Edith (Kleiman) Dorman; m. Kevin Boyle, Nov. 26, 1960; children: David Eric, Paul Coleman. BA in English with honors, U. Calif., Berkeley, 1957; JD, UCLA, 1960. Bar: Calif. 1961, N.Y. 1964, U.S. Supreme Ct. 1964. Atty. bus. affairs dept, corp. asst. sec. Am. Internat. Pictures, L.A., 1960-65; ptnr. Cohen & Boyle, L.A., 1967-74; exec. v.p., gen. counsel, chief op. officer New World Pictures, L.A., 1974-82; sr. v.p. prodn. Orion Pictures Corp., L.A., 1982-85; exec. v.p. prodn. RKO Pictures, L.A., 1986-87; pres. Sovereign Pictures, Inc., L.A., 1988-92, Boyle and Taylor Prodns., 1993—; lectr. in field. Exec. prodr. (film) Eight Men Out, 1987, Battle Rocket, 1995; prodr. (film) Mrs. Munck, 1995. Bd. dirs. UCLA Law Fund Com., Ind. Feature Project/West, L.A. Women's Campaign Fund; founding mem. entertainment adv. coun. sch. law UCLA, co-chmn. 1979-80; mem. adv. bd. Am. Film Inst., Womens Directing Workshop. Mem. Acad. Motion Picture Arts and Scis., Women in Film (pres. 1977-78), Hollywood Women's Polit. Com., Women Entertainment Lawyers Assn., Calif. Bar Assn., N.Y. State Bar Assn. Office: Boyle-Taylor Prodns 5200 Lankershim Blvd Ste 700 North Hollywood CA 91601-3100

BOYLE, CAROLYN MOORE, public relations executive, marketing communications manager; b. Los Angeles, Jan. 29, 1937; d. Cory Orlando Moore and Violet (Brennan) Baldock; m. Robert J. Ruppelt, Oct. 8, 1954 (div. Aug. 1964); children: Cory Robert, Traci Lynn; m. Jerry Ray Boyle, June 1, 1970 (div. 1975). AA, Orange Coast Coll., 1966; BA, Calif. State U., Fullerton, 1970; student, U. Calif., Irvine, 1970-71. Program coordinator Newport Beach (Calif.) Cablevision, 1968-70; dir. pub. relations Fish Communications Co., Newport Beach, 1970-74; mktg. rep. Dow Pharm. div. Dow Chem. Co., Orange County, Calif., 1974 77, Las Vegas, Nev., 1980-81; mgr. product publicity Dow Agrl. Products div. Dow Chem. Co., Midland, Mich., 1977-80; mgr. mktg. communications Dowell Fluid Services Region div. Dow Chem. Co. Houston, 1981-84; adminstr. mktg. communications Swedlow, Inc., Garden Grove, Calif., 1984-85; cons. mktg. communications, 1985-86; mgr. mktg. communications Am. Convertors div. Am. Hosp. Supply, 1986-87; mgr. sales support Surgidev Corp., Santa Barbara, Calif., 1987-88; owner Barrel House, Victorville, Calif., 1988-91, Saratoga Fences, Las Vegas, 1991; pub. info. officer nuclear waste divsn. Clark County Comprehensive Planning, Las Vegas, 1992—; guest lectr. Calif. State U., Long Beach, 1970; seminar coordinator U. Calif., Irvine, 1972; mem. Western White House Press Corps, 1972; pub. relations cons. BASF Wyandotte, Phila., 1981-82. Author: Agricultural Public Relations/Publicity, 1981; editor Big Mean AG Machine (internal mag.), 1977; contbr. numerous articles to trade publs.; contbg. editor Dowell Mktg. Newsletter, 1983; creator, designer Novahistine DMX Trial Size nat. mktg. program, 1977. Com. mem. Dow Employees for Polit. Action, Midland, 1978-80; bd. dirs. Dowell Employees for Polit. Action Com., Houston, 1983-84. World Campus Afloat scholar, U. Seven Seas, 1966-67; recipient PROTOS award, 1985. Mem. Pub. Relations Soc. Am. (cert.), Soc. Petroleum Engrs., Internat. Assn. Bus. Communicators. Episcopalian. Recipient first rights to televise President Nixon in Western White House. Office: 6340 Lanning Ln Las Vegas NV 89108-2605

BOYLE, FRANCIS WILLIAM, JR., computer company executive, chemistry educator; b. El Paso, Tex., Oct. 16, 1951; s. Francis William and Betty Lou Boyle; m. Sharon Marie McGuire; 1 child, Steven; m. Donna Marie Mader, Mar. 21, 1978; children: Richard, Genevieve, Veronica. BS in Chemistry, N.Mex. State U., 1973, MS in Soil Physics, 1979; PhD in Soil Chemistry, Colo. State U., 1984. Rsch. assoc. N.Mex. State U., Las Cruces, 1971-80, rsch. specialist, asst. prof., 1986-88, vis. prof. chemistry and agr., 1986—; rsch. specialist Colo. State U., Ft. Collins, 1980-84; asst. prof. Calif. State U., Fresno, 1984-85; dir. CATI field rsch. lab. Calif. Agrl. Tech. Inst., Fresno, 1985-86; chief fin. officer Software & Systems Techs., Las Cruces, 1986—; v.p. Internat. Safwater, Las Cruces, 1988-89; environ. cons. Buchanan Cons., Ltd., las Cruces, 1989—; mem. Reseller adv. coun. Everex Systems, Inc., Fremont, Calif., 1991—. Contbr. articles to profl. jours. Computer coord. field days Future Farmers Am., Fresno, 1984-86; judge So.N.Mex. State Sci. Fair, Las Cruces, 1987—. Grantee Kerley Chem. Co., 1985, Hewlett Packard Corp., 1986; N.Mex. eminent scholar N.Mex. Commn. on Higher Edn., 1989-90. Mem. Am. Soc. Agronomy, Soil Sci. Soc. Am., Western Soil Sci. Soc., Sigma Xi, Gamma Sigma Delta. Home: 1708 Calle Feliz Las Cruces NM 88001-4332 Office: NMex State U Dept Chemistry Las Cruces NM 88003

BOYLE, (CHARLES) KEITH, artist, educator; b. Defiance, Ohio., Feb. 15, 1930. Student, Ringling Sch. Art; B.F.A., U. Iowa. Prof. painting and drawing Stanford U., Calif., 1962-88. Group shows include Stanford U. Mus., 1964, San Francisco Mus. Art, 1965, Ann Arbor, Mich., 1965, Joslyn Art Mus., Omaha, 1970, San Jose Mus. Art, Calif., 1978; represented in permanent collections: San Francisco Mus. Art, Stanford U. Mus., Mead paper Corp., Atlanta, Nat. Fine Arts Collection, Washington, Oakland Mus., Continental Bank, Chgo., Seton Med. Ctr., Daily City, Calif., Schneider Mus., Ashland, Oreg. Grantee NEA, 1981-82, Pew Meml. Trust, 1986-87. Address: 6285 Thompson Creek Rd Applegate OR 97530-9639

BOYLE, LARRY LEON, environmental affairs professional, educator; b. Long Beach, Calif., Dec. 8, 1941; s. Lawrence Leon and Josephine (Risser) B.; m. Carol Mellick, Aug. 29, 1964 (dec. May 1988); children: Karleen Ann, Karen Ann; m. Susan Bennion, June 23, 1993; children: Luke, Lona. BA,

Whittier Coll., 1964, MEd, 1967. Registered environ. assessor, Calif. Jr. coll. tchr. Cerritos, Calif., 1968-80; h.s. tchr. Bellflower, Calif., 1964-80; sr. scientist, mgr. environ. div., environ. affairs mgr. Crosby & Overton, Long Beach, 1982—; mem. external rev. com. for emergency response Calif. EPA, 1990. Methodist. Home: 18903 Alexander Ave Cerritos CA 90703-6312

BOYLE, MARYLOU OLSEN, nursing administrator; b. Butte, Mont., Aug. 8, 1937; d. Paul Bogvang and Rose Patricia Olsen; m. John Anthony Boyle, July 8, 1978. Diploma, Sacred Heart Sch. Nursing, Spokane, Wash., 1958; BSN, U. Wash., 1969, M. Nursing, 1971; MS in Counseling Psychology, Pepperdine U., Quantico, Va., 1978. Dir. perioperative nursing Alexandria (Va.) Hosp., 1982-87; dir. surg. svcs. Arroyo Grande (Calif.) Community Hosp., 1987-89; DON Cottage Care Ctr., Santa Barbara, Calif., 1989-90, Marian Extended Care Ctr., Santa Maria, Calif., 1990-91; crisis intervention specialist, psychiat. assessment team Vista Del Mar Hosp., 1992—. Religious edn. tchr. St. Mary's Assumption Ch. Mem. Assn. Oper. Rm. Nurses (past pres. Coastal Valley chpt., mem. No. Va. chpt.), Naval Res. Assn. (life), The Ret. Officers Assn. (life), Marine Corps Assn. (life), U. Wash. Alumni Assn. (life). Office: CPC Vista del Mar Hosp 801 Seneca St Ventura CA 93001-1411

BOYLES, GARY EDWARD, protective services official; b. San Diego, Apr. 18, 1951; s. Calvin Ray Boyles and Alice Irene (Lane) Bilbrey; m. Jolene Young, July 17, 1971; children: Jeffrey, Gregory. AS in Police Sci., Chaffey Coll., 1971, AS in Fire Sci., 1975; BA in Mgmt., U. Redlands, 1984; MPA, Calif. State U., San Bernardino, 1991. Cert. state fire officer, Calif. Firefighter Central Valley Fire Dist., Fontana, Calif., 1972-77; engr. Central Valley Fire Dist., Fontana, 1977, capt., 1977-84, fire prevention supr., 1984-85, battalion comdr., 1985-88; div. chief, fire prevention San Bernardino County Fire Agy., Fontana, 1988-89, divsn. chief tng., 1989-94, asst. fire chief, 1994—. Mayor pro tem City of Fontana, 1986-89, mayor, 1992, councilman, 1984—, chmn. redevel. agy., 1987—, mem. redevel. agy., 1984—; bd. dirs. Omnitrans, 1984—; v.p. Ctrl. Valley Firefighters, 1984-88; sec. Internat. Assn. Firefighters Local 935, 1977-79. Completed L.A. Marathon, 1987, 88, 90, 91, 92, 93, 94. Mem. San Bernardino Associated Govts., Rotary Internat., Elks. Home: 9616 Kempster Ave Fontana CA 92335-5840 Office: San Bernardino County Fire 157 W 5th St 2nd Fl San Bernardino CA 92415-0450

BOYLES, LARRY WAYNE, computer scientist, consultant; b. Bay City, Tex., Mar. 23, 1948; s. Floyd Stewart and Vivienne Beach (Hetz) B.; m. Terri Dawn Merrell, Sept. 26, 1979 (div. Sept. 1989); children: Stewart Wayne, Patricia Faith. BA in Info. Systems, St. Martin's Coll., Lacey, Wash., 1988; postgrad., U. So. Calif. Served to 1st sgt. U.S. Army, various locations, 1968-88; programmer, analyst State of Wash., Olympia, 1988-89; systems mgr. U.S. Bur. of Census, San Diego, 1989-90; computer scientist Computer Scis. Corp., Edwards AFB, Calif., 1991—; MIS cons. on pvt. practice, So. Calif., 1989—; dir. MIS Jesus Christ Light & Power Ch., California City, 1993—. Decorated Bronze Star. Mem. Digital Equipment Corp. User Soc. Republican. Home: 20361 86th St California City CA 93505-5506 Office: CSC PO Box 446 Edwards CA 93524

BOYNTON, BRUCE RYLAND, pediatrician, neonatologist, educator; b. Richmond, Va., Feb. 1, 1948; s. Douglas Raymond and Meta Tutwiler (Hill) B.; m. Carole Ann Gillis, Dec. 23, 1974; children: William James Frederick, Benjamin Christian, Geoffrey Cabell. BA, U. Chgo., 1973; MD, MPH, Yale U., 1977; grad., Air Command and Staff Coll., 1994. Diplomate Am. Bd. Pediatrics, Am. Bd. Neonatal-Perinatal Medicine. Intern U. Ky. Med. Ctr., Lexington, 1977-78; resident Stanford (Calif.) U., 1981-82; fellow U. Calif., San Diego, 1982-85; asst. prof. Tufts U. Sch. Medicine, Boston, 1985-88; assoc. prof. pediatrics U. Ky. Coll. Medicine, Lexington, 1988-92; chief div. neonatology U. Ky. Med. Ctr., 1988-92; neonatologist, rsch. coord. dept. pediatrics Naval Med. Ctr., San Diego, 1992—; assoc. clin. prof. U. Calif., San Diego, 1993—; med. dir. Appalachian Dist. Health Dept., Boone, N.C., 1978-81. Editor: Bronchopulmonary Dysplasia, 1988, New Therapies for Neonatal Respiratory Failure, 1994; contbr. numerous articles and abstracts to med. jours., chpts. to books. With USN, 1966-70, 92—, comdr. M.C., USNR. Grantee Charlton Fund, 1986-87, Whitaker Found., 1988-91. Fellow Am. Acad. Pediatrics; mem. Soc. for Pediatric Rsch., Am. Physiol. Soc., So. Soc. for Pediatric Rsch., Nat. Perinatal Assn., Ky. Pediatric Soc., Phi Beta Kappa. Roman Catholic. Home: 11350 Swan Canyon Rd San Diego CA 92131-3538 Office: Naval Med Ctr Dept Pediatrics San Diego CA 92134

BOYNTON, DONALD ARTHUR, title insurance company executive; b. Culver City, Calif., Sept. 6, 1940; s. A.A. and Margaret Lena (Slocum) B.; m. Jean Carolyn Ferrulli, Nov. 10, 1962; children: Donna Jean, Michael Arthur; m. Sharon C. Burns, Nov. 18, 1984; children: Cynthia, David, Sharie. Student, El Camino Jr. Coll., 1960-62, Antelope Valley Jr. Coll., 1963-64, Orange Coast Coll., 1969-72; BA, Bradford U., 1977. With Title Ins. & Trust Co., 1958-63; sales mgr. Title Ins. & Trust Co., Santa Ana, Calif., 1980-81; dep. sheriff County of Los Angeles, 1963-65; with Transamerica Title Ins. Co., L.A., 1965-69, state coord., 1981-82; sr. title officer Calif. Land Title Co., L.A., 1969-72; asst. sec., systems analyst Lawyers Title Ins. Corp., 39 states, 1972-77; county mgr. Am. Title Co., Santa Ana, Calif., 1977-79; v.p., mgr. Orange County ops. Chgo. Title Ins. Co., Tustin, Calif., 1979-80; pres. Stewart Title Co. of Fresno, 1985-86; supr. builder svcs. Orange Coast Title Co., Santa Ana, 1986-89; sr. title officer TSG dept. Orange Coast/Record Title, Whittier, Calif., 1990-94; sr. title officer, ednl. coord. State of Calif. for Orange Coast Title, 1993; sr. nat. coord. Chgo. Title and Ins., Irvine, Calif., 1993—. Mem. Calif. Trustees Assn., Orange County Escrow Assn., Optimists (sec.-treas.), Elks (life, chaplain), Rotary. Home: 9061 Bermuda Dr Huntington Beach CA 92646-7812 Office: Chicago Title Ins Co 16969 Von Karman Irvine CA 92714

BOYNTON, ROBERT GRANVILLE, computer systems analyst; b. North Bend, Oreg., Aug. 11, 1951; s. Granville Clarence Jr. and Leatrice Anne (Yoder) B.; m. Sandra Lynn Harrold, Aug. 17, 1991. Student, Central Oreg. Community Coll., 1969-70. cert. career data processing Heald Coll. Bus., 1972. Computer operator Coca-Cola Bottling Co. Calif., San Francisco, 1973-76, data processing mgr., 1977-78; computer operator Warn Industries, Milwaukie, Oreg., 1979-81, computer programmer, 1981-85, analyst, 1983-85, computer systems analyst, 1985-90, info. systems team leader, 1990—. Vol. Oreg. Spl. Olympics, 1985-86. Democrat. Home: 5712 SE 130th Pl Portland OR 97236-4175 Office: Warn Industries 13270 SE Pheasant Ct Portland OR 97222-1277

BOYNTON, WILLIAM LEWIS, electronic manufacturing company official; b. Kalamazoo, May 31, 1928; s. James Woodbury and Cyretta (Gunther) B.; ed. pub. schs.; m. Kei Ouchi, Oct. 8, 1953. Asst. mgr. Speigel J & R, Kalamazoo, 1947-48; with U.S. Army, 1948-74, ret., 1974; with Rockwell/Collins div., Newport Beach, Calif., 1974-78, supr. material, 1978-81, coord., 1981-88; supr. coord. Rockwell/CDC, Santa Ana, Calif., 1981—, coord. investment recovery, 1982-86, shipping and material coord., 1987-88, material coord., 1988, environ. coord. Rockwell/DCD, Newport Beach, 1988-89, ret.; mem. faculty Western Mich. U., 1955-58. Trustee Orange County Vector Control Dist., 1980—, bd. sec. 1991, bd. v.p. 1992—; pres., 1993; v.p. Calif. Mosquito and Vector Control Assn. Trustee Corp. Bd., 1993, pres., 1993-94, mem. exec. bd. dirs., 1994, mem. bd.; mem. adv. panel for bus./econ. devel. Calif. State Legislature, 1979-86. Decorated Bronze Star. Mem. Assn. U.S. Army, Assn. U.S. Army, Non-Commd. Officers Assn., Nat. Geog. Soc. Republican. Roman Catholic. Home and Office: 5314 W Lucky Way Santa Ana CA 92704-1048

BOYSEN, LARS, financial consultant; b. Vejle, Denmark, Aug. 23, 1948; came to U.S., 1975; s. Svenn and Erna (Thomsen) B. BS in Bus. Adminstrn., The Aarhus Sch. Bus., Denmark, 1973, MS in Econs., 1975; postgrad., U. Wash., 1981-82. Mktg. research analyst Santa Fe Fed., San Bernardino, Calif., 1975-77, mktg. research mgr., 1977-79, v.p., mktg. dir., 1979-81; v.p., office adminstrn. mgr. Pacific Fed. Savs. & Loan Assn., Costa Mesa, Calif., 1981-82; v.p., human resources and corp. research dir. Pacific First Bank (formerly Pacific Savs. Bank), Costa Mesa, 1982-86, sr. v.p. corp. services, 1986-89; sr. v.p. adminstrn. Pacific First Bank (formerly Pacific Savs. Bank), Costa Mesa, Calif., 1989-90; v.p. client svcs. TBG Fin., Inc., L.A., 1991—. Recipient First award The Advt. Club, Los Angeles, 1979, Andy award of merit The Advt. Club, N.Y.C., 1980. Office: TBG Fin 2029 Century Park E Ste 3720 Los Angeles CA 90067-3023

BOZANICH, LAWRENCE ANTHONY, school system administrator; b. San Pedro, Calif., Aug. 20, 1937; s. Anthony Frank and Elizabeth (Bosnich) B.; m. Patricia Lee Dowell, June 20, 1959; children: Dennis, Maureen, Kathleen, Kevin, Patrick, Brian, Colleen. BS in Econs., Loyola U., L.A., 1959, postgrad., 1964-66; MS in Edn. Bus. Adminstrn., Mount St. Mary's Coll., 1974. Cert. edn. adminstr., Calif. Ship ops. agt. Gen. Steamship Corp., L.A., 1959-61; adminstrv. officer City of L.A., 1961-66; adminstrv. svcs. mgr. L.A. Sch. Dist., 1966-80; gen. mgr. Fishermen's Coop. Assoc., San Pedro, 1980-86; fin. svcs. officer Long Beach (Calif.) Sch. Dist., 1986—; cons. Republic of Mex., Mexico City, 1986—; mem. Pacific Fishery Adv. Coun., Washington, 1982-86. Mem. fin. com. Campfire Boys and Girls, Long Beach, 1992—. Mem. Calif. Assn. Sch. Bus. Ofcls., San Pedro C. of C. (dir. 1981-86). Democrat. Roman Catholic. Office: Long Beach Unified Sch Dist Fin Divsn 701 Locust Ave # 202 Long Beach CA 90813-4316

BRACEWELL, RONALD NEWBOLD, electrical engineering educator; b. Sydney, Australia, July 22, 1921; s. Cecil Charles and Valerie Zilla (McGowan) B.; m. Helen Mary Lester Elliott; children: Catherine Wendy, Mark Cecil. BS in Math. and Physics, U. Sydney, 1941, B in Engring., 1943, M. in Engring. with 1st class honors, 1948; PhD, Cambridge (Eng.) U., 1951. Sr. rsch. officer Radiophysics Lab., Commonwealth Sci. and Indsl. Rsch. Orgn., Sydney, 1949-54; vis. asst. prof. radio astronomy U. Calif., Berkeley, 1954-55; mem. elec. engring. faculty Stanford U., 1955—, Lewis M. Terman prof. and fellow in elec. engring., 1974-79, now Terman prof. emeritus elec. engring.; Pollock Meml. lectr. U. Sydney, 1978; Tektronix Disting. Visitor, summer 1981; Christensen fellow St. Catherine's Coll., Oxford, autumn 1987; sr. vis. fellow Inst. Astronomy, Cambridge, U., autumn 1988; mem. adv. panels NSF, Naval Rsch. Lab., Office Naval Rsch., NAS, Nat. Radio Astronomy Obs., Jet Propulsion Lab. Adv. Group on Radio Experiments in Space, Advanced Rsch. Projects Agy. Author: The Fourier Transform and Its Applications, 1965, rev. edit., 1986, The Galactic Club: Intelligent Life in Outer Space, 1974, The Hartley Transform, 1986, Two-Dimension Imaging, 1995; co-author: Radio Astronomy, 1955; translator: Radio Astronomy (J.L. Steinberg and J. Lequeux); editor: Paris Symposium on Radio Astronomy, 1959; mem. editl. adv. bd. Planetary and Space Sci.; former mem. editl. adv. bd. Proceedings of the Astron. Soc. Pacific, Cosmic Search, Jour. Computer Assisted Tomography; mem. bd. ann. rev. Astronomy and Astrophysics, 1961-68; contbr. articles and revs. to jours., chpts. to books; patentee in field. Recipient Duddell Premium, Instn. Elec. Engrs., London, 1952, Inaugural Alumni award Sydney U., 1992; Fulbright travel grantee, 1954, William Gurling Watson traveling fellow, 1978, 86. Fellow IEEE (life, Heinrich Hertz Gold medal 1994), AAAS, Royal Astron. Soc.; mem. Inst. Medicine of NAS (fgn. assoc.), Astron. Soc. Pacific (life), Am. Astron. Soc. (past councilor), Astron. Soc. Australia, Internat. Astron. Union, Internat. Sci. Radion Union, Internat. Acad. Astronautics. Home: 836 Santa Fe Ave Stanford CA 94305-1023 Office: Stanford U 329A Durand Bldg Stanford CA 94305

BRACHER, GEORGE, radiologist; b. Portland, Oreg., Mar. 20, 1909; s. George Michael and Anna (Ris) B.; m. Helen Arndt, Oct. 6, 1936; children: Randall W., Ann Louise. BS, U. Oreg., 1932, MD, 1934. Diplomate Am. Bd. Radiology. Intern St. Vincent's Hosp., Portland, 1935; resident fellow U. Chgo., 1936-38; asst. prof. radiology U. Oreg. Med. Sch., Portland, 1938-39; radiologist King County Hosp. System, Seattle, 1939-41, Hilo (Hawaii) Hosp., 1960-85, Lucy Henriques Med. Ctr., Kamuela, Hawaii, 1985—; pvt. practice Seattle and Spokane (Wash.), 1941-60; cons. radiologist Honokaa (Hawaii) Hosp., 1960—, Kohala (Hawaii) Hosp., 1960—, Kau Hosp., Pahala, Hawaii, 1960—; attending physician U. Hawaii Peace Corps Project, 1962-70. Pres. Hawaii County unit Am. Cancer Soc., Hilo, 1970, Hawaii Pacific div. Honolulu, 1972, chmn. Pacific and related islands com., 1975; founder Hawaii County Med. Soc. Scholarship Fund, Cancer Care Trust, Hilo. Mem. AMA, Hawaii Med. Assn., Hawaii County Med. Soc. (pres. 1969), Am. Coll. Radiology, Hawaii Radiologic Soc., Wash. Athletic Club, Hilo Yacht Club. Home: 134 Puako Beach Dr Kamuela HI 96743-9709 Office: Lucy Henriques Med Ctr PO Box 1108 Kamuela HI 96743-1108

BRACKBILL, JEREMIAH UHLER, physicist, educator; b. Harrisburg, Pa., Jan. 19, 1941; s. Martin Hervin and Elizabeth Uhler (Fager) B.; m. Isabel Maria-del-Carmen Mueller, June 11, 1965; children: Lise Mueller, John Fager. BS in Engring. Physics, Lehigh U., 1963; MS, U. Wis., 1970, PhD in Physics, 1971. Mem. staff Los Alamos (N.Mex.) Nat. Lab., 1971-78, 80-94; rsch. prof. Courant Inst., NYU, N.Y.C., 1978-80; prof. applied math. Brown U., Providence, 1985-86; vis. prof. math. and stats. U. N.Mex., Albuquerque, 1988-89, disting. prof. math. and stats., 1992—; lab. fellow Los Alamos Nat. Lab., 1983—. Editor: Multiple Time Scales, 1985; editor-in-chief Jour. of Computational Physics, 1994—; contbr. articles to profl. jours. Served to capt. USAF, 1964-68. Mem. AAAS, Am. Phys. Soc., Am. Geophys. Union. Office: Los Alamos Nat Lab T-3 MS B216 Los Alamos NM 87545

BRACKETT, LOUIS VINCENT, recreation and park administration educator; b. Price, Utah, Apr. 7, 1942; s. Louis Brackett and Renaun (Pace) Hansen; m. Judith Lynne Searle, Aug. 25, 1948; children: Heather Lynne, Louis Todd, Shannon, Nicole Marie. BS, U. Utah, 1966, MS, 1971; postgrad., Ill. State U., 1981. Cert. c.c. tchr., Ariz., cert. therapeutic recreation counselor; lic. ins. agt., Utah. Therapist Utah State Hosp., Provo, 1967-69; instr., therapist U. Utah Med. Ctr., Salt Lake City, 1969-72; therapist Salt Lake Comty. Mental Health Ctr., Salt Lake City, 1972-74; asst. prof., dir. Moraine Valley C.C., Palos Hills, Ill., 1974-81; instr. Ill. State U., Normal, 1981-84; col. U.S. Army, Ft. Benning & Ft. Monroe, Ga. & Va., 1984-92; agt. N.Y. Life Ins. and Am. Western Life, Provo and Salt Lake City, 1992-93; landscaper Stanworth & Landscaping, Inc., Orem, Utah, 1993; instr., trainer Salt Lake C.C., Salt Lake City, 1993—; cons. to aging Extended Care Facilities, Ill., 1976-84; advisor, bd. dirs. Spl. Populations, Utah, 1970-72. Co-author: Activities that Serve a Purpose, 1984. Camp dir. Easter Seal Soc., Normal, 1981-84; civil affairs officer civic projects Ill. NG, Chgo., 1981-84; coun. tng. chair Boy Scouts Am., 1992—. Col. U.S. Army, 1984-92, USAR, 1993—. Faculty devel. grantee Ill. State U., 1982-83. Fellow Nat. Recreation and Parks Assn. (pres. Ill. sect. 1978); mem. NG Assn. U.S. (life, com. mem. 1987—), Assn. U.S. Army, U.S. Army War Coll. (alumni life mem.). Republican. Reorganized Ch. of Jesus Christ of Latter-day Saints. Office: Salt Lake C C 4600 S Redwood Rd Salt Lake City UT 84123-3145

BRADBURY, JOHN WYMOND, sales executive; b. Grants, N.Mex., July 8, 1960; s. John Platt and Ellen Adel (Wilder) B. BA with distinction, U. Colo., 1983. Area mgr. Premiere Wine Mchts., San Francisco, 1984-85; mgr. of fine wines Premiere Wine Mchts., Costa Mesa, Calif., 1985-88; dir. of fine accts. Premiere Wine Mchts., Walnut Creek, Calif., 1988-90; western div. mgr. Parducci Wine Cellars, 1991-92; gen. sales mgr. Western Wine Merchants-Western Distbg. Co., Denver, 1992-93; regional mgr. Prisms Group, Rocky Mountain, 1993-94; fine wine mgr. Palace Brands, L.A., 1994—.

BRADBURY, STEPHEN DOUGLAS, judge, rancher; b. Long Beach, Calif., Jan. 25, 1950; m. Karen Lee Taylor, Aug. 14, 1971; children: William, Michael, Amedee. BA with honors, San Diego State U., 1973; JD, U. Calif., San Francisco, 1976. Bar: Calif. 1976, U.S. Dist. Ct. (ea. dist.) Calif. 1977, U.S. Supreme Ct. 1982. Ptnr. Harvey & Bradbury, Susanville, Calif., 1977-79, Bradbury, Kellison and Cady, PC, Susanville, 1979-84; v.p., gen. counsel Five Dot Land & Cattle Co., Inc., Susanville, 1984-86; judge Lassen Consolidated Jud. Dist., Lassen County, Calif., 1986—; mem. jud. faculty Calif. Jud. Coll., U. Calif., Berkeley (mcpl. ct. seminar leader 1992, rural cts. course 1993, 94), Calif. Rural Cts. Conf. (ethics session 1992, 93, mem. planning com. 1992, 93, 94), Mcpl. and Justice Cts. Inst., San Diego (contempt and sanctions 1993, jud. chairperson 1993, mem. planning com. 1992); apptd. by chief justice to standing com. jud. performance Jud. Coun. Calif., 1994—. Trustee Lassen C.C. Dist., 1978-86, Shaffer Union Sch. Dist., 1980-86; bd. chairperson City of Susanville Mcpl. Energy Corp., 1981-82; capt. Lassen County Sheriff's Posse, 1984; active Nev. area coun. Boy Scouts Am. With USAF, 1968-70. Recipient Dist. award of Merit, Boy Scouts Am., 1993. Mem. Calif. Judges Assn. (justice cts. mgmt. com. 1987-93, jud. chairperson rural mcpl. and justice cts. forum 1993-94), Lassen County Cattlemens Assn., Lassen County Farm Bur., Rotary Club (bd. dirs. Susanville chpt. 1990-94, pres. 1994—), Pi Sigma Alpha, Phi Delta Phi. Office: Courthouse 200 S Lassen St Susanville CA 96130

BRADBURY, WILLIAM CHAPMAN, III, state senator; b. Chgo., May 29, 1949; s. William L. and Lorraine (Patterson) B.; m. Betsy Harrison (Sept. 1984); children: Abby, Zoe; m. Kathleen P. Eymann, June 7, 1986. Student, Antioch Coll., 1967-69. Dir. pub. affairs Sta. KMPX-TV, San Francisco, 1970; mem. video prodn. group Optic Nerve, San Francisco, 1970-73; project dir. Coos Country TV, Bandon, Oreg., 1973-75; reporter, anchor Sta. KVAL-TV, Eugene, Oreg., 1975-76; news dir. Sta. KCBY-TV, Coos Bay, Oreg., 1976-78; prodr., writer, editor video news feature svc. Local Color, Langlois, Oreg., 1978-79; field prodr. PM Mag., Sta. KGW-TV, Portland, Oreg., 1979-80; mem. Oreg. Ho. of Reps., Salem, 1980-84; mem. Oreg. Senate, Salem, 1984—, pres., 1993-95; former videographer TVTV, L.A.; chmn. Western Legis. Conf., Coun. State Govs., 1991, mem. ocean resources com.; founder, former chmn. Pacific Fishery Legis. Task Force. Prodr. documentaries Gorda Ridge—Boom or Bust for the Oregon Coast?, The Tillamook Burn—From Ruin to Rejuvenation, Not Guilty by Reason of Insanity, Child as Witness, Local Color, Salmon on the Run, The First Perennial Poetic Hoohaw, TV Town Hall Meetings, Common Sense, also prodr. mktg. videos and commls. for polit. candidates, hosp. Democrat. Mem. Soc. of Friends. Home: PO Box 1499 Bandon OR 97411-1499 Office: State Capitol Oreg Senate S 311 Salem OR 97310-3445

BRADEN, GEORGE WALTER, II (LORD OF CARRIGALINE), company executive; b. L.A., Sept. 1, 1936; s. Paul Sumner and Evelyn Widney (Traver) B.; m. Trina Rose Thomas, July 3, 1964; children: Barbara Diane, Beverly Eileen Braden Christensen. BS, Calif. State U., 1963; grad. cert., U. So. Calif., 1990, Harvard U., 1991; postgrad., UCLA, 1990—; MBA, Chadwick U.; JA, Blackstone Law Sch. Mgr. western region vet. div. Bristol-Myers, Syracuse, N.Y., 1970-79; pres. Braden Sales Assocs. Internat., Apple Valley, Calif., 1980—. Mem. Friends of Hoover Inst., Stanford, Calif.; charter mem. Rep. Presdl. Task Force, Washington, 1989—; commr. Rep. Presdl. Adv. Com., Washington, 1991—; active Nat. Rep. Senatorial Com. Capt. USMC, 1985-93, maj., 1993—. Recipient Presdl. order Of Merit, Heritage Found., Rep. Presdl. award, 1994; numerous awards Boy Scouts of Am. Mem. Am. Mktg. Assn., Tex. A&M U. Internat. Assn. of Agri-Bus., Meml. Soc. of Great Britain, Pres.'s Club. Mem. LDS Ch.

BRADFORD, CRAIG SNOW, city official; b. San Francisco, Feb. 10, 1944; s. Lowell W. and Mauvia S. (Tracy) B.; m. Sharon A. Cokely, July 27, 1973; children: Matthew, Daniel, Anna-Marie. B.S. in Biol. Scis., U. Utah, 1968; M.A. In Internat. Law, U. So. Calif., Cambridge, Eng., 1980. Commd. 2d lt. USAF, 1968, advanced through grades to col., 1987; U.S. diplomat, Chief Aviation, Office Mil. Cooperation USAF, Cairo, 1988-90; chief staff 57th Fighter Weapons Wing, dep. inspector gen. USAF, Nellis AFB, Nev., 1990-91, dir. quality improvement Fighter Weapons Ctr., 1991-93; pres. Bradford & Assocs Internat., Las Vegas, Nev., 1993—; dir. project adminstrn. City of North Las Vegas, Nev., 1992-93, dep. city mgr., 1994—; bd. dirs. Quality and Productivity Inst., Nev., 1991—; mem. Gov.'s Task Force for Reinstating Govt., Nev., 1993—. Author, producer video Rebirth of a City: A Total Quality Challenge, 1994. Mem. election bd. Clark County, Nev., 1993; Eagle Scout advisor, mem. com. Boy Scouts Am., 1993-94. Decorated Legion of Merit, DFC (7), Bronze Star with "V", Purple Heart, Air medals (16), Vietnamese Cross of Gallantry with bronze star, Vietnamese Cross of Gallantry with Gold Palm. Mem. Indsl. Rels. Rsch. Assn. Republican. Mem. LDS Ch. Home: 323 Oliveiro Ct Henderson NV 89014-5100

BRADFORD, DAVID PAUL, judicial assistant; b. Lynwood, Calif., Mar. 23, 1955; s. William H. and Barbara E. (O'Leary) Johnson. AA, Citrus Coll., Azusa, Calif., 1975; BA in Polit. Sci., UCLA, 1978; postgrad., Calif. State U., L.A., 1984-85, U. W. L.A., 1990-91. Prin. clerk UCLA Brain Rsch. Inst., 1977-81; adminstrv. asst., supr. UCLA Hosp. and Clinics, 1977-81; dep. to atty. in residence matters office of registrar UCLA, 1981-85; office of clerk L.A. County Bd. Suprs., L.A., 1987-88; judicial asst., ct. clerk L.A. Superior Ct., L.A., 1988—; founder Bradford & Assocs., L.A., 1987—; rsch. dir. citizens Protection Alliance, Santa Monica, 1992—. Active L.A. County Domestic Violence Coun. Recipient Cert. of Appreciation, Domestic Violence Coun., 1990, Commendation, L.A. County Bd. Suprs., 1993. Mem. AAAS, N.Y. Acad. Scis., L.A. County Superior Ct. Clerks Assn. (local 575 AFSCME, pres. 1993, 94), N.Y. Acad. Polit. Scis. Office: LA County Superior Ct Rm 215 Dept 2 111 N Hill St Ste 215 Los Angeles CA 90012-3106

BRADKOWSKI, KEITH A., patient services administrator; b. Chgo., July 18, 1956; s. Frank J. and Violet (Reshel) Bradkowski. BSN, Rush U., 1983; MS, U. Ill., Chgo., 1984. RN, Ill., Calif.; cert. nursing adminstrn. advanced ANCC. Tng. Nat. Inst. Mental Health, 1983-84; clin. nurse mgr. Northwestern Meml. Hosp., Chgo., 1986-90, clin. nurse mgr. II, 1990-92; clin. dir. surg. nursing Cedars-Sinai Med. Ctr., L.A., 1992-93; adminstrv. dir. patient care svcs. Santa Monica (Calif.) Hosp. Med. Ctr., 1993-95; assoc. dir. patient care svcs. Santa Monica-UCLA Med. Ctr., 1995—; mem. adv. bd. RN Times; instr. psychiat.-mental health nursing Lewis U., 1985-86; mem. adj. faculty med.-surg. nursing U. Ill., Chgo., 1986-92; adj. grad. clin. preceptor Rush U. Coll. Nursing, Chgo., 1986-88; mem. clin. specialist task force Calif. Bd. Registered Nursing, Sacramento, 1994. Mem. Am. Orgn. Nurse Execs. (exec. task force 1995), Calif. Orgn. Nurse Execs., Sigma Theta Tau. Home: 7660 Beverly Blvd Apt 452 Los Angeles CA 90036-2747 Office: Santa Monica Hosp Med Ctr 1250 16th St Santa Monica CA 90404-1249

BRADLEY, CHARLES WILLIAM, podiatrist, educator; b. Fife, Tex., July 23, 1923; s. Tom and Mary Ada (Cheatham) B.; m. Marilyn A. Brown, Apr. 3, 1948 (dec. Mar. 1973); children: Steven, Gregory, Jeffrey, Elizabeth, Gerald. Student, Tex. Tech., 1940-42; D. Podiatric Medicine, Calif. Coll. Podiatric Medicine U. San Francisco, 1949, MPA, 1987, D.Sc. (hon.). Pvt. practice podiatry Beaumont, Tex., 1950-51, Brownwood, Tex., 1951-52, San Francisco, San Bruno, Calif., 1952—; assoc. clin. prof. Calif. Coll. Podiatric Medicine, 1992—; chief of staff Calif. Podiatry Hosp., San Francisco; mem. surg. staff Sequoia Hosp., Redwood City, Calif.; mem. med. staff Peninsula Hosp., Burlingame, Calif.; chief podiatry staff St. Luke's Hosp., San Francisco; chmn. bd. Podiatry Ins. Co. Am.; cons. VA; assoc. prof. podiatric medicine Calif. Coll. Podiatric Medicine. Mem. San Francisco Symphony Found.; mem. adv. com. Health Policy Agenda for the Am. People, AMA; chmn. trustees Calif. Coll. Podiatric Medicine, Calif. Podiatry Coll., Calif. Podiatry Hosp.; mem. San Mateo Grand Jury, 1989. Served with USNR, 1942-45. Mem. Am. Podiatric Med. Assn. (trustee, pres. 1983-84), Calif. Podiatry Assn. (pres. No. div. 1964-66, state bd. dirs., pres. 1975-76, Podiatrist of Yr. award 1983), Nat. Coun. Edn. (vice-chmn.), Nat. Acads. Practice (chmn. podiatric med. sect.), Am. Legion, San Bruno C. of C. (bd. dirs. 1978-91, v.p. 1992, bd. dir. grand jury assoc. 1990), Olympic Club, Commonwealth Club Calif., Elks, Lions. Home: 2965 Trousdale Dr Burlingame CA 94010-5708 Office: 560 Jenevein Ave San Bruno CA 94066-4408

BRADLEY, JAMES ALEXANDER, software engineer, researcher; b. Van Nuys, Calif., May 16, 1965; m. Alyson Wait, July 11, 1992. BA in Math., Computer Sci., U. Colo., 1988, postgrad., 1991—. Software developer Sci. Computer Systems, Inc., Boulder, Colo., 1982-84; teaching asst. Boulder Valley Pub. Schs., Boulder, Colo., 1984-87; software engr. Martin Marietta Aerospace, Littleton, Colo., 1988-94; dir. software engring. Intelligent Energy Corp., Golden, Colo., 1994—. Recipient NASA New Tech. award, Martin Marietta Aerospace, 1990. mem. Am. Math. Soc., Math. Assn. Am., Golden Key Honor Soc. Office: Intelligent Energy Corp 607 10th St Ste 203 Golden CO 80401-5828

BRADLEY, JEAN ELEANOR, newspaper executive, public relations consultant; b. North York, Ontario, Can., Apr. 14, 1928; d. Archer and Eleanor (Aitkin) Wardle; m. Kenneth Gordon Bradle, Nov. 26, 1949; children: Jill (dec. 1964), Anne Marjorie Bradley Jaeger. Grad., Earl Haig Coll., North York, Ontario, Can., 1945; student bus. mgmt., Portland (Oreg.) C.C., 1981-85; student computer sci., U. Oregon, Rock Creek, 1987-88. Underwriter, office mgr. A.B. Ferguson, Ins., Toronto, Ontario, Can., 1946-55; asst. editor, co-owner Estevan (Saskatchewan) Mercury, 1964-66; pub. rels. mgr. Kaiser Permanente N.W. region, Portland, Oreg., 1966-88; v.p., co-owner Daily Shipping News, Portland, 1985—; exec. com. Kaiser Permanente Retirees, Portland, 1989—. Contbg. author: Oregon Writers Colony

Anthology, 1993; contbr. articles to various newspapers and mags. Bd. Dirs. Vol. Ctr., Portland, 1989-95. Recipient 1st pl. fiction Nat. Fedn. Press Women, 1990, 1st pl. brochure Oreg. Press Women, 1994; named Outstanding Profl. of Yr., Women in Comms., Portland, 1986. Mem. Pub. Rels. Soc. Am. (accredited, chpt. pres. 1980, dist. chmn. 1985, president's citation 1985, William Marsh lifetime achievement award Columbia River chpt. 1988), Oreg. Press Women (various coms.), Oreg. Writers Colony (bd. dirs. 1994), Colored Pencil Soc. Am., Daus. Brit. Empire (v.p. state bd. dirs. 1989-93). Office: Daily Shipping News 7831 SE Stark St Ste 200 Portland OR 97215-2357

BRADLEY, MARK CHARLES, defender; b. Detroit, Dec. 28, 1965; s. Roger Wilson and Phyllis Marian (Readhead) B. BA, Hope Coll., 1988; JD, Northwestern U. Sch. of Law, 1993. Bar: Wash. Info. systems cons. Andersen Consulting, Detroit, 1988-90; community organizer North River Commn., Chgo., 1990; asst. pub. defender The Defender Assn., Seattle, 1993—. Mem. ACLU, Nat. Lawyers Guild. Home: 1519 3rd Ave Apt 501 Seattle WA 98101-1623 Office: The Defender Assn 810 3rd Ave Fl 8 Seattle WA 98104-1614

BRADLEY, WADE HARLOW, acquisitions specialist; b. Mpls.; s. Robert Douglas and Florence (Wells) B.; m. Alessandra Maria Benitez, June 30, 1984; children: Isabella Andrea, Francesca Alessandra. BS, U. Minn., 1983; postgrad., LaJolla Acad. Advt., 1984. Bus. cons. A.B.A. Investment Corp., LaJolla, Calif., 1987-88; pres. The Harlow Co., San Diego, 1987—; acquisitions specialist Pacific Capital Ptnrs., San Diego, 1989-90; sr. v.p. corp. devel. Sundance Resources Inc., San Diego, 1990-95, sr. v.p., 1995—; design cons. Forty Five Metro, LaJolla, 1983-85. Republican. Roman Catholic. Office: Sundance Sys Inc 12526 High Bluff Dr Ste 300 San Diego CA 92130-2067

BRADSHAW, CARL JOHN, investor, lawyer, consultant; b. Oelwein, Iowa, Nov. 1, 1930; s. Carl John and Lorraine Lillian (Thiele) B.; m. Katsuko Anno, Nov. 5, 1954; children: Carla K., Arthur Herbert, Vincent Marcus. BS, U. Minn., 1952, JD, 1957; LLM, U. Mich., 1958; MJur, Keio U., Tokyo, 1962. Bar: Minn. 1960, U.S. Supreme Ct., 1981, Calif. 1985,. Assoc. Graham, James & Rolph, Tokyo, 1961-63; assoc. prof. law U. Wash., Seattle, 1963-64; sr. v.p. Oak Industries, Inc., Crystal Lake, Ill., 1964-84, dir. internat. ops., 1964-70, dir. corp. devel., 1970-72, pres. communications group, 1972-78, chief legal officer, 1979-84; counsel Seki & Jarvis, L.A., 1985-87, Bell, Boyd & Lloyd, L.A., 1987; prin. The Pacific Law Group, L.A., Tokyo and Palo Alto, Calif., 1987—, The Asian Mktg. Group, Torrance, Calif., 1992—; participant Japanese-Am. program for cooperation in legal studies, 1957-61. Contbr. articles to legal and bus. jours. Bd. dirs. Japan-Am. Soc., Chgo., 1966-72; bd. dirs., fin. dir. San Diego Symphony Orch. Assn., 1980-81. Served to lt. (j.g.) USN, 1952-55. Fulbright scholar, 1958-59, Ford Found. scholar, 1960-61. Fellow Radio Club Am.; mem. Minn. Bar Assn., Calif. Bar Assn., Am. Soc. Internat. Law, Internat. Fiscal Assn., San Diego Bar Assn., Westwood Bar Assn., Regency Club, Order of Coif, Internat. House of Japan. Home: 12958 Robleda Cv San Diego CA 92128-1126 Office: Pacific Law Group 12121 Wilshire Blvd Fl 2 Los Angeles CA 90025-1123

BRADSHAW, RALPH ALDEN, biochemistry educator; b. Boston, Feb. 14, 1941; s. Donald Bertram and Eleanor (Dodd) B.; m. Roberta Perry Wheeler, Dec. 29, 1961; children: Christopher Evan, Amy Dodd. BA in Chemistry, Colby Coll., 1962; PhD, Duke U., 1966. Asst. prof. Washington U., St. Louis, 1969-72, assoc. prof., 1972-74, prof., 1974-82; prof., chair dept. U. Calif., Irvine, 1982-93, prof., 1993—; study sect. chmn. NIH, 1979, mem., 1975-79, 80-85; mem. sci. advisory bd. Hereditary Disease Found., 1983-87, ICN Nucleic Acids Research Inst., 1986-87; research study com. physiol. chem. Am. Heart Assn., 1984-86, mem. Council on Thrombosis, 1976-90; fellowship screening com. Am. Cancer Soc. Calif., 1984-87; chmn. adv. com. Western Winter Workshops, 1984-88; dir., chmn., mem. organizing com. numerous symposia, confs. in field including Proteins in Biology and Medicine, Shanghai, Peoples Republic China, 1981, Symposium Am. Protein Chemists, San Diego, 1985, chmn. exec. com. Keystone Symp. Mol. Cell. Biol., 1991-94, bd. trustees, 1991—, Internat. Union Biochem. Mol. Biol., 1991—, U.S. Nat. Commn. Biochem., 1987—, chmn., 1992—. Mem. editorial bd. Archives Biochemistry and Biophysics, 1972-88, Jour. Biological Chemistry, 1973-77, 78-79, 81-86, assoc. editor, 1989—, Jour. Supramolecular Structure/Cellular Biochemistry, 1980-91, Bioscience Reports, 1980-87, Peptide and Protein Reviews, 1980-86, Jour. Protein Chemistry, 1980-90, IN VITRO Rapid Communication in Cell Biology, 1984—; editor Trends in Biochemical Sciences, 1975-91, editor-in-chief, 1986-91, J. Neurochem, 1986-90, Proteins: Structure, Functions & Genetics, 1988-92, Growth Factors, 1989—; assoc. editor: Protein Science, 1990-92, mem. editl. bd., 1992—; contbr. numerous articles to scientific jours. Recipient Young Scientist award Passano Found., 1976. Fellow AAAS; mem. Am. Chem. Soc. (Sect. award 1979), Am. Soc. Biol. Chemists (coun. 1987-90, treas. 1991—), Am. Peptide Soc., N.Y. Acad. Scis., Protein Soc. (acting pres. 1986-87), Am. Soc. Neurochemistry, Am. Soc. for Cell Biology, Soc. for Neuroscience, The Endocrine Soc., Sigma Xi. Home: 25135 Rivendell Dr Lake Forest CA 92630-4134 Office: U Calif Irvine Dept Biol Chemistry CCM D240 Irvine CA 92717

BRADY, DORSEY RAY, hotel executive; b. Long Beach, Calif., Apr. 20, 1942; s. Arnold Ray and Dora Della (Helzer) B.; m. Patricia Dip Sheong Hoo, Aug. 25, 1968; children: Diana, Dawn, Dane. Student, UCLA, 1959-63. Cert. hotel adminstr. Asst. mgr. Deauville Country Club, Tarzana, Calif., 1963-65, Playboy Club, Hollywood, Calif., 1965-66; mgr. Hawaii Kai Golf Course, Honolulu, 1966—; asst. Kauai Surf, Lihue, Hawaii, 1966-70, resident mgr., 1972-75; gen. mgr. Kaanapali Beach Hotel, Lahaina, Hawaii, 1970-71, Kona Inn, Kailua-Kona, Hawaii, 1971-72, The Whaler, Kaanapali Beach, Hawaii, 1975; various positions Del Webb Hotels, various cities, 1975-83; sr. v.p., staff ops. Del Webb Hotels, Las Vegas, Nev., 1981, v.p. hotel ops., 1981-83; v.p. western region Quality Hotels and Resorts, Anaheim, Calif., 1983-84; gen. mgr. Surf and Sand Hotel, Laguna Beach, Calif., 1985; exec. v.p. ops. Continental Inns Inc., La Jolla, Calif., 1985-87; Western regional v.p. Tollman-Hundley Hotels, Santa Ana, Calif., 1988-90; v.p. ops. Outrigger Hotels Hawaii, Honolulu, 1990—; lectr. Kauai Community Coll., Lihue, 1968, mem. adv. bd., 1974, Maui Community Coll., Kahului, Hawaii, 1970-71. Bd. dirs. Kauai Visitor Industry Orgn., Lihue, 1973. Served with USMC, 1960-62. Mem. Confrerie De La Chaine Des Rotisseurs, Calif. Hotel Assn., Hawaii Hotel Assn. (bd. dirs. 1974, 94, 95), Skal (exec. com. 1984, v.p. 1994, pres. 1995), Am. Hotel and Motel Assn., Kailua Kona C. of C. (bd. dirs. 1971), UCLA Alumni Assn. (life). Republican. Office: Outrigger Hotels Hawaii 69-275 Waikoloa Beach Dr Kamuela HI 96743-9763

BRADY, JOHN PATRICK, JR., electronics educator, consultant; b. Newark, Mar. 20, 1929; s. John Patrick and Madeleine Mary (Atno) B.; m. Mary Coop, May 1, 1954; children: Peter, John P., Madeleine, Dennis, Mary G. BSEE, MIT, 1952, MSEE, 1953. Registered profl. engr., Mass. Sect. mgr. Hewlett-Packard Co., Waltham, Mass., 1956-67; v.p. engring. John Fluke Mfg. Co., Inc., Mountlake Terrace, Wash., 1967-73; v.p. engring. Dana Labs., Irvine, Calif., 1973-77; engring. mgr., tech. advisor to gen. mgr. Metron Corp., Upland, Calif., 1977-78; ptnr. Resource Assocs., Newport Beach, Calif., 1978-86; prof. electronics Orange Coast Coll., Costa Mesa, Calif., 1977—, faculty fellow, dean technology, 1983-84, chmn. electronics tech. dept., 1994—; instr. computers and electrinc engring. Calif. State U., Long Beach, 1982-84. Mem. evaluation team Accrediting Commn. for Community and Jr. Colls., 1982-92; mem. blue ribbon adv. com. on oversees technology transfer U.S. Dept. of Commerce, 1974-76. With USN, 1946-48. Mem. Measurement Sci. Conf. (dir. 1982-83), MIT (L.A.). Contbr. articles in field to profl. jours.; mem. Eta Kappa Nu, Tau Beta Pi, Sigma Xi. Office: Orange Coast Coll Costa Mesa CA 92626

BRADY, LEE BURNETT, columnist, playwright; b. Seminole, Okla., Oct. 30, 1932; d. William and Arlie (Jones) Burnett; m. Charles Edward Brady, Dec. 8, 1952; children: Michael Sean, Joseph Patrick, Kathryn Linn. BA in English Lit., Towson State U., 1969; MA in Theatre, U. Hawaii, 1973; MA in English and Creative Writing, San Francisco State U., 1983. Playwright San Francisco, 1980—; columnist, critic Pacific Sun Newspaper, Mill Valley, Calif., 1982—; instr. creative writing Monterey (Calif.) Peninsula Coll., 1975—; artist-in-residence Ft. Lewis Coll., Durango, Colo., 1985, San Francisco Performing Arts High sch., 1990-91. Workshop coord. Bay Area Playwrights Festival, San Francisco, 1982-83. Recipient Best Script and Musical award Bay Area Theatre Critics, 1992, Best Script and Children's Play award Columbia Entertainment Co., 1993, Best Script award U. Ark. "Kernodle" competition, 1994. Democrat. Office: Pacific Sun Newspaper 21 Corte Madera Ave Mill Valley CA 94941-1800

BRADY, MARY ROLFES, music educator; b. St. Louis, Nov. 26, 1933; d. William Henry and Helen Dorothy (Slavick) Rolfes; m. Donald Sheridan Brady, Aug. 29, 1953; children: Joseph William, Mark David, Douglas Sheridan, John Rolfes, Todd Christopher. Student, Stanford U., 1951-54, UCLA, 1967, U. So. Calif., 1972-73; pvt. studies with, Roxanna Byers, Dorothy Desmond, and Rudolph Ganz. Pvt. practice tchr. piano L.A., 1955—; TV and radio performer; pres. Jr. Philharmonic Com. L.A., 1975-76; legis. coord., bd. dirs. Philharmonic Affiliates, L.A., 1978-80. Life mem. Good Samaritan Hosp., St. Vincent Med. Ctr., L.A., The Amazing Blue Ribbon, 1979—; bd. dirs. Hollygrove-L.A. Orphans Home, Inc.; trustee St. Francis Med. Ctr., 1984-88. Mem. Am. Coll. Musicians Club, Stanford Women's Club (past bd. dirs., pres. L.A. chpt. 1977—), The Muses, Springs Country Club.

BRADY, RODNEY HOWARD, broadcast company executive, former college president, former government official; b. Sandy, Utah, Jan. 31, 1933; s. Kenneth A. and Jessie (Madsen) B.; m. Carolyn Ann Hansen, Oct. 25, 1960; children: Howard Riley, Bruce Ryan, Brooks Alan. BS in Acctg. with high honors, U. Utah, MBA with high honors, 1957; DBA, Harvard U., 1966; postgrad., UCLA, 1969-70; PhD (hon.), Weber State Coll., 1986, Snow Coll., 1991. Missionary Ch. Jesus Christ of Latter-day Saints, Great Britain, 1953-55; teaching assoc. Harvard U. Bus. Sch., Cambridge, Mass., 1957-59; v.p. Mgmt. Systems Corp., Cambridge, 1962-65, Center Exec. Devel., Cambridge, 1963-64; v.p., dir. Center Exec. Devel., Boston, 1964-65; v.p. Tamerand Reef Corp., Christiansted, St. Croix, V.I., 1963-65; v.p., dir. Am. Inst. Execs., N.Y.C., 1963-65; v.p., mem. exec. com. aircraft div. Hughes Tool Co., Culver City, Calif., 1966-70; asst. sec. adminstrn. and mgmt. Dept. HEW, Washington, 1970-72; chmn. subcabinet exec. officers group of exec. br., 1971-72; exec. v.p., chmn. exec. com., dir. Bergen Brunswig Corp., Los Angeles, 1972-78; chmn. bd. Uni-mgrs. Internat., Los Angeles, 1974-78; pres. Weber State Coll., Ogden, Utah, 1978-85; pres., CEO Bonneville Internat. Corp., Salt Lake City, 1985—, also dir.; bd. dirs. Bergen Brunswig Corp., 1st Security Bank Corp., Smith's Food & Drug, Inc., Mgmt. and Tng. Corp., Deseret Mut. Benefit Assn., Maximum Svc. Telecasters, Intermountain Health Care Found.; bd. advisors Mountain Bell Telephone, 1983-87; chmn. Nat. Adv. Com. on Accreditation and Instl. Eligibility, 1984-86, mem., 1983-87; chmn. Utah Gov.'s Blue Ribbon Com. on Tax Recodification, 1984-90; cons. Dept. Def., Dept. State, Dept. Commerce, HEW, NASA, Govt. of Can., Govt. of India (and indsl. firms), 1962—. Author: An Approach to Equipment Replacement Analysis, 1957, Survey of Management Planning and Control Systems, 1962, The Impact of Computers on Top Management Decision Making in the Aerospace and Defense Industry, 1966, (with others) How To Structure Incentive Contracts—A Programmed Text, 1965, My Missionary Years in Great Britain, 1976, An Exciting Start Along an Upward Path, 1978; contbr. articles to profl. jours. Mem. exec. com. nat. exec. bd. Boy Scouts Am., 1977—; chmn. nat. Cub Scout commn., 1977-81, pres. Western region, 1981-83, chmn. nat. ct. of honor, 1984-88; mem. adv. com. program for health systems mgmt. Harvard U., 1973-78, mem. nat. adv. coun. U. Utah, 1971—, chairperson, 1974-76, nat. adv. bd. Coll. Bus., 1985—, chmn., 1989-93, mem. adv. com. Brigham Young U. Bus. Sch., 1972—; mem. dean's round table UCLA Grad. Sch. Mgmt., 1973-78; trustee Ettie Lee Homes for Boys, 1973-79; mem. governing bd. McKay Dee Hosp., Ogden, Utah, 1979-87; bd. dirs. Utah Endowment for Humanities, 1978-80, Nat. Legal Ctr. for the Pub. Interest, 1991-94, vice chmn., 1994—, Utah Shakespeare Festival, 1992—, Ogden C. of C., 1978-83. 1st lt. USAF, 1959-62. Recipient Silver Antelope award Boy Scouts Am., 1976; recipient Silver Beaver award Boy Scouts Am., 1979, Silver Buffalo award Boy Scouts Am., 1982, Disting. Alumni award U. Utah, 1990. Mem. Am. Mgmt. Assn. (award 1969), Am. Def. Preparedness Assn., Nat. Indsl. Security Assn., U.S. Army Assn., Air Force Assn., Am. Helicopter Soc., L.A. C. of C. (tax structure com. 1969-70), Salt Lake Area C. of C. (bd. dirs. 1985-88), SAR (pres. Utah chpt. 1986-87), Sons of Utah Pioneers, Freedoms Found. at Valley Forge (nat. bd. dirs. 1986—), Nat. Legal Ctr. Pub. Interest (nat. bd. dirs. 1991—, chmn. 1995—), L.A. Country Club, Ft. Douglas Country Club, Alta Club, Rotary, Phi Kappa Phi, Tau Kappa Alpha, Beta Gamma Sigma. Mem. LDS Ch. (past pres. L.A. stake). Office: Bonneville Internat Corp PO Box 1160 Salt Lake City UT 84110-1160

BRADY, TIMOTHY SCOTT, health care administration educator, management consultant; b. Canton, Ohio. BA, Tex. Luth. Coll., 1967; MBA, U. N.Mex., 1978; PhD, Columbia Pacific U., 1980. Dep. div. mgr. ARC, Albuquerque, 1973-78; gen. mgr. Ednl. Systems, Albuquerque, 1979-83; exec. dir. Panhandle Emergency System, Amarillo, Tex., 1983-84; pres. San Joaquin Health Care, Fresno, Calif., 1985-88; assoc. prof. Calif. State U., Bakersfield, 1988-94; prin. cons. Health Svcs. Inc., Tucson, 1994—; cons., prin. Brahms and Assocs., Albuquerque, 1978-83. Editor: Positive Pressure Ventilation, 1991; patentee in field. Bd. dirs. Bakersfield Native Am. Coun., Bakersfield, 1989-93, Ammonia Safety Tng. Inst., Watsonville, Calif., 1990—. Capt. U.S. Army, 1968-72. Recipient Hazardous Gases grant Tempest Tech., 1992, Health Care grant Kaiser Permanente, 1993. Mem. Am. Coll. Health Care Execs., Pi Alpha Alpha. Home: PO Box 41376 Bakersfield CA 93384-1376 Office: PO Box 31584 Tucson AZ 85751

BRAGDON, LYNN LYON, library administrator; b. Kansas City, Mo., Dec. 22, 1944; d. Chester Willard and Frances Helen (Bechtold) Lyon; m. James Albert Bragdon, Jr., June 16, 1969. BS in Edn., Central Mo. State U., 1967; cert., U. Paris at Sorbonne, 1966; MLS, U. Okla., 1968. Rsch. libr. E.I. DuPont de Nemours, Wilmington, Del., 1968-72; asst. libr. North Cobb H.S., Marietta, Ga., 1972-74; head cataloging U. Miss. Med. Ctr., Jackson, 1975-76, assoc. dir. libr. ops., 1976-77; mgr. reference svcs. Miss. R & D Ctr., Jackson, 1977-79; chief libr. svc. VA Med. Ctr., Grand Junction, Colo., 1980—; mem. governing bd. Pathfinders Regional Libr. System, 1985—; mem. regional adv. com. Midcontinental Regional Med. Libr. Program, Omaha, 1988-92; mentor new chiefs libr. svc. Dept. Vets. Affairs, Washington, 1992—. Mem. Jr. Svc. League/Colo. Riverfront Commn., Grand Junction,, 1984—, bd. dirs., 1986-94, sec., 1988-90, coord. park, 1991-94; active Western Colo. Mus., 1984—. Mem. Acad. Health Info. Profls. (sr.), Med. Libr. Assn., Colo. Coun. Med. Librs., Colo. Nat. Monument Assn. (v.p., bd. dirs. 1986-87, mem. bd. dirs. 1986-92), Grand Junction Gem and Mineral Soc. (libr. 1983), Western Colo. Botanic Soc. Methodist. Avocations: travelling, wildflower photography, cross-country skiing, music. Home: 610 Broken Spoke Rd Grand Junction CO 81504-5270 Office: Library Service 142D VA Med Ctr 2121 North Ave Grand Junction CO 81501-6428

BRAGG, ALBERT FORSEY, retired airline captain; b. Providence, Oct. 25, 1932; s. Horatio Frederick Roy and Olive Lavinia (Bardsley) B.; m. Anne Dana Bernard, Mar. 22, 1955 (div. 1977); children: Steven Keith, Gail Marie; m. Anita Bürki, Aug. 6, 1983. Student, Duke U., 1950-53. Lic. air transport pilot, flight engr., FAA, numerous ratings. First officer-capt. N.Y. Airways, Inc., N.Y.C., 1959-64; flight ops. instr. United Air Lines, Denver, 1964-65; flight engr. United Air Lines, Chgo., 1965-66; co-pilot United Air Lines, N.Y.C., Denver, 1967-83; capt. United Air Lines, 1983-92; check airman United Air Lines, Denver, 1984-85, 86-89, flight check mgr., 1985-86; pilot Boeing 747 United Air Lines, N.Y.C., 1991-92; aerospace edn. officer Civil Air Patrol, Boonton, N.J., 1972-74, Denver, 1974-79. Designer, builder dome for astronomic obs., Sheep Hill Obs., Boonton, N.J., 1973. Mem. sch. bd. Town of Boonton, 1972-75; active Colo. Motor Sports Coun. Comdr. USN, 1954-59. Recipient life saving award Civil Air Patrol, Denver, 1977, first place short take off contest Nat. Stearman Fly-In, Galesburg, Ill., 1992, 93, 94. Mem. Exptl. Aircraft Assn. (safety lectr., tech. counselor Rocky Mountaing Builder Forum), Tail Hook Assn., Antique Aircraft Assn., Stearman Restorers Assn., Mercedes Benz Club (bd. dirs. 1989—, treas. 1992-94, pres. 1994—, Mem. of Yr. 1991, Otto Saborsky award 1994), Ret. United Pilots Assn. Republican. Home: 10695 W Rowland Ave Littleton CO 80127-2941

BRAGG, DARRELL BRENT, nutritionist, consultant; b. Sutton, W.Va., May 24, 1933; s. William H. and Gertrude (Perrine) B.; m. Elizabeth Hosse, Dec. 28, 1957; children: Roger, Larry, Teresa. BSc, W.Va. U., 1959, MSc, 1960; PhD, U. Ark., 1966. Instr. dept. animal sci. U. Ark., Fayetteville, 1965-67; asst. prof. U. Man., Winnipeg, Can., 1967-68, assoc. prof., 1970-74; assoc. prof. dept. poultry sci. U. B.C., Vancouver, Can., 1970-74, prof., head dept., 1975-86; industry cons., Vancouver, 1986-89; nutritionist, dir. quality assurance Rangen Aquaculture Feeds, Buhl, Idaho, 1990-92; sr. rsch. scientist Rangen Aquaculture Rsch. Ctr., Hagerman, Idaho, 1991-92; indsl. biochem. cons. Deutrel Labs. Inc., Palmdale, Calif., 1991—. Contbr. numerous articles to sci. jours. With U.S. Army, 1954-56. Recipient numerous rsch. grants from industry, univs. and govts. Mem. Poultry Sci. Assn. (nat. bd. dirs., v.p., pres. 1978-84), World Poultry Sci. Assn. (bd. dirs., v.p. 1975-86), Sigma Xi, numerous others. Home: PO Box 902521 Palmdale CA 93590-2521

BRAGG, DAVID GORDON, physician, radiology educator; b. Portland, Oreg., May 1, 1933; s. George Tully and Edith (Lee) B.; m. Marcia Robertson, Aug. 19, 1955; children: Eric Allan, Daniel Robert, James Tully, Anne Elizabeth. AB in History, Stanford U., 1955; MD, U. Oreg., 1959. Intern Phila. Gen. Hosp., 1959-60; resident in radiology Columbia-Presbyn. Med. Ctr., Coll. Physicians and Surgeons, N.Y.C., 1962-64, chief resident, 1964-65, instr., 1965-66; asst. prof. Cornell U. Med. Coll., N.Y.C., 1966-70, assoc. prof., 1970; chmn. diagnostic radiology Meml. Sloan-Kettering Cancer Ctr., N.Y.C., 1967-70; prof., chmn. dept. radiology U. Utah Med. Ctr., Salt Lake City, 1970—; cons. Salt Lake City VA Hosp., Meml. Sloan-Kettering Cancer Soc., 1970—; mem. Nat. Cancer Adv. Bd., 1988—; trustee Am. Bd. Radiology, 1988—. Editor: Oncologic Imaging; mem. editorial bds. Internat. Jour. Radiation Oncology, Biol. Physics, Current Problems in Diagnostic Radiology, Postgrad. Radiology, Cancer. Mem. AMA, Assn. Univ. Radiologists (pres. 1980-81), Soc. Chmn. Acad. Radiology Depts. (pres. 1979-80), Radiol. Soc. N.Am., Soc. for Cancer Imaging (founder). Home: 4403 Covecrest Dr Salt Lake City UT 84124-4009 Office: U Utah Dept Radiology 1A-71 50 N Medical Dr Salt Lake City UT 84132-0001

BRAGG, DOUGLAS E., lawyer; b. Denver, Oct. 18, 1942; s. Earl E. and Helen B. (Bean) B.; married; children: Michelle, Christopher, Elizabeth, James. BA in History, Stanford U., 1964; JD, U. Colo., 1968. Bar: Colo. Supreme Ct. 1968, U.S. Dist. Ct. (D.C. dist.) 1968, Ct. of Appeals (10th cir.) 1970, Ct. of Appeals (4th cir.) 1986. Seldon, Nordmark & Bayer, Denver, 1969-70, Kripke, Carrigan & Duffy, P.C., Denver, 1970-72, Carrigan & Bragg, P.C., Denver, 1973-76, Bragg & Dusofsky, P.C., Denver, 1976-89, Bragg, Baker & Cederberg, P.C., Denver, 1989-93, Bragg & Baker, P.C., Denver, 1993—; lectr., tchr. U. Colo. Sch. Law, U. Denver Coll. of Law, annual conventions of the ATLA, Colo. Trial Lawyers Assn., Colo. Bar Assn., Western Trial Lawyers Assn., Nat. Inst. for Trial Advocacy and numerous others. Contbr. articles to profl. jours. With Air Force, 1967-69, Korea. Fellow Colo. Bar Fdn.; mem. ATLA (bd. govs. 1984-90, state delegate 1982-83, co-chair Dalkon Shield litigation section 1986—, chair sci. & tech. com. 1991-92, mem. insurance practicescom. 1987-89, liability insurance co. liaison com. 1988-89, com. on insurance abuses, 1988-90, products liability adv. com. 1989-92, nat. coll. of advocacy adv. com. 1989-91, orgn. rev. com. 1990-91, section and litigation group oversight com. 1991-94, litigation group coordination counsel, 1992-95), Am. Bd. of Trial Advocates, Internat. Soc. of Barristers (adminstrv. dir. 1976-81, bd. govs. 1982-85), Colo. Bar Assn. (bd. govs. 1979-81, 85-86, chair litigation section 1977-78, vice chair 1976-77, sec. negligence section 1975-76, mem. interprofessional com. 1975-76, nominating com. 1975-76, legal assts. com. 1971-73, ethics com. 1984-89), Colo. Trial Lawyers Assn. (pres. 1982-83, pres. elect 1981-82, sec, treas. 1978-79, legislative chmn. 1978-81, bd. dirs. 1976-78, chair long range planning com. 1976-77, by laws com. 1975-76, 88-89, consumer protection com. 1974-75, best article in Trial Talk award 1990), Boulder County Bar Assn. (mem. interprofessional com. 1973-76, chmn. 1973-74, 75-76), Denver Bar Assn. (mem. interprofessional com. 1976-79), Western Trial Lawyers Assn. (bd. dirs. 1976-94, parliamentarian 1994-95); Order of the Coif. Democrat. Office: Bragg & Baker PC 600 17th St Ste 1700 N Denver CO 80202

BRAHMA, CHANDRA SEKHAR, civil engineering educator; b. Calcutta, India, Oct. 5, 1941; came to U.S., 1963; s. Nalinia Kanta and Uma Rani (Bose) B.; m. Purnima Sinha, Feb. 18, 1972; children: Charanjit, Barunashish. B in Engring., Calcutta U., 1962; MS, Mich. State U., 1965; PhD, Ohio State U., 1969. Registered profl. engr. Calif., Utah, N.H., Tex., Wis. Asst. engr. Pub. Works Dept., Calcutta, 1962-63; rsch. asst. Mich. State U., East Lansing, 1963-65; teaching and rsch. assoc. Ohio State U., Columbus, 1965-69; project engr. Frank H. Lehr Assocs., East Orange, N.J., 1969-70; sr. soils engr. John G. Reutter Assocs., Camden, N.J., 1970-72; asst. prof. Worcester (Mass.) Poly. Inst., 1972-74; prin. soils engr. Daniel, Mann, Johnson & Mendenhall, Balt., 1974-79; sr. engr. Sverdrup Corp., St. Louis, 1979-80, cons., 1980—; prof. Calif. State U., Fresno, 1980—; cons. Expert Resources, Inc., Peoria Heights, Ill., 1981—, The Twining Labs., Inc., Fresno, 1982—, Law Offices Marderosian and Swanson, Fresno, 1985—, Law Offices Hurlbutt, Clevenger, Long and Vortmann, Visalia, Calif., 1988—, Tech. Adv. Svcs. for Attys., Blue Bell, Pa., 1992—. Author: Fundaciones y Mechanica de Suelos, 1986; contbr. articles to profl. jours. Head sci. judge Calif. Cen. Valleys Sci. and Engring. Fairs, Fresno, 1988—. Recipient Outstanding Prof. of Yr. award Calif. State U., 1989, Halliburton award Calif. State U., 1991, Calif. Ctrl. Valley Outstanding Profl. Engr. award Calif. Soc. Profl. Engrs., 1993, Disting. Svc. award, 1994, Claude C. Laval Jr. award Innovative Tech. and Rsch. Calif. State U., 1991, 92; Brahma St. named in City of Bakersfield, Calif., 1989; Fulbright scholar, 1984; Hugh B. William fellow, Assn. Drilled Shaft Contractors, 1986. Fellow ASCE (v.p. 1983-84, pres. 1984-85, Outstanding Engr. award 1985, Disting Svc. award, 1986, Outstanding Prof. award 1985, Edmund Friedman Profl. Recognition award 1993); mem. ASTM, Am. Soc. Engring. Edn. (AT&T Found. award 1991), Rotary (chair Clovis club 1986—, chair pub. rels. 1987, chair youth svcs. 1989, bd. dirs. 1989). Democrat. Hindu. Home: 561 Houston Ave Clovis CA 93611-7032 Office: Calif State U Maple And Shaw Ave Fresno CA 93740

BRAHTZ, JOHN FREDERICK PEEL, civil engineering educator; b. St. Paul, Jan. 29, 1918; s. John Henry August Brahtz and Charlotte Beatrice Peel; m. Lise Vetter, May 11, 1991. BA, Stanford U., 1939, MS, 1948, PhD, 1951. Registered profl. civil and mech. engr., Calif. Various engring. positions Calif., 1939-53; assoc. prof. UCLA, 1953-57; v.p., dir. engring. J.H. Pomeroy & Co. Inc., San Francisco, L.A., 1957-60; mgr. constrn. scis. dvsn. Stanford Rsch. Inst., Menlo Park, Calif., 1960-63; staff cons. U.S. Naval Civil Engring., U.S. Naval Elec. Labs., Port Hueneme, San Diego, Calif., 1963-70; lectr. UCLA, 1963-70; dir. constrn. systems inst. Calif. State U., San Diego, 1970-73; vis. prof. ocean engring. U. Calif., San Diego, 1986-87; cons. rsch. prof. Civil Engring. Ctr. for Study of Infrastructure Sys., Stanford U., 1987—; cons., mem. gen. ocean engring. panel nat. coun. marine resources and engring. exec. offices of Pres. U.S., Washington, 1964-68; cons. various orgns., San Francisco, N.Y.C., San Diego, Chgo., 1964—; cons. to Devel. Engring. and Rsch. Inst., Carmel, Calif. Co-author, editor: (books) Ocean Engineering: System Planning and Design, 1968, Coastal Zone Management: Multiple Use with Conservation, 1972; editor (book series) Construction Management and Engineering Series, 1976—; patentee in field. Comdr. USN, WWII, ret. Nat. Ocean Rsch. and Exploration Ctr. fellow. Fellow ASCE; mem. Am. Soc. for Engring. Edn., Old Capital Club (Monterey, Calif.), Beach and Tennis Club (Pebble Beach, Calif.), Sigma Xi. Home: 800 Prospect St La Jolla CA 92037-4202 Office: 2740 16th Ave Carmel CA 93923-9212

BRAIDEN, ROSE MARGARET, art educator, illustrator, calligrapher; b. Los Angeles, Nov. 25, 1922; d. Sylvester and Margaret Mary (Hines) B.; B.A., Mt. St. Mary's Coll., Los Angeles; M.F.A., Calif. Coll. Arts and Crafts. Chmn. art dept. Bishop Montgomery High Sch., Torrance, Calif., 1958-68; chmn. humanities Mt. St. Mary's Coll., Los Angeles, 1968-70; prof. art Santa Barbara City Coll., 1970—; chmn. photo art dept. Brooks Inst. Photo, 1970-82; chmn. photo dept. Cate Sch., Carpinteria, Calif., 1982-89; founder Los Padres Water Color Soc., 1990. Illustrator: Choices, 1983, Leah, 1986, The Mystical Ferryboat, 1986, A Mother's Journal, 1990. Democrat. Roman Catholic. Address: 2929 Paseo Tranquillo Santa Barbara CA 93105-2932

BRAITHWAITE, CHARLES HENRY, chemist, chemical engineering consultant; b. Chgo., Dec. 16, 1920; s. Charles Henry and Wilhelmina (Hoth) B.; m. Bernice May Hyde, Apr. 29, 1949; children: Charles Henry

III, Betty Susan Braithwaite Artman. AB, UCLA, 1941; BS in Chem. Engring., U. Mich., 1943; MS, Carnegie Inst. Tech., 1948, DSc, 1949. Registered profl. engr., Calif. Materials engr. Westinghouse Electric, East Pittsburgh, Pa., 1943-46; rsch. chemist Shell Oil Co., Wood River, Ill., 1949-51; dir. rsch. FMC Corp.-Chlor-Alkali div., South Charleston, W.Va., 1951-57; dir. R & D Productol Co., Santa Fe Springs, Calif., 1957-59; pres. Cal-Colonial Chemsolve, La Habra, Calif., 1960-87; forensic cons. Braithwaite Cons., Whittier, Calif., 1987—; forensic cons., 1987—. Patentee in field; contbr. articles on elec. insulation to tech. publs. Mem. Am. Chem. Soc., Am. Inst. Chem. Engrs., Soc. Plastics Engrs., Western Plastics Pioneers. Office: 11232 Tigrina Ave Whittier CA 90603-3241

BRAITHWAITE, WALT WALDIMAN, aircraft manufacturing company executive; b. Kingston, Jamaica, Jan. 19, 1945; s. Ivanhoe Alexander and Ivy Mary (Green) B.; m. Edwina Gerell Patrick, Apr. 7, 1967 (div. March 1976); 1 child, Charlene Maria; m. Rita Cecelia Wood, May 4, 1974; children: Catherine Cecelia, Rachel Christine. BS in Electromech. Engring., Am. Inst. Engring. & Tech., Chgo., 1965; MS in Computer Sci., U. Wash., Seattle, 1975; SM in Mgmt., MIT, Cambridge, 1981. Cert. computer tech. Systems engr. engring. div. The Boeing Co., Renton, Wash., 1979-80; Sloan fellow MIT The Boeing Co., 1980-81; program mgr. bus. planning and commitments 7/7/7 div. The Boeing Co., Renton, Wash., 1981-82, mgr. CAD/CAM integration engring. div., 1982-83; dir. program tech. mgmt. Nat. Airspace Systems Co. div. Boeing/Lockheed, Kent, Wash., 1983-84; chief engr. CAD/CAM integration engring. div. The Boeing Co., Renton, Wash., 1984; chief engr. engring. ops. 747/767 div. The Boeing Co., Everett, Wash., 1984-85, dir. computing systems 747/767 div., 1985-86; dir. program mgmt. 707/737/757 div. The Boeing Co., Renton, 1986-91, v.p. info. systems Boeing Comml. Airplane Group, 1991—; initial graphics exchange specification Nat. Bur. Standards, Calif., 1980. Author: Design and Implementation of Interpreters, 1978. Bd. dirs. City Art Works, Seattle, 1981-85. Recipient Joseph Marie Jacquare Meml. award Am. Inst. Mfg. Tech., Mass., 1987, leadership award Computer and Automated Systems Assn., Seattle, 1987, Black Achievers award YMCA, Seattle, 1990. Mem. Soc. Mfg. Engrs., Greater Renton C. of C. (pres. 1990-91), Boeing Mgmt. Assn. (pres. 1994, Black Engr. of Yr. 1995). Episcopalian. Office: The Boeing Co PO Box 3707 Seattle WA 98124-2207

BRAKHAGE, JAMES STANLEY, filmmaker, educator; b. Kansas City, Mo., Jan. 14, 1933; s. Ludwig and Clara (Dubberstein) B.; m. Mary Jane Collom, Dec. 28, 1957 (div. 1987); children: Myrrena, Crystal, Neowyn, Bearthm, Rarc; m. Marilyn Jull, Mar. 30, 1989; children: Anton, Vaughn. Ph.D., San Francisco Art Inst., 1981; Doctorate (hon.), Calif. Arts, 1994. Lectr. Sch. Art Inst. Chgo., 1969-81; prof. U. Colo., Boulder, 1981; mem. Filmmakers Coop., N.Y.C., Canyon Cinema Coop., San Francisco, London Filmmakers Coop., Can. Filmmakers' Distbn. Ctr., Toronto, Lightcome, Paris, France; Faculty lectr. U. Colo., 1990-91. Films include Interim, 1952, Anticipation of the Night, 1958, The Dead, 1960, Blue Moses, 1962, Dog Star Man, 1964, Songs in 8mm, 1964-69, Scenes from Under Childhood, 1967-70, The Weir Falcon Saga, 1970, The Act of Seeing with One's Own Eyes, 1971, The Riddle of Lumen, 1972, Sincerity and Duplicity, 1973-80, The Text of Light, 1974, Desert, 1976, The Governor, 1977, Burial Path, 1978, Nightmare Series, 1978, Creation, 1979, Made Manifest, 1980, Salome, 1980, Murder Psalm, 1980, Roman Numeral Series, 1979-81, the Arabic series, 1980-82, Unconscious London Strata, 1982, Tortured Dust, 1984, The Egyptian Series, 1984, The Loom, 1986, Nightmusic, 1986, The Dante Quartet, 1987, Faust, parts I-IV, 1987-89, Marilyn's Window, 1988, Visions in Meditation, 1989-90, City Streaming, 1990, Glaze of Cathexis, 1990, Babylonian Series, 1989-90, Passage Through: A Ritual, 1990, A Child's Garden and the Serious Sea, 1991, Delicacies of Molten Horror Synapse, 1991, Christ Mass Sex Dance, 1991, Crack Glass Eulogy, 1992, Boulder Blues and Pearls and For Marilyn, Interpolations 1-5, 1992, Blossom Gift Favor, The Harrowing, Tryst Haunt, Study in Color and Black and White, Stellar, Atumnal, 1993, Three Homerics, 1993, Naghts, Chartres Series, Ephemeral Solidity, Elementary Phrases, Black Ice, First Hymn to the Night—Novalis, 1994, In Consideration of Pompeii, 1994, The Mammals of Victoria, 1994, Paranoia Corridor, 1994, Can Not Exist, 1994, Can Not Not Exist, 1994, I Take These Truths, 1994, We Hold These, 1994, I..., 1995, Earthen Aerie, 1995, Spring Cycle, 1995; author: Metaphors on Vision, 1963, A Moving Picture Giving and Taking Book, 1971, The Brakhage Lectures, 1972, Seen, 1975, Film Biographies, 1977, Brakhage Scrapbook, 1982, Film at Wits End, 1989, I...Sleeping, 1989. Recipient Brussels Worlds Fair Protest award, 1958, Brandeis citation, 1973, Colo. Gov.'s Award for Arts and humanities, 1974, Jimmy Ryan Morris Meml. Found. award, 1979, Telluride Film Festival medallion, 1981 Maya Deren award Am. Film Inst., 1986, medal U. Colo., 1988, Outstanding Achievement award Denver Internat. Film Festival, 1988, MacDowell medal, 1989, Libr. Cong. Nat. Film Registry, 1992, Anthology Film Archives honor, 1993, The Colo. 100 certificate of Recognition, 1993, Disting. Prof. award U. Colo., 1994; grantee Avon Found. 1965-69, NEA, 1974-75, 77, 80, 83, 88, U. Colo. Coun. Rsch. and Creative Work, 1983, Rocky Mountain Film Ctr., 1985; Rockefeller fellow, 1967-69, Guggenheim fellow, 1978. Democrat. Home: 2142 Canyon Blvd Apt 203 Boulder CO 80302-4517 Office: U Colo Film Studies Hunter 102 Campus Box 316 Boulder CO 80309

BRALEY, JEAN (J. MCNEIL SARGENT), artist, educator; b. North Wilkesboro, N.C., 1925; d. Sargent Duffield and Agnes A. Student, Sch. Profl. Art, N.Y.C., 1942-45, Art Students League, 1957, La Reparata Graphic Ctr., Florence, Italy, 1975, Pratt Graphic Ctr., N.Y.C., 1976. Dir. Atelier for Calif. Printmakers; instr. art C.C. San Diego, Mira Costa Coll., Oceanside, Calif., Corcoran Mus., Washington; cons. Calif. Art Commn.; founder, 1st pres. Artists Equity Assn. San Francisco; comml. illustrator, N.Y.C. and Washngton. Exhibited in one-person shows at Yogesh Gallery, Bombay, Spectrum Gallery, San Diego, Prestige Gallery, Boston, Riverside (Calif.) Mus., The Gallery, Washington, others; mus. shows include Long Beach (Calif.) Mus., Palm Springs Desert Mus., San Diego Mus., Palace of Fine Arts, Mexico City, Smithsonian Inst., Washington, De Young Mus., San Francisco; group exhbns. include Art Nold, Nice, France, Galerie Cezanne, Laguna Beach, Calif., Plaza Gallery, N.Y.C., Agra Gallery, Washington;. Recipient awards San Diego Art Inst., S.W. Annual Art Festival, Washington, Fairfax (Va.) Art Ann., Ajax Nat. Art Exhibit, numerous others. Mem. Nat. Assn. Women Artists. Address: 12245 Carmel Vista Rd Apt 193 San Diego CA 92130-2532

BRAMAN, DONALD WILLIAM, public relations consultant; b. Mpls., June 19, 1917; s. Maurice I. and Ida (Garber) B.; m. Sally Davidson, June 16, 1946; children: Stuart, Sandra, Richard. BA cum laude, U. Minn., 1937. With Mpls. Star, 1937-41; dir. public relations Manson-Gold Advt. Agy., Mpls., 1946-47; public relations staff, publs. editor Toni Co., St. Paul, 1947-49; assoc. dir. public relations Olmsted & Foley, Mpls., 1950-58; co-founder, pres. Don Braman & Assos., Inc., Mpls., 1958-77; v.p. Doremus & Co., N.Y.C. 1977-82; pub. relations cons., 1982—; cons. Internat. Exec. Service Corps., Service Corps Retired Execs.; teaching asst., lectr. Sch. Journalism U. Minn.; dir. Minn. Advt. Fedn. Chmn. Mayor's Com. for Employment of Handicapped, 1950's; chmn. Mpls. Symphony Orchestra Guaranty Fund Campaign, 1960's; fin. com. Mpls. LWV, 1970's; dir. Am.-Israel Chamber of Commerce & Industry of Minn., 1980's; bd. dirs. Keep Sedona Beautiful. Served with USMC, 1941-45. Mem. Public Relations Soc. Am. (dir., pres. Minn. chpt., mem. exec. com. counselors acad., Disting. Service award 1973, accredited fellow), Nat. Investor Rels. Inst. (dir., pres. Minn. chpt.), Mpls. Area C. of C. (chmn. coms. various dates), Marine Corps Combat Correspondents Assn., Nat. Audubon Soc., Ariz. Archeol. Soc., Masons, Scottish Rite, Shrine, Zeta Beta Tau. Contbr. articles in field to profl. publs., travel articles to popular publs. Home and Office: 1865 Gun Fury Rd Sedona AZ 86336-3948

BRAME, MARILLYN A., hypnotherapist; b. Indpls., Sept. 17, 1928; d. David Schwalb and Hilda (Riley) Curtin; 1 child, Gary Mansour. Student, Meinzinger Art Sch., Detroit, 1946-47, U. N.Mex., 1963, Orlando (Fla.) Jr. Coll., 1964-65, El Camino Coll., Torrance, Calif., 1974-75; PhD in Hypnotherapy, Am. Inst. Hypnotherapy, 1989. Cert. and registered hypnotherapist. Color cons. Pitts. Plate Glass Co., Albuquerque, 1951-52; owner Signs by Marillyn, Albuquerque, 1952-53; design draftsman Sandia Corp., Albuquerque, 1953-56; designer The Martin Co., Orlando, 1957-65; pres. The Arts, Winter Park, Fla., 1964-66; supr. tech. publs. Gen. Instrument Corp., Hawthorne, Calif., 1967-76; pres. Camart Design, Westminster, Calif., 1977-86, Visual Arts, El Toro, Calif., 1978—; mgr. tech. publs. Archive Corp., Costa Mesa, Calif., 1986-90; adj. instr. Orange Coast Coll., Costa Mesa, 1985-90; hypnotherapist, Lake Forest, 1986—; bd. dirs. Orange County chpt. Am. Bd. Hypnotherapy. Author: Lemon and Lime Scented Herbs, 1994, (textbook) Folkdancing is for Everybody, 1974; inventor, designer dance notation sys. MS Method. Mem. bd. govs. Lake Forest II Showboaters Theater Group, 1985-88, 90-95. Mem. Soc. Tech. Communication (v.p. programs, 1987, newsletter editor 1986-87, newsletter prodn. editor 1985-86).

BRAMHALL, EUGENE HULBERT, lawyer; married; 5 children. BS, U. Calif., Berkeley, 1954, LLB, 1960. Bar: Calif. 1960, Guam, 1968, Trust Ter. Pacific Islands 1968, U.S. Supreme Ct. 1972, Utah 1981. Assoc. Best, Best & Krieger, Riverside, Calif., 1960-63; from assoc. to ptnr. Blade, Farmer & Bramhall, Oroville, Calif., 1964-68; ptnr. Ferenz, Bramhall, Paul & Nolan (and predecessor ptnrships), Oakland, Calif. and Agana, Guam, 1968-77; from assoc. gen. counsel Provo (Utah) campus to gen. counsel Hawaii campuses Brigham Young U., 1977-86, adj. prof. bus. law MBA program, 1981-89; asst. to pres., gen. counsel Brigham Young U., Provo, 1986—; ptnr. Ray Quinney & Nebeker, Salt Lake City, 1980-86; lectr. Am. Assn. Coll. Admissions and Records Officers, Am. Bankers Assn., Utah Edn. Assn., Pacific Coast Coll. Health Assn., Western Assn. Coll. and Univ. Bus. Officers, Collegium Aesculapium, Am. Assn. Pres. Ind. Colls. and Univs., Stetson Law Conf., Nat. Assn. Coll. and Univs. Attys. Maj. Walter Dinkelspiel scholar, Ford Found. scholar. Mem. ABA, Nat. Assn. Coll. and Univ. Attys., Maritime Law Assn., Utah Bar Assn., Calif. Bar Assn. Home: 163 E 1575 S # 7 Orem UT 84058-7692 Office: Brigham Young U ASB # A357 Provo UT 84602

BRANCH, BARBARA LEE, elementary education educator; b. Baton Rouge, Sept. 6, 1948; d. Robert Lee and Dorothy Lee (Niquette) B. AB, U. Calif., Davis, 1970, MA, 1976; cert. computer sci., Calif. State U., Sacramento, 1986. Cert. adminstrv. svcs., 1993. Tchr. grades 1-3 Sacramento City Unified Sch. Dist., 1970-81, curriculum and rsch. asst., 1974-90, tchr. 6th grade, 1981-90, mentor tchr., 1986—, math./computer resource specialist, 1990—; tchr. algebra Acad. Talent Search, Sacramento, 1984-86; instr. Nat. U., Sacramento, 1987—; tchr. 7th grade math. and sci. Leonardo da Vinci Sch., Sacramento, 1992-93; prin. elem. sch. Lisbon Elem. Sch., Sacramento, 1993—; cons. math./computers, Sacramento, 1975—. Named Tchr. of Yr., Sacramento City Unified Sch. Dist., 1990-91; Woodrow Wilson fellow Princeton U. Fellow No. Calif. Math. Project; mem. Nat. Coun. Tchrs. Math., Assn. Sch. Curriculum Devel., Assn. Calif. Sch. Administrs., Math. Alliance for Access and Equity, Calif. Tchrs. Assn., PTA (hon. life). Republican. Methodist. Home: 9296 Linda Rio Dr Sacramento CA 95826-2250 Office: Lisbon Elem Sch 7555 S Land Park Dr Sacramento CA 95831-3863

BRANCH, TAYLOR, writer; b. Atlanta, Jan. 14, 1947; s. Franklin T. and Jane (Worthington) B.; m. Christina Macy; 2 children. AB, U. N.C., 1968; postgrad., Princeton U., 1968-70. Staff member Washington Monthly mag., Washington, D.C., 1970-73, Harper's mag., N.Y.C., 1973-75, Esquire mag., N.Y.C., 1975-76. Author: (with Bill Russell) Second Wind: The Memoirs of an Opinionated Man, 1979, The Empire Blues, 1981, (with Eugene M. Propper) Labyrinth, 1982, Parting the Waters: America in the King Years, 1954-63, 1988 (Pulitzer Prize for history 1989, Nat. Book Critics Circle award for non-fiction 1988, Christopher award 1988, Nat. Book award nomination 1989); editor, contbr.: (with Charles Peters) Blowing the Whistle: Dissent in the Public Interest, 1972. Office: care George Diskant 1033 Gayley Ave Ste 202 Los Angeles CA 90024-3417

BRANCH, TURNER WILLIAMSON, lawyer; b. Houston, Aug. 22, 1938; s. James Alexander and Juanita (Wilson) B.; m. Margaret Moses; children: Brian Kern, Rebecca Claire. BA, U. N.Mex., 1960; JD, Baylor U., 1965. Bar: N.Mex. 1966; U.S. Dist. Ct. N.Mex. 1968; U.S. Ct. Appeals (10th cir.), U.S. Supreme Ct. 1972; Tex., Colo., U.S. Dist. Ct. (wc. and so. dist.) Tex. 1988; U.S. Dist. Ct. Colo. 1988, D.C. 1989, U.S. Ct. Appeals (9th cir.), U.S. Dist. Ct. (no. dist.) Tex. 1992, U.S. Dist. Ct. (ea. dist.) Tex. 1993. Ptnr. The Branch Law Firm, Albuquerque, 1965—; bd. dir. liquor control State of N.Mex., 1966-68; atty. City of Gallup, 1970-72; mem. ho. judiciary com. and ho. corp. and banking com. N.Mex. Ho. of Reps., 1968-74. Author: Branch on Constrn. Pleading and Practice; sect. editor Baylor U. Law Rev., 1964-65; contbr. articles to jours. 1st lt. USMC, 1960-63. Fellow Internat. Acad. Trial Lawyers; mem. ABA (torts vice chmn. ins. practice sect.), Nat. Inst. Trial Advisors, Am. Arbitration Assn. (negligence adv. com.), Am. Soc. Law & Medicine, Am. Judicature Soc., Am. Bd. Trial Advs. (bd. dirs., pres. Albuquerque chpt. 1983-84), N.Mex. Bar Assn. (chmn. fee arbitration com. 1982—, legal med. rev. com.), Albuquerque (chmn. other professions com. 1969), N.Mex. Trial Lawyers Assn. (bd. dirs. 1969-73, 91—), State Bar of Tex., Tex. Trial Lawyers Assn., Colo. Trial Lawyers Assn., Assn. Trial Lawyers Am. (state committeeman 1970-74, sustaining 1978—), Nat. Advance Coll. Trial Advisors (vice chmn. 1984-85, The Best Lawyer in Am.), Nat. Coll. Advocacy (trustee), Pa. and N.Y. Trial Lawyers, Nat. Bd. Trial Advs. (cert.), D.C. Bar Assn., Internat. Acad. Trial Lawyers. Office: 2025 Rio Grande Blvd NW Albuquerque NM 87104-2525

BRAND, LEONARD ROY, biology educator; b. Harvey, N.D., May 17, 1941; s. George Edward and Clara Leona (Kingsfield) B.; m. Kim Kwangho, Aug. 8, 1974; children—Dennis, Jenelle. B.A., La Sierra Coll., Riverside, Calif., 1964; M.A., Loma Linda U., 1966; Ph.D., Cornell U., 1970. Asst. prof. biology Loma Linda U., Loma Linda and Riverside, Calif., 1969-74, assoc. prof. biology, 1974-78, prof. biology, 1978-90, chmn. dept. biology, 1971-86, 88-90, chmn. dept. natural scis., 1990—, prof. biology and paleontology, 1990—. Contbr. articles to profl. jours. Recipient Zapara award for disting. teaching Loma Linda U., 1989; NSF grad. fellow, 1964-69. Mem. Animal Behavior Soc., Am. Soc. Mammalogists (A. Brazier Howell award 1967), Soc. Vertebrate Paleontologists, Geol. Soc. Am., Sigma Xi (Grant-in-Aid of Rsch. 1968, Rsch. Project Merit award 1993). Seventh-Day Adventist. Home: 1413 Magnolia Ave Redlands CA 92373-4921 Office: Loma Linda U Dept Natural Scis Loma Linda CA 92350

BRAND, MALCOLM LEIGH, lawyer; b. Inglewood, Calif., Mar. 5, 1935; s. Robert L. and Jeannette E. (Schureman) B.; m. Myra Jean Friesen, Sept. 19, 1958; children: Martin L., Janice E. BA in Econs., Willamette U., 1957, JD, 1964. Bar: Oreg. 1964. Atty. examiner Salem (Oreg.) Title Co., 1964-68; asst. city atty. City of Salem (Oreg.), 1968-69; ptnr. Rhoten, Rhoten et al, Salem, 1969-84; sole practice Salem, 1984—. Served with USAF, 1960-61. Mem. ABA, Oreg. Bar Assn., Marion County Bar Assn. (pres. 1976), Assn. Trial Lawyers Am., Oreg. Trial Lawyers Assn., Oreg. Assn. Def. Counsel. Republican. Presbyterian. Home: 720 Mcgilchrist St SE Salem OR 97302-3749 Office: 100 High St SE # 183 Salem OR 97301-3607

BRANDAUER, NANCY ELLSWORTH, resource center executive; b. N.Y.C., Oct. 14, 1934; d. Ralph Oliver Ellsworth and Mary Dexter (Grosvenor) Behrend; m. Peter Matthews Spackman, July 14, 1958 (div. Apr. 1968); children: Thomas Matthews, John Grosvenor; stepchildren: Jennifer Mode, Phoebe Proctor; m. Carl Martin Brandauer, Nov. 28, 1969; stepchildren: Peter Carl, Aline Chipman. AA with honors, Monticello Coll., 1955; BA in English and Philosophy, Vassar Coll., 1957; postgrad., Princeton U., 1965-68, U. Colo., 1973-74. Rsch. asst. dept. psychology Princeton (N.J.) U., 1969; feature writer, photographer Longmont Daily Times-Call, 1972; stringer news writing and photography Denver Post, 1972; mus. assoc. U. Colo. Mus., Boulder, 1974-89; mollusk identification cons. Marathon Oil Co., 1985; mollusk identification, vol. trainer Denver Mus. Natural History, 1985; bus. assoc. Malacological Rev., 1983-89; vol. Boulder County AIDS Project, 1988-89, resource ctr. mgr., vol. coord., 1989—. Contbr. articles to sci. publs. Chmn. Sch. Bd. Election Dist., Princeton, N.J.; vol. tchg. asst. Head Start and pub. schs. Mem. Am. Malacological Union, Western Soc. Malacologists, Dirs. Vols. in Orgns. Home: 1760 Sunset Blvd Boulder CO 80304-4243

BRANDENBURGH, DONALD CARTER, literary agent; b. Stuart, Iowa, July 4, 1931; s. Wilbur Hager and Esther Hadley (Carter) B.; m. Mary Isabelle Moore, June 5, 1953; children: Gregory, Curtis, Brenda. BA, William Penn Coll., 1953; MA, Whittier Coll., 1960; MDiv, Talbot Sch. Theology, La Mirada, Calif., 1970. Ordained minister Soc. of Friends, 1956; Pastor Paton (Iowa) Friends Ch., 1955-57; clk. So. Calif. Gas Co., L.A., 1958-59; minister Christian edn. Alamitos Friends Ch., Garden Grove, Calif., 1959-68; bus. adminstr. Calif. Yearly Meeting Friends Ch., Whittier, Calif., 1968-73; exec. dir. Nat. Sunday Sch. Assn., Whittier, 1973-74, Evang. Christian Publs. Assn., La Habra, Calif., 1974-80; assoc. pub., owner Home & Land mag., La Habra, 1981-85; lit. agt., owner, mgr. Brandenburgh & Associates, Murrieta, Calif., 1986—. Bd. dirs. Friends Ctr., Azusa, Calif., 1986-87; vestryman St. John's Episcopal Ch., Fallbrook, Calif, 1992-95. Mem. Greater L.A. Sunday Sch. Assn. (bd. dirs. 1962-82). Republican. Home and Office: 24555 Corte Jaramillo Murrieta CA 92562-3819

BRANDES, STANLEY HOWARD, anthropology educator, writer; b. N.Y.C., Dec. 26, 1942; s. Emanuel Robert and Annette (Zalisch) B.; divorced; children: Nina Rachel, Naomi Carla. BA, U. Chgo., 1964; MA, U. Calif., Berkeley, 1969, PhD, 1971. Asst. prof. anthropology Mich. State U., East Lansing, 1971-75; asst. prof. anthropology U. Calif., Berkeley, 1975-78, assoc. prof., 1978-82, prof. anthropology, 1982—, chmn. dept., 1990-93; dir. Barcelona Study Ctr., U. Calif. and Ill., Spain, 1981-82, Mexico City Study Ctr., U. Calif. Author: Migration, Kinship and Community, 1975, Metaphors of Masculinity, 1980, Forty: The Age and the Symbol, 1985, Power and Persuasion, 1988; co-editor: Symbol as Sense, 1980. NIH fellow, 1967-71; NICHD Rsch. fellow, 1975-77; fellow John Carter Brown Libr., 1994; Am. Council Learned Socs. grantee, 1977. Fellow Am. Anthrop. Assn.; mem. Am. Ethnological Soc., Soc. for Psychol. Anthropology. Office: U Calif Dept Anthropology Berkeley CA 94720

BRANDIN, ALF ELVIN, retired mining and shipping company executive; b. Newton, Kans., July 1, 1912; s. Oscar E. and Agnes (Larsen) B.; m. Marie Eck, June 15, 1936 (dec. 1980); children: Alf R., Jon, Erik, Mark.; m. Pamela J. Brandin, Jan. 28, 1983. A.B., Stanford U., 1936. With Standard Accident of Detroit, 1936-42; bus. mgr. Stanford U., Calif., 1946-52; bus. mgr., exec. officer for land devel. Stanford U., 1952-59, v.p. for bus. affairs, 1959-70; sr. v.p., dir., mem. exec. com. Utah Internat. Inc., San Francisco, from 1970; pres. Richardson-Brandin, 1964-86, also bd. dirs.; bd. dirs. Hershey Oil Co.; vice chmn. bd. dirs. Doric Devel. Inc. Bd. govs. San Francisco Bay Area Council; trustee Reclamation Dist. 2087, Alameda, Calif.; bd. overseers Hoover Instn. on War, Revolution and Peace, Stanford; mem. VIII Olympic Winter Games Organizing com., 1960. Served as comdr. USNR, 1942-46. Mem. Zeta Psi. Clubs: Elk, Stanford Golf, Bohemian, Pauma Valley Country, Silverado Country; Royal Lahaina. Home: 668 Salvatierra St Stanford CA 94305-8538 Office: 550 California St San Francisco CA 94104-1006

BRANDIN, MARK SEMPLE, financial services executive; b. San Francisco, Sept. 20, 1950; s. Alf and Marie Brandin; m. Elizabeth Brandin; children: Heather, Tucker, Will. BA, Stanford U., 1972; MBA, U. Chgo., 1976. Cons. dept. HEW 1st Nat. Bank Chgo., Washington, 1973-74; loan officer 1st Nat. Bank Chgo., Chgo., 1973-77; v.p. banking adminstrn. Crocker Nat. Bank, San Francisco, 1977-81, sr. v.p. consumer svc., 1981-84, exec. v.p. specialized bus., 1984-86; fin. cons. Shearson Lehman Hutton, San Francisco, 1986-88; exec. v.p. specialized bus. Charles Schwab & Co., Inc., San Francisco, 1988-90, exec. v.p. mktg. and sales, 1990-92, exec. v.p. capital markets/trading, 1992—; mem. com. SIA Sales & Mktg., N.Y.C., 1990-92; mem. San Francisco Traders Assn., 1992—; bd. dirs. Option Clearing Corp., Chgo. Mem. Stanford Golf Club. Office: Charles Schwab & Co Inc 101 Montgomery St San Francisco CA 94104-4122

BRANDLIN, THOMAS E., nonprofit association consultant; b. L.A., Mar. 9, 1950; s. William T. and Nancy L. (O'Neal) B. BA in History, U. Calif., Santa Barbara, 1974; M in Nonprofit Adminstrn., U. San Francisco, 1991. Fin. dir. spl. svcs. coord. St. Vincent's, Santa Barbara, 1971-86; dir. corp. sec. Seton Sch.-Developmentally Disabled, Santa Barbara, 1980-83; bus. mgr. Brier Oak Care Ctr., L.A., 1986-87; exec. dir. Women's Legal Clinic, L.A., 1987-88; adminstr. Sunset Hall, L.A., 1988-90, St. Lawrence Martyr Parish, Redondo Beach, Calif., 1990-91; cons. Not-for-Profit Counsel, L.A., 1992—; mem. adj. faculty St. John's Sch. Theology, Camarillo, Calif., 1980-86. Mem. spiritual adv. com. AIDS Svc. Ctr., Pasadena, 1992—; mem. exec. com. Cath. League Religious and Civil Rights, Pasadena, 1991-93; v.p. South Coast Spl. Olympics, Santa Barbara, 1978-86; deacon Roman Cath. Ch. Mem. Nat. Soc. Fund Raising Execs. (faculty fund raising day 1993, Pres.'s award 1993), Wilshire C. of C. (capital campagin advisor 1994), Serra Club of L.A. (pres. 1990-91, chaplain 1992—). Roman Catholic. Home: 1162 5th Ave Los Angeles CA 90019-3440 Office: Not-for-Profit Coun 1162 5th Ave Los Angeles CA 90019-3440

BRANDON, JEFFREY CAMPBELL, physician, interventional radiologist, educator; b. Reynoldsville, Pa., Dec. 5, 1953; s. Milton Boyd and Patricia Alfreda (Steele) B. BS, Allegheny Coll., 1975; MD, Jefferson Med. Coll., 1979. Diplomate Am. Bd. Radiology, Nat. Bd. Med. Examiners. Intern gen. surgery Bryn Mawr (Pa.) Hosp., 1979-80, resident gen. surgery, 1980-81; resident in diagnostic radiology Hahnemann U. Hosp., Phila., 1983-86; fellow interventional radiology, abdominal imaging Hahnemann U. Hosp., 1986-87; clin. instr. Hahnemann U. Hosp., Phila., 1987-88; asst. prof. U. Calif., Irvine, 1988-94, assoc. prof., chmn. radiol. scis., 1994—; mem. adv. bd. Baxter Health Care Tech. and Ventures Div., Irvine, 1990-92, Laparomed Corp., Irvine, 1991-94, Visioneering, Fullerton, Calif., 1993—. Author: (chpt.) Common Problems in Gastrointestinal Radiology, 1989, Critical Care Imaging, 1990, Textbook of Gastrointestinal Radiology, 1991, Textbook of Diagnostic Imaging, 1994; contbr. articles to books and profl. jours. Recipient S. Macuen Smith Otolaryngology award Jefferson Med. Coll., 1979, Baxter Healthcare grant Baxter Corp., 1990, Faculty Rsch. grant U. Calif., Irvine Coll. of Medicine, 1990. Mem. Am. Bd. Radiology (bd. examiner 1994—), Am. Coll. Radiology, Assn. Univ. Radiologists, Soc. Gastrointestinal Radiologists (lectr. 1989—), Am. Inst. Ultrasound in Medicine, Soc. Cardiovascular and Interventional Radiologists, Calif. Med. Assn. (bd. dirs., sci. adv. panel on radiology 1993—), Phi Beta Kappa. Office: Univ Calif Irvine Med Ctr 101 City Dr Rt 140 Orange CA 92668

BRANDON, KATHRYN ELIZABETH BECK, pediatrician; b. Salt Lake City, Sept. 10, 1916; d. Clarence M. and Hazel A. (Cutler) Beck; MD, U. Chgo., 1941; BA, U. Utah, 1937; MPH, U. Calif., Berkeley, 1957; children: John William, Kathleen Brandon McEnulty, Karen (dec.). Intern, Grace Hosp., Detroit, 1941-42; resident Children's Hosp. Med. Center No. Calif., Oakland, 1953-55, Children's Hosp., L.A., 1951-53; pvt. practice, La Crescentia, Calif., 1946-51, Salt Lake City, 1960-65, 86—; med. dir. Salt Lake City public schs., 1957-60; dir. Ogden City-Weber County (Utah) Health Dept., 1965-67; pediatrician Fitzsimmons Army Hosp., 1967-68; coll. health physician U. Colo., Boulder, 1968-71; student health physician U. Utah, Salt Lake City, 1971-81; occupational health physician Hill AFB, Utah, 1981-85; child health physician Salt Lake City-County Health Dept., 1971-82; cons. in field; clin. asst. U. Utah Coll. Medicine, Salt Lake City, 1958-64; clin. asst. pediatrics U. Colo. Coll. Medicine, Denver, 1958-72; active staff emeritus Primary Children's Hosp., LDS Hosp., and Cottonwood Hosp., 1960-67. Diplomate Am. Bd. Pediatrics. Fellow Am. Pediatric Acad., Am. Pub. Health Assn., Am. Sch. Health Assn.; mem. Utah Coll. Health Assn. (pres. 1978-80), Pacific Coast Coll. Health Assn., AMA, Utah Med. Assn., Salt Lake County Med. Soc., Utah Public Health Assn. (sec.-treas. 1960-66), Intermountain Pediatric Soc. Home and Office: PO Box 58482 Salt Lake City UT 84158-0482

BRANDSNESS, DAVID R., hospital administrator; b. Stanley, Wis., Mar. 27, 1936; married. BA, U. Oreg., 1958; MA, U. Minn., 1960. Adminstrv. resident San Jose (Calif.) Hosp. and Health Ctr., 1959-60; adminstrv. officer William Beaumont Army Med. Ctr., El Paso, Tex., 1960-62; adminstr. Elko (Nev.) Gen. Hosp., 1962-64, Nev. State Hosp., Sparks, 1964-65; exec. dir. Sunrise Hosp., Las Vegas, 1965-80; pres. Sparks (Nev.) Family Hosp., 1980-84; CEO U. Med. Ctr., Las Vegas, 1984—. Mem. Am. Hosp. Assn., Nev. Hosp. Assn. (del. 1970-78, bd. dirs. 1974-78). Office: Univ Med Ctr 1800 W Charleston Blvd Las Vegas NV 89102-2329

BRANDT, ALAN ERWIN, insect biotechnology company executive, consultant; b. Norfolk, Va., Jan. 13, 1944; s. Erwin L. and Ruth I. (Prescott) B.; m. Susan J. Rapport, June 10, 1983; 1 child, Aaron E. BS in Chemistry, U. Mich., 1966, PhD in Biochemistry, 1971. Postdoctoral fellow U. Calif., Davis, 1972-73; sr. biochemist SRI Internat., Menlo Park, Calif., 1973-86; pres., CEO, Growth Source, Woodside, Calif., 1985—; chmn., CEO, Insect Biotech., Redwood City, Calif., 1992—. Contbr. articles to sci. jours.; patentee in field. Mem. Nat. Ski Patrol, San Francisco Peninsula, 1981—, patrol dir., 1988-90, sect. chief Bay Area region, 1992-94. Grantee NIH, 1981. Mem. Am. Chem. Soc.

BRANDT, BEVERLY KAY, university administrator, educator; b. Evanston, Ill., Aug. 26, 1951; d. Richard Charles Brandt and Edith Elaine (Uhrenholdt) Littler. BFA, U. Mich., 1973; MA, Mich. State U., 1977; PhD, Boston U., 1985. Cert. designer Nat. Coun. Interior Design Qualification. Asst. prof. Iowa State U., Ames, 1984-87; asst. prof. Ariz. State U., Tempe, 1987-92, assoc. prof., 1992—, dir., 1992-95; cons. Phoenix Art Mus., 1993; dir.-at-large Ariz. Design Inst., Tempe, 1992-93. Book reviewer; author (chpts.) Encyclopedia of Arts and Crafts, 1989; contbr. articles to profl. jours. Fellow Wakonse Fellowship, 1992; recipient Faculty Achievement award Burlington Resources Found., 1991, Travel-to-Collections grant NEH, 1985-86. Mem. Am. Soc. Interior Designers (Attingham grant-in-aid 1987), Decorative Arts Soc., Furniture History Soc., Nat. Trust for Hist. Preservation, Soc. Archtl. Historians, Victorian Soc. Am., Kappa Omicron Nu. Office: Arizona State U Sch of Design PO Box 872105 Tempe AZ 85287-2105

BRANDT, IRA KIVE, pediatrician, medical geneticist; b. N.Y.C., Nov. 9, 1923; s. Charles Zachary and Hilda Eleanor (Moss) B.; m. Dorothy Godfrey, Nov. 26, 1947; children—Elizabeth, Laura, William, Rena. A.B., NYU, 1942; M.D., Columbia U., 1945. Diplomate Am. Bd. Pediatrics, Am. Bd. Med. Genetics. Intern Morrisania City Hosp., N.Y.C., 1945-46; resident Lincoln Hosp., N.Y.C., 1948-50; fellow pediatrics Yale U., New Haven, 1955-57, asst. prof., 1957-61, assoc. prof., 1961-68; chmn. dept. pediatrics Children's Hosp., San Francisco, 1968-70; clin. prof. pediatrics U. Calif., San Francisco, 1970; prof. pediatrics and med. genetics Ind. U. Sch. Medicine, Indpls., 1970-89, prof. emeritus, 1989—. Served to capt. U.S. Army, 1946-47, 52. Mem. Am. Pediatric Soc., Am. Acad. Pediatrics, Soc. Pediatric Rsch., Soc. Inherited Metabolic Disorders, Am. Soc. Human Genetics, Am. Coll. Med. Genetics. Office: Ind U Sch Medicine Dept Pediatrics 702 Barnhill Dr # 0907 Indianapolis IN 46202-5128

BRANDT, MARYCLARE, interior designer, educator; b. Winona, Minn., Aug. 30, 1950; 1 child, Laran Clare. Student, Academie DePort Royal, Paris, France, 1970-71; BA in Art, Coll. St. Teresa, Winona, 1972; MA in Interior Design, Kans. State U., 1976. Cert. interior designer, Calif. V.p., designer Environ. Concepts, San Marcos, Tex., 1980-86; owner, designer M.C. Brandt, La Jolla, Calif., 1986—; instr. S.W. Tex. State U., San Marcos, 1985-86, U. Calif., San Diego, 1990-93. Works have appeared in numerous mags. including Austin Homes and Gardens, Designer Mag., Better Homes and Gardens. Mem. Am. Soc. Interior Designers (bd. dirs. 1988-90, 94—, Outstanding Design award 1990, 1st place award 1990, 3rd place award 1994). Office: MC Brandt Interior Design PO Box 8276 La Jolla CA 92038-8276

BRANDT, WILLIAM CARL, sports memorabilia store owner, chaplain; b. L.A., Nov. 16, 1954; s. William C. Sr. and Ruth Ellen (Halsey) B.; m. Sherry Lynne Quinlivann, Aug. 25, 1978 (div. Apr. 1991); children: Krystal Lynne, Krystin Michelle. BA, Life Bible Coll., 1977; MA, Azusa Pacific U., 1979; postgrad., Iliff Theol. Sem., 1988. Lic. minister. Minister, staff mem., basketball coach Life Bible Coll., L.A., 1977-81; min. Angeles Temple, L.A., 1978-81; pastor New Life Foursquare Ch., Loveland, Colo., 1981-89; basketball coach Dayspring H.S., Greeley, Colo., 1982-83; chaplain Loveland Police Dept., 1983—; owner The Collectory, Loveland, 1983—; ethics com. Midwest Dist. Chs., Colorado Springs, 1984-89; dir. Hope Inst. Ministry, Greeley, 1994. Coach Loveland Athletic League, 1989, Immanuel Luth. Sch., Loveland, 1993-94. Office: The Collectory 1051 E Highway 402 Loveland CO 80537-8800

BRANDWAJN, ALEXANDRE, software company executive; b. Hohne, Fed. Republic of Germany, Apr. 13, 1948; came to U.S., 1978; s. Rachmiel and Liba (Goldziuk) B.; m. Marlene Francette Chabbat, May 22, 1974; children: Elise Sophie, Xavier Marc. Telecommunications Engring. Diploma, ENST, Paris, 1971; D of Engring., U. Paris, 1972, BA in Lit., 1973, Docteur d'Etat, 1975. Researcher Inst. Rsch. Automatique and Informatique, Rocquencourt, France, 1971-75; prof. computer sci. Ecole Nat. Superieure des Telecommunications, Paris, 1975-79; sr. computer architect Amdahl Corp., Sunnyvale, Calif., 1979-82, mgr. performance analysis, 1982-85; pres. Pallas Internat. Corp., San Jose, Calif., 1983—; prof. computer engring. U. Calif., Santa Cruz, 1985—; cons. UCCEL Corp., Dallas, 1986-87, MCC, Austin, Tex., 1986-87, Amdahl Corp., Sunnyvale, 1985—. Contbr. articles to profl. jours. Mem. Assn. for Computing Machinery, Computer Measurement Group. Office: Pallas Internat Corp 1763 Valhalla Ct San Jose CA 95132-1653

BRANKOVICH, MARK J., restaurateur; b. Rijeka, Yugoslavia, Mar. 4, 1922; came to U.S., 1951; s. Joseph M. and Rose (Haydin) B.; m. Marilyn J. Severin, Jan. 4, 1957; children: Mark, Laura. BA in Philosophy, U. Zurich, 1944; student, U. Geneva, 1945, U. Padua, Italy, 1947. Owner The Golden Deer, Chgo., 1953-55; mgr. Gaslight Club, N.Y.C., 1955-57; gen. mgr., exec. v.p., dir. Gaslight Club, Chgo., 1959-63; owner, mgr. Franchise Gaslight Club, L.A., 1963-66; owner Monte Carlo Italian Deli, Burbank, Calif., 1969—, Pinocchio Restaurant, Burbank, 1970—, Pinocchio West, Santa Monica, 1972—, Pinocchio Westwood (Calif.), 1978, Italia Foods Wholesale, Burbank, 1972. Mem. Presdl. Task Force, Washington, 1980—, Rep. Senatorial Inner Circle, 1986. Mem. Internat. Platform Assn. Serbian Orthodox. Home: 1250 Hilldale Ave West Hollywood CA 90069-1826 Office: Monte Carlo Italia Foods Inc 3103 W Magnolia Blvd Burbank CA 91505-3046

BRANN, ALTON JOSEPH, oil field services executive; b. Portland, Maine, Dec. 23, 1941; s. Donald Edward and Marjorie Margaret (Curran) B. B.A., U. Mass., 1969. Mgr. advanced programs Dynamics Research Corp., Wilmington, Mass., 1969-73; dir. engring. Litton Guidance & Control Systems, L.A., 1973-79, dir. program mgmt., 1979-81, v.p. engring., 1981-83, pres., 1983-86; group exec. Navigation Guidance and Control Systems Group, Beverly Hills, Calif., 1986-88; sr. v.p. Components and Indsl. Products Group Litton Industries, Beverly Hills, 1988-90, pres., COO, 1990-92, CEO, 1992-94, chmn., 1994—; chmn., CEO Western Atlas Inc., Beverly Hills, 1994—; trustee Mfrs. Alliance Productivity and Innovation, coun. fgn. diplomacy, U.S.-Russia bus. coun. Mem. IEEE (sr. mem.), Soc. Petroleum Engrs., Optical Soc. Am., L.A. World Affairs Coun., Town Hall of L.A. Office: Western Atlas Inc 360 N Crescent Dr Beverly Hills CA 90210-4802*

BRANSBY, ERIC JAMES, muralist, educator; b. Auburn, N.Y., Oct. 25, 1916; s. Charles Carson and Lillian Holland (Dowsett) B.; m. Mary Antoinette Hemmie, Nov. 23, 1941; 1 dau., Fredericka Jo. Profl. cert., Kansas City Art Inst., 1938-42; BA, Colo. Coll., 1947, MA, 1949; MFA, Yale U., 1952. Instr. U. Ill., Urbana, 1950-52; asst. prof. art Western Ill. U., Macomb, 1963-65; assoc. prof. art U. Mo., Kansas City, 1965-70; prof. U. Mo., 1970—; authority on history and theory of mural painting. One-man shows include, Okla. Art Center, Oklahoma City, 1973, U. Mo., Kansas City, 1971, 77, Denver U., 1966, Brigham Young U., 1966, Colorado Springs (Colo.) Fine Arts Center, 1968, U. Mo., Columbia, 1979, nat. and internat. group shows, murals include, U.S. Command and Gen. Staff Sch., 1945, Mech. Engring. Bldg., U. Ill., 1953, NORAD Hdqrs., Colorado Springs, 1956, Brigham Young U., 1958, Mcpl. Bldg., Liberty, Mo., 1982 (Nat. Mural Competition award), Luth. Ch., Mo. Synod, Internat. Ctr., St. Louis, 1983 (Nat. Mural Competition award), planetarium, USAF Acad., Colorado Springs, 1961-70, Western Ill. U., Macomb, 1965, Rockhurst Coll., Kansas City, 1968, F.D. Roosevelt Meml. Competition, 1961, HUD Nat. Community Art Competition, 1974, U. Mo., Kansas City, 1973-75, Mcpl. Bldg., Sedalia, Mo., 1977, Kans. State Capitol Nat. Mural Competition, 1978, St. Paul Sch., Chgo., 1985, Colo. Springs Fine Arts Ctr., 1986, Kans. State U., 1986, Loveland (Colo.) Mus., 1988, Park Coll., Kansas City, 1991, City of Colorado Springs (Colo.) Mus., 1994; producer of video tapes in field; represented in permanent collections. Served with inf. AUS, 1942-45. Edwin Austin Abbey Found. mural painting fellow, 1952; grantee applied and theoretical studies in mural painting field U.S., Turkey, Mex., Italy; recipient Veatch award U. Mo., 1977. Mem. Nat. Soc. Mural Painters, Phi Kappa Phi. Home: 9080 S State Highway 115 Colorado Springs CO 80926-9716 Office: Univ Mo Dept Art Kansas City MO 64110

BRANSON, ALBERT HAROLD (HARRY BRANSON), magistrate judge, educator; b. Chgo., May 20, 1935; s. Fred Brooks and Marie (Vowell) B.; m. Siri-Anne Gudrun Lindberg, Nov. 2, 1963; children: Gunnar John, Gulliver Dean, Hanna Marie, Siri Elizabeth. BA, Northwestern U., 1957; JD, U. Chgo., 1963. Bar: Pa. 1965, Alaska 1972. Atty. Richard McVeigh law offices, Anchorage, 1972-73; ptnr. Jacobs, Branson & Guetschow, Anchorage, 1973-76, Branson & Guetschow, Anchorage, 1976-82; pvt. practice Law Offices of Harry Branson, Anchorage, 1982-84, 85-89; atty. Branson, Bazeley & Chisolm, Anchorage, 1984-85; U.S. magistrate judge U.S. Dist. Ct., Anchorage, 1989—; instr., adj. prof. U. Alaska Justice Ctr., 1980-93; U.S. magistrate, Anchorage, 1975-76. With U.S. Army, 1957-59. Mem. Alaska Bar Assn. (bd. dirs., v.p. bd. govs. 1977-80, 83-86, pres. bd. govs. 1986, Disting. Svc. award 1992, Spl. Svc. award 1988, editor-in-chief Alaska Bar Rag 1978-86), Anchorage Bar Assn. (bd. dirs., bd. govs. 1982-86), Anchorage Inn of Ct. (pres. 1995). Democrat. Office: US Dist Ct # 33 222 W 7th Ave Unit 33 Anchorage AK 99513-7504

BRANSON, HARLEY KENNETH, lawyer, finance executive; b. Ukiah, Calif., June 10, 1942; s. Harley Edward and Clara Lucile (Slocum) B.; 1 child, Erik Jordan. BS in Acctg. and Fin., San Jose State U., 1965; JD, Santa Clara U., 1968. Bar: Calif. 1969. Law clk. to judge U.S. Ct. Appeals (9th cir.), San Diego, 1968-69; pvt. practice San Diego, 1969-78; div. counsel Ralston Purina Co., San Diego, 1978-83; group gen. counsel Castle & Cooke, Inc., San Diego, 1983-85; gen. counsel, corp. sec. Bumble Bee Seafoods, Inc., San Diego, 1985-89, 90-95; bd. dirs., asst. corp. sec. Network Resources Corp., San Jose, Calif., 1990, Flying Palms LLC, San Diego, 1990-95. Editor Santa Clara Law Rev., 1967-68. Bd. dirs. Installation Gallery, 1992-94, San Diego Civic Light Opera, 1993-95, U. C. Univ. Art Gallery, 1995—. Office: PO Box 6250 San Diego CA 92166-0250

BRANSON, LISA JANE, controller; b. Anchorage, Mar. 8, 1961; d. Mitchell Andrew and Helen Ester (Piesik) Webber; m. Kevin Edward Branson, May 17, 1986; children: Melissa Jo, Jerry Alan. Student, U. Alaska, Spokane Falls C.C., Alaska Bus. Coll., 1980. Bookeeper Bush Air, Anchorage, 1982; receptionist Thomas Heads Greisen, Anchorage, 1982-83, Coopers & Lybrand, Anchorage, 1983-84; budget analyst Westmark Hotels, Anchorage, 1984-91; contr. Penco Alaska, Anchorage, 1991—. Pres. St. Mark Ch. Coun., Anchorage, 1993—; asst. to chmn. Kenai River Sportfishing, Soldotna, Alaska, 1994; adv. bd. Food Bank of Alaska, 1994—. Republican. Lutheran. Office: Penco Alaska 3620 Penland Pkwy Anchorage AK 99508

BRANSON, ROBERT DALE, farm owner; b. Cottonwood, Idaho, Aug. 14, 1950; s. Dale Robert and Alice Arleen (Johnson) B.; m. Kathleen Joan Gunning, Feb. 16, 1974; children: Greg, Julie, Kari. Student, U. Idaho, 1969-73. Ptnr. Branson Farms, Nezperce, Idaho, 1974-88, owner, operator, 1988—; commr. Idaho Wheat Commn., Boise, 1988—, Prairie Hwy, Nezperce, 1988—. Mem. Agrl. Cons. Coun. (pres. 1988—), Idaho State Wheatgrower's Assn. (presdl. leadership award 1984). Lutheran. Home: Rt 1 Box 22B Nezperce ID 83543

BRANTHAVER, JAN FRANKLIN, research chemist; b. Davenport, Iowa, Mar. 12, 1936; s. Franklin Inglis and Ruth Matilda (Doering) B. BA, Millikin U., 1958; PhD, N.D. State U., 1976. Rsch. aide N.D. State U., Fargo, 1964-76; rsch. chemist Laramie (Wyo.) Energy Tech. Ctr., 1976-83; program mgr. Western Rsch. Inst., Laramie, 1983—. Editor Metal Complexes in Fossil Fuels, 1987; contbr. numerous articles to profl. publs. With U.S. Army, 1959. Mem. Am. Chem. Soc. (sec. Wyo. sect. 1986-87, treas. 1990-95), Sigma Xi. Lutheran. Home: 1000 E Garfield St Apt 17 Laramie WY 82070-4065 Office: Western Rsch Inst 365 N 9th St Laramie WY 82070-3380

BRANTINGHAM, CHARLES ROSS, podiatrist, ergonomics consultant; b. Long Beach, Calif., Feb. 14, 1917; m. Lila Carolyn Price; children: Paul Jeffery, John Price, Charles Ross, James William. Student, Long Beach City Coll., 1935; D in Podiatric Medicine, Calif. Coll. Podiatric Medicine, 1939, postdoctoral student surgery, 1947. Diplomate Am. Bd. Podiatric Pub. Health. Resident in podiatry Podiatry Clinics, San Francisco, 1939-40; pvt. practice podiatry Long Beach, 1946-56; podiatrist, dir. Podiatric Group, Long Beach, 1956-71, Los Alamitos (Calif.) Podiatric Group, 1971-90; chief podiatry sect., dept. orthopedics Los Alamitos Med. Ctr., 1983-90; ergonomics educator and cons. Nipomo, Calif., 1990—; adj. prof. Calif. State U., Long Beach, 1972-89; vol. faculty Sch. Medicine U. So. Calif., L.A., 1965-94; cons. Specified Products Co., El Monte, Calif., 1969-91, Armstrong World Industries, Lancaster, Pa., 1983-91, Cert. Carpet Svcs., Lancaster, 1991-94. Contbr. chpts. to books, articles to profl. jours. Patentee in field. Bd. dirs. Diabetes Assn. So. Calif., L.A., 1964-67; cons., bd. dirs. Comprehensive Health Planning Assn., L.A., 1969-72; pub. improvement and adv. cons. Long Beach City Coun. and Office of Mayor, 1957-67. With USN, 1942-46, to lt. comdr. (ret.) USNR. Fellow Am. Assn. Hosp. Podiatrists (pres. 1958-60), Am. Pub. Health Assn. (sect. coun. pres. 1986, Steven Toth award 1982), Am. Soc. Podiatric Medicine, Internat. Acad. Standing and Walking Fitness (pres. 1963—); mem. Am. Podiatric Med. Assn. (mem. nat. coun. 1953-55, bd. trustees 1957-59, exec. coun. 1957-59, Hall of Sci. award 1973), Calif. Podiatric Med. Assn. (life, pres. 1951), Assn. Mil. Surgeons U.S. (life), Res. Officers Assn. U.S. (life), Exch. Club (local pres. 1948-49), Ind. Bus. Club (pres. 1958), Nat. Acad. Practice (Disting. Practioner Podiatric Medicine award 1983, Founders Honor Roll 1993). Republican. Mem. LDS Ch. Home and Office: 1541 Los Padres Dr Nipomo CA 93444-9625

BRASSELL, ROSELYN STRAUSS, lawyer; b. Shreveport, La., Feb. 19, 1930; d. Herman Carl and Etelka (McMullan) Strauss. BA, La. State U., 1949; JD, UCLA, 1962. Bar: Calif. 1963. Atty. CBS, Los Angeles, 1962-68, sr. atty., 1968-76, asst. gen. atty., 1976-83, broadcast counsel, 1983-91; pvt. practice law L.A., 1991—; instr. TV Prodn. Bus. and Legal Aspects, UCLA Extension, 1992. Co-writer: Life After Death for the California Celebrity, 1985; bd. editors U. Calif. Law Rev., 1960-62. Named Angel of Distinction Los Angeles Cen. City Assn., 1975. Mem. Calif. Bar Assn., L.A. County Bar Assn. (exec. com. 1970—, sect. chmn. 1980-81), Beverly Hills Bar Assn., L.A. Copyright Soc. (treas. 1977-78, sec. 1978-79, pres. 1981-82), Am. Women in Radio and TV (nat. dir.-at-large 1971-73, nat. pub. affairs chmn. 1977-78, Merit award So. Calif. chpt. 1989), NATAS, Women in Film, Orange County World Affairs Coun. (trustee 1995-96), U. Calif. Law Alumni Assn. (dir. 1971-74), Order of Coif, Alpha Xi Delta, Phi Alpha Delta. Republican. Home: 33331 Gelidum Cir Monarch Beach CA 92629-4451 Office: 645 Wilcox Ave Ste 1-d Los Angeles CA 90004-1131

BRATMAN, DAVID STEPHEN, librarian; b. Chgo., Mar. 31, 1957; s. Robert Louis and Nancy Ellin (Bylan) B.; m. Bernadette Cecile Phillips, June 12, 1994. BA, U. Calif. Berkeley, 1979; MLS, U. Wash., 1983. Cataloger Stanford U., Stanford, Calif., 1983-89, Santa Clara U., Santa Clara, Calif., 1989-91, Coll. of Notre Dame, Belmont, Calif., 1992-93; libr. cons. Hillel Found., Stanford, Calif., 1991—. Editor: (periodical) Mythprint, 1980-95; contbr. articles to profl. jours. Mem. The Mythopoeic Soc. (bd. dirs. 1980—, chmn. 1986-87, 93, conf. chair 1988, awards adminstr. 1992—), The World Sci. Fiction Soc. (awards adminstr. 1993-94), The Tolkien Soc., Friends of the English Regency, No. Calif. Tech. Processing Group. Home: 1161 Huntingdon Dr San Jose CA 95129

BRATTON, HOWARD CALVIN, federal judge; b. Clovis, N.Mex., Feb. 4, 1922; s. Sam Gilbert and Vivian (Rogers) B. B.A., U. N.Mex., 1941, LL.D., 1971; LL.B., Yale U., 1947. Bar: N.Mex. 1948. Law clk. U.S. Cir. Ct. Appeals, 1948; ptnr. Grantham & Bratton, Albuquerque, 1949-52; spl. asst. U.S. atty. charge litigation OPS, 1951-52; assoc., then ptnr. Hervy, Dow & Hinkle, Roswell, N.Mex., 1952-64; judge U.S. Dist. Ct. N.Mex., Las Cruces, 1964—, chief judge, 1978-87, sr. judge, 1987—; chmn. N.Mex. Jr. Bar Assn., 1952; pres. Chaves County (N.Mex.) Bar Assn., 1962; chmn. pub. lands com. N.Mex. Oil and Gas Assn., 1961-64, Interstate Oil Compact Commn., 1963-64; mem. N.Mex. Commn. Higher Edn., 1962-64, Jud. Conf. of U.S. Com. on operation of jury system, 1966-72, 79—, Jud. Conf. U.S. Com. on Ethics, 1987-92; ad hoc com. on internat. jud. rels., 1992—. Bd. regents U. N.Mex., 1958-68, pres., 1963-64; bd. dirs. Fed. Jud. Ctr., 1983-87. Served to capt. AUS, 1942-45. Mem. Trial Judges Assn. 10th Circuit (pres. 1976-78), Nat. Conf. Fed. Trial Judges (exec. com. 1977-79), Sigma Chi. Home: 6760 Via Emma Dr Las Cruces NM 88005-4977 Office: US Dist Ct 200 E Griggs Ave Las Cruces NM 88001-3523*

BRAUCH, GARY JAMES, pilot; b. Evanston, Ill., July 25, 1943; s. Walter Greig and Marilyn Jean (Stube) B.; m. Diane Afton Davis, Aug. 7, 1964; 1 child, Derek Gary. BS in Polit. Sci., Calif. State U., Long Beach, 1964. Flight officer United Airlines, Newark, N.J., 1964-65; flight officer United Airlines, San Francisco, 1965-80, capt., 1980—. Producer Kaleidoscope Pub. TV, Los Altos, Calif., 1993-94.

BRAUDY, LEO BEAL, English language educator, author; b. Phila., June 11, 1941; s. Edward and Zelda (Smith) B.; m. Dorothy Wood McGahee, Dec. 24, 1974. B.A., Swarthmore Coll., 1963; M.A., Yale U., 1964, Ph.D., 1967. Instr. English Yale U., New Haven, 1966-68; asst. prof. Columbia U., N.Y.C., 1968-70; assoc. prof. Columbia U., 1970-73, prof., 1973-76; prof. English Johns Hopkins U., Balt., 1977-83; prof. English, chmn. dept. U. So. Calif., Los Angeles, 1983-86; Leo S. Bing prof. English U. So. Calif., 1986—. Author: Narrative Form in History and Fiction: Hume, Fielding, and Gibbon, 1970, Jean Renoir: The World of His Films, 1972, 2d edit., 1989, The World in a Frame: What We See in Films, 1976, 2d edit., 1984, The Frenzy of Renown: Fame and Its History, 1986, Native Informant: Essays on Film, Fiction and Popular Culture, 1992; editor: Norman Mailer: A Collection of Critical Essays, 1972, Focus on Truffaut's Shoot the Piano Player, 1972, (with Morris Dickstein) Great Film Directors: A Critical Anthology, 1978, (with Gerald Mast and Marshall Cohen) Film Theory and Criticism, 4th edit., 1992; mem. editorial bd. ELH, 1976—, PMLA, 1979-82, Raritan Rev, 1979—, Prose Studies, 1979—, Film Quar., 1984—. Guggenheim fellow, 1971-72; grantee Am. Council Learned Socs., 1971, NEH, 1978, 79, 86; Rockefeller Found. fellow, Bellagio, Italy, 1986. Mem. MLA, Am. Soc. for Eighteenth-Century Studies, Nat. Book Critics Cir., PEN Ctr.-USA West (bd. dirs. 1989-92, 94-95). Office: U So Calif Dept English Los Angeles CA 90089-0354

BRAULT, G(AYLE) LORAIN, healthcare executive; b. Chgo., Jan. 3, 1944; d. Theodore Frank and Victoria Jean (Pribyl) Hahn; m. Donald R. Brault, Apr. 29, 1971; 1 child, Kevin David. AA, Long Beach City Coll., 1963; BS, Calif. State U.-Long Beach, 1973, MS, 1977. RN, Calif. Dir. nursing Canyon Gen. Hosp., Anaheim, Calif., 1973-76; dir. faculty critical care masters degree program Calif. State U., Long Beach, 1976-79; regional dir. nursing and support svcs. Western region Am. Med. Internat., Anaheim, Calif., 1979-83; v.p. Hosp. Home Care Corp. Am., Santa Ana, Calif., 1983-85; pres. Hosp. Home Health Care Agy. Calif., Torrance, 1986-92; v.p. Hosp. Coun. So. Calif., L.A., 1993—; invited lectr. China Nurses Assn., 1983; cons. AMI, Inc., Saudi Arabia, 1983; advisor dept. grad. nursing Calif. State U., L.A., 1988, advisor Nursing Inst., 1990-91; guest lectr. dept. pub. health UCLA, 1986-87; assoc. clin. prof. U. So. Calif., 1988-93; advisor RN Times, Nurseweek, 1988—. Contbr. articles to profl. jours., chpts. to books. Commr. HHS, Washington, 1988. HEW advanced nurse tng. grantee, 1978. Mem. Women in Health Adminstrn. (sec. 1989, v.p. 1990), Nat. Assn. Home Care, Am. Orgn. Nursing Execs., Calif. Assn. Health Svcs. at Home (task force chmn. 1988, bd. dirs. 1988-93, chmn. bd. dirs. 1990-93), Calif. League Nursing (bd. sec. 1983, program chmn. 1981-82), Am. Coll. Health Care Execs., ASAE, AONE, Phi Kappa Phi, Sigma Theta Tau. Republican. Methodist. Home: 1032 E Andrews Dr Long Beach CA 90807-2406

BRAULT, MARGUERITTE BRYAN, theatre organization administrator; b. Hutchinson, Kans., Sept. 18, 1930; d. George Wilson and Maude Alice (Vancil) Bryan; m. James William Brault, June 27, 1952 (div. May 1986); children: Stephen Michael, Lisa Lynn, Jennifer Elaine. BS with high honors, U. Wis., 1952; BA with highest distinction, U. Ariz., 1975, MA, 1979. Adminstrv./rsch. asst. Ednl. Testing Svc., Princeton, N.J., 1959-64; cons., scorer trainer Ednl. Testing Svc., Tucson, 1964-65; psychometrician Sunnyside Sch. Dist., Tucson, 1965-66; psychometrician U. Ariz., Tucson, 1966, rsch. asst., 1984-86; prodr., writer Sci-Expo, Tucson, 1985; program dir., writer Sci. Alive!/Discovery Alive, Inc., Tucson, 1986—; actor, 1988—; mem. Arts Edn. Working Group, Tucson, 1992. Writer video: An Apple Did Not Fall on My Head, 1985; co-author drama/musical prodn. The Fate of the Earth, 1982; writer, dir. plays: How Do We Discover?, the Fascinating World of Electricity, Secrets of the Heart, What is the World Made Of?; contbr. poetry to profl. publs. Bd. dirs. LifeQuest Interfaith Cmty., Tucson, 1990—; toy project dir. Am. Friends Svc. Com., Tucson, 1983-90. Mem. Ariz. Reading Assn., Tucson Area Reading Coun., Inst. Noetic Scis., Phi Beta Kappa. Office: Sci Alive!/Discovery Alive! 3331 N Wilson Tucson AZ 85719

BRAUMAN, JOHN I., chemist, educator; b. Pitts., Sept. 7, 1937; s. Milton and Freda E. (Schlitt) B.; m. Sharon Lea Kruse, Aug. 22, 1964; 1 dau., Kate Andrea. B.S., Mass. Inst. Tech., 1959; Ph.D. (NSF fellow), U. Calif., Berkeley, 1963. NSF postdoctoral fellow U. Calif., Los Angeles, 1962-63; asst. prof. chemistry Stanford (Calif.) U., 1963-69, assoc. prof., 1969-72, prof., 1972-80, J.G. Jackson-C.J. Wood prof. chemistry, 1980—, chmn. dept., 1979-83; cons. in phys. organic chemistry; adv. panel chemistry div. NSF, 1974-78; adv. panel NASA, AEC, ERDA, Rsch. Corp., Office Chemistry and Chem. Tech., NRC; coun. Gordon Rsch. Confs., 1989—, trustee, 1991—. Mem. editorial adv. bd. Jour. Am. Chem. Soc., 1976-83, Jour. Organic Chemistry, 1974-78, Nouveau Jour. de Chimie, 1977-85, Chem. Revs., 1978-80, Chem. Kinetics, 1987-89, Accts. Chem. Rsch., 1995—; dep. editor for phys. scis. Sci., 1985—. Fellow Alfred P. Sloan, 1968-70, Guggenheim, 1978-79; Christensen, Oxford U., 1983-84. Fellow AAAS (chmn-elect, sec. 1995—), Calif. Acad. Scis. (hon.); mem. NaT, Am. Acad. Arts Sci., Am. Chem. Soc. (award in pure chemistry 1973, Harrison Howe award 1976, R.C. Fuson award 1986, James Flack Norris award 1986, Arthur C. Cope scholar 1986, exec. com. phys. chemistry divsn., com. on sci. 1992—), Brit. Chem. Soc., Sigma Xi, Phi Lambda Upsilon. Home: 849 Tolman Dr Palo Alto CA 94305-1025 Office: Stanford U Dept Chemistry Stanford CA 94305-5080

BRAUN, GERALD CURTIS, rehabilitation administrator; b. Red Wing, Minn., Aug. 24, 1946; s. Quentin Vernon and Marian (Stumpf) B.; m. Donna Susan Gustafson Nordin, Nov. 7, 1970 (div. July 1987); children: Eric, Kirsten, Rebecca, Joanna; m. Deborah Ann Chinnock, July 27, 1990;. BA, St. Cloud State U., 1968, MS, 1971; DEd, U. Nev., 1981. Cert. rehab. counselor; nat. cert. counselor. Rehab. counselor State of Minn. Svcs. to the Blind, St. Paul, 1971-72; vocat. rehab. specialist VA Regional Office, St. Paul, 1972-74; counseling psychologist trainee VA Regional Office, Chgo., 1974-75; counseling psychologist VA Regional Office, St. Paul, 1975-77; supervisory counseling psychologist VA Regional Office, Reno, 1977-80, vocat. rehab. adminstr., 1980—; profl. adv. mem. No. Nev. Multiple Sclerosis Soc., Reno, 1979—; apptd. mem. Govs. Com. on Employment of People with Disabilities, State of Nev., 1993—. Editor: VR&C Profl. Rev., 1988—. Curriculum advisor U. Nev., Reno, 1987. With U.S. Army, 1968-70, Vietnam. Lutheran. Office: VA Regional Office 1201 Terminal Way Reno NV 89520-0118

BRAUN, STANLEY, insurance company executive; b. N.Y.C., July 2, 1937; s. Herman and Gussie (Cigler) B.; m. Madeline Joan Littman, Dec. 25, 1959 (div. Jan. 1984); children: Cindy Karen, Dina Jill, Suzanne Alyse; m. Ardis Nadine Knoppel, May 11, 1985. BS in Banking and Fin., NYU, 1959. V.p. CNA Ins. Co., N.Y.C., Chgo., Los Angeles, 1959-74; sr. v.p. Harbor Ins. Co., Los Angeles, 1974-76; pres. Mission Ins. Co., Los Angeles, 1976-84; exec. v.p. Fairmont Fin., Inc. and Fairmont Ins., Burbank, Calif., 1984-86; pres., chief exec. officer Fairmont Ins. Co., Burbank, Calif., 1986—; bd. dirs. Am. Capitol Ins. Co., Los Angeles, Chase World Info. Corp., Los Angeles, Fairmont Ins. Co., Chiltar Ins. Co., Continental Surety and Fidelity Ins. Co. Founder Raritan Valley Civic Assn., Hazlet, N.J., 1965. Served as sgt. U.S. Army, 1961-67. Mem. Calif. Workers' Compensation Inst. (bd. dirs. 1983-84). Republican. Jewish. Clubs: Los Angeles Athletic; Calabasas Golf and Country (Calabasas Park, Calif.). Home: 4640 Dunas Ln Tarzana CA 91356-4602

BRAUN, STEPHEN BAKER, academic administrator; b. Cleve., Nov. 3, 1942; s. William B. and Louise M. (Baker) B.; m. Retta F. Kriefall, June 16, 1974; children: Elizabeth Rachel, Christopher Baker. BS, Xavier U., 1964; MBA, Fairleigh Dickinson U., 1976. Regional mgr. Northwest Airlines, Inc., St. Paul, Minn., 1967-72; v.p. Inflight Motion Pictures, Inc., N.Y.C., 1972-78; v.p., gen. mgr. Columbia Pipe & Supply, Inc., Portland, Oreg., 1978-79; exec. v.p. Golby Mfg. Co., Portland, 1979-80; v.p. fin. Timberline Systems, Inc., Portland, 1980-82; pres., founder Systems Supplyware, Inc., Portland, 1982-87; dean Coll. Bus. Concordia U., Portland, 1987-92, exec.

v.p., 1993—; CEO Concordia U. Found., Portland, 1993—; vice chmn., dir. CCNW Found., Portland, 1985—; bd. regents Concordia U., 1986-87, 92—; bd. dirs. Alameda Resources Co., Tigard, Oreg. Com. chmn. United Way, Boston, 1966; bd. dirs. German Am. Found., 1990—. With USN, 1964-67. Mem. Oreg. Ctr. for Entrepreneurship (pres., founder, 1986), Am. Mktg. Assn. (panelist 1985-88), Assn. Data Processing Systems Orgn., Rotary (long-range planning com. 1985—). Lutheran. Office: Concordia Coll 2811 NE Holman St Portland OR 97211-6067

BRAUN, STEPHEN HUGHES, psychologist; b. St. Louis, Nov. 20, 1942; s. William Lafon and Jane Louise B.; BA, Washington U., St. Louis, 1964, MA, 1965; PhD (USPHS fellow in Clin. Psychology), U. Mo., Columbia, 1970; 1 son, Damian Hughes. Asst. prof. psychology Calif. State U., Chico, 1970-71; dir. social learning div. Ariz. State Hosp., Phoenix, 1971-74; chief bur. planning and evaluation Ariz. Dept. Health Svcs., Phoenix, 1974-79; pres. Braun and Assocs., human svc. program cons.'s, Scottsdale, Ariz., 1979—; v.p. Ariz. Healthcare, 1991—; asst. prof. psychology Ariz. State U., 1971-79, vis. asst. prof. Ctr. of Criminal Justice, 1974-79, Ctr. for Pub. Affairs, 1979-81; cons. Law Enforcement Assistance Adminstrn., NIMH, Alcohol, Drug Abuse, and Mental Health Adminstrn., Ariz. Dept. Health Svcs., Ariz. Dept. Corrections, Ariz. Dept. Econ. Security, local and regional human svc. agys. NIMH rsch. grantee, 1971-74; State of Calif. rsch. grantee, 1971; lic. clin. psychologist, Ariz. Mem. Am. Psychol. Assn., Sigma Xi. Editorial cons.; contbr. articles to profl. publs. Office: 4540 N 44th St # 63 Phoenix AZ 85018

BRAUNSTEIN, GLENN DAVID, physician, educator; b. Greenville, Tex., Feb. 29, 1944; s. Mervin and Helen (Friedman) B.; m. Jacquelyn D. Moose, July 5, 1965; children: Scott M. Braunstein, Jeffrey T. Braunstein. BS summa cum laude, U. Calif. San Francisco, 1965, MD, 1968. Diplomate Am. Bd. Internal Medicine, subspecialty endocrinology, diabetes, metabolism. Intern, resident Peter Bent Brigham Hosp., Boston, 1968-70; clin. fellow in medicine Harvard U. Med. Sch., Boston, 1969-70; clin. assoc., reproduction rsch. br. NIH, Bethesda, Md., 1970-72; chief resident in endocrinology Harbor Gen. Hosp. UCLA, 1972-73; dir. endocrinology Cedars-Sinai Med. Ctr., L.A., 1973-86, chmn., dept. medicine, 1986—; asst. prof. medicine UCLA Sch. Medicine, 1973-77, assoc. prof., 1977-81, prof., 1981—, vice chair dept. medicine, 1986—; cons. for AMA drug evaluations, 1990—; mem. internat. adv. com. Second World Conf. on Implantation and Early Pregnancy in Human, 1994; mem. endocrinologic and metabolic drugs adv. com. FDA, 1991—, chmn. 1995-96, bd. dirs. Editl. bd. Jour. Clin. Endocrinology & Metabolism, 1978-80, editor, 1980-83; editl. bd. Mt. Sinai Jour. Medicine, 1984-88, Early Pregnancy: Biology and Medicine, 1994, Am. Family Physician, 1995. Bd. dirs. Israel Cancer Rsch. Fund, 1991—; mem. Jonsson Comprehensive Cancer Ctr., 1991—. Recipient Gold Headed Cane Soc. award U. Calif. San Francisco Med. Ctr., 1968, Merck scholarship, 1968, Mosby scholarship, 1968, Soc. of Hacham award Cedars-Sinai Med. Ctr., 1976, Morris Press Humanism award Cedars-Sinai Med. Ctr., 1984. Fellow ACP (mem. adv. com. to gov., So. Calif. region 1989—, credentials com. So. Calif. region 1993); mem. AAAS, Am. Diabetes Assn., Cross Town Endocrine Club (chmn. 1982-83), Endocrine Soc. (publs. com. 1983-89, long range planning com. 1986-87, recent progress hormone rsch. com. 1993—, ann. meeting steering com. 1993-95), Pacific Coast Fertility Soc. (pres. 1988), Western Soc. for Clin. Rsch., Am. Fedn. for Clin. Rsch., Am. Fertility Soc., Western Assn. Physicians, Assn. Am. Physicians, Am. Soc. Clin. Investigations (mem. nom. com. 1989), USCF Sch. Medicine Alumni Faculty Assn. (regional v.p. so. Calif., mem. bd. dirs. Israel Cancer Rsch. Fund, 1991—, mem. Jonsson Comprehensive Cancer Ctr., 1991—), Phi Delta Epsilon, Alpha Omega Alpha. Office: Cedars Sinai Med Ctr Dept Med Pla Level B118 8700 Beverly Blvd Los Angeles CA 90048-1804

BRAUNSTEIN, RUTH, art dealer, gallery owner; b. Mpls., July 20, 1923; m. Tod Braunstein, July 13, 1943; children: Mark, Marna. Dance instr. Dance Theatre, Washington, 1950-60; owner art gallery Braunstein/Quay Gallery, San Francisco, 1961—. Mem. San Francisco Art Dealers Assn. (pres. 1974-76, 95—), Art Table, Inc. (bd. dirs. 1990-92).

BRAUNSTEIN, TERRY MALIKIN, artist; b. Washington, Sept. 18, 1942; d. Hiram and Dorothy (Malakoff) Malikin; m. David R. Braunstein, Jan. 17, 1965; children: Samantha, Matthew. BFA, U. Mich., 1964; MFA, Md. Inst. Art, 1968. vis. prof. Calif. State U., Long Beach, 1989; asst. prof. Corcoran Sch. Art, 1978-86; lectr. in field. One-woman shows include Franklin Furnace, N.Y.C., 1977-79, Fendrick Gallery, Washington, 1980, Washington Project for Arts, 1976-82, Marcuse Pfeifer, N.Y.C., 1987, Tartt Gallery, Washington, 1986, 88, U. Mich., Ann Arbor, 1990, Hampshire Coll., Amherst, Mass., 1990, Hampshire Coll., Amherst, Mass., 1990, Almediterranea '92, Almeria, Spain, 1990, Long Beach (Calif.) Mus. of Art, 1991, Turner/Krull Gallery, L.A., 1992, Troyer, Fiktzpatrick, Lassman Gallery, Washington, 1994, Craig Krull Gallery, L.A., 1994; exhibited in group shows at Bronx Mus., 1976, Corcoran Gallery of Art, 1973, 85, Gallery Miyzazki, Osaka, Japan, 1983, Bertha Udang Gallery, N.Y.C., 1985, Calif. State U., Long Beach, Calif., 1987, Ctr. Georges Pompidou, Paris, 1985, Calif. Mus. Photography, Riverside, 1990, Long Beach Mus. Art., 1992, Sala Arcs Gallery, Barcelona, Spain, 1990, Salas de Arenal and travelling exhibition, Seville, Madrid, Spain and Marseille, France, 1992—; represented in permanent collections at Mus. Modern Art, N.Y.C., Corcoran Gallery of Art, Washington, Long Beach Mus. Art, Mus. Contemprary Art, Chgo. Bibliotheque Nationale, Paris, Libr. of Congress, Washington, Bruce Peel Spl. Collections Libr., U. Alberta, Can., Nat. Mus. Am. Art, Washington, Mills Coll. Spl. Collections Libr., Oakland, Calif., U. Art Mus., Calif. State U., Long Beach, Metro Rail Met. Transp. Authority. Recipient Visual Artists fellowship Nat. Endowment for Arts, 1985, Disting. Artist award City of Long Beach, 1992, video grant Long Beach Mus. Art, 1992, Nat. Artist's Book award Nat. Mus. Women in Arts, 1994; named disting. Vis. Prof., Calif. State U., 1989. Home: 262 Belmont Ave Long Beach CA 90803-1522

BRAUNSTEIN, YALE MITCHELL, economist, educator; b. Phila., Jan. 12, 1945; s. Oscar Samuel and Betty E. (Seidman) B.; m. Elizabeth Susan Huebner, June 23, 1968; 1 child, Alex Jacob. BS, Rensselaer Poly. Inst., 1966; MA, Stanford U., 1968, PhD, 1975. Mem. faculty NYU, 1974-77; asst. prof. econs. Brandeis U., Waltham, Mass., 1977-83; prof. U. Calif., Berkeley Sch Info. Mgmt. and Sys., 1983—; bd. dirs. Kalba Bowen Assocs. (now Kalba Internat., Inc.); trustee Engring, Info., Inc., 1981-84; cons. in field. Contbr. articles, reports to profl. jours. NSF grantee, 1972-82. Mem. Am. Econs. Assn., Am. Soc. Info. Sci., Am. Lancia Club, Lancia Motor Club U.K. Home: 1467 Olympus Ave Berkeley CA 94708-2207 Office: U Calif Berkeley CA 94720

BRAVERMAN, DONNA CARYN, fiber artist; b. Chgo., Apr. 4, 1947; d. Samuel and Pearl (Leen) B.; m. William Stanley Knopf, Jan. 21, 1990. Student, U. Mo., 1965-68; BFA in Interior Design, Chgo. Acad. Fine Arts, 1970. Interior designer Ascher Dental Supply-Healthco., Chgo., 1970-72, Clarence Krusinski & Assocs. Ltd., Chgo., 1972-74, Perkins & Will Architects, Chgo., 1974-77; fiber artist Fiber Co-op Fibrecations, Chgo., 1977, Scottsdale, Ariz., 1977—. Exhibited in group shows at Mus. Contemporary Crafts, N.Y.C., 1977, James Prendergast Library Art Gallery, Jamestown, N.Y., 1981, Grover M. Herman Fine Arts Ctr., Marietta, Ohio, 1982, Okla. Art Ctr., 1982, Middle Tenn. State U., Murfreesboro, 1982, Redding (Calif.) Mus., 1983, Tucson Mus. Art, 1984, 86, The Arts Ctr., Iowa City, 1985, The Wichita Nat., 1986; in traveling exhibitions Ariz. Archtl. Crafts, 1983, Clouds, Mountains, Fibers, 1983; represented in permanent collections Phillips Petroleum, Houston, Metro. Life, Tulsa, Directory Hotel, Tulsa, Keys Estate Ariz. Biltmore Estates, Phoenix, Sohio Petroleum, Dallas, Reichold Chem., White Plains, N.Y., Rolm Telecommunications, Colorado Springs, Mesirow & Co., Chgo., Exec. House Hotel, Chgo., Cambell Estate, Ariz., Dictaphone Worldhead Quarters, Stratford, Conn., Davenport Bldg., Boston; contbr. articles to profl. jours. Home and Office: 1041 E Glenrosa Ave Phoenix AZ 85014-4435

BRAVERMAN, ROBERT ALLEN, lawyer; b. Oakland, Calif., July 9, 1940; s. Joseph Braverman and Elton Pearl Briggs Rayhill; m. Frances Ternus, Sept. 19, 1967 (div. 1974). BS in Bus. Adminstrn., U. Calif., Berkeley, 1963; JD, U. Calif., San Francisco, 1966. Bar: Calif. Legis. counsel Calif. Legislature, Sacramento, 1966-68; asst. pub. defender Pub Defender of Alameda County, Oakland, 1968-71; atty. in pvt. practice Oakland, 1972—; dir. Ct. Apptd. Atty. Program, Oakland, 1975; hearing officer Alameda County. dir. Ct. Apptd. Atty. Program, Oakland, 1975—; hearing officer Alameda County. Pres. Alameda County Dem. Lawyers, Oakland, 1988. With U.S. Army, 1959-63. Mem. Alameda County Bar Assn. (bd. dirs.), Sierra Club, Commonwealth Club, World Affairs Coun., Calif. Attys. for Criminal Justice, Calif. Pub. Defenders Assn., Lawyers Club of Alameda County, Nat. Wildlife Fedn., World Wildlife Fund, Nature Conservancy, Nat. Travel Club, Nat. Audubon Soc. Presbyterian. Office: Law Offices 1611 Telegraph Ave Ste 1100 Oakland CA 94612-2146

BRAWLEY, EDWARD ALLAN, social work educator; b. Edinburgh, Scotland, Nov. 20, 1935; came to U.S., 1964; s. Edward and Elizabeth Swan Berwick (Allan) B.; m. Emilia Esther Martinez, Nov. 9, 1963; children: Stephen, Ewan. Cert., Heriot-Watt U., Edinburgh, 1958, Langside Coll., Glasgow, Scotland, 1960, Strathclyde U., Glasgow, Scotland, 1963; DSW, U. Pa., 1973. Cert. social worker. Social worker Larchgrove House, Glasgow, 1960-61, Dr. Guthrie's Boys Sch., Edinburgh, 1963-64; dir. residential life The Glen Mills (Pa.) Schs., 1965-68; div. dir. social scis. Community Coll. Phila., 1968-78; prof. social work Pa. State U., University Park, 1978-92, Ariz. State U. W, Phoenix, 1992—; cons. Bur. Labor Stats., Washington, 1986-88, Nat. Inst. Alcohol Abuse and Alcoholism, Rockville, Md., 1978-81; vis. prof. U. Regina (Can.) Faculty Social Work, 1983; vis. rsch. fellow U. East Anglia Sch. Econ. and Social Studies, Norwich, Eng., 1985; scholar-in-residence Bar-Ilan U., Ramat-Gan, Israel, 1987. Co-author: Community and Social Service Education in the Community College, 1972, Social Care at the Front Line, 1987; author: The New Human Service Worker, 1975, Mass Media and Human Services, 1983, Human Services and the Media, 1995. Mem. Pa. Transp. Adv. Com., Harrisburg, 1986-92; mem. Gov. of Pa. Task Force on Human Svcs., Harrisburg, 1970-71; mem. Pa. Legis. Audit Adv. Commn., Harrisburg, 1978. Mem. Nat. Assn. Social Workers, Coun. Social Work Edn., Internat. Coun. Social Welfare, Internat. Assn. Schs. Social Work. Home: 4523 E La Mirada Way Phoenix AZ 85044-7510 Office: Ariz State U 4701 E Thunderbird Rd Phoenix AZ 85032-5540

BRAY, ABSALOM FRANCIS, JR., lawyer; b. San Francisco, Nov. 24, 1918; s. Absalom Francis and Leila Elizabeth (Veale) B.; m. Lorraine Cerena Paule, June 25, 1949; children: Oliver, Brian, Margot. BA, Stanford U., 1940; JD, U. So. Calif., 1949. Bar: Calif. 1949, U.S. Supreme Ct. 1960. Sr. ptnr. Bray & Baldwin and successive firms to Bray & Bray, Martinez, Calif., 1949—, now pres.; founder, bd. dirs. John Muir Nat. Bank, Martinez. Chmn. Martinez Recreation Commn., 1949-54; chmn. nat. bd. dirs. Camp Fire Girls, 1959-61, 1969-71; pres. Contra Costa County (Calif.) Devel. Assn., 1959-60; pres. Contra Costa County Hist. Soc., 1995. Lt. USNR, 1942-46. Mem. State Bar Calif. (chmn. adoption com. 1955-56), Martinez Hist. Soc. (pres. 1984), John Muir Meml. Assn. (pres. 1989-92), Navy League U.S. (pres. Contra Costa Coun. 1981-83), Martinez High Twelve Club (pres. 1987). Republican. Episcopalian. Lodges: Masons, Rotary (pres. Martinez chpt. 1970-71). Home: 600 Flora St Martinez CA 94553-3268 Office: Ward and Ferry Sts Martinez CA 94553-1697

BRAY, JONATHAN DONALD, engineering educator, consultant; b. Kennett, Mo., Aug. 17, 1958; s. Andrew Bernard and Marlea C. (Hoheisel) B.; m. Mary Elizabeth Painton, Aug. 9, 1986; children: David Painton, Caroline Anne, Madeleine Claire. BS, U.S. Mil. Acad., 1980; MS, Stanford U., 1981; PhD, U. Calif., Berkeley, 1990. Registered profl. engr., Calif., Va. Sr. project engr. Balt. dist. Corps of Engrs., 1985-86; project engr. Dames & Moore, San Francisco, 1990; asst. prof. Purdue U., West Lafayette, Ind., 1990-93, U. Calif., Berkeley, 1993—; consulting engr., 1988—. Contbr. articles to profl. jours. Capt. U.S. Army Corps Engrs., 1980-86, Korea. USAR, 1987-91. NSF fellow Stanford U., 1980-81, U. Calif. Berkeley, 1986-89; Packard Found. fellow, 1992; NSF Presdl. Young Investigator, 1991. Mem. ASCE (Geotech. bd. 1993—), Seismol. Soc. Am., Internat. Soc. for Soil Mechanics and Found. Engring., Can. Geotech. Soc., Earthquake Engring. Rsch. Inst. Republican. Roman Catholic. Office: U Calif 437 Davis Hall Berkeley CA 94720

BRAY, R(OBERT) BRUCE, music educator; b. LaGrande, Oreg., July 24, 1924; s. Ernest C. and Leta M. (Haight) B.; m. Donna Marie Siegman, July 2, 1949 (div. 1980); children: Stephen Louis, Ruth Elizabeth, Katherine Ernestine, Anne-Marie. BA, U. Oreg., 1949, MMus, 1955; cert., U. Strasbourg, France, 1951; postgrad., U. Wash., 1960-61. Music tchr. Helen McCune Jr. High Sch., Pendleton, Oreg., 1951-54; dir. choral music Albany (Oreg.) Union High Sch., 1954-56; elem. music supr. Ashland (Oreg.) Public Schs., 1956-57; asst. prof. music Cen. Wash. U., Ellensburg, 1957-60; asst. prof. U. Idaho, Moscow, 1961-67, assoc. prof., 1967-74, prof., 1974-89, prof. emeritus, 1989—, sec. faculty, 1968-88. Editor: Oreg. Music Educator, 1954-57, Wash. Music Educator, 1957-60, U. Idaho Music, 1961-68, Idaho Music Notes, 1963-68, U. Idaho Register, 1974-88 ; editorial bd. Music Educators Jour., 1964-68. With USNR, 1942-46. Mem. AAUP, Music Educators Nat. Conf. (bd. dirs., pres. N.W. div. 1963-65, nat. exec. com. 1964-66), Phi Mu Alpha Sinfonia. Democrat. Episcopalian. Home: W 2411 2d Ave Apt 2 Spokane WA 99204-1191 Office: U Idaho Brink Hall Rm M6 Moscow ID 83844

BRAZEEL, DALE MICHAEL, food products executive; b. 1965. With Bravo Inc., Brawley, Calif., 1982—; pres. Frontier Harvesting Inc., Brawley, 1986—; with La Mina Vegetable Co., Phoenix, 1988—. Office: Frontier Harvesting Inc 561 W Main St Brawley CA 92227-2246*

BRAZIER, JOHN RICHARD, lawyer, physician; b. Olean, N.Y., Mar. 11, 1940; s. John R. and Edith (Martin) B.; children: Mark, Jennifer. AAS, SUNY, Alfred, 1960; BS in Engring. Physics, U. Colo., 1963, MD, 1969; JD, Santa Clara U., 1989. Bar: Calif., 1989. Intern in surgery Downstate Med. Ctr., Bklyn., 1969-70; resident in surgery U. Colo., Denver, 1970-75; fellowship thoracic and cardiovascular surgery NYU, 1975-77; asst. prof. surgery UCLA, 1977-78; pvt. practice Northridge, 1978-84, Newport News, Va., 1984-86, Sacramento, 1989—. Fellowship NIH, UCLA, 1972-74. Mem. AMA, ACS, Am. Coll. Chest Physicians, Calif. Bar, Sacramento County Bar Assn. Home: 1401 36th St Sacramento CA 95816-6606 Office: 915 21st St Sacramento CA 95814-3117

BRAZIER, ROBERT G., transportation executive. Student, Stanford U. With Airbone Aircraft Service Inc., 1953-63; v.p. ops. Pacific Air Freight Inc., 1963-68; sr. v.p. ops. Airbone Freight Corp., Seattle, 1968-73, exec. v.p., 1973-78, COO, 1973—, pres., dir, COO, 1978—. Office: Airborne Freight Corp PO Box 662 Seattle WA 98111-0662*

BREAKER, RICHARD CARROLL, construction company executive; b. Cambridge, Nebr., Nov. 19, 1926; s. William C. and Clara (Ogorzolka) B.; m. Virginia C. Driscoll, Jan. 30, 1954; children: Kathryn, John, William, Michael. BS in Civil Engring., U. Colo., 1951. Registered profl. engr., Colo. Draftsman U.S. Geological Survey, Denver, 1946-47; engr. Colo. State Hwy. Dept., Denver, 1948-52; engr., estimator Peter Kiewit Sons Co., Denver, 1952-55; project mgr. Webb & Knapp Construction Corp., Denver, 1955-61; estimator Gerald H. Phipps, Inc., Denver, 1961-64, chief estimator, 1964-67, v.p., 1967-84, pres., CEO, 1984-92, also bd. dirs., vice chmn. bd. dirs., 1992-94; chmn. bd. Geral H. Phipps, Inc., Denver, 1994—; dir. Gerald H. Phipps, Inc., Denver, 1967—. With USAF, 1944-46. Mem. Am. Arbitration Assn., Associated Gen. Contractors of Colo. (sec. 1986-87, treas. 1987-88), Rolling Hills Country Club, Denver Athletic Club, Denver Country Club. Roman Catholic.

BRECHBILL, SUSAN REYNOLDS, lawyer, educator; b. Washington, Aug. 22, 1943; d. Irving and Isabell Doyle (Reynolds) Levine; B.A., Coll. William and Mary, 1965; J.D., Marshall-Wythe Sch. Law, 1968; children—Jennifer Rae, Heather Lea. Admitted to Va. bar, 1969, Fed. bar, 1970; atty. AEC, Berkeley, Calif., 1968-73, indsl. relations specialist AEC, Las Vegas, 1974-75; atty. ERDA, Oakland, Calif., 1976-77; atty. Dept. Energy, Oakland, 1977-78, dir. procurement div. San Francisco Ops. Office, 1978-85, asst. chief counsel for gen. law, 1985-93, acting asst. mgr. environ. mgmt. and support, 1992, acting asst. mgr. def. programs, 1993; chief counsel Dept. Energy Richland Ops. Office, 1994—; mem. faculty U. Calif. Extension; speaker Nat. Contract Mgmt. Assn. Ann. Symposiums, 1980, 81, 83, 84, 88; speaker on doing bus. with govt. Leader Girl Scouts U.S.A., San Francisco area. Named Outstanding Young Woman Nev., 1974; recipient Meritorious Svc. award Dept. Energy, 1992. Mem. NAFE, Va. State Bar Assn., Fed. Bar Assn., Nat. Contract Mgmt. Assn. (pres. Golden Gate chpt. 1983-84, N.W. regional v.p. 1984-86). Contbr. articles to profl. jours.

BRECHT, ALBERT ODELL, library and information technology administrator; b. Dallas, Nov. 19, 1946. BA in Govt. and Sociology, North Tex. State U., 1969; JD, U. Houston, 1972; LLM, U. Wash., 1973. Bar: Tex. 1972. Asst. law libr. U. So. Calif., L.A., 1973-74, asst. law libr. in-charge Law Libr., 1975, lab libr., asst. prof. law, 1975-77, dir. Law Libr., 1977—, assoc. prof., 1977-79, prof., 1979—, interim dep. univ. libr. for ctrl. libr. sys., 1984-85, assoc. dean Law Libr. and Info. Tech.; pres. Libraria Sodalitas, 1980; mem. Westlaw Acad. Adv. Bd., 1988-92. Author: (with A. Holoch and K. Pecarovich) Medical Malpractice Insurance and Its Alternatives: The Legal, Medical, and Insurance Literature—A Bibliography, 1975; contbr. articles and book revs. to profl. jours. Mem. Am. Assn. Law Librs. (audio-visual com. 1975, chmn. nominations com. 1978, recruitment com. 1975-76, placement com. 1979-81, cons. law librs. of correctional instns., chmn. program com. ann. meeting 1983, v.p. 1986-87, pres. 1987-88, moderator program on law librs. 1991), Spl. Librs. Assn., So. Calif. Assn. Law Librs. (v.p. 1974-75, pres. 1975-76, bd. dirs. 1978, chmn. com. on cons. for non-law librs. 1981). Office: U So Calif Law Libr University Park MC 0072 Los Angeles CA 90007

BRECKENRIDGE, KLINDT DUNCAN, architect; b. Iowa City, Apr. 24, 1957; s. Jack Duncan and Florence (Kmiecik) B.; m. Nancy Ann Dernier, Apr. 19, 1986; children: Wilson Reid, Lauren Alessandra. BArch, U. Ariz., 1981. Registered architect, Ariz., Calif.; cert. NCARB. Architect Finical & Dombrowski, Tucson, 1981-84; pres. The IEF Group, Inc., Tucson, 1984—; assoc. faculty Pima Community Coll. Bd. dirs. Mirical Square; pres.-elect bd. dirs. Leadership Tucson. Mem. AIA, Leadership Tucson Alumni (bd. dirs.). Democrat. Episcopalian. Home: 5535 N Waterfield Dr Tucson AZ 85715-6473 Office: The IEF Group 705 N 7th Ave Tucson AZ 85705-8306

BRECKENRIDGE, REBECCA K., nurse consultant; b. Greenville, Miss., May 13, 1946; d. Louis Hardie and Frances Mildred (Wiggs) Kent; m. George E. Breckenridge, Jan. 7, 1966; children: Louis Kent, Benjamin Ellis. AA, Miss. Delta Jr. Coll., 1966. Cert. nursing adminstrn. RN supr. Calhoun County Hosp., Bruce, Miss.; dir. nurses, asst. adminstr. Yalousha County Nursing Home, Water Valley, Miss., pub. health nurse; ind. nurse cons. North Miss. Med. Sonographers, Water Valley; office nurse DCIM, Las Vegas. Named Mother of Yr., 1984; recipient recognition Medicaid Commn. and Health Care Commn. Mem. ANA, Miss. Nurses Assn., Nev. Nurses Assn., Am. Cancer Soc., NRA. Home: 8155 W Charleston Blvd Apt 56 Las Vegas NV 89117-1262

BREDA, MICHAEL ALEXANDER, surgeon; b. Vienna, Austria, Dec. 18, 1959; came to the U.S., 1963; m. Susan A. Huang; 1 child, Sonja Breda. BS in Chemistry magna cum laude, U. Wash., 1981; MD, Johns Hopkins U., 1985; postgrad., UCLA, 1992. Diplomate Am. Bd. Surgery, Am. Bd. Surgery Critical Care; lic. physician, Calif, Oreg.; cert. ACLS. From jr. to chief resident in surgery U. Calif., L.A., 1985-92; fellowship liver transplantation and hepatobiliary surgery Cedars-Sinai Med. Ctr., L.A., 1992-94; staff surgeon Met. Clinic, Portland; clin. faculty Oreg. Health Scis. U.; researcher Fred Hutchinson Cancer Rsch. Ctr. Dept. Tumor Virology, Seattle, 1979-80, U. Wash. Dept. Biochemistry, Seattle, 1981, Johns Hopkins U. Div. Cardiothoracic Surgery, Balt., 1984-85, UCLA div. cardiothoracic surgery, 1987-89; instr. UCLA Program Endovascular Surgery, 1989; presenter in field. Co-author: (with H. Lakes) Thoracic and Cardiovascular Surgery, 1991; contbr. articles to profl. jours. Biomed. Rsch. Support grantee; Nat. Rsch. Svcs. scholar; recipient Philip K. Caves award Internat. Soc. for Heart Transplantation, 1985, Paul C. Samson prize Western Thoracic Surg. Assn., 1989. Mem. ACS, Phi Beta Kappa, Alpha Omega Alpha. Office: Met Clinic 1130 NW 22nd Ave Ste 520 Portland OR 97210-2976

BREDDAN, JOE, systems engineering consultant; b. N.Y.C., Sept. 18, 1950; s. Hyman and Sylvia (Hauser) B. BA in Math. and Psychology, SUNY, Binghamton, 1972; MS in Ops. Research, U. Calif., Berkeley, 1975; PhD in Systems Engring., U. Ariz., 1978. Teaching and research assoc. Dept. Systems and Indsl. Engring. U. Ariz., Tucson, 1975-79; project engr. B.D.M. Services Co., Tucson, 1979-80; mem. tech. staff Bell Labs., Am. Bell, AT&T Info. Systems, Denver, 1980-86; staff mgr. AT&T, Denver, 1986-91; pvt. practice cons. Boulder, Colo., 1991—. Patentee in field. Home and Office: 2120 Goddard Pl Boulder CO 80303-5616

BREDFELDT, JAMES EDWARD, gastroenterologist; b. Spearville, Kans., Feb. 17, 1948; s. Everett I. and Evelyn Mary (Stehwien) B.; m. Elaine Marie Riley, Aug. 28, 1982. B.A., U. Kans.-Lawrence, 1970; M.D., U. Kans.-Kansas City, 1974. Diplomate Am. Bd. Internal Medicine and Gastroenterology. Intern U. Kans.-Kansas City, 1974-75; resident in internal medicine, 1975-77; fellow in gastroenterology U. Mo., Columbia, 1977-79; fellow in hepatology Yale U., New Haven, 1979-81, instr. in medicine, 1981-83; gastroenterologist Lovelace Med. Ctr., Albuquerque, 1983-88, Va. Mason Med. Ctr., Seattle, 1988—; research assoc. VA, Med. Ctr., West Haven, Conn., 1981-83; clin. asst. prof. medicine U. N.Mex., Albuquerque, 1983-88. Contbr. articles, abstracts to profl. publs. Fellow ACP, Am. Coll. Gastroenterology; mem. Am. Gastroenterol. Assn., Am. Assn. for Study Liver Diseases, Am. Soc. Gastrointestinal Endoscopy, Alpha Omega Alpha. Office: Virginia Mason Clinic 1100 9th Ave Seattle WA 98101-2756

BREDLOW, THOMAS GAYLE, metals designer, craftsman; b. Pontiac, Mich., Oct. 18, 1938; s. Warren Kenneth and Elizabeth (La Ponsa) B. BA in Math., Tex. A&M U., 1960; postgrad., U. Ariz., 1960-61. Machinist, designer physics dept. Tex. A&M U., 1958-60, U. Ariz., Tucson, 1960-61, 64; owner, sole craftsman Tom Bredlow's Blacksmith Shop, Tucson, 1964-86; designer, craftsman, preservationist Tucson, 1986—; guest speaker Sch. Arch., U. Ariz., Tucson, 1964-86, Sch. Anthropology, 1964-86. Prin. woirks include Washington Cathedral, Mt. St. Albans, Washington, 1968, Barrio to Historico, Tucson, 1970, Pima County Parks and Recreation, Tucson, 1981, Fred Harvey Bldgs., Grand Canyon, Ariz., 1983-91, McCormick residence entry, Houston, 1978, Santa Fe, 1993. Mem. Mountain Oyster Club (hon. artist life mem.). Home: 3524 N Olive Rd Tucson AZ 85719-1830

BREECHER, SHEILA RAE, lawyer; b. Nephi, Utah, Aug. 14, 1953; d. Leo Neil and Jeannine (Cole) Van Ausdal; children: Michael Erin, Anthony Edward, Kelsey Nichole. BS, Utah State U., 1974, MS, 1974; JD, Brigham Young U., 1984. Bar: Ariz. 1985, U.S. Dist. Ct. Ariz. 1985, U.S. Ct. Appeals (9th cir.) 1985. Speech pathologist Maricopa Spl. Svcs. Consortium, Buckeye, Ariz., 1974-75; speech pathologist Phoenix Union High Sch. Dist. (Ariz.), 1975-81; assoc. Charles, Smith & Bellah, Glendale, Ariz., 1986; speech pathologist Phoenix Union High Sch. Dist., 1986-88; judge pro tem City of Peoria (Ariz.) Mcpl. Ct., 1987—; of counsel Smith & Breecher, Scottsdale, Ariz., 1987—; tchr. Legal Magnet High Sch. Program Phoenix Union High Sch. Dist., 1988-89; coord. policy and legal assistance, spl. edn. sect. Ariz. Dept. Edn., Phoenix, 1989-94, dir. adult edn., 1995—; legal cons. Flagstaff (Ariz.) Pub. Schs., 1987-89, Phoenix Union High Sch. Dist., 1986-89; mem. legis. team Ariz. Dept. Edn., Phoenix, 1991-95; mem. ednl. policy fellowship program Inst. for Ednl. Leadership, 1991-92. Editor: Criminal Procedure, 1983. Precinct committeeperson Dem. Party, Glendale, Ariz., 1979-81; adv. Ariz. Dept. Edn., Phoenix, 1988-90; dep. registrar Maricopa County Elections Dept., Phoenix, 1987-92; authorized pub. lobbyist, 1989-95; mem. Edn. Policy Fellowship Program, 1991-92; v.p., bd. dirs. Phoenix Day, 1993—; pres. bd. dirs. Cmty. Info. and Referral, 1993—; mem. hon. bd. Tempe Ctr. Habilitation, 1994—; mem. adv. bd. Inst. Cultural Affairs, 1995—. Mem. ABA, Ariz. Bar Assn., Valley Leadership Class XII (Phoenix), Soroptimist Internat. Home: 4512 E Thistle Landing Phoenix AZ 85044 Office: Ariz Dept Edn Adult Edn Divsn 1535 W Jefferson St Phoenix AZ 85007-3209

BREEDLOVE, JAMES FELMAN, real estate broker; b. L.A., June 12, 1961; s. James and Annetta (Cato) B.; m. Crystal Marie Prowtle, Dec. 27, 1986; children: Kelly, Christopher. BSBA, Calif. State U., Long Beach, 1985; MPA, Calif. State U., 1993. Cert. real estate broker, Calif; cert. rangemaster, Calif. Youth counselor Dept. Youth Auth. State of Calif., Chino, 1980-87; owner, mng. broker Breedlove & Assocs., Beverly Hills, Calif., 1988—; parole agt. Dept. Corrections, State of Calif., L.A., 1987—; owner Rosewood Adult Resdl. Facilities, Long Beach, Carson & Compton,

Calif., 1989—. Mem. NAACP, Calif. Correctional Peace Officers Assn., Phi Kappa Phi, Pi Alpha Alpha. Office: Breedlove & Assocs 433 N Camden Dr Ste 400 Beverly Hills CA 90210-4408

BREEDLOVE, S. MARC, psychology educator; b. Springfield, Mo., June 20, 1954; s. John T. and Lula (Collins) B.; m. children: Benjamin, Nicholas, Tessa, Christopher. BA, Yale U., 1976; MA, UCLA, 1978, PhD, 1982. Prof. psychology U. Calif., Berkeley, 1982—. Cons. editor Hormones and Behavior; assoc. editor Jour. Neurosci.; co-editor: Behavioral endocrinology, 1991; contbr. articles to profl. jours. Recipient Angier prize, Yale U., 1976, Franz award, UCLA, 1979, Lindsley prize, Soc. for Neursci., 1982, Early Career award, Am. Psychol. Assn., 1987; named. Presdl. Young Investigator, NSF, 1985. Mem. Am. Psychol. Soc., Am. Psychol. Assn., Soc. for Neurosci., Soc. for Sci. Study of Sex. Office: University of California Dept Psychology Berkeley CA 94720-1650

BREEZLEY, ROGER LEE, banker; b. Williston, N.D., Apr. 1, 1938. B.B.A., U. N.D. C.P.A., Oreg. Acct. Haskins & Sells, 1960-68; pres. Moduline Internat. Inc., 1968-77; with U.S. Bancorp, Portland, Oreg., 1977—, with corp. devel. and fin. analysis depts., 1977-79, sr. v.p. fin. analysis planning, 1979-80, exec. v.p., 1980-82, treas., 1980-87, vice chmn., 1982-87, COO, 1983-87, past dir., chmn., CEO, 1987—. Office: US Bancorp PO Box 4412 111 SW 5th Ave # 8837 Portland OR 97208*

BREGGIN, JANIS ANN, lawyer; b. Rochester, N.Y., Mar. 5, 1955; d. Arnold H. and Eleanor (Wingo) B.; children: Rachel Tyler, Cadiz Safira, Theo Socrates. BA, U. Denver, 1976, JD, 1980. Bar: Colo. 1980, U.S. Ct. Appeals (10th cir.) 1980. Assoc. Sherman & Howard, Denver, 1980-82, Jeffrey M. Nobel & Assocs., Denver, 1982-84; assoc. in house counsel Bill L. Walters Cos., Englewood, Colo., 1984-85; assoc. Deutsch & Sheldon, Englewood, 1985-87; ptnr. Breggin & Assocs. P.C., Denver, 1987—. Mem. Denver Women's Commn., 1990-93, chmn. 1991-92. Mem. ABA, Colo. Bar Assn., Denver Bar Assn., Colo. Women's Bar Assn. Office: The Breggin Law Firm PC # 204 1546 Williams Denver CO 80218

BREHOVE, THERESA M., physician; b. Burbank, Calif., Oct. 3, 1959; d. Stephen and Joan (Froelich) McDonough; m. Richard S. Brehove, July 9, 1983; children: Matthew Steven, Christina Marie, Lisa Ann. BS in Biology, Loyola Marymount U., 1980; MD, St. Louis U., 1984. Diplomate Am. Bd. Family Practice. Resident in family medicine Glendale (Calif.) Adventist Hosp., 1984-87; family physician Bay Shores Med. Group, San Pedro, Calif., 1987—. Mem. Am. Acad. Family Physicians. Roman Catholic.

BREITENBACH, MARY LOUISE MCGRAW, psychologist, drug rehabilitation counselor; b. Pitts., Sept. 26, 1936; d. David Evans McGraw and Louise (Schoch) Neel; m. John Edgar Breitenbach, Apr. 15, 1960 (dec. 1963); m. Joseph George Piccoli III, Aug. 15, 1987; 1 dau. Kirstin Amethyst. Postgrad., Oreg. State Coll., 1960-61; BA, Russell Sage Coll., Troy, N.Y., 1958; MEd, Harvard U., 1983. Lic. profl. counselor, Wyo.; lic. chem. dependency specialist, Wyo.; cert. addiction specialist, level III; nat. cert. addiction counselor II. Paraprofessional psychologist St. John's Episc. Ch., Jackson, Wyo., 1963-94; pvt. practice Wilson, Wyo., 1983-94; counselor Curran/Seeley Found. Addiction Svcs., Jackson, 1989-91, Van Vleck House/Tri-County Group Home, Jackson, 1986-89, others. Trustee Teton Sci. Sch., Kelly, Wyo, 1960-76; pres. bd. govs. Teton County Mus. Bd., Jackson; vestry mem. St. John's Ch., Jackson. Mem. Am. Psychol. Assn., Wyo. Psychol. Assn., Wyo. Assn. Counseling and Devel., Wyo. Assn. Addiction Specialists. Democrat. Episcopalian. Home and Office: Star Rte Wilson WY 83014

BREITMEYER, JO ANNE, sales and marketing executive; b. Ann Arbor, Mich., Mar. 25, 1947; d. Philip and Joan Clista (Thomas) B. Student, U. Tex., 1965-66, Boston U., 1966-67, U. Md., 1967-68; AA, BA, Canada Coll., Redwood City, Calif., 1970. Mktg. sec. Fairchild Camera & Instrument Co., Mountain View, Calif., 1969-70; sec. to v.p. Optimum Systems, Inc., Palo Alto, Calif., 1970-72; sec. to pres. Advanced Memory Systems, Sunnyvale, Calif., 1972-74; asst. to pres. Ness Time, Inc., Mountain View, 1974-75; art dir. Collage, Inc., Mountain View, 1975-76; owner, mgr. Briteday, Inc., Mountain View, 1976-87; with mktg. communications dept. PANAGEA, Cupertino, Calif., 1987-89; with Hewlett Packard Co., Palo Alto, 1989; mgr. adminstrn. Micro Integration Corp., San Jose, Calif., 1989-92; cons. Breitmeyer & Assocs., Mountain View, Calif., 1992-93; v.p. sales and mktg. Aries Trading Co. Ltd., Cupertino, Calif., 1993—. Bd. dirs. Peninsula Little Club, Palo Alto, 1981-87, pub. rels. com., 1984-87; bd. dirs. Peninsula Children's Ctr., Palo Alto, 1984-87, printing chmn. charter aux., 1984—; sec. Cypress Point Homeowners Assn., Mountain View, 1978-80, treas., 1988; mem. Arthritis Found., 1970—, mem. No. calif. chpt. adv. bd., devel. com., printing chmn., nominating com., telethon chmn., 1990-93, v.p. fund devel. South Bay br., 1991—; active Menlo Circus Club Charity Horse Show, 1983-89, Festival of Trees, 1984—; sec. Japanese-Am. Vets. Meml. Campaign com., San Jose/Santa Clara Valley; mem. Japanese Am. Campaign Com., Japanese Nat. Historical Mus.; vol. JACL. Recipient Disting. Svc. award No. Calif. Arthritis Found. South Bay Br., 1993. Mem. Bus. Profl. Advt. Assn., Peninsula Mktg. Assn., Mountain View Women in Bus. (steering com. 1986-87), Am. Electronics Assn., Environ. and Occupational Health Com., Tech. Employment Coop. Silicon Valley, Am. Biog. Inst. (rsch. bd. advisors), Ayres Ski Club (publs. com., Outstanding Svc. award), Far West Skiing Assn. (Outstanding Publ. award), Alpha Omicron Pi (chpt. advisor 1988—, pres. Palo Alto Alumnae Chpt. 1992-94, region X advisor inst., 1992—, del. 1992 Leadership conf., Alumnae svc. award 1992, cert. of honor, 1988, 92, del. internat. conv. 1985, 87, 89, 93, Rose award 1993, Outstanding Chpt. Pres., 1993, Outstanding Pub./Newsletter award 1993, mem. regional pubs. com.). Home: 209 Horizon Ave Mountain View CA 94043-4718

BREMEN, RONALD DAVID, lawyer; b. Indpls., Feb. 12, 1950; s. Julius and Bernice (Arshop) B.; m. Jenny Lynn Stephenson, June 9, 1973; children: Jonathan, Brandon. BA, Ind. U., 1972; JD, Western State U., 1981. Bar: Calif. 1982, U.S. Dist. Ct. (cen. dist.) Calif. 1983, U.S. Ct. Appeals (9th cir.) 1983. Pvt. practice law Anaheim, Calif., 1983-84; counsel State Compensation Ins. Fund, Cerritos, Calif., 1985-86, Mission Ins. Co., Orange, Calif., 1985-86; assoc. Mercer Gallagher & Zinder, Santa Ana, Calif., 1986-87, Gray & Prouty, Santa Ana, 1987-90, Stockwell, Harris, Anderson & Widom, San Bernardino, Calif., 1990-95, Warner & Assocs, Sacramento, Calif., 1995—; atty./advisor U.S. Small Bus. Adminstrn., Sacramento, 1994-95. Staff sgt. USAFR, 1972-78. Mem. Calif. Bar Assn. Office: Warner & Assocs 1540 River Park Dr Sacramento CA 95815

BREMER, ROBERT JAMES, aerospace industry executive; b. Chgo., Apr. 30, 1941; s. Algot Henning and Cecelia Ann (Skrobot) B.; m. Maude Gertude Williams, July 13, 1974. BS in Aero. Engring., Purdue U., 1963, MS in Engring., 1964; MBA, U. So. Calif., 1973. Propulsion systems analyst Rockwell Internat., L.A., 1964-73; market rsch. specialist Lockheed, Burbank, Calif., 1973-83, corp. planner, 1983-87; assoc. dir. bus. rsch. Lockheed, Calabasas, Calif., 1987-95, dir. competitive assessment, 1995—. Mem. AIAA (chmn. air transp. systems tech. com. 1982-84, internat. air transp. conf. 1983, Shuttle Flag award 1984), The Planning Forum, Soc. of Competitive Intelligence Profls. Home: 239 Argonne Ave Long Beach CA 90803-1739 Office: Lockheed Corp 4500 Park Granada Woodland Hills CA 91399-0001

BREMS, DAVID PAUL, architect; b. Lehi, Utah, Aug. 10, 1950; s. D. Orlo and Gearldine (Hitchcock) B.; m. Johna Devey Brems; 1 child, Stefan Tomas Brems. B.S., U. Utah, 1973, M.Arch., 1975. Registered arch., Utah, Calif., Colo., Ariz., Wyo., N.Mex., Idaho, Mont., Wash. Draftsman, Environ. Assocs., Salt Lake City, 1971-73; draftsman/architect intern Environ. Design Group, Salt Lake City, 1973-76; architect/intern Frank Fuller AIA, Salt Lake City, 1976-77; prin. Edwards & Daniels, Salt Lake City, 1978-83; pres. David Brems & Assocs., Salt Lake City, 1983-86; prin. Gillies, Stransky, Brems, Smith P.C., Salt Lake City, 1986—; adj. prof. U. Utah Grad. Sch. Architecture, 1990-93; mem. urban design com. Assist, Inc., Salt Lake City, 1982—, Salt Lake County Planning Commn., 1991—, chmn., 1992—; invited lectr. Wyo Soc. Archs., 1992, sch. engring. U. Utah, 1993, 95, VA, 1993, Utah Soc. Archs., 1994, Utah Power and Light, 1994, Utah Soc. Archts., 1994; juror U. Utah Grad. Sch. Architecture, 1975—, Utah Soc. Am. Planning Assn., 1994—. Prin. works include solar twin homes Utah Holiday, (Best Solar Design award), Sun Builder, Daily Jour., Brian Head Day Lodge, Easton Aluminum, Four Seasons Hotel, Gore Coll. Bus., CMF Tooele, Utah Regional Corrections Facility, St. Vincents De Paul Ctr., Steiner Aquatic Ctr., U. Utah Football Support Facility, Sports Medicine West, West Jordan Community Water Park, Utah Nat. Guard Apache Helicopter Hangar & Armory, Kashmitter I Residences, St. Thomas More Cath. Ch., Spanish Fork Cmty. Water Park, Natures Herbs, ABC Office Bldg. Divsn. of Natural Resources Bldg., Kashmitter II Residence, Litton Residence, and others; mem. Leadership Utah. Recipient 3 awards Am. Concrete Inst., 1993, Chief Engrs. Honor award U.S. Army Corps Engrs., 1994; Bronze medalist Utah Summer Games, 1991, Silver medalist, 1992, Gold medalist, 1994, Design award Dept. Def., 1995; named Best Pvt. Project by Intermountain Architecture, 1994. Mem. AIA (pres. Salt Lake chpt. 1983-84, pres. Utah Soc. 1987, chmn. Western Mountain Region conf., 1986, com. on design 1990—, chmn. com. on environment AIA Utah 1993, chmn. Design for Life Workshop at Sundance, 1993, Honor awards 1983, 88, Merit awards 1983, 85, 88, 93, chmn. Western Mountain Region honor awards 1983, 88, PCI award 1988, IFRAA award 1988, 94, Juror Colo. West awards 1992), Am. Planning Assn. (juror awards 1994), Utah Soc. Architects, Am. Solar Energy Soc., Hobie Fleet 67 (commodore 1985-86), Great Salt Lake Yacht Club, Illuminating Engring. Soc. (assoc.). Home: 161 Young Oak Rd Salt Lake City UT 84108-1645

BREMS, JOHN JOSEPH, surgeon; b. Cedar Rapids, Iowa, Sept. 21, 1954; s. George Frederick and Anne Delores (Kennedy) B.; m. Catherine Susan Edwards, June 27, 1980; children: Daniel Edward, Julie Ann, Mark Joseph. BS in Chemistry, Rockhurst Coll., 1979; MD, St. Louis U., 1981. Gen. surgery resident Sch. Medicine St. Louis U., 1981-86, dir. liver transplantation dept. surgery, 1988-90; transplant fellow UCLA, 1986-87, asst. prof. surgery, asst. dir. liver transplantation, 1987-88; dir. multi organ transplantation program Scripps Clinic, La Jolla, Calif., 1990—; med. dir. Organ and Tissue Ctr. of So. Calif., San Diego, 1992-94; mem. sci. bd. Exten Corp., San Diego, 1993-94. Co-developer artificial liver; contbr. chpts. to books. Bd. dirs. Am. Liver Found., San Diego, 1990-94; mem. adv. panel on transplantation Calif. Med. Assn., Sacramento, 1992; mem. nat. edn. com. United Network Organ Sharing, Richmond, Va., 1992-93; active environ. and social issues San Diego County Med. Soc., 1992-94. Fellow ACS, Southwestern Surg. Congress (program 1992-94), Pacific Coast Surg. Soc.; mem. San Diego Surg. Soc. (v.p. 1993-94), Am. Soc. Transplant Surgeons (chmn. bylaws com. 1993-94), Am. Assn. for Study of Liver Diseases. Roman Catholic. Home: 3719 Newcrest Pt San Diego CA 92130-2033 Office: Scripps Clinic & Rsch Found 10666 N Torrey Pines Rd La Jolla CA 92037-1027

BREMSER, GEORGE, JR., electronics company executive; b. Newark, May 26, 1928; s. George and Virginia (Christian) B.; m. Marie Sundman, June 21, 1952 (div. July 1979); children: Christian Fredrick II, Priscilla Suzanne, Martha Anne, Sarah Elizabeth; m. Nancy Kay Woods, Oct. 27, 1983 (div. Feb. 1989). BA, Yale U., 1949; postgrad., U. Miami, 1959; MBA, NYU, 1962. With McCann-Erickson Inc., N.Y.C., 1952-61; asst. gen. mgr. McCann-Erickson Inc., Bogota, Columbia, 1955, gen. mgr., 1955-57; account supr. McCann-Erickson Inc., N.Y.C., 1958; v.p., mgr. McCann-Erickson Inc., Miami, Fla., 1959-61; with Gen. Foods Corp., White Plains, N.Y., 1961-71; v.p., gen. mgr. internat. div. Gen. Foods Europe, White Plains, N.Y., 1967; pres. Gen. Foods Internat., White Plains, 1967-71; group v.p. Gen. Foods Corp., White Plains, 1970-71; chmn., pres., chief exec. officer Texstar Corp., Grand Prairie, Tex., 1971-81; exec. v.p. Shaklee Corp., San Francisco, 1981-82; chmn., pres., chief exec. officer Etak Inc., Menlo Park, Calif., 1983-88, chmn., 1989—; bd. dirs. PBI Industries Inc. Trustee Union Ch., Bogota, 1956-57; Dem. county committeeman, Ridgewood, N.J., 1962-63; mem. New Canaan (Conn.) Town Council, 1969-73; founder, past pres. Citizens Com. for Conservation, New Canaan; mem. coun. Save the Redwoods League, 1987—. Served to 2d lt. USMC 1950-52, capt. Res. Mem. New Canaan Country Club, Brook Club, Yale Club (N.Y.C.), Block Island Club, Casino Club (Nantucket, Mass.), Explorers Club, Phi Beta Kappa, BBeta Gamma Sigma, Beta Theta Pi. Congregationalist. Clubs: New Canaan Country; Brook, Metropolitan, Yale (N.Y.C.); Block Island; Casino (Nantucket, Mass.); Explorers. Home: 535 Everett Ave Palo Alto CA 94301-1547 also: Mansion Beach Rd Block Island RI 02807 Office: care Etak Inc 1430 Obrien Dr Menlo Park CA 94025-1432

BRENNAN, CIARAN BRENDAN, accountant, independent oil producer, real estate developer; b. Dublin, Ireland, Jan. 28, 1944; s. Sean and Mary (Stone) B. BA with honors, Univ. Coll., Dublin, 1966; MBA, Harvard U., 1973; MS in Acctg., U. Houston, 1976. Lic. real estate broker, Calif.; CPA, Tex. Auditor Coopers & Lybrand, London, 1967-70; sr. auditor Price Waterhouse & Co., Toronto, Ont., Can., 1970-71; project acctg. specialist Kerr-McGee Corp., Oklahoma City, 1976-80; contr. Cummings Oil Co., Oklahoma City, 1980-82; CFO Red Stone Energies, Ltd., 1982, Leonoco, Inc., 1982-87; treas., chief fin. officer JKJ Supply Co., 1983-87, Saturn Investments Inc., 1983-87, JFL Co., 1984-87, Little Chief Drilling & Energy Inc., 1984-85; pres. Ciaran Brennan Corp., 1990, Rathgar Securities, Inc., 1989-90; CFO Nationwide Industries, 1991-93, Cinema Internat. Inc., 1993—; bd. dirs., cons. small oil cos.; adj. faculty Oklahoma City U., 1977-86; vis. faculty Ctrl. State U., 1977-86. Contbr. articles to profl. jours. Mem. AICPA, Inst. Chartered Accts. Eng. and Wales, Inst. Chartered Accts. Can., Inst. Chartered Accts. Ireland, Tex. Soc. CPAs, Clif. Soc. CPAs. Democrat. Roman Catholic.

BRENNAN, JERRY MICHAEL, economics educator, statistician, reseacher, clinical psychologist; b. Grosse Pointe, Mich., July 17, 1944; s. Walter X. and Aretta May (Gempler) B. Student Kalamazoo (Mich.) Coll., 1962-64, Pasadena (Calif.) City Coll., 1966-67; B.A., UCLA, 1969; M.A., U. Hawaii, 1973, Ph.D., 1978. Researcher, UCLA, 1968-69; researcher U. Hawaii, 1972, 74-78, cons., 1975, 77, 78, data analyst and statis. cons., 1979-80, lectr., 1976-80, asst. prof. econs., 1980—; pres. Sugar Mill Software, 1986—; cons. WHO; v.p. Forest Inst. Profl. Psychology. Light scholar, 1964-66. Mem. Am. Psychol. Assn., Soc. Multivariate Exptl. Psychology, Psychometric Soc., Western Psychol. Assn., AAUP, Hawaii Ednl. Research Assn. Contbr. psychol. articles to profl. jours. Address: 651 Kaumakani St Honolulu HI 96825-1827

BRENNAN, MICHAEL JOSEPH, news service executive; b. Grand Rapids, Mich., Dec. 25, 1952; s. Joseph R. and Patricia Jean (Doherty) B.; m. Laurel Ruth Strand, Aug. 31, 1985 (div. Apr. 1994); 1 child, Lillian Ruth. A, Grand Rapids Jr. Coll., 1974; B, U. Mich., 1976; M, U. Mo., 1980. Reporter The Daily Missourian, Columbia, Mo., 1979-80, Punta Gorda (Fla.) Daily Herald, 1981, CMP Pubs., Great Neck, N.Y., 1981-83, The San Jose (Calif.) Bus. Jour., 1983-84; bus. and labor reporter The Comml. Appeal, Memphis, 1984-88; sr. bus. reporter The Herald, Everett, Wash., 1988-93; exec. v.p. Pacific Run News Svc., Seattle, 1993—. Recipient 1st pl. Wash. Press Assn., 1989, Labor News Reporting award Snohomish County Labor Coun., 1992; Mich. Journalism fellow, 1992-93. Mem. Soc. Profl. Journalists (v.p. programs 1990-91, pres. West Wash. chpt. 1991-92, region 10 co-chair 1993-94). Roman Catholic. Office: Pacific Run News Svc 2400 E Roy St Seattle WA 98112-4126

BRENNEN, STEPHEN ALFRED, international business consultant; b. N.Y.C., July 7; s. Theodore and Margaret (Pembroke) B.; m. Yolanda Alicia Romero, Sept. 28, 1957; children: Stephen Robert, Richard Patrick. AB cum laude, U. Americas, Mexico City, 1956; MBA, U. Chgo., 1959. Supr. Montgomery Ward, Chgo., 1956; credit mgr. Aldens, Chgo., 1956-59; gen. mgr. Purina de Guatemala, 1964-66; pres. Purina Colombiana, Bogotá, 1967-69; founding pres. Living Marine Resources, Inc., San Diego, 1969-70; mng. dir. Central and S. Am. Ralston Purina, Caracas, Venezuela, Coral Gabels, Fla., 1970-74; pres. Van Camp Seafood Co., San Diego, 1974-79; chmn. P.S.C. Corp., Buena Park, Calif., 1979-81; pres. Inter-Am. Cons. Group, San Diego, 1981-85; chmn. Beta Enterprises Inc., 1986-89; advisor Nat. Productivity Exch.; spl. asst. C.A.O., County of San Diego, Calif., 1987-95; mng. ptnr. Interam. Cons. Group, 1983-95; ptnr. Acad. Interpreting & Translations, Internat., 1995; assoc., owner the Montgomery Group, Inc., La Jolla. Author: Successfully Yours. Mem. adv. bd. Mexican-Am. Found. Served with USAF. Mem. Am. Soc. Profl. Cons. Roman Catholic. Club: U. Chgo. in San Diego (past pres.).

BRENNER, ARNOLD S., electronics company executive; b. Chgo., Apr. 1, 1937; s. Leo and Freida (Polland) B.; m. Anita E. Kleifield, Mar. 26, 1961; children—Ira, Glenn, Karen. B.S.E.E., Ill. Inst. Tech., 1958; M.S.E.E., U. Ill., 1959. Vice pres., gen. mgr. Mobile Products div. Motorola Inc., Schaumburg, Ill., 1976-77, v.p., dir. internat. products ops., 1977-81, corp. v.p. internat. products div., 1981-84, sr. v.p. comml. internat. group, 1984-85, sr. v.p., chief staff ops., 1985—. Bd. dirs. Jr. Engrng. Tech. Soc., Urbana, Ill., 1981-84. Mem. IEEE (sr.), Vehicular Tech. Soc., Tau Beta Pi. Office: Motorola Inc Japanese Operations 1303 E Algonquin Rd Schaumburg IL 60196-4041

BRENT, JEFFREY ALAN, physician; b. N.Y.C., Jan. 15, 1946; s. Robert I. and Lea (Tobacowitz) B.; m. Janet Seeley (div. 1982); 1 child, Zackary Robert Boureshaw Brent; m. Laura J. Klein, Aug. 31, 1992. BA, MA, Hunter Coll., 1970; PhD in Biochemistry, Mt. Sinai Sch. Medicine, 1976; MD, SUNY, Buffalo, 1980. Diplomate Am. Bd. Emergency Medicine, Am. Bd. Med. Toxicology. Postdoctoral staff assoc. Inst. Cancer Rsch., N.Y.C., 1977-78; rsch. affiliate dept. experimental therapeutics Roswell Park Meml. Inst., Buffalo, 1978-79; intern in gen. surgery New Eng. Deaconess Hosp., Boston, 1980-81; resident in ob-gyn. Sch. Medicine, U. Conn., Farmington, Conn., 1982; resident in emergency medicine Grady Meml. Hosp., Atlanta, 1982-87; fellow in clin. toxicology Rocky Mountain Poison Ctr., Denver, 1987-89, asst. med. dir., 1989-91, acting med. dir., 1991-92, med. toxicology fellowship dir. U. Colo. Health Scis. Ctr., 1991-93; attending physician dept. medicine divsn. clin. toxicology Denver Gen. Hosp., 1989-93, acting dir. divsn. clin. toxicology, 1991-92; attending physician dept. surgery divsn. emergency medicine U. Colo. Health Scis. Ctr., Denver, 1987—, attending physician dept. medicine divsn. clin. pharmacology, 1990—, attending physician Occupational Health Clinic, 1991—, aviation medicine cons. Aviation Medicine Clinic, 1992—; attending physician regional poison treatment ctr. Porter Meml. Hosp., Denver, 1987—, attending physician divsn. hyperbaric medicine, 1989—; ptnr. Toxicology Assocs., 1993—; adj. prof. emergency medicine Springfield (Mass.) Coll., 1985-86; instr. dept. cmty. medicine Sch. Medicine Tufts U., Boston, 1984-86; asst. prof. dept. biochemistry U. Mass., Amherst, 1983-86; clin. instr. dept. surgery in trauma and emergency medicine U. Colo. Health Sci. Ctr., Denver, 1987-89, asst. prof. dept. pediatrics, 1989-93, asst. prof. dept. surgery, 1989-93, asst. clin. prof. dept. pediatrics, 1993—, asst. clin. prof. dept. surgery, 1993—; aviation med. examiner FAA, 1991—; cons. in field; lectr. in field. Asst. editor Micromedex, 1992—; consulting editor: Genium Pub. Co.; mem. editl. bd. Current Trends in Drug Therapy, 1987-89; reviewer Ann. Emergency Medicine, 1989—; contbr. articles, papaers to profl. jours. Recipient AZT Overdose Study award Burroughs-Wellcome Pharm., 1988-90, Career Devel. award Emergency Medicine Found., Antidepressant Drug Overdose Studty award Eli Lilly Inc., 1990-92. Fellow Am. Coll. Emergency Physicians (chmn. Mass. rsch. com. 1985-86, mem. nat. rsch. com. 1989—, editor Toxicology Sect. Newsletter 1990-91, mem. pediatric emergency medicine com. 1991-92, chair sect. toxicology 1991—, mem. sect. affairs com. 1992—), Am. Acad. Clin. Toxicology (mem. edn. com. 1989—, chmn. 1990—, mem. ann. meeting oversight com. 1990—, course dir. 1990, 91, 93, bd. trustees 1991—, chair abstract rev. com. 1991—, mem. com. on med. practice 1993-94, mem. ad hoc com. on position statements 1993-94, Postdoctoral Fellowship award 1989-90); mem. Am. Coll. Occupational and Environ. Medicine, Aviation Med. Assn., Physicians for Social Responsibility, Soc. Acad. Emergency Medicine, Undersea and Hyperbolic Med. Soc., Civil Aviation Med. Assn. Office: Toxicology Assocs 805 Colorow Rd Golden CO 80401-9509

BRENT, RICHARD SAMUEL, manufacturing company executive; b. Pitts., July 30, 1949; s. Irving J. and Sarah Evelyn (Weiss) B.; m. Sharon I. Levine, Aug. 17, 1969; children: Andrew, Sarah, Kirah. BA, Sonoma State Coll., 1972, teaching cert., 1973. Gen. mgr. Solar Warehouse, El Cajon, Calif., 1980-82; plant mgr., program mgr. Jet Air, Inc., El Cajon, 1982-85; program mgr. Solar Turbines, Inc., San Diego, 1985—. Editor: (booklet) Who Says You Can't Do Anything?, 1970. V.p. United Cerebral Palsy of San Diego, 1984; vice chmn. Nat. Kidney Found. of So. Calif., San Diego, 1989-90, chmn., 1990-91; loaned exec. United Way Am. of San Diego, 1986; mem. exec. adv. com. U. Phoenix. Named Outstanding Vol. of Yr., Combined Health Agys., 1989. Mem. Solar Profl. Mgmt. Assn. (pres. bd. dirs. 1989), Keeper's Club-Zool. Soc. San Diego. Home: 5402 Redland Pl San Diego CA 92115-2217

BRERETON, ALYN ROBERT, behavioral primatologist, researcher; b. Turlock, Calif., June 29, 1948; s. Robert Young and Gladine Harriet (Unger) B. BA, Stanislaus State Coll., Turlock, 1971; MA, Calif. State U., Sacramento, 1976; PhD, U. Stirling, Scotland, 1989. Rschr. Cayo Santiago, P.R., 1977; observer Gilgil, Kenya, 1982; rschr. Tanaxpillo, Catemaco, Mex., 1983-84; observer Arashiyama West, Dilley, Tex., 1989-90, Cayo Santiago, P.R., 1991-92; ind. scholar Modesto, Calif., 1992-94; adj. asst. prof. anthropology Calif. State U., Stanislaus, Turlock, 1994—. Author articles on primates. Sigma Xi grantee, 1981; L.S.B. Leakey Found. grantee, 1982. Mem. Am. Anthrop. Assn., Internat. Primatological Soc., Am. Soc. Primatologists, Animal Behavior Soc. Democrat. Home: 913 Carrigan Ave Modesto CA 95350-3608

BRES, PHILIP WAYNE, automotive executive; b. Beaumont, Tex., Mar. 6, 1950; s. Roland Defrance Bres and Edna Gene (Griffith) Seale; m. Janet Vivian Meyer, May 16, 1987; children: Rachel Elizabeth, Rebecca Claire. BA, Lamar U., Beaumont, Tex., 1972; MBA, Stephen F. Austin State U., 1973. Distbn. mgr., bus. mgmt. mgr. Mazda Motors of Am., Houston, 1973-75; analyst, cons. C.H. McCormack and Assocs., Houston, 1975-76; assoc. Frank Gillman Pontiac/GMC/Honda, Houston, 1976-79, David Taylor Cadillac Co., Houston, 1979-80; pres. Braintrust Inc., Houston, 1980-83; sales mgr. Mossy Oldsmobile, Inc., Houston, 1983-84; gen. mgr. Mossy Nissan/Ford, Bellevue, Wash., 1984-86; dir. ops. Mossy Co., Encinitas, Calif., 1986-91; gen. mgr. Performance Nissan, Duarte, Calif., 1991—; seminar lectr. Rice U., Houston, 1980-83. Author: The Entrepreneurs Guide for Starting a Successful Business., 1982; contbr. (book) Business Planning for the Entrepreneur, 1983. Mem. Houston C. of C. (small bus. coun.), Opt Astron. Soc., Univ. Club, Phi Eta Sigma, Phi Kappa Phi. Office: Performance Nissan PO Box 1500 Duarte CA 91009-4500

BRESLAUER, GEORGE WILLIAM, political science educator; b. N.Y.C., Mar. 4, 1946; s. Henry Edward and Marianne (Schaeffer) B.; m. Yvette Assia, June 5, 1976; children: Michelle, David. BA, U. Mich., 1966, MA, 1968, PhD, 1973. Asst. prof. polit. sci. U. Calif., Berkeley, 1971-79, assoc. prof., 1979-90, prof., 1990—, chmn. dept., 1993—, chmn. Ctr. for Slavic and East European Studies, 1982-94; vice chmn. bd. trustees Nat. Coun. for Soviet and East European Rsch., Washington, 1988-91. Author: Khrushchev and Brezhnev as Leaders, 1982, Soviet Strategy in the Middle East, 1989; editor: Can Gorbachev's Reforms Succeed?, 1990, Learning in U.S. and Soviet Foreign Policy, 1991. Grantee Ford Found., 1982-84, Carnegie Corp., 1985-94. Mem. Am. Assn. for Advancement Slavic Studies (bd. dirs., exec. com. 1990-93). Office: U Calif Dept Polit Sci 210 Barrows Hall Berkeley CA 94720

BRESLOW, NORMAN EDWARD, biostatistics educator, researcher; b. Mpls., Feb. 21, 1941; s. Lester and Alice Jane (Philp) B.; m. Gayle Marguerite Bramwell, Sept. 7, 1963; children: Lauren Louise, Sara Jo. BA, Reed Coll., 1962; PhD, Stanford U., 1967. Trainee Stanford U., 1965-67; vis. research worker London Sch. Hygiene, 1967-68; instr. U. Wash., Seattle, 1968-69, asst. prof., 1969-72, assoc. prof., 1972-76, prof., 1976—, chmn. dept. biostats., 1983-93; statistician Internat. Agy. Research Cancer, Lyon, France, 1972-74; mem. Hutchinson Cancer Ctr., Seattle, 1982—; statistician Nat. Wilms' Tumor Study, 1969—; cons. Internat. Agy. Research Cancer, Lyon, 1978-79, Stats. and Epidemiology Research Corp., Seattle, 1980—; assoc. prof. U. Geneva, 1994—. Recipient Spiegelman Gold medal Am. Pub. Health Assn., 1978, Preventive Oncology Acad. award, NIH, 1978-83; research grantee NIH, 1984—; sr. U.S. Scientist, Alexander Humboldt Found., Fed. Republic Germany, 1982; sr. Internat. fellowship Fogarty Ctr., 1990. Fellow AAAS, Am. Statis Assn., Royal Statis. Soc.; mem. Internat. Statis. Inst., Inst. Medicine-Nat. Acad. Scis., Internat. Biometric Soc. (regional com. 1975-78, coun. 1994—). Office: Univ of Wash Dept Biostatistics Seattle WA 98195-7232

BRESSAN, PAUL LOUIS, lawyer; b. Rockville Centre, N.Y., June 15, 1947; s. Louis Charles Bressan and Nance Elizabeth Batteley. BA cum laude, Fordham Coll., 1969; JD, Columbia U., 1975. Bar: N.Y. 1976, Calif. 1987, U.S. Dist. Ct. (so., ea. and no. dists.) N.Y. 1976, U.S. Dist. Ct. (no.

and ctrl. dists.) Calif. 1987, U.S. Ct. Appeals (2d cir.) 1980, U.S. Supreme Ct. 1980, U.S. Ct. Appeals (1st and 4th cirs.) 1981, U.S. Ct. Appeals (11th cir.) 1982, U.S. Ct. Appeals (9th cir.) 1987, U.S Ct. Appeals (7th cir.) 1991, U.S. Dist. Ct. (ea. dist.) Calif. 1995. Assoc. Kelley, Drye & Warren, N.Y.C., 1975-84; ptnr. Kelley, Drye & Warren, N.Y.C. and Los Angeles, 1984—. Served to lt. USNR, 1971-72. Named one of Outstanding Coll. Athletes of Am., 1969; Harlan Fiske Stone scholar. Mem. ABA, N.Y. Bar Assn., Calif. Bar Assn. Republican. Roman Catholic. Office: Kelley Drye & Warren 515 S Flower St Ste 1100 Los Angeles CA 90071-2213

BRESSAN, ROBERT R., accountant; b. Yonkers, N.Y., Feb. 8, 1945; s. Alfred D. and Antionette (Desivo) B.; m. Florence L. Vigna, June 9, 1968; children: Anne Marie, Robert A., Tiffany L. BBA in Acctg., Iona Coll., 1967. CPA; cert. tax profl. Staff to sr. Coopers & Lybrand, N.Y.C., 1967-70; sr. to audit mgr. Fox & Co., Colorado Springs, 1970-80; ptnr., owner Robert R. Bressan, Colorado Springs, 1980—. Mem. Sertoma, AICPA, Inst. Mgmt. Accts., Govtl. Fin. Officers Assn., Colo. Govtl. Fin. Officers, Nat. Assn. Counties. Office: 829 N Circle Dr Ste 214 Colorado Springs CO 80909-5008

BREST, PAUL A., law educator; b. Jacksonville, Fla., Aug. 9, 1940; s. Alexander and Mia (Deutsch) B.; m. Iris Lang, June 17, 1962; children: Hilary, Jeremy. AB, Swarthmore Coll., 1962; JD, Harvard U., 1965; LLD (hon.), Northeastern U., 1980, Swarthmore Coll., 1991. Bar: N.Y. 1966. Law clk. to Hon. Bailey Aldrich U.S. Ct. Appeals (1st cir.), Boston, 1965-66; atty. NAACP Legal Def. Fund, Jackson, Miss., 1966-68; law clk. Justice John Harlan, U.S. Supreme Ct., 1968-69; prof. law Stanford U., 1969—, Kenneth and Harle Montgomery Prof. pub. interest law, Richard E. Lang prof. and dean, 1987—. Author: Processes of Constitutional Decisionmaking, 1992. Mem. Am. Acad. Arts and Scis. Home: 814 Tolman Dr Palo Alto CA 94305-1026 Office: Stanford U Sch Law Nathan Abbott Way at Alvarado Row Stanford CA 94305

BRETERNITZ, CORY DALE, archaeological company executive, consultant; b. Tucson, Apr. 9, 1955; s. David Alan and Barbara Blair (Myers) B.; m. Adrian Sue White, May 21, 1981; children: Jessie Lynn, Dylan Blair. BA, U. Ariz., 1978; MA, Wash. State U., 1982. Archaeologist Mus. No. Ariz., Flagstaff, 1973; lab. technician Lab. of Tree-Ring Rsch., Tucson, 1973-78; archaeologist Ariz. State Mus., Tucson, 1978, Nat. Pk. Svc., Albuquerque, 1976-79, Dolores (Colo.) Archaeol. Program, 1980-81; project dir. Navajo Nation Archaeology Program, Window Rock, Ariz., 1981-82, Profl. Svc. Industries, Inc., Phoenix, 1982-84; pres. Ctr. for Indigenous Studies in Ams., Phoenix, 1991—; pres., owner Soil Systems, Inc., Phoenix, 1984—. Mem. Ariz. Archaeol. Coun. (exec. com. 1976, editor 1989-94), N.Mex. Archaeol. Coun., Colo. Coun. Profl. Archaeologists, Utah Profl. Archaeol. Coun., Am. Quaternary Assn., Soc. for Am. Archaeology, Am. Anthrop. Assn. Office: Soil Systems Inc 1121 N 2nd St Phoenix AZ 85004-1807

BREUER, MELVIN ALLEN, electrical engineering educator; b. L.A., Feb. 1, 1938; s. Arthur and Bertha Helen (Friedman) B.; m. Sandra Joyce Scalir, Apr. 7, 1967; children: Teri Lynn, Jeffrey Steven. BS in Engring., UCLA, 1959, MS in Engring., 1961; PhD in Elec. Engring., U. Calif., Berkeley, 1965. Asst. prof. U. So. Calif., L.A., 1965-71; assoc. prof. U. So. Calif., Los Angeles, 1971-80, prof., 1980—, chmn. elect. engring. systems dept., 1991-94; Charles Lee Powell prof. U. So. Calif., L.A., 1995—. Co-author: Diagnosis and Reliable Design, 1976, Digital Systems Testing and Testable Design, 1990; editor, co-author: Design Automation, 1972; editor: Digital Systems Design Automation, 1975; editor-in-chief Jour. Design Automation, 1980-82; co-editor: Knowledge Based Systems for Test and Diagnosis, 1990; contbr. articles to profl. jours. Recipient Assocs. award U. So. Calif., 1991; Fulbright-Hays scholar, 1972. Fellow IEEE (Taylor Booth award for edn. 1993); mem. Sigma Xi, Tau Beta Pi, Eta Kappa Nu. Democrat. Home: 16857 Bosque Dr Encino CA 91436-3530 Office: U So Calif University Park Los Angeles CA 90089-2562

BREUER, STEPHEN ERNEST, temple executive; b. Vienna, Austria, July 14, 1936; s. John Howard and Olga Marion (Haar) B.; came to U.S., 1938, naturalized, 1945; BA cum laude, UCLA, 1959, gen. secondary credential, 1960; m. Gail Fern Breitbart, Sept. 4, 1960 (div. 1986); children: Jared Noah, Rachel Elise; m. Nadine Bendit, Sept. 25, 1988. Tchr. L.A. City Schs., 1960-62; dir. Wilshire Blvd. Temple Camps, Los Angeles, 1962-86; exec. dir. Wilshire Blvd. Temple, 1980—; dir. Edgar F. Magnin Religious Sch., Los Angeles, 1970-80. Instr. Hebrew Union Coll., Los Angeles, 1965-76, 92—, U. Judaism, 1991; field instr. San Francisco State U., 1970-80, Calif. State U., San Diego, Hebrew Union Coll., 1977-81, U. of Judaism UCLA extension. Vice pres. Los Angeles Youth Programs Inc., 1967-77; youth adviser Los Angeles County Commn. Human Relations, 1969-72. Bd. dirs. Community Relations Conf. So. Calif., 1965-85; regional bd. mem. Union Am. Hebrew Congregations, 1986-88; bd. dirs. Alzheimer's Disease and Related Disorders Assn., 1984-95, v.p. L.A. County chpt., 1984-86, pres., 1986-88, nat. exec. com., 1987-95, nat. devel. chair, 1992-95, Calif. state coun. pres. 1987-92, chmn. of Calif. gov.'s adv. com. on Alzheimer's disease, 1988—; mem. goals program City of Beverly Hills, Calif., 1985-91; bd. dirs. Pacific SW regional Union Am. Hebrew Congregations, 1985-88, mem. nat. bd. , exec. com., 1993—; bd. dirs. Echo Found., 1986-88, Mazon-Jewish Response to Hunger, 1993—, Wilshire Stakeholders, exec. com., 1987-94; treas. Wilshire Community Prayer Alliance, 1986-88; active United Way. Recipient Service awards Los Angeles YWCA, 1974, Los Angeles County Bd. Suprs., 1982, 87, Ventura County Bd. Suprs., 1982, 87, Weinberg Chai Lifetime Achievement award Jewish Fed. Council Los Angeles, 1986, Nat. Philanthropy Day L.A. Medallion, 1993, L.A. County Redevel. Agy. recognition, 1994; Steve Breuer Conference Ctr. in Malibu named in his honor Wilshire Blvd. Temple Camps. Mem. So. Calif. Camping Assn. (dir. 1964-82), Nat. Assn. Temple Adminstrs. (nat. bd. dirs. 1987—, v.p. 1991-93, pres. 1993—, Svc. to Judaism award 1989, Svc. to the Community award 1990), Nat. Assn. Temple Educators, Los Angeles Assn. Jewish Edn. (dir.), Profl. Assn. Temple Adminstrs. (pres. 1985-88), Assn. Supervision and Curriculum Devel., Am. Mgmt. Assn., So. Calif. Conf. Jewish Communal Workers, Jewish Profl. Network, Amnesty Internat., Jewish Resident Camping Assn. (pres. 1976-82), World Union for Progressive Judaism, UCLA Alumni Assn., Wilderness Soc., Center for Environ. Edn., Wildlife Fedn., Living Desert, Maple Mental Health Ctr. of Beverly Hills, Los Angeles County Mus. Contemporary Art, People for the Am. Way, Assn. Reform Zionists Am. Office: Wilshire Blvd Temple 3663 Wilshire Blvd Los Angeles CA 90010-2703

BREUER, WERNER ALFRED, plastics company executive; b. Sinn, Hessia, Germany, Jan. 30, 1930; came to U.S., 1959; s. Christian and Hedwig (Cunz) B.; m. Gertrud Ackermann, June 21, 1950; children: Patricia, Julia, Eva-Maria. BS in Human Rels. and Orgnl. Behavior, U. San Francisco, 1983; MS in Bus. Mgmt., U. La Verne, 1985, DPA, 1988. Musician, bandleader BBT Dance Orch., various cities, Germany, 1950-54; lab. technician Firma E. Leitz GMBH, Wetzlar, Germany, 1954-59; lab. supr. Dayco Corp. (Am. latex divsn.), Hawthorne, Calif., 1959-65; tech. ops. mgr. Olin Corp., Stamford and New Haven, Conn., 1965-69; gen. mgr., exec. v.p. Expanded Rubber and Plastics Corp., Gardena, Calif., 1969—; gen. mgr. Schlobohm Co. Inc., Dominguez Hills, Calif., 1989—; cons. human resources Stabond Corp., Gardena, 1988—. Author/composer various popular and sacred recordings, 1970s; contbr. articles to jours. Active Town Hall of Calif., L.A., 1972—, World Affairs Coun., L.A., 1975—. Recipient William of Orange Gymnasium scholarship, Dillenburg, Germany, 1940, Portfolio award U. San Francisco, 1983-84. Mem. ASTM, ASCAP, Am. Soc. for Metals, Soc. for Plastics Engrs., N.Y. Acad. Scis., U. La Verne Alumni Assn. Republican. Home: 17761 Anglin Ln Tustin CA 92680-1903

BREUNIG, ROBERT HENRY, foundation executive; b. Phila., May 12, 1926; s. Robert Henry and Gertrude Florence (Burke) B.; m. Ruth Carolyn Cole, Aug. 30, 1947; children: Lynn Carol, Mark Robert, Christopher John, Eric Martin. BA, Ind. U., 1950; MA, Goddard Coll., 1979; PhD, Union Inst., 1981. Dir. pub. affairs Calif. State U., Long Beach, 1974-85; co-founder, exec. dir. Found. for the 21st Century, San Diego, 1985-87; sec. Found. for Pvt. Sector, San Diego, 1987—; dep. chmn. Sammis Co., San Diego, 1987-90. Cons. Pres.'s Coun. on Phys. Fitness and Sports, 985, Am. for the Reagan Agenda, 1985-87; U.S. exec. dir. Pacific Intercultural Exch.-Japan, World Intercultural Network. With U.S. Army, 1943-46. Decorated Bronze star, Belgian Fourragere, Presdl. Citation. Episcopalian. Home and Office: 3372 Cortese Dr Los Alamitos CA 90720-4306

BREWER, DAVID L., sociologist; b. Tucson, Mar. 11, 1933; s. Leslie O. and Nina (Brinkerhoff) B.; m. Sue Mansfield; children: Phillip, Brent, Robin. BS in Sociology, Brigham Young U., 1957; MS in Sociology, Purdue U., 1959; PhD in Sociology, U. Utah, 1966. Various teaching and rsch. positions including Fresno (Calif.) State U., Calif. State U./Hayward, Newark, State Coll., others, 1964-77; various to assoc. govtl. program analyst Calif. Dept. Corrections, Sacramento, 1982-88, correctional counselor, 1988-89; correctional counselor Calif. Dept. Corrections, Chino, 1989-90, clin. sociologist, 1990-92, correctional counselor, 1992-94; rsch. assoc. Dem. Processes Ctr., Tucson, 1995—. Contbr. articles to profl. jours., publs. Mem. Am. Sociol. Assn., Assn. Criminal Justice Rsch., Soc. for Study of Symbolic Interaction, Calif. Sociol. Assn., Sociol. Practice Assn., John Dewey Soc. Office: Calif Inst for Men Calif Dept of Corrections PO Box 128 Chino CA 91710

BREWER, JANICE KAY, state legislator, property and investment firm executive; b. Hollywood, Calif., Sept. 26, 1944; d. Perry Wilford and Edna Clarice (Bakken) Drinkwine; m. John Leon Brewer, Jan. 1, 1963; children: Ronald Richard, John Samuel, Michael Wilford. Med. asst. cert. Valley Coll., Burbank, Calif., 1963, practical radiol. technician cert., 1963; D in Humanities (hon.) L.A. Chiropractic Coll., 1970. Pres., Brewer Property & Investments, Glendale, Ariz., 1970—; mem. Ariz. Ho. of Reps., Phoenix, 1983-86, Ariz. Senate, 1987—, majority whip, 1993—. State committeeman, Rep. Party, Phoenix, 1970, 1983; legis. liaison Ponderosa Rep. Women, Phoenix, 1980; bd. dirs. Motion Picture & TV Commn. Active NOW. Recipient Freedom award Vets. of Ariz., 1994; named Woman of Yr., Chiropractic Assn. Ariz., 1983, Legislator of Yr., Behaviour Health Assn. Ariz., 1991, NRA, 1992. Mem. Nat. Fedn. Rep. Women, Am. Legis. Exch. Coun. Lutheran. Home: 6835 W Union Hills Dr Glendale AZ 85308-8058 Office: Ariz State Senate State Capitol Phoenix AZ 85007

BREWER, LIA HARPER, marriage and family therapist; b. San Luis Obispo, Calif., June 4, 1962; d. Jeremy More and Althea (Harper); m. David Wayne Brewer, Oct. 15, 1988; 1 child, Alyssa Michelle; stepchildren: Anthony, Rebecca. Student, Lewis and Clark Coll., 1980-82; BA in Devel. Psychology, U. Calif., Santa Barbara, 1984; MA in Counseling, Calif. Family Study Ctr., Burbank, 1986. Lic. marriage, family, and child counselor. Play therapy intern Internat. Inst. for Transpersonal Studies, Ojai, Calif., 1986-87; marriage, family, and child counseling intern Interface Family Svcs., Ventura, Calif., 1986-87; intern, assoc. play therapist Ventura Family Ctr., 1986-93; pvt. practice Ventura, Ojai, 1993-94; pvt. practice, sch. cons. Taft, Calif., 1994—. Author: Digger Gets Help - A Story About Sexual Abuse for Children, 1992, Digger's Secret Fear - A Story About Divorce for Children, 1993. Mem. Am. Assn. Marriage, Family Therapists, Am. Psychotherapy Assn., Step-Family Assn., Calif. Assn. Marriage, Family Therapists. Republican. Mem. Christian Ch. Office: 503 6th St Taft CA 93268-2704

BREWER, MICHAEL ALAN, dentist. BA in Psychology, Creighton U., 1980, DDS, 1984. mem. med. staff Bess Kaiser Hosp., Portland, Oreg., 1986-92, Sunnyside Hosp., Portland, 1986-92; mem. dental hygiene adv. com. Clark Coll., 1989-94. Various local, state, nat. and internat. positions Boy Scouts Am., 1966—. Fellow Acad. Gen. Dentistry; mem. Wash. State Dental Assn chmn. membership svcs. and ins. com. 1990-91, ho. of dels. 1990—, exec. coun., 1991-95, ADA del. 1991-95, sec. 1993-94, pres.-elect 1994—), Clark County Dental Soc. (chmn. membership svcs. 1989-95, recruitment and retention 1990-95, ins. com. 1990-95, exec. coun. 1990-95, del. 1990-93), Creighton U. Alumni Assn., Sports Car Club Am., Nat. Eagle Scout Assn. (life), Sigma Alpha Epsilon. Home: PO Box 2952 Vancouver WA 98668-2952

BREWER, THOMAS BOWMAN, retired university president; b. Fort Worth, July 22, 1932; s. Earl Johnson and Maurine (Bowman) B.; m. Betty Jean Walling, Aug. 4, 1951; children: Diane, Thomas Bowman Jr. B.A., U. Tex., 1954, M.A., 1957; Ph.D., U. Pa., 1962. Instr. St. Stephens Episcopal Sch., Austin, Tex., 1955-56, S.W. Tex. State Coll., San Marcos, 1956-57; from instr. to asso. prof. N. Tex. State U., Denton, 1959-66; asst. prof. U. Ky., 1966-67; asso. prof. Iowa State U., 1967-68; prof. history, chmn. dept. U. Toledo, 1968-71; dean Tex. Christian U., Fort Worth, 1971-72, vice chancellor, dean univ., 1972-78; chancellor E. Carolina U., Greenville, N.C., 1978-82; v.p. acad. affairs Ga. State U., Atlanta, 1982-88; pres. Met. State Coll. of Denver, 1988-93. Editor: Views of American Economic Growth, 2 vols, 1966, The Robber Barons, 1969; gen. editor: Railroads of America Series. Mem. Econ. History Assn., Bus. History Assn., Am. Assn. Higher Edn. Home: 104 Javelin Dr Austin TX 78734-5016

BREWSTER, ELIZABETH WINIFRED, English language educator, poet, novelist; b. Chipman, N.B., Can., Aug. 26, 1922; d. Frederick John and Ethel May (Day) Brewster. B.A., U. N.B., 1946; M.A., Radcliffe U., 1947; B.L.S., U. Toronto, Ont., Can., 1953; Ph.D., Ind. U., 1962; D.Litt., U. N.B., 1982. Cataloger Carleton U., Ottawa, Ont., 1953-57; cataloger Ind. U. Library, Bloomington, 1957-58, N.B. Legis. Library, 1965-68, U. Alta. Library, Edmonton, Can., 1968-70; mem. English dept. Victoria U., B.C., 1960-61; reference libr. Mt. Allison U. Libr., Sackville, N.B., 1961-65; vis. asst. prof. English U. Alta., 1970-71; mem. faculty U. Sask., Saskatoon, Can., 1972—, asst. prof. English, 1972-75, assoc. prof., 1975-80, prof., 1980-90, prof. emeritus, 1990—. Author: East Coast, 1951, Lilloot, 1954, Roads, 1957, Passage of Summer, 1969, Sunrise North, 1972, In Search of Eros, 1974, Sometimes I Think of Moving, 1977, The Way Home, 1982, The Sisters, 1974, It's Easy to Fall on the Ice, 1977, Digging In, 1982, Junction, 1982, A House Full of Women, 1983, Selected Poems 1944-84, 2 vols., 1985, Visitations, 1987, Entertaining Angels, 1988, Spring Again, 1990, The Invention of Truth, 1991, Wheel of Change, 1993. Recipient E.J. Pratt award for poetry U. Toronto, 1953, Pres. medal for poetry U. Western Ont., 1980, Lit. award Can. Broadcasting Corp., 1991, Lifetime Excellence in the Arts award Sash-Arts Bd., 1995. Mem. League Can. Poets (life), Writers' Union Can., Assn. Can. Univ. Tchrs. English. Office: U Saskatchewan, Dept English, Saskatoon, SK Canada S7N 0W0

BREWSTER, JOHN WELDON, SR., librarian, consultant; b. Arlington, Tex., Jan. 3, 1944; s. Weldon and Margaret Lee (Howard) B.; m. Pamela Diane Crittenden, Mar. 27, 1965; children: John Weldon Jr., Patricia Anne, Elizabeth Leigh. BA, U. Tex., 1966; MS, La. State U., 1967; postgrad., U. North Tex., Denton, 1970-80. Libr. Libr. of Congress, Washington, 1967-68; libr. mgr. U. North Tex., Denton, 1969-81; econ. libr. Republic Bank Corp., Dallas, 1981-85; securities analyst Underwood Neuhaus, Dallas, 1985-86; v.p., CFO Sander Textiles, Dallas, 1987-89; libr. mgr. N.Mex. State Libr., Santa Fe, 1989—; book reviews in hist. jours., 1972-78. Contbr. articles to profl. jours. Bd. dirs. Leadership Santa Fe, 1993, Arthritis Found., Tex., 1975-78. Mem. N.Mex. Libr. Assn. (dir. 1990-94), Lions Internat. (dir. 1994—). Democrat. Roman Catholic. Office: NMex State Libr 325 Don Gaspar Santa Fe NM 87501

BREWSTER, RUDI MILTON, federal judge; b. Sioux Falls, S.D., May 18, 1932; s. Charles Edwin and Wilhemina Therese (Rud) B.; m. Gloria Jane Nanson, June 27, 1954; children: Scot Alan, Lauri Diane (Alan Lee), Julie Lynn Yahnke. AB in Pub. Affairs, Princeton U., 1954; JD, Stanford U., 1960. Bar: Calif. 1960. From assoc. to ptnr. Gray, Cary, Ames & Frye, San Diego, 1960-84; judge U.S. Dist. Ct. (so. dist.) Calif., San Diego, 1984—. Served to capt. USNR, 1954-82 Ret. Fellow Am. Coll. Trial Lawyers; mem. Am. Bd. Trial Advs., Internat. Assn. Ins. Counsel, Am. Inns of Ct. Republican. Lutheran. Office: US Dist Ct 940 Front St San Diego CA 92101-8994

BRICKEN, WILLIAM MARION, scientist; b. Melbourne, Victoria, Australia, Apr. 27, 1945; s. William M. Sr. and Lois D. (Hickman) B.; m. Meredith S. VanNess Williams, Aug. 16, 1967; children: Ian, Colin. MS in Stats., Stanford U., 1983, PhD in Edn., 1987. Cert. tchr. Prin. Coonara Sch., Melbourne, 1972-75; asst. prof. State Coll. of Victoria, Melbourne, 1973-75; prin. scientist Advanced Decision Systems, Mountain View, Calif., 1984-88; dir. Autodesk Rsch. Lab, Sausalito, Calif., 1988-89; prin. scientist Human Interface Tech. Lab./Univ. Wash., Seattle, 1990-94; chief tech. officer InWorld, Seattle, 1994; co-founder Oz... Internat., Seattle, 1991—. Creator: Boundary Mathematics, 1983; designer: (computer program) VEOS, 1990; assoc. editor: Presence, Boston, 1991—. Mem. IEEE, AAAI, Assn. Computing Machinery, Spl. Interest Group on Computer Graphics.

BRICKER, SEYMOUR (MURRAY), lawyer; b. N.Y.C., May 19, 1924; s. Harry and May (Glick) B.; m. Darlene M. Mohilef, July 29, 1951 (dec. Mar. 1987); children: Andrea Helene, Phillip Alan, Julie Ellen. Student, U. Okla., 1943-44; AB, U. Calif., Los Angeles, 1947; LLB, U. So. Calif., 1950. Bar: Calif. 1951. Atty. Calif. Jud. Coun., 1951-52; with legal dept. Universal Pictures, 1952-56; ptnr. Cohen & Bricker, 1956-68, Kaplan, Livingston, Goodwin, Berkowitz & Selvin, 1968-81, Mitchell, Silberberg & Knupp, 1982—; exec. v.p. Ed Friendly Prodns. Inc.; pres. Friendly/Bricker Prodns. Bd. dirs. Acad. TV Arts and Scis. Found. Served with inf. AUS, 1943-46. Fellow Am. Bar Assn. Found.; mem. ABA (mem. coun. patent, trademark and copyright sect., past chmn. copyright divsn., past chmn. forum com. on entertainment and sports industries, mem. com. on Bicentennial program), L.A. Copyright Soc. (past pres.), Copyright Soc. U.S. (trustee), Calif. Copyright Conf. (past pres.), Acad. TV Arts and Scis. Found. (bd. dirs.). Home: 10445 Wilshire Blvd Los Angeles CA 90024-4634 Office: Mitchell Silberberg & Knupp 11377 W Olympic Blvd Los Angeles CA 90064-1625

BRICKMAN, HARRY RUSSELL, psychiatrist, psychoanalytic institute dean; b. N.Y.C., Feb. 16, 1924; s. Lewis and Rose (Oxman) B.; m. Beatrice Helen Krane, May 29, 1948; children: Mark, Marianne. BS, NYU, 1944, MD, 1947; PhD, So. Calif. Psychoanalytic Inst., 1972. Intern Fresno (Calif.) County Hosp., 1947-48; resident in psychiatry Menninger Found., Topeka, 1948-50, Palo Alto (Calif.) Hosp., 1950-51, Langley Porter Clinic, San Francisco, 1950-51; dir. Riverside (Calif.) State Mental Hygiene Clinic, 1951-52; pvt. practice L.A., 1951—; dir. So. Calif. Reception Ctr., Calif. Youth Authority, Norwalk, 1954-56; dir. outpatient svcs. dept. psychiatry UCLA Sch. Medicine, 1956-60; dir. Los Angeles County Mental Health Dept., L.A., 1960-76; dean So. Calif. Psychoanalytic Inst., L.A., 1991—. Contbr. articles to profl. jours. Lt. USNR, 1950-52. Fellow Am. Psychiat. Assn. (life). Office: 1100 Glendon Ave Ste 1210 Los Angeles CA 90024-3516

BRIDGE, SHERRY, clinical dietitian; b. Magrath, Alta., Can., Apr. 4, 1952; came to U.S., 1954; d. Malcolm Ririe and Elizabeth (McBride) B. BS, Utah State U., 1974. Registered dietitian, Utah. Dietitian/supr. Lakeview Hosp., Bountiful, Utah, 1975-76; dietitian/food svc. dir. Brigham City (Utah) Cmty. Hosp., 1977-79; adminstrv. dietitian Lakeview Hosp., an affiliate of HealthTrust, Inc., Bountiful, 1978-93, clin. dietitian, 1993—; cons. dietitian Davis County Coun. on Aging, Farmington, Utah, 1979-81; adj. prof. Brigham Young U., Provo, Utah, 1992—. Organist LDS Ch., Bountiful, 1974—; data entry operator LDS Geneol. Soc., Salt Lake City, 1990-93. Mem. Utah Dietetic Assn. (coun. on practice 1981-89, sec. 1989-91, 92, pres. 1994—), Am. Heart Assn. (Davis County affiliate).

BRIDGES, EDWIN MAXWELL, education educator; b. Hannibal, Mo., Jan. 1, 1934; s. Edwin Otto and Radha (Maxwell) B.; m. Marjorie Anne Pollock, July 31, 1954; children: Richard, Rebecca, Brian, Bruce. BS, U. Mo., 1954; MA, U. Chgo., 1956, PhD, 1964. English tchr. Bremen Community High Sch., Midlothian, Ill., 1954-56; asst. prin. Griffith (Ind.) High Sch., 1956-60, prin., 1960-62; staff assoc. U. Chgo., 1962-64, assoc. prof., 1967-72; assoc. dir. Univ. Coun. for Edn. Adminstrn., Columbus, Ohio, 1964-65; asst. prof. Washington U., St. Louis, 1965-67; assoc. prof. U. Chgo., 1967-72; prof. U. Calif., Santa Barbara, 1972-74; prof. edn. Stanford (Calif.) U., 1974—; mem. nat. adv. panel Ctr. for Rsch. on Ednl. Accountability and Tchr. Evaluation, 1990—; external examiner U. Hong Kong, 1990-92; cons. World Bank, China, 1986, 89; dir. Midwest Adminstrn. Ctr., Chgo., 1967-72. Author: Managing the Incompetent Teacher, 1984, 2d edit., 1990, The Incompetent Teacher, 1986, 2d edit., 1991, Problem Based Learning for Administrators, 1992; co-author: Introduction to Educational Adminstration, 1977, Implementing Problem-based Leadership Development, 1995; contbr. articles to profl. jours. Named Outstanding Young Man of Ind., C. of C., 1960; named hon. prof. and cert. of honor So. China Normal U., 1989. Mem. Am. Ednl. Rsch. Assn. (v.p. 1974-75). Office: Stanford U Sch Edn Stanford CA 94305

BRIDGES, JOHN ALBERT, archaeologist, educator; b. Balt., Dec. 9, 1949; s. Hilbert Patton and Catherine Regina (Marzi) B.; m. Donna Lee Lind, July 3, 1971. BA in Social Scis., U. No. Colo., Greeley, 1972; student, Met. State Coll., Denver, 1989-90. Asst. mgr. H.M. Woods Bldg. Materials, Thornton, Colo., 1974-86; field worker numerous archaeology firms, 1986—; field worker Colo. Hwy. Dept., Denver, 1990—; tchr. Thornton Middle Sch., 1990—, Belmar Village Mus., Lakewood, Colo., 1992—. Author site reports. Tchr. Colo. Literacy Project, Westminster, 1987; coach, judge, problem capt. Odyssey of the Mind, 1984-93. Mem. Colo. Coun. Profl. Archaeologists, Colo. Archaeol. Soc., Colo. Hist. Soc. (Stephen H.Hart award 1992), Denver Mus. Natural History, Golden Key Nat. Honor Soc. Office: Thornton Mid Sch 9451 Hoffman Way Thornton CO 80229-3535

BRIDGES, KATHLEEN ERICKSON, communication disorders specialist; b. Mojave, Calif., June 3, 1944; d. John Stahlberg and Evelyn Lyle (Shriver) Erickson. BA cum laude, U. Utah, 1968, MA, 1969. Lic. speech pathologist, Utah, Calif. Resource tchr. Salt Lake City Schs., 1971-76, communication disorders specialist, 1969-70, 76-89; communication disorders specialist Orange (Calif.) Unified Schs., 1970-71, 89-91, Tustin Unified Schs., 1991-93; spl. day class tchr. Capistrano Unified Sch. Dist., 1993—; clin. instr. U. Utah Dept. Communication Disorders, Salt Lake City, 1976-89, mem. adv. bd.; chmn. com. for practical examination speech pathology licensure Utah Dept. Bus. Regulations, Salt Lake City, 1984, 86. Mem. Salt Lake Jr. League, 1973-85, rec. sec., 1980-81, project chmn., 1976-77; chmn. Youth Services Adv. Bd., 1976-78; treas., trustee Parent Support Inc., 1976-89; bd. dirs., coms. chmn. Salt Lake Jr. Achievement, 1974-78, 85-87; tchr. specialist Salt Lake Dist. Career Ladder, 1987-88, faculty rep., 1987-89; mem. Pi Beta Phi alumnae adv. bd. U. Calif., Irvine, 1993-95. Named Vital Vol., Salt Lake County Commn., 1986. Mem. NEA, Calif. Tchrs. Assn., Am. Speech Lang. Hearing Assn. (cert.), Calif. Speech Lang. Hearing Assn., Capistrano Unified Tchrs. Assn., Pi Beta Phi Alumnae Club (sec. 1971-72, chmn. 1972-73, philanthropy chmn. 1973-75, pledges advisor 1978-80, house advisor 1985-86, adv. com. chmn. 1986-88), PSI (province coord. 1988-89), Golden Key, Phi Kappa Phi. Democrat. Mem. Christian Scientist Ch. Home: 15 Telura Rcho Station Marg CA 92688-3024 Office: Moulton Elementary 29851 Highlands Ave Laguna Niguel CA 92677-2008

BRIDGES, ROBERT MCSTEEN, mechanical engineer; b. Oakland, Calif., Apr. 17, 1914; s. Robert and Josephine (Hite) B.; BS cum laude in Mech. Engring., U. So. Calif., 1940; postgrad. UCLA; m. Edith Brownwood, Oct. 26, 1945; children: Ann, Lawrence, Robert. Engr. Nat. Supply Co., Torrance, Calif., 1940-41; design engr. landing gear and hydraulics Lockheed Aircraft Corp., Burbank, Calif., 1941-46; missile hydraulic controls design engr. Convair, San Diego, 1946-48; sr. staff engr. oceanic systems mech. design Bendix Corp., Sylmar, Calif., 1948—; adv. ocean engring. U.S. Congress. Com. chmn. Boy Scouts Am., 1961. Recipient award of Service Am. Inst. Aero. Engrs., 1965. Mem. Marine Tech. Soc. (charter; com. cables, connectors 1969), Tau Beta Pi. Republican. Patentee in field of undersea devices (54 internat., 14 U.S.), including deep ocean rubber band moor; inventor U.S. Navy sonobuoy rotochute; contbr. articles to profl. jours. and confs. Home: 10314 Vanalden Ave Northridge CA 91326-3326 Office: Allied Signal Ocean Systems Corp Bendix Sylmar Divsn 15825 Roxford St San Fernando CA 91342-3537

BRIDGES, ROY DUBARD, JR., career officer; b. Atlanta, July 19, 1943; s. Roy D. and Elizabeth A. (Roberson) B.; m. Benita L. Allbaugh, Mar. 26, 1967; children: Tanya M., Brian N. BS in Engring. Sci., USAF Acad., 1965; MS in Astronautical Engring., Purdue U., 1966. Commd. 2d lt. USAF, 1965, advanced through grades to maj. gen., 1992; test pilot Air Force Flight Test Ctr., Edwards AFB, Calif., 1970-75; student Air Command and Staff Coll., Maxwell AFB, Ala., 1975-76; staff officer Hdqrs. USAF, Pentagon, Washington, 1976-79; dep. dir. plans Detachment 3, Air Force Flight Test Ctr., Henderson, Nev., 1979-80; astronaut (pilot) Johnson Space Ctr., NASA, Houston, 1980-86; comdr. 6510th Test Wing, Edwards AFB, Calif., 1986-89; comdr., Ea. Space and Missile Ctr., Patrick AFB, Fla., 1989-90; dep. chief of staff for test and resources Air Force Systems Command, Andrews AFB, Md., 1990-91; comdr. Air Force Flight Test Ctr. Edwards AFB, Edwards AFB, Calif., 1991-93; dir. requirements Air Force Materiel Command, Wright Patterson AFB, Ohio, 1993—; pilot space shuttle Challenger, NASA,1985. Named to Ga. Aviation Hall of Fame, 1995; recipient Space Flight award Am. Astronautical Soc., 1986, Astronaut Engring. Alumnus award Purdue U., 1990. Fellow Soc. Exptl. Test Pilots (assoc.);

mem. Air Force Assn., Soc. of Space Explorers. Methodist. Office: Wright Patterson AFB Materiel Command DR 4375 Chidlaw Rd Ste 6 Dayton OH 45433-5066

BRIDGEWATER, NORA JANE, medical/surgical nurse; b. Rodgers, Tex., Feb. 27, 1924; d. Wiley Levi and Phoebajane (Owens) Shelgren; m. Joe Garland Bridgewater, Aug. 7, 1940; children: Garland, Janie William Clayton, Richard, Allen, Paula, Shewanna, Russell. AA in Psychology, Bakersfield Coll., 1970, BSN, 1978. Med. nurse Kern Med. Hosp., Bakersfield, Calif., 1964-68, Mercy Hosp., Bakersfield, 1969-78, Sherrif's Dept., Laredo, Calif., 1978-87; nurse Sheriff Facility, Bakersfield, 1986-87. Sgt. U.S. Army Nurses Corps, 1938-40. Mem. Calif. Nursing Assn. Democrat. Baptist. Home: 2104 Bedford Way Bakersfield CA 93308

BRIDGFORTH, ROBERT MOORE, JR., aerospace engineer; b. Lexington, Miss., Oct. 21, 1918; s. Robert Moore and Theresa (Holder) B.; student Miss. State Coll., 1935-37; BS, Iowa State Coll., 1940; MS, MIT, 1948; postgrad. Harvard U., 1949; m. Florence Jarnberg, November 7, 1943; children: Robert Moore, Alice Theresa. Asst. engr. Standard Oil Co., of Ohio, 1940; teaching fellow M.I.T., 1940-41, instr. chemistry, 1941-43, research asst., 1943-44, mem. staff div. indsl. cooperation, 1944-47; asso. prof. physics and chemistry Emory and Henry Coll., 1949-51; rsch. engr. Boeing Airplane Co., Seattle, 1951-54, rsch. specialist 1954-55, sr. group engr., 1955-58, chief propulsion systems sect. Systems Mgmt. Office, 1958-59, chief propulsion rsch. unit, 1959-60; founder, chmn. bd. Rocket Rsch. Corp., 1960-69, Explosives Corp. Am., 1966-69. Fellow AIAA (assoc.), Brit. Interplanetary Soc., Am. Inst. Chemists; mem. AAAS, Am. Astronautical Soc. (dir.), Am. Chem. Soc., Am. Rocket Soc. (pres. Pacific NW 1955), Am. Ordnance Assn., Am. Inst. Physics, Am. Assn. Physics Tchrs., Tissue Culture Assn., Soc. for Leukocyte Biology, N.Y. Acad. Scis., Combustion Inst., Sigma Xi. Achievements include U.S. patents for rocket tri-propellants and explosives. Home: 4325 87th Ave SE Mercer Island WA 98040-4127

BRIDWELL, C. JOSEPH, computer systems analyst; b. Greenville, S.C., Feb. 4, 1955; s. Gordon William and Vera Mae (Whisenant) B.; m. Clemeth Ray Saylor, May 2, 1987 (dec. July 1994). BS, Furman U., 1977; MA, Ga. State U., 1983. Programmer, analyst Daniel Internat., Greenville, S.C., 1977-80, C&S Nat. Bank, Atlanta, 1980-83; DBA So. Motor Carriers, Atlanta, 1983-87; analyst, cons. Options Clearing Corp., Chgo., 1987-88, Seafirst Nat. Bank, Seattle, 1988-91, Ernst, Seattle, 1991—; sec. Urdd Arleisiau'r Ddraig, Seattle, 1993-94, bd. dirs. Contbr. articles to mags. Mem. Hands Off Washington, Seattle, 1994, Human Rights campaign, Washington, 1994. Fellow TRUST; mem. ACLU, NWGRA, Nat. Leather Assn. Home: 1104 E Fir St Seattle WA 98122-5416

BRIEGER, STEPHEN GUSTAVE, management consultant; b. Marburg, Ger., Sept. 7, 1935; came to U.S., naturalized, 1945; s. Heinrich and Kate L. (Steitz) B.; B.Sc., Springfield (Mass.) Coll., 1955; M.S., Fla. State U., 1970, Ph.D., 1972; m. Karen L. Jentes, Nov. 27, 1968; children: Jennifer B., Benjamin A. Tchr., Calif. schs., 1954-69; indsl. cons. mgmt. tng., 1960-70; mgmt. cons. Nebr. Criminal Justice System, 1972; research criminologist Stanford Research Inst., 1972-74; evaluation cons. Office Gov. Calif., 1974-76; mgmt. devel. assoc. Am. Electronics Assn., 1976-80; mgr. employee and mgmt. devel. ISS Sperry Univac, Santa Clara, Calif., 1980-83; mgr. tng. recruiting and devel. Lawrence Livermore Nat. Lab., U. Calif., 1983-95; mem. faculty U.S. Internat. U., St. Mary's Coll., U. San Francisco. Mem. Am. Soc. Tng. and Devel., Am. Mgmt. Assn., Am. Electronics Assn. Author studies, reports in field. Home: 1665 Fairorchard Ave San Jose CA 95125-4935 Office: PO Box 5508 Livermore CA 94551-5508

BRIERLEY, JAMES ALAN, research administrator; b. Denver, Dec. 22, 1938; s. Everette and Carrie (Berg) B.; m. Corale Louise Beer, Dec. 21, 1965. BS in Bacteriology, Colo. State U., 1961; MS in Microbiology, Mont. State U., 1963, PhD, 1966. Research scientist Martin Marietta Corp., Denver, 1968-69; asst. prof. biology N.Mex. Inst. Mining and Tech., Socorro, 1966-68, from asst. prof. to prof. biology, chmn. dept. biology, 1969-83; research dir. Advanced Mineral Techs., Golden, Colo., 1983-88; chief biologist Newmont Metall. Svcs., Salt Lake City, 1988—; vis. fellow U. Warwick, Coventry, Eng., 1976, vis. prof. Catholic U., Santiago, Chile, 1983; adj. prof. dept. metallurgy U. Utah, 1994—; cons. Mountain State Mineral Enterprises, Tucson, 1980, Sandia Nat. Lab., Albuquerque, 1976, Bechtel Civil and Minerals, Scottsdale, Ariz., 1984. Contbr. numerous articles to profl. jours.; patentee in field. Served to staff sgt. Air N.G., 1956-61. Recipient 32 research grants. Fellow AAAS; mem. Am. Soc. Microbiology, Soc. Gen. Microbiology, Sigma Xi. Home: 2872 Elk Horn Ln Sandy UT 84093-6595 Office: Newmont Metall Svcs 417 Wakara Way Ste 210 Salt Lake City UT 84108-1255

BRIERLEY, RICHARD GREER, business consultant; b. Kearney, N.J., July 1, 1915; s. Josiah Richards and Castella Sophia (Parker) B.; m. Margaret Jean LaLone, Aug. 24, 1940; children: Linda, Sandra, Martha, Ann. AB, Dartmouth Coll., 1936; MBA, Tuck Sch., 1937; AMP, Harvard U., 1952. Salesman Armstrong Cork Co., Lancaster, Pa., 1937-40; with Archer-Daniels-Midland Co., Mpls., 1940-64; exec. v.p. Arcaer-Daniels-Midland Co., Mpls., 1979-61, Drackett Co., Cin., 1961-66; pres., chief exec. officer Bristol Myers Can., Toronto, Ont., 1966-68; v.p. corp. planning Bristol Myers Co., N.Y.C., 1968-70; pres., chief exec. officer Stearns & Foster, Cin., 1970-75, chmn. bd. dirs., 1975-76; pres., chmn. bd. dirs. Brierley Assocs., Carefree, Ariz., 1976—; bd. dirs. Transcapital Fin. Corp., Cleve., Galleon Beach Club, Antiqua, W.I. Office: Brierley Assocs PO Box 2659 34 Easy St Carefree AZ 85377

BRIGGS, DINUS MARSHALL, agriculturist; b. Stillwater, Okla., Mar. 5, 1940; s. Hilton Marshall and Lillian (Dinusson) B.; m. June Elaine Wolf, Sept. 2, 1962; children: Denise, Deborah. BS, S.D. State U., 1962; MS, Iowa State U., 1969, PhD, 1971. Asst. pastor Stroudsburg (Pa.) Meth. Ch., 1962-64; grad. asst. Iowa State U., Ames, 1964-66, research assoc., 1966-70; asst. prof. N.C. State U., Raleigh, 1970-75; asst. dir. Ark. Agrl. Expt. Sta., Fayetteville, 1976-82; assoc. dir. N.Mex. Agrl. Expt. Sta., Las Cruces, 1982—. Co-author: Modern Breeds of Livestock, 1980. Mem. Poultry Sci. Assn. (resolutions com. 1972-73), Am. Assn. Animal Sci., World's Poultry Sci., Sigma Xi. Lodge: Rotary. Home: 1927 Francine Ct Las Cruces NM 88005-5509 Office: NMex Agrl Experiment Sta PO Box 30003 # 3bf Las Cruces NM 88003-8003

BRIGGS, JAMES HENRY, II, engineering administrator; b. San Francisco, Dec. 25, 1953; s. James Henry and Barbara (Cordes) B.; m. Niwana Page, Sept. 1, 1979; children: Melanie Shannon, James Henry III. AA in Bus. Adminstrn., Albany (Ga.) Jr. Coll., 1976; BS in Computer Sci., U. N.C., Wilmington, 1979; BSEE, So. Tech., Marietta, Ga., 1985. Lic. 1st class radio telephone; registered profl. engr., Calif. Asst. chief engr. WECT-TV, Wilmington, 1978-82; maintenance supr. Cable News Network, Atlanta, 1982-85; mgr. engring. ops. KCOP-TV, L.A., 1985-87; sr. product support engr. Abekas Video Systems, Redwood City, Calif., 1987-92; dir. engring. D.T.S., Union City, Calif., 1991—. Editor: Video Prodn. in the 90's. Mem. Soc. Motion Picture and TV Engrs., Soc. Broadcast Engrs., Greenpeace, Toastmasters Club, Lions. Office: DTS 3200 Lenox Rd NE Apt E203 Atlanta GA 30324-2635

BRIGGS, ROBERT NATHAN, electrical engineer; b. Miami Beach, Fla., Dec. 22, 1946; s. Donald Hickes and Harriett Martha (Mercer) B.; m. Polly Elizabeth Partridge, Dec. 22, 1970; children: Nathan Michael, Carey Robert, Christopher Alan. BSEE, Northrop Inst. Tech., 1974; postgrad. in Physics, U. Nev., Las Vegas, 1978-81. Electronics engr. U.S. Dept. Energy Telcom Inc., Las Vegas, 1974-75; sr. fiber optics engr. U.S. Dept. Energy Holmes & Narver, Las Vegas, 1975-81; dir. quality assurance Am. Fiber Optics, Signal Hill, Calif., 1981-83; sr. staff engr. command and data handling lab. TRW, Inc., Redondo Beach, Calif., 1983-84, sr. sect. head telecommunications lab., 1984-85, sr. staff engr. electro-optic rsch. ctr., 1985-86, Tracking and Data Relay Satellite System Telemetry, Tracking and Command systems engr. spacecraft electronics system lab., 1986-91, AXAF-I on-board computer mgr., 1991—. Mem. Am. Inst. Aeronautics and Astronautics, Inc., Optical Soc. Am. Home: 6532 Verde Ridge Rd Palos Verdes Peninsula CA 90275-4632 Office: TRW Inc Space & Electronics Group One Space Park Redondo Beach CA 90278

BRIGHAM, JOHN ALLEN, JR., financial executive, environmentalist; b. San Francisco, June 17, 1942; s. John Allen, Sr. and Susan (Endberg) B.; m. Patricia Katherine Carney, Feb. 4, 1968; 1 child, Jennifer. BS in Acctg., San Jose State U., 1967. Acct. Shell Oil Co. Data Ctr., Palo Alto, Calif., 1963-66; asst. plant controller Brown Co., Santa Clara, Calif., 1966-68; budget mgr. Varian Assocs., Palo Alto, 1968-80; cost acctg. mgr. Adac Labs., San Jose, Calif., 1980-86; contr. Crystal Tech., Palo Alto, 1986-90, GV Contractors, Healdsburg, Calif.; environ. stock analyst, environ. industry stock newsletter, owner Brigham Investment Advisory Svc., 1990-94; controller GV Contractors, Heraldsburg, Calif., 1994—; part-time sci. tchr. Insects and Dinosaurs, 1994—. Del. League Calif. Cities, 1974-78; mem. Saratoga (Calif.) City Council, 1974-78; vice-chmn. Santa Clara County Polity Planning Use Commn., 1975-78; chmn. Santa Clara Com. on Mass Transit, 1976-78; chmn. Open Space Bond Issue, 1976; treas. Calif. State Solar Bond Issue, 1976; mem. Castle Rock State Pk. Com., 1972-74; vice-chmn. Saratoga Hillside Com. 1978-79. Recipient 10 Yr. Sierra Club Activist award, 1989, Chpt. Svc. award, 1990, Spl. Achievement award, 1990; Local Outstanding Young Man of Am. award, 1974, Siemens USA Personality of the Month award, Jan. 1990. Mem. Am. Entomol. Soc., Archeol. Inst. Am., Nat. Acctg. Assn., Sierra Club (vice chmn., treas. Loma chpt. 1985-94, treas. Redwood chpt. 1994—, internat. chmn. 1989—, Centennial chmn. 1990-92, liaison to USSR and Mex., co-chair Earth Day 1990, taskforce 1989, chmn. fin. commn. 1985—), Am. Diabetes Soc. (treas., bd. dirs. Santa Clara County chpt.), Nat. Wildlife Fedn., Cousteau Soc., Planetary Soc., Nat. Audubon Soc. Republican. Roman Catholic.

BRIGHAM, SAMUEL TOWNSEND JACK, III, lawyer; b. Honolulu, Oct. 8, 1939; s. Samuel Townsend Jack, Jr. and Betty Elizabeth (McNeil) B.; m. Judith Catherine Johnson, Sept. 3, 1960; children: Robert Jack, Bradley Lund, Lori Ann, Lisa Katherine. B.S. in Bus. magna cum laude, Menlo Coll., 1963; J.D., U. Utah, 1966. Bar: Calif. 1967. Asso. firm Petty, Andrews, Olsen & Tufts, San Francisco, 1966-67; accounting mgr. Western sales region Hewlett-Packard Co., North Hollywood, Calif., 1967-68; atty. Hewlett-Packard Co., Palo Alto, Calif., 1968-70; asst. gen. counsel Hewlett-Packard Co., 1971-73, gen. atty., asst. sec., 1974-75, sec., gen. counsel, 1975-82, v.p., gen. counsel, 1982-85, v.p. corp. affairs, gen. counsel, mgr./dir. law dept., 1985—; lectr. law Menlo Coll.; speaker profl. assn. seminars. Bd. dirs. Palo Alto Area YMCA, 1974-81, pres., 1978; bd. govs. Santa Clara County region NCCJ; trustee Menlo Sch. and Coll.; bd. dirs. Just Say No. Served with USMC, 1957-59. Mem. ABA, Calif. Bar Assn., Peninsula Assn. Gen. Counsel, MAPI Law Council, Am. Corp. Counsel Assn. (chmn. 1985, bd. dirs. 1983—), Am. Soc. Corp. Secs. (pres. No. Calif. Chpt. 1983—), Assn. Gen. Counsel (sec.-treas. 1991—). Home: 920 Oxford Dr Los Altos CA 94024-7032 Office: Hewlett-Packard Co 3000 Hanover St Palo Alto CA 94304-1112*

BRILES, JUDITH, writer, speaker, consultant; b. Pasadena, Calif., Feb. 20, 1946; d. James and Mary Tuthill; MBA, Pepperdine U., 1980; PhD Nova U., 1990; children: Shelley, Sheryl, Frank (dec.), William (dec.). Brokers asst. Bateman, Eichler, Hill, Richards, Torrance, Calif., 1969-72; account exec. E. F. Hutton, Palo Alto, Calif., 1972-78; pres. Judith Briles & Co., Palo Alto, 1978-85, Briles & Assocs., Palo Alto, 1980-86; ptnr. The Briles Group, Inc., 1987—; instr. Menlo Coll., 1986-87, Skyline Coll., 1981-86; instr. U. Calif.-Berkeley Sch. Continuing Edn., U. Calif.-Santa Cruz Sch. Continuing Edn., U. Hawaii; mem. adv. coun. Miss Am. Pageant, 1989—, No-nonsense Panty Hose, 1989—, Colo. Women's News, 1993—. Pres., v.p., sec., bd. dirs. Foothill-DeAnza Coll. Found., Los Altos Hills, Calif., 1979-90, bd. dirs. Col. Nurses Task Force, Col. League Nursing; mem. adv. bd. Flint Ctr., Cupertino, Calif. Mem. NAFE (adv. bd. bus. woman's mag. 1981-86), Peninsula Profl. Women's Network, Nat. Speaker's Assn. (bd. dirs.). Republican. Club: Commonwealth. Author: The Woman's Guide to Financial Savvy, 1981; Money Phases, 1984, Woman to Woman: From Sabotage to Support, 1987, Dollars and Sense of Divorce, 1988, Faith and Savvy Too!, 1988, When God Says No, 1990, The Confidence Factor, 1990, Money Guide, 1991, The Workplace: Questions Women Ask, 1992, Financial Savvy for Women, 1992, The Briles Report on Women in Healthcare, 1994, Money Sense, 1995, Gender Traps, 1995.

BRILL, YVONNE THERESA, marketing research company executive, consultant; b. Redwood City, Calif., Oct. 13, 1960; d. Fred and Hedy (Buhler) Schneider; m. Michael Clark Brill, May 1, 1982; children: Laura, Katherine, Jeff. BS in Biol. Scis., U. Calif., Davis, 1982; MBA, Santa Clara U., 1987. Biologist I Syntex, Palo Alto, Calif., 1982-84, biologist II, 1984-85, regulatory affairs assoc., 1985-87, regulatory affairs project adminstr., 1987-89, regulatory affairs group mgr., 1989-90, product devel. mgr., 1990-91; mgr. strategic devel. Nycomed Salutar, Sunnyvale, Calif., 1991-92, dir. mktg., 1992-93; dir. ops. MedSearch, Los Altos, Calif., 1993-94, v.p., 1994—. Sunday sch. tchr. Queen of Apostles Ch., San Jose, Calif., 1990-95. Office: 11625 Par Ave Los Altos CA 94024

BRILLINGER, DAVID ROSS, statistician, educator; b. Toronto, Ont., Can., Oct. 27, 1937; s. Austin Carlyle and Winnifred Elsie (Simpson) B.; m. Lorie Silber, Dec. 17, 1960; children: Jef Austin, Matthew David. B.A., U. Toronto, 1959; M.A., Princeton U., 1960, Ph.D., 1961. Lectr. math Princeton U. and; mem. tech. staff Bell Labs., 1962-64; lectr. stats. London Sch. Econs., 1964-66, reader, 1966-69; prof. stats. U. Calif., Berkeley, 1970—; chmn. dept. U. Calif., 1979-81. Author: Time Series: Data Analysis and Theory, 1975; editor Internat. Statis. Rev., 1988-91. Recipient R.A Fisher award, 1991; Woodrow Wilson fellow, 1959; Bell Telephone Labs. fellow, 1960; Social Sci. Research Council postdoctoral fellow, 1961; Miller prof., 1973; Guggenheim fellow, 1975-76, 82-83. Fellow AAAS (mem.-at-large statistics sect.), Am. Acad. Arts and Scis., Royal Soc. Can., Am. Statis Assn., Inst. Math. Stats.; mem. Internat. Statis. Inst., Royal Statis Soc., Can. Statis. Soc. (Gold medal 1992), Seismol. Soc. Am., Inst. Math. Statistics (pres.-elect), Bernoulli Soc., Biometric Soc., Can. Math. Soc. Office: Univ Calif Dept Stats Berkeley CA 94720

BRIM, ARMAND EUGENE, healthcare executive; b. South Bend, Wash., July 23, 1930; s. Thomas Armand and Mary May (Leonard) B.; m. Evona Harford, Aug. 28, 1955; children: Susan C., Elizabeth J., Julia A., Thomas E. B.S., U. Wash., 1952; M.Hosp. Adminstrn., U. Minn., 1954. Bus. mgr. Good Samaritan Hosp., Portland, Oreg., 1956-61; adminstr. Madera County Hosp., Calif., 1962-63, Woodland Park Hosp., Portland, Oreg., 1963-71; pres. Brim, Inc., Portland, 1972—. Pres. Fedn. Oreg. Hosps., Portland, 1966; trustee, chmn. Pacific U., Forest Grove, Oreg., 1984—; pres. Pacific Found., 1987-92. lst lt. USAF, 1954-56. Mem. Am. Coll. Hosp. Adminstrs., Am. Hosp. Assn., Toastmasters (pres. 1960), Arlington Club, Optimist (Portland, Oreg., pres. 1959). Home: 6666 SE Yamhill St Portland OR 97215-2030 Office: Brim Inc 305 NE 102nd Ave Portland OR 97220-4170

BRIMACOMBE, JAMES KEITH, metallurgical engineering educator, researcher, consultant; b. Windsor, N.S., Can., Dec. 7, 1943; s. Geoffrey Alan and Mary Jean (MacDonald) B.; m. Margaret Elaine Rutter, Feb. 6, 1970; children: Kathryn Margaret, Jane Margaret. B of Applied Sci. with honors, U. B.C., 1966; PhD, U. London, 1970, DSc in Engring., 1986; D in Engring. (hon.), Colo. Sch. Mines, 1994. Registered profl. engr., B.C. Asst. prof. metall. engring. U. B.C., Vancouver, Can., 1970-74, assoc. prof., 1974-79, prof., 1979-80, Stelco prof., 1980-85, Stelco/Nat. Scis. and Engring. Rsch. Coun. Can. prof., 1985-91; Alcan chair in materials process engring.; dir. Ctr. for Metall. Process Engring. U. B.C., Vancouver, Can., 1985—; Arnold Markey lectr. Steel Bar Mill Assn., 1981; retained cons. Hatch Assocs., Toronto, 1984-89; cons. over 60 metall. cos. Author: Continuous Casting, vol. II, 1984, The Mathematical and Physical Modeling of Primary Metals Processing Operations, 1988; contbr. numerous articles to profl. jours.; patentee in field. Capt. Can. Air Force, 1961-70. Recipient B.C. Sci. and Engring. Gold medal Sci. Coun. B.C., 1985, Ernest C. Manning Prin. award The Manning Trust, 1987, Izaak Walton Killam Meml. prize in engring. The Can. Coun., 1989, Corp. Higher End. Forum award, 1989, Commemorative medal for 125th Anniversary of Can. Confedn., numerous awards for publs.; Can. Commonwealth fellow Brit. Coun., 1966, E.W.R. Steacie fellow Nat. Scis. and Engring. Rsch. Coun. Can., 1980; Officer Order of Can. Fellow Can. Inst. Mining, Metallurgy and Petroleum Engrs., Canadian Acad. of Engring., Royal Soc. Can., Minerals, Metals and Materials Soc. (founding chmn. extraction and processing div. 1989-92, extractive metallurgy lectr. 1989, pres. 1993-94); mem. Metall. Soc. of Can. Inst. Mining and Metallurgy (pres. 1985-86, Alcan award 1988), Iron and Steel Soc. (disting. mem., bd. dirs. 1989—, Howe Meml. Lectr. 1993, pres. 1995—), Inst. Materials, Am. Soc. Metals (now ASM Internat., Can. Coun. lectureship 1986), Iron and Steel Inst. Japan, Sigma Tau Xi, (UBC hon. frat.). Roman Catholic.

BRIMHALL, DENNIS C., hospital executive; b. Provo, Utah, Sept. 8, 1948; s. Delbert and Elinor (Brockbank) B.; m. Linda Christensen. BS in Zoology, Brigham Young U., 1972; MBA, Northwestern U., 1974. Evening adminstr. Evanston (Ill.) Hosp., 1973-74; asst. adminstr. U. Utah Hosp., Salt Lake City, 1974-79, assoc. adminstr., 1979-83; assoc. dir. Med. Ctr., U. Calif., San Francisco, 1983-88; pres. univ. hosp. Health Scis. Ctr., U. Colo., Denver, 1988—. Bd. dirs. Univ. Hosp. Consortium, Chgo., 1988—, Colo. Children's Campaign, Denver, 1989—, Colo. Hosp. Assn., 1990—, Nat. Conf. Christians and Jews, 1993—; active Spl. Commn. on AIDS, 1987—. Mem. Am. Coll. Hosp. Adminstrn., Colo. Hosp. Assn. (chmn. 1994—), Assn. Practitioner in Inf. Control Rsch. Found. (pres. 1993—), Rotary Club. Mem. LDS Ch. Home: 5339 S Kenton Ct Englewood CO 80111-3829 Office: Univ Hosp 4200 E 9th Ave Box A020 Denver CO 80262

BRIMM, LARRY EUGENE, counseling psychologist; b. Belknap, Ill., Aug. 7, 1946; s. Christopher Columbus and Eva Ruth (Canada) B.; 1 child, Eric Neil; m. Debra Dean Belt, Dec. 21, 1985; stepchildren: Jeffrey, Melinda. BS in Rehab. Counseling, U. Ariz., 1991, MA in Rehab. Counseling, 1993. Cert. rehab. counselor. Police officer City of Cape Girardeau (Mo.), 1969-71; supr. vets. affairs Kankakee C.C., 1973-78; vocat. rehab. counselor Ariz. Rehab. Svc. Adminstrn., Tucson, 1987-93, Dept. Vets. Affairs, Tucson, 1993%—; cons., counselor Comin' Home, Tucson, 1990-92, chairperson, 1991; spkr. post-traumatic stress disorder, 1991, 92. Organizer Salute to Desert Storm Vets., Tucson, 1992, Homeless Vet. Facility Comin' Home, Tucson, 1989, 90, 91, Prisoner of War/Missing in Action Meml., Tucson, 1991; mem. support counseling staff Vietnam Vets. Am. Nam Jam, Tucson, 1993. Sgt. USMC, 1964-68, Vietnam. Recipient Svcs. to Vets. award Am. Ex-Prisoners of War Assn., 1994, Copper Letter City of Tucson Vets. Commn., 1992. Mem. Nat. Rehab. Assn., Ariz. Rehab. Assn. (pres. 1988—, Counselor of Yr. 1991, Sarah Folsum award 1993), Nat. Rehab. Counselors Assn., Disabled Am. Vets., Vietnam Vets. Am., Am. Legion. Home: 1445 W Cool Dr Tucson AZ 85704-2102 Office: Dept Vet Affairs VAMC BLDG 13/28 VR Tucson AZ 85723

BRIMMER, CLARENCE ADDISON, federal judge; b. Rawlins, Wyo., July 11, 1922; s. Clarence Addison and Geraldine (Zingsheim) B.; m. Emily O. Docken, Aug. 2, 1953; children: Geraldine Ann, Philip Andrew, Andrew Howard, Elizabeth Ann. B.A., U. Mich., 1944, J.D., 1947. Bar: Wyo. 1948. Pvt. practice law Rawlins, 1948-71, mcpl. judge, 1948-54; U.S. commr., magistrate, 1963-71; atty. gen. Wyo. Cheyenne, 1971-74; U.S. atty., 1975; chief judge U.S. Dist. Ct. Wyo., Cheyenne, 1975-92, dist. judge, 1975—; mem. panel multi-dist. litig., 1992—; mem. Jud. Conf. of U.S., 1995—, exec. com., 1995—. Sec. Rawlins Bd. Pub. Utilities, 1954-66, Wyo. Rep. Com., chmn., 1967-71, Rep. gubernatorial condidate, 1974; trustee Rocky Mountain Mineral Law Found., 1963-7 5. With USAAF, 1945-46. Mem. ABA, Wyo. Bar Assn., Am. Judicature Soc., Laramie County Bar Assn., Carbon County Bar Assn. Episcopalian. Clubs: Masons, Shriners. Office: US Dist Ct PO Box 985 Cheyenne WY 82003-0985

BRINDLEY, ROBERT E., food products executive; b. 1937. Student, Union Coll.; grad., Harvard Bus. Sch., 1979. Mktg. mgr. Union Carbide Corp., Danbury, Conn., 1958-75; area prodn. mgr. Hong Kong area Union Carbide Eastern, 1975-79, v.p. Hong Kong area, 1979-85; v.p., gen. mgr. electronics divsn. Union Carbide Corp., Danbury, Conn., 1985-87, retired, 1987; pres. Getz Bros & Co., Inc., San Francisco, 1987—. With USMC, 1960-66. Office: Getz Bros & Co Inc 150 Post St Ste 500 San Francisco CA 94108-4707

BRINK, GLEN ARTHUR, publisher, wholesaler; b. Boulder, Colo., Mar. 26, 1944; m. Gloria Jean Savage, 1979 (div. 1983); 1 child, Holly Francesca; m. Alice Lorraine O'Dell. BS in Applied Math., U. Colo., 1967, MS in Computer Sci., 1977. Statistician U. Colo. Med. Ctr., Denver, 1967-69; food mgr. K-Mart, Cheyenne, Wyo., 1971-72; computer cons. CIBAR, Colorado Springs, 1977-83; wholesaler The Radiant Expression, Colorado Springs, 1981—; pub. The Fly Fishing Catalog, Boulder, 1991—. Author: (booklets) The Bidding Apercu', 1977, Mail Order Multilevel Marketing, 1992, How to Get Anything You Want, 1993. With U.S. Army, Vietnam, 1969-70. Recipient Tipton scholarship U. Colo., 1962. Mem. Stars Edge Rsch., Wisdom Soc., Four Sigma, Sigma Tau. Office: The Fly Fishing Catalog PO Box 6101 Boulder CO 80306-6101

BRINKERHOFF, DERICKSEN MORGAN, art history educator; b. Phila., Oct. 4, 1921; s. Robert Joris and Marion (Butler) B.; m. Mary Dean Weston, Dec. 20, 1946; children: Derick W., Elizabeth, Jonathan D., Caroline. BA, Williams Coll., 1943; AM, Yale U., 1947; postgrad., U. Zurich, Switzerland, 1948-49; Ph.D., Harvard U., 1958. Teaching fellow Harvard U., 1949-50; instr. Brown U., 1952-55; assoc. prof., head history dept. R.I. Sch. Design, 1955-59, chmn. div. liberal arts, 1956-59; assoc. prof. Pa. State U., 1961-62, Tyler Sch. Art, Temple U., Phila., 1962-1965; chmn. dept. art U. Calif. Riverside, 1965-71, 80-85, prof., 1967—. Author monograph on classical and early medieval art; contbr. articles to profl. jours. Trustee Riverside Art Assn., 1968-72. Served with AUS, World War II. Recipient U. Calif. Humanities Inst. award, 1971-72; Summer fellow Belgian Am. Ednl. Found., 1959; sr. fellow classical studies Am. Acad. in Rome, 1959-61; Am. Philos. Soc. grantee, 1960-61. Mem. Archaeol. Inst. Am., Art Historians So. Calif. (pres. 1982-83), Coll. Art Assn. Am., Internat. Assn. Classical Archaeology. Home: 4985 Chicago Ave Riverside CA 92507-5859

BRINNER, WILLIAM MICHAEL, near eastern studies educator; b. Alameda, Calif., Oct. 6, 1924; s. Fred Kohn and Sadie (Weiser) B.; m. Lisa Johanna Kraus Brinner, Sept. 23, 1951; children: Benjamin E., Leyla A., Rafael J. BA, U. Calif., Berkeley, 1948, MA, 1950, PhD, 1956; DHL (hon.), Hebrew Union Coll., 1992. Asst. prof. U. Calif., Berkeley, 1957-61, assoc. prof., 1961-64, prof., 1964-91, prof. emeritus, 1991; vis. prof. U. San Francisco, 1985; prof. emeritus U. Wash., 1991; dir. Ctr. for Arabic Study Abroad, Cairo, Egypt, 1967-70, Study Ctr. U. Calif., Jerusalem, Israel, 1973-75; acting dir. Annenberg Rsch. Inst., Phila., 1992-93. Editor, translator: A Chronicle of Damascus, 2 vols., 1963; translator: An Elegant Composition Concerning Relief After Adversity, 1978 (Jewish Book Coun. award 1979), History of Al-Tabari vols. 2 and 3, 1987, 91; editor, contbr.: Studies in Islamic & Judaic Traditions 2 vols., 1986, 89. Commentator World Press Pub. Broadcasting, 1967-77; mem. Steering Com. World Affairs Coun., Oakland, Calif., 1979-82, Bd. Trustees Judah Magnes Mus., Berkeley, Calif., 1981-95; chmn. Steering Com. Bay Area Academic Consortium, San Francisco, 1989—. Guggenheim Fellowship Guggenheim Fdn., 1965-66. Mem. Am. Oriental Soc. (pres. 1976), Am. Acad. for Jewish Rsch. (exec. com. 1992—), Am. Hist. Assn., Middle East Studies Assn. (pres. 1970), Assn. for Jewish Studies (bd. dirs. 1986-92), Soc. for Judeo-Arabic Studies (bd. dirs. 1984—). Home: 753 Santa Barbara Rd Berkeley CA 94707 Office: U Calif Dept of Near Eastern Studies 250 Barrows Hall Berkeley CA 94720

BRINTON, BYRON CHARLES, publishing executive, editor; b. Fessenden, N.D., Jan. 28, 1912; s. Charles Mackay and Elizabeth Rose (Mueller) B.; m. Roberta Lee Wright, Sept. 14, 1935 (dec. Jan. 1993); children: Lynn Ann, Ross Burr, Byron Dorsy, Alice Kathleen, Greg Charles. Jr. cert. with honors, U. Oreg., 1933. Co-owner, co-editor Weekly North Powder News and Haines Record, Haines, Oreg., 1928-34; co-owner, co-editor Record-Courier, Baker City, Oreg., 1934-57, owner, 1957—, editor, 1934—; bd. dirs. Oreg. Geographic Names, Oreg. Trail Regional Mus.; pres., organizing exec. Anthony Lakes Ski Area Corp., 1961-64. Active Bonneville Adv. Bd., 1940—, Oreg. State Water Bd., 1958-59; com. sec. City of Baker Mgr. Charter Form Govt., 1950-57; co-founder, dir. Sumpter Valley R.R. Restoration, Baker City, 1980; sec. Hells Canyon Devel. Assn., Baker City, 1944—. With USN, 1944-46. Recipient Baker County Cattlemens Assn. Svc. plaque, 1993, Outstanding Svc. plaque Baker County Fair, 1993, Oreg. State Coll. Diamond Agr. Achievement Registry award, 1993; named Baker County Man of Yr., 1995. Mem. Baker County Mus. Commn., Oreg. Cattlemens Assn., Baker County Livestock Assn. (Outstanding Svc. plaque), Future Farmers Am. (hon.), Kiwanis (life), Powder River Sportsmens Club (life). Democrat. Baptist. Home: PO Box 70 2517 Valley Ave Baker City

OR 97814 Office: The Record Courier 1718 Main St Baker City OR 97814-3447

BRINTON, RICHARD KIRK, marketing executive; b. Hanover, Pa., Apr. 21, 1946; s. James Henry and Mabel (Adelung) B.; m. Joan Marita Ayo, Mar. 21, 1970; children: Katherine, Mark, Michael. BA in Liberal Arts, BS in Indsl. Engring., Pa. State U., 1968. Registered profl. engr., Ohio. From systems engr. to dir. mktg. AccuRay/ABB, Columbus, Ohio, 1968-82; group mktg. dir. AccuRay/ABB, London, 1982-84; internat. sales mgr. Flow Systems, Seattle, 1984, v.p. sales and mktg., 1985-87; dir. mktg. and bus. devel. UTILX Corp., Seattle, 1987-90, v.p. mktg. and bus. devel., 1990-93, v.p. internat. ops., 1993—; chmn. Nippon FlowMole, Tokyo, 1991-93. Mem. World Trade Club Seattle (bd. dirs. 1993-95). Home: 18137 149th Ave SE Renton WA 98058-9654 Office: UTILX Corp 22404 66th Ave S Kent WA 98032-4843

BRISBIN, ROBERT EDWARD, insurance agency executive; b. Bklyn., Feb. 13, 1946; m. Sally Ann Tobler-Norton. BSBA, San Fancisco State U., 1968. Cert. safety exec. Field rep. Index Research, San Mateo, Calif., 1969-82; mgr. loss control Homeland Ins. Co., San Jose, Calif., 1982-87; ins. exec. Morris and Dee Ins. Agy., San Luis Obispo, Calif., 1987—; prin., cons. Robert E. Brisbin & Assocs., Pismo Beach, Calif., 1972—; mgt. cons.; pres. Profl. Formulas Amino Acid Food Supplements, 1987-90. Author: Amino Acids, Vitamins and Fitness, 1986, Loss Control for the Small- to Medium-Sized Business, 1989, (with Carol Bayly Grant) Workplace Wellness, 1992; composer: Country Songs and Broken Dreams, 1978, America the Land of Liberty, 1980. Mem. Am. Soc. Safety Engrs., World Safety Orgn. (cert. safety exec.), UN Roster Safety Cons. Republican. Office: PO Box 341 Pismo Beach CA 93448-0341

BRISCOE, AGATHA DONATTO, data processing executive, instructor; b. Liberty, Tex., Feb. 21, 1947; d. Alton Peter and Audrey Mary (Broussard) Donatto; m. Edward Gans Briscoe, Jan. 23, 1976; 1 child, Allison Marie. BS in Math. summa cum laude, Tex. So. U., 1969; student, UCLA, 1967-68, 69-70. Cert. secondary tchr., Tex. Scientific programmer The Aerospace Corp., El Segundo, Calif., 1971-73; tech. staff TRW Def. and Space Systems Group, El Segundo, 1973-76; instr. data processing Hawaii C.C., Hilo, 1979-86; analyst, programmer Cayman Islands Govt., Grand Cayman, 1986-87; dir. mgmt. info. svcs. V.I. Dept. Health, St. Thomas, 1987-89; systems analyst V.I. Telephone Co., St. Thomas, 1989-90; sr. applications specialist InfoTech (Kapioloni Health Care Systems), Honolulu, 1990-93, new projects coord., 1993-95; sr. programmer/analyst Sutter Health, Sacramento, 1995—; pres. Hawaii Vocat. Assn., Hilo, 1983-85; coord. data processing program Hawaii C.C., Hilo, 1979-86. Supr. com. mem. Big Island Ednl. Fedn. Credit Union, Hilo, 1979-86; troop leader Girl Scouts Am., Hilo, 1984-85; cmty. rep. African-Am. adv. com. U. Hawaii, Manoa, 1994; vol. tutor, Honolulu, 1991—. Equipment grantee U. Hawaii Pres.'s Fund, Honolulu, 1985. Home: 2964 Bridlewood Dr Cameron Park CA 95682 Office: Sutter Health 2901 L St Sacramento CA

BRISCOE, BARBARA JUNE, nurse; b. Newark, Ohio, Nov. 20, 1938; d. Eugene Harvey Cooper and Eileen (Pierce) Roche; m. Robert William Briscoe, Feb. 4, 1961 (div. Feb. 1973); children: Michael Edward, Kimberly Anne. BSN, Ohio State U., 1960; MA in Psychology, Calif. Grad. Inst., 1981; M of Nursing, UCLA, 1992. Cert. nurse adminstr.; cert. clin. nurse specialist-adult psychiat. mental health. Sr. psychiatric nurse Fairview State Hosp., Costa Mesa, Calif., 1960-64; instr. Orange Coast Jr. Coll., Costa Mesa, Calif., 1964-65; head nurse, adminstrv. nurse II U. Calif. Med. Ctr., Orange, 1965-82, assoc. dir. nursing, 1982-85, clin. nurse specialist, 1985—; clin. faculty dept. psychiat. human behavior U. Calif. Irvine; part-time nursing faculty Cerretos Jr. Coll. Author: (chpt.) Contemporary Strategies in Nursing, 1986. Group leader Vital Options, L.A., 1990. Mem. Sigma Theta Tau. Presbyterian. Home: 20025 Baywood Ct Yorba Linda CA 92686-6761 Office: U Calif Med Ctr 101 The City Dr S Orange CA 92668-3201

BRISCOE, JOHN, lawyer; b. Stockton, Calif., July 1, 1948; s. John Lloyd and Doris (Olsen) B.; divorced; children: John Paul, Katherine. JD, U. San Francisco, 1972. Bar: Calif. 1972, U.S. Dist. Ct. (no. and ea. dists.) Calif. 1972, U.S. Supreme Ct. 1976. Dep. atty. gen. State of Calif., San Francisco, 1972-80; ptnr. Washburn and Kemp, San Francisco, 1980-88; ptnr. Washburn, Briscoe and McCarthy, San Francisco, 1988—, chmn., 1990-93; bd. dirs. San Francisco Bay Planning Coalition, 1982—; vis. scholar U. Calif., Berkeley, 1990—. Author: Surveying the Courtroom, 1984; editor: Reports of Special Masters, 1991; contbr. articles to profl. and lit. jours. Mem. ABA, San Francisco Bar Assn., Law of the Sea Inst. Roman Catholic. Office: Washburn Briscoe & McCarthy 55 Francisco St San Francisco CA 94133-2122

BRISTOW, JOHN TEMPLE, minister, writer; b. Dallas, Oreg., Aug. 20, 1945; s. Selden Temple and Helen Dorothy (Overholser) B.; m. Christy Clare Olson, Mar. 20, 1966; children: Sheila Gail, Erica Elizabeth. BTh, N.W. Christian Coll., 1967; MDiv, Lexington (Ky.) Theol. Sem., 1970, DMin, 1972. Ordained to min. Disciples of Christ Ch., 1970. Min. Bethany Christian Ch., Louisville, 1972-74, Lake City Christian Ch., Seattle, 1974-93, Murray Hills Christian Ch., Beaverton, Oreg., 1993—; adj. prof. Fuller Sem. Ext., Seattle, 1992; lectr. various chs. and colls., 1988—. Author: What Paul Really Said about Women, 1988, What the Bible Really Says about Love, Marriage and Family, 1994, (play) Tobit, 1977. Recipient award Excellence in Pub. Speaking, Am. Bible Soc., 1969. Home: 165 SE 33rd Ave Hillsboro OR 97123-7101 Office: Murray Hills Christian Ch PO Box 7096 Beaverton OR 97007-7096

BRITT, ANNE BAGG, geneticist; b. Bronxville, N.Y., Oct. 16, 1958; d. Thomas Graham and Joyce (Maynard) Bagg; m. Ralph David Britt, Sept. 6, 1986. SB, MIT, 1981; PhD, U. Calif., Berkeley, 1986. Postdoctoral rschr. dept. biol. scis. Stanford (Calif.) U., 1986-89; asst. rsch. geneticist sect. plant biology U. Calif., Davis, 1990-94, asst. prof., 1994—. Contbr. articles to sci. jours. NSF Eukaryotic Genetics grantee, 1991, NSF Nucleic Acids grantee, 1993, USDA grantee, 1994. Mem. Genetics Soc. Am., Am. Soc. Plant Physiologists. Office: U Calif Sect Plant Biology Davis CA 95616

BRITTAN, JOHN SCOTT, cultural exchange society executive; b. Bozeman, Mont., Mar. 12, 1921; s. Homer and Aurelia Brittan. BA, U. Mont., 1942; MA, UCLA, 1947. Instr. U. Nev., Reno, 1947-48, Glendale (Calif.) Coll., 1948-51; ind. ins. agt. Group Adminstrs. Pres., L.A., 1952-65; mgr., gen. agt., pres. Com. Nat. Securities Svc., L.A., 1966-73; pres. U.S. Cultural Exch. & Sports Soc., L.A., 1977-92, U.S. Cultural Exch. Soc., Thousand Oaks, Calif., 1993—. With USN, 1942-45. Ryman fellow U. Mont., 1942. Office: US Cultural Exch Soc 787 Woodlawn Dr Thousand Oaks CA 91360-2571

BRITTINGHAM, JAMES CALVIN, nuclear engineer; b. Hamlet, N.C., Apr. 6, 1942; s. James Calvin and Elizabeth (McCanless) B.; m. Margaret Kitchen, Feb. 12, 1978; 1 child, James Robert. BS in Nuclear Engring., N.C. State U., 1964, MS in Nuclear Engring., 1966; PhD in Nuclear Engring., U. Calif., Berkeley, 1975. Registered nuclear engr., Calif. Engr. Rockwell Internat., Canoga Park, Calif., 1975-80; engr. Pacific Gas and Electric, San Francisco, 1981-85; sr. consulting engr. Ariz. Pub. Svc., Phoenix, 1986—; assoc. faculty Ariz. State U., 1991-93. Contbr. articles to profl. jours. Recipient Talent for Svc. scholarship N.C. State U., 1960-63, AEC fellowship, 1964-66, NSF traineeship, 1967-69. Mem. Am. Nuclear Soc. Republican. Home: 3367 W Grandview Rd Phoenix AZ 85023-2953 Office: Palo Verde Nuclear Generation Sta Mail Sta 7693 5801 S Wintersburg Rd Tonopah AZ 85354-7529

BRITTO, CHARLOTTE MARY, dietitian, educator; b. Lafayette, La., Dec. 20, 1937; d. Charles R. and Hannah Jane (Fisk) Flack; m. Edward F. Schwyn, Sept. 15, 1962 (div. May 1987); m. John Britto, May 23, 1987; children: Kent, Kirk, Darren, Gilbert, Debbie. BS, Pa. State U., 1959; MS, Ohio State U., 1960. Registered dietitian. Supr. dietary Ohio State, Columbus, 1960-62; dietitian Ohio U., Athens, Ohio, 1962-64; univ. dietitian U. Pacific, Stockton, Calif., 1966-77; instr. San Joaquin Delta Coll., Stockton, Calif., 1979—; cons. dietitian Jene Wah, Stockton, Calif., 1993—; pres. Golden Empire Dietitic, Sacramento, 1979. Commr. Parks & Recreation, Stockton, 1976-87; vol. swim instr. Red Cross, Stockton, 1969-87. Recipient numerous grants Chancellor's Office, Sacramento, 1987-91. Mem. Coun. Hotel, Rest Inst. Educators, Am. Dietetic Assn., Nat. Restaurant Assn., Calif. Restaurant Assn. Republican. Roman Catholic. Home: 3148 W Swain Rd Stockton CA 95219-3911

BRITTON, THOMAS WARREN, JR., management consultant; b. Pawhuska, Okla., June 16, 1944; s. Thomas Warren and Helen Viola (Haynes) B.; BS in Mech. Engring., Okla. State U., 1966, MS in Indsl. Engring. and Mgmt., 1968; m. Jerlyn Kay Davis, 1964 (div. 1970); 1 child, Natalie Dawn; m. Deborah Ann Mansour, Oct. 20, 1973; 1 child, Kimberly Ann. Cons., Arthur Young & Co., Los Angeles, 1968-72, mgr., 1972-76, prin., 1976-79, ptnr., 1979—, office dir. mgmt. svcs. dept., Orange County, Calif., 1980-87; ptnr. West Region Mfg., 1987-88, Price Waterhouse; ptnr.-in-charge west coast mfg. cons. practice, Nat. Aerospace and Def. Industry, 1988-95; part-in-charge west coast products and supply chair practice, 1995—; lectr. in field. Mem. City of San Dimas Creative Growth Bd., 1976-77, chmn. planning commn., 1977-83; trustee World Affairs Council of Orange County, 1980; benefactor, founders com., v.p. ann. fund, pres., chair long range planning, trustee South Coast Repertory Theater; trustee Providence Speech and Hearing Ctr.; mem. devel. com. U. Calif.-Irvine Med. Sch.; chmn. Costa Mesa Arts Council. Served to capt. USAR, 1971-86. Cert. mgmt. cons. Mem. Los Angeles Inst. CPAs, Mgmt. Adv. Svcs. Com., Am. Prodn. and Inventory Control Soc., Am. Inst. Indsl. Engrs., Greater Irvine Indsl. League, Okla. State Alumni Assn., Kappa Sigma Alumni Assn. Clubs: Jonathan, Ridgeline Country, Santa Ana Country. Home: 18982 Wildwood Cir Villa Park CA 92667-3137

BRIXEY, LORETTA SANCHEZ, strategic management consultant; b. Lynwood, Calif., Jan. 7, 1960; d. Ignacio Sandoval and Maria Socorro (Macias) S.; m. Stephen Simmons, May 5, 1990. BS in Econs., Chapman U., 1982; MBA, Am. U., 1984. Spl. projects mgr. Orange County Transp. Authority, Santa Ana, Calif., 1984-87; asst. v.p. Fieldman, Rolapp & Assocs., Irvine, Calif., 1987-90; assoc. Booz, Allen & Hamilton, L.A., 1990-93; pres. Amiga Advisors, Inc., L.A., 1993—; cons. Migrant Workers Edn., Santa Ana, 1991—. Bd. dirs. Providence Speech and Hearing Ctr., Santa Ana, Calif.; Hispanic adv. coun. Pepperdine U., Malibu, Calif. Orange County Rotary Found. scholar, 1984. Mem. Nat. Soc. Hispanic MBAs (pres. L.A. chpt.), Dem. Found. Orange County. Roman Catholic. Office: Booz Allen & Hamilton Inc 523 W 6th St Ste 616 Los Angeles CA 90014-1224

BROAD, ELI, financial services executive; b. N.Y.C., June 6, 1933; s. Leon and Rebecca (Jacobson) B.; m. Edythe Lois Lawson, Dec. 19, 1954; children: Jeffrey Alan, Gary Stephen. BA in Acctg. cum laude, Mich. State U., 1954. CPA, Mich. 1956. Co-founder SunAmerica Inc. (formerly Kaufman & Broad, Inc.), L.A., 1957—; chmn. Sun Life Ins. Co. Am., Anchor Nat. Life Ins. Co., Balt., 1976—; chmn. exec. com. Kaufman and Broad Home Corp., L.A., 1986-93, 1993-95; chmn. Stanford Ranch Co.; co-owner Sacramento Kings and Arco Arena, 1992—; active Calif. Bus. Rountable, 1986—, Com. for Econ. Devel.; trustee Com. for Econ. Devel., 1993-95. Mem. bd. dirs. L.A. World Affairs Coun., 1988—, chmn., 1994—, DARE Am., 1989-95; founding trustee Windward Sch., Santa Monica, Calif., 1972-77; bd. trustees Pitzer Coll., Claremont, Calif., 1970-82, chmn. bd. trustees, 1973-79, life trustee, 1982—, Haifa U., Israel, 1972-80, Calif. State U., 1978-82, vice chmn. bd. trustees, 1979-80, trustee emeritus, 1982—, Mus. Contemporary Art, L.A., 1980-93, founding chmn., 1980, Archives Am. Art, Smithsonian Instn., Washington, 1985—, Am. Fedn. Arts, 1988-91, Leland Stanford Mansion Found., 1992—, Calif. Inst. Tech., 1993—; pres. Calif. Non-Partisan Vote Registration Found., 1971-72; chancellor's assoc. UCLA, 1971—, mem. vis. com. Grad. Sch. Mgmt., 1972-90, trustee UCLA Found., 1986—; assoc. chmn. United Crusade, L.A., 1973-76; chmn. Mayor's Housing Policy Com., L.A., 1974-75; del., spkr. Fed. Econ. Summit Conf., 1974, State Econ. Summit Conf., 1974; mem. contemporary coun. L.A. County Mus. Art, 1973-79, bd. trustees acquisitions com., 1978-81; bd. fellows, mem. exec. com. The Claremont (Calif.) Colls., 1974-79; nat. trustee Balt. Mus. Art, 1985-91; mem. adv. bd. Boy Scouts Am., 1982-85, L.A. Bus. Jour., 1986-88; mem. adv. coun. Town Hall of Calif., 1985-87; trustee Dem. Nat. Com. Victory Fund, 1988, 92; mem. painting and sculpture com. Whitney Mus., N.Y.C., 1987-89; chmn. adv. bd. ART/LA, 1989; bd. overseers The Music Ctr. of L.A. County, 1991-92; mem. contemporary art com. Harvard U. Art Mus., Cambridge, Mass., 1992—; mem. internat. dirs. coun. Guggenheim Mus., N.Y.C., 1993—; active Nat. Indsl. Pollution Control Coun., 1970-73, Maeght Found., St. Paul de Vence, France, 1975-80, Mayor's Spl. Adv. Com. on Fiscal Adminstrn., L.A., 1993-94. Recipient Man of Yr. award City of Hope, 1965, Golden Plate award Am. Acad. Achievement, 1971, Housting Man of Yr. award Nat. Housing Coun., 1979, Humanitarian award NCCJ, 1977, Am. Heritage award Anti Defamation League, 1984, Pub. Affairs awad Coro Found., 1987, Honors award visual arts L.A. Arts Coun., 1989; Eli Broad Coll. Bus. and Eli Broad Grad. Sch. Bus. named in his honor Mich. State U., 1991; knighted Chevalier in Nat. Order Legion of Honor, France, 1994. Mem. Beta Alpha Psi, Regency Club and Hillcrest Country Club (L.A.). Home: 75 Oakmont St Los Angeles CA 90049-1901 Office: SunAmerica Inc 1 SunAmerica Ctr Los Angeles CA 90067

BROADBENT, AMALIA SAYO CASTILLO, graphic arts designer; b. Manila, May 28, 1956; came to U.S., 1980, naturalized, 1985; d. Conrado Camilo and Eugenia de Guzman (Sayo) Castillo; m. Barrie Noel Broadbent, Mar. 14, 1981; children: Charles Noel Castillo, Chandra Noel Castillo. BFA, U. Santo Tomas, 1978; postgrad. Acad. Art Coll., San Francisco, Alliance Francaise, Manila, Karilagan Finishing Sch., Manila, Manila Computer Ctr.; BA, Maryknoll Coll., 1972. Designer market research Unicorp Export Inc., Makati, Manila, 1975-77; asst. advt. mgr. Dale Trading Corp., Makati, 1977-78; artist, designer, pub. relations Resort Hotels Corp., Makati, 1978-81; prodn. artist CYB/Young & Rubicam, San Francisco, 1981-82; freelance art dir. Ogilvy & Mather Direct, San Francisco, 1986; artist, designer, owner A.C. Broadbent Graphics, San Francisco, 1982—; faculty graphic design & advt. depts. Acad. Art Coll., San Francisco. Works include: Daing na Isda, 1975, (Christmas coloring) Pepsi-Cola, 1964 (Distinctive Merit cert.), (children's books) UNESCO, 1973 (cert.). Pres. Pax Romana, Coll. of Architecture and Fine Arts, U. Santo Tomas, 1976-78, chmn. cultural sect., 1975; v.p. Atelier Cultural Soc., U. Santo Tomas, 1975-76; mem. Makati Dance Troupe, 1973-74. Recipient Merit cert., Inst. Religion, 1977. Mem. NAFE, Alliance Francaise de San Francisco, Internat. Platform Assn., San Francisco Bus. & Profl. Women's Prayer Group. Roman Catholic.

BROADHEAD, RONALD FRIGON, petroleum geologist, geology educator; b. Racine, Wis., July 22, 1955; s. Ronald Leslie and Thereise (Frigon) B. BS, N.Mex. Tech. U., 1977; MS, U. Cin., 1979. Geologist, Cities Svc. Oil Co., Oklahoma City and Tulsa, 1979-81; sr. petroleum geologist, asst. dir. N.Mex. Bur. Mines, Socorro, 1981—, asst. dir., 1984—; mem. adj. faculty N.Mex. Tech. Coll., 1983—; mem. potential gas com. Potential Gas Agy. Union Oil Co. summer fellow Duke U. Marine Lab., 1977. Mem. Am. Assn. Petroleum Geologists (Ho. of Dels.), Soc. Econ. Paleontologists and Mineralogists, N.Mex. Geol. Soc., Roswell Geol. Soc., Four Corners Geol. Soc., West Tex. Geol. Soc., Sigma Xi. Office: NMex Bur Mines Campus Sta Socorro NM 87801

BROADHURST, NORMAN NEIL, foods company executive; b. Chico, Calif., Dec. 17, 1946; s. Frank Spencer and Dorothy Mae (Conrad) B.; BS, Calif. State U., 1969; MBA, Golden Gate U., 1975; m. Victoria Rose Thomson, Aug. 7, 1976; 1 child, Scott Andrew. With Del Monte Corp., San Francisco, 1969-76, product mgr., 1973-76; product mgr. Riviana Foods, Inc., div. Colgate Palmolive, Houston, 1976-78; new products brand devel. mgr. foods div. Coca Cola Co., Houston, 1978-79, brand mgr., 1979-82, mktg. dir., 1982-89, v.p. mktg. Beatrice Foods Co., Chgo., 1983-86; pres., COO Famous Amos Chocolate Chip Cookie Co., Torrance, Calif., 1986-88; corp. sr. v.p., gen. mgr. Kerr Group Inc., L.A., 1988-92, corp. sr. v.p., pres. Kerr Group Consumer Products, 1992-95; chmn. dir. Double Eagle Holdings, Inc., 1995—. Chmn. youth soccer program Cystic Fibrosis; pres., chmn. South Coast Symphony, 1985-88; vice chmn. Lit. Vol. Am., Inc., 1992—. Recipient Cystic Fibrosis Community Svcs. award, 1982; vice-chmn. bd. dirs. Literacy Vols. Am., Inc., 1987—. Mem. Am. Mgmt. Assn., Am. Mktg. Assn., Toastmasters Internat. (past chpt. pres.). Home: 5009 Queen Victoria Rd Woodland Hills CA 91364-4757 Office: Double Eagle Holdings Inc 19528 Ventura Blvd #420 Tarzana CA 91356

BROADLEY, HUGH T., art history educator; b. Sacramento, Calif., June 5, 1922; s. Harold S. and Isabella J. (Taylor) B.; m. Jean V. Brown, May 31, 1946; children: Hugh T., Jr., Mark A. AB, Park Coll., 1947; MA, Yale U., 1949; PhD, NYU, 1961. Mus. curator and lectr. Nat. Gallery of Art, Washington, 1954-61; asst. prof. art Bowling Green (Ohio) State U., 1961-65; curator Univ. Art Collections/assoc. prof. art Ariz. State U., Tempe, 1965-67, prof. art, 1969-88, prof. art emeritus, 1988, faculty assoc., 1992; dir. Phoenix Art Mus., 1967-69; mem. numerous acad. coms., including Fulbright-Hays screenin com., 1974-81, faculty senate, others. Contbr. articles to profl. jours. Vis. com. mem. Am. Assn. Mus., 1970—, sr. examiner, 1980—; adv. bd. Alliance of Ariz. Opera Guilds, 1968-78; mem. commn. Ariz. Gov.'s Ariz.-Mexico Commn., 1972-75; past treas. Ariz. Humanities Coun., 1973-79; numerous others. With U.S. Army, 1942-46. Mem. Am. Assn. Mus., Coll. Art Assn. Am., Internat. Coun. Mus., Phi Kappa Phi.

BROADWAY, NANCY RUTH, landscape design and construction company executive, consultant, model and actress; b. Memphis, Dec. 20, 1946; d. Charlie Sidney and Patsy Ruth (Meadows) Adkins. BS in Biology and Sociology cum laude, Memphis State U., 1969; postgrad., Tulane U., 1969-70; MS in Horticulture, U. Calif.-Davis, 1976. Lic. landscape contractor, Calif. Claims adjuster Mass. Mut. Ins., San Francisco, 1972-73; community garden coord. City of Davis, Calif., 1976; seed propagation supr. Bordier's Wholesale Nursery, Santa Ana, Calif., 1976-78; owner, founder Calif. Landscape Co., 1978-88, Design & Mgmt. Consultare, 1988—. Actress: Visions of Murder, 1993, Eyes of Terror, 1994. NDEA fellow Tulane U., 1969-70. Fellow Am. Hort. Soc.; mem. Nat. Assn. Gen. Contractors, Calif. Native Plant Soc., Stockton C. of C. Democrat. Home and Office: 220 Atlantic Ave Unit 112 Santa Cruz CA 95062-3800

BROCA, LAURENT ANTOINE, aerospace scientist; b. Arthez-de-Bearn, France, Nov. 30, 1928; came to U.S., 1957, naturalized, 1963; s. Paul L. and Paule Jeanne (Ferrand) B.; B.S. in Math., U. Bordeaux, France, 1949; Lic. es Scis. in Math. and Physics, U. Toulouse (France), 1957; grad. Inst. Technique Professionnel, France, 1960; Ph.D. in Elec. Engring., Calif. Western U., 1979; postgrad. Boston U., 1958, MIT, 1961, Harvard U., 1961; m. Leticia Garcia Guerra, Dec. 18, 1962; 1 dau., Marie-There Yvonne. Teaching fellow physics dept. Boston U., 1957-58; spl. instr. dept. physics N.J. Inst. Tech., Newark, 1959-60; sr. staff engr. advanced research group ITT, Nutley, N.J., 1959-60; examiner math. and phys. scis. univs. Paris (France) and Caen, Exam. Center, N.Y.C., 1959-69; sr. engr. surface radar div. Raytheon Co., Waltham, Mass., 1960-62, Hughes Aircraft Co., Culver City, Calif., 1962-64; asst. prof. math. Calif. State U., Northridge, 1963-64; prin. engr. astrionics lab. NASA, Huntsville, Ala., 1964-65; fellow engr. Def. and Space Center, Westinghouse Electric Corp., Balt., 1965-69; cons. and sci. adv. electronics, phys. scis. and math. to indsl. firms and broadcasting stations, 1969-80; head engring. dept. Videocraft Mfg. Co., Laredo, Tex., 1974-75; asst. prof. math. Laredo State U., summer, 1975; engring. specialist dept. systems performance analysis ITT Fed. Electric Corp., Vandenberg AFB, Calif., 1980-82; engring. mgr. Ford Aerospace and Communications Corp., Nellis AFB, Nev., 1982-84; engring. mgr. Arcata Assocs., Inc., North Las Vegas, Nev., 1984-85; sr. scientific specialist engring. and devel. EG&G Spl. Projects, Inc., Las Vegas, 1985—. Served with French Army, 1951-52. Recipient Published Paper award Hughes Aircraft Co., 1966; Fulbright scholar, 1957. Mem. IEEE, Am. Nuclear Soc. (vice chmn. Nev. sect. 1982-83, chmn. 1983-84), Am. Def. Preparedness Assn., Armed Forces Communications and Electronics Assn., Air Force Assn. Home: 5040 Lancaster Dr Las Vegas NV 89120-1445 Office: EG&G Spl Projects Inc PO Box 93747 Las Vegas NV 89193-3747

BROCCHINI, RONALD GENE, architect; b. Oakland, Calif., Nov. 6, 1929; s. Gino Mario and Yoli Louise (Lucchesi) B.; m. Myra Mossman, Feb. 3, 1957; 1 child, Christopher Ronald. B.A. in Architecture with honors, U. Calif., Berkeley, 1953, M.A. in Architecture with honors, 1957. Registered architect, Calif., Nev. Architect, designer SMP, Inc., San Francisco, 1948-53, designer, assoc., 1956-60; assoc. architect Campbell & Wong, San Francisco, 1961-63; prin. architect Ronald G. Brocchini, Berkeley, Calif., 1964-67, Worley K Wong & Ronald G Brocchini Assocs., San Francisco, 1968-87, Brocchini Architects, Oakland, Calif., 1987—; lectr. Calif. Coll. Arts and Crafts, Oakland, 1981-83; commr. Calif. Bd. Archtl. Examiners, 1961-89; mem. exam. com. Nat. Coun. Archtl. Registration Bds., 1983-85. Author: Long Range Master Plan for Bodega Marine Biology, U. Calif., 1982; prin. works include San Simeon Visitor Ctr., Hearst Castle, Calif., Mare Island Med.-Dental Facillity, IBM Ednl. and Data Processing Hdqrs., San Jose, Calif., Simpson Fine Arts Gallery, Calif. Coll. Arts, Ceramics and Metal Crafts, Emery Bay Pub. Market Complex, Analytical Measurement Facility, U. Calif., Berkeley, Bodega Marine Biology Campus, U. Calif., Berkeley, Fromm & Sichell (Christian Bros.) Hdqrs., The Nature Co., Corp. Offices, Berkeley, Merrill Coll., Athletic Facilities, U. Calif., Santa Cruz, Coll. III Housing, U. Calif., San Diego, Ctr. Pacific Rim Studies, U. San Francisco, married student housing Escondido II, III, IV, Stanford (Calif.) U. With U.S. Army, 1953-55. Recipient Bear of Yr. award U. Calif., Berkeley, 1987, Alumni Citation, 1988. Fellow AIA (bd. dirs. Calif. coun., pres. San Francisco chpt. 1982); mem. Bear Backers Club (bd. dirs. U. Calif.-Berkeley athletic coun.), Berkeley Breakfast Club (bd. govs.), Order of the Golden Bear, Chi Alpha Kappa. Republican. Roman Catholic. Office: Brocchini Architects Inc 407-49th St Oakland CA 94609

BROCE, DOROTHY DIANE, real estate broker, interior designer; b. Liberal, Kans., Jan. 25, 1933; d. Howard Clark and Emogene (Davis) Nash; m. Ray C. Broce, Nov. 30, 1963 (div. Dec. 1971); 1 child, Kimberly Tesitor Van Wormer. Student, Pomona Coll., 1951. Owner Diane's Interiors, Dodge City, Kans., 1959—, Cuchara, Colo.; broker Spoon River Real Estate, Cuchara, 1975—; pub. rels. cons. McCall's Mag., Congress for Better Living, N.Y.C. and Washington, 1959. Reader radio Sun Sounds for the Blind, Tucson, 1993-94; pres. Cuchara Assn., 1995-94; deaconess Presbyn. Ch., 1970; active PEO Women's Ednl. Orgn. Mem. Am. Soc. Interior Designs (allied mem.). Home: 574 Community Rd Cuchara CO 81055 Office: Dianes Interiors 3900 E Alvernon Cir Tucson AZ 85718-2402

BROCK, JAMES MELMUTH, engineer, futurist; b. Brockton, Mass., Jan. 12, 1944; s. James Melmuth and Ruth Eleanor (Copeland) B.; student U. Hawaii, 1964-65, 1982, Taiwan Normal U., 1969; m. Mary Soong, June 24, 1964; 1 dau., Cynthia. Survey apprentice Malcolm Shaw, Hanson, Mass., 1959-62; with Peace Corps, N. Borneo, 1962-64; engr. Austin, Smith & Assocs., Honolulu, 1964-65, Trans-Asia Engrs., Vietnam, 1965-67; ops. mgr. Teledyne, Bangkok, Thailand, 1967-69; chief surveys Norman Saito Engrs. Hawaii, 1970-73; sr. prin. Brock and Assocs., Maui, Hawaii, 1973-82; pres. Honolulu Cons. Group, Honolulu, 1982-88; dir. Koolau Brewery, Inc., 1985-88; pres., dir. First Pacific Capital, Inc., 1984-88; v.p., dir., ceo, Seaculture Inc., 1988-90; prin. ECM, Inc., 1989-92; v.p., dir., and ceo, USA-China Tech. Corp., 1992—; Del. White House Conf. Small Bus., 1980, 86. Registered land surveyor, Hawaii, registered profl. engr.; mem. NSPE, ASCE, World Futures Studies Fedn. Address: PO Box 4586 Honolulu HI 96812-4586

BROCK, JAMES WILSON, drama educator, playwright, researcher; b. Greensfork, Ind., May 23, 1919; s. Virgil Prentiss and Blanche (Kerr) B.; m. Martha Faught, June 1942 (div. Mar. 1956); m. Patricia Anne Clemons, Mar. 1956 (div. Nov. 1966); children: Lisa Anne, Tamsen Lee, Julie Michele; m. Marjorie Mellor, Feb. 1, 1969. AB, Manchester Coll., 1941; MA, Northwestern U., 1942, PhD, 1950. Assoc. prof. Albion (Mich.) Coll., 1946-56; asst. prof. Mich. State U., East Lansing, 1956-57, U. Mich., Ann Arbor, 1957-58; assoc. prof. Fla. State U., Tallahassee, 1958-59; prof. Calif. State U., Northridge, 1959-89; mng. dir. Plymouth (Mass.) Drama Festival, 1956-58. Author: (plays) Modern Chancel Dramas, 1964, (musical dance drama) The Summons, 1964; contbr. articles to profl. jours. Sgt. USAAF, 1942-45, Middle East, ETO. Decorated Bronze Star; fellow Ch. Soc. for Coll. Work, Eng., 1964; rsch. grantee Calif. State U. Found., 1964, 66, 67. Mem. Am. Soc. for Theatre Rsch., Nat. Theatre Conf., Theta Alpha Phi (sec.-treas. 1952-57), Delta Sigma Rho. Democrat. Episcopalian. Home: 55 E 700 S Apt 51 Saint George UT 84770-3915

BROCKE, STEFAN, physician, researcher; b. Essen, Germany, Sept. 10, 1958; came to U.S., 1990; s. D. and R. Brocke; m. Lihi Brocke, Nov. 2, 1963;

1 child, Maya. MD, Free U., Berlin, 1985. Scientist Free U., Berlin, 1985-86, resident, 1989-90; postdoctoral fellow in neurology Stanford (Calif.) U., 1990—; vis. scientist Weizmann Inst. of Sci., Rehovot, Israel, 1986-88. Contbr. articles to profl. jours. Mem. German State Bd. Physicians, Berlin State Bd. Physicians, German Immunol. Soc. Home: 15 Kent Pl Menlo Park CA 94025-3547 Office: Stanford U Med Ctr Dept Neurology Stanford CA 94305

BROCKERT, JOHN EARL, state official; b. Madison, Wis., Feb. 11, 1934; s. Claude O. and Geneva C. (Smith) B.; m. Mary O'Connor, May 19, 1962; children: Mary C., Chris S. BS, Ariz. State U., 1956; MS, U. Idaho, 1958; MPH, U. Calif., 1965. Clk. unemployment ins. claims Ariz. Dept. Employment Security, Casa Grande, 1958-59; survey field mgr. Ariz. Dept. Employment Security, Phoenix, 1959; statistican vital records Ariz. Dept. Pub. Health, Phoenix, 1960; statistician health statistics Alaska Dept. Health & Welfare, Juneau, 1960-64; statistician vital records Calif. Dept. Pub. Health, Sacramento, 1965-66, statistician, cons., 1966-67, asst. dir. vital records, 1968-69; dir. vital records and health statistics Utah Dept. of Health, Salt Lake City, 1969—. Commr. Not-Too Serious Softball League, Salt Lake City, 1972-92; mgr. beverage booths Carmelite Fair, Salt Lake City, 1974—; mem. Nat. Com. for Vital Records and Health Statistics, Washington, 1979-82; chair birth cert. sub-com. Panel to Revise U.S. Standard Ctrs., Washington, 1983-86. Fellow Am. Pub. Health Assn. (sect. rep. 1965—, Disting. Svc. award 1985); mem. Utah Pub. Health Assn. (pres. 1972-74, Betty award 1987), Utah Child Abuse and Neglect Coun. (chair, trust com. 1986—, Recognition Cert. 1989), Assn. Vital Records and Health Stattistics (pres. 1978-80, Halbert Dunn award 1988), Hibernian Soc. (founding mem., trustee, pres. 1982-83, chair 1st st. Patrick's day parade 1979, Grand marshall parade 1985, Hibernian of Yr. award 1984), Friends of St. Joseph's Villa (chair 1990—). Home: 2183 Evergreen Ave Salt Lake City UT 84109-2940 Office: Utah Dept Health Bur Vital Records PO Box 16700 Salt Lake City UT 84116

BROCKMEIER, ALAN LEE, protective services official; b. Freeport, Ill., July 7, 1948; s. Lowell Lee and Barbara Jean (Lang) B.; m. LaQuane L. Kilpatrick, July 12, 1969 (div. Jan. 1987); 1 child, Deedra Michelle; m. Suzanne L. Carroll, July 8, 1994. AS in Criminal Justice, Ea. N.Mex., 1987. Cert. command N.Mex. Law Enforcement Acad. Patrolman N.Mex. State Police, Clovis, 1969-78, sgt., 1978-85, lt., 1985-93; capt. N.Mex. State Police, Tucumcari, N.Mex., 1994—; instr. Ea. N.Mex. U., Clovis, 1984-90, Clovis C.C., 1990-93, adv. bd. law enforcement, 1992-94; acad. instr., Santa Fe, 1974—. Instr. ARC, Clovis; mem. Clovis Safety Com., Pleasent Hill (N.Mex.) Fire Dept.; EMT instr., N.Mex. (Outstanding EMT award 1984). Mem. Am. Assn. State Troopers. Republican. Episcopalian. Office: NMex State Police PO Box 646 Tucumcari NM 88401

BRODERICK, DONALD LELAND, electronics engineer; b. Chico, Calif., Jan. 5, 1928; s. Leland Louis and Vera Marguerite (Carey) B.; m. Constance Margaret Lattin, Sept. 29, 1957; children: Craig, Eileen, Lynn. BSEE, U. Calif., Berkeley, 1950; postgrad., Stanford U., 1953-54. Jr. engr. Boeing Co., Seattle, 1950-52; design engr. Hewlett-Packard Co., Palo Alto, Calif., 1952-59; sr. staff engr. Ampex Computer Products, Culver City, Calif., 1959-60; dir. engring. Kauke & Co., Santa Monica, Calif., 1960-61; program mgr. Space Gen. Corp., El Monte, Calif., 1961-68, Aerojet Electronics Div., Azusa, Calif., 1968-89; prin. D.L. Broderick, Arcadia, Calif., 1989—. Contbr. articles to profl. jours. Mem. Jr. C. of C., Woodland Hills, Cailf., 1963-64. With USN, 1945-46. Fellow Inst. for Advancement of Engring.; mem IEEE (chmn. profl. group on audio 1955-59, mem. exec. com. San Francisco sect. 1957-59, chmn. San Gabriel Valley sect. 1964-71, chmn. sects. com. L.A. coun. 1971-72, chmn. L.A. coun. 1972-76, chmn. bd. WESCON conv. 1976-80, bd. dirs. IEEE Electronics Conv. Inc. 1981-84, 1995—, Centennial medal 1984), AIAA (sec. L.A. sect. 1986-88, sec. nat. tech. com. on command control comm. and intelligence, Washington, 1985-89, chmn. devel. com. L.A. coun. 1986-94). Home: 519 E La Sierra Dr Arcadia CA 91006-4321

BRODERICK, GLEN REID, engineer, consultant; b. Delta, Utah, Aug. 14, 1943; s. Cloy Lenord and Anna (Mortensen) B.; m. Mary (div. Oct. 1970); m. Liwliwa Bradago Manuel, Nov. 2, 1970; 1 child, Reid M. BS in Bus. Adminstrn., U. Redlands, 1983; MS in Telecommunications Mgmt., Golden Gate U., 1986. Test engr. GTE, Northlake, Ill., 1969-76; staff engr. GTE, Thousand Oaks, Calif., 1976-82; sr. planning analyst GTE, Thousand Oaks, 1982-86, mktg. product mgr., 1986-90; cons. engr. Infonet, El Segundo, Calif., 1990—. Coach Conejo Valley Little League, Thousand Oaks, 1985-90. Sgt. USAF, 1965-68. Latter Day Saints.

BRODERICK, HAROLD CHRISTIAN, interior designer; b. Oakland, Calif., Apr. 8, 1925; s. Harold Christian and Laura Jane (Lloyd) B. BA, U. Tex., 1947. A founder Arthur Elrod Assos., Inc., Palm Springs, Calif., 1954, now pres.; bd. dirs. The Living Desert. Mem. Planning Commn., City of Palm Springs, 1972-74; trust Palm Springs Desert Mus.; mem. devel. com. Barbara Sinatra Children's Ctr. Mem. Am. Soc. Interior Designers. Republican. Office: Arthur Elrod Assocs Inc PO Box 2890 Palm Springs CA 92263-2890

BRODERICK, JON PALMER, geologist, mining company executive; b. Sheboygan, Wis., Dec. 23, 1941; s. John James Broderick and Viola Madelaine (Maigret) Walsh; m. Margaret Carol Bobo, June 7, 1969 (div. Mar. 15, 1995); children: Amy Erin, Cristopher Kelly, Jeffry Palmer. BSc, Union Coll., Schenectady, N.Y., 1964; MSc, U. Ariz., 1967. Cert. profl. geologist. Exploration geologist The Hanna Mining Co., various locations, 1966-69; sr. geologist NL Industries, Inc., various locations, 1969-78, Labrador Mining & Exploration, various locations, 1978-85; cons. geologist Reno, Nev., 1985-92; pres. Silver Eagle Resources Ltd., Reno, 1992—; dir. Silver Eagle Resources Ltd., Vancouver, B.C., Reno, Reese River Resources, Inc., Battle Mountain, Nev.; dir., pres. Exploration Mgmt. Svcs., Inc., Reno, 1990—. Fellow Soc. Econ. Geologists; mem. Am. Assn. Petroleum Geologists, Am. Inst. Profl. Geologists, Geol. Soc. Nev. (membership chair 1984-85, v.p. 1985, pres. 1985-86), Assn. Exploration Geochemists (organizing com. and treas. Reno Symposium 1983-85), Reno C. of C. Office: Silver Eagle Resources Ltd PO Box 71569 Reno NV 89570

BRODIE, HOWARD, artist; b. Oakland, Calif., Nov. 28, 1915; s. Edward and Anna (Zeller) B. Student, Art Inst. San Francisco, Art Student's League, N.Y.C., U. Ghana, Accra; LHD (hon.), Acad. Art Coll., San Francisco, 1984. Mem. staff Life mag., Yank: the Army Weekly, Collier's, AP, CBS News, 1969-89; freelance artist, journalist, 1990—. Author: (book) Howard Brodie War Drawings, 1963; art journalist: (major wars) World War II, Korea, French Indo-China, Vietnam, (trials) Jack Ruby, Ray, Sirhan, My Lai, Charles Manson, Chicago Seven, Watergate, John Hinckley, Klaus Barbie of France, (famous people) John Wayne, Pres. Kennedy, James Jones; art at White House, 1946, 48; work represented in permanent collections Calif. Palace of the Legion Hon., San Francisco, Soc. Illustrators, N.Y., Libr. Congress, Washington, Air Force Acad., Colo.; prints, books: U.S. Army Infantry Mus., Ft. Benning, Ga., U.S. Army Mus., Presidio, Monterery, Oreg. Nat. Mil. Mus., The Hoover Instn. on War, Revolution and Peace, Anne S.K. Brown Mil. Collection Brown U. Libr., The Mus. of Books, Lenin Libr., Moscow, Gorky Sci. Libr., Moscow State U., Admiral Nimitz State Hist. Pk., Tex., Henry E. Huntington Libr. (award), San Marina, New Britain Mus. Am. Art, Conn., West Point Libr., N.Y., Brown U. Libr., R.I.; guest on Merv Griffin Show, Charles Kuralt Sunday Morning program, Ted Koppel program, Night Line; featured Andy Rooney CBS Sunday Morning program. Sgt., U.S. Army. Decorated Bronze Star; recipient honor medals Freedom Found., 1957, 58, 60, 61.

BRODSKY, BART LOU, publisher; b. Toledo, Ohio, Nov. 3, 1949; s. Robert L. and Anne M. (Shoched) B.; m. Janet E. Geis, Feb. 14, 1985; 1 child, Audrey Lane Geis. BA, U. Calif., Berkeley, 1974. Exec. dir. Community Resource Inst., Berkeley, 1973—; founder, pub. Open Exch. Mag., Berkeley, 1974—. Author: The Teaching Marketplace, 1991, Finding Your Niche...Marketing Your Professional Service, 1992. Office: Open Exch Mag 1442-A Walnut # 51 Berkeley CA 94709-1405

BRODSKY, JAY BARRY, medical educator; b. N.Y.C., Nov. 11, 1946; s. Irving and Ann (Sapir) B.; m. Solveg Jensen, Aug. 12, 1973; children: Sonja Brodsky, Noah Brodsky. BS, CCNY, 1967; MD, Upstate Med. Ctr., Syracuse, N.Y., 1971. Diplomate Am. Bd. Anesthesiology. Asst. prof. Stanford U. Sch. Medicine, Stanford, Calif., 1977-82; assoc. prof. Stanford U. Sch. Medicine, Stanford, 1982-88, prof., 1988—; bd. dirs. Interplast, Inc., Palo Alto, 1984-86. Editor: (books) Oxygen--a Drug, The Pregnant Surgical Patient, Thoracic Anesthesia; contbr. 80 articles to profl. jours.; author 20 book chpts. Maj. U.S. Army, 1975-77. Mem. Am. Soc. Anesthesiologists, Calif. Soc. Anesthesiologists, Internat. Anesthesia Rsch. Soc., Assn. Univ. Anesthesiologists. Jewish. Home: 852 Pine Hill Rd Stanford CA 94305-1018 Office: Dept Anesthesia Stanford U Med Ctr Stanford CA 94305

BRODY, ARTHUR, industrial executive; b. Newark, June 30, 1920; s. Samuel A. and Ruth (Marder) B.; m. Sophie Mark, Mar. 5, 1944; children: Janice, Donald. Student, Columbia U., 1939-42. Organizer, operator Library Service, 1940-42; exec. buyer L. Bamberger & Co., Newark, 1942-43; chmn. Brodart Co., Williamsport, Pa., 1946—, BDI Investment Corp., San Diego, Tura Inc., Lake Success, N.Y.; past mem. adv. panel study on librs. and industry Nat. Adv. Com. on Librs.; past pres. Friends of N.J. Librs. Past trustee Newark Symphony Hall., Ctr. for Book, Libr. of Congress, L.A. County Libr. Found., Friends of Libr. USA, San Diego Community Found.; past commr. San Diego Pub. Libr. With AUS, 1943-46. Mem. ALA, NEA, Green Brook Country Club, San Diego Yacht Club, Rancho Sante Fe Golf Club, Masons, Shriners. Office: Brodart Co 990 Highland Dr Ste 100 Solana Beach CA 92075-2409

BRODY, ARTHUR WILLIAM, artist, educator; b. N.Y.C., Mar. 2, 1943; s. Joshua and Evelyn Charlotte (Edelberg) B.; m. Anne Loring Sullivan, Aug. 1964 (dec. Feb. 1968); m. Bonnie Ann Mechlowe, June 22, 1969. BS, Harvey Mudd Coll., 1965; MFA, Claremont Grad. Sch., 1967. Instr. U. Alaska, Fairbanks, 1967-69, from asst. to assoc. prof., 1977-83, prof., 1985—; from instr. to asst. prof. Ripon (Wis.) Coll., 1970-75; prof. Ea. Conn. State Univ., Willimantic, Conn., 1990-91; vis. prof. Harvey Mudd Coll., Claremont, Calif., 1983-84; lectr. Scripps Coll., Claremont, 1983-84. Author (computer program) Edpaint, 1986, Merge 1987, Print 1988, Scoot 28, Merge 28, 1989. Individual Artist grantee Alaska State Arts Council, 1985. Mem. Fairbanks Art Assn. (bd. dirs. 1985—), Coll. Art Assn., The Print Club, N.W. Print Coun., L.A. Printmakers. Home: 1650 Black Sand Rd Fairbanks AK 99712-2057 Office: U Alaska Art Dept Fine Arts Complex Fairbanks AK 99775-5640

BRODY, JACOB JEROME, art history educator; b. Bklyn., Apr. 24, 1929; s. Aladar and Esther (Kraiman) B.; m. Jean Lindsey, Feb. 13, 1956; children: Jefferson, Jonathan, Allison. Cert. fine arts, Cooper Union, 1950; B.A., U. N.Mex., 1956, M.A., 1964, Ph.D., 1970. Curator of art Everhart Mus., Scranton, Pa., 1957-58; curator collections Isaac Delgado Mus. Art, New Orleans, 1958-60; Mus. Internat. Folk Art, Santa Fe, 1960-61; prof. anthropology U. N.Mex., 1965-85, prof. art history, 1972-89; prof. emeritus, 1989—; curator Maxwell Mus., U. N.Mex., Albuquerque, 1962-72; dir. Maxwell Mus., U. N.Mex., 1972-85; mem. adv. bd. Ghost Ranch Mus., N.Mex. Mus. Natural History, 1981-84, Wheelwright Mus. of the Am. Indian, 1989-92, Zuni Pueblo Mus., 1992—; rsch. curator Maxwell Mus., Sch. of Am. Rsch., Lab. of Anthropology; mem. fine arts bd. City of Albuquerque, vice chmn., 1970-74; mem. Gov. N.Mex. Task Force Paleontol. Resources, 1978-79. Author: Indian Painters and White Patrons, 1971, Mimbres Painted Pottery, 1977, Between Traditions, 1977, Yazz: Navajo Painter, 1982, The Chaco Phenomenon, 1983, The Anasazi, 1990, Beauty From the Earth, 1990, Anasazi and Pueblo Painting, 1991. Recipient Tom L. Popejoy Dissertation award U. N.Mex., 1970, Gov.'s award of honor N.Mex. Hist. Com., 1978; Non-Fiction award Border-Regional Library Assn., 1972; Art Book award, 1979; resident scholar Sch. Am. Research, 1980-81; honoree Archeol. Soc. N.Mex., 1990. Mem. Am. Assn. Museums, Soc. Am. Archaeology, Council Mus. Anthropology, N.Mex. Mus. Assn.

BRODY-WATTS, STELLA, nurse; b. Athens, Greece, Oct. 15, 1939; came to U.S., 1965; d. Isaac Leon and Alice (Levy) Leontsini; m. William Brody, June 11, 1963 (div. 1977); children: Suzanne, David, Alexia; m. Dan Pike Watts III, Nov. 19, 1977. AA in Nursing, El Camino Coll., Torrance, Calif., 1974. RN, Calif. Operating room nurse Bay Harbor Hosp., Lomita, Calif., 1974-76, Kaiser Hosp., Harbor City, Calif., 1976-78, Dr. Sheldon Thorrens, Torrance, 1978-79, Long Beach (Calif.) Meml. Hosp., 1979-85; recreational nurse Am. Travel Cons., Redondo Beach, Calif., 1985-89; pres. Lela Tours, Inc., Redondo Beach, 1990—; part time nurse South Bay Hosp., Redondo Beach, 1989—. Editor newsletter South Bay Women in Travel, 1988—. Mem. Assn. Oper. Rm. Nurses (editor newsletter South Bay chpt., pres. 1982-83), Opera Guild So. Calif. (bd. dirs. 1989—). Democrat. Jewish. Home: 513 Via La Selva Redondo Beach CA 90277-6506 Office: Lela Tours Inc 757 Deep Valley Dr Rolling Hills Estates CA 90274

BROER, ROGER L., artist; b. Omaha, Nov. 9, 1945; s. Ludwig and Frieda B.; m. Merlene Julie Good, May 31, 1970; children: Juli Jyll, Zame Stockton. BA, Ea. Mont. Coll., 1974; postgrad., Cen. Wash. U., 1974-76. Artist in residence Alaska Arts Artist in the Schs., various towns, 1978-81, Wash. State Arts, 6 schs. in Wash., 1985-89; artist in the prisons, Wash. State Arts, 4 prisons in Wash., 1987-91; lectr. in field. One man and group shows throughout the U.S., Can. and Europe. Mem. Oglala Sioux tribe. With USAF, 1964-68. Over 25 nat. and internat. awards. Mem. Dream Catchers Artist Guild. Office: PO Box 6412 Kent WA 98064-6412

BROESAMLE, JOHN JOSEPH, history educator; b. Long Beach, Calif., Feb. 10, 1941; s. Otto Albert and Josephine (Young) B.; m. Katharine Sue Warne, June 12, 1963; children: Carolyn Jo, Robert Alan. BA, U. of the Pacific, Stockton, Calif., 1964; MA, Columbia U., 1965, PhD, 1970. Prof. history Calif. State U., Northridge, 1968—. Author: William Gibbs McAdoo 1863-1917, 1973, Reform and Reaction in 20th Century American Politics, 1990, Suddenly a Giant, 1993. Coord. Growth Control Initiative, Thousand Oaks, Calif., 1979-80; vol. reading tutor Ojai (Calif.) Unified Sch. Dist., 1993—; exec. com. mem. Ojai Valley Land Conservancy, 1994—; active Dem., 1968—. Woodrow Wilson fellow, 1964-65, Woodrow Wilson Dissertation fellow, 1966-67; Columbia U. fellow, 1965-67. Mem. AAUP, Am. Hist. Assn., Orgn. Am. Historians, Acad. Polit. Sci., Nat. Parks and Conservation Assn., Danforth Assn., Phi Kappa Phi. Home: 3945 Thacher Rd Ojai CA 93023-9368 Office: Calif State U Northridge Dept History 18111 Nordhoff St Northridge CA 91330-0001

BROGAN, MAURICE KENNETH, visual media consultant, photographer; b. Dinuba, Calif., Nov. 23, 1954; s. Maurice K. and Dama Day (Hill) B. BFA, Calif. Inst. Arts, 1983. Photographer Stubbings Studio, Lancaster, Calif., 1976-79; photographic printer Spectra Am., Sun Valley, Calif., 1983-84; reproduction, duplication tchr. Alexander & Ishara Color Lab., L.A., 1984-89; video & film archiving Cosgrove Meurer Prod., L.A., 1989—. With photographic intelligence U.S. Navy, 1972-76. Home: 1412 N Kingsley Dr Apt 307 Hollywood CA 90027-5759 Office: Cosgrove Meurer Prod 3255 Cahuenga Blvd W Los Angeles CA 90068-1375

BROGDEN, STEPHEN RICHARD, library administrator; b. Des Moines, Sept. 26, 1948; s. Paul M. and Marjorie (Kueck) B.; m. Melinda L. Raine, Jan. 1, 1983; 1 child, Nathan. BA, U. Iowa, 1970, MA, 1972. Caretaker Eya Fechin Branham Ranch, Taos, N.Mex., 1970-72; dir. Harwood Found. U. N.Mex., Taos, 1972-75; vis. lectr. U. Ariz., Tucson, 1975-76; rd. mgr. Bill and Bonnie Hearne, Austin, Tex., 1976-79; head fine arts Pub. Libr. Des Moines, 1980-90; dep. dir. Thousand Oaks (Calif.) Libr., 1990—. Author book revs., Annals of Iowa, 1980; columnist Taos News, 1973. Mem. Am. Libr. Assn., Calif. Libr. Assn., Films for Iowa Librs. (pres. 1983-86), Metro Des Moines Libr. Assn. (pres. 1980). Office: Thousand Oaks Libr 1401 E Janss Rd Thousand Oaks CA 91360

BROGLIATTI, BARBARA SPENCER, television and motion picture executive; b. L.A., Jan. 8, 1946; d. Robert and Lottie (Goldstein) Spencer; m. Raymond Haley Brogliatti, Sept. 19, 1970. BA in Social Scis. and English, UCLA, 1968. Asst. press. info. dept. CBS TV, L.A., 1968-69, sr. publicist, 1969-74; dir. publicity Tandem Prodns. and T.A.T. Comm. (Embassy Comm.), L.A., 1974-77, corp. v.p., 1977-82, sr. v.p. worldwide publicity, promotion and advt. Embassy Comm., L.A., 1982-85; sr. v.p. worldwide corp. comm. Lorimar Telepictures Corp., Culver City, Calif., 1985-89; pres., chmn. Brogliatti Co., Burbank, Calif., 1989-90; sr. v.p. worldwide TV publicity, promotion and advt. Lorimar TV, 1991-92; sr. v.p. worldwide TV publicity, promotion and pub. rels. Warner Bros. Inc., Burbank, 1992—. Mem. bd. govs. TV Acad., L.A., 1984-86; bd. dirs. KIDSNET, Washington, 1987—, Nat. Acad. Cable Programming, 1992-94; vice chmn. awards com. TV Acad.; mem. Hollywood Women's Polit. Com., 1992-93. Recipient Gold medallion Broadcast Promotion and Mktg. Execs., 1984. Mem. Am. Diabetes Assn. (bd. dirs. L.A. chpt. 1992-93), Am. Cinema Found. (mem. bd. dirs. 1994—), Dirs. Guild Am., Publicists Guild, Acad. TV Arts and Scis. (vice chmn. awards com.). Office: Warner Bros Studios 4000 Warner Blvd Ste 1057 Burbank CA 91552

BROKAW, NORMAN ROBERT, talent agency executive; b. N.Y.C., Apr. 21, 1927; s. Isadore David and Marie (Hyde) B.; children—David M., Sanford Jay, Joel S., Barbara M., Wendy E., Lauren Quincy. Student pvt. schs., Los Angeles. With William Morris Agy., Inc., Beverly Hills, Calif., 1943—, sr. agt. and co. exec., 1951-74, v.p. world-wide ops., 1974-80, exec. v.p., dir., 1980—, co-chmn. bd., 1986-91, pres., CEO, 1989-91, chmn. bd., CEO, 1991—. Pres. Betty Ford Cancer Center, Cedars-Sinai Med. Center, Los Angeles, 1978—; bd. dirs. Cedars-Sinai Med. Center; industry chmn. United Jewish Welfare Fund, 1975. With U.S. Army, World War II. Mem. Acad. Motion Picture Arts and Scis. Clubs: Hillcrest Country (Los Angeles). Home: 710 N Alta Dr Beverly Hills CA 90210-3506 Office: William Morris Agy 151 El Camino Dr Beverly Hills CA 90212-2704 also: William Morris Agy Inc 1325 Avenue Of The Americas New York NY 10019-4701

BROM, LIBOR, journalist, educator; b. Ostrava, Czechoslovakia, Dec. 17, 1923; came to U.S., 1958, naturalized, 1964; s. Ladislav and Bozena (Bromova) B.; m. Gloria S. Mena, Aug. 31, 1961; 1 son, Rafael Brom. Ing., Czech Inst. Tech., 1948; JUC, Charles U. Prague, 1951; postgrad., San Francisco State Coll.; MA, U. Colo., 1962, PhD, 1970. V.p. Brom, Inc., Ostrava, 1942-48; economist Slovak Magnesite Works, Prague, Czechoslovakia, 1948-49; economist, chief planner Vodostavba, Navika, Prague, 1951-56; tchr. Jefferson County Schs., Colo., 1958-67; prof., dir. Russian area studies program U. Denver, 1967-91, prof. emeritus, 1992—; journalist, mem. editorial staff Denni Hlasatel-Daily Herald, Chgo., 1978-92; editorial staff Jour. of Interdisciplinary Studies, 1988—; Pres. Colo. Nationalities Council, 1970-72; comptroller Exec. Bd. Nat. Heritage Groups Council, 1970-72; mem. adv. bd. Nat. Security Council, 1980-85; acad. bank participant Heritage Found; adv. bd. Independence Inst. Author: Ivan Bunin's Proteges, Leonid Zurov, 1973, Alexander Zinoviev's Concept of the Soviet Man, 1991; co-author: Has the Third World War Already Started, 1983, Christianity and Russian Culture in Soviet Society, 1990, The Search for Self-Definition in Russian Literature, 1991; translator: Problems of Geography, 1955; author: (in Czech) In the Windstorm of Anger, 1976, Time and Duty, 1981, Teacher of Nations and Our Times, 1982, The Way of Light, 1982, On the Attack, 1983, Between the Currents, 1985, Homeland After 50 Years Nazi & Communist Occupation, 1992. V.p. Colo. Citizenship Day, 1968-69; pres. Comenius World Coun., 1976-85, World Representation of Czechoslovak Exiles, 1976-85; pres. Czech World Union, 1985-94; gen. sec. Czechoslovak Republican Movement, 1980-91. Recipient Americanism medal DAR, 1969, Disting. Service award Am. by Choice, 1968, Kynewisbov Pioneer award Denver U., 1989; named Tchr. with Superlative Performance MLA, 1961, Outstanding Faculty mem. Omicron Delta Kappa, 1972, The Order of M.R. Stefanik Provisional Czechoslovak Govt. in Exile. Mem. Econ. Inst. Rsch. and Edn., Am. Assn. Tchrs. Slavic and Eastern European Langs. (v.p. 1973-75), Intercollegiate Studies Inst., Rocky Mountain Assn. Slavic Studies (sec. treas. 1975-78, v.p. 1978-81, pres. 1982-83), Rocky Mountain Modern Lang. Assn., Nat. Assn. Scholars, Czechoslovak Christian Democratic Movement in Exile (central com. 1970-79), Dobro Slovo (hon.), Slava (hon.), Aleksandr Solzhenitsyn Soc., Shavano Inst. Nat. Leadership, Nat. Rep. Nationalities Coun. (co-chmn. human rights com. 1979-81), Phi Beta Kappa (hon.). Republican. Roman Catholic. Home: 39 Hillside Dr Lakewood CO 80215-6639 Office: U Denver Denver CO 80208-0293

BROM, ROBERT H., bishop; b. Arcadia, Wis., Sept. 18, 1938. Ed., St. Mary's Coll., Winona, Minn., Gregorian U., Rome. Ordained priest Roman Catholic Ch., 1963, consecrated bishop, 1983. Bishop of Duluth Minn., 1983-89; coadjutor bishop Diocese of San Diego, 1989-90, bishop, 1990—. Office: Diocese of San Diego Pastoral Ctr PO Box 85728 San Diego CA 92186-5728

BROMM, ROBERT DALE, nuclear engineer; b. San Pedro, Calif., Nov. 13, 1950; s. Robert and Olive Genevive (Hart) B.; m. Linda Suzanne Owens, June 30, 1973 (div. June 1986); children: Christina Ann, Ryan David; m. Margaret Rose Meusborn, Jan., 14, 1989; 1 adopted child, Mindy Christine. BSME, Calif. State Poly. U., 1973; MBA, Idaho State U., 1985. Registered profl. engr., Calif. Engr. Bechtel Power Corp., Norwalk, Calif., 1973-76; engring. specialist EG&G Idaho Inc., Idaho Falls, 1977-85; sr. remote systems and robotics engr. Fluor Daniel, Irvine, Calif., 1985—. Mem. Am. Nuclear Soc. (chmn. L.A. 1989), Mensa (loc. sec. SE Idaho chpt. 1985), Toastmasters (pres. Irvine 1988). Office: Flour Daniel 3333 Michelson Dr Irvine CA 92715

BROMMER, GERALD FREDERICK, artist, writer; b. Berkeley, Calif., Jan. 8, 1927; s. Edgar C. and Helen (Wall) B.; m. Georgia Elizabeth Pratt, Dec. 19, 1948. BS in Edn., Concordia Coll., Nebr., 1948; MA, U. Nebr., 1955; postgrad., UCLA, U. So. Calif., Otis Art Inst., Chouinard Art Inst.; D.Litt., Christ Coll., 1985. Instr., St. Paul's Sch., North Hollywood, Calif., 1948-55, Lutheran High Sch., Los Angeles, 1955-76; one-person shows throughout country; exhibited in numerous group shows including Am. Watercolor Soc., NAD, Royal Watercolor Soc., London; represented in permanent collections Claremont Colls. (Calif.), Pacific Telesis, Epcot Ctr., Orlando, Hilton Hotels, Inc., Reno, Anaheim, San Francisco, Intercontinental Hotel, L.A., Harvey Muod Coll., Claremont, Calif., Laguna Beach Mus. Art, TRW, Cola Cola Co., Ky., Concordia Coll., Nebr., Ill., Mo., Utah State U., Provo; books include: College Techniques, 1994, Discovering Art History, 1981, 3rd edit., 1995, The Art of Collage, 1978, Drawing, 1978, Understanding Transparent Watercolor, 1993, Landscapes, 1977, Art in your World, 1977, Watercolor and Collage Workshop, 1986, Exploring Painting, 1989, Exploring Drawing, 1990, Art: Your Visual Environment, 1977, Movement and Rhythm, 1975, Space, 1974, Transparent Watercolor, 1973, Relief Printmaking, 1970, Wire Sculpture, 1968, Careers in Art, 1984, and others; editor: The Design Concept Series, 10 vols., 1974-75, Insights to Art series, 1977—; various texts; 8 video art presentations for Crystal Prodns., Inc.; set of 14 design posters fro schs. for Crystal Prodns., Inc.; assoc. Hewitt Painting Workshops, Artist Workshop Tour Agy. Grand Strand Watercolor workshops, Jade Fun Watercolor Workshops, Hudson Valley Art Workshops. Recipient prizes Am. Watercolor Soc., 1965, 68, 71, Watercolor U.S.A., 1970, 73, Los Angeles City Art Festival, 1970, 75, Calif. State Fair, 1975. Mem. Nat. Watercolor Soc. (treas., v.p., pres., awards 1972, 74, 78, 80), West Coast Watercolor Soc., Nat. Arts Club, Rocky Mountain Nat. Watermedia Soc., Watercolor USA Honor Soc., Nat. Art Edn. Assn., Nat. Arts (N.Y.C.), Phila. Water Color Club, La. Watercolor Soc. Republican. Lutheran. Address: 11252 Valley Spring Ln North Hollywood CA 91602-2611

BRON, WALTER ERNEST, physics educator; b. Berlin, Jan. 17, 1930; came to U.S., 1939, naturalized, 1946; s. Arthur and Edith (Seidel) B.; m. Ann Elisabeth Berend, June 1, 1952; children: Karen Susanne, Michelle Elise. B.M.E., N.Y. U., 1952; M.S., Columbia, 1953, Ph.D., 1958. Research assoc. IBM Watson Lab., Yorktown Heights, N.Y., 1957-58; research physicist IBM Watson Lab., 1958-66; assoc. prof. physics Ind. U., Bloomington, 1966-69; prof. Ind. U., 1969-86; prof. dept. physics U. Calif., Irvine, 1986—, chmn., 1989-92; lectr. George Washington U., 1955-56, Columbia, 1957, adj. lectr., 1964; vis. prof. Physikalisches Institut der Technischen Hochschule, Stuttgart, Germany, 1966-67; vis. scientist Max Planck Inst. for Solid State Research, Stuttgart, Germany, 1973-74, 81-82, 83. Contbr. articles sci. jours. Mem. Bloomington Environ. Quality and Conservation Commn., 1972-81, chmn., 1974-76. Served with AUS, 1954-56. Gen. Electric fellow, 1952-53; W. Campbell fellow, 1953-54, 56-57; Guggenheim fellow, 1966-67; sr. Scientist award Alexander von Humboldt Found., 1973. Fellow Am. Phys. Soc.; mem. Optical Soc. Am., Sassafras Audubon Soc. (pres. 1976-78), Sigma Xi, Tau Beta Pi, Pi Tau Sigma. Home: 20 Mendel Ct Irvine CA 92715-4039 Office: U Calif Irvine Dept Physics Irvine CA 92717

BRONSTEIN, ARTHUR J., linguistics educator; b. Balt., Mar. 15, 1914; s. Gershon and Bessie B.; m. Elsa Meltzer, May 15, 1941; children: Nancy

Ellen, Abbot Alan. B.A., CCNY, 1934; M.A., Columbia U., 1936; Ph.D., NYU, 1949. Vis. scholar and rsch. assoc. in linguistics U. Calif., Berkeley, 1987—; prof. Queens Coll., N.Y.C., 1938-67; Fulbright prof. U. Tel Aviv, (Israel), 1967-68, U. Trondheim, (Norway), 1979; prof. linguistics Lehman Coll. and Grad. Sch., CUNY, 1968-83, prof. emeritus, 1983—; exec. officer PhD program in speech and hearing scis. CUNY, 1969-72; exec. officer Ph.D. program in linguistics Grad. Sch., CUNY, 1981-83; cons. in field; with dept. linguistics U. Calif., Berkeley. Author: Pronunciation of American English, 1960, Essays in Honor of C.M. Wise, 1970, Biographical Dictionary of the Phonetic Sciences, 1977; project dir.: Dictionary of American English Pronunciation. Served with Signal Corps and AGD USAA, 1942-46. Fellow Am. Speech and Hearing Assn., Internat. Soc. Phonetic Scis., N.Y. Acad. Sci.; mem. MLA, Linguistics Soc. Am., Am. Dialect Soc., Am. Assn. Phonetic Scis., Dictionary Soc. N.Am., Phi Beta Kappa. Office: U Calif Dept Linguistics Berkeley CA 94720

BROOK, WINSTON ROLLINS, audio-video design consultant; b. Cameron, Tex., Aug. 20, 1931; s. Winston Marshall and Maude Katherine (Woody) B. BA, U. Denver, 1955. Lic. radiotelephone operator, FCC. Engr. Sta. WKNO-TV, Memphis, 1965-67; instr. Memphis State U., 1967-69; audio-visual dir. So. Coll. Optometry, Memphis, 1968-73; sr. cons. Bolt Beranek and Newman, Chgo. and L.A., 1973-87; prin. RB Sys., L.A., 1987—; instr. various seminars and workshops; assoc. editor Theater Design & Tech. mag., N.Y.C., 1981-87; tech. cons. Sound & Video Contractor mag., Overland, Kans., 1987—. Co-author: Handbook for Sound Engineers, 1987; contbr. articles to profl. jours., 1978—. Mem. Audio Engring. Soc., Acoustical Soc. Am., U.S. Inst. for Theatre Tech. Democrat. Mormon. Home and Office: 5715 Calvin Ave Tarzana CA 91356-1108

BROOKBANK, JOHN W(ARREN), retired microbiology educator; b. Seattle, Apr. 3, 1927; s. Earl Bruce and Louise Sophia (Stoecker) B.; m. Marcia Ireland, Sept. 16, 1950 (div. 1978); children: Ursula Ireland, John W. Jr., Phoebe Bruce; m. Sally Satterberg Cahill, Aug. 6, 1983. BA, U. Wash., 1950, MS, 1953; PhD, Calif. Inst. Tech., 1955. Asst. prof. U. Fla., Gainesville, 1955-58, assoc. prof., 1958-68, prof. microbiology and cell sci., 1968-85, prof. emeritus, 1985—; vis. assoc. prof. U. Fla. Coll. Medicine, Gainesville, 1961-63, U. Wash., Seattle, 1965; cons. in field, Friday Harbor, Wash. 1986—. Author: Developmental Biology, 1978, (with W. Cunningham) Gerontology, 1988; editor: Improving Quality of Health Care of the Elderly, 1977, Biology of Aging, 1990; contbr. articles to profl. jours. Pres. Griffin Bay Preservation Com., Friday Harbor, 1985—, Bridge Council on Narcotics Addiction, Gainesville, 1974, Marine Environ. Consortium, 1986—; founding pres. Gainesville Regional Council on Alcoholism, 1976. Research grantee NIH, 1957-80, NSF, 1972-73. Mem. Gerontol. Soc. Am., Seattle Tennis Club. Republican. Episcopalian. Home: PO Box 2688 Friday Harbor WA 98250-2688

BROOKE, EDNA MAE, retired business educator; b. Las Vegas, Nev., Feb. 10, 1923; d. Alma Lyman and Leah Mae (Ketcham) Shurtliff; m. Bill T. Brooke, Dec. 22, 1949; 1 child, John C. BS in Acctg., Ariz. State U., 1965, MA in Edn., 1967, EdD, 1975. Grad. teaching asst. Ariz. State U., Tempe, 1968-69; prof. bus. Maricopa Tech. Coll., Phoenix, 1967-72, assoc. dean instl. services, 1972-74; prof. bus. and acctg. Scottsdale (Ariz.) Community Coll., 1974-93; ret., 1993; cons. in field. Author: The Effectiveness of Three Techniques Used in Teaching First Semester Accounting Principles to Tech. Jr. College Students, 1974. Mem. Nat. Bus. Edn. Assn., Western Bus. Edn. Assn., Ariz. Bus. Edn. Assn., Am. Acctg. Assn., Delta Pi Epsilon. Home: 1330 E Calle De Caballos Tempe AZ 85284-2404 Office: Scottsdale CC 9000 E Chaparral Rd Scottsdale AZ 85250-2614

BROOKE, TAL (ROBERT TALIAFERRO), company executive, author; b. Washington, Jan. 21, 1945; s. Edgar Duffield and Frances (Lea) B. BA, U. Va., 1969; M in Theology/Philosophy, Princeton (N.J.) U., 1986. V.p. pub. rels. nat. office Telecom Inc., 1982-83; pres., chmn. Spiritual Counterfeits Project, Inc., Berkeley, 1989—; guest lectr. Cambridge U., Eng., 1977, 86, Oxford and Cambridge U., 1979, 84. Author: Lord of the Air, 1990, When the World Will Be As One, 1989 (bestseller 1989-90), Riders of the Cosmic Circuit, 1986, Avatar of Night, 1987 (bestseller in India 1981-84), The Other Side of Death, Lord of the Air: The International Edition, 1976. Mem. Internat. Platform Assn., Soc. of The Cincinnati. Office: SCP Inc PO Box 4308 Berkeley CA 94704-0308

BROOKE, VIVIAN M., state legislator; b. N.Y.C., Feb. 6, 1943; m. Joseph Brooke; 4 children. Attended, U. South Fla.; BA, Carroll Coll. Mem. Mont. Ho. of Reps.; office mgr. Mont. Com. Humanities. Democrat. Home: 1610 Madeline Ave Missoula MT 59801-5806 Office: Mt State Senate State Capitol Helena MT 59620-0001

BROOKES, VALENTINE, retired lawyer; b. Red Bluff, Calif., May 30, 1913; s. Langley and Ethel (Valentine) B.; m. Virginia Stovall Cunningham, Feb. 11, 1939; children: Langley Brookes Brandt, Lawrence Valentine, Alan Cunningham. A.B., U. Calif., Berkeley, 1934, J.D., 1937. Bar: Calif. 1937, U.S. Supreme Ct. 1942. Asst. franchise tax counsel State of Calif., 1937-40; dep. atty. gen. Calif., 1940-42; spl. asst. to U.S. atty. gen., asst. to solicitor gen. U.S., 1942-44; partner firm Kent & Brookes, San Francisco, 1944-70, Alvord & Alvord, Washington, 1944-50, Lee, Toomey & Kent, Washington, 1950-79; partner firm Brookes and Brookes, San Francisco, 1971-88, of counsel, 1988-90; legal cons. Orinda, Calif., 1990—; lectr. Hastings Coll. Law, U. Calif., 1941-48, U. Calif. Law Sch., Berkeley, 1948-70; cons. fed. taxation. Author: The Continuity of Interest Test in Reorganizations, 1946, The Partnership Under the Income Tax Laws, 1949, The Tax Consequences of Widows Elections in Community Property States, 1951, Corporate Trasactions Involving Its Own Stock, 1954, Litigation Expenses and the Income Tax, 1957. Bd. dirs. Children's Hosp. Med. Center of N. Calif., 1963-74, v.p., 1968-70; trustee Oakes Found., 1957-70; regent St. Mary's Coll., Calif., 1968-88, pres. bd., 1970-72, emeritus mem., 1988—. Fellow Am. Bar Found. (life); mem. Am. Law Inst., ABA (chmn. com. on statute of limitations 1954-57, mem. council, tax sect. 1960-63), Calif. Bar Assn. (chmn. com. on taxation 1950-52, 60-61), Soc. Calif. Pioneers (v.p. 1964, 1975-86), Am. Coll. Tax Counsel, Phi Kappa Sigma, Phi Delta Phi. Republican. Clubs: Pacific Union, Orinda Country, World Trade. Home and Office: 7 Sycamore Rd Orinda CA 94563-1418

BROOKLER, HARRY AARON, physician; b. Winnipeg, Man., Can., Jan. 16, 1915; came to U.S., 1954; s. Samuel David and Rachel (Farbstein) B.; m. Gertrude Mandel, Jan. 1, 1941; children: Jerome, Rickey, Jackie, Resa, Maxwell. MD, Man. U., 1938. Diplomate Am. Bd. Anesthesiology. Resident in surgery Winnipeg Gen. Hosp., 1937-39; pvt. practice Lemberg, Sask., 1940-41, Weyburn, Sask., 1941-54, San Diego, 1954-59, 61-85; resident in anesthesia Harbor Gen. Hosp.-UCLA, Torrance, 1959-61; med. dir. Casa Blanca Corp., San Diego, 1976-86; surg. cons. Weyburn Mental Hosp., Sask., 1942-54; chief of staff Weyburn Gen. Hosp., Sask., 1945-50, Doctors (Sharp Cabbillo) Hosp., San Diego, 1964-66; coroner Sask. Govt., 1944-54; cons. Can. Pacific Railway, Weyburn, 1941-54. Bd. dirs. Beth Jacob Congregation, San Diego, 1958-60, Jewish Family Svc., San Diego, 1960-62; workshipful master Masons, Weyburn, 1952; chmn. bd. dirs. Bd. Jewish Fedn., San Diego, 1961. Recipient Isbister scholarships Man. Govt., 1931, 32, 33. Fellow Am. Geriatrics Soc., Am. Coll. Anesthesia; mem. AMA, Calif. Med. Assn., San Diego County Med. Assn. (chmn. skilled nursing com. 1961-66, staff survey com. 1967—), Calif. Assn. Med. Dirs. (bd. dirs., founder 1980—, treas. 1980-85). Home and Office: 5310 Prosperity Ln San Diego CA 92115-2145

BROOKMAN, ANTHONY RAYMOND, lawyer; b. Chgo., Mar. 23, 1922; s. Raymond Charles and Marie Clara (Alberg) B.; m. Marilyn Joyce Brookman, June 5, 1982; children: Meribeth Brookman Farmer, Anthony Raymond, Lindsay Logan Christensen. Student, Ripon Coll., 1940-41; BS, Northwestern U., 1947; JD, U. Calif., San Francisco, 1953. Bar: Calif. 1954. Law clk. to presiding justice Calif. Supreme Ct., 1953-54; ptnr. Nichols, Williams, Morgan, Digardi & Brookman, 1954-68; sr. ptnr. Brookman & Talbot, Inc. (formerly Brookman & Hoffman, Inc.), Walnut Creek, Calif., 1969-92, Brookman & Talbot Inc., Sacramento, 1992—. Pres. Young Reps. Calif., San Mateo County, 1953-54. 1st lt. USAF. Mem. ABA, Alameda County Bar Assn., State Bar Calif., Lawyers Club Alameda County, Alameda-Contra Costa County Trial Lawyers Assn., Assn. Trial Lawyers Am., Calif. Trial Lawyers Assn., Athenian Nile Club, Crow Canyon Country Club, Masons, Shriners. Republican. Office: 901 H St Ste 200 Sacramento CA 95814-1808 also: 1990 N California Blvd Walnut Creek CA 94596-3742 also: 1746 Grand Canal Blvd Ste 11 Stockton CA 95207-8111

BROOKS, EDWARD HOWARD, college administrator; b. Salt Lake City, Mar. 2, 1921; s. Charles Campbell and Margery (Howard) B.; m. Courtaney June Perren, May 18, 1946; children: Merrillee Brooks Runyan, Robin Anne (Mrs. R. Bruce Pollock). B.A., Stanford U., 1942, M.A., 1947, Ph.D., 1950. Mem. faculty, adminstrn. Stanford U., 1949-71; provost Claremont (Calif.) Colls., 1971-81; v.p. Claremont U. Center, 1979-81; sr. v.p. Claremont McKenna Coll., 1981-84; provost Scripps Coll., 1987-89, pres., 1989-90; ret., 1990. Trustee EDUCOM, 1978-80, Webb Sch. of Calif., 1979-90, Menlo Sch. and Coll., 1985-88; bd. overseers Hoover Instn., 1972-78; bd. dirs. Student Loan Mktg. Assn., 1973-77; mem. Calif. Student Aid Commn., 1984-88, chmn., 1986-88. Served with AUS, 1942-45. Clubs: Manhattan Country. Home: 337 8th St Manhattan Beach CA 90266-5629

BROOKS, JAMES SPRAGUE, retired national guard officer; b. Los Angeles, Feb. 16, 1925; s. Julian Chesney and Louise Heegaard (Sprague) B.; m. Loa Mae Woolf, June 17, 1947; children—Georgia Lee (stepdau.), Kerri Louise (dec.), James Patrick. B.C.E., Oreg. State Coll., 1951. Commd. lt. Idaho N.G., 1947, advanced through grades to maj. gen., 1975; engring. staff officer Idaho Mil. Dept. Idaho N.G., Boise, 1951-64, engr. Budget and Property Office, 1953-64, chief staff, 1965-74, adj. gen., chief Bur. Disaster Svcs., state dir. Selective Svc., 1975-85; chmn. army res. forces policy com. Dept. Army, 1979. Contbr. articles to Aviation Digest. Nat. Guard Mag. Mem. Boise Mcpl. Airport Commn., 1963-90, Idaho Law Enforcement Planning Commn., 1975, Boise Met. Plan Steering Com., 1976, Boise County Comprehensive Planning Task Force, 1989—, Idaho Pub. Transp. Adv. Coun., 1994—; chmn. Boise Mayor's Transit Adv. Com., 1991-94. With USAAF, 1943-46. Decorated Legion of Merit, D.S.M.; recipient Idaho Safe Pilot award, 1974; named Disting. Citizen, Idaho Statesman, 1977. Mem. N.G. Assn., U.S. Army, AF Assn., Retired Officers Assn., Tau Beta Pi, Sigma Tau.

BROOKS, JEANNE FREEMAN, journalist; b. Canton, N.C., Sept. 30, 1945; d. Joseph Earl and Jamia Carter (Massey) Moore; m. Clark Alan Brooks, May 29, 1992; children by previous marriage: Robert Dane Freeman Jr., Cortney Grey Freeman. BA in English, U. N.C., Greensboro, 1967. Tchr. English Hendersonville (N.C.) City Schs., 1967-68, Spartanburg (S.C.) City Schs., 1970-73; tchr. English Sch. Dist. of Greenville County, Greenville, 1973-77, dir. community and media rels., 1987; English instr. Michelin Tires Inc., Greenville, 1977-84; feature writer, columnist The Greenville News, 1984-87, 88, San Diego Tribune, 1988-92; feature writer San Diego Union-Tribune, 1992—. Recipient Ring of Truth award Copley Newspapers, 1993, media awards San Diego County Med Soc., 1992, awards S.C. Press Assn., 1985, 86, others. Mem. Soc. Profl. Journalists (award 1991-94), Alliance Francaise, San Diego Press Club (best column writing award 1991, 92, best feature writing award 1993). Office: San Diego Union Tribune PO Box 191 San Diego CA 92112-4106

BROOKS, RAYMOND, protective services official. AA in Applied Fire Sci., Ind. Vocat. Tech. Coll.; BS in Fire Sci. Mgmt., So. Ill. U.; grad. in mgmt. studies, Purdue U.; postgrad., Calif. State U., Northridge. Fire chief City of Alhambra, Calif., City of Evanston, Ill., City of Michigan City, Ind., City of San Jose, Calif., 1994—; adj. instr. Carl Holmes Exec. Inst. Fla. A&M U. Named Outstanding Young Man of Am., 1981. Mem. Internat. Assn. Fire Chiefs, Ill. Fire Chiefs Assn. (former mem. legis. liaison), Ind. Fire Chiefs' Assn. (former 1st v.p.), Internat. Assn. Black Profl. Fire Fighters Assn. (chairperson black chief officers com.), Nat. Forum Black Pub. Adminstrs. Office: San Jose Fire Dept 4 N Second St Ste 1100 San Jose CA 95113-1305*

BROOKS, SAMUEL EVERETT, purchasing agent; b. Connellsville, Pa., Jan. 19, 1946; s. J. Melvin and Ruth Pearl (Firestone) B.; m. Martha Jane Peters, May 28, 1966; children: Kristine, Kimberly, Kerrie, Jason. Student, W.Va. U., 1963-64, Ann Arundel C.C., 1964-66. Data compiler Westinghouse, Balt., 1965-70; buyer, dept. head Leggetts, Waynesboro, Va., 1970-74; asst. mgr. Cranes Men's Shop, Connellsville, 1974-77; buyer Volkswagen of Am., New Stanton, Pa., 1977-88; mgr. indirect purchasing New United Motors Mfg. Inc., Fremont, Calif., 1988—; bd. dirs. No. Calif. Purchasing Coun. Youth worker local ch., Balt., 1965-70, Waynesboro, 1971-74. Republican. Home: 4844 Sterling Hill Dr Antioch CA 94509-7667 Office: New United Motors Mfg Inc 45500 Fremont Blvd Fremont CA 94538-6326

BROOKS, SCOTT DAVID, medical research analyst; b. Burbank, Calif., Aug. 22, 1962. BA, UCLA, 1985; MA, Calif. Grad. Inst., 1990. From rsch. asst. to dir. HIV Intervention Project Edelman Health Ctr., L.A., 1988-92; program asst. Children's Hosp. L.A., 1993-94; adminstrv. analyst clin. rsch. unit UCLA, 1994—; dir. cmty. adv. bd. Edelman Health Ctr., 1990-92. Mem. Am. Psychol. Assn., Am. Counseling Assn., Calif. Psychol. Assn., L.A. Gay Psychotherapists Assn. Home: 1337 N Sierra Bonita Ave # 302 Los Angeles CA 90046

BROOKS, STEPHEN VOLUME, foundation executive; b. Fresno, Calif., July 19, 1942; s. Dan C. and Rachel Ann (Patterson) B.; m. Edna J. Charles Bradford, 1964 (div. 1977); children: Stephanie, Karen, Stephen Jr., Nya; m. Delores D. Washington, June 27, 1977. AA, Coll. of Sequoias, 1962; BA in Zoology, U. Calif., Berkeley, 1971; MPA, Calif. State U., Hayward, 1978. Co-dir. Western Student Movement, Richmond, Calif., 1964-65; v.p. Worldwide Educators, Oakland, Calif., 1965-67; dep. dir. Oakland Econ. Devel. Coun., 1967-71; assoc. exec. dir. United Way of Bay Area, San Francisco, 1971-79; pres., CEO, founder Bay Area Black United Fund, Oakland, 1979-85; pres. Stephen Brooks & Assocs., Livermore, Calif., 1985—; exec. dir. Tri-Valley Comty. Fund, Pleasanton, Calif., 1990—. Office: Tri-Valley Cmty Fund PO Box 1018 Pleasanton CA 94566

BROOKS, TEMPE BOYCE-SMITH, manufacturing company executive; b. Summit, N.J., May 26, 1941; d. John III and Lee Ellis (Wootten) Boyce-Smith; m. John Emmert Brooks, June 14, 1963; children: Christine Brooks Macdonald, Cynthia, John Emmert Jr. BA in Zoology, Pomona Coll., 1963. Sec.-treas. Adams & Brooks, Inc., L.A., 1985—. Pres. bd. dirs. Jr. League of Pasadena, Calif., 1977-78, Pasadena Pub. Libr. Found., 1986-90, Project D.A.Y. Found., 1992—; pres. bd. trustees Westridge Sch. for Girls, Pasadena, 1985-88; vice chmn. United Way Planning Coun. Region II, San Gabriel Valley, 1978-88; bd. dirs. Calif. Coun. on Alcoholism, 1980-83; del. White House Conf. on Aging, 1981. Recipient 20th Century award Pasadena YWCA, 1982, Gold Key award L.A. United Way, 1985; named to Outstanding Young Women in Am., 1970. Mem. Pasadena Garden Club (treas. 1986-88), Cal Tech Assocs. Republican. Presbyterian. Home: 1118 Wellington Ave Pasadena CA 91103-2763 Office: Adams & Brooks Inc 1915 S Hoover St Los Angeles CA 90007-1322

BROOKS, WILLIAM JAMES, osteopathic physician, educator; b. Ft. Wayne, Ind., Sept. 7, 1952; s. James Edward and Anne (Waterfield) B.; m. Barbara Lynn Campbell, Nov. 1986; 1 child, James Campbell. Student, Earlham Coll., 1970-73, Life Rsch. Ctr. for Studies, Brantford, Ont., Can., 1973-75; DO, Chgo. Coll. Osteo. Medicine, 1980. Cert. spl. proficiency in osteo. manipulative medicine Am. Osteo. Bd. Intern Tucson Gen. Hosp., 1980-81, 91, surg. asst., attending physician in alcohol and drug rehab., 1981-83; pvt. practice, Tucson, 1981-85, St. Paul, 1985-88; assoc. staff mem. Univ. Med. Ctr., Tucson, 1989—; instr. clin. surgery U. Ariz. Coll. Medicine, Tucson, 1989-92, asst. prof. clin. surgery (orthopedic), 1992—, asst. clin. scientist Arthritis Ctr., 1991—; cons. physician U. Ariz. Wildcat Athletic Teams, Tucson, 1993—; cons. biomechanics clinic dept. orthopedic surgery Park Nicollet Med. Ctr., Mpls., 1986-88; med. dir. Univ. Physicians Orthopedic and Sports Medicine Ctr., Tucson, 1992-93; presenter, lectr. in field, 1986—. Grantee Tucson Osteo. Med. Found., 1988-89, U. Ariz. Arthritis Ctr., 1993-94, U. Ariz. Coll. Medicine, 1993-94, Wallace Genetics Found., 1994. Mem. Am. Osteo. Assn., Am. Acad. Osteopathy, Cranial Acad., Ariz. Acad. Osteopathy, Complementary Medicine Assn., U. Ariz. Collaborative Pain Mgmt. Group, Am. Coll. Sports Medicine, Am. Osteo. Acad. Sports Medicine, Am. Assn. Orthopedic Medicine. Office: U Ariz Health Scis Ctr Dept Surgery Orthopedic Tucson AZ 85724

BROOM, GLEN MARTIN, communication educator; b. Anna, Ill., Nov. 2, 1940; s. Ralph Curvella and Wanda Audrey (Broadway) B.; m. Betty Lou Bollinger, Aug. 31, 1963. BS in Agrl. Communication, U. Ill., 1963, MS in Advt., 1967; PhD in Mass Communication, U. Wis., 1977. Asst. extension editor U. Ill. Coop. Extension Service, Urbana, 1963-68; v.p., dir. pub. relations Applied Behavioral Sci., Inc., Chgo., 1969-72; asst. prof. communications U. Wis., Madison, 1975-79; from assoc. prof. to prof. San Diego State U., 1979—; vis. prof. U. Tex., Austin, 1985-86. Author: (with others) Effective Public Relations, 1985, 94, Using Research in Public Relations, 1990; contbr. articles to profl. jours. Served with USAR, 1960-66. Mem. Pub. Relations Soc. Am., Assn. Edn. in Journalism and Mass Communication, Arthur W. Page Soc. Office: San Diego State U Sch Comm San Diego CA 92182

BROOME, JOHN WILLIAM, retired architect; b. Middle Haddam, Conn., Mar. 7, 1923; s. Bertram Clinton and Helen Millington (Connery) B.; m. Althea Pratt, May 31, 1980; children: Bertram Vedeler, Sheryl Lynn. B.Arch., U. Oreg., 1951. Archtl. work in Oslo, Norway, 1951-54; planning technician Vancouver (Wash.) Housing Authority, 1954-56; archtl. designer Edmundson, Kochendoerfer & Kennedy, Portland, Oreg., 1956-58; ptnr. Broome, Oringdulph, O'Toole & Rudolf & Assos., Portland, 1958-85, ret., 1985. Mem. Gov. Oreg. Com. for Livable Oreg., 1967-71; commr. Oreg. Coastal Conservation and Devel. Commn., 1971-75; pres. The Wetlands Conservancy; trustee Meridian Park Hosp., Healthlink, Inc. Served with USMC, 1942-46. Decorated Air medal with 2 gold stars; recipient Regional Conservation award U.S. Fish & Wildlife Svc., 1990, Nat. Conservation award Environ. Law Inst., 1991, State Disting. Svc. award Oreg. Shores Conservation Coalition, 1992. Fellow AIA (pres. Portland 1966, Oreg. council 1967); mem. Phi Kappa Psi. Democrat. Address: PO Box 236 Tualatin OR 97062-0236

BROPHY, DENNIS RICHARD, psychology and philosophy educator, administrator, clergyman; b. Milw., Aug. 6, 1945; s. Floyd Herbert and Phyllis Marie (Ingram) B.; BA, Washington U., St. Louis, 1967, MA, 1968; M.Div., Pacific Sch. Religion, 1971; PhD in Indstrl. and Orgnl. Psychology, Texas A & M U., 1995. Cert. coll. tchr., Calif. Edn. researcher IBM Corp., White Plains, N.Y., 1968-71; edn. minister Cmty. Congl. Ch., Port Huron, Mich., 1971-72, Bethlehem United Ch. of Christ, Ann Arbor, Mich., 1972-73, Cmty. Congl. Ch., Chula Vista, Calif., 1974; philosophy instr. Southwestern Coll., Chula Vista, 1975; assoc. prof. psychology and philosophy Northwest Coll., Powell, Wyo., 1975—, chmn. social sci. divsn., 1992-95; religious edn. cons. Mont.-No. Wyo. Conf. United Ch. of Christ. Mem. Wyo. Coun. for Humanities, Am. Psychol. Assn., Soc. Indsl. Orgnl. Psychology, Yellowstone Assn. of United Ch. of Christ, Phi Kappa Phi, Phi Beta Kappa, Sigma Xi, Omicron Delta Kappa, Theta Xi, Golden Key Nat. Honor Soc. Home: 533 Avenue C Powell WY 82435-2401 Office: Northwest Coll 231 W 6th St Powell WY 82435-1898

BRORBY, WADE, federal judge; b. 1934. BS, U. Wyo., 1956, JD with honor, 1958. Bar: Wyo. County and prosecuting atty. Campbell County, Wyo., 1963-70; ptnr. Morgan Brorby Price and Arp, Gillette, Wyo., 1961-88; judge U.S. Ct. Appeals (10th cir.), Cheyenne, Wyo., 1988—. With USAF, 1958-61. Mem. ABA, Campbell County Bar Assn., Am. Judicature Soc., Def. Lawyers Wyo., Wyo Bar Assn. (commr. 1968-70). Office: US Ct Appeals 10th Cir O'Mahoney Fed Bldg Rm 2016 PO Box 1028 Cheyenne WY 82002-0001*

BROSELOW, STANLEY DAVID, electrical engineer; b. Phila., Aug. 3, 1925; s. Herman George and Dorothy Edyth B.; m. Bernyce Helene Shulman, Mar. 27, 1949; children: Stephen Mark, Hope Gail. BSEE, Drexel U., 1946. Construction mgmt. engr. U.S. Army Engr. Dist., Balt., 1946-61; chief, contract adminstrn. Corps of Engrs. Ballistic Missile Construction Office, Norton AFB, Calif., 1961-66; chmn. Western Regional Renegotiation Bd., L.A., 1966-79; procurement mgr. Hughes Aircraft Co., El Segundo, Calif., 1979-89. Mem. IEEE, Soc. Am. Mil. Engrs., ASCE, Nat. Contract Mgmt. Assn., Sigma Alpha Mu. Democrat. Jewish. Home: 7357 Paradiso Ct Las Vegas NV 89129-6481

BROSNAN, PETER LAWRENCE, documentary filmmaker; b. Bklyn., July 6, 1952; s. John Joseph and Audrey Barbara (Holran) B. BFA, NYU, N.Y.C., 1974; MA, U. So. Calif., 1979, Pepperdine U., 1995. Documentary filmmaker, writer L.A., 1980—; dir. DeMille Project, Hollywood Heritage, L.A., 1988—. Author: (screenplays) Heart of Darkness, 1992, The Ark, 1994; co-author: (book) PML Report, 1989; writer: (documentary film) Ghosts of Cape Horn, 1980 (World Ship Trust award); prodr., dir.: (TV documentary) The Lost City, 1992; writer, segment prodr.: (PBS series) Faces of Culture, 1983-84 (Emmy award 1984), Writer Marketing, 1984 (Emmy award 1985); dir.: (documentary) Sand Castles, 1995. Democrat. Home: 1709 N Fuller Ave Apt 25 Los Angeles CA 90046-3012

BROTMAN, CAROL EILEEN, adult education educator, advocate; b. L.A., Feb. 17, 1955; d. Hyman and Beverly Joanne (Krause) B. AA, L.A. Pierce Coll., 1977; BA, U. So. Calif., L.A., 1984; postgrad., UCLA, 1990, cert. legal asst., 1991. Cert. adult edn. tchr., Calif. Tchr. L.A. Unified Sch. Dist., 1986—; tchr. adult edn. and ESL North Hollywood (Calif.) Adult Sch., 1987-94, dept. chair, 1990-91. Founder Families for Quality Care, San Fernando Valley, Calif., 1983-86; mem. com. L.A. Pub. Libr. Ctrl. Libr., internat. langs. dept. Langs. Expertese and Resources Network, 1991; vol. paralegal Harriet Buhai Ctr. for Family Law, 1992-94; organizer adult-student cmty. group Thanksgiving dinner for new immigrants St. Patrick's Ch., North Hollywood, 1987-90. Recipient Mayor's Commendation, 1984, Older Women's League, 1985, Cert. of Tribute, Harriet Buhai Ctr. for Family Law, 1992, 93, Cert. of Appreciation for Outstanding Vol. Work, Family Law Sect., L.A. County Bar Assn. and Superior Ct. of L.A., 1993, L.A. Unified Adult and CAreer Edn. Divsn., 1994. Mem. AAUW, NAFE, United Tchrs. of L.A., Rare Fruit Gardenrs Assn. Home: 10921 Reseda Blvd Northridge CA 91326-2803

BROTMAN, JEFFREY H., variety stores executive; b. 1942. JD, U. Wash., 1967. Ptnr. Lasher-Brotman & Sweet, 1967-74; with ENI Exploration Co., 1975-83; co-founder Costco Wholesale Corp., 1983, chmn. bd., chief exec. officer, 1983-88; chmn. bd. Price/Costco, 1988—. Office: Price/Costco 10809 120th Ave NE Kirkland WA 98033-5030*

BROTMAN, RICHARD DENNIS, counselor; Detroit, Nov. 2, 1952; s. Alfred David and Dorothy G. (Mansfield) B.; m. Debra Louise Hobold, Sept. 9, 1979. AA, E. L.A. Jr. Coll., 1972; AB, U. So. Calif., 1974, MS, 1976. Instructional media coord. Audio-Visual Div., Pub. Library, City of Alhambra, Calif., 1971-78; clin. supr. Hollywood-Sunset Community Clinic, L.A., 1976—; client program coord. N. L.A. County Regional Ctr. for Developmentally Disabled, 1978-81; sr. counselor Eastern L.A. Regional Ctr. for Developmentally Disabled, 1981-85; dir. community svcs. Almansor Edn. Ctr., 1985-87; tng. and resource devel. Children's Home Soc. Calif., 1987-90; program supr. Pacific Clinics-East, 1990-94; dir. clin. svcs. Alma Family Svcs., 1994—; intern student affairs div., U. So. Calif., 1976. Corp. dir. San Gabriel Mission Players, 1973-75. Lic. marriage, family and child counselor, Calif.; cert. counselor Calif. Community Coll. Bd. Mem. Am. Assn. For Marriage and Family Therapy (approved supr.), Calif. Personnel and Guidance Assn. (conv. participant, 1976, 77, 79), Calif. Rehab. Counselors Assn. (officer), San Fernando Valley Consortium of Agys. Serving Developmentally Disabled Citizens (chmn. recreation subcom.), L.A. Aquarium Soc. Democrat. Home: 3515 Brandon St Pasadena CA 91107-4542 Office: Alma Family Svcs 6505 Rosemead Blvd Ste 300 Pico Rivera CA 90660-3544

BROTZMAN, AMY JEAN, health facility administrator; b. Hilo, Hawaii, Oct. 17, 1951; d. Wing You and Lillian Y.E. (Ching) Chong; m. Frederick Llewelyn Palea, Dec. 21, 1970 (div. June 1981); children: Karl, Stacey; m. Paul David Brotzman, Jan. 1, 1984. BS, U. Wash., 1973, BA in Home Econs., 1974; MS in Healthcare Adminstrn., Calif. State U., Northridge, 1991. Clin. dietitian Kaiser Found. Hosp., Walnut Creek, Calif., 1976-77; dir. food svcs. Kaiser Found. Hosp., Martinez, Calif., 1977-85; dir. food and nutrition Kaiser Found. Hosp., Woodland Hills, Calif., 1986-93; asst. hosp. adminstr. Kaiser Found. Hosp., L.A., 1993—; mgr. food svcs. dept. Cedars Sinai Med. Ctr., L.A., 1985-86; adj. prof. family and environ. svcs. Calif. State U., Northridge, 1991—, prof. health sci., 1994—. Bd. dirs. West

Hollywood (Calif.) Homeless Orgn., 1994—. Mem. Am. Coll. Healthcare Execs. (assoc.), Am. Dietetic Assn. (registered, Recognized Young Dietitian of Yr. 1980), Calif. Dietetic Assn., L.A. Dist. Dietetic Assn. Democrat. Home: 2573 Laurel Pass Los Angeles CA 90046-1403 Office: Kaiser Found Hosp 4747 W Sunset Blvd Los Angeles CA 90027-6021

BROUDY, VIRGINIA CONSTANCE, hematologist, educator; b. Stockholm, Sweden, Nov. 7, 1954; came to U.S., 1955; d. Lloyd Hollingsworth and Margaret Constance (Avery) Smith; m. David Robert Broudy, June 19, 1983; children: Sarah, Laura, Daniel. BA in Biochemistry cum laude, Harvard U., 1976; MD, U. Calif., San Francisco, 1980. Diplomate in internal medicine, hematology and oncology Am. Bd. Internal Medicine. Med. intern Oreg. Health Scis. U., Portland, 1980-81, resident in medicine, 1981-83, fellow in oncology, 1983-85; fellow in hematology U. Wash., Seattle, 1985-87, asst. prof. medicine, 1987-92, assoc. prof. medicine, 1992—; mem. biol. response modifiers adv. com. FDA, Bethesda, Md., 1994—; mem. pers. for rsch. sci. adv. com. Am. Cancer Soc., Atlanta, 1994—. Contbr. more than 50 articles to profl. jours. Mem. U.S. Nat. Championship Team, U.S. Rowing Assn., 1973; Am. Cancer Soc. grantee, 1991, NIH grantee, 1992. Mem. Am. Soc. Hematology (chair membership com. 1994), Am. Soc. Clin. Oncology, Western Soc. for Clin. Investigation. Office: U Wash Div Hematology RM-10 Seattle WA 98195

BROUGH, BRUCE ALVIN, public relations and communications executive; b. Wayland, N.Y., Nov. 22, 1937; s. Alvin Elroy and Marjorie Huberta (McDowell) B.; m. Jane Virginia Koethen, Aug. 9, 1958; children: John David, Pamela Marjorie, Robert Bruce. BS in Pub. Rels., U. Md., 1960; MS in Mass Communications, Am. U., Washington, 1967. Comm. mgr. IBM Corp., various locations, 1965-74; owner, pres. Bruce Brough Assocs., Inc., Boca Raton, Fla., 1974-75; worldwide press rels. rep. Tex. Instruments Inc., 1975-76; v.p. pub. rels. Regis McKenna Inc., 1976-77; pres., prin. Pease/Brough Assocs., Inc., Palo Alto, Calif., 1978-80, Franson/Brough Assocs., Inc., San Jose, Calif., 1980-81; sr. v.p., dir. Advanced Tech. Network Hill and Knowlton, Inc., San Jose, 1981-86; sr. v.p., gen. mgr. Hill and Knowlton, Inc., Santa Clara, Calif., 1989; mgr. corp. pub. rels. Signetics Corp., 1986-87; mktg. comm. mgr. Corp. Ctr. Philips Components divsn. Philips Internat., B.V., Eindhoven, The Netherlands, 1987-89; dir. corp. comm. Centigram Comm. Corp., San Jose, Calif., 1989-90; prin. Brough Comm., Santa Cruz, Calif., 1994—; lectr. San Jose State U., 1977-83, 91—; cons. comm. and pub. rels., 1986—. Author: Publicity and Public Relations Guide for Business, 1984, revised edit., 1986, The Same Yesterday, Today and Forever, 1986; contbg. editor Family Bible Ency., 1973. Recipient Sustained Superior Performance award NASA, 1964, award Freedom's Found., 1963. Mem. Pub. Rels. Soc. Am. (accredited), Soc. Tech. Comm., Nat. Press Club, Sigma Delta Chi. Republican. Roman Catholic. Home: 155 Rabbits Run Rd Santa Cruz CA 95060-1526 Office: Brough Communications 155 Rabbits Run Rd Santa Cruz CA 95060-1526

BROUGHER, CRAIG WILLIAM, geologist; b. Spokane, Wash., May 23, 1962; s. Gayle Kermit and Carol Ann (Hodge). BS, Wash. State U., 1987. V.p. Brougher Ranch Inc., Wilbur, Wash., 1985—; rsch. asst. Wash. State U., Pullman, 1986-88; cons. Brougher Earth Resources, Pullman, 1988-89; rsch. assoc. People to People Internat., Spokane, Wash., 1989-90; pres., owner Pangaea Internat. export import trading and cons. co., Wilbur, 1990—; ind. rschr. computer, satellite and remote sensing applications to field of geology, Wash. State U., Pullman, 1986-89; prin. investigator sci. rsch. including Russian nuclear disaster at Kyshtym; submitted proposals to NSF, NASA, Dept. Energy for advanced radar and remote sensing applications to the field of geology. Candidate Wilbur City Coun., 1991. Mem. Am. Geophys. Union, Geologic Soc. of Am., Am. Soc. for Photogrammetric Engrng. and Remote Sensing, Wilbur C. of C. Lutheran. Office: Pangaea Internat SW 107th Pope St Wilbur WA 99185

BROUGHTON, JOSEPH OTIS, physician; b. Wilmington, N.C., Jan. 3, 1939; s. Joseph Otis and Clara Maude (Bissinger) B.; m. Linda Ann Kinaman Broughton, Feb. 17, 1968; children: Jody Elizabeth, Lindsay Simmons. MD, Duke U., Durham, N.C., 1963. Cert. internal medicine, pulmonary disease, critical care, Am. Bd. Internal Medicine, 1969. Pulmonary physician Colo. Pulmonary Assocs., Denver, 1987—; sr., founding ptnr. Colo. Pulmonary Assocs., Denver, 1987—; med. dir. respiratory therapy Mercy Med. Ctr., Denver, 1969—. Author: Understanding Blood Gases, 1970. Capt. USAF, 1967-69. Fellow Am. Coll. Chest Physicians; mem. Am. Thoracic Soc. Office: Colorado Pulmonary Assocs 1721 E 19th Ave Ste 366 Denver CO 80218-1235

BROUGHTON, RAY MONROE, economic consultant; b. Seattle, Mar. 2, 1922; s. Arthur Charles and Elizabeth C. (Young) B.; BA, U. Wash., 1947, MBA, 1960; m. Margret Ellen Ryno, July 10, 1944 (dec.); children: Linda Rae Broughton Silk, Mary Catherine Broughton Boutin; m. Carole Jean Packer, 1980. Mgr. communications and managerial devel. Gen. Electric Co., Hanford Atomic Products Ops., Richland, Wash., 1948-59; mktg. mgr., asst. to pres. Smyth Enterprises, Seattle, 1960-62; dir. rsch. Seattle Area Indsl. Council, 1962-65; v.p., economist (mgr. econ. rsch. dept.) First Interstate Bank of Oreg., N.A., Portland, 1965-87; ind. economic cons., 1987—; mem. econ. adv. com. to Am. Bankers Assn., 1980-83; mem. Gov.'s Econ. Adv. Council, 1981-88; dir. Oregonians for Cost Effective Govt., 1989-90; instr. bus. communications U. Wash., Richland, 1956-57. Treas., dir. Oreg. affiliate Am. Heart Assn., 1972-78, chmn., 1980-81, dir., 1980-84. Served to 1st lt. U.S. Army, 1943-46; ETO. Mem. Western Econ. Assn., Pacific N.W. Regional Econ. Conf. (dir. 1967-94), Nat. Assn. Bus. Economists (co-founder chpt. 1971), Am. Mktg. Assn. (pres. chpt. 1971-72), Alpha Delta Sigma. Episcopalian. Author: Trends and Forces of Change in the Payments System and the Impact on Commercial Banking, 1972; contbg. editor Pacific Banker and Bus. mag., 1974-80.

BROUSSARD, CAROL MADELINE, writer, literary consulting agent, photographer; b. Albany, Calif.; d. Roy E. Avila and Adele (Belfils) Cazet; m. Marvin E. Broussard; children: Valerie Madeline, Sean Hunter Rutledge. Student, West Hill Coll., Coalinga, Calif., Coll. Sequoias, Visalia, Calif., Inst. Metaphysics, La Brea, Calif. Former pub. and investigative journalist; pub. TV Watch, Tyler, Tex., 1969-74; resource sec. John C. Fremont Sch., Corcoran, Calif., 1974-77; editor Coalinga (Calif.) Record, 1978-81; pub., prodn. mgr. Kern Valley Chronicle, Lake Isabella, Calif., 1981-84; freelance writer, 1990—; featured TV show Writing Procedures, 1992; instr. home pub. Calif. State U., Fresno, 1992, 95; instr. photography Clovis (Calif.) Adult Edn., 1993—, instr. ethnic watercolors, 1993-94, instr. investigative journalism. 1994, instr. freelance journalism, 1995; tchr. photog. lab. Clovis Teen Summer Sch., 1992-94. Author poetry; composer lyrics for Cajun Hoedown Man Century, summer 1990, theme song Karma for Cinnimin Skin, Lance Mungia film, 1994. Vol., Literacy Progra for WIN/WIN, Fresno Unified Sch. Dist., 1992. Recipient Photo-Journalist award Calif. Newspaper Assn., 1983, Best Feature Photo award Calif. Justice System, 1984, World of Child Photo award Fresno City and County Offices, 1980, Poetic Achievement award Amherst Soc., 1990, award of merit World of Poetry, 1990, Golden Poet award, 1990, 91, Iliad Literary award, 1990, Poetry Editor's Choice award, 1992-93; spotlight interview Writers' Journal, 1992. Mem. Writers Internat. Network (speaker 1991, 92, coord. Vols. Conf. awards 1991). Republican.

BROUSSARD, FREDERICK, sales executive; b. Chgo., Aug. 26, 1937; s. A.B. and V. B.; m. Mildred Broussard, July 10, 1980. BS, Calif. State U., Long Beach, 1989; MA, West Coast U., L.A., 1992. Commd. ensign USN, 1957-79; test engr. Hughes Aircraft, El Segundo, Calif., 1979-89; system analyst McDonald Douglas, Long Beach, Calif., 1989-91; tech. writer Northrup, Pico Rivera, Calif., 1991-92; dir. ops. Freeway Engine Sales, Gardena, Calif., 1992—. Mem. Elks, Fleet Reserve, VFW. Office: Freeway Engine Sales 190 West Sierra Madre Azusa CA 91702

BROWER, DAVID ROSS, conservationist; b. Berkeley, Calif., July 1, 1912; s. Ross J. and Mary Grace (Barlow) B.; m. Anne Hus, May 1, 1943; children: Kenneth David, Robert Irish, Barbara Anne, John Stewart. Student, U. Calif., 1929-31; DSc (hon.), Hobart and William Smith Colls., 1967; DHL (hon.), Claremont Colls. Grad. Sch., 1971, Starr King Sch. for Ministry, 1971, U. Md., 1973; PhD in Ecology (hon.), U. San Francisco, 1973, Colo. Coll., 1977; other hon. degrees, New Sch. for Social Rsch., 1984, Sierra Nev. Coll., 1985, Unity Coll., Maine, 1989. Editor U. Calif. Press, 1941-52; exec. dir. Sierra Club, 1952-69, bd. dirs., 1941-43, 46-53, 83-88, mem. editorial bd., 1935-69, hon. v.p., 1972—; dir. John Muir Inst. Environ. Studies, 1969-71, v.p., 1968-72; pres. Friends of the Earth, 1969-79; founder, chmn. Friends of the Earth Found., 1972-84, bd. dirs.; founder Environ. Liaison Ctr., Nairobi, 1974; founder, chmn. Earth Island Inst., San Francisco, 1982—; founder, pres. Earth Island Action Group, 1989; founder biennial Fate and Hope of the Earth Confs., N.Y.C., 1982, Washington, 1984, Ottawa, 1986, Managua, 1989; activist in conservation campaigns, Kings Canyon Nat. Pk., 1938-40, Dinosaur Nat. Monument, 1952-56, Alaska parks and forests, 1954—, North Cascades Nat. Pk., 1955-94, Cape Cod, Fire Island, Point Reyes nat. seashores, 1960-68, Redwood Nat. Pk., 1963-68, Great Basin Nat. Park, 1965, Galapagos Islands World Heritage, 1965-68, Grand Canyon 1952-68, Snowdonia Nat. Park, 1970, 71, population and growth control and nuclear proliferation issues, Nat. Wilderness Preservation System, 1951-64, James Bay defense, 1991-94, conservation lectr., U.S., 1939—, Finland, 1971, Sweden, 1972, Kenya, 1972, 74, Italy, 1972, 74, 79, 82, 91, 94, Australia and N.Z., 1974, Japan, 1976, 78, 90, 92, U.K., 1968, 70, 93, USSR, 1985, 88, 90, 91, 92, France, 1970, 90-91, Fed. Republic Germany, 1989, Berlin, 1990, Nicaragua, 1988, 89, Brazil, 1992, The Netherlands, 1993-94; founder Trustees for Conservation, 1954, sec., 1960-61, 64-65; founder Sierra Club Found., 1960; bd. dirs. Citizens Com. Natural Resources, 1955-78; chmn. Natural Resources Coun. Am., 1955-57; bd. dirs. North Cascades Conservation Coun., from 1957, Rachel Carson Trust for Living Environment, 1966-72, cons. expert, from 1973; founder, steering com. League Conservation Voters, 1969-80; founder Les Amis de la Terre, Paris, 1970; founder, guarantor Friends of the Earth U.K., 1970-88; chmn. Earth Island Ltd., London, 1971-74; active Restoring-the-Earth movement, from 1986, founder Global CPR Svc., 1990, leader del. to Lake Baikal, Siberia, 1988, 90, 91, 92, mem. various adv. bds. including Found. on Econ. Trends, Nat. Strategy, Coun. Econ. Priorities, Zero Population Growth, Yosemite Concessions Svc., Earth Day 1990, 94; mem. Com. on Nat. Security. Initiator, designer, gen. editor: Sierra Club Exhibit Format Series, 20 vols., 1960-68, Friends of the Earth series The Earth's Wild Places, 10 vols., 1970-77, Celebrating the Earth series, 3 vols., 1972-73; numerous other films and books, biographee in Encounters with the Archdruid (John McPhee), 1970; (autobiography) Vol. 1, For Earth's Sake: The Life and Times of DAvid Brower, 1990, Vol. 2, Work in Progress, 1991; co-author: (Steve Chapple) Let the Mountains Talk, Let the Rivers Run, 1995; contbr. articles to nat. mags., profl. publs., others; subject video documentary produced for Sta. KCTS, Seattle, shown nationally on PBS; contbr. to U.S. Army mountain manuals, instruction, 1943-45. Participant in planning for 1992 UN Conf. on Environment, Rio de Janiero, 1987-92. Served as 1st lt. with 10th Mountain div. Inf. AUS, 1943-45; maj. Inf.-Res. ret. Decorated Bronze Star; recipient awards Calif. Conservation Coun., 1953, Nat. Parks Assn., 1956, Bklyn. Coll. Libr. Assn., 1970, also Carey-Thomas award, 1964, Paul Bartsch award Audubon Naturalist Soc. of Cen. Atlantic States, 1967, Golden Ark award the Prince of The Netherlands, 1979, Golden Gadfly award Medlliance, San Francisco, 1984, Rose award World Environment Festival, Ottawa, Can., 1986, Strong Oak award New Renaissance Ctr., 1987, Lewis Mumford award Architects Designers Planners for Social Responsibility, 1991, Robert Marshall award, 1994; hon. fellow John Muir Coll., U. Calif., San Diego, 1986. Nominated Nobel Peace Prize, 1978, 79. Mem. Nat. Parks and Conservation Assn. (hon.), The Mountaineers (hon.), Appalachian Mountain Club (hon.), Sierra Club (1933—, John Muir award 1977), Am. Alpine Club (hon.). Address: Earth Island 300 Broadway St San Francisco CA 94133-4545

BROWER, LESTER MAYER, physical therapist; b. Chgo., May 29, 1929; m. Patricia L.; children: Jordan Al, Kirk J, Shaun Z. BA, State U. Iowa, MA; BS, Western Mich. U. Registered phys. therapist, occupl. therapist. Tchr. Codo Parish Sch. Dist., Shreveport, La., 1953-54; dir. sch. for spl. edn. Hammond (Ind.) Pub. Schs., 1957-62; owner phys. therapy practice Lester M. Brower, Highland Pk., Ill., 1962-74; owner Hi-Desert Therapy Ctr., Yucca Valley, Calif., 1975—. Contbr. articles to profl. jours. 1st lt. USAF, 1951-53. Mem. Am. Phys. Therapy Assn. (pvt. practice sect. 1959—, orthopedic and sports medicine sect. 1960—), Am. Occupl. Therapy Assn., Airplane Pilot and Owners Assn. Home: 7253 Balsa Ave Yucca Valley CA 92284-5941 Office: Hi-Desert Therapy Ctr 58471 29 Plams Hwy Ste 101 Yucca Valley CA 92284

BROWN, ALAN JOHNSON, chemicals executive; b. Alnwick, Eng., June 18, 1951; came to U.S., 1987; s. George and Margaret Mary (Johnson) B.; m. Cathy Sturlis, May 14, 1988 (div. Feb. 1993). BS in Chemistry, U. East Anglia, Eng., 1974; MS in Enzymology, U. Warwick, Eng., 1975, PhD in Molecular Sci., 1977. Chartered chemist. Group leader ICI Corp. Rsch., Runcorn, Eng., 1977-81; group leader ECC Internat. Cen. Rsch., St. Austell, Eng., 1981-87; rsch. mgr. ECC Internat. Tech. Ctr., Sandersville, Ga., 1987-92; tech. dir. Columbia River Carbonates, Woodland, Wash., 1993—. Patentee in field. Mem. Royal Soc. Chemistry (S.W. Region com. 1986-87), Am. Chem. Soc., Clay Minerals Soc., Tech. Assoc. Pulp and Paper Inst., Chem. Mfrs. Assn. (chmn. analytical methods group 1991, 92). Office: Columbia River Carbonates PO Box D Woodland WA 98674-1103

BROWN, ALISON K., aeronautics company executive; b. Edinburgh, Scotland, Jan. 14, 1957; came to the U.S., 1980; d. Kenneth Robson and Margery (Kay) B.; m. Bruce Graham Johnson, June 26, 1993. BA, MA in Engrng., Cambridge U., 1979; MS in Aero. Engrng., MIT, 1981; PhD in Mechanics and Aerospace, UCLA, 1985. Draper fellow Draper Lab., Cambridge, Mass., 1980-81; mem. tech. staff Litton Industries, Woodland Hills, Calif., 1981-86; pres. NAVSYS Corp., Monument, Colo., 1986—; bd. dirs. Ctr. for Mapping Ohio State U., Columbus. Patentee in field; contbr. articles to profl. jours. Mem. com. USAF Scientific Adv. Bd., Washington, 1994. Scholar Sidney Sussex Coll., 1979, DuPont scholar, 1980; recipient Sir George Nelson prize Cambridge U., 1979, Cert. of Appreciation Radio Tech. Com. for Aviation. Mem. Inst. Navigation (coun. mem., conf. chair), IEEE, AIAA. Office: NAVSYS 14960 Woodcarver Rd Colorado Springs CO 80921-2370

BROWN, ALLEN LEON, JR., computer scientist, educator; b. Washington, Nov. 8, 1946; s. Allen Leon and Martha Ada (Drake) B.; m. Susan Jane Foster, Sept. 4, 1969 (div. Oct. 1972); m. Karen Laree Taylor, Jan. 1, 1986. SB, MIT, 1967, PhD, 1975. *. Rsch. assoc. Columbia U., N.Y.C., 1968-69, MIT, Cambridge, 1969-72; mem. rsch. staff T. J. Watson Rsch. Ctr. IBM, Yorktown Heights, N.Y., 1975-79; section mgr. Office Systems div. Xerox, Palo Alto, 1979-84; computer scientist R&D div. GE, Schenectady, N.Y., 1984-88; prin. scientist Webster Rsch. Ctr. Xerox, Webster, N.Y., 1988-92; dir. tech., XSoft fellow XSoft divsn. Xerox Corp., Palo Alto, 1993—; prof. computer and info. sci. Syracuse (N.Y.) U., 1989-95; vis. fellow Math. Scis. Inst., Cornell U., Ithaca, N.Y., 1992-94; James Clark Welling prof. The George Washington U., Washington, 1995—. Contbr. articles to profl. jours. Rsch. grantee Def. Advanced Rsch. Projects Agy., 1985. Mem. Soc. Indsl. and Applied Math. Home: 425 Glenmont Dr Solana Beach CA 92075-1310 Office: Xerox Corporation XSoft Divsn 3400 Hillview Ave MS PAHV-127 Palo Alto CA 94304

BROWN, ANTHONY B., finance executive; b. Mpls., Apr. 5, 1922; s. Wayland Hoyt and Adele (Birdsall) B.; m. Mary Alice Ann Anderson, July 28, 1956. BS, Rutgers U., 1949; postgrad. U. So. Calif., 1968-69; PhD, U. Beverly Hills, 1986. Cert. data processing systems profl. Sr. system analyst Thrifty Corp., L.A., 1957-69; system engr. Informatics Gen., Inc., L.A., 1969-73; contract instr. computer software York U., 1970, McGill U., U. Victoria, 1971, USMC, Boston U., W.Va. U., U. Guelph, 1972; sr. system engr. Jet Propulsion Lab., La Canada, Calif., 1974-76; sr. system engr. Informatics Gen., Inc., Anchorage, L.A., Washington, 1976-78; supr. project control Hughes Aircraft Co., L.A., 1978-81; contr. western ops. Contel Corp., Redondo Beach, Calif., 1981-88. Author: A Century of Blunders—America's China Policy 1844-1949. Rep. precinct capt., presdl. election, 1964; vol. Reason Found.; chmn. bd. govs. La Brea Vista Townhouses, 1967-68; active numerous animal welfare orgns. Served with Finance Corps, U.S. Army, 1951-57. Decorated Bronze Star. Fellow Brit. Interplanetary Soc.; mem. AAAS, The Planetary Soc., Nature Conservancy, Town Hall of Calif., Assn. Computer Machinery (chpt. sec. 1973-74), Assn. Systems Mgmt., Mensa, Intertel, Armed Forces Communications and Electronics Assn., Assn. Inst. Cert. Computer Profls., Am. Assn. Fin. Profls., Am. Def. Preparedness Assn., Washington Legal Found., Am. Security Council (mem. nat. adv. bd.), Calif. Soc. SAR, Mil. Order World Wars, Aircraft Owners and Pilots Assn., Internat. Platform Assn., Theodore Roosevelt Assn., Res. Officers Assn., Delta Phi Epsilon. Republican. Club: Los Angeles Athletic. Lodges: Masons, Shriners, Nat. Sojourners. Home: 4333 Redwood Ave Marina Del Rey CA 90292

BROWN, ARTHUR CARL, JR., retired minister; b. Stockton, Calif., Dec. 16, 1915; s. Arthur Carl and Maud (Twitchings) B.; m. Inez Lundquist, May 10, 1940 (dec. Aug. 1982); 1 child, Arthur Carl III. BA, Coll. of the Pacific, 1937; MA, San Francisco Theol. Sem., 1939, BD with honors, 1940; postgrad., Stanford U., 1949-50. Ordained to ministry Presbyn. Ch., 1940. Pastor Presbyn. Ch., Sedro Woolley, Wash., 1940-44, Community Ch., Santa Clara, Calif., 1944-46; assoc. pastor First Presbyn. Ch., San. Jose, Calif., 1946-49; minister edn. First Presbyn. Ch., Palo Alto, Calif., 1949-51; organizing pastor Covenant Presbyn. Ch., Palo Alto, 1951-74; pastor Trinity Presbyn. Ch., Santa Cruz, Calif., 1974-78; outreach assoc. Los Gatos (Calif.) Presbyn. Ch., 1978-81; commr. to gen. assembly United Presbyn. Ch., 1947, 52, 59; moderator San Jose Presbytery, 1950, chmn. various coms., 1950-78; mem. Synod Golden Gate and Synod of Pacific coms. Synod of Calif., 1947-82; pastor emeritus Covenant Presbyn. Ch.; moderator Bellingham Prebytery-Synod of Wash., 1943. Treas., chmn. fin. com., bd. dirs. Internat. House, Davis, Calif., 1984-90, chmn. internat. house nominating com., 1990-95, mem. internat. devel. com., 1991—. Home: 4414 San Ramon Dr Davis CA 95616-5018

BROWN, BARBARA BLACK, publishing company executive; b. Eureka, Calif., Dec. 11, 1928; d. William Marion and Letitia (Brunia) Black; m. Vinson Brown, June 18, 1950; children—Tamara Pinn, Roxana Hodges, Keven. B.A., Western State Coll., Gunnison, Colo. Owner, mgr. Naturegraph Pubs., Inc., Los Altos, Calif., 1950-53, San Martin, Calif., 1953-60, Healdsburg, Calif., 1960-76, Happy Camp, Calif., 1976—. Author: Barns of Yesteryear; co-author: Sierra Nevadian Wildlife Region. Mem. Baha'i World Faith. Office: Naturegraph Pubs Inc 3543 Indian Creek Rd Happy Camp CA 96039-9706

BROWN, BART A., JR., consumer products company executive; b. Louisville, 1933. LLB, U. Louisville, 1955; LLM, Georgetown U., 1957, JD. With Irs, 1970-76, with Keating, Muething, Klekamp, Brown & Gardner, 1976-90; past CEO Circle K. Corp., Phoenix, 1971—, chmn., also bd. dirs. *

BROWN, BENJAMIN ANDREW, journalist; b. Red House, W.Va., Apr. 30, 1933; s. Albert Miller and Mary Agnes (Donegan) B.; m. Joanne Gretchen Harder, May 22, 1956; children: Benjamin Andrew, Gretchen, Mark, Betsy Brown Larson. BS in Journalism, Fla. State U., 1955. Sportswriter Charleston (W.Va.) Daily Mail, 1955-57; with AP, 1957-93; gen. exec. AP, N.Y.C., 1976-78, 82-93; chief bur. AP, Los Angeles, 1978-82; assoc. Am. Newspapers Cons., Ltd., Milw., 1993—; bd. dirs. Last Chance Press Club, Helena, Mont., 1969; v.p. Minn. Press Club, 1975. Office: PO Box 3012 Paso Robles CA 93447-3012

BROWN, CAROL ELIZABETH, management educator; b. Boise, Idaho, Jan. 26, 1950; d. Mason Oliver Brown and Hazel (Metcalf) Henderson; m. Richard Bruce Wodtli, Aug. 16, 1989. BS in Art, U. Wis., 1972; MS in Acctg., U. Oreg., 1977; PhD in Computer Sci., Oreg. State U., 1989. CPA. Bookkeeper Stone Fence Inc., Madison, Wis., 1972-74; staff acct. Baillies, Denson, Erickson & Smith, Madison, 1974-75, Minihan, Kernutt, Stokes & Co., Eugene, 1977-78; instr. Oreg. State U., Corvallis, 1978-89, asst. prof., 1989-92, assoc. prof., 1992—. Assoc. editor Jour. Info. Sys., 1989-92; mem. editl. rev. bd. Internat. Jour. Intelligent Sys. in Acctg., Fin. and Mgmt., 1991—, Internat. Jour. Applied Expert Sys., 1994—; guest editor Expert Sys. With Applications, 1991, 95; contbr. articles to profl. jours. Bd. dirs. United Way of Benton County, Corvallis, 1989—, sec.-treas., 1993—; vol. acct., 1982-86. Recipient Outstanding Vol. Svc. award United Way of Benton County, 1986, 93; rsch. grant Oreg. State U., 1988, 90, Scholarship award, 1992, 93; rsch. grant TIAA-CREF, 1990, 91. Mem. IEEE Computer Soc., Am. Acctg. Assn. (program adv. com. 1990-91, artificial intelligence/expert sys. sect., vice chairperson 1991-92, chairperson-elect 1992-93, chairperson 1993-94, Pioneer Svc. award 1994), Am. Assn. Artificial Intelligence, Inst. Mgmt. Accts. (dir. manuscripts Salem, Oreg. area 1990—, bd. dirs. 1990—, Merit cert. 1990-91, Rsch. grantee 1993), Oreg. Soc. CPA (com. mem. 1989-94, vice chmn. computer svcs. com. 1990-91, Recognition cert. for Leadership Excellence 1989-90, Outstanding Svc. award 1990-91), Assn. Computer Machinery, others. Home: 1145 NW 20th St Corvallis OR 97330-2509 Office: Oreg State U Coll Bus Bexell Hall # 200 Corvallis OR 97331-2603

BROWN, CAROLYN SMITH, communications educator, consultant; b. Salt Lake City, Aug. 12, 1946; d. Andrew Delbert and Olive (Crane) Smith; m. David Scott Brown, Sept. 10, 1982. BA magna cum laude, U. Utah, 1968, MA, 1972, PhD, 1974. Instr. Salt Lake Ctr., Brigham Young U., Salt Lake City, 1976-78; vis. asst. prof. Brigham Young U., Provo, 1978; asst. prof. Am. Inst. Banking, Salt Lake City, 1977—; prof., chmn. English, communication and gen. edn. depts. Latter Day Saints Bus. Coll., Salt Lake City, 1973—, acad. dean, 1986—; founder, pres. Career Devel. Tng., Salt Lake City, 1979—; field mktg. dir. Systems Internat./Prformax Inc., Mpls., 1978—, Carlson Learning Co., Mpls., 1978—; cons. in-house seminars 1st Security Realty Svcs., USDA Soil Conservation Svc., Utah Power & Light, Utah Soc. Svcs., Adminstrv. Office of Cts., HUD, Intermountain Health Care, Continental Bank. Author: Writing Letters & Reports That Communicate, 6 ed., 1985; contbr. articles to profl. jours. Demi-soloist Utah Civic Ballet (now Ballet West), Salt Lake City, 1964-68; active Mormon Ch. Named Tchr. of Month, Salt Lake City Kiwanis, 1981; NDEA fellow, U. Utah, 1972. Mem. Am. Bus. Communications Assn. (lectr. West/N.W. regional chpt. 1987), Delta Kappa Gamma (2d v.p. 1977-79), Lambda Delta Sigma (Outstanding Woman of Yr. 1983), Kappa Kappa Gamma (Outstanding Alumnus in Lit. 1974). Republican. Clubs: Alice Louise Reynolds Literary (Salt Lake City) (v.p. 1978-79, sec. 1985-86). Office: LDS Bus Coll 411 E South Temple Salt Lake City UT 84111-1302

BROWN, CHARLES SIDNEY, SR., consultant to restaurant and computer industries; b. New Orleans, Dec. 6, 1946; s. Charles L. and Lorraine (Larsen) B.; m. Linda Moore (div.); children: Charles S. Jr., Lori M. Student, La. State U., 1969. Owner Brown & Assocs., New Orleans, 1969-76; area mgr. Pizza Hut, New Orleans, 1976-81; dir. ops. Pizza Hut, Dallas, 1981-86; internat. dir. ops. AFC, Inc., Atlanta, 1986-93; pres. Brown Enterprises, Las Vegas, Nev., 1993—. Mem. Jaycees (New Orleans chpt. sec. 1972). Republican. Home: 2823 Laplace St Chalmette LA 70043 Office: Brown Enterprises PO Box 98378 Las Vegas NV 89193-8378

BROWN, CHRISTOPHER PATRICK, health care administrator, educator; b. Phoenix, June 7, 1951; s. Charles Francis and R. Patricia (Quinn) B.; m. Tracey Ann Wallenberg, May 23, 1987; 1 child, Ryan Matthew. AA in Biol. Scis., Shasta Coll., Redding, Calif., 1976; AS in Liberal Arts, SUNY, Albany, 1977; grad. Primary Care Assoc. Program, Stanford U., 1978; BA in Community Svcs. Adminstrn., Calif. State U., Chico, 1982; M. in Health Svcs., U. Calif., Davis, 1984. Gen. mgr. Pacific Ambulance Svc., El Cajon, Calif., 1974; primary care assoc. Family Practice, Oregon-Calif., 1978-82; cons. Calif. Health Profls., Chico, 1982-84; bus. ops. mgr. Nature's Arts, Inc., Seattle, 1985-86; instr. North Seattle C.C., 1984-89, program dir., 1986-89; asst. dir. Pacific Med. Clinic North, Seattle, 1990-92; dir. Pacific Med. Clinic Renton (Wash.), Pacific Med. Ctr., 1992-95; dir. ops./physician svcs. St. Luke's Regional Med. Ctr., Boise, 1995—. Mem. Butte County Adult Day Care Health Coun., Chico, 1982-84; bd. dirs., pres. Innovative Health Care Svcs., Chico, 1982-84; bd. dirs. Highline W. Seattle Mental Health Ctr., 1985-90, v.p. 1988-90; tech. adv. com. North Seattle C.C., 1992-93, With U.S. Navy, 1970-74. Mem. Adult Day Care Alliance (bd. dirs.), Med. Group Mgmt. Assn., Multispecialty Group Exec. Soc. Home: 2902 Crane Creek Rd Boise ID 83702 Office: St Lukes Regional Med Ctr 190 E Bannock Boise ID 83712

BROWN, CLINT M., geologist, oil company executive; b. Dallas, Jan. 12, 1964; s. Burton M. and Sylba Corene (Busby) B.; m. Janelle Linnea Campbell. BS, E. Tex. State U., 1991; MS, Utah State U., 1995. Exploration geologist Basin Exploration, Inc., Dallas, 1982-91; rsch. asst. dept. geology Utah State U., Logan, 1991—. Contbr. article to jour. in field. Mem. Am. Assn. Petroleum Geologists, Geol. Soc. Am., Delta Chi (house mgr. 1983-84). Episcopalian. Home: 577 E 200 N Logan UT 84321

BROWN, DANIEL WARREN, public relations executive; b. Portchester, N.Y., Oct. 26, 1930; s. Malcolm Doughty and Helen Ann (Warren) B.; m. Helen June Sproule, Mar. 15, 1953 (div. 1958); 1 child, Peter; m. Jean Frances High, Aug. 2, 1958; 1 child, Daniel Warren; stepchildren: Carole Hoppe, Fredric Hoppe, Catherine Hoppe. BA, Columbia U., 1952; MA in Journalism, U. Wis., 1971. Reporter Sun-Tattler, Hollywood, Fla., 1956-57, Miami Herald, Fla., 1957-61; dir. Combined Fed. Campaign, San Diego, 1980-82; dir. pub. affairs Aerojet, Sacramento, 1982-91; owner Hartman Brown & Assocs., Sacramento, 1991—. Lt. Col. USMC, 1952-55, 61-80. Decorated Legion of Merit, Joint Svcs. Commendation medal, Navy Commendation medal. Mem. Pub. Rels. Soc. Am. (chpt. pres. 1988). Republican. Office: Hartman Brown & Assocs 11447 Hesperian Cir Gold River CA 95670-7651

BROWN, DARMAE JUDD, librarian; b. Jefferson City, Mo., Sept. 14, 1952; d. William Robert and Dorothy Judd (Curtis) B. BA, W.Va. Wesleyan Coll., 1974; MA, U. Denver, 1975; M of Computer Info. Systems, U. Denver, 1992. Searching assoc. Bibliog. Ctr. for Rsch., Denver, 1975-76; libr. N.E. Colo. Regional Libr., Wray, 1976-81; head tech. svcs. Ector County Libr., Odessa, Tex., 1981-84, Waterloo (Iowa) Pub. Libr., 1984-89; systems coord. Aurora (Colo.) Pub. Libr., 1989—. Mem. ALA, Iowa OCLC Users Group (pres. 1986-87), Colo. Libr. Assn., Libr. & Info. Tech. Assn., Beta Phi Mu, Sigma Alpha Iota. Home: 12010 E Harvard Ave Aurora CO 80014-1808

BROWN, DAVID A., computer hardware company executive; b. 1945. Formerly with Shugart Assocs.; pres., COO Quantum Corp., Milpitas, Calif., 1987—, also bd. dirs. Office: Quantum Corp 500 Mccarthy Blvd Milpitas CA 95035-7908

BROWN, DAVID R., academic administrator. Pres., dir. Art Ctr. Coll. Design, Pasadena, Calif. Office: Art Ctr Coll of Design Office of Pres 1700 Lida St Pasadena CA 91103-1924

BROWN, DAVID RICHARD, school system administrator, minister; b. Manhattan, Kans., Oct. 22, 1929; s. Marion Arthur and Dorothy (Bailey) B.; m. Jeanette Christine Phoenix, July 28, 1962; children: David M., Mark, Thomas. BA, U. So. Calif., 1951; MDiv, U. Chgo., 1955; postgrad., U. So. Calif., 1956, 57. Ordained minister, Presbyn. Ch. Assoc. pastor Federated Community Ch., Flagstaff, Ariz., 1957-59; minister of edn. Lakeside Presbyn. Ch., San Francisco, 1959-62; pastor of edn. 1st Presbyn. Ch., Medford, Oreg., 1962-69; pastor 1st Presbyn. Ch., Newark, Calif., 1969-75; founder, pastor Community Presbyn. Ch., Union City, Calif., 1975-89; founder, supt. Christian Heritage Acad., Fremont, Calif., 1984—; organizing pastor New Life Presbyn. Ch., Fremont, 1989—; asst. prof. Chabot Coll., Hayward, Calif., 1975-80; moderator Presbytery of No. Ariz., 1959. Dir. various Shakespearian theatrical prodns., 1982-84 (Thesbian award 1984). Pres. Boys Christian League, L.A., 1953-54, Coconino Assn. for Mental Health, Flagstaff, 1958-59; chaplain Mozumdar YMCA Camp, Crestline, Calif., 1952-56; chmn. Tri-City Citizens Action Com., 1986-90. Recipient plaque KC, 1989. Mem. Rotary (chpt. pres. 1988-89, Paul Harris fellow 1989). Office: Christian Heritage Acad PO Box 7688 Fremont CA 94537

BROWN, DEBORAH ELIZABETH, television producer, marketing professional; b. Aledo, Ill., Nov. 29, 1952; d. Kenneth M. and Mary Esther (Gilmore) B.; m. K. J. Lester, Nov. 28, 1975 (dec. Mar. 1982); children: Rebekah Jean, Aaron Mark, Jonathan Caleb. Student, Letourneau Coll., 1970; BA in Theater Arts, Sterling Coll., 1974; MA in Comm., Wheaton Coll., 1977. Producer, dir. Sta. WCFC-TV, Chgo., 1978-80; sales mgr. SNG Enterprises, St. Charles, Ill., 1980-82; pres., CEO Circle Family Video Stores, Niles, Mich., 1982-87; exec. producer Picture Radio Pictures, Lakeland, Fla., 1987-93; mgr. Computer Keyboard, Portland, Oreg., 1993—; vis. prof. comm. Wheaton (Ill.) Coll., 1980; video cons. Spring Arbor Distbrs., Belleville, Mich., 1985, Gospel Films, Muskegan, Mich., 1985. Producer, dir., writer (TV program and book) Crafts With Emilie, 1979 (Spl. Emmy nomination); video contbg. editor Christian Booksellers Assn. jour., 1984-85; set decorator Cindy Williams Comedy Spl., 1993. Corp. sponsor Pregnancy Care Ctr., Niles, 1985-87; producer Four Flags Area Apple Festival, Niles, 1987. Mem. Fellowship of Christians in Arts, Media and Entertainment, Christian Video Retailers Assn. (exec. dir. 1985-87), Fla. Motion Picture and TV Assn. Baptist. Office: Computer Keyboard 12000 SE 82nd Ave Ste 1121 Portland OR 97266-7736

BROWN, DEE ALEXANDER, author; b. La., 1908; s. Daniel Alexander and Lulu (Cranford) B.; m. Sara B. Stroud, Aug. 1, 1934; children—James Mitchell, Linda. B.S., George Washington U., 1937; M.S., U. Ill., 1951. Librarian Dept. Agr., Washington, 1934-42, Aberdeen Proving Ground, Md., 1945-48; agrl. librarian U. Ill. at Urbana, 1948-72, prof., 1962-75. Author: Wave High the Banner, 1942, Grierson's Raid, 1954, Yellowhorse, 1956, Cavalry Scout, 1957, The Gentle Tamers: Women of the Old Wild West, 1958, The Bold Cavaliers, 1959, They Went Thataway, 1960, (with M.F. Schmitt) Fighting Indians of the West, 1948, Trail Driving Days, 1952, The Settler's West, 1955, Fort Phil Kearny, 1962, The Galvanized Yankees, 1963, Showdown at Little Big Horn, 1964, The Girl from Fort Wicked, 1964, The Year of the Century, 1966, Action at Beecher Island, 1967, Bury My Heart at Wounded Knee, 1971, Andrew Jackson and the Battle of New Orleans, 1972, The Westerners, 1974, Tepee Tales, 1979, Creek Mary's Blood, 1980, The American Spa, 1982, Killdeer Mountain, 1983, Conspiracy of Knaves, 1987, Wondrous Times on the Frontier, 1991, When the Century Was Young, 1993, The American West, 1994; contbr.: Growing Up Western, 1990; editor: Agricultural History, 1956-58, Pawnee, Blackfoot and Cheyenne, 1961. Served with AUS, 1942-45. Recipient A.L.A. Clarence Day award, 1971, Christopher award, 1971, Illinoisian of Yr., Ill. News Broadcasters Assn., 1972, W.W.A. Golden Saddleman award, 1984. Mem. Authors Guild, Soc. Am. Historians, Western Writers Am., Beta Phi Mu. Home: 7 Overlook Dr Little Rock AR 72207-1619

BROWN, DONALD MALCOLM, plastic surgeon; b. Nelson, N.Z., May 28, 1945; came to U.S., 1947; s. Donald Roland and Edna M. (McPherson) B.; m. Susan E. Boeing, Sept. 3, 1989. MD, U. B.C., 1970. Diplomate Am. Bd. Otolaryngology and Plastic Surgery. Resident in otolarngology Manhattan Eye and Ear Hosp., N.Y.C., 1976; resident in plastic surgery Columbia U., N.Y.C., 1980; pvt. practice San Francisco, 1981—; vis. prof. plastic surgery U. Liberia, Africa, 1980-81. Mem. AMA, Calif. Med. Assn., San Francisco Med. Assn., Am. Soc. Plastic and Reconstructive Surgery, Am. Soc. Aesthetic Surgery, Pacific Union Club, St. Francis Yacht Club. Office: 2100 Webster St Ste 429 San Francisco CA 94115-2380

BROWN, E. LYNN, minister; b. Jackson, Tn., Apr. 2, 1936; s. Willie T. and Ocie (Royal) B.; m. Gladys Deloris Stephens, Aug. 10, 1963; children: A. Victor, Cheronda Patrice. BD and MDiv, Interdenominational Theol. Ctr., 1963; BS, Lane Coll., 1960; DD (hon.), Tex. Coll., 1987, Miles Coll., 1979. Min. Phillips Chapel Christ Meth. Episc. Ch., Milan, Tn., 1963, Greenwood Christ Meth. Episc. Ch., Memphis, 1963-67, Mt. Pisgah Christ Meth. Episc. Ch., Memphis, 1967-78; gen. sec. Christ MEth. Episc. Nat. Hdqrs., Memphis, 1978-86; bishop 9th Episc. Dist., L.A., 1986—; bd. dirs. South Cen. Organizing Com., SCLC, Atlanta. Mem. NAACP (bd. dirs.), Nat. Coun. Chs. (bd. dirs.). Office: 9th Episc Dist 3844 W Slauson Ave Ste 1 Los Angeles CA 90043-2935

BROWN, ERIC, developer; b. Columbus, Ohio, July 31, 1959; s. David Evan and Kay Elinor (Klayman) B.; m. Katherine Marie Logan, May 26, 1990; 1 child, Julian Logan. BA in Urban Planning, U. Wash.; M in City Planning, MIT. Asst. projects dir. Wash. Pub. Interest Rsch. Group, Seattle, 1982-83; rsch. asst. Nat. Endowment for the Arts/MIT, Cambridge, Mass., 1984-85; cons. City of Boston, Mass., 1986; housing developer Common Ground, Seattle, 1987-92; exec. dir. St. Andrew's Housing Group, Bellevue, Wash., 1993—; planning cons. St. Andrew's Luth. Ch., Bellevue, 1994; presenter in field. State bd. dirs. Washington Pub. Interest Rsch. Group, Seattle, 1983-84; active Seattle (Wash.) City Light Resources Planning Citizens Adv. Com., 1983-84, Seattle (Wash.) Design Rev. Adv. Com., 1990-93. Office: St Andrews Housing Group 2650 148th Ave SE Bellevue WA 98007-6452

BROWN, FREDERICK CALVIN, physicist, educator; b. Seattle, July 6, 1924; s. Fred Charles and Rose (Mueller) B.; m. Joan Schauble, Aug. 9, 1952; children—Susan, Gail, Derek. B.S., Harvard U., 1945, M.S., 1947, Ph.D., 1950. Physicist Systems Research Lab., Harvard (NDRC), 1945-46; staff physicist Naval Research Lab., Washington, 1950; physicist Applied Physics Lab., U. Wash., 1950-51; asst. prof. Reed Coll., Portland, Oreg., 1951-55, U. Ill., Urbana, 1955-58; assoc. prof. U. Ill., 1958-61, prof., 1961-87, prof. emeritus, 1987—; assoc. Center for Advanced Study, 1969-70; prin. scientist, area mgr. Xerox Palo Alto Research Center, 1973-74; prof. U. Wash., Seattle, 1987; cons. prof., applied physics dept. Stanford, 1973-74. Author: The Physics of Solids-Ionic Crystals, Lattice Vibrations and Imperfections, 1967; Contbr. articles profl. jours. Recipient Alexander von Humboldt sr. scientist award U. Kiel, 1978; NSF sr. postdoctoral fellow Clarendon Lab., Oxford, 1964-65. Fellow Am. Phys. Soc. Home: 2414 E Discovery Pl Langley WA 98260 Office: U Wash Dept Physics Box 351560 Seattle WA 98195-1560

BROWN, GARY HUGH, artist, art educator; b. Evansville, Ind., Dec. 19, 1941. BA, DePauw U., 1963; MFA, U. Wis., 1966. Prof. art U. Calif., Santa Barbara, 1966—; mem. faculty Coll. Creative Studies, 1984-85, Courtyard of Hope and Fountain of Tears Aids Home, 1994, Venice Biennale: Art Against AIDS, 1993; judge 9th ann. competition Bristol-Myers Squibb Co., 1991. One-man shows include Colmsley, Beverley Hills, 1974, United Arts Club, Bublin, Ireland, 1975, Source, San Francisco, 1976, New Harmony Gallery of Contemporaty Art, 1977, Santa Barbara City Coll. Art Gallery, 1979, Atelierhaus, Worpswede, Germany, George Eastman House, Hewitt Mus., N.Y.C., 1980, Life Gallery Santa Barbara, 1982, The Frameworks and De La Guerra Gallery, Santa Barbara, 1984, Art Space, Nishunomiya, Japan, 1980, Allan Hancock Coll. Art Gallery, Santa Maria, Calif., 1991, Gallery 2, Ventura Coll., Calif., 1992; Evansville Mus. Arts & Scis., 1988, De La Guerra Gallery, 1989,. Bd. dirs. Santa Barbara Contemporary Arts Forum, 1988; statewide liaison com. Creative Arts, 1971-73. Recipient purchase prize Nat. Endowment for Arts, 1971; fellow U. Calif. Inst. Creative Art, 1977-78; grantee E.T. Greenshields Found., 1963-64. Home: 8 W Mountain Dr Santa Barbara CA 93103-1624 Office: U Calif Art Studio Dept Santa Barbara CA 93106-7120

BROWN, GAY WEST, school psychologist; b. L.A., Nov. 20, 1953; d. James Dale and Ola Maye (Daniels) West; m. Lorenzo Hubbard, Nov. 26, 1977 (dec. Feb. 1990); 1 child, Loren Rochelle; m. Fred Lyndle Brown, Jr., Dec. 28, 1992. BA, Calif. State U., Dominguez Hills, 1975; MS, U. So. Calif., 1976; PhD, UCLA, 1991. Lic. ednl. psychologist; cert. sch. psychologist. Student counselor Dignity Ctr. for Drug Abuse, L.A., 1974-76; community health worker Am. Indian Free Clinic, Compton, Calif., 1974-76; student psychologist Martin Luther King Hosp., L.A., 1976-77; counselor aide Washington High Sch., L.A., 1974-77; vocat. counselor Skill Ctr., L.A., 1977-78; sch. psychologist L.A. Unified Sch. Dist., 1978—, tchr., advisor, 1988-90; psychol. asst. Verdugo Hills (Calif.) Mental Health, 1984-85; counselor, coord. Crenshaw High Sch., L.A., 1985-87; asst. behavior sci. cons. Coalition Mental Profls., L.A., 1992-93; psychol. asst. Martin Luther King Hosp., L.A., 1992-93; part-time prof. Calif. State U., L.A. Mem. APA, Nat. Assn. Sch. Psychologists, Calif. Assn. Sch. Psychologists, L.A. Assn. Sch. Psychologists, Assn. Black Psychologists (sec. 1992-93), Pan African Scholars Assn., United Tchrs. L.A., Delta Sigma Theta. Democrat. United Methodist. Office: Sch Mental Health Clinic 439 W 97th St Los Angeles CA 90003 Office: Sch Mental Health Svcs 439 W 97th St Los Angeles CA 90003-3968

BROWN, GEORGE, research forester and educator; b. Warrensburg, Mo., Jan. 31, 1939; married, 1964; 2 children. BS, Colo. State U., 1960, MS, 1962; PhD in Forsest Hydrology, Oreg. State U., 1967. Head dept. forest engring., 1973-86, assoc. dean rsch., 1986-90; prof. forest hydology Oreg. State U., 1966—; cons. hydrologist Weyerhaeuser Co., 1973; prin. engr. Forest Svc. USDA, 1981. Mem. Soc. Am. Foresters, Forest Prod. Soc. Office: Oreg State U Coll Forestry Forest Rsch Lab Corvallis OR 97331-5704

BROWN, GEORGE EDWARD, JR., congressman; b. Holtville, Calif., Mar. 6, 1920; s. George Edward and Bird Alma (Kilgore) B.; 4 children. B.A., UCLA, 1946; grad. fellow, Fund Adult Edn., 1954. Mgmt. cons. Calif., 1957-61; v.p. Monarch Savs. & Loan Assn., Los Angeles, 1960-68; mem. Calif. Assembly from 45th Dist., 1959-62; former mem. 88th-91st congresses from 29th Dist. Calif., 93d Congress from 38th Dist. Calif.; mem. 94th-104th Congresses from 36th (now 42nd) Dist. Calif.; mem. standing com. on agr., chmn. sci. space and tech. com. 94th-101st Congresses from 36th Dist. Calif., 1987; mem. agriculture com., ranking minority mem. sci. com.; chmn. Office of Tech. Assessment; coll. lectr., radio commentator, 1971. Mem. Calif. Gov.'s Adv. Com. on Housing Problems, 1961-62; mem. Mayor Los Angeles Labor-Mgmt. Com., 1961-62, Councilman, Monterey Park, Calif., 1954-58, mayor, 1955-56; candidate for U.S. Senate, 1970. Served to 2d lt., inf. AUS, World War II. Recipient Chairman's award Am. Assn. Engring. Socs., 1993. Mem. Am. Legion, Colton C. of C., Urban League, Internat. Brotherhood Elec. Workers, AFL-CIO, Friends Com. Legislation, Ams. for Dem. Action. Democrat. Methodist. Lodge: Kiwanis. Office: US Ho of Reps 2300 Rayburn HOB Washington DC 20515-0542*

BROWN, GEORGE STEPHEN, physicist; b. Santa Monica, Calif., June 28, 1945; s. Paul Gordon and Frances Ruth (Moore) B.; m. Nohema Fernandez, Aug. 8, 1981 (div. 1992); 1 child, Sonya. BS, Calif. Inst. Tech., 1967; MS, Cornell U., 1968, PhD, 1973. Mem. tech. staff Bell Labs., Murray Hill, N.J., 1973-77; sr. research assoc. Stanford (Calif.) U., 1977-82, rsch. prof. applied physics, 1982-91; prof. physics U. Calif., Santa Cruz, 1991—; assoc. dir. Stanford Synchrotron Radiation Lab., Stanford, 1980-91. Mem. editorial bd. Rev. Sci. Instruments, 1983-86; contbr. articles to profl. jours. Fellow Am. Phys. Soc. Home: 10699 Empire Grade Santa Cruz CA 95060-9474 Office: U Calif Dept Physics Santa Cruz CA 95064

BROWN, GREGORY DONALD, sportswriter, author; b. Houston, Feb. 23, 1957; s. McDonald G. and Rosemary (Poe) B.; m. Stacy K. Barnes, Aug. 8, 1980; children: Lauren, Benji. BA in Journalism, U. Wash., 1979. Sportswriter Anacortes (Wash.) Am., 1979-80; sportswriter Skagit Valley Herald, Mt. Vernon, Wash., 1980-85, sports editor, 1985-88; sportswriter Seattle Post-Intelligencer, 1988—. Co-author: (children's books) Edgar Martinez: Patience Pays, 1992, Kirby Puckett: Be the Best You Can Be, 1993, Troy Aikman: Things Change, 1995. Home and Office: 20912 33rd Ave SE Bothell WA 98021-3528

BROWN, H. DOUGLAS, English language educator; b. Ntondo, Zaire, July 26, 1941; came to U.S., 1959; s. Henry D. and Ethel D. (White) B.; m. Mary Bjornson, June 3, 1963; children: Stefanie Diana, Jeffrey Douglas. BA, Linfield Coll., 1963; MDiv, Am. Bapt. Sem., 1966; MA, UCLA, 1968, PhD, 1970. Asst. prof. U. Mich., Ann Arbor, 1970-75, assoc. prof., 1975-78; assoc. prof. U. Ill., Urbana, 1978-81, prof., 1981-83; prof. San Francisco State U., 1983—; dir. Am. Lang. Inst., San Francisco, 1983—. Author: Principles of Language Learning and Teaching, 1980, 3d edit., 1994, A Practical Guide to Language Learning, 1989, Breaking the Language Barrier, 1991, (series) Vistas, 1991, Teaching by Principles, 1994. Mem. Am. Bapt. Community Ch., Walnut Creek, Calif., 1983—. Mem. Tchrs. of English to Speakers of Other Langs. (pres. 1979-81, Disting. Svc. award 1986), Calif. Tchrs. of English to Speakers of Other Langs., Am. Coun. on Teaching Fgn. Langs., Am. Assn. Applied Linguistics. Office: San Francisco State U Dept English 1600 Holloway Ave San Francisco CA 94132-1722

BROWN, H. WILLIAM, urban economist, private banker; b. L.A., Sept. 6, 1931; s. Homer William Brown and Carol Lee (Thompson) Weaver; m. Verlee Nelson, Aug. 1951 (div. 1953); 1 child, Shirlee Dawn; m. Shirley Rom, Jan. 18, 1953 (div. 1962). BA in Pub. Adminstrn., Calif. State U., 1956; MA in Bus. Adminstrn., Western States U., 1983, Phd in Urban Econs., 1984. Pres. Real Estate Econs., Sacramento, 1956-60; dir. spl. projects Resource Agy. Calif., Sacramento, 1960-65; program planning officer U.S. Dept. Housing and Urban Devel., Washington, 1965-66; asst. dir. regional planning U.S. Dept. Commerce, Washington, 1967-69; dir. internat. office Marshall and Stevens, Inc., L.A., 1970-72; vice chmn., CEO Investment Property Econ. Cons., 1972—; chmn., CEO The Northpoint Investment Group, San Francisco, 1986—; chmn. Trade and Devel. Ctr. For UN, N.Y. 1983-88, pres. Ctr. for Habitat and Human Settlements, Washington 1977-90. Author: The Changing World of the Real Estate Market Analyst-Appraiser, 1988. Mem. Appraisal Inst., Le Groupe (charge d'affaires, pvt. bankers club). Office: Northpoint Investment Group 350 Bay St Ste 100-111 San Francisco CA 94133-1902

BROWN, HANK, senator; b. Denver, Feb. 12, 1940; s. Harry W. and Anna M. (Hanks) B.; m. Nana Morrison, Aug. 27, 1967; children: Harry, Christy, Lori. BS, U. Colo., 1961, JD, 1969; LLM, George Washington U., 1986, M in Tax Law, 1986. Bar: Colo. 1969; CPA, Colo. Tax acct. Arthur Andersen, 1967-68; asst. pres. Monfort of Colo., Inc., Greeley, 1969-70; corp. counsel Monfort of Colo., Inc., 1970-71; v.p. Monfort Food Distbg., 1971-72, v.p. corp. devel., 1973-75, v.p. internat. ops., 1975-78, v.p. lamb div., 1978-80; mem. 97th-101st Congresses from Colo. 4th dist., 1981-90; mem. Colo. State Senate, 1972-76, asst. majority leader, 1974-76; U.S senator from Colo. Washington, 1991—; mem. Budget Com.; chmn. Fgn. Rel. subcom. Near Ea. and South Asian affairs; mem. Nat. Rep. Senatorial Com. With USN, 1962-66. Decorated Air medal. Mem. Colo. Bar Assn. Republican. Congregationalist. Office: US Senate 716 Hart Senate Bldg Washington DC 20510

BROWN, HERMIONE KOPP, lawyer; b. Syracuse, N.Y., Sept. 29, 1915; d. Harold H. and Frances (Burger) Kopp; m. Louis M. Brown, May 30, 1937; children—Lawrence D., Marshall J., Harold A. BA, Wellesley Coll., 1934; LLB, U. So. Calif., 1947. Bar: Calif. 1947. Story analyst 20th Century-Fox Film Corp., 1935-42; assoc. Gang, Kopp & Tyre, Los Angeles, 1947-52; ptnr. to sr. ptnr. Gang, Tyre, Ramer & Brown, Inc., Los Angeles, 1952—; lectr. copyright and entertainment law U. So. Calif. Law Sch., 1974-77. Contbr. to profl. publs. Fellow Am. Coll. Trust and Estate Coun.; mem. Calif. Bar Assn. (chair probate law cons. group nd. legal specialization 1977-82, trust and probate law sect., exec. com. 1983-86, advisor 1986-89), L.A. Copyright Soc. (pres. 1979-80), Order of Coif, Phi Beta Kappa. Office: Gang Tyre Ramer & Brown Inc 132 S Rodeo Dr Beverly Hills CA 90212

BROWN, ILENE DE LOIS, special education educator; b. Wichita, Kans., Aug. 17, 1947; d. Homer DeWitt and Estella Lenora (Cleland) Rusco; m. Gale Robert Aaroe, Nov. 23, 1967 (div. July 1983); 1 child, Candice Yvonne. BEd in Elem. Edn., Washburn U., Topeka, 1969; MS, Nazareth Coll. Rochester, 1979. Cert. tchr. Idaho. Emotionally disturbed trainer Rochester Mental Health Ctr., Greece, N.Y., 1970-71, West Ridge, Greece, 1971-72; tutor kindergarten through grades 6 Craig Hill, Greece, 1978-79; resource rm. tchr. math. English Village, Greece, 1979-80; resource rm. tchr. grades 4-6 Lakeshore, Greece, 1980; tutor, translator Guadalajara, Mex., 1980-82; tchr. grade 1 English John F. Kennedy Sch., Guadalajara, 1982-83; tchr. various grades Greenleaf (Idaho) Friends Acad., 1983-89; resource tchr., high sch. spl. edn. community work coord. Middleton (Idaho) Primary Sch., 1989-91, tchr., 1991—, tchr. 2d grade, 1990—. Sunday sch. tchr. Mem. Coun. for Exceptional Children, Coun. for Children with Behavior Disorders and Learning Disabilities (officer,sec. state chpt. 1991-92), Middleton Profl. Devel. Com. (chairperson PDC 1992—), Idaho Edn. Assn., Middleton Edn. Assn., Phi Delta Kappa. Office: Middleton Primary Sch 115 W Main St Middleton ID 83644-5565

BROWN, JACK, magazine editor; b. Los Angeles, Aug. 6, 1927; s. George Wesley and Harriett Isabel (Barton) B.; m. Arlyne Reddick, 1950 (div. 1962); children: Gregg Richard (dec.), Jeffrey Loren, Jan Patrice; m. Patricia Willard, 1963 (div. 1976); 1 child, Jack B. Jr.; m. Lynn Johannsen, 1986. AS, Los Angeles City Coll., 1948; BA, UCLA, 1950. Asst. polit. editor Los Angeles Examiner, 1960-62; exec. asst. Office Mayor, Los Angeles, 1962-69; polit. editor Los Angeles Herald Examiner, 1970-77; assoc. pub. Met. News, Los Angeles, 1977-81; editor Western Outdoors, Costa Mesa, Calif., 1981—; faculty Reader's Digest Writers Workshops. Co-editor: Outdoor Writers Association of America Style Manual, 1992, rev. 1995; contbr. articles to profl. jours. With USN, 1945-46. Recipient Resolution Commendation award Calif. State Senate, 1962. Mem. Outdoor Writers Assn. Am., Outdoor Writers Calif. (bd. dirs. 1990-91), Soc. Outdoor Mag. Editors (founding pres. 1990-91). Home: 3515 Landsford Way Carlsbad CA 92008-7047

BROWN, JAMES CARRINGTON, III (BING BROWN), public relations and communications executive; b. Wilmington, Del., May 17, 1939; s. James Carrington Jr. and Virginia Helen (Miller); m. Carol Osman, Nov. 3, 1961. Grad. security mgmt. group, Indsl. Coll. of the Armed Forces; BBA, Ariz. State U., 1984. Accredited, Pub. Rels. Soc. Am., 1988. Newsman, disc jockey, program dir. various radio stas., Ariz., 1955-60; morning news editor Sta. KOY, Phoenix, 1960-61; staff writer, photographer Prescott (Ariz.) Evening Courier, 1961; bus. editor, staff writer, photographer Phoenix Gazette, 1961-65; various communications positions Salt River Project, Phoenix, 1965-89; pres. Carrington Communications, Phoenix, 1989—; cons. comm., freelance writing, photography The Browns, Phoenix, 1965—; pub. info. officer Water Svcs. Dept., City of Phoenix, 1991—; instr. Rio Salado C.C., Phoenix, 1989—; guest lectr. various colls. and univs., 1975—; prof. Walter Cronkite Sch. Journalism and Telecomm., Ariz. State U., 1990—. Bd. dirs Grand Canyon coun. Boy Scouts Am., 1985-89, mem. adv. coun., 1990—; mem. environment com. Phoenix Futures Forum, 1991-93; deacon Meml. Presbyn. Ch., 1980-82, elder, 1985-87; spl. gifts com. United Way, Phoenix, 1986-89. Recipient Golden Eagle award Boy Scouts Am., 1992. Mem. Western Systems Coordinating Coun. (chmn. pub. info. com. 1969-89), Ariz. Newspapers Assn. (Billy Goat award, Allied Mem. of Yr. 1985), Ariz. Broadcasters Assn., Western Coalition Arid States (chmn. comm. subcom. 1991-93, co-chmn. com. and mem. com. 1993—, editor WESTCAS News 1991—), Western Energy Supply and Transmission Assocs. (mem. pub. info. com. 1967-89), Phoenix Press Club (pres. 1982-83), PRSA, Nat. Acad. TV Arts/Scis., Ariz. Zool. Soc., Heart Mus. Anthropology And Primitive Art. Republican. Home and Office: Carrington Comm 3734 E Campbell Ave Phoenix AZ 85018-3507 also: Phoenix Water Svcs Dept 200 W Washington St Phoenix AZ 85003-1611

BROWN, JAMES CHANDLER, college administrator; b. Garden City, N.Y., Aug. 5, 1947; s. Harry Chandler and Lillian Marie (Cutter) B. BA, Susquehanna U., Selinsgrove, Pa., 1970; License es Lettres, Geneva U., 1978; postgrad., Stanford U., 1984. Rsch. asst. Geneva (Switzerland) U., 1972-79; asst. Galerie Jan Krugier, Geneva, 1978-81; coord. pubs. So. Oreg. State Coll., Ashland, 1982-84; dir. pubs. So. Oreg. State Coll., 1984—; cons. in field. Author: How to Sharpen Your Publications (brochure, Case award) 1985, College Viewbook (booklet), 1985. Sec. bd. dirs. Schneider Mus. Art, Ashland, 1985-94. Canton of Geneva grantee, 1974-79; awardee, Coun. for Advancement and Support of Edn., 1987-88, 95. Mem. Coun. for Advancement and Support of Edn., Omicron Delta Kappa Leadership Soc. Methodist. Home: 385 Guthrie St Ashland OR 97520-3023 Office: So Oreg State Coll 1250 Siskiyou Blvd Ashland OR 97520-5001

BROWN, JAMES COOKE, nonprofit organization administrator, game inventor, educational administrator, writer; b. Tagilarin, Bohol, The Philippines, July 21, 1921; came to U.S., 1929; s. Bryan Burtis and Violet Mary (Cooke) B.; m. Evelyn Ruth Hamburger, July 21, 1985; children: Jefferson O'Reilly, Jill O'Reilly, Jennifer Fuller. BA in Philosophy and Math., U. Minn., 1946, PhD in Sociology, Philosophy and Math. Stats., 1952. Instr. sociology Wayne State U., Detroit, 1949-50; asst. prof. Ind. U., Bloomington, 1950-52; dir. statis. controls Inst. for Motivation Rsch., Croton-on-Husdon, N.Y., 1954-55; asst. prof. sociology and humanities, assoc. prof. sociology, philosophy U. Fla., Gainesville, 1955-63, 70; dir., then chmn. Loglan Inst., Inc., Gainesville and San Diego, 1964—. Author: Loglan 1: A Logical Language, 1966, 4th edit., 1989; (novel) The Troika Incident, 1970; inventor game Careers, 1956, Loglan lang., 1960. Home and Office: 3009 Peters Way San Diego CA 92117-4313

BROWN, JAMES WILLIAM, information systems development executive; b. Pitts., Dec. 27, 1946; s. Vincent J. and Rose C. Brown; m. Macrine Yee, June 24, 1972; children: Teresa C., Christine M. BS, Villanova (Pa.) U., 1968; PhD, Calif. Inst. of Tech., 1974. Mem. tech. staff Bell Labs., Holmdel, N.J., 1973-77; mem. tech. staff Calif. Inst. Tech.-Jet Propulsion Lab., Pasadena, 1977-84, tech. group supr., 1984-85; tech. sect. mgr. Calif. Inst. Tech.-Jet Propulsion Lab., 1985-87, tech. mgr., 1987—. With USAF, 1973, USAF Res., 1973-81. Recipient Exceptional Svc. medal NASA, 1983, Group Achievement award, 1980, 85, 93. Mem. Assn. for Computing Machinery. Republican. Roman Catholic. Home: 3605 Fairmeade Rd

Pasadena CA 91107-3015 Office: Jet Propulsion Lab 4800 Oak Grove Dr Pasadena CA 91109-8001

BROWN, J'AMY MARONEY, journalist, media relations consultant; b. L.A., Oct. 30, 1945; d. Roland Francis and Jeanne (Wilbur) Maroney; m. James Raphael Brown, Jr., Nov. 5, 1967 (dec. July 1982); children: James Roland Francis, Jeanne Raphael. Attended U. So. Calif., 1963-67. Reporter L.A. Herald Examiner, 1966-67, Lewisville Leader, Dallas, 1980-81; editor First Person Mag., Dallas, 1981-82; journalism dir. Pacific Palisades Sch., L.A., 1983-84; free-lance writer, media cons., 1984-88; press liaison U.S. papal visit, L.A., 1987; media dir., chief media strategist Tellem Inc., communication cons., issues mgr. 1990-94. Auction chmn. Assn. Pub. Broadcasting, Houston, 1974, 75; vice chmn. Dallas Arts Council, 1976-80; vice chmn. Met. March of Dimes, Dallas, 1980-82; del. Dallas Council PTAs, 1976-80; coord. specialist World Cup Soccer Organizing Com. Recipient UPI Editors award for investigative reporting, 1981. Mem. NAFE, Pub. Rels. Soc. Am. (accredited), Women Meeting Women, Women in Comm., Am. Bus. Women's Assn. Republican. Roman Catholic. Home: 13101 Nimrod Pl Los Angeles CA 90049-3632

BROWN, JANIECE ALFREIDA, pilot; b. Ellensburg, Wash., May 23, 1956; d. Don Elmer and LaRhee Deloris (Montgomery) Lewis; m. David E. Brown, Oct. 10, 1993. AA, Big Bend Community Coll., Moses Lake, Wash., 1980-82; BS, Cen. Wash. U., 1982-84. Pilot AAR Western Skyways, Troutdale, Oreg., 1984-87; airline capt. N.P.A., Inc., Pasco, Wash., 1987-89; flight engr. airline pilot Alaska Airlines, Seattle, 1989—, 1st officer Boeing 727 and MD-80; bus. mgr. David Brown & Assocs., 1994—. Lobbyist Save Our Watershed, Roslyn, Wash., 1978-80. Recipient Scholastic award CleElum (Wash.) High Sch., 1974. Mem. Airline Pilot Assn. (mem. dangerous goods com.), Alpha Eta Rho (pres. Ctrl. Wash. U. chpt. 1983-84). Home: 20912 NE Interlachen Ln Troutdale OR 97060-8731 Office: Alaska Airlines PO Box 61900 Seattle WA 98178

BROWN, JOAN MAZZAFERRO, telephone company executive; b. Greenport, N.Y., Jan. 1, 1956; d. Joseph Anthony and Sophia (Kroleski) M. BS, SUNY-Brockport, 1978; MS, Purdue U., 1980; grad. Fuqua Sch. Bus., 1988. Sr. tech. assoc. Bell. Tel. Labs., Whippany, N.J., 1978-79, mem. tech. staff, 1979-83; staff analyst Pacific Bell Co., San Francisco, 1983-84, staff mgr., 1984-85, dist. staff mgr., San Ramon, Calif., 1985-94, divsn. mgr., 1994—. Kodak scholar, 1978. Mem. NAFE. Roman Catholic. Avocations: skiing, sailing, aerobics, theatre, dance. Office: Pacific Bell 2600 Camino Ramon # 4104E San Ramon CA 94583-5041

BROWN, JOHN LAFAYETTE, III, civil engineer; b. Midwest, Wyo., Mar. 31, 1926; s. John L. Jr. and Alma Ruby (Ray) B.; m. Faye D. Converse, Oct. 10, 1958; children: Kevin D., Steven G. BS, McPherson Coll., 1949; BSCE, Kans. State Coll., 1951. Registered profl. engr., Kans., Ariz. Engr. Bartlett and West, Topeka, 1952-61; ptnr. Grove-Brown Consulting Engrs., Marysville, Kans., 1961-70; project mgr. Neosho Constrn. Co., Inc., Council Grove, Kans., 1971-80; hwy. engr. Ariz. Dept. Transp., Phoenix and Tucson, 1981—. Cubmaster Boy Scouts Am., Marysville, 1966-80, scoutmaster, 1969-80. Cpl. U.S. Army, 1944-46, PTO. Mem. Am. Legion, Masons. Home: 7425 E Serenity Ln Tucson AZ 85750 Office: Ariz Dept Transp 1739 W Jackson St Phoenix AZ 85007-3218

BROWN, JOHN VINCENT, gynecologic oncologist; b. Kansas City, Mo., Feb. 11, 1958; s. John Vincent and Celia Ann (Kilgore) B.; m. Katharine Virginia Fry, May 19, 1984; children: Michael Overton, Katharine Kilgore, Sarah Elizabeth. BS, U. Kans., 1980, MD, 1980-84. Diplomat Am. Bd. Ob.-Gyn.; cert. spl. qualification ob./gyn. Intern/resident U. Wash., Seattle, 1984-88; fellow Divsn. of Gynecology/Oncology, UCLA, 1988-90; ptnr. Gyn Oncology Assocs., Newport Beach, Calif., 1990—; asst. clin. prof. UCLA Harbor Sch. Medicine, Torrance, 1990—. Contbr. articles to profl. jours. Recipient J. George Moore award Western Assn. Gynecologic Oncologists, 1990; U. Kans. Summerfield scholar, 1977; Bristol Myers Pharm. Co. grantee, 1994. Fellow ACOG, ACS (assoc.); mem. AMA, Soc. Gynecologic Oncologists (cand. mem.), Am. Soc. Clin. Oncologists, Phi Kappa Phi. Office: Gynecologic Oncology Assocs 351 Hospital Rd Newport Beach CA 92663-3509

BROWN, JOSEPH E., landscape architecture executive; b. 1947. BA, Cath. U., 1970; M in Landscape Architecture and Urban Design, Harvard U., 1972. With Edaw, Inc., San Francisco, 1973—, now pres. Office: Edaw Inc 753 Davis St San Francisco CA 94111-1405*

BROWN, JUDITH ELLEN, community relations executive; b. Newark, Jan. 10, 1950; d. Richard Warren and Miriam (Laskowitz) B.; m. Terence Randolph Pitts, Oct. 21, 1979; children: Jacob, Rebecca. BA, Boston U., 1972, MA, 1975. Coord. program Boston Community Music Sch., 1975-76; coord. conf. U. Ariz., Tucson, 1976-83; dir. community relations City of Tucson, 1983—. Host and producer TV and radio show Topic of Tucson, 1983—. Mem. exec. bd. office cultural affairs U. Ariz., Tucson, 1990—; bd. mem. Tucson Unified Sch. Dist. "4th R". Mem. Internat. Assn. of Bus. Communicators, Govt. Communicators, Pub. Rels. Soc. Am. (treas. Tucson chpt. 1985—, pres. 1990, accredited). Office: City Mgrs Office 255 W Alameda Tucson AZ 85701-1508

BROWN, KATE, state legislator; b. Torrejon de Ardoth, Spain, 1960. BA, U. Colo.; JD, Lewis and Clark Northwestern. Mem. Oreg. Ho. of Reps., 1991—; atty. Democrat. Office: Oreg Ho of Reps State Capitol Salem OR 97310

BROWN, KAY (MARY KATHRYN BROWN), state official; b. Ft. Worth, Tex., Dec. 19, 1950; d. H.C., Jr. and Dorothy Ruth (Ware) B.; m. William P. Dougherty, Dec. 15, 1978 (div. 1984); m. Mark A. Foster, Aug. 24, 1991. B.A., Baylor U., 1973. Reporter, UPI, Atlanta, 1973-76; reporter, feature writer Anchorage Daily Times (Alaska), 1976-77; reporter, co-owner Alaska Advocate, Anchorage, 1977; aide, researcher Alaska State Legislature, Juneau, 1979-80; dep. dir. div. of oil and gas (formerly div. minerals and energy mgmt.) Alaska Dept. Natural Resources, Anchorage, 1980-82, dir., 1982-86; elected Alaska Ho. of Reps., 1986; del. White House Conf. Libr. and Info. Svcs., 1991. Co-author: Geographic Information Systems: A Guide to the Technology, 1991. Office: House of Representatives State Capitol Juneau AK 99811

BROWN, KENNETH RAY, minister; b. Quincy, Mass., Sept. 14, 1946; s. Kenneth Minor and Ruth Dorothy Marie (Hedman) B.; m. Thompson O'Sullivan, Sept. 17, 1968; 1 child, Sara Beth. BA, Bethel Coll., St. Paul, 1968; postgrad., Bridgewater State Coll., 1970-71, Calif. State U., L.A., 1989—; MDiv, Andover-Newton Theol. Sem., 1974. Ordained to ministry Unitarian Universalist Assn. , 1974. Min. 1st Unitarian Soc., Exeter, N.H., 1975-78, North Shore Unitarian Universalist Soc., Plandome, N.Y., 1978-84; exec. dir. Interfaith Hunger Coalition, L.A., 1985-87, Community Rels. Conf., L.A., 1987-89; interim min. Unitarian Universalist Soc. Verdugo Hills, La Crescenta, Calif., 1990-92; min. 1st Unitarian Ch., L.A., 1994—; producer, host Cambridge Forum West Radio Sta. KPFK-FM, Pacifica Radio, L.A., 1990—; bd. dirs. Interfaith Ctr. for Corp. Responsibility, N.Y.C., 1978-84, Unitarian Universalist Peace Fellowship, 1981-95; co-chmn. Unitarian Universalist Urban Ch. Coalition, 1982-85, chair, 1992—; mem. steering com. Religous Community Against the War in the Gulf, L.A., 1990-91—. Editor UNIPAX newsletter, 1982-85. Bd. dirs. Family Planning Assn., Exeter, 1975-78, Exeter Sch. Bd., 1976-78, ACLU, N.H., 1976-78, Clergy and Laity Conferned So. Calif., L.A., 1985-87. Mem. Unitarian Universalist Mins. Assn., Phi Alpha Theta, Phi Kappa Phi. Democrat. Home: 421 S Sparks St Burbank CA 91506-2745 Office: 1st Unitarian Ch 2936 W 8th St Los Angeles CA 90005-1524

BROWN, LARITA EARLY DAWN MA-KA-LANI, publisher; b. Santa Monica, Calif., Dec. 21, 1937; d. Robert Walter and Lela Shirley (Sims) B. AA, Santa Monica City Coll., 1956; BA, L.A. State U., 1973; PhD (hon.), Boston U., 1977; Masters, LaSalle U., 1988, D in Sociology/Technology, 1989. Tchr. parochial sch. Gardena, Calif., 1968-70; supr. Early Childhood programs/tchr. L.A. City Schs.-Headstart Program, 1970-72; project asst. Mayor's Office Job Devel., L.A., 1972-76; community svcs. specialist U.S. Dept. Commerce, Washington, 1976-81; owner, founder N & Out Pub. Co., Richardson, Tex., 1982—; dir. tutorial programs resource learning ctrs.; cons. human resources, Dallas area, 1985—; contractor Reading Is Fundamental assn., 1984; robot programmer; computer scis. specialist, cons.; founder, dir. Skooter Sam Ednl. Software Co., Dallas; founder Electronics Tech. Consortium; founder (pvt. sch.) Skooter Sam New Age Space Sch.; lectr. Cultural Hertiage, Intenat. Speaker in field. Author: Ginalyn's Surprise, 1983, Skooter Sam in Texas, 1985, Skooter Sam Series, Queens/Kings of Afrikan Heritage, Afrikan American Inventors, Skooter Sam: Key to the Future, Skooter Sam: Parents Guide, Princess Ebony, Queens and Kings Crowns, Queens and Kings of Afrika, Collectible Dolls, vol. 1 and 2, Skooter Sam: Esteem Team, Skooter Sam Whiz Scholar in Texas and others; patentee numerous childrens' computer product novelties. Active Dallas PTA Bd.; supr. various polit. campaigns, Calif. and Tex., 1970—; advisor youth and coll. student div. NAACP, 1981-82; media cons. Nat. Womens Polit. Caucus, Hollywood, Calif., 1976; vol. Bridge Over Troubled Waters project for homeless. Recipient trophy from L.A. County Community, 1980, Svc. award U. So. Calif., 1970, Dallas Kiwanis Clubs, 1984, Silver Poet award, 1986, Sesquicentennial Tex. Logo award, 1986, Gold Seal award Gov. State of La., Mayor City of New Orleans, Plaque of Dedication award Jeffries St. Learning Ctr., Cert. of recognition City of Dallas; named hon. citizen S. Dallas. Mem. Internat. Speakers Bureau (commd. writer), Anthropological Assn., Phi Beta Alpha Gamma. Methodist. Office: N & Out Pub-Mfg PO Box 43-507 Los Angeles CA 90043-0507

BROWN, LEONID S., biophysicist researcher; b. Moscow, Jan. 9, 1966; came to U.S., 1992; s. Sergey I and Nina I (Slutskaya) B.; m. Mariya N Kozhevnikova, Jun. 9, 1990. MS in Biology, Moscow State U., Russia, 1988, PhD in Biophysics, 1991. Rschr. Moscow State U., Russia, 1991-92, U. Calif., Irvine, 1992—. Contbr. articles to profl. jours. Mem. Am. Biophysical Soc. Office: U Calif Coll Medicine Dept Physiology and Biophysics Irvine CA 92717

BROWN, LEWIS MARVIN, biologist, renewal energy laboratory official; b. Bklyn., June 9, 1950; s. Sigmund and Mollie Brown; m. Candice Anne Evin; children: Seth Andrew, Joanna Gail. BS in Biol. Scis., SUNY, Stony Brook, 1972; MA in Botany, U. South Fla., 1974; PhD in Botany, Biochemistry-Biophysics, U. Toronto, Ont., Can., 1978. Vis. fellow Atlantic Rsch. Lab., Nat. Rsch. Coun. Can., Halifax, N.S., 1978-80; asst. prof. microbiology U. Western Ont., 1980-87; vis. scientist Nat. Cancer Inst. Can. Rsch. Lab., London, Ont., 1987-88; project mgr. applied biol. scis. br. Nat. Renewable Energy Lab., Golden, Colo., 1988—; mem. grant rev. panel Nat. Cancer Inst., NIH, Rockville, Md., 1990; proposal reviewer Small Bus. Innovative Rsch. Grants Program; reviewer U.S.-Israel Binat. Agrl. R & D Fund, numerous sci. jours. Contbr. articles to sci. jours. Recipient exceptional performance dir.'s award Nat. Renewable Energy Lab., 1989, 91, cert. of appreciation, 1991; N.Y. State Regents scholar, 1968-72; open fellow U. Toronto, 1975-76, doctoral fellow, 1977-88; rsch. fellow U. Western Ont., 1980-82, Natural Scis. and Engring. Rsch. Coun. Can., 1982-85. Office: Nat Renewal Energy Lab 1617 Cole Blvd Golden CO 80401

BROWN, LILLIAN ERIKSEN, retired nursing administrator, consultant; b. Seattle, Feb. 7, 1921; d. Peter Louis and Lena (Lien) Eriksen; m. Jan. 21, 1942 (div. Nov. 1963); children: Patricia Lee, Michael Gregory, Kevin William. Student, U. Calif., Berkeley, 1939-40; diploma, St. Luke's Hosp. Sch. Nursing, San Francisco, 1943; AB, Calif. State U., San Francisco, 1952; MPA, U. So. Calif., 1975. RN, Calif. Pub. health nurse San Francisco Dept. Health, 1946-50; asst. dir. nursing San Francisco Gen. Hosp., 1950-56; dir. nursing Weimar (Calif.) Med. Ctr., 1956-62, Orange County Med. Ctr., Orange, Calif., 1962-76; assoc. dir. hosp. and clins., dir. nursing, lectr. U. Calif. Med. Ctr., Irvine, 1976-82; assoc. hosp. adminstr. King Khalid Eye Specialist Hosp., Riyadh, Saudi Arabia, 1982-86; cons. AMI-Saudi Arabia Ltd., Jeddah, 1986-90; chmn. Western Teaching Hosp. Coun. Dirs. Nursing, 1972-75, 80-81; mem. planning project com. Calif. Dept. Rehab., 1967-69, mem. adv. com., 1970-73; mem. ad hoc president's com. on hosp. governance U. Calif., 1981-82; pres. dirs. nursing coun. Hosp. Coun. So. Calif., 1972-74, mem. pers. practices com., 1976-78, 80-83, area rep., 1975-82; mem. dept. nursing adv. com. to establish baccalaureate program U. So. Calif., 1980-82; mem. adv. bd. various coll. nursing programs. Contbr. articles to profl. jours. Sec. Olive (Calif.) Little League, 1967-72; mem. com. on emergency med. svcs. Orange County Health Planning Coun., 1977-78, mem. health promotion task force, 1978-79. 2d lt. Nurse Corps, U.S. Army, 1944-45. Recipient Lauds and Laurels award U. Calif., Irvine, 1981. Fellow Am. Acad. Nurses; mem. ANA (cert. nurse adminstr. advanced), Nat. League for Nursing, APHA, Am. Orgn. Nurse Execs., Nat. Critical Care Inst. Edn., Calif. Nurses Assn. (Lillian E. Brown award named in her honor 1989), Calif. Orgn. for Nurse Execs. (hon.), Calif. Soc. for Nursing Svc. Adminstr., NOW. Republican. Home: 1806 N Nordic Pl Orange CA 92665-4637

BROWN, LILLIE MCFALL, elementary school principal; b. Feb. 29; d. Clayton and Septertee (Dewberry) McFall; m. Charles Brown, Oct. 4, 1958; 1 child, Eric McFall. BA in Home Econ., Sci., Langston Univ., 1956; MA in Spl. Edn., Chgo. Tchrs. Coll., 1964; MA in Adminstrn., Seattle Univ., 1976. Home econ. tchr. Altue (Okla.) Separate Pub. Schs., 1955-56, first grade tchr., 1956-57, fourth grade tchr., 1957-60; middle sch. tchr. Chgo. Pub. Sch.s, 1960-64; spl. edn. primary tchr. Seattle Pub. Schs., 1966-67, spl. edn. intermediate tchr., 1967-68, program coord., 1968-71, elem. asst. prin., 1971-76, elem. prin., 1976—; Mem. Project READ, Seattle, 1968. Contbr. articles to profl. jours. Treas. African Am. Alliance, 1980—; historian Wash. Alliance Black Sch. Educators, 1991—; vol. Olympic Games, Seattle, 1990. Recipient Sears Found. grant., 1967. Mem. NAACP, Nat. Assn. Elem. Sch. Prins., Elem. Prins. Assn. Seattle Pub. Schs., Prins. Assn. Wash. State, Prin. Assn. Seattle Pub. Schs., Educational Leadership, Phi Delta Kappa, Kappa Delta Pi, Delta Sigma Theta. Democrat. Baptist. Home: 2736 34th Ave S Seattle WA 98144-5561

BROWN, LORRAINE ANN, administrative services coordinator; b. Providence, Mar. 15, 1947; d. Leonard Francis and Elaine Frances (Pettis) Millen; m. Jeffrey Schofield Brown, May 22, 1976 (div. 1983); 1 child, Kaneeta Sage; m. Dieter Paul Wuennenberg, July 14, 1965; 1 child, Desiree Jacqueline Wuennenberg. Student, Manhattan Sch. Printing, 1972, L.A. Trade Tech. Coll., 1981-83. Communications rep. TransAmerica Occidental, Los Angeles, 1973-77; owner, jewelry designer The Lorraine Brown Co., El Segundo, Calif., 1979-83; mgr. Silk Lingerie Outlet, Sherman Oaks, Calif., 1982-83; office mgr. Am. Silk Label, L.A., 1984; asst. prodn. coordinator Pacific Coast Mills, L.A., 1984-85; asst. designer jr. wear Judy Knapp Inc., L.A., 1986-87; sales exec. Integrated Aquatic Systems, Marina Del Rey, Calif., 1987-88; adminstrv. svcs. coord. GTE Svcs., El Segundo, Calif., 1988-94. Asst. leader Girl Scouts U.S., El Segundo, 1985-87; P.V.P. leader 4-H, 1991-94; vol. Tree Muskateers and Swift Project. Mem. Svcs. Employees Assn. (pres.), Young Exec. Singles, Advanced Degrees, Sierra Singles. Home: 756 Main St El Segundo CA 90245-3051

BROWN, MARIAN VAN DE WATER, utilities executive; b. Oakland, Calif., June 28, 1946; d. Gilbert Raymond and Florence (Culbertson) Van de Water; m. Kenneth Spiers Brown, June 16, 1968; children: Monica Suzanne, Patricia Hawley. BA in Econs. cum laude, Pomona Coll., 1968; PhD in Econs., Stanford U., 1979. Vol. Peace Corps, Ghana, 1968-70; sr. rsch. analyst Nat. Bur. Econ. Rsch., West Stanford, Calif., 1975-77; asst. prof. econs. Pomona Coll., Claremont, Calif., 1977-86; sr. analyst market rsch. and program evaluation So. Calif. Edison, San Dimas, 1986-89, mgr. measurement and evaluation Energy Efficiency Divsn., 1989—; vis. scholar Divsn. Econ. Rsch., Social Security Adminstrn., Washington, 1984-85; chair Calif. Demand-Side Mgmt. Measurement Adv. Com., 1993, Edison rep., 1994—; bd. dirs., treas. Assn. Energy Svcs. Profls., 1994—; bd. dirs. Clinebell Inst. Vol.; bd. dirs. United Campus Christian Movement, Stanford U., 1970-73; Lay leader Claremont United Meth. Ch., 1991—, chair adminstrv. bd., 1986-88, chair various coms., 1981-91; bd. dirs., alumni coun. Pomona Coll., 1989-90; sec.-treas. involvement corps Palo Alto (Calif.) 1st United Meth., 1975-77, youth leader, 1971-73. NSF fellow, 1970-73. Mem. Am. Econ. Assn., Assn. Energy Svc. Profls., Nat. Coun. Returned Peace Corps Vols., Stanford Profl. Women L.A., Phi Beta Kappa. Democrat. Methodist. Home: 434 W 12th St Claremont CA 91711-3835 Office: So Calif Edison 300 N Lone Hill Ave San Dimas CA 91773-1741

BROWN, MARK STEVEN, medical physicist; b. Denver, July 12, 1955; s. Clarence William and Gail Margaret (Farthing) B.; m. Mary Linda Avery, Oct. 9, 1988. Student, Northwestern U., 1973-74; BS, Colo. State U., 1977; PhD in Phys. Chemistry, U. Utah, 1984. GE postdoctoral fellow Yale U. Sch. Medicine, New Haven, 1984-86, assoc. rsch. scientist, 1986-87; rsch. asst. prof. U. N.Mex. Sch. Medicine, Albuquerque, 1987-89; med. physicist Swedish Med. Ctr. Porter Meml. Hosp., Englewood, Colo., 1989-92; instr. C.C. Denver, Denver, 1990, 91; asst. clin. prof. radiology U. Colo. Sch. Medicine, Denver, 1991-92, asst. prof. radiology, 1992—. Author: (with others) NMR Relaxation in Tissues, 1986; contbr. articles to profl. jours. Mem. Am. Chem. Soc., Soc. Magnetic Resonance. Home: 3190 Vance St Wheat Ridge CO 80215 Office: Univ Colo Health Scis Ctr Dept Radiology Box A034 4200 E 9th Ave Denver CO 80220-3706

BROWN, MERLINDE MARIA, elementary school educator; b. Oct. 2, 1936; d. Carlos Augusto and Lizzie Coleta (Oliveira) D'Assumpcao; m. Ronald Peter Brown; children: Bridgette Maria, Michael Peter. BA, 1960, diploma in edn., 1961; MA, U. San Francisco, 1968. Cert. elem. tchr.; cert. secondary teaching; cert. supr.; cert. lang. devel. specialist. Tchr. San Francisco Archdiocese, 1967-68, San Francisco Unified Sch. Dist., 1968-94. Contbr. articles to profl. publs. Co-chairperson Don Underwood for City Coun., Danville, 1985, City Coun. campaign com.; exec. bd. dirs., crime prevention com. Danville Assn., 1978-79. Mem. AAUW, Calif. Retired Tchrs. Assn., Smithsonian. Republican. Roman Catholic. Home: 893 El Cerro Blvd Danville CA 94526-2704

BROWN, PAUL FREMONT, aerospace engineer, educator; b. Osage, Iowa, Mar. 10, 1921; s. Charles Fremont and Florence Alma (Olson) B.; m. Alice Marie Culver, Dec. 5, 1943; children—Diane, Darrell, Judith, Jana. BA in Edn. and Natural Sci., Dickinson State Coll., 1942; BS in Mech. Engring., U. Wash., 1948; MS in Cybernetic Systems, San Jose State U., 1971. Profl. quality engr., Calif., 1978; cert. reliability engr., Am. Soc. Quality Control, 1976. Test engr., supr. Boeing Aircraft Corp., Seattle, 1948-56; design specialist, propulsion systems, Lockheed Missiles and Space Co., Sunnyvale, Calif., 1956-59; supr. system effectiveness, 1959-66, staff engr., 1966-76, mgr. product assurance Hubble Space Telescope Program, 1976-83; v.p. research, devel. Gen. Agriponics Inc. of Hawaii, 1971-76; owner Diversatek Engring. and Product Assurance Conss., 1983—; coll. instr., lectr., San Jose State U. Active in United Presbyn. Ch., 1965—; scoutmaster, Boy Scouts Am., 1963-65. Served to 1st lt., USAF, 1943-46. Recipient awards for tech. papers, Lockheed Missiles and Space Co., 1973-75. Mem. Am. Soc. Quality Control, AIAA. Clubs: Toastmasters (Sunnyvale, Calif.), Calif. Writers' (pres. South Bay br. 1993-94). Author: From Here to Retirement, 1988; contbr. articles to profl. jours. Home and Office: 19608 Braemar Dr Saratoga CA 95070-5046

BROWN, RANDALL EMORY, geologist; b. Eugene, Oreg., May 28, 1917; s. Percy Walker and Zula (Correll) B.; m. Helene Kerr, Jan. 21, 1950; children: Derek Jeffrey, Kevin Randall. AB, Stanford U., 1938; MA, Yale U., 1941. Registered geologist. Chief sampler, resident geologist M.A. Hanna Co., Darrington, Wash., 1941; geologist Oreg. Dept. Geology and Mineral Industries, Portland, 1941-42, U.S. Geol. Survey, 1942-45, U.S. Army, Corps Engrs., Portland, 1945-47, Gen. Electric Co. Hanford Works, Richland, Wash., 1947-65; sr. rsch. scientist Battelle Meml. Inst., Richland, 1965-71; asst. prof. Cen. Wash. U., Ellensburg, Wash., 1971-72; instr. Columbia Basin Coll., Pasco, Wash., 1972-73; cons. Pasco, 1973—; panelist radio and TV sci. program Hanford Sci. Forum, 1954, 56. Contbr. articles to profl. jours. Asst. supr. Franklin County Conservation Dist., Pasco, 1972—. Fellow AAAS, Geol. Soc. Am.; mem. Assn. Ground Water Scientists and Engrs., Nat. Water Well Assn., N.W. Sci. Assn. (pres. 1969-70), Sigma Xi. Republican. Episcopalian (lay reader). Home: 504 N Road 49 Pasco WA 99301-3042

BROWN, RANDY LEE, systems engineer; b. Yakima, Wash., Oct. 9, 1963; s. Jack Leroy Brown and Carol Ann (Litchtenburg) Myers. Student, Yakima Valley Vocat. Skills Ctr., 1980-82, Phoenix Inst. Tech., 1982-83. Electronic technician Easy Enterprises Amusements, Yakima, 1983-84; svc. mgr. Cliff Miller's Computers Inc., Yakima, 1984—. Named State Champion radio TV repair Vocat. Industries Clubs Am., 1982. Home: 608 S Yakima Ave Wapato WA 98951-1261 Office: Cliff Millers Computers Inc 22 N 2nd St Yakima WA 98901-2612

BROWN, RICHARD ELWOOD, educator; b. Kansas City, Mo., Feb. 11, 1946; s. Lester J. and Frances M. (Brizendine) B. AB, Stanford U., 1968; PhD, Cornell U., 1972. Asst. to assoc. to prof. U. Nev., Reno, 1972—. Author: Chester's Last Stand, 1988, (short story collection) Fishing for Ghosts, 1994. Office: U Nev Reno English Dept 098 Reno NV 89557

BROWN, RICHARD M., professional baseball team executive; b. Chgo., Nov. 16, 1942; m. Sandra Spellman; children: Scott, Todd. BA, UCLA, 1964, JD, 1967. With legal staff FTC, Xerox Corp.; div. counsel Bechtel Power Corp., 1974-79; v.p., gen. counsel Avery Internat.; v.p., gen. counsel, sec. Golden West Broadcasters, 1981-83; legal counsel Calif. Angels, from 1981, mem. bd. dirs., 1986—, pres., chief exec. officer, 1990—; ptnr. Jeffer, Mangels, Butler & Marmano, Century City, Calif., 1989-90. Capt. U.S. Army JAGC, 1968-71. Mem. ABA, State Bar Calif., Sports Lawyers Assn., Acad. TV Arts and Scis. Office: Calif Angels Anaheim Stadium Anaheim CA 92806*

BROWN, ROBERT FREEMAN, mathematics educator; b. Cambridge, Mass., Dec. 13, 1935; s. Irving and Charlotte (Frankel) B.; m. Brenda Webster, June 16, 1957; children: Geoffrey, Matthew. AB, Harvard Coll., 1957; postgrad., Am. U., 1959; PhD, U. Wis., 1963. Asst. prof. UCLA, 1963-68, assoc. prof., 1968-73, prof., 1973—. Author: Lefschetz Fixed Point Theorem, 1970, Applied Finite Math, 1977, Essentials of Finite Math, 1990, Finite Mathematics, 1992, A Topological Introduction to Nonlinear Analysis, 1993. Mem. Am. Math. Soc., Math. Assn. Am. (gov. 1986-89, Lester Ford award 1983). Democrat. Episcopalian. Office: Univ Calif Dept Math Los Angeles CA 90007

BROWN, ROBERT HENRY, physics educator; b. Sioux Falls, S.D., Aug. 27, 1915; s. Harry Joseph and Isabel E. (Ross)B.; m. Ruth Frances Miler, May 26, 1942; children: Rebecca Sue, Judith Ann. BA, Union Coll., Lincoln, Nebr., 1940; MS, U. Nebr., 1942; PhD, U. Wash., 1950. Asst. instr. physics U. Nebr., 1940-42; rsch. engr. Sylvania Electronic Products Co., 1942-45; head sci. dept. Can. Union Coll., Lacombe, Alta., 1945-47; instr. physics U. Wash., 1948-49; mem. faculty Walla Walla Coll., 1947-70, prof. physics, 1954-70, v.p., 1961-70; pres., prof. Union Coll., Lincoln, 1970-73; dir. Geosci. Rsch. Inst., Berrien Springs, Mich., 1973-80; prof. geophysics Andrews U., Berrien Springs, 1973-80; prof. physics Loma Linda (Calif.) U., 1980-88. Mem. Am. Phys. Soc., Am. Geophys. Union, Sigma Xi. Republican. Seventh-day Adventist. Home: 12420 Birch St Yucaipa CA 92399-4218

BROWN, ROBERT MUNRO, museum director; b. Riverside, N.J., Mar. 4, 1952; s. James Wendell and Janet Elizabeth (Munro) B.; m. Mary Ann Noel, June, 1973 (div. 1977); m. Claudia Leslie Haskell, Jan. 14, 1978. BA in Polit. Sci. cum laude, Ursinus Coll., 1973; MA in Social Scis., Rivier Coll., 1978; PhD in Early Am. History, U. N.H., 1983. Grad. asst. dept. history U. N.H., Durham, 1979-83, instr., 1983-84; site curator T.C. Steele State Hist. Site Ind. State Mus. System, Nashville, Ind., 1984-91; dir. Hist. Mus. at Ft. Missoula, Mont., 1991—; hist. interpreter Strawberry Banke, Portsmouth, N.H., 1980-83; instr. Rivier Coll., Nashua, N.H., 1986-91, N.H. Coll., Nashua and Salem, 1986-91; supr. pub. programs Mus. Am. Textile History, North Andover, Mass., 1985-91; sec.-treas. We. Mont. Heritage Ctr./No. Rockies Heritage Ctr., 1992-93; mem. grad. com. U. Mont., 1993; mem. steering com. Ft. Missoula, 1993; reviewer Inst. Mus. Svcs., 1993, 94; lectr., presenter, chair panels in field. Contbr. articles to profl. jours. Trustee Historic Harrisville, N.H., 1989-91; bd. dirs. United Peoples Found., 1991-93, v.p., 1993; mem. planning com. Western Mont. Heritage Ctr., 1991, U. Mont. Centennial Celebration, 1992, Leadership Missoula, 1992; active open space, parks and resource planning and mgmt. project team City of Missoula, 1993; mem. blue ribbon task force Five Valleys Luth. Retirement Community Planning Com., 1994. Scholar U. N.H., 1979-83, Rsch. grantee, 1982; grantee Mass. Coun. on Arts and Humanities, 1986, 87, 88, Int. Mus. Svcs., 1988, 89, 90, 91, AT&T, 1988, Am. Wool Coun., 1988, BayBank, 1989, Am. Yarn Assn., 1989, North Andover Arts Lottery Coun., 1989, 90, Mass. Cultural Coun., 1990, Greater Lawrence Community Found., 1991,

Mass. Arts Lottery Coun., 1991, Gallery Assn. for Greater Art, 1991, 92, Mont. Com. for Humanities, 1991, 92, 93, 94, Sinclair Oil Co., 1991, Mont. Rail Link, 1992, U. Mont. Found., 1992, Pepsi-Cola Co., 1992, 93, U.S. WEST Found., 1992, The Missoulan, 1992, Champion Internat., 1992, Mont. Cultural Trust, 1993, Missoula Rotary, 1993, Tex. Assn. Mus., 1993, Inst. Mus. Svcs., 1993, Zip Beverage Co., 1994, Bitterroot Motors, 1994, Grizzly Hackle, 1994; Kellogg Found. fellow, 1987. Mem. Am. Assn. Mus., Am. Assn. State and Local History, Am. Hist. Assn., Assn. Records Mgrs. and Adminstrs. (charter Big Sky chpt. 1992-94), Mont. Hist. Soc., Mus. Assn. Mont. (panelist 1994), We. Mont. Fundraisers Assn. (charter 1991, v.p. 1993-95), Mountain Plains Mus. Assn., Greater Boston Mus. Educator's Roundtable (steering com. 1988-90), Masons (Missoula chpt.), Kiwanis (Sentinel chpt.), Phi Alpha Theta (Psi Pi chpt.). Democrat. Home: 216 Woodworth Ave Missoula MT 59801-6052 Office: Hist Mus at Ft Missoula Ft Missoula Bldg 322 Missoula MT 59801

BROWN, ROBERT STEPHEN, JR., gastroenterologist; b. N.Y.C., Sept. 14, 1963; s. Robert Stephen and Judith (Kaufman) B.; m. Susan Marie Wilson, June 26, 1993. AB cum laude, Harvard Coll., 1985; MD, NYU, 1989. Diplomate Nat. Bd. Med. Examiners, Am. Bd. Internal Medicine; lic. physician, Calif., Mass. Intern Beth Israel Hosp., Boston, 1989-90, resident in medicine, 1991-92; clin. fellow in medicine Harvard Med. Sch., Boston, 1989-92; fellow in gastroenterology and Hepatology U. Calif., San Francisco, 1992—, clin. instr. medicine, 1994—; preceptor intro. to clin. medicine U. Calif., San Francisco, 1993—. Contbr. articles to profl. jours. Nat. Merit scholar, 1980, Harvard Coll. scholar, 1981-85. Mem. ACP, Am. Gastroenterol. Assn., Am. Soc. Gastrointestinal Endoscopists, Am. Assn. for the Sudy Liver Diseases, Mass. Med. Soc., Alpha Omega Alpha. Democrat. Office: Univ Calif Med Ctr Box 0538 The GI Unit S-357 San Francisco CA 94143-0538

BROWN, RODNEY JAY, dean, consultant; b. Coalville, Utah, Oct. 6, 1948; s. John Parley and Vera (Bisel) B.; m. Sandra Claire Wood, May 28, 1971; children: Shauna Marie, Carla Rae, David Michael. BS, Brigham Young U., 1972; MS, Utah State U., Logan, 1973; PhD, N.C. State U., Raleigh, 1977. Rsch. assoc. Weizmann Inst. of Sci., Rehovot, Israel, 1977-79; asst. prof. dept. nutrition and food scis. Utah State U., 1979-83, assoc. prof. dept. nutrition and food scis., 1983-84, assoc. prof., head dept. nutrition and food scis., 1985-87, prof., head dept. nutrition and food scis., 1987-91; dean Coll. Agr. Utah State U., Logan, 1991—, acting v.p. rsch., 1994. Contbr. numerous articles to profl. jours. Mem. AAAS, Am. Chem. Soc., Am. Dairy Sci. Assn. (mem. editorial bd. Jour. Dairy Sci. 1981-91, chair dairy foods div. 1993-94), Inst. Food Technologists (chair dairy tech. div. 1991-92), Rotary, Phi Kappa Phi. LDS. Home: 615 Circle Pl Providence UT 84332-9435 Office: Utah State U Coll Agr Logan UT 84322

BROWN, RONALD MALCOLM, engineering corporation executive; b. Hot Springs, S.D., Feb. 21, 1938; s. George Malcolm and Cleo Lavonne (Plumb) B.; m. Sharon Ida Brown, Nov. 14, 1964 (div. Apr. 1974); children: Michael, Troy, George, Curtis, Lisa, Brittney. AA, Southwestern Coll., 1970; BA, Chapman Coll., 1978. Commd. USN, 1956, advanced through grades to master chief, 1973, ret., 1978; engring. mgr. Beckman Inst., Fullerton, Calif., 1978-82; mech. engring. br. mgr. Northrop Corp., Hawthorne, Calif., 1982-83; dir. of ops. Transco, Marina Del Rey, Calif., 1983-85; v.p. ops. Decor Concepts, Arcadia, Calif., 1985—; design dir. Lockheed Aircraft Corp., Ontario, Calif. Mem. Soc. Mfg. Engrs., Inst. Indsl. Engrs., Nat. Trust for Hist. Preservation, Fleet Res. Assn., Am. Film Inst., Nat. Mgmt. Assn.

BROWN, SAUL LEON, psychiatrist, educator; b. Gunnison, Utah, Oct. 13, 1922; s. Benjamin and Clara (Horowitz) B.; children: Janine, Jonathan, Gordon, Emily; m. Helen Reid, May 15, 1970. BA, U. Calif., Berkeley, 1943; MD, U. Calif., San Francisco, 1946. Diplomate Am. Bd. Psychiatry and Neurology, Am. Bd. Child and Adolescent Psychiatry. Intern L.A./U. So. Calif. County Hosp., 1947-48; resident in psychiatry St. Elizabeth Hosp., Washington, 1948, Langley Porter Inst./U. Calif. Med. Sch., San Francisco, 1948-49; fellow in child psychiatry Mt. Sinai Hosp., L.A., 1959-61; dir. dept. child psychiatry Cedars Sinai Med. Ctr., L.A., 1962-73; dir. dept. psychiatry Cedards Sinai Med. Ctr., L.A., 1973-92; clin. asst. prof. psychiatry U. So. Calif. Med. Sch., L.A., 1962-73; clin. prof. psychiatry UCLA Med. Sch., L.A., 1973—; supervising psychoanalyst So. Calif. Psychoanalytic Inst., Beverly Hills, 1965—, tng. psychoanalyst, 1968—; founder, chief clin. cons. Early Childhood Ctr., Cedars Sinai Med. Ctr., L.A., 1992—. Contbr. over 30 articles to profl. jours. Capt. U.S. Army, 1951-53. Recipient Outstanding Achievement award So. Calif. Psychiat. Soc., L.A., 1990. Fellow Am. Psychiat. Assn., Am. Orthopsychiat. Assn.; mem. Am. Psychoanalytic Assn. Democrat. Office: Cedars Sinai Med Ctr Thalians E-215 PO Box 48750 Los Angeles CA 90048

BROWN, SHEILA DENISE, medical/surgical nurse; b. St. Louis, Jan. 1, 1959; d. William Edward and Alice Olivia (Goods) Esters; m. Gerald Richard Brown, Feb. 14, 1986; children: Gerald Richard Jr., Kimberly Denise. BSN, St. Louis U., 1982. RN, Mo. Staff nurse Barnes Hosp., 1982—, head nurse, 1989-92; nurse mgr. Palomar/Pomerado Home Care, Escondido, Calif., 1992—, dir., 1994—. Mem. Police Wives Assn. (pres. 1990-91), Am. Coll. Healthcare Execs., Calif. Assn. Health Svcs. at Home, San Diego Coun. Home Care. Presbyterian. Home: 1608 Calle Las Casas Oceanside CA 92056-6535 Office: Palomar/Pomerado Home Care 225 E 2nd Ave Ste 200 Escondido CA 92025-4238

BROWN, SPENCER L., surgeon; b. Boston, July 30, 1954; s. Samuel and Phyllis Lillian (Perlman); m. Lauren Carole Pinter, May 25, 1980; children: Joshua Samuel, Benjamin Harrison. BA, Brandeis U., 1972; MD, Boston U., 1986. Mem. staff UCLA Med. Ctr., 1980-87; surgeon Century City Surg. Assocs., 1987—. Mem. AMA, Am. Coll. Surgeons. Office: 2080 Century Park E Ste 1807 Los Angeles CA 90067-2021

BROWN, STEPHAN MARK, international fundraising and resource development executive, consultant; b. Glendale, Calif., Mar. 7, 1943; s. Mackey Elbert and Grace (Ferguson) B.; m. Janet Eyre Brookhart, Feb. 11, 1968; chidlren: Theodore Mark, Stephen Thomas. Student, Wash. State U., 1961-64, Eastern Wash. U., 1964-68; BA in Ministry, Melodyland Sch. Theology, 1978. Ordained to ministry Bapt. Ch., 1978. Sales and ops. mgr. Bon Marche Dept. Store, Seattle and other cities, Wash., 1966-74; devel. svcs. coord. Melodyland Sch. Theology, Anaheim, Calif., 1974-78; min. Renton (Wash.) First Bapt. Ch., 1978-80; dir. seminars Christian Broadcasting Network, Virginia Beach, Va., 1980-83; dir., sr. cons. Devel. Assn. for Christian Instns., McConkey Johnston Inc., Dallas, 1983-86; resource devel. cons. Spokane, Wash., 1986-89; dir. of direct mkgt. Christian Broadcasting Network, Virginia Beach, 1989-93; sr. cons. Crossroads Comms., Toronto, 1994—, Maridian Group, Skye Village, Centralia, Wash., 1994—; CEO, chmn. bd. Scottish Merc., ltd. Bd. dirs. Teen-Aid Inc., Spokane, 1988-89; com. mem., campaign vol. Rep. Party, Spokane, 1987-88. With U.S. Army N.G., 1966-72. Mem. Devel. Assn. for Christian Instns., Tidewater Pipes and Drums (pres. 1991-94, Grad. 3 awards 1993, Piper at the Inn-Founders Inn, Virginia Beach 1991-93), Rotary Internat. Republican. Home: 1000 S Pearl # 6 Centralia WA 98531 Office: Scottish Merc Ltd 107 N Tower Ste 11 Centralia WA 98531

BROWN, STEPHANIE DIANE, psychologist, consultant, researcher; b. Mpls., July 19, 1944; d. Samuel Benjamin and Stephanie (Sanko) B.; m. Robert Francis Harris, Sept. 9, 1978; 1 child, Makenzie. BS, U. Calif., Berkeley, 1966; MS, Calif. State U., San Jose, 1974; PhD, Calif. Sch. Profl. Psychology, 1977. Advt. rep. Koratron Co., San Francisco, 1966-68; rsch. asst. Stanford Rsch. Inst., Menlo Park, Calif., 1968-69; rsch. analyst Baumeister & Dole, Palo Alto, Calif., 1969-70; rsch. assoc. dept. psychiatry Stanford (Calif.) U. Med. Sch., 1972-75; founder, dir. Stanford Alcohol Clinic, 1977-85; cons. psychologist, Menlo Park, 1986—; rsch. assoc. Mental Rsch. Inst., Palo Alto, 1989—; dir. The Addictions Inst., Menlo Park, 1989—; cons. Monte Villa Hosp., Gilroy, Calif., 1977-80, O'Connor Hosp., Campbell, Calif., 1984-87, Kids Are Spl., San Jose, Calif., 1986-88, Merritt Peralta Inst., Oakland, Calif., 1988-89. Author: Treating the Alcoholic, 1985, Treating adult Children of Alcoholics, 1988, Adult Children of Alchohlics in Treatment, 1989, Safe Passage, 1991, Treating Alchoholism, 1995. Recipient Outstanding Instr. award Stanford U., 1980, Community Svc. award Calif. Soc., 1986; Bronze Key award Nat. Coun. on Alcoholism, 1983, Humanitarian award, 1984; Academic Specialist grantee, 1991. Mem. APA, Am. Group Psychotherapy Assn., Assn. for Med. Edn. and Rsch. in Substance Abuse, No. Calif. Group Psychotherapy Assn., Nat. Assn. for Children Alcoholics (adv. bd.). Democrat. Office: The Addictions Inst 445 Burgess Dr Menlo Park CA 94025-3442

BROWN, STEVEN BRIEN, radiologist; b. Ft. Collins, Colo., Jan. 18, 1952; s. Allen Jenkins and Shirley Irene (O'Brien) B.; m. Susan Jane DiTomaso, Sept. 10, 1983; children: Allison Grace, Laura Anne. BS, Colo. State U., 1974; MD, U. Calif., San Diego, 1978. Diplomate Am. Bd. Radiology, Radiol. Soc. N. Am. Intern U. Wash., Seattle, 1978-79; resident in radiology Stanford (Calif.) U., 1979-82; fellow in interventional and neuro-radiology Wilford Hall, USAF Med Ctr., San Antonio, 1982-83; staff radiologist Wilford Hall, USAF Med Ctr., 1983-86, Luth. Med. Ctr., Wheat Ridge, Colo., 1986—; chief angiography and interventional radiology Luth. Med. Ctr., 1987-94, chief dept. med. imaging, 1994—; pres. Luth. Med. Ctr. Joint Venture, 1992-93. Contbr. articles to profl. jours. Mem. Rep. Nat. Com., Washington, 1984—, Nat. Rep. Senatorial Com., 1985—, Rep. Presdl. Task Force, 1986—. Maj. USAF, 1982-86. Fellow Radiol. Soc. N.Am.; mem. Rocky Mt. Radiol. Soc. (pres. 1994-95), Am. Coll. Radiology, Soc. Cardiovascular and Interventional Radiology, Western Neuroradiol. Soc., Am. Soc. Neuroradiology, Colo. Preferred Physicians Orgn. (bd. dirs. 1987-89), World Wildlife Orgn., Colo. Angio Club. Republican. Presbyterian. Office: Luth Med Center 8300 W 38th Ave Wheat Ridge CO 80033-6005

BROWN, THEOPHILUS, artist; b. Moline, Ill., 1919. BA, Yale U., 1941; MA, U. Calif., Berkeley, 1952; studied with Ozenfant, New York, 1948; studied with Leger, Paris, 1949. Instr. U. Calif., Berkeley, 1954-56, San Francisco Art Inst., 1955-57, U. Calif., Davis, 1956-60, 75-76, U. Kans., Lawrence, 1967, Stanford U., 1967. One man shows include San Francisco Mus. Modern Art, 1957, Felix Landau Gallery, L.A., 1958, 60, 63, 65, 67, Kornblee Gallery, N.Y.C., 1961, Barone Gallery, N.Y.C., 1961, Crocker Art Gallery, Sacramento, 1965, Hollis Gallery, San Francisco, 1965, Ester Bear Gallery, Santa Barbara, Calif., 1965, U. Kans. Art Mus., 1967, Landau Alan Gallery, N.Y.C., 1968, Charles Campbell Gallery, San Francisco, 1972, 75, 78, Smith Gallery U. Calif., Santa Cruz, 1982, John Berggruen Gallery, San Francisco, 1983, 87, Maxwell Davidson Gallery, N.Y., 1989, Koplin Gallery, L.A., 1989, 91, 94, Tatistcheff & Co., Inc., N.Y., 1990, 92, Natsoulas Gallery, Davis, Calif., 1991, Harcourts Gallery, San Francisco, 1993; included in public collections at Metropolitan Mus. Art, Joseph H. Hirshhorn Mus., U. Kansas, Oakland Art Mus., San Francisco Mus. Modern Art, Sheldon Mus. U. Nebr., Capitol Records Inc., Commerce Trust Co., Davenport Mcpl. Art Gallery, Readers Digest Assn.

BROWN, THOMAS ADAMS, aviation executive; b. Phoenix, May 3, 1948; s. James Granville and Billie Kathryn (Adams) B.; m. Christine Ann Hajjar; children: Mark, Adam, Matthew. Student in aero. engring., U. Colo., 1966-69; BS in Bus., U. Tex., 1970. Regional dir. sales and svcs. Tex. Internat. Airlines, Houston, 1968-79; dir. material sys. and controls Tiger Internat., Burbank, Calif., 1979-81; exec. v.p. Aerotron AirPower, Inc., Long Beach, Calif., 1981—; pres. Long Beach Airport Assn. Mem. Nat. Aviation Assn., Aero Club of So. Calif., Nat. Bus. Aircraft Assn., Aero. Repair Sta. Assn., Long Beach Area C. of C. (bd. dirs.). Home: 880 Whitebook Dr La Habra CA 90631-6410 Office: Aerotron AirPower 2955 Redondo Ave Long Beach CA 90806-2445

BROWN, THOMAS JOSEPH, immunologist; b. Washington, Iowa, Feb. 6, 1947; s. William Wright and Margory Louise (Walker) B.; 1 child, Erinn Alysia. BS, Iowa State U., 1971. Registered microbiologist. Rsch. assoc. U. Iowa Hosp. and Clinic, Iowa City, 1972-85; rsch. scientist Bristol-Myers Squibb Pharm. Rsch. Inst., Seattle, 1985—. Author: book chpt., 1990; contbr. articles to profl. jours. Patentee in field. Mem. Am. Soc. Microbiology, Inflammation Rsch. Assn. Office: Bristol Myers Squibb Co 3005 1st Ave Seattle WA 98121-1010

BROWN, THOMAS RAYMOND, marketing company executive; b. Hammond, Ind., Nov. 6, 1947; s. Harvey Raymond and Cristina (Frunzio) B.; m. Constance Gladys, June 17, 1972; children: Katherine, Elizabeth Anne. BA in Letters and Sci., U. Calif., Berkeley, 1972. Pvt. practice comml. photographer Tom Brown Photography, Oakland, Calif., 1972-78; various oper. dept. positions Western Pacific RR, San Francisco, 1978-80, gen. mgr., 1980-82; sr. v.p. intermodal Western Pacific RR, Oakland, Calif., 1982-83; pres. Riss Intermodal, Alameda, Calif., 1983—.

BROWN, TIMOTHY CHARLES, social science professional; b. June 9, 1938; s. Gilbert Edgar Brown and Frances G. (Shaw) Milum; m. Leda Moraima Zuniga Fernandez, Sept. 11, 1958; children: Barbara, Rebecca, Tamara, Timothy Patrick. BA in Internat. Rels., U. Nev., 1965; MA in Internat. Trade & Econs., Fgn. Svc. Inst. Dept. State, 1974; PhD, N.Mex. State U., 1995. Staff state dept. Internat. Energy Agy., NATO, 1965-80; Orgn. Econ. Coop. desk Orgn. Economic Coop. & Devel., 1980-81; dep. coord. for Cuban affairs Dept. State, Coord. Cuban Embargo and Radio Marti, Washington, 1981-83; U.S. consul gen. French Caribbean Depts., Martinique, 1983-87; sr. liaison in C.Am. Nicaraguan Dem. Resistance, Tegucigalpa, Honduras, 1987-90, UN Observer Force in C.Am. and OAS Internat. Commn. Cease-Fire Verification and Assistance, 1989-90; sr. fellow Border Rsch. Inst. N.Mex. State U., Las Cruces, 1990-92; ind. scholar, trade cons., internat. and nat. lectr., 1992-94; rsch. fellow Hoover Instn. on War, Revolution and Peace, Stanford U., 1994; trustee S.W. Inst.; presenter in field. Contbr. articles to profl. jours. Sgt. USMC, 1954-64. Recipient Marine Corps. Commendations, Nicaragua, 1959, Thailand, 1963, State Dept. Commendations, Disting. Svc. award, Vietnam, 1967, Meritorious Honor awards, 1978, 82, Commendation Dir. Gen.s' Reporting awards, 1985, 89, Superiour Honor medal, 1990. Mem. Rotary Club, Marine Corps Assn. Home: 1025 Marilissa Ln Las Cruces NM 88005-3816 Office: Ctrl Am Found PO Box 1266 Mesilla NM 88046-1266

BROWN, TIMOTHY DONELL, professional football player; b. Dallas, July 22, 1966. BA, U. Notre Dame, 1988. Wide receiver L.A. Raiders, 1988—. Recipient Heisman trophy, 1987; named Wide Reciever on The Sporting News Coll. All-Am. team, 1986, 87; Coll. Football Player of the Yr. The Sporting News, 1987, Kick Returner The Sporting News NFL All-Pro Team, 1988. Office: LA Raiders 332 Center St El Segundo CA 90245-4047*

BROWN, TOD DAVID, bishop; b. San Francisco, Nov. 15, 1936; s. George Wilson and Edna Anne (Dunn) B. BA, St. John's Coll., 1958; STB, Gregorian U., Rome, 1960; MA in Theology, U. San Francisco, 1970, MAT in Edn., 1976. Dir. edn. Diocese of Monterey, Calif., 1970-80, vicar gen., clergy, 1980-82, chancellor, 1982-89, vicar gen., chancellor, 1983-89; pastor St. Francis Xavier, Seaside, Calif., 1977-82; bishop Roman Catholic Diocese of Boise, Idaho, 1989—; chair com. on laity Nat. Conf. Cath. Bishops. Named Papal Chaplain Pope Paul VI, 1975. Mem. Cath. Theol. Soc. Am., Cath. Biblical Assn., Canon Law Soc. Am., Equestrian Order of the Holy Sepulchre in Jerusalem. Office: Diocese of Boise 303 Federal Way Boise ID 83705-5925*

BROWN, TONI CYD, secondary education educator; b. Billings, Mont., Apr. 22, 1950; d. Alec Wilbert and Ruth Isabel (Uline) Brown; m. Mark A. Higdon; children: Marykitt, Elizabeth. BA, U. Wyo., 1972; MA, 1979, BA in Elem. Edn., 1988, postgrad., 1979-80. Cert. flight instr. Tchr. Billings Sch. Dist. #2, 1973-77; admissions counselor Rocky Mt. Coll., Billings, 1977-78; tchr. Gillette Campus No. Wyo. Community Coll., 1979-80, dir. Region III Developmentally Delayed Presch. Prog., 1980; tchr. various grades Campbell County Sch. Dist., Gillette, Wyo., 1980-88; tchr. gifted resource rm. Campbell County Sch. Dist., Gillette, 1988-89; tcrh. mid. sch. English comm., career, acad. competition, 1989—; cons. in field; lectr. in aerospace edn. Chairman bd. dirs. High Plains Energy Tech. Ctr. Found. Named Campbell County Am. Legion Educator of the Yr., 1988, Outstanding Educator of Yr. Fed. Aviation Adminstrn., 1990; Space Acad. grantee Internat. Ninety-Nines, 1987; Wyo. Christa McAuliffe fellow, 1990. Mem. Campbell County Reading Assn., Wyo. Assn. Gifted Edn., Wyo. Coun. Tchrs. Math., Nat. Sci. Tchrs. Assn., Nat. Coun. Tchrs. Math., Nat. Coun. Tchrs. English, Wyo. Reading Assn., Wyo. Sci. Tchrs. Assn. (Elem. Sci. Tchr. of the Yr. 1988), Aircraft Owners and Pilots Assn., CAP, Exptl. Aircraft Assn., Nat. Space Soc., Ninety Nines, Inc., Planetary Soc., Soc. Children's Book Writers, U. Wyo. Alumni Assn., Women's Sports Found., Wyo. Writers/Poets, Young Astronauts Am., Wyo. Aerospace Assn. (chmn.). Home: PO Box 396 Gillette WY 82717-0396

BROWN, VALERIE, state legislator; b. Kansas City, Mo., Oct. 30, 1945; divorced; 1 child, Lisa Davis. BS, U. Mo., 1972, MA, 1978. Former mayor City of Sonoma; mem. Calif. State Assembly, 1993—; marriage, family and child counselor. Mem. Sonoma Valley C. of C. (v.p.). Democrat. Presbyterian. Home: 299 1st St West Sonoma CA 95476 Office: State Capitol Rm 2130 Sacramento CA 95814-4906

BROWN, WALTER CREIGHTON, biologist; b. Butte, Mont., Aug. 18, 1913; s. D. Frank and Isabella (Creighton) B.; m. Jeanette Snyder, Aug. 20, 1950; children: Pamela Hawley, James Creighton, Julia Elizabeth. AB, Coll. Puget Sound, 1935, MA, 1938; PhD, Stanford U., 1950. Chmn. dept. Clover Park High Sch., Tacoma, Wash., 1938-42; acting instr. Stanford U., Calif., 1949-50; instr. Northwestern U., Evanston, Ill., 1950-53; dean sci. Menlo Coll., Menlo Park, Calif., 1955-66, dean instrn., 1966-75; rsch. assoc., fellow Calif. Acad. Sci., San Francisco, 1978—; lectr. Sillman U., Philippines, 1954-55, dir. rsch. Program on Ecology and Systematics of Philippine Amphibians and Reptiles, 1958-74; ; vis. prof. biology Stanford U., 1962, 64, 66, 68, Harvard U., Cambridge, Mass., 1969, 72. Author: Philippine Lizards of the Family Gekkonidae, 1978, Philippine Lizards of the Family Scincidae, 1980, Lizards of the Genus Emoia (Scincidae) with Observations of Their Evolution and Biogeography, 1991; contbr. 79 articles to profl. jours. Served with U.S. Army, 1942-46. Fellow AAAS; mem. Am. Soc. Ichthyologists and Herpetologists, Am. Inst. Biol. Scis., Sigma Xi. Office: Calif Acad Scis Dept Herpetology Golden Gate Park San Francisco CA 94118

BROWN, WILLIAM CARROLL, plastic surgeon, microsurgeon; b. St. Paul, Mar. 16, 1954; s. Jerry W. and M. Suzanne (Stussi) B.; m. Sandra J. Hansen Brown, Nov. 12, 1977; children: Amanda B., Ryan W. BS and BA in biochemical genetics and physiological psychology magna cum laude, U. Minn., 1976, student, 1978, postgrad., 1978-79; MD CM, McGill U. Faculty of Medicine, Montreal, Que., Can., 1983. Diplomate Am. Bd. Plastic Surgery in Surgery of the Hand, Am. Bd. Plastic Surgery, Am. Bd. Surgery, Nat. Bd. of Med. Examiners. Resident, gen. surgery Boston's Beth Israel Hosp. Dept. of Surgery, 1983-88; postdoctoral tng. Boston Mass Dept. of Surgery, 1984-86, Royal Cornwall Hosp., Truro, Cornwall, England, 1986-88; resident, fellow Duke U. Med. Ctr. Dept of Plastic Surgery, Durham, N.C., 1988-91; resident, hand and microsurgery fellow Christine M. Kleinert Inst. for Hand and Microsurgery, Louisville, 1989; rsch. Plastic and Reconstructive Surgery Duke U. Med. Ctr., Physiological Psychology U. Minn., 1973-76, Biochemical Genetics U. Minn., 1974-76, Gastrointestinal Physiology U. Minn., 1977-78, Microciculatory Physiology U. Minn., 1978-82. Contbr. articles to profl. jours. Capt. M.C., U.S. Army, 1990—. Mem. AMA, ACS, Am. Soc. of Plastic and Reconstructive Surgeons, Am. Soc. for Surgery of the Hand, Am. Cleft Palate-Craniofacial Assn., Colo. State Soc. Plastic and Reconstructive Surgeons, Colo. Cleft Palate Assn., Denver Med. Assn., Rose Cleft Palate Assn. Office: Plas Surg Clinic 1578 Humboldt St Denver CO 80218-1638

BROWN, WILLIAM EDWIN, construction executive, educator; b. Belknap, Ill., Jan. 11, 1934; s. Samual Edwin and Sarah Elizabeth (Kean) B. BS, So. Ill. U., 1956, MS, 1957; PhD, Ohio State U., 1964. Asst. instr. So. Ill. U., Carbondale, 1955-56; instr. U. Tenn., Knoxville, 1956-57; asst. prof. Ohio Sate U., Columbus, 1957-64, asst. to dean, 1964-67; prof. Trenton State Coll., N.J., 1967-76; regional dir. State of Calif., Sacramento, 1976-80; owner Dial One Bear Tavern Construction, Inc., Sacramento, 1979—; seminar dir. Dial One of No. Calif., 1985—; part-time prof. Calif State U., Sacramento, 1986—. Adv. Phi Alpha Delta, Trenton State Coll. Served with USAR, 1955-62. Mem. Am. Soc. Engring. Educators, Optimist (v.p. 1965-67), Phi Delta Kappa, Epsilon Phi Tau. Republican. Methodist. Home: 1110 Sierra Dr Sacramento CA 95864

BROWN, WILLIAM OSCAR, retired railroad executive; b. El Paso, Tex., May 16, 1915; s. Benjamin McCulloch and Alice Lillian (Drisdale) B.; m. Phyllis Ann Disano, July 6, 1940; children: William Drisdale, Marcia Jean. BSME, Rice U., 1937; postgrad., Stanford U., 1958, MIT, 1964. Registered profl. engr. With So. Pacific Transp. Co., 1937—; asst. supt. motive power So. Pacific Transp. Co., Sacramento, 1955-58, supt. mech. dept., 1959-67; asst. chief mech. officer So. Pacific Transp. Co., San Francisco, 1968-69, chief mech. officer, 1970-78, ret., 1978; mech. adv. mem. Trailer Train Corp., Chgo., 1970-78, Assn. Am. R.R. mech. divsn., Washington, 1970-78. Mem. ASME, So. Pacific Ret. Execs. club (pres. 1987-88), Green Hills Country Club. Republican. Baptist. Address: 1130 Murchison Dr Millbrae CA 94030-2919

BROWN, WILLIE LEWIS, JR., state legislator, lawyer; b. Mineola, Tex., Mar. 20, 1934; s. Willie Lewis and Minnie (Boyd) B.; children: Susan, Robin, Michael. B.A., San Francisco State Coll., 1955; LL.D., Hastings Coll. Law, 1958; postgrad. fellow, Crown Coll., 1970, U. Calif.-Santa Cruz, 1970. Bar: Calif. 1959. Mem. Calif. State Assembly, Sacramento, 1965—; speaker Calif. State Assembly, 1980—, chmn. Ways and Means Com., 1971-74; chmn. revenue and taxation com., 1976-79; Democratic Whip Calif. State Assembly, 1969-70, majority floor leader, 1979-80, chmn. legis. black caucus, 1980, chmn. govtl. efficiency and economy com., 1968-84. Mem. U. Calif. bd. regents, 1972, Dem. Nat. Com., 1989-90; co-chmn. Calif. del. to Nat. Black Polit. Conv., 1972, Calif. del. to Nat. Dem. Conv., 1980; nat. campaign chmn. Jesse Jackson for Pres., 1988. Mem. State Legis. Leaders Found. (dir.), Nat. Conf. State Legislatures, NAACP, Black Am. Polit. Assn. Calif. (co-founder, past chmn.), Calif. Bar Assn., Alpha Phi Alpha, Phi Alpha Delta. Democrat. Methodist. Office: Calif Assembly Office of Speaker 219 State Capitol Sacramento CA 95814 also: 1388 Sutter St Ste 820 San Francisco CA 94109-5453

BROWNE, GRETCHEN LYNN, interior designer; b. Seattle, Dec. 6, 1969; d. Ivan Len and Judy Lynn (Gott) A. BA, We. Wash. U., 1992. Interior designer Village Interiors, Inc., Issaquah, Wash., 1992—. Mem. Associated Soc. Interior Designers. Home: 10005 NE 201st St Bothell WA 98011-2437 Office: Village Interiors Inc 10522 238th Way SE Issaquah WA 98027-4816

BROWNE, JOSEPH PETER, retired librarian; b. Detroit, June 12, 1929; s. George and Mary Bridget (Fahy) B.; A.B., U. Notre Dame, 1951; S.T.L., Pontificium Athenaeum Angelicum, Rome, 1957, S.T.D., 1960; MS in L.S., Cath. U. Am., 1965. Joined Congregation of Holy Cross, Roman Cath. Ch., 1947, ordained priest, 1955; asst. pastor Holy Cross Ch., South Bend, Ind., 1955-56; libr., prof. moral theology Holy Cross Coll., Washington, 1959-64; mem. faculty U. Portland (Oreg.), 1964-73, 75—, dir. libr., 1966-70, 76-94, dean Coll. Arts and Scis., 1970-73, assoc. prof. libr. sci. 1967-95, prof. emeritus, 1995—, regent, 1969-70, 77-81, chmn. acad. senate, 1968-70, 1987-88; prof., head dept. libr. sci. Our Lady of Lake Coll., San Antonio, 1973-75; chmn. Interstate Libr. Planning Coun., 1977-79. Mem. Columbia River chpt. Huntington's Disease Soc. Am., 1975-90, pres., 1979-82; pastor St. Birgitta Ch., Portland, 1993—; chmn. Archdiocesan Presbyteral Coun., 1994—. Recipient Culligan award U. Portland, 1979. Mem. Cath. Libr. Assn. (life, pres. 1971-73), ALA, Cath. Theol. Soc. Am., Pacific N.W. Libr. Assn. (pres. 1985-86), Oreg. Libr. Assn. (life, pres. 1967-68), Nat. Assn. Parliamentarians, Oreg. Assn. Parliamentarians (pres. 1985-87), Archdiocesan Hist. Commn. (pres. 1985-90), Mensa Internat., All-Ireland Cultural Soc. Oreg. (pres. 1984-85). Democrat. Club: KC. Home: 11820 NW Saint Helens Rd Portland OR 97231-2319

BROWNE, MILLARD CHILD, former newspaper editor; b. Sprague, Wash., Feb. 7, 1915; s. Clarence Swain and Irma Josephine (Child) B.; m. Jane Sweet, Aug. 25, 1939; children: Katherine Anne Browne Kunkle, Millard Warren, Jeffrey Child, Barbara Jane Browne Atlas. AB, Stanford U., 1936, MA, 1939; postgrad. (Nieman fellow), Harvard U., 1942-43. Reporter, Columnist, editorial writer Calif. newspapers Santa Paula Chronicle, Santa Ana Jour., Sacramento Union, 1936-42; asso. editor Sacramento Union, 1943-44; editorial writer Buffalo Evening News, 1944-80, chief editorial writer, 1953-66, editorial page editor, 1966-80; sr. mem. Wolfson Coll., Cambridge (Eng.) U., 1980-81. Mem. Nat. Conf. Editorial Writers (pres. 1962-63), Am. Soc. Newspaper Editors, Internat. Press Inst., World Press Freedom Com., Soc. Profl. Journalists, Sigma Alpha Epsilon. Unitarian. Home: 2140 Santa Cruz Ave Apt D301 Menlo Park CA 94025-6346

BROWNHILL, H. BUD, small business owner, canine behavior therapist; b. Fort Erie, Ont., Can., May 22, 1941; came to U.S., 1958; s. Charles V. and June M. (Ott) B. Student, Fullerton (Calif.) Coll., 1960-62, Fanshaw Coll., London, Ont. Can., 1971-73, Brock U., Ont., Can., 1977. Cert. canine behavior therapist in aggression solving, trainer, Calif. Owner Brownhill Basics Dog Tng., N.Y., Ariz., Calif., Can., Dogs-Calif. Tng., Anaheim, 1988—; presenter seminars to dog tng. assns. in U.S. and Can.; speaker on dog-bite prevention to various orgns.; puppy expert, gen. problem solving tnr., specialist in competition tng.; instr. other profl. dog trainers for pvt. bus. and govt.; legal cons. dog aggression in & out of court. lectr. seminars on dog tng. anti-aggression to tng. assns. and pvt. industry, U.S. A. and Can.; contbr. articles to profl. jours. Active Smithsonian, Habitat for Humanity. Recipient High in Trials awards Am. Kennel Club, Can. Kennel Club, Bermuda Kennel Club, Mex. Kennel Club; winner High in Trials U.S. Chesapeake Obedience Nat., 1989, Shuffle Bd. Champion, 1980; 1st pl. Gaines Western U.S. Obedience Championship, 1985, 3d pl. tie World Series Obedience Competition, 1985; recipient Calif. State award, Golden State award. Mem. NRA, Am. Assn. Ret. Persons, Calif. Handlers Advanced Obedience Soc., Internat. Platform Assn., Am. Amateur Trap-Shooting Assn. (class winner 1977, 78, 79, 80, 83, 84, 85), Long Beach German Shepherd Dog Club (obedience chmn. 1985-90, 94-95), Nat. Fishing Assn., Nat. Hunting Assn., Dog Owners Internat. Travel (founder, internat. chmn. 1987-90, 94), Doberman Club (Santa Ana, obedience cons. 1984-86), Orange Coast Obedience Club (program dir. 1984), Can. Nat. Assn. (provincial rep. 1980). Home: 2147 W Avon Cir Anaheim CA 92804-4306 Office: Dogs-Calif Tng 2230 W Colchester Dr # 14 Anaheim CA 92804-4286

BROWNING, JAMES ROBERT, federal judge; b. Great Falls, Mont., Oct. 1, 1918; s. Nicholas Henry and Minnie Sally (Foley) B.; m. Marie Rose Chapell. BA, Mont. State U., Missoula, 1938; LLB with honors, U. Mont., 1941, LLD (hon.), 1961; LLD (hon.), Santa Clara U., 1989. Bar: Mont. 1941, D.C. 1950, U.S. Supreme Ct. 1952. Spl. atty. antitrust div. Dept. Justice, 1941-43, spl. atty. gen. litigation sect. antitrust div., 1946-48, chief antitrust dept. N.W. regional office, 1948-49; asst. chief gen. litigation sect. antitrust div. Dept. Justice (N.W. regional office), 1949-51, 1st asst. civil div., 1951-52; exec. asst. to atty. gen. U.S., 1952-53; chief U.S. (Exec. Office for U.S. Attys.), 1953; pvt. practice Washington, 1953-58; lectr. N.Y.U. Sch. Law, 1953, Georgetown U. Law Center, 1957-58; clk. Supreme Ct. U.S., 1958-61; judge U.S. Ct. Appeals 9th Circuit, 1961—, chief judge, 1976-88; mem. Jud. Conf. of U.S., 1976-88, exec. com. of conf., 1978-87, com. on internat. conf. of appellate judges, 1987-90, com. on ct. adminstrn., 1969-71, chmn. subcom. on jud. stats., 1969-71, com. on the budget, 1971-77, adminstrn. office, subom. on budget, 1974-76, com. to study U.S. jud. conf., 1986-88, com. to study the illustrative rules of jud. misconduct, 1985-87, com. on formulation of standard of conduct of fed. judges, 1969, Reed justice com. on cont. edn., tng. and adminstrn., 1967-68; David T. Lewis Disting. Judge-in-residence, U. Utah, 1987; Blankenbaker lectr. U. Mont., 1987, Sibley lectr. U. Ga., 1987, lectr. Human Rights Inst. Santa Clara U. Sch. Law, Strasbourg. Editor-in-chief, Mont. Law Rev. Dir. Western Justice Found.; chmn. 9th Cir. Hist. Soc. 1st lt. U.S. Army, 1943-46. Decorated Bronze Star; named to Order of the Grizzly, U. Mont., 1973; scholar in residence Santa Clara U., 1989, U. Mont., 1991; recipient Devitt Disting. Svc. to Justice award, 1990. Fellow ABA (judge adv. com. to standing com. on Ethics and Profl. Responsibility 1973-75); mem. D.C. Bar Assn., Mont. Bar Assn., Am. Law Inst., Fed. Bar Assn. (bd. dirs 1945-61, Nat. council 1958-62), Inst. Jud. Adminstrn., Am. Judicature Soc. (chmn. com. on fed. judiciary 1973-74, bd. dirs. 1972-75), Herbert Harley award 1984), Am. Soc. Legal History (adv. bd. jour.), Nat Lawyers Club (bd. govs. 1959-63). Office: US Ct Appeals 9th Cir 121 Spear St Fl 2 San Francisco CA 94105-1558*

BROWNING, JESSE HARRISON, entrepreneur; b. Kingsville, Mo., July 27, 1935; s. Jesse Harrison and Anna Love (Swank) B.; m. Vicki Carol Thompson, Dec. 21, 1957; children: Caroline Kaye, Marcia Lynn, Nanci Ann, Susan Louise. MPA, U. So. Calif.; $D; PhD, U. Wash. Cert. mfg. engr. Field engr. The Boeing Co., Los Angeles, 1961-64; gen. mgr. SPI, Los Angeles, 1964-70; chmn. Browning Inc., Los Angeles, 1970—, Indsl. Systems, Los Angeles, 1979-87, Vapor Engring., Los Angeles, 1979-87. Patentee in field. Mem. ASPA, World Coun. on Internat. Trade, World Affairs Coun., Am. Helicopter Soc., Am. Assn. Geographers, Soc. Mgr. Engrs. Lutheran. Home and Office: 16301 Inglewood Rd NE Bothell WA 98011-3908

BROWNING, NORMA LEE (MRS. RUSSELL JOYNER OGG), journalist; b. Spickard, Mo., Nov. 24, 1914; d. Howard R. and Grace (Kennedy) B.; m. Russell Joyner Ogg, June 12, 1938. A.B., B.J., U. Mo., 1937; M.A. in English, Radcliffe Coll., 1938. Reporter Los Angeles Herald-Express, 1942-43; with Chgo. Tribune, from 1944, Hollywood columnist, 1966-75; Vis. lectr. creative writing, editorial cons., mem. nat. adv. bd. Interlochen Arts Acad., Northwood Inst. Author: City Girl in the Country, 1955, Joe Maddy of Interlochen, 1963, (with W. Clement Stone) The Other Side of the Mind, 1965, The Psychic World of Peter Hurkos, 1970, (with Louella Dirksen) The Honorable Mr. Marigold, 1972, (with Ann Miller) Miller's High Life, 1972, Peter Hurkos: I Have Many Lives, 1976, Omarr: Astrology and the Man, 1977, (with George Masters) The Masters Way to Beauty, 1977, (with Russell Ogg) He Saw A Hummingbird, 1978, (with Florence Lowell) Be A Guest At Your Own Party, 1980, Face-Lifts: Everything You Always Wanted to Know, 1981, Joe Maddy Of Interlochen: Portrait of A Legend, 1991; Contbr. articles to nat. mags. Recipient E.S. Beck award Chgo Tribune. Mem. Theta Sigma Phi, Kappa Tau Alpha. Address: 226 E Morongo Rd Palm Springs CA 92264-8402

BROWNING, WILLIAM DOCKER, federal judge; b. Tucson, May 19, 1931; s. Horace Benjamin and Mary Louise (Docker) B.; m. Courteny Browning (div.); children: Christopher, Logan, Courtenay; m. Zerilda Sinclair, Dec. 17, 1974; 1 child, Benjamin. BBA, U. Ariz., 1954, LLB, 1960. Bar: Ariz. 1960, U.S. Dist. Ct. Ariz. 1960, U.S. Ct. Appeals (9th cir.) 1965, U.S. Supreme Ct. 1967. Pvt. practice Tucson, 1960-84; judge U.S. Dist. Ct., Tucson, 1984—; mem. jud. nominating com. appellate ct. appointments, 1975-79. Del. 9th Cir. Jud. Conf., 1968-77, 79-82; trustee Inst. for Ct. Mgmt., 1978-84; mem. Ctr. for Pub. Resources Legal Program. 1st lt. USAF, 1954-57, capt. USNG, 1958-61. Recipient Disting. Citizen award U. Ariz., 1995. Fellow Am. Coll. Trial Lawyers, Am. Bar Found.; mem. ABA (spl. com. housing and urban devel. law 1973-76, com. urban problems and human affairs 1978-80), Ariz. Bar Assn. (chmn. merit selection of judges com. 1973-76, bd. gove. 1968-74, pres. 1972-73, Outstanding Mem. 1980), Pima County Bar Assn. (exec. com. 1964-68, med. legal screening panel 1965-75, pres. 1967-68), Am. Bd. Trial Advocates, Am. Judicature Soc. (bd. dirs. 1975-77), Fed. Judges Assn. (bd. dirs.). Office: US Dist Ct US Courthouse Rm 301 55 E Broadway Blvd Tucson AZ 85701-1719*

BROWNLEE, WILSON ELLIOT, JR., history educator; b. Lacrosse, Wis., May 10, 1941; s. Wilson Elliot Sr. and Pearl (Woodings) B.; m. Mary Margaret Cochran, June 25, 1966; children: Charlotte Louise, Martin Elliot. BA, Harvard U., 1963; MA, U. Wis., 1965, PhD, 1969. Asst. prof. U. Calif., Santa Barbara, 1967-74, assoc. prof., 1974-80, prof. history, 1980—, spl. advisor to provost, 1995—; vis. prof. Princeton (N.J.) U., 1980-81; chmn. dept. history U. Calif., Santa Barbara, 1984-87, acad. senate, 1983-84, 88-90, systemwide acad. senate, 1992-93; dir. U. Calif.-Santa Barbara Ctr., Washington, 1990-91; chmn. exec. com. dels. Am. Coun. Learned Socs., N.Y.C., 1988-90, bd. dirs.; bd. dirs. Nat. Coun. on Pub. History, Boston; bicentennial lectr. U.S. Dept. Treasury, 1989; faculty rep. U. Calif. Bd. Regents, 1991-93. Author: Dynamics of Ascent, 1974, 79, Progressivism and Economic Growth, 1974; co-author: Women in the American Economy, 1976, Essentials of American History, 1976, 80, 86, America's History, 1987, 93; contbr. numerous articles to profl. jours., chpts. to books. Chair schs. com. Harvard Club, Santa Barbara, 1971-80, 85, 86; pres. Assn. for Retarded Citizens, Santa Barbara, 1982-84; 1st v.p. Assn. for Retarded Citizens Calif., Sacramento, 1983-84; pres. Santa Barbara Trust for Hist. Preservation, Santa Barbara, 1986-87, 95; bd. trustees Las Trampas Inc., 1994—. Charles Warren fellow Harvard U., 1978-79, fellow Woodrow Wilson Ctr., Washington, 1987-88; recipient Spl. Commendation, Calif. Dept. Parks and Recreation, 1988. Mem. Am. Hist. Assn., Orgn. Am. Historians, Econ. History Assn., Am. Tax Policy Inst. Office: U Calif Dept History Santa Barbara CA 93106

BROWNSON, JACQUES CALMON, architect; b. Aurora, Ill., Aug. 3, 1923; s. Clyde Arthur and Iva Kline (Felter) B.; m. Doris L. Curry, 1946; children—Joel C., Lorre J., Daniel J. BS in Architecture, Ill. Inst. Tech., 1948, MS, 1954. Instr., asst. prof. architecture Ill. Inst. Tech., 1949-59; prof. architecture, chmn. dept. U. Mich., 1966-68; chief design C.F. Murphy Assocs., Chgo., 1959-61; project architect, chief designer Chgo. Civic Ctr. Architects, 1961-68; dir. state bldg. div. State of Colo., Denver, 1986-88; pvt. practice Denver, 1988—; former mng. architect Chgo. Pub. Bldg. Commn.; past dir. planning and devel. Auraria Ctr. for Higher Edn., Denver; bd. dirs. Capital Constrn., Denver; guest lectr. architecture in U.S. and Europe. Prin. works include Chgo. Civic Ctr., Lake Denver, Colo., 1985, Chgo. Tribune/Cabrini Green Housing, 1993. Recipient award for Geneva House Archtl. Record mag., 1956; Design award for steel framed factory Progressive Architecture mag., 1957. Home and Office: 659 Josephine St Denver CO 80206-3722

BROWN-STIGGER, ALBERTA MAE, nurse; b. Columbus, Ohio, Nov. 11, 1932; d. Sylvester Clarence and Malinda (Mason) Angel; grad. Antelope Valley Coll., 1961; AA, L.A. Valley Coll., 1975; BS, Calif. State U., Dominguez Hills, 1981; m. Norman Brown, Dec. 29, 1967 (dec. Jan. 1989); children: Charon, Charles, Stevan, Carole; m. A.C. Stigger, June 14, 1992. RN, Calif.; lic. vocat. nurse. Nurses aid, vocat. nurse, respiratory therapist St. Bernardines Hosp., 1965-69, Good Samaritan Hosp., L.A., 1969-70, Midway Hosp., L.A., 1973-81; allergy nurse, instr. respiratory therapy VA Hosp., L.A., 1970-93, also acting dept. head; nurse, respiratory splty. unit Jerry L. Pettis Meml. Hosp., Loma Linda, Calif., 1984-93; with Wadley Regional Med. Ctr., Texarkana, Tex., 1993-94; rehab. nurse Robert H. Ballard Rehab. Hosp., San Bernardino, Calif., 1994—; instr. L.A. Valley Med. Technoogists Sch., Compton Coll. seminar instr., 1979. Active Arrowhead Allied Arts Coun. of San Bernardino; CPR instr. Am. Heart Assn. Mem. Am. Assn. Respiratory Therapy, Nat. Honor Soc., Eta Phi Beta. Democrat. Baptist. Clubs: Social-Lites, Inc. of San Bernardino, Order Ea. Star. Patentee disposable/replaceable tubing for stethoscope. Home: Orangewood Estates 1545 Hancock St San Bernardino CA 92411-1667

BROWN-VAN HOOZER, STEFANIA ALENKA, electrical engineer, human factor specialist; b. Trieste, Italy, Feb. 26, 1953; (parents Am. citizens); d. Charles and Liliana Maria (Clemente) Brown; married, Feb. 10, 1973; 1 child, Daniel S. VanHoozer. Assocs. degree, European divsn. U. Md., Germany, 1982; BS in Computer Sci., U. Md., 1985; MSEE, U. Colo., 1990; PhD, Columbia Pacific U., 1995. Lab. asst. U. Tex., San Antonio, 1983-84; rsch. engr. Micro Rsch., Inc., Falls Church, Va., 1984-86; R&D instrumentation and control engr. Rockwell Internat., Golden, Colo., 1986-90; elec. engr. Rockwell Internat., Idaho Nat. Engring. Lab., 1990-91, Babcock & Wilcox, Idaho Nat. Engring. Lab., 1991-92; elec. engr., human factors specialist Argonne (Ill.) Nat. Lab., 1992—; bd. dirs. Display Motion, Inc., Boulder, Colo.; condr. seminars on recognizing learning styles. Contbr. papers to profl. jours. Debate judge Southeastern H.S., Idaho, 1994-95; trustee Idaho Acad. Scis.; mem. adv. bd. Post Register Newspaper, Idaho Falls, 1994; chair Scholastic Tournament for Rigby Jr. H.S., 1993-94. Mem. Am. Nuclear Soc. (news editor for human factors divsn. 1994-95), Soc. Women Engrs. (pres. 1991-93, Outstanding Mem. 1992-93), Young Women's Conf. (chair 1993, Outstanding Leadership award 1993), Am. Bus. (advisor 1990-92). Office: Argonne Nat Lab MS 6000 PO Box 2528 Idaho Falls ID 83403

BRUBAKER, CRAWFORD FRANCIS, JR., government official, aerospace consultant; b. Fruitland, Idaho, Apr. 23, 1924; s. Crawford Francis and Cora Susan (Flora) B.; m. Lucile May Christensen, May 5, 1945; children: Eric Stephen, Alan Kenneth, Craig Martin, Paul David. BA, Pomona Coll., 1946; MBA, U. Pa., 1948. Office mgr. Lockheed Calif. Co., Burbank, 1948-54, sales adminstr., 1954-57, with fighter contracts div., field office rep., 1959-65, asst. dir. fighter sales, 1965-69, dep. mgr. bid and proposals, 1969-74, mgr. govt. sales, 1974-76; dir. internat. mktg. devel. and policy Lockheed Corp., Burbank, 1976-83; dep. asst. sec. for aerospace U.S. Dept. Commerce, Washington, 1983-87; internat. aerospace cons., 1987—; vice chmn. Industry Sector Adv. Com., Washington, 1979-83; mem. Aero. Policy Rev. Com., Washington, 1983-87. Vice chmn. So. Calif. Dist. Export Coun., L.A., 1980-83, 88-91, chmn., 1992-93. Lt. (j.g.) USN, 1943-45, PTO. Mem. AIAA, Am. Defense Preparedness Assn., Kiwanis, Sigma Alpha Epsilon. Republican. Presbyterian.

BRUBAKER, JOHN E., bank executive; b. 1941. CEO 1st Bank Ill., Chgo., 1967-89; chmn. bd., pres., CEO, dir. Ctrl. Bank Walnut Creek, Calif., 1989-92; past COO, sr. exec. v.p., now pres., CEO Bay View Fed. Bank, San Mateo, Calif., 1992—. Office: Bay View Fed Bank Ste 1111 2121 S El Camino Real San Mateo CA 94403-1819*

BRUBAKER, WILLIAM ROGERS, sociology educator; b. Evanston, Ill., June 8, 1956; s. Charles William and Elizabeth (Rogers) B. BA summa cum laude, Harvard U., 1979; MA, Sussex U., Eng., 1980; PhD, Columbia U., 1990. Prof. UCLA, 1994—, assoc. prof. sociology, 1991-94. Author: The Limits of Rationality, 1984, Citizenship and Nationhood in France and Germany, 1992; editor: Immigration and Politics of Citizenship in Europe and North America, 1989. Jr. fellow Soc. Fellows Harvard U., 1988-91, MacArthur fellow MacArthur Found., 1994-99; grantee NSF, 1994-99. Office: U Calif Dept Sociology 405 Hilgard Ave Los Angeles CA 90024-1301

BRUCE, JOHN ALLEN, foundation executive, educator; b. Kansas City, Mo., Sept. 17, 1934; BA, Wesleyan U., Middletown, Conn., 1956; MDiv, Gen. Theol. Sem., N.Y.C., 1959; PhD, U. Minn., 1972. Ordained to ministry Episcopal Ch., 1959. Clergyman, 1959-68; prof. U. Ala., Tuscaloosa, 1972-74; exec. dir. E.C. Brown Found., Portland, Oreg., 1974—; cons. to philanthropies and corp. programs; clin. prof. community medicine Sch. Medicine, Oreg. Health Scis. U., Portland, 1976—. Author, editor various scholarly publs. Exec. producer various ednl. films on family life, health and values. Bd. dirs. various community orgns. Served to lt. USN, 1964-67. Recipient various awards and grants from med. orgns. and related groups. Mem. Nat. Coun. on Family Rels. (Disting. Service to Families award 1979), Oreg. Coun. on Family Rels. (pres. 1981), Cosmos Club. Republican. Office: EC Brown Found 101 SW Main St Ste 500 Portland OR 97204-3228

BRUCE, ROBERT KIRK, college administrator; b. Evanston, Ill., Nov. 7, 1942; s. Robert Kirk and Irma Bertha (Roese) B.; m. Judith Lee Chjlopecki, July 13, 1968; children: Michael, James, Suzanne, Gary, Meredith. BS in Edn., No. Ill. U., DeKalb, 1967; MA, Ctrl. Mich. U., Mt. Pleasant, 1972, EdS, 1974. Edn. writer Rockford (Ill.) Morning Star, 1969-70; coord. News Bur. Ctrl. Mich. U., Mt. Pleasant, 1970-75; dir. News Bur. U. Oreg., Eugene, 1975-78; dir. univ. rels. Kans. State U., Manhattan, 1978-82; dir. univ. info. U. Nebr., Lincoln, 1982-89; asst. v.p. Oreg. State U., Corvallis, 1989-94, interim chief instl. advancement officer, 1994—; cons. U. Ariz., Tucson, 1984, Barton County C.C., Great Bend, Kans., 1984, Glassboro (N.J.) State Coll., 1988. Mem. Mayor's Task Force on Pub. Artwork, Manhattan, Kans., 1981; bd. dirs. Lincolnfest Celebration, Lincoln, Nebr., 1983-87, Oreg. Spl. Olympics, 1976-78. With USNR, 1965-73. Recipient Pub. Rels. awards ACPRA, AAC, Washington, 1971-74. Mem. Coun. for Advancement and Support of Edn. (medal awards 1980—), Am. Legion, Lincoln C. of C. (chmn. com. 1983-89), Century Club (bd. dirs. 1990—). Democrat. Roman Catholic. Home: 1075 NW Charlemagne Pl Corvallis OR 97330-3643 Office: Oreg State U Ads # 524 Corvallis OR 97331

BRUCE, THOMAS EDWARD, thanatologist, psychology educator; b. Vinton, Iowa, Dec. 3, 1937; s. George Robert and Lucille Etta (Aurner) B.; m. Joan Lynne Thompson-Zimmerman, Nov. 19, 1993; children: Scott Thomas and Suzanne Laura (twins), Mark Adam Zimmerman, John Wesley Zimmerman. BA, U. No. Iowa, 1961, MA, 1964; postgrad., U. Colo., 1968-71; MA, U. San Francisco, 1985. Lic. psychology educator, counselor, Calif. Tchr. various Iowa high schs., 1961-65; sociologist, counselor Office Econ. Opportunity, Denver, 1965-66; social sci. educator Arapahoe Coll., Littleton, Colo., 1966-69; lectr. U. Colo., Boulder, 1968-71; psychology educator Sacramento City Coll., Calif., 1972—; thanatology cons. for hospices, survivor support groups, No. Calif., 1984—. Author: Grief Management: The Pain and the Promise, 1986, Thanatology: Through the Veil, 1992; contbr. articles to profl. pubs. Co-founder, bd. dirs. Bereavement Resources Network, Sacramento, 1983-87; profl. dir. Children's Respite Ctr., Sacramento, 1985-88; pres.-elect., bd. dirs. Hospice Care of Sacramento, 1979-85. With U.S. Army, 1955-58. Recipient Pres.'s award Nat. Hospice Orgn., 1985. Mem. Sacramento Mental Health Assn. (Vol. Svc. award 1985, 87), Assn. for Death Edn. and Counseling, Thanatology Found., Am. Fedn. Tchrs., Faculty Assn. Calif. C.C.'s, Pi Gamma Mu, Phi Delta Kappa. Presbyterian. Office: Sacramento City Coll 3835 Freeport Blvd Sacramento CA 95822-1318

BRUCH, JOHN CLARENCE, JR., engineer, educator; b. Kenosha, Wis., Oct. 11, 1940; m. Susan Jane Tippett, Aug. 19, 1967. BCE, U. Notre Dame, 1962; MCE, Stanford U., 1963, PhD in Civil Engring., 1966. Acting instr. engring. Stanford (Calif.) U., 1966; asst. prof. engring. U. Calif., Santa Barbara, 1966-74, assoc. prof. engring., 1974-78, prof. engring., 1978—. NSF grantee, 1987-93; U. Calif. faculty grantee, 1968. Mem. ASCE, Am. Sci. Affiliation, Sigma Xi, Tau Beta Pi. Office: U Calif Mech Engring Dept Santa Barbara CA 93106

BRUCKER, CONNIE, police officer, consultant; b. Detroit, June 29, 1946; d. Joseph Schwenk and Errawanna Coates; 1 child, Debra June Huegel. Student San Jose State Coll., 1980, East Los Angeles Coll., 1978. Legal sec. Lapin & Chester, West Los Angeles, Calif., 1972-75; police officer Santa Monica Police Dept., Calif., 1977—, mem. "K9 bite" rev. bd., mem. various award coms.; instr. Santa Monica Jr. Coll.; speaker, lectr. Lady Beware Programs, Los Angeles Area; cons. Safety Products, Calgary, Can., Calif. Council Hosps., Los Angeles, TV movies and spls. and interviews, Los Angeles. Author writings in field. Bd. dirs. ARC, Santa Monica, 1984—. Recipient Medal of Courage, City of Santa Monica, 1979, Mayor's Commendation, 1982, medal of Merit, 1994. Mem. Internat. Police Assn., Women Peace Officers Assn., Los Angeles Peace Officers Assn., Santa Monica Police Officers Assn., Sexual Assault Investigators Assn., Calif. Sexual Assault Investigators Assn. (pres. 1987). Office: Santa Monica Police Dept 1685 Main St Santa Monica CA 90401-3248

BRUDER, WILLIAM PAUL, architect; b. Milw., Aug. 28, 1946; s. Daniel R. and June (Luepke) B.; m. J. Simon Dumoulin, Jan. 28, 1968. BFA in Sculpture, U. Wis., Milw., 1969. Registered arch., Ariz., Calif., Utah, Colo., Wyo., Mass. Archtl. apprentice to William P. Wenzler, Michael P. Johnson, Paolo Soleri, Gunnar Birkerts, Michael and Kemper Goodwin; pvt. practice architecture New River, Ariz., 1974; vis. studio critic Ariz. State u. Sch. Architecture, U. Ariz., Taliesin, Yale U., Helsinki U. Tech., Tampere U. Tech. Prin. works include Phoenix Mesquite, 1983, Cholla Br. Librs., Phoenix, 1990, Phoenix Cen. Libr., 1995, Deer Valley Rock Art Mus., 1994, Riddell Bldg., 1995, (in books) The Prairie Tradition, 1979, Designing Your Clients House, Whitney, 1983, A Guide to the Architecture of Metro Phoenix, 1983, The Desert Southwest, 1987, others, (local publs.) Ariz. Republic, 1974-95, Sunset, 1975—, Artspace, 1982-83, Phoenix Home/Garden, 1981-95, others; exhibits include Archives Milw. Art Ctr., Sunset Western Home Awards Traveling Exhibit, 1977-78, Fine Arts Ctr. Tempe, 1983, The So. Calif. Inst. Arch., Santa Monica, 1984, The Graham Found., 1985, Am. Acad. Rome, 1987, Prescott Fine Arts, 1989, others. Recipient 1st Honor award Am. Plywood Assn., 1977, Record Home award, 1977, 93, Sunset Western Home award, 1977, 81, 87, 89, 91, 1st Pl. award The Ariz. Passive Solar Design Competition, 1981, Phoenix Home and Garden award, 1987, 88, 89, 91, 92, 93, 94, Domino's 30 award, 1990; Rome Prize Advanced Design fellow Am. Acad. Rome, 1987. Home: 1314 W Circle Mountain Rd New River AZ 85027-7194

BRUDVIG, GLENN LOWELL, retired library director; b. Kenosha, Wis., Oct. 14, 1931; s. Lars L. Brudvig and Anna Elizabeth (Hillesland) B. Lovejoy; m. Myrna Winifred Michael, Oct. 1, 1953; children—Gary Wayne, Lee Anthony, James Lowell, Kristin Elizabeth. B.A. in Edn., U. N.D., 1954, M.A., 1956; M.A.L.S., U. Minn., 1962. Tchr. pub. schs. Mahnomen and Herman, Minn., 1954-55, 56-58; librarian, archivist U. N.D., Grand Forks, 1958-62; asst. librarian U. N.D., 1962-63; supr. dept. libraries U. Minn., Mpls., 1964; dir. bio-med. libr. U. Minn., 1964-83; dir. librs. Calif. Inst. Tech., Pasadena, 1983-95, ret., 1995; instr. library sci. U. N.D., Grand Forks, 1962-63; asst. dir. for research and devel. U. Minn., Mpls., 1968-79, instr. library sci., 1968-71, dir. Inst. Tech. Libraries, 1982-83; cons. Nat. Library of Medicine, Bethesda, Md., 1971-75. Contbr. articles to profl. jours. Served with U.S. Army, 1951-52. Nat. Library of Medicine grantee, 1967-79. Home: 15 Eagle Ridge Rd North Oaks MN 55127

BRUE, STANLEY LEONARD, economics educator; b. Sioux Falls, S.D., Feb. 3, 1945; s. Esther (Ekberg) B.; m. Terryl L. Buzek, Apr. 11, 1970; 1 child, Craig. BA, Augustana Coll., Sioux Falls, S.D., 1967; PhD, U. Nebr., 1971. Prof. econs. Pacific Luth. U., Tacoma, Wash., 1971—. Co-author: Economic Scenes, 5th edit., 1992, Economics, 12th edit., 1993, Evolution of Economic Thought, 5th edit., 1994, Contemporary Labor Economics, 4th edit., 1995. Mem. Omicron Delta Epsilon (nat. pres. 1994—). Office: Pacific Luth U Dept Econs Tacoma WA 98447

BRUECKNER, BONNIE LICHTENSTEIN, security administrator; b. Chgo., Mar. 5, 1936; d. Ralph Henry and Hazel May (Mullens) Lichtenstein; m. Keith Allen Brueckner, June 18, 1988; children: Deborah Norwood, J. Patrick Klavas. BA in Psychology, San Diego State U., 1981. Security mgr. Phys. Dynamics, La Jolla, Calif., 1980-86, security cons., 1986—; sr. security coord. Lockheed, Burbank, Calif., 1986-87, United Tech., San Diego, 1987-89; div. adminstr. security Inst. for Def. Analyses Ctr. for Comm. Rsch. La Jolla, San Diego, 1989—. Mem. Nat. Classification Mgmt. Soc. Home: 3120 Almahurst Row La Jolla CA 92037-1162

BRUGGEMAN, LEWIS LEROY, radiologist; b. N.Y.C., Sept. 9, 1941; s. Louis LeRoy and Edwina Jane (Mickel) B.; m. Ann Margaret Kayajan, May 28, 1966; children: Gretchen Ann, Kurt LeRoy. AB, Dartmouth Coll., 1963, B in Med. Sci., 1965; MD, Harvard U., 1968. Intern Los Angeles County Harbor Gen. Hosp., Torrence, Calif., 1968-69; resident in diagnostic radiology Columbia Presbyn. Med. Ctr., N.Y.C., 1969-72; chief dept. radiology Bremerton (Wash.) Naval Regional Med. Ctr., 1972-74; pvt. practice diagnostic radiology South Coast Med. Ctr., South Laguna, Calif., 1974—, dir. dept. radiology, 1983—, hosp. bd. trustees, 1985-87; pvt. practice diagnostic radiology Saddleback Community Hosp., Laguna Hills, Calif., 1974—; pres., chmn. bd. dirs. South Coast Med. Group Inc., South Laguna, Calif., 1983—; pres. So. Coast Radiol. Med. Group Inc., South Laguna, 1986—; vice-chmn. and bd. trustees South Coast Med. Ctr. Found., 1993—. Lt. comdr. Med. Corps USN, 1972-74. Mem. AMA, Radiol. Soc. N.Am., Am. Coll. Radiology, Calif. Med. Assn., Calif. Radiol. Soc., Dartmouth Club Orange County. Office: S Coast Radiol Med Group 28 Monarch Bay Plz Ste J Dana Point CA 92629-3455

BRUGGER, PAUL RAYMOND, gaming professional; b. Glendale, Calif., July 31, 1942; s. Paul Joseph and Rita Marie (Wirth) B.; m. Carol Ann Tarleton, May 12, 1965; children: John-Paul, Eric, Joel, Beth, Dann, Elyn, KayCee. Student, Glendale Coll., 1960-64, L.A. City Coll., 1961, Western Nev. Community Coll., 1978-79, U. Nev., Las Vegas, 1981. Enging. asst. Nev. Controls, Inc., Minden, 1968; prodn. test technician Raven Electronics, Reno, 1968-69; electronics specialist Nev. Gaming Control Bd., Carson City, 1969-81; mgr. field support Summit Systems, Inc., Las Vegas, 1981-82; dist. mgr. Cal-Omega, Inc., Las Vegas, 1982-83; project engr. Sierra Control Systems, Carson City, 1983-85; electronics engr., mktg. mgr. Bally Systems, Reno, 1985-89; account exec. Computerland, Carson City, 1990-91; sys. & govt. liaison mgr. Aristocrat, Inc., Reno, 1991—; owner, gaming cons. Paul R. Brugger Cons. Svcs., Carson City, 1979—. Adult leader Nev. Area coun. Boy Scouts Am., 1971—. With USN, 1964-68. Mem. IEEE (sr., sect. chmn. 1988-90). Republican. Mormon. Office: Aristocrat Inc 750A S Rock Blvd Reno NV 89502-4114

BRULOTTE, BENNETT, agricultural products executive; b. 1944. With A/B Hop Farms, Inc., Prosser, Wash., 1968—, now sec. With U.S. armed forces, 1965-68. Office: A/B Hop Farms Inc 4456 Evans Rd Prosser WA 99350*

BRUMMETT, ROBERT EDDIE, pharmacology educator; b. Concordia, Kans., Feb. 11, 1934; s. Gordon Legonia and Gladys Leona (Anderson) B.; m. Naomi Deen Weaver, Dec. 19, 1955; children: Randall, Wendy, Robin, Philip. BS, Oreg. State U., 1959, MS, 1960; PhD, U. Oreg., 1964. Registered pharmacist, Oreg. Asst. prof. pharmacology Oreg. State U., Corvallis,

1961-62; asst. prof. otolaryngology Oreg. Health Scis. U., Portland, 1964-70, assoc. prof. otolaryngology and pharmacology, 1970-80, prof. otolaryngology and Pharmacology, 1981—; mem. Oreg. Coun. on Alcohol and Drug Problems, Salem, 1979-85; instr. Am. Acad. Otolaryngology, Washington, 1964—; mem. adv. panel otorhinolaryngology U.S. Pharmacopeia, 1985—, mem. drug info. adv. panel, 1988—, mem. coun. on naturopathic physicians formulary, 1990—. Contbr. more than 100 articles to profl. jours.; patentee in field. Comdr. U.S. Power Squadron, Portland, 1988-89, adminstrv. officer, 1986—, dist. ednl. officer, 1991-94, dist. exec. officer, 1995-96. Grantee NIH, 1969—, Deafness Research Found., 1970, Med. Research Found., 1979, 83. Mem. AAAS, Am. Acad. Otolaryngology (instr. 1964—), Head and Neck Surgery, Associated Rschrs. in Otolaryngology, Hayden Island Yacht Club, Elks, Sigma Xi. Republican. Home: 2366 N Menzies Ct Portland OR 97217-8219 Office: Oreg Health Scis U 3181 SW Sam Jackson Park Rd Portland OR 97201-3011

BRUN, CHRISTIAN MAGNUS FROM, university librarian; b. Trondheim, Norway, Oct. 3, 1920; came to U.S., 1923; s. Aage and Petra Christine (From) B.; m. Jane Carey Fristoe, June 1, 1958; 1 child, Erik From. BA in Econs. and Bus., U. Wash., 1948; BLS, U. N.C., 1950; AM in L.S., U. Mich., 1952, MA in History, 1956. Asst. curator U. Pa. Library, Phila., 1950-51; bibliog. asst. U. Mich., Ann Arbor, 1951-52, asst. curator, 1952-55, resident advisor, 1955-63; head spl. coll. library U. Calif., Santa Barbara, 1963-90; archivist U. Calif., 1963-90, preservation officer, 1988-90; curator William Wyles Coll., U. Calif., 1963-90; cons., 1990—. Author: Guide to the MSS Maps, 1959, Wm. L. Clements Lib. Maps and Charts Pub. in Am. before 1800, 1969; author (with others): new edition, 1978. Decorated Bronze Star, 1945; recipient Acorn Found. award, Acorn Found., 1969, Bicentennial Citation City of Santa Barbara, 1982. Mem. Am. Scandinavian Found., Santa Barbara Hist. Soc., Map Soc. Calif., Soc. Calif. Archivists, Am. Printing Hist. Assn., Soc. History Discoveries, Friends UCBS Library. Democrat. Home: 5667 Via Trento Goleta CA 93117 Office: U Calif Libr Dept Spl Collections Santa Barbara CA 93106

BRUN, KIM ERIC, photographer; b. San Diego, Jan. 31, 1947; s. Henry Milton and Laurel Elizabeth (Von Heeringen) B.; m. Susan Eileen Headley, Nov. 5, 1990; children: Brittany Nicole, Blaine Eric. BA, Humboldt State U., 1973; MBA, San Diego State U., 1976. Asst. rsch. physyologist Naval Personal Rsch. and Devel. Ctr., San Diego, 1973-76; sales rep. Sparkletts Water Co., San Diego, 1977-78; photographer Kim Brun Photography, San Diego, 1978-84, Kim Brun Studios, Inc., San Diego, 1984-94; dir. photography PhotoGroup, Inc., Portland, Oreg., 1994—. Co-author: Computer-Based Management Info Systems and Organization Behavior, 1980; photographer 23 nat. mag. covers, 7 interior design books. Bd. dirs. San Diego Oceans Found., 1993—. Sgt. U.S. Army, 1968-70, Vietnam. Decorated Bronze star for valor with two oak leaf clusters. Mem. Am. Soc. Mag. Photographers (treas. 1985-87, bd. dirs. 1987-88), Sierra Club.

BRUN, MARGARET ANN CHARLENE, buyer, planner; b. Toledo, Ohio, June 19, 1945; d. John Joseph and Maude Elizabeth (Harrell) Bartos; m. Paul Joseph Brun, June 17, 1967. Student, Phoenix Coll., 1964-67, Glendale C.C., 1991-93, Mosa C.C., 1995—. Cert. purchasing mgr. Contr. material inventory Digital Equipment Corp., Phoenix, 1975-76, contr. prodn. inventory, 1976-77, prodn. control planner, 1977-79, inventory control planner, 1979, buyer, 1979-91; buyer, planner ASM Am., Inc., 1991—. Named Buyer of Yr., Purchasing World mag., 1987. Mem. Purchasing Mgmt. Assn. Ariz. affiliate of Nat. Assn. Purchasing Mgmt. Democrat. Methodist.

BRUNACINI, ALAN VINCENT, fire chief; b. Jamestown, N.Y., Apr. 18, 1937; s. John N. and Mary T. Brunacini; B.S., Ariz. State U., 1970, M.P.A., 1975; m. Rita McDaugh, Feb. 14, 1959; children—Robert Nicholas, John Nicholas, Mary Candice. Mem. Phoenix Fire Dept., 1959—, bn. chief, then asst. fire chief, 1971-78, fire chief, 1978—; condr. nat. seminar on fire dept. mgmt., 1970—. Redford scholar, 1968. Mem. Am. Soc. Public Adminstrn. (Superior Service award 1980), Nat. Fire Protection Assn. (chmn. fire service sect. 1974-78, dir. 1978), Internat. Assn. Fire Chiefs, Soc. Fire Service Instrs. Author: Fireground Command; also articles in field. Office: Office of Fire Chief 520 W Van Buren St Phoenix AZ 85003-1632*

BRUNDIN, BRIAN JON, lawyer; b. St. Paul, Oct. 11, 1939; s. Milton E. Brundin and LuVerne (Johnson) Roddan; m. Carolyn Bagley, June 30, 1961; children: Iana L. Sayer, Ian S., Dane E. BBA in Acctg. cum laude, U. Alaska, 1961; JD, Harvard U., 1964. Bar: Alaska 1966, U.S. Ct. Appeals (9th cir.) 1966, U.S. Supreme Ct. 1986; CPA, Alaska. Assoc. Hughes, Thorsness, Gantz, Powell & Brundin, Anchorage, 1966-70, ptnr., 1970—, prin. ptnr., 1975—, chair comml. div. and corp. sect., 1970—, from vice-chmn. to chmn., 1972-82, group, 1994—; instr. acctg. and law U. Alaska, 1965-69; bd. dirs., pres. Brundin, Inc., 1979—, Kyak Oil, Inc., 1985-90; bd. dirs., sec. Far North Fishermen, Inc., 1981-85; trustee Humana Hosp. Alaska, 1982-83; adv. bd. World Trade Ctr. Alaska, 1992—. Chmn. subcom. on sales taxes Operation Breakthrough, Anchorage, 1968; mem. U. Alaska Bd. Regents, 1969-77, chmn. fin. com., 1970-75, v.p. 1973-75, pres., 1975-77; mem. Alaska Postsecondary Commn., 1973-75; founder, trustee U. Alaska Found., 1974—, pres., 1974-77, mem. exec. com., 1987—, chmn. Bullock prize for execellence com., 1989—; Alaska chmn. Harvard U. Law Sch. Fund, 1975-78; mem. adv. bd. alaska Ctr. for Internat. Bus., 1986-88. Capt. U.S. Army, 1964-66. Mem. ABA, AICPA, Anchorage Bar Assn. (legis com.), Alaska Bar Assn. (ethics and client security, corp. banking, bus. law and taxation WICHE, higher edn.), Am. Acad. Hosp. Attys., Am. Soc. Atty./CPAs, Alaska Soc. CPAs, U. Alaska Alumni Assn, (pres. Anchorage chpt. 1968-69), Sons of Norway, Pioneers of Alaska Igloo 15, Am. Legion, Amvets, Lions, Rotary, Ancient Teachings of Masters (bd. dirs., treas.).

BRUNEAU, BILL, architect; b. Phila., May 29, 1948; s. William Francis and Mabel Frances (Quiroli) B.; children: Nicole Domenique, Mercedes Angelina, William Robert, Michelangelo Joseph. BArch., Pa. State U., 1970; MArch., U. Colo., 1971; M. of Urban Design, Harvard U., 1974; Cert. in City Planning, U. Florence, Italy, 1969; Cert. in Urban Econs., MIT, 1970. Registered architect Colo., Calif., Mo., Mass., Wyo., Minn. Urban designer planning dept. City of Aurora, Colo., 1977-80; project interior architect Cannell & Chaffin, Denver, 1980-82; dir. architecture URS Co., Denver, 1982-84; mgr. facilities Frontier Airlines, Denver, 1984-86, United Airlines, Chgo., 1986-87; sr. aviation planner Burns & McDonnell, Denver, 1987-91; dir. facilities Continental Airlines, 1991-94; v.p. aviations facilities HOK, San Francisco, 1994-95; LHR-T5 Airport, London, 1995—; instr. U. Colo., Denver, 1972, Community Coll. Denver, Red Rocks, Colo., 1975-80, Boston Archtl. Ctr., 1972-74; prin. Bruneau Urban Design and Architecture Assocs., Denver, 1980-87; pres. Rocky Mountain Constrn. Mgmt., Inc., Aurora, 1982. Contbr. articles to profl. jours. Vol. YMCA, Colo., Denver Art Mus., Denver Nat. History Mus., Zoological Soc., Math Counts; lectr. career days Colo.; Sunday sch. tchr., counselor and planning commr. Harvard U. fellow, 1973; recipient award of Merit City and County of Denver, 1972; named Outstanding Young Man of Am., 1976. Mem. AIA, AAAE, AOCI, Am. Soc. Interior Designers, Am. Inst. Certified Planners, Illuminating Engring. Soc. Presbyterian. Home: 58 Cornwall Gardens Flat 1, London SW7 4BE, England Office: 71 Stevenson St Ste 2200 San Francisco CA 94105-2934

BRUNEAUX, DEBRA LOUISE, costume designer; b. Orange, Calif., Oct. 19, 1953; d. James Fredricksen and Carol Gwen (Cashner) B. BA in Exptl. Psychology, U. Calif., Santa Barbara, 1975. Residents women's cutter/draper Ctr. Theatre Group, Los Angeles, 1978-79; asst. to resident costume designer Oreg. Shakespearean Festival Assn., Ashland, 1980-82; costume shop supr. Sacramento Theatre Co., Calif., 1982-83; resident costume designer Sacramento Theatre Co., 1983-88; costume designer, costume mgr. Oreg. Shakespeare Festival, Portland, 1988—, costume mgr., 1988-94; costume shop mgr., cons. Berkeley Repertory Theatre, Calif., 1979; costumer TV series Mr. Holland's Opus, McKenna, 1994. Home: 2020 SW Main St Apt 702 Portland OR 97205-1535 Office: Oreg Shakespeare Festival PO Box 9008 Portland OR 97207-9008

BRUNELL, DAVID H., information systems specialist; b. 1948. BA in History, U. N.Mex., 1970, MA in European History, 1974. Rsch. asst. U. Mich., Ann Arbor, 1974-76; sys. specialist U. N.Mex., Albuquerque, 1976-79; network libr. Libr. Congress, Washington, 1979-83; exec. dir., sec., treas. Bibliog. Ctr., Aurora, Colo., 1983—. Office: Bibliog Ctr 14394 E Evans Ave Aurora CO 80014*

BRUNELLO-MCCAY, ROSANNE, sales executive; b. Cleve., Aug. 26, 1960; d. Carl Carmello and Vivan Lucille (Caranna) B.; divorced, 1991; m. Walter B. McCay, Feb. 26, 1994; 1 child, Angela Breanna. Student, U. Cin., 1978-81, Cleve. State U., 1981-82. Indsl. sales engr. Alta Machine Tool, Denver, 1982; mem. sales./purchases Ford Tool & Machine, Denver, 1982-84; sales/ptnr. Mountain Rep. Enterprises, Denver, 1984-86; pres., owner Mountain Rep. Ariz., Phoenix, 1986—; pres. Mountain Rep. Oreg., Portland, 1990—, Mountain Rep. Wash., 1991—; sec. Computer & Automated Systems Assoc., 1987, vice chmn., 1988, chmn., 1989. Active mem. Rep. Party, 1985—; mem. Phoenix Art Mus., Grand Canyon Minority Coun., 1994; vol. Make-A-Wish Found., 1995. Mem. NAFE, Soc. Mfg. Engrs. (pres. award 1988), Computer Automated Assn. (sec. 1987, vice chmn. 1988 chmn. 1989), Nat. Hist. Soc., Italian Cultural Soc., Tempe C. of C., Vocat. Ednl. Club Am. (mem. exec. bd., pres. 1987—). Roman Catholic. Office: Mountain Rep Ariz 410 S Jay St Chandler AZ 85224-7668

BRUNER, CINDY HULL, judge; b. Waterbury, Conn., Apr. 26, 1949; d. Harry Garfield Jr. and Ella Betsey (Houghton) Hull (dec.); m. Jack Dennis Bruner, Sept. 24, 1988; children. BS, U. Vt., 1979; JD, U. Colo., 1984. Bar: Colo. 1984, U.S. Dist. Ct. Colo., 1985. Law clk. U.S. Dist. Ct., Denver, 1984-85; dep. dist. atty. Adams County, Brighton, Colo., 1985-91; count. ct. judge 17th Jud. Dist., Brighton, 1991—. Mem. Colo. Bar Assn. (criminal law sect. exec. coun. 1993—), , Adams County Bar Assn. Office: Hall of Justice 17th Jud Dist 1931 E Bridge St Brighton CO 80601-1940

BRUNETT, ALEXANDER J., bishop; b. Detroit, MI, Jan. 13, 1958. ordained priest July 13, 1958. Ordained bishop Diocese of Helena, 1994. Office: Chancery Diocesan Pastoral Office 515 North Ewing PO Box 1729 Helena MT 59624

BRUNETTI, MELVIN T., federal judge; b. 1933; m. Gail Dian Buchanan; children: Nancy, Bradley, Melvin Jr. Student, U. Nev.; JD, U. Calif., San Francisco, 1964. Mem. firm Vargas, Bartlett & Dixon, 1964-69, Laxalt, Bell, Allison & Lebaron, 1970-78, Allison, Brunetti, MacKenzie, Hartman, Soumbeniotis & Russell, 1978-85; judge U.S. Ct. Appeals (9th cir.), Reno, 1985—. Mem. Council of Legal Advisors, Rep. Nat. Com., 1982-85. Served with U.S. Army N.G., 1954-56. Mem. ABA, State Bar of Nev. (pres. 1984-85, bd. govs. 1975-84), Washoe County Bar Assn., Carson City Bar Assn. Office: US Ct Appeals c/o US Marshal 300 Booth St 1st Fl Reno NV 89509-1356

BRUNK, PATRICK CHARLES ROY, mental health professional, counselor; b. Tonasket, Wash., June 5, 1959; s. Charles H. and Margie J. (Stockham) B. BS in Psychology, Warner Pacific Coll., 1983; MEd, Heritage Coll., 1991. Cert. counselor, child and adolescent treatment specialist, Wash. Social worker, mental health counselor II Carondeler Psychiat. Care Ctr., Richland, Wash., 1985-88, county designated mental health profl., 1988-91; co-therapist Inner Directions Counselling, Kennewick, Wash., 1990-94; county designated mental health profl. Benton County, Kennewick, Wash., 1992—; employee assistance counselor Personal Counselling Svc., Hermiston, Oreg., 1994—; pvt. practitioner Umatilla County Anger Mgmt. Program, Hermiston, Oreg., 1994—; co-instr. psychology Yakima Valley C.C., Grandview, Wash., 1990-91, Columbia Basin Coll., Pasco, Wash., 1990-93. Mem. ACA, Assn. Specialists in Group Work. Office: Personal Counselling Svc 955 W Orchard Ave Hermiston OR 97838

BRUNNER, HOWARD WILLIAM, professional land surveyor; b. Mobile, Ala., July 24, 1946; s. Joseph Edward and Beaulah (Howard) B.; m. Linda Marie Parker, Dec. 20, 1963 (div. June 1978); children: Leah Marie, Anne Marie; m. Catherine Cecilia Byrnes, June 27, 1981; children: Jordan, Thomas, Howard. Grad. high sch., Santa Rosa, Calif. Lic. profl. land surveyor. Survey technician Roemer & Estes, Mill Valley, Calif., 1964-65, Ken Frost & Assocs., Mill Valley, 1965-66; engring. aide County of Marin, San Rafael, Calif., 1966-75; pres. Engring. Field Svcs., San Rafael, 1975-77, Brunner, Phelps & Assocs., Inc., Cotati, Calif., 1977-80; v.p. Ray Carlson & Assocs., Inc., Santa Rosa, Calif., 1980—; expert examiner, Profl. Land Surveyor/Tech. Adv. Com. mem., expert witness Bd. Registration for Profl. Engrs. and Land Surveyors, Sacramento, 1985-91. Mem. Geysers Geothermal Assn. (bd. dirs. 1985-92), Calif. Land Surveyors Assn. (treas. 1987-88, sec. 1988-89, pres. 1990). Roman Catholic. Home: 1161 Valley View Dr Healdsburg CA 95448-4540 Office: Ray Carlson & Assocs Inc 411 Russell Ave Santa Rosa CA 95403-2219

BRUNO, JUDYTH ANN, chiropractor; b. Eureka, Calif., Feb. 16, 1944; d. Harold Oscar and Shirley Alma (Farnsworth) Nelson; m. Thomas Glenn Bruno, June 1, 1968; 1 child, Christina Elizabeth. AS, Sierra Coll., 1982; D of Chiropractic, Palmer Coll. of Chiropractic West, Sunnyvale, Calif., 1986. Diplomate Nat. Bd. Chiropractic Examiners. Sec. Bank Am., San Jose, Calif., 1965-67; marketer Memorex, Santa Clara, Calif., 1967-74; order entry clk. John Deere, Milan, Ill., 1977; system analyst Four Phase, Cupertino, Calif., 1977-78; chiropractic asst. Dr. Thomas Bruno, Nevada City, Calif., 1978-81; chiropractor Chiropractic Health Care Ctr., Nevada City, 1987-91; pvt. practice Cedar Ridge, Calif., 1991—. Area dir. Cultural Awareness Coun., Grass Valley, Calif., 1977—; vol. Nevada County Libr., Nevada City, 1987-88, Decide Team III, Nevada County, 1987-92, Active Parenting of Teen Facilitator Nev. Union High Sch. Mem. Am. Chiropractic Assn., Women Health Practitioners of Nevada County (founder 1993—), Nevada County C. of C. (vol. task force health care 1993), Toastmasters (sec. 1988, pres. 1989, edn. v.p. 1990). Republican. Office: Chiropractor Health Care PO Box 1718 Cedar Ridge CA 95924-1718

BRUNO, KATHLEEN MCGINN, management consultant; b. Castro Valley, Calif., Mar. 28, 1957; d. Raymond Edward and Nancy Lee (Beamer) McGinn; m. Richard Bruce Bruno, Sept. 28, 1991; 1 child, Nicole Pearl. BA, St. Mary's Coll. Calif., Moraga, 1979; MBA, Georgetown U., Washington, 1990. Asst. v.p. cash mgmt. Crocker Bank/Wells Fargo Bank, San Francisco, 1979-86; cash mgmt. cons. Amdahl Corp., Sunnyvale, Calif., 1987; mgr. fin. analysis Fed. Res. Bd. of Govs., Washington, 1988; prin. Am. Mgmt. Sys. Inc., Redwood City, Calif., 1990—. Home: 47 Bayview Ave Mill Valley CA 94941-1847 Office: Am Mgmt Sys Inc 3 Twin Dolphin Dr Redwood City CA 94065-1516

BRUNO, PETER JACKSON, counselor, consultant, pastor; b. White Plains, N.Y., Dec. 27, 1945; s. Charles Fredrick and Barbara (Jackson) B.; m. Barbara Suesens; 1 child, Linda; 2d m. Corky Jean Brown, July 3, 1976; children: Benjamin, Elizabeth. BA in Psychology, Brown U., 1968; MEd in Counseling, Mont. State U., 1978. Lic. profl. counselor, Mont.; nat. cert. counselor; cert. clin. mental health counselor. Addictive disease counselor Mont. State Hosp., Galen, 1973-76; tchg. asst. Mont. State U., Bozeman, 1977-78; psychologist V Ea. Mont. Mental Health, Miles City, 1979-92; pvt. practice counselor Glendive, Mont., 1992—; clin. cons. Dept. Family Svcs., Miles City, Home on the Range, Sentinel Butte, N.D., Pine Hills Sch., Miles City, all 1992—; lead clin. staff Big Sky Ranch, Glendive, 1993—. Author: New Ways Workbook, 1992. Pres. Montanans for Children, Youth and Families, Inc.; leader, tchr. Evangelical Ch. Named Mont.'s Outstanding Direct Svc. Provider, Mental Health Assn. Mont., 1982. Mem. Am. Profl. Soc. on the Abuse of Children, Assn. for the Treatment Sex Abusers (clin. mem.), Mont. Sex Offender Treatment Assn. (clin. mem.), Great Plains Counseling Assocs. (dir.), Toastmasters Internat. Glendive (membership chmn.). Office: Great Plains Counseling PO Box 684 513 N Merrill Ave Glendive MT 59330

BRUNSON, KATHLEEN KAY, elementary educator; b. Newcastle, Wyo., Oct. 13, 1944; d. William Nathaniel and Lorraine Maryanne (Peterson) Popham; children: Lyle, Chris, Melanie. BA in Elem. Edn., U. Wyo., 1989, MA in Curriculum and Instrn., 1993. Cert. tchr., Wyo. Tchr. Platte County Sch. Dist., Wheatland, Wyo., 1983—. Chmn. bd. Platte County Resource Dist., Wheatland, 1995. Named Wyo. Conservation Tchr. of Yr. Wyo. Assn. Conservation Dists., 1993. Mem. Platte County Edn. Assn. (past pres., sec.-treas., chmn. pub. rels.), Wyo. Edn. Assn. (Exceptional Svc. award 1988), NEA, ASCD (Wyo. del. to internat. leadership conf. 1988), Phi Kappa Phi, Kappa Delta Pi.

BRUST, DAVID, physicist; b. Chgo., Aug. 24, 1935; s. Clifford and Ruth (Klapman) B.; BS, Calif. Inst. Tech., 1957; MS, U. Chgo., 1958, PhD, 1964. Rsch. assoc. Purdue U., Lafayette, Ind., 1963-64; rsch. assoc. Northwestern U., Evanston, Ill., 1964-65, asst. prof. physics, 1965-68; theoretical rsch. physicist U. Calif., Lawrence Radiation Lab., Livermore, Calif., 1968-73; cons. Bell Telephone Lab., Murray Hill, N.J., 1966. Campaign co-ordinator No. Calif. Scientists and Engrs. for McGovern, 1972. NSF travel grantee, 1964; NSF rsch. grantee, 1966-68. Mem. Am. Phys. Soc., Am. Assn. Coll. Profs., Internat. Solar Energy Soc., Astron. Soc. of Pacific, Nature Conservancy, Calif. Acad. Sci., World Affairs Coun. No. Calif. Anza Borrego Desert, Natural History Assn., Planetary Soc., Sierra Club, Sigma Xi. Office: PO Box 13130 Oakland CA 94661-0130

BRUTTING, THOMAS CHARLES, architect; b. N.Y.C., July 8, 1954; s. Charles Christian and Dorothy Martha (Kasil) B.; m. Laura Jean Kinzie, June 24, 1978 (div. Apr. 12, 1986); 1 child, Michael; m. M.W. Henderson, Sept. 30, 1986; step-children: Matthew, Sarah. BArch, Tulane U., 1977. Registered profl. architect. Architect Russo & Sonder, N.Y.C., 1977-78, Leibowitz & Bodouva, N.Y.C., 1978-80, HSR Architects, Madison, Wis., 1980-82, Strang Ptnrs., Madison, Wis., 1983-86, Engelbrecht & Griffin, Des Moines, 1986-89, Hardison, Komatsu, Ivelich & Tucker, San Francisco, 1989—. Pres. Old Market Pl. Neighborhodd Assn., Madison, 1981-84; bd. dirs. Bethel Outreach, Madison, 1984-86; mem. budget com. Unified Sch. Dist., San Francisco, 1994. Recipient John Lawrence fellowship AIA, 1976. Mem. AIA. Episcopalian. Home: 795 Buena Vista Ave W San Francisco CA 94117-4133 Office: Hardison Komatsu Ivelich & Tucker 400 Second St Ste 200 San Francisco CA 94107

BRYA, WILLIAM JOHN, anesthesiologist; b. Chgo., Mar. 30, 1938; s. William George and Julie Anne (Mikalansky) B.; m. Catherine Anne Froehlich, June 26, 1965; children: Jacqueline Anne, Lara Michele, Jennifer Rene, Kristen Elisabeth. B of Engring. Sci., Johns Hopkins U., 1960, PhD, 1966; MD, U. Miami, 1975. Diplomate Am. Bd. Anesthesiology. Postdoctoral fellow Bell Tel. Labs., Murray Hill, N.J., 1966-69; staff scientist Sandia Labs., Albuquerque, 1969-73; intern U. Calif., San Diego, 1975-76, resident in anesthesiology, 1976-78; pvt. practice, Albuquerque, 1978—. Mem. AMA, Tau Beta Pi, Eta Kappa Nu, Omicron Delta Kappa. Republican. Roman Catholic. Office: Surgery Ctr Albuquerque 1720 Wyoming Blvd NE Albuquerque NM 87112-3855

BRYAN, A(LONZO) J(AY), service club official; b. Washington, N.J., Sept. 17, 1917; s. Alonzo J. and Anna Belle (Babcock) B.; student pub. schs.; m. Elizabeth Elfreida Koehler, June 25, 1941 (div. 1961); children: Donna Elizabeth, Alonzo Jay, Nadine; m. Janet Dorothy Onstad, Mar. 15, 1962 (div. 1977); children: Brenda Joyce, Marlowe Francis, Marilyn Janet. Engaged as retail florist, Washington, N.J., 1941-64. Fund drive chmn. ARC, 1952; bd. dirs. Washington YMCA, 1945-55, N.J. Taxpayers Assn., 1947-52; mem. Washington Bd. Edn., 1948-55. Mem. Washington Grange, Sons and Daus. of Liberty, Soc. Am. Florists, Nat. Fedn. Ind. Businessmen, Florists Telegraph Delivery Assn., C. of C. Methodist. Clubs: Masons, Tall Cedars of Lebanon, Jr. Order United Am. Mechanics, Kiwanis (pres. Washington (N.J.) 1952, lt. gov. internat. 1953-54, gov. N.J. dist. 1955, sec. N.J. dist. 1957-64, sec. S.E. area Chgo. 1965-74; editor The Jersey Kiwanian 1958-64, internat. staff 1964-85); Breakfast (pres. 1981-82) (Chgo.); sec., treas. Rocky Mtn. Kiwanis Dist., 1989; pres. South Denver, 1990-91; editor Rocky Mountain Kiwanian, 1990—. Home: 8115 S Poplar Way Englewood CO 80112-3174 Office: 1192 Aberdeen Dr Broomfield CO 80020-2410

BRYAN, GORDON REDMAN, JR., nuclear power engineering consultant; b. Cleve., Dec. 1, 1928; s. Gordon Redman and Iola (Schecter) B.; m. Janet Louise McIntyre, Aug. 1, 1951 (div. Oct. 1986); children: Gordon L., Steven G.; m. Judith Hager, July 5, 1987. BA, Brown U., 1951; MS, George Washington U., 1970. Commd. ensign USN, 1951, advanced through grades to capt., 1971; comdg. officer 4 navy ships and 5 shore commands, 1965-78, submarine squadron, 1972-74; ret., 1978; marine design cons. various aerospace and engring. cos., Seattle, 1979-81; engring. cons. U.S. Nuc. Regulatory Commn. and U.S. Dept. Energy, Seattle, 1982-95. Decorated Legion of Merit. Mem. Am. Nuclear Soc., Am. Radio Relay League, N.Y. Acad. Scis., Rotary. Republican. Home and Office: Saddle Brook Country Club 37810 S Rolling Hills Dr Tucson AZ 85737 also: PO Box 1285 Bay View MI 49770

BRYAN, JOHN RODNEY, management consultant; b. Berkeley, Calif., Dec. 29, 1953; s. Robert Richard and Eloise (Anderson) Putz; m. Karen Nelson, Jan. 20, 1990. BA in Chemistry, U. Calif., San Diego, 1975; MBA, Rutgers U., 1985. Agt. Prudential, San Diego, 1975-79; sales mgr. Herman Schlorman Showrooms, L.A., 1980-83; pvt. practice mgmt. cons. Basking Ridge, N.J., 1983-85; mgmt. cons. Brooks Internat. Corp., North Palm Beach, Fla., 1985-88; pvt. practice San Diego, 1988—; with Western Productivity Group, 1990—. Elder La Jolla Presbyn. Ch., 1991—. Mem. ASPA, Inst. Indsl. Engring., Rutgers Club So. Calif., Beta Gamma Sigma. Office: Applied Control Mgmt Effectiveness Sys 6265 Hurd Ct San Diego CA 92122

BRYAN, KEVAN FRED, treasurer; b. Peoria, Ill., Apr. 15, 1959; s. Robert Louie and Marjorie Jane (Flocken) B.; m. Cynthia Jo Tavolacci, Sept. 12, 1981; children: Keith, Gregory, Jennifer. BSBA in Acctg. Option, Mont. State U., Billings, 1981. CPA, Mont. Staff acct. McGladrey, Hendrickson & Co., CPAs, Billings, 1981-82; asst. dvisn. acct., dir. office svcs. Super Valu Stores, Inc., Billings, 1982-88; county treas. Yellowstone County, Billings, 1989—. Bd. dirs. Family Svc., Inc., Billings, 1991-94; divsn. chmn. United Way, Billings, 1991. Mem. AICPAs, Mont. Soc. CPAs, Mont. Fedn. Pachyderm Clubs (pres. 1993-94), Mont. State U. Alumni Assn. (Billings chpt. v.p., bd. dirs. 1994—, Outstanding Young Alumnus award 1991). Republican.

BRYAN, RICHARD H., senator; b. Washington, July 16, 1937; married; 3 children. B.A., U. Nev., 1959; LL.B., U. Calif.-San Francisco, 1963. Bar: Nev. 1963. Dep. dist. atty. Clark County, Nev., 1964-66; public defender Clark County, 1966-68; counsel Clark County Juvenile Ct., 1968-69; mem. Nev. Assembly, 1969-73, Nev. Senate, 1973-79; atty. gen. State of Nev., 1979-83, gov. Nev., 1983-89, U.S. Senator from Nevada, 1989—; mem. U.S. Senate coms. on commerce, sci. and transp.; mem. Dem. Policy Com.; mem. armed svcs. com.; mem. Banking, Housing and Urban Affiars Com.; v. chmn. Ethics Com.; mem. Sen. Nom. Steering and Coor. Com.; chmn. western region Dem. Senate Campaign Com.; chmn. Senate Consumer Subcom. Bd. dirs. March of Dimes; former v.p. Nev. Easter Seal Soc.; former pres. Clark County Legal Aid Soc. Served with U.S. Army, 1959-60. Recipient Disting. Svc. award Vegas Valley Jaycees. Mem. ABA, Clark County Bar Assn., Am. Judicature Soc., Nat. Gov.'s Assn. (com. econ. devel. and technol. innovation, com. internat. trade and fgn. relations, task force on adult literacy, task force on jobs growth and competitiveness, chmn. subcom. tourism), Council of State Govts. (past pres.), Phi Alpha Delta, Phi Alpha Theta. Democrat. Clubs: Masons, Lions, Elks. Office: US Senate 364 Russell Senate Bldg Washington DC 20510*

BRYAN, ROBERT J., federal judge; b. Bremerton, Wash., Oct. 29, 1934; s. James W. and Vena Gladys (Jensen) B.; m. Cathy Ann Welander, June 14, 1958; children: Robert James, Ted Lorin, Ronald Terence. BA, U. Wash., 1956, JD, 1958. Bar: Wash. 1959, U.S. Dist. Ct. (we. dist.) Wash. 1959, U.S. Tax Ct. 1965, U.S. Ct. Appeals (9th cir.) 1985. Assoc., then ptnr. Bryan & Bryan, Bremerton, 1959-67; judge Superior Ct., Port Orchard, Wash., 1967-84; ptnr. Riddell, Williams, Bullitt & Walkinshaw, Seattle, 1984-86; judge U.S. Dist. Ct. (we. dist.) Wash., Tacoma, 1986—; mem. State Jail Comm., Olympia, Wash., 1974-76, Criminal Justice Tng. Com., Olympia, 1978-81, State Bd. on Continuing Legal Edn., Seattle, 1984-86; mem., sec. Jud. Qualifications Commn., Olympia, 1982-83. Author: (with others) Washington Pattern Jury Instructions (civil and criminal vols. and supplements), 1970-85, Manual of Model Criminal Jury Instructions for the Ninth Circuit, 1992, Manual of Model Civil Jury Instruction for the Ninth Circuit, 1993. Chmn. 9th Ct. Jury Com., 1991-92. Served to maj. USAR. Office: US Dist Ct 1717 Pacific Ave Rm 4427 Tacoma WA 98402-3234

BRYAN, SHARON ALLEN, writer, humanities educator; b. Salt Lake City, Feb. 10, 1943; d. Glen and Shirley (Storrs) Allen. BA in Philosophy, U. Utah, 1965; MA in Anthropology, Cornell U., 1969; MFA in Poetry, U. Iowa, 1977. Acting asst. prof. U. Wash., Seattle, 1980-87; assoc. prof.

Memphis State U., 1987-93; vis. prof. Darmouth Coll., Hanover, N.H., 1994-95, U Houston, 1995—; poet-in-residence The Frost Pl, Franconia, N.H., 1993. Author: Salt Air, 1983 (award 1985), Objects of Affection, 1987; editor: Where We Stand, 1994. Poetry fellow Nat. Endowment for Arts, 1987, Tenn., 1992. Mem. Poetry Soc. Am., Associated Writing Programs, Acad. Am. Poets, Modern Lang. Assn. Home: 1254 W 1000 N Salt Lake City UT 84116 Office: Dartmouth Coll Dept English Hanover NH 03755

BRYANS, RICHARD W., lawyer; b. Denver, May 29, 1931; s. William A. and Ruth W. (Waldron) B.; m. Carol Jean, Feb. 17, 1955; children—Richard W., Bridget Ann. B.S., Denver U., 1954, J.D., 1955. Bar: Colo., U.S. Supreme Ct. 1971. Sole practice, Boulder, Colo., 1958-63; ptnr. Kelly, Stansfield & O'Donnell, Denver, 1963-92, Bryans & Bryans, Denver, 1993—. Served to lt. (j.g.) USNR, 1955-58. Mem. ABA, Colo. Bar Assn., Denver Bar Assn. Office: 1700 Broadway Ste 414 Denver CO 80290-0401

BRYANT, CAROL LEE, public health educator, psychotherapist, consultant; b. L.A., Aug. 17, 1946; d. John Thomas and Janice Hathaway (Haislip) B.; m. Norman Alexander, June 4, 1966 (div. 1975); children: Ian Alexander, Colin Alexander; m. Reinhard Alexander Fritsch, June 14, 1983. AA, Diablo Valley Jr. Coll., Pleasant Hill, Calif., 1975; BA, San Francisco State U., 1978; MA in Transpersonal Counseling, John F. Kennedy U., Orinda, Calif., 1982, MA in Clin. Psychology, 1982; PhD in Clin. Psychology, Sierra U., 1986. Lic. marriage, family, and child counselor, Calif. Instr., tchr. Community Recreation YWCA, Walnut Creek, Calif., 1970-80, John F. Kennedy U., Orinda, Calif., 1980-81; adminstrv. dir. Touchstone Counseling Svc., Walnut Creek, 1981-83; tchr. Diablo Valley Jr. Coll., 1984; exec. dir. Battered Women's Alternatives, Concord, Calif., 1984-85, Child Abuse Prevention Coun., Walnut Creek, 1985-90; psychotherapist InVision Assocs., Lafayette, Calif., 1984—; pub. health educator Mariposa (Calif.) Health Dept., 1990—; cons. Computer Using Educators, Menlo Park, Calif., 1988-90; lectr. in field; mem., chairperson Mariposa Mental Health Adv. Bd.; vice chairperson Mariposa Drug and Alcohol Adv. Bd., maternal child health adv. bd. John C. Fremont Hosp. Found. Contbr. articles to profl. jours. and books. Chmn. No. Calif. Legis. Children and Family Coalition, Berkeley, 1987-90; adv. bd., chmn. Women's Recovery Ctr., Bass Lake, Calif., 1990-92; coord./mem. No. Calif. Child Death Review Coalition, San Francisco, 1988-90, Children and Family Trust Fund Com., Concord, 1989-90. Mem. Assn. Marriage Family Therapists. Home: 4821 Crystalaire Dr Mariposa CA 95338-9663 Office: Mariposa Pub Health Dept PO Box 5 Mariposa CA 95338-0005

BRYANT, DON ESTES, economist, scientist; b. Truman, Ark., May 18, 1917; s. James Monroe and Olivia (Mayfield) B.; m. Jess Ann Chailer, Jan. 27, 1956; children: Stephen Williamson (dec.), Patrice Ann. Student, Cass Tech. Trade Coll., 1938-41. Pres., founder Consol. Aircraft Products, El Segundo, Calif., 1949-57, Trilan Corp., El Segundo, 1957-62, The Am. Inventor, Palos Verdes Estates, Calif., 1962-68; chmn., founder Message Control Crop., Palos Verdes Estates, 1968-70; scientist Econ. Rsch., Palos Verdes Estates and Lake Arrowhead, Calif., 1970—; cons. Svc. Corps. Ret. Execs. Assn.-SBA, L.A., 1965-67; founder Bryant Inst. and Club U.S.A. (United to Save Am.), 1991, J. Ayn Bryant and Assocs., 1991. Inventor missle and satellite count-down systems for USAF, 1958; formulator sci. of human econs.; host TV talk show World Peace Through Free Enterprise, 1985; author: 10-book children's series The 1, 2, 3's of Freedom and Economics, 1988. Served with USN, 1935-37. Republican. Roman Catholic. Home: 282 S Sunset Lake Arrowhead CA 92352 Office: Econ Rsch PO Box 1023 Lake Arrowhead CA 92352-1023

BRYANT, JANET HOUGH, actress, voice teacher, performing artist; b. Rockford, Ill.; d. Roy Arthur and Ida Elissa Bertha (Bergman) Hough; m. Charles Herbert Bryant Jr., Dec. 28, 1938 (dec. 1942); 1 child, Janna Lee Wright. Student, U. Iowa, 1931; AM, Stephens Coll., 1934; BE, Drake U., 1937; student, Vassar Experimental Theatre, 1935, Am. Conservatory Music, Chgo., 1942; MS in Music Edn., U. So. Calif., 1961; cert., Ecole d'Art Am., Fontainebleau, France, 1965; student, Am. Inst. Musical Studies, Graz, Austria, 1979. Tchr. music Los Angeles Schs., 1955-76; pvt. voice tchr. Newport Beach, Calif., 1955—. Appeared in plays Born Yesterday, Rumpelstiltskin, Stage Door, The Heiress, Darling Delinquent, You Can't Take It With You, So You Want To Be A Mother; appeared in operas Dance of Death, La Boheme, Faust, Rape of Lucretia, La Traviata, Stabat Mater; performed as guest artist throughout Orange County, Calif.; exhibited in art shows at Lido Village, Bullock's Dept. Store, Jewel Court, City Hall of Newport, Orange County, Calif., Orange Coast Plaza; appeared in movies Sister Act II, Kangaroo Man, Strange Days; performer Hats, Hats, Hats, 1993-94. Pres. Musical Arts Orange County, 1980-82, chmn. program, 1978-80, rec. sec., 1977-78; chmn. program Orange County Philharm. Soc., 1984-86, 88-89, chmn. ways means, 1986-88, chmn. publicity, 1980-82; chmn. program Musical Theatre Guild Orange County, 1978-80; founder Opera Pacific; charter mem. Rep. Nat. Task Force, Nat. Mus. of Women in Arts, 1988—. Mem. Nat. Assn. Tchrs. Singing (exec. bd. dirs. 1984-89), Music Tchrs. Assn., Music Tchrs. Assn. Calif., Costa Mesa Art league, South Coast Repertory Theatre Guild, Internat. Congress Voice Tchrs., Camelot Chpt. Performing Arts Ctr., Soc. Mil. Widows of Orange County (pres. 1993-95, fundraiser), Delta Gamma. Home and Studio: 2022 Barranca Newport Beach CA 92660-4528

BRYANT, NANCY DRU, physician; b. Roswell, N.Mex., May 4, 1952; d. Abner Hill and Natalie (Williams) B.; m. Ronny Michael Simmons, Nov. 29, 1986. BA, Trinity U., 1973; MD, U. Tex., Galveston, 1977. Diplomate Am. Bd. Ob.-Gyn. Intern, resident Geisinger Med. Ctr., Danville, Pa., 1977-81; pvt. practice, 1988-94, Clovis, N.Mex., 1994—. Maj. USAF, 1981-87. Mem. AMA, ACOG, Am. Med. Women's Assn., Assn. Women Surgeons. Lutheran.

BRYANT, RICHARD LEWIS, historic preservation specialist, archaeologist; b. Buffalo, Feb. 21, 1943; s. Gordon Rex and Elizabeth Jane (Masters) B. BA in Anthropology, Wash. State U., 1973. Cultural resource program mgr. Pro-Lysts Inc., Eugene, Oreg., 1978-80; mgr. rev. and compliance program Wyo. State Hist. Preservation Office, 1981-92; hist. preservation officer F.E. Warren AFB, Cheyenne, Wyo., 1992—; mem. Wyo. State Cultural Resource task force, 1992-94. Vol. Spl. Olympics, Cheyenne, 1982; County Search and Rescue Team, Whitman County, Wash., 1978-79; leader cub scout den Boy Scouts Am., Cheyenne, 1993—; mem. Mayor's MX Missile Impact Planning Com., Cheyenne, 1983-85. With USMC, 1962-68. Mem. Soc. Profl. Archaeologists (cert.), Wyo. Assn. Profl. Archaeology, Soc. Am. Mil. Engrs., Warren Mil. Hist. Assn. (pres. 1993—), USMC Hist. Found. Office: FE Warren AFB Office of Hist Preservation Cheyenne WY 82005

BRYANT, STEVEN BRADLEY, management consultant; b. Oceanside, Calif., July 9, 1963; s. Cottery Lee and Rose Jeannen (Sumner) B. BS in Computer Sci., San Diego State U., 1986; MBA in Internat. Bus., U. San Diego, 1990. Sr. software engr. Sci. Applications Internat., San Diego, 1984-90; pres. Insight Resources, San Diego, 1987-88; sr. cons. Andersen Cons., San Francisco, 1990-94; pres. Avitel Cons., Inc., San Francisco, 1994—. Mem. Assn. Computing Machinery, IEEE. Home: 2410 Montcliff Rd San Diego CA 92139-3904

BRYANT, THOS LEE, magazine editor; b. Daytona Beach, Fla., June 15, 1943; s. Stanley Elson and G. Bernice (Burgess) B.; m. Patricia Jean Bryant, June 30, 1979. BA in Polit. Sci., U. Calif., Santa Barbara, 1965, MA in Polit. Sci., 1966. Fgn. svc. officer U.S. Dept. State, Washington, Buenos Aires, 1967-69; radio broadcaster KDB Sta., Santa Barbara, Calif., 1969-72; magazine editor Road & Track, Newport Beach, Calif., 1972—. Mem. Internat. Motor Press Assn., Motor Press Guild, Sports Car Club of Am. Office: Road & Track 1499 Monrovia Ave Newport Beach CA 92663-2752

BRYANT, WOODROW WESLEY, architect; b. San Jose, Calif., June 5, 1949; s. Foy Eldean and Loraine (McKee) B.; m. Becky Ann Hoffmaster, June 27, 1981; 1 stepson: Jeremy Saul Martin. Student, Am. River Coll., Sacramento, Calif., 1968; BArch, Calif. State Polytechnic U., 1973. Registered architect, Calif., Nev., Utah, Idaho, Ariz. Designer, project mgr. Angello & Vitiello Assoc., Sacramento, 1971-75; draftsman Caywood, Nopp & Ward, Sacramento, 1975; architect W. Bryant Enterprises, Sacramento, 1975-76, Wright, Bryant & Johnson, Ketchum, Idaho, 1976—; bd. dirs. Elkhorn Archtl. Design Commn., Uniform Bldg. Code Bd. Appeals, Ketchum, Uniform Fire Code Bd. Appeals, Ketchum, Blaine County, Idaho. Recipient Best Archtl. Interior Detailing award, Custom Builder mag., 1993. Mem. AIA. Office: Wright Bryant & Johnson PO Box 21 Sun Valley ID 83353-0021

BRYCHEL, RUDOLPH MYRON, engineer; b. Milw., Dec. 4, 1934; s. Stanley Charles and Jean Ann (Weiland) B.; m. Rose Mary Simmons, Sept. 3, 1955; children: Denise, Rita, Rudolph Myron Jr., Patrick, Bradford, Matthew. Student, U. Wis., Stevens Point, 1953, U.S. Naval Acad., 1954-55, U. Del., 1957, Colo. State U., 1969, North Park Coll., Chgo., 1973, Regis U., Denver, 1990-91. Lab. and quality tech. Thiokol Chem. Co., Elkton, Md., 1956; final test insp. Martin Aircraft Co., Middle River, Md., 1956-57; system final insp. Delco Electronics Co., Oak Creek, Wis., 1957-58; test equipment design engr. Martin Marietta Co., Littleton, Colo., 1958-64; prodn. supr. Gates Rubber Co., Denver, Colo., 1964-65; freelance mfr., quality and project engr. Denver and Boulder, Colo., Raton, N.Mex., 1965-67; quality engr. IBM, Gaithersburg (Md.), Boulder (Colo.), 1967-73; sr. quality engr. Abbott Labs., North Chicago, Ill., 1973-74; instrumentation and control engr. Stearns Roger Co., Glendale, Colo., 1974-81; staff quality engr. Storage Tech., Louisville, Colo., 1981-83; sr. quality engr. Johnson & Johnson Co., Englewood, Colo., 1983-84; quality engr., cons. Staodynamics Co., Longmont, Colo., 1984-85; sr. engr. for configuration and data mgmt. Martin Marietta Astronautics Group, Denver, 1985-91; freelance cons. Littleton, Colo., 1991—. With USN, 1953-56. Mem. Am. Soc. Quality Control (cert. quality engr.), Regulatory Affairs Profl. Soc., Soc. for Tech. Communications (regional chpt. chmn. 1970), KC. Democrat. Roman Catholic. Home and Office: 203 W Rafferty Gardens Ave Littleton CO 80120-1710

BRYDON, HAROLD WESLEY, entomologist, writer; b. Hayward, Calif., Dec. 6, 1923; s. Thomas Wesley and Hermione (McHenry) B.; m. Ruth Bacon Vickery, Mar. 28, 1951 (div.); children: Carol Ruth, Marilyn Jeanette, Kenneth Wesley. AB, San Jose State Coll., 1948; MA, Stanford U., 1950. Insecticide sales Calif. Spray Chem. Corp., San Jose, 1951-52; entomologist, fieldman, buyer Beech-Nut Packing Co., 1952-53; mgr., entomologist Lake County Mosquito Abatement Dist., Lakeport, Calif., 1954-58; entomologist, adviser Malaria Eradication Programs AID, Kathmandu, Nepal, 1958-61, Washington, 1961-62, Port-au-Prince, Haiti, 1962-63; dir. fly control research Orange County Health Dept. Santa Ana, Calif., 1963-66; free-lance writer in field, 1966—; research entomologist U. N.D. Sch. Medicine, 1968; developer, owner Casierra Resort, Lake Almanor, Calif., 1975-79; owner Westwood (Calif.) Sport Shop, 1979-84; instr. Lassen Community Coll., Susanville, Calif., 1975—; bio control cons., 1980—. Mem. entomology and plant pathology del. People to People Citizen Ambassador Program, China, 1986; citizen ambassador 30th Anniversary Caravan to Soviet Union, 1991, Vietnam Initiative Del., 1992. Contbr. profl. jours. and conducted research in field. Served with USNR, 1943-46. Recipient Meritorious Honor award for work in Nepal, AID, U.S. Dept. State, 1972. Mem. Entomol. Soc. Am., Am. Mosquito Control Assn., Pacific Coast Entomol. Soc., Am. Legion. Republican. Methodist. Club: Commonwealth of California. Lodges: Masons, Rotary. Home: PO Box 312 Westwood CA 96137-0312

BRYDON, RUTH VICKERY, history educator; b. San Jose, Calif., June 2, 1930; d. Robert Kingston and Ruth (Bacon) Vickery; m. Harold Wesley Brydon, Mar. 28, 1951 (div.); children: Carol Ruth Brydon Koford, Marilyn Jeanette, Kenneth Wesley. BA, Stanford U., 1952; student San Jose State Coll., 1964-65, MA, Calif. State Coll., Chico, 1987. Cert. tchr., Calif., cert. sch. adminstr. Tchr., Lincoln Sch., Kathmandu, Nepal, 1959-60; tchr. Am. Sch., Port-au-Prince, Haiti, 1962-63; tchr. social studies Norte Vista High Sch., Riverside, Calif., 1965-67, chmn. social studies dept., 1966-67; tchr. home econs., social studies Westwood (Calif.) H.S., 1967-90, mentor tchr., 1984-85; media specialist Lake Havasu H.S., 1990-91; history instr. Mohave C.C., Lake Havasu Campus, 1990—; instr. Elderhostel, 1992—; coord. extended day classes Lassen Coll., 1977-84. Author: Westwood, California: A Company Town in Comparative Perspective, 1900-1930. Co-chairperson Almanor Art Show, 1980-84. NDEA grantee, 1967. Mem. Internat. Platform Assn. Episcopalian. Home: 2681 N Cisco Dr Lake Havasu City AZ 86403-5020

BRYNES, RUSSELL KERMIT, pathologist, educator; b. N.Y.C., May 7, 1945; s. Kermit and Lore (Brunn) B.; m. Angelita Sales Cordero, May 31, 1970; children: Barbara, Erica. BA, U. Mass., 1967; MD, Tufts U., 1971. Diplomate Am. Bd. Pathology, Nat. Bd. Med. Examiners; lic. physician, Calif. Intern then resident U. Chgo. Hosps. and Clinics, 1971-73, USPHS fellow, 1973-75; resident U. Minn. Hosps., 1975-77; dir. clin. hematology lab. Emory U. Hosp., Atlanta, 1979-86; from asst. to assoc. prof. pathology Emory U., Atlanta, 1979-86; dir. clin. hematology U. So. Calif. Med. Ctr., L.A., 1986-91; assoc. prof. pathology U. So. Calif., L.A., 1986-91, clin. prof. pathology, 1993—; dir. dept. clin. pathology City of Hope Nat. Med. Ctr., Duarte, Calif., 1991—. Editor, assoc.: Hematology: Clinical and Laboratory Practice, 1993; contbr. over 60 articles to profl. jours. Maj. U.S. Army Med. Corp, 1977-79. Fellow Coll. Am. Pathologists; mem. Am. Soc. Clin. Pathologists (dep. commr. 1991—), Am. Soc. Hematology, U.S. and Can. Acad. Pathology, L.A. Soc. Pathologists (v.p. 1994-95), Soc. Hematopathology. Office: City of Hope Dept Clin Pathology 1500 Duarte Rd Duarte CA 91010-3012

BRYNGELSON, JIM, educational administrator; b. Billings, Mont., Mar. 8, 1941; s. Ivan Carl and Clarie (Ellingwood) B.; m. Judy Bryngelson, June 29, 1969; children: Joy, Nick. BS, U. Mont., 1959; MS, Purdue U., 1967; EdS, U. No. Colo., 1974, EdD, 1976. Tchr. sci. Littleton Pub. Schs., Colo., 1964-66, sch. counselor, 1967-73, sch. psychologist, 1974-75; spl. edn. cons., Steamboat Springs, Colo., 1975-78; dir. edn. Yellowstone Edn. Ctr., Billings, Mont., 1978-90, supr. treatment team, 1990—; pres. Self Esteem Assocs., Billings, 1980—. Bd. dirs. Tumbleweed Foster Homes, Billings, 1980-84, Rocky Mountain Little League, Billings, 1982, Mental Health Assn., Billings, v.p., 1986-87, pres. 1987-88. Recipient Disting. Educator award Charles Kettering Found., 1983; named U.S. Cultural Exchange Delegate to Republic of China, 1986. Fellow Assn. Supervision and Curriculum Devel., Sch. Adminstrs. Mont., Council Exceptional Children, Council for Children with Behavior Disorders, Mont. Assn. Supervision and Curriculum Devel. (bd. dirs. 1987-89), Council for Adminstrs. Spl. Edn., Albert Schweitzer Soc., John Dewey Soc., Phi Delta Kappa (v.p. 1984-85, pres 1985-86); mem. Mont. Educators Emotionally Disturbed (charter). Democrat. Lutheran. Home: 1144 Henry Rd Billings MT 59102-0811 Office: Youth Dynamics 2601 Uir Ln Billings MT 59102

BRYSON, DOROTHY PRINTUP, retired educator; b. Britton, S.D., Dec. 2, 1894; d. David Lawrence and Marion Harland (Gamsby) Printup; m. Archer Butler Hulbert, June 16, 1923 (dec. Dec. 1933); children: Joanne Woodward, Nancy Printup; m. Franklin Fearing Wing, Oct. 15, 1938 (dec. Mar. 1942); m. Arthur Earl Bryson, Feb. 15, 1964 (dec. Apr. 1979). AB, Oberlin Coll., 1915; AM, Radcliffe Coll., 1916; LHD (hon.), Colo. Coll., 1989. Instr. Latin, Tenn. Coll., Murfreesboro, 1916-18; tchr. Latin, prin. high sch., Britton, 1918-20; instr. classics Colo. Coll., Colorado Springs, 1921-22, 23-25, sec., instr., head resident, 1951-60; tchr. latin San Luis Prep. Sch., Colorado Springs, 1934-36, 41-42, Sandia Sch., Albuquerque, 1937-39, Westlake Sch., L.A., 1946-49; exec. dir. YWCA, Colorado Springs, 1942-46, 49-51; editor western history Stewart Commn., Colorado Springs, 1934-41; ret., 1960. Editor: Overland to the Pacific, 5 vols., 1934-41. Bd. dirs. Day Nursery, Colorado Springs 1933-37. Fellow Aelioian Lit. Soc., 1920-21; scholar U. Chgo., 1920-21. Mem. LWV (v.p., bd. dirs. Colorado Springs 1943-45), Women's Edn. Soc. Colo. Coll. (pres., bd. dirs. 1955—), Reviewers Club, Tuesday Discussion Club, Pikes Peak Posse Westerners, Women's Literary Club, Phi Beta Kappa, Gamma Phi Beta. Republican. Episcopalian. Home: 107 W Cheyenne Rd Apt 610 Colorado Springs CO 80906-2509

BRYSON, GARY SPATH, cable television and telephone company executive; b. Longview, Wash., Nov. 8, 1943; s. Roy Griffin and Marguerite Elizabeth (Spath) B.; children: Kelly Suzanne, Lisa Christine. A.B., Dartmouth Coll., 1966; M.B.A., Tuck Sch., 1967. With Bell & Howell Co., Chgo., 1967-79; pres. consumer and audio-visual group Bell & Howell Co., 1977-79; chmn. bd., chief exec. officer Bell & Howell Mamiya Co., Chgo., 1979-81; exec. v.p. Am. TV & Communications Corp., subs. Time, Inc., Englewood, Colo., 1981-88; v.p. diversified group US West, Englewood, 1988-89, pres. cable communications div., 1989-92; pres., CEO TeleWest Internat., 1992-93; pres. SkyConnect, Boulder, 1994—. Mem. Phi Beta Kappa, Sigma Alpha Epsilon. Republican. Lutheran. Home: 2221 Carriage Hills Dr Boulder CO 80302-9476 Office: Sky Connect 6285 Lookout Rd Boulder CO 80301

BRYSON, JOHN E., utilities company executive; b. N.Y.C., July 24, 1943; m. Louise Henry. B.A. with great distinction, Stanford U., 1965; student, Freie U. Berlin, Federal Republic Germany, 1965-66; J.D., Yale U., 1969. Bar: Calif., Oreg., D.C. Asst. in instrn. Law Sch., Yale U., New Haven, Conn., 1968-69; law clk. U.S. Dist. Ct., San Francisco, 1969-70; co-founder, atty. Natural Resources Def. Council, 1970-74; vice chmn. Oreg. Energy Facility Siting Council, 1975-76; assoc. Davies, Biggs, Strayer, Stoel & Boley, Portland, Oreg., 1975-76; chmn. Calif. State Water Resources Control Bd., 1976-79; vis. faculty Stanford U. Law Sch., Calif., 1977-79; pres. Calif. Pub. Utilities Commn., 1979-82; ptnr. Morrison & Foerster, San Francisco, 1983-84; sr. v.p. law and fin. So. Calif. Edison Co., Rosemead, 1984; exec. v.p., chief fin. officer SCEcorp. and So. Calif. Edison Co., 1985-90; chmn. of bd., CEO SCE Corp. and So. Calif. Edison Co., Rosemead, 1990—; lectr. on pub. utility, energy, communications law.; former mem. exec. com. Nat. Assn. Regulatory Utility Commrs., Calif. Water Rights Law Rev. Commn., Calif. Pollution Control Financing Authority; former mem. adv. bd. Solar Energy Research Inst., Electric Power Research Inst., Stanford Law Sch.; bd. dirs. Pacific Am. Income Shares Inc. Mem. bd. editors, assoc. editor: Yale U. Law Jour. Bd. dirs. World Resources Inst., Washington, Calif. Environ. Trust, Claremont U. Ctr., Grad. Sch., Stanford U. Alumni Assn.; trustee Stanford U., 1991. Woodrow Wilson fellow. Mem. Calif. Bar Assn., Oreg. Bar Assn., D.C. Bar Assn., Nat. Assn. Regulatory Utility Commrs. (exec. com. 1980-82), Stanford U. Alumni Assn. (bd. dirs. 1983-86), Phi Beta Kappa. Office: SCE Corp 2244 Walnut Grove Ave Rosemead CA 91770-3714*

BRYSON, VERN ELRICK, nuclear engineer; b. Woodruff, Utah, May 28, 1920; s. David Hyrum and Luella May (Eastman) B.; m. Esther Sybil de St Jeor, Oct. 14, 1942; children: Britt William, Forrest Lee, Craig Lewis, Nadine, Elaine. Commd. 2d lt. USAAF, 1941; advanced through grades to lt. col. USAF, 1960, ret., 1961; pilot, safety engr., civil engr., electronic engr., nuclear engr., chief Aeronaut. Systems div., Aircraft Nuclear Propulsion Program, Wright-Patterson AFB, Ohio, 1960-61; chief Radiation Effects Lab., also chief Radiation Effects Group Boeing Airplane Co., Seattle, 1961-65; nuclear engr. Aerospace Corp., San Bernardino, Calif., 1965-68; service engr., also head instrumentation lab., Sacramento Air Logistic Ctr. USAF, McClellan AFB, Calif., 1968-77; owner, mgr. Sylvern Valley Ranch, Calif., 1977—; Mem. panel Transient Radiation Effects on Electronics, Weapon Effects Bd., 1959-61. Contbr. research articles on radiation problems to profl. pubs. Decorated D.F.C. with oak leaf cluster, Air medal with 12 oak leaf clusters. Mem. IEEE. Mem. Ch. Jesus Christ of Latter-day Saints. Home: 1426 Caperton Ct Penryn CA 95663-9515

BRYSON, YVONNE J., pediatrician, virologist; b. Dublin, Ireland; came to U.S., 1960; d. Charles Joseph and Gladys (Clarke) Bryson; m. Michael Lovett, Mar. 28, 1981; children: Bryson Lovett, Ryan Lovett. BS, U. Tex., 1966; MD, U. Tex., Dallas, 1970. Diplomate Am. Bd. Pediatrics. Postdoctoral fellow in infectious disease U. Calif., San Diego, 1971-73, resident and chief resident in pediatrics, 1974-76; asst. prof. pediatrics UCLA Sch. Medicine, 1976-82, assoc. prof., 1982-88, prof., 1988—; bd. dirs Nat. Found. for Infectious Diseases, L.A., 1984-89; mem. health adv. bd. Pediatric AIDS Found., Santa Monica, Calif., 1989—; bd. dirs. L.A. Pediatric AIDS Consortium, 1988—; bd. dirs. L.A. Venereal Disease Coun.; cons. Herpes Rsch. Ctr., 1980—; co-dir. Maternal Child Immunology Clinic, UCLA, 1988—; mem. exec. bd. Ariel Project; speaker in field. Contbr. numerous articles to profl. jours. Recipient grants in field. Mem. AMA, Am. Soc. for Microbiology, We. Soc. for Pediatric Rsch., Am. Fedn. for Clin. Rsch., Soc. for Pediatric Rsch., Infectious Diseases Soc., Am. Soc. for Virology, Soc. for Exptl. Biology and Medicine, Am. Pediatric Soc. Office: UCLA Sch Medicine Pediatrics Rm 22-442 10833 Le Conte Ave Los Angeles CA 90095

BUCCIGROSSI, DAVID ERIC, internist; b. Riverside, Calif., Sept. 12, 1956; s. Sam Anthony and Geraldine (Ligman) B.; m. Debbie Lee Winkelbauer, Sept. 7, 1985. BA, U. Calif., San Diego, 1979, MD, 1984. Diplomate Am. Bd. Internal Medicine with added qualifications in geriatric medicine. Guitar instr. San Diego, 1973-78; chemistry instr. U. Calif., San Diego, 1978-81; chemistry reasearcher Scripps Inst. Oceanography U. Calif., 1978-80; intern, then resident U. Wash., Seattle, 1984-87; ptnr. specializing in internal medicine So. Calif. Permanente Med. Group, San Diego, 1990—. Family practice preceptorship grantee U. Calif., 1981. Mem. Am. Coll. Physicians, A. Baird Hasting Soc. Democrat. Roman Catholic. Office: So Calif Permanente Med Group 6860 Avenida Encinas Carlsbad CA 92009-3201

BUCCOLA, VICTOR ALLAN, physical education educator, sports association executive; b. L.A., June 20, 1933; s. Carl and Josephine (Canzoneri) B.; m. Sally Louise Ward, Jan. 17, 1959; children: David, Anna, Victoria. BS in Phys. Edn., Calif. Polytechnic State U., 1956, MS in Edn., Phys. Edn., 1957; EdD, Ariz. State U., 1972. Phys. edn. instr., football, boxing and track coach Coll. Idaho, Caldwell, 1958-61; health and sci. instr., asst. football and track coach Mark Keppel High Sch., Alhambra, Calif., 1961-62; phys. edn. instr., asst. football coach Calif. Polytechnic State U., San Luis Obispo, 1962—, prof. phys. edn., 1981—; commr. Western Football Conf., San Luis Obispo, 1982-93, Am. W. Conf., 1993—; chair divsn. II Football Com. NCAA, 1980-83, mem. championship com. divsn. II, 1986-92. Contbr. articles to jours. in field. Mem. bd. dirs. SESLOC Fed. Credit Union, San Luis Obispo, 1980-90, v.p. 1984-90; mem. Youth Football Bd., San Luis Obispo, 1972; asst. coach Little League Baseball Team, San Luis Obispo, 1971-73. Capt. Artillary, 1957. Mem. AAHPERD, Calif. Assn. Health, Phys. Edn., Recreation and Dance. Office: Cal Poly San Luis Obispo CA 93407

BUCHANAN, LEE ANN, public relations executive; b. Albuquerque, July 6, 1955; d. William Henry Buchanan and Juanita Irene (Pilgrim) Wood; m. Charles Stanton Wood, Jan. 17, 1987. BA, U. Calif., Irvine, 1977. Exec. asst. to Congressman William Thomas, U.S. Ho. of Reps., Washington, 1979-83; dep. chief staff Gov. George Deukmejian, Sacramento, 1983-84; sr. v.p., ptnr. Nelson Comm., Costa Mesa, Calif., 1985-95. Bd. govs. Rep. Assocs. of Orange County, 1985—; founding sec. Orange County Young Reps., 1985. Mem. Internat. Assn. Bus. Communicators, Am. Assn. Polit. Cons., Pub. Relations Soc. Am., U. Calif.-Irvine Alumni Assn. Address: PO Box 1741 Mammoth Lakes CA 93546-1741

BUCHANAN, PAUL WILLIAM, English language educator; b. Belfast, Ireland, Oct. 4, 1959; s. William and Ruth (Lowry) B.; m. Revelation Versoza, Aug. 15, 1981; children: Ryan, Heather, Dylan. BA, Biola U., 1981; MA, U. Calif., Riverside, 1985. Lectr. in English Biola U., La Mirada, Calif., 1989—; chief editor Biola U., 1991—; prin. Petersen & Buchanan Graphic Design, Whittier, Calif., 1993—. Author: Return of the Eagle, 1992; editor Connections Magazine, La Mirada, 1991—; assoc. editor South Coast Poetry Jour., Fullerton, Calif., 1993—; fiction and poetry editor Ratio: Essays in Christian Thought, Fullerton, 1994—. Dir. campus chpt. Habitat for Humanity, Whittier, 1993—. Recipient awards for distinction and excellence Coun. for Advancement and Support of Edn., 1993. Mem. PEN. Democrat. Office: Biola U 13800 Biola Ave La Mirada CA 90639-0002

BUCHANAN, TERI BAILEY, communications executive; b. Long Beach, Calif., Feb. 24, 1946; d. Alton Hervey and Ruth Estelle (Thompson) Bailey; m. Robert Wayne Buchanan, Aug. 14, 1964 (div. May 1979). BA in English with highest honors, Ark. Poly. Coll., 1968. With employee communications AT&T, Kansas City, Mo., 1968-71; freelance writer Ottawa, Kans., 1971-73; publs. dir. Ottawa U., 1973-74; regional info. officer U.S. Dept. Labor, Kansas City, 1974; owner, operator PBT Communications, Kansas City, 1975-79; sr. pub. affairs rep., sr. editor, exhibit supr., communications specialist Standard Oil/Chevron, San Francisco, 1979-84; owner The Resource Group/Mktg. Comm., Yountville, Calif., 1984—; mem. faculty pub. rels. master's program Golden Gate U., San Francisco, 1987. Pub. rels. trainer Bus. Vols. for Arts, San Francisco, 1985-93; mem. Napa Conf. and Visitors Bur. Recipient Internat. Assn. Bus. Communicators Bay Area Gold and Silver awards, 1984. Mem. Napa C. of C., Yountville C. of C. (mktg.

com.). Democrat. Episcopalian. Office: The Resource Group 6516 Yount St Yountville CA 94599-1269

BUCHER, ANITA MARIE, investigations specialist; b. Fairfield, Calif., Dec. 21, 1952; d. Donald Glen and Loretta Mae (Muller) B. BS in Bus. Adminstrn., U. No. Colo., Greeley, 1975. Collateral audit clk. United Bank of Denver, N.A., 1975-78; loan review analyst, audit and compliance coord. United Bank of Skyline, N.A., Denver, 1978-83; loan review mgr. Guaranty Bank & Trust, Denver, 1983-85; investigations specialist Fed. Deposit Ins. Corp., Denver, 1985-94. Recipient FDIC Spl. Group Svc. award Denver, 1987, Letter of Commendation Mike Carey Asst. U.S. Atty., denver, 1988, FDIC Spl. Commendation Denver, 1989.

BUCHER, GLENN RICHARD, academic administrator; b. Mechanicsburg, Pa., May 20, 1940; s. K. Ezra and Esther (Markley) B.; m. Mary K. Gladfelter, June 12, 1963; children—Christina Hope, Timothy Jon. A.B., Elizabethtown (Pa.) Coll., 1962; M.Div., Union Sem., N.Y.C., 1965; Ph.D., Boston U., 1968. Vis. instr. Emerson Coll., Boston, 1967-68; asst. prof. Howard U., 1968-70; vis. scholar Union Sem., N.Y.C., 1975-76; acting dir. Austin Coll. Ctr. for Program and Instl. Renewal, Sherman, Tex., 1980-82; Lincoln prof. religion Coll. of Wooster, 1970-85, dean of faculty, 1985-89; v.p. acad. affairs, dean faculty Columbia Theol. Sem., 1989-92; pres., prof. religion and soc. Grad. Theol. Union, 1992—; higher edn. cons. Assn. Am. Colls., 1980-92, Assn. Theol. Schs., 1992-93. Author, editor: Straight/White/Male, 1976, Confusion and Hope, 1974; contbr. articles to profl. jours. Mem. UN 50th Anniversary Com.; trustee acad. affairs com. Elizabethtown Coll., 1968—. Fellow Soc. Values in Higher Edn., Am. Acad. Religion; mem. Calif. Bus.-Higher Edn. Forum, Univ. Club San Francisco. Home: 1344 Rifle Range Rd El Cerrito CA 94530-2505 Office: Grad Theol Union 2400 Ridge Rd Berkeley CA 94709-1212

BUCHI, KENNETH NORMAN, medical director, educator; b. Salt Lake City, July 28, 1951. BS in Psychology, U. Utah, 1973, MD, 1978. Diplomate Am. Bd. Internal Medicine. Intern then resident U. Utah, Salt Lake City, 1978-81, fellow, 1981-83, instr. internal medicine, 1984, asst. prof. medicine, 1984-90, assoc. prof. medicine, 1990-92, adj. asst. prof. foods and nutrition, 1987—, adj. assoc. prof. medicine, 1992—; cheif resident in internal medicine Salt Lake Vet.'s Adminstrn. Med. Ctr., 1983; med. dir. Holy Cross Hosp., Salt Lake City, 1992-94; assoc. chief staff ambulatory care Salt Lake VA Med. Ctr., Salt Lake City, 1994—; staff physician VA Med. Ctr., Salt Lake City, 1984-86, Pioneer Valley Hosp., Salt Lake City, 1988—, Holy Cross Jordan Valley Hosp., Salt Lake City, 1993—; cons. in field. Contbr. articles to profl. jours. Founding trustee Salt Lake County Clean Air Coalition, 1990—, chair, 1991—; mem. Salt Lake County Environ. Quality Adv. Commn., 1991—, Salt Lake Cmty. Health Agenda Com., 1992-94; mem. quality mgmt. com. Blue Cross/Blue Shield Utah, 1993—; mem. quality com. Utah Health Cost Mgmt. Found., 1993—; mem. clean air task force Utah 2d Congrl. Dist., 1990-92; mem. interim health com. Office Legis. Rsch. and Gen. Counsel, 1991—; mem. emergency dept. task force Utah Dept. Health, 1992-93, others. Grantee NIH, 1982-88, VA RAG, 1984-86, Serono Labs., 1986-87, Smith, Kline and French Labs., 1986-87, Glaxco, Inc., 1987-88, Merck, Sharp and Dohme Rsch. Labs., 1987-88, Richard Wolf Med. Instruments Corp., 1988-90, Am. Cyanamid Co., 1988-90, U.S. Dept. of Def., 1990-93. Fellow ACP, Am. Coll. Gastroenterology; mem. AMA, Am. Gastroenterology Assn., Am. Soc. Laser Medicien and Surger, Am. Coll. Physician Execs., Am. Hosp. Assn. (del. 1993—), Utah Acad. Preventative Medicine, Utah Soc. Internal Medicine, Utah Med. Assn. (trustee 1986—, del. 1987-93), Internat. Soc. Chronobiology, Intermountain Gut Club (charter). Home: 2944 Saint Marys Way Salt Lake City UT 84108-2044

BUCHSER, JOHN ROBERT, computer scientist; b. Fairbanks, Alaska, Feb. 25, 1954; s. Robert D. Buchser and Alberta (Rumpp) Allesandro; m. Linda W. Dutcher, July 4, 1985. BS in Basic Scis., N.Mex. Inst. Mining and Tech., 1982. Software engr. Los Alamos (N.Mex.) Nat. Lab., 1977-87, Sandia Nat. Lab., Albuquerque, 1988-92; systems analyst Lincoln Lab. MIT, Socorro, N.Mex., 1993-94; mgmt. analyst State of N.Mex. Dept. of Health, Santa Fe, 1994—; v.p. engring. Mentron, Santa Fe, 1992—; mem. summer sci. tng. program Fla. State U., Tallahassee, 1971. Mem. IEEE, AAAS, Assn. for Computing Machinery (v.p. 1985-87, 93, pres. 1990-91), Sierra Club. Home: 1225 Vitalia St Santa Fe NM 87505-3278 Office: Pub Health Office 605 Letrado St Santa Fe NM 87505-4162

BUCHTA, EDMUND, engineering executive; b. Wostitz, Nikolsburg, Czechoslovakia, May 11, 1928; came to U.S., 1979; Kaufmann, Deutsche Wirtschaftoberschule, Bruenn, Czechoslovakia, 1942-45. Shop foreman Messerklinger, Ernsting, Austria, 1949-51; constrn. foreman Hinteregger, U.S. Mil. Project, Salzburg, Siezenheim, Austria, 1951-52, Auserehl Constrn. Corp., N.Y.C., 1963; pres. Grout Concrete Constrn. Ltd., Edmonton, Alta., Can., 1966-73; pioneer & explorer Canol Project Parcel B and Land Ownership N.W. Can., 1968—; pres. Barbarosa Enterprises Ltd., Yellowknife, Can., 1971—; owner (with Barbarosa Enterprises Ltd.) Canol Project Parcel B, 1968—. Mem. Dem. Senatorial Campaign Com. With German Mil., 1943-45. Named Emperor of the North, McLean Mag., Can., 1976. Mem. Internat. Platform Assn., Dem. Senatorial Campaign Com. Home: PO Box 7000-713 Redondo Beach CA 90277

BUCHTEL, MICHAEL EUGENE, optical mechanical engineer; b. Denver, Jan. 29, 1939; s. William Paxton and Lorraine Edith (Hammond) B.; m. Gloria Jean Guerrero, Sept. 29, 1967. BS, West Coast U., Compton, Calif., 1972. Sr. engr. Ford Aerospace Corp., Newport Beach, Calif., 1972-92; pres. The Techtel Co., Costa Mesa, Calif., 1992—; cons. Internat. Orgn. for Standards, Pforzheim, Switzerland, 1993—. Patentee for optical scanner in U.S. and Japan. With U.S. Army, 1962-64. Mem. Internat. Soc. for Optical Engrs., Am. Soc. Design Engrs. Republican. Roman Catholic. Office: The Techtel Co 1666 Newport Blvd Costa Mesa CA 92627-3776

BUCK, ALAN CHARLES, forensic investigator; b. Chgo., Oct. 26, 1931; s. Axel Harris and Mabel Anna (Kleutgen) B.; m. Kay Collins, Mar. 27, 1992. BS, U. Ill., 1954, MS, 1959; PhD, U. Hawaii, 1967; postgrad., Stanford U., 1961-63. Sr. lectr. Kampala (Uganda), Makerere U., 1967-69; sr,. researcher NASA, Houston, 1969-75; mgr. environ. affairs Gulf Interstate Eng. Co., Houston, 1975-78; pres. Practical Scis., Inc., Cypress, Calif., 1978-87, Chem. Applications Techs., Cypress, Calif., 1987—; sr. scientist Environ. Forensics, Cypress, Calif., 1990—; pres. Detroit Testing Labs., 1980-81; sr. scientist Am. Stas. Testing Bur., N.Y.C., 1984-86; sr. cons. Ecoserve, Pitts., 1990-91; spl. cons. Nat. Tech. Svcs., Fullerton, Calif., 1992—. Patentee in field. With U.S. Army, 1950-52. USPH PhD Tng. grantee, 1961-63; U. Ill. Alumni scholar, 1950-52. Mem. Am. Chem. Soc. (pub. rels. com. dir. 1987), Aerospace Medicine (edit. review 1970-74), Undersea Med. Soc. (Edit. review 1971-75). Home: 6073 Nauru St Cypress CA 90630-5644

BUCK, ANNE MARIE, library director, consultant; b. Birmingham, Ala., Apr. 12, 1939; d. Blaine Alexander and Marie Reynolds (McGeorge) Davis; m. Evan Buck, June 17, 1961 (div. Apr. 1977); children: Susan Elizabeth Buck Rentko, Stephen Edward. BA, Wellesley (Mass.) Coll., 1961; MLS, U. Ky., 1977. Bus. mgr. Charleston (W.Va.) Chamber Music Soc., 1972-74; dir. Dunbar (W.Va.) Pub. Libr., 1974-76; tech. reference libr. AT&T Bell Labs., Naperville, Ill., 1977-79; group supr. libr. AT&T Bell Labs., Reading, Pa., 1979-83; group supr. support svcs. AT&T Bell Labs., North Andover, Mass., 1983; dir. libr. network Bell Communications Rsch. (Bellcore), Morristown, N.J., 1983-89; dir. human resources planning Bell Communications Rsch. (Bellcore), Livingston, N.J., 1989-91; univ. libr. N.J. Inst. Tech., Newark, 1991-95, Calif. Inst. of Tech., Pasadena, 1995—; adj. prof. Rutgers U., New Brunswick, N.J., 1989—; instr. U. Wis., Madison, 1988—; v.p. Engring. Info. Found., N.Y.C., 1994; mem. Engring. Info. Inc. (bd. dirs.), Castle-Point-on-the-Hudson, Hoboken, N.J., 1988—; speaker profl. assn. confs., 1982—; libr. cons. North Port (Fla.) Area Libr., 1990-91. Mem. editorial adv. bd. Highsmith Press, 1991—; contbr. articles to profl. jours. Sect. mgr. United Way of Morris County, Cedar Knolls, N.J., 1984-95; advisor Family Svc. Transitions Coun., Morristown, 1987-90; libr. trustee Lisle (Ill.) Pub. Libr. Dist., 1978-80; bd. dirs. Kanawha County Bicentennial Commn., Charleston, W.Va., 1974-76. Recipient Vol.'s Gold award United Way, 1991. Mem. ALA (Grolier Nat. Libr. Week grantee 1975), Am. Soc. Info. Sci. (chpt. chmn. 1987-89, Chpt. of Yr. award 1988, treas. 1992—), Conf. Bd. Inc. (chmn. info. svcs. adv. coun. 1987-89), Spl. Libr. Assn., Am. Soc. Engring. Edn., Calif. Libr. Assn., Archons of Colophon, Indsl. Tech. Info. Mgrs. Group, Wellesley Coll. Alumni Assn. (class rep. 1986-91), N.J. Wellesley Club (regional chmn. 1986-89, corr. sec. 1994-95), Beta Phi Mu. Unitarian. Home: 2254 Loma Vista Pasadena CA 91104 Office: Calif Inst of Tech Mail Stop 1-32 Pasadena CA 91125

BUCK, CHRISTIAN BREVOORT ZABRISKIE, independent oil operator; b. San Francisco, Oct. 18, 1914; s. Frank Henry and Zayda Justine (Zabriskie) B.; student U. Calif., Berkeley, 1931-33; m. Natalie Leontine Smith, Sept. 12, 1948; children—Warren Zabriskie, Barbara Anne. Mem. engring. dept. U.S. Potash Co., Carlsbad, N.Mex., 1933-39; ind. oil operator, producer, Calif., 1939-79, N.Mex., 1939—; owner, operator farm, ranch, Eddy County, N.Mex., 1951-79; dir. Belridge Oil Co. until 1979; dir. Buck Ranch Co. (Calif.). Served with RAF, 1942-45. Democrat. Episcopalian. Club: Riverside Country (Carlsbad). Home: PO Box 5368 599 Lariat Cir # 2 Incline Village NV 89450 Office: PO Box 2183 Santa Fe NM 87504-2183

BUCK, G. WENDELL, library director; b. Medford, Oreg., Jan. 7, 1950; s. Gilbert Wallace and Mildred Fern (Miracle) B.; m. Judy Ann Syphers, Aug. 17, 1975; children: Emily Rose, Geoffrey Wycliffe. BA, Walla Walla Coll., 1973; M Libr. Info. Scis., U. Alt., Edmonton, Can., 1991. Tchr., libr. Columbia Acad., Battleground, Wash., 1975-78, Broadview Acad., La Fox, Ill., 1978-80; asst. libr. Can. Union Coll., College Heights, Alta., 1980-88; libr. technician Lacombe (Alta.) Composite H.S., 1989-91; tech. svcs. libr. Wapiti Regional Libr., Prince Albert, Sask., 1992; libr. dir. Oreg. Trail Libr. Dist., Boardman, 1993—. V.p. Ctrl. Alta. AIDS Network, Red Deer, 1990. Mem. ALA, Oreg. Libr. Assn. Democrat. Home: 700 Wilson Rd SW # D2 Boardman OR 97818-9776 Office: Oregon Trail Libr Dist 203 1st St NW Boardman OR 97818

BUCK, LAWRENCE RICHARD, fundraising executive; b. Albuquerque, Jan. 31, 1953; s. Richard Arthur and Mary Farris (Van Allen) B. BS in Phys. Sci., Colo. State U., 1976; MBA in Mktg., Calif. State U., San Bernardino, 1983. Ordained minister Evang. Ch. Alliance, 1991. Asst. to the dean Internat. Sch. of Theology, San Bernardino, 1977-78, asst. to the pres., 1978-80, deve. adminstr., 1980-82, donor rels. coord., 1982-83, asst. planning officer, 1983-84, dir. mktg., 1984-86; devel. adminstr. The JESUS Film Project, Campus Crusade for Christ Internat., San Bernardino, 1986-87, assoc. devel. officer, 1987—; cons., com. mem. ann. fund com. Calif. State U., San Bernardino, 1987-88; bd. dirs. Genesis Counseling Svc., 1992—. Mem. bd. councillors Calif. State U. Sch. Bus. and Pub. Adminstrn., San Bernardino, 1984-94. Named one of Outstanding Young Men in Am., U.S. Jaycees, 1984. Mem. Nat. Soc. Fund Raising Execs. (cert. fund raising exec. Orange County, 1994—). Republican. Office: The Jesus Film Project PO Box 72007 San Clemente CA 92674-2007

BUCK, LINDA DEE, recruiting company executive; b. San Francisco, Nov. 8, 1946; d. Sol and Shirley D. (Setterberg) Press; student Coll. San Mateo (Calif.), 1969-70; divorced. Head hearing and appeals br. Dept. Navy Employee Rels. Svc., Philippines, 1974-75; dir. human resources Homestead Savs. & Loan Assn., Burlingame, Calif., 1976-77; mgr. VIP Agy., Inc., Palo Alto, Calif., 1977-78; exec. v.p., dir. Sequent Personnel Svcs., Inc., Mountain View, Calif., 1978-83; founder, pres. Buck & Co., San Mateo, 1983-91. Publicity mgr. for No. Calif., Osteogenesis Imperfecta Found. Inc., 1970-72; cons. Am. Brittle Bone Soc., 1979-88; active Florence (Oreg.) Area Humane Soc., 1994—, Friends of Libr., Florence, 1994—; mem. steering com. Florence Festival Arts, 1995—; mem. Florence Area C. of C.; bd. dir., dir. women Rhododendron Scholarship Program, Florence, Oreg., 1995—. Jewish.

BUCK, LOUISE BRYDEN, psychiatrist; b. St. Louis, Mo., Apr. 26, 1943; d. Robert Ervin and Jane Bookings (Bryden) Buck; m. Adolph Pfefferbaum, June 11, 1967 (div. Feb. 1973); m. Randolph Seville Charlton, Feb. 14, 1975; children: Genevieve Lynn, Blake Randolph. BS, U. Calif., San Francisco, 1965, MD, 1968. Diplomate Am. Psychoanalytic Assn. Internal medicine intern Barnes Hosp.-Washington U., St. Louis, 1968-69; gen. practice Olney, Md., 1969-70; resident in psychiatry U. Md., Balt., 1970-72, Stanford U., Palo Alto, Calif., 1971-73; pvt. practice specializing in psychiatry Palo Alto, 1974—; mem. clin. fculty Stanford U., 1973—. Mem. Am. Psychoanalytic Assn., Peninsula Psychoanalytic Group (chmn.), San Francisco Psychoanalytic Inst. Office: 690 Waverley St Palo Alto CA 94301-2549

BUCKELS, MARVIN WAYNE, savings and loan executive; b. Sterling, Colo., Feb. 11, 1929; s. Harvey and Myrl (Tarr) B.; m. Doris Torrance, Aug. 1, 1959; children: Lisa K., Devon Carol. BA, U. Denver, 1951; MS, U. Wis., 1952. Trainee Beatrice Foods, Denver, 1952-53, mgr. sales devel., 1953-54, sales mgr., 1954-55; loan counselor Midland Fed. Savs. and Loan Assn., Denver, 1955-56, asst. treas., 1956-58, treas., 1958-60, v.p., treas., 1960-62, exec. v.p., 1962-85; exec. v.p. Western Capital Investment Corp., Denver, 1985-91. Vice chmn. Colo. Bd. for Community Colls. and Occupational Edn., 1967-75, chmn., 1975-78; vice chmn. Colo. Bd. Vocat. Edn., 1967; chmn. task force on employment Met. Denver Urban Coalition, 1970; pres. Adult Edn. Coun. Met. Denver, 1970; bd. dirs. Denver Opportunity, 1965-68, Downtown Denver, Inc., 1979-81; bd. dirs. Auraria Higher Edn. Ctr., 1975-79, vice chmn. bd., 1977-78; bd. dirs. Rocky Mountain Hosp., 1979, pres., 1980; chmn. Colo. Postsecondary Edn. Facilities Authority, 1981—; mem. Denver Civic Ventures Inc., 1986, chmn. 1987-90; mem. legis. policy com. Colo. Assn. Commerce and Industry, 1986-89; treas. Colo. Pub. Affairs Council, 1987-89; bd. dirs., treas. Colo. Symphony Orch., 1990—; chmn. The Denver Partnership, 1991-92. With U.S. Army, 1946-48. Mem. U.S. Savs. and Loan League, Colo. Savs. and Loan League (legis. com.), Am. Savs. and Loan Inst. (past pres. Denver chpt.), Contrs. Soc. (past pres. Denver chpt., nat. bd. govs.), Systems and Procedures Assn. (past pres. Denver chpt.), Adminstrv. Mgmt. Soc. (past pres. Denver chpt.), Greater Denver C. of C. (past chmn. spl. task force studying sch. bond issue, mem. legis. action coun. 1991, loaned exec. Nat. Alliance Businessmen's program), Phi Beta Kappa. Democrat.

BUCKINGHAM, JERRY L., hospital administrator; b. Lake Arthur, La., May 19, 1931; married. Bachelors degree, McNeese State U., 1956; masters degree, U. Chgo., 1959. Adminstrv. asst. Lake Charles (La.) Meml. Hosp., 1955-57; adminstrv. rschr. Parkland Hosp., Dallas, 1958-59; asst. adminstr. Santa Rosa Health Care Corp., San Antonio, 1959; supt. Dr. Walter Olin Moss Regional Hosp., Lake Charles, 1959-66; assoc. adminstr. NYU Med. Ctr., N.Y.C., 1966-68, v.p. adminstrn., 1968-74; exec. dir. Touro Infirmary, New Orleans, 1974-85; exec.-in-residence Tulane U. Hosp. and Clinics, New Orleans, 1985-86; exec. dir. LAC/U. So. Calif. Med. Ctr., L.A., 1986—. Contbr. articles to profl. jours. Mem. AHA. Home: 1200 Brookmere Rd Pasadena CA 91105

BUCKINGHAM, MICHAEL JOHN, oceanography educator; b. Oxford, Eng., Oct. 9, 1943; s. Sidney George and Mary Agnes (Walsh) B.; m. Margaret Penelope Rose Barrowcliff, July 15, 1967. BSc with hons., U. Reading (Eng.), 1967, PhD, 1971. Postdoctoral rsch. fellow U. Reading, 1971-74; sr. sci. officer Royal Aircraft Establishment, Farnborough, Eng., 1974-76; prin. sci. officer Royal Aircraft Establishment, 1976-82; exchange scientist Naval Rsch. Lab., Washington, 1982-84; vis. prof. MIT, Cambridge, 1986-87; sr. prin. sci. officer Royal Aircraft Establishment, 1983-86, 1987-90; prof. oceanography Scripps Instn. of Oceanography, La Jolla, Calif., 1990—; vis. prof. Inst. Sound and Vibration rsch., Southampton, Eng., 1990—; cons. Commn. of European Communities, Brussels, Belgium, 1989—; dir. Arctic rsch. Royal Aerospace Establishment, Farnborough, 1990—. Author: Noise in Electronic Devices and Systems, 1983; sr. editor Jour. Computational Acoustics; editor Phys. Acoustics; contbr. articles to profl. jours.; patentee in field. Recipient Clerk Maxwell Premium, Inst. Electronic and Radio Engrs. London, 1972, A.B. Wood Medal, Inst. Acoustics, Bath, Eng., 1982, Alan Burman Pub. award, Naval Rsch. Lab., 1988, Commendation for Disting. Contbns. to ocean acoustics Naval Rsch. Lab., 1986. Fellow Inst. Acoustics (U.K.), Inst. Elec. Engrs. (U.K.), Acoustical Soc. Am. (chmn. acoustical oceanography tech. com. 1991—); mem. Am. Geophys. Union, Sigma Xi. Home: 7921 Caminito Del Cid La Jolla CA 92037-3404 Office: Scripps Inst Oceanography Marine Phys Lab La Jolla CA 92093-0213

BUCKLEY, JAMES W., librarian; b. Los Angeles, Aug. 16, 1933; s. George W. and Alta L. (Hale) B.; m. Margaret Ann Wall, Aug. 7, 1965; children: Kathleen Ann, James William, John Whitney. AA, Los Angeles Harbor Coll., 1953; BA, Calif. State U., Long Beach, 1960; MLS, U. So. Calif., 1961, M in Pub. Adminstrn., 1974. Cert. tchr., Calif. Libr. West Gardena br. Los Angeles County Pub. Libr., 1961-62, librarian Carson br., 1962-63; libr. Montebello (Calif.) Regional Libr., 1963-68; regional librarian Orange County (Calif.) Pub. Libr., 1968, dir. pub. services, 1969-74; county librarian San Mateo County (Calif.) Libr., 1974-77, Marin County (Calif.) Libr., 1978; city librarian Torrance (Calif.) Pub. Libr., 1979—; exec. dir. Calif. Nat. Libr. Week, 1970; tchr. pub. svc. Coll. San Mateo, 1975; chmn. Met. Coop. Libr. System, 1989-90, Calif. Libr. Assn. Assembly, 1993—. Served with U.S. Army, 1955-57. Mem. ALA, Am. Soc. Pub. Adminstrn., Calif. Libr. Assn., Rotary. Office: Torrance Pub Libr 3301 Torrance Blvd Torrance CA 90503-5014

BUCKLEY, LINDA ANNE, critical care, psychiatric-mental health, chemical dependency nurse; b. Kewanee, Ill., Sept. 11, 1945; d. Kenneth Leybourne and Rose Marie (Schlitz) B.; divorced; 1 child, Kael Damian Buckley. Lic. vocat. nurse diploma, Vocat. Nursing Sch. Calif., 1970; AA in Nursing, L.A. City Coll., 1978; BS, Calif. State U., Northridge, 1980, Ryan Credential Authorizing Service in California Public Schools, 1981; grad. in chem. dependency studies, L.A. Mission Coll., 1992. RN, Calif., Ill. Nurse pediatric and adult walk in clinic and emergency room Kaiser Hosp. West L.A., 1978-79; nurse operating room and perioperative unit Children's Hosp. L.A., 1978-80; hospice team nurse Vis. Nurses Assn., L.A., 1980; critical care nurse, charge nurse chem. dependency-psychiat. Henry Mayo Newhall Meml. Hosp., Valencia, Calif., 1982—; diabetes educator for endocrinologist Dr. Steven Baron, Newhall, Calif., 1990—; nurse adolescent psychiatry Olive View, UCLA Med. Ctr., 1991—.

BUCKLEY, VIKKI, state official. Sec. of state State of Colo., 1995—. Office: Office of the Sec of State 1560 Broadway Ste 200 Denver CO 80202-5135

BUCKLIN, LOUIS PIERRE, business educator, consultant; b. N.Y.C., Sept. 20, 1928; s. Louis Lapham and Elja (Barricklow) B.; m. Weylene Edwards, June 11, 1956; children: Randolph E., Rhonda W. Student, Dartmouth Coll., 1950; MBA, Harvard U., 1954; PhD, Northwestern U., 1960. Asst. prof. bus. U. Colo., Boulder, 1954-56; instr. in bus. Northwestern U., Evanston, 1958-59, assoc. dean Grad. Sch. Bus. Adminstrn., 1981-83; prof. bus. adminstrn. U. Calif., Berkeley, 1960-93, prof. emeritus, 1993—; vis. prof. Stockholm Sch. Econs., 1983, INSEAD, Fontainebleau, France, 1984, Erasmus U., Rotterdam, Netherlands, 1993-94, Cath. U. Leuven, Belgium, 1994; prin. Bucklin Assocs., Lafayette, Calif., 1975—;mem. adv. bd. Gemini Cons., San Francisco, 1987-94. Author: A Theory of Distribution Channel Structure, 1966, Competition Evolution in The Distributive Trades, 1972, Productivity in Marketing, 1979; editor: Vertical Marketing Systems, 1971, Channels and Channel Institutions, 1986. Mem. City of Lafayette Planning Commn., 1990-93. Capt. USMC, 1951-53, Korea. Recipient Alpha Kappa Psi Found. award for best paper in Jour. Mktg., 1993. Mem. Am. Mktg. Assn. (Paul D. Converse award 1986), Inst. for Ops. Rsch. and Mgmt. Scis., European Acad. Mktg., Lafayette-Langeac Soc. (bd. dirs. 1988-92). Democrat. Office: U Calif Haas Sch Bus Berkeley CA 94720-1900

BUCKNER, KAY LAMOREUX, artist; b. Seattle, Dec. 26, 1935; d. H.D.W. and Eunice (Coble) Lamoreux; m. Paul Buckner, Aug. 15, 1959; children: Matthew, Nathan. BA, U. Wash., 1958; MFA, Claremont Grad. Sch., 1961. One-woman shows include Frye Art Mus., Seattle, 1979, Oreg. Mus. Art, Eugene, 1981, Jadite Galleries, N.Y.C., 1988; exhibited in group shows at Marietta (Ohio) Coll., 1974, 76, Ea. N.Mex. U., Portales, 1981 (1st prize), U. Wash., Seattle, 1984, Austen Peay U., Clarksville, Tenn., 1989, Md. Fedn. Art, Annapolis, 1991, U. Md., Balt., 1994; rep. in permanent collections Olympic Coll., Bremerton, Wash., Georgia-Pacific Co., Portland, Oreg., Wash. State Dept. Corrections, Emanuel Hosp., Portland.

BUCKNER, MATTHEW ERIC, sculptor; b. Pomona, Calif., Jan. 15, 1961; s. Paul Eugene and Kay Shirley (Lamoreux) B. BA, SUNY, N.Y.C., 1984; MFA, Boston U., 1988. Apprentice carver Intagliatori Bertolozzi, Florence, Italy, 1980-81; carving restorer Regency Restorations, Ltd., N.Y.C., 1983-86; supervisor gilding, painting Fine Art Decorating Co., N.Y.C., 1986; sculpture finisher Tallix Sculptuer Foundry, N.Y.C., 1988-91; art instr. U. Oreg., Eugene, 1991—; gallery dir. Howland Art Ctr., Beacon, N.Y., 1990. Collections include Mugar Meml. Libr., Boston, 1988, Lawrence Hall, U. Oreg., 1991, Thunderbird Sch., Phoenix, 1994. Mem. Nat. Sculpture Soc. (Louis Bennett prize 1989, Gloria medal 1988). Home and Studio: 2332 Rockwood St Eugene OR 97405-1413

BUCKNER, PHILIP FRANKLIN, newspaper publisher; b. Worcester, Mass., Aug. 25, 1930; s. Orello Simmons and Emily Virginia (Siler) B.; m. Ann Haswell Smith, Dec. 21, 1956 (div. Nov. 1993); children: John C., Frederick S., Catherine A. AB, Harvard U., 1952; MA, Columbia U., 1954. Reporter Lowell (Mass.) Sun, 1959-60; pub. East Providence (R.I.) Post, 1960-62; asst. to treas. Scripps League Newspapers, Seattle, 1964-66, div. mgr., 1966-71; pres. Buckner News Alliance, Seattle, 1971—, 2 newspapers, York, Pa. and Pecos, Tex. Office: Buckner News Alliance 2101 4th Ave Ste 2300 Seattle WA 98121-2317

BUCY, RICHARD SNOWDEN, aerospace engineering and mathematics educator, consultant; b. Washington, July 20, 1935; s. Edmond Howard and Marie (Glinke) B.; m. Ofelia Teresa Rivva, Aug. 25, 1961; children: Phillip Gustav, Richard Erwin. B.S. in Math., MIT, 1957; Ph.D. in Math. Stats., U. Calif.-Berkeley, 1963. Researcher in math. Rsch. Inst. Advanced Studies, Towson, Md., 1960-61, 63-64; rsch. asst. U. Calif., Berkeley, 1961-63; asst. prof. math. U. Md., College Park, 1964-65; assoc. prof. aerospace engring. U. Colo., Boulder, 1965-66; prof. aerospace engring. and math. U. So. Calif., Los Angeles, 1966—; professeur associe French Govt., Toulouse, 1973-74, Nice, 1983-84, 90-91; vis. prof. Technische Universität Berlin, 1975-76; codir. NATO Advanced Study Inst. on Non-linear Scholastic Problems, Algarve, Portugal; cons. to industry. Author: Filtering for Stochastic Processes, 1968, 2d edit., 1987, Nonlinear Stochastic Problems, 1984, Lectures on Discrete Filtering Theory, 1994; editor Jour. Info. Scis., Jour. Math. Modelling and Sci. Computing; founding editor (jour.) Stochastics, 1971-77; contbr. numerous articles to profl. publs. Recipient Humboldt prize Govt. W. Germany, Berlin, 1975-76; Air Force Office Sci. Sch. grantee, 1965-81, NATO Rsch. grantee, 1979—. Fellow IEEE (del. to Soviet Acad. of Scis. Info. Theory Workshop); mem. Am. Math. Soc. Republican. Home: 240 S Juanita Ave Redondo Beach CA 90277-3438 Office: U So Calif Dept Aerospace Engring Los Angeles CA 90089-1191

BUDD, NANCY J., lawyer; b. Glendale, Calif., Dec. 28, 1951; d. Arthur Richard Budd and Claire (Jorgensen) Budd Brooks; m. Joe F. Calhoun, Aug. 14, 1982; 1 child, Lauren Noelani. BA magna cum laude, Calif. State U., Chico, 1974; JD, U. Calif., Davis, 1979. Bar: Hawaii 1980, Calif. 1980, U.S. Dist. Ct. Hawaii 1980, U.S. Ct. Appeals (9th cir.) 1982. Prin. Law Offices Nancy J. Budd, Lihue, Hawaii, 1980-82, 87—; mng. lawyer Legal Aid Soc. Hawaii, Lihue, 1982-87; pres., v.p. for legislation King Kaumauali'i Elem. Sch., Hanamaulu, Hawaii, 1989—; arbitrator ct. annexed arbitration program Circuit Ct. of 5th Cir., State of Hawaii, 1987—. Co-producer video on sch. reform. Bd. dirs. Kauai (Hawaii) Cmty. Housing Resource Be., 1986—, Hawaii State Parent Tchr. Student Assn. Bd. Mgrs., Honolulu, 1989-92, Salvation Army Adv. Bd., Lihue, 1991—; vice chair, bd. dirs. Kauai Housing Devel. Corp., 1992—; bd. dirs., pres. Kauai Children's Fund, Inc., Lihue, 1989—; pres., bd. dirs. Kauai Dist. Parent Tchr. Student Assn., Lihue, 1989—; mem. legacy planned giving com. Am. Cancer Soc., Kauai, 1991—; of counsel Kauai Acad. of Creative Arts; cmty. rep. State Found. on Culture and the Arts in Public Places Project King Kaumualii Elem. Sch., 1993—. Mem. ABA, Hawaii Bar Assn., Kauai Bar Assn. (v.p. 1983-84, pres. 1985-86). Office: 4374 Kukui Grove St Ste 103 Lihue HI 96766-2007

BUDEK, ALLIN ALLA, artist; b. Kiev, Ukraine, June 19, 1923; came to U.S., 1948; d. Igor W. and Olga G. (Intelman) Domansky; m. Herbert E. Budek, June 1, 1946; 2 children. BA in Creative Studies, U. Calif., Santa Barbara, 1981. Exhibited in group shows at COAL Art Gallery, Carlsbad, Calif., 1993-94, San Dieguito Art Guild, Leucadia, Calif., 1993-95 (1st pl. award 1993, 94, 95), La Jolla (Calif.) Art Assn. Gallery, 1993-94, Hellenic Arts Inst., N.Y.C., 1993-94, Musee D'Art Moderne de la Commanderie, Unets, France, 1994; represented in permanent collections Stockholm Royal

Collection, Madrid Royal Collection, Vatican, Gerald R. Ford Libr., Notre Dame U., U. Colo.; represented in numerous pvt. collections. Recipient 1st Pl. award Art Vision, 1993, 94, COAL Spring Show, 1993. Home: 133 Smart Ct Encinitas CA 92024-2934

BUDHU, MUNIRAM, soil mechanics educator; b. Windsor Forest, Demerara, Guyana, Dec. 4, 1947; s. George and Ramdulari (Sawh) B.; m. Shanta Surujdai Bookram, July 9, 1972; children—Anuradha, Ravi. B.Sc., U. W.I., 1974; Ph.D., U. Cambridge, 1979. Asst. prof. McMaster U., Hamilton, Ont., Can., 1982-83; asst. prof. soil mechanics SUNY-Buffalo, 1983—; lectr. U. Guyana, 1974-76, sr. lectr., 1979-82. Author: Fundamental Principles of Soil Mechanics and Foundation Engineering. Mem. ASCE. Address: U Ariz Dept Civil Engring Tucson AZ 85721

BUDINGTON, WILLIAM STONE, retired librarian; b. Oberlin, Ohio, July 3, 1919; s. Robert Allyn and Mabel (Stone) B.; m. Irma Johnson. B.A., Williams Coll., 1940, L.H.D., 1975; B.S. in L.S, Columbia U., 1941, M.S., 1951; B.S. in Elec. Engring, Va. Poly. Inst., 1946. Reference librarian Norwich U., 1941-42; librarian, engring. and phys. scis. Columbia, 1947-52; asso. librarian John Crerar Library, Chgo., 1952-65; librarian John Crerar Library, 1965-69, exec. dir., librarian, 1969-84; Mem. U.S.-USSR Spl. Libraries Exchange, 1966; bd, dirs. Center for Research Libraries, 1970-72, chmn., 1972; mem. vis. com. on libraries Mass. Inst. Tech., 1972-77. Served with AUS, 1942-46. Fellow AAAS, Med Library Assn.; mem. ALA, Am. Soc. Info. Sci., Spl. Libraries Assn. (pres. 1964-65, Hall of Fame 1984), Am. Soc. Engring. Edn., Assn. Research Libraries (dir. 1970-74, pres. 1973), Assn. Coll. and Research Libraries (Acad. Research Librarian of Year 1982), Phi Beta Kappa, Tau Beta Pi, Eta Kappa Nu. Clubs: Caxton, Arts. Home: 211 Wood Terrace Dr Colorado Springs CO 80903-2337

BUDKEVICS, GIRTS JANIS, financial planner; b. Bklyn., July 10, 1952; s. Boriss and Ilga (Prods) B. BA in Communications, Hofstra U., 1975. Cert. fin. planner. Sales rep. Martin L. Stroll, Inc., Hartsdale, N.Y., 1976-79; asst. mgr. Nassau Splty. Steel, Garden City, N.Y., 1979-82; sales rep. Smith Corona, Anaheim, Calif., 1982-83, Royal Consumer Bus. Products, L.A., 1983-87; fin. adviser Am. Express Fin. Advisors, Inc., Long Beach, Calif., 1987—; mem. Internat. Bd. Cert. Fin. Planners. Mem. Internat. Assn. Fin. Planners, Internat. Soc. Retirement Planners (bd. dirs. 1989, 91-94, treas. 1992-94), Am. Latvian Assn. (bd. dirs. 1992—, pres. sports coun. 1993, v.p. fin. 1993), Latvian Assn. So. Calif. (bd. dirs. 1987—, pres. 1991—), West Coast Latvian Athletic Assn. (pres. 1986-88), Latvian Folk Dance Ensemble Club (bd. dirs. 1986-87), Latvian Freedom Found. (pres. 1993-95), Sports Club Riga So. Calif. (pres. 1986—), Riga Volleyball Club (pres. 1985-86), Lettonia (pres. So. Calif. 1987-90). Republican. Lutheran. Home: 660 The Village # 310 Redondo Beach CA 90277 Office: IDS Fin Svcs 5000 E Spring St Ste 200 Long Beach CA 90815-1271

BUDLONG, THEODORE WARREN, insurance company executive; b. N.Y.C., Mar. 16, 1946; s. Theodore W. and Ware (Torrey) B. BA, Amherst Coll., 1968; PhD, Cornell U., 1973. Asst. prof. Purdue U., West Lafayette, Ind., 1972-76; underwriting mgr. Workmen's Auto Ins. Co., L.A., 1976-78; facultative underwriter Gen. Reins. Corp., San Francisco, 1978-79; v.p. underwriting Workmen's Auto Ins. Co., L.A., 1979-82; regional controller CNA Ins.Cos., Woodland Hills, Calif., 1982-90; sr. v.p. ops. Workmen's Auto Inst. Co., L.A., 1990—. Office: Workmen's Auto Ins Co 714 W Olympic Blvd Los Angeles CA 90015-1425

BUDZINSKI, JAMES EDWARD, interior designer; b. Gary, Ind., Jan. 4, 1953; s. Edward Michael and Virginia (Caliman) B. Student U. Cin., 1971-76. Mem. design staff Perkins & Wills Architects, Inc., Chgo., 1973-75, Med. Architectonics, Inc., Chgo., 1975-76; v.p. interior design Interior Environs., Inc., Chgo., 1976-78; pres. Jim Budzinski Design, Inc., Chgo., 1978-80; dir. interior design Robinson, Mills & Williams, San Francisco, 1980-87, dir. design, interior architecture Whisler Patri, San Francisco, 1987-90; v.p. design sales and mktg. Deepa Textiles, 1990—; instr. design Harrington Inst. Design, Chgo.; cons. Chgo. Art Inst., Storwal Internat., Inc.; speaker at profl. confs. Designs include 1st Chgo. Corp. Pvt. Banking Ctr., 1st Nat. Bank Chgo. Monroe and Wabash Banking Ctr., 1978, IBM Corp., San Jose, Deutsch Bank, Frankfort, Crowley Maritime Corp., San Francisco, offices for Brobeck, Phleger and Harrison, offices for chmn. bd. Fireman's Fund Ins. Cos., Nob Hill Club, Fairmont Hotel, San Francisco, offices for Cooley, Godword, Castro, Huddleson, and Tatum, Palo Alto, Calif, offices for Pacific Bell Acctg. div., San Francisco, showroom for Knoll Internat., San Francisco, lobby, lounge TransAm. Corp. Hdqrts, San Fransisco, offices for EDAW, San Francisco, showroom for Steelcase Inc., Bally of Switzerland, N.Am. Flagship store, San Francisco; corp. Hqrs. Next Inc., Redwood City, Calif., Schafer Furniture Design, Lobby Renovation 601 California, San Francisco, Bennedetti Furniture Inc. Furniture Design. Pres. No. Calif. chpt. Design Industries Found. for AIDS. Office: Deepa Textiles 333 Bryant St San Francisco CA 94107-1421

BUEHLER, MARILYN KAY HASZ, secondary education educator; b. Garden City, Kans., July 19, 1946; d. Benjamin Bethel and Della Marie (Appel) Hasz; m. Brice Edward Buehler, July 23, 1966. BA in English, Washburn U., 1970; MA in Reading Edn., Ariz. State U., 1976; DHL (hon.), No. Ariz. U., 1989. Cert. tchr. English and secondary edn. Vol. probation officer, co-facilitator Maricopa County Probation Office, Phoenix, 1972; adult edn. tchr. Phoenix Union High Sch., 1972-73; tchr. English Trevor G. Browne High Sch., Phoenix, 1973; tchr. Title I Carl Hayden High Sch., Phoenix, 1974; tchr. English Camelback High Sch., Phoenix, 1975, Central High Sch., Phoenix, 1976-85, North High Sch., Phoenix, 1985—; internat. baccalaurate English instr., 1986—; chmn. awareness facilitator Phoenix Union High Sch. System, 1986-95; speaker Partnrships in Edn., Phoenix, 1991—, adv. bd. Phoenix Coll. Creative Writing, 1995. Bd. dirs. Ariz. Edn. Found., Phoenix, 1990-95, North High-Ariz. Pub. Svc. Partnership Com., 1991-95. Named Ariz. State Tchr. of Yr., State of Ariz./AEF, 1989; recipient award of honor for outstanding contbns. to edn. Nat. Sch. Pub. Rels. Assn., 1989, others. Mem. NEA, Nat. Coun. Tchrs. English, Classroom Tchrs. Assn., Nat. Writers Club, Nat. State Tchrs. of Yr., Ariz. State Tchrs. of Yr. (pres. 1993—), Phoenix Zoo Bd. (edn. com, 1995—). Democrat. Office: North High Sch 1101 E Thomas Rd Phoenix AZ 85014-5447

BUEHRER, ROGER DEAN, communications executive utility company; b. Toledo, Ohio, July 12, 1946; s. Charles Donald and Esther Estelle (Sheidler) B.; m. Lana Kay Blythe, Aug. 25, 1973; children; Aaron Christopher, Nicholas Charles. BS, Bowling Green State U., 1968; MA, Am. Univ., 1972. Tchr. English, journalism Continental (Ohio) High Sch., 1968-72; city editor Crescent News Pub. Co., Defiance, Ohio, 1972-76; dir. media rels. Toledo Edison Co., 1974-83; dir. media rels S.W. Gas Corp., Las Vegas, 1983-86, dir. consumer and cmty. affairs., 1986-89, dir. employee comms., 1989- . Bd. dirs. Clark County (Nev.) Chpt. ARC, 1986-91, pres. 1989-90, mem. awards com. mountain west region, 1993, Nev. Svc. Coun., 1993; bd. dirs. Las Vegas Exchange Club, 1993, bd. chair 1995—; mem. Clark County Rep. Ctrl. Com., Las Vegas, 1988-89. Named to Outstanding Young Men in Am. Jaycees, Toledo, Ohio, 1981; recipient Golden Bear svc. award Calif.-Nev. Region ARC, 1991, Spl. Citation for Svc. Nat. ARC, 1992, Cert. Spl. Recognition, U.S. Senate, Wash., 1992. Mem. Pub. Rels. Soc. Am. (accredited pub. rels. profl., mem. at large Desert Sands chpt., Las Vegas), Internat. Assn. Bus. Communicators, Soc. Profl. Journalists. Methodist. Office: SW Gas Corp PO Box 98510 Las Vegas NV 89193-8510

BUEL, JAMES WES, food service executive; b. Long Beach, Calif., May 21, 1937; s. James Buel and June (von Opperman) B.; m. Renee J. Ellis; children: Frank, Roddy, Tammy, Ty, Wesley, Elise. BS, Calif. Poly. State U., 1963. Cert. food exec. Internat. Food Svc. Execs. Assn. Food svc. mgr. Dole Philippines, 1964-69; dir. food and beverage Hyatt Hotels Asia, Philippines, 1969-79; food svc. dir. Western Innkeepers, L.A., 1979-83; food service dir. Svc. Am., Long Beach, Calif., 1983-88; food svc. mgr. Lucky Food Stores, Redlands, Calif., 1988-90; food and beverage dir. Newport Diversified, Santa Fe Springs, Calif., 1990—; cons. in field. Author: Food Service in the Philippines, 1977, Food Service in Asia, 1978, Food Service Software, 1991. Coun. bd. dirs. Boy Scouts Am., 1987-90; v.p. Am. Assn., Manila, 1977; mem. Buena Park Vision 2010 Commn. Recipient Cert. of Leadership, Cornell U., 1979; named Fulbright exch. student, 1958. Mem. James Beard Found., Internat. Found. Svc. Execs. Assn. (life), Calif. Poly. Alumni Assn., Global Holelies Club (life). Republican.

BUELL, THOMAS ALLAN, lumber company executive; b. Toronto, Ont., Can., Nov. 14, 1931; s. Allan Foster and Jessie L. (Stayner) B.; m. Phyllis Ann Lee, Aug. 27, 1955; children: Elizabeth, Christopher, Michael, Robert. BSCF in Forestry, U. Toronto, 1956. Forester Kimberly Clark of Can., 1956-61; mgr. No. Plywoods Co., 1961-64; with Weldwood of Can. Ltd., Vancouver, B.C., 1964—; v.p. mfg. Weldwood of Can. Ltd., 1970-75, pres., chief exec. officer, 1975-79, chmn., pres., CEO, 1979-92, chmn., 1992—, CEO, 1992-93, ret. CEO, 1993; co-chmn. Canfor-Weldwood Distbn. Ltd.; bd. dirs. B.C. Gas Inc., Placer Dome Inc., Swiss Bank Corp. (Can.), Mayne Nickless Can. Inc., Lafarge Corp. Chmn. dean's adv. coun. faculty of forestry U. B.C., mem. adv. coun. faculty of commerce and bus. adminstrn.; mem. citizens bd. Forest Alliance B.C.; mem. forestry sector adv. coun., chmn. Can. Forest Industries Coun. Mem. Royal Vancouver Yacht Club, Vancouver Club. Office: Weldwood of Can Ltd, 1055 West Hastings, Vancouver, BC Canada V6B 3V8

BUENVIAJE, ROSALINDA TAGLE, dietitian, consultant; b. Manila, Philippines, Mar. 13; came to U.S., 1969; d. Jose V. and Victoria S. Tagle; divorced; children: Lelynda Jane, Brian Jay. BS in Foods and Nutrition, Centro Escolar U., Manila, 1969. Food svc. dir. Habilitative & Rehab. Ctr., Hartford, Conn., 1984-87; adminstrv./clin. asst. dir. S.W. Healthcare, Santa Fe, 1987-88; food and nutrition dir. Vista Hill Found., Albuquerque, 1988-90, Beverly Enterprise, Melrose, Mass., 1990-91; food svc. dir. Beverly Enterprise, Laguna Hills, Calif., 1991-92; adminstr./clin. dir. NME-Yorba Linda (Calif.) Psychiat. Ctr., 1991-92; healthcare mkgt. assoc. Sterling Healthcare, Bellflower, Calif., 1992-94; food svc. dir. Sterling Healthcare, Bellevue, Wash., 1992-94; food svc. mgr. Newport Bay Hosp., Newport Beach, Calif., 1994—; cons. Park Superior Healthcre, Newport Beach, 1993—; cons., nutritionist Villa Luren Healthcare, Whittier, 1993—, Beverly Enterprise, Cape Ann, Mass. Mem. Am. Dietetic Assn., Calif. Dietetic Assn., Am. Hosp. Food Svc. Assn. Office: Newport Bay Hosp 1501 E 16th St Newport Beach CA 92663

BUESCHER, BERNARD, air transportation executive; b. 1949. Attended, U. Colo., 1970-73. With Williams, Turner & Holmes P.C., Grand Junction, Colo., 1973-87; ptnr. Buescher Family Ltd. Partnership, Grand Junction, 1982—; officer West Star Engine Corp., Grand Junction, 1987-92; pres. West Star Aviation, Grand Junction, 1987—. Office: West Star Aviation Inc 768 Heritage Way Grand Junction CO 81506-8643*

BUESCHER, LOUIS, airport service executive. With Mesa Beverage Co., Grand Junction, Colo., 1971-82; gen. ptnr. Buescher Family L.P., Grand Junction, Colo., 1982—; with Pipeline Service, Inc., Grand Junction, Colo., 1983-87; officer West Star Engine Corp., Grand Junction, Colo., 1987-92; with West Star Aviation, Inc., Grand Junction, Colo., 1987—. Office: West Star Aviation Inc 796 Heritage Way Grand Junction CO 81506-8643*

BUFFINGTON, LINDA BRICE, interior designer; b. Long Beach, Calif., June 21, 1936; d. Harry Bryce and Marguerite Leonora (Tucciarone) Van Bellehem; student El Camino Jr. Coll., 1955-58, U. Calif., Irvine, 1973-75; children: Lisa Ann, Phillip Lynn. Cert. interior designer and gen. contractor, Calif.; lic. gen. contractor, Calif. With Pub. Fin., Torrance, Calif., 1954-55, Beneficial Fin., Torrance and Hollywood, Calif., 1955-61; interior designer Vee Nisley Interiors, Newport Beach, Calif., 1964-65, Leon's Interiors, Newport Beach, 1965-69; ptnr. Marlind Interiors, Tustin, Calif., 1969-70; owner, designer Linda Buffington Interiors, Villa Park, Calif., 1970—, LBI, Contractors, 1993—; cons. builders, housing developments. Mem. Bldg. Industry Assn. (past pres. Orange County chpt. 1989, 90), Internat. Soc. Interior Designers, Nat. Assn. Home Builders. Republican. Office: 17853 Santiago Blvd Ste 107 Villa Park CA 92667-4105

BUFFMIRE, JUDY ANN, state representative, psychologist, consultant; b. Salt Lake City, June 5, 1929; d. William Henry Broyles and Audrey Francis (Cook) Ballinger; m. LaMar Lee Buffmire, Nov. 28, 1948; children: Kathryn Ann, Shanna Lee. B.S. cum laude, U. Utah, 1966, M.S., 1967, Ph.D., 1969. Asst. prof. dept. spl. edn. U. Utah, 1967-76; state program specialist Utah State Office Edn., Salt Lake City, 1976-77; dep. dir. Utah Social Services, Salt Lake City, 1978-80; dir. State Div. Family Services, Salt Lake City, 1981-82, dir. State Div. Registration, Salt Lake City, 1982-83, dir. State Div. Rehab., Salt Lake City, 1983-87, exec. dir. Utah State Office of Rehab., 1987-91; rep. Utah House of Reps., 1992—. Contbr. articles to profl. publs. Mem. Presdl. Adv. Council on Ednl. and Profl. Devel., 1974-77; chmn. Utah Adv. Com. on Handicapped, 1975-77, chmn. State Mental Health Adv. Com., Salt Lake City, 1977-78, Regional VIII Adoption Resource Ctr., Salt Lake City, 1980; mem. State Bd. Fin. Instns., Salt Lake City, 1981-83; vol. therapist Parents United, Inc., Salt Lake City, 1982-84. Utah State Bd. Edn. scholar 1967; NDEA scholar, 1968-69; recipient Disting. Grad. award Wasatch Acad., 1976, Cmty. Svc. award for lifelong pub. contbn. Cath. Cmty. Svcs. Utah, 1988, Light of Learning award Utah State Bd. Edn., 1991, Outstanding Svc. award Great Plains Region Nat. Rehab. Assn., 1992, Leadership award 1993, Vol. award Utah Assn. Substance Abuse, 1994, Co-Legislator of the Yr. award NASW, 1994, Legislative Svc. award Utah Psychol. Assn., 1995, Hero on the Hill award The Gov. Coun. for People with Disabilities and the Legislative Coalition for People With Disabilities, 1995; named Bureaucrat of Yr., Utah Issues, 1982; Pub. Service Adminstr. of Yr., Nat. Assn. Social Workers, 1983. Mem. Utah Psychol. Assn., Am. Psychological Assn. (Karl F. Heiser Advocacy award 1995), Delta Kappa Gamma (pres. 1983-84). Democrat. Presbyterian. Avocations: cooking; camping; fishing; running rivers; traveling.

BUFFORD, SAMUEL LAWRENCE, federal judge; b. Phoenix, Ariz., Nov. 19, 1943; s. John Samuel and Evelyn Amelia (Rude) B.; m. Julia Marie Metzger, May 13, 1978. BA in Philosophy, Wheaton Coll., 1964; PhD, U. Tex., 1969; JD magna cum laude, U. Mich., 1973. Bar: Calif., N.Y., Ohio. Instr. philosophy La. State U., Baton Rouge, 1967-68; asst. prof. Ea. Mich. U., Ypsilanti, 1968-74; asst. prof. law Ohio State U., Columbus, 1975-77; assoc. Gendel, Raskoff, Shapiro & Quittner, L.A., 1982-85; atty. Paul, Weiss, Rifkind, Wharton & Garrison, N.Y.C., 1974-75, Sullivan Jones & Archer, San Francisco, 1977-79, Musick, Peeler & Garrett, L.A., 1979-81, Rifkind & Sterling, Beverly Hills, Calif., 1981-82, Gendel, Raskoff, Shapiro & Quittner, L.A., 1982-85; U.S. bankruptcy judge Ctrl. Dist. Calif., 1985—; bd. dirs. Fin. Lawyers Conf., L.A., 1987-90, Bankruptcy Forum, L.A., 1986-88; lectr. U.S.-Romanian Jud. Delegation, 1991, Internat. Tng. Ctr. for Bankers, Budapest, 1993, Bankruptcy Technical Legal Assistance Workshop, Romania, 1994, Comml. Law Project, Ukraine, 1995; cons. Calif. State Bar Bd. Bar Examiners, 1989-90. Editor-in-chief Am. Bankruptcy Law Jour., 1990-94; contbr. articles to profl. jours.; columnist Norton Bankruptcy Adviser, 1988—. Younger Humanist fellowship NEH. Mem. ABA, L.A. County Bar Assn. (past chmn. ethics com.), Order of Coif. Office: US Bankruptcy Ct 255 E Temple St Ste 1582 Los Angeles CA 90012-3334

BUGBEE-JACKSON, JOAN, sculptor; b. Oakland, Calif., Dec. 17, 1941; d. Henry Greenwood and Jeanie Lawler (Abbot) B.; m. John Michael Jackson, June 21, 1973; 1 child, Brook Bond. BA in Art, U. Calif., San Jose, 1964, MA in Art/Ceramics, 1966; student Nat. Acad. Sch. Fine Arts, N.Y.C., 1968-72, Art Students League, N.Y.C., 1968-70. Apprentice to Joseph Kiselewski, 1970-72; instr. art Foothill (Calif.) Jr. Coll., 1966-67; instr. design De Anza Jr. Coll., Cupertino, Calif., 1967-68; instr. pottery Greenwich House Pottery, N.Y.C., 1969-71, Craft Inst. Am., N.Y.C., 1970-72, Cordova (Alaska) Extension Center, U. Alaska, 1972-79, Prince William Sound Community Coll., 1979—; one-woman exhbns. in Maine, N.Y.C., Alaska and Calif.; group exhbns. include Allied Artists Am., 1970-72, Nat. Acad. Design, 1971, 74, Nat. Sculpture Soc. Ann., 1971, 72, 73, Alaska Woman Art Show, 1987, 88, Cordova Visual Artists, 1991, 92, 93, 94, 95, Alaska Artists Guild Show, 1994, Am. Medallic Sculpture Nat. Travelling Exhbn., 1994-95; pres. Cordova Arts and Pageants Ltd., 1975-76; commns. include Merle K. Smith Commemorative plaque, 1973, Eyak Native Monument, 1978, Anchorage Pioneer's Home Ceramic Mural, 1979, Alaska Wildlife Series Bronze Medal, 1980, sculpture murals and portraits Alaska State Capitol, 1981, Pierre De Ville Portrait commn., 1983, Robert B. & Evangeline Atwood, 1985, Armin F. Koernig Hatchery Plaque, 1985, Cordova Fishermen's Meml. Sculpture, 1985, Alaska's Five Govs., bronze relief, Anchorage, 1986, Reluctant Fisherman's Mermaid, bronze, 1987, Charles E. Bunnell, bronze portrait statue, Fairbanks, 1988, Alexander Baranof Monument, Sitka, Alaska, 1989, Wally Noerenberg Hatchery Plaque, Prince William Sound, Alaska, 1989, Russian-Alaskan Friendship Plaque (edit. of 4), Kayak Island, Cordova, Alaska and Vladivostok & Petropavlovsk-Kamchatskiy, Russia, 1991, Sophie-Last Among Eyak Native People, 1992, Alaska Airlines Medal Commn. 1993, Hosp. Aux. plaque, 1995; also other portraits. Bd. dirs. Alaska State Coun. on the Arts, 1991-95. Scholarship student Nat. Acad. Sch. Fine Arts, 1969-72; recipient J.A. Suydam Bronze medal, 1969; Dr. Ralph Weiler prize, 1971; Helen Foster Barnet award, 1971; Daniel Chester French award, 1972; Frishmuth award, 1971; Allied Artists Am. award, 1972; C. Percival Dietsch prize, 1973; citation Alaska Legislature, 1981, 82, Alaskan Artist of the Yr., 1991. Fellow Nat. Sculpture Soc. Address: PO Box 374 Cordova AK 99574-0374

BUGHER, ROBERT DEAN, association executive; b. Lafayette, Ind., Oct. 17, 1925; s. Walter Earl and Lillie Victoria (Feldner) B.; m. Patricia Jean McConnell, Sept. 7, 1945; children: Vickie Leigh, Robert James. Student, Millsaps Coll., 1943, Miami U., Oxford, Ohio, 1944; B.S. in Civil Engring, Purdue U., 1948; M.P.A., U. Mich., 1951. Staff engr. Mich. Mcpl. League, 1948-53; mgr. Mcpl. Purchasing Svc., 1951-53; sec.-treas. Mich. Mcpl. Utilities Assn., 1951-53; asst. dir. Am. Pub. Works Assn., 1953-58, exec. dir., 1958-89, exec. dir. emeritus, 1990—; Lectr. Internat. Seminar on Ekistics, Athens, Greece, 1970; chmn. nat. adv. coun. Keep Am. Beautiful, Inc., 1974-75; chmn. Nat. Conf. on Solid Waste Disposal Sites, Washington, 1971; advisor pub. mgmt. program Northwestern U., 1977-82; bd. dirs. Pub. Adminstrn. Svc., Chgo., 1958-73; trustee Nat. Acad. Code Adminstrs.; chmn. Coun. Internat. Urban Liaison, 1982-84; trustee Nat. Tng. and Devel. Svc., Am. Consortium for Internat. Pub. Adminstrn.; adv. com. internat. divsn. GAO, 1979-80. Editor: pub. works sect. Municipal Yearbook Internat. City Mgmt. Assn., 1953-58; cons. editor pub. works sect., Mcpl. Pub. Works Adminstrn., 1957; chmn. adv. bd. Internat. Ctr. Acad. State and Local Govts., 1985-87. Served to 1st lt. USMCR, 1943-45. Mem. ASCE (life), Am. Pub. Works Assn. (hon.), Internat. Pub. Works Fedn. (treas. 1985-89, sec.-gen. 1990), Am. Soc. Assn. Execs., Am. Soc. Pub. Adminstrn., Internat. Union Local Authorities (pres. U.S. sect. 1977-79, v.p. 1968-70, 75-77), Internat. Solid Wastes and Pub. Cleansing Assn. (v.p. 1968-70), Internat. Fedn. Mcpl. Engrs. (treas. 1976-79), Pub. Works Hist. Soc. (hon., treas. 1975-89), Sigma Alpha Epsilon. Baptist. Home: 8238 E Del Cadena Dr Scottsdale AZ 85258-2319 Office: 21st Fl 106 W 11th St Fl 21 Kansas City MO 64105-1831

BUHLER, JILL LORIE, editor, writer; b. Seattle, Dec. 7, 1945; d. Oscar John and Marcella Jane (Hearing) Younce; 1 child, Lori Jill Kelly; m. John Buhler, 1990; stepchildren: Christie, Cathie Vsetecka, Mike. AA in Gen. Edn., Am. River Coll., 1969; BA in Journalism with honors, Sacramento State U., 1973. Reporter Carmichael (Calif.) Courier, 1968-70; mng. editor Quarter Horse of the Pacific Coast, Sacramento, 1970-75, editor, 1975-84; editor Golden State Program Jour., 1978, Nat. Reined Cow Horse Assn. News, Sacramento, 1983-88, Pacific Coast Jour., Sacramento, 1984-88, Nat. Snaffle Bit Assn. News, Sacramento, 1988; pres., chief exec. officer Communications Plus, Port Townsend, Wash., 1988—; mag. cons., 1975—. Interviewer Pres. Ronald Regan, Washington, 1983; mng. editor Wash. Thoroughbred, 1989-90. Mem. 1st profl. communicators mission to USSR, 1988; bd. dirs. Carmichael Winding Way, Pasadena Homeowners Assn., 1985-87; mem. scholarship com. Thoroughbred Horse Racing's United Scholarship Trust; hosp. commr. Jefferson Gen. Hosp., 1995—. Recipient 1st pl. feature award, 1970, 1st pl. editorial award Jour. Assn. Jr. Colls., 1971, 1st pl. design award WCHB Yuba-Sutter Counties, Marysville, Calif., 1985. Mem. Am. River Jaycees (Speaking award 1982), Am. Horse Publs. (1st Pl. Editorial award 1983, 86), Port Townsend C. of C. (trustee, v.p. 1993, pres. 1994, officer 1995), Mensa (bd. dirs., asst. local sec., activities dir. 1987-88, membership chair 1988-90), Kiwanis Internat. (chair MEP com., treas. 1992—), 5th Wheel Touring Soc. (v.p. 1970). Republican. Roman Catholic. Home: 440 Adelma Beach Rd Port Townsend WA 98368-9605

BUI, EUGENE LEE, justice consultant; b. Redding, Calif., Sept. 5, 1936; s. Elmer Nixon and Marguerite Daisy Bui; m. Nancy Esther Dent, Jan. 29, 1970 (div. June 1992); children: David E., Bettina M. BA, Calif. State U., Chico, 1959; postgrad., Police Standards Acad., Salem, Oreg., 1978. Cert. probation and parole officer; cert. tchr., Calif., Oreg. Probation officer Shasta County, Redding, 1964-67; probation supr. Shasta County, Redding, Calif., 1967-68; chief. juv. probation officer Clatsop County, Astoria, Oreg., 1968-70; county adminstr. Clatsop County, 1976-78; crime cons. Nat. Coun. on Crime, Portland, Oreg., 1970-72; justice system coord. Bd. of Commrs., Portland, 1972-74, exec. asst., 1974-76; ptnr. All Am. Security & Investigation, 1993; chief Oreg. Probation/Parole, Portland, 1978-80; nat. traffic safety profl. Portland Police, 1970-80, cons., 1980-81. Bd. dirs. Cmty. Block Grant, Portland, 1986-93, Cmty. Action Agy., Portland, 1985-88; mayor, councilor City of Troutdale, Oreg., 1980-93; 1st v.p. LWV East Multnomah County, 1995; v.p. Oreg. State Law Enforcement Coun., 1968-73; mem. adv. com. Nat. Assn. Counties Justice, 1974-75. Named Outstanding Citizen, Redding C. of C., 1967, Astoria Newspaper, 1970, Outstanding Alumnus, Shasta Coll., 1973. Mem. Oreg. State Sheriff Assn., League of Oreg. Cities, Nat. Assn. Counties, East County Shelter Project, Lions (pres. Troutdale club 1985, Plaque 1986).

BUI, TUAN SY, biomedical company executive, researcher; b. Thanh Hoa, Vietnam, Oct. 16, 1950; came to U.S., 1991; s. Thi Sy and Kim Yen (Tran) B.; m. Chau Bich Phan, Nov. 6, 1973; 1 child, Tuan Huy. BE, Canterbury U., Christchurch, New Zealand, 1972, PhD in Electronics, 1979; MBA, MacQuarie U., Sydney, Australia, 1984. Group leader Ausonics, Sydney, 1980-83, prodn. mgr., 1983-84, chief rsch. engr., 1984-87, mktg. exec., 1987-89; group product mgr. Telectronics, Sydney, 1989-91; internat. product mgt. Telectronics Pacing Systems, Denver, 1991-92, project mgr., 1992-93, dir. ops., 1993—. Patentee in field. Colombo scholar New Zealand Govt., 1968-78. Mem. IEEE (sr.). Office: Telectronics Pacing Systems 7400 S Tucson Way Englewood CO 80112-3938

BUIDANG, GEORGE (HADA BUIDANG), education educator, administrator, consultant, writer; b. Danang, Vietnam, Dec. 30, 1924; came to U.S., 1981; s. Bui Dang Do and Ha Thi Yen; m. Pham Thi Hong, Feb. 25, 1951; children: Bui Tu Long, Bui Nguyen Khanh, Bui Minh Hoang, Bui Thi Tuong Vi. Grad., Providence Inst., Vietnam, 1944. Head translator USMC, 1956-61; dep. employment officer Hdqrs. Support Activity Saigon USN, 1962-65; asst. dir. Cen. Tng. Inst. U.S. Army, Vietnam, 1966; pers. dir. Foremost Dairies Vietnam of Foremost-McKesson Internat., 1966-75; instr. of French Un Bateau Pour L'Asie Du Sud-Est, Brussels, Belgium, 1980; asst. dir. edn. Career Resources Devel. Ctr., Inc., San Francisco, 1981-93; ind. cons. San Francisco, 1993—. Author: Using WordPerfect 5.0, 1989, Using Lotus 1-2-3 Release 2.2., 1991, Using WordPerfect 5.1, 1991, Using Microsoft Windows 3.1, 1993, Using WordPerfect 6.0 for DOS, 1994, Using Lotus 1-2-3 for Windows, 1995, Using WordPerfect for Windows, 1996. Recipient Outstanding Performance award Bd. Dirs., 1987; nominated Internat. Man of Yr. for 1992/1993 Internat. Biographical Centre of Cambridge, Eng. Republican. Roman Catholic. Home: 565 Geary St Apt 411 San Francisco CA 94102-1660 Office: 655 Geary St San Francisco CA 94102-1646

BUIST, NEIL ROBERTSON MACKENZIE, medical educator, medical administrator; b. Karachi, India, July 11, 1932; m. Sonia Chapman; children: Catriona, Alison, Diana. Degree with commendation, U. St. Andrews, Scotland, MB, ChB, 1956; Diploma of Child Health, London U., England, 1960. Diplomate Am. Bd. Med. Genetics, Am. Bd. Clinical Genetics. House physician internal medicine Arbroath Infirmary, 1956-57; house physician externe cardiopulmonary dept. Hosp. Marie Lannelongue, Paris, 1957; house surgeon Royal Hosp. Sick Children, Edinburgh, Scotland, 1957; commd. far east med. officer Regimental Military Svc., 1957-60; house physician Royal Infirmary, Dundee, Scotland, 1960; registrar internal medicine Maryfield Hosp., Dundee, Scotland, 1960-62; lectr. child health U. St. Andrews, Edinburgh, Scotland, 1962-64; rsch. fellow pediatric microchemistry, Sch. Health Sci. U. Colo., Denver, 1964-66; asst. prof. pediatrics, Sch. Medicine U. Oreg., Portland, 1966-70; dir. Pediatrics Metabolic Lab, Oreg. Health Sci. U., Portland, 1966-93, Metabolic Birth Defects Ctr., Oreg. Health Sci. U., Portland, 1966—; assoc. prof. pediatrics and med. genetics Health Sci Ctr., U. Oreg., Portland, 1970-76; prof. pediatrics and med. genetics Oreg. Health Scis. U., 1976—; med. cons. Northwest Regional

Newborn Screening Program, Portland, 1970—; vis. prof. World Health Organization, China, 1988, U. Colo., 1990, Wesley Med. Ctr., Kans., 1991, Phoenix Children's Hosp., Ariz., 1991, Tucson Med. Ctr., Ariz., 1991, U. Ill., Chgo., 1991, Kapoiolani Med. Ctr., Hawaii, 1992, Shriners Hosp. for Crippled Children., Hawaii, 1992,, Ark. Children's Hosp., 1993, Australasian Soc. for Human Genetics, New Zealand, 1994; rsch. com. Oreg. Diabetes Assn., Portland, 1977-88. Author: (with others) Textbook of Pediatrics, 1973, Inherited Disorders of Amino Acid Metabolism, 1974, 1985, Clinics in Endocrinology and Metabolism: Aspects of Neonatal Metabolism, 1976, Textbook of Pediatrics, 1978, Practice of Pediatrics, 1980, Management of High-Risk Pregnancy, 1980, Current Occular Therapy, 1980, Practice of Pediatrics, 1981, Clinics in Endocrinology and Metabolism: Aspects of Neonatal Metabolism, 1981, Textbook of Pediatrics, 1984, SDisorders of Fatty Acid Metabolism in the Pediatric Practice, 1990, Birth Defects Encyclopedia, 1990, 1991, Treatment of Genetic Disease, 1991, Pediatric Clinics of North Americs Medical Genetics II, 1992, Forfar & Arneil's Textbook of Paediatrics, 1992, Galactosemia New Frontiers in Research, 1993, New Horizons in Neonatal Screening, 1994, New Trends in Neonatal Screening, 1994, Alpha-1-Antitrypsin Deficiency, 1994, Diseases of the Fetus and Newborn, 1995, Inborn Metabolic Diseases: Diagnosis and Treatment, 1995; cons. editor: Inborn Metabolic Disease Text, 1995; editorial bd. mem.: Jour. of Inherited Metabolic Diseases, 1977—, Kelley Practice of Pediatrics, 1980-87, Screening, 1991—; jour. reviewer: Am. Jour. of Human Genetics, Jour. of Pediatrics, Pediatric Rsch., Screening. Adv. com. Tri County March of Dimes, Portland, 1977—; physician Diabetic Children's Camp, 1967—, Muscle Biopsy Clinic Shriners Hosp., 1989—; bd. dirs. Mize Info. Enterprises, Dallas, 1987—. Fellow Royal Coll. Physicians, Fogarty Internat. Vis. Scientist; mem. Brit. Med. Assn., Western Soc. Pediatric Rsch. (coun. mem. 1966—), Pacific North West Pediatric Soc., Am. Pediatric Soc., Soc. for the Study of Inborn Errors of Metabolism, Soc. for Inherited Metabolic Disorders (treas. 1977—), Oreg. Pediatric Soc., Oreg. Diabetes Assn., Portland Acad. Pediatrics, Internat. Newborn Screening Soc. Coun. (founding mem. 1988—). Office: Oreg Health Sci U 3181 SW Sam Jackson Pk Rd L473 Portland OR 97201-3098

BUKOWINSKI, MARK STEFAN TADEUSZ, geophysics educator; b. Trani, Italy, Oct. 17, 1946; came to U.S., 1962; s. Stanley K. and Jadwiga Teresa (Jezierski) B.; m. Halina V. Mudy, June 20, 1970; children: Katherine, Anne, John, Christopher. BS in Physics, UCLA, 1969, PhD in Physics, 1975. Asst. rsch. geophysicist Inst. Geophysics and Planetary Physics, UCLA, 1975-78; asst. prof. U. Calif., Berkeley, 1978-82, assoc. prof., 1982-89, prof., 1989—. Assoc. editor Jour. Geophys. Rsch., 1988-91; mem. bd. editors Phys. Earth Planetary Interiors, 1992—; contbr. over 50 articles to sci. jours. NSF grantee, 1976—, Inst. Geophysics and Planetary Physics. Mem. AAAS, Am. Geophys. Union (mem. mineral physics com. 1988-90), Mineralog. Soc. Am. (mem. publs. com. 1988-91, chair 1991-92). Home: 5738 Laurelwood Pl Concord CA 94521-4807 Office: U Calif Berkeley Dept Geology and Geophysics Berkeley CA 94720

BULICK, WILLARD JAMES, project management and safety engineer; b. Adrain, Minn., Nov. 5, 1935; s. Russell W. and Minta (Thompson) B.; m. Nellie W. Mitchell, Feb. 21, 1960 (div. May 1979); children: Debra, James; m. Susan B. Beucler, Feb. 22, 1982; children: Allen, Daniel, Sandra. B in Mineral Engring., U. Minn., 1964. From project mgr. to asst. project dir. Morrison-Knudsen Co., Boise, 1974-76; project svcs. mgr. Exxon Minerals Co., Houston, 1976-85; cons. engr., 1986-87; cost engr. Tex. Eastern Gas Pipeline Co., Houston, 1987-89; project controls mgr. PATSCO, Anchorage, Alaska, 1989—. Author: Project Scheduling Manual, 1981, Investment Estimate Classification System, 1981, Project Evaluation Procedures, 1992. Pres. Southpark Homeowners Assn., Anchorage, Alaska, 1991-93, v.p. 1993-94. Served in U.S. Army, 1958-60. Mem. Am. Inst. Mining Engrs., Project Mgmt. Inst. (certification com. 1991-93), Am. Soc. Safety Engrs. (prof. mem.), Am. Assn. Cost Engrs. (cert. 1992). Home: 500 Stenton Ave Plymouth Meeting PA 19462-1231

BULL, BRIAN STANLEY, pathology educator, medical consultant, business executive; b. Watford, Hertfordshire, Eng., Sept. 14, 1937; came to U.S., 1954, naturalized, 1960; s. Stanley and Agnes Mary (Murdoch) B.; m. Maureen Hannah Huse, June 3, 1963; children: Beverly Velda, Beryl Heather. B.S. in Zoology, Walla Walla Coll., 1957; M.D., Loma Linda (Calif.) U., 1961. Diplomate: Am. Bd. Pathology. Intern Yale U., 1961-62, resident in anat. pathology, 1962-63; resident in clin. pathology NIH, Bethesda, Md., 1963-65; fellow in hematology and electron microscopy NIH, 1965-66, staff hematologist, 1966-67; research asst. dept. anatomy Loma Linda U., 1958, dept. microbiology, 1959, asst. prof. pathology, 1968-71, assoc. prof., 1971-73, prof., 1973—, chmn. dept. pathology, 1973—, assoc. dean for acad. affairs sch. medicine, 1993-94, dean sch. medicine, 1994—; cons. to mfrs. of med. testing devices; mem. panel on hematology FDA; mem. Nat. Com. on Clin Lab. Standards; mem. Internat. Commn. for Standards in Hematology. Bd. editors Blood Cells, Molecules and Diseases; contbr. chpts. to books and numerous articles to med. jours.; patentee in field. Served with USPHS, 1963-67. Nat. Inst. Arthritis and Metabolic Diseases fellow, 1967-68; recipient Daniel D. Comstock Meml. award Loma Linda U., 1961, Merck Manual award, 1961, Mosby Scholarship Book award, 1961; Ernest B. Cotlove Meml. lectr. Acad. Clin. Lab. Physicians and Scientists, 1972. Fellow Am. Soc. Clin. Pathologists, Am. Soc. Hematology, Nat. Com. on Clin. Lab. Stds., Internat. Commn. for Stds. in Hematology, N.Y. Acad. Scis.; mem. AMA, Calif. Soc. Pathologists, San Bernardino County Med. Soc., Acad. Clin. Lab. Physicians and Scientists, Am. Assn. Pathologists, Sigma Xi, Alpha Omega Alpha. Seventh-day Adventist. Office: Loma Linda U Sch Medicine 11234 Anderson St Loma Linda CA 92354-2804

BULL, HENRIK HELKAND, architect; b. N.Y.C., July 13, 1929; s. Johan and Sonja (Geelmuyden) B.; m. Barbara Alpaugh, June 9, 1956; children: Peter, Nina. B.Arch., Mass. Inst. Tech., 1952. With Mario Corbett, San Francisco, 1954-55; pvt. practice, 1956-68; ptnr. Bull, Field, Volkmann, Stockwell, Calif., 1968-82, Bull, Volkmann, Stockwell, Calif., 1982-90, Bull Stockwell and Allen, Calif., 1990-93, Bull, Stockwell, Allen & Ripley, San Francisco, 1993—; Vis. lectr. Syracuse U., 1963; Mem. adv. com. San Francisco Urban Design Study, 1970-71. Works include Sunset mag. Discovery House, Tahoe Tavern Condominiums, Lake Tahoe, Calif., Snowmass Villas Condominiums, Aspen, Colo., Northstar Master Plan Village and Condominiums, Moraga Valley Presbyn. Ch., Calif., Spruce Saddle Restaurant and Poste-Montane Hotel, Beaver Creek, Colo., Bear Valley visitor ctr., Point Reyes, Calif., The Inn at Spanish Bay, Pebble Beach, Calif., Taluswood Cmty., Whistler, B.C. Served as 1st lt. USAF, 1952-54. Winner competition for master plan new Alaska capital city, Willow, 1978. Fellow AIA (pres. N. Calif. chpt. 1968, Firm award Calif. chpt. 1989). Democrat. Office: Bull Stockwell Allen Ripley 350 Pacific Ave San Francisco CA 94111-1708

BULL, JOHN CARRAWAY, JR., plastic surgeon; b. Raleigh, Sept. 21, 1934; s. John Carraway and Coralee Bull; m. Ann Bull, June 28, 1958; children: Virginia S., Kristin L., Natalie E., John C. III. MD, Harvard U., 1960. Diplomate Am. Bd. Surgery, Am. Bd. Plastic Surgery. Intern med. sch. hosp. U. Oreg.; resident in gen. surgery U. Calif., San Francisco; resident in plastic surgery Johns Hopkins; pvt. practice specializing in plastic surgery Phoenix, 1970-86; v.p. med. affairs St. Joseph Hosp. & Med. Ctr., Phoenix, 1986—. Lt. USN, 1961-64. NIH awardee, 1970. Fellow ACS; mem. Am. Coll. Physician Execs., Am. Coll. Health Care Execs., Ariz. Med. Assn. (Disting. Svc. award 1986), Maricopa County Med. Soc. (Disting. Svc. award 1981), Harvard Club. Office: Saint Joseph Hosp & Med Ctr 350 W Thomas Rd Phoenix AZ 85013-4409

BULL, NANCY ANN, publishing executive; b. Muskegon, Mich., Nov. 9; d. Kenneth Earnest and Pauline Fern (Morrison) B. Ed. Kalamazoo Coll. UCLA, Detroit Inst. Tech. Customer mgr. Styker Corp., Kalamazoo; mktg. mgr. Circon Corp., Santa Barbara, Calif.; prod. mgr. Hall Surg. Systems, Santa Barbara; now pres. Vet. Practice Pub. Co., Santa Barbara; mem. feline adv. bur. Cornell U., Ithaca, N.Y. Mem. comml. revitalization task force East Beach Homeowners Assn. Mem. Am. Vet. Exhibitors Assn. (past pres.), Mission Canyon Homeowners Assn., Am. Animal Hosp. Assn. (assoc.), various other local, state and nat. profl. and civic orgns. Clubs: Coral Casino Beach (Santa Barbara). Home: PO Box 5101 Santa Barbara CA 93150-5101 Office: PO Box 4457 Santa Barbara CA 93140

BULLARD, DONALD LEE, health facility administrator; b. Gary, Ind., Oct. 12, 1951; s. Donald Elvin and Mary Evelyn (Maris) B.; 1 child, Trinity Ann. AB, U. Calif., Berkeley, 1978, MPH, 1980. Commd. 2d lt. USAF, 1980, advanced through grades to lt. col., 1995; aeromed. staging officer USAF, Travis AFB, Calif., 1980-81; intern-in-tng. AFELM HFO-WR Air Force Element, Health Facilities Office, Western Region, San Francisco, 1981-82; project health facilities officer USAF, George AFB, Calif., 1982-86, Osan AB, Republic of Korea, 1986-87; sr. health facilities officer USAF, Travis AFB, 1987-89; regional health facilities officer USAF, San Francisco, 1989-90; sr. health facilities programmer OASD (HA) DMFO Office of Asst. Sec. Def., Def. Med. Facilities Office, Falls Church, Va., 1990-93; sr. health facilities programmer Office of Asst. Sec. Def., Resource Mgmt. Office, Falls Church, Va., 1993-94; managed health care intern SAIC, San Diego, 1994-95; ops. officer Med. Support Squadron, Sheppard AFB, Tex., 1995—; assoc. adminstr. 82d Med. Group, Sheppard AFB, 1995—. Author: California License and Certification Guide, 1978. Belknap Fund scholar Howard Inst., 1975. Fellow Health Facilities Inst.; mem. Nat. Fire Protection Assn., Am. Soc. for Hosp. Engring. Byzantine Catholic. Office: SAIC 149 Hart St Ste 1 Sheppard AFB TX 76311

BULLARD, RICHARD FORREST, mathematics educator; b. Seattle, July 3, 1937; s. Harold C. and Hazel (Andersen) B.; m. Mary E. Day, June 29, 1963; children: Elizabeth, Lisa, Christopher. BS, U. Wash., 1959, MS, 1961; postgrad., Calif. State U., Sacramento, 1967. Instr. math. San Joaquin Delta Coll., Stockton, Calif., 1964-67, rsch. asst., 1967-69, dir. fin. aid, 1969-80, instr. math., 1980-94. Pres. bd. dirs. 1st Unitarian Ch., Stockton, 1980-82; exec. sec. Weberstown Homes Assn., Stockton, 1982-94. Recipient Disting. Faculty award San Joaquin Delta Coll., 1994. Mem. San Joaquin Delta Coll. Found. (exec. sec. 1975-80), Calif. Assn. of Student Aid Adminstrs. (treas. 1976-77), Calif. Community Coll. Student Aid Adminstrs. (pres. 1977-78), San Joaquin Delta Coll. Tchrs. Assn. (pres. 1986-87), Masons, Order DeMolay (Legion of Honor 1962). Democrat.

BULLARD, SHARON WELCH, librarian; b. San Diego, Nov. 4, 1943; d. Dale L. and Myrtle (Sampson) Welch; m. Donald H. Bullard, Aug. 1, 1969. B.S.Ed., U. Central Ark., 1965; M.A., U. Denver, 1967. Media specialist Adams County Sch. Dist. 12, Denver, 1967-69; tchr., libr. Humphrey pub. schs., Ark., 1965-66, libr., 1969-70; catalog libr. Ark. State U., Jonesboro, 1970-75; head documents cataloging Wash. State U., Pullman, 1979-83; head serials cataloging U. Calif.-Santa Barbara Davidson Libr., 1984-88, head circulation dept., 1988—; cons. Ctr. for Robotic Systems Microelectronics Rsch. Libr., Santa Barbara, 1986, Calif. State Libr. retrospective conversion project, 1987, Ombudsman's Office U. Calif., Santa Barbara, 1988; distributor Amway, 1985-91. Canvasser, Citizens for Goleta Valley, 1985-86. Mem. ALA, Calif. Libr. Assn. (tech. svcs. chpt. southern Calif. sect.), Libr. Assn. U. Calif.-Santa Barabara (mem. subcom. on advancement and promotion 1987-91), NAFE, So. Calif. Tech. Processes Group (membership com. 1987), Assn. Coll. and Rsch. Librs. (intern membership com. 1993-94), Libr. Adminstrn. and Mgmt. Assn. (mem. circulation/access svcs. systems and svcs. sect. 1993—, mem. equipment com. bldg. and equipment sect. 1993—), Notis Users Circulation Interest Group (presenter meeting 1992, mem. CIRC SIG steering com. 1993—, moderator meeting 1993—, chair elect 1994—), Pi Lambda Theta (exec. bd., sec. Santa Barbara chpt. 1990-91, hospitality com. 1991-92). Avocations: t'ai chi, walking, camping, boogey boarding, swimming.

BULLICK, KAREN FAYE, dietitian; b. L.A., Aug. 11, 1964; d. Ralph and Pearl Ellen (Harris) B. BS in Psychology, Brigham Young U., 1987; BS in Nutrition summa cum laude, Calif. State U., Long Beach, 1990; MS in Nutrition, U. Wash., 1993. Registered dietitian. Nutrition specialist Evans-Kraft Advt. and Pub. Rels. Agy., Seattle, 1991-92; cons. dietitian in pvt. practice Huntington Beach, Calif., 1992—; cons. dietitian for long-term health care facilities Huntington Beach, 1992—; speaker in field. Brigham Young U. scholar, 1983-87, U. Wash. scholar, 1993. Mem. Am. Dietetic Assn. (legis. network 1992-93), Am. Soc. Parenteral and Enteral Nutrition, Sierra Club, Toastmasters Internat., Phi Kappa Phi. Mormon. Home: 34026 Selva Rd Unit 66 Dana Point CA 92629-3762

BULLIS, MICHAEL A., hotel executive; b. Pensacola, Fla., Aug. 24, 1947; s. Jerell W. Sr. and W. Joyce (Watson) B.; children: Shannon Renee Bullis Ray, Katrina Celeste. BBA, Sam Houston State U., 1969. Gen. mgr. Nat. Hotel Co., Galveston, Tex., 1969-74, Hospitality Mgmt. Corp., Dallas, 1974-78; mng. dir. Claremont Resort Hotel & Tennis Club, Oakland, Calif., 1978-82; pres. Wrather Hotels & Wrather Mgmt. Co., Anaheim, Calif., 1982-89, Destination Properties, Inc., Newport Beach, Calif., 1989-94; v.p. Hanjin Internat., gen. mgr. Omni L.A. Hotel & Ctr., 1995—. Dir. Gov.'s Coun. on Tourism, Calif.; mem. Calif. Tourism Bd.; dir. Disney Pigskin Classic and Freedom Bowl. 1st lt. U.S. Army Nat. Guard. Mem. Calif. Hotel & Motel Assn. (pres., chmn., co-chmn. polit. action com., mem. strategic planning com., mem. ednl. inst. audit com., chmn. mktg. task force and membership com.), Orange County Sports Assn., Anaheim Visitor & Convention Bur. (chmn.), Huntington Beach Conf. & Visitors Bur. (dir.), Huntington Beach C. of C. Republican. Home and Office: 2133 Miramar Dr Newport Beach CA 92661 Office: Destination Properties 2133 Miramar Dr Balboa CA 92661-1518

BULLOCK, DONALD WAYNE, elementary education educator, educational computing consultant; b. Tacoma Park, Md., Mar. 24, 1947; s. B.W. and Margaret (Harris) B.; m. Pamela Louise Hatch, Aug. 7, 1971. AA in Music, L.A. Pierce Coll., Woodland Hills, Calif., 1969; BA in Geography, San Fernando Valley State Coll., 1971; Cert. Computer Edn., Calif. Luth. U., 1985, MA in Curriculum-Instrn., 1987. Tchr. music Calvary Luth. Sch., Pacoima, Calif., 1970-71; elem. tchr. 1st Luth. Sch., Northridge, Calif., 1971-73; elem. tchr. Simi Valley (Calif.) Unified Sch. Dist., 1973—, computer insvc. instr., 1982-85, computer mentor tchr., 1985-87, mentor tchr. ednl. tech., 1992-95; lectr. Calif. Luth. U., Thousand Oaks, 1985-92; ednl. computer cons. DISC Ednl. Svcs., Simi Valley, 1985—; speaker profl. confs. Contbr. articles to profl. publs. Pres. Amen Choir, Van Nuys, Calif., 1981-83. Recipient Computer Learning Month grand prize Tom Snyder Prodns., 1988, Computer Learning Found., 1990, Spl. Commendation of Achievement, Learning mag. profl. best tchr. excellence awards, 1990, Impact II Disseminator award Ventura County Supt. of Schs. and Ventura County Econ. Devel. Assn., 1995; grantee Tandy-Radio Shack, Inc., 1985, Calif. Dep. Edn., 1985. Mem. NEA, ASCD, Internat. Soc. Tech. in Edn., Computer Using Educators Calif., Gold Coast Computer Using Educators (bd. dirs. 1988-89), Basset Hound Club Am., Basset Hound Club So. Calif. (bd. dirs. 1994—). Home: 2805 Wanda Ave Simi Valley CA 93065-1528 Office: Garden Grove Elem Sch 2250 Tracy Ave Simi Valley CA 93063

BULLOCK, GAYLE NELSON, healthcare executive; b. Mpls., Sept. 16, 1952; d. Leslie A. and Joyce (Olson) Nelson; m. William J. Bullock; children: Leslie, Kendall. Student, U. Santa Clara, 1970-72; BA, UCLA, 1974; MPA, U. So. Calif., 1976. Rsch. assoc. Tech. Systems Inst., L.A., 1975-76; asst. adminstr. Cedars-Sinai Med. Ctr., L.A., 1976-79; assoc. adminstr. South Bay Hosp., Redondo Beach, Calif., 1979-84; sr. v.p. corp. devel. Robert F. Kennedy Med. Ctr., Hawthorne, Calif., 1984-85; pres., chief exec. officer St. Jude Hosp., Yorba Linda, Calif., 1985-89; regional v.p. St. Joseph Health System, Orange, Calif., 1989; sr. v.p. Long Beach (Calif.) Meml. Med. Ctr., 1989-90; pres., chief exec. officer Neurocare of Orange County, Inc., Irvine, Calif., 1991—. Fellow Am. Coll. Healthcare Execs. (Calif. regents adv. com., Robert S. Hudgens Meml. award com. 1989-90); mem. Health care Execs. So. Calif. (bd. dirs.), Hosp. Coun. So. Calif. (bd. dirs.), Hosp. Home Health Care Agy. Calif. (bd. dirs.), Women in Health Adminstrn. So. Calif. (bd. dirs.), Delta Gamma Alumnae. Republican. Roman Catholic. Home: 136 Starcrest Irvine CA 92715-3627

BULLOCK, JAMES BENBOW, sculptor; b. St. Louis, Feb. 6, 1929; s. James Absalom and Rosalind Julia (Hausberger) B.; m. Jean Audrey Peageans, May 31, 1952; children: Richard Benbow, Sarah Jean, Carol Ann. BA, Wesleyan U. Prin. works exhibited in numerous one-man and group shows including Gensler & Assocs., 1993, Marathon Plaza, San Francisco, 1993, Art Concepts Gallery and Contra Costa Coun., Walnut Creek, Calif., 1992, Pacific Design Ctr., L.A., 1992, Contract Design Ctr., San Francisco, 1991, Palm Springs Desert Mus., 1994, SOMAR Gallery, San Francisco, 1993, others; works represented in numerous collections including AT&T, San Francisco, Gov.'s Mansion, Santa Fe, N.Mex., Bramalea Pacific Corp., Oakland, Calif. With USCG, 1951. Recipient Royal Mus. award Hakone Open Air Mus., 1989, 2d prize Festival des Arts, France, 1994. Home: 12 Sandy Beach Rd Vallejo CA 94590-8122

BULLOCK, LOUISE ANN, information consultant; b. Phila., Dec. 20, 1942; d. Robert W. and Helen E. (Melvin) Marley; m. Lawrence A. Laurich, Oct. 29, 1993. BS, Pa. State U., 1964; MEd, Tufts U., 1967; MBA, San Jose State U., 1985. Nutritionist Harvard Sch. Pub. Health, Roxbury, Mass., 1966; nutritionist Frances Stern Nutrition Clinic New Eng. Med. Ctr. Hosps., Boston, 1966; nutritionist Boston Hosp. for Women, 1966; dir. dept. edn. New Eng. Dairy and Food Coun., Boston, 1967-72; dir. dietetic internship and insvc. program Presbyn. Hosp. Dallas, 1972-81; founder, pres., chief exec. officer Custom Info. Searches, Inc., San Jose, Calif., 1986—; ptnr. OMT Group, Santa Clara, Calif., 1993—. Author: Dietetic Internship, 1981. Fed. Govt. grantee, 1981. Mem. Am. Dietetic Assn. (chmn. ednl. standards 1978-79, chmn. coun. edn. 1980-81), Calif. Dietetic Assn., Silicon Valley Entrepreneurs Club. Republican. Episcopalian. Office: OMT Group 2700 Augustine Dr Ste 242 Santa Clara CA 95054-2911 Office: Custom Info Searches Inc 2700 Augustine Dr Ste 242 Santa Clara CA 95054-2911

BULLOCK, MOLLY, educator; d. Wiley and Annie M. Jordan; m. George Bullock; children: Myra A. Bauman, Dawn M. BS in Edn., No. Ariz. U., 1955, postgrad., 1958; postgrad., LaVerne U., 1962, Claremont Grad. Sch., 1963, Calif. State U. L.A., 1966. Tchr. Bur. Indian Affairs, Kaibeto, Ariz., 1955-56, Crystal, N.Mex., 1956-59; tchr. Covina (Calif.) Valley Unified Sch. Dist., 1961—, supervising master tchr. for trainees of LaVerne U. and Calif. State U. - L.A., 1961-71, mem. curriculum devel. adv. bd., 1977-79. Poet: A Tree (Golden Poet 1991), What is Love (Golden medal of honor). Mini grantee Hughes/Rotary Club/Foothill Ind. Bank, Covina, 1986-90. Mem. ASCD, NEA, NAFE, AAUW (treas. 1972), Internat. Platform Assn., Internat. Soc. Poets (hon. charter mem.), Calif. Tchrs. Assn. Home: 2175 Victoria Way Pomona CA 91767-2371

BULLOCK, RICHARD LEE, mining engineer; b. Kansas City, Mo., July 24, 1929; s. Royce Franklin and Ruby Lee (Dyer) B.; m. Jacqueline Hyer Leavitt, Nov. 11, 1951 (div. 1970); children: Richard Leavitt, Denise Muriel; m. Janice Fay Walker; 1 stepdaughter, Jeliane Prentise Wiseman. BS in Mining Engring., Mo. Sch. Mines, 1951, MS, 1955; D of Engring. in Mining, U. Mo., Rolla, 1975. Registered profl. engr., Mo., Nev. Mine engr. N.J. Zinc Co., Gilman, Colo., 1951-52; from mine rsch. engr. to corp. dir. mine R&D St. Joe Mineral Corp., various cities, 1955-77; mgr. mine evaluation and devel. Exxon Minerals Co. USA, Houston, 1977-80; v.p. engring., tech. and rsch. Exxon Mineral Corp., Houston, 1980-82, mgr. mine engring., sr. staff advisor, 1983-86; project exec. Los Bronces project La Desputada Lia Mineria (Exxon), Houston, Santiago, Chile, 1982-83; tech. advisor, project mgr. Raytheon Svc. Nev., Las Vegas, 1986-94, ret., 1994; mining cons., 1995; mem. operating com. Tenn. Consol. Coal Co., Jasper, 1976-77, Carthage (Tenn.) Zinc Co., 1976-77; mem. adv. bd. generic rsch. com. U.S. Bur. Mines and Va. Poly. Inst. and State U., Blacksburg, 1983-94. Contbr. articles to profl. jours. and chpts. to books. Pres. Iron County (Mo.) Sch. Bd., 1968-74; mem. C-4 Dist. Sch. Bd., Viburnum, Mo., 1970-74; mem. Nat. Def. Exec. Res. U.S. Dept. Interior, Washington, 1972-82. Cpl. U.S. Army, 1952-54. Mem. Soc. Mining Engrs. (Disting. Svc. award 1991), Soc. Explosive Engrs., Internat. High Level Radioactive Waste Mgmt. Conf. (steering com. 1990-94). Home: 9548 World Cup Dr Las Vegas NV 89117-0813

BULLOUGH, VERN LEROY, nursing educator, historian, sexologist, researcher; b. Salt Lake City, July 24, 1928; s. D. Vernon Bullough and Augusta Rueckert; m. Bonnie Uckerman, Aug. 2, 1947; children: David, James, Steven, Susan, Michael. BSN, Calif. State U., Long Beach, 1981; BS, U. Utah, 1951; MA, U. Chgo., 1951, PhD, 1954. Dean, faculty of nat. and social scis. SUNY, Buffalo, disting. prof. emeritus; vis. prof. U. So. Calif., 1994—. Author, co-author of more than 40 books; sr. editor Free Inquiry; contbr. more than 200 articles to profl. jours. With U.S. Army Security Agy., 1946-48. Named Oustanding Prof. Calif. State U. sys., Disting. Prof., SUNY; recipient Kinsey award. Fellow Am. Acad. Nursing, Soc. Sci. Study Sex (past pres.), Acad. Humanism (laureate); mem. Internat. Humanist and Ethical Union (pres.).

BULMER, CONNIE J., film librarian; b. Seattle, Jan. 22, 1931; d. George Arthur and Helen Harriet (Braman) Bulmer. Librarian Republic Studios, Studio City, Calif., 1950-54; head librarian Revue Prodns.-Universal Studios, Studio City, 1954-61, Twentieth Century Fox, Beverly Hills, Calif., 1961-62, Selmur Prodns., Culver City, Calif., 1963-68, Hope Enterprises, Burbank, Calif., 1968-71, Paramount Studios, Hollywood, 1972—. Mem. Acad. TV Arts and Scis., Motion Picture-Videotape Editors, Am. Film Inst. Office: Paramount Pictures 5555 Melrose Ave Los Angeles CA 90038-3149

BULTMANN, WILLIAM ARNOLD, historian; b. Monrovia, Calif., Apr. 10, 1922; s. Paul Gerhardt and Elsa (Johnson) B.; AB, UCLA, 1943, PhD, 1950; m. Phyllis Jane Wetherell, Dec. 28, 1949; 1 child, Janice Jane. Assoc. prof. history Central Ark. U., Conway, 1949-52, prof., 1954-57; assoc. prof. Ohio Wesleyan U., Delaware, 1957-61, prof., 1961-65; prof. Western Wash. U., Bellingham, 1965-87, chmn. dept., 1968-70, dean arts and scis., 1970-72, provost, 1971-73; vis. assoc. prof. U. Tex., Austin, 1952-53; vis. prof. U. N.H., summers 1965, 66; acad. cons. Wash. Commn. for Humanities, 1973-87, Nat. Endowment for Humanities, 1976-87; reader Ednl. Testing Service Princeton, 1973-85. Bd. dirs. Bellingham Maritime Heritage Found., 1980-85; mem. The Nature Conservancy, 1992—, Washington Arboretum Found., 1992—; adminstrv. officer Bellingham Power Squadron, 1981-82, comdr., 1982-84. Fulbright sr. lectr. Dacca (Bangladesh) U., 1960-61; Ohio Wesleyan U. rsch. fellow, 1964; Fund for Advancement Edn. fellow for fgn. study, 1953-54; recipient rsch. award Social Sci. Rsch. Coun., 1957. Mem. AAUP. Am. Hist. Assn., Nat. Tropical Botanical Garden Soc., Nat. Boating Fedn., Wash. Arboretum Found., Ch. Hist. Soc., Conf. Brit. Studies, Pacific, Pacific N.W. confs. Brit. studies, Mystery Writers of Am., Interclub Boating Assn. Washington, Seattle Power Squadron, Phi Beta Kappa, Phi Delta Kappa, Pi Gamma Mu. Episcopalian. Clubs: Park Athletic Recreation, Bellingham Yacht (chmn. pub. rels. com. 1981-86), Squalicum Yacht (trustee 1979-82), Birch Bay Yacht; Wash. Athletic. Co-author: Border Boating, 1978; co-founder, mem. editorial bd. Albion, 1968-84; mng. editor Brit. Studies Intelligencer, 1973-80; co-editor Current Research in British Studies, 1975; editor Jib Sheet, 1981-86; feature writer, columnist Sea mag., 1974—; feature writer Venture mag., 1981-85, Poole Publs., 1988—. Home: 1600 43rd Ave E Apt 101 Seattle WA 98112-3245

BUMBAUGH, ROBERT WARREN, SR., oil industry executive; b. L.A., Sept. 8, 1937; s. Warren Herbert and Nina May (Browning) B.; m. Betty Jean Harkless, Apr. 14, 1956; children: Robert Warren Jr., Scott Arthur, Cheryllyn Jean. Student, Santa Ana (Calif.) Jr. Coll., 1960-62, Orange Coast Coll., 1965-66, Kenai Peninsula Coll., 1989-92. Cert. journeyman painter, CPR, internat. coating inspector. Painter Garden Grove (Calif.) Unified Sch. Dist., 1964-67, Kent (Ohio) U., 1968-69, Nicholas and Nicholas Painting, Orange, Calif., 1969-70, Stockwell Painting Contractors, 1970-71; owner, operator Bumbaugh's Painting, 1971-79; painter Sledge & Son Painting, 1979-81; painter, foreman Roger's Alaskan Painting, 1981-83; owner, operator Bumbaugh's Alaskan Enterprises, 1983-86; foreman Wade Oilfield Svc. Co., Inc., 1986-89; supr. Alaska Petroleum Contractors, Nikiski, 1989—. Bd. dirs. Ch. of Nazarene, Coeur d' Alene, Idaho, 1947-94. Home: PO Box 3727 Soldotna AK 99669-3727 Office: Alaska Petroleum Contractor PO Box 8113 Nikiski AK 99635-8113

BUMGARDNER, LARRY G., foundation administrator, communications educator; b. Chattanooga, June 10, 1957; s. Walter G. and Kathryn (Hamrick) B. BA, David Lipscomb Coll., 1977; JD, Vanderbilt U., 1981. Bar: Tenn. 1981, U.S. Dist. Ct. (cen. dist.) Tenn. 1982, Calif. 1984, U.S. Dist. Ct. (cen. dist.) Calif. 1985. From reporter to copy editor Nashville (Tenn.) Banner, 1975-79; editor Tenn. Attorneys Memo, Tenn. Jour., Nashville, 1979-83; dir. founds. Pepperdine U., Malibu, Calif., 1983-85, asst. v.p. comm. and grants, 1985-92, assoc. vice chancellor for founds. and rsch., asst. prof. comms., 1992-94, adj. prof. of law, 1994—; dep. dir. Ronald Reagan Presdl. Found., Simi Valley, Calif., 1994—. Contbr. numerous articles to various publs. Mem. ABA, Calif. Bar Assn. Home: 2700 Westham Cir Thousand Oaks CA 91362 Office: 40 Presidential Dr Simi Valley CA 93065

BUMILLER, TRINE ROBERTS, artist; b. Cin., Mar. 12, 1959; d. Theodore Roberts Bumiller and Gunhild Elken Møller Rose; m. Kurt Raymond Monigle, May 25, 1985; children: Elspeth, Kora. BFA, R.I. Sch. Design, 1981. Exhbn. curator Seibu Art Mus., Tokyo and N.Y.C., 1981-82; art gallery asst. Betty Parsons Galley, N.Y.C., 1982-83; asst. dir. Jack Tilton Gallery, N.Y.C., 1983-85; fine art printer Jeryl Parker Edits., N.Y.C., 1985-86; artist, specializing in oil painting Denver, 1986—; artist-in-residence Yaddo, Saratoga Springs, N.Y., 1991, Walden (Colo.) Elem. Sch., 1994, Park Hill Elem. Sch., Denver, 1994; guest art critic Art Students League, Denver, 1994; assoc. artist Rocky Mountain Women's Inst., Denver, 1992-93. Commd. artist Colo. Icons, 1994. Mentor, Denver Pub. Schs., 1994; instr. art Montessori Sch., Denver, 1993-94. Recipient Arts Innovation award Colo. Fedn. Arts, 1994. Mem. Alliance for Contemporary Art. Home: 1701 Forest Pky Denver CO 80220-1333

BUNCHMAN, HERBERT HARRY, II, plastic surgeon; b. Washington, Feb. 23, 1942; s. Herbert H. and Mary (Halleran) B.; m. Marguerite Fransioli, Mar. 21, 1963 (div. Jan. 1987); children: Herbert H. III., Angela K., Christopher. BA, Vanderbilt U., 1964; MD, U. Tenn., 1967. Diplomate Am. Bd. Surgery, Am. bd. Plastic Surgery. Resident in surgery U. Tex., Galveston, 1967-72, resident in plastic surgery, 1972-75; practice medicine specializing in plastic surgery Mesa, Ariz., 1975—; chief surgery Desert Samaritan Hosp., 1978-80. Contbr. articles to profl. jours. Eaton Clin. fellow, 1975. Mem. AMA, Am. Soc. Plastic and Reconstructive Surgery, Am. Soc. Aesthetic Plastic Surgery, Singleton Surgical Soc., Tex. Med. Assn., So. Med. Assn. (grantee 1974), Ariz. Med. Assn. Office: Plastic Surgery Cons PC 1520 S Dobson Rd Ste 314 Mesa AZ 85202-4727

BUNDESEN, FAYE STIMERS, investment and management company owner, educator; b. Cedarville, Calif., Sept. 16, 1932; d. Floyd Walker and Ermina Elizabeth (Roberts) Stimers; m. Allen Eugene Bundesen, Dec. 27, 1972 (dec. 1991); children: William, David, Edward Silvius; Ted, Eric Bundesen. BA, Calif. State U.-Sacramento, 1955; MA, Calif. State U.-San Jose, 1972. Licensed real estate broker, Calif. Elem. sch. tchr. San Francisco Pub. Schs., 1955-60; elem. and jr. h.s. tchr., lang. arts specialist Sunnyvale (Calif.) Schs., 1978-83; cons. Santa Clara County Office of Edn. and Sunnyvale Sch. Dist., 1983-86; v.p. Bundesen Enterprises, Elk Grove, Calif., 1975-81, pres., 1981—. Bd. dirs. Sunnyvale Sch. Employees' Credit Union, 1983-86, v.p., 1984-86; co-chmn. Elk Grove Taxpayers Assn. for Incorporation, 1994; pres. Elk Grove/Laguna Civic League, 1994—; pers. chmn. Bethany Presbyn. Ch., 1992-95; mem. City of San Jose Tenant/Landlord Hearing Com., 1983-86, v.p., 1984-85. Mem. Assn. Supervision and Curriculum Devel., Calif. Scholarship Fedn. (life), AAUW, Calif. Apartment Assn., Nat. Apartment Assn., Calif. Assn. Realtors, Nat. Assn. Realtors, Sacramento Assn. Realtors, Sacramento Valley Apt. Assn., Soroptimist Internat. Rio Cosumnes, Elk Grove C. of C. Presbyterian. Office: PO Box 2006 Elk Grove CA 95759-2006

BUNGE, RUSSELL KENNETH, writer; b. Long Beach, Calif., Apr. 28, 1947; s. Kenneth Duncan Bunge and Mona Irene (Deleree) Coker. BA in Creative Writing, Calif. State U., Long Beach, 1972; MA in Humanities, Calif. State U., Dominguez Hills, 1985. Cert. C.C. tchr., Calif. Spl. svcs. cons. AT&T Comms., San Luis Obispo, Calif., 1973-90; info. cons. Obispo Info. Group, San Luis Obispo, 1990-95; mem. adv. bd. Calif. Online Resources for Edn., Long Beach, 1993-94. Author: Double Lives: Poems 1984-85, 1985; contbr. poems to profl. publs. Founding mem. AIDS Support Network, San Luis Obispo, 1984. Mem. MLA, Assn. for Computers and Humanities. Office: SLONET Cmty Edn PO Box 15818 San Luis Obispo CA 93406-5818

BUNKER, JOHN BIRKBECK, cattle rancher, retired sugar company executive; b. Yonkers, N.Y., Mar. 28, 1926; s. Ellsworth and Harriet (Butler) B.; m. Emma Cadwalader, Feb. 27, 1954; children: Emma, Jeanie, Harriet, John C., Lambert C. BA, Yale U., 1950. With Nat. Sugar Refining Co., 1953-62; pres. Gt. Western Sugar Co., Denver, 1966; pres., CEO Holly Sugar Co., Colorado Springs, Colo., 1967-81, chmn., CEO, 1971-81; pres., CEO Calif. and Hawaiian Sugar Co., San Francisco, 1981-88, vice chmn., 1988-89, ret., 1989; gen. ptnr. Bunker Ranch Co., 1989—; chmn. Wheatland Bankshares and First State Bank of Wheatland, 1992—. Trustee Colo. Coll., 1973-94, Asia Found., 1985-94. Mem. Wyo. Nature Conservancy, Wyo. Stockgrowers Assn., Wyo. Heritage Found., Wyo. Farm Bur., Colo.-Wyo. Nat. Farmers Union. Home: 1451 Cottonwood Ave Wheatland WY 82201-3412

BUNKIS, JURIS, plastic surgeon; b. Lubeck, Germany, Aug. 27, 1949; came to the U.S., 1974; s. Janis and Jadviga (Buzinskis) B.; m. Ruta Sternbergs, Oct. 12, 1974; children: Justin S., Jessica S. Degree, U. Toronto, 1970, MD, 1974. Intern gen. surgery Mary Imogene Bassett Hosp., Columbia U., Cooperstown, N.Y., 1974-75, jr. resident gen. surgery, 1975-76; jr. resident surgery Beth Israel Hosp., Mass. Gen. Hosp. & Shriner's Burn Inst., Harvard U., Boston, 1976-77; sr. resident gen. surgery Mary Imogene Bassett Hosp., Columbia U., Cooperstown, 1977-78, chief resident gen. surgery, 1978-79; sr. resident, chief resident plastic surgery Peter Bent Brigham & Children's Hosps., Harvard U., Boston, 1979-81; clin. instr. in surgery Harvard U., 1979-81; asst. prof. surgery divsn. plastic surgery U. Calif., San Francisco, 1981-83, asst. clin. prof. surgery, 1983-85; asst. chief plastic surgery San Francisco Gen. Hosp. U. Calif., 1981-82, chief plastic surgery, 1983; chmn. bd. dirs., pres. Juris Bunkis M.D., Inc., Danville, Calif., 1983—; chmn. bd. dirs., pres., med. dirs. Blackhawk Surgery Ctr., Inc., Danville, 1989—; chmn. bd. dirs., pres., sec. United Bridges, Inc., 1994—; invited lectr. numerous confs. Contbr. chpts. to books and articles to med. jours. Mem. Am. Assn. Hand Surgery (mem. program com. 1983-84, socioecons. com. 84-85), Am. Soc. Plastic and Reconstructive Surgery (mem. Tel Med subcom. 1986-87), Am. Soc. Aesthetic Surgery, Calif. Med. Soc., Calif. Soc. Plastic Surgeons (mem. program com. 1984-85, mem. ethics com. 86-87, mem. newsletter com. 87-89, mem. B.M.Q.A. liaison com. 87-89), Alameda-Contra Costa Med. Assn., Lipoplasty Soc. N.Am., Internat. Soc. Aesthetic Plastic Surgery, Pan Pacific Surg. Assn., Latvian Med. and Dental Assn., Plastic Surgery Rsch. Coun. Office: United Bridges Inc 4165 Blackhawk Plz Cir Ste 150 Danville CA 94506-4691

BUNN, CHARLES NIXON, strategic business planning consultant; b. Springfield, Ill., Feb. 8, 1926; s. Joseph Forman and Helen Anna Frieda (Link) B.; student U. Ill., 1943-44; BS in Engring., U.S. Mil. Acad., 1949; MBA, Xavier U., Cin., 1958; m. Cecine Cole, Dec. 26, 1951 (div. 1987); children: Sisene, Charles; m. Marjorie Fitzmaurice, Apr. 5, 1988. Flight test engr. Gen. Electric Co., Cin., also Edwards AFB, Calif., 1953-59; sr. missile test engr., space systems div. Lockheed Aircraft Corp., USAF Satellite Test Center, Sunnyvale, Calif., 1959-60, 63-70, economist, advanced planning dept., 1961-63; economic and long-range planning cons., Los Altos, Calif., 1970-73; head systems planning, economist, strategic bus. planning, Western Regional hdqrs. U.S. Postal Service, San Bruno, Calif., 1973-78; strategic bus. planning cons., investment analysis cons., 1978-79; strategic bus. planning Advanced Reactor Systems dept. Gen. Electric Co., Sunnyvale, Calif., 1979-84; strategic planning cons., 1984—. Served with inf. paratroops U.S. Army, 1944-45, with inf. and rangers, 1949-53, Korea. Decorated Battle Star (5). Mem. Nat. Assn. Bus. Economists, World Future Soc., Sigma Nu. Episcopalian. Home and Office: 222 Incline Way San Jose CA 95139-1525

BUNN, DOROTHY IRONS, court reporter; b. Trinidad, Colo., Apr. 30, 1948; d. Russell and Pauline Anna (Langowski) Irons; m. Peter Lynn Bunn; children: Kristy Lynn, Wade Allen, Russell Ahearn. Student No. Va. Community Coll., 1970-71, U. Va., Fairfax, 1971-72. Registered profl. reporter; cert. shorthand reporter. Pres., chief exec. officer Ahearn Ltd., Springfield, Va., 1970-81, Bunn & Assocs., Glenrock, Wyo., 1981—; cons. Bixby Hereford Co., Glenrock, 1981-89, co-mgr., 1989—. Del., White House Conf. on Small Bus., Washington, 1986, 95—. Mem. NAFE, Am. Indian Soc., Nat. Ct. Reporters Assn., Nat. Fedn. Ind. Bus., Xcel Internat. (1st v.p., 1994-95, dir. 1995—), Wyo. Shorthand Reporters Assn. (chmn. com. 1984-85), Nat. Cattlewomen, Wyo. Cattlewomen (Converse County), Nat. Fedn. Ind. Businesses (guardian 1991—), Nat. Fedn. Bus. and Profl. Women (1st v.p. Casper 1994-95, pres. 1995—, pub. rels. chair, Choices chair), Nat. Cattlewomen. Avocations: art, music. Home: PO Box 1602 Bixby Hereford Co Glenrock WY 82637 Office: Bunn & Assocs 81 Bixby Rd Glenrock WY 82637

BUNN, JAMES LEE, congressman; b. McMinnville, Oreg., Dec. 12, 1956; s. Benjamin Adam and Viola Mae (Fulgham) B.; m. Cindy Lou Mishler, Sept. 9, 1978; children: James Jr., Matthew, Phillip, Malachi, Caleb. AA, Chemeketa Community Coll., Salem, Oreg., 1977; BA in Biology, N.W. Nazarene Coll., Nampa, Idaho, 1979. Farmer Oreg.; senator from dist. 15 Oreg. State Senate, 1987-95, Rep. whip, 1990-95; mem. 104th Congress from 5th Oreg. dist., 1995—; exec. dir. Oreg. Rep. Party.; mem. appropriations com., interior, water and energy, fgn. ops. subcom. U.S. Congress. With Oreg. Criminal Justice Coun., Commn. Hispanic Affairs, Oreg. Hunger Task Force, Yamhill Cmty. Action Program Bd. Dirs., Oreg. N.G. Res. Recipient Minuteman citation Non-Commd. Officers Assn. U.S.A., 1989, cert. of appreciation Cmty. Action Agy. Yamhill County, 1990, Nat. Sr. Citizen Hall of Fame award, 1992, cert. of appreciation County Planning Dirs. Assn. Oreg., 1993. Mem. Nazarene Ch. Office: 738 Hawthorne Ave NE Salem OR 97301 also: 1517 Longworth HOB Washington DC 20515

BUNN, PAUL A., JR., oncologist, educator; b. N.Y.C., Mar. 16, 1945; s. Paul A. Bunn; m. Camille Ruoff, Aug. 17, 1968; children: Rebecca, Kristen, Paul H. BA cum laude, Amherst Coll., 1967; MD, Cornell U., 1971. Diplomate Nat. Bd. Med. Examiners, Am. Bd. Internal Medicine, Am. Bd. Med. Oncology. Intern U. Calif., H.C. Moffitt Hosp., San Francisco, 1971-72, resident, 1972-73; clin. assoc. medicine br. Nat. Cancer Inst., NIH, Bethesda, Md., 1973-76; sr. investigator med. oncology br. Nat. Cancer Inst., Washington VA Hosp., 1976-81; asst. prof. medicine med. sch. Georgetown U., 1978-81; head cell kinetic sect., Navy med. oncology br. Nat. Cancer Inst., Bethesda, 1981-84; assoc. prof. medicine uniformed svcs. Univ. Health Scis., Bethesda, 1981-84; prof. medicine health scis. ctr. U. Colo., Denver, 1984—, head divsn. med. oncology, 1984-94, dir. cancer ctr., 1987—; mem. instl. rev. bd. NIH, Nat. Cancer Inst., 1982-84; mem. intramural support contract rev. com. Nat. Cancer Inst., 1982-84; cons. Coulter Immunology, 1984-89, Abbott Labs., 1992-94, Seragen, 1993—, others; mem. cancer com. U. Colo., 1984—, mem. faculty senate health scis. ctr., 1985-94, mem. exec. com. sch. medicine, 1987—; mem. fin. com. Univ. Physicians, Inc., 1986-91; mem. med. bd. Univ. Hosp., 1987—; external sci. advisor cancer ctr. U. Miami, 1988-92, U. Ark., 1989-94, U. Va., 1991-94, others; mem. oncology drug adv. com. FDA, 1992—; mem. sci. secretariat 7th World Conf. Lung Cancer, 1994; bd. dirs. Univ. Hosp. Resource Coun.; mem. oncology drug adv. com. FDA, 1993—. Author: Carboplatin (JM-8) Current Perspectives and Future Directions, 1990, Clinical Experiences With Platinum and Etoposide Therapy in Lung Cancer, 1992, (with M.E. Wood) Hematology/Oncology Secrets, 1994; assoc. editor Med. and Pediatric Oncology, 1984—, Jour. Clin. Oncology, 1991—, Cancer Rsch., 1992—, others; contbr. chpts. to books and articles to profl. jours. Bd. dirs. Colo. divsn. Am. Cancer Soc., 1989—, Leukemia Soc. Am., 1991—; bd. dirs. The Cancer Venture, 1993-94, Fair Share Colo., 1993-94. With USPHS, 1973-84. Decorated Medal of Commendation; recipient Sci. of Yr. award Denver chpt. ARCS, 1992; named one of 400 Best Drs. in Am., Good Housekeeping Mag., 1991, 92; grantee Schering Plough, 1988-89, Burroughs Wellcome, 1991—, Bristol-Myers Squibb, 1993—, others. Fellow ACP; mem. AAAS, Am. Soc. Hematology (mem. sci. subcom. neoplasia 1989-92), Am. Assn. Cancer Rsch., Am. Soc. Clin. Oncology (chair program subcom. 1985-86, 90), Am. Fedn. Clin. Rsch., Am. Assn. Cancer Insts. (bd. dirs. 1992—), Internat. Assn. Study Lung Cancer (bd. dirs. 1988—, pres. 1994—), Western Assn. Physicians, S.W. Oncology Group (mem. lung and leukemia com. 1986—, mem. biologic response modifier com. 1987—), Lung Cancer Study Group, Alpha Omega Alpha. Office: U Colo Cancer Ctr Box B188 4200 E 9th Ave Denver CO 80220-3706*

BUNTAIN, JEANNINE, agricultural products executive; b. 1939. Various positions Inland Fruit & Produce Co., Wapato, Wash., 1968-92, pres., 1992—. Office: Inland Fruit & Produce Co Frontage Rd Wapato WA 98951*

BUNTEN, JUDITH ANN, perinatal nurse, educator; b. Logan, Utah; d. Glenn and Bess Bunten. AA with honors, Antelope Valley Coll., 1963; BS with honors, UCLA, 1966; MS, U. Colo., 1968. RN, Calif.; cert. pub. health nurse, Calif.; cert. instr. community colls., Calif.; cert. basic cardiac life support; cert. neonatal resuscitation. Rsch. asst. U. Colo. Sch. of Nursing, Denver, 1969; instr. Mount St. Mary's Coll., L.A., 1973-76, St. John's Hosp., Santa Monica, 1974; instr., asst. dir. nursing edn. Cedars-Sinai Med. Ctr., L.A., 1976-78; clin. nurse, adminstrv. nurse UCLA Med. Ctr., L.A., 1966-68, 69-73, clin. nurse, 1978-83, adminstrv. nurse, 1983—; adj. faculty Coll. of the Canyons, Santa Clarita, Calif., 1986-91, 93; clin. nurse Holy Cross Hosp., Mission Hills, Calif., 1984-87; mgmt. preceptor UCLA Sch. of Nursing, 1990, Calif. State U., 1990; guest lectr. cmty. hosps., 1989-90; guest spkr. vocat. nurse graduation L.A. Sch. Dist., 1989. Contbr. to Maternity Nursing, 18th edit., 1995. Mem. ARC, Santa Clarita, 1990-91, co-organizer child's health fair, 1990. Regents scholar U. Calif., 1964-66. Mem. Perinatal Adv. Coun. of L.A. Office: UCLA Med Ctr Dept Nursing 10833 Le Conte Ave Los Angeles CA 90024

BUNTING, DAVID CUYP, economics educator, consultant; b. Chgo., Sept. 22, 1940; s. Van Asmus and Jane (Whitemore) B.; m. Susan Jean Wilkins, Oct. 28, 1978; children: Maxwell C., N. Henri. BS, Ohio State U., 1962, MA, 1964; MS, U. Wis., 1966; PhD, U. Oreg., 1972. Asst. prof. Ea. Wash. U., Cheney, 1971-76, assoc. prof., 1976-80, prof., 1980—; cons. Bonneville Power Adminstrn., Spokane, Wash., 1985—. Author: Rise of Large American Corporations, 1987; contbr. articles to profl. jours. Soccer coach Spokane Youth Sports Assn., 1985—. Mem. Am. Econ. Assn., Am. Statis. Assn., Western Social Sci. Assn., Bus. History Conf., Econ. History Assn. Democrat. Home: 2311 E 17th Ave Spokane WA 99223-5121 Office: Ea Wash U Dept Economics Cheney WA 99004

BUNTON, CLIFFORD ALLEN, chemist, educator; b. Chesterfield, Eng., Jan. 4, 1920; came to U.S., 1963, naturalized, 1978; s. Arthur and Edith (Kirk) B.; m. Ethel Clayton, July 28, 1945; children—Julia Margaret, Claire Jennifer. B.Sc., Univ. Coll., London, 1941, Ph.D., 1945; hon. degree, U. Perugia, Italy, 1986. Successively asst. lectr., lectr., reader Univ. Coll., 1944-63; prof. chemistry U. Calif., Santa Barbara, 1963-90, prof. emeritus, 1990—, chmn. dept., 1967-72; Commonwealth Fund fellow U. Columbia, 1948-49; Brit. Coun. vis. lectr., Chile and Argentina, 1960; vis. prof. UCLA, 1961, U. Toronto, 1962, U. Sao Paolo, Brazil, 1973, U. Lausanne, Switzerland, 1976, 79; adj. prof. U. Chile, Santiago, 1990—; mem. policy com. U. Chile-U. Calif. Coop. Program, chmn. sci. and engring. sub-com., 1969—; mem. sci. com., U.S.-Mexico Found. for Sci., 1993—. Contbr. articles to profl. jours. Recipient Tolman medal, So. Calif. sect. Am. Chem. Soc., 1987. Fellow AAAS; mem. N.Y. Acad. Sci., Am. Chem. Soc. (Calif. sect.), Chem. Soc. (London); corr. mem. Chilean Acad. Scis. (1974). Home: 935 Cocopah Dr Santa Barbara CA 93110-1204

BUNZEL, JOHN HARVEY, political science educator, researcher; b. N.Y.C., Apr. 15, 1924; s. Ernest Everett and Harriett (Harvey) B.; m. Barbara Bovyer, May 11, 1963; children—Cameron, Reed. A.B., Princeton U., 1948; M.A., Columbia U., 1949; Ph.D., U. Calif.-Berkeley, 1954; LL.D., U. Santa Clara, 1976. Mem. faculty San Francisco State U., 1953-56, 63-70, vis. scholar Ctr. Advanced Study in Behavioral Scis., 1969-70; mem. faculty Mich. State U., East Lansing, 1956-57, Stanford U., Calif., 1957-63; pres. San Jose State U., Calif., 1970-78; sr. research fellow Hoover Inst. Stanford U., Calif., 1978—; mem. U.S. Commn. on Civil Rights, 1983-86. Author: The American Small Businessman, 1962; Anti-Politics in America, 1967; Issues of American Public Policy, 1968; New Force on the Left, 1983, Challenge to American Schools: The Case For Standards and Values, 1985, Political Passages: Journeys of Change Through Two Decades 1968-1988, 1988, Race Relations on Campus: Stanford Students Speak, 1992; contbr. articles to profl. jours., popular mags., newspapers. Weekly columnist San Jose Mercury-News. Bd. dirs. No. Calif. Citizenship Clearing House, 1959-61; mem. Calif. Atty. Gen.'s Adv. Com., 1960-61; del. Calif. Democratic Conv., 1968; del. Dem. Nat. Conv., 1968. Recipient Presdl. award No. Calif. Polit. Sci. Assn., 1969, cert. of Honor San Francisco Bd. Suprs., 1974, Hubert Humprey Pub. Policy award Policy Studies Orgn., 1990; grantee Ford Found., Rockefeller Found., Rabinowitz Found. Mem. Am. Polit. Sci. Assn. Home: 1519 Escondido Way Belmont CA 94002-3634 Office: Stanford U Hoover Inst Stanford CA 94305

BURAS, NATHAN, hydrology and water resources educator; b. Barlad, Romania, Aug. 23, 1921; came to U.S., 1947; s. Boris and Ethel (Weiser) B.; m. Netty Stivel, Apr. 13, 1951; 1 child, Nir H. BS with highest honors, U. Calif., Berkeley, 1949; MS, Technion, Haifa, Israel, 1957; PhD, UCLA, 1962. Registered profl. engr., Israel. Prof. hydrology and water resources Technion, 1962-80, dean, 1966-68; vis. prof. Stanford (Calif.) U., 1976-81; prof., head of dept. hydrology and water resources U. Ariz., Tucson, 1981-89, prof. hydrology and water resources, 1989—; cons. Tahal, Ltd., Tel Aviv, 1963-73, World Bank, Washington, 1972-76, 79-81, Regional Municipality of Waterloo, Ont., Can., 1991-93, U.S. AID, Washington, 1992-93, Great No. Paper Co., 1992—. Author: Scientific Allocation of Water Resources, 1972; editor: Control of Water Resources Systems, 1976. Mem. Israel-Mex. Mixed Commn. on Sci. Cooperation, 1976, So. Ariz. Water Resource Assn., 1982—; active Pugwash Workshops, 1991, 92, 93. Named Laureat du Congres, Internat. Assn. Agrl. Engring., 1964; recipient Cert. of Appreciation, USDA., 1970. Fellow Ariz.-Nev. Acad. Sci., ASCE (life), Am. Geophys. Union, Am. Water Resources Assn. (charter). Jewish. Home: 5541 E Circulo Terra Tucson AZ 85715-1003 Office: U Ariz Dept Hydrology and Water Resources Tucson AZ 85721

BURBACK, RONALD LEROI, computer scientist; b. Brush, Colo., Feb. 1, 1952; s. William and Pauline (Cook) B.; m. Sandra Ann Rockwell, Aug. 14, 1971; children: Jennifer, Christy, Katy. BA, U. Colo., 1974; MS in Engring., Stanford U., 1982, postgrad., 1993. Physicist Los Alamos (N.Mex.) Labs., 1974-78, Stanford Rsch. Inst., Menlo Park, Calif., 1978-82; prin. engr. Digital, Colorado Springs, Colo., 1982-86; artificial intelligence rschr. Lawrence Livermore (Calif.) Labs., 1987; sr. corp. cons. TDS Healthcare, San Jose, Calif., 1988-90; researcher Stanford (Calif.) U., 1991, tchr., 1993—; CEO Tableau Software, Stanford, 1988-92; dir. engring. Oceania Healthcare, Palo Alto, Calif., 1992-93; pres. Object Plus Software, Pleasanton, Calif., 1993—. Author: Using the Tableau System, 1991; patentee in field. Bloodorn Found. scholar, 1970, Phi Beta Kappa scholar, 1974; recipient Outstanding Artificial Intelligence Rschr. award U.S. Pentagon, 1988. Mem. AAAI, IEEE. Home: 1944 Paseo Del Cajon Pleasanton CA 94566-5913 Office: Stanford U Computer Sci Dept Stanford CA 94305-3068

BURBIDGE, E. MARGARET, astronomer, educator; b. Davenport, Eng.; d. Stanley John and Marjorie (Stott) Peachey; m. Geoffrey Burbidge, Apr. 2, 1948; 1 child, Sarah. B.S., Ph.D., U. London; Sc.D. hon., Smith Coll., 1963, U. Sussex, 1970, U. Bristol, 1972, U. Leicester, 1972, City U., 1973, U. Mich., 1978, U. Mass., 1978, Williams Coll., 1979, SUNY, Stony Brook, 1985, Rensselaer Poly. Inst., 1986, U. Notre Dame, 1986, U. Chgo., 1991. Mem. staff U. London Obs., 1948-51; rsch. fellow Yerkes Obs. U. Chgo., 1951-53, Shirley Farr fellow Yerkes obs., 1957-59, assoc. prof. Yerkes Obs., 1959-62; rsch. fellow Calif. Inst. Tech., Pasadena, 1955-57; mem. Enrico Fermi Inst. for Nuclear Studies, 1957-62; prof. astronomy dept. physics U. Calif. San Diego, 1964—, univ. prof., 1984—; dir. Royal Greenwich Obs. (Herstmonceaux Castle), Hailsham, Sussex, Eng., 1984-90; rsch. prof. dept. physics U. Calif., San Diego, 1990—; Lindsay Meml. lectr. Goddard Space Flight Ctr., NASA, 1985; Abby Rockefeller Mauze prof. MIT, 1968; David Elder lectr. U. Strathclyde, 1972; V. Gildersleeve lectr. Barnard Coll., 1974; Jansky lectr. Nat. Radio Astronomy Observatory, 1977; Brode lectr. Whitman Coll., 1986. Author: (with G. Burbidge) Quasi-Stellar Objects, 1967; editor: Observatory mag., 1948-51; mem. editorial bd.: Astronomy and Astrophysics, 1969—. Recipient (with husband) Warner prize in Astronomy, 1959, Bruce Gold medal Astronomy Soc. Pacific, 1982; hon. fellow Univ. Coll., London, Girton Coll., Lucy Cavendish Coll., Cambridge; U.S. Nat. medal of sci., 1984; Sesquicentennial medal Mt. Holyoke Coll., 1987, Einstein medal World Cultural Coun., 1988. Fellow Royal Soc., Nat. Acad. Scis. (chmn. sect. 12 astronomy 1986), Am. Acad. Arts and Scis., Royal Astron. Soc.; mem. Am. Astron. Soc. (v.p. 1972-74, pres. 1976-78; Henry Norris Russell lectr. 1984), Internat. Astron. Union (pres. commn. 28 1970-73), Grad. Women Sci. (nat. hon. mem.). Office: U Calif-San Diego Ctr Astrophysics Space Scis Mail Code # 0111 La Jolla CA 92093

BURCH, HAMLIN DOUGHTY, III, retired sheet metal professional; b. Oakland, Calif., June 14, 1939; s. Hamlin D. Burch II and Bernice I. (Ingerski) Bortscheller; m. Zettie A. Honeycutt, Nov. 16, 1957 (div. 1974); children: Paula Christine Grothaus, Victoria Jaylee Alberti, Hamlin D. IV. Grad., Modesto (Calif.) High Sch. Sheet metal worker Fred L. Hill., Modesto, 1960-62, Olson's Plumbing, Turlock, 1962-64, Hansen's Inc., Modesto, 1964-74; Lang's Engerprises, Modesto, 1974-87; sheet metal worker Mendenhall, Sacramento, 1987, South Valley Mech., San Juan Baptiste, 1987-88, Brott Mech., Tulare, 1988; ret. Brott Mech. Mem. flag com. Boy Scouts of Am. Mem. Mem. Sheet Metal Workers Internat. Assn., Nat. Rifle Assn., Wilderness Soc., Nat. Park and Conservation Assn., Nat. Wildlife Fedn., Nat. Trust for Hist. Preservation, World Wildlife Fund. Republican. Mem. LDS Ch.

BURCH, MARY LOU, organization consultant, housing advocate; b. Billings, Mont., Apr. 4, 1930; d. Forrest Scott Sr. and Mary Edna (Hinshaw) Chilcott; m. J. Sheldon Robinson, June 18, 1949 (div. 1956); m. G. Howard Burch, Nov. 27, 1957 (div. 1984); children: Julie Lynne Scully, Donna Eileen, Carol Marie Kimball, Alan Robert, Christine Philips Spruill Enomoto. AA, Grant Tech. Coll., Sacramento, 1949; AB, Sacramento State Coll., 1955; student, U. Alaska, 1976-78, Santa Rosa (Calif.) Jr. Coll., 1987. Diagnostic tchr. Calif. Youth Authority, Perkins, 1955-57; com. chmn. on pub. info. Sequoia Union High Sch. Dist., So. San Mateo County, Calif., 1970-72; exec. dir. Presbyn. Hospitality House, Fairbanks, Alaska, 1979-80; realtor Century 21 Smith/Ring, Renton, Wash., 1980-81; cons. Fairbanks, Alaska, 1981-84; exec. dir. Habitat for Humanity of Sonoma County, Santa Rosa, Calif., 1986-89, Affordable Housing Assoc., Santa Rosa, Calif., 1989-90; pvt. cons. in housing and orgn. Scottsdale, Ariz., 1991-92, Prescott and Dewey, Ariz., 1992—; bd. dirs. Hosp. Chaplainey Svcs, Santa Rosa, Villa Los Alamos Homeowners Assn.; cons. Access Alaska, Anchorage, 1983; contractor Alaka Siding, Fairbanks, 1982-83. Local coord. fgn. exch. student program Acad. Yr. in Am., 1993-94; acad. coord. fgn. exch. student program Cultural Homestay Internat., 1994; vol. Habitat for Humanity coms. Named vol. of the year, Hosp. Chaplaincy Svcs., 1987. Democrat. United Ch. of Christ. Home and Office: 1288 Tapadero Dr # D-pcc Dewey AZ 86327-5823

BURCH, ROBERT DALE, lawyer; b. Washington, Jan. 30, 1928; s. Dallas Stockwell and Hepsy (Berry) B.; m. Joann D. Hansen, Dec. 9, 1966; children—Berkeley, Robert Brett, Barrett Bradley. Student, Va. Mil. Inst., 1945-46; B.S., U. Calif. at Berkeley, 1950, J.D., 1953. Bar: Calif. bar 1954. Since practiced in Los Angeles and Beverly Hills; ptnr. Gibson, Dunn & Crutcher, 1961—; lectr. U. So. Calif. Inst. Fed. Taxation, 1960, 62, 65, 75; guest lectr. U. Calif.-L.A. Law Sch., 1959; lectr. C.E.B. seminars U. Calif.; founder Robert D. Burch Ctr. for Tax Policy and Pub. Fin., U. Calif., Berkeley. Author: Federal Tax Procedures for General Practitioners; Contbr. profl. jours., textbooks. Bd. dirs. charitable founds.; founder Robert D. Burch Ctr. for Tax Policy and Pub. Fin., U. Calif., Berkeley. With AUS, 1945-47. Mem. Beverly Hills Bar Assn. (bd. govs., chmn. probate and trust com.), Law Trust, Tax and Ins. Council (past czar), Los Angeles World Affairs Council. Home: 1301 Delresto Dr Beverly Hills CA 90210-2100 Office: Gibson Dunn & Crutcher 2029 Century Park E Los Angeles CA 90067-2901 also: 333 S Grand Ave Los Angeles CA 90071-1504

BURCIAGA, JUAN RAMON, physics educator; b. Ft. Worth, June 24, 1953; s. Ramon Medellin and Aurora (Vega) B. BS in Physics, U. Tex., 1975, MA in Physics, 1977; PhD, Tex. A&M U., 1986. Asst. prof. Austin Coll., Sherman, Tex., 1986-93, Colo. Coll., Colo. Springs, 1993—. Contbr. articles to profl. jours. including Jour. of Molecular Spectroscopy, Proc. of the Workshop on Comp. Physics, Phys. Rev. A, Jour. Physics B. Advisor Grayson C.C., Sherman, 1987-93, Sherman Pub. Libr., 1991-93. Mem. Am. Astron. Soc., Am. Assn. of Physics Tchrs., Am. Phys. Soc., Soc. of Physics Students, Sigma Pi Sigma. Office: Colorado Springs Coll Dept Physics 14 E Cache La Poudre St Colorado Springs CO 80903-3294

BURD, STEVE, food service executive; b. 1949. BS, Carroll Coll., 1971; MA in Econs., U. Wis., 1973. With fin. and mktg. So. Pacific Transp. Co., San Francisco; with Arthur D. Little, N.Y.C., 1982-87; mgmt. cons., 1986-91; cons. Stop & Shop Cos., Boston, 1988-89, Fred Meyer Inc., Portland, Oreg., 1989-90, Safeway Inc., Oakland, Calif., 1986-87, 91—; pres., CEO Safeway Inc., 1992—. Office: Safeway Inc 201 4th St Oakland CA 94660

BURDEN, JAMES EWERS, lawyer; b. Sacramento, Oct. 24, 1939; s. Herbert Spencer and Ida Elizabeth (Brosemer) B.; m. Kathryn Lee Gardner,

Aug. 21, 1965; children: Kara Elizabeth, Justin Gardner. BS, U. Calif., Berkeley, 1961; JD, U. Calif., Hastings, 1964; postgrad., U. So. Calif., 1964-65. Bar: Calif. 1965, Tax Ct. U.S. 1969, U.S. Supreme Ct. 1970. Assoc. Elliott and Aune, Santa Ana, Calif., 1965, White, Harbor, Fort & Schei, Sacramento, 1965-67; assoc. Miller, Starr & Regalia, Oakland, Calif., 1967-69, ptnr., 1969-73; ptnr. Burden, Aiken, Mansuy & Stein, San Francisco, 1973-82, James E. Burden, Inc., San Francisco, 1982—; bd. dirs. Roofing Equipment, Inc., Indsl. Products, San Leandro, Calif., Zigo, Inc.; pres. Austex, Oil and Gas Co., Inc., Luling, Tex.; underwriting mem. Lloyds of London, 1986-93; instr. U. Calif., Berkeley, 1968-74, Merritt Coll. Contbr. articles to profl. jours. Mem. ABA, Lutine Golf Soc. (London), Claremont Country Club, San Francisco Grid Club, Commonwealth of Calif., The Naval Club (London). Office: 200 California St 5th fl San Francisco CA 94111-4344

BURDEN, JEAN (PRUSSING), poet, writer, editor; b. Waukegan, Ill., Sept. 1; d. Harry Frederick and Miriam (Biddlecom) Prussing; m. David Charles Burden, 1940 (div. 1949). BA, U. Chgo., 1936. Sec. John Hancock Mutual Life Ins. Co., Chgo., 1937-39, Young & Rubicam, Inc., Chgo., 1939-41; editor, copywriter Domestic Industries, Inc., Chgo., 1941-45; office mgr. O'Brion Russell & Co., Los Angeles, 1948-55; adminstr. pub. relations Meals for Millions Found., Los Angeles, 1955-65; editor Stanford Research Inst., South Pasadena, Calif., 1965-66; propr. Jean Burden & Assocs., Altadena, Calif., 1966-82; lectr. poetry to numerous colls. and univs., U.S., 1963—; supr. poetry workshop Pasadena City Coll., Calif., 1960-62, 66, U. Calif. at Irvine, 1975; also pvt. poetry workshops. Author: Naked as the Glass, 1963, Journey Toward Poetry, 1966, The Cat You Care For, 1968, The Dog You Care For, 1968, The Bird You Care For, 1970, The Fish You Care For, 1971, A Celebration of Cats, 1974, The Classic Cats, 1975, The Woman's Day Book of Hints for Cat Owners, 1980, 84, Taking Light from Each Other, 1992; poetry editor: Yankee Mag, 1955—; pet editor: Woman's Day Mag, 1973-82; contbr. numerous articles to various jours. and mags. MacDowell Colony fellow, 1973, 74, 76; Recipient Silver Anvil award Pub. Relations Soc. of Am., 1969, 1st prize Borestone Mountain Poetry award, 1963, Gold Crown award for lit. achievement, 1989. Mem. Poetry Soc. Am., Acad. Am. Poets, Authors Guild. Address: 1129 Beverly Way Altadena CA 91001-2517

BURDETTE, ROBERT SOELBERG, accountant; b. Salt Lake City, Apr. 28, 1955; s. Grant Edward and Jewel Irene (Soelberg) B.; m. Marne Marie Erekson, June 21, 1977 (div. May 1985); children: Aaron Edward, Melissa Marie, Barton Allen; m. Conna Lee Jolley, Feb. 1, 1990; children: Seth Robert, Mark Jacob. BA, U. Utah, 1979; M in Taxation, Wash. Inst. Grad. Studies, 1993. CPA, Utah. Staff acct. Huber & Assocs., Salt Lake City, 1979-80; acctg. mgr. Huntsman-Christensen Corp., Salt Lake City, 1980-81; supervising tax specialist Leverich & Co., Salt Lake City, 1982-83; tax. ptnr. Burdette & Hymas CPAs, Salt Lake City, 1983-93, pres., 1993-94; compt. Art Beats, Inc., Salt Lake City, 1988-90; prof. law in taxation Washington Sch. Law, 1991; tax ptnr. Hansen, Barnett & Maxwell CPA, 1994—. Conv. del. Salt Lake County Rep. Party, 1980, Utah State Rep. Party, 1992; missionary Ch. Jesus Christ of Latter-Day Saints, 1974-76; basketball coach Salt Lake Boys & Girls Club, 1989; scout master Boy Scouts Am., Sandy, Utah, 1986-87. Mem. AICPA, Utah Assn. CPAs (taxation com. 1983), Intermountain Soc. Practicing CPAs (exec. com.), CPA Law Forum (bd. adv.). Home: 1756 Wilson Ave Salt Lake City UT 84108-2917 Office: 345 E 300 S Salt Lake City UT 84111

BURE, PAVEL, professional hockey player; b. Moscow, Mar. 31, 1971. Wing Vancouver (Can.) Canucks. Recipient Calder Meml. trophy, 1991-92; regular season and playoff Top Goal Scorer, 1993-94. Office: Vancouver Canucks, 100 N Renfrew St, Vancouver, BC Canada V5K 3N7

BURFORD, RICHARD S., agricultural products executive; b. 1931. Graduate, U. Tenn., 1953. Pvt. practice Fresno, Calif., 1957-79; with Richard S. Burford, Inc., Fresno, Calif., 1967—. With U.S. Army, 1953-57. Office: 1443 W Sample Ave Fresno CA 93711-1948*

BURG, ANTON BEHME, chemist, retired educator; b. Dallas City, Ill., Oct. 18, 1904; s. Frank Winchester and Sadie Quinton (Hornby) B. BS, U. Chgo., 1927, MS, 1928, PhD, 1931. Researcher Kimberley-Clark Co., Neenah, Wis., 1928-29; rsch. asst. U. Chgo., 1929-31, instr., 1931-39; from asst. prof. to prof. U. So. Calif., L.A., 1939-74, dept. head, 1940-50, prof. emeritus, 1974—; cons. in field. Contbr. numerous articles to profl. jours. Fellow AAAS; mem. Am. Chem. Soc. (Mallinckrodt award Tolman medal 1969), AAUP, Sigma Xi, Phi Beta Kappa. Home: 459 W 38th St Los Angeles CA 90037-1325 Office: U So Calif Los Angeles CA 90089-0744

BURG, BARRY RICHARD, history educator, writer; b. Denver, Aug. 2, 1938; s. H.D. and Florence Burg; m. Kathleen Semrau, June 12, 1965 (div. 1980); children: Jenny Anne, John Eliot; m. Judith Marie Harbour, July 17, 1982. BA, U. Colo., 1960; MA, Western State Coll., Gunnison, Colo., 1963; PhD, U. Colo., 1967. Lectr. U. Colo., Denver, 1965-67; with Ariz. State U., Tempe, 1967—, dir. honors program, 1978-82, prof. history, 1977—; dir. Am. studies Rsch. Ctr., Hyderabad, India, 1995—. Author: Richard Mather of Dorchester, 1976, Sodomy and The Pirate Tradition, 1982, An American Seafarer in the Age of Sail: The Erotic Diaries of Philip C. Van Buskirk, 1851-1870, 1994. Lt. U.S. Army, 1961-62. Fulbright scholar Pakistan, 1982-83, Indonesia, 1989-90, India, 1995—; Ford Found. fellow Mass. Hist. Soc., 1969-70. Office: Ariz State U History Dept Tempe AZ 85287

BURG, GARY G., vocational expert; b. L.A., Aug. 24, 1956; s. George J. and Kathleen A. (Doheny) B.; m. Diane Teresa Giliotti, Aug. 5, 1978; children: Sean Douglas, Anthony Christian. BA in Psychology, Calif. State U., Los Angeles, 1978, MS in Rehab. Counseling, 1982. Diplomate Am. Bd. Vocat. Experts; cert. vocat. evaluation specialist, cert. ins. rehab. specialist, cert. work adjustment specialist, cert. rehab. economist. Counselor East Valley Community Health Ctr., West Covina, Calif.; evaluation and tng. counselor Goodwill Industries So. Calif., L.A.; vocat. counselor, evaluator PAR Services, Santa Fe Spring, Calif.; exec. dir. West Mountain Community Services, Crestline, Calif.; vocat. evaluator, mgr. Anfuso Work Evaluation Ctr. Inc., Pasadena, Calif.; owner, dir. Testing, Evaluation And Mgmt., El Monte, Riverside and Temecula, Calif., forensic vocat. expert; former assoc. prof. Calif. State U., L.A.; lectr. in field. Past bd. dirs. Crestline Area Presch., Contact the Helpline, San Bernardino, Calif., East Valley Community Health Ctr., South Hills Little League, West Covina, Assn. Retarded Citizens, San Gabriel Valley, Calif., West End Industry Edn. Coordination Counsel, San Bernardino County, bd. dirs. Arts Coun. of Temecula Valley. Mem. Am. Bd. Vocat. Experts (membership chair 1991-93, bd. dirs. 1992—), Calif. Assn. Rehab. Profl., Inland Empire Rehab. Group, Nat. Rehab. Assn., Nat. Assn. Rehab. Profl. Pvt. Sector, Calif. Vocat. Evaluators and Work Adjustment Assn. (bd. dirs. 1987-94, pres. 1989). Office: Testing Evaluation and Mgmt 3600 Lime St Ste 611 Riverside CA 92501-2975

BURG, GERALD WILLIAM, religious organization administrator; b. Pitts., Oct. 16, 1923; s. Julius Samuel and Anna (Shapiro) B.; student Walsh Inst., 1940-43; m. Flavia Kafton, Aug. 12, 1945; children—Cindy, Melinda, Andrew. Engring. rep. U.S. Rubber Co., 1943-45; adminstr. Beverly Hills (Calif.) B'nai B'rith, 1945-52, Univ. Synagogue, Brentwood, 1952-55; exec. dir. Wilshire Blvd. Temple, Los Angeles, 1956-80; mgmt. and fin. cons., 1980-85; adminstr. Sinai Temple, 1985—. Mem. Jewish relations com. Los Angeles council Boy Scouts Am., 1959-85; mem. Mayor's Adv. Com. on Community Activities, Los Angeles, 1963-73; chmn. Crime Prevention Fifth Councilmanic Dist., Los Angeles, 1968-73. Bd. dirs. McCobb Home for Boys, Los Angeles Psychiat. Service, Maple Ctr. for Crises Intervention, Save a Heart Found., Didi Hirsch Community Mental Health Services, pres., 1975-77; bd. dirs., chmn. finances, chmn. adminstrv. com. Community Care and Devel. Services, 1975-92. Mem. Nat. (bd. dir., pres. 1975-77), Western (pres. 1969-71, bd. dirs.), So. Calif. (pres. 1958-60) assns. temple adminstrs., NCCJ (bd. dirs. brotherhood anytown 1966-82), Los Angeles Jewish Communal Execs. (dir.). Mem. B'nai B'rith (youth dir. 1945-82, Akiba award 1950, Beverly Hills pres. 1953-54). Club: Sertoma (v.p. 1971-72). Home: 5115 Kester Ave Apt 202 Sherman Oaks CA 91403-1365 Office: Sinai Temple 10400 Wilshire Blvd Los Angeles CA 90024-4602

BURG, JEROME STUART, financial planning consultant; b. N.Y.C., Aug. 2, 1935; s. Norman and Ruth (Schkurman) B.; m. Janis Elaine Lyon, May 26, 1974; children: Jeffrey Howard, David Matthew, Audree, Harriet, Robert, Stephanie. Student, Temple U., 1953-56; CLU, Am. Coll., 1973, chartered fin. cons., 1984; cert. fin. planner, Coll. Fin. Planning, 1983. Pres., CEO Jerome Burg Assoc., Inc., Cherry Hill, N.J., 1963-79, Contemporary Fin. Planning, Scottsdale, Ariz., 1979-89; sr. acct. mgr. Acacia Group, Phoenix, 1989—; instr. Glendale and Scottdale C.C., 1983—, Nat. Inst. Fin., N.J., 1984-90. Host (radio program) Money Talks Sta. KFNN, Phoenix, 1993—. Pres. N.J. Assn. Life Underwriters, Trenton, 1963-65; instr. Jr. Achievement, Scottsdale, 1985-89; 1st v.p. Pres. Cabinet-Acacia Group, Washington, 1991, 93, co-pres., 1992. With U.S. Army, 1956-58. Mem. Internat. Assn. Fin. Planning (bd. dirs. Greater Phoenix chpt. 1982—), Inst. Cert. Fin. Planners. Office: Acacia Group 3200 E Camelback Rd Ste 245 Phoenix AZ 85018-2320

BURG, WALTER A., airport terminal executive. Gen. manager, ceo Tucson Airport Authority, Ariz., 1966—. Office: Tucson Internat Airport 7005 S Plumer Ave Tucson AZ 85706-6926*

BURGAR, RUBY RICH, college health service nurse; b. Boardman, N.C., Sept. 29, 1908; d. William Hardy and Lena (Carter) Rich; m. William Edward Burgar, June 29, 1935 (div. 1940). Diploma, Baker Sanatorium Sch. Nursing, 1929; BA in Sociology, Occidental Coll., 1955; postgrad., UCLA, 1957-64. RN, Calif. Indsl. nurse Manville-Jenkes Co., Gastonia, N.C., 1929-30; pub. health nurse Hampshire County Dept. Health, W.Va., 1931-32; staff nurse USPHS, San Francisco, 1932-35, Emergency Hosp., Washington, 1940-41, Queen's Hosp., Honolulu, 1941, St. Francis Hosp., San Francisco, 1941, Monterey (Calif.) Hosp., 1941-42; staff nurse, then head nurse Emmons Student Health Svc., Occidental Coll., L.A., 1942-66, nurse dir., 1966-74, relief nurse, 1976-77. Active L.A. chpt. ARC, 1952-91. Staff nurse USN, 1930-31; jr. nurse officer res. USPHS, 1954-74. Recipient Clara Barton medallion ARC, 1977, 40 Yr. pin, 1992; named Vol. of Yr. Am. Bapt. Home, 1992-93. Fellow Am. Coll. Health Assn. (emeritus; Ruth E. Boyington award 1968, Edward E. Hitchcock award 1971, Cert. of Appreciation 1993); mem. ANA, Pacific Coast Coll. Health Assn. (exec. dir. emeritus 1987, Ruby Rich Burgar Svc. award established 1977), Calif. Nurses Assn., Nat. League Nursing (charter), Calif. League for Nursing, L.A. Lung Assn., L.A. County Heart Assn., L.A. Art Mus., Alpha Tau Delta. Presbyterian.

BURGARINO, ANTHONY EMANUEL, environmental engineer, consultant; b. Milw., July 20, 1948; s. Joseph Francis Burgarino and Mardelle (Hoeffler) T.; m. Gail Fay DiMatteo, Mar. 13, 1982; children: Paul Anthony, Joanna Lynn. BS, U. Wis., 1970; MS, Ill. Inst. Tech., 1974, PhD, 1980. Registered profl. engr., Ariz. Sales engr. Leeds & Northrup, Phila., 1970-72; rsch. asst. Ill. Inst. Tech., Chgo., 1972-75; chemist City of Chgo., 1975-79; instr. Joliet (Ill.) Jr. Coll., 1978-79; project engr. John Carollo Engrs., Walnut Creek, Calif., 1980—; cons. City of Clovis, Calif., 1981-83, City of Fresno, Calif., 1983—, City of Phoenix, 1981-90, City of Yuma, Ariz., 1989—, City of Santa Maria, Calif., 1991—, City of Vallejo, Calif., 1992—. Contbr. articles to profl. jours. EPA grantee, 1970-72; NSF fellow, 1973, Ill. Inst. Tech. Rsch. Found. fellow, 1974. Mem. Am. Water Works Assn. Roman Catholic. Home: 2321 Lafayette Dr Antioch CA 99509 Office: John Carollo Engrs # 300 2700 Ygnacio Valley Rd Walnut Creek CA 94598

BURGE, DAVID RUSSELL, concert pianist, composer, piano educator; b. Evanston, Ill., Mar. 25, 1930; s. Russell David and Sylvia (Swensen) B.; m. Liliane Choney, 1993; 1 child, Russell David. Mus.B., Northwestern U., 1951, Mus.M., 1952; D.Mus. Arts artists diploma, Eastman Sch. Music, 1956; student, Cherubini Conservatory, Florence, Italy, 1956-57; D.F.A., Bucknell U., 1980. Instr. piano Northwestern U., 1949-52; assoc. prof. music, composer-pianist in resident Whitman Coll., 1957-62; dir. MacDowell Hall Concert Series at coll., 1959-62; organist Ch. of Christ Scientist, Walla Walla, 1958-62; asst. prof. music U. Colo., 1962-64, assoc. prof., 1964-68, prof., 1968-75; chmn. piano dept. Eastman Sch. Music, U. Rochester, N.Y., 1975-87, prof., 1975-93, Kilbourn prof., 1978-79; artist-in-residence U. Calif., Davis, 1975; guest prof. composition U. Pa., 1977; guest prof. music history U. Gothenberg, Sweden, 1980, 92; guest prof. piano U. Stockholm, Sweden, 1981, 92, Banff Ctr., Can., 1983, 84, 86; guest prof. piano U. Auckland, New Zealand, 1988, Seoul, S. Korea, 1993. Rec. artist, Mercury, Advance, Candide, Nonesuch (grammy nomination 1974), CRI Records, Mus. Heritage Soc. Records, Vox Records, Proviva Records; composer: opera Intervals, 1961, Trio; trio for violin, cello, piano, 1962; work for piano Eclipse, 1963; for flute-piano Sources I, 1964; for violin-celeste-piano Sources II, 1965; for piano Eclipse II, 1966; for clarinet-percussion Sources III, 1967; for soprano-piano A Song of Sixpence, 1967; for flute-clarinet-violin-cello-piano-tape Aeolian Music, 1968; for piano Sources IV, 1969; String Quartet, 1969, Twone in Sunshine, an Entertainment for Theater, 1969; for violin-orch. that no one knew, 1969, Songs of Love and Sorrow, 1989; also songs, anthems.; contbr. more than 200 articles to periodicals; regular columnist: Keyboard Mag., Clavier Mag., Piano Quar.; music reviewer: Music Library Assn. Notes; first major postarmistice concert, Seoul, Korea, 1953, New York debut playing all-modern program, 1961; toured, Korea, 1953-54, Europe, 1956-57, U.S.A., annually, 1960—, Eastern Europe, 1974, Far East, Australia, N.Z., 1984, 88; author: Twentieth-Century Piano Music, 1990. Served with AUS, 1952-54, Korea. Decorated by U.S. Army for cultural relations work in Korea, 1954; recipient Alumni Merit award Northwestern U., 1974, Colo. Gov.'s award, 1975, Distinguished Alumni award Eastman Sch. Music, 1975, Deems Taylor award for mus. journalism ASCAP, 1978, 79; Fulbright fellow in Italy, 1956-57; Faculty Research lectr. U. Colo., 1972. Mem. Internat. Webern Soc. (charter), Am. Soc. Univ. Composers (founder, nat. chmn. 1970-74), Pi Kappa Lambda. Address: 5243 Caminito Apartado San Diego CA 92108-4204

BURGE, HENRY CHARLES, architect; b. Peyton, Somerset, Eng., May 28, 1911; came to U.S., 1923, naturalized, 1930; s. Charles Henry and Gladys (Chedgey) B.; m. Doris Greener, Jan. 12, 1932; children: Charles Henry, Evilaura (Mrs. Lalo Codona-Hus), William Temple. B.Arch., U. So. Cal., 1935. With Clifford A. Truesdell, 1927-32, Samuel Lunden, 1934, Meyer & Holler, 1935-40, Risly & Gould, 1944-45; layout artist Walt Disney Prodns., Burbank, Calif., 1943-44; with Douglas Aircraft Interiors, Los Angeles, 1944; with U. So. Calif., 1945-62, acting dean, 1962-63; with Burge-Roach (and successor firm Urban Architects), Irvine, Calif., 1945—; pres. Burge-Roach (and successor firm Urban Architects), 1969—; dir. Atlantic Savs. & Loan Assn., Los Angeles, Universal Sav. and Loan Assn., Rosemead, Calif.; cons. Calif. Bd. Architecture, Los Angeles Civil Service. Bd. dirs. La Canada Youth House. Recipient nat. better neighborhood award Nat. Assn. Home Builders, 1951; many A.I.A. and A.R.A. awards. Fellow A.I.A., A.R.A.; mem. Pasadena Fine Arts Club, Montebello C. of C. Home: 2068 E Mission Rd Fallbrook CA 92028-1837

BURGE, WILLARD, JR., software company executive; b. Johnson City, N.Y., Oct. 2, 1938; s. Willard Sr. and Catherine Bernice (Matthews) B.; m. Carol Crockenberg, June 16, 1961; children: Willard III, Pennie Lynn. Registered profl. engr., Ohio. Indsl. engr. Harnischfeger Corp., Escanaba, Mich., 1966-67; sr. indsl. engr. Gen. Electric, Ladson, S.C., 1968-74; advanced mfg. engr. Gen. Electric, Mentor, Ohio, 1971-74; corp. staff engr. Eaton Corp., Willoughby Hills, Ohio, 1974-79, supr. N/C programming, 1979-80, supr. mfg. engring., 1980-82, mgr. mfg. systems engring., 1982-87; bus. unit mgr. MSC Products, Eaton Corp., Costa Mesa, Calif., 1987-91; pres., CEO CAM Software, Inc., Provo, Utah, 1991-93; chief exec. officer Key Svcs., Cypress, Calif., 1993—; bd. dirs. CAM Software, Inc.; presenter in field. With U.S. Army, 1957. Mem. Soc. Mfg. Engrs. Republican. Home and Office: Key Svcs Unit 256-1 13280 St Andrew's Dr Seal Beach CA 90740

BURGER, EDMUND GANES, architect; b. Yerington, Nev., Mar. 28, 1930; s. Edmund Ganes and Rose Catherine (Kobe) B.; m. Shirley May Pratini, Jan. 21, 1968; 1 dau., Jane Lee. B.M.E., U. Santa Clara, 1951; B.Arch., U. Pa., 1959. Engr. Gen. Electric Co., 1951-52; design engr. U. Calif. Radiation Lab., 1952-57; John Stewardson fellow in architecture, 1959; architect Wurster, Bernardi & Emmons, San Francisco, 1960-63; founder Burger & Coplans, Inc. (Architects), San Francisco, 1964; pres. Burger & Coplans, Inc. (Architects), 1964-79; owner Edmund Burger (Architect), 1979—; guest lectr. U. Calif., Berkeley. Important works include Acorn Housing Project, Oakland, Calif., Crescent Village Housing Project, Suisun City, Calif., Coplans residence, San Francisco, Betel Housing Project, San Francisco, Grand View Housing Project, San Francisco, Albany (Calif.) Oaks Housing, Grow Homes, San Pablo, Calif., Mariposa Housing, Dunleavy Plaza Housing, Potrero Ct. Housing, San Francisco, Lee residence, Kentfield, Calif., Burger residence, Lafayette, Calif., Burger residence, Oceanside, Oreg., Yamhill Valley Vineyards Winery, McMinneville, Oreg., Portico De Mar, shop and restaurant complex, Barcelona, Spain, Hendrickson residence, Newport Beach, Calif., Hamilton residence, Winters, Calif.; author: Geomorphic Architecture, 1986. Recipient citation for excellence in community architecture AIA, 1969, award of merit AIA, award of merit Homes for Better Living, 1970, 79, 1st Honor award, 1973, 81, Holiday award for a beautiful Am., 1970, Honor award 4th Biennial HUD awards for design excellence, 1970, Bay Area awards for design excellence, 1969, 74, 78, Apts. of Year award Archtl. Record, 1972, Houses of Year award, 1973, Calif. Affordable Housing Competition award, 1981, HUD Building Value into Housing award, 1981, Community Design award Calif. Council AIA, 1986; design grant Nat. Endowment for Arts, 1980, HUD, 1980; constrn. grant HUD, 1981. Office: PO Box 10193 Berkeley CA 94709-5193

BURGER, EMIL FERDINAND, allergist, medical group executive; b. Dallas, June 7, 1934; s. Emil Ferdinand and Florance Helen (Hays) B. BA, Rice U., 1955; MD, U. Tex., 1961. Diplomate Am. Bd. Allergy and Immunology. Pediatrician Kaiser Permanente Med. Group, L.A., 1964-66, 68-70; pvt. practice allergy, Downey, Calif., 1970—; med. dir. Am. Techs., Paramount, Calif., 1993—; guest prof. Chulalongkorn U. Sch. Dentistry, Bangkok, 1992. Capt. U.S. Army, 1966-68. Fellow Am. Acad. Allergy, Am. Coll. Allergy. Office: 8301 Florence Ave Ste 104 Downey CA 90240-3946

BURGESS, DAVID BRUCE, pediatrician; b. Waukegan, Ill., Apr. 15, 1947; s. Samuel George and Jane Catherine (Menzel) B.; 1 child, Sarah Elizabeth. BS, U. Ill., 1969; MD, U. Wis., 1973. Resident Tulane U., New Orleans, 1973-77, asst. prof., 1977-78, 1980-85; fellow in child development U. Colo., Denver, 1978-80; med. dir. Exceptional Family Member Program Fitzsimons Army Med. Ctr., Aurora, Colo., 1985—. Mem. Soc. for Devel. Pediatrics, Soc. for Behavioral Pediatrics, Soc. for Pediatric Rsch., Am. Acad. for Cerebral Palsy and Devel. Medicine. Office: Fitzsimons Army Med Ctr Bldg 506 Aurora CO 80045-5501

BURGESS, HAYDEN FERN (PŌKĀ LAENUI), lawyer; b. Honolulu, May 5, 1946; s. Ned E. and Nora (Lee) B.; m. Puanani Sonoda, Aug. 28, 1968. B in Polit. Sci., U. Hawaii, JD, 1976. Bar: Hawaii 1976, U.S. Tax Ct., U.S. Ct. Appeals (9th cir.). Pvt. practice Waianae, Hawaii, 1984-90; pres. Hawaii Coun. for 1993 and Beyond, Honolulu, 1991—; v.p. World Coun. Indigenous Peoples before UN, 1984-90; human rights adv., writer, speaker in field; pres. Pacific and Asia Coun. Indigenous Peoples; cons. on indigenous affairs, 1984; indigenous expert to ILO Conv.; expert UN seminar on effects of racism and racial discriminations on social and econ. rels. between indigenous peoples and states, 1989—. Trustee Office Hawaiian Affairs, Honolulu, 1982-86; mem. Swedish Nat. Commn. on Mus., 1986; leader Hawaiian Independence Movement; mem. Hawaiian Sovereignty Elections Coun. Mem. Law Assn. Asia and Western Pacific (steering com. on human rights 1988), Union of 3d World Journalists.

BURGESS, JOSEPH JAMES, JR., artist, educator; b. Albany, N.Y., July 13, 1924; s. Joseph James and Marie (Southwell) B.; m. Anna Kang, Aug. 25, 1959; children: Ian Tai Kyung, Dana Tai Soon. BA, Hamilton Coll., Clinton, N.Y., 1947; MA, Yale U., 1948; postgrad., Pratt Inst., Bklyn., 1950-52; MFA, Cranbrook Acad. Art, Bloomfield Hills, Mich., 1954. Asst. prof. fin arts, dept. head St. Lawrence U., Canton, N.Y., 1954-55; instr. art, chmn. art dept. Flint (Mich.) Community Jr. Coll., 1956-65, dir. DeWaters Art Ctr., 1956-65; asst. prof. design Ariz. State U., Tempe, 1965-66; instr. dept. continuing edn. Coll. of Santa Fe (N.Mex.), 1977-82; lectr. audio visual dept. Santa Fe Pub. Libr., 1981-82; asst. prof. art Highlands U., Las Vegas, N.Mex., 1982-83; instr. art Santa Fe Community Coll., 1987-90; instr. art workshops Valdes Corp., Santa Fe, 1988—; owner design studio and retail outlet Origins, Carmel, Calif., 1966-75, K/B Designs, 1960—; dir. Blair Galleries, Santa Fe, 1976-80. One man shows: Albany Inst. History and Art, 1958; group shows: Ball State Tchrs. Coll., 1958, Palace of Legion of Honor, San Francisco, 1959, DeWaters Art Ctr., 1964, Pasadena Art Mus., 1968, Santa Fe Festival of Arts, 1979, 80; group shows include Detroit Inst. Arts, 1956, Mus. Modern Art, N.Y.C., 1956, Flint Inst. Arts, 1956-65, Albany Inst. of History and Art, 1957; author: Three Chinese Poems, 1962, Four Chinese Poems, 1961, A Random Poem, 1973, others; contbr. articles to profl. jours. With USNR, 1943-46. Mem. Phi Beta Kappa. Home: PO Box 2151 Santa Fe NM 87504-2151 Office: K/B Designs PO Box 2151 Santa Fe NM 87504-2151

BURGESS, LARRY LEE, aerospace executive; b. Phoenix, May 13, 1942; s. Byron Howard and Betty Eileen (Schook) B.; m. Sylvia Wynnell, Sept. 30, 1964 (div. Dec. 1984); children: Byron, Damian; m. Mary Jane Ruble, Mar. 10, 1985; children: Christopher, Patrick. BSEE, MSEE, Naval Postgrad. Sch. Officer USN, Washington, 1964-85; corp. exec. Lockheed-Martin, Denver, 1985—; pres. L & M Capital Investments, Denver, 1987—; pub. 2 papers 4th Internat. Conf. on Tethers, 1995. Coach Youth Activities, Corpus Christi, Tex., 1976-78; coach youth basketball Littleton (Colo.) YMCA; speaker in local schs., Littleton, 1987-90. Inducted into the Kans. Basketball Hall of Fame, 1993. Mem. AIAA (dir.), SASA, Armed Forces Comm. and Electronic Agy. Republican. Home: 3 Red Fox Ln Littleton CO 80127-5710 Office: Martin Marietta PO Box 179 # 4001 Denver CO 80201-0179

BURGESS, MARY ALICE (MARY ALICE WICKIZER), publisher; b. San Bernardino, Calif., June 21, 1938; d. Russell Alger and Wilma Evelyn (Swisher) Wickizer; m. Michael Roy Burgess, Oct. 15, 1976; children from previous marriage: Richard Albert Rogers, Mary Louise Rogers Reynnells. AA, Valley Coll., San Bernardino, 1967; BA, Calif. State U., San Bernardino, 1975, postgrad., 1976-79; postgrad., U. Calif., Riverside, 1976-79. Lic. real estate salesman, Calif.; real estate broker, Calif. Sec.-treas. Lynwyck Realty & Investment, San Bernardino, 1963-75; libr. asst. Calif. State U., San Bernardino, 1974-76, purchasing agt., 1976-81; co-pub. The Borgo Press, San Bernardino, 1975—. Co-pub: (with Robert Reginald) Science Fiction and Fantasy Book Review, 1979-80; co-author (with M.R. Burgess) The Wickizer Annals: The Descendents of Conrad Wickizer of Luzerne County, Pennsylvania, 1983, (with Douglas Menville and Robert Reginald) Futurevisions: The New Golden Age of the Science Fiction Film, 1985, (with Jeffrey M. Elliot and Robert Reginald) The Arms Control, Disarmament and Military Science Dictionary, 1989, (with Michael Burgess) The House of the Burgesses, 2d edit., 1994; author: The Campbell Chronicles: A Genealogical History of the Descendants of Samuel Campbell of Chester County, Pennsylvania, 1989, (with Boden Clarke) The Work of Katherine Kurtz, 1992-93, (with Michael Burgess and Daryl F. Mallett) State and Province Vital Records Guide; editor: Cranberry Tea Room Cookbook, Still The Frame Holds, Defying the Holocaust, Risen from the Ashes: A Story of the Jewish Displaced Persons in the Aftermath of World War II, Being a Sequel to Survivors (Jacob Biber), 1989, Ray Bradbury: Dramatist (Ben P. Indick), 1989, Across the Wide Missouri: The Diary of a Journey from Virginia to Missouri in 1819 and Back Again in 1821, with a Description of the City of Cincinnati, (James Brown Campbell), Italian Theatre in San Francisco, Into the Flames: The Life Story of a Righteous Gentile, Jerzy Kosinski: The Literature of Violation, The Little Kitchen Cookbook, Victorian Criticism of American Writers, 1990, The Magic That Works: John W. Campbell and The American Response to Technology, 1993, Libido into Literature: The "Primēra Época" of Benito Pérez Galdós, 1993, A Triumph of the Spirit: Stories of Holocaust Survivors, 1994, A Way Farer in a World in Upheaval, 1993, William Eastlake: High Desert Interlocutor, 1993, The Price of Paradise: The Magazine Career of F. Scott Fitgerald, 1993, The Little Kitchen Cookbook, rev. edit., 1994, An Irony of Fate: William March, 1994, Hard-Boiled Heretic: Ross Macdonald, 1994, We The People!, 1994, The Chinese Economy, 1995, Voices of the River Plate, 1995, Chaos Burning on My Brow, 1995; co-editor and pub. (with Robert Reginald) of all Borgo Press publs.; also reviewer, indexer, researcher and editor of scholarly manuscripts. Chmn. new citizens Rep. Women, San Bernardino, 1967; libr. San Bernardino Geneal. Soc., 1965-67; vol. Boy Scout Am., Girl Scouts U.S., Camp Fire Girls, 1960s. Recipient Real Estate Proficiency award Calif. Dept. Real Estate, San Bernardino, 1966. Mem.

City of San Bernardino Hist. and Pioneer Soc., Calif. State U. Alumni Assn., Cecil County (Md.) Hist. Soc., Gallia County (Ohio) Hist. and Geneal. Soc., DAR (membership and geneal. records chmn. 1964-66, registrar and vice regent San Bernardino chpt. 1965-67). Office: The Borgo Press PO Box 2845 San Bernardino CA 92406-2845

BURGESS, ROBERT JOHN, marketing consultant, writer, educator; b. Metarie, La., Aug. 4, 1961; s. John Jacob and Doris Claire (Keating) B. BSBA summa cum laude, U. Denver, 1983; MBA, Loyola U., Chgo., 1984. Rsch. analyst United Bank Denver, 1984-85; sr. rsch. analyst Adolph Coors Co., Golden, Colo., 1985-88; sr. mgr. market rsch. U.S. West, Englewood, Colo., 1988-90; pres. Mktg. Advs., Inc., Englewood, 1990—. Author: Blitzed, 1992; columnist monthly mktg. jour. Quick Consult, 1992; inventor Keystone Beer, 1988. Mem. Colo. Rep. Party, Denver, 1983—. Mem. Am. Mktg. Assn. (pres. Colo. chpt. 1990-92, Outstanding Mktg. Rschr.-Peak awards 1992, grantee 1992), Market Rsch. Assn., South Metro Denver C. of C. (counselor 1992—), Colo. State U. Mktg. Club (hon.), Beta Gamma Sigma, Mu Kappa Tau (lifetime). Roman Catholic. Office: Mktg Advs Inc 6702 S Ivy Way Apt B1 Englewood CO 80112-6291

BURGESS, STEPHEN ANDREW, company executive; b. San Francisco, May 6, 1951; s. Roy Walter and Betty Jane (Kapel) B.; m. Gina Rae Mann, Mar. 16, 1974; children: Allison Renae, Andrew Ryan. BS in Biology, So. Oreg. State U., 1975. Br. mgr. Transamerica, Beaverton, Oreg., 1976-77; field mgr. Southland Corp., Portland, Oreg., 1977-79; bus. mgr. Clark Bros. Equipment Co., Portland, 1979-83; franchising/bus. cons. B & B Enterprises, San Diego, 1983-84; br. mgr. Businessland Inc., San Diego, 1984; corp. tng. mgr. Businessland Inc., San Jose, Calif., 1985-86; dir. bus. ops. Businessland Inc., San Jose, 1987-89; v.p. ops. Krause's Sofa Factory, Fountain Valley, Calif., 1989-91; sr. v.p. sales and ops. Krause's Sofa Factory/Castro Convertibles, Brea, Calif., 1991—; sr. v.p. franchise ops. Krause's Furniture Inc., Brea, 1994—. Contbr. articles to profl. jours. Contbr., vol. Olive Crest Homes for Children, Newport Beach, 1989—, City of Hope, L.A., 1990—. Mem. Canyon Crest Country Club, Gonzaga Preparatory Alumni Club. Home: 5360 Via Zopapo Yorba Linda CA 92687-3130 Office: Krauses Sofa Factory Castro Convertibles 200 N Berry St Brea CA 92621-3903

BURGOYNE, DAVID SIDNEY, psychiatrist; b. Montpelier, Idaho, Mar. 28, 1923; s. Sidney Eynon and Beatrice (Holmes) B.; m. Helen Louise Seewer, Nov. 15, 1945; children: David Sidney II, Rhoda Lee, James Carl (dec.), Steven John. Student, Utah State U., 1941-42, 46-47; MD, Cornell U., 1951. Med. intern LDS Hosp., Salt Lake City, 1951-52; gen. practice medicine Coolidge, Ariz., 1952-59; commd. ens. USN, 1960, advanced through grades to comdr.; resident in psychiat. medicine U.S. Naval Hosp., Oakland, Calif., 1960-62; chief neuropsychiatry USN-Pearl Harbor (Hawaii) Shipyard, 1963-65; chief of psychiatry U.S. Naval Hosp., Camp Pendleton, Calif., 1965-66; resigned USN, 1966; pvt. practice psychiatry Phoenix, 1966—; chief of staff Camelback Hosp., Phoenix, 1975-76, Scottsdale, Ariz., 1989. Author: Psychiatric Disorders - Identification and Emergency Care Aboard Submarines, 1964; contbr. articles to profl. jours. Lt. USN, 1942-46, PTO. Fellow Am. Psychiat. Assn. (life, Ariz. rep. 1972-77, dep. regional rep. area 7, 1977-79); mem. Ariz. Psychiat. Soc. (pres. 1971-72), Pinal County Med. Assn. (pres. 1958). Home: 4523 E Orange Dr Phoenix AZ 85018-1714 Office: 4630 E Indian School Rd Phoenix AZ 85018-5416

BURK, GARY MAURICE, health care facility planner; b. Dallas, Nov. 8, 1943; s. Houston Maurice and Evelyn (Howell) B. BArch, Tex. Tech U., 1968; MArch, U. Ill., 1970. Registered architect; NCARB cert. Asst. prof. Tex. Tech U., Lubbock, 1970-79; project designer Hellmuth, Obata & Kassabaum, Dallas, 1979-80; assoc. Richard Ferrara, Architect, Dallas, 1980-83; cons. designer Myrick, Newman, Dahlberg, Dallas, 1982-83; assoc. prof. Calif. State U., Pomona, Calif., 1983-85; sr. facility planner Am. Med. Internat., L.A., 1985-86; dir. facilities planning URS Cons., Cleve., 1986-88, URS Consultants, N.Y. and N.J., 1988-91; sr. med. planner Ellerbe Becket, Inc., L.A., 1991-95; v.p. Ellerbe Becket, Inc., San Francisco, 1995—; cons. City Hosp./St. Thomas Med. Ctr., Merger Task Force, Akron, 1988-89, L.A. County Pub. Health Programs and Svcs., 1992-94, Palo Alto (Calif.) Med. Found., 1992—, U. Tex. med. branch, Galveston, 1994—; dir. Hosp. of the Future research studio, 1985. Mem. Dallas Civic Chorus, 1980-83, St. Alban's Parish Choir, Cleveland Heights, Ohio, 1987-88, All Saints Parish Choir, Hoboken, N.J., 1988-90, Cleve. Opera Assocs., 1987-88; mem. steering com. Judith Resnik Women's Health Ctr., Summa Health System, Akron, 1989-91, Friends of N.Y. Philharm, 1990-91. Research grantee Tex. Tech U., 1976. Mem. AIA (ednl. fellow 1968, Calif. coun.), Am. Soc. for Testing Materials, AIA Acad. on Architecture for Health. Democrat. Episcopalian. Home: 155 Jackson St Apt 2204 San Francisco CA 94111 Office: Ellerbe Becket Inc 435 Market St 20th Fl San Francisco CA 94104

BURKART, JORDAN V., financial consultant; b. Marshall, Tex., Dec. 7, 1935; s. William Jordan and Lois (Vincent) B.; m. Marcia Marcotte, Aug. 24, 1969; children: Ashley, Frazer. BS, So. Meth. U., 1958; MBA, Harvard U., 1963. Assoc. Glore Forgan, William R. Staats, Inc., L.A., 1964-67; 1st v.p. Blyth Eastman Dillon & Co., L.A., 1967-74; v.p. Crocker Nat. Bank, L.A., 1974-79, sr. v.p., 1979-85; sr. v.p., treas. Crocker Nat. Corp., L.A., 1982-85; corp. fin. cons. L.A., 1986—. Served to lt. (j.g.) USNR, 1958-61. Club: Jonathan (Los Angeles).

BURKE, ARLENE L., osteopath, surgeon; b. Long Beach, Calif., Jan. 20, 1947; d. Luster B. and Margaret E. (Rives) Larch; children: David T. Burke, Christiene M. Burke, Sandra A. Hinsdale; m. Ronald H. Lloyd, Nov. 21, 1993. BA with honors, Loma Linda U., 1976; DO, U. Health Sci. Osteo. Medicine, Kansas City, Mo., 1981; MPH, The Johns Hopkins U., 1987. Commd. 2d lt. U.S. Army, 1977, advanced through grades to lt. col., 1993; resident in family practice Silas B. Hayes Army Cmty. Hosp., Fort Ord, Calif., 1981-83; family practice physician Weed Army Cmty. Hosp., Fort Irwin, Calif., 1983-85; med. dir. Med. Clinic, South Korea, 1985-86; resident in preventive medicine Madigan Army Med. Ctr., Tacoma, 1987-88; physician, occupl. health cons. Blanchfield Army Cmty. Hosp., Fort Campbell, Ky., 1988-91; preventive medicine physician Operation Desert Storm, 1990-91; occupl. health cons. Pueblo (Colo.) Health Clinic, 1991-93; physician, occupl. health cons. Evans Army Cmty. Hosp., Fort Carson, Colo., 1991-93; med. dir., staff physician several hosps., 1988-93; pvt. practice occupational medicine & adult primary care Colorado Springs, 1994—. Contbr. articles to profl. jours. Mem. APHA, Am. Osteo. Assn., Am. Coll. Preventive Medicine, Colo. Soc. Osteo. Physicians, Colo. Pub. Health Assn., Colo. Med. Soc., El Paso County Med. Soc. Republican. Seventh Day Adventist. Office: Arlene L Burke DO MPH PO Box 5499 Woodland Park CO 80866-5499

BURKE, ARTHUR THOMAS, engineering consultant; b. Pueblo, Colo., Nov. 26, 1919; s. Daniel Michael and Naomi Edith (Brashear) B.; BS, U.S. Naval Acad., 1941; postgrad. UCLA; m. Regina Ahlgren Malone, June 15, 1972; children: Arthur Thomas, Craig Timothy, Laura Ahlgren, Scott Ahlgren. With USN Electronics Lab. Center, San Diego, 1947-72, sr. satellite communications cons., 1964-72, satellite communications engring. cons., 1974—. Sweepstakes judge, San Diego Sci. Fair, 1960—. With USN, 1938-46; comdr. Res., ret. Recipient Presdl. Unit citation, 1942, Superior Performance award USN Electronics Lab. Center, 1967. Mem. IEEE (mem. San Diego membership com. 1958-68), AAAS, San Diego Astronomy Assn., San Diego Computer Assn., Am. Radio Relay League. Patentee electronic bathythermograph. Home and Office: 4011 College Ave San Diego CA 92115-6704

BURKE, EDMOND WAYNE, retired judge; b. Ukiah, Calif., Sept. 7, 1935; s. Wayne P. and Opal K. B.; children from previous marriage: Kathleen R., Jennifer E.; m. Anna M. Hubbard, Dec. 29, 1990. A.B., Humboldt State Coll., 1957, M.A., 1958; J.D., U. Calif., 1964. Bar: Calif., Alaska, Mont. Individual practice law Calif. and Alaska, 1965-67; asst. atty. gen. State of Alaska, 1967; asst. dist. atty. Anchorage, Alaska, 1968-69; judge Superior Ct., Alaska, 1970-75; justice Supreme Ct. State of Alaska, Anchorage, 1975-93, chief justice, 1981-84; of coun. Bogle & Gates, 1994—. Republican. Presbyterian. *

BURKE, GARY PALMER, historian, educator, coach; b. Grand Junction, Colo., Dec. 27, 1942; s. Granville Thomas and Blossom Ozelle (Palmer) B.; m. Patricia Ruth Armstrong, Apr. 7, 1966; children: Michael Palmer, Michelle Renee, Mitchell Alan. AA, Mesa Jr. Coll., 1962; BA, Western State Coll., 1964, MA, 1967. Cert. tchr., Colo. Tchr. Fowler (Colo.) H.S., 1965-67; tchr., coach Delta (Colo.) Mid. Sch., 1967—; sports editor Delta County Ind., 1968—; bd. dirs. Old Timers Assn. Youth Baseball, Delta, 1970-78; mem. adv. bd. Ft. Robidoux Hist. Site, Delta, 1994—. Author: History of Delta High School Football, 1974, Palisade: A Wrestling History, 1994, Colorado High School Wrestling Record Book, 1994. Recipient Nat. Sportswriter of Yr. award USA Wrestling Mag., 1992, Outstanding Media Coverage of H.S. Sports award Colo. Athletic Dirs. Assn., 1994, Gaskill award Colo. H.S. Coaches Assn., 1995. Mem. NEA, Am. Numismatic Assn., Colo. Edn. Assn., Delta Edn. Assn. Home: 1103 Catherine Pl Delta CO 81416-2499 Office: Delta Mid Sch 822 Grand Ave Delta CO 81416-2031

BURKE, JOHN CHARLES, social worker; b. N.Y.C., May 11, 1946; s. Charles John and Mary Rosalma (DeMott) B.; m. Kathleen Killough, Aug. 4, 1972; children: Eric John, Colleen Lee. BA in Sociology, Siena Coll., 1970; MS in Counseling, Laverne U., 1989; MBA, Chapman U., 1990. Owner, mgr. Burke's Apts., Saugerties, N.Y., 1973-76; owner, operator, tchr. Burke's Studio and Sch. Photography, Saugerties, 1973-76; outdoor recreation expert PM Mag., Channel 8 WFAA TV, Dallas, 1978; child placement worker Tex. Dept. Human Resources, Dallas, 1976-79; social worker State of Alaska Div. Family and Youth Svcs., Anchorage, 1979—; pres., CEO Internat. Bus. Devel. Corp., Anchorage, 1992; instr. Am. Inst. Banking, Am. Bankers Assn.; speaker in field. Contbr. articles to profl. publs. With U.S. Army, 1970-71. Roman Catholic. Home: 7500 Chalet Ct Anchorage AK 99516-1155

BURKE, KRISTIN MARIE, costume designer; b. Orange, Calif., Mar. 20, 1970; d. Bruce Lemont and Patricia Ann (Mullin) B. Grad., Northwestern U., 1991. Owner, designer KB Creates Fashion Design, Chico, Calif., 1982—; wardrobe runner Tri-Star Hudson Hawk, L.A., 1990—, asst. prodn. coord., 1990—; prodn. designer Niteskool, Northwestern U., 1987, 88, 89, 90, exec. producer, 1989—. Dir. La Madeleine, 1990 (Judge's Pick Seattle Video Shorts); costume designer (5 episodes) Varsity Cafe, 1989; (feature films) The Skate Board Kid, 1992, Street Wise, 1992, Carnosaur, 1992, Human Target, 1993, The Unborn II, 1993, Furious Angel, 1993, Revenge of the Red Baron, 1993, Blind Trust, 1993, Ground Zero, 1993, Munchie Strikes Back, 1993, Sweet Dreams, 1994, Force on Force, 1994, Red Ribbon Blues, 1995; (short films) Lucky Peach, 1992, Showdown on Rio Road, 1992, Judgement, 1994; also music videos; wardrobe asst. Dracula, 1991; writer screenplay Mes Jours San Popcorn, 1990; writer, dir. Ascent, 1990, To Whom It May Concern, 1990, I Am A Red Cat Flipping, 1990. Calif. State art scholar, 1987; finalist USA-Dallas Filmfest, 1991. Mem. Costume Designers Guild (local IATSE 892 designer category). Office: PO Box 492553 Los Angeles CA 90049-8553

BURKE, MARIANNE KING, state agency administrator, financial executive; b. Douglasville, Ga., May 30, 1938; d. William Horace and Evora (Morris) King; divorced; 1 child, Kelly Page. Student, Ga. Inst. Tech., 1956-59, Anchorage C.C., 1964-66, Portland State U., 1968-69; BBA, U. Alaska, 1976. CPA, Alaska. Sr. audit mgr. Price Waterhouse, 1982-90; v.p. fin., asst. sec. NANA Regional Corp., Inc., Anchorage, 1990-95; v.p. fin. NANA Devel. Corp., Inc., Anchorage, 1990-95; sec.-treas. Vanguard Industries, J.V., Anchorage, 1990-95, Alaska United Drilling, Inc., Anchorage, 1990-95; treas. NANA/Marriott Joint Venture, Anchorage, 1990-95; v.p. fin. Arctic Utilities, Inc., Anchorage, 1990-95, Tour Arctic, Inc., Anchorage, 1990-95, Purcell Svcs., Ltd., Anchorage, 1990-95, Arctic Caribou Inn, Anchorage, 1990-95, NANA Oilfield Svcs., Inc., Anchorage, 1990-95, NANA Corp. Svcs., Inc., Anchorage, 1992-95; dir. divsn. ins. State of Alaska, 1995—; mem. State of Alaska Medicaid Rate Commn., 1985-88, State of Alaska Bd. Accountancy, 1984-87. Bd. dirs. Alaska Treatment Ctr., Anchorage, 1978, Alaska Hwy. Cruises; treas. Alaska Feminist Credit Union, Anchorage, 1979-80; mem. fund raising com. Anchorage Symphony, 1981. Mem. AICPA, Alaska Soc. CPAs, Govtl. Fin. Officers U.S. and Can., Fin. Execs. Inst. (bd. dirs.). Home: 7241 Foxridge Cir Anchorage AK 99518-2702 Office: State Office Bldg PO Box 110805 333 Willoughby Ave Juneau AK 99811-0805 also: 3601 C St Ste 1324 Anchorage AK 99503-5948

BURKE, PAMELA ANN, systems engineer; b. Syracuse, N.Y., Mar. 20, 1952; d. Martin Michael and Eleanor Bernedette (Mahoney) B. AS in Aerospace Engring., Miami Dade Jr. Coll., 1971; BS in Aviation Mgmt. summa cum laude, Embry Riddle Aero. U., Daytona Beach, Fla., 1974; MBA in Quantative Methods, Fla. State U., 1978; Cert. Computer & Info. Systems, U. Colo., 1985. Vol. coord. Com. to Re-elect the Pres., Bethesda, Md., 1971-72; aviation specialist Office Info. and Trade Devel. Balt.-Washington Internat. Airport, Balt., 1975; aviation systems planner Howard, Needles, Tammen and Bergendoff, Alexandria, Va., 1975; engr. Fla. Dept. Transp., Tallahassee, 1976-78; instr. Coll. Bus. Fla. State U., Tallahassee, 1978-79; strategic planner, rsch. engr. Gen. Dynamics, San Diego, 1979-81; sr. systems engr. Martin Marietta, Denver, 1981-84, group systems engr., 1984-85, sr. group systems engr., 1981-93; sr. scientist, info. defence and space system cons. Colo. Office Space Advocacy, Colorado Springs, 1994—; prin. owner Red Star Arabians Equestrian Gift Horse Sense, Sedalia, Colo., 1987—. Author newsletter Pub. Policy Report/Column, 1985-93. Mem. AIAA (chmn. sect. pub. policy 1980-86, mem. nat. pub. policy com. 1985-93, dep. dir. region V pub. policy 1985-93, award pub. policy sect. 1983), NAFE, Colo. Office Space Advocacy/Colo. Space Bus. Roundtable (vice chmn. membership 1994—), Colo. Arabian Horse Club/Internat. Arabian Horse Assn., Am. Warmblood Soc., U.S. Humane Soc., N.Am. Riding for Handicapped Assn., other conservation, humane and preservation founds. Office: PO Box 486 Sedalia CO 80135-0486

BURKE, ROBERT BERTRAM, lawyer, political consultant, lobbyist; b. Cleve., July 9, 1942; s. Max and Eve (Miller) B.; m. Helen Choate Hall, May 5, 1979 (div. Oct. 1983). B.A., UCLA, 1963, J.D., 1966; LL.M., London Sch. Econs., 1967. Bar: D.C. 1972, Calif. 1978, U.S. Supreme Ct. 1977. Exec. dir. Lawyer's Com. Civil Rts. under Law, Washington, 1968-69; ptnr. Fisk, Wolfe & Burke, Paris, 1969-71; assoc. O'Connor & Hannan, Washington, 1972-74; sole practice, Washington, 1974-79, Los Angeles, 1978—; cons. Commonwealth Pa., Harrisburg, 1973. Chmn. So. Calif. Hollings for Pres., 1984; pres. Bldg. and Appeals Bd. City of Los Angeles, State Adv. Bd. on Alcohol Related Problems; bd. dirs. Vols. of Am. Mem. ABA, Am. Inst. Architects (profl. affiliate), UCLA Law Alumni Assn. (pres.). Jewish. Home: 10450 Wilshire Blvd Apt 11D Los Angeles CA 90024-4611

BURKEE, IRVIN, artist; b. Kenosha, Wis., Feb. 6, 1918; s. Omar Lars and Emily (Quardokas) B.; diploma Sch. of Art Inst. Chgo., 1945; m. Bonnie May Ness, Apr. 12, 1945; children: Brynn, Jill, Peter (dec.), Ian (dec.). Owner, silversmith, goldsmith Burkee Jewelry, Blackhawk, Colo., 1950-57; painter, sculptor, Aspen, Colo., 1957-78, Pearce, Ariz., Pietrasanta, Italy, 1978—; instr. art U. Colo., 1946, 50-53, Stephens Coll., Columbia, Mo., 1947-49. John Quincy Adams travel fellow, Mex., 1945. Executed copper mural of human history of Colo. for First Nat. Bank, Englewood, Colo., 1970, copper mural of wild birds of Kans. for Ranchmart State Bank, Overland Park, Kans., 1974; exhibited Art Inst. Chgo., Smithsonian Instn. (award 1957), Milw. Art Inst., Krannert Mus., William Rockhill Nelson Gallery, St. Louis Art Mus., Denver Art Mus.; represented in southwestern galleries, also pvt. collections throughout U.S.; work illustrated in books Design and Creation of Jewelry, Design through Discovery, Walls. Mem. Nat. Sculpture Soc., Sedona Chamber Music Soc. Address: PO Box 5361 Lake Montezuma AZ 86342-5361

BURKETT, JOHN DAVID, professional baseball player; b. New Brighton, Mass., Nov. 28, 1964. With San Francisco Giants, 1983-94, Tex. Rangers, 1994—. Office: Tex Rangers 1000 Ball Park Way Arlington TX 76011*

BURKETT, WILLIAM ANDREW, banker; b. nr. Herman, Nebr., July 1, 1913; s. William H. and Mary (Dill) B.; m. Juliet Ruth Johnson, Oct. 5, 1940 (dec. Mar. 1976); children: Juliet Ann Burkett Hooker, Katherine C. Burkett Congdon, William Cleveland; m. Nancy Shallert Morrow, June 20, 1992. Student, U. Nebr., 1931-32, Creighton U. Law Sch., 1932-33; LL.B., U. Omaha, 1936. Exec. trainee Bank Am., 1937-38; Sr. spl. agt., intelligence unit Treasury Dept., 1945-50; exec. v.p. Calif. Employers Assn. Group, Sacramento, 1950-53; dir. Calif. Dept. Employment, 1953-55; chmn. Calif. Employment Stabilization Commn., 1953-55; supt. banks, chmn. Dept. Investments Calif., 1955-59; dir. Liquidation Yokohama Specie Bank; also Sumitomo Bank, San Francisco, 1955-59; cons. Western Bancorp, San Francisco, 1959-61; chmn. bd., pres. Security Nat. Bank Monterey County, Monterey-Carmel, Calif., 1961-66, Burkett Land Co., Monterey, 1966—; chmn. bd. Securities Properties Corp., Monterey; witness Calif. Crime Com., U.S. Senate Kefauver Crime Com., 1950-52, U.S. Congress Banking Com., 1991; nat. chmn., founder Bank Savs. & Loan Depositor's League, 1991. Author: Mount Rushmore National Memorial's History of America, 1776-1904, 1971. Elected nominee Nebr. Sec. State, 1936; witness Calif. Crime Commn. and U.S. Senate Kefauver Crime Commn., 1950-52, U.S. Congress Banking Com., 1991; dir. banking and investments, cabinet gov., Calif., 1953-59; dir. Calif. Emergency Manpower Commn., 1953-55; chmn. Gov. Calif. Com. Refugee Relief, 1953-55; mem. Calif. Securities Commn., 1955-59; mem. financial bd. Pine Manor Jr. Coll., Chestnut Hill, Mass., 1967—; mem. Monterey County Hist. Commn., Nat. Trust Found., Royal Oak Found.; bd. dirs. Monterey Symphony Assn.; chmn. bd. trustees Nat. Hist. Found.; trustee Monterey Mus. Art, Bishop Kip Sch., Carmel Valley, Calif.; co-chmn., trustee Mt. Rushmore Hall of Records Commn., 1987; mem. adv. bd. Robert Louis Stevenson Sch., Pebble Beach, Calif., 1971-74, candidate for gov. Calif., 1978 . Served as officer USCGR, 1943-45. Mem. Am., Calif., Ind. bankers assns., Nat. Assn. Supts. State Banks (pres. 1958-59), Monterey History and Art Assn., Mt. Rushmore Nat. Meml. Soc. (life mem., trustee), Amvets (dept. comdr. Calif. 1947, nat. vice comdr. 1948), Soc. Calif. Pioneers, Bank and Savs. and Loan Depositor's League (nat. chmn. 1991—), Monterey Peninsula Mus. Art, Mt. Rushmore Hall of Records Commn. Inc. (nat. co-chmn.1990—). Episcopalian. Clubs: Monterey Peninsula Golf and Country (Pebble Beach), Beach and Tennis (Pebble Beach), Stillwater Yacht (Pebble Beach); Carmel Valley Golf and Tennis; Commonwealth (San Francisco), Rotary (San Francisco); Sutter Lawn (Sacramento). Home: PO Box 726 Pebble Beach CA 93953-0726 Office: Viscaino Rd Pebble Beach CA 93953

BURKHART, BRAD JOHN, horticulturist, landscape architect; b. Ann Arbor, Mich.. BA in Fine Art, Kalamazoo Coll., 1971; student, Washington U., St. Louis, 1972-74; cert. completition horticulture, City Coll. San Francisco, 1979; M Landscape Architecture, U. Mich., 1982. Mgr. Weber Native Plant Nursery, San Diego County, 1983-86, Habitat Restoration and Mgmt. Group, San Diego, 1987-94; tchr. native plant lendscaping 3 colls., San Diego County, 1984-93; lectr. on habitat restoration and native plant landscaping; presenter Soc. Ecol. Restoration confs., 1989—. Prin. works include 1st San Diego River Improvement Project Horticultural Supervision and Monitoring, La Paloma Brodiaea Filifolia Mitigation Program - Baldwin Co., Twin Oaks Valley Ranch Riparian Mitigation Plans - Brock Devel., North Mission Valley Interceptor Sewer Riparian Mitigation Plans - City of San Diego Water Utilities Dept., Black Mountain Rd. San Diego Thornmint Mitigation - Pardee Devel., Sabre Springs Disturbed Hillside Chaparral Revegetation Program - Pardee Constrn.; contbr. articles to profl. jours. Recipient San Diego Xeriscape award, 1990. Mem. Soc. Ecol. Restoration, Assn. Wetland Mgrs., Internat. Erosion Control Assn., Jepson Herbarium, Brit. Ecol.Soc. Indsl. Ecol. Group, Calif. Native Plant Soc., Native Grassland Assn. Calif. Home: 9836 Rimpark Way San Diego CA 92124-1627 Office: Ogden Environ & Energy Svcs 5510 Morehouse Dr San Diego CA 92121-3720

BURKHAUSER, TERESA ELAINE, company planning executive; b. Enid, Okla., Oct. 18, 1955; d. Cleo Veryl and Gladys Elaine (West) Winter; m. Ralph Ottokar Burkhauser, Sept. 30, 1978; 1 child, Cody Steven. Diploma, Altus High Sch., 1973. Tour and travel mgr. Caesars Tahoe Hotel and Casino, Stateline, Nev., 1980-82, sales mgr., 1982-85, nat. sales mgr., 1985-89, convention svcs. mgr., 1989-90; owner, meeting and conv. planner Mountain View Planners, Garnerville, Nev., 1990—. Mem. Sac. Soc. Assn. Execs., No. Calif. Soc. Assn. Execs., Am. Soc. Assn. Execs., So. Calif. Soc. Assn. Execs., Tahoe Douglas C. of C. Office: Mountain View Planners PO Box 2273 Gardnerville NV 89410-2273

BURKHEAD, VIRGINIA RUTH, rehabilitation nurse; b. Marlow, Okla., Apr. 11, 1937; d. Norvin Woodrow Whitehead and Harriet Louise (Pittman) Mayes; m. Marvin Vern Foster, Oct. 16, 1956 (div. 1964); children: Deborah, Marcia, Marva, Laurie, Sheila; m. Robert Burdett Burkhead, Apr. 11, 1987. ADN, Casper Coll., 1971; BSN, Wash. State U., 1994. RN, Wash. Staff nurse, house supr., enterostomal therapy nurse Meml. Hosp. Natrona County, Casper, Wyo., 1971-79; enterostomal therapy nurse, coord. ostomy program Holy Family Hosp., Spokane, 1979—, coord. neurol. rehab. program, 1985—. Deaconess 1st Christian Ch., Spokane, 1986—. Mem. Assn. Rehab. Nurses, Wound, Ostomy and Contence Nurses Soc., Jacks and Jennys Square Dance Club (coun. del. 1992), Sigma Theta Tau. Mem. Christian Ch. (Disciples of Christ). Home: 2116 E Lincoln Rd Spokane WA 99207-7723 Office: Holy Family Hosp 5633 N Lidgerwood St Spokane WA 99207-1224

BURKHOLDER, GRACE ELEANOR, educator, archeologist; b. Sumas, Wash., Sept. 21, 1920; d. George Lewis and Leah (Benke) Welch; m. Warren Stanford Burkholder, June 4, 1938 (div. Apr. 1957); children: Warren Stanford, Carol Joyce Brackett. BEd cum laude, U. Miami, Fla., 1956; MEd, U. Okla., 1980. Tchr., Laurel Sch., Oceanside, Calif., 1956-58; elem. tchr. U.S. Navy, Kwajalein, M.I., 1958-59, Transport Co. Tex., Kwajalein, 1959-60, Arabian Am. Oil Co., Dhahran, Saudi Arabia, 1960-80. Author: An Arabian Collection: Artifacts from the Eastern Province, 1984, Perceptions of the Past: Solar Phenomena in Southern Nevada, 1995; author: (with others) Rock Art Papers, vol. 7, 1990, vol. 8, 1991, vol. 9, 1992, vol. 10, 1993, American Indian Rock Art, vol. 17, 1992; rsch., publs. on Ubaid sites and pottery in Saudi Arabia. Active San Diego Mus. Man, Mus. No. Ariz., Clark County Heritage Mus., Lost City Mus. Mem. Am. Rock Art Rsch. Assn., Nev. Archael. Assn.

BURKHOLDER, JOYCE LYNN, clinical social worker; b. Phila., Oct. 28, 1951; d. J. Edward and Mae Elizabeth (Wood) B.; m. Dirk Denier Vandergon, May 31, 1983; children: Austin Edward, Alexandra Mae. BSW, Temple U., 1975; MSW, Calif. State U., Sacramento, 1985. Lic. clin. social worker, Nev. Caseworker Silver Springs Martin Luther Sch., Plymouth Meeting, Pa., 1974-76; counselor Turning Point Youth Svc., Ambler, Pa., 1976-77; dir., counselor Aquarian Effort Alternative House, Sacramento, Calif., 1978-81; dir. social svcs., case mgr. Truckee Meadows Hosp., Reno, 1983-84; clin. social worker U. Calif. Davis Med. Ctr., Sacramento, 1985-86; cons. Greater Nev. Home Health Care, Revo, 1988-90; sec., bd. dirs. Pathways, Reno, 1990—; pvt. practice, 1993—; instr. U. Nev., Reno, 1991. Bd. dirs. Aux. to Washoe County Med. Soc., Reno, 1989-90; vol. Planned Parenthood of No. Nev., Reno, 1990. Mem. Nat. Assn. Social Workers. Home: 4288 Bitterroot Rd Reno NV 89509-0617

BURKLE, RONALD W., food service executive; b. 1953. Pvt. practice, 1975-88; pres. Jurgensen's, Pasadena, Calif., 1986-88; prin. Yucaipa Mgmt. Co., Claremont, Calif., 1986—; chmn. Food 4 Less Supermarkets, La Habra, Calif., 1989—. Office: Food 4 Less Supermarkets 777 S Harbor Blvd La Habra CA 90631-6839

BURKLUND, PATRICIA HELEN, marketing professional; b. Chgo., Mar. 12, 1944; d. John Lawrence and Virginia Mae (Brader) Stackpool; m. Sidney Andrew Burklund. Student, Shoreline Community Coll., 1972-76; BA, U. Puget Sound, 1981. Lic. refrigeration operating engr. Mgr. service Genesee Fuel Co., Seattle, 1976-79; asst. service mgr. MacDonald Miller Co., Seattle, 1979-81, mgr. constrn. project, 1981-83; mgr. service Hill Refrigeration, Tukwila, Wash., 1983-84; gen. mgr. Care Co., Bellevue, Wash., 1984-85; pres. P. Burklund and Assocs., Bothell, Wash., 1985—. Mem. Wash. State Refrigeration Contractors Assn. (sec. 1983-84), Nat. Assn. Female Execs., Am. Assn. Profl. Cons., Womens Network. Roman Catholic. Club: W.S. Yacht. Office: P Burklund & Assocs Inc 23525 SE # 3D Bothell WA 98021

BURLAND, BRIAN BERKELEY, novelist, poet, artist, scenarist, playwright; b. Paget, Bermuda, Apr. 23, 1931; s. Gordon Hamilton and Honor Alice Croydon (Gosling) B.; m. Charlotte Ann Taylor, 1952 (div. 1957); children: Susan, Anne, William; m. Edwina Ann Trentham, 1962 (div. 1979); 1 child, Benjamin; m. Isabella Petrie, 1990. Grad., Aldenham Sch., Elstree, Eng., 1948; student, U. Western Ont., Can., 1948-51. Mng. dir. Burland Estates, Ltd., Gosling Estates, Ltd.; 1st v.p. G.H. Burland & Co., Ltd., 1951-56; assoc. editor Bermudian Mag., 1957; lectr. Am. Sch., London, 1974, Washington and Lee U., Va., 1973; writer in residence So. Sem., Va.,

1973, Bermuda Writers Conf., 1978, U. Hartford, Conn., 1981-82; guest fellow Yale U., 1982-83; vis. prof. Conn. Coll., 1986-87; judge P.E.N. Syndicated Fiction Project, 1985; narrator stories and poems BBC, 1968—; condr. poetry and fiction readings Yale U., Washington and Lee U., U. Hartford, U. Mass., Amherst, Arts coun. Princeton, 1990-93; writer, painter-in-residence Melville Coll., 1992, Schotts (Scotland) Prison, 1995; lectr. BDA Coll. Author: A Fall from Aloft, 1968, A Few Flowers for St. George, 1969, Undertow, 1970, The Sailor and the Fox, 1973, Surprise, 1975, Stephan Decatur, 1976, The Flight of the Cavalier, 1980, Love is a Durable Fire, 1985 (children's book), St. Nicholas the Tub, 1964; (poetry) To Celebrate a Happiness That is America, 1971; represented in various pvt. collections. Mem. Princeton Arts coun. With Brit. Mcht. Svc., 1944. Recipient Lifetime Achievement award Bermuda Arts Coun., 1993. Fellow Royal Soc. Lit., Acad. Am. Poets; mem. PEN, Poetry Soc. Am., Author's Guild, Am. Ctr. Soc., Acad. of Am. Poets, Princeton Writers Group (founder), Royal Yacht Club (Bermuda), Chelsea Yacht Club (London). Mem. Bah'ai World Faith. Office: c/o Mary Cunnane W W Norton & Co 550 5th Ave New York NY 10036-5001

BURLEIGH-SPARKS, DIANA LEE, infection control nurse, healthcare consultant; b. Stibnite, Idaho, May 14, 1946; d. Ernest Edmund and Carol Alice (Hamburg) Oberbillig; m. John Sparks; children: Tracy Joy, Alyson Dawn. ASRN, Boise (Idaho) Coll., 1968; BS, U. San Francisco, 1980; MEd, U. Idaho, 1992. Nurse St. Agnes Hosp., Fresno, Calif.; pub. health nurse Merced (Calif.) County Med. Ctr., Merced County Health Dept.; infection surveillance and AIDS coord. St. Luke's Regional Med. Ctr., Boise, cons. infection control. Mem. Am. Practitioners in Infection Control, Sigma Theta Tau. Home: 3703 E Shady Glen Dr Boise ID 83706-5778

BURLESKI, JOSEPH ANTHONY, JR., information services professional; b. Poughkeepsie, N.Y., June 30, 1960; s. Joseph Anthony Burleski Sr. and Fredeline Cyr; m. Judith Ann Lezon, June 10, 1989; 1 child, Joseph Anthony III. BSBA, Marist Coll., 1982; MBA Mktg., U. Phoenix, 1992; grad. in human rels. and effective speaking, Dale Carnegie, 1990. Computer operator IBM Corp., Poughkeepsie, 1982-83, lead/sr. computer operator, 1983-84, systems programmer, 1984-85, assoc. systems programmer, 1985-86, mgr. offshift computer ops., 1986-87; mgr. info. processing IBM Corp., Boulder, Colo., 1987-88, mgr. MVS systems programming, 1988-91; mgr. location and field svcs. devel. Integrated Systems Solutions Corp. (subs. IBM), Boulder, 1991-93, mgr. location and field svc. devel. ind. test, 1992-93; mgr. VM/VSE svcs. Integrated Sys. Solutions Corp. subs. IBM Corp., Boulder, 1993-94; account mgr. Integrated Sys. Solutions Corp., Boulder, 1994—; mem. IBM Data Processing Ops. Coun., Poughkeepsie, 1983-92; grad. asst. Dale Carnegie Inst., Boulder, 1990—. Coach Spl. Olympics, 1987—; mem. Order of the Arrow Hon. Soc., sec., editor, 1976-77, pres. 1977-78, treas. 1980-81; patrol leader, store dir., asst. camp dir. Boy Scouts Am., Cub Scouts Summer Camp, 1985-87. Mem. Marist Coll. Alumni Assn. (contbr.), Vigil Nat. Honor Soc., IBM Runners' Club. Roman Catholic. Home: 1826 Lashley St Longmont CO 80501-2061 Office: ISSC Corp 5600 63rd St Boulder CO 80301-9269

BURLINGAME, ALMA LYMAN, chemist, educator; b. Cranston, R.I., Apr. 29, 1937; s. Herman Follett Jr. and Rose Irene (Kohler) B.; children: Mark, Walter; m. Marilyn F. Schwartz. BS, U. R.I., 1959; PhD, MIT, 1962. Asst. prof. U. Calif., Berkeley, 1963-68, assoc. chemist, 1968-72, rsch. chemist, 1972-78; prof. U. Calif., San Francisco, 1978—; vis. prof. Ludwig Inst. for Cancer Rsch., London, 1993-94. Editor: Topics in Organic Mass Spectrometry, 1970, Mass Spectrometry in Health and Life Science, 1985, Biological Mass Spectrometry, 1990, Mass Spectrometry in the Biological Sciences, 1995; contbr. articles to profl. jours. With USAR, 1954-62. Guggenheim Found. fellow, 1970. Fellow AAAS. Office: U Calif Dept Pharm San Francisco CA 94143

BURLINGHAM, ARAGON, aerospace engineer; b. Ipswich, Eng., Feb. 25, 1968; came to U.S., 1986; s. Richard and Haleh (Mojibi) B. BS in Aeronautics/Astronautics, U. So. Calif., L.A., 1990; MS in Aerospace Engring., Stanford U., 1992. Rsch. technologist GEC-Alsthom, Whetstone, Eng., 1990-91; customer support engr. RASNA Corp., San Jose, Calif., 1992-93; cons. engr. Food & Machinery Corp., San Jose, 1993; engr. Modeling & Computing Svcs., Boulder, Colo., 1993—. Contbr. papers to tech. publs. Mem. AIAA (events coord. U. So. Calif. chpt. 1989), ASME (assoc.), Bakersfield Coll. Engrs. Club (v.p. 1987-88), Tau Beta Pi.

BURNETT, ERIC STEPHEN, environmental consultant; b. Manchester, Eng., Apr. 5, 1924; s. William Louis and Edith Winifred (Gates) B.; came to U.S., 1963; naturalized, 1974; BSc in Physics (with honors), London U., 1954; MS in Environ. Studies, Calif. State, Dominguez Hills, 1976; PhD in Environ. Engring., Calif. Coast U., 1982; Reg. Environ. Auditor. children: Diana, Ian, Brenda, Keith. Program mgr. Brit. Aircraft Corp., Stevenage, Eng., 1953-63; sr. systems engr. RCA, Princeton, N.J., 1963-66; project mgr. Gen. Electric Co., Valley Forge, Pa., 1966-67; dept. head TRW systems Group, Redondo Beach, Calif., 1967-72; dir. energy and pollution control ARATEX Svcs., Inc., Calif., 1974-81, dir. tech. devel., 1981-83, staff cons., 1983-91; cons., lectr. in spacecraft sensor tech., energy conservation, environ. and contamination controls. With Royal Air Force, 1942-47. Assoc. fellow AIAA; mem. Inst. Environ. Scis. (sr.). Contbr. articles in field to profl. jours. Home and Office: 3423 Excalibar Rd Placerville CA 95667-5418

BURNETT, GARY BOYD, lawyer, real estate consultant; b. Huntington Park, Calif., Mar. 19, 1954; s. A. Boyd Burnett and Betty J. (Koontz) Wiggins; m. Shelli Green, June 23, 1977 (div. June 1984); 1 child, Justin; m. Lisa D. Parker, May 14, 1988; children: Garrett, Kara. BA, Calif. State U., Fullerton, 1978; JD, Brigham Young U., 1980. Bar: Utah 1990, U.S. Dist. Ct. Utah 1990. Staff atty. Am. Land Devel. Assn., Washington, 1981-83; corp. counsel Preferred Equities Corp., Las Vegas, Nev., 1983-84, Real Corp., Las Vegas, 1984-85; real estate cons. Las Vegas, 1985-86; corp. counsel Ridgeview Pk., Inc., Las Vegas, 1986—; real estate broker Las Vegas, 1986—; corp. counsel S.W. Oasis Constrn., Inc., Las Vegas, 1990—. Contbr. articles to profl. jours. Del. Rep. State Ctrl. Com., Sacramento, Calif., 1976; coach Green Valley Little League, Henderson, Nev., 1992; leader Boy Scouts Am., Henderson, 1992. Mem. ABA, Assn. Trial Lawyers Am. Mem. LDS Ch. Office: 4045 S Eastern Ave Las Vegas NV 89119

BURNETT, GEORGE, professional hockey coach. Head coach Edmonton Oilers, 1994—. Office: Edmonton Oilers, Northlands Coliseum, Edmonton, AB Canada T5B 4M9

BURNETT, JOHN LAURENCE, geologist; b. Wichita, Kans., Aug. 28, 1932; s. Virgil Milton and Bertha Maurine (Van Order) L.; m. Annetta J. Saywell, July, 2, 1954 (div. 1975); children: John Forrester, Laurence Gregory. AB in Geology, U. Calif., Berkeley, 1957, MS in Mining, 1960. Cert. engring. geologist; registered geologist. Geologist Calif. Div. Mines and Geology, Sacramento, Calif., 1958—; courts expert superior ct. of L.A., 1967-71; instr. geology U. Calif. Extension, Berkeley, 1967-75, Cosumnes River Coll., 1981-88. Pvt. U.S. Army, 1955. Fellow Geol. Soc. of Am.; mem. Assn. of Engring. Geologists, Soc. of Mining Metallurgy and Exploration. Unitarian. Office: Calif Div Mines and Geology 801 St Ms 12 # 31 Sacramento CA 95814

BURNETT, LYNN BARKLEY, health science educator; b. Reedley, Calif., Oct. 20, 1948; s. Charles Erbin and Ruth Clarice (Erickson) B. BS, Columbia Pacific U., MSc; diploma in nat. security mgmt. Nat. Def. U. of U.S.; PhD in Physiology and Psychology, Columbia Pacific U.; EdD in Higher Edn. Nova Southeastern U.; Faculty of Laws, U. London. Cert. community coll. tchr., Calif., instr. in emergency care, basic CPR, ACLS, Pediatric ALS. Med. advisor Fresno County Sheriff's Depart., 1972—, assoc. dir. Cen. Valley Emergency Med. Svcs. System, Fresno, Calif., 1974-75; faculty Fresno City Coll., 1978—, prof. health sci., 1981-87, dir. continuing edn. in health, Calf. State U. Fresno, 1981—, adj. faculty West Coast Christian Coll., 1989-92, med. and health commentator Sta. KVPR-FM Valley Pub. Radio, 1990— lectr., cons. in field; co-dir. conjoint rsch. program of Stanford U. Sch. Medicine and Dept. Health Sci. Calif. State U., Fresno, 1986; established pilot paramedic program Fresno County, 1974-75; dir. Cent. Valley's Inaugural Paramedic Tng. Program, 1975; established CPR tng. Programs Fresno Fire Dept., 1968, Fresno Police Dept., 1972, Fresno County Sheriff's Dept., 1973. Chmn. Fresno County steering com. The Chem. People, 1983-86, Generation at Risk, 1987; mem. Emergency Med. Care Com. Fresno County, 1979-85, vice chmn., 1984-85; mem. Calif. State Commn. Emergency Med. Services, 1974-75; mem. Fresno County Adv. Bd. on Drug Abuse, 1984-92, chmn. drug adv. bd., 1985-88; bd. dir. First Baptist Ch. of Fresno, 1994—, vice chmn., 1995—; chmn. pub. edn. Fresno County unit Am. Cancer Soc., 1984-87, 90-92, bd. dirs. 1984—, v.p., 1985-87, pres. elect 1987-88, pres. 1988-90, past. pres., 1990-92, chmn. nominations and leadership devel. Fresno County unit, 1990-92, task force cancer and under-served populations Fresno County unit, 1992—, youth and cancer, Calif. Divsn. Am. Cancer Soc., 1992-94; com. mem. Early Detection and Treatment, Prevention and Risk Reduction, Fresno County Unit Am. Cancer Soc., 1993;; chmn. Alcohol, Drug adv bd. Fresno County, 1992—; pres. Fresno County Safety Coun., 1985—; mem. steering com. Fresno Health Promotion Coalition, chmn. com. on crime, violence and safety, 1987-89; chmn. bd. Fresno County Drug and Alcohol Prevention Coalition, Inc., 1991-92; mem. med. staff, steering com. All-Star Football Game. 1965—; emergency med. cons. Dept. Intercollegiate Atheltics Calif. State U., Fresno, 1982—; mem. Community Collaborative of Fresno Tomorrow, Inc., com. Juvenile Crime Benchmarks, 1990-91; mem. core com. Student Assistance Program for Substance Abuse and Related Problems Fresno City Coll., 1989—; mem. coms. on bus. and industry and govt. Fresno County Master Plan Adv. Body for Comprehensive Coordination of Substance Abuse Svcs.; faculty advanced trauma life support and trauma nurse tactics Valley Med. Ctr., 1982—; bd. dirs. Calif. div. Am. Cancer Soc., 1990-92; chmn. com. pub. policy Fresno County Drug, Alcohol Prevention Coalition, Inc., 1992—; mem. cancer svcs. adv. bd., Calif. Cancer Ctr., 1992-94; mem. com. biomedical ethics Fresno Community Hosp. and Med. Ctr., 1992—; subcom. mem. Resuscitation Status, Advance Directives, and Organ Donation, Protocol for Consultations and Med. Records, Intramural and Extramural Bioethics Edn., 1993; mem. com. emergency cardiac care, Central Valley Divsn. of Am. Heart Assn., 1992—; mem.steering com., subcom. neighborhood revitalization and svc. coord., Oper. "Weed and Seed", office of U.S. attorney gen. eastern dist. Calif., 1992-93; chmn. master plan adv. body to reduce alcohol and other drug abuse in Fresno County. Recipient State Service medal Calif. Mil. Dept., 1980; Bronze medal Am. Heart Assn., 1974, Appreciation award Am. Cancer Soc., 1985. Mem. AAAS, Am. Coll. Preventive Medicine, Am. Acad. Forensic Scis. (alt. del. People's Republic of China, citizen ambassador program People to People Internat. 1986), Am. Assn. Suicidology, N.Y. Acad. Scis., Internat. Platform Assn., Fresno Counublican. Baptist. Avocations: reading, musical conducting, writing screenplays. Co-author: manuscript for motion picture Quarantine. Home: PO Box 4512 Fresno CA 93744-4512

BURNEY, VICTORIA KALGAARD, business consultant, civic worker; b. Los Angeles, Apr. 12, 1943; d. Oscar Albert and Dorothy Elizabeth (Peterson) Kalgaard; children: Kim Elizabeth, J. Hewett. BA with honors, U. Mont., 1965; MA, U. No. Colo., 1980; postgrad. Webster U., St. Louis, 1983-84. Exec. dir. Hill County Community Action, Havre, Mont., 1966-67; community orgn. specialist ACCESS, Escondido, Calif., 1967-68; program devel. and community orgn. specialist Community Action Programs, Inc., Pensacola, Fla., 1968-69; cons. Escambia County Sch. Bd., Fla., 1969-71; pres. Kal Kreations, Kailua, Hawaii, 1974-77; instr., dir. office human resources devel. Palomar Coll., San Marcos, Calif., 1978-81; chief exec. officer IDET Corp., San Marcos, 1981-87; cons. County of Riverside, Calif., 1983. Mem. San Diego County Com. on Handicapped, San Diego, 1979; cons. tribal resource devel., Escondido, Calif., 1979; mem. exec. com. Social Services Coordinating Council, San Diego, 1982-83; mem. pvt. sector com. and planning and rev. com. Calif. Employment and Tng. Adv. Council, Sacramento, 1982-83; bd. mgrs. Santa Margarita Family YMCA, Vista, Calif., 1984-86; bd. dirs. North County Community Action Program, Escondido, 1978, Casa de Amparo, San Luis Rey, Calif., 1980-83; mem. San Diego County Pub. Welfare Adv. Bd., 1979-83, chairperson, 1981; mem. Calif. Rep. Cen. Com., Sacramento, 1989—; ofcl. San Diego County Rep. Cen. Com., 1985-93, exec. com., 1987-92, 2nd vice-chmn. 1991-92; chmn. 74th Assembly Dist. Rep. Caucus, 1989-90; chmn. Working Ptnrs., 1987-90; trustee Rancho Santa Fe Community Ctr., 1991-92; active Nat. Assistance League, 1993—; bd. dirs. Assistance League North Coast, 1994—, mem. 1993—. Mem. Nat. Assn. County Employment and Tng. Adminstrs. (chairperson econ. resources com. 1982-85), Calif. Assn. Local Econ. Devel., San Diego Econ. Devel. Corp., Oceanside Econ. devel. Council (bd. dirs. 1983-87), Oceanside C. of C., San Marcos C. of C. (bd. dirs. 1982-85), Carlsbad C. of C. (indsl. council 1982-85), Escondido C. of C. (comml. and indsl. devel. council 1982-87), Vista C. of C. (vice chairperson econ. devel. com. 1982-83), Vista Econ. Devel. Assn., Nat. Job Tng. Partnership, San Diego County Golden Eagle Club.

BURNHAM, WILLIAM A., wildlife protection society administrator; b. Pueblo, Colo., Oct. 5, 1947; s. William H. and Bertha (Nemier) B.; m. Patricia Ann Wood, July 9, 1966; 1 child, Kurt Kristopher. BS, U. So. Colo., 1973; MS, Brigham Young U., 1975; PhD, Colo. State U., 1984. Tech. assoc. Cornell U., Colo. and Idaho, 1974-88; dir. World Ctr. for Birds of Prey, Boise, Idaho, 1984—; pres. The Peregrine Fund Inc., Boise, Idaho, 1986—; adj. faculty Boise State U., 1986—, trustee, 1985—; bd. dirs. The Raptor Fund Inc., Chgo. Contbr. articles to profl. jours. Mem. Cooper Ornithological Soc., Am. Ornighologists' Union, Wilson Ornithological Soc., Raptor Research Found., The Avicultural Soc., Internat. Council for Bird Preservation, Arctic Inst. of N. Am., The Ottawa Field-Naturalists' Club, The Wildlife Soc., Sigma Xi. Office: Peregrine Fund Inc 5666 W Flying Hawk Ln Boise ID 83709-7289

BURNINGHAM, KIM RICHARD, former state legislator; b. Salt Lake City, Sept. 14, 1936; s. Rulon and Margie (Stringham) Burningham; m. Susan Ball Clarke, Dec. 19, 1968; children: Christian, Tyler David. BS, U. Utah, 1960; MA, U. Ariz., 1967; MFA, U. So. Calif., 1977. Cert. secondary tchr., Utah. Tchr. Bountiful (Utah) High Sch., 1960-88; mem. Utah Ho. of Reps., Salt Lake City, 1979-94; cons. Shipley Assocs., Bountiful, 1989—; gubernatorial appointee as exec. dir. Utah Statehood Centennial Commn., 1994—. Author dramas for stage and film, also articles. Mem. state strategic planning com. Utah Tomorrow, 1979—. Mem. NEA, PTA (life), Utah Edn. Assn., Davis Edn. Assn., Nat. Forensic League (dist. chair). Republican. Mem. LDS Ch. Home: 932 Canyon Crest Rd Bountiful UT 84010-2002

BURNISON, BOYD EDWARD, lawyer; b. Arnolds Park, Iowa, Dec. 12, 1934; s. Boyd William and Lucile (Harnden) B.; m. Mari Amaral; children: Erica Lafore, Alison Katherine. BS, Iowa State U., 1957; JD, U. Calif., Berkeley, 1961. Bar: Calif. 1962, U.S. Supreme Ct. 1971, U.S. Dist. Ct. (no. dist.) Calif. 1962, U.S. Ct. Appeals (9th cir.) 1962, U.S. Dist. Ct. (ea. dist.) Calif. 1970, U.S. Dist. Ct. (ctrl. dist.) Calif., 1992. Dep. counsel Yolo County, Calif., 1962-65; of counsel Davis and Woodland (Calif.) Unified Sch. Dists., 1962-65; assoc. Steel & Arostegui, Marysville, Calif., 1965-66, St. Sure, Moore & Hoyt, Oakland, 1966-70; ptnr. St. Sure, Moore, Hoyt & Sizoo, Oakland and San Francisco, 1970-75; v.p. Crosby, Heafey, Roach & May, P.C., Oakland, 1975—, also bd. dirs. Adviser Berkeley YMCA, 1971—; adviser Yolo County YMCA, 1962-65, bd. dirs. 1965; bd. dirs. Easter Seal Soc. Crippled Children and Adults of Alameda County, Calif., 1972-75, Moot Ct. Bd., U. Calif., 1960-61; trustee, sec., legal counsel Easter Seal Found., Alameda County, 1974-79, hon. trustee, 1979—. Fellow ABA Found. (life); mem. ABA (labor rels. and employment law sect., equal employment law com. 1972—), Nat. Conf. Bar Pres.'s, State Bar Calif. (spl. labor counsel 1981-84, labor and employment law sect. 1982—), Alameda County Bar Assn. (chmn. memberships and directory com. 1973-74, 80, chmn. law office econs. com. 1975-77, assn. dir. 1981-85, pres., 1984, vice chmn. bench bar liaison com. 1983, chmn. 1984, Disting. Svc. award 1987), Alameda County Bar Found. (bd. dirs. 1993—), Yolo County Bar Assn. (sec. 1965), Yuba Sutter Bar Assn., Bar Assn. San Francisco (labor law sect.), Indsl. Rels. Rsch. Assn., Sproul Assoc. Boalt Hall Law Sch. U. Calif. Berkeley, Iowa State Alumni Assn., Order Knoll, Round Hill Country Club, Rotary (Paul Harris fellow), Pi Kappa Alpha, Phi Delta Phi. Democrat. Home: PO Box 743 2500 Caballo Ranchero Dr Diablo CA 94528 Office: Crosby Heafey Roach & May 1999 Harrison St Oakland CA 94612-3517

BURNS, ALEXANDRA DARROW (SANDRA BURNS), health program administrator; b. West Point, Ky., Mar. 28, 1946; d. Eugene Alexander and Phyllis Anna (Kedroski) Darrow; m. Maurice Edward Burns Jr., Sept. 8, 1966 (div. May 1985); 1 child, Megan Alexandra. BS in Journalism, U. Colo., 1967, MA in Guidance and Counseling, 1974. Cert. rehab. counselor. Probation and parole officer Office of Probation and Parole, Olympia, Wash., 1969-70; employment counselor Div. Employment, Denver, 1971-73; rehab. counselor Colo. Div. Rehab.-Blind Svcs., Denver, 1973-77; rehab. supr. Colo. Div. Rehab., Denver, 1978-81, program supr. rehab. ins. svcs. for employment, 1981-91; program adminstr. Americans With Disabilities Act, Denver, 1991-94; supr. mktg. and resource acquisition Colo. Div. Rehab., Denver, 1994-95, tng. adminstr., 1995—. Vice chmn. Juvenile Parole Bd., Denver, 1982-91, acting chmn., 1987, chmn., 1988-91; del. Dem. County Caucus, Aurora, Colo., 1986; coun. del. Girl Scouts U.S.A., 1988-90, co-leader Brownie troop, 1988-9-, mem. area svc. team, 1989-90; mem. adv. bd. Indsl. Commn., 1983-86; mem. Jr. Symphony Guild, 1986-87; sec., bd. dirs. Mission Viejo Homeowners Assn., 1989-90. Mem. Nat. Rehab. Assn., Nat. Rehab. Adminstrn. Assn., Colo. Rehab. Adminstrn. Assn. (bd. dirs. 1988—, pres.-elect pvt. sector div. 1989, pres. 1990-91), Zonta (corr. sec. 1984-86). Episcopalian. Home: 15770 E Mercer Pl Aurora CO 80013-2559 Office: Colo Div Rehab 110 16th St Fl 2 Denver CO 80202-5202

BURNS, BRENDA, state legislator; b. LaGrange, Ga., Nov. 22, 1950; m. Bruce Burns; 3 children. Rep. dist. 17 State of Ariz.; vice chmn. judiciary com.; mem. econ. devel., internat. trade & tourism, ways & means, appropriations, edn. coms.; bus. mgr. Republican. Home: 8220 W Orange Dr Glendale AZ 85303-6006 Office: State Capitol 1700 W Washington St Phoenix AZ 85007-2812

BURNS, BRENT EMIL, electrical engineer; b. Wynnewood, Okla., Dec. 3, 1952; s. Frank Brent and Dorothy Esther (Westberg) B. BSEE, U. Okla., 1978, MSEE, 1979; PhD of Elec. Engring., Stanford U., 1987. Mgr. Northrop Grumman Integrated Micro Sensors Group, Palos Verdes, Calif., 1985—. Patentee on micro-electro-mechanical systems/silicon micromachining. With U.S. Army, 1972-74. Scholarship NSF 1979-82. Mem. IEEE, Electrochem. Soc., Tau Beta Pi, Eta Kappa Nu. Home: 26566 Basswood Ave Rancho Palos Verdes CA 90275-2269 Office: Northrop Grumman ESID PO Box 5032 Hawthorne CA 90251-5032

BURNS, CATHERINE ELIZABETH, art dealer; b. Winnipeg, Man., Can., June 21, 1953; came to U.S., 1955; d. Robert Franklin and Claire Margaret (Lillington) B. BA, U. Calif., Davis, 1975; MA in Museology, U. Minn., 1978. Adj. prof., curator univ. gallery U. Mass., Amherst, 1978-80; curator gallery of art Washington U., St. Louis, 1981-82; dealer in 19th and early 20th century prints and drawings Catherine E. Burns Fine Prints, Oakland, Calif., 1982—; also appraiser Catherine E. Burns Fine Prints, Oakland. Organizer San Francisco Fine Print Fair; mem. Nat. Trust for Hist. Preservation, Oakland Heritage Alliance. Grantee Nat. Endowment for Arts, 1981-82. Mem. Graphic Arts Coun., Art Deco Soc. Calif. Office: PO Box 11201 Oakland CA 94611-0201

BURNS, CONRAD RAY, senator; b. Gallatin, Mo., Jan. 25, 1935; s. Russell and Mary Frances (Knight) B.; m. Phyllis Jean Kuhlmann; children: Keely Lynn, Garrett Russell. Student, U. Mo., 1952-54. Field rep. Polled Hereford World Mag., Kansas City, Mo., 1963-69; pub. rels. Billings (Mont.) Livestock Com., 1969-73; farm dir. KULR TV, Billings, 1974; pres., founder No. Ag-Network, Billings, 1975-86; commissioner Yellowstone County, Billings, 1987-89; U.S. Senator from Montana, 1989—; Mem. Aging Com., Small Bus. Com., Nat. Rep. Senatorial Com., chmn. Appropriations Subcom. of Military Constrn., Chmn. Com. Sci. and Transp. Subcom. of Sci. Tech. and Space, chmn. Energy and Nat. Rescs. Subcom. of Energy Rsch & Devel. With USMC, 1955-57. Mem. Nat. Assn. Farm Broadcasters, Am. Legion, Rotary, Masons, Shriners. Republican. Lutheran. Office: US Senate 183 Dirksen Bldg Washington DC 20510*

BURNS, DAN W., manufacturing company executive; b. Auburn, Calif., Sept. 10, 1925; s. William and Edith Lynn (Johnston) B.; 1 child, Dan Jr. Dir. materials Menasco Mfg. Co., 1951-56; v.p., gen. mgr. Hufford Corp., 1956-58; pres. Hufford div. Siegler Corp., 1958-61; v.p. Siegler Corp., 1961-62, Lear Siegler, Inc., 1962-64; pres., dir. Electrada Corp., Culver City, Calif., 1964; pres., chief exec. officer Sargent Industries, Inc., L.A., 1964-85, chmn. bd. dirs., 1985-88; now chmn. bd. dirs., chief exec. officer Arlington Industries, Inc.; bd. dirs. Gen. Automotive Corp., Dover Tech. Internat., Inc. Bd. dirs. San Diego Aerospace Mus., Smithsonian Inst., The Pres.'s Cir., Nat. Acad. Scis., Atlantic Coun. of U.S., George C. Marshall Found. Capt. U.S. Army, 1941-47; prisoner of war Japan; asst. mil. attache 1946, China; adc to Gen. George C. Marshall 1946-47. Mem. OAS Sports Com. (dir.), L.A. Country Club, St. Francis Yacht Club, Calif. Club, Conquistador del Cielo. Home: 10851 Chalon Rd Los Angeles CA 90077-3206

BURNS, DANIEL MICHAEL, manufacturing company financial executive; b. Phila., Sept. 18, 1927; s. Michael John and Louise Ruth (Haun) B.; m. Margery Fay Mueller, Apr. 23, 1966; children: Jeremy Michael, Elizabeth Louise. Cert. in fin., U. Pa., 1957. Mgr. cost acctg. Electric Storage Battery Co., Phila., 1953-58; asst. treas., contr. Eversharp, Inc., Culver City, Calif., 1958-70; dir. corp. fin. analysis Warner-Lambert Co., Morris Plains, N.J., 1970-73; treas., contr. Schick Electric, Inc., Lancaster, Pa., 1973-76; v.p. fin. Chloride Power Electronics, Laguna Hills, Calif., 1976-91; chief fin. officer Altus Corp., Laguna Hills, 1991-93, also bd. dirs.; bd. dirs. UP Systems, Inc., Caledonia, N.Y., CHC Holding Corp., Burgaw, N.C., Chloride Power Electronics, Inc., Burgaw. Sgt. 1st class U.S. Army, 1950-52. Mem. Fin. Execs. Inst., Inst. Mgmt. Accts., Saddlebrook Resorts Country Club. Home: 27441 Via Caudaloso Mission Viejo CA 92692-2415 Office: Burns Travel Ind 27660 Marguerite Pky Mission Viejo CA 92692-3606

BURNS, DAVID M., medical educator; b. Boston, May 6, 1947; s. John J. and Catherine (Riley) B.; m. Diane Marie Lischio, May 26, 1990; 1 child, David P. BS in Biology, Boston Coll., 1968; BMS in Medicine, Dartmouth U., 1970; MD, Harvard U., 1972. Intern Boston City Hosp., 1972-73, resident, 1973-74; pulmonary fellow U. Calif. San Diego Med. Ctr., 1976-79, asst. prof. medicine, 1979-85, assoc. prof., 1985-91, prof., 1993—, med. dir. respiratory therapy, 1993—, coord. clin. rsch., 1993—; cons. U.S. Consumer Product Safety Commn. on Fire-Safe Cigarettes, 1992-93, indoor air quality adv. com. EPA, 1990-91; mem. rsch. adv. bd. Inst. for Study of Smoking Behavior and Policy Harvard U., 1984—. Sr. reviewer Surgeon Gen.'s Reports on Smoking and Health, 1987—; contbr. articles to profl. jours. Mem. policy adv. com. Community Intervention Trial for Smoking Cessation Nat. Cancer Inst., 1987—; pres. Am. Cancer Soc., San Diego, 1992-93, bd. dirs.; chair San Diego County Tobacco Control Coalition. Recipient Surgeon Gen.'s Medallion, 1989, Life and Breath award for Disting. Community Svc. Am. Lung Assn., 1989. Fellow Am. Coll. Chest Physicians; mem. Am. Thoracic Soc., Calif. Thoracic Soc., San Diego Pulmonary Soc., Am. Assn. for Respiratory Care, Nat. Coord. Com. for Tobacco-Related Rsch., Lung Assn. San Diego (bd. dirs. 1979-83). Office: U Calif San Diego Med Ctr 200 W Arbor Dr San Diego CA 92103-1911

BURNS, DENISE RUTH, artist; b. Bellville, N.J., Oct. 17, 1943; d. A. Richard and Ruth Jean (Landers) Culkin; m. Robert P. Burns Jr., Apr. 8, 1960; children: Michael R, David R. Studied, Sergei Bonjart Sch. Art, 1971-73; studied with Dan McCaw, Scottsdale Sch. Art, 1980, 89, studied with, 1988; studied with, Harley Brown, 1994, Michael Lynch and, Ovanes Berberian, 1995. One-woman shows include Off White Gallery, 1984, 85, 86, 93; two-woman show May Gallery, 1993; group shows include May Galleries, Scottsdale, Ariz., 1987-92, 94-95, Roy Miles Gallery, London, 1993, Art du Monde, Japan, 1993, N.C. Mus. History, 1995; featured in Swart Mag., 1992. Instr. Chambersburg (Pa.) Art Alliance, 1985-86, 87-89, Omaha Artist Group, 1988, Pocono Pines (Pa.), 1994, Catalina Art Assn., Avalon, Calif., 1990-91; dir. Plein Ait Painters Show, Catalina Island, 1986-95; judge Big Bear Art Festival, 1986, Children's Show, L.A. County Libr., Avalon, 1990. Recipient 2nd Pl. award Scottsdale Art Sch., 1991; named Emerging Artist by Am. Artist Mag., 1984, Best of Show by Catalina Art Festival, 1984, 86, 87, 89-91, Oil Painters of Am. Regional Best of Show, 1994; Gold medal artist award May Galleries, 1994. Mem. Plein Air Painters Am. (dir., founder), Catalina Art Assn. (pres. 1985, 86), Oil Painters of Am., Calif. Art Club, Palos Verdes Art Ctr. Home: PO Box 611 Avalon CA 90704-0611

BURNS, DENVER P., forestry research administrator; b. Bryan, Ohio, Oct. 27, 1940; married; 1 child. BS, Ohio State U., 1962, MS, 1964, PhD in Entomology, 1967; MPA, Harvard U., 1981. Asst. entomologist So. Forest Experiment Sta., 1962-68, rsch. entomologist, 1968-72, asst. dir., 1972-74; staff asst. to dep. chief for rsch. U.S. Forest Svc., 1974-76; dep. dir. North

Ctrl. Experiment Sta., 1976-81; dir. Northeastern Forest Experiment Sta., Radnor, Pa., 1981-92, Rocky Mountain Sta., 1992—. Mem. AAAS. Office: US Forest Service 240 W Prospect Rd Fort Collins CO 80526-2002

BURNS, DONALD SNOW, registered investment advisor, financial and business consultant; b. Cambridge, Mass., July 31, 1925; s. Jules Ian and Ruth (Snow) B.; m. Lucy Lee Keating, July 15, 1947 (div.); childen: Julie Ann Wrigley, Patti B. Boyd, Laurie Bidegain, Wendi Collins, Loni Monahan, Robin Alden. Student, Williams Coll., 1943-44; M in Baking, Am. Inst. of Baking, 1947. Baker O'Rourke Baking Co., Buffalo, 1946-49; gen. mgr. Glaco Co. of So. Calif., L.A., 1949-51; regional mgr. Glaco Div. of Ekco Prodn. Co., Chgo., 1951-53, gen. mgr., 1953-56; pres. McClintock Mfg. Div. Ekco Prodn. Co., Chgo., 1956-61; v.p. Ekco Products Co., Chgo., 1961-67; pres., chmn. Prestige Automotive Group, Garden Grove, Calif., 1967-78; chmn. Prestige Holdings Ltd., Newport Beach, Calif., 1978—; chmn. bd. Newport Nat. Bank, Newport Beach, 1961-67; bd. dir. Securitas Trust, Monte Carlo, Monaco, Am. Safety Equipment Co., Glendale, Calif., Internat. Tech. Corp., Torrance, Calif., Escorp, San Luis Obispo, Calif.; dir. Internat. Rectifier, El Segundo. Author: (short story) The Goose that Neighed, 1967, (books) Two and a Half Nickels, 1970, Light My Fire, 1979. Mem. Calif. State U. Adv. Bd., Fullerton, 1973-76; bd. dirs. Santiago Coll. Found., Santa Ana, Calif., 1989-90, Orange County Sheriff's Adv. Coun., Calif., 1978—, pres., 1987-88; chmn. bd. trustees Orme Sch. Mayer Ariz., 1976-78. With USNR, 1943-46. Mem. Jonathan Club. Office: Prestige Holdings Ltd 16 Tech Way Ste 114 Irvine CA 92718

BURNS, FRANCIS RAYMOND, biofeedback administrator; b. Ogden, Utah, Oct. 13, 1935; s. Gerald Eugene and Lucy Marie (Sargent) B.; m. Wendy Purdom Crooks, Jan. 16, 1973 (div. 1980); m. Lucia Esperanza Gaitan, Sept. 19, 1993. AA, San Francisco City Coll., 1961; BA, San Francisco State U., 1968. Dir. biofeedback clinic Noogenesis Inc., San Francisco, 1968-81, dir. clinic, head rsch. and devel., 1968—. Vol. coord. San Francisco Neighborhood Park Renovation Group, San Francisco, 1972-74. Home and Office: Noogenesis Inc 27920 Manon Ave Apt 20 Hayward CA 94544-5239

BURNS, GILBERT ALEXANDER, science educator; b. Ionia, Mich., Jan. 24, 1949; s. Arthur and Hedwig B.; m. Marilyn J. Edwards, June 13, 1970. BA magna cum laude, Mich. State U., 1971; DVM, Cornell U., 1987, PhD, 1991. Cert. veterinarian, Vt., N.H., Mass. Cert. physician's asst., Wis., N.H. Lab. technician Colorado Springs, Colo., 1972-76; physician's asst. Murphy Clinic, Park Falls, Wis., 1978-79, Newport (N.H.) Cmty. Health Clinic, 1979-83; veterinarian Wendell Veterinary Clinic, Sunapee, N.H., 1987-88; grad. student Cornell U., Ithaca, N.Y., 1988-91; asst. prof. Wash. State U., Pullman, 1991—. Assoc. editor: The Cornell Veterinarian, 1992—; contbr. articles to profl. jours. Mem. Latah County Human Rights Task Force, Moscow, Idaho, 1991—. Recipient Grant Sherman Hopkins award, Ane Besse award Cornell U., 1987. Mem. Am. Assn. Anatomists, Am. Assn. Veterinary Anatomists, Am. Veterinary Med. Assn., Soc. for Neurosciences, Phi Beta Kappa, Phi Zeta Veterinary Honor Soc.

BURNS, JAMES M., federal judge; b. Nov. 24, 1924. BA in Bus. Adminstrn., U. Portland, 1947; JD cum laude, Loyola U., Chgo., 1950. Pvt. practice Portland, 1950-52; dist. atty. Harney County, Oreg., 1952-56; assoc. Black, Kendall, Tremaine, Boothe and Higgins, Portland, 1956-60; ptnr. Beason, Whitely McCleanan and Burns, 1960-66; judge Oreg. Cir. Ct., Multnomah County, 1966-72; mem. faculty Nat. Jud. Coll., 1972—; judge U.S. Dist. Ct. Oreg., Portland, 1972—, chief judge, 1979-84; Mem. Oreg. Criminal Law Revision Commn., 1967-72; chmn. continuing legal edn. com. Oreg. State Bar, 1965-66; faculty advisor Nat. Jud. Coll., 1971. Mem. Oreg. Cir. Judges Assn. (pres. 1967-70), U.S. Jud. Conf. (com. on adminstrn. of probation system 1978-87). Office: US Dist Ct 602 US Courthouse 620 SW Main St Portland OR 97205-3037

BURNS, JANE CARY, molecular biologist, educator, physician; b. San Francisco, Sept. 30, 1952; d. Milton Dearlove and Vivian (Curtis) B.; m. John Benett Gordon III, Apr. 16, 1977; children: Elizabeth Curtis Gordon, Catherine Tileston Gordon. BA, Wesleyan U., 1974; MD, U. N.C., 1978. Diplomate Am. Bd. Pediats.; lic. physician, Calif. Pediat. intern and resident U. Colo., Denver, 1978-81, pediat. chief resident, 1981-82, pediat. infectious disease fellow, 1982-83; pediat. infectious disease fellow Children's Hosp., Boston, 1983-86; instr. Harvard Med. Sch., Boston, 1986-89, asst. prof., 1989-90; asst. prof. U. Calif., San Diego, 1990—; dir. Kawasaki Disease Rsch. Program, U. Calif., San Diego, 1991—. Contbr. rsch. articles to profl. jours. Recipient ICAAC Young Investigator award Am. Soc. Microbiology, 1987, Shannon award NIH, 1992. Fellow Pediat. Infectious Disease Soc.; mem. Soc. Pediat. Rsch., Western Soc. Pediat. Rsch. Home: 6505 El Camino Del Teatro La Jolla CA 92037-6337 Office: U Calif Dept Pediats 0609-D 9500 Gilman Dr La Jolla CA 92093-5003

BURNS, LOUIS FRANCIS, retired history educator; b. Elgin, Kans., Jan. 2, 1920; s. Lee Robert and Bessie Pearl (Tinker) B.; m. Ruth Blake, Apr. 24, 1945; children: Alice Bettie Burns Thomas, Keith Lee. BS in Edn., Kans. State U., 1949, MS, 1950. Cert. secondary educator, jr. coll. educator, Kans., Mo., Calif. Teaching fellowship Kans. State U., Emporia, 1950; instr. geography, U.S. history Shawnee-Mission (Kans.) Sr. High Sch., 1950-60; instr. U.S. history Santa Ana (Calif.) Coll., 1965-76; author, speaker self-employed Fallbrook, Calif., 1977-94; ret., 1994; presenter and speaker in field; advisor Osage Tribal Mus., Pawhuska, Okla., 1990-94. Author: (book) Osage Indian Customs & Myths, 1984, A History of the Osage People, 1989, Symbolic & Decorative Art of the Osage People, 1994 and related books; editor Osage News, 1982-84; contbr. related articles to profl. jours. Rep. Osage Indian Nation, Montauban, France, 1990, 92. Sgt. USMC, 1942-45. Recipient Chevalier de L'Hypocras du Foix, Companions of L'Hypocras, 1992; named in Mottled Eagle Clan, Osage Indian Tribe, 1988; admitted to I'n Lon Schka, Pawhuska Camp, Osage Tribe, 1988. Mem. NEA, Okla. Hist. Soc., Kans. State Hist. Soc., Western History Assn. Democrat. Roman Catholic. Home: 654 Golden Rd Fallbrook CA 92028-3452

BURNS, MARVIN GERALD, lawyer; b. Los Angeles, July 3, 1930; s. Milton and Belle (Cytron) B.; m. Barbara Irene Fisher, Aug. 23, 1953; children: Scott Douglas, Jody Lynn, Bradley Frederick. BA, U. Ariz., 1951; JD, Harvard U., 1954. Bar: Calif. 1955. Bd. dirs., v.p. Inner City Arts for Inner City Children. With AUS, 1955-56. Clubs: Beverly Hills Tennis, Sycamore Park Tennis. Home: 10350 Wilshire Blvd Ph 4 Los Angeles CA 90024-4734 Office: 4th Fl 10390 Santa Monica Blvd Los Angeles CA 90025-5058

BURNS, MARY FERRIS, society administrator; b. Corpus Christi, Tex., Aug. 24, 1952; d. Wilbur Glenn and Lena (Faught) Ferris; m. Douglas Keith Burns, Dec. 26, 1975. BA, Baylor U., 1974; MLS, U. Tex., Austin, 1975; BS, U. Tex., Dallas, 1982; MA, U. Fla., 1978. CPA, Tex., Wash. Reference libr., Latin Am. collection U. Fla., Gainesville, 1975-78; reference libr., Fondren Libr. So. Meth. U., Dallas, 1978-79; libr. Tex. A&M U., College Station, 1979-81; auditor, provider reimbursement div. Blue Cross & Blue Shield of Tex., Dallas, 1983-84; internal auditor U. Tex. Health Sci. Ctr. at Dallas, 1984-85, adminstrv. svcs. officer Biomed. Comm. Resource Ctr., 1985-87; adminstrv. svcs. mgr. Div. of Lab. Animal Medicine Stanford U., 1988-89, adminstrv. svcs. mgr. Dept. of Microbiology and Immunology, 1989; dir. adminstrn. RIDES for Bay Area Commuters, Inc., San Francisco, 1989-93; CFO Children's Home Soc. Wash., Seattle, 1993—; cons. Centro Intenacional de Desarrollo Humano en America Latina, Cuernavaca, Mex., 1975. Contbg. editor: Hispanic American Periodicals Index, 1975, 76. Mem. AICPA, Wash. Soc. of CPA's., Soc. for Human Resource Mgmt.

BURNS, MICHAEL EDWARD, technology company executive; b. Long Beach, Calif., July 11, 1943; s. Troy A. Burns and Vivian F. (Clay) Clifton; m. Jane K. Slothower, Apr. 18, 1965; 1 child, Heather Anne. BA, Western State Coll., 1966; exec. cert., U. Va., 1976. Dir. pro ski patrol Crested Butte (Colo.) Ski Area, 1966-70; sales rep. The North Face, Berkeley, Calif., 1970-85; cons. Learning Internat., Washington, 1985-90; N.Am. sales mgr. Patagonia, Ventura, Calif., 1990-92; dir. sales and mktg. The North Face, Berkeley, 1992-93; v.p. sales Sweetwater, Inc., Boulder, Colo., 1993—. Contbr. articles to profl. mags. Republican. Office: Sweetwater Inc 2505 Trade Center Ave Boulder CO 80501

BURNS, PAUL ANDREW, sports editor; b. Costa Mesa, Calif., Apr. 26, 1958; s. Jack Sharples and Benice Dorthea (Calkins) B.; m. Jill Elaine Schaunaman, May 17, 1987; children: Andrew Hamilton, Peter Schaunaman. BS in Stats., Mont. State U., 1983. Sports intern Bozeman (Mont.) Chronicle, 1988-89, sports writer, 1989-93, sports editor, 1993—. Recipient Best Humor Writing award Soc. Profl. Journalists, 1989, Best Feature award Soc. Profl. Journalists, 1991, Best Sports Pages award Soc. Profl. Journalists, 1992, Best Sports Story award Soc. Profl. Journalists, 1993. Home: 1010 E Babcock St Bozeman MT 59715-3833 Office: Bozeman Daily Chronicle PO Box 1188 32 S Rouse Bozeman MT 59771

BURNS, ROBERT IGNATIUS, historian, educator, clergyman; b. San Francisco, Aug. 16, 1921; s. Harry and Viola Marie (Whearty) B. B.A., Gonzaga U., 1945, M.A., 1947; M.A., Fordham U., 1949; Phil.B., Jesuit Pontifical Faculty, Spokane, Wash., 1946, Phil.Lic., 1947; S.Th.B., Jesuit Pontifical Faculty, Alma, Calif., 1951, S.Th.Lic., 1953; postgrad., Columbia U., 1949, Oxford (Eng.) U., 1956-57; Ph.D. summa cum laude, Johns Hopkins U., 1958; Doc.ès Sc.Hist., Fribourg (Switzerland) U. (double summa cum laude), 1961; hon. doctorates, Gonzaga U., 1968, Marquette U., 1977, Loyola U., Chgo., 1978, Boston Coll., 1982, Georgetown U., 1982, U. San Francisco, 1983, Fordham U., 1984, U. Valencia, 1985. Mem. Jesuit order; ordained priest Roman Catholic Ch., 1952. Asst. archivist Jesuit and Indian Archives Pacific N.W., Province, Spokane, 1945-47; instr. history dept. U. San Francisco, 1947-48, asst. prof., 1958-62, assoc. prof., 1963-66, prof., 1967-76; sr. prof. dept. history UCLA, 1976—, named overscale (chair), 1987—; dir. Inst. Medieval Mediterranean Spain, 1976—; prof. methodology, faculty history Gregorian U., Rome, 1955-56; guest lectr. humanities honors program Stanford U., 1960; vis. prof. Coll. of Notre Dame, Belmont, Calif., 1963; James chair Brown U., Providence, 1970; faculty mem. Inst. Advanced Study, Princeton, N.J., 1972; Levi della Vida lectr. UCLA, 1973; vis. prof., Hispanic lectr. U. Calif. at Santa Barbara, 1976; staff UCLA Near Eastern Center, 1979—, UCLA Center Medieval-Renaissance Studies, 1977—; Humanities Coun. lectr. NYU, 1992; Columbus Quincentennial Commn. of Calif. State Legislature, 1992. Author: The Jesuits and the Indian Wars of the Northwest, 1966, reprinted, 1985, The Crusader Kingdom of Valencia: Reconstruction on a Thirteenth-Century Frontier, 1967, Islam Under the Crusaders: Colonial Survival in the Thirteenth-Century Kingdom of Valencia, 1973, Medieval Colonialism: Post-Crusade Exploitation of Islamic Valencia, 1975, Morrs and Crusaders in Mediterranean Spain, 1978, Jaume I i els Valencians del segle XIII, 1981, Muslims, Christians and Jews in the Crusader Kingdom of Valencia, 1983, El reino de Valencia en el siglo XIII, 1983, Society and Documentation in Crusader Valencia, 1985, The Worlds of Alfonso the Learned and James the Conqueror, 1985, Emperor of Culture: Alfonso X, 1990, Foundations of Crusader Valencia, 1991, El Regne Croat de Valencia, 1994; bd. editors: Trends in History, 1979—, Anuario de Estudios Medievales (Spain), 1985—, Bulletin of the Cantigueiros, 1986—, Catalan Rev., 1986—; co-editor: Viator, 1980-93; assoc. editor Ency. of Medieval Iberia; mem. editl. bd. U. Calif. Press, 1985-88, chair, 1987-88, mem. bd. of control, 1987-88; contbr. articles to profl. jours. Trustee Hill Monastic Manuscript Library, 1977-81; mem. adv. bd. Am. Bibliog. Center, 1982—. Recipient Book award Am. Hist. Assn. Pacific Coast Br., 1968, Am. Assn. State Local History, 1967, Am. Cath. Hist. Assn., 1967, 68, Book award Inst. Mission Studies, 1966, Am. Cath. Press Assn., 1975, Phi Alpha Theta, 1976; Haskins medal Medieval Acad. Am., 1976; Premi de la Critica, 1982; Premi Catalonia, 1982, Premi Internacional Llull, 1988; Cross of St. George Catalan Govt., 1989; Guggenheim fellow, 1963-64; Ford Found. and Guggenheim grantee, 1980; NEH fellow, 1971, 73, 75-83, 88, Am. Coun. Learned Socs. fellow, 1972; travel grantee, 1975; Robb Publ. Grantee, 1974; Darrow Publ. grantee, 1975; Consejo Superior de Investigaciones Cientificas (Spain) travel grantee, 1975, 82; Valencia province and Catalan region publ. grantee, 1981; Del Amo Grantee, 1983; U.S.-Spain treaty grantee, 1983-85; grantee Consejo Superior de Investigaciones Cientificas (Spain), 1985; Mellon Publ. grantee, 1985. Fellow Medieval Acad. Am. (trustee 1975-77, prize com. 1980, scribe 1987—), Accio Cultural del Pais Valencia; mem. Hispanic Soc. Am. (hon.), Am. Cath. Hist. Assn. (pres. 1975, coun. 1976—), Soc. Spanish Portuguese Hist. Studies (exec. coun. 1974-77), Am. Hist.n. (del. Internat. Congress Hist. Scis. 1975, 80, pres. Pacific Coast br. 1979-80, exec. coun. 1981-83), Medieval Assn. Pacific (exec. coun. 1975-77), Acad. Rsch. Historians Medieval Spain (pres. 1976), N.Am. Catalan Soc., Tex. Medieval. Office: UCLA History Dept Los Angeles CA 90024

BURNS, SCOTT FRIMOTH, geology educator; b. Portland, Ore., Oct. 7, 1947; s. Jack Hancock and Phyllis Gwen (Frimoth) B.; m. Glenda Marie Stemmler, Aug. 6, 1974; children: Lisa, Doug, Tracy. BS, Stanford U., 1969, MS, 1970; PhD, U. Colo., 1980. Registered geologist Ore. Prof., dept. chair Am. Coll. Switzerland, Leysin, 1970-75; vis. prof. Lincoln Coll., Christchurch, New Zealand, 1980-81; prof. La. Tech. U., Ruston, 1982-90, Portland State U., 1990—; vis. prof. Western Wash. U., Bellingham, 1981-82, U. Colo., Boulder, 1982; cons. in field, 1984—; nat. engring. geology com. NAS, Washington, 1989—. Basketball coach Leysin Basketball Club, 1970-75, Lincoln Basketball Club, Christchurch, 1980-81, Tigard (Ore.) Basketball Assn., 1993-94. Kellogg Found. fellow, 1990. Mem. Assn. Engring. Geologists (pres.-elect 1989—), Oreg. Soc. Soil Scientists (pres. 1990-94), Geol. Soc. N.Am., Sigma Xi (chpt. sec. 1985—). Home: 21502 SW Christensen Ct Tualatin OR 97062-8910 Office: Portland State U Geology Dept PO Box 751 Portland OR 97207

BURNSIDE, MARY BETH, biology educator, researcher; b. San Antonio, Apr. 23, 1943; d. Neil Delmont and Luella Nixon (Kenley) B. BA, U. Tex., 1965, MA, 1967, PhD in Zoology, 1968. Instr. med. sch. Harvard U., Boston, 1970-73; asst. prof. U. Pa., Phila., 1973-76; asst. prof. U. Calif., Berkeley, 1976-77, assoc. prof., 1977-82, prof., 1982—, dean biol. scis., 1984-90; mem. nat. adv. eye coun. NIH, 1990-94; mem. sci. adv. bd. Lawrence Hall of Sci., Berkeley, 1983—, Whitney Labs., St. Augustine, Fla., 1993—; mem. bd. sci. councillors Nat. Eye Inst., 1994—. Mem. editl. bd. Invest. Ophthalmol. Vis. Sci., 1992-94; contbr. numerous articles to profl. jours. Scientific adv. bd. Mills Coll., Oakland, Calif., 1986-90; trustee Bermuda Biol. Sta., St. George's, 1978-83; exec. bd. Miller Inst., Berkeley, Calif., 1993—. Recipient Merit award NIH, 1989—, rsch. grantee, 1972—; rsch. grantee NSF. Fellow AAAS; mem. Am. Soc. Cell Biology (coun. 1980-84). Office: U Calif Dept Molecular & Cell Biology 335 Life Scis Addn Berkeley CA 94720-3200

BURR, CAROL ELIZABETH, English language educator; b. Hackensack, N.J., Jan. 16, 1943; d. Frank White and Marie (Barnitt) B. BA, Middlebury Coll., 1965; MA, Columbia U., N.Y.C., 1968; PhD, Case Western Res. U., 1975. Instr. Cleve. State U., 1966-68; teaching fellow Case Western Res. U., Cleve., 1968-70; from asst. prof. to prof. Calif. State U., Chico, 1970—; dir. Univ. Honors Program Calif. State U., 1984-89; co-chair Women's Coun. State U., 1986-91; chair Dept. of English, 1985-94; dir. Ctr. for Multicultural and Gender Studies, 1995—. Chancellor's grantee Calif. State U., 1984-86; recipient Outstanding Leadership award Carnegie Inst. Chancellor's grantee Calif. State U., 1984-86. Mem. MLA, AAUW. Office: Calif State U English Dept 1st and Normal St Chico CA 95929

BURR, JOHN CHARLES, software engineer; b. Ft. Huachuca, Ariz., May 16, 1934; s. John Charles and Willa Victoria (Walker) B.; m. Caroline Janet O'Shaughnessy, Aug. 26, 1961; children: Elizabeth, Michael. BS, Colo. State U., 1957; PhD, U. Minn., 1969. R&D coord. Redstone arsenal U.S. Army, Huntsville, Ala., 1964-66; chemist B.F. Goodrich Rsch. Ctr., Brecksville, Ohio, 1966-69; air quality mgr. Ohio EPA, Columbus, 1969-76; sr. environ. scientist Dames & Moore, North Ridge, Ill., 1976-82; postdoctoral fellow Colo. State U., Ft. Collins, 1982-84; software test & quality assurance mgr. ITT FSI, Colorado Springs, 1984-87; sr. software engr. Sci. Applications Internat. Corp., Boulder, Colo., 1987-92; prin. Sagatech, Boulder, 1992-94; software engr. Inst. Tel. Sci., Boulder, 1994—. Capt. U.S. Army, 1963-65. GE fellow, 1960. Mem. IEEE, Kappa Mu Epsilon, Phi Kappa Phi. Democrat. Episcopalian. Home: 8343 Westfork Rd Boulder CO 80302 Office: ITS/DOC 325 S Broadway St Boulder CO 80303-3464

BURR, JOHN CLARENCE, physician; b. Tonkawa, Okla., Jan. 27, 1931; s. Clarence E. and Gladys (Jones) B.; student No. Okla. Jr. Coll., 1949-50; B.S., Tulsa U., 1953; M.D., U. Okla., 1957; m. Mary Patricia Casey, May 29, 1956; children—Andrea, John David. Intern, St. Lukes and Denver Gen. hosps., 1957-58; resident U. Okla. Med. Center, 1958-61; practice medicine, specializing in gen., adolescent, diagnostic and forensic psychiatry, Denver, 1963-83, Santa Fe, 1984-86, Las Cruces, N.Mex., 1986, Tucson, Ariz., 1987—; clin. med. dir. forensic div. N.Mex. State Hosp., Las Vegas, chmn. dept. psychiatry, 1983-84; med. dir. Mt. Airy Hosp., 1967-68, youth dir., 1969; mem. staff St. Lukes Hosp., Mount Airy Psychiat. Center, Bethesda Hosp., St. Joseph Hosp. Chmn. bd., mng. dir. Gallery of Fine Art Ltd., 1973-74. Pres. bd. trustees, chmn. bd. dirs. Colo. Orgn. for Drug Abuse Control, 1970-71. Past prin., past chmn. bd. trustees St. Anne's Episcopal Sch.; trustee Mount Airy Found., 1967-83, trustee emeritus, 1983—, past mem. exec. com., chmn. staff edn. program, 1972-74; cons. Jorgensen Healthcare and FHP, 1990-93, state Ariz. cmty. mental health programs, 1987; adult dir. Tucson Psychiat. Hosp., 1987; med. dir. Valley View Hosp., Las Cruces, 1986-87, Tucson Psychiat. Hosp., 1987—, Charter Hosp., 1988, Kino Cmty. Hosp., 1990—, Carondolet St. Joseph's, 1987—, St. Mary's, 1993—. Served to capt. AUS, 1961-63. Mem. Am. Psychiat. Assn. (life), Ariz. Psychiat. Soc., Pima County Med. Soc., Central Neuropsychiat. Assn., Phi Beta Pi, Sigma Chi. Republican. Episcopalian. Home: 2928 N Orlando Ave Tucson AZ 85712-1247

BURR, ROBERT LYNDON, library director; b. Boonville, N.Y., May 9, 1944; s. James Isaac and Virginia Ellen (Davidson) B.; m. Angela Delores Tucci, June 26, 1965; 1 son, Robert Anthony. Student, U. Rochester, 1962-65; A.B., Canisius Coll., 1972; M.S. in L.S, Case-Western Res. U., 1973; Ed.D., Gonzaga U., 1981. Asst. prodn. mgr., purchasing mgr. Carleton Controls Corp., Buffalo, 1966-71; asst. to pres. Audn Corp., Buffalo, 1971-72; circulation services librarian Coll. William and Mary, Williamsburg, Va., 1973-77; dir. libraries Gonzaga U., Spokane, Wash., 1977—; adj. asso. prof. edn. Gonzaga U., 1979—; library cons. Contbr. articles to profl. jours. Trustee Mus. Native Am. Cultures, 1979—. Served with AUS, 1967-69. Mem. ALA (nat. research award 1974), Nat. Libraries Assn., Wash. Library Assn., Pacific N.W. Library Assn., AAUP, Mensa. Club: University (Spokane). Office: Gonzaga U Foley Ctr 502 E Boone Ave Spokane WA 99258-1774

BURRELL, CALVIN ARCHIE, minister; b. Fairview, Okla., June 22, 1943; s. Lawrence Lester and Lottie Edna (Davison) B.; m. Barbara Ann Mann, May 29, 1966; children: Debra, Darla, Donna. BS, Northwestern State U., 1965; M.A., So. Nazarene U., Bethany, Okla., 1978. Ordained to ministry Ch. of God. tchr., prin., dean of boys, Spring Vale Acad., Owosso, Mich., 1964-76; Pastor Ch. of God (Seventh Day), Ft. Smith, Ark., 1970-73, Shawnee, Okla., 1976-78, Denver, 1978-88; pres. Gen. Conf. of Ch. of God (Seventh Day), Denver, 1987—; instr. Summit Sch. Theology, Denver, 1978-94; officer Bible Sabbath Assn., 1983-95. Office: Ch of God 330 W 152nd Ave PO Box 33677 Denver CO 80233-0677

BURRELL, GARLAND E., JR., federal judge; b. L.A., July 4, 1947. BA in Sociology, Calif. State U., 1972; MSW, Washington U., Mo., 1976; JD, Calif. Wes. Sch. Law, 1976. Bar: Calif. 1976, U.S. Dist. Ct. (ea. dist.) Calif. 1976, U.S. Ct. Appeals (9th cir.) 1981. Dep. dist. atty. Sacramento County, Calif., 1976-78; dep city atty. Sacramento, 1978-79; asst. U.S. atty., dep. chief civil divsn. Office of U.S. Atty. for Ea. Dist. Calif., 1979-85, asst. U.S. atty., chief civil divsn., 1990-92; litigation atty. Stockman Law Corp., Sacramento, Calif., 1985-86; sr. dep. city atty. Office of City Atty., Sacramento, 1986-90; judge U.S. Dist. Ct. (ea. dist.) Calif., Sacramento, 1992—. With USMC, 1966-68. Office: Dist Ct 650 Capitol Mall Sacramento CA 95814-4708*

BURRI, BETTY JANE, research chemist; b. San Francisco, Jan. 23, 1955; d. Paul Gene and Carleen Georgette (Meyers) B.; m. Kurt Randall Annweiler, Dec. 1, 1984. BA, San Francisco State U., 1976; MS, Calif. State U., Long Beach, 1978; PhD, U. Calif. San Diego, La Jolla, 1982. Research asst. Scripps Clinic, La Jolla, 1982-83, research assoc., 1983-85; research chemist Western Human Nutrition Rsch. Ctr., USDA, San Francisco, 1985—; adj. prof. nutrition dept. U. Nev., 1993—; mem. steering com. Carotenoid Rsch. Interaction Group, 1994—. Co-editor Carotenoid News; contbr. articles to profl. jours. Grantee NIH, 1982, 85, USDA, 1986-95; affiliate fellow Am. Heart Assn., 1983, 84. Mem. Assn. Women in Sci. (founding dir. San Diego chpt.), N.Y. Acad. Sci., Carotenoid Rsch. Interaction Group, Am. Inst. Nutrition, Am. Soc. Clin. Nutrition. Office: Western Human Nutrition Rsch Ctr PO Box 29997 San Francisco CA 94129-0997

BURRI, GLENN ALAN, middle school educator; b. L.A., Feb. 12, 1955; s. Paul Martin and Bev (Rozner) B.; m. Wanda LaRock, Nov. 11, 1983 (div. July 1985). BA, Calif. State U., Northridge, 1989. Cert. lang. devel. specialist; cert. tchr., Calif. Tchr. mid. sch. L.A. Unified Sch. Dist., Van Nuys, Calif., 1992—. Grantee L.A. Edn. Program, 1994. Mem. Calif. Social Studies Found. Office: 5435 Vesper Ave Van Nuys CA 91411-3738

BURRIS, HARRISON ROBERT, computer and software developer; b. Phila., July 13, 1945; s. Harrison Roosevelt and Mabel Eynon (Bosler) B. BS in Elec. Engring., Pa. State U., 1967, MS in Computer Sci., 1969; MBA in Mgmt., Fairleigh Dickinson U., 1973. Chief technologist U.S. Army Office Project Mgr. for Army Tactical Data Systems, Fort Monmouth, N.J., 1970-74; mgr. advanced computing Systems Engring. & Integration Divsn TRW, Redondo Beach, Calif., 1974-84, mgr. engring. operation Electron Systems Divsn., 1984-86, mgr. NASA Spaceborne Computing, Electronic Systems Group, 1986-90; pres. Neotechnic Industries Inc., Redondo Beach, 1980—; lectr. computer sci. Grad. Sch. Calif. State U., Fullerton, 1977-82. Editor microprogramming Simulation mag., 1982—. Recipient Am. Spirit Honor medal Assn. U.S. Army, 1970. Mem. IEEE, Assn. Computing Machinery, Res. Officers Assn. (v.p. Army Dept. Calif. 1993). Republican. Baptist. Office: 620 Via Monte Doro Redondo Beach CA 90277-6651

BURROWES, CARL PATRICK, communications educator; b. Monrovia, Liberia, Oct. 29, 1952; came to U.S., 1980; s. Cecil Augustus and Hyacinth Aletha (Campbell) B.; m. Adjoa Deborah Jackson, Sept. 26, 1981; children: Kassahun, Hyacinth Bendu. BA in Journalism, Howard U., 1976; MA in Comm., Syracuse U., 1979; PhD in Comm., Temple U., 1994. Corr. West Africa, Monrovia, Liberia, 1979-80, New African, Monrovia, 1979-80; instr. U. Liberia, Monrovia, 1979-80, Hampton (Va.) Inst., 1980-81; asst. prof. Calumet Coll., Whiting, Ind., 1981-84, Glassboro (N.J.) State Coll., 1984-90; assoc. prof. Calif. State U., Fullerton, 1990—; exec. dir. Liberia Rsch. & Info. Project, Glassboro, 1984-90; bd. mem. Assn. Constl. Democracy in Liberia, Washington, 1988-90. Mng. editor Lone Star Newsletter, Fullerton, 1994—. Mem. Soc. Profl. Journalists, Assn. Edn. in Journalism and Mass Comm., Liberia Studies Assn., Frederick Douglass Soc. Office: Calif State U Fullerton CA 92634-9480

BURROWS, GATES WILSON, retired architect; b. Santa Paula, Calif., Apr. 17, 1899; s. Hubert Gates and Sallie Josephine (Wilson) B.; m. Lucinda Margaret Griffith; 1 child, Gates Wilson Jr. Student, Stanford U., 1918-21; BS, MIT, 1925; student, Fontainbleau Sch. Fine Arts, France, 1926. Prin. Gates W. Burrows, Architect, Laguna Beach, Calif., 1937-42, Santa Ana, Calif., 1945-62; prin. Burrows and Allen Architects, Santa Ana, 1962-73. Pres. Laguna Beach Art Mus., 1945-46; mem. Episcopal Bishops Archtl. Commn., L.A., 1953-90. Fellow AIA (pres. Orange County chpt. 1955-56); mem. Laguna Beach Art Assn. (life), Marine Meml. (life), University Club (L.A.). Republican. Episcopalian. Home: 5193 Duenas Laguna Hills CA 92653-1814

BURROWS, JAMES, television and motion picture director, producer; b. L.A., Dec. 30, 1940; s. Abe Burrows. BA, Oberlin Coll.; MFA, Yale U. Dir. Off-Broadway prodns.; dir. (motion picture) Partners, 1982, (TV film) More Than Friends, 1978, (TV series episodes) Mary Tyler Moore Show, Bob Newhart, Rhoda, Phyllis, Taxi, Lou Grant, Dear John, (pilot) Night Court, Wings (pilot), Roc (pilot); co-creator, co-exec. producer, dir. (TV series) Cheers. Recipient Dirs. Guild Am. award for comedy direction, 1984, 91, 94, Emmy awards NATAS for dir. in comedy series Taxi, 1979-80, 81-82 seasons, Cheers, 1982-83, 90-91 seasons; Emmy award as co-producer Cheers, 1982-83, 83-84, 89-90, 90-91 seasons; Emmy award as director of a Comedy Series for Fraiser, 1994. Office: c/o Paramount TV Prodns 5555 Melrose Ave Los Angeles CA 90038-3149

BURRY, KENNETH ARNOLD, physician, educator; b. Monterrey Park, Calif., Oct. 2, 1942; s. Frederick H. and Betty Jean (Bray) B.; m. Mary Lou

Tweedy, June 4, 1964 (div. 1981); 1 child, Michael Curtis; m. Katherine A. Johnson, Apr. 3, 1982; 1 child, Lisa Bray. BA, Whittier Coll., 1964; MD, U. Calif.-Irvine, 1968. Diplomate Am. Bd. Ob-Gyn, Am. Bd. Reproendocrine. Intern, Orange County Med. Ctr., Calif.; resident U. Oreg. Med. Sch.; sr. rsch. fellow U. Wash., Seattle, 1974-76; asst. prof. Oreg. Health Sci. U., Portland, 1976-80, assoc. prof., 1980-89, prof., 1989—; dir. Oreg. Reproductive Rsch. and Fertility Program, Portland, 1982—; dir. Fellowship Program, Portland, 1984—, asst. chmn. Dept. Ob-Gyn, 1986—, dir. divsn. Reproendocrine, 1992—; sci. presentations to profl. assns. Author: In Vitro Fertilization and Embryo Transfer, Oregon Health Sciences University Patient Handbook, 1984 (with others). Contbr. abstracts, articles to profl. publs. Served to capt. U.S. Army, 1969-71. Decorated Bronze Star, Air medal, Army Commendation medal oak leaf cluster; recipient Combat Med. badge. Fellow Am. Coll. Ob-Gyn; mem. Endocrine Soc., Am. Fertility Soc., Am. Fedn. Clin. Rsch., Soc. Reproductive Endocrinologists, Soc. Reproductive Surgeons, Pacific Coast Obstet. and Gynecol. Soc. Republican. Lutheran. Home: 8630 SW Pacer Dr Beaverton OR 97008-6980 Office: Oreg Health Scis U 3181 SW Sam Jackson Park Rd Portland OR 97201-3011

BURSTEIN, DAVID, astronomy educator; b. Englewood, N.J., May 19, 1947; s. Bernard and Mildred (Mindlin) B.; m. Gail Kelly, June 19, 1971; children: Jonathan, Elizabeth. BS in Physics with honors, Wesleyan U., Middletown, Conn., 1969; PhD in Astronomy, U. Calif., Santa Cruz, 1978. Research fellow dept. terrestrial magnetism Carnegie Instn., Washington, 1977-79; research assoc. Nat. Radio Astronomy Obs., Charlottesville, Va., 1979-82; asst. prof. dept. physics Ariz. State U., Tempe, 1982-88, assoc. prof., 1988-94; prof., 1994—. Contbr. more than 145 articles to astronomy and astrophysics jours. Named Outstanding Tchr. Ariz. State Golden Key, 1989, Ariz. State Faculty of Yr., Disabled Student Resources, 1990. Mem. Am. Astron. Soc., Internat. Astron. Union, Sigma Xi. Office: Ariz State U Dept Physics Tempe AZ 85283

BURTNER, ROGER LEE, research geologist; b. Hershey, Pa., Mar. 31, 1936; s. Bruce Lemmuel and Bernetta Viola (Quigle) B.; m. Carol Ann Spitzer, Aug. 1, 1965; 1 child, Pamela Sue. BS cum laude, Franklin and Marshall Coll., 1958; MS, Stanford U., 1959; PhD, Harvard U., 1965. Assoc. research geologist Calif. Research Corp. div. Standard Oil Co. of Calif., La Habra, 1963-64, research geologist, 1964-68; exploration geologist Tex. div. Standard Oil Co. of Calif., Corpus Christi and Houston, 1968-69; research geologist Chevron Oil Field Research Co. div. Chevron Corp., La Habra, 1969-74, sr. research geologist, 1974-77, sr. research assoc., 1977-92, petrology group project leader, 1975-80, supr. electron microscopy lab., 1977-82; sr. assoc. TerraSpec Assocs., La Habra, 1992—; mem. Pres. west coast regional adv. coun. Franklin & Marshall Coll., 1992—; adj. prof. Case Western Reserve U., Cleveland, 1992—. Contbr. articles to sci. jours. Founder Concordia U., Irvine, 1976, Orange County Performing Arts Ctr., Costa Mesa, Calif., 1979; trustee Concordia U. Found., 1989—, found. sec., 1990, v.p., 1991—, chmn. found., 1992-95; mem. Friends of Concordia U., Cmty. Chorale, 1983—; mem. Fullerton Arboretum, 1983—, Orange County Master Chorale, 1978-81; bd. dirs. Luth. H.S. Assn., Orange County, Calif., 1975-81, 88-94, pres., 1977-79, v.p., 1979-81, 92-94; v.p. Prince of Peace Luth. Ch., Anaheim, Calif., 1980-86, 89-91, 93-95, pres., 1972-74, 86-89, 95—; mem. energy and resource mgmt. com. City of Fullerton, 1995—. NSF fellow, 1958-60. Fellow Geol. Soc. Am.; mem. Am. Assn. Petroleum Geologists, Soc. Sedimentary Geology, Clay Minerals Soc. (councilor 1981-84), Geochem. Soc., Los Angeles Basin Geol. Soc., Audubon Soc., Rocky Mountain Assn. Geologists, South Coast Geological Soc., Sierra Club, Internat. Assn. Geochemistry and Cosmochemistry, Sigma Xi, Phi Beta Kappa. Republican. Home: 721 E Harmony Ln Fullerton CA 92631-1865

BURTON, AL, producer, director, writer; b. Chgo.; s. D. Chester and Isabelle (Olenick) G.; m. Sally Lou Lewis, Jan. 8, 1956; 1 dau., Jennifer. BS cum laude, Northwestern U. Exec. v.p. creative affairs Norman Lear-Embassy Communications, Inc., 1973-83; exec. producer-cons. Universal TV, 1983-92; exec. prodr., v.p. syndication Castle Rock Entertainment, 1992-95; pres. Al Burton Prodns., Beverly Hills, Calif., 1995—; bd. dirs. Pilgrim Group Funds; mem. Second Decade council Am. Film Inst., adv. bd. Samantha Smith Found. Producer Johnny Mercer's Mus. Chairs, 1952-55, Oscar Levant Show, 1955-61; creative producer Teen-Age Fair, 1962-72; exec. producer Charles in Charge, CBS-TV, 1984-85, Tribune Entertainment, 1986-91, Together We Stand, CBS-TV, 1986-87, Nothing Is Easy, 1987-88, The New Lassie, The Family Channel, 1989-92 (Outstanding Family Classic award Youth in Film 1994), Out of the Blue, Tribune Entertainment, 1995—; creative supr. Mary Hartman, Mary Hartman, Fernwood 2Night, America 2Night; prodn. supr. One Day At a Time, Facts of Life, Silver Spoons, The Jeffersons, Square Pegs, Different Strokes; composer-lyricist theme songs for Facts of Life, Different Strokes, Charles in Charge, The New Lassie (Genesis award, 1992), Together We Stand, Nothing Is Easy; cons. Domestic Life CBS-TV, 1983-84, Alan King Show, 1986. Shared Emmy award for outstanding comedy series All in the Family, 1978-89, Producers award Nat. Coun. for Families and TV, 1984, Jackie Coogan award for Oustanding Contbn. to Youth through Entertainment, 1991; honored for Different Strokes, NCCH, 1979-80; honored by Calif. Gov.'s Com. for employment of the handicapped for Facts of Life, 1981-82, for Charles in Charge, 1988; recipient Youth in Film award Charles in Charge, 1990, The New Lassie, 1994, Genesis award for portrayal animal issues The New Lassie, 1992; spl. commendation Entertainment Industries Coun. for The New Lassie and Charles in Charge, 1990. Mem. AFTRA, Chmn.'s Coun. of Caucus for Producers, Writers and Dirs., Dirs. Guild Am., Writers Guild Am., Acad. TV Arts and Scis., Acad. Magical Arts. Office: Al Burton Prodns 5900 Wilshire Blvd Los Angeles CA 90036

BURTON, CHARLES EDWARD, electrical engineer, systems engineer; b. Colorado Springs, Colo., Jan. 4, 1946; s. Charles Richard and Easter Drees (Kuettner) B.; m. Linda Ruth Robinson, Jan. 27, 1969; children: Heather Marie, Stephanie Anne. BSEE, Tex. Tech. U., 1969; MSEE, Tex. Tech U., 1971, PhD EE, 1973. Sr. rsch. engr. S.W. Rsch. Inst., San Antonio, 1973-75; rsch. engr. NCR Corp., Dayton, Ohio, 1975-76; sr. systems engr. Systems Rsch. Labs., Dayton, 1976-81; chief engr. Profl. Geophysics Inc., Denver, 1981-84; sr. staff engr. Hughes Aircraft Co., Denver, 1984-94; sr. engr. Info. Mechanics, 1994—; adj. prof. U. Tex., San Antonio, 1974-75, Wright State U., Dayton, 1976-78, U. Colo., Denver, 1984—; cons. various orgns. Designer copyrighted software; contbr. over 16 articles to profl. jours. Asst. coach Lakewood Soccer Assn., Denver, 1982; judge U.S. Swimming Assn., Denver, 1984-86. Mem. IEEE (sr., various offices), Assn. Computing Machinery, Am. Assn. for Artificial Intelligence, Internat. Neural Net Soc., Sigma Alpha Epsilon. Home: 13284 W Utah Cir Lakewood CO 80228-4228

BURTON, CLIFTON ALLEN, manufacturing company executive; b. Elwood, Ind., July 29, 1933; s. Joseph Melvin and Florence P. (Knotts) B.; m. Joyce Lorraine Emerson, Sept. 22, 1957; children: Keith Allen, Phillip Glenn, Catharine Lorraine, Michael Scott. Student, Purdue U., 1956-59. Registered profl. engr., Calif.; cert. mfg. engr. Tool design engr. Delco Remy div. Gen. Motors Corp., Anderson, Ind., 1959-61; mfg. engr. ACF Industries, Albuquerque, 1961-64, Automation Industries, Abilene, Tex., 1964-66, 69-71, Hughes Aircraft, Tucson, Ariz., 1966-69; mgr. prodn. engring. Hughes Tool Co., Houston, 1971-77; v.p. mfg. Eastman Whipstock, Houston, 1977-86; dir. mfg. Eastman Christensen, Salt Lake City, 1986-90; v.p. mfg. Baker Hughes, Houston, 1990-92; mfg. cons. Bayfield, Colo., 1992—; lectr., tchr. Coll. Tech., U. Houston, 1976-85; mem. bd. indsl. advisors U. Houston, 1981-87, chmn., 1984-85. Patentee in field. With USAF, 1952-56. Recipient Teaching Excellence award Coll. Tech., U. Houston, 1977. Mem. Soc. Mfg. Engrs. (chpt. chmn. 1984-85, Chmn.'s award 1985). Presbyterian. Home: 16 Forest Lakes Dr Bayfield CO 81122-9756

BURTON, EDWARD LEWIS, educator, industrial procedures and training consultant; b. Colfax, Iowa, Dec. 8, 1935; s. Lewis Harrison and Mary Burton; m. Janet Jean Allan, July 29, 1956; children: Mary, Cynthia, Katherine, Daniel. BA in Indsl. Edn., U. No. Iowa, 1958; MS in Indsl. Edn., U. Wis.-Stout, 1969; postgrad., Ariz. State U., 1971-76. Tchr. apprentice program S.E. Iowa Community Coll., Burlington, 1965-68; tchr. indsl. edn. Keokuc (Iowa) Sr. High Sch., 1965-68, Oak Park (Ill.)-River Forest High Sch., 1968-70; tchr. Rio Salado Community Coll., Phoenix, 1972-82; tchr. indsl. edn. Buckeye (Ariz.) Union High Sch., 1970-72; cons. curriculum Westside Area Career Opportunities Program - Ariz. Dept. Edn.; instr. vocat. automotive Dysart High Sch., Peoria, Ariz., 1979-81; tng. adminstr. Ariz. Pub. Service Co., Phoenix, 1981-90; tng. devel. cons. NUS Corp., 1991—; mem. dispatcher tng. com. Western Systems Coord. Coun., Salt Lake City, 1986-90; owner Aptitude Analysis Co., 1987—; mem. IEEE Dispatcher Tng. Work Group, 1988-91. Editor: Bright Ideas for Career Education, 1974, More Bright Ideas for Career Education, 1975. Mem. Citizens Planning Com., Buckeye, 1987-90, Town Governing Coun., Buckeye, 1990-91. NDEA grantee, 1967. Mem. NEA (life), NRA (life, endowment), Ariz. Indsl. Edn. Assn. (life), Personnel Testing Council of Ariz., Cactus Combat League, Mensa (test proctor 1987—), Masons. Republican. Methodist. Home: 19845 W Van Buren St Buckeye AZ 85326-5601

BURTON, FREDERICK GLENN, laboratory director; b. Greensburg, Pa., Nov. 30, 1939; s. Frederick Glenn and Vivian Baird (Chambers) B.; m. Jeanne Marie Nesper, May 29, 1968. BA, Coll. Wooster, 1962; MA, Wesleyan U., 1966; PhD, U. Rochester, 1971. Instr. Ohio Agrl. Experiment Sta., Wooster, 1962-64; postdoctoral fellow Salk Inst., San Diego, 1971-73; from rsch. scientist to sr. rsch. scientist Battelle N.W., Richland, Wash., 1974-85; project mgr. Battelle Meml. Inst., Columbus, Ohio, 1985-89; lab dir. Battelle Tooele (Utah) Ops., 1990—; project mgr., 1994—; cons. Immunodiagnostics Inc., Oceanside, Calif., 1973-74. Mayor City of West Richland, 1976-81. With USAR, 1964-70. Recipient honor Fed. Lab. Consortium, 1986. Mem. Am. Chem. Soc., Controlled Release Soc. Home: 90 Lakeview Tooele UT 84074-9668 Office: Battelle Tooele Ops 11650 Stark Rd Tooele UT 84074-9712

BURTON, JOHANNA KING, journalist; b. Bronx, N.Y., June 23, 1964; d. William Joseph and Carmela (Licenziato) King; m. Vaughn Eugene Burton Jr.; 1 child, Alicia Clair. BA in Journalism and Econs., U. N.Mex., 1986. Zone reporter Albuquerque Jour., 1986-87, county govt. reporter, 1987-89, gen. assignment reporter, 1989-92, religion reporter, 1992-93, police reporter, 1993—. Coach Spl. Olympics, Albuquerque, 1986. Democrat. Presbyterian. Home: 7829 Bursera Dr NW Albuquerque NM 87120-5213

BURTON, JOHN PAUL (JACK BURTON), lawyer; b. New Orleans, Feb. 26, 1943; s. John Paul and Nancy (Key) B.; m. Anne Ward; children: Jennifer, Susanna, Derek, Catherine. BBA magna cum laude, La. Tech. U., 1965; LLB, Harvard U., 1968. Bar: N.Mex. 1968, U.S. Dist. Ct. N.Mex. 1968, U.S. Ct. Appeals (10th cir.) 1973, U.S. Supreme Ct. 1979. Assoc., Rodey, Dickason, Sloan, Akin & Robb, Albuquerque, 1968-74, dir., 1974—, chmn. comml. dept., 1980-81, mng. dir. Santa Fe, N.Mex., 1986-90. Coauthor: (book) Boundary Disputes in New Mexico, 1992, Unofficial Update on the Uniform Ltd. Liab. Co. Act., 1994. Mem. Nat. Coun. Commrs. on Uniform State Laws, 1989—, drafting com. UCC Article 5, 1990—, UCC Article 9, 1993—, Uniform Ltd. Liability Co. Act, 1993—, legis. coun., 1991—, divsn. chair, 1993—; liaison for exec. com. to joint editorial bd. Unincorporated Bus. Orgns., 1994—; com. on liaison with Nat. Bankruptcy Review Commn., 1995—; pres. Brunn Sch., 1987-89. Fellow Am. Coll. Real Estate Lawyers, Lex Mundi Coll. of Mediators, State Bar Found.; mem. ABA, N.Mex. State Bar Assn. (chmn. comml. litigation and antitrust sect. 1985-86), Am. Law Inst. (rep. to UCC Article 5 drafting com. 1992—), Am. Coll. Mortgage Attys., Am. Arbitration Assn. (panel arbitrators), Am. Bankruptcy Inst., Internat. Bar Assn. Office: Rodey Dickason Sloan Akin & Robb PA PO Box 1357 Santa Fe NM 87504-1357

BURTON, LOREN G., school system administrator; b. Ogden, Utah, June 16, 1939; s. Dale Shirtliff and Belva Ginger (Marriott) B.; m. Annette Jean Laughlin, June 22, 1962; children: Stephen, Greg, Lori, Brad, Jeanine, Becky, John, Mike. AS, Weber State Coll., 1959; BS, U. Utah, 1964, MS, 1967, EdD, 1975. Supt. Granite Sch. Dist., Salt Lake City, 1987—, tchr., coach, counselor, 1964-68, asst. prin., 1968-74, 75-77, intern adminstrv. asst., 1977-78, prin. Kennedy Jr. High Sch., 1978-81, dir. west area, 1981-82, asst. supt. west area, 1982-87, asst. supt. adminstrv. svcs., 1987; chmn. Consortium of Supts., Salt Lake City, 1990—; mem. State Adv. Com. on Tchr. Edn., Salt Lake City, 1988-89. Del. polit. conventions, Utah, 1966, 69, 71; leader Boy Scouts Am., Utah, 1967—; leader community athletic programs, 1968—; leader Ch. of Jesus Christ of Latter-Day Saints, Utah, 1959—; mem. exec. bd. Jr. Achievement, Salt Lake City, 1988; mem. Utah Partnership, Salt Lake City, 1990-94. Recipient Fellow's award U. Utah, 1985, Exec. Educator 100 award 1993, Utah Supt. of Yr. award 1995. Mem. Granite Assn. Sch. Adminstrs., Am. Assn. Sch. Adminstrs., Nat. Fedn. Urban Suburban Sch. Dists., Utah State PTA (v.p. 1988—), Utah High Sch. Activities Assn., Utah Sch. Supt. Assn. (v.p.), Phi Delta Kappa. Republican. Home: 4985 S 1645 E Salt Lake City UT 84117-5972 Office: Granite Sch Dist 340 E 3545 S Salt Lake City UT 84115-4615

BURTON, MICHAEL WEBSTER, secondary education educator; b. Vancouver, B.C., Can., Jan. 24, 1947; came to U.S., 1955; s. Alfred Webster and Margret Ann (Ryan) B. AA, Clark Coll., 1967; B of Edn., Pacific Luth. U., 1969, M of English, 1974. Instr. debate, English White River High Sch., Buckley, Wash., 1969-74; tchr. English, speech Olympic Jr. High Sch., Auburn, Wash., 1974-83; dir. forensics, English Auburn Sr. High Sch., 1983—. Chmn. Auburn Wash. Edn. Assn. Pulse Com., 1981. Recipient Bruno E. Jacob Dist. Svc. award N.F.L., 1994, Nat. Fedn. Speech, Debate and Drama Coach of the Yr. award section 8, 1995; named Coll. Alumni of Yr. Clark Coll., 1994. Mem. NEA (Auburn pres. 1978, 80), Nat. Forensic League (dist. chmn. 1991—), Nat. Fedn. Interscholastic Ofcls. Assn. (bd. dirs. 1994, Meritorius Svc. award 1993), Northwest Collegiate Assn. (coll. football ofcl. 1975—), Western Wash. Football Ofcls. Assn. (pres. 1978, 85, 90, 94), Wash. State Forensic Assn. (v.p. 1986—). Episcopalian. Office: Auburn Sr High Sch 800 4th St NE Auburn WA 98002-5018

BURTON, PAUL FLOYD, social worker; b. Seattle, May 24, 1939; s. Floyd James and Mary Teresa (Chovanak) B.; BA, U. Wash., 1961, MSW, 1967; m. Roxanne Maude Johnson, July 21, 1961; children: Russell Floyd, Joan Teresa. Juvenile parole counselor Div. Juvenile Rehab. State of Wash., 1961-66; social worker VA, Seattle, 1967-72, social worker, cons. Work Release program King County, Wash., 1967-72; supr., chief psychiatry sect. Social Work Svc. VA, Topeka, Kans., 1972-73; pvt. practice, Topeka and L.A., 1972—; chief social work svc. VA, Sepulveda, Calif., 1974—, EEO coord. Med. ctr., 1974-77. Mem. Nat. Assn. Social Workers (newsletter editor Puget Sound chpt. 1970-71), Acad. Cert. Social Workers, Ctr. for Studies in Social Functioning, Am. Sociol. Assn., Am. Public Health Assn., Am. Hosp. Assn., Soc. Hosp. Social Work Dirs., Assn. VA Social Work Chiefs (founder 1979, charter mem. and pres. 1980-81, newsletter editor 1982-83, 89-91, pres. elect 1993-95, pres. 1995—). Home: 14063 Remington St Arleta CA 91331-5359 Office: 16111 Plummer St Sepulveda CA 91343-2036

BURTON, RANDALL JAMES, lawyer; b. Sacramento, Feb. 4, 1950; s. Edward Jay and Bernice Mae (Overton) B.; children: Kelly Jacquelyn, Andrew Jameson; m. Kimberly D. Rogers, Apr. 29, 1989. BA, Rutgers U., 1972; JD, Southwestern U., 1975. Bar: Calif. 1976, U.S. Dist. Ct. (ea. dist.) Calif. 1976, U.S. Dist. Ct. (no. dist.) Calif., 1990, U.S. Supreme Ct, 1991. Assoc. Brekke & Mathews, Citrus Heights, Calif., 1976; pvt. practice, Sacramento, 1976-93; ptnr. Finch, Burton, White & Drack, Sacramento, 1993—; judge pro tem Sacramento Small Claims Ct., 1982—. Bd. dirs. North Highlands Recreation and Park Dist., 1978-86, Family Svc. Agy. of Sacramento, 1991—; active Local Bd. 22, Selective Svc., 1982—, Active 20-30 Club of Sacramento, 1979-90, pres., 1987. Recipient Disting. Citizen award, Golden Empire Council, Boy Scouts Am. Mem. Sacramento Bar Assn., Sacramento Young Lawyers Assn. Presbyterian. Lodge: Rotary (pres. Foothill-Highlands club 1980-81). Office: 1540 River Park Dr Ste 224 Sacramento CA 95815-4609

BURTON, THOMAS ROGHAAR, English language educator; b. Ogden, Utah, Oct. 7, 1933; s. Laurence S. and Marguerite E. (Roghaar) B.; m. Sharon Slater, June 11, 1959; children: Thomas, Julie, Matthew, James. AS, Weber Coll., 1953; BS, Brigham Young U., 1959, MA, 1960; PhD, U. Wash., 1967. Chair English dept. Weber State U., Ogden, 1972-74, assoc. v.p. for acad. affairs, 1974-80, prof. English dept., 1963—, chair faculty senate, 1989—; treas., bd. dirs. Weber State Credit Union; chair, bd. dirs. Utah State Divsn. of Youth Correction, Salt Lake City; active numerous coms. including salary com., strategic planning task force and steering com., deans coun., search com. for pres., Weber State U., chair gen. edn. com., curriculum com., admissions, stds. and student affairs com. Contbr. articles to profl. jours. With USN, 1953-55. Mem. AAUP (pres. Utah conf.), Assn. for Mormon Letters (exec. bd.), Phi Kappa Phi. Republican. Mem. Ch. LDS. Home: 839 Vista Dr Ogden UT 84403-3038 Office: Weber State U 3800 Harrison Blvd Ogden UT 84403-2027

BUSBOOM, LARRY D., food products company executive; b. 1942. CPA. With Deloitte Haskins & Sells, Crown Zellerbach Corp., San Francisco, 1972-86; v.p., contr. Crown Zellerbach Corp.; CFO, sr. v.p. Sun Diamond Growers of Calif., Pleasanton, 1986-89, pres., 1989—, also bd. dirs. Office: Sun-Diamond Growers Calif 5568 Gibraltar Dr Pleasanton CA 94588-8544*

BUSCH, ANN MARIE HERBAGE, medical/surgical clinical nurse specialist; b. Roseburg, Oreg., Jan. 24, 1958; d. Robert Canfield and Magdaline Mary (Tuchscherer) Herbage; m. John Patrick Busch, June 27, 1981; children: Rebecca Ann, Michael Robert. BSN summa cum laude, U. Portland, 1980; MSN, U. Calif., San Francisco, 1985. RN, Oreg., Calif.; cert. clin. specialist in med.-surg. nursing; cert. enterostomal therapy nurse; cert. CPR instr. Staff nurse IV Stanford (Calif.) U. Hosp., 1981-88, acting nursing ednl. coord., 1986-87; coord./educator RN refresher program DeAnza Coll., Cupertino, Calif., 1986-88; med-surg. clin. nurse specialist Cmty. Hosp. Los Gatos (Calif.), 1988-92; surg. clin. nurse specialist Palo Alto VA Med. Ctr., 1992-95; liver transplant clin. nurse specialist Vet. Affairs Med. Ctr., Portland, Oreg., 1995—; cons. for patient pathways U. So. Calif. Hosp., 1990-91; asst. clin. prof. dept. physiol. nursing U. Calif., San Francisco, 1993—. Recipient dist. nursing rsch. utilization award VA, 1993. Mem. ANA (coun. nurses advanced practice), Wound, Ostomy and Continence Nurses Soc., Am. Soc. Parenteral and Enteral Nutrition, Nat. League for Nursing, Oreg. Nurses Assn., No. Calif. Clin. Nurse Specialists Group (pres.), Blue Key, Sigma Theta Tau, Delta Epsilon Sigma. Home: 1310 Stonehaven Dr West Linn OR 97068-1867 Office: Portland Vet Affs Med Ctr PO Box 1034 3710 SW US Veterans Hosp Rd Portland OR 97207

BUSCH, JOYCE IDA, small business owner; b. Madera, Calif., Jan. 24, 1934; d. Bruno Harry and Ella Fae (Absher) Toschi; m. Fred O. Busch, Dec. 14, 1956; children: Karen, Kathryn, Kurt. BA in Indsl. Arts & Interior Design, Calif. State U., Fresno, 1991. Cert. interior designer Calif. Stewardess United Air Lines, San Francisco, 1955-57; prin. Art Coordinates, Fresno, 1982—, Busch Interior Design, Fresno, 1982—; art cons. Fresno Community Hosp., 1981-83; docent Fresno Met. Mus., 1981-84. Treas. Valley Children's Hosp. Guidance Clinic, 1975-79, Lone Star PTA, 1965-84,; mem. Mothers Guild Jan Joaquin Mem. Hosp., 1984-88. Mem. Am. Soc. Interior Designers, Illuminating Engring. Soc. N.Am. Republican. Roman Catholic. Club: Sunnyside Garden (pres. 1987-88).

BUSCH, MORGAN DAVID, health care executive; b. Vallejo, Calif., July 20, 1955; s. Morgan Maxfield and Sorina Jane (Pedersen) B.; m. Diane Louise Walker, Apr. 27, 1978; children: Angelina, Diane, Morgan, Charles, Sorina. BS in Bus. Mgmt., Brigham Young U., 1979, MPA, 1981. Dir. planning Idaho Falls (Idaho) Consol. Hosps., 1981-84; mgr. corp. planning Intermountain Health Care, Salt Lake City, 1984-86, dir. adminstrv. svcs. ctrl. region, 1986-89, dir. adminstrv. svcs. rural region, 1989—; alt. mem. Utah Rural Health Adv. Com., Salt Lake City, 1990-91; com. mem. Mountain West Rural Health Conf., Salt Lake City, 1993—. Fellow Am. Coll. Healthcare Execs. Democrat. Mem. LDS Ch.

BUSH, JUNE LEE, real estate executive; b. Philippi, W.Va., Sept. 20, 1942; d. Leland C. and Dolly Mary (Costello) Robinson; m. Jerry Lee Coffman, June 15, 1963 (div. 1970); 1 child, Jason Lance; m. Richard Alfred Bush, May 20, 1972. Grad., Fairmont State Coll., 1962, Dale Carnegie, Anaheim, Calif., 1988. Exec. sec. McDonnell Douglas, Huntington Beach, Calif., 1965-72; adminstrv. asst. Mgmt. Resources, Inc., Fullerton, Calif., 1978-80; bldg. mgr. Alfred Gobar Assocs., Brea, Calif., 1980—; treas. Craig Park East, Fullerton, 1982, bd. dirs., 1982-84. Author instrn. manual Quality Assurance Secretarial Manual, 1971. Sec. PTA, La Palma, 1974. Mem. Gamma Chi Chi. Home: 6600 E Canyon Hills Rd Anaheim Hills CA 92807-4239 Office: Alfred Gobar Assocs Inc 721 W Kimberly Ave Placentia CA 92670-6343

BUSH, MARY ELIZABETH, mechanical engineer; b. Gary, Ind., June 11, 1963; d. Charles L. and Margaret A. (LaVoy) Schoenborn; m. William H. Bush, Aug. 10, 1984. BS in Mech. Engring., Purdue U., 1984, MS in Biology, 1986. Registered profl. engr., Calif. Registered patent agt., U.S. Patent Office. Anatomy and Physiology teaching asst. Purdue U., West Lafayette, Ind., 1984-85; Neuro Biology teaching asst. Purdue U., West Lafayette, 1986; rsch. asst. Purdue U. Biomed. Engring. Ctr., West Lafayette, 1985-86; mech. engr. Pacesetter Systems, Inc., Sylmar, Calif., 1986-89; mech. devel. engr. Siemens-Pacesetter, Inc., Sylmar, 1989; leads engr. Ventritex, Inc., Sunnyvale, Calif., 1989-91; sr. mech. engr. Ventritex, Inc., Sunnyvale, 1991—. Patentee implantation of leads, apparatus for attaching implanted materials to body tissue, multiple electrode deployable lead. Recipient Pres.'s Honor award Purdue U., 1981. Mem. Assn. for the Advancement of Med. Instrumentation. Home: 2068 Mento Dr Fremont CA 94539-4625

BUSH, REX CURTIS, lawyer; b. Longview, Wash., Oct. 21, 1953; s. Rex Cole Bush and Arline (Quanstrom) Fitzgerald; m. Joy Ann Pallas, July 22, 1977 (div.); children: Alicia, Angela, Carrie; m. Janet Rae Hicks July 2, 1988; children: Jeni, Mykal. BA cum laude, Brigham Young U., 1980; JD, U. Utah, 1983. Bar: Utah 1983, U.S. Dist. Ct. (no. dist.) Utah 1983, U.S. Tax Ct. 1985. Tax atty. Arthur Andersen & Co., Houston, 1983-84; assoc. Mortensen & Neider, Midvale, Utah, 1984-85; in-house counsel Fin. Futures, Salt Lake City, 1985-87; registrar Hollander Cons., Portland, Oreg., 1987-88; in-house counsel Bennett Leasing, Salt Lake City, 1987-88; pres. Bush Law Firm, Sandy, Utah, 1988—; judge pro tempore 3d Cir. Ct., Salt Lake City, 1985-87. Author: (booklet) What To Do in Case of an Automobile Accident, 1994. Mayor University Village, U. Utah, 1981-82; Rep. candidate Utah state senate, 1992; Rep. voting dist. sec., treas., 1992. Recipient Meritorious Leadership award, Nat. Com. for Employer Support of Guard and Reserve, 1990. Mem. Am. Trial Lawyers Assn., Utah Trial Lawyers Assn., Utah State Bar (chmn. small firm and solo practitioners com.). Office: Bush Law Firm 9615 S 700 E Sandy UT 84070-3557

BUSH, SARAH LILLIAN, historian; b. Kansas City, Mo., Sept. 17, 1920; d. William Adam and Lettie Evelyn (Burrill) Lewis; m. Walter Nelson Bush, June 7, 1946 (dec.); children: William Read, Robert Nelson. AB, U. Kans., 1941; BS, U. Ill., 1943. Clk. circulation dept. Kansas City Pub. Library, 1941-42, asst. librarian Paseo br., 1943-44; librarian Kansas City Jr. Coll., 1944-46; substitute librarian San Mateo County Library, Woodside amd Portola Valley, Calif., 1975-77; various temporary positions, 1979-87; owner Metriguide, Palo Alto, Calif., 1975-78. Author: Atherton Lands, 1979, rev. edition 1987. Editor: Atherton Recollections, 1973. Pres., v.p. Jr. Librarians, Kansas City, 1944-46; courtesy, yearbook & historian AAUW, Menlo-Atherton branch (Calif.) Br.; asst. Sunday sch. tchr., vol. Holy Trinity Ch., Menlo Park, 1955-78; v.p., membership com., libr. chairperson, English reading program, parent edn. chairperson Menlo Atherton High Sch. PTA, 1964-73; founder, bd. dirs. Friends of Atherton Community Library, 1967—, oral historian, 1968—, chair Bicentennial event, 1976; bd. dirs. Menlo Park Hist. Assn., 1979-82, oral historian, 1973—; bd. dirs. Civic Interest League, Atherton, 1978-81; mem. hist. county commn. Town of Atherton, 1980-87; vol. Allied Arts Palo Alto Aux. to Children's Hosp. at Stanford, 1967—, oral historian, 1978—, historian, 1980—; vol. United Crusade, Garfield Sch., Redwood City, 1957-61, 74-88, Encinal Sch., 1961-73, program dir., chmn. summer recreation, historian, sec.; vol. Stanford Mothers Club, 1977-81, others; historian, awards chairperson Cub Scouts Boy Scouts Am.; founder Atherton Heritage Assn. 1989, bd. dirs., 1989—; mem. Guild Gourmet, 1971—. Recipient Good Neighbor award Civic Interest League, 1992. Mem. PTA (life). Episcopalian.

BUSH, STANLEY GILTNER, secondary education educator; b. Kans. City, Mo., Nov. 4, 1928; s. Dean Thomas and Sallie Giltner (Hoagland) B.; m. Barbara Snow Adams, May 23, 1975 (dec. Mar. 1994); stepchildren: Deborah Gayle Duclon, Douglas Bruce Adams. BA, U. Colo., 1949, MA, 1959, postgrad., 1971; postgrad., U. Denver, 1980, 85, 90. Tchr. Gering (Nebr.) Pub. Schs., 1949-51, 54-57, Littleton (Colo.) Pub. Schs., 1957-91; emergency plan dir. City of Littleton, 1961—; safety officer Littleton Pub. Schs., 1968—; founder, chief Arapahoe Rescue Patrol, Inc., Littleton, 1957-92; pres. Arapahoe Rescue Patrol, Inc., 1957—, Expedition, Inc., Littleton, 1973—. Contbr. chpts. to Boy Scout Field Book, 1984; co-author: Managing

Search Function, 1987; contbr. articles to profl. jours. Safety advisor South Suburban Parks Dist., Littleton, 1985—; advisor ARC, Littleton, 1987—, Emergency Planning Com., Arapahoe County, Colo., 1987—; coord. search and rescue Office of Gov., Colo., 1978-82. Sgt. U.S. Army, 1951-54. Shell Oil Co. fellow, 1964; recipient Silver Beaver award Boy Scouts Am., 1966, Vigil-Order of Arrow, 1966, Award of Excellence Masons, 1990. Mem. Nat. Assn. for Search and Rescue (life, Hall Foss award 1978), Colo. Search and Rescue Bd., NEA (life). Methodist. Home: 2415 E Maplewood Ave Littleton CO 80121-2817 Office: Littleton Ctr 2255 W Berry Ave Littleton CO 80120-1151

BUSHARA, MOHAMED N., geologist, oil industry executive; b. Nyala, Sudan, Jan. 2, 1956; s. Nurein L. and Zahara Bushara; m. Catherine Ruth Bushara, July 7, 1993; 1 child, Nasrene Kelley. BSc with honors, U. Khartoum, 1980; MS in Geology, U. Washington, 1987; PhD, U. Wis., 1991. Geologist Geol. Survey Dept., Sudan, 1980-84; rsch. asst. dept. geol. scis. U. Washington, 1986-87; geologist Exxon Prodn. Rsch. Co., Houston, 1989, ARCO Alaska Inc., 1991—. Contbr. articles to scientific jours. Grantee German Acad. Exchange Svc., 1982, U.S. Dept. Energy, 1983; Patricia Roberts Harris Doctoral fellow U. Wis., 1988-91; recipient Minority Edn. Divsn. award U. Washington D.C., 1985-86, Grad. Rsch. Fund dept. Geol. Scis. U. Washington, 1986, Corp. Fund, 1986. Mem. Am. Geophysical Union, Am. Assn. Petroleum Geologists (recipient Grant-in-Aid 1989), Geol. Soc. of Am., Sigma Xi. Home: 3016 Brittany Pl Anchorage AK 99504-3986 Office: ARCO Alaska Inc 700 G St Anchorage AK 99510

BUSHMAN, EDWIN FRANCIS ARTHUR, engineer, plastics consultant, rancher; b. Aurora, Ill., Mar. 16, 1919; s. George J. and Emma (Gengler) B.; B.S., U. Ill., 1941, postgrad., 1941-42, Calif. Inst. Tech., 1941; m. Louise Kathryn Peterson, Jan. 3, 1946; children: Bruce Edwin, Gary Robert, Joan Louise, Karen Rose, Mary Elisabeth, Paul George. Jr. engr, Gulf Refining Co. Gulf Oil Corp., Mattoon, Ill., 1940-41; engr. radio and sound lab. war rsch. div. U. Calif. at Navy Electronics Lab., Pt. Loma, San Diego, 1942-45; project engr. Bell and Howell Co., Lincolnwood, Ill., 1945-46; research cons., Scholl Mfg. Co., Inc., Chgo., 1946-48; project engr. deepfreeze div. Motor Products Corp., North Chicago, Ill., 1948-50; research and product design engr. Bushman Co., Aurora, Ill. also Mundelein, Ill., 1946-55; with Plastics div. Gen. Am. Transp. Corp., Chgo., 1950-68, tech. dir., 1950-55, mgr. sales and sales engring. Western states, Compton, Calif., 1955-68, sales and sales engring. research and devel. div., 1962-64; with USS Chems., 1968-70; plastics cons. E.F. Bushman Co., 1970—, Tech. Conf. Assocs., 1974-80. Program mgr. Agriplastics Symposium Nat. Agrl. Plastics Conf., 1966; program mgr. Plastics in Hydrospace, 1967; originator Huisman Plastics awards, 1970, Un-Carbon Polymer prize and Polymer Pool Preserve Plan, 1975, Polymer Independence award, 1977, 78. Bd. dirs. Coastal Area Protective League, 1958-66, Lagunita Community Assn., 1959-66 (pres. 1964-65), Calif. Marine Parks and Harbors Assn., 1959-69. Sr. editor Plastic Trends mag., 1985-90. Recipient Western Plastics Man of Yr. award, 1972. Mem. Soc. Plastics Industry Inc. (chpt. pres. 1971-72), Soc. Plastic Engrs. (Lundberg award 1981), Western Plastics Pioneers, Western Plastics Mus. and Pioneers, Plastics Pioneers Assn., Sunkist Growers, Cal. Citrus Nurserymen's Soc., Calif. Farm Bur. Fedn. U. Ill. Alumni Assn., Soc. for Advancement Materials and Process Engring., Geopolymers Inst. Roman Catholic. Author various profl. and strategic resource papers. Patentee in field of plastics, carbon and colored glass fibers, process, and applications. Home: 19 Lagunita Ln Laguna Beach CA 92651-4237 Office: PO Box 581 Laguna Beach CA 92652-0581

BUSHNELL, KENNETH WAYNE, artist, educator; b. L.A., Oct. 16, 1933; s. George Lilburn and Luella Mae (Bivens) B.; m. Reneé Hazel Loufer, Mar. 15, 1956 (div. 1973); children: Blake, Dale. BA, UCLA, 1956; MFA, U. Hawaii, 1961. Prof. art U. Hawaii at Manoa, Honolulu, 1961—; exch. prof. in painting L.I. U., C.W. Post Ctr., 1979-80, 83. Shows include Mus. Modern Art, N.Y., 1962, Balt. Mus. Art, 1962, Gima's Gallery, Honolulu, 1963, 66, 69, 72, 75, Pa. Acad. Fine Arts, 1963, United Fedn. Graphic Arts, Phila., 1964, Contemporary Arts Ctr, Honolulu, 1965, 77, 86, Honolulu Acad. Arts Mus., 1968, 73, 74, 82,85, Ariel Gallery, Milan, 1976, N.Y. Horticultural Soc. Gallery, N.Y.C., 1980, Wallnut Gallery, Phila., 1980, 81, Galerie Meissner Editions, Hamburg, West Germany, 1984, Taller Fort Gallery, Cadaques, Spain, 1984, 90, 91, Sande Webster Gallery, Phila., 1985, 88, Maronier Gallery, Kyoto, Japan, 1986, Wacoal Ginza Gallery, Tokyo, 1986, Richards Gallery, Boston, 1986, The Contemporary Mus., Honolulu, 1992, others; exhibited in group shows at Contemporary Arts Ctr., 1977, 78, Honolulu Internat. Ctr., Honolulu Acad. Arts, 1963-75, 78, 79, 82, 84, 86, 89, 91, Honolulu Hale, 1979, Beretania Coop. Gallery, Contemporary Museum, 1990, Queen Emma Gallery, Honolulu, 1990, Galerie Karin Fesel, Dusseldorf, West Germany, 1990, Sande Webster Gallery, 1992, others; represented in permanent collections Portland Museum, Contemporary Art Ctr., The Honolulu Acad. Arts Museum, Bibliotheque Nationale, Corcoran Museum, Library of Congress, numerous others. Drawing sessions in studio open to Community, 1986—; chmn. dept. pers. com. U. Hawaii, 1986, dept. curriculum com., 1987; mem. Manoa Writing Bd.; juror in field. Lt. USNR, 1956-60. Recipient Honolulu Acad. of Arts Purchase award, 1973, Hawaii State Found. on Culture and Arts puchase award, 1973, 75, 79, 81, Bibliotheque Nationale purchase award, 1976; paintings commissioned by Harmonie Club of N.Y., 1980, Mr. and Mrs. Alan Hunt of Honolulu, 1983; print commissioned by Hawaiian Diptych for Waiohai Gallery; site specific relief painting commissioned by Sande Webster Gallery, 1986 and others. Mem. AAUP, Coll. Art Assn., Honolulu Printmakers Assn. (pres. of the bd. 1961). Democrat. Home: 2081 Keeaumoku Pl Honolulu HI 96822-2553 Office: U Hawaii at Manoa 2535 The Mall Honolulu HI 96822-2233

BUSHNELL, RODERICK PAUL, lawyer; b. Buffalo, Mar. 6, 1944; s. Paul Hazen and Martha Atlee B.; m. Suzann Yvonne Kaiser, Aug. 27, 1966; 1 child, Arlo Phillip. BA, Rutgers U., 1966; JD, Georgetown U., 1969. Bar: Calif. 1970, U.S. Supreme Ct. 1980. Atty. dept. water resources Sacramento, 1969-71; ptnr. Bushnell, Caplan & Fielding, San Francisco, 1971—; adv. bd. dirs. Bread & Roses, Inc., Mill Valley, Calif. Bd. dirs. Calif. Lawyers for the Arts, Ft. Mason, San Francisco, 1985—. Mem. Assn. Trial Lawyers Am., San Francisco Bar Assn. (arbitrator), San Francisco Superior Ct. (arbitrator), Calif. Bar Assn., Lawyers Club of San Francisco, Calif. Trial Lawyers Assn., San Francisco Trial Lawyers Assn., No. Calif. Criminal Trial Lawyers Assn., San Francisco Bay Club, Commonwealth Club. Democrat. Office: Bushnell Caplan & Fielding 901 Market St Ste 230 San Francisco CA 94103-1735

BUSIG, RICK HAROLD, mining executive; b. Vancouver, Wash., June 21, 1952; s. Harold Wayne and Ramona (Riley) B. AA, Clark Coll., Vancouver, 1972; BA in Econs., U. Wash., 1974. CPA, Wash. Acct., Universal Svcs., Seattle, 1975-78; acct., acctg. mgr., controller Landura Corp., Woodburn, Oreg., 1978-80; asst. controller Pulte Home Corp., Laramie, Wyo., 1980-81; treas., controller Orcal Cable, Inc., Sparks, Nev., 1981-82; controller Saga Exploration Co., Reno, Nev., 1982—; acct. Sterling Mine Joint Venture, Beatty, Nev., 1982-95. Del. Nev. State Dem. Conv., Reno, 1984, 94, Las Vegas, 1988. Recipient Spaatz award CAP. Mem. AICPA, Wash. Soc. CPA's, Oreg. Soc. CPA's. Home: 2735 Lakeside Dr # A Reno NV 89509-4203 Office: Saga Exploration Co 2660 Tyner Way Reno NV 89503-4926

BUSINGER, STEVEN, meteorology educator; b. Utrecht, The Netherlands, May 17, 1953; came to U.S., 1956; s. Joost Alois and Judith (Swart) B.; m. Susan Coleen Lewis; children: Aaron, Paul. BS, U. Washington, PhD; MS, Colo. U. Rsch. asst. U. Colo., Boulder, 1975-78; avalanche forecaster Forest Svc., Seattle, 1978-82; rsch. asst. U. Washington, Seattle, 1982-86; asst. prof. N.C. State U., Raleigh, 1986-93; assoc. prof. U. Hawaii, Honolulu, 1993—; chmn. U. Corp. Atmospheric Rsch. U. Rels. Comm., Boulder, 1989—; outside expert Nat. Oceanographic Atmospheric Adminstrn, Nat. Weather Svc., Disaster Survey Team, 1991; mem. steering com. U. Navigational Consortium, Boulder, 1994—; organizer, instr. Project Globe-Net, NSF. Contbr. articles to profl. jours. Mem. AAAS, Am. Meteorol. Soc. (chmn. local chpt. 1990), Am. Geophysical Union, Sigma Xi, Phi Beta Kappa, Phi Eta Sigma. Home: 108 Kekaha Pl Honolulu HI 96825-2116 Office: Univ Hawaii Dept Meteorology 2525 Correa Rd Honolulu HI 96822-2219

BUSS, JERRY HATTEN, real estate executive, sports team owner; children: John, Jim, Jeanie, Jane. BS in Chemistry, U. Wyo.; MS, PhD in Chemistry, U. So. Calif., 1957. Chemist Bur. Mines; past mem. faculty dept. chemistry U. So. Calif.; mem. missile div. McDonnell Douglas, Los Angeles; partner Mariani-Buss Assos.; former owner Los Angeles Strings; chmn. bd., owner Los Angeles Lakers (Nat. Basketball Assn.); until 1988 owner Los Angeles Kings (Nat. Hockey League). Office: care LA Lakers PO Box 10 3900 W Manchester Blvd Inglewood CA 90305-2200

BUSS, TERESA THACKER, software engineer; b. Canton, Ga., Jan. 4, 1957; d. Paul Reed and Geneva (McWhorter) Thacker; m. Samuel Rudolph Buss, June 7, 1980; children: Stephanie Samantha, Ian Paul. BS, Oglethorpe U., 1976. Programmer analyst Emory U. Computing Ctr., Atlanta, 1976-80; contract programmer Sellers Software Co., Atlanta, 1979-80; sr. programmer analyst Proximity Tech. Inc., Ft. Lauderdale, 1980-82; software engr. Exxon Office Systems, Princeton, N.J., 1982-85; sr. systems analyst U. Calif., Berkeley, 1985-88, Sci. Applications Internat. Corp., San Diego, 1988—. Pres. Wyman Club Princeton U., 1983-85; mem. PTA, San Diego, 1990—. Shell Cos. Found. scholar Oglethorpe U., 1975-76; recipient Sally Hull Welter award, 1976. Mem. San Diego Zool. Soc. Democrat. Baptist. Office: Sci Applications Internat Corp 5550 Oberlin Dr San Diego CA 92121

BUSS, WILLIAM CHARLES, research pharmacology educator; b. Bremerton, Wash., Aug. 13, 1938; s. William Edward and Olga Sophia (Thorwick) B. BS in Chemistry, Portland State U., 1965; MS in Pharmacology, U. Alta., Edmonton, Can., 1967; PhD in Pharmacology, U. Oreg., 1971. Postdoctoral fellow U. Calif., San Francisco, 1971-72; asst. prof. pharmacology U. N.Mex. Sch. Medicine, Albuquerque, 1973-79, assoc. prof., 1979-89, prof., 1989—, acting chmn. dept. pharmacology, 1981, 86-92; chair, dept. pharmacology U N.Mex. Sch. Medicine, Albuquerque, 1992—. Contbr. articles to profl. jours. Research grantee NIH, NSF, Am. Heart Assn., others. Mem. AAAS, Am. Soc. Pharmacology and Exptl. Therapeutics, Am. Soc. Biochem. and Molecular Biology. Home: PO Box 1185 Corrales NM 87048-1185 Office: U NMex Sch Medicine Dept Pharmacology Albuquerque NM 87131

BUSSE, MICHAEL CLIFFORD, newspaper advertising executive; b. Milw., Dec. 28, 1942; s. Clifford August and Lucille Minnie (Retzlaff) B.; Gloria Jean Olsen, June 8, 1968; children: Bradford Michael, Kurtis Mountaine. Student, Chapman U., 1960-61, Fullerton (Calif.) Coll., 1961-62, El Camino Coll., 1971-72, Cerrtius Coll., 1972-73. Yellow pages sales rep. Gen. Telephone and Electronics, Long Beach, Calif., 1968-70; account exec. L.A. Times, 1970-73, L.A. Times/N.Y. Advt. Bur., N.Y.C., 1973-78; co-op advt. L.A. Times, 1978-83; display advt. mgr. west side edit. L.A. Times, Santa Monica, Calif., 1983-85; display advt. mgr. Orange County L.A. Times, Costa Mesa, Calif., 1985-89; new bus. devel. group mgr. L.A. Times, 1989—; pres., founder Western States Co-op Advt. Newspaper Network, 1989—. Author: (video) Newspaper Co-Op Network, 1990 (Achievement award 1990), Newspaper Advertising Co-Op Network, 1990 (Achievement award 1991), The Non-Traditional Sell, 1991; contbr. articles to profl. jours. With U.S. Army, 1965-67, Vietnam. Recipient Outstanding Leadership/Promotions and Advt. Chmn. Orange County Centennial Commn., 1989, Ann. Leadership award Newspaper Advt. Bur., 1990; named Regional Dir. fo Yr. Newspaper Co-Op Network, 1991. Mem. Am. Legion, Newspaper Advt. Co-Op Network (bd. dirs. 1990-92, regional dir. 1989—, pres. 1983-84, John Maione award 1986, 94), Purple Heart Assn., Newspaper Assn. Am. (mktg. ops. com. 1992-93, chmn. co-op fedn. 1992-94, bd. govs. 1992-94), Western States Co-op Newspaper Network (pres.), Dealer Newspaper Advt. Sys. (chmn. 1994—). Republican. Lutheran. Office: LA Times Mirror Square Los Angeles CA 90053

BUSSEWITZ, M. WALTER, writer; b. Horicon, Wis., Nov. 23, 1919; s. Walter Richard and Addie Mae (Rupnow) B.; m. Marjorie E. Veness, June 12, 1943; children: Stephen, Gerald. BA, U. Wis., 1941. CLU; chartered fin. cons. Writer radio news Transradio Press, Chgo., 1941-42, UPI, Milw. and St. Paul, 1942-43; writer bus. news AP, N.Y.C., 1943-58; mgr. press relations Equitable Life Assn. Soc. of U.S., N.Y.C., 1959-69, dir. info. svcs., 1970-73; asst. v.p. office of corp. responsibility N.Y. Life, N.Y.C., 1973-74; spl. staff writer Inst. Life Ins., N.Y.C., 1974-77; regional dir. life ins. media relations Am. Council Life Ins., Washington, 1977-85; contbg. editor Life Assn. News, Washington, 1986-90; columnist Nat. Underwriter, Washington, 1986-90, N.W. corr., 1990—. Author numerous booklets on personal fin., 1980-85; contbr. articles on ins. related subjects to profl. publs. Treas. Housing Help, Huntington, N.Y., 1970-77. Mem. Soc. Profl. Journalists (editor newspaper N.Y. chpt. 1969-74, Pres.' award 1972), N.Y. Fin. Writer's Assn., Am. Soc. CLUs, Pub. Rels. Soc. Am., Nat. Press Club, Silurians, U. Wis. Alumni Assn.

BUSSEY, GEORGE DAVIS, psychiatrist; b. Salta, Argentina, Apr. 14, 1949; s. William Harold and Helen (Wygant) B.; m. Moira Savage, July 26, 1975; children: Andrew Davis, Megan Elizabeth. BS, U. Denver, 1969; MD, Ea. Va. Med. Sch., 1977; JD, U. Hawaii, 1993. Intern Eastern Va. Grad. Sch. Medicine, 1977-78; resident Ea. Va. Grad. Sch. Medicine, 1978-79, Vanderbilt U. Hosp., Nashville, 1979-81; staff psychiatrist Hawaii State Hosp., Kaneohe, 1981-82; asst. prof. dept. psychiatry U. Hawaii, Honolulu, 1982-84; dir. adult svcs. Kahi Mohala Hosp., Ewa Beach, Hawaii, 1983-89; clin. dir. Queens Healthcare Plan, Honolulu, 1988-94; med. dir. Managed Care Mgmt., Inc., 1994—; clin. assoc. prof. Dept. Psychiatry U. Hawaii, Honolulu, 1990—. Mem. U. Hawaii Law Rev., 1991-93; contbr. articles to profl. jours. Fellow Am. Psychiat. Assn., Hawaii Psychiat. Soc. (treas. 1982-83, pres. 1985-87).

BUSSIERE, JEANINE LOUISE, toxicologist; b. Winona, Minn., May 29, 1962; d. Eugene Albert and Ruth Margaret (Utecht) B. BS, U. Idaho, 1984; MS, Western Wash. U., 1986; PhD, Wash. State U., 1989. Diplomate Am. Bd. Toxicology. Rsch. asst. U. Idaho, Moscow, 1982-84, Western Wash. U., Bellingham, 1985-86; rsch. aide U. Idaho, Moscow, 1986-89; postdoctoral fellow Temple U., Phila., 1990-92; toxicologist Genentech, Inc., San Francisco, 1992—; tng. program lectr. SmithKline Beecham, Phila., 1991; peer rev. on Boron Neutron Capture Therapy, Dept. Energy, Chgo., 1992; in vitro toxicology task force Pharm. Mfrs. Assn., Bethesda, Md., 1993-94. Contbr. chpt. to book and articles to profl. jours. Recipient Travel awards Nat. Inst. Drug Abuse, 1991, Comm. Problems of Drug Dependence, 1992; postdoctoral fellow Nat. Inst. Drug Abuse, Temple U., 1990-92. Mem. Am. Soc. for Pharmacology and Exptl. Therapeutics, Soc. for Neurosci., Soc. Environ. Toxicology and Chemistry, Soc. Toxicology (Travel award 1988). Office: Genentech Inc Dept Pathobiol & Toxicology 460 Point San Bruno Blvd San Francisco CA 94080

BUSSINGER, ROBERT EUGENE, service executive; b. Dayton, Ohio, Jan. 26, 1932; s. Albert G. and Louise B. (Hoffman) B.; m. Doreen L. Fine, Jan. 25, 1957 (div. 1978); children: Leslie E., Daniel M., David M. Student, U. Dayton, 1955-56, U. Redlands, 1957-59. Broker Bussinger Ins., Carmel, Calif., 1962-69; broker, dealer Esper Corp., Carmel, 1969-72; owner Esperanto Coffee House, Carmel, 1971-75; gen. mgr. Gen. Store Restaurant, Carmel, 1976-77; food svc. dir. Lodge at Pebble Beach (Calif.), 1977-79; resort v.p., gen. mgr. Ventana Inn Resort, Inc., Big Sur, Calif., 1979-95; dir. cmty. planning Rancho San Carlos Partnership, Carmel Valley, Calif., 1995—. Bd. dirs. Pacific Repertory Theater, Monterey, 1990—, chmn., 1991-92; bd. dirs. Monterey Peninsula Mus. Art, 1990—. With USN, 1951-55. Mem. Nat. Restaurant Assn., Calif. Hotel Assn., Monterey County Hospitality Assn. (bd. dirs.), Carmel Bus. Assn., Calif. Hotel Sales Mktg. Assn., Monterey County Restaurant Assn. (bd. dirs.), Bug Sur C. of C. (bd. dirs. 1984—, pres. 1984-89), Am. Inst. Wine and Food (bd. dirs. 1990-95), Monterey Advt. Club (v.p. 1985-87), KAZU Radio (bd. dirs.). Home and Office: Ventana Big Sur CA 93920

BUSTER, EDMOND BATE, metal products company executive; b. Whitt, Tex., Oct. 20, 1918; s. Edmond Bate and Emma Lee (Johnston) B.; m. Beatrice Keller, Oct. 24, 1939; children: John Edmond, Robert William, Susan Lynn, Steven K., James L., Brian R. A.A., Menlo Jr. Coll., 1937; B.S. in Mining Engring, U. Calif. at Berkeley, 1940. With Tex. Co., Santa Paula, Calif., 1937-40, Tidewater Asso. Oil Co., Ventura, 1940-42; supr. mfg. and engring. Douglas Aircraft Co., Long Beach, 1942-45; pres. Pacific Rivet and Machine Co., Alhambra, 1945-52, Pacific Fasteners, inc., Alhambra, 1951-54; v.p. Milford Rivet and Machine Co., Alhambra, 1952-54; sales mgr. S & C Electric Co., Chgo., 1954-56; v.p. West Coast ops. Townsend Co., Santa Ana, 1956-67; exec. v.p. West Coast ops. Townsend Co., 1967-82; pres. Cherry Textron, 1982-85, chmn., 1985-86; pres. Camalisa, Panama, 1965—; dir. Morehouse Engring. Corp., 1968-74, Orange County regional bd. U.S. Nat. Bank, 1969-73, First Fed. Savs. & Loan Assn., 1974-82; mem. regional bd. Calif. Fed. Bank, 1982-92; cons., bd. dirs. Airdrome Parts Co., Long Beach, Calif., 1987—. Mem. adv. bd. Calif. State U., Fullerton, 1961-81, chmn., 1971-81; chmn. Disneyland awards com., 1971-72; trustee St. Joseph Found., 1970-76, 78-82, chmn., 1982; trustee Chapman U., Orange, 1972—, exec. vice chmn., 1976—; trustee Calif. Coll. Medicine of U. Calif. at Irvine, 1973—, vice chmn., 1976-79, chmn., 1979-91; chmn. Community Airport Coun., 1974-86. Recipient Outstanding Humanitarian award NCCJ, 1980. Mem. IEEE, Nat. Aeros. Assn., Mchts. and Mfrs. Assn. (v.p., bd. dirs., chmn. 1985, chmn. exec. com. 1986), Airplane Owners and Pilots Assn., Nat. Pilots Assn., Am. Mgmt. Assn., Theta Tau. Clubs: Santa Ana Country, Balboa Bay, Pacific. Home: 1841 Beverly Glen Dr Santa Ana CA 92705-3383 Office: 1224 E Warner Ave Santa Ana CA 92705-5414

BUSWELL, DEBRA SUE, small business owner, programmer, analyst; b. Salt Lake City, Apr. 8, 1957; d. John Edward Ross and Marilyn Sue (Patterson) Potter; m. Randy James Buswell, AUg. 17, 1985; 1 child, Trevor Ryan. BA, U. Colo., Denver, 1978. Programmer, analyst Trail Blazer Systems, Palo Alto, Calif., 1980-83; data processing mgr. Innovative Concepts, Inc., San Jose, Calif., 1983-86; owner Egret Software, Milpitas, Calif., 1986—. Mem. IEEE, No. Calif. Pick Users. Home and Office: 883 Del Vaile Ct Milpitas CA 95035-4518

BUTCHART, RONALD EUGENE, social foundations educator, researcher, administrator; b. Nampa, Idaho, Apr. 16, 1943; s. Roy A. and Mary Lou (Speakes) B.; m. Sandra Kay Kahl, July 15, 1967; 1 child, Joshua Karl. BA, Northwest Nazarene Coll., 1967; MA, Northern Ariz. U., 1974; PhD, SUNY, 1976. Tchr. Capital High Sch., Boise, ID, 1967-70; asst. prof. SUNY, Cortland, 1974-80, assoc. prof., 1980-86, prof., 1986-92; prof., dir. edn. program U. Wash., Tacoma, 1992—; abstractor Hist. Abstracts, Santa Barbara, Calif., 1978-85; reader, table leader advanced placement exam. Coll. Bd., Princeton, N.J., 1982—; reviewer NEH, Washington, 1980—; guest curator Onondaga Hist. Assn., Syracuse, N.Y., 1989-90. Author: Northern Schools, Southern Blacks and Reconstruction, 1980, Local Schools: Exploring Their History, 1986; mem. editl. bd. History Edn. Quar., 1987-90, Teaching History: A Jour. Methods, 1975—; contbr. articles to profl. jours. Mem. Am. Ednl. Rsch. Assn., Am. Ednl. Studies Assn. (pres. 1993-94), History of Edn. Soc., Orgn. Am. Historians, So. Hist. Assn. Office: U Wash Edn Program 5th fl 917 Pacific Ave Fl 5 Tacoma WA 98402-4421

BUTCHER, DUANE CLEMENS, economist, consultant; b. Okla. City, Sept. 12, 1939; s. Cecil E. and Helen Louise (Clemens) B.; m. Barbara Needham, Feb. 2, 1963; children: Duane C. Jr., Christopher N. BA in Polit. Sci., Okla. State U., 1961; MA in Econs., Princeton U., 1970. Various positions foreign svc. U.S. Dept. State, Washington, 1962-74; econs. officer U.S. Embassy, Jidda, Saudi Arabia, 1974-76, Stockholm, Sweden, 1976-80; counselor for econ. affairs U.S. Embassy, Nairobi, Kenya, 1980-83; spl. asst. to gov. Office of the Gov., Denver, 1983-84; econ. counselor U.S. Embassy, Bonn, Germany, 1984-86, New Delhi, India, 1986-89; coord. Kuwait Task Force, 1989; sr. fellow Ctr. Study Fgn. Affairs, Washington, 1989-91; coord. Kuwait Task Force, 1989; cons. Global Bus. Assocs., Grand Junction, Colo., 1991—. Author (booklet) Campaign for Quality, 1984; (with others) Computer Integrated Manufacturing, 1992. Democrat. Home and Office: 408 1/2 Ridgeway Dr Grand Junction CO 81503-1652

BUTCHER, JACK ROBERT, manufacturing executive; b. Akron, Ohio, Dec. 10, 1941; s. William Hobart and Marguerite Bell (Dalton) B.; m. Gloria Jean Hartman, June 1, 1963; children: Jack R. II, Charlotte Jean. BA in Math., Jacksonville U., 1964; cert. mgmt. consulting, Akron U., 1979; cert. paralegal, CCT Inst., 1990; cert. radio broadcasting, Chaffey Coll., 1994. Pres. Portableacher Corp., Hesperia, Calif., 1977—; v.p. Nice Day Products, Hesperia, 1980-85; pres. The Mark of Profl. Mgmt. and Design Co., Hesperia, 1983—, Nice Day Products, Hesperia, 1985—; co-owner JB Scale Co., Hesperia, Calif., 1991—. Author: (poem) Something Good, 1978; patentee in field. Mem. Internat. Platform Assn., Masons, Shriners, Royal Order of Jesters. Address: 11177 Hesperia Rd Hesperia CA 92345-2129

BUTCHER, RICHARD KENT, local market manager; b. Scottsbluff, Nebr., June 20, 1949; s. Richard Walter and Donna Beth (Winchell) B.; m. Cheryl Ann Morton, June 8, 1969; children: James William, Shelly Rene, Sherry Rene. BS in Agronomy, Agrl. Econs., U. Nebr., 1971. Agriculturalist Gt. Western Sugar Co., Lovell, Wyo., 1972-75; farmer Butcher Farms, Morrill, Nebr., 1975-78; sr. sales rep. Monsanto Agrl. Co., Sterling, 1978-83; sales specialist Monsanto Agrl. Co., Ft. Collins, Colo., 1983-89, sr. sales specialist, 1989-93; local market mgr., team facilitator, 1993—; trainer co. internal Monsanto Agrl. Col., Sterling, Ft. Collins, 1979—, regional mgr. adv. team, Ft. Collins, 1987-93, gen. mgr. adv. bd., Sterling, Ft. Collins, 1983-87. Author: (pamphlet) Colorado Conservation Tillage Guide, 1980 (Achievement award 1980, Master Salesman award 1989); co-prodr. (video) Low Rate Application Guidelines, 1989. Coach Sterling Soccer Assn., 1980-83, Sterling Baseball Assn., 1982-83, Ft. Collins Soccer Assn., 1984-86, Ft. Collins Baseball League, 1984-87. 2d lt. U.S. Army, 1971-72. Mem. Colo. Conservation Tillage Assn. (founding/bd. mem. 1988—), Rocky Mountain Plant Food and Agrl. Chem. Assn. (v.p. 1986, bd. dirs. 1980-86), Residue Mgmt. Work Group USDA-Soil Conservation Svc. (adv. bd. 1991-94), Colo. Aerial Applicators Assn., Colo. Assn. Wheat Growers, Colo. Corn Growers Assn. Home: 2212 Ouray Ct Fort Collins CO 80525-1847 Office: Monsanto Agrl Co 2212 Ouray Ct Fort Collins CO 80525-1847

BUTENHOFF, SUSAN, public relations executive; b. N.Y.C., Jan. 13, 1960. BA with honors in Internat. Rels., Sussex U., Eng.; MPhil, Wolfson Coll., Cambridge U., Eng. Account exec. Ellen Farmer Prodns., 1984-85; account exec. Ketchum Pub. Rels., N.Y.C., 1988-90, v.p., account supr., 1990-91; prin. Access Pub. Rels., San Francisco, 1991—. Mem. Pub. Rels. Soc. Am. Office: Access Pub Rels 101 Howard St San Francisco CA 94105-1629

BUTH, DONALD GEORGE, biology educator; b. Chgo., Feb. 23, 1949; s. Werner George and Arlene Dolores (Kreier) B. BS in Zoology, U. Ill., 1971, AB in Anthropology, 1972, MS in Zoology, 1974, PhD in Ecology, Ethol. and Evolution, 1978. Research, teaching asst. U. Ill., Urbana, 1971-78; postdoctoral researcher UCLA, 1978-79, instr. biology, 1980, asst. prof., 1980-86, assoc. prof., 1986-92, prof., 1992—. Contbr. articles to profl. jours. Fellow AAAS, Willi Hennig Soc. (councilor 1981-82); mem. Am. Soc. Ichthyologists and Herpetologists (bd. govs. 1984—, exec. com. 1983-86, assoc. editor COPEIA, 1985-93, editl. bd. 1993—, editor Isozyme Bull. 1991-93, System Biol., 1994—), So. Calif. Acad. Sci. (bd. dirs. 1992—, editl. bd. bull. 1995—). Office: UCLA Dept Biology Los Angeles CA 90095-1606

BUTLER, ANNE M., history educator; b. Somerville, Mass., Dec. 4, 1938; d. Thomas Francis Maroney and Katherine Jean (Atkins) Posey; divorced, 1970; children: Daniel Ryan Porterfield, Katherine Anne Porterfield. BS, Towson State U., 1973; MA, U. Md., 1975, PhD, 1979. Assoc. editor/historian U.S. Capitol Hist. Soc., Washington, 1980-81; assoc. prof. history Gallaudet U., Washington, 1981-88; assoc. prof., then prof. Utah State U., Logan, 1989—; co-editor Western Hist. Quar., Logan, 1989—. Author: Daughters of Joy, Sisters of Misery: Prostitutes in the American West, 1985; contbr. chpt. to: Oxford History of the American West, 1994; contbr. articles to hist. publs.; mem. editorial bd. Western Hist. Quar., 1987-89. Mem. Am. Hist. Assn., Orgn. Am. Historians, Western History Assn., Phi Kappa Phi. Office: Western Hist Quar Utah State Univ Logan UT 84322

BUTLER, A(RTHUR) BATES, III, lawyer; b. N.Y.C., Aug. 17, 1944; s. A. Bates Jr. and Mary Katherine (Wiley) B.; m. Ann Kathleen Johnson, Nov. 29, 1974; children: Robert Bates, Elizabeth Ann. BA, Trinity U., 1966; JD, George Washington U., 1969. Bar: Ariz. 1969, U.S. Dist. Ct. Ariz. 1969, U.S. Ct. Appeals (9th cir.) 1974, U.S. Supreme Ct. 1977, Colo. 1990. Dep. atty. Pima County Atty., Tucson, 1970-77; 1st asst. U.S. atty. Dept. Justice, Tucson, 1977-80, U.S. atty., 1980-81; ptnr. Butler & King, Tucson, 1981-84; pvt. practice, Tucson, 1984-85; ptnr. Butler & Stein, P.C., Tucson, 1985—. Bd. dirs. Family Counseling Agy., 1988-89, Cmty. Orgn. for Drug Abuse Control, Tucson, 1977-81, chmn., 1981-82; bd. dirs. Tucson Ariz. Boys Chorus, 1989—, pres., 1992-94. Recipient Spl. award ACLU So. Calif., 1987, Charles Ares award ACLU So. Ariz., 1994; named one of Outstanding Young Men Am., 1979. Founding fellow Ariz. Bar Found.; mem. Ariz. Bar Assn., Pima County Bar Assn., Nat. Assn. Criminal Def. Attys., Ariz.

Criminal Def. Assn. (founding), Assn. Former U.S. Attys. Democrat. Club: Ducks Unltd. Home: 2702 E 4th St Tucson AZ 85716-4420 Office: Butler & Stein PC 110 S Church Ste 9300 Tucson AZ 85701

BUTLER, BYRON CLINTON, physician, cosmologist, gemologist, scientist; b. Carroll, Iowa, Aug. 10, 1918; s. Clinton John and Blance (Prall) B.; m. Jo Ann Nicolls; children: Marilyn, John Byron, Barbara, Denise; 1 stepdau., Marrianne. MD, Columbia Coll. Physicians and Surgeons, 1943; ScD, Columbia U., 1952; G.G. grad. gemologist, Gemol. Inst. Am., 1986. Intern Columbia Presbyn. Med. Ctr.; resident Sloane Hosp. for Women; instr. Columbia Coll. Physicians and Surgeons, 1950-53; dir. Butler Rsch. Found., Phoenix, 1953-86, pres., 1970—; pres. World Gems/G.S.G., Scottsdale, Ariz., 1979—, World Gems Software, 1988, World Gems Jewelry, 1990—; cosmologist, jewelry designer Extra-Terrestrial-Alien Jewelry & Powerful Personal Talismans, 1992—, 3rd Mellineum Line of Tektite Jewelry, 1994—. Featured in Life mag. for discovery of cause of acute fibrinolysis in premature separation of the placenta in humans; designer Extra Terrestrial Alien jewelry line. Bd. dirs. Heard Mus., Phoenix, 1965-74; founder Dr. Byron C. Butler, G.G., Fund for Inclusion Research, Gemol. Inst. Am., Santa Monica, Calif., 1987. Served to capt. M.C. AUS, 1944-46. Grantee Am. Cancer Soc., 1946-50, NIH, 1946-50. Fellow AAAS; mem. Ariz. Soc. Astrologers, Mufon, Mutual UFO Networks. Home: 6302 N 38th St Paradise Valley AZ 85253

BUTLER, EDWARD EUGENE, plant pathology educator; b. Wilmington, Del., Dec. 8, 1919; s. Edward Harry and Julia (Ennis) B.; m. Mildred Norene Godden, Dec. 20, 1947; children: David, Stephen, Susan, Thomas, James. BS, U. Del., Newark, 1943; MS, Mich. State U., 1948; PhD, U. Minn., 1954. Instr. plant pathology U. Minn., St. Paul, 1951-54; jr. plant pathologist U. Calif., Davis, 1955-56; asst. plant pathologist U. Calif., 1957-61, assoc. prof. plant pathology, 1961-68, prof. plant pathology, 1968-90, prof. emeritus, 1990—; vis. prof. U. P.R., 1966-67; vis. scientist Rancho Santa Ana Bot. Garden, Claremont, Calif., 1983-84. Assoc. editor Phytopathology, 1973-76; editorial bd. Mycologia, 1978-88, Mycopathologia, 1992—; contbr. to profl. jours. Capt. U.S. Army, 1943-46; PTO. Fellow AAAS; mem. Mycol. Soc. Am. (W.H. Weston award 1981), Am. Phytopathol. Soc., Brit. Mycol. Soc. Democrat. Home: 402 12th St Davis CA 95616-2023 Office: U Calif Dept Plant Pathology Davis CA 95616

BUTLER, EVELYN ANNE, writer, educator, editor; b. Norfolk, Va., Aug. 17, 1940; d. James Timothy and Janette Laura (Boardman) Kelly; m. Gerald Joseph Butler, Feb. 14, 1964; children: James Dale, Marian Margaret Cade, Wayne Anthony. BA, U. Calif., Berkeley, 1963; PhD, U. Calif., San Diego, 1985; MA, NYU, 1966. Mem. faculty lit. Chapman Coll., Orange, Calif., 1972-81, San Diego State U., 1984-90, U. Paris-Dauphine, 1990-91; reviewer children's lit. Author: (novels) Fire, 1987, Going Away, 1992; editor jour. Recovering Lit., 1970—; asst. editor jour. Fiction Internat., 1985-89. Fellow Woodrow Wilson Fellowship Com., 1963-64, NDEA U. Calif., San Diego, 1968-72. Mem. AAUP, MLA, Phi Beta Kappa. Home and Office: PO Box 805 Alpine CA 91903-0805 also: 39 Quai de Valmy, 75010 Paris France

BUTLER, GEOFFREY SCOTT, systems engineer, educator, consultant; b. Jacksonville, Fla., July 19, 1958; s. George Lauritzen and Mary Elizabeth (Cox) B.; m. Diana Lynn Martin, Aug. 29, 1987. BS in Aerospace Engring., U. Fla., 1981; MS in Aerospace Engring., San Diego State U., 1986; MS in Aerospace Systems, West Coast U., 1988. Engr. Lockheed Missiles & Space Co., Sunnyvale, Calif., 1981-83; engring. specialist Convair div. Gen. Dynamics, San Diego, 1983-92; project mgr. Horizons Tech., Inc., San Diego, 1992—; tech. program chmn. 13th Applied Aerodynamics Conf.; cons. WEB Engring., San Diego, 1992—. Contbr. articles to profl. publs. Speaker Scott's Valley Homeowners Assn., Encinitas, Calif., 1992. Mem. AIAA (sr. mem., tech. com. mem. 1992). Republican. Roman Catholic. Office: Horizons Tech Inc 3990 Ruffin Rd San Diego CA 92123-1826

BUTLER, GERALD JOSEPH, English and comparative literature educator; b. San Francisco, Feb. 24, 1942; s. Dale and Marian Elizabeth (Watchler) B.; m. Evelyn Anne Kelly, Feb. 3, 1964; children: James Dale, Marian Margaret, Wayne Anthony. AA, San Francisco City Coll., 1961; AB with honors, U. Calif., Berkeley, 1963; PhD, U. Wash., 1969. Prof. English & comparative lit. San Diego State U., 1968—; maitre de conf. U. Nice, France, 1987-88; prof. U. Orleans, France, 1990-91; mem. exec. com. Inst. for History of Mentalities, Hamilton, New Zealand, 1992—. Author: Love and Reading, 1989, Henry Fielding and Lawrence's Old Adam, 1991; editor: Recovering Literature, 1972—; contbr. articles to profl. jours. Mem. Phi Beta Kappa. Home: PO Box 805 Alpine CA 91903-0805 Office: San Diego State U Dept English and Comparative Lit San Diego CA 92182

BUTLER, GRANGER HAL, hospital administrator; b. Long Beach, Calif., Feb. 26, 1960; s. James Russell and Brenda Patricia (Wilson) B.; m. Anne Carroll Wilson, Jan. 16, 1982 (div. 1989); 1 child, Geneva Dorothy; m. Irma Canelo Lara, Apr. 27, 1991; children: Rebekah Abigail, Seraih Abigail. AB with honors, U. Calif., Berkeley, 1983; M Health Adminstrn., U. So. Calif., 1987. Lic. nursing home adminstr., Calif., Ohio. Adminstrv. resident Am. River Hosp., Sacramento, 1984-86; asst. adminstr. Roseville (Calif.) Convalescent Hosp., 1986-88; adminstr. Orange Park Convalescent Ctr., Orange, Calif., 1988-90, Sierra Convalescent Hosp., Davis, Calif., 1990-91; adminstr. USAF Hosp., Grissom AFB, Ind., 1991-93, Cannon AFB, N.Mex., 1993-95; managed care specialist Ohio U., Athens, 1995—; adviser on long-term care Chapman Hosp., Orange, 1990. Contbr. articles to newspapers. Helper Dayton (Ohio) Spl. Olympics, 1979; vol. Orange County Rep. party, Santa Ana, Calif., 1987-90. Capt. USAF, 1991—. Mem. Am. Coll. Healthcare Adminstrs., U. So. Calif. Alumni Assn., U. Calif. Alumni Assn., Kokomo C. of C. (cmty. coun. 1992), Pi Sigma Alpha, Sigma Phi Epsilon. Roman Catholic. Home: 21 W 2d St The Plains OH 45780

BUTLER, JAMES ROBERTSON, JR., lawyer; b. Cleve., May 29, 1946; s. James Robertson and Iris David (Welforn) B. AB magna cum laude, U. Calif., Berkeley, 1966, JD, 1969. Bar: Calif. 1970, U.S. Tax Ct. 1977, U.S. Supreme Ct. 1980. Sr. corp. ptnr., chmn. Hospitality Industry Group Jeffer, Mangels, Butler & Marmaro, L.A., L.A., San Francisco, 1982—; founder, chmn. JMBM Hospitality Forum, 1991—; expert panelist on hospitality industry topics NYU Hospitality Industry Investment Conf., UCLA Hospitality Investment Conf., Calif. Soc. CPAs ann. hospitality confs., 1992, 93, 94, 95; spkr., panelist Robert Morris Assocs. Nat. Conf., Chgo., 1989, nat. ann. conf. Ind. Bankers Assn. Am., 1992; frequent guest expert securities, real estate and banking various TV programs, 1985—; participant comml. real estate workouts workshop FDIC & RTC Nat. Tng. Conf., San Antonio, 1989, San Diego, 1990; adv. bd. Bur. Nat. Affairs, Washington. Author: Arbitration in Banking, A Robert Morris Associates State of the Art Book, 1988, Lender Liability: A Practical Guide, A BNA Special Report, 1987; editor Banking Law Report Capital Adequacy series, 1985, Calif. Law Rev.; co-chmn. adv. council Money and Real Estate: The Jour. of Lending, Syndication, Joint Ventures, and the Third Market; contbr. chpt., Mapping the Minefield--Lender's Liability, The Workout Game, Solutions to Problem Real Estate Loans, 1987; contbr. over 50 articles to profl. jours. Mem. Am. Arbitration Assn., Comml. Arbitration Panel; founding dir. Liberty Nat. Bank; Charter Adv. bd. dirs., Adv. Council of the Banking Law Inst. Recipient Kraft Prize U. Calif., 1966; Bartley Cavenaugh Crum scholar U. Calif. Sch. Law, 1969. Mem. ABA (corp., banking and bus. law sect., taxation sect.), L.A. County Bar Assn., Century City Bar Assn. (chmn. fin. instn. sect. 1990-91), Beverly Hills Bar Assn., Calif. League of Savs. Instns. (chmn. arbitration com. 1987, 88), Order of Coif, Phi Beta Kappa, Pi Sigma Alpha. Office: Jeffer Mangels Butler & Marmaro 2121 Avenue Of The Stars Los Angeles CA 90067-5010 also: 1 Sansome St Fl 12 San Francisco CA 94104-4430 also: 620 Newport Center Dr Ste 450 Newport Beach CA 92660-8004

BUTLER, JOHN MICHAEL, II, international business consultant; b. Arlington, Tex., Apr. 1, 1969; s. Ronald Ray Butler and Lou Ann (Owen) Brown. BA in Polit. Sci. and Russian Studies, U. Denver, 1992; student, Leningrad State Polytechnic U., 1992. Law clk. Bourke Jacobs Luber, Denver, 1989-90; presdl. advanceman The White House, Washington, 1989-91; intern Interfax Russian News Agy., Denver, 1992-93; govt. accounts exec. UNISYS Corp., Denver, 1995—; cons. Baltic Commodities Co., St. Petersburg, Russia, 1992, Western Govs. Assn., Denver, Colo., 1993. Precinct committeeman Denver County Rep. Com., 1990; mem. exec. bd. Colo. Rep. Party, 1990; state chmn. Coll. Reps. Colo., 1990-91. Coors scholar, Milliken scholar, Woodward scholar U. Denver, 1989; named Outstanding Young Men of Am., 1989. Mem. Russian-Am. C. of C., Sigma Iota Rho, Pi Sigma Alpha, Beta Theta Pi. Baptist. Office: UNISYS Corp 6025 S Quebec Ste 200 Englewood CO 80111

BUTLER, LESLIE ANN, advertising agency owner, artist; b. Salem, Oreg., Nov. 19, 1945; d. Marlow Dole and Lala Ann (Erlandson) Butler. Student Lewis and Clark Coll., 1963-64; BS, U. Oreg, 1969; postgrad. Portland State U. 1972-73, Lewis & Clark Coll., 1991. Creative trainee Ketchum Advt., San Francisco, 1970-71; asst. advt. dir. Mktg. Systems, Inc., Portland, Oreg., 1971-74; prodn. mgr., art dir., copywriter Finzer-Smith, Portland, 1974-76; copywriter Gerber Advt., Portland, 1976-78; freelance copywriter, Portland, 1983-84, 83-85; copywriter McCann-Erickson, Portland, 1980-81; copy chief Brookstone Co., Peterborough, N.H., 1981-83; creative dir. Whitman Advt., Portland, 1984-87; prin. L.A. Advt., 1987—. Co-founder, v.p., newsletter editor Animal Rescue and Care Fund, 1972-81; Bd. dir. Big Brothers Big Sisters of Am.; active mem. Oregon Ballet Theatre, Portland Art Mus., Oreg. Humane Soc. Recipient Internat. Film and TV Festival N.Y. Finalist award, 1985, 86, 87, 88, Internat. Radio Festival of N.Y. award, 1984, 85, 88, Hollywood Radio and TV Soc. Internat. Broadcasting award, 1981, TV Comml. Festival Silver Telly award, 1985, TV Comml. Festival Bronze Telly, 1986, AVC Silver Cindy, 1986, Los Angeles Advt. Women LULU, 1986, 87, 88, 89 Ad Week What's New Portfolio, 1986, N.W. Addy award Seattle Advt. Fedn., 1984, Best of N.W. award, 1985, Nat. winner Silver Microphone award, 1987, 88, 89. Mem. ASPCA, Portland Advt. Fedn. (Rosey Finalist award 1986), , People for Ethical Treatment of Animals. Home and Office: 7556 SE 29th Ave Portland OR 97202-8827

BUTLER, LILLIAN CATHERINE, biochemistry educator; b. Chgo., Dec. 1, 1919; d. William Joseph and Lillian Eleanor (Kennedy) B. BS, U. Ill., 1941; MS in Biochemistry, U. Tex., 1945; PhD in Nutrition, U. Calif.-Berkeley, 1953. Assoc. prof. U. Ill., Champaign/Urbana, 1956-58; vis. scientist NIH, Endocrinology Sect., Bethesda, Md., 1958-60; rsch. biochemist and supr. VA Hosp., Diabetes Rsch. Unit, Birmingham, Ala., 1960-63; assoc. prof. rsch. Coll. Medicine, U. Ala., Birmingham, 1963-66; assoc. prof. nutrition U Md., College Park, 1967-78; ret. Author/editor: Nutrition from Infancy Through the Geriatric, 1976; contbr. articles to profl. jours. Nat. Inst. Cancer postdoctoral fellow, 1953-55, Nat. Inst. Arthritis and Metabolic Diseases fellow, 1949-53. Mem. Am. Chem. Soc., Am. Inst. Nutrition, Ariz. Watercolor Guild, Sigma Xi, Iota Sigma Pi, Sigma Delta Epsilon.

BUTLER, MERRILL, bank executive. Sr. exec. v.p. Am. Savs. & Loan Assn., 1986—; exec. v.p. Fin. Corp. of Am., Irvine, Calif., 1986—. Office: Fin Corp Am 18401 Von Karman Ave Irvine CA 92715-1542

BUTLER, VIGGO M., airport terminal executive; b. 1942. BBD, Calif. State Poly U., 1964; MBA, Pepperdine U., 1980. Ops. mgr. Kansas City (Mo.) Internat. Airport, 1969-73; various positions Lockheed Air Terminal Inc., Burbank, Calif., 1973—, now pres. With USAF, 1964-69. Office: Lockheed Air Terminal Inc 2550 N Hollywood Way Burbank CA 91505-1055*

BUTTERWORTH, ROBERT ROMAN, psychologist, researcher, media therapist; b. Pittsfield, Mass., June 24, 1946; s. John Leon and Martha Helen (Roman) B. BA, SUNY, 1972; MA, Marist Coll., 1975; PhD in Clin. Psychology, Calif. Grad. Inst., 1983. Asst. clin. psychologist N.Y. State Dept. Mental Hygiene, Wassaic, 1972-75; pres. Contemporary Psychology Assocs., Inc., L.A. and Downey, Calif., 1976—; cons. L.A. County Dept. Health Svcs.; staff clinician San Bernardino County Dept. Mental Health, 1983-85; staff psychologist State of Calif. Dept. Mental Health, 1985—; media interviews include PA, L.A. Times, N.Y. Times, USA Today, Wall St. Jour., Washington Post, Redbook Mag., London Daily Mail and many others; TV and radio interviews include CBS, NBC and ABC networks, Oprah Winfrey Show, CNN Newsnight, Can. Radio Network, Mut. Radio Network and many others. Served with USAF, 1965-69. Mem. Am. Psychol. Assn. for Media Psychology, Calif. Psychol. Assn., Nat. Accreditation Assn. Psychoanalysis. Office: Contemporary Psychology Assocs Inc PO Box 76477 Los Angeles CA 90076-0477

BUTTS, EDWARD PERRY, civil engineer, environmental consultant; b. Ukiah, Calif., July 29, 1958; s. Edward Oren Butts and Orvilla June (Daily) Hutcheson; m. JoAnne Catherine Zellner, Aug. 14, 1978; children: Brooke C., Adam E. Cert. continuing studies in Irrigation Theory and Practices, U. Nebr., 1980. Registered profl. engr., Oreg., Wash.; cert. water rights examiner, Oreg. Technician Ace Pump Sales, Salem, Oreg., 1976; technician Stettler Supply Co., Salem, 1976-78, assoc. engr., 1978-86, chief engr., 1986-90, v.p. engring., 1990—; profl. engr. exam. question reviewer Nat. Coun. Engring. Examiners, Clemson, S.C., 1989—; profl. engr. exam. supr. Oreg. State Bd. Engring. Examiners, Salem, 1986—; lectr. various water works profl. groups; mem. Marion County Water Mgmt. Coun., 1993—. Contbr. articles to Jour. Pub. Works Mag., AWWA Opflow, Water Well Jour. Coach Little League Cascade Basketball Leage, Turner, Oreg., 1990—. Recipient Merit award Am. City and County Mag., 1990. Mem. ASCE, Prof. Engrs. Oreg. (mid-Willamette chpt. v.p. 1990-91, pres. 1992-93, state v.p. 1993-95, state pres.-elect 1995-96, Young Engr. of Yr. award 1993-94), Am. Water Works Assn. Republican. Office: 1810 Lana Ave NE Salem OR 97303-3116

BUURSMA, WILLIAM F., architect. BArch, U. Mich., 1964; MArch, U. Pa., 1965. Lic. arch. With various archtl. design firms; joined John Graham Assocs/DLR Group, Seattle, 1976—, prin.; tchg. fellow U. Tenn., also assoc. prof. France program. Prin. works include Madigan Army Med. Ctr., Ft. Lewis, Wash., Clackamas Town Ctr., Portland, Oreg., Kauai Hilton Resort and Condominium Complex, Hawaii, high-rise office bldgs., retail shopping malls, and numerous other complexes. Mem. AIA. Office: John Graham Assocs/DLR Group 520 Pike St Ste 100 Seattle WA 98101-4001

BUUS, LINDA LEE PANNETIER, secondary education educator; b. Rapid City, S.D., Aug. 23, 1949; d. Max Pannetier and Pansy A. (Francisco) Robison; m. David V. Buus, Aug. 1, 1970 (div. Apr. 1988); children: Baend J., Yuri D. BS in Secondary Edn., Black Hills State, 1973; MEd, Lesley Coll., 1988. Cert. tchr. English, social studies, libr.-media specialist, Wyo. Tchr.'s aide Taipei (Taiwan) Am. Sch., 1971-72; 7th and 8th grade social studies tchr. Our Lady of Perpetual Help Sch., Rapid City, 1973-74; 7th and 8th grade English and spelling tchr. Newcastle (Wyo.) Jr. H.S., 1974-75; 9th grade social studies, English tchr. Campbell County Jr. H.S., Gillette, Wyo., 1975-76; 9th grade social studies tchr. Twin Spruce Jr. H.S., Gillette, 1976-81, Sage Valley Jr. H.S., Gillette, 1982—; chairperson dept. social studies Twin Spruce Jr. H.S. and Sage Valley Jr. H.S., 1979-91, 94—; mem. liaison task force Campbell County Sch. Dist., 1983-86, mem. curriculum coordinating coun., 1987-90; student tchr. supr. U. Wyo., Laramie, 1980-93. Participant Wyo. Gov.'s Youth Conf./Legis. Youth Forum, Cheyenne, 1979-81. Fellow Taft Inst. Govt., 1985, Nat. Humanities Summer History, 1991. Mem. NEA (del. to rep. assembly 1986), Campbell County Edn. Assn. (faculty rep. 1983-88, v.p. 1986-87, mem. leadership team 1994—), Wyo. Edn. Assn. (senate liaison legis. dinner 1985, mem. profl. standards and practices commn. 1994—), Wyo. Coun. of Social Studies, Nat. Coun. of Social Studies, Kappa Delta Pi, Sigma Kappa (pres. 1970), Phi Kappa Phi (mem. Wyo. chpt.). Roman Catholic. Home: 415 Sisson Ave Moorcroft WY 82721 Office: Sage Valley Jr H S 1000 W Lakeway Rd Gillette WY 82718-5633

BUXTON, RICHARD MILLARD, financial planning executive; b. Denver, July 8, 1948; s. Charles Roberts and Janet (Millard) B.; m. Consuelo Gonzalez, June 15, 1974; 1 child, Richard Fernando. B.A. with distinction, Stanford U., 1970; M.B.A., Harvard U., 1975. Mgr. ops. planning Western Fed. Savs., Denver, 1975-78; sr. fin. analyst Rocky Mountain Energy Co., Denver, 1978-83; dir. fin. analysis, treas. Frontier Devel. Group, Inc., Denver, 1983-85; treas. Frontier Holdings, Inc., Denver, 1985-86; dir. fin. svcs. K N Energy, Inc., Denver, 1986-91, v.p. strategic planning and fin. svcs., 1991—. Mem. Nat. Investor Rels. Inst., Fin. Execs. Inst., Colo. Harvard Bus. Sch. Club, Rocky Mountain Stanford Club, Columbine Country Club. Home: 17 Wedge Way Littleton CO 80123-6629 Office: KN Energy Inc PO Box 281304 Lakewood CO 80228-8304

BUXTON, SUSAN ELAINE, critical care nurse; b. Carlisle, Pa., Mar. 30, 1960; d. Paul Justin and Shirley Ann (Snader) Smith; divorced; children: Sara Ann, Ashley Elizabeth. BSN summa cum laude, York Coll. Pa., 1982; postgrad., Calif. State U., 1990—. CCRN, ACLS, neonatal ALS, pediatric ALS. Rsch. asst. U.S. Army War Coll., Carlisle, 1980-81; nurse surg. ICU Polyclinic Med. Ctr., Harrisburg, Pa., 1982-83, Mansfield (Ohio) Gen. Hosp., 1983-84; nurse emergency dept. Gordon Hosp., Calhoun, Ga., 1986-88; nurse surg. ICU Kern Med. Ctr., Bakersfield, Calif., 1988—. Recipient Furber Marshall Scholarship, 1978. Mem. Sigma Theta Tau (Eta Eta chpt.). Home: 2225 Steven Ct Bakersfield CA 93306-3448

BUYERS, JOHN WILLIAM AMERMAN, agribusiness and specialty foods company executive; b. Coatesville, Pa., July 17, 1928; s. William Buchanan and Rebecca (Watson) B.; m. Elsie Palmer Parkhurst, Apr. 11, 1953; children: Elsie Buyers Viehman, Rebecca Watson Buyers-Basso, Jane Palmer Buyers-Russo. B.A. cum laude in History, Princeton U., 1952; M.S. in Indsl. Mgmt., MIT, 1963. Div. ops. mgr. Bell Telephone Co. Pa., 1964-66; dir. ops. and personnel Gen. Waterworks Corp., Phila., 1966-68; pres., chief exec. officer Gen. Waterworks Corp., Phila, 1971-75; v.p. adminstrn. Internat. Utilities Corp., Phila., 1968-71; pres., chief exec. officer, dir. C. Brewer and Co., Ltd., Honolulu, 1975—, chmn. bd., 1982—; chmn. Calif. and Hawaiian Sugar Co., 1982-84, 86-90; pres. Buyco, Inc., 1986—; mem. U.S. Army Civilian Adv. Group, Hawaii Joint Coun. Econ. Edn., Japan-Hawaii Econ. Coun.; bd. dirs. 1st Hawaiian Inc., John B. Sanfilippo & Sons, Inc.; chmn. bd. C. Brewer Homes, Inc. Trustee U. Hawaii Found., Hawaii Prep. Acad., 1986—; chmn. bd. dirs. Hawaii Visitors Bur., 1990-91; mem. Gov.'s Blue Ribbon Panel on the Future of Healthcare in Hawaii; bd. dirs. Hawaii Sports Found., 1990—; mem. adv. group to U.S. Dist. Ctr., Hist. Palace Theatre. With USMC, 1946-48. Sloan fellow, 1963. Mem. Hawaiian Sugar Planters Assn. (chmn. bd. dirs. 1980-82, dir.), c. of C. Hawaii (chmn. bd. dirs. 1981-82), Nat. Alliance Bus. (chmn. Hawaii Pacific Metro chpt. 1978), Cap and Gown Club (Princeton), Hilo Yacht Club, Oahu County Club, Pacific Club, Waialae county Club, Prouts Neck (Maine) County Club, U.S. C. of C. (mem. food and gr. com. 1991—), Beretania Tennis Club. Presbyterian. Clubs: Cap and Gown (Princeton); Hilo Yacht, Oahu Country, Pacific, Waialae Country; Prouts Neck (Maine) Country. Home: Grand Penthouse West 1080 S Beretania St Honolulu HI 96814-1400 Office: C Brewer & Co Ltd PO Box 1826 Honolulu HI 96805-1826 also: Buyco Inc 827 Fort Street Mall Honolulu HI 96813-4317*

BUZUNIS, CONSTANTINE DINO, lawyer; b. Winnipeg, Man., Can., Feb. 3, 1958; came to U.S., 1982; s. Peter and Anastasia (Ginakes) B. BA, U. Man., 1980; JD, Thomas M. Cooley Law Sch., 1985. Bar: Mich. 1986, U.S. Dist. Ct. (ea. and we. dists.) Mich. 1986, Calif. 1986, U.S. Dist. Ct. (so. dist.) Calif. 1987, U.S. Supreme Ct. 1993. Assoc. Church, Kritselis, Wyble & Robinson, Lansing, Mich., 1986; assoc. Neil, Dymott, Perkins, Brown & Frank, San Diego, 1987-94, ptnr., 1994—. Sec., treas. Sixty Plus Law Ctr., Lansing, 1985; active Vols. in Parole, San Diego, 1988—; bd. dirs. Hellenic Cultural Soc., 1993—. Mem. ABA, FBA, ATLA, Mich. Bar Assn., Calif. Bar Assn., San Diego County Bar Assn., San Diego Trial Lawyers Assn., So. Calif. Def. Counsel, State Bar Calif. (gov. 9th dist. young lawyers div. 1991-94, 1st v.p. 1993-94, pres. 1994-95, bd. govs. 1995—), San Diego Barristers Soc. (bd. dirs. 1991-92), Pan Arcadian Fedn., Order of Ahepa (chpt. bd. dirs., v.p. 1995—), Phi Alpha Delta. Home: 3419 Overpark Rd San Diego CA 92130-1865 Office: Neil Dymott Perkins Brown & Frank 1010 2nd Ave Ste 2500 San Diego CA 92101-4913

BYAM, M(ARIE) ELIZABETH, data processing management consultant; b. Cooperstown, N.Y., Oct. 31, 1949; d. Harmon Leigh and Elizabeth Virginia (Baldo) B. BA, Ga. State U., 1972; postgrad., Columbia So. Sch. Law, 1976-78. Cert. Systems Profl. Programmer Coastal States Life Ins. Co., Atlanta, 1973-75; programmer, analyst So. Airways, Atlanta, 1975-76; cons. computer programming Atlanta, 1978-82; sr. cons., field mgr. Computer Dynamics, Woodland Hills, Calif., 1983-84; owner, prin. cons. MEB Assocs., Canoga Park, Calif., 1984-92; cons. Intel Corp., Rio Rancho, N.Mex., 1992—; frequent speaker on career planning and info. processing techs. for schs., profl. confs. and meetings. Guest co-host Ms. Biz radio show, 1987. Bd. dirs. Opera Guild So. Calif., Los Angeles, 1984-88. Mem. Data Processing Mgmt. Assn. (publs. dir. L.A. chpt. 1988, treas. 1989, pres. 1990, nat. chair legis. affairs com. 1990-91), Assn. Women in Computing (pres. L.A. chpt. 1985-87, nat. conf. chmn. 1986), Sierra Club. Republican. Office: PO Box 3492 Albuquerque NM 87190-3492

BYBEE, JOAN LEA, linguistics educator; b. New Orleans, Feb. 11, 1945; d. Robert William and Elizabeth Mai (Rachal) B.; divorced; 1 child, Brody. BA in Spanish and English, U. Tex., 1966; MA in Linguistics, San Diego State U., 1970; PhD in Linguistics, UCLA, 1973. Prof. linguistics SUNY, Buffalo, 1973-89; prof. linguistics U. N.Mex., Albuquerque, 1989—, assoc. dean Coll. Arts and Scis., 1992-93; dir. 1995 Linguistic Inst., U. N.Mex., 1995. Author: Introduction to Natural Generative Phonology, 1976, Morphology, 1985, The Evolution of Grammar, 1994, Modality in Grammar and Discourse, 1995. Fellowship Guggenheim Meml. Found., 1987-88, Netherlands Inst. of Advanced Study, 1983-84; recipient Disting Alumni award San Diego State U., 1976. Mem. Linguistic Soc. of Am. (chair program com. 1982-83, exec. com. 1988-91). Office: Dept Linguistics Humanities 526 Albuquerque NM 87131

BYBEE, PAUL RALPH, psychiatrist; b. Cin., Sept. 5, 1931; s. Earl Lee and Sara Frances (Hays) B.; m. Margaret Pauline Knepper Brooks, Aug. 13, 1955 (div. Mar. 1972); children: Paul Daniel, Victoria Lynn, Tammy Lou, Guy Adam; m. Matilda Gaio, June 15, 1985. BS, E. Ky. U., 1954; MD, Ohio State U., 1958. Diplomate Am. Bd. Psychiatry and Neurology. Intern St. Joseph's Hosp., Phoenix, 1958-59; psychiat. resident Walter Reed Army Hosp., Washington, 1959-62; chief of psychiatry Ft. Campbell Army Hosp., Ky., 1962-66; pvt. practice Phoenix, 1966-85; chief psychiat. svcs. VA Hosp., Cheyenne, Wyo., 1985-86, Prescott, Ariz., 1986-87, Temple, Tex., 1987-91. Author: What's Psychotherapy?, 1977. Maj. U.S. Army, 1957-66. Mem. APA (life). Home: 8101 N 12th Pl Phoenix AZ 85020-3867 Office: 4105 N 20th St Ste 280 Phoenix AZ 85016

BYBEE, RODGER WAYNE, science education administrator; b. San Francisco, Feb. 21, 1942; s. Wayne and Mary Genevieve (Mungon) B.; m. Patricia Ann Brovsky, May 28, 1966. BA, Colo. State Coll., 1966; MA, U. No. Colo., 1969; PhD, NYU, 1975. Tchr. sci. Greeley (Colo.) Pub. Schs., 1965-66; instr. sci. U. No. Colo., Greeley, 1966-70; teaching fellow NYU, N.Y.C., 1970-72; instr. edn. Carleton Coll., Northfield, Minn., 1972-75, asst. prof., 1975-81, assoc. prof., chmn. dept., 1981-85; assoc. dir. Biol. Scis. Curriculum Study, Colorado Springs, 1986—, acting dir., 1992-93; mem. adv. bd. for sci. assessment Nat. Assessment Ednl. Progress, Princeton, N.J., 1987-89, 92-93, 95-96; mem. adv. bd. Social Sci. Edn. Consortu=ium, Boulder, Colo., 1987-90; chairperson working group on curriculum NRC project on Nat. Sci. Ednl. Stds., 1993-95. Author: numerous books; contbr. numerous articles to profl. jours. NSF grantee, 1986—. Fellow AAAS (mem.-at-large 1987-90, chair sect. Q 1993-94), Nat. Assn. Rsch. Sci. Teaching (rsch. coord. 1986-89). Home: PO Box 563 Frisco CO 80443-0563

BYDALEK, DAVID ALLEN, education educator; b. Kankakee, Ill., June 14, 1943; s. Paul Daniel and Earleen Doris (Shrontz) B.; m. Karen Mildred Gebauer, Jan. 24, 1968; children: Karin, Peggy, Gabriel. BS in Edn., Ea. Ill. U., 1965; MS in Edn., No. Ill. U., 1967; EdD, Ariz. State U., Tempe, 1979. Instr. Ind. U., Ft. Wayne, 1967-69; instr., dept. chair Gateway C.C., Phoenix, 1969-90; instr. Mesa (Ariz.) C.C., 1990—, chair dept., 1992—. Author: A Means for Individualized Progression in Bookkeeping, 1972, A Supplement to Teach Accounting Principles, 1977. Mem. Maricopa County Colls. Faculty Assn. (pres. 1979), Delta Pi Epsilon (pres. 1978). Office: Mesa CC 1833 W Southern Ave Mesa AZ 85202-4866

BYE, ROSEANNE MARIE, marketing professional; b. Chgo., Nov. 27, 1946; d. Paul David and Gwendalynn Luciell (Hipp) Forrester; BS in Foods and Nutrition, Western Ill. U., 1969; m. Richard Wayne Bye, June 14, 1969. Banquet mgr. Western Ill. U., 1967-69; new product home economist Hunt/Wesson Foods, Fullerton, Calif., 1969-73; retail and restaurant home economist Lawry's Foods, L.A., 1973-74; mgr. product devel. Carl Karcher Enterprises, Anaheim, Calif., 1974-81; v.p. R & D Denny's Restaurants, La Mirada, Calif., 1981-88; owner, cons. Roseanne Bye & Assocs., Orange, Calif., 1988-89; v.p. foodsvc. div. TG Mktg. and Advt., Inc., Anaheim,

1989—; mem. speakers bur. mktg. fast food Industry/Edn. Coun. Mem. food svc. adv. com., Calif. State U., Long Beach, Chapman U., adv. com. Santa Ana Jr. Coll., Garden Grove Sch. Dist; moderator, program chmn. printed materials So. Calif. Food Industry Conf. Recipient Nat. Mktg. award for devel. of Charbroiler Steak Sandwich, 1975-76, serve-yourself salad bar, 1978-79. Mem. Am. Home Econs. Assn., Calif. Home Econs. Assn. (Outstanding Economist in Bus. 1977, 79, 86, pres. 1977-79, pres., treas., del. and newsletter editor Orange dist. 1993—), Home Economists in Bus. (award of excellence, Western regional adv. 1976-78, nat. pub. rels. chmn. 1983-85, chmn.-elect 1991-92, chmn. 1992-94, Hall of Fame 1980-91, program chmn. 1991-92, newsletter chmn. 1992-95, chmn. 1992—), So. Calif. Food Industry Coun. (chmn. 1994-95, steering com., session chair, printing chair), Women in Mgmt., Nat. Restaurant Assn. (chmn. mktg. rsch. div., nat. conf. speaker), NOW, Anaheim C. of C. (publicity chmn. 1977-78), Soc. Advancement Food Svc. Rsch. (bd. dirs. 1986-88, co-chair regional meetings 1988-92, sec. 1990-92, treas. 1992-94, newsletter editor 1993—, Fellowship award 1987), Internat. Food Svc. Editorial Coun., So. Calif. Culinary Guild (newsletter editor 1992—, bd. dirs. 1993—), Multi Unit Food Svc. Ops., Chain Ops. Execs., Internat. Platform Assn. Republican. Presbyterian. Clubs: Tennis and Swim, Gourmet/Wine, Teddy Bear Boosters (treas. 1988—), Lit. Guild, Newport Harbor Art Mus., Bower's Art Mus., Gem Theatre Guild, Shakespeare Orange County Guild (fundraising 1991—). Office: TG Mktg & Advt Inc 3943 E La Palma Ave Anaheim CA 92807-1741

BYERS, BRECK EDWARD, geneticist educator; b. St. Louis, July 4, 1939; s. F. Donald and Melba Constance (Boothman) B.; m. Margaret Tyler Read, Nov. 26, 1964; children: Mark Andrew, Carl Bradford. BS, U. Colo., 1961; MS, Harvard U., 1963, PhD, 1967. Researcher Univ. of Geneva, Geneva, Switzerland, 1968-70; asst. prof. dept. genetics U. Washington, Seattle, 1970—, chair., prof. dept. genetics, 1990—. Contbr. articles to profl. jours. Recipient Merit award Nat. Inst. Health, 1993. Democrat. Office: U Wash Dept Genetics # Sk-50 Seattle WA 98195

BYERS, CHARLES FREDERICK, public relations executive, marketing executive; b. Johnstown, Pa., Jan. 30, 1946; s. Walter Hayden and Mary Ann Elizabeth (Succop) B.; m. Vicki Louise Beard, June 3, 1967 (div. Apr. 1992); children: Natalie L., Tamara N., Valerie A.; m. Janet Lenora Buck, Apr. 23, 1993. BS in Journalism, Ohio U., 1968; MA in Mass Comms., U. Tex., 1969. Accredited pub. rels. practitioner. Gen. reporter Springfield (Ohio) Daily News, 1967-68; promotion specialist Gen. Electric Co., Chgo., 1969-71; account supr. Burson-Marsteller, Chgo., 1971-78; group v.p. Carl Byoir & Assocs., Chgo., 1978-82; gen. mgr. Carl Byoir & Assocs., Atlanta, 1982-85; pres. Camp-Byers Pub. Rels., Atlanta, 1985-91; client svc. dir. Kalman Comm., L.A., 1991-92; v.p., COO Hayes Pub. Rels., San Jose, Calif., 1992-95; mktg. comms. mgr. Actel Corp., San Jose, Calif. Pres. Hoffman Estates (Ill.) Jaycees, 1976; dir., treas. Brookcliffe Home Owners Assn., 1988-89; comm. chair Ga. Heart Assn., Atlanta, 1990. Recipient Golden Trumpet, Chgo. Publicity Club, 1980. Mem. Pub. Rels. Soc. Am. (dir. Silicon Valley chpt. 1993, v.p. Silicon Valley chpt. 1994, pres.-elect 1995, dir. L.A. chpt. 1992, Silver Anvil 1978). Office: Actel Corp 955 E Arques Ave Sunnyvale CA 94086

BYRD, MARC ROBERT, florist; b. Flint, Mich., May 14, 1954; s. Robert Lee and Cynthia Ann (Poland) B.; m. Bonnie Jill Berlin, Nov. 25, 1975 (div. June 1977). Student, Ea. Mich. U., 1972-75; grad., Am. Floral Sch., Chgo., 1978. Gen. mgr., dir. flowers shop; designer Olive Tree Florist, Palm Desert, Calif., 1978-79, Kayo's Flower Fashions, Palm Springs, 1979-80; owner, designer Village Florist, Inc., Palm Springs, 1980-85; pres. Mon Ami Florist, Inc., Beverly Hills, 1986-87; gen. mgr. Silverio's, Santa Monica, 1987; gen. mgr., hotel florist, creative dir. Four Seasons Hotel, Beverly Hills, 1988-90; owner, ptnr. Marc Fredericks, Inc., Beverly Hills, 1990—. Author: Celebrity Flowers, 1989. Del., Dem. County Conv., 1972, Dem. County Conv., 1972, Dem. State Conv., 1972, Dem. Nat. Conv., 1972. Mem. Soc. Am. Florists, So. Calif. Floral Assn., Desert Mus., Robinson's Gardens. Republican. Mem. Dutch Reformed Ch. Home: 2350 N Vermont Ave Los Angeles CA 90027-1239 Office: Marc Fredericks Inc 8445 Warner Dr Culver City CA 90232-2428

BYRD, RONALD DALLAS, civil engineer; b. Reno, Nov. 30, 1934; s. Eugene Richard and Helen Madelyn (Hursh) B.; m. Irene Josephine Phenix, Sept. 19, 1953; children: Kevin Gregory, Helen Christine, Stephanie Irene. BSCE, U. Nev., 1960. Registered profl. engr., Nev., Calif., Oreg., Wash., Idaho., Wyo. Staff engr. Sprout Engrs., Sparks, Nev., 1960-64, design engr., 1964-67; office mgr. Sprout Engrs., Seattle, 1967-70; exec. v.p. Sea, Inc., Seattle, 1970-72, Sparks, 1972—; also bd. dirs. SE&A Engrs.; bd. dirs. ABS Land Co.; bd. dirs. Am. Cons. Engrs. Coun. Nev., 1987-95, pres., 1993-94, nat. dir. 1994-95; cons. Pres.-elect Engrs. Council of Nev., 1992-93. Fellow ASCE (sec. 1966-67); mem. NSPE (bd. dirs. 1983-86), Am. Pub. Works Assn., U. Nev. Reno Engring. Alumni Assn. (sec. 1985-86), U. Nev. Reno Alumni Assn. (pres. 1989-90), Kiwanis (pres. Sparks club 1971-72), Rotary (pres. Federal Way, Wash. club 1971-72, bd. dirs. Reno Sunrise 1992—), Elks, Masons. Republican. Methodist. Home: 50 Rancho Manor Dr Reno NV 89509-3956 Office: SEA Inc 950 Industrial Way Sparks NV 89431-6092

BYRNE, GEORGE MELVIN, physician; b. San Francisco, Aug. 1, 1933; s. Carlton and Esther (Smith) B.; BA, Occidental Coll., 1958; MD, U. So. Calif., 1962; m. Joan Stecher, July 14, 1956; children: Kathryne, Michael, David; m. Margaret C. Smith, Dec. 18, 1982. Diplomate Am. Bd. Family Practice, 1971-84. Intern, Huntington Meml. Hosp., Pasadena, Calif., 1962-63, resident, 1963-64; family practice So. Calif. Permanente Med. Group, 1964-81, physician-in-charge Pasadena Clinic, 1966-81; asst. dir. Family Practice residency Kaiser Found. Hosp., L.A., 1971-73; clin. instr. emergency medicine Sch. Medicine, U. So. Calif., 1973-80; v.p. East Ridge Co., 1983-84, sec., 1984; dir. Alan Johnson Porsche Audi, Inc., 1974-82, sec., 1974-77, v.p., 1978-82. Bd. dirs. Kaiser-Permanente Mgmt. Assn., 1976-77; mem. regional mgmt. com. So. Calif. Lung Assn., 1976-77; mem. pres.'s circle Occidental Coll., L.A. Drs. Symphony Orch, 1975-80; mem. profl. sect. Am. Diabetes Assn. Fellow Am. Acad. Family Physicians (charter); mem. Am., Calif., L.A. County Med. Assns., Calif. Acad. Family Physicians, Internat. Horn Soc., Quarter Century Wireless Assn., Am. Radio Relay League (Pub. Service award), Sierra (life), So. Calif. Dx Club. Home: 528 Meadowview Dr La Canada Flintridge CA 91011-2816

BYRNE, JOHN VINCENT, academic administrator; b. Hempstead, N.Y., May 9, 1928; s. Frank E. and Kathleen (Barry) B.; m. Shirley O'Connor, Nov. 26, 1954; children: Donna, Lisa, Karen, Steven. AB, Hamilton Coll., 1951, LLD (hon.), 1994; MA, Columbia U., 1953; PhD, U. So. Calif., 1957; LLD (hon.), Hamilton Coll., 1994. Research geologist Humble Oil & Refinery Co., Houston, 1957-60; assoc. prof. Oreg. State U., Corvallis, 1960-66, prof. oceanography, 1966—, chmn. dept., 1968-72, dean Sch. Oceanography, 1972-76, acting dean research, 1976-77, dean research, 1977-80, v.p. for research and grad. studies, 1980-81, pres., 1984—; adminstr. NOAA, Washington, 1981-84; Program dir. oceanography NSF, 1966-67. Recipient Carter teaching award Oreg. State U., 1964. Fellow AAAS, Geol. Soc. Am., Am. Meteorol. Soc.; mem. Am. Assn. Petroleum Geologists, Am. Geophys. Union, Sigma Xi, Chi Psi. Club: Arlington (Portland, Oreg.). Home: 3520 NW Hayes Ave Corvallis OR 97330-1746 Office: Oreg State U Office of Pres Corvallis OR 97331

BYRNE, NOEL THOMAS, sociologist, educator; b. San Francisco, May 11, 1943; s. Joseph Joshua and Naomi Pearl (Denison) B.; m. Dale W. Byrne, Aug. 6, 1989. BA in Sociology, Sonoma State Coll., 1971; MA in Sociology, Rutgers U., 1975, PhD in Sociology, 1987. Instr. sociology Douglass Coll., Rutgers U., New Brunswick, N.J., 1974-76, Hartnell Coll., Salinas, Calif., 1977-78; from lectr. to assoc. prof. depts. sociology and mgmt. Sonoma State U., 1978—; chmn. Dept. of Mgmt. Sonoma State U., Rohnert Park, Calif., 1990-91; cons. prof. Emile Durkheim Inst. for Advanced Study, Grand Cayman, Brit. West Indies, 1990-93. Contbr. articles and revs. to profl. lit. Recipient Dell Pub. award Rutgers U. Grad. Sociology Program, 1976, Louis Bevier fellow, 1977-78. Mem. AAAS, Am. Sociol. Assn., Pacific Sociol. Assn., N.Y. Acad. Sci., Soc. for Study Symbolic Interaction (rev. editor Jour. 1980-83), Soc. for Study Social Problems, Commonwealth Club. Democrat. Home: 4773 Ross Rd Sebastopol CA 95472-2114 Office: Sonoma State U Dept Sociology Rohnert Park CA 94928

BYRNE, WILLIAM MATTHEW, JR., federal judge; b. Los Angeles, Sept. 3, 1930; s. William Matthew Sr. and Julia Ann (Lamb) B. BS, U. So. Calif., 1953, LLB, 1956; LLD, Loyola U., 1971. Bar: Calif. Ptnr. Dryden, Harrington & Schwartz, 1960-67; asst. atty U.S. Dist. Ct. (so. dist.) Calif., 1958-60; atty. U.S. Dist. Ct. (cen. dist.) Calif., Los Angeles, 1967-70, judge, 1971—; exec. dir. Pres. Nixon's Commn. Campus Unrest, 1970; instr. Loyola Law Sch., Harvard U., Whittier Coll. Served with USAF, 1956-58. Mem. ABA, Fed. Bar Assn., Calif. Bar Assn., Los Angeles County Bar Assn. (vice chmn. human rights sect.), Am. Judicature Soc. Office: US Dist Ct 312 N Spring St Los Angeles CA 90012-4701*

BYRNES, JAMES BERNARD, museum director emeritus; b. N.Y.C., Feb. 19, 1917; s. Patrick J.A. and Janet E. (Geiger) B.; m. Barbara A. Cecil, June 10, 1946; 1 son, Ronald L. Student, N.A.D., 1936-38, Am. Artist Sch., 1938-40, Art Students League, 1940-42, U. Perugia, Italy, 1951, Istituto Meschini, Rome, 1952. Art tchr. mus. activity program N.Y.C. Bd. Edn., 1936-40; indsl. designer Michael Saphier Assos., N.Y.C., 1940-42; docent Los Angeles County Mus., 1946-47, assoc. curator modern contemporary art, 1947-48, curator, asst. to dir., 1948-53; dir. Colorado Springs Fine Arts Center, 1954-55; assoc. dir. N.C. Mus. Art, 1956-58, acting dir., 1958-59, dir., 1959-60; dir. New Orleans Mus. Art, 1961-71, dir. emeritus, 1989—; dir. Newport Harbor Art Mus., Newport Beach, Calif., 1972-75; vis. lectr. U. Fla., 1961, Newcomb Coll., Tulane U., 1963; art cons. Author: Masterpieces of Art, W.R. Valentiner Memorial, 1959, Tobacco and Smoking in Art, 1960, Fetes de la Palette, 1963, Edgar Degas, His Family and Friends in New Orleans, 1965, Odyssey of an Art Collector, 1966, Art of Ancient and Modern Latin America, 1968, The Artist as Collector of Primitive Art, 1975, also numerous mus. catalogs. Decorated knight Order Leopold II, Belgium. Mem. Am. Soc. Interior Design (hon. life), Am. Soc. Appraisers (sr., internat. examining bd.), Appraisers Assn. Am. Office: James B Byrnes and Assocs 7820 Mulholland Dr Hollywood CA 90046-1223

BYSTROM, ARNE, architect; b. Seattle, June 8, 1927; s. Albin Petrus and Martha (Hammerose) B.; m. Valerie Anne Broze, Sept. 10, 1960; children: Ashley Allen Bystrom McConnaughey, Carl Arnold Jr. BArch, U. Wash., 1951. Registered architect, Wash., Calif., Ariz., Oreg., Alaska, Idaho. Project architect Paul Thivy Architect, Seattle, 1951-56; ptnr. Bystrom & Greco Architects, Seattle, 1957-66; prin. Arne Bystrom Architect, Seattle, 1967—; vis. critic, chair selection com., asst. prof. architecture Wash. Sch. Architecture; tchr., lectr., critic U. Wash. Creator software program MacArchitect; designer bath houses for Seattle Parks Dept., 1968, Black Restaurant chain, Tiki Hut, Costacos, Straw Hat Pizza; work featured on covers of Architecture, Progressive Architecture, Sunset Mag., Hist. Preservation, Popular Sci., and Archtl. Furniture at Linda Farris Gallery, Seattle. Mem. Seattle Planning Commn., 1975-82; founding mem. Pike Pl. Market Hist. Commn. Tech. sgt. U.S. Army, 1946-47. Recipient. Mem. AIA (treas. 1978, pres.-elect 1983, pres. 1984, nat. design com. 1987, various awards, including 2 nat. honor awards, mem. nat. housing com. 1988—), N.W. Inst. Architecture and Urban Studies in Italy (pres. 1988). Office: Arne Bystrom Architect 1617 Post Aly Seattle WA 98101-1569

CABANYA, MARY LOUISE, software development executive, rancher; b. Denver, Nov. 3, 1947; d. Dareo and Hellen Etta (Charley) Mattivi; m. Robert L. Cabanya, Jan. 6, 1978. BS in Math., U. So. Colo., 1969; postgrad., Regis U., 1985. Flight test engr. Boeing Co., Seattle, 1969-75; computer scientist Telephone Computing Service, Seattle, 1975-77; support engr. Digital Equipment Corp., Denver, 1977-79; cons. computer systems Colorado Springs, Colo., 1979-92; program mgr. Digital Equipment Corp., Colorado Springs, 1980-92; owner, operator ostrich ranch Little Pines Ranch, Colorado Springs. Mem. Rocky Mountain Ratite Assn., Am. Ostrich Assn., Aircraft Owners Pilots Assn. Republican. Roman Catholic.

CABLE, GARY DEAN, physicist; b. Tucson, Ariz., Oct. 21, 1947; s. Lowell Dean and Martha Virginia (Burton) C.; m. Celia Arias, May 25, 1974; children: Nefe Martin, Adam Noel, Orlando Gary, Alfonso Ruben. BS in Physics, Calif. Tech., 1969; MS in Physics, U. Chgo., 1971; PhD in Physics, U. Ariz., 1973; postgrad., N.Mex. Highland U., 1979-81. Rsch. asst. dept. physics U. Ariz., Tucson, 1968-69; asst. resident head U. Chgo., 1970-71; rsch. assoc. Enrico Fermi Inst. U. Chgo., 1970-73; prin. scientist, tech. dir. Computer Scis. Corp., Albuquerque, 1978-88; analyst res. Air Force Weapons Lab. (now Phillips Lab.), Kirtland AFB, N.Mex., 1978-94; sr. reservist Phillips Lab., Edwards AFB, Calif., 1994—; sr. mem. tech. staff Sandia Nat. Labs., Albuquerque, 1988—. Developer, instr. coop. minority honors program Luna Vocat. Tech. Inst., Las Vegas, N.Mex., 1982—. Capt. USAF, 1973-78, col. USAF Res., 1978—. Mem. Am. Geophys. Union, Am. Phys. Soc., Assn. Computing Machinery, Air Force Assn., Res. Officers Assn. Democrat. Roman Catholic. Office: Sandia Nat Labs MS 0576 PO Box 5800 Albuquerque NM 87185-0576

CABOT, HUGH, III, painter, sculptor; b. Boston, Mar. 22, 1930; s. Hugh and Louise (Melanson) C.; m. Olivia P. Taylor, Sept. 8, 1967; student Boston Museum, 1948, Ashmolean Mus., Oxford, Eng., 1960, Coll. Ams., Mexico City, 1956, San Carlos Acad., Mexico City. Portrait, landscape painter; sculptor in bronze; one-man shows: U.S. Navy Hist. and Recreation Dept., U.S. Navy Art Gallery, The Pentagon, Nat. War Mus., Washington, La Muse de la Marine, Paris; group shows include: Tex. Tri-state, 1969 (1st, 2d, 3d prizes), Starmont Vail Med. Ctr. Topeka, Kans., Tucson Med. Ctr. Ariz., Harwood Found. Taos, N.Mex., Washburn U. Topeka, Kans., U. Ariz. Tucson, Ariz. Served as ofcl. artist USN, Korean War. Named Artist of Yr., Scottsdale, Ariz., 1978, 30th ann. Clubs: Salmagundi (N.Y.C.). Author, illustrator: Korea I (Globe).

CACHOLA, ROMY MUNOZ, state representative; b. Vigan, Philippines, Mar. 8, 1938; m. Erlinda Cachola; children: Lyla, Earl. Mem. State Ho. of Reps., 1984—; chair com. on tourism Ho. of Reps. Bd. govs. Kalihi YMCA; bd. dirs. Susannah Wesley Cmty. Ctr.; hon. chmn. Statewide Sakada Com.; pres. St. Anthony's Sch. Bd. Recipient Pub. Servant of Yr. Community Advocate Mag., 1990, Disting. Legislator award Dem. State Legis. Leaders Assn., 1990. Mem. Filipino C. of C., Ilocos Surian Assn. of Hawaii, St. Anthony's Filipino Cath. Club, Waipahu Bus. Assn. (past. pres.), Kalakaua Lions Club, Kalihi Bus. Assn. (bd. dirs.). Office: Ho of Reps Rm 1207 State Office Tower Honolulu HI 96813

CACIOPPO, PETER THOMAS, government bank liquidator; b. N.Y.C., Jan. 31, 1947; s. Joseph Eugene and Sistina Elizabeth (Attardo) C.; m. Rhonda Jean Thomas, Nov. 12, 1983. BSBA, U. Mo., 1969. Cert. fin. planner. Examiner FDIC, St. Louis, 1972-82, Nat. Assn. of Securities Dealers, Kansas City, Mo., 1983-84; fin. cons. Merrill Lynch, Overland Park, Kans., 1984-87; pres. Centrex Fin., Kansas City, 1987-88; v.p. S.W. Bank, Vista, Calif., 1988-89; bank liquidation specialist, account officer FDIC, Irvine, Calif., 1990—. Mem. Phi Kappa Psi (treas. 1973-79). Home: 12642 Hinton Way Santa Ana CA 92705-1433

CADD, GARY GENORIS, molecular biologist; b. Richland, Wash., Sept. 2, 1953; s. Robert Milton and Pauline Helen (Bybee) C.; m. Debra Jean Mastrude, Aug. 27, 1982. BS with honors, Western Wash. U., Bellingham, 1982; MS, U. Calif., Davis, 1984; PhD, U. Wash., 1990. Sr. fellow Hughes Med. Rsch. Inst., Seattle, 1990-92; mem. staff dept. physiology and biophysics U. Wash., Seattle, 1992—. Contbr. articles to profl. jours. Bd. dirs. Amnesty Internat., Puget Sound, Wash., 1990—, pres., 1993—, UN Assn., Seattle, 1988, pres., 1990—, mem. nat. coun., N.Y.C., 1990—. With USN, 1972-75, Viet Nam. Fellow Andrew Mellon Found., 1992—. Mem. AAAS, Viet Nam Vets. Leadership Program. Home: 1212 NE Ballinger Pl Seattle WA 98155-1138

CADDY, EDMUND HARRINGTON HOMER, JR., architect; b. N.Y.C., Apr. 17, 1928; s. Edmund Harrington Homer and Glenna Corinne (Garratt) C.; m. Mary Audrey Ortiz, Dec. 22, 1951; children—Edmund Harrington Homer III, Mary Elizabeth. B.A., Princeton, 1952, M.F.A. (grad. sch. fellow), 1955. With Louis E. Jallade, N.Y.C., 1949-53, Eggers & Higgins, N.Y.C., 1953-55; dir. design Dalton-Dalton Assocs., Cleve., 1955-60; assoc. Raymond & Rado, N.Y.C., 1960-68; gen. ptnr. Raymond & Rado and Ptnrs., N.Y.C., 1968-72, Raymond, Rado, Caddy & Bonington, P.C., N.Y.C., 1972-80; pres. Raymond, Rado, Caddy & Bonington, P.C., 1980-83; project mgr. Robinson, Mills & Williams, San Francisco, 1983-87, McCue, Boone, Tomsick, San Francisco, 1987-88, O'Brien-Kreitzberg, San Francisco, 1988-90; Sverdrup Corp., 1990—; apptd. by Pres. John F. Kennedy to adv. com. arts John F. Kennedy Ctr. Performing Arts, 1963-70; mem. archtl. adv. commn. N.Y.C. C.C., CUNY, 1979-83. Works include Suburban Hosp, Cleve., 1957, J.M. Smucker Co, Salinas, Cal., 1957, Brookpark (Ohio) City Hall, 1959; Cleve. Transit System addition, 1959, administrn. bldg., Met. Water Treatment System, Saigon, 1960, Franklin D. Roosevelt High Sch, N.Y.C., 1963, Crown Heights Intermediate Sch, N.Y.C., 1966, engring. complex, Stony Brook Campus, State U. N.Y., 1970, Sibley's dept. stores, Syracuse, N.Y., 1973, Rochester Downtown Devel. Study, 1975, R.H. Macy & Co. dept. store, Stamford, Conn., 1979; project mgr. Main Postal Facility, San Francisco, 1985, Univ. Ctr., U. Calif., Irvine, 1987, Santa Clara (Calif.) County CourtHouse. Pres. bd. trustees Montclair (N.J.) Community Hosp., 1973-80. Served with USMC, 1946-48; Served with USMCR, 52-53. Mem. AIA, Architects Soc. Calif., N.J., Ohio, N.Y. State Architects Assn. Clubs: Tower (Princeton); Racquet and Tennis (N.Y.C.). Home: PO Box 22 Dillon Beach CA 94929-0022 Office: Sverdrup Corp 1340 Treat Blvd Walnut Creek CA 94596

CADIEUX, ROBERT D., chemical company executive; b. 1937; married. BS in Econs. and Acctg., Ill. Inst. Tech., 1959; MBA, U. Chgo., 1969. Mgr. adminstrv. ctr. Amoco Oil Co., Chgo., 1972-74; mgr. budgets and control reports Amoco Corp. (formerly Standard Oil Co. of Ind.), Chgo., 1971-74, div. contr. petroleum ops., 1974; with Amoco Chems. Co., Chgo., 1959—, v.p. adminstrn. and planning, 1975-81, v.p. plastic products and ventures mgmt., 1977-81, exec. v.p., dir., 1981-83, pres., 1983—; bd. dirs. Amoco Corp., 1989—. With USAR, 1957-61. Office: Air Liquide 2121 N California Blvd Ste 350 Walnut Creek CA 94596-7305

CADWALADER, GEORGE LYELL, lawyer; b. San Francisco, Jan. 16, 1919; s. George L. and Charlotte (Wilson) C.; m. Louise Gathe, Oct. 28, 1950 (div. Jan. 1979); 1 child, Marilyn Lindquist (dec.); m. Joy Marie Johnson, Apr. 22, 1979. AB, Stanford U., 1939; JD, U. Calif.-Hastings Coll. Law, San Francisco, 1948. Bar: Calif. 1960, U.S. Dist. Ct. (no. dist.) Calif. 1960, U.S. Tax Ct. 1968. Trust officer Crocker Anglo Bank, San Francisco, 1955-63; pvt. practice San Francisco, 1963-66; assoc. Gavin McNab Schmulowitz, San Francisco, 1966-67, Behr, Colangelo & Imlay, San Francisco, 1967-68; sr. ptnr. Cadwalader & Black, San Francisco, 1968-83. Co-author: Probate in California, 1966. Bd. dirs. Marshal Hale Hosp., San Francisco, 1986-87, chmn. bd., 1977-82; bd. dirs., v.p. Calif. Heritage Coun., San Francisco, 1976. Col. USAF, 1941-45, ETO. Fellow Am. Coll. Trust and Estate Counsel; mem. ABA, San Francisco Bar Assn., State Bar Calif. (Pro Bono Legal Svc. award 1986-87), Bohemian Club (chmn. chorus 1986-87), St. Francis Yacht Club. Republican. Episcopalian. Home: 245 Pacheco St San Francisco CA 94116-1458 Office: 22 Battery St San Francisco CA 94111-5505

CADY, JOSEPH HOWARD, management consultant; b. Dallas, Feb. 2, 1959. BSBA, San Diego State U., 1981, MBA, 1988. Cert. profl. cons. to mgmt. Project coord. Mitsubishi Bank of Calif., Escondido and L.A., 1979-82; ind. mgmt. cons. San Diego, 1985-87; sr. cons. Deloitte & Touche, San Diego, 1989-90; mng. ptnr. CS Cons. Group, San Diego, 1990—; guest lectr. U. San Diego, 1987-94, Southwestern Coll., Chula Vista, Calif., 1990; speaker in field. Contbr. articles to profl. jours. Mem. Cons. Roundtable of San Diego. Office: CS Cons Group 3150 Sandrock Rd San Diego CA 92123-3064

CAEN, HERB, newspaper columnist, author; b. Sacramento, Calif., Apr. 3, 1916; s. Lucien and Augusta (Gross) C.; m. Sally Gilbert, Feb. 15, 1952 (div. 1959); m. Maria Theresa Shaw, Mar. 9, 1963 (div. 1982); 1 son, Christopher. Student, Sacramento Jr. Coll., 1934. Daily newspaper columnist San Francisco Chronicle, 1936-50, 1958—; columnist San Francisco Examiner, 1950-58. Author: The San Francisco Book, 1948, Baghdad-by-the-Bay, 1949, Baghdad 1951, 1950, Don't Call It Frisco, 1953, Caen's Guide to San Francisco, 1957, Only in San Francisco, 1960, (with Dong Kingman) City on Golden Hills, 1968, The Cable Car and the Dragon, 1972, One Man's San Francisco, 1976, The Best of Herb Caen, 1960-75, 1991, Herb Caen's San Francisco-1976-1991, 1992. Served from pvt. to capt. USAAF, 1942-45. Decorated Medaille de la Liberation France, 1949. Democrat. Club: Calif. Tennis. Office: Chronicle Pub Co 901 Mission St San Francisco CA 94103-2905

CAESAR, CAROL ANN, psychologist, consultant; b. Jacksonville, Fla., June 10, 1945; d. David Union and Helen Claudia (Casper) Richards; m. Vance Ray Caesar, Apr. 22, 1967; 1 child, Eric Roy. BS in Edn. and Biology, U. Fla., 1968; M in Edn. Guidance and Counseling, Fla. Atlantic U., 1975; PhD, Calif. Sch. of Profl. Psychology, 1987. Lic. psychologist, Calif. Instr. in sci. Palm Springs Jr. High Sch., Hialeah, Fla., 1968-71; therapist Long Beach (Calif.) Counseling Ctr., 1986; chief behavioral scientist Long Beach Meml. Hosp. Family Practice, 1987-90; owner Carol Ann R. Caesar Psychologist, Seal Beach, Calif., 1989—; psychoanalyst St. Mary Med. Ctr., Long Beach, 1987-90; bd. dirs. Long Beach chpt. Am. Heart Assn. Bd. dirs. House for Abuse Children/Women, Long Beach, 1987-88, Am. Cancer Soc., Long Beach, 1989-90; officer, bd. dirs. Family Svcs., Long Beach, 1988-89. Mem. APA, Calif. Psychol. Assn., Fla. Oceanographic Soc., Indian River Plantation Soc., South Fla. Humane soc., Stuart Animal Shelter, Long Beach Psychol. Assn., Long Beach Yacht Club, Olo Ranch Country Club. LDS. Home: 110 Ocean Ave Seal Beach CA 90740-6027 Office: 550 Pacific Coast Hwy Ste 200 Seal Beach CA 90740-6601

CAETANO, RAUL, epidemiologist, educator; b. São Paulo, Brazil, May 5, 1945; came to U.S., 1978; s. Silvestre Vieira and Vera Vieira (Barbosa) C.; m. Elizabeth Angela Caetano, Dec. 16, 1972 (div.); 1 child, Izabel. MD, U. Rio de Janeiro, 1969, diploma in psychiatry, 1971; MPH, U. Calif., Berkeley, 1979, PhD, 1983. Psychiatrist Pine Hosp., Rio de Janeiro, 1969-73; asst. prof. State U., Rio de Janeiro, 1969-73; rsch. psychiatrist Inst. Psychiatry U. London, 1973-76; asst. prof. Inst. Psychiatry, Rio de Janeiro, 1976-78; vis. scholar Alchohol Rsch. Group, Berkeley, 1978-83, assoc. scientist to sr. scientist, 1983-94, dir., 1992—; assoc. adj. prof. Sch. Pub. Health, U. Calif., Berkeley, 1991—; assoc. dir. Calif. Pacific Med. Ctr. Rsch. Inst., San Francisco, 1992-93. Contbr. numerous sci. papers to profl. jours. WHO fellow, 1973-76; rsch. grantee Nat. Inst. Alcohol Abuse and Alcoholism, 1985—. Mem. APHA, Am. Coll. Epidemiology, Rsch. Soc. Alcoholism. Roman Catholic. Office: Alcohol Rsch Group 2000 Hearst Ave Berkeley CA 94709-2130

CAHALAN, MARIANNE TROY, nurse; b. Vallejo, Calif., July 2, 1946; d. Jerry and Maryanne Cecile (DeBonis) Troy; m. Michael Kermit Cahalan, Aug. 13, 1978. AA, Solano Coll., 1966; RN, Contra Costa Coll., 1969. Staff RN Broadway Hosp., Vallejo, 1969-72, Queens Hosp., Honolulu, 1972-75; pvt. scrub nurse Queens Med. Ctr., Honolulu, 1975-76; staff RN U. Calif., San Francisco, 1976-78, head nurse cardiac surgery, 1978—. Mem. Assn. of Operating Rm. Nurses. Republican. Roman Catholic. Home: 8 Midden Ln Tiburon CA 94920-2114 Office: Univ Calif San Francisco 505 Parnassus Ave # 0220 San Francisco CA 94122-2722

CAHAN, ROBERT BARMACH, psychiatrist, educator; s. Jacob Morris and Hilda G. (Barmach) C.; m. Bernice Alpert, Mar. 20, 1955; 1 child, James Samuel. AB, Syracuse U., 1949, MA, 1950, JD; MD, Jefferson Med. Coll., 1954. Diplomate Am. Bd. Psychiatry and Neurology, Am. Bd. Forensic Psychiatry. Intern Nazareth (Pa.) Hosp., 1954-55; resident in psychiatry Norristown (Pa.) State Hosp., 1955-60; pvt. practice San Francisco, 1960—; sr. psychiatrist, cons. geriatrics rsch. project, U. Calif., San Francisco, 1960-65; dir. Immediate Psychiat. Aid and Referral Ctr., 1961-67; mem. clin. faculty U. Calif., San Francisco, 1961—; clin. assoc. San Francisco Psychoanalytic Inst., 1962-74; psychiat. cons. Jail Med. Svc., San Francisco, 1974-76; med. dir. Consulting Med. Specialists, San Francisco, 1987—; adj. prof. U. Calif. San Francisco Mt. Zion Med. Ctr., 1964—; dir. Worker's Compensation Psychiat. Evaluation Program, 1983; faculty expert Hastings Coll. Advocacy, 1984—; mem. forensic panel U.S. Dist. Ct., U.S. Atty., Fed. Pub. Defender, U.S. Dept. Labor, U.S. Dept. Commerce, U.S. Dept. Interior, FAA, Calif. Med Bd., Nev. Med. Bd., Retirement System City and County San Francisco. Mem. AMA, San Francisco Ind. Practice Assn. (bd. dirs., ins. mediation com.), San Francisco Med. Soc., Calif. Med. Assn., Calif. Psychiat. Assn., No. Calif. Psychiat. Soc., Am. Acad. Psychiatry and Law (pres. No. Calif. chpt. 1984-90, dir. psychiat. cross-examination video workshop 1988, 90, 91), Calif. Soc. Indsl. Medicine and Surgery (exec. bd. dirs. 1982-88). Office: 825 Van Ness Ave 401 San Francisco CA 94109

CAHILL, EILEEN MARY, secondary education educator; b. Norwich, N.Y., Nov. 3, 1950; d. Kevin Tracey and Martha Sue (Eckard) C. BA, D'Youville Coll., Buffalo, 1972; MA, U. Toronto, 1974; PhD, SUNY, Buffalo, 1987. Cert. tchr., N.Y. English tchr. North Collins (N.Y.) Ctrl. Sch., 1972-85; curator of lit. Rosenbach Mus. and Libr., Phila., 1988-89; instr. English Temple U., Phila., 1987-88, Bryn Mawr (Pa.) Coll., 1987-88; English tchr. Marlborough Sch., L.A., 1989—; mem. Stanford (Calif.) Ctr. for Rsch. on Women, 1990-94. Author articles. Coun. for BAsic Edn. Nat. fellow for ind. study in humanities, 1993. Mem. MLA, Am. Conf. for Irish Studies, Irish Am. Cultural Inst. Democrat. Home: 427 Westminster Ave Apt 312 Los Angeles CA 90020-4687 Office: Marlborough Sch 250 S Rossmore Ave Los Angeles CA 90004-3739

CAHILL, LAWRENCE GLENN, JR., investigation firm owner; b. Modesto, Calif., Aug. 13, 1934; s. Lawrence Glenn and Marjorie Ellen (Malone) C.; m. Vera Louise Bettes, Apr. 11, 1955; children: Edwin James, Larry Allan, Joseph Lloyd, John Michael. AS, Modesto Jr. Coll.; BS, Stanislaus State U., Turlock, Calif., 1977; postgrad., FBI Acad./U. Va., 1978. Lic. pvt. investigator, Calif. Enlisted USAF, 1953, rose through ranks to master sgt., intelligence analyst, 1953-73, retired, 1973; sr. criminal investigator Dist. Atty.'s Office, Modesto, 1973-89; ret.; owner, investigator, cons. Larry Cahill & Assocs., Modesto, 1989—. Fellow Internat. Coll. Pvt. Police Practitioners, FBI Acad. Grads. Assn., Calif. Assn. Lic. Investigators, Calif. Pub. Defenders Assn., Nat. Assn. Investigative Specialists, Calif. Inst. Profl. Investigators, K.C. Office: Larry Cahill & Assocs PO Box 3150 Modesto CA 95353-3150

CAHILL, RICHARD FREDERICK, lawyer; b. Columbus, Nebr., June 18, 1953; s. Donald Francis and Hazel Fredeline (Garbers) C.; m. Helen Marie Girard, Dec. 4, 1982; children: Jacqueline Michelle, Catherine Elizabeth, Marc Alexander. Student, Worcester Coll., Oxford, 1973; BA with highest honors, UCLA, 1975; JD, U. Notre Dame, 1978. Bar: Calif. 1978, U.S. Dist. Ct. (ea. dist.) Calif. 1978, U.S. Dist. Ct. (cen. dist.) Calif. 1983, U.S. Dist. Ct. (so. dist.) Calif. 1992, U.S. Ct. Appeals (9th cir.) 1992. Dep. dist. atty. Tulare County Dist. Atty., Visalia, Calif., 1978-81; staff atty. Supreme Ct. of Nev., Carson City, 1981-83; assoc. Acret & Perochet, Brentwood, Calif., 1983-84, Thelen, Marrin, Johnson & Bridges, L.A., 1984-89; ptnr. Hammond Zuetel & Cahill, Pasadena, Calif., 1989—. Mem. Pasadena Bar Assn., Los Angeles County Bar Assn., Assn. So. Calif. Defense Counsel, Notre Dame Legal Aid and Defender Assn. (assoc. dir.), Phi Beta Kappa, Phi Alpha Delta (charter, v.p. 1977-78), Pi Gamma Mu, Phi Alpha Theta (charter pres. 1973-74), Phi Eta Sigma, Sigma Chi. Republican. Roman Catholic. Home: 2015 Fox Ridge Dr Pasadena CA 91107-1009 Office: Hammond Zuetel & Cahill Ste 540 180 S Lake Ave Pasadena CA 91101-2619

CAHN, ROBERT NATHAN, physicist; b. N.Y.C., Dec. 20, 1944; s. Alan L. and Beatrice (Geballe) C.; m. Frances C. Miller, Aug. 22, 1965; children: Deborah, Sarah. BA, Harvard U., 1966; PhD, U. Calif., Berkeley, 1972. Rsch. assoc. Stanford (Calif.) Linear Accelerator Ctr., 1972-73; rsch. asst. prof. U. Wash., Seattle, 1973-76; asst. prof. U. Mich., Ann Arbor, 1976-78; assoc. rsch. prof. U. Calif., Davis, 1978-79; sr. staff physicist Lawrence Berkeley Lab., 1979-91, div. dir., 1991—. Author: Semi Simple Lie Algebras and Their Representations, 1984; co-author: Experimental Foundations of Particle Physics, 1989. Fellow Am. Phys. Soc. (sec.-treas. divsn. particles and fields 1992-94).

CAI, XING YI, art historian, educator; b. Zhongshan, China, May 30, 1939; came to U.S., 1988; s. Jun Guang and Ling Fang (Huang) C.; m. Kock Wah Lum, Oct. 1, 1970; children: Franklin Cai, Lance Cai. BA, Tchr's. U. of South China, 1963; MA, The Art Acad. of China, 1981. Vice chief editor History and Theory of the Fine Arts, Beijing, 1981-83; dir. ancient art divsn. The Art Acad. of China, Beijing, 1983-85; dean dept. of art history grad. sch. The Art Acad. of China, Beijing, 1985-87; vis. scholar, prof. U. Belgium, 1987-88, U. Kans., 1988-89, Stanford U., 1989-90, U. Calif. Berkeley, 1989-90; honor rsch. fellow Fine Arts Inst., Art Acad. of China, Beijing, 1990—; art cons., Oakland, 1993—. Author, editor: Dictionary of Connoisseur of Caligraphy and Painting, 1988; contbr. to Great Ency. of China, 1986-90; contbr. articles to profl. jours. Mem. Artists Assn. of China. Office: 1208 Webster St Oakland CA 94612-3919

CAI, YANG, software engineer, computer scientist; b. Shanton, Guangdong, China, Aug. 22, 1964; came to the U.S., 1987; s. Zangxin and Iqian (Huang) C. BS, Beijing (China) U., 1985; MS, U. Kans., 1988; PhD, U. Tex., 1992. Contbr. articles to profl. jours. Mem. IEEE, Assn. Computing Machinery. Office: AscSys Inc 1208 E Arques Ave Sunnyvale CA 94086-5401

CAIN, PATRICIA JEAN, accountant; b. Decatur, Ill., Sept. 28, 1931; d. Paul George and Jean Margaret (Horne) Jacka; m. Dan Louis Cain, July 12, 1952; children: Mary Ann, Timothy George, Paul Louis. Student, U. Mich., 1949-52, Pasadena (Calif.) City Coll., 1975-76; BS in Acctg., Calif. State U., L.A., 1977, MBA, 1978; M in Taxation, Golden Gate U., Los Angeles, 1988; Diploma in Pastry, Hotel Ritz, France, 1991. CPA, Calif.; cert. personal fin. planner; cert. advanced fin. planner. Tax supr. Stonefield & Josephson, L.A., 1979-87; chief fin. officer Loubella Extendables, Inc., L.A., 1987—; participant program in bus. ethics U. So. Calif., L.A., 1986; trainer for A-Plus in house tax Arthur Andersen & Co., 1989-90; instr. Becker CPA Rev. Course, 1989-93. Bd. dirs. Sierra Madre coun. Girl Scouts U.S.A., 1968-73, treas., 1973-75, nat. del., 1975; mem. Town Hall, L.A., 1987—, L.A. Bus. Forum, 1991—. Listed as one of top six tax experts in L.A. by Money mag., 1987. Mem. AICPA (chair nat. tax teleconf. 1988, taxation com./forms subcom. 1994—), Am. Women's Soc. CPAs (bd. dirs. 1986-87, v.p. 1987-90), Calif. Soc. CPAs (chair free tax assistance program 1983-85, high road com. 1985-86, chair pub. rels. com. 1985-89, microcomputer users discussion group taxation com., fin. com./speaker computer show and conf. 1987-93, planning com. and speaker San Francisco Tax and Microcomputer show 1988, state com. on taxation 1991—, speaker Tax Update 1992, dir. L.A. chpt. 1993-95, v.p. 1995—), Internat. Arabian Horse Assn., Wrightwood Country Club, Beta Alpha Psi. Democrat. Episcopalian. Office: Loubella Extendables Inc 5540 Harbor St Commerce CA 90040-1419

CAIN, RAYMOND FREDERICK, landscape architect, planning company executive; b. Harrisburg, Ill., Sept. 13, 1937; s. Raymond Ransome and Edna (Kirkham) C.; m. Galen S. Short, Sept. 13, 1965 (div. 1971); m. Lois A. Kiehl, Dec. 27, 1981. B.A., U. Ill., 1959, M.A., 1962. Cert. profl. landscape architect, Md., Hawaii. Landscape architect W.J. Spear & Assoc., Houston, 1962-66; landscape architect Belt, Collins & Assoc., Honolulu, 1966-76, dir. landscape architecture, 1976—, v.p., 1981—; speaker Urban Devel. Seminar, Singapore, 1980, Fiji Hotel Assn., Nandi, Fiji, 1981; lectr. Tourist Mgmt. Sch., Honolulu, 1978. Mem. Hawaii Year 2000, Honolulu, 1971; advisor Outdoor Cir., Honolulu, 1976; mem. Waikiki Improvement Assn., Honolulu, 1973. Recipient Nat. Landscape award Mauna Kea Beach Hotel, Hawaii, 1976; Nat. Design award Kona Surf Hotel, Hawaii, 1980, Mauna Lani Golf course, 1982, Aga Khan award Tanjong Jara Hotel, Malaysia, 1983. Fellow Am. Soc. Landscape Architects (treas. 1975-76); mem. Am. Planning Assn. (assoc.). Clubs: Outrigger (ground chmn. 1976-77), Honolulu, Oahu Country (ground chmn. 1972-73). Office: Belt Collins & Assocs 680 Ala Moana Blvd Honolulu HI 96813-5406

CAIN, ROBERT JOSEPH, elementary school educator; b. Floral Park, N.Y., June 18, 1947; s. Edwin Thomas and Cecilia Marie (Dunn) C. BA in English, Hofstra U., 1972; BA in Edn., Ariz. State U., 1978, MEd, 1988. Cert. elem. tchr. Auditor Williamsburgh Savs. Bank, Bklyn., 1973-74; skip tracer, adjuster Ariz. Bank, Phoenix, 1974-75; 1st grade tchr. Paradise Valley Unified Sch. Dist. #69, Phoenix, 1979—. Actor City of Phoenix Shakespeare, 1978, Janus Theatre, Phoenix, 1980-81; actor, dir. Glendale Little Theatre, 1974-80; cantor St. Joseph's Ch., 1974—; benefactor Ariz. Opera, 1989—; supporter Met. Opera, 1980—. With U.S. Army, 1968-69. Republican. Roman Catholic. Home: 11012 N 45th St Phoenix AZ 85028-3013 Office: Arrowhead Elem Sch 3820 E Nisbet Rd Phoenix AZ 85032-4639

CAIN, SEYMOUR, historian, philosopher and writer; b. Chgo., May 1, 1914; s. Michael Max and Sarah Annabelle (Rabinowitz) Caann; m. Betty Jean Binder, Oct. 27, 1951; children: Henry George Binder, Robert Victor Binder, Michael Soren. PhD, U. Chgo., 1956. Mem., editor Inst. for Philos. Rsch., San Francisco, 1958-63; cons. to pres. Ctr. for Study of Dem. Instns., Santa Barbara, Calif., 1963-65; contbg. editor Annals of Am., Chgo., 1965-67; sr. editor Ency. Britannica, Chgo., 1967-73; humanist emeritus Tri-Coll. Univ., Moorhead, Minn., 1974-75; asst. prof. Indiana U. of Pa., 1977-78; ind. scholar and writer, San Diego, 1978—; vis. scholar U. Calif.-San Diego, La Jolla, 1990—; vis. prof. Western Mich. U., Kalamazoo, 1975-76, Kalamazoo Coll., 1975-76; organizer, participant Internat. Interdisciplinary Conf. on Martin Buber's Impact on Human Scis., San Diego State U., 1991; columnist Light Newspapers, San Diego, 1983-85. Author: Gabriel Marcel, 1963, 79, Gabriel Marcel's Theory of Religious Experience, 1995; assoc. editor, contbr. Martin Buber and the Human Sciences, 1995; author guides to classic texts in theology, philosophy, lit., ethics, 1961-63; poetry pub. in Midstream, Christian Century, others; short stories pub. in Cosmopolitan, San Diego Writers monthly, others. Organizer, active various civil rights groups, Pacifica, Calif.; organizer, publicist University City Residents for Equity, San Diego. With Signal Corps, USAAF, 1941-45. U. Chgo. fellow, 1954-55, NEH fellow, 1978-79, 94. Mem. Am. Acad. Religion, Am. Soc. for Study of Religion, Soc. for Sci. Study of Religion, Mormon History Assn., San Diego Ind. Scholars, Nat. Writers Union. Democrat. Jewish. Home and Office: 2845 Arnoldson Ave San Diego CA 92122-2132

CAIN, STEPHEN MICHAEL, city official; b. Bridgeport, Calif., Oct. 14, 1957; s. Walter B. and Patricia A. (Lowden) C. BA in Comm. and Sociology, U. Calif., Santa Barbara, 1980, MA in Govt., 1987; PhD in Polit. Sci., Claremont Coll., 1995. Legis. asst. to Bd. Suprs. and County Counsel County of Mono, Bridgeport, Calif., 1980-84; legis. asst. to Assemblyman Norman Waters State of Calif., Sacramento, 1984-85; asst. to pres. and dean of students Harvey Mudd Coll., Claremont, Calif., 1985-92; mgmt. analyst dept. pub. works and transp. City of Pasadena, Calif., 1993—. Author: Chips of the Same Block? Majority and Minority Group Political Activities, 1987, Constructing the Invisible: Clean Air, Federal Legislation and the Media, 1995; editor Pub. Works and Transp. Happenings, 1993-95. Vol. L.A. Marathon, World Cup Soccer Tournament; mem. Pasadena Police Vol. Exec. Com., Pasadena Citizens' Police Acad., L.A. Mcpl. Elections Commn. Mem. ASPA, ACLU, Mcpl. Mgmt. Assts. So. Calif., Pasadena Hist. Soc., Mono County Hist. Soc., Pi Sigma Alpha. Episcopalian.

CAINE, CAROL WHITACRE, business owner; b. Vandergrift, Pa., Mar. 14, 1925; d. Guy Alvin and Genevra Madeline (Lash) Whitacre; m. Charles Clyde Caine, Dec. 27, 1948; children: Christopher, Charles Lash. BS, Ohio State U., 1951. Part-time med. and x-ray technician Internal Medicine Lab., 1950-70; co-owner Transceiver Ctrs. of Columbus, Ohio, 1968-79, PIP Printing, Cheyenne, Wyo., 1981-94; ret., 1994. Mem. AAUW (bd. dirs. Cheyenne chpt. 1984-86), Wyo. Media Profls., Am. Soc. Radiol. Technologists, Am. Soc. Med. Tech., Nat. Fedn. Press Women, Zonta (bd. dirs. Cheyenne chpt. 1988-92), Order of Eastern Star, Alpha Phi (life). Home: 3304 Sunrise Hills Dr Cheyenne WY 82009-4528

CAINE, SIMON BARAK, neuroscientist, researcher; b. Jerusalem, Israel, July 30, 1962; s. Ivan Willard and Deborah (Taylor) C. BA in Biologic Basis Behavior, U. Pa., 1985; PhD in Neurosci., U. Calif. San Diego, La Jolla, 1994. Pre-doctoral fellow U. Calif., La Jolla, 1989-94, Scripps Rsch. Inst., La Jolla, 1989-94; post-doctoral fellow Cambridge (Eng.) U., 1994—. Contbr. articles to profl. jours. Recipient Individual Nat. Rsch. Svc. award Nat. Inst. Drug Abuse, La Jolla, 1991-94, EBPS award, Cambridge, England, 1992, ISGIDAR award, Palm Beach, Fla., 1994, Human Frontier Sci. Program Fellowship award Cambridge, 1994—. Mem. Soc. for Neurosci. Democrat. Jewish. Office: The Scripps Rsch Inst CVN-7 10666 N Torrey Pines Rd La Jolla CA 92037-1027

CAINE, STEPHEN HOWARD, data processing executive; b. Washington, Feb. 11, 1941; s. Walter E. and Jeanette (Wenborne) C. Student Calif. Inst. Tech., 1958-62. Sr. programmer Calif. Inst. Tech., Pasadena, 1962-65, mgr. systems programming, 1965-69, mgr. programming, 1969-70; pres. Caine, Farber & Gordon, Inc., Pasadena, 1970—; lectr. applied sci. Calif. Inst. Tech., Pasadena, 1965-71, vis. assoc. elec. engring., 1976, vis. assoc. computer sci., 1976-84. Dir. San Gabriel Valley Learning Ctrs., 1992—. Mem. Pasadena Tournament of Roses Assn., 1976—. Mem. AAAS, Nat. Assn. Corrosion Engrs., Am. Ordnance Assn., Assn. Computing Machinery, Athanaeum Club (Pasadena), Houston Club. Home: 77 Patrician Way Pasadena CA 91105-1039

CAINES, KENNETH L.D., management consulting executive; b. N.Y.C.; s. Clarence and Monica C.; BS in Psychology and Sociology, NYU; postgrad. Calif. State Coll., UCLA, ; m. Josephine A. Robinson. pres. People Oriented Systems, Santa Ana, Calif., 1969—; v.p. Band Aide, 1984-87; dir. Joken Human Factors Assocs 1967-76. lectr. civil and social systems U. Calif.-Irvine, 1970-71. V.p. tech. adv. com. on testing Calif. Fair Employment Practices Commn., 1967-71; mem. U. Calif. at Irvine-Project 21 Com. on Population Growth, 1971-72; pres. Orange YMCA, 1973; mem. exec. bd. Orange County coun. Boy Scouts Am., 1970-73; mem. Orange County Grand Jury, 1980-81. Mem. Orange Planning Commn., 1973-76. Bd. dirs. Orange County United Way, 1971-73, Orange County Community Housing Corp., 1986—. Served with USAAF. Named Citizen of Year Orange YMCA, 1972. Mem. IEEE, Am. Mgmt. Assn., Serenity Foster Care Homes (treas.), Assn. Profl. Cons. Office: People Oriented Systems PO Box 10728 Santa Ana CA 92711-0728

CAIRNS, DIANE PATRICIA, motion picture literary agent; b. Fairbanks, Alaska, Mar. 2, 1957; d. Dion Melvin and Marsha Lala (Andrews) C. BBA, U. So. Calif., 1980. Literary agt. Sy Fischer Agy., L.A., 1980-85; sr. v.p. Internat. Creative Mgmt., L.A., 1985—. Mem. Acad. Motion Picture Arts and Scis., Women in Film, Hollywood Women's Polit. Com., NOW, Amnesty Internat., L.A. County Mus. of Art, Mus. of Contemporary Art (L.A.).

CAIRNS, ELTON JAMES, chemical engineering educator; b. Chgo., Nov. 7, 1932; s. James Edward and Claire Angele (Larzelere) C.; m. Miriam Esther Citron, Dec. 26, 1974; 1 dau., Valerie Helen; stepchildren: Benjamin David, Joshua Aaron. B.S. in Chemistry, Mich. Tech. U., Houghton, 1955; B.S. in Chem. Engring, 1955; Ph.D. in Chem. Engring. (Dow Chem. Co. fellow, univ. fellow, Standard Oil Co. Calif. grantee, NSF fellow), U. Calif., Berkeley, 1959. Phys. chemist Gen. Electric Co. Research Lab., Schenectady, 1959-66; group leader, then sect. head chem. engring. div. Argonne (Ill.) Nat. Lab., 1966-73; asst. head electrochemistry dept. Gen. Motors Corp. Research Labs., 1973-78; assoc. lab. dir., dir. energy and environment div. Lawrence Berkeley (Calif.) Lab., 1978—; prof. chem. engring. U. Calif., Berkeley, 1978—; Croft lectr. U. Mo., 1979; McCabe lectr. U. N.C., 1993; cons. in field, mem. numerous govt. panels. Author: (with H.A. Liebhafsky) Fuel Cells and Fuel Batteries, 1968; mem. editor bd. Advances in Electrochemistry and Electrochm. Engring., 1974—; div. editor Jour. Electrochem. Soc., 1968-91; regional editor Electrochimica Acta, 1984—; contbr. articles to profl. jours. Recipient IR-100 award, 1968, Centennial medal Case Western Res. U., 1980, R&D 100 award, 1992; named McCabe lectr. U. N.C., 1993; grantee DuPont Co., 1956. Fellow Am. Inst. Chemists, Electrochem. Soc. (chmn. phys. electrochem. divsn. 1981-84, v.p. 1986-89, pres. 1989-90, Francis Mills Turner award 1963); mem. AIChE (chmn. energy conversion com. 1970-94), AAAS, Am. Chem. Soc., Internat. Soc. Electrochemistry (chmn. electrochem. energy conversion divsn. 1977-85, U.S. nat. sec. 1983-89, v.p. 1984-88), Intersoc. Energy Conversion Engring. Conf. (steering com. 1970—, gen. chmn. 1976, 90, program chmn. 1983—). Home: 239 Langlie Ct Walnut Creek CA 94598-3615 Office: Lawrence Berkeley Lab 1 Cyclotron Rd Berkeley CA 94720

CAISSE, JEANNE MAE, city official; b. Concord, N.H., Oct. 26, 1948; d. Charles R. and Alta M. (Dickerson) Hammett; m. Charles Alejandro Sebastian de la Vega-Cordoba y Trevino, 1972 (dec. 1972); m. Albert Robert Caisse, June 16, 1984. AA in Bus., Daytona Beach (Fla.) Community Coll., 1976; student, Fla. State U., 1977-78; BS in Pers., Franklin Pierce Coll., Rindge, N.H., 1988; postgrad., Keene (N.H.) State Coll., 1991—. Cert. paralegal, justice of peace, notary pub., N.H. Br. libr. Concord (N.H.) Pub. Libr., 1969-74; exec. sec. Conf. Ctr. United Ch. of Christ, Concord, 1978-80; exec. sec. to v.p. trust dept. Bank of N.H., Concord, 1980-82; summer asst., libr., computer programer State of N.H., 1982-84; from paralegal to mgr. pers. Brighton, Fernald, Taft & Hampsey PA, Peterborough, N.H., 1984-89; asst. pers. mgr. Internat. Data Group, Peterborough, 1989; mgr. adminstrv. svcs. Schleicher & Schuell, Inc., Keene, N.H., 1990-92; pres. Lost River Travel, Inc., 1992-94; paralegal, cons. Am. Paralegal Group, 1984-94; grants adminstr. City of Bullhead, Ariz., 1994—; cmty. devel. specialist, 1984-95, fed. "rural encourager", Idaho, 1992-94; cons., seminar spkr., trainer Interwest Svcs., 1992-94. Entertainer for elderly, shut-ins and hospitalized, Concord, 1980-81; dir., founder Rainbow Hope, Loudon, N.H., 1985—; trustee Peterborough (N.H.) Pub. Libr., 1988-90; mem. Peterborough Recreational Com., 1988-90. Recipient outstanding svc. award Loudon (N.H.) Bicentennial Parade Com., 1976; fellow Rotary Club Internat., State of Fla., 1976-77; President's scholar Daytona Beach Community Coll., 1976. Mem. Grange (sec. Louden 1978—). Republican. Home: PO Box 10130 Golden Valley AZ 86413-2130 Office: City of Bullhead City 1255 Marina Blvd Bullhead City AZ 86442-5733

CAJERO, CARMEN, state legislator; b. Morenci, Ariz.. State rep. dist. 10 Ariz. Ho. of Reps.; mem. appropriations com., natural resources com., agr. and rules com.; businesswoman. Democrat. Home: 104 W District St Tucson AZ 85714-2528 Office: Office of State Senate 1700 W Washington St Phoenix AZ 85007-2812

CALAS, NAPOLEON EVANS, medical laboratory administrator; b. Pontiac, Mich., June 12, 1951; s. Angelo and Anna Louise (O'Brien) C.; m. Carolyn Ann Cooper, Sept. 24, 1977 (div. 1992); children: Megan Ann, Christopher Evans; m. Lonna Rae Bernhard, Aug. 7, 1992; 1 child, Hannah Beth. BS in Zoology, Mich. State U., 1973, BS in Med. Tech., 1974; med. tech. cert., Beaumont Hosp., Royak Oak, Mich., 1975; MBA, U. Mich., 1979. Fin. analyst Hospital Affiliates, Nashville, 1979-80; adminstr. Rogers City (Mich.) Hosp., 1980-84; divsn. pres. Internat. Clin. Labs., Seattle, 1984-88; area v.p. Metpath, Inc., Denver, 1988-89; divsn. mgr. Nat. Health Labs., Kent, Wash., 1989-94; v.p., owner Sterilchek Laboratories, 1995—. Home: 20314 42nd Ave NE Lk Forest Park WA 98155

CALDER, CLARENCE ANDREW, mechanical engineer, educator, researcher; b. Baker, Oreg., Oct. 30, 1937; s. Clarence Leroy and Viola Mary (Lucas) C.; m. Judy Lee Wood, Dec. 15, 1961; children: Brian Andrew, Gregory Clarence, Kaylene Ellen, Chad Warner, Jared Lucas. BSME, Oreg. State U., Corvallis, 1960; MS, Brigham Young U., 1962; PhD, U. Calif., Berkeley, 1969. Registered profl. engr., Oreg., Calif. Project engr. Sandia Corp., Albuquerquqe, 1962-64; asst. prof. mech. engr. Wash. State U., Pullman, 1969-74; sr. rsch. engr. Lawrence Livermore (Calif.) Nat. Lab., 1974-78; assoc. prof. Oreg. State U., Corvallis, 1978-94, prof., 1994—; vis. sr. lectr. U. Auckland, N.Z., 1986; tech. cons. Lawrence Livermore Nat. Lab., 1978-88. Contbr. articles to profl. jours. Mem. Philomath Sch. Bd., 1993. Mem. ASME, Am. Soc. Engring. Edn., Soc. for Exptl. Mechs. (treas. 1982-85, pres. 1987-88). Republican. LDS. Office: Oreg State U Dept Mech Engring Corvallis OR 97331

CALDER, ROBERT MAC, aerospace engineer; b. Vernal, Utah, Oct. 16, 1932; s. Edwin Harold and Sydney (Goodrich) C.; m. Yoshiko Iemura, Feb. 14, 1959; children: Suzanne, Alexis, Irene, John. BSChemE, U. Utah, 1956, M.S. in Math. and Geology (NSF grantee), 1967; postgrad., U. Wash., 1964, Utah State U., 1965, U. Iowa, 1966. Cert. secondary tchr., Utah. Tchr. Utah Pub. Schs., 1958-79. V.p. Sydney Corp., Bountiful, Utah, 1958-82; sr. engr. aero. div. Hercules Inc., Magna, Utah, 1979—; owner RMC Enterprises, Nations Imports; cons. in field, 1960—; cultural exchange participant to Israel, Egypt, 1983, 87. Active Boy Scouts Am., 1945-75, instr., Philmont Scout Ranch, 1972, asst. scoutmaster Nat. Jamboree Troop, 1973; instr. hunter safety and survival, Utah Dept. Fish and Game, 1964-74; state advisor U.S. Congl. Adv. Bd., 1982—; mem. Rep. Nat. Com. Capt. USAF, 1956-70. Mem. AIAA, NRA (life), Am. Quarter Horse Assn., Internat. Platform Assn., Oratorio Soc. Utah, The Planetary Soc., Hercules Toastmasters Club (treas. 1980, v.p. edn. 1981, pres. 1982), N.Am. Fishing Club (life). Mormon. Home: PO Box 268 Bountiful UT 84011-0268 Office: PO Box 194 Kaysville UT 84037-0194

CALDERON, REBECA FRANCO, judiciary interpreter; b. Guadalajara, Jalisco, Mexico, July 17, 1951; came to the U.S., 1976; d. Otilio Franco and Maria De Jesus (Roman) C.; m. June 29, 1974 (dec. Mar. 1991); children: Elizabeth, Diana Sophia. BA in Law, Bus, Adminstrn., Lang., Art, U. de Guadalajara, 1988. Cert. ct. interpreter, U.S. cts. judiciary interpreter, Calif. Lang. instr. Latin Am. Lang. Ctr., Guadalajara, 1971-73, Berlitz, San Diego, 1976-78; freelance interpreter San Diego, 1978—; ct. interpreter KNSD Ch. 39, San Diego, 1988-91, U.S. Cts., San Diego, 1988—. Mem. Nat. Assn. Judiciary Interpreters, Am. Translators Assn. Roman Catholic. Home: 382 Surrey Dr Bonita CA 91902-2350

CALDERWOOD, NEIL MOODY, retired telephone traffic engineer, consultant; b. Vinalhaven, Maine, June 19, 1910; s. Austin Shirley and Eliza Louise (Carver) C.; m. Katherine Foster Mariani, Oct. 13, 1940; children: John Carver, James Foster, Bruce Glidden. BSCE, U. Maine, Orono, 1932, MS in Math., 1935. Sr. engr. Resettlement Adminstrn., Camden, Maine, 1935-37; sr. engr. Pacific Telephone, San Francisco, 1937-42, staff engr., dist. traffic engr., gen. traffic engr., staff dir. network ops., 1946-75; telecom. expert Internat. Telecom. Union, UN, Geneva, 1975-76; cons. telephone numbering plans Libyan Govt., Benghazi, Tripoli, 1976; traffic engring. cons. Las Vegas Telephone Co., 1952, Hawaiian Telephone Co., 1963; expert witness Public Utilities Commn. of Calif. hearings on all number calling cases, San Francisco and L.A., 1962-64. Lt. comdr. USNR, 1942-46. Mem. Am. Rose Soc., Pierce-Arrow Soc., Telephone Pioneers, Phi Gamma Delta. Republican. Home: 49 Dolores Way Orinda CA 94563-4154

CALDERWOOD, WILLIAM ARTHUR, physician; b. Wichita, Kans., Feb. 3, 1941; s. Ralph Bailey and Janet Denise (Christ) C.; m. Nancy Jo Crawford, Mar. 31, 1979; children: Lisa Beth, William Arthur II. MD, U. Kans., 1968. Diplomate Am. Bd. Family Practice. Intern Wesley Med. Ctr., Wichita, 1968-69; gen. practice family medicine Salina, Kans., 1972-80, Peoria, Ariz., 1980—; med. dir. First Am. Home Care, 1994—; pres. staff St. John's Hosp., Salina, 1976; 28th jud. dist. coroner State of Kans., Salina, 1973-80; clin. instr. U. Kans., Wichita, 1978-80; cons. in addiction medicine VA Hosp., 1989-94. Inventor, patentee lighter-than-air-furniture. Bd. dirs. Pelms House, Peoria, Ariz., 1995—. Lt., M.S., USN, 1969-70. Fellow Am. Acad. Family Physicians; mem. AMA, Ariz. Med. Soc. (physicians med. health com., exec. com. 1988-92), Maricopa County Med. Soc., Ariz. Acad. Family Practice (med. dir. N.W. Orgn. Vol. alternatives 1988-91), Am. Med. Soc. on Alcoholism and Other Drug Dependencies (cert.), Shriners. Home: 7015 W Calavar Rd Peoria AZ 85381-4706 Office: 14300 W Granite Valley Dr Sun City West AZ 85375-5783

CALDWELL, COURTNEY LYNN, lawyer, real estate consultant; b. Washington, Mar. 5, 1948; d. Joseph Morton and Moselle (Smith) C. Student, Duke U., 1966-68, U. Calif., Berkeley, 1967, 1968-69; BA, U. Calif., Santa Barbara, 1970, MA, 1975; JD with highest honors, George Washington U., 1982. Bar: D.C. 1984, Wash. 1986, Calif. 1989. Jud. clk. U.S. Ct. Appeals for 9th Cir., Seattle, 1982-83; assoc. Arnold & Porter, Washington, 1983-85, Perkins Coie, Seattle, 1985-88; dir. western ops. MPC Assocs., Inc., Irvine, Calif., 1988-91, sr. v.p., 1991—. Bd. dirs. Univ. Town Ctr. Assn., 1994; bd. dirs. Habitat for Humanity, Orange County, 1993-94, chair legal com., 1994. Named Nat. Law Ctr. Law Rev. Scholar, 1981-82. Mem. Calif. Bar Assn., Wash. State Bar Assn., D.C. Bar Assn., Urban Land Inst. Office: MPC Assocs Inc 1451 Quail St Ste 212 Newport Beach CA 92660-2741

CALDWELL, DAN EDWARD, political science educator; b. Oklahoma City, May 12, 1948; s. John Edward and Hester Evelyn (Kiehn) C.; m. Lora Jean Ferguson, Mar. 21, 1970; children: Beth Christine, Ellen Claire, John Ferguson. BA in History, Stanford U., 1970, MA in Polit. Sci., PhD in Polit. Sci., 1978; MA in Internat. Rels., Tufts U., 1971. Staff mem. Office Emergency Preparedness, Exec. Office of Pres., Washington, 1972; rsch. and teaching fellow Stanford (Calif.) U., 1975-78; assoc. dir. Ctr. for Fgn. Policy Devel., Brown U., Providence, 1982-84; prof. polit. sci. Pepperdine U., Malibu, Calif., 1978-82, 84—, pres. faculty orgn., 1980-81, 89-90; dir. Forum for U.S.-Soviet Dialogue, Washington, 1984—, pres., 1989-91. Author: American-Soviet Relations, 1981, The Dynamics of Domestic Politics and Arms Control, 1991; editor: Henry Kissinger, 1985. Elder Pacific Palisades

(Calif.) Presbyn. Ch.; co-chmn. Ground Zero, L.A., 1982. With USN, 1971-74. Named Prof. of Yr., Pepperdine U. Student Alumni Assn., 1992.; rsch. fellow U.S. Inst. Peace, 1987, Pew faculty fellow Harvard U. Kennedy Sch. Govt., 1990. Mem. Internat. Inst. Strategic Studies (London), Am. Polit. Sci. Assn., Internat. Studies Assn. (sect. exec. com. 1982-87, dir. sect. on Am.-Soviet rels. 1984-86, fellow 1977), Coun. on Fgn. Rels. Home: 654 Radcliffe Ave Pacific Palisades CA 90272-4331 Office: Pepperdine U Social Sci Div 24255 Pacific Coast Hwy Malibu CA 90263-0001

CALDWELL, DAVID ORVILLE, physics educator; b. Los Angeles, Jan. 5, 1925; s. Orville Robert and Audrey Norton (Anderson) C.; m. Miriam Ann Planck, Nov. 4, 1950 (div. Apr. 1978); children: Bruce David, Diana Miriam; m. Edith Helen Anderson, Dec. 29, 1984. BS in Physics, Calif. Inst. Tech., 1947; postgrad., Stanford U., 1947-48; MA in Physics, UCLA, 1949, PhD in Physics, 1953. From instr. to assoc. prof. physics MIT, Cambridge, 1954-63; vis. assoc. prof. physics Princeton U., N.J., 1963-64; lectr. physics dept. U. Calif., Berkeley, 1964-65; prof. physics U. Calif., Santa Barbara, 1965—; cons. U. Calif. Radiation Lab., Berkeley, 1957-58, 64-67, Am. Sci. and Engring., Boston, 1959-60, Inst. Def. Analysis, Washington, 1960-67, U.S. Dept. Def., Washington, 1966-70; dir. U. Calif. Inst. for Nuc. and Particle Astrophysics and Cosmology, 1984, 95—, U. Calif. Inst. for Rsch. at Particle Accelerators, 1984-95. Contbr. numerous articles to profl. jours. Served to 2d lt. USAAF, 1943-46. Recipient von Humboldt Sr. Disting. Sci. award, 1987; research grantee Dept. Energy, 1966—; Ford Found. fellow, 1961-62, NSF fellow, 1953-54, 1960-61, Guggenheim fellow, 1971-72. Fellow Am. Phys. Soc.; mem. Phys. Soc. (exec. com. 1976-78). Democrat. Office: U Calif Santa Barbara Dept Physics Santa Barbara CA 93106

CALDWELL, HOWARD BRYANT, English language educator; b. London, Ky., Jan. 28, 1944; s. Stratton and Linda Emily (Bryant) C. BA, Berea (Ky.) Coll., 1966; MA, U. Calif., Berkeley, 1977. Cert. adult edn. tchr. Tchr. L.A. Unified Sch. Dist., 1977—. Mem. L.A. County Mus. Art, N.Y. Met. Mus. Art, L.A. World Affairs Coun. With USAF, 1966-70, The Philippines. Mem. United Tchrs. L.A., London Victory Club. Republican. Baptist.

CALDWELL, JONI, psychology educator, small business owner; b. Chgo., Aug. 8, 1948; d. Bruce Wilber and Eloise Ethel (Ijams) C. BS in Home Econs. Edn., Mich. State U., 1970; MA in Psychology, U. San Francisco, 1978. Cret. high sch. and coll. tchr., Mich. Instr. Northwestern Mich. Coll., Traverse City, 1972-78, Mott Community Coll., Flint, Mich., 1974-78; tchr. Grand Blanc (Mich.) High Sch., 1970-73, Clio (Mich.) High Sch., 1974-78; parent educator, vol. coord. Family Resource Ctr., Monterey, Calif., 1981-82; owner, gen. mgr. Futons & Such, Monterey, 1982—; instr. psychology Hartnell Coll., Salinas, Calif., 1993—. Bd. dirs., v.p., pres. Ch. Religious Sci., Monterey, 1984-87; mem. bd. stewards Pacific Coast Ch., Monterey, 1988-92, v.p.; bd. dirs. YWCA, Monterey, 1986-88; vol., fund raiser Buddy Program, 1992—; membership com. Profl. Womens Network, 1989—. Mem. New Monterey Bus. Assn. (past pres., bd. dirs. 1984—, v.p. 1993—), Monterey C. of C. (cons. workshop com. 1985-87, Small Bus. Excellence award 1990). Home: 29 Portola Ave Monterey CA 93940-3731 Office: Futons & Such 484 Lighthouse Ave Monterey CA 93940-1457

CALDWELL, PETER DEREK, pediatrician, pediatric cardiologist; b. Schenectady, N.Y., Apr. 16, 1940; s. Philip Graham and Mary Elizabeth (Glockler) C.; m. Olga Hoang Hai Miller, May 31, 1969. BA, Pomona Coll., 1961; MD, UCLA, 1965. Intern King County Hosp., Seattle, 1965-66; resident in pediatrics U. Wash., 1969-71, fellow in pediatric cardiology, 1971-73; pvt. practice Hawaii Permanente Med. Group, Honolulu, 1973—. Author: Bac-Si: A Doctor Remembers Vietnam, 1990, Adventurer's Hawaii, 1992; contbr. articles to profl. jours. Lt. comdr. USNR, 1966-69. Fellow Am. Acad. Pediatrics; mem. Am. Coll. Sports Medicine, Wilderness Med. Soc., Internat. Soc. Mountain Medicine. Office: Kaiser Punawai Clinic 94-235 Leoku St Waipahu HI 96797-1906

CALDWELL, STRATTON FRANKLIN, kinesiologist; b. Mpls., Aug. 25, 1926; s. Kenneth Simms and Margaret Mathilda (Peterson) C.; m. Mary Lynn Shaffer, Aug. 28, 1955 (div. May 1977); children: Scott Raymond, Karole Elizabeth; m. Sharee' Deanna Ockerman, Aug. 6, 1981; 1 stepchild, Shannon Sharee' Calder. Student, San Diego State Coll., 1946-48; BS in Edn. cum laude, U. So. Calif., 1951, PhD in Phys. Edn., 1966; MS in Phys. Edn., U. Oreg., 1953. Teaching asst. dept. phys. edn. UCLA, 1953-54, assoc. in phys. edn., 1957-65, vis. asst. prof. phys. edn., 1967; dir. phys. edn. Regina (Sask., Can.) Young Men's Christian Assn., 1954-56; tchr. sec. grades, dir. athletic Queen Elizabeth Jr.-Sr. High Sch., Calgary, Alta., Can., 1956-57; asst. prof. phys. edn. San Fernando Valley State Coll., Northridge, Calif., 1965-68, assoc. prof., 1968-71; prof. phys. edn. dept. kinesiology Calif. State U., Northridge, 1971-90, prof. kinesiology, 1990-92, prof. kinesiology emeritus, 1992; vis. asst. prof. phys. edn. UCLA, 1967; vis. assoc. prof. phys. edn. U. Wash., Seattle, 1968, U. Calif., Santa Barbara, 1969. Author (with Cecil and Joan Martin Hollingsworth) Golf, 1959, (with Rosalind Cassidy) Humanizing Physical Education: Methods for the Secondary School Movement Program, 5th edit., 1975; also poetry, book chpts., articles in profl. jours., book revs. With USN, 1944-46. Recipient Meritorious Performance and Profl. Promise award Calif. state U., 1986, 87, 89, Disting. Teaching award, 1992; AAPHERD fellow, 1962, Am. Coll. Sports Medicine fellow, 1965, Can. Assn. for Health, Phys. Edn., and Recreation fellow, 1971. Fellow Am. Alliance for Health, Phys. Edn., Recreation and Dance (Centennial Commn. 1978-85, cert. appreciation 1985), Am. Coll. Sports Medicine; mem. Calif. Assn. for Health, Phys. Edn., Recreation and Dance (pres. L.A. coll. and univ. unit 1969-70, v.p. phys. edn. com. 1970-71, mem. editorial bd. CAHPER Jour. 1970-71, mem. forum 1970-71, Disting. Svc. award 1974, Honor award 1988, Verne Landreth award 1992), Nat. Assn. for Phys. Edn. in Higher Edn. (charter), Sport Art Acad., Nat. Assn. for Sport and Phys. Edn., N.Y. Acad. Scis., N.Am. Soc. for Sports History, Sport Lit. Assn., Acad. Am. Poets, Phi Epsilon Kappa (Svc. award 1980), Alpha Tau Omega (charter,Silver Circle award 1976), Phi Delta Kappa, Phi Kappa Phi, others. Republican. Mem. Christian Ch. Home: 80 N Kanan Rd Oak Park CA 91301-1105

CALDWELL, THOMAS MICHAEL, facilities director; b. Beardstown, Ill., June 29, 1946; s. Carl and E. Lou (Bullard) C.; children: Tamera Lynn, Thomas Adam, Elizabeth R., Benjamin T. BS, U. N.Mex., 1975. Ptnr. Solar Retrofit Inc., Albuquerque, N.Mex., 1978-81; maint. data collections W.B.C. Consultants, Tucson, 1981-82; facilities dir. EG&G, Albuquerque, 1983-90; owner T's Weldry, Los Lunas, N.Mex., 1988-; ptnr. D&T Solar Lazers, Albuquerque, 1983; exec. v.p. Solar Detox. Corp., Albuquerque, 1990—. Co-designer human powered vehicle, Boing 888. With USN, 1965-69. Mem. Rio Grande Human Powered Vehicle Assn. (pres.). Democrat. Roman Catholic. Home: 329 Gorman Ave Belen NM 87002-6004

CALDWELL, WALTER EDWARD, editor, small business owner; b. L.A., Dec. 29, 1941; s. Harold Elmer and Esther Ann (Fuller) C.; m. Donna Edith Davis, June 27, 1964; 1 child, Arnie-Jo. AA, Riverside City Coll., 1968. Sales and stock professional Sears Roebuck & Co., Riverside, Calif., 1963-65; dispatcher Rohr Corp., Riverside, Calif., 1965-67; trainee Aetna Fin., Riverside, 1967-68; mgr. Aetna Fin., San Bruno, Cal., 1968-70, Amfac Thrift & Loan, Oakland, Calif., 1970-74; free lance writer San Jose, Calif., 1974-76; news dir. Sta. KAVA Radio, Burney, Cal., 1977-79; editor-pub. Mountain Echo, Fall River Mills, Calif., 1979—. Contbg. author Yearbook of Modern Poetry, 1976. Del. Farmers and Ranchers' Congress, St. Louis, 1985; participant Am. Leadership Conf., San Diego, 1989; pres. United Way, Burney, Calif., 1979, co-chmn., 1977, chmn., 1979; disaster relief worker ARC, Redding, Calif., 1988-91, disaster action team leader, 1991—; bd. dirs. Shasta County Women's Refuge, Redding, 1988-91; bd. dirs. Shasta County Econ. Devel. Task Force, Redding, 1985-86, exec. bd. dirs., 1988; bd. dirs. Shasta County Econ. Devel. Corp., 1986-90; pres. Intermountain Devel. Corp., 1989; leader Girl Scouts U.S., San Jose, 1973-76; announcer various local parades; trustee Mosquito Abatement Dist., Burney, 1978-87, 89—, chmn., 1990—; commr. Burney Fire Protection Dist., 1987-91, v.p., 1990, pres. 1991; bd. dirs. Crossroads, 1985; past chmn. Burney Basin Days Com., 1984—; candidate Shasta County Bd. Suprs., 1992. Cpl. USMC, 1959-63. Mem. Burney Basin C. of C. (advt. chmn. 1982, Community Action award 1990, 93), Fall River Valley C. of C. (bd. dirs. 1991), Internat. Platform Assn., Am. Legion (Citation of Recognition 1987, Community Action award 1989, 93), Calif. Newspaper Pubs. Assn., Profl. Journalism Assn., Rotary (pres. 1977-78, chmn. bike race 1981-85), Lions (student speaker chmn. Fall River club 1983—, 1st v.p. 1991, pres. 1992, co-chmn. disaster com., newsletter chmn. dist. 4-C1 1989-91), Moose, Masons, Shriners (sec.-treas. Intermountain club). Republican. Home: 20304 Elm St Burney CA 96013-4028 Office: Mountain Echo Main St Fall River Mills CA 96028 also: PO Box 224 Fall River Mills CA 96028-0224

CALDWELL, WILLIAM MACKAY, III, business executive; b. Los Angeles, Apr. 6, 1922; s. William Mackay II and Edith Ann (Richards) C.; BS, U. So. Calif., 1943; MBA, Harvard U., 1948; m. Mary Louise Edwards, Jan. 16, 1946 (dec. 1980); children: William Mackay IV, Craig Edwards, Candace Louise; m. Jean Bledsoe, Apr. 27, 1985. Sec.-treas., dir. Drewry Photocolor Corp., 1957-60, Adcolor Photo Corp., 1957-60; treas., dir. Drewry Bennetts Corp., 1959-60; sr. v.p., chief fin. officer Am. Cement Corp., 1960-67; sr. v.p. corp., 1966-70, pres. cement and concrete group, 1967-70; pres., chmn. bd., chief exec. officer Van Vorst Industries, 1969; pres. Van Vorst Corp., Washington, 1969-77; chmn. bd., pres. So. Cross Industries, U.S. Bedding Co., 1979-84, St. Croix Mfg. Co., 1979-81, Hawaiian Cement Corp.; pres. Englander Co., 1979-84; v.p., dir. Am. Cement Internat. Corp., Am. Cement Properties; chmn. Kyco Industries Inc., 1982—; pres. BHI Inc., 1984—; cons. prof. U. So. Calif. Mem. men's com. Los Angeles Med. Center; bd. dirs. Commerce Assocs., Calif. Mus. Sci. and Industry, U. So. Calif. Assocs., bd. dirs. Pres.'s Circle; bd. dirs. Am. Cement Found. Served to lt. USNR, 1943-46. Mem. Newcomen Soc., Friends Huntington Library, L.A. Country Club, Town Hall Club, Calif. Club (L.A.), Trojan Club, Annandale Golf Club, Eldorado Country Club, Chaparell Golf Club, Harvard Bus. Sch. of So. Calif. (dir. 1960-63), Kappa Alpha, Alpha Delta Sigma, Alpha Pi Omega. Presbyterian. Office: PO Box 1151 Pasadena CA 91102-1151

CALDWELL-PORTENIER, PATTY JEAN GROSSKOPF, advocate, educator; b. Davenport, Iowa, Sept. 28, 1937; d. Bernhard August and Leontine Virginia (Carver) Grosskopf; m. Donald Eugene Caldwell Mar. 29, 1956 (dec. Feb. 1985); children: John Alan, Jennifer Lynn Caldwell Lear; m. Walter J. Portenier, Oct. 3, 1992. BA, State U. Iowa, 1959. Hearing officer Ill. State Bd. Edn., Springfield, 1979-91, Appellate Court, 1986-91; pres., bd. dirs. Tri-County Assn. for Children With Learning Disabilities, Moline, Ill., 1972-79; adv. vol., Iowa and Ill., 1979-91; mem. adv. coun. Prairie State Legal Svcs., Inc., Rock Island, Ill., 1984-91; mem. profl. svcs. com. United Cerebral Palsy N.W. Ill., Rock Island, 1986-88; arbitrator Am. Arbitration Assn., Chgo., 1986-91, Better Bus. Bur., Davenport, 1986-91. Founder, pres. Quad Cities Diabetes Assn., Moline, 1969-72, bd. dirs., 1973—; mem. com. Moline Internat. Yr. Disabled, 1981; mem. Assn. for Retarded Citizens, Rock Island, 1987; mem. vol. Coun. on Children at Risk, Moline, 1988-91; reader for the blind Sta. WVIK, Rock Island, 1989-91. Mem. Ill. Assn. for Children with Learning Disabilities (bd. dirs., adv. 1980-83). Methodist. Home and Office: 2443 La Condessa Dr Los Angeles CA 90049-1221

CALHOUN, GORDON JAMES, lawyer; b. Pitts., Sept. 3, 1953; s. Bertram Allen and Dorothy Mae (Brown) C.; m. Jane Ann Walchli, May 7, 1982; children: Andrew Michael, Megan Jane. BA with honors, John Hopkins U., 1975; JD, Stanford U., 1978. Bar: Calif. 1978, U.S. Dist. Ct. (no., cen., ea. and so. dists.) Calif. 1979, U.S. Ct. Appeals (9th cir.) 1980. Assoc. Long & Levit, 1978-83, Parkinson & Wolf, 1983-84; ptnr. Wolf & Leo, 1984-91, Lewis, D'Amato, Brisbois & Bisgaard, 1991—. Mem. ABA (real property, probate and trust law sect., litigation sect., tort and ins. practice sect.), Am. Trial Lawyers Assn., So. Calif. Def. Counsel, L.A. County Bar Assn., Phi Beta Kappa, Omicron Delta Kappa. Office: Lewis D'Amato Brisbois & Bisgaard 221 N Figueroa St Los Angeles CA 90012-2601

CALHOUN, JOHN JOSEPH, advertising executive; b. Lafayette, Ind., May 27, 1964; s. Robert James and Elizabeth (Callaghan) C. BS, Purdue U., 1987; MBA, Harvard, 1992. Asst. brand mgr. Procter & Gamble, Cin., 1987-90; cons. Corp. Decision, Boston, 1991; asst. brand mgr. Procter & Gamble, Hunt Valley, Md., 1992-93; mktg. mgr. Levi Strauss & Co., San Francisco, 1993-94; acct. supr. Foote, Conc & Belding, San Francisco, 1994—.

CALIENDO, THEODORE JOSEPH, pediatrician, neonatalogist; b. Bklyn., Nov. 9, 1941; s. Leo J. and Anna C.; m. Arlene Mann, Jan. 7, 1970 (div. Aug. 1984); children: Michael, Robert, Barbra, David. BS, St. John's U., Bklyn., 1962; MD, N.Y. Med. Coll., 1966. Intern, resident Cedars Sinai Med. Ctr., L.A., 1966-69; pediatrician, neonatalogist Kaiser-Permanente, Mission Viejo, Calif., 1973—; attending physician Cedars Sinai Med. Ctr., L.A., 1971-81, Kaiser Hosp., Anaheim, Calif., 1979—; asst. prof. pediatrics UCLA Med. Sch., 1971-82. Lt. comdr. USN, 1969-71. Fellow Am. Acad. Pediatrics; mem. L.A. Pediatric Soc., Ritz Bros., Monarch Bay Club, Rancho Niquel Club, Ferarri Club Am. Office: Kaiser Permanente 23781 Maquina Mission Viejo CA 92691-2716

CALKINS, JERRY MILAN, anesthesiologist, educator, administrator, biomedical engineer; b. Benkelman, Nebr., Sept. 10, 1942; s. Robert Thomas and Mildred Rachel (Stamm) C.; m. Connie Mae Satterfield, Oct. 17, 1964; children: Julie Lynn, Jenifer Ellan. BSChemE, U. Wyo., 1964, MSChemE, 1966; PhD in Chem. Engring., U. Md., 1971; MD, U. Ariz., 1976. Diplomate Am. Bd. Anesthesiology. Lectr. engring. U. Md., College Park, 1970-71; asst. prof. engring. Ariz. State U., Tempe, 1971-73; asst. prof. anesthesiology U. Ariz., Tucson, 1979-84, assoc. prof., 1984; assoc. prof., vice chmn. dept. U. N.C., Chapel Hill, 1984-86; clin. assoc. U. N.Mex., Albuquerque, 1986-88, chmn. dept. anesthesiology Lovelace Med. Ctr., 1986-88; chmn. dept. anesthesiology Maricopa Med. Ctr., Phoenix, 1988—; clin. prof. anesthesiology U. Ariz., 1988—; adj. assoc. prof. indsl. engring. N.C. State U., 1984-86; dir. med. engring. lab. Harry Diamond Labs., Washington, 1968-71; cons. Bur. Med. Devel., FDA, Washington, 1977-86; asst. prof. engring., bd. dir. advanced biotech. Lab. Ariz. Health Sci. Ctr., Tucson, 1979-84. Co-author: Future Anesthesia Delivery Systems, 1984, High Frequency Ventilation, 1986; editor Annals Biomed. Engring., 1979, Clin. Monitoring, 1984—; contbr. numerous articles to profl. jours., chpts. to books. Recipient Outstanding Tchr. award Upjohn Co., 1979; spl. fellow NIH, 1970. Mem. AMA, AICE, Am. Soc. Anesthesiologists, Am. Soc. Artificial Internal Organs, Closed and Lowflow Anesthesia Systems Soc. (pres. 1986-88), Soc. Tech. Anesthesia (pres. 1993—), Ariz. Med. Assn., Ariz. Soc. Anesthesiology, Maricopa County Med. Assn., Masons, Sigma Xi. Republican. Office: Maricopa Med Ctr Phoenix AZ 85010

CALKINS, ROBERT BRUCE, aerospace engineer; b. Pasadena, Calif., Apr. 10, 1942; s. Bruce and Florence May (Bennit) C.; m. Dana B. Ericson. BS in Aerospace Engring., Calif. State Polytech., 1965; BA in Applied Math., San Diego State U., 1970; MS in Computer Sci., Wright State U., 1984. Project engr. U.S. Air Force Flight Test Ctr., El Centro, Calif., 1965-75; sr. engr. U.S. Air Force Aero. Systems Div., Dayton, Ohio, 1975-85; prin. engr. Douglas Aircraft Co., Long Beach, Calif., 1985-90; project engr. McDonnell Douglas Missile Systems Co., Long Beach, 1990—. Recipient U.S. Presidential citation, Fed. Govt., 1967. Fellow AIAA (Disting. Svc. award 1992, assoc., chmn. tech. standards com.); mem. SAFE Assn. (sec. chpt. 1 1991, pres. chpt. 1 1992). Home: 7901 Southwind Cir Huntington Beach CA 92648-5458 Office: McDonnell Douglas 3855 N Lakewood Blvd Long Beach CA 90846-0003

CALL, JOSEPH RUDD, accountant; b. Pensacola, Fla., Oct. 18, 1950; s. Melvin Eliason and Doris Mae (Rudd) C.; m. Nola Jean Pack, Dec. 20, 1973; children: Benjamin, Jeremy, Joshua, Rebecca, Jacob, James. BS, Brigham Young U., 1974. CPA, Calif., Idaho; cert. fin. planner, 1986. Small bus. specialist Deloitte, Haskins & Sells, L.A., 1974-78; audit mgr. Rudd, DaBell & Hill, Rexburg, Idaho, 1978-80, audit ptnr. Rudd & Co., 1980-82, ptnr. in charge Idaho Falls office, 1982—. Mem. task force Small Bus. High Tech. Devel. State of Idaho, 1983; pres. Bonneville-Idaho Falls Crimestoppers, Inc., 1984-85; bd. dirs. Idaho Falls symphony Soc., 1988-91. Mem. Am. Inst. CPAs (hon. mention on CPA exam 1975, exec. coms. pvt. cos. 1989-92, continuing profl. edn. exec. com. 1992—), Calif. Soc. CPAs., Idaho Soc. CPAs (pres. S.E. Idaho chpt. 1983-84, state bd. dirs. 1984-88, pres.-elect 1987, pres. 1988-89), Idaho Falls C. of C. (bd. dirs. 1984-90, chmn. bd. dirs. 1986-87), Rexburg C. of C. (dir. 1981-82), Eastern Idaho Sailing Assn. (rear commodore 1983-89). Mormon. Office: Rudd & Co/Chartered 725 S Woodruff Ave Idaho Falls ID 83401-5286

CALLAGHAN, KATHLEEN MARIE, family nurse practitioner, nursing educator; b. Omaha, Feb. 25, 1950; d. Ambrose James and Marie J. (La Fontaine) C. BSN, Creighton U., 1972; MSN, U. Wyo., 1983, cert. FNP, 1984. Pub. health nurse State of Wyo., Worland, 1979-81; nursing instr. Cen. Wyo. Coll., Riverton, 1984-87; assoc. prof. nursing U. Wyo., Casper, 1987-88; asst. prof. nursing Boise (Idaho) State U., 1988-94; psychiat. nurse practitioner in pvt. practice Boise, 1994—; field coord. Idaho Interdiciplinary Health Rural Tng. Grant, Rural, Idaho, 1992; presenter in field. Mem. adv. bd. dirs. Terry Reilly and Boise Clinic for the Homeless, 1990—, coord. nursing vol. Clinic for Homeless Shelter, 1990—. Malmquist Nursing scholar, 1982. Mem. ANA, Primary Care Nurses Assn., Nat. League for Nursing (instr. test rev. Wyo. and Idaho divs. 1988-92), Idaho Nurses Assn. (chair edn. com. 1990), Soroptomists (Woman of Yr. Worland chpt. 1980), Sigma Theta Tau, Phi Kappa Phi. Home: 5995 Anna St Boise ID 83709-1077 Office: North Edn Ctr Health Resources 1015 W Hays Boise ID 83702

CALLAHAN, MARILYN JOY, social worker; b. Portland, Oreg., Oct. 11, 1934; d. Douglas Q. and Anona Helen (Bergemann) Maynard; m. Lynn J. Callahan, Feb. 27, 1960 (dec.); children: Barbara Callahan Baer, Susan Callahan Sewell, Jeffrey Lynn. BA, Mills Coll., 1955; MSW, Portland State U., 1971, secondary teaching cert., 1963. Bd. cert. diplomate in clin. social work. Developer, adminstr. ednl. program Oreg. Women's Correctional Ctr., Oreg. State Prison, Salem, 1966-67; mental health counselor Benton County Mental Health, Corvallis, Oreg., 1970-71; inst. tchr. Hillcrest Sch., Salem, Oreg., 1975-81; social worker protective svcs. Mid Willamette Valley Sr. Svcs. Agy., Salem, 1981-88; psychiat. social worker dept. forensics Oreg. State Hosp., 1988-93; pvt. practice specializing of adult sexual offenders Salem, 1993—; pvt. practice in care/mgmt. of elderly, 1993—; panel mem. Surgeon Gen.'s N.W. Regional Conf. on Interpersonal Violence, 1987; speaker in field; planner, organizer Seminar on Age Discrimination, 1985. Mem. NASW (bd. dirs. Oreg. chpt.), Acad. Cert. Social Workers (lic. clin. social worker), Oreg. Gerontol. Assn., Catalina 27 Nat. Sailing Assn. Office: Ste 304 780 Commercial St SE Salem OR 97301-3455

CALLAHAN, RONALD, federal investigator, historian; b. San Francisco, Jan. 8, 1947; s. Raymond Edward and Camille (Masucci) C.; m. Delores Leona Cody Callahan, Nov. 15, 1986; children: Randell James Stowe, Miranda Dawn Stowe, Christopher Ronald Callahan, Kimberly Ann Callahan. BS, Calif. State U., 1973, student, 1987-91. Cert. spl. agt. Air traffic controller USAF, Davis-Monthan AFB, Ariz., 1967-68; air trafic controller USAF, Kadena AB, Japan, 1968-70; clk. Franchise Tax Bd., Sacramento, 1973; acct. clk. Employment Devel. Dept., Sacramento, 1973-74; air cargo specialist 82nd Aerial Port Squadron, Travis AFB, Calif., 1978-80; adjudicator VA, San Francisco, 1974-82; historian 349th Mil. Airlift Wing, Travis AFB, Calif., 1980-82, Fourth Air Force, McClellan AFB, Calif., 1986-90; investigator Def. Investigative Svc., Sacramento, 1982—. Author: Annual Histories of McClellan and Travis Air Bases, 1980-82, 86-90, Airpower Journal, 1991-93. Vol. El Dorado County Juvenile Svc. Coun., Placerville, Calif., 1992-93, Calvary Refuge, Sacramento, Marysville, Calif., 1992—, Grace Cmty. Ch., Pleasant Valley, Calif., 1993—; adult literacy tutor El Dorado County Literacy Action Coun., Placerville, 1994—. Sgt. USAF, 1966-70. Named Dean's Honors list Calif. State U., Sacramento, 1971, 72; recipient Spl. Act award Def. Investigative Svc., Sacramento, 1983, Air Force Commendation medal USAF, McClellan AFB, Calif., 1989. Mem. Air Force Assn., Orgn. Am. Historians, Am. Christian History Inst., Friends of Libr., Grace Cmty. Ch., Calvary Refuge, Phi Alpha Theta. Republican. Home: 1640 Glen Dr Placerville CA 95667-9302 Office: Defense Investigative Svc 2973 Fulton Ave Sacramento CA 95821-4909

CALLAN, JOSI IRENE, museum director; b. Yorkshire, Eng., Jan. 30, 1946; came to U.S., 1953; d. Roger Bradshaw and Irene (Newbury) Winstanley; children: James, Heather, Brett Jack; m. Patrick Marc Callan, June 26, 1984. BA in Art History summa cum laude, Calif. State U., Dominguez Hills, 1978, MA in Behavioral Scis., 1981. Dir. community rels./alumni affairs Calif. State U., Dominguez Hills; adminstrv. fellow office chancellor Calif. State U., Long Beach, assoc. dir. univ. svcs. office chancellor, 1979-85; dir. capital campaign, assoc. dir. devel. Sta. KVIE-TV, Sacramento, 1985-86; dir. project devel. Pacific Mountain Network, Denver, 1986-87; dir. mktg. and devel. Denver Symphony Orch., 1988-89; assoc. dir. San Jose (Calif.) Mus. Art, 1989-91, dir., 1991—; asst. prof. sch. social and behavioral scis. Calif. State U., Dominguez Hills, 1981—; mem. adv. com. Issues Facing Mus. in 1990s JKF U., 1990-91. Mem. com. arts policy Santa Clara Arts Coun., 1990-92; chair San Jose Arts Roundtable, 1992-93; active ArtTable, 1992—, Community Leadership San Jose, 1992-93, Am. Leadership Forum, 1994; mem. adv. bd. Bay Area Rsch. Project, 1992—; mem. Calif. Arts Coun., Visual Arts Panel, 1993, Santa Clara Arts Coun. Visual Arts Panel, 1993; bd. dirs. YWCA, 1993—. Recipient Leadership award Knight Found., 1995; fellow Calif. State U., 1982-83. Mem. AAUW, Am. Assn. Mus., Nat. Soc. Fund Raising Execs. (bd. dirs. 1991), Colo. Assn. Fund Raisers, Art Mus. Devel. Assn., Assn. Art Mus. Dirs., We. Mus. Assn., Calif. State U. Alumni Coun. (pres. 1981-83), Rotary Internat., Knight Found. (leadership award, 1995). Office: San Jose Mus Art 110 S Market St San Jose CA 95113-2383

CALLAN, PATRICK M., educational executive, educator; b. Tacoma, Wash., Oct. 7, 1942; s. Mark and Mary Callan; m. Josi I. Bradshaw. BA in History, U. Santa Clara, 1964, MA in History, 1966; postgrad., UCLA, 1968-71, Stanford U., 1989—. Staff dir. joint legis. com. on master plan for higher edn. Calif. State Legislature, Sacramento, 1971-73; dir. Mont. Commn. on Postsecondary Edn., Helena, 1973-74; exec. dir. Wash. State Coun. for Postsecondary Edn., Olympia, 1975-78, Calif. Postsecondary Edn. Commn., Sacramento, 1978-86; v.p. Edn. Commn. of States, Denver, 1986-89, sr. cons., 1989-91; dir. Calif. Higher Edn. Policy Ctr., San Jose, 1991-92, exec. dir., 1992—; pres. Higher Edn. Policy Inst., San Jose, Calif., 1992—; mem. faculty Far East Divsn.-U. Md., 1966, 67, Grad. Sch. Edn. Syracuse U., 1974, Grad. Sch. Edn.-Inst. Edn. Mgmt. Harvard U., 1982, 83, 91; commr. Edn. Commn. of States, 1975-78, mem. nat. working party on effective action to improve undergrad. edn., 1985-86, mem. nat. task force for minority in achievement in higher edn., 1989-91; commr. Western Interstate Commn. for Higher Edn., Wash., 1975-78, Calif., 1978-82, 84-86, chair, 1982, 93, mem. western tech. manpower coun., 1981-82; mem. adv. coun. area higher edn. U. Wash., 1975-78; mem. nat. bd. Fund for Improvement Postsecondary Edn., 1979-82; mem. panel on governance and control of higher edn. Carnegie Found. for Advancement of Tchg., 1979-82; bd. advisors Servicemembers Opportunity Colls., 1986-89, Ctr. for Studies in Higher Edn. U. Calif-Berkeley, 1989—; spl. cons. Calif. State Legislature, Sacramento, 1981; mem. dean's adv. coun. Sch. Edn. U. Colo., Denver, 1987-89; mem. nat. adv. panel Nat. Ctr. for Postsecondary Governance and Fin., 1987-91; lectr. Sch. Edn. Stanford (Calif) U., 1992; active Joint Com. on Future of Self-Regulation in Higher Edn., 1993; cons. in field. Author: (with Calvin Fraser) What State Leaders Can Do to Help Change Teacher Education, 1990, (with Joni E. Finney) By Design or Default?, 1993, The California Higher Education Policy Vacuum, 1993; editor Environ. Planning for Strategic Leadership, New Directions for Higher Edn., 1986; contbg. editor Perspectives on Postsecondary Edn.: An Annotated Bibliography, 1981; mem. editl. bd. Planning for Higher Edn., 1975-80; contbr. articles to profl. jours. Bd. trustees Stanford Homes Found., Sacramento, Calif., 1979-84; bd. dirs. Eleanor McClatchy Ctr. for Performing Arts, Sacramento, 1979-81; commr. Calif. Pub. Broadcasting Commn., 1978-83; active Calif. Student Loan Authority, 1978-84. 1st lt. USAR, 1967-69. Recipient Outstanding Young Man in Am. award, 1977, 78; named One of Top One Hundred Young Leaders, Change Mag., 1978. Mem. Western Assn. Schs. and Colls. (mem. accrediting commn. for sr. colls. and univs.). Office: Calif Higher Edn Policy Ctr 160 W Santa Clara St Ste 704 San Jose CA 95113-1700

CALLAWAY, LINDA MARIE, special education educator; b. Upland, Calif., June 21, 1940; d. Elwyn T. and Fladger Idell (Flake) Bice; m. David Barry Callaway, May, 1957 (div. sept. 1962); children: Tess Callaway Tyler, Darren Francis. B in English, Calif. State U., Fullerton, 1975; MEd Adminstrn., Calif. State U., L.A., 1991. Cert. tchr., Calif. Tchr. multiply-handicapped children L.A. County Office Edn., Downey, 1984-88; tchr. spl. day class Pomona (Calif.) Unified Sch. Dist., 1988-90, resource specialist spl. edn., 1990-93; resource specialist Spl. Edn. Mt. Baldy Joint Sch. Dist., 1994-95; mem. subcom. Master Plan, Claremont, Calif., 1994. Writer, editor Tempo Jour. Inland Valley, 1993, 94. Calif. State U. monetary grantee, 1990-91. Mem. Am. Inst. Wine and Food (assoc.). Republican. Soc. of

Friends. Home: 1071 E Alvarado Pomona CA 91767-5137 Office: Etiwanda Sch Dist P O Box 248 Rancho Cucamonga CA 91739

CALLEMAN, CARL JOHAN, toxicologist; b. Stockholm, May 15, 1950; came to U.S., 1985; s. Carl Birger and Eva Margareta Calleman. BS, U. Stockholm, 1976, PhD, 1984. Rsch. asst. U. Stockholm, 1974-85; acting head dept. environ. carcinogenesis Pacific N.W. Rsch. Found., Seattle, 1986; sr. rsch. fellow dept. environ. health U. Wash., Seattle, 1986—; vis. scientist dept. medicinal chemistry U. Wash., Seattle, 1987; mem. adv. panel ethylene oxide Chem. Industry Inst. Toxicology, Research Triangle Park, N.C., 1990—; sci. expert Internat. Agy. on Rsch. in Cancer, Lyon, France, 1993-94. Author: The Maya Hypothesis, 1994. Home: 525 S Washington St Seattle WA 98104 Office: U Wash SC-34 Dept Environ Health Seattle WA 98195

CALLEN, ELNORA STOLLER, nurse, mental retardation professional; b. Lewistown, Mont., Feb. 11, 1935; d. Edward T. and Hilja Alice (Hannula) Stoller; (div. 1965); children: Susan M., John M., Shirley A., Thomas E. (dec.), William F., Katherine E. Student, Great Falls (Mont.), Sch. Practical Nursing, 1966; ADN, No. Mont. Coll., 1970; BA in Psychology and Health Scis., Ft. Wright Coll. Holy Names, 1974. RN, Wash. LPN Deaconess Hosp., Great Falls, Mont., 1966-68; RN staff nurse Deaconess Hosp., Great Falls, 1970; staff nurse Deaconess Hosp., Spokane, 1970-72, Holy Family Hosp., Spokane, 1972-74; RN therapist Community Mental Health Ctr., Spokane, 1975; alcoholism counselor, nurse Community Personal Guidance Ctr., Community Alcohol Bd., Spokane, 1977; skilled lab. instr. ADN nursing program Lewis-Clark State Coll., Lewiston, Idaho, 1978-79; RN II, qualified mental retardation profl. State of Wash., Dept. Social and Health Svcs., Medical Lake, 1982—; coll. health ctr. RN Fort Wright Coll. of the Holy Names, Spokane, 1971-74; part time RN charge nurse newborn/premature nursery St. Joseph's Hosp., Lewiston, summer 1978, part time RN float, summer 1979; mem. bd. dirs. Am. Heart Assn., Spokane, 1980-82; RN cons. Social Detoxification Ctr., Spokane (Wash.) Alcoholism Care Ctr., 1981-82. vol. RN disaster nursing Washington Red Cross, 1978-82; visual and hearing screening, vol. worker ARC-Pub. Elem. Schs., Spokane, 1982; campaign worker Rep. Party, Spokane, 1985-86. Recipient scholarship No. Mont. Coll., 1969, George B. Boland Nurses scholarship Gonzaga U., 1979. Mem. Eagles Aux., Sisters of Holy Names (assoc.), Alpha Chi. Roman Catholic. Home: 2010 E 12th Ave Spokane WA 99202-3519

CALLEN, LON EDWARD, county official; b. Kingman, Kans., Mar. 31, 1929; s. Cleo Paul and Josephine Nell (Mease) C.; BA in Math. and Physics, U. Wichita (Kans.), 1951; m. Barbara Jean Sallee, Oct. 12, 1954; children: Lon Edward, Lynnette J. Commd. 2d lt. USAF, 1951, advanced through grades to lt. col., 1968; comdr. Tuslog Detachment 93, Erhac, Turkey, 1966-67; sr. scientist Def. Atomic Support Agy., Washington, 1967-71; ret., 1971; dir. emergency preparedness City-County of Boulder, Colo., 1976—; bd. dirs. Boulder County Emergency Med. Svcs. Coun., 1977, Boulder County Amateur Radio Emergency Svcs., 1978—. Mem. hon. awards com. Nat. Capital Area council Boy Scouts Am., 1971; chmn. Boulder County United Fund, 1976-82; mem. asst. staff Indian Princesses and Trailblazer programs Boulder YMCA, 1974-78. Decorated Joint Svc. Commendation medal; recipient cert. achievement Def. Atomic Support Agy., 1970. Mem. AAAS, Am. Ordnance Soc., Am. Soc. Cybernetics, Planetary Soc., Math. Assn. Am., N.Y. Acad. Scis., Fedn. Am. Scientists, Nat. Assn. Atomic Vets., Union Concerned Scientists, Boulder County Fire Fighters Assn., Colo. Emergency Mgmt. Assn., Ret. Officers Assn., Colo. Front Range Protective Assn., Mensa, Sigma Xi, Pi Alpha Pi. Clubs: Boulder Knife and Fork, Boulder Gunbarrel Optimists, Denver Matrix, U. Colo. Ski, U. Wichita. Author articles in field. Home: 4739 Berkshire Ct Boulder CO 80301-4055 Office: Box 471 County Courthouse Boulder CO 80306

CALLENDER, JONATHAN FERRIS, environmental consultant; b. L.A., Nov. 7, 1944; s. Robert Ford and Ruth Merigold (Ferris) C.; m. Cynthia E. Bennett, Aug. 16, 1967 (div. Apr. 1982); children: Katherine, Elizabeth, Jennifer, Sarah. BS, Calif. Inst. Tech., 1966; AM, Harvard U., 1968, PhD in Geology, 1975. Asst. prof. U. N.Mex., Albuquerque, 1972-77, assoc. prof., 1977-84, asst. chmn. geology dept., 1979-81, adj. prof. geology, 1985-90; chief sci. programs N.Mex. Mus. Natural History, Albuquerque, 1983-84, dir., 1984-90, also bd. dirs.; v.p., prin. Adrian Brown Cons., Denver, 1990—; adj. prof. geology N.Mex. Inst. Mining and Tech., Socorro, 1985-90. Editor numerous books on N.Mex. geology; author numerous tech. papers in field. Active N.Mex. First, 1986-90, Hispanic Cultural Found., Albuquerque, 1986-90; bd. dirs. N.Mex. Mus. Found., 1984-90. Nat. Sci. Found. fellow, 1971-72; recipient Presdl. Recognition award U. N.Mex., 1982. Fellow Geol. Soc. Am.; mem. AAAS (sect. bd. mem. 1988-92), Am. Assn. Petroleum Geologists, Am. Geophys. Union (chmn. transl. bd. 1985—), N.Mex. Geol. Soc. (hon., pres. 1977). Home and Office: Callender Enterprises 2525 S Dahlia St Denver CO 80222-6557

CALLIES, QUINTON CARL, allergist; b. Lomira, Wis., Sept. 16, 1930. MD, U. Wis. Intern Metro Gen. Hosp., Cleve., 1960-61; immunologist U. Mich. Hosp., Ann Arbor, 1961-64, fellow in allergy medicine, 1964-66; now allergist Scottsdale (Ariz.) Meml. Hosps.; asst. prof. medicine Mayo Med. Sch. Office: 13400 E Shea Blvd Scottsdale AZ 85259-5404*

CALLISON, JAMES R., plastic surgeon; b. Columbia, Ky., 1933. MD, Vanderbilt U., 1958. Intern Vanderbilt Hosp., Nashville, 1958-59; surgeon Mass. Gen. Hosp., Boston, 1959-60, 62-65; plastic surgeon Pitts. Med. Ctr., 1965-67; now plastic surgeon St. Joseph's Hosp., Phoenix. Fellow ACS. Office: 2218 N 3rd St Phoenix AZ 85004-1401*

CALLISON, NANCY FOWLER, nurse; b. Milw., July 16, 1931; d. George Fenwick and Irma Esther (Wenzel) Fowler; m. B.G. Callison, Sept. 25, 1954 (dec. Feb. 1964); children: Robert, Leslie, Linda. Diploma, Evanston Hosp. Sch. Nursing, 1952; BS, Northwestern U., 1954. RN, Calif.; cert. case mgr. Staff nurse, psychiat. dept. Downey VA Hosp., 1954-55; staff nurse Camp Lejeune Naval Hosp., 1955, 59-61; obstet. supr. Tri-City Hosp., Oceanside, Calif., 1961-62; pub. health nurse San Diego County, 1962-66; sch. nurse Rich-Mar Union Sch. Dist., San Marcos, Calif., 1966-68; head nurse San Diego County Community Mental Health, 1968-73; dir. patient care services Southwood Mental Health Ctr., Chula Vista, Calif., 1973-75; program cons. Comprehensive Care Corp., Newport Beach, Calif., 1975-79; dir. Manpower Health Care, Culver City, Calif., 1979-80; dir. nursing services Peninsula Rehab. Ctr., Lomita, Calif., 1980-81; clinic supr., coordinator utilization and authorizations, acting dir. provider relations Hawthorne (Calif.) Community Med. Group, 1981-86; mgr. Health Care Delivery Physicians of Greater Long Beach, Calif., 1986-87; cons. Quality Rev. Assocs., West L.A., 1988-93; case mgr. Mercy Physicians Med. Group, 1992-93; med. mgmt. specialist The Zenith Ins., 1993—; clin. coord., translator Flying Samaritans, 1965—, mem. internat. bd. dirs., 1975-77, 79-86, 89—, dir. San Quentin project, 1991-93, pres. South Bay chpt., 1975-81, v.p., 1982-85, bd. dirs. San Diego chpt., 1987-90, pres. San Diego chpt. 1991-92, adminstr. Clinica Esperanza de Infantil Rosarito Beach 1990-93. Mem. Rehab. Nurse Coord. Network, U.S.-Mex. Border Health Assn., Calif. Assn. of Quality Assurance Profls., Cruz Roja Mexicana (Delegacion Rosarito 1986-92), Baja Bush Pilots.

CALLISON, RUSSELL JAMES, lawyer; b. Redding, Calif., Sept. 4, 1954; s. Walter M. and Norma A. (Bruce) C. BA in Polit. Sci., U. of Pacific, 1977, JD cum laude, 1980. Bar: Calif. 1980, U.S. Dist. Ct. (ea. dist.) Calif. 1981, U.S. Dist. Ct. (no. dist.) Calif. 1986, U.S. Ct. Appeals (9th cir.) 1989. Assoc. Memering & DeMers, Sacramento, Calif., 1980-85; pres. DeMers, Callison & Donovan, P.C., Sacramento, 1985—, 1994—; spl. master Calif. State Bar, 1991—; arbitrator, judge pro tem Sacramento County Superior Ct., 1986—. Capt. fund raising Met. YMCA, Sacramento, 1986—. Mem. ABA (litigation sect.), SAR (chpt. pres. 1992-93), Am. Arbitration Assn. (panel of arbitrators), Sacramento County Bar Assn., Assn. Def. Counsel No. Calif., Commonwealth Club, Rio Del Oro Racquet Club, Order ofCoif, Phi Alpha Delta. Republican. Episcopalian. Home: 1891 11th Ave Sacramento CA 95818-4142 Office: DeMers Callison & Donovan 7919 Folsom Blvd Ste 210 Sacramento CA 95826-2617

CALLISTER, LOUIS HENRY, JR., lawyer; b. Salt Lake City, Aug. 11, 1935; s. Louis Henry and Isabel (Barton) C.; m. Ellen Gunnell, Nov. 27, 1957; children: Mark, Isabel, Jane, Edward, David, John Andrew, Ann. BS, U. Utah, 1958, JD, 1961. Bar: Utah 1961. Asst. atty. gen. Utah, 1961; sr. ptnr. Callister Nebeker & McCullough (formerly Callister, Duncan & Nebeker), Salt Lake City, 1961—; bd. dirs. Am. Stores Co., Quailbluff Devel. Co. Vice-chmn. Salt Lake City Zoning Bd. Adjustment, 1979-84; bd. govs. Salt Lake Valley Hosps., 1983-91; treas. exec. com. Utah Rep. Com., 1965-69; chmn. Utah chpt. Rockefeller for Pres. Com., 1964-68; sec., trustee Salt Lake Police/Sheriff Hon. Cols., 1982—; trustee, mem. exec. com. Utah Econ. Devel. Corp., 1992—, U. Utah, 1987—, vice-chmn., 1989—, bd. dirs. U. Utah Hosp., 1993—. Mormon. Home: 1454 Tomahawk Dr Salt Lake City UT 84103 Office: Callister Nebeker & McCullough 900 Kennecott Building Bldg Salt Lake City UT 84133-1102

CALLISTER, MARION JONES, federal judge; b. Moreland, Idaho, June 6, 1921; m. Nina Lynn Hayes, June 7, 1946; children—Nona Lynn Callister Haddock, Lana Sue Callister Meredith, Jenny Ann Callister Thomas, Tamara Callister Banks, Idonna Ruth Callister Andersen, Betty Patricia Callister Jacobs, Deborah Jean Hansen, Mary Clarice Fowler, David Marion, Nancy Irene Callister Garvin, Michelle, Kimberly Jane. Student, Utah State U., 1940-41; B.S.L., U. Utah, 1950, J.D., 1951. Bar: Idaho 1951. Dep. pros. atty. Bingham County, Idaho, 1951-52; asst. U.S. atty. Dist. of Idaho, 1953-57, U.S. atty., 1975-76; pvt. practice, 1958-69; judge Idaho Dist. Ct. 4th Jud. Dist., 1970-75; judge U.S. Dist. Ct. Idaho, Boise, 1976—, chief judge, 1981-88. Served with U.S. Army, 1944-46. Decorated Purple Heart. Republican. Mormon. Office: US Dist Ct MSC 040 550 W Fort St Boise ID 83724-0101

CALLOS, JOHN DOUGLAS, banker; b. Long Beach, Calif., May 23, 1962; s. John P. and Lynda Jean (Lathrop) C.; m. April Dawn Callos, July 6, 1990; 1 child, Connor William Lathrop. BS in Bus., U. So. Calif., 1985. Lic. contractor, Calif. Comml. loan officer Bank of Am., L.A., 1984-86; asst. v.p. Wells Fargo Bank, El Monte, Calif., 1986-88, Bank of Boston, L.A., 1988-89; v.p. Security Pacific Bank, L.A., 1989-92; sr. v.p. Calif. United Bank, Encino, 1992—. Vice chair retail subcom., chmn. comml. and retail devel. Long Beach (Calif.) Econ. Partnership, 1992; bd. dirs. area coun. Boy Scouts Am., Long Beach, 1992-93; vice chmn. Long Beach Econ. Devel. Commn., 1992—; bd. mem. Long Beach Cert. Devel. Corp., 1993. Republican. Home: 5300 E El Prado Ave Long Beach CA 90815-3909 Office: Calif United Bank NA 16030 Ventura Blvd Encino CA 91436-2731

CALLOW, KEITH MCLEAN, judge; b. Seattle, Jan. 11, 1925; s. Russell Stanley and Dollie (McLean) C.; m. Evelyn Case, July 9, 1949; children: Andrea, Douglas, Kerry. Student, Alfred U., 1943, CCNY, 1944, Biarritz Am. U., 1945; BA, U. Wash., 1949, JD, 1952. Bar: Wash. 1952, D.C. 1974. Asst. atty. gen. Wash., 1952; law clk. to justice Supreme Ct. Wash., 1953; dep. pros. atty. King County, 1954-56; ptnr. Little, LeSourd, Palmer, Scott & Slemmons, Seattle, 1957-62, Barker, Day, Callow & Taylor, 1964-68; judge King County Superior Ct., 1969-71, Ct. of Appeals Wash., Seattle, 1972-84; presiding chief judge Ct. of Appeals Wash., 1985-90; justice State Supreme Ct. Wash., Olympia, 1985-90, chief justice, 1989-90; 2d v.p. Conf. of Chief Justices; Bonneville Power Admin. Rate Hearings Officer, 1995—; lectr. bus. law U. Wash., 1956-62, Shefelman Disting. lectr., 1991; faculty Nat. Jud. Coll., 1980, Seattle U. Environ. Law, 1992, 94, 95—; co-organizer, sec. Coun. of Chief Judges of Cts. of Appeals; Rep. of Estonia, 1993, 94, 95, advisor Nat. Ct. and Ministry of Justice. Editor-in-chief Commercial Law Desk Book, 1992—; editor works in field. Chief Seattle coun. Boy Scouts Am.; adviser Gov. Health Care Commn. State of Washington, 1991-92; pres. Young Men's Rep. Club, 1957. With AUS, 1943-46. Decorated Purple Heart; recipient Brandeis award Wash. State Trial Lawyers Assn., 1981, Douglas award, 1990. Fellow Am. Bar Found.; mem. ABA (chmn. com. on judiciary 1984-90), Wash. State Bar Assn. (mem. exec. com., appellate Judges Conf.), D.C. Bar Assn., Seattle-King County Bar Assn., Estate Planning Coun., Navy League, Rainier Club (sec. 1978, trustee 1989-92), Coll. Club, Forty Nine Club (pres. 1972), Masons, Rotary, Psi Upsilon, Phi Delta Phi.

CALLOWAY, COLIN GORDON, historian educator; b. Keighley, U.K., Feb. 10, 1953; came to U.S., 1982; BA in History, U. Leeds, 1974, PhD of History, 1978. Grad. asst., tutor U. Leeds, Eng., 1976-79; asst. prof. history and Am. studies Coll. Ripon and York St. John, Eng., 1979-82; adj. history lectr. Keene State Coll., N.H., 1982-83; tchr. Springfield (Vt.) H.S., 1983-85; asst. dir., editor Newberry Libr., Chgo., 1985-87; asst. prof. history U. Wyo., Laramie, 1987-91, assoc. prof. history, 1991—; adj. faculty mem. Union Inst., 1992—; vis. assoc. prof. Dartmouth Coll., N.H., 1990, 91, 93; lectr. Wakefield Coll. Tech. and Arts, Eng., 1978-79; cons. N.H. Hist. Soc., 1993—, New Eng. Found. for Humanities, 1989-91. Author: The Western Abenakis of Vermont, 1600-1800: War, Migration and the Survival of an Indian People, 1990, Crown and Calumet: British-Indian Relations, 1783-1815, 1987, The Abenaki, 1989, The Indians of the Northeast, 1991, The AmericanRevolution in Indian Country, 1995; edited works: The World Turned Upside Down: Indian Voices From Early America, 1994, Revolution and Confederation, 1775-1789, 1994, North Country Captives: Selected Narratives of European Captivity Among Ntive Americans in Vermont and New Hampshire, 1992, Dawnland Encounters: Indians and Europeans in Northern New England, 1991, paper, 1992, New Directions in Indian History: A Bibliography of Recent Writings in American Indian History, 1988, paper, 1992; assoc. editor Ethnohistory, 1993—; co-editor series The Indians of the Northeast; contbr. book chpts., ency. entries, articles to profl. jours.; book reviewer in field. Archie K. Davis rsch. grantee N. Caroliniana Soc., 1993, Phillips fund grantee Am Philos. Soc., 1992; grantee NEH, 1985, 87; fellow Yale U., 1989, David Libr. of Am. Revolution, 1989, Vt. Hist. Soc., 1984, NEH, 1989, 83. Mem. Am. Soc. Ethnohistory (chair Heizer prize com. 1992, nominating com. 1991), We. Hist. Assn., Wyo. State Hist. Soc. Office: Dept History Univ Wyoming Laramie WY 82071

CALLOWAY, LARRY, columnist; b. Lovell, Wyo., Nov. 21, 1937; s. Joseph Charles and Frances (Linda) C.; children: Lara, Maia. BA, U. Colo., 1962. Staff writer United Press Internat., 1963-69; gov. and polit. writer The Associated Press, Santa Fe, 1969-79; bureau chief, zoned-edition editor The Albuquerque Jour., 1980-88, featured columnist, 1988—. Stanford U. fellow, 1979-80. Home: PO Box 1534 Santa Fe NM 87504-1534 Office: Albuquerque Jour 328 Galisteo St Santa Fe NM 87501-2606

CALMAN, CRAIG DAVID, writer, actor; b. Riverside, Calif., June 11, 1953. Student, Pacific U., Forest Grove, Oreg., 1971-72, U. de Querétaro, Mex., 1972-73; BA in Motion Picture/TV, UCLA, 1975. Sr. admitting worker UCLA Med. Ctr., 1974-76; actor/playwright Old Globe Theatre, San Diego, 1977-78, Off Broadway and regional, N.Y.C. and East Coast, 1979-86; exec. asst. various film/TV studios and law firms, L.A., 1986-89, Orion Pictures Corp., L.A., 1989-90; Actor with starring roles (TV and film) ADP Industrial, Teamwork, Dog Days, Macbeth, A Trashy Affair, Flesteron in Amazonia, co-starring roles in Commercial Break, Sullivan's Travels; actor with co-starring/lead roles (theatre) in Book of the Dead, Dark Lady of the Sonnets, Hamlet, Rosencrantz and Guildenstern are Dead, Much Ado About Nothing, Too True to be Good, Henry V, The Counterfeit Rose, Richard III, The Rivals, Merchant of Venice, A Day for Surprises, The Tavern, many others. Author play/screenplays: The Turn of the Century, 1982, 89, Strangled Nocturne, 1977, 91, Skidoo Ruins, 1987, 92; author novel: The Turn of the Century, 1994; author one-act plays, screenplays, full-length plays, poetry; writer asst. Hal Roach, Bel Air, Calif., 1987-88. Vol. book reader Recording for the Blind, L.A., 1991—. Recipient Old Globe Theatre Atlas award for best actor in a comedy role for Too True to be Good, 1977-78; Helene Wurlitzer Found. of N.Mex. Writers Residency grantee, 1988. Mem. Screen Actors Guild, Actors Equity Assn. Office: 6632 Lexington Ave Ste 77 Los Angeles CA 90038-1306

CALVERT, KEN, congressman; b. Corona, Calif., June 8, 1953. AA, Chaffey Coll., 1973; BA Econs., San Diego State U., 1975. Corona/ Norco youth chmn. for Nixon, 1968, 82; county youth chmn. rep. Vesey's Dist., 1970, 43d dist., 1972; congl. aide to rep. Vesey, Calif., 1975-79; gen. mgr. Jolly Fox Restaurant, Corona, Calif., 1975-79, Marcus W. Meairs Co., Corona, Calif., 1979-81; pres., gen. mgr. Ken Calvert Real Properties, Corona, Calif., 1981—; Reagan-Bush campaign worker, 1980; co chmn. Wilson for Senate Campaign, 1982, George Deukmejian election, 1978, 82, 86, George Bush election, 1988, Pete Wilson senate elections, 1982, 88, Pete Wilson for Gov. election, 1990; mem. 104th Congress from 43rd Calif. dist., 1993—; mem. natural resources com., sci., space and tech. com., 1993—, also mem. ag. com.; former v.p. Corona/ Norco Rep. Assembly; chmn. Riverside Rep. Party, 1984-88, County Riverside Asset Leasing; bd. realtors Corona/ Norco. Exec. bd. Corona Community Hosp. Corp. 200 Club; mem. Corona Airport adv. commn.; adv. com. Temescal/ El Cerrito Community Plan. Mem. Riverside County Rep. Winners Circle (charter), Lincoln Club (co-chmn., charter, 1986-90), Corona Rotary Club (pres. 1991), Elks, Navy League Corona Norco, Corona C. of C. (pres. 1990), Noroco C. of C., Monday Morning Group, Corona Group (past chmn.), Econ. Devel. Ptnrship., Silver Eagles (March AFB support group, charter). Office: US Ho of Reps 1034 Longworth HOB Washington DC 20515*

CALVERT, PATRICIA VIOLA, dietitian; b. Richmond, Oreg., Apr. 28, 1940; d. Oliver Raymond Trent and Clara Hester (Brooks) Reynolds; m. Lyle Lavern Calvert, Sept. 9, 1962; children: Lyla Dalene Calvert Stensrud. BS, Walla Walla Coll., 1961. Registered dietitian, Oreg. Intern Loma Linda U., 1962; clin. rsch. dietitian, chief Good Samaritan Hosp., Portland, Oreg., 1963-68; food and nutrition supr., clin. rsch. dietitian, chief St. Charles Med. Ctr., Bend, Oreg., 1971—; food and nutrition cons. Pioneer Meml. Hosp., Prineville, Oreg., 1968-74, 87-92, Ctrl. Oreg. Dist. Hosp., Redmond, 1974-75, Batchelor Butte Nursing Home, Bend, 1968-70, Harney Dist. Hosp., Burns, Oreg., 1987-92; menu cons. Soroptimist Sr. Mealsite, Prineville, Oreg., 1992—. City budget com. Redmond City Coun., 1970, 71; deaconess Powell Butte Christian Ch., 1994—. Mem. Am. Dietetic Assn., Oreg. Dietetic Assn. (treas., pres.-elect, pres., nominating chair 1963—). Office: St Charles Med Ctr 2500 NE Neff Rd Bend OR 97701-6015

CALVIN, ALLEN DAVID, psychologist, educator; b. St. Paul, Feb. 17, 1928; s. Carl and Zelda (Engelson) C.; m. Dorothy VerStrate, Oct. 5, 1953; children—Jamie, Kris, David, Scott. B.A. in Psychology cum laude, U. Minn., 1950; M.A. in Psychology, U. Tex., 1951, Ph.D. in Exptl. Psychology, 1953. Instr. Mich. State U., East Lansing, 1953-55; asst. prof. Hollins Coll., 1955-59, assoc. prof., 1959-61; dir. Britannica Center for Studies in Learning and Motivation, Menlo Park, Calif., 1961; prin. investigator grant for automated teaching fgn. langs. Carnegie Found., 1960; USPHS grantee, 1960; pres. Behavioral Research Labs., 1962-74; prof., dean Sch. Edn., U. San Francisco, 1974-78; Henry Clay Hall prof. Orgn. and leadership, 1978—; pres. Pacific Grad. Sch. Psychology, 1984—. Author textbooks. Served with USNR, 1946-47. Mem. Am. Psychol. Assn., AAAS, Sigma Xi, Psi Chi. Home: 1645 15th Ave San Francisco CA 94122-3523 Office: U San Francisco San Francisco CA 94117

CALVIN, DOROTHY VER STRATE, computer company executive; b. Grand Rapids, Mich., Dec. 22, 1929; d. Herman and Christina (Plakmyer) Ver Strate; m. Allen D. Calvin, Oct. 5, 1953; children: Jamie, Kris, Bufo, Scott. BS magna cum laude, Mich. State U., 1951; MA, U. San Francisco, 1988; EdD, U. San Francisco, 1991. Mgr. data processing. Behavioral Rsch. Labs., Menlo Park, Calif., 1972-75; dir. Mgmt. Info. Systems Inst. for Prof. Devel., San Jose, Calif. 1975-76; systems analyst, programmer Pacific Bell Info. Systems, San Francisco, 1976-81; staff mgr., 1981-84; mgr. applications devel. Data Architects Inc., San Francisco, 1984-86; pres. Ver Strate Press, San Francisco, 1986—. Instr., Downtown C.C., San Francisco, 1980-84, Cañada C.C., 1986-92, Skyline Coll., 1988-92, City Coll. of San Francisco, 1992—; mem. computer curriculum adv. coun. San Francisco City Coll., 1982-84. V.p. LWV, Roanoke, Va., 1956-58; pres. Bulliss Purissima Parents Group, Los Altos, Calif., 1962-64; bd. dirs. Vols. for Israel, 1986-87. Mem. NAFE, ACM, IEEE Computer Soc., Assn. Systems Mgmt., Assn. Women in Computing, Phi Delta Kappa. Democrat. Avocations: computing, gardening, jogging, reading. Office: Ver Strate Press 1645 15th Ave San Francisco CA 94122-3523

CALVIN, MELVIN, chemist, educator; b. St. Paul, Minn., Apr. 8, 1911; s. Elias and Rose I. (Hervitz) C.; m. Genevieve Jemtegaard, 1942; children: Elin, Karole, Noel. BS, Mich. Coll. Mining and Tech., 1931, DSc, 1955; PhD, U. Minn., 1935, DSc, 1969; hon. rsch. fellow, U. Manchester, Eng., 1935-37; Guggenheim fellow, 1967; DSc, Nottingham U., 1958, Oxford (Eng.) U., 1959, Northwestern U., 1961, Wayne State U., 1962, Gustavus Adolphus Coll., 1963, Poly. Inst. Bklyn., 1962, U. Notre Dame, 1965, U. Gent, Belgium, 1970, Whittier Coll., 1971, Clarkson Coll., 1976, U. Paris Val-de-Marne, 1977, Columbia U., 1979, Grand Valley U., 1986. With U. Calif., Berkeley, 1937—; successively instr. chemistry, asst. prof., prof., Univ. prof., dir. Lab. Chem. Biodynamics U. Calif., 1963-80, assoc. dir. Lawrence Berkeley Lab., 1967-80; Peter Reilly lectr. U. Notre Dame, 1949; Harvey lectr. N.Y. Acad. Medicine, 1951; Harrison Howe lectr. Rochester sect. Am. Chem. Soc., 1954; Falk-Plaut lectr. Columbia U., 1954; Edgar Fahs Smith Meml. lectr. U. Pa. and Phila. sect. Am. Chem. Soc., 1955; Donegani Found. lectr. Italian Nat. Acad. Sci., 1955; Max Tishler lectr. Harvard U., 1956; Karl Folkers lectr. U. Wis., 1956; Baker lectr. Cornell U., 1958; London lectr., 1961, Willard lectr., 1982; Vanuxem lectr. Princeton U., 1969; Disting. lectr. Mich. State U., 1977; Prather lectr. Harvard U., 1980; Dreyfus lectr. Grinnell Coll., 1981, Berea Coll., 1982; Barnes lectr. Colo. Coll., 1982; Nobel lectr. U. Md., 1982; Abbott lectr. U. N.D., 1983; Gunning lectr. U. Alta., 1983; O'Leary disting. lectr. Gonzaga U., 1984; Danforth lectr. Dartmouth Coll., 1984, Grinnell Coll., 1984; R.P. Scherer lectr. U. S. Fla., 1984; Imperial Oil lectr. U. Western Ont., Can., 1985; disting. lectr. dept. chemistry U. Calgary, Can., 1986; Melvin Calvin lectr. Mich. Tech. U., 1986; Eastman prof. Oxford (Eng.) U., 1967-68. Author: (with G.E.K. Branch) The Theory of Organic Chemistry, 1940, (with others) Isotopic Carbon, 1949, (with Martell) Chemistry of Metal Chelate Compounts, 1952, (with Bassham) Path of Carbon in Photosynthesis, 1957, (with Bassham) Photosynthesis of Carbon Compounds, 1962, Chemical Evolution, 1969, Following the Trail of Light: A Scientific Odyssey, 1992; contbr. articles to chem. and sci. jours. Recipient prize Sugar Research Found., 1950, Flintoff medal prize Brit. Chem. Soc., 1953, Stephen Hales award Am. Soc. Plant Physiologists, 1956, Nobel prize in chemistry, 1961, Davy medal Royal Soc., 1964; Virtanen medal, 1975, Priestley medal, 1978, Am. Inst. Chemists medal, 1979, Feodor Lynen medal, 1983, Sterling B. Hendricks medal, 1983, Melvin Calvin Medal of Distinction Mich. Tech. U., 1985, Nat. Medal of Sci., 1989, John Ericsson Renewable Energy award U.S. Dept. Energy, 1991. Mem. Britain's Royal Soc. London (fgn. mem.), Am. Chem. Soc. (Richards medal N.E. chpt. 1956, Nichols medal N.Y. chpt. 1958, award for nuclear applications in chemistry, pres. 1971, Gibbs medal Chgo. chpt. 1977, Priestley medal 1978, Desper award Cin. chpt. 1981), Am. Acad. Arts and Scis., Nat. Acad. Scis., Royal Dutch Acad. Scis., Japan Acad., Am. Philos. Soc., Sigma Xi, Tau Beta Pi, Phi Lambda Upsilon. Office: U Calif Dept Chemistry Berkeley CA 94720

CALVO, DEBRA LEE GOFF, public relations executive; b. Inglewood, Calif., May 21, 1957; d. Francis Lee and Grace Mae (Finfrock) Goff; m. Angel Luis Calvo, Sept. 15, 1990. BA, UCLA, 1981. V.p. The Dolphin Group, L.A., 1981-87, 88—; asst. mgr. govt. rels. First Interstate Bank, L.A., 1987-88. Coord.: (resource notebook) Medfly Task Force Resource Book, 1990, Disaster in The Wings: Medfly Threat, 1994; contbg. writer World Cup Curriculum, 1994; editor Issues in Food Safety, 1990-94. Adminstrv. asst. to campaign mgr. Deukmejian for Gov., L.A., 1981-82; mem. steering com. govt. rels. UCLA, 1981—, bd. dirs. UCLA Prytanean, 1987—; mem./sponsor Results, 1982-88; mgr. Crime Victims for Ct. Reform, L.A., 1983-86; campaign mgr. No On K Campaign, Newport Beach, Calif., 1988; exec. dir. Alliance for Food & Fiber, L.A., 1989—; mem. Gov. Wilson's Women's Adv. Com., Calif., 1990—; mem. Jr. League of L.A., 1991—; mem. internat. adv. coun. World Food Day, 1992—; bd. dirs. Friends of Coro Found., L.A., 1993—. Named one of Outstanding Young Women of Am. Republican. Presbyterian. Office: The Dolphin Group 10866 Wilshire Blvd Ste 550 Los Angeles CA 90024

CALZA, ROGER ERNEST, animal science genetics and cell biology educator; b. Meriden, Conn., July 10, 1951; m. Stella Margaret Caesar; children: Gina Marguerite, Laura Elizabeth, Paula Therese, Olivia Mary. BS, U. N.H., 1974; PhD, Wash. State U., 1981. Teaching asst. Wash. State U., Pullman, 1976-81; grad. rsch. asst. Yale U., 1977, 80; rsch. asst. Cornell U., 1983-85, French Nat. Rsch. Inst., 1985-86; grad. faculty Wash. State U., 1990, asst. prof., 1986-92, assoc. prof., 1992—. Contbr. 25 articles to profl. jours. Coach Greater Ithaca Activity Ctr. Boxing Program, 1983-84; bd. dirs., mem. steering com. St. Mary's Cath. Sch., 1989-92, mem. parish coun., 1994—. Postdoctoral Rsch. fellow, Albert Einstein Sch. Medicine, 1982-83; Rsch. grantee 1987. Mem. Am. Soc. Animal Sci., KC (4th degree), Phi Sigma, Alpha Zeta. Office: Wash State U Dept Animal Sci Genetics & Cell Biol Pullman WA 99164-6320

CALZOLARI, ELAINE, sculptor; b. Albertson, N.Y., Dec. 30, 1950; d. Oswald Henry and Edith (Jackson) C.; m. Robert A. Paley, May 2, 1986; 1

child, Miranda. Student, Sarah Lawrence Coll., Lacoste, France, 1972; BA magna cum laude, Hofstra U., 1973. artist design team New Denver Airport, 1990, artful cities panelist pub. art symposium Urban Design Forum, Denver, 1990; rules and regulations com. art in pub. places program Colo. Coun. on Arts, Denver, 1991-92; cons. CityTime, 1992—; guest critic pub. art course Colo. Coll., Colorado Springs, 1993. Exhbited in two-person shows and group shows at Denver Art Mus., 1980, 82, Sante Fe Festival of Arts, 1983, Mus. of N.Mex., Santa Fe, 1985, Robinschon Gallery, Denver, 1986, The New Gallery, Houston, 1986, The Aspen (Colo.) Inst., 1986, Gerald Peters Gallery, Dallas, 1986, Internat. Symposium on Electronic Art, Mpls., 1993, etc.; represented in permanent collections including Colo. State U., Ft. Collins, Bosher Assocs., Palm Springs, Calif., Mesa Coll., Grand Junction, Colo., Denver Art Mus., Auraria Higher Edn. Complex, Denver, Piper Jaffary, Mpls., City and County of Denver, etc. Vol. Community Caring Project, Denver, 1991—. Fellow Eagle Valley Arts Coun., 1974, Colo. Coun. on Arts and Humanities, 1984. Mem. Internat. Sculpture Ctr., Urban Design Forum.

CAMARA, JORGE DE GUZMAN, ophthalmologist, educator; b. Ann Arbor, Mich., May 21, 1950; s. Augusto A. and Feliciana (de Guzman) C.; m. Virginia Valdes, June 23, 1977; 1 child, Augusto Carlos. BS in Pre-Medicine, U. Philippines, 1972, MD cum laude, 1976. Diplomate Am. Bd. Ophthalmology. Surg. intern U. Tex, Houston, 1977-78; resident in ophthalmology Baylor Coll. Medicine, Houston, 1978-81, fell in ophthalmic plastic and reconstructive surgery, 1981-82; ophthalmologist Straub Clinic and Hosp., Honolulu, 1982-88; pvt. practice Honolulu, 1988—; asst. prof. U. Hawaii Sch. Medicine, Honolulu, 1982—; cons. Tripler Army Hosp., Honolulu, 1982—; chmn. dept. ophthalmology and otorhinolaryngology St. Francis Med. Ctr., bd. dirs. Bd. dirs. Aloha Med. Mission, Honolulu, 1988—. Fellow Am. Acad. Ophthalmology; mem. AMA, Nawaii Ophthal. Soc. (pub. rels. officer 1984-85), Philippine Med. Assn. Hawaii (pres. 1988—), Hawaii Ophthal. Soc. (pres. 1992). Roman Catholic. Office: 2228 Liliha St Ste 106 Honolulu HI 96817

CAMARILLO, RICHARD JON, professional football player; b. Whittier, Calif., Nov. 29, 1959. Student, Cerritos Jr. Coll., Washington U. With New England Patriots, 1981-87, L.A. Rams, 1988; punter Phoenix Cardinals, 1989-93, Houston Oilers, 1994—. Elected to All Century team U. Wash., Sporting News NFL All-Pro Team, 1983. Office: Houston Oilers 6910 Fannin St Lower Level Houston TX 77030*

CAMBRE, ATHLEO LOUIS, JR., plastic surgeon; b. L.A., Feb. 21, 1954. MD, Case Western Res. U., 1981. Intern U. Colo. Sch. Medicine, Denver, 1981-82, gen. surgeon, 1982-86; burn surgery fellow Cornell-N.Y. Hosp., N.Y.C., 1986-87; plastic surgeon UCLA, 1987-89, Cedars-Sinai Hosp., L.A., 1989—; asst. clin. prof. plastic surgery UCLA. Office: Plastic and Recostruction Surgery 436 N Roxbury Dr Ste 207 Beverly Hills CA 90210-5017*

CAMENZIND, MARK J., research chemist; b. Palo Alto, Calif., Nov. 17, 1956; s. Paul V. and Mildred Martha Camenzind; m. Dorothy L. Hassler. SB in Chemistry, MIT, 1978; PhD in Inorganic Chemistry, U. Calif., Berkeley, 1983. Postdoctoral fellow U. B.C., Vancouver, 1983-86; rsch. chemist Salutar, Inc., Sunnyvale, Calif., 1987, Balazs Analytical Lab., Sunnyvale, 1987—. Contbr. rsch. papers to profl. jours. Mem. ASTM, Semicondr. Equipment and Materials Internat., Am. Chem. Soc., Am. Soc. Mass Spectroscopy, Am. Vacuum Soc. Office: Balazs Analytical Lab 252 Humboldt Ct Sunnyvale CA 94089-1315

CAMERON, BRUCE ANDREW, textile science educator; b. Melbourne, Victoria, Australia, Sept. 23, 1960; came to the U.S., 1986; s. Alexander Cameron and Elizabeth Smith (Gauld) C.; m. Donna Marie Brown, July 4, 1987; 1 child, Christopher William. BSc in Textile Tech. with honors, U. NSW, 1983, PhD in Textile Tech., 1986. Rsch. asst. Bradmill Ltd. Cotton Spinners, Newcastle, Australia, 1981, Australian Wool Corp., Melbourne, Australia, 1982; lab. demonstrator in textile dyeing and finishing U. NSW, Dept. Textile and Tech., 1983-85, profl. officer, 1986; vis. asst. prof. textile sci. U. Wyo., Dept. Home Econs., 1986-92, asst. prof. textile sci., 1992—; ad hoc reviewer grant proposals Nat. Rsch. Initiative Competitive Grants progra USDA, Textile Rsch. Jour.; mem. various coms. U. Wyo.; presenter in field. Contbr. articles to profl. jours. Recipient Australian Wool Corp. Textile Tech. scholarship, 1979-82, U. NSW Chem. Soc. George Wright prize for best performance in organic chemistry, 1982, Commonwealth Australia Postgrad. Rsch. award, 1983-86, Paul Stock Found. Work Study award, 1990, 91, 93; grantee U. Wyo., 1987-88, Wyo. Dept. Agr., 1988-89, Gen. Motors Corp., 1990, USDA Nat. Rsch. Initiative Competitive Grants Program, 1993—, U. Wyo. Major Equipment Fund. Mem. Gamma Sigma Delta, Phi Upsilon Omicron. Office: Univ Wyo PO Box 3354 Laramie WY 82071-3354

CAMERON, CHARLES HENRY, petroleum engineer; b. Greeley, Colo., Oct. 21, 1947; s. Leo Leslie and Naomi Tryphena (Phillips) C.; m. Cheryl Christine Debelock, Aug. 30, 1969; 1 child, Ericka Dawn. AS, Mesa State Coll., 1968; BS in Geology, Mesa Coll., 1978; AS in Hazardous Materials Tech., Front Range C.C., Wesminister, Colo., 1990. Retardation technician Colo. State Home and Tng. Sch., Grand Junction, 1967-69; journeyman carpenter Brotherhood of Carpenters and Joiners, Grand Junction, 1969-76; hydrocompaction mgr. Colo. Dept. Hwys., Grand Junction, 1975-77; rsch. geologist Occidental Oil Shale, Inc., Grand Junction, 1977-78; geol. engr. Cleveland Cliffs Iron Co., Morgantown, W.Va., 1978-81; tech. advisor Ute Indian Tribe, Ft. Duchesne, Utah, 1981-86; natural resources officer U.S. Dept Interior/Bur. Indian affairs, Ft. Duchesne, 1990—; ops. mgr. Charging Ute Corp., Golden, Colo., 1986-87; cons. Golden, 1987-90; natural resources officer, petroleum engr. U.S. Dept. Interior/Bur. of Indian Affairs, Ft. Duchesne, 1990—, hazardous material mgr., freedom of info./privacy act coord., 1990—. Contbr. articles to profl. jours. Mem. Colo. Oil Field Investigators Assn. Home: 255 E 200 N Vernal UT 84078-1713 Office: Bia Uintah Ouray Agy Fort Duchesne UT 84026

CAMERON, JUDITH LYNNE, secondary education educator, hypnotherapist; b. Oakland, Calif., Apr. 29, 1945; d. Alfred Joseph and June Estelle (Faul) Moe; m. Richard Irwin Cameron, Dec. 17, 1967; 1 child, Kevin Dale. AA in Psychol., Sacramento City Coll., 1965; BA in Psychol., German, Calif. State U., 1967; MA in Reading Specialization, San Francisco State U., 1972; postgrad., Chapman Coll.; PhD, Am. Inst. Hypnotherapy, 1987. Cert. tchr., Calif. Tchr. St. Vincent's Catholic Sch., San Jose, Calif., 1969-70, Fremont (Calif.) Elem. Sch., 1970-72, LeRoy Boys Home, LaVerne, Calif., 1972-73; tchr. Grace Miller Elem. Sch., LaVerne, Calif., 1973-80, resource specialist, 1980-84; owner, mgr. Pioneer Take-out Franchises, Alhambra and San Gabriel, Calif., 1979-85; resource specialist, dept. chmn. Bonita High Sch., LaVerne, Calif., 1984—; mentor tchr. in space sci. Bonita Unified Sch. Dist., 1988—, rep. LVTV; owner, therapist So. Calif. Clin. Hypnotherapy, Claremont, Calif., 1988—; bd. dirs., recommending tchr., asst. dir. Project Turnabout, Claremont, Calif.; Teacher-in-Space cons. Bonita Unified Sch. Dist., LaVerne, 1987—; advisor Peer Counseling Program, Bonita High Sch., 1987—; advisor Air Explorers/Edwards Test Pilot Sch., LaVerne, 1987—; mem. Civil Air Patrol, Squadron 68, Aerospace Office, 1988—; selected amb. U.S. Space Acad.-U.S. Space Camp Acad., Huntsville, Ala., 1990; named to national (now internat.) teaching faculty challenger Ctr. for Space Edn., Alexandria, Va., 1990; regional coord. East San Gabiel Valley Future Scientists and Engrs. of Am.; amb. to U.S. Space Camp, 1990; mem. adj. faculty challenger learning ctr. Calif. State U., Dominguez Hills, 1994; rep. ceremony to honor astronauts Apollo 11, White House, 1994. Vol. advisor Children's Home Soc., Santa Ana, 1980-81; dist. rep. LVTV Channel 29, 1991; regional coord. East San Gabriel Valley chpt. Future Scientists and Engrs. of Am., 1992; mem. internat. investigation Commn. UFOs, 1991. Recipient Tchr. of Yr., Bonita H.S., 1989, continuing svc. award, 1992; named Toyolaa Tchr. of Yr., 1994. Mem. NEA, AAUW, Internat. Investigations Com. on UFOs, Coun. Exceptional Children, Calif. Assn. Resource Specialists, Calif. Elem. Edn. Assn., Calif. Tchrs. Assn., Calif. Assn. Marriage and Family Therapists, Planetary Soc., Mutual UFO Network, Com. Sci. Investigation L5 Soc., Challenger Ctr. Space Edn., Calif. Challenger Ctr. Crew for Space Edn., Orange County Astronomers, Chinese Shar-Pei Am., Concord Club, Rare Breed Dog Club (L.A.). Republican. Home: 3257 N La Travesia Dr Fullerton CA 92635-1455 Office: Bonita High Sch 115 W Allen Ave San Dimas CA 91773-1437

CAMERON, MINDY, newspaper editor; m. Bill Berg; 2 children; 1 stepchild. B in Journalism, Pacific U. Exec. prodr./anchor, writer pub. TV Rochester, N.Y. and Boise, Idaho; newspaper reporter Boise and Lewiston, Idaho; assoc. city editor Seattle Times, 1981-83, city editor, 1983-89, dep. editorial page editor, 1989-90, editorial page editor, 1990—; leader workshops Am. Press Inst.; writer, reporter PBS documentary, 1978. Bd. dirs. Pacific U., Northwest Pub. Affairs Network. Mem. Nat. Conf. Editorial Writers (bd. dirs. 1993—), Am. Soc. Newspaper Editors, Soc. Profl. Journalists. Office: Seattle Times Fairview Ave N & John PO Box 70 Seattle WA 98111-0070

CAMERON, PAUL DRUMMOND, research facility administrator; b. Pitts., Nov. 9, 1939; s. Nelson Drummond and Veronica (Witco) C.; m. Virginia May Rusthoi. BA, L.A. Pacific Coll., 1961; MA, Calif. State U., L.A., 1962; PhD, U. Colo., 1966. Asst. prof. psychology Stout State U., Menomonie, Wis., 1966-67, Wayne State U., Detroit, 1967-69; assoc. prof. psychology U. Louisville, Ky., 1970-73, Fuller Grad. Sch. Psychology, Pasadena, Calif., 1976-79; assoc. prof. marriage and family therapy U. Nebr., Lincoln, 1979-80; pvt. practice psychologist Lincoln, 1980-83; chmn. Family Rsch. Inst., Washington, 1982-95, Colo. Springs, 1995—; reviewer Am. Psychologist, Jour. Gerontology, Psychol. Reports; presenter, witness, cons. in field. Author: Exposing the AIDS Scandal, 1988, The Gay 90's, 1993; contbr. articles to profl. jours. Mem. Ea. Psychol. Assn., Nat. Assn. for Rsch. and Treatment of Homosexuality. Republican. Lutheran. Office: Family Rsch Inst PO Box 62640 Colorado Springs CO 80962-2640

CAMMALLERI, JOSEPH ANTHONY, security firm executive, retired air force officer, academic administrator; b. Bronx, N.Y., Feb. 2, 1935; s. Leo Anthony and Angela Marie (Mirandi) C.; BS, Manhattan Coll., 1956; M.S., Okla. State U., 1966; postgrad. Golden Gate U., 1974; children: Anthony R., Aaron L., Thomas K., Jeffrey A. Cert. life ins. instr., Calif. Commd. 2d lt. USAF, 1956, advanced through grades to lt. col., 1973; trainee flight crew, 1956-58; crew mem. B-52, 1958-64; behavioral scientist Aerospace Med. Rsch. Labs., Wright-Patterson AFB, Ohio, 1966-68; EB-66 crew mem. Tahkli AFB, Thailand, 1968-69; faculty mem. dept. life and behavioral scis. USAF Acad. (Colo.), 1969-74, assoc. prof., dir. operational psychology div., 1972-74, B-1 human factors engring. mgr. Air Force Flight Test Center, Edwards AFB, Calif., 1974-76, chief handbook devel., 1976-77; ret., 1977; account exec. Merrill Lynch, Pierce, Fenner & Smith, Sherman Oaks, Calif., 1977-80; acad. program rep. U. Redlands (Calif.), 1980-84, regional dir. admissions assessment, 1984—, mem. faculty Whitehead Ctr., 1979—, assoc. dean admissions, 1986-89; faculty Golden Gate U., 1975-80; account exec. Humanomics Ins., 1989-90; corp. dir. tng. and edn. Fin. West Group, 1990-92, prin. CEO Spectrum Securities, Inc., Westlake Village, Calif., 1992—; adj. faculty Calif. Luth. U., 1990—, Antioch U., 1992—; sec., 7th Ann. Narrow Gauge Conv. Com., Pasadena, Calif., 1986. Contbr. articles to profl. jours. Sec. com. centennial celebration Rio Grande So. Ry., Dolores, Colo., 1991; USAF Acad. Liason Officer, North Los Angeles County, 1992—. Decorated D.F.C., Air medal (5), Meritorious Service medal. Mem. Nat. Ry. Hist. Soc., Ry. and Locomotive Hist. Soc., Rocky Mountain R.R. Club, L.A. Live Steamers, Nat. Model R.R. Assn., Colo. R.R. Hist. Found. (life), Santa Fe Ry. Hist. Soc., USAF Acad. Athletic Assn. (life), DAV, Psi Chi. Home: 601 Hampshire Rd #550 Westlake Village CA 91361-4927 Office: Spectrum Securites Inc 2977 Willow Ln #200 Thousand Oaks CA 91361-4927

CAMMANS, STEPHEN CHARLES, finance executive, former controller; b. Nephi, Utah, Sept. 9, 1954; s. Francis Carolus and Helen (Lunt) C.; m. Victoria Payne, Nov. 17, 1979; children: Miriam, Joseph Lemar. B, Calif. State Polytechnic U., 1978. CPA. Acct. Schultz, Meggelin, et al, Covina, Calif., 1977-87, jr. partner, 1987-89; controller Ameritec Corp., Covina, 1989-92, v.p., 1992—; dir. Hollfelder Found., Covina, 1988—. Asst. scoutmaster Boy Scouts of Am., Covina, 1977-78, scoutmaster, Pomona, Calif., 1982; scout coord. Cub Scouts of Am., Chino, 1989-92. Republican. Home: 11923 Roswell Ave Chino CA 91710-1549 Office: Ameritec Corp 760 Arrow Grand Cir Covina CA 91722-2147

CAMMERMEYER, MARGARETHE, nurse; b. Oslo, Mar. 24, 1942; came to U.S., 1951; d. Jan and Margrethe (Grimsgaard) C.; m. Harvey H. Hawken, Aug. 1965 (div. 1980); children: Matthew, David, Andrew, Thomas. BS, U. Md., 1963; MA, U. Wash., 1976, PhD, 1991. RN, Wash. Enlisted U.S. Army, 1961, advanced through grades to capt., 1965, resigned, 1968; staff nurse VA Hosp., Seattle, 1970-73, clin. nurse specialist in neurology, epilepsy, 1976-81; clin. nurse specialist in neuro-oncology VA Med. Ctr., San Francisco, 1981-86; clin. nurse specialist in neuroscis., nurse rschr., col. VA Med. Ctr., Tacoma, Wash., 1986—; capt. to col. U.S. Army Res., 1972-88; asst. chief nurse, supr. Army Res. Hosp., Oakland, Calif., 1985-88; col. Wash. Army N.G. and N.G. Hosp., Tacoma, 1988—. Coauthor: Neurological Assessment for Nursing Practice, 1984 (named Book of Yr. ANA), Serving in Silence, 1994; co-editor, contbg. author: Core Curriculum for Neuroscience Nursing, 1990; contbr. articles to profl. publs. Decorated Bronze Star medal; recipient presdl. cert. for outstanding community achievement of Vietnam era vets., 1979, "A" Proficiency designation Office of Surgeon Gen. Dept. of Army, 1986, Woman of Power award NOW, 1993; named Woman of Yr. Woman's Army Corps Vets. Assn., 1984, Nurse of Yr. VA, 1985. Mem. Feminist Majority Found., Am. Assn. Neurosci. Nursing (chair core task force), Am. Nurses Assn. (hon. human rights award 1994), Wash. State Nurses Assn., Assn. Mil. Surgeons of U.S., Sigma Theta Tau. Home: 1715 S 234th St Seattle WA 98198-7522 Office: Am Lake VA Med Ctr Tacoma WA 98493

CAMPBELL, ADDISON JAMES, JR., writer; b. Dilliner, Pa., Dec. 16, 1933; s. Addison James Campbell and Nora Lee (Marshall) Reynolds; m. Fumie Murashige, Oct. 13, 1962; 1 child, Gary Clark Campbell. Author: Nanci's World, Ukulele Lil of Lihue, The Object; contbr. numerous articles to profl. jours. Sgt. USMC, 1952-55.

CAMPBELL, ALICE DEL CAMPILLO, biochemist, researcher; b. Santurce, Puerto Rico, May 30, 1928; d. José Adrian and Julia Pilar (Rivera) del Campillo; m. Allan McCulloch Campbell, Sept. 5, 1958; children: Wendy Alice, Joseph Lindsay. AB, Columbia U., 1947; MS, NYU, 1953; PhD, U. Mich., 1960. Research asst. Pub. Health Research Inst., N.Y.C., 1947-48, NYU, 1948-54; instr. biochemistry Sch. Medicine, San Juan, Puerto Rico, 1954-56; research assoc. U. Rochester, N.Y., 1960-68; sr. research assoc. Stanford U., Calif., 1968—. Contbr. articles to sci. jours. Fellow Am. Inst. Chemists; mem. Am. Chem. Soc., Sigma Xi (sec., treas. 1985-86, v.p. Stanford chpt. 1986-87), Phi Sigma (Beta chpt.). Home: 947 Mears Ct Stanford CA 94305-1041 Office: Stanford U Dept Biol Scis Stanford CA 94305

CAMPBELL, ARTHUR WALDRON, lawyer, educator; b. Bklyn., Mar. 29, 1944; s. Wilburn Camrock and Janet Louise (Jobson) C.; m. Drusilla Newlon Green, June 7, 1969; children: Wilburn Camrock, Matthew Patrick. BA, Harvard U., 1966; JD, W.Va. U., 1971; M in Criminal Justice, Georgetown U., 1975. Bar: W.Va. 1971, D.C. 1971, Calif. 1974. Asst. U.S. atty. U.S. Justice Dept., Washington, 1971-73; clin. instr. D.C. Consortium Univs., 1973-76; law prof. Calif. Western Sch. Law, San Diego, 1976—; cons. W.Va. State Legis. Com. to Rewrite Criminal Code, 1972-73; chmn. Va. sect. Nat. Assn. Criminal Def. Lawyers Strike Force on Grand Jury Abuse, 1975-76; mem. ABA Com. on Privacy, Washington, 1974, D.C. Bar Landlord and Tenant Com., 1975, Neighborhood Legal Svcs., San Diego, 1982; pvt. prac. 1976—; chief exec. officer Trudar Prodns. Inc., San Diego, 1981—; devel. real estate Trudar Prodns. Inc., 1982—. Author: (legal treatise) Law of Sentencing, 1978, 2d edit., 1991, (coursebook) Entertainment Law, 1993, (books) Discoveries of a Workaholic, 1988, Meditations for Recovering Workaholics, 1990. Pres. Peace Store, San Diego, 1986. Recipient Harvard Nat. scholarship, 1962-63, Am. Jurisprudence awrd Lawyers Coop. Pub. Co., 1970-71, Prettyman Fellowship, Georgetown U., 1971-73; middle weight boxing champion Harvard U., 1964-65. Mem. Fed. Defenders, Appellate Defenders, Peace Through Law Inst., World Svc. Orgn. for Workaholics Anonymous (sec. 1990-91), San Diego Workaholics Anonymous (founder). Home: 4891 Sparks Ave San Diego CA 92110-1358 Office: Calif Western Sch Law 225 Cedar St San Diego CA 92101-3046

CAMPBELL, BARBARA ANN, state official, director; b. Trenton, N.J., July 12, 1957; d. Peter Francis and Adele Virgina (Osiecki) C. BA, Lewis U., 1978; MA, Ea. Ill. U., 1979. Legis. liaison Alliance of Am. Insurers, Schamburg, Ill., 1983-86; mgr. tech. and product devel. Ill. State Dept. of Commerce and Cmty. Affairs, Chgo., 1986-90; spl. asst. tech. transfer Wash. State Dept. of Trade and Econ. Devel., 1990—. Dir. small bus. and govt. affairs Chgo. C. of C., 1980-83. Home and Office: 12318 NE 100th Pl Kirkland WA 98033-4675

CAMPBELL, BEN NIGHTHORSE, senator; b. Auburn, Calif., Apr. 13, 1933; m. Linda Price; children: Colin, Shanan. BA, Calif. U., San Jose, 1957. Educator Sacramento Law Enforcement Agy.; mem. Colo. Gen. Assembly, 1983-86, U.S. Ho. Reps., 1987-93; U. S. Senator from Colorado, 1993—; rancher, jewelry designer, Ignacio, Colo. Chief No. Cheyenne Tribe. Named Outstanding Legislator Colo. Bankers Assn., 1984, Man of Yr. LaPlata Farm Bur., Durango, Colo., 1984; named one of Ten Best Legislators Denver Post/Channel 4, 1986. Mem. Am. Quarter Horse Assn., Am. Brangus Assn., Am. Indian Edn. Assn. Republican. Office: US Senate 380 Russell Senate Bldg Washington DC 20510

CAMPBELL, CAROLE ANN, sociology educator; b. Gallup, N.Mex., July 6, 1949; d. Albert James and Dorothy Elaine (Kauzlarich) Baumgardner; m. John H. Campbell (div.); 1 child, Jameel. BA summa cum laude, U. Albuquerque, 1978; MA, U. Colo., Denver, 1979; PhD, U. Colo., Boulder, 1984. Teaching and rsch. asst. U. Albuquerque, 1976-78; teaching and rsch. asst. U. Colo., Denver, 1978-79, Boulder, 1980-84; instr. sociology U. Nev., Las Vegas, 1985-86; assoc. prof. sociology Calif. State U., Long Beach, 1986—. Contbr. articles to profl. jours. AIDS educator, field placement coord. Calif. State U., Long Beach, 1986—. Mem. Am. Med. Writers Assn. Democrat. Office: Calif State U Dept Sociology 1250 N Bellflower Blvd Long Beach CA 90840-0006

CAMPBELL, CAROLYN MARGRET, communications consultant; b. Washington, Sept. 11, 1949; d. Donald Herman and Josephine Anne (Conrad) C. BA in Interior Design summa cum laude, Md. Inst. Coll. Art, 1971. Dir. spl. events Corcoran Gallery Art, Washington, 1977-79, dir. pub. rels., 1977-83; pub. rels. cons. Washington, 1983-85; dir. pub. info. Am. Film Inst., L.A., 1985; v.p. Josh Baran & Assocs., Venice, Calif., 1986-88; pres. Campbell Communications, L.A., 1988—. Named one of Outstanding Young Women Am., 1982, 83. Mem. Pub. Rels. Soc. Am. (Thoth Cert. Excellence 1979), ArtTable (membership and program coms.), Calif. & West Coast New Art Assn. (founder 1985, bd. dirs. 1985-90). Home and Office: 8530 Holloway Dr Apt 226 Los Angeles CA 90069-2477

CAMPBELL, CHARLES CURTIS, healthcare consultant; b. Orange, Calif., Dec. 16, 1944; s. J.M. Bill Campbell and Elizabeth M. (Burnham) Davis; m. Grace Lyn Buttermore, Nov. 7, 1965 (div. 1969); m. Sara Moores, Mar. 2, 1970; children: Brett James, Thomas Edward. BA, U. N.C., Asheville, 1974; postgrad., Harvard U., 1975-80. Dir. admissions Warren Wilson Coll., Asheville, N.C., 1974-79; dir. admissions Sch. Pub. Health Harvard U., Boston, 1979-82; ptnr. Burnham-Campbell, Greenport, N.Y., 1982-86; dir. MidAtlantic Med. Svcs., Inc.-Healthcare, Rockville, Md., 1986-89, Am. Psychmgmt., Arlington, Va., 1989-91; ptnr. Campbell & Assocs., Santa Barbara, Calif., 1991—; cons. numerous hosps., Md., Va., 1986-91. Trustee L.I. Hosp., Greenport, 1982-86; mem. exec. com. Santa Barbara Hospice, 1992—. Mem. Univ. Club (Santa Barbara). Unitarian-Universalist. Home: 2330 Skyline Way Santa Barbara CA 93109 Office: Campbell & Assocs 2330 Skyline Way Santa Barbara CA 93109

CAMPBELL, C(HARLES) ROBERT, architect. BS in Archtl. Engring., U. N.Mex., 1958. Registered architect, N.Mex., Tex., Ariz., Colo., Okla. With SMPC Architects, Albuquerque, 1955—, prin., 1969—, pres., CEO, 1991—; mem. State Bd. Examiners Architects, 1992-93, vice chmn., 1994; mem. adv. com. sch. architecture U. N.Mex.; vis. critic U. N.Mex. Profl. mem. Bernalillo County Bd. Appeals; bd. dirs. Presbyn. Healthcare Found. Mem. AIA (corp., pres., v.p., sec. Albuquerque chpt., mem. joint practices com. 1989—), Am. Arbitration Assn., Nat. Coun. Archtl. Registration Bd. (cert., juror/grader architecture registration exam, mem. architecture registration exam com. 1993-94), N.Mex. Soc. Architects (sec. 1974, pres. 1975-76). Office: Campbell 115 Amherst Dr SE Albuquerque NM 87106-1425

CAMPBELL, CHARLES TAYLOR, chemistry educator; b. Beaumont, Tex., Apr. 30, 1953; married; 1 child. BS, U. Tex., 1975, PhD, 1979. Postdoctoral rsch. assoc. U. Munich, 1979-81; staff mem. Los Alamos (N.Mex.) Nat. Lab., 1981-86; assoc. prof. Ind. U., Bloomington, 1986-89; assoc. prof. U. Wash., Seattle, 1989-92, prof. chemistry, 1992—; presenter in field. Mem. editl. bd. Jour. of Catalysis, 1991-93; patentee in field; contbr. articles to profl. jours. Recipient DuPont Young Faculty award, 1988-89, Camille and Henry Dreyfus Found. Tchr./Scholar award, 1988-92, John Yarwood Meml. award Brit. Vacuum Coun., 1989; NSF NATO postdoctoral fellow U. Munich, 1979-80, Alexander von Humboldt fellow U. Munich, 1980-81, Alfred P. Sloan rsch. fellow, 1986-88; Lubrizol Found. scholar U. Tex., 1973-74, Alcoa and Dean's Office scholar U. Tex., 1974-75. Mem. Am. Chem. Soc. (treas. colloid & surface divsn. 1984-89, co-chmn. continuing symposium on surface and colloid chemistry of advanced materials 1988-91, vice-chmn. 1991, chmn.-elect 1992, chmn. 1993), Am. Vacuum Soc. (exec. com. N.Mex. chpt. 1983-84), Phi Eta Sigma (pres. Lamar U. chpt. 1971). Office: U Wash Dept Chemistry Brg Bldg 10 Seattle WA 98195

CAMPBELL, CHRISTOPHER MARK, artist, singer, songwriter. Student, Western Res. Acad., 1973, Kent State U., 1973, Cranbrock Art Acad., 1974; BFA, Calif. Inst. Arts, 1979. Contest coord. tv game show Tic-Tac-Dough, 1981; graphic animator for films including Star Trek, Poltergeist I and II, Space Camp and various videos. One-man show Wailoa Art Ctr., Hilo, Hawaii, 1994; exhibited in group shows R.I. Sch. art and Design, Calif. Inst. Arts, U. Mich., L.A. Contemporary Exhbns. Gallery, L.I.C.A. Gallery, L.A., Sounding Drum Gallery, Hilo, Lepad Gallery, Pahoa, Hawaii; portraits commd. for pvt. collections, including Pres. Clinton for Virginia Clinton Kelly; appeared in movie Waterworld and Michelob commls. Mem. SAG, Am. Soc. Portrait Artists. Home: PO Box 357 Kurtistown HI 96760-0357

CAMPBELL, CINDY IRENE, social service administrator; b. Alameda, Calif., Jan. 27, 1955; d. Reginald Marvin Corum and LeOsa Riley; m. David James Campbell, June 12, 1977. BS in Psychology and Social Work, Gallaudet U., Washington, 1977; MS in Rehab. Counseling, U. Md., 1992. Vocat. evaluation supr. Ctrs. for the Handicapped, Silver Spring, Md., 1978-81; outreach specialist Ardmore Industries, Hyattsville, Md., 1981-82; vocat. evaluator Nat. Assn. of the Deaf, Silver Spring, 1982-85; vocat. rehab. specialist Md. State Divsn. of Vocat. Rehab., Landover, Md., 1985-90; asst. dir. Inst. on Deaf-Blindness, Hyattsville, 1990-91; placement specialist Electronics Industries Found., Washington, 1991-92; exec. dir. S.W. Wash. Ctr. of the Deaf and Hard of Hearing, Vancouver, Wash., 1992—. Cons. to Am. Deafness Assn. gov.'s coms. on ADA compliance, Olympia, Wash., 1992—, com. on employment, 1992; cons. Clark County Steering Com. on Social Health Svcs., Vancouver, 1992—, Columbia River Mental Health Svcs., Vancouver, 1993—. Named Counselor of the Yr., Md. Divsn. of Vocat. Rehab., 1987; mem. Nat. Disting. Svc. Registry, Libr. of Congress, 1987, 89. Mem. Nat. Assn. Rehab., Wash. Assn. Rehab., Am. Deafness and Rehab. Assn., Order Ea. Star. Office: SW Wash Ctr Deaf/Hard Hear 1715 Broadway St Vancouver WA 98663-3436

CAMPBELL, COLIN HERALD, former mayor; b. Winnipeg, Man., Can., Jan. 18, 1911; s. Colin Charles and Aimee Florence (Herald) C.; m. Virginia Paris, July 20, 1935; children: Susanna Herald, Corinna Buford, Virginia Wallace. BA, Reed Coll., 1933. Exec. sec. City Club of Portland, 1934-39; alumni sec., dir. endowment adminstrn. Reed Coll., 1939-42, exec. sec. N.W. Inst. Internat. Rels. 1940-42, instr. photography, 1941-42; contract engr. Kaiser Co., Inc., 1942-45; asst. pers. dir. Portland Gas & Coke Co., 1945-48; dir. indsl. rels. Pacific Power & Light Co., Portland, 1948-76. Mem. Oreg. Adv. Com. on Fair Employment Practices Act, 1949-55; trustee, chmn., pres. Portland Symphonic Choir, 1950-54; trustee Portland Civic Theater, 1951-54; bd. dirs. Portland Symphony Soc., 1957-60, Community Child Guidance Clinic, 1966-68; active United Way, 1945-75; bd. dirs. Contemporary Crafts Assn., 1972-76, treas., 1975-76; bd. dirs. Lake Oswego Corp., 1961-65, 71-73, 74-76, corp. sec., 1964, pres., 1973-74, treas., 1975-76; mem. Com. on Citizen Involvement, City of Lake Oswego, 1975-77; chmn. Bicentennial Com., Lake Oswego; sec.-treas. Met. Area Communications Commn., 1980-85; treas. Clackamas County Community Action Agy., 1980-82, chmn., 1982-85; mem.

fin. adv. com. W. Clackamas County LWV, 1974-76, 78-80; councilman City of Lake Oswego, 1977-78, mayor, 1979-85, chmn. libr. growth task force, 1987-89, chmn. hist. rev. bd., 1990-92; chmn. energy adv. com. League Oreg. Cities, 1982-84; mem. adv. bd., chmn. fin. com. Lake Oswego Adult Community Ctr. 1985-88; pres. Oswego Heritage Coun., 1992-95, sec., 1995—; active county Blue Ribbon Com. on Law Enforcement, 1987-89. Mem. Edison Electric Inst. (exec. com.), N.W. Electric Light and Power Assn., Lake Oswego C. of C. (v.p. 1986-87, chmn. Land Use com. 1990-91), Nat. Trust for Hist. Preservation, Hist. Preservation League Oreg., Portland Art Mus., Pacific N.W. Pers. Mgmt. Assn. (past regional v.p.), St. Andrews Soc., Oreg. Hist. Soc., Rotary (treas. Lake Oswego chpt. 1990-93). Republican. Presbyterian. Home: 398 Furnace St Lake Oswego OR 97034-3917

CAMPBELL, DAVID ALAN, retail store manager; b. Berkeley, Calif., Oct. 20, 1954; s. Percy Ralph and Margaret Ann (Lawrence) C.; m. Diana Kay Pritchard, Aug. 31, 1977; children: Esther Jean, David Lawrence. BS, Calif. State U., Hayward, Calif., 1976. Store mgr. K Mart Corp., Great Falls, Mont., 1974—. Office: K Mart 7454 4400 10th Ave S Great Falls MT 59405-5627

CAMPBELL, DAVID CHARLES, economist; b. Edmonton, Alberta, Can.; s. Gordon Alexander Campbell and Margaret Rosemary (Lacroix) Forbes; m. Joyce Claire Berney, June 13, 1964; children: Allan Douglas, Michael-Ramsey. B Commerce, U. B.C., Vancouver, Can., 1965; MA, San Francisco State U., 1967; MS, U. Calif., Berkeley, 1969, PhD, 1972. Acct. Sagadahoc Oil & Gas Corp., San Francisco, 1959-71; assoc. prof. econs. U. Idaho, Moscow, 1972-80; econ. advisor OAS, Port of Spain, Trinidad, 1973-74; vis. assoc. prof. govt. and pub. adminstrn. The Am. U., Washington, 1978-79; sr. economist U.S. Water Resources Coun., Washington, 1979-82; staff economist Nat. Wildlife Fedn., Washington, 1982-93. Mem. Am. Water Resource Assn. (nat. capital sec., pres. 1988-89). Office: 2126 Mayview Dr Los Angeles CA 90027-4636

CAMPBELL, DAVID MARTIN, bank executive; b. San Rafael, Calif., Oct. 19, 1961; s. John Kelly and Mary Lou (Payette) C.; m. Danee Lynn Collins, June 4, 1983; children: Geoffrey David, Christopher Ryan. BSBA, U. Nev., 1983, MBA, 1992. CFP. Trust officer Valley Bank of Nev., Las Vegas, 1984-86, asst. v.p., 1986-87, v.p., mgr., 1987-89, regional v.p., 1989-91; mgr. fiduciary svcs. group Bank of Am., Nev. (formerly Valley Bank of Nev.), Las Vegas, 1991-92; mgr. fin. mgmt. and trust svcs. client exec. SEI Corp., San Francisco, 1992—. Bd. dirs. Bridge Counseling Assocs., Las Vegas, 1989, Nev. Community Found., Las Vegas, 1992, Nev. Arthritis Found. Planned Giving Com. mem., Las Vegas, 1992. Mem. So. Nev. Estate Planning Coun. (pub. rels. com. 1985-86, v.p. 1987-88), Internat. Assn. of Fin. Planners. Office: SEI Corp 9001 Ridgepointe Way Henderson NV 89014-6960

CAMPBELL, DAVID RANDALL, equipment manufacturing company executive; b. Rupert, Idaho, Aug. 26, 1928; s. Charles Newton and Rhoda (Randall) C.; m. Mary Elizabeth May, Jan. 3, 1951; children: Colin, Heather, Anne, Catherine, Bonnie, Allison, Rebecca. Student, Utah State U., 1946-48, U. Utah, 1951-53, 57-59. Salesman Home Furniture Co., Rupert, 1951-57; ptnr. Kenyon Farms, Oakley, Idaho, 1952-57; pres. Campbell Mfg. Inc., Salt Lake City, 1958-59; mgr. Cambelt div. Eimco Corp. Campbell Mfg. Inc., 1969-74; pres., owner Cambelt Internat. Corp., 1974-89, chmn. bd., CEO, 1989—. Numerous patents in field. Pres. Internat. Visitors-Utah Coun., Salt Lake City, 1974-75, 88, bd. dirs., 1990—; commr. Clan Campbell, Utah, 1990-92, trustee Clan Campbell USA, 1989-93, v.p. Clan Campbell N.Am., 1993—; former high councilman and bishop LDS Ch.; former dist. chmn., dist. rep. to county, dist. chmn. to state Nat. Rep. Com.; singer Utah Chorale. Recipient award of merit Internat. Visitors-Utah Coun., 1990. Mem. Utah Scottish Assn. (pres. 1987-88). Home: 8800 Kings Hill Dr # B Salt Lake City UT 84121-6162 Office: Cambelt Internat Corp 2420 W 1100 S Salt Lake City UT 84104-4513

CAMPBELL, DEMAREST LINDSAY, artist, designer, writer; b. N.Y.C.; d. Peter Stephen III and Mary Elizabeth (Edwards) C.; m. Dale Gordon Haugo. BFA in Art History, MFA in S.E. Asian Art History, MFA in Theatre Design. Art dir., designer murals and residential interiors Campbell & Haugo, 1975—. Designed, painted and sculpted over 200 prodns. for Broadway, internat. opera, motion pictures. Mem. NOW, Asian Art Mus. Soc., San Francisco. Mem. United Scenic Artists, Scenic & Title Artists and Theatrical Stage Designers., Sherlock Holmes Soc. London, Amnesty Internat., Nat. Trust for Hist. Preservation (Gt. Brit. and U.S.A. chpt.), Shavian Malthus Soc. (charter Gt. Brit. chpt.).

CAMPBELL, DIANE RITA, biologist, educator; b. Washington, Jan. 25, 1956; m. Theodore Mark Porter, Aug. 19, 1979; 1 child, David Campbell Porter. BS in Biology, Stanford U., 1977; PhD in Zoology, Duke U., 1983. Postdoctoral fellow U. Calif., Riverside, 1983-84; asst. prof. U. Va., Charlottesville, Va., 1984-89; asst. prof. U. Calif., Irvine, 1989-93, assoc. prof., 1993—. Contbr. articles to profl. jours. Mem. Am. Soc. Naturalists, Bot. Soc. Am., Ecol. Soc. Am., Soc. Study Evolution (assoc. editor 1992-94), Rocky Mountain Biol. Lab. Office: U Calif Dept Ecology & Evolutionary Biology Irvine CA 92717

CAMPBELL, DRACE ALLAN, psychiatric technician, student; b. Coffeyville, Kans., July 4, 1969; s. Jerry Lee and Sandra Sue (Wilson) C. Student, Pima C.C., Tucson, 1992—, No. Ariz. U., 1995—. Psychiatric technician Palo Verde Hosp., Tucson, 1990-95. Vol. Ariz. Greyhound Rescue, Tucson, 1993—, Voices for Animals, Tucson, 1994—. Mem. Phi Theta Kappa. Home: 4232 E Pima St Apt C Tucson AZ 85712-3127 Office: 2695 N Craycroft Rd Tucson AZ 85712-2243

CAMPBELL, FREDERICK HOLLISTER, lawyer, historian; b. Somerville, Mass., June 14, 1923; s. George Murray and Irene Ivers (Smith) C.; A.B., Dartmouth, 1944; J.D., Northwestern U., 1949; postgrad. Indsl. Coll. Armed Forces, 1961-62; M.A. in History, U. Colo., 1984, PhD in History, 1993; m. Amy Holding Strohm, Apr. 14, 1951; 1 dau., Susan Hollister. Served with USMCR, 1944-46; joined USMC, 1950, advanced through grades to lt. col., 1962; admitted to Ill. bar, 1950, U.S. Supreme Ct. bar, 1967, Colo. bar, 1968; judge adv. USMC, Camp Lejeune, N.C., Korea, Parris Island, S.C., El Toro, Calif., Vietnam, Washington, 1950-67; asso. editor Callaghan and Co., Chgo., 1949-50; practiced law, Colorado Springs, Colo., 1968-88; ptnr. firm Gibson, Gerdes and Campbell, 1969-79; pvt. practice law, 1980-88; gen. counsel 1st Fin. Mortgage Corp., 1988—, vice chmn., corp. sec., 1993—; hon. instr. history U. Colo., Colorado Springs, 1986—; vis. instr., Colo. Coll., 1993—. Mem. Estate Planning Coun., Colorado Springs, 1971-81, v.p., 1977-78. Rep. precinct committeeman, 1971-86; del. Colo. Rep. State Conv., 1972, 74, 76, 80, alt., 1978; trustee Frontier Village Found., 1971-77; bd. dirs. Rocky Mountain Nature Assn., 1975—, pres., 1979-92, Rocky Mountain Nat. Park Assocs. 1986—, v.p. 1986-92, sec. 1992—. Mem. Colo. Bar Assn., El Paso County Bar Assn., Am. Arbitration Assn., Marines Meml. Club, Phi Alpha Theta. Congregationalist. Author: John's American Notary and Commissioner of Deeds Manual, 1950. Contbr. articles to profl. jours. Home and Office: 2707 Holiday Ln Colorado Springs CO 80909-1217

CAMPBELL, GAYLON SANFORD, soil physicist; b. Blackfoot, Idaho, Aug. 20, 1940; s. Hazelton Sanford and Rosalie (Barrus) C.; m. Judith Harris, Aug. 5, 1964; children: Tamsin, Julia Bee, Karine, Colin, Cecily, Scott, Nigel, Stuart, Gillian. BS in Physics, Utah State U., 1965, MS in Soil Physics, 1966; PhD in Soils, Wash. State U., 1968. Asst. prof. soils Wash. State U., Pullman, 1971-75; assoc. prof. soils Wash. State U., 1975-80, prof. soils, 1980—; vis. prof. U. Nottingham, England, 1984-85. Author: Introduction to Environmental Biophysics, 1977, Soil Physics with BASIC, 1985; contbr. articles to profl. jours; patentee Krypton hygrometer. NSF fellow 1966-68, Sr. Vis. fellow British Sci. Rsch. Coun., Nottingham, England, 1977-78. Fellow Am. Soc. Agronomy, Soil Sci. Soc. Am. Mem. LDS Ch. Office: Pullman WA 99164-6420 Office: Wash State U Dept Crop & Soil Scis Pullman WA 99164

CAMPBELL, GEOFFREY HAYS, materials scientist; b. Berkeley, Calif., Aug. 16, 1962; s. Graham Hays and Patricia Helen (Gregory) C.; m. Andrea Regina Berger, Aug. 20, 1992. BS, MIT, 1984; MS, U. Calif., Berkeley, 1986; PhD, U. Calif., Santa Barbara, 1990. Postdoctoral fellow Max Planck Inst. fur Metallforschung, Stuttgart, Germany, 1990-91; postdoctoral assoc. Lawrence Livermore (Calif.) Nat. Lab., 1991-93, metallurgist, 1993—. Mem. Am. Ceramic Soc., Materials Rsch. Soc., Microscopy Soc. Am., Inst. Mechanics and Materials (Young Investigator adv. com. 1993—). Democrat. Office: Lawrence Livermore Nat Lab L-356 Livermore CA 94551

CAMPBELL, GORDON MUIR, mayor; b. Vancouver, B.C., Can., Jan. 12, 1948; s. Charles Gordon and Margaret Janet (Muir) C.; m. Nancy J. Chipperfield, July 4, 1970; children: Geoffrey Gordon, Nicholas James. AB, Dartmouth Coll., 1970; MBA, Simon Fraser U., 1978. Tchr. Can. Univ. Service Overseas, Yola, Nigeria, 1970-72; exec. asst. to mayor City of Vancouver, 1972-76, alderman, 1984-86, mayor, 1986-94; project mgr. Marathon Realty Devel. Co., Vancouver, 1976-81; pres. Citycore Devel. Corp., Vancouver, 1981-86. Recipient Outstanding Alumni award Simon Fraser U., 1987. Office: Ste 907 865 Hornby St, Vancouver, BC Canada V6Z 2G3

CAMPBELL, HARRY WOODSON, geologist, mining engineer; b. Carthage, Mo., Jan. 14, 1946; s. William Hampton and Elizabeth Verle (LeGrand) C. BSEE, Kans. State U., 1969; MBA, U. Oreg., 1973, BS in Geology, 1975; MS in Geology, Brown U., 1978. Registered profl. engr., Wash.; cert. profl. geologist, Va. Geologist, mining engr. and phys. scientist U.S. Bur. Mines, Spokane, 1980—. Served with U.S. Army, 1969-71. Recipient Spl. Achievement award U.S. Bur. Mines, 1983, 86, 88. Mem. Geol. Soc. Am., Soc. Mining Engrs. Office: US Bur Mines 360 E 3rd Ave Spokane WA 99202-1413

CAMPBELL, IAN DAVID, opera company director; b. Brisbane, Australia, Dec. 21, 1945; came to U.S., 1982; m. Ann Spira; children: Benjamin, David. BA, U. Sydney, Australia, 1966. Prin. tenor singer The Australian Opera, Sydney, 1967-74; sr. music officer The Australia Council, Sydney, 1974-76; gen. mgr. The State Opera of South Australia, Adelaide, 1976-82; asst. artistic adminstr. Met. Opera, N.Y.C., 1982-83; gen. dir. San Diego Opera, 1983—; guest lectr. U. Adelaide, 1978; guest prof. San Diego State U., 1986—; cons. Lyric Opera Queensland, Australia, 1980-81; bd. dirs. Opera Am., Washington, 1986-95; chmn. judges Met. Opera Auditions, Sydney, 1989, Masterclasses, Music Acad. of the West, 1993—. Producer, host San Diego Opera Radio Program, 1984—, At the Opera with Ian Campbell, 1984—. Recipient Peri award Opera Guild So. Calif., 1984; named Headliner of Yr., San Diego Press Club, 1991. Assoc. fellow Australian Inst. Mgmt.; mem. Kona Kai Club, Rotary, San Diego Press Club (Headliner award 1991). Office: San Diego Opera PO Box 988 San Diego CA 92112-0988

CAMPBELL, JAMES EDWARD, physicist, consultant; b. Kingsport, Tenn., Jan. 13, 1943; s. Edward Montroe and Iola (Church) C.; m. Judy Priscilla Cameron, June 12, 1966; children: Jennifer Marie, James Kyle. BA in Math., Physics, Catawba Coll., 1965; PhD in Physics, Va. Tech. Inst., 1969. Nuclear radiation expert Naval Weapons Evaluation Facility, Albuquerque, 1970-76; mem. tech. staff Sandia Nat. Labs., Albuquerque, 1976-80; v.p. Intera Techs., Inc., Denver, 1980-88; disting. mem. tech. staff Sandia Nat. Labs., Albuquerque, 1988—; bd. dirs. TechLaw, Inc., Denver, 1983-88. Contbr. articles to profl. jours. Recipient IEEE Outstanding Paper award, 1991, NDEA fellowship, 1965-68, Acad. Honors scholarship, Catawba Coll., 1961-65. Mem. AAAS, Am. Phys. Soc. Republican. Lutheran. Office: Sandia Nat Labs Ms 0746 # 6613 Albuquerque NM 87185

CAMPBELL, JOHN ARTHUR, geology educator, researcher; b. Muskogee, Okla., Nov. 2, 1930; s. John Cope and Leda (Diffendaffer) C.; m. Patricia B. Bartlett, May 26, 1953; children: Keith, Allyn, Karyn. B of Geology, U. Tulsa, 1955; MS, U. Colo., 1957, PhD, 1966. Instr. geology Colo. State U., Ft. Collins, 1957-60, asst. prof., 1960-66, assoc. prof., 1966-74; rsch. geologist U.S. Geol. Survey, Denver, 1974-81; prof. geology Ft. Lewis Coll., Durango, Colo., 1981—, dept. chair, 1986-89; rsch. geologist U.S. Geol. Survey, Durango, Colo., 1981-85, 91-94; hon. prof. U. Colo., Denver, 1978-80; appointed by Gov. of Colo. to Minerals, Energy, Geology Adv. Bd., State of Colo., 1992-94, Oil and Conservation Com., 1990-94. Contbr. over 85 articles to profl. jours. Commr. Oil and Gas Conservation Commn., 1990-94. Served with USN, 1952-56. Recipient NSF Faculty fellowship, 1962-63, fellowship U. Colo., 1963. Fellow Geol. Soc. Am.; mem. Am. Assn. Petroleum Geologists, Soc. Econ. Paleontologists and Mineralogists, RMAG, Four Corners Geol. Soc., Sigma Xi. Home: 195 Aspen Ln # Fcr Durango CO 81301-8594 Office: Ft Lewis Coll Dept Geology Durango CO 81301

CAMPBELL, JOHN D., religious organization administrator, religious publication editor. Media contact, coord. ch. svc. mission Ch. God. Editor: The Gospel Contact. Office: Ch God We Can Assembly, 4717 56th St, Camrose, AB Canada T4V 2C4

CAMPBELL, LAURENCE JOSEPH, physicist; b. Belmont, W.Va., Feb. 26, 1937; s. Joseph Hayes and Genevieve Naomi (Masters) C.; married; 1 child, Elizabeth Laurel. SB, MIT, 1961, SM, 1961; PhD, U. Calif., San Diego, 1965. Rsch. assoc. U. Ill., Champaign, 1965-67; staff mem. Los Alamos (N.Mex.) Nat. Lab., 1967—; dir. pulsed fields Nat. High Magnetic Field Lab., Tallahassee, Fla., 1992—. Mem. Am. Phys. Soc., Materials Rsch. Soc. Office: Los Alamos Nat Lab MS-K765 Los Alamos NM 87545

CAMPBELL, LEE ANN, microbiology educator; b. Altoona, Pa., Sept. 12, 1955; d. Ronald Charles Crain and Ruth Ann Hooper Crain Saleme. BS in Microbiology, Pa. State U., 1977, MS in Microbiology, 1979, PhD in Microbiology, 1982. Grad. teaching asst. dept. microbiology Pa. State U., 1977-82; postdoctoral fellow U. Rochester, N.Y., 1982-83; scientist dept. microbiology U. Rochester, 1984-85; asst. prof. dept. pathobiology U. Wash., Seattle, 1985-91, mem. grad. sch. faculty, 1985—, faculty mem. interdisciplinary molecular/cell biology prog., 1990—, assoc. prof. dept. pathobiology, 1991—; ad hoc grant reviewer The Wellcome Trust, London, 1992, The Israel Sci. Found., 1993; ad hoc grant reviewer Dept. Vets. Affairs, 1994; ad hoc mem. site visit com. BM-1 Study Sect., NAIAD/NIH, 1992, ad hoc mem. BM-1 Study Sect., 1995; cons. Microprobe, Bothel, Wash., 1989-90; lectr. in field. Contbr. numerous articles to profl. jours.; patentee in field; reviewer Jour. Clin. Microbiology, Gene, Am. Jour. Vet. Medicine, Jour. Immunology, Jour. Infectious Disease, Clin. Infectious Disease, European Jour. Epidemiology, European Jour. Clin. Microbiology and Infectious Diseases; mem. Wash. Pub. Health Editl. Bd., 1987—. Pa. State U. Alumnae Award scholar, 1975; grantee N.Y. State Health Rsch. Coun., 1982-83, Edna McConnell Clark Found., 1985-87, 88, 89-90, NIH, 1986-91, 88-93, 90-91, 91—, 92—, 93—, USDA, 1992-94, Pfizer Labs., 1991-94. Mem. Am. Soc. Microbiology, Sigma Xi, Phi Kappa Phi. Home: 17515 8th Ave NE Seattle WA 98155-3603 Office: Univ of Wash Dept Pathobiology Box 357238 Seattle WA 98195

CAMPBELL, MICHAEL LEE, computer science researcher; b. L.A., Nov. 25, 1958; s. Earl J. and Lee (Fitch) C.; m. Asya Glozman, Jan. 23, 1961; children: Sasha Madeline, Alice Edie. BS in Math., U. Calif., Riverside, 1980; MS in Computer Sci., UCLA, 1982, PhD in Computer Sci., 1986. Mem. tech. staff electro-optical and data systems group Hughes Aircraft, El Segundo, Calif., 1982-88; sr. staff computer scientist Hughes Rsch. Labs., Malibu, Calif., 1988-92; section mgr. computer systems divsn. Aerospace Corp., El Segundo, 1992—; lectr. dept. computer sci. UCLA, 1987-88. Contbr. articles to profl. jours. Mem. AIAA Computer Sys. Tech. Com., Computer Soc. of IEEE, Assn. for Computing Machinery, Sigma Xi (chpt. pres.). Office: Aerospace Corp PO Box 92957 Los Angeles CA 90009-2957

CAMPBELL, PATRICK MILTON, internist, educator; b. Vancouver, Wash., Mar. 17, 1955; s. Robert Owen Campbell and Phyllis June (Mattison) Lindsley; m. Carolyn Ann Lintner, May 23, 1989; children: Thomas S., Jessica M. Student, Lewis and Clark Coll., 1973-75; BA in Chemistry and Biology, U. Calif., Santa Cruz, 1981; MD, U. Calif., Irvine, 1988. Diplomate Am. Bd. Internal Medicine. Resident primary care internal medicine program U. Calif., Davis, 1988-91; assoc. med. dir. MED Ctr., Sacramento, 1991-92; pvt practice in internal medicine Redding, Calif., 1993—; staff dept. Medicine Redding Med. Ctr., Redding Splty. Hosp., Redding, 1993—; staff Mercy Med. Ctr., Redding, Calif., 1993—; clin. instr. U. Calif. Davis, Sacramento, 1991-92; staff dept. Medicine Sutter Cmty. Hosps., Sacramento, 1992—. Contbr. articles to profl. jours. U. Calif. MacKenzie scholar, 1986-88, Fight for Sight Inc. fellow, summer 1982, 83. Mem. ACP, Am. Heart Assn. Home: 8250 Muscat Ct Redding CA 96001-9575 Office: 1555 East St Ste 300 Redding CA 96001-1153

CAMPBELL, RICHARD ALDEN, electronics company executive; b. Bend, Oreg., July 31, 1926; s. Corlis Eugene and Lydia Amney (Peck) C.; m. Edna Mary Seaman, June 12, 1948; children: Stephen Alden, Douglas Niall (dec.), Carolyn Joyce. B.S. in Elec. Engring., U. Ill., 1949, M.S. in Elec. Engring., 1950. With TRW Inc., Redondo Beach, Calif., 1954-87, exec. v.p., 1979-87; bus. cons., profl. co. dir. Rolling Hills Estates, Calif., 1987—; bd. dirs. Novadyne Computer Systems, Inc. Patentee in radio communications. Bd. dirs. U. Ill. Found., Hugh O'Brian Youth Found. With USN, 1944-46. Recipient Alumni Honor award U. Ill. Coll. Engring. Mem. IEEE (sr.), Am. Electronics Assn. (pres. 1969, dir. 1970), Phi Kappa Phi, Tau Beta Pi, Eta Kappa Nu, Sigma Tau, Pi Mu Epsilon, Phi Eta Sigma, Rolling Hills Country Club, Rancheros Visitadores Club, Los Caballeros Club. Republican.

CAMPBELL, ROBERT ALLEN, pediatrician; b. Toledo, Dec. 21, 1924; s. Glenn Harold and Harriet Mae (Kintzley) C.; m. Mary Christine Muchka, Sept. 21, 1949; children: Robert Perry, Mary Ellen, Catherine Anne. BA, U. Calif., Berkeley, 1954; MD, U. Calif., San Francisco, 1958. Rsch. asst. dept. zoology U. Calif., Berkeley, 1950-54; intern. resident U. Calif., San Francisco, 1954-58; instr. pediatrics U. Oreg. Med. Sch., Portland, 1961-63, asst. prof., 1963-67, assoc. prof., 1967-72, prof., 1972-91, prof. emeritus, 1991—; dir. pediat. renal-metabolic rsch. lab. OHSU, Portland, 1963—. Editor: Advances in Polyamine Research, 1978; contbr. articles to profl. jours., chpts. to books. Mem. World Coun., Portland, 1988—, Am. Chinese Orgn., Portland, 1988—; trustee, dir. Cystic Fibrosis Soc. Oreg., Kidney Assn. Oreg., Kerr Ctr. for Children, Portland. USPHS fellow U. Oreg. Med. Sch., 1961-63, Am. Pediat. Soc., Wyeth fellow, 1960-61. Fellow Am. Acad. Pediatrics, Am. Pediatric Soc., Am. Soc. Nephrology, Am. Soc. Pediat. Nephrology, Internat. Soc. Nephrology, Internat. Pediat. Nephrology Assn. Office: Oreg Health Sci U 3181 SW Sam Jackson Park Rd Portland OR 97201-3011

CAMPBELL, ROBERT CHARLES, clergyman, religious organization administrator; b. Chandler, Ariz., Mar. 9, 1924; s. Alexander Joshua and Florence (Betzner) C.; m. Lotus Idamae Graham, July 12, 1945; children: Robin Carl, Cherry Colleen. AB, Westmont Coll., 1944; BD, Eastern Bapt. Theol. Sem., 1947, ThM, 1949, ThD, 1951, DD (hon.), 1974; MA, U. So. Calif., 1959; postgrad., Dropsie U., 1949-51, U. Pa., 1951-52, NYU, 1960-62, U. Cambridge, Eng., 1969; DLitt (hon.), Am. Bapt. Sem. of West, 1972; HHD (hon.), Alderson-Broaddus Coll., 1979; LHD (hon.), Linfield Coll., 1982; LLD (hon.), Franklin Coll., 1986. Ordained to ministry Am. Bapt. Ch., 1947; pastor 34th St. Bapt. Ch., Phila., 1945-49; instr. Eastern Bapt. Theol. Sem., Phila., 1949-51; asst. prof. Eastern Coll., St. Davids, Pa., 1951-53; assoc. prof. N.T. Am. Bapt. Sem. of West, Covina, Cal., 1953-54, dean, prof., 1954-72; gen. sec. Am. Bapt. Chs. in U.S.A., Valley Forge, Pa., 1972-87; pres. Eastern Bapt. Theol. Sem., Phila., 1987-89, ret.; Vis. lectr. Sch. Theology at Claremont, Calif., 1961-63, U. Redlands, Calif., 1959-60, 66-67, Fuller Theology Seminary, Calif., 1992—; Bd. mgrs. Am. Bapt. Bd. of Edn. and Publ., 1956-59, 65-69; v.p. So. Calif. Bapt. Conv., 1967-68; pres. Am. Bapt. Chs. of Pacific S.W., 1970-71; Pres. N.Am. Bapt. Fellowship, 1974-76; mem. exec. com. Bapt. World Alliance, 1972-90, v.p., 1975-80; mem. exec. com., gov. bd. Nat. Council Chs. of Christ in U.S.A., 1972-87; del. to World Council of Chs., 1975, 83, mem. central com., 1975-90. Author: Great Words of the Faith, 1965, The Gospel of Paul, 1973, Evangelistic Emphases in Ephesians, Jesus Still Has Something To Say, 1987. Home: 125 Via Alicia Santa Barbara CA 93108-1769

CAMPBELL, ROBERT HEDGCOCK, investment banker; b. Ann Arbor, Mich., Jan. 16, 1948; s. Robert Miller and Ruth Adele (Hedgcock) C.; m. Katherine Kettering, June 17, 1972; children: Mollie DuPlan, Katherine Elizabeth, Anne Kettering. BA, U. Wash., 1970, JD, 1973. Bar. Wash. 1973, Wash. State Supreme Ct. 1973, Fed. 1973, U.S. Dist. Ct. (we. dist.) Wash. 1973, Ct. Appeals (9th cir.) 1981. Assoc. Roberts & Shefelman, Seattle, 1973-78, ptnr., 1978-85; sr. v.p. Shearson Lehman Bros., Inc., Seattle, 1985-87, mng. dir., 1987—; dir., treas. Nat. Assn. Bd. Lawyers, Hinsdale, Ill., 1982-85; pres., trustee Wash. State Soc. Hosp. Attys., Seattle, 1982-85. Contbr. articles to profl. jours. Trustee Bellevue (Wash.) Schs. Found., 1988-91, pres., 1989-90; nation chief Bellevue Eastside YMCA Indian Princess Program, 1983-88; trustee Wash. Phikeia Found., 1983-91; mem. Wash. Gov.'s Food Processing Coun., 1990-91. Republican. Home: 8604 NE 10th St Bellevue WA 98004-3915 Office: Lehman Bros Columbia Seafirst Ctr 701 5th Ave Ste 7101 Seattle WA 98104-7016

CAMPBELL, ROBERT MADISON, university program director; b. Princeton, N.J., Dec. 26, 1954; s. Jackson Justice and Margarita (Monal) C.; m. Elizabeth Carol Trupin, May 20, 1984; children: Jared, Nicholas. BA, Yale U., 1977; MusM, U. Ill., 1979; DMA, Stanford U., 1985. Rsch. assoc. Stanford U., Palo Alto, Calif., 1983-85; asst. prof. Music U. Wis., Kenosha, 1985-89; dir. choral activities U. San Diego, San Diego, 1989—; dir. choral scholars U. San Diego, 1989—; dir. Parkside Chorale and Chamber Singers, 1985-89, West Towns Chorus, Lombard, Ill., 1987-89, R.I. Sound, Providence, 1979-81; mem. faculty Harmony Coll., St. Joseph, Mo., Dirs. Coll., Kenosha, Wis. Author various choral editions, vocal arrangements; editor Cantate California newsletter, 1991—, FYI; contbr. articles to profl. jours. Assoc. dir. Sun Harbor Chorus, 1990—. Fellow Stanford U., 1981-84, Minority Rsch. grantee U. Wis., Madison, 1988. Home: 6569 Reflection Dr San Diego CA 92124-3105 Office: U San Diego Alcala Park San Diego CA 92110

CAMPBELL, SCOTT ROBERT, lawyer, former food company executive; b. Burbank, Calif., June 7, 1946; s. Robert Clyde and Jenevieve Anne (Olsen) C.; m. Teresa Melanie Mack, Oct. 23, 1965; 1 son, Donald Steven. BA, Claremont Men's Coll., 1970; JD, Cornell U., 1973. Bar: Ohio 1973, U.S. Dist. Ct. (so. dist.) Ohio 1974, Minn. 1976, Calif. 1989, U.S. Dist. Ct. (no. dist.) Calif. 1989, U.S. Ct. Appeals (9th cir.) 1989, U.S. Dist. Ct. (cen. and so. dists.) Calif. 1990, U.S. Ct. Appeals (5th cir.) 1991, U.S. Tax Ct. 1991. Assoc. Taft, Stettinius & Hollister, Cin., 1973-76; atty. Mpls. Star & Tribune, 1976-77; sr. v.p., gen. counsel, sec. Kellogg Co., Battle Creek, Mich., 1977-89; ptnr. Furth Fahrner Mason, San Francisco, 1989—; U.S. del. ILO Food and Beverage Conf., Geneva, 1984; participant, presenter first U.S.-USSR Legal Seminar, Moscow, 1988; speaker other legal seminars. Mem. ABA, Ohio Bar Assn., Minn. Bar Assn., Calif. Bar. Assn., Am. Soc. Corp. Secs. Office: Furth Fahrner & Mason 1000 Furth Bldg 201 Sansome St San Francisco CA 94104-2303

CAMPBELL, THOMAS J., legislator, chiropractor; b. Bklyn., Oct. 27, 1954; s. Charles Marvin and Edna Mary (Sacer) C.; m. C. Lynn Hearn, July 2, 1983. AA in Social Scis., Fla. Tech. U., 1974; BA in Police Sci. and Adminstrn., Seattle U., 1977; DC, Life Chiropractic Coll., 1983; postgrad. in orthopedics, L.A. Chiropractic Coll., 1984-90. Diplomate Am. Acad. Pain Mgmt.; cert. chiropractic rehab. dr. Nat. Bd. Chiropractic Examiners-Physiotherapy; lic. chiropractor, Wash., Fla. Pvt. practice Chiropractic Spinal Care, Inc., 1984—. Mem. Wash. State Ho. of Reps., 1993—. With U.S. Army, 1977-79, capt. USAR/ARNG, 1979-85. Recipient Appreciation for Svc. award Chiropractic Disciplinary Bd., 1989-93, Gov. Appreciation Certificate Wash. State Disciplinary Bd. Fellow Internat. Coll. of Chiropractors; mem. Am. Chiropractic Assn. (alt. del. House of Dels. 1988-92), Wash. State Chiropractic Assn. (chmn. mem. com. 1984-85, dist. 4A 1985-86, dir. exec. bd. 1985-88, v. chmn. disciplinary bd. 1990-93, pres. award outstanding achievement in the mem. com. 1985, legislative affairs com. 1986, Dist. of the Yr. award 1985-86, named Chiropractor of the Yr. 1987, 89, 90, 91, Appreciation award for outstanding svc to the profession, 1994, Exceptional Svc. award 1994), Fla. Chiropractic Assn., Pierce County Chiropractic Assn., Chiropractic Rehabilitation Assn. (bd. dirs.), Elks (Tacoma Lodge # 174), Am. Legion. Republican. Home: PO Box 443 Spanaway WA 98387-0443

CAMPBELL, TIMOTHY L., municipal official; b. Fullerton, Calif., Sept. 17, 1960; s. Robert E. Lee and Jean Dorn (Blaska) C.; m. Rosa Maria Alvarez, Aug. 8, 1987. BA in Polit. Sci., Calif. State U., Fullerton, 1983, MPA, 1985. Exec. dir. Coll. Legal Clinic, Inc., Fullerton, 1982-84; grad. asst. univ. outreach program Calif. State U., 1984-85; facility coord. City of Santa Ana, Calif., 1987; ctr. adminstr. City of Fullerton, 1987-89, adminstrv. asst., 1989-90, sr. adminstrv. analyst, 1990—; sec. bd. North Orange County credit Union, Fullerton. Vol. ARC, Santa Ana, Calif., 1978-83; trustee Coll. Legal Clinic, Inc., 1984— (Cmty. Svc. award 1984). Mem. Mcpl. Mgmt. Assn. So. Calif. Democrat. Roman Catholic. Office: City of Fullerton 116 S Basque Ave Fullerton CA 92633-2715

CAMPBELL, WILLIAM JOSEPH, academic director; b. Bklyn., N.Y., Nov. 26, 1944; s. William Joseph and Loretta Jane (Graessle) C. BA in Philosophy, U. Dayton, 1966; MS in Edn., Fordham U., 1972; MA in Theology, St. John's U., 1977; MA in Pvt. Sch. Adminstrn., U. San Francisco, 1986; EdD in Ednl. Mgmt., U. LaVerne, 1990. Cert. sch. adminstr., Calif.; cert. guidance counselor, N.Y. Tchr., dean students Most Holy Trinity High Sch., Bklyn., 1966-68; tchr., coach Charlotte (N.C.) Catholic High Sch., 1968-69; tchr., dir. freshman guidance Chaminade High Sch., Mineola, N.Y., 1969-82; tchr., counselor Jumpero Serra High sch., Gardena, Calif., 1982-84; academic asst. prin. Archbishop Riordan H.S., San Francisco, 1984-87; prin. Chaminade Coll. Preparatory, West Hills, Calif., 1987-90; dir. edn. Marianists, Cupertino, Calif., 1990—; bd. dirs. Chaminade U., Honolulu, Marianist Ctr., Honolulu, Archbishop Riordan H.S., Chaminade Coll. Prep. Sch. Trustee St. Louis High Sch., Honolulu, 1991—. Mem. ASCD, Nat. Assn. Secondary Sch. Prins., Nat. Catholic Edn. Assn., World Future Soc., Assn. for Religious and Values Issues in Counseling, Phi Delta Kappa. Office: Marianist Provincialate PO Box 1775 Cupertino CA 95015-1775

CAMPER, JOHN SAXTON, public relations and marketing executive; b. Trenton, N.J., Apr. 24, 1929; s. Thomas Emory and Mildred Ruth (Burke) C.; m. Ferne Arlene Clanton; children: Susan Jennifer, John Saxton III. BS in History and Econs., U. Nebr., 1968. Enlisted U.S. Army, 1948, commd. to 1st lt., advanced through ranks to maj., 1972, ret., 1972; regional mktg. officer First Bank System, Mont., 1978-83; lectr., instr. mktg. and advt. pub. rels.; pres. Camper Comm., Helena, 1983—; dir. Profl. Devel. Ctr., Mont., 1984-91. Decorated Legion of Merit. Mem. Helena Advt. Fedn. (1st pres., founder), Rotary Internat. Republican. Methodist.

CAMPESE, VITO MICHELE, nephrologist; b. May 23, 1942; m. Stefania; 1 child, Paola. MD, U. Bari, Italy, 1966. Diplomate Am. Bd. Nephrology, Am. Bd. Internal Medicine; cert. in nephrology, Italy. Internship, residency Policlinico, Bari, Italy, 1966-67, 67-69; fellowship in nephrology U. Bari, Italy, 1971-73, asst. prof. Inst. of Nephrology, 1973-74; fellowship hypertension svc. U. So. Calif., 1974-75; asst. prof. hypertension svc. L.A. County-U. So. Calif. Med. Ctr., L.A., 1975-77, asst. prof. divsn. nephrology, 1977-80, assoc. prof. divsn. nephrology, 1980-85, prof. medicine divsn. nephrology, 1985—, assoc. chief divsn. nephrology, 1987—; physician specialist L.A. County-U. So. Calif., L.A.; reviewer for various journs. in field; invited speaker in field. Mem. editorial bd. Hypertension, Jour. of the Am. Soc. of Nephrology, Clin. and Exptl. Pharmacology and Physiology, Jour. of Nephrology, Jour. of Human Hypertension, Clin. Advances in the Treatment of Hypertension, Hypertension: Index and Reviews; asst. editor Am. Jour. of Nephrology; contbr. numerous articles to profl. jours. Mem. adv. coun. Kidney Found. of So. Calif., 1977—; mem. promotion com. U. So. Calif., 1982—; mem. promotion com. dept. medicine U. So. Calif., 1989—, mem. grievance com., 1990—, mem. med. student rsch. com., 1990—; mem. Nat. High Blood Pressure Edn. Program, 1991—. Recipient The Domenico Cotungo medal and award in Nephrology, 1988, The Regione Puglia Targa D'oro award for contbn. to Sci., 1991; grantee NIH, 1988-92, 92-95, 91-95, Baxter, 1994-97, Pfizer Lab, 1991-93. Mem. Internat. Soc. Nephrology, Internat. Soc. Hypertension, Coun. for High Blood Pressure Rsch., Am. Soc. Nephrology, Am. Fedn. Of Clin. Rsch., Am. Soc. Internat. Medicine, Am. Soc. Renal Biochemistry and Metabolism, The Endocrine Soc., Western Soc. Clin. investigation, Italian-Am. Soc. Nephrologists, Am. Soc. Hypertension. Office: U So California Nephrology 2025 Zonal Ave # 4250 Los Angeles CA 90033-4526

CAMPOBASSO, CRAIG, casting director; b. Sun Valley, Calif., Oct. 5, 1959; s. Fred Vierow and Marie Donna King Campobasso; stepson of Louis V. Campobasso. Acting coach L.A., 1987—; casting dir. for motion pictures: Dickwad--A Comedy, 1993, The Silence of the Hams, 1993, Innocent Adultery, 1993, Prancer, 1994, Red Palms, 1995, Stigmata. 44, 1994, Stick Fighter, 1994, L.A.'s Finest--To Protect and Serve, 1994, McNelly's Rangers, 1994, Timebomb, Endless Descent, 1994, Watch the Skies, 1995; TV credits include Cinemax's Payback, 1994; assoc. casting dir. for TV, Steven Spielberg's Amazing Stories. Author: Autobiography of an Estraterrestrial: The Star-Seed Journals, 1995—. Vol. Babies with AIDS, L.A., 1992.

CAMPOS, JOAQUIN PAUL, III, chemical physicist, regulatory affairs analyst; b. L.A., Feb. 16, 1962; s. Joaquin Reyna and Maria Luz (Chavez) C.; m. Barbara Ann Esquivel, Oct. 31, 1987; children: Courtney Luz, Nathaniel Alexander. Student, U. Calif., Santa Cruz, 1980-85, UCLA, 1985-86. Tutor U. Calif., Santa Cruz, 1980-82, admissions liaison, 1982-84; chem. teaching assoc. L.A. Unified Sch. Dist., 1985-87; pvt. tutor Santa Clara, L.A., 1987-89; tech. specialist Alpha Therapeutics Corp., L.A., 1989-95; regulatory affairs analyst II Gensia Labs., Ltd., Irvine, Calif., 1995—; cons. L.A. Unified Sch. Dist., 1985-87. Docent in tng. L.A. Mus. of Sci. and Industry, 1989. Scholar, grantee So. Calif. Gas Co., L.A., 1980-84, Sloan Rsch. fellow, 1981-82. Mem. Am. Chem. Soc., N.Y. Acad. Sci., Am. inst. Chemists, am. Assn. Physics Tchrs., AAAS, Fed. Am. Scientists, Internat. Union of Pure and Applied Chemistry, Drug Info. Assn., Math. Assn. Am., Soc. Hispanic Profl. Engrs., IEEE. Office: Gensia Labs Ltd 19 Hughes St Irvine CA 92718-1902

CAMPOS, LEONARD PETER, psychologist; b. Arecibo, P.R., Dec. 24, 1932; s. Joseph Gervasio Campos and Emma (Roman) Crespi; m. Mary Lois Cole, Oct. 1, 1961 (div. 1976); children: David, Elizabeth, Barbara; m. Lee Barrett, June 13, 1986 (div. 1992). BA cum laude, CCNY, 1955; PhD, Mich. State U., 1963. Diplomate Am. Bd. Profl. Psychology, Am. Bd. Forensic Psychology. Asst. prof. U. of Pacific, Stockton, Calif., 1963-66; staff psychologist Calif. Youth Authority, Stockton, 1966-70; cons. psychologist Sacramento, 1970—. Author: You Can Redecide Your Life, 1989, Introduce Yourself to Transactional Analysis,1992. With U.S. Army, 1955-57. Mem. Am. Psychol. Assn., Calif. Psychol. Assn., Sacramento Valley Pscyhol. Assn. (pres. Div. I 1988-89, pres. Divsn. II 1992), Nat. Hispanic Psychol. Assn. Office: 1820 Professional Dr # 5 Sacramento CA 95825-2120

CAMPOS, MARK HENRY, cartoonist; b. Reno, Nev., Oct. 24, 1962; s. Felix and Lucy (Arreygue) C.; m. Jeri L. Leckron, Mar. 28, 1987. Student, Willamette U., Salem, Oreg., 1980-81. Editor: (with Marshall Gooch) Uncorrected Personality Traits, 1986; author: El Mago Szazbo!, 1991, Greenland Whale Fisheries, 1992, Bombast, 1993, Tumz: June One, 1994, Places That Are Gone, 1994, Mere Bits of Shame, 1995; contbr. articles to profl. jours. Mem. Cartoon Loonacy (co-editor 1994—). Office: PO Box 95234 Seattle WA 98145-2234

CAMPOS, SANTIAGO E., federal judge; b. Santa Rosa, N.Mex., Dec. 25, 1926; s. Ramon and Miquela Campos; m. Patsy Campos, Jan. 27, 1947; children: Theresa, Rebecca, Christina, Miquela Feliz. J.D., U. N.Mex., 1953. Bar: N.Mex. 1953. Asst., 1st asst. atty gen. State of N.Mex., 1955-57; judge 1st Jud. Dist. N.Mex., 1971-78; judge U.S. Dist. Ct. N.Mex., Santa Fe, 1978—, sr. judge, 1992—. Served as seaman USN, 1944-46. Mem. State Bar of N.Mex., First Jud. Dist. Bar Assn. (hon.), Hon. Order of Coif. Office: US Dist Ct PO Box 2244 Santa Fe NM 87504-2244

CAMRON, ROXANNE, editor; b. Los Angeles; d. Irving John and Roslyn (Weinberger) Spiro; m. Robert Camron; children: Ashley, Jennifer, Erin Jessica. B.A. in Journalism, U. So. Calif. West Coast fashion and beauty editor, Teen mag., Los Angeles, 1969-70; sr. editor Teen mag., 1972-75, editor, 1976—; pub. relations rep. Max Factor Co., 1970; asst. to creative dir. Polly Bergen Co., 1970-71; lectr. teen groups; freelance writer. Active Homeowners Assn. Mem. Am. Soc. Exec. Women. Office: Teen Mag 6420 Wilshire Blvd Los Angeles CA 90048-5502

CANADA, STEPHEN ANDREW, writer; b. Portland, Maine, Apr. 20, 1941; s. Andrew Jackson and Hazel Maude (Archibald) C.; divorced. Student, Upsala (Sweden) U., 1964-65, Alliance Francaise, Paris, 1967; BA, Calif. State Coll., 1969; MA, Calif. State U., L.A., 1977. lcetr. in field. Author: Crop Circle Language 10 vols., 1990-91, UFOs' Origin Identified, 1993, The Mars Structures--Who Made Them?, 1993, UFOs Crop Circles and Mars Structures--Their Common Origin, 1993, Crop Circles Series, Communication, 4 vols., 1993, and 26 other books; also poetry; paintings exhibited at various group shows, 1969-86. Home: Box 4961 Salinas CA 93912

CANADA, WILLIAM H., plastic surgeon; b. Huntington, W.Va., Sept. 5, 1930. MD, W.Va. U., 1956. Intern Meml. Hosp., Charleston, W.Va., 1956-57, gen. surgeon, 1957-59; plastic surgeon Baylor U. Med. Ctr., Houston, 1959-61; chief plastic surgeon Las Vegas Surgery Ctr., 1987—; attending surgeon Univ. Med. Ctr., Las Vegas; clin. instr. plastic surgery Baylor U., Houston. Fellow ACS. Office: 8068 W Sahara Ave Ste G Las Vegas NV 89117-1973*

CANADAY, NICHOLAS, retired English educator; b. N.Y.C., Dec. 22, 1928; s. Nicholas and Nadine (Mueller) C.; m. Amelia Crossland, Mar. 1, 1952; children: Ellen, Nicholas III, Thomas. BA, Princeton U., 1950; MA, U. Fla., 1955, PhD, 1957. Instr. English, asst. prin. The Bolles Sch., Jacksonville, Fla., 1952-54; grad. tchg. asst. U. Fla., Gainesville, 1954-57; instr. English La. State U., Baton Rouge, 1957-59, asst. prof. English, 1959-65, assoc. prof. English, 1965-73, prof. English, 1973-86, prof. emeritus English, 1986—; Fulbright Lectr. in Am. lit. Kanazawa (Japan) U., 1963-64, Trondheim (Norway) U., 1977-78, Shandong U., Jinan, China, 1986-87; Danforth Black Studies fellow Yale U., New Haven, 1970-71. Author: Melville and Authority, 1968; contbr. articles to profl. jours. Vol. Downtown Emergency Svc. Ctr., Seattle, 1987-93; precinct com. officer Dem. Party, Seattle, 1988—; vestry mem. St. Mark's Cathedral, Seattle, 1993—. Cpl. U.S. Infantry, 1950-52. Episcopalian. Home: 228 11th Ave E Apt 301 Seattle WA 98102-5784

CANADY, GLORIA DIANE, secondary education educator, business owner; b. Fresno, Calif., Feb. 10, 1953; d. Louis Anthony and Patricia Ann (Cagle) Ghidelli; m. Laurence E. Canady, Jan. 19, 1974; children: Jarod, Shanda, Brock. AA in Liberal Studies, Coll. Sequoias, 1973; BSBA, Calif. State U., Fresno, 1990, MA in Edn. and Counseling, 1994. Cert. single subject secondary tchr., multiple subject elem. tchr., pupil pers. counseling, Calif. Office mgr., bookkeeper Vincent Outdoor Adv., Hanford, Calif., 1971-78; owner Canady Ag. Svc., Hanford, 1980-89, Western Underground Surveys, Hanford, 1989—; tchr. bus. Roosevelt High Sch., Fresno, 1992—. Mem. Alpha Mu Alpha, Delta Pi Epsilon. Home: 2856 N Spalding Dr Hanford CA 93230

CANALES, FRANCISCO LUIS, hand surgeon; b. Mexico City, July 20, 1957. MD, Stanford U., 1982. Intern Stanford (Calif.) U. Hosp., 1982-83, surgeon, 1983-87, plastic surgeon, 1987-90; microsurgery fellow Davies Med. Ctr., San Francisco, 1989; hand surgery fellow San Francisco Hand Fellowship, 1988; now hand surgeon Santa Rosa (Calif.) Meml. Hosp. *

CANALIS, RINALDO FERNANDO, surgeon, educator, researcher; b. Peru, Sept. 15, 1938; came to U.S., 1965; s. Fernando and Andreina (Oneto) C.; m. Sandra Ciotola, Apr. 5, 1970; childrn: John, Elizabeth. BS, U. Nacional Mayor San Marcos, Lima, Peru, 1959, MD, 1965. Asst. chief otolaryn. Harbor-UCLA Med. Ctr., Torrance, Calif., 1973-78, assoc. chief otolaryn., 1979, chief otolaryn., 1979—; vice chief head and neck surgery UCLA Sch. Medicine, 1979—; acting chair surgery, Harbor-UCLA Med. Ctr., Torrance, 1992-93; acting vice chair surgery UCLA Sch. Medicine, 1992-93, prof. surgery, 1981—; cons. phys. anthropology lab. San Diego Mus. of Man, 1980—. Contbr. chpt. to book, numerous sci. papers to profl. jours. Prin. advisor Meniere's Patients Support Group, West L.A., 1985—. Mem. ACS, Am. Acad. Otolaryn./Head and Neck Surgery (Honor award 1983, cert. of appreciation 1979, 82), Am. Laryngological, Rhinological and Otological Soc., Am. Laryngological Assn., Am. Otological Soc., N.Am. Base of the Skull Soc. (funding mem.). Democrat. Roman Catholic. Home: 457 15th St Santa Monica CA 90402-2231 Office: Harbor-UCLA Med Ctr PO Box 2910 Torrance CA 90509-2910

CANBY, WILLIAM CAMERON, JR., federal judge; b. St. Paul, May 22, 1931; s. William Cameron and Margaret Leah (Lewis) C.; m. Jane Adams, June 18, 1954; children—William Nathan, John Adams, Margaret Lewis. A.B., Yale U., 1953; LL.B., U. Minn., 1956. Bar: Minn. 1956, Ariz. 1972. Law clk. U.S. Supreme Ct. Justice Charles E. Whittaker, 1958-59; asso. firm Oppenheimer, Hodgson, Brown, Baer & Wolff, St. Paul, 1959-62; asso., then dep. dir. Peace Corps, Ethiopia, 1962-64; dir. Peace Corps, Uganda, 1964-66; asst. to U.S. Senator Walter Mondale, 1966; asst. to pres. SUNY, 1967; prof. law Ariz. State U., 1967-80; judge U.S. Ct. Appeals (9th cir.), Phoenix, 1980—; chief justice High Ct. of the Trust Ter. of the Pacific Islands, 1993-94; bd. dirs. Ariz. Center Law in Public Interest, 1974-80, Maricopa County Legal Aid Soc., 1972-78, D.N.A.-People's Legal Services, 1978-80; Fulbright prof. Makerere U. Faculty Law, Kampala, Uganda, 1970-71. Author: American Indian Law, 1988; also articles; note editor: Minn. Law Rev, 1955-56. Precinct and state committeeman Democratic Party Ariz., 1972-80; bd. dirs. Central Ariz. Coalition for Right to Choose, 1976-80. Served with USAF, 1956-58. Mem. State Bar Ariz., Minn. Bar Assn., Maricopa County Bar Assn., Phi Beta Kappa, Order of Coif. Office: US Ct Appeals 9th Cir 6445 US Courthouse 230 N 1st Ave Phoenix AZ 85025-0230

CANCIAN, FRANK (FRANCIS ALEXANDER CANCIAN), anthropology educator; b. Stafford Springs, Conn., Apr. 14, 1934; s. Frank and Emma (Lazzerin) C. AB in Philosophy, Wesleyan U., 1956; PhD in Social Anthropology, Harvard U., 1963. Reporter, photographer The Providence (R.I.) Jour. Co., 1957-58; instr. in social anthropology Harvard U., 1963-64; asst. prof. anthropology Stanford (Calif.) U., 1964-66, chmn. dept. anthropology, 1967-69, prof. anthropology, 1969-76; assoc. prof. anthropology Cornell U., Ithaca, N.Y., 1966-69; prof. anthropology, chmn. social rels. program U. Calif., Irvine, 1979-81, chmn. dept. anthropology, 1991-94; field work includes White Mountain Apache, Ariz., 1955, Peasant Community in So. Italy, 1956-57, Zinacantan, Chiapas, Mexico, 1960-90; cons. and lectr. in field. Author: The Decline of Community in Zinacantan: The Economy, Public Life, and Social Stratification, 1960-87, 1992, The Innovator's Situation: Upper Middle Class Conservatism in Agricultural Communities, 1979, Another Place: Photographs of a Maya Community, 1974, Change and Uncertainty in a Peasant Economy: The Maya Corn Farmers of Zinacantan, 1972, Economics and Prestige in a Maya Community: The Religious Cargo System in Zinacantan, 1965; contbr. articles to profl. jours.; mem. editorial bds. Fulbright scholar, Italy, 1956=57; post-doctoral fgn. area fellowship in Latin Am. Studies, 1966-68; fellow Ctr. for Advanced Sutdy in the Behavioral Scis., Palo Alto, Calif., 1970-71; rsch. grantee NIMH, 1963-64, Wenner-Gren Found., 1971, 81, Ford Found., 1975-77, Rockefeller Found., 1976-78, USAID, 1977-79, 80-82, UCMexus Program, 1983-84, NSF, 1983-88. Fellow Am. Anthropol. Assn., Soc. Applied Anthropology, AAAS; mem. Am. Ethnol. Soc., Soc. Econ. Anthropology.

CANDELARIA, JUDITH (WATT), nursing administrator; b. South Bend, Ind., Jan. 2, 1940; d. William Smale and June Edna (Harrison) Lenhard; m. Michael R. Watt, Nov. 12, 1960 (div. Sept. 1990); children: Steven, Karen Watt Rodriguez, Christopher; m. John Joseph Candelaria, Dec. 24, 1991. BSN, Ind. U., Bloomington, 1961; MSN, Ind. U., 1985. RN, N.Mex. Pub. health nurse Marion County Health Dept., 1961-62, 79, nurse epidemiologist, 1979-83, coord. communicable disease control and immunization programs, 1983-85; from staff nurse to supr. Vis. Nurse Assn., 1977-79; asst. dir. med. svcs. People's Health Ctr., 1985-87, dir. community oriented care, 1987-91; part-time lectr. dept. community health nursing Ind. U., 1987-88, adj. asst. prof., 1990-91; clin. specialist U. Tex. at El Paso Coll. Nursing and Allied Health, 1991; asst. prof. part-time N.Mex. State U., 1991—; chief nurse pub. health div. N.Mex. Dept. Health, 1991, presenter and researcher in field. Contbr. articles to profl. jours. Mem. adv. bd. Tech Teen Clinic, 1985-90, Teen Community Coun., 1985-90, health adv. com. N.Mex. Sch., 1992—, quality adv. bd. N.Mex. Health Resources, 1991—, Ind. Healthy Mothers, Healthy Babies Coalition, 1984-88, Marion County Healthy Mothers and Healthy Babies Coalition, 1984-88, Indpls. Alliance for Health Promotion, 1988-89, case rev. com. ISBH Infant Mortality, 1989-90, Sch. #15 PTO Bd., 1990-91, Parents and Babies Adv. Bd., 1985-90, elder alternative adv. bd. NESMC, 1985-90; bd. dirs. Indpls. Campaign for Healthy Babies, 1989-90; vice chair Homeless Network Indpls., 1989-90; chpt. dir. Pathways to Recovery, 1990-91. Mem. ANA, APHA, Am. Assn. for Practitioners in Infection Control (Ind. chpt. 1980-85), Ind. Pub. Health Assn. (legis. and pub. policy com., v.p., pres.-elect, pres. 1983-91), Nat. Assn. Community Health Ctrs., N.Mex. Nurses Assn., Ind. Pub. Health Assn. (Pres's. award 1982, 83), Sigma Theta Tau. Home: 2N Sandia Trl Corrales NM 87048 Office: NMex Dept Health Runnells Bldg 1190 S Saint Francis Dr Santa Fe NM 87505-4182

CANDELARIA, MICHAEL RICHARD, religious studies educator; b. Roswell, N.Mex., Apr. 15, 1955; s. Eddie Fresquez and Ernestina (Navarette) C.; m. Penny Ann Garcia King, Apr. 2, 1979 (div. Mar. 1989); children: Andrea Misha, Candice Nicole; m. Cheryl Lee Stephens, Aug. 29, 1994. BS, So. Bible Coll., 1981; MDiv, Southwestern Bapt. Theol. Sem., 1983; ThD, Harvard U., 1987. Pastor First Spanish Bapt. Ch., Sulphur Springs, Tex., 1981-83, Chelsea, Mass., 1983-87; tchg. fellow Harvard U., Cambridge, 1984-87; asst. prof. Calif. State U., Bakersfield, 1987-95; tutor St. John's Coll., Santa Fe, 1995—. Author: Popular Religion and Liberation, 1990. With U.S. Army, 1973-76. Fellow Fund for Theol. Edn., Harvard U., 1983-85, NEH, U. So. Calif., 1988, NEH, Grad. Theol. U., Berkeley, 1992, Rockefeller Found., U. N.Mex., 1992-94. Mem. Assn. for the Philosophy Liberation.

CANDIA, TANYA MARIE, marketing executive; b. Great Bend, Kans., Feb. 14, 1949; d. Robert Eugene and Margaret Anice (Bellinger) Bair; m. Xavier Andre Candia, June 24, 1979; children: Cathleen Stael, Alexandra Anice. BA in English (Linguistics), U. Calif., Davis, 1971; MA in Intercultural Comm., Monterey Inst.Internat.Studies, 1977; MS in Sys. Mgmt., U. So. Calif., Pasadena, 1984. Prof. U. De Las Americas, Cholula, Puebla, Mexico, 1977-79; systems analyst Memorex, Santa Clara, Calif., 1979-80; mgr. MIS cons. Hood & Strong, San Jose, 1980-82; quality S.W. mgr. Amdahl Corp., Sunnyvale, Calif., 1982-84; product mgr. ASK, Los Altos, Calif., 1984-86; dir. ops. AIDA Corp., Santa Clara, Calif., 1986-89; dir. customer svc. Qronos Tech., Santa Clara, 1989; v.p. mktg. Demax Software, San Mateo, Calif., 1989-93, Unison Software, Sunnyvale, 1993—. Editor Security Mgmt. Jour., 1992-93, Americarum, 1976-79. Mem. IEEE. Office: Unison Software 5101 Patrick Henry Dr Santa Clara CA 95051

CANDLIN, FRANCES ANN, psychotherapist, social worker, educator; b. Phila., July 18, 1945; d. Francis Townley and Wilma (David) C. BA magna cum laude, Loretto Heights Coll., Denver, 1967; MSW, St. Louis U., 1971. Diplomate Am. Bd. Clin. Social Work; cert. social worker; lic. clin. social worker, Colo. Recreational therapist trainee Jewish Hosp., St. Louis, 1970-71; social worker trainee Jefferson Barracks VA Hosp., St. Louis, 1970-71; social worker Adams County Juvenile Probation, Brighton, Colo., 1972-74, Boulder (Colo.) County Social Svcs., 1974-75; sch. social worker Adams County Sch. Dist. #50, Westminster, Colo., 1975-80; workshop presenter Human Enrichment Cons., Denver, 1980-90; pvt. practice Denver, 1980—; dir. Madison St. Counseling Ctr., Denver, 1991—; cons. Mountain Plains Regional Ctr., Denver, 1981-85, Dept. Edn., Topeka, 1981-87, Dept. Spl. Edn., Nebr., Colo., Mo., N.Mex., Utah, 1982-86. Bd. dirs. Denver Sch. for Gifted, 1982-86, Weaver Found., 1985-86, St. Mary's Acad., Englewood, Colo., 1985-88. Recipient stipend NIMH, 1969, VA Social Work Trainee, 1970. Mem. NASW, NOW, Acad. Cert. Social Workers, Assn. Humanistic Psychology, Assn. Transpersonal Psychology, Colo. Assn. Clin. Social Workers, County Assn. Clin. Social Workers, Vajra Soc. (bd. dirs. 1990—). Office: Madison St Counseling Ctr 123 Madison St Denver CO 80206-5417

CANE, WILLIAM EARL, nonprofit organization executive; b. San Francisco, Aug. 15, 1935; s. Joseph Earl and Mae M. (McDermott) C.; m. Patricia Ann Mathes. MDiv, St. Patrick's Sem., 1973; ThD, San Francisco Theol., 1976. Assoc. pastor St. Joseph Ch., Cupertino, Calif., 1960-65; dir. St. Benedict Ctr., San Francisco, 1966-72; prof. Grad. Theol., Berkeley, Calif., 1973-79; dir. IF, Santa Cruz, Calif., 1975—; editor Integrities, Santa Cruz, 1985—; pres. Assn. Priests Union, San Francisco, 1970-72; bd. dirs. Gaia Ctr., Santa Cruz, Friends of Cantera, Santa Cruz; lectr. in field. Author: Thru Crisis to Freedom, 1980, Circles of Hope, 1992; contbr. articles to profl. jours. Founder Friends of the Deaf, San Francisco, 1970; co-founder Santa Cruz (Calif.) Sanctuary, 1987. Grantee Rascob Found., San Francisco, 1970, Santa Cruz (Calif.) Cmty. Found., 1988, Meruyn's Found., 1988, Eschaton Found., Santa Cruz, 1994. Home and Office: 3015 Freedom Blvd Watsonville CA 95076-0436

CANFIELD, BRIAN A., communications company executive; b. New Westminister, B.C., Canada, July 9, 1938; s. Orra Wells and Effie Beatrice (Dunham) C.; m. Beverly Irene Gillies, Apr. 15, 1961; children: Brian Robert, Bruce Martin, Nancy Susan. Area gen. mgr. B.C. Telephone Co., Burnaby, 1983-85, v.p. tech. support, 1985-88, exec. v.p. tel. ops., 1988-89, pres., COO, 1989-91, pres., chief exec. officer, 1991—, chmn., CEO, 1993—; chmn. bd. Microtel Ltd., MPR Teltech Ltd., BC TEL Svcs, Inc., Can. Telephones and Supplies Ltd., BC TEL Mobility-Cellular Inc., BC TEL Mobile Ltd.; dir. Telesat Can., BC TEL, Telecom Leasing Can.; mem. adv. coun. faculty commerce and bus. adminstrn. U.B.C., Stentor Coun. CEOs; bd. govs. Bus. Coun. B.C. Bd. dirs. Royal Columbian Hosp. Found., Royal Trust, Vancouver Bd. of Trade; chmn. Bus. Coun. of B.C., Stentor Coun. of CEOs. Office: BC Telecom Inc, 3777 Kingsway, 21st fl, Burnaby, BC Canada V5H 3Z7

CANFIELD, GRANT WELLINGTON, JR., management consultant; b. L.A., Nov. 28, 1923; s. Grant Wellington and Phyllis Marie (Westland) C.; m. Virginia Louise Bellinger, June 17, 1945; 1 child, Julie Marie. BS, U. So. Calif., 1949, MBA, 1958. Personnel and indsl. relations exec., L.A., 1949-55; employee relations cons., regional mgr. Mchts. and Mfrs. Assn. L.A., 1955-60; v.p., orgnl. devel. cons. Hawaii Employers Council, Honolulu, 1960-75; pres., dir. Hawaiian Ednl. Council, 1969-92, chmn., CEO, 1989-92, chmn. emeritus, 1992; prin. cons. Grant W. Canfield CMC, 1993—; faculty assignments Calif. State U., L.A., 1957-59, U. So. Calif., 1958-59, U. Hawaii, 1963-72; exec. v.p. Hawaii Garment Mfrs. Assn., 1965-75, Assn. Hawaii Restaurant Employers, 1966-75; exec. dir. Hawaii League Savs. Assns., 1971-78; exec. dir. Pan-Pacific Surg. Assn., 1980-81, exec. v.p., 1982-83; exec. dir. Hawaii Bus. Roundtable, 1983-89; sec., treas. Econ. Devel. Corp. Honolulu, 1984-85; sec., treas. Hawaii Conv. Park Council, Inc., 1984-86, hon. dir., 1986-88. Co-author: Resource Manual for Public Collective Bargaining, 1973. Bd. dirs. Hawaii Restaurant Assn., 1974-76, bd. dirs. Hawaii chpt. Nat. Assn. Accts., 1963-67, nat. dir., 1965-66; bd. dirs. Vol. Service Bur. Honolulu, 1965-66, pres., 1966-68; bd. dirs. Vol. Info. and Referral Service Honolulu, 1972-75, Goodwill Vocat. Tng. Ctrs. of Hawaii, 1973-81, Girl Scout council Pacific, 1961-65, 71-72; bd. dirs. Hawaii Com. Alcoholism, 1962-71, co-chmn., 1964-68; pres., dir. Friends of Punahou Sch., 1972-75; mem. community adv. bd. Jr. League Honolulu, 1968-70; exec. bd. Aloha council Boys Scouts Am., 1962-65; bd. regents Chaminade U., 1983-85. Served to 1st lt. inf. AUS, 1943-46. Decorated Bronze Star, Purple Heart, Combat Inf. badge. Mem. ASTD, Am. Soc. Assn. Execs. (cert. assn. exec.), Inst. Mgmt. Cons. (cert.), Soc. for Human Resource Mgmt., Pacific Club, Healdsburg Mus. and Hist. Soc. (chmn. exec. com. 1993—, v.p. dir. 1994—), Santa Rose Symphony Assn. (bd. dirs. 1993—, mem. exec. com. 1995—, exec. com. 1995—), Rotary, Masons. Home: 1950 W Dry Creek Rd Healdsburg CA 95448-9747 Office: PO Box 637 Healdsburg CA 95448-0637

CANFIELD, J(OHN) DOUGLAS, English language educator; b. Washington, Feb. 4, 1941; s. Austin Francis and Gertrude (MacBride) C.; m. Pamela Eden Crotty, Sept. 7, 1963; children: Robert Alan, Bret Douglas, Colin Geoffrey. BA, U. Notre Dame, 1963; MA in Tchg., Yale U., 1964; MA, Johns Hopkins U., 1966; PhD, U. Fla., 1969. Tchr. Radnor (Pa.) Sr. H.S., 1964-65; grad. asst. tchg. Johns Hopkins U., Balt., 1965-66; asst. prof. U. Calif., L.A., 1969-74; assoc. prof. U. Ariz., Tucson, 1974-79, prof., 1979-94, Regents' prof., 1994—. Author: Nicholas Rowe and Christian Tragedy, 1977, Word as Bond in English Literature from the Middle Ages to the Restoration, 1989; co-editor: Rhetorics of Order/Ordering Rhetorics, 1989, Cultural Readings of Restoration and Eighteenth-Dencuty-English Theater, 1995; contbr. articles to profl. jours. Coach, referee Am. Youth Soccer Orgn., Tucson, 1984—. Recipient Excellence in Tchg., Burlington Resources Found., 1991; named Ariz. Prof. of the Yr., Coun. for the Advancement and Support of Edn., Washington, 1993. Mem. MLA (chair divsn. restoration and early eighteenth century English lit. 1994), Am. Soc. for Eighteenth Century Studies (chair 1990-91, Clifford prize com.). Office: Dept English Univ Ariz Tucson AZ 85721

CANFIELD, JUDY OHLBAUM, psychologist; b. N.Y.C., May 15, 1947; d. Arthur and Ada (Werner) Ohlbaum; m. John T. Canfield (div.); children: Oran David, Kyle Danya. BA, Grinnell Coll., 1963; MA, New Sch. Social Rsch., 1967; PhD, U.S. Internat. U., 1970. Psychologist Mendocino State Hosp., Talmage, Calif., 1968-69, Douglas Coll., New Westminster, BC, Can., 1971-72, Family & Childrens Clinic, Burnaby, BC, Can., 1971-72; psychologist, trainer, cons. VA Hosp., Northampton, Mass., 1972-75; dir. New England Ctr., Amherst, Mass., 1972-76; dir., psychologist Gateways, Lansdale, Pa., 1977-78; asst. prof., psychologist Hahnemann Med. Ctr., Phila., 1978-84; pres., dir. Inst. Holistic Health, Phila., 1978-85; psychologist, cons. Berkeley, Calif., 1986—. Mem. task force, tng. com. Berkeley Dispute Resolution Svc., 1986-89; mem. measure H com. Berkeley United Sch. Dist., 1987-88. Mem. APA, Nat. Register Health Svc. Providers in Psychology, Nat. Assn. Advancement Gestalt Therapy (steering com. 1990), Calif. Psychol. Assn., Alameda County Psychol. Assn. (info.-referral svc. 1989—), Assn. Humanistic Psychology. Office: 2031 Delaware St Berkeley CA 94709-2121

CANN, WILLIAM HOPSON, former mining company executive; b. Newark, June 17, 1916; s. Howard W. and Ruth (Hopson) C.; m. Mildred E. Allen, Mar. 7, 1942 (dec. 1982); children: William Hopson, Sharon Lee, John Allen, Lawrence Edward; m. Nancy B. Barnhart, Nov. 17, 1984. A.B. magna cum laude, Harvard, 1937; LL.B., 1940. Bar: N.Y. 1941, Calif. 1947. Assoc. Chadbourne, Parke, Whiteside & Wolfe (and predecessors), N.Y.C., 1940-53; asst. to pres. Rockwell Internat. Corp., 1953-60, v.p., sec., 1960-75; coordinator for stockholder relations Cyprus Mines Corp., Los Angeles, 1975-76; corp. sec. Cyprus Mines Corp., 1977-85, ret., 1985. Former mem. adv. bd. Family Svc. of Los Angeles. Served to 1st lt. USAAF, 1942-45. Mem. Am. Soc. Corp. Secs. (past pres.), Phi Beta Kappa. Episcopalian. Club: Rocky Mountain Harvard (Denver). Home: 24575 Palace Ct Aliso Viejo CA 92656-5307

CANNON, CHRISTOPHER JOHN, lawyer; b. Milw., Feb. 12, 1954; s. John and Delphine (Bruckwick) C.; m. Anne E. Libbin, July 20, 1985; children: Abigail, Rebecca. Student, U. Sophia, Tokyo; BA, U. Notre Dame; JD, Southwestern U., 1979. Bar: Calif. 1979, U.S. Dist. Ct. (so. and no. dists.) Calif. 1979, U.S. Ct. Appeals (9th cir.) 1979, U.S. Dist. Ct. (cen. and ea. dists.) Calif. 1990, U.S. Supreme Ct. 1992. Law clk. to Hon. William J. Swiegart U.S. Dist. Ct., San Francisco, 1979-81; asst. pub. defender Santa Clara (Calif.) Cts., 1981-82; asst. fed. pub. defender San Francisco Cts., 1982-89; ptnr. Sugarman & Cannon, San Francisco, 1989—. Contbr. articles to profl. jours. Recipient Cert. of Appreciation Fed. Practice Program, San Francisco, 1989. Mem. Fed. Bar Assn., Nat. Assn. Criminal Def. Lawyers, ACLU, Calif. Attys. Criminal Justice Assn., San Francisco Bar Assn. Democrat. Home: 18 Mateo Dr Belvedere Tiburon CA 94920-1046 Office: Sugarman & Cannon 600 Harrison St Ste 535 San Francisco CA 94107-1370

CANNON, GRANT WILSON, physician; b. Salt Lake City, June 17, 1953; m. Sandra Lee Warner; children: Christine, Lisa, Janae, Karen, Suzanne. BA, U. Utah, 1975, MD, 1979. Diplomate Am. Bd. Internal Medicine, sub-specialty rheumatology. Intern U. Utah Affil. Hosp., 1979-80, resident, 1980-82, fellowship, 1982-84; instr. internal medicine U. Utah Sch. of Medicine, 1984-86, asst. prof. internal medicine, 1986-91, assoc. prof. internal medicine, 1991—; assoc. chief of staff for edn. VA Med. Ctr., Salt Lake City, 1988—; dir. clin. studies, divsn. of rheumatology U. Utah, 1988—, dir. student edn., divsn. of rheumatology, 1988—; adj. asst. prof. phys. therapy, U. Utah, 1987-91, adj. assoc. prof., 1987-91; mem. numerous coms. in field. Contbr. articles to profl. jours. Bd. dirs. Arthritis Found., 1988-92. Recipient Young Investigator award The Upjohn Co., 1985; winner clin. paper/poster competition, Assocs. Am. Coll. Physicians, 1984. Fellow Am. Coll. Physicians, Am. Coll. Rheumatology; mem. Utah Med. Assn. (gov. coun. 1987-91, ho. of dels. 1980-81, 88-90), Salt Lake County Med. Soc., Am. Fedn. for Clin. Rsch.

CANNON, JAMES DEAN, accountant, division controller, financial analyst, military officer; b. Ariz., May 27, 1964; s. Ronald Dean Cannon and Laureen Day (Snyder) White; 1 child, Patricia Ann. BA, U. Ariz., 1987; MBA, Nat. U., San Diego, 1989. Financial analyst Lockheed Missiles and Space, Sunnyvale, Calif., 1987-90; contr. Corning-Metwest Inc., Phoenix, 1990-92; divsn. controller The Dial Corp., Phoenix, 1992—. Mem. Young Reps., 1987-90; officer Ariz. Nat. Guard, Phoenix, 1992—. Capt. Med. Svc. Corp., commdr., 1994—. Mem. Inst. for Cert. Mgmt. Accts. (contr. coun.), Nat. Guard Assn.(U.S., Ariz., and Calif.). Office: The Dial Corp 6263 N Scottsdale Rd Ste 340 Scottsdale AZ 85250-5402

CANNON, KEVIN FRANCIS, sculptor; b. N.Y.C., Nov. 27, 1948; s. Connell and Maud (Brogan) C. AA, CCNY, 1971. One-man shows include Willard Gallery, N.Y.C., 1982, James Corcoran Gallery, L.A., 1984, Charles Cowles Gallery, N.Y.C., 1985-86, Rena Bransten Gallery, San Francisco, 1987, New Gallery, Houston, 1987, and others; exhibited in group shows Ft. Worth Gallery, 1984, Am. Crafts Mus., N.Y.C., 1986, Charles Cowles Gallery, N.Y.C., 1987, Modern Objects Gallery, L.A., 1987 and others; represented in permanent collections Lannan Found., Cin. Mus., Bklyn. Mus., Am. Crafts Mus., JB Speed Art Mus., Albuquerque Mus. Nat. Endowment for the Arts grantee, 1986.

CANNON, LOUIS SIMEON, journalist, author; b. N.Y.C., June 3, 1933; s. Jack and Irene (Kohn) C.; m. Virginia Oprian, Feb. 2, 1953 (div. 1983); children: Carl, David, Judy, Jack; m. Mary L. Shinkwin, Sept. 7, 1985. Student, U. Nev., 1950-51, San Francisco State U., 1951-52. Reporter Lafayette Sun, Calif., 1957; editor Newark (Calif.) Sun, 1957-58, Merced Sun Star, Calif., 1958-60, Contra Costa Times, Calif., 1960-61, San Jose (Calif.) Mercury News, Calif., 1961-69; Sacramento corr. San Jose Mercury News, Calif., 1965-69; Washington corr. Ridder Pubs., Washington, 1969-72; reporter The Washington Post, Washington, 1972—; western bur. chief The Washington Post, L.A., 1990—. Author: President Reagan: the Role of a Lifetime, 1991, Reagan, 1982, Ronnie and Jesse, 1969, Reporting: An Inside View, 1977, The McCloskey Challenge, 1972. Recipient Gerald R. Ford prize Gerald Ford Libr., 1988, Merriman Smith award White House Corrs. Assn., 1986, Aldo Beckman award, 1984, Washington Journalism Rev. award, 1985, Disting. Reporting of Pub. Affairs award Am. Polit. Sci. Assn., 1968. Mem. Soc. of Profl. Journalists, Authors Guild. Home: PO Box 436 Summerland CA 93067-0436 Office: Washington Post 10 100 Santa Monica Blvd # 745 Los Angeles CA 90067

CANNON, SAMANTHA KARRIE, management consultant, entrepreneur; b. Dayton, Ohio, Aug. 27, 1948; d. Emerson Lee and Elizabeth Ann (Riecken) Poppler; m. Peter Marcellus Cannon, Oct. 30, 1988. BA in Psychology, Calif. State U., Sacramento, 1977, MPA, MSW, 1982. Editor, pub. Equitable Life, Sacramento, 1972-76; mgmt. cons. State of Calif., Sacramento, 1976—; pvt. practice mgmt. cons. Sacramento, 1990—; founder, owner Your Best Friend, Sacramento, 1991—; mgmt. cons. United Way, Sacramento, 1985-88. Editor, pub.: (jour.) The Westerner, 1972-76. Past bd. dirs. Aquarian Effort; vol. comty. rape, suicide, family crisis, substance abuse and ex-offender programs; bd. dirs. Diogenes Youth Svcs., 1992-94. Recipient numerous local, state and nat. poetry awards. Lutheran. Office: Calif Dept Alcohol & Drug Programs 1700 K St Sacramento CA 95814-4022

CANOFF, KAREN HUSTON, lawyer; b. Medford, Oreg., May 15, 1954; d. Loyd Stanley and Donna Lou (Wall) Huston; m. Lawrence Scott Canoff, May 30, 1981; children: Vincent Jared, Alyssa Rae. BS, U. Oreg., 1977; JD cum laude, Lewis & Clark Coll., 1981. Bar: Oreg. 1981, U.S. Dist. Ct. Oreg. 1982, U.S. Ct. Appeals (9th cir.) 1985, Calif. 1985, U.S. Dist. Ct. (so. dist.) Calif. 1985, U.S. Dist. Ct. (cen. dist.) Calif. 1986, U.S. Ct. Appeals (fed. cir.) 1991. Fin. cons. Stretch & Sew, Inc., Eugene, Oreg., 1975-78; assoc. Margaretta Eakin P.C., Portland, Oreg., 1981-82, 83, Gary M. Bullock, Portland, 1982-83, Markowitz & Herbold, Portland, 1983-86; ptnr. Dorazio, Barnhorst & Bonar, San Diego, 1986-89, shareholder, 1989; ptnr. Hyde & Canoff, San Diego, 1990—; instr. People's Law Sch., Eugene, Oreg., 1978. Author: (with others) Legal Resource Guide, 1983; contbr. articles to profl. jours. Mem. Multnomah County Vol. Lawyers, Portland, Oreg., 1982-83, San Diego Vol. Lawyers Program, 1985—, Vols. in Parole, San Diego, 1986-87, Charlotte Baker Soc., 1992-93; judge pro tem San Diego County Mcpl. Ct., 1988—, San Deigo Superior Ct., 1991—; mem. nat. panel comml. arbitrators Am. Arbitration Assn., 1991—. Recipient Am. Jurisprudence award, 1979. Mem. Calif. State Bar Assn., San Diego County Bar Assn. (appellate ct. com. 1987—, editor It's the Law 1987, alternative dispute resolution sec. 1990—, arbitration com. 1990—, client rels. com. 1990—, editor Bar Briefs 1992), Lawyers Club San Diego (bd. dirs. 1988-91, editor Lawyers Club News 1986-88), Assn. Bus. Trial Lawyers, Women in Comml. Real Estate, Nat. Assn. Women Bus. Owners (bd. dirs. 1993—), Phi Beta Kappa.

CANOVA-DAVIS, ELEANOR, biochemist, researcher; b. San Francisco, Jan. 18, 1938; d. Gaudenzio Enzio and Catherine (Bordisso) Canova; m. Kenneth Roy Davis, Feb. 10, 1957; children: Kenneth Roy Jr., Jeffrey Stephen. BA, San Francisco State U., 1968, MS, 1971; PhD, U. Calif., San Francisco, 1977. Lab. asst. Frederick Burk Found. for Edn., San Francisco, 1969-71; rsch. tchg. asst. U. Calif., San Francisco, 1972-77, asst. rsch. biochemist, 1980-84; NIH postdoctoral fellow U. Calif., Berkeley, 1977-80; sr. scientist Liposome Tech., Menlo Park, Calif., 1984-85, Genentech, Inc., South San Francisco, 1985—. Contbr. articles to profl. jours. Recipient Nat. Rsch. Svc. award NIH, 1977-80; grantee Chancellor's Patent Fund, U. Calif., San Francisco, 1976, Earl C. Anthony Trust, 1975; grad. div. fellow U. Calif., San Francisco, 1972-73. Mem. Am. Chem. Soc., Calif. Scholarship Fedn., Sequoia Woods Country Club, Protein Soc., Am. Peptide Soc., Am. Soc. Mass Spectrometry. Roman Catholic. Home: 2305 Bourbon Ct South San Francisco CA 94080-5367 Office: Genentech Inc 460 Point San Bruno Blvd South San Francisco CA 94080-4918

CANTER, BARRY MITCHELL, electronics specialist, musician; b. Mineola, N.Y., Feb. 24, 1950; s. Robert Ackley and Lillian Georgette (Cook) C.; m. Janice Marie Cantone, Aug. 25, 1974; children: Eric Vincent, Laura Marie. Student, Nassau C.C., 1968-70, Clark County C.C., 1980-82, Nat. U., 1987, Mesa Coll., 1991-92. Lic. FCC Gen. Radio Telephone Operator, 1994, FCC amateur tech., 1994, FCC radar endorsement, 1995. Rec. producer, engr., musician Accutrack Rec. Studios, Garden City, N.Y., 1971-73; musical dir., performer Assoc. Booking Corp., N.Y.C., 1973-75; entertainer, performer various major hotels, San Diego and Las Vegas, Nev., 1975—; electronics repair technician Wilson Electronics, Inc., Las Vegas, 1980-83, Motorola Comms., Inc., Las Vegas, 1986-87; nat. tech. svc. advisor Regency Landmobile, Inc., Las Vegas, 1983-86; nat. customer svc. mgr. Celltronics-Neutec-Trilectric, San Diego, 1987-89, asst. nat. sales mgr., 1989-90; nat. customer svc. mgr. Hitec RCD Inc., Santee, Calif., 1991—; music tchr., San Diego, 1990—; band leader Third Degree, San Diego, 1991—, Material Witness, San Diego, 1995—. Composer various songs; contbr. articles to profl. publs. Vol. Sundance Elem. Sch., 1989-90, Deer Canyon Elem. Sch., 1990-91, disabled children's basketball and baseball league, San Diego, 1991—. Mem. Musicians Union of Las Vegas. Office: Hitec RCD 10729 Wheatlands Ave Santee CA 92071-2887

CANTERBURY, LESLIE JOHN, librarian; b. Hancock, Mich., June 9, 1958; s. Leslie Blaine and Ellen Ann (Järvenpää) C.; m. Alisa Marie Slaughter, July 20, 1991. BA, U. Ariz., 1986, MLS, 1988. Librarian U. Ariz. Main Libr., Tucson, 1989-90, U. Redlands (Calif.) Armacost Libr., 1990—. Mem. ALA (various coms.), Calif. Libr. Assn. (various coms.), Ariz. State Libr. Assn. (various coms.). Democrat. Office: Univ Redlands Armacost Libr 1200 E Colton Ave Redlands CA 92374-3755

CANTO, DIANA CATHERINE, nurse; b. Antioch, Calif., Mar. 20, 1939; d. William Light and Emma Catherine (Disher) Clark; children: Paul Petroni, Peter Petroni, Patrick Canto, Alexander Canto. AS with honors, Contra Costa Coll., San Pablo, Calif., 1982; BSN summa cum laude, Holy Name Coll., Oakland, Calif., 1984; MS, U. Calif., San Francisco, 1987. RN, Calif.; cert. PNP, FNP, CPR. RN Children's Hosp. Oakland, Calif., 1984-86, Merrithew Meml. Hosp., Martinez, Calif., 1986-87; family nurse practitioner Contra Costa County Detention Facility, Martinez, Calif., 1987, Berkeley (Calif.) City Pub. Health Dept., West Berkeley (Calif.) Health Clin., 1987-88, Maxicare Health Svcs., Calif., 1988-90, Homeless Program Alameda, San Leandro, Calif., 1989-90; nurse practitioner, founder student health svcs. U. San Francisco, 1989-90; with San Francisco Pub. Health Dept., 1989-91; ind. nurse practitioner family, pediatrics, family planning, women's health care, 1991—; researcher Contra Costa County P.H.D., Pitts., 1984, Ctr. for New Americans, Concord, Calif., 1985, UCSF, 1986-87, edn. program developer, Children's Hosp. Oakland, 1984-85, other ctrs. Mem. Walnut Creek Com. on Aging. Mem. AAUW, LWV, NOWA, ANA, APHA, Calif. Nurses Assn., Calif. Coalition Nurse Practitioners, Wash. State Nurses Assn., Nat. Assn. Pediatric Nurse Practitioner Assn., Coun. Nursing and Anthropology, Intercultural Interest Group of the Bay Area, Kappa Gamma Pi, Sigma Theta Tau. Home: 618 Avenue A Snohomish WA 98290-2416 Office: Sky River Health Ctr 615 W Stevens Ste D Sultan WA 98294

CANTOR, ALAN BRUCE, management consultant, computer software developer; b. Mt. Vernon, N.Y., Apr. 30, 1948; s. Howard and Muriel Anita Cantor; m. Judith Jolanda Szarka, Mar. 1, 1987; 1 child, Alec Brandon. BS in Social Scis., Cornell U., 1970; MBA, U. Pa., 1973. Mgmt. cons. M & M Risk Mgmt. Services, N.Y.C., 1974-78, nat. services officer, spl. projects div. Marsh & McLennan, Inc., 1978-80, asst. v.p., mgr. Marsh & McLennan Risk Mgmt. Services, Los Angeles, 1980-81; sr. v.p. sr. cons. prin. Warren, McVeigh & Griffin, Inc., 1981-82, sr. v.p., prin., 1982; founder, pres. Cantor & Co., 1982—; co-mgr. Air Travel Rsch. Group, N.Y.C., 1977-79; instr. risk mgmt. program Am. Mgmt. Assn.; lectr. Risk and Ins. Mgmt. Soc. Conf., 1975-87; seminars How to Use Spreadsheets in Risk Mgmt., 1986-89, How to Use Computers in Risk Mgmt., 1989-93. Cons., vol. Urban Cons. Group, N.Y.C.; elder Beverly Hills Presbyn. Ch., 1991—. Mem. Cornell Alumni Assn. N.Y.C. (bd. govs., program chmn.), Cornell Alumni Assn. So. Calif. Clubs: Wharton Bus. Sch. (N.Y.C.); Los Angeles, Wharton of Los Angeles (chmn., mem. adv. bd.) Los Angeles Athletic (Los Angeles). Copyright airline industry model, 1975. Contbr. articles to profl. jours.; creator, developer, copyright RISKMAP risk mgmt. software products, 1982-95; copyright airline industry model, 1975, Exposure Base Mgmt. System (EBMS), 1985, 86, patient care monitoring system, 1985-92, Med. Quality Mgmt. Systems Plus, 1991-95, MQMS Plus, COLTS, corp. overall legal tracking system, 1983, hosp. risk info. mgmt. system, 1984, 86, 87, 89, 90, 91, 93, 94, RISKMAP ins. schedules system, 1989. Office: Cantor & Co 9100 Wilshire Blvd Beverly Hills CA 90212-3415

CANTOR, MARA JUDITH, human resources executive, management consultant; b. N.Y.C., July 24, 1940; d. William and Phyllis Shirley (Schiff) C.; children: Charles Cohen, Leslie Kalish, Kim Biggio. AA, Monterey Peninsula Jr. Coll., 1974; BA, U. Calif., Santa Cruz, 1978; MA, San Francisco State U., 1981. Adminstrv. v.p. Accurate Diamond Tool Corp., Hackensack, N.J., 1964-71; sales rep. Dictaphone Corp., Santa Clara, Calif., 1972-76; archaeologist various projects Nat. Geographic, Harvard Peabody Mus., also others, Belize, 1978-84; cons., Carmel, Calif., 1984-87; owner, mgr. LeGrand Travel, Monterey, Calif., 1987-93; mgr. human resources Highlands Inn, Carmel, 1988-92; v.p. human resources The Homestead, Hot Springs, Va., 1993-94; trustee Culinary Ins. Trust, Pacific Grove, Calif., 1990-93; cons., ptnr. Expanding Horizons. Author: Belize—Frommer's Mexico on $25 a Day; newspaper travel columnist, 1989. Mem. Leadership Monterey Peninsula, 1986; del. Monterey County Social Svcs., Salinas, Calif., 1987; bd. dirs. Personal Empowerment Ctr., 1985, Carmel Valley (Calif.) Property Owners, 1988. Named One of Top 10 Businesswomen, N.J. Bus. mag., 1971. Mem. Monterey County Hospitality Assn. (edn. com. 1991-92).

CANTWELL, MARIA E., congresswoman. Grad., Miami U. Former rep. Dist. 44 State of Wash.; mem. 103rd Congress from 1st Wash. dist., Washington, D.C., 1993—; owner pub. rels. firm. Office: US Ho Reps Office Ho Mems Washington DC 20515*

CAO, DAC-BUU, software engineer; b. Ninh Hoa, Khanh Hoa, Vietnam, Feb. 21, 1949; came to U.S., 1980; s. Thuan and Tiep Thi (Le) C.; m. Amy My-Hao Luong, Nov. 11, 1967; children: Valerie Phuong-Bao, Jesse Chau, Mike Minh-Chau. B of Law, U. Saigon, Vietnam, 1972; BS in Computer Sci., U. Calif., Irvine, 1985; MS in Computer Sci., West Coast U., L.A., 1991. Spl. corr. Progress Daily News, Saigon, 1965-69, mng. editor, 1969-72; asst. editor Dem. Daily News, Saigon, 1973-74; programmer, analyst Eaton Corp., Costa Mesa, Calif., 1981-85; system design engr. EPC Internat., Newport Beach, Calif., 1985-89; sr. application specialist McDonnell Douglas System Integration, Cypress, Calif., 1989-91; sr. systems engr. Unigraphics div. EDS Corp., 1991—. Author: (Vietnamese) Tien Don Yeu Dau, 1969, Ngon Doi Tuyet Vong, 1970; inventor protector for motor vehicles; designer Cellular Air Time Tracking Sys. Recipient Vietnamese Journalism award Nat. Press Coun., U.S. Govt., 1966, Systems Integration MVP award McDonnell Douglas Corp., 1990. Mem. IEEE Computer Soc., Acad. of Am. and Internat. Law, Assn. for Computing Machinery, Am. Assn. for Artificial Intelligence, N.Y. Acad. Scis. Republican. Buddhist. Office: Electronic Data Systems Corp 10824 Hope St Cypress CA 90630-5214

CAO, THAI-HAI, industrial engineer; b. Saigon, Republic of Vietnam, July 8, 1954; came to U.S., 1975; s. Pho Thai and Anh Ngoc (Nguyen) C.; m. Hue Thi Tran, June 29, 1979; children: Quoc-Viet Thai, Quoc-Nam Thai, Huyen-Tran Thai. BS in Indsl. Engring., U. Wash., 1980; grad., Gen. Electric Mfg. Mgmt. Prgm., 1982. Mfg. engr. GE, San Jose, Calif., 1980-82; mgr. mfg. engring. and quality assurance Broadcast Microwave div. Harris Corp., Mountain View, Calif., 1982-85; mgr. mfg. engring. John Fluke Mfg. Co., Everett, Wash., 1986-90; mgr. quality engring. Advanced Tech. Labs., Bothell, Wash., 1990-91; prin. electronic process engr. Olin Aerospace Co.; cons. total quality mgmt. Vinatek. Mem. Am. Soc. Quality Control (chmn. membership com. 1987-88), Soc. Vietnamese Profls. (pres. 1988), Soc. Mfg. Engrs., Inst. Indsl. Engrs., Am. Prodn. and Inventory Control. Home: 23502 22nd Ave SE Bothell WA 98021-9553

CAPANNA, ALBERT HOWARD, neuroscientist, neurosurgeon; b. Utica, N.Y., May 12, 1947; m. Dawn McLouth; children: Christine, Alicia, Albert II, Danielle, Gabriella, Guy, Brianna, Gianna. BA, U. Tex., 1970; MD, Wayne State U., 1974. Med. intern St. John Hosp., Detroit, 1974, resident in gen. surgery, 1974-75; resident in neurosurgery Wayne State U., Detroit, 1975-79; fellow in microneurosurgery U. Zurich, 1979; stereotactic fellow U. Paris, 1980; fellow in pediatric neurosurgery Hosp. for Sick Children, Toronto, 1980; pvt. practice Internat. Neurosci. Cons., Las Vegas, 1983—; chief staff Sunrise Hosp., Las Vegas; chief neurosurgery Univ. Med. Ctr., Las Vegas; clin. prof. U. Nev. Sch. Medicine. Office: 2040 W Charleston Blvd Ste 403 Las Vegas NV 89102-2231

CAPE, RONALD ELLIOT, biotechnology company executive; b. Montreal, Que., Can., Oct. 11, 1932; came to U.S., 1967, naturalized, 1972; s. Victor and Fan C.; m. Lillian Judith Pollock, Oct. 21, 1956; children: Jacqueline R., Julie A. AB in Chemistry, Princeton U., 1953; MBA, Harvard U., 1955; PhD in Biochemistry, McGill U., Montreal, 1967; postgrad., U. Calif., Berkeley, 1967-70. Customs, purchasing and advt. clk. Merck and Co., Ltd., Montreal, 1955-56; pres. Profl. Pharm. Corp., Montreal, 1960-67; chmn. bd. Profl. Pharm. Corp., 1967-73; pres. Cetus Corp., Emeryville, Calif., 1972-78; chmn. bd. Cetus Corp., 1978-91; chmn. Darwin Molecular Coirp., 1992—; mem. adv. coun. dept. molecular biology Princeton U.; adj. prof. bus. adminstrn. U. Pitts.; vis. prof. biochemistry Queen Mary Coll., U. London; bd. dirs. Neutrogena Corp., The Found. Nat. Medals of Sci. & Tech., 1992—, Advanced Bioconcept, Inc., Interactive Scis., Inc.; founder, bd. dirs. Bay Area Biosci. Ctr., 1989—; mem. bus. affairs com. Ann. Revs., Inc., 1975-80; mem. impacts of applied genetics adv. panel to Office Tech. Assessment; mem. adv. com. on life scis. Natural Scis. and Engring. Rsch. Coun. Can.; bus. adv. com. Neurobiol. Techs., Inc. Mem. Rockefeller U. Coun.; bd. dirs. U. Calif. Art Mus. Coun., Berkeley, 1974-76; trustee Head-Royce Schs., Oakland, Calif., 1975-80, Rockefeller U., 1986-90, San Francisco Conservatory Music, The Keystone Ctr., 1987-93; bd. dirs. San Francisco Opera Assn., mem. budget and fin. com., 1992—, U. Waterloo Inst. for Biotech. Rsch.; mem. bus. adv. com. U. Calif., Berkeley; mem. Berkeley Roundtable on Internat. Economy; mem. sci. adv. bd. Bio-Technology Mag., 1987—; trustee Princeton U., 1989-93; mem. bd. regents Nat. Libr. of Medicine, 1989-92; scientific adv. bd. Med. Rsch. Coun., Can., standing com. bus. devel. Fellow AAAS, Am. Acad. Arts and Scis., Am. Soc. Microbiology (Found. for Microbiology lectr. 1978-79); mem. Can. Biochem. Soc., Fedn. Am. Scientists, Royal Soc. Health, Soc. Indsl. Microbiology, Indsl. Biotech. Assn. (founding mem., pres. 1983-85, dir.), N.Y. Acad. Scis., Princeton Club of N.Y., Commonwealth Club of Calif., Sigma Xi. Jewish.

CAPELL, CYDNEY LYNN, editor; b. Jacksonville, Fla., Dec. 20, 1956; d. Ernest Clary and Alice Rae (McGinnis) Capell; m. Garrick Philip Martin, July 16, 1983 (div. Jan. 1988). BA, Furman U., 1977. Mktg. rep. E.C. Capell & Assocs., Greenville, S.C., 1977-80; sales rep. Prentice-Hall Publs., Cin., 1980-81; sales, mktg. rep. Benjamin/Cummings, Houston, 1981-83; sales rep. McGraw-Hill Book Co., Houston, 1983-85, engring. editor, N.Y.C., 1985-87; acctg. and infosystems editor Bus. Pubs., Inc., Plano, Tex., 1988-89; sr. editor Gorsuch Scarisbrick Pubs., Scottsdale, Ariz., 1989-90; editor-in-chief rsch. dept. Rauscher, Pierce, Refsnes Stock Brokers, 1990-94; editor-in-chief Marshall & Swift, L.A., 1994—; editor lit. mag. Talon, 1972; news editor Paladin newspaper, 1977. Named Rookie of Yr., McGraw-Hill Book Co., 1985. Mem. NOW, NAFE, Women in Pub., Women in Communications, Mensa. Republican. Avocations: tennis, ballet.

CAPELLE, MADELENE CAROLE, opera singer, educator, music therapist; b. Las Vegas, Nev., July 29, 1950; d. Curtis and Madelene Glenna (Healy) C. BA, Mills Coll., 1971; MusM, U. Tex., 1976; postgrad., Ind. U., 1976-77; diploma cert., U. Vienna, Austria, 1978; postgrad. in creative arts, Union Coll. Cert. K-12 music specialist, Nev. Prof. voice U. Nev. Clark County C.C., Las Vegas, 1986—; music therapist Charter Hosp., Las Vegas, 1987—; pvt. practice music therapy, Las Vegas, 1989—; music specialist Clark County Sch. Dist., Las Vegas, 1989—; contract music therapist Nev. Assn. for Handicapped, Las Vegas, 1990; guest voice coach U. Basel, Switzerland, 1992; presenter concerts in Kenya, self-esteem workshops for children and adult women; artist-in-residence, Nev., Wyo., S.D., Oreg., Idaho, N.D., Utah, 1988—; mem. cons. roster Wyo. Arts Cou., 1988—; cons. U.S. rep. Princess Margaret of Romania Found.; workshops in music therapy and humor therapy Germany, Austria, Switzerland; workshop day treatment program dir. Harmony Health Care; judge Leontyne Price Nat. Voice Competition. Opera singer, Europe, Asia, S.Am., U.S., Can., Australia, 1978—; roles include Cio Cio San in Madama Butterly, Tosca, Turandot and Fidelio, Salome Electra; community concerts artist; featured PBS artist Guess Who's Playing the Classics; featured guest All Things Considered PBS radio, 1985; co-writer (one-woman show) The Fat Lady Sings, 1991 (Women's Awareness award); concerts Africa, Kenya, Somalia; concerts for Jugaslavian Relief throughout Europe; guest soloist national anthem San Francisco 49ers. Pres., founder, cons. Children's Opera Outreach, Las Vegas, 1985—; artist Musicians Emergency Found., N.Y.C., 1978-82; vol. Zoo Assn., Allied Arts, Ziegfeld Club (first Junior Ziegfeld Young Woman of Yr.), Las Vegas, 1979—; clown Very Spl. Arts, Nev., Oreg., S.D., 1989-90; goodwill and cultural amb. City of Las Vegas, 1983; panelist Kennedy Ctr., Washington, 1982; artist Benefit Concerts for Children with AIDS; mem. Nev. Arts Alliance, Make a Wish Found., Lyric Opera of Las Vegas. Named Musician of Yr. Swiss Music Alliance, 1993. Mem. Internat. Platform Assn., Nat. Assn. Tchrs. Singing (featured guest speaker), Performing Arts Soc. Nev., Brown Bag Concert Assn. (bd. dirs.), Make a Wish Found., Las Vegas Lyric Opera (bd. dirs.). Democrat. Home: 3266 Brentwood St Las Vegas NV 89121-3316

CAPELLI, MARK HENRI, coastal planner, university lecturer; b. San Buenaventura, Calif., Sept. 1, 1946; s. Henry F. and Rosalie (Colla) C.; m. Elaine Wesley, FEb. 19, 1992; 1 child, Aaron Wolfson Capelli. BA with honors, U. Calif., Santa Barbara, 1969; MLS, U. Calif., Berkeley, 1973; MA in History, U. Calif., Santa Barbara, 1973, postgrad., 1974-77. Calif. coastal program analyst Calif. Coastal Commn., 1976—; lectr. environ. studies program U. Calif., Santa Barbara, 1991—; mem. Beacon Erosion Authority for and Control Ops. and Nourishment; mem. wetlands policy com. Calif. Coastal Commn. Contbr. numerous articles to profl. jours. Mem. Ventura County Fish and Game Commn., 1972-74; exec. dir. Friends of the Ventura River, 1974—. Recipient Pres.'s Streamkeeper award Calif. Trout, Inc., 1976, Golden Trout award, 1994; Planner of Yr. award Citizens Planning Assn. Santa Barbara County, 1994; John and Ina Campbell scholar; U. Calif. Regents grad. rsch. grantee, 1972. Office: U Calif Santa Barbara Environ Studies Program Santa Barbara CA 93106

CAPENER, REGNER ALVIN, minister, electronics engineer; b. Astoria, Oreg., Apr. 18, 1942; s. Alvin Earnest and Lillian Lorraine (Lehtosaari) C.; divorced; children: Deborah, Christian, Melodie, Ariella; m. Della Denise Melson, May 17, 1983; children: Shelley, Danielle, Rebekah, Joshua. Student, U. Nebr., 1957-58, 59-60, Southwestern Coll., Waxahachie, Tex., 1958-59, Bethany Bible Coll., 1963-64. Ordained minister Full Gospel Assembly Ch., 1971. Rsch. engr. Lockheed Missiles & Space Corp., Palo

Alto, Calif., 1962-64; engr., talk show host Sta. KHOF-FM, Glendale, Calif., 1966-67; youth min. Bethel Union Ch., Duarte, Calif., 1966-67; pres. Intermountain Electronics, Salt Lake City, 1967-72; assoc. pastor Full Gospel Assembly, Salt Lake City, 1968-72, Long Beach (Calif.) Christian Ctr., 1972-76; v.p. Refuge Ministries, Inc., Long Beach, 1972-76; pres. Christian Broadcasting Network-Alaska, Inc., Fairbanks, 1977-83; gen. mgr. Action Sch. of Broadcasting, Anchorage, 1983-85; pres., pastor House of Praise, Anchorage, 1984-93; chief engr. KTBY-TV, Inc., Anchorage, 1988-93; pres. R & DC Engring., Anchorage, 1993—; area dir. Christian Broadcasting Network, Virginia Beach, 1977-83; cons., dir. Union Bond and Trust Co., Anchorage, 1985-86; author, editor univ. courses,1 984-85; dep. gov. Am. Biog. Inst. Rsch. Assn., 1990—; adviser Anchorage chpt. Women's Aglow Internat., 1990-91. Author: Spiritual Maturity, 1975, Spiritual Warfare, 1976, The Doctrine of Submission, 1988, A Vision for Praise, 1988, Ekklesia, 1993; author, composer numerous gospel songs; creator numerous broadcasting and electronic instrument inventions. Sec., Christian Businessmen's Com., Salt Lake City, 1968-72; area advisor Women's Aglow Internat., Fairbanks, 1981-83; local co-chmn. campaign Boucher for Gov. Com., Fairbanks, 1982; campaigner for Boucher, Anchorage, 1984, Clark Gruening for Senate Com., Barrow, Alaska, 1980; TV producer Stevens for U.S. Senate, Barrow, 1978; fundraiser City of Refuge, Mex., 1973-75; statewide rep. Sudden Infant Death Syndrome, Barrow, 1978-82; founder Operation Blessing/Alaska, 1981; mem. resch. bd. advisors Am. Biog. Inst., 1990—; advisor Anchorage chpt. Women's Aglow Internat., 1990-91. Mem. Soc. Broadcast Engrs., Internat. Soc. Classical Guitarists (sec. 1967-69), Alaska Broadcaster's Assn., Nat. Assn. Broadcasters, Anchorage C. of C. Republican. Office: R & DC Engring 3960 S State Line Rd Post Falls ID 83854-8245

CAPIZZI, MICHAEL ROBERT, lawyer; b. Detroit, Oct. 19, 1939; s. I.A. and Adelaide E. (Jennelle) C.; m. Sandra Jo Jones, June 22, 1963; children: Cori Anne, Pamela Jo. BS in Bus. Adminstrn., Eastern Mich. U., 1961; JD, U. Mich., 1964. Bar: Calif. 1965, U.S. Dist. Ct. (so. dist.) Calif. 1965, U.S. Ct. Appeals (9th cir.) 1970, U.S. Supreme Ct. 1971. Dep. dist. atty. Orange County, Calif., 1965-68, head writs, appeals and spl. assignments sect., 1968-71, asst. dist. atty., dir. spl. ops., 1971-86; legal counsel, mem. exec. bd. Interstate Organized Crime Index, 1971-79, Law Enforcement Intelligence Unit, 1971-95, chief asst. dist. atty., 1986-90, dist. atty., 1990—; instr. criminal justice Santa Ana Coll., 1967-76, Calif. State U., 1976-87. Commr. City Planning Commn., Fountain Valley, Calif., 1971-80, vice chmn., 1972-73, chmn., 1973-75, 79-80. Fellow Am. Coll. Trial Lawyers; mem. Nat. Dist. Attys. Assn. (bd. dirs. 1995), Calif. Dist. Attys. Assn. (outstanding prosecutor award 1980, v.p. 1995), Calif. Bar Assn., Orange County Bar Assn. (chmn. cts. com. 1977, chmn. coll. of trial advocacy com. 1978-81, bd. dirs. 1977-81, sec.-treas. 1982, pres. 1984). Office: Orange County Dist Atty 700 Civic Center Dr W Santa Ana CA 92701-4045

CAPLAN, EDWIN HARVEY, university dean, accounting educator; b. Boston, Aug. 24, 1926; s. Henry and Dorothy (Nathanson) C.; m. Ramona Hootner, June 20, 1948; children—Gary, Dennis, Jeffrey, Nancy. B.B.A., U. Mich., 1950, M.B.A., 1952; Ph.D., U. Calif., 1965. C.P.A., Calif., Mich. Ptnr. J.J. Gotlieb & Co., C.P.A.s, Detroit, 1953-56; prof. acctg. Humboldt State U., 1956-61, U. Oreg., 1964-67; prof. U. N.Mex., Albuquerque, 1967—, assoc. dean Sch. Mgmt., 1982-83, dean Sch. Mgmt., 1989-90; cons. in field. Contbr. articles to profl. jours. Served to 1st lt. U.S. Army, 1944-46. Mem. Am. Acctg. Assn., AICPA, Nat. Assn. Accts. Home: 8201 Harwood Ave NE Albuquerque NM 87110-1517 Office: Univ N Mex Anderson Sch Mgmt Albuquerque NM 87131

CAPLAN, JOHN ALAN, executive search company executive; b. San Mateo, Calif., Aug. 24, 1945; s. Julian and Sylvia Yetta (Peterman) C.; m. Andrea Illyne Wiener, June 25, 1967; children: Jay Wesley, Cynthia Rochelle. BS, San Jose State U., 1967; MBA, U. Calif., Berkeley, 1968. With Shell Oil Co., 1970-73; mgr. Mattel, Inc., Hawthorne, Calif., 1972-73; v.p. Syntex Corp., Palo Alto, Calif., 1973-85, Valid Logic Systems, San Jose, 1985-86; exec. v.p. Howe-Lewis Internat., Menlo Park, 1986—. Bd. dirs. Jr. Achievement, Santa Clara, Calif., 1987; mem. MBA adv. bd. U. Santa Clara, 1986-89. With USAR, 1968-72. Democrat.

CAPLIN, ABIGAIL BETH, allergist; b. Rochester, N.Y., July 5, 1955. MD, Tex. Tech U., 1981. Resident physician U. Tex. Health Scis. Ctr., Houston, 1981-84; allergy and immunology fellow U. Calif., San Francisco, 1984-86; now allergist and immunologist Peninsula Hosp., Burlingame, Calif. Office: Peninsula Allergy Assocs 1828 El Camino Real Ste 703 Burlingame CA 94010*

CAPORASO, KAREN DENISE, financial planner; b. Alhambra, Calif., May 23, 1953; d. Robert S. and Vivian J. (Scharff) Kuhle; m. Fredric Caporaso, Dec. 5, 1981; children: Allison Marie, Eric Duncan. BS in Fin., Chapman U., 1988, BS in Bus. Econs., 1988. CFP. Supr. payroll and acctg. Am. Med. Optics, Irvine, Calif., 1983-85; acct. Liberty Capital Markets, Newport Beach, Calif., 1985-89; stock broker Baraban Securities, Inc., Anaheim, Calif., 1990-92; registered rep. First Fin. Planners/FFP Securities, Tustin, Calif., 1992-95; with Orange Capital Mgmt., Orange, Calif., 1995—; registered rep. FFP Adv. Svcs., Inc. Mem. Internat. Assn. Fin. Planners, Orange County Soc. of Inst. CFPs, So. Calif. Profl. Women in Bus. Office: Orange Capital Mgmt 333 S Anita Dr # 625 Orange CA 92668

CAPOZZI, ANGELO, surgeon; b. Solvay, N.Y., Apr. 20, 1933; s. Angelo and Daminana (Pirro) C.; m. Louise Armanetti, June 18, 1960; children: Angelo III, Leonard, Jeanne. BS, U. Notre Dame, 1956; MD, Loyola U., Chgo., 1960. Diplomate Am. Bd. Plastic Surgery. Intern St. Francis Hosp., Evanston, Ill., 1960-61, resident in gen. surgery, 1962-64; resident in plastic surgery U. Wis., Madison, 1964-66; chief plastic surgery USAF, Travis AFB, Calif., 1966; chief dept. plastic surgery St. Marys Hosp., San Francisco, 1974-77; assoc. clin. prof. dept. surgery U. Calif., San Francisco; chmn. dept. plastic and reconstructive surgery St. Francis Meml. Hosp., San Francisco, 1987—, dir. plastic surgery residency program, 1987—; mem. tchg. staff St. Francis Meml. Hosp., Bothin Burn Ctr., San Francisco, 1968—; cons. Shriners Hosp., San Francisco. Author: Change of Face, 1984; contbr. articles to profl. jours. Mem. parks and recreation com. City of Tiburon, Calif., 1973. Capt. USAF, 1966-68. Recipient Alumni citation Loyola U., 1983; named Man of Yr., U. Notre Dame Alumni, 1983. Mem. San Francisco Olympic Club, San Francisco Rotary (Outstanding Svc. award 1993). Office: 1199 Bush St Ste 640 San Francisco CA 94109-5977

CAPPELLO, A. BARRY, lawyer; b. Bklyn., Feb. 21, 1942; s. Gus and Ann (Klukoff) C.; children: Eric Rheinschild, Blythe, Brent. AB, UCLA, 1962, JD, 1965. Bar: Calif. 1966, U.S. Dist. Ct. (cen. dist.) Calif. 1966, U.S. Ct. Appeals (9th cir.) 1974, U.S. Dist. Ct. (no. dist.) Calif. 1981, U.S. Ct. Appeals (7th cir.) 1985, U.S. Supreme Ct. 1985, U.S. Dist. Ct. (ea. dist.) Calif. 1986, U.S. Ct. Appeals (10th cir.) 1986. Dep. atty. gen. State of Calif., L.A., 1965-68; chief trial dep. Santa Barbara County, 1968-70, asst. dist. atty., 1970-71; city atty. Santa Barbara, 1971-77; pvt. practice, mng. ptnr., 1977-85; with Cappello & McCann, Santa Barbara, 1977—; lectr. complex bus. litigation, lender liability, adv. trial techniques. Author: Lender Liability, 2d edit., 1994, Lender Liability: A Practical Guide, 1987, AmJur Model Trials and Proofs of Facts; contbr. more than 100 articles to profl. legal and bus. jours. Mem. ABA, ATLA, Consumer Attys. of Calif. Office: Cappello & McCann 831 State St Santa Barbara CA 93101-3227

CAPPELLO, EVE, business educator, writer, international business consultant; b. Sydney, Australia; d. Nem and Ethel Shapira; children: Frances Soskins, Alan Kazdin. AA, Santa Monica City Coll., 1972; BA, Calif. State U.-Dominguez Hills, 1974; MA, Pacific Western U., 1977, PhD, 1978. Singer, pianist, L.A., 1956-76; profl. devel., mgmt./staff tng., 1976—; instr. Calif. State U. Extension, Dominguez Hills, 1977-90; counselor Associated Tech. Coll., L.A., 1994—. instr. Mt. St. Mary's Coll., U. of Judaism, U. So. Calif., Loyola Marymount U.; founder, pres. A-C-T Internat.; invited speaker World Congress Behavior Therapy, Israel, Melbourne U., Australia. Mem. Internat. Platform Assn., Book Publicists So. Calif., Zonta Internat., Alpha Gamma. Author: Let's Get Growing, 1979, The New Professional Touch, 1988, 2d edit., 1988, Dr. Eve's Garden, 1984, Act, Don't React, 1985, 3d edit., 1988, The Game of the Name, 1985, The Perfectionist Syndrome, 1990, Why Aren't More Women Running The Show?, 1994; newspaper columnist, 1976-79; contbr. articles to profl. jours. Home: 10600 Eastborne Ave Apt 16 Los Angeles CA 90024-5971 Office: PO Box 25544 Los Angeles CA 90025-0544

CAPPS, ANTHONY THOMAS (CAPOZZOLO CAPPS), international public relations executive; b. Pueblo, Colo.; s. Nicola and Anna (Solomone) Capozzolo; married, Dec. 1945. Student, L.A. Bus. Coll.; pvt. studies in arts, music. Dance dir., choreographer, producer motion pictures for TV and radio; featured profl. dance team Biltmore Bowl, Cocoanut Grove, Los Angeles, St. Catherine Hotel, Catalina, Calif., 1939-42; dance dir., producer NBC, ABC, Sta. KCOP-TV, Columbia Pictures, 20th Century Fox, Calif. Studios, 1940-60; exec. dir. activities Lockheed and Vega Aircraft Co., various locations, 1942-44; internat. pub. rels. dir. Howard Manor, Palm Springs Key Club, 1960—, Palm Springs Ranch Club, 1970-71, Kedes Radio, Cameron Ctr., 1971-73, Cameron Ent.rprises, Murietta Hot Springs Hotel, Health and Beauty Spa, 1972-73; numeruos TV interviews on religion and politics, history of ballet and opera of last 500 yrs.; founder, pres., dir. Tony Capps Enterprises, Inc., Palm Springs, Calif., 1959—, chmn., exec. dir. golf and tennis tournaments, benefit dinners, govt. ofcls., various fund-raising events; mem. research council Scripps Clinic and Research Found.; chmn., founder NAAPS St. Martins Abbey and Coll. Columnist Desert Sun Newspapers, 1959—. Founder, co-chmn. Nat. Football Found. and Hall of Fame Golf Classic, Palm Springs; founder, pres. Capps-Capozzolo Art Gallery, City of Hope, Duarte, Calif.; exec. dir. Alan Cranston for Senator Dinner, 1963, Edmund G. (Pat) Brown Testimonial Dinner, 1964, Progressive Jet Set Party-Nat.Cystic Fibrosis Research Found. fund raising, 1968, United Fund Gala Premier Ball, 1971; mem. Assistance League Palm Springs Desert Area, Desert Hosp., Palm Springs Desert Mus., Desert Art Ctr. of Coachella Valley, Mary and Joseph League, Eisenhower Med. Ctr, Women's Aux. Internat. Found., Boys Club of Palm Springs, Children Charity of the Desert; founder, pres. City of Hope Duarte; founder Nat. Artists Art Patrons Soc. St. Martins Abbey and Coll., Lacey, Wash., Capps Capozzolo Art Gallery, 1988; pres., found. sponsor Rep. Presdl. Task Force, 1993—; devel. scholarship fund St. Martins Abbey and Coll., 1994. Mem. Am. Film Inst., Nat. Cystic Fibrosis Found. and Hall of Fame in Calif. (founder, pres. Tri-county chpt., founder, co-chmn. golf classic at Palm Springs), Internat. Platform Assn., Nat. Hist. Soc. Gettysburg, Nat. Trust for Historic Preservation, Smithsonian Instn., Jacques Cousteau Soc., Palm Springs Pathfinders (life), Internationale Philanthropique Societe de Gourmet (founder), Century Club, Rep. Senatorial Inner Cir., U.S. Senatorial Club (life, Washington), Presdl. Task Force (life). Home: 2715 N Junipero Ave Palm Springs CA 92262-1816

CAPURRO, FRANK L., food products executive; b. 1945. Ptnr. Watsonville (Calif.) Produce, 1974—; treas. Ocean Organic Produce, Inc., Castroville, Calif., 1988—, now ptnr. Office: 2250 Salinas Rd Watsonville CA 95076-9232*

CAPUTO, GARY RICHARD, radiology educator; b. Newark, Nov. 26, 1951. AB in Chemistry, Coll. of the Hoy Cross, 1973; MD, Mt. Sinai Sch. Medicine, 1977. Diplomate Am. Bd. Internal Medicine, Am. Bd. Nuclear Medicine. Intern in internal medicine Mt. Sinai Hosp., 1977-78, resident in internal medicine, 1978-79; fellow in cardiology U. Wash., Seattle, 1979-81, 82-83; resident in internal medicine St. Vincent's Hosp. & Med. Ctr., Portland, Ore., 1981-82; resident in nuclear medicine U. Wash., 1983-85; fellow in cardiovascular imaging U. Calif., San Francisco, 1985-86; asst. prof. U. Utah Sch. Medicine, Salt Lake City, 1986-89, U. Calif., San Francisco, 1989-92; assoc. prof. U. Calif., 1992—; clin. instr. U. Wash., 1982-83; adj. asst. prof. U. Utah, 1987-89, dir. advanced cardiac imaging svc. LDS Hosp., Salt Lake City, 1986-89; clin. instr. U. Calif. San Francisco, 1985-86, supr. clin. cardiovascular magnetic resonance rsch. program and vis. fgn. scholars, 1989—, adminstr. NIH tng. grant, 1989—, coord. in-svc. tng. program, 1990-91, clin. magnetic resonance vis. fellow, 1990—, com. on human rsch., 1991-93; lectr. Fla. Radiol. Soc., 1988—; cons. Gen. Electric Med. Sys., Milw., 1991—; dir. nuclear cardiology fellowship tng. program U. Utah Sch. of Medicine, 1987-89, mem. PhD candidate com. dept. med. informatics, 1987-91; apptd. bioengring. grad. group U. Calif., Berkeley, San Francisco, 1992—, staff scientist Lawrence Berkeley Lab., 1992—, Magnetic Resonance Sci. Ctr. and PET Ctr., San Francisco, 1993—, assoc. dir., 1993—. Grantee Deseret Found., 1987, Am. Heart Assn., 1988, Richards Meml. Med. Found., 1988, Merritt-Peralta Rsch. Found., 1990, NIH, 1986—, numerous others. Fellow Am. Heart Assn. Coun. Cardiovascular Radiology; mem. AAAS, Radiol. Soc. N.Am., N.Am. Soc. Cardiac Imaging, Soc. Nuclear Medicine, San Francisco Radiol. Soc. Office: U Calif Dept Radiology Box 0628 San Francisco CA 94143-0628

CARATAN, ANTON G., food products executive; b. 1955. With Anton Caratan & Son, Delano, Calif., 1976—, ptnr., 1984—. Office: Anton Caratan & Son Ave 16 RR 160 Delano CA 93215*

CARATAN, GEORGE, food products executive; b. 1929. With Anton Caratan & Son, Delano, Calif., 1952—. Office: Anton Caratan & Son Ave 16 RR 160 Delano CA 93215*

CARD, STUART KENT, psychologist; b. Detroit, Dec. 21, 1943; s. Stuart Llewellyn and Kathleen Marie (Wolfe) C.; m. Josefina Bulatao Jayme, Jan. 26, 1972; children: Gwyneth Megan, Tiffany Heather. AB, Oberlin (Ohio) Coll., 1966; MS, Carnegie Mellon U., 1970, PhD, 1978. Acting dir. Oberlin Coll. Computer Ctr., 1967; mem. rsch. staff Xerox Palo Alto (Calif.) Rsch. Ctr., 1974-86, prin. scientist, 1986-90, mgr. user interface rsch., 1988—, rsch. fellow, 1990—; cons. Psychol. Svc. of Pitts., 1968-73; affiliated assoc. prof. dept. psychology Stanford (Calif.) U., 1983—; chmn. human factors summer study on automation in combat aircraft for the 1990s Air Force/NRC, Woods Hole, Mass., 1980; charter mem. Bd. on Army Sci. and Tech., NRC, Washington, 1982-85; group leader NATO Advanced Workshop on Man-Machine Sys., Loughborough, Eng., 1983; mem. blue ribbon com. on Army aviation aircrew integration NASA/Army, Moffitt Field, Calif., 1983. Editorial bd. Behavioral and Info. Tech., London, 1984—, Human-Computer Interaction, 1984—, ACM Transactions on Office Info. Sys., 1988-90, Cambridge U. Press, 1991—; assoc. editor ACM Transactions on Human-Computer Interaction, 1992—; co-author: The Psychology of Human-Computer Interaction, 1983; co-editor: Human Performance Models for Computer-Aided Engineering, 1990; co-designer computer system: Rooms, 1986, Information Visualizer, 1991. Troop leader Girl Scouts U.S., Palo Alto, Calif., 1985-86; coach Odyssey of the Mind, Palo Alto, 1993-94; chair cognition models Nat. Acad. Scis. Panel on Pilot Performance Models for Computer-Aided Engring., Washington, 1987-89. Mem. ACM (program chair conf. on human factors in software 1991, program com. mem., 1983-94, faculty doctoral consortium 1985, 88), IEEE, Cognitive Sci. Soc., Human Factors Soc., Sigma Xi. Office: Xerox Palo Alto Rsch Ctr 3333 Coyote Hill Rd Palo Alto CA 94304-1314

CARDEN, JOY CABBAGE, educational consultant; b. Livermore, Ky., Dec. 15, 1932; d. Henry L. and Lillie (Richardson) Cabbage; m. Donald G. Carden, Dec. 19, 1954; children: Lynn Kehlenbeck, Tom Carden, Bob Carden, Jan Blount, Jim Carden. BA, Ky. Wesleyan, 1955; MA, U. Ky., 1975. Instr. music Owensboro (Ky.) City Schs., 1955-57; founder, dir. Musical Arts Ctr., Lexington, Ky., 1980-88; edn. specialist Roland Corp., L.A., 1989, dir. edn., 1990-94, edn. cons., 1994—. Author: Music in Lexington Before 1840, 1980, Guide to Electronic Keyboards, 1988; editor, author: Carden Keyboard Ensemble Series; editor: Ensemble the Resource of Keyboard Instructors; composer ensembles for electronic keyboards. Mem. Music Tchrs. Nat. Assn. (coord. composer 1987), Nat. Guild Piano Tchrs. (state chmn. 1980-88), Nat. Conf. Piano Pedagogy (com. chmn. 1990-94), Ky. Music Tchrs. Assn. (state chmn. 1980-88), Music Tchrs. Calif. Home and Office: 112 La Fontenay Ct Louisville KY 40223-3020

CARDEN, THOM(AS) RAY, psychologist; b. Indpls.; s. Howard Ray Carden and Mary Ola Eacret; m. Shirley A. Towles, 1953 (div. 1968); m. Anita Van Natter, May 26, 1973; children: Thom H., Kevin L., Shawn D., Dennis P., Suzanne M., Marlene, Cindy, Lorrie, Linda, Alayne. AA in Psychology, Cerritos Coll., 1973; BA in Psychology, Calif. State U., Northridge, 1975; MS in Psychology, U. So. Calif., 1976; PhD in Psychology, Walden U., 1980. Tchr. spl. edn. L.A. Unified Schs., 1976-81; spl. developmental disabilities resource cons. Torrance (Calif.) Unified Sch. Dist., 1977-78; founder, educator, counselor Western Inst. for Sexual Edn. and Rsch., Northridge, Calif., 1977-84; pvt. practice, 1977—; devel. workshops for Calif. Coun. on Adult Edn., L.A., Santa Barbara, 1977-78; mem. Calif. State Coun. for Devel. Disabled. Author: Birth Control for Disabled, 1977, V.D. is Very Dangerous, 1977, Sexuality Tutoring for Developmentally Disabled Persons, 1976, (computer program) Personality Index Spectral Analysis, 1987; contbr. articles to profl. jours. With USN, 1950-51. Republican. Mormon.

CÁRDENAS, ANTHONY J., foreign language educator. BA, U. N.Mex., 1968; MA, U. Wis., 1969, PhD, 1974. Asst. prof. Wichita State U., 1975-81, assoc. prof., 1981-90; prof. U. N.Mex., Albuquerque, 1990—, orientation com. for new faculty, grad. tchg./awards com., 1991, 92, provost's libr. evaluation com., 1993; vis. prof. U. Wis., summer, 1986; project assoc. Dictionary of the Old Spanish Lang. Project, 1974-75, summers 1975-77, 85-87; presented papers at numerous confs. and symposiums, 1978—; session chmn. Rocky Mt. Medieval Renaissance Assn. Conf., 1978, 72nd Annual Meeting AATSP, Fla., 1990, 75th, 1993, 76th, 1994; guest speaker U. Colo., 1984, U. Houston, 1984, U. Okla., 1990, U. Ky., 1990, U. Denver, 1992; lectr. in the field. Author: Bibliography of Old Spanish Texts, Edit. 1, 1975, Edit., 2, 1977; assoc. editor: Concordances and Texts of the Royal Scriptorium Manuscripts of Alfonso X, el Sabio, 1978, The Text and Concordance of Biblioteca Nacional Manuscript Reservado, 1987; contbr. articles to profl. jours. Recipient Novus award Ball State U., 1978, 79, Am. Philos. Soc. award, 1980, 86; fellow Newberry Libr., 1979, UCLA, 1978, Andrew W. Mellon/Vatican Microfilm Libr., 1980, 90, Ford Found., 1981-82, NEH, 1983, 89, Com. Internat. Exch. Scholars, 1983, Rsch. Allocation Com. U. N.Mex., 1991, 94; grantee Am. Coun. of Learned Socs., 1983. Mem. MLA (exec. com. Spanish medieval lang. and lit. 1991—), Am. Acad. Rsch. Historians of Medieval Spain (treas. 1991-92), Renaissance Soc. Am., Am. Assn. Tchrs. Spanish and Portuguese (exec. coun. 1988-90, pres. Kans. South Ctrl. chpt. 1982-83; N.Mex. Cibola chpt.), Mid-Am. Medieval Assn., Asociacion Internacional de Hispanistas, Asociacion Hispanica de Literatura Medieval, Rocky Mountain Medieval and Renaissance Assn. Office: U NMex Dept Spanish and Portuguese Albuquerque NM 87131-1146

CARDENAS, DIANA DELIA, physician, educator; b. San Antonio, Tex., Apr. 10, 1947; d. Ralph Roman and Rosa (Garza) C.; m. Thomas McKenzie Hooton, Aug. 20, 1971; children: Angela, Jessica. BA with highest honors, U. Tex., 1969; MD, U. Tex., Dallas, 1973; MS, U. Wash., 1976. Diplomate Nat. Bd. Med. Examiners, Am. Bd. Phys. Medicine & Rehab., Am. Bd. Electrodiagnostic Medicine. Asst. prof. dept. rehab. medicine Emory U., Atlanta, 1976-81; instr. dept. rehab. medicine U. Wash., Seattle, 1981-82, asst. prof. dept. rehab. medicine, 1982-86, assoc. prof. dept. rehab. medicine, 1986-92, prof. rehab. medicine, 1992—; med. dir. rehab. medicine clinic U. Wash. Med. Ctr., Seattle, 1982; project dir. N.W. Regional Spinal Cord Injury System, Seattle, 1990—. Editor: Rehabilitation & The Chronic Renal Disease Patient, 1985, Maximizing Rehabilitation in Chronic Renal Disease, 1989; contbr. articles to profl. jours. Co-chairperson Lakeside Sch. Auction Student Vols., Seattle, 1991; bd. dirs. CONSEJO Counseling & Referral Svc., 1994. Mem. Am. Spinal Injury Assn. (chairperson rsch. com. 1991), Am. Acad. Phys. Medicine and Rehab., Am. Congress of Rehab. Medicine (chairperson rehab. practice com. 1980-84, Ann. Essay Contest winner 1976), Am. Assn. Electrodiagnostic Medicine. Office: Univ Wash RJ-30 Dept Rehab Medicine 1959 NE Pacific St Seattle WA 98195-0004

CARDINALE, ROBERT LEE, foundation executive, art administrator; b. Pueblo, Colo., Sept. 8, 1939; s. Salvator R. and Agnes (Costanza) C.; m. Patricia Miller, June 7, 1966; children: Christopher, Anthony. AA in Engring., Pueblo Coll., 1959; BA in Math. and Philosophy, St. Benedict's Coll., Atchison, Kans., 1963; MA in Art Edn., U. No. Colo., 1965; cert. in advanced art edn., U. Ill., 1972; EdD Art Edn., Ariz. State U., 1977. Asst. prof. U. No. Colo., Greeley, 1968-69, Ohio State U., Columbus, 1970-74; assoc. prof. U. Ariz., Tucson, 1974-81; prof., dir. program in artisanry Boston U., 1981-85; prof., inst. pres. San Antonio Art Inst., 1985-90; pres., chief exec. officer Mus. N.Mex. Found., Santa Fe, 1990-92; v.p. devel. Southwestern Coll., Santa Fe, N.Mex., 1993—; monk Holy Cross Abbey, Canon City, Colo., 1959-64; photographer Ford Found., U. Ill., Princeton U., Morgantina, Sicily, 1968; dir. oral history conf. Smithsonian Instn., 1982. Contbr. articles to profl. jours.; participant metal art and drawings exhbns. Exhbn. grantee Nat. Endowment for Arts, 1977, 80. Mem. Soc. N.Am. Goldsmiths, Nat. Soc. Fund Raising Execs., Am. Assn. Mus., Rotary. Democrat. Mem. Soc. of Friends. Office: Southwestern Coll PO Box 4788 Santa Fe NM 87502-4788

CARDINE, GODFREY JOSEPH, state supreme court justice; b. Prairie Du Chien, Wis., July 6, 1924; s. Joseph Frederick and Mary (Kasparck) C.; m. Janice Irene Brown, Sept. 14, 1946; children: Susan, John, Lisa. BS in Engring., U. Ill., 1948; JD with honors, U. Wyo., 1954. Bar: Wyo. 1954, U.S. Dist. Ct. Wyo. 1954, U.S. Ct. Appeals (10th cir.) 1954. Assoc. Schwartz, Bon & McCrary, Casper, Wyo., 1954-66; dist. atty. Natrona County, Wyo., 1966-70; ptnr. Cardine, Vlastos & Reeves, Casper, 1966-77; prof. law U. Wyo., Laramie, 1977-83; justice Wyo. Supreme Ct., Cheyenne, 1983-88, 90-94, chief justice, 1988-90; mem. Wyo. State Bd. Law Examiners, 1973-77; faculty dir. Western Trial Advocacy Inst., Laramie, 1981—; bd. advisors Land and Water Law Rev., 1985-90; mem. ad hoc com. to rev. bar assn. rules and by-laws, 1987-88; jud. assoc. editor Georgetown U. Cts., Health Sci. and the Law, 1989-91; adj. prof. trial advocacy Harvard U. Law Sch., 1991;. Contbr. articles to profl. jours. Active Little League Baseball, Casper, 1960-62; mem. Gov.'s Com. on Dangerous Drugs, 1968-71; initiator Alternative Dispute Resolution Program State of Wyo., 1989, chmn., 1990—. Fellow Internat. Soc. Barristers; mem. ABA (jud. adminstrn. divsn.), Assn. Trial Lawyers Am., Wyo. State Bar (pres. 1977-78), Phi Alpha Delta, Potter Law Club (pres. 1953-54), Rotary. Home: 2040 Rustic Dr Casper WY 82609-3405 Office: Wyo Supreme Ct Supreme Ct Bldg Cheyenne WY 82002

CARDON, LON RAY, geneticist researcher; b. Bremerton, Wash., Oct. 11, 1965; s. Kenneth R. Cardon and Patricia A. (Waddle) Ploium; m. Debbie L. Cardon, Aug. 22, 1987. BA in Psychology, U. Puget Sound, 1988; MA in Behavior Genetics, U. Colo., 1991, PhD in Behavior Genetics, 1992. Rsch. assoc. Inst. for Behavioral Genetics, Boulder, Colo., 1988-92; mem. faculty dept. math. Stanford (Calif.) U., 1992—; computer cons. Rsch. Group Inc., Bremerton, 1988, U. Colo., 1988-92, invited lectr., 1989; statis. con. U. Puget Sound, 1988; invited lectr. NATO Twin Methodology, Leuven, Belgium, 1989, vis. lectr., 1990; biostatis. cons. SRI Internat., 1992—. Co-author (with M.C. Neale) Methodology for Genetic Studies of Twins and Families, 1992; contbr. articles to profl. jours. Grantee NIH, NICHD, NATO. Mem. Am. Soc. Human Genetics, Behavior Genetics Assn., Phi Beta Kappa, Phi Kappa Phi. Office: SRI Internat 333 Ravenswood Ave Menlo Park CA 94025-3453

CARDONA-LOYA, OCTAVIO, plastic surgeon; b. San Diego, Nov. 28, 1946. MD, Med. U. of Guadalajara, Mex., 1972. Intern Regina Grey Nuns Hosp., 1972-73; plastic surgeon Tulane U., New Orleans, 1979-81; now plastic surgeon Sharp, Chula Vista, Calif.; clin. asst. prof. U. Calif., San Diego. Surgeon USPHS, 1975-79. Fellow ACS. Office: 750 Med Ctr Ct # 4 Chula Vista CA 91911-6634*

CARDWELL, KENNETH HARVEY, architect, educator; b. Los Angeles, Feb. 15, 1920; s. Stephen William and Beatrice Viola (Duperrault) C.; m. Mary Elinor Sullivan, Dec. 30, 1946; children: Kenneth William, Mary Elizabeth, Ann Margaret, Catherine Buckley, Robert Stephen. A.A., Occidental Coll.; A.B., U. Calif.-Berkeley; postgrad., Stanford U. Lic. architect, Calif. Draftsman Thompsen & Wilson Architects, San Francisco, 1946-48, Michael Goodman, Architect, Berkeley, Calif., 1949; architect W.S. Wellington, Architect, Berkeley, 1950-59; prin. Kolbeck, Cardwell, Christopherson, Berkeley, 1960-66; prof. dept. arch. U. Calif.-Berkeley, 1950-82; prin. Kenneth H. Cardwell Architect, Berkeley, 1982—. Author: Bernard Maybeck, 1977. Pres. Civic Art Commn., Berkeley, 1963-65; mem. Bd. Adjustments, 1967-69, Alameda County Art Commn., 1969-72. Served to 1st lt. USAAF, 1941-45. Decorated D.F.C.; decorated Air medal with 3 oak leaf clusters; Rehman fellow, 1957; Graham fellow, 1961; recipient Berkeley citation U. Calif., 1958. Fellow AIA; mem. Alpha Rho Chi. Home and Office: 1210 Shattuck Ave Berkeley CA 94709-1413

CAREN, ROBERT POSTON, aerospace company executive; b. Columbus, Ohio, Dec. 25, 1932; s. Robert James and Charlene (Poston) C.; m. Linda Ann Davis, Mar. 27, 1963; children: Christopher Davis, Michael Poston. B.S., Ohio State U., 1953, M.S., 1954, Ph.D., 1961. Sr. physicist N.Am. Aviation, Columbus, 1959-60; assoc. research scientist research and devel. div. Lockheed Missiles and Space Co., Inc., Palo Alto, Calif., 1962-63, research scientist, 1963-66, sr. mem. research lab., 1966-69, mgr. def. systems space systems div., 1969-70, mgr. infared tech. R & D div., 1970-71, research dir., 1972-76, chief engr., 1976-86, v.p. gen. mgr. R & D div., 1986—, corp. v.p. sci. and engring., 1987—; bd. dirs. Software Productivity Consortium, Superconducting Tech. Inc. Contbr. articles to profl. jours. Mem. dean's adv. coun. Ohio State U., Calif. Poly. State U.-St. Louis Obispo, U. So. Calif., U. Calif., L.A., U. Calif., Davis. Fellow AIAA, AAAS, AAS; mem. NAE, IEEE (sr.), Am. Astron. Soc., Am. Def. Preparedness Assn. (past chmn. rsch. divsn.), Am. Phys. Soc., Aerospace Industries Assn. (chmn. tech. and ops. coun.), Sigma Pi Sigma, Pi Mu Epsilon. Home: 5616 Blackbird Ave Thousand Oaks CA 91362-5019 Office: 4500 Park Granada Calabasas CA 91399-0001

CARESWELL, LORI SUE, dietitian; b. Devils Lake, N.D., Nov. 6, 1956; d. Clayton Harris and Ruth Darline (Johnson) Nelson; m. Monty Allen Careswell, Oct. 27, 1990; 1 child, Amy Elizabeth. BS, Colo. State U., 1979. Registered dietitian, Colo. Dietary dir. Eventide South Nursing Home, Ft. Collins, Colo., 1979-80; chief clin. and clin. dietitian Presbyn. Denver Hosp., 1980-88; cholesterol ctr. dietitian Humana Hosp.-Mountain View, Thornton, Colo., 1988-90; clin. dietitian Humana Hosp.-Aurora, Colo., 1990-92; pediatric nutritionist U. Colo. Health Scis. Ctr., Denver, 1992—; nutrition cons. Denver, 1988—. Mem. Denver Dietetic Assn. (pres. 1993-94, nominating com. chair 1994—), Am. Diabetes Assn. (Colo. affiliate pres. 1989-90), Cons. Nutritionists Practice Group, Diabetes Care and Edn. Practice Group (state worker 1990-95), area 4 coord. 1995—). Republican. Christian Ch. Home: 13603 W 66th Way Arvada CO 80004-2004

CAREY, JAMES C., JR., plastic surgeon; b. Chgo., 1932. MD, Northwestern U., 1957. Intern Cook County Hosp., Chgo., 1957-58, resident in gen. surgery, 1958-63; plastic surgeon U. Mo., Kansas City, 1980-82; now plastic surgeon Twin Cities Cmty. Hosp., Templeton, Calif. Office: 959 Las Tablas Rd Ste B3 Templeton CA 93465-9703*

CAREY, KATHRYN ANN, advertising and public relations executive, editor, consultant; b. Los Angeles, Oct. 18, 1949; d. Frank Randall and Evelyn Mae (Walmsley) C.; m. Richard Kenneth Sundt, Dec. 28, 1980. BA in Am. Studies with honors, Calif. State U., L.A., 1971. Cert. commercial pilot instrument rated. Tutor Calif. Dept. Vocat. Rehab., L.A., 1970; teaching asst. U. So. Calif., 1974-75, UCLA, 1974-75; claims adjuster Auto Club So. Calif., San Gabriel, 1971-73; corp. pub. rels. cons. Carnation Co., L.A., 1973-78; cons., adminstr. Carnation Community Svc. Award Program, 1973-78; pub. rels. cons. Vivitar Corp., 1978; sr. advt. asst. Am. Honda Motor Co., Torrance, Calif., 1978-84; exec. dir. Am. Honda Found., 1984—; adminstr. Honda Matching Gift and Vol. Program, Honda Involvement Program; mgr. Honda Dealer Advt. Assns., 1978-84; cons. advt., pub. rels., promotions. Editor: Vivitar Voice, Santa Monica, Calif., 1978, Rod Machado's Instrument Pilots' Survival Manual, c. 1991; editor Honda Views, 1978-84, Found. Focus, 1984—; asst. editor Friskies Research Digest, 1973-78; contbg. editor Newsbriefs and Momentum, 1978—, Am. Honda Motor Co., Inc. employees publs. Calif. Life Scholarship Found. scholar, 1967. Mem. Advt. Club L.A., Pub. Rels. Soc. Am., So. Calif. Assn. Philanthropy, Coun. on Founds., Affinity Group on Japanese Philanthropy (pres.), Ninety-Nines, Am. Quarter Horse Assn., Aircraft Owners and Pilots Assn., Los Angeles Soc. for Prevention Cruelty to Animals, Greenpeace, Ocicats International., Am. Humane Assn., Humane Soc. U.S., Elsa Wild Animal Appeal. Office: Am Honda Found 1919 Torrance Blvd Torrance CA 90501-2722

CAREY, MARGARET THERESA LOGAN, newspaper education consultant; b. Phila., May 8, 1931; d. Michael Francis and Margaret Mary (Meehan) Logan; m. William Emmett Carey, June 21, 1952; children: William Edward, Michael Patrick, Peggy Ann. AA, Bucks County Community Coll., 1968; student, Temple U., 1968-69; BS, U. Bridgeport, 1971; MEd in Reading, U. N.C., 1973. Reading resource tchr. Wake County Sch. Dist., Raleigh, N.C., 1971-76; newspaper in edn. cons. The News & Observer, Raleigh, 1976-77; ednl. cons. U.S. News and World Report, Washington, 1977-78; newspaper in edn. cons. N.Y. Times, N.Y.C., 1978, Times Newspaper, Trenton-Princeton, N.J., 1979-91, Mitchellville, Md., 1991-93; cons. N.J. Dept. Edn., Trenton, 1978-79, Newspaper Assn. Am., 1992-93, Washington Post, 1992-93. Author: The Aft Summer Learning Calendar, 1992, 93; editor, founder (children's page) Funtimes, 1981-88, (supplement) Create-An-Ad, 1984-88. Newspaper in Edn. State rep. for N.J. Am. Newspaper Pubs. Assn. Found., Reston, Va., 1983-91; active Reading is Fundamental, Mercer County, N.J., 1984-91. Mem. AAUW, Internat. Reading Assn. (literacy 1986), N.J. Reading Assn. (award 1986), Tri-County Reading Assn. (award 1986), N.J. Press Assn. (chmn. newspaper in edn. com. 1983-91), Denver Lyric Opera Guild, Denver Botanic Gardens, Nat. Wildflower Rsch. Ctr., U.S. Golf Assn., Nat. Trust for Historic Preservation, Am. Hort. Soc., Country Club Castle Pines. Roman Catholic.

CAREY, PETER KEVIN, reporter; b. San Francisco, Apr. 2, 1940; s. Paul Twohig and Stanleigh M. (White) C.; m. Joanne Dayl Barker, Jan. 7, 1978; children: Brendan Patrick, Nadia Marguerite. BS in Econs., U. Calif., Berkeley, 1964. Reporter San Francisco Examiner, 1964; reporter Livermore (Calif.) Ind., 1965-67, editor, 1967; aerospace writer, spl. projects and investigative reporter San Jose (Calif.) Mercury, 1967—. Recipient Pulitzer prize for internat. reporting Columbia U., 1986, George Polk award L.I. U., 1986, Investigative Reporters and Editors award, 1986, Jessie Meriton White Svc. award Friends World Coll., 1986, Mark Twain award Calif.-Nev. AP, 1983, staff team Pulitzer prize for gen. reporting, Columbia U., 1990, Thomas L. Stokes award Washington Journalism Ctr., 1991, Malcolm Forbes award Overseas Press Club of Am., 1993, Gerald Loeb award UCLA Grad Sch. Mgmt., 1993, Best of the West Immigration and Minority Reporting award First Amendment Funding Inc., 1993; profl. journalism fellow NEH, 1983-84. Mem. Soc. Profl. Journalists, Investigative Reporters and Editors. Office: San Jose Mercury-News 750 Ridder Park Dr San Jose CA 95131-2432

CAREY, STAN, sports administrator, football coach; b. Atlanta, June 17, 1955; s. Morris Stanton Sr. and Dorothy (Kirkman) C.; m. Kathy; 1 Child, Michael. Student, DeKalb C.C., Decatur, Ga., 1975-77, Atlanta Tech., 1976, Gallaudet Coll., 1979. Coaching aide Atlanta Falcons, 1971-78, Washington Redskins, 1979, Ga. Tech., Atlanta, 1981-82, L.A. Rams, 1983, UCLA, 1983, U. So. Calif., 1984; assoc. gen. mgr., asst. head coach Gainesville (Ga.) Rams, 1983-86; gen. mgr., spl. teams coach Seattle Raiders, 1989; pres., CEO Am. Pacific N.W. Sports, Seattle, 1989—; asst. gen. mgr., player Sno-King Blue Knights, Edmonds, Wash., 1990; v.p. Seattle Panthers, 1991; v.p. exec. ops., football dir., asst. head coach Seattle Skyhawks, 1992-93; head coach, exec. v.p., dir. football ops. N.W. Huskys; cons. United Cerebral Palsy, Seattle, 1990. Worker Jerry Lewis MDA Telethon, 1973—; charity golfer United Cerebral Palsy, 1974—, Ga. Spl. Olympics, 1974; campaign aide Reagan-Bush, Atlanta, 1980, 84, campaign worker Bush-Quayle, Atlanta, 1988, Seattle, 1992; active Rep. Cen. Com., 1992; elected 2d term as Rep. CPO, 1994. Mem. NFL Players Assn., Kiwanis Internat. Episcopalian. Address: Am Pacific NW Sports PO Box 21481 Seattle WA 98111-3481

CARGILL, CARL FREDERICK, standards strategist; b. Denver, Feb. 28, 1948; s. Everett and Elizabeth Cargill; children by previous marriage: Helen, Adam. BA in History and Philosophy, U. Colo., 1969; MS in Adminstrn., George Washington U., 1975. Point of Sales specialist Gold Circle Stores Federated Dept. Stores, 1975-76; mktg. systems analyst NCR Corp., 1976-78; mktg. mgr. Point of Sale Terminals Datatrol, Inc., 1978-80; mgr.strategic planning/pricing mgr. Digital Equipment Corp., 1980-83, sr. programs and products bus. cons., 1983-92; stds. strategist SunSoft Sun Microsystems, Inc., Mountain View, Calif., 1992—. Author: Information Technology Standardization: Theory, Process and Organization, 1989; editor-in-chief ACM Jour. Standard View; contbr. articles to profl. jours., chpt. to book. Capt. USAF, 1969-75, Korea. Office: SunSoft MTV 18-122 2550 Garcia Mountain View CA 94043-1109

CARINO, LINDA SUSAN, financial software company executive; b. San Diego, Nov. 4, 1954; d. DeVona (Clarke) Dungan. Student, San Diego Mesa Coll., 1972-74, 89-90. Various positions Calif. Can. Bank, San Diego, 1974-77, ops. supr., 1977-80, ops. mgr., 1980-82; asst. v.p. ops. mgr. First Comml. Bank (formerly Calif. Can. Bank), San Diego, 1982-84; v.p. data processing mgr. First Nat. Bank, San Diego, 1984-91; v.p. conversion adminstr. Item Processing Ctr. Svc. Corp., Denver, 1991-92; mgr. computer ops. FIserv, Inc., Van Nuys, Calif., 1992-93; v.p., data processing mgr. So. Calif. Bank, La Mirada, Calif., 1993-94, v.p. tech. support mgr., 1994—. Democrat. Home: 255 S Vista Del Monte Anaheim CA 92807-3832 Office: So Calif Bank PO Box 588 La Mirada CA 90637-0588

CARL, JOAN STRAUSS, sculptor, painter; b. Cleve., Mar. 20, 1926. Student, Cleve. Sch. Art, Chgo. Art Inst., New Sch. Art, L.A. Lectr. Fed. Visual Arts Program, Title Three, 1961-64; faculty Valley Ctr. of the Arts, 1960-64; tchr. Univ. of Judaism. One-woman shows inlcude Paideia Gallery, L.A., Bel Air Ext. Gallery, Beverly Hills, Calif., Laguna Beach (Calif.) Art Mus., Courtney Collins Gallery, Raleigh, N.C., Linden-Kicklighter Gallery, Cleve., Muskegon (Mich.) C.C., Bakersfield (Calif.) Coll., Fresno (Calif.) Art Ctr. Mus., Brand Libr. Gallery, Glendale, Calif., Thinking Eye, L.A., Courtright Gallery, L.A.; group shows include Cerritos (Calif.) Coll., L.A. Art Assn., So. Calif. Exposition, San Diego, Santa Cruz (Calif.) Art Show, West End Gallery, N.Y.C., Stuart Kingston Galleries, Naples, Fla., Laguna Beach Art Mus., Mint Mus., Charlotte, N.C., Paideia Gallery, Oborn Gallery, Kansas City Kans., Gallery Judaica, L.A., Feldheim Libr. Gallery, San Bernardino, Calif., Feingood Gallery, Milkin Ctr., Northridge, Calif.; comms. and collections include Zinkal Ltd., Tel Aviv, Raleigh (N.C.) Mus., No. Ohio Mus., Cleve., Sinai Meml. Pk., L.A., Govt. of Japan, Internat. Cultural Ctr. Youth, Jerusalem, others. Recipient Design award Ceramic Tile Inst. Mem. Calif. Confedn. of Arts (founding mem.), Artists Equity Assn. (past pres. L.A. chpt.), L.A. Art Assn. (pres.). Home and Office: 4808 Mary Ellen Ave Sherman Oaks CA 91423-2120

CARLE, HARRY LLOYD, social worker, career development specialist; b. Chgo., Oct. 26, 1927; s. Lloyd Benjamin and Clara Bell (Lee) C.; BSS, Seattle U., 1952; MSW, U. Wash., 1966; m. Elva Diana Ulrich, Dec. 29, 1951 (div. 1966); adopted children: Joseph Francis, Catherine Marie; m. Karlen Elizabeth Howe, Oct. 14, 1967 (dec. Feb. 1991); children: Kristen Elizabeth and Sylvia Ann (twins), Eric Lloyd; m. Diane Wyland Gambs, May 23, 1993. Indsl. placement and employer rels. rep. State of Wash., Seattle, 1955-57, parole and probation officer, Seattle and Tacoma, 1957-61, parole employment specialist, 1961-63, vocat. rehab. officer, 1963-64; clin. social worker Western State Hosp., Ft. Steilacoom, Washington and U.S. Penitentiary, McNeil Island, Wash., 1964-66; exec. dir. Shohomish County Community Action Council/Social Planning Council, Everett, Wash., 1966-77; employment and edn. counselor Pierce County Jail Social Services, Tacoma, 1979-81; dir. employment devel. clinic, coord. vocat. program North Rehab. Facility, King County Div. Alcoholism & Substance Abuse, Seattle, 1981-90; counselor Northgate Outpatient Ctr. Lakeside Recovery , Inc., Seattle, 1991; staff devel. cons. Counseling for Ind. Living, Newport, R.I., 1992; community orgn./gy. problems mgmt. cons., 1968—; mem. social service project staff Pacific Luth. U., Tacoma, 1979-81. Cons. to pres. Geneal. Inst., Salt Lake City, 1974-78. Served with USN, 1944-46. U.S. Office Vocat. Rehab. scholar, 1965-66, named First Honoree Hall of Success Iowa Tng. Sch. for Boys, 1969. Mem. NASW, Seattle Geneal. Soc. (pres. 1974-76), Soc. Advancement Mgmt. (chpt. exec. v.p. 1970-71), Acad. Cert. Social Workers, Pa. German Soc., Henckel Family Nat. Assn., various hist. and geneal. socs. in Cumberland, Perry and Lancaster counties, Pa., Peoria and Fulton Counties, Ill., Seattle Japanese Garden Soc. (v.p. 1993—), Hakone Found. (Saratoga, Calif.), Olympia-Yashiro Sister City Assn., Puget Sound Koi Soc., Dr. Sun Yat-sen Garden Soc. Vancouver (B.C., Can.), Kubota Garden Found. (Seattle), Bloedel Reserve (Banbridge Island, Wash.). Roman Catholic. Home: Karlensgarten Retreat 1425 10th Pl N Edmonds WA 98020-2629

CARLEONE, JOSEPH, aerospace executive; b. Phila., Jan. 30, 1946; s. Frank Anthony and Amelia (Ciaccia) C.; m. Shirley Elizabeth Atwell, June 29, 1968; children: Gia Maria, Joan Marie. BS, Drexel U., 1968, MS, 1970, PhD, 1972. Civilian engring. trainee, mech. engr. Phila. Naval Shipyard, 1963-68; grad. asst. in applied mechanics Drexel U., Phila., 1968-72, postdoctoral rsch. assoc., 1972-73, NDEA fellow, 1968-71, adj. prof. mechanics, 1974-75, 77-82; chief rsch. engr. Dyna East Corp., Phila., 1973-82; chief scientist warhead tech. Aerojet Ordnance Co., Tustin, Calif., 1982-88. v.p., gen. mgr. warhead systems div. GenCorp. Aerojet Precision Weapons, Tustin, 1988-89; v.p., dir. armament systems, Aerojet Electronics Systems Divsn., Azusa, Calif., 1989-94, v.p. tactial def. and armament products., Aerojet, Calif. 1994—. Editor: Tactical Missile Warheads, 1993. Mem. ASME, Sigma Xi, Tau Beta Pi, Pi Tau Sigma, Phi Kappa Phi. Contbr. articles to profl. jours.; rschr. explosive and metal interaction, ballistics, projectile penetration, impact of plates. Home: 2112 Campton Cir Gold River CA 95670 Office: Aerojet PO Box 13222 Sacramento CA 95813-6000

CARLESIMO, P. J. (PETER J. CARLESIMO), former college basketball coach, professional basketball coach; b. Scranton, Pa.. Grad., Fordham U., 1971. Asst. basketball coach Fordham U., Bronx, N.Y., N.H. Coll., Manchester; mem. staff Wagner Coll., Staten Island, N.Y.; head coach Seton Hall U., South Orange, N.J., 1982-94, Portland Trailblazers, 1994—. Office: Portland Trailblazers 700 NE Multnomah St Portland OR 97232-2131

CARLESON, ROBERT BAZIL, public policy consultant, corporation executive; b. Long Beach, Calif., Feb. 21, 1931; s. Bazil Upton and Grace Reynolds (Wilhite) C.; m. Betty Jane Nichols, Jan. 31, 1954 (div.); children: Eric Robert, Mark Andrew, Susan Lynn; m. Susan A. Dower, Feb. 11, 1984. Student, U. Utah, 1949-51; B.S., U. So. Calif., 1953, postgrad., 1956-58. Adminstrv. asst. City of Beverly Hills, Calif., 1956-57; asst. to city mgr. City of Claremont, Calif., 1957-58; sr. adminstrv. asst. to city mgr. City of Torrance, Calif., 1958-60; city mgr. City of San Dimas, Calif., 1960-64, Pico Rivera, Calif., 1964-68; chief dep. dir. Calif. Dept. Public Works, 1968-71; dir. Calif. Dept. Social Welfare, 1971-73; U.S. commr. welfare Washington, 1973-75; pres. Robert B. Carleson & Assocs., Sacramento, Calif. and Washington, 1975-81; chmn. Robert B. Carleson & Assocs., Washington, 1987-93, San Diego, 1993—; pres. Innovative Environ. Svcs. Ltd., Vancouver, B.C., Can., 1992; spl. asst. to U.S. pres. for policy devel. Washington, 1981-84; prin., dir. govt. rels. Main Hurdman KMG, Washington, 1984-87; dir. transition team Dept. Health & Human Services, Office of Pres.-Elect, 1980-81; spl. adviser Office of Policy Coordination; sr. policy advisor, chmn. welfare task force Reagan Campaign, 1980; bd. dirs. Fed. Home Loan Bank of Atlanta, 1987-90, I.E.S., Ltd., Can., Transenviro Co., USA, Churchill Co., USA; adv. com. Fed. Home Loan Mortgage Corp., 1985-87; pres. Nat. Tax Limitation Found., Washington, 1991—; mem. strengthening family policy coun. Nat. Policy Forum, Washington, 1994—. Adv. coun. gen. govt. Rep. Nat. Com., Washington, 1980-81; sr. fellow Free Congress Found., 1994—. Officer USN, 1953-56. Clubs: Masons, Rotary (pres. 1964), Army & Navy (Washington), Capitol Hill, Fairfax Hunt. Home and Office: 1911 Willow St San Diego CA 92106-1823

CARLETON, MARY RUTH, television news anchor, consultant; b. Sacramento, Feb. 2, 1948; d. Warren Alfred and Mary Gertrude (Clark) Case; m. Bruce A. Hunt, Jan. 21, 1989. BA in Polit. Sci., U. Calif.-Berkeley, 1970, MJ, 1974. TV news anchorwoman, reporter Sta. KXAS-TV, Ft. Worth, 1974-78, Sta. KING-TV, Seattle, 1978-80, Sta. KOCO-TV, Oklahoma City, 1980-84; news anchor, reporter Sta. KTTV-TV, L.A., 1984-87; news anchor Sta. KLAS-TV, Las Vegas, Nev., 1987-91, KTNV-TV, 1991-93, Sta. UNLV-TV, 1993—; broadcast instr. Okla. Christian Coll., 1981-84, UCLA, 1985-87, U. Nev.-Las Vegas, 1991—; pub. speaking cons.; dir. UNLV Women's Ctr., 1991—; news dir. univ. news Sta. UNLV-TV, 1992—. Bd. dirs. World Neighbors, Oklahoma City, 1984-89, Allied Arts Coun. So. Nev.-Las Vegas, 1988—, Nev. Inst. for Contemporary Art, 1988—; bd. dirs. United Way, Las Vegas, 1991—, secret witness bd., 1991—, Las Vegas Women's Coun., 1993—, Friends of Channel 10, 1991—. Named Best Environ. Reporter, Okla. Wildlife Fedn., 1983, Disting. Woman of So. Nev., Woman of Achievement Las Vegas Women's Coun., 1990; recipient Broadcasting award UPI, 1981, Nat. award for best documentary, 1990, Tri-State award for best newscast, 1990, Emmy award, L.A., 1986, L.A. Press Club award 1986, 90, Nat. award for documentaries UPI, 1990, Woman of Achievement Media award Las Vegas C. of C., 1990. Mem. AARP (mem. nat. econ. issues team 1992—, state legis. com.)Women in Comm. (Clarion award 1981, Best Newscaster 1990), Soc. Prol. Journalists, Press Women, Investigative Reporters, Sigma Delta Chi. Democrat. Roman Catholic. Avocations: tennis, gourmet cooking. Office: Sta KTNV-TV 3355 S Valley View Blvd Las Vegas NV 89102-8216

CARLEY, JOHN BLYTHE, retail grocery executive; b. Spokane, Wash., Jan. 4, 1934; s. John Lewis and Freida June (Stiles) C.; m. Joan Marie Hohenleitner, Aug. 6, 1960; children: Christopher, Kathryn, Peter, Scott. AA, Boise Jr. Coll., 1955; student, U. Wash., 1956-57, Stanford U. Exec. Program, 1973. Store dir. Albertson's Inc., Boise, Idaho, 1961-65, grocery merchandiser, 1965-70, dist. mgr., 1970-73, v.p. gen. mdse., 1973, v.p. corp. merchandising, 1973-75, v.p. retail ops., 1975-76, sr. v.p. retail ops., 1976-77, exec. v.p. retail ops., 1977-84, pres., 1984-91; pres., COO Albertson's Inc., Boise, 1991—; also bd. dirs. Albertson's Inc., Boise, Idaho. Republican. Roman Catholic. Clubs: Arid, Hillcrest Country (Boise). Office: Albertson's Inc PO Box 20 Boise ID 83726-0020*

CARLEY, PATRICK CLARE, physician; b. Aurora, Ill., Sept. 8, 1944. BS, Spring Hill Coll., Mobile, Ala., 1967; MD, U. Ill., 1971. Diplomate Am. Bd. Internal Medicine; lic. physician, Tex., Wash., N.Mex. Intern Bapt. Meml. Hosp., Memphis, 1971-72; resident William Beaumont Army Med. Ctr., El Paso, Tex., 1972-75, chief hematology svc., 1978-82; fellow Walter Reed Army Med. Ctr., Washington, 1975-78; asst. prof. Tex. Tech. U. Health Scis. Ctr., El Paso, 1982-87; staff physician VA Med. Ctr., Phoenix, 1988-89; assoc. prof. internal medicine U. Health Scis. Ctr., El Paso, Tex., 1989-93; clin. fellow bone marrow tranplantation, program dir. Fred Hutchinson Cancer Rsch. Ctr., Seattle, 1993—; attending physician R.E. Thomason Gen. Hosp., El Paso, 1989-93, chmn. cancer com., 1982-88; exec. subcom. faculty coun. Tex. Tech. U., El Paso, 1986—. Contbr. articles and abstracts to profl. jours. Vol. St. Vincent De Paul Soc., 1983—. Fellow ACP; mem. Am. Soc. Clin. Oncology, Am. Soc. Hematology, Am. Cancer Soc. (prof. edn. com. 1983—, hispanic task force 1985—, pres. 1992—), Tex. Med. Assn., S.W. Oncology Group, El Paso County Med. Soc., Hospice El Paso (bd. dirs. 1990—). Office: U Wash Mercer Hall 247 Seattle WA 98105

CARLIN, JEAN EFFAL, psychiatrist; b. Hibbing, Minn., July 24; d. Earl William and Effal OCtavia (Anderson) C. BA, U. Minn., 1950, BS, 1952, MA, 1953, MD, 1954; PhD, 1959. Faculty North Park Coll., Chgo., 1956-58, Long Beach (Calif.) U., 1958-61; physican pvt. practice, 1961-67; faculty U. Calif., Irvine, 1969-80, assoc. dean med. sch., 1974-78; dir. psychiatry resident edn. Martin Luther King Med. Sch., L.A., 1978-80; mem. faculty/staff Fairview Hosp. for Devel. Disabled, Costa Mesa, Calif., 1969-75, 78-80; dir. resident edn. U. Okla., Oklahoma City, 1982-86; fellowship in forensic psychiatry U. So. Calif., L.A., 1986-87; psychiatrist So. regional office Conditional Release Program State of Calif., L.A., 1987-88; cons. L.A. County Mental Health Dept., 1979-80. Contbr. chpts. to books and articles to profl. jours. Col. U.S. Army Nat. Guard, Okla., 1982-86, Calif., 1980-82, 86—. Recipient Am. Bus. Women's Assn. award, Cambodian Assn. Am. awards, 1976-78, Vietnam Govt. awards, 1969, 72. Mem. Covenant Ch. Office: 500 Pacific Coast Hwy Ste 208 Seal Beach CA 90740-6601

CARLQUIST, JOHN FREDERICK, microbiologist, immunologist; b. Salt Lake City, May 25, 1948; s. John Howard and Beatrice (Degenkolbe) C.; m. Pamela Woodbury, Aug. 22, 1975; children: John David, William Christopher. BS, U. Utah, 1971, PhD, 1977. Rsch. asst. dept. microbiology U. Utah Coll. of Medicine, Salt Lake City, 1967-69; microbiologist Utah State Dept. Health, Salt Lake City, 1970-71; microbiologist, curator Pure Culture Lab. U. Utah Coll. of Medicine, Salt Lake City, 1972-73, teaching asst. Dept. Microbiology, 1973-75, teaching fellow Dept. Microbiology, 1976-77; postdoctoral fellow Dept. Bioengring. U. Utah, Salt Lake City, 1977-78; rsch. asst. Dept. Pathology LDS Hosp., Salt Lake City, 1979-82, rsch. assoc. Dept. Medicine Divsn. Cardiology, 1982-86, rsch. scientist head cardiology rsch. lab., sci dir., 1986—, 92—; rsch. instr., rsch. asst. prof. Dept. Internal Medicine U. Utah Sch. of Medicine, Salt Lake City, 1988-91, 91—. Contbr. numerous articles to profl. jours. English instr. Guadalupe Cultural Ctr., Salt Lake City, 1971; youth councilor, chaperone St. Mary's Cath. Ch., Park City, Utah, 1979; dist. rep. Park City Cmty. Citizens Coun., 1980. Recipient Am. Soc. for Microbiology Student Rsch. award, 1976, 77, Frat. Order of Eagles award for Cardiovascular Rsch., 1990, Grad. fellowship U. Utah, 1973; grantee Deseret Found. Rsch., 1980, 85, 88, Am. Heart Assn., 1984, 87, 90, NIH, 1989, 90. Mem. AAAS, Am. Soc. for Microbiology, Transplantation Soc., Park City Ski Patrol (avalanche advisor 1990—, Outstanding Patroller award 1990, 91), Nat. Ski Patrol. Office: LDS Hosp Divsn of Cardiology 8th Ave C St Salt Lake City UT 84060

CARLSEN, JANET HAWS, insurance company owner, mayor; b. Bellingham, Wash., June 16, 1927; d. Lyle F. and Mary Elizabeth (Preble) Haws; m. Kenneth M. Carlsen, July 26, 1952; children: Stephanie L. Chambers, Scott Lyle, Sean Preble, Stacy K., Spencer J. Cert., Armstrong Bus. Sch., 1945; student, Golden Gate Coll., 1945-46. Office mgr. Cornwall Warehouse Co., Salt Lake City, 1950-55, Hansen's Ins., Newman, Calif., 1969-77; owner Carlsen Ins., Gustine, Calif., 1978—. Mem. city coun. City of Newman, 1980-82, mayor, 1982-94; bd. dirs. ARC, Stanislaus, Calif., 1982-83, Tosca, 1993—, Stanislaus County Area on Aging, 1995—, Ctrl. Valley Opportunity Ctr., 1995—; grand marshall Newman Fall Festival, 1989; v.p. ctrl. divsn. League of Calif. Cities, 1989-90, pres., 1990, 91; dir. Ctrl. Valley Opportunity Ctr., 1990—, Sr. Opportunity Svc. Ctr., 1993—. Named Soroptimist Woman of Achievement, 1987, Soroptimist Woman of Distinction, 1988, Outstanding Woman, Stanislaus County Commn. for Women, 1989, Newman Rotary Club Citizen of Yr., 1993-94, Woman of Yr. Calif. State Assembly Dist. 26, 1994. Morman. Club: Booster (Newman). Lodge: Soroptimist. Home: 1215 Amy Dr Newman CA 95360-1003 Office: 377 5th St Gustine CA 95322-1126

CARLSEN, MARY BAIRD, clinical psychologist; b. Salt Lake City, Utah, Aug. 31, 1928; d. Jesse Hays and Susannah Amanda (Bragstad) Baird; m. James C. Carlsen, May 1, 1949; children: Philip, Douglas, Susan, Kristine. Student, St. Olaf Coll., 1946-47; BA, Whitworth Coll., 1950; MA, U. Conn., 1967; PhD, U. Wash., 1973. Profl. organist, piano tchr. Wash., Oreg., Ill., Conn., 1949-68; staff counselor Presbyn. Counseling Svc., Seattle, 1976-79; pvt. practice clin. psychologist, marriage therapist, cognitive, devel. psychology, career devel. Seattle, 1978—; chmn. sr. adult adv. coun. Seattle Parks Dept., 1975-76; adv. bd. Inst. Successful Aging, 1995—. Author: Meaning-Making: Therapeutic Processes in Adult Development, 1988, Creative Aging: A Meaning-Making Perspective, 1991, Transformational Meaning-Making and the Practices of Career Counseling, 1991; editl. bd. Jour. Constructivist Psychology, 1994—. Grantee PEO Rsch., 1972, U. Wash. Women's Guidance Ctr., 1972. Mem. APA, ACA, Am. Soc. Aging, Assn. Humanistic Psychology, N.Am. Personal Construct Network.

CARLSON, CURTIS EUGENE, orthodontist, periodontist; b. Mar. 30, 1942; m. Dona M. Seely; children: Jennifer Ann, Gina Christine, Erik Alan. BA in Divisional Scis., Augustana Coll., 1965; BDS, DDS, U. Ill., 1969; cert. in periodontics, U. Wash., 1974, cert. in orthodontists, 1976. Dental intern Oak Knoll Navy Hosp., Oakland, Calif., 1969-70; dental officer USN, 1970-72; part-time dentist VA Hosp., Seattle, 1972-73; part-time periodontist Group Health Dental Coop., Seattle, 1973-76, part-time orthodontist, 1976-78; clin. instr. U. Wash., 1976; prin. Bellevue (Wash.) Orthodontic and Periodontic Clinic, 1976—; clin. instr., trainer Luxar Laser Corp., Bothell, Wash., 1992—; presenter in field. Master of ceremonies Auctioneer Friendship Fair, Augustana Coll., 1965, orientation group leader, 1965, mem. field svcs. com. for high sch. recruitment, 1965. Fellow Am. Coll. Dentists; mem. ADA, Am. Acad. Periodontology, Am. Assn. Orthodontics, Western Soc. Periodontology (bd. dirs. 1984-85, 86, program chmn. 1986, v.p. 1988, pres. elect 1989, pres. 1990), Seattle King County Dental Soc. (grievance, ethics and pub. info. coms.), Wash. State Dental Assn., Wash. State Soc. Periodontists (program chmn., pres. elect 1987, pres. 1988, 89), Wash. Assn. Dental Specialists (com. rep. 1987, 88, 89), Omicron Kappa Upsilon (dental hon. fraternity), Pi Upsilon Gamma (social chmn. 1964, pres. 1965). Home: 16730 Shore Dr NW Seattle WA 98155-5634 Office: Bellevue Orthodontic Periodontic Clinic 1248 112th Ave NE Bellevue WA 98004-3712

CARLSON, DEVON MCELVIN, architect, educator; b. Topeka, Dec. 1, 1917; s. Gustave Elvin and Gertrude M. (Swanson) C.; m. Mary E. Ackley, June 14, 1949; children: Mitchell Lans, Martha Sue, Judith Ann, Peter DeVon. BS in Architecture, U. Kans., 1941; BS in Archtl. Engring. with honors, U. Colo., 1947; MS in Architecture, Columbia U., 1949. Mem.

faculty U. Colo., 1943-81, prof., chmn. dept. architecture and archtl. engring., 1959-62, dean Sch. Architecture, 1962-70, dean Coll. Environ. Design, 1970-71, dean emeritus, 1981—, mem. steering com. Creative Arts Program, 1959-80; lectr. civic and profl. groups; past mem. Colo. Bd. Examiners Architects, pres., 1964-65. Co-author: An Approach to Architectural Design, 1950, Architecture/Colorado, 1966; contbr. articles to profl. jours. Past mem. Boulder Landmarks Bd.; advisor emeritus Nat. Trust for Hist. Preservation; mem. Colo. Hist. Preservation Rev. Bd., 1980-84, 85—. Recipient Stearns award 1972, Disting. Alumnus award U. Kans., 1984; Columbia U. scholar, 1948. Fellow AIA (bd. dirs. Colo. chpt. 1966-67, pres. 1969, nat. scholarship com. chmn. 1977-78, mem. nat. com. on hist. resources 1978—, Silver medal Western Mountain region 1980, Carlson Lecture series established in his honor 1981); mem. Nat. Coun. Archtl. Registration Bds. (exam-devel. com. 1962-76, 87-93, chmn. 1975, editor Handbook 1976), Colo. Soc. Architects (pres. 1980), Assn. Coll. Schs. Architecture, Am. Soc. Engring. Edn. (past chmn. Colo. chpt.), Boulder C. of C., Rocky Mountain Liturg Art Assn., Hist. Boulder, Hist. Denver, Soc. Archtl. Historians, Scarab Club, Triangle Club, Rotary (bd. dirs.), Tau Beta Pi, Delta Phi Delta, Chi Epsilon. Address: 502 Mapleton Ave Boulder CO 80304-3986

CARLSON, DORIS CATHERINE, art educator, retired publications specialist; b. Wilmot, S.D., Apr. 11, 1923; d. Maurice A. and Rose Christine (Madsen) Carlson. Student, Mpls. Art Inst., 1940s, Sch. of Magic Art, 1981. Accredited art instr. Editor, pvt. sec. Wesley News, Wesley Ch., Mpls., 1942-48; portrait artist Donaldson Portrait Studio, Mpls., 1948; singer, schedule dir. Radio Sta. KEYD, Mpls., 1948-52; sec. Tidewater Oil Co., L.A., 1952-57; sec., legal sec. Hunt Foods, Inc., L.A., 1957-59; publs. specialist The Rand Corp., Santa Monica, Calif., 1959-88; instr. arts Rand Recreation Club, Santa Monica, 1975-88; instr. oil painting various locations, 1970-88; instr. art, lectr. and demonstrator oil painting L.A. area, also Ventura, Calif., 1975—. Author 4 booklets, 1986-88; composer, lyricist (anthem) Evening of Excellence, 1991. Dir. Just For Fun Singers, Oxnard, Calif., 1983—; vol. R.S.V.P., Oxnard. Mem. Ventura County Artists Guild (exhbit coord.), Santa Paula Soc. Arts, Smithsonian Inst. (porcelain Christmas ornament on dispay), Nat. Soc. Tole and Decorative Painters. Mormon. Home: 430 Raspberry Pl Oxnard CA 93030-1525

CARLSON, FREDERICK PAUL, electronics executive; b. Aberdeen, Wash., May 26, 1938; s. Edwin Gustaf and Anna Amelia (Anderson) C.; m. Alice A. Mercer, July 20, 1960 (div. Dec. 1969); 1 child, David Michael; m. Judith Kathryn Maxner, Dec. 12, 1970; children: Paul John, Britt Anna, Corrie Kathryn. Cert. advanced nuclear engring., Bettis Reactor Engring. Sch., 1962; BSEE, U. Wash., 1960, PhD, 1967; MS, U. Md., 1964; cert. exec. program, Stanford U., 1987, Aspen Inst., 1990, MIT, 1991. Registered profl. engr., Oreg., Wash. Rsch. engr. Boeing Aerospace Co., Seattle, 1965-66; prof. elec. engring. U. Wash., Seattle, 1967-77; pres., chief exec. officer Oreg. Grad. Ctr. Corp., Beaverton, 1977-88; v.p. strategy and bus. devel. Honeywell, Inc., Mpls., 1988-91; pres., chief exec. officer Carlson Cons., Inc., Tacoma, 1991—, pres., 1991—; bd. dirs. Synektron, Inc., Portland, Oreg., Tektronix, Inc., Beaverton, Logic Automation, Inc., Portland, Cascade Microtech, Inc., Portland, Frank Russell Trust Co., Tacoma, Wash.; vis. prof. elec. engring. Stanford (Calif.) U., 1975-76; mem. Commn. for Internat. Union Radio Sch., NRC. Author: Introduction to Applied Optics for Engineers, 1977; editor: Man, His Capabilities and Limitations in Systems, 1968; patentee low-frequency detection system, 1978, blood cell analyzer, 1979. Mem. Gov.'s Task Force on Econ. Recovery, Portland, 1982, Bus. Task Force on Trasnp. Systems, Portland, 1988. Officer electronics command USN, 1960-64; capt. USNR, 1964-83. Recipient High Tech. Industry's Good Scout award, Boy Scouts Am., Portland, 1986. Mem. IEEE, Optical Soc. Am. (chpt. pres. 1976), Arlington Club, Waverly Club, Tacoma Club.

CARLSON, GARY LEE, public relations executive, director, producer; b. Yakima, Wash., Oct. 15, 1954; s. Glenn Elmer and Helen Mary (McLean) Carlson. AA, Yakima Community Coll., 1975; BA in Communications, U. Wash., 1977. Dir. pub. affairs Sta. KCMU, Seattle, 1976-77; dir. programming and promotions Sta. KAPP-TV, Yakima, 1978-80; dir. promotions Sta. WBZ-TV, Boston, 1980-84; producer Sta. KCBS-TV, Los Angeles, 1985; dir. creative services Metromedia Producers, Los Angeles, 1985-86; dir. promotion publicity 20th Century Fox, Los Angeles, 1986—. Co-prodr. (TV movie) Coaching a Murder, 1994; prodr., dir. M*A*S*H* 15th Ann. Campaign, 1987 (Internat. Film and TV Festival N.Y. award), The Fox Tradition, 1988 (Internat. Film and TV Festival N.Y. award, Clio finalist award 1988, Telly award 1988, B.P.M.E. award 1988); prodr., writer, dir. Consumer Reports, 1983 (Internat. Film and TV Festival N.Y. award, Houston Internat. Film and TV award). Mem. Broadcast Promotion and Mktg. Execs., Nat. Assn. TV Program Execs., Beta Theta Pi. Home: 1510 Rock Glen Ave Glendale CA 91205-2063 Office: 20th Century Fox Film Corp PO Box 900 Beverly Hills CA 90213-0900

CARLSON, GREGORY DALE, geologist; b. Portland, Oreg., May 20, 1950; s. Dale Keith and Dorothy Elaine (Moyer) C.; m. Diane Elaine Borrego, May 1, 1982; children: Brett Alan, Ashley Marie. BS, U. Oreg., 1972; MS, U. S.C., 1978. Registered profl. geologist, Wyo. Geologist Arco, Denver, 1973-76, Rocky Mountain Energy Co., Denver, 1978-79; geologist, supr. Mobil, Denver, 1979-90; geosci. supr. Mobil, Liberal, Kans., 1990-92; sr. geologist Mobil, Bakersfield, Calif., 1992—. Contbr. articles to profl. jours. State of Oreg. scholar, 1968. mem. Am. Assn. Petroleum Geologists, Soc. Sedimentary Geology (Rocky Mountain sect.). Republican. Office: Mobil Oil Corp 10000 Ming Ave Bakersfield CA 93311-1301

CARLSON, HERB, state legislator. Senator 14th Dist. State of Idaho. Home: PO Box 1238 1812 Hill Rd Eagle ID 83616-5352

CARLSON, KATHLEEN BUSSART, law librarian; b. Charlotte, N.C., June 25, 1956; d. Dean Allyn and Joan (Parlette) Bussart; m. Gerald Mark Carlson, Aug. 15, 1987. BA in Polit. Sci., Ohio State U., 1977; JD, Capital U., 1980; MA in Libr. and Info. Sci., U. Iowa, 1986. Bar: Ohio 1980 (inactive). Editor Lawyers Coop. Pub. Co., Rochester, N.Y., 1980-83; asst. state law libr. State of Wyo., Cheyenne, 1987-88, state law libr., 1988—. Elder Highlands Presbyn. Ch., Cheyenne, 1990-93; 2d v.p. bd. dirs. Wyo. coun. Girl Scouts U.S., Casper, 1990-92, 1st v.p. bd. dirs., 1993—. Mem. Am. Assn. Law Librs. (sec., treas., state, ct. and county SIS 1992-95, edn. com. 1991-92, indexing legal periodical lit. adv. com. 1993-96, chair 1994-96), We. Pacific Assn. Law Librs. (pres.-elect 1995-96), Wyo. Libr. Assn. (sec. acad. and spl. librs. sect. 1990-92, pres. 1994-95), Bibliographic Ctr. for Rsch. (trustee 1991-95), Kappa Delta, Beta Phi Mu, Zonta. Home: 911 E 18th St Cheyenne WY 82001-4722 Office: State Law Libr Supreme Ct Bldg Cheyenne WY 82002

CARLSON, NANCY LEE, English language educator; b. Spokane, Wash., June 1, 1950; d. Catherine Esther Paight. BS, Wash. State U., 1973; MEd, curriculum specialist, Ea. Wash. U., 1987. Tchr. Stevenson-Carson Sch. Dist., Wash., 1973-74, Spokane Sch. Dist., 1974—; vis. faculty Ea. Wash. U., 1989-91, 93—; active steering com. Spokane County Children's Alliance, 1992—. Spokane County co-chmn. Sen. Slade Gorton campaign, 1988, mem. adv. bd., 1989—; Rep. precinct committeeperson, 1988-90, 92-94; bd. dirs. West Ctrl. Cmty. Ctr., Spokane Civic Theater, sec., 1992-94; mem. affordable housing com. Spokane County, 1990-91; treas. Inland Empire for Africa, Spokane, 1985-86; vice chmn. Ea. Wash. phone bank for Sen. Dan Evans, Spokane, 1984; mem. Mayor's Task Force on the Homeless, 1987-88; mem. Spokane County adv. bd. City of Spokane Cmty. Ctr., 1990-92; lay min. First Presbyn. Ch., deacon, 1994—, sec. bd. deacons, 1994—. Mem. NEA, ASCD, Nat. Coun. Tchrs. English, Wash. Coun. Tchrs. English, Wash. Edn. Assn., Spokane Edn. Assn., Wash. State U. Alumni Assn. (area rep. 1987-90). Republican. Presbyterian. Office: Rogers High Sch Sch Dist # 81 1622 E Wellesley Ave Spokane WA 99207-4261

CARLSON, NATALIE TRAYLOR, publisher; b. St. Paul, Feb. 15, 1938; d. Howard Ripley and Maxine (Johnson) Smith; m. James S. Carlson, Oct. 6, 1990; children: Drew Michael, Dacia Lyn, Dana Ann. BA, Jacksonville (Ala.) State U., 1975. Dir. Madison County Assn. of Mental Health, Huntsville, Ala., 1966-67; campaign mgr. U.S. Senatorial Race, No. Ala., 1968; pub. rels. Anniston Acad., 1970-76; journalist The Anniston Star, 1970-74, The Birmingham News, 1972-76; dir. Ala. affiliate, Am. Heart Assn., Birmingham, 1976-77; mgr. San Vincent New Home div., San Diego County Estates Realty, 1978-79; dir. sales Blake Pub. Co., San Diego, 1980-86; pres. Century Publ., San Diego, 1986—. Alternate del. at large Rep. Nat. Conv., San Francisco, 1964; fin. chmn. Madison County Rep. Exec. Com., Huntsville, Ala., 1966-69; pres. Madison County Rep. Women, Huntsville, 1967, 68; Diocesan Conv. del. Grace Episcopal Ch., Ala., 1975; active Nat. Rep. Party, 1962—; mem. St. James Episcopal Ch., Newport Beach, 1990—. Recipient 1st Pl. Newswriting award AP, 1971, 72, 73; nominee Outstanding Woman of Yr., Huntsville Area Jaycees, 1967. Mem. Long Beach Area C. of C., Palm Springs C. of C., Greater Del Mar C. of C., Huntington Beach C. of C., Kappa Kappa Gamma.

CARLSON, PAULA JEAN, publishing executive; b. Little Rock, Nov. 9, 1944; d. Eugene and Mary Pauline (Golleher) Harden; m. Gregory T. Carlson, Feb. 22, 1964; children: Stephanie Diane, Christina L. Carlson-Hirshberger. AS, Clackamas C.C., 1981; BA, Portland State U., 1984. Pres. Handprint Signature, Inc., Portland, Oreg., 1988—. Pub.: (greeting card designs) Little Taxi, 1992, Cars, 1993. Mem. Mensa. Office: Handprint Signature Inc PO Box 22682 Portland OR 97269-2682

CARLSON, RALPH WILLIAM, JR., food products company executive; b. Oak Park, Ill., Dec. 28, 1936; s. Ralph W. and Evelyn Marie (Benson) C.; m. Donna Drevs, Feb. 9, 1963; children: Daniel, Karen Carlson Lombardi, Susan Carlson Franklin, Robert, Kathleen. B.A., Mich. State U., 1958; M.B.A., U. Chgo., 1965; J.D., De Paul U., 1976. Bar: Ill. Group product mgr. The Kendall Co., Chgo., 1966-70; dir. mktg. Ovaltine Products Co. div. Sandoz, Inc., Chgo., 1970-76; mgr. new products Arco Polymers, Inc. subs. Atlantic Richfield Co., Chgo., 1976-78; mgr. internat. fleet ops. Arco Transp. Co., Long Beach, Calif., 1978-81; dir. mktg. planning Arco Solar Industries, Woodland Hills, Calif., 1981-85; mgr. trademark licensing Sunkist Growers, Inc., Ontario, Calif., 1986—. part-time instr. mktg. UCLA, 1989—; judge CORO So. Calif., 1995—. Mem. Oak Park (Ill.) Sch. Bd., 1976-78; bd. dirs. Phila. Maritime Exchange, 1978-79; trustee Cornelia Connelly Sch., 1990-94. Served to lt. USNR, 1958-63. Mem. ABA, Am. Mktg. Assn., Calif. Solar Energy Soc. (dir. 1983-85), U.S. Naval Inst., Delta Chi. Republican. Roman Catholic. Club: Economic (Chgo.); Newfoundland of So. Calif. (bd. dirs. 1985-93). Office: Sunkist Growers Inc 720 E Sunkist St Ontario CA 91761-1861

CARLSON, REVEANN JODI, radon technologist; b. Fargo, N.D., May 29, 1959; d. Robert Edward and Jorjann Reve (Vaala) C. Student, Pierce Coll., Reseda, Calif., 1979-80, Am. U., Washington, 1981. Svc. mgr. F&F Heating & Air Conditioning, Camarillo, Calif., 1982-91; owner Radon Testing Svcs., Westlake Village, Calif., 1991—. Mem. Am. Assn. Radon Scientists and Technologists. Republican. Roman Catholic.

CARLSON, ROBERT CODNER, industrial engineering educator; b. Granite Falls, Minn., Jan. 17, 1939; s. Robert Ledin and Ada Louise (Codner) C.; children: Brian William, Andrew Robert, Christina Louise. BSME, Cornell U., 1962; MS, Johns Hopkins U., 1963, PhD, 1976. Mem. tech. staff Bell Tel. Labs., Holmdel, N.J., 1962-70; asst. prof. Stanford (Calif.) U., Stanford, 1970-77; assoc. prof. Stanford (Calif.) U., 1977-82, prof. indsl. engring., 1982—; program dir., lectr., cons. various spl. programs U.S., Japan, France, 1971—; cons. Japan Mgmt. Assn., Tokyo, 1990—, Raychem, Menlo Park, Calif., 1989—, GKN Automotive, London, 1989—, Rockwell Internat., L.A., 1988—; vis. prof. U. Calif., Berkeley, 1987-88, Dartmouth Coll., Hanover, N.J., 1978-79; vis. faculty Internat. Mgmt. Inst., Geneva, 1984, 88. Contbr. articles to profl. jours. Recipient Maxwell Upson award in Mech. Engring. Cornell U., 1962; Bell Labs. Systems Engring. fellow, 1962-63, Bell Labs. Doctoral Support fellow, 1966-67. Mem. Ops. Rsch. Soc. Am. (chmn. membership com. 1981-83), Inst. Mgmt. Scis., Inst. Indsl. Engrs., Am. Soc. Engring. Edn., Am. Prodn. and Inventory Control Soc. (bd. dirs. 1975-81), Internat. Material Mgmt. Soc., Tau Beta Pi, Phi Kappa Phi, Pi Tau Sigma, Soc. of Enophiles Club (Woodside, Calif.). Office: Stanford Univ Dept Indsl Engring/Enging Mgmt Stanford CA 94305

CARLSON, ROBERT ERNEST, freelance writer, architect, lecturer; b. Denver, Dec. 6, 1924; s. Milton and Augustine Barbara (Walter) C.; m. Jane Frances Waters, June 14, 1952 (div. June 1971); children: Cristina, Bob, Douglas, Glenn, James. BS in Archtl. Engring., U. Colo., 1951. Registered architect, Colo. Architect H.D. Wagener & Assocs., Boulder, Colo., 1953-75; pvt. practice architect Denver, 1975-82; health and promotion cons. Alive & Well Cons., Denver, 1982-85; freelance writer Denver, 1985—; mem. Colo. Gov.'s Coun. for Fitness, Denver, 1975—; state race walking chmn. U.S. Track & Field, Denver, 1983—; bd. dirs. Colo. Found. for Phys. Fitness, Denver, 1987—; lectr. in field. Author: Health Walk, 1988. Vol. Colo. Heart Assn., 1985—, Better Air Campaign, 1986-87, Cystic Fibrosis, 1989-91, Multiple Sclerosis Soc., 1988-91, Qualife, 1989—, March of Dimes, 1989, United Negro Coll. Fund, 1989, bd. trustees, 1990. With U.S. Army, 1943-46, ETO. Decorated Bronze Star; named One of Ten Most Prominent Walking Leaders in U.S.A., Rockport Walking Inst., 1989. Mem. Colo. Author's League, Phidippides Track Club (walking chmn. 1981-85), Rocky Mountain Rd. Runners (v.p. 1983-84), Front Range Walkers Club (founder, pres. Denver chpt. 1985—), Lions (bd. dirs. 1965-72). Episcopalian. Home and Office: 2261 Glencoe St Denver CO 80207-3834

CARLSON, ROBERT MICHAEL, artist; b. Bklyn., Nov. 19, 1952; s. Sidney Carlson and Vickey (Mihaloff) Woodward; m. Linda Schneider; m. Mary Elizabeth Fontaine, Feb. 24, 1984; 1 child, Nora. Student, CCNY, 1970-73; studied with Flora Mace and Joey Kirkpatrick, Pilchuck Glass Sch., 1981, studied with Dan Dailey, 1982. Teaching asst. Pilchuck Sch., Stanwood, Wash., 1986, 88, mem. faculty, 1989, 90, 92; mem. faculty Pilchuck Sch., 1995, Pratt Fine Arts Ctr., Seattle, 1988-90, Penland (N.C.) Sch. Crafts, 1994; mem. artists adv. com. Pilchuck Sch., 1989, 90; vis. artist Calif. Coll. Arts and Crafts, Oakland, 1989, Calif. State U., Fullerton, 1991, blossom summer program Kent State U., Ohio, 1991, U. Ill., Urbana-Champaign, 1993, Toledo Mus. of Art Sch., 1994; visual-artist-in-residence Centrum Found., Port Townsend, Wash., 1992. One-man shows include Foster White Gallery, Seattle, 1987, 90, 92, The Glass Gallery, Bethesda, Md., 1988, Heller Gallery, N.Y.C., 1989, Betsy Rosenfield Gallery, Chgo., 1991, 92, MIA Gallery, Seattle, 1994, others; exhibited in group shows at Traver Gallery, Seattle, 1984, 89, Mindscape Gallery, Evanston, Ill., 1984, 86, Tucson Mus. Art., 1984 (Purchase award), 86 (Award of Merit), Hand and Spirit Gallery, Scottsdale, Ariz., 1985, 86, Craftsman Gallery, Scarsdale, N.Y., 1985, Robert Kidd Gallery, Birmingham, Mich., 1985, 88, Gazebo Gallery, Gatlinburg, Tenn., 1985, The Glass Gallery, Bethesda, Md., 1986 (Jurors award), 91, 92, 94, Artists Soc. Internat., San Francisco, 1987 (Critics Choice award), William Traver Gallery, Seattle, 1987, 90, 91, 92, Japan Glass Artcrafts Assn., Tokyo, 1987, Heller Gallery, 1988, 89, 90, 91, 93, 94, 95, Washington Sq. Ptnrs., 1988, Foster White Gallery, 1988, 90, Bellvue Art Mus., Wash., 1988, 91, 94, Am. Arts and Crafts Inc., San Francisco, 1989, Mus. Craft and Folk Art, San Francisco, 1989, Great Am. Gallery, Atlanta, 1989, Dorothy Weiss Gallery, San Francisco, 1989, Habitat Gallery, Farmington Hills, Mich., 1990, 93, Philabaum Gallery, Tucson, 1990, Greg Kucera Gallery, Seattle, 1990, Connell Gallery, Atlanta, 1990, Net Contents Gallery, Bainbridge Island, Wash., 1991, Seattle Tacoma Internat. Airport Installation, 1991, 95, Pratt Fine Arts Ctr., Seattle, 1991, Crystalex, Novy Bor, Czechoslovakia, 1991, Whatcom County Mus., Bellingham, Wash., 1992, Art Gallery West Australia, 1992, 1004 Gallery, Port Townsend, 1992, Bainbridge Island Arts Coun., 1992, MIA Gallery, 1993, Betsy Rosenfield Gallery, Chgo., 1993, Blue Spiral Gallery, Asheville, N.C., 1995; represented in permanent collections Corning (N.Y.) Mus. Glass, Tucson Mus. Art, Glasmuseum Frauenau, Germany, Glasmuseum Ebeltoft, Denmark, Valley Nat. Bank, Phoenix, Fountain Assocs., Portland, Oreg., Iceland Air Co., Reykjavik, Iceland, Crocker Banks, L.A., Davis Wright Tremain, Seattle, Meiwa Trading Co., Tokyo, Safeco Ins. Corp., Seattle, Crystalex, L.A. County Mus. Art. Fellow Tucson Pima Arts Coun., 1987, NEA, 1990. Mem. Glass Art Soc. (conf. lectr. 1991, bd. dirs. 1992-94, v.p. 1993-94, pres. 1995). Office: PO Box 11590 Bainbridge Island WA 98110

CARLSON, RONALD FRANK, educator, fiction writer; b. Logan, Utah, Sept. 15, 1947; s. Ed and Verna (Mertz) C.; m. Georgia Elaine Craig, June 14, 1969; children: Nicholas George Carlson, Colin Edwin. BA, U. Utah, 1970, MA, 1972. English tchr. Hotchkiss Sch., Lakeville, Conn., 1971-81; artist in edn. Utah Arts Coun., Salt Lake City, 1982-87, Idaho Arts Com., Boise, 1983-89, Alaska Arts Com., Anchorage, 1984-87; instr. continuing edn. U. Utah, Salt Lake City, 1982-86; writer-in residence Ariz. State U., Tempe, 1986-87, asst. prof. English, 1987-88, assoc. prof. English, 1988-94, prof. English, 1994—, dir. creative writing, 1989—, prof. Eglish, 1994—. Author: (novels) Betrayed by F. Scott Fitzgerald, 1977, Truants, 1981, (collection of stories) The News of the World, 1987, Plan B for the Middle Class, 1992, (story) Milk (Best Am. Stories 1987). Bd. dirs., founder Class of '65 West High Schlarship Fund, Salt Lake City, 1985—. Mem. Writers Guild of Am. West. Office: Ariz State Univ Dept English Tempe AZ 85287

CARLSON, SYDNEY ANNE, secondary school educator and counselor; b. San Francisco, May 8, 1943; d. Charles Edward and Geraldine Theresa (Melton) Stoeckle; m. Martin Richard Carlson, Oct. 1, 1965; children: Bartly Timothy, Daniel Martin. AA, City Coll. San Francisco, 1964; BA, San Francisco State U., 1967; Grad. Cert. Alcohol Studies, U. Calif., Berkeley, 1978; MAV, San Francisco Theol. Sem., 1993. Counselor Nat. Coun. on Alcoholism, San Mateo, Calif., 1978-82; alcoholism counselor and lectr. Peninsula Hosp., Burlingame, Calif., 1988-91; math instructional aide Aragon High Sch., San Mateo, Calif., 1983—; counselor in pvt. practice Naptime Counseling, Millbrae, Calif., 1994—. Author: Chaplains' Support Service: A Volunteer's Guide to Hospital Ministry at Peninsula Hosp., 1993. Mem. chaplain's support svc. Peninsula Hosp. Aux., Burlingame, 1980—, past chair; mem. 12 Step Groups, 1978—. Mem. AAUW (chair bridge). Methodist. Home: 503 Hemlock Ave Millbrae CA 94030-2633

CARLSTROM, R. WILLIAM, retired special education educator; b. Seattle, Oct. 22, 1944; s. Roy Albert Carlstrom and Dorothy (Anderson) Hart; m. Ann Scheffer, July 29, 1967; children: Trina Anderson Schmoll, Paul Scheffer. BA, Lewis & Clark Coll., 1967; MA, U. Wash., 1970. Tchr. Shoreline Pub. Schs., Seattle, 1968-71; program coordinator fo adult handicapped City of Seattle, 1971-72; spl. edn. tchr. South Shore Middle Sch., Seattle, 1972-75, Sharples Jr. High, Seattle, 1975-78, Ryther Child Ctr., Seattle, 1978-89; sec., treas., bd. dirs. Glaser Found., Inc., Edmonds, Wash., 1974-86, exec. dir. 1983-91, trustee, 1983—; dir. of adminstrn. First Place Sch. for Homeless Children, 1994; adv. com. mem. U. Wash. Dentistry for Handicapped, Seattle, 1979—; pres., cons. Funding Resources Group, Inc., Edmonds, 1984—; co-founder, trustee Snohomish County Youth Comty. Found., 1992-93; pres. Current Health Techs., Inc., 1992-93, N.P. Mktg.; trustee St. Regis Clinics, 1992-93. Coun. mem. U. Wash. Grad. Sch. for Dentistry, 1979—; trustee Edmonds Unitarian Ch., 1980-81, Pub. Edn. Fund, Dist. 15, Edmonds, 1986-88, Home Care Wash.; pres. Madrona Middle Sch. PTA, Edmonds, 1983-84. Grantee Seattle Masonic Temple, 1974-75, Fed. Govt., 1970-71. Mem. Pacific N.W. Grantmakers Forum. Democrat. Office: NP Mktg 144 Railroad Ave Ste 109 Edmonds WA 98020-4121

CARLTON, THOMAS GRANT, psychiatrist; b. San Diego, Nov. 9, 1943; s. Edwin Thomas and Theda Miriam (Waddell) C. BA, San Jose State U., 1966; MD, U. Wis., 1970. Commd. ensign USN, 1969, advanced through grades to capt., 1985, ret., 1993; pvt. practice psychiatry Moses Lake, Wash., 1993-95; med. dir. Ctr. for Emotional Trauma Recovery, Lake Chelan Cmty. Hosp., 1995—; asst. prof. Eastern VA Med. Sch., Norfolk, Va., 1979-83, George Washington U., Washington, 1979-83, Chgo. Med. Sch., 1988-90. Mem. AMA, Am. Psychiatric Assn., Am. Profl. Soc. on Abuse of Children, Internat. Soc. for Study of Dissociation, Am. Soc. Clin. Hypnosis, Rotary. Office: Ctr for Emotional Trauma Recovery Lake Chelan Cmty Hosp PO Box 908 Chelan WA 98816

CARLTON-ADAMS, GEORGIA M., psychotherapist; b. Kansas City, Mo.; d. George Randolph Carlton and Harriett Marie (Smith) Carlton-Witt; m. John Adams; 1 child, J.J. II. Student, Kansas City (Mo.) Jr. Coll., Rockhill Coll., Trinity Coll., Dublin, Ireland, 1973, City U. of London (Eng.), 1978. Owner Pure White Electric Light and Magic, Lakewood, Calif., 1985—; dir., owner Trauma Buddy's, Lakewood, 1988—; clin. hypotherapist Inner Group Mgmt., Cerritos, Calif., 1989—; cons. Rockwell, McDonnell Douglas, Long Beach, Calif., 1987-90; owner In Print mag., 1990—; staff counselor FHP. Author: Who Calls on Pandora, 1969, Jupiter in Scorpio, 1974, Burma Route, 1989, Counterstrike: Dimitri Manulski, 1990, Kitty-Mophis, 1982, Mouse Tails, 1991, Bookish Miss Emma, 1993, A Little Trip Through the Universe, 1993, Handbook for the Living, 1990. Adv. Greater Attention Victims Violent Crimes; active Animal Rights Pet Protection Soc., Calif. Preventive Child Abuse Orgn., Sierra Club. Mem. Calif. Astronomy Assn., Acoustic Brain Rsch., Inner Group Mgmt., NLP Integration Soc. (pres. 1988-89), British Psychol. Assn., C. of C. Home and Office: 744 Chestnut Ave Apt 11 Long Beach CA 90813-4157

CARMAN, JOHN ELWIN, journalist; b. Des Moines, Nov. 25, 1946; s. Paul Herbert and Trace Emma (Becker) C.; m. Leslie Debbs Hill, Feb. 15, 1975 (div. 1982); m. Janice Faller, Sept. 21, 1985. B.A., Kenyon Coll., 1968; M.S. in Journalism, Northwestern U., 1970. Reporter, Des Moines Register, 1967, Duluth News-Tribune (Minn.), 1968-69, Milw. Jour., 1970-72; reporter, columnist Mpls. Star, 1972-82; columnist Atlanta Jour. and Constitution, 1982-86, San Francisco Chronicle, 1986—. Recipient Page One award Twin Cities Newspaper Guild, 1975; AP Ann. award Minn. AP, 1977; Green Eyeshade award Sigma Delta Chi, 1985. Mem. TV Critics Assn. (mem. nat. bd., George Peabody award 1985-90). Office: Chronicle Pub Co 901 Mission St San Francisco CA 94103-2905

CARMAN, LAURALEE, writer, personal development coach, speaker; b. Phoenix, May 28, 1964; d. John W. Peters and Janet May (Muder) Hiscoe; m. Brian S. Carman, July 23, 1983 (div. Sept. 1994); 2 adopted children. Student, Portland (Oreg.) Community Coll., 1980-82, City U., 1994. Asst. project mgr. No. Telecom, Santa Maria, Calif., 1981-82; customer svc. Savenet, Portland, 1982-84; acct. exec. Finzer Bus., Portland, 1984-86; western sales mgr. Abaton Tech., San Francisco, 1986-87; prin. DTP Cons., San Francisco, 1986-87; western sales mgr. DEST Corp., San Francisco, 1987-88; founder, pres. Adelphi Corp., San Ramon, Calif., 1988-92; owner Decorating Den Franchise, Tigard, Oreg., 1991—; pres., founder Kyklos, Inc., Lake Oswego, Oreg., 1993—. Home and Office: 3601 Red Cedar Way Lake Oswego OR 97035-3525

CARMEL, RALPH, hematologist, educator; b. Riga, Latvia, Aug. 8, 1940; came to U.S., 1948; s. Herman and Ida (Paul) C.; m. Martha, July 20, 1967; children: Rina, Abigail. BA, Yeshiva U., 1959; MD, NYU, 1963. Diplomate Am. Bd. Internal Medicine in medicine and hematology. Intern, resident Maimonides Med. Ctr., Bklyn., 1963-65, Univ. Hosp., Madison, Wis., 1965-66; USPHS rsch. fellow Mt. Sinai Sch. Medicine, N.Y.C., 1966-68; fellow MRC Exptl. Hematology Unit, St. Mary's Hosp., London, 1971; asst. prof. medicine Wayne State U., Detroit, 1972-75; assoc. prof. medicine U. So. Calif., L.A., 1975-81, prof. medicine and pathology, 1981—; vis. investigator Inserm, Hosp. Henri Mondor, Creteil, France, 1982-83; vis. scientist Weizmann Inst., Rehovot, Israel, 1991-92; ad hoc cons. NIH/FASEB, Bethesda; mem. VA Merit Rev. Bd. for Hematology, 1988-91; chmn. Sci. Subcom. on Nutritional Anemia, Am. Soc. Hematology, 1982; cons. FDA, 1993, Ctr. Disease Control, 1994. Contbr. more than 100 articles to sci. jours. and 20 chpts. to various books. Maj. USAF, 1968-70. Mem. Am. Soc. Hematology, Am. Inst. Nutrition, Am. Soc. for Clin. Investigation, Internat. Soc. for Exptl. Hematology. Office: U So Calif 2025 Zonal Ave Los Angeles CA 90033-4526

CARNAHAN, ORVILLE DARRELL, state legislator, retired college president; b. Elba, Idaho, Dec. 25, 1929; s. Marion Carlos and Leola Pearl (Putnam) C.; m. Colleen Arrott, Dec. 14, 1951; children: Karen, Jeanie, Orville Darrell, Carla. B.S., Utah State U., 1958; M.Ed., U. Idaho, 1962, Ed.D., 1964. Vocat. dir., v.p. Yakima Valley Coll., Yakima, Wash., 1964-69; chancellor Eastern Iowa Community Coll. Dist., Davenport, 1969-71; pres. Highline Coll., Midway Wash., 1971-76; assoc. Utah Commr. for Higher Edn., Salt Lake City, 1976-78; pres. So. Utah State Coll., Cedar City, 1978-81, Salt Lake Community Coll., Salt Lake City, 1981-90; pres. emeritus Salt Lake Community Coll. (formerly Utah Tech. Coll.), Salt Lake City, 1990—; mem. Utah Ho. of Reps.; cons. to various orgns. Active Boy Scouts Am. Served with U.S. Army, 1952-54, Korea. Mem. Am. Vocat. Assn., NEA, Idaho Hist. Soc., Utah Hist. Soc., Alpha Tau Alpha, Phi Delta Kappa, Rotary Internat. Mem. Ch. of Jesus Christ of Latter-Day Saints. Home: 2112 Quailbrook Dr Salt Lake City UT 84118-1120 Office: Salt Lake Community Coll 4600 S Redwood Rd Salt Lake City UT 84123-3145

CARNEY, HEATH JOSEPH, aquatic ecologist, educator; b. Lyon, France, Aug. 7, 1955; s. Stephen McLure and June (Kempf) C. BS, Coll. William and Mary, 1979; MS, U. Mich., 1981; PhD, U. Calif., Davis, 1987. Rsch. asst. U. Mich., Ann Arbor, 1979-82; aquatic ecology fellow U. Calif., Davis, 1982-87, rsch. ecologist, 1989—; asst. prof., rsch. fellow dept. biology Ind. U., Bloomington, 1987—; cons. U. Mich., 1980-81, Harvard U., 1988—, U. Calif. Berkeley, 1989—. Contbr. articles to profl. jours. Grantee EPA, NOAA, NSF, MAB/UNESCO. Mem. AAAS, Am. Soc. Limnology and Oceanography, Ecol. Soc. Am. Phycol. Soc. Am., Soc. Internat. Limnologiae, Internat. Assn. Ecology, Union Concerned Scientists, Sierra Club, Sigma Xi, Phi Beta Kappa. Office: U Calif Inst Ecology Davis CA 95616

CARNEY, RICHARD EDGAR, foundation executive; b. Marshall, Tex., Dec. 11, 1923; s. Edgar Lester and Lillian (Sansom) C.; m. Adrienne McAndrews, 1973 (div. 1981). Student, Culver-Stockton Coll., 1942, 46, Washington U., St. Louis, 1946-48; Taliesin fellow, Spring Green, Wis. and Scottsdale, Ariz., 1948-55. Aide to Frank Lloyd Wright, 1952-59; asst. to sec.-treas. Frank Lloyd Wright Found., Scottsdale, 1959-62, exec. asst. to pres., 1962-85, treas., 1962—, mng. trustee, ceo, 1985—; dir. admissions, student adviser Frank Lloyd Wright Sch. Architecture, Scottsdale, 1962—; treas. Taliesin Architects, Scottsdale, 1962—; exhbn. com. Scottsdale Ctr. for Arts, 1985-91; mem. Gov.'s Commn. on Taliesin, State of Wis., 1988-89; organizer, bd. dirs. Taliesin Preservation Commn., Spring Green, 1990—, pres., 1991—. Set designer, performer theatrical prodns., Taliesin, Spring Green, 1960—. Trustee Unity Chapel, Inc., Spring Green, 1980—; mem. Task Force on Higher Edn., Scottsdale, 1991—. Sgt. U.S. Army, 1942-46, ETO. Recipient Alumni of Yr. award Culver-Stockton Coll., 1962. Home and Office: Frank Lloyd Wright Found Taliesin W Scottsdale AZ 85261

CARNICKE, SHARON MARIE, drama educator, theatre specialist and director; b. Bridgeport, Conn., July 28, 1949; d. Stephen J. and Evelyn (Furjesz) C. Cert. Russian Lang., Moscow U., USSR, 1970; AB, Barnard Coll., 1971; MA, NYU, 1973; PhD, Columbia U., 1979. Asst. prof. Sch. Visual Arts, N.Y.C., 1980-83; coord. core curriculum Columbia U., N.Y.C., 1978-83; asst. dean curriculum NYU, 1983-86, asst. prof. English, 1984-87; assoc. prof. theatre U. So. Calif., L.A., 1987—; Russian evaluator, NEA, Washington, 1984-87; cons. core curriculum Sch. Visual Arts, N.Y.C., 1980-83; interpretor Soviet Dirs. at Actors Studio, N.Y.C., 1978. Contbr. articles to profl. jours.; author: The Theatrical Instinct, 1989; translator plays from Russian, Chekhov and New Soviet, 1970—; adaptor, trans. plays: The Storm, Blackforest, 1978, 89; head editor project to publish English translation of Collected Works of Stanislavsky. Interpretor Am. Soviet Youth Forum, USA, USSR, 1973-74. Fellowship Am. Coun. Learned Socs., 1988-89, Rockefeller Found., U. Wis., Madison, 1988, Mogilat-Mihaly fellowship, USSR, 1978; grantee Institut d'etudes slaves, La Sorbonne, France, 1979. Mem. MLA, Am. Lit. Translators Assn., Dramatists Guild. Office: U So Calif MC0791 Divsn Theatre Drc Los Angeles CA 90089

CARO, MIKE, writer, editor, publisher; b. Joplin, Mo., May 16, 1944; s. Peter Klaus and Marguerite (Zuercher) C.; m. Bonita Marie Polniak, June 6, 1965 (div. June 1972); m. Phyllis Marsha Goldberg. Gen. mgr. Huntington Park (Calif.) Casino, 1985; chief strategist Bicycle Club, Bell Gardens, Calif., 1984-85; editor, pub. Mike Caro's Pro Poker monthly, 1993; founder Mad Genius Brain Trust; actor, instr. video tape Play to Win Poker, 1988. Author: Caro on Gambling, 1984, Mike Caro's Book of Tells: The Body Language of Poker, 1985, Poker for Women: A Course in Destroying Male Opponents at Poker and Beyond, 1985, New Poker Games, Gambling Times Quiz Book, Bobby Baldwin's Winning Poker Secrets, Caro's Fundamental Secrets of Poker, 1991; editor-in-chief Poker Player; poker editor Gambling Times; mng. editor B&G Pub.; contbr. articles to gambling mags.; programmer ORAC: Artificially Intelligent Poker Player, 1983; developer programming tools Mike Caro's Poker Engine, audio tapes Real Life Strategy, Positive Poker, Pro Poker Secrets, Pro Hold on Secrets, 1992, four-color deck, 1992; video Caro's Power Poker Seminar, 1995. Address: 4535 W Sahara Ave Ste 105 Las Vegas NV 89102-3733

CARPARELLI, PETER LOUIS, school system administrator; b. Passaic, N.J., Sept. 7, 1943; s. Peter N. and Frances Anne (Scarfo) C.; m. Mary Louise DuPont, June 18, 1966; children: Keith Allen Carparelli, Lisa Maria Schuma Carparelli. BA, Montclair State U., 1966; MS, Mich. State U., 1971; EdD, U. Mont., 1979. Cert. sci. tchr., N.J., N.D., sch. adminstr., Mont. Sci., phys. edn. tchr., coach Red Cloug Indian Sch., Pine Ridge, S.D., 1964-65; sci. tchr., coach West Morris Regional H.S., Chester, N.J., 1966-69; sci. tchr., sci. dept. chmn. U.S. Bur. Indian Affairs, Belcourt, N.D., 1970-72; tchr. supr. U.S. Bur. Indian Affairs, Belcourt, 1972-75; sci. methods instr. U. Mont., Missoula, 1975-76; vice prin. Helena (Mont.) H.S., 1976-79, prin., 1979-84; prin. Helena Mid. Sch., 1984-87; supt. Butte (Mont.) Pub. Schs., Bozeman, 1987-90, Billings (Mont.) Pub. Schs., 1990—; prin. ptnr. Synergetics Consulting Svcs., Billings, 1992—; bd. dirs. N.W. Regional Edn. Lab., Portland, Oreg., 1992—; mem. Gov.'s Edn. Adv. Com., Helena, 1989-91. Editor: (jour.) Big Sky Administrator, 1985; contbr. articles to profl. jours. Bd. dirs. Billings Family YMCA, 1993—, Job Svc. Employers Com., Billings, 1990-94, Jobs for Mont.'s Grads., Helena, 1989-93, Yellowstone United Way, Billings, 1990-93. Recipient G.V. Erickson award Sch. Adminstrs. Mont., 1994, Excellence award Mont. State U.-Billings, 1993, Golden Apple award Butte Area C. of C., 1990; named Outstanding Adminstr. Yr. Billings Edn. Assn., 1994. Mem. Mont. Assn. Sch. Supts. (membership com. 1987—), Am. Assn. Sch. Adminstrs. (com. on state nat. rels. 1994-95), Elks. Roman Catholic. Home: 1731 Augsburg Dr Billings MT 49105 Office: Mont State Univ 116 Reid Hall Bozeman MT 59717

CARPENTER, ARTHUR ESPENET, furniture designer; b. N.Y.C., Jan. 20, 1920; s. Flora Dunn (Welch) C.; children: Victoria, Arthur III. BA, Dartmouth Coll., 1942. Furniture craftsman, 1948—; tchr. San Francisco State U., 1975-79, Anderson Ranch, Snowmass, Colo., 1976-88; workshop tchr. in field. Pres. Sch. Bd., Bolinas, 1960-63. NEA fellow, 1976; Fulbright lectr. tour, 1985. Fellow Am. Craft Coun.; mem. Calif. Craft Assn. (hon.). Home: 1100 Olema Bolinas Rd Bolinas CA 94924-9615

CARPENTER, DIANE ELLEN, small business owner; b. Chgo., Dec. 17, 1951; d. Alex F. and Helen E. (Tuholski) Wirkus; 1 child, Chelsea Carpenter. BA in English, Calif. State U., Long Beach, 1984; MAT, Loyola Marymont U., L.A., 1987. Cert. tchr., Calif. Flight attendant United Airlines, L.A., 1972-87; county clk. San Luis Obispo (Calif.) County, 1989; office mgr. Almond Country R.E., Paso Robles, Calif., 1990-92; tchr. St. Rose Sch., Paso Robles, 1992; owner Chelsea Bookshop and Cafe, Paso Robles, 1992—; adv. bd. San Luis Obispo County Psychiat. Bd., 1989-90. Author: (book) Depression: Ways to Recover, (poetry) Animal Husbandry, 1993. Mem. Paso Robles C. of C., San Luis Obispo C. of C., Paso Robles Art Assn., Am. Bookseller Assn., No. Calif. Bookseller Assn. Office: Chelsea Bookshop and Cafe 701 6th St Paso Robles CA 93446

CARPENTER, DONALD BLODGETT, real estate appraiser; b. New Haven, Aug. 20, 1916; s. Fred Donald and Gwendolen (Blodgett) C.; m. Barbara Marvin Adams, June 28, 1941 (dec. Aug. 1978); m. 2d, Lee Burker McGough, Dec. 28, 1980 (div. Apr. 1987); children—Edward G., John D., William V., Andrew J., Dorothy J. and James J. McGough. PhB, U. Vt., 1938; postgrad., Sonoma State U., 1968-69, Mendocino Community Coll., 1977, Coll. of Redwoods, 1984-85. Reporter Burlington (Vt.) Daily News, 1938-39; guide chair operator Am. Express Co., N.Y. World's Fair, 1939; underwriter G.E.I. Corp., Newark, 1939-40; sales corr. J. Dixon Crucible Co., Jersey City, 1940-41, asst. office mgr., priorities specialist, 1941-42; sales rep. J. Dixon Crucible Co., San Francisco, 1946-52; field supr. Travelers Ins. Co., San Francisco, 1952-58; gen. agt. Gen. Am. Life Ins. Co., San Francisco, 1958-59; western supr. Provident Life & Accident Ins. Co., San Francisco, 1959-60; brokerage supr. Aetna Life Ins. Co., San Francisco, 1960-61; maintenance cons. J.I. Holcomb Mfg. Co., Mill Valley, Calif., 1961-68; ednl. svc. rep. Marquis Who's Who, Inc., 1963-68; sales rep. Onox, Inc., Mendocino, Calif., 1965-68; tchr., coach Mendocino Jr.-Sr. High Sch., 1968; real property appraiser Mendocino County, 1968-81; instr. Coll. of Redwoods, 1985-87; real estate appraiser Carpenter Appraisal Svcs., 1982-88, ret. Active numerous civic orgns.; co-chmn. Citizens for Sewers, 1971-72; mem. Mendocino County Safety Coun., 1981; sponsor mem. Mendocino Art Ctr., 1965—. With USNR, 1942-46; lt. comdr., comdg. officer res. unit, 1967-68, ret., 1968. Sec. of Navy Commendation with ribbon, 1946, other awards, certificates; companion Mil. Order World Wars (life); named Cmty. Sportsman of Yr., 1971. Mem. Res. Officers Assn. U.S. (life, chpt. pres. 1954, 56, state v.p. 1958-61), Ret. Officers Assn. (life, chpt. survivors assistance area counselor 1979—, chpt. scholarship com. 1986-91), Save-the-Redwoods League, Marines Meml. Assn., Mendocino County Employees Assn. (dir. 1981), Mendocino County Hist. Soc., Mendocino Hist. Rsch. Inc. (docent 1982-88), Nat. Assn. Uniformed Svcs. (life), Mendocino Coast Geneal. Soc. (pres. 1991-93), Nat. Ret. Tchrs. Assn., Calif. Ret. Tchrs. Assn., Naval Order of U.S. (life), Naval Res. Assn. (life), Navy League of U.S. (life), U.S. Naval Inst. (life), Am. Diabetes Assn., Alumni Assn. U. Vt. (founding pres. San Francisco Alumni Club 1964), Mendocino Coast Stamp Club (charter, dir. 1983-93, pres. 1994, v.p. 1995), Rotary Internat. (club pres. 1975-76, dist. gov. area rep. 1977-78, Dist. Gov. awards 1974, 76, dist. amg. scholarship com. 1978-81, 89-90, dist. group study exchange com. 1981-88, 90-93, dist. foun. alumni com. 1991-92, Paul Harris fellow 1979—, Rotarian of the Yrs. 1969-88, club historian 1989—, Cert. Achievement for oustanding svc. 1993-94), Am. Legion (post comdr. 1972-73, state citation for outstanding cmty. svc. 1972, past comdrs. Calif., life), Mendocino Coast Land Devel. Corp. (dir. 1991—, exec. v.p. 1995), Mendocino Cardinal Booster Club (charter, life, pres. 1971), U. Vt. Catamount Club (charter), Old Mill Club, Kappa Sigma (Scholarship-Leadership award 1937-38). Republican. Congregationalist. Home: PO Box 87 10801 Gurley Ln Mendocino CA 95460-0087

CARPENTER, FRANK CHARLES, JR., retired electronics engineer; b. L.A., June 1, 1917; s. Frank Charles and Isobel (Crump) C.; A.A., Pasadena City Coll., 1961; B.S. in Elec. Engring. cum laude, Calif. State U.-Long Beach, 1975, M.S. in Elec. Engring., 1981; m. Beatrice Josephine Jolly, Nov. 3, 1951; children—Robert Douglas, Gail Susan, Carol Ann. Self-employed design and mfgr. aircraft test equipment, Los Angeles, 1946-51; engr. Hoffman Electronics Corp., Los Angeles, 1951-56, sr. engr., 1956-59, project mgr., 1959-63; engr.-scientist McDonnell-Douglas Astronautics Corp., Huntington Beach, Calif., 1963-69, spacecraft telemetry, 1963-67, biomed. electronics, 1967-69, flight test instrumentation, 1969-76; lab. test engr. Northrop Corp., Hawthorne, Calif., 1976-82, spl. engr., 1982-83; mgr. transducer calibration lab. Northrop Corp., Pico-Rivera, Calif., 1983-86. Served with USNR, 1941-47. Mem. IEEE (sr.), Amateur Radio Relay League. Contbr. articles to profl. jours. Patentee transistor squelch circuit; helicaland whip antenna. Home: 2037 Balearic Dr Costa Mesa CA 92626-3514

CARPENTER, JEANNINE NUTTALL, nurse; b. Safford, Ariz., Feb. 10, 1934; d. Joseph Heber and Alma (Woolsey) Nuttall; m. Jerry K. Carpenter, Apr. 1, 1953; children: Jeffrey, Joe, Jan, Jason, Julie. ADN, Mesa Community Coll., 1973; BSN, U. Phoenix, Tucson, Ariz., 1990. Cert. Profl. Health Care Quality, RN, Ariz. Dental asst. Safford, Ariz., 1952-69; staff nurse Maricpa Med. Ctr., Phoenix, 1973, Mt. Graham Community Hosp., Safford, 1973-75; dance instr. Ea. Ariz. Coll., Thatcher, 1978-91, instr. cert. nursing asst., 1984-90; nurse supr. Mt. View Nursing Ctr., Safford, 1975-77; RN/EMT Caldwell's Ambulance, Safford, 1974-86; nurse supr. No. Cochise Hosp., Willcox, Ariz., 1977-79; dir. nurses Safford Care Ctr., 1986-87; swing bed coord. Mt. Graham County Hosp., Safford, 1987—; quality coord. nursing Mt. Graham Hosp., Safford, 1989—, interim dir. nursing, 1994, quality resources dept. dir., 1993—; v.p. Ariz. Bd. Adminstrs., Phoenix, 1987-90; clin. preceptor U. Phoenix, Tucson, 1990—; publ. bd. Ariz. Assn. Healthcare Quality, Tucson, 1990-93; coord. Joint Commn. Accreditation and State Dept. of Health Svcs. Licensure, 1991—. Actress mus. theater, 1974. Sec. Am. Heart Assn., Safford. Republican. Mormon. Office: Mt Graham Community Hosp 1600 S 20th Ave Safford AZ 85546-4011

CARPENTER, JOHN EVERETT, retired principal, educational consultant; b. Tarrytown, N.Y., Nov. 27, 1923; s. Everett Birch and Mary (Avery) C.; student Union Coll., 1943; B.A., Iona Coll., 1946; M.A., Columbia, 1949, profl. diploma, 1961; m. Marie F. McCarthy, Nov. 14, 1944; 1 son, Dennis Everett. Tchr., Blessed Sacrament High Sch., New Rochelle, N.Y., 1946-50; tchr., adminstr. Armonk (N.Y.) pub. schs., 1950-62; dir. guidance Ridge Street Sch., Port Chester, N.Y., 1962-64; counselor Rye (N.Y.) High Sch., 1964-66, prin., 1966-78, ret.; guest lectr. Served to lt. USNR; now lt. comdr. ret. Res. Decorated Bronze Star medal. Mem. Middle States Assn. Colls. and Schs. (commn. on secondary schs.), Am. (life), Westchester-Putnam-Rockland (past pres.) personnel and guidance assns., NEA, Am. Legion (past comdr.), Phi Delta Kappa, Kappa Delta Pi. Rotarian (past pres., Paul Harris fellow). Clubs: Tarrytown Boat (past commodore), Green Valley Elks. Home: 321 N Paseo De Los Conquistadores Green Valley AZ 85614-3140

CARPENTER, PETER ROCKEFELLER, social services agency administrator; b. Sunbury, Pa., Apr. 18, 1939; s. Alvin Witmer and Katherine (Rockefeller) C.; m. Janet Ross Buck, Aug. 24, 1963; children: Karen Louise Althaus, Jean Ellen Chronis, Peter Alvin. BA, Pa. State U., 1962. Mgr. dept. J.C. Penney Co., Menlo Park, N.J., 1964-67; ops. mgr. Allstate Ins. Co., Summit, N.J., 1967-73; adminstrv. mgr. Prudential Property & Casualty, Scottsdale, Ariz., 1973-75; v.p. Fortune Properties, Scottsdale, 1975-76; life underwriter Conn. Mutual Life, Phoenix, 1976-81; v.p. and dir. sales and mktg. No. Trust Bank, Phoenix, 1981-89; v.p. M&I Marshall & Ilsley Trust Co., 1989-94; dir. planned giving Luth. Social Svcs. of the S.W. Sec. exec. bd. Samuel Gompers Rehab. Ctr., 1981-84, chmn. bd., 1984-91; div. chmn. Phoenix United Way, 1981, 82, 86, 90; Rep. committeeman, Phoenix, 1978-86; bd. dirs. Scottsdale Boys Club, Scottsdale Cultural Coun. Adv., Herberger Theatre Ctr. With USN, 1962-64. Mem. Nat. Assn. Planned Giving Roundtable, Pa. State U. Alumni Assn. (dir. 1979-86), Son of Am. Revolution, Ariz. Club, U.S. Navy League, Kiwanis (Disting. lt. gov.), Sigma Alpha Epsilon. Lutheran. Home: 11684 E Terra Dr Scottsdale AZ 85259-5900 Office: Luth Social Svcs of the SW 919 N 1st St Phoenix AZ 85004

CARPENTER, RICHARD NORRIS, lawyer; b. Cortland, N.Y., Feb. 14, 1937; s. Robert P. and Sylvia (Norris) C.; m. Elizabeth Bigbee, Aug. 1961 (div. June 1975); 1 child, Andrew Norris; m. Leslie Nordby, July, 1992. BA magna cum laude, Syracuse U., 1958; LLB, Yale U., 1962. Bar: N.Y. 1962, N.Mex. 1963, U.S. Dist. Ct. (no. dist.) N.Y., U.S. Dist. Ct. N.Mex., U.S. Ct. Appeals (D.C. and 10th cirs.), U.S. Supreme Ct. Assoc. Breed, Abbott & Morgan, N.Y.C., 1962-63, Bigbee & Byrd, Santa Fe, 1963-67; ptnr. Carpenter, Comeau, Maldegan, Nixon & Templeman, Santa Fe, 1967—; spl. asst. atty. gen., State of N.Mex., 1963-74, 90—; sec. Bokum Corp., Miami, Fla., 1969-70. Mem. adv. bd. Interstate Mining Compact, N.Mex., 1981-88; elder 1st Presbyn. Ch., Santa Fe, 1978-80, 86-89, trustee, 1975-77, pres., 1977; bd. dirs. Santa Fe Community Coun., 1965-67, St. Vincent Hosp. Found., Santa Fe, 1980-84; trustee Santa Fe Prep. Sch., 1981-84, pres., 1982-84; trustee St. Vincent Hosp., 1980-86, 87—, chmn. 1985-86, 90-93; bd. dirs. Santa Fe YMCA, 1964-69, pres., 1969; trustee Santa Fe Prep. Permanent Endowment Fund., 1987-90. Rotary Found. fellow, Panjab U., Pakistan, 1959-60. Mem. ABA, N.Mex. Bar Assn., 1st Jud. Bar Assn., N.Y. State Bar Assn., Phi Beta Kappa, Pi Sigma Alpha, Phi Beta Phi. Home: 1048 Bishops Lodge Rd Santa Fe NM 87501-1009

CARR, JACQUELYN B., psychologist, educator; b. Oakland, Calif., Feb. 22, 1923; d. Frank G. and Betty (Kreiss) Corker; children: Terry, John, Richard, Linda, Michael, David. BA, U. Calif., Berkeley, 1958; MA, Stanford U., 1961; PhD, U. So. Calif., 1973. Lic. psychologist, Calif; lic. secondary tchr., Calif. Tchr. Hillsdale High Sch., San Mateo, Calif., 1958-69, Foothill Coll., Los Altos Hills, Calif., 1969—; cons. Silicon Valley Companies, U.S. Air Force, Interpersonal Support Network, Santa Clara County Child Abuse Council, San Mateo County Suicide Prevention Inc.,Parental Stress Hotline, Hotel/Motel Owners Assn.; co-dir. Individual Study Ctr.; supr. Tchr. Edn.; adminstr. Peer Counseling Ctr.; led numerous workshops and confs. in field. Author: Learning is Living, 1970, Equal Partners: The Art of Creative Marriage, 1986, The Crisis in Intimacy, 1988, Communicating and Relating, 1984, 3d edit., 1991, Communicating with Myself: A Journal, 1984, 3d edit., 1991; contbr. articles to profl. jours. Mem. Mensa. Club: Commonwealth. Home: 837 Miller Ave Cupertino CA 95014-4642 Office: Foothill College 12345 El Monte Ave Los Altos CA 94022-4504

CARR, JAMES PATRICK, lawyer; b. Cheverly, Md., Apr. 13, 1950; s. Lawrence Edward Jr. and agnes (Dyer) C.; m. Mona L. Kyle, May 28, 1986; children: James P. Jr., Kristin, Kevin, Sean. BA, U. Notre Dame, 1972, JD, 1976. Bar: Md. 1976, Calif. 1977, U.S. Dist. Ct. (cen. dist.) Calif. 1977, U.S. Dist. Ct. (so. dist.) Calif. 1986. Assoc. Carr, Jordan et al, Washington, 1976-77; ptnr. Breidenbach, Swainston et al, L.A., 1977-84, Harney, Wolfe, Shaller & Carr, L.A., 1984-88, Carr & Shaller, L.A., 1988-89; pvt. practice law L.A., 1989—. Mem. Am. Bd. Trial Advs., Assn. Trial Lawyers Am., Calif. Trial Lawyers Assn. Democrat. Roman Catholic. Office: 11755 Wilshire Blvd Ste 1170 Los Angeles CA 90025-1517

CARR, NOEL, food products executive; b. 1943. BS in Farm Mgmt., Calif. State Poly U., 1967. Mgr. Spreckels Sugar, Salinas, Calif., 1967-71; sales mgr. Bruce Church, Inc., Salinas, 1971-75, harvest mgr., 1975-81; v.p. Fresh Western Marketing, Salinas, 1981—; pres. Harvest Tek Inc., Salinas, 1981—; v.p. Pacific Freezers, Salinas, 1989-94. Office: Harvest Tek Inc 1156 Abbott St Salinas CA 93901-4503*

CARR, PETER EMILE, publisher; b. La Habana, Cuba, Oct. 16, 1950; came to U.S., 1962; s. Pedro Emilio Carr and Carmen Emelina Luaces. BA in Anthropology, Calif. State U., Long Beach, 1986. Asst. mgr. Hides & Skins Unltd., L.A., 1976-85; archaeol. cons. Archaeol. Enterprises, L.A., 1985-91; pres. The Cuban Index, San Luis Obispo, Calif., 1991—; cons. Soc. for Hispanic Hist. and Ancestral Rsch., Westminster, Calif., 1992—, Calif. Geneal. Alliance, San Francisco, 1992—. Author: Guide to Cuban Genealogical Research, 1991 (reference book series) San Francisco Passenger Departure Lists, Vols. I-IV, 1992, 93, 94; author, editor jours. Caribbean Hist. and Geneal. Jour., 1993-94. Recipient Spl. Honor award Anthropology Students Assn., 1985, Gold Poet award Internat. Poetry, 1988. Mem. Calif. Libr. Assn., Nat. Geneal. Soc., Coun. for Genealogy Columnists, Inc. (co-editor newsletter 1992—), Manchester and Lancashire Family History Soc., Cercle Genealoguique de la Brie, Mortar Bd. Honor Soc. Mem. Humanist Party. Roman Catholic. Office: The Cuban Index PO Box 15839 San Luis Obispo CA 93406-5839

CARR, ROY ARTHUR, agricultural products applied research, development & communication processing organization executive; b. Toronto, Ont., Can., Aug. 21, 1929; s. Arthur Edwin and Ruth Adelaide (Milligan) C.; m. Elizabeth Anne Gladman, Aug. 23, 1958; 1 son, Robert A. BASc in Chem. Engring. with first class honors, U. Toronto, 1952. Supr. quality control Procter and Gamble Co., 1952-55, supr. applied devel., 1955-58, quality control mgr., 1958-61, plant chem. engr., 1961-66; sect. head process engring. Anderson-Clayton Foods, Tex., 1966-68, div. head process engring., 1968-70, asst. tech. dir., 1970-71, plant mgr., 1971-72; mgr. engring. devel. Hunt-Wesson Foods, Calif., 1972-74, assoc. rsch. dir., 1974-75, dir. quality assurance, 1975-78, dir. consumer rels., 1976-78; dir. mfg. Canbra Foods, Alta., Can., 1978-80, v.p. ops., 1980-84; exec. dir. POS Pilot Plant Corp., Saskatoon, Sask., Can., 1984-85, pres., 1985—; pres. Internat. Oil Mill Supts., 1991-92; chmn. bd. dirs. AgWest Biotech., 1990-93; vice chmn. bd. dirs. Internat. Ctr. Agrl. Sci. and tech., 1991; chmn., bd. dirs. Nuvotech Ventures Internat., 1993—; bd. dirs. Canamino, Inc. Contbr. papers to profl. confs., articles to jours. Served to lt. COTC RCEME Corp, 1948-51. Mem. Am. Oil Chemists Soc. (pres. 1989-90), Can. Inst. Food Sci., Inst. Food Technologists, Canola Coun. Can. (tech. com.). Office: POS Pilot Plant Corp, 118 Veterinary Rd, Saskatoon, SK Canada S7N 2R4

CARR, RUTH MARGARET, plastic surgeon; b. Waco, Tex., July 2, 1951. MD, U. Okla., 1977. Intern U. Okla. Med. Sch., Oklahoma City, 1977-78; resident U. Okla. Health Sci. Ctr., Oklahoma City, 1978-81, UCLA, 1981-83; plastic surgeon St. John's Hosp., 1989—, Santa Monica (Calif.) Hosp., 1989—; clin. asst. prof. UCLA, 1983—. Office: 1301 20th St Ste 470 Santa Monica CA 90404-2050*

CARR, THOMAS JEFFERSON, JR., gaming executive; b. Memphis, Aug. 19, 1942; s. Thomas J. Sr. and Emily K. (Draper) C.; m. Jean N. Simpkins, May 10, 1984; children: Jeff, Tricia, Ashley. BBA, Memphis State U., 1967. C.P.A., Tenn. Asst. controller Holiday Corp., Memphis, 1965-81; v.p., controller Harrah's, Reno, 1981-85, v.p. devel., 1986, sr. v.p. devel., 1987—; mem. adv. bd. Arkwright Ins. Mem. AICPA, Tenn. C.P.A. Soc. Office: Harrahs 300 E 2nd St Reno NV 89501-1510

CARRARA, PAUL EDWARD, geologist, researcher; b. San Francisco, Sept. 16, 1947. BA in Geology, San Francisco State Coll., 1969; MSc in Quaternary Geology, U. Colo., 1972. Snow avalanche cons. Inst. Arctic and Alpine Rsch., U. Colo., Boulder, 1972-74; geologist U.S. Geol. Survey, Denver, 1974—. Contbr. articles to profl. jours. Recipient Antarctic Svc. medal NSF, 1980. Fellow Geol. Soc. Am.; mem. Am. Quaternary Assn., Colo. Sci. Soc., N.W. Sci. Assn. Office: US Geol Survey Denver Fed Ctr Mail Stop 913 Denver CO 80225

CARRELL, HEATHER DEMARIS, educational consultant; b. Bryn Mawr, Pa., Jan. 4, 1951; d. Jeptha J. and J. Demaris (Affleck) C.; m. Peter F. Brazitis, June 27, 1981; children, Evan, Victoria. BA, Oberlin Coll., 1973; MEd, U. Wash., 1976, PhD, 1982. Cert. tchr., Wash. Head tchr., trainer Exptl. Edn. Unit U. Wash., Seattle, 1976-80, tchr. trainer, 1976-80, supr. early childhood and spl. edn. tchrs. in tng., 1980, coord. classrooms behavior disorders, 1980-81, coord. interdisciplinary tng., 1979-82, asst. prin., 1981-82, cons. Transition Rsch. Problems Handicapped Youth, 1986-88; self-employed cons., 1983—; cons. North Kitsap Sch. Dist., Poulsbo, Wash., 1984; presenter edn. and spl. edn. various groups from U.S., Can., Australia, 1977-82; pres., co-founder Hansville (Wash.) Coop. Presch., 1982, 84-89; mem. diversity and multicultural advocacy team Wash. State Sch. Dirs. Assn.; rep. to U. Wash. Tchr. Profl. Edn. Adv. Bd., 1992-95; mem. WSSDA Fin. Task Force, 1994; mem. Intertribal Coun. Com. on Racism, North Kitsap, Wash., 1993-94. Author: (with others) The Experimental Education Training Program, 1977; contbr. articles to profl. publs. Commr. North Kitsap Dept. Parks and Recreation, 1983-84; dir. North Kitsap Sch. Bd., 1990—, v.p., 1992-93, pres., 1993—; trustee North Kitsap Tchr. of Yr. Found., 1989-90; bd. dirs. North Kitsap Juvenile Diversion Bd., 1987-91; co-founder, v.p. Kitsap Cmty. Found., 1993—. Bur. Edn. Handicapped fellow, 1974-75, 77-78.

CARREY, NEIL, lawyer, educator; b. Bronx, N.Y., Nov. 19, 1942; s. David L. and Betty (Kurtzburg) C.; m. Karen Krysher, Apr. 9, 1980; children: Jana, Christopher; children by previous marriage: Scott, Douglas, Dana. BS in Econs., U. Pa., 1964; JD, Stanford U., 1967. Bar: Calif. 1968. Mem. firm, v.p. corp. DeCastro, West, Chodorow & Burns, Inc., L.A., 1967—; instr. program for legal paraprofls. U. So. Calif., 1977-89; lectr. U. So. Calif. Dental Sch., 1987—. Author: Nonqualified Deffered Compensation Plans-The Wave of the Future, 1985. Officer, Vista Del Mar Child Care Center, Los Angeles, 1968-84; treas. Nat. Little League of Santa Monica, 1984-85, pres., 1985-86, coach, 1990—, coach Bobby Sox Team, Santa Monica, 1986-88, bd. dirs. 1988, umpire in chief, 1988; referee, coach Am. Soccer Youth Orgn., 1989—; curriculum com. Santa Monica-Malibu Sch. Dist., 1983-84, community health adv. com., 1988-95, chmn., 1989-95, athletic adv. com., chmn., 1993—, dist. com. for sch. based health ctr., 1991-94, gender equity com., chmn., 1992—, athletic study com., chmn., 1989-91, fin. adv. com., 1994; dir. of The Santa Monica Youth Athletic Found., 1995—; dir. The Small Bus. Coun. of Am.; pres. Gail Dorin Music Found., 1994—. Mem. U. Pa. Alumni Soc., So. Calif. (pres. 1971-79, dir. 1979-87), Alpha Kappa Psi (disting. life). Republican. Jewish. Club: Mountaingate Tennis (Los Angeles). Home: 616 23rd St Santa Monica CA 90402-3130 Office: 10960 Wilshire Blvd Fl 18 Los Angeles CA 90024-3702

CARRICA, XAVIER, health and fitness professional; b. Grants, N.Mex., Oct. 8, 1961; s. John Baptiste and Lorenza (Trujillo) C. BBA, N.Mex. State U., 1983. Aerobics instr. The Body Shop for Women, 1986; membership sales & aerobics instr. The Midlander Club, 1986; membership sales & promotion mgr. Herald Square Fitness Ctr., 1987-88; personal trainer, ptnr. C & C Fitness Cons., 1987-88; master instr. Molly Fox Studios and Instr. Trainer Ctr., 1987-88; program cons. numerous spas, 1989-91; dir. fitness & mktg. The Phoenix Spa at the Houstonian, Houston, 1989-91; Step Reebok/ high-low impact/sculpting instr. Martin Henry Fitness Studio, L.A., 1992; top personal trainer Body Sculpting, L.A., 1992—. Exec. prodr. (exercise videos) Xavier's Workout for Everyone, A Workout from the Phoenix Spa. Office: Fitsource PO Box 691856 Los Angeles CA 90069-8856

CARRICO, DONALD JEFFERSON, public transit system manager; b. Dallas, June 15, 1944; s. Ivan and Helen Mae (Jefferson) C.; m. Prudence Louise Cornish, Aug. 17, 1968; children: Bryan Jefferson, Alan Jefferson. BSBA, Ohio State U., 1967; MA in Bus. Mgmt., Cen. Mich. U., 1977. Commd. 2d lt. USAF, 1967, advanced through grades to maj., 1979; various supervisory positions USAF Air Freight Terminals, 1967-72; mgr. passenger travel and cargo br. USAF Transp. Div., Rickenbacker AFB, Ohio, 1972-74; transp. and air terminal insp. USAF Insp. Gen. Team, Hawaii, 1974-76; liaison officer US Naval Supply Ctr., Pearl Harbor, Hawaii, 1976-78; transp. staff officer USAF Hdqrs. Tactical Air Command, Langley AFB, Va., 1978-83; chief transp. USAF Transp. Div., Incirlik AB, Turkey, 1983-85, Williams AFB, Ariz., 1986-88; vehicle fleet mgr. V&B Svcs., Phoenix, 1989-91; asst. mgr. dispatch svcs. Phoenix Transit System, 1991-92, ops. mgr., 1993—. Logistics chief Gilbert Food Bank Cmty. Food Dr., Gilbert, Ariz., 1987, chmn., 1988; asst. cubmaster Pack 282 Boy Scouts Am., Gilbert, 1987; mem. Town of Gilbert Gen. Plan Rev. Task Force, 1992-93, total quality mgmt. rsch. panel Transp. Rsch. Bd., Washington, 1992—. Decorated Bronze Star. Home: 683 E Washington Ave Gilbert AZ 85234-6401

CARRICO, STEPHEN J., construction company executive; b. 1954. Grad., Ctrl. Mich. U., 1977. CPA. With Straka, Jarackas & Co., Detroit, 1977-84; various positions Hensel Phels Constrn. Co., Greeley, Colo., 1984—, now v.p. fin. Office: Hensel Phelps Construction Co 420 6th Ave Greeley CO 80631-2332*

CARRIGAN, CHARLES ROGER, geophysicist; b. Altadena, Calif., Sept. 7, 1949; s. Charles Francis and Alyce (Krosley) C.; m. Suzanne Lundin, Feb. 21, 1976; children: Alisa Lynn, Charles Jonathan. BA in Astronomy and Physics, UCLA, 1971, MS in Geophysics, 1973, PhD in Geophysics, 1977. Rsch. assoc. UCLA, 1979-80; tech. staff mem. Sandia Nat. Labs., Albuquerque, 1980-89; physicist Lawrence Livermore Nat. Lab., Livermore, Calif., 1989—. Patentee in field; contbr. articles to profl. jours. Deacon Grace Bapt. Ch., Tracy, Calif., 1993-94, chmn. bd. 1994-95. Fellow Cambridge (Eng.) U., 1977-79, NATO, 1977. Mem. Am. Geophys. Union, Sigma Xi, Sigma Pi Sigma. Office: Lawrence Livermore Nat Lab PO Box 808 Livermore CA 94551-0808

CARRIGAN, JIM RICHARD, federal judge; b. Mobridge, S.D., Aug. 24, 1929; s. Leo Michael and Mildred Ione (Jaycox) C.; m. Beverly Jean Halpin, June 2, 1956. Ph.B., J.D., U. N.D., 1953; LL.M. in Taxation, NYU, 1956; LLD (hon.), U. Colo., 1989, Suffolk U., 1991. Bar: N.D. 1953, Colo. 1956. Asst. prof. law U. Denver, 1956-59; vis. assoc. prof. NYU Law Sch., 1958, U. Wash. Law Sch., 1959-60; jud. adminstr. State of Colo., 1960-61; individual practice law Denver, 1961-62; prof. law U. Colo., 1961-67; partner firm Carrigan & Bragg (and predecessors), 1967-76; justice Colo. Supreme Ct., 1976-79; judge U.S. Dist. Ct. Colo., 1979—; mem. Colo. Bd. Bar Examiners, 1969-71; lectr. Nat Coll. State Judiciary, 1964-77; bd. dirs. Nat Bd. Trial Advocacy, 1978-91; adj. prof. law U. Colo., 1984, 1991—; chmn. bd. dirs. Nat. Inst. Trial Advocacy, 1986-88, also mem. faculty, mem. exec. bd., trustee. Editor-in-chief: N.D. Law Rev., 1952-53, Internat. Soc. Barristers Quar., 1972-79; editor: DICTA, 1957-59; contbr. articles to profl. jours. Bd. regents U. Colo., 1975-76; bd. visitors U. N.D. Coll. Law, 1983-85. Recipient Disting. Svc. award Nat. Coll. State Judiciary, 1969, Outstanding Alumnus award U. N.D., 1973, Regent Emeritus award U. Colo., 1977, B'nai Brith Civil Rights award, 1986, Thomas More Outstanding Lawyer award Cath. Lawyers Guild, 1988, Oliphant Disting. Svc. award Nat. Inst. Trial Advocacy, 1992, Disting. Svc. award Nat. Assn. Blacks in Criminal Justice (Colo. chpt.), 1992, Amiens award Assn. Trial Lawyers Am., 1994, Disting. Svc. award Colo. Bar Assn., 1994, Amicus Curiae award ATLA, 1994. Fellow Colo. Bar Found., Boulder County Bar Found.; mem. ABA (action com. on tort system improvement 1985-87, TIPS sect. long range planning com. 1986-90, coun. 1987-91, task force on initiatives and referenda 1990—, size of civil juries task force 1988-90), Am. Law Inst., Colo. Boulder Denver County Bar Assns., Cath. Lawyers Guild, Inns of Ct., Internat. Soc. Barristers, Internat. Acad. Trial Lawyers, Fed. Judges Assn. (bd. dirs. 1985-89), Am. Judicature Soc. (bd. dirs. 1985-89), Tenth Cir. Dist. Judges Assn. (sec. 1991-92, v.p. 1992-95, pres. 1994—), Order of Coif, Phi Beta Kappa. Roman Catholic. Office: US Courthouse 1929 Stout St Denver CO 80294-2900

CARRIKER, ROBERT CHARLES, history educator; b. St. Louis, Aug. 18, 1940; s. Thomas B. and Vivian Ida (Spaunhorst) C.; m. Eleanor R. Gualdoni, Aug. 24, 1963; children: Thomas A., Robert M., Andrew J. BS, St. Louis U., 1962, AM, 1963; PhD, U. Okla., 1967. Asst. prof. Gonzaga U., Spokane, Wash., 1967-71, assoc. prof., 1972-76, prof. history, 1976—. Author: Fort Supply, Indian Territory, 1970, 91, The Kalispell People, 1973, Father Peter De Smet, 1995; editor: (with Eleanor R. Carriker) Army Wife on the Frontier, 1975; book rev. editor Columbia mag., 1987—. Mem. Wash. Lewis and Clark Trail Com., 1978—; commr. Wash. Maritime Bicentennial, Olympia, 1989-92; bd. dirs. Wash. Commn. for Humanities, Seattle, 1988-94. Burlington No. Found. scholar, 1985; recipient Disting. Svc. award Lewis and Clark Trail Heritage Found., 1989. Mem. Wash. State Hist. Soc. (trustee 1981-90, v.p. 1993—), Western Hist. Assn., Phi Alpha Theta (councilor 1985-87). Roman Catholic. Office: Gonzaga U 502 E Boone Ave Spokane WA 99258-1774

CARRILLO, GILBERTO, engineer; b. San Diego, Sept. 22, 1926; s. Manuel C. and Francisca (Ruiz) C.; m. Maria de Lourdes Paez, Jan. 21, 1957; children: Gilbert A., Elizabeth, Evelyn, Fernando, Mary Lou. BS with honors, San Diego State U., 1951. Materials and process engr. Convair Div. Gen. Dynamics, San Diego, 1950-56, Douglas Aircraft Co., El Segundo, Calif., 1956-60; tech. dir. Torco Products, Inc., Mexico City, 1960-68; mgr., environ. engr. Rohr Industries, Riverside, Calif., 1969-92; founder, CEO Enviro-Safe Systems, Riverside, 1992—; gen. chmn. First Soc. Advancement Materials and Process Engring. Internat. Environ. Symposium and Tech. Conf., 1991. Contbr. articles to profl. jours.; patentee in field. Served as sgt. USAAF, 1945-46, Japan. Mem. Soc. for Advancement Materials and Process Engring. (nat. chpt.: gen. chmn., internat. symposium and tech. conf. 1988; Inland Empire chpt.: chmn. arrangements com. 1972-76, chmn. scholarships 1976-82, gen. chmn. 1982-83, Best Paper award, 1983), VFW. Republican. Roman Catholic. Home: 5535 Montero Dr Riverside CA 92509-5608

CARROLL, BONNIE, publisher, editor; b. Salt Lake City, Nov. 20, 1941. Grad. high sch., Ogden, Utah. Owner The Peer Group, San Francisco, 1976-78; pub., editor The Reel Directory, Cotati, Calif., 1978—. Pub., editor The Reel Thing newsletter, San Francisco, 1977-78. Mem. Assn. Visual Communicators (bd. dirs. 1987-90), No. Calif. Women in Film, San Francisco Film Tape Council (exec. dir. 1979-81). Office: The Reel Directory PO Box 866 Cotati CA 94931-0866

CARROLL, DAVID TODD, computer engineer; b. West Palm Beach, Fla., Apr. 8, 1959; s. David Irwin and Lois Ellen (Spriggs) C. Student, U. Houston, 1978-81. Lab. technician Inst. for Lipid Rsch., Baylor Coll. Medicine, Houston, 1978-81; software specialist Digital Equipment Corp., Colorado Springs, Colo., 1982-86, systems engr., 1986-91, systems support cons., 1991-94; systems cons. Mentel, Inc., Colorado Springs, 1994—. Mem. AAAS, Digital Equipment Corp. Users Soc. Home: 7332 Aspen Glen Ln Colorado Springs CO 80919-3024 Office: Mentec Inc 305 S Rockrimmon Blvd Colorado Springs CO 80919-2303

CARROLL, EARL HAMBLIN, federal judge; b. Tucson, Mar. 26, 1925; s. John Vernon and Ruby (Wood) C.; m. Louise Rowlands, Nov. 1, 1952; children—Katherine Carroll Pearson, Margaret Anne. BSBA, U. Ariz., 1948, LLB, 1951. Bar: Ariz., U.S. Ct. Appeals (9th and 10th cirs.), U.S. Ct. of Claims, U.S. Supreme Ct. Law clk. Ariz. Supreme Ct., Phoenix, 1951-52; assoc. Evans, Kitchel & Jenckes, Phoenix, 1952-56, ptnr., 1956-80; judge U.S. Dist. Ct. Ariz., Phoenix, 1980—; spl. counsel City of Tombstone, Ariz., 1962-65, Maricopa County, Phoenix, 1968-75, City of Tucson, 1974, City of Phoenix, 1979; designated mem. U.S. Fgn. Intelligence Surveillance Court by Chief Justice U.S. Supreme Ct., 1993—. Mem. City of Phoenix Bd. of Adjustment, 1955-58; trustee Phoenix Elem. Sch. Bd., 1961-72; mem. Gov.'s Council on Intergovtl. Relations, Phoenix, 1970-73; mem. Ariz. Bd. Regents, 1978-80. Served with USNR, 1943-46; PTO. Recipient Nat. Service awards Campfire, 1973, 75, Alumni Service award U. Ariz., 1980, Disting. Citizen award No. Ariz. U., Flagstaff, 1983, Bicentenial award Georgetown U., 1988, Disting. Citizen award U. Ariz., 1990. Fellow Am. Coll. Trial Lawyers, Am. Bar Found.; mem. ABA, Ariz. Bar Assn., U. Ariz. Law Coll. Assn. (pres. 1975), Phoenix Country Club, Sigma Chi (Significant Sig award 1991), Phi Delta Phi. Democrat. Office: US Dist Ct US Courthouse & Fed Bldg 230 N 1st Ave Ste 6000 Phoenix AZ 85025-0005

CARROLL, JEREMIAH PATRICK, II, auditor; b. Akron, Ohio, Feb. 9, 1955; s. Jeremiah Patrick and Kathleen Mary (Kilroy) C.; m. Anne Marie Mollica; children: Dawn Renee, Patricia Eileen, Bridget Kathleen, Jeremiah Joseph. BS in Acctg., U. Akron, 1979. CPA, Nev., Mont. Benefits supr. Roadway Express, Akron, Ohio, 1976-80; auditor Clark County Nev., Las Vegas, 1980-86, dir. internal audit, 1986—. Contbr. articles to profl. jours. Mem. Am. Soc. Pub. Adminstrs., Nat. Assn. Local Govt. Auditors, Nev. State Bd. Accountancy, Nev. Soc. CPAs, Nat. Assn. Local Govt. Auditors, Western Intergovtl. Audit Forum, Sons of Erin (pres. 1984-86). Republican. Roman Catholic. Home: 7185 Del Rey Ave Las Vegas NV 89117-1526 Office: Clark County Nev Internal Audit 301 Clark Ave Ste 265 Las Vegas NV 89101-6533 also: PO Box 551120 Las Vegas NV 89155-1120 also: 500 S Grand Central Pkwy Las Vegas NV 89106

CARROLL, JON, newspaper columnist. Columnist San Francisco Chronicle. Office: Chronicle Pub Co 901 Mission St San Francisco CA 94103-2905

CARROLL, PAT, actress; b. Shreveport, La., May 5, 1927; d. Maurice Clifton and Kathryn Angela (Meagher) C.; children: Sean, Kerry, Tara. Student, Immaculate Heart Coll., 1944-47, Catholic U., 1950; Litt.D. (hon.), Barry Coll., Miami, Fla., 1969. pres. Sea-Ker, Inc., Beverly Hills, Calif., 1979—; pres. CARPA Prodns., Inc., N.Y.C. Profl. debut in stock prodn. A Goose for the Gander, 1947; supper club debut at Le Ruban Bleu, N.Y.C., 1950; appeared on numerous television shows, 1950—, including: Red Buttons Show, 1951, Caesar's Hour, 1956-57 (Emmy award), Danny Thomas Show, 1961-63, Getting Together, 1971-72, Busting Loose, 1977, The Ted Knight Show, 1985, She's the Sheriff, 1987-1988; (TV movie) Second Change, 1972; Broadway debut in Catch a Star, 1955 (Tony nomination); appeared in motion picture With Six You Get Eggroll, 1968, The Brothers O'Toole, 1973; producer, actress: Gertrude Stein Gertrude Stein Gertrude Stein for colls. and univs. (Grammy award 1980, Drama Desk award, Outer Critics Circle award); Shakespeare debut as nurse in Romeo and Juliet and Falstaff in The Merry Wives of Windsor (Helen Hayes award, 1990), Shakespeare Theater at the Folger, 1986 (Helen Hayes award 1987); voice of Ursula, the Wicked Squidwitch, in The Little Mermaid, 1989; appeared in The Show-Off, 1992, Roundabout Theater Company. Pres. Center of Films for Children, 1971-73; bd. regents Immaculate Heart Coll., Hollywood, Calif., 1970. Mem. AFTRA, SAG, Actors Studio, Actors Fund (life), Actors Equity Assn., Acad. TV Arts and Scis. (trustee 1958-59), Am. Youth Hostel (life), Del. and Hudson Canal Hist. Soc., The Players, George Heller Meml. Fund. Office: care Judy Schoen and Assoc 606 N Larchmont Blvd Ste 309 Los Angeles CA 90004-1309*

CARROLL, PETE, professional football coach. Head coach N.Y. Jets, 1994-95; defensive coordinator San Francisco 49ers, 1995—. Office: San Fransisco 49ers 4949 Centennial Santa Clara CA 95054-1229

CARROLL, STEPHEN GRAHAM, university publications administrator, writer; b. St. Joseph, Mo., July 18, 1942; s. Lecil R. and Lelah M. (Ketchum) C.; m. Sharon Ann Kelly, Sept. 9, 1962; children: Stephen G., Kathryn; m. Louise Ann Purrett, Feb. 18, 1978. BJ, U. Mo., 1964; MA, Drake U., 1968; PhD, U. Colo., 1970. Asst. prof. Mo. Western State Coll., St. Joseph, 1970-74; sr. ptnr. R&D Cons., Boulder, Colo., 1974-77; corp. editor Storage Tech. Corp., Louisville, Colo., 1977-79; comms. project leader Solar Energy Rsch. Inst., Golden, Colo., 1979-81; exec. mgr. Market Media Svcs., Inc., Boulder, 1981-87; dir. engring. publs. Coll. Engring. and Applied Sci. U. Colo., Boulder, 1987-94, dir. engring. comm. Coll. Engring. and Applied Sci., 1995—; cons. CU Comms. Roundtable, Boulder, 1993—; co-instr. Sch. Journalism and Mass Comms., Boulder, 1994-95, mem. chancellor's pubs. commn., 1995. Co-author: The Rushing Tide, 1983; reviewer IEEE Transactions on Tech. Comms., 1990—; newsletter editor Boys' Club of Boulder, 1974-79. Cons. Meals on Wheels of Boulder, 1992—; bd. dirs., sec. Boulder Press Club, 1988-89. Recipient APEX Nat. awards of excellence Comms. Concepts, Inc., 1991, 92, 93, 94. Mem. Soc. for Tech. Comm. (sr. mem., Disting., Excellence and Merit awards), Am. Soc. for Engring. Edn., Coun. for Advancement and Support of Edn. (Nat. Bronze medal awards 1990, 93, Exceptional Achievement award 1992, award for Excellence 1994), IEEE Profl. Comm. Soc. Home: 3331 Sentinel Dr Boulder CO 80301-5474 Office: U Colo Coll Engring & Applied Sci Campus Box 422 Applied Sci Regents Dr and Colorado Ave Boulder CO 80309-0422

CARROLL, WALLACE B., allergist, immunologist; b. Oakland, Calif., 1946. MD, U. Autonoma de Guadalajara, Mex., 1975. Intern Valley Med. Ctr., Fresno, Calif., 1976-77, resident pediatrician, 1977-79; resident in allergy and immunology Children's Hosp., Stanford, Calif., 1979-81; now allergist and immunologist Meml. Hosp., Modesto, Calif. Office: Gould Med Group 600 Coffee Rd Modesto CA 95355*

CARROTT, JOHN ARDEN, manufacturing executive; b. Columbus, Ohio, Dec. 18, 1947; s. Donald Forwein and Marion Randall (Miller) C.; m. Nancy Elizabeth Loftus, Oct. 2, 1970 (div. Sept. 1986); children: Andrew Alan, Christopher Thomas; m. Jerri Lynn Stetler, May 22, 1987. ASEE, Capital Radio Engring. Inst., Washington, 1973; B of Tech. in Computer Tech., N.Y. Inst. Tech., Old Westbury, 1976; AS in Computer Sci., R.I. Jr. Coll., Warwick, 1981; postgrad., Kennedy-Western U. Research specialist U. R.I. Sch. Oceanography, Narragansett, 1974-78; sr. engr. Data Gen., Providence, 1978-81; pres. Sequoia Computers, Cranston, R.I., 1981-83; dir. research & devel. SCI, Inc., Huntsville, Ala., 1983-84; pres. Diversified Digital Systems, Huntsville, 1984, Universal Systems of Ala., Albertville, 1985; dir. engring. Mets, Inc., Pompano Beach, Fla., 1985-87; v.p. Fairview, Inc., Orlando, Fla., 1987; chief exec. officer Ocean Electronic Systems, Sunnyvale, Calif., 1988—; cons. John A. Carrott & Assocs., 1989—. Patentee security monitoring and tracking systems. Served with USN, 1967-73. Mem. World Trade Ctr., VFW, Smithsonian Assn. Roman Catholic.

CARROZZO, GUY A., former school principal, mayor; b. McKeesport, Pa., Mar. 25, 1932; s. Guy Sr. and Mary (Porecco) C.; m. Dolores Ann Chaverini, June 23, 1954; children: Guy Anthony, Kimberly. BA, Calif. State U., Long Beach, 1959; MA, Calif. State U., Fullerton, 1965. Teacher Westminster (Calif.) Sch. Dist., sch. principal; councilman City of Fountain Valley, Calif., 1990—, mayor pro-tem, 1994-95, mayor, 1995—, re-elected mayor, 1994—; mem. bd. dirs. Am. Cancer Soc., Fountain Valley, 1995—; alcohol and drug awareness com. mem., 1992—; past pres. Westminster Edn. Leadership Assn., 1976-77; past mem. Adv. Com. For the Disabled, 1991-92. del. Orange County League of Cities, 1995; mem. Fountain Valley Ednl. Allocation Com., 1991, 95, Inter-Jurisdicational Planning Forum, 1992, 95. 1st class airman USAF, 1951-55. Mem. AARP, Italian Catholic Fedn (past pres. 1990—), Vets. of Fgn. Wars, Knights of Columbus (dir. cmty. activities 1990—). Republican. Roman Catholic. Office: Fountain Valley City Mall 10200 Slater Ave Fountain Valley CA 92708

CARR-RUFFINO, NORMA, management educator; b. Ft. Worth, Dec. 15, 1932; d. Robert L. and Lorene D. (Dickeson) Carr; m. Randell H. Smith, July 20, 1951 (div. Jan. 1973); children: Randell H. II, Brian F., Carrie F.; m. Alfredo Ruffino, Jan. 6, 1979. BBA, Tex. Wesleyan U., 1968; M Bus. Edn., U. North Tex., 1969, PhD, 1973. V.p. Randy's, Inc., Ft. Worth, 1965-69; vocat. office edn. coord. Ft. Worth Pub. Schs., 1969-72; prof. mgmt. San Francisco State U., 1973—. Author: Writing Short Business Reports, 1980, Promotable Woman, 1982, rev. edit., 1985, 2d edit., 1993, Business Student Guide, 1987, 2d edit., 1991, Managing Cultural Differences, 1995. Referee Calif. State Bar Ct., 1985—. Named Alumna of Yr. Tex. Wesleyan U., 1988, one of Top 100 Women Alumna (100th anniversary), 1991. Mem. Acad. of Mgmt., Women's Leadership Forum of Dem. Party, World Future Soc., Internat. Assn. of Bus. and Soc., 21st Century World. Home: 1414 Alameda San Mateo CA 94402 Office: San Francisco State U Coll of Bus 1600 Holloway San Francisco CA 94132

CARRUTHERS, PETER AMBLER, physicist, educator; b. Lafayette, Ind., Oct. 7, 1935; s. Maurice Earl and Nila (Ambler) C.; m. Jean Ann Breitenbecher, Feb. 26, 1955; children: Peter, Debra, Kathryn; m. Lucy J. Marston, July 10, 1969; m. Cornelia B. Dobrovolsky, June 20, 1981; m. Lucy Marston Carruthers, Mar. 3, 1990. BS, Carnegie Inst. Tech., 1957, MS, 1957; PhD, Cornell U., 1960. Asst. prof. Cornell U., Ithaca, N.Y., 1961-63, assoc. prof., 1963-67, prof. physics, atomic and solid state physics, nuclear studies, 1967-73; leader theoretical divsn. Los Alamos (N.Mex.) Sci. Lab., 1973-80, group leader of elem. particles and field theory, 1980-85, sr. fellow, 1980-86; prof. U. Ariz., Tucson, 1986—, head dept. physics, 1986-93, dir. Ctr. for Study Complex Systems, 1987—; vis. assoc. prof. Calif. Inst. Tech., 1965, vis. prof., 1969-70, 77-78; vis. prof. U. Frankfurt, Germany, 1993-94; mem. physics adv. panel NSF, 1975-80, chmn., 1978-80; trustee Aspen Ctr. for Physics, 1976-82, chmn. exec. com., 1977-79, chmn. bd. trustees, 1979-82; mem. com. on U.S.-USSR cooperation in physics NAS, 1978-82; cons. SRI Internat., 1976-81, MacArthur Found., 1981-82, 84-88, Inst. for Def. Analysis, 1985-89; chmn. Ariz. Superconducting Super Collider Tech. Com., 1986-89. Author: (with R. Brout) Lectures on the Many-Electron Problem, 1963, Introduction to Unitary Symmetry, 1966, Spin and Isospin in Particle Physics, 1971; editor: (with D. Strottman) Hadronic Matter in Collision, 1986, Hadronic Multiparticle Dynamics, 1988, (with J. Rafelski) Hadronic Matter in Collision, 1988; editor Multiparticle Prodn. Dynamics, 1988; cons. editor Harwood Soviet Physics Series. Trustee Santa Fe Inst., 1984-86, v.p., 1985-86, mem. sci. bd. 1986-93. Recipient Merit award Carnegie-Mellon U., 1980; Alfred P. Sloan rsch. fellow, 1963-65, NSF sr. postdoctoral fellow U. Rome, 1967-68, Alexander von Humboldt sr. fellow, 1987-94. Fellow AAAS, Am. Phys. Soc. (mem. panel on pub. affairs 1984-86), Univs. Rsch. Assn. (mem. Superconducting Super Collider bd. overseers 1990-93). Home: 2220 E Camino Miraval Tucson AZ 85718-4939 Office: Univ Ariz Dept Physics Tucson AZ 85721

CARSON, EDWARD MANSFIELD, banker; b. Tucson, Nov. 6, 1929; s. Ernest Lee and Earline M. (Mansfield) C.; m. Nadine Anne Severns, Dec. 13, 1952; children: Dawn, Tod. BSBA, Ariz. State U., 1951; grad. in banking, Rutgers U., 1963. With First Interstate Bank of Ariz., Phoenix, 1951-85, exec. v.p., 1969-72, chief adminstrv. officer, 1972-75, vice chmn. bd., 1975-77, pres., chief exec. officer, 1977-85, also bd. dirs.; pres. First Interstate Bancorp, L.A., from 1985, now chmn. bd., chief exec. officer, also bd. dirs.; bd. dirs. Inspiration Resources Corp., Ramada Inns, Inc., First Interstate Bank of Oreg. Bd. fellows Am. Grad. Sch. Internat. Mgmt. Recipient Service award Ariz. State U. Alumni Assn., 1968; named to Ariz. State U. Alumni Assn. Hall of Fame, 1977. Mem. Assn. Res. City Bankers, Assn. Bank Holding Cos. (bd. dirs.). Clubs: Paradise Valley Country, Thunderbirds, Los Angeles Country, Calif.; Phoenix Country. Office: 1st Interstate Bancorp PO Box 54068 633W 5th St Los Angeles CA 90071*

CARSON, ELIZABETH LORRAINE NEAL, small business owner, civilian military employee; b. Glendale, Calif., Oct. 2, 1958; d. Harold Dean and Viola Gertrude (Neal) Donaldson; m. Robert Lawrence Chally, Aug. 7, 1981 (div. Sept. 1985); m. Richard Wayne Carson, Oct. 5, 1992. BS, Spring Arbor Coll., 1979; MS, Air Force Inst. Tech., 1988. Loan sec. Sacramento (Calif.) Savs. and Loan, 1979, acctg. clk., 1979-81; equipment specialist trainee Civil Svc. USAF, McClellan AFB, 1981-84, equipment specialist, 1984-86; logistics specialist Civil Svc. USAF, L.A. AFB, 1986-88; dep. systems program mgr. Civil Svc. USAF, Sacramento, 1988-89, chief, resource and plans, 1989-90, program mgr., 1990-93, integrated weapon system mgr., program mgmt. process action team rep., 1991-92; adj. prof. Colo. Tech. Coll., Colorado Springs, 1989-91; advisor Logistics Adv. Bd., Colorado Springs, 1988-92; integrated weapon sys. mgmt. program mgr., process action team mem. Air Force Materiel Command, 1991-93; co-owner Colors of Natura Gallery, Chapel Hills Mall, Antler's Palmer Ctr. Organist/pianist Orangevale Free Meth. Ch., 1971-76, fin. com. 1981-82, music com., 1971-76, 80-85, chmn. music com., 1984. Mem. Soc. Reliability Engrs., Soc. Logistics Engrs., Sigma Iota Epsilon. Republican. Office: Colors of Nature Gallery 1710 Briargate Blvd Ste 428 Colorado Springs CO 80920-3460 also: Colors of Nature Gallery 50 S Cascade Ave Colorado Springs CO 80903-1609

CARSON, RICHARD TAYLOR, JR., economics educator; b. Jackson, Miss., Feb. 24, 1955; s. Richard Taylor and Alice Helen (Goldthwaite) C. BA, Miss. State U., 1977; MA, George Washington, 1979, U. Calif., Berkeley, 1985; PhD, U. Calif., Berkeley, 1985. Staff mem. Resources for the Future, Washington, 1979-82; prof. U. Calif. San Diego, La Jolla, Calif., 1985—; prin. Natural Resource Damage Assessment, Inc., La Jolla, Calif., 1990—. Author: Energy Oriented Input-Output Models, 1984, Using Surveys to Value Public Goods, 1989, A Contingent Valuation Study of Lost Passive Use Values Resulting From the Exxon Valdez Oil Spill, 1992. Grantee EPA, 1988, 89, 90, Electric Power Rsch. Inst., 1988, 89, Alaska Dept. Fish and Game, 1987, Met. Water Dist., L.A., 1987, City of L.A., 1992, 93, NOAA ,1991, 92, 93, 94, 95, Calif. Dept. Game and Fish, 1992, 95. Fellow Nat. Bur. Econ. Rsch. Office: U Calif San Diego Dept Econs La Jolla CA 92093

CARSON, WALLACE PRESTON, JR., state supreme court chief justice; b. Salem, Oreg., June 10, 1934; s. Wallace Preston and Edith (Bragg) C.; m. Gloria Stolk, June 24, 1956; children: Scott, Carol, Steven (dec. 1981). BA in Politics, Stanford U., 1956; JD, Willamette U., 1962. Bar: Oreg. 1962, U.S. Dist. Ct. Oreg. 1963, U.S. Ct. Appeals (9th cir.) 1968, U.S. Supreme Ct. 1971, U.S. Ct. Mil. Appeals 1977; lic. comml. pilot FAA. Pvt. practice law Salem, Oreg., 1962-77; judge Marion County Cir. Ct., Salem, 1977-82; assoc. justice Oreg. Supreme Ct., Salem, 1982-92, state chief justice, 1992—. Mem. Oreg. Ho. of Reps., 1967-71, maj. leader, 1969-71; mem. Oreg. State Senate, 1971-77, minority floor leader, 1971-77; dir. Salem Area Community Council, 1967-70, pres., 1969-70; mem. Salem Planning Commn., 1966-72, pres., 1970-71; co-chmn. Marion County Mental Health Planning Com., 1965-69; mem. Salem Community Goals Com., 1965; Republican precinct commiteeman, 1963-66; mem. Marion County Rep. Central Exec. Com., 1963-66; com. predinct edn. Oreg. Rep. Central Com., 1965; vestryman, acolyte, Sunday Sch. tchr., youth coach St. Paul's Episcopal Ch., 1935—; task force on cts. Oreg. Council Crime and Delinquency, 1968-69; trustee Willamette U., 1970—; adv. bd. Cath. Ctr. Community Services, 1976-77; mem. comporehensive planning com. Mid-Willamette Valley Council of Govts., 1970-71; adv. com. Oreg. Coll. Edn. Tchr. Edn., 1971-75; pres. Willamette regional Oreg. Lung Assn., 1974-75, state dir., exec. com., 1975-77; pub. relations com. Williamette council Campfire Girls, 1976-77; criminal justice adv. bd. Chemeketa Community Coll., 1977-79; mem. Oreg. Mental Health Com., 1979-80; mem. subcom. Gov's Task Force Mental Health, 1980; you and govt. adv. com. Oreg. YMCA, 1981—. Served to col. USAFR, 1956-59. Recipient Salem Disting. Svc. award, 1968; recipient Good Fellow award Marion County Fire Svc., 1974, Minuteman award Oreg. N.G. Assn., 1980; fellow Eagleton Inst. Politics, Rutgers U., 1971. Mem. Marion County Bar Assn. (sec.-treas. 1965-67, dir. 1968-70), Oreg. Bar Assn., ABA, Willamette U. Coll. Law Alumni Assn. (v.p. 1968-70), Salem Art Assn., Oreg. Hist. Soc., Marion County Hist. Soc., Stanford U. Club (pres. Salem chpt. 1963-64), Delta Theta Phi. Home: 1309 Hillendale Dr SE Salem OR 97302-3347 Office: Oreg Supreme Ct Supreme Ct Bldg Salem OR 97310*

CARSTEN, ARLENE DESMET, financial executive; b. Paterson, N.J., Dec. 5, 1937; d. Albert F. and Ann (Greutert) Desmet; m. Alfred John Carsten, Feb. 11, 1956; children: Christopher Dale, Jonathan Glenn. Student Alfred U., 1955-56; Exec. dir. Inst. for Burn Medicine, San Diego, 1972-81, adv. bd. mem., 1981 92; founding trustee, bd. dirs. Nat. Burn Fedn., 1975-83; chief fin. officer A.J. Carsten Co. Inc., San Diego, 1981-91; chief fin. officer A.J. Carsten Co., Ltd., Powell River, B.C., Can., 1992—. Contbr. articles to profl. jours. Organizer, mem. numerous community groups; chmn. San Diego County Mental Health Adv. Bd., 1972-74, mem., 1971-75; chmn. community relations subcom., mem. exec. com. Emergency Med. Care Com., San Diego, Riverside and Imperial Counties, 1973-75; pub. mem. psychology exam. com. Calif. State Bd. Med. Quality Assurance, 1976-80, chmn., 1977; mem. rep. to Health Services Agy. San Diego County Govt., 1980; mem. Calif. Dem. Cen. Com., 1968-74, exec. com., 1971-72, 73-74; treas. San Diego Dem. County Cen. Com., 1972-74; chmn. edn. for legislation com. women's div. So. Calif. Dem. Com., 1972; dir. Muskie for Pres. Campaign, San Diego, 1972; organizer, dir. numerous local campaigns; councilwoman City of Del Mar, Calif., 1982-86, mayor, 1985-86; bd. dirs. Gentry-Watts Planned Indsl. Devel. Assn., 1986-90, pres., 1987-90; commencement speaker Alfred U., 1984. Recipient Key Woman award Dem. Party, 1968, 72, 1st Ann. Community award Belles for Mental Health, Mental Health Assn. San Diego, 1974, citation Alfred U. Alumni Assn., 1979. Office: RR# 2 Malaspina Rd C-13, Powell River, BC Canada V8A 4Z3

CARSTEN, GARY A., city manager; b. Greeley, Colo., Apr. 10, 1953; s. Alvin Herman and Mary Lou (Lindgren) C.; m. Roxanne Foster, Aug. 20, 1976; children: T.J., Tara Kae. BS in Fin., Colo. State U., 1976. City mgr. City of Eaton, Colo., 1976—. Scout leader Cub Scouts, Eaton, 1990-91.

Mem. Internat. City Mgrs. Assn. Home: 440 Cherry Ave Eaton CO 80615-3678 Office: 223 1st St Eaton CO 80615-3479

CARTÉ, GEORGE WAYNE, geophysicist, mayor; b. Buhl, Idaho, Sept. 8, 1940; s. Harold D. Carte and Reba E. (Lammert) Magoon; m. Katherine I. Williams, Sept. 8, 1962; children: Charles M., Theresa L., Jeannette M., Suzanne E. AAS, Columbia Basin Coll., Wash., 1962; BS in Geol. Engring., U. Idaho, 1964; postgrad. U. Hawaii, 1978-79. Hydraulic engr. U.S. Geol. Survey, Anchorage, 1964-66; seismologist AK Tsunami Warning Ctr., Palmer, Alaska, 1966—; instr. Mat-Su Community Coll., Palmer, 1971-72, 81. Mayor City of Palmer, 1981—; chmn. Palmer Planning and Zoning Commn., 1968-78; mem. Mat-Su Borough Planning Commn., 1975-78. Mem. Alaska Conf. of Mayors, 1982—, Mat-Su Borough Econ. Devel. Commn., 1989—; chmn. Palmer-Saroma Japan Sister City. Recipient cert. of achievement Anchorage Fed. Exec. Assocs., 1981, 87. Mem. Alaska Mcpl. League (bd. dirs. 1983—, chmn. bd. dirs. 1992—, pres. 1986-87, trustee joint ins. arrangement 1989—, trustee 1989—), Earthquake Engring. Rsch. Inst., Am. Geophys. Union, Tsunami Soc., Alaska Geol. Soc. Mem. Pentecostal Ch. Home: 367 N Valley Way Palmer AK 99645-6137 Office: 910 S Felton St Palmer AK 99645-6552

CARTER, DAVID MACCORMICK, management consultant; b. Oakland, Calif., Nov. 22, 1964; s. Robert Melvin and Marjorie Claire (Lee) C.; m. Vickie Williams, Feb. 9, 1991. BS in BA, U. So. Calif., 1986, MBA in Fin., 1991. Mktg. rep. L.A. Athletic Club, 1987-88, L.A. Clippers, 1988-89; sports mgmt. cons. Redondo Beach, Calif., 1989—; Author: You Can't Play the Game if You Don't Know the Rules, 1994, Keeping Score, 1995. Author: You Can't Play the Game if You Don't Know the Rules, 1994, Keeping Score, 1994. Bd. dirs. Help the Homless Help Themselves, Palos Verdes, Calif., 1992-93. Republican. Roman Catholic.

CARTER, DOROTHY LINNEA, child psychiatrist, cultural anthropologist; b. Newark, Mar. 10, 1937; d. Edward Callahan and Eva Hilda Linnea (Johnson) C.; m. John Henry Lueck, June 11, 1967 (div. 1972); 1 child, Samantha Christine Lueck Mitchell. BA, Northwestern U., 1960; MD, Temple U., 1966; MA, U. Colo., 1987. Diplomate Am. Bd. Psychiatry and Neurology. Rsch. asst. G.D. Searle and Co., Skokie, Ill., 1960, Wyeth Labs., Radnor, Pa., 1960-62; emergency rm. physician Pima County Hosp., Tucson, Ariz., 1968-70; staff psychiatrist C.F. Menninger Meml. Hosp., Topeka, 1975-77; clin. asst. prof. U. Calif. Davis, Sacramento, 1977-78; dir. adolescent svcs. Boulder (Colo.) Psychiat. Inst., 1978-86; consulting child psychiatrist Mental Health Ctr. Boulder County, 1989-92; supervision, pvt. practice Boulder, 1978—. Precinct committee person Dem. Party, Boulder County, 1992—. Home: PO Box 458 Allenspark CO 80510-0458

CARTER, EDWARD WILLIAM, retail executive; b. Cumberland, Md., June 29, 1911; s. S. and Rose P. C.; m. Christine Dailey; children: William Dailey, Ann Carter Huneke; m. Hannah Locke Caldwell, 1963. AB, UCLA, 1932; MBA cum laude, Harvard, 1937; LLD (hon.), Occidental Coll., 1962. Account mgr. Scudder, Stevens & Clark, L.A.; mdse. mgr. May Co., L.A.; chmn. emeritus bd. dirs. Carter Hawley Hale Stores, Inc., L.A.; emeritus bd. dirs. Stanford Rsch. Inst., Palo Alto, Calif., Businessmen's Coun., N.Y.C.; emeritus chmn. bd. regents U. Calif., Berkeley. Emeritus trustee Occidental Coll., Brookings Instn., Los Angeles County Mus. Art, Nat. Humanities Ctr. Com. Econ. Devel.; emeritus bd. dirs. Assocs. Harvard Grad. Bus. Sch., Santa Anita Found., L.A. Philharm Assn.; mem. vis. com. UCLA Grad. Sch. Mgmt.; mem. Woodrow Wilson Internat. Ctr. Coun., Coun. on Fgn. Rels. Mem. Bus. Coun., Harvard U. Bus. Sch. Alumni Assn. Clubs: Calif. (Los Angeles), Los Angeles Country; Pacific Union, Bohemian, Burlingame Country (San Francisco); Cypress Point (Pebble Beach). Office: Ste 320 12233 W Olympic Blvd Los Angeles CA 90064-1060

CARTER, GARY LEE, artist; b. Hutchinson, Kans., Mar. 12, 1939; s. Phillip M. and Louise E. (Sloan) C.; m. MarLys Taylor, Feb. 6, 1976; children: Jeffrey T., Suzanne. AA, Southwestern Coll., 1968; BFA with honors, Art Ctr. Coll. of Design, 1971. Staff artist Art Works Design Studio, La Jolla, Calif., 1971-72; Western artist Tucson, 1972-75; prin., owner Gary Carter Wester Art Lithography, West Yellowstone, Mont., 1975—. Featured in numerous mags. Adopted into Crow Tribe, 1991. Mem. Cowboy Artists of Am. (pres. 1986-87, Gold Medal award for Drawing 1990). LDS. Office: 12075 Marina Loop West Yellowstone MT 59758-9717

CARTER, GEORGE KENT, oil company executive; b. Toledo, Ohio, Nov. 5, 1935; s. Fred S. and Charlotte J. (Horen) C.; children from previous marriage: Caitlin, Seth; m. Kathleen Anne McKenna, July 22, 1990. AB, Stanford U., 1957, MBA, 1961. Various fin. positions Standard Oil of Calif., San Francisco, 1962-74, asst. treas., 1974, asst. comptroller, 1974-81; comptroller Chevron U.S.A., Inc., San Francisco, 1981-83, v.p. fin., 1986-89; comptroller Chevron Corp. (formerly Standard Oil of Calif.), San Francisco, 1983-86, v.p. and treas., 1989—. Mem. Stanford Bus. Sch. Assn., Stanford U. Alumni Assn., Bankers Club. Office: Chevron Corp 225 Bush St San Francisco CA 94104-4207 Office: Chevron Corp PO Box 7137 San Francisco CA 94120-7137

CARTER, HAROLD O., agricultural economics educator; b. Eaton Rapids, Mich., Dec. 13, 1932; s. Ola Gay and Lillian Darlene (Fox) C.; m. Janet M. Edger, June 21, 1952; children: Teresa, Lisa, Brian, Michael, Alison. BS, Mich. State U., 1954, MS, 1955; PhD, Iowa State U., 1958. From asst. prof. to assoc. prof. agrl. econs. U. Calif., Davis, 1958-66; prof. U. Calif., 1966—; chmn. dept. U. Calif., Davis, 1970-76, 87-89, dir. Agrl. Issues Ctr., 1985—; vis. prof. Agrl. Coll. Sweden, Uppsala, 1967, Ctr. Agrl. Econs. U. Naples, Italy, 1972, dept. agrl. econs U. Sydney, Australia, 1984; economist Giannini Found. Agrl. Econs. Fellow Am. Agrl. Econs. Assn. (Outstanding Rsch. awards 1963, 67, 71, 75, 89, Best Jour. Article award 1968), Western Agrl. Econs. Assn. (Outstanding Extension award 1975, Outstanding Rsch. award 1962, 69, 71). Republican. Home: 550 Oak Ave Woodland CA 95695-3945 Office: U Calif Dept Agrl Econs Davis CA 95616

CARTER, JACK RALPH, broadcasting administrator, television personality; b. Pueblo, Colo., Nov. 4, 1948; s. Jack R. Sr. and Billie Carter; m. Virginia Carter, May 10, 1988. BS, U. Southern Colo., 1970. Sta. mgr. KDZA TV, Pueblo, Colo., 1967-76; sales program mgr. Cetec Broadcast Group, Goleta, Calif., 1976-77; gen. mgr. Sta. KSPN-FM, Aspen, Colo., 1977; weatherman KOAA-TV, Pueblo and Colorado Springs, 1979-87; cons. KCCY-FM, Pueblo, 1980-86, v.p., gen. mgr., 1986—; host program "Matchwits" Sta. KTSC-TV, Pueblo, 1980-84, 86—; broadcasting and bus. cons. Pueblo, 1981—; instr. U. So. Colo., Pueblo, 1970-76, 77-82. Home: 2429 7th Ave Pueblo CO 81003-1726 Office: Sta KCCY-FM 106 W 24th St Pueblo CO 81003-2408

CARTER, JAMES EDWARD, judge; b. Phoenix, Apr. 9, 1935; s. Charles Albert Carter and Edna Ruth (Edwards) Woehler; m. Virginia N. Jenkins, Mar. 7, 1958; children: Tonya Elise Carter Zeien, Tiffany Jaye Carter, Heath. BS, Grand Canyon Coll., 1957; MA in Edn., Ariz. State U., 1960; JD, U. Ariz., 1964. Bar: Ariz. 1964, U.S. Dist. Ct. Ariz. 1965, U.S. Ct. Appeals (9th cir.) 1986. Tchr., coach Sunnyslope H.S., Phoenix, 1957-61; assoc. Cox and Hedberg, Phoenix, 1964-65; asst. city prosecutor City of Phoenix, 1965-72, city prosecutor, 1972-74, asst. city atty. (civil), 1974-86; assoc. DeConcini McDonald et al, Phoenix, 1986-88; ptnr. Heron Burchette et al, Phoenix, 1988-90; pvt. practice Phoenix, 1990-91; city mcpl. judge City of Phoenix, 1991—; mem. faculty for new judge orientation, 1994—; mentor New Judges Ltd. Jurisdiction, 1994—. Bd. dirs. Bapt. Hosp. and Health Sys., Phoenix, Phoenix Bapt. Hosp., 1965—; trustee Grand Canyon U., Phoenix. Mem. State Bar Ariz., Maricopy County Bar Assn. Republican. Baptist. Office: Mcpl Ct Divsn 12 400 N 7th St Phoenix AZ 85006

CARTER, JANE FOSTER, agriculture industry executive; b. Stockton, Calif., Jan. 14, 1927; d. Chester William and Bertha Emily Foster; m. Robert Buffington Carter, Feb. 25, 1952 (dec. Dec. 1994); children: Ann Claire Carter Palmer, Benjamin Foster. BA, Stanford U., 1948; MS, NYU, 1949. Pres. Colusa (Calif.) Properties, Inc., 1953—; owner Carter Land and Livestock, Colusa, 1965—; sec.-treas. Carter Farms, Inc., Colusa, 1975-94, pres., 1994—. Author: If the Walls Could Talk, Colusa's Architectural Heritage, 1988; author, editor: Colusa County Survey and Plan for the Arts, 1981, 82, 83, Implementing the Colusa County Arts Plan, 1984, 85, 86. Mem. Calif. Gov.'s Commn. on Agr., Sacramento, 1979-82, Calif. Rep. Cen. Com., 1976—; del. Rep. Nat. Conv., Kansas City, Mo., 1976, Detroit, 1980, Dallas, 1984; trustee Calif. Hist. Soc., 1979-89, regional v.p., 1984-89; mem. Calif. Reclamation Bd., 1983—, sec., 1986—; mem. Calif. Hist. Resources Comm., 1994—; Heritage Preservation Com. City of Colusa, 1976—, chmn., 1977-83, vice chmn., 1983-91; bd. dirs. Colusa Comty. Theatre Found., 1980—, English Speaking Union, San Francisco, 1992—, pres., 1993-95; bd. dirs. Leland Stanford Mansion Found., Sacramento, 1992—; trustee Calif. Preservation Found., 1989-95. Recipient award of Merit for Historic Preservation Calif. Hist. Soc., 1989, Design award Calif. Preservation Found., 1990. Mem. Sacramento River Water Contractors Assn. (sec. 1992—, exec. com. 1974—), Francisca Club, Kappa Alpha Theta. Episcopalian. Home and Office: 4746 River Rd Colusa CA 95932-4200

CARTER, JANICE JOENE, telecommunications executive; b. Portland, Oreg., Apr. 17, 1948; d. William George and Charline Betty (Gilbert) P.; m. Ronald Thomas Carter, June 13, 1968; children: Christopher Scott, Jill Suzanne. Student, U. Calif., Berkeley, 1964, U. Portland, 1966-67, U. Colo., Boulder, 1967-68; BA in Math, U. Guam, 1970. Computer programmer Ga.-Pacific Co., Portland, 1972-74; systems analyst ProData, Seattle, 1974-79; systems analyst, mgr. Pacific Northwest Bell, Seattle, 1979-80; data ctr. mgr. Austin Co., Renton, Wash., 1980-83; developer shared tenent svcs. Wright-Runstad, Seattle, 1983-84; system adminstr. Hewlett-Packard, Bellevue, Wash., 1984; telecom. dir. Nordstrom, Inc., Seattle, 1984—; mem. large customer panel AT&T, Seattle, 1987—. Ski instr. Alpental, Snoqualmie Pass, Wash., 1984-87; bd. dirs. Educationally Gifted Children, Mercer Island, Wash., 1978-80; mem. curriculum com. Mercer Island Sch. Bd., 1992—; mem. Sweet Adelines. Mem. Telecom. Assn., Internat. Comm. Assn., System 85/ETN User Group. Office: Nordstrom Inc 1904 3rd Ave Seattle WA 98101-1126

CARTER, JOY EATON, electrical engineer, consultant; b. Comanche, Tex., Feb. 8, 1923; d. Robert Lee and Carrie (Knudson) Eaton; m. Clarence J. Carter, Aug. 22, 1959; 1 child, Kathy Jean. Student, John Tarleton Agrl. Coll., 1939-40; B Music cum laude, N. Tex. State Tchrs. Coll., 1943, postgrad., 1944-45; postgrad., U. Tex., 1945; MSEE, Ohio State U., 1949, PhDEE and Radio Astronomy, 1957. Engr. aide Civil Service Wright Field, Dayton, Ohio, 1945-46; instr. math. Ohio State U., Columbus, 1946-48, asst., then assoc. Rsch. Found., 1947-49, from instr. to asst. prof. elec. engring., 1949-58; rsch. engr. N.Am. Aviation, Columbus, 1955-56; mem. tech. staff Space Tech. Labs. (later TRW Inc.), Redondo Beach, Calif., 1958-68; sect. head, staff engr. electronics rsch. labs. The Aerospace Corp., El Segundo, 1968-72, staff engr. and mgr. system and terminals, USAF Satellite Communications System Program Office, 1972-77, mgr. communications subsystem Def. Satellite Communications System III Program Office, 1978-79; cons. Mayhill, N.Mex., 1979—. Active Mayhill Vol. Fire Dept.; bd. dirs. Mayhill Cmty. Assn., 1988—, sec. bd. dirs., 1988—; co-chair music com. Mayhill Bapt. Ch., 1988—, trustee, 1989-92, 94—; bd. dirs. Otero County Farm Bur., 1987—. Named Cow Belle of Yr. Otero Cow Belles, 1988. Mem. IEEE (sr., life), Am. Astron. Soc., Am. Nat. Cattle Women (sec. otero CowBelles chpt. 1986-87, 1st v.p. 1988, historian 1989), Calif. Rare Fruit Growers, Native Plant Soc. N.Mex., Sacramento Mountains Hist. Soc. (bd. dirs. 1986—), High Country Horseman's Assn., Sigma Xi (life), Eta Kappa Nu (life), Sigma Alpha Iota (life), Alpha Chi, Kappa Delta Pi, Pi Mu Epsilon, Sigma Delta Epsilon. Home and Office: PO Box 23 Mayhill NM 88339-0023

CARTER, LARRY ALEXANDER, brokerage firm executive; b. Joplin, Mo., Nov. 9, 1940; s. Samuel E. and Laura L. (House) C.; m. Jan. 24, 1962 (div.); children: Larry Vince, Donna Diane, Mitchell Alexander. Student, Cerritos Coll., Long Beach State Coll., UCLA, Calif. Orange Coast Coll. Police officer South Gate (Calif.) Police Dept., 1963-65; narcotics expert Long Beach (Calif.) Police Dept., 1965-75; pvt. practice constrn., 1975-76; v.p., office mgr. Diversified Securities, Inc., El Toro, Calif., 1976-89; v.p. Diversified Securities, Inc., Crestline, 1989—; speaker in field. Recipient Calif. Commn. on Police Officer Standards and Tng. Advanced cert., 1974; named DSI Top Ten Mem., 1977—. Mem. Saddleback C. of C., Lake Arrowhead C. of C., Crestline C. of C., Narcotics Officers Assn., Crest Forest Community Assn. (dir.), Rotary. Republican. Baptist. Address: PO Box 3271 Crestline CA 92325-3271 Office: 396 Hartman Cir # A Cedarpines Park CA 92322

CARTER, LAURA LEE, academic librarian, psychologist; b. Iowa City, Apr. 9, 1955; d. Jack L. and Martha Ann (Shelton) C. BA in East Asia Studies magna cum laude, U. Colo., 1977; M of Librarianship, U. Washington, 1979; grad. FALCON program, Cornell U., 1983; tng. in Chinese lang., Stanford Ctr., Taipei, Taiwan, 1983-84; MA in Third World History, U. Colo., 1988; MA in Transpersonal Counseling Psychol., Naropa Inst., Boulder, Colo., 1995. Internat. documents libr., asst. libr. Documents Divsn. Marriott Libr., U. Utah, Salt Lake City, 1979-82; original cataloger, instr. original cataloging dept. Norlin Libr., U. Colo., Boulder, 1986-89; internat. documents libr., asst. prof. Govt. Publs. Libr., U. Colo., Boulder, 1989-94; part-time instr. Chinese and Japanese history dept history U. No. Colo., Greeley, 1987; invited participant/libr. cons. collection devel. tour S.E. Asia, China and Japan, 1982; judge Most Notable Documents sect. Libr. Jour., 1994; mem. exec. bd. tech. svcs. and automation divsn. Colo. Libr. Assn., 1989-90; co-chair state plan for documents com. Utah Libr. Assn., 1981-82; mem. del. Commn. European Communities Workshop for Depository Librs., Washington, 1990; organizer programs and confs.; lectr. and presenter in field. Contbr. book revs. to profl. publs., articles to periodicals. Participant Boulder County Big Sisters Program, 1992; book evaluator Boulder Pub. Libr. Co-recipient READEX/GODORT/ALA Catherine Reynolds award, 1991, Univ. Colo. Program grant, 1990-91; Japan Found. Libr. Support grantee U. Utah, 1980-81; Nat. Resource fellow for Chinese lang. study Cornell U., 1982-83; tuition scholar Inter-Univ. Program for Advanced Chinese Lang. Studies, 1983-84. Mem. ALA (coord. internat. documents task force 1992-93, program chmn. internat. documents task force 1991 ann. conf., conf. leader 1989, 90, 91, 92, 93), Colo. Libr. Assn. (chair cataloging sect. tech. svcs. and automation divsn. 1989-90). Home: 1180 Edinboro Dr Boulder CO 80303-6430

CARTER, MELVIN WHITSETT (MEL CARTER), artist, educator; b. Ill., Nov. 19, 1941; s. Mallory and Claudia (Whitsett) C. BFA, U. Ill., 1963; MFA, U. Gunajuato, Mex., 1968. Tchr. art Denver Pub. Schs., 1963-68; instr. Fine Arts Community Coll., Denver, 1968-71; coord. Fine Arts Community Auraria, Denver, 1971-89; artist, instr. Art Students League Denver, 1987—; guest prof. art Western N.Mex. U., summer 1994; artist cons., bd. dirs. Cherry Creek Arts Festival, Denver, 1991-92. Numerous one-man shows and group exhbns., 1964-90, including residence U.S. amb. to Austria, Vienna; illustrator: Occupational Communications, 1969; artist (withothers) Figure Drawing Workshop, 1985; featured artist New Choices mag., 1995. Commr. art Mayors Commr. Art, Culture, Film, 1992; artist advisor, bd. dirs. Cherry Creek Arts Festival, Denver, 1991. Sgt. USAF, 1959-61. Named Prof. Art, Colo. Community Colls. Abroad, Rome, Paris, London, 1970, Outstanding Educator Am., Bd. Dirs., Washington, 1974, State of Colo., 1987; recipient medal Excellence in Higher Edn., U. Tex., Austin, 1989; Fulbright scholar USIA, Netherland Am. Agy., 1987. Home: 1330 Gilpin St Denver CO 80218-2511 Office: Art Students League Denver 200 Grant St Denver CO 80203-4020

CARTER, MICHAEL RAY, freelance artist, singer, composer; b. L.A., Dec. 2, 1953; s. Richard Eugene and Sarah Ann (Carter) C.; m. Janet Lynette Siefman, Sept. 15, 1978 (div. Apr. 1987). Student, Cypress (Calif.) Coll., 1976-77. Ind. collector, appraiser memorabilia and Am. oak antiques San Diego, 1965—, freelance artist,, 1976—; pres., founder M.R. Carter's Am. Character Co., San Diego, 1988—; co-chair programming and mktg. New Year's Live '91, Sea World, San Diego, 1990. Author poetry; songwriter, storyteller. Charter, founding mem. Gene Autry Western Heritage Mus., L.A., 1988; mem. Buffalo Bill Hist. Ctr., Cody, Wyo.; asst. nat. foreman Buck Jones Western Corral 1, Lompoc, Calif., 1989-90. Recipient 2d place award Ft. Verde Days Assn., Inc., 1985, art placement award Roy Rogers-Dale Evans Mus., 1986, 94, best of show award UNISYS Corp., 1987, 90. Mem. Western Music Assn. (founding, voting mem. 1988), N.Am. Hunting Club (life, charter, founding), State of Liberty-Ellis Island Found. (charter). Internat. Platform Assn., Am. Lyceum Assn. Republican. Office: PO Box 27464 San Diego CA 92198-1464

CARTER, MICHELLE ADAIR, editor; b. El Paso, Tex., Dec. 2, 1944; d. Theodore Edwin and Dorothy (Terwilliger) Grimm; m. Laurence Roy Carter, Jan. 28, 1967; children: Robyn Adair, David Brian. BJ, U. Mo., 1966. Copy editor Kansas City (Mo.) Star, 1966-67; reporter San Mateo (Calif.) Times, 1967-82, news editor, 1982-88, mng. editor, 1988—. Co-author: Children of Chernobyl: Raising Hope From The Ashes, 1993. Bd. dirs. San Mateo County Gen. Hosp. Found., 1990—, bd. exec., 1991—; founder Children of Chernobyl Project, Belmont, Calif., 1990—. Recipient numerous writing awards AP, UPI, San Francisco Bar Assn., Calif. Tchrs. Assn. Mem. Am. Soc. Newspaper Editors, Nat. Fedn. Press. Women, Soc. Profl. Journalists, Peninsula Press Club. Mem. United Ch. Christ. Office: San Mateo Times PO Box 5400 San Mateo CA 94402-0400

CARTER, MILDRED BROWN, executive assistant; b. Leo, S.C., Feb. 22, 1927; d. Eddie Washington and Hester Lessie Lee (Poston) Brown; m. Richard Bert Carter, Sept. 6, 1952; children: Paul, Mark, Janis, David. Student Pace Seminar, 1977, Dale Carnegie, 1977, Am. Mgmt. Assn., 1977. Various secretarial positions, FBI, Washington, 1943-48, adminstrv. asst., 1948-51; adminstrv. asst., office asso. dir., 1952; with Bellevue (Wash.) Sch. Dist., 1965-75; sec., registrar Hyak Jr. High Sch., 1971-75; asst. to exec. v.p. Bonneville Internat. Corp., Salt Lake City, 1975-83, exec. asst. to pres., 1983-92. Mem. PTA Bd., Yakima, Wash., 1963; treas. PTA, Bellevue, 1973. Recipient Hon. Paul Harris Fellow award Rotary Internat., 1985, Martha Washington medal SAR, 1993. Mem. Soc. Former FBI Women, Beta Sigma Phi. Mormon. Clubs: Women's Century. Lodge: Soroptimists. Home: 2180 Elaine Dr Bountiful UT 84010-3120

CARTER, NANCY CAROL, legal educator, law librarian; b. Tacoma, Wash., Nov. 12, 1942; d. Walter Martin and Lois (Wilson) Schwebel. BS, Tex. A&I, 1963, MS, 1967; MLS, U. Okla., 1965, JD, 1975. Asst. acquisitions libr. U. Okla., Norman, 1967-71; law libr. dir., prof. law Golden Gate U., San Francisco, 1975-86; legal rsch. ctr. dir., prof. law U. San Diego, 1987—. Mem. Am. Assn. Law Librs., Okla. State Bar Assn. Office: U San Diego Legal Rsch Ctr 5998 Alcala Park San Diego CA 92110-2429

CARTER, PETER LENN, electrical engineer; b. Albany, Calif., Sept. 28, 1938; s. Lennard James and Emogene (West) C.; m. Barbara Randolph, Apr. 1959 (div. June 1969); children: Kimberly, Kiersten, Katherine, James. AA, Contra Costa (Calif.) Coll., 1961; BS, U. Calif., Berkeley, 1963. Registered profl. engr., Calif. Engring. positions Bechtel Corp., San Francisco, 1966-73; project engr. Bechtel Corp., Beruit, Lebanon, 1973-75; chief engr. Bechtel Corp., San Francisco, 1975-79; owner Pacific Bldg., Oakland, Calif., 1979—; real estate developer and investor, Calif., 1979—. Lt., Alameda County (Calif.) Underwater Rescue Unit, 1963-70. Mem. IEEE, NSPE, Calif. Soc. Profl. Engrs., Augustan Soc. (bd. dirs.), Def. Orientation Conf. Assn., Soc. Mayflower Decendants, Pilgrim Soc., Order of Wash., Shriners, Magna Charta Barons (Somerset chpt.), Commonwealth Club, Tahoe Yacht Club.

CARTER, RICHARD BERT, retired church official, retired government official; b. Spokane, Wash., Dec. 2, 1916; s. Richard B. and Lula Selena (Jones) C.; BA in Polit. Sci., Wash. State U., 1939; postgrad. Georgetown U. Law Sch., 1941, Brown U., 1944, Brigham Young U. Extension, 1975-76; m. Mildred Brown, Sept. 6, 1952; children: Paul, Mark, Janis, David. Advt. credit mgr. Elec. Products Consol., Omaha, 1939-40; pub. affairs ofcl., investigator FBI, Washington, 1940-41, Huntington, W.Va., 1941, Houston, 1942, Boston, 1943, S. Am., 1943, Providence, 1944-45, N.Y.C., 1945, Salt Lake City, 1945, P.R., 1946-48, Phoenix, 1948-50, Washington, 1950-51, Cleve., 1952-55, Seattle, 1955-75, ret., 1975; assoc. dir. stake and mission pub. affairs dept. Ch. Hdqrs., Ch. of Jesus Christ of Latter-day Saints, Salt Lake City, 1975-77. Dist. chmn. Chief Seattle coun. Boy Scouts Am., 1967-68, coun. v.p., 1971-72, coun. commr., 1973-74, nat. coun. rep., 1962-64, 72-74, area II, Eagle Scout Assn., 1984—. Mem. Freedoms Found. Valley Forge, Utah chpt., 1988—; bd. dirs. Salvation Army, 1963, United Way, 1962-63, mem. allocations com., 1962, 1987-88, JayCees, Omaha, Neb., 1939-40. Served to 1st lt., Intelligence Corps, U.S. Army, 1954. Recipient Silver Beaver award Boy Scouts Am., 1964, Vigil Honor, 1971; named Nat. Media Man-of-Month Morality in Media, Inc., N.Y.C., 1976. Mem. Profl. Photographers Am., Internat. Assn. Bus. Communicators, Am. Security Council (nat. adv. bd.), Internat. Platform Assn., Sons Utah Pioneers (pres. 1982, Disting. Svc. award 1985), SAR (pres. Salt Lake City chpt. 1987-88, Law Enforcement Commendation medal 1987, Meritorious Svc. medal 1989, Pres.-Gen.'s Program Excellence award, Oliver R. Smith medal 1990, Grahame T. Smallwood award 1990, Liberty medal 1991, Patriot medal 1992), Utah State Soc. (pres. 1989-90), Amicus Club of Deseret Found., chmn. membership com. 1988—, Gold Caduceus award, 1993), World Sr. Games (adv. com, 1987—), William Carter Family Orgn. (nat. pres.), Nat. Assn. Chiefs of Police (Am. Police Hall of Fame, John Edgar Hoover Distin. Pub. Svc. medal 1991, Nat. Patriotism medal 1993), Scabbard and Blade, Crimson Circle, Am. Media Network (nat. adv. bd.), Assn. Former Intelligence Officers, Soc. Profl. Journalists, Alpha Phi Omega, Pi Sigma Alpha, Phi Delta Theta. Mem. LDS Ch. (coord. pub. communications council Seattle area 1973-75, br. pres. 1944-45, seventies quorum pres. 1952, dist. pres. 1954-55, high priest 1958—, stake pres. counselor 1959-64, stake Sunday Sch. pres. 1980-81, temple staff 1987—). Clubs: Bonneville Knife and Fork (bd. dirs. 1982-85), Rotary (dir., editor The Rotary Bee, 1982-83, Paul Harris fellow 1982, Richard L. Evans fellow 1987, Best Club History in Utah award 1988, Best Dist. Newsletter award 1983, Rotarian of Month 1988). Author: The Sunbeam Years-An Autobiography, 1986; assoc. editor FBI Investigator, 1965-75; contbg. author, editor: Biographies of Sons of Utah Pioneers, 1982; contbr. articles to mags. Home: 2180 Elaine Dr Bountiful UT 84010-3120

CARTER, ROBERT SPENCER, private investor; b. Oakmont, Pa., Aug. 18, 1915; s. Robert Spencer and Adele Rebecca (Crowell) C.; m. Cynthia Root, Dec. 31, 1937; children—Lief Hastings, Delight Carter Willing. B.A., Harvard U., 1937. Underwriter, Atlantic Mutual Ins. Co., N.Y.C., 1939-51; marine mgr. Gen. Ins. Co. of Am., Seattle, 1951-59; pvt. investor, Medina, Wash., 1959—. Author: Sail Far Away, 1978. Contbr. articles to profl. jours. Trustee, Archaeol. Inst. Am. Boston, 1980-87. Clubs: Cruising of Am., Seattle Yacht, Corinthian, Explorers.

CARTER, ROBERTA ECCLESTON, therapist, counselor; b. Pitts.; d. Robert E. and Emily B. (Bucar) Carter; divorced; children: David Michael Kiewlich, Daniel Michael Kiewlich. Student Edinboro State U., 1962-63; BS, California State U. of Pa., 1966; MEd, U. Pitts., 1969; MA, Rosebridge Grad. Sch., Walnut Creek, Calif., 1987. Tchr., Bethel Park Sch. Dist., Pa., 1966-69; writer, media asst. Field Ednl. Pub., San Francisco, 1969-70; educator, counselor, specialist Alameda Unified Sch. Dist., Calif., 1970—; master trainer Calif. State Dept. Edn., Sacramento, 1984—; personal growth cons., Alameda, 1983—. Author: People, Places and Products, 1970, Teaching/Learning Units, 1969; co-author: Teacher's Manual Let's Read, 1968. Mem. AAUW, NEA, Calif. Fedn. Bus. and Profl. Women (legis. chair Alameda br. 1984-85, membership chair 1985), Calif. Edn. Assn., Alameda Edn. Assn., Charter Planetary Soc., Oakland Mus., Exploratorium, Big Bros. of East Bay, Alameda C. of C. (svc. award 1985). Avocations: aerobics, gardening, travel. Home: 1516 Eastshore Dr Alameda CA 94501-3118

CARTER, STEVEN RAY, computer programmer, analyst; b. Provo, Utah, Aug. 2, 1954; s. Ray L. and Marjorie Louise C.; m. Pamela Jean Beard, Dec. 17, 1977; children: Tanylle Marie, Phillip Ray, Heidi, Timothy Steven, April Lynn, Daniel. BS, Brigham Young U., Provo, Utah, 1979. Programmer analyst DHI Computing Svc., Provo, Utah, 1977-82, sr. programmer anslyst, 1982-87, v.p., 1987-92, sr. v.p., 1992—; computer sci. adv. bd. Utah Valley State Coll., Orem, Utah, 1988-94. Zone Commr., 1993—, scoutmaster 1987-93, Boy Scouts, American Fork, Utah. Republican. Mem. LDS Ch. Office: DHI Computing Svc 1525 W 820 N Provo UT 84601

CARTER, WILLIAM GEORGE, III, army officer; b. Buffalo, June 18, 1944; s. William George Jr. and Elaine Ruth (Weber) C.; m. Linda Fay Yener, Oct. 2, 1965; children: Kris Ann, William George. BS, U. Tampa, 1972; MA, U. Shippensberg, 1982; MPE, U. Pitts., 1984. Commd. 2d. lt. U.S. Army, 1965, advanced through grades to maj. gen., 1992; various command and staff positions, 1964-77; exec. officer 3d Brigade, 1st Armored

Div., Bamberg, Fed. Republic Germany, 1977-79; comdr. 1st Bn., 52d Inf., Bamberg, 1979-81, G3 1st Armored Div., VII U.S. Corps, Ansbach, Fed. Republic Germany, 1981-83; chief Plans and Integration Office, Hdqrs. U.S. Army, Washington, 1983-86; comdr. 1st Brigade, 4th Inf. Div., Ft. Carson, Colo., 1986-88; exec. asst. Office Chief of Staff Army, Washington, 1988-89; asst. div. comdr. 1st Inf. Div., Ft. Riley, Kans., 1989-91; comdr. Nat. Tng. Ctr., Ft. Irwin, Calif., 1991-93, 1st Armored Divsn., 1993-95. Decorated Legion of Merit with six oak leaf clusters, Bronze Star with V device and two oak leaf clusters, Purple Heart with oak leaf cluster. Mem. Soc. of the Big Red One, Alpha Chi. *

CARTERETTE, EDWARD CALVIN HAYES, psychologist; b. Mt. Tabor, N.C., July 10, 1921; s. John Calvin and Alma Olivia (Fowler) C.; m. Patricia Spidel Blum, Jan. 18, 1955 (dec. Jan. 1977); 1 son, Christopher Edward; m. Noël McSherry, Sept. 27, 1980. Diploma, U.S. Army Command and Gen. Staff Coll., 1943; A.B., U. Chgo., 1949; A.B. cum laude, Harvard U., 1952; M.A., Ind. U., 1954, Ph.D. (NSF predoctoral fellow), 1956. Served as enlisted man U.S. Army, 1937-42; commd. 2d lt., 1942, advanced through grades to lt. col., 1946; served in Hawaii, 1937-41; dep. dir. personnel Hampton Roads Port of Embarcation, Newport News, Va., 1942-45; adj. gen. 32d Inf. Div., Philippines and, Japan, 1945-46; ret., 1946; mem. research staff acoustics lab. M.I.T., 1952; instr. UCLA, 1956-58, asst. prof. psychology, 1958-63, asso. prof., 1963-68, prof., 1968—, adj. prof. ethnomusicology and systemic musicology, 1988—; vis. assoc. prof. U. Calif., Berkeley, 1966; NSF postdoctoral fellow in physics Royal Inst. Tech., Stockholm and Cambridge (Eng.) U., 1960-61; NSF sr. postdoctoral fellow Inst. Math. Studies in Social Scis., Stanford U., 1965-66; cons. neuropsychology VA Wadsworth Hosp. Center, 1978—; chmn. selection com. Woodrow Wilson Nat. Fellowship Found., 1963-72, chmn., 1966-72; mem. editorial com. U. Calif. Press, 1970-77, co-chmn., 1973-77, mem. bd. control, 1973-77; Disting. visitor Am. Psychol. Assn., 1979—, disting. lectr. 1982—; bd. dirs. Packard Humanities Inst., 1987—; rsch. prof. psychology U. Va., Charlottesville, 1991—, adj. prof., Coll. of William and Mary, Williamsburg, Va., 1991—. Author: Brain Function: Speech, Language and Communication, 1966, (with Margaret Hubbard Jones) Informal Speech, 1974; editor: (with M.P. Friedman) Handbook of Perception, 11 vols., 1973-78, Academic Press Series in Cognition and Perception, 1973, Handbook of Perception and Cognition, 17 vols., 1994—; assoc. editor: Perception and Psychophysics, 1972—, Music Perception, 1981—; exec. adv. bd.: Dictionary of Biology, 1987—, Dictionary of Science and Technology, 1989—. Co-pres. 1st Internat. Conf. on Music Perception and Cognition, 1989. Fellow Acoustical Soc. Am., AAAS (electorate nominating com. 1981-84, chmn. 1984), Am. Psychol. Assn., Am. Psychol. Soc., Soc. Exptl. Psychologists (sec.-treas., mem. exec. com. 1982-87, co-chmn. 1977); mem. Psychonomic Soc., Soc. Music Perception and Cognition (v.p. 1990-91, bd. dirs. 1991—), Soc. Math. Psychology, Sigma Xi (sec. UCLA chpt. 1983-86, pres. 1988-89), Harvard Radcliffe Club of Soc. Calif. (bd. dirs. 1982-85, v.p. 1985-87, 91—, pres. 1987-89), Harvard Club of Va. (v.p. 1991-95). Home: 456 Greencraig Rd Los Angeles CA 90049 Office: U Calif Dept Psychology Los Angeles CA 90024

CARTER-GOLDSTON, CATHERINE ANGOTTI, principal; b. Grove City, Pa., Nov. 21, 1943; d. Thomas Gratian and Helena Viola (Tonti) Angotti; m. Robert Leroy Carter Jr., Dec. 15, 1967 (div. May 1977); m. Richard Neil Goldston Sr., Apr. 4, 1982; children: Patricia Ann Carter-Griggs, Richard N. Goldston Jr., Shell Lyn Goldston. BS, Edinboro State Coll., 1966; MEd, U. Fla., 1969; EdD, U. So. Calif., 1982. Cert. tchr., sch. adminstr., Calif. Tchr. Clay County Bd. Pub. Instrn., Green Cove Springs, Fla., 1966-69, U.S. Dept. Def. Dependent Schs., Fed. Republic Germany, 1969-75; sch. prin. Dept. Def. Dependent Schs., Fed. Republic Germany, 1975-77, Rowland Unified Sch. Dist., Rowland Heights, Calif., 1977—; assoc. prof. Whittier (Calif.) Coll., 1983—; ednl. cons. Carter & Assocs., L.A., 1988—; mem. adv. bd. Whittier Coll., 1985—. Mem. L.A. County Park Planning Commn., Hacienda Heights, Calif., 1985-86; bd. dirs. CWPHA # 2, Hacienda Heights, 1979-82. Named Woman of Achievement, YWCA, 1987. Mem. ARA (treas. 1979-80), ACSA, Rotary (treas. 1990-92, pres. 1993-94). Home: 1743 Orchard Hill Ln Hacienda Hgts CA 91745-3844 Office: Hollingworth Sch 3003 E Hollingworth St West Covina CA 91792-3229

CARTIER, CAROL JEAN MCMASTER, social worker; b. Spokane, Wash., Sept. 11, 1954; d. Gilbert Clayton and Thelma L. (Wentworth) McMaster; m. Robert Alan Cartier, Sept. 20, 1986. AA, Green River Community Coll., Auburn, Wash., 1976; BSW, Ea. Wash. U., 1981, MSW, 1983. Cert. social worker, Wash. Counselor Family Counseling Svcs., Spokane, 1983-84; med. social worker Harbors Home Health and Hospice, Hoquiam, Wash., 1984—; case mgr. AIDS prevention program and maternity support svc. Grays Harbor County Health Dept., Aberdeen, 1989—; social worker III Wash. State Dept. Health Svc., Aberdeen, 1989-90; cons. Grays Harbor County Health Dept., 1989-90. Vol. sta. supr. Sr. Companion Program, Aberdeen, 1986—, mem. adv. bd., 1985-92; facilitator People Living with AIDS Support Group, Aberdeen, 1989-94. Fellow Ea. Wash. U. Alumni Assn.; mem. NASW, Ocean Shores C. of C., Ocean Shores Community Club. Home: PO Box 1352 Ocean Shores WA 98569-1352 Office: Grays Harbor County Health Dept 2109 Sumner Ave Aberdeen WA 98520-3600

CARTWRIGHT, MARY LOU, laboratory scientist; b. Payette, Idaho, Apr. 5, 1923; d. Ray J. and Nellie Mae (Sherer) Decker; B.S., U. Houston, 1958; M.A., Central Mich. U., 1976; m. Chadwick Louis Cartwright, Sept. 13, 1947. Med. technologist Methodist Hosp., Houston, 1957-59, VA Hosp., Livermore, Calif., 1960-67, Kaiser Permanente Med. Center, Hayward, Calif., 1967-71, United Med. Lab., San Mateo, Calif., 1972-73; sr. med. technologist Oakland (Calif.) Hosp., 1974-86; cons. med. lab. tech. Oakland Public Schs. Chmn., Congressional Dist. 11 steering com. Common Cause, 1974-77; consumer mem. Alameda County (Calif.) Health Systems Agy., 1977-78. Served with USNR, 1945-53. Mem. Calif. Soc. Med. Tech., Calif. Assn. Med. Lab. Tech. (Technologist of Yr. award 1968, 78, Pres.'s award 1977, Service award chpt. 1978, 79), Am. Soc. Med. Tech. (by-laws chmn. 1981-83), Disabled Am. Veterans (adjutant treas. of chpt. 122, 1993-95), Am. Bus. Women's Assn., Nat. Assn. Female Execs. Democrat. Home and Office: 350 Bennett St Apt 9 Grass Valley CA 95945-6870

CARUSO, MARK JOHN, lawyer; b. L.A., Apr. 27, 1957; s. John Mondella and Joyce Dorothy (Baldi) C.; m. Judy F. Velarde, Aug. 15, 1987. BA, Pepperdine U., 1979, JD, 1982. Bar: Calif. 1982, U.S. Dist. Ct. (cen. dist.) Calif. 1982, U.S. Ct. Appeals (9th cir.) 1983, N.Mex. 1987, U.S. Dist. Ct. N.Mex. 1987, U.S. Ct. Appeals (10th cir.) 1987. Pvt. practice, Burbank, Calif., 1982—, Albuquerque, 1987—; mem. House labor com., House consumer and pub. affairs com., workers compensation oversight interim com., ct., correction and justice interim com.; state rep. N.M. House of Reps., 1990-94. Col., aide-de-camp to gov. State of N.Mex., 1987; chmn. N.Mex. Mcpl. Boundary Commn., 1988—; del. Rep. Nat. Conv., 1988, 92; mem. jud. com. house labor com., workers compensation oversight com. N.Mex. Ho. of Reps., 1990, 92, 93, 94. Recipient platinum award N.Mex. Free Enterprise Adv., 1986. Mem. Albuquerque Hispano C. of C., Greater Albuquerque C. of C. Office: 4302 Carlisle Blvd NE Albuquerque NM 87107-4811

CARVER, DARREL R., computer engineer; b. Caldwell, Idaho, Dec. 3, 1959; s. William Hoyt and Mary Francis (Mayhew) C. Student, Wash. State U., 1979-82. Libr. tech. Wash. State U., Pullman, 1979-83; sr. sys. programmer Commtek Pub., Boise, Idaho, 1985-88; sr. sys. analyst Computer Scis., Piscataway, N.J., 1988-89; tech. prodn. mgr. Commtek Pub., Vienna, Va., 1989-90; computer tech. III HFS, Inc., Vienna, 1990-92; computer engr. Bull WW Info. Sys., Phoenix, 1992—. Co-author: Palouse Bibliography, 1982. Mem. IEEE, AAAS, Assn. Computing Machinery, Planetary Soc. Office: Bull WW Info Systems 13430 N Black Canyon Hwy Phoenix AZ 85029-1310

CARVER, DOROTHY LEE ESKEW (MRS. JOHN JAMES CARVER), retired educator; b. Brady, Tex., July 10, 1926; d. Clyde Albert and A. Maurine (Meadows) Eskew; student So. Ore. Coll., 1942-43, Coll. Eastern Utah, 1965-67; B.A., U. Utah, 1968; M.A., Cal. State Coll. at Hayward, 1970; postgrad. Mills Coll., 1971; m. John James Carver, Feb. 26, 1944; children—John James, Sheila Carver Bentley, Chuck, David. Instr., Rutherford Bus. Coll., Dallas, 1944-45; sec. Adolph Coors Co., Golden, Colo., 1945-47; instr. English, Coll. Eastern Utah, Price, 1968-69; instr. speech Modesto (Calif.) Jr. Coll., 1970-71; instr. personal devel. men and women Heald Bus. Colls., Oakland, Calif., 1972-74, dean curricula, Walnut Creek, Calif., 1974-86; instr. Diablo Valley Coll., Pleasant Hill, Calif., 1986-87, Contra Costa Christian High Sch.; ret., 1992; communications cons. Oakland Army Base, Crocker Bank, U.S. Steel, I. Magnin, Artec Internat.; presenter in field. Author: Developing Listening Skills. Mem. Gov.'s. Conf. on Higher Edn. in Utah, 1968; mem. finance com. Coll. Eastern Utah, 1967-69; active various community drives. Judge election Republican party, 1960, 64. Bd. dirs. Opportunity Center, Symphony of the Mountain. Mem. AAUW, Bus. and Profl. Womens Club, Nat. Assn. Deans and Women Adminstrs., Delta Kappa Gamma. Episcopalian (supt. Sunday Sch. 1967-69). Clubs: Soroptimist Internat. (pres. Walnut Creek 1979-80 sec., founder region 1978-80); Order Eastern Star. Home: 20 Coronado Ct Walnut Creek CA 94596-5801

CARVER, FRANK GOULD, theology educator; b. Crookston, Nebr., May 27, 1928; s. Frank Alonzo and Greeta G. (Gould) C.; m. Betty Joan Ireland, Mar. 31, 1949; children: Mark Erwin, Carol Denise. BA, Taylor U., 1950; BD, Nazarene Theol. Sem., 1954; MTh, Princeton Theol. Sem., 1958; PhD, New Coll., U. Edinburgh, Scotland, 1964. Pastor Ch. of Nazarene, Kimball, Nebr., 1954-56, Edison, N.J., 1956-58, Edinburgh, Scotland, 1959; from asst. to full prof. Pasadena/Point Loma (Calif.) Nazarene Coll., 1961—, chmn. dept. philosophy and religion, 1967-82, 1991—, dir. grad. programs in religion, 1981—, dir. summer ministries, faculty officer, 1986-89; Mem. numerous coms. including curricular exceptions, academic policy, coun. on ednl. policy and program, graduate studies, profl. devel., rank and tenure and many others Point Loma Nazarene Coll., San Diego, Calif.; guest prof. Olivet Nazarene Coll., fall 1972, Nazarene Theol. Sem., 1976, 79, 81, 85, Nazarene Theol. Coll., S. Africa, 1979, Inst. Biblico Nazareno Ensenada, Mex., 1987; mem. Ch. Growth Symposium, 1978-79; mem. curriculum com. Enduring Word Series, 1976-80; many lecturing positions. Author: Peter the Rock Man, 1973, Matthew Part One: To Be a Disciple, 1984, Matthew Part Two: Come...and Learn From Me, 1986, The Cross and the Spirit: Peter and the Way of the Holy, 1987; editor: Thank God and Take Courage, 1992; contbr. articles to profl. jours. and chpts. to books. Tchr. adult Sunday Sch. Pasadena First Ch. Nazarene, San Diego First Ch. Nazarene, 1961-89. Mem. Inst. Biblical Rsch. (West Coast chmn. 2 terms, nat. exec. com. 2 terms), Soc. Biblical Lit., Wesleyan Theol. Soc. (1st v.p. 1985-86, pres. 1986-87), Evangel. Theol. Soc. Home: 403795 Porte De Palmas San Diego CA 92122 Office: Point Loma Nazarene Coll 3900 Lomaland Dr San Diego CA 92106-2810

CARVER, JOHN GUILL, physicist; b. Mt. Juliet, Tenn., Feb. 10, 1924; s. Henry Gilliam and Inez (Cook) C.; m. Elva Emily Kattelman, Apr. 21, 1956; children: John Jr., Linda Lee, Karen Emily, Susan Aline. BS in Physics, Ga. Inst. Tech., 1950; MS, Yale U., 1951, PhD, 1955. Registered profl. elec. engr., Ohio, registered profl. nuclear engr., Calif. Field svc. engr. Philco Corp., Phila., 1946-48; nuclear engr. dept. atomic power equipment Gen. Electric, Cin., 1955-60; nuclear engr., mgr. irradiations physics Gen. Electric, San Jose, Calif., 1960-67; mgr. advanced rsch. Rockwell Internat., Downey, Calif., 1967-72; supr. electro-optics Rockwell Internat., Seal Beach, Calif., 1972-78; prin. engr. Rockwell Internat., Downey, 1978-84; prin. cons. Rockwell Internat., Seal Beach, 1984-89; cons. in electro-optical physics Karsulin Enterprises, Orange, Calif., 1989—. Contbr. articles to profl. jours. Elder Forest Dale Ch. of Christ, Cin., 1957-60, Valley Ch. of Christ, Livermore, Calif., 1964-67, East Anaheim (Calif.) Christian Ch., 1969—. 1st lt. USAAF, 1943-46. Rockefeller Found. fellow, 1955-56. Fellow AAAS, AIAA (assoc.); mem. Am. Phys. Soc., Soc. Photo-Optical Instrumentation Engrs., N.Y. Acad. Scis., Am. Nuclear Soc. Office: Karsulin Enterprises PO Box 3774 Orange CA 92665-0774

CARVER, JUANITA ASH, plastic company executive; b. Indpls., Apr. 8, 1929; d. Willard H. and Golda M. Ashe; children: Daniel Charles, Robin Lewis, Scott Alan. Cons. MOBIUS, 1983—; pres. Carver Corp., Phoenix, 1977—. Bd. dirs. Scottsdale Meml. Hosp. Aux., 1964-65, now assoc. Republican. Methodist. Patentee latch hook rug yarner, Pressure Lift. Home: 9866 Reagan Rd Apt 126 San Diego CA 92126-3143

CARVER, LOYCE CLEO, clergyman; b. Decaturville, Tenn., Dec. 13, 1918; s. Oscar Price and Mae Joanne (Chumney) C.; m. Mary Rebecca Frymire, Dec. 14, 1940; children—Judith Ann Carver Tyson, Linda Carver Sheals, Rebecca Carver Bishop. Ordained to ministry Apostolic Faith, 1947; real estate appraiser, dep. county tax assessor Klamath County, Oreg., 1943-44; bookkeeper Pacific Fruit Co., Los Angeles, Klamath Falls, Oreg., 1945-47; pastor Apostolic Faith Ch., Dallas, Oreg., 1948-49, San Francisco, 1949-52, Los Angeles, 1952-56, Medford, Oreg., 1956-65; chmn. bd. dirs. Apostolic Faith, Portland, Oreg., 1965-93; chmn. bd. dirs. World-Wide Movement, 1965-93, trustee, 1959—, pres., 1993. Served with USNR, 1944. Home: 5411 SE Duke St Portland OR 97206-6841 Office: 6615 SE 52nd Ave Portland OR 97206-7660

CASABURI, RICHARD, respiratory and critical care physician; b. Queens, N.Y., Apr. 28, 1947; m. Mary Jane Molitor, July 3, 1976; children: James, Anne. BSEE, Rensselaer Poly. Inst., 1968, M of Engring. in Biomed. Engring., 1969, PhD in Biomed. Engring., 1971; MD, U. Miami, 1980. Bd. cert. in internal medicine and pulmonary medicine. Rsch. asst. dept. surgery Albany (N.Y.) Med. Coll., 1968-69, rsch. asst. dept. physiology, 1969-71; rsch. assoc. dept. biomed. engring. U. So. Calif., L.A., 1971-73, postdoctoral fellow in biomed. engring., 1971-73; rsch. assoc. divsn. respiratory physiology and medicine Harbor-UCLA Med. Ctr., Torrance, Calif., 1973-74, asst. prof. medicine divsn. respiratory physiology and medicine, 1974-78, 84-88, intern, 1980-81, resident in internal medicine, 1981-83, pulmonary fellow divsn. respiratory and critical care physiology and medicine, 1983-84, dir. clin. respiratory physiology lab., 1986—, assoc. prof. medicine divsn. of respiratory and critical care physiology and medicine, 1988-94, prof. medicine, 1994—, assoc. chief divsn. of respiratory and critical care physiology and medicine, 1989—; lectr. in field. Mem. editl. rev. bd. Jour. Cardiopulmonary Rehab., 1992—; mem. editl. bd. Jour. Applied Physiology, 1993—; contbr. articles to profl. jours. Pres. Pulmonary Edn. and Rsch. Found., 1993—; mem. cardiopulmonary coun. Am. Heart Assn. Tng. fellow Am. Lung Assn., 1983-85, Trudeau scholar, 1985-88; investigator Am. Lung Assn. Calif., 1991-93. Fellow Am. Coll. Chest Physicians; mem. Am. Physiol. Soc., Am. Thoracic Soc. (respiratory and structure function assembly program com., chmn. long-range planning com. and nominating com. 1992—, co-chmn. combined Am. Thoracic Soc./Calif. Thoracic Soc. blood gas proficiency testing program 1989-94, mem. com. on proficiency stds. for clin. pulmonary function labs.), Calif. Thoracic Soc. (blood gas proficiency testing program 1987—, treas. 1994-95, sec. 1995—), Sigma Xi, Tau Beta Pi, Eta Kappa Nu. Office: Harbor-UCLA Med Ctr Divsn Resp & Crit Care PO Box 2910 Torrance CA 90509-2910

CASADY, TIMOTHY PHILIP, medical-surgical nurse; b. Hollywood, Calif., Aug. 1, 1947; s. Philip Miller Casady and Peggy (Payne) Breuning; m. Karen Bram, Mar. 19, 1989; children: Philip, Emma Rose. BS, MIT, 1969; AA in Nursing with honors, Santa Monica (Calif.) Coll., 1991. Cert. phacoemulsification technician. Orderly St. John's Hosp., Santa Monica, 1970-74, cystoscopy tech., phaco-emulsification tech., 1974-91; oper. rm. orthopedic nurse St. John's Hosp., Santa Monica, 1991—, 1991-93; ambulatory surgery nurse Northridge Hosp. Med. Ctr., 1993—. Counselor Diabetes Youth Found. Camp, 1982-85. Leonard J. Marmor scholar Santa Monica Coll., 1989. Home: 14251 Chandler Blvd Sherman Oaks CA 91401-5713

CASALS, ROSEMARY, professional tennis player; b. San Francisco, Sept. 16, 1948. Profl. tennis player, 1968—; nat. championships and major tournaments include U.S. Open singles (finalist), 1970, 71, U.S. Open doubles, 1967, 71, 74, 82, U.S. Open mixed doubles, 1975, Wimbledon doubles, 1967, 68, 70, 71, 73; nat. championships and major tournaments include Wimbledon mixed doubles, 1971, 73, finalist with Dick Stockton, 1976; finalist with Dick Stockton Italian doubles, 1967, 70; finalist with Dick Stockton Family Circle Cup (winner), 1973, Wightman Cup, 1967, 76-81; Wightman Cup Bridgeston doubles championships (finalist), 1975, Spalding mixed doubles, 1976, 77, U.S. Tennis Assn. Atlanta doubles, 1976, Fedn. Cup, 1967, 76-81; winner 1st Virginia Slims tournament, 1970; 3d place Virginia Slims Championships, 1976, 4th place, 1977, 78; winner Murjani-WTA championship, 1980; Fla. Fed. Open doubles, 1980; pres. sports promotion co. Sportswoman, Inc., Sausalito, Calif., 1981—; Mem. Los Angeles Strings team, World Team Tennis, 1975-77. Virginia Slims Event tennis winner, 1986, doubles winner (with Martina Navratilova), 1988, 89. Mem. Women's Internat. Tennis Assn. (bd. dirs.). Office: Sportswoman Inc PO Box 537 Sausalito CA 94966-0537

CASANO, SALVATORE FRANK, physician; b. Chgo., Aug. 16, 1948; s. Salvatore and Rose Mary Casano; m. Freda Lois, Aug. 19, 1978; children: Ashley Rae, Sebastian Ross. BS in Biology, John Carroll U.; MD, Automous U., Guadalajara, Mex., 1975. Diplomate in gen. surgery and surg. critical care Am. Bd. Surgery. Intern Maricopa County Med. Ctr., Phoenix, 1977, resident in gen. surgery, 1978-82; pvt. practice in gen. surgery Phoenix, 1982—; trauma surgeon St. Joseph's Hosp., Phoenix, 1985—, Good Samaritan Hosp., Phoenix, 1989—. Fellow ACS, Southwestern Surg. Congress; mem. Phoenix Surg. Soc. (pres. 1993-94), Maricopa County Med. Soc., Ariz. Med. Assn. Democrat. Roman Catholic. Home: 600 W Berridge Ln Phoenix AZ 85013 Office: 333 E Virginia Ave Ste 201 Phoenix AZ 85004-1210

CASAZZA, RALPH ANTHONY, architect; b. Reno, May 12, 1926; s. Anthony T. and Rena Katherine (Lagomarsino) C.; m. Eileen Kathryn Cole, Feb. 4, 1954; children: Thomas, Richard, Kathryn, Marianne, Susan, Elizabeth. Student, U. Nev., Calif. State U., San Francisco. Pvt. practice architecture Reno, 1948-49; ptnr. Lockard & Casazza, Reno, 1949-72; pres. Casazza, Peetz & Assocs., Reno, 1972—; owner, v.p., mgr. Tore & Casa, Ltd., Reno, 1963-86; pres. Triangle Devel. Co., Reno, 1982-86. Mem. Boosters Club U. Nev., 1984—, U. Nev. Found., 1984—, Econ. Devel. Authority Western Nev., 1984—; del. to Rep. Nat. Conv., San Francisco, 1956; Nev. state chmn. Young Reps., 1956-58. Mem. AIA (legis. com. 1986), Nev. Inst. Architects (pres.1960-62, pres. N. Nev. chpt. 1956-58, Bradley B. Kidder award 1965), Associated Gen. Contractors, Inter Council Shopping Ctrs. (state dir. 1972-74, legis. dir. 1986—), Western Indsl. Nev. Roman Catholic. Club: Prospectors (Reno). Lodges: KC (dep. grand knight 1965-67), Italian Benevolent Soc. (v.p. 1962-65). Home: 2395 Crescent Cir Reno NV 89509-3512 Office: Casazza Peetz & Hancock Architects 1745 S Wells Ave Reno NV 89502-3306

CASE, CHARLES CALVIN, anthropology educator; b. Tulare, Calif., Oct. 20, 1922; s. Charles Calvin and Evelyn K. (Sells) C.; m. Ramona Davis (div. 1972); children: Lisa, Cosette. BA, UCLA, 1947; MA, U. So. Calif., 1961; PhD, U. Oreg., 1968. Prof. anthropology No. Ariz. U., 1963—, U.S. Internat., Calif., 1970—. Author: Culture: The Human Plan, 1977, The Yankee Generations, 1982. With USAF, 1942-43. Fellow Am. Anthropol. Assn., Current Anthropology; mem. Am. Inst. Archeology, Etruscan Soc. Home: D-10 7858 Cowles Mountain Ct San Diego CA 92119-2543

CASE, DANIEL HIBBARD, III, investment banker; b. Honolulu, July 27, 1957; s. Daniel Hibbard and Carol Mary (Holmes) C.; m. Stacey Black; children: Alexander, Winston. BA in Econ. and Pub. Policy, Princeton U., 1979; postgrad., U. Oxford (Eng.), 1979-81. Cert. series 7 and 24 NASD. Legis. aide govt. affairs com. U.S. Senate, Washington, 1977; rsch./corp. fin. asst. Hambrecht & Quist, San Francisco, 1979, assoc. corp. fin., 1981-83, prin. corp. fin., 1983-84, gen. ptnr. venture capital, 1984-86, co-head mergers and acquisitions, 1986-87, mng. dir., head investment banking, 1987-89, exec. v.p., head investment banking, 1989-92, pres., CEO, 1992—, also bd. dirs.; mng. ptnr., founder Hambrecht & Quist Guaranty Fin., San Francisco, 1984—. Co-author: Start-Up Companies, 1985. Rhodes scholar Rhodes Com., U. Oxford, 1979-81. Mem. Commonwealth Club. Office: Hambrecht & Quist 1 Bush St San Francisco CA 94104-4425

CASE, DAVID LEON, lawyer; b. Lansing, Mich., Sept. 22, 1948; s. Harlow Hoyt and Barbara Jean (Denman) C.; m. Cynthia Lou Rhinehart, Jan. 28, 1968; children: Beau, Ryan, Kimberly, Darren, Stephanie. BS with distinction, Ariz. State U., 1970, JD cum laude, 1973. Bar: Calif. 1973, U.S. Dist. Ct. (cen. dist.) Calif. 1973, U.S. Tax Ct. 1974, Ariz. 1976. Assoc. Willis, Butler & Scheifly, Los Angeles, 1973-75; from assoc. to mem. Ryley, Carlock & Applewhite, Phoenix, 1975—. Fellow Ariz. Bar Found.; mem. ABA (tax sect., corp. sect., probate and trust sect.), Ariz. Bar Assn., Ctrl. Ariz. Estate Planning Coun. (bd. dirs., pres. 1988-89), Beta Gamma Sigma. Republican. Presbyterian. Office: Ryley Carlock & Applewhite 101 N 1st Ave Ste 2700 Phoenix AZ 85003-1911

CASE, JAMES BOYCE, physical scientist; b. Lincoln, Ill., Oct. 26, 1928; s. Richard Warren and Blanch Irene (Boyce) C.; m. Clare Karlin Criger, Sept. 20, 1958 (dec. Mar. 1983); 1 child, James Christian. Student, Oreg. State Coll., 1946-47; BS, Stanford U., 1950; MS, Ohio State U., 1957, PhD, 1959. Cartographer Inter-Am. Geodetic Survey, Costa Rica, Brazil, 1950-55; photogrammetrist Broadview Rsch. Corp., Washington, 1960-61; prin. scientist Autometric Corp., Alexandria, Va., 1961-71; physical scientist Def. Mapping Agy., Washington, 1971-89; editor in chief Am. Soc. for Photogrammetry and Remote Sensing, Bethesda, Md., 1975—. Co-author (books) Manual of Photogrammetry, 1966, Manual of Photogrammetry, 1980, Handbuch der Vermessunskunde, 1972. Chair Iron County Dem. Com., Cedar City, Utah, 1991—. Am. Geographical Soc. rsch. fellow, 1957-58; NSF rsch. grantee, 1959. Fellow The Royal Geographical Soc.; mem. AAAS, AARP (pres. Cedar City chpt. 1992-93), Kiwanis (div. lt. gov. 1994-95), The Photogrammetric Soc. (hon.); mem. emeritus The Soc. of the Sigma Xi, Am. Soc. for Photogrammetry and Remote Sensing. (hon.). Home: PO Box 1669 Cedar City UT 84721-1669

CASE, LEE OWEN, JR., retired academic administrator; b. Ann Arbor, Mich., Nov. 5, 1925; s. Lee Owen and Ava (Comin) C.; m. Dolores Anne DeLoof, July 1950 (div. Feb. 1958); children: Lee Douglas, John Bradford; m. Maria Theresia Breninger, Feb. 27, 1960; 1 adopted dau., Ingrid Case Dunlap. AB, U. Mich., 1949. Editor Washtenaw Post-Trib, Ann Arbor, 1949; dir. pub. rels. Edison Inst., Dearborn, Mich., 1951-54; field rep. Kersting, Brown, N.Y.C., 1954-58; campaign dir. Cumerford Corp., Kansas City, Mo., 1958-59; v.p. devel., pub. rels. U. Santa Clara, 1959-69; v.p. planning, devel., Occidental Coll., L.A., 1969-90, ret., 1990; interim v.p. Inst. Advance Calif. State U., L.A., 1994.Mem. Sr. Cons. Network. Chmn. Santa Clara City Proposition A, 1966; mem. Santa Clara County Planning Com. on Taxation and Legis., Santa Clara, 1968. Served to 1st lt. USAAF, 1943-46. Mem. Am. Coll. Pub. Relations Assn. (bd. dirs. 1968-74), Council for Advancement and Support Edn. (founding bd. dirs. 1974-75), 1st Tribute for Distinction in Advancement, Dist. VII, 1985), Santa Clara C. of C. (pres. 1967), Santa Clara County C. of C. (founding bd. dirs. 1968), Aviation Pioneers Assn. Republican. Lodge: Rotary. Home and Office: 2633 Risa Dr Glendale CA 91208-2355

CASE, PATRICIA SULLIVAN, mental health counselor, educator; b. Ft. Worth, Aug. 1, 1946; d. Elmer Dudley Sullivan and Minnie Jo Crittenden Bennett; m. John Philip Case, July 5, 1985. AA, Scottsdale (Ariz.) C.C., 1978; BS, Ariz. State U., 1980, M of Counseling, 1984; PhD, Walden U., Mpls., 1993. Diplomate Nat. Bd. Cert. Counselors; cert. counselor, Ariz.; cert. cmty. coll. counselor. Counselor in pvt. practice Scottsdale, 1984-88; adj. faculty Maricopa C.C.s, Phoenix, 1984-90; area ctrl. cons. Rio Salado C.C., Phoenix, 1987-89, adminstr. asst., 1989-90, faculty, counselor, dept. chair., 1990—; treas. Ariz. Behavioral Health Credentialing Task Force, 1987-89, chair, 1989-91. Mem. ACA, Ariz. Counselors (pres. Ctrl. chpt. 1986-87, govt. liaison 1987-88, pres.-elect 1989), Outstanding Contbn. to Counseling Profession award 1987), Ariz. Mental Health Counselors Assn. (treas. 1985-86), Rio Salado C.C. Faculty Assn. (pres. 1994—). Office: Rio Salado CC 640 N 1st Ave Phoenix AZ 85003-1515

CASE, ROCKY CECIEL, finance company executive; b. Worland, Wyo., Aug. 12, 1949; s. Leslie Charles and Helen Jewel (Williams) C.; m. Judy Ann Agee, Aug. 25, 1971; children: Tiffany Jo Mossey, Eric William Case, Rocky Shane. AA, Laramie County C.C., Cheyenne, Wyo., 1986. CFP, Wyo. Plant mgr. Cheyenne Cable TV, 1969-84; v.p. Wyo. Deferred Compensation, Inc., Cheyenne, 1985—; chmn. publicity com. U.S.S. Cheyenne. Author numerous poems and short stories. Mem. Nat. Assn. Life Underwriters, Cheyenne C. of C. (chmn. publicity com. 1994), Rotary (chmn. youth exch. 1992-95, bd. dirs. 1995—). Home: 1201 W 8th Ave Cheyenne WY 82001

CASERIO, MARJORIE CONSTANCE, academic administrator; b. London, Feb. 26, 1929; came to U.S., 1953; d. Herbert C. and Doris May (House) Beckett; m. Frederick F. Jr. Caserio, Mar. 9, 1957; children: Brian, Alan. BSc in Chemistry, U. London, 1950; MA in Organic Chemistry, Bryn Mawr Coll., 1951, PhD in Organic Chemistry, 1956. Rsch. chemist Fulmer Rsch. Inst., Buckinghamsnire, Eng., 1952-53; post-doctoral fellow Calif. Inst. Tech., Pasadena, 1956-59, sr. rsch. fellow, 1959-65; from. asst. prof. to prof. chemistry U. Calif., Irvine, 1965-90, chair dept. chemistry, 1987-90; vice-chancellor academic affairs U. Calif., San Diego, 1990—. Contbr. articles to profl. jours. Recipient Cert. of Achievement, Leadership of Women Orange County, 1983; Sir John Dill scholar, 1950; Fulbright travel award, 1950; Guggenheim fellow, 1975-76. Fellow AAAS; mem. Am. Chem. Soc. (Garvan medal 1975) Grad. Women in Sci. (hon.), Sigma Xi. Office: U Calif San Diego Acad Affairs 0001 La Jolla CA 92093

CASEY, BARBARA A. PEREA, state representative, educator; b. Las Vegas, N.Mex., Dec. 21, 1951; d. Joe D. and Julia A. (Armijo) Perea; m. Frank J. Casey, Aug. 5, 1978. BA, N.Mex. U., 1972; MA, Highland U., Las Vegas, N.Mex., 1973. Instr. N.Mex. Highlands U., Las Vegas, 1972-74; tchr. Roswell Ind. Schs., Roswell, N.Mex., 1974—; mem. N.Mex. Ho. of Reps., 1984—; instr. N.Mex. Mil. Inst., Roswell, 1977-82, Roswell Police Acad., 1984. Mem. NEA (Adv. of of Yr.), AAUW, Am. Bus. Women's Assn., N.Mex. Endowment for Humanities. Democrat. Roman Catholic. Home: 1214 E 1st St Roswell NM 88201-7960

CASEY, DANIEL E., psychiatrist, educator; b. West Springfield, Mass., Jan. 24, 1947; s. Arthur and Gloria Casey; m. Lenka Casey. BA in Psychology, U. Va., 1969, MD, 1972. Resident in psychiatry U. Oreg., Portland, 1973-74, Brown U., Providence, 1974-76; affiliate sci. Oreg. Regional Primate Rsch. Ctr., Portland, 1980—; staff psychiatrist VA. Med. Ctr., Portland, 1980—, chief psychiatry rsch., psychopharmacology, 1980—; prof. psychiatry Oreg. Health Scis. U., Portland, 1985—, prof. neurology, 1992—; pres., bd. dirs. Danicas Found., Portland. Author books; Contbr. over 150 articles to profl. jours. Office: VA Med Ctr Psychiatry Svc 3710 SW Us Veterans Hospital Rd Portland OR 97201-2964

CASEY, JOSEPH T., corporate executive; b. 1931; married. B.S., Fordham U. With Arrow Surgical Supply Co., 1947-51, Am. Lumberman's Mutual Casualty Co. of Ill., 1951-52, Thoroughbred Racing Protective Bur. Inc., 1952-55; mgr. audits Touche, Ross, Bailey & Smart, 1955-63; controller Litton Industries Inc., Beverly Hills, Calif., 1963-67, v.p. fin., 1967-69, sr. v.p. fin., 1969-76, exec. v.p. fin., 1976-91, CFO, 1991-94, chmn. exec. com., 1994—, also bd. dirs.; vice chmn. and CFO Western Atlas, Inc., Beverly Hills, Calif., 1994—; bd. dirs., chmn. exec. com. Litton Industries, Inc. Office: Western Atlas Inc 360 N Crescent Dr Beverly Hills CA 90210-4802

CASEY, PATRICK ANTHONY, lawyer; b. Santa Fe, Apr. 20, 1944; s. Ivanhoe and Eutimia (Casados) C.; m. Gail Marie Johns, Aug. 1, 1970; children: Christopher Gaelen, Matthew Colin. BA, N.Mex. State U., 1970; JD, U. Ariz., 1973. Bar: N.Mex. 1973, U.S. Dist. Ct. N.Mex. 1973, Ariz. 1973, U.S. Ct. Appeals (10th cir.) 1979, U.S. Supreme Ct. 1980. Assoc. firm Bachicha & Corlett, Santa Fe, 1973-75; assoc. firm Bachicha & Casey, Santa Fe, 1975-77; pvt. practice law, Santa Fe, 1977—. Bd. dirs. Santa Fe Sch. Arts and Crafts, 1974, Santa Fe Animal Shelter, 1975-81, Cath. Charities of Santa Fe, 1979-82, Old Santa Fe Assn., 1979-88; bd. dirs. United Way, 1986-89, N.Mex. State U. Found., 1985-93. With USN, 1961-65; Vietnam. Mem. Assn. Trial Lawyers Am. (state del. 1988-89, bd. govs. 1990-91, 93-95), ABA, Western Trial Lawyers Assn. (bd. dirs. 1988-91, parlimentarian 1990-91, gov. 1987-90, treas. 1991—, sec. 1991-92, pres. elect 1995—), N.Mex. Trial Lawyers Assn. (dir. 1977-79, 85—, treas. 1979-83, pres. 1983-84), Bar Assn. 1st Jud. Dist. (pres. 1980), Am. Legion, VFW, Vietnam Vets. of Am., Elks. Office: 1421 Luisa St Ste Q Santa Fe NM 87505-4073

CASH, DEANNA GAIL, nursing educator; b. Coatesville, Pa., Nov. 28, 1940. Diploma, Jackson Meml. Hosp., 1961; BS, Fla. State U., 1964; MN, UCLA, 1968; EdD, Nova U., Ft. Lauderdale, Fla., 1983. Staff and relief charge nurse Naples (Fla.) Community Hosp., 1961-62; staff nurse Glendale (Calif.) Community Hosp., 1964-65; instr. Knapp Coll. Nursing, Santa Barbara, Calif., 1965-66; staff nurse, team leader Kaiser Found. Hosp., Bellflower, Calif., 1968-69; prof. nursing El Camino Coll., Torrance, Calif., 1969—; coord., instr. Internat. RN Rev. course, L.A., 1974-76; mentor statewide nursing program, Long Beach, Calif., 1981-88; clin. performance in nursing exam. evaluator Western Performance Assessment Ctr., Long Beach, 1981—. Mem. ANA.

CASH, R. D., natural gas and oil executive; b. Shamrock, Tex., 1942. BSIE, Tex. Tech U., 1966. With Amoco Prodn. Co., 1966-76; v.p. Mountain Fuel Supply Co. subs. Questar Corp., 1976-79, pres., CEO, 1980-84, now also chmn. bd.; pres. Wexpro Co., 1979-80; pres., CEO Questar Corp., 1984—, also chmn. bd., 1985—. Office: Questar Pipeline Co 79 S State St Salt Lake City UT 84111-1517*

CASH, R(OY) DON, gas and petroleum company executive; b. Shamrock, Tex., June 27, 1942; s. Bill R. and Billie Mae (Lisle) C.; m. Sondra Kay Burleson, Feb. 20, 1966; 1 child, Clay Collin. BSIndslE, Tex. Tech U., 1966. Former engr. Amoco Prodn. Co.; v.p. Mountain Fuel Supply, Salt Lake City, 1976-79; pres. Wexpro Co., Salt Lake City, 1979-80; pres., chief exec. officer Mountain Fuel Supply Co., Salt Lake City, 1980-84; pres., chief exec. officer Questar Corp., Salt Lake City, 1984-85, pres., chmn., chief exec. officer, 1985—, also bd. dirs.; bd. dirs. Zions Bancorp., Zions First Nat. Bank, FuelMaker Corp., 1989-91; trustee Inst. Gas Technology, Chgo., 1986—; chmn. 1993-94. Trustee Holy Cross Hosp., 1987-90; bd. dirs. Utah Symphony Orch., Salt Lake City, 1983-86, 93—; Gas Rsch. Inst., 1991-93. Mem. Soc. Petroleum Engrs., Rocky Mountain Oil and Gas Assn. (bd. dirs., pres. 1982-84), Utah Mfrs. Assn. (bd. dirs. 1983-89, chmn. 1986), PAcific Coast Gas Assn. (bd. dirs. 1981-85, 87—, chmn. 1993-94), Am. Gas Assn. (bd. dirs. 1989—), Am. Petroleum Inst. (bd. dirs. 1986-91), Nat. Petroleum Coun., Ind. Petroleum Assn. of Am., Salt Lake Area C. of C. (bd. dirs. 1981-84, 89-92, chmn. 1991-92), Alta Club, Ft. Douglas Country Club. Office: Questar Corp 180 1st Ave Salt Lake City UT 84103-2301

CASH, WILLIAM, correspondent, columnist; b. London, Sept. 1, 1966; s. William Nigel Paul and Bridget Mary (Lee) C. MA, Cambridge (England) U., 1989. West Coast corr. The Times of London, 1990-93; Am. corr. Daily Mail, 1993-94; Hollywood corr. Daily Telegraph, L.A., 1994—; columnist Daily Express, 1991, Harpers & Queen Mag., 1992—. Author: Memoirs of a Hollywood Correspondent, 1993; journalist The Spectator, The New Republic. Home: 7357 Woodrow Wilson Dr Los Angeles CA 90046-1320

CASHATT, CHARLES ALVIN, retired hydro-electric power generation company executive; b. Jamestown, N.C., Nov. 14, 1929; s. Charles Austin and Ethel Buren (Brady) C.; m. Wilma Jean O'Hagan, July 10, 1954; children: Jerry Dale, Nancy Jean. Grad. high sch., Jamestown. Bldg. contractor, Jamestown, 1949-50; 1954-58; powerhouse foreman Tri-Dam Project, Strawberry, Calif., 1958-66; power project mgr. Merced Irrigation Dist., Calif., 1966-92; ret. 1992; mem. U.S. com. large dams, 1988-92. Contbr. articles to ASCE pub. and books. Pres. Merced County Credit Union, 1981-82. Served with USAF, 1950-54. Mem. Am. Legion. Republican. Lodge: Elks, Odd Fellows.

CASHMAN, MICHAEL RICHARD, small business owner; b. Owatonna, Minn., Sept. 26, 1926; s. Michael Richard and Mary (Quinn) C.; m. Antje Katrin Paulus, Jan. 22, 1972 (div. 1983); children: Janice Katrin, Joshua Paulus, Nina Carolin. BS, U.S. Mcht. Marine Acad., 1947; BA, U. Minn., 1951; MBA, Harvard U., 1953. Regional mgr. Air Products & Chems., Inc., Allentown, Pa., 1959-64; then pres. so. div. Air Products & Chems., Inc., Washington, 1964-68; mng. dir. Air Products & Chems., Inc Europe, Brussels, 1968-72; internat. v.p. Airco Indsl. Gasses, Brussels, 1972-79; pres. Continental Elevator Co., Denver, 1979-81; assoc. Moore & Co., Denver, 1981-84; prin. Cashman & Co., Denver, 1984—. Committeeman Denver Rep. Com., 1986—, congl. candidate, 1988; chmn. "Two Forks or Dust" Ad Hoc Citizens Com.. Lt. (j.g.) USN, 1953-55. Mem. Bldg. Owners and Mgrs. Assn., Colo. Harvard Bus. Sch. Club, Am. Rights Union, Royal Golf de Belgique, Belgian Shooting Club, Rotary, Soc. St. George, Phi Beta Kappa. Home: 2512 S University Blvd Apt 802 Denver CO 80210-6152

CASILLAS, MARK, lawyer; b. Santa Monica, Calif., July 8, 1953; s. Rudolph and Elvia C.; m. Natalia Settembrini, June 2, 1984. BA in History, Loyola U., L.A., 1976; JD, Harvard U., 1979. Bar: N.Y. 1982, Calif. 1983. Clk. to chief judge U.S. Ct. Appeals (10th cir.), Santa Fe, 1979-80; assoc. Breed, Abbott & Morgan, N.Y.C., 1980-82; counsel Bank of Am. Nat. Trust and Savs. Assn., San Francisco, 1982-84; assoc. Lillick & Charles, San Francisco, 1984-87, ptnr., 1988-95; ptnr. Russin & Vecchi, San Francisco, 1995—; counsel Internat. Bankers Assn. in Calif., L.A., 1984-89, 94—. Co-author: California Limited Liability Company: Forms and Practice Manual, 1994; mng. editor Harvard Civil Rights-Civil Liberties Law Rev., 1978-79. Mem. ABA (apptd. mem. airfin. subcom. 1991—), N.Y. Bar Assn., Calif. Bar Assn. (vice-chmn. fin. instn. com. 1987-88), Internat. Bar Assn., The Japan Soc., Bankers Club.

CASKIE, WILLIAM WIRT, accountant, securities broker; b. N.Y.C., May 9, 1945; s. John Minor and Rosa Maria (Marchese) C.; BS in Physics, Georgetown U., 1967; MBA in Ops. Research, NYU, 1970; BS magna cum laude in Acctg., Golden Gate U., 1976. Tchr. math. N.Y.C. pub. schs., 1968-71; statistician Fed. Res. Bank of San Francisco, 1972-74; pvt. practice acctg., Marina Del Rey, Calif., 1977—; registered rep. Fin. Network Investment Corp., 1986-92, H.D. Vest Fin. Svcs., 1993—. Mem. Assn. Bus. and Tax Cons., Nat. Assn. Enrolled Agts., Calif. Soc. Enrolled Agts., Mensa, H.D. Vest Fin. Svcs. Home and Office: 557-1/2 Washington Blvd Marina Del Rey CA 90292-5438

CASPE, NAOMI, children's entertainer, educator; b. Colorado Springs, Colo., Apr. 21, 1954; d. Leonard and Neva Jean (Hayutin) C.; m. Douglas Kim Kipping, Aug. 26, 1990. BA, Mills Coll., 1987. Cert. storyteller Dominican Coll. Owner Jester Enterprises and The Magic Makers, Oakland, Calif., 1982—; tchr. Oakland Mus., 1992—. Artist: (book) Facepainting, 1991 (Parents Choice award 1991), video mime Bodybonding, 1990. Nat. Women's Book grantee, San Francisco, 1987. Mem. Nat. Storytelling Assn., Nat. Assn. for Perpetuation of Storytelling, World Clown Assn. Office: Magic Makers 564 Melrose Ave San Francisco CA 94127-2220

CASPER, SCOTT E, historian; b. Bellefont, Pa., Nov. 20, 1964. AB, Princeton U., 1986; MA, Yale U., 1990, MPhil, 1990, PhD, 1992. Asst. prof. History U. Nev., Reno, 1992—. Contbr. articles to profl. jours. Recipient Field Dissertation prize Yale U., 1992; Mellon fellow in the humanities Woodrow Wilson Found., 1986-92, Peterson fellow Am. Antiquarian Soc., 1990-91, Kahrl fellow Houghton Library Harvard U., 1993-94. Mem. Am. Studies Assn., Am. Historical Assn., Orgn. Am. Historians. Office: Dept History U Nevada Reno NV 89557

CASPERS, CORLYN MARIE, adult nurse practitioner; b. Breckenridge, Minn., Aug. 24, 1964; d. Wilbur Richard Caspers and Coralee Meredith (Warner) Fries; m. Rodney Ralph Kolkow, May 1, 1993; children: Megan, Laura. BSN, Oreg. Inst. Tech., 1986; MS, U. Portland (Oreg.), 1994. RN, registered adult nurse practitioner. Hospice primary care nurse Klamath (Oreg.) Hospice, 1985-93; clin. mgr. Merle West Med. Ctr., Klamath Falls, 1989, primary care nurse, 1986-94; home health nurse Merle West Med. Ctr., 1988-94; clinician at coll. health svcs. Oreg. Inst. Tech., Klamath Falls, 1994—; sub-chmn. quality assurance and standards com., 1989, nursing edn. coun., preceptor Merle West Med. Ctr., 1988-94.

CASPY, BARBARA JANE, social worker; b. N.Y., Jan. 11, 1945; d. Harold Brooks Mandel and Lillian (Metzger) Rost; m. Avram Caspy, Apr. 24, 1966; children: Nick Walker, Karen Caspy Nielsen. BA, Bklyn. Coll., 1966; MSW, Rutgers U., 1984. Lic. clin. social worker, Nev. Family counselor Family Svc. Agy. Princeton, N.J., 1984; pvt. practice clin. social work Princeton, 1985-87; social worker Trenton (N.J.) Psychiat. Hosp., 1987-89; clin. social worker So. Nev. Adult Mental Health Svcs., Las Vegas, Nev., 1989-92, Apogee, Inc., Las Vegas, 1992—; social work cons. Family Infant Resource Ctr., Princeton, 1985-88; group facilitator Rutgers Med. Sch. Sexuality Seminar, Piscataway, N.J., 1984-87. Mem. Nat. Assn. Social Workers (diplomate clin. social work), Nat. Rifle Assn. (life).

CASSEL, RUSSELL NAPOLEON, retired clinical research psychologist; b. Harrisburg, Pa., Dec. 18, 1911; s. Herman I. and Sallie (Hummer) C.; m. Lan Dam, Oct. 5, 1964; children—Louis A., Angelica V., Gary R., Lynn V., Gail J., Sallie M., Susie L. Student Pa. State U., 1929-32; B.S., Millersville State Coll., 1937; M.Ed., Pa. State U., 1939; D.Ed., U. So. Calif., 1949; grad. Air War Coll., 1963-65. Diplomate Am. Bd. Profl. Psychology. Tchr. rural sch., North Twp., Pa., 1935-38; tchr. Dauphin (Pa.) Jr. High Sch., 1938-40; personnel cons. U.S. Army Air Force, 1940-46; prof. ednl. psychology U. San Diego, 1949-51; research psychologist U.S. Air Force, San Antonio, 1951-57; sch. psychologist Phoenix Schs., 1957-59; dir. pupil personnel services Lompoc Unified Schs., Calif., 1959-61; cons. to schs. Dept. State, Viet-Nam also Liberia, 1961-67; prof. ednl. psychology U. Wis.-Milw., 1967-74; editor Project Innovation, Chula Vista, Calif., 1969—. Contbr. articles to profl. jours.; author books in field, psychol. tests, computerized programs. Served to col. USAF, 1951-57. Fellow Am. Psychol. Assn., Assn. Correctional Psychology (past pres.), San Diego Computer Soc. (past pres.), Phi Delta Kappa. Republican. Lutheran. Home: 1362 Santa Cruz Ct Chula Vista CA 91910-7114

CASSEL, SUSIE LAN, humanities educator; b. Monrovia, Liberia, Sept. 30, 1966; d. Russell Napoleon and Lan Mieu (Dam) C. BA, U. So. Calif., 1986, U. So. Calif., 1987; MA in English, Harvard U., 1988; PhD in English Lit., U. Calif., Riverside, 1996. Tchg. asst., lectr. U. Calif., Riverside, 1991—. Capt. USAF, 1988-91, res. Mem. Mod. Lang. Assn., Asian Am. Studies Assn., Chinese Hist. Soc. Am., Multi-ethnic Lit. of U.S. Assn.

CASSELL, BEVERLY ANNE, artist, art association executive; b. Montgomery, Ala., Jan. 20, 1936; d. William Duhenfort and Mildred Lucile (Taylor) Bach; m. Dennis Don Cassell, May 17, 1968 (div. Mar. 1972); m. Jesiah C. Venger, Aug. 30, 1989; stepchildren: Jamie Lewis, Tad, Ty Venger. BA, Birmingham So. Coll., 1958; MFA, U. Ga., 1960; postgrad., NYU, 1963. Tchr. drawing and painting U. Colo., Denver, 1967-69, Temple-Buell Coll., Denver, 1968-71; tchr. drawing and painting U. Calif., Santa Cruz, 1972-81, L.A., 1986-89; founder, dir. Artist Conf. Network, 1983—; lectr. art Getty Mus. Edn. Series, L.A., 1992. Works have appeared in shows including Art Mus. of Santa Cruz, Calif., 1984, 85, Taiwan Mus. Art, Taichung, 1989, Nagasaki (Japan) Mus. Art, 1992, 93, 94, L.A. (Calif.) County Mus. Art, 1992, Hanlim Gallery, Tae Jeon, Korea, 1994; spl. guest: (tv show) Women in Contemporary Art, L.A., 1988; set design: Disney Studios, 1990. Bd. dirs. Judson Arts Coun., N.Y.C., 1961-64, L.A. Artcore, 1990-92; mem. L.A. (Calif.) Arts Coun., 1986-89; youth enrollment team Youth at Risk, L.A., 1987-89; dir. L.A. (Calif.) Inner-City Youth Water Sculpture Project, 1990-92. Mem. Mortar Bd. Home and Office: Artist Conf Network 2202 W 20th St Los Angeles CA 90018-1408

CASSENS, NICHOLAS, JR., ceramics engineer; b. Sigourney, Iowa, Sept. 8, 1948; s. Nicholas and Wanda Fern (Lancaster) C.; B.S. in Ceramic Engring., Iowa State U., 1971, B.S. in Chem. Engring., 1971; M.S. in Material Sci. and Engring., U. Calif., Berkeley, 1979; m. Linda Joyce Morrow, Aug. 30, 1969; 1 son, Randall Scott, Jr. research engr. Nat. Refractories and Minerals Corp., Livermore, Calif., 1971-72, research engr., 1972-74, sr. research engr., 1974-77, staff research engr., 1977-84, sr. staff research engr., 1984—. Mem. Am. Ceramic Soc. Democrat. Patentee in field, U.S., Australia, S.Am., Japan, Europe. Home: 4082 Suffolk Way Pleasanton CA 94588-4117 Office: 1852 Rutan Dr Livermore CA 94550-7635

CASSIDY, ADRIAN CLYDE, telephone company executive; b. Polar, Wis., Jan. 27, 1916; s. William Thomas and Ethel (Jenkins) C.; m. Elizabeth Bevans, Mar. 24, 1945; children: David Bevans, Leigh Sheridan, Lynne Porter, Laurie Bevans. BA, U. Wis., 1939, LLB, 1942. Bar: Wis. 1945., N.Y. 1947, Minn. 1951, N.J. 1962. Atty. N.Y. Telephone Co., 1946-50, Am. Tel. & Tel. Co., 1950, 56-61; Minn. atty. Northwestern Bell Telephone Co., 1950-56; gen. atty. N.J. Bell Telephone Co., 1961-63, v.p., 1963-66; v.p. Pacific Tel. & Tel. Co., San Francisco, 1966-81, chief fin. officer, 1972-81; bd. dirs. Datron Systems, Inc., Clemente Global Growth Fund, Inc., First Philippine Fund, Inc. Served to lt. USCGR, 1942-46. Mem. ABA, Am. Judicare Soc., Order of Coif, Menlo Country Club (Woodside, Calif.), Wigwam Country Club (Litchfield Park, Ariz.

CASSIDY, DONALD LAWRENCE, former aerospace company executive; b. Stamford, Conn., May 26, 1933; s. John Dingee and Ursula Agnes (Lynch) C. BS, MIT, 1954; grad. mgmt. policy inst., U. Southern Calif., L.A., 1973. Jr. exec. Johns-Manville Corp., N.Y.C., 1954-55; contracting officer U.S. Army Signal Corps Electric Lab., Ft. Monmouth, N.J., 1955-57; with contract dept. field svc. and support div. Hughes Aircraft Co., L.A., 1957-69, mgr. contracts support systems, 1969-78; dir. contracts Hughes Aircraft Co., Long Beach, Calif., 1978-87, group v.p. bus. ops., 1987, v.p., chief contracts officer, 1987-92. 1st lt. U.S. Army, 1955-57. Mem. Am. Def. Preparedness Assn. (L.A. chpt. bd. dirs.), Nat. Contract Mgmt. Assn., Nat. Security Indsl. Assn., Aerospace Industries Assn. (procurement finance coun. exec. group). Republican.

CASSIDY, RICHARD ARTHUR, environmental engineer, governmental water resources specialist; b. Manchester, N.H., Nov. 15, 1944; s. Arthur Joseph and Alice Ethuliette (Gregoire) C.; m. Judith Diane Maine, Aug. 14, 1971; children: Matthew, Amanda, Michael. BA, St. Anselm Coll., 1966; MS, U. N.H., 1969, Tufts U., 1972. Field biologist Pub. Service Co. of N.H., Manchester, 1968; jr. san. engr. Mass. Div. Water Pollution Control, Boston, 1968-69; aquatic biologist Normandeau Assocs., Bedford, N.H., 1969-70; hydraulic engr. New Eng. div. U.S. Army C.E., Waltham, Mass., 1972-77, environ. engr., Portland Dist., Oreg., 1977-81, supr., environ. engr., 1981—. Contbr. articles to books and profl. jours. Den leader Pack 164 and 598 Columbia Pacific council Cub Scouts Am., Beaverton, Oreg., 1982-83, Webelos leader, 1984-85, 90-91, troop 764 committeeman, 1985-87, asst. scoutmaster, 1992, scoutmaster, 1993-94 troup 598 scoutmaster, 1995—, Columbia Pacific council Boy Scouts Am., 1985-87; mem. Planning Commn. Hudson, N.H., 1976-77. Recipient commendation for exemplary performance Mo.-Miss. flood, 1973, commendation for litigation defense, 1986, commendation for mgmt. activities, 1987, 91. Mem. Am. Inst. Hydrology (cert., profl. ethics com. 1986, v.p. Oreg. sect. 1987-89, pres. Oreg. sect. 1990-92, nat. treas. 1995—), Internat. Tng in Communication (pres. West Way Club 1989-90), N.Am. Lake Mgmt. Soc. Democrat. Roman Catholic. Office: Portland Dist CE Chief Reservoir Reg and Water Quality Sect-PO Box 2946 Portland OR 97208

CASSIDY, SAMUEL H., lawyer, lieutenant governor, state legislator; m. Jillian Jacobellis; children: Rachael Kathryn, Sarah Woyneve, Alexandra, Samuel H. IV. BA, U. Okla., 1972; JD, U. Tulsa, 1975; postgrad., Harvard U., 1991. Bar: Okla., 1975, U.S. Supreme Ct. 1977, U.S. Ct. Appeals (10th cir.), 1977, Colo. 1982. Ptnr. Cassidy, Corely & Ganem, Tulsa, 1975-77, Seigel, Cassidy & Oakley, Tulsa, 1977-79, Beustring, Cassidy, Faulkner & Assocs., Tulsa, 1979-82; pvt. practice Pagosa Springs, Colo., 1982—; mem. Colo. State Senate, 1991-94; lt. gov. State of Colo., 1994—; bd. dirs. Capital Reporter; instr. U. Tulsa, 1978-81, Tulsa Jr. Coll., 1979; owner High Country Title Co.; developer Townhome Property, Mountain Vista; ptnr. Hondo's Inc.; pres., Sam Cassidy, Inc.; mem. agriculture and natural resources com. 1991-92, state, military and vet. affairs com., 1991-92, local govt. com. 1991, legal svcs. com. 1991-92, hwy. legislative review com. 1991-93, nat. hazards mitigation coun., 1992-93, appropriations com., 1993, judiciary com., 1993 ; adv. bd. Colo. Econ. Devel., 1993; exec. com. legis. coun., 1993-94, senate svcs. com. 1993; elected Senate Minority Leader, exec. com. Colo. Gen. Assembly. Mem. State Dem. Ctr. Com., 1987—; mem. steering com. Clinton/Gore campaign. Named Outstanding Legislator for 1991 Colo. Bankers Assn., ACLU Outstanding Legis. 1994; recipient Outsatnding Legis. Efforts award Colo. Counties, Guardian of Small Bus. award, NFIB, 1992, 94; fellow Gates Found., 1991. Mem. Colo. Bar Assn. (bd. gov., 1993—, S.W, Colo. Bar Assn., Nat. Conf. State Legis. (Colo. rep., task force on state-tribe rels.), Rotary (hon. mem., sustaining Paul Harris fellow), Club 20 (bd. dir.), San Juan Forum (chmn., bd. dir.). Office: 1390 Ash St Denver CO 80220-2409

CASTAGNETTO, PERRY MICHAEL, retail sales executive; b. San Francisco, Jan. 22, 1959; s. William Joseph and Patricia Mary (Williams) C. BA, San Jose State U., 1985. Lic. real estate agt., Calif. Asst. mgr. Emerald Hills Golfland, San Jose, 1978-85; dept. mgr. Orchard Supply Hardware, San Jose, 1987—; owner, pres. Castagnetto Enterprises, San Jose, 1991—. Mem. Kappa Sigma (Outstanding alumni 1985, 87). Home: 450 Avenida Arboles San Jose CA 95123-1428

CASTAIN, RALPH HENRI, physicist; b. L.A., Nov. 23, 1954; s. Henry Ulrich and Anni (Springmann) C.; m. Cynthia Ellen Nicholson, Dec. 28, 1976; children: Kelson, Alaric. BS in Physics, Harvey Mudd Coll., 1976; MS in Physics, Purdue U., 1978, MSEE in Robotics, PhD in Nuclear Physics, 1983. Sr. engr. Harris Semiconductor, Palm Bay, Fla., 1978-79; mem. staff Jet Propulsion Lab., Pasadena, Calif., 1983-84; mem. staff Los Alamos (N.Mex.) Nat. Lab., 1984-92, chief scientist nonproliferation and arms control, 1992-93, project leader advanced prosthetics project, 1994, indsl. fellow, 1994-95; mgr. strategic forecasting Eaton Corp., Southfield, Mich., 1995—; cons. Jet Propulsion Lab., Pasadena, 1984-91. Editor, contbr. to Dept. Energy Office Arms Control publs. Recipient Maths. award Bank of Am., 1972, Gold Seal, State of Calif., 1972; Calif. State scholar, 1972-76. Mem. IEEE, Am. Phys. Soc., Internat. Neural Network Soc., VLSI Spl. Interest Group (chmn. electronics com.). Home: 3346 Tiquewood Cir Commerce MI 48382-9999 Office: Eaton Corp 26201 Northwestern Hwy Southfield MI 48037

CASTALDI TODDRE, GWEN, journalist; b. Cleve., Mar. 15, 1952; d. John Wilson and Anna Marie (Dawley) Rupert; m. Ralph Anthony Toddre, May 9, 1981 (div. 1988). Student, Cleve. State U., 1970-71. Reporter, photographer Euclid (Ohio) News Jour., 1971; musician, pianist, singer, 1971-74; reporter, copy editor Sta. KBMI All News Radio, Las Vegas, 1975-76, reporter, assignment editor, 1976; reporter, news anchor Sta. KSHO TV, Las Vegas, 1976; promotion asst. Las Vegas Rev.-Jour., 1977; news dir. Sta. KNUUS All News Radio, Las Vegas, 1977; news reporter, pub. affairs show host Sta. KLAS TV, Las Vegas, 1977-80; news reporter Sta. WBBM-TV, Chgo., 1980; news reporter, anchor Sta. KVBC-TV, Las Vegas, 1981—. Contbr. articles to newspapers and mags. Judge Bicentennial Com., Las Vegas, 1987—; bd. dirs. Arthritis Found., Las Vegas, 1986-87; mem. historic preservation com. City of Las Vegas, 1993—; mem. mus. and history bd. State of Nev., 1992-93; panel moderator Gov.'s Conf. on Victim's Rights, 1986; panelist numerous orgns.; speaker, host for numerous community groups including United Blood Svcs., Am. Cancer Soc., Am. Heart Assn., C. of C.,, Children's Miracle Network Telethons, United Way, others. Recipient numerous awards for journalism So. Nev. Journalism awards, UPI, AP, Emmy, 1995, NATAS (San Diego chpt.). Mem. NATAS (San Diego chpt.), Women in Comm., Profl. Soc. Journalists, Sigma Delta Chi (past pres., v.p.). Office: Sta KVBC TV 3 1500 Foremaster Ln Las Vegas NV 89101-1103

CASTANEDA, CARLOS, anthropologist, author; b. Sao Paulo, Brazil, Dec. 25, 1931; s. C.N. and Susana (Aranha) C. BA, UCLA, Los Angeles, 1962; MA, UCLA, 1964, PhD, 1970. Apprentice to Yaqui Indian sorcerer, five years; now anthropologist. Author: The Teachings of Don Juan: A Yaqui Way of Knowledge, 1968, A Separate Reality: The Phenomenology of Special Consensus, 1971, Journey to Ixtlan, 1974, Tales of Power, 1975, The Second Ring of Power, 1977, The Eagle's Gift, 1982, The Fire from Within, 1984, The Power of Silence: Further Lessons of Don Juan, 1987, The Art of Dreaming, 1993. Office: TOHCC Artists 813 N Martel Ave Los Angeles CA 90036

CASTANES, JAMES CHRISTOPHER, architect; b. Vallejo, Calif., Jan. 12, 1951; s. James Christopher and Helen C.; m. Diane Allenbach, June 22, 1991. BArch, U. Ark., Fayetteville, 1975. Apprentice Schmidt, Garden, Erickson, Chgo., 1969-71; staff architect Ibsen Nelsen & Assocs., Seattle, 1975-76, Jouce, Copeland, Vaughn & Nordfors, Seattle, 1976-80; project architect Jean Fraley & Assocs., Seattle, 1980-85; pvt. practice architect Seattle, 1985-87; ptnr. Castanes/Gibson Architects, Seattle, 1987—. Recipient Home of Yr. award Seattle Am. Inst. Architects/Seattle Times Newspaper, 1987. mem. N.F.G. 1969—. Office: Castanes/Gibson Architects 1932 1st Ave Ste 928 Seattle WA 98101-1040

CASTBERG, EILEEN SUE, construction company owner; b. Santa Monica, Calif., Mar. 12, 1946; d. George Leonard and Irma (Loretta) Conroy; m. David Christopher Castberg, Oct. 27, 1967; children: Eric, Christopher. Grad. high sch., U. High Sch., L.A., 1964; certificate, Anthony

Schs., 1990. Lic. real estate agt., Calif. Exec., co-founder Advanced Connector Telesis, Inc., Santa Ana, Calif., 1986-87; exec. Western Energy Engrs., Inc., Costa Mesa, Calif., 1987-89; owner Dave Castberg and Assoc., Inc., Ramona, Calif., 1989 --; cons. Watt Asset Mgmt., Santa Monica, 1990-91. Mem. choir Ramona Luth. Ch.; 3d v.p. Holy Cross Luth. Ch. Women's League, Cypress, Calif., 1983. Mem. San Diego Bd. Realtors, Ramona Real Estate Assn., Intermountain Rep. Women's Fedn. (pres.), Ramona Christian Women's Club. Republican.

CASTEEL, CHERYL THEODORA, security officer; b. Dallas, Oct. 11, 1955; d. Richard Lee Taylor and Robbie Roy (Collins) Bowling; m. James A. Grade, June 18, 1977 (div. 1980); 1 child, James Robert Grade; m. James L. Casteel, Dec. 13, 1980 (dec. 1991); children: Janice, Marjeen, Sabrina, Thresea, Terris (dec.); adopted children: Dawn, Toni, Jason; 1 stepchild, Shawna. AA, Cochise Coll., Sierra Vista, Ariz., 1981. Sec. Batchelder Ins., Sierra Vista, 1973-77; truck driver J&C Trucking, Sierra Vista, 1977-79; sec. Dental Clinic, Fort Huachuca, Ariz., 1979-81; bus. mgr. Mr. Photo, Sierra Vista, 1980; paraprofl. Buena High Sch., Sierra Vista, 1981-89, day security officer, 1989—. Actress Tombstone Vigilantes and Tombstone Vigilets, 1986—. Coach Spl. Olympics, Sierra Vista, 1982-88; sec., treas. Anonymous Program, 1984-86; foster parent for Cochise County, 1983-86; advisor Vocat. Industries of Am., Sierra Vista, 1980-91; chmn. Jim Casteel Scholarship Fund, Sierra Vista, 1991—. Named Outstanding Vocat. Industries Clubs Am. advisor for Ariz., 1983, Nat. Outstanding VICA advisor for Ariz., 1985. Mem. NEA, NAFE, Ariz. Ednl. Assn. (Outstanding Young Woman of Am. 1987). Democrat. Baptist. Home: PO Box 937 Sierra Vista AZ 85636-0937

CASTELLANO, MICHAEL ANGELO, research forester; b. Bklyn., June 26, 1956; s. Biagio and Mildred Anne (Cucco) C.; m. Elizabeth Marie Phillips, July 14, 1979; children: Nicholas Aaron, Daniel Robert Feller, Kelly Marie, Katlyn Morgan. AAS, Paul Smiths Coll., 1978; BS, Oreg. State U., 1982, MS, 1984, PhD, 1988. Forest technician Weyerhauser Co., Columbus, Miss., 1979; forester trainee USDA Forest Svc., Pacific N.W., Corvallis, Oreg., 1980-84, forester, 1984-87, rsch. forester, 1987—; cons. CSIRO, Div. of Forestry, Australia, 1988-95, Spanish-Am. Binational Prog., Barcelona, 1987, 91. Author: Key to Hypogeous Fungi, 1989, (agr. handbook) Mycorrhizae, 1989; contbr. articles to profl. jours. Bishop LSD Ch. Named one of Outstanding Young Men, Am. JayCees, 1984. Mem. Soc. Am. Foresters, N.Am. Truffling Soc. (advisor), Soil Ecology Soc., Mycol. Soc. of Am. (nomenclature 1986), Sigma Xi. Home: 1835 NW Garfield Ave Corvallis OR 97330-2535 Office: USDA Forest Svc 3200 SW Jefferson Way Corvallis OR 97331-8550

CASTELLANO, OLIVIA GUERRERO, English language educator; b. Del Rio, Tex., July 25, 1944; d. Secundino Peña and Cruz (Guerrero) C. BA in French and English, Calif. State U., Sacramento, 1966, MA in Social Anthropology, 1970; PhD fellow in Modern Thought and Lit., Stanford U., 1976. Cert. H.S. tchr., C.C. tchr., Calif. H.S. tchr. English, French and Spanish San Juan and Grant Unified Sch. Dist., Sacramento, 1967-69; instr. Mex.-Am. studies Sacramento City Coll., 1969-72; prof. English Calif. State U., Sacramento, 1972—; cons. Alameda Sch. Dist., Oakland, Calif., 1980-85, Sacramento City Coll., 1969-85. Author (poems): Blue Mandolin: Yellow Field, 1980, Blue Horse of Madness, 1983, Spaces That Time Missed, 1986. Cmty. organizer Sacramento Concilio, 1969-80. Fellow Ford Found., 1976, Mex. Am. Experienced Tchrs., 1969-70. Mem. MLA. Democrat. Office: Calif. State U 6000 J St Sacramento CA 95819-2605

CASTELLINI, PATRICIA BENNETT, business management educator; b. Park River, N.D., Mar. 25, 1935; d. Benjamin Beekman Bennett and Alice Catherine (Peerboom) Bennett Breckinridge; m. William McGregor Castellini; children: Bruce Bennett Subhani, Barbara Lea Ragland. AA, Allan Hancock Coll., Santa Maria, Calif., 1964; BS magna cum laude, Coll. Great Falls, 1966; MS, U. N.D., 1967, PhD, 1971. Fiscal acct. USIA, Washington, 1954-56; pub. acct., Bremerton, Wash., 1956; statistician USN, Bremerton, 1957-59; med. svcs. accounts officer U.S. Air Force, Vandenberg AFB, Calif., 1962-64; instr. bus. adminstrn. Western New Eng. Coll., 1967-69; vis. prof. econs. Chapman Coll., 1970; vis. prof. U. So. Calif. systems Griffith AFB, N.Y., 1971-72; assoc. prof., dir. adminstrv. mgmt. program Va. State U., 1973-74; assoc. prof. bus. adminstrn. Oreg. State U., Corvallis, 1974-81, prof. mgmt., 1982-90, emeritus prof. mgmt., 1990—, univ. curriculum coord., 1984-86, dir. adminstrv. mgmt. program, 1974-81, pres. Faculty Senate, 1981, Interinstl. Faculty Senate, 1986-90, pres., 1989-90; exec. dir. Bus. Enterprise Ctr., 1990-92, Enterprise Ctr. L.A., Inc., 1992-95, W.M. Castellini Co., 1995—; commr. Lafayette Econ. Devel. Authority, 1994—; cons. process tech. devel. Digital Equipment Corp., 1982. Pres., chmn. bd. dirs. Adminstrv. Orgnl. Svcs., Inc., Corvallis, 1976-83, Dynamic Achievement, Inc., 1983-92; bd. dirs. Oreg. State U. Bookstores, Inc., 1987-90, Internat. Trade Adv. Group, 1992—, BBB of Acadiana, 1994—, sec., 1995—, Internat. Trade Devel. Group; exec. dir. Bus. Enterprise Ctr., Inc., 1990-92; dir., cons. Oregonians in Action, 1990-91; commr. Lafayette Econ. Devel. Authority, 1994—. Cert. adminstrv. mgr. Pres. TYEE Mobil Home Park, Inc., 1987-92. Fellow Assn. Bus. Communication (mem. internat. bd. 1980-83, v.p. Northwest 1981, 2d v.p. 1982-83, 1st v.p. 1983-84, pres. 1984-85); mem. Am. Bus. Women's Assn. (chpt. v.p. 1979, pres. 1980, named Top Businesswoman in Nation 1980, Bus. Assoc. Yr. 1986), Assn. Info. Systems Profls., Adminstrv. Mgmt. Soc., AAUP (chpt. sec. 1973, chpt. bd. dirs. 1982, 84-89, pres. Oreg. conf. 1983-85), Am. Vocat. Assn. (nominating com. 1976), Associated Oreg. Faculties, Nat. Bus. Edn. Assn., Nat. Assn. Tchr. Edn. for Bus. Office Edn. (pres. 1976-77, chmn. public relations com. 1978-81), La. Bus. Incubation Assn. (sec.-treas. 1993-95), Corvallis Area C. of C. (v.p. chamber devel. 1987-88, pres. 1988-89, chmn. bd. 1989-90, Pres.' award 1986), Boys and Girls Club of Corvallis (pres. 1991-92), Sigma Kappa, Rotary (bd. dirs. 1990-92, 94—, pres.-elect 1992, treas. 1995—). Roman Catholic. Contbr. numerous articles to profl. jours. Office: Wm Castellini Co 109 Silver Medal Dr Lafayette LA 70506-3420

CASTER, RONALD LYNN, fire chief; b. Medford, Oreg., May 16, 1954; s. Otto R. and Patricia A. (Hopkins) C.; m. Rosanne D. Green, Nov. 15, 1975 (div. 1991); children: Amanda M., Anna L. AA in fire sci., Rogue Cmty. Coll., Grants Pass, Oreg., 1990. Firefighter U.S. Air Force, Mountain Home AFB, Idaho, 1975-79; fire dept. crew chief U.S. Air Force, RAF Fairford, Eng., 1979-81; fire chief U.S. Air Force, Calumet AFS, Mich., 1981-84; firefighter U.S. Army, Hermiston, Oreg., 1984-85; fire chief Medford/Jackson County Airport, Medford, Oreg., 1985-90; trainer Oreg. State Fire Marshal's Office, Medford, Oreg., 1990-91; fire chief Grays Harbor Fire Dist. 2, Aberdeen, Wash., 1991—; adv. fire sci. South Puget Sound Cmty. Coll., Olympia, Wash., 1992—. Mem. Nat. Fire Protection Assn., Internat. Assn. Fire Chiefs, Washington State Fire Chiefs Assn., Twin Harbor Fire Chiefs Assn. (v.p. 1991-94). Democrat. Office: Grays Harbor Fire Dist #2 6317 Olympic Hwy Aberdeen WA 98520-5723

CASTILLO, RICHARD JOSEPH, psychiatric anthropologist, educator; b. Long Beach, Calif., Aug. 17, 1951; s. Celestino Ledesma and Elvira Alarcon (Gloria) C. BA in Philosophy magna cum laude, U. Hawaii, 1983, MA in Asian Religions, 1985; MA in Psychiat. Anthropology, Harvard U., 1989, PhD in Psychiat. Anthropology, 1991. Tchg. fellow Harvard U., Cambridge, Mass., 1986-88, resident tutor, 1987-89; vis. colleague U. Hawaii Manoa, Honolulu, 1989-90; lectr. psychiat. anthropology U. Hawaii West Oahu, Pearl City, 1990-93, asst. prof., 1993-95, assoc. prof., 1995—; advisor Diagnostic & Statis. Manual Mental Disorders, 4th edit. task force Am. Psychiat. Assn., Washington, 1992-94; mem. cultural study group, dept. of psychiatry U. Hawaii Sch. of Medicine. Ford Found. dissertation fellow, 1989-90; grad. fellow NSF, 1986-89, Harvard U., 1985-91. Fellow Am. Anthrop. Assn.; mem. NIMH (mem. group on culture and diagnosis 1992—), Am. Ethnol. Soc., Internat. Soc. for Study of Dissociation, Soc. for Anthropology of Consciousness (Volney Stefflre award 1993), Soc. Med. Anthropology, Phi Beta Kappa. Office: Univ Hawaii West Oahu 96-043 Ala Ike Pearl City HI 96782

CASTLE, ALFRED, administrator; b. Washington, Dec. 22, 1948; m. Mary Ann Slagle (div. 1979). BA, Colo. State U., 1971, MA, 1972; postgrad., U. N.Mex., Columbia U., 1980, U. N.Mex. Chmn., div. humanities Sunset Hill Sch., Kansas City, 1973-75; teaching asst. U. N.Mex., Alburquerque, 1975; prof., history N.Mex. Mil. Inst., Roswell, 1976-83; exec. dir. NMMI Fedn. N.Mex. Mil. Inst., 1983-87; v.p. devel. Hawaii Pacific U., Honolulu, 1987-95; v.p. U. advancement Calif. State U., San Marcos, 1995—; trustee Samuel N. and Mary Castle Found., Honolulu, 1987—, pres.-elect, 1992—; trustee Acad. Pacific, Honolulu, 1987—, Hawaiian Hist. Soc., Honolulu, 1988—. Author: Century of Philanthropy, 1992; contbr. articles to profl. jours., chpts. to books. Trustee Hawaii Food Bank, Honolulu, 1987—, Hawaii Sch. Girls, Honolulu, 1987—, Henry Dorothy Castle Fund, Robert Black Meml. Trust, Trimble Charitable Trust; trustee, pres. Samuel N. and Mary Castle Found. NEH fellow, 1978, 79-80, 81, 86, 91, Hoover fellow, 1983, 86, 90, 93, Coolidge fellow, 1988. Mem. Assn. Grantmakers Hawaii, Govrs. Coun. Children Youth, Coun. Founds. Episcopalian. Home: 206 Alta Mesa Dr Vista CA 92084

CASTLE, EMERY NEAL, agricultural and resource economist, educator; b. Eureka, Kans., Apr. 13, 1923; s. Sidney James and Josie May (Tucker) C.; m. Merab Eunice Weber, Jan. 20, 1946; 1 dau., Cheryl Diana Delozier. B.S., Kans. State U., 1948, M.S., 1950; Ph.D., Iowa State U., 1952. Agrl. economist Fed. Res. Bank of Kansas City, 1952-54; from asst. prof. to prof. dept. agrl. econs. Oreg. State U., Corvallis, 1954-65; dean faculty Oreg. State U., 1965-66, prof., head dept. agrl. econs., 1966-72, dean Grad. Sch., 1972-76, Alumni disting. prof., 1970, prof. univ. grad. faculty econs., 1986—; v.p., sr. fellow Resources for the Future, Washington, 1976-79; pres. Resources for the Future, 1979-86; vice-chmn. Environ. Quality Commn. Oreg., 1988—. Author: U.S.-Japanese Agricultural Trade Relations, 1982, Global Natural Resources: Energy, Minerals and Food, 1984; mem. editl. bd. Land Econs., 1969—. Recipient Alumni Disting. Service award Kans. State U., 1976; Disting. Service award Oreg. State U., 1984. Fellow AAAS, Am. Assn. Agrl. Economists (pres. 1972-73), Am. Acad. Arts and Scis. Home: 1112 NW Solar Pl Corvallis OR 97330-3640 Office: Oreg State U 307 Ballard Extension Hall Corvallis OR 97331-8538

CASTLE, TIMOTHY JAMES, food products executive; b. Richmond, Va., Mar. 2, 1955; s. Alexander James and Diane Marie Castle. BS in Pub. Health, UCLA, 1979, profl. designation internat. bus. mgmt., 1985, profl. designation internat. trade, 1985. V.p. Inter Trade Co., San Francisco, 1978-87; pres. Castle & Co., Santa Monica, Calif., 1987-91, Timothy J. Castle, Inc., Santa Monica, 1991—. Author: The Perfect Cup, 1991; contbr. articles to profl. jours., mags. and newspapers. Mem. Am. Inst. Wine and Food (bd. dirs. L.A. chpt. 1984—, newsletter editor), Am. Inst. Wine and Food (charter founder), Splty. Coffee Assn. Am. (past pres. 1990-91, v.p. 1989-90, sec. 1987-89, bd. dirs. 1986-87). Home and Office: Timothy J Castle Inc and Castle Comm 2118 Wilshire Blvd #634 Los Angeles CA 90403

CASTLE, TRIS SPEAKER, physician assistant; b. Cleve., July 10, 1942; s. Edward Balzhiser and Betty (Witt) C.; m. Kathryn Joan Burroughs, June 1964 (div. Oct. 1971); 1 child, Edward Joseph; m. Judith Arthelia Hatcher, July 7, 1977; 1 child, Kathleen Marie. Student, Oreg. State U., 1961-64; AAS, Big Bend C.C., 1977, Cuyahoga C.C., 1980; postgrad., Ea. Wash. U., 1977-78. Cert. physician asst., advanced cardiac life support. Physician asst. Ariz. Dept. Corrections, Florence, Ariz., 1986-92, West Pinal Family Health Ctr., Casa Grande, Ariz., 1992—; mem. P&T com. Regional Health Svcs., Casa Grande, Ariz., 1992-94. Patentee instrument to cure ingrown toenails. Chief warrant officer U.S. Army, 1980-85. Fellow Ariz. State Assn. Physician Assts., Am. Acad. Physician Assts. Office: Policlinica San Xavier 809 E Washington St Ste 106 Phoenix AZ 85034

CASTLEBERRY, ARLINE ALRICK, architect; b. Mpls., Sept. 19, 1919; d. Bannona Gerhardt and Meta Emily (Veit) Alrick; m. Donald Montgomery Castleberry, Dec. 25, 1941; children: Karen, Marvin. B in Interior Architecture, U. Minn., 1941; postgrad., U. Tex., 1947-48. Designer, draftsman Elizabeth & Winston Close, Architects, Mpls., 1940-41, Northwest Airlines, Mpls., 1942-43, Cerny & Assocs., Mpls., 1944-46; archtl. draftsman Dominick and Van Benscotten, Washington, 1946-47; ptnr. Castleberry & Davis Bldg. Designers, Burlingame, Calif., 1960-65; prin. Burlingame, 1965-90. Recipient Smith Coll. scholarship. Mem. AIA, Am. Inst. Bldg. Designers (chpt. pres. 1971-72), Commaisini, Alpha Alpha Gamma, Chi Omega. Democrat. Lutheran. Home and Office: 3004 Canyon Rd Burlingame CA 94010-6019

CASTLES, JOHN WILLIAM, healthcare company executive; b. Portland, Oreg., Dec. 13, 1947; s. James B. and Ruth (Lintz) C.; m. Sarah E. Boylston, Dec. 27, 1985. Student U. Wash., 1966, 67, Linfield Coll., 1968, Portland State U., 1969-72. Comml. loan officer, br. mgr. Oreg. Bank, Portland, 1972-76; mgr. fin. mgmt. div. Capital Cons., Inc., Portland, 1976-80; fin. cons., Portland, 1981-91; chmn. Vital Choice, Inc., Portland, 1991-93; pres. and CEO Mutual Health Systems, Inc., Vancouver, Wash., 1993—; bd. dirs. ASN Ventures, Inc., Portland, Mut. Health Sys. Inc.; trustee U. Mont. Found., Missoula; mem. Craighead Wildlife-Wildlands Inst., Ecotrust, Sunset Presbyn. Ch. Mem. Multnomah Athletic Club, West Hills Racquet Club. Home: 11725 SW Lynnridge St Portland OR 97225-4510 Office: 7725 NE Highway 99 Ste B Vancouver WA 98665-8834

CASTON, JONATHON CRAIG, radio producer; b. McCloud, Calif., Dec. 13, 1948; s. John Harding and Joanne Louise (Maddock) C.; m. Lucy V. Palkina, July 12, 1991; 1 child, Irina G. BA in Polit. Sci., Calif. State U., Northridge, 1972, BA in Journalism, 1977. Staff mem. Sta. KEDC-FM Pub. Radio Broadcasting, Northridge, 1969-72; intern pub. affairs dept. Sta. KCET-TV Pub. TV, L.A., 1971-72; early morning anchor, reporter Sta. KORK-TV, Las Vegas, 1976; talk radio producer, engr. KIEV Radio, Glendale, L.A., Calif., 1984—; cons. Caston Internat., Littlerock, Calif., 1992—; owner, co-founder Orion Bus. Internat., Canoga Park, Calif., 1985-90. Active Littlerock Town Coun., 1992-93. Mem. Am. Radio Relay League (life), Amateur Radio Satellite Orgn. (life). Democrat. Office: Caston Internat PO Box 74 Littlerock CA 93543-0074

CASTOR, JON STUART, management consultant; b. Lynchburg, Va., Dec. 15, 1951; s. William Stuart and Marilyn (Hughes) C.; m. Stephanie Lum, Jan. 7, 1989; 1 child, David Jon. BA, Northwestern U., 1973; MBA, Stanford U., 1975. Mgmt. cons. Menlo Park, Calif., 1981—. Dir. Midwest Consumer Adv. Bd. to FTC, 1971-73; v.p., bd. dirs. San Mateo coun. Boy Scouts Am., 1991-93; bd. dirs. Pacific Skyline Coun. Boy Scouts Am., 1994—; trustee Coyote Point Mus. Environ. Edn., San Mateo, 1992-95. Office: 830 Menlo Ave Menlo Park CA 94025-4734

CASTOR, WILBUR WRIGHT, futurist, author, consultant; b. Harrison Twp., Pa., Feb. 3, 1932; s. Wilbur Wright and Margaret (Grubbs) C.; m. Donna Ruth Schwartz, Feb. 9, 1963; children: Amy, Julia, Marnie. BA, St. Vincent Studies, 1959; PhD, Calif. U. Advanced Studies, 1990. Sales rep. IBM, Pitts. and Cleve., 1959-62; v.p. data processing ops. Honeywell, Waltham, Mass., 1962-80; pres., chief exec. officer Aviation Simulation Tech., Lexington, Mass., 1980-82; sr. v.p. Xerox Corp., El Segundo, Calif., 1982-89; freelance cons., 1989—. Author: (play) Un Certaine Soirire, 1958, (mus. comedy) Breaking Up, 1960, (book) The Information Age and the New Productivity, 1990; contbr. articles to profl. jours. Mem. Presdl. Rep. Task Force; pres., bd. dirs. Internat. Acad., Santa Barbara; active Town Hall Calif. Served to capt. USN, 1953-58, with USAFR, 1958-76. Recipient Disting. Alumnus of Yr. award St. Vincent Coll., 1990. Mem. World Bus. Acad., The Strategy Bd., U. Denver "Netthink", World Future Soc., Aircraft Owners and Pilots Assn., Caballeros Country Club, Rolling Hills (Calif.) Club, Tennis Club, U.S. Senator's Club. Home: 19 Georgeff Rd Rolling Hills CA 90274-5272

CASTRO, DAVID ALEXANDER, construction executive; b. L.A., Dec. 30, 1950; s. Victor A. and Guadalupe (Valadez) C.; m. Katherine Winfield Taylor, Sept. 30, 1990; children: Sarah Taylor, Kyle Christian. A Liberal Arts, U. Md., 1976, BS in Bus. and Mgmt., 1978; A Engring. Asst., C.C. USAF, 1986; MS in Systems Mgmt., Golden Gate U., 1991. Enlisted USAF, 1970, advanced through grades to Chief Master Sgt., 1989; quality control mgr. 6950 security wing USAF, Royal AFB Chicksands, U.K., 1976-79; supr. engring. support 2851 civil engring. squadron USAF, McClellan AFB, Calif., 1979-82, inspector major projects 2851 civil engring. squadron, 1982-85, supt. engring. svcs. 2851 civil engring. squadron, 1985-87; dep. dir. pub. works tech. assistance team USAF, Beni Seuf, Egypt, 1987-88; contract mgr., then program mgr. 60 civil engring squadron USAF, Travis AFB, Calif., 1988-91; ret. USAF, 1991; acct. rep. Met. Life Ins. Co., Fairfield, Calif., 1991-92; construction mgr. Pacifica Svcs. Inc., Travis AFB, Calif., 1992—; mem. USAF Enlisted Coun., Washington, 1984-86. Group leader Neighborhood Watch, North Highlands, Calif., 1983-86; vol. Loaves and Fishes, Sacramento, 1984-86, Christman Promise, Sacramento, 1983-85; coach Little League Baseball, U.K. and Sacramento, 1976-81. Mem. Air Force Assn. (named Outstanding Airman 1985), Air Force Sgts. Assn., Travis Chiefs Group (treas. 1990-92), Am. Legion. Republican. Roman Catholic. Home: 1354 James St Fairfield CA 94533-6451

CASTRO, JOSEPH ARMAND, music director, pianist, composer, orchestrator; b. Miami, Ariz., Aug. 15, 1927; s. John Loya and Lucy (Sanchez) C.; m. Loretta Faith Haddad, Oct. 21, 1966; children: John Joseph, James Ernest. Student, San Jose State Coll., 1944-47. Mus. dir. Herb Jeffries, Hollywood, Calif., 1952, June Christy, Hollywood, 1959-63, Anita O'Day, Hollywood, 1963-65, Tony Martin, Hollywood, 1962-64, Tropicana Hotel, Las Vegas, Nev., 1980—, Desert Inn, Las Vegas, 1992-93; orch. leader Mocambo Night Club, Hollywood, 1952-54; soloist Joe Castro Trio, L.A., N.Y.C., Honolulu, 1952-65, Sands Hotel, Desert Inn, Las Vegas, 1975-80; mus. dir. Folies Bergere, 1980-89. Recs. include Cool School with June Christy, 1960, Anita O'Day Sings Rodgers and Hart, 1961, Lush Life, 1966, Groove-Funk-Soul, Mood Jazz, Atlantic Records, also albums with Teddy Edwards, Stan Kenton, Jimmy Borges with Joe Castro Trio, 1990, Loretta Castro with Joe Castro Trio, 1990, Honolulu Symphony concerts; command performance, Queen Elizabeth II, London Palladium, 1989, Concerts with Jimmy Borges and Honolulu Symphony Pops Concerts, 1991; jazz concert (with Nigel Kennedy) Honolulu Symphony, 1990; jazz-fest, Kailua-Kona, Hawaii, 1990; leader orch. Tropicana Hotel, 1989-94. With U.S. Army, 1946-47. Roman Catholic. Home: 2812 Colanthe Ave Las Vegas NV 89102-2026 Office: Tropicana Hotel 3801 Las Vegas Blvd S Las Vegas NV 89109-4325

CASTRO, LEONARD EDWARD, lawyer; b. L.A., Mar. 18, 1934; s. Emil Galvez and Lily (Meyers) C.; 1 son, Stephen Paul. A.B., UCLA, 1959, J.D., 1962. Bar: Calif. 1963, U.S. Supreme Ct. 1970. Assoc. Musick, Peeler & Garrett, Los Angeles, 1962-68, ptnr., 1968—. Mem. ABA, Internat. Bar Assn., Los Angeles County Bar Assn. Office: Musick Peeler & Garrett 1 Wilshire Blvd Ste 2000 Los Angeles CA 90017-3806

CASTRO, TERESA HARPER, small business owner; b. Chgo., July 18, 1956; d. Jene Paul and June Edith (Aleff) Harper; m. Oscar Armando Rodriguez (div. 1981); 1 child, Avelina; m. Jorge Castro, Jan. 9, 1988; 1 child, Pablo. AA in Opera, Fleming Coll., Florence, Italy, 1975; BA in Spanish and Portuguese cum laude, U. N.Mex., 1979. Adminstrv. asst. Latin Am. Inst., Albuquerque, 1981-83; law office mgr. Camacho & Hinkle, San Francisco, 1983; owner, founder, pres. Access Word Processing, San Francisco and Viña del Mar, Chile, 1983—; tech. translator Red de Television Universitaria (RTU), Santiago, Chile, 1983—, Municipality of Valparaiso, Office of the Gov., Chile, 1983—; freelance computer and word processing systems analyst, San Francisco and Phoenix, 1985-89. State coord. Truth Seekers in Adoption of Calif., San Francisco, 1985-89; vol. notary pub. People With AIDS/ARC, 1985-91, The AIDS Found./Shanti Project, San Francisco, 1986-90; chairperson bilingual adv. bd. Buena Vista Sch., San Francisco, 1986; bd. dirs. Escola Nova de Samba, San Francisco, 1987; vol. working on reunification searches for adoptees and birth parents, Calif., N.Y., Latin Am.; tchr. Spanish law enforcement pers. San Francisco Police Acad., 1988-89, Spanish for med. pers. Kaiser Permanente Med. Ctr., San Francisco, 1988-89. Mem. NAFE, Nat. Notary Assn. Home and Office: 884 Minnesota Ave San Jose CA 95125-2418

CASTRUITA, RUDY, school system administrator. BA in Social Sci., Utah State U., 1966, MS in Sch. Adminstrn., 1967; EdD, U. So. Calif., 1983. Cert. adminstrv. svcs., std. secondary, pupil svcs. Dir. econ. opportunity program City of El Monte, Calif., 1966-67; secondary tchr., counselor, program coord. El Monte Union High Sch. Dist., 1967-75, asst. prin. Mountain View High Sch., 1975-80; prin. Los Alamitos (Calif.) High Sch. Los Alamitos Unified Sch. Dist., 1980-85; asst. supt. secondary divsn. Santa Ana (Calif.) Unified Sch. Dist., 1985-87, assoc. supt. secondary divsn., 1987-88, supt., 1988—; adj. prof. Calif. State U., Long Beach, 1981-88, mem. adv. com. dept. ednl. adminstrn., 1983-86; adj. prof. U. San Francisco, 1984-88; mem. State Tchr. of Yr. Selection Com., 1988, Student Tchr. Edn. Project Coun., SB 620 Healthy Start Com., SB 1274 Restructuring Com., Joint Task Force Articulation, State High Sch. Task Force; mem. Latino eligibility study U. Calif., mem. ednl. leadership inst.; mem. state adv. coun. Supt. Pub. Instrn.; Delta Epsilon lectr. U. So. Calif.; rep. Edn. Summit; mem. selection com. Calif. Ednl. Initiatives Fund; co-chair subcom. at risk youth Calif. Edn. Com., 1989; mentor supt. Harvard Urban Supt.'s Program, 1993—. Chair Orange County Hist. Adv. Coun., South El Monte Coordinating Coun.; mem. exec. coun. Santa Ana 2000; mem. articulation coun. Rancho Santiago C.C. Dist.; active Hacienda Heights Recreation and Pks. Commn., Santa Ana City Coun. Stadium Blue Ribbon Com.; exec. dir. Orange County coun. Boy Scouts Am.; mem. adv. com. Bowers Mus.; mem. exec. bd. El Monte Boys Club; hon. lifetime mem. Calif. PTA; bd. dirs. Santa Ana Boys and Girls Club, Orange County Philharm. Soc., Santa Ana Pvt. Industry Coun., El Monte-South El Monte Consortium, Drug Use is Life Abuse, EDUCARE sch. edn. U. So. Calif. Named Supt. of Yr. League United Latin Am. Citizens, 1989; state finalist Nat. Supt. Yr. award, 1992. Mem. ASCD, Assn. Calif. Sch. Adminstrs. (rep. region XVII secondary prins. com. 1981-85, presenter region XVII 1984, Calif. Supt. of Year award 1991, Marcus Foster award 1991), Calif. Sch. Bds. Assn. (mem. policy and analysis com.), Assn. Calif. Urban Sch. Dists. (pres. 1992—), Orange County Supts. (pres.), Santa Ana C. of C. (bd. dirs.), Delta Epsilon (pres. 1990-91), Phi Delta Kappa. Office: Santa Anna USD 1405 French St Santa Ana CA 92701-2414*

CASTY, ALAN HOWARD, author, retired humanities educator; b. Chgo., Apr. 6, 1929; s. Louis and Gertrude (Chaden) C.; m. Marilyn McPheeters, Aug. 10, 1956 (div. Dec. 1970); children: Lisa, David, Erica; m. Jill Herman, Jan. 7, 1971. BA, U. Calif., Berkeley, 1950; MA, U. Calif., L.A., 1956, PhD, 1973. Sports reporter The Richmond (Calif.) Ind., 1950-51; publicist Natural Vision Film Corp., Hollywood, Calif., 1953-54; prof. English and cinema Santa Monica (Calif.) Coll., 1956-92, prof. emeritus, 1992—. Author: Robert Rossen, 1967, The Shape of Fiction, 1967, 2d edit., 1973, Mass Media and Mass Man, 1968, 2d edit., 1973, 3d edit., 1975, The Films of Robert Rossen, 1969, A Mixed Bag, 1970, 2d edit., 1975, Building Writing Skills, 1971, The Dramatic Art of the Film, 1971, Development of the Film: An Interpretive History, 1973, Let's Make It Clear, 1977, Improving Writing, 1981, The Writing Project, 1983, others; contbr. articles to profl. jours. Sgt. U.S. Army, 1951-53. Jewish. Home: 225 17 Mile Dr Pacific Grove CA 93950 Office: Santa Monica Coll 1900 Pico Blvd Santa Monica CA 90405-1628

CATALANO, JOHN GEORGE, management consultant; b. Rockford, Ill., Jan. 28, 1950; s. Francis Richard and Angela C.; m. Kathryn Swaney, Sept. 20, 1980; 1 child, F. Richard. BSBA, U. Ill., 1972. Sales rep. Metal Fabricators, Inc., Rockford, Ill., 1972-76; v.p. sales/mktg. Metal Fabricators, Inc., 1976-82, pres., chief exec. officer, 1982-86; pres. Catalano & Co., Rockford, 1986-88, Greenbrae, Calif., 1988-91; CEO, pres. Casa Blanca Works, Greenbrae, 1991—; CEO, ProLine Distbn., Inc., 1994—. Pub. (monthly newsletter) BusinessMac, (directory) Chicago Computer Training Directory, 1987; contbr. articles to profl. jours. Recipient Silver Beaver award, Boy Scouts Am., 1988, Silver Wreath, 1986. Mem. Am. Mgmt. Assn., Apple Profl. Exch. (gen. mgr. 1989-90), Apple Cons. Rels. Bd., Marin County C. of C. Republican. Office: 148 Bon Air Shopping Ctr Greenbrae CA 94904-2417

CATALDO, RENZO MARIO, cardiologist; b. Bklyn., Aug. 6, 1962; s. Calogero and Lidia (Parovel) C. MD, U. Trieste, 1987. Intern St. Vincent's Med. Ctr., Staten Island, N.Y., 1988-89; resident L.I. Jewish Hosp., New Hyde Park, N.Y., 1989-91; fellow in cardiology U. Utah, Salt Lake City, 1991—. Grantee Am. Heart Assn., 1993-94. Mem. Utah Med. Assn., Am. Coll. Cardiology Affiliates in Tng. Democrat. Roman Catholic. Office: U Utah Divsn Cardiology 50 N Medical Dr Salt Lake City UT 81132-0001

CATANESE, PETER ANTHONY, military officer; b. Kittanning, Pa., Jan. 9, 1965; s. Peter and Mary Ann (Gundy) C. BS in Bus. Mgmt., Ind. U. of Pa., 1987. Commd. 2d lt. U.S. Army, 1987; advanced through grades to capt.; surveyor platoon leader F Battery, 333d Field Artillery, Hanau, Germany, 1988-89, counterfire officer, 1989-91, radar platoon leader, 1991; supply and svcs. officer 68th Corps Support Bn., Fort Carson, Colo., 1992-94; comdr. 73d maintenance co. Fort Carson, 1994—. Decorated Bronze

Star, 1991. Mem. U.S. Field Artillery Assn., Assn. Quartermasters, Armed Forces Comm. Electronics Assn., Assn. US Army, VFW. Roman Catholic. Home: 1410 Michelle Ct Apt A Colorado Springs CO 80916-1917 Office: 73d Maintenance Co Fort Carson CO 80913-5000

CATE, BENJAMIN WILSON UPTON, journalist; b. Paris, France, Sept. 28, 1931; s. Karl Springer and Josephine (Wilson) C.; children: Christopher, Stephanie. B.A., Yale U., 1955. Reporter St. Petersburg (Fla.) Times, 1955-60; corr. Time mag., Los Angeles, 1960-61, Detroit, 1961-65; chief Houston bur. Time mag., 1965-68; corr. Time mag., Paris, 1968-69; chief Bonn. (Fed. Republic of Germany) bur. Time mag., 1969-72; dep. chief of corrs. Time mag., N.Y.C., 1972-75; chief Midwest bur. Time mag., Chgo., 1975-81; chief West Coast bur. Time mag., Beverly Hills, Calif., 1981-85; spl. asst. to pub. Time mag., Los Angeles, 1985-86, sr. corr., 1987; polit. editor Sta. KCRW-FM, Santa Monica, Calif., 1987-88; freelance writer, 1989—. Served with U.S. Army, 1955-57. Mem. Sigma Delta Phi. Club: Chgo. Press. Home: 10583 Dunleer Dr Los Angeles CA 90064-4317

CATE, FLOYD MILLS, electronic components executive; b. Norfolk, Va., Aug. 2, 1917; s. Floyd Mills and Ellen (Lewis) C.; m. Ann Willis, Jan. 31, 1943; 1 child Carol Cate Webster. B.A. U. Tenn., 1940; student exec. program UCLA, 1958; B.A. (hon.) Calif. Inst. Tech., 1947. With special sales dept. Cannon Electric Co., Los Angeles, 1940-46, western sales mgr., 1946-50, with internat. sales dept., 1950-57, v.p. sales, mktg., 1957-62, pres. internat. sales, 1958-62, v.p. sales and mktg. electronics, 1962-69; v.p. sales, mktg. divsn. Japan Aviation Electronics Zemco, Irvine, Calif., 1977-80, cons., 1977-80; pres., owner F.E.S. Cons., San Clemente, Calif., 1968-94; 2R engrng. cons. dir., San Marcos, Calif., 1987-94; consulting agent LHC Shorecliff Golf Club; U.S.A. agent Ocean Resources Engr. Co-chmn. Ron Packard for Congress, San Clemente, 1984; chmn. ad hoc com. Sea Sade Village, 1986-94; pres. Assn. Shorecliffs Residence, San Clemente, 1986-94; dir. La Christianitos pagents Samaritan Hosp. Guild. Mem. IEEE, Internat. Electric Electronic Engrs., San Clemente C. of C., San Clemente Hist. Soc. Democrat. Roman Catholic. Club: Shorecliff Golf (bd. dirs. San Clemente). Office: 205 Via Montego San Clemente CA 92672-3625

CATER, JUDY JERSTAD, librarian; b. San Francisco, Jan. 20, 1951; d. Theodore S. and Estelle E. (Christian) Jerstad; m. Jack E. Cater, Nov. 24, 1973; children: Joanne Jerstad, Jennifer Jerstad. AB, Mount Holyoke Coll., 1973; MS, Simmons Coll., 1974; MA, U. San Diego, 1984. Cert. libr., libr. tech., supr. chief adminstrv. officer. Cataloging libr. Palomar Coll., San Marcos, Calif., 1975-76, fine arts, evening reference libr., 1976-77, acquisitions libr., 1977-86, media svcs., acquisitions libr., 1988-90, chair, v.p. instrn. search, 1987-88, dir. libr. media ctr., 1986-88, 90-92, media svcs. libr., 1993—; cons., manuscript asst. Presidio Army Mus., Calif. Hist. Soc., San Francisco, 1974-75; rschr. Charles H. Brown Archaeol. Site, San Diego, 1977; adj. faculty mem. history dept., 1990—. Pres. Mount Holyoke Club of San Diego, 1982-86. Recipient stipend Simmons Coll. Sch. Libr. Sci., 1979, Girl Scouts of San Diego and Imperial Counties Disting. Leader award, 1990, Faculty Svc. award Palomar Coll., 1990, NISOD Excellence award, 1991. Mem. ALA, Calif. Libr. Assn. (sec. treas. 1986, membership chair 1987, minority scholarship com. 1991-93, awards and scholarships com. 1993—), Calif. Tchrs. Assn. (pres. Palomar Coll. chpt. 1979-80), Faculty Assn. Calif. Cmty. Colls., Am. Assn. Women in Cmty. and Jr. Colls. Episcopalian. Office: Palomar Coll Libr 1140 W Mission Rd San Marcos CA 92069-1415

CATHERWOOD, HUGH ROBERT, public administration consultant; b. Chgo., July 6, 1911; s. Robert and Lucy Cotton (Morris) C.; m. Frances Maughs, May 31, 1941 (dec. 1963); children: Jane, Nancy; m. Jean Williams, Sept. 5, 1967. BA, Yale U., 1933. Project dir. Griffenhagan Assocs., 1935-42; dir. budget and pers. City of Denver, 1947-53; pres. Western Wood Preserving, Denver, 1954-60, Shannon (Ireland) Repair Svcs., 1960-64; ptnr., pub. adminstrn. cons. Kansas-Denver Assocs., Denver, 1967—; clients include cities of Houston, Amarillo, El Paso, Texarkana, Tex., Boulder, Colorado Springs, Denver, Colo., states of Mont., La., Mich., Va., numerous counties and individual corps.; chief of party J.L. Jacobs Co., Govt. of Saudi Arabia, Riyadh, 1966-67; arbitrator Fed. Mediation and Conciliation Svc. Contbr. articles and opinion pieces to various publs. Lt. comdr. USNR, 1947-92. Mem. Univ. Club N.Y., Univ. Club Chgo., Univ. Club Denver, Denver Country Club, Denver City Club, Colo. Physicians for Social Responsibility (bd. dirs.) SCORE (officer). Democrat. Episcopalian. Home and Office: 130 Lafayette St Denver CO 80218-3923

CATLIN, JAMES C., conservationist, land use planner, electrical engineer; b. Evanston, Ill., Dec. 11, 1947; s. James MacKenzie and Mary Jane (Carr) C. BS in Electrical Engring., Oreg. State U., 1971; MS in Civil Engring., U. Utah, 1980; PhD, U. Calif., Berkeley, 1995. Tchr. Peace Corps., The Gambia, West Africa, 1971-73; field svc. engr. Internat. Computers Ltd., London, 1974-76; field svc. supr. Evans & Sutherlund, Salt Lake City, 1977-90. Co-editor, co-pub., cartography team leader, contbg. photographer Wilderness at the Edge, A citizen Proposal to Protect Utah's Canyons and Deserts, 1990; contbg. photographer, asst. editor Utah's Unprotected Wilderness, 1991. Recipient Conservation award Souther Utah Wilderness Alliance, 1989; Switzer fellow San Francisco, 1992, Sigma Xi grantee Sci. Rsch. Soc. N.C., 1993. Mem. Soc. Am. Foresters, Soc. Range Mgmt., Sierra Club (chmn. conservation Utah chpt. 1981-89, chair BLM subcom. pub. lands com. 1986-93, regional v.p. southwest 1988-89, John Muir award 1992), Utah Wilderness Coalition (bd. dirs. 1986-90). Office: U Calif Berkeley Environ Sci Policy & Mgmt Dept Berkeley CA 94720

CATRAMBONE, EUGENE DOMINIC, public relations consultant; b. Chgo., June 5, 1926; s. Nicola and Maria Theresa (Catrambone) C.; m. Mary Gloria Gaimari, Mar. 26, 1951; children: Mary, Eugene Jr., Jane, David, Jill. BA, St. Benedict Coll., 1950; postgrad., Kans. State U., 1952-54; MA, DePaul U., 1960; postgrad., UCLA, 1962-63. Cert. secondary tchr., coll. instr., Calif. Tchr. high schs. Chgo., 1950-62, L.A., 1963-88; cons. pub. rels. Westlake Village, Calif., 1986—; tech. writer U. Chgo., 1956-59, Douglas Missile div. USN, L.A. and Ventura, Calif., 1962-75; reporter, editor Las Virgenes Enterprise, Calabasas, Calif., 1968-75; evening instr. L.A. City Coll., 1965-68. Author: Requiem for a Nobody, 1993, The Golden Touch: Frankie Carle, 1981; poem "Exit dust", 1982; contbr. articles on edn. to profl. publs., 1959-60, feature stories to local newspapers, 1968-75. Sgt. U.S. Army, 1944-46. Recipient Fostering Excellence award L.A. Unified Sch. Dist., 1986-87, nominee Apple award, 1986. Mem. NEA (life), Calif. Tchrs. Assn., Book Publicists So. Calif., United Tchrs. L.A., Am. Legion, Westlake Village Men's Golf Club (pub. rels. editor 1986—, bd. dirs., pres. 1989—). Democrat. Roman Catholic. Home: 31802 Tynebourne Ct Westlake Village CA 91362 Office: Golden Touch Assocs 31802 Tynebourne Ct Westlake Village CA 91362-4132

CATTANACH, RICHARD L., contractor; b. Stanley, Wis., Feb. 28, 1942; s. Bert Cornwall and Katherine Mary (Lamont) C.; m. Mary M. Cattanach, May 7, 1976; children: Thomas Burke, Shaun Eric, Eric Lamont. BBA, U. Wis., Whitewater, 1964; MSBA, U. Denver, 1966; PhD, Ariz. State U., 1971. CPA, Alaska, Ariz. Asst. prof. U. Miss., Oxford, 1971-73, U. Denver, 1973-74; contr. Alaska Bank of Commerce, 1974-77; asst. to v.p. Nat. Tech. Inst. for the Deaf, Rochester, N.Y., 1977-80; v.p. Unit Co., Anchorage, 1980—; dir. Workers Compensation Com. of Alaska, 1980-91; chmn. Mgmt./Labor Ad Hoc Workers Compensation Com., 1983-92; chmn. Alaskans for Liability Reform, 1992—. Recipient Alaska Hard Hat award for contbns. to constrn. industry, 1994. Mem. Assoc. Gen. Contractors (sec.-treas. 1991, v.p. 1992, pres. 1993, bd. dirs. 1986—), Fin. Execs. Inst. (sec. to pres. 1985-88). Episcopalian. Home: 2103 Sorbus Way Anchorage AK 99518 Office: Unit Co 8101 Old Seward Hwy Anchorage AK 99518-3359

CATTANEO, JACQUELYN ANNETTE KAMMERER, artist, educator; b. Gallup, N.Mex., June 1, 1944; d. Ralph John and Gladys Agnes (O'Sullivan) Kammer; m. John Leo Cattaneo, Apr. 25, 1964; children: John Auro, Paul Anthony. Student Tex. Woman's U., 1962-64. Portrait artist, tchr. Gallup, N. Mex., 1972; coord. Works Progress Adminstrn. art project renovation McKinley County, Gallup, Octavia Fellin Performing Arts wing dedication, Gallup Pub. Library; formation com. mem. Multi-modal/Multi-Cultural Ctr. for Gallup, N.Mex.; exch. with Soviet Women's Com., USSR Women Artists del., Moscow, Kiev, Leningrad, 1990; Women Artists del. and exch. Jerusalem, Tel Aviv, Cairo, Israel; mem. Artists Del. to Prague, Vienna and Budapest.; mem. Women Artists Del. to Egypt, Israel and Italy, 1992, Artist Del. Brazil, 1994. One-woman shows include Gallup Pub. Libr., 1963, 66, 77, 78, 81, 87, Gallup Lovelace Med. Clinic, Santa Fe Station Open House, 1981, Gallery 20, Farmington, N.Mex., 1985—, Red Mesa Art Gallery, 1989, Soviet Restrospect Carol's Art & Antiques Gallery, Liverpool, N.Y., 1992, N.Mex. State Capitol Bldg., Santa Fe, 1992, Lt. Govt. Casey Luna-Office Complex, Women Artists N.Mex. Mus. Fine Arts, Carlsbad, 1992, Rio Rancho Country Club, N.Mex., 1995; group shows include: Navajo Nation Library Invitational, 1978, Santa Fe Festival of the Arts Invitational, 1979, N.Mex. State Fair, 1978, 79, 80, Catharine Lorillard Wolfe, N.Y.C., 1980, 81, 84, 85, 86, 87, 88, 89, 91, 92, 4th ann. exhbn. Salmagundi Club, 1984, 90, 3d ann. Palm Beach Internat., New Orleans, 1984, Fine Arts Ctr. Taos, 1984, The Best and the Brightest O'Brien's Art Emporium, Scottsdale, Ariz., 1986, Gov.'s Gallery, 1989, N.Mex. State Capitol, Santa Fe, 1987, Pastel Soc. West Coast Ann. Exhbn. Sacramento Ctr. for Arts, Calif., 1986-90, gov.'s invitational Magnifico Fest. of the Arts, Albuquerque, 1991, Assn. Pour La Promotion Du Patrimone Artistique Français, Paris, Nat. Mus. of the Arts for Women, Washington, 1991, Artists of N.Mex., Internat. Nexus '92 Fine Art Exhbn., Trammell Corw Pavilion, Dallas, Carlsbad (N.Mex.) Mus. Fine Art; represented in permanent collections: Zuni Arts and Crafts Ednl. Bldg., U. N.Mex., C.J. Wiemar Collection, McKinley Manor, Gov.'s Office, State Capitol Bldg., Santa Fe, Historic El Rancho Hotel, Gallup, N.Mex., Sunwest Bank. Fine Arts Ctr., En Taos, N.Mex., Armand Hammer Pvt. Collection, Wilcox Canyon Collections, Sadona, Ariz., Galaria Impi, Netherlands, Woods Art and Antiques, Liverpool, N.Y., Stewarts Fine Art, Taos, N.Mex. Mem. Dora Cox del. to Soviet Union-U.S. Exchange, 1990. Recipient Cert. of Recognition for Contbn. and Participation Assn. Pour La Patrinome Du Artistique Français, 1991, N.Mex. State Senate 14th Legislature Session Meml. # 101 for Artistic Achievements award, 1992, Award of Merit, Pastel Soc. West Coast Ann. Membership Exhbn., 1993. Mem. Internat. Fine Arts Guild, Am. Portrait Soc. (cert.), Pastel Soc. of W. Coast (cert.), Mus. N.Mex. Found., Mus. Women in the Arts, Fechin Inst., Artists' Co-op. (co-chair), Gallup C. of C., Gallup Area Arts and Crafts Council, Am. Portrait Soc. Am., Pastel Soc. N.Mex., Catharine Lorillard Wolfe Art Club of N.Y.C. (oil and pastel juried membership), Chautaugua Art Club, Soroptimists (Internat. Woman of Distinction 1990). Address: 210 E Green St Gallup NM 87301-6130

CATTELL, MARGUERITA BRIANA, veterinarian, researcher; b. Boston, Dec. 25, 1961; d. William Channing Cattell and Joan Leonard Chadbourne. BS, Colo. State U., 1987, DVM, 1991. Cons. DDX Inc., Boulder, Colo., 1992-94; staff veterinarian Duo Dairy Ltd., Loveland, Colo., 1992-94; rsch. dir. Dairy Rsch. & Tech., Loveland, 1994—; instr. Colo. State U., 1993-94. Contbr. articles to profl. jours. Fellow Fulbright Found., 1987-88. Mem. Am. Vet. Medicine Assn., Am. Assn. Bovine Practioners, Nat. Mastitis Coun., Am. Minor Breed Conservancy. Home: PO Box 430 Windsor CO 80550-0430 Office: Dairy Rsch & Tech 6875 NCR 9 Loveland CO 80538

CATTELL, RODERIC GEOFFREY GALTON, computer scientist; b. Urbana, Ill., May 4, 1953; s. Raymond Bernard and Alberta Karen (Schuettler) C.; m. Nancy Worner, Aug. 11, 1973 (div. 1981); 1 child, Eric; m. Susan Gail Fraenkel, Feb. 14, 1987; children: Aaron, Elliott. BS in Computer Sci. and Psychology, U. Ill., 1974; PhD in Computer Sci., Carnegie-Mellon U., 1978. Rsch. scientist Carnegie-Mellon U., Pitts., 1978, Xerox PARC, Palo Alto, Calif., 1978-84; 2d level mgr. Sun Microsystems, Mountain View, Calif., 1984-88, disting. engr., 1988—; mem. tech. adv. bd. several object-oriented software cos., 1988—; chmn. Object Data Mgmt. Group, 1991—. Author: Formalization and Automatic Derivation of Code Generators, 1978, Object Data Management, 1991, The Object Database Standard ODMG-93, 1993; also articles. Mem. IEEE, Assn. for Computing Machinery. Office: Sun Microsystems 2550 Garcia Ave Mountain View CA 94043-1109

CATTERTON, MARIANNE ROSE, occupational therapist; b. St. Paul, Feb. 3, 1922; d. Melvin Joseph and Katherine Marion (Bole) Maas; m. Elmer John Wood, Jan. 16, 1943 (dec.); m. Robert Lee Catterton, Nov. 20, 1951 (div. 1981); children: Jenifer Ann Dawson, Cynthia Lea Uthus. Student, Carleton Coll., 1939-41, U. Md., 1941-42; BA in English, U. Wis., 1944; MA in Counseling Psychology, Bowie State Coll., 1980; postgrad., No. Ariz. U., 1987-91. Registered occupational therapist, Occupational Therapy Cert. Bd. Occupational therapist VA, N.Y.C., 1946-50; cons. occupational therapist Fondo del Seguro del Estado, Puerto Rico, 1950-51; dir. rehab. therapies Spring Grove State Hosp., Catonsville, Md., 1953-56; occupational therapist Anne Arundel County Health Dept., Annapolis, Md., 1967-78; dir. occupational therapy Eastern Shore Hosp. Ctr., Cambridge, Md., 1979-85; cons. occupational therapist Kachina Point Health Ctr., Sedona, Ariz., 1986; regional chmn. Conf. on revising Psychiat. Occupational Therapy Edn., 1958-59; instr. report writing Anne Arundel Community Coll., Annapolis, 1974-78. Editor Am. Jour. Occupational Therapy, 1962-67. Active Md. Heart Assn., 1959-60; mem. task force on occupational therapy Md. Dept. of Health, 1971-72; chmn. Anne Arundel Gov. Com. on Employment of Handicapped, 1959-63; mem. gov.'s com. to study vocat. rehab., Md., 1960; com. mem. Annapolis Youth Ctr., 1976-78; mem. ministerial search com. Unitarian Ch. Anne Arundel County, 1962; curator Dorchester County Heritage Mus., Cambridge, 1982-83; v.p., officer Unitarian-Universalist Fellowship Flagstaff, 1988-93; co-moderator, founder Unitarian-Universalist Fellowship of Sedona, 1994—, respite care vol., 1994—; citizen interviewer Sedona Acad. Forum, 1993, 94. Mem. P.R. Occupational Therapy Assn. (co-founder 1950), Am. Occupational Therapy Assn. (chmn. history com. 1958-61), Md. Occupational Therapy Assn. (del. 1953-59), Ariz. Occupational Therapy Assn., Pathfinder Internat., Dorchester County Mental Health Assn. (pres. 1981-84), Internat. Platform Assn., Ret. Officers Assn., Air Force Assn. (Barry Goldwater chpt., sec. 1991-92, 94-95), Severn Town Club (treas. 1965, sec. 1991-92, 94-95), Internat. Club (Annapolis, publicity chmn. 1966), Toastmasters, Newcomers (Sedona, pres. 1986), Zero Population Growth, Delta Delta Delta. Republican. Home: 415 Windsong Dr Sedona AZ 86336-3745

CATZ, BORIS, endocrinologist, educator; b. Troyanov, Russia, Feb. 15, 1923; s. Jacobo and Esther (Galbmilion) C.; came to U.S., 1950, naturalized, 1955; m. Rebecca Schechter; children: Judith, Dinah, Sarah Lea, Robert. BS, Nat. U. Mexico, 1941, MD, 1947; MS in Medicine, U. So. Calif., 1951. Intern, Gen. Hosp., Mexico City, 1945-46; prof. adj., sch. medicine U. Mexico, 1947-48; research fellow medicine U. So. Calif., 1949-51, instr. medicine, 1952-54, asst. clin. prof., 1954-59, assoc. clin. prof., 1959-83, clin. prof., 1983—; pvt. practice, Los Angeles, 1951-55, Beverly Hills, Calif., 1957—; chief Thyroid Clinic Los Angeles County Gen. Hosp., 1955-70; sr. cons. thyroid clin. U. So. Calif.-Los Angeles Med. Center, 1970—; clin. chief endocrinology Cedars-Sinai Med. Ctr., 1983-87. Served to capt. U.S. Army, 1955-57. Boris Catz lectureship named in his honor Thyroid Research Endowment Fund, Cedars Sinai Med. Ctr., 1985. Fellow ACP, Am. Coll. Nuclear Medicine (pres. elect 1982), Royal Soc. Medicine; mem. AMA, AAAS, Cedars Sinai Med. Ctr. Soc. for History of Medicine (chmn.), L.A. County Med. Assn., Calif. Med. Assn., Endocrine Soc., Am. Thyroid Assn., Soc. Exptl. Biology and Medicine, Western Soc. Clin. Research, Am. Fedn. Clin. Research, Soc. Nuclear Medicine, So. Calif. Soc. Nuclear Medicine, N.Y. Acad. Scis., L.A. Soc. Internal Medicine, Collegium Salerni, Cedar Sinai Soc. of History of Medicine, Beverly Hills C. of C., Phi Lambda Kappa. Jewish. Mem. B'nai B'rith. Club: The Profl. Man's (past pres.). Author: Thyroid Case Studies, 1975, 2d edit., 1981. Contbr. numerous articles on thyroidology to med. jours. Home: 300 S El Camino Dr Beverly Hills CA 90212-4212 Office: 435 N Roxbury Dr Beverly Hills CA 90210

CAUDILL, SAMUEL JEFFERSON, architect; b. Tulsa, June 5, 1922; s. Samuel Jefferson and Maymie Starling (Boulware) C.; m. Joy Maxwell, May 31, 1952; children: Jody Caudill Cardamone, Julie, Samuel Boone, Robert Maxwell, Anne Goertzen,. BArch, Cornell U., Ithaca, N.Y., 1946. Registered architect, Colo., Calif., Ind., Idaho., Wyo., Ariz., N.Mex. Prin. architect Samuel J. Caudill, Jr., Aspen, Colo., 1954-59, Caudill Assocs. Architects, Aspen, 1959-80; pres. Caudill Gustafson & Assocs. Architects, P.C., Aspen, 1980-87, Caudill Gustafson Ross & Assocs., Architects, P.C., Aspen, 1987-92, Caudill Gustafson & Assocs., Architects, P.C., Aspen, 1992—; mem. Pitkin County Planning and Zoning Commn., Colo., 1955-58; mem. outdoor edn. com. Colo. Dept. Edn., 1966-68; chmn. Pitkin County Bd. Appeals, 1970; mem. Colo. Water Quality Control Commn., 1977-80. Wildlife rep. adv. bd. Bur. Land Mgmt. Dept. Interior, Grand Junction, Colo., 1969-75, 80-85; chmn. citizens adv. com. Colo. Hwy. Dept. for I-70 through Glenwood Canyon, 1975-92; chmn. Colo. Wildlife Commn., 1978-79. Recipient Outstanding Pub. Service Bur. Land Mgmt., 1975. Fellow AIA (Community Svc. award 1976, Architect of Yr. award 1992); mem. Colo. Soc. Architects (pres. 1983), Colo. Coun. on Arts and Humanities, Aspen C. of C. (pres. 1956-57), Masons, Shriners (Denver). Home: Maroon Creek Aspen CO 81612 Office: Caudill Gustafson & Assocs Architects PC 234 E Hopkins Ave Aspen CO 81611-1938 also: Caudill Gustafson & Assoc PO Box Ff Aspen CO 81612-7433

CAUDLE, JONES RICHARD, III, marketing and management consultant; b. Houston, Sept. 11, 1954; s. J.R. and Mary Ann C.; married; children: Madeline, Tessa. BA with honors, U. Tex., 1976; MBA, Am. Grad. Sch. Internat. Mgmt., Phoenix, 1977. Account exec. Ogilvy & Mather Advt., Houston, 1976-78; brand mgr. Coca-Cola Foods, Houston, 1978-81; cons. Gemini Cons., L.A., 1981-83; dir. mktg. Celestial Seasonings, Boulder, Colo., 1983-87; owner Caudle Assocs., Denver, 1987-89, 91—; v.p. mktg. and sales Keystone (Colo.) Resort, 1989-91. Bd. dirs. Nat. Reporatory Orch., Keystone, 1990-92. Mem. Denver Athletic Club. Office: Caudle Associates 630 Vine St Denver CO 80206-3738

CAUDRON, JOHN ARMAND, accident reconstructionist, technical forensic investigator; b. Compton, Calif., Sept. 26, 1944; s. Armand Robert and Evelyn Emma (Hoyt) C.; m. Marilyn Edith Fairfield, Mar. 16, 1968; children: Melita, Rochelle. AA, Ventura Coll., 1965; BA, Calif. State U., Fullerton, 1967; postgrad., U. Nev., 1975-78; MS, U. So. Calif., 1980. Dist. rep. GM, Reno, 1969-75; mgr. Snyder Rsch. Lab., Reno, 1976-78, v.p., El Monte, Calif., 1978-82, pres., 1982-85; prin. Fire and Accident Reconstruction, Rowland Heights, Calif., 1985—. Pub. accident reconstrn. newsletter. With U.S. Army, 1967-69. Mem. ASCE, Am. Soc. Safety Engrs., Nat. Fire Protection Assn., Geol. Soc. Am., Firearms Rsch. and Identification Assn. (pres. 1978—), Am. Soc. Metals, Nat. Safety Coun., Nat. Soc. Profl. Engrs., Nat. Assn. Profl. Accident Redonstruction Specialists, Ft. Tejon Hist. Assn. (info. adviser 1983—). Republican. Baptist. Avocations: hiking, traveling, photography. Office: Fire & Accident Reconstrn 17524 E Colima Rd Ste 360 La Puente CA 91748-1750

CAUFIELD, MARIE CELINE, religious organization administrator; b. Chgo., Aug. 11, 1929; d. John Patrick and Anna Marie (Clear) C. MA in Religious Edn., Fordham U., 1975; DMin in Creative Ministry (hon.), Grad. Theol. Found., Bristol, Ind., 1989. Elem. prin. St. Martin's Sch., Kankakee, Ill., 1952-64; missionary Congregation de Notre Dame, Guatemala, Ctrl. Am., 1964-71; dir. religious edn. St. Colomba, N.Y.C., 1971-75, St. Bernard, Pirtleville, Ariz., 1975-76; dir. Hispanic ministry Diocese of Providence (R.I.), Central Falls, 1976-81; dir. of the Office of Hispanic ministry Roman Cath. Diocese of Boise, 1981—. Author numerous poems; contbr. articles to profl. jours. Bd. dirs. Cath. Migrant Farmworkers' Network, Toledo, 1992—; founder Idaho's Cath. Golden Age Chpt., Boise, 1983-87. Grantee Am. Bd. Cath. Missions, 1991. Mem. Nat. Writers Assn., Fedn. of Returned Overseas Missioners (N.W. contact person 1990-94). Roman Catholic. Home: 1111 N 17th St Boise ID 83702-3306 Office: Roman Cath Diocese of Boise 303 Federal Way Boise ID 83705-5925

CAUGHEY, CYNTHIA LOUISE, agency executive director; b. Harrisburg, Pa., Aug. 25, 1958; d. Robert Walter and Dorothy Birtha (Sharpless) C. Grad. in Liberal Arts, Roberts U., 1981; MA, Fuller Sem., 1987. Counselor Shadow Mountain Inst., Okla., 1981-82, personnel coord./quality assurance coord., 1982-84; program dir. women's concerns com. Fuller Grad. Sch., Pasadena, Calif., 1985-87; dir. YWCA Hestia House, Pasadena, Calif., 1988-91; exec. dir. Women's Care Cottages, San Fernando Valley, Calif., 1991—; fundraising cons. L.A. Women's Arts Bldg. Active numerous homelessness coalitions, women's and feminist orgns. Named Women of Yr., Bus. and Profl. Women's Club, 1993. Democrat. Episcopalian. Office: Womens Care Cottage 12828 Victory Blvd # 294 North Hollywood CA 91606-3013

CAUGHLIN, STEPHENIE JANE, organic farmer; b. McAllen, Tex., July 23, 1948; d. James Daniel and Betty Jane (Warnock) C. BA in Family Econs., San Diego State U., 1972, MEd, 1973; M. in Psychology, U.S. Internat. U., San Diego, 1979. Cert. secondary life tchr., Calif. Owner, mgr. Minute Maid Svc., San Diego, 1970-75; prin. Rainbow Fin. Svcs., San Diego, 1975-78; tchr. San Diego Unified Sch. Dist., 1973-80; mortgage broker Santa Fe Mortgage Co., San Diego, 1980-81; commodity broker Premex Commodities, San Diego, 1981-84; pres., owner Nationwide Futures Corp., San Diego, 1984-88; owner, sec. Nationwide Metals Corp.; owner, gen. mgr. Seabreeze Organic Farm, 1984—. Sec. Arroyo Sorrento Assn., Del Mar, Calif., 1978—. Mem. Greenpeace Nature Conservancy, DAR, Sierra Club, Jobs Daus. Republican. Avocations: horseback riding, swimming, skiing, gardening. Home and Office: 3909 Arroyo Sorrento Rd San Diego CA 92130-2610

CAULFIELD, CARLOTA, education educator; b. Havana, Cuba, Jan. 16, 1953; came to U.S., 1981; d. Francis and Ada (Robaina) C.; m. Servando Gonzalez, May 1973; 1 child, Franco Caulfield Gonzalez. BA, U. Havana, 1979; MA, San Francisco State U., 1986; PhD, Tulane U., 1992. Lectr. San Francisco State U., 1985-86; publ., editor Literary Gazette/El Gato Tuerto, San Francisco, 1984-88; from teaching asst. to rsch. asst. Tulane U., New Orleans, 1988-92; asst. prof. Hispanic studies Mills Coll., Oakland, Calif., 1992—; free-lance acquisitions editor Mercury House, San Francisco, 1988-90; free-lance copy editor John Wiley & Sons, Inc., N.Y.C., 1988. Author: Visual Games for Words and Sounds, 1993, (poems) Angel Dust, 1990, Oscurita Divina, 1990, 34th Street, 1987. Cintas fellow, 1988, Quigley fellow Mills Coll., 1994; Nat. Hispanic scholar, 1991; Mellon Summer Rsch. grantee Tulane U., 1990; recipient Honorable Mention Premio Plural, Mex., 1993, Internat. Poetry prize Ultimo Novecento, 1988. Mem. MLA, Latin Am. Jewish Studies Assn., Philol. Assn. the Pacific Coast, PEN Internat., Gruppo Internat. Lettura (hon., pres. U.S. chpt. 1988—), Libera Acad. Galileo Galilei (hon.). Office: Mills Coll 5000 Macarthur Blvd Oakland CA 94613-1301

CAULFIELD, W. HARRY, health care industry executive, physician; b. Waverly, N.Y., Aug. 22, 1936; m. Mary Sisk; children: Mary, Harry, James, Michael. AB, Harvard U., 1957, postgrad., 1976; MD, U. Pa., 1961. Diplomate Am. Bd. Internal. Medicine, Am. Bd. Cardiology. Rotating intern Hosp. U. Pa., 1961-62; resident Pa. Hosp., 1962-64; fellow in cardiology Georgetown U. Hosp., 1964-66; dir. ICU Kaiser Found. Hosp., San Francisco, 1969-75, asst. chief of staff, 1971-75, chief of staff, 1975-80; physician-in-chief, mem. exec. com. Permanente Med. Group, San Francisco, 1975-80, mem. internal medicine staff cardiology, 1968—, from exec. dir.-elect to exec. dir., 1990—; assoc. clin. prof. medicine U. Calif., San Francisco. Capt. U.S. Army Med. Corps, 1966-68. Fellow Am. Coll. Cardiology, Am. Heart Assn.; mem. AMA (adv. com. on group practice physicians 1994—, fedn. study consortium 1994—), San Francisco Med. Soc. (alt. del. to Calif. Med. Assn. 1992, del. 1993-94, managed care task force, leadership devel. com.), Calif. Med. Assn., Calif. Hosp. Assn. (membership com. 1987), Am. Hosp. Assn., Calif. Acad. Medicine, Am. Group Practice Assn. (trustee 1994—, vice chmn. bylaws com. 1994—), Soc. Med. Adminstrs., Group Health Assn. Am. (bd. dirs. 1994—). Office: Permanente Med Group Inc 1950 Franklin St Oakland CA 94612-5103

CAVAGNARO, EDMUND WALTER, radio station executive; b. San Francisco, Feb. 25, 1952; s. Walter John and Loretta (Monahan) C.; m. Barbara Ann Goode, June 10, 1978; 1 child, Elizabeth. BA, U. Calif., Berkeley, 1974; MJ, Northwestern U., 1975. Adminstrv. asst. San Francisco Bd. Suprs., 1976-77; editor KCBS Radio, San Francisco, 1978-81, asst. mng. editor, 1981-83, mng. editor, 1984-85, asst. dir. news and programming, 1985-88, dir. news and programming, 1988—. Chmn. Bay Region Emergency Broadcast System Com., San Francisco, 1991—; mem. fire task force City of Oakland, Calif., 1991-92; vol. basketball and baseball coach YMCA, San Francisco, 1991-92. Recipient Peabody award U. Ga., 1990, duPont-Columbia award Columbia U., 1990. Mem. Radio-TV News Dirs. Assn. (Edward R. Murrow award 1990, 94, 95). Office: KCBS-AM 1 Embarcadero Ctr San Francisco CA 94111-3607

CAVALLI-SFORZA, LUIGI LUCA, genetics educator; b. Genoa, Italy, Jan. 25, 1922; came to U.S., 1970; s. Pio and Attilia (Manacorda) C.; m. Albamaria Ramazzotti, Jan. 12, 1946; children: Matteo, Francesco, Tommaso, Violetta. MD, U. Pavia (Italy), 1944; MA, Cambridge U. (Eng.), 1950; DSc (hon.), Columbia U., 1980. Asst. rsch. Istituto Sieroterapico Milanese, Milan, Italy, 1945-48, dir. rsch., 1950-57; prof. genetics U. Parma, 1951-62; prof. genetics, dir. Istituto di Genetica, U. Pavia, 1962-70; prof. genetics Stanford (Calif.) U., 1970-92, chmn., 1986-90, chmn. emeritus, 1992—. Vice-pres. Internat. Congress Genetics, Tokyo, Japan, 1968. Served as med. officer, Italian Army, 1947-48. Recipient T.H. Huxley award in anthropology, 1972, Weldon award in biometry, 1975, Allen award Human Genetics Premio Acad. Lincei, 1982, Catalonia award, 1993. Fellow Gonville and Caius Coll. Cambridge U. (hon.); mem. Am. Soc. Human Genetics (pres. 1989), Accad. dei Lincei (nat.), Am. Acad. Arts and Scis. (fgn. hon.), Japanese Soc. Human Genetics (fgn. hon.), Royal Soc. London (fgn. hon.), U.S. Nat. Acad. Sci. (fgn. hon.). Author: (with W. Bodmer) The Genetics of Human Populations, 1971; Genetics, Evolution and Man, 1976; (with M. Feldman) Cultural Transmission and Evolution, 1981, (with A. Ammerman) The Neolithic Transition in Europe, 1984; editor: African Pygmies, 1986, (with Francesco Cavalli-Sforza, in Italian) Chi Siamo? A History of Human Diversity, 1993, (with P. Menozzi and A. Piazza) History and Geography of Human Genes, 1994. Office: Stanford U Dept Genetics Stanford CA 94305

CAVANAGH, JOHN CHARLES, advertising agency executive; b. San Francisco, Dec. 19, 1932; s. John Timothy and Alicia Louise (McDowell) C.; m. Mary Ann Anding, Apr. 10, 1959; children: Karen, Brad. Student, U. Hawaii, 1950; BS, U. San Francisco, 1954. Pub. rels. rep. Kaiser Industries Corp., Oakland, Calif., 1956-58; pub. rels. mgr. Kaiser Cement & Gypsum Corp., Oakland, 1958-63; pub. relations dir. Fawcett-McDermott Assos. Inc., Honolulu, Hawaii, 1964-66; ops. v.p. Fawcett-McDermott Assos. Inc., 1966-69, exec. v.p., 1969-73, pres., dir., 1973-75; pres., dir. Fawcett McDermott Cavanagh Inc., Honolulu, 1975-87, Fawcett McDermott Cavanagh Calif., Inc., San Francisco, 1975-87; pres. The Cavanagh Group/Advt. Inc., Honolulu, 1987—. Served to 1st. lt. 740th Guided Missile Bn. AUS, 1954-56. Named Advt. Man of Yr. Honolulu Advt. Fedn., 1985. Mem. Pub. Rels. Soc. Am. (accredited, v.p. 1970, pres. Hawaii chpt. 1971), Advt. Agy. Assn. Hawaii (pres. 1973), Am. Assn. Advt. Agys. (chmn. Hawaii coun. 1980-81), Affiliated Advt. Agys. Internat. (chmn. 1984-85), Sonoma County Ad Club, Fountaingrove Country Club, Outrigger Canoe Club, Commonwealth Club of Calif. Home and Office: 3750 Saint Andrews Dr Santa Rosa CA 95403-0945 also: 1142 Auahi St Ste 3007 Honolulu HI 96814-4900

CAVANAUGH, MICHAEL ARTHUR, secondary education educator, retired sociologist; b. Tacoma, Feb. 16, 1953; s. Robert Paul and Lorraine Florence Bertha (Teske) C. AA, Fla. Keys C.C., Key West, 1973; BA in Religion, Fla. State U., 1975, MA in Religion, 1977; PhD in Sociology, U. Pitts., 1983. Instr. Temple U., Phila., 1983-85; co-adjutant prof. Rutgers U., Camden, N.J., 1983-85; sr. wine cons. Emissary/Aura Ltd., Orange, Calif., 1986; instr. L.A. (Calif.) Cmty. Coll. Dist., 1986—, Calif. State U., Northridge, 1988-90; certificated employee L.A. (Calif.) Unified Sch. Dist., 1989—. Contbr. articles to profl. jours. Charles E. Merrill fellow Fla. State U., 1975-76, Andrew W. Mellon fellow U. Pitts., Pa., 1981-83, Vis. fellow UCLA, L.A., 1985-86. Mem. Assn. for Sociology Religion. Home: 1851 W 11th Pl Los Angeles CA 90006-4101

CAVE, ALAN WAYNE, psychologist; b. Muscatine, Iowa, June 19, 1958; s. Wayne L. and Marlene L. (Schoeneman) C. Student, Kirkwood Coll., Cedar Rapids, Iowa, 1979-81; PhB, U. Iowa, 1982, M Health Sci., 1985, D of Psychology, 1989. Juvenile detention officer Linn County Juvenile Detention, Cedar Rapids, 1979-81; counselor, advocate Tommy Dale Meml. Hosp., Cedar Rapids, 1981-82; rsch. assoc. U. Iowa Hosps., Iowa City, 1982-84; staff therapist Hartgrove Hosp., Chgo., 1984-87; pvt. practice Chgo., 1987—; cons. Planning Collective, L.A., 1989-91. Co-author: (textbook) Client Variables in Psychotherapy, 1989. Bd. dirs. Concerned Citizen's Youth Ctr., Chgo., 1990-91. Lutheran.

CAVERS-HUFF, DASIEA YVONNE, philosopher; b. Cleve., Oct. 24, 1961; d. Lawrence Benjamin and Yvonne (Warner) Cavers; m. Brian Jay Huff, July 26, 1986. BA, Cleve. State U., 1984, MA, 1988; postgrad., U. Md., 1986-90, U. Calif., Riverside, 1995. Teaching asst. Cleve. State U., 1983-86; instr. Upward Bound program Case Western Res. U., Cleve., 1986; instr. U. Md., Coll. Park, Md., 1987-89; mem. faculty Charles County Community Coll., 1989-90; asst. prof. Riverside Community Col., 1990—. U. Md. grad. fellow, 1986-87; Ford Found. predoctoral fellow, 1987-89. Mem. Am. Philos. Assn., Minority Grad. Student Assn. (co-chmn. U. Md. 1987-88). Democrat. Home: 25969 Andre Ct Moreno Valley CA 92553-6824 Office: Riverside City Coll Humanities and Social Scis Div Riverside CA 92506

CAVEZZA, CARMEN JAMES, career officer; b. Scranton, Pa., Nov. 15, 1937; s. James Vincent and Rose (Verdetto) C.; m. Joyce Mae Mathews, Apr. 30, 1960; 1 child, Peggy Joi Cavezza Anders. BA in Polit. Sci., The Citadel, 1961; MA in Govt., U. Miami, 1961; MS in Internat. Affairs, George Washington U., 1977, PhD, 1993, PhD in Polit. Sci., 1993; grad. inf. officers' basic course, Fort Benning, 1961, grad. inf. officers' advanced course, 1967; grad., USM Corps. Commd. and Staff Coll., 1972, U.S. Nat. War Coll., 1977. Commd. 2d lt. U.S. Army, 1961, advanced through grades to lt. gen.; bn. comdr. 2d Inf. Div. U.S. Army, Republic of Korea, 1975-76; div. chief mil. pers. U.S. Army, Alexandria, Va., 1977-81; comdr. 197th Inf. Brigade (mech.) U.S. Army, Fort Benning, Ga., 1981-84; asst. div. comdr. 82d Airborne Div. U.S. Army, Fort Bragg, N.C., 1986-87; comdg. gen. 7th Inf. Div. (light) and Fort Ord, Calif. U.S. Army, 1987-89; comdg. gen. Inf. Ctr. U.S. Army, Fort Benning, 1989-91; comdg. gen. I Corps and Fort Lewis, Wash. U.S. Army, 1991—; exec. dir. Columbus 96 Support Com. for Olympic Games. Decorated D.S.M., Silver Star with oak leaf cluster, D.F.C. with oak leaf cluster, Bronze Star with four oak leaf clusters, Purple Heart, Legion of Merit with two oak leaf clusters, Meritorious Svc. medal with two oak leaf clusters, Army Commendation medal with three oak leaf clusters. Mem. Assn. of U.S. Army, The Citadel Alumni Assn., Rotary (Columbus, Ga.). Home: 6301 Cape Cod Dr Columbus GA 31904-2915 Office: Columbus 96 PO Box 1519 Columbus GA 31902-1519

CAVIGLI, HENRY JAMES, petroleum engineer; b. Colfax, Calif., Mar. 14, 1914; s. Giovanni and Angelina (Giachi) C.; m. Ruth Loree Denton, June 11, 1942; children: Henry James Jr., Robert D., Paul R., Loree Ann McIntire. BS in Petroleum Engring., U. Calif., Berkeley, 1937, MS in Mech. Engring., 1947. Sr. engr. Chevron Corp., Rio Vista, Calif., 1954-57, supt. No. Calif., 1958-69; mgr. non operated joint ventures Chevron Corp., LaHabra, Calif., 1970-76; cons. Cavigli & Mee, petroleum cons., Sacramento, Calif., 1976—. Author: Escapades in the Blue, 1995. Mem. sch. bd. Rio Vista High Sch., 1962-67. Maj. USAF, 1942-47. Decorated Bronze Star with 4 oak leaf clusters. Mem. Soc. Petroleum Engrs., Petroleum Prodn. Pioneers, Calif. Conservation Commn. Oil Producers (chmn. 1971-72), Sutter Club, C. of C., Lion, Sigma Xi, Theta Tau Epsilon. Republican. Roman Catholic. Home: 6271 Eichler St Sacramento CA 95831-1864 Office: Cavigli & Mee PO Box 22815 Sacramento CA 95822-0815

CAVNAR, MARGARET MARY (PEGGY CAVNAR), business executive, former state legislator, nurse, consultant; b. Buffalo, July 29, 1945; d. James John and Margaret Mary Murtha Nightengale; BS in Nursing, D'Youville Coll., 1967; MBA, Nat. U., 1989; m. Samuel M. Cavnar, 1977; children: Heather Anne Hicks, Heide Lynn Gibson, Dona Cavnar Hambly, Judy Cavnar Bentrim. Utilization rev. coord. South Nev. Meml. Hosp., Las Vegas, 1975-77; v.p. Ranvac Publs., Las Vegas, 1976—; ptnr. Cavnar & Assocs., Reseda, Calif., 1976—, C & A Mgmt., Las Vegas, 1977—; pres. PS Computer Svc., Las Vegas, 1978—; bd. mem. Nev. Eye Bank, 1987-89, exec. dir., 1990-91; dir. of health fairs Centel & CH13TV, 1991-94; pres., bd. dirs. Bridge Counseling Assocs. Mem. Clark County Republican Cen. Com., 1977-87, Nev. Rep. Cen. Com., 1978-80; mem. Nev. Assembly, 1979-81; Rep. nominee for Nev. Senate, 1980; Rep. nominee for Congress from Nev. 1st dist., 1982, 84; bd. dirs., treas. Nev. Med. Fed. Credit Union; v.p. Cmty. Youth Activities Found., Inc., Civic Assn. Am.; mem. utilization rev. bd. Easter Seals; trustee Nev. Sch. Arts, 1980-87; nat. adviser Project Prayer, 1978—; co-chmn. P.R.I.D.E. Com., 1983—; co-chmn. Tax Limitation Com., 1983, Personal Property Tax Elimination Com., 1979-82, Self-Help Against Food Tax Elimination Denial Com., 1980; mem. nat. bd. dirs., co-chmn. Nev. Pres. Reagan's Citizens for Tax Reform Com., 1985-88; mem. Nev. Profl. Stds. Rev. Orgn., 1984; co-chmn. People Against Tax Hikes, 1983-84; bd. dirs. Nev. Eye Bank, 1988-90. Mem. Nev. Order Women Legislators (charter, parliamentarian 1980—), Cosmopolitanly Hers Info. (pres.), Sigma Theta Tau.

CAVNAR, SAMUEL MELMON, author, publisher, activist; b. Denver, Nov. 10, 1925; s. Samuel Edward and Helen Anita (Johnston) C.; m. Peggy Nightengale, Aug. 14, 1977; children by previous marriage: Dona Cavnar Hambly, Judy Cavnar Bentrim; children: Heather Anne Hicks, Heide Lynn. Student pub. schs., Denver. Dist. mgr. U.S. C. of C., various locations, 1953-58; owner Cavnar & Assocs., mgmt. cons., Washington, Las Vegas, Nev., Denver and Reseda, Calif., 1958—; v.p. Lenz Assoc. Advt., Inc., Van Nuys, Calif., 1960—; dist. mgr. Western States Nu-Orm Plans, Inc., Los Angeles, 1947-52; cons. to architect and contractor 1st U.S. Missile Site, Wyo., 1957-58; prin. organizer Westway Corp. and subsidiaries, So. Calif. Devel. Co., 1958—; chmn. bd. Boy Sponsors, Inc., Denver, 1957-59; pres. Continental Am. Video Network Assn. Registry, Inc., Hollywood, Calif., 1967—; pres. United Sales Am., Las Vegas and Denver, 1969—; sr. mgmt. cons. Broadcast Mgmt. Cons. Service, Hollywood, Las Vegas, Denver, Washington, 1970—; pres., dir., exec. com. Am. Ctr. for Edn., 1968—; pub. Nat. Ind., Washington, 1970—, Nat. Rep. Statesman, Washington, 1969—, Nat. Labor Reform Leader, 1970—, Nat. Conservative Statesman, 1975—; owner Ran Vac Pub., Las Vegas and Los Angeles, 1976—; ptnr. P.S. Computer Services, Las Vegas, 1978—, C & A Mgmt., Las Vegas, 1978—, Westway Internat., 1983—; lectr. in field; spl. cons. various U.S. senators, congressmen, 1952—. Author: Run, Big Sam, Run, 1976, The Girls on Top, 1978, Big Brother Bureaucracy, The Cause and Cure, 1977, Kiddieland West, 1980, Games Politicians Play: How to Clean Up Their Act, 1981, A Very C.H.I.C. President, 1981, How to Clean Up Our Act, 1982, Assassination By Suicide, 1984, How to Get Limited Government, Limited Taxes, 1985, Tax Reform or Bust, 1985, At Last: Real Tax Reform, 1986, On the Road to a Real Balanced Budget, 1989, It's Time for Term Limitation, 1990, Clinton's "Investments": Just More Taxes, 1993, Hillary-Billary's New Road to Socialism, 1993. Nat. gen. chmn. Operation Houseclean, 1966-81; nat. candidate chmn. Citizens Com. To Elect Rep. Legislators, 1966, 68, 70, 72-74, 85—; mem. Calif. and Los Angeles County Rep. Cen. Coms., 1964-70; nat. gen. chmn. Project Prayer, 1962—; exec. dir. Project Alert, 1961—; nat. chmn. Nat. Labor Reform Com., 1969—; sustaining mem. Rep. Nat. Com., 1964—; Western states chmn. and nat. cochmn. Am. Taxpayers Army, 1959—; area II chmn. Calif. Gov.'s Welfare Reform Com., 1970; chmn. Com. Law and Order in Am., 1975; mem. Nev. State Rep. Com., 1972—; mem. Clark County Rep. Com., 1972—; bd. dirs. Conservative Caucus, Las Vegas, 1974, 76, 82, 92; Rep. candidat for U.S. Senate from Nev., 1976, 82, 92; Rep. nominee for U.S. Congress from 30th dist. Calif., 1968, 70; nat. chmn. Return Pueblo Crew, 1968, Citizens League for Labor Reform, 1984—; nat. co-chmn. U.S. Taxpayers Forces, 1985—; pres., trustee Community Youth Activities Found., 1977—; nat. chmn. Operation Bus Stop, 1970—, P.R.I.D.E. Com., 1981—, Positivics Program, 1982—; co-chmn. Question 8 Com., 1980-82, S.H.A.F.T.E.D. Tax Repeal Com., 1982 C.H.I.C. Polit. Edn. Com., 1977—, People Against Tax Hikes Com., 1983—; bd. dirs., Nev. co-chmn. Pres. Reagan's Citizen's Com. for Tax Reform, 1985-86; nat. chmn. Term Limitation Com., 1988—; nat. chmn. Combined Coms. for Republican's Contract With Am., 1994—; chmn. Citizen's To Return Barloon and Daliberti, 1995—. Served with USN, 1942-45, USAF, 1950-53, Korea; comdr. USCG Aux., 1959-60. Recipient Silver medal SAR. Mem. Am. Legion (comdr. 1947-48, mem. nat. conv. disting. guest com. 1947-52), DAV, VFW, Am. Security Council (nat. adviser 1966—), U.S. C. of C. (sr. mem. rep. 1986—). Home: 301A Misty Isle Ln Las Vegas NV 89107-1117 Office: 1615 H St NW Washington DC 20062-0001

CAWLEY, LEO PATRICK, pathologist, immunologist; b. Oklahoma City, Aug. 11, 1922; s. Pat Bernard and Mary Elizabeth (Forbes) C.; m. Joan Mae Wood, May 20, 1948; children: Kevin Patrick, Karin Patricia, Kary Forbes. BS in Chemistry, Okla. State U., 1948; MD, Okla. Sch. Medicine, 1952. Diplomate Am. Bd. Pathology, Am. Bd. Nuclear Medicine, Am. Bd. Allergy and Immunology, Am. Bd. Med. Lab. Immunology, Am. Bd. Med. Genetics. Intern Wesley Med. Ctr., Wichita, 1952-53, resident in pathology, 1953-54; resident in pathology Wayne County Gen. Hosp., Eloise, Mich., 1954-56, chief resident in pathology, 1956-57; clin. pathologist, asst. dir. lab. Wesley Med. Ctr., Wichita, Kans., 1957-69, dir. sci., 1965-86, dir. labs., 1969-77, dir. clin. immunology, 1979-86; med. dir. Roche Biomed. Lab., Wichita, Kans., 1979-86; dir. clin. labs. Iatric Corp., Tempe, Ariz., 1988—; pres. Kilcawley Enterprises, 1986—. Author: Electrophoresis/Immunoelectric Phoresis, 1969; editor series Lab Med Little Brown, 1965-81; contbr. 210 articles to profl. jours. Pfc. USM, 1942-45. Fellow Am. Soc. Clin. Pathologist (bd. dirs. 1968, Disting. Svc. award 1980), Coll. Am. Pathologist; mem. AAAS, ACS, Am. Assn. Clin. Chemists, Alpha Pi Mu, Phi Lambda Upsilon, Alpha Omega Alpha. Office: KilCawley Enterprises 133 W San Francisco St Santa Fe NM 87501-2111

CAWOOD, ELIZABETH JEAN, public relations executive; b. Santa Maria, Calif., Jan. 6, 1947; d. John Stephen and Gertrude Margaret (Shelton) Dille; m. Neil F. Cawood, Jan. 4, 1975; 1 child, Nathan Patrick. BA, Whitworth Coll., 1964-68. Dir. pub. info. Inland Empire Goodwill, Spokane, Wash., 1967-72; adminstrv. asst. N.W. Assn. Rehab. Industries, Seattle, 1973-74; pres., counselor Cawood Comm., Eugene, Oreg., 1974—; pres. Women in Comm., Inc., 1981-83; advisor U. Oreg. chpt. Pub. Rels. Soc. Am., 1987-91; active Benton Lane Lincoln Linn Region Stragegy Bd., 1993—, chair, 1993-94. Editor: Dictionary of Rehabilitation Acronyms, (newsletters) INTERCOM, Family Communicator, Oreg. Focus, (dictionary) Work-Oriented Rehabilitation Dictionary and Synonyms, 1st and 2nd edits. Bd. dirs. Laurel Hill Ctr., Lane County Boy Scouts Am., Eugene Action Forum, 1981-86, Birth-to-Three, 1982-85, Lane County chpt. ARC, 1982-83, 84-89, Lane County chpt. Am. Cancer Soc., 1984-87, Eugene Opera, 1985-88, Joint Com. Econ. Diversification, 1985-89, 91-93, Lane County United Way, 1987-93, Lane Econ. Com., vice chmn., 1990—; bd. dirs. So. Willamette Pvt. Industry Coun., 1985-88, pres., 1988; chmn. Eugene Pvt. Industries Coun., 1981-83, vice chmn., 1983-84; chmn. Bus. Owners Network, Eugene, 1980-81; advisor Eugene Jr. League. Mem. LWV (bd. dirs. 1979), Pub Rels. Soc. Am. (bd. dirs. Columbia River chpt. 1987-88, pres. Greater Oreg. chpt. 1991-92, bd. dirs. 1991-93), Nat. Rehab. Assn. (pres. 1980-81), Profl. Women's Network (bd. dirs. Oreg. chpt. 1982), Eugene C. of C. (bd. dirs. 1980-87, 92—, chmn. econ. devel. 1982-83, bd. dirs. exec. com. 1984-87, v.p. 1987, 93, chmn. edn. com., pres.-elect 1994, pres. 1995), Mid-Oreg. Advt. Club (bd. dirs. 1985-87), Oreg. Sales and Mktg. Execs. (bd. dirs. 1985-87), Eugene/Springfield Assn. Quality and Performance (chmn. 1991-93, bd. dirs. 1991-94), Internat. Assn. Sports and Human Performance (bd. dirs. 1993), Eugene City Club (bd. dirs. 1992—, pres.-elect 1995). Office: Cawood Communications 1200 High St Ste 21 Eugene OR 97401-3222

CAYETANO, BENJAMIN JEROME, governor, former state senator and representative; b. Honolulu, Nov. 14, 1939; s. Bonifacio Marcos and Eleanor (Infante) C.; m. Lorraine Gueco, Sept. 20, 1958; children: Brandon, Janeen, Samantha. B.A., UCLA, 1968; J.D., Loyola U., 1971. Bar: Hawaii 1971. Practiced in Honolulu, 1971-86; mem. Hawaii Ho. of Reps., 1975-78, Hawaii Senate, 1979-86; lt. gov. State of Hawaii, 1986-95, gov., 1994—; bar examiner Hawaii Supreme Ct., 1976-78, disciplinary bd., 1982-86; arbitration panel 1st Cir. Ct. State of Hawaii, 1986; adv. U. Hawaii Law Rev., 1982-84. Mem. bd. regents Chaminade U., 1980-83; mem. adv. council U. Hawaii Coll. Bus. Adminstrn., 1982-83. Recipient Excellence in Leadership Medallion Asia-Pacific Acad. Consortium for Pub. Health, 1991, UCLA Alumni award for excellence in pub. svc., 1993. Democrat. Office: Office of Gov State Capitol 5th Fl Honolulu HI 96813

CAYNE, DOUGLAS ANDREW, computer company executive; b. Cambridge, Mass., Mar. 8, 1958; s. Bernard Stanley and Helen Marie (Burgard) C.; m. Madoka Etoh, Aug. 20, 1977 (div. 1981). BA, Stanford U., 1980. Analyst Hudson Inst., Croton-on-Hudson, N.Y., 1978-80; rsch. analyst McKinsey & Co., L.A., 1980-81; v.p. Gartner Group, Inc., Stamford, Conn., 1981-91; group v.p., gen. mgr. Gartner Group, Inc., Santa Clara, Calif., 1992—. Office: Gartner Group Inc 5201 Great America Pky Ste 219 Santa Clara CA 95054-1126

CAYSE, PHYLLIS, federal mediator; b. Newark, N.J., Oct. 7, 1930; d. Isadore Helen (Blackman) Smith; m. Aaron H. Schectman, Dec. 24, 1950 (div. Apr. 1973); children: David, Hal; m. Raymond T. Cayse, July 25, 1976. BA, Douglass Coll., 1952. Cert. tchr., N.J.; commd. Fed. Mediation and Conciliation. Libr. asst. Newark Pub. Libr., 1952-54; tchr. Metuchen (N.J.) Pub. Schs., 1954-56, Woodbridge Pub. Schs., Colonia, N.J., 1964-67, Ocean Twp. Pub. Schs., Ocean Twp., N.J., 1967-68; hearing officer N.J. Pub. Employee Rels., Trenton, 1968-72; field agt. Nat. Labor Rels. Bd., Newark, 1973-74; commr. Fed. Mediation and Conciliation Svc., St. Louis and L.A., 1974—; nominating com. mem. Soc. for Profls. in Dis. Res., St. Louis, L.A., 1974-80. Mem. Indsl. Rels. Rsch. Assn. (exec. bd. mem., sec.-treas. L.A. 1990-93), Nat. Trust for Historic Preservation, Smithsonian, Holocaust Mus. Office: Fed Mediation/Conciliation Svc 225 W Broadway Glendale CA 91204

CAYWOOD, THOMAS ELIAS, business educator, consultant; b. Lake Park, Iowa, May 9, 1919; s. Harry E. and Alice A. (Bollenbach) C.; m. Mary E. Miller, June 6, 1941; children: Ann, Beth, Kay Dee. AB, Cornell Coll., Mt. Vernon, Iowa, 1939; MA, Northwestern U., 1940; PhD, Harvard U., 1947. Sr. mathematician Inst. Air Weapons Rsch. U. Chgo., 1947-50, coord. rsch., 1950-52; supr. ops. rsch. Armour Rsch. Found., Chgo., 1952-53; mng. ptnr. Caywood-Schiller Assocs., Chgo., 1953-70; v.p. Caywood-Schiller div. A.T. Kearney and Co., Chgo., 1970-78; lectr. grad. sch. bus. U. Chgo., 1953-58, 78-86, sch. bus. econs. Calif. State U., Hayward, 1981—; pres. Investigacion de Operaciones S.A. (Mex.), 1959-60; mem. R & D bd. Dept. Def., 1952-53, chmn. panel on ordinance transport and supply, 1959-64, def. sci. bd., 1960-64. Bd. dirs. Cornell Coll. Alumni Assn., 1962-65, trustee, 1964—, pres. bd. trustees 1970-73. Mem. Am. Math. Assn., Am. Inst. Indsl. Engrs., Am. Math. Soc., Ops. Rsch. Soc. Am. (editor 1961-68, pres. 1969-70). Home: 704 Argyle Ave Flossmoor IL 60422-1204 Office: Calif State U Sch Bus & Econs Hayward CA 94542

CAZARES, HECTOR ROBERT, county executive, director of animal control; b. San Diego, Jan. 22, 1945; s. Carlos Barboa and Norberta (Amaya) C.; m. Sandra Mae Callahan, Mar. 21, 1967; children: Tish, Ron, Jeremy, Corey, Joel. AA, Southwestern Cmty. Coll., 1969; BA, San Diego State U., 1972. Asst. dir. animal control County of San Diego, 1983-93, dir. animal control, 1993—. V.p. Sweetwater Valley Civic Assn., Bonita, Calif., 1993; mem. VFW, San Diego, 1994. Named Highest Ranking Hispanic in Animal Control in U.S. Mem. Calif. Animal Control Dirs. Assn. (v.p., bd. dirs. 1982—), Soc. Animal Welfare Adminstrs., County of San Diego Exec. Assn., San Diego County Latino Assn. (exec. bd. mem. 1985—). Office: County Dept Animal Control 5480 Gaines St San Diego CA 92110-2624

CAZARES, ROGER, community improvement executive. AA in Applied Scis., Southwestern Coll., Chula Vista, Calif., 1966; BA in Social Scis., San Diego State U., 1969. Supr. electronic data processing dept. San Diego Trust and Savs. Bank, 1965-69; OJT developer, counselor MAAC Project, National City, Calif., 1969-71; asst. dir. CASA Justicia, National City, 1971-72; planning dir. MAAC Project, National City, 1972-75, exec. dir., pres., CEO, 1975—; bd. dirs. San Diego BanCorp. Mem. San Diego County Charter Rev. Com., San Diego Literacy Coun., Mayor's Hispanic Adv. Com., Calif. Urban Forestry Bd., Com. on Racial and Ethnic Balance, Adv. Com. on Adult Detention, San Diego Gas & Electric PEP Com., Communities Untied for Econ. Justice; chair San Diego Job Corps; bd. dirs. Am. Youth Soccer Orgn.; numerous others. Served with U.S. Army, 1960-62. Mem. Nat. City C. of C. (pres.), Chula Vista C. of C., Hispanic C. of C.

CAZIER, BARRY JAMES, electrical engineer, software developer; b. Phoenix, May 10, 1943; s. James Henry and Dorothy Marie (Lynton) C.; m. Susan Arline Shewey, June 13, 1964 (dec. July 1979); children: Suzanne, Bryan; m. Illene D. Miller, Dec. 19, 1994. Student, Colo. Sch. Mines, 1961-62; BSEE, U. Colo., 1965; student advanced bus. adminstrn., Ariz. State U., 1974-77. Mfg. mgmt. Gen. Electric, Richland, Wash., 1965-66, Warren, Ohio, 1966-67; system engr. Gen. Electric, Schenectady, N.Y., 1967-69; project mgr. Honeywell, Phoenix, 1970-80, dir. field ops., 1980-85, program mgr., 1985—; prin. Cazier Software Designs, Scottsdale, Ariz., 1985—. adv. Jr. Achievement, Phoenix, 1972. Club: IBM PC Users (Phoenix). Home: 8508 E Via Montoya Scottsdale AZ 85255-4936 Office: Honeywell 16404 N Black Canyon Hwy Phoenix AZ 85023-3033

CEBRICK, JOAN ALICE, fitness educator; b. Swoyersville, Pa., Dec. 13, 1964; d. Andrew Henry and Dolores Jean (Warick) C. BS, King's Coll., 1986; MS, Colo. State U., 1989, postgrad., 1989—. Cert. CPR, first aid and water safety instr. ARC. Personal fitness trainer, aerobic instr. Hollywood (Fla.) Beach Resort Health Spa, 1986; adult fitness staff swim program Colo. State U., Ft. Collins, 1987-90, instr. exercise and sports sci., 1987-92, 94, faculty instr., univ. wellness coord., 1992-94; med. officer Wildwoodcrest Beach Patrol, 1990; nutrition cons., adult fitness staff Colo. State U., Ft. Collins, 1991-92; aerobic and swimming instr., fitness cons. Ft. Collins Pulse Health Club, 1990—. Contbr. articles to profl. jours. Mem. Byzantine Catholic Ch. Mem. Am. Dietetic Assn. (registered dietitian), Internat. Sports Med. Assn. (faculty instr.), Aerobic Assn. Internat. (faculty instr.), Am. Coll. Sports Medicine, Soc. for Nutrition Edn. Democrat. Roman Catholic. Home: 1117 City Park Ave Apt H9 Fort Collins CO 80521-4474

CECH, THOMAS ROBERT, chemistry and biochemistry educator; b. Chicago, Ill., Dec. 8, 1947; m. Carol Lynn Martinson; children: Allison E., Jennifer N. BA in Chemistry, Grinnell Coll., 1970, DSc (hon.), 1987; PhD in Chem., U. Calif., Berkeley, 1975; DSc (hon.), U. Chgo., 1991; Drury Coll., 1994. Postdoctoral fellow dept. biology MIT, Cambridge, Mass., 1975-77; from asst. prof. to assoc. prof. chemistry U. Colo., Boulder, 1978-83, prof. chemistry and biochemistry also molecular cellular and devel. biology, 1983—, disting. prof., 1990—; research prof. Am. Cancer Soc., 1987—; investigator Howard Hughes Med. Inst., 1988—; co-chmn. Nucleic Acids Gordon Conf., 1984; Phillips disting. visitor Haverford Coll., 1984; Vivian Ernst meml. lectr. Brandeis U., 1984, Cynthia Chan meml. lectr. U. Calif., Berkeley; mem. Welch Found. Symposium, 1985; Danforth lectr. Grinnell Coll, 1986; Pfizer lectr. Harvard U., 1986; Verna and Marrs McLean lectr. Baylor Coll. Medicine, 1987; Harvey lectr., 1987; Mayer lectr. MIT, 1987; Martin D. Kamen disting. lectureship, U. Calif., San Diego, 1988; Alfred Burger lectr. U. Va., 1988; Berzelius lectr. Karolinska Inst., 1988; Osamu Hayaishi lectr. Internat. Union Biochemistry, Prague, 1988; Beckman lectr. U. Utah, 1989, HHMI lectr. MIT, 1989; Max Tishler lectr. Merck, 1989; Abbott vis. scholar U. Chgo., 1989; Herriott lectr. Johns Hopkins U., 1990; J.T. Baker lectr., 1990; G.N. Lewis lectr. U. Calif., Berkeley, 1990; Sonneborn lectr. Ind. U., 1991; Sternbach lectr. Yale U., 1991; W. Pauli lectr., Zürich, 1992; Carter-Wallace lectr. Princeton U., 1992; Hastings lectr. Harvard U., 1992; Stetten lectr. NIH, 1992; Dauben lectr. U. Wash., 1992; Marker lectr. U. Md., 1993; Hirschmann lectr. Oberlin Coll., 1993; Beach lectr. Purdue U., 1993; Abe White lectr. Syntex, 1993; Robbins lectr. Pomona Coll., 1994; T.Y. Shen lectr. MIT, 1994; Bren lectr. U. Calif., Irvine, 1994. Assoc. editor Cell, 1986-87, RNA Jour.; mem. editl. bd. Genes and Development; dep. editor Sci. mag. NSF fellow, 1970-75, Pub. Health Service research fellow Nat. Cancer Inst. 1975-77, Guggenheim fellow, 1985-86; recipient medal Am. Inst. Chemists, 1970, Research Career Devel. award Nat. Cancer Inst., 1980-85, Young Sci. award Passano Found., 1984, Harrison Howe award, 1984, Pfizer award, 1985, U.S. Steel award, 1987, V.D. Mattia award, 1987, Louisa Gross Horowitz prize, 1988, Newcombe-Cleveland award AAAS, 1988, Heineken prize Royal Netherlands Acad. Arts and Scis., 1988, Gairdner Found. Internat. award, 1988, Lasker Basic Med. Rsch. award, 1988, Rosenstiel award, 1989, Warren Triennial prize, 1989, Nobel prize in Chemistry, 1989, Hopkins medal Brit. Biochemical Soc., 1992, Feodor Lynen medal, 1995; named to Esquire Mag. Register, 1985, Westerner of Yr. Denver Post, 1986. Mem. AAAS, Am. Soc. Biochem. Molecular Biology, NAS, Am. Acad. Arts and Scis., European Molecular Biology Orgn., RNA Soc. (v.p. 1993—). Office: U Colo Dept Chemistry & Biochemistry Boulder CO 80309

CECI, JESSE ARTHUR, violinist; b. Phila., Feb. 2, 1924; s. Luigi Concezio and Catherine Marie (Marotta) C.; m. Catherine Annette Stevens, Aug. 5, 1979. BS, Juilliard Sch. Music, 1951; license de concert, L'Ecole Normale de Musique, Paris, 1954; MusM, Manhattan Sch. Music, 1971. Assoc. concertmaster New Orleans Philharm. Orch., 1953-54; violinist Boston Symphony Orch., 1954-59, N.Y. Philharm. Orch., N.Y., 1959-62, Esterhazy Orch., N.Y.C., 1962-68; concertmaster Denver Symphony Orch., 1974-89, Colo. Symphony Orch., 1989—; over 50 solo performances of 22 major works; mem. Zimbler Sinfonietta, Boston, 1957-59; participant Marlboro

Festival Chamber Orch. Vt., summmers 1960-62, 65, Marlboro Festival Chamber Orch. European-Israeli tour, 1965, Grand Teton Festival, Wyo., 1972, N.Mex. Festival, Taos, 1980, Carmel (Calif.) Bach Festival, 1987—, Whistler (B.C., Can.) Mozart Festival, 1989-90; mem. faculty N.Y. Coll. Music, 1961-71, NYU, 1971-74, U. Colo., 1975-79; guest faculty Univ. Denver, 1986; mem., assoc. concertmaster Casals Festival Orch., San Juan, P.R., 1963-77; violinist Cleve. Orch. fgn. tours, 1967, 73, 78, Cin. Symphony Orch. world tour, 1966; 1st violinist N.Y. String Quartet in-residence at U. Maine, Orono, summer 1969; concertmaster Minn. Orch., summers 1970-71; guest concertmaster Pitts. Symphony Orch., Pitts., L.A., 1988, mem. N.Y. Philharmonia Chamber Ensemble in-residence at Hopkins Ctr., Dartmouth U., summer 1973; recitalist, Paris, 1963, Amsterdam, 1963, recitalist Carnegie Recital Hall, N.Y.C., 1963, Town Hall, N.Y.C., 1968, 70, Alice Tully Hall, N.Y.C., 1972; fgn. tour Pitts. Symphony Orch., 1989. Concertmaster Denver Chamber Orch., 1985-90; faculty Congress of Strings, Dallas, 1985. Served to cpl. U.S. Army, 1943-46, PTO. Fulbright fellow Paris, 1951-52. Democrat. Roman Catholic. Office: Colo Symphony Orch 1031 13th St Denver CO 80204-2156

CEDERBERG, DOLORES KATHERINE, elementary education educator, school administrator; b. Chgo., May 5, 1929; d. Robert Olen and Margaret Russell (Merrifield) Dunn.; m. Donald Wesley Cederberg, Aug. 21, 1953 (dec. Feb. 1986); children: Katherine Christine, Robert Wesley. BA, Macalester Coll., St. Paul, 1951; student, Nat. U. Mex., 1953, Columbia U., 1960-62, U. Oxford, Eng., 1972; MA, Stony Brook (N.Y.) U., 1972. Art tchr. Omaha Pub. Schs., 1951-53; art supr. Edina (Minn.) Pub. Schs., 1953-54; jr. high art tchr. Union Free Sch. Dist. #16, Elmont, N.Y., 1954-58; third grade tchr. Union Free Sch. Dist. #4, Northport, N.Y., 1958-60; second grade tchr. Half Hollow Hill Sch. Dist. #5, Dix Hills, N.Y., 1964-87; adminstr. Clark Fork Sch., 1994-95. Mem. Half Hollow Hills Tchrs. Assn. (exec. bd. del.-at-large 1972-87, negotiator 1971-86, profl. standard chairperson 1973-87); elected to sch. bd. dist. #1, Missoula, Mont., 1988-94; bd. dirs. YWCA, 1991-95; instr. U. Mont. Art Edn., summer 1993, 94, 95; pres. Art Assocs., Missoula Mus. of Arts, 1992, Unitarian/Universalist fellowship, 1992-94. Mem. Am. Fedn. Tchrs. (citation for svc. 1987, del. 1984-87), Half Hollow Hills Tchrs. Assn. (svc. award 1987), N.Y. State United Tchrs. (del. retirement bd. 1979-81), Western Mont. Ret. Tchrs. Assn. (pres. 1990-92).

CEDOLINE, ANTHONY JOHN, psychologist; b. Rochester, N.Y., Sept. 19, 1942; s. Peter Ross and Mary J. (Anthony) C.; m. Clare Marie De Rose, Aug. 16, 1964; children: Maria A., Antonia C., Peter E. Student, U. San Francisco, 1960-62; BA, San Jose State U., 1965, MS, 1968; PhD in Ednl. Pscyhology, Columbia Pacific U., 1983. Lic. ednl. psychologist, sch. adminstr., marriage, family, child counselor, sch psychologist, sch. counselor, social worker, Calif.; Lic. real estate broker, Calif. Mng. ptnr. Cienega Valley Vineyards and Winery (formerly Almaden Vineyards) and Comml. Shopping Ctrs., 1968—; coord. psychol. svcs. Oak Grove Sch. Dist., San Jose, Calif., 1968-81, asst. dir. pupil svcs., 1977-81; dir. pupil svcs. Oak Grove Sch. Dist., San Jose, 1981-83; pvt. practice, ednl. psychologist Ednl. Assocs., San Jose, 1983—; co-dir. Biofeedback Inst. of Santa Clara County, San Jose, 1976-83; ptnr. in Cypress Ctr.-Ednl. Psychologists and Consultancy, 1978—; cons., program auditor for Calif. State Dept. Edn.; instr. U. Calif., Santa Cruz and LaVerne Coll. Ext. courses; guest spkr. San Jose State U.; lectr., workshop presenter in field. Author: Occupational Stress and Job Burnout, 1982, A Parents Guide to School Readiness, 1971, The Effect of Affect, 1975; contbr. articles to profl. jours. and newspapers. Founder, bd. dirs. Lyceum of Santa Clara County, 1971—. Mem. NEA, Calif. Tchrs. Assn., Calif. Assn. Sch. Psychologists, Nat. Assn. Sch. Psychologists, Council for Exceptional Children, Calif. Assn. for Gifted, Assn. Calif. Sch. Adminstrs., Calif. Personnel & Guidance Assn., Biofeedback Soc. Am., Nat. Assn. Realtors, Calif. Assn. Realtors, San Jose Realty Bd., Tau Delta Phi. Home and Office: 1183 Nikulina Ct San Jose CA 95120-5441

CELLA, JOHN J., freight company executive; b. 1940; married. BBA, Temple U., 1965. Regional mgr. Japan ops. Airborne Freight Corp., Seattle, 1965-71, v.p. Far Ea. ops., 1971-72, sr. v.p. internat. div., from 1982, now exec. v.p. internat. div. Office: Airborne Freight Corp 3101 Western Ave Seattle WA 98121-1024

CENARRUSA, PETE T., secretary of state; b. Carey, Idaho, Dec. 16, 1917; s. Joseph and Ramona (Gardoqui) C.; m. Freda B. Coates, Oct. 25, 1947; 1 son, Joe Earl. B.S. in Agr., U. Idaho, 1940. Tchr. high sch. Cambridge, Idaho, 1940-41, Carey and Glenns Ferry, Idaho, 1946; tchr. vocat. agr. VA, Blaine County, Idaho, 1946-51; farmer, woolgrower, nr. Carey, 1946-95; mem. Idaho Ho. of Reps., 1951-67, speaker, 1963-67; sec. state Idaho, 1967-90, 91-94; mem. Idaho Bd. Land Commrs., Idaho Bd. Examiners; pres. Idaho Flying Legislators, 1953-63; chmn. Idaho Legis. Council, 1964—, Idaho Govt. Reorgn. Com.; Idaho del. Council State Govts., 1963—. Elected ofcl., mem. BLM Adv. Coun., Boise Dist.; Rep. adminstr. Hall of Fame, 1978. Maj. USMCR, 1942-46, 52-58. Named Hon. Farmer Future Farmers Am., 1955; named to Agrl. Hall of Fame, 1973; Idaho Athletic Hall of Fame, 1976, Basque Hall of Fame, 1983. Mem. Blaine County Livestock Mktg. Assn., Blaine County Woolgrowers Assn. (chmn. 1954), Carey C. of C. (pres. 1952), U. Idaho Alumni Assn., Gamma Sigma Delta, Tau Kappa Epsilon. Republican. Office: Office of Sec State State Capital Rm 203 Boise ID 83702

CENTER, ELIZABETH MERCY, biology educator; b. Sterling, Ill., Aug. 11, 1928; d. Ernest W. and Florence A. (Neary) Moothart; m. Hugh Lipton Center, Sept. 9, 1951; 1 child, Hugh Stuart. AB in Biology, Augustana Coll., Rock Island, Ill., 1950; PhD in Biology, Stanford U., 1957. Lectr., asst. prof., assoc. prof., prof. biology Coll. Notre Dame, Belmont, Calif., 1977—, advisor preprofl. med. program, 1980—, head dept. biology, 1980-89, chair divsn. natural scis. and math., 1984—, head dept. life scis., 1989-93; presenter Johns Hopkins U., Santa Cruz, Calif., 1990, Conf. on Talented Youth, Berkeley, Calif., 1991, 92, 93; rsch. asst. dept. anatomy Stanford U. Sch. Medicine, 1951-61, guest lectr. embryology and histology, 1966-67, rsch. assoc. dept. anatomy, 1961-69, instr. dept. biol. scis., 1968-71, lectr., 1971-75, sr. lectr., 1975-78, vis. asst. prof., vis. prof., 1979-89; vis. scientist divsn. anatomy U. Calif., San Diego, 1984; hon. rsch. fellow dept. genetics and biometry U. Coll., London, 1984. Contbr. articles to profl. jours. Mem. AAUP, Genetics Soc. Am., Am. Genetic Assn., Am. Soc. Zoologists, Am. Assn. Anatomists, Histochem. Soc., Teratology Soc., N.Y. Acad. Scis., Sigma Xi. Methodist. Home: 502 Greer Rd Palo Alto CA 94303-3017 Office: Coll Notre Dame 1500 Ralston Ave Belmont CA 94002

CENTERWALL, WILLARD RAYMOND, physician; b. Missoula, Mont., Jan. 16, 1924; s. Willard Raymond Centerwall, Sr. and Charlotte Amanda (Brandon) Wood; m. Siegried Louise Achom Centerwall, Sept. 2 , 1949 (dec. July 1992); children: Theodore, Brandon, Krista, Alison, Jennifer, Rebecca; m. Arlene Rudd Centerwall, Aug. 27, 1994. BS in Zoology, Yale U., 1949, MD, 1952; MPH in Maternal & Child Health, U. Mich., 1967, MS in Human Genetics, 1968; D in Cultural Anthropology (hon.), World U., 1983. Diplomate Am. Bd. Pediatrics, Am. Bd. Preventive Medicine, Am. Bd. Med. Genetics. Rotating internship White Meml. Hosp., L.A., 1952-53; first yr. pediatric residency White Meml. Hosp., L.A. County Gen. Hosp., 1953-54; sr. yr. pediatric residency L.A. Children's Hosp., 1953-55; instr., asst. clin. prof., asst. prof. pediatrics Coll. Med. Evangelists Sch. of Medicine, L.A., 1955-61; lectr., reader, assoc. prof. pediatrics Christian Med. Coll., Vellore, South India, 1961-66; organizer, first head of dept. pediatrics Miraj Med. Sch., Maharashtra State, India, 1965; assoc. prof. pediatrics Loma Linda U. Sch. Medicine, 1968, prof. pediatrics, 1970-78; assoc. prof. pub. health Loma Linda U. Sch. Health, Calif., 1968, prof. maternal & child health, 1970-78, gen. cons., 1982—; prof. anthropology Loma Linda U. Grad. Sch., Calif., 1976-78; prof. emeritus of pediatrics and genetics Loma Linda U. Sch. Medicine, 1986; prof. pediatrics and genetics U. Calif. Sch. Medicine, Davis, 1978-85; prof. in residence dept. reproduction U. Calif. Sch. Veterinary Medicine, Davis, 1981-85; prof. emeritus of pediatrics and genetics U. Calif., Davis, 1986; clin. prof. depts. med. genetics & pediatrics Oreg. Health Scis. U. & Sch. Medicine, Portland, 1986—; ret.; dir. Satellite Genetic Diagnostic and Counseling Clinic, Reno, 1983-85, State Newborn Metabolic Screening Program at U. Calif., Davis, 1980-85, Chico-Oroville (Calif.) Satellite Genetic Diagnostic and Counseling Clinic, 1980-85, Satellite Genetic Diagnostic & Counseling Clinic, Redding, Calif., 1980-83, Genetic Disorders and Birth Defects Clinic Alta Regional Ctr., Sacramento, Calif., 1978-83; civilian med. specialist cons. in pediatrics David Grant USAF Med. Ctr., Travis AFB, 1982-85; organizer, 1st med. dir. Birth Defects and Genetics Clinic, Lakeport, Calif., 1978-84, Birth Defects and Genetics Diagnostic and Counseling Svc. Riverside County Health Dept., Calif., 1978, Birth Defects and Genetics Diagnostic and Counseling Svc. Loma Linda U. Med. Ctr., Calif., 1969-78, Birth Defects and Genetics Svc. Clarke County Dept. Pub. Health, Las Vegas, 1972, Birth Defects and Chromosome Lab. Svcs. Loma Linda U. Med. Ctr., Calif., 1969-78; organizer, 1st dir. Birth Defects and Genetics Clinic at Regional Ctr. for Devel. Disabilities, San Bernardino, Calif., 1976-78; spl. cons. to genetic disease section maternal & child health branch State Calif. Dept. Health, 1977-85, mem. adv. com. on inherited disorders, 1976; med. dir. Orthopedically Handicapped Clinic, Redlands, Calif., 1971-78; med. cons. Calif. Sch. for the Deaf, Riverside, Calif., 1969-78; pediatric cons. Pacific State Hosp. for Mentally Retarded, Pomona, Calif., 1955-60, 69-78, Sch. for Cerebral Palsied Children of Southern Calif., Altadena, 1956-60, and numerous others. Med. editor: Introduction series of booklets, 1958—; speaker in field. 1st lt. U.S. Army Corps of Engrs., 1943-47. Recipient of rsch. grants NIH, U.S. Pub. Health Svc., Meda Johnson & Co., Alumni Assn. of the Coll. of Med. Evangelists, Nat. Assn. for Retarded Children, Walter E. MacPherson Soc., The Nat. Found. March of Dimes, The Nat. Cancer Inst. and HEM Rsch., Inc., Calif. State Dept. Health; recipient Outstanding Svc. award for Excellence in the Provision of Med. Svcs. to Mentally Retarded Sacramento Assn. for the Retarded, Inc., 1982, 1st J.B.S. Haldane Oration medal Soc. Bionaturalists, 1985, Children's Bur. fellowship in Pub. Health and Human Genetics U. Mich., Ann Arbor, 1966-68. Home: 101 Silverwood Ln Silverton OR 97381

CEPPOS, JEROME MERLE, newspaper editor; b. Washington, Oct. 14, 1946; s. Harry and Florence (Epstein) C.; m. Karen E. Feingold, Mar. 7, 1982; children: Matthew, Robin. B.S. in Journalism, U. Md., 1969; postgrad., Knight-Ridder Exec. Leadership Program, 1989-90. Reporter, asst. city editor, night city editor Rochester (N.Y.) Democrat & Chronicle, 1969-72; from asst. city editor, to nat. editor, to asst. mng. editor The Miami (Fla.) Herald, 1972-81; assoc. editor San Jose (Calif.) Mercury News, 1981, mng. editor, 1983-94, exec. editor, sr. v.p., 1995—; mem. nat. adv. bd. Knight Ctr. Specialized Reporting, U. Md.; mem. Accrediting Coun. on Edn. in Journalism and Mass Comm. Mem. AP Mng. Editors (bd. dirs.), Am. Soc. Newspaper Editors, Calif. Soc. Newspaper Editors (bd. dirs., pres.), Soc. Profl. Journalists, Assn. for Edn. in Journalism and Mass Comm., Silicon Valley Capital Club. Home: 14550 Pike Rd Saratoga CA 95070-5359 Office: San Jose Mercury News 750 Ridder Park Dr San Jose CA 95131-2432

CERBONE, ROBERT, sales executive; b. Bklyn., Jan. 29, 1960; s. Frank James Sr. and Margaret (Castore) C.; m. Deborah Sue Boyle, Sept. 23, 1989. BA in Physics, Adelphi U., 1982; MBA in Mktg., L.I. U., 1985. Sales engr. Logitek, Farmingdale, N.Y., 1981-82; systems support specialist Porta Systems Corp., Syosset, N.Y., 1982-83; sales engr. Rhode & Schwarz, New Hyde Park, N.Y., 1983-84; regional sales rep. Chyron Corp., Melville, N.Y., 1984-86; sales engr. Ampex Systems Corp., Redwood City, Calif., 1986-87, dist. mgr., 1987-89, dir. southcentral region, 1989-91, mgr. hdqs. sales programs, 1991, dir. eastern region, 1991-93; mgr. group sales Dynatech Video Group, Salt Lake City, 1993-94; regional sales mgr. Leitch Inc., Chesapeake, Va., 1994-95; mktg. mgr. Tektronix, Inc., Beaverton, Oreg., 1995—. Mem. Soc. Broadcast Engrs. Roman Catholic.

CEREGHINO, JAMES JOSEPH, health facility administrator, neurologist; b. Portland, Oreg., Oct. 27, 1937; s. Joseph Thomas and Amelia E. (Arata) C. BS, Portland State Coll., 1959; MD, U. Oreg., 1964; MS in Neurophysiology, Linfield U., 1971. Intern Good Samaritan Hosp., Portland, 1964-65; resident Good Samaritan Hosp. and Med. Ctr., Portland, 1965-68; rotating resident in neuropathology Sch. of Medicine U. Wash., 1967; rotating resident in child neurology U. Calif. Med. Ctr., San Francisco, 1968; rotating resident in psychiatry Med. Sch. U. Oreg., 1968; nerol. cons. pub. health svc.-health svcs. and mental health adminstrn.-neurol. and sensory disease control program HEW, Rockville, Md., 1968-70; staff neuroglogist epilepsy br. NIH HEW, Bethesda, Md., 1970-85; chief epilepsy br. convulsive, devel. and neuromuscular disorders program Nat. Inst. Neurol. Disorders and Stroke, Bethesda, Md., 1985-93; dir. rsch. Epilepsy Ctr. Oreg. Health Scis. U., Portland, 1993—; prof. dept. neurology Oreg. Health Scis. U., 1993—; attending neurologist VA Med. Ctr., Portland, 1993—; speaker in field. Editor-in-chief Epilepsia, 1986-94, emeritus, 1994—, supplements editor, 1994—; contbr. numerous articles to profl. jours. Capt. USPHS, ret. Fellow Am. Electroencephalographi Soc. (pub. rels. com. 1980-81); mem. Am. Acad. Neurology, Am. Epilepsy Soc. (constn. com. 1970-74, chmn. 1975, membership com. 1975, chmn. 1976, 77 chmn. edn. com. 1978, 79, 80, dir. continuing med. edn. 1981-83, 1st v.p. 1982-83, pres. 1983-84, v.p. to ILAE 1985-86, coun. 1985-94), Am. Neurologic Assn., Epilepsy Found. of Am. (profl. adv. bd. Washington chpt. 1969-93, v.p. 1973-75, speaker's bur. 1972-93, Epilepsy Internat. (libr. devel. com. 1981, chmn. 1981-85), U. Oreg. Med. Sch. Alumni Assn., Internat. League Against Epilepsy (edn. com. 1985-94, coun. 1985-94), Med. Soc. D.C. (sect. neurology and neurol. surgery 1971-94), Uniformed Svcs. Orgn. Neurologists (chmn. awards com. 1984-85), Epilepsy Assn. Oreg. (sec. 1993—), World Fedn. Neurology (epidemiology rsch group 1978—), Alzheimer's Rsch. Alliance Oreg. (exec. coun. 1994—). Home: 525 SE 65th Ave Portland OR 97215-2038 Office: Oreg Health Scis Univ Epilepsy Ctr CDW-3 3181 SW Sam Jackson Park Rd Portland OR 97201-3011

CEREPAK, JULIA LEE, poet, writer; b. Akron, Ohio, Apr. 28, 1962; d. Irvin Dow Jr. and Peggy Lee (Hoskins) Nichols; m. Edward Andrew Cerepak, Sept. 1, 1984; children: Cara Marie, Raymond Andrew. Student, Akron U., 1980-81. Saleswoman E.J. Thomas Performing Arts Ctr., Akron, Crab Tree and Evelyn Notions, San Mateo, Calif., Royal Dalton China, Pacific Grove, Calif.; featured guest, poetry reader Minatour Press Poetry Series, Burlingame, Calif., poetry forums, San Francisco, Pacific Grove, Big Sur, San Mateo, Calif. Author: (poetry) A Poet's Dream, 1989, Modern Day Minstrel, 1991; art pub. in various publs. Recipient Editor's Choice award Nat. Libr. Poetry, 1993. Mem. Coyote Point Mus., Monterey Bay Aquarium, United Meth. Ch. Women. Home: 103 Grand Blvd San Mateo CA 94401-2313

CERNAK, KEITH PATRICK, health care and financial consultant; b. Northampton, Mass., Mar. 17, 1954; s. Samuel and Geraldine (Dykstra) C.; m. Kristin Freedman, Sept. 10, 1983; children: Emily Samantha, Melanie Kristin. BA magna cum laude, U. Mass., 1976; MPH, U. Hawaii, 1980; MBA, UCLA, 1984. Healthcare researcher U. Hawaii, Honolulu, 1978; health planning cons. Guam Health Planning Agy., Agana, 1979; rsch. dir. Hawaii Dept. Health, Honolulu, 1980-81; grad. instr. UCLA Sch. Pub. Health, 1981; mgmt. cons. Am. Med. Internat., Beverly Hills, Calif., 1982; asst. v.p. Crocker Bank, L.A., 1984-86; v.p. fin. Weyerhaeuser, San Francisco, 1986-90; cmty. partnership intervention dir. Evergreen Med. Ctr., Seattle, 1992—; health care cons.; nat. presenter in field. Author papers in field. Cabinet mem. Shepherd of the Hills Ch., Berkeley, Calif., 1988-90. Health Svc. scholar U. Hawaii, 1978. Mem. UCLA Sch. Mgmt., Beta Gamma Sigma. Home: 24509 SE 43rd Pl Issaquah WA 98027-9518

CERNY, CHARLENE ANN, museum director; b. Jamaica, N.Y., Jan. 12, 1947; d. Albert Joseph and Charlotte Ann (Novy) Cerny; children: Elizabeth Brett Cerny-Chipman, Kathryn Rose Cerny-Chipman. BA, SUNY, Binghamton, 1969. Curator Latin-Am. folk art Mus. Internat. Folk Art, Santa Fe, 1972-84, mus. dir., 1984—; adv. bd. C.G. Jung Inst., Santa Fe, 1990—. Mem. Mayor's Commn. on Children and Youth, Santa Fe, 1990-93, adv. bd. Recipient Exemplary Performance award State of N.Mex., 1982, Internat. Ptnr. Among Mus. award; Smithsonian Instn. travel grantee, 1976; Florence Dibell Bartlett Meml. scholar, 1979, 91; Kellogg fellow, 1983. Mem. Am. Assn. Mus. Internat. Coun. Mus. (bd. dirs. 1991—, exec. bd. 1991-95), Am. Folklore Soc., Mountain-Plains Mus. Assn., N.Mex. Assn. Mus. (chair membership com. 1975-77). Office: Mus Internat Folk Art PO Box 2087 Santa Fe NM 87504-2087

CERNY, JOSEPH, III, chemistry educator, scientific laboratory administrator, university dean and official; b. Montgomery, Ala., Apr. 24, 1936; s. Joseph and Olaette Genette (Jury) C.; m. Barbara Ann Nedelka, June 13, 1959 (div. Nov. 1982); children: Keith Joseph, Mark Evan; m. 2d Susan Dinkelspiel Stern, Nov. 12, 1983. BS in Chem. Engring., U. Miss.-Oxford, 1957; postgrad. Fulbright scholar, U. Manchester, Eng., 1957-58; PhD in Nuclear Chemistry, U. Calif.-Berkeley, 1961; PhD in Physics (hon.), U. Jyväskylä, Finland, 1990. Asst. prof. chemistry U. Calif., Berkeley, 1961-67, assoc. prof., 1967-71, prof., 1971—, chmn. dept. chemistry, 1975-79, head nuclear sci. div., 1979-84, assoc. dir. Lawrence Berkeley Lab., 1979-84, dean grad. div., 1985—, provost for research, 1986-94, vice chancellor for rsch., 1994—; mem. Nat. Acad. Scis. Physics Commn., chair nuclear physics panel, 1983-86; mem. NASA Adv. Coun., Univ. Rels. Task Force, 1991-93, NRC Study of Rsch. Doctorates, 1992-95. Editor: Nuclear Reactions and Spectroscopy, 4 vols., 1974; contbr. numerous articles to field to profl. jours. Served with U.S. Army, 1962-63. Recipient E.O. Lawrence award AEC, 1974, A. von Humboldt sr. scientist award, 1985; named to U. Miss. Alumni Hall of Fame, 1988. Fellow AAAS, Am. Phys. Soc.; mem. Am. Chem. Soc. (Nuclear Chemistry award 1984), Assn. Grad. Schs. (v.p., pres. 1992-94). Democrat. Home: 860 Keeler Ave Berkeley CA 94708-1324 Office: U Calif 309 Sproul Hall Berkeley CA 94720

CERVANTES, JAMES VALENTINE, English language educator; m. Leilani Wright, Mar. 31, 1995. BA, U. Wash., 1972; MFA, U. Iowa, 1974. Tchng. asst. U. Iowa, 1972-74; tchr. humanities dept. C.C. of Vt., Brattleboro, 1974-76; lectr., English dept. Ariz. State U., 1978-81; instr. English dept. Yavapai C.C., 1987-88, No. Ariz. U., 1985-88; asst. prof. Learning Skills Ctr., English dept. Calif. State U., Sacramento, 1988-92; prof. English dept. Mesa C.C., 1992—; poet-in-residence Ariz. Commn. on the Arts, 1994-95; presenter confs. in field; presenter poetry readings; cellist, Air Force Orchestra, 1963-67; psychiat. aide at pvt. mental hosp., 1974-75. Author: The Headlong Future, 1990, The Year is Approaching Snow, 1981, The Firesin Oil Drums, 1980; editor Porch Mag., 1977-81; contbr. poetry to anthologies; contbr. articles to profl. jours. Bd. dirs. Cochise Fine Arts, Bisbee, Ariz., 1982-83. Recipient Outstanding Writer award/Pushcart prize III, 1977, tchng. fellowship U. Iowa Writer's Workshop, 1972-74, writer's fellowship in poetry, Ariz. Commn. on the Arts, 1981, faculty profl. devel. mini-grantee, Calif. State U., Sacramento, 1990-91; recipient The Capricorn award The Writer's Voice and the West Side Y Writer's Ctr., N.Y.C., 1987. Office: Mesa CC 1833 W Southern Ave Mesa AZ 85202-4866

CERVANTEZ, GIL LAWRENCE, venture capital company executive; b. Concord, Calif., July 14, 1944; s. Val J. and Laura E. (Verduguа) C.; m. Pamela A. Richmond, Feb. 14, 1965; children: Jeffrey, Thomas. BS, U. Oreg., 1965; MBA, U. Calif., Berkeley, 1972. V.p. Gt. Western Nat. Bank, Portland, Oreg., 1971-74, Heller Internat., San Francisco, 1975-76; dir. Control Data, San Francisco, 1976-79; sr. v.p. Century Bank, San Francisco, 1979-85; dir. syndications Pacificorp Ventures, Portland, 1988-90; pres. Latipac Fin., San Francisco, 1985-90; pres. A, G & T Investments, Inc., Walnut Creek, Calif., 1990—, also bd. dirs.; exec. v.p. Terameth Industries, Inc., Walnut Creek, 1990—, also bd. dirs. Lt. comdr. USN, 1965-71, Vietnam. Mem. Robert G. Sproul Assocs., U. Calif. Alumni Assn., Libr. Assocs., Smithsonian Assocs., Bear Backers, Commonwealth Club Calif. Republican. Roman Catholic. Home: 177 Ardith Ct Orinda CA 94563-4344 Office: A G & T Investments Inc 1331 N California Blvd Ste 730 Walnut Creek CA 94596-4536

CHABOT-FENCE, DENE, industrial engineer; b. Long Beach, Calif., Dec. 20, 1932; s. Marvin Carl and Jessica May Castleberry (Albrecht) Fence. AA, Am. River Coll., Sacramento, 1965; BS, Calif. Inst. Tech., 1966, U. San Francisco, 1983; MS, U. San Francisco, 1985. Research technician Calif. Inst. Tech., Pasadena, 1960-66; engr. various firms, Calif., 1966-80; design engr. J.R. Simplot, Helm, Calif., 1980-85; project engr. J. Oakley & Assocs., Fresno, Calif., 1985-86; prin. engr. Handypersons, Fresno, 1986-87; design engr. Heublein Wines, Madera, Calif., 1987-88, Bruce Industries, Dayton, Nev., 1988-95; bus. entrepreneur Vitamin Villa, Carson City, Nev. Patentee in field. Mission pilot Airlifeline, Sacramento. Served with USAF, 1950-54, Korea. Mem. Am. Assn. Indsl. Hygiene (cert.), 99's (chmn. local chpt. 1985-86). Democrat. Home: 5959 Sedge Rd Carson City NV 89701-9303

CHACKO, GEORGE KUTTICKAL, systems science educator, consultant; b. Trivandrum, India, July 1, 1930; came to U.S., 1953.; s. Geevarghese Kuttickal and Thankamma (Mathew) C.; m. Yo Yee, Aug. 10, 1957; children: Rajah Yee, Ashia Yo Chacko Lance. MA in Econs. and Polit. Philosophy, Madras (India) U., 1950; postgrad., St. Xavier's Coll., Calcutta, India, 1950-52; B in Commerce, Calcutta U., 1952; cert. postgrad. tng., Indian Stat. Inst., Calcutta, 1951; postgrad., Princeton U., 1953-54; PhD in Econometrics, New Sch. for Social Rsch., N.Y.C., 1959; postdoctoral, UCLA, 1961. Asst. editor Indian Fin., Calcutta, 1951-53; comml. corr. Times of India, 1953; dir. mktg. and mgmt. rsch. Royal Metal Mfg. Co., N.Y.C., 1958-60; mgr. dept. ops. rsch. Hughes Semicondr. div., Newport Beach, Calif., 1960-61; cons., 1961-62; ops. research staff cons. Union Carbide Corp., N.Y.C., 1962-63; mem. tech. staff Research Analysis Corp., McLean, Va., 1963-65, MITRE Corp., Arlington, Va., 1965-67; sr. staff scientist TRW Systems Group, Washington, 1967-70; cons. def. systems, computer, space, tech. systems and internat. devel. systems, assoc. in math. test devel. Ednl. Testing Service, Princeton, N.J., 1955-57; asst. prof. bus. adminstrn. UCLA, 1961-62; lectr. Dept. Agr. Grad. Sch., 1965-67; asst. professorial lectr. George Washington U., 1965-68; professorial lectr. Am. U., 1967-70, adj. prof., 1970; vis. prof. def. systems Mgmt. Coll., Ft. Belvoir, Va., 1972-73; vis. prof. U. So. Calif., 1970-71, prof. systems mgmt., 1971-83, prof. systems sci., 1983-93, prof. emeritus, 1993—; sr. Fulbright prof. Nat. Chengchi U., Taipei, 1983-84, sr. Fulbright rsch. prof., 1984-85; prin. investigator and program dir. Tech. Transfer Project, Taiwan Nat. Sci. Coun., 1984-85; disting. fgn. expert lectr. Taiwan Ministry Econ. Affairs, 1986; sr. vis. rsch. prof. Taiwan Nat. Sci. Coun. Nat. Chengchi U., Taipei, 1988-89; sr. vis. rsch. prof. Dah-Yeh Inst. Tech., Dah-Tsuen, Chang-Hwa, Taiwan, 1993-94, sr. research prof. 1996—; vis. prof. Nat. Chengchi U., Taipei, 1993-94; v.p. program devel. Systems and Telecom. Corp., Potomac, Md., 1987-90; chief sci. cons. RJO Enterprises, Lanham, Md., 1988-89; cons. Med. Svcs. Corp. Internat., vector biology and control project U.S. Agy. for Internat. Devel., 1991; guest lectr. Tech. Univs. Tokyo, Taipei, Singapore, Dubai, Cairo, Warsaw, Budapest, Prague, Bergen, Stockholm, Helsinki, Berlin, Madras, Bombay, London, 1992, Yokohoma, Taipei, Hong Kong, Kuala Lampur, Madras, Bombay, Alexandria, Jerusalem, Cairo, Paris, London, 1993-94, Madrid, Bologna, Milan, Monte Carlo, Amsterdam, Vienna, Austria, Kuala Lampur, Bangkok, 1994; USIA sponsored U.S. sci. emissary to Egypt, Burma, India, Singapore, 1987; USIA sponsored U.S. expert on tech. transferand military conversion 1st Internat. Conf. on Reconstrn. of Soviet Republics, Hannover, Germany, 1992; keynote speaker 2d annual conf. on mgmt. edn. in China, Taipei, Taiwan, 1989, worldconf. on transition to advanced market economies, Warsaw, Poland, 1992, annual conv. Indian Inst. Indsl. Engring., Hyderabad, India, 1993, First Sino-South Africa Bilateral Symposium on Tech. Devel., Taipei, 1994; mem. internat. adv. com. on restructuring strategies for electronics info. industry Asian Inst. Tech. Workshop, 1994. Author: 22 books in field, including Applied Statistics in Decision-Making, 1971, Computer-aided Decision-Making, 1972, Systems Approach to Public and Private Sector Problems, 1976, Operations Research Approach to Problem Formulation and Solution, 1976, Management Information Systems, 1979, Trade Drain Imperative of Technology Transfer: U.S. Taiwan Concomitant Coalitions, 1985, Robotics/Artificial Intelligence/Productivity-U.S.-Japan Concomitant Coalitions, 1986, Technology Management: Applications to Corporate Markets and Military Missions, 1988, The Systems Approach to Problem-Solving: From Corporate Markets to National Missions, 1989, Toward Expanding Exports Through Technology Transfer: IBM-Taiwan Concomitant Coalions, 1989, Dynamic Program Management: From Defense Experience to Commercial Application, 1989, Decision-Making under Uncertainty: An Applied Statistics Approach, 1991, Operations Research/Management Science: Case Studies in Decision-Making under Structured Uncertainty, 1993; contbr. articles to profl. publs.; editor contbr. 22 books including The Recognition of Systems in Health Services, 1969, Reducing the Cost of Space Transportation, 1969, Systems Approach to Environmental Pollution, 1972, National Organization of Health Services-U.S., USSR, China, Europe, 1979, Educational Innovation in Health Services-U.S., Europe, Middle East, Africa, 1979, Management Education in the Republic of China: Second Annual Conference, 1989, Expert Systems: 1st World Congress Proceedings, 1991, Transition to Advanced Market Economies: Internat. Conf. Proceedings, 1992, Industrial Engineering Interfaces: Indian Nat. Conv. Proceedings, 1993, Technological Development: 1st Sino-South Africa Bilateral Symposium Proceedings, 1994; guest editor Jour. Rsch. Comm. Studies, 1978-79; assoc. editor Internat.

Jour. Forecasting, 1982-85; mem. internat. editl. bd. Malaysian Jour. Mgmt. Scis., 1993—. Active Nat. Presbyn. Ch., Washington, 1967-84, mem. ch. coun., 1969-71, mem. chancel choir, 1967-84, co-dean ch. family camp, 1977, coord. life abundant discovery groups, 1979; chmn. worship com. Taipei Internat. Ch., 1984, mem. adult choir, 1983-85, 88-89, 93—, chmn. membership com., 1985, chmn. stewardship and fin. com., 1985, chmn. com. Christian edn., 1988, Sunday Sch. supt., 1989, adult Sunday sch. leader, 1993; founder-dir. Prayer Power Partnership, 1994; adult Sunday Sch. leader 4th Presbyn. Ch., Bethesda, Md., 1986-87, mem. santuary choir, 1985—; participant 9th Internat. Ch. Mus. Festival, Coventry Cathedral, 1992; mem. Men's Ensemble, 1986-93; mem. Ministry Com., 1990—; founder, dir. Prayer Power Partnership, 1990—. Recipient Gold medal Inter-Collegiate Extempore Debate in Malayalam U. Travancore, Trivandrum, India, 1945, 1st pl. Yogic Exercises Competition U. Travancore, 1946, Jr. Lectureship prize Physics Soc. U. Coll., 1946, 1st prize Inter-Varsity Debating Team Madras, 1949, NSF internat. sci. lectures award, 1982, USIA citation for invaluable contbr. to America's pub. diplomacy, 1992, Commendation for 2 books on U.S. - Taiwan Technology Transfer by Presidential Palace, Taipei, 1993; Coll. scholar St. Xavier's Coll., 1950-52; Inst. fellow Indian Stat. Inst., 1951, S.E. Asia Club fellow Princeton U., 1953-54, Univ. fellow UCLA, 1961. Fellow AAAS (mem. nat. coun. 1968-73, chmn. or co-chmn. symposia 1971, 72, 74, 76, 77, 78), Am. Astronautical Soc. (v.p. publs. 1969-71, editor Tech. Newsletter 1968-72, mng. editor Jour. Astronautical Scis. 1969-75); mem. Ops. Rsch. Soc. Am. (vice chmn. com. of representation on AAAS 1972-78, mem. nat. coun. tech. sect. on health 1966-68, editor Tech. Newsletter on Health 1966-73), Washington Ops. Rsch. Coun. (trustee 1967-69, chmn. tech. colloquia 1967-68, editor Tech. Newsletter 1967-68, Banquet chmn. 1992-93), Inst. Mgmt. Scis. (rep. to Internat. Inst. for Applied Systems Analysis in Vienna, Austria 1976-77, session chmn. Athens, Greece 1977, Atlanta 1977), World Future Soc. (editorial bd. publs. 1970-71), N.Y. Acad. Scis., Soc. Scientific Mgmt. and Ops. Rsch. (Egypt, 1st hon. fgn. mem.), Kiwanis (charter 1st v.p.), Costa Mesa North Club (charter pres.), Friendship Heights Club (charter dir.), Taipei Yang Min Club (disting. divsn. one svc. award, 1968, 70, capital dist. chmn. 1967, 69-70m 71-72, inter divsn. chmn. Green Candle of Hope Dinner, 1965-82), Friendship Heights Club (Outstanding svc. award 1972-73, Life mem. award) Capital dist. Found. 1982, Taipei-Keystone Club (disting. dir., spl. rep. of internat. pres. and counselor to dist. of Republic of China 1983-86, Pioneer Premier Project award Asia-Pacific conf. 1986, Legion of Honor 1985), Bethesda Club (dir., chmn. internat. rels. 1991-95, chmn. hon. 1992, mem. numerous coms. 1966—). Democrat. Office: U So Calif Inst Safety and Systems Mgmt Los Angeles CA 90089-0021

CHACON, MICHAEL ERNEST, computer networking specialist; b. L.A., Feb. 14, 1954; s. Ernest Richard and Teresa Marie (Venegas) C.; m. Virginia Marie; children: Mylan Graham, Aubrie Sarah, Christina Nabseth, Caitlyn Nabseth, Julia Anna. Student, Pierce Coll., 1972-74, Boise State U., 1980-82. Systems cons. MEC & Assocs., Riverside, Calif., 1986-91; regional mgr. Inacom Corp., Garden Grove, Calif., 1991—; cons. in field; lectr. Microsoft Corp., Bellvue, Wash., 1990-92. Author: Understanding Networks, 1991; contbr. articles to profl. jours. Named to Dean's List, Pierce Coll., 1973, 74. Mem. Lake Elsinore Sportsman Assn., L.A. World Affairs Coun., 3Com Adv. Coun. (pres. tech. adv. bd. 1986-92). Office: Inacom Corp 11842 Monarch St Garden Grove CA 92641-2113

CHADEY, HENRY F., museum director; b. Superior, Wyo., Feb. 20, 1924; s. Frank and Anna (Glogovsek) C.; m. Helen Putz, Aug. 3, 1957; children: Michael, Katherine, Mary Jo, Jeanne. BA, U. Wyo., 1949, MA, 1955. Tchr. Dist. No. 7, Reliance, Wyo., 1956; sch. supt. Dist. No. 7, Reliance, 1956-59; asst. supt. Wyo. State Dept. Edn., Cheyenne, Wyo., 1959-61; high sch. prin. Dist. No. 8, Glenrock, Wyo., 1961-62, Dist. No. 4, Rock Springs, Wyo., 1962-67; mus. dir. Sweetwater City Mus., Green River, Wyo., 1967-90; ret., 1990; instr. in field. Author: Rock Springs Chinese, 1985; author jour. Wyoming Geological Assistant Guidebook, 1973, Annals of Wyoming, 1978. Clk. Sch. Dist. No. 1, Sweetwater County, 1967—; pres. Wyo. State Hist. Soc., 1972-73; chmn. Wyo. Sch. Bd. Assn., 1977-78; mem. Wyo. State Sch. Bd., 1977-78. Mem. Am. Assn. Mus., Am. Assn. for State and Local History, Mt. Plains Mus. Assn., Colo.-Wyo. Mus. Assn. (dir. 1986-88), Lions (pres. 1976-77, clk. 1980—), Wyo Ret. Tchrs. (v.p.). Democrat. Roman Catholic. Home: 413 Fremont St Rock Springs WY 82901-6627

CHADWICK, SHARON STEVENS, librarian; b. Syracuse, N.Y., June 1, 1951; d. Robert Harold and Melba Frances (Hurlburt) Stevens; m. Gary Robert Chadwick, May 27, 1972. BS in Chemistry, Clarkson Coll. Tech., 1973; MSLS, Syracuse U., 1975; MS in Chemistry, SUNY, Oswego, 1980. Asst. librarian SUNY, Oswego, 1977-78; chemistry, physics bibliographer Syracuse U., 1978-79; sci. librarian Humboldt State U., Arcata, Calif., 1980—. Mem. ALA, Am. Chem. Soc., Med. Libr. Assn., N.Y. Acad. Scis., Self-Help for Hard of Hearing, Nat. Captioning Inst., Humane Soc. U.S. Home: 190 Willow Ln Arcata CA 95521-9210 Office: Humboldt State U The Libr Arcata CA 95521

CHAFE, WALLACE LESEUR, linguist, educator; b. Cambridge, Mass., Sept. 3, 1927; s. Albert J. and Nathalie (Amback) C.; m. Mary Elizabeth Butterworth, June 23, 1951 (div. 1980); children—Christopher, Douglas, Stephen; m. Marianne Mithun, Jan. 25, 1985. B.A., Yale U., 1950, M.A., 1956, Ph.D., 1958. Asst. prof. U. Buffalo, 1958-59; linguist Bur. Am. Ethnology, Smithsonian Instn., 1959-62; mem. faculty U. Calif.-Berkeley, 1962-86, prof. linguistics, 1967-86; prof. linguistics U. Calif., Santa Barbara, 1986-91, prof. emeritus, 1991—. Author: Seneca Thanksgiving Rituals, 1961, Seneca Morphology and Dictionary, 1967, Meaning and the Structure of Language, 1970, The Pear Stories, 1980, Evidentiality, 1986, Discourse, Consciousness, and Time, 1994. Served with USNR, 1945-46. Mem. Linguistic Soc. Am., Am. Psychol. Assn., Am. Anthrop. Assn. Office: Univ Calif Dept Linguistics Santa Barbara CA 93106

CHAFEE, JUDITH DAVIDSON, architect; b. Chgo., Aug. 18, 1932; d. Percy Bernard and Christina (Affeld) D.; adopted d. Benson Bloom; m. Richard Spofford Chafee, 1959 (div. 1964). BA, Bennington Coll., 1954; BArch, Yale U., 1960, MArch, 1960. Lic. architect, Conn., N.Y., Ariz.; cert. Nat. Coun. Archtl. Registration Bds. Draftsperson Paul M. Rudolph, Architect, New Haven, 1960-61; draftsperson, design The Architects Collaborative, Cambridge, Mass., 1962-63; job capt., design Eero Saarinen and Assocs., Hamden, Conn., 1963-65; project architect Edward Larrabee Barnes, Architect, New Haven, 1965-69; prin. Judith Chafee, Architect, Hamden, Conn., 1966-69, Tucson, 1969—; vis. critic U. Ariz. Coll. Architecture, 1973-76, adj. prof., 1977—; guest architect, critic to advanced students U. Tex. Coll. Architecture, 1976; vis. prof. disting. visitor's studio, advanced studio MIT Dept. Architecture, fall semesters, 1986, 88, advanced design studio Washington U. Sch. Architecture, St. Louis, spring semester, 1988; mem. jury We. Home awards Sunset mag., 1979, Ariz. Solar Energy Commn. Western Solar Utilization Network, Ariz. Passive Solar Design Competition, 1981, Design and Environ. awards program Dept. of Navy, 1983, Rancho San Miguel Design Competition, Sante Fe, 1987, Ariz. Homes of Yr. Competition, 1992, The Environ. Showcase Home, 1992; guest speaker Princeton U., 1989, Mont. State U., 1990, S.W. Ctr. U. Ariz., 1990; mem. vis. com. MIT Sch. Architecture and Planning, 1990—. Contbr. numerous articles to jours. and mags. in field. Nat. Endowment for the arts/Am. Acad. in Rome mid-career fellow, 1977; recipient award of excellence Archtl. Record mag., 1970, 75, 79, Outstanding Use of Concrete award Am. Concrete Inst. 1978, 84, Mortar Bd. Citation award for archtl. edn. Ariz. Mortar Bd., 1988. Fellow AIA (First Honor award Housing mag. 1978, com. on design 1986-89, jury mem. Honor awards, N.Mex. Soc. Architects, Concrete Masonry Design awards Calif. Coun., Concrete Masonry Assn. Calif., Nev. 1988, Ariz. Homes of Yr. awards 1989, Orange County Ann. Design awards 1989, del. to Internat. Conf. on Architecture, Urban Planning and Design, Finland, 1989), Amer. Acad. in Rome; mem. Nature Conservancy, Nat. Trust for Hist. Preservation, Old Fort Lowell Neighborhood Assn., El Presidio Neighborhood Assn., Tucson Mountain Assn. Office: Judith Chafee Architect 317 N Court Ave Tucson AZ 85701-1016

CHAFFEE, JAMES ALBERT, protective services official; b. Balt., Aug. 14, 1952; s. John Dempster and Elizabeth May (Holden) C.; m. Virginia Rose Braun, Oct. 4, 1980; children: Andrew James, Thomas John, Elizabeth Mary. AA, Alan Hancock Coll., 1973; BA, Chapman Coll., 1980; MBA, St. [illegible] Coll., 1986. Lic. EMT, L.A. County; lic. police officer, Minn. Police officer Minnetonka (Minn.) Police Dept., 1976-87, police supr., 1982-87; pub. safety dir. City of Chanhassen, Minn., 1987-90; dir. security Walt Disney Studios, Burbank, Calif., 1990—; dir. S.W. Metro Drug Task Force, Chanhassen, 1988-90; adv. com. 1991 U.S. Open, Chaska, Minn., 1989-90. Founding mem. Chanhassen Rotary Club, 1987, v.p., 1990; pres. Emblem Sch. Site Coun., Saugus, Calif., 1992. With USAF, 1972-76. Mem. Chief Spl. Agts. Assn. (dir. 1991—), Am. Soc. for Indsl. Security, Community Police and Security Team. Republican. Roman Catholic. Office: Walt Disney Studios 500 S Buena Vista St Burbank CA 91521-0001

CHAFFEE, STEVEN HENRY, communications educator; b. South Gate, Calif., Aug. 21, 1935; s. Edwin Wilbur and Nancy Marion (Kinghorn) C.; m. Sheila M. McGoldrick, Sept. 20, 1958 (div. Apr. 1987); children: Laura, Adam, Amy; m. Debra Lieberman, Mar. 25, 1989; 1 child, Eliot. BA, U. Redlands, 1957; MS, U. Calif., 1962; PhD, Stanford U., 1965. News editor Angeles Mesa News Advertiser, L.A., 1957; reporter Santa Monica (Calif.) Evening Outlook, 1962; rsch. assoc. Stanford (Calif) U., 1963-65, prof. communication, 1981—, Janet M. Peck prof., 1986—; asst. prof. to assoc. prof. U. Wisconsin, Madison, 1965-72, prof., 1972-82, 85-86, Vilas rsch. prof., 1974-81; mem. com. on mass communication and polit. behavior Soc. Sci. Rsch. Coun., N.Y.C., 1973-77; sci. adv. com. on TV and behavior NIMH, Washington, 1979-82. Author: Communication Concepts I: Explication, 1991; co-author: Television and Human Behavior, 1978, To See Ourselves, 1994; author, editor: Political Communication, 1972; co-author, editor: Handbook of Communication Science, 1986; contbr. numerous articles to profl. jours. Campaign pollster Dem. Party, Dane Co., Wis., 1966-84. Lt (j.g.) USNR, 1958-61. Fellow Internat. Communication Assn. (pres. 1982-83); Assn. for Edn. in Journalism and Mass Communication (mem. exec. com. 1971-72, 86-87), Am. Assn. Pub. Opinion Rsch. Democrat. Office: Stanford U Dept Communication Bldg 120 Stanford CA 94305-2050

CHAFFEE, WILBER ALBERT, political science educator; b. L.A., Oct. 17, 1930; s. Wilber Albert Chaffee and Elene (Graham) Chaffee-Loebbecke; m. Alice Blake (div.); children: Graham Stewartson, Lyman Blake; m. Edivanir Fontanelli. BA, Occidental Coll., L.A., 1952; MA, U. Tex., 1970, PhD, 1975. Asst. prof. U. Tex., Austin, 1975-77; asst. prof. St. Mary's Coll., Moraga, Calif., 1978-82, assoc. prof., 1982-88, prof., 1988—; chair dept. govt. St. Mary's Coll., Moraga, 1991—, dir. internat. studies, 1992—. Author, editor: Cuba: a Different America, 1989; author: Economic of Violence, 1992. Sgt. U.S. Army, 1953-55, Korea. Fulbright grantee, Latin Am., 1985. Mem. Am. Polit. Sci. Assn., Latin Am. Studies Assn., Pan Am. Soc. Calif. (chair acad. adv. com. 1991—). Presbyterian. Office: St Mary's Coll Calif PO Box 3356 SMC Moraga CA 94575

CHAGALL, DAVID, journalist, author; b. Phila., Nov. 22, 1930; s. Harry and Ida (Coopersmith) C.; m. Juneau Joan Alsin, Nov. 15, 1957. Student, Swarthmore Center Coll., 1948-49; B.A., Pa. State U., 1952; postgrad., Sorbonne, U. Paris, 1953-54. Social caseworker State of Pa., Phila., 1955-57; sci. editor Jour. I.E.E., 1959-61; pub. relations staff A.E.I.-Hotpoint Ltd., London, 1961-62; mktg. research assoc. Chilton Co., Phila., 1962-63; mktg. research project dir. Haug Assos., Inc. (Roper Orgn.), Los Angeles, 1964-74; research cons. Haug Assos., 1976-79; investigative reporter for nat. mags., 1975—; host TV series The Last Hour, 1994—. Author: Diary of a Deaf Mute, 1960, The Century God Slept, 1963, The Spieler For The Holy Spirit, 1972, The New Kingmakers, 1981, The Sunshine Road, 1988; pub.: Inside Campaigning, 1983; contbr. syndicated column, articles, revs., stories and poetry to mags., jours., newspapers; contbg. editor: TV Guide, Los Angeles Mag. Apptd. to Selective Svc. Bd., 1991; bd. dirs. Chosen Prophetic Ministries, 1991. Recipient U. Wis. Poetry prize, 1971; nominee Nat. Book award in fiction, 1972, Pulitzer prize in letters, 1973, Disting. Health Journalism award, 1978; Presdl. Achievement award, 1982; Carnegie Trust grantee, 1964. Home: PO Box 85 Agoura Hills CA 91376-0085

CHAGOYA, JANINE ELAINE, religious organization administrator, consultant; b. San Rafael, Calif., Oct. 10, 1950; d. Justus John and Jean Theodora (Reuter) Craemer; m. Enrique Chagoya Flores, May 25, 1977 (div. June 1990). BA in Psychology, BA in Sociology, U. Calif. Davis, 1972. Group counselor Sacramento County Juvenile Probation Dept., 1972-74; counseling program dir. Berkeley (Calif.) Emergency Food project, 1974-76; program staff Centro de Estudios Migratorios, Mexico City, 1976-78; rsch. dir. Data Ctr., Oakland, Calif., 1979-84, program dir No. Calif. Ecumenical Coun., San Francisco, 1984—. Mem. Youth and Edn. Commn., San Francisco, 1991—; program dir. San Francisco/Estelli Sister City Assn., 1991—; founding bd. mem. Inter-Am. Health Found., 1987-91. Mem. Nat. Assn. Ecumenical Staff, Nat. Rainbow Coalition. Democrat.

CHAHINE, MOUSTAFA TOUFIC, atmospheric scientist; b. Beirut, Lebanon, Jan. 1, 1935; s. Toufic M. and Hind S. (Tabbara) C.; m. Marina Bandak, Dec. 9, 1960; children: Tony T., Steve S. B.S., U. Wash., 1956, M.S., 1957; Ph.D., U. Calif., Berkeley, 1960. With Jet Propulsion Lab., Calif. Inst. Tech., Pasadena, 1960—; mgr. planetary atmospheres sect. Jet Propulsion Lab., Calif. Inst. Tech., 1975-78, sr. research scientist, mgr. earth and space scis. div., 1978-84, chief scientist, 1984—; vis. scientist MIT, 1969-70; vis. prof. Am. U., Beirut, 1971-72; regent's lectr. UCLA, 1989-90; mem. NASA Space and Earth Sci. Adv. Com., 1982-85; mem. climate rsch. com. Nat. Acad. Scis., 1985-88, bd. dirs. atmospheric scis. and climate, 1988—; chmn. sci. steering group Global Energy and Water Cycle Experiment World Meteorol. Orgn., 1988—; cons. U.S. Navy, 1972-76. Contbr. articles on atmospheric scis. to profl. jours. Recipient medal for exceptional sci. achievements NASA, 1969, NASA Outstanding Leadership medal, 1984, William T. Pecora award, 1989, Jule G. Charney award, 1991, Losey Atmospheric Scis. award AIAA, 1993. Fellow AAAS, Am. Phys. Soc., Royal Soc., Am. Meteorol. Soc.; mem. Internat. Acad. Astronautics, Sigma Xi. Office: 4800 Oak Grove Dr Pasadena CA 91109-8001

CHAI, WINBERG, political science educator, foundation chair; b. Shanghai, China, Oct. 16, 1932; came to U.S., 1951, naturalized, 1973; s. Ch'u and Mei-en (Tsao) C.; m. Carolyn Everett, Mar. 17, 1966; children: Maria Maylee, Jeffrey Tien-yu. Student, Hartwick Coll., 1951-53; BA, Wittenberg U., 1955; MA, New Sch. Social Rsch., 1958; PhD, NYU, 1968. Lectr. New Sch. Social Rsch., 1957-61; vis. asst. prof. Drew U., 1961-62; asst. prof. Fairleigh Dickinson U., 1962-65; asst. prof. U. Redlands, 1965-68, assoc. prof., 1969-73, chmn. dept., 1970-73; prof., chmn. Asian studies CCNY, 1973-79; disting. prof. polit. sci., v.p. acad. affairs, spl. asst. to pres. U. S.D., Vermillion, 1979-82; prof. polit. sci., dir. internat. programs U. Wyo., Laramie, 1988—; chmn. Third World Conf. Found., Inc., Chgo., 1982—; pres. Wang Yu-fa Found., Taiwan, 1989—. Author: (with Ch'u Chai) The Story of Chinese Philosophy, 1961, The Changing Society of China, 1962, rev. edit., 1969, The New Politics of Communist China, 1972, The Search for a New China, 1975; editor: Essential Works of Chinese Communism, 1969, (with James C. Hsiung) Asia in the U.S. Foreign Policy, 1981, (with James C. Hsiung) U.S. Asian Relations: The National Security Paradox, 1983, (with Carolyn Chai) Beyond China's Crisis, 1989, In Search of Peace in the Middle East, 1991, (with Cal Clark) Political Stability and Economic Growth, 1994, China Mainland and Taiwan, 1994; co-translator: (with Ch'u Chai) A Treasury of Chinese Literature, 1965. Haynes Found. fellow, 1967, 68; Ford Found. humanities grantee, 1968, 69, Pacific Cultural Found. grantee, 1978, 86, NSF grantee, 1970, Hubert Eaton Meml. Fund grantee, 1972-73, Field Found. grantee, 1973, 75, Henry Luce Found. grantee, 1978, 80, S.D. Humanities Com. grantee, 1980, Pacific Culture Fund grantee, 1987, 90-91. Mem. Am. Assn. Chinese Studies (pres. 1978-80), AAAS, AAUP, Am. Polit. Sci. Assn., N.Y. Acad. Scis., Internat. Studies Assn., NAACP. Democrat. Home: 1071 Granito Dr Laramie WY 82070-5045 Office: PO Box 4098 Laramie WY 82071-4098

CHAIM, ROBERT ALEX, academic administrator, educator; b. Stockton, Calif., Oct. 25, 1947; s. Alex Jr. and Carmen Lorraine (Rodriques-Lopez) C.; m. Diane Leonora Gregonis, May 30, 1971 (dec. 1973); m. Linda Jean Riley, Dec. 22, 1976. AA, San Joaquin Delta Coll., 1967; BA, Sacramento State Coll., 1970; cert. in secondary teaching, U. Pacific, 1972, ArtsD, 1980. Instr. English lang. U. Pacific, Stockton, 1973-77; lectr. lang. of law U. Pacific, Sacramento, 1977—; asst. to dean McGeorge Sch. Law, Sacramento, 1977-81, asst. dean students, 1981—; cons. grammar, usage and linguistics numerous law orgns. and pvt. law firms, Calif., 1978—; mem. curriculum com. law sch. U. San Fernando, Calif., 1979; mem. ABA/Assn. Am. Law Schs./Law Sch. Admission Coun. Joint Task Force on Fin. Aid, 1991-93. Editor-in-chief Stauffer Legal Rsch. Series, 1978—; contbr. articles to scholarly books and profl. jours. Mem. Elk Grove (Calif.) Community Planning Adv. Couns., 1986-88, vice-chmn., 1987; mem. scholarship com. Centro Legal de Calif., Sacramento, 1987-90, curriculum adv. com. Elk Grove Unified Sch. Dist., 1988, scholarship com. Sacramento Country Day Sch., 1988; lectr., campus coord. Oak Park Sports and Edn. Found., Inc., 1989—; bd. advisors St. Hope Acad. Youth Orgn., 1991—. Recipient Meritorious Svc. award Asian-Am. Law Students Assn., Sacramento, 1986, 87, Outstanding Svc. award La Raza Law Students Assn., 1988. Mem. ABA (assoc., legal edn. and bar admissions sect.), Nat. Assn. Fgn. Student Affairs, Assn. Am. Law Schs. (mem. legal rsch. and writing sect., student svcs. sect., student svc. com. 1990-91, law admission coun. joint task force on fin. aid 1991-94), Lions Club (judge 53rd ann. multiple dist. four, final spkr. contest, 1990). Office: U of Pacific McGeorge Sch Law 3200 5th Ave Sacramento CA 95817-2705

CHAKRABARTI, AJOY CHUNI, biochemist, educator; b. Baton Rouge, La., Apr. 28, 1964; came to U.S., 1993; s. Chuni Lal and Vimal C. BSc in Biochemistry with honors, Carleton U., Ottawa, Ontario, Can., 1986, MSc, 1988; PhD in Biochemistry, U. British Columbia, Can., 1992. NASA Planetary Biology Intern U. Calif., Davis, 1991, fellow, 1993-94; fellow Scripps Rsch. Inst., La Jolla, Calif., 1993—, U. Santa Cruz, Calif., 1994—. Contbr. articles to profl. jours.; patentee; lipid encapsulation of enzymes; accumulation of peptides into liposomes; metal ion accumulation in liposomes. Recipient summer rsch. award Nat. Sci. & Engring. Rsch. Coun., Can., 1984, grad. fellowship U. British Columbia, 1989-91, grad. award Sci. Coun. Br. Columbia, 1990-91, NASA internship U. Calif. Davis, 1991, postdoctoral fellowship NASA exobiology, 1993—, MRC of Can., 1993—; fellow Human Frontiers of Sci. Rsch. Program, 1995. Mem. AAAS, Bioencapsulation Rsch. Group. Office: U Calif Santa Cruz Chemistry Dept Santa Cruz CA 95064

CHALK, EARL MILTON, retired art director; b. Deerlodge, Mont., Sept. 14, 1927; s. Forrest A. and Jeanette Curtis (Robinson) C.; m. Carole Estelle, Feb. 9, 1963 (div. 1974); children: Teri, Kevin, Quinn. BFA, U. Wash., 1953. Artist Facilities Boeing, Seattle, 1954-57; writer, artist Facilities Boeing, Renton, Wash., 1957-60; supr. mfg. Facilities Boeing, Seattle, 1960-65; sr. supr. planning Facilities Boeing, Auburn, Wash., 1965-71, art dir. mfg. engring., 1971-87; painter in oils, 1987—; artist and writer fabrication divsn. Auburn, 1954-87; co-mgr., owner Art Galary, 1967-74. Artist Puget Sound Group of North West Painters, Seattle, 1968-78, artist Puyallup, Wash., 1987—. 1st class petty officer USN, 1945-49. Recipient Rotary scholarship U. Wash., 1953. Mem. Grapha Techna. Home and Office: 1803 7th Ave SE Puyallup WA 98372

CHALLEM, JACK JOSEPH, editor, health, advertising and public relations writer; b. Montreal, Quebec, Can., May 29, 1950; came to U.S., 1954; s. Alex and Sara Bella (Novak) C.; m. Renate Lewin, Sept. 30, 1977; 1 child, Evan G. BA, Northeastern Ill. U., 1972. Advt. mgr. J.R. Carlson Labs., Arlington Heights, Ill., 1973-78; editor-in-chief Physician's Life Mag., Evanston, Ill., 1978; contbg. editor Health Quarterly, New Canaan, Conn., 1979-83, Your Good Health Rev., New Canaan, 1979-83; graphics mgr. Eberline Instrument Corp., Santa Fe, 1979-81; sci. writer, media rels. specialist Los Alamos (N.Mex.) Nat. Lab., 1981-88; contbg. editor Let's Live Mag., L.A., 1978—; writer KVO Advt. & Pub. Rels., Portland, Oreg., 1988-94; pres. The Virtual Writer. Author: What Herbs Are All About, 1979, Vitamin C Updated, 1983, Getting the Most out of Your Vitamins and Minerals, 1993; contbr. Natural Health Mag., 1992—; editor, pub.: The Nutrition Reporter Newsletter, 1992—; contbr. articles to profl. jours. Home: 6782 SW 167th Pl Beaverton OR 97007-6310

CHALMERS, JAMES A., consulting company executive; b. Ithaca, N.Y., Jan. 10, 1942. BA in Econs., U. Wyo., 1963; PhD in Econs., U. Mich., 1969. Cert. real estate counselor. Asst. prof. econs. Amherst (Mass.) Coll., 1966-70; field staff Rockefeller Found., Bangkok, 1970-72; assoc. prof. econs. Ariz. State U., Tempe, 1972-79; prin., pres. Mountain West, Inc., Phoenix, 1974—, chmn. bd. dirs. Bd. dirs., sec. East Valley Partnership, Ariz., Phoenix City Club. Mem. Am. Soc. of Real Estate Counselors, Lambda Alpha (pres. 1987-88). Office: Mountain W Rsch SW Inc 2901 N Central Ave Ste 1000 Phoenix AZ 85012-2730

CHAMBERLAIN, ADRIAN RAMOND, state agency executive; b. Detroit, Nov. 11, 1929; s. Adrian and Leila (Swisher) C.; m. Melanie F. Stevens, May 19, 1979; children: Curtis (dec.), Tracy, Thomas (dec.). BS, Mich. State U., 1951, D Engring., 1971; MS, Wash. State U., 1952; PhD, Colo. State U., 1955; LittD, Denver U., 1974. Registered profl. engr., Colo. lic. real estate broker, Colo., 1981-91. Rsch. engr. Phillips Petroleum Co., 1955; rsch. coord., civil engr. Colo. State U., 1956-57, chief civil engr. sect., 1957-61, acting dean engring., 1959-61, v.p., 1960-66, exec. v.p., treas., governing bd., 1966-69, pres., 1969-80; chmn. bd. dirs. Univ. Nat. Bank, 1964-69, dir., 1964-74; pres., dir. Mitchell & Co., Inc., 1981-85; exec. v.p. Simons, Li & Assocs., Inc., 1985-87; pres., chief exec. officer Chemagnetics, Inc., Ft. Collins, Colo., 1987-89; exec. dir. Colo. Dept. Hwys., Denver, 1987-91, Colo. Dept. Transp., 1991-94; chmn. NSF Commn. Weather Modification, 1964-66; mem. Nat. Air Quality Criteria Adv. Com., 1967-70; vice chmn. rsch. and tech. coord. com. Fed. Hwy Admiinstrn. of Transp. Rsch. Bd., NRC, 1991-94. Colo. commr. Western Interstate Commn. on Higher Edn., 1974-78; pres. State Bd. Agr. System, 1978-80; trustee Cystic Fibrosis Found., 1971-84; trustee Univ. Corp. for Atmospheric Rsch., 1967-72, 74-81, chmn. bd. trustees, 1977-79; pres. Black Mountain Ranch, Inc., 1969-85; bd. dirs. Nat. Ctr. for Higher Edn. Mgmt. Systems, 1975-80, chmn. bd. dirs., 1977-78; bd. visitors Air U., USAF, 1973-76, chmn., 1975-76; exec. com. Nat. Assn. State Univs. and Land Grant Colls., 1976-80, pres.-elect, 1978-79, chmn., 1979-80; mem. adv. coun. to dir. NSF, 1978-81; chmn. Ft. Collins-Loveland Airport Authority, 1983-86; bd. dirs. Synergetics Internat. Inc., 1987-90; mem. exec. com. strategic hwy. rsch. commn. Transp. Rsch. Bd. NRC, 1989-93, chmn. strategic transp. rsch. study hwy. safety, 1989-90, exec. com., 1991—, vice-chmn. 1992, chmn. 1993; mem. Gov.'s Cabinet, State of Colo., 1987-94; mem. Info. Mgmt. Commn., 1988-93. Fulbright student U. Grenoble, 1955-56. Mem. ASCE, Am. Assn. State Hwy. and Transp. Ofcls. (policy com. 1987-92, v.p. 1990-91, pres. 1991-92, bd. dirs. 1992-94, chmn. standing com. on adminstrn. 1993-94), Am. Trucking Assn. (v.p. for freight policy 1994—), Order of Aztec Eagle, Mex., Sigma Xi, Tau Beta Pi, Phi Kappa Phi, Chi Epsilon. Home: 124 Idlewild Ln Winter Park CO 80482 Office: Am Trucking Assns 2200 Mill Rd Alexandria VA 22314-4686

CHAMBERLAIN, BARBARA KAYE, small business owner; b. Lewiston, Idaho, Nov. 6, 1962; d. William Arthur and Gladys Marie (Humphrey) Greene; m. Dean Andrew Chamberlain, Sept. 13, 1986; children: Kathleen Marie, Laura Kaye. BA in English cum laude, BA in Linguistics cum laude, Wash. State U., 1984. Temp. sec. various svcs., Spokane, Wash., 1984-86; office mgr. Futurepast, Spokane, 1986-87; dir. mktg. and prodn. Futurepast: The History Co., Melior Publs., Spokane, 1987-88, v.p., 1988-89; founder, owner PageWorks Publ. Svcs., Post Falls, Idaho, 1989—; mem. dist. 2 Idaho State Ho. of Reps., 1990-92; mem. Idaho State Senate, 1992-94; adj. faculty North Idaho Coll., 1995. Author North Idaho's Centennial, 1990; editor Washington Songs and Lore, 1988. Bd. dirs. Mus. North Idaho, Coeur d'Alene, 1990-91, Ct. Apptd. Spl. Advocates, 1993—, Northwest Water Watch, 1992-94. Named Child Advocate Legislator of Yr., Idaho Alliance for Children, Youth and Families, 1993. Mem. AAUW, NOW, LWV, Nat. Women's Polit. Caucus, Idaho Women's Network, No. Idaho Pro-Choice Network, Idaho Conservation League, Mensa, Post Falls C. of C. Democrat. Office: PageWorks Publ Svcs PO Box 1893 Post Falls ID 83854

CHAMBERLAIN, OWEN, nuclear physicist; b. San Francisco, July 10, 1920; divorced 1978; 4 children; m. June Steingart, 1980 (dec.). AB (Cramer fellow), Dartmouth Coll., 1941; PhD, U. Chgo., 1949. Instr. physics U. Calif., Berkeley, 1948-50, asst. prof., 1950-54, assoc. prof., 1954-58, prof., 1958-89, prof. emeritus, 1989—; civilian physicist Manhattan Dist., Berkeley, Los Alamos, 1942-46. Recipient Nobel prize (with Emilio Segrè) for physics, for discovery anti-proton, 1959, The Berkeley citation U. Calif., 1989; Guggenheim fellow, 1957-58; Loeb lectr. at Harvard U., 1959. Fellow Am. Phys. Soc., Am. Acad. Arts and Scis.; mem. Nat. Acad. Scis., Berkeley Fellows. Office: U Calif Physics Dept Berkeley CA 94720

CHAMBERLAIN, WILLIAM EDWIN, JR., management consultant; b. St. Louis, June 8, 1951; s. William Edwin Sr. and Grace (Salisbury) C. AA in Bus. Mgmt., Mesa (Ariz.) Community Coll., 1983; BBA, U. Phoenix, 1988. Tng. and human resources devel. specialist Motorola, Inc., Phoenix, 1979-87; pres., seminar speaker Chamberlain Cons. Svcs., Chino Valley, Ariz., 1987—. Curator, dir. ops. U.S. Wolf Refuge and Adoption Ctr. Mem. ASTD, Network for Profl. Devel.

CHAMBERLAIN, WILTON NORMAN, retired professional basketball player; b. Phila., Aug. 21, 1936. Student, U. Kans., 1954-58. Player Harlem Globetrotters, 1958-59, Phila. (later San Francisco) Warriors, 1959-65, Phila. 76ers, 1965-68, Los Angeles Lakers, 1968-73; coach San Diego Conquistadors, Am. Basketball Assn., 1973-74. Actor, Conan The Destroyer, 1982; author: A View from Above, 1991. Player, Nat. Basketball Assn. All-Star Game, 1960-69, 71-73; rookie of yr. Nat. Basketball Assn., 1960; Most Valuable Player, Nat. Basketball Assn., 1960, 66-68, Nat. Basketball Assn. Playoffs, 1972; inducted Naismith Meml. Basketball Hall of Fame, 1978; named to Nat. Basketball Assn. 35th Anniversary All-Time Team, 1980; mem. Nat. Basketball Assn. Championship Team, 1967, 72; holder Nat. Basketball Assn. record for most points scored in one game with 100. Office: care Seymour Goldberg 11111 Santa Monica Blvd Los Angeles CA 90025-3344*

CHAMBERLIN, EUGENE KEITH, historian, educator; b. Gustine, Calif., Feb. 15, 1916; s. Charles Eugene and Anina Marguerite (Williams) C.; B.A. in History, U. Calif. at Berkeley, 1939, M.A., 1940, Ph.D., 1949; m. Margaret Rae Jackson, Sept. 1, 1940; children—Linda, Thomas, Rebecca, Adrienne (dec.), Eric. Tchr. Spanish, Latin, Lassen Union High Sch. and Jr. Coll., Susanville, Calif., 1941-43; tchr. history Elk Grove (Calif.) Joint Union High Sch., 1943-45; teaching asst. history U. Calif., Berkeley, 1946-48; instr. history Mont. State U., Missoula, 1948-51, asst. prof., 1951-54; asst. prof. to prof. San Diego City Coll., 1954-78; cab driver San Diego Yellow Cab Co., 1955-74, 79, 86; vis. prof. history Mont. State Coll., Bozeman, summer 1953, U. Calif. Extension, 1965-68, San Diego State Coll., 1965-68, others; instr., coordinator history lectures San Diego Community Colls.-TV, 1969-77; prof. San Diego Miramar Coll., 1978-83; prof. history San Diego Mesa Coll., 1983-86; mem. adv. com. Quechan Crossing Master Plan Project, 1989-90. Huntington Library-Rockefeller Found. grantee, 1952; Fulbright-Hays grantee, Peru, 1982; recipient merit award Congress of History San Diego County, 1978; Outstanding Educator award, San Diego City Coll., 1970; recipeint award for dedicated svc. to local history San Diego Hist. Soc., 1991. Mem. AAUP (various coms., nat. council 1967-70, pres. Calif. conf. 1968-70, acting exec. sec. 1970-72), San Diego County Congress of History (pres. 1976-77, newsletter editor 1977-78), Am. Hist. Assn. (life, Beveridge-Dunning com. 1982-84, chmn. 1984), Pacific Coast Council on Latin-Am. Studies, Cultural Assn. of the Californias, The Westerners (Calif., S.D. chpts.), E Clampus Vitus (historian 1970—, chpt. pres. 1972-73, dir. 1983-89, grand council mem. 1972-93, dir. T.R.A.S.H 1979-93, pres. 1983-84), Phi Alpha Theta (sec. U. Calif. Berkeley chpt. 1947-48, organizer and faculty adv., Mont. State U. chpt. 1948-54). Democrat. Mem. Ch. of the Brethren (del. 200th Annual Conf. 1986). Author numerous booklets on SW Am. history and numerous articles on Mexican NW to profl. jours. Home: 3033 Dale St San Diego CA 92104-4929

CHAMBERLIN, JOHN HOWARD, economic and management consultant; b. Alameda, Calif., Aug. 14, 1950; m. Joanne Louise Kinsman, May 25, 1985; children: Jennifer, Elizabeth, John, Andrew. BA in Econs., Calif. State U., Chico, 1972; MA in Econs., Wash. State U., 1975, PhD in Econs., 1976. Economist Hanford Engring. Devel. Lab., Washington, 1975-77; project mgr. Electric Power Rsch. Inst., Palo Alto, Calif., 1977-79, ICF, Inc., Washington, 1979-82; sr. project mgr. Electric Power Rsch. Inst., Palo Alto, Calif., 1982-85; exec. v.p. Barakat & Chamberlin, Inc., Oakland, Calif., 1985—; instr. Cybernetic System program San Jose (Calif.) U., 1979-80; bd. dirs. Creston Fin. Group, Oakland, 1991—, Hasting Coll. of Law for Trial and Appellate Advocacy, 1987, 88. Co-author: DSM Concepts and Methods, 1988, Demand-Side Management Planning, 1992; contbr. (book) Strategic Marketing, 1988; contbr. articles to profl. jours. Mem. Calif. Scholastic Fedn. (life 1968), Assn. Demand-Side Mgmt. Prof. (treas. 1989-91), Pacific Coast Electrical Assn., Pacific Coast Gas Assn., Am. Econ. Assn., Omocron Delta Epsilon. Office: Barakat & Chamberlin Inc 1800 Harrison St Fl 18 Oakland CA 94612-3429

CHAMBERLIN, SUSAN BURT, health facility administrator; b. Buffalo, N.Y., Oct. 14, 1945; d. Phillip Allister and Loyal Elizabeth (McClatchey) Burt; m. Richard H. Chamberlin, Sept. 16, 1967 (div. Jan. 1970); 1 child, Laura Elizabeth. BA in English, St. Lawrence U., 1967; M in English, SUNY, Oswego, 1972; MLS, SUNY, Albany, 1973. Asst. libr. for interlibr. loan, info. svcs. SUNY, Buffalo, 1973-75, head info. dissemination svc. Health Scis. Libr., 1975-77, asst. dir. Health Scis. Libr., 1977-79; asst. dir. program and resource devel. Med. Ctr. Libr. U. N.Mex., Albuquerque, 1979-82; dir. program devel./adminstr. for planning and devel. U. N.Mex. Cancer Ctr., Albuquerque, 1982—, mem. Cancer Ctr. internal adv. com., 1987—, mem. Cancer Ctr. exec. com., 1982—; mem. Med. Ctr. ambulatory care mktg. com. Med. Ctr. mktg. com., Albuquerque, 1986—; mem. Cancer Ctr. edn. com. U. N.Mex. Cancer Ctr., Albuquerque, 1982—; adj. asst. prof. comms. Sch. Nursing, SUNY, Buffalo, 1974-79; presenter to numerous groups including Rotary, Kiwanis, VFW, U.S. West Employee groups throughout the state, Optimists' Club, TV and radio talk shows, among others. Bd. dirs. Casa Esperanza, Inc., Albuquerque, 1986-93; bd. advisers Living Through Cancer, Inc., Albuquerque, 1985—, bd. dirs., 1983-85. Home: 6047 Redlands Rd NW Albuquerque NM 87120-1362 Office: U N Mex Cancer Rsch and Treatment Ctr 900 Camino de Salud NE Albuquerque NM 87131

CHAMBERS, CAROLYN SILVA, communications company executive; b. Portland, Oreg., Sept. 15, 1931; d. Julio and Elizabeth (McDonnell) Silva; widowed; children: William, Scott, Elizabeth, Silva, Clark. BBA, U. Oreg. V.p., treas. Liberty Comm., Inc., Eugene, Oreg., 1960-83; pres. Chambers Comm. Corp., Eugene, 1983—; chmn., bd. dirs. Chambers Constrn. Co., 1986—; bd. dirs., dep. chair bd. Fed. Res. Bank, San Francisco, 1982-92; bd. dirs. Portland Gen. Corp.; bd. dirs. U.S. Bancorp. Mem. Sacred Heart Med. Found., 1980—, Sacred Heart Gov. Bd., 1987-92, Sacred Heart Health Svcs. Bd., 1993—; mem. U. Oreg. Found., 1980—, pres., 1992-93; chair U. Oreg. Found. The Campaign for Oreg., 1988-89; pres., bd. dirs. Eugene Arts Found.; bd. dirs., treas., dir. search com. Eugene Symphony; mem. adv. bd. Eugene Hearing and Speech Ctr., Alton Baker Park Commn., Pleasant Hill Sch. Bd.; chmn., pres., treas. Civic Theatre, Very Little Theatre; negotiator, treas., bd. dirs., mem. thrift shop Jr. League of Eugene. Recipient Webfoot award U. Oreg., 1986, U. Oreg. Pres.'s medal, 1991, Disitng. Svc. award, 1992, Pioneer award, 1983, Woman Who Made a Difference award Internat. Women's Forum, 1989, U. Oreg. Found. Disting. Alumni award, 1995. Mem. Nat. Cable TV Assn. (mem. fin. com., chmn. election and by-laws com., chmn. awards com., bd. dirs. 1987—, Vanguard award for Leadership 1982), Pacific Northwest Cable Comm. Assn. (conv. chmn., pres.), Oreg. Cable TV Assn. (v.p., pres., chmn. edn. com., conv. chmn., Pres.'s award 1986), Calif. Cable TV Assn. (bd. dirs., conv. chmn., conv. panelist), Women in Cable (charter mem., treas., v.p., pres., recipient star of cable recognition), Wash. State Cable Comm. Assn., Idaho Cable TV Assn., Community Antenna TV Assn., Cable TV Pioneers, Eugene C. of C. (first citizen award, 1985). Home: PO Box 640 Pleasant Hill OR 97455-0640 Office: Chambers Comm Corp PO Box 7009 Eugene OR 97401-0009

CHAMBERS, CLYTIA MONTLLOR, public relations consultant; b. Rochester, N.Y., Oct. 23, 1922; d. Anthony and Marie (Bambace) Capraro; m. Joseph John Montllor, July 2, 1941 (div. 1958); children: Michele, Thomas, Clytia; m. Robert Chambers, May 28, 1965. BA, Barnard Coll., N.Y.C., 1942; Licence en droit, Faculte de Droit, U. Lyon, France, 1948; MA, Howard U., Washington, 1958. Assoc. dir. dept. rsch. Coun. for Fin. Aid to Edn., N.Y.C., 1958-60; asst. to v.p. indsl. rels. Sinclair Oil Corp., N.Y.C., 1961-65; writer pub. rels. dept. Am. Oil Co., Chgo., 1965-67; dir. editorial svcs., v.p. Hill & Knowlton Inc., N.Y.C., 1967-77; sr. v.p., dir. spl. svcs. Hill & Knowlton Inc., L.A., 1977-90; sr. cons. Hill & Knowlton Inc., 1990—; cons. and trustee Childen's Inst. Internat., L.A., 1988-93. Co-author: The News Twisters, 1971; editor: Critical Issues in Public Relations, 1975. Mem. Calif. Rare Fruit Growers (editor Fruit Gardener 1979—). Home: 11439 Laurelcrest Dr Studio City CA 91604-3872

CHAMBERS, GARY LEE, lawyer; b. Inglewood, Calif., June 6, 1953; s. George Edmund and Beverly Jean (Shuler) C.; m. Dalyn Valerie Myhra, Dec. 7, 1985; children: Garrett Ryan, Brendan Kyle, Danielle Christine. BA, U. Redlands (Calif.), 1975; JD, Western State U., Fullerton, Calif., 1978. Bar: Calif. 1979, U.S. Dist. Ct. (cen. dist.) Calif. 1979, U.S. Supreme Ct. 1982. Assoc. Law Offices of Murray Palitz, Westminster, Calif., 1979; pvt. practice law Orange, Calif., 1979-80; assoc. Law Offices Giles, Callahan et al, Tustin, Calif., 1980-81, Law Offices of Mark E. Edwards, Tustin, 1981-82; ptnr. Edwards, Chambers & Hoffman, Tustin, 1983-88, Chambers, Hoffman & Noronha, Santa Ana, Calif., 1989-92, Chambers, Noronha & Lowry, Santa Ana, Calif., 1992—; mem. tech. adv. staff Impact Gen., 1990—. Editorial adv. bd. James Pub. Co., 1988—. Named to Hall of Fame, Western State U., 1994. Mem. Orange County Trial Lawyers Assn. (bd. govs. 1984-92, pres. 1990), Calif. Trial Lawyers Assn. (bd. govs. 1986-93, sec. 1991-93, v.p. 1994-95, Chpt. Pres. of Yr. 1990, Presdl. award of merit 1987, 92, 93). Democrat. Christian Ch. Office: Chambers Noronha & Lowry 2070 N Tustin Ave Santa Ana CA 92705-4042

CHAMBERS, HENRY GEORGE, orthopaedic surgeon; b. Portsmouth, Va., June 22, 1956; s. Walter Charles and Teresa Frances (Fernandez) C.; m. Jill Annette Swanson, June 10, 1978; children: Sean Michael, Reid Christopher. BA summa cum laude in Biochemistry, U. Colo., 1978; MD, Tulane U. Sch. Medicine, 1982. Diplomate Am. Bd. Orthopaedic Surgery. Commd. 2d lt. U.S. Army, 1978; advanced through grades to maj.; intern Fitzsimmons Army Med. Ctr., Aurora, Colo., 1982-83; orthopaedic surgery resident Brooke Army Med. Ctr., Ft. Sam Houston, Tex., 1983-87, chief resident, 1986-87, staff orthopaedic surgeon to asst. residency program dir., 1987-89, asst. chief surgeon orthopaedic surgery svc., 1990-92; staff orthopaedic surgeon DeWitt Army Hosp., Ft. Belvoir, Va., 1987; pediatric orthopaedic fellow San Diego Children's Hosp., 1989-90; adj. prof. natural scis. Incarnate Word Coll., San Antonio, 1986—; asst. prof. surgery Uniformed Svcs. U. Health Scis., Bethesda, Md., 1987—; asst. program dir. Brooke Army Med. Ctr. Orthopaedic Surgery, 1987-92; asst. prof. U. Calif. San Diego Med. Ctr., 1989—. Co-author: Long Distance Runner's Guide to Training, 1983; contbr. various articles to profl. jours. Physician St. Vincent de Paul Clinic for Homeless, San Diego, 1989-92; bd. dirs. United Cerebral Palsy. Recipient Comdrs. award for oustanding rsch. Brooke Army Med. Ctr., 1987. Fellow Acad. Cerebral Palsy Devel. Medicine; mem. Pediatric Orthopedic Soc. N.Am., Am. Acad. Pediatrics, Acad. Orthopedic Soc., Orthopedic Rsch. Soc., Am. Acad. Orthopedic Surgeons, Physicians for Social Responsibility, Physicians Coun. for Responsible Medicine, We. Orthopedic Soc., Earth Island Inst., World Wildlife Fedn., Wilderness Soc., Union Concerned Scientists, Friends of Earth, Handgun Control, Phi Beta Kappa. Democrat. Unitarian. Home: 5458 Sandburg Ave San Diego CA 92122-4128

CHAMBERS, JOAN LOUISE, dean of libraries; b. Denver, Mar. 22, 1937; d. Joseph Harvey and Clara Elizabeth (Carleton) Baker; m. Donald Ray Chambers, Aug. 17, 1958. B.A. in English Lit., U. No. Colo., Greeley, 1958; M.S. in Library Sci., U. Calif.-Berkeley, 1970; M.S. in Systems Mgmt., U. So. Calif., 1985. Librarian U. Nev., Reno, 1970-79; asst. univ. librarian U. Calif., San Diego, 1979-81; univ. librarian U. Calif., Riverside, 1981-85; dir. libraries Colo. State U., 1985—; mgmt. intern. Duke U. Libr., Durham, N.C., 1978-79; sr. fellow UCLA, summer, 1982; cons. tng. program Assn. of Rsch. Libraries, Washington, 1981; libr. cons. Calif. State U., Sacramento, 1982-83, U. Wyo., 1985-86, U. Nebr., 1991-92, Calif. State U. System, 1993-94. Contbr. articles to profl. jours., chpts. to books. U. Calif. instl. improvement grantee, 1980-81; State of Nev. grantee, 1976, ARL grantee, 1983-84. Mem. ALA, Assn. Coll. and Rsch. Librs. IFLA (com. mem.) CNI, Libr. Adminstrn. and Mgmt. Assn., Colo. Libr. Assn., Assn. Rsch. Librs., United Way, Sierra Club, Beta Phi Mu, Phi Lambda Theta, Kappa Delta Phi. Home: 4470 S Lemay Ave Apt 1305 Fort Collins CO 80525-4844 Office: Colo State U William E Morgan Libr Fort Collins CO 80523

CHAMBERS, JONATHAN GOETZ, film producer; b. Wilmington, Del., Sept. 24, 1955; s. David Everett and Marie Louise (Goetz) C. BS in Film, Syracuse U., 1977. Prin. Chambers Co., L.A., 1980-90; pres. Chambers Co. Enterprises, Inc., Altadena, Calif., 1990—. Assoc. producer (films) Taste of Hemlock, 1988, One Cup of Coffee, 1991. Recipient Silver award Film & Tape Festival, 1979. Office: Chambers Co Enterprises Inc 1171 E Mendocino St Altadena CA 91001-2524

CHAMBERS, KENNETH CARTER, astronomer; b. Los Alamos, N.Mex., Sept. 27, 1956; s. William Hyland and Marjorie (Bell) C.; m. Jeanne Marie Hamilton, June 28, 1986; children: Signe Hamilton, William Hamilton. BA in Physics, U. Colo., 1979, MS in Physics, 1982; MA in Physics and Astronomy, Johns Hopkins U., 1985, PhD in Physics and Astronomy, 1990. Rsch. asst. dept. physics U. Colo., Boulder, 1982-83; rsch. asst. dept. physics and astronomy Johns Hopkins U., Balt., 1983-86; mem. instrument team Hopkins Ultraviolet Telescope, Balt., 1983-86; rsch. asst. Space Telescope Sci. Inst., Balt., 1986-90; postdoctoral fellow Leiden (The Netherlands) Obs. Leiden U., 1990-91; asst. prof. Inst. Astronomy U. Hawaii, Honolulu, 1991—; Contbr. articles to Astrophys. Jour., Nature mag., Phys. Rev.; contbr. conf. procs. in field. Mem. Am. Astron. Soc. (Chretein award 1989), Am. Phys. Soc. Office: Inst Astronomy U Hawaii 2680 Woodlawn Dr Honolulu HI 96822-1839

CHAMBERS, LOIS IRENE, insurance automation consultant; b. Omaha, Nov. 24, 1935; d. Edward J. and Evelyn B. (Davidson) Morrison; m. Peter A. Mscichowski, Aug. 16, 1952 (div. 1980); 1 child, Peter Edward; m. Frederick G. Chambers, Apr. 17, 1981. Clk. Gross-Wilson Ins. Agy., Portland, Oreg., 1955-57; sec., bookkeeper Reed-Paulsen Ins. Agy., Portland, 1957-58; office mgr., asst. sec., agt. Don Biggs & Assocs., Vancouver, Wash., 1958-88, v.p. ops., 1988-89, automation mgr., 1989-91, mktg. mgr., 1991-94; automation cons. Chambers & Assocs., Tualatin, Oreg., 1985—; chmn. adv. com. Clark Community Coll., Vancouver, 1985-93, adv. com., 1993-94. Mem. citizens com. task force City of Vancouver, 1976-78, mem. Block Grant rev. task force, 1978—. Mem. Ins. Women of S.W. Wash. (pres. 1978, Ins. Woman of Yr. 1979), Nat. Assn. Ins. Women, Nat. Users Agena Systems (charter; pres. 1987-89), Soroptimist Internat. (Vancouver)(pres. 1978-79, Soroptimist of the Year 1979-80). Democrat. Roman Catholic. Office: Chambers & Assocs 8770 SW Umatilla St Tualatin OR 97062-9338

CHAMBERS, MILTON WARREN, architect; b. L.A., Aug. 5, 1928; s. Joe S. and Barbara N. (Harris) C.; m. Elizabeth M. Smith, Nov. 27, 1949; children: Mark, Michael, Daniel, Matthew. Student, Coll. of Sequoias, 1948-49, Harvard U., 1990. Lic. architect, Calif., Nev., Colo., Hawaii, Mont.; cert. Nat. Coun. Archtl. Registration Bds. Apprentice architect Kastner & Kastner Architects, Visalia, Calif., 1950-57; project architect Wurster, Bernardi & Emmons, Architects, San Francisco, 1958-63, Claude Oakland, Architect, San Francisco, 1964-65; chief architect Bank of Am., San Francisco, 1965-68; pres., owner Milton W. Chambers, Architect, San Rafael, Calif., 1969-82, The Chambers Group, Architects, Rancho Mirage, Calif., 1983—. Architect, designer St. Margaret's Episcopal Church, 1988. Foreman Marin County Grand Jury, San Rafael, 1976; mem. Archtl. Design Rev. Bd., Rancho Mirage, 1986—; trustee Marywood Sch., Rancho Mirage, 1990—. Cpl. U.S. Army, 1946-48, PTO, 50-51. Mem. AIA (pres. Calif. Desert chpt. 1986-87, dir. Calif. Coun. 1989-90), Rotary Internat., Terra Linda Rotary Club (pres. 1975-76, dist. gov. 1993-94), Rancho Mirage Rotary Club (pres. 1986-87). Republican. Episcopalian. Office: The Chambers Group 70390 Highway 111 Ste 101 Rancho Mirage CA 92270

CHAMBERS, STEPHEN L.E., university official; b. Flagstaff, Ariz., July 24, 1956; s. LeRoy O. and Geraldine (Fisher) C.; m. Mary Elizabeth Elliott, May 4, 1991. BS in Polit. Sci., No. Ariz. U., 1977, MA in Sociology, 1979, PhD in History and Polit. Sci., 1985; student, Calif. West Sch. Law, 1977. Rsch. analyst No. Ariz. U., Flagstaff, 1978-80, rsch. asst., 1980-82, program dir., 1982-83, mgmt. rsch. analyst, 1983-87, interim dir. inst. rsch., 1987-88, asst. dir. inst. rsch., 1988-89, assoc. dir. univ. planning analysis, 1989-94; interim dir. univ. planning, analysis, 1994—; invited speaker on campus preservation planning, Tex. Tech. U., 1990, Clemson U. and Nat. Park Svc., 1995; expert in field; mem. Ariz. Hist. Sites Rev. Com., 1986—. Contbr. articles to profl. jours. Elections marshall Coconino County, Flagstaff, 1978-82; active Big Sisters No. Ariz., Flagstaff, 1987—; vice chmn. adv. com. Ariz. Hist. Preservation, 1991—; chmn. tech. support com. Ariz. Bd. Regents, 1991-92, mem. commn. on status of women, 1989-91, mem. enrollment mgmt. task force, 1992—, mem. ethnic minority student goal setting tech. assistance com., 1993—; mem. Flagstaff Main St. Found. Recipient cert. award DAR, 1986; named One of Handful of Nat. Experts on Resolving Sticky Issues of Campus Planning, Hist. Preservation News, Nat. Trust for Hist. Preservation, 1995; acad. scholaara R.O. Raymond Found., Phoenix, 1974-76; rsch. grantee Navajo and Hopi Rels. Com.-U.S. Govt., 1982, program grantee U.S. Dept. Edn., 1979-82. Mem. Mus. No. Ariz., Flagstaff Symphony Assn., Assn. for Study of Higher Edn., Am. Assn. for Higher Edn., Ariz. Assn. Instl. Rsch. (founder 1987-88), Ctr. for Study of Presidency, Nat. Trust Historic Preservation, Ariz. Hist. Soc., Assn. for Instl. Rsch., Soc. Coll. and Univ. Planning, Phi Alpha Theta. Democrat. Roman Catholic. Office: No Ariz U PO Box 4132 Flagstaff AZ 86011

CHAMBERS, VIRGINIA ELLEN, community volunteer, retired photographer; b. St. Paul, Apr. 17, 1927; d. Carlton Gardner and Lillian (Cox) Annable; m. Newell LeMoine Bradley, Oct. 26, 1946 (dec. Aug. 1968); children: Rosalind (dec.), Newell Jr., Lawrence, Stephan; m. Stanley Lancaster Chambers, July 22, 1979. Student, Morningside Coll., Sioux City, Iowa, 1945, Nebr. U., 1961-62. Telephone operator Northwestern Bell, Sioux City, 1946-48, Norfolk, Nebr., 1949-52, Des Moines, 1962-67; owner cocktail lounge Tucson, 1968-72; photographer Jones & Presnell, Charlotte, N.C., 1975-79. Treas. Gen. Fedn. Women's Clubs-Ariz., 1990-92, recording sec., 1992-94; pres. Gen. Fedn. Women's Clubs-Southwestern dist., 1986-88, 3d v.p., 1994—; founder London Bridge Woman's Club, Lake Havasu, pres. 1981-83, treas., 1984-86, pres.-elect, 1992-94, pres., 1994—; v.p. Homemaker's Extension Club, Lake Havasu, 1988; vol. Festival Arts Assn., Lake Havasu, Cancer Soc., Easter Seal Soc., Heart Fund, Jazz Festival, Hosp. Aux.-Havasu Samaritan Regional Hosp.; mem. state legis. com. Am. Assn. Ret. Persons, Friends of Libr.; sec. Mohave County (Ariz.) Dem. Cen. Com., 1988-91; mem. Dem. Assn. of Havasu. Mem. Lake Havasu Hist. Soc. Home: PO Box 297 Lake Havasu City AZ 86405-0297

CHAMBERS-SWEENEY, LINDA J., association administrator, small business owner; b. Glendale, Calif., Jan. 29, 1954; d. Thomas Bowden and Barbara Lenore (Hutton) Chambers; m. Robert Sandt, Oct. 25, 1986 (div.); m. Michael Joseph Sweeney, Feb. 8, 1992; children: Deanna Perry, Sean Sandt, Cara Underwood. Grad., Am. Sch. in Switzerland, 1972. Buyer children's clothing The Yellow Brick Rd., Torrance, Calif., 1977-82; owner catering business and gift baskets Fantastique Food, Dana Point, Calif., 1983-88; owner gift basket service and specialty foods Spl. Request, Park City, Utah, 1989-92; founder, acting dir. Campaign for Prevention of Head Injury, Bozeman, Mont., 1992—; owner, chef, designer Spl. Request Catering & Gift Baskets, Bozeman, 1993—, acting dir., chair, 1992-94. Office: Campaign Prevention Head Injury PO Box 6425 Bozeman MT 59771

CHAMBON, CHARLES WILLIAM, electrical engineer; b. Colorado Springs, Colo., Apr. 15, 1954; s. George William and Myrtle Ines (Elliott) C. BSEE, U. Colo., 1982, MSEE, 1985, postgrad., 1985—. Asst. prof. engrng. graphic design, instr. physics U. Colo., Colorado Springs, 1981-82; rschr. with Robert Burton and Ronald M. Sego Defense Advanced Rsch. Project, 1979-85. Active Pikes Peak Jaycees, Colorado Springs Jaycees, Colorado Springs Police Dept. Named Community Fund Raiser of Yr., Colo. Jaycees, 1984, Jaycee of Yr., Pikes Peak Jaycees, 1982, 84, Outstanding Young Coloradan, Colo. Jaycees and JCI Senate, 1984, Outstanding Young Man Am., U.S. Jaycees, 1983; recipient Award of Appreciation, Rocky Mountain Multiple Sclerosis Ctr. Denver, 1983, Cert. of Merit, Colo. Engring. Coun., 1982. Mem. IEEE, Acoustics, Speech and Signal Processing Soc. of IEEE, Automatic Control Soc. of IEEE, Aerospace and Electronic Systems Soc. of IEEE, AAAS (disabled resource group 1981—), Am. Radio Relay League, Denver Radio League, Lookout Mountain Repeater Group, Squaw Mountain Ham Club, Pueblo Ham Club, Telstar Ham Club, Amateur Radio Emergency Svc., Pikes Peak FM Assn., Wilderness on Wheels Found., Cheyenne Mountain Repeater Group (pres., founder 1981—), Rocky Mountain Pedals and Chords Organ Club, Eta Kappa Nu (Theta Chi chpt., pres. 1982-83, Award of Appreciation 1984). Home: 2823 W Vintah St Colorado Springs CO 80904-2429

CHAMPAGNE, DUANE WILLARD, sociology educator; b. Belcourt, N.D., May 18, 1951; m. Liana Marie Bruce, Aug. 16, 1973; children: Talya, Gabe, Demelza. BA in Math., N.D. State U., 1973, MA in Sociology, 1975; PhD in Sociology, Harvard U., 1982. Teaching fellow Harvard U., Cambridge, Mass., 1981-82, rsch. fellow, 1982-83; asst. prof. U. Wis., Milw., 1983-84; asst. prof. UCLA, 1984-91, assoc. prof., 1991—; publs. dir. Am. Indian Studies Ctr., UCLA, 1986-87, assoc. dir., 1990, acting dir., 1991, dir., 1991—; adminstrv. co-head interdepartmental program for Am. Indian studies UCLA, 1992-93; mem. grad. rsch. fellowship panel NSF, 1990-92, minority fellowship com. ASA; cons. Energy Resources Co., 1982, No. Cheyenne Tribe, 1983, Realis Pictures, Inc., 1989-90, Sta. KCET-TV, L.A., 1990, 92, Salem Press, 1992, Book Prodns. Systems, 1993, Readers Digest, 1993, Rattlesnake Prodns., 1993. Author: American Indian Societies, 1989, Social Order and Political Change, 1992; editor: Native North American Almanac, 1994, Chronology of Native North American, 1994, Native American of the Peoples Portrait, 1994; editor Native Am. Studies Assn. Newsletter, 1991-92; bok rev. editor Am. Indian Culture and Rsch. Jour., 1984-86, editor, 1986-95; book reviewer Contemporary Sociology, Am. Indian Quarterly, Cultural Survival Quarterly, Am. Ethnologist, Ethnohistory; reviewer Am. Sociol. Rev., Am. Indian Culture and Rsch. Jour., Social Sci. Quarterly, Social Problems, Am. Ethnologist, Families in Society, Am. Indian Quarterly, Demography, Ethnohistory, NSF, U. Calif. Press, Oxford U. Press; contbr. over 20 articles to profl. jours. Mem. City of L.A. Cmty. Action Bd., 1993, L.A. County/City Am. Indian Commn., 1992—, chair, 1993-95; mem. subcom. for cultural and econ. devel. L.A. City/County Native Am. Commn., 1992-93; bd. dirs. Ctr. for Improvement of Child Caring, 1993-95, Greater L.A. Am. Indian Culture Ctr., Inc., 1993, Incorporator, 1993. Grantee Rockefeller Found., 1982-83, U. Wis. Grad Sch. Rsch. Com., 1984-85, Wis. Dept. Edn., 1984-85, 87-88, 88-89, NSF, 1985-88, 88-89), Nat. Endowment for Arts, 1987-88, 91-92, NRC, 1988-89, Nat. Sci. Coun., 1989-90, John D. and Catherine T. MacArthur Found., 1990-91, Hayes Found., 1990-91, 92-93, Calif. Coun. for Humanities, 1991-92, Ford Found., 1990-92, Gale Rsch. Inc., 1991-93, 93-95, Rockwell Corp., 1991-93, GTE, 1992-93; Am. Indian scholar, 1973-75, 80-82, Minority fellow Am. Sociol. Assn., 1975-78, RIAS Seminar fellow, 1976-77; Rockefeller Postdoctoral fellow, 1982-83, NSF fellow, 1985-88, Postdoctoral fellow Ford Found., 1988-89. Office: UCLA Am Indian Studies Ctr 3220 Campbell Hall PO Box 951548 Los Angeles CA 90095-1548

CHAMPOUX, JAMES JOSEPH, biochemist, educator; b. Seattle, Nov. 6, 1942; s. Louis and Alice Louise (Stafford) C.; m. Esther Arceo, Aug. 30, 1968 (div. Sept. 1992); children: Angie Farmer, Erik; m. Sharon Schultz, June 25, 1994. BS in Chemistry, U. Wash., 1965; PhD in Biochemistry, Stanford U., 1970. Postdoctoral fellow The Salk Inst., La Jolla, Calif., 1970-72; asst. prof. U. Wash., Seattle, 1972-78, assoc. prof., 1978-82, prof., 1982—; vis. scientist MIT, Cambridge, Mass., 1980-81; mem. study sect. Am. Cancer Soc., N.Y.C., 1979-84; sabbatical leace ISREC, Lausanne, Switzerland, 1992-93. Co-author: (book) Medical Microbiology-An Introduction to Infectious Diseases, 2d edit., 1990, 3rd edit., 1994; contbr. articles to profl. jours. Recipient Guggenheim fellowship Guggenheim Found., 1980-81, Disting. Teaching award U. Wash., 1985. Home: 4101 NE 186th St Seattle WA 98155-2851 Office: U Wash Dept Microbiology Seattle WA 98195

CHAN, ALLEN FONG, protective services official; b. Union City, Calif., Mar. 9, 1957; s. Herbert Quai and Christine (Lee) C.; m. Cimberly Chu. Student, Ohlone Coll., Fremont, Calif., 1975-79; BS in Recreation Adminstrn., Calif. State U., Hayward, 1979. Recreation specialist City of Newark (Calif.) Recreation Dept., 1973-79, police aide, 1981-83, police officer, 1983—; instr. Ohlone Coll., Fremont; supervising recreation coordinator City of Fremont (Calif.) Community Services, Recreation, 1978-79, park ranger, 1979-83; communication operator City of Hayward (Calif.) Police Dept., 1980-81. Advisor Newark Police Explorers, Boy Scouts Am., 1983—; coordinating officer, Sch. Safety Patrol, Newark, 1987—; basketball ofcl. Mission Valley Athletic League, Fremont, Calif., 1975-79; site ofcl. Cath. Youth Orgn., Fremont, 1975-79; active Alameda County (Calif.) Spl. Olympics, 1981; chmn. local chpt. Internat. Spl. Olympic Winter Games, 1989; chmn. law enforcement torch run Calif. Spl. Olympics, 1989; bd. dirs.

Fremont Softball League, 1979-80. Named Outstanding Young Men. Am., 1982. Mem. Police Officers Rsch. Assn. Calif., Calif. Orgn. Police and Sheriffs, Calif. Parks and Recreation Soc., Newark Police Assn. (sec. 1985-88, pres. 1988-90), Calif. Law Enforcement Adminstrn. (bd. dirs. 1988—). Democrat. Office: City of Newark Police Dept 37101 Newark Blvd Newark CA 94560-3727

CHAN, DANIEL CHUNG-YIN, lawyer; b. Kowloon, Hong Kong, June 5, 1948; came to U.S., 1969; s. David Chi-Kwong and Betty Wai-Lan (Kwok) C.; m. Mary Ching-Fay Wong, June 11, 1977; children: Pamila Wai-Sum (dec.), Derrick Ming-Deh. BA cum laude, Azusa Pacific U., 1972; postgrad., Calif. State U., L.A., 1973-75; JD, U. West L.A., 1983. Bar: Calif. 1984, U.S. Dist. Ct. (cen. dist.) Calif. 1984, U.S. Ct. Appeals (9th cir.) 1984, U.S. Dist. Ct. (so. dist.) Calif. 1985, U.S. Dist. Ct. (no. dist.) Calif. 1986. Mgr. Elegant Sewing Co., L.A., 1977; legal asst. Otto Frank Swanson Law Office, Marina Del Ray, Calif., 1978-84, assoc., 1984-87; pvt. practice, Pasadena, Calif., 1987—; legal counsel Chinese Grace Missions Internat., Inc., Duarte, Calif., 1984—, Diao Jiou Chinese Christian Ch. L.A., Highland Park, Calif., 1988—, Ruth Hitchcock Found. Mem. ABA, Assn. Trial Lawyers Am., So. Calif. Chinese Lawyers Assn., Am. Immigration Lawyers Assn., Delta Epsilon Chi, Alpha Chi. Office: 283 S Lake Ave Ste 219 Pasadena CA 91101-3007

CHAN, LOREN BRIGGS, technical writing specialist; b. Palo Alto, Calif., Sept. 10, 1943; s. Shau Wing and Anna Mae (Chin) C.; m. Frances Anastasia Chow, Apr. 19, 1975 (div. Jan. 1988); children: Karen Monique, Pierre Bénédict, Marc Henri. AB, Stanford U., 1965, AM, 1966; MS, Golden Gate U., 1988; PhD, UCLA, 1971. Teaching asst. UCLA, 1968-69, teaching assoc., 1969-70; lectr. in history Calif. State U., Northridge, 1970-71; lectr. in history San Jose (Calif.) State U., 1971-72, asst. prof. history, 1972-76, assoc. prof. history, 1976-80; lectr. history Calif. State U., Hayward, 1980-81; prodn. test technician Nicolet Paratronics Corp., Fremont, Calif., 1982; computer svc. technician Bell-Northern Rsch., Mountain View, Calif., 1982-83; rsch. analyst Bell-No. Rsch., Mountain View, 1984-85, tech. writer, 1985-87; sr. tech. writer StrataCom, Inc., Campbell, Calif., 1987-88; tech. writer Sun Microsystems, Mountain View, 1988-90, sr. tech. writer, 1990—. Author: Sagebrush Statesman, 1973, SPARCstation 1 Installation Guide, 1989, Collected Technical Support Notes, 1988, SPARCstation 2 Installation Guide, 1990, Desktop Storage Pack Installation Guide, 1989-90, SPARCstation 10 Installation Guide, 1992, SPARCstation 10 Networking and Communication Guide, 1993, SPARCstation 10SX VSIMMs Installation, 1993, SPARCstation 20 HyperSPARC Module Upgrade, 1995, SPARCstation 20 SuperSPARC-II Module Upgrade, 1995; editor: Chinese-American History Reader, 1976; contbr. articles to profl. jours. Radio sta. trustee ARC, Menlo Park, Calif., 1975-80. Recipient Presdl. Sports award Pres.'s Coun. on Phys. Fitness and Sports, 1973. Mem. Nat. Geog. Soc., Chinese Inst. Engrs., Am. Radio Relay League, Confederate Stamp Alliance, Buick Club of Am., San Jose Aquatics Masters Swim Club. Democrat. Christian Scientist. Home: 5719 Makati Cir Apt D San Jose CA 95123-6211

CHAN, MICHAEL CHIU-HON, chiropractor; b. Hong Kong, Aug. 31, 1961; came to U.S., 1979; s. Fuk Yum and Chun Wai (Ma) C. D of Chiropractic, Western States Chiropractic Coll., 1985; fellow, Internat. Acad. Clin. Acupuncture, 1986. Assoc. doctor Widoff Chiropractic Clinic, Phoenix, 1986, Horizon Chiropractic Clinic, Glendale, Ariz., 1986-88; dir. North Ranch Chiropractic Assoc., Scottsdale, Ariz., 1988-91; pvt. practice Phoenix, 1991—; dir. Neighborhood Chiropractic, Phoenix, 1988-89. Contbr. articles to profl. jours. Mem. Am. Chiropractic Assoc., Internat. Platform Assn., Coun. on Diagnostic Imaging, Paradise Valley Toastmaster Club. Office: 6544 W Thomas Rd Ste 37 Phoenix AZ 85033-5741

CHAN, PETER WING KWONG, pharmacist; b. L.A., Feb. 3, 1949; s. Sherwin T.S. and Shirley W. (Lee) C.; m. Patricia Jean Uyeno, June 8, 1974; children: Kristina Dionne, Kelly Alison, David Shoichi. BS, U. So. Calif., 1970, D in Pharmacy, 1974. Lic. pharmacist, Calif. Clin. instr. U. So. Calif., 1974-76; staff clin. pharmacist Cedars-Sinai Med. Ctr., L.A., 1974-76; 1st clin. pharmacist in ophthalmology Alcon Labs., Inc., Ft. Worth, 1977—, formerly in Phila. monitoring patient drug therapy, teaching residents, nurses, pharmacy students, then assigned to Tumu Tumu Hosp., Karatina, Kenya, also lectr. clin. ocular pharmacology tng. course, Nairobi, Cairo, Athens, formerly dist. sales mgr. Alcon/BP, ophthal. products div. Alcon Labs., Inc., Denver; v.p., gen. mgr. Optikem Internat., Sereine Products Div., Optacryl, Inc., Denver, 1980-91; product mgr. hosp. pharmacy products Am. McGaw div. Am. Hosp. Supply Corp., 1981-83; internat. market mgr. IOLAB subs. Johnson & Johnson, 1983-86, dir. new bus. devel. Iolab Pharms., 1986-87, dir. Internat. Mktg., 1987-89, dir. new products mktg., 1989; bus. and mktg. strategies cons. to pharm. and med. device cos. Chan & Assocs., Northridge, Calif., 1989—; ptnr., chmn., CEO PreFree Techs., Inc., 1992—; ptnr. Vitamin Specialties Corp., 1993—, JSP Ptnrs., Ltd., 1992—; bd dirs. SUDCO Internat., L.A. Del. Am. Pharm. Assn. House of Dels., 1976-78; bd. dirs. Calif. Youth Theatre at Paramount Studios, Hollywood 1986-87, 91-95. Recipient Hollywood-Wilshire Pharm. Assn. spl. award for outstanding svc., 1974. Mem. Chinese Am. Pharm. Assn., Am. Pharm. Assn., Calif. Pharm. Assn., Hollywood-Wilshire Pharm. Assn. (bd. dirs. 1972-76), Am. Soc. Hosp. Pharmacists, Am. Pharm. Assn. Acad. of Pharmacy Practice, U. So. Calif. Assocs. (life), U. So. Calif. Gen. Alumni Assn., U. So. Calif. (steering com. lifescis. info. networking coun.), Granada Hills High Sch. Highlanders Booster Club (bd. dirs. 1991, 92, 93, chmn.-Project 2000), QSAD Centurions, U. So. Calif. Lifetime Assocs., Gamma Epsilon Omega Alumni Assn. (bd. dirs.), Phi Delta Chi, NRA (life), Golden Eagle, Calif. Rifle and Pistol Assn. (life mem.). Republican. Home: 10251 Vanalden Ave Northridge CA 91324-1240 Office: Chan & Assocs PO Box 7398 Northridge CA 91327-7398 also: PreFree Techs. Inc 18600 Von Karman Ave Irvine CA 92715-1513 also: JSP Ptnrs Ltd 2646 Dupont Dr Ste 20-455 Irvine CA 92715-1688

CHANCE, KENNETH DONALD, engineer; b. Denver, July 27, 1948; s. John Jefferson and Evelyn Pauline (Jacobs) C. AA, Red Rocks Coll., Golden, Colo., 1982. Stationery operating engr. EG&G Rocky Flats, Golden, 1980—. Office: EG&G Rocky Flats Rocky Flats Util Bldg 707 Golden CO 80402

CHAND, KRISHNA, surgeon; b. Chgo., Feb. 6, 1960; s. Ramesh and Alma (Ambrosio) C. BS, U. Mich., 1979; MD, Wayne State U., 1983. Bd. cert. Am. Bd. Surgery. Intern, then resident Wayne State U. Affiliated Hosps., Detroit, 1983-89; gen. surgeon Sunnyside (Wash.) Comty. Hosp., 1990—, Providence Hosp., Toppenish, Wash., 1990—. Fellow ACS (assoc.); mem. AMA, Am. Soc. Gastrointestinal Endoscopy, Soc. Laparoendoscopal Surgeons, Soc. Critical Care Medicine, Wash. State Med. Assn., Yakima County Med. Soc. Office: 1017 Tacoma Ave Sunnyside WA 98944-2262

CHANDLER, ALLEN, food products executive; b. 1942. With Northwest Wholesale, Wenatchee, Wash., 1964-68; with No. Fruit Co., Wenatchee, Wash., 1968—, now v.p. Office: Northern Fruit Co 220 3rd St NE Wenatchee WA 98802-4856*

CHANDLER, BRIDGETT ANN, urban planner; b. Spokane, Wash., Sept. 18, 1961; d. Leo Michael and Patricia Mae (Sterling) C.; m. Bear Silverstein, Aug. 13, 1993. BA in Comparative Lit., Seattle U., 1983, BA in Fgn. Lang., 1983; license sciences economiques, Université Paul Valéry, Montpellier, France, 1985; M in Internat. Studies, Claremont U., 1987. Rsch. asst. Seattle City Light, 1982-83; paralegal King County Prosecuting Atty., Seattle, 1979-82, Wash. Atty. Gen., Seattle, 1984; statistics teaching asst. Claremont Grad. Sch., 1986-87; rsch. asst. U.S. EPA, Washington, 1984; planning and devel. specialist City of Seattle, Washington, 1987-91, sr. planner human svcs., 1992, sr. planner rapid transit, 1993, sand point base closure mgr., 1993-95; chair-steering com. Student Conservation Assn., Seattle, 1993—, Earthwork. Contbg. author: Framework Policies, 1991; editor: Fragments, 1983; radio talk show host: Talking Book and Braille Libr., Seattle, 1990—. Pres. Seattle Women in Gov., 1989-90, program chair, 1988-89; panel discussion facilitator Seattle Women's Commn., 1992-93; grad. Leadership Tomorrow, Seattle, 1990-91; judicial candidate review Mcpl. League, Seattle, 1992; City of Seattle AIDS Walk Coord. NW Aids Found., Seattle, 1992—. Named Outstanding Grad., Coll. Arts and Scis. Seattle U., 1983; Claremont Grad. Sch. fellow, 1985-87, Internat. scholar Rotary Internat., 1984-85. Mem. Am. Planning Assn., Seattle Women in Govt., Seattle Mgmt. Assn. Democrat. Home: 5436 48th Ave SW Seattle WA 98136-1009 Office: City of Seattle Mayor's Office Mgmt and Planning 600 Fourth Ave Rm 200 Seattle WA 98104

CHANDLER, BRUCE FREDERICK, internist; b. Bohemia, Pa., Mar. 26, 1926; s. Frederick Arthur and Minnie Flora (Burkhardt) C.; m. Janice Evelyn Piper, Aug. 14, 1954; children: Barbara, Betty, Karen, Paul, June. Student, Pa. State U., 1942-44; MD, Temple U., 1948. Diplomate Am. Bd. Internal Medicine. Commd. med. officer U.S. Army, 1948, advanced through grades to col., 1967; intern Temple U. Hosp., Phila., 1948-49; chief psychiatry 7th Field Hosp., Trieste, Italy, 1950; resident Walter Reed Gen. Hosp., Washington, 1949-53; battalion surgeon 2d Div. Artillery, Korea, 1953-54; chief renal dialysis unit 45th Evacuation Hosp. and Tokyo Army Hosp., Korea, Japan, 1954-55; various assignments Walter Reed Gen. Hosp., Fitzsimons Gen. Hosp., Letterman Gen. Hosp., 1955-70; comdg. officer 45th Field Hosp., Vicenza, Italy, 1958-62; pvt. practice internist Ridgecrest (Calif.) Med. Clinic, 1970-76; chief med. svc. and out-patients VA Hosps., Walla Walla, Spokane, Wash., 1976-82; med. cons. Social Security Adminstrn., Spokane, Wash., 1983-87; ret. Panel mem. TV shows, 1964-70; lectr.; contbr. numerous articles to med. profl. jours. Decorated Legion of Merit. Fellow ACP, Am. Coll. Chest Physicians; mem. AMA, Am. Thoracic Soc., N.Y. Acad. Scis., So. European Task Force U.S. Army Med. Dental Soc. (pres., founder 1958-62). Republican. Methodist. Home: 6496 N Callisch Ave Fresno CA 93710-3902

CHANDLER, COLSTON, physics educator; b. Boston, June 7, 1939; s. William Knox and Margaret Belle (Colston) C.; m. Seeley Dole, Jan. 30, 1965 (div. Feb. 1987); children: Andrew, Martin, Thomas; m. Susan Craig, Apr. 17, 1994. BS in Applied Math., Brown U., 1961; PhD in Physics, U. Calif., Berkeley, 1967. Asst. prof. U. N.Mex., Albuquerque, 1966-68, 70-73, assoc. prof., 1973-78, prof. physics, 1978—; vis. prof. U. Bonn, Fed. Republic Germany, 1978; NAS Exch. scientist East German Acad. Scis., 1983; faculty scientist-in-residence Argonne Nat. Lab., 1984-85; vis. scientist CRIP Inst. for Particle and Nuclear Physics, 1977-78, 85—; Fulbright sr. scholar Flinders U., Adelaide, Australia, 1994-95. Contbr. articles to profl. publs. Recipient Meml. medal Ctrl. Rsch. Inst. for Physics, 1988. Fellow Am. Phys. Soc.; mem. AAUP, AAAS, Internat. Assn. Math. Physics, Sigma Xi. Office: U NMex Dept Physics And Astro Albuquerque NM 87131

CHANDLER, DAVID, scientist, educator; b. Bklyn., Oct. 15, 1944. SB, MIT, 1966; PhD, Harvard U., 1969. Research assoc. U. Calif., San Diego, 1969-70; from asst. prof. to prof. U. Ill., Urbana, 1970-83; prof. U.Pa., Phila., 1983-85, U. Calif., Berkeley, 1986—; vis. prof. Columbia U., N.Y.C., 1977-78; vis. scientist IBM Corp., Yorktown Heights, N.Y., 1978, Oak Ridge Nat. Lab., 1979; cons. Los Alamos Nat. Labs., 1986-90; Miller rsch. prof., 1991; dir. de recherche Ecole Normale Superieure de Lyon, France, fall 1992; Christensen vis. fellow Oxford U., winter 1993, Hinshelwood lectr., 1993. Editor Chem. Physics, 1985—; mem. editl. bd. Jour. Statis. Physics, 1976-78, 94—, Jour. Chem. Physics, 1978-80, Chem. Physics Letters, 1980-82, 91—, Molecular Physics, 1982-88, Jour. Phys. Chemistry, 1987-92; author books in field; contbr. articles to profl. jours. Recipient Bourke medal Faraday Div. Royal Chem. Soc., Eng., 1985, Joel Henry Hildebrand award Am. Chem. Soc., 1989; fellow Alfred P. Sloan Found., 1972-74, Guggenheim Found., 1981-82. Fellow AAAS, Am. Phys. Soc.; mem. Nat. Acad. Scis., Am. Acad. Arts and Scis., Am. Chem. Soc. (chmn. divsn. theoretical chemistry 1984, chmn. divsn. phys. chemistry 1990). Office: U Calif Dept Chemistry Berkeley CA 94720

CHANDLER, DOUGLAS EDWIN, zoology educator; b. Oak Park, Ill., Oct. 1, 1945; s. Herbert Edwin and Jeannette (Willard) C. BS in Chemistry, U. Rochester, 1967; MA in Biochemistry, Johns Hopkins U., Balt., 1969; PhD in Physiology, U. Calif., San Francisco, 1977. Postdoctoral fellow U. Calif., San Francisco, 1977-79, U. Coll. Sch. Medicine, London, 1979-80; asst. prof. Ariz. State U., Tempe, 1980-85; assoc. prof. Ariz. State U., 1985-90, prof. zoology, 1990—. Contbr. articles to profl. jours.; guest editor Microscopy Rsch. & Technique, 1988—, mem. editorial bd., 1990—. With USN, 1969-73. NIH rsch. career devel. awardee, 1985-90; NSF grantee, 1981—. Mem. Am. Soc. Cell Biology, Soc. for Developmental Biology. Office: Arizona State Univ Dept Zoology Tempe AZ 85287

CHANDLER, FLOYD COPELAND, fine arts educator; b. San Diego, Dec. 5, 1920; s. Floyd Fedrick and Benadah (Sullivan) C. Cert., S.D. Acad. Fine Arts, 1937, Otis Art Inst., L.A., 1941, Art Students League N.Y., N.Y.C., 1950; BA, San Diego State U., 1964; MA, Claremont Grad. Sch., 1969. Designer Farr Screen Prossing Corp., N.Y.C., 1950; advt., art dept. Preferred Utilities Mfg. Corp., N.Y.C., 1951-54; free-lance mural work and porature N.Y.C., 1947-53; head art dept. Desert Sun High Sch., Idyllwild, Calif., 1954; fine arts instr. adult sch. San Diego Unified Sch. Dist., 1955-71; dept. head continuing edn. div. San Diego C.C., 1971-79, fine arts instr., 1980-95; curator San Diego Art Inst., 1960-70; chmn. city-wide art shows Adult Educator of San Diego, 1969-75; curator Balboa Park, San Diego, 1960-70. Exhibited in group shows at Chapellier Studio Gallery, N.Y.C., 1950, Mus. Natural History, San Diego, 1969, Thackeray Fine Arts Gallery, San Diego, 1969-80, The Jerome Ariz. Hist. Mine Mus., 1970-92, Southwestern Arts Ltd. Art Gallery, Carmel, Calif., 1975-77, Pratt Gallery, San Diego, 1992—, Antiques West Mall and Gallery, 1993-95; contbr. paintings to mags. With USCG, 1942-46. Recipient Grumbacher Golden Palette award. Mem. Art Students League N.Y. (life), Calif. Coun. Adult Edn., San Diego Adult Educators Assn., Fine Arts Assn. San Diego, Del Gardens Art Assn. Republican. Christian Scientist. Home: 4121 Texas St San Diego CA 92104-1615

CHANDLER, KRIS, computer consultant, educator; b. Cleveland Heights, Ohio, June 26, 1948; d. Gerhard A. and Hanna R. (Rittmeyer) Hoffmann; children: Karen, Heidi. BSBA with honors and spl. distinction U. So. Colo., 1984, postgrad., 1984-85; MBA, U. Ark., 1987; PhD in C.C. Adminstrn. Colo. State U, 1993. Owner, mgr. V&W Fgn. Car Svc., Canon City, Colo., 1970-80; prin. The Chandlers, Computer Cons., Pueblo, Colo., 1982-88; ptnr. Jak Rabbit Software, 1989—; faculty Pikes Peak Community Coll., chair computer info. systems dept., U. So. Colo., also mgr. Sch. Bus. microcomputer lab. Bd. dirs. Canon City Community Svc. Ctr., 1978-80, Canon City chpt. ARC, 1978-81. Mem. Assn. for Computing Machinery, Data Processing Mgmt. Assn. (advisor student chpt. Pikes Peak Community Coll. 1989—), U. So. Colo. Honors Soc. (pres.), U. So. Colo. Grad. Assn. (founder), Alpha Chi, Sigma Iota Epsilon. Home and Office: 401 S Neilson Ave Pueblo CO 81001-4238

CHANDLER, PAUL MICHAEL, Spanish and Portuguese educator, homeless advocate; b. Flora, Ill., Nov. 15, 1954; s. John Paul and Doris (O'Dell) C. BA, Ind. Purdue U., Ft. Wayne, 1983; MA in Tchg., Ind. U., Bloomington, 1985, PhD, 1992. Instr. Spanish, Ind. U., 1983-89, coord. Spanish, 1989-90; asst. prof. San Jose (Calif.) State U., 1990-92; instr. Portuguese, Mission Coll., Santa Clara, Calif., 1992; asst. prof. and coord. Spanish, U. Hawaii, Honolulu, 1992—; vis. lectr. U. Seville, Spain, 1985-86; Portuguese translator Gen. Telephone, Honolulu, 1993. Editor, author: HALT Selected Papers and Language Teaching Ideas from Paradise, 1994; contbr. articles to profl. publs. Travel grantee Ind. U., 1989-90, San Jose State U., 1990-92, U. Hawaii, 1992. Mem. MLA, Nat. Reading Conf., Am. Coun. on Tchg. Fgn. Langs. (nat. award com. for outstanding tchr. of culture 1993), Am. Assn. Tchrs. of Spanish and Portuguese, Calif. Fgn. Lang. Tchrs. Assn., Hawaii Assn. Lang. Tchrs., Acad. Alliance (treas. 1992—). Office: U Hawaii Moore Hall 483 1890 E West Rd Honolulu HI 96822-2318

CHANDLER, RICHARD HILL, medical products company executive; b. N.Y.C., Mar. 25, 1943; s. Marvin and Carmen (Arguedas) C.; m. Linda Boerner, Aug. 21, 1965; Children: Lauren, Christy, Karen. BA, Princeton U., 1964; MBA, U. Chgo., 1966; Masters Internat. Econs., U. Louvain, Belgium, 1967. Various exec. positions Bell & Howell Co., Chgo., 1967-72; pres. retail div. Harvey Group, Melville, N.Y., 1972-74; v.p. planning & devel. Sara Lee Corp., Chgo., 1974-77, pres. Abbey Rents div., 1977-78, group v.p., 1979; chmn., pres. Abbey Med. Inc., 1979-82; pres. Sunrise Med. Inc., Torrance, Calif., 1983—; founder, vice chmn. Chgo. Community ventures, Inc., 1970-73. Del. White House Conf. Youth, 1970; trustee Chadwick Sch., Palos Verdes, Calif., 1983-89. Mem. Young Pres.'s. Orgn., 1980—, Princeton Club of N.Y., J. Kramer Tennis. Republican. Episcopalian. Office: Sunrise Med Inc 2355 Crenshaw Blvd Ste 150 Torrance CA 90501-3341

CHANDOR, STEBBINS BRYANT, pathologist; b. Boston, Dec. 18, 1933; s. Kendall Stebbins Bryant and Dorothy (Burrage) C.; m. Mary Carolyn White, May 30, 1959; children: Stebbins Bryant Jr., Charlotte White. B.A., Princeton U., 1955; M.D., Cornell U., 1960. Diplomate Am. Bd. Pathology. Intern Bellevue Hosp., N.Y.C., 1960-61, resident, 1965-66; resident Stanford U. Med. Ctr., Palo Alto, Calif., 1962-65; instr. Cornell U., Ithaca, N.Y., 1966; asst. prof. U. So. Calif. Med. Ctr., Los Angeles, 1969-73, assoc. prof., 1974-76; assoc. prof. SUNY, Stony Brook, 1976-80; prof., chmn. dept. pathology Marshall U. Sch. Medicine, Huntington, W.Va., 1981-91; assoc. dean for clin. affairs Marshall U. Sch. Medicine, 1990-91; prof., vice chmn. Sch. Medicine U. So. Calif., L.A., 1991—; pathologist Tripler Army Med Ctr, Honolulu, 1966-69; dir. immunopathology U. So. Calif., Los Angeles County Med. Ctr., 1969-76; dir. clin. lab. Univ. Hosp., Stony Brook, N.Y., 1978-80; dir. JMMS Labs., Huntington, W.Va., 1981-91; dir.labs. U. So. Calif. U. Hosp., L.A., 1991—. Contbr. articles to profl. jours. Pres. San Marino Tennis Found., 1975. Served to maj. USAR, 1966-69. Decorated Army Commendation medal; recipient Physicians Recognition award AMA, 1983, 86, 89, 93. Fellow Am. Soc. Clin. Pathologists (project dir. commr. continuing edn., bd. dirs. 1990—, chair by-law com.), Coll. Am. Pathologists (state commr. I&A program 1987-91, dist. commr. 1991—); mem. Calif. Soc. Pathologists (sec.-treas. 1974-75, pres. elect. 1975-76), Assn. Am. Pathologists, W.Va. Assn. Pathologists (pres. 1985-86), Assoc. Pathol. Chmn. Acad. Clin. Lab. Physicians and Scientists (rep. CAS 1991—), Princeton Club, Valley Club (v.p. 1975, bd. dirs. 1993), City Club (v.p. 1988-89, pres. 1989-90), San Gabriel Country Club. Republican. Episcopalian. Home: 855 S Oak Knoll Ave Pasadena CA 91106-4419 Office: U So Calif Sch Medicine 2011 Zonal Ave Los Angeles CA 90033-1034

CHANDRA, ABHIJIT, engineering educator; b. Calcutta, India, Jan. 4, 1957; came to U.S., 1980; s. Ramesh Kumar and Sandhya (Dey) C.; m. Dolly Day, June 4, 1984; children: Koushik, Shoma. B of Tech. with honors, Indian Inst. Tech., Kharagpur, India, 1978; MS, U. N.B., Fredericton, Can., 1980; PhD, Cornell U., 1983. Sr. rsch. engr. GM Rsch. Labs., Warren, Mich., 1983-85; asst. prof. U. Ariz., Tucson, 1985-89, assoc. prof. engring., 1989-95; prof. Mich. Tech. U., Houghton, 1995—; cons. Goodyear Tire and Rubber Co., Akron, Ohio, 1988-89, Advanced Ceramic Rsch., Tucson, 1990—, ALCOA, Pitts., 1990—. Editor: Developments in Boundary Element Method, 1991; contbr. articles to tech. publs. Alexander von Humboldt fellow, 1991; recipient Presdl. Young Investigator award NSF, 1987, Arc Welding Achievement award J. F. Lincoln Arc Welding Found., 1989. Mem. ASME (sec. So. Ariz. sect. 1988-89), SME, Sigma Xi.

CHANDRAMOULI, RAMAMURTI, electrical engineer; b. Sholinghur, Madras, India, Oct. 2, 1947; s. Ramamurti and Rajalakshmi (Ramamurti) Krishnamurti; m. Ranjani, Dec. 4, 1980; children: Suhasini, Akila. BSc, Mysore U., 1965, BE, 1970, MEE, Pratt Inst., 1972; PhD, Oreg. State U., 1978. Instr., Oreg. State U., Corvallis, 1978; sr. engr. R & D group, mem. tech. staff spacecraft datasystems sect. Jet Propulsion Lab., Pasadena, Calif., 1978-81; staff engr., design automation group Am. Microsystems Inc., Santa Clara, Calif., 1982-83; staff software engr. corp. computer-aided design Intel, Santa Clara, 1983-86; project leader computer-aided design Sun Microsystems, Mountain View, Calif., 1986-93; tech. mktg. engr. Mentor Graphics, San Jose, Calif., 1993-95; dir. Esta Products Logicvision, San Jose, 1995—; adj. lectr. Calif. State U.-Fullerton, 1987—. Sec., South India Cultural Assn., L.A., 1980-81; bd. dirs. Am. Assn. East Indians. Mem. IEEE, IEEE Computer Soc., Sigma Xi, Eta Kappa Nu. Home: 678 Tiffany Ct Sunnyvale CA 94087-2439 Office: LV Software Inc 1735 N First St San Jose CA 95112

CHANDRARATNA, PREMINDRA ANTHONY N., physician; b. Ceylon, July 27, 1941; came to U.S., 1971; m. Frances Roanne; children: Nirmal, Previn. MD, U. Ceylon, 1964. Diplomate Am. Bd. Internal Medicine, Am. Bd. Cardiovascular Disease. Rsch. fellow in cardiology U. Rochester Sch. Medicine; staff cardiologist Mt. Sinai Med. Ctr., Miami Beach, Fla., 1973-75; assoc. prof. medicine U. Okla. Health Scis. Ctr., 1975-77, U. Calif., Irvine, 1977-80; chief echocardiography lab., divsn. cardiology Los Angeles County/U.So. Calif. Med. Ctr., 1990—; Bauer and Bauer Rawlins prof. cardiology, prof. medicine U. So. Calif. Sch. Medicine. Mem. editl. bd. Am. Jour. Non-Invasive Cardiology and Echocardiography; contbr. more than 180 articles to profl. jours. Fellow ACP, Am. Coll. Cardiology, Am. Heart Assn. (coun. clin. cardiology), Royal Coll. Physicians; mem. Western Soc. for Clin. Investigation. Home: 30923 Marne Dr Rancho Palos Verdes CA 90274

CHANDY, KANIANTHRA MANI, computer sciences educator, consultant; b. Kottayam, Kerala, India, Oct. 25, 1944; came to U.S., 1965; s. Kanianthra Thomas and Rebecca (Mani) C.; m. Jean Marie Collaco, May 5, 1969; children: Christa Rebecca, Mani K. B.Tech., Indian Inst. Tech., Madras, 1965; M.S., Poly. Inst. Bklyn., 1966; Ph.D., MIT, 1969. Engr. Honeywell, Waltham, Mass., 1966-67; scientist IBM Cambridge Sci. Ctr., Mass., 1969-70; asst. prof. computer scis. U. Tex., Austin, 1970-73, assoc. prof., 1973-78, prof., 1978—, chmn. computer sci. dept., 1984-86; cons. in field; bd. regents Inst. for Software engring., Sunnyvale, Calif.; program chmn. Internat. Symposium on Computer Performance Modelling, Yorktown Heights, N.Y., 1977; sr. cons. scientist Boole and Babbage. Author: Computer Systems Performance Modeling, 1980; co-editor: Computer Performance, 1977, Current Trends in Programming Methodology, 1978, Parallel Program Design: A Foundation, 1989, An Introduction to Parallel Programming, 1991; editorial bd.: IEEE Transactions on Software Engring., 1984. Grantee NSF, 1974—; grantee USN, 1979-81, USAF, 1981—, IBM, 1981—; recipient A.A. Michelson award of Computer Measurement Group, 1985; Sherman Fairchild Disting. scholar Calif. Inst. Tech., 1987-88. Fellow IEEE (K.M. Chandy); mem. Assn. Computing Machinery. Home: 2015 Tulip Tree Ln La Canada Flintridge CA 91011-1528 Office: Calif Inst Tech Computer Sci Dept 256-80 Pasadena CA 91125

CHANEN, STEVEN ROBERT, lawyer; b. Phoenix, May 15, 1953; s. Herman and Lois Marion (Boshes) C. Student, UCLA, 1971-73; BS in Mass Communications, Ariz. State U., 1975, JD, 1979. Bar: Ariz. 1980, U.S. Dist. Ct. Ariz. 1980, U.S. Ct. Appeals (9th cir.) 1980, Calif. 1981, U.S. Dist. Ct. (no. dist.) Calif. 1982. Ptnr. Wentworth & Lundin, Phoenix, 1980-86, of counsel, 1986-87; appointed bd. dirs. Ariz. Gov.'s Commn. on Motion Pictures and TV, 1986, chmn., 1990; appointed bd. dirs., exec. v.p. Chanen Corp.; fin. intermediary, chmn. bd. dirs. S.R. Chanen and Co, Inc.; pres. Chanen Constrn. Co., Inc. Bd. dirs. Anytown, Am., Phoenix, 1986—, COMPAS, Inc., Phoenix, 1986—, Ariz. Mus. Sci. and Tech., Phoenix, 1987—, Mus. Theater Ariz., Phoenix, 1988-89, Temple Beth Isreal, Ariz. Politically Interested Citizens, Jewish Fedn.; v.p. bd. dirs. Community Forum, Phoenix, Phoenix Children's Hosp., Maricopa County C.C. Dist. Found. Mem. ABA (forum com. entertainment and sports industries 1981—), Ariz. Bar Assn., Calif. Bar Assn., Maricopa County Bar Assn., Assn. Trial Lawyers Am. Republican. Jewish. Office: 3300 N 3rd Ave Phoenix AZ 85013-4304

CHANEY, RONALD CLAIRE, environmental engineering educator, consultant; b. Tulsa, Okla., Mar. 26, 1944; s. Clarence Emerson and Virginia Margaret (Klinger) C.; m. Patricia Jane Robinson, Aug. 11, 1984. BS, Calif. State U., Long Beach, 1969; MS, Calif. State U., 1970; PhD, UCLA, 1978. Prof. engr., Calif.; geotech. engr., Calif. Structural engr. Fluor Corp. Ltd., L.A., 1968-70; rsch. engr. UCLA, 1972-74; lab. mgr. Fugro Inc., Long Beach, 1974-79; assoc. prof. Lehigh U., Bethlehem, Pa., 1979-81; dir. Telonicher Marine Lab. Humboldt State U., Trinidad, Calif., 1984-90; prof. Humboldt State U., Arcata, Calif., 1981—; geotech. engr. LACO ASsocs., Eureka, Calif., 1988-95; panel mem. Humboldt County Solid Waste Appeals, Eureka, 1992-95; mem. shipboard measurement panel Joint Oceanog. Instn., Washington, 1991-95. Co-editor: Marine Geotechnology and Nearshore/Offshore Structures, 1986, Symposium on Geotechnical Aspects of Waste Disposal in the Marine Environment, 1990, Suympossium on Dredging, Remediation and Containment of Contaminated Sediments, 1995; editor Marine Geotech. jour., 1981-92; co-editor Marine Georesources and Geotech. jour., 1992—. Fellow ASTM (Hogentogler award 1988, Std. Devel. award 1991, Outstanding Achievement award 1992, Dudley medal 1994, Award of Merit 1995, vice chmn. D18), Seismological Soc. Am., Earthquake Engring. Rsch. Inst., Sigma Xi, Phi Kappa Phi. Office: Humboldt State U Dept Environ Engring Arcata CA 95521

CHANEY, VICTOR HARVEY, secondary education educator, historical dramatist; b. Chgo., Nov. 11, 1940; s. Charles and Libby (Siegel) C.; m. Meta Bowman, July 14, 1973; 1 child, Dana; stepchildren: Gary, Rick, Randy. BA in Polit. Sci., UCLA, 1963; MEd, Calif. State U., Northridge, 1973. Tchr. Simi Valley (Calif.) Unified Sch. Dist., 1972-89, Beaverton (Oreg.) Sch., 1989—. Author: (poetry volume) Passing Through, 1984; (novel) The Bernstein Projections, 1991; creator and actor of one man plays and guest speaker presentations. Mem. Oreg. Tchrs. Assn., Nat. Audubon Soc., Nature Conservancy. Home: 6940 SW 160th Ave Beaverton OR 97007-4883

CHANG, DONALD S. M., fire department chief; b. Honolulu, Mar. 16, 1934; s. Thomas and Rose (Lee) C.; m. Frances M. Spencer, Dec. 28, 1957; children: Kathy, Kimberly, Randall. Diploma fire adminstrn., U. Hawaii, 1952-54, 57-58. Fire fighter Honolulu Fire Dept., 1957-62, fire equiptment operator I, 1963, fire equipment operator II, 1963-69, fire lieutenant, 1969-71, fire capt., 1971-76, fire battalion chief, 1976-88, fire asst. chief, 1988-90, fire dep. chief, 1990-92, fire chief, 1993—; field rep. Hawaii Fire Fighters Assn.; mem bd. dirs. Hon. Fire Dept. Fed. Credit Union, 1968-79; pres. Hon. Fire Dept. Fireman's Fund, 1966-76. Mem. exec. coun. Boy scouts of Am. (Aloha coun.). Mem. Western Fire Chief's Assn., Hawaii Fire Chiefs Assn., Hawaii State Fire Coun. (pres.), Internat. Assn. Fire Chiefs. Home: 98-324 Ponohale St Aiea HI 96701-2111 Office: Honolulu Fire Dept 3375 Koapaka St Ste H425 Honolulu HI 96819-1869

CHANG, HENRY CHUNG-LIEN, library administrator; b. Canton, China, Sept. 15, 1941; came to U.S., 1964, naturalized, 1973; s. Ih-ming and Lily (Lin) C.; m. Marjorie Li, Oct. 29, 1966; 1 dau., Michelle. LL.B., Nat. Chengchi U., 1962; M.A., U. Mo., 1966; M.A. in L.S, U. Minn., 1968; Ph.D., 1974. Book selector Braille Inst. Am., Los Angeles, 1965-67; reference librarian U. Minn., Mpls., 1968-70, instr., librarian, 1970-72, asst. head govt. document div., 1972-74; library dir., lectr. in social scis. U. of the V.I., St. Croix, 1974-75; dir. div. libraries, museums and archeol. services, 1975-88; dir. V.I. Library Tng. Inst., 1975-76; coordinator, chmn. V.I. State Hist. Records Adv. Bd., 1976-88; pres., libr. cons., 1988-89; dir. libr. svcs. Braille Inst. Am., L.A., 1990—; chmn. microfilm com. ACURIL, 1977-88; coordinator V.I. Gov.'s Library Adv. Council, 1975-87; mem. V.I. Bicentennial Commn., 1975-77, Ft. Frederik Commn., 1975-76; mem. adv. com. on research tng. Caribbean Research Inst., 1974-75; coordinator Library Conf., 1977-87; project dir. cultural heritage project Nat. Endowment for Humanities, 1979-83. Author: A Bibliography of Presidential Commissions, Committees, Councils, Panels and Task Forces, 1961-72, 1973, Taiwan Democraphy, 1964-71: A Selected Annotated Bibliography of Government Documents, 1973, A Selected Annotated Bibliography of Caribbean Bibliographies in English, 1975, A Survey of the Use of Microfilms in the Caribbean, 1978, Long-Range Program for Library Development, 1978, Institute for Training in Library Management and Communications Skill, 1979; also needs assessments and reports; contbr. numerous articles and book revs. on library sci. to profl. jours. Served to 2d lt. Taiwan Army, 1962-63. Recipient Libr. Adminstrs. Devel. Program fellowship award, 1972, L.A. Internat. Lions Club award, 1992, Cert. of Appreciation, Govt. V.I., 1985, Driver Safety award, 1993; named Mem. Staff of Yr., Coll. V.I., 1974-75; Nat. Commn. on Librs. and Info. Sci. grantee. Mem. ALA (counselor 1980-84), AAUP, Asian Pacific Am. Libr. Assn. (chmn. fin. com. 1993—), Population Assn. Am., Am. Sociol. Assn., Chinese Am. Profl. Soc. Home: 7839 Svl Box Victorville CA 92392-5161 Office: Braille Inst Am 741 N Vermont Ave Los Angeles CA 90029-3514

CHANG, HSU HSIN (SIDNEY H. CHANG), history educator; b. Wuchang, China, Jan. 1, 1934; came to U.S., 1957; s. Chung-ning C.; m. Elaine Pardue; children: Chi-chung, Chi-tung. BA, Nat. Taiwan U., 1956; MA, U. Mo., 1959; MS, Fla. State U., 1961; PhD, U. Wis., 1967. Asst. prof. history Calif. State U., Fresno, 1966-69, assoc. prof. history, 1969-74, prof. history, 1974—; post-doctoral fellow Harvard U., Cambridge, Mass., 1969-70. Co-author: Sun Yat-sen and His Revolutionary Thought, 1991; co-editor: Bibliography of Sun Yat-sen in China's Republican Revolution, 1885-1925, 1990, The Storm Clouds Clear over China: Memoir of Ch en Li-fu, 1900-93, 1994. Mem. Rep. Presdl. Task Force, 1984—. Mem. Am. Hist. Assn., Assn. for Asian Studies. Office: Calif State U Dept History Cedar and Shaw Fresno CA 93726

CHANG, I-SHIH, aerospace engineer; b. Taipei, Taiwan, Dec. 2, 1945; came to U.S., 1968; s. I-H. and T.-C. Chang; mem. O.J. Chang, May 25, 1974; children: Anna, Brandon. ME, Taipei Inst. Tech., 1965; MS, U. Kans., 1969; PhD, U. Ill., 1973. Assoc. rsch. scientist Lockheed Missile & Space, Huntsville, Ala., 1973-76; mem. tech. staff Rockwell Internat., Anaheim, Calif., 1976-77; mem. tech. staff Aerospace Corp., El Segundo, Calif., 1977-80, engring. specialist, 1980-90, sr. engring. specialist, 1990-91, prin. engring. specialist, 1991-92, disting. engr., 1992—; PhD thesis examiner Indian Inst. Sci., Bangalore, 1990; tech. paper reviewer Jour. Fluid Mechanics, N.Y.C., 1983. Contbr. articles to sci. jours. Mem. AIAA (tech. paper reviewer AIAA Jour. 1981-86, Jour. Propulsion and Power 1985-94), Phi Kappa Phi. Democrat. Office: Aerospace Corp M4/967 2350 E El Segundo Blvd El Segundo CA 90245

CHANG, KUANG-YEH, microelectronics technologist; b. Nanjing, China, Sept. 1, 1948; came to U.S., 1971; s. Yi and Wen-Teh (Tang) C.; m. Huey-Lian Ding, June 30, 1975; children: Fen, Wendy, Sherry, Sean. BSEE, Nat. Taiwan U., 1970; MSEE, U. Tenn., 1973; PhD, U. Pitts., 1978. Mem. tech. staff Hughes Aircraft Co., Newport Beach, Calif., 1978-83; mem. tech. staff Advanced Micro Devices, Sunnyvale, Calif., 1983-85, tech. integration mgr., 1994—; device mgr. Motorola, Austin, Tex., 1985-89; engring. mgr. VLSI Tech., San Jose, Calif., 1989-91; fellow Compass Design Automation, San Jose, 1991-94; com. mem. ASIC Conf., Rochester, 1993-94. Patentee in field. 2d lt. Chinese Army, 1970-71. Mem. IEEE, Phi Kappa Phi. Home: 125 Forest Hill Dr Los Gatos CA 95032-4023 Office: AMD PO Box 3453 M/S 117 Sunnyvale CA 94088-3453

CHANG, RODNEY EIU JOON, artist, dentist; b. Honolulu, Nov. 26, 1945; s. Alfred Koon Bo and Mary Yet Moi (Char) C.; m. Erlinda C. Feliciano, Dec. 4, 1987; children: Bronson York, Houston Travis, Rochelle Jessica. BA in Zoology, U. Hawaii, 1968; AA in Art, Triton Coll., 1972; DDS, Loyola U., 1972; MS in Edn., U. So. Calif., 1974; MA in Painting and Drawing, U. No. Ill., 1975; MA in Community Leadership, Cen. Mich. U., 1976; BA in Psychology, Hawaii Pacific U., 1977; MA in Psychology of Counseling, U. No. Colo., 1980; PhD in Art Psychology, The Union Inst., 1980; MA in Computer Art, Columbia Pacific U., 1989. Pvt. practice dentist Honolulu, 1975—; dir. SOHO too Gallery and Loft, Honolulu, 1985-89; freelance artist Honolulu, 1982—; founder Pygoya Internat. Art Group, 1990—; founder Art Cap Group, Slap Caps Co., Honolulu, 1993; columnist Milk Cap News; dir. ann. Honolulu City Hall Hawaiian Computer Art Exhbn., 1990-92; speaker on art psychology and computer art, also numerous TV and radio interviews. Author: Mental Evolution and Art, 1980, Rodney Chang: Computer Artist, 1988, Commentaries on the Psychology of Art, 1980; host (radio show) Disco Doc Hour, Sta. KISA; one-man shows include Honolulu Acad. Arts, 1986, Shanghai State Art Mus., People's Republic of China, 1988, Retrospective Exhbn. 1967-87, Ramsay Gallery, Honolulu, 1987, Visual Encounters Gallery, Denver, 1987, The Bronx Mus. of the Arts, N.Y.C., 1987, Nishi Noho Gallery, N.Y.C., 1987, Eastern Wash. U. Gallery of Art, 1988, Salon de la Jeune Peinture, Paris, 1989, Holter Art Mus., Mont., 1989, Las Vegas Art Mus., 1990, Forum Art Sch. Gütershoh, Fed. Republic of Germany, 1990, Siggraph-Dallas, 1990, Tartu State Art Mus., Estonia/USSR, 1990, U. Oregon Continuation Ctr., Portland, 1991—, Kauai Art Mus., Hawaii, 1993, RC Gallery of Computer Art, Honolulu, 1994, Archtl. Design of the Pygoya Home Mus., 1994; conceived, produced 1st milk cap art exhbn., Arts of Paradise Gallery, Waikiki Beach, 1993. Judge Jr. Miss Contest, Honolulu, 1981. Served to capt., U.S. Army, 1973-74. Mem. ADA, Hawaii Dental Assn., Assn. of Honolulu Artists (pres. 1989), Nat. Computer Graphics, Acad. Gen. Dentistry, Hawaii Space Soc., Bernice Bishop Mus. Honolulu. Roman Catholic. Office: 2119 N King St Ste 206 Honolulu HI 96819-4550

CHANG, SHENG-TAI, English language educator; b. Shanghai, Dec. 12, 1951; came to the U.S., 1986; s. Shucheng and Miaoxin (Xu) C. BA in English, East China Normal U., 1982; MA, U. Calgary, 1986; PhD in Comparative Lit., U. So. Calif., 1993, MA in East Asian Langs. and Cultures, 1994. English tchr. East China Normal U., Shanghai, 1982-84; instr. Chinese L.A. Trade-Tech. Coll., 1991; asst. lectr. in Chinese U. So. Calif., L.A., 1991; adj. asst. prof. Occidental Coll., L.A., 1993; lectr. U. So. Calif., L.A., 1994; instr., prof. South Puget Sound C.C., Olympia, Wash., 1994—. Editor, translator: The Tears of Chinese Immigrants, 1990; contbr. articles to profl. jours. Grantee Can. Ministry Multiculturalism, 1986. Mem. MLA, Philological Assn. Pacific Coast, Am. Assn. for Asian Studies, Am. Comparative Lit. Assn., Internat. Soc. for Comparative Study Civilizations, Phi Kappa Phi. Office: South Puget Sound CC 2011 Mottman Rd SW Olympia WA 98512-6218

CHANG, SYLVIA TAN, health facility administrator, educator; b. Bandung, Indonesia, Dec. 18, 1940; came to U.S., 1963.; d. Philip Harry and Lydia Shui-Yu (Ou) Tan; m. Belden Shiu-Wah Chang, Aug. 30, 1964; children: Donald Steven, Janice May. Diploma in nursing, Rumah Sakit Advent, Indonesia, 1960; BS, Philippine Union Coll., 1962; MS, Loma Linda (Calif.) U., 1967; PhD, Columbia Pacific U., 1987. Cert. RN, PHN, ACLS, BLS instr., cmty. first aid instr. Head nurse Rumah Sakit Advent, Bandung, Indonesia, 1960-61; critical care, spl. duty and medicine nurse, team leader White Meml. Med. Ctr., L.A., 1963-64; nursing coord. Loma Linda U. Med. Ctr., 1964-66; team leader, critical care nurse, relief head nurse Pomona (Calif.) Valley Hosp. Med. Ctr., 1966-67; evening supr. Loma Linda U. Med. Ctr., 1967-69, night supr., 1969-79, adminstrv. supr., 1979-94; sr. faculty Columbia Pacific U., San Rafael, Calif., 1986-94; dir. health svc. La Sierra U., Riverside, Calif., 1988—; site coord. Health Fair Expo La Sierra U., 1988-89; adv. coun. Family Planning Clinic, Riverside, 1988-94; blood drive coord. La Sierra U., 1988—. Counselor Pathfinder Club Campus Hill Ch., Loma Linda, 1979-85, crafts instr., 1979-85, music dir., 1979-85; asst. organist U. Ch., 1982-88. Named one of Women of Achievement YWCA, Greater Riverside C. of C., The Press Enterprise, 1991, Safety Coord. of Yr. La Sierra U., 1995. Mem. Am. Coll. Health Assn., Assn. Seventh-day Adventist Nurses, Pacific Coast Coll. Health Assn., Loma Linda U. Sch. Nursing Alumni Assn. (bd. dir.), Adventist Student Pers. Assn., Sigma Theta Tau Internat. Republican. Seventh-day Adventist. Home: 11466 Richmont Rd Loma Linda CA 92354-3523 Office: La Sierra U Health Svc 4700 Pierce St Riverside CA 92505-3331

CHANG, TAIPING, marketing executive, magazine publisher; b. Tainan, Taiwan, Apr. 20, 1949; came to U.S., 1975; d. Lanfeng Chang and Shuchun Liu; m. David R. Knechtges, June 7, 1976; 1 child, Jeanne Y. BA, Tunghai U., 1971, MA, 1974; PhD, U. Wash., 1981. Lectr. Tunghai U., Taichung, Taiwan, 1974-75; asst. prof. Pacific Luth. U., Tacoma, 1986-88; pub. Asia Pacific Bus. Jour., Seattle, 1988-94; pres. Asia Media Group, Inc., Seattle, 1989-94; asst. prof. Asian studies program U. Puget Sound, Tacoma, Wash., 1994—; bd. dirs. Chong-Wa Benevolent Assn., Seattle, No. Seattle (Wash.) C.C.; chmn. World Trade Club-Taiwan Forum, Seattle, 1991—. Editor: Editor-in-Chief, 1988. Named Woman of Yr., Asia Am. Soc., Seattle, 1990. Mem. Rotary Club. Office: U Puget Sound Pac-Rim Studies Tacoma WA 98416 also: U Puget Sound Asian Studies Program Tacoma WA 98416-0110

CHANG, WUNG, business advisor; b. Kang-Kyea, Korea, Apr. 24, 1942; came to the U.S., 1973; s. Jae Sun and Kye Bok (Yoo) C.; m. Han Jin Yang, Nov. 14, 1970; children: Min, Won. MPA, Yon-Sei U., 1971; PhD in Bus. Mgmt., Union U., 1983. Editor-in-chief Korea Photo Times, Seoul, 1970-73; sec.-gen. Wum Found., L.A., 1986-87; sr. analyst Pacific Rsch. Inst., L.A., 1988—; advisor Korea Travel News, Seoul, 1988-90; controller U.S. Top Capital Corp., L.A., 1991—; vice chmn. Mid-Wilshire Vocat. Tng. Ctr. divsn. Adult and Career Edn. LAUSD Adv. Coun., L.A., 1994—; vice chmn. Mid-Wilshire Vocat. Tng. Ctr. divsn. Adult and Career Edn., L.A. Unified Sch. Dist. Adv. Coun., 1994—; nat. campaign advisor Rep. Senatorial Inner Cir., Washington, 1995—. Adv. mem. Rep. Presdl. Adv. Commn., Washington, 1991; active Rep. Senatorial Com., Washington, 1991; at-large del. Rep. Ctrl. Com. Platform Planning Com., 1992. Capt. Korean Army, 1966-70. Recipient Presdl. Order of Merit, 1991, Rep. Presdl. Task Force Wall of Honor, 1992. Home: 7625 Radford Ave Los Angeles CA 91605

CHAO, CHIH HSU, research mechanical engineer; b. Shantung, China, Aug. 2, 1939; s. Ching Fung and Ching Chih (Lin) C.; BS, Nat. Taiwan U., 1962; MS, U. Calif.-Berkeley, 1965, PhD, 1972; m. Grace Yng Chu, Apr. 15, 1967; children: Henry Shaw, Lily Yuin. Rsch. asst., applied mechanics U. Calif.-Berkeley, 1965-72; rsch. engr. Boeing Co., Seattle, 1966-67; rsch. scientist, mgr. engring. analysis, chief engr. dir. TQM facilitator, v.p. and dir. quality mgmt. Physics Internat. Co., San Leandro, Calif., 1969—; cons. engr. Registered profl. engr., Calif. Bd. dirs. and judge Chinese Am. Polit. Assn., San Francisco Bay Area Sci. Fair. Mem. ASME (sect. chmn.), Nat. Soc. Profl. Engrs., Calif. Soc. Profl. Engrs. (chpt. v.p.), Nat. Apt. and Property Owners Assn. Democrat. Roman Catholic. Contbr. research papers in field to profl. jours. Home: 1018 Contra Costa Dr El Cerrito CA 94530-2710

CHAO, JAMES MIN-TZU, architect; b. Dairen, China, Feb. 27, 1940; s. T. C. and Lin Fan (Wong) C.; came to U.S., 1949, naturalized, 1962; m. Kirsti Helena Lehtonen, May 15, 1968. BArch, U. Calif., Berkeley, 1965. Registered architect, Calif., Ariz.; cert. instr. real estate, Calif. Intermediate draftsman Spencer, Lee & Busse, Architects, San Francisco, 1966-67; asst. to pres. Import Plus Inc., Santa Clara, Calif., 1967-69; job capt. Hammaberg and Herman, Architects, Oakland, Calif., 1969-71; project mgr. B A Premises Corp., San Francisco, 1971-79; constrn. mgr. The Straw Hat Restaurant Corp., 1979-81, mem. sr. mgmt., dir. real estate and constrn., 1981-87; mem. mktg. com. Straw Hat Coop. Corp., 1988-91; pvt. practice architect, Berkeley, Calif., 1987—; pres. Food Svc. Cons. Inc., 1987-89; pres., CEO Stratsac, Inc., 1987-92; prin. architect Alpha Cons. Group Inc., 1991—; v.p. Intersyn Industries Calif., 1993—; nat. tng. dir. Excel Telecommunications, Inc., 1995—; lectr. comml. real estate site analysis and selection for profl. real estate seminars; coord. minority vending program, solar application program Bank of Am.; guest faculty mem. N.W. Ctr. for Profl. Edn.; bd. dirs Ambrosia Best Corp., 1992—. Patentee tidal electric generating system; author first comprehensive consumer orientated performance specification for remote banking transaction. Recipient honorable mention Future Scientists Am., 1955. Mem. AIA, Encinal Yacht Club (bd. dir. 1977-78). Republican.

CHAO, RONALD J., communications executive; b. Sydney, Australia, Mar. 8, 1959; s. Hsin Min Chao and Yu Ho; m. Kathryn M.S. Kahn, Dec. 27, 1987; 1 child, Stephanie E. Chao. BS, Nat. Chiaotung U., Taiwan, 1978; MS, Carnegie Mellon U., 1982, U. Pitts., 1984; PhD, U. Pitts., 1989. Engr. IBM T.J. Watson Rsch., Yorktown Height, N.Y., 1982-88, Compunetix, Inc., Monroeville, Pa., 1988-94; pres. TCG Telecom, Ltd., Honolulu, 1994—; v.p. for rsch. Pacific Telecomms. Coun., Honolulu, 1994—. Mem. IEEE Comms. Soc. (chmn. cons. network 1994—).

CHAPELLE, GREGORY PHILIPPE, electronics engineer, researcher; b. Vitoria, Spain, July 28, 1961; came to U.S., 1963; s. Rene Adrien and Glenda Mae (Padgett) C.; m. Sonja Wischow, Aug. 8, 1986. BSEE, U. Calif. San Diego, 1985; MSEE, Purdue U., 1986; CPhil, U. Calif., San Diego, 1994. Lic. amateur radio operator, FCC. Teaching asst. U. Calif. San Diego, 1984-85; assoc. engr. La Jolla Scis., Solana Beach, Calif., 1984-85; mem. tech. staff TRW Mil. Electronics and Avionics Divsn., San Diego, 1987—. Author: The Birdcage Review, 1985; author, editor: (newspaper) Hiatus, 1985. Radio merit badge counselor Boy Scouts Am., San Diego, 1993—; chmn. Friends of Canyon Country, San Diego, 1993—. Recipient TRW Doctorate fellowship, 1989. Mem. IEEE, IEEE Comm. Soc. (vice chmn. San Diego sect. 1988-90), Eta Kappa Nu, Tau Beta Pi. Presbyterian. Home: 10984 Canyon Hill Ln San Diego CA 92126-2056 Office: TRW Mil Electronics andAvionics Divsn One Rancho Carmel San Diego CA 92126

CHAPGIER, PIERRE ANDRE, financing company executive; b. Perigueux, Dordogne, France, Jan. 18, 1941; came to U.S., 1979; s. Andre and Jeanne (Duclos) C.; m. Florence Baumgartner, Apr. 18, 1980; children: Julie, Kevin, Dylan. Degree engring., French Naval Acad., 1960-62, Ecole Centrale Paris, 1962-65; MBA, Institut Europeen D'Administration Des Enterprises, Fontainebleau, France, 1969. Dept. head Societe Centrale Pour L'Equipement Du Territoire, Paris, 1965-69; assoc. McKinsey and Co., Paris, 1969-72; ptnr. Interfinexa, Paris, 1972-74; exec. v.p. Meridien Hotels, Paris, 1974-79; pres. Meridien Hotels Investment Group, Inc., N.Y.C., 1980-85; founder, pres. Jukedy, Inc., L.A., 1986—. Translator: Managing By Results, 1969. Roman Catholic. Home: 1891 Kimberly Ln Los Angeles CA 90049-2221 Office: Jukedy Inc 15th fl 1999 Avenue Of The Stars Fl 15 Los Angeles CA 90067-6022

CHAPIN, DWIGHT ALLAN, columnist, writer; b. Lewiston, Idaho, June 16, 1938; s. Don Merle and Lucille Verna (Walker) C.; m. Susan Enid Fisk, Feb. 14, 1963 (div. 1973); children—Carla, Adam; m. Ellen Gonzalez, Aug. 10, 1983. B.A., U. Idaho, 1960; M.S. in Journalism, Columbia U., 1961. Reporter Lewiston Morning Tribune, Idaho, 1956-62; reporter, editor Vancouver Columbian, Wash., 1962-65; sportswriter Seattle Post-Intelligencer, 1965-67, Los Angeles Times, 1967-77; columnist San Francisco Examiner, 1977—. Co-author: Wizard of Westwood, 1973; contbr. numerous articles to popular mags. Served with USNG, 1962-68. Recipient Sports Writing award AP, Calif./Nev., 1968-69; Baseball Writing award Am. Assn. Coll. Baseball Coaches. Mem. Sigma Delta Chi (sports writing award Wash. state 1964, 65, 66). Democrat. Office: San Francisco Examiner 110 5th St San Francisco CA 94103-2918

CHAPIN, NED, information systems consultant; b. Port Gamble, Wash., Aug. 8, 1927; s. Manellus C. and Rose A. (Smallwood) C.; m. June Roediger, June, 12, 1954; children: Suzanne, Elaine. MBA, U. Chgo., 1949; PhD, Ill. Inst. Tech., 1959. Registered profl. engr., Calif. From lectr. to asst. prof. various schs., Chgo., 1953-56; systems analyst SRI Internat., Menlo Park, Calif., 1956-61; assoc. prof. San Francisco State U., 1961-64; data processing cons. InfoSci Inc., Menlo Park, 1964-89, info. systems cons., 1989—, also bd. dirs.; prof. Calif. State U., Hayward, 1987-93; session chmn. Nat. Computer Conf.; bd. dirs. CTS Time Sharing Corp., Palo Alto, Calif., 1967-69. Author: Computers: A Systems Approach, 1971; editor, computer sci. series Van Nostrand Reinhold Co., N.Y.C., 1967—; rschr. for invention; editor Jour. of Software Maint., 1992—; author articles and conf. procs. Officer Home Owners Assn., Menlo Park. Served with U.S. Army, 1951-53. Mem. N.Y. Acd. Scis., Software Maintenance Assn. (pres. 1986-88), Inst. Indsl. Engrs., Info. Systems Audit and Control Assn. (cert.), Soc. Gen. Systems Rsch., Ops. Rsch. Soc. Am., Internat. Soc. Tech. in Edn., Assn. Computing Machinery, Data Processing Mgmt. Assn., Soc. Info. Mgmt., Computers and Humanities, Am. Econ. Assn., Sigma Xi, Delta Sigma Rho. Home: 1190 Bellair Way Menlo Park CA 94025-6611 Office: InfoSci Inc PO Box 7117 Menlo Park CA 94026-7117

CHAPLIN, GEORGE, newspaper editor; b. Columbia, S.C., Apr. 28, 1914; s. Morris and Netty (Brown) C.; m. Esta Lillian Solomon, Jan. 26, 1937; children: Stephen Michael, Jerry Gay. BS, Clemson Coll., 1935; Nieman fellow, Harvard U., 1940-41; HHD (hon.), Clemson U., 1989; LHD (hon.), Hawaii Loa Coll., 1990. Reporter, later city editor Greenville (S.C.) Piedmont, 1935-42; mng. editor Camden (N.J.) Courier-Post, 1946-47, San Diego Jour., 1948-49; mng. editor, then editor New Orleans Item, 1949-58; asso. editor Honolulu Advertiser, 1958-59, editor in chief, 1959-86, editor at large, 1986—; mem. selection com. Jefferson fellowships East-West Ctr.; chmn. Gov.'s Conf. on Year 2000, 1970; chmn. Hawaii Commn. on Year 200, 1971-74; co-chmn. Conf. on Alt. Econ. Futures for Hawii, 1973-75; charter mem. Goals for Hawaii, 1979—; alt. U.S. rep. South Pacific Commn., 1978-81; chmn. search com. for pres. U. Hawaii, 1983; chmn. Hawaii Gov.'s Adv. Coun. on Fgn. Lang. and Internat. Studies, 1983—; rep. of World Press Freedom Com. on missions to Sri Lanka, Hong Kong, Singapore, 1987. Editor, officer-in-charge: Mid-Pacific edit. Stars and Stripes World War II; Editor: (with Glenn Paige) Hawaii 2000, 1973. Bd. dirs. U. Hawaii Rsch. Corp., 1970-72, Inst. for Religion and Social Change, Hawaii Jewish Welfare Fund; bd. govs. East-West Ctr., Honolulu, 1980-89, chmn., 1983-89, Pacific Health Rsch. Inst., 1984-90, 93—, Straub Med. Found., 1989—, Hawaii Pub. Schs. Found., 1986-87; trustee Clarence T.C. Ching Found., 1986-95; Am. media chmn. U.S.-Japan Conf. on Cultural and Ednl. Interchange, 1978-86; co-founder, v.p. Coalition for Drug-Free Hawaii, 1987-90; panelist ABA Conv., 1989; mem. Hawaii Jud. Salary Commn., 1994—; mem. civilian adv. group U.S. Army, Hawaii, 1985—. Capt. AUS, 1942-46. Decorated Star Solidarity (Italy), Order Rising Sun (Japan), Prime Minister's medal (Israel). Recipient citations Overseas Press Club, 1961, 72, Headliners award, 1962, John Hancock award, 1972, 74, Distinguished Alumni award Clemson U., 1974, E.W. Scripps award Scripps-Howard Found., 1976, Champion Media award for Econ. Understanding, 1981, Judah Magnes Gold medal Hebrew U. Jerusalem, 1987, Herbert Harley award Am. Judicature Soc., 1991; inductee Honolulu Press Club Hall of Fame, 1987. Mem. Soc. Nieman Fellows, Honolulu Symphony Soc., Pacific and Asian Affairs Council (dir.), Internat. Press Inst., World Future Soc., Japan-Am. Soc. Honolulu, Am. Soc. Newspaper Editors (dir., treas. 1973, sec. 1974, v.p. 1975, pres. 1976), Friends of East-West Ctr. Clubs: Pacific, Waialae Country. Home: 4437 Kolohala St Honolulu HI 96816-4938 Office: care Honolulu Advertiser PO Box 3110 Honolulu HI 96802-3110

CHAPLINE, CLAUDIA BEECHUM, artist, art dealer; b. Oak Park, Ill., May 23, 1930; d. Jacob Burwell and Lillian Estella (Schell) C.; m. James Nicol Hood, Nov. 1956 (div. 1972); children: Craig Chapline Hood, Randall Jameson Hood; m. Harold Chambers Schwarm, Feb. 14, 1989. BA in Drawing and Painting cum laude with spl. honors, George Washington U., 1953; MA in Dance Therapy, Washington U., St. Louis, 1956. Instr. dance Washington U., St. Louis, 1953-56, U. Mo., Columbia, 1956-57, Alhambra (Calif.) High Sch., 1959-60, El Camino Coll., L.A., 1960-61; dir. Shatto Drama Ctr., L.A., 1958-59; assoc. prof. dance UCLA, 1960-67; asst. prof. dance Calif. State U., Northridge, 1961-64; founder, dir. Inst. for Design/Dance and Exptl. Art, Santa Monica/Sacramento, 1974-88; lectr. dance U. Calif. ext., L.A., 1981-82; owner Claudia Chapline Gallery & Sculpture Garden, Stinson Beach, Calif., 1987—; coord. Artists in Social Instns., Calif. Arts Coun., 1982-84, program mgr. Art in Pub. Bldgs., 1984-90; dir. Bolinas (Calif.) Mus. Devel., 1989. One-woman shows include Humanist Ctr., St. Louis, 1956, Hobart Gallery, 1966, 67, E.B. Crocker Art Gallery, Sacramento, 1967, Humboldt Galleries, San Francisco, 1969, Jacqueline Anhalt Gallery, L.A., 1973, Palos Verdes Mus. Art, 1975, Inst. for Dance and Experimental Art, Santa Monica, Calif., 1976, 78, 79, Shackelford and Sears Gallery, Davis, Calif., 1986, IDEA, Sacramento, 1990, Wilder Gallery, Los Gatos, Calif., 1992, Claudia Chapline Gallery, Stinson Beach, Calif., 1994, JFK U., Orinda, Calif., 1994, Galerie Im Gassla, Erlangen, Germany, 1995, Anagma Arte Contemporaneo, Valencia, Spain, 1995; exhibited in group shows at Corcoran Gallery of Art, Washington, 1952, Hobart Gallery, 1965, Ryder Gallery, L.A., 1967, Zachary Waller Gallery, L.A., 1970, Long Beach Mus. Art, 1971, L.A. County Mus. Art, 1973, L.A. Inst. Contemporary Art, 1975, Pasadena Artists Concern, 1976, Gray Whale, Sacramento, 1985, Bolinas Mus., Calif., 1990, 92, 93, 94, Marin Arts Coun., 1993, 94, Artisan's Gallery, Mill Valley, Calif., 1994, Somar Gallery, San Francisco, 1994, Falkirk Cultural Ctr., San Rafael, Calif., 1994, 95, Pub. Art Works (bd. dirs. 1995—); represented in numerous pub. and pvt. collections. Mem. San Francisco Art Dealers Assn., ArtTable (bd. dirs. 1993-95). Office: Claudia Chapline Gallery & Sculpture Garden PO Box 946 3445 Shoreline Stinson Beach CA 94970

CHAPMAN, ALGER BALDWIN, III, pediatrician, researcher; b. N.Y.C., June 13, 1957; s. Alger B. Chapman Jr. and Pauline Badham Pinto; m. Trina McKean, Sept. 25, 1988; children: Ryan, Samantha. BS cum laude, Yale U., 1979; PhD, Stanford U., 1986, MD, 1987. Diplomate Am. Bd. Pediatrics. Pediatric intern U. Calif., San Francisco, 1987-88, residnet in pediatrics, 1988-89, fellow in pediatric infectious disease, 1989-92, adj. asst. prof. pediatrics, 1992—. Contbr. articles to profl. jours. NIH fellow, 1979-88, 90-95. Fellow Am. Acad. Pediatrics; mem. Infectious Disease Soc. Am. (assoc.), Pediatric Infectious Disease Soc., Am. Soc. Tropical Medicine and Hygiene. Democrat. Office: U Calif San Francisco Box 1204 LHTS Ste 150 San Francisco CA 94143

CHAPMAN, DONALD BRENT, computer network security consultant; b. Prescott, Ariz., July 23, 1968; s. Timothy James and Diana Patricia (Beasley) C. BS, U. Calif., Berkeley, 1989. Computer ops. mgr. Capital Market Tech., Berkeley, 1985-89; UNIX ops. mgr. Xerox Palo Alto (Calif.) Rsch. Ctr., 1989-90; computer ops. mgr. Ascent Logic Corp., San Jose, Calif., 1990-91; cons., owner Great Circle Assocs., Mountain View, Calif., 1988—. Mission coord., search & rescue pilot Civil Air Patrol, Palo Alto, 1991—. Mem. IEEE, Sys. Adminstrs. Guild (charter), Bay Area Large Installation Sys. Adminstrs., Assn. for Computing Machinery. Office: Great Circle Assocs 1057 W Dana St Mountain View CA 94041-1222

CHAPMAN, ELAINE GRACE, engineer; b. St. Johnsbury, Vt., Dec. 30, 1956; d. Frederick Elmer and Marie Louise (Warner) Chapman; m. Richard Dale Smith, Jan. 5, 1985; 1 child, Jeffrey. BS, Rensselaer Poly. Inst., Troy, N.Y., 1978; M.Eng., Rensselaer Poly. Inst., 1980. Student intern engr. Stauffer Chem. Co., Dobbs Ferry, N.Y., 1977; engr. Battelle Pacific N.W. Labs., Richland, Wash., 1980-81; rsch. engr. Battelle Pacific N.W. Labs., 1981-83, sr. rsch. engr., 1983—. Contbr. articles to profl. jours. Mem. Lower Columbia Basin Audubon Soc. (pres. 1981-82, 86-87). Office: Battelle Pacific NW Labs PO Box 999 Richland WA 99352-0999

CHAPMAN, GEORGE J., agricultural products executive; b. 1936. With Magi Inc., Brewster, Wash., 1966—, now pres. Office: Magi Inc 26049 State Hwy 97 Brewster WA 98812*

CHAPMAN, JUDI, Indian tribes and organizations consultant, lobbyist; d. Francis Andrew and Leona Phyllis (Cook) Larson. Student, St. Olaf Coll., 1963, U. Mont., 1975. Dir. Edn.-Social Svcs. Mt. Plains, Glasgow, Mont., 1970-72; legis. asst. Congressman Pat Williams, Washington, 1979-91; cons., 1991-92; cons. Nat. Commn. on Librs., Info. Sci., Washington, 1991—; reviewer Head Start, Washington, 1992—; contract work with Blackfeet Tribe, Affiliated Tribes NW Indians, Spokane Tribe, Colleville, Sinte Glaska U., Salish-Kootenai Coll., Ft. Bellnap Coll., Dull Knife Coll., Nat. Comsn. Native Am., Alaska Natives, Native Hawaiian Housing, Kauffman & Assocs. Reader Adminstrn. for Native Ams., 1992—; state Dem. Committeewoman, Missoula County; coord. Discover the Indian Vote, 1992; county coord. Williams for Congress, Missoula, 1978; mem. Missoula Women for Peace, 1991—; mem. precinct com. Dem. Party, Missoula, 1991—, mem. issues com., 1991—, Clinton del. Dem. Nat. Conv., 1992; bd. dirs. City-County Health Bd., Missoula, 1992—, City-County Water Quality Dist., City-County Air Pollution Control Bd., Missoula Indian Ctr., 1992—. Mem. Mont. Indian Edn. Assn., Nat. Congress-Am. Indians. Home and Office: 2300 Hilda Ave Missoula MT 59801-7015

CHAPMAN, LORING, psychologist, educator, neuroscientist; b. L.A., Oct. 4, 1929; s. Lee E. and Elinore E. (Gundry) Scott; children: Robert, Antony, Pandora (dec.). BS, U. Nev., 1950; PhD, U. Chgo., 1955. Lic. psychologist, Oreg., N.Y., Calif. Rsch. fellow U. Chgo., 1952-54; rsch. assoc., asst. prof. Cornell U. Med. Coll., N.Y.C., 1955-61; rsch. dir. Music Rsch. Found., N.Y.C., 1958-61; assoc. prof. in residence Neuropsychiat. Inst., UCLA, 1961-65; rsch. prof. U. Oreg., Portland, 1965; br. chief NIH, Bethesda, Md., 1966-67; prof., chmn. dept. behavioral biology Sch. Medicine U. Calif., Davis, 1967-81; prof. psychiatry Sch. Medicine U. Calif., 1977-91, prof. emeritus, 1991—, prof. neurology, 1977-81, prof. human physiology, 1977-81; vice chmn. div. of sci. basic to medicine, 1976-79; condr. rsch. in field of behavioral and sensory physiology, brain function, neuropharmacology; vis. prof. U. Sao Paulo, Brazil, 1959, 77, Univ. Coll., London, 1969-70, U. Florence, Italy, 1979-80; clin. prof. Georgetown U., 1966-67; mem. Calif. Primate Rsch. Ctr., 1967-81; dir. rsch. Fairview Hosp., 1965-66; cons. Nat. Inst. Neurol. Disease and Stroke, 1961—, Nat. Cancer Inst., 1977—; Nat. Inst. Child Health & Human Devel., 1967—, mem. rsch. and tng. com., 1968-72. Author: Pain and Suffering, 3 vols, 1967, Head and Brain 3 vols, 1971, (with E.A. Dunlap) The Eye, 1981; assoc. editor courtroom medicine series updates, 1965—; contbr. sci. articles to publs. Fogarty Sr. Internat. fellow, 1980; grantee NASA, 1969-80; grantee NIH, 1956-91; grantee Nat. Inst. Drug Abuse, 1971-80; recipient Thorton Wilson prize, 1958, Career award USPHS, 1964, Commonwealth Fund award, 1970. Mem. Am. Acad. Neurology, Am. Physiol. Soc., Am. Psychol. Assn., Royal Soc. Medicine (London)., Am. Neurol. Assn., Am. Assn. Mental Deficiency, Aerospace Med. Assn., Soc. for Neurosci. Home: 205 Country Pl Apt 188 Sacramento CA 95831-2076 Office: U Calif Med Ctr Dept Psychiatry 2315 Stockton Blvd Sacramento CA 95817-2201

CHAPMAN, ORVILLE LAMAR, chemist, educator; b. New London, Conn., June 26, 1932; s. Orville Carmen and Mabel Elnora (Tyree) C.; m. Faye Newton Morrow, Aug. 20, 1955 (div. 1980); children: Kenneth, Kevin; m. Susan Elizabeth Parker, June 15, 1981. B.S., Va. Poly. Inst., 1954; Ph.D., Cornell U., 1957. Prof. chemistry Iowa State U., 1957-74; prof. chemistry UCLA, 1974—; Cons. Mobil Chem. Co. Recipient John Wilkinson Tchg. award Iowa State U., 1968, Nat. Acad. Scis. award, 1974, Founders prize Tex. Instruments, George and Freda Halpern award in photochemistry N.Y. Acad. Scis., 1978, Outstanding Patent of Yr. Mobil Corp, 1992, Edn. award ComputerWorld Smithsonian Inst., 1995. Mem. Am. Chem. Soc. (award in pure chemistry 1968, Arthur C. Cope award 1978, Midwest award 1978, Havinga medal 1982, McCoy award UCLA, 1985). Home: 1213 Roscomare Rd Los Angeles CA 90077-2202 Office: UCLA Dept Chemistry 405 Hilgard Ave Los Angeles CA 90024-1301

CHAPMAN, RICHARD LEROY, public policy researcher; b. Yankton, S.D., Feb. 4, 1932; s. Raymond Young and Vera Everette (Trimble) C.; m. Marilyn Jean Nicholson, Aug. 14, 1955; children: Catherine Ruth, Robert Matthew, Michael David, Stephen Raymond, Amy Jean. BS, S.D. State U., 1954; postgrad., Cambridge (Eng.) U., 1954-55; MPA, Syracuse U., 1958, PhD, 1967. With Office of Sec. of Def., 1958-59, 61-63; dep. dir. rsch. S.D. Legis. Rsch. Coun., 1959-60; mem. staff Bur. of the Budget, Exec. Office of Pres., Washington, 1960-61; profl. staff mem. com. govt. ops. U.S. Ho. of Reps., Washington, 1966; program dir. NIH, Bethesda, Md., 1967-68; sr. rsch. assoc. Nat. Acad. Pub. Adminstrn., Washington, 1968-72, dep. exec. dir., 1973-76, v.p., dir. rsch., 1976-82; sr. rsch. scientist Denver Rsch. Inst., 1982-86; mem. adv. com. Denver Rsch. Inst. U. Denver, 1984-86; ptnr. Milliken Chapman Rsch. Group Inc., Denver, 1986-88; v.p. Chapman Rsch. Group, Inc., Littleton, 1988—; cons. U.S. Office Pers. Mgmt., Washington, 1977-81, Denver, 1986—; cons. CIA, Washington, 1979, 80, 81, Arthur S. Fleming Awards, Washington, 1977-81; exec. staff dir., cons. U.S. Congressman Frank Denholm; lectr. on sci., tech., govt. and pub. mgmt. Author: (with Fred Grissom) Mining the Nation's Braintrust, 1992; contbr. over 60 articles and revs. to profl. jours. and congl. staff reports. Mem. aerospace com. Colo. Commn. Higher Edn., Denver, 1982-83; chmn. rules com. U. Denver Senate, 1984-85; bd. dirs. S.E. Englewood Water Dist., Littleton, 1984-88, pres., 1986-88; mem. strategic planning com. Mission Hills Bapt. Ch., 1986; bd. dirs. Lay Action Ministry Program, 1988—, chmn., 1992—; established Vera and Raymond Chapman Scholarship Fund, S.D. State U.; mem. Fairfax County Rep. Ctrl. Com., Va., 1969-71, Fairfax County Com. of 100, 1979-82. With U.S. Army, 1955-57, Korea, capt. Res. Syracuse U. Maxwell Sch. fellow, 1957-58, 63-64, Brookings Inst. fellow, 1964-65. Mem. AAAS, Engring. Mgmt. Soc., Tech. Transfer Soc. (bd. dirs. 1987-95, Pres.'s award 1991, founder Colo. chpt.), Fed. Lab. Consortium (nat. adv. com. 1989—), S.D. State U. Found. (bd. dirs. 1992—, vice chmn. 1994—), Masons, Order of DeMolay (Cross of Honor 1982), Rotary (fellow Internat. Found. 1954-55, Paul Harris fellow 1989), K.T. Republican. Office: Chapman Rsch Group 6129 S Elizabeth Way Littleton CO 80121-2647

CHAPMAN, ROBERT DALE, research chemist; b. Glendale, Calif., June 4, 1955; s. Forrest Dale and Berta (Jäger) C.; m. Debra Jay Cullen, Dec. 5, 1981. BA in Chemistry, U. Calif., Irvine, 1977, PhD, 1980. Research assoc. U. Colo., Boulder, 1981; research chemist Naval Weapons Ctr., China Lake, Calif., 1981-82; rsch. chemist Astronautics Lab., Edwards AFB, Calif., 1982-89; sr. rsch. chemist Fluorochem Inc., Azusa, Calif., 1989-91; staff scientist Unidynamics, Phoenix, 1991-92; sr. scientist TPL Inc., Albuquerque, 1992-95; rsch. chemist Naval Air Warfare Ctr., China Lake, Calif., 1995—. NRC fellow, 1981. Mem. Am. Chem. Soc., Internat. Pyrotechnics Soc., Sigma Xi. Methodist. Office: NAWC Code 0235 China Lake CA 93555

CHAPMAN, ROBERT GALBRAITH, retired hematologist, administrator; b. Colorado Springs, Colo., Sept. 29, 1926; s. Edward Northrop and Janet Galbraith (Johnson) C.; m. Virginia Irene Potts, July 6, 1956; children: Lucia Tully Chapman Chatzky, SArah Northrop Chapman Bohrer, Robert Bostwick. Student, Westminster Coll., 1944-45; BA, Yale U., 1947; MD, Harvard U., 1951; MS, U. Colo., 1958. Diplomate Am. Bd. Internal Medicine and Pathology. Intern Hartford (Conn.) Hosp., 1951-52; resident in medicine U. Colo. Med. Ctr., Denver, 1955-58; fellow in hematology U. Wash., Seattle, 1958-60; chief resident in medicine U. Colo., Denver, 1957-58, instr. medicine, 1960-62, asst. prof. medicine, 1962-68, assoc. prof., 1968-91; chief staff VA Hosp., Denver, 1968-70; dir. Belle Bonfils Meml. Blood Ctr., Denver, 1977-91; mem. regionalization com. Am. Blood Commn., Washington, 1985-87, Colo.sickle cell com., Denver, 1978-91, gov.'s AIDS Coun., 1987-88; trustee Coun. Community Blood Ctrs., v.p., 1979-81, pres., 1989-91, mem. rsch. inst. bd. Palo Alto Med. Found., 1991—. Contbr. articles to profl. jours. Served as capt. USAF, 1953-55. USPHS fellow, 1958-60. Fellow ACP; mem. Am. Assn. Blood Banks, Mayflower Soc., Denver Med. Soc., Colo. Med. Soc., Western Soc. Clin. Rsch., Denver Country Club, Am. Radio Relay League. Mem. United Ch. Christ. Home: 47 La Rancheria Carmel Valley CA 93924-9424

CHAPMAN, VAUGHN VICKERS, dentist; b. Seattle, Mar. 14, 1921; s. Asa B. and Emma (Woodhouse) C.; m. Mildred Fyfe, Dec. 28, 1949; 1 child, Melissa. Student, Wheaton (Ill.) Coll., 1939-41, U. Wash., 1941; BS, U. Ill., 1942, DDS, 1944. Gen. practice dentistry Seattle, 1944-90; bd. dirs. Worldwide Dental Health Service, Seattle, 1950—, Missionary Dentists Overseas Tng. Seminars, 1957—. Editor News Report, 1950—, Dental Evangelism Heartbeat, 1983—; editor: Missionary Dentistry, 1969; producer radio broadcast The Dental Story, 1955-59. Bd. dirs. Internat. New Life Ministries, 1986—. Served to capt. U.S. Army, 1942-47, ETO. Named Man of Year Wash. Acad. Gen. Dentistry, 1988. Mem. Christian Med. Soc. (house of dels.), ADA, Seattle-King County Dental Soc. , Wash. State Dental Assn., Internat. Assn. for Orthodontics. Presbyterian. Club: Wash. Athletic. Office: Worldwide Dental Health Svc PO Box 7002 Seattle WA 98133-2002

CHAPPELL, DAVID WELLINGTON, religion educator; b. Saint John, N.B., Can., Feb. 3, 1940; came to U.S., 1966; s. Hayward Lynsin and Mary Elvira (Mosher) C.; m. Bertha Vera Bidulock, Aug. 23, 1960 (div. Jan. 1976); children: Cynthia Joan, Mark Lynsin David; m. Stella Quemada, July 11, 1981. BA, Mt. Allison U., Sackville, N.B., 1961; BD, McGill U., Montreal, Que., Can., 1965; PhD, Yale U., 1976. Min. United Ch. Can., Elma, Ont., Can., 1964-66; prof. U. Hawaii, Honolulu, 1971—; asst. prof. U. Toronto, Toronto, Ont., 1977-78; vis. prof. U. Pitts., 1982; vis. lectr. Taisho U., Tokyo, 1986-88; dir. East West Religions Project, Honolulu, 1980—, Buddhist Studies Program, U. Hawaii, 1987-92. Editor: T'ien-t'ai Buddhism, 1983, Buddhist and Taoist Practice, 1987; editor Buddhist-Christian Studies jour., 1980—. Mem. Am. Acad. Religion, Assn. Asian Studies, Internat. Assn. Buddhist Studies, Soc. Buddhist-Christian Studies (pres.). Democrat. Home: 47-696 Hui Kelu St Apt 1 Kaneohe HI 96744-4636

CHAPSON, LOIS JESTER, interior designer; b. Plumas County, Calif., May 18, 1922; d. Lewis and Agda Edwards (Olsson) Jester; m. Elmer Donald Chapson, Nov. 7, 1959. AB, U. Calif., Berkeley, 1954; BS, San Jose State U., 1977. Pvt. practice interior designer Los Gatos, Calif., 1978—. Planning commr. Town Los Gatos, Calif., 1978-84. Mem. Am. Soc. Interior Designers (allied mem.), Calif. Coun. of the Blind. Democrat. Home and Office: 323 Pennsylvania AVe Los Gatos CA 95030

CHAR, CARLENE, writer, publisher, editor; b. Honolulu, Oct. 21, 1954; d. Richard Y. and Betty S.M. (Fo) C. BA in Econs., U. Hawaii, 1977; MA in Bus. Adminstrn., Columbia Pacific U., 1984, PhD in Journalism, 1985, B in Gen. Studies in Computer Sci., Roosevelt U., 1986. Freelance writer, Honolulu, 1982—; editor Computer Book Rev., Honolulu, 1983—; info. developer Sprint, 1988—.

CHARBONNEAU, JOANNE ADRIENNE, literature and humanities educator; b. Worcester, Mass., Sept. 9, 1950; d. Philip Paul and Stasia Marie (Poltorak) C.; m. Richard Eugene Rice, June 9, 1972. Student, St. John's Coll., Annapolis, Md., 1968-70; BA, U. Mass., 1972; MA, U. Mont., 1974; PhD, Mich. State U., 1981. Instr., writing specialist Mich. State U., East Lansing, 1978-79, asst. prof., English, 1981-82; mem. faculty, English dept. Md. Inst. Coll. of Arts, Balt., 1983-84; asst. prof. English Butler U., Indpls., 1984-88, dir. freshman English, 1986-89, assoc. prof. English, 1988-90; chmn. English dept. Fayetteville (N.C.) State U., 1990-91; vis. assoc. prof. U. Mont., Missoula, 1991—. Co-editor: Smart jour., Missoula, 1994—; freelance editor; contbg. author: (book) Riverside Chaucer; author: (book) ME Romance: Annotated Bibliography, 1982; contbr. ency. entries, articles to profl. jours. Mem. Medieval Acad. of Am., MLA, Rocky Mountain Medieval and Renaissance Assn. Office: U Mont Liberal Studies Dept Missoula MT 59812

CHARBONNEAU, RALPH GRAY, air cargo leasing company executive; b. Osborne, Kans., Jan. 4, 1929; s. Alvarez Emery and Jessie Lucinda (Haskins) C.; m. Martha Habegger, May 19, 1957; children: Eric Gray, Christine Rebecca. BA, Doane Coll., Crete, Nebr., 1950; postgrad., Army Lang. Sch., Monterey, Calif., 1952, Pacific Coast Banking Sch., Seattle, 1968-69. Trainee Mercantile Bank & Trust Co., Kansas City, Mo., 1955-56; loan officer City Nat. Bank & Trust Co., Kansas City, 1956-63; mgr. ICD Seattle-First Nat. Bank, 1963-69; mng. dir. Seattle-First Nat. Bank Switzerland, Zurich, 1969-74; v.p. internat. Seattle First Nat. Bank, 1974-78, v.p., mgr. Europe, Can. and Australasia, 1980-88; gen. mgr. Seattle-First Nat. Bank Switzerland, 1978-80; v.p., mgr. Transiplex, Seattle, 1988—; prof. internat. banking Am. Inst. Banking, Seattle, 1984-94. Advisor book, Internat. Banking, 1987, 90. With USAF, 1951-55. Mem. Canadian Soc. (bd. dirs. 1989), Australian-N.Z. Am. Soc. (bd. dirs. 1989), Swiss Soc. Congregationalist. Home: 1531 Sunset Ave SW Seattle WA 98116-1648 Office: Transiplex Inc 2580 S 156th St PO Box 68515 Seattle WA 98168

CHARBONNEAU, ROBERT BRUCE, university official, natural resourcess consultant; b. Worcester, Mass., Oct. 4, 1960; s. Philip Paul and Statia Marie (Polturak) C. BS in Environ. Scis. cum laude, U. Mass., 1983; M City Planning, U. Calif., Berkeley, 1988. Registered environ. assessor, Calif. 2firefighter, EMT, Northboro Fire Dept., Northborough, Mass., 1978-86; sr. san. engr.'s aide div. water pollution control Mass. Dept. Environ. Quality Engring., Westboro, 1981; biologist, water qualaity specialist IEP Inc., Northborough, 1984-86; environ. resstoration project coord., environ. planner U. Calif. Office Environ. Health and Safety, Berkeley, 1987-89, cons. on Strawberry Creek restoration project, 1989-92; environ. assessment coord. Office of Pres., U. Calif. Office Environ. Health and Safety, Oakland, 1992—; coord. Environ. Assessment program, Systemwide Emergency Preparedness program Office of Pres., U. Calif., 1989—; mem. Calif. Statewide Emergency Planning Com., 1992—. Author: (booklet) Walking Tour of Campus Natural History, U. Calif., Berkeley, 1990. Coord. disaster svcs. ARC, Northborough, 1976-78; charter mem. Berkeley Citizens for Creek Restoration, 1989. Grantee U. Calif., Berkeley, 1987. Mem. Assn. Environ. Profls., Soc. for Ecol. Restoration and Mgmt., Watershed Mgmt. Assn., Bay Area Resource Mgrs. Assn., Sierra Club, Berkeley Hiking Club (bd. dirs. 1987-91). Office: U Calif Environ Protection Svcs Office of Pres 300 Lakeside Dr Fl 12 Oakland CA 94612-3524

CHARD, CHESTER STEVENS, archaeologist, educator; b. N.Y.C., Sept. 15, 1915; s. Walter Goodman and Kathleen (Stevens) C.; m. Jeanne W. Bell, Apr. 16, 1974; children by previous marriage—Carleton S., Kenneth W., Frederick H., Robert L., Alan D., Susan L. A.B., Harvard, 1937; Ph.D., U. Calif. at Berkeley, 1953. Vis. lectr. anthropology U. Wash., 1954-56; faculty U. Wis., 1958—, prof. anthropology, 1963—, chmn. dept., 1962-64; founder, editor Arctic Anthropology, 1962-74; cons. Russian translation program Arctic Inst. N.Am., 1960—. Author: Kamchadal Culture, 1961, Northeast Asia in Prehistory, 1974, Man in Prehistory, 1969. Served to lt. USNR, 1942-46. Fellow Am. Anthrop. Assn., AAAS, Royal Anthrop. Inst., Explorers Club of N.Y.; mem. Prehistoric Soc., Soc. Am. Archaeology, Arctic Inst. N.Am., Far Eastern Prehistory Assn., Sigma Xi. Address: 4891 Searidge Dr, Victoria, BC Canada V8Y 2B3

CHARLES, ANNE H., communications executive; b. Bethlehem, Pa., May 3, 1941; d. Clement Richard and Ethel Eve (Grein) Hanlon; m. Peter Charles, Nov. 18, 1939; children: Eric, Susan, Jeffrey, Leslie. BA magna cum laude, Marymount Coll., 1969. Exec. dir. Marin Arts Coun., San Rafael, Calif., 1979-83; pub. rels. specialist Anne Charles & Assocs., Kentfield, Calif., 1975-85; dir. comm. State Bar of Calif., San Francisco, 1985—. Bd. dirs. No. Calif. Mediation Ctr., Corte Madera, Calif., 1984—; Dem. nominee for Calif. State Assembly, 1980; mem. cost control commn. Calif. State Senate, Sacramento, 1986—; pres. Calif. Nat. Women's Polit. Caucus, 1979. Recipient Women Making a Difference award Women's Campaign Fund, San Francisco, 1988. Mem. Nat. Assn. Bar Execs. (mem. exec. com. pub. rels. sect. 1992—). Roman Catholic. Home: 33 Terrace Ave Kentfield CA 94904-1528

CHARLES, BLANCHE, retired elementary education educator; b. Spartanburg, S.C., Aug. 7, 1912; d. Franklin Grady and Alice Florida (Hatchette) C. BA, Humboldt State U., 1934; adminstrv. cert., U. So. Calif., 1940. Tchr. Jefferson Elem. Sch., Calexico (Calif) Unified Sch. Dist., 1958-94; libr. Calexico Pub. Libr., El Centro Pub. Libr. Elem. sch. named in her honor, 1987. Mem. NEA, ACT, Calif. Tchrs. Assn., Nat. Soc. DAR, Nat. Soc. Daus. of Confederacy, Delta Kappa Gamma. Home: 337133 Hwy 94 Campo CA 91906-2809

CHARLES, FREDERICK C., publisher, editor, writer; b. N.Y.C., Jan. 22, 1933; m. Mary Asebrook, 1956 (div. 1964); children: Christine Anne, Mark Charles; m. Beatrice Frayer, Sept. 1966 (div. Feb. 1975); 1 child, Dorian Leslie; m. Josephina Bilaro, May 12, 1984. AA, Pierce Coll., 1955; BA in Polit. Sci., U. Northridge, 1966. Br. mgr. Van Nuys Savs. & Loan Assn., 1956-66; ops. mgr. Gen. Ins. of Am., 1966-67; exec. dir. Calif. Employment Assn., 1967-72; pub. rels. dir. Multnomah County Dept. Pub. Safety, Portland, Oreg., 1973-75; engring. adminstr. Paradyne Corp., Largo, Fla., 1978-84; staff writer Las Vegas Sun Newspaper, 1986-88; editor Constrn. Connection Mag. Associated Gen. Contractors, Las Vegas, 1989-94; editor The Aggregate Wells Cargo, Inc., Las Vegas, 1989—; feature writer The Grogan Report, Denver, 1989—; pub. Nev. Constrn. and Mining Newspaper, 19956. Contbr. more than 800 feature articles to various newspapers and mags. Cpl. USMC, 1949-52. Recipient award Calif. Gov. Ronald Regan. Libertarian. Office: Charles & Assocs PO Box 81571 Las Vegas NV 89180-1571

CHARLES, LYN ELLEN, marketing executive, commercial artist, photographer; b. Little Falls, N.Y., Sept. 1, 1951; d. Searle and Barbara (Yount) C. Student So. Conn. State U., 1969-70, Lake Placid Sch. Art, 1975-76; BA, U. Conn., 1970-73; A.I.S., Art Instrn. Schs., Inc., 1974-76; student employee ECSU Libr., 1969-70; Vanda beauty counselor, divsn. Dart Industries, Orlando, Fla., 1972-73; with Sechs., Inc. 1974-76; rsch. asst. Conn. State U., New Britain, 1974; comml. artist Conn. Community Colls., Hartford, 1978; market rschr. Karen Assocs., Farmington Valley Mall, Simsbury, Conn., 1981; market rsch. operator Consumer Surveys Telemarketing, Inc., Dedham, Mass., 1981-87; receptionist and file clerk Jobpro Temp. Svcs., 1987-88; field rep. Actnow, Westhampton Beach, N.Y., 1987-88; with Inventory Control Co., S. Hasckensack, N.J., 1988—; artist, vol. Farmington Valley Arts, Avon, Conn., 1982-84; freelance artist West Hartford Art League, 1978-81, Northwestern Conn. Art Assn., 1979-81, Wadsworth Atheneum, 1980-82. Vol. med. receptionist Hosp. and Clinical Info. Desk, U. Conn. Health Ctr., 1976-78, 75, Office Cultural Affairs, Pub. Survey to Select Artist for Art Work at Coliseum, Hartford Civic Ctr., 1979; mem. Childreach Sponsorship of PLAN Internat. USA, 1992—; Corvallis Arts Ctr., 1995—. Recipient Alice Collins Dunham prize, 69th Ann. Exhbn. of Conn. Acad. Fine Arts, 1980. Mem. Christian Ch. Avocations: hiking, swimming, bicycling, horseback riding, skiing.

CHARLES, MARY LOUISE, newspaper columnist, photographer, editor; b. L.A., Jan. 24, 1922; d. Louis Edward and Mabel Inez (Lyon) Kusel; m. Henry Loewy Charles, June 19, 1946; children: Susan, Henry, Robert, Carol. AA, L.A. City Coll., 1941; BA, San Jose (Calif.) State U., 1964. Salesperson Bullock's, L.A., 1940-42, Roos Bros., Berkeley, Calif., 1945-46; ptnr. Charles-Martin Motors, Marysville, Calif., 1950-54; farm editor Indep. Herald, Yuba City, Calif., 1954-55; social worker Sutter County, Yuba City, 1955-57; social worker Santa Clara County, San Jose, 1957-61, manual coordinator, 1961-73, community planning specialist, 1973-81; columnist Sr. Grapevine various weekly newspapers, Santa Clara County, 1981-86; editor Bay area Sr. Spectrum Newspapers, Santa Clara, 1986-90; columnist, 1990-94; columnist Santa Clara Valley edit. Senior Mag., 1994-95; columnist San Jose Mercury News, 1994—, Prime Times Mo. Mag., 1994—; founder, pres. Triple-A Coun. Calif., 1978-80. Vice chmn. Santa Clara County Sr. Care Commn., 1987-89, chmn., 1989-91, mem. social svcs. com., 1993—; mem. adv. coun. Coun. on Aging of Santa Clara County, 1995—. Served with WAVES, USNR, 1942-45. Recipient Social Welfare award Daniel E. Koshland Found., 1973, Friends of Santa Clara County Human Rels. Commn. award, 1992, first ann. Angelina Aguilar Yates Humanitarian award, 1995; named 24th State Assembly Dist. Woman of Yr., 1990. Mem. NASW, LWV (San Jose/Santa Clara Bd. 1993—), Nat. Coun. Sr. Citizens (bd. dirs. 1988—), Svc. Employees Internat. Union (mem. local 535, state exec. bd. dirs. 1973—, pres. sr. mems. and retiree chpt. 1982—), Congress of Calif. Srs. (bd. dirs. 1987—, region IV pres. 1992—, trustee 1993—), Older Women's League (bd. dirs. 1980-84), Older Women's League of Calif. (edn./resource coord. 1987-89, pres. 1990-91), Am. Soc. on Aging (co-chair women's concerns com. 1985-86, awards com. 1990-93), Nat. Coun. on the Aging., Calif. Specialists on Aging (treas. 1985-93), Calif. Srs. Coalition (chmn. 1986, treas. 1993—), Calif. Writers Club. Home and Office: 2527 Forbes Ave Santa Clara CA 95050-5547

CHARLESTON, STEVE, bishop. Bishop Diocese of Alaska, Fairbanks, 1991—. Office: Diocese of Alaska PO Box 441 1205 Derali Way Fairbanks AK 99701-4137*

CHARLTON, JOHN KIPP, pediatrician; b. Omaha, Jan. 26, 1937; s. George Paul and Mildred (Kipp) C. A.B., Amherst Coll., 1958; M.D., Cornell U., 1962; m. Susan S. Young, Aug. 15, 1959; children: Paul, Cynthia, Daphne, Gregory. Intern, Ohio State U. Hosp., Columbus, 1962-63; resident in pediatrics Children's Hosp., Dallas, 1966-68, chief pediatric resident, 1968-69; nephrology fellow U. Tex. Southwestern Med. Sch., Dallas, 1969-70; pvt. practice medicine specializing in pediatrics, Phoenix, 1970; chmn. dept. pediatrics Maricopa Med. Ctr., Phoenix, 1971-78, 84-93, assoc. chmn. dept. pediatrics, 1979-84, med. staff pres., 1991; med. dir., bd. dirs. Crisis Nursery, Inc., 1977—; dir. Phoenix Pediatric Residency, 1983-85, Phoenix Hosps. affiliated pediatric program, 1985-88; clin. assoc. prof. pediatrics U. Ariz. Coll Medicine. Pres. Maricopa County Child Abuse Coun., 1977-81; bd. dirs. Florence Critenton Svcs., 1980-83, Ariz. Children's Found, 1987-91; mem. Gov.'s Coun. on Children, Youth and Families, 1984-86. Officer M.C., USAF, 1963-65. Recipient Hon Kachina award for volunteerism, 1980, Jefferson award for volunteerism, 1980, Horace Steel Child Advocacy award, 1993. Mem. Am. Acad. Pediatrics, Ariz. Pediatric Soc., Maricopa County Pediatric Soc. (past pres.). Author articles, book rev. in field. Home: 6230 E Exeter Blvd Scottsdale AZ 85251-3060 Office: Maricopa Med Ctr 2601 E Roosevelt St Phoenix AZ 85008-4973

CHARLTON, RANDOLPH SEVILLE, psychiatrist, educator; b. Salt Lake City, Nov. 16, 1944; s. Randolph Seville and Patricia Joy (Jensen) C.; m. Louise Bryden Buck, Feb. 14, 1975; children: Genevieve, Blake. BA, Wesleyan U., 1966; MD, Cornell U., 1970. Diplomate Am. Acad. Psychoanalysis. Intern U. Calif., San Francisco, 1970-71; resident psychiatry Stanford U., 1971-74; clin. faculty Standford Med. Sch., Palo Alto, Calif., 1974—; prof. clin. psychiatry Stanford (Calif.) U. Med. Ctr., 1990—; pvt. practice psychiatrist Palo Alto, 1974—. Contbr. chpt. to book and articles to profl. jours. Bd. trustees Castilleja Sch., Palo Alto, 1992—; bioethics com. Recovery Inn, Menlo Park, Calif., 1994—. Fellow Am. Acad. Psychoanalysis; mem. C.G. Jung Inst. (tng. analyst 1978—). Democrat. Office: 690 Waverley St Palo Alto CA 94301-2549

CHARLTON, VALERIE E., pediatrics professor, neonatologist, researcher; b. N.Y.C., Jan. 2, 1947; m. Devron H. Char. BA, Harvard U., 1967, MD, 1971; MPH, U. Calif., Berkeley, 1994. Diplomate Am. Bd. Neonatal-Perinatal Medicine. From asst. prof. to prof. pediatrics U. Calif., San Francisco, 1976—, dir. admission, recovery nurseries, 1976-88, dir. extracorporeal life support program, 1988—, mem. Cardiovascular Rsch. Inst., 1985—; mem. maternal and child health resch. com. Nat. Inst. Child Health and Human Devel., Bethesda, Md., 1990-94; mem. state neonatal intensive care adv. com. Calif. Children's Svc., Sacramento, 1993—. Contbr. numerous articles to profl. jours., also book chpts. and revs. Recipient numerous grants NIH, 1976—, Rsch. Career Devel. award, 1985-89; Teaching and Rsch. scholar ACP, 1976-78; Hartford Found. fellow, 1978-80. Mem. APHA, Am. Pediatric Soc., Soc. for Critical Care Medicine, Perinatal Rsch. Soc., Soc. for Pediatric Rsch., Extracorporeal Life Support Orgn.

CHARTIER, VERNON LEE, electrical engineer; b. Ft. Morgan, Colo., Feb. 14, 1939; s. Raymond Earl and Margaret Clara (Winegar) C.; m. Lois Marie Schwartz, May 20, 1967; 1 child, Neal Raymond. BSEE, BS in Bus., U. Colo., 1963. Registered profl. engr., Pa.; cert. electromagnetic compatibility engr. Rsch. engr., cons. Westinghouse Electric Co., East Pittsburgh, Pa.,

1963-75; principal engr. high voltage phenomena Bonneville Power Adminstrn., Vancouver, Wash., 1975—. Contbr. articles to profl. jours. Fellow IEEE (mem. fellow com., Herman Halperin Transmission and Distribution award 1995); mem. IEEE Power Engrng. Soc. (chmn. transmission and distribution com. 1987-88, chmn. fellows com. 1990-92), Internat. Conf. Large High Voltage Electric Systems (U.S. rep. to study com. 36 on power system electromagnetic compatibility), Acoustical Soc. Am., Bioelectromagnetics Soc., Internat. Electrotech. Commn. (U.S. rep. to subcom. on High Voltage Lines & Traction Systems), Chartier Family Assn. Baptist. Home: 5190 SW Dover Ln Portland OR 97225-1021 Office: Bonneville Power Adminstrn PO Box 491 Vancouver WA 98666-0491

CHARVET, KATHY DELAINE, counselor, psychologist; b. Toppenish, Wash., Dec. 19, 1954; d. Don and Lorraine Jeannette (Allen) Camp; m. Vincent Lee Charvet, June 5, 1993; 1 child, Danielle; 1 stepchild, Alissa. AA, Yakima (Wash.) C.C., 1987; BA magna cum laude, U. Wash., 1989; MS, Ctrl. Wash. U., 1992. Registered counselor, Wash. Grad. rsch. asst. Ctrl. Wash. U., Ellensburg, 1989-91; new accounts rep. Seafirst Bank, Sunnyside, Wash., 1975-78; fixed income asst. Seafirst Bank, Seattle, 1980-85; counselor Brookhaven Group Home, Woodinville, Wash., 1990; rsch. asst. U. Wash., Seattle, 1987-89; career counselor People for People, Yakima, 1991—; poster presenter in field. Sexual assault adv. Ctrl. Wash. Comprehensive Mental Health, Yakima, 1991-92. Mem. ACA, Wash. Sch. Counseling Assn., Phi Beta Kappa, Psi Chi. Democrat. Home: 761 Belma Rd Grandview WA 98930-9755 Office: People for People 2201 E Edison Rd Sunnyside WA 98944-9214

CHASE, GAIL ANNE, geriatrics nurse, nursing executive; b. Lowell, Mass., Dec. 13, 1953; d. Normand A. and Theresa M. (Mello) Pinette; children: Eric George, Nicole Mary. LPN, Lowell Vocat.-Tech. Coll., 1974; AAS, Maricopa Community Coll., 1986. Lic. nursing home adminstr., Ariz., Mich.; RN, Ariz., Mich. Dir. nursing svc. Plaza del Rio Care Ctr., Peoria, Ariz., 1986-88, adminstr., 1988—; tchr. Gateway Community Coll., Phoenix, 1990-94; exec. dir. Freedom Plaza Life Care, Peoria, Ariz., 1994—; bd. dirs. Gov. Symington Nursing Care Instn. Adminstrs., Phoenix, 1992-94, pres., 1994, 95; mem. adv. bd. Gateway C.C., Phoenix, 1990—. Recipient Ednl. award Peoria C. of C., 1992, Athena award State of Ariz., 1995. Mem. Am. Coll. Health Care Adminstrs., Nat. League for Nursing, Kiwanis.

CHASE, JACOLINE B., designer, career consultant, educator; b. Richmond Heights, Mo., Oct. 10, 1953; d. Thomas Joseph and Dorothea Mae (Pilgrim) S. B of Liberal Studies, magna cum laude, St. Louis U., 1978; MA, UCLA, 1991. Cert. tchr., Calif. Office mgr., sec. Investors Planning Group, Clayton, Mo., 1978; substitute tchr. Vashon High Sch., St. Louis, 1978; pres., creative dir. Chase and Assocs., Goleta, Calif., 1979-81; CEO Personal Packaging, Inc., Santa Barbara, Calif., 1981—, Seraphim, Cherubim, Sweet Angels & More, Inc., 1990—; cons. Ventura (Calif.) Unified Sch. Dist., 1986; instr. adult edn. Santa Barbara (Calif.) City Coll., 1984; pub. speaker, conductor seminars and chief designer in field. Producer ednl. video tapes; tech. writer, editor numerous govt. proposals; author, writer: Santa Barbara News-Press, The Minority Engineer, Carpinteria Herald, and others. Pub. rels. dir. United Boys' Clubs Greater Santa Barbara, 1980; vol. coach Spl. Olympics, Santa Barbara, 1979—. Grad. Fellow State of Calif., 1987-89. Home: 712 Deerfield Ln Apt 8 Paso Robles CA 93446-3623

CHASE, JUDITH HELFER, librarian, educator, musician; b. Elizabethton, Tenn., Feb. 19, 1939; d. Edward Conley and Faith (Clemons) Helfer; m. William Clark Chase, Aug. 8, 1970. BS in Music Edn., East Tenn. State U., 1962; postgrad., Bradley U., 1963-64, U. Tenn., Knoxville, 1968; student, German Ctr. for Internat. Music Edn., 1969-70; postgrad., Oreg. Inst. Tech., 1975-77; M in Music, U. Oreg., 1984; ML, U. Wash., 1986. Music specialist Morristown (Tenn.) City Schs., 1962-63, Peoria (Ill.) County Schs., 1963-64, Anne Arundel County Bd. Edn., Annapolis, 1964-69, 70-73; ch. organist, pvt. practice piano tchr. Elizabethton, Tenn. and Klamath Falls, Oreg., 1973-77; with med. records dept. Merle West Med. Ctr., Klamath Falls, 1977-79; media svcs. cataloger, libr. aide, music specialist Klamath County Sch. Dist., 1977-85; med. libr. aide of aux., 1987-89; asst. prof., reference and documents librarian Oreg. Inst. Tech., Klamath Falls, 1986-89; asst. catalog libr. Francis Marion Coll., Florence, S.C., 1989-90, Klamath County Pub. Libr., Klamath Falls, 1992; catalog libr. Weyerhaeuser Corp. Libr., Tacoma, Wash., 1992-93; bassoonist, counselor Brevard (N.C.) Music Ctr., summer 1961; unit leader Nat. Music Camp, Interlochen, Mich., summer 1964. Dir. youth choir St. Paul's Episcopal Ch., Klamath Falls., 1975-84; mem. aux. Klamath Arts Coun., 1976-84; mem. online coord. com. Interinstitnl. Libr. Coun. Oreg. State Systems Higher Edn., 1989; soprano Klamath Symphonic Choir, 1977-84; libr. Plum Ridge Symphony, Klamath Falls, 1979-84, v.p. guild, 1980-82; bd. dirs., libr. Klamath Youth Symphony, 1983-89; mem. FMC Artist Series Com., 1989-90; alto Masterworks Choir, Florence, S.C., 1990. Bassoon scholar, 1957, 58-62, 63, 63-64. Mem. ALA (govt. documents roundtable 1987—, resources and tech. svcs. div. 1988—), AAUW, Med. Libr. Assn. (ednl. media and tech. svcs. sect. 1988-92), Music Libr. Assn., Pacific N.W. Libr. Assn., Online Audiovisual Catalogers, MacDowell Evening Music Club, Nat. Fedn. Music Clubs, Delta Omicron (pres. alumni chpt. 1967-68, Mae Chenoweth Grannis grantee 1984), Kappa Delta Pi. Episcopalian. Office: Weyerhaeuser Corp Libr 33663 Weyerhaeuser Way S Tacoma WA 98477-0001

CHASE, KRISTINE LOUISE, economics educator, academic administrator; b. Oakland, CA, Jan. 16, 1949; d. Keith E. and Dorothea L. (Lodi) Terrill; m. Daniel P. Chase, June 9, 1973; children: Karen L., Michael S. BA in Econs., U. Calif., Davis, 1970, MA in Econs., 1972; PhD in Econs., U. Md., 1981. Instr. and asst. chair econs. dept. U. Md., College Park, 1973-79; vis. asst. prof. U.S. Naval Acad., Annapolis, Md., 1979-81; asst. prof. U. Md., Balt., 1981-82; assoc. prof. St. Mary's Coll., Moraga, Calif., 1985-93; prof., acting dean sch. econs. and bus. St. Mary's Coll., Moraga, 1993-94, prof., 1994—; cons. Irwin, Inc. Publishers, Homewood, Ill., 1988—. Contbr. articles to profl. jours., chpts. to books. Mem. planning commn. City of Larkspur, Calif., 1983-84; pres. Orinda (Calif.) Assn. Mem. Am. Econs. Assn., Western Econs. Assn., Contra Costa Coun. Home: 37 Van Ripper Ln Orinda CA 94563-1117 Office: Saint Mary's Coll Econs Dept Moraga CA 94575

CHASE, RICHARD BARTH, operations management educator; b. L.A., May 4, 1939; s. Louis R. and Sally (Barth) C.; m. Harriet Levine, Jan. 27, 1962; children: Laurie, Andrew, Glenn. BS, UCLA, 1962, MBA, 1963, PhD, 1966. Asst. prof. UCLA, 1966-68; assoc. prof. Pa. State U., University Park, 1968-69; assoc. prof. U. Ariz., Tucson, 1970-75, prof., 1975-85; prof. ops. mgmt. U. So. Calif. Sch. Bus., L.A., 1985—; vis. prof. Inst. for Mgmt. Devel., Lausanne, France, 1976-77, Harvard U., Boston, 1988-89; dir. Ctr. for Ops. Mgmt., L.A., 1985—; examiner Malcolm Baldridge Nat. Quality Award, 1989; bd. govs. Acad. Mgmt., 1985-87. Co-author: Management: A Life Cycle Approach, 1981, Production and Operations Management, 1989, Service Management Effect, 1990. Fellow Decision Scis. Inst., Acad. Mgmt.; mem. Ops. Mgmt. Assn. (bd. dirs. 1985-87), Beta Gamma Sigma, Omega Rho. Office: U So Calif Sch Bus Ctr Ops Mgmt Los Angeles CA 90089-1421

CHATARD, PETER RALPH NOEL JR., aesthetic surgeon; b. New Orleans, June 25, 1936; s. Peter Ralph Sr. and Alberta Chatard; m. Patricia Myrl White, Jan. 31, 1963; children: Andrea Michelle, Faedra Noelle, Tahra Deonne. BS in Biology, Morehouse Coll., 1956; MD, U. Rochester, 1960. Diplomate Am. Bd. Plastic Surgery, Am. Bd. Otolaryngology. Intern Colo. Gen. Hosp., 1960-61; asst. resident in gen. surgery Highland Gen. Hosp., Rochester, N.Y., 1963-64; resident in otolaryngology Strong Meml. Hosp., Rochester, 1964-67; resident in plastic and reconstructive surgery U. Fla., 1980-82; staff otolaryngologist Group Health Corp. of Puget Sound, Seattle, 1967-68; practice medicine specializing in otolaryngology Seattle, 1968-80, practice medicine specializing in plastic surgery, 1982—; clin. asst. prof. otolaryngology, head and neck surgery U. Wash., Seattle, 1975—; plastic surgery cons. western sec. Maxillofacial Rev. Bd. State of Wash., 1982—, cons. Conservation of Hearing Program, 1968-80; trustee Physicians and Dentist Credit Bur., 1974-80, 84-87, pres. 1976-77, 84-85; chief subspecialty surgery and active staff mem. Northwest Hosp., Seattle; courtesy staff Swedish Hosp., Children's Hosp. Med. Ctr., Seattle, Providence Hosp., Seattle, Stevens Meml. Hosp., Edmond, Wash., St. Cabrini Hosp., Seattle, Fifth Ave. Med. Ctr., Seattle, and others. Capt. USAF, 1961-63. Fellow Am. Rhinologic Soc., Seattle Surg. Soc., ACS, Am. Acad. Facial Plastic and Reconstructive Surgery, Am. Acad. Otolaryngology-Head and Neck Surgery, Northwest Acad. Otolaryngology and Head and Neck Surgery, Soc. for Ear, Nose and Throat Advances in Children, Pacific Oto-Ophthalmological Soc.; mem. AMA, Am. Soc. Plastic and Reconstructive Surgeons, Lipoplasty Soc. N. Am., Wash. Soc. Plastic Surgeons, Nat. Med. Assn., King County Med. Soc., Wash. Med. Assn., N.W. Soc. of Plastic Surgeons. Home: 20914 39th Ave SE Bothell WA 98021-7904 Office: Chatard Plas Surg Ctr 1200 N Northgate Way Seattle WA 98133-8916

CHATFIELD, CHERYL ANN, nonprofit organization executive, educator; b. King's Park, N.Y., Jan. 24, 1946; d. William David and Mildred Ruth (King) C.; m. Gene Allen Chasser, Feb. 17, 1968 (div. 1979); m. James Bernard Arkebauer, Apr. 16, 1983 (div. 1987). BS, Cen. Conn. Coll., 1968, MS, 1972; PhD, U. Conn., 1976. Cert. gen. prin. securities. Tchr. Bristol East High Sch., Conn., 1968-77; adminstr. New Britain Schs., Conn., 1977-79; prof. Ariz. State U., Phoenix, 1979; stockbroker J. Daniel Bell, Denver, 1980-83, Hyder and Co., Denver, 1983-84; stockbroker; chief exec. officer Chatfield Dean & Co., Denver, 1984-90, Women Securities Internat., 1990-92; exec. dir. Visitor Hospitality Ctr., Santa Fe, N.Mex.; instr. Ctr. Entrepreneurship U. N.Mex., 1992—; tchr. investment seminars Front Range Community Coll., Denver, 1984-86; speaker women's groups, Denver, 1983-86. Author: Low-Priced Riches, 1985, Selling Low-Priced Riches, 1986, (newspaper columns) For Women Investors, 1982-84, Commentary, 1985-86; editor, founder (newsletter) Women in Securities . Project bus. cons. Jr. Achievement, Denver, 1986; exec. dir., visitor Hopitality Ctr. at State Penitentary. Mem. NAFE, AAUW, Aircraft Owners and Pilots Assn., Internat. Women's Forum, Kappa Delta Pi. Republican. Roman Catholic. Avocation: flying. Office: 2801 W Rodeo Rd Ste B-217 Santa Fe NM 87505-6503

CHATHAM, JOSEPH CHRISTOPHER, financial executive; b. Glendale, Calif., July 23, 1965; s. Harold Stell Chatham and Carol Jo Kopietz Brown. BA, Pitzer Coll., Claremont, Calif., 1989. Account exec. Household Fin. Corp., Long Beach/La Puente, Calif., 1989-91; br. sales mgr. Household Fin. Corp., Brea/La Habra, Calif., 1991-93; asst. v.p. Campbell Fin. Svcs., Riverside, Calif., 1993—. Mem. elect Riverside County Rep. Ctrl. Com., 1994—; regional co-chmn. Pete Wilson for Gov., Riverside/Corona, 1994—; mem. Congressman Ken Calvert's Steering Com., Corona, 1994—. Mem. Riverside C. of C. (govt. affairs com. 1993—), Pitzer Coll. Alumni Assn. (class rep. 1990—). Roman Catholic. Office: Campbell Fin Svcs 2900 Adams St Ste C110 Riverside CA 92504-4336

CHATROO, ARTHUR JAY, lawyer; b. N.Y.C., July 1, 1946; s. George and Lillian (Leibowitz) C.; m. Christina Daly, Aug. 6, 1994. BChemE, CCNY, 1968; JD cum laude, New York Law Sch., 1979; MBA with distinction, NYU, 1982. Bar: N.Y. 1980, Ohio 1992, Calif. 1993. Process engr. Standard Oil Co. of Ohio, various locations, 1968-73; process specialist BP Oil, Inc., Marcus Hook, Pa., 1974-75; sr. process engr. Sci. Design Co., Inc., N.Y.C., 1975-78; mgr. spl. projects The Halcon SD Group, N.Y.C., 1978-82; corp. counsel, tax and fin. The Lubrizol Corp., Wickliffe, Ohio, 1982-85; sr. counsel spl. investment projects The Lubrizol Corp., Wickliffe, 1989-90; gen. counsel Lubrizol Enterprises, Inc., Wickliffe, 1985-89; chmn. Correlation Genetics Corp., San Jose, Calif., 1990-91; gen. counsel Agrigenetics Co., Eastlake, Ohio, 1990-92; gen. counsel, dir. comml. contracting Agrigenetics, L.P., San Diego, 1993—, Mycogen Plant Scis. (formerly Agrigenetics L.P.), San Diego, 1993—. Mem. Met. Parks Adv. com., Allen County, Ohio, 1973. Mem. ABA, Am. Inst. Chem. Engrs., N.Y. State Bar Assn., Cleve. Bar Assn., Am. Corp. Counsel Assn., Jaycees (personnel dir. Lima, Ohio chpt. 1972-73), Omega Chi Epsilon, Beta Gamma Sigma. Club: Toastmasters. Home: 3525 Del Mar Hts Rd # 285 San Diego CA 92130 Office: Mycogen Plant Scis 4980 Carroll Canyon Rd San Diego CA 92121-1736

CHAUDHURI, SURAJIT, computer scientist, researcher; b. Calcutta, India, Jan. 1960; came to U.S., 1985; B Tech., India Inst. Tech., 1983, MS, 1985; PhD, Stanford U., 1992. Rsch. asst. Stanford U., Stanford, Calif., 1985-91; mem. tech. staff Hewlett Packard Labs., Palo Alto, Calif., 1992—. Contbr. articles to profl. jours. Mem. Assn. for Computing Machinery. Home: PO Box 6870 Palo Alto CA 94309-6870

CHAUVIN, YVES, cognitive scientist; b. Cholet, France, Dec. 20, 1956; came to U.S., 1982; s. Rene and Marie-Therese (Provost) C. BS in Engring., INPG, 1980; BA in Psychology, U. Calif., San Diego, 1983, PhD in Cognitive Sci., 1988. Rsch. scientist Thomson-CSF, Palo Alto, Calif., 1986-90, Stanford U., Palo Alto, Calif., 1986-90, Net-ID, Inc., San Francisco, 1991—; founder, pres. NEt-ID, Inc., 1991—. Author/editor: Back-Propagation: Theory, Architecture and Applications, 1995.

CHAVEZ, ALBERT BLAS, financial executive; b. L.A., Jan. 1, 1952; s. Albert Blas and Yolanda (Garcia) C. BA, U. Tex., El Paso, 1979; MBA, Stanford U., 1985. CPA, Calif. Mem. profl. staff Deloitte Haskins and Sells, L.A., 1980-83; planning analyst corp. fin. planning Boise (Idaho) Cascade Co., 1984; treasury analyst corp. treasury RCA Corp., N.Y.C., 1985; asst. contr. RCA/Ariola Records, Mexico City, 1986; fin. analyst corp. exec. office GE Co., Fairfield, Conn., 1987-90; fin. cons. Entertainment Industry and Litigation Support Svcs., L.A., 1990-91; co-founder, sr. v.p., CFO El Dorado Comm., Inc., L.A., 1991—, also bd. dirs. Bd. dirs., treas. L.A. Conservation Corps, 1990—. Mem. AICPA, Calif. Soc. CPAs. Democrat. Home: 11701 Texas Ave Apt 312 Los Angeles CA 90025-1667 Office: El Dorado Comm Inc 2130 Sawtelle Blvd Ste 307 Los Angeles CA 90025-6250

CHAVEZ, EDWARD, police chief; b. Stockton, Calif., Mar. 22, 1943; m. Nancy Chavez; children: Eric, Jill. AA, San Joaquin Delta Coll.; BA, Calif. State U.; MS, Calif. Polytechnic Pomona; grad., POST Command Coll., Delinquency Control Inst., Leadership Stockton Program, FBI Nat. Acad. With USAF, 1962-70; officer Stockton Police Dept., 1973, sgt., 1980, lt., 1986, capt., 1990, dep. chief of police, 1990, acting chief of police, 1993, chief of police, 1993; mem. bd. dirs. Greater Stockton C. of C., United Way of San Joaquin, Coun. for Spanish Speaking, Lilliput Children's Svcs.; active Hispanics for Political Action. Mem. Calif. Peace Officers Assn., Hispanic Am. Police Command Officer's Assn., Mexican Am. C. of C., Stockton E. Rotary. Office: 22 E Market St Stockton CA 95202-2802*

CHAVEZ, GILBERT ESPINOZA, bishop; b. Ontario, Calif., Mar. 19, 1932; ed. St. Francis Sem., El Cajon, Calif., Immaculate Heart Sem., San Diego, U. Calif., San Diego. Ordained priest Roman Cath. Ch., 1960; titular bishop of Magarmel and aux. bishop Diocese of San Diego, 1974—. Office: 1535 3rd Ave San Diego CA 92101-3101*

CHÁVEZ-SILVERMAN, SUZANNE, Chicano/Latino and Latin American literature educator; b. L.A., Mar. 21, 1956; d. Joseph Herman and June Audrey (Chávez) Silverman; 1 child, Etienne Joseph Strauss. BA magna cum laude, U. Calif., Irvine, 1977; MA, Harvard U., 1979; PhD, U. Calif., Davis, 1991. Permanent lectr. U. South Africa, Pretoria, 1982-84; asst. prof. Spanish and L.Am. lit. Pomona Coll., Claremont, Calif., 1989—. Contbr. articles to profl. jours. and anthologies. NEH rsch. asst. grantee Pomona Coll., summers 1992, 93. Mem. MLA, Am. Studies Assn., Nat. Assn. for Chicano Studies, Am. Lit. Assn., Am. Assn. Tchrs. Spanish and Portuguese, Latin Am. Studies Assn. Office: Pomona Coll Modern Langs Dept 550 Harvard Ave Claremont CA 91711

CHAYKIN, HOWARD VICTOR, cartoonist, screenwriter; b. Newark, Oct. 7, 1950; s. Leon and Rosalind (Pave) C. Freelance cartoonist, 1971—; TV writer, script cons. Warner Bros. TV., Burbank, Calif., 1990-91, Paramount TV, L.A., 1993. Mem. Writers Guild of Am. West, Soc. Illustrators. Democrat. Jewish.

CHAYKIN, ROBERT LEROY, manufacturing and marketing executive; b. Miami, Fla., May 2, 1944; s. Allan Leroy and Ruth (Levine) C.; m. Patty Jean Patton, Feb. 1971 (div. May 1975); m. Evalyn Marcy Slodzina, Sept. 3, 1989; children: Michelle Alee, Catrina Celia, Ally Sue. BA in Polit. Sci., U. Miami, Fla., 1965, LLB, 1969. Owner, operator Serrating Svcs. Miami, 1969-71, Serrating Svcs. Las Vegas, Nev., 1971-84; pres. Ser-Sharp Mfg., Inc., Las Vegas, 1984—; nat. mktg. dir. Coserco Corp., Las Vegas, 1987—. Patentee in mfg. field. With U.S. Army, 1962. Recipient 2d degree black belt Tae Kwon Do, Profl. Karate Assn., 1954-61.

CHAZEN, MELVIN LEONARD, chemical engineer; b. St. Louis, Sept. 26, 1933; s. Saul and Tillie (Kramer) C.; m. Dorothea Glazer, June 29, 1958; children: Jamie Lynn, Avery Glazer. BS in Chem. Engring., Washington U., St. Louis, 1955. Registered profl. engr., Mo. Thermodynamics engr. Bell Aerospace Textron, Buffalo, 1958-59; devel. engr. Bell Aerospace Textron, 1959-62, project engr., 1962-65, chief sec. rocket engines, 1965-72, prog. mgr., tech. dir., 1972-74, project engr., 1974-84, chief engr. rocket devel., 1984-87; sr. staff engr. Space and Tech. div. TRW, Redondo Beach, Calif., 1987—; bd. dirs. Unimed Corp., Rochester. Contbr. articles to profl. jours. Recipient Enterprise Development Inc. Innovation award 1994, NASA Innovation Cert. of Recognition, 1994. Mem. Alpha Chi Sigma. Home: 12522 Inglenook Ln Cerritos CA 90703-7837 Office: TRW Space and Tech Divsn One Space Park Redondo Beach CA 90278

CHAZIN, WALTER J., structural biology researcher and educator; b. Lackawanna, N.Y., Nov. 7, 1954; m. Christiane Martel; children: Sara Helene, Daniel Max. BS in Chemistry, McGill U., Montreal, Que., Can., 1975; PhD in Phys. Organic Chemistry, Concordia U., Montreal, Can., 1983. Postdoctoral fellow E.T.H.-Zürich, Switzerland, 1983-85; rsch. assoc. Scripps Rsch. Inst., La Jolla, Calif., 1986-87; asst. prof. Rsch. Inst. of Scripps Clinic, La Jolla, Calif., 1987-92, assoc. prof. structural biology, 1992—; mem. internat. adv. bd. Internat. Jour. Macromolecules, 1990—; mem. drug devel., hematology and pathology com. Am. Cancer Soc. Contbr. articles to profl. jours. Recipient Jr. Faculty Rsch. award Am. Cancer Soc., 1990-93, Faculty Rsch. award, 1993-98; grantee NIH, 1988—, NSF, 1991—, Am. Cancer Soc., 1992—; traveling fellow NAS, 1990. Mem. AAAS, Internat. Union Pure and Applied Chem., Am. Chem. Soc., Protein Soc., Biophys. Soc., Scripps Rsch. Inst. Office: The Scripps Rsch Inst 10666 N Torrey Pines Rd La Jolla CA 92037-1027

CHEAH, KEONG-CHYE, psychiatrist; b. Georgetown, Penangt, West Malaysia, Mar. 15, 1939; came to U.S., 1959; s. Thean Hoe and Hun Kin (Keong) C.; m. Sandra Massey, June 10, 1968; children: Chylynn, Maylynn. BA in Psychology, U. Ark., 1962; MD, U. Ark., Little Rock, 1967, MS in Microbiology, 1968. Diplomate Am. Bd. Psychiatry and Neurology (examiner 1982, 85); cert. Ark. State Sci. Bd., Ark. State Med. Bd. Intern U. Ark. Med. Ctr., 1967-68; resident VA Med. Ctr. and U. Ark. Med. Ctr., Little Rock, 1968-72; chief addiction sect. Little Rock (Ark.) VA Med. Ctr., 1972-73, staff psychiatrist, 1975-80; chief psychiatry Am. Lake VA Med. Ctr., Tacoma, Wash., 1981-86; chief consultation, liason Am. Lake VA Med. Ctr., Tacoma, 1986—; asst. prof. medicine, psychiatry U. Ark., Little Rock, 1975-81; asst. prof. psychiatry and behavioral scis. U. Wash., Seattle, 1981-86, clin. assoc. prof., 1987—; mem. dist. br. com. The CHAMPUS, 1977-91; site visitor AMA Continuing Med. Edn., 1979-83; book reviewer Jour. Am. Geriatrics Soc., 1984-85; mem. task force alcohol abuse VA Med. Dist. 27, 1984, survey mem. Sytematic External Rev. Process, 1985; mem. mental health plan adv. com. State of Ark., 1976-81, chmn. 1979-81, chmn. steering com., 1979; mem. Vietnamese Resettlement Program, 1979; many coms. Am. Lake VA Med. Ctr. including chmn. mental health coun. 1981-84, utilization rev. com., 1981-86. Contbr. articles and abstracts to profl. jours.; presenter to confs. and meetings of profl. socs. Mem. Parents Adv. Com., Lakes H.S., Wash., 1987-91; mem. Mayor's Budget and Fin. Foresight Com., 1992—, chmn. 1990-92; sch. cons. Child Study Ctr. U. Ark., 1972-74; bd. dirs. Crisis Ctr. Ark., 1974-79, chmn. pub. rels. com., 1975-79, mem. pers. com. 1974, vice chmn. bd. 1977; pres. Chinese Assn. Ctrl. Ark., 1977; mem. gifted edn. adv. coun. Clover Park Sch. Dist. 400, Wash., 1983-85, Parent Tchr. Student Orgn.,. Recipient U.S. Govt. scholarship 1959, cert. merit State of Ark., 1973, Leadership award, Mental Health Svcs. Divsn., State of Ark., 1980. Fellow Am. Psychiat. Assn. (sec. treas. Asian Am. caucus 1985-87, pres. 1987—); mem. Assn. Mil. Surgeons U.S., Wash. State Psychiat. Assn. (mem. peer rev. com. 1982-92, chmn. pub. psychiatry com. 1985-93, exec. coun. 1985-93), N. Pacific Soc. Neurology and Psychiatry, S. Puget Sound Psychiat. Assn., Assn. Chinese-Am. Psychiatrists, Ark. Caduceus Club, Alpha Epsilon Delts, Psi Chi, Phi Beta Kappa. Office: VA Med Ctr Am Lake Tacoma WA 98493

CHEAL, MARYLOU, experimental psychologist; b. St. Clair County, Mich.; d. Marion Louis Fast and Leda Eleanor (Shaw) Martin; m. James Cheal, Apr. 13, 1946; children: Thomas James, Catheryn Leda, Robert David. BA in Psychology with honors, Oakland U., 1969; PhD in Psychology, U. Mich., 1973. Rsch.investigator dept. zoology U. Mich., Ann Arbor, 1973-75, rsch. investigator dept. oral biology, 1975-76, lectr. dept. psychology, 1973-76; Charles A. King rsch. fellow Harvard U. Med. Sch., Boston, 1976-77; lectr. on psychology dept. psychiatry Harvard U. Sch. Medicine, Boston, 1977-83; asst. psychologist McLean Hosp., Belmont, Mass., 1977-81, assoc. psychologist, 1981-83; faculty rsch. assoc. dept. psychology Ariz. State U., Tempe, 1983-87, mem. faculty Women's Studies program, 1986; rsch. psychologist U. Dayton Rsch. Inst.-Williams AFB, Higley, Ariz., 1986-94; sr. rsch. psychologist U. Dayton Rsch. Inst.-Armstrong Laboratory, Mesa, Ariz., 1994-95; vis. prof. Air Force Systems Command U. Resident Rsch. Program appointment, Williams AFB, Airz., 1986-88; adj. assoc. prof. psychology Ariz. State U., 1987-91, adj. prof., 1993—; sr. rsch. psychologist U. Dayton Rsch. Inst. Armstrong Lab., Ariz., 1994-95; reviewer CUNY, NIMH, NSF, Ont. Mental Health Found., Tufts U. Sch. Medicine, Internat. Sci. Found. Referee Internat. Jour. Aging and Human Devel., Pharmacology Biochemistry and Behavior, Jour. Exptl. Psychology: Animal Behavioral Processes, Jour. Comparative Psychology, Animal Behavior, Physiology and Behavior, Sci., Behavioral Brain Rsch., Acta Psychologica, Perception and Psychophysics, Jour. Exptl. Psychology: Human Perception and Performance, Human Factors (editorial bd. 1993—), Psychol. Sci., Quarterly Jour. Exptl. Psychology, others; cons. editor Jour. Gen. Psychology, 1995—; contbr. articles to profl. jours. Recipient numerous rsch. awards. Fellow AAAS, APA (program com. 1985, chmn. symposium 1985, 87, fellow physiol. and comparative psychology and psychopharmacology 1986-90, mem. and fellow com. 1986-90), Am. Psuchol. Soc.; mem. Internat. Brain Rsch. Orgn., Soc. Neurosci., Psychonomics Soc., Sigma Xi. Office: Ariz State U Dept Psychology Tempe AZ 85287-1104

CHEAVENS, THOMAS HENRY, chemistry educator; b. Dallas, May 19, 1930; s. Tom H. and Sarah (Newsom) C.; m. Eleanor Louise Seemar, Dec. 30, 1955; children: Suzanne Cheavens Wontrobski, Tom Jr., Jeff W. BS in Chemistry, U. Tex., 1950, PhD in Chemistry, 1955. Rsch. chemist Am. Cyanamid Co., Bound Brook, N.J., 1955-57; group leader Am. Cyanamid Co., Stamford, Conn., 1957-67; rsch. supr. W.R. Grace & Co., Clarksville, Md., 1967-72; rsch. dir. W.R. Grace & Co., Clarksville, 1972-75; contract officer Energy R & D Adminstrn., Washington, 1976-78; rsch. dir. Quest Rsch. and Engring., Tyler, Tex., 1978-82; pres. Quest Rsch. and Engring., Tyler, 1982-86; rsch. assoc. chemistry U. Tex., Austin, 1986-89; assoc. prof. chemistry N.Mex. Highland U., Las Vegas, 1989—; v.p. Improtec, Inc., Tyler, 1981-86. Inventor in field. Rsch. grantee NSF, 1991, NIH, 1992—. Fellow AAAS, Am. Inst. Chemists; mem. Am. Chem. Soc., Sigma Xi, Phi Kappa Phi. Office: N Mex Highlands Univ National Ave Las Vegas NM 87701

CHECINSKI, JADWIGA, JOANNA, computer company executive, electrical engineer; b. Janòu Polesu, Poland, Dec. 6, 1928; came to U.S., 1973; d. Kazimierz and Honorata (Niedbalska) Wisniewski; m. Stanley S. Checinski, July 4, 1954; children: Margaret E., George R. BSEE, Wroceaw (Poland) U., 1957. Engr. Elect. Zaklady Naukowe, Wrogeaw, 1972; pvt. practice as engr. Chgo., 1974-85; system, software engr. Honeywell, Inc., Phoenix, 1985-90; pres. Surface Mounted Device Tech., Phoenix, 1991—. Editor: Pal Bulletin, 1986, Ch. Bulletin, 1988, Pol-Am. Women Voice, 1994; contbr. articles to newspapers. Sec. Polish Am. Congress, Phoenix, 1985, pres., 1990; pres., founder Polish Am. Women in Ariz., Phoenix, 1992; treas. Phoenix Diocesan Coun. Cath. Women, 1994. Mem. Soc. Women Engrs. Republican. Roman Catholic. Home and Office: Surface Mounted Device Tech 1739 W Banff Ln Phoenix AZ 85023-5156

CHEDID, JOHN G., bishop; b. Eddid, Lebanon, July 4, 1923. Educated, Sems. in Lebanon and Pontifical Urban Coll., Rome. Ordained priest Roman Cath. Ch., 1951. Titular bishop of Callinico and aux bishop St. Maron of Bklyn., 1981. Office: Aux Bishop of St Maron 333 S San Vicente Blvd Los Angeles CA 90048-3313*

CHEE, JASON S.I., product marketing management; b. Honolulu, Nov. 8, 1962; s. William K.Y. and Dorothy K. C.; m. Julie C. Kong, Mar. 12, 1994. BS in computer sci., U. S. Calif., 1984; MBA, Pepperdine U., 1991. Sr. engr. GTE, Thousand Oaks, Calif., 1984-88; st. tech. support engr. Harris Corp., Camarillo, Calif., 1988-91; product marketing. mgr. Tekelec, Calabasas, Calif., 1991—. Mem. IEEE. Office: Tekelec 26580 Agoura Rd Calabasas CA 91302-1921

CHEE, PERCIVAL HON YIN, ophthalmologist; b. Honolulu, Aug. 29, 1936; s. Young Sing and Den Kyau (Ching) C.; m. Carolyn Tong, Jan. 27, 1966; children: Lara Wai Lung, Shera Wai Sum. BA, U. Hawaii, 1958; MD, U. Rochester, 1962. Intern Travis AFB Hosp., Fairfield, Calif., 1962-63; resident Bascom Palmer Eye Inst., Miami, Fla., 1965-68, Jackson Meml. Hosp., Miami, 1965-68; partner Straub Clinic, Inc., Honolulu, 1968-71; practice medicine specializing in ophthalmology, Honolulu, 1972—; mem. staffs Queen's Med. Center, St. Francis Hosp., Kapiolani Children's Med. Center, Honolulu; clin. assoc. prof. surgery U. Hawaii Sch. Medicine, 1971—; cons. Tripler Army Med. Center. Mem. adv. bd. Services to Blind; bd. dirs. Lions Eye Bank and Makana Found. (organ bank), Multiple Sclerosis Soc. Served to capt. USAF, 1962-65. Fellow Am. Acad. Ophthalmology, ACS; mem. AMA, Pan Am. Med. Assn., Pan Pacific Surg. Assn., Am. Assn. Ophthalmology, Soc. Eye Surgeons, Hawaii Ophthal. Soc. Pacific Coast Ophthal. Soc., Am. Assn. for Study Headache, Pan Am. Ophthal. Found. Contbr. articles to profl. pubs. Home: 3755 Poka Pl Honolulu HI 96816-4409 Office: Kukui Pla 50 S Beretania St Ste C116 Honolulu HI 96813-2222

CHEESEMAN, DOUGLAS TAYLOR, JR., wildlife tour executive, photographer, educator; b. Honolulu, July 16, 1937; s. Douglas Taylor Cheeseman and Myra (Bettencourt) Ehrlich; m. Gail Macomber, Apr. 7, 1963; children: Rosie M., Ted F. BA, San Jose (Calif.) State U., 1959, MA, 1964. Cert. secondary tchr., Calif. Naturalist Crater Lake (Oreg.) Nat. Park, summers 1959-60; tchr. biology Woodside High Sch., Redwood City, Calif., 1961-65; teaching asst. U. Colo., Boulder, 1966-67; prof. biology De Anza Coll., Cupertino, Calif., 1967—, dir. environ. study area, 1970—, dir. Student Ecology Rsch. Lab., 1990—; pres. Cheeseman's Ecology Safaris, Saratoga, Calif., 1981—; instr. wildlife and natural history photography, Saratoga, 1984—; rsch. cooperator Fish and Wildlife Svc., 1972—, guest lectr. numerous conservation groups, No. Calif., 1978—; spkr. on rainforest destruction, zone depletion, global warming; participant, spkr. to save planet; spkr. Calif. Acad. Antarctic Ecology; expdn. leader Sengey Vavilov, Antarctic, 1994; active in saving flora and fauna in third world; expdn. leader, Antarctice, 1996. Photographs represented in books and on calendars. Recipient Outstanding Svc. and Tchr. award, Pres.'s award De Anza Coll., 1988, Nat. Leadership award U. Tex., Austin, 1989; NSF fellow, 1969, 71; NEDA Title III grantee, 1970. Mem. Ecol. Soc. Am., Am. Ornithologists Union, Am. Soc. Mammalogists, Brit. Trust Ornitology, Brit. Ornithologists Union, AfricanWildlife Soc., Marine Mammal Soc. (founding), Calif. Native Plants Soc., Bay Area Bird Photographers (co-founder), Santa Clara Valley Audubon Soc. (bd. dirs., v.p., program chmn. 1983—), Cooper Soc. Home: 20800 Kittridge Rd Saratoga CA 95070-6322 Office: De Anza Coll Dept Biology Cupertino CA 95014

CHEIFETZ, LORNA GALE, psychologist; b. Phoenix, Mar. 22, 1953; d. Walter and Ruth Cheifetz. BS, Chapman Coll., Orange, Calif., 1975; D of Psychology, Ill. Sch. Profl. Psychology, 1981. Psychology intern Cook County Hosp., Chgo., 1979-80; clin. psychologist City of Chgo., 1980-84, Phoenix Inst. for Psychotherapy, 1984-87; pvt. practice Phoenix, 1987—; cons. to judges, attys., cts., 1984—; adj. faculty Met. U., Phoenix, 1984-88, Ill. Sch. Profl. Psychology, 1982-86. Contbr. chpt. to book Listening and Interpreting, 1984; contbg. editor Internat. Jour. Communicative Psychoanalysis and Psychotherapy, 1991-93. Cons., vol. Ariz. Bar Assn. Vol. Lawyer Program, 1985—; co-coord. Psychology Info. Referral Svc., Maricopa County, Ariz., 1984—. Named Psychologist of Yr. Ariz. Bar Assn., 1987. Mem. Am. Psychol. Assn. (activist 1981—), Ariz. Psychol. Assn. (activist 1989—), Maricopa Psychol. Soc., Nat. Register Health Svc. Providers in Psychology, Internat. Soc. for the Study of Dissociative Disorders. Office: 2211 E Highland Ave Ste 135 Phoenix AZ 85016-4833

CHEITLIN, MELVIN DONALD, physician, educator; b. Wilmington, Del., Mar. 25, 1929; s. James Cheitlin and Mollie Budman; m. Hella Hochschild, Aug. 4, 1952; children: Roger, Kenneth, Julie. AB, Temple U., 1950, MD, 1954. Intern, resident internal medicine Walter Reed Army Med. Ctr., Washington, 1954-59, cardiology fellow, 1959-60, chief cardiology, 1971-74; chief cardiology Madigan Army Med. Ctr., Tacoma, Wash., 1960-64, Tripler Army Med. Ctr., Honolulu, 1964-68, Letterman Army Med. Ctr., San Francisco, 1968-71; assoc. chief cardiology San Francisco Gen. Hosp., 1974-91, chief cardiology, 1991—; prof. medicine U. Calif., San Francisco, 1974—. Author: Clinical Cardiology, 1994; editor: Cardiology, 1988, rev. edit., 1993. Mem. ACP. Democrat. Jewish. Home: 224 Castenada Ave San Francisco CA 94116 Office: San Francisco Gen Hosp 1001 Potrero Avee San Francisco CA 94110

CHEMSAK, JOHN ANDREW, entomologist; b. Ambridge, Pa., Feb. 19, 1932; s. Andrew and Mary C.; m. Mary Ann McHenry, Sept. 19, 1959 (div. 1980); children: Sheryl, Laurie, John M.; m. Hatsue W. Katsura, Aug. 5, 1985. BS, Penn State U., 1954, MS, 1956; PhD, U. Calif, Berkeley, 1961. Rsch. entomolgist U. Calif., Berkeley, 1961-64, specialist in entomology, 1964—; rsch. assoc. Calif. Acad. Scis., San Francisco, 1965—. Editor jour. Pan-Pacific Entomologist, 1984-89. Fellow Calif. Acad. Scis; mem. Pacific Coast Entomol. Soc. (pres. 1972-73), Coleopterists Soc. (coun. mem.). Office: Essig Mus of Entomol University of Calif Berkeley Berkeley CA 94720

CHEN, BASILIO, engineering executive; b. Panama, Republic of Panama, Mar. 10, 1953. BEE, Calif. State Poly. U., 1974; MAS, U. Brit. Columbia, Vancouver, 1976. Engr. Nat. Inst. Tech., Panama, 1970, Wescom, Inc., Santa Clara, Calif., 1978-79; engring. mgr. Rolm, Corp., Santa Clara, 1979-81; cons. Engring. Mgmt. cons., Daly City, Calif., 1981—; pres. Evotech, Inc., Burlingame, Calif., 1984—. Life mem. Gway Sen Assn., San Francisco, 1990. Mem. IEEE, Profl. Assn. Tech. Cons., Internat. Computer Cons. Assn., Asian Am. Mfrs. Assn., Eta Kappa Nu, Tau Beta Pi. Office: Evotech Inc 875 Cowan Rd Ste 203B Burlingame CA 94010-1204

CHEN, EVE Y.V., city official; b. Hong Kong, Oct. 7, 1958; came to U.S., 1975; d. George W.Y. and Ven-Yah E. (Szw) Chow; m. Yaw-Hwang Henry Chen, June 17, 1982; children: Ryan, Alan. BS in Bus. Adminstrn., Colo. State U., Ft. Collins, 1991. Budget technician Intel Corp., Santa Clara, Calif., 1983-84; budget analyst City of Loveland, Colo., 1985-93, budget officer, 1994—. Mem. Govt. Fin. Officers Assn. (budget reviewer 1990—), Colo. Mcpl. League. Christian. Office: City of Loveland 500 E 3d St Loveland CO 80537

CHEN, HAO, biochemist, researcher; b. China, Dec. 13, 1957; s. Dong-Ting and Feng (Hao) C.; m. Qiang Bin, Dec. 20, 1990; 1 child, Irena Beverly. BS, Portland State U., 1984; MS, Wash. State U., 1986, PhD, 1989. Lipid chemist N.C. State U., Raleigh, 1989-91; rsch. biochemist dept. food sci. U. Calif., Davis, 1991-93; rsch. biochemist dept. pharmacology U. Wash., Seattle, 1993—. Contbr. articles to profl. jours. Mem. AAAS, Sigma Xi. Office: U Wash Dept Pharmacology SJ 30 Health Sci Bldg Seattle WA 98034

CHEN, JAMES JEN-CHUAN, electrical engineer; b. Hsinchu, Taiwan, July 30, 1964; came to U.S. 1968; s. Yung C. and Lily L. (Lin) C. BA, U. Calif., Berkeley, 1985; MS, U. Ill., 1987, PhD, 1991. Rsch. asst. U. Ill., Urbana, 1985-91; device engr. Intel Corp., Hillsboro, Oreg., 1991—. Contbr. articles to profl. jours. Mem. IEEE, Am. Phys. Soc. Home: 222 SW Harrison St Apt 16A Portland OR 97201-5316 Office: Intel Corp 5200 NE Elam Young Pky Hillsboro OR 97124-6463

CHEN, JOHN CALVIN, child and adolescent psychiatrist; b. Augusta, Ga., Apr. 30, 1949; s. Calvin Henry Chen and Lora (Lee) Liu. BA, Pacific Union Coll., 1971; MD, Loma Linda U., 1974; PhD in Philosophy, Claremont Grad. Sch., 1984; JD, UCLA, 1987. Bar: Calif. 1987, U.S. Dist. Ct. (ctrl. dist.) Calif. 1988; diplomate Am. Bd. Psychiatry and Neurology, Child and Adolsecent Psychiatry. Gen. resident in psychiatry Loma Linda U. Med. Ctr., 1975-77; fellow in child and family psychiatry Cedars-Sinai Med. Ctr., L.A., 1977-78; psychiat. cons. San Bernardino (Calif.) County Mental Health Dept., 1979-83; pvt. practice psychiatry Claremont, Calif., 1980-84; fellow in child and adolescent psychiatry U. So. Calif., L.A., 1983-84; law clk. to Hon. William P. Gray U.S. Dist. Ct., L.A., 1987-88; mental health psychiatrist L.A. County Mental Health Dept., L.A., 1988-94, Alameda County Health Care Svcs. Agy., Fremont, Calif., 1994—; adj. instr. philosophy Fullerton (Calif.) Coll., 1989-90. Recipient Cert. Recognition Pub. Svc. L.A. County Mental Health Dept., 1993; univ. fellow Claremont Grad. Sch., 1980-81. Mem. ABA, Am. Philos. Assn. Office: 39270 Paseo Padre Pky # 346 Fremont CA 94538-1616

CHEN, LYNN CHIA-LING, librarian; b. Peking, China, Dec. 3, 1932; came to U.S., 1955; d. Shu-Peng Wang; m. Di Chen, June 14, 1958; children: Andrew A., Daniel T. BA, Nat. Taiwan U., 1955; MLS, U. Minn., 1957. Cataloger Hennepin County Libr., Edina, Minn., 1972-80; libr./programmer Prorodeo Hall of Champions, Colorado Springs, Colo., 1981-83; ref. libr. Meml. Hosp., Colorado Springs, 1983-85; asst. libr. Am. Numismatic Assn., Colorado Springs, 1985-90, head libr., 1991—. Mem. Colo. Libr. Assn., Spl. Libr. Assn. Home: 302 Sunbird Cliffs Ln W Colorado Springs CO 80919-8017 Office: American Numismatic Assn 818 N Cascade Ave Colorado Springs CO 80903-3208

CHEN, MARY YUN-CHUN, research engineer; b. Shanghai, China, Sept. 4, 1949; came to U.S., 1981; d. Donald Zhi-Chu and Grace (Fang) Chen; m. Paul D. Elliott. AA, Shanghai Tchr.'s Coll., China, 1980; BA magna cum laude, Mount Holyoke Coll., 1983; PhD, Cornell U., 1988. Rsch. asst. Cornell U., Ithaca, N.Y., 1983-87; sr. rsch. engr. Rsch Triangle Inst., Research Triangle Park, N.C., 1987-91; sr. mem. tech. staff Comsat Lab., Clarksburg, Md., 1991-93; rsch. staff Hughes Rsch. Labs., Malibu, Calif., 1993—; reviewer several proposals, NSF, 1992. Contbr. articles to profl. jours. Mem. IEEE, Phi Beta Kappa. Office: Hughes Rsch Labs 3011 Malibu Canyon Rd Malibu CA 90265-4737

CHEN, NAI-FU, finance educator; b. Hong Kong, Nov. 24, 1950; came to U.S., 1968; s. Lee (Wong) Chen;m. Victoria Ma, Feb. 1, 1975; children: Nicole, Ellen. AB in Math., U. Calif., Berkeley, 1972, PhD in Math., 1975; PhD in Finance, UCLA, 1981. Asst. prof. math. U. So. Calif., L.A., 1976-78; asst. prof. econs. U. Calif., Santa Barbara, 1980-81; asst. prof. finance U. Chgo., 1981-85, assoc. prof. finance, 1985-89; prof. finance U. Calif., Irvine, 1989—; prof., head fin. Hong Kong U. Sci. and Tech., 1990—; docent fin. Swedish Sch. Econs. and Bus. Adminstrn., Helsinki, 1991—; exec. cons. Roll & Ross Asset Mgmt., Culver City, Calif., 1989—. Contbr. articles to profl. jours. Mem. Am. Finance Assn.

CHEN, PETER WEI-TEH, mental health services administrator; b. Fuchow, Fukien, Republic of China, July 20, 1942; came to U.S., 1966; s. Mao-Chuang and Sheu-Lin (Wang) C.; m. Lai-Wah Mui, Nov. 8, 1969; children: Ophelia Mei-Chuang, Audrey Mei-Hui. BA, Nat. Chung Hsing U., Taipei, Taiwan, Republic of China, 1964; MSW, Calif. State U., Fresno, 1968; D of Social Work, U. So. Calif., 1976. Case worker Cath. Welfare Bur., L.A., 1968-69; psychiat. social worker L.A. County Mental Health Svcs., 1969-78, mental health svcs. coordinator, 1978; sr. rsch. analyst Jud. and Legis. Bur. L.A. County Dept. Mental Health, 1978-79; Forensic In-Patient Program dir. L.A. County Dept. Mental Health, 1979-86, chief Jail Mental Health Svcs., 1986-89, asst. dep. dir. Adult Svc. Bur., 1989, dir. specialized commnunity programs, 1989—; pres. Orient Social and Health Soc., Los Angeles, 1973-75; bd. dirs. Am. Correctional Health Assn., 1986-87. Author: Chinese-Americans View Their Mental Health, 1976. Bd. dirs. San Marino (Calif.) Cmty. Chest, 1986-87; trustee San Marino Schs. Found., 1987-90; advisor San Marino United Way, 1989-92, AIDS Commn. L.A. County, 1993; bd. dirs. Chinese Am. Profl. Soc., 1984. 2d lt. Chinese Marine Corps, Taiwan, Republic of China, 1964-65. Recipient several cmty. svc. awards, 3 spl. awards Nat. Assn. County Orgn. Mem. Nat. Assn. Social Workers (bd. dirs. Calif. chpt. 1979-80), Nat. Correctional Health Assn., Forensic Mental Health Assn. Calif., L.A. World Affairs Coun. Clubs: Chinese of San Marino (pres. 1987-88), San Marino City. Home: 2161 E California Blvd San Marino CA 91108-1348 Office: LA County Dept Mental Health 505 S Virgil Ave Los Angeles CA 90020-1403

CHEN, STEPHEN SHAU-TSI, psychiatrist, physiologist; b. Tou-Nan, Yun-Lin, Taiwan, Aug. 18, 1934; s. R-Yue and Pi-Yu (Huang) C.; m. Clara Chin-Chin Liu, Sept. 7, 1936; children: David, Timothy, Hubert. MD, Nat. Taiwan U., Taipei, 1959; PhD, U. Wis., 1968. Diplomate Am. Bd. Psychiatry and Neurology, also sub. bd. Geriatric Psychiatry. Intern Nat. Taiwan U. Hosp., 1959; instr. dept. physiology U. Wis., Madison, 1968-71, asst. prof., 1971-75; resident in psychiatry SUNY, Stony Brook, 1975-78; asst. prof. psychiatry dept. psychiatry U. Pitts., 1978-80; asst. prof. psychiatry dept. psychiatry and behavioral sci. U. Wash., Seattle, 1981-86, clin. asst. prof. psychiatry, 1986—; chief mental health clinic VA Med. Ctr., Tacoma, 1981-85. Contbr. articles to Am. Jour. Physiol., Jour. Physiology, Can. Jour. Physiology and Pharmacology, Acta Physiol. Fellow Wis. Heart Assn., 1966-68. Mem. APA, North Pacific Soc. Neurology and Psychiatry, Formosan Assn. for Pub. Affairs (pres. Seattle chpt. 1986-88, bd. dir. Washington chpt. 1988-89). Presbyterian. Office: VA Med Ctr Psychiatry Svc Tacoma WA 98493

CHEN, YEA MOW, finance educator; b. Kao Hsiung, Taiwan, Apr. 12, 1953; came to U.S., 1978; s. Shien and Yang-Yung (Hsieh) C.; m. SuRu Chiang, Aug. 8, 1980; children: Elaine, Allen, Edward. BA in Econs., Nat. Taiwan U., Taipei, 1976; MA in Econs., Ohio State U., 1980, PhD in Econs., 1984. Prof. fin. San Francisco State U., 1984—; vis. prof. Tamkang U. Taipei, Taiwan, 1990-91; dir. U.S. Chinese Bus. Inst., San Francisco, 1991—; adviser Yunnan (China) Assn. of Internat. Pers. Exchange, 1993—; cons. banks and securities cos.. Mem. San Francisco-Shanghai Sister Com., 1993—. Recipient Competitive Rsch. award, Chgo. Bd. of Trade, Hong Kong, 1991; named fellow Pacific-Basin Rsch. Ctr. Univ. R.I., 1991-92. Mem. Am. Econs. Assn., Am. Fin. Assn., Assn. Asian-Am. Bankers, Taiwanese Assn. Cs. of C. Home: 655 Ulloa St San Francisco CA 94127-1142 Office: San Franciso State U Sch of Bus 1600 Holloway Ave San Francisco CA 94132-1722

CHEN, YUANWEI, chemist; b. Quxian, Sichuan, China, Sept. 16, 1963; s. Wenqing Chen and Renging Li; m. Ying Liu, Sept. 27, 1987. BS, Sichuan U., 1983, MS, 1986; PhD, U. Lausanne, Switzerland, 1993. Rsch. scientist Chengdu (People's Republic of China) Inst. Organic Chemistry, 1986-89; rsch. assoc. Scripps Rsch. Inst., La Jolla, Calif., 1993—. Contbr. articles to profl. pubs.; patentee in field. Mem. Am. Chem. Soc. Office: Scripps Rsch Inst 10666 N Torrey Pines Rd La Jolla CA 92037-1027

CHEN, YU-CHENG JEFFREY, cardiologist; b. Taipei, China, 1958; came to U.S., 1985; MD, Nat. Taiwan U., 1983. Diplomate Am. Bd. Internat. Medicine in cardiovascular disease. Resident in internal medicine U. Calif., Irvine, 1985-89; fellow in cardiology U. So. Calif., L.A., 1989-92, asst. prof. clin. medicine, 1992-93; asst. dir. cardiologic catherder lab. U. Soc. Calif., L.A., 1992-93; pvt. practice South Pasadena, Calif., 1993—. Fellow Am. Coll. Cardiology, Am. Coll. Angiology.

CHENEY, ERIC SWENSON, geology educator; b. New Haven, Nov. 17, 1934; s. Kimberly and Margreta Curtis (Swenson) C.; m. Olga Marie Campaine, Sept. 20, 1958 (dec. Nov. 1983); children: Eric, Kathryn, Jamison, Lois. BS in Geology, Yale U., 1956, PhD in Geology, 1964. Asst. prof. U. Wash., Seattle, 1964-69, assoc. prof., 1969—; pres. Cambria Corp., Seattle, 1981-91, Kaupbaal Corp., 1993—; vis. assoc. prof. Stanford (Calif.) U., 1974; vis. research prof. U. Pretoria, South Africa, 1984-85, Rand Afrikaans U., South Africa, 1987-89; cons. ore deposits and regional geology, 1963—. Contbr. articles to profl. jours. Served with USNR, 1956-58. Grantee Am. Chem. Soc., 1967-70, Wash. Mining Mineral Inst., 1980, 85, 87. Fellow Geol. Soc. Am.; mem. AIME (best paper award 1971), Soc. Econ. Geologists (councilor 1984-87), NW Mining Assn., NW Geol. Soc. (pres. 1970, 87). Office: U Wash Dept Geol Scis Box 351310 Seattle WA 98195

CHENG, CARL FU KANG (JOHN DOE CO.), artist; b. San Francisco, Feb. 8, 1942; s. Theodore and Sung Yuan (Kwan) C. BA, UCLA, 1963; postgrad., Folkwang Sch. Art, Essen, Germany, 1964-65; MA, UCLA, 1967. instr. Otis Art Inst., L.A., 1977-80; vis. lectr. UCLA, 1980-84, Claremont (Calif.) Grad. Sch., 1984-85. Pub. art commns. for City of Santa Monica, Calif., San Francisco, Tempe, Ariz., MTA, L.A., Kaiser Permanente, L.A. Getty Museum fellow, L.A., 1990; grantee L.A. Cultural Affairs, 1990; recipient award NEA, 1986, 92. Mem. Internat. Sculpture Ctr., Mus. Contemporary Art, L.A.C.E. Studio: 1518 17th St Santa Monica CA 90404-3402

CHENG, HENG-DA, computer scientist; b. Shenyang, Liaoning, China, May 1, 1944; came to U.S., 1980; s. Ji Cheng and Yu-Zhi Pan; m. Xiaohong Hao (Haybina Hao); children: Yang-Yang, Yue-Yue, Lydia. BS, Harbin (China) Inst. Tech., 1967; MS, Wayne State U., 1981; PhD, Purdue U., 1985. Instr. Harbin Shipbuilding Inst., 1971-76; rschr., technician Harbin Railway Sci. and Tech. Rsch. Inst., Harbin, 1976-78, Computing Tech. Inst., 1978-80; vis. asst. prof. U. Calif., Davis, 1985-86; asst. prof. Concordia U., Montreal, Que., Can., 1987-88; assoc. prof. Tech. U. Nova Scotia, Halifax, Can., 1988-91, Utah State U., Logan, 1991—; co-chair Visioon Interface '90, The Fourth Can. Conf., Halifax, 1990; com. mem. Vision Interface '92, 1992; panelist 2nd Internat. Conf. Fuzzy Theory & Tech., 1993; mem. Best Paper Award Evaluation Com., Internat. Joint Conf. on Info. Scis., 1994, session chair, 1994, com. mem. Internat. Conf. on Tools With Artificial Intelligence, 1995; lectr. in field. Co-editor: Pattern Recognition: Architectures, Algorithms and Applications, 1991; assoc. editor Pattern Recognition, Info. Scis.; contbr. articles to profl. jours. and confs.; reviewer sci. jours. and confs. Grantee Natural Scis. and Engring. Rsch. Coun. Can., NSF, 1987—, NSERC, 1989-93; Utah State U. grantee, 1992-93, others. Mem. IEEE Soc. (sr.), IEEE Computer Soc., IEEE Circuits and System Soc., IEEE Geosci. and Remote Sensing Soc., IEEE Robotics and Automation Soc., IEEE System, Man and Cybernetics Soc., IEEE Signal Processing Soc., IEEE Engring. in Medicine and Biology Soc., Assn. for Computing Machinery. Office: Utah State Univ Dept Computer Sci Logan UT 84322-4205

CHENG, MEILING, theatre arts educator; b. Taipei, Taiwan, Dec. 15, 1960; came to U.S., 1986; d. Shu-King Cheng and Yu-Jen Su; m. Nonchi Wang. BA in English summa cum laude, Nat. Taiwan U., 1983; MFA in Dramaturgy cum laude, Yale U., 1989, DFA in Dramaturgy, 1993. Teaching asst. fgn. lang. and lit. dept. Nat. Taiwan U., 1983-86; rsch. asst. Sch. Drama Yale U., New Haven, 1987-89, instr. and teaching fellow dept. theater studies, 1990-93; asst. prof. dept. theatre arts Mt. Holyoke Coll., South Hadley, Mass., 1993-94; asst. prof. Sch. of Theatre U. So. Calif., L.A., 1994—; lectr. in field; vis. dramaturg The Guthrie Theater, Mpls., 1991-93; dramaturg/lit. cons. Pan Asian Repertory Theatre, N.Y.C., 1992-93, lit. mgr. 1990; dramaturg Le MaMa e.t.c., N.Y.C., 1990, Bklyn. Acad. Music, 1988, Yale Repertory Theatre, 1987, 88, Yale Sch. Drama, 1986-88; artistic cons. The Naked Angel, N.Y.C., 1989, Circle Rep Studio, N.Y.C., 1986; dir., designer various prodns. Nat. Taiwan U., 1982-83, Yale U., 1987. Contbr. articles to profl. jours.; translator: The Emerald Bodhisattva (Chinese into English), 1987. Recipient Lit. award for poetry Nat. Taiwan U., 1983, Lit. award for prose, 1981, Lit. award for fiction, 1983, Taita Lit. award for prose, 1980;; Ministry of Edn. scholar, ROC, 1980-83, Mayer Found. scholar, 1987-88, Lord Meml. scholar, 1987-88; Asian Oceanic fellow, 1988-89, Asian Cultural Coun. fellow, 1989-93, Bass fellow, 1991-92, Newhouse fellow, 1992-93. Mem. MLA, Assn. for Theatre in Higher Edn., Am. Soc. for Theatre Rsch., Phi Tau Phi. Home: 1835 Bentley Ave # 2 Westwood Los Angeles CA 90025-4324 Office: U So Calif Sch of Theatre University Park CA 90089-0791

CHENG, PING, engineering educator; b. Canton, China; m. Sabrina H.T. Yuen; children: Albert H., Bonnie J. BS in Mech. Engring., Okla. State U., 1958; MS in Mech. Engring., MIT, 1960; PhD in Aeronautics & Astronautics, Stanford U., 1965. Vis. prof. Nat. Taiwan U., Taipei, 1968-70; assoc. prof. U. Hawaii, Honolulu, 1970-74; vis. prof. Stanford U., Palo Alto, Calif., 1976-77; guest prof. Tech. U. Munich, Germany, 1984; prof. mech. engring. U. Hawaii, 1974-94, chmn. dept. mech. engring., 1989-94. Editor: (jour.) AAIA Jour. of Thermophysics & Heat Transfer, 1988—; contbr. articles to scientific jours. including Internat. Jour. Heat Mass Transfer, Jour. Heat Transfer. Recipient Dist. Scientific Achievement award Chung Shan Found., 1969. Fellow ASME. Office: Dept Mech Engring U Hawaii 2540 Dole St Honolulu HI 96822-2303

CHENG, XUECHENG, chemist, research scientist; b. Lalin, China, May 4, 1955; came to U.S., 1982; s. Liangjun and Shuzhen (Gao) C.; m. Xiaolin Zhang, July 23, 1984; 1 child, Sarah Ye. BS in Chemistry, Peking U., Beijing, 1982; PhD in Chemistry, Harvard U., 1989. Rsch. assoc. Harvard U., Cambridge, Mass., 1988-91, U. Md., Balt., 1991-92; rsch. assoc. Batelle Pacific N.W. Lab., Richland, Wash., 1992-94, sr. rsch. scientist, 1994-95; sr. mass spectroscopist Abbott Labs, Abbott Park, Ill., 1995—; vis. scientist U. Calif., Riverside, 1989. Contbr. articles to profl. jours. Mem. Am. Chem. Soc., Internat. Union Pure and Applied Chemistry, Am. Soc. for Mass Spectrometry (ICMS Travel award 1991). Office: Abbott Labs Abbott Park IL 60064-3537

CHENHALL, ROBERT GENE, former museum director, consultant, author; b. Maurice, Iowa, Jan. 24, 1923; s. Raymond Ernest and Lillian Georgia (Clark) C.; m. Carol Ann Vandercook, Feb. 26, 1943 (div. 1972); children: Raymond E., Donald R., Doris Chenhall Flenniken; m. Barbara Phyliss Von Lenz, Nov. 16, 1972. BA, San Diego State U., 1946; MA, Ariz. State U., 1965, PhD, 1972. Accountant Price Waterhouse & Co. (C.P.A.'s), Los Angeles, 1951-55, Fisher Contracting Co., Phoenix, 1955-63, Del E. Webb Corp., Phoenix, 1963-66; mem. faculty dept.anthropology U. Ark., Fayetteville, 1969-74; mem. staff Strong Museum, Rochester, N.Y., 1974-79; dir. Buffalo Mus. Sci., 1979-80, N.Mex. Mus. Natural History, Albuquerque, 1980-82; mus. cons., author, 1982—; mem. commn. archaeol. data banks Internat. Union Prehistoric and Protohistoric Scis., 1977-80; mem. trustees vis. com. Internat. Mus. Photography, Rochester, 1978-80; treas. N.E. Museums Conf., 1979-80; mem. mus. aid panel N.Y. State Council Arts, 1979-80; reviewer operating support grants Inst. Mus. Services, 1980-81. Author: Computers in Anthropology and Archeology, 1971, Museum Cataloging in the Computer Age, 1975, Nomenclature for Museum Cataloguing: A System for Classifying Man-Made Objects, 1978, rev. edit. 1988, (with David Vance) Museum Collections and Today's Computers, 1988, (with Michael Yergin) Wealth Building in the 90s, 1991; also articles, revs., chpts. in books; founder, editor: Newsletter Computer Archaeology, 1965-71; editor: archaeol sect. Computers and the Humanities, 1967-70; corr. editor: archaeol sect. Computers in the Humanities, 1968-71. Served with AUS, 1944-46. Fellow Am. Anthrop. Assn.; mem. Soc. Am. Archaeology, Am. Assn. Museums, Internat. Council Museums (dir. documentation com. 1971-80), Assn. Sci. Mus. Dirs., Council Mus. Anthropology.

CHENOWETH, WILLIAM LYMAN, consulting geologist; b. Wichita, Kans., Sept. 16, 1928; s. Bertrum and Bessie (Lyman) C.; m. Miriam Bernadine Pawlicki, Jan. 6, 1955; children: Mary, Martin, Peter, Paul. AB, Wichita State U., 1951; postgrad., N.Mex. Sch. of Mines, 1949; MS, U. N.Mex., 1951. Registered profl. geologist Wyo. Geologist AEC, Navajo Indian Reservation, Ariz., 1953-55, project geologist, 1955-57, area geologist, 1957-62; project geologist AEC, Grand Junction, Colo., 1962-74, staff geologist, 1975-77; staff geologist U.S. Dept. of Energy, Grand Junction, 1977-81, chief geologist, 1981-83; pvt. practice cons. geologist Grand Junction, 1984—; rsch. assoc. N.Mex. Bur. Mines, Socorro, 1984—. Editor: Colorado Uranium, 1981. Staff sgt. USNG, 1955-59. Fellow Geol. Soc. Am.; mem. Am. Assn. Petroleum Geologists (chmn. nuclear minerals com. 1982—), Rocky Mountain Assn. Geologists (Cert. of Recognition 1980), N.Mex. Geol. Soc. Democrat. Roman Catholic. Home: 707 Brassie Dr Grand Junction CO 81506-3911

CHERESKIN, VALERIE LEE, marketing professional; b. Chgo., Aug. 2, 1954; d. Samuel and Rosalie (Marks) C.; m. John William Hansen Jr., July 18, 1987. MusB, Eastern Ill. U., 1976; MBA, San Diego State U., 1995. Sales rep. Wurlitzer Piano and Organ, Westchester, Ill., 1976-77; office mgr. Carl Fischer, Inc., Chgo., 1977-78; regional tng. mgr. Motorola, Inc., Schaumburg, Ill., 1979-81, account mgr., 1981-83; sales engr. Motorola-Codex, Schaumburg, Ill., 1983-84; account exec. Computer Intelligence, La Jolla, Calif., 1984-87; dir. mktg. Chereskin Designs, La Jolla, 1987-90; prin. and owner Valerie Chereskin Mktg. Strategies, Carlsbad, Calif., 1990—. Mem. Pub. Rels. Soc. Am., Carlsbad C. of C., Am.-Russian Bus. Coun. of So. Calif. (bd. dirs.), Pub. Rels. Club. Democrat. Club: San Diego (Calif.) Flute Guild. Home: 1364 Calle Christopher Encinitas CA 92024-5511 Office: Ste 2B 7750 El Camino Real Carlsbad CA 92009-8519

CHERINGTON, MICHAEL, neurologist, educator; b. Pitts., Nov. 24, 1934; s. Maurice and Sybil (Young) C.; children: Claire, David, Jennifer. BS in Chemistry summa cum laude, U. Pitts., 1956, MD, 1960. Diplomate Am. Bd. Neurology and Psychiatry, Am. Bd. Electrodiagnostic Medicine. Intern Montefiore Hosp., Pitts., 1961; resident in internal medicine U. Colo. Med. Ctr., 1961-62, resident in neurology, 1963-66; instr. neurology U. Colo. Med. Ctr., Denver, 1966-68, asst. clin. prof. neurology, 1968-76, assoc. clin. prof. neurology, 1976-88, clin. prof. neurology, 1988—; dir. med. edn. Mercy Hosp., Denver, 1968-71; pres. staff Spalding Rehab. Ctr., 1976-77; chmn., founder Lightning Data Ctr., St. Anthony Hosp., Denver, 1992—. Contbr. articles to profl. jours. With M.C., U.S. Army, 1962-63, hon. discharge. Fellow ACP, Am. Acad. Neurology, Am. Geriatric Soc., Am. Assn. Electromyography and Electrodiagnosis; mem. Am. Neurol. Assn., Phi Beta Kappa, Alpha Omega Alpha, Phi Eta Sigma. Office: St Anthony Hosp Lightning Data Ctr 4231 W 16th Ave Denver CO 80204-1335

CHERKAS, MARSHALL S., psychiatrist, psychoanalyst; b. Savannah, Calif., Jan. 5, 1929; s. Meyer L. and Fanye (Robinson) C.; m. Patricia Mae Clemens, Dec. 20, 1958; children: Karen, Brian, Jonathan. BA, U. Ill., 1948; MS in Hosp. Adminstrn., Northwestern U., 1952, MD, 1959; PhD, So. Calif. Psychoanalytic Inst. Diplomate Am. Bd. Psychiatry and Neurology. Intern Cedars of Lebanon Hosp., L.A., 1959-60; resident VA Ctr., Mt. Sinai Hosp., L.A., 1960-63; pres. M.S. Cherkas, M.D. Med. Corp., L.A., 1963—; panel psychiatrist L.A. County Superior Ct., 1967—; cons. L.A. County Dept. Mental Health, 1965-73. Fellow APA (life), Am. Coll. Forensic Psychiatry (bd. dirs. 1980—); mem. AMA, Am. Soc. Adolescent Psychiatry (L.A. chpt. pres. 1966—). Address: Marshall S Cherkas Med Corp 12304 Santa Monica Blvd Los Angeles CA 90025

CHERKIN, ADINA, interpreter, translator; b. Geneva, Nov. 22, 1921; came to U.S., 1940; d. Herz N. and Genia (Kodriansky) Mantchik; m. Arthur Cherkin, Mar. 14, 1943 (div. Sept. 1980); children: Della Peretti, Daniel Craig. BA, UCLA, 1942, MA in Russian Linguistics, 1977. Pvt. practice med. interpreter L.A., 1942-80; translator UCLA Med. Sch., 1970-79; pres. acad. forum Jewish studies Herz Mantchik Amity Cir., L.A., 1973—. Author numerous poems. Active L.A. Internat. Vis. Coun., 1991—; pub. rels. Judge Stanley Mosk's Campaign, L.A., 1960; vol. Gov. Cranston's Campaign, 1960. Recipient Community Svc. award L.A. City Coun., 1992. Mem. Am. Soc. for Technion Israel Inst. Tech. (nat. bd. regents 1991—). Home and Office: 2369 N Vermont Ave Los Angeles CA 90027-1253

CHERMAK, GAIL DONNA, audiologist, speech and hearing sciences educator; b. N.Y.C., Sept. 30, 1950; d. Martin I. Chermak and Zelda (Kessler) Lax; children: Isaac Martin, Aljwa Marta. BA in Communication Disorders, SUNY, Buffalo, 1972; MA in Speech and Hearing Sci., Ohio State U., 1973, PhD in Speech and Hearing Sci., 1975. Cert. clin. competency in audiology. Asst. prof. speech So. Ill. U., Edwardsville, 1975-77; assoc. prof. and dir., communication disorders program Wash. State U., Pullman, 1977-89, prof., chmn. dept. speech and hearing scis., 1990—, coord. grad. program dept. speech and hearing scis., 1983-89; feature edutor Am. Jour. Audiology, 1991—; editorial cons. Ear and HEaring Jour., Cin., 1984, 88, 89, 90, 91, 92, 93, 94, Internat. Jour. Disability Devel. and Edn., 1991, Lang. Speech and Hearing Svcs. in Schs., 1993, 94, Jour. of Communication Disorders, 1994; profl. advisor Palowe chpt. Self-Help for Hard of Hearing, Moscow, Idaho, 1984-89. Author: Handbook of Audiological Rehabilitation, 1981; feature editor Am. Jour. Audiology, 1991—; contbr. articles to profl. jours. Kellogg nat. fellow, 1986-89; Fulbright scholar, 1989-90. Fellow Soc. Ear, Nose and Throat Advances in Children; mem. AAAS, AAUW, Am. Assn. for Higher Edn., Am. Speech, Lang. and Hearing Assn. (cert. clin. competence in audiology), Acoustical Soc. Am., Am. Acad. Audiology, Am. Auditory Soc., Internat. Soc. Audiology, NOW (v.p. Moscow chpt. 1985-86), ACLU (human rights com.), Phi Beta Kappa. Office: Wash State U Dept Speech and Hearing Scis Pullman WA 99164-2420

CHERN, SHIING-SHEN, mathematics educator; b. Kashing, Chekiang, China, Oct. 26, 1911; s. Lien Ching and Mei (Han) C.; m. Shih-ning Chern, July 28, 1939; children—Paul, May. B.S., Nankai U., Tientsin, China, 1930; hon. dr., Nankai U., 1985; M.S., Tsing Hua U., Peiping, 1934; D.Sc., U. Hamburg, Germany, 1936, D.Sc. (hon.), 1972; D.Sc. (hon.), U. Chgo., 1969, SUNY-Stony Brook, 1985; LL.D. honoris causa, Chinese U., Hong Kong, 1969; Dr. Math (hon.), Eidgenossische Technische Hochschule, Zurich, Switzerland, 1982; DSc (hon.), U. Notre Dame, 1994. Prof. math. Nat. Tsing Hua U., China, 1937-43; mem. Inst. Advanced Study, Princeton, N.J., 1943-45; acting dir. Inst. Mathematics, Academia Sinica, China, 1946-48; prof. math. U. Chgo., 1949-60, U. Calif., Berkeley, 1960-79; prof. emeritus U. Calif., 1979—; dir. Math. Scis. Rsch. Inst., 1981-84, dir. emeritus, 1984—; dir. Inst. Mathematics, Tianjin, P.R., China. hon. prof. various fgn. univs.; Recipient Chauvenet prize Math. Assn. Am., 1970, Nat. Medal of Sci., 1975, Wolf prize Israel, 1983-84. Fellow Third World Acad. Sci. (founding mem. 1985); mem. NAS, Am. Math. Soc. (Steele prize 1983), Am. Acad. Arts and Scis., N.Y. Acad. Scis. (hon. life), Am. Philos. Soc., Indian Math. Soc. (hon.), Brazilian Acad. Scis. (corr.), Academia Sinica, Royal Soc. London (fgn.), Academia Peloritana (corr. mem. 1986), London Math. Soc. (hon.), Acad. des sciences Paris (fgn. mem.), Acad. der Lincei Rome (stranieri). Home: 8336 Kent Ct El Cerrito CA 94530-2548 Office: Univ Calif Berkeley Dept of Mathematics Berkeley CA 94720

CHERNISS, DAVID ALAN, lawyer; b. L.A., Apr. 24, 1954; s. Howard Lee and Marilyn Janet (Kaminsky) C. BA in Psychology, UCLA, 1976; JD, Calif. Western U., 1979. Bar: Calif. 1979. Assoc. Kellner, Mitten, Ybarrondo, Hemet, Calif., 1979-80, Jacoby & Meyers, Riverside, Calif., 1981-82, Grant Carner, Riverside, 1982-83; pvt. practice Moreno Valley, Calif., 1983-86; ptnr. Ellis & Cherniss, Moreno Valley, 1986—; prof. law Citrus Belt Law Sch., Riverside, 1983-88, Mt. San Jacinto Jr. Coll., Hemet, 1979-80. Bd. dirs. Inland AIDS Project, Riverside, 1987-93. Mem. Riverside County Bar Assn., Moreno Valley C. of C. (treas. 1983-84, v.p. 1984-85), Lions. Office: Ellis & Cherniss 23025 Atlantic Cir Ste E Moreno Valley CA 92553 also: 225 S Cabrillo Hwy Ste 201C Half Moon Bay CA 94019

CHERNOFF-PATE, DIANA, interior designer, small business owner; b. San Mateo, Calif., Apr. 7, 1942; d. Fred Eugene and Nadine (Chernoff) Pate; 1 child, Kim Renee. BA in Design, U. Calif., Berkeley. Lic. cosmetologist, Calif. Owner, mgr. Diana Interiors/Design, Napa, Calif.; co-owner, v.p., mgr. ops. Stickney Enterprises, Redwood, Calif., Stickney Restaurants and Bakeries, Redwood; pub. rels. specialist, coord. passenger svc. tng. TWA, San Francisco; adminstr. Internat. Fed. Employees Benefits, 1973, Pension Funds, 1982. Author: Cooking for Profit. Co-sponsor Stanford Athletic Fund, Stanford U.; mem. Frank Lloyd Wright Found. Mem. LWV (Carmel br.), NAFE, Internat. Platform Assn., Am. Soc. Phys. Rsch., Am. Assn. Ret. Persons, Embroiderers Guild Am. (founder San Mateo and Santa Clara chpts.), Internat. Parliament Safety & Peace, Maison Internat. Intellectuels Acad. Midi, London Inst. Applied Rsch., World Affairs Coun., Designers Lighting Forum, Inst. Noetic Scis., San Francisco De Young Mus., San Francisco Asian Mus., San Francisco Ballet, Commonwealth Club Calif. Home: 1220 Cayetano Dr Napa CA 94559-4263

CHERRY, JAMES DONALD, physician; b. Summit, N.J., June 10, 1930; s. Robert Newton and Beatrice (Wheeler) C.; m. Jeanne M. Fischer, June 19, 1954; children—James S., Jeffrey D., Susan J., Kenneth C. B.S., Springfield (Mass.) Coll., 1953; M.D., U. Vt., 1957; M.Sc. in Epidemiology, London Sch. Hygiene and Tropical Medicine, 1983. Diplomate: Am. Bd. Pediatrics. Intern, then resident in pediatrics Boston City Hosp., 1957-59; resident in pediatrics Kings County Hosp., Bklyn., 1959-60; research fellow in medicine Harvard U. Med. Sch.-Thorndike Meml. Lab., Boston City Hosp., 1961-62; instr. pediatrics U. Vt. Coll. Medicine, also asst. attending physician Mary Fletcher DeGoesbriand Meml. hosps., Burlington, Vt., 1960-61; asst. prof., then assoc. prof. pediatrics U. Wis. Med. Sch., Madison, 1963-66; assoc. attending physician Madison Gen., U. Wis. hosps., 1963-66; dir. John A. Hartford Research Lab., Madison Gen. Hosp., 1963-66; mem. faculty St. Louis U. Med. Sch., 1966-73, prof. pediatrics, 1969-73, vice chmn. dept., 1970-73; mem. staff Cardinal Glennon Meml. Hosp. Children, St. Louis U. Hosp., 1966-73; prof. pediatrics, chief divsn. infectious diseases UCLA Med. Ctr. UCLA Sch. Medicine, 1973—; acting chmn. dept. pediatrics UCLA Med. Ctr., 1977-79; attending physician, chmn. infection control com. UCLA Med. Ctr.; cons. Project Head Start; vis. worker dept. cmty. medicine Middlesex Hosp. and Med. Sch., London, 1982-83; vis. worker Common Cold Rsch. Unit, 1969-70; mem. immunization adv. com. Los Angeles County Dept. Health Svcs., 1978—. Co-editor Textbook of: Pediatric Infectious Diseases, 1981, 2d edit., 1987, 3rd edit., 1992; assoc. editor: Clin. Infectious Diseases, 1990—; Am. regional editor: Vaccine, 1991—; author numerous papers in field; editorial reviewer profl. jours. Bd. govs. Alexander Graham Bell Internat. Parents Orgn., 1967-69. Served with USAR, 1958-64. John and Mary R. Markle scholar acad. medicine, 1964. Mem. Am. Acad. Pediatrics (exec. com. Calif. chpt. 2 1975-77, mem. com. infectious diseases 1977-83, assoc. editor 19th Red Book 1982), Am. Soc. Microbiology, Am. Fedn. Clin. Research, AAAS, Soc. Pediatric Research, Infectious Diseases Soc. Am., Am. Epidemiological Soc., Am. Pediatric Soc., Los Angeles Pediatric Soc., Soc. Exptl. Biology and Medicine, Internat. Orgn. Mycoplasmologists, Am. Soc. Virology, Soc. Hosp. Epidemiologists Am., Am. Pub. Health Assn., Pediatric Infectious Diseases Soc. (pres. 1989-91), Alpha Omega Alpha. Home: 1402 San Vicente Blvd Santa Monica CA 90402-2204 Office: UCLA Sch Medicine Los Angeles CA 90024

CHERWIN, SUNAH CAROLINE, publisher, editor; b. San Francisco, Aug. 4, 1957; d. Edward Mailhouse and Bobby Jean (Cherwin) Lane. AA, Laney Coll., Oakland,, 1993. Circulation mgr. More! Productions, Santa Cruz, San Francisco, 1990—; copy editor Smart Drugs and Nutrients, Stop the FDA, Santa Cruz, Menlo Park, Calif., 1990, 91; assoc. book editor Smart Drugs II, Menlo Park, 1993; style editor Anything That Moves, San Francisco, 1990-93; publisher, editor in chief Slippery When Wet, Berkeley, Calif., 1991—; panelist Outwrite, San Francisco, 1992. Producer Points of View, 1992; mem. dance troupe Note Nice Girls, 1991-92. Mem. San Francisco Street Patrol, 1990-92; staff San Francisco Sex Info., 1992-93. Libertarian.

CHESHIRE, WILLIAM POLK, newspaper columnist; b. Durham, N.C., Feb. 2, 1931; s. James Webb and Anne Ludlow (McGehee) C.; m. Lucile Geoghegan, Aug. 1, 1959; children—William Polk, Helen Wood Cheshire Elder, James Webb. A.B., U. N.C., Chapel Hill, 1958. Reporter Richmond News Leader, Va., 1958-61; assoc. editor Canton (N.C.) Enterprise, 1961-62, Charleston Evening Post, S.C., 1963-68, The State, Columbia, S.C., 1968-72; editorial dir. Capital Broadcasting Co., Raleigh, N.C., 1972-75; editorial page editor Greensboro Record, N.C., 1975-78; editor-in-chief Charleston Daily Mail, W.Va., 1978-84; editor, editorial pages Washington Times, 1984-87; editor, editorial pages The Ariz. Republic, Phoenix, 1987-93, sr. editorial columnist, 1993—; prof. journalism U. Charleston, 1979-83; commentator Voice of Am., 1986-87. Dir. comm. N.C. Senate Campaign, 1972; bd. dirs. Sunrise Mus., Charleston United Way, 1978-84. With USCG, 1952-56. Recipient Council for the Def. of Freedom award, 1980, George Washington Honor medal Freedoms Found., 1975; named Disting. Fellow in Journalism, Heritage Found., 1987; Media fellow Hoover Instn., 1991. Mem. N.C. Soc. Cin. (pres. 1988-91), Phila. Soc., Nat. Press Club, Phoenix Country Club, Ariz. Club, Sigma Delta Chi (pres. Piedmont chpt. 1978). Anglican. Office: The Ariz Republic 120 E Van Buren St Phoenix AZ 85004-2227

CHESNEY, SUSAN TALMADGE, human resources specialist; b. N.Y.C., Aug. 12, 1943; d. Morton and Tillie (Talmadge) Chesney; m. Donald Lewis Freitas, Sept. 17, 1967 (div. May 1976); m. Robert Martin Rosenblatt, Apr. 9, 1980. AB, U. Calif., Berkeley, 1967. Placement interviewer U. Calif., Berkeley, 1972-74, program coord., 1974-79; pers. adminstr. Hewlett-Packard Co., Santa Rosa, Calif., 1982-84; pres. Mgmt. Resources, Santa Rosa, 1984—; human resources mgr. BioBottoms Inc., Petaluna, Calif., 1990-91; human resources adminstr. Parker Compumotor, Rohnert Park, Calif., 1991-93; cons. Kensington Electronics Group, Healdsburg, Calif., 1984-85, Behavioral Medicine Assocs., Santa Rosa, 1985-86, M.C.A.I., Santa Rosa, 1986-87, Bowdon Designs, Santa Rosa, 1987-88, Bass & Ingram, Santa Rosa, 1988—, Eason Tech., Inc., Healdsburg, 1995—. Mem. Nat. Soc. Performance Instrn., No. Calif. Human Resources Coun., Pers. Assn. Sonoma County. Avocations: cooking, gardening, music.

CHESNUT, CAROL FITTING, economist; b. Pecos, Tex., June 17, 1937; d. Ralph Ulf and Carol (Lowe) Fitting; m. Dwayne A. Chesnut, Dec. 27, 1955; children: Carol Marie, Stephanie Michelle, Mark Steven. BA magna cum laude, U. Colo., 1971; JD, U. Calif., San Francisco, 1994. Rsch. asst. U. Colo., 1972; head quality controller Mathematica, Inc., Denver, 1973-74; cons. Mincome Man., Winnipeg, Can., 1974; cons. economist Energy Cons. Assocs. Inc., Denver, 1974-79; exec. v.p. tng. ECA Intercomp, 1980-81; gen. ptnr. Chestnut Consortium, S.F., 1981—; sec., bd. dirs. Critical Resources, Inc., 1981-83. Rep. Lakehurst Civic Assn., 1968; staff aide Senator Gary Hart, 1978; Dem. precinct capt., 1982-88. Mem. ABA, ACLU, AAUW (1st v.p. 1989-90), Am. Mgmt. Assn., Soc. Petroleum Engrs., Am. Nuclear Soc. (chmn. conv. space activities for 1989, chair of spouse activities 1989), Am. Geophys. Union, Assn. Women Geoscientists (treas. Denver 1983-85), Associated Students of Hastings (rep. 1994), Calif. State Bar, Phi Beta Kappa, Phi Chi Theta, Phi Delta Phi. Unitarian. Office: 7537 Dry Pines Cir Las Vegas NV 89129

CHESNUT, TANYA LYNN, dietitian; b. Spokane, Wash., Mar. 30, 1950; d. Peter Dominic and Elsie Agnes (Absec) Rinaldi; 1 child, Cameron David. BS in Food, Nutrition, Wash. State U., 1972. Supr., dietary Meml. Hosp., Pullman, Wash., 1974-78; women, infants and children prog. coord. No. Central Dist. Health, Lewiston, Idaho, 1976-78; women, infants, children prog. supr. Panhandle Health Dept., Coeur d'Alene, Idaho, 1978—; cons. dietitian Pinecrest Psychiatric Hosp., Coeur d'Alene, 1987, Headstart Prog., others, 1978—. Contbr. articles to profl. jours. Chmn. food activities Am. Heart Assn., Coeur d'Alene, 1987. Recipient Women Helping Women award, Soroptomists, 1987, Career Excellence award Women's Forum Health, 1992. Mem. Moscow Dietetic Assn. (pres. 1974-75), Idaho Dietetic Assn. (fellow, treas. 1990-92), Am. Dietetic Assn. (fellow), Coeur d'Alene Dietetics Practice Group, Alpha Lambda Delta, Omicron Nu. Roman Catholic. Home: 230 S Rivercrest Dr Post Falls ID 83854-9619 Office: Panhandle Health Dept 1106 Ironwood Pky Coeur D Alene ID 83814-2649

CHESSER, STEVEN BRUCE, public relations executive; b. Lakeland, Fla., Sept. 28, 1951; s. Gordon Stuart and Shirley (Hoff) C.; m. Mary Sennholtz, 1972 (div. 1989); children: Bethany, Michelle; m. Karole Gwen Sense, Feb. 28, 1993. BA, U. S.C., 1973; MA, U. Okla., 1985. Commd. ensign USN, 1973, advanced through grades to lt. comdr., served on U.S.S. N.J., 1986-88, served with Naval Surface Group at Long Beach, Calif., 1988-93, ret., 1993; media rels. specialist Met. Transp. Authority, L.A., 1993—. Tech. advisor films Marine Mammals: Navy Undersea Partners, 1986, The Hunt for Red October, 1989, Flight of the Intruder, 1990, Family of Spies, 1990, Heroes of Desert Storm, 1991. Event chmn. Am. Cancer Soc., Long Beach, Calif., 1992-93; publicity dir. The Crossing Homeless Shelter, San Pedro, Calif., 1992-93; pres. Drug Abuse Resistance Edn., Long Beach, 1993-94. Recipient Key to the City, City of Long Beach, 1993. Mem. Internat. Assn. of Bus. Communicators, Drug Abuse Resistance Edn. (bd. dirs.). Office: Met Transp Authority PO Box 194 Los Angeles CA 90053-0194

CHESSICK, CHERYL ANN, psychiatrist; b. Ft. Collins, Colo., July 30, 1960. BA, Colo. Coll., 1982; MD, U. Colo., 1986. Med. technologist, rsch. asst. Children's Hosp., Denver, 1983; intern U. Colo., Denver, 1986-87, resident in psychiatry, 1987-90; on-call physician Ft. Logan State Hosp., Denver, 1988-89; on-call psychiatrist Denver Gen. Hosp., 1989—; staff psychiatrist Colo. State Hosp., Pueblo, 1990-91, med. dir. psychiat. emergency rm., 1991-92; psychiatrist in pvt. practice Denver, 1992—; expert witness Denver Civil Ct., Pueblo Civil Ct., Logan County Criminal Ct., El Paso Civil Ct., Adams County Criminal Ct., 1987—; presenter at profl. confs. co-coord. seminar on battered women U. Colo. Health Sci. Ctr., Denver, 1986; guest lectr. Boulder Community Hosp., 1989, Hosp. & Community Psychiat. Ctr., 1990; curriculum cons. Colo. AIDS Edn. and Tng. Ctr., Denver, 1989—. Mem. Am. Psychiat. Soc., Colo. Psychiat. Soc., Phi Gamma Mu. Office: 950 S Cherry St # 200 Denver CO 80222

CHESTER, ELFI, artist; b. Cologne, Rheinland/Westfalen, Germany, Aug. 7, 1952; came to the U.S., 1977; d. Adolf and Elsbeth Bollert; m. Marvin Chester, July 30, 1977; children: Chaim Peter, Sadye Vera. Degree in Art Edn., Pädagogische Hochschule Berlin, 1976. Founder "Odd Thursday" group of figurative artists in Venice, Calif., 1990; co-founder COOP Fine Art Gallery, Occidental, Calif., 1993. Exhibits include: Collector's Choice, Laguna Beach, Calif., 1982, The House, Santa Monica, Calif., 1982, Arts in Motion, Laguna Beach Arts Commn. Alliance, Calif., 1982, Sculpture in the Park '83, '84, Peter Strauss Ranch, Agoura, Calif., Pierce Coll., Mainstage Theatre, Woodland Hills, Calif., 1983, Designs in Motion, San Francisco, 1983, Don Conrad Mobiles, Ghiradelli Square, 1983, Meditate Centrum DE KOSMOS, Amsterdam, 1983, Agoura Hills City Gallery, 1984, Exploratorium, San Francisco, Deplana Einrichtungshaus, Berlin, 1984, Star Magic, N.Y. and San Francisco, 1984, Gallo, Rome, 1986, Tropical Palm Gallery, Maui, 1988, Talpa Trangle Gallery, Taos, New Mexico, 1988, Santa Monica Main Library, 1990, Claudia Chapline Gallery, Stinson Beach, Calif., 1991, Sebastopol Ctr. for the Arts, 1992, Coop. FINE ART, Occidental, 1993, Small Works, Calif. Mus. of Art, 1993; numerous pvt. collections; prodr. art performance Laguna Beach Arts Commn. Alliance and L.A. Choreographers and Dancers, 1982. Recipient Agoura Hills Art Contbn. award City of Agoura Hills, 1983. Mem. Sebastopol Ctr. for the Arts, Cultural Arts Coun. of Sonoma County. Home: PO Box 324 Occidental CA 95465-0324

CHESTER, LYNNE, foundation executive, artist; b. Fargo, N.D., May 29, 1942; d. Harry Batton and Margaret Emily (White) Welliver; m. R. Craig Chester, Feb. 25, 1984; 1 child, Benjamin. BA, Hillsdale Coll., 1964; MA, Mich. State U., 1965; PhD, U. Mich., 1971. Tchr. Warren (Mich.) Consol. Schs., 1965-70; curriculum advisor Royal Oak (Mich.) Pub. Schs., 1974-75; co-founder, exec. dir. Peace Rsch. Found., Carmel, Calif., 1993—; assoc. Hillsdale Coll., 1989—; guest lectr. ceramics James Milliken U., Decatur, Ill., 1991; guest lectr. creative convergence Carl Cherry Ctr. for Art, Carmel, 1991; co-founder, bd. mem. Monterey (Calif.) Peninsula Coll. Art Gallery, 1991—; fundraiser Monterey (Calif.) Peninsula Coll. Student Art Gallery, 1992-94. Artist of three commd. sculptures for pvt. collections; author of poetry. Pres., bd. dirs. Carl Cherry Ctr. for Arts, Carmel, 1988-94; bd. dirs. Carmel Pub. Libr. Found., 1992-93, Monterey Inst. for Rsch. in Astronomy, 1985-95, Monterey County Cultural Commn., Salinas, Calif., 1994—; bd. dirs. Monterey Peninsula Mus. Art, 1991-93; co-founder, bd. dirs. Monterey Bay Artists Day. Recipient Citizens Adv. Coun. award City of Royal Oak, Mich., 1978-83, Best of Show award for monoprint Monterey Peninsula Coll., 1990, Poetry prizes Carl Cherry Ctr. for Arts, Carmel, 1990, 94, Benefactor of Arts award Monterey County Cultural Coun., Salinas, 1992, 93, 94. Mem. Internat. Sculpture Ctr., Nat. Mus. Women in Art (charter mem.). Home: 3037 Forest Way Pebble Beach CA 93953-2904 Office: Peace Rsch Found 225 Crossroads #145 Carmel CA 93923

CHESTER, MARVIN, physics educator; b. N.Y.C., Dec. 29, 1930; s. Herman and Sadye Chester; m. Sandra (div. 1963); children: Lisa, Karen; m. Elfi Bollert, July 30, 1977; children: Chaim Peter, Sadye Vera. BS, CCNY, 1952; PhD, Calif. Inst. Tech., 1961. Prof. physics U. Calif., L.A., 1961-92, prof. emeritus, 1992—; sr. rsch. fellow U. Sussex, Eng., 1973. Author: Primer of Quantum Mechanics, 1987; contbr. articles to profl. jours. Recipient Alexander von Humboldt award, Von Humboldt Stifftung, 1974-75. Mem. Am. Phys. Soc., N.Y. Acad. Sci. Office: UCLA Dept Physics Los Angeles CA 90024

CHESTER, SHARON ROSE, photographer, natural history educator; b. Chgo., July 12, 1942; d. Joseph Thomas and Lucia Barbara (Urban) C. BA, U. Wis., 1964; grad., Coll. San Mateo, 1972-74; postgrad., U. Calif., Berkeley, 1977; grad., San Francisco State U., 1989. Flight attendant Pan Am. World Airways Inc., San Francisco, 1965; free lance photographer San Mateo, Calif., 1983—; stock photographer Comstock, N.Y.C., 1987—; lectr. Soc. Expdns., Seattle, 1985-91, Abercrombie & Kent, Chgo., 1992-94, Seven Seas Cruise Line, San Francisco, 1994—; owner Wandering Albatross, 1993. Author (checklist) Birds of the Antarctic and Sub-Antarctic, 1986, revised, 1994, Antarctic Birds and Seals: A Pocket Guide, 1993, South to Antarctica, 1994, The Northwest Passage, 1994, Illustrated Birds of Chile, Aves de Chile, 1995; translator: Field Guide to the Birds of Chile, 1989; co-author: The Birds of Chile, 1993; photos featured in Sierra Club Book: Mother Earth Through the Eves of Women Photographers and Writers, 1992; photographer mag. cover King Penguin and Chick for Internat. Wildlife Mag., 1985, Sierra Club Calendar, 1986; exhibited photos at Royal Geog. Soc., London, 1985. Mem. Calif. Acad. Sci. Home: 724 Laurel Ave Apt 211 San Mateo CA 94401-4131

CHESTERFIELD, MARY, editor; b. New London, Conn.; d. William Young and Alice (Aarons) Minkus; m. Jerome Rowitch, Sept. 1959 (div. Oct. 1968); children: David Rowitch, Douglas Rowitch, Janine Davis. BA, UCLA, 1970, Tchr.'s Credential, 1971. Art dir. "An American City" documentary film, 1973; artist, fiber sculpture L.A., 1973-80; extension design instr. UCLA, 1977-81; spl. features editor Architectural Digest, L.A., 1980-88; freelance writer/editor L.A., 1988-92; editor Phoneix Home and Garden mag., Phoenix, 1992—. Recipient Excellence award Knapp Comms. Corp., L.A., 1984, 85. Office: Phoenix Home and Garden 4041 N Central Ave Ste A-100 Phoenix AZ 85012

CHESTERFIELD, RHYDONIA RUTH EPPERSON, financial company executive; b. Dallas, Tex., Apr. 23, 1919; d. Leonard Lee and Sally E. (Stevenson) Griswold; m. Chad Chesterfield, Apr. 21, 1979. BS Southwestern U., 1952; BS, North Tex. U., 1954, ME, 1956; PhD, Bernardean U., 1974, Calif. Christian U., 1974, LLD (hon.), 1974. Evangelist with Griswold Trio, 1940-58; tchr., counselor Dallas public schs., 1952-58, L.A. pub. schs., 1958-74; pres. Griswold-Epperson Fin. Enterprise, L.A., 1974—; pres. GEC Enterprises, 1979—; guest speaker various schs., chs. and civic orgns. in U.S. and Can. Author: Little Citizens series, Cathedral Films; contbr. articles on bus. to profl. publs. Fellow Internat. Naturopathic Assn.; mem. L.A. Inst. Fine Arts, Assn. of Women in Edn. (hon.), Internat. Bus. and Profl. Women, Calif. C. of C., L.A. C. of C., Pi Lambda Theta (hon.), Kappa Delta Pi (hon.). Office: 10790 Wilshire Blvd Apt 202 Los Angeles CA 90024-4426

CHESTON, MICHAEL GALLOWAY, airport executive; m. Laurie; children: Kenny, Geoffrey. AA in Gen. Edn., Catonsville (Md.) C.C., 1975; BA in English, St. Mary's Coll. of Md., 1977; MBA in Real Estate Devel., George Washington U., 1994. Cert. air traffic control specialist. Corporate recruiting supr., computer resource acquisition specialist Electronic Data Sys., Inc., Bethesda, Md., 1984-86; dir. European ops. Corporate Devel. Sys., Inc., Wellesley, Mass., 1986-87; acting mgr., ops. officer, bus. analyst Met. Washington Airports Authority, Alexandria, Va., 1987-93; airport mgr. Portland (Oreg.) Internat. Airport, 1993—. Comdr. USMC, 1977-84; maj., USMCR. Mem. Am. Assn. Airports Execs., Airports Coun. Internat., Portland Highland Games Assn. (pub. safety mgr.), Marine Corps Assn., Marine Corps Res. Officers Assn. (chpt. pres.). Office: Portland Internat Airport PO Box 3529 Portland OR 97208-3529*

CHETWYND, LIONEL, screenwriter, producer, director; b. London, Jan. 29; s. Peter and Betty (Dion) C.; m. Gloria Carlin, June 2; children: Michael Anthony, Joshua Stephen. BA with honors, Sir George Williams U., Montreal, Que., 1963; B in Civil Law, McGill U., Montreal, Que., 1967; postgrad., Trinity Coll. of Oxford (Eng.) U., 1968. Bar: PQ 1967. With acquisition/distbn. dept. Columbia Pictures, London, 1968-72; screenwriter, 1971—; mem. faculty Grad. Film Sch., NYU; lectr. screenwriting Frederick Douglass Ctr., Harlem; appointed pres.. Am. Cinema Found. Writer: (stage prodns.) Maybe That's Your Problem, 1971, Bleeding Great Orchids, 1971, (feature films) The Apprenticeship of Duddy Kravitz, 1974 (also adaptor, Acad. award nomination 1974), Morning Comes, 1975 (also dir.), Two Solitudes, 1978 (also producer, dir., Grand award Salonika 1979), Quintet, 1978, Hot Touch, 1981 (Genie nomination), The Hanoi Hilton, 1987 (also dir.), (TV films) Johnny, We Hardly Knew Ye, 1976 (also producer, George Washington Honor medal Freedom Found. 1976), It Happened One Christmas, 1977 (citation Am. Women in Film and TV 1979), Goldenrod, 1977 (also producer), A Whale for the Killing, 1980, Miracle on Ice, 1981 (Christopher award 1981), Escape From Iran: The Canadian Caper, 1981, Sadat, 1983 (NAACP Image award 1983), Children in the Crossfire, 1984 (Prix D'Association Mondiale des Amis de L'Enfants 1985, award Monte Carlo Internat. TV Festival 1985), To Heal a Nation, 1988 (also producer, Vietnam Vets. Meml. Fund Patriots award, George Washington Honor medal Freedom Found. 1989), The American 1776 (official U.S. bicentennial film), (cable film) The Doom's Day Gun; co-writer, co-producer (stage prodn.) We The People...200, 1987; exec. producer (TV film) Evil in Clear River, 1988 (Spl. award Am. Jewish Com., Christopher award); writer, dir., exec. producer So Proudly We Hail (Bnai Zion Creative Achievement award 1990), Heroes of the Desert Storm, 1991; exec. prodr., writer, creator (PBS documentary series) Reverse Angle, 1993, (HBO) Doom's Day Gun, The

Bible-Jacob, The Bible-Joseph, The Bible-Moses. Co-chair Arts and Entertainment Commn. for Reagan/Bush, L.A., 1978-80; exec. bd. dirs. Can. Ctr. for Advanced Cinema Studies, Toronto, 1986—; mem. exec. bd. L.A. chpt. Am. Jew Com.; named to panel on sexuality and social policy Am. Enterprise Inst.; bd. dirs. Profl. Friends of Dept. Film and Theatre UCLA. Mem. Acad. Motion Picture Arts and Scis., Acad. TV Arts and Scis., Am. Cinema Found. (pres.), Writers Guild Am. (exec. bd. 1972-76, nat. exec. 1975, Writers Guild award 1974), Writers Guild Britain, Can. Bar Assn., Dirs. Guild Am., Broadcast Music, Inc., Assn. Can. TV and Radio Artists, UCLA Film TV and Edn. Assn. (bd. dirs.). Jewish. Office: care Gang Tyre Raymer & Brown 6400 W Sunset Blvd Los Angeles CA 90028-7307

CHEUNG, JEFFREY, sales and marketing professional; b. June 18, 1950. BA in Psychology and Econ., Ind. U., Bloomington, 1972; MBA in Fin. and Mgmt., 1974. Loan officer The First Nat. Bank of Chgo., 1974-78; v.p. No. Calif. Corp. Banking Dept., 1978-80; v.p., E. Bay regional mgr. No. Calif. Div., 1980-82; v.p., mgr. No. Calif. Pvt. Banking Div., 1983-85; sr. v.p., mgr. No. Calif. Div., Comml. Banking Group, 1985-89; sr. v.p. The Bank of Calif., San Francisco, 1989-90; exec. v.p., nat. sales mgr. Omega, San Francisco, 1990-91; sr. v.p., gen. mgr. The Bank of Calif., San Francisco, 1991—; com. mem. Small Bus. Banking Com., Consumer Bankers Assn., panel participant Bus. Banking Adv. Bd., VIP Forum of Coun. of Fin. Competition; assoc. Omega, Miller-Heiman Client. Recipient Bryon L. Willford award, Children's Hosp., 1991, Bank of Calif. chmn.'s award, Bambino award, Children's Hosp. Office: Bank of California 400 California St San Francisco CA 94104-1302

CHEUNG, JOHN B., research and development executive; b. 1943. COO Quest Integrated, Inc., Kent, Wash. Office: Quest Intergrated Inc 21414 68th Ave S Kent WA 98032-2416*

CHEUNG, KING-KOK, English language educator; b. Hong Kong, Jan. 11, 1954; came to U.S., 1973; m. Gerard M. Maré, Feb. 17, 1984. BA, Pepperdine U., 1975, MA, 1976; PhD, U. Calif., Berkeley, 1984. Asst. prof. English dept. UCLA, 1984-91, assoc. prof., 1991—. Author: Articulate Silences, 1993; editor: Asian American Literature: An Annotated Bibliography, 1988; mem. editl. bd. Asian America, Santa Barbara, Calif., 1991—. Recipient Rsch. fellowship Am. Coun. Learned Socs., 1987-88, Ctr. for Advanced Study in Behavioral Scis., Stanford U., 1995-96. Mem. MLA (chair publs. com. 1992-93, exec. com. divsn. of ethnic studies 1991-93, com. on the lit. and lang. of Am., 1995—), Soc. for the Study of Multi-Ethnic Lits. of the U.S. Office: Dept English UCLA Los Angeles CA 90024-1530

CHEVELDAE, TIM, professional hockey player; b. Melville, Sask., Can., Feb. 15, 1968. Goalie Detroit Red Wings, 1986-94, Winnipeg Jets, 1994—; player NHL All-Star game, 1992. Named to WHL All-Star 1st Team, 1987-88. Office: Calgary Flames, PO Box 1540 Sta M, Calgary, AB Canada T2P 3B9

CHEVERS, WILDA ANITA YARDE, probation officer; b. N.Y.C.,; d. Wilsey Ivan and HerbertLee (Perry) Yarde; m. Kenneth Chevers, May 14, 1950; 1 child, Pamela Anita. BA, CUNY, 1947; MSW, Columbia, 1959; PhD, NYU, 1981. Probation officer, 1947-55; supr. probation officer, 1955-65; br. chief Office Probation for Cts. N.Y.C., 1965-72, asst. dir. probation, 1972-77, dep. commr. dept. probation, 1978-86; prof. pub. adminstrn. John Jay Coll. Criminal Justice CUNY, 1986-91; conf. faculty mem. Nat. Council Juvenile and Family Ct. Judges; mem. faculty N.Y.C. Tech. Coll., Nat. Coll. Juvenile Justice; mem. adv. com. Family Ct., First Dept. Sec. Susan E. Wagner Adv. Bd., 1966-70. Sec., bd. dirs. Allen Community Day Care Ctr., 1971-75; bd. dirs. Allen Sr. Citizens Housing, Queensboro Soc. for Prevention Cruelty to Children; chairperson, bd. dir. Allen Christian Sch., 1987-91. Named to Hunter Coll. Hall of Fame, 1983. Mem. ABA (assoc.), N.Y. Acad. Pub. Edn., Nat. Council on Crime and Delinquency, Nat. Assn. Social Workers, Acad. Cert. Social Workers. Middle Atlantic States Conf. Correction, Alumni Assn. Columbia Sch. Social Work, N.Y.U. Alumni Assn., NAACP, Am. Soc. Pub. Adminstrn. (mem. council), Counseliers, Hansel and Gretel Club (pres. 1967-69, Queens, N.Y.). Delta Sigma Theta. Home: 9012 Covered Wagon Ave Las Vegas NV 89117-7010

CHEVERTON, RICHARD E., newspaper editor. BSJ, Northwestern U., 1964, MSJ, 1965. Reporter Chgo. Today, 1970; editor Sunday Mag. Detroit Free Press, 1970-71; asst. editor Sunday Mag., editor review & opinion sect. Phila. Inquirer, 1972-75; mng. editor The New Paper, Phila., 1975; freelance Phila., 1975-76; features editor Phila. Daily News, 1976-79; newsfeatures editor Seattle Times, 1979-81; asst. mng. editor, features Orange County Reporter, Santa Ana, Calif., 1982-90, asst. mng. editor strategy and adminstrn., 1990-91, mng. editor strategy and adminstrn., 1991—; guest lectr. Poynter Inst., Am. Press Inst. Media mgr. Gray for Cong. campaign; speechwriter Friedman for Mayor campaign, Chgo., 1970. With US Army, 1967-69, Vietnam. Decorated Bronze Star; edited series that won Pulitzer Prize for Spl. Local Reporting, 1982. Mem. Am. Assn. Sunday and Feature Editors. Home: 7211 Monterey Ln La Palma CA 90623-1143 Office: The Orange County Register 625 N Grand Ave Santa Ana CA 92701-4347

CHEVERTON, WILLIAM KEARNS, science corporation executive, consultant; b. Corpus Christi, Tex., Dec. 20, 1944; s. Milton Robbins and Pauline (Kearns) C. Student, San Diego State Coll., 1962-65, Chapman Coll., 1965-68; PhD, LaJolla U., 1980. Lic. ins. broker, Calif. Chmn., CEO WYBSQUIZ Sci., La Jolla, 1980—. Contbr. articles to profl. publs. Cons./vol. YMCA, C. of C., Ednl. Insts.; scoutmaster Boy Scouts Am., 1968-78; dir. Am. Congress Internat. Execs. Named Kiwanian of Yr., Kiwanis Club, 1986. Mem. Camelopard High Intelligence Group, Mensa High Intelligence Group, DRONK Radio Network. Republican.

CHEW, LINDA LEE, fundraising management consultant; b. Riverside, Calif., Mar. 3, 1941; d. LeRoy S. and Grace (Ham) Olson; m. Dennis W. Chew, July 23, 1965; children—Stephanie, Erica. B.Mus., U. Redlands, 1962. Cert. fund raising exec. Dir. pub. events U. Redlands (Calif.), 1962-69; dir. fin. and communications San Gorgonio council Girl Scouts U.S.A., Colton, Calif., 1969-71; exec. dir. United Cerebral Palsy Assn. Sacramento-Yolo Counties, 1972-73; fin. devel. dir. San Francisco Bay coun. Girl Scouts U.S.A., 1973-76; chief devel. and pub. info. East Bay Regional Park Dist., Oakland, Calif., 1976-86; cons. Chew & Assocs., Alamo, Calif., 1986—; pres. Providence Hosp. Found., Oakland, 1991-92. Bd. dirs. Planned Parenthood Contra Costa County, 1980-82, San Ramon Valley Edn. Found., 1984-88; Calif. Conservation Corps Bay Area Ctr. Adv. Bd., 1988-89; Mem. AAUW (pres. Redlands br. 1968-69), Nat. Soc. Fund Raising Execs. (nat. bd. dirs. 1981-90, nat. vice chmn. 1982-84, pres. Golden Gate chpt. 1979-80, bd. dirs. 1987-90, Abel Hanson Meml. award 1977, Outstanding Fund Raising Exec. 1988), Assn. Healthcare Philanthropy (Region 11 cabinet mem. 1991-94), Am. Guild Organists (dean Riverside-San Bernardino chpt. 1969-71), Pub. Rels. Soc., Alamo Rotary, Lamorinda Volleyball Club (pres. 1994—). Office: 170F Alamo Plz Ste 400 Alamo CA 94507-1550

CHI, HONG, English as Second Language and Chinese educator; b. Shanghai, Apr. 19, 1955; came to U.S., 1985; s. Zhi-Qiang Chi and Wen-Ying Hu; m. Cheng-Ying Xie, Dec. 23, 1993; 1 child, Shawn Xi-ang. Diploma, Shanghai Inst. Fgn. Langs., 1977; MS, SUNY, Albany, 1985, MA, 1988; PhD, La. State U., 1991. Instr. English Shanghai Inst. of Fgn. Langs., 1977-78, Shanghai U., China, 1978-84; instr. ESL and Chinese Cypress (Calif.) Coll., 1991—. Wenner Gren Found. fellow, 1986-88. Mem. Calif. Tchrs. of English to Speakers of Other Langs., Linguistic Soc. Am. Home: 76 Bridgeport Irvine CA 92720-3209 Office: Cypress Coll 9200 Valley View St Cypress CA 90630-5805

CHIANG, ALBERT CHIN-LIANG, electrical engineer; b. Putai, Taiwan, Jan. 25, 1937; s. San Chi and Chiu (Hsu) C.; BS in Elec. Engring., Nat. Taiwan U., 1959; MS in Elec. Engring., Chiaotung U., Taiwan, 1963; PhD, U. So. Calif., 1968; m. Steffie F.L. Huang, Dec. 24, 1966; children: Margaret, Stacy, Kathy, George. Came to U.S., 1963, naturalized, 1973. Research asst. U. So. Calif., Los Angeles, 1963-68; engr. specialist Litton Industries, Woodland Hills, Calif., 1968-70; dir. internat. sales Macrodata Co., Woodland Hills, Calif., 1970-77; pres. Tritek Internat. Co., Woodland Hills, Calif., 1977—. Mem. IEEE, Sigma Xi, Eta Kappa Nu. Home: 24132 Lupin Hill Rd Hidden Hills CA 91302-2430 Office: Tritek Internat Co 5000 N Parkway Calabasas Calabasas CA 91302

CHIANG, SAMUEL EDWARD, theological educator, humanities educator; b. Taipei, Taiwan, Republic of China, Oct. 20, 1959; s. William L. and Gladys (Chao) C.; m. Roberta Jean Bush, Dec. 31, 1987; children: Zachariah Asa, Micah Kaleem, Joni Abigail. B. Commerce, U. Toronto (Can.), 1982; MA in Bibl. Studies, Dallas Theol. Sem., 1989. Ordained minister Peoples' Ch., 1990. Writer, researcher Can. Broadcasting Co., Toronto, Ont., Can., 1980-81; audit automation coord. Can. nat. office Ernst & Young, Toronto, 1982-86; asst. to the pres. Dallas Sem. Found., 1988-91; East Asia regional dir. Ptnrs. Internat., San Jose, Calif., 1991—; tchr. Applied Principle of Learning-Walk Thru the Bible, 1990—. Contbr. articles to profl. jours.; editor, contbr. World Christian Perspective, 1988-91. Youth dir. jr. high The Peoples' Ch., Toronto, 1980-82; youth pastor Korean Philadelphia Presbyn. Ch., Toronto, 1983-85; youth dir. Dallas Chinese Fellowship Ch., 1987-90; bd. dirs. Dallas Chinese Ch. Youth Camps, 1987-91; adv. bd. dirs. I Too Have A Dream, Harare, Zimbabwe, 1989—, Foyer Fraternal, Ndjamena, Chad, 1990—, Student Christian Outreach for China, U.S., 1991; bd. dirs. Asian Impact Ministries, 1992—, Kingdom Trust, 1992—; cons. The Tear Found., U.K., 1994—. Mem. Evang. Messiological Soc. Office: PO Box 98583, TST Kowloon Hong Kong

CHIARELLA, PETER RALPH, corporate executive; b. Bklyn., Dec. 6, 1932; s. C. Ralph and Catherine (Zinzi) C.; m. Frances M. Crane, Oct. 10, 1953; children: Ralph, Thomas, John, Karen. B.B.A., St. John's U., 1957. C.P.A., N.Y. Sr. accountant Peat, Marwick, Mitchell & Co., N.Y.C., 1957-61; asst. controller Bonwit Teller, N.Y.C., 1961-62; accounting mgr. plastics div. Celanese Corp., Newark, 1963-67; v.p., controller Clairol, Inc., N.Y.C., 1967-72; pres., dir. Kleinert's, Inc., Kutztown, Pa., 1972-77; v.p., corp. controller United Brands Co., N.Y.C., 1977-79; sr. v.p., chief fin. officer Max Factor & Co., Hollywood, Calif., 1979-83; sr. v.p. fin. and adminstrn. Syncor Internat., Sylmar, Calif., 1983-85; exec v.p. Doctors' Co., Napa, Calif., 1985-92; pres. Cakebread Cellars, Inc., Rutherford, Calif., 1992—, also bd. dirs.; lectr. Am. Mgmt. Assn. Mem. budget com. United Fund, Stamford, Conn., 1970; bd. dirs. Vis. Nurse Assn., L.A., 1983-90, Napa Valley Opera House, Napa Valley Coll. Found., 1991—, Napa Valley Fair Bd. With USN, 1952-54. Mem. AICPA, Fin. Execs. Inst., Delta Mu Delta. Home: 1051 Borrette Ln Napa CA 94558-9702

CHIASSON, ROBERT BRETON, veterinary science educator emeritus; b. Griggsville, Ill., Oct. 9, 1925; s. Placid Nelson and Anna Marie Chiasson; m. Frances Marguirete Kientzle, Oct. 24, 1944; children: Phyllis, Robert, Sarah, John, William, Mary, Annette, Laura. AB, Ill. Coll., 1949; MS, U. Ill., 1950; PhD, Stanford U., 1956. Spl. supr. Ill. State Mus., Springfield, 1949-50; instr. in zoology U. Ariz., Tucson, 1951-55, asst. prof. in zoology, 1956-60, assoc. prof. in zoology, 1960-65, prof. in zoology and biology, 1965-75, prof. in vet. sci., 1975-93, prof. emeritus, 1993—; vis. scientist U. Edinburgh, Scotland, 1976-77, U. Lueven, Belgium, 1985; cons. editor Wm. C. Brown Co. Pubs., Dubuque, Iowa, 1968—. Author (lab. texts): Laboratory Anatomy of the White Rat, 5th edit., 1988, Labortory Anatomy of the Cat, 8th edit., 1989, Laboratory Anatomy of the Shark, 5th edit., 1988, various others; contbr. articles to profl. jours. Air quality advisor County of Pima, Tucson, 1978-87; bd. dirs. Ariz. Consumers Coun., 1974-85; sr. arbitrator Better Bus. Bur., Tucson, 1980—. With U.S. Army, 1944-46, ETO. Named Fulbright Prof., 1969-70. Mem. Am. Assn. Vet. Anatomists, Am. Physiol. Soc., Am. Soc. Zoologists, World Assn. Vet. Anatomists, N.Y. Acad. Sci., Sigma Xi, Gamma Sigma Delta (award of merit 1984). Home: 6941 E Calle Jupiter Tucson AZ 85710-5437 Office: U Ariz Dept Vet Sci Tucson AZ 85721

CHIAT, JAY, advertising agency executive; b. N.Y.C., Oct. 26, 1931; s. Sam and Min (Kretchmer) C.; children: Debra, Marc, Elyse. BS, Rutgers U. Prodn. asst. NBC, New York, 1953-54; mgr. of recruit advertising Aero-Jet General Corp., Sacramento & Azusa, CA, 1956-57; v.p. & dir. Leland Oliver Co., Santa Ana, CA, 1957-62; founder, pres. Chiat & Associates, Inc., 1963-68; Chm. Bd., CEO Chiat Day Inc. Advertising, Venice, CA, 1968—. Served with USAF, 1956-57. Office: Chiat/Day Inc Advt 340 Main St Venice CA 90291-2524 Office: Chiat/Day/Mojo Advt 340 Main St Venice CA 90291-2524*

CHIAVERINI, JOHN EDWARD, construction company executive; b. Providence, Feb. 6, 1924; s. John and Sadie (Ginsberg) C.; m. Cecile Corey, Mar. 31, 1951; children: Caryl Marie, John Michael. Cert. advanced san. engring. U. Ill., 1945; BS in Civil Engring., U. R.I., 1947. Registered profl. engr., Mass., R.I. Project engr. Perini Corp., Hartford, Conn., 1950-51, project mgr., 1951-55, asst. project mgr., Pitts. and Que., 1955-61, v.p., Framingham, Mass., 1965-84, sr. v.p., San Francisco, 1984—; pres., dir. Compania Perini S.A., Colombia, 1961—; v.p., exec. mgr. Perini Yuba Assocs., Marysville, Calif., 1966-70, v.p. Western ops., 1970-78, 79-84, group v.p., 1978-79; sr. v.p. spl. projects Perini Corp., 1984-90, dir., asst. to chmn., 1991—; mem. U.S. com. Internat. Commn. on Large Dams.; bd. dirs. Building Futures Coun., 1990—, vice chmn., 1993, chmn., 1994—; active Civil Engring. Rsch. Found., 1990—, mem. corp. adv. bd., 1992—. Served to 2d lt. USAAF, 1944-46. Recipient Golden Beaver award Supervision San Francisco Bay Area coun. Boy Scouts Am., 1989, Good Scout award, 1989. Fellow ASCE (mem. exec. com. constrn. dvsn., vice chmn. 1994-95, chmn. 1995—); mem. NSPE (life), Am. Arbitrators Assn., Calif. Soc. Profl. Engrs., Soc. Am. Mil. Engrs. (pres. San Francisco post 1991-92, bd. dirs.), Beavers (bd. dirs.), Moles, Commonwealth Club of Calif., KC, Rotary. Democrat. Roman Catholic. Home: 37 Dutch Valley Ln San Anselmo CA 94960-1045 Office: Perini Corp 601 Calif St Ste 950 San Francisco CA 94108

CHICO, RAYMUNDO JOSÉ, mining and oil executive; b. Hernando, Cordoba, Argentina, Sept. 17, 1930; came to U.S., 1954; s. Jesus and Magdalena (Giraudo) C.; m. Beverly Ann Berghaus, July 25, 1959; children: Christian, Gregory, R. Matthew, Marta. D in Geology, U. Nacional Cordóba, Argentina, 1953; MS in Mining Geology, Mo. Sch. Mines and Metallurgy, 1959; MA in Econ. Geology, Harvard U., 1962. Cert. profl. geologist, Idaho. Geologist Direccion Gen. Engrs., Argentina, 1953, Cerro de Pasco Corp., Peru and N.Y.C., 1954-58, Four Corners Uranium Corp., Peru and N.Y.C., 1956-75; cons. Internat. Basic Economy Corp., N.Y.C., 1959, U.S. Ltd. War Lab., Alberdeen, 1963-65; adminstrn. staff Nat. Oceanographic Data Ctr., Washington, 1965, U.S. Army C.E., Balt., 1966; pres. Raymundo J. Chico, Inc., Balt., 1968—, Denver, 1974—; pres. Raymundo J. Chico Overseas, Denver, 1985—; pres., chmn. bd. Am. Gold Minerals Corp., Denver, 1978-85; chmn. bd. No. Iron Ore Mines Ltd., Toronto, Ont., Can., 1988—; pres. Amada Mineral Corp., Denver, 1985—; ind. cons. 1966-68; cons. USAF Cambridge Research Lab. 1960; mem. Emergency Minerals Adminstrn. U.S. Govt., Washington, 1983—; U.S. del. Advanced Inst. of Uranium, NATO and U.K. group. Fellow The Geol. Soc. Am.; mem. AIME, Am. Assn. Petroleum Geologists, Sigma Xi. Club: Petroleum (Denver). Home: 9600 E Grand Ct Englewood CO 80111-1343

CHICOREL, MARIETTA EVA, publisher; b. Vienna, Austria; came to U.S., 1939, naturalized, 1945; d. Paul and Margaret (Gross) Selby. AB, Wayne State U., 1951; MALS, U. Mich., 1961. Asst. chief library acquisitions div. U. Wash., Seattle, 1962-66; project dir. Macmillan Info. Scis., Inc., N.Y.C., 1968-69; pres. Chicorel Library Pub. Corp., N.Y.C., 1969-79, Am. Library Pub. Co., Inc., 1979—; pub. cons. Creative Solutions Co., 1986—; asst. prof. dept. libr. sci. CUNY (Queens Coll.), 1986—; mem. edn. com. Gov.'s Commn. on Status of Women, Wash., 1963-65; instr. libr. scis. No. Ariz. U., Flagstaff, 1990; bd. dirs. Skills Devel. Tng. counseling; pub. cons. creative solutios. Chief editor: Ulrich's International Periodicals Directory, 1966-68; editor, pub.: Chicorel Indexes, 1969—; founding editor: Jour. Reading, Writing and Learning Disabilities International, 1985-90; contbr. chpt. on univs. to Library Statistics: A Handbook of Concepts, Definitions and Terminology, 1966. Mem. ALA (exec. bd. tech. svcs. divsn. 1965-68, chmn. libr. materials price index com. 1968-69, councillor 1969-73), Am. Assn. Profl. Cons., Am. Book Prodrs. Assn., Book League N.Y. (bd. govs. 1975-79), Am. Soc. for Info. Sci., Can. Libr. Assn., Pacific N.W. Libr. Assn., N.Y. Libr. Club, N.Y. Tech. Svcs. Librarians. Home and Office: PO Box 4272 Sedona AZ 86340-4272

CHIKALLA, THOMAS DAVID, science facility administrator; b. Milw., Sept. 9, 1935; s. Paul Joseph and Margaret Ann (Dittrich) C.; m. Ruth Janet Laun, June 20, 1960; children: Paul, Mark, Karyn. BS in Metallurgy, U. Wis., 1957, PhD in Metallurgy, 1966; MS in Metallurgy, U. Idaho, 1960. Research scientist Gen. Electric Co., Richland, Wash., 1957-62; sr. research scientist Battelle Pacific N.W. Labs., Richland, 1964-72, sect. mgr., 1972-80, programs mgr., 1980-83, dept. mgr., 1983-86, assoc. dir., 1986—; tchr. U. Wis., Madison, 1962-64. Contbr. articles to profl. jours. Fellow AEC. Fellow Am. Ceramic Soc. (counselor 1974-80); mem. AAAS, Am. Nuclear Soc., Sigma Xi. Republican. Roman Catholic. Clubs: Desert Ski (pres. 1958-59), Alpine. Home: 2108 Harris Ave Richland WA 99352-2021 Office: Battelle Pacific NW Labs Battelle Blvd Richland WA 99352

CHILCOAT, DALE ALLEN, artist, visual and performing arts educator; b. Phoenix, Ariz., Aug. 16, 1938; s. Robert Polk and Martha Viola (Barton) C.; m. Sharon Fernandez, Dec. 27, 1965; children: Jennifer Lee, Joshua Fernandez. BA, Ariz. State U., 1961; postgrad., U. Florence, 1963; MA, Calif. State U., Northridge, 1967. Cert. tchr., N.Y., Calif. Art tchr. Needles (Calif.) Pub. Schs., 1961-62; chmn. art dept. North Shore Schs., Glen Head, N.Y., 1962-70; chmn. dept. visual arts San Leandro (Calif.) High Sch., 1970-84; dir. collective antiques San Mateo (Calif.) Antique Corp., 1984-86; dir. visual and performing arts San Leandro Schs., 1986—; state mentor tchr. San Leandro Unified, 1984-94; cons. Greater Bay Area, San Mateo, 1981-94; chmn. art curriculum San Leandro Schs., 1988-94; arts dir. North Shore Sch., 1962-70. Author Calif. state art curriculum, 1989. Named Outstanding Artist Operation Democracy Am., 1963. Mem. Calif. Art Educators Assn. (no. state rep. 1994), San Leandro Tchrs. Assn., Nat. Tchrs. Assn. (rep. 1962). Republican. Presbyterian. Home: 62 Broadmoor Blvd San Leandro CA 94577-1818 Office: San Leandro Schs 2200 Bancroft Ave San Leandro CA 94577-6108

CHILD, CARROLL CADELL, research nursing administrator; b. Vicksburg, Miss., Nov. 10, 1949; s. John Clifton and Marie Adelaide (Gerwig) C.; m. Nicole Louise Child, Feb. 11, 1984; children: Dylan Christopher, Brendan Thomas. BA in Philosophy, So. Ill. U., 1972; BSN with honors, U. Calif., San Francisco, 1980; MSc with honors, San Francisco U., 1994. RN, Calif. Nurse supr. USDA/U. Calif., Berkeley; clin. rsch. supr. drug studies unit U. Calif., San Francisco; rsch. nurse educator Stanford (Calif.) U.; clin. trials coord. Community Consortium U. Calif., San Francisco; participant, co-presenter V Internat. Conf. on AIDS, Montreal, Que., Can., 1989, VI Internat. Conf. on AIDS, San Francisco, 1990, VIII Internat. Conf. on AIDS, Amsterdam, 1992; co-presenter univ.-wide task force on AIDS conf. U. Calif., Berkeley, 1990. Contbr. to profl. jours. Mem. Internat. AIDS Soc., Assn. Nurses in AIDS Care, Assn. Rsch. Nurses.

CHILDERS, CHARLES EUGENE, potash mining company executive; b. West Frankfort, Ill., Oct. 29, 1932; s. Joel Marion and Cora E. (Choate) C.; m. Norma A. Casper, June 8, 1952; children: Joel M., Katrina K. BS, U. Ill., 1955; LLD (hon.), U. Saskatchewan, 1994. With Duval Corp., Carlsbad, N.Mex., 1955-62, Internat. Minerals Corp. (IMC), 1963-77; v.p. Esterhazy oper. IMC, 1977-79; pres. IMC Coal, Lexington, 1979-81; v.p. potash oper. IMC, 1981-82, v.p. expansion and devel., 1982-87; pres., chief exec. officer Potash Corp. of Sask., Inc., Saskatoon, Can., 1987-90, chmn., pres., chief exec. officer, 1990—; bd. dirs., past chmn. bd. Canpotex Ltd., Sask., Found. for Agronomic Rsch.; past chmn. bd. The Fertilizer Inst.; bd. dirs. QUNO Corp., Battle Mountain Gold Corp.; chmn. Potash and Phosphate Inst.; mem. fertilizer industry adv. com. to FAO; mem. Can. ops. adv. bd. Allendale Mut. Ins. Co. Dir. at large Jr. Achievement of Can. 1st lt. U.S. Army, 1955-57. Mem. AIME, Can. Inst. Mining and Metallurgy, Sask. Potash Producers Assn. (past. chmn.), Internat. Fertilizer Industry Assn. (pres.). Republican Baptist. Home: 102 Lakeshore Terr, Saskatoon, SK Canada S7J 3X6 Office: Potash Corp of Sask, 122 1st Ave S, Saskatoon, SK Canada S7K 7G3

CHILDS, JOHN DAVID, computer hardware and services company executive; b. Washington, Apr. 26, 1939; s. Edwin Carlton and Catherine Dorothea (Angerman) C.; m. Margaret Rae Olsen, Mar. 4, 1966 (div.); 1 child, John-David. Student Principia Coll., 1957-58, 59-60; BA, Am. U., 1963. Jr. adminstr. Page Communications, Washington, 1962-65; account rep. Friden Inc., Washington, 1965-67; Western sales dir. Data Inc., Arlington, Va., 1967-70; v.p. mktg. Rayda, Inc., Los Angeles, 1970-73, pres., 1973-76, chmn. bd., 1976-84; v.p. sales Exec. Bus. Systems, Encino, Calif., 1981-87, sr. v.p. sales and mktg., 1987—; sr. assoc. World Trade Assocs., Inc., 1976—. Pres. Coll. Youth for Nixon-Lodge, 1959-60, dir. state fedn.; mem. OHSHA policy formulation com. Dept. Labor, 1967. Served with USAFR, 1960-66. Mem. Assn. Data Ctr. Owners and Mgrs. (chmn. privacy com. 1975, sec. 1972-74, v.p. 1974). Democrat. Christian Scientist. Office: 3089 Clairemont Dr # 213 San Diego CA 92117-6802

CHILDS, MARIAN TOLBERT, nutritionist, educator; b. Twin Falls, Idaho, Nov. 18, 1925; d. Edward and Helen (Mills) Tolbert; m. Morris Elsmere Childs, Nov. 26, 1952; children: Robert E., Mary E., Ruth E., Amy E. BS, U. Calif., Berkeley, 1946; PhD, U. Calif., 1950. Asst. prof. U. Ill., 1950-54; asst. prof. nutrition U. Wash., Seattle, 1969-81; assoc. prof. medicine U. Wash., 1981-90, assoc. prof. emeritus, 1990—. Contbr. articles to profl. jours. NIH fellow, 1976-78; recipient Borden award, 1943. Mem. Am. Inst. Nutrition, Sigma Xi, Iota Sigma Xi. Home: 7857-56th Pl NE Seattle WA 98115 Office: Univ Wash DL10 Seattle WA 98195

CHILES, WILTON RICHARDSON, electrical engineer; b. Greenville, S.C., Aug. 15, 1936; s. Wilton Richardson and Margaret Elizabeth (Skinner) C.; m. Dorothy Mae Stoky, Mar. 29, 1958; children: Derek Wilton, Devin Richardson. B in Elec. Engring. magna cum laude, U. Fla., 1960; MS in Elec. Engring., U. Pa., 1966. Design engr. RCA, Camden, N.J., 1960-66; sr. design engr. Gen. Elec., Phoenix, 1966-70; design engring. exec. Honeywell, Phoenix, 1970-88; sr. cons. engr. AT&T, San Diego, 1988—; referee, session chair Internat. Test Conf., Washington, 1992—. Holder patent in field. Mem. IEEE (tech. working group 1991—). Republican. Home: 12658 Hickory Ct Poway CA 92064-3239 Office: AT&T Global Info Solutions 17095 Via Del Campo San Diego CA 92127-1711

CHIN, ALBERT KAE, research physician; b. Spokane, Wash., May 5, 1953; s. Ting H. and Beatrice Y. (Lui) C.; m. Jeanne Yee, Aug. 6, 1977; children: Jennifer, Lisa, Stephanie. BSME, MIT, 1975; MSME, Stanford U., 1976; MD, U. Calif., San Francisco, 1983. Resident in gen. surgery U. Tex. Southwestern, Dallas, 1983-85; dir. rsch. Fogarty Rsch., Portola Valley, Calif., 1985-89; founder, v.p. rsch. Origin Medsystems, Inc., Menlo Park, Calif., 1989—; cardiovascular cons. Baxter Edwards LIS Divsn., Irvine, Calif., 1988; expert witness Advanced Cardiovascular Systems, Santa Clara, Calif., 1989. Contbr. articles to profl. publs.; 51 patents in field. Bd. dirs. YMCA, Palo Alto, Calif., 1987-89. Mem. AMA, Soc. of Laparoendoscopic Surgeons, Internat. Soc. Endovascular Surgery, FF Fraternity (chmn. San Francisco lodge 1986). Home: 2021 Newell Rd Palo Alto CA 94303-3424 Office: Origin Medsystems Inc 135 Constitution Dr Menlo Park CA 94025-1118

CHIN, JANET SAU-YING, data processing executive, consultant; b. Hong Kong, July 27, 1949; came to U.S., 1959; d. Arthur Quock-Ming and Jenny (Loo) C. BS in Math, U. Ill., Chgo., 1970; MS in Computer Sci., U. Ill., Urbana, 1973. System programmer Lawrence Livermore (Calif.) Lab., 1972-79; sect. mgr. Tymshare Inc., Cupertino, Calif., 1979-83, Fortune Systems, Redwood City, Calif., 1983-85; div. mgr. Impell Corp, Berkeley, Calif., 1985; pres. Chin Assocs., Oakland, Calif., 1985-88; bus. devel. mgr. Sun Microsystems, Mountain View, Calif., 1988-92; engring. dir. Cadence Design Systems, San Jose, Calif., 1992-94, quality dir., 1994—; Vice-chmn. Am. Nat. Standards Inst. X3H3, N.Y.C., 1979-82, internat. rep. X3H3, 1982-88. Co-author: The Computer Graphics Interface, 1991; contbr. tech. papers to profl. publs. Mem. Assn. Computing Machinery, Sigma Xi.

CHIN, KELVIN HENRY, legal association executive, mediator, consultant; b. Boston, Jan. 7, 1951; s. Henry W.F. and King (Lee) C.; m. Peggy Abbott, July 26, 1987; children: Jesse, Samantha. Student, U. Strasbourg, France, 1971; AB cum laude, high distinction in French, Dartmouth Coll., 1973; MA, Yale U., 1974; JD, Boston Coll., 1983. Dir. in East Asia Found. for Creative Intelligence, Seelisberg, Switzerland, 1974-76; asst. dir. admissions Newbury Coll., Boston, 1976-78; founding dir., corp. sec. Microtex Corp., Cambridge, Mass., 1978-83; life ins. agent Sun Life of Canada, Wellesley, Mass., 1979-81; law clerk Bingham, Dana & Gould, Boston, 1980-83;

summer assoc. to assoc. Choate, Hall & Stewart, Boston, 1982-84; employee benefits cons. Hicks Pension Svcs., Lexington, Mass., 1984-86; founder The Mediation Office of Kelvin Chin, Boston, San Diego, 1986-92; mediation coord. AAA Ctr. for Mediation, Am. Arbitration Assn., San Diego, 1992-93; regional v.p., alt. dispute resolution, ptnr. facilitator Am. Arbitration Assn., Las Vegas, Nev., 1993—; assoc. dir. Ctr. for Med. Ethics and Mediation, San Diego, 1992—; cons. Area Agy. on Aging, San Diego, 1991-93, San Diego Mediation Ctr., 1990-93, Continuing Edn. of the Bar, Calif. 1992—, Mediation Action Guide, 1993—, Bus. Practice Group, 1993—, Litigation Group, 1993—. Editor: International Law Dictionary, 1983. Ombudsman Calif. Dept. on Aging, San Diego, 1991-93; com. mem. Waldorf Sch. of San Diego PTA, 1992-93; vol. mediator Ctr. for Mcpl. Dispute Resolution City Atty.'s Office, San Diego, 1990-93. Rufus Choate scholar Dartmouth Coll., 1971-73; Nat. Def. Fgn. Language fellow U.S. Dept. Edn., 1973-74. Mem. ABA (dispute resolution sect.), Am. Arbitration Assn. (blue ribbon mediator panel 1992—), So. Nev. Mediation Assn., San Diego County Bar Assn. (treas. alternative dispute resolution sect. 1991-93), Soc. Profls. in Dispute Resolution, Dispute Resolution Forum, So. Calif. Mediation Assn., The Ombudsman Assn. Office: Am Arbitration Assn 4425 Spring Mountain Rd Ste 310 Las Vegas NV 89102-8741

CHIN, MARJORIE SCARLETT YEE, controller, business executive; b. Reno, Mar. 24, 1941; d. Wing Yee and Jessie (Wong) Echavia; m. Manford Jeffrey Chin, Dec. 26, 1969. AA, Contra Costa Coll., 1969; BS, John F. Kennedy U., 1988. Treas., contr. Maya Corp., South San Francisco, 1977-78; fin. and pers. coord. Garretson-Elmendorf-Zinov, San Francisco, 1978-82; bus. mgr. Cyclotomics, Berkeley, Calif., 1982-85; contr. JTS Leasing Corp., South San Francisco, 1985-88; contr., office mgr. Barbary Coast Steel Corp., Emeryville, Calif., 1988-90; cons. WAM, 1990-91, U. Calif., Berkeley, 1992-94; sr. acct. San Francisco, 1993—; contr. X.Clusiv Vending Corp., San Francisco, 1994—; bd. dirs. Experience Unlimited, Pleasant Hill, Calif. Vol. driver ARC, Richmond, Calif., 1978; vol. UNICEF, San Francisco, 1980. Mem. NAFE, AAUW, Nat. Assn. Accts. (bd. dir.), Calif. Fedn., Bus. & Profl. Women Club (sec. 1980—).

CHIN, SUE SOONE MARIAN (SUCHIN CHIN), conceptual artist, portraitist, photographer, community affairs activist; b. San Francisco; d. William W. and Soo-Up (Swebe) C. Grad. Calif. Coll. Art, Mpls. Art Inst., (scholar) Schaeffer Design Ctr.; student, Yasuo Kuniyoshi, Louis Hamon, Rico LeBrun. Photojournalist, All Together Now show, 1973, East-West News, Third World Newscasting, 1975-78, Sta. KNBC Sunday Show, L.A., 1975, 76, Live on 4, 1981, Bay Area Scene, 1981; graphics printer, exhbns. include Kaiser Ctr., Zellerbach Pla., Chinese Culture Ctr. Galleries, Capricorn Asunder Art Commn. Gallery (all San Francisco), Newspace Galleries, New Coll. of Calif., L.A. County Mus. Art, Peace Pla. Japan Ctr., Congress Arts Communication, Washington, 1989; SFWA Galleries, Inner Focus Show, 1989—, Calif. Mus. Sci. and Industry, Lucien Labaudt Gallery, Salon de Medici, Madrid, Salon Renacimento, Madrid, 1995, Life Is a Circus, SFWA Gallery, 1991, 94, Sacramento State Fair, AFL-CIO Labor Studies Ctr., Washington, Asian Women Artists (1st prize for conceptual painting, 1st prize photography), 1978, Yerba Buena Arts Ctr. for the Arts Festival, 1994, UN Exhibit Bayfront Galleries, San Francisco, 1995; represented in permanent collections L.A. County Fedn. Labor, Calif. Mus. Sci. and Industry, AFL-CIO Labor Studies Ctr., Australian Trades Coun., Hazeland and Co., also pvt. collections; author (poetry) Yuri and Malcolm, The Desert Sun. 1994 (Editors Choice award 1993-94). Del. nat., state convs. Nat. Women's Polit. Caucus, 1977-83, San Francisco chpt. affirmative action chairperson, 1978-82, nat. conv. del., 1978-81, Calif. del., 1976-81. Recipient Honorarium AFL-CIO Labor Studies Ctr., Washington, 1975-76; award Centro Studi Ricerche delle Nazioni, Italy, 1985; bd. advisors Psycho Neurology Found. Bicentennial award L.A. County Mus. Art, 1976, 77, 78. Mem. Asian Women Artists (founding v.p., award 1978-79, 1st award in photography of Orient 1978-79), Calif. Chinese Artists (sec.-treas. 1978-81), Japanese Am. Art Coun. (chairperson 1978-84, dir.), San Francisco Women Artists, San Francisco Graphics Guild, Pacific/Asian Women Coalition Bay Area, Chinatown Coun. Performing and Visual Arts. Chmn., Full Moon Products; pres., bd. dir. Aumni Oracle Inc. Address: PO Box 421415 San Francisco CA 94142-1415

CHIN, WANDA WON, graphics designer; b. L.A., July 10, 1952; d. John Ah and Lui Shui (Leung) Chin; m. Terry Paul Dickey, Feb. 3, 1982; children: Emile, Pierre. BA, UCLA, 1974. Graphic designer KCOP-13 TV, L.A., 1977-78, KTTV-11 TV, L.A., 1978; exhibits designer U. Alaska Mus., Fairbanks, 1979-84, coord. exhibits, 1984—. Artist fiber sculptures: Trading Ways, 1983, Magnetic Forces, 1985, Vuelo, 1986, Thrust Away, 1990; artist metal sculpture: Transformations, 1991. Panelist Dept. Natural Resources, Art in Pub. Places, Fairbanks, 1988-89; mem. State of Alaska Coun. on Arts, 1991—; bd. dirs. Dance Omnium, 1982; mem. gov.'s tourism coord. com. State of Alaska, 1992; organizer, designer Arctic Winter Games, 1986. Fellow Kellogg Found., 1982, 87, NEA/Rockefeller Found., 1976. Mem. Fairbanks Arts Assn., Am. Assn. of Mus., Mus. Alaska, Western States Arts Fedn. (trustee 1994—), Inst. Alaska Native Arts, North Star Borough Chinese Assn., Asian Am. Women in Am. Office: Univ of Alaska Mus 907 Yukon Dr Fairbanks AK 99775

CHIÑAS, BEVERLY NEWBOLD, anthropologist, retired educator; b. Minden, Nebr., Sept. 1, 1924; d. Lewis Francis and Glennie Athel (Shoemaker) Newbold; m. Carlos Chiñas, Aug. 27, 1969. BA in Anthropology/Sociology, Fresno State Coll., 1963; MA in Anthropology, UCLA, 1965, PhD in Anthropology, 1968. Faculty dept. anthropology Calif. State U., Chico, 1968-94, prof. emerita, 1994—; vis. prof. dept. anthropology UCLA, 1981; vis prof. Oberlin (Ohio) Coll., 1981; organizer, chair various symposia. Author: Las Mujeres de San Juan: Los Papeles Economicos de Las Mujeres Zapotecas del Istmo de Tehuantepec, Mexico, 1975, The Isthmus Zapotecs, revised edit., 1992, La Zandunga: Of Fieldwork and Friendship in Southern Mexico, 1993; contbr. articles to profl. jours. John and Dora Haynes grad. fellow UCLA, 1963, NSF grad. fellow, 1966; NSF doctoral dissertation rsch. grantee, 1966, travel grantee Am. Coun. Learned Socs., Lima, Peru, 1970, Wenner-Gren Found. field rsch. grantee, 1982, NEH grantee, 1982. Mem. Southwestern Anthropol. Assn. (pres. 1984-85), Sigma Xi (chpt. pres. 1984-85). Office: Calif State U Dept Anthropology Chico CA 95929

CHINCHINIAN, HARRY, pathologist, educator; b. Troy, N.Y., Mar. 7, 1926; s. Ohaness and Armen (Der Arakelian) C.; m. Mary Corcoran, Aug. 22, 1952; children: Armen, Marjorie, Matthew. BA, U. Colo., 1952; MS, Marquette U., 1956, MD, 1959. Cert. anatomic and clin. pathologist. Co-dir. Pathologists Regional Labs., Lewiston, Idaho, 1964—; chief of staff Tri-State Hosp., Clarkston, Wash., 1967, St. Joseph's Hosp., Lewiston, 1971; assoc. prof. pathology Wash. State U., Pullman, 1972—. Author: Antigens To Melanoma, 1957, Parasitism and Natural Resistance, 1958; co-author: Malakoplakia, 1957, Pneumocystis, 1965. Pres. Am. Cancer Soc., Asotin County, Wash., 1968, Lewiston Roundup, 1972-73, N.W. Soc. Blood Banks, 1973-74. Sgt. U.S. Army, 1944-46. Fellow Am. Coll. Pathologists (cert., lab. inspector 1970—); mem. Idaho Soc. Pathologists (pres. 1970). Home: 531 Silcott Rd Clarkston WA 99403 Office: Pathologists Regional Labs PO Box 956 Lewiston ID 83501-0956

CHING, ERIC SAN HING, health care and insurance administrator; b. Honolulu, Aug. 13, 1951; s. Anthony D.K. and Amy K.C. (Chong) C. BS, Stanford U., 1973, MS, MBA, 1977. Fin. analyst Mid Peninsula Health Service, Palo Alto, Calif., 1977; acting dep. exec. dir. Santa Clara County Health Systems Agy., San Jose, Calif., 1977-78; program officer Henry J. Kaiser Family Found., Menlo Park, Calif., 1978-84; dir. strategic planning Lifeguard Health Maintenance Orgn., Milpitas, Calif., 1984-90; v.p. strategic planning and dir. ops. Found. Life Ins. Co., Milpitas, 1986-90; sr. planning analyst Kaiser Found. Health Plan, Oakland, Calif., 1990-94, coord. product and competition analysis, 1994—; adj. faculty Am. Pistol Inst., 1991-94. Mem. vol. staff Los Angeles Olympic Organizing Com., 1984; mem. panel United Way of Santa Clara County, 1985, panel chmn., 1986-87, mem. com. priorities and community problem solving, 1987-90, Project Blueprint, 1988-90. Mem. NRA, ACLU, Am. Soc. Law Enforcement Trainers, Internat. Assn. Law Enforcement Firearms Instrs., Soc. Competitive Intelligence Profls., Stanford Alumni Assn., Stanford Bus. Sch. Alumni Assn., Stanford Swordmasters (pres. 1980-89). Office: Kaiser Found Health Plan Inc One Kaiser Pla 25th Fl Oakland CA 94612

CHING, LAWRENCE LIN TAI, retail executive; b. Hanalei, Hawaii, July 23, 1920; s. Young and Ah Har (Dang) C.; student St. Louis Coll., 1936-40; m. Jennie Kim Pang, Dec. 27, 1947; children: Steven L., Michael G. Dir. Kauai Realty, CKKS Corp.; pres., dir. Can Corp.; 1946—; owner, pres., mgr. Ching Young Store; founder, dir. Kauai Times Newspaper, 1976-81; bd. dirs. Na Pali Properties. Mem. Kauai Charter Commn., 1964-65. With Mil. Police U.S. Army, 1944-46. Democrat. Buddhist. Office: PO Box 426 Hanalei HI 96714-0426

CHING, STEFANIE W., realtor; b. Honolulu, Oct. 29, 1966; d. Norman K.H. and Jocelyn C. H. (Lee) C. BBA in Fin., U. Hawaii at Manoa, 1988; postgrad., U. Hawaii, Manoa, 1992—. Realtor Grad. Realtor Inst. Fin. analyst Am. Savs. Bank, F.S.B., Honolulu, 1988-89; realtor Herbert K. Horita Realty, Inc., Honolulu, 1989—; part-time auditor Kahala Hilton, Honolulu, 1990-92; mem. project sales team Herbert K. Horita Realty, Inc., Honolulu, 1993—. Mem. NAFE, NAR, HAR, Honolulu Bd. Realtors, Internat. Platform Assn., Million Dollar Club, Phi Kappa Phi, Beta Gamma Sigma, Phi Eta Sigma. Home: 5339 Manauwea St Honolulu HI 96821-1917

CHINN, PHYLLIS ZWEIG, mathematics educator; b. Rochester, N.Y., Sept. 26, 1941; d. Julian and Gladys Elizabeth (Weinstein) Z.; m. Daryl Ngee Chinn, Dec. 31, 1968; children: Allison Hai-Ting, Wesley Chee. BA, Brandeis U., 1962; MAT, Harvard U., 1963; MS, U. Calif., San Diego, 1966, PhD, Santa Barbara, 1969. Asst. prof. Towson State Coll. Balt., 1969-75; assoc. prof. Humboldt State U., Arcata, Calif., 1975-83, prof., 1984—; exch. prof. U. Cen. Fla., Orlando, 1983-84. Dir. Redwood Area Math Project, 1988—. Author: (bibliography) Women in Science and Math, 1979, 3rd edit., 1988; also monograph. Contbr. articles to profl. jours. Conf. coord. Nat. Women's Studies Assn., Arcata, 1982, Expanding Your Horizons in Sci. and Math, Arcata and Orlando, 1980-89. Calif. State U. grantee, 1977. Mem. Assn. for Women in Math., Women and Math., Assn. for Women in Sci., Nat. Council of Tchrs. of Math., Math. Assn. Am., Profs. Rethinking Options in Math. for Prospective Tchrs. (dir. project 1992—), Assn. Math. Tchr. Educators, Phi Beta Kappa, Phi Kappa Phi. Office: Humboldt State U Math Dept Arcata CA 95521

CHINN, THOMAS WAYNE, typographic company executive; b. Marshfield, Oreg., July 28, 1909; s. Wing Chin and Shee Lee; student U. Calif.; m. Daisy Lorraine Wong, June 8, 1930; 1 son, Walter Wayne Chinn. Propr., Chinn Linotype Co., San Francisco, 1937-42; owner Calif. Typesetting Co., 1949-56; typographer, 1956-71; pres. Gollan Typography, Inc., San Francisco, 1971-80. Mem. San Francisco Mayor's Citizens Com., 1958-93; mem. San Francisco Twin Bicentennial History Com., 1974-76; mem. Nat. Am. Revolution Bicentennial Advisory Com. on Racial, Ethnic and Native Am. Participation, 1974-76; governing mem. San Francisco YMCA, 1972-82; founding pres., Chinese Hist. Soc. Am., San Francisco, 1963, pres., 1964-66, 75; foreman Civil Grand Jury, City and County of San Francisco, 1983-84. Author: Bridging the Pacific: San Francisco Chinatown and Its People, 1989, A Historian's Reflections of Chinese American Life in San Francisco 1919-91, 1993. Recipient awards of merit Conf. Calif. Socs., 1976, 81, Am. Assn. State and Local History, 1976, San Francisco Laura Bride Powers Meml. award, 1987. Mem. Calif. Hist. Soc. (award of merit 1970, trustee 1981-83), E Clampus Vitus, The Westerners. Clubs: Masons (32 deg.) (past master lodge), Shriners. Editor: A History of the Chinese in California-A Syllabus, 1969; editor, co-pub. Chinese Digest, 1st newspaper in English for Chinese-Ams., 1935-37; contbr. articles to hist. jours.

CHINN-HECHTER, MAMIE MAY, nonprofit organization executive; b. Oakland, Calif., Aug. 20, 1951; d. Bing T. and Georgia S. (Ong) C.; m. Marc S. Hechter. BS in Bus., U. Nev., 1974. Loan processor First Fed. Savs. and Loan, Reno, 1974-75, loan processor supr., 1975-76, sr. loan counselor, affirmative action officer, 1977-78; jr. loan officer First Fed. Savs. and Loan, Carson City, Nev., 1976-77; loan officer State of Nev. Housing Divsn., Carson City, 1978-79, loan adminstr., 1979-83, dep. adminstr., 1983-93; pres., CEO Nev. Comty. Reinvestment Corp., Las Vegas, 1993—; mem. exec. com. Housing and Devel. Fin., Ethics Com., Media and Comms. Com., Carson City, 1987-93. Mem. Carson City Women's Polit. Caucus, Nev. Women's Polit. Caucus; bd. mem. Nev. Cmty. Reinvestment Corp., 1991—; adv. com. Nev. Housing and Neighborhood Devel., Inc., 1994—; adv. com. state low income housing trust fund, 1994—; mem. United Way Planning Coun., 1995—. Mem. NAFE, Capitol City (Carson City sec. 1984-88), Women's Bowling Assn. (bd. dirs. 1983-84), Nat. 600, Asian C. of C. Office: Nev Comty Reinvestment Corp 5920 W Flamingo Rd Ste 8 Las Vegas NV 89103-0109

CHIOLIS, MARK JOSEPH, television executive; b. Walnut Creek, Calif., Dec. 29, 1959; s. Richard Spiro and Muriel Marie (Kottinger) C. Student aeronautics, Sacramento Community Coll., 1980-82; student, American River Coll., 1982. With on-air ops. Sta. KRBK-TV, Sacramento, 1979-81; on-air ops. trainer, crew chief Sta. KVIE-TV, Sacramento, 1981-85; trainer on air ops., ops. crew chief Sta. KRBK-TV, Sacramento, 1981-84; producer, dir., ops. crew chief Sta. KVIE-TV, Sacramento, 1985-87, Sta. KRBK-TV, Sacramento, 1984-87; prodn. mgr., producer, dir. Sta. KVIE-TV, Sacramento, 1987—; production mgr., producer, dir. spl. programs, comml. productions Sta. KRBK-TV, Sacramento, 1987—; with on-air ops. Sta. KVIE-TV, Sacramento, 1980-82; regional sales mgr. BTS-Broadcast T.V. Systems, Inc., 1992—; promotion chmn. Capital Concour d'Elegance, Sacramento, 1984—, gen. chmn., 1987-89. Producer (music videos) Running Wild, Running Fee, 1984, Rocket Hot-/The Image, 1984 (Joey award 1985); producer, dir. (music video) Haunting Melodies, 1991; dir. (documentary) Behind Closed Doors, 1984; producer, dir. FLIGHTLOG, The Jerry Reynolds Show, CountryMile country music show, 1991; dir. (video camera) Reno Nat. Championship Air Races, 1992, 93, 94, Monty Insights, 1993; tech. video dir. for state franchise bd. Tax Talk, 1992, 93, 94, Teleconf. uplinks. Video producer Calif. N.G., 1980-82; video trainer Am. Cancer Soc., Sacramento, 1983-85; cons. Sacramento Sheriff's Dept., Sacramento, 1984—, United Way-WEAVE, Sacramento, 1984-85; bd. dirs. Woodside Homeowners Assn., 1989—. Recipient Gold Addy award, 1986, 87, Addy award, 1989. Mem. Am. Advt. Fedn., Sacramento Advt. Club (awards video producer 1984—, chmn. judging 1988-89, bd. dirs. 1989—, co-chair awards banquet 1989-90), Aircraft Owners and Pilots Assn., Computer Users Group. Republican. Office: BTS-Broadcast TV Systems 111 N First St Ste 100 Burbank CA 91505

CHIPMAN, HAROLD HASTINGS, psychology educator; b. Nassau, Bahamas, June 27, 1947; came to U.S., 1987; s. Harold Hastings and Eva Madeleine (Duschnitz) C. BA in Devel. Psychology, U. Sussex, Brighton, Eng., 1969; MA in Psychology, U. Geneva, 1970, PhD in Exptl. and Genetic Psychology, 1974. Head of rsch. U. Geneva, 1974-80, assoc. prof. of psychology, 1980-83; lectr. in psycholinguistics U. Fribourg, Switzerland, 1976-83; prof. of psychology Webster U., Geneva, 1978-83, U. Munich, 1985-87; researcher in pediatrics UCLA, 1988; prof. psychology Pepperdine U., L.A., 1989-95; vis. prof. edn. So. Ill. U., Edwardsville, 1972; vis. lectr. and rschr. U. Tasmania, Hobart, Tasmania, Australia, 1984; exec. dir. Intra-Mind Learning Systems, L.A., Chipman/Barry Internat., L.A.; vis. prof. Max Planck Inst. of Psychiatry, Munich, 1986. Author/editor books in field; contbr. articles to profl. jour. Vice-pres. Profl. Tng. Orgns., Bern, Switzerland, 1976-83, Swiss Com. of Spl. Edn., Lucerne, 1976-83; pres. Com. of Experts in Spl. Edn./Ministry, Bern, 1978-83. Alexander von Humboldt Found. scholar, Bonn, West Germany, 1984. Mem. APA, Am. Psychol. Soc., Swiss Am. C. of C.

CHIPMAN, JACK ERNEST, artist; b. L.A., Oct. 31, 1943; s. George Geotz and June Naomi (Hanson) C. BFA, Calif. Inst. Arts, 1966. Dealer Calif. pottery Calif. Spectrum, Redondo Beach, 1980-90; cons. Schroeder Pub., Paducah, Ky., 1982—. Author: Complete Collectors Guide Bauer Pottery, 1982, Collectors Ency. California Pottery, 1992 (periodicals) Antique Trader Weekly, 1981-83, Am. Clay Exch., 1982-88. Bd. dirs. Angels Gate Cultural Ctr., San Pedro, Calif., jour. editor, 1990-93. Office: Calif Spectrum PO Box 1079 Venice CA 90294-1079

CHIROT, DANIEL, sociology and international studies educator; b. Bélâbre, Indre, France, Nov. 27, 1942; came to U.S., 1949; s. Michel and Hélène C.; m. Cynthia Kenyon, July 19, 1974; children: Claire, Laura. BA in Social Studies, Harvard U., 1964; PhD in Sociology, Columbia U., 1973. Asst. prof. sociology U. N.C. Chapel Hill, 1971-74; asst. prof. to prof. internat. studies and sociology Henry M. Jackson sch. U. Wash., 1975—; mem. joint com. Ea. Europe of Am. Coun. Learned Socs. and Social Sci. Rsch. Coun., 1976-77, 1982-88, acad. adv. bd. E. European program Woodrow Wilson Ctr., 1990—; chair Russian and E. European studies program U. Wash., 1988-91; vis. prof. sociology Nat. Taiwan U., 1989; vis. prof. polit. sci. Northwestern U., 1993. Author: Social Change in a Peripheral Society, 1976, Social Change in the Twentieth Century, 1977, translations: Korean, 1984, Italian, 1985, Social Change in the Modern Era, 1986, translations: Korean, 1987, Chinese, 1991; co-author: Modern Tyrants: The Power and Prevalence of Evil in Our Age, 1994, How Societies Change, 1994; translator: (with Holley Coulter Chirot) Traditional Romanian Villages (Henri H. Stahl), 1980; editor: The Origins of Backwardness in Eastern Europe, 1989, The Crisis of Leninism and the Decline of the Left, 1991; consulting editor Am. Jour. Sociology, 1986-88; founder and editor Ea. European Politics and Socs., 1986-89. Cons. for Radio Free Europe, 1985. John Simon Guggenheim fellow 1991-92; guest scholar Rockefeller Found. Study Ctr., Bellagio, Italy, 1992; vis. fellow Institut für die Wissenschaften vom Menschen, Vienna, 1992. Office: U Wash Russian/East European Studies Ctr 503 Thompson Hall DR 05 Seattle WA 98195

CHIRUMBOLO, PAUL, arts organization executive; b. Binghamton, N.Y., Apr. 24, 1954; s. Paul and Lena Elizabeth (Domiano) C. BS, Ithaca Coll., 1976. Advt. and mktg. profl. Riger Advt. Agy., N.Y., 1976-81, So. Tier Adworks, N.Y., 1976-81; fellow Am. Film Inst.'s Ctr. for Advanced Film Studies, L.A., 1981; story editor IndieProd Co.; with Happy Go Lucy Film Corp.; founding dir., CEO, The Cmty. Arts Ctr., 1992. Editor: (TV and theatrical releases) Nobody's Child, The Memory Boy, The Young Toscannini; co-writer The Florentines; author: (screenplays) O Pioneers!, The Royal Road; exhibitor art shows in N.Y., N.C., L.A., Washington, San Francisco, others.

CHISHOLM, DAVID HOLLISTER, German studies educator; b. New Rochelle, N.Y., Aug. 30, 1940; s. Robert Kerr and Margaret Sale (Covey) C.; m. Ana Carmen Valdés-Estay, May 9, 1971; children: Claudia Carmen, Andrew David. BA, Oberlin Coll., 1962; postgrad., U. Erlangen, Germany, 1962-63; MA, U. Chgo., 1965; PhD, Ind. U., 1971. Postdoctoral fellow U. Cin., 1971-72; vis. asst. prof. U. Ill., Urbana, 1972-73; asst. prof. German studies U. Ariz., Tucson, 1973-77, assoc. prof., 1977-83, prof., 1983—; vis. prof. German Summer Sch. of N.Mex., Taos, 1985, 86, 90, 93; lectr. U. Hamburg, Germany, 1967-68. Author: Goethe's Knittelvers, 1975; co-editor/compiler: Verse Concordance: C.F. Meyer, 1982, Concordance to Goethe's Faust, 1986; mem. editorial bd. Lit. and Linguistic Computing, 1986—. Alexander von Humboldt rsch. grantee, 1979-80, 81-82; Fulbright grantee, 1977, 82; Ctr. for Interdisciplinary Studies grantee, Bielefeld, Germany, 1983; ACLS grantee, 1973-74, 83. Mem. MLA, Am. Assn. Tchrs. German (tech. com. 1993—), Assn. for Computers and the Humanities, Assn. for Lit. and Linguistic Computing, Text-Encoding Initiative, Fulbright Alumni Assn. Office: U Ariz Dept German Studies Tucson AZ 85721

CHISHOLM, TOM SHEPHERD, environmental engineer; b. Morristown, N.J., Nov. 28, 1941; s. Charles Fillmore and Eileen Mary (Fenderson) C.; m. Mary Virginia Carrillo, Nov. 7, 1964; children: Mark Fillmore, Elaine Chisholm. Student, Northeastern U., Boston, 1959-61; BS in Agrl. Engring., N.Mex. State U., 1964; MS in Agrl. Engring., S.D. State U., 1967; PhD in Agrl. Engring., Okla. State U., 1970. Registered profl. engr., Ariz., La.; cert. Class A indsl. wastewater operator. Agrl. engr. U.S. Bur. Land Mgmt., St. George, Utah, 1964-65; asst. prof. U. P.R., Mayaguez, 1970-74, La. State U., 1974-77; assoc. prof. S.D. State U., 1977-81; environ. engr. Atlantic Richfield Subsidiary, Sahuarita, Ariz., 1981-86, Ariz. Dept. Environ. Quality, Phoenix, 1986-88; environ. mgr. Galactic Resources, Del Norte, Colo., 1988-91; v.p. M&E Cons., Inc., Phoenix, 1991-94; pres. Chisholm & Assocs., Phoenix, 1991—; v.p. 3R Resources, Tucson, 1994—; cons. various mfrs., Calif., Tex., Ill., Mex., 1980-91. Contbr. articles to profl. jours. NSF fellow, 1965-66, 68-69. Mem. Am. Soc. Agrl. Engrs. (faculty advisor student chpt. 1978-79), Phi Kappa Phi, Sigma Xi, Alpha Epsilon, Beta Gamma Epsilon. Home: 738 E Joan D Arc Ave Phoenix AZ 85022-5328 Office: Chisholm & Assocs 738 E Joan D Arc Ave Phoenix AZ 85022-5328

CHISHTI, NADEEM AHMAD, physician; b. Faisalabad, Pakistan, Aug. 15, 1961; came to U.S., 1988; s. Mumtaz A. and Zubeda B. (Begum) C.; m. Fazi Tubusam, Jan. 20, 1988 (div. Nov. 1993). Student, Govt. Coll., Pakistan, 1976-78; MD, Punjab Med. Sch., Pakistan, 1985. Rsch. asst. U. Calif. Davis Med. Ctr., Sacramento, 1989-90; intern U. So. Calif. Med. Ctr., L.A., 1990-91, resident, 1991-93, chief resident, 1993-94; fellow U. Calif. Irvine Med. Ctr., Orange, 1994—. Mem. AMA, ACP, Am. Coll. Chest Physicians. Home: 8623 E Canyon Vista Dr Anaheim CA 92808-1621 Office: 101 The City Dr S Orange CA 92668-3201

CHITTICK, ARDEN BOONE, steamship agency executive; b. Sunnyside, Wash., Aug. 5, 1936; s. Herbert Boone and Maude Ellen (George) C.; m. Nina Sorensen, Apr. 16, 1960; children: Kyle, Kirsten. BS, Wash. State U., 1964. Ops. mgr. Kerr Steamship Co. Inc., Seattle, 1979-81, marine mgr. PNW, 1981-84; dist. ops. mgr. Merit Steamship Agy. Inc., Seattle, 1984-86, Pacific N.W. ops. mgr., 1986-87; ops. mgr. Internat. Shipping Co. Inc., Seattle, 1987-89, v.p. ops., 1989-91, regional v.p. ops., 1991—; v.p. Internat. Shipping Co. Inc., Portland, Oreg., 1991—; v.p. Marine Exch. of Puget Sound, Seattle, 1982-88; pres. Puget Sound Steamship Operators Assn., Seattle, 1987, v.p., 1983, 86, 95. Troop com. mem. Boy Scouts Am., Bainbridge Island, Wash., 1984. Capt. USMCR, 1957-64; comdr. USCG, 1964-79. Mem. Puget Sound Coast Guard Officers Assn. (pres. 1978), Propeller Club of U.S. (gov. Seattle chpt. 1984-87, 89—). Republican. Methodist. Home: 8380 NE Blakely Heights Dr Bainbridge Is WA 98110-3200 Office: Internat Shipping Co Inc 1111 3rd Ave Ste 1825 Seattle WA 98101-3207

CHIU, CHU-TSEN, surgeon; b. Tainan, Taiwan, Republic of China, Dec. 19, 1947; came to U.S. 1975; s. Ping-Hong and Li-Chu Chiu; m. Susan Wu, Jan. 10, 1974; 1 child, Alice. MD, Taipei Med. Coll., 1973. Diplomate Am. Bd. Surgery, Am. Bd. Colon and Rectal Surgery. Resident Meth. Hosp., Bklyn., 1976-80; fellow U. Tex. Med. Sch., Houston, 1980-81; pvt. practice surgery Monterey Park, Calif., 1981—; dir. Gen. Bank, L.A., 1985—. Fellow ACS, Am. Soc. Colon and Rectal Surgeons. Office: 500 N Garfield Ave # 311 Monterey Park CA 91754-1242

CHIU, JOHN TANG, physician; b. Macao, Jan. 8, 1938; s. Lan Cheong and Yau Hoon C.; m. Bonnie Doolan, Aug. 28, 1965 (div. Apr. 1986); children: Lisa, Mark, Heather. Student, Harvard U., 1959; BA, U. Vermont, 1960, MD, 1964. Diplomate Am. Bd. Allergy & Immunology. Pres. Allergy Med. Group, Inc., Newport Beach, Calif., 1969-72, 1972—; assoc. clin. prof. medicine U. Calif., Irvine, 1975—. Contbr. articles to profl. jours. Active Santa Ana Heights Adv. Commn., 1982-83; life mem. Orange County Sheriff's Adv. council, 1987—. Recipient Freshman Chem. Achievement award, Am. Chem. Soc., 1958. Fellow Am. Acad. Allergy and Immunology, Am. Coll. Allergy and Immunology, Am. Coll. Chest Physicians (sec. steering com. allergy 1977-81), Orange County Med. Assn. (chmn. communications com. 1985—, communications com.), Newport Med. Plaza Assn. (bd. dirs.). Office: Allergy Med Group Inc 400 Newport Center Dr Newport Beach CA 92660-7601

CHIU, PETER YEE-CHEW, physician; b. China, May 12, 1948; came to U.S., 1965; naturalized, 1973; s. Man Chee and Yiu Ying (Cheng) C. BS, U. Calif., Berkeley, 1969, MPH, 1970, DrPH, 1975; MD, Stanford U., 1983. Diplomate Am. Bd. Family Practice; registered profl. engr., Calif.; registered environ. health specialist, Calif. Asst. civil engr. City of Oakland, Calif., 1970-72; assoc. water quality engr. Bay Area Sewage Services Agy., Berkeley, 1974-76; prin. environ. engr. Assn. Bay Area Govts., Berkeley, 1976-79; intern San Jose (Calif.) Hosp., 1983-84, resident physician, 1984-86; ptnr. Chiu and Crawford, San Jose, 1986-89, Good Samaritan Med. Group, San Jose, 1989-90, The Permanente Med. Group, 1991—; adj. prof. U. San Francisco, 1979-83; clin. asst. prof. Stanford U. Med. Sch., 1987—. Contbr. articles to profl. publs.; co-authored one of the first comprehensive regional environ. mgmt. plans in U.S.; composer, pub. various popular songs Southeast Asia, U.S. mem. Chinese for Affirmative Action, San Francisco, 1975—; bd. dirs. Calif. Regional Water Quality Control Bd.,Oakland, 1979-84, Bay Area Comprehensive Health Planning Coun., San Francisco, 1972-76; mem. Santa Clara County Ctrl. Dem. Com., 1987—; mem. exec. bd. Calif. State Dem. Ctrl. Com.; commr. U.S. Presdl. Commn. on Risk Assessment and Risk Mgmt., Washington, 1993—. Recipient Resident Tchr. award Soc. Tchrs. Family Medicine, 1986, Resolution of Appreciation award Calif. Regional Water Quality Control Bd., 1985. Fellow Am. Acad. Family Physicians; mem. Am. Pub. Health Assn., Chi Epsilon, Tau Beta Pi. Democrat. Office: The Permanente Med Group 770 E Calaveras Blvd Milpitas CA 95035-5491

CHO, DEAN DEUK, computer company executive; b. Teajon, South Korea, Oct. 27, 1963; came to the U.S., 1972; s. Seog Whan and Sahng Chun (Lee) C. BS, U. Calif., Riverside, 1986. Cert. Novell network adminstrn., Calif. Network sys. mgr. Managed Health Network, L.A., 1988-89; programmer analyst Blue Cross, Woodland Hills, Calif., 1989-91; dir. computing Lab. Structural Biology and Molecular Medicine, UCLA, 1991—; pres., owner Advanced Micro Sys., Torrance, Calif., 1988—. Pres., founder Korean Student Assn., U. Calif., Riverside, 1985-86. Recipient Outstanding Alumnus award U. Calif., Riverside, 1992, Svc. award U. Calif., Riverside, 1992. Mem. Asian Pacific Alumni Assn. (pres., founder U. Calif. Riverside 1991—, Svc. award 1992), UCLA Adminstrs. and Suprs. Assn., South Bay Network. Home: 4323 Artesia Blvd Torrance CA 90504-3107 Office: Univ Calif LA 11252 Bunche Hall Los Angeles CA 90024

CHO, LEE-JAY, social scientist, demographer; b. Kyoto, Japan, July 5, 1936; came to U.S., 1959; s. Sam-Soo and Kyung-Doo (Park) C.; m. Eun-Ja Chun, May 20, 1973; children: Yun-Kyong, Sang-Mun, Ham-Jae. BA, Kookmin Coll., Seoul, Korea, 1959; MA in Govt., George Washington U., 1962; MA in Sociology (Population Council fellow), U. Chgo., 1964, PhD in Sociology, 1965; D in Econs. (hon.), Dong-A U., 1982; DSc in Demography, Tokyo U., 1983; D in Econs., Keio U., Tokyo, 1989. Statistician Korean Census Council, 1958-61; research assoc., asst. prof. sociology Population Research and Tng. Center, U. Chgo., 1965-66; asso. dir. Community and Family Study Center, 1969-70; sr. demographic adv. to Malaysian Govt., 1967-69; assoc. prof. U. Hawaii, 1969-73, prof., 1973-78; asst. dir. East-West Population Inst., East-West Center, Honolulu, 1971-74; dir. East-West Population Inst., East-West Center, 1974-92; pres. pro tem East-West Center, 1980-81, v.p., 1987—; cons. in field; mem. Nat. Acad. Scis. Com. on Population and Demography; mem. U.S. 1980 Census Adv. Com., Dept. Commerce. Author: (with others) Differential Current Fertility in the United States, 1970; editor: (with others) Introduction to Censuses of Asia and the Pacific: 1970-74, 1976, (with Kazumasa Kobayashi) Fertility Transition in East Asian Populations, 1979, (with Suharto, McNicoll and Mamas) Population Growth of Indonesia, 1980, The OWN Children of Fertility Estimation, 1986, (with Y.H. Kim) Economic Development of Republic of Korea: A Policy Perspective, 1989, (with Kim) Korea's Political Economy: An Institutional Perspective, 1994, (with Yada) Tradition and Change in the Asian Family, 1994; contbr. numerous articles on population and econ. devel. to profl. jours. Bd. dirs. Planned Parenthood Assn., Hawaii, 1976-77. Ford Found. grantee, 1977-79; Population Council grantee, 1973-75; Dept. Commerce grantee, 1974-78; recipient Award of Mugunghwa-Jang, govt. Republic of Korea, 1992. Mem. Internat. Statis. Inst. (tech. adv. com. World Fertility Survey), Internat. Union Sci. Study Population, Population Assn. Am., Am. Statis. Assn., Am. Sociol. Assn., N.E. Asia Econ. Forum (founding chmn.). Home: 1718 Halekoa Dr Honolulu HI 96821-1027 Office: 1777 East-West Rd Honolulu HI 96848

CHO, SUNG-NEI CHARLES, physician; b. Kaesong, Korea, Nov. 10, 1934; came to U.S., 1954; naturalized, 1967; s. In-Jei and Kum-Sun (Kim) C.; m. Kyung-Jai Lee, Apr. 16, 1959; children: Irene, Wesley. BS magna cum laude, Piedmont Coll., 1957, D of Humanities, 1982; MD, U. Kans., 1962. Diplomate Am. Bd. Family Practice. Intern St. Joseph Hosp., Wichita, Kans., 1962-63, resident in pathology, 1963-64; resident in gen. practice Ventura (Calif.) County Med. Ctr., 1964-66; pvt. practice in family medicine, 1969—; attending and teaching staff family practice residency program Ventura County Med. Ctr., 1966-86, also courtesy staff mem., chmn. dept. family practice, 1976-77; mem. active staff St. John's Regional Med. Ctr., Oxnard, Calif., chmn. dept. ob-gyn., 1975-76, chmn. dept. family practice, 1980-81; pres., CEO Ventura County Ind. Physicians-IPA subs., 1981-93, med. cons. Found. Health, 1993—; founder, CEO Ventura County HMO, 1979-90, also bd. dirs. Bd. trustees Piedmont Coll., Demorest, Ga., 1984—. Lt. comdr. USN, 1967-69. Mem. AMA, Am. Acad. Family Physicians, Am. Acad. Physician Execs., Am. Coll. Occupational and Environ. Medicine, Calif. Med. Assn., Ventura County Med. Soc. (bd. govs. 1973-75, 81-83, treas. 1981-83), Kiwanis (pres. 1989-90). Home: 4372 Clubhouse Dr Somis CA 93066-9708

CHO, ZANG HEE, physics educator; b. Seoul, Korea, July 15, 1936; came to U.S., 1972; p. Byung-Soon Cho and Kang Ae Yu. BSc, Seoul Nat. U., 1960, MSc, 1962; PhD, Uppsala (Sweden) U., 1966. Assoc. prof. Stockholm U., 1971-76, UCLA, 1972-78; prof. Columbia U., N.Y.C., 1979-85, U. Calif., Irvine, 1985—; hon. chair prof. Korea Acad. Indsl. Tech., 1990—; assoc. dir. Imaging Rsch. Ctr., Columbia U., 1979-84; dir. Nucl. Magnetic Resonance rsch. U. Calif., Irvine, 1985—; chmn. symposia in field. Author: Foundation of Medical Imaging, 1993; editor-in-chief Internat. Jour. Imaging Sys. and Tech., 1994—; guest editor IEEE Nucl. Sci., 1974, 84, Computers Medicine and Tech., 1989; edtl. bd. Phys. in Medicine & Biology, Inst. Phys., U.K., 1993, Magnetic Resonance in Medicine, U.S.A., 1984, Computerized Med. Imaging and Graphics, U.S.A., 1989; contbr., author over 200 articles to various refereed internat. sci. jours. Named Disting. Scientist, Asilomar, 1982; recipient Grand Sci. prize Seoul, 1984, Sylvia Sorkin Greenfield award Am. Assn. Med. Physicists, 1989, Nat. Applied Sci. prize Korea Sci. Found., 1995. Fellow IEEE, Inst. Elec. Engring, Third World Acad. Scis.; mem. Korean Acad. Sci. & Tech (life). Home: 29 Harbor Pointe Dr Corona Del Mar CA 92625-1333 Office: Univ Calif Dept Radiological Sci Irvine CA 92717

CHOATE, WAYNE D., protective services official; b. Puerto Rico, Oct. 3, 1953; s. Bobby Dewayne and Jean Arlene (Fagerstedt) C.; m. Cheryl Lee Baldwin, Apr. 11, 1983; children: Bobby Leland, Andrew Wayne. BS in Agrl. Bus., Calif. State U., 1980. Police officer U. Calif., Davis, 1985-89; dep. sheriff County of Sacramento, Calif., 1989—. Dir. Galt (Calif.) Fire Protection Dist., 1991—. With USN, 1974-76. Mem. Theta Chi. Republican. Roman Catholic.

CHOBOTOV, VLADIMIR ALEXANDER, aerospace engineer, educator; b. Zagreb, Yugoslavia, Apr. 2, 1929; came to U.S., 1946; s. Alexander M. and Eugenia I. (Scherbak) C.; m. Lydia M. Kazanovich, June 22, 1957; children: Alexander, Michael. BSME, Pratt Inst., 1951; MSME, Bklyn. Poly. Inst., 1956; PhD, U. So. Calif., 1963. Dynamics engr. Sikorsky Aircraft, Bridgeport, Conn., 1951-53, Republic Aviation, Farmingdale, N.Y., 1953-57, Ramo-Wooldridge, Redondo Beach, Calif., 1957-62; mgr. The Aerospace Corp., El Segundo, Calif., 1962—; adj. prof. Northrop U., L.A., 1982-91; instr. UCLA, 1984—; cons. Univ. Space Rsch. Assn., Washington, 1984-85; ad hoc advisor USAF Sci. Adv. Bd., Washington, 1985-87; cons. NASA Space Sta. Adv. Com., Washington, 1990-91; course leader Space Debris, Washington, 1990-91. Author: Spacecraft Attitude Dynamics and Control, 1991; author, editor: Orbital Mechanics, 1991; contbg. author: Space Based Radar Handbook, 1989, Earth, Sea and Solar System, 1987; contbr. numerous articles and reports to profl. publs. Fellow AIAA (assoc., Achievement award 1993); mem. Internat. Acad. of Astronautics. Office: The Aerospace Corp PO Box 92957 Los Angeles CA 90009-2957

CHOCK, CLIFFORD YET-CHONG, family practice physician; b. Chgo., Oct. 15, 1951; s. Wah Tim and Leatrice (Wong) C. BS in Biology, Purdue U., 1973; MD, U. Hawaii, 1978. Intern in internal medicine Loma Linda (Calif.) Med. Ctr., 1978-79, resident in internal medicine, 1979; resident in internal medicine U. So. Calif.-L.A. County Med. Ctr., L.A., 1980; physician Pettis VA Clinic, Loma Linda, Calif., 1980; pvt. practice Honolulu, 1981—; physician reviewer St. Francis Med. Ctr., Honolulu, 1985—, chmn. peer/credentials family practice care, 1990-93, 95—, chmn. utilization rev., 1990-91, 95—, acting chmn. credentials com., 1992; physician reviewer Peer Rev. Orgn. Hawaii, Honolulu, 1987-93; chmn. dept. family practice St. Francis Med. Ctr., Liliha, 1994—. Mem. Am. Acad. Family Physicians. Office: 321 N Kuakini St Ste 513 Honolulu HI 96817-2361

CHODERA, JERRY, mechanical engineer; b. Medina, Ohio, May 19, 1947; s. Joseph John and Marcella Ellaine (Damon) C.; m. Marie Grace Buonocore, June 29, 1972; children: John Damon, Kristin Ann. BS in Mech. Engring., Case Inst. Tech., 1969; postgrad., U. fla., 1969-70. Registered profl. engr., Calif., Ohio. Apollo launch crew engr. Boeing Atlantic Test Ctr., Cape Canaveral, Fla., 1969-70; sr. plant engr. B. F. Goodrich Co., Akron, Ohio, L.A., 1970-75; sr. project engr. AMF-Tire Equipment Div., Santa Ana, Calif., 1975-78; v.p. Wescal Industries, Rancho Dominguez, Calif., 1978—. Committeeman Boy Scouts of Am., 1988—. Recipient Bausch and Lomb Sci. award, 1965. Mem. ASME, Case Inst. Tech. Alumni Assn., Mensa. Presbyterian. Office: 18033 S Santa Fe Ave East Rancho Dominguez CA 90221

CHODOROW, NANCY JULIA, sociology educator; b. N.Y.C., Jan. 20, 1944; d. Marvin and Leah (Turitz) C.; m. Michael Reich, June 19, 1977; children: Rachel Esther Chodorow-Reich, Gabriel Issac Chodorow-Reich. BA, Radcliffe Coll., 1966; PhD, Brandeis U., 1975; grad., San Francisco Psychoanalytic, 1993. From lectr. to assoc. prof. U. Calif., Santa Cruz, 1974-86; from asst prof. sociology to prof. U. Calif., Berkeley, 1986—; faculty San Francisco Psychoanalytic Inst., 1994—. Author: The Reproduction of Mothering, 1978 (Jessie Bernard award 1979), Feminism and Psychoanalytic Theory, 1989, Femininities, Masculinities, Sexualities, 1994; contbr. articles to profl. jours. Fellow Russell Sage Found., NEH, Ctr. Advanced Study Behavioral Scis., ACLS, Guggenheim fellow. Mem. Am. Sociol. Assn., Am. Psychoanalytic Assn., San Francisco Psychoanalytic Soc. Office: U Calif Dept Sociology Barrows Hall Berkeley CA 94720

CHOI, JAI JOON, scientist, researcher, educator; b. Kyung-Joo, South Korea, Mar. 2, 1958; came to U.S., 1985; s. Byung-Ha and Kun-Sook (Lee) C.; m. Janice Chinki Min, June 23, 1985; children: Laura, Kathryn. BSE, Inha U., Inchon, Korea, 1979, MSE, 1981; MSEE, U. Wash., 1987, PhD in Elec. Engring., 1990. Mem. faculty Korean Air Force Acad., Seoul, 1981-85; sr. prin. scientist Boeing Computer Svcs., Seattle, 1990—; affiliate asst. prof. and grad. faculty U. Wash., Seattle, 1992—; adj. faculty Cogswell Coll. North, Kirkland, Wash., 1991—; cons. Flaw Industry, Kent, Wash., 1988; session chair World Congress on Computational Intelligence, Orlando, Fla., 1994, Internat. Symposium on Circuits and Sys., Seattle, 1995. Northcon Conf., Seattle, 1992. Assoc. editor: Fuzzy Logic Technology and Applications, 1994; contbr. articles to profl. jours.; 3 invention disclosures. Capt. Korean Air Force, 1981-85. Mem. IEEE (mem. tech. program com. Internat. Symposium on Circuits and Systems 1995, assoc. editor Trasn. on Neural Networks 1994), Eta Kappa Nu. Home: 24623 SE 37th St Issaquah WA 98027-6558 Office: Boeing Computer Svcs PO Box 24346 7L-44 Seattle WA 98124

CHOMKO, STEPHEN ALEXANDER, archaeologist; b. Bklyn., Nov. 18, 1948; s. Paul and Lucy Isabella (Bisaccio) C.; m. Leslie M. Howard, Aug. 1972 (div. 1980). BA in Anthropology cum laude, Beloit Coll., 1970; MA in Anthropology, U. Mo., 1976, PhD in Anthropology, 1995. Mem. rsch. staff Nassau County Mus. Natural History, Glen Cove, N.Y., 1969-71; grad. rsch. asst. U. Mo., Columbia, 1972-74, 75-78; rsch. asst. Ill. State Mus., Springfield, 1974-75; dist. archaeologist Bur. Land Mgmt., Rawlins, Wyo., 1978-80; archaeologist Office of Fed. Inspector, Denver, 1980-82; dir. Paleo Environ. Cons., Wheat Ridge, Colo., 1980-86; archaeologist Interagy. Archaeol. Svcs., Denver, 1982-92; chief rsch. and resource mgmt. Mesa Verde (Colo.) Nat. Park, 1992—; chief tng. mgmt. Fort Carson, 1994—. Writer, dir. (video program) Our Past Our Future, 1992; contbr. articles to profl. jours. Grantee Cave Rsch. Found., Yellow Springs, Ohio, 1976; recipient Anthropology Scholarship U. Mo., Columbia, 1978, Quality Performance award Nat. Park Svc., Denver, 1992, 93. Mem. Soc. Am. Archaeology, Am. Anthropol. Assn., Am. Quaternary Assn., Wyo. Assn. Profl. Archaeologists (exec. com. 1979-82), Mont. Archaeol. Soc., Plains Anthropol. Soc. (v.p. 1988-89, bd. dirs. 1986-89). Home: 1144 Rock Creek Canyon Rd Colorado Springs CO 80926-9772 Office: Decam Attn AFZC-ECM-TM Bld 302 Fort Carson CO 80917

CHOMSKY, MARVIN J., director; b. N.Y.C., May 23, 1929. B.S., Syracuse U.; M.A., Stanford U. Dir. films including Evel Knievel, 1971, Murph the Surf, 1974, MacKintosh and T.J., 1975, Good Luck, Miss Wycoff, 1979, Tank, 1983; dir. TV movies Assault on the Wayne, 1971, Mongo's Back in Town, 1971, Family Flight, 1972, Fireball Forward, 1972, Female Artillery, 1973, The Magician, 1973, The FBI Story--Alvin Karpis, 1974, Mrs. Sundance, 1974, Kate McShane, 1975, Victory at Entebbe, 1976, Brink's: The Great Robbery, 1976, Law and Order, 1976, A Matter of Wife...and Death, 1976, Danger in Paradise, 1977, Little Ladies of the Night, 1977, Hollow Image, 1979, Inside Attica, 1980 (Emmy award), King Crab, 1980, I Was a Mail Order Bride, 1982, My Body, My Child, 1982, Nairobi Affair, 1984, Anastasia, 1986, Billionaire Boys Club, 1987, Angel Green, 1987, Telling Secrets, 1992, Hurricane Andrew, 1993; dir. TV mini-series including Attack on Terror, 1975, Roots, 1977, Holocaust, 1978 (Emmy award), Evita Peron, 1981, Inside the Third Reich, 1982 (Emmy award), RFK and His Times, 1985, The Deliberate Stranger, 1986, Peter the Great, 1986 (Emmy award), Brotherhood of the Rose, 1988, Strauss Dynasty, 1990, Catherine the Great, 1994. Office: care Savitsky Satin & Geibelson Ste 1450 1901 Avenue Of The Stars Los Angeles CA 90067-6015

CHOOK, EDWARD KONGYEN, academic administrator, disaster medicine educator; b. Shanghai, China, Apr. 15, 1937; s. Shiu-heng and Shuiking (Shek) C.; m. Ping Ping Chew, Oct. 30, 1973; children by previous marriage: Miranda, Bradman. MD, Nat. Def. Med. Ctr., Taiwan, 1959; MPH, U. Calif., Berkeley, 1964, PhD, 1969; ScD, Phila. Coll. Pharmacy & Sci., 1971; JD, La Salle U., 1994. Assoc. prof. U. Calif., Berkeley, 1966-68; dir. higher edn. Bay Area Bilingual Edn. League, Berkeley, 1970-75; prof., chancellor United U. Am., Oakland and Berkeley, Calif., 1975-84; regional adminstr. U. So. Calif., L.A., 1984-90; provost Armstrong U., Berkeley, Calif., 1994—; vis. prof. Nat. Def. Med. Ctr., Taiwan Armed Forces U., 1982—, Tongji U., Shanghai, 1992—, Foshan U., China, 1992—; founder, pres. United Svc. Coun., Inc., 1971—; pres. Pan Internat. Acad., Changchun, China, San Francisco, 1992—; pres. U.S.-China Gen. Devel. Corp., 1992—; pub. Power News, San Francisco, 1979—; provost Armstrong U., Berkeley, Calif., 1994—; mem. Nat. Acad. Scis./NRC, Washington, 1968-71. Contbr. articles to profl. jours. Trustee Rep. Presdl. Task Force, Washington, 1978—; mem. World Affairs Coun., San Francisco, 1989—; deacon Am. Bapt. Ch.; sr. advisor U.S. Congl. Adv. Bd.; mem. Presdl. Adv. Commn., 1991—; hon. deputy Sec. State Calif., 1990-93; spl. advisor Calif. Sec. State, 1991—. Mem. Rotary (chmn. cm. 1971—).

CHOOLJIAN, LEO, food products executive; b. 1911. Now pres. Chooljian Bros. Packing Co., Inc., Sanger, Calif., 1949—. Office: 3192 S Indianola Ave Sanger CA 93657-9716*

CHOOLJIAN, MEHRAN, food products executive; b. 1918. Now v.p., sec. Chooljian Bros. Packing Co., Inc., Sanger, Calif., 1949—. Office: 3192 S Indianola Ave Sanger CA 93657-9716*

CHOPRA, INDER JIT, physician, endocrinologist; b. Gujranwala, India, Dec. 15, 1939; came to U.S., 1967; s. Kundan Lal and Labhwati (Bagga) C.; m. Usha Prakash, Oct. 16, 1966; children: Sangeeta, Rajesh, Madhu. B of Medicine and BS, All India Inst. Med. Scis., New Delhi, India, 1961, MD, 1965. Intern All India Inst. Med. Scis., New Delhi, 1961-62, clin. resident, 1962-65, registrar in medicine, 1966-67; resident Queens Med. Ctr., Honolulu, 1967-68; fellow in endocrinology Harbor Gen. Campus UCLA Sch. Medicine, 1968-71; asst. prof. of medicine UCLA, 1971-74, assoc. prof., 1974-78, prof., 1978—; mem. VA Merit Review Bd in Endocrinology, 1988-91. Contbr. over 230 rsch. articles, revs. and book chpts. to profl. lit. Recipient Rsch. Career Devel. award, NIH, 1972. Fellow Am. Coll. Physicians; mem. Endocrine Soc. (Ernst Oppenheimer award 1980), Am. Thyroid Assn. (Van Meter-Armour award 1977, Parke-Davis award 1988), Am. Soc. Clin. Investigation, Assn. of Am. Physicians, Western Assn. Physicians, Am. Fed. for Clin. Rsch. Office: UCLA Sch Medicine Ctr for Health Scis 10833 Le Conte Ave Los Angeles CA 90024

CHORLTON, DAVID, writer; b. Spittal-An-Der-Drau, Carinthia, Austria, Feb. 15, 1948; came to U.S., 1978; s. Frederick and Ernestine (Eder) C.; m. Roberta, June 21, 1976. Student, Stockport Sch. of Art, 1966-69. Graphic designer Pifco Co. Ltd., Manchester, Eng., 1969-71, Steinbock & Co., Vienna, Austria, 1971-72, Persil Ges-MBH, Vienna, 1972-75; editor The Current, Phoenix, 1991-93. Author: (poetry books) Outposts, 1994, Forget the Country You Came From, 1992; co-editor: (mag.) The Signal, 1986-92; dir. Alwun House Poetry Series, Phoenix, 1979-83. Bd. dirs. Ariz. Ctr. to Reverse the Arms Race, Phoenix, 1990-92, Ariz. Composers Forum, Phoenix, 1987-89; pres. Phoenix Early Music Soc., 1987-88. Home: 118 W Palm Ln Phoenix AZ 85003-1176

CHOU, CHUNG-KWANG, bio-engineer; b. Chung-King, China, May 11, 1947; came to U.S. 1969, naturalized 1979; s. Chin-Chi and Yu-Lien (Hsiao) C.; m. Grace Wong, June 9, 1973; children: Jeffrey, Angela. BSEE, Nat. Taiwan U., 1968; MSEE, Washington U., St. Louis, 1971; Ph.D., U. Wash., Seattle, 1975. Postdoctoral fellow U. Wash., Seattle, 1976-77, asst. prof., 1977-81, rsch. assoc. prof., 1981-85; rsch. scientist, head biomed. engring. sect., dir. dept. radiation rsch., div. radiation oncology, City of Hope Nat. Med. Ctr., Duarte Calif., 1985—; cons. Nat. Coun. Radiation Protection and Measurement, 1978—, vice chmn., 1989-95, med. tech. policy com., 1995—. Assoc. editor Jour. of Bioelectromagnetics, 1988—; contbr. 130 articles to profl. jours. Served to 2d lt. Army of Taiwan, 1968-69. Recipient Curtis CArl Johnson Meml. award 1995. Fellow IEEE (com. on man and radiation 1990—, standard coordinating com., subcoms. 1979—, ad hoc task force on health care reform 1993—); mem. Internat. Microwave Power Inst. (1st spl. award of decade 1981, Outstanding Paper award 1985), N.Am. Hyperthermia Soc., Bioelectromagnetics Soc. (bd. dirs. 1981-84), Radiation Rsch. Soc., Electromagnetic Acad., Internat. Radio Sci. Union, Commn. K, Sigma Xi, Tau Beta Pi. Mem. Christian Ch. Office: City of Hope Nat Med Ctr Divsn Radiation Oncology Duarte CA 91010

CHOU, TAI-YU, electrical engineer; b. Heng-Chun, Taiwan, China, Apr. 27, 1959; came to U.S., 1987; s. I-Kuan and Kue-Mei (Tseng) C.; m. Chi-Ho Wang, July 26, 1986; 1 child, Robin Meng-Zoo. BSEE, Nat. Cheng-Kung U., Tainan, Taiwan, 1982; MSEE, Nat. Tsing-Hua U., Hsinchu, Taiwan, 1984; PhD, Carnegie Mellon U., 1991. Product and test engr. MOS Electronic Corp., Hsinchu, 1986-87; devel. engr. Ansoft Corp., Pitts., 1991-93; sr. staff engr. LSI Logic Corp., Fremont, Calif., 1993—; conf. session chmn. 1st Internat. Symposium on Microelectronic Package and PCB Tech.; reviewer 1995 IEEE/ACM Design Automation Conf.; spkr. in field. Contbr. articles to profl. jours. Lt. Chinese Navy, 1982-84. Mem. IEEE, Internat. Electronic Packaging Soc., Chinese Inst. Engrs. (electronic packaging and mfg. com. mem. Bay Area chpt. 1993—), Circuit and System Soc., Microwave Technique and Tech. Soc. Home: 2371 Meadowlark Dr Pleasanton CA 94566-3116 Office: LSI Logic Corp 48580 Kato Rd # K-300 Fremont CA 94538-7338

CHOU, YUE HONG, education educator, researcher; b. Taipei, Taiwan, Oct. 14, 1952; came to U.S., 1978; s. Chang Shong and Chin-Lien (Cheng) C.; m. Grace Minn-Chue Liau, Aug. 11, 1978; children: Jason Hsun, Jonathan Wayne. BS, Nat. Taiwan U., Taipei, 1975; MA, Ohio State U., 1979, PhD, 1983. Asst. prof. Northwestern U., Evanston, Ill., 1984-87; assoc. prof. U. Calif., Riverside, 1987—; prin. investigator U.S. Forest Svc., Riverside, 1989—, U.S. Dept. Navy, Riverside, 1990—, So. Calif. Assn. of Govts., L.A., 1990—; co-investigator County of Riverside, 1990—. Contbr. articles to profl. jours. Moderator Internat. Symposium on the Role of Taiwan, L.A., 1988, Enviorn. Systems Rsch. Inst., Palm Springs, Calif., 1990—; invited speaker U.S. Forest Svc., Riverside, 1990—. U.S. Forest Svc. grantee, 1990—, USMC grantee, 1991—, grant Calif. Dept. of Forestry, 1994—, Calif. Dept. of Fish and Game, 1994—. Mem. Am. Assn. Geographers, Am. Congress on Surveying and Mapping, Am. Soc. for Photogrammetry and Remote Sensing, Am. Cartographic Assn., Urban and Regional Info. Systems Assn. Presbyterian. Office: U Calif Earth Scis Dept Riverside CA 92521

CHOW, BILLY YING-JUNG, software development executive; b. Hong Kong, 1956; came to the U.S., 1968; BS in Indsl. Engring. and Ops. Rsch., U. Calif., Berkeley, 1978; MS in Ops. Rsch., Stanford U., 1982. Indsl. engr. Nat. Semiconductor Corp., Santa Clara, Calif., 1978-80; pvt. practice cons. Fremont, Calif., 1980-82; software devel. engr. Consilium, Inc., Palo Alto, Calif., 1982-84; sr. devel. engr. Consilium, Inc., Mountain View, Calif., 1984-86; project mgr. Consilium, Inc., Mountain View, 1986-88, mgr. software devel., 1989-92, dir. software devel., 1992—. Mem. Am. Prodn. and Inventory Control Soc., Calif. Alumni Assn. (life), Phi Beta Kappa, Tau Beta Pi (sec.-treas. U. Calif. Berkeley chpt. 1978), Alpha Pi Mu (pres., v.p. U. Calif. Berkeley chpt. 1978). Republican. Mem. Christian Ch. Office: Consilium Inc 640 Clyde Ct Mountain View CA 94043-2239

CHOW, CHUEN-YEN, engineering educator; b. Nanchang, Jiangsi, China, Dec. 5, 1932; came to U.S., 1956; s. Pan-Tao and Huei-Ching (Yang) C.; m. Julianna H.S. Chen, June 26, 1960; children: Chi Hui, Chi Tu, Chi An. BSME, Nat. Taiwan U., 1954; MS in Aero. Engring., Purdue U., 1958; SM in Aeronautics and Astronautics, MIT, 1961; PhD in Aero. and Astro. Engring., U. Mich., 1964. Asst. prof. U. Notre Dame, Ind., 1965-67, assoc. prof., 1967-68; assoc. prof. U. Colo., Boulder, 1968-76, prof. engring., 1976—; aeronautics curriculum adv. com. USAF Acad., Colorado Springs, Colo., 1980—, disting. vis. prof., 1979-80. Author: An Introduction to Computational Fluid Mechanics, 1979; co-author: Foundations of Aerodynamics, 1986. Fellow AIAA (assoc.); mem. Sigma Xi. Office: Univ of Colorado Dept Aerospace Engring Sci Boulder CO 80309-0429

CHOW, FRANKLIN SZU-CHIEN, obstetrician-gynecologist; b. Hong Kong, Apr. 15, 1956; came to U.S., 1967; s. Walter Wen-Tsao and Jane Ju-Hsien (Tang) C. BS, CCNY, 1977; MD, U. Rochester, 1979. Diplomate Am. Bd. Ob-Gyn. Intern Wilmington (Del.) Med. Ctr., 1979-80, resident in ob-gyn, 1980-83; practice medicine specializing in ob-gyn Vail (Colo.) Valley Med. Ctr., 1983—, chmn. obstetrics com., 1984-85, 86-87, chmn. surg. com., 1987-88, vice chief of staff, 1989-91, chief of staff, 1991-92. Named to Athletic Hall of Fame, CCNY, 1983. Fellow Am. Coll. Ob-Gyn's; mem. AMA, Colo. Med. Soc., Intermountain Med. Soc. (pres. 1985-86), Internat. Fedn. Gynecol. Endoscopists, Am. Assn. Gynecol. Laparoscopists, Gynecologic Laser Soc., Am. Soc. Colposcopy and Cervical Pathology. Home: PO Box 5657 # 6 Persimman Woods Vail CO 81658-5657 Office: Vail Valley Med Ctr 181 W Meadow Dr Ste 600 Vail CO 81657-5058

CHOW, JUDY, library studies educator; b. Taipei, Taiwan, Feb. 13, 1954; came to U.S., 1964; d. Charles and Lucy (Chu) C.; m. Steve Lee, July 3, 1982; children: Andrew Chow Lee, Mike Chow Lee. BA, UCLA, 1975, MLS, 1977. Libr. L.A. County Pub. Libr., 1979-84, L.A. Pub. Libr., 1984-90; faculty mem. L.A. C.C., 1990—. Mem. Calif. Libr. Assn., Faculty Assn. of Calif. C.Cs. Buddhist. Office: LA CC 4800 Freshman Dr Culver City CA 90230-3519

CHOW, WINSTON, engineering research executive; b. San Francisco, Dec. 21, 1946; s. Raymond and Pearl C.; m. Lilly Fah, Aug. 15, 1971; children: Stephen, Kathryn. BSChemE, U. Calif. Berkeley, 1968; MSChemE, Calif. State U., San Jose, 1972; MBA cum laude, Calif. State U., San Francisco, 1985. Registered profl. chem. and mech. engr.; instr.'s credential Calif. Community Coll. Chem. engr. Sondell Sci. Instruments, Inc., Mountain View, Calif., 1971; mem. R & D staff Raychem Corp., Menlo Park, Calif., 1971-72; supervising engr. Bechtel Power Corp., San Francisco, 1972-79; sr. project mgr. water quality and toxic substances control program Electric Power Rsch. Inst., Palo Alto, Calif., 1979-89, program mgr., 1990—. Editor: Hazardous Air Pollutants: State-of-the-Art, 1993; co-author: Water Chlorination, vols. 4, 6; contbr. articles to profl. jours. Pres., CEO Directions, Inc., San Francisco, 1985-86, bd. dirs., 1984-87, chmn. strategic planning com., 1984-85; industry com. Am. Power Conf., 1988—; chmn. Dist. Cen. Com., 1992-94; strategic long-range planning and restructuring com. Sequoia Union H.S. Dist., 1990-93. Recipient Grad. Disting. Achievement award, 1985; Calif. Gov.'s Exec. fellow, 1982-83. Mem. ASME, AIChE (profl. devel. recognition award), NSPE, Calif. Soc. Profl. Engrs. (pres. Golden Gate chpt. 1983-84, v.p. 1982-83, state dir.), Calif. Water Pollution Control Assn., Air and Waste Mgmt. Assn. (mem. electric utility com. 1990—), Calif. State U. Alumni Assn. (bd. dirs., treas. 1989-91), Calif. Alumni Assn., Beta Gamma Sigma. Democrat. Presbyterian. Office: Electric Power Rsch Inst 3412 Hillview Ave Palo Alto CA 94304-1395

CHOWDHARY, SULTAN ALEEM, hematologist, oncologist; b. Punjab, Pakistan, July 15, 1957; came to U.S., 1984; s. Abdul-Rehman and Batool R. Chowdhary; m. Humera Arif, June 4, 1987; children: Hira B., Amal R. BS, U. Punjab, 1976, MBBS, 1981. Diplomate Am. Bd. Internal Medicine and Pathology. House officer Mayo Hosp., Lahore, Pakistan, 1981-82; instr.

dept. anatomy Punjab Med. Coll., Faisalabad, Pakistan, 1983-84; resident in anatomic pathology U. Mass. Med. Ctr., Worcester, 1986-89; resident in internal medicine The Med. Ctr. Ctrl. Mass., Worcester, 1989-92; clin. and rsch. fellow Ariz. Cancer Ctr.-U. Ariz., Tucson, 1992-95; pvt. practice hematology/oncology, 1995—. Mem. ACP, Am. Assn. Cancer Rsch. (assoc.). Office: Cancer Ctr Assocs Inc Ste 620 5959 Harry Hines Blvd Dallas TX 75235

CHOWDHURY, DEBRA COFER, photographer, administrative assistant; b. L.A., Feb. 5, 1961; d. Ruben Lewis and Alma Lee (Smith) Cofer; married, 1988 (div. 1993); 1 child, Devonn Christopher Chowdhury. Student, El Camino Coll., Cerritos Coll., Man Power Trade Sch. Owner, photographer Deco Photography, Hawthorne, Calif., 1981-85; travel photographer Am. Beauty Products Co., Inc., Inglewood, Calif., 1985-87; portrait sales cons., photographer trainee, mgr. trainee, portrait salesperson, photographer May Co. Portrait Studios, Westwood, Calif., 1987-88; order dept. mgr., asst. photographer The Portrait Gallery, Anaheim, Calif., 1988-90; acctg. clk., word processor Truman Van Dyke Co., Hollywood, Calif., 1990—; propr. Deco Photography & Enterprises, Inglewood, 1994—. Active Women's Referral Svc., Inglewood C. of C., 1994—.

CHOWNING, ORR-LYDA BROWN, dietitian; b. Cottage Grove, Oreg., Nov. 30, 1920; d. Fred Harrison and Mary Ann (Bartels) Brown; m. Kenneth Bassett Williams, Oct. 23, 1944 (dec. Mar. 1945); m. Eldon Wayne Chowning, Dec. 31, 1959. BS, Oreg. State Coll., 1943; MA, Columbia U., 1950. Dietetic intern Scripps Metabolic Clinic, LaJolla, Calif., 1944; sr. asst. dietitian Providence Hosp., Portland, Oreg., 1945-49; contact dietitian St. Lukes Hosp., N.Y.C., summer 1949; cafeteria food svc. supr. Met. Life Ins. Co., N.Y.C., 1950-52; set up food svc. and head dietitian McKenzie-Willamette Meml. Hosp., Springfield, Oreg., 1955-59; foods dir. Erb Meml. Student Union, Eugene, Oreg., 1960-63; set up food svc. and head dietitian Cascade Manor Retirement Home, Eugene, 1967-68; owner, operator Veranda Kafe, Inc., Albany, Oreg., 1971-80; owner, operator, sec.-treas. Chownings Adult Foster Home, Albany, 1984—. Contbr. articles to profl. jours. Linn County Women's chmn. Hatfield for Senator Spaghetti Rally, Albany H.S., 1966; food preparation chmn. Yi for You, Mae Yih for State Senate, Albany Lebanon, Sweet Home, 1982; Silver Clover Club sponsor Oreg. 4-H Found., Oreg. State U., Corvallis, 1994. Recipient coll. scholarship Nat. 4-H Food Preparation Contest, Chgo., 1939. Mem. Am. Dietetic Assn. (registered dietitian, gerontol. nutritionist dietetic practice group 1988—), Oreg. Dietetic Assn. (diet therapy chairperson, newsletter editor 1963-64), Willamette Dietetic Assn., Kappa Delta Pi (Kappa chpt.), Mu Beta Beta. Republican. Mem. Disciples of Christ. Home and Office: Chownings Adult Foster Home 4440 Woods Rd NE Albany OR 97321-7353

CHOY, CLEMENT KIN-MAN, research scientist; b. Fukien, China, Aug. 4, 1947; came to U.S., 1970.; s. Yick-Chu and Hui-Keng (Sy) C.; m. Anna K. Chan, Oct. 4, 1975; 1 child, Jennifer. Diploma, Hong Kong Baptist Coll., 1970; MS, Cleve. State U., 1972; PhD, Case Western Reserve U., 1976. Technician Univ. Hosps., Cleve., 1974-76; asst. dir. Gen. Med.Labs, Warrensville, Ohio, 1974-76; tech. staff Procter and Gamble, Cin., 1976-80; scientist Clorox, Pleasanton, Calif., 1980-81, sr. scientist, 1981-82, project leader, 1982-89, sr. rsch. assoc., 1989-93; tech. mgr. Asia Pacific region Clorox Internat. Co., Hong Kong, 1993-94; rsch. assoc. Clorox Tech. Ctr., 1994—. Pres. Chinese Assn. of Greater Cleve., 1972-74. Mem. Am. Chem. Soc., Am. Soc. Oil Chemists, Am. Assn. Clin. Chemists. Home: 1345 Sugarloaf Dr Alamo CA 94507-1238 Office: Clorox Tech Ctr 7200 Johnson Dr Pleasanton CA 94588-8005

CHOY, HERBERT YOUNG CHO, federal judge; b. Makaweli, Kauai, Hawaii, Jan. 6, 1916; s. Doo Wook and Helen (Nahm) C.; m. Dorothy Helen Shular, June 16; 1945. B.A., U. Hawaii, 1938; J.D., Harvard U., 1941. Bar: Hawaii 1941. Law clk. City and County of Honolulu, 1941; assoc. Fong & Miho, 1946; ptnr. Fong Miho & Choy, Honolulu, 1947-57; atty. gen. Ter. of Hawaii, 1957-58; ptnr. Fong, Miho, Choy & Robinson, 1958-71; judge U.S. Ct. Appeals, 9th circuit, Honolulu, 1971—. Trustee Hawaii Loa Coll., 1963-79. Served with Hawaii Territorial Guard, 1941-42, AUS, 1942-46, lt. col. USAR, ret. Decorated Order Civil Merit (Korea), 1973. Fellow Am. Bar Found.; mem. Am., Hawaii bar assns. Office: US Ct Appeals PO Box 50127 Honolulu HI 96850

CHOYKE, GEORGE RAYMOND, safety educator, consultant; b. Ferndale, Mich., July 2, 1929; s. George Francis Choyke and Blanche Marie (Archambeau) Gordon; m. Ruth Marion Whaley, Jan. 8, 1982; children: Kip Noble Hayes, Falene Darby. Student, U. Mich., 1951-54, San Diego State U., 1967-70, U. Calif., La Jolla, 1961-63, 64-65; BS in Liberal Arts, Regents Coll., U. State N.Y., 1994. Spanish interpreter County of San Diego, 1959-67; bus. mgr. Gemstar Co., LaJolla, Calif., 1967-76, bus. owner, 1976-86; educator Nat. Safety Coun., San Diego, 1986-92, Robinsons May Sch., San Diego, 1986—; cons. Automobile Assn. of So. Calif., 1990-94. Contbr. articles to profl. jours. Mem. Rep. Ctrl. Com., San Diego, 1964. With U.S. Army, 1951-54. Bus. scholarship AIESEC, 1968; grantee U. Mich., 1953; recipient Achievement award Nat. Safety Coun., San Diego, 1988. Mem. Am. Numismatic Assn., Clements Libr. of Am. History, Regents Coll. Alumni Assn., Heartland Numismatic Assn., Spinal Cord Soc. (asst. dir. regional 1988—), Mt. Helix Improvement Assn., Numismatic Soc. Mex., S.D. Numismatic Soc. Clubs: U. Mich. Republican. Roman Catholic. Home: 4410 Shade Rd La Mesa CA 91941-6953 Office: Robinson's May Sch 111 W Pomona Blvd Monterey Park CA 91754-7208

CHRISMAN, JAMES JOSEPH, management educator; b. Kansas City, Mo., Oct. 11, 1954; s. James John and Mildred Fay (Nelson) C.; m. Karen Waller, June 11, 1991. AA, Ill. Cen. Coll., 1977; BB, Western Ill. U., 1980; MBA, Bradley U., 1982; PhD, U. Ga., 1986. Machinst WABCO, Peoria, Ill., 1974-78; asst. prof. U. S.C., Columbia, 1986-91; assoc. prof. La. State U., 1991-93; prof. U. Calgary, Can., 1993—; cons. UN Devel. Program, 1989-90, Internat. Civil Aviation Orgn., 1990, La. Lottery Corp., 1992, Assn. Small Bus. Devel. Ctres., 1993—. Assoc. editor Case Rsch. Jour., 1984-87, mem. editl. bd., 1988-94, Case Collection editor McGraw-Hill; assoc. editor Strategic Planning Mgmt., 1987-88; advt. and circulation editor Am. Jour. Small Bus., 1986-88; promotions editor Entrepreneurship Theory and Practice, 1989, mem. editl. bd., 1990-94, editor 1994—; mem. editl. bd. Jour. Small Bus. Mgmt., 1986-87, Jour. Bus. Venturing, 1990—, Jour. Bus. Strategies, 1993—, Acad. Mgmt. Jour., 1994—, Jour. Mgmt., 1995—; ad hoc reviewer Jour. Mgmt. Studies, 1986, 90, Acad. Mgmt. Rev., 1991-92, Acad. Mgmt. Jour., 1991-94, Jour. Internat. Bus. Studies, 1992, 94, 95, Jour. Mgmt., 1993, Jour. Internat. Mgmt., 1993-94, Jour. Bus. Rsch., 1993, 95; contbr. numerous articles to profl. publs., also cases, book revs. and monographs. Fellow U.S. Assn. Small Bus. and Entrepreneurship (competitive papers chmn. 1988, v.p. corp. entrepreneurship 1989, bd. dirs. 1989-93, program chmn. 1991, v.p. rsch. 1992, pres. elect 1993, hon. pres. 1994); mem. N.Am. Case Rsch. Assn. (v.p. publs. 1987, proc. editor 1987, v.p. membership 1988-89), Internat. Coun. Small Bus. (competitive papers chmn. 1988, v.p. programs 1989, dep. program chmn. 1990), Ea. Casewriters Assn. (bd. dirs. 1990), Acad. Mgmt. (exec. com. Entrepreneurship div. 1991-92). Republican. Roman Catholic. Office: U Calgary, Faculty of Mgmt, Calgary, AB Canada T2NIN4

CHRISTENSEN, ALBERT SHERMAN, federal judge; b. Manti, Utah, June 9, 1905; s. Albert H. and Jennie (Snow) C.; m. Lois Bowen, Apr. 4, 1927; children: A. Kent, Karen D., Krege B. Student, Brigham Young U., intermittently 1923-27; J.D., Nat. U., 1931. Bar: D.C. 1932, Utah 1933. Asst. bus. specialist U.S. Dept. Commerce, 1930-32; practiced in Provo, Utah, 1933-42, 45-54; U.S. dist. judge Dist. of Utah, Salt Lake City, 1954—; sr. fed. judge, 1972—; mem. com. on revision laws Jud. Conf. U.S., 1960-68, com. on ct. adminstrn., 1968-75, adv. com. rules of civil procedure, 1972-82, rev. com., 1977-78, jud. ethics com., 1978-82, Temporary Emergency Ct. Appeals, 1972-93; bd. Utah Bar Examiners, 1939-42; chmn. Ad Hoc Com. Am. Inns of Ct. 1983-85. Republican congressional candidate, 1939. Served from lt. to lt. comdr. USNR, 1942-45. Recipient Chmn.'s award Am. Inns of Ct. Found., 1988; Fulbright award Nat. Law Ctr., George Washington U., 1990. Mem. ABA (awarded medal 1990), Utah Bar Assn. (pres. 1951-52, Judge of Yr. award 1977), Utah Jr. Bar Assn. (pres. 1937-38), Utah County Bar Assn. (pres. 1936-37, 47-48). Mem. Ch. Jesus Christ of Latter-day Saints.

CHRISTENSEN, ARNOLD, state senator, electrical contractor; b. Salt Lake City, July 26, 1936; s. Walter A. and Joyce (Pierce) C.; m. Necia Ann Larsen, May 10, 1956; children—Valerie Ann, Cheryl Ann, Kathy Ann, Bruce Arnold. Student, U. Utah, 1954-56; D in Vocat. Tech. (hon.), Utah Tech. Coll., 1986. Mem. Utah Senate, Salt Lake City, 1978—, majority whip, 1980-84, pres., 1985—; owner, pres. Christensen Electric. Leader Boy Scouts Am., Salt Lake City; mem. adv. bd. Utah Symphony; bd. dirs. Cottonwood Hosp., Salt Lake City; leader Latter Day Saints Ch., Salt Lake City. Named Legislator of Yr., Assoc. Builders and Contractors of Utah, 1982. Republican. Home: 891 E 8600 S Sandy UT 84094-1235

CHRISTENSEN, CAROLINE, vocational educator; b. Lehi, Utah, Oct. 5, 1936; d. Byam Heber and Ruth (Gardner) Curtis; m. Marvin Christensen, June 16, 1961; children: Ronald, Roger, Robert, Corlyn, Richard, Chad. BS, Brigham Young U., 1958, MS, 1964. Sec. Brigham Young U., Provo, Utah, 1954-58; instr. bus. Richfield (Utah) High Sch., 1958-61, Sevier Valley Applied Tech. Ctr., Richfield, 1970-92, dept. chairperson, 1988-92. Historian, Sevier Sch. Dist. PTA, 1968, 69; chmn. Heart Fund Dist., 1983, Voting Dist., 1988-90; dist. chmn. Am. Cancer Drive, 1994-95. Mem. Utah Edn. Assn., Am. Vocat. Assn., Utah Vocat. Assn., Nat. Bus. Edn. Utah Bus. Edn. Assn. (sec. 1986-87), NEA, Western Bus. Edn. Assn., Sevier Valley Tech. Tchrs. Assn. (sec. 1971-92, pres. 1986-87), Delta Pi Epsilon (historian), Delta Kappa Gamma (treas. 1975-90, pres. 1990-92, state nominating com. 1993-95, chmn. 95—, state treas. 1993-95), Phi Beta Lambda (advisor 1988-92).

CHRISTENSEN, C(HARLES) LEWIS, real estate developer; b. Laramie, Wyo., June 3, 1936; s. Raymond H. and Elizabeth C. (Cady) C.; m. Sandra Stadheim, June 11, 1960; children: Kim, Brett. BS in Indsl. Engring., U. Wyo., 1959. Mgmt. trainee Gen. Mills, Chgo., 1959, Mountain Bell, Helena, Mont., 1962-63; data communications mgr. Mountain Bell, Phoenix, 1964-66, dist. mktg. mgr., So. Colo., 1970-73; seminar leader AT&T Co., Chgo., 1966-68, mktg. supr., N.Y.C., 1968-70; land planner and developer Village Assocs., Colorado Springs, Colo., 1973, exec. v.p., 1975-77; v.p. Cimarron Corp., Colorado Springs, 1974-75; pres. Lew Christensen & Assocs., Inc.; ptnr., gen. mgr. Briargate Joint Venture, 1977-90; pres. Vintage Communities, Inc. 1982—. Bd. dirs. Pikes Peak council Boy Scouts Am., Citizens Goals, Colo. Council on Econ. Edn., Cheyenne Mountain Zoo, 1987-92; chmn. Colorado Springs Econ. Devel. Coun., 1977, 89 (named Colo. Springs Bus. Citizen of the Yr. 1993). Served with USAF, 1959-62. Mem. Colorado Springs Home Builders Assn. (bd. dirs.), Urban Land Inst., Colorado Springs C. of C. (bd. dirs. chmn. bd.). Republican. Presbyterian. Colorado Springs Country Club (bd. dirs.). Developer of 10,000-acre New Town area, east of USAF Acad., Colorado, 1,000-acre Peregrine planned cmty., south of USAF Acad. Home: 2948 Country Club Dr Colorado Springs CO 80909-1021 Office: Lew Christensen & Assocs Inc 7710 N Union Blvd Colorado Springs CO 80920-4079

CHRISTENSEN, CHRISTINA MARIE, newspaper columnist; b. Lima, Ohio, Feb. 24, 1948; d. Louis Frank Guagenti and Josephine A. (Zerante) Coffman; m. R. Michael Davis, June 24, 1967 (div. Mar. 1981); children: Michael, Gayle; m. Kim Martin Christensen, Dec. 20, 1986. Student, Ohio State U. Writer for women's sect. Lima News, 1966-73, women's editor, 1973-79; copy editor Neighborhood News dept. Dayton (Ohio) Daily News, 1979-83; copy editor combined features dept. Dayton Daily News and Jour. Herald, 1983-86, lifestyle editor, 1986-87; sr. editor Creators Syndicate, Inc., L.A., 1987; freelance writer, 1987-89; copy editor Entertainment dept. Press-Telegram, Long Beach, Calif., 1989, food editor, 1989-94, local columnist, 1994—. Office: Twin Coast Newspapers Inc 604 Pine Ave Long Beach CA 90844-0003

CHRISTENSEN, DAVID EARL, architect; b. Seattle, Sept. 9, 1953; s. Poul and Jette Malka C.; m. Jean Renae Christensen; 1 child, Hannah. Student, Washington State U., 1971-72, Huxley Coll., 1973; BS in Indsl. Design, Western Wash. U., 1975; postgrad., U. Hawaii, 1978, Harvard U., 1985, 95, Urban Land Inst., 1987, 92. Registered architect, Wash. Civil engring. documentation Island County Engrs., 1969-71; constn. documents G.A. Davison Design, Mt. Vernon, Wash., 1971-72; project mgr., designer Stradling & Stewart Architects, 1972-77; project architect Wimberly, Allison, Tong & Goo, 1977-78; ptnr. in charge design Zervas Group Architects, 1978-87; project designer, marketer The Callison Partnership, 1985-87; owner Christensen Design Mgmt., Bellingham, Wash., 1988—; v.p. devel. Trillium Corp., 1990-91; mem. adv. com. Bellingham Internat. Airport; guest lectr. Western Washington U. Bd. dirs. Internat. Cleche, 1994; chmn., land use com. Port of Bellingham. Recipient Commendation award Bellingham Arts Commn., 1985, Excellence award Nat. Assn. Housing & Redevel. Officials, 1986, Nat. Judges Choice award Wolverine Technologies & Architecture Mag., 1992, Retail Store of Yr. award Chainstore Age Exec., 1992-93, Hotel of Yr. award Holiday Inn Worldwide, 1994, Nat. Grand award Best in Am. Remodeling Awards/Adaptive Reuse, 1994. Mem. N.W. AIA (bd. dirs., Merit award 1993, Citation award 1992-93, Honor award 1980, 93), Urban Land Inst., Nat. Assn. Indsl. & Office Parks. Office: Christensen Design Mgmt 1151 Old Marine Dr Bellingham WA 98225

CHRISTENSEN, DAVID WILLIAM, mathematician, engineer; b. San Francisco, Jan. 19, 1937; s. Christopher Drost and Wilma (Hallowell) C.; m. Felicity Ann Bush, Nov. 2, 1963; children: Karen Anne, Paul Thomas. Student, MIT, 1954-58; BA, BS in Math., U. Calif., Santa Barbara, 1960; MIM in Internat. Mgmt. with honors, Am. Grad. Sch., Glendale, Ariz., 1973. Registered profl. engr., Calif. Project engr. North Am. Rockwell, Anaheim, Calif., 1963-70, Litton Ingalls Ships, Pascagoula, Miss., 1970-73; coord. of fin. Sonatrach Oil Co., Algiers, Algeria, 1975-78; revenue cons. Saudi Arabian Bechtel, Jubail, Saudi Arabia, 1978-80; sr. planner Arabian Am. Oil Co., Dhahran, Saudi Arabia, 1980-86; strategic planning and project controls Bechtel Power Corp., San Francisco, 1987—; mem. (from Jubail) Saudi Royal Commn. Com. on Indsl. Devel., Riyadh, Saudi Arabia, 1978-80; lectr. U. Calif., Santa Barbara, 1964. Contbr. articles to profl. publs. Mem. Charcot-Marie-Toothe Assn., Balt., 1987—, Gertrude Herbert Art Inst., Augusta, Ga., 1990—, Jr. C. of C., Santa Barbara, Calif., 1960-64. Recipient Boit prize, 1957. Mem. NSPE (power group 1990), Soc. Am. Mil. Engrs. Republican. Episcopalian. Office: Bechtel Inc 50 Beale St San Francisco CA 94105-1813

CHRISTENSEN, DON M., general contractor, realtor; b. Hinckley, Utah, Jan. 3, 1929; s. Joseph M. and Lula (Payne) C.; m. Arda Jean Warnock, Oct. 8, 1953; children—Jean Larie, Jolene, Mary Kaye, Martin Don, Evan Warnock, Rachel, Glenn Leroy, Ruth Angela. Student agr. Utah State U., 1951-53, student bldg. Brigham Young U., 1955-56. Ptnr. Christensen Bros. Constrn. Co., Salt Lake City, 1956-59; pres. Constrn. Realty, Inc., Salt Lake City, 1959—, Don M. Christensen Constrn. Co., Salt Lake City, 1965—, Bountiful Constrn. Co., Salt Lake City, 1960-65, Advanced Reprodns., Inc., Salt Lake City, 1960-61, Land Investors, Inc., Salt Lake City, 1960-63. Co-author: Yours Can Be a Happy Marriage, 1983, You Can Have Happy Obedient Children, 1989. Co-editor: Precious Testimonies, 1976. Bishop's counselor Ch. of Jesus Christ of Latter Day Saints, Salt Lake City, 1960-66, bishop, 1966-76, high councilman, 1976-85, counselor to stake pres., 1985-91, patriarch, 1992—. Served with U.S. Army, 1954-55. Named Missionary of Yr., Mormon Finland Mission, 1951. Mem. Home Builders Assn. Republican. Home: 1630 Olive Dr Salt Lake City UT 84124-2529 Office: Constrn Realty Inc 345 E 33rd S # D Salt Lake City UT 84115-4110

CHRISTENSEN, DONN WAYNE, insurance executive; b. Atlantic City, Apr. 9, 1941; s. Donald Frazier and Dorothy (Ewing) C.; BS, U. Santa Clara, 1964; m. Marshella Abraham, Jan. 26, 1963 (div.); children: Donn Wayne, Lisa Shawn; m. Mei Ling Fill, June 18, 1976 (div.); m. Susan Kim, Feb. 14, 1987; stepchildren: Don Kim, Stella Kim. West Coast div. mgr. Ford Motor Co., 1964-65; agt. Conn. Mut. Life Ins. Co., 1965-68; pres. Christensen & Jones, Inc., L.A., 1968—; v.p. Rsch. Devel. Systems Inc.; investment advisor SEC, 1985—. Pres. Duarte Community Drug Abuse Coun., 1972-75; pres. Woodlyn Property Owners Assn., 1972-73; mem. L'Ermitage Found., 1985-90, Instl. Rev. Bd. White Meml. Hosp., L.A., 1975—, Friend's Med. Rsch., 1992—. Recipient Man of Yr. award L.A. Gen. Agts. and Mgrs. Assn., numerous. Mem. Nat. Life Underwriters Assn., Calif. State Life Underwriters Assn., Investment Co. Inst. (assoc.), Soc. Pension Actuaries, Foothill Community Concert Assn. (pres. 1970-73). Registered investment advisor, SEC, 1984. Office: 77 N Oak Knoll Ave Ste 101 Pasadena CA 91101-1812

CHRISTENSEN, JOE DAVID, religious organization executive, architect; b. Salt Lake City, Nov. 12, 1950; s. David Christen and Dona Fern Christensen; m. Leslee Joann Cusick, Aug. 16, 1975; children: Emily, Russ, Andrew, Melissa. BArch, U. Oreg., 1977. Registered architect, Oreg., Wash., Idaho. Arch.-in-tng., office mgr. Harrison Fagg & Assocs., Billings, Mont., 1977-79; draftsman Skidmore Owings & Merrill, Portland, Oreg., 1979-80; ins. asst. Bonneville Gen. Agcy., Portland, 1980; owner, arch. Joe D. Christensen—Arch., Portland, 1981-83; area arch. phys. facilities LDS Ch., Boise, Idaho, 1984-85, region mgr. phys. facilities, 1985-87; region mgr. phys. facilities LDS Ch., Salt Lake City, 1987—. Scoutmaster Boy Scouts Am., Boise, 1984-87, Orem, Utah, 1987-88, Centerville, Utah, 1990-93, chmn. troop com., Orem, 1989-90. Home: 2006 N 150 E Centerville UT 84014-1087 Office: LDS Ch Phys Facilities 50 E North Temple Salt Lake City UT 84150

CHRISTENSEN, JOHN STANLEY, management executive; b. Salt Lake City, Aug. 4, 1960; s. Thayer and Sue (Douglas) C.; m. Joan Stevens; children: Rachel, Paige, Michael. BA in Econs., U. Utah, 1984; M of Internat. Mgmt., Am. Grad. Sch. Internat. Mgmt., Glendale, Ariz., 1985. Analyst Electronic Data Systems, Dallas and Washington, 1986-87; v.p. Western Savs., Phoenix, 1987-90, Southwest Savs., Phoenix, 1991-92; sr. cons. Coopers & Lybrand, Phoenix, 1992-93; Phoenix ops. mgr. Sunchase Capital, Phoenix, 1993—. Mem. Ariz. State Deans Bd. of Excellence, Valley Partnership. Mem. Urban Land Inst., Phoenix C. of C.

CHRISTENSEN, JON ALLAN, journalist; b. Northfield, Minn., May 17, 1960; s. Lauritz Christian and Barbara (Sheldon) C.; m. Carson Ann Miller, May 23, 1987; children: Annika Wesley, Lucia Rachel. Student, Stanford U., 1977-81; BA, San Francisco State U., 1985. Pub. affairs co-dir. KZSU-FM, Stanford, Calif., 1981-82; news and features producer KPFA-FM, Berkeley, Calif., 1983-85; news and info. asst. San Francisco State U., 1983-85; news and info. dir. Inst. for Food & Devel. Policy, San Francisco, 1985-87; assoc. editor Pacific News Svc., San Francisco, 1988; Brazil corr. Pacific News Svc., Rio de Janeiro, 1989; western corr. Pacific News Svc., Carson City, Nev., 1990-92; corr. Great Basin High Country News, Carson City, Nev., 1990-92, regional editor Great Basin, 1993—. Contbr. articles to profl. jours. Mem. Soc. Environ. Journalists. Home: 6185 Franktown Rd Carson City NV 89704-8529 Office: High Country News 6185 Franktown Rd Carson City NV 89704-8529

CHRISTENSEN, ROBERT WAYNE, JR., financial and leasing company executive; b. Chester, Calif., Nov. 11, 1948; s. Robert Wayne and Ann (Forsyth) C.; m. Debra Schumann, Dec. 6, 1988; 1 child, Heather. BA with honors, Coll. Gt. Falls, 1976; MBA, U. Puget Sound, 1978. Cert. flight instr. Corp. pilot Buttrey Food Stores, Gt. Falls, Mont., 1972-74; asst. to pres. Pacific Hide & Fur, Gt. Falls, 1974-76; fin. analyst Olympia Brewing Co., Olympia, Wash., 1977; pres., CEO Republic Leasing, Olympia, 1978—; pres. PacWest Fin. Corp., Olympia, 1984—; bd. dirs. Republic Leasing, Olympia, Wash. Independent Bancshares, Olympia, 1982—, PacWest Fin. Corp., Olympia. Trustee CASR Trust, 1993—. Served to sgt. USAF, 1969-72. Mem. Nat. Vehicle Leasing Assn. (bd. dirs. 1978-88, 2d. v.p. 1984, pres. 1986), Western Assn. Equipment Lessors, Western Leasing Conf., Mensa, Rotary (bd. dirs. 1982-89, v.p. 1986-88, pres. 1988-89). Office: Republic Leasing The Republic Bldg PO Box 919 Olympia WA 98507-0919

CHRISTENSEN, STEVEN BRENT, data processing executive; b. Salt Lake City, Feb. 26, 1959; s. Raymond David and Marlene Kay (Manheim) C. BA in Human Resource Devel. cum laude, Brigham Young U., 1983, MLS, 1990. Tng. specialist Am. Express Co., N.Y.C., 1983; mgr. C&J Clark Inc., Orem, Utah, 1984-86; mgr. computer svc. Valcom Computers, Provo, Utah, 1987; cons. Castle Computer Systems, Orem, 1988-91; systems mgr. tech. libr. Dugway (Utah) Proving Ground, 1991—. Vol. asst. Found. Ancient Rsch., Provo, 1987-88. Named one of Outstanding Young Men Am., 1983. Mem. ALA, Spl. Librs. Assn., Am. Soc. Tng. and Devel., Internat. Platform Assn. Republican. Home: 1579 E 8730 S Sandy UT 84093-1550 Office: US Army Dugway Proving Ground Tech Libr AHN JOD-I Dugway UT 84022-5000

CHRISTENSEN, THOMAS CRAIG, engineering executive; b. Visalia, Calif., Feb. 22, 1953; s. Marvin Charlton and Charlotte Marie (Humbarger) C.; m. Elizabeth Monica Macias; children: Tristan James, Trevor John. AA in Auto Tech., Coll. of Sequoias, Visalia, 1977; BS in Mech. Engring., Calif. State Poly. Coll., 1978; MS in Mech. Engring., Stanford U., 1990. Registered mech. engr., safety engr., Calif. Staff engr. Chevron USA, Bakersfield/Concord, Calif., 1978-81; weapons engr. Lawrence Livermore Nat. Lab., Livermore, Calif., 1981-88; devel. engr. Hewlett-Packard, Palo Alto, Calif., 1988-91; owner, prin. San Ramon, Calif., 1990—; cons. Hewlett-Packard Bay Analytical Operation, Palo Alto, 1993—. Mem. ASME, Am. Soc. Safety Engrs., Society Automotive Engrs., Soc. Forensic Engrs. and Scientists. Republican. Home and Office: Thomas C Christensen PE 601 Royal Coach Ct San Ramon CA 94583-5644

CHRISTENSON, ANDREW LEWIS, archaeologist; b. Seattle, Feb. 15, 1950; s. Carl James and Geraldine (Beleu) C. BA in Anthropology, UCLA, 1973, MA in Anthropology, 1976, PhD in Anthropology, 1981. Curator, archaeology Mus. of Cultural History, UCLA, L.A., 1980-83; assoc. scientist So. Ill. Univ., Carbondale, Ill., 1983-87; adj. faculty Prescott (Ariz.) Coll., 1988—; archaeologist CSWTA, Inc., Tuba City, Ariz., 1990-93; archaeology cons. U.S. Army, Washington, 1980, Zuni (N.Mex.) Archaeology Program, 1989-90, Nat. Park Svcs., 1990-93; assoc. editor Western U.S., Bull. of History of Archaeology, 1990—. Co-editor: (book) Modeling Change in Prehistoric Subsistence Economies, 1980; Co-author: (book) Prehistoric Stone Technology on Northern Black Mesa Arizona, 1987; editor: (book) Tracing Archaeology's Past, 1989. Grantee Am. Philosophical Soc., 1985, NEH, 1985, S.W. Pks. and Monuments Assn., 1987. Mem. Soc. for Am. Archaeology (com. on the history of archaeology). Home and Office: 746 Redondo Rd Prescott AZ 86303-3724

CHRISTENSON, CHARLES ELROY, art educator; b. Gary, Ind., Jan. 2, 1942; s. Christian Monroe and Violet May (Kirkland) C.; m. Coral Yvette Demar, Feb. 26, 1966 (div. May 1990); children: Michael Eric, Tessa Diahann, Leah Renee. Student, U. Tex., 1960-63; BFA, San Francisco Art Inst., 1966; MFA, U. Wash., Seattle, 1970. Staff artist Taylor Press, Dallas, 1962-63; freelance artist San Francisco, 1963-64, 65-66; comml. artist The Emporium, San Francisco, 1964-65; art educator U. Wash., 1970-71; art instr. Shoreline C.C., Seattle, 1971-75, North Seattle C.C., Seattle, 1971—; acting chmn. humanities div. North Seattle Community Coll., Seattle, 1978-79, gallery dir., 1977—; advisor art group North Seattle C.C., 1978—; juror Equinox Arts Festival, Everett, Wash., 1981; curator exhbns. Wash. C.C. Humanities Conv., Bellevue, 1986, 87; bd. advisors Noon Star Prodns., Seattle, 1992—; co-owner, tour leader Sketching and Touring Through France, Seattle, 1992—. Writer, illustrator: Simple Crafts for the Village, 1968; author poems. Vol. Am. Peace Corps, Andra Pradesh, India, 1966-68; beef leader Riverview Champs-4-H Club, Everett, 1980-81; coach Snohomish (Wash.) Youth Soccer, 1982-88; mem. Seattle Art Mus. Recipient Beyond War Found. award, 1987, Gov.'s Faculty Recognition award, 1987; Seattle C.C. Dist. grantee, 1988, Fulbright grantee India, 1990—, Indonesia, 1994; named to Humanities Exemplary Status, Wash. C.C. Humanities Assn., 1987. Mem. Wash. C.C. Humanities Assn., Smithsonian Inst., Artist's Trust, Seattle C.C. Fedn. Tchrs. (human div. rep. 1977-78), Nat. Coun. for Social Studies, Nat. Campaign for Freedom Expression, Amnesty Internat. Office: North Seattle CC 9600 College Way N Seattle WA 98103-3514

CHRISTENSON, DANIEL PAUL, biologist, conservationist; b. Montrose, Calif., Apr. 30, 1933; s. Clarence and Cecil Edna (Wells) C.; m. Maxine LaVon Parrish, Feb. 1, 1954 (div. Aug. 1980); children: Paul Daniel, Kenneth James, Glen Roger, Carl Edward, Julie Ann; m. Jennifer Lee Babcock, Jan. 10, 1981. AA, Glendale Coll., 1953; BS, Humboldt State Coll., 1956. Fish hatchery asst. Calif. Dept. Fish and Game, Bishop, 1956-57; from fisheries biologist to assoc. fisheries biologist Calif. Dept. Fish and Game, Fresno, 1957-84; biologist Calif. Dept. Fish and Game, Kernville, 1984—; endangered species coord. Region 4 Calif. Dept. Fish and Game, Fresno, 1978-81; charter mem. Threatened Salmonids Com., Sacramento, 1972—; mgr. Allen South Fork Preserve, Onyx, Calif., 1993—; prin. mgr. Little Kern Golden Trout Recovery Program, 1965—. Co-author: Blunt-nosed Leopard Lizard Recovery Plan, 1980. Founder Golden Valley Ecolog. Soc., Fresno,

1978-82; cmty. theater dir., pres. Kern Valley Players, Kernville, 1988—; conservation advisor Forest Alliance, Kernville, 1986—. Mem. Kern Valley Wildlife Assn. (conservation advisor 1983—), Sequoia Orgn. Llama Ownes (founder, bd. dirs. 1988—). Office: Calif Dept Fish and Game PO Box X 14591 Sierra Way Kernville CA 93238-1276

CHRISTIAENS, CHRIS (BERNARD FRANCIS CHRISTIAENS), financial analyst, state senator; b. Conrad, Mont., Mar. 7, 1940; s. Marcel Jules and Virgie Jeanette (Van Spyk) C. BA in Chemistry, Coll. Gt. Falls, 1962, M in human svcs., 1994. Fin. and ins. mgr. Rice Motors, Gt. Falls, Mont., 1978-84; senator State of Mont., 1983-87, 1991—, majority whip 49th legis., 1985-86; fin. planner Jack Stevens CPA, Gt. Falls, 1984-85; adminstr., fin. analyst Gt. Falls Pre-Release, 1986-92; owner Old Oak Inn-Bed and Breakfast, 1989—. Chmn. Balance of State Pvt. Industry Council, Mont. 1984—; mem. Mont. Human Rights Commn., 1981-84; bd. dirs. St. Thomas Child and Family Ctr., Gt. Falls, 1983—, Coll. Gt. Falls, 1984—, Salvation Army; mem. adv. bd. State Drug and Alcohol Coun., State Mental Health Coun.; bd. dirs., treas. Gt. Falls Community Food Bank, 1984-86; Dem. committeeman, Cascade County, Mont., 1976-82; Mont. del. to Nat. Rules Conv., 1980; pub. chmn. Cascade County chpt. ARC, 1986; mem. adv. bd. Cambridge Court Sr. Citizen Apt. Complex, 1986; bd. dirs. Cascade County Mental Health Assn., 1986—; treas. Cascade County Mental Health Ctr.; vice-chmn. Gov.'s Task Force on Prison Overcrowding; mem. regional jail com.; mem. Re-Leaf Great Falls com., 1989—, mem. steering com. Named one of Outstanding Young Men of Am., Jaycees, 1976; recipient Outstanding Young Alumni award Coll. Gt. Falls, 1979, Hon. Alumni Achievement award 1994. Roman Catholic. Clubs: Gt. Falls Ski, Toastmasters. Lodge: Optimists. Home and Office: Old Oak Inn Bed & Breakfast 709 4th Ave N Great Falls MT 59401-1509

CHRISTIAN, ANN SEGER, lawyer; b. Waterloo, Iowa, Oct. 11, 1954; d. David Edmund and Dorothy Ann (Reinhart) Seger; m. Thomas Embree Christian, July 21, 1978. BA in Social Work, U. Iowa, 1976, JD magna cum laude, 1980. Bar: Oreg. 1981. Worker income maintenance Iowa Dept. of Welfare, Cedar Rapids, 1976-77; assoc. Multnomah Defenders, Inc., Portland, Oreg., 1982-86, asst. dir., 1986-88; dir. Indigent Def. Svcs. divsn. Office of State Ct. Adminstrn., Salem, Oreg., 1988—. Bd. dirs. Vancouver (Wash.) Humane Soc., 1988-89. Mem. Oreg. Bar Assn., Phi Beta Kappa.

CHRISTIAN, ROLAND CARL (BUD CHRISTIAN), retired English and speech communications educator; b. LaSalle, Colo., June 7, 1938; s. Roland Clyde and Ethel Mae (Lattimer) C.; m. Joyce Ann Kincel, Feb. 15, 1959; children: Kathleen Marie, Kristine May Sweet. BA in English and Speech, U. No. Colo., 1962, MA, 1966. Cert. tchr., N.Y., Colo. Tchr. Southside Jr. High Sch., Rockeville Ctr., N.Y., 1962-63, Plateau Valley High Sch., Collbran, Colo., 1963-67; prof. English Northeastern Jr. Coll., Sterling, Colo., 1967-93, prof. emeritus, 1993—; presenter seminars, workshops, Sterling, 1967—; emcee/host Town Meeting of Am., Sterling, 1976. Author: Be Bright! Be Brief! Be Gone! A Speaker's Guide, 1983, Potpourrivia, A Digest of Curious Words, Phrases and Trivial Information, 1986, Nicknames in Sports: A Quiz book, 1986; lit. adv. New Voices mag., 1983—; contbr. Ways We Write, 1964, The Family Treasury of Great Poems, 1982, Our Twentieth Century's Greatest Poems, 1982, Anti-War Poems; vol. II, 1985, Impressions, 1986, World Poetry Anthology, 1986, American Poetry Anthology, 1986, Chasing Rainbows, 1988, The Poetry of Life, 1988, Hearts on Fire, 1988, Wide Open Magazine, 1986, 87, 88; columnist South Platte Sentinel, 1988—. Served with U.S. Army, 1956-59. Recipient Colo. Recognition of Merit scholarship, 1956, Merit cert. Poets Anonymous, 1983, Award of Merit (9), 1985, 86, Golden Poet of Yr. award World of Poetry Press, 1985, 86, 87, 88, Joel Mack Tchr. of Yr. award Northeastern Jr. Coll., 1986; Jr. Coll. Found. grantee, 1986, 87. Mem. NEA, AAUP, Jr. Coll. Faculty Assn. (sec./treas. 1970-72), Colo. Edn. Assn., Nat. Council Tchrs. of English, Poets of Foothills. Roman Catholic. Home: 1027 Park St Sterling CO 80751-3753

CHRISTIAN, SUZANNE HALL, financial planner; b. Hollywood, Calif., Apr. 28, 1935; d. Peirson M. and Gertrude (Engel) Hall; children: Colleen, Carolyn, Claudia, Cynthia. BA, UCLA, 1956; MA, Redlands U., 1979; cert. in fin. planning, U. So. Calif., 1986. CFP. Instr. L.A. City Schs., 1958-59; instr. Claremont (Calif.) Unified Schs., 1972-84, dept. chair, 1981-84; fin. planner Waddell & Reed, Upland, Calif., 1982—, sr. account exec., 1986; corp. mem. Pilgrim Place Found., Claremont; lectr. on fin., estate and tax planning for civic and profl. groups. Author: Strands in Composition, 1979; host Money Talks with Suzanne Christian on local TV cable, 1993—. Mem. legal and estate planning com. Am. Cancer Soc., 1988—; profl. adv. com. YWCA-Inland Empire, 1987; treas. Fine Arts Scripps Coll., 1993-94. Mem. Inst. CFP's, Internat. Assn. Fin. Planners, Pllanned Giving Roundtable, Estate Planning Coun. Pomona Valley, Claremont C. of C. (pres., bd. dirs. 1994-95), Curtain Raisers Club Garrison (pres. 1972-75), Circle of Champions (president's coun. 1994-95, Silver Crest award 1985-87, 94, 95), Rotary, Kappa Kappa Gamma (pres. 1970-74). Home: PO Box 1237 Claremont CA 91711-1237 Office: Waddell & Reed 1317 W Foothill Blvd Ste 222 Upland CA 91786-3673

CHRISTIANSEN, ERIC ALAN, software development executive; b. Salt Lake City, May 14, 1958; s. Don Parley and Lilian Patricia (Clegg) C.; m. April Gay Willes, Jan. 9, 1988; children: Amber, Carly. BS in Computer Sci., West Coast U., L.A., 1981. Software engr. Lear Siegler Astronics, Santa Monica, Calif., 1980-82; sr. software specialist Digital Equipment Corp., Culver City, Calif., 1982-83; software cons. L.A., 1983-84; v.p. Mindcode Devel. Corp., Salt Lake City, 1984-85; software cons. Van Nuys, Calif., 1985-89; sr. software engr. ITT Gilfillan, Van Nuys, 1989-90; prin. Wells Fargo Nikkop Investment Advisors, San Francisco, 1990—; strategic advisor Tri-Pacific Cons. Corp., Alameda, Calif., 1991-93; guest lectr. George Mason U. and Joint Tactical Command, Control, and Comm. Agy., 1991; mem. rsch. team devel. quantitive stock market investment model. Developer (comml. software program) Structurer preprocessor enhancing command interface and language for VAX/VMS, 1989; contbr. articles to profl. jours. Sunday sch. tchr. Ch. of LDS, Concord, Calif., 1992. Mem. IEEE, Assn. for Computing Machinery, Digital Equipment Computer Users Soc. (local user group bd. 1988-90). Republican. Office: Wells Fargo Nikko Investment Advisors 45 Fremont St San Francisco CA 94105

CHRISTIANSON, LISA, biomedical researcher; b. 1966. Student, Naruto (Japan) U., 1987-89. With Otuska Pharm. Co. Ltd., Tokushima, Japan, 1989-90; sec. Oncomembrane Inc., Seattle, 1987-89. Office: Oncomembrane Inc 1201 3rd Ave Ste 3010 Seattle WA 98101-3000*

CHRISTIANSON, ROGER GORDON, biology educator; b. Santa Monica, Calif., Oct. 31, 1947; s. Kyle C. and Ruby (Parker) C.; m. Angela Diane Rey, Mar. 3, 1967; children: Lisa Marie, David Scott, Stephen Peter. BA in Cell and Organismal Biology, U. Calif., Santa Barbara, 1969, MA in Biology, 1971, PhD in Biology, 1976. Faculty assoc. U. Calif., Santa Barbara, 1973-79, staff rsch. assoc., 1979-80; asst. prof. So. Oreg. State Coll., Ashland, 1980-85, assoc. prof., 1985-93, prof., 1993—; coord. gen. biology program So. Oreg. State Coll., 1980—; instr. U. Calif., Santa Barbara, summers 1976, 78, 80. Contbr. articles to profl. jours. Active Oreg. Shakespeare Festival Assn., Ashland, 1983-87; mem. bikeway com. Ashland City Coun., 1986-88; coord. youth program 1st Bapt. Ch., Ashland, 1981-85, mem. ch. life commn., 1982-88, mem. outreach com., 1994, 95; organizer Bike Oreg., 1982-92, Frontline staff, 1985—, Mex. Orphanage short-term mission work, 19886—, bd. deacons, 1993—; ofcl. photographer Ashland H.S. Booster Club, 1987-92; youth leader jr. and sr. h.s. students Grace Ch., Santa Barbara, Calif., 1973-80. Mem. AAAS (chair Pacific divsn. edn.s ect. 1985—, coun. mem. Pacific divsn. edn. sect. 1985—, coun. mem. Pacific divsn.1985—), Am. Mus. natural History, Oreg. Sci. Tchrs. Assn., Assn. for Biology Lab. Edn., Beta Beta Beta, Sigma Xi. Republican. Home: 430 Reiten Dr Ashland OR 97520-9724 Office: So Oreg State Coll Dept Biology 1250 Siskiyou Blvd Ashland OR 97520-5010

CHRISTIE, BRADLEY SCOTT, mental health services professional; b. Tacoma, Wash., May 20, 1964; s. Bradley Ralph and Carol Ann (DeTienne) C.; m. Cinda Marie Reimer, May 31, 1986; children: Benjamin Scott, Rebecca Marie, Elena Danielle. BS, U. Nev., 1988, MA, 1991. Cert. marriage and family therapist, Nev. Cert. drug/alcohol counselor, Nev. Cert. gambling addiction specialist, Oreg. Exec. dir. Hands & Hearts to the World, Reno, Nev., 1986-89; marriage/family therapist Reno, 1991-94; clin. dir. Suicide Prevention/Crisis Call Ctr., Reno, 1992-94; mental health specialist Jackson County HHS, Medford, Oreg., 1994—; spkr. gambling, marriage/family issues, 1992—. Mem. Am. Counseling Assn., Phi Kappa Phi. Home: 2468 Springbrook Rd Medford OR 97504-1716 Office: Jackson County Mental Health 1005 E Main Medford OR 97504

CHRISTIE, HANS FREDERICK, retired utility company subsidiaries executive, consultant; b. Alhambra, Calif., July 10, 1933; s. Andreas B. and Sigrid (Falk-Jorgensen) C.; m. Susan Earley, June 14, 1957; children: Brenda Lynn, Laura Jean. BS in Fin., U. So. Calif., 1957, MBA, 1964. Treas. So. Calif. Edison Co., Rosemead, 1970-75, v.p., 1975-76, sr. v.p., 1976-80, exec. v.p., 1980-84, pres., dir., 1984-87; pres., chief exec. officer The Mission Group (non-utility subs. SCE Corp.), Seal Beach, Calif., 1987-89, ret., 1989, cons., 1989—; bd. dirs. Gt. Western Fin. Corp., L.A., Ducommun Inc., L.A., Southwest Water Co., L.A., Untramar Corp., N.Y., Am. Mut. Fund, Inc., Am. Variable Ins., I.H.O.P. Corp., AECom Tech., L.A., Internat. House of Pancakes, Inc., Smallcap World Fund, L.A., Bond Fund Am., Inc., L.A., Tax-Exempt Bond Fund Am., L.A., Ltd. Term Tax-Exempt Bond Fund Am., Am. High Income Mcpl. Bond Fund, Capital Income Builder, L.A., Capital World Bond Fund, L.A., Capital World Growth Fund, Capital World Growth and Income Fund, Intermediate Bond Fund Am., L.A., Intermediate Tax-Exepmt Bond Fund Am., Capital World Growth 2d Income Fund, L.A.; trustee Cash Mgmt. Trust Am., New Economy Fund, L.A., Am. Funds Income Series, L.A., The Am. Funds Tax-Exempt Series II, Am. High Income Trust, L.A., Am. High Inc Mun. Board Fund, Am. Variable Ins. Trust, U.S. Treasury Fund Am., L.A. Trustee Occidental Coll., L.A.; pres. Nat. History Mus. L.A. County; bd. councillor sch. pub. adminstrn. U. So. Calif. With U.S. Army, 1953-55. Named Outstanding mem. Arthritis Found., L.A., 1975, Outstanding Trustee, Multiple Sclerosis Soc. So. Calif., 1979. Mem. Pacific Coast Elec. Assn. (bd. dirs. 1981-87, treas. 1975-87), L.A. C. of C. (bd. dirs. 1983-87), Calif. Club. Republican. Home: 548 Paseo Del Mar Palos Verdes Estates CA 90274 Office: PO Box 144 Palos Verdes Estates CA 90274

CHRISTMAN, ALBERT BERNARD, historian; b. Colorado Springs, Colo., May 18, 1923; s. James S. and Olga Emelia (Nelson) C.; m. Kate Gresham, July 1945 (div. July 1952); 1 child, Lloyd James; m. Jean Stewart, Apr. 4, 1954 (dec. Sept. 1984); children: Neil Stewart, Laura Elizabeth. BA, U. Mo., 1949, BJ, 1950; MA, Calif. State U., Dominguez Hills, 1982. Reporter Comml. Leader, North Little Rock, 1950-51; tech. editor, writer Naval Ordnance Test Sta., China Lake, Calif., 1951-55, head presentation divsn., 1956-63; historian, info. specialist Naval Weapons Ctr., China Lake, Calif., 1963-72, head pubs., 1973-79; historian Navy Labs., San Diego, 1979-82; freelance historian, writer San Marcos, Calif., 1982—. Author: Sailors, Scientists and Rockets, 1971, Naval Innovators, 1776-1900, 1989; co-author: Grand Experiment at Inyokern, 1979; contbr. articles to profl. jours. Founding mem. Red Rock Canyon State Park Adv. Com., Tehachapi, Calif., 1969-74. Pvt. U.S. Army, 1942-45; maj. USAFR, ret. Recipient Robert H. Goddard Meml. award nat. Space, 1972, Superior Civilian Svc. award Dept. of The Navy, 1982, Helen Hawkins Meml. Rsch. grant, 1994. Mem. Matarango Mus. (trustee-sec. 1973-76), Naval Hist. Found., USN Inst., OX-5 Aviation Pioneers, Smithsonian Inst. (assoc.). Democrat. Unitarian. Home and Office: 1711 Birchwood Dr San Marcos CA 92069-9609

CHRISTMAN, HELEN DOROTHY NELSON, resort executive; b. Denver, Nov. 25, 1922; d. Hector C. and Dorothy C. (Hansen) Russell; m. James Ray Christman, Aug. 7, 1942 (dec. June 1986); children: J. Randol, Linda Rae. Student, Colo. U., 1940-42. Producer Sta. KRMA-TV, Denver, 1960-62; resident mgr. Mana Kai Maui, Maui, Hawaii, 1974-76, exec. coord., 1976-78; pres. Resort Apts., Inc., 1986—; bd. dirs. Kihei Cmty. Assn. Pres. Stephen Knight PTA, Denver, 1957; radio and TV chmn. Colo. PTA, 1958-59; producer ednl. TV programs for PTA, Denver County, 1960-61; bd. dirs. Maui United Way, 1983—, Am. Lung Assn., chmn. Maui sect., 1995—, Hawaii State bd., 1995—; precinct pres. Maui Reps.; chmn. Maui County Rep. Com., 1989-91; mem. adv. bd. State of Hawaii Reapportionment Com., Maui, 1991—; bd. dirs. Hale Makua Found., 1994—. Mem. Delta Delta Delta, Women's Golf Club (chmn. Silverswood chpt.), Maui Country Club (chmn. women's golf assn. 1987), Waiehu Women's Golf Assn. (pres. 1992-93), Maui Liquor Commn. Address: 3448 Hookipa Pl Kihei HI 96753-9216

CHRISTOPHER, LEE NEIL, investment company executive, author; b. Hartwell, Ga., June 14, 1940; d. Neil and Ressie Mae (Locke) C.; m. Allen Hermann, May 19, 1979; children: Miriam, Mary, Neil, Scott. BA, Loretto (Colo.) Heights Coll., 1962; MEd, Tulane U., 1980; MFA in Poetry and Prose, Naropa Inst., 1993. V.p. So. Small Bus. Investment Co., Inc., New Orleans, 1962—, Fidelity Band & Mktg. Co. Inc., New Orleans, 1962—; tchr. Barnes Bus. Coll., Denver, 1984-85, 89-91; prof. English Metropolitan State Coll. Denver, 1994—. Author: Sonnets for a Sunday Afternoon, 1992, A Workshop With Anne, 1992, Experiments, 1992, Apollinaire Inspirations, 1992, Translations, Apollinaire a Beginning, 1992; co-editor: Bombay Gin, 1993, Hyena, 1994—; assoc. editor: The New Censorship, 1993—; contbr. articles to profl. jours. Mem. Assn. Retarded Citizens, Nat. Writers Assn.

CHRISTY, THOMAS PATRICK, human resources executive, educator; b. Urbana, Ill., May 18, 1943; s. Edward Michael and Iona Theresa (Rogers) C.; m. Marjorie Anne McIntyre, June 1966 (div. May 1973); children: Thomas Patrick Jr., Derek Edward; m. Sandra Allen Stern, May 19, 1984 (div. Mar. 1995); children: Patrick Edward, Margaret Allen. BA in Psychology, Adams State Coll., 1965. Tchr. Colorado Springs Pub. Sch., 1965-69; regional personnel dir. Forest Service USDA, Washington, 1969-81; sr. account exec. Mgmt. Recruiters Inc., Costa Mesa, Calif., 1981-84; v.p. Coleman & Assoc. Inc., Santa Monica, Calif., 1984; asst. v.p. Union Bank, Los Angeles, 1984-88; v.p., human resources dir. TOPA Savs. Bank, Los Angeles, 1988-89, Cenfed Bank, Pasadena, Calif., 1989-91; v.p., regional human resources mgr., nat. dir. tng. Tokio Marine Mgmt., Inc., Pasadena, 1991-94; assoc. prof. Coll. Bus. Mgmt., Northrop U., L.A., 1985-91; adj. prof. Coll. Bus. Mgmt., UCLA, 1991—; bd. dirs. Human Resources Mgmt. Inst., L.A. (pres. 1994—); mem. editorial rev. bd. Calif. Labor Letter, L.A. Arbitrator Bus. and Consumer Arbitrator program Better Bus. Bur., Los Angeles and Orange County; mem. Calif. Lincoln Clubs. Mem. AAUP, Pers. and Indsl. Rels. Assn. (pres.), Soc. Human Resources Mgmt. (Calif. state legis. affairs dir.), Employment Mgmt. Assn., Soc. Profls. in Dispute Resolution, The Employers Group (bd. dirs.), Am. Compensation Assn., Japanese Am. Soc. So. Calif., Adams State Coll. Alumni Assn. (Calif. state pres.), Town Hall Calif., Valley Hunt Club, L.A. Athletic Club, Beach Club, Sigma Pi Alumni Assn. Episcopalian. Home: 2275 Huntington Dr # 131 San Marino CA 91108-2640 Office: UCLA Coll Bus & Mgmt 2275 Huntington Dr Ste 330 San Marino CA 91108

CHRITTON, GEORGE A., film producer; b. Chgo., Feb. 25, 1933; s. George A. and Dorothea (Goergens) C.; m. Martha Gilman, Aug. 26, 1956 (div. May 26, 1978); children: Stewart, Andrew, Douglas, Laura, Neil, Lyle. BA, Occidental Coll., 1955; postgrad., Princeton U., 1955-57. With CIA & various U.S. govt. agys., 1960-89; gen. ptnr. Margeo Investment Co., L.A., 1963-76; pres. Wildacre Prodns., Inc., L.A., 1990—; pres., CEO Fin. Svcs. Bancorp, Reno, 1990—; pres. Sycamore Prodns. Ltd., Nev. and Calif., 1994—. Mem. Am. Fgn. Svc. Assn., Washington, 1960—; chmn. bd. Neighborhood Learning Ctr., Capitol Hill, Washington, 1985-87; vol. Options House, Hollywood, Calif.; vol. coord. Rebuild L.A. Maj. USAF, 1957-60. Named Princeton Nat. Fellow, 1955-56, Vis. Fellow & Lectr. U. Calif., 1987-88. Mem. AFTRA, Am. Film Inst., Nat. Assn. Ind. Film & T.V. Prodrs., Phi Beta Kappa, Phi Gamma Delta, Alpha Mu Gamma, Alpha Phi Gamma, Princeton Club (So. Calif.). Office: Wildacre Prodns Inc PO Box 719 Beverly Hills CA 90213-0719

CHRYSTAL, WILLIAM GEORGE, minister; b. Seattle, May 22, 1947; s. Francis Homer and Marjorie Isabell (Daubert) C.; m. Mary Francis King, Aug. 24, 1970; children: Shelley, Sarah, John, Philip. BA, U. Wash., 1969, MEd, 1970; MDiv, Eden Theol. Sem., 1978; MA, Johns Hopkins U., 1984. Ordained to ministry, United Ch. of Christ, 1977. Learning resources specialist Seattle C.C. Dist., 1970-71; dir. learning resources ctr. Whatcom C.C., Ferndale, Wash., 1971-73; minister St. Peter's United Ch. of Christ, Granite City, Ill., 1978-79; sr. minister 1st Congl. Ch., Stockton, Calif., 1979-83; minister Trinity United Ch. of Christ, Adamstown, Md., 1983-85; sr. minister Edwards Congl. Ch., Northampton, Mass., 1985-86, 1st Congl. Ch., Reno, Nev., 1991—; hosp. chaplain Washoe Med. Ctr., Reno, 1993—. Author: Young Reinhold Niebuhr: His Early Writings, 1911-1931, 1977, 2d edit., 1982, A Father's Mantle: The Legacy of Gustav Niebuhr, 1982, The Fellowship of Prayer, 1987; author monographs; contbr. articles to profl. jours. V.p. Reno-Sparks Met. Ministry, Reno, 1994—; Chautauqua scholar Great Basin Chautauqua, Reno, 1993, 94. Lt. comdr. USN, 1986-91, maj. Nev. Army N.G., 1992—. Decorated Meritorious Svc. medal. Mem. Am. Soc. Ch. History, Nev. Soc. Mayflower Descs. (gov.), Am. Legion, Disabled Vets. (life). Home: 3820 Bluebird Cir Reno NV 89509-5601 Office: 1st Congl Ch 627 Sunnyside Dr Reno NV 89503-3515

CHRYSTIE, THOMAS LUDLOW, investor; b. N.Y.C., May 24, 1933; s. Thomas Witter and Helen (Duell) C.; m. Eliza S. Balis, June 9, 1955; children: Alice B., Helen S., Adden B., James MacD. BA, Columbia U., 1955; MBA, NYU, 1960. With Merrill Lynch, Pierce, Fenner & Smith, Inc., N.Y.C., 1955-75, dir. investment banking div., 1970-75; sr. v.p. Merrill Lynch & Co., 1975-78, chief fin. officer, 1976-78; chmn. Merrill Lynch White Weld Capital Markets Group, 1978-81, Merrill Lynch Capital Resources, 1981-83; adv. on strategy Merrill Lynch & Co. Inc., 1983-88; pvt. investor Jackson, Wyo., 1988—; bd. dirs. Consumer Portfolio Svcs., Inc., Titanium Industries, Eeonyx corp. Trustee emeritus Columbia U.; trustee Presbyn. Hosp., Nat. Wildlife Art Mus., Middleton Place Found. Capt. USAF, 1955-58. Mem. Down Town Assn., N.Y. Athletic Club. Home and Office: PO Box 640 Wilson WY 83014

CHU, ALLEN YUM-CHING, automation company executive, systems consultant; b. Hong Kong, June 19, 1951; arrived in Can., 1972; s. Luke King-Sang and Kim Kam (Lee) C.; m. Janny Chu-Jen Tu, Feb. 27, 1993. BSc in Computer Sci., U. B.C., Vancouver, Can., 1977; BA in Econs., U. Alta., Edmonton, Can., 1986. Rsch. asst. dept. neuropsychology and rsch. Alta. Hosp., Edmonton, 1977-78; systems analyst dept. agr. Govt. of Alta., Edmonton, 1978-81; systems analyst for computing resources City of Edmonton, 1981-86; pres. ANO Automation Inc., Vancouver, 1986-92; v.p., bd. dirs. ANNOVA Bus. Group, Inc., Can., 1993—. Mem. IEEE Computer Soc., N.Y. Acad. Sci. Office: ANO Automation Inc, 380 W 2d Ave 2d Flr, Vancouver, BC Canada V5Y 1C8

CHU, CHRISTOPHER KAR FAI, graphic designer; b. Hong Kong, July 20, 1955; came to U.S., 1957; s. Joseph K. Woo and Marion Sui Sin Pau; m. Faye Allison Mark, July 30, 1988; children: Bethany Joy, Hannah Lynne. AA, City Coll. San Francisco, 1981; BS, San Jose State U., 1984. Journeyman clk. Safeway Stores, Inc., San Francisco, 1974-85; creative dir. Neumeier Design Team, Palo Alto, Calif., 1985—. Recipient Silver award, Murphy awards, 1987, certificate of Distinction, N.Y. Creativity Show, 1988, 89, 90, 91, 92, 93, 94, 95, award of Excellence, Print Regional Design Ann., 1988, 91, 92, 93, Print Computer Art & Design Ann., 1991, 92, 93, Distinctive Merit award, N.Y. Art Dirs. Club, cert. of Design Excellence, Print Mag., award of Merit Brit. Designers & Art Dirs., and others. Home: 868 Boardwalk Pl Redwood City CA 94065 Office: Neumeier Design Team 120 Hawthorne Ave Ste 102 Palo Alto CA 94301-2742

CHU, ESTHER BRINEY, retired history educator; b. Bluff City, Ill., Jan. 27, 1911; d. John and Charlotte (Shaw) Briney; m. H.T. Chu, Apr. 19, 1935 (dec. May 1983); children: David S.C., Edna S.C., George S.T. BA, U. Ill., 1935, MA, 1936; PhD, Northwestern U., 1942. Prof. history Hunter Coll., N.Y.C., 1943-45, 55-58; prof. history Jersey City (N.J.) State Coll., 1959-75, prof. emeritus, 1976; pres., faculty assoc. day coun., exec. com. Jersey City State Coll., 1960-75; founder Can. studies program, New Jersey Colls. Author: Briney Families, 1976, Briney Patriots Pioneers and Families, 1979, Briney Families Coast to Coast, 1989. Past pres. YWCA, Mt. Vernon, N.Y.; bd. dirs. Pilgrim Place, Claremont, Calif., 1984-92; chmn. Young People's Dem. Club, Schuyler County, Ill., 1932-33, UN Women's Guild, Westchester County, N.Y., 1951-60. Named Outstanding Educator of Am., 1971, Ill. Coll. scholar, 1931; Northwestern U. fellow, 1938. Mem. Am. Hist. Assn. (life), AAUP (pres. coll. chpt. 1970-72, nat. com. W 1972-75), AAUW, Assn. Can. Studies in U.S., LWV (pres. 1982-83), Phi Alpha Theta. Democrat. Episcopalian. Home: 2734 Mountain View Dr La Verne CA 91750-4312

CHU, JULIA NEE, artist; b. Shanghai, China, Dec. 10, 1943; came to U.S., 1960; d. James and Chu-Non (Yang) Nee; m. Wesley W.C. Chu, 1961; children: Milton W., Christin M. BA, UCLA, 1978, MFA, 1981. curator Artistas Chineses da Calif., Leal Senado de Macau, Galeria de Exposicoe s Temporarias, Macau, 1992; grad. teaching fellow UCLA, 1980-81; lectr. UCLA Ext., Brandeis U. Women's Com., Orange Coast Coll., Westside Arts Ctr., L.A. County Mus. Art, Far Eastern Arts Coun.; panelist L.A. Dept. Cultural Affairs Grants. One-woman shows include Richard Green Gallery, Santa Monica, Calif., 1992, Galley Q, Tokyo, 1992, Memory Gallery, Nagoya, Japan, 1992, Occidental Coll., Glendale, Calif., 1993, Pierce Coll. Art Gallery, Woodland Hills, Calif., 1993, Tsubaki Gallery, Tokyo, 1994, Mandarin Oriental Fine Arts, Hong Kong, 1994, Bunkamura Gallery, Tokyo, 1995; exhibited in group shows at Richard Green Gallery, Santa Monica, Calif., 1992, Andres Shire Gallery, L.A., 1992, Gallery Q, Tokyo, 1992; represented in permanent collections at Hong Kong Mus., Macau Mus.; also pub. and pvt. collections. Ford Found. travel grantee, 1980; recipient award GTE, 1975. Home and Studio: 1520 17th St Santa Monica CA 90404-3402

CHU, K. DAVID, engineer; b. Hualien, Taiwan, Republic of China, Oct. 25, 1957; came to U.S., 1984; s. Shih-Yi and Pao-Li (Lee) C. BSEE, Chiaotung U., 1980; MSEE, U. Mo., 1985. Application engr. United Microelectronics, Taiwan, 1982-84; design engr. Am. Computers, Santa Ana, Calif., 1987; electronic engr. Mitsubishi Electronics, Cypress, Calif., 1987-90; design engr. Trend Micro Devices, Torrance, Calif., 1990-91; electronic engr. Caltron Systems, Carson, Calif., 1991-92; design engr. CMD Tech., Irvine, Calif., 1992-95, Abekas Video, Redwood City, Calif., 1995—. Office: 101 Galveston Redwood City CA 94063

CHU, SALLY CHEN, medical librarian; b. Taiwan, China, 1939; came to U.S., 1963; MLS, Tex. Women's U., 1965. Children's libr. San Diego Pub. Libr., 1965-66, San Bruno (Calif.) Pub. Libr., 1966-70; dir. med. libr. Yang-Ming Med. Coll., Taipei, Taiwan, China, 1976-79; clin. med. libr. U. Mo., Kansas City, 1980-82, audio-visual libr., 1982-84; chief libr. svcs. Peninsula Hosp., Burlingame, Calif., 1984-86, Mills-Peninsula Hops., Burlingame, Calif., 1986—. Mem. Med. Libr. Assn., Acad. Health Info. Profls. (sr.), Chinese-Am. Librs. Assn. Office: Peninsula Hosp Health Scis 1783 El Camino Real Burlingame CA 94010-3205

CHU, VALENTIN YUAN-LING, author; b. Shanghai, Republic of China, Feb. 14, 1919; came to U.S., 1956, naturalized, 1961; s. Thomas V.D. and Rowena S.N. (Zee) Tsu; m. Victoria Chao-yu Tsao, Sept. 25, 1954; 1 child, Douglas Chi-hua. BA, St. John's U, Shanghai, 1940. Asst. Shanghai Mcpl. Coun., 1940-42; asst. mgr., pub., printer Thomas Chu & Sons, Shanghai, 1943-45; chief reporter China Press, Shanghai, 1945-49; pub. rels. officer Cen. Air Transport Corp., Shanghai and Hong Kong, 1949; Hong Kong corr. Time & Life mags., Shanghai and Hong Kong, 1949-56; with Time, Inc., N.Y.C., 1956-76; writer, asst. editor Time-Life Books, N.Y.C., 1968-76; assoc. editor Reader's Digest Gen. Books, N.Y.C., 1978-83; lectr. on China. Author: Ta Ta, Tan Tan---Fight Fight, Talk Talk, 1963, Thailand Today, 1968, (with others) U.S.A., A Visitor's Handbook, 1969, The Yin-Yang Butterfly---Ancient Chinese Sexual Secrets for Western Lovers, 1993; contbr. articles to popular mags. Recipient spl. award UN Internat. Essay Contest, 1948. Mem. Authors League Am., Authors Guild, China Inst. in Am., Inst. Noetic Scis. Presbyterian. Home: 4520 Wildcat Cir Antioch CA 94509-7149

CHUA, KOON MENG, civil engineering educator; b. Singapore, Apr. 23, 1955; came to the U.S., 1982; s. Kim Yeow and Poh Choo Chua. BCE, U. Singapore, 1980; MS, Tex. A&M U., 1983, PhD, 1986. Registered profl. engr., Tex. Civil and structural engr. marine divsn. Brown & Root, Singapore, 1980-82; rsch. engr. Tex. Transp. Inst., College Station, 1986-88; prof. U. N.Mex., Albuquerque, 1988—; cons. Westinghouse Electric Corp., 1991—, N.Mex. State Hwy. and Transp. Dept., 1988—, NASA, 1990—. Contbr. articles to profl. jours. Mem. ASCE (chair subcom., mem. com. 19876), Transp. Rsch. Bd. (com. mem. 1988—), ASTM (com. mem. 1988—), SPIE (hon.). Methodist. Office: U NMex Dept Civil Engring Albuquerque NM 87131

CHUA, LEON O., electrical engineering and computer science educator; b. June 28, 1936; m. Diana Chua; children: Amy Lynn, Michelle Ann, Katrin Faye, Cynthia Mae. SM, MIT, 1961; PhD, U. Ill., 1964; D honoris causa, Ecole Poly. Lausanne, Switzerland, 1983; honorary doctorate, U. Tokushima, Japan, 1984; D hon. causa, Tech. U. Dresden, Germany, 1992, Tech. U. Budapest, Hungary, 1993. Asst. prof. Purdue U., Lafayette, Ind., 1964-67, assoc. prof., 1967-70; prof. U. Calif., Berkeley, 1972—; cons. various electronic industries; Miller Rsch. prof. Miller Inst., 1976. Author: Introduction to Nonlinear Network Theory, 1969; co-author: Computer Aided Analysis of Electronic Circuits: Algorithms and Computational Techniques, 1975, Linear and Nonlinear Circuits, 1987; dep. editor Internat. Jour. Circuit Theory and Applications; editor Internat. Jour. Bifurcation and Chaos; contbr. numerous articles to profl. jours. Patentee in field. Recipient Frederick Emmons Terman award, 1974, Alexander von Humboldt Sr. U.S. Scientist award Tech. U. Munich, 1982-83, Vis. U.S. Scientist award Japan Soc. for Promotion Sci., 1983-84, Myril B. Reed Best Paper prize, 1985, Prof. Invite Internat. award French Ministry Edn., 1986; Cambridge (Eng.) U. sr. vis. fellow, 1982. Fellow IEEE (Browder J. Thompson Meml. Prize award 1967, W.R.G. Baker Prize award 1973, Centennial medal 1985, Guillemin-Cauer prize 1985); mem. Soc. Circuits and Systems IEEE (editor Trans. on Cirs. and Systems 1973-75, pres. 1976). Office: Univ Calif Dept Elec Engring & Computer Sci Berkeley CA 94720

CHUAN, RAYMOND LU-PO, scientific researcher, consultant; b. Shanghai, China, Mar. 4, 1924; came to U.S., 1941; s. Peter Shao-Wu and Katherine (Tao) C.; m. Norma Nicoloff, Dec. 21, 1951 (dec. 1973); m. Eugenia Nishimine Sevilla, Apr. 23, 1982; children: Jason, Alexander. BA, Pomona Coll., 1944; MS, Calif. Tech. U., 1945, PhD, 1953. Rsch. assoc., then dir. Engring. Ctr. U. So. Calif., L.A., 1953-63, adj. prof. Sch. Engring., 1957-63; pres. Celestial Rsch. Corp., South Pasadena, Calif., 1963-68; staff scientist Atlantic Rsch., Costa Mesa, Calif., 1968-72, Celesco, Costa Mesa, 1972-76, Brunswick Corp., Costa Mesa, 1976-88; v.p. Femtometrics, Costa Mesa, 1985-93; ret., 1993; cons. NASA, Hampton, Va., 1972-82. Patentee in field; contbr. papers to sci. jours. Co-founder, chmn. bd. dirs. Sequoyah Sch., Pasadena, Calif., 1958-72. Mem. AAAS, Am. Geophys. Union. Home: PO Box 1183 Hanalei HI 96714-1183

CHUCK, WALTER G(OONSUN), lawyer; b. Wailuku, Maui, Hawaii, Sept. 10, 1920; s. Hong Yee and Aoe (Ting) C.; m. Marian Chun, Sept. 11, 1943; children: Jamie Allison, Walter Gregory, Meredith Jayne. Ed.B., U. Hawaii, 1941; J.D., Harvard U., 1948. Bar: Hawaii 1948. Navy auditor Pearl Harbor, 1941; field agt. Social Security Bd., 1942; labor law insp. Terr. Dept. Labor, 1943; law clk. firm Ropes, Gray, Best, Coolidge & Rugg, 1948; asst. pub. prosecutor City and County of Honolulu, 1949; with Fong, Miho & Choy, 1950-53; ptnr. Fong, Miho, Choy & Chuck, 1953-58; pvt. practice law Honolulu, 1958-65, 78-80; ptnr. Chuck & Fujiyama, Honolulu, 1965-74; ptnr. firm Chuck, Wong & Tonaki, Honolulu, 1974-76, Chuck & Pai, Honolulu, 1976-78; pres. Walter G. Chuck Law Corp., Honolulu, 1980-94; pvt. practice Honolulu, 1994—; dist. magistrate Dist. Ct. Honolulu, 1956-63; gen. ptnr. M & W Assocs., Kapalama Investment Co.; bd. dirs. Aloha Airlines, Inc., Honolulu Painting Co., Ltd. Chmn. Hawaii Employment Rels. Bd., 1955-59; bd. dirs. Nat. Assn. State Labor Rels. Bds., 1957-58, Honolulu Theatre for Youth, 1977-80; chief clk. Hawaii Ho. of Reps., 1951, 53, Hawaii Senate, 1959-61; govt. appeal agt. SSS, 1953-72; former mem. jud. coun. State of Hawaii; mem. exec. com. Hawaiian Open; former dir. Friends of Judiciary History Ctr. Inc., 1983-94; former mem. bd. dirs. YMCA. Capt. inf. Hawaii Terr. Guard. Fellow Internat. Acad. Trial Lawyers (founder, dean, bd. dirs., state rep.), Am. Coll. Trial Lawyers; mem. ABA (former chmn. Hawaii sr. lawyers divsn., former mem. ho. of dels.), Hawaii Bar Assn. (pres. 1963), Am. Trial Lawyers Assn. (former editor), U. Hawaii Alumni Assn. (Disting. Svc. award 1967, dir., bd. govs.), Law Sci. Inst., Assoc. Students U. Hawaii (pres.), Am. Judicature Soc., Internat. Soc. Barristers, Am. Inst. Banking, Chinese C. of C., U. Hawaii Founders Alumni Assn (v.p., bd. dirs., Lifetime Achievement award). Republican. Clubs: Harvard of Hawaii, Waialae Country (pres. 1975), Pacific, Oahu Country. Home: 2691 Aaliamanu Pl Honolulu HI 96813-1216 Office: Pacific Tower 1001 Bishop St Ste 2750 Honolulu HI 96813

CHUN, LOWELL KOON WA, architect, land planner, consultant; b. Honolulu, Sept. 2, 1944; s. Kwai Wood and Sara Lau C. BA in Eng., U. Hawaii, 1967; BArch, Cornell U., 1971. Registered profl. architect, Hawaii. Archtl. designer Wilson, Okamoto & Assocs., Honolulu, 1972-74; architect, planner Aotani & Assocs., Inc., Honolulu, 1974-82; design planner Daniel, Mann, Johnson & Mendenhall, Manila and Honolulu, 1982-84; architect, planner Alfred A. Yee div. Leo A. Daly Co., Honolulu, 1984-87; prin. Lowell Chun Planning & Design, Honolulu, 1987-89; dir. planning Daniel, Mann, Johnson & Mendenhall, Honolulu, 1989; assoc. AM Ptnrs., Inc., Honolulu, 1989-92; planning svcs. officer Hawaii Community Devel. Authority, Honolulu, 1992-94; pres. LPC Internat., 1993—; rsch. bd. advisors Am. Biog. Inst., Raleigh, S.C., 1990—; dep. dir. gen. The America's, 1990—; mem. IBC adv. coun. Internat. Biog. Centre, Cambridge, Eng., 1990—. Prin. author: Kauai Parks and Recreation Master Plan, 1978, Hawaii State Recreation Plan (Maximum Fed. Eligibility award 1980), Maui Community Plans, 1981, Pauahi Redevel. Project, Honolulu, 1974, State Tourism Plan, Physical Resources Element, 1977, City & County of Honolulu Urban & Regional Design Plans, 1979, Hilo Civic Center Master Development Plan, 1989, New Communities, U. Petroleum and Minerals, Dhahran, Saudi Arabia, 1982, Lake Pluitt Resdl./Comml. District, Jakarta, Indonesia, 1982, Destination Resorts: Key Biscayne, Fla., Sint Maarten, Netherlands Antilles, St. Croix, U.S. Virgin Islands, Palm Springs, Calif., 1988, The Imperial Plaza Residential Commercial Complex, 1989, Kailua Elderly Housing Community Master Plan, 1990, Waimano Ridge Master Development Plan, 1991, Bishop Estate Urban Design Strategies for Ksksako Lands, 1992, Ksksako Cmty. Devel. Dist. Maues Area Regulations Review and Update, 1994, and others. Advisor, locations officer Maitreya Inst., Honolulu, 1983-84; v.p., treas. Kagyu Theg Chen Ling Tibetan Ctr., Honolulu, 1982, 84; rep. Environ. Coalition to Hawaii State Legislature, 1974; mem. Waikiki Improvement Assn., Phys. Improvement Task Force, 1990, Hawaii Soc. Corp. Planners, 1991. Recipient Master Plan award Nat. Assn. Counties, 1975. Mem. AIA, Am. Planning Assn. (local exec. com. mem.-at-large 1987-88), Sierra Club (local vice-chmn. 1974-76), Cornell Club of Hawaii (Honolulu), Kiwanis (2d v.p. 1993-94), Rotary Club of Honolulu Sunrise. Buddhist. Office: 456 N Judd St Honolulu HI 96817-1754 Home: 47-510 Hui Iwa St Kaneohe HI 96744-4615

CHUN, WENDY SAU WAN, investment company executive; b. China, Oct. 17, 1951; came to U.S., 1975, naturalized, 1988; d. Siu Kee and Lai Ching (Wong) C.; m. Tan Ng Wong, Jan. 1992; children: Sze Ho, Sze Man. BS, Hong Kong Bapt. Coll., 1973; postgrad. U. Hawaii-Manoa, 1975-77. Real estate saleswoman Tropic Shores Realty Co., Honolulu, 1977-80; pres., prin., broker Advance Realty Investment Co., Honolulu, 1980—; owner Video Fun Centre, Honolulu, 1981-83; pres. Asia-Am. Bus Cons., Inc., Can., 1983—; bd. dirs., exec. dir. B.P.D. Internat., Ltd., Hong Kong; exec. dir. Asia-Am. Bus. Cons., Inc., Hong Kong br., 1985—; pres. Asia-Am. Internat., Ltd., Honolulu, 1989; pres. Maurey Internat., Ltd., Hong Kong, 1990, Century 21 G & W Holdings Ltd., Hong Kong, 1994. Mem. Nat. Assn. Realtors. Avocations: singing, dancing, swimming, dramatic performances. Home: 25th Flr Flat B Tregunter Tower 3, 14 Tregunter Path Midlevels, Hong Kong Hong Kong

CHUNG, CRAWFORD, physician; b. Canton, China, Dec. 16, 1947; came to U.S., 1972; s. William and Louise (Cheung) C.; m. Jane Ann Chung; 1 child, Holly. MB BS, U. Hong Kong, 1971. Diplomate Am. Bd. Internal Medicine, also sub-bds. pulmonary disease and critical care medicine; lic. physician, Calif. Intern U. Hong Kong, 1971-72; resident in medicine St. Louis U., 1972-75; fellow in pulmonary disease Washington U., St. Louis, 1975-76, U. Calif. Davis/VA Hosp., Martinez, 1976-77; med. dir. internsive care unit Calif. Pacific Med. Ctr., San Francisco, 1977—; pvt. practice pulmonary disease San Francisco, 1977—. Office: 3838 California St San Francisco CA 94118-1522

CHUNG, HEON HWA, research and development executive; b. 1948. BEE, Younsai U.; M in Computer Sci., Mich. U., 1982. Engr. Signitic Korea, Seoul, Korea, 1973-77; mgr. PABC design Samsung GTE, Seoul, 1977-81; engr. hardware design Mohawk Data, 1983-84, ITT, 1984-87; with Samsung Info. Sys. Am., San Jose, Calif., 1990—, pres., 1994—. Office: Samsung Info Systems Am 3655 N 1st St San Jose CA 95134-1707*

CHUNG, HSIN-HSIEN, electronics company executive, electrical engineer; b. Pingtung, Taiwan, Apr. 6, 1949; came to U.S., 1978; s. Pi-Kuang and Hsien-Mei (Lin) C.; m. Yueh-Ying Liu, Mar. 4, 1976; children: Josephine, Joy. BS in Elec. Engring., Tatung Inst. Tech., Taipei, Taiwan, 1972; MSc, Ohio State U., 1980, PhD, 1983. Elec. engr. Taiwan Power Co., 1974-78; rsch. assoc. Ohio State U., Columbus, 1979-83; sr. engr. Teledyne Micronetics, San Diego, 1983-85; sr. scientist, group leader Teledyne Ryan Electronics, San Diego, 1985-90; sr. staff engr., R&D mgr. TRW, Inc., San Diego, 1990-94; pres. SatCom Electronics, Inc., San Diego, 1994—. Patentee in field. Recipient Cert. of Recognition, NASA, 1989. Mem. IEEE (sr.), Am. Phys. Soc. Home: PO Box 720068 San Diego CA 92172-0068

CHUN OAKLAND, SUZANNE NYUK JUN, state legislator; b. Honolulu, June 27, 1961; d. Philip Sing and Mei-Chih (Chung) Chun; m. Michael Sands Chun Oakland, June 11, 1994; 1 child, Mailene Nohea Pua Oakland. BA in Psychology and Comm., U. Hawaii, 1983. Adminstrv. asst. Au's Plumbing and Metal Works, Hawaii, 1979-90; community svc. specialist Senator Anthony Chang, Hawaii, 1984; adminstrv. asst. Smolenski and Woodell, Hawaii, 1984-86; rsch. asst., office mgr. City Coun. Mem. Gary Gill, Hawaii, 1987-90; mem. Hawaii Ho. of Reps., 1990—. Named Legis. of Yr. Hawaii Long Term Care Assn., 1993, Healthcare Assn. Hawaii, 1993, 95, Hawaii Psychiat. Med. Assn., 1994, Autism Soc. Hawaii, 1994; recipient Friend of Social Workers award NASW, 1995. Democrat. Episcopalian. Office: State House Reps State Capitol Honolulu HI 96813-2437

CHUR, DANIEL ERIC, lawyer; b. Honolulu, July 22, 1956; s. Emery B.D. and Mitoko (Shukuta) C. BA, U. Hawaii, 1978, JD, 1981. Bar: Hawaii, 1981, U.S. Dist. Ct. Hawaii 1981, Supreme Ct. 1994, U.S. Ct. Appeals (9th cir.) 1982. Officer, dir. Robinson and Chur, Honolulu, 1981—. Moot Ct. judge, U. Hawaii, 1983-88. Mem. ABA, Hawaii Bar Assn., Assn. Trial Lawyers Am., Assn. of Plaintiffs Lawyers Hawaii (bd. dirs. 1989—), Hawaii Trial Lawyers Assn., Hawaii Trial Lawyers Assn. (advocate), Roscoe Pound Found., Phi Delta Phi, Phi Kappa Phi, Mortar Bd. Democrat. Home: 2271 Halakau St Honolulu HI 96821 Office: Robinson & Chur 912 Nuuanu Ave Honolulu HI 96817-5114

CHURCH, ALONZO, mathematics and philosophy educator; b. Washington, June 14, 1903; s. Samuel Robbins and Mildred Hannah Letterman (Parker) C.; m. Mary Julia Kuczinski, Aug. 25, 1925 (dec. Feb. 1976); children—Alonzo, Mary Ann, Mildred Warner. A.B., Princeton U., 1924, Ph.D., 1927, D.Sc. (hon.), 1985; D.Sc. (hon.), Case Western Res. U., 1969, SUNY, Buffalo, 1990. Faculty Princeton U., 1929-67, prof. math., 1947-61, prof. math. and philosophy, 1961-67; prof. philosophy and math. UCLA, 1967-90, ret. Author: Introduction to Mathematical Logic, vol. I, 1956; editor: Jour. Symbolic Logic, 1936-79; contbr. articles to math. and philos. jours. Mem. Am. Acad. Arts and Scis., Assn. Symbolic Logic, Am. Math. Soc., AAAS, Nat. Acad. Scis., Brit. Acad. (corr.), Am. Philos. Assn. (pres. Pacific div. 1973-74).

CHURCH, LORENE KEMMERER, retired government official; b. Jordan, Mont., Oct. 18, 1929; d. Harry F. and Laura (Stoller) Kemmerer; m. Scott Johnston, Sept. 8, 1948 (div. 1953); children: Linda M., Theodore O.; m. Fred C. Church, May 9, 1956; children: Ned B., Nia J. Student, Portland Community Coll., 1973-76, Portland State U., 1978-79. Sec. intelligence div. IRS, Portland, Oreg., 1973-75; trade asst. Internat. Trade Adminstrn., U.S. Dept. Commerce, Portland, 1975-84, internat. trade specialist, 1984-94; ret., 1995. Mem. NAFE, World Affairs Coun., N.W. China Coun., Portland C. of C. (Europe 1992 com. 1988-89, internat. trade adv. bd. 1988-89). Democrat. Roman Catholic. Home: 19725 SW Pike St Beaverton OR 97007-1446 Office: US Dept Commerce US&FCS 121 SW Salmon St Portland OR 97204-2901

CHURCH, TOM, food products executive; b. 1944. BS in Mgmt., Calif. Polytech. State U., 1969. Sales mgr. Bruce Church, Inc., Salinas, Calif., 1969-81; pres. Pacific Freezers, Inc., Salinas, Calif., 1989-94, Fresh We. Mktg., Inc., Salinas, Calif., 1981—; with Harvest Tek, Inc., Salinas, Calif., 1981—. Office: Harvest Tek Inc 1156 Abbott St Salinas CA 93901-4503*

CHURCHILL, WILLIAM DELEE, retired education educator, psychologist; b. Buffalo, Nov. 4, 1919; s. Glenn Luman and Ethel (Smith) C.; AB, Colgate U., 1941; MEd, Alfred U., 1951; EdD, U. Rochester, 1969; m. Beulah Coleman, Apr. 5, 1943; children: Cherylee, Christie. Tchr. secondary sci., Canaseraga, N.Y., 1947-56; dir. guidance Alfred-Almond Sch., Almond, N.Y., 1956-63; grad. asst. U. Rochester, 1963-65; asst. prof. psychology Alfred (N.Y.) U., 1965-66; assoc. prof. edn. Ariz. State U., Tempe, 1966-86. Lt. col. USAAF, 1942-79, PTO. Mem. Ariz. Psychol. Assn. Author: Career Survey of Graduates, 1973. Home: 11454 N 85th St Scottsdale AZ 85260-5727

CHURCHYARD, JAMES NOHL, engineer, consultant; b. Douglas, Ariz., Feb. 18, 1935; s. Harry L. and Miriam F. (Best) C.; m. Martha Orr, May 31, 1959; (div. Feb. 1979); children—Henry, Ruth Kendrick, Elizabeth Emily; m. Alberta J. Parker, July 28, 1979. B.A. in Edn., U. Ariz., 1957, M.A., 1965, B.A., 1966; Ph.D., Kensington U., Glendale, Calif., 1984. Cert. community coll. inst. Tchr., Ariz., 1959-63; engr. Gen. Dynamics Corp., San Diego, 1963-64; engr. Def. div. Brunswick Corp., Costa Mesa, Calif., 1964—; prin. Fortran Doctor, Costa Mesa, 1984—; adj. prof. Orange (Calif.) Coast Coll., 1982-85. Contbr. articles to profl. jours. Fellow AIAA (assoc.); mem. Soc. Indsl. and Applied Math., Soc. Colonial Wars (sec. 1976-83, gov. 1984-86). Unitarian. Club: Cincinnati (N.Y.C.). Home: 1783 Hawaii Cir Costa Mesa CA 92626-2015

CHUTE, PHILLIP BRUCE, management consultant; b. Saugus, Mass., Aug. 19, 1938; s. Ernest Yorke and Dorothy (Bruce) C.; m. Elizabeth Boyd; children: Brian, Elaine. Student, Northeastern U., Boston, 1961-62; AA, Pasadena City Coll., 1965; BS, Calif. State U., L.A., 1977. Fin. reporter Dun & Bradstreet, L.A., 1961-62; mgr. Crocker Citizens Bank, L.A., 1962-64; acct. Cons. Rock Prod., L.A., 1965-74; pres. Phillip B. Chute, Corp., Riverside, Calif., 1974-95; prin., office supervisory jurisdiction mgr. Keogler Morgan & Co., Riverside, 1991; pres. Pacific Fin. Advisors Corp., 1992—. Author: American Independent Business, 1984, AIB Handbook, 1988. Pres. Riverside County Tax Commn. Assn., 1978; active Calif. Bapt. Coll., Riverside, 1990-93. With U.S. Army, 1957-60, Germany. Recipient Clyde Hurley writing award Kiwanis Internat., 1988, 89, Writing award, 1990. Republican. Home: 6710 Mountain Laurel Ct Highland CA 92346-5207 Office: Phillip B Chute Corp 4100 Central Ave Riverside CA 92506-2930

CHVANY, ELLEN, organizational development consultant, writer; b. Buffalo, Nov. 17, 1940; d. Thomas Hugh and Clara Louise (Dennis) Jameson; divorced; children: Peter Andre, Alexander Colin, Stephen Michael. BA, Radcliffe Coll., 1962. Devel. asst. fund office Radcliffe Coll., Cambridge, Mass., 1971-73; dir. devel. Wheaton Coll., Norton, Mass., 1973-76; asst. dean Tucker Found. Dartmouth Coll., Hanover, N.H., 1976-83; dir. devel. Harvard Divinity Sch., Cambridge, 1983-87; sr. devel. officer Boston U., 1987; dir. devel. Educators Social Responsibility, Cambridge, 1987-88, Ctr. Contemporary Arts, Santa Fe, 1990-93; ind. cons. orgnl. devel. Las Vegas, N.Mex., 1993—; screenwriter, film and sound editor Film Assocs. New Eng., Watertown, Mass., 1967-72, Chvany Assocs., Lebanon, N.H., 1976-84. Contbr. articles to profl. jours., newspapers. Class marshal 350th anniversary Harvard U., Cambridge, 1986. Mem. Harvard-Radcliffe Club N.Mex. (past pres., pres.). Home: 506 Columbia St Las Vegas NM 87701-4355

CIA, MANUEL LOPEZ, artist; b. Las Cruces, N.Mex., Jan. 4, 1937; s. Anastacio Cea Lopez and Mercedes Rivera. Student, Am. Acad. Art, Chgo., 1958-61, Art Inst. San Francisco, 1962, L.A. Trade Tech., 1963-64, U. N.Mex., 1990. Author: Color Quest, 1991, Theory of Sophisticism, 1993; Exhibited in group shows at The Fundacion Teleton de Honduras, Teguicigalpa, 1989, France-USA, Paris, 1991, Arts and the Quincentennial, Albuquerque, 1992, U.S. Artists, Phila., 1993, State of the Art, Boston, 1993, Miniatures 1993, Albuquerque, 1993, Montserrat Gallery, N.Y.C., 1995; one man shows include El Prado Galleries, Sedonia, Ariz. and Santa Fe, N.Mex., 1989, 90, 95. With USAF, 1954-57. Recipient Outstanding Individual award Youth Devel., Albuquerque, 1991. Mem. Internat. Assn. Contemporary Art, Soc. Am. Impressionists. Home: PO Box 7332 Albuquerque NM 87194-7332

CIAMPI, MARIO JOSEPH, architect, planner; b. San Francisco, Apr. 27, 1907; s. Guido and Palmira (DiVita) C.; m. Loretta Keane, Sept. 26, 1939 (dec. 1972); m. Carolyn Smith, June 1, 1983. Grad., Harvard Sch. Architecture, 1932; D.F.A. (hon.), Calif. Sch. Arts and Crafts, 1980. Lic. architect, Calif. Design critic San Francisco Archtl. Club, 1935-40; practice architecture Mario J. Ciampi and Assos. (Urban Design Consultants), San Francisco, 1945—; lectr. various orgns. and univs. Urban cons. San Francisco projects including, Market St. Devel. Plan, 1963-79, Waterfront Study, 1958, Golden Gateway Project, 1958, Freeway Study, 1966, Market St. Beautification Project, 1968-79, Yerba Buena Center Study, 1973-75, N.Waterfront, Port Commn., 1980, South of Market Design Plan, 1983. Bd. trustees San Francisco Art Inst.; bd. regents St. Mary's Coll.; mem. Marin Opera Co. Recipient honors and awards including; collaborative medal of honor Archtl. League N.Y., 1960; gold medal of honor, 1962; Albert John Evers Environ. award San Francisco, 1972; San Francisco Art Festival award, 1973; one man show of works winner nat. competition Arts Center U. Calif., 1965; recipient certificate of honor Bd. Suprs. City of San Francisco, 1973. Fellow AIA (mem. nat., state, local orgns., first honor awards state and nat. awards programs, awards for Market St. Beautification, 1970-79, Univ. Art Mus., Berkeley, San Francisco Junipero Serra Freeway, Seton House, Los Altos, Inst. Noetic Scis., Harvard Alumni Assn., various schs. and churches San Francisco area). Clubs: Harvard, Olympic, Serra, Laqunitas, Plam Springs Tennis, San Francisco Archtl. Lodge: Rosecrucians. Home and Office: 409 Crown Rd San Rafael CA 94904-2723

CICCHETTI, CHARLES JOSEPH, economist, educator; b. Jersey City, July 31, 1943; s. Agnes Cicchetti; m. Sally Karshner, July 19, 1991; children: Kristin Deasy, Colleen Cicchetti Westerfield, Skip. BA in Econs., Colo. Coll., 1965; PhD in Econs., Rutgers U., 1969. Instr. Rutgers U., 1968-69; with Resources for the Future, Washington, 1969-72; vis. assoc. prof. econs. and environ. studies U. Wis., Madison, 1972-74, assoc. prof. econs. and environ. studies, 1974-79, prof. econs. and environ. studies, 1979-86; sr. v.p. Nat. Econ. Rsch. Assocs., 1984-87; dep. dir. Energy and Environ. Policy Ctr. John F. Kennedy Sch. Govt., Harvard U., 1987-90; mng. dir. Putnam, Hayes & Bartlett, Inc., 1988-91, co-chmn., 1991-92; mng. dir. Arthur Andersen Econ. Consulting, 1992—; assoc. lectr. Sch. Natural Resources of the U. Mich., 1972; dir. Wis. Energy Office and spl. energy counselor Govt. Patrick J. Lucey, State Wis., 1975-76; chmn. Pub. Svc. Commn. Wis., 1977-79; co-founder, ptnr. Madison Consulting Group, 1980-84; lectr. econs. U. So. Calif., 1990—; adv. bd. Alliance for Energy Security; exec. com., program com., former mem. Assn. Environ. and Resource Econs.; energy rsch. adv. bd. Rutgers U., others. Author: (with W. Gillen and P. Smolensky) The Marginal Cost and Pricing of Electricity: An Applied Approach, 1977, (with V.K. Smith) The Costs of Congestion: An Econometric Analysis of Wilderness Recreation, 1976, A Primer for Environmental Preservation: The Economics of Wild Rivers and Other Natural Wonders, 1973, others; editorial bd.: Land Econs., Energy Sys. and Policy, Jour. Environ. Econs. and Mgmt.; contbr. articles to profl. jours. Office: Arthur Andersen Econ Cons 633 W 5th St # 2600 Los Angeles CA 90071

CICCIARELLI, JAMES CARL, immunology educator; b. Toluca, Ill., May 26, 1947; s. Maurice Cicciarelli and Helen Ippolito; divorced; 1 child, Nicola. BS, Tulane U., 1969; PhD, So. Ill. U., 1977. Lic. clin. lab. dir., Calif. Postdoctoral fellow dept. surgery UCLA, 1977-79, asst. prof. immunology, 1980-87, assoc. prof., 1987-91; prof. urology and microbiology U. So. Calif., L.A., 1992—; lab. dir. Metic Transplant Lab., Inc., L.A., 1984—; bd. dirs.. So. Calif. Organ Procurement Agy., 1987—; clin. lab. dir. Am. Bd. Bioanalysis, 1991—; mem. histocompatibility com. United Network Organ Sharing, 1991-94. Contbr. articles to sci. jours., chpts. to books. NIH rsch. grantee, 1985-88. Mem. Am. SOc. Histocompatibility and Immunogenetics, Internat. Transplant Soc., Am. Soc. Transplant Physicians, Internat. Soc. Heart Lung Transplantation. Libertarian. Roman Catholic. Home: 2524 Manhattan Ave Hermosa Beach CA 90254-2543 Office: USC Dept Urology Metic Transplant Lab 2100 W 3rd St Ste 280 Los Angeles CA 90057-1922

CICCONE, AMY NAVRATIL, art librarian; b. Detroit, Sept. 19, 1950; d. Gerald R. and Ruth C. (Kauer) Navratil. BA, Wayne State U., 1972; AM in Library Sci., U. Mich., 1973. Rsch. libr. Norton Simon Mus., Pasadena, Calif., 1974-81; chief libr. Chrysler Mus., Norfolk, Va., 1981-88; head libr. Architecture and Fine Arts Libr. U. So. Calif., L.A., 1988—, acting asst. univ. libr. pub. svcs., 1993-95. Contbr. articles to profl. jours.; cons. editor Art Reference Svcs., 1990—. Mem. Art Libraries Soc. N.Am. (moderator Decorative Arts Roundtable, 1991-93, facilities standards com. 1986-91, chmn. strategic planning task force 1994—, vice-chmn. So. Calif. chpt. 1989, chmn. 1990) Rsch. Librs. Group, Art & Architecture Group (steering com. 1992-94). Office: U So Calif Libr Los Angeles CA 90089-0182

CICHANSKI, GERALD, golf course architect. B in Architecture and Engring., Ohio State U.; M in Architecture and Urban Planning, U. Wash. Registered arch., Wash. Prin. Mithun Ptnrs., Seattle; spkr., panelist Nat. Club Mgrs. Conv. Prin. works include Point Roberts (Wash.) Marina and Clubhouse, The Summit Athletic Club, Bellevue, Wash., Everett (Wash.) Gold & Country Club, Sunset Club, Seattle, Carnation (Wash.) Club, Snoqualmie (Wash.) Ridge Golf Club, Allen Island Resort & Clubhouse, San Juan Islands, Wash., Broadmoor Golf Club, Seattle, Newcastle Golf Club, Bellevue, Indian Summer Golf Club, Olympia, Wash., Meriwood at Hawks Prairie Golf Club, Olympia, Summer Golf & Country Club, Lacey, Wash., others. Mem. AIA, Nat. Golf. Found., Club Mgrs. Assn. Office: Mithun Partners Inc 414 Olive Way Ste 500 Seattle WA 98101-1122

CICHOKE, ANTHONY JOSEPH, JR., chiropractor, writer, health consultant; b. Peoria, Ill., Nov. 23, 1931; s. Anthony Joseph Sr. and Margaret Mary (Conwell) C.; m. Margaret A. Kovner, Feb. 24, 1962; children: Anthony Joseph III, Michael David, William F., Margaret Kathleen. BS in Social Sci., John Carroll U., 1954; student, Army Lang. Sch., Monterey, Calif., 1955; MA in Speech and Theater, St. Louis U., 1964; MA in Speech Sci. Pathology and Audiology, U. Minn., 1967; postgrad., Case Western Res. U., 1969; D. Chiropractic, Nat. Coll. Chiropractic, Lombard, Ill., 1973; postgrad., Western States Chiropractic Coll., 1975. Diplomate Am. Chiropractic Bd. Nutrition. Actor, promoter Schubert Orgn., N.Y.C., 1960-61; entertainment dir., producer U.S. Army and 2d Army, Ft. Eustis, Va., 1961-62; actor, tchr. radio announcer U. Minn., Mpls., 1964-67; tchr., researcher Eastman Dental Ctr., Rochester, N.Y., 1967-68; team physician Portland State U. Amateur Athletic Union, 1975-84; instr. and lectr. on sports medicine, nutrition, and chiropractic medicine at seminars, convs. and various colls. and univs; researcher. Contbr. over 100 articles to profl. journals; editor Nutritional Prospectives mag, 1979; producer Blockheads, London, 1984-85, This was Burlesque, L.A., 1985. Chmn. sports medicine com. Amateur Athletic Union, 1975—; mem. postgrad. faculty numerous chiropractic colls. 1st lt. U.S. Army, 1955-59. Grantee U.S. Office Edn., 1965-67, Case We. Res. U., 1968-69, U. Minn., 1965-67, NIH, 1968-69. Fellow Internat. Assn. Study of Pain (diplomate), Internat. Coll. Chiropractic; mem. Am. Chiropractic Assn. (coun. orthopedics, 3 man posture com., coun. sports injuries, past pres. and v.p. coun. nutrition), N.Y. Acad. Scis., Orthomolecular Med. Soc., Acad. Orthomolecular Psychiatry, Acad. Sports Medicine, U.S. Sports Acad., Found. Chiropractic Edn. and Rsch., Metabolic Rsch. Found. Republican. Roman Catholic. Office: PO Box 16189 Portland OR 97216-0189

CICIORA, JOHN A., research and development executive; b. 1945. BS in Product Design, Ill. Inst. Tech., 1967, postgrad., 1969-70; postgrad., Hochschule fur Gestaltung, Ulm, Germany, 1967-68. Indsl. designer Martin Marietta Corp., Denver, 1970-75; with Johnson Engring. Corp., Boulder, Colo., 1975—, v.p., 1990—. Office: Johnson Engring Corp 3055 Center Green Dr Boulder CO 80301*

CICORA, MARY ANGELA, researcher, author; b. Ridgewood, N.J., Sept. 21, 1957; d. Samuel M. and Cecelia Cicora. BA, Yale U., 1979; MA, Cornell U., 1982, PhD, 1985. Vis. scholar Stanford (Calif.) U., 1986—. Author: Parsifal Reception, 1987, From History to Myth, 1992; contbr. articles to profl. jours. Mem. Phi Beta Kappa. Home: #1333 707 Continental Cir Apt 1333 Mountain View CA 94040-3313

CILEK, JEFFREY ROBERT, nonprofit executive; b. Iowa City, June 5, 1958; s. Joseph Francis Cilek and Jean (Wilson) Adler; m. Katherine Ann Peck, Nov. 24, 1994; 1 child, Joseph Francis. BBA, U. Iowa, 1980. Legis. dir. U.S. Senator James A. McClure, Washington, 1982-84; staff dir. interior subcom. U.S. Senate, Washington, 1984-90; exec. The Peregrine Fund, Boise, Idaho, 1992—; mem. adv. com. Nat. Fish and Wildlife Found., Washington, 1990-92. Editor: Congressional Candidates Briefing Book, 1984, Almanac of the Unelected, 1989-90. Del. Bush for Pres., Iowa City, 1980. Roman Catholic.

CIMIKOWSKI, ROBERT JOHN, computer scientist; b. Norwich, Conn., Apr. 23, 1949; s. Stephen and Sophie (Sudik) C.; m. Linda E. Sankoski, Feb. 11, 1983. BA in Math., Fordham U., 1972; MS in Computer Sci., Worcester Poly., 1974; PhD in Computer Sci., N.Mex. State U., 1990. Systems analyst Burroughs Corp., East Hartford, Conn., 1974-77, Martin-Marietta Data Systems, Denver, 1978-81, AT&T Info. Systems, Denver, 1981-83; asst. prof. Mont. State U., Bozeman, 1990—. Contbr. articles to Computers & Math. with Applications, Info. Processing Letter, Jour. Combinatorial Math. & Computing, Discrete Applied Math., Pattern Recognition Letters, others. Recipient Engring. Experiment Sta., Mont. State U., 1990, 91. Mem. Assn. for Computing Machinery, Spl. Interest Group on Automata Theory, European Assn. for Theoretical Computer Sci., Golden Key Honor Soc. Office: Computer Sci Dept Montana State U Bozeman MT 59717

CINGO, RALPH PAUL, aerospace executive; b. Cleve., Mar. 2, 1932; m. Lois I. Rosebrock, June 4, 1955; children: Denise Diane, David Alan. BSE, Purdue U., 1954, MSE, 1955; M of Bus.-Econs., Claremont Colls., 1972, MA in Mgmt., 1974. Project and analysis engr. Lockheed Propulsion Co., Redlands, Calif., 1960-65; mgr. prodn. engring. TRW Sys., San Bernardino, Calif., 1965-75; dep. to ops. mgr. Computer Scis. Corp., Huntsville, Ala., 1975-77; mgr. advance programs planning and tech. support Rockwell Internat. Nat. Ctr. for Wind Energy Devel., Golden, Colo., 1977-82; exec. v.p. SEAN Inc., Beverly Hills, Calif., 1982-83; v.p. Calif. Energy Group, Irvine, Calif., 1983-84; v.p. engring. and procurement Pollution Control Engring., Downey, Calif., 1984-85; sr. program mgr. United Techs. Corp., San Jose, Calif., 1985—. Contbr. articles to profl. jours. Lt. USN, 1955-60. Home: 6139 Montgomery Pl San Jose CA 95135-1428

CIOC, MARK, history educator; b. Havre, Mont., May 3, 1952; s. Charles John and Beatrice Devona (Watson) C. BA in History, U. Wyo., 1974, MA in History, 1978; PhD in History, U. Calif., Berkeley, 1986. Asst. prof. history U. Mass., Amherst, 1987-89; assoc. prof. history U. Calif., Santa Cruz, 1989—; provost Stevenson Coll., U. Calif., Santa Cruz, 1994—. Author: Pax Atomica, 1988. Grantee Fulbright Commn., 1978-79, 1993-94; peace fellow Hoover Inst., 1990-91. Home: Stevenson Provost House 101 McLaughlin Dr Santa Cruz CA 95064-1013 Office: U Calif 101 Mclaughlin Dr Santa Cruz CA 95064-1080

CIPRIANO, PATRICIA ANN, secondary education educator, consultant; b. San Francisco, Apr. 24, 1946; d. Ernest Peter and Claire Patricia (Croak) C. BA in English, Holy Names Coll., Oakland, Calif., 1967; MA in Edn. of Gifted, Calif. State U.-L.A., 1980. Cert. tchr., tchr. gifted, adminstrv. svc., lang. devel. specialist, Calif. Tchr. English, math. Bancroft Jr. High Sch., San Leandro, Calif., 1968-79, 83-85, coord. gifted edn., 1971-79; tchr. English, math., computers San Leandro High Sch., 1979-83, 85—, mentor tchr., 1991-94, chmn. English dept., 1992—, coord. gifted and talented edn., 1981-83; cons. Calif. State Dept. Edn., various Calif. sch. dists.; dir. Calif. Lit. Project Policy Bd. Recipient Hon. Svc. award Tchr. of Yr., Bancroft Jr. High Sch. PTA, 1973; bd. dirs. Calif. Curriculum Correlating Coun. Mem. NEA, Calif. Assn. for Gifted, World Coun. Gifted and Talented, Cen. Calif. Coun. Tchrs. English (past pres.), Calif. Assn. Tchrs. English (bd. dirs., past pres.), Nat. Coun. Tchr. English (bd. dirs.), San Leandro Tchrs. Assn., Calif. Tchrs. Assn., Computer Using Educators, Assn. for Supervision and Curriculum Devel., Calif. Math. Coun., Nat. Coun. Tchrs. Math., Curriculum Study Commn., Delta Kappa Gamma (past pres.). Roman Catholic. Avocations: reading, piano, calligraphy, tennis, photography. Contbr. articles to profl. jours. Office: San Leandro HS 2200 Bancroft Ave San Leandro CA 94577-6108

CIRESE, ROBERT CHARLES, economist, real estate investment counselor; b. Oak Park, Ill., Feb. 25, 1938; s. Ferd Louis and Ruth (Olson) C.; m. Sarah Jane Williams, Apr. 3, 1965 (div. 1973); children: Lesley Caren, Jeffrey Robert. BS, DePaul U., 1961; MS, U. Ill., 1963; postgrad., U. Calif., Berkeley, 1964. Lic. real estate broker Calif.; cert. gen. real estate appraiser Calif.; cert. coll. tchr. Calif. Economist State of Calif. Employment Divsn., San Francisco, 1965-67; assoc. prof. Golden Gate U., San Francisco, 1967-72; v.p. Larry Smith & Co., San Francisco, 1972-77; dir. Coopers & Lybrand, San Francisco, 1977-79; v.p. Rubloff Inc., San Francisco, 1979-85; pres. Cirese Assocs., Sausalito, Calif., 1985—; prin. real estate econ. Dept. Interior Presidio Project Nat. Park Svc., San Francisco, 1994—; guest lectr., speaker in field; economic, fin. and real estate investment counselor to corps., govt. agys. and pvt. insts. Contbr. articles to profl. jours. Active Stanford U. Buck Fund, U. Calif. Berkeley Bear Backer, Berkeley Repertory Theater, Calif. Shakespeare Festival; bd. dirs. San Francisco Camp Fire Inc., 1988-92. With Ill. Nat. Guard, 1956-63. U. Calif. Berkeley scholar, 1963; Cert. Appreciation Golden Gate U., 1973, U.S. Postal Svc., 1987, San Francisco Bay Area Camp Fire Inc., 1991; Letter Commendation Am. Acat. Ophthalmology, 1986, San Mateo County Bd. Edn., 1991, Univ. Calif., 1993.. Mem. Am. Soc. Real Estate Counselors (past chmn. no. Calif. chpt. 1988-89, bd. dirs. no. Calif. chpt. 1986—), San Francisco Planning and Urban Rsch. Assn., Urban Land Inst., Stanford Alumni Assn., U. Calif. Berkeley Alumni Assn., San Francisco Commonwealth Club, San Francisco Ballet Assn., Am. Conservatory Theater, Sierra Club (San Francisco, Marin Group), Sierra Singles. Home: 54 Buckelew St Sausalito CA 94965-1120 Office: Presidio of San Francisco San Francisco CA 94129

CISAR, CATHERINE ANN, special education educator; b. LaGrange, Ill., Mar. 2, 1968; d. Alan E. and Nancy (Smith) C. BS in Edn., Western Ill. U., 1990. Spl. edn. tchr. Charter Rehab. Hosp., Scottsdale, Ariz., 1991—; student tchr., behavior disorders, Villa Park, Ill., 1990, educatable mentally handicapped, Romeoville, Ill., 1990. Mem. Coun. Exceptional Children. Home: 11819 E Mission Ln Scottsdale AZ 85259-5946

CITRON, RONALD SETH, physician consultant; b. N.Y.C., Dec. 28, 1940. BS, CCNY, 1961; MD, NYU, 1965; postgrad., San Fernando Valley Coll. Law, 1986-87. Lic. physician Calif., N.Y., Ind. Intern Bklyn. Jewish Hosp., 1965-66, resident, 1966-67; resident U. So. Calif., L.A., 1965-66; med. dir. L.A. Free Clinic, 1969-70; physician internal medicine pvt practice, L.A., 1969-71, physician oncology, hematology, 1976—; asst. clin. prof. medicine divsn. med. oncology & hematology UCLA-VA Med. Ctrs., 1977-84; cons. Med. Bd. Calif., Divsn. Med. Quality, 1988—; tech. cons. 30 Something, 1989-90; researcher in field. Contbr. articles to profl. jours. U. So. Calif. Med. Oncology.Hematology fellow, 1974-76; Zinkoff Found. Anatomical Rsch. award, 1959. Mem. AAAS, Am. Soc. Internal Medicine, Am. Soc. Law & Medicine, Am. Soc. Preventive Incology, Am. Preventive Care Assn., Am. Bd. Forensic Experts, Am. Soc. Clin. Oncology, N.Y. Acad. Sci., So. Calif. Acad. Clin. Oncology, The Hastings Ctr., Phi Delta Epsilon. Office: 21531 Viewridge Rd Topanga CA 90290-4476

CIURCZAK, ALEXIS, librarian; b. Long Island, N.Y., Feb. 13, 1950; d. Alexander Daniel and Catherine Ann (Frangipane) C. BA Art History magna cum laude, U. Calif., L.A., 1971; MA Libr. Sci., San Jose State U., 1975; cert. tchr. ESL, U. Calif., Irvine, 1985. Intern IBM Rsch. Libr., San Jose, Calif., 1974-75; tech. asst. San Bernardino Valley Coll. Libr., Calif., 1975; tech. svcs. librarian Palomar Coll., San Marcos, Calif., 1975-78, pub. svcs. librarian, 1978-81, libr. dir., 1981-86, pub. svcs. librarian, 1987—, instr. Libr. Technology Cert. Program, 1975—; exchange librarian Fulham Pub. Libr., London, 1986-87; coord. San Diego C.C. Consortium Semester-in-London Am. Inst. Fgn. Study, 1988-89. Mem. ALA, San Diego Libr. Svcs. com., Calif. Libr. Media Educators Assn., Patronato por Niños, Kosciuszko Found., So. Calif. Tech. Processes Group, Pacific Coast Coun. Latin Am. Studies, Libros, Reforma, Libr. Assn. (British), Calif. Libr. Assn., Calif. Tchrs. Assn., Phi Beta Kappa, Beta Phi Mu. Office: Palomar CC 1140 W [illegible] Rd San Marcos CA 92069-1415

CLABAUGH, ELMER EUGENE, JR., lawyer; b. Anaheim, Calif., Sept. 18, 1927; s. Elmer Eugene and Eleanor Margaret (Heitshusen) C.; m. Donna Marie Organ, Dec. 19, 1960 (div.); children: Christopher C., Matthew M. BBA cum laude, Woodbury U.; BA summa cum laude, Claremont McKenna Coll., 1958; JD, Stanford U., 1961. Bar: Calif. 1961, U.S. Dist. Ct. (cen. dist.) Calif., U.S. Ct. Appeals (9th cir.) 1961, U.S. Supreme Ct. 1971. With fgn. svc. U.S. Dept. State, Jerusalem and Tel Aviv, 1951-53, Pub. Adminstrn. Svc., El Salvador, Ethiopia, U.S., 1953-57; dep. dist. atty. Ventura County, Calif., 1961-62; pvt. practice, Ventura, Calif., 1962—; mem. Hathaway, Clabaugh, Perrett and Webster and predecessors, 1962-79, Clabaugh & Perloff, Ventura, 1979—; state inheritance tax referee, 1968-78. Bd. dirs. San Antonio Water Conservation Dist., Ventura Community Meml. Hosp., 1964-80; trustee Ojai Unified Sch. Dist., 1974-79; bd. dirs. Ventura County Found. for Parks and Harbors, 1982—, Ventura County Maritime Mus., 1982-94. With USCGR, 1944-46, USMCR, 1946-48. Mem. NRA, Calif. Bar Assn., Am. Arbitration Assn., Safari Club Internat., Mason, Shriners, Phi Alpha Delta. Republican. Home: 241 Highland Dr Oxnard CA 93035-4412 Office: 1190 S Victoria Ave Ventura CA 93003-6507

CLABOTS, JOSEPH PAUL, cardiothoracic surgeon; b. Milw., May 2, 1951; s. Thomas F. and Mary Jane (Graves) C.; m. M. Teresa Garcia Otero, May 29, 1976. BA, St. Louis U., 1973; MD, Washington U., St. Louis, 1977. Diplomate Am. Bd. Thoracic Surgery. Mem. staff St. Joseph Hosp., Tacoma, Wash., 1986—. Fellow ACS; mem. Soc. Thoracic Surgeons. Office: 314 S K St Ste 306 Tacoma WA 98405-4292

CLAES, DANIEL JOHN, physician; b. Glendale, Calif., Dec. 3, 1931; s. John Vernon and Claribel (Fleming) C.; AB magna cum laude, Harvard U., 1953, MD cum laude, 1957; m. Gayla Christine Blasdel, Jan. 19, 1974. Intern, UCLA, 1957-58; Bowyer Found. fellow for rsch. in medicine, L.A., 1958-61; pvt. practice specializing in diabetes, L.A., 1962—; v.p. Am. Eye Bank Found., 1978-83, pres., 1983—, dir. rsch., 1980—; pres. Heuristic Corp., 1981—. Mem. L.A. Mus. Art, 1960—. Mem. AMA, Calif. Med. Assn., L.A. County Med. Assn., Am. Diabetes Assn., Internat. Diabetes Fedn., Internat. Pancreas & Islet Transplant Assn. Clubs: Harvard and Harvard Med. Sch. of So. Calif.; Royal Commonwealth (London). Contbr. papers on diabetes mellitus, computers in medicine to profl. lit. Office: Am Eyebank Found 15327 W Sunset Blvd Ste 236 Pacific Palisades CA 90272-3674

CLAES, GAYLA CHRISTINE, writer, editorial consultant; b. L.A., Oct. 17, 1946; d. Henry George and Glorya Desiree (Curran) Blasdel; m. Daniel John Claes, Jan. 19, 1974. AB magna cum laude, Harvard U., 1968; postgrad., Oxford (Eng.) U., 1971; MA, McGill U., Montreal, 1975. Adminstrv. asst. U. So. Calif., L.A., 1968-70; teaching asst. English lit. McGill U., Montreal, 1970-71; editorial dir. Internat. Cons. Group, L.A., 1972-78; v.p. Gaylee Corp., L.A., 1978-81, CEO, 1981-88; writer, cons. L.A. and Paris, 1988—; dir. pub. rels. Centre Internat. for the Performing Arts, Paris and L.A., 1991—. Author: (play) Berta of Hungary, 1972, (novel) Christopher Derring, 1990; contbr. articles to lit. and sci. jours. Mem. Harvard-Radcliffe Club of So. Calif., Commonwealth Trust (London).

CLAIR, THEODORE NAT, educational psychologist; b. Stockton, Calif., Apr. 19, 1929; s. Peter David and Sara Renee (Silverman) C.; A.A., U. Calif. at Berkeley, 1949, A.B., 1950; M.S., U. So. Calif., 1953, M.Ed., 1963, Ed.D., 1969; m. Laura Gold, June 19, 1961; children: Shari, Judith. Tchr., counselor Los Angeles City Schs., 1957-63; psychologist Alamitos Sch. Dist., Garden Grove, Calif., 1963-64, Arcadia (Calif.) Unified Sch. Dist., 1964-65; head psychologist Wiseburn Sch. Dist., Hawthorne, Calif., 1966-69; asst. prof. spl. edn., coordinator sch. psychology program U. Iowa, Iowa City, 1969-72; dir. pupil personnel services Orcutt (Calif.) Union Sch. Dist., 1972-73; adminstr. Mt. Diablo Unified Sch. Dist., 1973-77; program dir., psychologist San Mateo County Office of Edn., Redwood City, 1977-91; assoc. prof. John F. Kennedy U. Sch. Mgmt., 1975-77; pvt. practice as ednl. psychologist and marriage and family counselor, Menlo Park, Calif., 1978—, Menlo Park, Calif., 1977-93, dir. Peninsula Vocat. Rehab. Inst., 1978—; psychologist Coll. Counseling Svc., Menlo Pk., 1992—, Calif. Pacific Hosp., San Francisco, 1993—. Served with USNR, 1952-54. Mem. APA, Nat. Assn. Sch. Psychologists, Calif. Assn. Marriage and Family Counselors, Nat. Rehab. Assn, Palo Alto B'nai B'rith Club (pres.). Author: Phenylketonuria and Some Other Inborn Errors of Amino Acid Metabolism, 1971; editor Jour. Calif. Ednl. Psychologists, 1992-94; contbr. articles to profl. jours. Home and Office: 56 Willow Rd Menlo Park CA 94025-3654

CLAIRE, FRED, professional baseball team executive. A.A., Mt. San Antonio Coll.; B.A. in Journalism, San Jose State Coll., 1957. Formerly sports writer and columnist Long Beach Ind. Press Telegram and Whittier News; sports editor Pomo Progress-Bull, Calif., until 1969; dir. publicity Los Angeles Dodgers, Nat. League, 1969-75, v.p. pub. relations and promotions, 1975-82, exec. v.p., from 1982, now exec. v.p. player personnel, 1987—; bd. dirs. Major League Baseball Promotion Corp. Bd. dirs. Greater Los Angeles Vistors and Conv. Bur. Named The Sporting News Major League Exec. of Yr., 1988. Mem. Echo Park C. of C. Lodge: Los Angeles Rotary. Office: LA Dodgers 1000 Elysian Park Ave Los Angeles CA 90012-1199*

CLANCY, JUDITH MEYER, health facility administrator; b. Columbus, Ohio, Feb. 26, 1952; d. John Sherman and Aldyth Louise (Barber) Meyer; m. Michael James Clancy, Jan. 12, 1979 (div. 1991); children: Corinne Renee, Joanna Michelle. BSN, Ohio State U., 1975; cert., R.B. Turnbull Sch., 1977; MA, Cen. Mich. U., 1981; student, Ohio Wesleyan U., 1970-72. RN, Ohio. Staff nurse, charge nurse Children's Hosp., Columbus, 1977, enterostomal nurse clinician, 1977-89, dir. surg. nursing, 1981-89; dir. clin. ops. Nova Home Health Svcs., Phoenix, 1989-90, coord. programs and spl. projects corp. office, 1990-92; enterostomal nurse clinician Good Samaritan Regional Med. Ctr., Phoenix, 1992—. Named to Outstanding Young Women Am., 1982. Mem. Internat. Assn. Enterstomal Therapy, Sigma Theta Tau, Sigma Iota Epsilon. Home: 7106 N Via Nueva Scottsdale AZ 85258-3728

CLANON, THOMAS LAWRENCE, retired hospital administrator; b. Detroit, Sept. 17, 1929; s. William John and Wilhelmina T. (Francis) C.; m. Esther Theresa Giffin, June 11, 1955; children: John P., Kathleen A., Paul A., David L., Daniel J. BS, U. Detroit, 1951; MD, U. Mich., 1955. Diplomate: Am. Bd. Psychiatry and Neurology. Intern St. Mary s Hosp., Grand Rapids, Mich., 1955-56; grad. tng. Meninger Sch. Psychiatry, Topeka, 1956-59; resident psychiatrist in tng. Kans. Boys Indsl. Sch., Topeka, 1958-59; psychiatrist U.S. Med. Ctr. for Prisoners, Springfield, Mo., 1959-61; mem. staff Calif. Med. Facility, Vacaville, 1961-66, 72—, asst. supt. psychiat. svcs., 1972, supt., 1972-80; med. asst. Broadmoor Spl. Security Hosp., Crowthorne, Eng., 1971-72; med. dir. mental health program St. Luke's Hosp., San Francisco, 1986-94; cons. on clin. and adminstrv. hosp. problems, 1994—; staff psychiatrist San Francisco Parole Outpatient Clinic; asst. clin. prof. U. Calif. Med. Sch., Davis, 1969-81. Contbr. articles to med. jours. Former mem. community adv. bd. dept. psychiatry San Francisco Gen. Hosp. Served with USPHS, 1958-61. Fellow Am. Psychiat. Assn.; mem. Am. Correctional Assn., San Francisco Med. Soc., No. Calif. Psychiat. Soc., Vacaville Kiwanis Club (past pres.).

CLANTON, PAUL DAVID, JR., management information systems director; b. Potsdam, N.Y., May 29, 1958; s. Paul David and JoAnne Carol (DeWitt) C.; m. Kimberly Jean Thuon, June 11, 1983; children: Ian, Adria. BA in Psychology, SUNY, Albany, 1980; AAS in Computer Sci., Parks Jr. Coll., 1986. Product integration mgr. Coral Group, Denver, 1986-92; sr. cons. Berger & Co., Denver, 1992-94; MIS dir. City of Thornton, Colo., 1994—. Mem. Data Processing Mgmt. Assn., Assn. Computer Machinery. Office: City of Thornton 9500 Civic Center Dr Thornton CO 80229-4326

CLAPP, JAMES FORD, JR., architect; b. Cambridge, Mass., Nov. 18, 1908; s. James Ford and Leonora (Fanshawe) C.; m. Grace G. FitzGerald, June 3, 1933 (dec. May 1988); children: James Ford III, Susan Fanshawe, Deborah FitzGerald; m. Natalie Rieder Brisco, July 21, 1989. AB cum laude, Harvard Coll., 1931; MArch, Harvard Grad. Sch. Design, 1935. Architect Coolidge Shepley Bulfinch & Abbott, Boston, 1934-53; assoc. architect Shepley, Bulfinch Richardson & Abbott, Boston, 1953-60; ptnr. Shepley, Bulfinch Richardson & Abbott, 1960-72; pres. Shepley Bulfinch Richardson & Abbott Inc., Boston, 1972-75; prin., v.p. Shepley Bulfinch Richardson & Abbott Inc., 1975-83, cons., 1983-88; archtl. cons. to Acadia U.; also to Keyes D. Metcalf for book Planning Academic and Research Library Buildings, 1965; pres. Boston Archtl. Ctr., 1955-56. Mem. Cambridge Hist. Commn., 1969-90; permanent sec. John Worthington Ames Scholarship, 1966-90. Recipient Centennial award Boston Archtl. Ctr., 1989. Fellow AIA, Am. Numis. Soc., Royal Numis. Soc.; mem. Boston Soc. Architects (sec. 1957-58, centennial chmn. 1967), Mass. State Assn. Architects (v.p. 1958-59), Boston Numis. Soc. (pres. 1949-50, 63-64), New Eng. Numis. Assn. (pres. 1956-57), Am. Numis. Assn. (gen. chmn. 1960, Numismatic Amb. award 1980). Home and Office: 4800 N 68th St Scottsdale AZ 85251

CLARK, ALICIA GARCIA, political party official; b. Vera Cruz, Mex.; came to U.S., 1970; d. Rafael Garcia Aully and Maria Luisa (Cobos) Garcia; m. Edward E. Clark, Oct. 20, 1970; 1 child, Edward E. MS in Chem. Engring., Nat. U. Mex., Mexico City, 1951. Chemist Celanese Mexicana, Mexico City, 1951-53, lab. mgr., 1951-53, sales promotion mgr., 1958-65, sales promotion and advt. mgr., 1965-70; nat. chmn. Libertarian Party, Houston, 1981-83, coord. coun. state chairs, 1987—; pres. San Marino (Calif.) Guild of Huntington Hosps., 1981-82, chmn. Celebrity Series, 1989-90, 90-91. Pres. Multiple Sclerosis Soc., San Gabriel Valley, Calif., 1977-78, San Marino Woman's Club, 1989-90; bd. dirs. L.A. Opera Guild, 1990—; founder, chmn. Hispanics for Opera, 1992—; bd. dirs. L.A. Opera Assn., 1994—, Guild Opera Co., 1994—; mem. Blue Ribbon of the L.A. Music Ctr. Recipient award La Mujer de Hoy mag., 1969. Mem. Fashion Group (treas. 1969-70, award 1970), San Marino Woman's Club (ways and means chmn. 1987-88).

CLARK, ANNE DELAIN WARDEN, health department executive; b. Cambridge, Mass., May 27, 1961; d. John Lehman and Phillis Ann (Rodgers) Warden; m. Blair Robert Clark, Mar. 5, 1954; children: Grace Sterling, Sawyer Riordan. Student, Antioch Coll., 1980-81; BA in Econs., U. N.Mex., 1985, MBA in Gen. Mgmt., 1987. Cons. corp. devel. GE Corp. Hdqrs., Fairfield, Conn., 1981; fin. instns. examiner Fin. Instn. Divsn, N.Mex. Regulation and Licensing Dept., Santa Fe, N.Mex., 1987-88; acctg. officer The Bank of Santa Fe, N.Mex., 1988-89; budget analyst III Adminstrv. Svc. Divsn., N.Mex. Dept. Health, Santa Fe, 1989-92; sect. head of budgets, budget analyst IV Adminstrv. Svc. Divsn., N.Mex. Environ. Dept., Santa Fe, 1992-93; bur. chief mgmt. svc. Divsn. Substance Abuse, N.Mex. Dept. Health, Santa Fe, 1993—; tutor U. Phoenix, 1992-93; tchr. Santa Fe (N.Mex.) C.C., 1993. Vol. Big Bros./Big Sisters of Albuquerque, 1983-87; mus. vol. Santa Fe (N.Mex.) Children's Mus., 1992-93. Office: N Mex Divsn Substance Abuse 1190 S Saint Francis Dr Santa Fe NM 87505-4182

CLARK, ARTHUR JOSEPH, JR., mechanical and electrical engineer; b. West Orange, N.J., June 10, 1921; s. Arthur Joseph and Marjorie May (Courter) C.; BS in Mech. Engring., Cornell U., 1943; MS, Poly. Inst. Bklyn., 1948; MS in Elec. Engring., U. N.Mex., 1955; m. Caroline Katherine Badgley, June 12, 1943; children: Arthur Joseph, III, Durward S., David P. Design engr. Ranger Aircraft Engines Co., Farmingdale, N.Y., 1943-46; sr. structures engr. propeller div. Curtis Wright Co., Caldwell, N.J., 1946-51; mgr. space isotope power dept., also aerospace nuclear safety dept. Sandia Labs., Albuquerque, 1951-71, mgr. environ. systems test lab., 1971-79, mgr. mil. liaison dept., 1979-86; pres. Engring. Svcs. Cons. Firm, 1987; mem. faculty U. N.Mex., 1971-75; invited lectr. Am. Mgmt. Assn. Pres. Sandia Base Sch. PTA, 1960-61; chmn. finance com. Albuquerque chpt. Am. Field Svc., 1964-66; chmn. Sandia Labs. div. U.S. Savs. Bond drive, 1972-74, chmn. employee contbn. drive, 1973-75; active local Boy Scouts Am., 1958-66. Recipient Order Arrow, Boy Scouts Am., 1961, Order St. Andrew, 1962, Scouters Key award, 1964; cert. outstanding service Sandia Base, 1964. Fellow ASME (nat. v.p. 1975-79, past chmn. N.Mex. sect.); mem. IEEE (sr.), Cornell Engring. Soc., Theta Xi. Clubs: Kirtland Officers, Four Hills Country. Home: 905 Warm Sands Trail Albuquerque NM 87123-4332

CLARK, BEVERLY WYONE, nutritionist; b. Seattle, Sept. 10, 1948; d. Dean Voris and Gail Wyone (Whittaker) Babst; m. Roberto Medina Bernardo, Dec. 18, 1970 (div. June 1977); 1 child, Dolores; m. Barry Allan Clark, Dec. 30, 1978; children: Marcelina, Kevin. BS in foods & nutrition, Stout State U., 1970; MPH in nutrition, U. Calif., 1972; student, Merrill Palmer Inst., 1969. Registered dietitian. Dietary cons. various convalescent hosps., Bay Area, Calif., 1972-73; nutrition cons. Solano County Head Start, Fairfield, Calif., 1973-75; instr. home econs. San Jose (Calif.) City Coll., 1973; nutritionist Contra Costa County, Martinez, Calif., 1974-75, CARE, Manila, Philippines, 1975-76; dir., nutritionist Alameda County, Oakland, Calif., 1976-94, Contra Costa County, Concord, Calif., 1994—; rep. Task Force State WIC, Sacramento, 1986-88, 90-92; bd. rep. Calif. WIC Assn., 1992—; apptd. to adv. bd. Cambodian New Generation, Oakland, 1983-94. Vol. Lamorinda Dem. Club, Orinda, Calif., 1990-94. Mem. Bay Region Dietetic Assn., Calif. Dietetic Assn., Am. Dietetic Assn., Diablo Valley Dietetic Assn. Home: 400 Read Dr Lafayette CA 94549-5617 Office: Contra Costa County Health Svcs Dept 2355 Stanwell Cir Concord CA 94520-4806

CLARK, BRIAN THOMAS, mathematical statistician, operations research analyst; b. Rockford, Ill., Apr. 7, 1951; s. Paul Herbert and Martha Lou (Schlensker) C.; m. Suzanne Drake, Nov. 21, 1992. B.S. cum laude, No. Ariz. U., 1973; postgrad. Ariz. State U., 1980-82. Math. aide Center for Disease Control, Phoenix, 1973-74, math. statistician, 1979-83; math. Statistician Ctrs. for Disease Control, Atlanta, 1983-84 ops. research analyst U.S. Army Info. Systems Command, Ft. Huachuca, Ariz., 1984—; math. statistician U.S. Navy Metrology Engring. Center, Pomona, Calif., 1974-79. Republican. Mormon. Office: US Army Info Systems Command Dep Chief Staff Resource Mgmt Chargeback Test Divsn Fort Huachuca AZ 85613

CLARK, BURTON ROBERT, sociologist, educator; b. Pleasantville, N.J., Sept. 6, 1921; s, Burton H. and Cornelia (Amole) C.; m. Adele Halitsky, Aug. 31, 1949; children: Philip Neil (dec.), Adrienne. B.A., UCLA, 1949, Ph.D., 1954. Asst. prof. sociology Stanford U., 1953-56; research asso., asst. prof. edn. Harvard U., 1956-58; asso. prof., then prof. edn. and asso. research sociologist, then research sociologist U. Calif. at Berkeley, 1958-66; prof. sociology Yale U., 1966-80, chmn. dept., 1969-72; chmn. Higher Edn. Research Group, 1973-80, Comparative Higher Edn. Research Group, 1980-91; Allan M. Cartter prof. higher edn. UCLA, 1980-91, prof. emeritus, 1991—. Author: Adult Education in Transition, 1956, The Open Door College, 1960, Educating the Expert Society, 1962, The Distinctive College, 1970, The Problems of American Education, 1975, Academic Power in Italy, 1977, The Higher Education System, 1983, The Academic Life, 1987, Places of Inquiry, 1995; co-author: Students and Colleges, 1972, Youth: Transition to Adulthood, 1973, Academic Power in the United States, 1976, Academic Power: Patterns of Authority in Seven National Systems of Higher Education, 1978; editor: Perspectives on Higher Education, 1984, The School and The University, 1985, The Academic Profession, 1987, The Research Foundations of Graduate education, 1993; co-senior editor: Encyclopedia of Higher Education, 1992. Served with AUS, 1942-46. Mem. Internat. Sociol. Assn., Am. Sociol. Assn., Am. Ednl. Rsch. Assn. (Am. Coll. Testing award 1979, Divsn. J. Disting. Rsch. award 1988, Outstanding Book award 1989), Assn. Study Higher Edn. (pres. 1979-80, Rsch. Achievement award 1985), Am. Assn. Higher Edn., Nat. Acad. Edn. (v.p. 1989-93), Consortium Higher Edn. Rschrs. Office: UCLA Dept Edn Los Angeles CA 90024

CLARK, CHARLES SUTTER, interior designer; b. Venice, Calif., Dec. 21, 1927; s. William Sutter and Lodema Ersell (Fleeman) C. Student Chouinard Art Inst., Los Angeles, 1950-51. Interior designer LM.H. Co., Gt. Falls, Mont., 1956-62, Andreason's Interiors, Oakland, Calif., 1962-66, Western Contact Furnishers Internat., Oakland, 1966-70, Design Five Assocs., Lafayette, Calif., 1972-73; owner, interior designer Charles Sutter Clark Interiors, Greenbrae, Calif., 1973-91, San Rafael, Calif., 1991—. Served with USAF, 1951-55. Recipient prizes Mont. State Fair, 1953-55. Mem. Am. Soc. Interior Designers. Home: 429 El Faisan Dr San Rafael CA 94903-4517

CLARK, DAVID CURTIS, lawyer; b. Prairie City, Oreg., July 9, 1943; s. Cleon L. and Wanda (Veatch) C.; m. Pamela Rae Farster, Apr. 25, 1981; children: Nathaniel D., Justin D. BS in History, Oreg. State U., 1967; JD, U. Calif., San Francisco, 1975. Pvt. practice Redmond, Oreg., 1975-84, Rock Springs, Wyo., 1986-87; city atty. City of Rawlins, Wyo., 1987—. Lt. (j.g.) USN, 1967-71.

CLARK, DONALD B., utilities executive; b. New Glasgow, N.S., Can., 1942. Dir. Conversion Industries, Inc., Pasadena, Calif.; bd. dirs. CVD Fin. Corp., N.Am. Recycling Sys., Inc., Perennial Energy, Inc., Statordyne Corp. Home: 501 E Del Mar Pasadena CA 91101 Office: Conversion Industries Inc 230 E Colorado Blvd Pasadena CA 91101-2203*

CLARK, DREW, secondary education educator, state legislator; b. Jacksonville, Ill., Dec. 7, 1946; s. Robert Donald and Roberta Ruth (Wheelan) C.; m. Lainie (Joyce Elaine) Peters, Aug. 6, 1970. BS in Math., Ill. Coll., 1968. Cert. math., physics tchr., Colo. Tchr. Elmwood (Ill.) High Sch., 1968-69, Adams County Sch. Dist. 12, Northglenn, Colo., 1973—; mem. Colo. Ho. of Reps., 1993—, mem. edn., transp. coms. Elder Rocky Mountain Christian Ch., Niwot, Colo., 1991—; host fgn. exch. students. With U.S. Army, 1969-71, Vietnam. Republican. Home: 876 Dearborn Pl Boulder CO 80303-3238 Office: Ho of Reps Stuart St # 271 Denver CO 80219-1133

CLARK, DWIGHT DELONG, voluntary organization administrator; b. Great Bend, Kans., Jan. 21, 1934; s. Dwight DeLong and Ruth (Bales) C. BA, Stanford U., 1956, MA, 1958. Dean freshman men Stanford (Calif.) U., 1961-64, asst. dean men, 1964-65; exec. dir. Vols. in Asia, Stanford, 1965-84, pres., 1984—; pres. Trans-Pacific Exch., Stanford, 1988—, Avia Travel, San Francisco, 1985—. Mem. Soc. of Friends. Home: 2510 Birch St Palo Alto CA 94306-1903 Office: Vols in Asia Inc PO Box 4543 Palo Alto CA 94309-4543

CLARK, EARL ERNEST, publisher; b. Corpus Christi, Tex., Nov. 1, 1958; s. Earl Rush and Erika Martha (Jacobs) C. BA, Oreg. State U., 1985. Pub. Horison Publs., Corvallis, Oreg., Avant-Garde Publs., Tigard, Oreg. Author: Magic of Credit Repair, 1994, (poetry) ...Bomb threat for general public, 1993 (award 1994). With USN, 1987-92. Mem. Masons. Home: 10000 SW Hall Blvd 9 Tigard OR 97223

CLARK, EARNEST HUBERT, JR., tool company executive; b. Birmingham, Ala., Sept. 8, 1926; s. Earnest Hubert and Grace May (Smith) C.; m. Patricia Margaret Hamilton, June 22, 1947; children: Stephen D., Kenneth A., Timothy R., Daniel S., Scott H., Rebecca G. BS in Mech. Engring, Calif. Inst. Tech., 1946, MS, 1947. Chmn., chief exec. officer Friendship Group, Baker Hughes, Inc. (formerly Baker Oil Tools, Inc.), L.A., 1947-89, v.p., asst. gen. mgr., 1958-62, pres., chief exec. officer, 1962-69, 75-79, chmn. bd., 1969-75, 79-87, 87-89, ret., 1989; ret. The Friendship Group, Newport Beach, Calif., 1989; bd. dirs. CBI Industries, Inc., Honeywell Inc., Kerr-McGee Corp., Beckman Instruments Inc., Regenesis Inc., Am. Mut. Fund. Chmn., bd. dirs. YMCA of U.S.A.; past chmn. bd. YMCA for Met. L.A.; mem. nat. coun. YMCA; trustee Harvey Mudd Coll. With USNR, 1944-46, 51-52. Mem. AIME, Am. Petroleum Inst., Petroleum Equipment Suppliers Assn. (bd. dirs.), Tau Beta Pi. Office: Friendship Group W Tower # 3000 5000 Birch St Newport Beach CA 92660-2127

CLARK, EDGAR SANDERFORD, insurance broker, consultant; b. N.Y.C., Nov. 17, 1933; s. Edgar Edmund, Jr., and Katharine Lee (Jarman) C.; student U. Pa., 1952-54; BS, Georgetown U., 1956, JD, 1958; postgrad. INSEAD, Fountainbleau, France, 1969, Golden Gate Coll., 1973, U. Calif., Berkeley, 1974; m. Nancy E. Hill, Sept. 13, 1975; 1 dau., Schuyler; children by previous marriages: Colin, Alexandra, Pamela. Staff asst. U.S. Senate select com. to investigate improper activities in labor and mgmt. field, Washington, 1958-59; underwriter Ocean Marine Dept., Fireman's Fund Ins. Co., San Francisco, 1959-62; mgr. Am. Fgn. Ins. Assn., San Francisco, 1962-66; with Marsh & McLennan, 1966-72, mgr. for Europe, resident dir. Brussels, Belgium, 1966-70, asst. v.p., mgr. captive and internat. div., San Francisco, 1970-72; v.p., dir. Risk Planning Group, Inc., San Francisco, 1972-75; v.p., dir. global constrn. group Alexander & Alexander Inc., San Francisco, 1975-94; exec. dir. The Surplus Line Assn. of Calif., 1995—; lectr. profl. orgns.; guest lectr. U. Calif., Berkeley, 1973, Am. Grad. Sch. Internat. Mgmt., 1981, 82, Golden Gate U., annually 1985-91. Served with USAF, 1956-58. Mem. Am. Mgmt. Assn., Am. Risk and Ins. Assn., Internat. Insurance Soc., Chartered Ins. Inst., Am. Soc. Internat. Law, Soc. Calif. Pioneers San Francisco, Meadow Club, Fairfax, Calif., World Trade San Francisco. Republican. Episcopalian. Mem. editorial adv. bd. Risk Mgmt. Reports, 1973-76. Home: 72 Millay Pl Mill Valley CA 94941-1501 Office: Surplus Line Assn of Calif 388 Market St Ste 1150 San Francisco CA 94111

CLARK, EZEKAIL LOUIS, chemical engineering consultant; b. Gomel, Russia, June 29, 1912, came to U.S., 1914, naturalized, 1919; s. Louis Elia and Pauline (Rapoport) C.; m. Freida Cohen, June 29, 1933; children: Alvin M., Charlotte S. Clark Landay. BSChemE, Northeastern U., 1937. Process engr. Cities Svc. Co., 1943-45; supr. coal hydrogenation research U.S. Bur. Mines, 1945-54; supr. pilot plant labs. Israel Mining Industries, 1954-56; self-employed cons., 1956-64; pres., founder Pressure Chem. Co., 1964-74; chief coal gasification br. Dept. of Energy, 1974-78; chem. engring. cons., Scottsdale, Ariz., 1978—; bd. dirs. Pressure Chem. Co., 1990; assoc. prof. chem. engring. Haifa Technion, 1955, U. Pitts., 1951-52; lectr. Cath. U., 1954. Recipient McAffee award Pitts. Sect. Am. Inst. Chem. Engrs., 1988. Fellow Am. Inst. Chem. Engrs. (chmn. Pitts. sect. 1973-74); mem. Am. Chem. Soc. Contbr. articles on coal conversion to gaseous and liquid fuels, oil shale utilization, petroleum tech. to profl. jours. Home and Office: 4200 N Miller Rd Scottsdale AZ 85251

CLARK, GARY C., football player; b. Radford, Va., May 1, 1962. Student, James Madison U. With Jacksonville Bulls, 1984-85, Washington Redskins, 1985-92, Phoenix (now Arizona) Cardinals, 1993-95, Miami Dolphins, 1995—. Named to Pro Bowl team, 1986, 87, 90, 91. Office: care Miami Dolphins 2269 NW 199th St Opa Locka FL 33056*

CLARK, GARY KENNETH, religious ministries executive; b. New Castle, Pa., June 17, 1936; s. Stanley Kenneth and Melba Sunshine (Brickner) C.; m. Dorothy Agnes MacGregor, Aug. 23, 1958; children: Bethany Jane, Nathan Douglas, David Stanley, Kathryn Joy. BA, Barrington (R.I.) Coll., 1958; MDiv, Gordon Sem., Wenham, Mass., 1965, M of Christian Edn., 1969; DDiv (hon.), Trinity Coll., Nigeria, 1990. Asst. pastor Woodlawn Bapt Ch., Pawtucket, R.I., 1958-61; pastor Calvary Covenant Ch., Cranston, R.I., 1961-63, 1st Bapt. Ch., Salem, N.H., 1963-85; pres. Holy Spirit Renewal Ministries, Pasadena, Calif., 1984—; internat. field coord. Assn. of Internat. Mission Svcs., Pasadena, 1989—; assoc. dir. of program Lausanne Congress of World Evangelism, Manila, Philippines, 1988-89; pastor Christian Ctr. Renewal Ch., Arcadia, Calif., 1991—; pres. Gordon-Cornwell Sem. Alumni, Wenham, 1978-84. Editor: (newsletter) Lausanne Internat., 1988-89, Refreshing Times, 1985—, AD2000, 1987-89. Mem. ABC Ministers Coun., Rotary Internat. Republican. Baptist. Home: 1386 N Sierra Bonita Ave Pasadena CA 91104-2647

CLARK, GLEN EDWARD, federal judge; b. Cedar Rapids, Iowa, Nov. 23, 1943; s. Robert M. and Georgia L. (Welch) C.; m. Deanna D. Thomas, July 16, 1966; children: Andrew Curtis, Carissa Jane. BA, U. Iowa, 1966; JD, U. Utah, 1971. Bar: Utah 1971, U.S. Dist. Ct. Utah 1971, U.S. Ct. Appeals (10th cir.) 1972. Assoc. Fabian & Clendenin, 1971-74, ptnr., 1975-81, dir., chmn. banking and comml. law sect., 1981-82; judge U.S. Bankruptcy Ct. Dist. Utah, Salt Lake City, 1982—; bd. govs. nat. Conf. Bankruptcy Judges, 1988-94; mem. com. on bankruptcy edn. Fed. Jud. Ctr., 1989-92; vis. prof. U. Utah, Salt Lake City, 1977-79, 83; pres. Nat. Conf. Bankruptcy Judges, 1992-93; chair bd. trustees Nat. Conf. Bankruptcy Judges Endowment for Edn., 1990-92. With U.S. Army, 1966-68. Finkbine fellow U. Iowa. Fellow Am. Coll. Bankruptcy; mem. Jud. Conf. U.S. (mem. com. jud. br. 1992—), Utah Bar Assn., Order of Coif. Presbyterian. Office: US Bankruptcy Ct US Courthouse Rm 361 350 S Main St Salt Lake City UT 84101-2106

CLARK, JAMES A., banker; b. 1930. Grad., Rutgers U. Stonier Grad. Sch. of Banking, 1963. With Citizens Bank of Clovis Clovis, N. Mex., 1948-55; with Southwest Nat. Bank El Paso, Tex., 1955-64; pres. Security Bank of Roswell, Roswell, N. Mex., 1964-73; exec. v.p. Albuquerque Nat. Bank, Albuquerque, N. Mex., 1973-74; pres. First Nat. Bank, Albuquerque, N. Mex., 1974-75, First City Bank of Dallas, Dallas, Tex., 1975-79; chmn. bd. First City Fin. Corp., Dallas, Tex., 1979-80; pres., chief exec. officer United N. Mex. Fin. Corp., Albuquerque, N. Mex., 1980-85; chmn. bd. United N. Mex. Bank of Albuquerque, Albuquerque, N. Mex.; pres., chief exec. officer First Interstate Bank, Albuquerque, N. Mex., 1985—, now also chmn. bd., dir.

CLARK, JEFFREY RAPHIEL, research and development company executive; b. Provo, Utah, Sept. 29, 1953; s. Bruce Budge and Ouida (Raphiel) C.; m. Anne Margaret Eberhardt, Mar. 15, 1985; children: Jeffrey Raphiel, Mary Anne Elizabeth. BS, Brigham Young U., 1977, MBA, 1979. CPA, Tex. Fin. analyst Exxon Coal USA, Inc., Houston, 1979-83; constrn. mgr. Gen. Homes, Inc., Houston, 1983-84; controller Liberty Data Products, Houston, 1984-86; v.p. Tech. Rsch. Assocs., Inc., Salt Lake City, 1987—; also dir. Tech. Rsch. Assocs., Inc. Scoutmaster Boy Scouts Am., Salt Lake City, 1989-91. Mem. AICPA, Utah Inst. CPAs, Salt Lake C. of C. (legis. action com.), Salt Lake Country Club. Republican. Mormon. Home: 1428 Michigan Ave Salt Lake City UT 84105-1609 Office: Technical Rsch Assocs 2257 S 1100 E Salt Lake City UT 84106-2379

CLARK, JOHN DESMOND, anthropology educator; b. London, Eng., Apr. 10, 1916; came to U.S., 1961, naturalized 1993; s. Thomas John Chown and Catherine (Wynne) C.; m. Betty Cable Baume, Apr. 30, 1938; children: Elizabeth Ann (Mrs. David Miall Winterbottom), John Wynne Desmond. B.A. Hons, Cambridge U., 1937, M.A., 1942, Ph.D., 1950, Sc.D., 1974; Sc.D. (hon.), U. Witwatersrand, Johannesburg, 1985, U. Cape Town, 1985. Dir. Rhodes-Livingstone Mus., No. Rhodesia, 1938-61; prof. anthropology U. Calif., Berkeley, 1961-86; prof. emeritus U. Calif., 1986—; faculty rsch. lectr. U. Calif., 1979; Raymond Dart lectr. Inst. for Study of Man, Africa, 1979; Sir Mortimer Wheeler lectr. Brit. Acad., 1981; J.D. Mulvaney lectr. Australian Nat. U., 1990. Author: The Stone Age Cultures of Northern Rhodesia, 1950, The Prehistoric Cultures of the Horn of Africa, 1954, The Prehistory of Southern Africa, 1959, Prehistoric Cultures of Northeast Angola, 1963, Distribution of Prehistoric Culture in Angola, 1966, The Atlas of African Prehistory, 1967, Kalambo Falls Prehistoric Site, Vol. I, 1968, Vol. II, 1973, The Prehistory of Africa, 1970; editor: Cambridge History of Africa, Vol. I, 1982, (with G.R. Sharma) Palaeo environment and Prehistory in the Middle Son Valley Madhya Pradesh, North Central India, 1983, (with S.A. Brandt) The Causes and Consequences of Food Production in Africa, 1984, Cultural Beginnings: Approaches to Understanding Early Hominid Life-ways in the African Savanna, 1991. Served with Brit. Army, 1941-46. Decorated comdr. Order Brit. Empire; comdr. Nat. Order Senegal; recipient Huxley medal Royal Anthrop. Inst., London, 1974, Ad personam internat. Gold Mercury award Addis Ababa, 1982, Berkeley citation U. Calif., 1986, Fellows medal Calif. Acad. Scis., 1987, Gold medal of Am. Archaeol. Inst., 1989. Fellow AAAS, Brit. Acad., Royal Soc. South Africa, Soc. Antiquaries London (Gold medal 1985); mem. NAS, Am. Anthropol. Assn. (disting. lectr. 1992), Pan-African Congress Prehistory, Geog. Soc. Lisbon, Instituto Italiano di Preistoria e Protostoria, Body Corporate Livingstone Mus. Office: U Calif Dept Anthropology Berkeley CA 94720

CLARK, JOHN DEWITT, retired fine arts educator, sculptor; b. Kansas City, Mo., Mar. 11, 1925; s. Walter Perry and Anna Mae (Eubank) C. MA in Fine Art and Sculpture, San Diego State U., 1959. Prof. Southwestern Coll., 25 yrs. Exhibited works in numerous shows on West Coast, in N.Y. and Mex., others; represented in museums and pvt. collections throughout U.S. Served with U.S. Army, 1943-45, ETO. Decorated Silver Star. Democrat. Home: 10514 San Carlos Dr Spring Valley CA 91978-1037

CLARK, LARAINE MARIE, maternal-child health nurse; b. Portland, Oreg., Sept. 10, 1956; d. William Gavern and Marilyn Ann (McLean) Sykes; m. Terrence A. Clark, May 28, 1977; children: Wendy, Thomas, Leah. BSN, U. N.D., 1978. Cert. low risk neonatal nursing; internat. bd. cert. lactation cons.; RN, Oreg., Wash. Childbirth educator Prepared Childbirth Assn., Portland, 1978-80; staff nurse newborn nursery Good Samaritan Hosp., Portland, 1979-92; pediatric office nurse Met. Clinic, Portland, 1984-88; nurse educator Women's Health Source-Good Samaritan Hosp., Portland, 1990-92; RN, obstetrical home care Legacy Vis. Nurse Assn., Portland, 1992—, RN infant home monitoring program, 1992—; mktg. com. Good Samaritan Hosp., Portland, 1989-90; infant nutrition task force Legacy Health Sys., Portland, 1994—. Troop leader, organizer Girl Scouts USA, Portland and Wilsonville, Oreg., 1986—; bd. mem. Parent Staff Assn., Wilsonville, 1991-93, pres., 1995—. Mem. Assn. Women's Health, Obstetrical and Neonatal Nurses (chpt. coord. Portland area 1993—), Internat. Lactation Cons. Assn., Sigma Theta Tau. Mormon. Home: 31460 SW Isle Way Ln West Linn OR 97068-9408

CLARK, LAURA CARROLL, dietitian, educator, consultant; b. Shawnee-Mission, Kans., July 14, 1970; d. Kelly Charles and Julie Helen (Sherard) Viets; m. Eldon Allen Clark, Sept. 20, 1992. BS in Dietetics magna cum laude, Kans. State U., 1992. Instr./cons. Am. Heart Assn., Denver, 1992—; nutrition coord. Health One Corp., Denver, 1992—; store coord. heart fest Am. Heart Assn., 1993. Mem. Am. Dietetic Assn. (registered dietitian), Am. Soc. Parenteral and Enteral Nutrition (cert. nutrition support dietitian), Am. Diabetes Assn., Am. Soc. Hsp. Food Svc. Adminstrn., Colo. Nutrition Coun., Internat. Food Svc. Execs. Assn. (cert. food mgr.), Colo. Dietetic Assn., Denver Dietetic Assn. (consumer issues chair 1993-94, fundraising chair 1994-95, pres.-elect 1995—), Phi Kappa Phi, Kappa Omicron Nu, Phi Upsilon Omicron. Home: 16056 E Harvard Ave Aurora CO 80013-1413 Office: Rocky Mountain Rehab Inst 900 Potomac Ave Aurora CO 80011

CLARK, LLOYD, historian, educator; b. Belton, Tex., Aug. 4, 1923; s. Lloyd C. and Hattie May (Taylor) C.; m. Jean Reeves, June 17, 1950; children: Roger, Cynthia, Candyce. BSJ, So. Meth. U., 1948; B in Fgn. Trade, Am. Grad. Sch. Internat. Mgmt., 1949; MPA, Ariz. State U., 1972. String corr. A.P., Dallas, 1941-42; editor, pub. Ex-Press, Arlington, Tex., 1945-48; publicity mgr. Advt. Counselors Ariz., Phoenix, 1949; reporter Phoenix Gazette, 1949-65; asst. pub. Ariz. Weekly Gazette, 1965-66; founder Council on Abandoned Mil. Posts-U.S.A., 1966; project cons. City of Prescott, Ariz., 1971-72; dep. dir. adminstrv. svcs. No. Ariz. Coun. Govts., Flagstaff, 1972-73; regional adminstr. South Eastern Ariz. Govts. Orgn., Bisbee, 1973-75; local govt. assistance coordinator Ariz. Dept. Transp., Phoenix, 1975-80, program adminstr., 1980-83; history instr. Rio Salado Community Coll., Phoenix, 1983-89; editor and pub. Clark Blog. Reference, 1956-62. Bd. dirs. Friends of Channel 8, 1984-86; mem. transit planning com. Regional Pub. Transit Authority, 1988, Phoenix Citizen's Bond Com., 1987; bd. dirs. Friends of Ariz. Highways Mag., 1989-92; mem. Ariz. State Geographic and Historic Names Bd., 1994—. Served to lt. AUS, 1942-46; maj., 1966-70; col. Res. Recipient Ariz. Press Clubs exemplary gen. news coverage award, 1960, outstanding news reporting, 1961; Lloyd Clark Journalism scholarship named in honor U. Tex. at Arlington Alumni Assn., 1992. Mem. Am. Grad. Sch. Internat. Mgmt. Alumni Assn. (pres. Phoenix chpt. 1965), Ariz. Hist. Soc. (bd. dirs. cen. Ariz. chpt. 1992-93, state bd. dirs. 1993—), Sharlot Hall Hist. Soc. (life), Res. Officers Assn. (life), Ex-Students Assn. U. Tex. at Arlington (pres. 1946-48), U. Tex. Arlington Alumni Assn. (life, bd. dir. 1994—), The Westerners (sheriff Phoenix Corral 1986-88), Sigma Delta Chi (pres. Valley of Sun chpt. 1964). Club: University (Phoenix). Author: Lloyd Clark's Scrapbook, Vol. 1, 1958, Vol. 2, 1960. Address: PO Box 1489 Surprise AZ 85374-1489

CLARK, LOYAL FRANCES, public affairs specialist; b. Salt Lake City, July 16, 1958; d. Lloyd Grant and Zina (Okelberry) C. Student, Utah State U., 1976-78. Human resource coord. U.S. Forest Svc., Provo, Utah, 1984—, fire info. officer, 1987—, pub. affairs officer, interpretive svcs. coord., edn. coord., 1988—; mem. Take Pride in Utah Task Force, Salt Lake City, 1989—; chairperson Utah Wildlife Ethics Com., Provo, 1989—. Instr. Emergency Svcs., Orem, Utah, 1990—. Recipient Presdl. award for outstanding leadership in youth conservation programs Pres. Ronald Reagan, 1985, Superior Svc. award USDA, 1987, Exemplary Svc. award U.S. Forest Svc., 1992, Nat. Eyes on Wildlife Achievement award USDA Forest Svc., 1993. Mem. Nat. Wildlife Fedn., Nat. Assn. Interpretation, Utah Soc. Environ. Educators, Utah Wildlife Fedn. (bd. dirs. 1981-85, v.p. 1985-87, Achievement award 1983, 85, 87), Utah Wilderness Assn., Am. Forestry Assn., Nature Conservancy, Women in Mgmt. Coun. Office: Uinta Nat Forest 88 W 100 N Provo UT 84601-4452

CLARK, MICHAEL PHILLIP, English educator; b. Marlin, Tex., May 27, 1950; s. Burton Francis and Nelda (Blount) C.; m. Kathleen Mack, 1971 (div. 1973); m. Katherine Weber, May 26, 1977. BA magna cum laude, Rice U., 1972; MA, U. Calif., Irvine, 1973, PhD, 1977. Asst. prof. U. Mich., Ann Arbor, 1977-83; prof. in English and comparative lit. U. Calif., Irvine, 1983—. Author: Michael Foucault, 1983, Jacques Lacan, 1989; contbr. articles to profl. publs. Mem. MLA, Rocky Mountain MLA. Office: U Calif Dept English & Comparative Lit Irvine CA 92717

CLARK, MICHAL CHARLES, social services director; b. Bakersfield, Calif., Apr. 30, 1945; s. Henry Benjamin and Betty Jean (Bray) C.; m. Norleen Smith, June 8, 1973; children: Matthew, Amanda, Marlana. BA, UCLA, 1966; PhD, Stanford U., 1969. Asst. prof. U. Tex., Austin, 1969-70, Ariz. State U., Tempe, 1970-72; assoc. prof. Calif. State U., Bakersfield, 1972-74, adj. lectr., 1978—; assoc. prof. St. John's U., Collegeville, Minn., 1974-76; coord. gen. edn. Coll. of St. Benedict, St. Joseph, Minn., 1975-77; ops. officer Owen Clark Plumbing, Bakersfield, Calif., 1977; self-employed speculative builder Bakersfield, 1977-87; exec. dir. Kern Regional Ctr., Bakersfield, 1986—; pres. Nat. Down Syndrome Congress, Chgo., 1990-93; pres. Assn. Regional Ctr. Agys., Sacramento, 1991-94; chair So. Calif. Conf. Regional Ctr. Dirs., L.A., 1989-91. Editor: Understanding Student Behavior, 1969; presenter in field; contbr. articles to profl. jours. Campaign mgr. City Coun. Election, Bakersfield, 1982; mem. Spl. Edn. Adv. Com., Bakersfield, 1988-91; pres. Found. for Advocacy, Conservatorship and Trusts, L.A., 1989-91. Mem. Am. Assn. Mental Retardation (regional v.p. 1994—), Assn. Severe Handicaps, Assn. Retarded Citizens, Kern Down Syndrome Parent Group (pres. 1984-88, founder 1984). Republican. Roman Catholic. Office: Kern Regional Ctr 3200 N Sillect Ave Bakersfield CA 93308-6333

CLARK, NANCY JO, publisher; b. Bemidji, Minn., Jan. 30, 1953; d. Billy Ray and Elsie Helen (Torgerson) C.; m. Nelson C. Krum Jr., Dec. 28, 1974 (div. Aug. 1989); children: Shaun, Jarod. BA cum laude with distinction, Wheaton Coll., 1975. Reporter, editor Littleton (Colo.) Ind., 1975-79; mng. editor Titsch Publishing, Denver, 1980-81; columnist, freelance writer various publs. and consumer trade mags., 1981-84; journalist, reporter Sentinel Newspaper, Littleton & Aurora, Colo., 1988-90; editor Denver mag. Tall Oaks Publishing, Littleton, 1990-92; editor Denver Corp. Connection Squire Publishing, Engelwood, Colo., 1992; publisher Denver Corp. Connection DCC Publishing, Denver, 1992—; speaker in field. Recipient numerous awards for writing, editing, design and brochures including Colo. Press Women, Nat. Fedn. Press Women, Colo. Press Assn. Office: DCC Publishing Inc 2601 Blake St # 301 Denver CO 80205

CLARK, PATRICIA SUE, antiques dealer; b. Roswell, N.Mex., Mar. 18, 1947; d. Leslie James and Mary Agnes (Ferns) Hix; m. Charles M. Clark, Apr. 18, 1968; children: Katherine Joy, Matthew James. B in Univ. Studies, U. N.Mex., 1965-67, 91-94. Flight attendant Tex. Internat. Airlines, Houston, 1967-68; small bus. owner Great Find Antiques, Albuquerque, 1994—. Treas. and bd. mem. All Faiths Receiving Home for Abuse Children, Albuquerque, 1975-86; child watch state program chmn. Children's Def. Fund, Albuquerque, Washington,1 983-84; coun. bd. mem. City of Albuquerque Anti-Child Abuse Coun., 1988-89; project chmn., bd. mem. Jr. League, Albuquerque, 1986-87. Republican. Episcopalian. Home: 3112 Camino De La Sierra NE Albuquerque NM 87111-5604 Office: Great Find Antiques 12020 Central Albuquerque NM 87111

CLARK, R. BRADBURY, lawyer; b. Des Moines, May 11, 1924; s. Rufus Bradbury and Gertrude Martha (Burns) C.; m. Polly Ann King, Sept. 6, 1949; children: Cynthia Clark Maxwell, Rufus Bradbury, John Atherton. BA, Harvard U., 1948, JD, 1951; diploma in law, Oxford U., Eng., 1952; D.H.L., Ch. Div. Sch. Pacific, San Francisco, 1983. Bar: Calif. 1952. Assoc. O'Melveny & Myers, L.A., 1952-62, sr. ptnr., 1961-93; mem. mgmt. com., 1983-90; of counsel O'Melveny & Myers, L.A., 1993—; bd. dirs. So. Calif. Water Co., Econ. Resources Corp., Brown Internat. Corp., Automatic Machinery & Electronics Corp., John Tracy Clinic, also pres. 1982-88. Editor: California Corporation Laws, 6 vols, 1976—. Chancellor Prot. Episcopal Ch. in the Diocese of L.A., 1967—, hon. canon, 1983—. Capt. U.S. Army, 1943-46. Decorated Bronze Star with oak leaf cluster, Purple Heart with oak leaf cluster; Fulbright grantee, 1952. Mem. ABA (subcom. on audit letter responses, com. on law and acctg., task force on legal opinions), State Bar Calif. (chmn. drafting com. on gen. corp. law 1973-81, drafting com. on nonprofit corp. law 1980-84, mem. exec. com. bus. law sect. 1977-78, 84-87, sec. 1986-87, mem. com. nonprofit corp. law 1991—), L.A. County Bar Assn., Harvard Club, Chancery Club, Alamitos Bay Yacht Club (Long Beach, Calif.). Republican. Office: O'Melveny & Myers 400 S Hope St Los Angeles CA 90071-2801

CLARK, RAMONA RICHLI, radiologist; b. Camden, N.J., Jan. 24, 1940; m. Richard Norman Roger, June 24, 1961 (div. Sept. 1968); children: Gregory, Douglas, Nicholas; m. Guy Storman Clark, Sept. 24, 1972; children: Laura, Warren. Student, La Sierra U., 1957-59; MD, U. So. Calif., 1963. Diplomate Am. Bd. Pediatrics, Am. Bd. Radiology. Intern Glendale Adventist Med. Ctr., 1964-65; resident Children's Hosp. of L.A., 1964-65, L.A. County-U. So. Calif. Med. Ctr., 1968-69, Cedars-Sinai Med. Ctr., L.A., 1969-73; radiologist Alaska Native Svc. Hosp., Anchorage, 1973-74, Cmty. Meml. Hosp., Ventura, Calif., 1975-80; radiologist Pueblo Radiology Med. Group, Santa Barbara, Calif., 1980—, also bd. dirs.; dir. med. staff edn. Cmty. Meml. Hosp., 1976-79; mem. quality care com. Goleta Valley Hosp., 1985—; chmn. Poeblo Radiology Pension Fund, 1987—; lectr. in field. Bd. dirs. Santa Barbara Chamber Orch., 1989-93, Monterey Bay Acad., 1992—; violinist with local cmty. groups; music dir. Seventh-Day Adventist Ch., 1988—. Mem. AMA, Calif. Med. Assn. (alt. del. 1992), Am. Coll. Radiology, Radiol. Soc. N.Am., Southcoast Radiol. Soc. (pres. 1988-89, sec.-treas. 1986-87), Santa Barbara County Med. Soc. (bd. dirs. 1990—, treas. 1993, sec. 1994, pres.-elect 1995), Monterey Bay Acad. Alumni Assn. (bd. dirs. 1991-94, 1st fundraising chmn.). Office: Pueblo Radiology 2305 De La Vina St Santa Barbara CA 93105-3873

CLARK, RAYMOND OAKES, banker; b. Ft. Bragg, N.C., Nov. 9, 1944; s. Raymond Shelton and Nancy Lee (McCormick) C.; m. Patricia Taylor Slaughter; children: Matthew Patrick, Geoffry Charles. BBA, U. Ariz., 1966; postgrad., U. Wash., 1984-86. Mgmt. trainee First Interstate Bank, Phoenix, 1966, credit analyst, 1968-69, asst. br. mgr., Scottsdale, Ariz., 1969-72, asst. v.p., br. mgr., Tempe, Ariz., 1972-90, v.p. br. mgr. Scottsdale, 1990-92, v.p. mgr. main office Phoenix, 1992—. Pres., bd. dirs. Sun Devil Club, Tempe, 1975—; bd. dirs. Valley Big Brothers/Big Sisters, 1994—; pres. Tempe Diplomats, 1979-89; pres. Tempe Diablos, 1975—; major chmn. Fiesta Bowl, Tempe, 1975-79; bd. dirs. Maricopa County Bd. Mgrs., Phoenix, 1973, YMCA, Tempe, 1974, Tempe Design Rev. Bd., 1983-87. Named one of Outstanding Young Men of Am., 1978. Bd. dirs., treas. East Valley divsn. Am. Heart Assn., 1989-92. Served with U.S. Army, 1966-68. Mem. Tempe C. of C. (pres. 1979-80). Republican. Episcopalian. Lodge: Kiwanis (dist. lt. gov. 1972-87), Phoenix 100 Rotary.

CLARK, RICHARD DOUGLAS, radiologist, research scientist; b. El Paso, June 23, 1946; s. Joseph Ernest and Anne Lois (Baker) C.; m. Yoko, M.J.B. Tomabechi, Oct. 25, 1975; children: Eiko Theodora, Toshimasa James. BA, U. Calif., Berkeley, 1969, PhD, 1975; MD, Columbia U., 1986. Diplomate Nat. Bd. Med. Examiners, Am. Bd. Radiology. Rsch. scientist dept physiology U. Colo. Med. Sch., Denver, 1978-82; intern Mary Imogene Bassett Hosp., Cooperstown, N.Y., 1986-87; resident St. Luke's/Roosevelt Hosp. Ctr., N.Y.C., 1987-91; fellow dept. radiol. scis. U. Wash., Seattle, 1991-92; staff radiologist, asst. sect. chief dept. radiology Group Health Coop., Tacoma, 1992—. Contbr. articles to profl. jours. Musician in Tacoma Concert Band, 1992—. With U.S. Merchant Marine, 1970. Mem. NRA, Am. Coll. Radiology, Radiol. Soc. Am., Soc. for Neurosci., Am. Soc. Zoologists,, Wash. State Civil War Re-enactment Assn., Phi Beta Kappa, Sigma Xi, Alpha Omega Alpha,. Republican. Episcopalian. Home: 11817 Gravelly Lake Dr SW Tacoma WA 98499-1410 Office: Group Health Coop 209 S K St Tacoma WA 98405-4265

CLARK, RICHARD WARD, food industry executive, consultant; b. N.Y.C., Oct. 23, 1938; s. Richard Leal and Dorothy Jane (Whittaker) C. BA with honors, U. Rochester, N.Y., 1960; MBA in Fin., U. Pa., 1962. Corp. planning analyst Campbell Soup Co., Camden, N.J., 1965-67; asst. product mgr. Gen. Mills, Inc., Mpls., 1967-70; sr. fin. analyst McKesson Corp., San Francisco, 1970-71, asst. div. controller, 1971-72, div. controller, 1972-78, gen. mgr. grocery products devel., 1978-79; v.p., controller McKesson Foods Group/McKesson Corp., 1979-85, dir. strategic planning

1985-87; v.p. fin., chief fin. officer Provigo Corp. (Market Wholesale Grocery Co.), San Rafael, Calif., 1987-89; cons. and hotel devel. Napa Valley Assocs., S.A., San Francisco, 1990-94, health care cons., 1994—; bd. dirs. Taylor Cuisine, Inc., San Francisco. Author: Some Factors Affecting Dividend Payout Ratios, 1962; musician (albums) Dick Clark at the Keyboard, I Love a Piano, 1990, I Play the Songs, 1993. Adv. bd. Salvation Army, San Francisco, 1984—, chmn., 1993—; bd. dirs. Svcs. for Srs., San Francisco, 1990-93. Lt. (j.g.) USNR, 1962-64, PTO. Sherman fellow U. Rochester, 1960. Mem. Bohemian Club, Beta Gamma Sigma. Republican. Presbyterian. Home: 2201 Sacramento St Apt 401 San Francisco CA 94115-2314

CLARK, RONALD RALPH, marketing executive; b. San Francisco, Apr. 1, 1952; s. Meredith Wallace and Carol Rose (Sherod) C.; m. Linda Sue Partin, June 24, 1972; 1 child, Raeghan Noelle. Student, Augusta Coll., 1970-73. Produce mgr. Piggly Wiggly So., Inc., Augusta, Ga., 1970-73; prodn. supr. Uniroyal, Inc., Thomson, Ga., 1973-74; sales merchandiser Sav-A-Stop Inc., Augusta, 1974-80; dist. mgr. Sav-A-Stop Inc., Atlanta, 1980-82; regional mgr. Sav-A-Stop Inc., Miami, Fla., 1982-85; retail merchandise svc. mgr. McLane/S.E., Athens, Ga., 1985-88; v.p. mktg. McLane/So., Brookhaven, Miss., 1988-90, McLane/S.W., Temple, Tex., 1990-92; div. pres. McLane/Pacific, Brookhaven, 1992-93, Merced, Calif., 1993—. Mem. Brookhaven (Miss.) C. of C., 1989-90; coord. Children's Miracle Network/McLane/S.W., Temple, 1990-91; vice chmn. bd. dirs. Temple Salvation Army. With U.S. Army, 1971. Mem. Tex. Oil Marketers Assn., Tex. Food Industry Assn. Republican. Methodist. Home: 1169 Ensenada Ct Merced CA 95348-1853 Office: McLane/Pacific PO Box 2107 Merced CA 95344-0107

CLARK, RUTH ANN, lay worker, educator; b. Columbus, Kans., July 18, 1935; d. Jacob Ellis Harold and Annie Lee Opal (Noel) Davidson; m. Ralph Francis Clark, July 10, 1965; children: Kristine Anna Jamison, Russell Kirk. BS, McPherson Coll., 1957; M in Religious Edn., Bethany Theol. Sem., Oak Brook, Ill., 1964. Commd. lay spkr. no. plains dist. Ch. of the Brethren. Vol. Brethren Vol. Svcs., Friedland, Kassel, Germany, 1957-60; youth fieldworker Cen. Region Youth Cabinet, North Manchester, Ind., 1960-62; dir. Christian edn. 1st Ch. of the Brethren, Roanoke, Va., 1964-65; substitute tchr. Froid/Medicine Lake (Mont.) Schs., 1984—. Sec., chair dist. bd. witness Ch. of Brethren, 1972-79, nat. standing com. 1978, 79, discipleship reconciliation, 1980-94, rep. to ch., local dist. for internat. heifer project, 1983—, Mon-Dak area com. chmn., 1979-89, recipient plaque of appreciation, 1989, mem. gen. bd., 1994—, no. plains dist. bd., 1994—, ex officio, 1994—, com. interch. rels. 1986—; sec. PTO/PTA Medicine Lake, 1984; chairperson Music Mothers, Medicine Lake, 1983-85; judge county elections, Sheridan County, Mont., 1980—. Recipient 15 Yrs. Leadership award 4-H, 1986, Class Agent of Yr. award McPherson Coll., 1987. Mem. Inst. for Peace Studies (bd. dirs. 1990—, vice chairperson 1990—), Assn. Christian Educators (curriculum trainer 1994). Home: HC 61 Box 36 Froid MT 59226-9601

CLARK, SHERI LYNN, public relations and marketing executive; b. Denver, Mar. 15, 1961; d. Edward G. and Virginia Ann (Legg) M.; m. Howard Allen Clark, Mar. 28, 1985; children: Allen Joseph, Michael Howard. BA in Journalism and Tech. Comm., Met. State Coll. Denver, 1983. Acct. coord. Tracy Locke Advt. & Pub. Rels., Denver, 1983-84, asst. acct. exec., 1984-85; mktg. dir. May Ctrs. Inc., Denver, 1985-87; dir. pub. rels. and mktg. Mile Hi coun. Girl Scouts U.S.A., Denver, 1987—. Mem. fund raising com. St. Thomas More Cath. Sch., 1994—. Mem. Pub. Rels. Soc. Am., Am. Mktg. Assn.

CLARK, SILVANA MARIE, professional speaker, author; b. Munich, Mar. 4, 1953; came to U.S., 1957; d. Richard and Helga (Viktora) Vranjes; m. Allan Richard Clark, Aug. 27, 1977; children: Trina, Sondra. AA, Yakima (Wash.) Valley Coll., 1973; BS in Recreation Adminstrn., San Diego State U., 1978. Recreation supr. Bellingham (Wash.) Parks and Recreation Dept., 1980-90; profl. speaker, Bellingham, 1990—. Author: Taming the Recreation Jungle, 1993; contbr. over 75 articles to mags.; patentee for Foot Friends. Recipient Outstanding Recreation Programmer award Wash. Recreation and Paarks Assn., 1990. Mem. Nat. Speakers Assn., Nat. Parks and Recreation Assn. Home and Office: 3024 Haggin St Bellingham WA 98226-9430

CLARK, TERESA WATKINS, psychotherapist, clinical counselor; b. Hobart, Okla., Dec. 18, 1953; d. Aaron Jack Watkins and Patricia Ann (Flurry) Greer and Ralph Gordon Greer; m. Philip Winston Clark, Dec. 29, 1979; children: Philip Aaron, Alisa Lauren. BA in Psychology, U. N.Mex., 1979, MA in Counseling and Family Studies, 1989. Lic. profl. counselor, N.Mex. Child care worker social svcs. divsn. Family Resource Ctr., Albuquerque, 1978-79; head tchr., asst. dir. Kinder Care Learning Ctr., Albuquerque, 1979-80; psychiat. asst. Vista Sandia Psychiat. Hosp., Albuquerque, 1980-87; psychotherapist outpatient clinic Bernalillo County Mental Health Ctr.-Heights, 1989-91; therapist adolescent program Heights Psychiat. Hosp., Albuquerque, 1991—. Mem. ACA, Am. Assn. Multicultural Counseling and Devel., N.Mex. Health Counselors Assn. (ctrl. regional rep. bd. dirs., bd. dirs.), Phi Kappa Phi. Democrat. Office: Heights Psychiat Hosp 103 Hospital Loop NE Albuquerque NM 87109-2115

CLARK, THOMAS RYAN, retired federal agency executive, business and technical consultant; b. Aberdeen, Wash., Sept. 16, 1925; s. George O. and Gladys (Ryan) C.; m. Barbara Ann Thiele, June 14, 1948; children: Thomas R. III, Kathleen Clark Sandberg, Christopher J.T. Student, U. Kans., 1943-44; BS, U.S. Mil. Acad., 1948; MSEE, Purdue U., 1955; cert., U.S. Army Command and Gen. Staff Coll., 1960, Harvard U., 1979. Commd. C.E., U.S. Army, 1948, advanced through grades to col., 1968; ret. U.S. Army, 1968; program mgr. U.S. AEC, Washington, 1968-75; dep. mgr. Dept. of Energy, Albuquerque, 1976-83; sr. exec. svc., 1977; mgr. Nev. ops. Dept. of Energy, Las Vegas, 1983-87, ret., 1987; cons. in field Las Vegas and Albuquerque, 1987—; mem. adv. bd. Dept. Chem. and Nuclear Engring., U. N.Mex., 1984—; mem. statewide adv. bd. Desert Research Inst., U. Nev., 1985-88. Editor, co-author: Nuclear Fuel Cycle, 1975. Trustee Nev. Devel. Authority, Las Vegas, 1984-88, Nat. Atomic Mus. Found., 1993—. Decorated Legion of Merit, Bronze Star; named Disting. Exec., Pres. of U.S., 1982. Mem. Las Vegas C. of C. (bd. dirs. 1983-87), Sigma Xi, Tau Beta Pi, Eta Kappa Nu, Rotary Club of Albuquerque (pres. 1993-94). Episcopalian. Lodge: Rotary.

CLARK, THOMAS SULLIVAN, lawyer; b. Bakersfield, Calif., Dec. 12, 1947; s. Walter J. and Ruth Virginia (Sullivan) C. BA in History, U. So. Calif., 1969, JD, 1973. Gen. counsel Income Equities Corp., Los Angeles, 1972-74; campaign cons. Huntington Beach, Calif., 1974-75; prosecutor Office of Kern County Dist. Atty., Bakersfield, 1975-78; ptnr. Arrache, Clark & Potter (formerly Rudnick, Arrache & Clark), Bakersfield, 1978—; cons. Vol. Attys. Program, Bakersfield, 1985—. Bd. dirs. Kern Bridges Youth Found., pres. 1987-89; bd. dirs. Bakersfield City Sch. Dist. Ednl. Found., Bakersfield Med. Found. Mem. Calif. Bar Assn., Kern County Bar Assn. (client cons. 1984—), Community Assns. Inst., Kern County Hist. Soc., Kern County U. So. Calif. Alumni Assn. (bd. dirs., v.p. 1985-88, pres. 1988—). Republican. Roman Catholic. Club: Petroleum. Lodge: Rotary (bd. dirs. Bakersfield club 1982), Seven Oaks Country Club. Stockdale Country Club. Office: Arrache Clark & Potter 5401 California Ave Ste 301 Bakersfield CA 93309

CLARK, WALTER W., construction executive; b. 1947. With Arthur Young, Edmonton, Alta., Can., 1969-72, Levi-Strauss, Edmonton, Alta., Can., 1971-79, Westcan Group, Edmonton, Alta., Can., 1979-80, PCL Constrn. Group, Inc., Edmonton, Alta., Can., 1980-84; v.p. fin. adminstrn., sec., treas. PCL Enterprises, Inc., Denver, 1984—. Office: PCL Enterprises Inc 2000 S Cook St Ste 400 Denver CO 80210-3609*

CLARK, WILL (WILLIAM NUSCHLER CLARK, JR.), professional baseball player; b. New Orleans, Mar. 13, 1964. Student, Miss. State U. Baseball player San Francisco Giants, 1986-93, Texas Rangers, 1994—; mem. U.S. Olympic baseball team, 1984. Recipient Golden Spikes award USA Baseball, 1985, Gold Glove award Nat. League, 1991, Silver Slugger, 1989, 91; named to Sporting News Nat. League All-Star team, 1988-89, 91, Coll. All-Am. Team Sporting News, 1984-85, Nat. League All-Star team, 1988-92, Am. League All-Star team, 1994; Nat. RBI leader, 1988. Office: Texas Rangers Arlington Stadium PO Box 1111 Arlington TX 76004*

CLARKE, GRETA FIELDS, dermatologist; b. Detroit; d. George William and Willa (Wright) Fields; B.S., U. Mich., 1962; 1 child, Richard Clement Clarke. MD, Howard U., 1967. Resident in dermatology NYU, 1969-72, clin. instr., 1972-77; practice medicine specializing in dermatology, N.Y.C., 1972-77; dermatologist Arlington Med. Group, Oakland, Calif., 1977-79; practice medicine specializing in dermatology, Berkeley, Calif., 1979—. Bd. dirs. Bay Area Black United Fund, 1985-90, Sequoyah Heights Homeowners Assn., 1994—; CEO, Fields Dermatologic Group, 1992—. Diplomate Am. Bd. Dermatology. Mem. Nat. Med. Assn. (chmn. coun. on concerns of women physicians 1983-88, chmn. region VI 1986-90, jud. coun. 1988-91, trustee 1990-92), Golden State Med. Assn., Am. Acad. Dermatology, Soc. Cosmetic Chemists, San Francisco Dermatol., Jack and Jill Club Am. (chpt. pres. 1984-85), Carrousels Club. Office: 2500 Milvia St Berkeley CA 94704-2636

CLARKE, JANICE CESSNA, principal; b. Inglewood, Calif., Sept. 8, 1936; d. Eldon W. and Helen V. (Parcels) Cessna; m. Jack F. Clarke, Mar. 30, 1958; children: Scott Alan, Kristin Ann, Kerry Suzanne. BA, U. of Redlands, 1958; MA in Teaching, Reed Coll., 1963; EdD, U. Nev., Reno, 1993. Cert. tchr., adminstr., Nev. Elem. tchr. Portland (Oreg.) Pub. Schs., 1959-62, Eugene (Oreg.) Pub. Schs., 1964-66; music tchr. Tempe (Ariz.) Pub. Schs., 1969-70; music tchr. Washoe County Sch. Dist., Reno, 1971-80, tchr. gifted and talented program, 1980-89, coord. gifted and talented program, 1989-93; prin. Brown Elem. Sch., Reno, 1993—; bd. dirs. Far West Lab. for Ednl. Rsch., San Francisco, 1983-90. Mem. Nev. State Bd. Edn., 1982-90, pres., 1984-86. Recipient Disting. Svc. award Washoe County Tchr. Assn., 1974, Tchr. of Month award Reno/Sparks C. of C., 1984; named to El Segundo High Sch. Hall of Fame, 1989. Mem. NEA, Nev. State Edn. Assn., Nev. Assn. Sch. Adminstrs., Nev. Sch. Bds. Assn. (bd. dirs. 1982-90), Nat. Assn. Elem. Sch. Prins., Phi Delta Kappa, Delta Kappa Gamma. Office: Brown Sch 13815 Spelling Ct Reno NV 89511-7232

CLARKE, JUNO-ANN KROHN, nutrition educator; b. Detroit, Mar. 3, 1935; d. Bernhard Jorgsen and Bertha (Van Schellen) K.; children: Ceres Aleida Yueh-Mei, Freya Inga Grayce. BS in Dietetics, Mich. State U., 1956; MS in Food Sci., U. Calif., Berkeley, 1960, PhD in Clin. Nutrition, 1969. Registered dietitian; RN Calif. Instr. Bakersfield (Calif.) Coll., 1959-60; prof. San Francisco State U., 1960—; cons. USAID, Liberia, 1969, Afghanistan, 1971, Am. Tech. Assistance Corp., Pakistan and Bangladesh, 1971, Ministry of Edn., Kuwait, 1980-82, Hosp. de la Familia, Guatemala, 1984, 93; head task force for specialist in gerontology, Gerontology Practice Group, 1991-93. Leader Girl Scouts Am., Peidmont, Calif., 1988-90. Ida Hyde postdoctoral fellow AAUW, 1970-71. Mem. Am. Dietetic Assn. (del. 1968-70, Mead Johnson fellow 1959, Mary Schwartz Rose fellow 1969), Calif. Dietetic Assn. (treas. 1994—, Grad. fellow 1968), Bay Area Dietetic Assn. (pres. 1968), Dietetic Educators Practitioners (treas. 1987-89, area 1 rep. 1985-87). Lutheran. Office: San Francisco State U Dept CFS/D Sch HHS 1600 Holloway Ave San Francisco CA 94132-1722

CLARKE, PAUL A., public relations professional; b. Mar. 27, 1946; married. Govt. and pub. adminstrn. student, American U., 1969. Broadcast journalist ABC, CBS, NBC and RKO broadcast assignments, Washington, Chgo., L.A.; ins. agt. Washington Nat. Ins. Co., 1973-76; ind. polit. cons., 1976-80; congl. chief of staff Offices Congresswoman Bobbi Fiedler, Washington, 1981-87; v.p. govt. rels. Donut Inns of Am., 1990—; bd. dirs., v.p. Donuts Inns Internat.; bd. dirs. Franchise Support Svcs., Inc.; strategic planning cons. numerous clients with environ. documents, others. Contbr. articles to profl. jours.

CLARKE, RICHARD ALAN, electric and gas utility company executive, lawyer; b. San Francisco, May 18, 1930; s. Chauncey Frederick and Carolyn (Shannon) C.; m. Mary Dell Fisher, Feb. 5, 1955; children: Suzanne, Nancy C. Stephen, Douglas Alan. AB Polit. Sci. cum laude, U. Calif., Berkeley, 1952, JD, 1955. Bar: Calif. 1955. Atty. Pacific Gas and Electric Co., San Francisco, 1955-60, sr. counsel, 1970-74, asst. gen. counsel, 1974-79, v.p., asst. to chmn., 1979-82, exec. v.p., gen. mgr. utility ops., 1982-85, pres., 1985-86, chmn. bd., CEO, 1986-94, chmn. bd., 1994-95; ptnr. Rockwell, Fulkerson and Clarke, San Rafael, Calif., 1960-69; bd. dirs. Pacific Gas & Electric Co., Potlach Corp., Bank Am. Corp.; mem. Bus. Coun. Pres' Coun. on Sustained Devel. Bd. dirs., past chmn. Bay Area Coun.; bd. dirs. Bay Area Econ. Forum; trustee Boalt Hall Trust, Sch. Law U. Calif., Berkeley; mem. adv. bd. Walter A. Haas Sch. Bus., U. Calif., Berkeley; bd. govs. San Francisco Symphony. Mem. Calif. C. of C. (past dir.), San Francisco C. of C. (past dir., v.p. econ. devel.), Marin Tennis Club. Office: Pacific Gas & Electric Co 123 Mission St San Francisco CA 94177

CLARKE, ROBERT F., utilities company executive; b. Oakland, Calif.. BA, U. Calif., Berkeley, 1965, MBA, 1966. Pres., CEO Hawaiian Electric, 1991—. Office: Hawaiian Electric Industries Inc 900 Richards St Honolulu HI 96813-2919

CLARKE, URANA, writer, musician, educator; b. Wickliffe-on-the-Lake, Ohio, Sept. 8, 1902; d. Graham Warren and Grace Urana (Olsaver) C.; artists and tchrs. diploma Mannes Music Sch., N.Y.C., 1925; cert. Dalcroze Sch. Music, N.Y.C., 1950; student Pembroke Coll., Brown U.; BS, Mont. State U., 1967, M of Applied Sci., 1970. Mem. faculty Mannes Music Sch., 1922-49, Dalcroze Sch. Music, 1949-54; adv. editor in music The Book of Knowledge, 1949-65; v.p., dir. Saugatuck Circle Housing Devel.; guest lectr. Hayden Planetarium, 1945; guest lectr., bd. dirs. Roger Williams Park Planetarium, Providence; radio show New Eng. Skies, Providence, 1961-64, Skies Over the Big Sky Country, Livingston, Mont., 1964-79, Birds of the Big Sky Country, 1972-79, Great Music of Religion, 1974-79; mem. adv. com. Nat. Rivers and Harbors Congress, 1947-58; instr. continuing edn. Mont. State U. Chmn. Park County chpt. ARC, 1967-92, chmn. emeritus 1992—, co-chmn. county blood program, first aid instr. trainer, 1941-93; instr. ARC cardio-pulmonary resuscitation, 1976-84; mem. Mont. Commn. Nursing and Nursing Edn., 1974-76; mem. Park County Local Govt. Study Com., 1974-76, chmn., 1984-86, vice-chair, 94—. Mem. Am. Acad. Polit. Sci., Am. Musicol. Soc., Royal Astron. Soc. Can., Inst. Nav., Maria Mitchell Soc. Nantucket, N.Am. Yacht Racing Union, AAAS, Meteoritical Soc., Internat. Soc. Mus. Research, Skyscrapers (sec.-treas. 1960-63), Am. Guild Organists, Park County Wilderness Assn. (treas.), Trout Unlimited, Nature Conservancy, Big Sky Astron. Soc. (dir. 1965—), Sierra Club. Lutheran. Club: Cedar Point Yacht. Author: The Heavens are Telling (astronomy), 1951; Skies Over the Big Sky Country, 1965; also astron. news-letter, View It Yourself, weekly column Big Skies, 1981—; contbr. to mags. on music, nav. and astronomy. Pub. Five Chorale Preludes for Organ, 1975; also elem. two-piano pieces. Inventor, builder of Clarke Adjustable Piano Stool. Address: Log-A-Rhythm 9th St Island Livingston MT 59047

CLARK-LANGAGER, SARAH ANN, director, curator, university official; b. Lynchburg, Va., May 14, 1943; d. James Thomas and Mary Whitworth (Cooper) Clark; m. Craig T. Langager, 1979. BA in Art History, Randolph-Macon Woman's Coll., 1965; postgrad., U. Md., 1968; MA in Art History, U. Wash., 1970; PhD in Art History, CUNY, 1988. Assoc. edn. dept., lectr. Yale U. Art Gallery, New Haven, 1965-67, Albright-Knox Art Gallery, Buffalo, 1967-68; asst. to dir. Richard White Gallery, Seattle, 1969-70; curatorial asst. to curators painting and sculpture San Francisco Mus. Modern Art, 1970; assoc. edn. dept., lectr. Seattle Art Mus., 1971-73, 74-75; asst. curator, and then assoc. curator modern art, lectr. Seatle Art Mus., 1975-79; curator 20th century art, lectr. Munson-Willaims-Proctor Inst., Utica, N.Y., 1981-86; asst. prof. art history, dir. Univ. Art Gallery, U. North Tex., Denton, 1986-88; dir. Western Gallery, curator outdoor sculpture collection Western Wash. U., Bellingham, 1988—, mem. adj. faculty, 1988—; lectr., cons. in edn. N.Y. Cultural Ctr., N.Y.C., 1973-74; editl. asst. October, MIT Press, N.Y.C., 1980; lectr. art history South Seattle C.C., 1975; lectr. 20th century art Cornish Inst. Fine Arts, Seattle, 1977-78; sole rep. for N.Y. State, Art Mus. Assn. Am., 1984-86; mem. Wash. Art Consortium, 1988—, v.p., 1989-90, pres., 1990-93; mem. ad hoc del. concerning issues confronting Nat. Endowment for Arts, Bellingham, 1990; cons. State of Wash. SOS (Save Outdoor Sculpture), 1994—; also others. Contbr. articles to profl. jours.; curator exhbns., 1970—, including Rodney Ripps traveling exhbn., 1983, Sculpture Space: Recent Trends, 1984, Order and Enigma: American Art Between the Two Ward, 1984, Stars over Texas: Top of the Triangle, 1988, Master Works of American Art from the Munson-Williams-Proctor Institute, 1989, Public Art/Private Visions, 1989, Drawing Power, 1990, Audiophone Tour for Sculpture Collection-20 Interview, 1991, Focus on Figure, 1992, Chairs: Embodied Objectr, 1993, Northwest Native American and First Nations People's Art, 1993, New Acquisitions, 1995, Stars and Stripes: American Prints and Drawings, 1995. Juror Arts in Pub. Places, Seattle Arts Commn., 1975, 78-79, Wash. State Arts Commn., 1976, 91, 92-93, King County Arts Commn., Seattle, 1979, Ctrl. N.Y. regional art exhbns., Syracuse, Utica, Rome, Potsdam, 1981-86, East Tex. State U., Commerce, 1987, Brookhaven C.C., Farmers Branch, Tex., 1988, Bellingham Mcpl. Arts Commn., 1989, 90; mem. adv. com. Steuben Park Fountain, Utica, 1985-86. Recipient Woman of Merit in Arts award Mohawk Valley C.C. and YWCA, Utica, 1985; Kress Found. fellow U. Wash., 1970; Helena Rubenstein Found. scholar CUNY Grad. Ctr., 1980. Office: Western Wash U Western Gallery Fine Arts Complex Bellingham WA 98225-9068

CLARKSON, LAWRENCE WILLIAM, airplane company executive; b. Grove City, Pa., Apr. 29, 1938; s. Harold William and Jean Henrietta (Jaxtheimer) C.; m. Barbara Louise Stevenson, Aug. 20, 1960; children: Michael, Elizabeth, Jennifer. BA, DePauw U., 1960; JD, U. Fla., 1962. Counsel Pratt & Whitney, West Palm Beach, Fla., 1967-72, program dep. dir., 1972-75, program mgr., 1974-75; v.p., mng. dir. Pratt & Whitney, Brussels, Belgium, 1975-78; v.p. mktg. Pratt & Whitney, West Palm Beach, 1978-80; v.p. contracts Pratt & Whitney, Hartford, Conn., 1980-82, pres. comml. products div., 1982-87; sr. v.p. Boeing Comml. Airplanes Group, Seattle, 1988-91; corp. v.p. planning and internat. devel. Boeing Co., Seattle, 1992-93, sr. v.p., 1994—; dir. Partnership for Improved Air Travel, Washington, 1988—. Trustee DePauw U., Greencastle, Ind., 1987—; overseer Tuck Sch. Dartmouth, Hanover, N.H., 1993—; corp. coun. Interlochen (Mich.) Ctr. for the Arts, 1987, trustee, 1988—, Seattle Opera, 1990—, chmn., 1991—; pres. Japan-Am. Soc., Wash., pres. Wash. State China Rels. com., chmn. Nat. Bur. of Asia Rsch., Coun. Fgn. Rels.; vice chmn. U.S. Pacific Econ. Corp. Coun., 1993—. Capt. USAF, 1963-66. Mem. Nat. Assn. Mfrs. (bd. dirs.), N.Y. Yacht Club, Seattle Yacht Club, Met. Opera Club, Wings Club (bd. govs., 1987-91). Episcopalian. Home: 13912 NE 31st Pl Bellevue WA 98005-1881 Office: The Boeing Co MS 1F-26 PO Box 3707 Seattle WA 98124-2207

CLARREN, STERLING KEITH, pediatrician; b. Mpls., Mar. 12, 1947; s. David Bernard and Lila (Reifel) C.; m. Sandra Gayle Bernstein, June 8, 1970; children: Rebecca Pia, Jonathan Seth. BA, Yale U., 1969; MD, U. Minn., 1973. Pediatric intern U. Wash. Sch. Medicine, Seattle, 1973-74, resident in pediatrics, 1974-77, asst. prof. dept. pediatrics, 1979-83, assoc. prof., 1983-88, prof., 1988, Robert A. Aldrich chair in pediatrics, 1989—; head divsn. congenital defects U. Wash. Sch. Medicine, 1987-95; dir. dept. congenital defects Children's Hosp. and Med. Ctr., Seattle, 1987—, dir. fetal alcohol syndrome clinic Child Devel. & Mental Retardation Ctr. U. Wash., 1992—, dir. FAS Network, 1995—. Contbr. articles to profl. jours.; patentee for orthosis to alter cranial shape. Cons. pediatrician Maxillofacial Rev. Bd., State of Wash., Seattle, 1984—, chmn. Health-Birth Defects Adv. Com., Olympia, 1980—; mem. gov.'s task force on FAS State of Wash., 1994-95; mem. fetal alcohol adv. com. Children's Trust Found., Seattle, 1988—; mem. adv. bd. Nat. Orgn. on Fetal Alcohol Syndrome; mem. fetal alcohol com. Inst. Medicine, NAS, 1994-95. Rsch. grantee Nat. Inst. Alcohol Abuse & Alcoholism, 1982—, Ctrs. for Disease Control, 1992—. Fellow AAAS; mem. Am. Acad. Pediatrics, Soc. for Pediatric Rsch., Teratology Soc., Rsch. Soc. on Alcoholism (pres. fetal alcohol study group 1993), Am. Cleft Palate Assn., N.Y. Acad. Scis. Home: 8515 Paisley Dr NE Seattle WA 98115-3944 Office: Children's Hosp and Med Ctr Divsn Congenital Defects PO Box C-5371 Seattle WA 98105

CLARY, DONALD RAY, minister; b. Seattle, Wash., July 3, 1937; s. John Clifton and Graldine Marguerite (Lowry) C.; m. Carol Ann Ferris, July 3, 1963; children: Ronald, Robert, John, Joy, Laura, Paul. BA in Divinity with honors, Adler Meml. U., 1966; D. of Divinity with honors, Am. Bible Inst., Kansas City, Mo., 1968. Pastor Five Mile Comty. Ch., Spokane, Wash., 1968-70; founder, counseling minister Christian Counseling Ctr., Spokane, 1968-84; interim pastor Open Bible Ch., Smelterville, Idaho, 1981-82; founder (name change) Family Living Ministies, Spokane, 1984—; exec. pastor Foursquare Ch., Millwood, Wash., 1991-93. Author: What About and Why, 1988, Counseling in Ministry, 1989, On Target--A Guide to Effective Christian Counseling, 1995. Fellow Internat. Assn. Christian Clin. Counselors (cert. counselor); mem. Nat. Assn. Evangelicals, Hosp. Chaplain Mins. of Am. (fully cert. chaplain), Am. Assn. Christian Counselors (cert. counselor), Spokane Full Gospel Pastors Assn. (v.p.1993-94), Greater Spokane Assn. Evangelicals, Alpha Kappa Omega. Home: 207 W Euclid Ave Spokane WA 99205-3022 Office: Family Living Ministries 207 W Euclid Ave Spokane WA 99205-3022

CLARY, PATRICIA MAY, nonprofit administrator; b. Oakland, Calif., Nov. 13, 1946; d. Jackson Temple and Barbara (Harrison) C.; divorced; children: Aisha Candrian, Thomas Jackson Candrian. Grad. h.s., Santa Rosa, Calif. Clothing designer, herbalist No. Calif., 1967-74; real estate developer No. Calif. and So. Oreg., 1978-89; exec. dir. Calif. for Alternatives to Toxics, Arcata, 1988—; cons. on toxic issues various attys., San Jose and Redway, Calif., 1991—. Author: (newspaper) Econews, 1989—, (jour.) Jour. Pesticide Reform, 1988—; editor: (newsletter) Drift Dodger, 1988—. Bd. dirs. Yurock Head Start, Klamath, Calif., 1994—; mem. Calif. Methyl Bromide Rsch. Task Force, Sacramento, 1993—, UN Environ. Program Methyl Bromide Tech. Options Com., Nairobi, Kenya, 1993—, Methyl Bromide Alternatives Network, San Francisco, 1993—. Recipient Giraffe award Giraffe Found., 1992. Mem. Nat. Coalition Against Misuse of Pesticides, Environ. Health Coalition (bd. dirs. 1986-92). Democrat. Office: Californians for Alt Toxics 860 1/2 11th St Arcata CA 95521-5853

CLARY, THOMAS CHARLES, bishop, psychologist; b. Joplin, Mo., Mar. 3, 1927; s. Thomas Clinton Clary and Ruby Catherine Smith Battese; children: Catherine, Ann, Margaret, Barbara, Hunter. BBA, Pace U., N.Y.C., 1965; MA, U. Okla., 1968; STL, Free Cath. Sem., Iowa City, Iowa, 1992; PhD in Psychology, Calif. Coast U., Santa Ana, 1978. Ordained priest Free Cath. Ch., 1992, elevated to bishop, 1994; diplomate Am. Bd. Sexology. Commd. 2d lt. U.S. Army, 1945, advanced through grades to lt. col., 1966, ret., 1968; v.p. St. Gregory's Coll., Shawnee, Okla., 1968-70; instr., course dir. U. Okla., Norman, 1970-72; assoc. Nat. Tng. and Devel. Svc., Washington, 1972-77; pres. TCI, Inc., Washington, also La Jolla, Calif., 1977—; presiding bishop Free Cath. Ch., La Jolla, 1994—; cons. Indian Health Svc., Washington, 1985—, Bur. Indian Affairs, Washington, 177-93, Nat. Assn. Counties, Washington, 1973-92, City of Burbank, Calif., 1972-77. Fellow Am. Acad. Clin. Secologists, Am. Assn. Profl. Hypnotherapists, D.C. Mental Health Counseling Assn. (pres.-elect 1993-94), Am. Soc. Sex Educators, Counselors and Therapists. Home and Office: PO Box 1439 La Jolla CA 92038-1439

CLAUS, CAROL JEAN, small business owner; b. Uniondale, N.Y., Dec. 17, 1959; d. Charles Joseph and Frances Meta (Fichter) C.; m. Armand Joseph Gasperettl, Jr., July 7, 1985. Student pub. schs., Uniondale. Asst. mgr. Record World, L.I., N.Y., 1977-82, mgr. Info. Builders Inc., N.Y.C., 1982-92; pres. Carol's Creations, Belen, N.Mex. Mem. NAFE, Nat. Organization for Women. Democrat. Roman Catholic.

CLAUSEN, BRET MARK, industrial hygienist, safety professional; b. Hayward, Calif., Aug. 1, 1958; s. Norman E. and Barbara Ann (Wagner) C.; m. Cheryl Elaine Carlson, May 24, 1980; children: Kathrine, Eric, Emily. BS, Colo. State U., 1980, MS, 1983. Diplomate Am. Acad. Indsl. Hygiene; cert. indsl. hygienist, safety profl., hazard control mgr., hazardous materials mgr. Assoc. risk mgmt., indsl. hygienist, safety rep. Samsonite Corp., Denver, 1980-83, mgr. loss prevention, 1984-88; health, safety and environment rep. Storage Tech., Longmont, Colo., 1984; sr. project cons. Occusafe Inc., Denver, 1988; indsl. hygiene and occpl. safety tech. and mgmt. assignments Rocky Flats Environ. Tech. Site, Golden, Colo., 1988—; mem. radiol. assistance program team U.S. Dept. Energy, Region VI, 1994—. Mem. Am. Indsl. Hygiene Assn. (pres. Rocky Mtn. sect. 1988-89), Am. Soc. Safety Engrs. (profl.), Am. Bd. Indsl. Hygiene (cert. in comprehensive practice), Bd. Cert. Safety Profls. (cert. in comprehensive practice and mgmt. aspects), Bd. Hazard Control Mgmt. (cert. master level), Inst. Materials Mgmt. (cert. sr. level), Ins. Inst. Am. (assoc. risk mgmt.), Am. Nat. Stds. Inst. (com. on confined spaces), Am. Acad. Indsl. Hygiene (acad. accreditation com. 1994—). Republican. Lutheran. Home: 16794 Weld County Rd

44 La Salle CO 80645 Office: Kaiser-Hill LLC Rocky Flats Inc PO Box 464 Mail Stop T452D Golden CO 80402-0464

CLAUSNER, MARLIN DAVID, JR., forest products company executive; b. San Juan, Puerto Rico, Dec. 26, 1941; s. Marlin David and Aida Margaret (Jordan) C.; m. Linda Marie Nuxoll, Feb. 4, 1984; children: Karin, Ronald. BS, U.S. Naval Acad., 1965; MBA, Dartmouth Coll., 1972. Commd. ensign USN, 1965, advance through grades to lt., 1970, surface warfare officer, 1965-70; mfg. mgr. Potlatch Corp., Lewiston, Idaho, 1974-82; resource mgr. Potlatch Corp., Lewiston, 1982-88, v.p. western wood products div., 1988-93; v.p. ops. south BMC West Corp., Boise, Idaho, 1993-94; v.p. mktg. Trus Joist Macmillan, Boise, 1994—. Active Idaho Cmty. Found., Boise, 1988-90. Mem. Western Wood Products Assn. (bd. dirs. 1988-93), Nat. Forest Products Assn. (bd. dirs. 1988-93), Intermountain Forest Industries Assn. (v.p. 1991-93). Office: Trus Joist Macmillan 200 E Mallard Dr PO Box 60 Boise ID 83706

CLAUSON, GARY LEWIS, chemist; b. Peoria, Ill., Feb. 25, 1952; s. Cecil Lewis and Virgie Grace (Shryock) C. AAS, Ill. Cen. Coll., East Peoria, 1974; BA in Chemistry, U. Calif., San Diego, 1977; MS in Chem., Bradley U., Peoria, 1981; PhD in Organic Chemistry, U. Ill., 1987. Engring. technician U.S. Naval Sta., San Diego, 1974-75; lab. analyst Lehn & Fink Products Co., Lincoln, Ill., 1978-79; part-time faculty Bradley U., Peoria, 1980-81; sci. asst. Ill. State Geol. Survey, Urbana, 1986-87; sr. chemist Ciba-Geigy Corp., McIntosh, Ala., 1987-92; rsch. scientist Gensia, Inc., San Diego, 1992-95. Mem. Am. Chem. Soc. Home: 3277 Berger Ave Apt 20 San Diego CA 92123-1933

CLAUSS, JAMES JOSEPH, classics educator; b. Scranton, Pa., Sept. 1, 1953; s. James J. and Marion A. (Lynch) C.; m. Louise M. Betti, Aug. 12, 1978; children: Gerard, Michael, Elizabeth. BA, U. Scranton, 1974; MA, Fordham U., 1976; PhD, U. Calif., Berkeley, 1983; postgrad., Am. Sch. Classical Studies, Athens, 1982-83. Asst. prof. classics Creighton U., Omaha, 1983-84; asst. prof. classics U. Wash., Seattle, 1984-90, assoc. prof., 1990—. Author: The Best of the Argonauts, 1993; author numerous articles and revs. Mem. Seattle Perugia Sister City ASsn., 1991—. Thomas Day Seymour fellow Am. Sch. Classical Study, 1982-83. Mem. Am. Philol. Assn. (chmn. editorial bd. for textbooks, 1993—), Classical Assn. Pacific N.W. (v.p. 1991-92, pres. 1992-93), Classical Assn. Middlewest and South, Am. Inst. Archaeology (v.p., pres. local chpt. 1990-92). Democrat. Roman Catholic. Office: U Wash Dept Classics DH-10 Seattle WA 98195

CLAUSSEN, BONNIE ADDISON, II, aerospace company executive; b. Pueblo, Colo., Jan. 11, 1942; s. Bonnie A. I and Gertrude A. (Poe) C.; m. Charlotte J. Dipert, July 11, 1961; children: Christopher Addison, Raymond Dale. BS in Math., U. So. Colo., 1967; postgrad., Pa. State U., King of Prussia, 1968-69. Programmer Gen. Electric Corp., King of Prussia, 1967-69, sr. programmer, 1969-71; project mgr. Martin Marietta Aerospace Co., Denver, 1971-79; co-founder, exec. v.p. CTA, Inc., Englewood, Colo., 1979—, also bd. dirs. Designer: (software) Real-Time Flight, 1967-78, Viking Mars Lander Flight, 1975; contbr: Real-Time Simulation Publs., 1975-78. Served with USAF, 1962-65. Recipient Pub. Service medal Nat. Aeronautics and Space Adminstrn., 1976. Republican. Office: CTA Inc 5670 Greenwood Plaza Blvd Englewood CO 80111-2448

CLAUSSEN, RONALD VERNON, marketing consultant; b. Davenport, Iowa, Feb. 6, 1938; s. Elmer Arthur and Mary Elizabeth (Negus) C.; m. Martha Elizabeth Walls, Jan. 26, 1961 (div. 1988); children: Terry, Traci; m. Angelita Bautista, July 20, 1993. AA in Bus. Adminstrn., Palmer Jr. Coll., 1970; BA in Pub. Adminstrn., Upper Iowa U., 1974; MBA, Cen. Mich. U., 1977. Police officer City of Davenport, Iowa, 1961-67; transp. specialist Rock Island (Ill.) Arsenal Activity U.S. Dept. Def., 1967-69, traffic mgr. Savanna (Ill.) Army Depot, 1969-70; storage specialist personal property U.S. Dept. Def., Chgo. and Atlanta, 1970-73; traffic mgmt. specialist Rock Island Arsenal U.S. Dept. Def., 1973-74; sr. storage specialist personal property U.S. Dept. Def., Falls Church, Va., 1974-82; chief of transp. Army Aviation Ctr. U.S. Dept. Def., Ft. Rucker, Ala., 1982-85; dep. dir. personal property U.S. Dept. Def., Oakland, Calif., 1985-88; dep. dir. inland traffic U.S. Dept. Def., Oakland, 1988-93; dep. asst. chief of staff ops. U.S. Dept. def., Oakland, 1993, ret., 1993; prin. Claussen Assocs., Inc., Carson City, Nev., 1993—; Oakland traffic curb dir., 1993-94; pres. Greater Bay Area Transp. Assn., 1995; instr. bus. Fairfax County (Va.) adult Edn., 1977-83; instr. seminar George Mason U., Fairfax, 1977-83; adj. faculty U. Va., Falls Church, 1977-83, Embry-Riddle Aero. U., Daytona Beach, Fla., 1983—; sole propr. Claussen Assoc. Bus. Mgmt. and Mktg. Co-author: Warehouse Emergency Operations, 1982; contbr. to profl. orgns. Mem. supervisory com. San Francisco Bay Area unit Internat. Longshoremen and Warehousemen Fed. Credit Union. Sgt. USAF, 1956-60. Recipient Commander's award/medal Oakland (Calif.) Army Base, Meritorious Civliaan Svc. award, 1993. Mem. Meeting Planners Internat., Nat. Def. Transp. Assn. (bd. dirs. 1987-93, chpt. pres.), Soc. Govt. Meeting Planners (nat. pres. 1987-89, chpt. pres. 1986-87, Sam Gilmer Award Excellence 1990, Members' Choice award 1992), No. Calif. Meeting Planners Internat., Am. Legion, Shriners, Mason, Scottish Rite, Delta Nu Alpha (chpt. pres., region v.p., Pres.'s citation 1991). Republican. Lutheran. Home: 1009 Cedar Ter San Pablo CA 94806-3798 Office: Claussen Assocs Inc Western Area 2533 N Carson St Ste C274 Carson City NV 89706-0147

CLAWSON, MARY, social services administrator; b. Belen, N.Mex., Apr. 29, 1950. Grad. high sch., Albuquerque. Youth activities leader Albuquerque, 1966-68; youth dance instr. Grants, N.Mex., 1968-70; head-start coord. Albuquerque, 1970-72; libr. Marquette, Mich., 1972-74; Sunday sch. tchr. Guam, 1974-76; various positions Eglin AFB, Fla., 1976-80; asst. coord. for Asian refugees Albuquerque, 1980-83; ward libr. Anchorage, 1983-88; founder, dir. Survivors Reaching Out, Sacramento, Calif., 1988—; owner, cultural arts dir. Home Spun; educator, rschr., cons. Recipient Clifford Beers award. Mem. Internat. Soc. for Study of Multiple Personality and Dissociative Disorders, Calif. Ritual Crime Investigators Assn., Sacramento-Placer Mental Health Assn., Orange County Chpt. for Study of Multiple Personality and Dissociation, Calif. Consortium for Prevention of Child Abuse, Soc. for Investigation, Treatment and Prevention of Ritual and Cult Abuse, Calif. Profl. Soc. on Abuse of Children, Coalition for Accuracy About Abuse. Home: 5513 Hammond Ct Citrus Heights CA 95621-7315

CLAY, JAMES RAY, mathematics educator; b. Burley, Idaho, Nov. 5, 1938; s. Charles Milton Clay and Dahlia LaRae Carlson; m. Carol Cline Burge, June 12, 1959; children: Thea Patricia, Christine Marie, Terri Susan. BS in Math., U. Utah, 1960; MS in Math., U. Wash., 1962, PhD in Math., 1966. Asst. prof. U. Ariz., Tucson, 1966-69, assoc. prof., 1969-74, prof., 1974—, assoc. head math. dept., 1969-72; guest prof. U. Tuebingen, Germany, 1972-73, Kings' Coll., U. London, 1973, Technische U. Muenchen, Munich, Germany, 1979-80, 87, U. Edinburgh, Scotland, 1980, U. Stellenbosch, South Africa, 1989, U. der Bundeswehr, Hamburg, Germany, 1990, Nat. Cheng Kung U., Tainan, Taiwan, 1991, Johannes Kepler Universitaet, Linz, Austria, 1994, Klagenfurt (Austria) Universitat, 1995; postdoctorate dir. Hubert Kiechle, Technische U. Muenchen, 1991-93; lectr. in field. Author: Trigonometry--A Motivated Approach, 1977, Nearrings: Geneses and Applications, 1992; contbr. 50 articles to profl. jours. With USN, 1956-59. Recipient Dist. Sr. U.S. Scientist award Humboldt Found., 1972-73, Am. Men of Sci. Mem. Am. Math. Soc. Mem. LDS Ch. Home: 2201 N Frannea Dr Tucson AZ 85712-2924 Office: U Ariz Dept Math Bldg 89 Tucson AZ 85721

CLAY, SEAN COCHRANE, software development company executive; b. Oklahoma City, May 4, 1956; s. Robert Almonton and Maxine (Jackson) C.; m. Sharon Barlow, July 14, 1984; 1 child, Colby. AA, Saddleback C.C., 1977; student, Calif. State U., Fullerton, 1978, Riverside C.C., 1991. Programmer, software engr. Mai/Basic Four, Tustin, Calif., 1979-88; owner Clayco, Yucca Valley, Calif., 1988—; cons. Priority Computer Sys., Irvine, Calif., 1988—, Paper Rush Secretarial, Yucca Valley, 1992—, Venus Ranches, Indio, Calif., 1991—. Author (software) Custom Password Utility, 1990, Bookstore Management Sys., 1994; inventor dynamic wheel balancer. Recipient Cert. of Appreciation Toastmasters Internat., 1983, Area Contest Highest Honors, 1982. Mem. Hi Desert Aero Batons (treas., membership), Yucca Mesa Improvement Assn., Channel Bandits. Office: Clayco 2572 Yucca Mesa Rd Yucca Valley CA 92284-9272

CLAYTON, BERNARD MILES, JR., insurance company executive; b. Ketchikan, Alaska, Jan. 26, 1953; s. Bernard Miles and June Ester (Thompson) C.; m. Elizabeth Harte Johnson, Mar. 12, 1982. AA in Bus. Adminstrn., El Camino Coll., 1974; BS in Bus. Adminstrn. cum laude, Calif. State U., Long Beach, 1976. Underwriter Gamble Alden Ins. Co., Century City, Calif., 1976-77; dir. mktg. Ruland and Mattingley, Irvine, Calif., 1977-83; v.p., gen mgr. Gen. Benefits Ins. Svcs. Corp., Orange, Calif., 1983—; bd. dirs. So. Calif. (Tustin) Health Resources Ctr.; del. Orange County Health Planning Council. Mem. Calif. Assn. Health Underwriters, Orange County Assn. Health Underwriters (exec. bd. dirs. 1987-89), Orange County Employee Benefit Coun. (bd. dirs. 1988—, v.p. 1989-90, pres. 1990-91), Orange County Life Underwriters Assn. (bd. dirs. 1992—). Republican. Office: Gen Benefits Ins Svcs Corp 333 City Blvd W # 110 PO Box 1046 Orange CA 92668

CLAYTON, CATHY J., healthcare marketing executive; b. Brenham, Tex., Sept. 21, 1951; d. Leslie D. and Kathryn (Durden) C. BA, Tex. A&M U., 1973, MA, 1975; MLS, U. Tex., 1974. Cert. paralegal, Nev. Dir. alcohol and drug edn. svcs. Coun. Govts., Midland, Tex., 1977-85; dir. mktg. Camelback Hosps., Midland, 1985-86, Charter Med. Corp.-So. Calif., 1986-89; account exec. Ad Tech Comms., Torrance, Calif., 1990; dir. mktg. Behavioral Healthcare of Nev., Inc., Reno, 1990—; adj. faculty Midland Coll., 1980-86; condr. mgmt., motivation, leadership and quality based mgmt. tng. workshops; presenter in field. Vol. rm. mother Glenn Duncan Elem. Sch., Reno, 1993-94; mem. "Adopt a Sch." program Ptnrs. in Edn., Reno, 1993-94; mem. Partnership for Health Beginnings, Reno, 1994; chair Youth Suicide Prevention Task Force, Reno, 1994; founding mem., govtl. liaison Nev. Mental Health Coalition; mem. county crtl. com. Dem. Party Nev.; lay minister, mem. vestry, instr. confirmation classes Trinity Episcopal Ch. Mem. Sierra Nev. Celtic Soc.

CLAYTON, WAYNE CHARLES, protective services official, educator; b. Topeka, Kansas, Dec. 16, 1932; s. Alford Henry and Anna Ellen (Lynch) C.; m. Donna Marie Corrigan, March 3, 1962; Mark Wayne, Leslie Marie. AA in Liberal Arts, Mt. San Antonio Coll., 1959; BS, Calif. State U., L.A., 1968. cert. tchr., Calif. From reserve police officer to dep. chief El Monte Police Dept., 1957-1978, chief, 1978—; mem. session FBINA, 1980. With U.S. Navy, 1952-56. Recipient Golden Apple award West San Gabriel Valley Adminstrs. Assn., 1982, Spl. Medallion award Boys Club Am., 1982, Disting. Svc. award Dept. Youth Authority, 1983, Outstanding Svc. award C. of C., 1983, Spl. Appreciation award El Monte Police Officers Assn., 1985, Calif. Police Chief Officer of the Yr. award Internat. Union Police Assns. AFL-CIO, 1986, Exec. of Yr. award Exec. Mag., 1986, Dr. Byron E. Thompson Disting. Scouter award El Monte Explorer Post # 522, 1988, Appreciation award, 1992, Outstanding Svc. award Internat. Footprint Assn., 1991, award for continuing concern and dedication to the well being of Officers of El Monte Police Dept. Calif. Orgn. of Police and Sheriffs, 1991, Police Chief of the Yr. Perpetual award First Annual Shriners Club, 1994, C. of C. Citizen of Yr., 1994, Coord. Coun. Lifetime Achievement award, 1995. Mem. FBI Nat. Acad. Assocs., L.A. County Police Chiefs Assn., San Gabriel Valley Police Chiefs Assn., San Gabriel Valley Peace Officers Assn. (past pres.), Boys and Girls Club of San Gabriel Valley (v.p.), Civitan of El Monte (internat., charter pres. 1973). Democrat. Roman Catholic. Office: Police Dept Box 6008 11333 Valley Blvd El Monte CA 91731-3210

CLEARY, SHIRLEY JEAN, artist, illustrator; b. St. Louis, Nov. 14, 1942; d. Frank and Crystal (Maret) C.; m. (Leo) Frank Cooper, June 18, 1982; stepchildren: Clay Cooper, Alicia Cooper, Curt Cooper. BFA, Wash. U., St. Louis, 1964; MFA, Tyler Sch. of Art of Temple U., Phila.. Rome, Italy, 1968; student, The Corcoran, Washington, 1967-71. mem. adv. coun. Mont. Trout Unlimited. Prin. works include illustrations in mags. Flyfishing Quar., Fly Fishers Magazine, Flyfishing News, Mont. Outdoors, Flyfisherman, Flyfishing Heritage; contbr. articles to profl. jours., 1986, 88; exhibited in Am. in Paint and Bronze, Mo. Hist. Soc., St. Louis, 1987, Women in Wildlife, Wild Wings, Mpls., 1985-87, Am. Miniatures, Settlers West Galleries, Tucson, 1984, Women Artists & The West, Tucson Mus. Art, 1995; artist 1990 Oreg. Trout Stamp (artist of yr. award 1992, Assn. N.W. Steelheaders print winner 1992). Bd, mem. Mont. State Arts Coun., Mont., 1973-81, Helena Civic Ctr., Mont., 1983-89, mem. leadership Helena, 1985. Grantee Apprenticeship Grant, Western Starts Art Found., Artist in Residence, River Meadow, Jackson, Wyo., 1989-95, Herning Hojskole, Herning, Denmark, 1981, Wyo. Artist in the Schools, Sheridan, Wyo., 1977; named Arts for Parks Top 100 Artist, 1989, 94, Jackson (Wyo.) One Fly Artist of Yr., 1990-92. Mem. Miniature Art Soc. of N.J., Mont. Assn. Female Execs., Pat Barnes Mo. River Chpt. of Trout Unlimited, Coll. Art Assn. Democrat. Home: 1804 Beltview Dr Helena MT 59601-5801

CLEARY, WILLIAM JOSEPH, JR., lawyer; b. Wilmington, N.C., Aug. 14, 1942; s. William Joseph and Eileen Ada (Gannon) C.; AB in History, St. Joseph's U., 1964; JD, Villanova U., 1967. Bar: N.J. 1967, U.S. Ct. Appeals (3d cir.) 1969, Calif. 1982, U.S. Ct. Appeals (9th cir.) 1983, U.S. Dist. Ct. (ctrl. dist.) Calif. 1983, U.S. Supreme Ct., 1992. Law sec. to judge N.J. Superior Ct. Jersey City, 1967-68; assoc. Lamb, Blake, H&D, Jersey City, 1968-72; dep. pub. defender State of N.J., Newark, 1972-73; 1st asst. city corp. counsel, Jersey City, 1973-76; assoc. Robert Wasserwald, Inc., Hollywood, Calif., 1984-86, 88-89, Gould & Burke, L.A., 1986-87; pvt. practice, 1989—. Mem. ABA, FBA, N.J. State Bar, Calif. Bar Assn., L.A. County Bar, Alpha Sigma Nu, Nat. Jesuit Honor Soc. Democrat. Roman Catholic. Office: 1853 1/2 Canyon Dr Los Angeles CA 90028-5607

CLECAK, DVERA VIVIAN BOZMAN, psychotherapist; b. Denver, Jan. 15, 1944; d. Joseph Shalom and Annette Rose (Dveirin) Bozman; m. Pete Emmett Clecak, Feb. 26, 1966; children: Aimée, Lisa. BA, Stanford U., 1965; postgrad., U. Chgo., 1965; MSW, UCLA, 1969. Lic. clin. social worker, Calif.; lic. marriage, family and child counselor, Calif. Social work supr. Harbor City (Calif.) Parent Child Ctr., 1969-71; therapist Orange County Mental Health Dept., Laguna Beach, Calif., 1971-75, area coordinator, 1975-79; pvt. practice psychotherapy Mission Viejo, Calif., 1979—; founder, exec. dir. Human Options, Laguna Beach, 1981—; mem, co-chmn. domestic violence com. Orange County Commn. on Status of Women, 1979-81; mem. mental health adv. com. extension U. Calif., Irvine, 1983, counseling psychologist, 1980, lectr., 1984-85; lectr. Saddleback Community Coll., Mission Viejo, 1981-82, Chapman Coll., Orange, 1979; field instr. UCLA, 1970-71, 77-78. Recipient Women Helping Women award Saddleback Community Coll., 1987, Cert. for child abuse prevention Commendation State of Calif. Dept. Social Svcs., 1988, Community Svc. award Irvine Valley Coll. Found., 1989; named Orange County Non-profit Exec. of Yr., 1994. Mem. NASW, Calif. Marriage Family and Child Counselors' Assn., Phi Beta Kappa. Office: 303 Broadway # 204 Laguna Beach CA 92651

CLEMENS, CHARLES JOSEPH, insurance agent; b. Phila., Mar. 1, 1942; s. Charles Wesley and Jane Elizabeth (Nesselhauf) C.; m. Keiko Kobayashi, Aug. 12, 1965 (div. 1994); 1 child, Charles S. BA, Calif. State U., Fullerton, 1970; MBA, U. So. Calif., 1972. CLU. Asst. mgr. ins. N.Y. Life Ins. Co., Anaheim, Calif., 1971-74; ins. agt. Santa Ana, Calif., 1974-77; brokerage mgr. Alliance Ins. Co., Santa Ana, 1977-79; regional mgr. CIGNA, Orange, Calif., 1979-87; ins. agt. Garden Grove, Calif., 1987-93; ins. agt., broker Anaheim, 1993—. Major USAF-ANG, 1961—. Mem. NALU (pres. 1976, 80, Nat. Quality award). Republican.

CLEMENT, BETTY WAIDLICH, literacy educator, consultant; b. Honolulu, Aug. 1, 1937; d. William G. Waidlich and Audrey Antoinette (Roberson) Malone; m. Tom Morris, Jan. 16, 1982; 1 child, Karen A. Bratesani. BA in Elem. Edn., Sacramento State U., 1960; MA in Elem. Reading, U. No. Colo., 1973, MA in Adminstrn., EdD in Edn. & Reading, 1980. Elem. sch. tchr. pub schs., Colo., Calif., 1960-66; reading specialist, title I European area U.S. Dependent Schs., various locations, 1966-75; grad. practicum supr. U. No. Colo. Reading Clinic, Greeley, 1976-77; grant cons. Colo. Dept. Edn., Denver, 1978-81; adult edn. tutor, cons. various orgns., Boulder, Colo., 1983-87; student tchr. supr. U. San Diego, 1989-90; adult literacy trainer for vols. San Diego Coun. on Literacy, 1988—; adj. prof. U. Colo., Denver, 1981-82, U. San Diego, 1994—; adj. prof. reading Southwestern Coll., Chula Vista, Calif., 1990—; presenter various confs. Co-author, editor: Adult Literacy Tutor Training Handbook, 1990. Grantee Fed. Right-to-Read Office Colo. Dept. Edn., 1979, Southwestern Coll., 1992. Fellow San Diego Coun. on Literacy (chair coop. tutor tng. com. 1991-93); mem. Whole Lang. Coun. San Diego, Calif. Reading Assn. Office: Southwestern Coll Communication Arts 900 Otay Lakes Rd Chula Vista CA 91910-7223

CLEMENT, G. BRUCE, lawyer; b. Yakima, Wash., June 10, 1943; s. Deward Stevens and Lois Hazel (Gano) C.; children: Jeremy, Bruce, Hunter Joseph. BA, U. Wash., 1967, JD, 1970; grad., U.S. Army Command & Gen. Staff, 1989. Bar: Wash. 1970, U.S. Dist. Ct. (we. dist.) Wash. 1971, U.S. Ct. Appeals (9th cir.) 1972, U.S. Supreme Ct. 1979, U.S. Dist. Ct. (ea. dist.) Wash. 1979, U.S. Ct. Mil. Appeals 1991). Vol. U.S. Peace Corps, The Philippines, 1962-64; asst. atty. gen. State of Wash., Seattle, 1974-90; pvt. practice Federal Way, Wash., 1990-95. Editor: Consumer Lawyer's Handbook, 1971; author: Child Abuse and Neglect Handbook, 1979; contbr. articles to profl. publs. Lt. col. USAR, 1970—. Mem. Wash. State Bar Assn., Wash. State Trial Lawyers, Bar of U.S. Supreme Ct., Seattle/King County Bar Assn. (chair lawyer assistance com. 1988-89). Office: 100 Merrill Lynch Bldg 31919 1st Ave S Federal Way WA 98003-5258

CLEMENT, SHIRLEY GEORGE, educational services executive; b. El Paso, Tex., Feb. 14, 1926; d. Claude Samuel and Elizabeth Estelle (Mattice) Gillett; m. Paul Vincent Clement, Mar. 23, 1946; children: Brian Frank, Robert Vincent, Carol Elizabeth, Rosemary Adele. BA in English, Tex. Western Coll., 1963; postgrad. U. Tex., El Paso, N.Mex. State U.; MEd in Reading, Sul Ross State U., 1987. Tchr. lang. arts Ysleta Ind. Schs., El Paso, 1960-62; tchr. adult edn., 1962-64, tchr. reading/lang. arts, 1964-77; owner, dir. Crestline Learning Systems, Inc., El Paso, 1980-90; dir. Crestline Internat. Schs. (formerly Crestline Learning Systems, Inc., now Internat. Acad. Tex. at El Paso), 1987-90; instr. Park Coll., Ft. Bliss, Tex., 1992-95, U. Phoenix, 1995; dir. tutorial for sports teams U. Tex., El Paso, 1984; bd. dirs. Southwest Inst., pres., 1993; dir. continuing edn. program El Paso Community Coll., 1985; mem. curriculum com. Ysleta Ind. Schs., El Paso, 1974; mem. Right to Read Task Force, 1975-77; mem. Bi-Centennial Steering Com., El Paso, 1975-76; presenter Poetry in the Arts, Austin, Tex., 1992; judge student poetry contest, Austin, Tex., 1995; Poetry Soc. Tex. program presenter Mesilla Valley Writers, 1993-94, El Paso Writers, 1994-95, Poetry Soc. Tex., 1993; instr. writing Paris Am. Acad., summer 1994, 95; cons. Ysleta Schs. 1995; lectr. on reading in 4 states. Author: Beginning the Search, 1979; contbr. articles to profl. jours.; contbr. poems to Behold Texas, 1983. Treas. El Paso Rep. Women, 1956; facilitator Goals for El Paso, 1975; mem. hospitality com. Sun Carnival, 1974, Cotton Festival, 1975. Mem. Internat. Reading Assn. (pres. El Paso County council 1973-74, presentor 1977-87), Assn. Children with Learning Disabilities (tchr. 1980), Poetry Soc. Tex. (Panhandle Penwomen's first place award 1981, David Atamian Meml. award 1991), Nat. Fedn. State Poetry Soc. (1st place award ann. contest 1988, 1st prize El Paso Historical Essay contest 1991), Chi Omega Alumnae (pres. 1952-53). Home: PO Box 1645 114 Casas Bellas Ln Santa Teresa NM 88008-1645

CLEMENT, STEPHEN LE ROY, agricultural researcher; b. Ventura, Calif., Aug. 25, 1944; s. Edward Le Roy and Eleanor Eileen (Summers) C.; m. Mary Anne Lindeman, Dec. 21, 1981; 1 child, Kevin Matthew. BS in Entomology, U. Calif., Davis, 1967, PhD in Entomology, 1976. Postdoctoral researcher U. Calif., Davis, 1977; asst. prof. entomology Ohio State U., Ohio Agrl. Rsch. Devel. Ctr., Wooster, 1977-81; rsch. entomologist USDA, Agrl. Rsch. Svc., Rome, Italy, 1982-86; mem. agrl. mission U.S. Embassy, Rome, 1982-86; rsch. entomologist USDA, Agrl. Rsch. Svc., Pullman, Wash., 1986—; seasonal ranger-naturalist U.S. Park Svc., Yellowstone Nat. Park, 1970-72; mem. peer rev. panel agrl. rsch. grants USDA Coop. States Rsch. Svc., Washington, 1987; mem. adv. team Food Agrl. Orgn. UN, Rome, 1982. Contbr. articles to profl. jours. 1st lt. U.S. Army, 1967-70, Vietnam. Decorated Bronze Star for Valor (Vietnam); Sigma Xi grantee, 1976, U.S. EPA grantee, 1977-81. Office: Wash State U USDA Agrl Rsch Svc 59 Johnson Hall Pullman WA 99164-6402

CLEMENT, WALTER HOUGH, retired railroad executive; b. Council Bluffs, Iowa, Dec. 21, 1931; s. Daniel Shell and Helen Grace (Hough) C.; AA, San Jose (Calif.) City Coll., 1958; PhD, World U., 1983; m. Shirley Ann Brown, May 1, 1953; children: Steven, Robert, Richard. Designer, J.K. Konerle & Assocs., Salt Lake City, 1959-62; with U.P. R.R. Co., 1962—, class B draftsman, Salt Lake City, 1971-75, sr. right of way engr. real estate dept., 1975-80, asst. dist. real estate mgr., 1980-83, asst. engr. surveyor, 1983-87; owner, pres. Clement Sales and Svc. Co., Bountiful, Utah, 1987—. Mem. Republican Nat. Com., Rep. Congl. Com. With USN, 1950-54, Korea. Lic. realtor, Utah. Mem. Am. Ry. Engring. Assn., Execs. Info. Guild (assoc.), Bur. Bus. Practice. Methodist. Home: 290 W 1200 N Bountiful UT 84010-6826

CLEMENTE, PATROCINIO ABLOLA, psychology educator; b. Manila, Philippines, Apr. 23, 1941; s. Elpidio San Jose and Amparo (Ablola) C.; came to U.S., 1965; BSE, U. Philippines, 1960; postgrad. Nat. U., Manila, 1961-64; MA, Ball State U., 1966, EdD, 1969; postgrad. U. Calif., Riverside, 1970, Calif. State Coll., Fullerton, 1971-72. High sch. tchr. gen. sci. and biology, div. city schs., Quezon City, Philippines, 1960-65; doctoral fellow dept. psychology Ball State U., Muncie, Ind., 1966-67, dept. spl. edn., 1967-68, grad. asst. dept. gen. and exptl. psychology, 1968-69; tchr. educable mentally retarded high sch. level Fontana (Calif.) Unified Sch. Dist., 1969-70, intermediate level, 1970-73, dist. sch. psychologist, 1973-79, bilingual edn. counselor, 1979-81; resource specialist Morongo (Calif.) Unified Sch. Dist., 1981-83, spl. day class tchr., 1983-90, tchr. math, sci., Spanish, English, 1990—; adj. assoc. prof. Chapman Coll., Orange, Calif., 1982-91. Adult leader Girl Scouts of Philippines, 1963-65; mem. sch. bd. Blessed Sacrament Sch., Twentynine Palms, Calif. State bd. scholar Ball State U., 1965-66. Fellow Am. Biographical Inst. (hon. mem. research bd. advisors, life); mem. ASCD, NEA, Coun. for Exceptional Children, Am. Assn. on Mental Deficiency, Nat. Assn. of Sch. Psychologists, Found. Exceptional Children, Assn. for Children with Learning Disabilities, Nat. Geographic Soc., Calif. Tchrs. Assn., Morongo Tchrs. Assn., Smithsonian Inst. Roman Catholic. Home: PO Box 637 Twentynine Palms CA 92277-0637

CLEMENTS, DAVID EUGENE, linguist; b. San Diego, Nov. 6, 1955; s. Donald Milton Clements and Patricia Ann (Smith) Marcoux. BA in English and French, U. San Diego, 1977; MA in English, U. Calif., San Diego, 1981, PhD in English, 1989. Linguist Microtac Software, San Diego, 1989—. Active Muscular Dystrophy Assn., San Diego. Recipient Outstanding Achievement award and Appreciation award Muscular Dystrophy Assn., 1993. Mem. U. San Diego Alumni Assn. (Bishop Buddy award 1983), U. Calif.-San Diego Alumni Assn. Roman Catholic. Home: 10179 Camino Ruiz Apt 73 San Diego CA 92126-6414 Office: Microtac Software 4375 Jutland Dr Ste 110 San Diego CA 92117-3610

CLEMENTS, GEORGE FRANCIS, mathematics educator; b. Colfax, Wash., Apr. 17, 1931; s. Harry Frank and Louise May (Schmidt) C.; m. Anna Bell, June 18, 1952; children: Ellen, Mark, Eric, Owen. BSME, U. Wis., 1953; MA, Syracuse U., 1957, PhD, 1962. Asst. prof. math. U. Colo., Boulder, 1962-68, assoc. prof. math., 1968-76, prof. math., 1976—. Contbr. articles to profl. jours. With U.S. Army, 1953-55. Mem. Am. Math. Soc. Unitarian. Home: 2954 3rd St Boulder CO 80304-3041 Office: U Colo Dept Math Box 395 Boulder CO 80309

CLEMENTS, JOHN ROBERT, real estate professional; b. Richmond, Ind., Nov. 2, 1950; s. George Howard and Mary Amanda (McKown) C. Grad. high sch., Phoenix. Sales assoc. Clements Realty, Inc., Phoenix, 1973-75; office mgr. Clements Realty, Inc., Mesa, Ariz., 1975-78; v.p., co-owner Clements Realty, Inc., Phoenix, 1978-80; broker, assoc. Ben Brooks & Assocs., Phoenix, 1980-88; pres. John R. Clements, P.C., 1984—; broker Keller Williams Realty, Phoenix and Mesa, Ariz., 1994—, Phoenix, 1994—. Real Estate dir. Circle K Corp., Western Region, 1989-92; bd. dirs., v.p. Big Sisters Ariz., Phoenix, 1974-80; trustee Ariz. Realtors Polit. Action Com., 1975-85, Realtors Polit. Action Com., Ill., 1985-88; appointee Govtl. Mall Co., Ariz., 1986—, commr. chair, 1991—. Mem. Ariz. Assn. Realtors (bd. dirs., pres. 1981), Mesa-Chandler-Tempe Bd. Realtors (past bd. dirs., pres., 1978), Nat. Assn. Realtors (past bd. dirs.), REsidential Sales Coun. Realtors, Nat. Mktg. Inst. (bd. govs. 1986—, v.p. 1990, pres. 1991), Ariz. Country Club. Republican. Presbyterian. Home: 3618 N 60th St Phoenix AZ 85018-6708 Office: Keller Williams Realty 4343 E Camelback Rd #240 Phoenix AZ 85018

CLEMONS, LYNN ALLAN, land use planner; b. New Orleans, Oct. 23, 1946; s. Gaylord Wilson and Jessica Monica (McDonald) C. BS, Colo. State U., 1973. Planner outdoor recreation Bur. Outdoor Recreation, Denver, 1974-75; planner outdoor recreation Bur. Land Mgmt., Golden, Co., 1975-77, Winnemucca, Nev., 1977—; pub. affairs officer Bur. Land Mgmt., Winnemucca, 1989-93. Co-author environ. impact statements. With USN, 1968-69, Vietnam. Recipient Spl. Achievement award Dept. of Interior, 1988, 91. Mem. Am. Radio Relay League, U.S. Chess Fedn., No. Nev. Amateur Radio Club (sec.-treas. 1992), Winnemucca Amateur Trap Assn. (sec.-treas. 1981), Assn. for Preservation Tech., Wilderness Soc., One Moccasin Toastmasters Club (officer, Competent Toastmaster award 1988). Roman Catholic. Office: Bur Land Mgmt 705 E 4th St Winnemucca NV 89445-2807

CLEVENGER, JEFFREY GRISWOLD, mining company executive; b. Boston, Sept. 1, 1949; s. Galen William and Cynthia (Jones) C. BS in Mining Engring., N.Mex. Inst. Mining & Tech., Socorro, 1973. Engr. Phelps Dodge, Tyrone, N.Mex., 1973-78, gen. mine foreman, 1979-81, mine supt., 1981-86; mine supt. Phelps Dodge, Morenci, Ariz., 1986, gen. supt., 1987; asst. gen. mgr. Chino Mines Co., Hurley, N.Mex., 1987-88; asst. gen. mgr. Phelps Dodge, Morenci, 1988-89, gen. mgr., 1989-92; pres. Phelps Dodge Morenci, Inc., 1989-92, Morenci Water & Electric Co., 1989-92; sr. v.p. Cyprus Copper Co., Tempe, 1992-93; pres. Cyprus Climax Metals Co., Tempe, 1993—; sr. v.p. Cyprus Amax Minerals Co., Littleton, Colo., 1993—. Contbr. articles to profl. jours. Bd. dirs. Valley of the Sun YMCA, Mining Hall of Fame. Recipient Disting. Achievement award N.Mex. Inst. Mining & Tech., 1988. Mem. AIME (chmn. S.W. N.Mex. chpt. 1982), Soc. Mining Engrs. (Robert Peele award 1984), Mining and Metall. Soc. Am., Rotary, Elks. Home: 4575 N Launfal Ave Phoenix AZ 85018-2961 Office: Cyprus Climax Metals Co PO Box 22015 1501 W Fountainhead Pky Tempe AZ 85282-1846

CLEWIS, CHARLOTTE WRIGHT STAUB, mathematics educator; b. Pitts., Aug. 20, 1935; d. Schirmer Chalfant and Charlotte Wright (Rodgers) Staub; student Memphis State Coll., 1953-54, U. Wis., 1957-59; BA, Newark State Coll., 1963; MAT, Loyola Marymount U., 1974; m. John Edward Clewis, Aug. 11, 1954; 1 dau., Charlotte Wright. Asst. to dir., housemother Leota Sch. and Camp, Evansville, Wis., 1957-59; tchr. math. Rahway Jr. H.S. (N.J.), 1963-70; tchr. math. Torrance (Calif.) Unified Sch. Dist., 1970-95, coord. math. dept., 1977-95, mem. math. steering com., 1978-83, 86-89, mem. proficiency exam writing com., 1977-91; mem. instructional materials rev. panel State of Calif., 1986; instr. Weekend Coll. Marymount-Palos Verdes, 1992-94; coach math. teams. Sec., pres. Larga Vista Property Owners Assn., 1975-84; mem. Rolling Hills Estates City Celebration Com., 1975-81; treas. adult leaders YMCA, Metuchen, N.J., 1967-69; bd. dirs. Peninsula Symphony Assn., 1978-84, sec., 1993—; commr. Rolling Hills Estates Parks and Activities, 1981—, chmn., 1985, 90. Named Tchr. of Yr., Rahway Jr. H.S., 1966; recipient Appreciation award PTA, 1984, Hon. Service award PTA, 1986. Mem. Nat. Coun. Tchrs. Math., Calif. Math. Coun. Avocations: bicycling, camping, reading, horseback riding, computers. Home: 1 Gaucho Dr Rolling Hills Estates CA 90274-5113

CLIFF, RONALD LAIRD, energy company executive; b. Vancouver, B.C., Can., Mar. 13, 1929; s. Ronald Lorraine and Georgina (Laird) C.; children: Diana Maughan, Leslie Cliff Tindle, Sheila Sharp, Ronald Jr.; m. Ardelle Faith Simpson, 1983. B.Commerce, U. B.C., 1949. Chartered acct., 1954. Chmn. BC Gas Inc., Vancouver, 1972—; bd. dirs. Canfor Corp., Vancouver, Royal Bank of Can., Montreal, Southam Inc., Toronto, Trans Mt. Pipe Line Co., Ltd., Vancouver. Fellow Inst. Chartered Accts.; mem. Royal Vancouver Yacht Club, Eldorado Country Club (Calif.), Thunderbird Country Club (Calif.). Anglican.

CLIFFORD, NATHAN JOSEPH, cardiologist; b. Denver, Apr. 19, 1929; s. Donald Francis and Anna (Karchmer) C.; m. Maryellen Baptist, June 12, 1954; 1 child, William Barnett. BS in Pharmacy, U. Colo., Boulder, 1951; MD, U. Colo., Denver, 1956. Diplomate Am. Bd. Internal Medicine. Physician USPHS Indian Hosp., Whiteriver, Ariz., 1957-58; med. officer in charge USPHS Indian Hosp., Owyhee, Nev., 1958-59; med. resident Kings County Hosp., Bklyn., 1959-61; cardiology fellow Mercy Hosp., San Diego, 1961-63; physician Buenaventura Clinic, Ventura, Calif., 1963-67, Internal Medicine and Cardiology P.C., Greeley, Colo., 1967-90; med. officer Phoenix Indian Med. Ctr., 1990—, chief of staff, 1992; clin. prof. medicine U. Colo., Denver, 1967—. Named Tchr. of Yr. No. Colo. Med. Ctr., 1974. Fellow ACP (Disting. Internist award Colo. chpt. 1988); mem. Am. Heart Assn. Roman Catholic. Home: 6302 N 73rd St Scottsdale AZ 85250-5500 Office: Phoenix Indian Med Ctr 4212 N 16th St Phoenix AZ 85016-5319

CLIFFORD, STEVEN FRANCIS, science research director; b. Boston, Jan. 4, 1943; s. Joseph Nelson and Margaret Dorothy (Savage) C.; children from previous marriage: Cheryl Ann, Michelle Lynn, David Arthur. BSEE, Northeastern U., Boston, 1965; PhD, Dartmouth Coll., 1969. Postdoctoral fellow NRC, Boulder, Colo., 1969-70; physicist Wave Propagation Lab., NOAA, Boulder, 1970-82, program chief, 1982-87, dir. lab., 1987—; mem. electromagnetic propagation panel, NATO, 1989-93; vis. sci. closed acad. city Tomsk, Siberia, USSR. Author: (with others) Remote Sensing of the Troposphere, 1978; contbr. 125 articles to profl. jours.; patentee in acoustic scintillation liquid flow measurement, single-ended optical spatial filter. Recipient 4 Outstanding publs. awards Dept. Commerce, 1972, 75, 89. Fellow Optical Soc. Am. (editor atmospheric optics 1978-84, advisor atmospheric optics 1982-84), Acoustical Soc. Am.; mem. IEEE (sr.), Internat. Radio Sci. Union, Am. Geophys. Union. Office: NOAA Environ Tech Lab 325 Broadway St Boulder CO 80303-3337

CLIFT, WILLIAM BROOKS, III, photographer; b. Boston, Jan. 5, 1944; s. William Brooks C. and Anne (Pearmain) Thomson; m. Vida Regina Chesnulis, Aug. 8, 1970; children: Charis, Carola, William. Free lance comml. photographer in partnership with Steve Gersh under name Helios, 1963-71; pres. William Clift Ltd., Santa Fe, 1980-85; cons. Polaroid Corp., 1965-67. Photographer one-man shows, Carl Siembab Gallery, Boston, 1969, Mus. Art, U. Oreg., Eugene, 1969, New Boston City Hall Gallery, 1970, U. Mass., Berkshire Mus., Pittsfield, Mass., William Coll., Addison Gallery of Am. Art, Wheaton Coll., Mass., Worcester Art Mus., 1971, Creative Photography Gallery, MIT, 1972, St. John's Coll. Art Gallery, Santa Fe, 1973, Wiggin Gallery, Boston Pub. Library, 1974, Australian Ctr. for Photography, Sydney, 1978, Susan Spiritus Gallery, Newport Beach, Calif., 1979, MIT Creative Photography Gallery, 1980, William Lyons Gallery, Coconut Grove, Fla., 1980, Eclipse Gallery, Boulder, Colo., 1980, Atlanta Gallery of Photography, 1980, Phoenix Art Mus., 1981, Jeb Gallery, Providence, 1981, Portfolio Gallery, 1981, Images Gallery, Cin., 1982, Boston Atheneum, 1983, Bank of Santa Fe, 1984, Susan Harder Gallery, N.Y.C., 1984, Cleve. Art Mus., 1985, Art Inst. Chgo., 1987, Amon Carter Mus., Ft. Worth, 1987, Clarence Kennedy Gallery, Cambridge, Mass., 1988, Equitable Gallery, N.Y.C., 1993, Vassar Coll. Art Mus., N.Y., 1994, Vassar Coll. Art Gallery, N.Y., 1995; exhibited in group shows Gallery 216, N.Y., N.Y. Grover Cronin Gallery, Waltham, Mass., 1964, Carl Seimbab Gallery, Boston, 1966, Lassall Jr. Coll., 1967, Hill's Gallery, Santa Fe, Tyler Mus. Art, Austin, Tex., Dupree Gallery, Dallas, 1974, Quindacqua Gallery, Washington, 1978, Zabriskie Gallery, Paris, 1978, Am. Cultural Ctr., Paris, 1978; photographer AT&T Project-Am. Images, 1978, Seagram's Bicentennial Project, Courthouse, 1975-77, Readers Digest Assn. Project, 1984, Hudson River Project, 1985-92; author: Photography Portfolios, Old Boston City Hall, 1971, Photography Portfolios, Courthouse, 1979, Photography Portfolios, New Mexico, 1975, Certain Places, Photographs, 1987, A Hudson Landscape, Photographs, 1993. Nat. Endowment for Arts photography fellow, 1972, 79; Guggenheim fellow, 1974, 80, N.Mex. Gov.'s Excellence in The Arts award, 1987. Home and Office: PO Box 6035 Santa Fe NM 87502-6035

CLIFTON, JUDY RAELENE, association administrator; b. Safford, Ariz., Nov. 8, 1946; d. Ralph Newton and Fayrene (Goodner) Johnson; student Biola Coll., 1964-65; BA in Christian Edn., Southwestern Coll., 1970; married. Editl. asst. Accent Publications, Denver, 1970-73; expediter Phelps Dodge Corp., Douglas, Ariz., 1974-78; exec. asst. So. Ariz. Internat. Livestock Assn., Inc., Tucson, 1978-81; supt.'s sec. Phelps Dodge Corp., 1981—; sec. exec. bd. PAC, Phelps Dodge, 1985-90. Mem. adv. bd. Ariz. Lung Assn.; mem. Silver City Arts Coun., 1986-90; mem. Am. Security Council, [illegible] 4-H Douglas; mem. Rep. Nat. Com., 1978—, Conservative Caucus, 1979-85; del. Quadrennial N.Mex. State Rep. Con., 1988, 92. Recipient Am. Legion Good Citizen award, 1964, DAR award, 1964. Mem. NAFE, DAR, Nat. Assn. Evangelicals, U.S. Tennis Assn., So. Ariz. Internat. Livestock Assn., AAUW, Eagle Forum, Freedom Found., N.Mex. Eagle Forum, Mus. N.Mex. Found., Lordsburg/Hidalgo County C. of C. (1st v.p bd. dirs. 1990-93), Sigma Lambda Delta. Baptist. Clubs: Trunk & Tusk, Pima County Republican, Centre Ct., Westerners Internat., So. Ariz. Depression Glass, Tucson Tennis, Rep. Senatorial. Home: Drawer M Playas NM 88009

CLIFTON, MARK STEPHEN, administrator; b. San Diego, May 25, 1955; s. Paul Clifford and Dorothy Jean (Gross) C.; m. Margaret Eileen Hower, July 20, 1985; 1 child, Casey Mariah. Student, Grossmont Coll., 1973-74, San Diego City Coll., 1981. Oper. supr. San Diego Unified Sch. Dist., 1979—; owner A Home Touch Housecleaning, San Diego, 1985—; speaker in field. Author: There Goes the Neighborhood, 1993; contbr. articles to profl. jours. Mem. Ocean Beach Town Coun., San Diego, 1993—. Recipient Hon. Svc. award PTA, Point Loma High Sch., 1989. Mem. San Diego Writers and Editor's Guild, Christian Writers Guild, Adminstrs. Assn., Maranatha Surfing Assn. (founder, pres. 1983-86), Christian Surfing Assn. (co-founder 1982-83). Republican. Office: San Diego Unified Sch Dist 8460 Ruffner St San Diego CA

CLIFTON, MICHAEL EDWARD, English language educator; b. Reedley, Calif., Jan. 6, 1949; s. Edward Eugene and Helen May (Peters) C.; m. Anita May Bernardi, June 22, 1973. BA, Calif. State U., Fresno, 1971, MA with distinction, 1977; PhD, Ind. U., 1984. Tchr. English Hoover High Sch., Fresno, 1971-74; assoc. instr. Ind. U., Bloomington, 1978-80; lectr. Calif. State U., Fresno, 1982—; reader, presenter Internat. Assn. Fantastic in Arts, Ft. Lauderdale, Fla., 1988, 93, Houston, Tex., 1987, Am. Imagery Assn., San Francisco, 1986, Eaton Conf., U. Calif. Riverside, 1985. Contbr. articles to popular mags. and profl. jours. Chair Landmarks Preservation Coun., Tower Dist. Design Rev. Com.; bd. dirs. Fresno City and County Hist. Soc., Tower Dist. Preservation Assn., Inc. Mem. MLA, AAUP. Democrat. Home: 921 N San Pablo Ave Fresno CA 93728-3627 Office: Calif State U Dept English Peters Bldg Fresno CA 93740

CLINARD, FRANK WELCH, JR., materials scientist, researcher; b. Winston-Salem, N.C., Aug. 4, 1933; s. Frank Welch and Hazel Helen (Hauser) C.; m. Elva Adams Hyatt, Apr. 2, 1968. BSME, N.C. State U., 1955, MSMetE, 1957; PhD, Stanford U., 1965. Staff mem. Sandia Corp., Albuquerque, N.Mex., 1957-61; research asst. Stanford U., Palo Alto, Calif., 1961-64; staff mem. Los Alamos (N.Mex.) Nat. Lab., 1964-77, sect. leader, 1977-89, lab. assoc., 1989-92, staff mem., 1992-94; cons. in field, Los Alamos, 1983—; prof. materials sci. N.Mex. Inst. Mining and Tech., Socorro, 1990—. Contbr. more than 90 articles to profl. jours. Bd. dirs. County Pub. TV Orgns., Los Alamos, N.Mex., 1981-82; state chmn. Libertarian Party N.Mex., 1986-88, candidate for State Senate in Dist. 22, 1992. Fellow Am. Ceramic Soc.; mem. AAAS, ACLU (bd. dirs. N.Mex. chpt. 1993—), Amnesty Internat., Am. Soc. Metals (chmn. local chpt. 1969-70), Am. Nuclear Soc., Materials Rsch. Soc., Rotary (v.p., pres. Los Alamos chpt. 1995—), Sports Car Club (del. Valle Rio Grande, pres. 1967), Sigma Xi, Phi Kappa Phi, Tau Beta Pi, Pi Tau Sigma. Unitarian. Home: 2940 Arizona Ave Los Alamos NM 87544-1512 Office: Los Alamos Nat Lab Mail Stop E546 Los Alamos NM 87545

CLINCH, HARRY ANSELM, former bishop; b. San Anselmo, Calif., Oct. 27, 1908. Educ., St. Joseph College, Mountain View, Calif, St. Patrick's Seminary, Menlo Park, Calif. ord. priest June 6, 1936; ord. titular bishop of Badiae and auxiliary bishop of Monterey-Fresno Feb. 27, 1957. Appointed first bishop of Monterey in Calif., installed Dec. 14, 1967,served to 1982. Address: 3400 Paul Sweet Rd C-119 Santa Cruz CA 95065

CLINCH, NICHOLAS BAYARD, III, business executive; b. Evanston, Ill., Nov. 9, 1930; s. Nicholas Bayard Jr. and Virginia Lee (Campbell) C.; m. Elizabeth Wallace Campbell, July 11, 1964; children: Virginia Lee, Alison Campbell. Student, N.Mex. Mil. Inst., Roswell, 1948-49; AB, Stanford U., 1952, LLB, 1955. Bar: Calif. 1959. Expedition leader First Ascent, Gasherbrum I (26,470 ft.), Pakistan, 1958, First Ascent, Masherbrum (25, 660 ft.), Pakistan, 1959-60; assoc. Voegelin, Barton, Harris & Callister, L.A., 1961-68; pvt. practice Washington, 1968-70; v.p., counsel Lincoln Savs. & Loan Assn., L.A., 1970-74; exec. dir. Sierra Club Found., San Francisco, 1975-81; environ. cons. Fluor Corp., Grass Valley, Calif., 1981-84; v.p., sec. CCA, Inc., Denver, 1984—; dir. Growth Stock Outlook Inc., Potomac, Md., Recreational Equipment Inc., Seattle. Author: A Walk in the Sky, 1982. Leader Am. Antarctic Mountaineering Expdn., Sentinel Range, 1966-67; co-leader Chinese Am. Ulugh Muztagh Expdn., Kun Lun Range, Xinjiang, 1985; co-founder, trustee Calif. League Conservation Voters, San Francisco, 1972—. 1st lt. USAF, 1956-57. Recipient John Oliver La Gorce medal Nat. Geog. Soc., Washington, 1967. Fellow Royal Geog. Soc., Explorers Club; mem. ABA, Am. Alpine Club (hon., pres. 1967-70), Appalachian Mountain Club (hon.), State Bar Calif., Alpine Club (London), Chinese Assn. Sci. Expdns. (hon.). Republican. Episcopalian. Home: 2001 Bryant St Palo Alto CA 94301-3714 Office: CCA Inc 4100 E Mississippi Ave Ste 1750 Denver CO 80222-3048

CLINE, BRYAN M., industrial engineer; b. Springfield, Oreg., Mar. 18, 1959; s. Charles Frederick and Ilse Maria (Rausch) C. AAS with honors, Shoreline Community Coll., 1981; student, U. Mont., 1982; BA, U. Wash., 1984; MBA, Seattle U., 1991. Lifeguard City of Seattle, 1978-85; indsl. engring. mgr. The Boeing Co., Seattle, 1985—. Seattle Milk Fund scholar, 1977. Mem. U.S. Postal Commemorative Soc., Beta Gamma Sigma. Democrat. Lutheran.

CLINE, CAROLYN JOAN, plastic and reconstructive surgeon; b. Boston; d. Paul S. and Elizabeth (Flom) Cline. BA, Wellesley Coll., 1962; MA, U. Cin., 1966; PhD, Washington U., 1970; diploma Washington Sch. Psychiatry, 1972; MD, U. Miami (Fla.) 1975. Diplomate Am. Bd. Plastic and Reconstructive Surgery. Rsch. asst. Harvard Dental Sch., Boston, 1962-64; rsch. asst. physiology Laser Lab., Children's Hosp. Research Found., Cin., 1964, psychology dept. U. Cin., 1964-65; intern in clin. psychology St. Elizabeth's Hosp., Washington, 1966-67; psychologist Alexandria (Va.) Community Mental Health Ctr., 1967-68; research fellow NIH, Washington, 1968-69; chief psychologist Kingsbury Ctr. for Children, Washington, 1969-73; sole practice clin. psychology, Washington, 1970-73; intern internal medicine U. Wis. Hosps., Ctr. for Health Sci., Madison, 1975-76; resident in surgery Stanford U. Med. Ctr., 1976-78; fellow microvascular surgery dept. surgery U. Calif.-San Francisco, 1978-79; resident in plastic surgery St. Francis Hosp., San Francisco, 1979-82; practice medicine, specializing in plastic and reconstructive surgery, San Francisco, 1982—. Contbr. chpt. to plastic surgery textbook, articles to profl. jours. Mem. Am. Soc. Plastic and Reconstructive Surgeons, Royal Soc. Medicine, Calif. Medicine Assn., Calif. Soc. Plastic and Reconstructive Surgeons, San Francisco Med. Soc. Address: 490 Post St Ste 735 San Francisco CA 94102-1408

CLINE, CLINTON CLIFFORD, art educator, printmaker; b. Grant City, Ill., Oct. 21, 1934; s. Clinton Amas and Ruth C.; divorced; children: Justin, Allison. AA, East L.A. Jr. Coll., 1963; BA, Calif. State U., Long Beach, 1965; MA, 1968. Student asst. East L.A. Coll., 1962-63; student asst. Calif. State U., Long Beach, 1963-65, teaching asst., 1965-68; vis. artist Pacific Northwest Graphic Workshop, Cheshire, Oreg., 1971; prof. printmaking U. Colo., Boulder, 1969—. vis. artist Photo Techniques, Edwardsville, Ill., 1975, Exhbn. and Demonstration on Lithography, Denver Art Mus., 1975; guest artist Viscosity and photo Techniques, U. So. Ill., 1975, Printmaking, Visual Arts Ctr., Anchorage, Alaska, 1978, Wichita State U., 1978, Gallery as Studio, Visual Arts Ctr., Calif. State U., 1978, ANderson ranch Arts Found., Aspen, Colo., 1979; juror 4th Nat. Small painting, drawing, and Print Exhbn., Ft. Hays State U., 1978; dir. Nat. Printmaking WOrkshop, 1980. With U.S. Army, 1952-57. Home: 930 Quince Ave Boulder CO 80304-0703 Office: U Colo Fine Arts Dept Boulder CO 80309

CLINE, FRED ALBERT, JR., librarian, conservationist; b. Santa Barbara, Calif., Oct. 23, 1929; s. Fred Albert and Anna Cecelia (Haberl) C. AB in Asian Studies, U. Calif., Berkeley, 1952, MLS, 1962. Resident Internat. House, Berkeley, 1950-51; trainee, officer Bank of Am., San Francisco, Düsseldorf, Fed. Republic Germany, Kuala Lumpur, 1954-60; adminstrv. reference libr. Calif. State Libr., Sacramento, 1962-67; head libr. Asian Art Mus. San Francisco, 1967-93; ret., 1993. Contbg. author: Chinese, Korean and Japanese Sculpture in the Avery Brundage Collection, 1974; author, editor: Ruth Hill Cooke, 1985. Bd. dirs. Tamalpais Conservation Club, 1990-94, chmn. Found., The Desert Protective Coun.; AIDS activist. Sgt. M.C., U.S. Army, 1952-54. Mem. Metaphys. Alliance (sec., bd. dirs. San Francisco chpt. 1988-91), Nature Conservancy, Sierra Club. Democrat. Home: 825 Lincoln Way San Francisco CA 94122-2369

CLINE, GLEN EDWIN, retired architect and planner; b. Fredonia, Kans., Feb. 8, 1920; s. Marion Edwin and Bernice E. Loomis (Griffin) C.; m. Kathryn Crain, Feb. 2, 1946; children: Larry Stephan, Christina Bernice. Student, James Milikin U., 1942, Boise Jr. Coll., 1947; BS in Architecture, Kans. State U., 1949. Registered architect Idaho, Utah, Mont., Oreg., Wash., Calif. Archtl. apprentice Wayland and Fennell, Boise, Idaho, 1949-54; chief architect Skaggs Drug Corp., Salt Lake City, 1954-55; ptnr. Wayland and Cline, Boise, 1955-61, Wayland, Cline and Smull, Boise, 1961-69; prin. Cline Smull Hamill Quintieri Assocs., Boise, 1969-85; pvt. practice cons. Glen E. Cline, Architect/Planner, Boise, 1985-94; sec., chmn. Idaho State Bd. Architect Examiners, Boise, 1956-69; chmn. Planning and Zoning Commn., Boise, 1956-74, chmn. Design Rev. Com., 1971-74. Co-author: Public Works Construction Guide, 1971; prin. architect, project mgmt. Kibbe Dome (ASCE award 1976), Boise State U. Pavilion, 1982 (Facility of Merit award 1983), Boise Air Terminal, 1985 (Honor award 1985). 2d lt. USAAF, 1943-46. Recipient commendation Mayor's Com. on Handicapped, Boise, 1977. Fellow AIA; mem. Idaho chpt. AIA (pres. 1960, medal 1985), Constrn. Specifications Inst. (pres. Idaho chpt. 1982, commendation N.W. region 1988), Boise C. of C. (bd. dirs. 1962-85), Hillcrest Country Club, Kiwanis (pres. Boise 1953-63), Masons. Republican. Home: 1805 S Roosevelt St Boise ID 83705-2801

CLINE, HAROLD J., medical physicist; b. Denver, Feb. 28, 1960. BSc, Colo. Sch. Mines, 1982; MSc, U. Colo., 1993. Geophysicist Noranda Exploration, Lakewood, Colo., 1982-84; project geophysicist Earth Tech. Corp., Lakewood, 1984-87; U.S. geophysicist Aquaterra Internat., Denver, 1987-92; med. physicist Luth. Med. Ctr., Wheat Ridge, Colo., 1993—; thesis advisor U. Colo. Health Sci. Ctr., Denver, 1993—; cons. radiation oncology Meml. Hosp., Colorado Springs, 1993. Contbr. articles to profl. jours. Mem. Am. Assn. Physicists in Medicine. Office: Luth Med Ctr Radiol Oncology 8300 W 38th Ave Wheat Ridge CO 80033-6005

CLINE, PAULINE M., educational administrator; b. Seattle, Aug. 25, 1947; d. Paul A. and Margaret V. (Reinhart) C. BA in Edn., Seattle U., 1969, MEd, 1975, EdD, 1983. Cert. tchr., prin., supt., Wash. Tchr., Marysville High Sch., Wash., 1969-70; tchr./adminstr. Blanchet High Sch., Seattle, 1970-78; asst. prin. Edmonds High Sch., Wash., 1978-84; prin. College Place Middle Sch., Edmonds, 1984-85, Mountlake Terrace High Sch., Wash., 1985-93; asst. supr., Mount Vernon Sch. Dist., 1993—. Recipient Washington award for excellence in edn. Gov. and Supt. Pub. Instruction, 1992. IDEA Kettering fellow, 1984, 86, 87, 90, 92, 93, 94, 95. Mem. Am. Assn. Sch. Adminstr., Assn. Supervision and Curriculum Devel., Phi Delta Kappa. Roman Catholic. Club: Women's University (Seattle). Lodge: Rotary (charter mem., past pres. Alderwood club). Avocations: skiing; kayaking; backpacking. Office: Mt Vernon Sch Dist 124 East Lawrence Mount Vernon WA 98273

CLINE, PLATT HERRICK, author; b. Mancos, Colo., Feb. 7, 1911; s. Gilbert T. and Jessie (Baker) C.; m. Barbara Decker, Sept. 11, 1934. Grad., N.Mex. Mil. Inst., 1930; student, Colo. U., 1930-31; LittD, No. Ariz. U., 1966, BS, 1982. Advt. solicitor Denver Post, 1931; with Civilian Conservation Corps., 1934-36; Nat. Monument ranger, 1936; pub. Norwood (Colo.) Post, 1937-38; advt. mgr. Coconino Sun, Flagstaff, Ariz., 1938-41; mng. editor Holbrook Tribune-News, 1941-45; editor Coconino Sun, 1945-46; mng. editor Ariz. Daily Sun, 1946-53, pub., 1953-69, pres., 1969-76, v.p., 1976—; rsch. assoc. Mus. No. Ariz., 1976—; adj. prof. history No. Ariz. U., 1983—. Author: They Came to the Mountain, 1976, Mountain Campus, 1983, The View From Mountain Campus, 1990, Mountain Town, Flagstaff in the 20th Century, 1994. Mem. Ariz. Commn. Indian Affairs, 1952-55, Norwood (Colo.) Town Coun., 1937-38; chmn. Flagstaff Citizen of Yr. Com., 1976—; bd. dirs., past pres. Raymond Edn. Found., No. Ariz. U. Found.; bd. dirs. Transition Found; trustee Flagstaff Community Hosp., 1954-58. Recipient Ariz. Master Editor-Pub. award, 1969, El-Merito award Ariz. Hist. Soc., 1976; named Flagstaff Citizen of Yr., 1976, Disting. Citizen, No. Ariz. U. Alumni, 1983, Outstanding Flagstaff Citizen of Century award, 1994; dedicatee No. Ariz. U. Libr., 1988. Mem. Ariz. Newspapers Assn. (past pres., Golden Svc. award 1989), No. Ariz. Pioneers Hist. Soc. (trustee 1972-75), Sigma Delta Chi, Phi Alpha Theta, Phi Kappa Phi, Masons. Home: PO Box 578 Flagstaff AZ 86002-0578 Office: 417 W Santa Fe Ave Flagstaff AZ 86001-5318

CLINE, ROBERT STANLEY, air freight company executive; b. Urbana, Ill., July 17, 1937; s. Lyle Stanley and Mary Elizabeth (Prettyman) C.; m. Judith Lee Stucker, July 7, 1979; children: Lisa Andre, Nicole Lesley, Christina Elaine, Leslie Jane. BA, Dartmouth Coll., 1959. Asst. treas. Chase Manhattan Bank, N.Y.C., 1960-65; v.p. fin. Pacific Air Freight Co., Seattle, 1965-68; exec. v.p. fin. Airborne Express (formerly Airborne Freight Corp.), Seattle, 1968-78, vice chmn., CFO, dir., 1978-84, chmn., CEO, dir., 1984—; bd. dirs. Seattle-First Nat. Bank, Metricom Corp., Seafirst Corp., Safeco Corp. Trustee Seattle Repertory Theatre, 1974-90, chmn. bd., 1979-83; trustee Children's Orthopedic Hosp. Found., 1983-91, Corp. Coun. of Arts, 1983—; bd. dirs. Washington Roundtable, 1985—; chmn. bd. dirs. Children's Hosp. Found., 1987-89; trustee United Way of King County, 1991-93. With U.S. Army, 1959-60. Home: 1209 39th Ave E Seattle WA 98112-4403 Office: Airborne Express PO Box 662 Seattle WA 98111-0662*

CLINE, WILSON ETTASON, retired administrative law judge; b. Newkirk, Okla., Aug. 26, 1914; s. William Sherman and Etta Blanche (Roach) C.; m. G. Barbara Verne Pentecost, Nov. 1, 1939 (div. Nov. 1960); children: William, Catherine Cline MacDonald, Thomas; m. Gina Lana Ludwig, Oct. 5, 1969; children: David Ludwig, Kenneth Ludwig. Student, U. Ill., 1932-33; A.B., U. Okla., 1935, B.S. in Bus. Adminstrn., 1936; J.D., U. Calif., Berkeley, 1939; LL.M., Harvard U., 1941. Bar: Calif. 1940, U.S. Ct. Appeals (9th cir.) 1941, U.S. Dist. Ct. (no. dist.) Calif. 1943, U.S. Supreme Ct. 1953. Atty. Kaiser Richmond Shipyards, 1941-44; pvt. practice Oakland, 1945-49; prof., asst. dean, dean Eastbay Div. Lincoln U. Law Sch., Oakland, 1946-50; atty., hearing officer, asst. chief adminstrv. law judge, acting chief adminstrv. law judge Calif. Pub. Utilities Commn., San Francisco, 1949-80, ret., 1981, dir. gen. welfare Calif. State Employees Assn., 1966-67, chmn. retirement com., 1965-66, mem. member benefit com., 1980-81, mem. ret. employees div. council dist. C, 1981-82; executor estate of Warren A. Cline. Past trustee Cline Ranch Trust, various family trusts. Mem. ABA, State Bar Calif., Conf. Calif. Pub. Utility Counsel (steering com. 1967-71), Am. Judicature Soc., Boalt Hall Alumni Assn., Harvard Club of San Francisco, Commonwealth Club San Francisco, Sleepy Hollow Swim and Tennis Club (Orinda, Calif.), Masons (Orinda lodge # 494 sec. 1951-55, past Master 1949), Sirs (Peralta chpt. 12), Phi Beta Kappa (pres. No. Calif. assn. 1969-70), Beta Gamma Sigma, Delta Sigma Pi (Key award 1936), Phi Kappa Psi, Phi Delta Phi, Pi Sigma Alpha. Democrat. Mem. United Ch. Christ. Home: 110 St Albans Rd Kensington CA 94708-1035 Office: PO Box 11120 3750 Harrison St Unit 304 Oakland CA 94611-0120

CLINTON, JOHN PHILIP MARTIN, communications executive; b. Sheffield, Eng., Apr. 30, 1935; came to U.S., 1967; s. John A.T. and Phyllis Mary (Fowler) C.; m. Margaret Rosemary Morgan, Aug. 26, 1961; children: Alaric, Ivan, James. BA, Oxford U., 1959, MA, 1962. Mgr. computer systems Stanford (Calif.) U., 1967-70; v.p. systems devel. Computer Curriculum Corp., Palo Alto, Calif., 1970-79; exec. v.p. Captec, Inc., Santa Clara, Calif., 1979-80; mgr. product devel. Siltec Corp., Menlo Park, Calif., 1980-82; cons. Instructive Tech., Palo Alto, 1982-83; mgr. software devel. Voicemail Internat., Inc., Santa Clara, 1983-85, v.p. engring., 1985-87, sr. v.p. engring., 1987-88; pres. In-Gate Tech., Sunnyvale, Calif., 1988—. Author: Begin Algol, 1966; editor (newsletter) Flat Tyre, 1982. Adv. com. Sunnyvale City Coun., 1994—. Hastings scholar Queens Coll., Oxford U., 1955-59. Mem. Info. Industry Assn., Modern Transit Soc., Oxford Soc. (No. Calif. com. 1993—), Ultra Marathon Cycling Assn., Western Wheelers Bicycle Club (pres. 1983), Oxford and Cambridge Club (London). Home: 2277

Bryant St Palo Alto CA 94301-3910 Office: In-Gate Tech 710 Lakeway Dr # 270 Sunnyvale CA 94086-4013

CLIPSHAM, ROBERT CHARLES, veterinarian; b. Kansas City, Kans., June 27, 1955; s. Robert Berkley and Diana Ruth (Jordan) C.; m. Priscilla Sue Harlan, June 27, 1990. BS in Vet. Sci., Kans. State U., 1978, DVM, 1980; Cert. of Internship, U. Calif., Davis, 1981. Intern avian medicine U. Calif. Teaching Hosp., Davis, 1980-81; clinician McClaves Vet. Hosp., Reseda, Calif., 1981-82, Animal Med. Ctr., Hawthorne, Calif., 1982-83, Capri Pla. Pet Clinic, Tarzana, Calif., 1983-85, Valley Vet. Clinic, SimiValley, Calif., 1985-87; owner In-Flight Avicultural Svc., SimiValley, 1987-88, Calif. Exotics Clinic, SimiValley, 1988—; guest instr. Moorpark (Calif.) Jr. Coll., 1987-92; aviculture advisor World Wildlife Fund, Washington, 1989-93; bd. dirs. Wildlife on Wheels, L.A., 1987-91. Author: Veterinary Clinics of North America, 1992; contbg. author: Diseases of Caged and Aviary Birds, 3d edit., 1994; contbr. articles to profl. jours. Mem. Am. Vet Med. Assn., Am. Fedn. Aviculture, Assn. Avian Vets., Calif. Vet. Med. Assn., Am. Assn. Avian Pathologists, Model Avicultural Plan (bd. dirs. 1989—), So. Calif. Vet. Med. Assn., Am. Assn. Zool. Parks & Aquariums, Am. Assn. Lab. Animal Practitioners, Am. Assn. Lab. Animal Sci., Am. Assn. Zool. Practitioners. Republican. Office: Calif Exotics Clinic 1464 Madera Rd Ste N-122 Simi Valley CA 93065-3077

CLOSE, SANDY, journalist; b. N.Y.C., Jan. 25, 1943. BA, U. Calif., Berkeley, 1964. Journalist, exec. editor Pacific News Svc., San Francisco. MacArthur fellow, 1995. Office: Pacific News Service 450 Mission St / Ste 506 San Francisco CA 94105

CLOUD, JAMES MERLE, university and hospital administrator; b. Winston-Salem, N.C., Feb. 16, 1947; s. Merle Vail and Jane Crawford (Moore) C.; B.A., U. N.C., 1970; Ph.D., Columbia Pacific U., 1979. Co-founder Wholistic Health and Nutrition Inst., Mill Valley, Calif., 1974, dir. edn., 1974-76, dir. health resource consultation, 1976-78; dir., v.p. No. Calif. Internat. Coop. Coun., 1975-77; admissions dir. Columbia Pacific U., 1978-84, sec.-treas., dir., 1978-84; v.p. Calif. U. for Advanced Studies, Novato, 1984-85; dir. Wholistic Health and Nutrition Inst., 1974-85; adminstr. Autumn Care Convalescent Hosp., 1989-90; founder Memorobics Seminars of Memory Skills for Fgn. Lang. Study, 1992, Speed Learning Systems, 1992, Learning Made Easy Study Skills Seminars. Author: The Foreign Language Memory Book, 1995, The Bible Memory Book, 1995. Sec., dir. Citizens of Marin Against Crime, 1983. Columnist Ukiah Penny Pincher, 1990. Mem. Assn. Holistic Health (v.p. 1976, dir.), Airplane Owners and Pilots Assn., Am. Assn. Active Srs. (v.p. 1988-89), Internat. Friends of the Iron Horse (founder, pres. 1990—), Internat. Assn. of Body Mechanics (pres. 1991—), Mendocino County Railway Soc. (dir. 1991), Nat. Assn. of Railway Passengers, Train Riders Assn. of Calif., Pacific Internat. Trapshooters Assn. Author: The Healthscription, 1979, Directory of Active Senior Organizations and Communications Resources, 1989; anthologies of poems: Aeolus, 1971, No One Loves With Solitude, 1970; columnist The New Penny Pincher, Ukiah, 1991. Home: 4286 Redwood Hwy San Rafael CA 94903-2645

CLOUGH, CHARLES MARVIN, electronics company executive; b. Chgo., Nov. 9, 1928; s. Charles Marvin and Margaret Cecile C.; m. Emma Marie Giachetto, Oct. 11, 1952; children: John, Susan, Margaret, Irene, Charles Marvin III, Melissa. BS, U. Ill., 1951. V.p. mktg. Tex. Instruments, Dallas, 1955-82; pres. Wyle Electronics Mktg. Group, Irvine, Calif., 1982-85; pres., COO Wyle Labs., El Segundo, Calif., 1985-88, pres., CEO, 1988—, chmn., 1991—, also bd. dirs.; dir. Farr Co., El Segundo. Served to 1st lt. USAF, 1950-55. Republican. Roman Catholic. Home: 15 Cherry Hills Ln Newport Beach CA 92660-5118 Office: Wyle Labs 128 Maryland St El Segundo CA 90245-4115

CLOUSE, VICKIE RAE, biology and paleontology educator; b. Havre, Mont., Mar. 28, 1956; d. Olaf Raymond and Betty Lou (Reed) Nelson; m. Gregory Scott Clouse, Mar. 22, 1980; 1 child, Kristopher Nelson. BS in Secondary Sci. Edn., Mont. State U., Northern, 1989; postgrad., Mont. State U., Bozeman, 1991-94. Teaching asst. biology and paleontology Mont. State U.-Northern, 1986-90; rsch. asst. dinosaur eggs and embryos Mus. of the Rockies, 1992-94; instr. biology and paleontology Mont. State U., Northern, 1990—. Bd. trustees H.E. Clack Mus., Havre, 1991-97, H.E. Clack Mus. Found., Havre, 1991-97, Mont. Bd. Regents of Higher Edn., Helena, 1989-90, Mont. Higher Edn. Student Fin. Assistance Corp., Helena, 1989-90; mem. Ea. Mont. Hist. Soc., 1993—. Named Young Career Woman of Yr., Bus. and Profl. Woman's Club, 1986. Mem. Soc. Vertebrate Paleontologists, Paleontol. Rsch. Instn., Mont. Geol. Soc. Office: Mont State U Hagener Sci Ctr Havre MT 59501

CLOWERS, MYLES LEONARD, history educator; b. Pine Bluff, Ark., Feb. 19, 1944; s. Myles Leonard and Bernice Lorene (Teague) C.; m. Catherine Jean Bouslog, Sept. 23, 1964 (div. 1974); 1 child, Lee William; m. Linda Diane Davis, Jan. 2, 1979. Student, Fullerton (Calif.) Jr. Coll., 1962-64; BA, Calif. State U., Fullerton, 1966; MA, Calif. State U., 1970, U. Calif., Riverside, 1968-69; MS in Edn. and Computers, National Univ., 1985. Prof. history San Diego City Coll., 1971—; cons. in field; participan Midwest/Far West Reg. Conf. on Ednl. Computing, 1985; policy bd. mem. Calif. History-Social Sci. Project, 1990—. Co-author: Understanding American History Through Fiction, 2 fols. (with Warren Beck), 1974, Understanding American Politics Through Fiction (with Lorin Letendre), 1973, 2d edit. 1977, Understanding Sociology Through Fiction (with Steve Mori), 1976; contbr. articles to profl. jours.; editor medial rev. sect. Community Coll. Social Sci. Quar., 1975-77; assoc. editor Community Coll. Social Sci. Quar., 1975-77; editorial adv. bd. in Western Civilizations, Collegiate Press, 1988. Mem. San Diego Italian Cultural Assn. Recipient Golden Apple awards, Alpha Gamma Sigma, 1983, 84, 85; Fulbright grantee, 1981-82, 87, 90; Julian virtue Fellow in Econ. and Entrepreneur History, Pepperdine U., 1980. Mem. Am. Historical Assn., Am. Political Sci. Assn., Nat. Conference on Higher Edn., Community Coll. Humanities Assn., Conf. on Italian Politics and Soc., Brit. Politics Grp., Fulbright Alumni Assn., Am. Cultural Assn., Phi Alpha Theta. Democrat. Home: 10279 Caminito Agadir San Diego CA 92131-1719 Office: San Diego City Coll 1313 12th Ave San Diego CA 92101-4787

CLOWES, ALEXANDER WHITEHILL, surgeon, educator; b. Boston, Oct. 9, 1946; s. George H.A. Jr. and Margaret Gracey (Jackson) C.; m. Monika Meyer. AB, Harvard U., 1968, MD, 1972. Resident in surgery Case Western Reserve, Cleve., 1972-74, 76-79; rsch. fellow in pathology Harvard Med. Sch., Boston, 1974-76; fellow in vascular surgery Brigham and Womens Hosp. Harvard Med. Sch., 1979-80; asst. prof. surgery U. Wash., Seattle, 1980-85, assoc. prof., 1985-90, prof., 1990—, assoc. chmn. dept., 1989-91, acting chmn. dept., 1992-93, adj. prof. pathology, 1992. Contbr. chpts. to books; author numerous sci. papers. Trustee Marine Biol. Labs., Woods Hole, Mass., 1989—, Seattle Symphony, 1994—; bd. dirs. Seattle Chamber Music Festival, 1990. Recipient NIH Rsch. Career Devel. award, 1982-87; NIH Tng. fellow, 1974-77; Loyal Davis Traveling Surg. scholar ACS, 1987. Mem. Am. Surg. Assn., Am. Assn. Pathologists, Am. Heart Assn. (coun. on arteriosclerosis), Am. Soc. Cell Biology, Internat. Soc. Applied Cardiovasc. Biology, Seattle Surg. Soc., Soc. Vascular Surgery, Cruising Club Am., Quisset Yacht Club, Sigma Xi. Episcopalian. Home: 702 Fullerton Ave Seattle WA 98122-6432 Office: U Wash Dept Surgery Rf # 25 Seattle WA 98195

CLOWES, GARTH ANTHONY, electronics executive, consultant; b. Didsbury, Eng., Aug. 30, 1926; came to U.S., 1957; s. Eric and Doris Gladys (Worthington) C.; m. Katharine Allman Crewdson, July 29, 1950; children: John Howard Brett, Peter Miles, Vicki Anne. BSc, Stockport Coll., Cheshire, Eng., 1953; postgrad., UCLA, 1965-66; higher nat. cert., Birmingham (Eng.) Coll. Tech., 1955-56. Gen. mgr., v.p., dir. Eldon Industries, Inc., El Segundo, Calif., 1962-69; CEO, founder Entex Industries, Inc., Compton, Calif., 1969-83; pres., founder Entex Electronics, Inc., Valley Ford, Calif., 1983—; pres., founder TTC, Inc., Carson, Calif., 1984-86; pres. Universal Telesis Electronics, Inc., Carson, 1986-87; gen. mgr. Matchbox Toys (U.S.A.) Ltd., Moonachie, N.J., 1987-88; dir. gen. Matchbox Spain, S.A., Valencia, 1988-89; cons. Matchbox Internat. Ltd., worldwide, 1986-89. Inventor electronic voice recognition devices, numerous others. Mem. pres.'s com. UNICEF, N.Y., 1972-74, Senate Adv. Bd., Washington, 1982-83; cons. Interracial Coun., L.A., 1967-69. Decorated Knight of Malta. Home: 13950 Coast Hwy 1 Valley Ford CA 94972

CLUSKEY, MARY MARSHALL, dietitian, educator; b. Chgo., June 29, 1954; d. Charles Burt and Virginia June (Youle) Marshall; m. Steven Allan Cluskey, Oct. 16, 1976; children: Blaine Elizabeth, Gwendolyn Leigh. BS in Foods, So. Ill. U., 1972; MS in Home Econs., Ill. State U., 1979; PhD in Nutrition and Food Mgmt., Oreg. State U., 1992. Registered dietitian; lic. dietitian, Oreg. Dietitian, cons. various cos., Ill., 1978-85; asst. prof. W.Va., Morgantown, 1985-87; instr. Oreg. State U., Corvallis, 1987-92; foodservice internship dir. Capital Manor, Salem, Oreg., 1992—. Recipient Heinz Fellowship award Nat. Restaurant Assn., Chgo., 1990. Mem. Am. Dietetic Assn., Oreg. Dietetic Assn. (awards chair 1993-94, nominating com. 1994—, Col. Manchester scholar 1988, Foodservice Rsch. grant 1989). Home: 1926 NW Crest Pl Albany OR 97321-1203

COAD, DENNIS L., marketing executive, management consultant; b. St. Louis, Mar. 16, 1959; s. Stanley Meredith and Olga Marie (Salarano) C.; m. Linda Marie Kasmarzik, June 20, 1980 (div. May 1982); 1 child, Jason Christopher. AA, Jefferson Coll., Pevely, Mo., 1979; BS, S.W. Mo. State U., 1988, MBA, 1990. Systems engr. Computer Task Group, St. Louis, 1981-84; owner, mng. dir. Sci. Resources Cons. Group, La Mirada, Calif., 1990—; dir. bus. devel. AGCT Inc., Irvine, Calif., 1993—. Co-editor Nature, 1994—, Genetic Engring. News, 1993—. Active United We Stand, Calif., 1992. With U.S. Army, 1984-87. Boatmen's Bank scholar, 1977. Mem. AAAS, Am. Mgmt. Assn., Smithsonian Inst., Regulatory Profl. Soc. Roman Catholic. Home: 223 Chandon Laguna Beach CA 92677-5738 Office: SRCG 2102 Business Center Dr Irvine CA 92715-1001

COATE, LESTER EDWIN, university administrator; b. Albany, Oreg., Jan. 21, 1936; s. Lester Francis and Mildred Roxana (Clarck) C.; m. Marilyn Nan Robinson (dec.); chidlren: Steven, David, Carol; m. Cheryl Diane Mizer, Dec. 20, 1973. BS, Oreg. State U., 1959; MS, San Diego State U., 1969; PhD, U.S. Internat. U., 1973; vis. scholar, U. Wash., 1985-86. Engr. Los Angeles County, L.A., 1959-61; mng. ptnr. Robinson & Coate, Valley Center, Calif., 1961-64; asst. to pres. White House, Washington, 1970-71; environ. dir. San Diego County, San Diego, 1971-73; dep. regional adminstr. U.S. EPA, Seattle, 1973-86; v.p. fin. and adminstrn. Oreg. State U., Corvallis, 1986-92; vice chancellor bus. and adminstrv. svcs. U. Calif., Santa Cruz, 1992—; bd. dirs. U. Calif. Santa Cruz, 1992—. Author: Regional Environmental Management, 1974; contbr. articles to profl. jours. Bd. dirs. U. Calif. Santa Cruz Found. Fellow Am. Acad. Environ. Engrs., White House Fellows, Salzburg Fellows; mem. Nat. Assn. Coll. and Univ. Bus. Officers (chmn. fin. com., Neil Hines award for publs. 1994), C. of C. (past v.p.), Rotary (past pres.), Phi Kappa Phi. Home: 217 Venetian Way Aptos CA 95003-4624 Office: Univ Calif Santa Cruz CA 95064

COATES, ROSS ALEXANDER, art educator; b. Hamilton, Ont., Can., Nov. 1, 1932; s. Ralph Mansfield and Dorothea (Alexander) C.; m. Agnes Dunn, 1955 (div. 1979); children: Meagan Scott, Arwyn Alexandra; m. Marilyn Kathleen Lysohir, Sept. 27, 1980. BFA, Sch. of the Art Inst. of Chgo., 1956; MA, NYU, 1960, PhD, 1972. Asst. prof. Montclair (N.J.) State Coll., 1965-68; art tutor Canon Lawrence Coll., Lira, Uganda, 1968-70; chair fine arts dept. Russell Sage Coll., Troy, N.Y., 1971-76; prof. Wash. State U., Pullman, 1976—, chair art dept., 1976-84; vis. instr. in art Kansas City (Mo.) Art Inst., 1963-64. Editor: Gods Among Us, 1990; numerous one man shows and group exhibitions. Idaho Arts Commn. fellow, 1990. Mem. Coll. Art Assn. Office: Wash State U Fine Art Dept Pullman WA 99164

COATES, WAYNE EVAN, agricultural engineer; b. Edmonton, Alta., Can., Nov. 28, 1947; came to U.S., 1981; s. Orval Bruce Wright and Leora (Raesler) C.; m. Patricia Louise Williams, Aug. 28, 1970. BS in Agr., U. Alta., 1969, MS in Agrl. Engring., 1970; PhD in Agrl. Engring., Okla. State U., 1973. Registered profl. engr., Ariz., Sask. Forage systems engr. Agr. Can., Melfort, Sask., 1973-75; project engr., tech. advisor, asst. sta. mgr. Prairie Agrl. Machinery Inst., Humboldt, Sask., 1975-81; cattle, grain farmer pvt. practice, Humboldt, 1975-81; assoc. prof. U. Ariz., Tucson, 1981-91, prof., 1991—; prof. titular ad honorem U. Nat. de Catamarca, Argentina, 1993—; cons. Vols. in Coop. Assts. and Ptnrs. of Ames., 1991—, Paraguayan Govt. UN Devel. Program, 1987-90, Argentine Govt., univs. and pvt. industry, 1991—, govt., univ. and agrl. orgns., Mid.. East agrl. projects; speaker at internat. confs., Australia, Paraguay, Argentina, U.S. Designer farm equipment primarily for alternative crops and tillage; contbr. articles to profl. jours. Pres. Sunrise Ter. Village Townhomes Homeowners Assn., Tucson, 1990-92. Grantee USDA, Washington, 1981—, Ariz. Dept. Environ. Quality, Phoenix, 1989—, U.S. Dept. of Energy, Washington, 1991—, agrl. industries western U.S., 1982—. Mem. AAAS, NSPE, Am. Soc. Agrl. Engrs. (chmn. Ariz. sect. 1984-85, vice-chmn. Pacific region 1988-89, dir. dist. 4 1991-93, rep. to AAAS Consortium of Affiliates for Internat. Programs 1992—, internat. dir. 1994—), Assn. for Advancement of Indsl. Crops (pres. 1994—), Am. Soc. Engring. Edn., Soc. Automotive Engrs., Air and Waste Mgmt. Assn., Can. Soc. Agrl. Engring., Australian Soc. for Agrl. Engring., Asian Assn. for Agrl. Engring., Sigma Xi. Office: U Ariz Office Arid Lands Studies 250 E Valencia Rd Tucson AZ 85706-6800

COATS, WILLIAM SLOAN, III, lawyer; b. Fresno, Calif., Mar. 31, 1950; s. William Sloan Jr. and Willa (Macdonell) C.; m. Sherri Lee Young, Aug. 3, 1980; children: Devin Roseanne, Allyn Elizabeth. AB, U. San Francisco, 1972; JD, U. Calif., San Francisco, 1980. Bar: Calif. 1980, U.S. Dist. Ct. (no. dist.) Calif. 1980, U.S. Dist. Ct. (cen. and so. dists.) Calif. 1982. Assoc. Bancroft, Avery & McAlister, San Francisco, 1980-82, Hopkins, Mitchell & Carley, San Jose, Calif., 1982-84, Gibson, Dunn & Crutcher, San Francisco, 1984-93; ptnr. Brown & Bain, Palo Alto, Calif., 1993—. Nat. Merit scholar, 1968. Mem. ABA, Calif. Bar Assn. (co-chair copyright comm. intellectual property sect.), Intellectual Property Leadership Forum (adv. bd.), Green and Gold Club, Univ. Club. Republican. Roman Catholic. Office: Brown & Bain 600 Hansen Way Palo Alto CA 94304-1024

COBB, JOHN BOSWELL, JR., clergyman, educator; b. Kobe, Japan, Feb. 9, 1925; s. John Boswell and Theodora Cook (Atkinson) C.; m. Jean Olmstead Loftin, June 18, 1947; children: Theodore, Cliford, Andrew, Richard. M.A., U. Chgo. Div. Sch., 1949, Ph. D., 1952. Ordained to ministry United Meth. Ch., 1950. Pastor Towns County Circuit, N.Ga. Conf., 1950-51; faculty Young Harris Coll., Ga., 1950-53, Candler Sch. Theology and Emory U., 1953-58, Sch. Theology, Claremont, Calif., 1958-90; Avery prof. Claremont Grad. Sch., 1973-90; ret., 1990; mem. commn. on doctrine and doctrinal standard United Meth. Ch., 1968-72; mem. commn. on mission, 1984-88. Author: A Christian Natural Theology, 1965, The Structure of Christian Existence, 1967, Christ in a Pluralistic Age, 1975, (with Herman Daly) For the Common Good, 1989. Dir. Center for Process Studies. Fulbright prof. U. Mainz, 1965-66; fellow Woodrow Wilson Internat. Ctr. for Scholars, 1976. Mem. Am. Acad. Religion, Am. Metaphys. Soc.

COBB, LUTHER FUSON, surgeon, educator; b. Little Rock, Apr. 24, 1952; s. Lewis Latane Cobb and Eulalia Anne-Belle (Fuson) Vaughn; m. Mary Ellen Mahoney, Apr. 24, 1983; 1 child, Kathleen R.M.; 1 stepchild, David J. Haffner. BS, Mich. State U., 1974; MD, Stanford U., 1978. Diplomate Am. Bd. Surgery. Resident surgery Stanford (Calif.) U. Dept. Surgery, 1978-85, clin. asst. prof. surgery, 1985—; staff surgeon Santa Clara Valley Med. Ctr., San Jose, Calif., 1985—; dir. trauma svcs. Santa Clara Valley Med. Ctr., San Jose, 1987—. Contbr. articles to profl. jours. Recipient Nat. Rsch. Svc. award NIH, 1980; Nat. Merit scholar Merit Scholarship Bd., 1970, Alumni Disting. scholar Mich. State U., 1970. Mem. AMA, Calif. Med. Assn. (del. 1993—), Santa Clara County Med. Assn. (v.p. 1986—), Sigma Xi, Phi Kappa Phi. Democrat. Office: Santa Clara Valley Med Ctr 751 S Bascom Ave San Jose CA 95128-2604

COBB, ROWENA NOELANI BLAKE, real estate broker; b. Kauai, Hawaii, May 1, 1939; d. Bernard K. Blake and Hattie Kanui Yuen; m. James Jackson Cobb, Dec. 22, 1962; children: Shelly Ranelle Noelani, Bret Kimo Jackson. BS in Edn., Bob Jones U., 196l; broker's lic., Vitousek Sch. Real Estate, Honolulu, 198l. Lic. real estate broker, Honolulu; cert. residential broker. Bus. mgr. Micronesian Occupational Ctr., Koror Palau, 1968-70; prin. broker Cobb Realty, Lihue, Hawaii, 1983—; sec. Neighbor Island MLS Svc., Honolulu, 1985-87, vice chmn., 1987-88; chmn. MLS Hawaii, Inc., Honolulu, 1988-90. Assoc. editor Jour Entymology, 1965-66. Sec. Koloa Cmty. Assn., 1981-89, pres., 1989; mem. Kauai Humane Soc., YWCA, Kauai Mus.; bd. dirs. Wong Care Home; adv. bd. dist. edn. adminstrn. Mem. Nat. Assn. Realtors (grad. Realtors Inst., cert. residential specialist), Hawaii Assn. Realtors (cert. tchr., state bd. dirs. 1984, v.p. 1985, dir. 1995), Kauai Bd. Realtors (v.p. 1984, pres. 1985, bd. dirs. 1995—, Realtor Assoc. of Yr. award 1983, Realtor of Yr. award 1986), Kauai Mus., Soroptimists (bd. dirs. Lihue 1986-89, treas. 1989). Office: PO Box 157 Koloa HI 96756-0157

COBB, ROY LAMPKIN, JR., computer sciences corporation executive; b. Oklahoma City, Sept. 23, 1934; s. Roy Lampkin and Alice Maxine (Ellis) C.; B.A., U. Okla., 1972; postgrad. U. Calif., Northridge, 1976-77; m. Shirley Ann Dodson, June 21, 1958; children—Kendra Leigh, Cary William, Paul Alan. Naval aviation cadet U.S. Navy, 1955, advanced through grades to comdr., 1970; ret., 1978; mktg./project staff engr. Gen. Dynamics, Pomona, Calif., 1978-80; mgr. dept. support svcs. Computer Scis. Corp., Point Mugu, Calif., 1980—. Decorated Navy Commendation medal, Air medal. Mem. Assn. Naval Aviators, Soc. Logistic Engrs. (editor Launchings 1990—). Republican. Christian. Club: Las Posas Country, Spanish Hills Country Club. Home: 2481 Brookhill Dr Camarillo CA 93010-2112 Office: Computer Scis Corp PO Box 42273 Port Hueneme CA 93044-4573

COBB, SHIRLEY ANN, public relations specialist, journalist; b. Oklahoma City, Jan. 1, 1936; d. William Ray and Irene (Fewell) Dodson; m. Roy Lampkin Cobb, Jr., June 21, 1958; children: Kendra Leigh, Cary William, Paul Alan. BA in Journalism with distinction, U. Okla., 1958, postgrad., 1972; postgrad., Jacksonville U., 1962. Info. specialist Pacific Missle Test Ctr., Point Mugu, Calif., 1975-76; corr. Religious News Svc., N.Y.C., 1979-81; splty. editor fashion and religion Thousand Oaks (Calif.) News Chronicle, 1977-81; pub. rels. cons., Camarillo, Calif., 1977—; media mgr. pub. info City of Thousand Oaks, 1983—. Contbr. articles to profl. jours. Trustee Ocean View Sch. Bd., 1976-79; pres. Point Mugu Officers' Wives Club, 1975-76, 90—, Calif. Assn. Pub. Info. Ofcls. (pres. 1989-90, Paul Clark Lifetime Achievement award 1993); bd. dirs. Camarillo Hospice, 1983-85; sec. Conejo Valley Hist. Soc., 1993-95. Recipient Spot News award San Fernando Valley Press Club, 1979. Mem. Pub. Rels. Soc. Am. (L.A. chpt. liaison 1991), Sigma Delta Chi, Phi Beta Kappa, Chi Omega. Republican. Clubs: Las Posas Country, Spanish Hills Country, Town Hall of Calif. Home: 2481 Brookhill Dr Camarillo CA 93010-2112 Office: 2100 E Thousand Oaks Blvd Thousand Oaks CA 91362-2903

COBB, WILLIAM THOMPSON, environmental consultant; b. Spokane, Wash., Nov. 10, 1942; s. Elmer Jean and Martha Ella (Napier) C.; m. Sandra L. Hodgson, Aug. 29, 1964 (div. 1988); children: Mike, Melanie, Megan, Bill II. BA, Ea. Wash. U., 1964; PhD, Oreg. State U., 1973. Cert. profl. agronomist, profl. plant pathologist. Mgr., agronomist Sun Royal Co., Royal City, Wash., 1970-74; sr. scientist Lilly Rsch. Labs., Kennewick, Wash., 1974-87; environ. cons. Cobb Cons. Svcs., Kennewick, Wash., 1988—; bd. dirs. Bentech Labs., Portland, Oreg., 1989; dir. spl. projects Bioremediation, Inc., Lake Oswego, Oreg., 1990-92; adv. bd. Adv. Coun. Tri-Cities, Wash., 1991. Contbr. articles to profl. jours. 1st lt. U.S. Army, 1964-67. Mem. Am. Phytopath. Soc., Weed Sci. Soc. Am., We. Soc. Weed Sci., Am. Soc. Agronomy, N.W. Assn. Environ. Profls., Nat. Assn. Environ. Profls., Rocky Mountain Soc. Quality Assurance, Hazardous Materials Control Rsch. Inst., Sigma Xi. Republican. Home and Office: Cobb Cons Svcs 815 S Kellogg St Kennewick WA 99336-9369

COBIANCHI, THOMAS THEODORE, engineering and marketing executive, educator; b. Paterson, N.J., July 7, 1941; s. Thomas and Violet Emily (Bazzar) C.; m. Phyllis Linda Asch, Feb. 6, 1964; 1 child, Michael. Student, Clemson U., 1963; BS, Monmouth Coll., 1968, MBA, 1972; postgrad., U. Pa., 1987; D Bus. Adminstrn., U.S. Internat. U., 1994. Sales mgr. Westinghouse Electric Corp., Balt., 1968-74; sr. internat. sales engr. Westinghouse Electric Corp., Lima, Ohio, 1975-77; program mgr. Westinghouse Electric Corp., Pitts., 1977-78, mgr. bus. devel., 1978-82; dir. mktg. Westinghouse Electric Corp., Arlington, Va., 1982-86; acting dir., engring. mgr. General Dynamics Corp., San Diego, 1986-89; dir. bus. devel. RPV Programs Teledyne Ryan Aero., San Diego, 1989-90; pres. Cobianchi & Assocs., San Diego, 1990; v.p. strategic planning and program devel. S-Cubed div. Maxwell Labs., Inc., San Diego, 1991—; instr., lectr. various ednl. instns. Active various polit. and ednl. orgns.; mem. bus. adv. coun. U.S. Internat. U.; bd. dirs. Cath. Charities San Diego; vol. exec., sect. chmn. United Way San Diego. Mem. Armed Forces Communications and Electronics Assn. (acting chmn. 1988), Princeton Club of Washington, Nat. Aviation Club, General Dynamics Health Club, Delta Sigma Pi. Home: 16468 Calle Pulido San Diego CA 92128-3249

COBLEY, JOHN GRIFFIN, biochemist and educator; b. London, Oct. 28, 1946; s. William Thomas and Olive Marion Cobley; m. Evelyn Rogers, Jan. 4, 1986; children: Allison Claire, Caitlin Amanda. BSc in Biochemistry, U. Bristol, U.K., 1968, PhD in Biochemistry, 1972. Postdoctoral scientist U. Calif., San Francisco, 1972-74, U. Dundee, Scotland, 1974-76; asst. prof. biochemistry U. San Francisco, 1977-84, assoc. prof., 1984-91, prof. biochemistry, 1991—, chmn. dept. chemistry, 1986-89; vis. faculty U. Utrecht, Netherlands, 1984. Contbr.: (book) Microbial Chemoautotrophy, 1984; contbr. articles to profl. jours. Recipient Disting. Rsch. award U. San Francisco, 1994. Mem. Am. Soc. Plant Physiologists, Am. Soc. Photobiology. Office: Univ of San Francisco Dept Chemistry 2130 Fulton St San Francisco CA 94117-1080

COBURN, MARJORIE FOSTER, psychologist, educator; b. Salt Lake City, Feb. 28, 1939; d. Harlan A. and Alma (Ballinger) Polk; m. Robert Byron Coburn, July 2, 1977; children: Polly Klea Foster, Matthew Ryan Foster, Robert Scott Coburn, Kelly Anne Coburn. B.A. in Sociology, UCLA, 1960; Montessori Internat. Diploma honor grad. Washington Montessori Inst., 1968; M.A. in Psychology, U. No. Colo., 1979; Ph.D. in Counseling Psychology, U. Denver, 1983. Licensed clin. psychologist. Probation officer Alameda County (Calif.), Oakland, 1960-62, Contra Costa County (Calif.), El Cerrito, 1966, Fairfax County (Va.), Fairfax, 1967; dir. Friendship Club, Orlando, Fla., 1963-65; tchr. Va. Montessori Sch., Fairfax, 1968-70; spl. edn. tchr. Leary Sch., Falls Church, Va., 1970-72, sch. administr., 1973-76; tchr. Aseltine Sch., San Diego, 1976-77, Coburn Montessori Sch., Colorado Springs, Colo., 1977-79; pvt. practice psychotherapy, Colorado Springs, 1979-82, San Diego, 1982—; cons. spl. edn., agoraphobia, women in transition. Mem. Am. Psychol. Assn., Am. Orthopsychiat. Assn., Phobia Soc., Council Exceptional Children, Calif. Psychol. Assn., San Diego Psychological Assn., The Charter 100, Mensa. Episcopalian. Lodge: Rotary. Contbr. articles to profl. jours.; author: (with R.C. Orem) Montessori: Prescription for Children with Learning Disabilities, 1977. Office: 826 Prospect St Ste 101 La Jolla CA 92037-4206

COBURN, ROBERT JAMES, music educator, composer; b. Montebello, Calif., Oct. 29, 1949; s. Tyler Hadley and Elizabeth Coburn; m. Jeanne Nadine Ashby, May 12, 1974; 1 child, Benjamin Tyler. MusB in Theory and Composition, U. of the Pacific, 1972; MA in Music Composition, U. Calif., Berkeley, 1974; PhD in Music Composition, U. Victoria, Can., 1992. Adj. faculty Lewis and Clark Coll., Portland, Oreg., 1978-84; chair music dept. Marylhurst Coll., Portland, 1984-90; asst. prof. music theory and composition U. of the Pacific, Conservatory of Music, Stockton, Calif., 1993—; dir. Group for New Music Portland, Oreg., 1975-81, Ctr. for Electronic Music, Lewis and Clark Coll., Portland, 1979-85; featured composer Portland (Oreg.) Composers Festival, 1985; mem. arts design team Oreg. Conv. Ctr., Portland, 1987-89. Composer, sound artist/designer in field; commd. by Bell Circles II, Oreg., 1987-90, Phila. Bell Project, 1994—; composer Time's Shadow for clarinet and ensemble, 1995, Shadowbox for clarinet, 1994, Luminous Shadows, 1993. Oreg. Artists fellow Oreg. Arts Commn., 1978, Grad. fellow U. Victoria, B.C., 1991-93; Composers grantee Met. Arts Commn., Portland, 1981. Mem. Internat. Soc. for the Arts, Scis. and Tech. (Leonardo rev. com. 1993—), World Forum for Acoustic Ecology (founding mem.), Internat. Computer Music Assn., Pi Kappa Lambda. Office: Conservatory Music Univ of the Pacific Stockton CA 95211

COBURN, TIMOTHY CRAIG, research statistician; b. Houston, May 10, 1951; s. Robert Reeves and Doris Madeline (Gardner) C. BS, BSE, Abilene Christian U., 1973; MS, Okla. State U., 1975, PhD, 1980. Cert. tchr., Tex., Colo. Grad. asst. dept. stats. Okla. State U., Stillwater, 1973-75, grad. asst., cons. statistician Statis. Lab., 1978-80; regional statistician [illegible]

Nutrition Service, Dallas, 1975-78; cons. statistician USDA-Food and Nutrition Service, Washington, 1977; statistician Phillips Petroleum Co., Bartlesville, Okla., 1980-83; research statistician Phillips Petroleum Co., Denver, 1983-85; sr. scientist Marathon Oil Co., Littleton, Colo., 1985-87, supr. quantitive geoscis., 1988-94; mgmt. and program analyst U.S. SBA, 1994; data ctr. statistician Nat. Renewable Energy Lab., Golden, Colo., 1995—; statis. cons. Carson and Tratner Attys., Oklahoma City, Okla., 1975; cons. statistician Miss. State U. Dept. Gen. Sci., Jackson, 1981-83, Ctr. Environ., Energy and Sci. Edn., Jackson; cons. in field, Dallas, 1975; lectr. Secondary Sch. Lecture Program, Dallas, 1977; industry participant Colo. Alliance Sci., 1987-91. Contbg. editor: Current Index to Statistics, 1985—; pub. referee Communications in Statistics, 1984, Jour. Official Stats. Sweden, 1986, Computer Contbn. Series Kansas Geol. Survey, 1990-94, Mathematical Geology, 1994-95; contbr. articles to profl. jours., books; mem. editl. bd. Nonrenewable Resources, 1991—. Mem. bd. visitors Abilene (Tex.) Christian U., 1985-91, eval. team Okla. State U. Ctr. Local Govt.Tech., 1975. Grantee Research Corp., 1973, USDA Food and Nutrition Service, Washington, 1979; recipient Carl Marshall award Okla. State U., 1980. Mem. AAAS, Am. Statis. Assn. (pres. Okla. chpt. 1983-84, mem. energy stats. com., adv. group for Energy Info. Adminstrn.), Internat. Assn. Math. Geology, Internat. Biometric Soc., Am. Soc. Quality Control, Inst. Math. Statistics, Sigma Xi. Democrat. Mem. Ch. Christ. Home: 7414 S Downing Cir E Littleton CO 80121 Office: Nat Renewable Energy Lab 1617 Cole Blvd Golden CO 80401

COCCHIARELLA, VICKI MARSHALL, state legislator; b. Livingston, Mont., Dec. 19, 1949; d. James and Ruth E. (Officer) Marshall; m. Larry Ray Cocchiarella, 1973; children: Cara Jo, Michael James. BA, U. Mont., 1978, MA, 1985. Property mgr., 1975—; teaching asst. U. Mont., 1979-80, adminstrv. clk., 1981—; mem. Mont. Ho. of Reps., 1989—, mem. interim com. state employee compensation. Bd. dirs. Child & Family Resource Coun. Mem. Mont. Pub. Employees Assn. (former bd. dirs., former 1st v.p., pres. 1987—). Democrat. Home: 535 Livingston Ave Missoula MT 59801-8003 Office: Mont State Senate State Capitol Helena MT 59620

COCHRAN, ANNE WESTFALL, public relations executive; b. Cairo, Ill., Sept. 16, 1954; d. Howard Thurston and Flora Isabelle (Stone) Westfall; m. Charles Eugene Cochran, June 14, 1975; 2 children. BA in Advt., So. Ill. U., 1974; MA in Communications, U. Wis., Milw., 1975. Dir. advt. Sight and Sound Systems Inc., Milw., 1975-76; nat. publicity/promotions mgr. 20th Century Fox Classics, L.A., 1981-85; nat. publicity dir. Cannon Films Inc., L.A., 1985-86; publicist, staff writer Warner Bros. Inc., Burbank, Calif., 1986-87; v.p. mktg. Cinetel Films, Inc., L.A., 1987; v.p. publicity and promotion U.S. U.S. Cineplex Odeon Films, Inc., L.A., 1987-89; ptnr. Jones Cochran Assocs., Beverly Hills, Calif., 1989-92; sr. v.p. corp. and motion picture divsns. Bender, Goldman & Helper, L.A., 1992-95; ptnr. The Cochran Co., L.A., 1995—; mktg. cons., L.A., 1976-81. Bd. dirs. Case de Rosas Sunshine Mission, L.A., 1990. Mem. Publicists Guild. Democrat. Mem. Ch. Religious Sci. Home: 3641 Shannon Rd Los Angeles CA 90027-1420

COCHRAN, JOHN HOWARD, plastic and reconstructive surgeon; b. Muncie, Ind., Sept. 6, 1946; s. John H. and Lois M. (Woolridge) C.; m. Elizabeth M. Cochran; 1 child, Ryan K. BS cum laude, Colo. State U., 1968; MD, U. Colo. Sch. Medicine, 1973. Intern surgery U. Calif., San Diego, 1973-74; resident head and neck surgery Stanford U., Palo Alto, Calif., 1974-77; resident plastic surgery U. Wis., Madison, 1979-81; pvt. practice plastic surgery Denver, 1981-90; chief plastic surgery St. Joseph Hosp., Denver, 1987-93, Colo. Med. Group, Denver, 1990-95; chmn. dept. surgery St. Joseph Hosp., 1993-95. Contbr. chpt. to book. Pres. bd. trustees Kilimanjaro Children's Hosp.. Tanzania, E. Africa, 1989-95. Fellow Am. Soc. Plastic and Reconstructive Surgery, Am. Coll. SUrgeons, Acad. Otolaryngology, Head and Neck Surgery; mem. Am. Assn. Plastic Surgeons. Office: 2045 Franklin St Denver CO 80205-5437

COCHRAN, LEIGHTON SCOTT, wind engineering consultant, research scientist; b. Melbourne, Victoria, Australia; s. Michael John and Majorie Joyce (Newham) C. BE, U. Queensland, Australia, 1979; MS, Colo. State U., 1986, PhD, 1992. Design engr. Bornhorst and Ward, Brisbane, Australia, 1979-81; site engr. Fluor Australia, Collinsville, 1981-83; flood cons. No. Territory Dept. Lands, Darwin, 1984; site engr. civil and civic Mt. Isa, 1985; grad. rsch. assoc. Colo. State U., Ft. Collins, 1985-86, 90-92, rsch. scientist, 1993—; wind tunnel mgr. Vipac Engrs. and Scientists, Melbourne, 1987-90; sr. project engr. Cermak Peterka Petersen, Inc., Ft. Collins, 1993—. Contbr. articles, tech. reports to profl. jours. and conf. procs. Recipient NASA summer scholarship, UCLA and Jet Propulsion Lab., 1991. Mem. ASCE (task force on outdoor human comfort 1993—), ASME, Instn. of Engrs. (Australia), U.S. Wind Engrng. Rsch. Coun., Australian Wind Engrng. Soc., Australia and New Zealand Archtl. Sci. Assn., Australian and New Zealand Solar Energy Soc., The Planetary Soc., Internat. Human Powered Vehicle Assn. Office: CPP 1415 Blue Spruce Dr Fort Collins CO 80524-2003

COCHRAN, VERLAN LEYERL, soil scientist; b. Declo, Idaho, Feb. 19, 1938; s. Harley Earl and Anna Helena (Christensen) C.; m. Diana Larraine Dennis, June 21, 1969; children: Dean Scott, Vincent Lee. BS in Soil Sci., Calif. Poly. U., 1966; MS in Soils, Wash. State U., 1971. Soil scientist USDA-ARS, Pullman, Wash., 1966-85; soil scientist USDA-ARS, Fairbanks, Alaska, 1985-89, supervisory soil scientist, 1989-94; supervisory soil scientist USDA-ARS, Sidney, Mont., 1994—. Contbr. chpt. to book and articles to profl. jours. Mem. Am. Soc. Agronomy, Soil Sci. Soc. Am., Am. Soc. Microbiologists (br. pres. 1989). Office: USDA-ARS No Plains Soil & Water Rsch Ctr PO Box 1104 Sidney MT 59270

COCHRAN, WENDELL, science editor; b. Carthage, Mo., Nov. 29, 1929; s. Wendell Albert and Lillian Gladys (Largent) C.; m. Agnes Elizabeth Groves, Nov. 9, 1963; remarried Corinne Des Jardins, Aug. 25, 1980. A.B., U. Mo., Columbia, 1953, A.M. in Geology, 1956, B.J., 1960. Geologist ground-water br. U.S. Geol. Survey, 1956-58; reporter, copyeditor Kansas City (Mo.) Star, 1960-63; editor Geotimes and Earth Sci. mags., Geospectrum newsletter, Alexandria, Va., 1963-84; v.p. Geol. Survey Inc., Bethesda, Md., 1984-86. Co-author: Into Print: A Practical Guide to Writing, Illustrating, and Publishing, 1977; sr. editor: Geowriting: A Guide to Writing, Editing and Printing in Earth Science, 1973; contbr. articles to profl. jours. and encys. Mem. geol. socs. Washington, London, Assn. Earth Sci. Editors (award Outstanding Contbns. 1982), Dog in the Night-time. Home: 4351 SW Willow St Seattle WA 98136-1769

COCHRAN, WILLIAM MICHAEL, librarian; b. Nevada, Iowa, May 6, 1952; s. Joseph Charles and Inez (Larson) C.; m. Diane Marie Ohm, July 24, 1971. BLS, U. Iowa, 1979, MA with distinction in Libr. Sci., 1983; MA in Pub. Adminstrn., Drake U., 1989. Dir. Red Oak (Iowa) Pub. Libr., 1984; patron svcs. libr. Pub. Libr. of Des Moines, 1984-87; program coord. LSCA State Libr. of Iowa, Des Moines, 1987-88, dir. libr. devel., 1988-89, asst. state libr., 1989-90; coord. South Ctrl. Fedn. Librs., Billings, Mont., 1990—; dir. Parmly Billings Libr., 1990—. Author: A Century of Iowa Libraries in Association: A History of the Iowa Library Association 1890-1990, 1990; contbr. articles to profl. jours. Bd. dirs. Billings Cmty. Cable Corp., 1994—. Mem. ALA, Mont. Libr. Assn. (bd. dirs. 1991-93, pub. libr. divsn. 1991—, chair 1991-92, legislative com. chair 1992-93, task force on lobbying chair 1992-93, ad hoc com. on Mont. Libr. edn. 1991-92), Mont. Libr. Svcs. Adv. Coun. (planning com. 1991), Mont. Ctr. for the Book (exec. com. 1990-93, fundraising com. chair 1991-92), White House Conf. on Libr. and Info. Svcs. (del.-at-large, elected mem. of conf. recommendations com.), Libr. Admnstrn. and Mgmt. Assn. (govtl. affairs com. 1992—, pub. rels. sect., govtl. advocacy skills com. 1992-94, program chair for 1994 Miami conf. 1992-94), Pub. Libr. Assn., Writer's Voice of the YMCA (Billings chpt. steering com. 1991—), U. Iowa Alumni Assn. (life), Rotary Internat. (rotarian com. 1992—), Beta Phi Mu. Office: Parmly Billings Library 510 N Broadway Billings MT 59101-1156

COCHRANE, BARRYMORE DONALD, oil industry executive; b. Creelman, Sask., Can., July 10, 1935; s. Samuel Henry and Rose Ellen (Apps) C.; m. Patricia Cochrane, Oct. 16, 1982; children: Brent, Lauri, Alix, Matthew, Justin, Sam; stepchildren: Andrea, David, Paula, Frank. BSc, U. Sask., 1956. Exploitation engr. Great Plains Devel., 1956-58; mgr. Banner Petroleum Trans Can. Pipe Lines Ltd., 1958-73, Can. Arctic Gas, 1973-74; mgr. w. ops. Northern and Ctrl. Gas, 1974-76; mgr. corp. planning Norcen Energy Resources Ltd., 1976, v.p. corp. planning, 1979-82, sr. v.p., 1982, pres., CEO, 1991—; bd. dirs. Progas Ltd. Mem. Can. Inst. Mining and Metallurgy, Alta. Assn. Profl. Engrs., Geologists and Geophysicists, Glencoe Club, Lambton Golf and Country Club, Earl Grey Golf Club. Office: Norcen Energy Resources Ltd, 715 5th Ave SW, Calgary, AB Canada T2P 2X7

COCHRANE, PEGGY, architect, writer; b. Alhambra, Calif., July 9, 1926; d. E. Elliott and Gladys (Moran) C.; B.A., Scripps Coll., 1945; postgrad., U. So. Calif., 1951-52, Columbia U., 1954; m. Hugh Bowman, Nov. 24, 1954 (div.). Job capt. Kahn and Jacobs, N.Y.C., 1954-55; project architect Litchfield, Whiting, Panero & Severud, Teheran, Iran, 1956; archtl. designer Daniel, Mann, Johnson and Mendenhall, Los Angeles, 1956-59; individual practice architecture, Sherman Oaks, Calif., 1966—. Recipient Architecture prize Scripps Coll., 1945. Mem. Am. Inst. Architects, Assn. Women in Architecture (life), Union Internationale des Femmes Architects, Travelers' Century Club. Republican. Episcopalian. Author (musical) Mayaland, 1979, (book) The Witch Doctor's Manual, 1984, The Witch Doctors' Cookbook, 1984, The Sorcerers Guide to Good Health, 1993; contbr. to Contemporary Architects. Office: Ste 1-626 15030 Ventura Blvd # 22 Sherman Oaks CA 91403

COCHRUN, JOHN WESLEY, insurance agent; b. Spencerville, Ohio, May 4, 1918; s. Paul Wesley and Laura Edna (McClure) C.; m. Shirley Bunnell Stephens, June 7, 1942; children: Timothea Jourdan, David Wesley. BS, Purdue U., 1940; diploma, U.S. Army Command and Gen. Staff Coll., 1944; MS in Fin. Svcs., Am. Coll., 1985. CLU, chartered fin. cons. Spl. apprentice Bendix-Westinghouse A.A.B. Co., Pitts., 1940-41; asst. svc. mgr. Bendix-Westinghouse A.A.B. Co., Elyria, Ohio, 1945-50; mgr. customer svc. DeVilbiss Co., Toledo, 1950-58; exec. v.p. Elec. Products R & D Co., Toledo, 1958-60; spl. agt. Northwestern Mut. and other ins. cos., Toledo, 1961-81, St. Petersburg, Fla., 1981-87, Las Cruces, N.Mex., 1987—; registered investment adviser SEC, State of N.Mex., 1989—; pres. Cochrun Inc., Sylvania, Ohio, 1976-81, Seminole, Fla., 1981-87. Author: Service of the Piece, 1945, Avoid Financial Shocks in Your Family's Future, 1976, Wills, Trusts, and Life Insurance Settlement Options, 1995. Pres. Community League Sylvania, 1954; lobbyist Ohio Pub. Expenditure Coun., Sylvania, 1955, Fed. Transp. Commn., Washington, 1947-50. Lt. col. U.S. Army, 1941-45. Mem. Am. Soc. CLU and Chartered Fin. Cons., Nat. Assn. Life Underwriters (Nat. Quality award 1963-89), Nat. Estate Planning Coun., Million Dollar Round Table (life), Res. Officers Assn., Phi Kappa Psi. Republican.

COCKERHAM, KIRBY LEE, JR., geological consultant; b. Biloxi, Miss., June 28, 1926; s. Kirby Lee and Carrie Jones (Doty) C.; m. Mary Eleanor Meeks, June 19, 1951; children: Rebecca, Catherine, Amanda, Carrie. BS, La. State U., 1950, MS, 1952. Prodn. geologist Humble Oil and Refining Co., Houston, 1951-54, exploration geologist, 1954-66; dist. geologist Humble Oil and Refining Co., Lafayette, La., 1966-67, New Orleans, 1967-70; sr. exploration geologist Exxon Co. U.S.A., Denver, 1970-76, Houston, 1976-77; exploration mgr. Tesoro Petroleum Corp., Denver, 1977-82; dist. explorationist Williams Exploration Co., Denver, 1982-85; pvt. practice cons. geologist Denver, 1985—. Contbr. articles to profl. jours. With USN, 1944-46, PTO. Fellow Explorers Club of N.Y. (chmn. Rocky Mountain chpt. 1991-92); mem. Am. Assn. Petroleum Geologists (cert.), Soc. Ind. Profl. Earth Scientists (treas. Denver chpt. 1988-89, treas. nat. conv. 1989, membership chair Denver chpt. 1994), Houston Geol. Soc., Rocky Mountain Assn. Geologists (assoc. editor The Mountain Geologist). Republican. Episcopalian. Home: 9865 E Crestline Cir Englewood CO 80111-3627

COCKRELL, FRANK BOYD, II, film production company executive; b. Redding, Calif., May 3, 1948; s. Alfred Marion Sr. and Blanche Delma (Webb) C.; m. Grace Marie Louise Whest, KSept. 20, 1986; children: Catherine, Francis Marion V, Ross, Sabrina, Brooke, Amanda, Richard Sears III. AA, Shasta Jr. Coll., 1968; BS, Sacramento (Calif.) State U., 1970; postgrad., U. Pacific, 1970-72. Pres., chmn. Als Towing & Storage Co., Sacramento, 1976-78, Compacts Only Rental Cars, Sacramento, 1976-78; film producer, actor, comedian Sacramento, L.A. and Las Vegas, Nev., 1976—; fin. cons., 1974—; pres., chmn. Cockrell Prodns., Inc., L.A., 1984—, Palm Spring Employment Agy., Inc., Palm Desert, Calif., 1986; chmn. Contractor's Surety and Fidelity Co., Ltd., CNR Constrn. Co., Inc., U.S. Mining Corp., 21st Century Ins. Group, Inc.-Nev., Hollywood, Calif., 1992—, 21st Century Travel, Inc., Camarillo, Calif., 1992—; CEO, 1st Am. Contractors Bonding Assn., Inc. Author: Vietnam History, 1970. Candidate Assembly 6th Dist. Rep. Party, Sacramento, 1974; mem. Sacramento Rep. Cen. Com., 1975-76, Calif. State Cen. Rep. Com., 1974-76. Bank of Am. scholar, 1966, Shasta Coll. scholar, 1967. Lodge: Optimists (pres. Sacramento chpt. 1975-76, lt. gov. 1976-77). Office: Cockrell Prodns Inc PO Box 1731 Studio City CA 91614-0731

COCKRELL, RICHARD CARTER, lawyer; b. Denver, Oct. 9, 1925; s. Harold Arthur Sweet and Mary Lynne Cockrell. AB, U. Denver, 1949, JD cum laude, 1950. Bar: Colo. 1950, U.S. Supreme Ct. 1954. Supr. real estate, tax and claims Standard Oil, Denver, 1950-52; from assoc. to ptnr. Cockrell, Quinn & Creighton and predecessor firms, Denver, 1952-91; of counsel Cockrell, Quinn & Creighton, 1992—. Mem. law com. Colo. State Bd. Law Examiners, Denver, 1958-79; mem. bd. mgrs. Nat. Conf. Bar Examiners, Chgo., 1965-69. With U.S. Army, 1943-46, USAR, 1946-51, maj. USAFR, 1951-67, ret. 1985. Mem. Denver Bar Assn., Colo. Bar Assn., Law Club of Denver (pres. 1963-64), University Club (bd. dirs. 1982-88), Phi Beta Kappa, Beta Theta Pi, Phi Delta Phi. Episcopalian. Home: 1155 Ash St Apt 1504 Denver CO 80220-3752

COCKRUM, WILLIAM MONROE, III, investment banker, consultant, educator; b. Indpls., July 18, 1937; s. William Monroe C. II and Katherine J. (Jaqua) Moore; m. Andrea Lee Deering, Mar. 8, 1975; children: Catherine Anne, William Monroe IV. AB with distinction, DePauw U., 1959; MBA with distinction, Harvard U., 1961. With A.G. Becker Paribas Inc., L.A., 1961-84, mgr. nat. corp. fin. div., 1968-71, mgr. pvt. investments, 1971-74, fin. and adminstrv. officer, 1974-80, sr. v.p., 1975-78, vice chmn., 1978-84, also bd. dirs.; prin. William M. Cockrum & Assocs., L.A., 1984—; mem. faculty Northwestern U., 1961-63; vis. lectr. grad. sch. mgmt. UCLA, 1984-88, adj. prof., 1988—. Mem. Monterey Club (Palm Desert, Calif.), Deke Club (N.Y.C.), UCLA Faculty Club, Alisal Golf Club (Solvang, Calif.), Bel-Air Country Club (L.A.), Delta Kappa Epsilon.

CODDING, GEORGE ARTHUR, JR., political science educator; b. Salem, Oreg., June 23, 1923; s. George Arthur and Maude Fern (Corlies) C.; m. Yolanda Celeste Legnini, June 17, 1961; children: Christine Diane, George Arthur III, William Henry, Jennifer Celeste. Student, Willamette U., 1940-42; B.A., U. Wash., 1943, M.A., 1948; D. Polit. Sci, U. Geneva, 1952. Lectr. dept. polit. sci. U. Pa., 1953-55, asst. prof., 1955-61; assoc. prof. polit. sci. U. Colo., Boulder, 1961-65, prof. polit. sci., 1965-93, chmn. dept., 1971-73, dir. B.A. in Internat. Affairs Program, 1977-93, prof. emeritus, 1993—; vis. prof. Grad. Inst. Internat. Studies U. Geneva, 1973-74; tech. sec. Internat. Telecommunications Union, 1949; cons. sec.-gen., 1964-65; cons. UNESCO, 1957-58, 73, Nat. Commn. Causes & Prevention of Violence, 1968-69, Australian Fedn. Comml. Broadcasters, 1973, Office Telecommunications, Dept. Commerce, 1975, Telecommunications Policy, Exec. Office of Pres., 1976-77, FCC, 1979, Internat. Inst. Communications, 1982, 84, 85, 88, 89, 92, 93, 94; mem. adv. bd. Gen. Elec. Space Broadcast, 1967-70. Author: The International Telecommunication Union, 1952, Broadcasting Without Barriers, 1959, The Federal Government of Switzerland, 1961, The Universal Postal Union, 1964, Governing the Commune of Veyrier: Politics in Swiss Local Government, 1967, (with William Safran) Ideology and Politics: The Socialist Party of France, 1979, (with Anthony M. Rutkowski) The International Telecommunication Union in a Changing World, 1982, The Future of Satellite Communications, 1990; editorial bd.: Monograph Series in World Affairs, 1964-78, Telecommunications Policy, 1987—; mem. adv. bd.: Denver Jour. Internat. Law and Policy, 1971—. Exec. bd. Southeastern Pa. chpt. Ams. for Democratic Action. Served with USNR, 1943-46. Guggenheim fellow, 1958-59; Faculty fellow U. Colo., 1965-66, 73-74; SSRC Behavioral Scis. Evaluation Panel; NSF grad. fellow, 1969-73; NSF grantee, 1979-80. Mem. Am., Internat. polit. sci. assns., Internat. Studies Assn. (mem. governing council 1972-73, pres. West 1972-73), Am. Soc. Internat. Law, Pi Sigma Alpha. Club: Trout Unlimited (pres. 1976). Home: 6086 Simmons Dr Boulder CO 80303-3032

CODY, PATRICIA HERBERT, health educator; b. New London, Conn., Sept. 14, 1923; d. John Newman and Rosalia Bertha (Harr) Herbert; m. Fred Cody, Aug. 24, 1946 (dec. July 1983); children: Martha, Anthony, Nora, Celia. BA in Edn., State Tchrs. Coll., 1943; MA in Econs., Columbia U., 1948. Staff writer Economist Intelligence Unit, London, Eng., 1952-72; co-founder Cody's Books, Berkeley, Calif., 1956-77; program dir. DES Action, Oakland, Calif., 1978—, also bd. dirs. Author: Cody's Books: The Life and Times of a Berkeley Bookstore, 1956-77, 1992. Bd. dirs. Civil Justice Found., Washington, 1992—; mem. steering com. Nat. Women's Polit. Caucus Alameda North, Oakland, 1991—. Recipient Meritorious Svc. award ATLA, 1987, Consumer Advocate of the Yr. award Calif. Trial Lawyers Assn., 1990. Home: 3021 Fulton St Berkeley CA 94705-1804 Office: DES Action 1615 Broadway Oakland CA 94612-2115

CODYE, CORINN, writer, editor; b. L.A., Sept. 16, 1950; d. Richard Charles and Juanita Corinne (Myers) Wahl; m. Graham G. Scott, Oct. 4, 1980 (div. Nov. 1984); children: Richard Graham, Peter William (twins). BA, U. Calif., Riverside, 1975; postgrad., UCLA, 1976. Author, editor, project mgr. Quercus Corp., 1980-86, exec. editor, 1986-87. Author: (children's books) Cairo, 1991, Queen Isabella, 1991, Luis W. Alvarez, 1991, Vilma Martinez, 1991 (Outstanding Merit award, Nat. Coun. for the Social Studies 1990), If You Are Sick, 1994, Do You Hear Music?, 1994, I Like Surprises, 1994; contbg. author, mng. editor: Raintree Illustrated Science Encyclopedia, 1991; pub. (Justin Stone books) Meditation for Healing, Justin Stone Speaks on T'ai Chi Chih, Spiritual Stories 1 and 2, T'ai Chi Chih! Joy Through Movement, 1984-91.

COE, ELIZABETH ANN, elementary education educator; b. El Paso, Tex., Feb. 25, 1944; d. Charles William Murray and Jeanne (Roman) Moore; children: Christopher E. Sanchez, Christine Angela Sanchez. BS in Edn., N.Mex. State U., 1968; postgrad., U. N.Mex., 1987-88; MA in Edn., N.Mex. State U., 1992; postgrad., East N.Mex. U., 1970-95, U. Phoenix, 1995, Ctr. for Bilingual Multicultural Studies, Cuernavaca, Mex., 1995. Cert. elem. educator, lang. arts. educator Kindergarten thru grade 12, social studies educator Kindergarten thru grade 12, N.Mex. Tchr. Hatch (N.Mex.) Schs., 1968-70, Ruidoso (N.Mex.) Mcpl. Schs., 1970-84; real estate agt., 1978-88; tchr. Tularosa (N.Mex.) Schs., 1988—; workshop leader Region IX, Ruidoso, 1989, 90; rep. Project L.E.A.D., U. N.Mex., Albuquerque, 1991, N.Mex. State BA Restructuring Conf., Albuquerque, 1990, Mesilla Valley Regional Coun. on Bilingual Edn., 1968-70; co-chair Internat. Reading Assn. Young Authors Conf., Tularosa, 1990-91; cons. N.Mex. State Writing Project, 1993; mem. task force on writing and portfolio assessment N.Mex. State Dept. Edn., 1993—; mem. com. for ednl. plan for student success Tularosa Mcpl. Schs. Author: (short story) Los Desesperados, 1989 (1st prize Tri-State award), Tortillitas Quemaditas, 1991 (Honorable Mention). Mem. N.Mex. State Dept. Edn. Task Force on Writing. Mem. NEA, LWV, Phi Kappa Phi. Home: PO Box 929 Ruidoso NM 88345-0929

COE, JEFFREY DEAN, orthopaedic surgeon; b. Lakehurst Naval Air Sta., N.J., Mar. 29, 1953; s. Mr. and Mrs. Walter R. Coe; m. Marlene Coe; children: Julia Carolyn, Jennifer Mariel, Rachel Helen, Michael Joseph. BSEE with high honors in Elec. Engring., U. Notre Dame, 1975; MD, Washington U., St. Louis, 1979. Diplomate Am. Bd. Orthopaedic Surgery, Nat. Bd. Med. Examiners; lic. Bd. Med. Quality Assurance, Calif., Dept. Health and Mental Hygiene, Md. Commd. 2nd lt. U.S. Army, 1975, advanced through grades to lt. col., 1991; intern Letterman Army Med. Ctr., San Francisco, 1979-80, resident, 1980-84; asst. chief orthopaedic surgery svc. 34th Gen. Hosp., Augsburg, 1984-87; fellow dept. orthopaedic surgery Johns Hopkins Hosp., Balt., 1987-88; staff orthopaedic surgeon, dir. spinal surgery Brooke Army Med. Ctr., Ft. Sam Houston, Tex., 1988-92; chief orthopaedic surgery 41st Combat Support Hosp., Saudi Arabia, 1991; pvt. practice Los Gatos (Calif.) Orthopaedic Assocs., 1992—; clin. asst. prof. surgery Uniformed Svcs. U. Health Scis., F. Edward Hebert Sch. Medicine, Bethesda, Md., 1988—; clin. asst. prof. orthopaedic surgery U. Tex. Health Sci. Ctr., San Antonio, 1990-92. Contbr. articles to profl. jours. Fellow Am. Acad. Orthopaedic Surgeons; mem. Cervical Spine Rsch. Soc., N.Am. Spine Soc., Scoliosis Rsch. Soc., Orthopaedic Rsch. Soc., Soc. Mil. Orthopaedic Surgeons. Roman Catholic. Office: Los Gatos Orthopaedic Assoc 800 Pollard Rd Los Gatos CA 95030-1415

COE, MARGARET LOUISE SHAW, community service volunteer; b. Cody, Wyo., Dec. 25, 1917; d. Ernest Francis and Effie Victoria (Abrahamson) Shaw; m. Henry Huttleston Rogers Coe, Oct. 8, 1943 (dec. Aug. 1966); children: Anne Rogers Hayes, Henry H.R., Jr., Robert Douglas II. AA, Stephens Coll., 1937; BA, U. Wyo., 1939. Asst. to editor The Cody Enterprise, 1939-42, editor, 1968-71. Chmn. bd. trustees Buffalo Bill Hist. Ctr., Cody, 1966—, Cody Med. Found., 1964—; commr. Wyo. Centenniel Commn., Cheyenne, 1986-91. Recipient The Westerner award Old West Trails Found., 1980, Gold Medallion award Nat. Assn. Sec. of State, 1982, disting alumni award U. Wyo., 1984, exemplary alumni award, 1994, Gov.'s award for arts, 1988; inducted Nat. Cowgirl Hall of Fame, 1983. Mem. P.E.O., Delta Delta Delta. Republican. Episcopalian. Home: 1400 11th St Cody WY 82414-4206

COE, TRACY L., internist; b. St. Peter, Minn., Dec. 28, 1962; d. F. Allen and Julie Mae (Tenold) C.; m. Mark Alan Kirkham, Mar. 27, 1993; children: Kira and Kindle Coe Kirkham (twins). Grad., Tex. A&M U., 1985, U. Tex., San Antonio, 1989. Diplomate Am. Bd. Internal Medicine. Intern, resident in internal medicine St. Joseph Hosp., Denver, 1989-92; fellow in hematology/oncology U. Calif. Davis Med. Ctr., 1992—; lab. rsch. asst. dept. microbiology U. Tex. Health Sci. Ctr., San Antonio, summer 1986; rsch. fellow Sacramento Med. Found. Blood Ctr.; mem. hospice programmatic subcom. U. Calif. Davis, 1993-95; presenter in field. Contbr. articles to profl. jours. Active Brian Mountain Ski Patrol, Capitol Area Ski Series. VA Fellow Rsch. grantee, 1994-95; Tex. A&M U. Coll. Agr. scholar, 1981. Mem. ACP (assoc.), AMA, NRA, Am. Med. Women's Assn., Am. Cancer Soc. (Fellowship grantee 1992), Nat. Wildlife Fedn., U.S. Volleyball Assn., U.S. Parachute Assn., Calif. Med. Assn., Arthritis Found., Audubon Soc. Republican. Lutheran. Office: U Calif Davis Cancer Ctr 4501 X St Sacramento CA 95817

COE, WILLIAM CHARLES, psychology educator; b. Hanford, Calif., Oct. 22, 1930; s. Bernard and Bertha (Vaughan) C.; m. Charlene L. Brown; children: Karen Ann, William Vaughan. B.S., U. Calif., Davis, 1958; postgrad., Fresno State Coll., 1960-61; Ph.D. (NSF fellow), U. Calif., Berkeley, 1964. Rsch. helper Fresno State Coll., 1960-61; rsch. asst. U. Calif., Berkeley, 1961-62, 63-64; NSF rsch. fellow U. Calif., 1963-64; clin. psychology trainee VA Hosp., San Francisco, 1962-63; staff psychologist Langley Porter Neuropsychiat. Inst., San Francisco, 1964-66; asst. clin. prof. med. psychology U. Calif. Sch. Medicine, San Francisco, 1965-66; instr. corr. div. U. Calif., Berkeley, 1967-76; asst. prof. psychology Fresno State Coll., 1966-68; assoc. prof. psychology Calif. State U., Fresno, 1968-72; prof. Calif. State U., 1972—, chmn. dept. psychology, 1979-84; instr. Calif. Sch. Profl. Psychology, Fresno, 1973, Northeastern U., Boston, 1974; research assoc. U. Calif., Santa Cruz, 1975; cons. Tulare and Kings County Mental Health Clinics, Kingsview Corp., 1966-68, Visalia Unified Sch. Dist., 1967-68; Head Start Program, Fresno, 1970-71, Fig Garden Hosp., Fresno, 1972-73, Concentrated Employment Program, Fresno, 1973-74, VA Hosp., Fresno, 1974; vis. prof.U. Queensland, Australia, 1982. Author: (with T.R. Sarbin) The Student Psychologists Handbook: A Guide to Source, 1969, Hypnosis: A Social Psychological Analysis of Influence Communication, 1972, Challenges of Personal Adjustment, 1972, (with L. Gagnon and D. Swiercinsky) instructors Manual for Challenges of Personal Adjustment, 1972, Psychology X118: Psychological Adjustment, 1973, (with T.R. Sarbin) Mastering Psychology, 1984; Contbr.: chpts. to Behavior Modification in Rehabilitation Settings, 1975, Helping People Change, 1975, 80, Encyclopedia of Clinical Assessment, 1980, Hypnosis: The Cognitive-Behavioral Perspective, 1989, Hypnosis: Current Theory, Research and Practice, 1990, Theories of Hypnosis: Current Models and Perspectives, 1991, Contemporary Hypnosis Research, 1992; contbr. articles to profl. jours. Served with USAF, 1951-55. Decorated D.F.C., Air medal with oak leaf cluster.; NSF grantee, 1967, 71. Fellow Am. Psychol. Assn. (pres. div. 30 psychol. hypnosis 1986-87), Soc.

for Clin. and Exptl. Hypnosis; mem. Western Psychol Assn., Calif. Psychol Assn., San Francisco Psychol Assn. (editor San Francisco Psychologist 1966), Central Calif. Psychol. Assn. (pres. 1969, dir. 1972-73), Assn. for Advancement Behavior Therapy, Phi Beta Kappa, Sigma Xi, Phi Kappa Phi, Psi Chi. Office: Calif State U Dept Psychology Fresno CA 93740-0011

COEN, DANA, playwright, TV and film scriptwriter; b. Leominster, Mass., Oct. 16, 1946; s. Lloyd Albert Coen and Beatrice (Furst) Pearlmutter; m. Victoria Zane Loveland, Nov. 13, 1994. BS in Broadcasting and Film, Boston U., 1969; student playwriting workshop, Arthur Kopit, 1984-87. mem. L.A. Playwrights Group, 1987—; pvt. acting coach, tchr., 1980-86. Scriptwriter for TV shows include Room for Two, staff writer Carol & Co., The Wonder Years, Silk Stalkings (story editor) Gen. Hosp., series devel. deal Walt Disney TV, 1988-90, 4 TV pilots for ABC, NBC, FOX Network and MCA; script doctor Neuromancer, Bells; playwright Speak, 1994, 95, Tinkle Time, 1994, Ali Baba, Is It You?, 1993, Bunches of Betty, 1989, Sympathy, 1983, Soul of Wood, 1979; literary mgr. Theatre of Open Eye; dir. 20 plays; actor 25 plays. Mem. Actor's Equity Assn., Dramatist's Guild, Writer's Guild West. Democrat. Jewish. Home and Office: 5706 Noble Ave Van Nuys CA 91411-3230

COEN, MICHAEL DWAIN, pastoral counselor; b. San Pedro, Calif., Sept. 4, 1948; s. Charles Samuel and Eugenia Gage (Hancock) C.; m. Dorothy Lee Gray, July 26, 1994; children: Candace, Christopher, Colby. BTh, Life Bible Coll., 1971; MA in Counseling, Liberty U., 1993. Nat. cert. counselor, lic. profl. counselor. Pharmacy helper L.A. County Hosps., 1969-70; personal property custodian L.A. County Sheriff's Dept., 1970-71; pastor Foursquare Ch., Akron, Colo., 1971-72, Salida, Colo., 1972-74, Scottsbluff, Nebr., 1974-79; camp dir. Foursquare Ch., Wondervu, Colo., 1979-82; bldg. contractor The Carpenter's Shop, Arvada, Colo., 1982-87; youth dir. Faith Bible Chapel, Arvada, Colo., 1987-89, dir. pastoral care, 1989-94, ministry administr., 1995—. Author: Group Process, 1990, Pastoral Counseling, 1994. Bd. dirs. Faith Bible Chapel Internat., Arvada, 1987—, corp. v.p., 1994—. Mem. Am. Counseling Assn., Am. Assn. Christian Counselors, Nat. Bd. Cert. Counselors, Parent Tchr. Student Assn. (pres. Coal Creek Canyon chpt. 1980-83), Kiwanis (pres. Coal Creek Canyon 1980-82). Home: 13308 W 68th Pl Arvada CO 80004-1101 Office: Faith Bible Chapel 12189 W 64th Ave Arvada CO 80004-4031

COFER, BERDETTE HENRY, public management consulting company executive; b. Las Flores, Calif.; s. William Walter and Violet Ellen (Elam) C.; m. Ann McGarva, June 27, 1954 (dec. Feb. 20, 1990); children: Sandra Lea Cofer-Oberle, Ronald William; m. Sally Ann Shepherd, June 12, 1993. AB, Calif. State U., Chico, 1950; MA, U. Calif., Berkeley, 1960. Tchr. Westwood (Calif.) Jr.-Sr. High Sch., 1953-54, Alhambra High Sch., Martinez, Calif., 1954-59; prin. adult and summer sch. Hanford (Calif.) High Sch., 1959-60, asst. supt. bus., 1960-67; dean bus. svcs. West Hills Coll., Coalinga, 1967-76; vice chancellor Yosemite Community Coll. Dist., Modesto, 1976-88; pres. BHC Assocs., Inc., Modesto, 1988—; chmn. Valley Ins. Program Joint Powers Agy., Modesto, 1986-88. Contbr. articles to profl. publs. Pres. Coalinga Indsl. Devel. Corp., 1972-74, Assn. for Retarded Citizens, Modesto, 1985; mayor City of Coalinga, 1974-76; foreman Stanislaus County Grand Jury, Modesto, 1987-88. 1st lt. USAF, 1951-53. Recipient Outstanding Citizen award Coalinga C. of C., 1976, Walter Starr Robie Outstanding Bus. Officer award Assn. Chief Bus. Officers Calif. Community Colls., 1988. Mem. Assn. Calif. C.C. Adminstrs. (life), Commonwealth Club Calif. (San Francisco) Elks, Lions (dist. gov. 1965-66), Phi Delta Kappa (pres. Kings-Tulare chpt. 1962-63), Am. Legion (40 and 8 Sons in Retirement). Democrat. Home and Office: 291 Leveland Ln # D Modesto CA 95350-2255

COFFEY, C. SHELBY, III, newspaper editor; m. Mary Lee Coffey. Ed., U. Va. With Washington Post, 1968-85, dep. mng. editor, asst. mng. editor for nat. news; editor U.S. News and World Report, 1985-86; sr. v.p., editor Dallas Times Herald, 1986; from dep. assoc. editor to exec. editor L.A. Times, 1986-89, editor, exec. v.p., 1989—. Named Editor of Yr., Nat. Press Found., 1994. Mem. Am. Soc. Newspaper Editors, Am. Press Inst., Internat. Press Inst., Coun. on Fgn. Rels., New Directions for News, Found. for Am. Comms., Assoc. Press Mng. Editors, Calif. Newspaper Pubs. Assn. Office: LA Times Times Mirror Co Times Mirror Sq Los Angeles CA 90053

COFFEY, DANIEL WAYNE, lawyer; b. L.A., Feb. 3, 1955; s. James M. and Virginia C.; m. Pepper Rae Bateman, Aug. 14, 1993. BS in Chem. Engring., U. Calif., Davis, 1980; JD, U. Pacific, 1987. Bar: Calif. 1987, U.S. Dist. Ct. (ea. dist.) 1987, (cen. dist.) 1993. Rsch. asst. chem. engring. dept. U. Calif., Davis, 1980-82; pvt. cons. Gov.'s Office Appropriate Tech., 1982; waste mgmt. engr. State of Calif. Superfund Program, Sacramento, 1982-83; owner Cal Data Assocs., 1983; clk., std. atty. Cmty. Legal Svcs. Clinic, Sacramento, 1986-87; engr. Toxic Substances Control Divsn., Alt.Tech.Sect. State Calif. Dept. Health, 1988-89; sr. assoc. Jaffe, Trutanich, Scatena and Blum, 1989-91; pvt. practice Redondo Beach, Calif., 1991—; pres. Environ. Law Forum, 1986-87; co-sponsor symposium Bus. Law Forum, 1986-87; co-sponsor program Dem. Forum, 1987. Trustee Yolo County Bd. Edn., 1987-91. Recipient Pres.'s award SBA, 1987, Friend of Divsn. award ABA, Law Student Divsn., 1987. Home: 1710 Esplanade St Apt H Redondo Beach CA 90277-5370

COFFILL, MARJORIE LOUISE, civic leader; b. Sonora, Calif., June 11, 1917; d. Eric J. and Pearl (Needham) Segerstrom; A.B. with distinction in Social Sci., Stanford U., 1938, M.A. in Edn., 1941; m. William Charles Coffill, Jan. 25, 1948, (dec.); children: William James, Eric John. Asst. mgr. Sonora Abstract & Title Co. (Calif.), 1938-39; mem. dean of women's staff Stanford, 1939-41; social dir. women's campus Pomona Coll., 1941-43, instr. psychology, 1941-43; asst. to field dir. ARC, Lee Moore AFB, Calif., 1944-46; partner Riverbank Water Co., Riverbank and Hughson, Calif., 1950-68. Mem. Tuolumne County Mental Health Adv. Com., 1963-70; mem. central advisory coun. Supplementary Edn. Ctr., Stockton, Calif., 1966-70; mem. advisory com. Columbia Jr. Coll., 1972-89, pres., 1980—; pres. Columbia Found., 1972-74, bd. dirs., 1974-77; mem. Tuolumne County Bicentennial Com., 1974—; active PTA, ARC. Pres., Tuolumne County Rep. Women, 1952—, assoc. mem. Calif. Rep. Central Com., 1950. Trustee Sonora Union High Sch., 1969-73, Salvation Army Tuolumne County, 1973—; bd. dirs. Lung Assn. Valley Lode Counties, 1974—, life 1986—. Recipient Pi Lambda Theta award, 1940, Outstanding Citizen award C. of C., 1974, Citizen of Yr. award, 1987; named to Columbia Coll. Hall of Fame, 1990; named Alumnus of Yr., Sonora Union High Sch., 1994. Mem. AAUW (charter mem. Tuolumne County br., pres. Sonora br. 1965-66). Episcopalian (mem. vestry 1968, 75). Home: 376 Summit Ave Sonora CA 95370-5728

COFFIN, THOMAS M., federal magistrate judge; b. St. Louis, May 30, 1945; s. Kenneth C. and Agnes M. (Ryan) C.; m. Penelope Teaff, Aug. 25, 1973; children: Kimberly, Laura, Colleen, Corey, Mary, Brendan, T.J. BA, St. Benedict's Coll., 1967; JD, Harvard, 1970. Bar: Mo. 1970, Calif. 1972, Oreg. 1982, U.S. Dist. Ct. (so. dist.) Calif. 1971, U.S. Dist. Ct. Oreg. 1980, U.S. Ct. Appeals (9th cir.) 1971. Asst. U.S. atty., chief criminal divsn. U.S. Attys. Office, San Diego, 1971-80; asst. U.S. atty., supr. asst. U.S. atty. U.S. Attys. Office, Eugene, Oreg., 1980-92; U.S. Magistrate judge U.S. Dist. Ct., Eugene, Oreg., 1992—; sr. litigation counsel U.S. Dept. Justice, 1984. Mem. Oreg. Bar Assn. Office: US Dist Ct 211 E 7th Ave Eugene OR 97401-2722*

COFFINGER, MARALIN KATHARYNE, retired air force officer, consultant; b. Ogden, Iowa, July 5, 1935; d. Cleo Russell and Katharyne Frances (McGovern) Morse. BA, Ariz. State U., 1957, MA, 1961; diploma, Armed Forces Staff Coll., 1972, Nat. War Coll., 1977; postgrad., Inst. for Higher Def. Studies, 1985. Commd. 2nd lt. USAF, 1963, advanced through grades to brig. gen., 1985; base comdr., dep. base comdr. Elmendorf AFB, Anchorage, Alaska, 1977-79; base comdr. Norton AFB, San Bernardino, Calif., 1979-82; chmn. spl. and incentive pays Office of Sec. Def., Pentagon, Washington, 1982-83; dep. dir. pers. programs USAF Hdqrs., Pentagon, Washington, 1983-85; command dir. NORAD, Combat Ops., Cheyenne Mountain Complex, Colo., 1985-86; dir. pers. plans USAF Hdqrs., Pentagon, Washington, 1986-89; ret. USAF, 1989. Keynote speaker, mem. dedication ceremonies Vietnam Meml. Com., Phoenix, 1990. Decorated Air Force D.S.M., Def. Superior Svc. medal, Legion of Merit, Bronze Star.; recipient Nat. Medal of Merit. Mem. NAFE, Air Force Assn. (vet./retiree coun., pres. Sky Harbor chpt. 1990), Natl. Officers Assn., Ret. Officers Assn., Internat. Platform Assn., Maricopa County Sheriff's Exec. Posse, Ariz. State U. Alumni Assn. (Profl. Excellence award 1981). Roman Catholic. Home: 8531 E San Bruno Dr Scottsdale AZ 85258-2577

COFIELD, PHILIP THOMAS, educational association administrator; b. Monmouth, Ill., July 3, 1951; s. Earl Crescant and Vera (Shunick) C.; divorced; children: Calla, Megan. BA in English, St. Ambrose U., 1973. Dir. Jr. Achievment of Quad Cities, Davenport, Moline, Iowa, Ill., 1980-83; account exec. Jr. Achievment Inc., 1983-85; pres., CEO Jr. Achievment of Utah, Salt Lake City, 1985—. Established Utah Bus. Hall of Fame, 1991. Mem. Utah Coun. on Economic Edn. (bd. dirs.), Salt Lake area C. of C., Rotary Club, (com. co-chmn. Salt Lake City). Office: Jr Achievement of Utah 182 S 600 E Salt Lake City UT 84102-1909

COGGIN, CHARLOTTE JOAN, cardiologist, educator; b. Takoma Park, Md., Aug. 6, 1928; d. Charles Benjamin and Nanette (McDonald) Coggin; BA, Columbia Union Coll., 1948; MD, Loma Linda U., 1952, MPH, 1987; DSc (hon.), Andrews U., 1994. Intern, L.A. County Gen. Hosp., L.A., 1952-53, resident in medicine, 1953-55; fellow in cardiology Children's Hosp., L.A., 1955-56, White Meml. Hosp., L.A., 1955-56; rsch. assoc. in cardiology, house physician Hammersmith Hosp., London, 1956-57; resident in pediatrics and pediatric cardiology Hosp. for Sick Children, Toronto, Ont., Can., 1965-67; cardiologist, co-dir. heart surgery team Loma Linda (Calif.) U., asst. prof. medicine , 1961-73, assoc. prof., 1973-91, prof. medicine, 1991—, asst. dean Sch. Medicine Internat. Programs, 1973-75, assoc. dean, 1975—, spl. asst. to univ. pres. for internat. affairs, 1991, co-dir., cardiologist heart surgery team missions to Pakistan and Asia, 1963, Greece, 67, 69, Saigon, Vietnam, 1974, 75, to Saudi Arabia, 1976-87, People's Republic China, 1984, 89-91, Hong Kong, 1985, Zimbabwe, 1988, Kenya, 1988, Nepal, 1992, 93, China, 1992, Zimbabwe, 1993; mem. Pres's. Advisory Panel on Heart Disease, 1972—; hon. prof. U. Manchuria, Harbin, People's Republic China, 1989, hon. dir. 1st People's Hosp. of Mundanjiang, Heilongjiang Province, 1989. Apptd. mem. Med. Quality Rev. Com.-Dist. 12, 1976-80. Recipient award for service to people of Pakistan City of Karachi, 1963, Medallion award Evangelismos Hosp., Athens, Greece, 1967, Gold medal of health South Vietnam Ministry of Health, 1974, Charles Elliott Weinger award for excellence, 1976, Wall Street Jour. Achievement award, 1987, Disting. Univ. Svc. award Loma Linda U., 1990; named Honored Alumnus Loma Linda U. Sch. Medicine, 1973, Outstanding Women in Gen. Conf. Seventh-day Adventists, 1975, Alumnus of Yr., Columbia Union Coll., 1984. Diplomate Am. Bd. Pediatrics. Mem. Am. Coll. Cardiology, AMA (physicians adv. com. 1969—) Calif. Med. Assn. (com. on med. schs., com. on member services), San Bernardino County Med. Soc. (chmn. communications com. 1975-77, mem. communications com. 1987-88, editor bull. 1975-76, William L. Cover, M.D. Outstanding Contbn. to Medicine award 1995), Am. Heart Assn., AAUP, Med. Research Assn. Calif., Calif. Heart Assn., AAUW, Am. Acad. Pediatrics, World Affairs Council, Internat. Platform Assn., Calif. Museum Sci. and Industry MUSES (Outstanding Woman of Year in Sci. 1969), Am. Med. Women's Assn., Loma Linda Sch. Medicine Alumni Assn. (pres. 1978), Alpha Omega Alpha, Delta Omega. Author: Atrial Septal Defects, motion picture (Golden Eagle Cine award and 1st prize Venice Film Festival 1964); contbr. articles to med. jours. Democrat. Home: 11495 Benton St Loma Linda CA 92354-3682 Office: Loma Linda U Magan Hall Rm 105 11060 Anderson St Loma Linda CA 92350

COGHILL, JOHN BRUCE, state official; b. Fairbanks, Alaska, Sept. 24, 1925; s. William Alexander and Winefred (Fortune) C.; m. Frances Mae Gilbert, 1948; children: Patricia, John Jr., James, Jerald, Paula, Jeffry. Grad. high sch., Nenana, Alaska. Ptnr. Coghill's Inc., Nenana, Alaska, 1948—; owner Tortella Lodge & Apts., 1951, J.B. Coghill Oil Co., 1958-87, Nenana Fuel Co., 1960-87; mem. from senate dist. J Alaska State Legislature, Juneau, 1959-64, 85-90; chmn. resources com., chmn. majority caucus, vice chmn. transp., mem. oil and gas com., spl. joint com. on tax policy, nre revenue work group and fin. budget subcommittees on DNR, DEC and fish & game; lt. gov. State of Alaska, 1990—; mayor City of Nenana, 1962-84; ptnr. Coghill's, Inc.; sec. Nenana Industries, Nenana Fuel Co. Mem. sch. bd., 1948-59; mem. Alaskan territorial Ho. of Reps., 1953, 57, Alaska Constl. Conv., 1955; spl. asst. to gov. State of Alaska, 1967; sec. North Commn., 1968-72; chmn. Alaska Statehood Commn., 1980-83. Sgt. Alaska Command U.S. Army, 1944-46. Mem. VFW, Am. Legion, Eagle Hist. Soc., Pioneers of Alaska, Lions Club, Masons, Eagles, Moose. Office: Office of Lt Gov PO Box 110015 Juneau AK 99811-0015

COGNATA, JOSEPH ANTHONY, football commissioner; b. Ashtabula, Ohio, Feb. 11, 1946; s. Joseph and Ella Jane (Dispense) C.; m. Betty Jean Jacobs, Dec. 17, 1978; children: Lisa Ann, Joseph Anthony Jr. Student, Kent State U., 1964-66. Sales rep. Endicott Buick, Pompano Beach, Fla., 1977-80; sales mgr. Fla. Chrysler Plymouth, West Palm Beach, Fla., 1980-82; owner, CEO So. States Football Club, Tequesta, Fla., 1982-85; backfield/spl. teams coach San Jose (Calif.) Bandits Minor League Football System, 1987-90; asst. head coach Calif. Outlaws Minor League Football System, Hayward, Calif., 1990-91; asst. to dir. and v.p. football ops. Profl. Spring Football League, Meadowlands, N.J., 1991-92; co-founder Golden West Football League, Sacramento, 1991—; commr. West Coast Amateur Football League, Mountain View, Calif., 1992—; pres., CEO, commr. Pacific Western Football Alliance, Sacramento, 1992—; pres. CEO U.S. Amateur Football Fedn., 1994—; pres., CEO U.S. Amateur Football Fedn., 1994—, West Coast Football Conf., 1994—. Author: Complete Football Playbook, 1989. Lutheran. Home and Office: 107 S Mary Ave Apt 33 Sunnyvale CA 94086-5851

COHEA, MELINDA RUTH, school business executive; b. Moscow, Idaho, July 9, 1961; d. Jack Stillwell and Dolores Ruth (Ferguson) C. BFA, Tex. Christian U., 1983; MA in Edn., Tex. Christian U., Ft. Worth, 1992. Prodn. coord. Tandy Advt., Ft. Worth, 1984; asst. sales mgr. Joshua's Christian Bookstores, Ft. Worth, 1985; tchr. art Lake Country Christian Sch., Ft. Worth, 1985-92, bus. mgr., 1993—; seminar lectr. Assn. Christian Schs. Internat. Calendar illustrator; set and mag. designer; oil painter. Republican. Mem. Ch. of Christ. Home: 10854 Etiwanda Ave Northridge CA 91326-2828

COHEN, ALAN JAY, psychiatrist; b. Phila., Aug. 30, 1956; s. Harry Wallace and Shirley Vita (Berman) C.; m. Shannon Ruth Bowman, June 25, 1989; children: Brendan Harris, Hallie Patricia. BA, Oberlin Coll., 1978; MD, Jefferson Med. Coll., Phila., 1982. Diplomate Am. Bd. Psychiatry and Neurology. Resident U. Calif., San Francisco, 1982-86; fellow Inst. Pa. Hosp., Phila., 1987; pvt. practice Comprehensive Psychiat. Svcs., Walnut Creek, Calif., 1989—; asst. prof. psychiatry U. Calif., San Francisco, 1982-86; fellow Inst. of Pa. Hosp., Phila., 1987; attending physician AIDS focus unit San Francisco Gen. Hosp., 1987-90, Brookside Hosp.; lectr. Franklin Inst. and Sci. Mus., Phila., 1975-76; med. rschr. Johns Hopkins U., 1976; dir. clin. rsch. East Bay Hosp., Richmond, Calif., 1991—, dir. lab. svcs., 1994—; prin. rsch. investigator Burroughs-Wellcome. Contbr. articles to profl. jours. Lectr., cons. Family Night Workshops, San Francisco, 1988-90; musician Friends of the River, San Rafael, Calif., 1990. NSF fellow, 1978, NIH fellow, 1979; recipient Baldwin Keyes Psychiatry prize Jefferson Med. Coll., 1982. Mem. Am. Psychiat. Assn., Am. Thyroid Found., Am. Soc. Clin. Psychopharmacology, No. Calif. Psychiat. Soc., Sigma Xi (assoc.). Office: Comprehensive Psychiat Svcs 37 Quail Ct Ste 200 Walnut Creek CA 94596-5565 also: 2340 Ward St Ste 201 Berkeley CA 94705-1147

COHEN, ANDREW NEAL, activist, writer, scientist; b. Boston, Dec. 21, 1954; s. Arthur I. and Florence (Goldberg) C. BA in Environ. Scis., U. Calif., Berkeley, 1985, MS in Energy and Resources, 1989. Exec. dir. Urban Creeks Coun., Berkeley, 1988-89; marine rschr. Maritime Studies/Mystic (Conn.) Seaport, 1993-94; v.p. East Bay Mcpl. Utility Dist., Oakland, Calif., 1991-94; mem. Com. for Water Policy Consensus, Sacramento, 1985-88, Tech. Adv. Com. San Francisco Estuary Project, Oakland, 1987-91, Rural Water Impact Network, Davis, Calif., 1993—, Citizens Alliance to Restore the Estuary, Oakland, 1989—. Author: Introduction to the Ecology of the San Francisco Estuary, 1990; contbr. articles to profl. jours. Pres. Calif. Water Policy Group, Oakland, 1987-91; chair Buckhorn Canyon Legal Def. Fund, Oakland, 1989-90; founding mem. Pub. Ofcls. for Water and Environ. Reform, Sacramento, 1991-92. Named Pub. Ofcl. of Yr. San Francisco Bay chpt. Sierra Club, Oakland, Calif., 1994; recipient Scholarship award U. Calif. Club, Berkeley, 1989, Grad. Student Rsch. award Nat. Audubon Soc., Washington, 1989. Office: Energy & Resources Group U Calif Rm 100 Bldg T-4 Berkeley CA 94720

COHEN, BENJAMIN JERRY, political economy educator; b. Ossining, N.Y., June 5, 1937; s. Abraham and Rachel (Grossman) C.; m. Jane DeHart, Sept. 20, 1986. BA, Columbia U., 1959, PhD, 1963. Economist Fed. Res. Bank N.Y., 1962-64; asst. prof. econs. Princeton (N.J.) U., 1964-71; assoc. prof. Tufts U. Fletcher Sch. of Law and Diplomacy, Medford, Mass., 1971-78; William L. Clayton prof. Internat. Econ. Affairs Fletcher Sch. Law and Diplomacy Tufts U., Medford, Mass., 1978-91; Louis G. Lancaster prof. Internat. Polit. Economy U. Calif., Santa Barbara, 1991—. Author: Organizing the World's Money, 1976, Banks and the Balance of Payments, 1981, In Whose Interest?, 1986, Crossing Frontiers, 1991. Mem. Am. Econ. Assn., Am. Polit. Sci. Assn., Coun. Fgn. Rels. Jewish. Office: U Calif Dept Polit Sci Santa Barbara CA 93106

COHEN, CLARENCE BUDD, aerospace engineer; b. Monticello, N.Y., Feb. 7, 1925; s. Isidor and Dora Cohen; m. Beatrice Sholofsky, Jan. 1, 1947; children: William David, Deborah Ann. BAE, Rensselaer Poly. Inst., 1945, MAE, 1947; MA, Princeton U., 1952, PhD, 1954. Aerospace research scientist NASA, Cleve., 1947-56; assoc. chief. spl. projects br. TRW Electronics and Def., Redondo Beach, Calif., 1957-87, head hypersonics research section, 1957-61; mgr. aerodynamics dept. TRW Electronics and Defense, Redondo Beach, Calif., 1961-63, mgr. aero scis. lab., 1966-69, dir. tech. application, 1970-80, dir. technology, 1980-87; cons. in field. Contbr. articles to profl. jours; patentee manned spacecraft with staged reentry. Trustee, vice chmn. Northrup U., 1991—; With USNR, 1943-46. Recipient Class of 1902 Rsch. Prize, Rensselaer Poly. Inst., 1945; Guggenheim fellow Princeton U., 1950-52. Fellow AIAA; mem. Licensing Execs. Soc., Research Soc. Am. (past pres.), Indsl. Research Inst. (emeritus), Sigma Xi. Club: King Harbor Yacht. Home: 332 Via El Chico Redondo Beach CA 90277-6756

COHEN, D. ASHLEY, clinical psychologist, assessment specialist; b. Omaha, Oct. 2, 1952; d. Cenek and Dorothy A. (Bilek) Hrabik; m. Donald I. Cohen, 1968 (div. 1976); m. Lyn J. Mangiameli, June 12, 1985. BA in Psychology, U. Nebr., Omaha, 1975, MA in Psychology, 1979; PhD in Clin. Psychology, Calif. Coast U., 1988. Lic. psychologist, Calif.; lic. marriage and family therapist, Nev.; cert. substance abuse counselor, Nev. Team mgr. Ea. Nebr. Human Svcs. Agy., 1976-79; family specialist Ea. Nebr. Human Svcs. Agy. Consultation & Edn., 1979-80; psychotherapist Washoe Tribe, Gardnerville, Nev., 1980; therapist Family Counseling Svc., Carson City, Nev., 1980-93; psychotherapist Alpine County Mental Health, Markleeville, Calif., 1981-89, dir., 1990-93; psychologist Golden Gate Med. Examiners, San Francisco, 1993—; conf. presenter and spkr. in field; presenter rsch. findings 7th European Conf. Personality, Madrid, 1994, Oxford (Eng.) U. ISSID Conf., 1991; site coord. nat. standardization Kaufmann brief intelligence test A.G.S., 1988-90. Vol. EMT, Alpine County, 1983-93. Recipient Svc. to Youth award Office Edn., 1991. Mem. APA, Internat. Neuropsychol. Soc., Internat. Soc. Study Individual Differences, Am. Psychol. Soc., Western Psychol. Assn., Calif. Psychol. Assn., Am. Critical Incident Stress Found. Office: PO Box 60501 Sunnyvale CA 94088-0501

COHEN, DANIEL MORRIS, museum administrator, marine biology researcher; b. Chgo., July 6, 1930; s. Leonard U. and Myrtle (Gertz) C.; m. Anne Carolyn Constant, Nov. 4, 1955; children—Carolyn A., Cynthia S. BA, Stanford U., 1952, MA, 1953, PhD, 1958. Asst. prof., curator fishes U. Fla., Gainesville, 1957-58; systematic zoologist Bur. Comml. Fisheries, Washington, 1958-60; dir. systematics lab. Nat. Marine Fisheries Service, Washington, 1960-81; sr. scientist Nat. Marine Fisheries Service, Seattle, 1981-82; chief curator life scis. Los Angeles County Mus. of Natural History, 1982-93, dep. dir. rsch. and collections, 1993—; adj. prof. biology U. So. Calif., 1982—. Contbr. numerous articles to profl. jours. Fellow AAAS, Calif. Acad. Sci.; mem. Am. Soc. Ichthyologists and Herpetologists (v.p. 1969, 70, pres. 1985), Biol. Soc. Washington (pres. 1971-72), Soc. Systematic Biology (mem. coun. 1976-78). Home: 3667 Greve Dr Rancho Palos CA 90275-6281 Office: LA County Mus of Nat History 900 Exposition Blvd Los Angeles CA 90007-4000

COHEN, DAVID EDWARD, publisher; b. Springfield, Mass., Nov. 17, 1950; s. Philip J. and Marjorie C.; m. Barbara Elia, Dec. 31, 1979; children: Daniel Elia, Dustin Elia. BA, Windham Coll., 1971; postgrad., Internat. Acad. Continous Edn., 1974. Advt. mgr. Valley Adv. Newspaper, Springfield, 1976-79; assoc. pub. L.A. Weekly, Los Angeles, 1979-85; co-chmn., pubr., chief operating officer Metro Newspapers, San Jose, Calif., 1985—. Pub. many newspapers including Los Gatos Weekly-Times, Saratoga News, San Jose City Times, Willow Glen Resident, Metro Santa Cruz, Cupertino Courier, Sunnyvale Sun, and Sonoma County Independent. Bd. dirs. San Jose Symphony Assn., 1986—. Mem. San Jose Jazz Soc. (adv. bd. 1986—), Assn. of Alternative News Weeklies (past bd. dirs., past pres. western divsn.), Rotary (San Jose chpt.). Office: Metro 550 S 1st St San Jose CA 95113-2806

COHEN, HARVEY JOEL, pediatric hematology and oncology educator; b. N.Y.C., July 4, 1943; s. Phillip and Ida (Teitel) C.; m. Ilene Verne Bookseger, Aug. 15, 1965; children: Philip Jason, Jonathan Todd. BS, CUNY, 1964; MD, PhD, Duke U., 1970. Intern Children's Hosp., Boston, 1970-71, resident, 1973-74; instr. pediatrics Harvard U. Med. Sch., Boston, 1974-76, asst. prof., 1976-79, assoc. prof., 1979-81; assoc. prof. pediatrics U. Rochester (N.Y.) Med. Ctr., 1981-84, prof., 1984-93, assoc. chmn. dept., 1987-93, chief pediatric hematology and oncology, 1981-93; prof., chmn. dept. pediatrics Stanford (Calif.) U. Sch. Medicine, 1993—; chief staff Lucile Salter Packard Children's Hosp. at Stanford, 1993—; med. advisor Montgomery Med. Ventures, San Francisco, 1984—; sci. advisor St. Jude Children's Rsch. Hosp., Memphis, 1985-90; chmn. hematology study sect. NIH, Washington, 1986-88. Editor: Hematology: Basic Principles and Practice, 1991. Med. dir. Camp Good Days and Spl. Times, Rochester, 1981-93, Monroe County chpt. Am. Cancer Soc., Rochester, 1983-93, Rochester br. Cooley's Anemia Found., 1984-93. Surgeon USPHS, 1971-73. Tng. grantee Nat. Inst. Gen. Med. Scis., 1983-90, Nat. Inst. Child Health and Human Devel., 1990-94. Mem. Soc. for Pediatric Rsch. (pres. 1988-89), Am. Soc. for Clin. Investigation, Am. Pediatric Soc. Democrat. Jewish. Office: Stanford U Sch Medicine Dept Pediatrics Rm H-310 Stanford CA 94305

COHEN, JEREMY PATRICK, lawyer; b. Grant, Nebr., Oct. 26, 1960; s. Gerald Morris and Carolyn (Ruth) C.; m. Mary Ellen Cohen, Dec. 19, 1987; 1 child, Maeve. BA, Creighton U., 1982; JD, U. Denver, 1986, LLM in Taxation, 1992. Bar: Colo. 1986, Nebr. 1992, U.S. Dist. Ct. Colo. 1987, U.S. Ct. Appeals (10th cir.) 1987. Assoc. Robinson, Waters, O'Dorisio & Rapson, Denver, 1986-89, Grant, McHendrie, Haines & Crouse, Denver, 1989-91, Kelley, Scritsmlr & Byrne, P.C., North Platte, Nebr., 1991-93; prin. Jeremy P. Cohen, P.C., Lakewood, Colo., 1993—. Mem. ABA, Colo. Bar Assn., Denver Bar Assn. Democrat. Roman Catholic. Office: 1490 S Pearl St Denver CO 80210-2227

COHEN, JONATHAN JACOB, furniture artist; b. Boston, Aug. 13, 1955; s. Peter Myron and Nancy Ellen (Levy) C. BA in Graphic Design, Cornell U., 1977. Furniture designer, maker, artist Jonathan Cohen Fine Woodworking, Seattle, 1977—; vis. critic/lectr. U. Wash., Seattle, 1988—. One-man shows include N.W. Gallery Fine Woodworking, Seattle, 1984, 89, 93; group shows include Signature Gallery, Boston, 1984, Am. Crafts Gallery, Cleve., 1984-87, Boise Art Mus., 1984, Springfield (Ill.) Art Mus., and others; corres. Fine Woodworking mag., 1982-84. Office: Jonathan Cohen Fine Woodworking 3410 Woodland Park Ave N Seattle WA 98103

COHEN, JOYCE E., state senator, investment executive; b. McIntosh, S.D., Mar. 27, 1937; d. Joseph and Evelyn (Sampson) Petik; children: Julia Jo, Aaron J. Grad., Coll. Med. Tech., Minn., 1955; student, UCLA, 1957-58, Santa Ana Coll., 1957-62. Med. rsch. technician dept. surgery U. Minn., 1955-58; dept. immunology UCLA, 1958-59; dept. bacteriology U. Calif., 1959-61; med. rsch. scientist Allergan Pharms., Santa Ana, Calif., 1961-70; ptnr. Co-Fo Investments, Lake Oswego, Oreg., 1978-84; mem. Oreg. Ho. of Reps., 1979-81, Oreg. State Senate, 1983-94. Chmn. trade amd econ. devel., govt. reorgn. and reinvention com., senate judiciary com.; mem. senate revenue and sch. fin. com.; vice-chair agr. & natural resources com., health care & bio-ethics com.; mem. bus., housing & fin. com., rules com.; co-chair joint task force on lottery oversight; mem. joint com. on asset forfeiture oversight adv.; mem. Senate Exec. Appointments; mem. joint com. on land use, alt. joint com. legis. audit; mem. Energy Policy Rev. Bd.; appointed to Oreg. Coun. Econ. Edn., Oreg. Criminal Justice Coun., adv. com. Ctr. for Rsch. on Occupational and Environ. Toxicology; mem. Jud. Br. State Energy Policy Rev. Com., 1979, Gov's. Commn. on Child Support. Woodrow Wilson Lecture series fellow, 1988. Mem. LWV, Assn. Family Conciliation Cts. (founding mem.), Oreg. Environ. Coun., Oreg. Women's Polit. Caucus. Democrat. Office: Oreg State Senate State Capitol Bldg Rm S218 Salem OR 97310

COHEN, LAWRENCE EDWARD, sociology educator, criminologist; b. L.A., July 20, 1945; s. Louis and Florence (White) C. BA, U. Calif., Berkeley, 1969; MA, Calif. State U., 1971; PhD, U. Wash., 1974; postdoctorate study, SUNY, Albany, 1973-75. Rsch. assoc. Sch. of Criminal Justice, SUNY, Albany, 1973-76; asst. prof. U. Ill., Urbana, 1976-80; assoc. prof. U. Tex., Austin, 1980-85; prof. Ind. U., Bloomington, 1985-88, U. Calif., Davis, 1988—. Cons. editor Social Forces, 1981-84, Jour. Criminal Law and Criminology, 1982—, Am. Sociol. Rev., 1982-84, Am. Jour. Sociology, 1990—; contbr. numerous articles to profl. jours. Sgt. USMC, 1963-66, Vietnam. Grantee NIMH, 1978-80, NSF, 1983-89. Mem. Am. Sociol. Assn., Am. Soc. Criminology, Acad. Criminal Justice Scis., Soc. for Study Social Problems. Office: U Calif Dept Sociology Davis CA 95616

COHEN, MANLEY, gastroenterologist; b. Johannesburg, South Africa, May 6, 1937; came to U.S., 1963; s. Tuvia and Frieda Cohen; m. Barbara Hazel Cohen, Aug. 30, 1961; children: Darien, Ronan, Gila. MB BCh, U. Witwatersrand, Johannesburg, South Africa, 1960; MS in Medicine, U. Minn., 1972. Diplomate Am. Bd. Internal Medicine, Am. Bd. Gastroenterology. Intern Saint Bartholomew's Hosp., Rochester, Eng., 1962, Passavant Meml. Hosp., Northwestern U., Chgo., 1963; fellow in medicine and gastroenterology Mayo Clinic and May Grad. Sch. Medicine, Rochester, Minn., 1963-69; chief edn. dept. medicine Long Beach (Calif.) Meml. Med. Ctr., 1969-94; clin. prof. medicine U. Calif., Irvine. Mem. So. Calif. Soc. for Gastrointestinal Endoscopy (pres.). Jewish. Home: 650 Flint Ave Long Beach CA 90814-2041

COHEN, MARK JEFFREY, real estate owner, broker; b. Stockton, Calif., Nov. 19, 1942; s. Samuel and Sadie (Tager) C.; m. Rose Marie McDaniel, May 31, 1990; 1 child, Eric S. Cert. residential specialist, real estate brokerage mgr. Owner, broker Mark J. Cohen, Santa Rosa, Calif., 1975—. Writer for comic strips including Gasoline Alley, Popeye, and Wee Pals, 1970—; author various comic books; contbr. articles to Real Estate Today and Cartoonists Profiles. Treas., pres. No. Calif. Cert. Residential Specialists, 1980-85; past pres. Optimists Club, Santa Rosa, 1985-86; merit badge counselor Boy Scouts, Santa Rosa, 1985—. Named Disting. pres. Optimists Internat., 1986, Realtor of Yr., Sonoma County Bd. Realtors, 1988, 10 Gallon donor Blood Bank of the Redwoods, 1989; recipient Merit award Cmty. Svc., City of Santa Rosa, 1988. Mem. Sonoma County Realtors Assn., Nat. Cartoonists Soc. (No. Calif. chpt. sec. 1989-94), Sonoma County Bd. Realtors (v.p., dir. 1978-91). Office: Mark J Cohen 589 Mendocino # 5 Santa Rosa CA 95401

COHEN, ROBERT F., lawyer, journalist; b. N.Y.C., Feb. 19, 1951; s. Abraham and Ruth Hope (Sunshine) C. BA, SUNY, Stony Brook, 1975; BS in Law, Glendale U., 1990, JD, 1992. Bar: Calif. 1992, U.S. Dist. Ct. (cen. dist.) Calif. 1992, U.S. Dist. Ct. (no. dist.) Calif. 1993. Radio news anchor, news dir. various radio stas., 1972-79; radio news reporter Sta. WCBS, N.Y.C., 1979-80; broadcast bus. journalist Wall St. Jour., Bus. Week, UPI, N.Y.C., 1980-86; systems supr. Dern, Mason & Floum, L.A., 1988-89; paralegal Perkins Coie, L.A., 1989-92; pvt. practice Law Office of Robert F. Cohen, Santa Monica, Calif., 1992—. Editor-in-chief Glendale Law Rev., 1991-92. Vol. fundraiser AIDS Project L.A., 1989—, vol. atty., 1993—; col. 1992 Voter Registration Drive, L.A.; vol. atty. Disaster Emergency Ctr., 1994. Mem. AFTRA, ACLU, State Bar Calif., Santa Monica Bar Assn., L.A. County Bar Assn., Lawyers for Human Rights. Democrat. Office: 854 Pico Blvd Santa Monica CA 90405

COHEN, SEYMOUR I., lawyer; b. N.Y.C., Apr. 15, 1931; s. Fred and Nettie (Sederer) C.; m. Rhoda Goldner, July 22, 1956; children: Cheryl Lynn, Marcy Ann, Lori Beth. BBA cum laude, CCNY, 1951; LLB, Bklyn. Law Sch., 1954, JD, 1967; MBA, NYU, 1960. Bar: N.Y. 1954, U.S. Tax. Ct. 1954, Calif. 1973, U.S. Dist. Ct. (cen. dist.) Calif. 1973, U.S. Ct. Appeals (9th cir.) 1973, U.S. Supreme Ct. 1976; CPA, Ohio, Calif. Staff acct. S.D. Leidesdorf, N.Y.C., 1958-61; mgr., acct. Rockwell, Columbus, Ohio, and L.A., 1961-69; mgr. contracts Logicon, L.A., 1970-71; mgr. internal audit Daylin, 1971-72; contr. NYSE Co., 1972-73; pvt. practice, Torrance, Calif., 1973—. Mem. AICPA, L.A. County Bar Assn. (appellate ct. com. 1979—, svcs. com. 1981-82), S. Bay Bar Assn. (pres. 1986-87, chmn. referral svc. 1977-81), State Bar Calif. (client trust fund commr. 1983, 84), Ohio Inst. CPAs, N.Y. Inst. CPAs, Calif. Inst. CPAs, Inst. Mgmt. Accts., L.A. Trial Lawyers Assn., N.Y. State Bar Assn., Calif. State Bar Assn. Jewish. Republican. Home: 30691 Via La Cresta Palos Verdes Peninsula CA 90275-5353 Office: 18411 Crenshaw Blvd Ste 411 Torrance CA 90504-5046

COHEN, SUSAN GLORIA, organizational researcher; b. N.Y.C., Apr. 22, 1952. BA, SUNY, Buffalo, 1972; MA, Whitworth Coll., 1977; MPhil, MA, Yale U., 1984, 86, PhD, 1988. Social worker Children's Home Soc., Spokane, Wash., 1972-74; dir. YWCA, Spokane, 1974-79; consumer analyst Group Health coop., Seattle, 1979-80; cons. Exec. Devel. Assoc., Westport, Conn., 1986-87; rsch. scientist U. So. Calif., L.A., 1988—. Contbr. articles to profl. jours. Mem. N.O.W., 1975—, N.A.R.A.L., 1988—. Mem. Brandeis Bardine, Acad. Mgmt. Office: U So Calif Ctr for Effective Orgns G S B A Los Angeles CA 90089-1421

COHEN, WARREN, musician, writer; b. Montreal, Quebec, Canada, July 2, 1954; came to U.S., 1976; s. Philip Stanley and Olive (Harrison) C. BA, Concordia U., Montreal, Quebec, 1976; MA, U. Hawaii, 1979. Music tchr. Trafalgar Sch., Montreal, Quebec, Can., 1973-76; pianist Honolulu City Ballet, 1978-79; tchr. U. Hawaii Lab. Sch., Honolulu, 1982—; adj. faculty Chaminade U., Honolulu, 1989—. Author: Ethics in Thought and Action, 1994; mus. dir. Kumu Kahua Theatre, 1984-91, The Best of Am. Mus. Theatre, 1993—; artistic dir.: Music We Listened to concert series, 1990-91; condr. Diamond Head Theatre, 1995, Manoa Valley Theatre, 1989-95, Hawaii Chamber Orch. Soc., 1994-95; condr., pianist: Morning Music Honolulu, 1980-95; composer: Sinfonia Concertante for Orch. and Piano, 1991-92, Just So Stories, 1992, Concerto Grosso string quartet and string orch., 1994. Prodn. grantee State Found. for Culture and the Arts, 1991, tour grantee Hawaii Bur. of Econ. Devel., 1991; recipient Po'okela award Hawaii State Theatre Coun., 1993, composition award ASCAP, 1994, 95. Mem. Musician's Assn. Hawaii. Home: 415 South St Honolulu HI 96813

COHEN, WILLIAM, construction executive; b. 1962. Graduate, Loyola U., 1974. Assoc. Monteleone & McCrory, L.A., 1974-80; v.p. Valley Crest Landscape, Inc., Calabasas, Calif., 1980—. Office: Valley Crest Landscape Inc 24121 Ventura Blvd Calabasas CA 91302-1449*

COHEN, WILLIAM B., vascular surgeon; m. Joy L. Cohen; 1 child, Lauren L. Student, Colgate U., 1959; grad., NYU, 1963. Diplomate Am. Bd. Surgery; spl. cert. in vascular surgery. Attending surgeon Cedars/Sinai Med. Ctr., L.A., St. Vincents Hosp. Med. Ctr., L.A. Maj. U.S. Amry, 1969-71. Mem. ACS, So. Calif. Vascular Surgery Soc., Internat. Soc. for Cardiovascular Surgery, Peripheral Vascular Surgery Soc., Clin. Soc. for Vascular Surgery. Office: 8631 W 3rd St Ste 925E Los Angeles CA 90048-5912

COHLBERG, JEFFREY A., biochemistry educator; b. Phila., Feb. 26, 1945; s. Raymond G. and Helen E. (Greenberg) C. AB in Chemistry, Cornell U., 1966; PhD in Biochemistry, U. Calif., 1972. Postdoctoral Inst. For Enzyme Rsch. U. Wis., 1972-75; prof. Calif. State U., Long Beach, 1975—. Contbr. articles to profl. jours. Mem. Am. Soc. Cell Biology. Office: Calif State U Dept Chemistry Biochem Long Beach CA 90840

COHN, DANIEL HOWARD, laboratory director; b. Santa Monica, Calif., Aug. 24, 1955; s. Sidney Lorber and Mynda Ellen (Zimmerman) C.; m. [illegible] Reiman, May 16, 1982; children: Zachary, Marissa, Rachel. BA, U. Calif., Santa Barbara, 1977; PhD, Scripps Inst. Oceanography, 1983. Rsch. scientist, asst. prof. Cedars-Sinai Med. Ctr./UCLA, 1988-93, assoc. prof., 1993—; postdoctoral fellow U. Wash., Seattle, 1983-88; mem. genetics tng. program UCLA, 1988—; reviewer various jours. and granting agys. Editorial bd. various jours.; contbr. articles to profl. jours. and books. Grants com. chair, bd. dirs. Concern Found. for Cancer Rsch., L.A., 1988—. Recipient Martin Kamen award U. Calif., San Diego, 1983, Eckhart prize Scripps Inst. Oceanography, 1983; postdoctoral award NIH, 1985-88, grantee, 1988—. Mem. AAAS, Phi Beta Kappa. Democrat. Jewish. Office: Cedars-Sinai Med Ctr 8700 Beverly Blvd Los Angeles CA 90048-1804

COHN, FREDERIC, business executive; b. N.Y.C., Nov. 18, 1935; s. Samuel M. and Sarah (Brock) C.; m. Lorraine Schwartz, Sept. 7, 1958; children: nancy Brotkin, Andrew Cohn, Daniel Cohn. BS in Commerce and Fin., Wilkes Coll., 1956; JD, N.Y. Law Sch., 1963. Pres. Aladdin Enterprises Inc., Las Vegas, Calif., 1988—, Assist-U-Law, Inc., L.A., 1991—, Diatec Recycling Techs., Inc., Santa Monica, Calif., 1993—; bd. dirs. Harcourt Industries Inc., Carritos, Calif. Office: # 225 1424 Fourth St Santa Monica CA 90401

COHN, LAWRENCE SHERMAN, marketing and sales executive; b. Providence, Dec. 4, 1954; s. Jerome Bernard and Shirley Elaine (Davidson) C. BA cum laude, New England Coll., 1977. Tchr. English Attleboro (Mass.) High Sch., 1977-79; area dir. Met. Mktg., Santa Clara, Calif., 1979-81; dir. 3 restaurants, v.p. Puckers & Co., Oakland, Calif., 1981-88; dir. inspections and reports, ethics officer Ch. of Scientology, San Francisco, 1985-90; COO U.S Mcht. Systems Inc., Newark, 1992—; coord. Attleboro High Literacy Mag., 1978-79,poetry workshop, Henniker, N.H., 1974. Author of poems. Home: 3515 Cecil Ave San Jose CA 95117-1013 Office: US Mcht Systems Inc 39899 Balentine Ste 312 Newark CA 94560

COHN, LAWRENCE STEVEN, physician, educator; b. Chgo., Dec. 21, 1945; s. Jerome M. and Francis C.; BS, U. Ill., 1967, MD, 1971; m. Harriett G. Rubin, Sept. 1, 1968; children: Allyson and Jennifer (twins). Intern, Mt. Zion Hosp., San Francisco, 1971-72, resident, 1972-73; resident U. Chgo., 1973-74; practice medicine specializing in internal medicine, Paramount, Calif.; pres. med. staff Charter Suburban Hosp., 1981-83; mem. staff Long Beach Meml. Hosp., Harbor Gen. Hosp; assoc. clin. prof. medicine UCLA. Maj. USAF, 1974-76. Recipient Disting. Teaching award Harbor-UCLA Med. Ctr., 1980, 90; diplomate Am. Bd. Internal Medicine. Mem. A.C.P., AMA, Calif. Med. Assn., L.A. County Med. Assn., Am. Heart Assn., Soc. Air Force Physicians, Phi Beta Kappa, Phi Kappa Phi, Phi Lambda Upsilon, Phi Eta Sigma, Alpha Omega Alpha. Home: 6608 Via La Paloma Palos Verdes Peninsula CA 90275-6449 Office: 16415 Colorado Ave Ste 202 Paramount CA 90723-5054

COHN, MICHAEL JAY, psychologist, consultant, educator; b. Chgo., Apr. 22, 1951; s. Myron and Jacqueline P. (Gollob) C.; m. Linda D. Cohn, Mar. 22, 1986. BA, Ariz. State U., 1973, M of Counseling, 1975; EdD, Ball State U., 1979. Lic. psychologist. Doctoral fellow Ball State U., Muncie, Ind., 1977-79; prevention cons. Ind. Dept. Edn., Indpls., 1980-83; staff therapist Tri-County Mental Health Ctr., Carmel, Ind., 1983; asst. adminstr. Fairbanks Hosp., Indpls., 1983-86; CEO Treatment Ctrs. of Am., Scottsdale, Ariz., 1986; pres. Michael Jay Cohn, P.C., Scottsdale, Ariz., 1986—; mem. faculty U. Phoenix, 1988—; faculty assoc. Ariz. State U., Tempe, 1988—; lectr. Internat. Conf. on Drugs, Atlanta, 1984-86. Author: Al K. Hall Talks About Alcohol and Your Safety, 1986, (chpt.) Psychological Maltreatment of Children and Youth, 1987. Mem. community adv. com. U. Phoenix Counseling Dept., 1990—; pres. Ind. Juvenile Justice Task Force, Indpls., 1985; prevention com. chair Ind. Mental Health Assn., Indpls., 1985. Recipient Key to City, City of Indpls., 1986, Placque of Appreciation, Fairbanks Hosp., 1986, Placque of Appreciation, Ind. Juvenile Justice Task Force, 1986; named Hon. Lt. Col., Ind. State Police, 1986. Mem. APA, Ariz. Psychol. Assn. (conv. co-chair 1985—), Am. Soc. Clin. Hypnosis, Am. Bd. Forensic Examiners. Office: Michael J Cohn PC 7330 E Earll Dr Scottsdale AZ 85251-7221

COHN, ROBERT GREER, literary arts educator; b. Richmond, Va., Sept. 5, 1921; s. Charles Alfred and Susan (Spilberg) C.; m. Dorrit Zucker-Hale, June 20, 1947 (div. 1963); children: Stephen A., Richard L.; m. Valentina Catenacci, Oct. 26, 1965. BA in Romance Langs., U. Va., 1943; PhD in French, Yale U., 1949. Instr. Yale U., New Haven, 1949-50; asst. prof. Swarthmore (Pa.) Coll., 1952-54, Vassar Coll., Poughkeepsie, N.Y., 1954-59; from asst. to full prof. French lit. Stanford (Calif.) U., 1959-91, prof. emeritus, 1992—. Author: L'Oeuvre de Mallarmé, 1951, The Writer's Way in France, 1960, Toward the Poems of Mallarmé, 1965, The Poetry of Rimbaud, 1973; founding editor Yale French Studies, 1948. Guggenheim Found. fellow, 1956, 1985, Nat. Found. for the Humanities fellow, 1969. Home: 6 Maywood Ln Menlo Park CA 94025-5357

COIT, R. KEN, financial planner; b. L.A., Aug. 26, 1943; s. Roger L. and Thelma D. C.; BS, U. Ariz., 1967; MBA, Pepperdine U., 1981; m. Donna M. Schemanske, Oct. 8, 1977; children: Kristin M., Shannon, Darren, Lauryn. Prin. Coit Fin. Group, 1981; mem. adj. faculty Coll. Fin. Planning, Denver, 1978-79; pres. Walnut Creek adv. bd. Summit Bank, 1987—; shareholder Sequoia Equities Securities Corp., Walnut Creek, Calif.; bd. dirs. R.H. Phillips Winey. Mem. dean's adv. bd. Pepperdine U., 1988-91; nat. bd. advisor Coll. Pharmacy U. Ariz.; bd. dirs., chmn. investment com. East Community Found. Recipient Outstanding Alumnus award Pepperdine U. Sch. Bus. and Mgmt., 1986. Mem. Internat. Assn. Fin. Planners (chpt. pres. 1978-79), Inst. Cert. Fin. Planners, East Bay Gourmet Club, Blackhawk Country Club. Office: 1655 N Main St Bldg 270 Walnut Creek CA 94596-4610

COLACE, JOSEPH J., agricultural products company executive; b. 1955. Officer Colace Bros., El Centro, Calif., 1976-83, pres., 1983—. Office: Five Crowns Inc 551 W Main St Ste 2 Brawley CA 92227-2246*

COLACE, WILLIAM M., food products executive; b. 1955. With Colace Bros., El Centro, Calif., 1980-83; v. p. Five Crowns, Inc., Brawley, Calif., 1987—. Office: Five Crowns Inc 551 W Main St Ste 2 Brawley CA 92227-2246*

COLANGELO, JERRY JOHN, professional basketball team executive; b. Chicago Heights, Ill., Nov. 20, 1939; s. Larry and Sue (Drancek) C.; m. Joan E. Helmich, Jan. 20, 1961; children: Kathy, Kristen, Bryan. B.A., U. Ill., 1962. Partner House of Charles, Inc., 1962-63; assoc. D.O. Klein & Assocs., 1964-65; dir. merchandising Chgo. Bulls basketball club, 1966-68; gen. mgr. Phoenix Suns basketball club, 1968-87, now also exec. v.p., until 1987, pres., chief exec. officer, 1987—. Mem. Basketball Congress Am. (exec. v.p., dir.), Phi Kappa Psi. Republican. Baptist. Clubs: University, Phoenix Execs. Office: Phoenix Suns 201 E Jefferson St Phoenix AZ 85004-2412*

COLBAUGH, RICHARD DONALD, mechanical engineer, educator, researcher; b. Pitts., Oct. 31, 1958; s. Richard Donald and Anne Marie (McCue); m. Kristin Lea Glass, July 18, 1987; 1 child, Allison Collette. BS in Mechanical Engring., Pa. State U., 1980, PhD in Mechanical Engring., 1986. Mechanical engr. McDonnell Douglas Corp., Long Beach, Calif., 1980-81; instr. mechanical engring. Pa. State U., State College, 1981-86; asst. prof. mechanical engring. N.Mex. State U., Las Cruces, 1986-90, assoc. prof. mechanical engring., 1990—; cons. Dept. Energy, Albuquerque, 1987-- Jet Propulsion Lab., Pasadena, Calif., 1988--. Assoc. editor Internat. Jour. of Robotics and Auto., 1991-93, editor-in-chief, 1993—; assoc. editor Internat. Jour. Environ. Conscious Mfg., 1992—, Intelligent Automation and Soft Computing, 1994; co-author: Robotics and Remote Systems in Hazardous Environ., 1992; contbr. articles to profl. jours.; editor numerous jours. Recipient NASA Space Act Tech Brief award, 1990, 91, 92, 93, 95, Best Paper award Am. Automatic Control Coun., 1990, 93; NASA/ASEE Summer Faculty fellow 1991, 92. Mem. IEEE, Am. Soc. Mechanical Engrs., Sigma Xi. Office: NMex State U Dept Mechanical Engring PO Box 30001 # 3450 Las Cruces NM 88003-8001

COLBORN, RICHARD MELVIN, city official; b. Long Beach, Calif., Mar. 11, 1950; s. Robert Emery and Joyce Lucille (Holt) C.; m. Nyla Christensen, Sept. 7, 1973; children: Robert John, Trevor Dale, Shayna, Richard Chesson. AS, Dixie Coll., St. George, Utah, 1973. Cert. mcpl. clk. Draftsman American Fork (Utah) City Corp., 1978-80, planning adminstr., 1980—, city recorder, 1986—; exec. dir. American Fork Redevel. Agy., 1986—. Firefighter American Fork Vol. Fire Dept., 1979—; scoutmaster Boy Scouts Am., 1989—. Mem. Am. Planning Assn., Utah Mcpl. Clks. Assn., Ctrl. Utah Recorders Assn. (pres. 1989), Internat. Inst. Mcpl. Clks., Nat. Fire Protection Assn. Office: American Fork City 31 Church St American Fork UT 84003-1636

COLBURN, GENE LEWIS, insurance and industrial consultant; b. Bismarck, N.D., July 12, 1932; s. Lewis William and Olga Alma (Feland) C.; PhD, City U. L.A., 1983. Pres., gen. mgr. Multiple Lines Ins. Agy., Auburn, Wash., 1953-79; ins. and risk mgmt. cons., Auburn, Wash., 1980—; pres. Feland Safe Deposit Corp.; bd. dirs. Century Svc. Corp. subs. Capital Savs. Bank, Olympia, Wash.; mem. exec. com. Great Repub. Life Ins. Co., Portland, Oreg., 1971-75; mem. Wash. State Ins. Commrs. Test Devel. Com., 1986-87. cons. indsl. risk mgmt. Councilperson Auburn City, 1982-85; mayor-pro tem, City of Auburn, 1984; co-incorporator, chmn. bd. SE Community Alcohol Ctr., 1971-75; mem. Wash. State Disaster Assistance Coun., 1981-82, founding mem.; pres. Valley Cities Mental Health Ctr., 1980; mem. instn. rev. com. Auburn Gen. Hosp., 1978—; prin. trustee Dr. R. B. Bramble Med. Rsch. Found., 1980-90; bd. dirs. Wash. Assn. Chs. (Luth. Ch. in Am.), Asian Refugee Resettlement Mgmt. div., 1981-83, Columbia Luth. Home, Seattle, 1985-87, Wash. Law Enforcement Officers and Fire Fighter's Pension Disability Bd., Auburn, 1980-84. Cert. ins. counselor, 1978. Recipient Disting. Alumni award Green River Community Coll., 1982. Fellow Acad. Producer Ins. Studies (charter); mem. Internat. Platform Assn. Lodge: Auburn Lions (past pres.). Office: 720 L St SE Auburn WA 98002-6219

COLBY, BARBARA DIANE, interior designer, consultant; b. Chgo., Dec. 6, 1932; d. Raymond R. and Mertyl Shirley (Jackson) C.; 1 son, Lawrence James. Student Wright Jr. Coll., 1950, Art Inst. Chgo., UCLA. Owner, F.L.S., Los Angeles, 1971-77; ptnr. Ambiance Inc., Los Angeles, 1976-77; owner Barbara Colby, Ltd., Los Angeles, 1977-81; bus. adminstr. Internat. Soc. Interior Designers, Los Angeles, 1982—; owner Chromanetics, Glendale, Calif., 1981—; instr. Otis/Parsons Sch. Design, Los Angeles Fashion Inst. Design and Merchandising; dir. color Calif. Coll. Interior Design, Costa Mesa, Calif., 1987; also lectr. in field. Author: Color and Light Influences and Impact, 1990; contbg. editor Giftware News. Instr. L.A. County Regional Occupation Program, 1990-94; tng. cons. United Edn. Inst., 1994—. Recipient award for Best Children's Room, Chgo. Furniture Show, 1969, award Calif. Design Show '76, 1976. Mem. Am. Soc. Interior Designers (cert.), Color Mktg. Group of U.S. Author: Color and Light: Influences and Impact, 1990; contbr. articles to profl. jours. Office: 245 W Loraine St Apt 309 Glendale CA 91202-1849

COLBY, BILL, artist; b. Beloit, Kans., Jan. 8, 1927; s. Albert Warren and Nellie Dell (Lawson) C.; m. Gertrude Ann Bednorz, June 19, 1955; children: Andrea Lee, Sara Louise, Lisa Lorraine, Celia Dee. BA, U. Denver, 1950; MA, U. Ill., 1954. Art tchr. Portland (Oreg.) High Schs., 1950-53, 55-56; prof. art U. Puget Sound, Tacoma, 1956-89; trustee Tacoma Art Mus., 1962—; lectr. Wash. Commn. of Humanities, Seattle, 1987-90; bd. dirs. Kittredge Gallery, Tacoma, 1958-66, 74-89. Exhibited in shows in Phila., San Francisco, N.Y.C., Pasadena, Wichita, Seattle, Portland, others; represntd in permanent collections at Tacoma Art Mus., Portland Art Mus., Henry Art Gallery at U. Wash., Seattle, Library of Congress, Washington, Wash. State Hist. Mus., Tacoma, Seattle Art Mus., Bradley U. Art Ctr., Peoria, Ill., Wichita Art Mus., First Interstate Bank, Portland, Salishan Lodge, Glenden, Oreg., Weyerhaeuser Corp., Federal Way, Wash., Seafirst Bank, Seattle, others. Pres., treas., bd. dirs. Campfire, Tacoma, 1967-73; mem., rschr. City Club, Tacoma. 1986-94; mem. City Urban Waterfront Com., Tacoma, 1989-92; mem. Sister City Com., Japan, 1990-93. Served to sgt. U.S. Army, 1945-47, Germany. Recipient Civic Achievement award Allied Arts of Tacoma, 1964, others. Mem. Tacoma Arts and Crafts Assn. (pres., bd. dirs.), Puget Sound Sumi Artists (b.p., bd. dirs.), N.W. Print Coun. (bd. dirs.). Home: 3706 N Union Ave Tacoma WA 98407-6141

COLBY, ROBERT LESTER, psychologist; b. N.Y.C., Jan. 21, 1941; came to Can., 1966; s. Allen Michael and Beatrice Dorethea (Kalkut) C.; m. Catherine Gray. BA, NYU, 1963; MS, L.I. U., 1965. Rsch. fellow Ctr. for Ednl. Disabilities, Guelph, Ont., Can., 1967-69; lectr. U. Guelph, 1967-69; dir., chief psychologist Psychol. Svcs. of County Sch. Bd., Brantford, Ont., Can., 1969-83; pvt. practice psychology Vancouver, B.C., Can., 1980—; clin. field placement supr. Simon Fraser U., Vancouver, 1984-86, lectr. Justice Inst. B.C., 1984-86; clin. dir. Personnel Inst. Can., Vancouver, 1984-89; pres. Grad. Tests Tng., Inc., Vancouver, 1984—, Colby Gallagler & Assocs., Inc., Vancouver, 1984—; cons. to govt. agys. and depts., Can., 1984—. Chmn. Interagy. Coordinating Com., Brantford, 1975-77; bd. dirs. Ont. Antipoverty Coordinating Com., Brantford, 1975-77. Mem. APA, Can. Psychol. Assn., Coll. Psychologists (bd. dirs., chmn. ethics com. 1985-89, sec.-treas. 1988, pres. 1990-92, past pres. 1992-93), B.C. Psychol. Assn. (bd. dirs.), N.S. Psychol. Assn., Hong Kong Psychol. Assn., Can. Mental Health Assn., Soc. for Psychol. Study of Social Issues.

COLE, CHARLES EDWARD, state attorney general; b. Yakima, Wash., Oct. 10, 1927; married; 3 children. BA, Stanford U., 1950, LLB, 1953. Law clk. Vets. Affairs Commn. Territory of Alaska, Juneau, 1954, Territorial Atty. Gen.'s Office, Fairbanks, Alaska, 1955-56, U.S. Dist. Ct. Alaska, Fairbanks, 1955-56; city magistrate City of Fairbanks, 1957-58; pvt. practice law, 1957-90; atty. gen. State of Alaska, 1990-94; pvt. law comml. litigation, 1995—; profl. baseball player, Stockton, Calif. and Twin Falls, Idaho, summers of 1950, 51, 53. With U.S. Army, 1946-47. Mem. Calif. State Bar, Washington State Bar Assn., Alaska Bar Assn. Office: Law Dept State of Alaska Office of Atty Gen PO Box 110300 Juneau AK 99811-0300 also: Law Offices of Charles E Cole 406 Cushman St Fairbanks AK 99701

COLE, DAVID WINSLOW, personal care industry executive; b. Toledo, Sept. 20, 1947; s. Robert Winslow and Marjorie Lucile (Rottman) C.; m. Nancy Carol Gerathy, July 3, 1971; 1 child, Kevin. BS, Miami U., Oxford, Ohio, 1969. From field sales rep. to unit mgr. Procter and Gamble Co., Chgo. and St. Louis, 1970-76; dist. mgr. frozen foods Quaker Oats Co., Detroit, 1976-78; ea. regional mgr. frozen foods Quaker Oats Co., Severna Park, Md., 1978-82; nat. sales mgr. confectionery products Quaker Oats Co., Chgo., 1982-85; mgmt. cons. Northeastern Orgn., Inc., Trumbull, Conn., 1985-86; dir. field sales Cadbury U.S.A. subs. Cadbury Schweppes PLC, Stamford, Conn., 1986-88; dir. sales Peter Paul Cadbury Products subs. Hershey (Pa.) Chocolate Co., 1988-89; v.p. sales Personal Care Products div. Weyerhauser Co., Federal Way, Wash., 1989, exec. v.p. sales, 1989, v.p., gen. mgr., 1990-93; pres., COO Paragon Trade Brands, Federal Way, Wash., 1993—. Mem. Nat. Food Brokers Assn. (mem. prin. adv. group 1987-88, contbr. articles to assn. publs., author tng. program), Twin Lakes Golf and Country Club (mem. bd. trustees 1990-91). Office: Paragon Trade Brands 33325 8th Ave S Federal Way WA 98003-6328

COLE, DERMOT MATTHEW, newspaper columnist, historian; b. Allentown, Pa., Sept. 23, 1953; s. William Patrick and Anne Cole; m. Debbie Carter, Aug. 4, 1980; children: Connor, Aileen, Anne. BA, U. Alaska, 1979. Journalist AP, Seattle, 1988-89; journalist Fairbanks (Alaska) Daily News-Miner, 1976-88, editor, columnist, 1989—. Author: Frank Barr: Bush Pilot in Alaska and the Yukon, 1986, Hard Driving: The 1908 Auto Race from New York to Paris, 1991. Fellow U. Mich., 1986-87. Roman Catholic. Office: Fairbanks Daily News-Miner 210 N Cushman St Fairbanks AK 99701-2832

COLE, GLEN DAVID, minister; b. Tacoma, Dec. 21, 1933; s. Ray Milton and Ruth Evelyn (Ranton) C.; m. Mary Ann Von Moos, June 6, 1953; children: Randall Ray, Ricky Jay. BA in Theology, Cen. Bible Coll., 1956; DD, Pacific Coast Bible Coll., 1983. Pastor Assembly of God, Marion, Ohio, 1957-60, Maple Valley, Wash., 1960-65; assoc. pastor Calvary Temple, Seattle, 1965-67; sr. pastor Evergreen Christian Ctr., Olympia, Wash., 1967-78, Capital Christian Ctr., Sacramento, 1978—; exec. presbyter Assemblies of God, Springfield, 1985—; trustee Bethany Bible Coll., Santa Cruz, Calif., 1979—; bd. dirs. Cen. Bible Coll., Springfield, Mo., 1988—; bd. dirs. Calif. Theol. Sem., Fresno, 1985-90. Mem. Rotary (pres. Olympia chpt. 1977-78).

Republican. Office: Capital Christian Ctr 9470 Micron Ave Sacramento CA 95827-2612

COLE, GUY, food products executive. With Amfac Agribusiness, Puna Sugar, Hi.; v.p. Hawaiian Sweet, Inc., Keaau, Hi., 1991—. Office: Hawaiian Sweet Inc Milo St Keaau HI 96749*

COLE, HAROLD SPENCER, engineer; b. Riverside, Calif., Dec. 16, 1941; s. Ward Martin and Ruby Alverda (Hill) C.; m. Karin Elizabeth Gunnarsson, Apr. 15, 1974 (div. Sept. 1978); 1 child, Derek Mathew; m. Joan Margaret Hungerford, June 27, 1981; 1 child, Ward Martin. BS, Kans. State U., 1964. Planner Striton Properties, Atlanta, 1973-75; civil engr. FAA, Atlanta, 1975-81; resident engr. VA Med. Ctr., Atlanta, 1981-82, project engr., 1982-89; asst. chief engr. VA Med. Ctr., Montrose, N.Y., 1989-90; asst. chief engr. VA Med. Ctr., Bronx, N.Y., 1990-91, chief engr., 1991-93; chief engr. VA Med. Ctr., L.A., 1993—; airport mgr. Well-Air Flying, Wellington, Kans., 1964-67. 2nd lt. USAF, 1967-68, 1st lt., 1968-69, Vietnam, capt., 1970-71, Vietnam. Mem. ASCE, Phi Delta Theta. Republican. Methodist. Home: 307 Hadley Ln Los Angeles CA 90025-7830 Office: VA Med Ctr 11301 Wilshire Blvd Los Angeles CA 90073

COLE, JULIE KRAMER, artist; b. Springfield, Ohio, June 9, 1949; d. Charles Michael Kramer and Phyllis Ellen (Wobbe) Taft; m. Mark Stevens Cole, May 18, 1973; 1 child, Zachary Mark. Student, Colo. State U.; grad., Colo. Inst. Art. Fashion illustrator, artist Neusteters Dept. Store, Denver, 1963-67; freelance illustrator Denver, 1968-80; Western artist Cole Fine Art, Inc., Loveland, Colo., 1981—. Named one of Top 25 Print Artists, U.S. Art mag., 1993, one of Top 5 Print Artists, 1994. Mem. Colo. Inst. Art (hon.). Office: Cole Fine Art Inc PO Box 7268 Loveland CO 80537-0268

COLE, KENNETH JAMES, advocate; b. Ft. Monmouth, N.J., July 26, 1953; s. Loyal Joseph and Ellen Mary (Van Wart) C.; m. Elizabeth B. McGarry, Oct. 27, 1978 (div. 1988); m. Joan Marie Snopkowski, Apr. 29, 1989; 1 child, Madeline. BSBA, City U., Seattle, 1981. Clin. records adminstr. Seattle Mental Health Inst., Seattle, 1974-79; program coord. emergency med. svcs. divsn. Seattle-King County Health Dept., Seattle, 1979-80; case mgr. Seattle Mental Health Inst., Seattle, 1980-83; exec. dir. Downtown Emergency Svc. Ctr., Seattle, 1983-88, Mcpl. League of King County, Seattle, 1988-89; mgr. Pioneer Human Svcs., Seattle, 1989-91; exec. dir. Pike Mkt. Sr. Ctr./Downtown Food Bank, Seattle, 1991—; mem. Seattle Housing Levy Oversight com., Seattle, 1987—, steering com. Seattle Human Svcs. Coalition, 1992—. Profiled "Street Angel" People mag., 1986. Mem. Gov. Booth Gardner taskforce on AIDS, 1984; bd. dirs., chair Spectrum Dance Theatre, 1986-92; spokesperson Seattle/King County Coalition for the Homeless, Seattle, 1983—; pres. Roman Cath. Parish Coun., 1993—. Cpl. USMC, 1971-73. Mem. Defender Assn. (bd. dirs. 1994). Democrat. Office: Pike Mkt Sr Ctr 1930 Post Aly Seattle WA 98101-1015

COLE, LECIL, agricultural products company executive. With Puna (Hi.) Sugar; pres. Hawaiian Sweet, Inc., Keaau, Hi., 1991—. Office: Hawaiian Sweet Inc Milo St Keaau HI 96749*

COLE, LEE ARTHUR, new product development executive; b. Pitts., May 2, 1953; m. Loni Kay Chestor, May 11, 1985. BS, Indiana U. Pa., 1975; PhD, Dartmouth Coll., 1979. Postdoctoral fellow physics dept. Tulane U., New Orleans, 1979-81; project mgr. Solar Energy Rsch. Inst., Dept. Energy, Golden, Colo., 1981-85; program mgr. Solid State Elec. div. Honeywell Co., Colorado Springs, Colo., 1985-87; mgr. R&D Unisys CAD-CAM, Inc., Boulder, Colo., 1987-91; v.p. rsch. and devel. Graftek, Inc., a Unisys Co., Boulder, 1991-92; dir. product devel. Hunter Douglas, Broomfield, Colo., 1992-94, dir. mkt. rsch., 1992—; founder, ptnr. Cole-Chestor & Co. Contbr. articles to profl. jours. Mem. Am. Phys. Soc. Home: 29937 Gigi Dr Evergreen CO 80439-7213 Office: Hunter Douglas Inc One Duette Way Broomfield CO 80020

COLE, MALVIN, neurologist, educator; b. N.Y.C., Mar. 21, 1933; s. Harry and Sylvia (Firman) C.; A.B. cum laude, Amherst Coll., 1953; M.D. cum laude, Georgetown U. Med. Sch., 1957; m. Susan Kugel, June 20, 1954; children: Andrew James, Douglas Gowers. Intern, Seton Hall Coll. Medicine, Jersey City Med. Ctr., 1957-58; resident Boston City Hosps., 1958-60; practice medicine specializing in neurology, Montclair and Glen Ridge, N.J., Montville, N.J., 1963-72, Casper, Wyo., 1972—; teaching fellow Harvard Med. Sch., 1958-60; Research fellow Nat. Hosp. for Nervous Diseases, St. Thomas Hosp., London, Eng., 1960-61; instr. Georgetown U. Med. Sch., 1961-63; clin. assoc. prof. neurology N.J. Coll. Medicine, Newark, 1963-72, acting dir. neurology, 1965-72; assoc. prof. clin. neurology U. Colo. Med. Sch., 1973-88, clin. prof., 1988—; mem. staff Wyo. Med. Ctr., Casper, U. Hosp., Denver. Served to capt. M.C., AUS, 1961-63. Licensed physician, Mass., N.Y., Calif., N.J., Colo., Wyo.; diplomate Am. Bd. Psychiatry and Neurology, Nat. Bd. Med. Examiners. Fellow ACP, Am. Acad. Neurology, Royal Soc. Medicine; mem. Assn. Research Nervous and Mental Disease, Acad. Aphasia, Am. Soc. Neuroimaging, Internat. Soc. Neuropsychology, Harveian Soc. London, Epilepsy Found. Am., Am. Epilepsy Soc., Am. EEG Soc., N.Y. Acad. Sci., Osler Soc. London, Alpha Omega Alpha. Contbr. articles to profl. jours. Office: 246 S Washington St Casper WY 82601-2921

COLE, RICHARD GEORGE, public administrator; b. Irvington, N.J., Mar. 11, 1948; s. Warner W. and Laurel M. (Wilson) C. AS in Computer Sci., Control Data Inst., Anaheim, Calif., 1972; BA in Sociology with high honor, Calif. State U., Los Angeles, 1974; MA in Social Ecology, U. Calif., Irvine, 1976; postgrad., So. Oreg. State Coll., 1979. Computer operator Zee Internat., Gardena, Calif., 1971; teaching asst. U. Calif., Irvine, 1974-75; planner Herman Kimmel & Assocs., Newport Beach, Calif., 1976-78; program analyst The Job Council, Medford, Oreg., 1980-81, compliance officer, 1981-82, mgr. adminstrv. svcs., 1982—; instr. credential Calif. C.C.; chmn. bd. trustees Job Coun. Pension Trust, Medford, 1982—; mem. curriculum adv. com. Rogue C.C., Grants Pass, Oreg., 1986; mgr. computer project State of Oreg., Salem, 1983-84; mem. Oreg. Occupational Info. Coordinating Com., Salem, 1982-84. Pres. bd. trustees Vector Control Dist., Jackson County, Oreg., 1985, treas., 1986, bd. dirs., 1984-87, mem. budget com., 1988—, sec., 1988-89; cand. bd. dirs. Area Edn. Dist., Jackson County, 1981; treas. Job Svc. Employer Com., Jackson County, 1987— (Spl. Svc. award 1991); dir. fin. joint pub. venture System Devel. Project, Salem, Oreg., 1986-89; mem. adv. bd. New Jobs Planning, Medford, Oreg., 1987-88, Fin. Audit and Risk Mgmt. Task Force, 1987—, chm., 1989-90. Fellow LaVerne Noyes, U. Calif., Irvine, 1974; Dr. Paul Doehring Found. scholar, Glendale, Calif., 1973; Computer Demonstration grantee State of Oreg., Salem, 1983; recipient Award of Fin. Reporting Achievement Govt. Fin. Officers Assn. of U.S. and Can., 1989-90, Fin. Ops. recognition Vector Control Dist., Jackson County, Oreg., 1990, Nat. 2d Pl. Chpt. award Jackson County Job Svc. Employer Com., 1989, Oreg. Job Svc. Employer Com. Stat award, 1991, Oreg. Individual Citation award Internat. Assn. Profls. in Employment Security, 1993. Mem. Soc. for Human Resources Mgmt., Assn. So. Oreg. Pub. Adminstrs., Oreg. Employment and Tng. Assn., Pacific N.W. Personnel Mgmt. Assn. (chpt. treas. 1985-87, orgnl. liaison dir. 1988-89, Appreciation award 1985), Govt. Fin. Officers Assn., Oreg. Mcpl. Fin. Officers assn., The Nature Conservancy. Home: 575 Morey Rd Talent OR 97540-9725 Office: The Job Council 673 Market St Medford OR 97504-6125

COLE, TERRI LYNN, organization administrator; b. Tucson, Dec. 28, 1951; m. James R. Cole II. Student, U. N.Mex., 1975-80; cert., Inst. Orgn. Mgmt., 1985. Cert. chamber exec. With SunWest Bank, Albuquerque, 1971-74, employment adminstr., 1974-76, communications dir., 1976-78; pub. info. dir. Albuquerque C. of C., 1978-81, gen. mgr., 1981-83, pres., 1983—; pres. N.Mex. C. of C. Execs. Assn., 1986-87, bd. dirs., 1980—; bd. regents Inst. for Orgn. Mgmt., Stanford U., 1988—, vice chmn., 1990-91, chmn., 1991; bd. dirs. Hosp. Home Health, Inc. Recipient Bus. Devel. award Expn. Mgmt. Inc., 1985, Women on Move award YWCA, 1986; named one of Outstanding Women of Am., 1984. Mem. Am. C. of C. Execs. Assn. (chmn. elect bd. 1992—). Republican. Office: Greater Albuquerque C of C PO Box 25100 Albuquerque NM 87125-0100

COLEMAN, ALAN BROUSE, financial management educator; b. San Francisco, Jan. 11, 1929; s. Alan Brouse and Hazel Virginia (Deane) C.; m. Janet M. Saville, July 4, 1953; children: Kathleen, Frances Jennifer. BA, U. San Francisco, 1952; MBA, Stanford U., 1956, PhD, 1960. Mem. faculty Grad. Sch. Bus. Harvard U., 1958-62, Stanford U., 1962-70; dean ESAN, Lima, Peru, 1963-66; v.p., treas. U.S. Natural Resources, Inc., 1970-71; pres., chief exec. officer Yosemite Park and Curry Co., Calif., 1971-73; pres., chief adminstrv. officer Sun Valley Co., Idaho, 1973-74; Caruth Prof. fin. mgmt. So. Meth. U., Dallas, 1974-88, pres., chief exec. officer S.W. Sch. Banking Found., 1980-88, dean Edwin L. Cox Sch. Bus., 1975-81; pres. Alan B. Coleman, Inc., Cons., 1981—; bd. dirs. Centex Corp., Dallas. Treas., trustee Family Svc. Assn. Mid-Peninsula; bd. dirs. Stanford Credit Union; adv. dir. Army and Air Force Exch. Svc. World Hdqrs., Dallas. 1st lt. U.S. Army, 1952-54. Recipient Palmas Magisteriales, Orden de Commendador (Peru); Ford Found. fellow, 1956-57; Am. Numis. Soc. fellow, 1980—. Mem. Beta Gamma Sigma. Author: (with Hempel and Simonson) Bank Management: Text and Cases, 1983, 86, 90, 94 (with Robichek) Management of Financial Institutions, 1967, 77, (with Vandell) Case Problems in Finance, 1962, (with Marks) Cases in Commerical Bank Management, 1962. Office: PO Box 35 The Sea Ranch CA 95497-0035

COLEMAN, ARLENE FLORENCE, nurse practitioner; b. Braham, Minn., Apr. 8, 1926; d. William and Christine (Judin) C.; m. John Dunkerken, May 30, 1987. Diploma in nursing, U. Minn., 1947, BS, 1953; MPH, Loma Linda U., 1974. RN, Calif. Operating room scrub nurse Calif. Luth. Hosp., L.A., 1947-48; indsl. staff nurse Good Samaritan Hosp., L.A., 1948-49; staff nurse Passavant Hosp., Chgo., 1950-51; student health nurse Moody Bible Inst., Chgo., 1950-51; staff nurse St. Andrews Hosp., Mpls., 1951-53; pub. health nurse Bapt. Gen. Conf. Bd. of World Missions, Ethiopia, Africa, 1954-66; staff pub. health nurse County of San Bernadino, Calif., 1966-68, sr. pub. health nurse, 1968-73, pediatric nurse practitioner, 1973—. Contbr. articles to profl. jours. Mem. bd. dist. missions Bapt. Gen. Conf., Calif., 1978-84; mem. adv. coun. Kaiser Hosp., Fontana, Calif., 1969-85, Bethel Sem. West, San Diego, 1987—; bd. dirs. Casa Verdugo Retirement Home, Hemet, Calif., 1985—; active Calvary Bapt. Ch., Redlands, Calif., 1974—; mem. S.W. Bapt. Conf. Social Ministries, 1993—. With USPHS, 1944-47. Calif. State Dept. Health grantee, 1973. Fellow Nat. Assn. Pediatric Nurse Assocs. and Practitioners; mem. Calif. Nurses Assn. (state nursing coun. 1974-76). Democrat.

COLEMAN, DENNIS G., conductor; b. Klamath Falls, Oreg., Aug. 28, 1948; s. Arthur Eugene Coleman and Mary Maxine (Donahue) Wilson. . BMus, U. Wash., 1971, BEd, 1971, MMus, 1983. Conductor Seattle Men's Chorus, 1981—; dir. Chorus Am., Phila., 1990-94. Office: Seattle Men's Chorus 319 12th Ave Seattle WA 98122-5504

COLEMAN, GILBERT ROBEY, economist, statistician; b. Elko, Nev., Feb. 5, 1955; s. Franklyn Robey and Gladys (Gilbert) C. BA, U. So. Calif., 1977; MS, Stanford U., 1980, PhD, 1983. Intern U.S. Senate Commerce Com., Washington, 1978, 79; rsch. asst. Rosse and Olszewski, Palo Alto, Calif., 1980-81; economist Merrill Lynch & BAR, Pasadena, Calif., 1981-83; asst. prof. U. Nev., Reno, 1983-86; economist, owner Gilbert Coleman PhD Econ. Cons., Reno, 1984—; adj. prof. U. Nev., Reno. Named Sloan fellow Stanford U., 1978; recipient Trustees award, U. So. Calif., 1977. Mem. Am. Econ. Assn., No. Nev. Assn. Bus. Econs., U. So. Calif. Assocs., U. So. Calif. No. Nev. Alumni Club (v.p. 1986-93, pres. 1993—). Democrat. Roman Catholic. Home: 7508 Lighthouse Ln Reno NV 89511-1092

COLEMAN, J.D., public relations executive, writer; b. Spokane, Wash., Dec. 16, 1930; s. Thomas Coleman and Lois Leona (LeBreche) Magar; m. Madeline T. Young, Sept. 14, 1952; children: Kathleen, Darrell, Roger, Michelle, Joseph. BA in Journalism, U. Montana, 1956; postgrad. mass comms., U. Ind., 1968. Reporter Columbia Basin News, Pasco, Wash., 1956-58; news dir. KOTE Radio, Missoula, Mont., 1958-61, WDZ Radio, Decatur, Ill., 1961-63; commd. lt. U.S. Army, 1963, advanced through grades to lt. col., retired, 1979; dir. comms. Atlanta C. of C., 1980-83; owner Creative Comms., Atlanta, 1983-86; dir. pub. affairs Ga. Dept. Pub. Safety, Atlanta, 1987-90; pub. affairs officer Flathead Nat. Forest, Kalispell, Mont., 1991—. Author: Pleieu: The Dawn of Helicopter Warfare in Vietnam, 1987, Incursion: From America's Chokehold on North Vietnamese Lifelines to the Sacking of Cambodian Sanctuaries, 1990. Active pub. rels. and mktg. coms. numerous civic and charitable orgns., Atlanta, 1980-86; mem. Nat. Resources Com. Kalispell C. of C., Mont., 1991—. Decorated Silver Star, U.S. Army, Vietnam, 1966, Legion of Merit, 1969, 71, 79; recipient mng. editor's award, Assoc. Press, Missoula, Mont. 1959, Grand award Total Comms., Am. C. of C., Atlanta, 1981. Mem. Pub. Rels. Soc. Am. (accredited pub. rels. profl.). Home: General Delivery Kalispell MT 59901-9999 Office: Flathead Nat Forest 1935 3rd Ave E Kalispell MT 59901-5759

COLEMAN, KENNETH WILLIAM, publishing company executive; b. Phila., Apr. 22, 1930; s. George Craig Coleman and Catherine Estelle (Irwin) Cohen; m. Seraphine Elizabeth Rinaudo, Aug.9, 1952; 1 child, Catherine Coleman Chambers Little. BA in History, Calif. State U., Los Angeles, 1957; MS in Ednl. Psychology, Calif. State U., Long Beach, 1975. Cert. tchr., Calif. Tchr. Los Angeles city schs., 1957-75; chief exec. officer Seraphim Press, Carlsbad, Calif., 1978—. Author, pub.: The Misdirection Conspiracy, 1982, 2d rev. edit., 1983, U.S. Financial Institutions in Crisis, 1982, 4th rev. edit., 1986, America's Endangered Banks, 1984, 2d rev. edit., 1986, Reality Theory, Fed Tracking and Money Flow Analysis, 1988, rev. edit., 1992, A Monetary Time Bomb is Ticking, Ticking, Ticking..., 1994, The Fed Tracker newsletter, 1982—; dir. Am. Monetary Found., 1987—; regular contbr. Am. Assn. Fin. Profls. mag., Orange County Bus. Jour., Smart Money Investor mag.; contbr. monthly column Personal Investing News, 1988—, also articles on fin. news to Bull and Bear Digest, Personal Investing News, Eyes on L.A.; numerous appearances on KWHY-TV, L.A., and CNBC-TV, radio talk shows. Pres. Chansall Mut. Water Co., Bell, Calif., 1961-65; assoc. advisor senate congl. banking com. U.S. Senate Adv. Bd., 1987. With U.S. Army, 1945-47. Mem. Elks. Home and Office: 4805 Courageous Ln Carlsbad CA 92008-3783

COLEMAN, LEWIS WALDO, bank executive; b. San Francisco, Jan. 2, 1942; s. Lewis V. and Virginia Coleman; m. Susan G.; children: Michelle, Gregory, Nancy, Peter. B.A., Stanford U., 1965. With Bank Calif., San Francisco, 1965-73; with Wells Fargo Bank, San Francisco, 1973-86, exec. v.p., chmn. credit policy com., until 1986; vice chmn., CFO, treas. Bank Am., San Francisco, 1986—.

COLEMAN, ROBERT TRENT, social worker, rehabilitation consultant; b. Gary, Ind., Feb. 4, 1936; s. Robert Clinton and Lucille Verna C.; m. Dorothy Agnes, Aug. 1957; children: Sean, Bryce, Daniel; m. 2d, Patricia Lou, June 13, 1976; m. 3d Polly Anderson, Sept. 15, 1984. BA in Speech Therapy, U. Wash., Seattle, 1962; postgrad. in speech U. Redlands, 1963-64; MS in Rehab. Counseling, U. Oreg., 1971. Cert. rehab. counselor, cert. ins. rehab. specialist. Social worker, San Bernardino City Welfare Dept., 1963-64; correctional counselor Calif. Rehab. Center, Norco, 1964-67; sr. counselor Job Corps, Clearfield, Utah, 1967; assoc. dir. Ednl. Systems Corp., Washington, 1968-69; ptnr. Black Fir Jade Mines, Big Sur, Calif., 1971-76; vocat. specialist Internat. Rehab. Assn., San Diego, 1976-77; vocat. rehab. counselor Sharp Hosp., San Diego, 1977-80; clin. coord. San Diego Pain Inst., 1981; cons. in rehab. counseling, career guidance, human rels., Carlsbad, Calif., 1981—; propr. R.T.C. Cons. Svcs., Escondido, 1983—; vocat. rehab. expert Civil Ct., 1983—. Commr., Handicapped Appeals Commn., San Marcos, Calif., 1981-83. Served with U.S. Army, 1955-58. Mem. ACA, San Diego Career Guidance Assn. (pres. 1984), Assn. Indsl. Rehab. Reps. (pres. 1983), Am. Rehab. Counseling Assn., Nat. Assn. Rehab. Profls. in Pvt. Sector (standards and ethics com. 1986—, chmn. 1988-90). Republican. Home: 538 Glenheather Dr San Marcos CA 92069-2005 Office: 218 E Grand Ave Ste 6 Escondido CA 92025-2819

COLEMAN, ROGER DIXON, bacteriologist; b. Rockwell, Iowa, Jan. 18, 1915; s. Major C. and Hazel Ruth Coleman; A.B., UCLA, 1937; postgrad. Balliol Coll., Oxford (Eng.) U., 1944; MS, U. So. Calif., 1952, PhD, 1957; m. Lee Aden Skov, Jan. 1, 1978. Sr. laboratorian Napa (Calif.) State Hosp., 1937-42; dir. Long Beach (Calif.) Clin. Lab., 1946-86, pres., 1980-86; mem. Calif. State Clin. Lab. Commn., 1953-57. Served as officer AUS, 1942-46. Diplomate Am. Bd. Bioanalysts. Mem. Am. Assn. Bioanalysts, Am. Assn. Clin. Chemists, Am. Soc. Microbiologists, Am. Chem. Soc., Am. Venereal Disease Assn., AAAS (life), Calif. Assn. Bioanalysts (past officer), Med. Research Assn. Calif., Bacteriology Club So. Calif., Sigma Xi, Phi Sigma (past chpt. pres.). Author papers in field. Home: 7 Laguna Woods Dr Laguna Niguel CA 92677-2829 Office: PO Box 7073 Laguna Niguel CA 92607-7073

COLEMAN, WILLIAM ROBERT, optometrist; b. Newport, R.I., Aug. 29, 1916; s. Frank and Mae Markel; m. Monique Coleman; children: Philippe Charles, Kevin Charles, Tina-Lise. BS, So. Calif. Coll. Optometry, L.A., 1948, OD, 1949. Pvt. practice San Bernardino, Calif., 1951—. Mem. San Bernardino County Mus. Commn., 1962-67; chmn. San Bernardino Bicentennial Commn., 1974-76; bd. dirs. nat. historic site Friends of Touro Synagogue, 1955—; v.p. Touch Am. History, 1985—. 1st lt. U.S. Army, World War II. Mem. Manuscript Soc. (treas. 1981-86, pres. 1986-88), Am. Antiquarian Soc., Grolier Club, Orange Belt Optometric Assn. (pres. 1976-77), So. Calif. chpt. Manuscript Soc. (pres. 1972-74, 83-84).

COLEMAN-LEVY, JACK ROBIN, photographic laboratory design consultant; b. Bklyn., Mar. 24, 1956; s. Paul and Eileen (Moyal) L.; m. Judith Angell Coleman, May 15, 1982; children: Angella Rose, Benjamin Herschell, Maggie Illana. Tng. mgr. Shelley's Audio, L.A., 1976-79; western regional mktg. dir. Photo Lab Fabrications, Central Islip, N.Y., 1979-88; owner Photolab Innovations, Lancaster, Calif., 1988—. Bd. dirs. Lancaster Cmty. Shelter, 1993—; chair Beth Knesset Bamidbar Social Action Com., 1991-94; bd. dirs. Beth Knesset Bamidbar Early Childhood Ctr., 1992-94. Jewish. Office: Photolab Innovations 3328 Monte Carlo Ct Lancaster CA 93536-4844

COLE-MCCULLOUGH, DANIEL, music educator; b. Portland, Oreg., May 22, 1946; s. John Virgle and Barbara Jean (Johnson) Cole; m. Maryl Marcelite, Apr. 21, 1979; 1 child, Erika Kristine. BA in Music, Marylhurst Coll., 1984; MMus in Conducting, U. Portland, 1987. Cert. music tchr., Oreg., Wash. Music instr., orch. conductor Clark Coll., Vancouver, Wash., 1975-89; music instr. Marylhurst (Oreg.) Coll., 1985-94; prof. music, prof. bands Warner Pacific Coll., Portland, Oreg., 1993—; conductor, music dir. Pacific Crest Wind Ensemble, Marylhurst, 1988—; guest conductor Pres.'s USCG Band, 1994. Author: Mardsan Guitar Method, 1979; editor Oreg. Music Educators Assn. mag., 1994. With USAR, 1966-73. Recipient Clark County Theater Art award, 1988. Mem. Am. Symphony Orch. League, Music Educators Nat. Conf., Conductors Guild, World Assn. of Symphonic Bands and Ensembles, Coll. Music Soc., Coll. Band Dirs. Nat. Assn. (sec.-treas. N.W. divsn.), Assn. Concert Bands (Wash. State rep.), Nat. Band Assn., Am. Legion, Am. Quarter Horse Assn., Phi Mu, Tau Kappa Epsilon. Lutheran. Home: 17806 NE Edmunds Rd Vancouver WA 98682 Office: Warner Pacific Coll Dept Music 2219 SE 68th St Portland OR 97215

COLES, BETTIE JOHNSON, emergency services nurse; b. Balt., Feb. 18, 1948; d. Willie and Ethel (Evans) Johnson; m. Leroy A. Coles III, Apr. 13, 1968; children: Leroy A. IV, Katherine M. RN diploma, St. Vincent's Sch. Nursing, L.A., 1969; BS in Mgmt., Pacific Christian Coll.; MS in Health Care Adminstrn., U. LaVerne, 1987. RN, Calif. Med.-surg. staff RN St. Vincents Hosp., L.A., 1968-69; allergy/immunology clinic RN Kaiser Permanente, L.A., 1972-74, emergency svcs. asst. supr.-mgr., 1974-81; dir. nursing Kaiser Permanente, Anaheim, Calif., 1981-87; regional ops. mgr. Kaiser Permanente, Kansas City, Kans., 1987-91; mgr. integrated planning/project mgmt. Kaiser Permanente, Pasadena, Calif., 1991—. Bd. dirs. Orange County (Calif.) Urban League, 1985-87; vol. nurse Boy Scouts Am., Orange County, 1982-84. Mem. Nursing Adminstrs. Coun. of Orange County (pres. 1985-86, Leadership Appreciation award 1986), Med. Group Mgmt. Assn., Black Nurses Assn. Calif. Roman Catholic. Office: Kaiser Permanente 393 E Walnut St Fl 7 Pasadena CA 91188-0001

COLFACK, ANDREA HECKELMAN, elementary education educator; b. Yreka, Calif., July 17, 1945; d. Robert A. Davis and June (Reynolds) Butler; m. David Lee Heckelman, Sept. 5, 1965 (div. Nov. 1982); children: Barbara, Julie; m. Neal Cleve, Jan. 1, 1984; 1 stepchild, Karl. AB, Calif. State U., L.A., 1966; MA, Calif. State U., Fresno, 1969. Life standard elem. credential, Calif. cert. competencs: Spanish, Calif.; ordained to ministry Faith Christian Fellowship Internat., 1987. Tchr. Tulare (Calif.) City Schs., 1966-67, Palo Verde Union Sch. Dist., 1967-70, Cutler-Orosi (Calif.) Union Sch. Dist., 1979-82, Hornbrook (Calif.) Union Sch. Dist., 1982-84; sales mgr. Tupperware, Fresno, Calif., 1973-79; bilingual tchr. West Contra Costa (Calif.) Unified Sch. Dist., 1984—; site mentor Bayview Elem. Sch., Richmond, 1990-91; ELD mentor, Richmond, 1992-94, mentor selection com., 1994-95; summer sch. prin. Grant Elem. Sch., Richmond, 1995. Coauthor: Project Mind Expansion, 1974. East Bay C.U.E. Tech. grantee, 1995. Mem. United Tchrs. Richmond, Calif. Assn. Bilingual Educators (sec. Richmond 1990-91), AAUW (pres. Tulare br. 1967-68). Democrat. Pentecostal. Home: 875 Redwood Ct Crockett CA 94525-1442 Office: Grant Elem Sch ELD/Bilingual Resource 2400 Downer Ave Richmond CA 94804-1458

COLGAN, MICHAEL, nutrition scientist, consultant, researcher; b. Exeter, Devon, Eng., May 10, 1939; came to U.S., 1980; s. Joseph Michael and Emily (Nolan) C.; m. Hazel Aloma, May 10, 1963 (div. June 5, 1978); children: Michael, Damian; m. Lesley Aileen Speight, May 6, 1979; children: Megan, Tammy. BA in Physiology and Psychology, Victoria U. of Wellington, New Zealand, 1970, MA in Physiology with distinction, 1972; PhD in Physiology, U. Auckland, New Zealand, 1979. Cert. nutritionist. Instr. mammal physiology Victoria U. of Wellington, New Zealand, 1970; rsch. fellow Wellington (New Zealand) Hosp., 1971; assoc. prof. human scis. U. Auckland, New Zealand, 1971-82; from. asst. dir. to dir. U. Auckland Clinic, 1972-74; dir. Colgan Clinic, Auckland, 1971-80, Colgan Inst. Nutritional Sci., San Diego, 1979—; vis. scholar Rockefeller U., N.Y.C., 1981-83, lectr. cont. med. edn. 1982—; guest lectr. summer sch. U. Oregon, Eugene, 1984-86. cont. med. edn., 1982—, cont. dental edn., 1985—; lectr. Nutrition Cert. Course for Chiropractors, 1991—; guest lectr. U. Calif., San Diego, 1993; researcher and cons. in field. Author: Electroderman Responses: A Teaching Manual, 1969, Your Personal Vitamin Profile, 1982, Les Vitamines, 1986, Prevent Cancer Now, 1990, Optimum Sports Nutrition, 1993, The New Nutrition, 1994, Sexual Potency, 1995; author numerous articles and reports. Nutrition legis. activist Colgon Inst. Mem. AAAS, Am. Coll. Sports Medicine, New Zealand Fedn. Sports Medicine, British Soc. Nutritional Medicine, U.S. Nat. Strength & Conditioning Assn., Internat. and Am. Assn. Clin. Nutritionists (coun. mem.), N.Y. Acad. Scis., Interant. Coll. Applied Nutrition, Acad. Orthomolecular Psychiatry, Orthomolecular Med. Soc. Office: Colgan Inst 523 Encinitas Blvd # 204 Encinitas CA 92024

COLINO, RICHARD RALPH, communications consultant; b. N.Y.C., Feb. 10, 1936; s. Victor and Caroline (Pauline) C.; m. Wilma Jane Rubinstein, June 10, 1962 (div. Oct. 1991); children: Stacey Anne, Geoffrey William. BA, Amherst Coll., 1957; JD, Columbia U., 1960. Assoc. Sargoy & Stein, N.Y.C., 1960-61; atty. FCC, Washington, 1962-64, U.S. Info. Agy., Washington, 1964-65; dir. internat. affairs Communications Satellite Corp., Washington, 1965-68; dir. Europe Communications Satellite Corp., Geneva, 1968-69; asst. v.p. Communications Satellite Corp., Washington, 1969-75, v.p. and gen. mgr. internat. ops., 1975-79; pres., chief exec. officer Continental Home Theatre, Burlingame, Calif., 1979-80, DynaCom Enterprises Ltd., Chevy Chase, Md., 1980-83; dir. gen., chief exec. officer Internat. Telecommunications Satellite Orgn., Washington, 1983-86; v.p., cons. W. L. Pritchard & Co., Inc., Cons. Engrs., Bethesda, Md., 1990-92; v.p. Jackson-Richards Cons. Ltd. Telecomm. Cons., Irvine, Calif., 1992—. Contbr. to more than 30 books and articles. Bd. dirs. Washington Opera, 1986-87, Overseas Devel. Coun., 1986-87, Internat. Inst. Communication, London, 1985-86, Big Bros., Washington, 1975-77; co-chmn., chmn. Fund Raisers, Washington, 1983-89; docent The Irvine Mus., 1994—. With U.S. Army, 1961-62. Named one of top 15 people in U.S. comms. Comms. Week, 1986; recipient Adam Thompson award Amherst Coll., 1982. Home: 326 Deerfield Ave Irvine CA 92714-7606 Office: Jackson Richards Cons Ltd 14252 Culver Dr Ste A715 Irvine CA 92714-1867

COLLAMER, SONJA MAE SOREIDE, veterinary facility administrator; b. Rapid City, S.D., Sept. 3, 1937; d. Louis Severin and Mae Marie (Barber) Soreide; m. John Harry Collamer, Dec. 30, 1959; children: Debra, Michael, Kenneth, Kerry. BS in Bacteriology, Colo. State U., 1959. Practice mgr. Saratoga (Wyo.) Vet. Clinic, 1966-94, ret., 1994; mem. Wyo. Bd. Medicine, 1995—. Pres., mem. Wyo. Jaycettes, 1962-70; elder, mem. First Presby-

Ch., Saratoga, 1966—; neighborhood chmn., leader Girl Scouts Am., Saratoga, 1967-77; sec., mem. Snowy Range Cattlewomen, Carbon County, Wyo., 1967—; active bd. of edn. Sch. Dist. # 9, Saratoga, 1968-72; chmn. treas. bd. of edn. Sch. Dist. # 2, Carbon County, 1972-81; mem. Carbon County Rep. Ctrl. Com., 1980—; vice chair, mem. Saratoga Sr. Ctr. Bd., 1982-86; pres., mem. Snowy Range Ambs., Saratoga, 1984—; chair Region VIII Child Devel. Program, Carbon County, 1985-90; mem., fundraiser Saratoga Community Choir, 1988—; mediator Wyo. Agrl. Mediation Bd., 1988—; co-chair Thomas for Congress Com., Carbon County, 1990; chair Saratoga Hist. and Cultural Assn. Bd., 1990—; active Planning & Devel. Commn., Carbon County, 1994. Mem. Am. Vet. Med. Assn. Auxiliary, Wyo. Vet. Med. Assn. Auxiliary (pres.), Kappa Delta. Republican. Presbyterian. Home: PO Box 485/806 Rangeview Saratoga WY 82331

COLLAR, LEO LINFORD, marine transportation company executive; b. Cleve., Nov. 27, 1930; s. Leo Webster and Martha Caroline (Guenther) C.; m. Gail Valine, May 27, 1949; children—Randy L., Gary L., Steven M., Susan L. Student, Golden Gate Coll. With Crowley Maritime Corp., San Francisco, 1948—, exec. v.p., 1975-87, pres., chief operating officer, 1987—; now also pres., dir. Delta Steamship Lines, Inc., subs. Crowley Maritime Corp., New Orleans. Mem. Nat. Maritime Council (vice chmn. 1984—), Council Am. Ship Operators (bd. dirs. 1983—. Republican. Mem. Ch. of the Nazarene. Office: Crowley Maritime Corp 101 California St San Francisco CA 94111-3002 also: Delta Steamship Lines Inc PO Box 50250 New Orleans LA 70150-0250

COLLARD, LORRAINE FULLMER, violin educator; b. Salt Lake City, Mar. 25, 1957; d. Merlin Don and Mary Suz Anne (Christensen) F.; m. Steven Robert Collard, June 26, 1981; children: Grant, Christopher, Michael, Richard. MusB, Brigham Young U., 1980; MA in Music, San Diego State U., 1986. Cert. music tchr., Calif., Utah. Instr. violin Calif., Utah, 1970—; tchr. string orch. Nebo Sch. Dist., Payson, Utah, 1980-81; substitute tchr. Poway, City Schs., Escondido Dists., San Diego, 1982-84; instr. group lessons in violin, San Diego, 1991—. Violinist San Jose State U. Chamber Orch., 1975-77, San Jose State U. Orch., 1975-77, San Diego State U. Quartet, 1976-77, Brigham Young U. Philharmonic, 1977-79, Brigham Young U. Chamber Orch., 1978-79, San Diego State U., 1982-85; concertmaster U. San Diego, 1981-82; active mem. LDS Ch.; den mother cub scouts Boy Scouts Am., San Diego, 1984-85; asst. concertmaster Palomar Orch., San Marcos, Calif., 1989-91; coord. Handel's Messiah Orch., San Diego, 1988-92. Rudolph Giskin Meml. scholar San Jose State U., 1975, Gov. scholar State of Calif., 1975, San Jose Tchr.'s Assn. scholar, 1975, music scholar Brigham Young U., 1977-79, grad. scholar San Diego State U., 1982-83; recipient music award Bank of Am., 1975, 3d runner-up award Miss Am. County Pageant, 1975, Swimsuit Competition award, 1975. Mem. Suzuki Assn. Am., Suzuki Music Assn. Calif., Am. Family Assn.

COLLAS, JUAN GARDUÑO, JR., lawyer; b. Manila, Apr. 25, 1932; s. Juan D. and Soledad (Garduño) C.; m. Maria L. Moreira, Aug. 1, 1959; children: Juan Jose, Elias Lopes, Cristina Maria, Daniel Benjamin. LLB, U. of Philippines, Quezon City, 1955; LLM, Yale U., 1958, JSD, 1959. Bar: Philippines 1956, Ill. 1960, Calif. 1971, U.S. Supreme Ct. 1967. Assoc., Sy Cip, Salazar & Assocs., Manila, 1956-57; atty. N.Y., N.H. & H. R.R., New Haven, 1959-60; assoc. Baker & McKenzie, Chgo., 1960-63, ptnr., Manila, 1963-70, San Francisco, 1970—. Contbr. articles to profl. jours. Trustee, sec. Friends of U. of Philippines Found. in Am., San Francisco, 1982—; co-chmn. San Francisco Lawyers for Better Govt., 1982—; chmn. San Francisco-Manila Sister City Com., 1986-92. Recipient Outstanding Filipino Overseas in Law award, Philippine Ministry Tourism Philippines Jaycees, 1979. Mem. ABA, Am. Arbitration Assn. (panelist), Ill. State Bar Assn., State Bar Calif., Integrated Bar of Philippines, Filipino-Am. C. of C. (bd. dirs. 1974-91, 94—, pres. 1985-87, chmn. bd. dirs. 1987-89, 95—). Republican. Roman Catholic. Clubs: World Trade, Villa Taverna (San Francisco). Office: Baker & McKenzie 2 Embarcadero Ctr Ste 2400 San Francisco CA 94111-3909

COLLEDGE, DEBORAH GAIL, gifted and talented elementary educator; b. Altoona, Pa., Aug. 9, 1956; d. Charles E. Sr. and Shirley J. (Bragonier) C. BS, Clarion (Pa.) State, 1977; MEd, Pa. State U., 1981, EdD, 1993; prins. cert., 1983. Cert. elem. and middle sch. tchr., prin., adminstr., reading specialist, tchr. gifted. Elem. tchr. gifted Altoona Area Sch. Dist., 1978-85; tchr. Tuscarora Intermediate 11, McVeytown, Pa., 1984-85; tchr. gifted grades 3-6 Mesa (Ariz.) Pub. Schs., 1985—. Numerous grants. Mem. Assn. for Supervision and Curriculum Devel., Nat. Assn. for Gifted Children, Phi Delta Kappa, Kappa Delta Pi. Home: 944 N Cholla St Chandler AZ 85224-4295 Office: Mesa Pub Schs 549 N Stapley Dr Mesa AZ 85203-7203

COLLENTINE, JOHN THOMAS, arbitrator, public art consultant; b. Madison, Wis., Dec. 14, 1920; s. Arthur Owen and Anna May (Blotz) C.; m. Mary Theresa Lavin, May 21, 1949; children: Sean, Dennis, Brian, Ann, Therese, Patrick, David. BS in econs., U. Wis., 1943, JD, 1948; CLU, Am. Coll., 1968. Bar: Wis. Lawyer Kiel, Wis., 1948-59; city lawyer City of Kiel, 1950-59; staff lawyer Horner Agy., Madison, 1959-65; supv. advanced underwriting Northwestern Mutual Life Ins. Co., Milw., 1965-68; gen. agt. Northwestern Mutual Life Ins. Co., Sacramento, Calif., 1968-73; asst. v.p., dir. of estate & bus. plans div. Pacific Mutual Life Ins. Co., Newport Beach, Calif., 1973-85; pub. art cons. Sacramento, 1986—; arbitrator Am. Arbitrator Assn., Sacramento, 1986—; cons., bd. dirs. Charitable Giving Spec., Inc., Sacramento, 1988—, coord. Save Outdoor Sculpture Project, Sacramento, 1992-95. Bd. dirs., treas. Solar Cookers Internat., Sacramento, 1992—. Lt. (j.g.) USNR, 1943-46, Europe TO. Mem. Internat. Sculpture Ctr., Rotary. Democrat. Roman Catholic. Home: 1431 3rd St Apt 18 Sacramento CA 95814-5305

COLLER, BETH-ANN GRISWOLD, molecular biologist, research scientist; b. Hartford, Conn., Nov. 1, 1959; d. Edward Wells and Dorothy (Allen) Griswold; m. John Coller, July 17, 1982. BS, Norwich U., 1981; diploma med. tech., U. Va., 1982; MS, U. Dayton, 1986; PhD, U. Nebr., 1993. Cert. med. tech. Am. Soc. of Clin. Pathologists. Med. tech. Va. Med. Ctr., Hampton, 1982-84; grad. tchg. asst. U. Dayton, Ohio, 1984-86; grad. rsch. asst. U. Nebr., Omaha, 1986-93; rsch. scientist Hawaii Biotech. Group, Aiea, 1993—. Contbr. articles to profl. jours. Mem. AAAS, Am. Soc. Virology, Sigma Xi (grant-in-aid of rsch. 1992, 93). Home: 98-1781 Kaahumanu St Apt C Aiea HI 96701-1818 Office: Hawaii Biotech Group Inc 99-193 Aiea Heights Dr Aiea HI 96701

COLLETT, FARRELL REUBEN, art educator; b. Bennington, Idaho, Nov. 13, 1907; s. Charles Merrill and Mary Elnora (Munk) C.; m. Martha Howard Collett, July 9, 1940; children: Collett, Michael Farrell, Howard Merrill. AB, Brigham Young U., 1932, MA, 1946; HHD, Weber State Coll., 1977; PhD in Humanities (hon.), Weber State U., 1976. Cert. tchr., Utah. Art tchr. Provo (Utah) High Sch., 1933-38, Ogden (Utah) High Sch., 1938-39; art tchr. Weber State U., Ogden, 1939-76, prof. emeritus, 1976—; art tchr. Brigham Young U., Provo, 1954; prof. art Utah State U., U. Calgary, 1966-67; illustrator Caru Art Svc., N.Y.C., 1955-57; freelance illustrator, graphic designer, N.Y.C., L.A., San Francisco, Chgo. Dir. Utah State Inst. Fine Arts, Salt Lake City, 1962-64. Lt. Comdr. USNR, 1942-46. Recipient Dixon Meml. award, 1973, nat., state and local art awards; Weber State U. art bldg. dedicated as F. R. Collett Art Bldg. & Gallery, 1982, 6th Ann. Gov.'s Art award State of Utah, 1994, Ohio Valley Art League award of Merit, 1994. Mem. Soc. Animal Artists, Color Country Art Assn. Mem. LDS Ch. Home: 1541 Navajo Dr Saint George UT 84770-7730

COLLETT, MERRILL JUDSON, management consultant; b. Winona Lake, Ind., Feb. 20, 1914; s. Charles Alfred and Dora (Jenkins) C. BA, Stanford (Calif.) U., 1934; MPA, Syracuse (N.Y.) U., 1938. Western rep. Pub. Adminstrn. Svcs., Chgo., 1940-43; U.S. Bur. of Budget, 1945-46; pers. dir. Bonneville Power Adminstrn., Portland, Oreg., 1946-50; dir. pers. and mgmt. prodn., mktg. adminstrn. USDA, Washington, 1950-52; dir. wartime organizational planning Office Def. Mobilization, Washington, 1954-58; co-owner Collett and Clapp, P.R., 1958-65; founder, pres. Exec. Mgmt. Svc., Arlington, Va., 1967-82; editor-at-large The Bureaucrat, Washingt, 1981—; cons. for mgmt. Tucson Met. Ministry, 1985-88. Contbr. articles to profl. jours. Moderator Calvary Bapt. Ch., Washington, 1981-83; bd. dirs. Efforts from Ex-Convicts, Washington, 1967-83, Bacone Coll., Muskogee, Okla., 1980-86, 91—, Tucson Met. Ministry, 1989-91. Lt. USNR, 1943-46. Mem. Internat. Pers. Mgmt. Assn. (hon. life, Stockberger award), Ariz. Pers. Mgmt. Assn. (hon. life).

COLLETT, ROBERT LEE, financial company executive; b. Ardmore, Okla., July 1, 1940; s. Pat (Dowell) Conway; m. Sue Walker Healy; 1 child, Catherine April. BA in Math., Rice U., 1962; MA in Econs., Duke U., 1963. Chief actuarial asst. Am. Nat. Ins. Co., Galveston, Tex., 1963-66; actuary Milliman & Robertson, Inc., Phila., 1966-70; prin. Milliman & Robertson, Inc., Houston, 1970-89, pres., 1990; pres., CEO Milliman & Robertson, Inc., Houston and Seattle, 1991-92, Seattle, 1992—. Bd. dirs. Seattle Symphony, 1992—. Fellow Soc. Actuaries (chmn. internat. sect. 1992—); mem. Rainier Club. Episcopalian. Office: Milliman & Robertson Inc 1301 5th Ave Ste 3800 Seattle WA 98101-2603

COLLIER, DAVID, political science educator; b. Chgo., Feb. 17, 1942; s. Donald and Malcolm (Carr) C.; m. Ruth Berins, Mar. 10, 1968; children: Stephen, Jennifer. BA, Harvard U., 1965; MA, U. Chgo., 1967, PhD, 1971. From instr. to assoc. prof. Ind. U., Bloomington, 1970-78; from assoc. prof. to prof. U. Calif., Berkeley, 1978—, chmn. dept. polit. sci., 1990-93; faculty fellow U. Notre Dame, 1986, 87; vis. prof. U. Chgo., 1989; chmn. Ctr. for Latin Am. Studies U. Calif., Berkeley, 1980-83; co-dir., co-founder Stanford-Berkeley Joint Ctr. for Latin Am. Studies, 1981-83. Author: Squatters and Oligarchs: Authoritarian Rule and Policy Change in Peru, 1976; co-author: Shaping the Political Arena, 1991 (Prize, Best Book on Comparative Politics Am. Polit. Scis. Assn. 1993—), editor: The New Authoritariansim in Latin America, 1979. Recipient Guggenheim fellowship, 1988-89; fellow Nat. Fellow Program Hoover Instn., Stanford, 1983-84, Ctr. for Advanced Studies in Behavioral Scis., Stanford, 1994-95; grantee NSF, 1975-77, 80-83. Mem. Latin Am. Studies Assn., Am. Polit. Sci. Assn., Coun. on Fgn. Rels. Office: Univ Calif Dept Polit Sci 210 Barrows Hall Berkeley CA 94702

COLLIER, DAVID HARRIS, rheumatologist; b. Fresno, Calif., June 8, 1951; s. Alan and Beatrice Emily (Raimondo) C.; m. Catherine Joyce Isom, Aug. 18, 1979; 1 child, Alison Elizabeth. BS in Chemistry, Calif. Inst. Technology, Pasadena, 1973; MD, Washington U., St. Louis, 1977. Diplomate Am. Bd. Internal Medicine, Am. Bd. Rheumatology, Diplomate Nat. Bd. Medical Examiners. Intern, resident Barnes Hosp., St. Louis, 1977-80; fellow in rheumatology U. Calif., San Francisco, 1980-83; asst. prof. medicine U. Colo., Denver, 1983-90; assoc. prof. medicine U. Colo., 1990—; chief of rheumatology Denver Gen. Hosp., 1985—; lectr. in field. Contbr. articles to profl. jours., chpts. to books in field. Bd. dirs. Arthritis Found., Rocky Mountain Chpt., Denver, 1994, chmn. advocacy com., 1993—; pres. Rocky Mountain Rheumatism Soc., Denver, 1994. Recipient Sidney J. Schwab Book prize, Washington U., Merck, Sharp and Dohme Sr. Rheumatology Fellow award for Rsch.; grantee Wash. U., 1974, No. Calif. Arthritis Found., 1981, 82, Rocky Mountain Arthritis Found., 1984, 87, U. Colo. Sch. Medicine, 1986, 89. Fellow Am. Coll. Rheumatology. Democrat. Roman Catholic. Office: Denver Gen Hosp 777 Bannock St Denver CO 80204

COLLIER, GAYDELL MAIER, library director, writer, rancher; b. Long Island, N.Y., June 28, 1935; d. Harry and Jean (Gaydell) Maier; m. Roy H. Collier, 1955; 4 children. Student, Middlebury Coll., U. Wyo. Circulation mgr. U. Wyo. Libr., Laramie, 1974; rancher Sundance, Wyo., 1971—; bookshop mgr. Backpocket Ranch Bookshop, Sundance, Wyo., 1977—; dir. Crook County Pub. Libr. System, Wyo., 1985—; mem. Wyo. State Adv. Coun. on Librs., 1971-72; del. Crook County to Wyo. Gov.'s Conf. on Libr. and Info. Svcs., Cheyenne, 1979. Co-author: Basic Horsemanship: English and Western, 1974, 2d edit., 1993, Basic Training for Horses: English and Western, 1979, paperback edit., 1989 (Best Non-fiction Book award 1980), Basic Horse Care, 1986, paperback edit., 1989, German translation, 1992; editor: The Western Horse: Its Types and Training, 5th edit., 1967; book reviewer; contbr. articles to profl. jours. Bd. dirs. Albany County Pub. Libr., 1968-74, Vore Buffalo Jump Found., 1991—. Recipient numerous awards Wyo. Writers Contest, 1981, 82, 83, 90. Mem. Wyo. Libr. Assn. (roundup adv. bd. 1973-75, Outstanding Dedication and Contbns. award 1974, Libr. of Yr. 1990), Western Writers Am., Wyo. Writers, Inc.(pres. 1987-88), Bear Lodge Writers. Office: Crook County Libr PO Box 910 414 Main St Sundance WY 82729

COLLIER, NORMA JEAN, public relations executive, advertising executive; b. Yankton, S.D.; d. Guy L. and Elizabeth J. (Donegan) C. Student George Washington U., L.A. City Coll., U. Md.-Seoul, Korea. Exec. sec. Universal Studios, Universal City, Calif., 1955-58, Leo Burnett Advt. Co., Hollywood, Calif., 1958-60; adminstrv. asst. Survey & Research Co., Seoul, 1960-63; exec. asst. John E. Horton Assocs., Washington, 1963-72; exec. asst. Doremus & Co., Washington, 1972-74; account exec. Doremus/West, L.A., 1974-79, v.p., 1979-85; v.p., acting mgr. Doremus/L.A. Advt., 1985-87; sr. v.p., gen. mgr. Doremus & Co. Adv. and Pub. Rels., 1987-89; pres. Collier Comm., Glendale, Calif., 1989—. Recipient Letter of Appreciation, Republic of Korea, 1963. Mem. L.A. Advt. Club, Women in Communications (dir. chpt.), Town Hall. Republican. Roman Catholic. Club: Hollywood Studio (pres. 1957-58, house council). Home: 11147 Huston St North Hollywood CA 91601-4435 Office: Collier Comms 620 N Brand Blvd Ste 402 Glendale CA 91203-1239

COLLIER, RICHARD BANGS, philosopher, foundation executive; b. Hastings, Nebr., Aug. 12, 1918; s. Nelson Martin and Stella (Butler) C. BA, U. Wash., 1951. Fgn. aid officer GS14, air traffic control supr. gen. & airway comms. engr., civil aviation Am. embassy, Bangkok, Thailand, 1958-63; founder, dir. Pleneurethics Society, Tacoma, 1985—; founder Inst. Ethics & Sci., Tacoma, 1988—, Pleneurethics Inst., 1995—. Carnegie fellow Inst. Pub. Affairs, Grad. Sch., U. Wash., 1950-51. Nat. adv. bd. Am. Security Council. Capt. USAF, 1965-66. Recipient Rep. Presdl. Legion of merit, Medal of Freedom, Rep. Senatorial, 1964. Mem. Assn. Supervision & Curriculum Devel., Soc. Health & Human Values, Senatorial Trust (U.S. Senatorial Medal of Freedom), Royal Inst. Philosophy (Eng.), Nat. Rep. Senatorial Inner Circle (Presdl. commn.), Rep. Nat. Com. (life). Author: Pleneurethic, 20 vols., 1964-93, Pleneurethics: A Philosophical System Uniting Body, Brain and Mind, 2d edit. 1990, contrb. to Journal of Pleneurethics. Home: PO Box 1256 Tacoma WA 98401-1256

COLLIER, RUTH BERINS, political science educator; b. Hartford, Conn., June 20, 1942; d. Maurice and Esther (Meyers) Berins; m. David Collier; children: Stephen, Jennifer. AB, Smith Coll., 1964; MA, U. Chgo., 1966, PhD, 1974. Asst. prof. rsch. Ind. U., Bloomington, 1975-78; asst. to assoc. rsch. polit. scientist U. Calif., Berkeley, 1979-83, lectr., 1983-90, assoc. prof., prof., 1990—. Author: Regimes in Tropical Africa, 1982, The Contradictory Alliance: Labor Politics and the Regime Change in Mexico, 1992 (Hubert Herring award, 1993); co-author: Shaping the Political Arena: The Labor Movement, Critical Junctures, and Regime Dynamics in Latin America, 1991 (Comparative Politics Sect. award Am. Polit. Sci. Assn., 1993). Named fellow Ctr. for Advanced Study in the Behavioral Scis., Stanford, 1994-95.

COLLIN, JONATHAN, physician; b. Flushing, N.Y., July 17, 1949; s. Jerome and Betty (Covo) C.; m. Deborah Margaret Nissen, Nov. 9, 1976; children: Affinity, Samuel. BS, Cornell U., 1971; MD, Albany Med. Coll., 1975. Diplomate Am. Bd. Chelation, Am. Coll. for the Advancement of Physicians. Lic. physician, Wash. Intern USPHS, Staten Island, N.Y., 1975-76; med. officer USPHS, Carville, La., 1976-77; pvt. practice Bellevue, Wash., 1977-81, Port Townsend, Wash., 1981—, Kirkland, Wash., 1985—; editor-in-chief Townsend Letter for Doctors, Townsend, Wash., 1983—. editor: (newsletter) Port Townsend Health Letter, 1981-92. Mem. adv. panel U.S. Congress, 1987-90, NIH, 1992-93. Mem. Am. Preventive Med. Assn. (treas. 1992-94), Am. Holistic Med. Assn., Citizens for Health. Office: Townsend Letter for Doctors 911 Tyler St Port Townsend WA 98368

COLLING, KENNETH FRANK, hospital administrator; b. Watertown, N.Y., Apr. 17, 1945. BA, Cornell U., 1967, M Hosp. Adminstrn., 1969. Adminstrv. res. New Britain (Conn.) Gen. Hosp., 1968; asst. prof. Baylor Army program Healthcare Adminstrn., San Antonio, 1971-73; asst. adminstr. Kaiser Found. Hosp., Fontana, Calif., 1973-75, assoc. adminstr., 1979-81; asst. adminstr. Kaiser Found. Hosp., Panorama City, Calif., 1975-79; adminstr. Kaiser Found. Hosp., San Diego, 1981—. Contbr. articles to profl. jours. Mem. Calif. Hosp. Assn. (exec. com., trustee). Home: 3024 Cadencia St Carlsbad CA 92009-8307 Office: Kaiser Found Hosp 203 Travelodge Dr El Cajon CA 92020-4125

COLLINGS, CELESTE LOUISE (SHORTY VASSALLI), marketing executive, professional artist; b. Highland Park, Ill., Dec. 9, 1948; d. Robert Zane Jr. and Laura (Vasaly) C.; m. John Austin Darden III, July 17, 1971 (div. July 1975); 1 child, Desiree Anne; m. John Cochran Barber, Dec. 13, 1984. BA, U. Ariz., 1970; postgrad., N.Mex. State U., 1975; completed mktg. mgr. seminar, U. Calif., Irvine, 1978; cert. of achievement, Wilson Learning Course, 1983. Art tchr. Devargas Jr. High Sch., Santa Fe, 1971; artist, pvt. tchr. Las Cruces, N.Mex., 1971-75; sales rep. Helpmates Temp. Services, Santa Ana, Calif., 1975-76; sales account mgr. Bristol-Myers Products, N.Y.C., 1976-82; sales mgr. Profl. Med. Products, Greenwood, S.C., 1982-85; mktg. mgr. med. products Paper-Pak Products, La Verne, Calif., 1985-88; owner Multi-Media West, Newport Beach, Calif., 1988—; mgmt. trainee Bristol-Myers, Kansas City, Mo., 1978; sales trainee Profl. Med. Products, Greenwood, 1983, product strategy, 1984, chmn. nat. adv. com., 1983-84; owner and pres. Accent Shoji Screens, Newport Beach, Calif., 1981—. Exhibited in one-woman shows at Nancy Dunn Studio and Gallery, San Clemente, Calif., 1980, The Collectables, San Francisco, 1980, Breeden Gallery, Orange Calif., 1992, Orange County Cen. for Contemporary Art, Santa Ana, Calif., Laguna Beach (Calif.) Festival of the Arts Art-A-Fair, 1981, Ariz. Inter-Scholastic Hon. Exhibit, 1st place award, 1962-66, Glendale Fed. Savs. Art Exhitibition, 1982; numerous others; represented by Patricia Corriea Art Gallery, Santa Monica, Calif., Breeden Gallery, Orange, Calif., L.A. Artcore. Mem. Orange County Performing Arts Ctr., Colona Del Mar, Calif., 1981, Orange County Visual Artists, 1990, Orange County Ctr. for Contemporary Art, 1993; asst. dir. Orange County Satelittle, Womens Caucus for Art, organizer, 1993. Recipient 10 sales awards Bristol-Meyers, 1976-82, Western Zone Sales Rep. award Profl. Med. Products, 1984, Gainers Club award, 1984, named Nat. Sales Rep. of Yr. Profl. Med. Products, 1984. Mem. Humanities Assocs., U. Ariz. Alumni Assn., Kappa Alpha Theta Alumni.

COLLINGS, CHARLES LEROY, supermarket executive; b. Wewoka, Okla., July 11, 1925; s. Roy B. and Dessie L. C.; m. Frances Jane Flake, June 28, 1947; children—Sandra Jean, Dianna Lynn. Student, So. Methodist U., 1943-44, U. Tex., 1945. Sec., contr., dir. Noble Meat Co., Madera, Calif., 1947-54; chief acct. Montgomery Ward & Co., Oakland, Calif., 1954-56; with Raleys, Sacramento, 1956—; sec. Raleys, 1958—, pres., 1970—, CEO, 1993—, also dir. Bd. dirs. Pro Athlete Outreach, Youth for Christ, Kevin Johnson's St. Hope Acad., Dave Dravecky Found. With USNR, 1943-46. Mem. Calif. Grocers Assn. (dir., officer, past chmn.), Calif Retailers Assn. (bd. dir.). Republican. Baptist. Home: 6790 Arabella Way Sacramento CA 95831-2325 Office: Raley's PO Box 15618 Sacramento CA 95852-1618

COLLINS, AMY DENISE, reporter; b. Bakersfield, Calif., Sept. 8, 1968. BA in English, U. Calif., Santa Barbara, 1991. Editor-in-chief Daily Nexus, Santa Barbara, 1989-90; bus. editor Prognosis, Prague, Czech Republic, 1991-92; City Hall reporter The Dispatch, Gilroy, Calif., 1992-94; freelance reporter Prague, Czech Republic and Croatia, 1994-95; copy editor Daily News, L.A., 1995—.

COLLINS, BRUCE ALAN, consultant, mining company executive; b. Greensboro, N.C., Dec. 27, 1944; s. Alan Charles and Beattrice (Irene) Bramble C.; m. Betty Jeanne Estes, Aug. 19, 1966; children: Brian Scott, Bethany Alana. BA, Coll. of Wooster, 1966; MS, Colo. Sch. of Mines, 1971, PhD, 1975. Cert. profl. geologist; registered profl. geologist, Ky. Geologist Ea. Associated Coal Corp., Pitts., 1971-73, Mid-Continent Coal & Coke Co., Carbondale, Colo., 1974-78; dir. prospect devel. Western Associated Coal Corp., Denver, 1978-81; supt. Blue Ribbon Coal Co., Paonia, Colo., 1981; dir. property devel. Western Assoc. Coal Corp., Delta, Colo., 1982-83; geology cons. Paonia, 1983-86; asst. to pres. Mid-Continent Resources, Inc., Carbondale, 1986-92; v.p. Colo. Pacific Resources, Inc., 1991—; mgr. mines Pitkin Iron Corp., 1992-93; natural resource cons., Glenwood Springs, 1986—. Contbr. articles to profl. jours. Contbr. mem. Colo. Railroad Hist. Found., Golden, 1981—. Gulf Oil Co. fellow, 1969-71. Mem. Soc. Mining Engrs., Geol. Soc. Am., Am. Inst. Profl. Geologists, Am. Assn. Petroleum Geologists, Rocky Mountain Assn. Geologists, Nat. Ry. Hist. Soc. Methodist. Office: Colo Pacific Resources Inc PO Box 2342 Glenwood Springs CO 81602-2342

COLLINS, CONCHITA RYAN, writer; b. N.Y.C., Feb. 13, 1931; d. Thomas Aloysius and Maria Luisa (de Heredia) Ryan; m. Eugene J. Collins, Jan. 10, 1958 (dec. Nov. 1988); children: Patrick, Eugenia, Andrew, Maria, Amanda, Kieran, Alicia. BA in English, Coll. St. Elizabeth, Madison, N.J., 1952. Reporter Newark (N.J.) News, 1953-58; editor Louis Berger Internat., East Orange, N.J., 1988-90. Author essays. Broadcaster Sun Sounds, Tucson, Ariz., 1993—. Roman Catholic. Home: 750 S Calle Del Sol Tucson AZ 85710-6633

COLLINS, DANE H., marketing executive; b. Champaign, Ill., Feb. 2, 1961; s. Ronald Milton Collins and Beverly Carolyn (Brown) Patnaude; m. Leigh Ann Paulsen, Oct. 4, 1989. Student, Iowa State U., 1979-82. Acct. exec. Phoenix Pub., Inc., 1982-83, advt. mgr., 1983-85; comml. artist Jackie Awerman Assocs., Phoenix, 1983-88; acct. svcs. supr. The Lutzker Group, Phoenix, 1985-86; advt. dir. Intersouth Communications, Scottscale, Ariz., 1986-87; mktg. dir. Ariz. Bus. & Devel., Phoenix, 1988-89; v.p. S.W. Communications, Phoenix, 1988-90, Balloon Buddies, Inc., Mesa, Ariz., 1988-90; mktg. dir. Orange-Sol, Inc., Gilbert, Ariz., 1989-91, art/mktg., 1993—; cons. Continental Am. Corp., Wichita, Kans., 1990-92, Ariz. Bus. & Devel., Phoenix, 1990-91. Illustrator: (books) Power, Influence, Sabotage: The Corporate Survivor's Coloring Book & Primer, 1986, Good Morning Mr. President, 1988; patentee decorative message display. Vol. DeNovo, Phoenix, 1984, Cystic Fibrosis Found., Scottsdale, 1985, Aid to Women's Ctr., Phoenix, 1987, Dayspring U.M.C. Missions for Homeless, Tempe, Ariz., 1990-93. Mem. Phoenix Soc. Communicating Arts. Republican. Methodist. Home: 2650 E South Fork Dr Phoenix AZ 85048-8976

COLLINS, DAVID MICHAEL, foundation administrator; b. Long Beach, Calif., July 3, 1939; s. Raymond and Margaret (Smith) C.; m. Ann Deasy, Apr. 20, 1963 (div. Apr. 1991); children: Laura, Michelle, Michael, Stephan, Gary, Kevin, Kenneth, Brian. Student, City Coll. of San Francisco. Pres., co-founder Kevin Collins Found. for Missing Children, San Francisco, 1984—; asst. families of stranger-abducted children, police and media; speaker women's and men's clubs, U.S.; cons. Calif. Coalition of Missing Children's Groups, 1987, Calif. Dept. Justice, 1985-94; leader of victim workshops. Mem. Nat. Crises Response Team for Kidnapped Victims, 1984, Legis. Com. Calif. State, 1984, Sen. Presleys Task Force, 1987. Recipient Merit award Nat. Crises Response Team for Kidnapped Victims, 1987, Salute award U.S. Congress, 1986, Cert. of Appreciation Nat. Victim Ctr., Houston, 1987, numerous proclamations, citations and resolutions from No. Calif. area, 1984—. Home and Office: PO Box 590473 San Francisco CA 94159-0473

COLLINS, DENNIS ARTHUR, foundation executive; b. Yakima, Wash., June 9, 1940; s. Martin Douglas and Louise Constance (Caccia) C.; m. Mary Veronica Paul, June 11, 1966; children: Jenifer Ann, Lindsey Kathleen. BA, Stanford U., 1962, MA, 1963; LHD, Mills Coll., 1994. Assoc. dean admissions Occidental Coll., Los Angeles, 1964-66, dean admissions, 1966-68, dean of students, 1968-70; headmaster Emma Willard Sch., Troy, N.Y., 1970-74; founding headmaster San Francisco U. High Sch., 1974-86; pres. James Irvine Found., San Francisco, 1986—; trustee Coll. Bd., N.Y.C., 1981-85, Ind. Ednl. Svcs., Princeton, N.J., 1981-85, Calif. Assn. Ind. Schs., L.A., 1982-86, Branson Sch., 1987-89, Aspen Inst. Nonprofit Sector rsch. Fund, 1992—; chmn. bd. So. Calif. Assn. Philanthropy, L.A., 1989-91, No. Calif. Grantmakers, 1987-90; dir. Rebuild L.A., 1992-93. Trustee Ind. Sector, Washington, 1987—, San Francisco Exploratorium, 1984-86, Marin Country Day Sch., Corte Madera, Calif., 1978-84, Cathedral Sch. for Boys, San Francisco, 1976-82, Am. Farmland Trust, Washington, 1992—; bd. dirs., vice chmn. Children's Hosp. Found., San Francisco, 1984-86; chmn. bd. dirs. Coun. for Cmty. Based Devel., Washington, 1989-92. Mem. Council on Founds. Democrat. Episcopalian. Clubs: World Trade, University; California (L.A.). Home: 432 Golden Gate Ave Belvedere Tiburon CA 94920-2447 Office: The James Irvine Found Spear Tower One Market St Ste 1715 San Francisco CA 94105-1019

COLLINS, DICK (RKC), artist; b. South Pittsburg, Tenn., Feb. 16, 1930; s. William Columbus and Flora James (Lee) C.; divorced; children: Michael Charles, Deborah Marie. BA, U. Tenn., Chattanooga, 1953; MFA, Calif. State U., Fullerton, 1993. Cert. secondary tchr., Tenn. Tech. editor/writer Bechtel Power Co., Norwalk, Calif., 1972-75, Parsons Engring., Pasadena, Calif., 1975-86; instr. life drawing Calif. State U., Fullerton, 1992-93; figurative artist, 1993—. Paintings include California Dreaming, No More Closets, Just As I Am; exhibited in group shows at Rose City Gallery, Pasadena, 1993-94, Da Gallery, Pomona, Calif., 1994, 95, Orlando Gallery, Sherman Oaks, Calif., 1994, 95. Staff sgt. USAF, 1946-50, Japan. Mem. Omicron Delta Kappa. Home: 18133 Northam St La Puente CA 91744

COLLINS, DOROTHY SMITH, librarian; b. Nacogdoches, Tex., July 25, 1934; d. A.V. and Betty (Yarborough) Smith; m. Julius A. Collins, Aug. 14, 1954 (dec.). BA in Sociology, Prairie View (Tex.) A&M U.; MA in Elem. Edn., Tex. So. U.; MLS, U. So. Calif. Tchr. U.S. Dependant Sch., Schwabisch, Fed. Republic Germany; tchr., librarian Cleve. Pub. Schs.; tchr. Westside Elem. Sch. Dist., Lancaster, Calif.; librarian Antelope Valley/Palmdale High Sch. Dist., Lancaster; coordinator research and reference ctr. San Diego County Office Edn. Chmn. edn. and speakers bur. Save Our Heritage Orgn., 1986-88; pres., bd. dirs. San Diego chpt. United Scleroderma Found., 1983-86, 93-94, v.p. 1995—; pres. San Diego Pres. Coun., 1988-94, alumni Leadership Edn. Awareness Devel., 1986—; mem. health contract Team #13 San Diego United Way; Bus. Vol. for the Arts, 1994—. Mem. Am. Ednl. Research Assn., Delta Kappa Gamma, Delta Sigma Theta. Home: 6267 Rockhurst Dr San Diego CA 92120-4607 Office: San Diego County Office Edn 6401 Linda Vista Rd San Diego CA 92111-7319

COLLINS, FUJI, mental health professional; b. Tokyo, Nov. 3, 1954; s. Boyd Leslie and Kimiko (Terayama) C.; 1 child, Lacey Nichole. BS, Ariz. State U., 1977; MS, Ea. Wash. U., 1989; MA, The Fielding Inst., 1993, PhD, 1994. Commd. 2d lt. U.S. Army, 1978, advanced through grades to maj., 1989, lt. platoon leader, adminstrv. officer, 1978-79; lt. bat. adjutant 509th Airborne Bat. Combat Team, 1977-80; capt., air def. fire coordination officer U.S. Army, 1981-83, capt. battery comdr., 1983-85, capt., 1985-86; clin. therapist Wash. State Patrol, 1986—; registered clin. therapist, coord. Wash. State Patrol Critical Incident/Peer Support Team, Wash. State Hostage Negotiator; mem. Thurston/Mason County Critical Incident Stress Debriefing Team. Vol. Thurston/Mason County Crisis Clinic; mem. steering com. Thurston/Mason County Critical Incident Team. Mem. ACA, APA, Wash. State Psychol. Assn., Asian Am. Psychol. Assn., Soc. for Psychol. Study of Ethnic Minority Issues, Am. Critical Incident Stress Found., Wash. State Hostage Negotiation Assn., Assn. Police Planning and Rsch. Officers. Home: 2006 8th Ct SW Olympia WA 98502-5132 Office: Wash State Patrol Rm G-130 Gen Adminstrn Bldg Olympia WA 98504

COLLINS, GEORGE TIMOTHY, computer software consultant; b. Connersville, Ind., Aug. 21, 1943; s. Robert Emerson and Oma (Richie) C.; m. Martha Elizabeth Holt, Apr. 30, 1966; children: Kirsten Stephanie, Eowyn Erika. BA in Math., Ind. U., 1966; MS in Computer Sci., Rensselaer Poly. Inst., 1971. Engr. program analyst Sikorsky Aircraft, Stratford, Conn., 1966-70; research mathematician Peter Eckrich, Ft. Wayne, Ind., 1970-75; sr. systems analyst Pyrotek Data Service, Ft. Walton Beach, Fla., 1975-77; sr. aerosystems engr. Gen. Dynamics, Ft. Worth, 1977-79; sr. specialist Electronic Data Systems, Las Vegas, Nev., 1979-81; sr. assoc. CACI Fed., San Diego, 1981-82; prin., gen. mgr. Structured Software Systems, Escondido, Calif., 1982-88; sr. software engr. Sci. Applications Internat. Corp., San Diego, 1988-94; pvt. practice cons. Escondido, 1994—; cons. Hi-Shear Corp., Los Angeles, 1973-75. Developer (computer model and data base) Aircraft Stores Interface, 1975, (computer model) TAC Disrupter, 1981; co-developer (computer model) Tactical Air Def., Battle Model, 1978, Tactical Air and Land Ops., 1980; prime contbr. (computer data collection and analysis sys.) Mobile Sea Range, 1988-90; contbr. (computer comm. sys.) Lightweight Deployable Comms., 1990, Joint Advanced Spl. Ops. Radio Sys., 1992, Orbital Scis. Corp.'s Maj. Constituent Analyzer Environ. Control/Life Scis. Sys. for Internat. Space Station Alpha (team received NASA Manned Fligh-Awarness award). Bd. dirs. Family and Children's Service, Ft. Wayne, 1974. Mem. N.Y. Acad. Scis., North County Chess Club. Unitarian. Home: 121 W 8th Ave Escondido CA 92025-5001

COLLINS, HAROLD JOHN, III, military career officer; b. New Orleans, Jan. 21, 1955; s. Harold John Jr. and Bennie Jo (Wallace) C.; m. Judith Marie Mengwasser, Jan. 29, 1983. BS in Psychology, La. State U., 1980; MBA, U. West Fla., 1992. Commd. ensign USN, 1981, advanced through grades to lt. cmdr., 1992; flight tng. student USN, Virginia Beach, Va., 1981-82, 83-84; F-14 naval flight officer, avionics armament divsn. officer Fighter Squadron 41, Virginia Beach, Va., 1985-88; rescue swimmer sch. model mgr., human resources officer Naval Aviation Schs. Command, Pensacola, Fla., 1988-90; tchr. Naval Aviation Schs. Command, Pensacola, 1988-92; flight tng. student fighter squadron 124 USN Naval Air Sta. Miramar, San Diego, Calif., 1992-93; F-14 naval flight officer, safety officer Fighter Squadron 111, San Diego, 1993—; instr. CPR and first aid ARC, Pensacola, 1988-92. Instr. CPR and first aid ARC, Pensacola, 1988-92. Mem. U.S. Naval Inst. Democrat. Roman Catholic. Home: PO Box 625 Morgan City LA 70381-0625 Office: Fighter Squadron 111 Unit 25429 FPO AP San Diego CA 96601-6118

COLLINS, JOAN EILEEN, computer graphics specialist; b. Seattle, Mar. 13, 1958; d. Thomas Arthur Collins and Sylvia Geneveve Monsebroten Collins Krumbholz. BA in Fine Art, Wash. State U., 1980, BS, 1981; postgrad., UCLA, 1981-83. Promoter Concerts West, Seattle, 1980-81; dir. programming and graphics Laser Media, L.A., 1981-85; sales mgr. Robert Abel & Assocs., Hollywood, Calif., 1985-87; prodr. Sidley Wright & Assocs., Hollywood, 1989-91; pres. Joan Collins & Assocs., Santa Monica, Calif., 1987—; computer graphics producer Lightspan Entertainment, Van Nuys, Calif., 1994; post-prodn. supr. Judge Dredd Mass. Ilussion, Lenox, 1995; lectr. on computer graphics, 1984—; prodr./cons., 1984—; bd. dirs. Events Internat., Inc., Santa Monica, Calif., On the Threshold, Inc., Hollywood; promoter International Visual Music Festival, UCLA, 1982, Concerts West and Seattle Music Hall, 1980-82, ASWSU Performing Arts, 1976-80; AV agt. Beyond the Threshold, 1989, Hollywood's Salute to MGM, 1987, 1st Internat. Visual Music Festival, 1982. Computer animator Omni Max film: The Magic Egg, 1984, Peacock, 1987; contbr. articles to profl. jours.; prodr. laser animations Stone Mountain Park, Disney World's EPCOT Ctr. Prodr. and stage mgr. Easter Sunrise Svc., Hollywood Bowl, 1987—; mem. Telecomm. Infrastructure Coalition, Calif., 1994—. Recipient Cindy award for outstanding achievement First Video Wall, Hollywood Indsl., 1986, Award of Appreciation, Soc. Women Engrs. So. Calif., 1989; Art Club scholar, 1976. Mem. ACM/SIGGRAPH (Award of Appreciation 1987, 89, 94, chmn. L.A. chpt. 1985-87, 93-94, chair electronic theatre 1987, 95, AV chair 1989, steering com. 1988, exec. bd. L.A. chpt. 1981—, chair 1985-87, 94—), IEEE, Nat. Computer Graphics Assn.

COLLINS, MATTHEW, poet; b. New Orleans, Aug. 21, 1944; s. Warren Ransom and Hattie (Aupied) C.; m. Mallary Ann Moran, May 13, 1977. BA in English, La. State U., New Orleans, 1973. Deck hand to pilot Ctrl. Gulf Lines, New Orleans, 1973-88; pres., adminstr. Collins & Assocs., Lacombe, La., 1988-93; poet Idaho Falls, Idaho, 1993—. Author: (books of poetry) When Metaphors Collide, 1993, Fission or Fusion, 1993, Frayed Collars, 1994, Wreaking Havoc, 1994, Cypress Knees, 1994, The Harvester, 1995. Bd. dirs. Bayou Lacombe C. of C., 1986-91. Served with USN, 1961-67. Home: PO Box 3731 Idaho Falls ID 83403-3731

COLLINS, MICHAEL PAUL, secondary school educator, earth science educator, consultant; b. Chula Vista, Calif., Jan. 2, 1959; s. William Henry and Linda Lee (Capron) C.; m. Helen Marie Wassmann, July 23, 1994; 1 child, P. Collins; children from a previous marriage: Christopher M., Matthew R. A in Gen. Studies, Clatsop Community Coll., Astoria, Oreg., 1983; BS in Sci. Edn., Oreg. State U., 1987, BS in Geology, 1987; MS, U. Alaska. Cert. tchr., Wash., Alaska. Emergency med. technician II, fireman Sitka (Alaska) Fire Dept., 1978-80; paramedic Medix Ambulance, Astoria, 1980-83; cartographer technician U.S. Geol. Survey, Grants Pass, Oreg., 1985; earth sci. tchr. Lake Oswego (Oreg.) Sch. Dist., 1987-88; sci. tchr. Gladstone (Oreg.) Sch. Dist., 1988-90; radon technician Radon Detection Systems, Portland, Oreg., 1988-90; mktg. dir. Evergreen Helicopters of Alaska, Inc., Anchorage, 1990-91; sci./math tchr. Anchorage Sch. Dist., 1991—; instr. geology Alaska Jr. Coll., Anchorage, 1992-93; cons. earth sci. edn. Project ESTEEM, ctr. astrophysics Harvard U., Cambridge, Mass., 1992—; field technician Water Quality Divsn., City of Anchorage, 1993; cons. Am. Meteorol. Assn., atmospheric ednl. resource agt. Project Atmosphere, 1994—, Project MicroObservatory Ctr. for Astrophysics, Harvard U., 1995; co-coord. Alaska State H.S. Sci. Olympics, 1994. Co-author: Merrill Earth Science Lab Activities, 1989. With USCG, 1977-81. Mem. NEA, Am. Assn. Petroleum Geologists, Geol. Soc. Am., Nat. Sci. Tchr. Assn., Am. Geol. Inst., Am. Meteorol. Soc., Alaska Geol. Soc. Inc., Nat. Assn. Geology Tchrs. Home: 9501 Morningside Loop Apt 4 Anchorage AK 99515-2187 Office: West Anchorage HS 1700 Hillcrest Dr Anchorage AK 99517-1347

COLLINS, MICHAEL SEAN, obstetrician-gynecologist; b. Yankton, S.D., Sept. 8, 1951; s. Edward Daniel and Joyce (Slatky) C.; m. Judy Furman, Sept. 20, 1975; children: Lauren, Sean, Carolyn. BS, Davidson Coll., 1973; MD, Med. U. S.C., 1977. Diplomate Am. Bd. Ob-Gyn. Chief resident in ob-gyn Med. U. S.C., Charleston, 1980-81; instr. in ob-gyn U. Oreg. Health Scis. Ctr., Portland, 1981—; chmn. dept. ob-gyn Good Samaritan Hosp., Portland, 1983-85; cons. Prepared Childbirth Assn., Portland, 1981—, Triplet Connection, L.A., 1985—. Fellow Am. Coll. Ob-Gyn.; mem. AMA, Oreg. Med. Assn., Oreg. Ob-Gyn. Soc., Pacific Coast Ob-Gyn. Soc., Pacific N.W. Ob-Gyn. Soc., Am. Fertility Soc., Porsche Club Am., Oreg. Ob-Gyn. Soc. (vice-chmn. 1991-94, chmn. 1995—), Am. Coll. Ob-Gyn. (adv. coun. 1991—, chmn. Oreg. sect.), Alpha Omega Alpha. Republican. Roman Catholic. Home: 716 NW Rapidan Ter Portland OR 97210-3129 Office: Portland Ob-Gyn Assocs 1130 NW 22nd Ave Ste 120 Portland OR 97210-2934

COLLINS, WILLIAM LEROY, telecommunications engineer; b. Laurel, Miss., June 17, 1942; s. Henry L. and Christene E. (Finnegan) C. Student, La Salle U., 1969; BS in Computer Sci., U. Beverly Hills, 1984. Sr. computer operator Dept. Pub. Safety, Phoenix, 1975-78, data communications specialist, 1978-79, supr. computer ops., 1981-82; mgr. network control Valley Nat. Bank, Phoenix, 1979-81; mgr. data communications Ariz. Lottery, Phoenix, 1982-85; mgr. telecommunications Calif. Lottery, Sacramento, 1985—; Mem. Telecomm. Study Mission to Russia, Oct. 1991. Contbr. to profl. publs. Served as sgt. USAF, 1964-68. Mem. IEEE, Nat. Sys. Programmers Assn., Centrex Users Group, DMS Centrex User Group, Accunet Digital Svcs. User Group, Telecomms. Assn. (v.p. edn. Sacramento Valley chpt. 1990-94, pres. 1995), Telecomm. Assn. (chmn. corp. edn. com. 1994-95), SynOptics User Group, Timeplex User Group, Assn. Data Comm. Users, Soc. Mfg. Engrs., Data Processing Mgmt. Assn., Am. Mgmt. Assn., Assn. Computing Machinery, K.C. Roman Catholic. Home: 116 Valley Oak Dr Roseville CA 95678-4378 Office: Calif State Lottery 600 N 10th St Sacramento CA 95814-0393

COLLMER, RUSSELL CRAVENER, data processing executive, educator; b. Guatemala, Jan. 2, 1924; s. G. Russell and Constance (Cravener) C.; B.S., U. N.M., 1951; postgrad. Calif. Inst. Tech., 1943-44; M.S., State U. Iowa, 1955; m. Ruth Hannah Adams, Mar. 4, 1950; 1 son, Reed Alan. Staff mem. Mass. Inst. Tech., Lincoln Lab., Lexington, 1955-57; mgr. systems modeling, computer dept. Gen. Electric, Phoenix, 1957-59; mgr. ARCAS Thompson Ramo Wooldridge, Inc., Canoga Park, Cal., 1959-62; assoc. mgr. tech. dir. CCIS-70 Bunker-Ramo Corp., 1962-64; sr. assoc. Planning Rsch. Corp., Los Angeles, 1964-65; pres. R. Collmer Assocs., Benson, Ariz., 1965—; pres. Benson Econ. Enterprises Corp., 1968-69. Lectr. computer scis. Pima Community Coll., Tucson, 1970—. Served with USAAC, 1942-46, to capt. USAF, 1951-53. Mem. IEEE, Am. Meteorol. Soc., Assn. for Computing Machinery, Phi Delta Theta, Kappa Mu Epsilon. Republican. Baptist. Office: R Collmer Assocs PO Box 864 Benson AZ 85602-0864

COLMAN, RONALD WILLIAM, computer science educator; b. L.A., Sept. 13, 1930; s. William Maynard Colman and Edna Eliza (Halford) Smith. BA in Math., UCLA, 1957; PhD in Computer Sci., U. Calif., Irvine, 1976. Electronics tech. Lockheed Aircraft Corp., Burbank, Calif., 1952-53; staff specialist Western Electric Co., N.Y.C., 1957-58; assoc. math. Burroughs Corp., Pasadena, Calif., 1958-60; sr. computer analyst Beckman Instruments, Inc., Fullerton, Calif., 1960-62; mgr. L.A. dist. Digital Equipment Corp., L.A., 1962-64; chmn. computer sci. Calif. State U., Fullerton, 1964-80; prof. computer sci. Calif. State U., Northridge, 1980-89; ptnr. Windward Ventures, Venice, Calif.; chmn. session on heuristic search Internat. Joint Conf. on Artificial Intelligence, Stanford, 1973; chmn. nat. symposium on computer sci. edn. Assn. Computing Machinery, Anaheim, Calif., 1976; chmn. registration Nat. Computer Conf., Anaheim, 1978, 80. With USN, 1948-52. Home: 770 W 26th St Apt C San Pedro CA 90731-6358

COLN, WILLIAM ALEXANDER, III, pilot; b. Los Angeles, Mar. 20, 1942; s. William Alexander and Aileen Henrietta (Shimfessel) C.; m. Lora Louise Getchel, Nov. 15, 1969 (div. July 1979); 1 child, Caryn Louise. BA in Geography, UCLA, 1966. Cert. airline transport pilot, flight engr. Commd. USN, Pensacola, Fla., 1966; pilot, officer USN, Fighter Squadron 102, 1969-71, Port Mugu, Calif., 1975-77; pilot, officer USNR, Port Mugu, Calif., 1971-75, advanced through grades to lt. comdr., 1978; ret. USNR, 1984; airline pilot Delta Airlines, Inc. (formerly Western Airlines Inc.), Los Angeles, 1972—. Recipient Nat. Def. medal USN, 1966. Mem. Nat. Aero. Assn., Airline Pilots Assn., Aircraft Owners and Pilots Assn., UCLA Alumni Assn., Am. Bonanza Soc., Internat. Platform Assn. Democrat. Club: Santa Barbara (Calif.) Athletic. Home: 519 W Quinto St Santa Barbara CA 93105-4829 Office: Delta Air Lines Inc LA Internat Airport Los Angeles CA 90009

COLSON, BRET STERLING, public information officer; b. Oakland, Calif., Aug. 9, 1959; s. Searle Garth and Alfreda Mae (Carr) C.; m. Teresa Colson, June 20, 1982. AA, Gaston C.C., Dallas, N.C., 1980; BA in Comms., U. N.C., 1982. Media mgr. West Pac Corp., Orange, Calif., 1982-84; asst. mktg. svcs mgr. Weiser Lock, Huntington Beach, Calif., 1985-87; publicist parks, recreation and cmty. svcs. dept. Anaheim, Calif., 1988-89; pub. info. specialist City Mgrs. Office City of Anaheim, 1989-91, pub. info. mgr., 1991—; prodn. intern WUAG-FM, Greensboro, N.C., 1980, WFMV-TV, Greensboro, 1981; correspondent Baker Comms., Newport Beach, Calif., 1985-89; publishing cons. Big Bear Today Mag., Big Bear, Calif., 1989—. Recipient 1st & 2d pla. spl. pubs. divsn. Orange County Fair Best Reporters Contest, 1986, 1st pl. newsletter divsn., 1990, award of excellence pub. comms. Calif. Soc. of Mcpl. Fin. Officers, 1994. em. Nat. Broadcasters Hall of Fame (relccation com.), Pub. Rels. Soc. Am., Calif. Assn. Pub. Info. Officers (1st pl. emp. newsletter 1989, 90), City-County Comms. and Mktg. Assn., Am. Mensa. Home: 10274 La Hacienda Ave Apt G 2 Fountain Vly CA 92708-3646 Office: City of Anaheim City Mgrs Office 200 S Anaheim Blvd Anaheim CA 92805-3820

COLSON, ELIZABETH FLORENCE, anthropologist; b. Hewitt, Minn., June 15, 1917; d. Louis H. and Metta (Damon) C. BA, U. Minn., 1938, MA, 1940; MA, Radcliffe Coll., 1941, PhD, 1945; PhD (hon.), Brown U., 1978, D of Sociology, 1979; D.Sc., U. Rochester, 1985, U. Zambia, 1992. Asst. social sci. analyst War Relocation Authority, 1942-43; research asst. Harvard, 1944-45; research officer Rhodes-Livingstone Inst., 1946-47, dir., 1948-51; sr. lectr. Manchester U., 1951-53; assoc. prof. Goucher Coll., 1954-55; research assoc., assoc. prof. African Research Program, Boston U., 1955-59, part-time, 1959-63; prof. anthropology Brandeis U., 1959-63; prof. anthropology U. Calif.-Berkeley, 1964-84, prof. emeritus, 1984—; vis. prof. U. Zambia, 1987; Lewis Henry Morgan lectr. U. Rochester, 1973; vis. rsch. assoc. Refugee Studies Program Queen Elizabeth House, Oxford, 1988-89. Author: The Makah, 1953, Marriage and the Family Among The Plateau Tonga, 1958, Social Organization of the Gwembe Tonga, 1960, The Plateau Tonga, 1962, The Social Consequences of Resettlement, 1971, Tradition and Contract, 1974, A History of Nampeyo, 1992; jr. author Secondary Education and the Formation of an Elite, 1980, Voluntary Efforts in Decentralized Management, 1983, sr. author For Prayer and Profit, 1988; sr. editor: Seven Tribes of British Central Africa, 1951; jr. editor People in Upheaval, 1987. AAUW travelling fellow, 1941-42, fellow Ctr. Advanced Study Behavioral Scis., 1967-68, Fairchild fellow Calif. Inst. Tech., 1975-76. Fellow Am. Anthrop. Assn., Brit. Assn. Social Anthropologists, Royal Anthrop. Inst. (hon.); mem. Nat. Acad. Sci., Am. Acad. Arts and Scis., Am. Assn. African Studies (Disting. Africanist award 1988), Soc. Applied Anthropology, Soc. Woman Geographers, Phi Beta Kappa. Office: U Calif Dept Anthropology Berkeley CA 94720

COLTHARP, HUGH NELSON, investor; b. Salt Lake City, May 3, 1952; s. Edward Hugh and Myrtle (Nelson) C. Student, U. Utah, 1970-74. Mgr. Silica & Gypsum Co., Salt Lake City, Helena, Mont., 1970-81; broker E.H. Coltharp & Co., Salt Lake City, 1970-74, Potter Investment Co., Salt Lake City, 1974—; cons. Nat. Assn. Securities Dealers, 1990-91. Com. mem. Concour's de Elegrance, Salt Lake City, 1988-94; revue com. Bonneville Salt Flats Study, U.S. Govt., 1990-94. Mem. Utah Salt Flats Racing Assn. (treas. 1979-91), Salt Lake Stock Exch. (sec.-treas. 1974-89). Republican. Home and Office: 1478 Roosevelt Ave Salt Lake City UT 84105-2616

COLTON, ROY CHARLES, management consultant; b. Phila., Feb. 26, 1941; s. Nathan Hale and Ruth Janis (Baylinson) C.; B.A., Knox Coll., 1962; M.Ed., Temple U., 1963. With Sch. Dist. of Phila., 1963-64; systems analyst Wilmington Trust Co., 1967-69; exec. recruiter Atwood Consultants Inc., Phila., 1969-71; pres. Colton Bernard Inc., San Francisco, 1971—; occasional lectr. Fashion Inst. Tech., Phila. Coll. Textiles and Scis. Served with AUS, 1964-66. Mem. San Francisco Fashion Industries, San Francisco C. of C., Calif. Exec. Recruiter Assn., Nat. Assn. Exec. Recruiters, Am. Apparel Mfrs. Assn., Am. Arbitration Assn. (panel arbitrators). Office: Colton Bernard Inc 870 Market St Ste 822 San Francisco CA 94102-2903

COLTON, STANLEY, landscape architecture company executive; b. 1936. With Norman Wyatte Co., L.A., 1957-63; v.p. Environ. Industries, Inc., Calabasas, Calif., 1963—; pres. We. Landscape Constrn., Calabasas. Office: Western Landscape Cnstr 24121 Ventura Blvd Calabasas CA 91302-1449*

COLUCCI, CHUCK ROGER, management consultant; b. Chgo., Dec. 17, 1955; s. Ralph Michael and Mary Ann (Dolfi) C. BA with honors, Calif. State U., 1980; MBA, U. Calif., Irvine, 1983. Sr. analyst Ford Motor Co., Newport Beach, Calif., 1984-89; internal cons. County of Orange, Santa Ana, Calif., 1990-91; mgmt. cons. John Goodman & Assocs., Las Vegas, 1991-94; pres. IPA, Costa Mesa, Calif., 1994—. Editor: (with others) Programmed Business Math, 1986. Bank of Am. scholar, 1979. Mem. Managed Care Cons. Assn. (adv. bd. 1994—), U. Calif. Irvine Grad. Sch. Mgmt. Alumni Assn. (pres. 1990-91), Phi Kappa Phi.

COLVIN, DONALD ANDREW, marketing consultant; b. Toronto, Ont., Can., Apr. 15, 1915; s. Norman Buchanan and Margaret Jean (Bone) C.; m. Ruth McMurtrie, June 17, 1950. BA in Econs., Princeton U., 1936. Dir. advt. Ametek Corp., N.Y.C., 1936-55; account exec. Ketchum Communications, Pitts., 1956-60; sr. v.p., gen. mgr. Ketchum Communications, Houston, 1960-78; pres. Don Colvin & Assocs., Houston, 1978-81, Sun City West, Ariz., 1981—. Bd. dirs. Houston Grand Opera Assn., 1969-71, Sun Cities Art Mus., 1991—; trustee Sun Cities Symphony Assn., 1986—. Vol. ambulance driver Am. Field Svc., 1943-45, NATOUSA, ETO. Mem. Briarwood Country Club. Home and Office: 12635 W Paintbrush Dr Sun City West AZ 85375-2525

COLVIN, DORISJEAN MITTMANN, artist, educator; b. Oak Park, Ill., Apr. 23, 1927; d. Louis John Kramer and Jeanette Anna (Boss) Edge; m. Clyde S. Colvin, June 23, 1945 (div. Mar. 1972); children: Brian Lee, Michael Lynn, Colleen Sue; m. Frederick Palmer (div.). Five year comml. art degree, Minn. Art Sch., 1964; student, Sergei Bongart Workshop, Bellevue, Wash. Founder, dir. Redmond (Wash.) Sch. Fine Art (now Redmond Sch. Fine Art Publs., Inc.), 1962-88; art tchr. Iwakuni, Japan, 1965-66, Shoreline C.C., Seattle, 1968-88; founder, pres. N.W. Artist Soc., Redmond, 1968-75, Minature Art Guild, Federal Way, Wash., 1972-74, N.W. Pastel Soc., Redmond, 1979-84. Author: (tech. book) A Creative Pastel Color Guide, 1994; exhibited in shows at Pastel Soc. Am., Salmagundi, N.Y.C., Iwakuni, numerous shows in Wash. and Oreg. Artist Soroptimists of Federal Way, Wash., 1987-94. Recipient 1st pl. N.W. Pastel Soc., Redmond, 1981, 1st pl. Creative Art Ctr., Kirkland, Wash., 1985, others. Mem. Nat. League Am. Pen Women, Pastel Soc. Am., Skagit Art Assn. Lutheran. Home: PO Box 954 Marysville WA 98270

COLVIS, JOHN PARIS, aerospace engineer, mathematician, scientist; b. St. Louis, June 30, 1946; s. Louis Jack and Jacqueline Betty (Beers) C.; m. Nancy Ellen Fritz, Mar. 15, 1969 (div. Sept. 1974); 1 child, Michael Scott; m. Barbara Carol Davis, Sept. 3, 1976; 1 child, Rebecca Jo; stepchildren: Bruce William John Zimmerly, Belinda Jo Zimmerly Little. Student, Meramec Community Coll., St. Louis, 1964-65, U. Mo., 1966, 72-75, Palomar Coll., San Marcos, Calif., 1968, U. Mo., Rolla, 1968-69; BS in Math., Washington U., 1977. Assoc. system safety engr. McDonnell Douglas Astronautics Co., St. Louis, 1978-81; sr. system safety engr. Martin Marietta Astronautics Group-Strategic Systems Co., Denver, 1981-87; sr. engr. Martin Marietta Astronautics Group-Space Launch Systems Co., Denver, 1987-95, Lockheed Martin Astronautics Co.-Space Launch Sys., Denver, 1995—; researcher in field. Precinct del., precinct committeeman, congl. dist. del., state del. Rep. Party. Lance cpl. USMC, 1966-68, Vietnam. Mem. VFW (post 4171), Colo. Home Educators' Assn. (pres. 1989), Khe Sahn Vet Incorp., Colo. Christian Coalition (state bd. dirs.). Evangelical. Home: 4978 S Hoyt St Littleton CO 80123-1988 Office: Lockheed Martin Astron Co SLS PO Box 179 Denver CO 80201-0179

COLWELL, JAMES LEE, humanities educator; b. Brush, Colo., Aug. 31, 1926; s. Francis Joseph and Alice (Bleasdale) C.; BA, U. Denver, 1949; MA, U. No. Colo., 1951; cert. Sorbonne, Paris, 1956; diploma U. Heidelberg (Ger.), 1957; A.M. (Univ. fellow), Yale U., 1959, PhD (Hale-Kilborn fellow), 1961; m. Claudia Alsleben, Dec. 27, 1957; children—John Francis, Alice Anne. Tchr. high sch., Snyder and Sterling, Colo., 1948-52; civilian edn. adviser U.S. Air Force, Japan, 1952-56; assoc. dir. Yale Fgn. Student Inst., summers 1959-60; asst. dir. European div. U. Md., Heidelberg, 1961-65; dir. Office Internat. Edn., assoc. prof. Am. lit. U. Colo., Boulder, 1965-72; prof. Am. studies, chmn. lit. U. Tex. Permian Basin, Odessa, 1977-82, dean Coll. Arts and Edn., 1972-77, 82-84, K.C. Dunagan prof. humanities, 1984-87, prof. emeritus, 1988—. Mem. nat. adv. council Inst. Internat. Edn., 1969-75. Vice pres. Ector County chpt. ARC, 1974-76; mem. Ector County Hist. Commn., 1973-75. Served with USAAF, 1945; brig. gen. USAF Res. Ret. Mem. AAUP, Am. Studies Assn., Western Social Sci. Assn. (life; pres. 1974-75), MLA, NEA (life), Orgn. Am. Historians (life), South Central MLA, Permian Basin Hist. Soc. (life; pres. 1980-81), Air Force Assn. (life), Air Force Hist. Found. (life), Res. Officers Assn. (life), Ret. Officers Assn. (life), Phi Beta Kappa. Unitarian-Universalist. Contbr. articles to learned jours. Home: 4675 Gordon Dr Boulder CO 80303-6747

COLWELL, STEPHEN D., travel industry executive, lawyer; b. San Francisco, Sept. 16, 1959; s. James M. and Mary Anna (Culleton) C.; m. Ann R. Shulman, May 5, 1991. AB in Pub. and Internat. Affairs, Princeton U., 1982; JD, U. Calif., Berkeley, 1985; MA in Tourism Adminstrn., George Washington U., 1993. Bar: Calif. 1985. Assoc. Bronson, Bronson & McKinnon, San Francisco, 1985-88; pres. Tourism Solutions, Berkeley, 1988—; atty. Donahue, Gallagher, Thomas and Woods, Oakland, Calif., 1990-93, Ecotourism Soc., Bennington, Vt., 1993-94, Assn. Gites Ruraux, Fontaine-Sur-Ay, France, 198-91; dir. Forum on Dispute Resolution Geoge Washington U., Washington, 1984—. Author: Guide to Traveler's Rights, 1995. Dir. Berkeley Law Found., 1985-88; precinct worker Dem. Party, Berkeley, 1988-94. Wilson scholar Princeton (N.J.) U., 1982; ind. rsch. grantee Coun. on Internat. Ednl. Exch., N.Y.C., 1982. Mem. Internat. Forum of Travel and Tourism Advocates (chmn. N.Am. sect. 1991-94), Ecotourism Soc. (program officer 1993-94), Adventure Travel Soc., State Bar of Calif., ABA, The Coral Reef Alliance (exec. dir. 1994—). Democrat. Office: Tourism Solutions 1030 Merced St Berkeley CA 94707

COMANN, TYLER KENT, investment banker; b. Chgo., Sept. 14, 1950; s. Richard Kent and Marilyn Day (Crosby) C. BA, Stanford U., 1972; MBA, Harvard U., 1978. Sr. assoc. Booz, Allen & Hamilton, San Francisco, 1978-82; dir. Golden West Fin. Corp., Oakland, Calif., 1982-83; v.p. Crocker Nat. Bank, San Francisco, 1983-86; ptnr. Comann, Howard & Flamen, San Francisco, 1986-92, Comann & Montague, San Francisco, 1993—; instr. sophomore seminar program Stanford U., 1982-85. Lt. USNR, 1972-75. Mem. San Francisco Tennis Club, Bay Club, Guardsmen of San Francisco.

Office: Comann & Montague 555 Montgomery St Ste 1221 San Francisco CA 94111-2544

COMANOR, WILLIAM S., economist, educator; b. Phila., May 11, 1937; s. Leroy and Sylvia (Bershad) C.; m. Joan Thall; children: Christine, Katherine, Gregory. Student, Williams Coll., 1955-57; BA, Haverford Coll., 1959; MA, PhD, Harvard U., 1963; postgrad., London Sch. Econs., 1963-64. Spl. econ. asst. to asst. atty. gen. Antitrust div. U.S. Dept. Justice, Washington, 1965-66; asst. prof. econs. Harvard U., Cambridge, Mass., 1966-68; assoc. prof. Stanford (Calif.) U., 1968-73; dir. bur. econs. FTC, Washington, 1978-80; prof. econs. U. Calif., Santa Barbara, 1975—, dept. chmn., 1984-87; prof. Sch. Pub. Health U. Calif., L.A., 1990—. Author: National Health Insurance in Ontario, 1980, Advertising and Market Power, 1974, Competition Policy in Europe and North America, 1990; contbr. articles to profl. jours. Mem. Am. Econ. Assn. Home: 621 Miramonte Dr Santa Barbara CA 93109-1428 Office: U of Calif Santa Barbara Dept Econs Santa Barbara CA 93106

COMAR, KANWAR DAVE, surgeon; b. Peshawar, India, Apr. 4, 1918; came to U.S., 1950; m. Bertha Sarmento Comar, Jan. 5, 1979; children: Dave Inder, Maadhevi C. BSc, U. Punjab, India, 1935; MD, King Edward Med. Coll., Lahore, India, 1941; postgrad., Royal Coll. Surgeons, Eng., 1948, Western Res. U., 1950. Diplomate Am. Bd. Surgery, Am. Bd. Thoracic Surgery. Intern Irwin Hosp., New Delhi, 1941-42; med. officer Japanese Internment Camp, 1942-44; med. officer tech. tng. scheme Govt. of India, 1942-46; resident, fellow West Middlesex, Guys and Hammersmith Postgrad. Hosps., London, 1946-50; fellow Huron Rd. Hosp., East Cleve., 1950-51, Cleve. Clinic, 1951-53, Hosp. of Good Samaritan and Children's Hosp., L.A., 1953-54; pvt. practice L.A., 1960—; chief surgeon So. Calif. Edison Co., 1960-75; examiner Calif. Bd. Med. License. Contbr. numerous articles, papers to profl. jours. and internat. med. confs. Chmn. L.A. County Met. Heart Assn., 1970; hospitality vol. L.A. World Affairs Coun. Recipient Internat. Pers. Rsch. Creativity award. Fellow ACS, Internat. Coll. Surgeons, Royal Soc. Medicine (Eng.), Am. Coll. Angiology; mem. Masons, Lions Club Internat. Hindu. Office: 1323 E 1st St Los Angeles CA 90033-3217

COMBS, CORA VICTORIA, chemist; b. Manila, Philippines, Oct. 10, 1950; came to U.S., 1975; d. Marcos Peña and Elisa (Ramos) Victoria; m. Albert Ronald Combs, Aug. 21, 1981. BS in Chemistry, Mapua Inst. Tech., Manila, 1972; MS in Chemistry, Western Mich. U., 1979. Chemist E.R. Squibb, Manila, 1972-73; chemist-in-charge Central Colls., Quezon City, Philippines, 1973-75; grad. asst. Western Mich. U., Kalamazoo, 1975-79; lead chemist Banner Pharmaceuticals, Chatsworth, Calif., 1979-83; sr. chemist/group leader 3M Pharmaceuticals, Northridge, Calif., 1983—; pres. Mapua Inst. Tech. Assn. of Chem. Students, Manila, 1971-72. Recipient Pres.'s Gold medal Mapua Inst. Tech., 1972; Western Mich. U. grantee, 1978. Mem. Am. Chem. Soc, Philippine Chem. Soc., 3M Club. Republican. Roman Catholic. Office: 3M Pharmaceuticals 19901 Nordhoff St Northridge CA 91324-3213

COMBS, DONALD STEVEN, physician assistant; b. Sullivan, Ind., Nov. 3, 1951; s. Bernard Nathan and Alice Mae (Wills) C.; m. Melissa Jane Arnett, Ovt. 26, 1974; children: Adam W., Jared A., Seth A. AS, Kirkwood C.C., 1976; BS, Ball State U., 1974; MS, Chapman U., 1985; PhD, Union Inst., 1988. Cert. physician asst. Med. adminstr. Rockwell Internat., Palmdale, Calif., 1983-89; physician asst. Western Med. Group, Palmdale, Calif., 1989—. Robert R. Lawrence MD, Lancaster, Calif., 1980—; arminstr., physicians asst. Boron (Calif.) Health Clinic, 1985—; asst. prof. Chapman U., Palmdale, 1989—. Author: An Occupational Substance Abuse Study, 1988; contbr. articles to profl. jours. Maj. U.S. Army Med. Res., 1985—. Fellow Am. Acad. Phuysicians Assts., Calif. Acad. Physicians Assts.; mem. Am. Pub. Health Assn., Am. Soc. Orthopedic Phusicians Assts., Am. Assn. Health Care Cons. Republican. Mem. Ch. of Christ. Home: 39860 27th St W Palmdale CA 93551-3414

COMBS, JOHN FRANCIS, manufacturing company executive; b. N.Y.C., Sept. 23, 1950; s. John Francis and Katherine (Lange) C.; m. Susanna Margaret Klein, Sept. 3, 1978; children: David, Daniel, Andrew. BA, NYU, 1972; MBA, Harvard U., 1975. Sr. credit analyst Bankers Trust Co., 1972-73; project fin. mgr. Inco Ltd., N.Y.C., 1975-78; fin. mgr. Inco Ltd., Tokyo, 1978-79; dir. corp. fin. Inco Ltd., N.Y.C., 1983-85; mgr. strategic planning Inco Alloy Products co., N.Y.C., 1979-81; group fin. mgr. Inco Alloy Products Ltd., Birmingham, Eng., 1981-83; sr. v.p. 1st Interstate Bank, L.A., 1985-89; v.p., treas. Fluor Corp., Irvine, Calif., 1989—. Office: Fluor Corp 3333 Michelson Dr Irvine CA 92715

COMBS, W(ILLIAM) HENRY, III, lawyer; b. Casper, Wyo., Mar. 18, 1949; s. William Henry and Ruth M. (Wooster) C.; divorced; 1 child, J. Bradley. Student, Northwestern U., 1967-70; BS, U. Wyo., 1972, JD, 1975. Bar: Wyo. 1975, U.S. Dist. Ct. Wyo. 1975, U.S. Ct. Appeals (10th cir.) 1990, U.S. Supreme Ct. 1990. Assoc. Murane & Bostwick, Casper, 1975-77, ptnr., 1978—. Mem. com. on resolution of fee disputes, 1988-92. Mem. ABA (tort and ins. practice, law office mgmt. sects.), Natrona County Bar Assn., Def. Rsch. Inst., Am. Judicature Soc., Wyo. Trial Def. Counsel, Assn. Ski Def. Attys., U.S. Handball Assn., Am. Water Ski Assn., Casper Boat Club, Casper Petroleum Club, Wyo. Athletic Club, Porsche Club Am., BMW Club Am., Sports Car Club Am. Republican. Episcopalian. Office: Murane & Bostwick 201 N Wolcott St Casper WY 82601-1922

COMEAU, JACK FRANCIS, lighting and photography director; b. Boston, Dec. 23, 1955; s. John Francis and Catherine (Fallon) C.; m. Shawn Canavan, May 31, 1980; children: Kitty, Maggie. Student, Orson Welles Film Sch., 1973-74, U. Bridgeport, 1975-77, Lee Strasburg Acting Inst., 1977, Internat. Film Workshops, 1980—. Freelance gaffer-lighting dir. Boston, 1979-89; lighting dir. WWOR-TV/MCA Broadcasting, Secaucus, N.J., 1989—; guest lectr. on lighting U. N.H., Durham, 1986, Emerson Coll., Boston, 1987-88; gaffer Internat. Film Workshop, Rockport, Maine, 1981. Home: 4440 Ambrose Ave Ste 202 Los Angeles CA 90027

COMEAUX, KATHARINE JEANNE, realtor; b. Richland, Wash., Jan. 18, 1949; d. Warren William and Ruth Irma (Remington) Gonder; m. Jack Goldwasser, May 25, 1992; 1 child, Thelma Morrow. AA, West Valley Coll., 1970; student, San Jose State U., 1970-71. Cert. realtor. Realtor Value Realty, Cupertino, Calif., 1975-79, Valley of Calif., Cupertino, 1979-81, Coldwell Banker, Cupertino, 1981-82, Fox & Carskadon, Saratoga, Calif., 1984-90. With Los Gatos-Saratoga Bd. Realtors Polit. Action, 1984-89; v.p. Hospice of Valley Svc. League, Saratoga, 1984-89; big. sister Big Bros./Big Sisters, San Jose, Calif., 1976-90; bd. dirs. Mountain Energy Inc., United Way of Josephine County, Energia Natural Honduras. Home: 4330 Fish Hatchery Rd Grants Pass OR 97527-9547

COMES, ROBERT GEORGE, research scientist; b. Bangor, Pa., July 7, 1931; s. Victor Francis and Mabel Elizabeth (Mack) C.; student U. Detroit, 1957-58, Oreg. State Coll., 1959-60, U. Nev., 1960, Regis Coll., 1961-62; m. Carol Lee Turinetti, Nov. 28, 1952; children: Pamela Jo, Robert G. II, Shawni Lee, Sheryl Lynn, Michelle Ann. Tech. liaison engr. Burroughs Corp., Detroit, 1955-60, mgr. reliability and maintainability engring., Paoli, Pa., 1962-63, Colorado Springs, Colo., 1963-67; sr. engr. Martin Marietta Corp., Denver, 1960-62; program mgr., rsch. scientist Kaman Scis. Corp., Colorado Springs, 1967-75; dir. engring. Sci. Applications, Inc., Colorado Springs, 1975-80; mgr. space def. programs Burroughs Corp., Colorado Springs, 1980-82; tech. staff Mitre Corp., Colorado Springs, 1982-85; dir. Colorado Springs opn. Beers Assoc., Inc., 1985; dir. space programs Electro Magnetic Applications, Inc., Colorado Springs, 1985-87; dir. Space Systems, Profl. Mgmt. Assocs., Inc., 1987-88; mgr. Computer Svcs., Inc., Colorado Springs, 1989—; dir. mktg. Proactive Techs., Inc., Colorado Springs, 1990—; chmn. Reliability and Maintainability Data Bank Improvement Program, Govt.-Industry Data Exch. Program, 1978-80—; cons. in field. Youth dir. Indian Guides program YMCA, 1963-64; scoutmaster Boy Scouts Am., 1972-73; chmn. bd. dirs. Pikes Peak Regional Sci. Fair, 1972-84. Served with USAF, 1951-55. Mem. AAAS, IEEE, Inst. Environ. Scis., Soc. Logistics Engrs., Am. Soc. Quality Control. Lutheran. Club: Colorado Springs Racquet. Author: Maintainability Engineering Principles and Standards, 1962. Inventor Phase Shifting aircraft power supply, 1957. Home: 4309 Tipton Ct Colorado Springs CO 80915-1034 Office: Proactive Tech Inc 4309 Tipton Ct Colorado Springs CO 80915-1034

COMINGS, DAVID EDWARD, physician, medical genetics scientist; b. Beacon, N.Y., Mar. 8, 1935; s. Edward Walter and Jean (Rice) C.; m. Shirley Nelson, Aug. 9, 1958; children: Mark David, Scott Edward, Karen Jean.; m. Brenda Gursey, Mar. 20, 1982. Student, U. Ill., 1951-54; B.S., Northwestern U., 1955, M.D., 1958. Intern Cook County Hosp., Chgo., 1958-59; resident in internal medicine Cook County Hosp., 1959-62; fellow in med. genetics U. Wash., Seattle, 1964-66; dir. dept. med. genetics City of Hope Med. Ctr., Duarte, Calif., 1966—; mem. genetics study sect. NIH, 1974-78; mem. sci. adv. bd. Hereditary Disease Found., 1975—, Nat. Found. March of Dimes, 1978—. Author: Tourette Syndrome and Human Behavior, 1990; editor: (with others) Molecular Human Cytogenetics, 1977; mem. editorial bd.: (with others) Cytogenetics and Cell genetics, 1979—; editor in chief Am. Jour. Human Genetics, 1978-86. Served with U.S. Army, 1962-64. NIH grantee, 1967—. Mem. Assn. Am. Physicians, Am. Soc. Clin. Investigation, AAAS, Am. Soc. Human Genetics (dir. 1974-78, pres. 1988), Am. Soc. Cell Biology, Am. Fedn. Clin. Research, Western Soc. Clin. Research, Council Biology Editors. Office: City of Hope Med Ctr 1500 Duarte Rd Duarte CA 91010-3012

COMPRONE, JOSEPH JOHN, dean; b. Lansdowne, Pa., Mar. 11, 1943; s. John Joseph and Anne Rita (Lombardo) C.; m. Pamela Jane Gay, June 5, 1965 (div. Mar. 1978); children: Raphael John, Angela Jane; m. Constance Ann Dugan, Nov. 2, 1978; children: Christopher Allan, Joseph Oliver. BA cum laude, Springfield Coll., 1965; MA, U. Mass., 1967, PhD, 1970. Asst. dir. freshman English U. Mass., Amherst, 1968-69; asst. prof. English U. Minn., Morris, 1969-72; assoc. prof. English U. Cin., 1972-76; dir. writing programs U. Louisville, 1976-81, 84-88, dir. grad. studies in English, 1981-84, prof. English, 1976-88; head dept. humanities Mich. Tech. U., Houghton, 1989-92; dean Coll. of Arts and Scis. Ariz. State U., West Phoenix, 1992—; vis. prof. Nat. U. Singapore, 1988-89; cons. Ednl. Testing Svc., Princeton, N.J., 1978—, TRIO Counselor Tng. Program, Cherry Hill, N.J., 1980; cons. in comms. Ky. Fried Chicken, Louisville, 1978; cons. in legal writing Ky. Judges Coll., Frankfort, 1986. Author: From Experience to Expression, 1974, 76, Form and Substance, 1976, Perspectives, 1987; co-author: Contexts and Communities, 1994. Campaign organizer McCarthy for Pres., Amherst, 1968; pub. sch. cons. English Jefferson County Pub. Schs., Louisville, 1978-82; chair U. Cin., C.C. Consortium, Cin., 1972-76; mem. City of Glendale (Ariz.) Arts Commn., 1994. Recipient Toward Greater Quality award, 1978; Study Abroad travel fellow U. Mass., 1969; co-grantee NEH, U. S.C., 1977. Mem. MLA, Nat. Coun. Tchrs. of English (com. chmn. 1969—), Rhetoric Soc. Am., Assn. Am. Colls. and Univs., Nat. Orgn. Writing Program Adminstrs. (sec.-treas. 1976—), Conf. on Col. Composition and Comm. (exec. com. 1969—). Home: 21495 N 65th Ave Glendale AZ 85308-6408 Office: Ariz State U West 4701 E Thunderbird Rd Phoenix AZ 85032-5540

COMPTON, ALLEN T., state supreme court justice; b. Kansas City, Mo., Feb. 25, 1938; m. Sue Ellen Tatter; 3 children. B.A., U. Kans.; LL.B., U. Colo. Staff atty. legal services office in Colo., later entered pvt. practice; supervising atty. Alaska Legal Services, Juneau, 1970-73; sole practice Juneau, 1973-76; judge Superior Ct., Alaska, 1976-80; assoc. justice Alaska Supreme Ct., Anchorage, 1980—. Mem. 4 bar assns. including Juneau Bar Assn. (past pres.). Office: Alaska Supreme Ct 303 K St Anchorage AK 99501-2013

COMPTON, JAMES VINCENT, history educator; b. Perth Amboy, N.J., July 5, 1928; s. Lewis Compton and Beatrice Camille (Vincent) Copsey. BA, Princeton U., 1950; MA, U. Chgo., 1952; postgrad., U. Munich, 1954-55; PhD, U. London, 1964. Lectr. European divsn. U. Md., 1954-60; lectr. U. London, 1961-64; lectr. U. Edinburgh, Scotland, 1964-68, chair Am. studies, 1964-68; assoc. prof. history Trinity Coll., Hartford, Conn., 1968-69; prof. history San Francisco State U., 1969-95; ret., 1995. Author: The Swastika and The Eagle, 1967, America and Origins of Cold War, 1970, (study unit) The New Deal, 1973; cons. editor: For the President: Personal Secret, 1972. Konrad Adenauer fellow German Govt., 1954-55. Mem. Orgn. Am. Historians, Brit. Assn. Am. Studies. Democrat. Roman Catholic. Home: 170 Diamond St San Francisco CA 94114-2414

COMPTON, MERLIN DAVID, Spanish language educator; b. Ogden, Utah, July 22, 1924; s. George Albert and Margaret Estella (Mattson) C.; m. Avon Allen Compton, June 17, 1950; children: Terry Ann Compton Harward, Todd Merlin, Tamara Jane Compton Hauge, Timothy George, Tina Louise. BA, Brigham Young U., 1952, MA, 1954; PhD, UCLA, 1959. Asst. prof. Adams State Coll., Alamosa, Colo., 1959-63; assoc. prof. Weber State Coll., Ogden, Utah, 1963-64; prof. Spanish Brigham Young U., Provo, Utah, 1964-89. Author: Ricardo Palma, 1982, Trayectoria de las Tradiciones de Ricardo Palma, 1989. Staff sgt. USAF, 1943-46. Mem. Phi Kappa Phi. Mem. LDS Ch. Home: 1015 S River Rd Apt 27 Saint George UT 84770-2220

COMPTON, MILES STUART, librarian; b. Bellingham, Wash., June 18, 1929; s. Miles W. and Catherine J. (Sterns) C. BA, Western Wash. State U., 1951; BTh, Simpson Coll., 1955; ML, U. Wash., 1964. Page Seattle Pub. Libr., 1953-55; head libr. Simpson Coll., San Francisco, 1955-89, Redding, Calif., 1989—. Editor: Guidelines for Bible College Libraries, 1986, 2d edit., 1991. Mem. Calif. Libr. Assn., Assn. Christian Librs. (bd. dirs. 1987-88). Office: Simpson Coll Libr 2211 College View Dr Redding CA 96003-8601

COMPTON, TAMARA LYNN, theatre director, educator; b. Burbank, Calif., Nov. 13, 1948; d. Russell Jay and Joan Ursula (Pilgrim) C.; m. David Jackson Cox, Nov. 26, 1983. BA, U. Calif., Santa Barbara, 1970; MA, Kans. State U., 1985; PhD, U. Nebr., 1992. Gen. mgr., stage mgr. San Diego Repertory Theatre, 1978-80; asst. prodn. mgr. Denver Ctr. Theatre Co., 1980; comptroller Circle In The Sq. Theatre, N.Y.C., 1981; dir. theatre Dakota State Coll., Madison, S.D., 1987-88; instr. Ohio No. U., Ada, 1988-90; dir. theatre Chadron (Nebr.) State Coll., 1991-93; asst. prof., dir. theatre Westminster Coll., Salt Lake City, 1993—; mem. adv. bd. Ft. Wayne (Ind.) Dance Collective, 1991—, bd. dirs., 1990-91; bd. dirs. Susan Warden Dancers, Manhattan, 1982-85, Manhattan Civic Theatre, 1983-85. Dir. prodns. including A Christmas Carol, Manhattan Civic Theatre, 1982, Talking with Kansas State U., 1984, Ripen Our Darkness, U. Nebr., 1987, The House of Blue Leaves, Ohio No. U., 1989, The Heidi Chronicles, Chadron State Coll., 1993; designer numerous prodns., 1979—; author: Mary Hunter Wolf: Building Communities Through Theatre, 1993. Mem. NOW, Assn. for Theatre in Higher Edn., Women and Theatre Program, Am. Alliance for Theatre and Edn., Nat. Women's Studies Assn., Actors Equity Assn., Theta Alpha Phi, Phi Kappa Phi. Home: 3711 Indiana Ave Fort Wayne IN 46807-2213

COMRIE, BERNARD STERLING, linguistics educator; b. Sunderland, England, May 23, 1947; came to U.S., 1979; s. Clifford Reginald Herbert and Ellen (Coulton) C.; m. Akiko Kumahira, Feb. 10, 1985; children: Amanda Mariko Kumahira Comrie, Michael Masaru Kumahira Comrie. BA, U. Cambridge, 1968, PhD, 1972. Rsch. fellow King's Coll., Cambridge, 1970-74; sr. asst. in rsch. U. Cambridge, 1972-74, univ. lectr. in linguistics, 1974-78; assoc. prof. linguistics U. So. Calif., L.A., 1978-81, prof. linguistics, 1981—. Author: Aspect, 1976, Language Universals and Linguistic Typology, 1981, Tense, 1985; editor: The World's Major Languages, 1987 (Outstanding Acad. Book 1987-88), Studies in Language, Amsterdam, Netherlands, 1991—. Recipient Rsch. grant Social Sci. Rsch. Coun., London, 1975-78, NSF, 1985-86, 90—. Mem. Linguistic Soc. Am., Linguistics Assn. Great Britain, Philological Soc. Office: Dept Linguistics Univ So Calif Los Angeles CA 90089-1693

COMSTOCK, DALE ROBERT, mathematics educator; b. Frederic, Wis., Jan. 18, 1934; s. Walter and Frances (Lindroth) C.; m. Mary Jo Lien, Aug. 18, 1956; children—Mitchell Scott, Bryan Paul. B.A., Central Wash. State Coll., 1955; M.S., Oreg. State U., 1962, Ph.D., 1966. Tchr. math. Kennewick (Wash.) High Sch., 1955-57, 59-60; instr. Columbia Basin Coll., Pasco, Wash., 1956-57, 59-60; programmer analyst Gen. Electric Co., Hanford Atomic Works, Richland, Wash., 1963; prof. math. Cen. Wash. U., Ellensburg, 1964—, dean Grad. Sch. and Research,, 1970-90; on leave as sr. program mgr. U.S. ERDA, also Presdl. interchange exec., 1976-77; mem. Pres.'s Commn. on Exec. Devel., 1976-77; on leave as dean in residence Council Grad. Schs. in U.S., 1984-85; cons. Indian program NSF, 1968, 69, USIA, India, 1985, NSF, Saudi Arabia, 1986; mem. grant proposal rev. panels NSF, 1970, 71, 76, 77, 89, 90; pres. Western Assn. Grad. Schs., 1979-80, sec.-treas. 1984-90; pres. N.W. Assn. Colls. and Univs. for Sci., 1988-89; Russian exch. prof., St. Petersburg, 1993. With U.S. Army, 1957-59. NSF fellow, 1960-61; grantee, summer 1964. Mem. Am. Math Soc., Math. Assn. Am., Assn. Computing Machinery (exec. com.), Soc. Indsl. and Applied Math., Northwest Coll. and Univ. Assn. for Sci. (pres. 1980-83). Methodist. Home: 1311 Brick Rd Ellensburg WA 98926-9562 Office: Cen Wash U Dept Math Ellensburg WA 98926

CONCEPCIÓN, DAVID ALDEN, arbitrator, educator; b. Carmel, Calif., Aug. 6, 1935; s. Don Dominador Cuales Concepción and Elma Elizabeth Davis; m. Ann Martin Worster, Dec. 3, 1960; children: Leslie Martin Concepción Mayns, David Worster. BA, U. Calif., Santa Barbara, 1959. Adminstrv. exec. Lawrence Berkeley Lab. U. Calif., Berkeley, 1962-70, dir. mgmt. analysis, 1970-75; assoc. dean adminstrn. Hastings Coll. Law U. Calif., San Francisco, 1975-80; pvt. practice Berkeley, 1980—; mem. adv. bd. Calif. Pub. Employee Rels. at U. Calif., Berkeley, 1978—. Contbr. articles to profl. jours. Capt. USMC, 1959-62. Mem. Nat. Acad. Arbitrators (mem. com. 1995—), Am. Arbitration Assn. (mem. No. Calif. Adv. Coun. 1980—, mem. nat. bd. dirs. 1980-86, Disting. Svc. award 1990), Soc. Profls. in Dispute Resolution, Indsl. Rels. Rsch. Assn., Soc. Fed. Labor Rel. Profls. Democrat. Mem. United Ch. Christ. Office: 65 Stevenson Ave Berkeley CA 94708-1732

CONDIE, CAROL JOY, anthropologist, research facility administrator; b. Provo, Utah, Dec. 28, 1931; d. LeRoy and Thelma (Graff) C.; m. M. Kent Stout, June 18, 1954; children: Carla Ann, Erik Roy, Paula Jane. BA in Anthropology, U. Utah, 1953; MEd in Elem. Edn., Cornell U., 1954; PhD in Anthropology, U. N.Mex., 1973; Quivira Rsch. Ctr. Edn. coordinator Maxwell Mus. Anthropology, U. N.Mex., Albuquerque, 1973, interpretation dir., 1974-77; asst. prof. anthropology U. N.Mex., 1975-77; cons. anthropologist, 1977-78; pres. Quivira Research Ctr., Albuquerque, 1978—; cons. anthropologist U.S. Congl. Office Tech. Assessment, chair Archeol. Resources Planning Adv. Com., Albuquerque, 1985-86; leader field seminars Crow Canyon Archeol. Ctr., 1986—; appointee Albuquerque dist. adv. coun., bur. land mgmt. U.S. Dept. Interior, 1989; study leader Smithsonian Instn. Tours, 1991; mem. Albuquerque Heritage Conservation Adv. Com., 1992. Author: The Nighthawk Site: A Pithouse Site on Sandia Pueblo Land, Bernalillo County, New Mexico, 1982, Five Sites on the Pecos River Road, 1985, Data Recovery at Eight Archeological Sites on the Rio Nutritas, 1992, Data Recovery at Eight Archeological Sites on Cabresto Road Near Questa, 1992, Archeological Survey in the Rough and Ready Hills/Picacho Mountain Area, Dona Ana County, New Mexico, 1993, Archeological Survey on the Canadian River, Quay County, New Mexico, 1994; co-editor: Anthropology of the Desert West, 1985. Mem. Downtown Core Area Schs. Com., Albuquerque, 1982. Ford Found. fellow, 1953-54; recipient Am. Planning Assn. award, 1985-86, Gov.'s award, 1986. Fellow Am. Anthrop. Assn.; mem. Soc. Am. Archeology (chmn. native Am. rels. com. 1983-85), N.Mex. Archeol. Coun. (pres. 1982-83, hist. preservation award 1988), Albuquerque Archeol. Soc. (pres. 1992), Maxwell Mus. Assn. (bd. dirs.), Las Arañas Spinners and Weavers Guild (pres. 1972). Democrat. Home and Office: Quivira Research Ctr 1809 Notre Dame Dr NE Albuquerque NM 87106-1011

CONDIT, GARY A., congressman; b. Apr. 21, 1948. AA, Modesto Jr. Coll.; BA, Calif. State Coll. Councilman City of Ceres, Calif., 1972-74, mayor, 1974-76; supr. Stanislaus County, Calif., 1976-82; assemblyman State of Calif., 1982-89; mem. 101st-104th Congresses from 15th (now 18th) Calif. Dist., 1989—; ranking minority mem. Ag. subcom. on nutrition & fgn. ag., mem. govt. reform & oversight. Democrat. Office: US Ho of Reps 2444 Rayburn Washington DC 20515*

CONDIT, PHILIP MURRAY, aerospace executive, engineer; b. Berkeley, Calif., Aug. 2, 1941; s. Daniel Harrison and Bernice (Kemp) C.; m. Madeleine K. Bryant, Jan. 25, 1963 (div. June 1982); children: Nicole Lynn, Megan Anne; m. Janice Condit, Apr. 6, 1991. BS MechE, U. Calif., Berkeley, 1963; MS in Aero. Engring., Princeton U., 1965; MS in Mgmt., MIT, 1975. Engr. The Boeing Co., Seattle, 1965-72, mgr. engring., 1973-83, v.p., gen. mgr., 1983-84, v.p. sales and mktg., 1984-86, exec. v.p., 1986-89, exec. v.p., gen. mgr. 777 div., 1989-92, pres., 1992—; mem. adv. coun. Dept. Mech. and Aerospace Engring., Princeton (N.J.) U., 1984—; chmn. aero. adv. com. NASA Adv. Coun., 1988-92; bd. dirs. The Fluke Corp., 1987—, Nordstom, Inc., 1993—. Co-inventor Design of a Flexible Wing, 1965. Mem. Mercer Island (Wash.) Utilities Bd., 1975-78; bd. dirs. Camp Fire, Inc., 1987-92; mem. exec bd. chief Seattle coun. Boy Scouts Am., 1988-90; trustee Mus. of Flight, Seattle, 1990—. Co-recipient Laurels award Aviation Week & Space Tech. magazine, 1990; Sloan fellow MIT, Boston, 1974. Fellow AIAA (aircraft design award 1984, Edward C. Wells tech. mgmt. award 1982), Royal Aero. Soc.; mem. NAE, Soc. Sloan Fellows (bd. govs. 1985-89), Soc. Automotive Engrs. Clubs: Rainier, Columbia Tower (Seattle). Office: The Boeing Co PO Box 3707 7755 E Marginal Way S Seattle WA 98124-2207

CONDON, STANLEY CHARLES, gastroenterologist; b. Glendale, Calif., Feb. 1, 1931; s. Charles Max and Alma Mae (Chinn) C.; m. Vaneta Marilyn Mabley, May 19, 1963; children: Lori, Brian, David. BA, La Sierra Coll., 1952; MD, Loma Linda U., 1956. Diplomate Nat. Bd. Med. Examiners, Am. Bd. Internal Medicine, Am. Bd. Gastroenterology. Intern L.A. County Gen. Hosp., 1956-57, resident gen. pathology, 1959-61; resident internal medicine White Meml. Med. Ctr., L.A., 1961-63, attending staff out-patient clinic, 1963-64; active jr. attending staff L.A. County Gen. Hosp., 1964-65; dir. intern-resident tng. program Manila Sanitarium and Hosp., 1966-71, med. dir., 1971-72; chief resident internal medicine out-patient clinic Loma Linda U. Med. Ctr., 1972-74; fellow in gastroenterology Washington U., St. Louis, 1974-76; attending staff, asst. prof. medicine Loma Linda U. Med. Ctr., 1976-91, assoc. prof. medicine, 1991—; med. dir. nutritional support team Loma Linda Med. Ctr., 1984—. Contbr. articles to profl. jours. Capt. U.S. Army, 1957-59. Fellow ACP; mem. AMA, San Bernardino County Med. Soc., Calif. Med. Assn., Am. Soc. for Parenteral and Enteral Nutrition, Am. Gastroenterological Assn., So. Calif. Soc. Gastroenterology, Inland Soc. Internal Medicine, So. Calif. Soc. Gastrointestinal Endoscopy. Republican. Seventh-day Adventist. Home: 11524 Ray Ct Loma Linda CA 92354-3630 Office: Loma Linda U Med Ctr 115234 Anderson St Loma Linda CA 92350

CONDRY, ROBERT STEWART, retired hospital administrator; b. Charleston, W.Va., Aug. 16, 1941; s. John Charles and Mary Louise (Jester) C.; m. Mary Purcell Heinzer, May 21, 1966; children: Mary-Lynch, John Stewart. BA, U. Charleston, 1963; MBA, George Washington U., 1970. Asst. hosp. dir. Med. Coll. of Va., Richmond, 1970-73, assoc. adminstr., 1973-75; assoc. hosp. dir. McGaw Hosp., Loyola U., Maywood, Ill., 1975-84, hosp. dir., 1984-93, ret., 1993; pres. Inter-Hosp. Planning Assn. of Western Suburbs, Maywood, 1983-93; bd. dirs. PentaMed, Inc., San Antonio. Bd. dirs. Met. Chgo. Healthcare Coun., 1985-93, mem. exec. com., 1989-93; bd. dirs. Cath. Hosp. Alliance, 1992, chmn. bd. dirs., 1992, mem. exec. com. 1988-94; mem. Ill. Gov.'s Adv. Bd. on Infant Mortality Reduction, 1988-93, Rev. Bd. on Emergency Medicine Svcs., 1989-93. With U.S. Army, 1964-66. Recipient preceptorship George Washington U., 1985, U. Chgo., 1984, St. Louis U., 1984, Tulane U., 1984, Yale U., 1991. Fellow Am. Coll. Healthcare Execs., Am. Acad. Med. Adminstrs.; mem. Am. Hosp. Assn., Cath. Hosp. Assn., Am. Mgmt. Assn. Republican. Roman Catholic.

CONE, LAWRENCE ARTHUR, research medicine educator; b. N.Y.C., Mar. 23, 1928; s. Max N. and Ruth (Weber) C.; m. Julia Haldy, June 6, 1947 (dec. 1956); m. Mary Elisabeth Osborne, Aug. 20, 1960; children: Lionel Alfred. AB, NYU, 1948; MD, U. Berne, Switzerland, 1954; DSc (hon.), Rocky Mountain Coll., 1993. Diplomate Am. Bd. Internal Medicine, Am. Bd. Infectious Diseases, Am. Bd. Allergy and Immunology, Am. Bd. Med. Oncology. Intern Dallas Meth. Hosp., 1954-55, resident internal medicine, 1955; resident Flower 5th Hosp., N.Y.C., 1957-59, Met. Hosp., N.Y.C., 1959-60; rsch. fellow infectious diseases and immunology NYU Med. Sch., N.Y.C., 1960-62; from asst. prof. to assoc. prof. N.Y. Med. Coll., N.Y.C., 1962-72, chief sect immunology and infectious diseases, 1962-72; assoc. clin. prof. medicine Harbor UCLA Med. Sch., 1984—; career scientist Health Rsch. Coun. N.Y.C., 1962-68; chief sect. immunology and infectious diseases

Eisenhower Med. Ctr., Rancho Mirage, Calif., 1973—, chmn. dept. medicine, 1976-78, pres. elect, pres., past pres. med. staff, 1984-90; cons. infectious disease Desert Hosp., Palm Springs, Calif., 1980-85. Contbr. articles to profl. jours. Bd. dirs. Desert Bighorn Rsch. Inst., Palm Desert, Calif., 1986—, pres. bd. dirs., 1995—; mem. nat. adv. coun. Rocky Mountain Coll., Billings, Mont.; mem. med. adv. staff Coll. of Desert, Palm Desert; active Desert Mus., Palm Springs, Calif., Idaho Conservation League Gilcrease Mus., Tulsa. Fellow ACP, Royal Soc. Medicine, Am. Coll. Allergy, Am. Acad. Allergy and Immunology, Am. Soc. Infectious Diseases, Am. Geriatric Soc. (founding fellow western div.); mem. Internat. AIDS Soc., Am. Soc. Microbiology, Am. Fedn. for Clin. Rsch., Faculty Soc. UCLA, Woodstock Artists Assn., Harvey Soc., N.Y. Acad. Scis., Tamamisk Country Club, Coachella Valley Gun and Wildlife Club Faculty Soc. UCLA Harbor Med. Ctr., Lotos Club (N.Y.C.), Living Desert Club. Republican. Home: 765 W Via Vadera Palm Springs CA 92262-4170 Office: Probst Profl Bldg # 308 39000 Bob Hope Dr Rancho Mirage CA 92270-3221

CONERLY, WILLIAM BOOTH, economist; b. San Diego, Jan. 12, 1952; s. Tom Byron and Lila (Faught) C.; m. U. Christina West, Nov. 29, 1985; children: Peter Ulysses, Thomas William. BA, New Coll., Sarasota, Fla., 1974; PhD, Duke U., 1980. Instr. St. Andrews Presbyn. Coll., Laurinburg, N.C., 1977-80; economist to sr. economist Pacific Gas & Elec. Co., San Francisco, 1980-84; dir. econ. planning NERCO, Inc., Portland, Oreg., 1984-87; v.p. and economist First Interstate Bank of Oreg., Portland, 1987-91; sr. v.p. First Interstate Bank NW Region, Portland, 1992—. Contbr. articles to profl. jours. Mem. Gov.'s Coun. of Econ. Advisors, State of Oreg., Salem, 1989—; pres. Oreg. Coun. on Econ. Edn., 1990-93; bd. dirs. Oreg. Tax Rsch. Mem. Nat. Assn. Bus. Economists (chpt. pres. 1987-88), Am. Bankers Assn. (econ. adv. com. 1989—), Am. Econs. Assn., Willamette Sailing Club. Office: First Interstate Bank PO Box 3131 Portland OR 97208-3131

CONEY, CAROLE ANNE, accountant; b. Berkeley, Calif., Aug. 11, 1944; d. Martin James and Ida Constance (Ditora) Skuce; m. David Michael Coney, June 20, 1964; children: Kristine Marie, Kenneth Michael. BS cum laude, Calif. State Poly. U., 1985, MBA, 1988. Tax cons., instr. H&R Block, Portland, Oreg., 1969-71; acct., asst. sec.-treas. Surety Ins. Co., La Habra, Calif., 1973-76; bookkeeper Homemakers Furniture, Downers Grove, Ill., 1976-79; office mgr., acct. Helen's Pl. Printing, Upland, 1979-80; bookkeeper Vanguard Cos., Upland, 1980-82; dir. acctg. Coll. Osteopathic Medicine of Pacific, Pomona, Calif., 1982-89; acctg. mgr. City of Ontario, Calif., 1989—. Pres. Brea/La Habra Newcomers, 1975; treas. Alta Loma (Calif.) Com. to Elect Robert Neufeld, 1981. Mem. NAFE, Nat. Assn. Coll. and Univ. Bus. Officers, Calif. Soc. Mcpl. Fin. Officers, Govt. Fin. Officers Assn., Assn. Coll. and Univ. Auditors, Coun. Fiscal Officers, Soroptomists, Ontario Kiwanis, Delta Mu Delta, Alpha Iota. Democrat. Roman Catholic. Home: PO Box 4910 24581 San Moritz Dr Crestline CA 92325-4910 Office: City of Ontario 303 E B St Ontario CA 91764-4105

CONGDON, MARSHA B., telecommunications executive; b. Omaha, Mar. 10, 1947; d. William Vincent and Jane Elizabeth (Christensen) Brooks; m. Frederick M. Congdon, Dec. 22, 1973; 1 child: Beth Ann Hiner, 1 stepchild, Christopher Congdon. BA, U. Nebr., 1973; MA in Bus. Mgmt., U. Mich., 1983. With U S West Inc., 1973—; mgmt. asst. N.W. Bell U S West Inc., Fargo, N.D., 1973; installation supr., N.W. Bell U S West Inc., Jamestown, N.D., 1973-75; various positions Northwestern Bell, Bismarck, N.D., 1975-82; gen. mgr. regulatory and pub. affairs, N.W. Bell U S West Inc., Sioux Falls, N.D., 1982-83; v.p. Northwestern Area, N.W. Bell U S West Inc., Omaha, 1983-84, v.p. U S West Direct, 1984-85; exec. v.p. Directory Publ. Corp. U S West Inc., Loveland, Colo., 1985-87; Oreg. v.p., chief exec. officer U S West Communications U S West Inc., Portland, Oreg., 1987—; bd. dirs. U.S. Nat. Bank Oreg., Bohemia Inc., Mentor Graphics Corp.; judge McKinsey award Harvard Bus. Rev., 1989; advisor Capital Cons., Portland, 1989-90. Mem. Housing, Ednl. and Cultural Facilities Authority, Oreg. Investment Coun.; trustee Maryhurst Coll.; bd. dirs., exec. com. Oreg. Bus. Coun., Oreg. Ind. Coll. Found; S.D. chmn. State Bd. Indsl. Devel.; bd. dirs. S.D. C. of C.; trustee Oreg. Mus. Sci. and Industry; pres.'s adv. bd. Portland State U.; chmn. fund raising United Negro Coll. Fund Inc. Named Woman of Distinction, Girl Scouts Am., 1987, Woman of Achievement, Oreg. Women's Commn., 1988, Rising Tide honoree, Nat. Women's Polit. Caucus, White Rose honoree March of Dimes, 1991. Mem. Internat. Women's Forum. Lutheran. Home: 1209 SW 6th Ave # 603 Portland OR 97204

CONGDON, ROGER DOUGLASS, theology educator, minister; b. Ft. Collins, Colo., Apr. 6, 1918; s. John Solon and Ellen Avery (Kellogg) C.; m. Rhoda Gwendolyn Britt, Jan. 2, 1948; children: Rachel Congdon Lidbeck, James R., R. Steven, Jon B., Philip F., Robert N., Bradford B., Ruth A. Mahner, Rebecca York Skones, Rhoda J. Miller, Marianne C. Potter, Mark Alexander. BA, Wheaton Coll., 1940; postgrad, Eastern Bapt. Sem., 1940-41; ThM, Dallas Theol. Sem., 1945; ThD, Dallas Theology Sem., 1949. Ordained to ministry Bapt. Ch., 1945. Exec. sec., dean Altanta Bible Inst., 1945-49; prof. theology Carver Bible Inst., Atlanta, 1945-49; prof. Multnomah Bible Coll., Portland, Oreg., 1950-87; pastor Emmanuel Bapt. Ch., Vancouver, Wash., 1985—; past dean of faculty, dean of edn., v.p., chmn. libr. com., chmn. achievement-award com., chmn. lectureship com., advisor grad. div. and mem. pres.'s cabinet Multnomah Bible Co.; chmn. Chil Evang. Fellowship of Greater Portland, 1978—; founder, pres. Preaching Print Inc., Portland, 1953—. Founder, speaker semi-weekly radio broadcast Bible Truth Forum, KPDQ, Portland, Oreg., 1989—; author: The Doctrine of Conscience, 1945. Chmn. Citizen's Com. Info. on Communism, Portland, 1968-75. Recipient Outstanding Educators of Am. award, 1972, Loraine Chafer award in Systematic Theology, Dallas Theol. Sem. Mem. Am. Assn. Bible Colls. (chmn. testing com. 1953-78), N.Am. Assn. Bible Colls. (N.W. rep. 1960-63), Near East Archaeol. Soc., Evang. Theol. Soc. Republican. Home: 16539 NE Halsey St Portland OR 97230-5607 Office: Emmanuel Bapt Ch 14810 NE 28th St Vancouver WA 98682-8357

CONGER, HARRY MILTON, mining company executive; b. Seattle, July 22, 1930; s. Harry Milton Jr. and Caroline (Gunnell) C.; m. Phyllis Nadine Shepherd, Aug. 14, 1949 (dec.); children: Harry Milton IV, Preston George; m. Rosemary L. Scholz, Feb. 22, 1991. D in Bus. Adminstrn. (hon.), S.D. Sch. Mines and Tech., 1983; D. in Engring. (hon.), Colo. Sch. Mines, 1988, hon. degrees. Registered profl. engr., Ariz., Colo. Shift foreman Asarco, Inc., Silver Bell, Ariz., 1955-64; mgr. Kaiser Steel Corp. Eagle Mountain Mine, 1964-70; v.p., gen. mgr. Kaiser Resources, Ltd., Fernie, B.C., Can., 1970-73, Consolidation Coal Co. (Midwestern div.), Carbondale, Ill., 1973-75; v.p. Homestake Mining Co., San Francisco, 1975-77; pres. Homestake Mining Co., 1977-78, pres., chief exec. officer, 1978-82, chmn., pres., chief exec. officer, 1982-86, chmn., chief exec. officer, 1986—; also bd dirs.; bd. dirs. CalMat, Inc., ASA Ltd., Pacific Gas & Electric Co., Baker Hughes Inc.; chmn. Am. Mining Congress, 1986-89, World Gold Coun., 1995—. Trustee Calif. Inst. Tech. With C.E., U.S. Army, 1956. Recipient Disting. Achievement medal Colo. Sch. Mines, 1978, Am. Mining Hall of Fame, 1990, Disting. Svc. award Am. Mining Congress, 1995. Mem. NAE, Am. Inst. Mining Engrs. (disting., Charles F. Rand gold medal 1990), Mining and Metallurgy Soc. Am., Mining Club, Bohemian Club, Commonwealth Club, Pacific Union Club, World Trade Club, Diablo Country Club. Republican. Episcopalian. Office: Homestake Mining Co 650 California St San Francisco CA 94108-2702

CONIGLIO, JOHN VINCENT, financial company executive; b. East Chgo., Ind., Dec. 21, 1963; s. George and Margaret Irene (Chovanec) C.; m. Stacey L. Coniglio, June 24, 1994. BA in journalism, U. Wis., 1986. Advt. salesman Orange Coast Mall Mags., Lake Forest, Calif., 1986-87; yellow pages acct. rep. Southwestern Bell Publs., St. Louis, 1987-89; pres., founder Burcon Financial, Inc., Brea, Calif., 1989—. Author: Rumors of Angels, 1994; appeared on numerous radio and TV talk shows including WORD Radio, Pitts., 1994, KSLR Radio, San Antonio, 1994 and others. Office: Burcon Fin Inc 1215 W Imperial Hwy Brea CA 92621-3738

CONKLIN, HAL (HAROLD CONKLIN), arts association executive; b. Oakland, Calif., Dec. 11, 1945; s. Ralph Harold and Stella (Garabedian) C.; m. Barbara Elaine Lang, Mar. 25, 1972; children: Nathaniel, Joseph Lucas, Zachary. Student, Calif. State U., Hayward, 1967-71. Editor New Focus Mag., Santa Barbara, Calif., 1969-72; co-dir. Community Environ. Coun., Santa Barbara, 1972-82; pres. Santa Barbara Renaissance Fund, 1983—. Councilman City of Santa Barbara, 1977-93, mayor, 1993—; bd. dirs. Santa Barbara Redevel. Agy., 1978—, Calif. Local Govt. Commn., Sacramento, 1979—, Nat. League of Cities, 1987-89; v.p. Nat. League of Cities, 1994. Mem. League of Calif. Cities (bd. dirs. 1986—, pres. 1991-92), Calif. Resource Recovery Assn. (pres. 1978-82). Methodist. Home: 214 El Monte Dr Santa Barbara CA 93109-2006 Office: City of Santa Barbara 735 Anacapa St Santa Barbara CA 93101-2203

CONLEY, GARY NELSON, economist; b. Cin., Mar. 12, 1949; s. William Paul and Geraldine Gay Conley; m. Patricia Ruggie, Oct. 1, 1992; 1 child, Aaron Conley. BA in Econs./Bus., Ctr. Coll., 1970; M of City Planning, U. Pa., 1972; M of Econs., Wright State U., 1975. Assoc. planner City Plan Bd., Dayton, Ohio, 1972-73; asst. dir. City Wide Devel. Corp., Dayton, 1973-78, dir., 1978-83; dir. econ. devel. City of Cleve., 1983-87; pres. North Coast Harbor Inc., Cleve., 1987-91, Econ. Devel. Corp. L.A. County, L.A., 1991—; cons. U.S. Depts. Commerce, Housing and Urban Devel., Cities of Chgo., St. Paul, Albuquerque, Toledo, Commonwealth of P.R., U.S. Conf. Bd. Contbr. articles to profl. jours. Pres. Nat. Coun. for Urban Econ. Devel., 1984-86; trustee Northwestern U., Evanston, Ill., 1986—, Calif. Econ. Devel. Assn., Cleve. Conv. and Vis. Bur., Cleve. State U. Coll. Urban Affairs Vis. com., Cleve. City-Devel. Corp. George Baker scholar, 1967, 70; recipient Wall Street Journal award, 1970. Office: Econ Devel Corp LA County 515 S Flower St # 32 Los Angeles CA 90071-2201

CONLEY, KEVIN EDWARD, biologist; b. Lake Bluff, Ill., Aug. 3, 1954. BA, Lake Forest (Ill.) Coll., 1976; PhD, U. Wis., 1983. Postdoctoral fellow Harvard U., Cambridge, Mass., 1983; exchange fellow U. Berne, Switzerland, 1983-85; rsch. fellow Harvard Med. Sch., Boston, 1986-88; rsch. asst. prof. radiology U. Wash., Seattle, 1988-94, rsch. assoc. prof., 1994—, assoc. prof., 1995—; vis. scientist Flinders U., Bedford, Australia, 1986-87; adj. assoc. prof. of bioengring., 1995—. Named NIH Nat. Rsch. Svc. awardee, 1985-88, Swiss Nat. Sci. Found. fellow, 1983; grantee Am. Heart Assn., 1990-93, USPHS, 1992—, NSF, 1993—. Mem. AAAS, Biophys. Soc., Am. Soc. Zoologists. Office: U Wash Med Ctr Dept Radiology Sb # 05 Seattle WA 98195

CONLEY, PHILIP JAMES, JR., retired air force officer; b. Providence, May 22, 1927; s. Philip James and Lillian Loretta (Burns) C.; m. Shirley Jean Andrews, Jan. 26, 1956; children: Sharon, Kathleen, Anne, James. BS, U.S. Naval Acad., 1950; MS, U. Mich., 1956, Rensselaer Poly. Inst., 1963. Commd. 2d lt. USAF, 1950, advanced through grades to maj. gen., 1979; dep. chief staff, ops. Air Force Systems Command, Andrews AFB, Washington, 1974-75; chief staff Air Force Systems Command, 1975-78; comdr. Air Force Flight Test Center, Edwards AFB, Calif., 1978-82, Hanscom AFB, Mass., 1983; ret., 1983. Decorated Legion Merit with oakleaf cluster, Air medal (2), D.F.C., D.S.M. (2). Mem. Air Force Assn., Order of Daedalians, U.S. Naval Acad. Alumni Assn., Am. Legion, Vikings Club (L.A.). Roman Catholic. Home: 930 Camino Viejo Santa Barbara CA 93108-1920

CONLEY, SUSAN BERNICE, medical school faculty pediatrician; b. Coldwater, Mich., Feb. 3, 1948; d. Kenneth D. and Mary F. (Spence) C. MD, U. Mich., 1973. Instr. Washington U. Med. Sch., St. Louis, 1977-78; asst. prof. pediatrics U. Tex. Med. Sch., Houston, 1978-84, dir. pediatric nephrology, 1983—, assoc. prof. pediatrics, 1984-91; dir. pediatric renal ctr. Calif. Pacific Med. Ctr., San Francisco, 1991-94; prof. pediatrics sch. medicine Stanford (Calif.) U., 1994—; chmn. med. adv. bd. No. Calif. chpt. Nat. Kidney Found., pres. region V western states. Fellow Am. Acad. Pediatrics; mem. Am. Soc. Nephrology, Am. Soc. Pediatric Nephrology, Soc. for Pediatric Rsch. Office: Sch Medicine Dept Pediatrics Stanford U Stanford CA 94305-5119

CONLEY, ZEB BRISTOL, JR., art gallery director; b. Andrews, N.C., Feb. 12, 1936; s. Zeb Bristol and A. Elizabeth (Faircloth) C.; student N.C. State Coll., 1954-55, Mars Hill Coll., 1955-57, Coll. William and Mary, 1957-61; m. Betty Ann Wiswall, May 25, 1974; stepchildren—Peter Wiswall Betts, Stephen Wood Betts, Frederick Beale Betts, III. Designer, Seymour Robins, Inc., N.Y.C., 1961; with First Nat. Bank, Las Vegas (N.Mex.), 1964-65; gen. mgr. Swanson's Inc., Las Vegas, 1965-73, v.p., 1969-86; dir. Jamison Galleries, Santa Fe, 1973—, guest curator Alfred Morang: A Retrospective at Mus. of S.W. Midland, Tex., 1985; sec. Marbasconi, Inc., d.b.a. Jamison Galleries, 1974-80, pres., 1980—. Republican. Office: c/o The Jamison Galleries 560 Montezuma Ave Ste 103 Santa Fe NM 87501-2590

CONLIN, RICHARD BYRD, association administrator; b. Washington, May 1, 1948; married; 3 children. BA in History, Mich. State U., 1968, MA in Polit. Sci., 1971. Systems rep. Burroughs Corp., 1969-73; projects dir. Pub. Interest Rsch. Group in Mich., 1973-77; lectr. in pub. adminstrn. U. Botswana and Swaziland, 1977-79; legis. network coord. Solar Lobby, 1979-81; energy mgmt. projects dir. Alcor Cmty. Oriented Devel., 1981-87; dir. cmty. and environ. project Metroctr. YMCA, Seattle, 1984—; dir. earth svc. corps Seattle YMCA, 1992—; speaker, presenter workshops in field; testifier for Mich. Pub. Svc. Commn. Author: Head 'em Up...Move 'em Out, 1987, Hazard Free Home Handbook, 1992, also brochures, articles, reports in field; editor, co-author: A Handbook on the Constitution, 1987; editor: Wealth and Well-Being, 1986; developer, editor newsletter N.W. Conservation Act Report, 1981-82. Mem. Ingham County Bd. Commrs., 1972-76; alternate del. Dem. Nat. Conv., 1976; mem. Seattle City Light Alternative Resources Planning Citizen Adv. Com., 1981-85; docent Woodland Park Zoo, 1982-85; co-chair Seattle City Light Rate Adv. Com., 1985-86; bd. dirs. Madrona Cmty. Coun., 1986-89, N.W. Conservation Act Coalition, 1992—, Puget Sound Alliance, 1987—, treas., 1988-92; co-chair action programs working group, edn. and pub. involvement adv. group Puget Sound Water Quality Authority, 1987-89; active Seattle Citizens Tech. Adv. Com. on Secondary Wastewater Treatment Alternatives, 1986-88, United Way Leadership Tomorrow, 1990-91, City of Seattle Environ. Priorities Project Adv. Com., 1990-92, Bonneville Power Adminstrn. Puget Sound Electric Reliability Plan Sounding Bd., 1990-92. Recipient award Nat. Assn. Counties for Innovative Programs, Environ. Quality award U.S. EPA, 1st prize Soc. for Human Ecology, 1989. Office: Metrocenter YMCA 909 4th Ave Seattle WA 98104-1108

CONLIN, WILLIAM PATRICK, computer company executive; b. Gardner, Mass., Dec. 15, 1933; s. William Patrick Conlin and Nora A. (Helow) Patriquin; stepfather: George A Patriquin; m. Laila Strott, May 30, 1957; children: Margo Ann, Patrick George. BBA, U. Mass., 1959; MBA, U. Calif., Berkeley, 1960. With Burroughs Corp., 1960-83; v.p. product mgmt. Burroughs Corp., Detroit, 1978-79, v.p., group exec. internat. group, 1979-81, sr. v.p., pres. industry systems group, 1982-83, sr. v.p., pres. large accounts devel. group, 1983; pres. CalComp Inc., Anaheim, Calif., 1983—; v.p. Lockheed Corp., Calabasas, Calif., 1986-92; bd. dirs. SDRC, Milford, Ohio. Bd. dirs. Orange County Philharm. Soc., Costa Mesa, 1985, pres., 1991-92; bd. dirs. Orange County coun. Boy Scouts Am., Costa Mesa, 1986-92, UCI Found.; active Opera Pacific, Costa Mesa, 1985. With USMC, 1953-56. Mem. Balboa Bay Club and Racquet Club, Center Club. Republican. Methodist. Office: CalComp Inc 2411 W La Palma Ave Anaheim CA 92801-2610

CONN, RICHARD GEORGE, retired art museum curator; b. Bellingham, Wash., Oct. 28, 1928; s. Bert Grover and Mary Ann (Slack) C. BA, U. Wash., 1950, MA, 1955. Curator history Ea. Wash. State Hist. Soc., Spokane, 1959-61, dir., 1961-66; chief human history Man. (Can.) Provincial Mus., Winnipeg, 1966-70; dir. Heard Mus., Phoenix, 1970-72; curator Indian art Denver Art Mus., 1955-59, curator native art, 1972-90, chief curator, 1990-93; ret., 1993; bd. dirs. Native Am. Art Studies, 1989-93. Author: (exhbn. catalogues) Robes of White Shell and Sunrise, 1974, Circles of the World, 1982, A Persistent Vision, 1986, (collection catalogue) American Indian in the Denver Art Museum, 1979. With U.S. Army, 1951-53. Recipient Excellence in Arts award Colo. Gov.'s Office, 1993, Rosenstock Lifetime Achievement award, 1994; fellow McCloy Found., Germany, 1979. Mem. Am. Assn. Mus., An. Anthrop. Assn., Westeners (Denver Posse). Democrat. Office: Denver Art Mus 100 W 14th Ave Denver CO 80204-2788

CONNELL, WILLIAM D., lawyer; b. Palo Alto, Calif., Apr. 1, 1955; s. Robert Charles and Audrey Elizabeth (Steele) C.; m. Kathy Lynn Mleko, Aug. 13, 1977; 1 child, Hilary Anne. BA in Polit Sci. with honors, Stanford U., 1976; JD cum laude, Harvard U., 1979. Bar: Calif. 1979, U.S. Dist. Ct. (cen., no. and ea. dists.) Calif. 1979, U.S. Ct. Appeals (9th cir.) 1979. Assoc. Gibson, Dunn & Crutcher, L.A., 1979-80; assoc. Gibson, Dunn & Crutcher, San Jose, Calif., 1980-87, ptnr., 1988—. Mem. Christian Legal Soc. Mem. Stanford Alumni Assn. (life), Commonwealth Club Calif., The Churchill Club, Silicon Valley Capital Club (founder), Sports Car Club Am., Phi Beta Kappa. Republican. Office: Gibson Dunn & Crutcher Telesis Tower 26th Flr 1 Montgomery St San Francisco CA 94104-4505

CONNELLAN, D. MICHAEL, health care finance executive; b. Washington, July 4, 1947; s. Gerald V. and Marjorie J. (Gunnels) C.; m. Suzanne D. Dochez, May 9, 1970; children: Jennifer Shannon, Christine Lauren. Student, U.S. Naval Acad., 1965-67; BA, U. Ky., 1970; MS, Ind. U., 1972; MBA in Fin. with Distinction, Am. U., 1976. Mgmt. cons. Booz, Allen and Hamilton, 1980-81; asst. treas. Coop. Fin. Corp., 1981-85; prin. Alex. Brown, Inc., 1985-90; sr. v.p. Nationwide Health Properties, 1991-93, Gran Care, Inc., Culver City, Calif., 1993—; bd. dirs. Brown Healthcare, Inc., Brown Healthcare Holding Cos. Bd. dirs. Mission Viejo Nadadores Found., Inc. Bd. dirs. Mission Viejo Nadadores Found., Inc., 1991—. Republican. Office: Gran Care Inc 300 Corporate Pointe Ste 400 Culver City CA 90230-7642

CONNELLY, DIANE MAUREEN, urology service coordinator; b. Springfield, Mass., Sept. 29, 1943; d. Paul A. and Catherine C. Connelly. Diploma, Framingham (Mass.) Union Hosp., 1964; BA, Am. Internat. Coll., 1967; MEd, Springfield Coll., 1971; MSN, U. San Diego, 1993. Emergency rm. nurse, utilization rev. nurse Wesson Meml. Hosp., Springfield, 1965-74; oper. rm. nurse Alvarado Community Hosp., San Diego, 1974-76; cardiac lab. nurse, oper. rm. nurse Beth Israel Hosp., Boston, 1976-83; from oper. rm. nurse to outpatient dept. nurse Children's Hosp., San Diego, 1989-93, oper. rm. nurse, 1993—. Mem. Assn. Oper. Rm. Nurses, Emergency Nurses Assn., Am. Heart Assn., Sigma Theta Tau. Home: 7974 Mission Center Ct # A San Diego CA 92108-1464

CONNELLY, JOHN WILLIAM, wildlife research biologist; b. Waterbury, Conn., June 7, 1952; s. John William and Katherine Marie (McHann) C.; m. Cheryl Ann Hinman, Aug. 24, 1974; children: Jennifer, Allison. AS, Paul Smiths Coll., 1972; BS, U. Idaho, 1974; MS, Wash. State U., 1977, PhD, 1982. Rsch. asst. Wash. State U., Pullman, 1974-80; biol. technician U.S. Fish and Wildlife Svc., Missoula, Mont., 1980-82; wildlife scientist EG&G Idaho Inc., Idaho Falls, 1982-84; regional wildlife biologist Idaho Dept. Fish & Game, Salmon, 1984-85; prin. wildlife rsch. biologist Idaho Dept. Fish & Game, Pocatello, 1985—; rschr. sage and sharp-tailed grouse Idaho Dept. Fish and Game, Pocatello, 1977—; state rep. Western States Grouse Workshop, Boise, 1985—, Prairie Grouse Tech. Conf., Boise, 1991—; mem. EPA Pesticide Adv. Panel, Seattle, 1990—; cons. Oreg. and Utah Fish and Wildlife, Blackfoot, Idaho, 1988—; lectr. R.O. Butler Lectures, S.D. State U., 1990-93; grad. faculty U. Idaho, Moscow, Idaho State U., Pocatello. Contbr. tech. papers to profl. jours. Soccer coach Blackfoot Youth Soccer Assn., 1992-94, Blackfoot AYSO, 1988-94; regional soccer coach AYSO, Blackfoot, 1994; merit badge counselor Boy Scouts Am., Blackfoot and Shelley, Idaho, 1988—. Recipient Ted Trueblood comms. award, 1991, Profl. and Tech. award Idaho Dept. Fish and Game, 1993, Tech. Rsch. award U.S. Forest Svc, 1995; rsch. grantee various funding sources, 1977—. Mem. Am. Ornithologists Union, The Wildlife Soc. (com. mem.), Idaho chpt. The Wildlife Soc. (pres. 1988-92, Wildlife Profl. of Yr. 1992), Cooper Ornithol. Soc., Soc. for Range Mgmt. (chpt. chmn. 1989). Methodist. Office: Idaho Dept Fish and Game 1345 Barton Rd Pocatello ID 83204-1847

CONNER, FINIS F., electronics company executive; b. Gadsden, Ala., July 28, 1943; s. William Otis and Vera Belle (Beasley) C.; m. Julie Machura, July 17, 1971. BS in Indsl. Mgmt., San Jose State U., 1969. Pres. Mastec Corp., Cupertino, Calif., 1969-71; original equipment mfr. market mgr. Memorex, Santa Clara, Calif., 1971-73; co-founder, western regional mgr. Shugart Assocs., Sunnyvale, Calif., 1973-79; co-founder, exec. v.p. sales and mktg., bd. dirs. Seagate Tech., Scotts Valley, Calif., 1979-85; co-founder, chmn., CEO Conner Peripherals Inc., San Jose, Calif., 1985—. With USN Air Res. Mem. Eldorado County Club, Quarry at La Quinta, Monterey Peninsula County Club, Preston Trail Golf Club, The Vintage Club, Big Horn County Club, Castle Pines Golf Club (Denvr). Democrat. Office: Conner Peripherals 3081 Zanker Rd San Jose CA 95134-2127

CONNER, JEANNE WILLIAMS, retired educator; b. Pitts., Aug. 10, 1930; d. John Scouten and Jean (Haggenjos) Williams; m. James Beynon Conner, Aug. 9, 1952; children: James Beynon Jr., David Hardwick, William Scouten. BS, Northwestern U., Evanston, 1952; postgrad., U. Calif., Santa Barbara, 1966-68. Rsch. asst. AMA, Chgo., 1952-54; tchr. The Harris Sch., Chgo., 1961-63, Laguna Blanca Sch., Santa Barbara, Calif., 1965-76; spl. edn. tchr. Santa Barbara Ctr. Ednl. Therapy, 1977-79; pvt. tutor Santa Barbara, 1979-80. writer Am. Jour. of Forensic Psychiatry, reviewer; writer Bur. of Med. Econ. Rsch. of AMA, 1952-54. Mem. AAUW, Phi Beta Kappa. Republican. Congregationalist. Home: 14409 W Futura Dr Sun City West AZ 85375-5931

CONNER, LINDSAY ANDREW, screenwriter, producer; b. N.Y.C., Feb. 19, 1956; s. Michael and Miriam (Mintzer) C. BA summa cum laude, UCLA, 1976; MA, Occidental Coll., 1977; JD magna cum laude, Harvard U., 1980. Bar: Calif. 1980, U.S. Dist. Ct. (cen. dist.) Calif. 1983. Assoc. Kaplan, Livingston, Goodwin, Berkowitz & Selvin, Beverly Hills, Calif., 1980-81, Fulop & Hardee, Beverly Hills, 1982-83, Wyman, Bautzer, Kuchel & Silbert, L.A., 1983-86; ptnr., entertainment dept. head Hill Wynne Troop & Meisinger, L.A., 1986-93. Author: (with others) The Courts and Education, 1977; editor: Harvard Law Rev., 1978-80. Trustee L.A. Community Coll., 1981—, bd. pres., 1989-90; pres. Calif. Community Coll. Trustees, 1992-93. Mem. ABA, L.A. County Bar Assn., UCLA Alumni Assn. (life), Harvard-Radcliffe Club, Phi Beta Kappa. Office: 54th St Prodns 10960 Wilshire Blvd Ste 1428 Los Angeles CA 90024

CONNER, NATALIE ANN, community health nurse specialist; b. Iowa City, May 6, 1962; d. Frederick Raymond and Sheila Ruth (Rapoport) Greenberg; m. Eric Lyle Conner, Sept. 12, 1987 (div. May 1995). BSN, U. Wash., 1984; MS, U. Calif., San Francisco, 1992. Cert. community health nurse, ANCC, pub. health nurse, State Calif., HIV counselor DHHS/ Oreg. State Health Div. Charge nurse Riverton Hosp. Care Unit., Seattle, 1985; community health nurse Sound Heart, Seattle, 1985-88; staff nurse Univ. Hosp., Seattle, 1986-88; nurse Portland (Oreg.) Indian Health Clinic, 1988-89; staff nurse San Francisco State U. Student Health Svc., 1989-92; clin. instr. U. California, San Francisco, 1992; rsch. nurse dept. pediatrics U. Wash., Seattle, 1992—; nurse cons. job corps program region X Dept. Labor, 1992—; sec. Grad. Nurses Student Coun., U. Calif., 1991-92; chairperson Nrusing Peer Rev. Com. Student Health Svcs. U. Calif., 1991-92; mem. commencement com. U. Calif., 1992-92. Delegate Washington State Democratic Convention, Seattle, 1984. Mem. Am. Nurses Assn., Am. Pub. Health Assn., King County Nurses Assn. (membership com. 1986-88), Sigma Theta Tau. Democrat. Jewish.

CONNOLLY, DAVID L., retail executive; b. Juntura, Oreg., May 27, 1934; s. Michael J. and Mae J. Connolly; m. Mary J. Lukesh, May 7, 1960; children: Michael, Kellie, Scott. BS, U. Oreg., 1957; postgrad. in fin., Harvard U., 1977. Staff acct. Albertson's, Boise, Idaho, 1959-61, mgr. accounts payable, 1963-66, asst. contr., 1966-72, contr., 1972-76, treas., 1976-77, v.p. fin., 1977—. Chmn. gen. employees Ada County United Way, 1975, bd. dirs., 1978, chmn. 1992-93 campaign. With Fin. Corps U.S. Army, 1957-59. Recipient award United Way, 1975. Mem. Nat. Assn. Accts., Adminstrv. Mgmt. Soc. (pres. 1974), Fin. Execs. Inst., Boise Area Econ. Devel. Coun. Republican. Roman Catholic. Office: Albertson's Inc PO Box 20 250 E Parkcenter Blvd Boise ID 83726-0001

CONNOLLY, JOHN EARLE, surgeon, educator; b. Omaha, May 21, 1923; s. Earl A. and Gertrude (Eckerman) C.; m. Virginia Hartman, Aug. 12, 1967; children: Peter Hart. John Earle, Sarah. A.B., Harvard U., 1945, M.D., 1948. Diplomate: Am. Bd. Surgery (bd. dirs. 1976-82), Am. Bd. Thoracic and Cardiovascular Surgery, Am. Bd. Vascular Surgery. Intern. in surgery Stanford U. Hosps., San Francisco, 1948-49, surg. research fellow, 1949-50, asst. resident surgeon, 1950-52, chief resident surgeon, 1953-54, surg. pathology fellow, 1954-55, 1957-60, John and Mary Markle Scholar in med. scis., 1957-62; surg. registrar professional unit St. Bartholomew's Hosp., London, 1952-53; resident in thoracic surgery Bellevue Hosp.,

N.Y.C., 1955; resident in thoracic and cardiovascular surgery Columbia-Presbyn. Med. Ctr., N.Y.C., 1956; from instr. to assoc. prof. surgery Stanford U., 1957-65; prof. U. Calif., Irvine, 1965—, chmn. dept. surgery, 1965-78; attending surgeon Stanford Med. Ctr., Palo Alto, Calif., 1959-65; chmn. cardiovascular and thoracic surgery Irvine Med. Ctr. U. Calif., 1968—; attending surgeon Children's Hosp., Orange, Calif., 1968—, Anaheim (Calif.) Meml. Hosp., 1970—; vis. prof. Beijing Heart, Lung, Blood Vessel Inst., 1990, A.H. Duncan vis. prof. U. Edinburgh, 1984; Hunterian prof. Royal Coll. Surgeons Eng., 1985-86; Kinmonth lectr. Royal Coll. Surgeons, Eng., 1987; mem. adv. coun. Nat. Heart, Lung, and Blood Inst.-NIH, 1981-85; cons. Long Beach VA Hosp., Calif., 1965—. Contbr. articles to profl. jours.; editorial bd.: Jour. Cardiovascular Surgery, 1974—, chief editor, 1985—; editorial bd. Western Jour. Medicine, 1975—, Jour. Stroke, 1979—, Jour. Vascular Surgery, 1983—. Bd. dirs. Audio-Digest Found., 1974—; bd. dirs. Franklin Martin Found., 1975-80; regent Uniformed Svcs. U. of Health Scis., Bethesda, 1992—. Served with AUS, 1943-44. Recipient Cert. of Merit, Japanese Surg. Soc., 1979, 90. Fellow ACS (gov. 1964-70, regent 1973-82, vice chmn. bd. regents 1980-82, v.p. 1984-85), Royal Coll. Surgeons Eng. (hon.), Royal Coll. Surgeons Ireland (hon.), Royal Coll. Surgeons Edinburgh (hon.); mem. Am. Surg. Assn., Soc. Univ. Surgeons, Am. Assn. Thoracic Surgery (coun. 1974-78), Pacific Coast Surg. Assn. (pres. 1985-86), San Francisco Surg. Soc., L.A. Surg. Soc., Soc. Vascular Surgery, Western Surg. Assn., Internat. Cardiovascular Soc. (pres. 1977), Soc. Internat. Chirurgie, Soc. Thoracic Surgeons, Western Thoracic Surg. Soc. (pres. 1978), Orange County Surg. Soc. (pres. 1984-85), James IV Assn. Surgeons (councillor 1983—). Clubs: California (Los Angeles); San Francisco Golf, Pacific Union, Bohemian (San Francisco); Cypress Point (Pebble Beach, Calif.); Harvard (N.Y.C.); Big Canyon (Newport Beach). Home: 7 Deerwood Ln Newport Beach CA 92660-5108 Office: U Calif Dept Surgery Irvine CA 92717

CONNOLLY, MICHAEL JOSEPH, priest, educator; b. Boston, Mar. 15, 1937; s. John Patrick and Agnes Christine (Concannon) C. BA, MA, Boston Coll., 1960, 1961, BD, 1968; MA in Law and Diplomacy, Fletcher Sch. Law & Diplomacy, Medford, Mass., 1973; PhD, Monash U., Australia, 1986. Ordained priest, Roman Cath. Ch., 1968; mem. Soc. Jesus. Sr. tutor in politics Monash U., Clayton, Vic, 1974-80; asst. prof. Gonzaga U., Spokane, 1983-90, assoc. prof., 1990—; chmn. polit. sci. dept. Gonzaga U., 1992-95; dir. internat. studies program, 1988-92. Author: Church Lands and Peasant Unrest in the Philippines, 1992. Bd. dirs. Sister Cities, Spokane, 1988-90. Mem. Am. Polit. Sci. Assn., Internat. Studies Assn. Democrat. Office: Gonzaga U 502 E Boone Ave Spokane WA 99258-1774

CONNOLLY, PHYLLIS MARIE, nursing educator, clinical specialist; b. Summit, N.J., Oct. 24, 1942; d. William James Connolly Sr. and Margaret Elizabeth Coughlin; m. Bruno E. Zorzi, Sept. 21, 1963 (div. June 1978); children: Michael K. Zorzi, Colleen Patricia Zorzi; m. G. Michael Northrup, Aug. 16, 1980. BA magna cum laude, Georgian Ct. Coll., 1974; MS, Rutgers U., 1981; PhD, Golden Gate U., 1987. RN, Calif., N.J.; cert. clin. specialist adult psychiat./mental health nursing ANCC. Staff nurse ICU Middlesex Gen. Hosp., New Brunswick, N.J., 1963-64; staff nurse Community Meml. Hosp., Toms River, N.J., 1966-67, staff nurse coronary care unit, 1967-68, evening supr., 1968-74, insvc. instr., 1974; pub. health nurse Ocean County Health Dept., Toms River, N.J., 1974-75; nursing care coord. emergency dept., mainland div. Atlantic Mental Health Ctr., Atlantic City, N.J., 1975-76; insvc. educator mainland div. Atlantic Mental Health Ctr., Pomona, N.J., 1976-78; mental health cons. Atlantic Mental Health Ctr., Atlantic City, 1978-81, adminstrv. asst. C.I.P., 1980-81; asst. prof. Stockton State Coll., Pomona, N.J., 1981-83; assoc. prof. San Jose (Calif.) State U., 1983-90, interim dept. chair, 1990, prof., 1991—; pvt. practice, 1982—, coord. transdisciplinary collaboration project, 1993—; facilitator, trainer Moller-Wer Simultaneous Patient Family Edn., 1994—; dir. Inst. Nursing Rsch. & Practice, 1995—; instr., mentor Consortium of Calif. State U. Nursing Program, 1984-86; psych. nurse cons., Vis. Nurses' Assn., Santa Clara, Calif., 1986-89; active in acad. governance local campus and statewide Calif. State U., 1987-94, chair personnel com., 1991-93; cons., content dir. Nat. Coun. Licensure exam, CTB McGraw-Hill Psych./Mental Health Nursing, 1988, 89; coord. nurse managed ctrs., 1988-92, semester 6 chair, 1984-88, 92-94, project dir. Los Gatos CDBG, 1989-92; presenter profl meetings, local, state, nat. and internat. Contbr. articles to profl. jours. Mem. Santa Clara County Alliance for the Mentally Ill, 1986—; curriculum and tng. network Spl. Com. of Nat. Alliance for Mentally Ill, 1989—; bd. dirs. ACT for Mental Health, San Jose, 1987—; chair profl. adv. com. ACT, 1987—. Recipient NIMH Grad. Tgn. grant, Rutgers U., 1979-80, Sigma Theta Tau scholarship, 1985, 86, 87, 90, 93. Fellow Am. Orthopsychiat. Assn.; mem. ASPA, ANA (cert. clin. specialist, govt. rels. com. 1984-94), Am. Psychiat. Nurses Assn. (chair of regional and state reps. 1991-94, regional rep. Calif. 1991—, co-chair The Consumer & Family Educators spl. interest group 1994—, chair task force on spl. interest groups 1995), Calif. Faculty Assn., Bay Area Nursing Diagnosis Assn. (sec. 1991-92), Calif. Alliance for the Mentally Ill (co-chair task force on families and mental illness 1991—, cons. to Bakersfield Alliance for Mentally Ill and Calif. State U. Bakersfield 1995), Sigma Theta Tau (nominating com. 1993-94). Republican. Roman Catholic. Office: San Jose U Sch Nursing San Jose CA 95192

CONNOLLY, THOMAS JOSEPH, bishop; b. Tonopah, Nev., July 18, 1922; s. John and Katherine (Hammel) C. Student, St. Joseph Coll. and St. Patrick Sem., Menlo Park, Calif., 1936-47, Catholic U. Am., 1949-51; JCD, Lateran Pontifical U., Rome, 1952; DHL (hon.), U. Portland, 1972. Ordained priest Roman Cath. Ch., 1947. Asst. St. Thomas Cathedral, Reno, 1947, asst., rector, 1953-55; asst. Little Flower Parish, Reno, 1947-48; sec. to bishop, 1949; asst. St. Albert the Gt., Reno, 1952-53; pastor St. Albert the Gt., 1960-68, St. Joseph Ch., Elko, 1955-60, St. Theresa's Ch., Carson City, Nev., 1968-71; bishop Baker, Oreg., 1971—; Tchr. Manogue High Sch., Reno, 1948-49; chaplain Serra Club, 1948-49; officialis Diocese of Reno; chmn. bldg. com., dir. Cursillo Movement; moderator Italian Cath. Fedn.; dean, mem. personnel bd. Senate of Priests; mem. Nat. Bishops Liturgy Com., 1973-76; region XII rep. to adminstrv. bd. Nat. Conf. Cath. Bishops, 1973-76, 86-89, mem. adv. com., 1974-76; bd. dirs. Cath. Communications Northwest, 1977-82. Club: K.C. (state chaplain Nev. 1970-71). Home: 63255 Overtree Rd Bend OR 97701-9759 Office: Bishop of Baker PO Box 5999 Bend OR 97708-5999*

CONNOLLY, TOM M., state legislator, lawyer; b. Toledo, Ohio, May 12, 1946; s. Thomas M. and Margaret Ann (Bodie) C.; m. Janet Connolly, Oct. 29, 1988. BA, Calif. State U., Northridge, 1971; JD, Pepperdine U., 1974. Bar: Calif., U.S. Supreme Ct., U.S. Ct. Mil. Appeals. Judge adv. USMC, Camp Pendleton, Calif., 1974-77; atty. Law Offices of David McKenzie, Oceanside, Calif., 1977-79; sole practice Carlsbad, Calif., 1979-88; child adv. atty. San Diego Pub. Defender, 1988-93; legislator Calif. State Assembly, Sacramento, 1993-94; child advocate atty. San Diego Pub. Defender, 1995—. Vice chmn. Community Adv. Bd. Calif. Conservation Corps, San Diego, 1991-94. Sgt. U.S. Army, 1968-70, Vietnam; capt. USMC, 1974-77. Decorated Vietnamese Cross Gallantry. Mem. C.C.C., VFW, Am. Legion. Democrat. Roman Catholic. Home: 8350 Golden Ave Lemon Grove CA 91945-2627 Office: Calif State Assembly State Capitol Sacramento CA 95814-4906

CONNOR, BRUCE J., construction company executive; b. 1929. With Cubbitt Wells, Auckland, New Zealand, 1961-72, Mainline Constrn., Melbourne, Australia, 1972-75, EA Watts, Melbourne, Australia, 1975-79; now pres. Fletcher Industries Ltd., 1979—. Office: Fletcher Chllnge Inds USA LTD 425 Pontius Ave N Ste 100 Seattle WA 98109-5451*

CONNOR, CHARLES PETER, psychiatrist, educator; b. Greenwich, Conn., Mar. 14, 1955; s. George Peter and Elline (Walther) C.; m. Yetty Croff; 1 child, Jetty Jane. BA, Calif. Luth. U., 1977; MD, Med. Coll. Wis., 1985; MA, U. Chgo., 1992. Asst. prof. clin. psychiatry U. Chgo., 1991-92; asst. clin. prof. U. Calif., San Francisco, 1992—. Mem. AMA, Am. Psychiatric Assn., Am. Soc. Addiction Medicine, Am. Assn. Psychiatrists in Alcoholism and Addiction, Calif. Psychiatric Assn., Calif. Med. Assn. Home: 2628 Greenwich St San Francisco CA 94123-3206 Office: San Francisco VA Med Ctr 4150 Clement St San Francisco CA 94121-1545

CONNOR, GARY EDWARD, manufacturing company marketing executive; b. S.I., N.Y., Nov. 13, 1948; s. Everett M. and Josephine (Amato) C.; B.S. in Elec. Engring., U. Md., 1973; M.B.A., U. Santa Clara (Calif.), 1979. Quality assurance engr. Frankford Arsenal, 1973; quality assurance engr., field service engr. Lockheed Electronics Co., 1973-74; group leader memory test engring. sect. head bipolar product engring. Nat. Semicondr. Corp., 1975-79; internat. mktg. mgr. Am. Microsystems Inc., 1979-80; mktg. mgr. GenRad-STI, Santa Clara, 1980-82; prodn. mktg. exec. AMD, Sunnyvale, Calif., 1982-86; dept. mgr. IDT, Santa Clara, Calif., 1986—. Mem. IEEE, Electronics Internat. Adv. Panel, Am. Security Council (nat. adv. bd.), Franklin Mint Collectors Soc. Republican. Home: 5121 Kozo Ct San Jose CA 95124-5527 Office: 2670 Seely Ave San Jose CA 95134-1929

CONNOR, PAUL LYLE, medical librarian; b. San Francisco, June 1, 1954; s. Harold Leon and Greta Frances (Holliger) C.; m. Martha Emily Bowman, Aug. 30, 1980; children: Laura, Erin, Rebecca, Daniel. BA, U. Calif., Berkeley, 1976, M Libr. Info. Svcs., 1981. Med. libr. VA Med. Ctr., Fresno, Calif., 1981-89, Valley Children's Hosp., Fresno, 1989—. Mem. Acad. Health Info. Profls., Med. Libr. Assn., No. Calif. and Nev. Med. Libr. Group, Med. Libr. Group So. Calif. and Ariz. Office: Valley Children's Hosp 3151 N Millbrook Ave Fresno CA 93703-1425

CONNORS, DENNIS MICHAEL, infosystems executive; b. Anaconda, Mont., June 13, 1943; s. Dennis Anthony and Vivian Helen (Mahaulos) C.; m. Sandra Lee Haubrich, Sept. 15, 1962; children: Brad, Kevin, Karrie, Timothy, Tricia. AA, El Camino Sch., 1966; Cert. in Tech. of Info. Mgmt., U. Calif., Long Beach, 1967; degree in bus. mgmt., U. Mont., 1963; postgrad., Stanford U. Sr. Exec. Program, 1985. Mgr. TRW Systems, Los Angeles, 1965-77; dir. Levi Strauss & Co., San Francisco, 1977-79; dir. Mervyn's, Hayward, Calif., 1979-81, v.p., 1981—; mem. info. systems adv. bd. Golden Gate U., San Francisco, 1984. Vice chmn. Bay Area Urban League, Oakland, Calif., 1983—. Mem. Data Processing Mgmt. Assn., Am. Mgmt. Assn., Nat. Retail Mchts. Assn. (bd. dirs. info. systems div. 1984—). Office: Mervyn's 22305 Foothill Blvd Hayward CA 94541-2709 Office: The Gap Inc 1 Harrison St San Francisco CA 94105-1602

CONOVER, MONA LEE, retired adult education educator; b. Lincoln, Nebr., Nov. 9, 1929; d. William Cyril and Susan Ferne (Floyd) C.; m. Elmer Kenneth Johnson, June 14, 1953 (div. 1975); children: Michael David, Susan Amy, Sharon Ann, Jennifer Lynne. AB, Nebr. Wesleyan U., 1952; student, Ariz. State U., 1973-75; MA in Edn., No. Ariz. U., 1985. Cert. tchr., Colo., Ariz. Tchr. Jefferson County R-1 Sch., Wheat Ridge, Colo., 1952-56, Glendale (Ariz.) Elem. Sch. # 40, 1972-92; dir. Glendale Adult Edn., 1987-92; ret., 1992. Author: ABC's of Naturalization, 1989. Mem. AAUW, Phoenix Bot. Gardens, Heard Mus., Phoenix Zoo, Order of Ea. Star. Republican. Methodist.

CONOVER, ROBERT WARREN, librarian; b. Manhattan, Kans., Oct. 6, 1937; s. Robert Warren and Grace Darline (Grinstead) C.; BA, Kans. State U., 1959; MA, U. Denver, 1961. Librarian, supervising librarian County of Fresno, Calif., 1961-66; county librarian County of Yolo, Woodland, Calif., 1967-68; dir. City of Fullerton (Calif.) Pub. Library, 1968-73, City of Pasadena (Calif.) Pub. Library, 1973-80, Palos Verdes Library Dist., Palos Verdes Peninsula, Calif., 1980-85, City of Commerce (Calif.) Pub. Library, 1985—. Recipient Pres.'s award Fresno Jaycees, 1963. Mem. ALA, Orange County Libr. Assn. (pres. 1971), Spl. Librs. Assn., Calif. Libr. Assn. (pres. Yosemite chpt. 1965, mem. coun. 1981), Santiago Libr. System Coun. (pres. 1972), Met. Coop. Libr. System (exec. com. mem., 1994, vice chair 1995), Univ. Club, Pi Kappa Alpha. Episcopalian. Home: 280 N Orange Grove Blvd Pasadena CA 91103-3536 Office: City of Commerce Pub Libr 5655 Jillson St Commerce CA 90040-1493

CONRAD, BARBARA ANN, association executive; b. El Paso, Tex., Aug. 2, 1942; d. Gordon Andrew and Jewel Charlotte (Wilbanks) Jones; m. Robert G. Conrad,. BA, U. Tex., Austin, 1965; postgrad., Tex. Women's U., 1970-73, So. Meth. U., 1974. Caseworker Austin State Hosp., 1965-66; floor mgr. Titche-Goettingen Dept. Store, Dallas, 1966-68; dir. adult activity ctr. Dallas Assn. Retarded Citizens, 1968-70; supr. adult svcs. San Antonio Assn. Retarded Citizens, 1970-71; recreation therapist Children's Devel. Ctr., Dallas, 1975-80; devel. specialist Idaho Dept. Health & Welfare, Nampa, 1980-83; exec. asst. to pres. Coll. of Idaho, Caldwell, 1982-83, dean students, 1983-86; field svc. dir. Silver Sage Girl Scouts, Boise, 1986-88; dir. Community Edn., Lewistown, Mont., 1988-91; program coord. Adult Literacy Ctr., Durango, Colo., 1991-92; dir. Durango Arts Coun., 1992—; lectr., cons. in field of non-profit adminstrn. Nat. trainer of trainers Girls Scouts U.S., 1989—; active in various charitable orgns. Named Ida. Vol. of the Yr., 1983, Woman of Distinction by Girl Scouts of Chaparral Coun., 1994; recipient Disting. Vol. award, HHS, 1984. Mem. AAUW, Soroptomist. Methodist. Home: 107 Crazy Horse Dr Durango CO 81301-3101 Office: Durango Arts Coun 835 Main Ave Ste 210 Durango CO 81301-5436

CONRAD, JOHN WILFRED, fine arts educator, ceramist; b. Cresson, Pa., Aug. 3, 1935; s. Wilfred L. and Elizabeth S. (Bouch) C.; m. Barbara J. Daugherty, 1963; children: William Thomas, Kristin Elizabeth. BS, Indiana U. of Pa., 1958; MFA, Carnegie Mellon U., 1963; PhD, U. Pitts., 1970. Tchr. art Penn-Hills Sr. High Sch., Pitts., 1959-64; part-time instr. Carnegie Mellon U., Pitts., 1960-64; prof. fine arts Mesa Coll., San Diego, 1966—, chmn. dept., 1980-82, 85-88; chief officer Falcon Co., San Diego, 1983—. Author: Ceramic Formulas: The Complete Compendium, 1973, Contemporary Ceramic Techniques, 1979, Contemporary Ceramic Formulas, 1980, Ceramic Windchimes, 1983, Advanced Ceramic Manual, 1988, Studio Potter's Dictionary, 1990, Cone Six Ceramics, 1994. Recipient Outstanding Alumni award Ind. U. Pa., 1993. Mem. Ceramic Artists San Diego, Nat. Coun. on Edn. for the Ceramic Arts (co-chair 1993 San Diego conf.), Mex.-Am. Educators Exch., Chinese-Am. Ceramic Educators Exch., Allied Artists San Diego. Home and Office: 770 Cole Ranch Rd Encinitas CA 92024-6611

CONRADY, JAMES LOUIS, audio visual technician; b. Santa Ana, Calif., May 22, 1933. AA in Electronics, Orange Coast Coll., 1953; BA in Social Sci., Chapman Coll., 1964. Audio visual technician Centralia Sch. Dist., Buena Park, Calif., 1960—. With USN, 1954-56. Mem. SAR, Assn. Audio Visual Technicians, The Soc. Photo-Technologists, Internat. Comm. Industries Assn., Gen. Soc. Mayflower Descendants. Presbyterian. Office: Centralia Sch Dist 6625 La Palma Ave Buena Park CA 90620-2859

CONRAN, JAMES MICHAEL, state government official; b. N.Y.C., Mar. 15, 1952; s. James Adrian and Mary Ellen (McGarry) C.; m. Phyllis Jean Thompson, Aug. 1, 1984; children: Michael O., Thomas O. BA, Calif. State U., Northridge, 1975; M in Urban Studies, Occidental Coll., 1978. Mgr. regulatory rels. Pacific Bell, San Francisco, 1985-88, mgr. pub. affairs & pub. issues, 1988-91; dir. State of Calif. Dept. Consumer Affairs, Sacramento, 1991-94; founder, pres. Consumers First, 1994—; bd. dirs. Consumer Interest Inst., TRW Consumer Adv. Coun., Great WEstern Fin. Corp., Consumer Adv. Panel, Electric Inst. Consumer Adv. Panel; mem. Coun. Licensing Enforcement and Regulation. Contbr. articles to profl. jours. Bd. dirs. Fight Back! Found., L.A., 1991—, Disabled Children's Computer Group, Orinda, Calif., Telecomm. Edn. Trust Fund-Calif. Pub. Utilities Commn., San Francisco, 1990-91; chair adminstrv. sect. United Calif. State Employees Campaign, Sacramento; mem. Stream Preservation Commn., Orinda, 1988-91, Calif. Rep. Party Cen. Com., Orinda, 1992; del. Rep. Nat. Conv., Houston, 1992; regional chair Bush-Quayle campaign, Orinda, 1992. Fellow Coro Found., 1977, Levere Meml. Found., 1976. Mem. Coro Assocs., Calif. Agenda for Consumer Edn., Sigma Alpha Epsilon. Roman Catholic. Home: 33 Southwood Dr Orinda CA 94563-3025

CONRON, JOHN PHELAN, architect; b. Brookline, Mass., Dec. 4, 1921; s. Carl Edward and Katherine (Phelan) C. Student, U. So. Calif., 1940-41; B.Arch., Yale U., 1948. Draftsmn. Whelan & Westman, Boston, 1948-52; owner, prin. John P. Conron (Architect), Santa Fe, N.Mex., 1952-61; ptnr. Conron-Lent Architects, Santa Fe, 1961-86, Conron-Muths (restoration architects), Santa Fe and Jackson Hole, Wyo., 1975-88, Conron-Woods Architects, Santa Fe, 1986—; pres. The Centerline, Inc., Santa Fe, 1952-86. Prin. works include Centerline, Inc., Santa Fe, KB Ranch, nr. Santa Fe, Henry R. Singlton residence, Lamy, N.Mex., Amtech Corp., Santa Fe, restorations Stephen W. Dorsey Mansion State Monument, Colfax County, N.Mex., Palace of Govs., Santa Fe, Pipe Spring Nat. Monument, Ariz.; editor La Cronica de Nuevo Mexico, 1976—; co-editor: N.Mex. Architecture mag., 1960-66, editor, 1966-91. Vice chmn. N.Mex. Cultural Properties Com., 1968-80; founder v.p. Las Trampas Found., 1967-80; trustee Internat. Inst. Iberian Colonial Art, Santa Fe, pres. 1978—; bd. dirs. Preservation Action, 1976-80; bd. dirs. Hist. Soc. N.Mex., 1976—, pres., 1982-86, Hope House, Santa Fe, 1994—. With USAAF, 1941-45. Recipient Merit award AIA, 1962, Spl. Commendation award, 1970. Fellow AIA, Am. Soc. Interior Designers (pres. N.Mex. chpt. 1966-68, 74-75, , 94-95, regional v.p. 1970-73, Historic Preservation award for restoration Palace of Govs. 1980, chpt. bd. dirs., 1994—), Am. Soc. Man Environ. Rels. (dir. 1973-86). Office: Conron & Woods Architects 1807 2nd St Ste 44 Santa Fe NM 87505-3509

CONSTANT, CLINTON, chemical engineer, consultant; b. Nelson, B.C., Can., Mar. 20, 1912; came to U.S., 1936, naturalized, 1942; s. Vasile and Annie (Hunt) C.; m. Margie Robbel, Dec. 5, 1965. BSc with honors, U. Alta., 1935, postgrad., 1935-36; PhD, Western Res. U., 1939. Registered profl. engr., Calif., Wis. Devel. engr. Harshaw Chem. Co., Cleve., 1936-38, mfg. foreman, 1938-43, sr. engr. semi-works dept., 1948-50; supt. hydrofluoric acid dept. Nyotex Chems., Inc., Houston, 1943-47, chief devel. engr., 1947-48; mgr. engring. Ferro Chem. Co., Bedford, Ohio, 1950-52; tech. asst. mfg. dept. Armour Agrl. Chem. Co. (name formerly Armour Fertilizer Works), Bartow, Fla., 1952-61, mfg. research and devel. div., 1961-63; mgr. spl. projects Research div. (co. name changed to USS Agri-Chems 1968), Bartow, Fla., 1963-65, project mgr., 1965-70; chem. adviser Robert & Co. Assocs., Atlanta, 1970-79; chief engr. Almon & Assocs., Inc., Atlanta, 1979-80; project mgr. Engring. Service Assocs., Atlanta, 1980-81; v.p. engring. ACI Inc., Hesperia, Calif., 1981-83; sr. v.p., chief engr. MTI (acquisition of ACI), Hesperia, 1983-86; engring. cons. San Bernardino County APCD, Victorville, Calif., 1986-90; instr. environ. chemistry Victor Valley C.C., 1990; pvt. cons. Victorville, Calif., 1991—; cons. in engring., 1992—. Author tech. reports, sci. fiction; patentee in field. Fellow AAAS, Am. Inst. Chemists, Am. Inst. Chem. Engrs., N.Y. Acad. Scis., AIAA (assoc.); mem. Am. Chem. Soc., Am. Astron. Soc., Astron. Soc. Pacific, Royal Astron. Soc. Can., NSPE, Am. Water Works Assn., Calif. Water and Pollution Control Assn., Air Pollution Control Assn., Soc. Mfg. Engrs., Calif. Soc. Profl. Engrs.

CONSTANTINEAU, CONSTANCE JULIETTE, banker; b. Lowell, Mass., Feb. 18, 1937; d. Henry Goulet and Germaine (Turner) Goulet-Lamarre; m. Edward Joseph Constantineau; children: Glen Edward, Alan Henry. Student, Bank Adminstrn. Inst. and Am. Inst. Banking, 1975-87. Mortgage sec. The Cen. Savs. Bank, Lowell, 1955-57; head teller First Fed. Savs. & Loan, Lowell, 1957-59, Lowell Bank & Trust Co., Lowell, 1973-74; br. mgr. Century Bank & Trust Co., Malden, Mass., 1975-78; v.p. purchasing, mgr. support svcs. First Security Bank of N.Mex. (formerly First Nat. Bank Albuquerque), 1983—; mem. planning purchasing mgr.'s conf. Bank Adminstrn. Inst., San Antonio, Orlando, Fla., New Orleans; treas. polit. action com. First Nat. Bank, 1986. Bd. dirs., historian Indian Pueblo Cultural Ctr., Albuquerque, 1986-89. Mem. Fin. Women Internat., In-Plant Mgmt. Assn. (charter). Home: 13015 Deer Dancer Trl NE Albuquerque NM 87112-4831 Office: 1st Security Bank NMex 40 First Plaza Ctr NW Albuquerque NM 87102-3355

CONSTENIUS, KURT NORMAN, geophysicist; b. Whitefish, Mont., Aug. 28, 1957; s. John Norman and Leona Marie (Logan) C.; m. Jennifer Susan Constenius, June 4, 1988; children: Matthew Logan, Lindsey Bowes. BS in Earth Sci., Mont. State U., 1979; MS in Geology, U. Wyo., 1981; postgrad., U. Ariz., 1992—. Exploration geophysicist Amoco Prodn. Co., Denver, 1981-92; rsch. assoc. Carnegie Mus., Pitts., 1985—, Denver Mus., 1988—. Contbr. articles to profl. jours. Mem. Am. Assn. Petroleum Geologists. Home: 1622 W Avenida de Tucson AZ 85704

CONTI, DANIEL JOSEPH, health science association administrator; b. Somerville, N.J., Feb. 22, 1949; s. Daniel A. and Helen (Glab) C.; m. Carolynn E. Frush, Aug. 10, 1982; children: Jonathan Daniel, Joshua Joseph. BS, St. Bonaventure U., 1970; MS, U. Ariz., 1979. Physiologist Los Angeles County Occupational Health Dept., 1979-80; program dir. Inst. Health Mgmt., San Francisco, 1980-82; owner, pres. Health Mgmt. Cons., San Francisco, 1982-86; v.p., chief ops. officer Nat. Inst. Cardiovascular Tech., Inc., Newport Beach, Calif., 1986-87; also bd. dirs. Nat. Inst. Cardiovascular Tech., Inc., Newport Beach; pres., chief exec. officer Nat. Inst. Cardiovascular Tech., Inc., Newport Beach, Calif., 1987-89; founder Health Resource Group, 1989—; chmn. heart at work com. Orange County chpt. Am. Heart Assn., 1988-90, state chmn. worksite subcom., 1989-91, bd. dirs., 1989-90. Pub. wellness newsletter The Pulse, 1989—; editor Health Mgmt. Newsletter, 1982-84. Coord. Orange County Men's Community Bible Study, 1993-95. Republican. Mem. Christian Ch. Office: Health Resource Group PO Box 196540166 Irvine CA 92713

CONTI, ISABELLA, psychologist, consultant; b. Torino, Italy, Jan. 1, 1942; came to U.S., 1964; d. Giuseppe and Zaira (Melis) Ferro; m. Ugo Conti, Sept. 5, 1964; 1 child, Maurice. J.D., U. Rome, 1966; Ph.D. in Psychology, U. Calif.-Berkeley, 1975. Lic. psychologist. Sr. analyst Rsch. Inst. for Study of Man, Berkeley, Calif., 1967-68; postgrad. rsch. psychologist Personality Assessment and Rsch. Inst., U. Calif.-Berkeley, 1968-71; intern U. Calif.-Berkeley and VA Hosp., San Francisco, 1969-75; asst. prof. St. Mary's Coll., Moraga, Calif., 1978-84; cons. psychologist Conti Resources, Berkeley, Calif., 1977-85; v.p. Barnes & Conti Assocs., Inc., Berkeley, 1985-90; pres. Lisardco, El Cerrito, Calif., 1989—; v.p. ElectroMagnetic Instruments, Inc., El Cerrito, Calif., 1985—. Author: (with Alfonso Montuori) From Power to Partnership, 1993; contbr. articles on creativity and mgmt. cons. to profl. jours. Regents fellow U. Calif.-Berkeley, 1972; NIMH predoctoral rsch. fellow, 1972-73. Mem. Am. Psychol. Assn. Office: Lisardco 1318 Brewster Dr El Cerrito CA 94530-2526

CONTO, ARISTIDES, advertising agency executive; b. N.Y.C., Feb. 10, 1931; s. Gus Dimitrios and Osee (Kenney) C.; BA, Champlain Coll., 1953; MS in Journalism, UCLA, 1958, certificate in indsl. rels., 1965; m. Phyllis Helen Wiley, June 22, 1957; 1 son, Jason Wiley. Reporter, City News Svc., L.A., 1958; dir. pub. rels. Galaxy Advt. Co., Los Angeles, 1959-60; news media chief Los Angeles County Heart Assn., 1960-61; pub. rels. assoc. Prudential Ins. Co., L.A., 1961-64; advt. mgr. Aerospace Controls Co., L.A., 1964-65; comml. sales promotion coord. Lockheed-Calif. Co., Burbank, 1965-73; pres. Jason Wiley Advt. Agy., L.A., 1973-92; dir. Tower Master, Inc., L.A. With U.S. Army, 1955-56. Recipient advt. awards. Mem. Nat. Soc. Published Poets, L.A. Press Club, Bus.-Profl. Advt. Assn. L.A.s, Pub. Rels. Soc. Author: The Spy Who Loved Me, 1962; The Diamond Twins, 1963, Edit Me Dead, 1992, I Marcus, 1994, A Short Life, 1995, (screenplays) Lannigan, 1973, Haunted Host, 1976, Captain Noah, 1977, Government Surplus, 1983. Office: PO Box 25546 Los Angeles CA 90025-0546

CONTOS, PAUL ANTHONY, engineer, investment consultant; b. Chgo., Mar. 18, 1926; s. Anthony Dimitrios and Panagiota (Kostopoulos) C.; m. Lilian Katie Kalkines, June 19, 1955 (dec. Apr. 1985); children: Leslie, Claudia, Paula, Anthony. Student, Am. TV Inst., Chgo., 1946-48, U. Ill., 1949-52, 53-56, Ill. Inst. Tech., 1952-53, U. So. Calif., 1956-57 Engr. J.C. Deagan Co., Inc., Chgo., 1951-53, Lockheed Missile and Space Co., Inc., Sunnyvale, Calif., 1956-62; engring. supr. Lockheed Missile and Space Co., Inc., Sunnyvale, 1962-65, staff engr., 1965-88; pres. PAC Investments, Saratoga, Calif., 1984-88; pres. PAC Investments, San Jose, Calif., 1988—, also advisor, 1984—. Mem. Pres. Coun. U. Ill., 1994—. With U.S. Army, 1944-46, ETO. Decorated Purple Heart. Mem. DAV (life, commdr. Chgo. unit 1948-51), VFW (life), Pi Sigma Phi (pres. 1951-53). Republican. Greek Orthodox. Home and Office: 1009 Blossom River Way Apt 105 San Jose CA 95123-6305

CONWAY, CASEY ANTHONY, health and safety manager; b. Portland, Oreg., Mar. 11, 1953; s. James William and Wanna Donna (Caspers) C. AA, Orange Coast Coll., 1974; BA in Bus. Adminstrn., Calif. State U.-Fullerton, 1976; MS in Safety, U. So. Calif., 1978. Cert. instr./trainer in surface/underground mine safety, mine foreman surface uranuim, safety profl.; registered environ. assessor Calif. EPA; lic. amateur radio operator (extra class). Safety and environ. technician energy mining div. Union Oil Co. Calif., 1979, Rawlins, Wyo., safety trainer, 1979-80, safety supr., 1980-82, regulatory compliance coord. oil shale ops., Parachute, Colo., 1983-85; safety supr. UNOCAL L.A. Refinery, Wilmington, Calif., 1986; mgr. regulatory compliance, refining and mktg. div. UNOCAL, L.A., 1986-89, mgr. health and safety compliance Refining Dept., 1989-91; sr. advisor health and safety compliance Unocal 76 Products Co., 1992—, speaker and writer in field; vol. examiner FCC amateur radio lics. profl. Mem. Am. Soc. Safety Engrs. (membership chmn. Wyo. chpt. 1981-82, Wyo. safety congress com. 1982, sec. 1982-83, Western Slope chmn. 1983-86, assembly del. Orange Coast chpt. 1990-94, v.p., 1992-94, pres. 1994-95, nat. govt. affairs com. 1991—, Culbertson Outstanding Vol. Svc. award), Calif. Mfrs. Assn. (chmn. safety and health com. 1989-92), Nat. Petroleum Refiners Assn. (fire and safety com., chmn. regulatory issues group), Orgn. Resource Counselors, Western Occupational Safety Health Steering Com., Am. Indsl. Hygiene Assn., Nat. Fire Protection Assn., Am. Radio Relay League (life, asst. dir. SW div. 1986-88) Soc. Advancement Mgmt. (Outstanding mem. 1975; v.p. membership 1976), Carbon County Amateur Radio Assn. (pres. 1980), Grand Mesa Contesters (sec.-treas. 1985), Southern Calif. DX Club, Univ. So. Calif. Inst. Safety and Systems Mgmt. Alumni Assn. (bd. dirs. 1990-91), So. Calif. Contest, Cactus Radio, Orange County Trojan Club (bd. dirs. 1988—, pres. 1991-93). Roman Catholic. Lodge: Elks. Home: 2000 Diana Ln Newport Beach CA 92660-4434 Office: Unocal 76 Products Co PO Box 7600 Los Angeles CA 90051-0600

CONWAY, JAMES F., writer, counselor, minister; b. Cleve., Jan. 11, 1932; m. Sally Ann Christon, June 2, 1954; children: Barbara Conway, Schneider, Brenda Conway Russell, Becki Conway Sanders. MDiv, Denver Seminary, 1957; MA in Psychology, Trinity Evangel. Divinity Sch., Ill., 1968; DMin in Theology, Fuller Theol. Seminary, Pasadena, Calif., 1979; PhD in Adult Devel., U. Ill., 1987. Ordained minister. Pastor Newton (Kans.) Bible Ch., 1958-63, Village Ch. of Carol Stream, Wheaton, Ill., 1963-69; instr. Coll. Christian Studies, Urbana, Ill., 1972-77; sr. pastor Twin City Bible Ch., Urbana, 1969-81; assoc. prof. Biola U., La Mirada, Calif., 1981-86, dir. D of Ministry Program, 1981-86; co-founder, pres. Mid-Life Dimensions, 1981—; counseling dir. Internat. Missions Convs. Urbana 76, Urbana 78; conf. and retreat leader; appearances on numerous TV and radio programs, including Focus on the Family, Mid-Morning LA, Michael Jackson Talk Radio, 700 Club, numerous CBN programs, others; adj. prof. U. Nebr., Gordon Coll., Mass., Sterling Coll., Kans., Taylor U., Ind., Spring Arbor Coll., Mich., Loma Linda (Calif.) U., Kettering Med. Sch., Ohio, Grace Bible Coll., Nebr., St. Paul Bible Coll., Minn., Columbia Sch. of the Bible, S.C., Fuller Theol. Sem., Calif., Denver Seminary, Covenant Sem., Mo. Author: Men in Mid-Life Crisis, 1978, Friendship, 1989, How to Make Real Friends in a Phony World, 1991, Adult Children of Legal or Emotional Divorce, 1990, Sexual Harassment No More, 1993; co-author: (with Sally Conway) Women in Mid-Life Crisis, 1983, Maximize Your Mid-Life, 1987, Your Marriage Can Survive Mid-Life Crisis, 1990, What God Gives When Life Takes, 1989, Moving On After He Moves Out, 1995, (with Sally Conway and Bill and Pam Farrel) Pure Pleasure, 1994, others; contbr. articles to profl. jours., books in field. Trustee Sterling (Kans.) Coll., 1984—, chmn. various coms. Recipient Disting. Parents' award Taylor U., 1980, Disting. Alumni award Sterling Coll., 1984. Mem. Phi Kappa Phi. Evangelical. Address: Mid-Life Dimensions PO Box 3790 Fullerton CA 92634

CONWAY, JOHN E., federal judge; b. 1934. BS, U.S. Naval Acad., 1956; LLB magna cum laude, Washburn U., 1963. Assoc. Matias A Zamora, Santa Fe, 1963-64; ptnr. Wilkinson, Durrett & Conway, Alamogordo, N.Mex., 1964-67, Durrett, Conway & Jordon, Alamogordo, 1967-80, Montgomery & Andrews, P.A., Albuquerque, 1980-86; city atty. Alamogordo, 1966-72; Mexico State Senate, 1970-80, minority leader, 1972-80; chief fed. judge U.S. Dist. Ct. N.Mex., Albuquerque, 1986—. 1st lt. USAF, 1956-60. Mem. ABA, Nat. Commrs. on Uniform State Laws, N.Mex. Bar Assn., N.Mex. Jud. Coun. (vice chmn. 1973, chmn. 1973-75, disciplinary bd. of Supreme Ct. on N.Mex., vice chmn. 1980, chmn. 1981-85), Albuquerque Bar Assn., Albuquerque Lawyers Club. Office: US Dist Ct PO Box 1160 Albuquerque NM 87103-1160

CONWAY, REBECCA ANN KOPPES, lawyer; b. Colorado Springs, Colo., May 18, 1952; d. Virgil Lee and Betty J. Koppes; children: Kelley, Kathrine; m. Sean P. Conway, Nov. 26, 1994. BA, U. Colo., 1975, JD, 1978. Bar: Colo. 1978, U.S. Dist. Ct. Colo. 1978. Atty. EEOC, Denver, 1978-79, Dist. Atty.'s Office, Adams County, Brighton, Colo., 1979-80; ptnr. Gutierrez & Koppes, Greeley, Colo., 1980-92; prin. Law Office of Rebecca Koppes Conway, Greeley, 1992—; chairperson Colo. Pub. Defenders Commn., 1985-95. Chmn. Placement Alternatives Commn., Weld County, Colo., 1987-89; dir. Our Saviors Luth. Ch., Greeley, 1989-90; chmn. bd. dirs. Colo. Rural Legal Svcs., Denver, 1984-85; vice chair Weld Child Care Network, 1988. Mem. ABA (House of Dels.), Colo. Bar Assn. (mem. various coms., mem. exec. coun. 1986-89, bd. govs. 1983-90, 94—, chmn. young lawyers divsn. 1988-89, Outstanding Young Lawyer 1988, v.p. 1989-90), Weld County Bar Assn. (pres. 1992-93, mem. various coms.). Home: 2595 56th Ave Greeley CO 80634-4503 Office: 912 8th Ave Greeley CO 80631-1112

CONWAY, ROBERT P., art dealer; b. San Diego, Oct. 31, 1946; s. Robert B. and Jane A. (Peabody) C.; m. Anne E. Rhodes, June 13, 1968 (div. 1977); 1 child, Satya; m. Tyrell C. Collins, Apr. 22, 1978; children: Evan, Alexander. BA, Williams Coll., 1967; MA, Princeton U., 1982. Gallery dir. David Tunick, Inc., N.Y.C., 1982-84; dir. Associated Am. Artists, N.Y.C., 1984-91; pvt. art dealer Oakland, Calif., 1992—; consulting curator Mills Coll. Art Gallery, 1994—. Dir. The Eichenberg Trust, 1994—.

CONWAY, SALLY, writer, lecturer, counselor; b. Pennington County, S.D., Mar. 23, 1934; m. Jim Conway, June 2, 1954; children: Barbara Conway Schneider, Brenda Conway Russell, Becki Conway Sanders. BS in Edn. magna cum laude, U. Ill., 1974, MS in Human Devel. & Family Ecology, 1986. Co-founder, v.p. Mid-Life Dimensions, Calif., 1981—; adj. instr., coord. women's concerns Talbot Sch. Theology, Biola U., La Mirada, Calif., 1981-86; adj. instr. or lectr. U. Nebr., Gordon Coll., Mass., Sterling Coll., Kans., Taylor U., Ind., Spring Arbor Coll., Mich., Loma Linda (Calif.) U., Kettering Med. Sch., Ohio, Grace Bible Coll., Nebr., St. Paul Bible Coll., Minn., Columbia Sch. Bibl. Edn., S.C., Fuller Theol. Sem., Calif., Denver Sem., Covenant Sem., Mo., Talbot Sem., Calif.; numerous TV and radio appearances including Focus on the Family, Mid-Morning L.A., Michael Jackson Talk Radio, 700 Club, numerous CBN programs, others. Author: Your Husband's Mid-Life Crisis, 1980, Menopause, 1990, When a Mate Wants Out, 1992, (with Jim Conway) Women in Mid-Life Crisis, 1983, Maximize Your Mid-Life, 1987, Your Marriage Can Survive Mid-Life Crisis, 1987, Traits of a Lasting Marriage, 1991, Sexual Harassment No More, 1993, Traits of a Lasting Marriage, 1991, Moving On After He Moves Out, 1995, (with Jim Conway and Bill and Pam Farrel) Pure Pleasure, 1994, (with Becki Conway Sanders & Jim Conway) What God Gives When Life Takes/Trusting God in a Family Crisis, 1989; contbg. author numerous other books; contbr. articles to various jours.; author tapes. Recipient Disting. Parents award Taylor U., 1980, Disting. Alumni award Sterling Coll., 1984. Mem. Kappa Delta Pi. Address: PO Box 3790 Fullerton CA 92634-3790

CONWAY, WALLACE XAVIER, SR., retired curator; b. Washington, June 11, 1920; m. Jessie Dedeaux, June 1, 1943. B.A., Miner Tchrs. Coll., 1941; postgrad. Cath. U., Washington, 1957, 58, 61, Trenton State Coll., 1977-78, U. Paris, Sorbonne, 1977, NYU, 1987, Mercer County Coll., 1975-76, MA. 1988; postgrad Venice, Italy, 1989, Art Inst. Chgo., 1990, NYU. Owner, dir. Co-Art Studios, Washington, 1950-64; graphic artist Dept. Commerce, U.S. Weather Bur., Washington, 1964-65; graphic supr. Smithsonian Inst., Washington, 1965-69; curator, chmn. exhibits bur. N.J. State Mus., Trenton, 1969-88; ret.; tech. cons. mural The Life of Martin Luther King, Washington, 1984-86; cons. Pa. Council on the Arts/Minority Arts; museum cons. Mother Bethel A.M.E. Ch., nat. hist. landmark, Phila.; mem. art com. Mercer Med. Ctr.; cons. Afro-Am. Hist. Soc. Mus., Jersey City. Mem. adv. bd. Minority Arts Council, Phila. Mem. Art Students League (co. chpt.), Kappa Alpha Psi, Beta Kappa. Lodge: Rotary Internat. Home: 2119 Olympic Dr Colorado Springs CO 80910-1262

COOK, ALBERT THOMAS THORNTON, JR., financial advisor; b. Cleve., Apr. 24, 1940; s. Albert Thomas Thornton and Tyra Esther (Morehouse) C.; m. Mary Jane Blackburn, June 1, 1963; children: Lara Keller, Thomas, Timothy. BA, Dartmouth Coll., 1962; MA, U. Chgo., 1966. Asst. sec. Dartmouth Coll., Hanover, N.H., 1972-77; exec. dir. Big Brothers, Inc., N.Y.C., 1977-78; underwriter Boettcher & Co., Denver, 1978-81; asst. v.p. Dain Bosworth Inc., Denver, 1981-82, Colo. Nat. Bank, Denver, 1982-84; pres. The Albert T.T. Cook Co., Denver, 1984—; arbitrator Nat. Assn. Securities Dealers, N.Y.C., 1985—, Mcpl. Securities Rulemaking Bd., Washington, 1987—. Pres. Etna-Hanover Ctr. Community Assn., Hanover, N.H., 1974-76; mem. Mayor's Task Force, Denver, 1984; bd. dirs. Rude Park Community Nursery, Denver, 1985-87, Willows Water Dist., Colo., 1990—, sec.; trustee The Iliff Sch. Theol., Denver, 1986-92; mem. Dartmouth Coll. Com. on Trustees, 1990-93. Mem. Dartmouth Alumni Coun. (exec. com., chmn. nominating and trustee search coms. 1987-89), University Club, Cactus Club (Denver), Dartmouth Club of N.Y.C., Yale Club, Lions (bd. dirs. Denver chpt. 1983-85, treas. 1986-87, pres. Denver Found. 1987-88), Delta Upsilon. Congregationalist. Home: 7099 E Hinsdale Pl Englewood CO 80112-1610 Office: One Tabor Ctr 1200 17th St Ste 1303 Denver CO 80202-5813

COOK, DIERDRE RUTH GOORMAN, school administrator, secondary education educator; b. Denver, Nov. 4, 1956; d. George Edward and Avis M. (Wilson) Goorman; m. Donald Robert Cook, Apr. 4, 1981; 1 child, Christen. BA in Theatre Arts, Colo. State U., 1980, MA in Adminstrn., MEd, 1995. Cert. secondary tchr. Tchr. Centennial High Sch., Fort Collins, Colo., 1983-87; educator Poudre High Sch., Fort Collins, 1987-95; asst. prin. Lesher Jr. H.S., Ft. Collins, 1995—; curriculum devel. com. Poudre R-1 Sch. Dist., Ft. Collins, 1984—, instrnl. improvement com., 1985—, trainer positive power leadership, 1986-87, profl. devel. com., 1994—; comm. cons. Woodward Gov. Co., Ft. Collins, 1991, 92, 95; evaluation visitation team North Ctrl. Evaluation, Greeley, Colo., 1991; dir. student activities Poudre H.S. Campaign worker Rep. Party, Littleton, Colo., 1980, Ft. Collins, 1984, 88; mem. Colo. Juvenile Coun., Ft. Collins, 1986, 88, loaned exec., 1987; bd. dirs. Youth Unltd., 1994—; mem. Leadership Ft. Collins, 1992-93; troop leader Girl Scouts U.S., 1991-94. NEH scholar, 1992; named Disting. Tchr. 1993 Colo. Awards Coun.; recipient Tchr. Excellence award Poudre High Sch., 1992. Mem. NEA, ASCD, Colo. Edn. Assn., Poudre Edn. Assn. (rep. 1989, 90, 91), Nat. Speech Comm. Assn., Nat. Forensics League (degree for outstanding distinction 1992), Nat. PTO, Nat. Platform Soc., Kappa Kappa Gamma (Epsilon Beta chpt., pres. 1985-90, mem. corporate houseboard). Home: 1600 Burlington Ct Fort Collins CO 80525 Office: Poudre R-1 Sch Dist 1400 Stover Fort Collins CO 80524

COOK, DONALD E., pediatrician; b. Pitts., Mar. 24, 1928; s. Merriam E. and Bertha (Gwin) C.; BS, Colo. Coll., 1951; MD, U. Colo., 1955; m. Elsie Walden, Sept. 2, 1951; children: Catherine, Christopher, Brian, Jeffrey. Intern, Fresno County Gen. Hosp., Calif., 1955-56; resident in gen. practice Tulare (Calif.) County Gen. Hosp., 1956-57; resident in pediatrics U. Colo., 1957-59; practice medicine specializing in pediatrics, Aurora, Colo., 1959-64, Greeley (Colo.) Med. Clin., Greeley Sports Medicine Clin., 1964-93; founder, dir. Greeley Children's Clinic, 1995—, mem. exec. com., 1990-92; med. adv. Centennial Develop. Svcs., Inc., clin. faculty U. Colo., clin. prof., 1977—; organizer, dir. Sports Medicine Px Exam Clinic for indigent Weld Co. athletes, 1990-95; mem. adv. bd. Nat. Center Health Edn., San Francisco, 1978-80; mem. adv. com. on maternal and child health programs Colo. State Health Dept., 1981-84, chmn., 1981-84; preceptor Sch. Nurse Practitioner Program U. Colo., 1978-88. Mem. Weld County Dist. 6 Sch. Bd., 1973-83, pres., 1973-74, 76-77, chmn. dist. 6 accountability com., 1972-73; mem. adv. com. dist. 6 teen pregnancy program, 1983-85; mem. Weld County Task Force on teen-aged pregnancy, 1986-89, Dream Team Weld County Task Force on sch. dropouts, 1986-92, Weld County Interagy. Screening Bd., Weld County Cmty. Ctr. Found., 1984-89, Weld County Task Force Speakers Bur. on AIDS, 1987—; mem. Weld County Task Force Adolescent Health Clinic; mem. Task Force Child Abuse, C. of C.; bd. dirs. No. Colo. Med. Ctr., 1993—, No. Colo. Med. Ctr. Found., 1994—; mem. Sch. Dist. 6 Health Coalition, Task Force on access to health care; group leader neonatal group Colo. Action for Healthy People Colo. Dept. Pub. Health, 1985-86; co-founder Colorodoans for seatbelts on sch. buses, 1985-90; co-founder, v.p. Coalition of primary care physicians, Colo., 1986; mem. adv. com. Greeley Cen. Drug and Alcohol Abuse, 1984-86, Rocky Mtn. Ctr. for Health Promotion and Edn., 1984—, bd. dirs., 1984—, v.p., 1992-93, pres. 1994; rep. coun. on med. specialty soc., AAP, 1988-89, mem. coun. pediatric rsch., 1988-89, oversight com. fin., oversight com. communications, rep. to nat. PTA, 1990-94, mem. coun. on govt. affairs, 1989-90, rep. to coun. sects. mgmt. com., mem. search com. for new exec. dir.; med. cons. Sch. Dist. 6, 1989—; adv. com. bd. comm., adv. com. bd. membership comm., adv. com. bd. finance, adv. com. bd. dirs. AAP 1990-95, AAP com. govt. affairs, 1990; bd. dirs. N. Colo. Med. Ctr., 1993—, United Way Weld County, 1993—; founder, med. dir. Greeley Children's Clinic, 1994. With USN, 1946-48. Recipient Disting. Svc. award Jr. C. of C., 1962, Disting. Citizenship award Elks, 1975-76, Svc. to Mankind award Sertoma Club, 1972, Spark Plug award U. No. Colo., 1981; Mildred Doster award Colo. Sch. Health Coun. for sch. health contbns., 1992. Diplomate Am. Bd. Pediatrics. Mem. Colo. Soc. Sch. Health Com. (chmn. 1967-78), Am. Acad. Pediatrics (alt. dist. chmn. 1987-93, dist. chmn. dist. VIII 1993, chmn. alt. dist. chmn. com. 1991-93, chmn. sch. health com. 1975-80, chmn. Colo. chpt. 1982-87, mem. task force on new age of pediatrics 1982-85, Ross edn. and award com. 1985-86, media spokesperson Speak Up for Children 1983—, mem. coun. sects. mgmt. 1991-92, mem. search com., exec. dir.), AMA (chmn. sch. and coll. health com. 1980-82, James E. Strain Community Svc. award 1987, 94, coun. pediatric practice), Adams Aurora Med. Soc. (pres. 1964-65), Weld County Med. Soc. (pres. 1968-69), Colo. Med. Soc. (com. on sports medicine, 1980-90, com. chmn. 1986-90, chmn. com. sch. health 1988-91, A.H. Robbins Community Svc. award 1974), Centennial Pediatric Soc. (pres. 1982-86), Rotary (bd. dirs. Greely chpt. 1988-91, mem. immunization com. 1994—, chmn. immunization campaign Weld county, 1994). Republican. Methodist. Home: 1710 21st Ave Greeley CO 80631-5143 Office: Greeley Sports Medicine Clinic 1900 16th St Greeley CO 80631-5114

COOK, DOUGLAS NEILSON, theatre educator, producer, artistic director; b. Phoenix, Sept. 22, 1929; s. Neil Estes and Louise Y. (Wood) C.; m. Joan Stafford Buechner, Aug. 11, 1956; children: John Richard, Peter Neilson, Stephen Barton. Student, Phoenix Coll., 1948-49, U. Chgo., 1949-50, UCLA, 1950-51, Los Angeles Art Inst., 1948; B.F.A., U. Ariz., 1953; M.A., Stanford U., 1955; postgrad., Lester Polakov Studio Stage Design, 1966-67. Instr. San Mateo (Calif.) Coll., 1955-57, Nat. Music Camp, Interlochen, Mich., 1961; asst. prof. drama U. Calif., Riverside, 1957-66; assoc. prof., chair theatre dept. U. Calif., 1967-70; head dept. Pa. State U., University Park, 1970-88, sr. prof. theatre arts, 1988-92; prof. emeritus Pa. State U., 1992—. Actor Corral Theatre, Tucson, 1952-53, Orleans (Mass.) Arena Theatre, 1953; dir., designer Palo Alto (Calif.) Community Theatre, 1954, Peninsula Children's Theatre, 1956-57; assoc. producer Utah Shakespearean Festival, Cedar City, 1964-90, producing artistic dir., 1990—; producer Pa. State Festival Theatre, State College, 1970-85, The Nat. Wagon Train Show, 1975-76. Instl. rep. Juniata Valley council Boy Scouts Am., 1973-77; bd. dirs. Central Pa. Festival Arts, 1970-75, 84-87, v.p., 1984-86; bd. dirs. Nat. theatre Conf., 1980-90, v.p. 1983-85, pres. 1987-88. Recipient disting. alumni award U. Ariz., 1990; named to Coll. of Fellows of the Am. Theatre, 1994. Mem. AAUP, Shakespeare Theatre Assn. Am. (v.p. 1990-92, pres. 1993-94), Nat. Assn. Schs. Theatre, Am. Theatre Assn. (bd. dirs. 1977-86, exec. com. 1979-80, pres. 1984-85), U.S. Inst. Theatre Tech., Am. Soc. Theatre Rsch., Univ. Resident Theatre Assn. (bd. dirs. 1970-88, v.p. 1975-79, pres. 1979-83), Theatre Assn. Pa. (bd. dirs. 1972-76). Home: PO Box 10194 Phoenix AZ 85064-0194 Office: Utah Shakespearean Festival 351 W Center St Cedar City UT 84720-2470

COOK, GALEN BRUCE, computer company executive; b. Independence, Mo., May 23, 1930; s. Galen B. and Elsie A. (Snow) C.; m. Dori Schober, Dec. 30, 1967. AB, Washington U., 1951, MD, 1955. Diplomate Am. Bd. Surgeons. Intern St. Louis City Hosp.; resident Barnes Hosp., St. Louis; assoc. prof. surgery U. Mo., Columbia, 1966-70; assoc. med. dir. FHP Internat., Long Beach, Calif., 1976-79; med. dir. S.C. Dept. of Health, Sumter, 1979-90; prof. pub. health S.C. U., Columbia, 1981-90; pres. Med. Logic Internat., Sumter, 1979—. Contbr. 48 articles to profl. jours.; patentee in field; author 56 clin. software applications. Capt. U.S. Army, 1956-59. Republican.

COOK, JUDITH ANN POLUS, art educator; b. Reedsburg, Wis., Apr. 16, 1943; d. Allan Milton and Leona Christina (Gadow) Jenkins; m. Gerald Edward Polus, Oct. 26, 1973 (div. 1987); 1 child, Jessica Lynette; m. Curtis Dillard Cook, July 7, 1994. BA, St. Olaf Coll., Northfield, Minn., 1964; postgrad., U. Iowa, 1965-66, U. Phoenix. Elementary art tchr., supr. Wauwatosa (Wis.) Pub. Sch. Sys., 1964-65; high sch. art tchr. Oakfield (Wis.) Pub. Sch. System, 1969-74; curator of edn. Leigh Yawkey Woodson Art Mus., Wausau, Wis., 1983-86; dir. Bemis Art Sch., Colo. Springs (Colo.) Fin Arts Ctr., 1987-89, 91-93, acting exec. dir., 1989-90, 94—; art juror 5th Congl. Dist. High Sch. Art Competition, Colorado Springs, 1988, Fred Wells 15-12 State Juried Competition, Lincoln, Nebr., 1990-91; juror Colo. Bus. Com. for the Arts, 1994; coord. Kennedy Ctr. Imagination Celebration, 1988, Robert Bateman Master Classes, Wausau, Wis., 1986, Colorado Springs, 1991; workshop presenter R.T. Peterson Inst., Jamestown, N.Y., 1992. Mem. steering com. Arts/Bus./Edn. Com., Colorado Springs, 1988—, Kennedy Ctr. Imagination Celebration, 1987—; mem. Colo. Springs Airport Art Commn. Recipient Pikes Peak Art Coun.'s Recognition award 1994. Mem. Nat. Art Edn. Assn., Colo. Art Edn. Assn., Met. Mus. Art (assoc. mem.), Nat. Mus. of Women in the Arts (charter mem.). Office: Bemis Art Sch Colorado Springs 30 W Dale St Colorado Springs CO 80903-3210

COOK, LODWRICK MONROE, petroleum company executive; b. Castor, La., June 17, 1928; married. B.S., La. State U., 1950, B.S. in Petroleum Engring., 1955; M.B.A., So. Meth. U., 1965. Petroleum engr. Union Producing Co., 1955-56; with Atlantic Richfield Co., Los Angeles, 1956-95; engring. trainee Atlantic Richfield Co., Inc., Los Angeles, 1956-61, adminstrv. asst., 1961-64, sr. personnel dept., then personnel mgr., 1964-67, labor reins. con., 1967-69, mgr. labor reins. dept., 1969-70, v.p., gen. mgr. product div. Western area, 1970-72, v.p. mktg. products div., 1972-73, v.p. corp. planning div., 1973-74, v.p. products div., 1974-75, v.p. transp. div., 1975-77, sr. v.p. transp. div., 1977-80, exec. v.p., dir., 1980-85, chief exec. officer, 1985-94, chmn., 1986-95;, 1995, ret. chmn., 1995. 1st lt. U.S. Army, 1950-53. Mem. Nat. Petroleum Council, Am. Petroleum Inst. (bd. dirs.). Office: Atlantic Richfield Co PO Box 2579 515 S Flower St Los Angeles CA 90071

COOK, LYLE EDWARDS, retired fund raising executive, consultant; b. Astoria, Oreg., Aug. 19, 1918; s. Courtney Carson and Fanchon (Edwards) C.; m. Olive Freeman, Dec. 28, 1940; children: James Michael, Ellen Anita Cook Otto, Mary Lucinda Cook Vaage, Jane Victoria. A.B. in History, Stanford U., 1940, postgrad., 1940-41. Instr. history Yuba Jr. Coll., Marysville, Calif., 1941-42; methods analyst Lockheed Aircraft Corp., 1942-45; investment broker Quincy Cass Assocs., Los Angeles, 1945-49; mem. staff Stanford U., 1949-66, asso. dean Sch. Medicine, 1958-65; sr. staff mem. Lester Gorsline Assos., Belvedere, Calif., 1966-72, v.p., 1967-70, exec. v.p., 1970-72; v.p. univ. relations U. San Francisco, 1973-75; fund-raising and planning cons., 1975; dir. fund devel. Children's Home Soc. Calif., 1976-78; exec. dir. That Man May See, Inc., San Francisco, 1978-87; co-founder, trustee, chmn. bd. The Fund Raising Sch., 1977-86; spl. cons. NIH, 1960-62. Mem. Marin County Grand Jury, 1987-88. Mem. Nat. Soc. Fund Raising Execs. (bd. dirs. 1976-88, chmn. certification bd. 1988-90, recipient first Nat. Chmn.'s award 1981, named Outstanding Fund Raising Exec. 1987), Stanford Assocs., Stanford Founding Grant Soc. (dir. 1994—), Belvedere Tennis Club, Theta Delta Chi. Democrat. Episcopalian. Home: 25 Greenwood Bay Dr Belvedere Tiburon CA 94920-2252

COOK, PAUL M., technology company executive; b. Ridgewood, N.J.. BSChemE, MIT, 1947. With Stanford Rsch. Inst., Menlo Park, Calif., 1948-53, Sequoia Process Corp., 1953-56; with Raychem Corp., Menlo Park, Calif., 1957—, founder, former pres., CEO, until 1990, now chmn., bd. dirs.; chmn., CEO CellNet Data Sys., San Carlos, Calif., 1990-94, now chmn., bd. dirs.; chmn., bd. dirs. SRI Internat., 1993—. Mem. exec. com. San Francisco Bay Area Coun., 1988-94, chmn., 1990-91. Recipient Nat. Medal Tech., 1988. Mem. NAE, Am. Acad. Sci., Environ. Careers Orgn. (chmn., bd. trustees), MIT Corp. (life). Office: SRI Internat 333 Ravenswood Ave Menlo Park CA 94025-3453*

COOK, QUENTIN LAMAR, healthcare executive; b. Sept. 8, 1940; s. J. Vernon and Bernice (Kimball) C.; m. Kathryn Cook Knight, Quentin Laurance, Joseph Vernon III. BS, Utah State U., 1963; JD, Stanford U., 1966. Bar: Calif. 1966. Assoc. Carr, McClellan, Ingersoll, Thompson & Horn, Burlingame, Calif., 1966-69, ptnr., 1969-93; interim pres., CEO Calif. Healthcare Sys., San Francisco, 1993-94, pres., CEO, 1994—; bd. dirs. Burlington Bank & Trust Co., Guittard Chocolate Co., Burlingame, Calif. Healthcare Sys.; mem. adv. bd. KOIT AM/FM, San Francisco, 1994. City atty. Town of Hillsborough, Calif., 1982-93; mem. adv. bd. Utah State U., Logan, 1985—; mem. bd. visitors Brigham Young U. Law Sch., Provo, 1994. Mem. Nat. Health Lawyers Assn., Am. Soc. Hosp. Attys. Republican. Mormon. Home: 595 Pullman Rd Hillsborough CA 94010-6748 Office: Calif Healthcare Sys 1 California St Fl 15 San Francisco CA 94111-5401

COOK, ROBERT P., psychiatrist; b. Cin., May 7, 1923; s. George Harvey and Lenore (Hartzell) C.; m. Marilyn Claassen Lucas, Aug. 10, 1944 (div. Aug. 1975); children: Suzanne Cook Barth, George Robert Cook, Cynthia Cook Cusator; m. Joretta Lou Shaegley. BA, Miami U., Oxford, Ohio, 1946; MD, U. Cin., 1950. Diplomate Am. Bd. Psychiatry and Neurology. Intern U. Tex., Galveston, 1951; resident in psychiatry U. Colo., Denver, 1952, U. So. Calif., L.A., 1953-54; pvt. practice psychiatry Riverside, Calif., 1954—; dir. Cook Psychiat. Med. Group, Riverside, 1969—; assoc. clin. prof. psychiatry Loma Linda U. Med. Sch., Calif., 1974-89; hon. civilian cons. March AFB, Riverside, 1971—. Lt. (j.g.) USNR, 1944-46, PTO. Life fellow Am. Psychiat. Assn.; mem. Calif. Med. Assn., So. Calif. Psychiat. Assn. (pres., co-founder 1964), Riverside County Med. Assn., Victoria Club, Phi Delta Theta. Home: 4850 Somerset Dr Riverside CA 92507-5705 Office: Cook Psychiat Med Group 3773 Tibbetts St Ste F Riverside CA 92506-2640

COOK, ROBERT P., software architect; b. Chattanooga, Aug. 30, 1947; s. Eddie Patterson and Cynthia (Hubble) C.; m. Kristina Payne, Aug. 30, 1975. BE, Vanderbilt U., 1969, MS, 1971, PhD, 1978. Instr. Vanderbilt U., Nashville, 1970-71, 76-78, U. Fla., Gainesville, 1973-76; asst. prof. U. Wis., Madison, 1978-83; assoc. prof. U. Va., Charlottesville, 1983-91; architect Microsoft, Redmond, Wash., 1991—. Mem. IEEE, Assn. for Computing Machinery. Home: 611 Austin Cv Oxford MS 38655-5455

COOK, ROBERT P., II, business development executive; b. Balt., Nov. 23, 1931; s. Edward Damerel Cook and Emma Elizabeth (Tagmyer) Amstutz; m. Jean Lee Whittle, Mar. 31, 1951 (div. Jan. 1977); children: Robert, Susan. BS in Biochemistry, Johns Hopkins U., 1960. Pharm. rep. Borden, Inc., N.Y.C., 1954-62, mktg. mgr., 1962-71; product mgr. Syntex Labs., Inc., Palo Alto, Calif., 1971-81, group product dir., 1981-85, dir. bus. devel., 1985-88, dir. generics bus., 1988-94; pres. Cook and Co., Los Altos, Calif., 1994—; seminar spkr. Inst. Internat. Rsch., 1990, 93, R.B.C., Inc., 1991, 92, Windhover Assocs., 1990. With USN, 1949-53, lt. comdr. USNR, 1953-64. Mem. Licensing Execs. Soc., Inst. Internat. Rsch. Republican. Home: 60 Doud Dr Los Altos CA 94022-2326 Office: 4906 El Camino Real Ste 208 Los Altos CA 94022

COOK, SHARON EVONNE, university official; b. Pocatello, Idaho, July 16, 1941; d. Willard Robert and Marian (Bartlett) Leisy; m. John Fred Cook, June 19, 1971 (div. Nov. 1980). BEd, No. Mont. Coll., 1970; M in Secondary Edn., U. Alaska, Juneau, 1980; EdD, U. San Francisco, 1987. Cert. secondary sch. tchr., Alaska. Loan officer 1st Nat. Bank, Havre, Mont., 1964-68; adminstrv. asst. Alaska State Legis., Juneau, 1970-71; tchr. Juneau Dist. High Sch., 1971-75; instr. Juneau Dist. Community Coll., 1975-79; assoc. prof. U. Alaska, Juneau, 1979-90, dean Sch. Bus. and Pub. Adminstrn., 1986-90; assoc. dean Coll. Tech., Boise (Idaho) State U., 1990—; editor in chief office tech. McGraw Hill Book Gregg Div., N.Y.C., 1983-84; mem. exec. bd. statewide assembly U. Region V Vocat. Assn., 1978-80, del. 1982. Treas. Alaska State Vocat. Assn., 1980-82, pres.-elect, 1986, pres., 1987; pres. U. Alaska Juneau Assembly, 1978-80, v.p., 1980-82. No. Mont. Coll. scholar, Havre, 1968-70; named Outstanding Tchr., U. Alaska, 1976. Republican. Home: 2551 S Swallowtail Ln Boise ID 83706-6150 Office: Boise State U Coll Tech Office of Assoc Dean 1910 University Dr Boise ID 83725-0001

COOK, STANLEY JOSEPH, English language educator, academic programs administrator, poet; b. Spicer, Minn., June 9, 1935; s. William Joseph and Lillie Esther (Feeland) C.; m. Janet Lucille Terry, Oct. 9, 1964 (div. June 1988); children: John Hildon, Laurel Erin; m. Michaela Dianne Higuera, Dec. 18, 1989; 1 step-child, Richard Scott. BA, U. Minn., 1957; MA, U. Utah, 1966, PhD (NDEA fellow), 1969. Project specialist in English, U. Wis., Madison, 1967; instr. English, U. Utah, Salt Lake City, 1968-69; prof. English and modern langs. Calif. State Poly. U., Pomona, 1969—; cons. communications. Served with USMCR, 1958-64. NSF grantee, 1966;

Calif. State U. and Colls. grantee, 1973-74. Mem. SUBUD, AAUP, NEA, Phi Beta Kappa. Democrat. Roman Catholic. Editor: Language and Human Behavior, 1973, Man Unwept: Visions from the Inner Eye, 1974; author: (with others) The Scope of Grammar: A Study of Modern English, 1980, Cal Poly through 2001: A Continuing Commitment to Excellence, 1987; fieldworker Dictionary of Am. Regional English, 1986—. Home: 1744 N Corona Ave Ontario CA 91764-1236 Office: Calif State Poly U 3801 W Temple Ave Pomona CA 91768-2557

COOK, STEPHEN CHAMPLIN, retired shipping company executive; b. Portland, Oreg., Sept. 20, 1915; s. Frederick Stephen and Mary Louise (Boardman) C.; m. Dorothy White, Oct. 27, 1945; children: Mary H. Cook Goodson, John B., Samuel D., Robert B. (dec.). Student, U. Oreg., 1935-36. Surveyor U.S. Engrs. Corp., Portland, Oreg., 1934-35; dispatcher Pacific Motor Trucking Co., Oakland, Calif., 1937-38; manifest clk. Pacific Truck Express, Portland, 1939; exec. asst. Coastwise Line, San Francisco, 1940-41, mgr. K-Line svc., 1945-56; chartering mgr. Ocean Svc. Inc. subs. Marcona Corp., San Francisco, 1956-75, ret., 1975; cons., San Francisco, 1976-78. Author 1 charter party, 1957. Mem. steering com. Dogwood Festival, Lewiston, Idaho, 1985-92; sec. Asotin County Reps., Clarkston, Wash., 1986-88; adv. bd. Pt. Clarkston Commrs., 1989-92. Lt. USN, 1941-45, PTO. Recipient Pres.'s award Marin (Calif.) coun. Boy Scouts Am., 1977, Order of Merit, 1971, 84, Skillern award Lewis Clark coun., 1982, Silver Beaver award 1987; Lewis-Clark Valley Vol. award, 1987, Youth Corps award Nat. Assn. Svc. and Conservation Corps., 1990. Mem. VFW, Clarkston C. of C. (pres.'s spl. award 1983), Asotin County Hist. Soc. (hon. life pres. 1982-83, bd. dirs.), Asotin C. of C. (v.p. 1994-95). Republican. Mem. Stand for United Ch. of Christ.

COOK, THOMAS EDWARD, federal agency administrator; b. Fresno, Calif., July 20, 1947; s. James Taylor and Mary Frances (Logue) C.; m. Alicia Hermina Guerra, Sept. 7, 1977; children: Thomas Edward Jr., Richard James. BA, San Deigo State U., 1974. Immigration officer Immigration & Naturalization Svc., Houston, 1976-79, immigration examiner, 1979-82; sr. immigration examiner Immigration & Naturalization Svc., Washington, 1982-90; deputi ctr. dir. Immigration & Naturalization Svc., Laguna Niguel, Calif., 1990—; v.p. Child Care Ctr., Laguna Niguel, 1991-93. Sgt. USAF, 1966-70, Vietnam. Mem. Am. Soc. Pub. Adminstrn., Internat. Personnel Mgmt. Assn., FOP, Am. Legion. Roman Catholic. Office: USINS Western Svc Ctr 24000 Avila Rd Aliso Viejo CA 92656-3405

COOK, TODD MCCLURE, health care executive; b. Frankfort, Ind., Nov. 3, 1962; s. Robert Eugene and Patricia (McKinney) C. Student Calif. State U., 1981-82; BA in Econs./English George Mason U., 1983; MBA in Health Care Administrn., Columbia Pacific U., 1990. Asst. dir./acting dir. This Way House, Alexandria, 1983-85; pvt. cons., 1985-86; bus. mgr. Falls Church (Va.) Med. Ctr., Va., 1986-88; adminstr., Neurology Svcs., Inc., Fairfax, Alexandria, Woodbridge, Va. and Washington, 1989-92; sr. ptnr. Cook & Miele Assocs., Alexandria and L.A., 1989-93; health care exec. RehabCare Corp., Rio Hondo Hosp., Downey, Calif., Valley Presbyn. Hosp., Van Nuys, Calif., Alhambra (Calif.) Hosp., 1993—; cons. St. Elizabeth's Hosp. Crisis Intervention Tng., Washington, 1985, Alexandria's Child Safety Day, 1984; Bd. dirs. Help in Emotional Trouble, Fresno, 1982, v.p., bd. dirs., 1983; bd. dirs. Mental Health Assn., Alexandria, 1984, v.p. bd., 1985; del. Nat. Network of Runaway and Youth Services Symposium, Bethesda, Md., 1985; v.p. Alexandria Mental Health Assn., 1983-86; active Nat. Head Injury Found., Va. Head Injury Found., Calif. Head Injury; vol. Alexandria Crisis Hot-Line. Grantee Youth Devel. Bur., 1984, 85, Alexandria City grantee, 1985. Mem. SAR, Am. Coll. Health Care Execs. (affiliate), Am. Coll. Med. Quality (affiliate), Am. Bd. Quality Assurance and Utilization Rev. Physicians (diplomate), Am. Acad. Med. Adminstrs., Am. Coll. Neuromusculoskeletal Adminstrs. Democrat. Presbyterian. Club: Entrepreneur Orgn. (Alexandria) (pres. 1985). Lodge: Demolay. Avocation: tennis.

COOKE, SUZETTE ALLEN, state representative; b. Bellingham, Wash., Aug. 27, 1949. BA, Western Wash. U., 1972. Recreation supr. City of Seattle, 1972-75; dir. Kent (Wash.) Parks and Recreation Dept. Sr. Activity Ctr., 1975-81; exec. dir. Kent C. of C., 1981-92; rep. 47th Dist. Washington State, 1993—; chair ho. human svcs. com., appropriations com., mem. joint com. on pension policy. Former ex-officio bd. mem. Wash. State Small Bus. Improvement Coun.; Fist Christian Ch. of Kent; former mem. King County Housing Rehab. Adv. Com., Valley Med. Ctr. Citizens Adv. Coun.; bd. dirs. Covington Cmty. Ctr. Adv. Coun., Am. Heart Assn., South King County Coun., South County Youth Violence Com. Mem. Wash. C. of C. Execs. (past pres.), Assn. Wash. Bus. (former bd. and exec. com. mem.), Wash. State Sr. Ctr. Dirs. Assn. (founding organizer), Rotary Club Kent, King County Sexual Assault Resource Ctr., Growth and Prevention Theatre. Home: 25307 144th Ave SE Kent WA 98042-3401 Office: 320 John L O'Brien Bldg Olympia WA 98504

COOL, THOMAS EDWARD, geophysicist; b. Auburn, Ind., Sept. 6, 1950; s. Philip and Suzanne Marian (Somers) C.; m. Iris Elaine Preas, Nov. 22, 1980; children: Jack Philip, Catherine Anna. B.S. in Geology, Ind. U., Ft. Wayne, 1972; M.S. in Oceanography, Tex. A&M U., 1976, Ph.D., 1979. Petroleum geophysicist Gulf Oil Co., Houston, 1980-82, sr. geophysicist, 1982-84, project geophysicist, 1984-85; devel. geophysicist Chevron Exploration North Sea, Ltd., 1985-87, sr. geophysicist, 1987-91, Angola bus. unit Chevron Overseas Petroleum, Inc., San Ramon, Calif., 1991—. Contbr. articles to profl. jours. Bd. dir., AAII; referee U.S. Soccer Fed. Grade V; den leader Boy Scots of Am. Mem. Am. Assn. Petroleum Geologists, Houston Geol. Soc., fellow Geol. Soc. London. Methodist. Club: Houston A&M. Avocations: tennis, history, travel. Home: 478 Bolero Dr Danville CA 94526-5007 Office: Chevron Overseas Petroleum Inc PO Box 5046 San Ramon CA 94583-0946

COOLBAUGH, CARRIE WEAVER, librarian; b. Pocatello, Idaho, Dec. 26, 1945; d. Elmer Dever and Pearl (Cutting) Weaver; (div. 1990); 1 child, Marc Harry Pachon; m. J.D. Coolbaugh, June 15, 1992. BA, Calif. State U. L.A., 1972; MS, U. So. Calif., 1974; DPA, U. La Verne, 1993. Reference librarian L.A. County Pub. Library, 1974; adminstrv. asst. Lansing (Mich.) Parks and Recreation, 1975-76; cons. Applied Mgmt. Systems, Silver Spring, Md., 1977; reference librarian Fairfax (Va.) County Pub. Library, 1978, children's librarian, 1979-81, regional children's librarian, 1981-83, br. mgr., 1983-88; coord. Downey (Calif.) City Library, 1987-88; asst. city librarian Commerce (Calif.) Pub. Library, 1988—. Mem. ALA, Calif. Libr. Assn., Libr. Adminstrn. and Mgmt. Assn., Pub. Libr. Assn., Met. Coop. Libr. System (chmn. adult svcs. com. 1988-89, Reforma, S.L.A.). Home: 404 Damien Ave La Verne CA 91750-4104 Office: Commerce Pub Library 5655 Jillson St Los Angeles CA 90040-1493

COOLEY, EDWARD H., castings manufacturer; b. 1922; grad. in mech. engring., Swarthmore Coll.; postgrad. Harvard U., 1947; married. With Dana Corp., 1947-49, Ore Saw Chain Corp., 1950-55; pres., dir. Precision Castparts Corp., Portland, Oreg., 1955—, now chmn. Office: Precision Castparts Corp 4600 SE Harney Dr Portland OR 97206-0825*

COOLEY, WES, Congressman; b. L.A., Calif., Mar. 28, 1932; married; 4 children. AA, El Camino C. C.; BS in Bus., U. So. Calif., 1958. Asst. to pres. Hyland Labs. divsn. Baxter Labs. Allergan Pharmaceuticals; asst. to pres., asst. to chmn. bd. ICN, divsn. mgr., dir. drug regulatory affairs; v.p. Virateck divsn.; founder, co-owner Rose Labs., Inc., 1981—; mem. Oregon State Senate, 1992-94; congressman 104 Congress from 2nd Oreg. dist., 1994—; mem. House Com. Agriculture, House Com. Resources, House Com. Veteran Affairs, Subcommittee Gen. Farm Commodities, Subcommittee on Livestock, Dairy and Poultry, Subcommittee on Nat. Pks., Forests and Lands, SubcommitteeWater and Power Resources. With U.S. Army, 1952-54, Korea. Home: 27430 Willard Rd Powell Butte OR 97753 Office: US House Reps 108 Cannon House Office Bldg Washington DC 20515-3702*

COOMBE, GEORGE WILLIAM, JR., lawyer, banker; b. Kearny, N.J., Oct. 1, 1925; s. George William and Laura (Montgomery) C.; A.B., Rutgers U., 1946; LL.B., Harvard, 1949; m. Marilyn N.Y. Ross, June 4, 1949; children—Susan, Donald William, Nancy. Bar: N.Y. 1950, Mich. 1953, Calif. 1976, U.S. Supr. Ct. Practice in N.Y.C., 1949-53, Detroit, 1953-69; atty., mem. legal-staff Gen. Motors Corp., Detroit, 1953-69, asst. gen. counsel, sec., 1969-75; exec. v.p., gen. counsel Bank of Am., San Francisco, 1975-90; ptnr. Graham and James, San Francisco, 1991—. Served to lt. USNR, 1942-46. Mem. Am., Mich., Calif., San Francisco, Los Angeles, N.Y.C. bar assns., Phi Beta Kappa, Phi Gamma Delta. Presbyterian. Home: 2190 Broadway St Apt 2E San Francisco CA 94115-1311 Office: Graham and James One Maritime Place San Francisco CA 94111

COOMBS, MICHAEL JOHN, research center administrator; b. London, June 2, 1946; came to U.S., 1986; s. George Henry and Doris Elvina (Richardson) C.; m. Margaret Thomson, Nov. 24, 1983. BA, U. London, 1969; PhD in Psychology, U. Liverpool, 1978. Group leader Man Machine Rsch. group U. Liverpool, Eng., 1978-82; rsch. fellow in computer sci. U. Strathclyde, Glasgow, Scotland, 1982-83, lectr. in computer sci., 1983-85; prin. scientist Computing Rsch. Lab., N.Mex. State U., Las Cruces, 1986-87, assoc. dir., 1987—; dir. Rsch. Ctr., Phys. Sci. Lab., N.Mex. State U., Las Cruces, 1992—; cons. U.S. Army Info. Processing Adv. Bds., 1987—. Mem. editorial bd. Internat. Jour. Man Machine Studies, 1983—, Jour. Exptl. and Theoretical Army Info., 1990—; contbr. numerous articles to profl. jours. Recipient Freedom award City of London, 1985. Mem. Cognitive Sci. Soc., Am. Assn. Artificial Intelligence, Phi Kappa Phi. Home: PO Box 3315-UPB Las Cruces NM 88003 Office: Phys Sci Lab PO Box 30002 Las Cruces NM 88003-8002

COOMER, JOHN HARNER, association administrator; b. Chgo., Oct. 4, 1954; s. Albert Monroe and Patricia (Romaine) C.; m. JoLayne Michele Good, June 30, 1984; children: Paul William, Michael Darius. BA in Spl. Edn., U. Ariz., 1976; MBA, No. Ariz. U., 1986. Job placement specialist Casa Grande (Ariz.) Rehab. Ctr., 1981-82; asst. dir. program and tng. Ariz. Spl. Olympics, Tempe, 1982-84; exec. dir. Ariz. Spl. Olympics, Phoenix, 1990—; grad. asst. No. Ariz. U., Flagstaff, 1984-86; gen. mgr. Perfect Type Co., Tucson, 1986-87; sr. area mgr. western U.S. Alpha Graphics, Tucson, 1987-90; mem. exec. adv. bd. SureGift, Phoenix, 1992—. V.p. Florence (Ariz.) Preservation Found., 1983—. Capt. U.S. Army, 1977-81. Mem. Nat. Assn. Spl. Olympics Profls., Phi Kappa Phi, Beta Gamma Sigma. Episcopalian. Office: Ariz Spl Olympics 3821 E Wier Ave Phoenix AZ 85040-2935

COOMES, LISA ANN, critical care nurse; b. Loma Linda, Calif., Nov. 21, 1966; d. Timothy Gerald and Peggy Jean (Thomas) C. ASN, Riverside Community Coll., 1988; BSN, U. Phoenix, San Bernardino, 1993. RN, Calif.; CEN; cert. mobile intensive care nurse, Calif. Staff nurse emergency rm. Riverside (Calif.) Community Hosp., 1988-92, shift coord. emergency rm., 1992-94; with critical care transport Goodhew Ambulance, Riverside, 1990-94; dir. critical care nurse transport Care Line Calif., 1994—; instr. pediatric advanced life support Riverside Cmty. Hosp., 1992—, instr. ACLS, 1992—; emergency relief nurse 1994 Northridge Earthquake, Calif. Mem. Emergency Nurses Assn. Home: 155 Chant St Perris CA 92571-4654 Office: Riverside Community Hosp 4445 Magnolia Ave Riverside CA 92501-4135

COONEY, DANIEL ELLARD, aeronautical engineer; b. Deland, Fla., Oct. 25, 1949; s. William P. and Ruth E. C.; m. Marguerite R. Williams, Nov 17, 1990; children: Michael, Aaron. BS in Aerospace Engring., U. Fla., 1972; MA in Counseling, A.G. Theological Sem., 1987. Registered aeronautical engr., Kans.; cert. airline pilot. Project engr. Bede Aircraft Inc., Newton, Kans., 1972-78; CAD mgr. Lear Avia Corp., Reno, 1978-82; CAD cons. Aerospace CAD/CAM Svcs., Reno, 1982-89; chief engr. Scaled Composites Inc., Mojave, Calif., 1989—. Patents in field. Office: Scaled Composites 1624 Flight Line Hngr 78 Mojave CA 93501-1663

COONEY, MIKE, state official; b. Washington, Sept. 3, 1954; s. Gage Rodman and Ruth (Brodie) C.; m. Dee Ann Marie Gribble; children: Ryan Patrick, Adan Cecelia, Colin Thomas. BA in Polit. Sci., U. Mont., 1979. State rep. Mont. Legislature, Helena, 1976-80; exec. asst. U.S. Sen. Max Baucus, Butte, Mont., 1979-82, Washington, 1982-85, Helena, Mont., 1985-89; sec. of state State of Mont., Helena, 1988—. Com. mem. Project Democracy Commn., Fed. Clearinghouse Adv. Panel, YMCA; chmn.Friends of Youth Campaign. Mem. Nat. Secs. of State. Home: PO Box 754 Helena MT 59624-0754 Office: Office Sec of State 225 State Capitol Helena MT 59620

COONS, DAVID JOEL, physician, psychiatrist; b. Oakland, Calif., Mar. 16, 1947; s. Harold S. Coons and Maxine Flowers; m. Jean Elizabeth Curtiss, Sept. 15, 1970; children: Daniel, Michael, Christine. BS, U. Utah, 1969, MD, 1973. Diplomate Am. Bd. Psychiatry and Neurology, Am. Bd. Forensic Psychiatry. Intern Good Samaritan Hosp., Phoenix, 1973-74, resident, 1977; dep. dir. psychiatry Indian Health Services, Anchorage, 1977-78; asst. supt. Alaska Psychiat. Inst., Anchorage, 1978-82; practice medicine specializing in psychiatry Anchorage, 1982-88; med. dir. Adult Services St. Luke's Behavioral Health Ctr., Phoenix, 1988-89; v.p. med. affairs St. Luke's Behavioral Health Ctr., 1989—; cons. South Cen. Counseling, Anchorage, 1982-88; assoc. clin. prof. U. Wash., Seattle, 1987-88; clin. supr., sr. cons. Ariz. State Hosp., 1987—. Contbr. articles to profl. jours. Den and pack officer Anchorage council Boy Scouts Am., 1985-86. Served as surgeon USPHS, 1977-78. Mem. Am. Psychiat. Assn., Alaska Psychiat. Assn. (legis. rep. 1950-83, pres. 1987), Ariz. Psychiat. Assn., AMA. Congregationalist. Address: PO Box 31990 Mesa AZ 85275-1990

COONS, ELDO JESS, JR., manufacturing company executive; b. Corsicana, Tex., July 5, 1924; s. Eldo Jess and Ruby (Allison) C.; m. Beverly K. Robbins, Feb. 6, 1985; children by previous marriage: Roberta Ann, Valerie, Cheryl. Student engring., U. Calif., 1949-50. Owner C & C Constrn. Co., Pomona, Calif., 1946-48; sgt. traffic div. Pomona Police Dept., 1948-54; nat. field dir. Nat. Hot Rod Assn., L.A., 1954-57; pres. Coons Custom Mfg., Inc., Oswego, Kans., 1957-68; chmn. bd. Borg-Warner Corp., 1968-71; pres. Coons Mfg., Inc., Oswego, 1971-84; pres. E.B.C Mgmt. Cons., Lake Havasu City, Ariz., 1984—. Mem. Kans. Gov.'s Adv. Com. for State Architects Assn. Served with C.E., AUS, 1943-46. Named to Exec. and Profl. Hall Fame, Recreational Vehicle/Mobile Homes Hall of Fame, Internat. Hot Rod Hall of Fame, 1961, Internat. Drag Racing Hall of Fame, 1991; recipient Paul Abel award Recreation Vehicle Industry Assn., 1978, 1st Ann. New Product award Kans. Gov.'s Office and Kans. Engring. Soc. 1982-83. Mem. Oswego C. of C. (dir.), Nat. Juvenile Officers Assn., Am. Legion, AIM (fellow pres.'s coun.), Mcpl. Officers Assn., Oswego C. of C., Young Pres.'s Orgn. Masons (K.T., Shriner), Rotary (pres. Oswego 1962-63). Originator 1st city sponsored police supervised dragstrip. Home and Office: EBC Mgmt Cons 2634 Diablo Dr Lake Havasu City AZ 86406-8450

COONTZ, STEPHANIE JEAN, history and family studies educator, author; b. Seattle, Aug. 31, 1944; d. Sidney Coontz and Patricia (McIntosh) Waddington; 1 child, Kristopher. BA with honors, U. Calif., Berkeley, 1966; MA, U. Wash., Seattle, 1970. Mem. faculty Evergreen State Coll., Olympia, Wash., 1975—; fellow The Nat. Faculty; lectr. Inquiring Minds Spkrs. program Wash. Humanities Commn., 1989-91. Author: The Way We Never Were: American Families and the Nostalgia Trap, 1992, The Social Origins of Private Life: A History of American Families, 1988, (with others) Women's Work, Men's Property: On the Origins of Gender and Class, 1986, History and Family Theory, vol. II, 1989; contbr. numerous articles to profl. jours. Woodrow Wilson Found. fellow, 1968-69; recipient Washington Gov's. Writer's award, 1989, Dale Richmond award Am. Acad. Pediatrics, 1995. Mem. Am. Studies Assn., Am. Hist. Assn., Orgn. Am. Historians. Office: Evergreen State Coll Olympia WA 98505

COOPER, ANNETTE CARLESTA, entrepreneur; b. Huntington Park, Calif., Feb. 20, 1949; d. Joette Clarina (Murin) C.; Ron Stokes, Jan. 27, 1969 (div.). Massage therapist Fabulous Faces, San Francisco, 1977-80, Shiseido, Manila, Phillipines, 1980-82; mgr. Says Who?, Oakland, San Francisco, Calif., 1984-87; pvt. practice Began Annette's Sizes 14 & Up, Santa Rosa, 1987—; pres., bd. mem. Montgomery Village Bd. Dirs., Santa Rosa, Calif., 1991-93. Columnist Ask Annette, 1991. hospice clothing drive, Santa Rosa, Calif., 1991—. Named Merchant Ambassador of Yr., Montgomery Village Coding Enterprises, Santa Rosa, Calif., 1993. Mem. C. of C. Office: Annette's Plus Sizes 2406 Magowan Dr Santa Rosa CA 95405-5006

COOPER, AUSTIN MORRIS, chemist, chemical engineer, consultant, researcher; b. Long Beach, Calif., Feb. 1, 1959; s. Merril Morris and Charlotte Madeline (Wittmer) C. BS in Chemistry with honors, Baylor U., 1981; BSChemE with honors, Tex. Tech U., 1983, MSChemE, 1985. Solar energy researcher U.S. Dept. Energy, Lubbock, Tex., 1983-85; advanced mfg. and process engring. mgr. McDonnell Douglas Space Systems Co., Huntington Beach, Calif., 1986-87, chem.-process line mgr., 1987-89, sr. material and process engr., 1989—. Contbr. articles to profl. jours. Mem. Am. Inst. Chem. Engrs., Am. Chem. Soc., Soc. Advancement of Materials and Process Engrs., Sigma Xi, Omega Chi Epsilon, Kappa Mu Epsilon, Beta Beta Beta.

COOPER, GINNIE, library director; b. Worthington, Minn., 1945; d. Lawrence D. and Ione C.; 1 child, Daniel Jay. Student, Coll. St. Thomas, U. Wis., Parkside; BA, S.D. State U.; MA in Libr. Sci., U. Minn. Tchr. Flandreau (S.D.) Indian Sch., 1967-68, St. Paul Pub. Schs., 1968-69; br. libr. Wash. County Libr., Lake Elmo, Minn., 1970-71, asst. dir., 1971-75; assoc. adminstr., libr. U. Minn. Med. Sch., Mpls., 1975-77; dir. Kenosha (Wis.) Pub. Libr., 1977-81; county libr. Alameda County (Calif.) Libr., 1981-90; dir. librs. Multnomah County Libr., Portland, Oreg., 1990—. Chair County Mgr. Assn.; county adminstr. Mayor's Exec. Roundtable. Mem. ALA (mem. LAMA, PLA and RASD coms., elected to coun. 1987, 91, mem. legislation com. 1986-90, mem. orgn. com. 1990—), Calif. Libr. Assn. (pres. CIL, 1985, elected to coun. 1986, pres. Calif. County Librs. 1986), Oreg. Libr. Assn. Office: Multnomah County Libr 205 NE Russell St Portland OR 97212-3708

COOPER, GLEN ALAN, financial planner; b. Torrance, Calif.; s. Edward and Mary Cooper; m. Linda Ten Lew, Aug. 4, 1991. BSBA with great distinction, Calif. State U., Long Beach, 1984; MBA with distinction, Calif. State U., Northridge, 1993. Jr. auditor Peat Marwick Main & Co., L.A., 1984-85; sr. auditor Grant Thornton, Irvine, Calif., 1985-88; tech. acctg. specialist Gibraltar Savs., 1988-89; asst. v.p. fin. Ea. divsn. retail Countrywide Funding Corp., L.A., 1989-93, v.p. fin. retail divsn., 1993-94, v.p. fin. planning, 1994—. Mem. Calif. State U. Long Beach (Pres.'s List scholar 1981-82), Golden Key, Beta Gamma Sigma, Beta Alpha Psi. Home: 134 S Gramercy Pl Apt 8 Los Angeles CA 90004-4920

COOPER, JACK KYLE, dentist; b. Beaumont, Tex., Sept. 15, 1932; s. Clio E. and Josephine Edwin (Fuller) C.; m. Nita Jeane Foster, June 5, 1955; children: Anne Kyle Cooper Gruensfelder, Lynne Carrell. Student, U. Tulsa, 1950-53; DDS, Wash. U., St. Louis, 1957. Lic. dentist, Colo. Pvt. practice Alamosa, Colo., 1959-90; dental dir. San Luis Valley Area Health Edn. Ctr., Alamosa, 1979-84, San Luis Valley HMO, Monte Vista, Colo., 1981—; clin. asst. prof. dept. applied chemistry Sch. Dentistry U. Colo., Denver, 1980—; instr. dept. biology Adams State Coll., Alamosa, 1962-94, instr. emeritus, 1994—. Author: (booklet) From Grubstakers, Tooth Carpenters and Travelers to Consumate Doctors of Dentistry—The Story of The Making of the Profession in the San Luis Valley, 1993; photographs represented in local exhbn., 1988, 94. Mem. coun. City of Alamosa; founder, mem. San Luis Valley Hist. Soc., 1968—, pres., 1968-70, 82-84. Capt. Dental Corps, U.S. Army, 1957-59. Fellow Internat. Coll. Dentists; mem. ADA, Colo. Dental Assn. (trustee, mem. coms. 1959—), San Luis Valley Dental Soc. (pres. 1962-66, 78-82, other offices), Kappa Sigma (pres. Tulsa U. chpt. 1952-53). Presbyterian. Home and Office: 64 El Rio Dr Alamosa CO 81101-2117

COOPER, JON HUGH, public television executive; b. Wynnewood, Okla., Aug. 6, 1940; s. John Hughes and Sarah Edna (Ray) C.; m. L. Ilene Batty, Dec. 16, 1961 (div. Jan. 1984); children: Jon Shelton, Geoffrey Harold; m. Patricia Carol Kyle, Jan. 28, 1989; children: Cynthia Lynne, Jennifer Jon Kyle. BA, Okla. State U., 1962; postgrad., U. Ariz., U. Denver, U. Colo., Denver. Mgmt. positions with Evening Star Broadcasting, Washington and Lynchburg, Va., 1962-67; producer, program mgr., dir. prodn. Sta. KUAT-AM-TV, Tucson, 1967-73; exec. dir. Rocky Mountain Network, Denver, 1973-77; exec. dir. Pacific Mountain Network, Denver, 1977-79, also bd. dirs.; gen. mgr. Sta. KNME-TV, Albuquerque, 1979—; lectr. speech and journalism U. Ariz., 1967-73; mem. interconnection com. PBS, 1983-92, bd. dirs., 1986-92, mem. exec. com., 1988-90, 91-92; bd. dirs. PBS Enterprises and Nat. Datacast, 1990-94; bd. dirs. Native Am. Pub. Broadcasting Consortium, Pacific Mountain Network Japan Survey Team. Bd. dirs., v.p., pres. Pueblo Los Cerros Homeowners Assn., 1987-88; bd. dirs. Samaritan Counseling Ctr., Albuquerque, 1987, N.Mex. Better Bus. Bur., 1991—; bd. advisors Pub. TV Outreach Alliance, 1992—; mem. N.Mex. Edn. Tech. Coun., 1992—; chmn. N.Mex. Commn. Pub. Broadcasting, 1992—; mem. steering com. Western Coop. on Ednl. Telecommunications. Named Govt. Bus. Adv. of Year U.S. Hispanic C. of C. Region II, 1990.

COOPER, LARRY S., cleaning network executive, textile consultant; b. Bklyn., June 14, 1957; s. Jack and Evelyn (Weinfeld) C.; m. Tryna Lee Giordano, Dec. 31, 1975;a children: Jonathan, Jennifer, Jillian. Student, U. Colo., 1975-78. Cert. master cleaner, sr. level carpet inspector. Owner Cooper's Carpet Cleaners, Boulder, Colo., 1975-79; pres. Profl. Cleaning Network, Denver, 1979—; owner Textiles Cons., Denver, 1986—. Chmn. Broomfield (Colo.) Connection, 1988-90; mayor pro-tem City of Broomfield, 1995—. Named Cleanfax Man of Yr., Clean Fax Mag., 1990. Mem. Profl. Carpet and Upholstery Cleaners Assn. (pres. 1980-81, 84-86), Internat. Inst. of Carpet and Upholstery Cert. (v.p. 1984-85, pres. 1985-87, chmn. bd. 1988, chmn. cert. bd. 1990—). Office: Profl Cleaning Network 6445 Downing St Denver CO 80229-7225

COOPER, LYNN DALE, minister, retired navy chaplain; b. Aberdeen, Wash., Aug. 11, 1932; s. Lindsey Monroe and Mattie Ann (Cattron) C.; m. Doris Marlene Aydelott, June 2, 1956; children: Kevin Dale, Kathy Cooper O'Briant, Karen Doris Cooper Henthorn. Student, Gray's Harbor Coll., 1950-51; BTh, Northwest Christian Coll., 1955; MDiv, Phillips U., 1961, D Ministry, 1977. Ordained to ministry Christian Ch., 1955. Commd lt. (j.g.) USN, 1965, advanced through grades to comdr., 1988, ret., 1988; assoc. pastor First Christian Ch., Olympia, Wash., 1955-57; minister First Christian Ch., Aline, Okla., 1957-61, Sumner, Wash., 1961-66; chaplain U.S. Navy, 1966-88; minister Cen. Christian Ch., Prosser, Wash., 1988—; bd. dirs. Jubilee Ministries, Prosser, Wash., 1988—. V.p. Prosser Sch. Bd. Recipient many Navy and Marine Corps awards and medals; decorated Bronze Star medal. Mem. Mil. Chaplains Assn. U.S.A. (life), Disciples of Christ Hist. Soc. (life), Navy League of U.S., Ret. Officers Assn. (life), Kiwanis (pres. Prosser, Wash. chpt.), De Molay (past master councillor 1950—). Home: 1818 Benson Ave Prosser WA 99350-1547 Office: Cen Christian Ch 1000 6th St Prosser WA 99350-1407

COOPER, RALPH SHERMAN, physicist, college dean; b. Newark, June 25, 1931; s. Morris David and Fay Bella (Gottfried) C.; m. Sandra Lenore Kleeman, Jan. 30, 1956; children: Laurie Mara, Brett Edward. B in Chem. Engring., Cooper Union U., 1953; MS in Physics, U. Ill., 1954, PhD in Physics, 1957. Chief scientist Douglas Labs., Richland, Wash., 1965-69; assoc. div. leader Los Alamos (N.Mex.) Sci. Lab., 1957-65, 69-75; dep. dir. research and devel. Physics Internat., San Leandro, Calif., 1975-82; dir. systems INESCO, Inc., San Diego, 1982-84; pres. Apogee Research Corp., San Diego, 1984-87; Long Beach, 1987—; assoc. dean research Coll. of Engring. Calif. State U., Long Beach, 1987-94; v.p. Creative Enterprises, Long Beach, Calif., 1987—; pres. Apogee Rsch. Corp., 1985—, Class, Inc., 1993—. Patentee in field. Recipient Young Author prize Am. Electrochemistry Soc., 1956. Mem. AIAA, Am. Soc. Engring. Edn., Nat. Sci. Tchrs. Assn., Am. Phys. Soc., Am. Nuclear Soc., Sigma Xi, Tau Beta Pi. Office: Creative Enters 5354 E 2nd St # 200 Long Beach CA 90803-5333

COOPER, STEVEN JON, health care management consultant, educator; b. Oct. 19, 1941; B.A., U. Calif., Los Angeles, 1966; M.Ed., Loyola U., 1973; postgrad. Union Sch., 1977—; m. Sharon M. Lepack; children: Robin E., Erik S. Ednl. coordinator dept. radiology Mt. Sinai Hosp. Med. Ctr., Chgo., 1969-72; chmn. dept. radiol. scis. U. Health Scis., Chgo. Med. Sch., VA Hosp., North Chicago, 1972-79; v.p. C&S Inc., Denver, 1980-81; pres. Healthcare Mktg. Corp., Denver, 1981-84; corp. officer Sharon Cooper Assocs. Ltd., Englewood, Colo., 1984—; cons. HEW; lectr. in field. Served with USAF, 1960-64, USAFR, 1964-66. Mem. W.K. Kellogg Found. grantee. Mem. Am. (mem. edn., curriculum review coms., task force), Ill. (chmn. annual meeting 1976, program Midwest conf., 1977) socs. radiol. tech., Coll. Radiol. Scis., Am. Hosp. Radiology Adminstrs. (mem. edn. com., treas. Midwest region, nat. v.p.), AMA (com. on allied health edn. and accreditation), Kiwanis (charter, pres.-elect), Sovereign Order of St. John of

Jerusalem, Knights of Malta, Inverness Club (bd. dirs.), Sigma Xi. Author numerous publs. in field. Home: 8522 E Dry Creek Pl Englewood CO 80112-2701 Office: 9085 E Mineral Cir Ste 160 Englewood CO 80112-3418

COOPER, SUSAN, artist; b. L.A., Apr. 25, 1947; d. Morris and Zelda (Lefkowitz) C.; m. Joseph C. Anderson, July 25, 1976 (div. 1990); children: Martha Cooper, David Gaylord; m. Richard A. Cohn, Jan. 25, 1992. BA in Art and Anthropology with honors, U. Calif., Berkeley, 1968, MA, 1970. Instr. Met. State Coll., Denver, 1987-89, U. Colo., Denver, 1990-91; bd. dirs. Ctr. for Idea Art, 1985-87; guest spkr. U. Denver, 1988, 89, No. Ky. U., 1979, Met. State Coll., 1989. One-woman shows include Foothills Art Ctr., Golden, Colo., 1995, Inkfish Gallery, Denver, 1993, 90, Galleria Expositum, Mexico City, 1992, Henri Gallery, Washington, 1989, Denver Art Mus., 1989, others; paintings represented in permanent collections at Denver Art Mus., City and County Bldg., Denver, Std. Oil of Ohio, Ea. N.Mex. State U., Sch. Am. Rsch., Santa Fe, N.Mex., St. Luke's Hosp., Denver, Denver Pub. Libr., Congress Park, Denver, City and County Bldg., Denver, 1993, others. Pres., dir. Rocky Mountain Women's Inst. U. Denver, 1977-87.

COOPER, SUSAN CAROL, environmental, safety and health professional; b. Milw., Dec. 25, 1939; d. Carroll Arthur and Edith Estelle (Hicks) Brooks; m. William Randall Cooper, June 20, 1964; children: Darin Benbrook, Carol Kimberly, Ryan Randall. BS in Biology, U. Wis., Milw., 1962; MS in Physiology, Wash. State U., 1966; PhD in Physiology, U. Idaho, 1972, MS in Geol. Engring., Hydrology, 1990. EIT. Sr. lab. technician Dept. Vet. Pathology, Wash. State U., Pullman, 1965-68; postdoctoral assoc. dept. chemistry U. Idaho, Moscow, 1972-74, vis. prof. chemistry, 1974; instr. facilitator for gifted/talented Highland Sch. Dist., Craigmont, Idaho, 1975-76; program dir. YWCA, Lewiston, Idaho, 1977-78; support asst. Exxon Nuclear Idaho Corp., Idaho Falls, 1983; engr. Exxon Nuclear Idaho Corp. and Westinghouse Idaho Nuclear Co. Inc., Idaho Falls, 1983-84; environ. engr., sr. environ. engr. Westinghouse Idaho Nuclear Co. Inc., Idaho Falls, 1984-86, mgr. environ., safety and health, SIS Project, 1986-90; mem. Environ. Compliance Office Dept. Energy Idaho Ops. Westinghouse Idaho Nuclear Co. Inc., 1989; mgr. environ. compliance, environ. permits and programs, adv. engr. Waste Isolation divsn., Westinghouse Electric Co., Carlsbad, N.Mex., 1990-92; sr. project mgr., regulatory compliance specialist S.M. Stoller Corp., Albuquerque, 1992-95; artist Albuquerque, 1993—; v.p. Sisneros-Cooper Environ. Corp., Albuquerque, 1995—; pres. Cooper Creations, Albuquerque, 1993-95; instr. hazardous waste mgmt. N.Mex. State U., Carlsbad, 1991; instr. Clean Air Act, Sch. Environ. Excellence, Westinghouse/Dept. Energy, 1990-91; mem. speaker's bur. Idaho Nat. Engring. Lab./Westinghouse Idaho Nuclear Co. Inc., 1988-90, Waste Isolation divsn. Westinghouse Electric Co., 1990-92; presenter profl. confs. Contbr. articles to profl. jours. Mem. presenting team Marriage Encounter, 1980-90; campaign group leader United Way, 1986-87, campaigner, 1985-86; mem., historian Mayor's Com. for Employment of Handicapped and Older Workers, Idaho Falls, 1985-86; singer Idaho Falls Opera Theater, 1983-85; lay preacher, lay reader, lay Eucharistic minister Episc. Ch., Idaho and N.Mex., 1984—; mem. choir St. John's Ch., Idaho Falls, 1983-85, Grace Episc. Ch., Carlsbad, 1990-92, Holy Trinity/St. Francis Ch., Albuquerque, 1992—; del. Dem. Conv., Boise, Idaho, 1975. NSF fellow, 1963, NDEA fellow, 1963-65, NASA trainee, 1968-70, Nat. Assn. Geology Tchrs. scholar, 1980. Mem. Toastmasters (past pres, founder 2 corp. clubs, adminstrv. v.p., Competent Toastmaster, Able Toastmaster). Home and Office: Sisneros-Cooper Environ Corp 3413 Dellwood Ct NE Albuquerque NM 87110-2203

COOPER, SUSAN J., dietitian, consultant; b. Maywood, Calif., May 12, 1954; d. Juan Mike and Josephine (Salias) Blanco; m. Monte Lloyd Cooper, Oct. 15, 1975, children: Leigh Ayn, Erin Jan. BA in Biology, U. Mo., St. Louis, 1978; MS in Dietetics, U. Arizona, 1982. Lic. dietitian, Mont. Faculty mem. Fla. State U., Panama City, 1984-86, Glendale (Ariz.) C.C., 1988-92; clin. dietitian Deaconess Med. Ctr., Great Falls, Mont., 1992-93; owner Consults in Nutrition, Great Falls, Mont., 1994—. Author, editor: Healthy Meals of Great Falls, 1994. With U.S. Army, 1973-75. Mem. Am. Dietetic Assn. (coun. on practice 1994—), Environ. Nutrition Dietetic Practice Group (chmn. 1994—), Mont. Dietetic Assn., Ctrl. Ariz. Dist. Dietetic Assn. (bd. dirs., editor 1986-88). Home and Office: Consults in Nutrition 3908 16th Ave S Great Falls MT 59405

COOPER, WILLIAM CLARK, physician; b. Manila, P.I., June 22, 1912 (father Am. citizen); s. Wibb Earl and Pearl (Herron) C.; MD, U. Va., 1934; MPH magna cum laude, Harvard U., 1958; m. Ethel Katherine Sicha, May 1, 1937; children: Jane Willoughby, William Clark, David Jeremy, Robert Lawrence. Intern, asst. resident U. Hosps., Cleve., 1934-37; commd. asst. surgeon USPHS, 1940, advanced through grades to med. dir., 1952; chief occupational health Field Hqrs., Cin., 1952-57; mem. staff div. occupational health USPHS, Washington, 1957-62, chief div. occupational health, 1962-63; ret., 1963; rsch. physician, prof. occupational health in residence Sch. Pub. Health, U. Calif.-Berkeley, 1963-72; med. cons. AEC, 1964-73; sec.-treas. Tabershaw-Cooper Asso., Inc., 1972-73, v.p., sci. dir., 1973-74; v.p. Equitable Environ. Health Inc., 1974-77; cons. occupational medicine, 1977-94. Served to 1st lt. M.C., U.S. Army, 1937-40. Diplomate Am. Bd. Internal Medicine, Am. Bd. Preventive Medicine, Am. Bd. Indsl. Hygiene. Fellow AAAS, Am. Pub. Health Assn., Am. Coll. Chest Physicians, Am. Coll. Occupational Medicine, Royal Soc. Medicine (London); mem. Internat. Commn. on Occupational Health, Western Occupational Med. Assn., Am. Indsl. Hygiene Assn., Cosmos Club. Contbr. articles to profl. jours. Home: 8315 Terrace Dr El Cerrito CA 94530-3060

COOPERMAN, OLIVER B(URTON), psychiatrist; b. Perth Amboy, N.J., Jan. 18, 1946; s. Eli Louis and Dorothy (Sallinger) C.; m. Corrie Boulden, Apr. 28, 1985; 1 stepson, Jason Corder. AB, Dartmouth Coll., 1966; MD, Harvard U., 1971. Diplomate Am. Bd. Psychiatry and Neurology, Am. Bd. Adolescent Psychiatry; lic. physician and surgeon, Wyo.; lic. MD and surgeon, Mont., N.Mex. Rotating internship Herrick Meml. Hosp., Berkeley, Calif., 1971-72; residency in psychiatry Mt. Zion Hosp. and Med. Ctr., San Francisco, 1972-75; rsch. assoc. dept. child devel. Inst. Edn., U. London, 1968-69; ward chief, staff psychiatrist Palo Alto (Calif.) VA Hosp., 1976, 76-77; asst. chief mental hygiene clinic San Francisco VA Hosp., 1977-78; pvt. practice adult and adolescent psychiatry San Francisco, Petaluma, Calif., 1976-88, Casper, Wyo., 1988-90, Santa Fe, 1991-93, Albuquerque, N.Mex., 1994—; assoc. med. dir. Pinon Hills Hosp., Santa Fe, N.Mex., 1991-93; assoc. clin. dir. Yellowstone Treatment Ctrs., Billings, Mont., 1993-94; clin. instr. dept. psychiatry Stanford (Calif.) U. Sch. Medicine, 1976-78, lectr. in psychiatry, 1978-81; asst. clin. prof. dept. psychiatry U. Calif. Sch. Medicine, San Francisco, 1978—; clin. faculty U. Wyo. Family Practice Residency Program, Casper, 1988-89; courtesy staff Deaconness Med. Ctr., Billings, 1994; speaker in field. Contbr. articles to profl. jours. Mem. GREX, affiliate of A. K. Rice Inst., 1975-90, bd. dirs., 1978-84, sec.-treas. bd. dirs., 1979-80, pres. bd. dirs., 1980-82; mem. Orgnl. Devel. Network. Recipient Spl. Merit Advancement award VA Ctrl. Office. Mem. Am. Psychiat. Assn., Am. Group Psychoterhapy Assn., Am. Soc. for Adolescent Psychiatry, N.Mex. Med. Soc., Mont. Psychiat. Assn. Office: Ste 215 101 Hospital Loop NE Albuquerque NM 87109

COOR, LATTIE FINCH, university president; b. Phoenix, Sept. 26, 1936; s. Lattie F. and Elnora (Witten) C.; m. Ina Fitzhenry, Jan. 18, 1964 (div. 1988); children: William Kendall, Colin Fitzhenry, Farryl MacKenna Witten; m. Elva Wingfield, Dec. 27, 1994. AB with high honors (Phelps Dodge scholar), No. Ariz. U., 1958; MA with honors (Univ. scholar, Universal Match Found. fellow, Carnegie Corp. fellow), Washington U., St. Louis, 1960, PhD, 1964; LLD (hon.), Marlboro Coll., 1977, Am. Coll. Greece, 1982, U. Vt., 1991. Adminstrv. asst. to Gov. Mich., 1961-62; asst. to chancellor Washington U., St. Louis, 1963-67, asst. dean Grad. Sch. Arts and Scis., 1967-69, dir. internat. studies, 1967-69, asst. prof. polit. sci., 1967-76, vice chancellor, 1969-74, univ. vice chancellor, 1974-76; pres. U. Vt., Burlington, 1976-89; prof. public affairs, and pres. Ariz. State U., Tempe, 1990—; cons. HEW; spl. cons. to commr. U.S. Commn. on Edn., 1971-74; chmn. Commn. on Govtl. Rels., Am. Coun. on Edn., 1976-80; dir. New Eng. Bd. Higher Edn., 1976-89; co-chmn. joint com. on health policy Assn. Am. Univs. and Nat. Assn. State Univs. and Land Grant Colls., 1976-89; mem. pres. commn. NCAA, 1984-90, chmn. div. I, 1989; mem. Ariz. State Bd. Edn., 1993—. Trustee Am. Coll. Greece. Mem. Nat. Assn. Stae Univs. and Land Grant Colls. (chmn. bd. dirs. 1991-92), New Eng. Assn. Schs. and Colls. (pres. 1981-82), Am. Coun. on Edn. (bd. dirs. 1991-93, chmn. Pacific 10 Conf. 1995—). Office: Ariz State U Office of President Tempe AZ 85287

COORS, PETER HANSON, beverage company executive; b. Denver, Sept. 20, 1946; s. Joseph and Holly (Hanson) C.; m. Marilyn Gross, Aug. 23, 1969; children: Melissa, Christien, Carrie Ann, Ashley, Peter, David. B.S. in Idsl. Engring., Cornell U., 1969; M.B.A., U. Denver, 1970. Prodn. trainee, specialist Adolph Coors Co., Golden, Colo., 1970-71, dir. fin. planning, 1971-75, dir. market research, 1975-76, v.p. self distbn., 1976-77, v.p. sales and mktg., 1977-78, sr. v.p. sales and mktg., 1978-82, div. pres. sales, mktg. and adminstrn., 1982-85, pres. brewing div.; pres. Coors Brewing Co., Golden, Colo., 1989—, Coors Distbn. Co., 1976-82, 1976-81, chmn., from 1981, dir.; dir. Adolph Coors Co., 1973—, asst. sec.-treas., 1974-76; dir. CADCO, 1975-85; exec. v.p. Adolph Coors Co., Golden, Colo., 1991—; vice-chmn., CEO Coors Brewing Co., Golden, Colo., 1991—. Bd. dirs. Nat. Wildlife Fedn., 1978-81, Wildlife Legis. Fund, 1987—; hon. bd. dirs. Colo. Spl. Olympics Inc., 1978—; trustee Colo. Outward Bound Sch., 1978—, Adolph Coors Found., Pres.'s Leadership Com., U. Colo., 1978—; chmn. Nat. Commn. on the Future of Regis Coll., 1981-82, chmn. devel. com., 1983—, now trustee. Mem. Nat. Indls. Adv. Council, Opportunities Ctrs. of Am., Young Pres.' Orgn., Ducks Unlimited (nat. trustee 1979, sr. v.p., mem. mgmt. com., exec. com. 1982—, dir. Can. 1982—, pres. 1984-85, chmn. bd. 1986—). Club: Met. Denver Exec. (dir 1979, pres. 1981—). Office: Adolph Coors Co BC350 Golden CO 80401*

COORS, WILLIAM K., brewery executive; b. Golden, Colo., Aug. 11, 1916. BSChemE, Princeton U., 1938, MSChemE, 1939. Pres. Adolph Coors Co., Golden, Colo., from 1956, Chmn. bd., 1970—, also corp. pres. Office: Adolph Coors Co 311 10th St Golden CO 80401-5811*

COPE, J. ROBERT, engineer; b. Deadwood, S.D., Feb. 6, 1937; s. Jake David and Lila Lucille (Brown) Otey; m. Jeanette Elaine Jones, July 26, 1958; children: James Eric, Joan Renea, John Richard. BSME, Colo. State U., 1960; BSEE, U. Colo., 1971. Registered profl. engr., Colo. Test engr. Pratt & Whitney Corp., West Palm Beach, Fla., 1963-65, Sundstrando Corp., Denver, 1965-66; adv. engr. IBM Corp., Boulder, Colo., 1966-78, Storagetek Corp., Louisville, Colo., 1978-85; prin. engr. Cipher Data Corp., San Diego, Calif., 1985-90; adv. engr. Exabyte Corp., Boulder, 1990-93; cons. engr. Louisville, 1993—. Patentee in field; contbr. articles to profl. jours. Capt. USAF, 1960-63. Home and Office: 470 Muirfield Cir Louisville CO 80027

COPELAND, LAWRENCE R., construction company executive; b. 1947. Graduate, U. Notre Dame. With Fluor Corp., Irvine, Calif., 1969-93; now pres. Fluor Constructors Internat., Irvine, Calif., 1993—. Office: Fluor Constructors Intl 3333 Michelson Dr Irvine CA 92715*

COPELAND, MARY ELLEN, nurse; b. Atlanta, Sept. 14, 1957; d. Harold William and Mary Liz (Jones) C. AA, Freed-Hardeman Coll., 1978; BS in Nursing, Harding U., 1981; MS, Pepperdine U., 1995. RN. Staff RN St. Vincent Infirmary, Little Rock, 1982, Piedmont Hosp., Atlanta, 1982-87, Hoag Meml. Hosp., Newport Beach, Calif., 1987—; wellness program mgr., Pepperdine U., 1987—, adj. prof. natural sci. divsn., 1988. Mem. AACN, NAFE, Am. Heart Assn., Am. Assn. Occupational Health Nurses, Nat. Wellness Assn., Sigma Theta Tau. Mem. Ch. Christ. Home: 30856 Agoura Rd # C-3 Agoura Hills CA 91301

COPELAND, PHILLIPS JEROME, former academic administrator, former air force officer; b. Oxnard, Calif., Mar. 22, 1921; s. John Charles and Marion Moffatt) C.; student U. So. Calif., 1947-49; BA, U. Denver, 1956, MA, 1958; grad. Air Command and Staff Coll., 1959, Indsl. Coll. Armed Forces, 1964; m. Alice Janette Lusby, Apr. 26, 1942; children: Janette Ann Copeland Bosserman, Nancy Jo Copeland Briner. Commd. 2d lt. USAAF, 1943, advanced through grades to col. USAF, 1964, pilot 8th Air Force, Eng., 1944-45; various flying and staff assignments, 1945-51; chief joint tng. sect. Hdqrs. Airsouth (NATO), Italy, 1952-54; asst. dir. plans and programs USAF Acad., 1955-58; assigned to joint intelligence, Washington, 1959-61; plans officer Cincpac Joint Staff, Hawaii, 1961-63; staff officer, ops. directorate, then team chief Nat. Mil. Command Center, Joint Chiefs Staff, Washington, 1964-67; dir. plans and programs USAF Adv. Group, also adviser to Vietnamese Air Force, Vietnam, 1967-68; prof. aerospace studies U. So. Calif., L.A., 1968-72, exec. asst. to pres., 1972-73, assoc. dir. office internat. programs, 1973-75, dir. adminstrv. services Coll. Continuing Edn., 1975-82, dir. employee relations, 1982-84. Decorated D.F.C., Bronze Star, Air medal with 3 clusters; Medal of Honor (Vietnam). Mem. Air Force Assn., Order of Daedalians. Home: 81 Cypress Way Palos Verdes Peninsula CA 90274-3416

COPELLO, ANGELO GENE, health services administrator; b. Passaic, N.J., Jan. 27, 1959; s. Angelo F. and Jean Constance (DeLorenzo) C. BA, Eckerd Coll., 1980; MS, U. Tenn., 1984; MDiv, Vanderbilt U., 1984, DDiv, 1985. Clin. social worker, rsch. ethics and social scis. specialist. Dir., asst. prof. AIDS project Vanderbilt U. Med. Sch., Nashville, 1985-90; dir. San Mateo (Calif.) AIDS Prog., 1990—; mem. San Francisco AIDS Planning Coun., 1990—; dir. Fifth Internat. Conf. on AIDS Edn., Budapest, 1991—; mem. ethics com. San Mateo County Gen. Hosp.; conf. chmn. Third Internat. Conf. on AIDS Edn., 1989; mem. FDA Monitoring Bd., 1988. Contbg. author: AIDS: Confronting the Issues, 1989, AIDS Benchbook, 1991; mem. editorial bd. Jour. of AIDS Edn. and Prevention, N.Y.C., 1987—; contbr. articles to profl. jours. Mem. Mayor's Task Force on AIDS, Nashville, 1989, Tenn. AIDS Coun., Nashville, 1985-90, AIDS com. Tenn. Med. Assn., Nashville, 1989; pres. Nashville CARES, Inc., 1987-89; bd. dirs. Alive Hospice, Inc., Nashville, 1989; liaison CAEAR Coalition, 1993—; active Nat. AIDS Prevention Working Group, 1993—; mem. health care adv. bd. Office of Congresswoman Anna Eschoo, 1993—; mem. nat. AIDS com. Office of Senator Dianne Fienstien, 1993—. Recipient Presdl. scholarship Eckerd Coll., St. Petersburg, Fla., 1976, Miller Community Svc. award, 1980, Svc. citation Nashville Mayor's Office, 1990, Svc. award Nashville CARES, Inc., 1990; nominated Social Worker of Yr. Tenn. chpt. Nat. Assn. Social Workers, 1988. Mem. APHA, Internat. Soc. AIDS Edn. (pres. 1988-89, chairperson pub. policy com. 1993—), Clin. Ethics Guild, Internat. AIDS Soc., Soc. Health and Human Values, Calif. Conf. Local AIDS Dirs. (mem. exec. com. 1991—, sec.-treas. 1991-92, pres.-elect 1992-93, pres. 1993-94), Calif. Assn. AIDS Agys. (bd. dirs.), Life AIDS Lobby (bd. dirs. 1993—, chairperson San Francisco Bay area AIDS intergovtl. com. 1993-94). Episcopalian. Office: San Mateo County AIDS Program 3700 Edison St San Mateo CA 94403-4462

COPENHAVER, LARRY JAMES, journalist; b. Independence, Iowa, Sept. 16, 1943; s. George Hugh and Winona Louise (Moline) C.; m. Shirley Anne Sondgeroth, Dec. 24, 1986. BA, U. Ariz., 1973. Tchr. English Sahuarita (Ariz.) Unified Sch. Dist., 1973-85; journalist Tucson Citizen Newspaper, 1985—. Recipient Unity Award in Media, Lincoln U., 1987, Ariz. Sch. Bd. Assn. award Flowing Well Unified Sch. Dist., 1988, Tucson Unified Sch. Dist., 1990, Award of Excellence, Ariz. Sch. Pub. Rels. Assn., 1992. Office: Tucson Citizen Newspaper 4850 S Park Ave Tucson AZ 85714-1637

COPI, IRVING MARMER, philosophy educator; b. Duluth, Minn., July 28, 1917; s. Samuel Bernard and Rose (Marmer) Copilowish; m. Amelia Glaser, Mar. 20, 1941; children: David Marmer, Thomas Russell, William Arthur, Margaret Ruth. B.A., U. Mich., 1938, M.S., 1940, M.A. (Univ. fellow 1946-47), 1947, Ph.D., 1948; postgrad., U. Chgo., 1938-39. Instr. philosophy U. Ill., 1947-48; faculty U. Mich., 1948-69, prof. philosophy, 1958-69, research assoc., 1951-52; research assoc. Engring. Research Inst., 1954-59; research logician Inst. Sci. and Tech., 1960-61; prof. philosophy U. Hawaii, Honolulu, 1969-91; research assoc. U. Calif., Berkeley, 1954; vis. lectr. Air Force U., 1958-66, Georgetown U. Logic Inst., 1960; vis. prof. Princeton, 1959-60, U. Hawaii, 1967; acad. visitor London Sch. Econs., 1975; Cons. Office Naval Research, 1952. Author: Introduction to Logic, 9th edit, 1994, Symbolic Logic, 5th edit, 1979, Introduccion a la Logica, 1962, Introduzione alla Logica, 1965, Theory of Logical Types, 1971, Li-tse Hsueh, 1972, Tarkasastra Ka Paricaya, 1973, Lo-chi-Kai-lun, 1973, Introducao a Logica, 1974, Mavo Lelogika, 1977, Lógica Simbólica, 1979, Einführung in die Logik, Kurseinheit 1, 1983, Einführung in die Logik, Kurseinheit 2, 1984, Informal Logic, 2d edit., 1992, Einführung in die Logic, Kurseinheit 3, 1987; also numerous essays. Editor: (Plato): Theaetetus, 1949, (with J.A. Gould) Readings in Logic, 1964, 2d edit., 1972, (with R.W. Beard) Essays on Wittgenstein's Tractatus, 1966, (with J.A. Gould) Contemporary Readings in Logical Theory, 1967, Contemporary Philosophical Logic, 1978. Faculty fellow Fund Advancement Edn., 1953-54; Guggenheim fellow, 1955-56; Fulbright sr. fellow, 1975. Mem. Am. Philos. Assn., Assn. Symbolic Logic, Mich. Acad. Letters, Arts and Scis., AAUP (chpt. pres. 1968-69), Phi Beta Kappa, Phi Kappa Phi. Democrat. Jewish (pres. congregation 1962-63). Home: 1618 Kamole St Honolulu HI 96821-1426

COPLEY, HELEN KINNEY, newspaper publisher; b. Cedar Rapids, Iowa, Nov. 28, 1922; d. Fred Everett and Margaret (Casey) Kinney; m. James S. Copley, Aug. 16, 1965 (dec.); 1 child, David Casey. Attended, Hunter Coll., N.Y.C., 1945. Assoc. The Copley Press, Inc., 1952—, chmn. exec. com., chmn. corp., dir., 1973—, chief exec. officer, sr. mgmt. bd., 1974—; chmn. bd. Copley News Svc., San Diego, 1973—; chmn. editorial bd. Union-Tribune Pub. Co., 1976—; pub. The San Diego Union-Tribune, 1973—; bd. dirs. Fox Valley Press., Inc. Chmn. bd., trustee James S. Copley Found., 1973—; life mem. Friends of Internat. Center, La Jolla, Mus. Contemporary Art, San Diego, San Diego Hall of Sci., Scripps Meml. Hosp. Aux., San Diego Opera Assn., Star of India Aux., Zool. Soc. San Diego; mem. La Jolla Town Coun. Inc., San Diego Soc. Natural History, YWCA, San Diego Symphony Assn.; life patroness Makua Aux.; hon. chmn., bd. dirs. Washington Crossing Found.; trustee, mem. audit and compensation com. Howard Hughes Med. Inst.; hon. chmn. San Diego Coun. Literacy. Mem. Inter-Am. Press Assn., Newspaper Assn. Am., Calif. Press Assn., Am. Press Inst., Calif. Newspaper Pubs. Assn., Calif. Press Inst., San Francisco Press Club, L.A. Press Club. Republican. Roman Catholic. Clubs: Aurora (Ill.) Country, Army and Navy (D.C.), Univ. Club San Diego, La Jolla Beach and Tennis, La Jolla Country. Office: Copley Press Inc 7776 Ivanhoe Ave La Jolla CA 92037-4520*

COPLEY, JOHN DUANE, civil engineer; b. Visalia, Calif., May 25, 1938; s. John Harrington and Emma Theresa (Gallistl) C.; m. Jeanette Sue Nunn, July 1, 1961; children: John Kent, Kari Lynne, Kevin Michael. AA, Coll. of Sequoias, Visalia; BSCE, Stanford U. Registered profl. engr., Calif. Sr. civil engr. City of Davis (Calif.) Pub. Works Dept., 1965—. Served with U.S. Army, 1961-63. Mem. ASCE, Am. Pub. Works Assn. (pres. Sacramento chpt. 1974). Home: 2901 Catalina Dr Davis CA 95616-0105 Office: City of Davis Pub Works Dept 23 Russell Blvd Davis CA 95616-3837

COPMAN, LOUIS, radiologist; b. Phila., Jan. 17, 1934; s. Jacob and Eve (Snyder) C.; m. Avera Schuster, June 8, 1958; children: Mark, Linda. BA, U. Pa., 1955, MD, 1959. Diplomate Am. Bd. Radiology; Nat. Bd. Med. Examiners. Commd. ensign Med. Corps USN, 1958; advanced through grades to capt. M.C. USN, 1975; ret.; asst. chief radiology dept. Naval Hosp., Pensacola, Fla., 1966-69; chief radiology dept. Doctors Hosp., Phila., 1969-73; radiologist Mercer Hosp. Ctr., Trenton, N.J., 1973-75; chmn. radiology dept. Naval Hosp., Phila., 1975-84; chief. radiology dept. Naval Med. Clinic, Pearl Harbor, Hawaii, 1984-89; pvt. practice radiologist Honolulu, 1989-92; cons. Radiology Services, Wilmington, Del., 1978-84, Yardley (Pa.) Radiology, 1979-84. Author: The Cuckold, 1974. Recipient Albert Einstein award in Medicine, U. Pa., 1959. Mem. AMA, Assn. Mil. Surgeons of the U.S., Royal Soc. Medicine, Radiol. Soc. N.Am., Am. Coll. Radiology, Photographic Soc. Am., Sherlock Holmes Soc., Phi Beta Kappa, Alpha Omega Alpha. Home: PO Box 384767 Waikoloa HI 96738-4767 Office: 68-1771 Makanahele Pl Waikoloa HI 96738-4767

COPPERMAN, WILLIAM H, value engineer, consultant; b. Cleve., Dec. 4, 1932; s. Jack Jason and Ruth (Rollnick) C.; m. Rena June Dorn, Dec. 26, 1954; children: Randy Lee, David Marc. BS, Duquesne U., 1954; MBA, U. So. Calif., L.A., 1962; JD, U. San Fernando, 1977. Cert. value specialist. Corp. mgr., value engr. Hughes Aircraft Co., L.A., 1957-89; pres. Copperman Assocs. in Value Engring., Inc., L.A., 1983—; bd. dirs. Miles Value Found., Washington; cert. bd. SAVE, Chgo., 1986-88. Author books, video tape series in value engring.; contbr. articles to profl. jours. Recipient Outstanding Achievement award U.S. Army, 1986, Value Engring. award Purchasing Mag., Washington, 1987, Achievement in Value Engring. U.S. Army, 1977, 78, 79, 80, 82. Mem. Soc. Am. Value Engrs. (exec. v.p. 1975—). Office: Copperman Assocs in Value Engring PO Box 5488 Playa Del Rey CA 90296-5488

COPPERSMITH, SAM, lawyer; b. Johnstown, Pa., May 22, 1955; m. Beth Schermer, Aug. 28, 1983; children: Sarah, Benjamin, Louis. AB in Econs. magna cum laude, Harvard U., 1976; JD, Yale Law Sch., 1982. Fgn. svc. officer U.S. Dept. State, Port of Spain, Trinidad, 1977-79; law clk. to Judge William C. Canby Jr. U.S. Ct. Appeals (9th cir.), Phoenix, 1982-83; atty. Sacks, Tierney & Kasen, P.A., Phoenix, 1983-86; asst. to Mayor Terry Goddard City of Phoenix, 1984; atty. Jones, Jury, Short & Mast P.C., Phoenix, 1986-88, Bonnett, Fairbourn & Friedman P.C., Phoenix, 1988-92; mem. 103d Congress from 1st Ariz. Dist., 1993-95; atty. Coppersmith & Gordon, PLC, 1995—. Former dir., pres. Planned Parenthood Cen. and No. Ariz.; former chair City of Phoenix Bd. of Adjustment; former dir. Ariz. Comty. Svc. Legal Assistance Found., 1986-89. Mem. ABA, State Bar of Ariz., State Bar of Calif., Maricopa County Bar Assn. Democrat. Office: Coppersmith & Gordon Plc 2633 E Indian School Rd Ste 300 Phoenix AZ 85016-6762

COPPIN, ANN STACY, information specialist; b. Pasadena, Mar. 2, 1944; d. Alvin W. and Inez T. (Thomason) Stacy; m. Frederic A. Coppin, July 9, 1969; children—Stacy M., Thomas A. B.S. in Geology, U. Redlands, 1966; M.S. in Geology, N.Mex. Inst. Mining and Tech., 1970; M.L.S., U. Ariz., 1974. Librarian Ariz.-Sonora Desert Mus., Tucson, 1973; supr. tech. info. service Chevron Oil Field Research Co., La Habra, Calif., 1974-92; team leader tech. info. svc. Chevron Petroleum Tech. Co., La Habra, 1992-93; reference libr. Sci. and Engring. Libr., U. So. Calif., L.A., 1993-94. Contbr. articles to profl. jours. NDEA fellow, 1968-69; Lunar Sci. Inst. vis. grad. fellow, 1974. Mem. Am. Soc. for Info. Sci., Spl. Libraries Assn., Assn. for Women Geoscientists (v.p. L.A. chpt. 1991), Western Assn. of Map Librs., So. Calif. On-Line Users Group, Geosci. Info. Soc., Beta Phi Mu. Office: U So Calif Sci & Engring Libr Los Angeles CA 90089-0481

COPPOCK, RICHARD MILES, nonprofit association administrator; b. Salem, Ohio, Mar. 17, 1938; s. Guy Lamar and Helen Angeline (Johnston) C.; m. Rita Mae McArtor, June 20, 1961 (div. 1973); 1 child, Carole; m. Trelma Anne Kubacak Hafer, Nov. 21, 1973; children: James, Lori. BS, USAF Acad., 1961; MSME, U. Colo., 1969. Commd. 2d lt. USAF, 1961, advanced through grades to lt. col., 1983, ret., 1983; pres., CEO Assn. Grads. USAF Acad., Colo., 1983—; bd. dirs. Air Acad. Nat. Bank, Colo.; v.p. Nat. Assns. in Colorado Springs. Decorated DFC (4), Air medal (29); named Outstanding Alumnus Salem H.S., 1980. Mem. Colorado Springs C. of C. (mil. affairs coun. 1985-90), VFW (life), Am. Legion, Air Force Assn., Ret. Officers Assn., Elks. Republican. Methodist. Home: 2513 Mirror Lake Ct Colorado Springs CO 80919-3515 Office: USAF Acad Assn Grads 3116 Academy Dr U S A F Academy CO 80840

CORAH, DEBORAH JEAN, respiratory therapist; b. L.A., May 27, 1960; d. Ronald Bruce and Dorothy Jean (Meier) Dahlstrom; m. Paul Frank Corah, June 26, 1982. Student, Oreg. State U., 1978-81; Assocs. of Respiratory Therapy, Mt. Hood Community Coll., 1986. Registered Respiratory Therapist, Oreg. Respiratory therapy asst. St. Vincent Med. Ctr., Portland, Oreg., 1981-83, respiratory therapy technician, 1983-86, cert. respiratory therapy technician, 1986-88; registered respiratory therapist St. Vincent Med. Ctr., Portland, 1988—; cert. respiratory therapy technician Portland Adventist Med. Ctr., Portland, 1986-88; respiratory therapy clin. instr. Mt. Hood Community Coll., Portland, 1987—. Mem. Am. Assn. Respiratory Care, Oreg. Edn. Assn. Republican. Roman Catholic.

CORAM, DAVID JAMES, marketing professional; b. San Diego, Oct. 17, 1962; s. Thomas Harry and Joan Catherine (Rueter) C.; m. Irma Elizabeth Aquino, Jan. 14, 1989 (dec. July 1991); children: Catherine May, Corinna Briann; m. Corinna Kay Wayd, May. 6, 1995. AS with honors, Miramar Coll., 1989; honor grad. sheriff acad. basic tng., Southwestern Coll., 1986. Computer oper. Cubic Data Systems, San Diego, 1981-83, Electronic Data Systems, San Diego, 1983-84; ct. svc. officer San Diego County Marshal, 1985-86, deputy marshal, 1986—; pres. Coram Consulting Group, 1994—. Mediator San Diego Community Mediation Ctr., 1990—. Awarded Gold medal soccer Ariz. Police Olympics, 1990, 91, Silver medal, 1993,

Marksmanship award San Diego Marshal, Outstanding Young Men Am. award, 1989; 2d pl. Mid. Weight San Diego Gold's Gym Classic, 1993, Bronze medal Bodybuilding Calif. Police Olympics, 1994. Mem. Calif. State Marshal's Assn. (dir. on state bd. 1994), San Diego County Marshal's Assn. (parliamentarian 1988, dir. 1989-91, 93-94), San Diego County Marshal's Athletic Fedn. (dir. 1993-95), Nat. Physique Com. (contest judge). Republican. Office: Coram Cons Group PO Box 0863 Temecula CA 92593-0863

CORAY, JEFFREY WARREN, assistant principal, instructor; b. Chgo., July 16, 1958; s. Warren George and Rose (Paul) C. Student, U. Calif., Berkeley, 1976-77; BA, Occidental Coll., 1980; postgrad., Calif. State U., San Bernardino, 1993—. Instr. Damien High Sch., La Verne, Calif., 1982—, dir. student activities, 1983-87, chair social sci. dept., 1986-88, asst. prin. student activities, 1987-88, asst. prin. acad. affairs, instr. social sci., 1988—; cons. advanced placement program N.J. Coll. Bd., 1987—, exam reader, 1988—. Mem. Omicron Delta Epsilon, Phi Kappa Phi. Republican. Roman Catholic. Home: PO Box 116 La Verne CA 91750-0116 Office: Damien High Sch 2280 Damien Ave La Verne CA 91750-5210

CORBIN, ROSEMARY MAC GOWAN, mayor; b. Santa Cruz, Calif., Apr. 3, 1940; d. Frederick Patrick and Lorena Maude (Parr) MacGowan; m. Douglas Tenny Corbin, Apr. 6, 1968; children: Jeffrey, Diana. BA, San Francisco State U., 1961; MLS, U. Calif., Berkeley, 1966. Libr. Stanford (Calif.) U., 1966-68, Richmond (Calif.) Pub. Libr., 1968-69, Kaiser Found. Health Plan, Oakland, Calif., 1976-81, San Francisco Pub. Libr., 1981-82, U. Calif., Berkeley, 1982-83; mem. coun. City of Richmond, 1985-93, vice mayor, 1986-87, mayor, 1993—; mem. Solid Waste Mgmt. Authority, 1985—, Contra Costa Hazardous Materials Commn., Martinez, Calif., 1987—, San Francisco Bay Conservation and Devel. Commn., 1987—; chair League of Calif. Cities Environ. Affairs Com., 1994—; mem. energy and environ. com. U.S. Conf. Mayors and Nat. League of Cities, 1993—. Contbr. articles to profl. publs. Mem. Calif. Libr. Assn., Local Govt. Commn., League Calif. Cities, Nat. League Cities, LWV, NOW, Nat. Women's Polit. Caucus. Democrat. Home: 114 Crest Ave Richmond CA 94801-4031 Office: Richmond City Hall 2600 Barrett Ave Richmond CA 94804-1654

CORBOY, JAMES MCNALLY, investment banker; b. Erie, Pa., Nov. 3, 1940; s. James Thomas and Dorothy Jane (Schluraff) C.; m. Suzanne Shaver, July 23, 1965; children: Shannon, James McNally. BA, Allegheny Coll., 1962; MBA, U. Colo., 1986. Sales staff Boettcher & Co., Denver, 1964-70; sales staff Blyth Eastman Dillon, Denver and Chgo., 1970-74, William Blair & Co., Chgo., 1974-77; mgr. corp. bond dept. Boettcher & Co., Denver, 1977-79; ptnr. in charge William Blair & Co., Denver, 1979-86; first v.p. Stifel, Nicolaus & Co., Denver, 1986-88; pres., chief exec. officer SKB Corboy Inc., Denver, 1988—; chmn., CEO Telluride (Colo.) Aero Ctr., Inc. With USMC, 1962-67. Mem. Nat. Assn. Securities Dealers (bd. arbitrators), Country Club at Castle Pines, Met. Club, Denver Athletic Club. Republican. Presbyterian. Home: Castle Pines Village 4212 Morning Star Dr Castle Rock CO 80104-9022 Office: 5251 Dtc Pky Ste 1200 Englewood CO 80111-2741

CORCORAN, GEORGE BARTLETT, pharmacologist/toxicologist; b. Madison, Wis., May 14, 1948; s. George Bartlett and Eleanor Martin (Cavanaugh) C.; m. Anna Karen Jordan, July 21, 1973; children: Sean Bartlett, Cavan Ryan. BA in Chemistry, Ithaca (N.Y.) Coll., 1970; MS in Chemistry, Bucknell U., Lewisburg, Pa., 1973; PhD in Pharmacology/Toxicology, George Washington U., 1980. Vis. chemist Sun Oil Co., Marcus Hook, Pa., 1970; guest worker NIH, Bethesda, Md., 1972-74; chemist NIH/NHLBI, Bethesda, Md., 1974-77; postdoctoral fellow Baylor Coll. Medicine, Houston, 1980-81; asst. prof. pharmaceutics SUNY, Buffalo, 1981-87; assoc. prof. pharmacology/toxicology U. N.Mex., Albuquerque, 1988-93, chair grad. programs in toxicology, 1989—, prof. pharmacology/toxicology, 1993—, prof. biochemistry, 1993—; toxicology cons. G.B. Corcoran, Albuquerque, 1988—. Contbr. articles to profl. jours. Vol. Albuquerque Youth Soccer Orgn., 1993—, Boy Scouts Am., Albuquerque, 1988—, Am. Cancer Soc., Buffalo, 1982-88. Rsch. grantee NIH, 1984—, Norwegian Marshall Fund, 1990-92, Pharmacia Inc., 1993—. Mem. Internat. Soc. Study of Xenobiotics (v.p. toxicology sect. 1994—), Soc. Toxicology (chair placement com., edn. com. 1991—), Am. Soc. Pharmacology and Exptl. Therapeutics, Mountain West Soc. Toxicology (sec.-treas. 1991-94), Am. Assn. Pharm. Scientists (charter), Am. Assn. Colls. of Pharmacy. Democrat. Presbyterian. Home: 8005 Pickard Ave NE Albuquerque NM 87110-1533 Office: U NMex Coll Pharmacy Albuquerque NM 87131

CORDES, FAUNO LANCASTER, retired nuclear medicine technologist; b. San Francisco, Nov. 3, 1927; d. Frederick Carl and Faun-Hope (Lancaster) C. AA, U. Calif. Berkeley, 1946, BA in Psychology, 1948; MA in Geography, San Francisco State U., 1991. Chief hematology rsch. technician NIH and U. Calif. Lab. of Exptl. Oncology, San Francisco, 1949-53, City of Hope Med. Ctr., Duarte, Calif., 1953-59; nuclear medicine technologist Mt. Zion Hosp., U. Calif., San Francisco, 1959-92; exec. com. Soc. Nuclear Medicine, No. Calif. Tech. Soc., San Francisco, 1968-81. Contbr. over 31 articles to profl. publs. Mem. AAAS, Soc. Nuclear Medicine, Soc. Woman Geographers, Calif. Acad. Scis., Antarctican Soc., Gleeson Libr. Assocs., The Explorers Club, Sigma Xi. Home: 355 Arballo Dr San Francisco CA 94132-2156

CORDINGLEY, MARY JEANETTE BOWLES (MRS. WILLIAM ANDREW CORDINGLEY), social worker, psychologist, artist, writer; b. Des Moines, Jan. 1, 1918; d. William David and Florence (Spurrier) Bowles; m. William Andrew Cordingley, Mar. 17, 1942; children: William Andrew, Thomas Kent, Constance Louise. Student, Stephens Coll., 1936; BA, Carleton Coll., 1939; postgrad. U. Denver, 1944-45; MA in Psychiat. Social Work, U. Minn., 1948; grad. art student, 1963; MA in Counseling Psychology Pepperdine U., 1985; Co-pub. Univ. News, 1939-40; with U.S.O. Travelers Aid Service, 1942-44; mem. Jr. League, Des Moines, 1943, bd. dirs., sec. Mpls., 1951-56; clinic psychiat. social worker U. Minn. Hosp., 1947-48; social worker community service project neuropediatrics U. Minn., 1964-65; med. dir. med. sch. svc. Mont. Deaconess Hosp., 1970-74; instigator, pres. Original Pioneer Prints Notepaper Co.; paintings in variety of galleries and traveling shows; exhibited in numerous one-man shows including Chas. Russell Gallery, Mont., Student Union U. Minn., Nat. Biennial League Am. Pen Women, 1968, 70, U. Mont., 1974, Mont. Traveling Exhibit, 1966-67, Mus. of the Rockies hist. show, 1976, Bergen Art Guild, 1976, 78, U.S. Traveling Show, 1987-89, Russell Auction, 1977, 91, Kessel Long Gallery, Scottsdale, 1991, Great Falls Pub. Libr. hist. art show oil exhibit 1992—, Artist's Kaleidoscope, 1995; Ariz. terrain show, Mayo Clinic, Scottsdale, 1991—; illustrator: The Tobacco Route, Geol. Soc. Guide Book, 1992; Mon. Artist Exhibit-Gov.'s Mansion, 1990; graphic artist in metal etchings; therapist Mental Health Center, 1977-82. Organizer, Hazeltine Nat. Golf Club Womens Assn., 1962-64, I. & R. Ctr., 1967; pres. adv. bd. Mont. State U.; past mem. bd. dirs. United Way, mem. arts adv. bd. Sierra Nev. Coll.; former mem. Youth Guidance Home Bd. Recipient various awards. Mem. NASW, State Arts Coun., Scottsdale Jr. League (sustainers 1986—), Am. Mus. Women in Arts (art instr.). Co-author: Series on Mont. Instns.; author: Art Show: Artist's Kaleidoscope, Speaking With a Brush. also (winter): 7878 E Gainey Ranch Rd Unit 47 Scottsdale AZ 85258-1770 Home: Box 4674 Incline Village NV 89450

CORDOVA, DONALD E., lawyer; b. Trinidad, Colo., Jan. 26, 1938. AB, Regis Coll., 1961; JD, U. Colo., 1964. Bar: Colo. 1964. Asst. U.S. atty. Colo., 1964-68, mem. Denver County Ct. Judicial Selection Commn., 1968-71; ptnr. Cordova, DeMoulin, Harris & Mellon, P.C., Denver; judge U.S. Bankruptcy Ct., Denver. Mem. ABA, Denver Bar Assn. (v.p. 1981-82, pres. 1987-88) Colo. Bar Assn. (v.p. 1978-79, mem. bd. govs 1970-72, 80-82, 86-89, Supreme Ct. com. on pattern jury instructions 1987-90), Nat. Conf. Bankruptcy Judges (mem. judicial conf. adv. com. bankruptcy rules 1994—), Hispanic Bar Assn. (pres. 1984), Denver Law Club (pres. 1977-78). Office: US Custom House 721 19th St Denver CO 80202-2513

CORDRAY, RICHARD LYNN, electronics engineering executive; b. Tulsa, Jan. 27, 1952; s. Austin Edwin and Barbara Lee (Kline) C.; m. Barbara Scott Lamb, May 9, 1975; children: Michael Scott, Carol Ann. BS in Elec. Engring., Rice U., 1974, MEE, 1975, PhD, 1978. Cert. forms cons. Rsch. engr. Tektronix, Inc., Beaverton, Oreg., 1978-81, program mgr., 1981; v.p. N.W. Instrument Systems, Beaverton, 1981-84; program mgr. Intel, Hillsboro, Oreg., 1984-85, Spacelabs, Inc., Redmond, Wash., 1985-89; pres. Image Tech., Redmond, 1989—. Bd. dirs. English Hill Homeowners Assn., Redmond, 1987-89. Mem. IEEE, Soc. for Info. Display, Bus. Forms Mgmt. Assn. Home: 17613 NE 142nd St Redmond WA 98052-1237 Office: Image Tech 16307 NE 83rd St Redmond WA 98052-3867

CORDTS, PAUL ROGER, surgeon; b. Cumberland, Md., Sept. 27, 1958; s. Harold J. and Jeanne (Moore) C. BA, Johns Hopkins U., 1980; MD, USUHS, 1984. Diplomate Am. Bd. Surgery, Am. Bd. Surg. Critical Care, Am. Bd. Gen. Vascular Surgery. Commd. med. officer U.S. Army, 1980; intern, resident in surgery William Beaumont Army Med. Ctr., El Paso, Tex., 1984-89; staff surgeon Munson Army Community Hosp., Ft. Leavenworth, Kans., 1989-90; fellow in vascular surgery Boston U. Med. Ctr., Boston, 1990-92; chief vascular surgery sect. Tripler Army Med. Ctr., Honolulu, 1992-93, chief gen. surgery svc., tng. dir. surg. residency program, 1993—. Fellow ACS (assoc.); mem. Uniformed Svcs. U. Health Scis. Surg. Assocs., Am. Venous Forum, Peripheral Vascular Surgery Soc., 38th Parallel Med. Soc., Soc. of Critical Care Medicine, Assn. of Mil. Surgeons of U.S., Am. Legion (Farrady Post 24), Omicron Delta Kappa Nat. Leadership Soc. Home: 98-1323 Kaonohi St Aiea HI 96701-2836 Office: Tripler Army Med Ctr Gen Surgery Svc Honolulu HI 96859-5000

COREY, JO ANN, management analyst; b. Methuen, Mass., Jan. 26, 1965; d. Joseph Augustine and Marie Ellen (Dowe) C. BA, Calif. State U., Fullerton, 1987, MPA, 1989. Adminstrv. intern City of Brea, Calif., 1987-90; mgmt. aide City of Mission Viejo, Calif., 1990-92, sr. mgmt. analyst, 1992—. Mem. Mcpl. Mgmt. Assts. So. Calif. (programming com. 1987—), Calif. Parks and Recreation Soc., Phi Alpha Theta. Democrat. Roman Catholic. Office: City of Mission Viejo 25909 Pala Mission Viejo CA 92691-2778

CORIELL, BRUCE RICHARD, clergy; b. Millington, N.J., Aug. 15, 1956; s. Richard and Kathleen Veronica (Franolich) C.; m. Eleanor Ann Sents, Aug. 19, 1978; children: Richard Bruce, Alyssa Kathleen. BA, Wheaton (Ill.) Coll., 1978; MDiv, Princeton Theol. Sem., 1981; postgrad., Vanderbilt U., 1989. Ordained to ministry Am. Bapt. Ch., 1981. Assoc. chaplain DePauw U., Greencastle, Ind., 1981-85; asst. chaplain Vanderbilt U., Nashville, 1986-88; coll. chaplain Colo. Coll., Colorado Springs, 1988—. Chair Martin Luther King Jr. Holiday Com., Colorado Springs, 1988:, bd. dirs. Citizen's Project, Colorado Springs, 1994—, Gay and Lesbian Cmty. Ctr., Colorado Springs, 1992, San Luis Valley Christian Cmty. Svcs., 1990—, United Way, others; mem. Pikes Peak Peace and Justice Commn., Colorado Springs, 1991—. Harold Vanderbilt scholar, 1985-88. Mem. Am. Acad. Religion, Nat. Assn. Coll. and Univ. Chaplains, Assn. Coll. and Univ. Religious Affairs (exec. bd.). Office: Colo Coll Shove Meml Chapel Colorado Springs CO 80903

CORKERN, ROBERT J., agricultural products company executive; b. 1944. Graduate, U. Nev., 1966. With Klein Bros., Stockton, Calif., 1971-92; pres. Klein-BergerCo., Stockton, Calif., 1992—. With U.S. Army, 1967-70. Office: Klein-Berger Co 1305 W Fremont St Stockton CA 95203-2625*

CORKRAN, JOHN ROGERSON, fundraising executive; b. Chgo., Dec. 16, 1936; s. David Hudson Jr. and Marion (Montgomery) C.; m. Carol Tonette Bender, Jan. 4, 1963; children: Carol, Susan, Timothy, Laurel. BA in History, Wesleyan U., 1958. Recreation technician U.S. Forest Svc., Estacada, Oreg., 1962-64; work supr. Job Corps U.S. Forest Svc., Roseburg, Oreg., 1964-65, asst. corpsmen supr. Job Corps, 1966; dir. ann. giving Wesleyan U., Middletown, Conn., 1966-69; dir. devel. Catlin Gabel Sch., Portland, Oreg., 1969-80, Fountain Valley Sch., Colorado Springs, Colo., 1980-86, The Bush Sch., Seattle, 1986-90; exec. dir. Bethany of N.W. Found., Everett, Wash., 1990—; chmn. dist. VIII, bd. dirs. Coun. for Advancement and Support of Edn., Washington, 1977-78. Mem. fin. com. Horn of Africa Svcs., Seattle, 1993-94; bd. dirs. Presbyn. Counselling Svc., Seattle, 1986-93, chair dirs. search com., 1991; mem. Shohomish County Estate Planned Giving Coun., 1991-94; sec. bd. dirs. Colo. Assn. Fundraisers, 1983. Recipient Robert Bell Crow award Coun. for Advancement and Support of Edn., 1984. Mem. Snohomish, Whatcom Island, Skagit County Devel. Officers (chair program com. 1993-94), No.w. Devel. Officers Assn., Washington Planned Giving Coun. Democrat. Lutheran. Home: 4715 44th Ave S Seattle WA 98118-1807 Office: Bethany of NW Found 3322 Broadway Everett WA 98201-4425

CORLESS, DOROTHY ALICE, nurse educator; b. Reno, Nev., May 28, 1943; d. John Ludwig and Vera Leach (Wilson) Adams; children: James Lawrence Jr., Dorothy Adele. RN, St. Luke's Sch. Nursing, 1964. Clinician, cons., educator, author, adminstr. Fresno County Mental Health Dept., 1970-94; pvt. practice mental health nurse Fresno, 1991-94; instr. police sci. State Ctr. Tng. Facility, 1991-94; owner, dir. Western Mental Health Assocs., Florence, Oreg., 1994—. Maj. USAFR, 1972-94. Mem. NAFE, Forensic Mental Health Assn. Calif., Calif. Peace Officer's Assn., Critical Incident Stress Found. Home: 1580 Kalla Kalla Ct Florence OR 97439-8963

CORMIE, DONALD MERCER, investment company executive; b. Edmonton, Alta., Can., July 24, 1922; s. George Mills and Mildred (Mercer) C.; m. Eivor Elisabeth Ekstrom, June 8, 1946; children: John Mills, Donald Robert, Allison Barbara, James Mercer, Neil Brian, Buce George, Eivor, Robert. BA, U. Alta., 1944, LLB, 1945; LLM, Harvard U., 1946. Bar: Alta. 1947. Queens counsel, 1964; sessional instr. faculty law U. Alta., 1947-53; sr. ptnr. Cormie, Kennedy, Edmonton, Barristers, 1954-87; instr. real estate law Dept. of Extension, U. Alta., 1958-64; pres., bd. dirs. Collective Securities, Ltd., Cormie Ranch, Inc., Sea Investors Corp.; With Can. Mcht. Marine, 1943-44. Recipient Judge Green Silver medal in law. Mem. Dean's Coun. of 100 Ariz. State U., World Pres.'s Orgn., Chief Execs. Orgn. (bd. dirs. 1976-79), Can. Bar Assn. (mem. coun. 1961-76, chmn. adminstrv. law 1963-66, chmn. taxation 1972-82, v.p. Alta. 1968-69), Found. Legal Rsch. Can. (hon. life). Home: 5101 N Casa Blanca Dr # 314 Scottsdale AZ 85253-6986 Office: 10405 Jasper Ave # 216-21, Edmonton, AB Canada T5J 3S2

CORNABY, KAY STERLING, lawyer, former state senator; b. Spanish Fork, Utah, Jan. 14, 1936; s. Sterling A. and Hilda G. C.; m. Linda Rasmussen, July 23, 1965; children: Alyse, Derek, Tara, Heather, Brandon. AB, Brigham Young U., 1960; postgrad. law Heidelberg (Ger.), 1961-63; JD, Harvard U., 1966. Bar: N.Y. 1967, Utah 1969, U.S. Patent and Trademark Office 1967. Assoc. Brumbaugh, Graves, Donahue & Raymond, N.Y.C., 1966-69; ptnr. Mallinckrodt & Cornaby, Salt Lake City, 1969-72; sole practice, Salt Lake City, 1972-85; mem. Utah State Senate, 1977-91, majority leader, 1983-84; shareholder Jones, Waldo, Holbrook & McDonough, Salt Lake City, 1985—; mem. adv. coun. Salt Lake Dist. SBA, 1984-91. Mem. Nat. Commn. on Uniform State Laws, 1988-93; mem. adv. bd. U. Mich. Ctr. For Study Youth Policy, 1990-93, Utah State Jud. Conduct Commn., 1983-91, chmn. 1984-85; bd. dirs. KUED-KUER Pub. TV and Radio, 1982-88, adv. bd. KUED, 1982—; bd. dirs. Salt Lake Conv. and Visitors Bur., 1985—. Mem. New York Bar, Utah Bar, Utah Harvard Alumni Assn. (pres. 1977-79), Harvard U. Law Sch. Alumni Assn. (v.p. 1979—); Alta Club. Office: Jones Waldo Holbrook & McDonough 1500 1st Interstate Plz 170 S Main St Salt Lake City UT 84101-1605

CORNAY, STACY SHELTON, public relations specialist; b. Laramie, Wyo., Oct. 18, 1961; d. Vern E. and Nancy A. (Reinhart) Shelton; m. Paul J. Cornay, Dec. 29, 1984; 1 child, Tanner. BS in Psychology, U. Wyo., 1984; MS in Comm., U. S.W. La., 1986. Panhellenic cons. U. S.W. La., Lafayette, 1984-86; account exec. Comm. Concepts, Lafayette, 1986-87; exec. dir. Vol. Ctr. of Lafayette, 1987-90; pub. rels. rep. ARC, Boulder, Colo., 1990-92; v.p. Longmont (Colo.) C. of C., 1992-94; pvt. cons., 1994—; pres., owner Comm. Concepts, Longmont, 1995—; cons. ARC, 1992—. Editor newsletter The Leader, 1992-94; editor La. Crawfish Farmers Jour., 1986-87. Bd. dirs. Rape Crisis Ctr., Lafayette, 1988-90, Festival Internat. de Louisiane, Lafayette, 1988-90, Longmont Coun. for the Arts, Tiny Tim Devel. Pre-sch.; mem. Existing Industry Task Force. Mem. Pub. Rels. Soc. Am. (newsletter, speakers com. 1990—), Twin Peaks Rotary Club (program chair 1992-93, vocat. chair 1995—), Boulder C. of C., Longmont C. of C., Econ. Devel. Assn. Longmont. Home: 1506 Frontier St Longmont CO 80501-2405

CORNELL, ANNIE AIKO, nurse, administrator, retired army officer; b. L.A., Sept. 23, 1954; d. George and Fumiko (Iwai) Okubo; m. Max A. Cornell, Dec. 10, 1990. BSN, U. Md., 1976. RN, Calif. Enlisted U.S. Army, 1972, advanced through grades to maj.; clin. staff nurse surg. ICU U.S. Army, Presidio of San Francisco; clin. head nurse ICU U.S. Army, Seoul, Korea; clin. head nurse gen. medicine ward U.S. Army, Ft. Ord, Calif., chief nursing adminstrn.; ret. U.S. Army, 1992; nursing supr. Home Health Plus; dir. patient svcs. Hollister Vis. Nurs Assn., Calif. Recipient Walter Reed Army Inst. nursing scholarship. Mem. Sigma Theta Tau. Home: 199 Linde Cir Marina CA 93933-2206

CORNELL, KENNETH LEE, lawyer; b. Palo Alto, Calif., Feb. 23, 1945; s. Clinton Burdette and Mildred Lucy (Sheafer) C.; m. Barbara J. Smith, June 26, 1966; children: Melinda Lee, Geoffery Mark. BBA, BA in Social Sci., Pacific Union Coll., 1966; JD, U. Wash., 1971. Bar: Wash. 1971, U.S. Dist. Ct. (we. dist.) Wash. 1971, U.S. Supreme Ct. 1974. Ptnr. Keller & Rohrback, Seattle, 1971-75, Richard, Rossano & Cornell, Seattle, 1975-77, Moren, Lageschulte (now Cornell, Hansen, Bugni & McConnell), Seattle, 1978-87, Cornell, Hansen, Bugni & McConnell PS (firm name change), 1995—; cons. atty. Town of Clyde Hill, Wash. 1980-87. Editor Wash. U. Law Rev., 1970-71. Bd. dirs. Kirkland (Wash.) Seventh Day Adventist Sch., 1972-78, Auburn (Wash.) Acad., 1974-80, Western Wash. Corp. Seventh Day Adventists, Bothell, 1974-80. Mem. ABA, Assn. Trial Lawyers Am., Christian Legal Soc., Wash. State Bar Assn., Wash. State Trial Lawyers Assn., Order of Coif. Republican. Office: Cornell Hansen Bugni & McConnell PS 11320 Roosevelt Way NE Seattle WA 98125-6228

CORNELL, SHERRY ELIZABETH, occupational health nurse; b. Harbor City, Calif., Apr. 9, 1957; d. Richard O. and Kathryn S. (Sorrell) Puckett; 1 child, Mary Kathryn Medina; m. Walter R. Cornell, Mar. 1995. Lic. Vocat. Nurse, Coll. of the Desert, 1978; BA in Psychology, Chapman Coll., 1995. LVN, Calif. Gerontol. nurse Moyle's Health Care, Yucca Valley, Calif., 1989-91; staff developer Hi-Desert Continuing Care Ctr., Joshua Tree, Calif., 1991-93; employee health nurse Desert Hosp., 1993—; owner Citrus Nursing Acad., 1993—; owner, founder Eloquence Creative Writing Svcs., Yucca Valley, 1985—; preceptor for Quality Care Health Found. Staff Developer Program, Sacramento, 1992. Creator, facilitator How to Teach Sex Edn. to Your Child, Friendly Hills Elem. Sch., 1990. Mem. Inland County Staff Developers Assn. (sec. 1991—). Republican. Home: 55525 Mira St Yucca Valley CA 92284 Office: Hi-Desert Star 56445 29 Palms Hwy Yucca Valley CA 92286

CORNETTE, WILLIAM MAGNUS, scientist, research director, company executive; b. San Francisco, Apr. 17, 1945; s. William Magnus and Elisabeth Louise (Stone) C.; m. Patricia Ruth King, Mar. 24, 1968 (div. Oct. 1981); children: Christopher Scott, David Warren; m. Sylvia Annette Martin, Jan. 6, 1982; 1 child, Jennifer Nicole. BS with high honors, U. Fla., 1967; MS, U. Chgo., 1969; PhD, U. Denver, 1973. Mathematician Naval Weapons Ctr., China Lake, Calif., 1973-77; specialist engr. Boeing Co., Seattle, 1977-80; v.p., dir. Photon Research Assocs., La Jolla, Calif., 1980—, Observables Tech., 1989, Adv. Phenomenologies and Models, 1992; cons. Denali Software Systems, San Diego, 1983-91. Contbr. articles to profl. jours. Active Congregation Beth El. With USAF, 1969-73. Mem. Optical Soc. Am., Wilderness Soc., Sierra Club, Am. Geophys. Union, German Philatelic Soc. (working group chmn. 1985-89), U.S. Figure Skating Assn., Phi Beta Kappa, Sigma Xi. Home: 7905 Port Royale Dr San Diego CA 92126-3514 Office: Photon Rsch Assocs 10350 N Torrey Pines Rd # 300 La Jolla CA 92037-1020

CORNISH, LINDA SOWA YOUNG, children's books author and illustrator, educator; b. Woodburn, Oreg., May 14, 1943; d. Cecil Edward and Marian Regina (Nibler) Sowa; m. Edmund Y.w. Young, June 11, 1966 (div. July 1988); children: Laura Young Engelmann, Amy L.H. Young, Kimberly L.F. Young; m. H.T. Cornish, Oct. 6, 1991. BA, U. Portland, 1966; EdM, Temple U., 1968. Tchr. spl. edn. Phila. Sch. System, 1966-69; tchr. elem. and spl. edn. North Clackamas Dist. 12, Milwaukie, Oreg., 1974-92; author, illustrator Cornish Hen, Hillsboro, Oreg., 1994—. Author, illustrator: (juvenile) Pong's Visit, 1994, Pong's Ways, 1994. Mem. AAUW, ASCD, Assn. for Childhood Edn. Internt., Oreg. Coun. Tchrs. English. Democrat. Methodist. Home: 1295 SW Brookwood Ave Hillsboro OR 97123-7593

CORNOG, ROBERT AIDEN, engineering consultant; b. Portland, July 7, 1912; s. Jacob Rodenbaugh and Emma Daisy (Ripley) C.; divorced; children: Ann, David. BS in Mech. Engring., U. Iowa, 1933; MS in Physics, U. Calif., Berkeley, 1939, PhD in Nuclear Physics, 1940. Physicist, engr. various organizations, 1940—; atomic bomb devel. Los Alamos, N.Mex., 1943-45; co-discover tritium; cons. in field. Contbr. articles to profl. jours.; patentee in field. Fellow British Interplanetary Soc. (life); mem. IEEE (sr.), Tau Beta Pi, Sigma Xi. Home: 2242 20th St Apt 4 Santa Monica CA 90405-1738 Office: Pacific Infrared Systems 6914 Canby Ave Ste 109 Reseda CA 91335-4313

CORNWALL, JOHN MICHAEL, physics educator, consultant, researcher; b. Denver, Aug. 19, 1934; s. Paul Bakewell and Dorothy (Zitkowski) C.; m. Ingrid Linderos, Oct. 16, 1965. AB, Harvard U., 1956, MS, U. Denver, 1959; PhD, U. Calif., 1962. NSF postdoctoral fellow Calif. Inst. Tech., Pasadena, 1962-63; mem. Inst. Advanced Study, Princeton, N.J., 1963-65; prof. physics UCLA, 1965—; vis. prof. Niels Bohr Inst., Copenhagen, 1968-69, Inst. de Physique Nucléaire, Paris, 1973-74, MIT, 1974, 87, Rockefeller U., N.Y.C., 1988; cons. Inst. Theoretical Physics, Santa Barbara, Calif., 1979-80, 82, bd. dirs., 1979-83; assoc. Ctr. Internat./Strategic Affairs, UCLA, 1987—; cons. MITRE Corp., Aerospace Corp., Los Alamos Nat. Labs., RAND Corp.; mem. dir's. adv. com. Lawrence Livermore Labs., 1991—; mem. Def. Sci. Bd., 1992-93; chmn. External Review com. Accelerator Oper. & Technol. Divsn., Los Alamos Nat. Labs, 1995—. Author: (with others) Academic Press Ency. of Science and Technology, other encys. and books; contbr. numerous articles to profl. jours. Mem. acad. adv. bd. RAND Grad. Sch., 1994—. With U.S. Army, 1956-58. Grantee NSF, NASA; NSF pre/postdoctoral fellow 1960-63, A.P. Sloan fellow, 1967-71. Fellow AAAS; mem. Am. Phys. Soc., Am. Geophys. Union, N.Y. Acad. Sci. Office: UCLA Dept Physics Los Angeles CA 90024

CORNWELL, RONALD WILLIAM, surgeon; b. Emmett, Idaho, June 20, 1958; s. David Leroy and Karen Jewell (Dobbs) C.; m. Patrice Mae Reimer, Sept. 4, 1982; children: Briana, Patrick, Austin, Kelsey. BS, Boise State U., 1982; MD, U. Nev., 1986. Diplomate Am. Bd. Surgery. Commd. 2d lt. USAF, 1982, advanced through grades to maj., 1992; staff gen. surgeon Med. Group USAF, Mountain Home AFB, Idaho, 1991-95; gen. surgeon West Valley Med. Ctr., Caldwell, Idaho, 1994—; resident in integrated surgery Wright State U., Dayton, Ohio, 1986-91; trainer, presenter in field. Health Professions scholar USAF, 1982-86. Fellow ACS; mem. Soc. Air Force Clin. Surgeons, Alpha Omega Alpha. Republican. Presbyterian. Office: 404 E Elm St Caldwell ID 83605

CORNYN, JOHN EUGENE, III, management consultant; b. Evanston, Ill., May 5, 1945; s. John Eugene and Virginia Ryder (Shannahan) C.; m. Patricia R. Benner, July 27, 1992; 1 child, Kelly. B.S. in Hotel and Restaurant Adminstrn., Okla. State U., 1968. Mgr. Indian Trail Restaurant, Winnetka, Ill., 1970-71; employee services mgr. Zenith Corp., Chgo., 1971-72; mgr. Red Lion Corp., Portland, Oreg., 1973; cons. Pannell, Kerr, Forster, Chgo., 1973-75; prin., ptnr. The Cornyn Fasano Group, Portland, 1976—; v.p. Seven Seas, Inc., Winnetka, Ill., 1978—, All Seas, Inc., Winneka, Ill., 1980—. Co-author: Noncommercial Foodservice-An Administrator's Handbook, 1994. Served to 1st lt. U.S. Army, 1968-70. Mem. Foodservice Cons. Soc. Internat. (chmn. mgmt. cons. com. 1983—), Inst. Mgmt. Cons. Republican. Club: Portland City. Home: 3350 NE Holladay St Portland OR 97232-2533 Office: The Cornyn Fasano Group 1618 SW 1st Ave Ste 315 Portland OR 97201-5708

CORNYN-SELBY, ALYCE PATRICIA, publishing company executive; b. Dayton, Ohio, Nov. 22, 1946; d.William Bain and Alice Ruth Sellers; 1 child, Kelly Alexandre. BA, Marylhurst Coll., Oreg. Prodn.mgr. Instrumentalist Pub., Evanston, Ill., 1971-72; visual communications mgr. Port of Portland, Oreg., 1976-85; owner AEnterprise, Portland, 1979-86; pres. AEnterprise, 1985-88; owner Paris Opera Co., Portland, 1988—; pub. Beynch Press Pub. Co., Portland, 1986—; speaker in field. Author: Procrastinator's Success Kit, 1986, Take Your Hands Off My Attitude!, 1987, Don't Have To & You Can't Make Me!, 1987, Making Your Mark: That's Marketing!, 1988, I'm Going To Change My Name & Move Away!, 1989, One Thing Worse Than Being Alone--Wishing You Were!, 1989, Selt-Sabotage: Solve It!, 1988; contbr. articles to profl. jours. Recipient numerous awards for script/copy writing, design, photography and film prodn. Mem. Pubrs. Mktg. Assn., N.W. Book Pubrs. Assn., Willamette Writers, Oreg. Writers Colony. Office: Beynch Press 1928 SE Ladd Ave Portland OR 97214-4737

CORPORON, NANCY ANN, marketing executive; b. Independence, Kans., Nov. 11, 1949; d. Lewis Leonard and Helen Maxine (Church) Corporon. BM in Music Performance, Oklahoma City U., 1971; MBA, NYU, 1985. French hornist, 1970-85; mgr. mktg. Am. Express Co., 1987-90, Wells Fargo Bank, 1991—; assoc. Mgmt. Practice Cons. Ptnrs., 1985-87; cons. Urban Bus. Assistance Corp., N.Y.C., 1981-83, v.p., 1983-84; artistic dir. San Francisco Winds Freedom, 1990—; music dir. N.Y Community Marching Band, N.Y.C., 1979-81; founder, pres. Trimusicangle, Inc., N.Y.C., 1979-82. Recipient Cardinal Key, Oklahoma City U., 1971, Sword of Honor Sigma Alpha Iota, 1971. Mem. Pi Kappa Lambda. Home: 178 Hearst Ave San Francisco CA 94131-3136

CORPRON, KAREN KAE, childhood education specialist; b. Yakima, Wash., Sept. 28, 1953; d. Walter Edison and Violet Irene Hanthorn; m. William Douglas Corpron, July 15, 1972; children: Jennifer, Lisa, Sarah. BA in Home Econs., Wash. State U., 1975. Preschool tchr. Jane's House Yakima Valley C.C., 1975-80, family life instr., parent educator Jane's House, 1979-94, family life instr., educator Parent Edn. Child Care Ctr., 1990-94, asst. coord. parent edn. coop. preschools, 1990-94; edn. cons. Through the Eyes of Children, Bell, Wash., 1994—. Author: She Dances With Me, 1992. Mem. Nat. Coun. Family Rels., Am. Home Econs. Assn. (cert.), Nat. Assn. Edn. Young Children, Wash. Coalition Sexual Assault, Coalition for Accuracy About Abuse, Wash. Home Econs. Assn., Yakima Home Econs. Assn., Wash. Assn. Edn. Young Children, Yakima Valley Assn. Edn. Young Children (founder local affiliate 1983-84, conf. com. 1987, treas. 1984-88, membership cahirperson 1984-88, co-chair workshops 1991, 93, pres. 1990-92, affiliate rep. to Wash. state assn. 1993—). Home: 4301 Bell St Yakima WA 98908-3314

CORRADINI, DEEDEE, mayor. Student, Drew U., 1961-63; BS, U. Utah, 1965, MS, 1967. Adminstrv. asst. for public info. Utah State Office Rehab. Svcs., 1967-69; cons. Utah State Dept. Community Affairs, 1971-72; media dir., press sec. Wayne Owens for Congress Campaign, 1972; press sec. Rep. Wayne Owens, 1973-74; spl. asst. to N.Y. Congl. Rep. Richard Ottinger, 1975; asst. to pres., dir. community rels. Snowbird Corp., 1975-77; exec. v.p. Bonneville Assocs., Inc., Salt Lake City, 1977-80; pres. Bonneville Assocs., Inc., 1980-89, chmn., CEO, 1989-91; mayor Salt Lake City, 1992—; mem. urban con. policy com. U.S. Conf. on Mayors, mem. unfunded fed. mandates task force, mem. crime and violence task force, trustee exec. com.; chair Mayor's Gang Task Force; mem. interngovtl. policy adv. com. U.S. Trade Rep., 1993-94; mem. transp. and comm. com. Nat. League of Cities, 1993-94. Bd. trustees Intermountain Health Care, 1980-92; bd. dirs., exec. com. Utah Symphony, 1983-92, vice chmn., 1985-88, chmn., 1988-92; dir. Utah chpt. Nat. Conf. Christians and Jews, Inc., 1988; bd. dirs. Salt Lake Olympic Bid Com., 1989—; chmn. image com. Utah Partnership for Edn. and Econ. Devel., 1989-92; co-chair United Way Success by 6 Program; pres. Shelter of the Homeless Com.; active Sundance Inst. Utah Com., 1990-92; disting. bd. fellow So. Utah U., 1991; active numerous other civic orgns. and coms. Mem. Salt Lake Area C. of C. (bd. govs. 1979-81, chmn. City/County/Govt. com. 1976-86). Office: Office of the Mayor City & County Bldg 451 S State St Rm 306 Salt Lake City UT 84111-3104

CORRIGAN, GERALD F., executive search consultant; b. Dublin, Ireland, Apr. 16, 1937; came to the U.S., 1959; s. Nicholas J. and Bridget (Donohue) C.; m. Virginia Tang, 1965; children: Peter, Elizabeth. AB, UCLA, 1963, MBA, 1965. Asst. dean adminstrn. and external affairs UCLA Grad. Sch. Mgmt., dean exec. edn.; mgmt. cons. Booz, Allen & Hamilton, Cresap, Inc.; exec. search cons., pres. The Corrigan Group, L.A., 1978—. Mem. N.Am. bd. Michael Smurfit Grad. Sch. Bus. U. Coll. Dublin. Mem. UCLA Alumni Assn. (life), Jonathan Club. Democrat. Roman Catholic. Home: 1057 Corsica Dr Pacific Palisades CA 90272-4013 Office: The Corrigan Group 1333 Ocean Ave Santa Monica CA 90401-1023

CORRIGAN, MARY KATHRYN, theatre educator; b. Mpls., July 11, 1930; d. Arthur Joseph Kolling and Hazel (Pierce) Colp; children: Michael Edward, Timothy Patrick. BA, U. Minn., Mpls., 1965, MA, 1967. Advisor, counselor Coll. Liberal Arts U. Minn., Mpls., 1964-65, instr. dept. theatre, 1966-69, asst. prof. dept. theatre, 1969-73; assoc. prof. dept. theatre Fla. State U., Tallahassee, 1973-75, U. Calif., San Diego, 1975-89, 92—; assoc. dir. U. Calif. Study Ctr. U.K., Ireland, 1989-91; master tchr. Brit. Am. Drama Acad., Balliol Coll., Oxford U., Eng., summers, 1987—, chair undergrad. & intermediate programs midsummer, 1992, 93. Actress nat. pub. radio Chopin, 1984, video film Ultrasonography, 1986. Mem. adv. com. United Ministeries, Mpls., 1968-73, Mpls. Sch. Bd., 1968-72. Recipient Tozier Found. award, Eng., 1967, Best Actress award Globe Theatre, San Diego, 1979, NEH award Folger Shakespeare Theatre, 1992-93; grantee Rockefeller Found., 1968, McMillan grantee U. Minn., Eng., 1968, U. Calif.-San Diego, 1982-87, NEH grantee Folger Inst., Washington, 1993-94, Stanford U., summer 1994, Ceravity LaJolla Conf., 1995. Mem. Am. Theatre Assn. (exec. com., v.p. performance tng. 1984-86), Voice and Speech Theater Assn. (bd. dirs. 1986-89). Democrat. Home: 2645 Gobat Ave San Diego CA 92122-3127 Office: U Calif San Diego Theatre Dept La Jolla CA 92093-0344

CORRIGAN, ROBERT ANTHONY, academic administrator; b. New London, Conn., Apr. 21, 1935; s. Anthony John and Rose Mary (Jengo) C.; m. Joyce D. Mobley, Jan. 12, 1975; children by previous marriage: Kathleen Marie, Anthony John, Robert Anthony; 1 stepdau., Erika Mobley. A.B., Brown U., 1957; M.A., U. Pa., 1959, Ph.D., 1967; LHD (hon.), 1995. Researcher Phila. Hist. Commn., 1957-59; lectr. Am. civilization U. Gothenburg, Sweden, 1959-62, Bryn Mawr Coll., 1962-63, U. Pa., 1963-64; prof. U. Iowa, 1964-73; dean U. Mo., Kansas City, 1973-74; provost U. Md., 1974-79; chancellor U. Mass., Boston, 1979-88; pres. San Francisco State U., 1988—. Author: American Fiction and Verse, 1962, 2d edit., 1970, also articles, revs.; editor: Uncle Tom's Cabin, 1968. Vice chmn. Iowa City Human Rels. Commn., 1970-72, Gov.'s Commn. on Water Quality, 1983-84; mem. Iowa City Charter Commn., 1972-73; chmn. Md. Com. Humanities, 1976-78, Assn. Urban Univs., 1988-92; mem. Howard County Commn. Arts, Md., 1976-79; bd. dirs. John F. Kennedy Libr.; trustee San Francisco Econ. Devel. Corp., 1989-92, Modern Greek Studies Found., Found. of Spain and U.S., Adv. Coun. of Calif. Acad. Scis., Bishop Desmond Tutu South African Refugee Scholarship Fund, Calif. Historical Soc., 1989-92; co-chmn., bd. dirs. Calif. Compact, 1990-93; exec. com. Campus Compact, 1991—; active Mayor's Blue Ribbon Commn. on Fiscal Stability, 1994-95. Smith-Mundt prof., 1959-60; Fulbright lectr., 1960-62; grantee Standard Oil Co. Found., 1968, NEH, 1969-74, Ford Found., 1969, Rockefeller Found., 72-75, Dept. State, 1977; recipient Clarkson Able Collins Jr. Maritime History award, 1956, Pa. Colonial Soc. Essay award, 1958, 59, William Lloyd Garrison award Mass. Ednl. Opportunity Assn., 1987; Disting. Urban Fellow Assn. Urban U., 1992. Mem. San Francisco C. of C. (bd. dirs.), San Francisco World Affairs Coun. (bd. dirs.), Pvt. Industry Coun. (bd. dirs. 1992—), Boston World Affairs Coun. (1983-88), Greater Boston C. of C. (v.p. 1987-89), Fulbright Alumni Assn. (bd. dirs. 1978-80), Univ. Club, City Club, World Trade Club, Phi Beta Kappa. Democrat. Office: San Francisco State U 1600 Holloway Ave San Francisco CA 94132-1722

CORRIGAN, WILFRED J., data processing and computer company executive; b. 1938. Divsn. dir. Motorola, Phoenix, 1962-68; pres. Fairchild Camera & Instrument, Sunnyvale, Calif., 1968-80; chmn. bd., CEO LSI Logic Corp., Milpitas, Calif., 1980—, also dir. Office: LSI Logic Corp 1551 Mccarthy Blvd Milpitas CA 95035-7424*

CORRY, LAWRENCE LEE, sugar company executive; b. Portland, Oreg., Oct. 31, 1939; s. Rowland Parry and Clara Hannah (Orton) C.; m. Rhea Kathleen Reeder, May 29, 1964; children—Kamille, Todd L., Matthew D., Jill, Steffani, Melanee. A.S. in Bus. Mgmt., Weber State Coll., 1959; B.A., Brigham Young U., 1963, M.B.A., 1965. Indsl. engr. Arabian Am. Oil Co., Saudi Arabia, 1958; fin. analyst Standard Oil Co. Calif., San Francisco, Houston, 1965-68; fin. analyst, asst. to pres. Amalgamated Sugar Co., Ogden, Utah, 1968-73, dist. agrl. mgr., Nampa, Idaho, 1973-75, dir. indsl. and pub. relations, Ogden, Utah, 1975-77, v.p., 1977-84, exec. v.p., 1984—; mem. Dept. Agrl. Mktg. Allotment Task Force, 1968-74; dir. Curtis Grain Co. Mem. North Ogden City Citizens Planning Commn., 1973. Mem. Am. Soc. Sugarbeet Technologists. Clubs: Rotary (Nampa); Kiwanis (Ogden); Ogden Golf and Country. Mormon. Office: Amalgamated Sugar Co PO Box 1520 Ogden UT 84402-1520

CORSER, KIRA DOROTHY, photographic artist; b. San Antonio, Tex., Feb. 27, 1951; d. William Franklin and Maria (McCarthy) Freeman; children: Robert William, Anna Katrina. BA in Journalism and Art, San Diego State U., 1984. dir. photography dept. KPBS TV and Radio Stas., 1979-89; lectr. in field. Co-author, produced (with Frances Payne Adler) Home Street Home, Struggle to be Borne, 1987, When the Bough Breaks Pregnancy and the Legacy of Addiction; photographs have appeared in numerous books and exhbns. Recipient Calif. State Senate award for artistic excellence and social collaboration, 1989; David Copley Art grantee, 1984, 87, 89, Combined Arts and Edn. grantee NEA, San Diego, 1987, Las Patronas grantee and March of Dimes Birth Defects Found. grantee, 1989, Monterey Cultural Arts Commn. grantee, 1991, Santa Clara County Arts Commn. grantee, 1992, Irvine Found. Art grantee, 1993, others. Home and Office: Art for Social Change 17467 Via Cielo Carmel Valley CA 93924-9169

CORSI, SANDRO, artist, educator; b. Rome, June 21, 1958; came to the U.S., 1983; s. Luigi and Adriana (De Simoni) C.; m. Elena Pascuzzi, Jan. 26, 1987. BFA, Sch. Art Inst. Chgo., 1984, MFA, 1986. Freelance illustrator Rome, 1979-83; animation intern David Alexovich Animation, Chgo., 1984-86; computer graphics cons. Northwestern U. Med. Libr., Chgo., 1987; faculty U. Wis., Oshkosh, 1987-92, Fullerton (Calif.) Coll., 1992—; speaker in field; guest lectr. Syracuse (N.Y.) U., 1989. Exhibited in numerous group shows including 1st Annual Art & Design Contest Computer Pictures Mag., No. Ill. U. Gallery, Chgo., 1992, Gallery 100, Cape Girardeau, Mo., 1992, Milw. Art Mus., 1991, U. of Arrts, Phila., 1990, Edna Carlsten Gallery U. Wis., Stevens Point, 1990, St. Louis C.C., 1989, Conn. Coll., New London, 1989, many others. Mellon fellow, 1985-86; scholar Sch. Art Inst. Chgo., 1985-86. Office: Fullerton Coll 321 E Chapman Ave Fullerton CA 92632-2011

CORSINI, RAYMOND JOSEPH, psychologist; b. Rutland, Vt., June 1, 1914; s. Joseph August and Evelyn Carolyn (Lavaggi) C.; m. Kleona Rigney, Oct. 10, 1965; 1 dau., Evelyn Anne. B.S., CCNY, 1939, M.S. in Edn, 1941; Ph.D., U. Chgo., 1955. Prison psychologist Auburn (N.Y.) Prison, 1941-45, San Quentin Prison, 1945-47, Wis. Prison System, 1947-50; research assoc. U. Chgo., 1955-57; pvt. practice indsl. psychology Alfred Adler Inst., Chgo., 1957-63; assoc. prof. Ill. Inst. Tech., 1964-65, U. Calif. at Berkeley, 1965-66; pvt. practice psychology Honolulu, 1965-89; faculty research affiliate Sch. Pub. Health, U. Hawaii, 1970—; affiliate grad. faculty dept. psychology, U. Hawaii; founder, sr. counselor Family Edn. Centers Hawaii, 1966—. Author: Methods of Group Psychotherapy, 1957, Roleplaying in Business and Industry, 1961, Roleplaying in Psychotherapy, 1966, The Family Council, 1974, The Practical Parent, 1975, Role Playing, 1980, Give In or Give Up, 1981, Individual Psychology: Theory and Practice, 1982, Effective Discipline in the Home and the School, 1989, Five Therapists and One Client, 1990, Coping With Your Teenager, 1990; editor: Critical Incidents in Psychotherapy, 1959, Adlerian Family Counseling, 1959, Critical Incidents in Teaching, 1965, Critical Incidents in School Counseling, 1972, Critical Incidents in Nursing, 1973, Current Psychotherapies, 1973, 77, 83, 89, 95, Current Personality Theories, 1977, Readings in Current Personality Theories, 1978, Great Cases in Psychotherapy, 1979, Alternative Educational Systems, 1979, Theories of Learning, 1980, Comparative Educational Systems, 1981, Handbook of Innovative Psychotherapies, 1981, Adolescence: The Challenge, Encyclopedia of Psychology, 1984, 2nd. edit. 1994, Condensed Encyclopedia of Psychology, 1987, Jour. Individual Psychology, 1974-76, Encyclopedia of Aging, 1987. Bd. dirs. Hawaii chpt. John Howard Assn., 1966-68. Recipient James McKeen Cattell award psychology Psychol. Corp., 1944; Sertoma award, 1980. Mem. Am. Psychol. Assn. (Significant Profl. Contbn. award Hawaii chpt. 1985), N.Am. Soc. Adlerian Psychology. Club: Waikiki Yacht (Honolulu). Address: 140 Niuiki Cir Honolulu HI 96821-2349

CORSON, KIMBALL JAY, lawyer; b. Mexico City, Sept. 17, 1941; came to U.S., 1942; s. Harland Jerry and Arleen Elizabeth (Jones) C.; m. Ann Dudley Wood, May 25, 1963 (div. Apr. 1978); 1 child, Claudia Ring; m. Joy Lorann Sligh, June 16, 1979; children: Bryce Manning, Jody Darlene. BA, Wayne State U., 1966; MA, U. Chgo., 1968, JD, 1971. Bar: Ariz. 1972, U.S. Dist. Ct. 1971, U.S. Supreme Ct. 1991. Assoc. Lewis & Roca, Phoenix, 1971-74, ptnr., 1974-90; ptnr. Horne Kaplan & Bistrow, Phoenix, 1990—. Co-author: Document Control: Organization, Management and Production, 1988; contbg. author: Litigation Support Using Personal Computers, 1989. Co-founder Desert Hills Improvement Assn., Phoenix, 1988—. With U.S. Army, 1961-64. Fellow Woodrow Wilson Found., 1966, 67. Mem. ABA (civil practice and procedures com. antitrust sect. 1988—), Ariz. Bar Assn. (spkr. 1991—), Maricipa County Bar Assn., Internat. Trademark Assn. (editl. bd. The Trademark Reporter 1993-94, mem. publs. com. 1995—, INTA Speaker's award 1988), Am. Sailing Assn., Phi Beta Kappa. Home: Summit Ranch 35808 N 15th Ave Phoenix AZ 85027 Office: Horne Kaplan & Bistrow 40 N Central Ave Ste 2800 Phoenix AZ 85004-4447

CORTELYOU, ROBERT J(OHN), civil engineer; b. Taft, Calif., July 2, 1937; s. John Taylor and Mildred Louise (Kessel) C.; m. Barbara Jean Watson, May 26, 1962; children: Robert John, Jr., John Charles. BS in Mech. Engring., Calif. State Poly. Coll., 1960. Registered profl. engr., Calif. Mech., civil engr. GE, Louisville, San Jose, Calif., 1960-61; mech. engr. Calif. State Dept. of Water Resources, Sacramento, 1965-70, Sonoma County Water Agy., Santa Rosa, Calif., 1970-78; supr. design engr. Western Water Dist. Riverside (Calif.) County, 1978-80; design engring. supr. Sonoma County Water Agy., 1980—. Lt. USN, 1961-64; capt. USNR, 1965-92. Decorated Navy Commendation medal, Nat. Def. medal; recipient Welding Design Contest 1st Pl. award Lincoln Electric Co., 1960. Mem. ASME, ASCE, San Francisco Bay Area Engrs. Coun. (scholarship com.), U.S. Navy League, Model A Ford Car Club, Tau Sigma. Home: 6640 Saint Helena Rd Santa Rosa CA 95404-9694 Office: Sonoma County Water Agy 2150 W College Ave Santa Rosa CA 95401-4442

CORTES, WILLIAM PATRICK, lawyer, telecommunications executive; b. Ellenville, N.Y., Apr. 23, 1955; s. Robert Paul and Joan Helen (Whitstock) C. AB, Stanford U., 1977; MBA, U. Wash., 1983, JD, 1984. Bar: Wash. 1984; CPA, Wash. Fin. instr. Sch. Bus. Adminstrn. U. Wash., Seattle, 1980-83; strategic planning analyst Burlington No., Inc., Seattle, 1982, 83; sr. cons. Ernst & Young Telecommunications Group, Tacoma, 1985-86; fin. mgr. spec. projects U S WEST NewVector Group Inc., Bellevue, Wash., 1986-88, dir. investor rels. and bus. analysis, 1988-90; dir. investor rels. U S WEST, Inc., Englewood, Colo., 1990; dir. bus. devel. U S WEST Internat. Inc., Paris, 1990-92; U S WEST Internat. Inc., London, 1992-93; dir. new opportunity devel. US West Comm., Denver, 1993-95, exec. dir. product devel. wireless group, 1995—. Mem. ABA, AICPAs, Wash. State Bar Assn., Fed. Comms. Bar Assn., Wash. Soc. CPAs. Democrat. Roman Catholic. Office: US West Comm 1999 Broadway 10th Fl Denver CO 80202

CORTESE, DOMINIC L., state legislator, farmer; b. San Jose, Calif., Sept. 27, 1932; s. Vincent and Rose (Carova) C.; m. Suzanne Donovan; children: David, Rosanne, Mary, Thomas, James. BS in Polit. Sci., U. Santa Clara, 1954. Farmer, businessman San Jose; mem. Calif. Assembly, Sacramento, 1980—, chmn. com. on water, parks and wildlife, chmn. select com. on Calif. wine prodn. and economy; mem. wine industry task force Nat. Conf. State Legislatures; chmn. Santa Clara County Transit Dist., 1976, 80, Com. on W.P. & W.; selection com. CA Wine Prodn. and Economy. Bd. fellows U. Santa Clara, Calif.; chmn. exec. bd. Calif. Assn. Local Agy. Formation Commn., 1972-73; mem. Santa Clara County Bd. Suprs., 1968-80, also past chmn.,; former chmn. Santa Clara County Transit Dist., Regional Criminal Justice Planning Bd., Santa Clara County Local Agy. Formation Commn.; instrumental in creation Santa Clara County commns. on drug abuse, alcoholism, consumer affairs, status of women, human rels., and Mobilehome Owners Task Force. With U.S. Army, 1954-56. Recipient award Ctr. for Employment Tng., 1982, Legislator of Yr. award League Calif. Cities, 1983, Am. Planning Assn., 1984, 89, Am. Cancer Soc., 1988, Calif. coun. AIA, 1990, Calif. Trucking Assn., 1994, Pres. award County Suprs. Assn. Calif., 1983, Disting. Svc. award, 1987, El Gran Matador award Calif. Contract Cities Assn., 1984, Blue Ribbon award Western Fairs Assn., 1986, Legislator's Merit award Assn. Calif. Water Agys., 1988, Committment to Children award Assn. for Edn. Young Children, 1988, Environ. Leadership commendation Sierra Club, 1992, others. Mem. Am. Planning Assn. (legislator of Yr. award Calif. chpt. 1984), Am. Legion, Italian Am. Heritage Found., Civic Club San Jose, Santa Clara County Bd. Suprs., Coms. on G.O., H. & C.D., Rev. and Tax. Office: Calif Assembly State Capitol PO Box 942849 Sacramento CA 94249-0001 also: 100 Paseo De San Antonio San Jose CA 95113-1402

CORTINEZ, VERONICA, language and literature educator; b. Santiago, Chile, Aug. 27, 1958; came to U.S. 1979; d. Carlos Cortinez and Matilde Romo. Licenciatura en Letras, U. Chile, 1979; MA, U. Ill., Champaign, Ill., 1981, Harvard U., 1983; PhD, Harvard U., 1990. Teaching asst. U. Chile, Santiago, 1977-79, U. Ill., Champaign, 1979-80; teaching fellow Harvard U., 1982-86, instr., 1986-89; asst. prof. colonial and contemporary Latin Am. lit. UCLA, 1989—; fgn. corres. Caras, Santiago, 1987—. Editorial bd. Mester/Dept. Spanish and Portuguese of UCLA, 1989—; editor Plaza mag., 1981-89, Harvard Rev., 1983-89; contbr. articles to profl. jours. Recipient Award for Teaching Excellence, Danforth Ctr., Harvard U., 1982, 83, 84, 85, 86; Teaching prize, Romance Lang. Dept., Harvard U., 1986; Whiting fellow. Mem. Cabot House, Phi Beta Phi. Office: UCLA Dept Spanish and Portuguese 5310 Rolfe Hall Los Angeles CA 90024

CORTNER, HANNA JOAN, science administrator, research scientist, educator; b. Tacoma, Wash., May 9, 1945; d. Val and E. Irene Otteson; m. Richard Carroll Cortner, Nov. 14, 1970. BA in Polit. Sci. magna cum laude with distinction, U. Wash., 1967; MA in Govt., U. Ariz., 1969, PhD in Govt., 1973. Grad. teaching and rsch. asst. dept. govt. U. Ariz., Tucson, 1967-70, rsch. assoc. Inst. Govt. Rsch., 1974-76, rsch. assoc. forest-watershed and landscape resources divsns. Sch. Renewable Natural Resources, 1975-82, adj. assoc. prof. Sch. Renewable Natural Resources, 1983-89; exec. asst. Pima County Bd. Suprs., 1985-86; adj. assoc. prof. renewable natural resources, assoc. rsch. scientist Water Resources Rsch. Ctr. U. Ariz., Tucson, 1988-89, prof., rsch. scientist Water Resources Rsch. Ctr., 1989-90, prof., rsch. scientist, dir. Water Resources Rsch. Ctr., 1990—; program analyst USDA Forest Svc., Washington, 1979-80; vis. scholar Inst. Water Resources, Corps of Engrs., Ft. Belvoir, Va., 1986-87; com. arid lands AAAS, 1986-89; com. natural disasters NAS/NRC, 1988-91, com. on planning and remediation of irrigation, 1994—; rev. com. nat. forest planning Conservation Found., Washington, 1987-90; chair adv. com. renewable resources planning techs. for pub. lands Office of Tech. Assessment, U.S. Congress, 1989-91; mem. policy coun. Pinchot Inst. Conservation Studies, 1991-93; co-chair working party on evaluation of forest policies Internat. Union Forestry Rsch. Orgns., 1990—; vice-chair Man and the Biosphere Program, Temperate Directorate, US Dept. of State, 1991—; cons. Greeley and Hansen, Consulting Engrs., U.S. Army Corps Engrs., Ft. Belvoir, U.S. Forest Svc., Washington, Portland, Oreg., Ogden, Utah. Author: (with others) New Dimensions to Energy Policy and Public Administration, 1980, Energy and the Western United States: Politics and Development, 1982, Borderlands Sourcebook, 1983, Climate Change and U.S. Water Resources, 1990, Public Policy in Arizona, 1993; assoc. editor Society and Natural Resources, 1992-94; book reviewer Western Polit. Sci. Quar., Am. Polit. Quar., Perspectives, Natural Resources Jour., Climatic Change, Society and Natural Resources, Jour. of Frestry; pub. papers and monographs; contbr. articles to profl. jours. Bd. dirs. Planned Parenthood So. Ariz., 1992-94, planning com., 1992, bd. devel. and evaulation com., 1994; bd. dirs. N.W. Homeowners Assn., 1982-83, v.p., 1983-84, pres., 1984; vice chmn., chmn. Pima County Bd. Adjustment Dist. 3, 1984; active Pima Assn. of Govts. Avra Valley Task Force, 1988-90, Tucson Tomorrow, 1984-88; environ. planning adv. com. Pina Assn. Govts., 1989-90, chmn., 1984, water quality subcom., 1983-84; bd. dirs. So. Ariz. Water Resources Assn., 1984-86, 87—, sec., 1987-89, com. alignment and terminal storage, 1990-94, CAP com., 1988-92, chair 1989-90, basinwide mgmt. com., 1983-86, chair, 1992-93; active Ariz. Interagy. Task Force on Fire and the Urban/Wildland Interface, 1990-92, wastewater mgmt. adv. com. Pima County, 1988-92, subcom. on effluent reuse Joint CWAC-WWAC, 1989-91, citizens water adv. com. Water Resources Plan Update Subcom., 1990-91; bd. dirs. Ctrl. Ariz. Water Conservation Dist., 1985-90, fin. com., 1987-88, spl. studies com., 1987-88, nominating com. 1987; mem. Colo. River Salinity Control, 1989-90; chair adv. com. Tucscon Long Range Master Water Plan, 1988-89; active water adv. com. City of Tucscon, 1984. Travel grantee NSF/Soc. Am. Foresters; Rsch. grantee US Geol. Survey, US Army Corps of Engrs., USDA Forest Svc., Soil Conservation Svc., Utah State U., Four Corners Regional Commn., Office of Water Rsch. & Tech.; Sci. & Engring. fellow AAAS, 1986-87; recipient Copper Letter Appreciation cert. City of Tucson, 1985, 89, SAWARA award, 1989. Mem. Am. Water Resources Assn. (nat. award com. 1987-90, statues and bylaws com. 1989-90, tech. co-chair ann. meeting 1993), Am. Forestry Assn. (forest policy ctr. adv. coun. 1991—), Soc. Am. Foresters (task force on sustaining long-term forest and productivity, 1991-92, com. forest policy 1994—), Am. Polit. Sci. Assn., Western Polit. Sci. Assn. (com. constrn. and by-laws 1976-80, chair 1977-79, exec. com. 1980-83, com. profl. devel. 1984-85, com. on the status of women 1984-85), Nat. Fire Prevention Assn. (tech. com. on forest and rural fire protection 1990-94), Phi Beta Kappa. Democrat. Home: 1425 W Calle Tiburon Tucson AZ 85704-1023 Office: U Ariz Water Resources Rsch Ctr 350 N Campbell Ave Tucson AZ 85721

CORTRIGHT, INGA ANN, accountant; b. Silver City, N.Mex., Sept. 30, 1949; d. Lester Richard and Claudia Marcella (Huckaby) Lee; m. Russell Joseph Cortright, June 25, 1987. BS in Acctg., Ariz. State U., 1976, MBA, 1978; postgrad., Walden U., 1991—. CPA, Ariz., Tex. Sole practice cert. pub. acctg. Ariz., 1981—; cons. in field. Mem. AICPA, Beta Alpha Psi. Republican. Episcopalian. Office: 9421 W Bell Rd Ste 108 Sun City AZ 85351-1361

CORUM, WILLIAM THOMAS, III, computer information systems executive; b. Yreka, Calif., Feb. 20, 1935; s. William Thomas II and Joyce Elizabeth (Stone) C.; m. Ellen Ardel Reiber, June 20, 1954; children: Steven Craig, Scott Andrew. AA, Compton Coll., 1954; student, Calif. State U., Long Beach, 1966-72; MBA, Calif. State U., Dominguez Hills, 1976. With Douglas Aircraft Info. Systems, Long Beach, 1961-71; mgr. tech. svcs. McAuto Tech. Svcs., Long Beach and St. Louis, 1971-77; dir. data ctr. ops. McAuto Health Systems, St. Louis, 1977-81, v.p. product devel., 1981-84, v.p., dep. gen. mgr., 1984-86, v.p. fed. systems div., 1986-88, v.p. patient care systems, 1988, v.p. advanced R & D, 1988-89; sr. v.p. tech. svcs. Profl. Healthcare Systems, L.A., 1989-92; v.p. info. mgmt. planning svcs. Healthcare Computing Strategies, L.A., 1993—. Contbr. articles to profl. publs., chpt. to book. Subject of case study Harvard U. Grad. Sch. Bus., 1969. Republican. Lutheran. Office: Healthcare Computing Strategies 1510 McCormick Pl Wheaton IL 60187

CORWIN, JACK B., holding company executive; b. N.Y.C., July 10, 1951; s. Howard Stanley and Sydelle (Friedman) C. BSBA, U. Md., 1978; M Pub. and Pvt. Mgmt., Yale U., 1980. Assoc. corp. fin. Advest, Inc., Hartford, Conn., 1980-82, Drexel Burnham, Lambert, N.Y.C., 1982-83; assoc. exec. corp. E.F. Hutton, N.Y.C., 1983-84; v.p. PruCapital, L.A., 1984-86; pres. Huntington Holdings, Inc., L.A., 1987—; chmn. Bianchi Holding, Temecula, Calif., 1987—; bd. dirs. FIPC Holding, Winston-Salem, N.C. Mem. Ketchum-Downtown YMCA (bd. dirs. 1991—), City Club Bunker Hill. Office: Huntington Holdings Inc 633 W 5th St Ste 6780 Los Angeles CA 90071 also: 99 Emerald Bay Laguna Beach CA 92651-1252

CORWIN, STANLEY JOEL, book publisher; b. N.Y.C., Nov. 6, 1938; s. Seymour and Faye (Agress) C.; m. Donna Gelgur; children: Alexandra, Donna, Ellen. AB, Syracuse U., 1960. Dir. subsidiary rights, v.p. mktg. Prentice-Hall, Inc., Englewood Cliffs, N.J., 1960-68; v.p. internat. Grosset & Dunlap, Inc., N.Y.C., 1968-75; founder, pres. Corwin Books, N.Y.C., 1975; pres., pub. Pinnacle Books, Inc., Los Angeles, 1976-79; pres. Stan Corwin Prodns. Ltd., 1980—; pres., chief exec. officer Tudor Pub. Co., N.Y.C. and Los Angeles, 1987-90; lectr. Conf. World Affairs, U. Colo., 1976, U. Denver, 1978, Calif. State U., Northridge, 1980, The Learning Annex; participant

Pubmart Seminar, N.Y.C., 1977, UCLA, 1985, 93; guest lectr. U. So. Calif., 1987—. Author: Where Words Were Born, 1977, How to Become a Best Selling Author, 1984, 2d edit., 1993; contbr. articles to L.A. Times, N.Y. Times, short stories to Signature Mag.; prodr. motion picture Remo Williams-The Adventure Begins, 1986; (golf video) How to Golf with Jan Stephenson, 1987; exec. prodr. The Elvis Files TV Show, 1991, The Marilyn Files, 1993; pub. The Movie Script Libr., 1994. Mem. Pres. Carter's U.S. Com. on the UN, 1977. Served with AUS, 1960. Nat. prize winner short story contest Writers' Digest, 1966. Mem. Assn. Am. Pubs., PEN. Home and Office: 1185 Coldwater Canyon Beverly Hills CA 90210-3605

CORY, ROLLAND WAYNE, business administrator; b. Camp Zama, Sagamihira, Japan, Feb. 7, 1957; s. Claude Charles Cory and Kyoko (Narasaki) Reibel; m. Victoria Athena Dale Plasting, Nov. 8, 1980. AS in Transp. and Bus. Adminstrn., Chaffey Coll., 1992. Crane tender Ameron Steel Producing Div., Etiwanda, Calif., 1976; structural fitter Kaiser Steel Fabricated Products Group, Fontana, Calif., 1976-81; retail camera salesman Fedco Inc., San Bernardino, Calif., 1981; elevator mechanic Exec. Elevator Co., Fontana, Calif., 1985; storekeeper TTX Co./Calpro div., Mira Loma, Calif., 1981-95; pres. United Steelworkers of Am. Local Union #8844, Mira Loma, 1992-94; legis. educator United Steelworkers of Am. Local Union # 8844, Mira Loma, 1985-95, safety chmn., 1983-88, rec. sec., 1985-88. Mem. Calif. Turtle and Tortoise Club (treas. Inland Empire chpt. 1990-95, Plaque 1991), Nat. Geographic Soc. (cert. 1982), Indsl. Rels. and Rsch. Assn. Democrat. Office: Calif Turtle & Tortoise Club PO Box 976 Fontana CA 92334-0976

COSAY, BENNETT WAYNE, photographer; b. Phoenix, June 21, 1966; s. Eugene Sr. and Myra (Hinton) C.; m. Mary Louise Lupe, June 1, 1965; children: Joseph Blaine, Kayleigh Jamie. Grad., high sch., 1984. Photographer Ft. Apache Scout, Whiteriver, Ariz., 1985-89, head photographer, 1989—. Contbr. photographs to Bur. of Cath. Newsletter, 1987, Arizona's Indian Country, 1989, Sun Life mag., 1992. Recipient Best Use of Photography award Ariz. Newspapers Assn., 1989, Deptl. News Coverage award, 1989; honorable mention Nat. Pre-Historic Preservation, 1989. Mem. Native Am. Journalist Assn. Home: PO Box 886 Whiteriver AZ 85941-0886 Office: Ft Apache Scout Newspaper PO Box 898 Whiteriver AZ 85941-0898

COSGROVE, CAMERON, insurance executive; b. Arcadia, Calif., July 25, 1957; s. Joseph Patrick Jr. and Marion (Barrons) C.; m. Marilee Jane Mann, Feb. 12, 1980; children: Christopher Farley, Steven Patrick. BS in Mgmt., Calif. State U., Long Beach, 1980. Asst. v.p. Pacific Mut. Life Ins. Co., Newport Beach, 1982—. Co-author city ordnance Regulation of Ozone, Depleting Compounds, 1989-90; contbr. articles to newspaper. Fin. commr. City of Irvine, Calif., 1983-87, planning commr. 1987-88, city councilman, 1988-90; bd. dirs. Irvine Transp. Authority, 1988-90.; founding advisor Irvine Conservancy, advisor, 1986-88, Irvine Infrastructure Authority, 1988-90; founder San Joaquin Marsh Adv. Com., chair 1988-90. Recipient Sea and Sage Audubon Conservation award, 1990. Republican. Office: Pacific Mut Life Ins 700 Newport Center Dr Newport Beach CA 92660-6307

COSH, JOHN MORTON, bank executive; b. Mimico, Ont., Can., Dec. 28, 1924; s. George Morton and Margaret (Brown) C.; m. Marjorie Bernice Cosh, Apr. 20, 1952; children: George M., John Michael, Jayne Ann, Robert Alan. Cert. banking, U. Wis., 1971. Asst. cashier First Nat. Bank Vista, Calif., 1946-51; escrow officer, asst. mgr., mgr. security First Nat. Bank Vista, 1951-70; exec. v.p., pres., vice chmn. W. Coast Nat. Bank, 1970-77; pres. Palomar Ind. & Comml. Realtors Inc., 1977-83; v.p. Torrey Pines Bank, 1983—; apptd. to fee arbitration com. Calif. State Bar. Bd. dirs., past pres. Tri-City Hosp.; vice chmn. Oceanside Econ. Devel. Corp.; bd. dirs. Overall Econ. Devel. Commn. San Diego County; past pres. Greater San Luis Rey Council; past bd. dirs., chmn. guarantors fund North County Concert Assn.; vol. Vista Boys Club, founder, past. pres.; pres. Vista Boys Club Found.; life mem. San Luis Rey Council PTA's. Served with USAAF, 1943-46. Recipient Silver Keystone, Golden Boy, Bronze Medallion, Man Behind the Boy awards Boys Clubs Am.; named Disting. Citizen Jaycees, Man of Yr. North County Associated C. of C.'s, 1965, Banker of Yr. Am. Bankers Assn., 1984, Hon. Officer Vista League Cancer Socs. Mem. Vista Hist. Soc., Vista C. of C. (bd. dirs.), Indsl. Devel. Bond Authority (past chmn.), Vista Econ. Devel. Assn. (past chmn.), Elks, Lions, Masons, Rotary. Republican. Presbyterian. Home: 1638 Alta Vista Dr Vista CA 92084-5708

COSSUTTA, RENÉE CLAIRE, graphic designer; b. N.Y.C., Oct. 6, 1955; d. Araldo Alfred and Thelma Claire (Bouchet) C. BA, Smith Coll., 1978; MFA, Yale U., 1982. Carl P. Rollins fellow Yale U. Printing Svc., New Haven, 1980-81; graphic designer Sussman Prejza, L.A., 1983-84; ptnr. Lausten/Cossutta Design, L.A., 1984—; mem. faculty graphic design dept. Calif. Inst. Arts; lectr. in field. Work published in Communication Arts Design Ann., 1990. Recipient award Am. Inst. Graphic Arts, 1985, Art Dirs. Club L.A., 1987, 88, Am. Mus. Assn., 1987. Office: 1724 Redcliff St Los Angeles CA 90026-1132

COST, BRUCE, cooking educator, writer; b. Hackensack, N.J., June 12, 1945; s. Robert Bruce Wilson and Eva June (Cost) St. Thomas; m. Lynn Murphy, Apr. 23, 1966 (div. Jan. 1987); children: Eliza, Jennifer; m. Catherine Shen, Aug. 1, 1989; 1 child, Benjamin Shen. BA, Wesleyan U., Middletown, Conn., 1966; postgrad., New Sch., Parsons Sch. of Design, N.Y. State U. Tchr., cook, writer, 1968—; ptnr. Monsoon Restaurant, San Francisco, 1989-92; chef ann. Chinese New Year's banquet Chez Panisse, Berkeley, Calif.; tchr. Calif. Culinary Acad., Mary Risely's Tante Marie; cooking demonstrator at De Gustibus at Macy's, N.Y.C., Food & Wine's ann. festival, Aspen, Colo.; lectr. on Asian food and history Smithsonian Inst., Washington, San Francisco Acad. Scis., U. Calif., Berkeley; panelist at food and nutrition confs. Author: Ginger East to West, 1984, Bruce Cost's Asian Ingredients, 1988; columnist for San Francisco Chronicle, Washington Post; contbr. articles to Food and Wine, Cook's, Cuisine Mag., Jour. of Gastronomy. Monsoon Restaurant named one of 6 Four-Star restaurants in Bay Area, San Francisco Chronicle, Best Chef in Calif. nominee James Beard awards. Home: 2985 Pacific Ave Apt 10 San Francisco CA 94115-1067

COST, JAMES PETER, artist; b. Phila., Mar. 3, 1923; s. Peter and Rose (Perry) C.; children: Curtis, Shelley, Janet, Nancy. B.A., U. Calif. at Los Angeles, 1950; M.S., U. So. Calif., 1959. Tchr. art Los Angeles City Sch. Dist., 14 years; lectr. art Northwood Insts., Midland, Mich., Dallas, 1971; mem. faculty of art Principia Coll., 1975. One-man shows, Northwood Inst., Midland, 1971, R.W. Norton Gallery, Shreveport, La., 1971; exhibited in group shows at, Artists Guild Gallery Am., Carmel, 1961-63, James Peter Cost Gallery, (1964), Mus. Fine Arts, Springfield, Mass., 1965, 73, Nat. Arts Club, N.Y.C., 1966; represented in permanent collection, R.W. Norton Mus., Shreveport, also numerous pvt. collections; commd. 12 paintings for golf courses, Kobe, Osaka and Tokyo, Japan, 1986-87. Pres. Carmel Bus. Assn., 1970, Republican candidate for La. State Assembly, 1982. Served with USCGR, 1942-45. Recipient gold medal Franklin Mint, 1973. Republican. Christian Scientist. Studio: 85 Heaaula St Haiku HI 96708-5903

COSTA, VINCENZO FRANCESCO, engineer; b. Santa Cruz, Calif., Jan. 7, 1956; s. Francesco Vincenzo Costa. BSME, U. Calif., Santa Barbara, 1980, MSME, 1981. Pres. Aluminum Unltd., Santa Clara, Calif., 1974-77; rider Cobar Racing, Sacramento, 1982-87; engr. Lockheed Missiles and Space Co., Sunnyvale, Calif., 1987-89; pres. Tigra, Milpitas, Calif., 1989—; explorer Triceratops Expeditions, Africa, 1982; cons. Mitek Med., San Jose, Calif., 1994; expert witness Boccada Law Firm, San Jose, 1986. Author: Suspension Set Up, 1990, Dinosaur Safari Guide, 1994, (photographs) Images from the Past, 1993; patentee in field. Recipient Most Creative Design award AIAA, 1981; Formula 1 Champion, AFM, 1985, 86, 750 Champion, AFM, 1985. Office: Tigra 449 Glenmoor Milpitas CA 95035

COSTA, WALTER HENRY, architect; b. Oakland, Calif., July 2, 1924; s. Walter H.F. and Mamie R. (Dunkle) C.; m. Jane Elisabeth Ledwich, Aug. 28, 1948; 1 dau., Laura. B.A., U. Calif., Berkeley, 1948, M.A., 1949. Designer Mario Corbett (architect), San Francisco, 1947-48, Ernst Born (architect), San Francisco, 1949; draftsman Milton Pflueger, San Francisco, 1950-51; designer Skidmore, Owings & Merrill, San Francisco, 1951-57, participating assoc., then assoc. ptnr., 1957-69, gen. prtnr., 1969-89, ret., 1990. Bd. dirs. East Bay Regional Park Dist., 1977-87, pres., 1984-85; mem. city council, Lafayette, Calif., 1972-76, mayor, 1973. Served with USSNR, 1943-46. Fellow AIA. Clubs: Olympic (San Francisco), Univ. (San Francisco), Lakeview (Oakland, Calif.). Home: 1264 Redwood Ln Lafayette CA 94549-2416 Office: Skidmore Owings & Merrill 333 Bush St San Francisco CA 94104-2806

COSTAMANGA, GARY, fire chief; b. Sacramento, Calif.. Office: Sacramento Fire Dept 1231 I St Ste 401 Sacramento CA 95814*

COSTANZO, PATRICK M., constuction executive. Sr. v.p., asst. sec. Granite Constrn. Inc., Watsonville, Calif. Office: Granite Construction Inc PO Box 50085 Watsonville CA 95077-5085*

COSTARINO, F. THOMAS, naval officer; b. Bklyn., Dec. 4, 1943; s. Frank T. and Eileen Marie (Maher) C.; m. Judy Beth Wilson, Jan. 31, 1976; 1 child, Jennifer Anne. BA, C.W. Post Coll., 1968; MA, U.S. Navy Postgrad. Sch., 1981. Enlisted U.S. Navy, 1969; patrol boat command Coastal Divsn. 13, 1969; naval spl. warfare group Dir. Intelligence, Coronado, Calif., 1970-74; asst. intelligence officer U.S.S. Kitty Hawk, 1974-76, Pacific Naval Air Force, San Diego, 1976-79; intelligence officer U.S.S. Kitty Hawk, 1981-84; commanding officer Naval Intelligence Sch., Key West, Fla., 1984-87; asst. chief staff intelligence Cmdr. Carrier Group One, 1987-89, Pacific Naval Air Force, San Diego, 1989-92; dir. intelligence Naval Strike Warfare Ctr., Fallon, Nev., 1992—. Recipient Bronze star U.S. Navy, 1969, Purple Heart, 1969, meritorious svc. medals, 1984, 87, 89, 92, Navy commendation medals, 1969, 84. Roman Catholic. Office: Naval Strike Warfare Ctr Fallon NV 89406

COSTA-ZALESSOW, NATALIA, foreign language educator; b. Kumanovo, Macedonia, Dec. 5, 1936; came to the U.S., 1951; d. Alexander P. and Katarina (Duric) Z.; m. Gustavo Costa, June 8, 1963; 1 child, Dora. BA in Italian, U. Calif., Berkeley, 1959, MA in Italian, 1961, PhD in Romance Langs. and Lits., 1967. Tchg. asst. U. Calif., Berkeley, 1959-63; instr. Mills Coll., Oakland, Calif., 1963; asst. prof. San Francisco (Calif.) State U., 1968-74, assoc. prof., 1974-79, prof., 1979—. Author: Scrittrici italiane dal XIII al XX secolo; Testi e critica, 1982; contbr. articles to profl publs. Sidney M. Ehrman scholar U. Calif., Berkeley, 1957-58, Gamma Phi Beta scholar U. Calif., Berkeley, 1958, Herbert H. Vaughan scholar U. Calif., Berkeley, 1959-60, Advanced Grad. Traveling fellow in romance lang. and lit. U. Calif., Berkeley, 1964-65. Mem. MLA, Am. Assn. Tchrs. Italian, Renaissance Soc. Am., Dante Soc. Am., Croatian Acad. Am. Roman Catholic. Office: Dept Fgn Lang & Lit San Francisco State Univ San Francisco CA 94132

COSTEA, ILEANA, civil engineer, educator, consultant, researcher; b. Bucuresti, Romania, May 20, 1947; came to U.S., 1973.; d. Paul and Ana (Ciumetti) Paunescu; m. Nicolas Vincent Costea, Apr. 20, 1973. MArch, Ion Mincu Inst., Bucuresti, 1972; MA in Indsl. Design, UCLA, 1974, PhD in Engring., 1982. Chief teaching asst. UCLA, 1981; scientist ground systems analysis sect. Hughes Aircraft Co., Fullerton, Calif., 1982; lectr. dept. mgmt. sci. Sch. Bus. Adminstrn. Calif. State U., Northridge, 1982-83; cons. CAE Office vehicle engring. div. Aerospace Corp., El Segundo, Calif., 1984; sr. scientist, cons. Perceptronics, Inc., Woodland Hills, Calif., 1985; asst. prof. dept. civil and indsl. engring. Calif. State U., Northridge, 1983-86; cons. Jet Propulsion Lab. Calif. Inst. Tech., Pasadena, 1986-87, assoc. prof. dept. civil and indsl. engring. and mechanics, 1986-89, prof. dept. civil and indsl. engring. and applied mech., 1989—; vis. prof. U. Calif., Davis, 1980, U. Metz, France, 1989-93, U. Claude Bernard, Lyon, France, U. Metz, U. Catholique de l'Ouest, Angers. France, Inst. Français du Petrole, France, Rueil Malmaison, France, 1989-93, Ecole Centrale de Lille, France, U. Milan, Italy, 1990-91; vis. rschr. Social Sci. Rsch. Inst., U. So. Calif., 1982. Author: Artificial Intelligence/Expert Systems/CAD/CAM and Computer Graphics; contbr. articles to profl. jours.; reviewer for NSF and IEEE Computer jours. Recipient Merit award San Fernando Valley Engrs.' Coun., 1986. Mem. AAAS, IEEE, AAUP, AIAA, Computer Soc. of IEEE, Nat. Computer Graphics Assn., Assn. for Computing Machinery, Inst. Mgmt. Sci., Ops. Rsch. Soc. Am., Calif. Faculty Assn., Am. Inst. for Decision Scis., Women in Sci. and Engring., Am. Assn. Artificial Intelligence, European Assn. for Computer Graphics, Am. Inst. Indsl. Engrs., Computer and Automated Systems Assn., Soc. Women Engrs. Home: 3651 Terrace View Dr Encino CA 91436-4019 Office: Calif State U 18111 Nordhoff St Northridge CA 91330-0001

COSTON, MALCOLM MCGREGOR, chemical engineer; b. Aug. 13, 1918; s. Walter Best and Grace Bell (Bourne) C.; m. Ruth Stengenga Coston, Nov. 15, 1941; children: Malcolm Bruce Coston, Elizabeth Anne Coston (Putnam). BSChemE, U. Mich., Ann Arbor, 1940; MSChemE, 1941. Dist. engr. Whiting Corp., Harvey, Ill., 1941-53; gen. mgr. Rodney Hunt Machine Co., Orange, Mass., 1953-55; dist. mgr. Whiting Corp., Harvey, Ill., 1955-81; cons. pvt. practice, Newport Beach, Calif., 1981-89; v.p. GLM Assocs., South Pasadena, Calif., 1989—; cons. GLM Assocs., South Pasadena, 1989—. Patentee: Special Crane Hook and Rigging, 1950. Mem. AIChE, Elks, U.S. Power Squadrons. Episcopalian. Home: 450 Belvue Ln Newport Beach CA 92661-1508 Office: GLM Assocs 823 Mission St South Pasadena CA 91030-3141

COTA, HAROLD MAURICE, educator; b. San Diego, Apr. 16, 1936. Educator engring. Calif. Poly. State U., Luis Obispo. Office: Calif Poly State U Dept Civil Environ Eng San Luis Obispo CA 93407

COTCHETT, JOHN CRAIG, obstetrician and gynecologist; b. N.Y.C., Sept. 21, 1948; s. John Pratt and Marilou (Gerhard) C.; m. Deborah Elizabeth Vallejo, Apr. 27, 1993; 1 child, Kyle. BA, U. Calif., Berkeley, 1970; MD, Northwestern U., Chgo., 1974. Intern Highland Hosp., Oakland, Calif., 1974-75; dir. emergency dept. Meml. Hosp., Modesto, Calif., 1975-78; resident in ob-gyn. Kaiser Hosp., San Francisco, 1978-81; pvt. practice ob-gyn. San Mateo, 1981—; chief dept. ob-gyn. Mills-Peninsula Hosps., San Mateo, 1991-93. Fellow ACOG; mem. Peninsula Gynecol. Soc., San Francisco Gynecol. Soc., San Mateo County Med. Soc., Calif. Med. Assn. Republican. Roman Catholic. Office: Ste 400 50 San Mateo Dr San Mateo CA 94401

COTCHETT, JOSEPH WINTERS, lawyer, author; b. Chgo., Jan. 6, 1939; s. Joseph Winters and Jean (Renaud) C.; children—Leslie F., Charles P., Rachael E., Quinn Carlyle, Camilla E. B.S. in Engring., Calif. Poly. Coll., 1960; LL.B., U. Calif. Hastings Coll. Law, 1964. Bar: Calif. 1965, D.C. 1980. Ptnr. Cotchett & Pitre, Burlingame, Calif., 1965—; mem. Calif. Jud. Coun., 1975-77, Calif. Commn. on Jud. Performance, 1985-89, Commn. 2020 Jud. Coun., 1991-94; select com. on jud. retirement, 1992—. Author: (with R. Cartwright) California Products Liability Actions, 1970, (with F. Haight) California Courtroom Evidence, 1972, (with A. Elkind) Federal Courtroom Evidence, 1976, (with Frank Rothman) Persuasive Opening Statements and Closing Arguments, 1988, (with Stephen Pizzo) The Ethics Gap, 1991, (with Gerald Uelmen) California Courtroom Evidence Foundations, 1993; contbr. articles to profl. jours. Chmn. San Mateo County Heart Assn., 1967; pres. San Mateo Boys and Girls Club, 1971; bd. dirs. U. Calif. Hastings Law Sch., 1981-93. With Intelligence Corps, U.S. Army, 1960-61; col. JAGC, USAR, ret. Fellow Am. Bar Found., Am. Bd. Trial Advs., Am. Coll. Trial Lawyers, Internat. Acad. Trial Lawyers, Internat. Soc. of Barristers, Nat. Bd. Trial Advs. (diplomate civil trial adv.), State Bar Calif. (gov. 1972-75). Clubs: Commonwealth, Press (San Francisco). Office: 840 Malcolm Rd Burlingame CA 94010-1401 also: Ste 1100 12100 Wilshire Blvd Los Angeles CA 90025-7111

COTÉ, RALPH WARREN, JR., retired mining engineer, nuclear engineer; b. Berkeley, Calif., Oct. 5, 1927; s. Ralph Warren and Clara Maria (Neves) C.; m. Lois Lydia Maddox, Aug. 8, 1950; children: Ralph Warren III, Michele Marie. BSME, N.Mex. Inst. Mining and Tech., 1952. Registered profl. nuclear engr., Calif. Resident engr. Am. Smelting and Refining Co., Page, Idaho, 1952-54; shift boss Bunker Hill Co., Kellogg, Idaho, 1954-57, gen. mine foreman, 1958-60; project engr. Union Carbide Nuclear Co., Grand Junction, Colo., 1957-58; shift supr. GE, Richland, Wash., 1960-63; shift supr. GE, Vallecitos, Calif., 1963-66, maintenance mgr., 1966-67; start-up shift supr. GE, San Jose, Calif., 1967-71; project start-up mgr. Bechtel Power Corp., San Francisco, 1971-89, retired, 1989. Served to 2d lt. U.S. Army and U.S. N.G., 1946-50. Mem. Am. Nuclear Soc., VFW. Republican. Home: 14610 W Sky Hawk Dr Sun City West AZ 85375-5925 Office: Bechtel Power Corp 50 Beale St San Francisco CA 94105-1813

COTE, RICHARD JAMES, pathologist, researcher; b. L.A., May 10, 1954; s. Richard Patrick and Kathrine (Bisbas) C.; m. Anne Louise Foxen, Feb. 8, 1992; children: Nicholas Foxen, Juliet Ann. BS in Biology, U. Calif., Irvine, 1976, BA in Chemistry, 1976; MD, U. Chgo., 1980. Diplomate Am. Coll. Pathologists. Intern in surgery U. Mich. Hosp., Ann Arbor, 1980-81; rsch. fellow, immunology Meml. Sloan-Kettering Cancer Ctr., N.Y.C., 1981-83; rsch. assoc., immunology Meml. Sloan-Kettering Hosp., N.Y.C., 1983-85, fellow, pathology, 1987-88, chief fellow, pathology, 1988-90; resident, pathology Cornell U. Med. Ctr., N.Y.C., 1985-87; asst. prof., pathology U. So. Calif., L.A., 1990-95, assoc. prof., 1995—; attending pathologist Kenneth Norris Cancer Ctr., L.A., 1990—; founder, dir. Impath Labs., N.Y.C., 1987—; scientific dir. Neoprobe Corp., Columbus, Ohio, 1992—. Author: Immunomicroscopy, 1994; contbr. scientific papers to profl. jours., book chpts. Patentee in field. Am. Cancer Soc. fellow, 1988; recipient rsch. grants, awards NIH, ACS, others, 1981—. Mem. Soc. for Basic Urologic Rsch., Internat. Soc. for Hematotherapy, Phi Beta Kappa. Office: U So Calif 1441 Eastlake Ave Los Angeles CA 90033-1048

COTÉ, ROBERT DEAN, social activist; b. Detroit, June 17, 1945; s. Robert Dean and Louise Marie (Sanger) C.; m. Susane Kinsmen, June 12, 1963 (div.); children: Shelle, Robert; m. Cherie Steinberg, Mar. 5, 1994. BSW, Hillsdale (Mich.) Coll., 1967; alcohol drug counselor degree, Colo. Dept. Health, 1984. Drug alcohol therapist Mile Stone Inc., Denver, 1980-83; founder, exec. dir. Step 13, Denver, 1983—; spkr. and cons. in field. Charter mem. Hertitage Found., Washington, 1990-94, Empower Am., Washington, 1993-94; mem. Hudson Internat. Inst., Indpls., 1993-94. Recipient Point of Light #540 award Pres. George Bush, Washington, 1991, commendation V.p. Dan Quayle, Washington, 1992, Achievement Against the Odds award Nat. Ctr. for Neighborhood Enterprise, 1993; Donner New Leadership fellow William Donner Found., N.Y.C., 1993. Mem. Sertoma Club (charter mem., Svc. to Mankind award 1990). Republican. Office: 2029 Larimer St Denver CO 80205-2014

COTLAR, MORTON, organizational scientist, educator; b. Phila., Feb. 19, 1928; s. Joseph and Henrietta B. (Klaits) C.; m. Gayle Epstein, Aug. 20, 1954; children: Geri Lynda, Gary Michael. B.S. in Mech. Engring., Drexel U., 1950, M.S. in Aero. Engring., 1955; Ph.D., U. Ga., 1969. Registered profl. engr. Engr., chief engr. Sunshine Sci. Instruments, Phila., 1953-56; sr. mgmt. engr. Sperry Rand, Great Neck, N.Y., 1956-67; adj. prof. systems mgmt. Poly. Inst. N.Y., N.Y.C., 1964-67; asst. prof. mgmt. U. Ga., Athens, 1967-70; prof., chmn. mgmt. dept. U. Hawaii, Honolulu, 1970-95, prof. emeritus, 1995—; L. J. Buchan Disting. prof. Colo. State U., 1977-78; vis. prof. Colo. State U., Fort Collins, 1974-75, 77-78, Boston U., 1981-82, U. Colo., Boulder, 1985; Dennis Ching Disting. prof., 1990; founder, exec. dir. Videodocumentary Clearinghouse; cons. comml. and instl. orgns.; lectr. mgmt. devel. programs. Author books jour. articles, monographs, films, videotapes in field. Mem. Acad. of Mgmt. (nat. officer 1975-76), Nat. Soc. Profl. Engrs., Acad. Ind. Scholars, Mensa, Beta Gamma Sigma (Nat. Disting. Prof. award), Phi Delta Kappa, Pi Tau Sigma. Home: Harbor Sq 700 Richards # 2201 Honolulu HI 96813

COTTER, JOHN CATLIN, marketing consultant; b. Monterey Park, Calif., Apr. 3, 1950; s. Frank Cotter and Duncanne (Kilday) Tyson; children: Chris, Lisa. BS in Mktg., Ariz. State U., 1972. Promotion mgr. Gillcable, San Jose, Calif., 1982-85; mktg. dir. Stas. KSJO/KHTT, San Jose, 1985-87, Heritage Cablevision, San Jose, 1987-89; mktg. cons. The Cotter Media Group, San Jose, 1989—.

COTTER, LAWRENCE RAFFETY, management consultant; b. Albany, Calif., Aug. 13, 1933; s. Malcolm Thompson Cotter and Una Elyse Raffety. AA, U. Calif., Berkeley, 1953, BA in Astronomy, 1956; MS in Bus. Adminstrn., The George Washington U., 1967; PhD in Mgmt. Theory, UCLA, 1977. Commd. 2nd lt. USAF, 1956, advanced through grades to col., 1975, ret., 1982; orbital analyst, network controller Project Space Track USAF, Bedford, Mass., 1958-61; staff scientist Hdqs. N.Am. Air Def. Command, Colorado Springs, Colo., 1962-66, Hdqrs. USAF, Washington, 1967-70; dir. test and deployment DEF. Support program USAF, Los Angeles, 1975-76; commdr. detachment 1 Electronic Systems Div. USAF, Tehran, Iran, 1976-78; system program dir. Electronic Systems div. USAF, Bedford, Mass., 1978-79; dep. commdr. network plans and devel. AF Satellite Control Facility USAF, Sunnyvale, Calif., 1979-82; mgmt. cons. Berkeley, 1982—; adminstrv. asst. Arnold Air Soc., Washington, 1959-72. Co-author: The Arnold Air Soc. Manual, 1956; (computer program) SPACE, 1970; editor: The Arnold Air Soc. Manual 1964-72. Recipient Departmental Citation U. Calif. Berkeley, 1955, Citation of Honor, Arnold Air Soc., 1967. Mem. AF Assn., The Royal AF Club, Beta Gamma Sigma.

COTTINGHAM, MARY PATRICIA, vocational rehabilitation counselor; b. Seattle, May 9, 1930; d. Carl Frank and Frances Mary (Keon) Fox; m. Ken Cottingham, Sept. 15, 1951 (div. Sept. 1982); children: Cathy Ann, David Carl, Susan Mary, Keith Bryan, Patricia Frances. BA, U. Wash., 1974, MEd in Psychology, 1977. Diplomate Am. Bd. Vocat. Experts; cert. mental health counselor, Wash.; cert. vocat. rehab. counselor, cons. Counselor Mental Health North, Seattle, 1974-77; vocat. rehab. counselor Counseling Svcs. Northwest, Lynnwood, Wash., 1977-79; owner, cons. People Systems Inc., Seattle, 1979—. Bd. dirs. King County Mental Health Bd., Seattle, 1982-84; guardian ad litem King County Juvenile Ct., Seattle, 1981-84. Mem. AACD, Am. Mental Health Counselors Assn., Nat. Rehab. Assn., Pvt. Rehab. Orgns. Wash. (sec. 1986-89), Wash. Mental Health Counselors Assn. (sec. 1983-85). Office: People Systems Inc 155 NE 100th St Ste 406 Seattle WA 98125-8012

COTTLE, CRAIG HANSEN, financial executive; b. Lewiston, Utah, July 11, 1943; s. Laurence Glen and Margaret (Hansen) C.; m. Sharon Elizabeth Dooley, June 25, 1969; children: Todd Alan, Sean Glen, Elizabeth Dawn, Jeremy Craig, Timothy Aaron, Darin Shea, Ayssa Shiree. BS, Weber State U., 1969; MBA, Utah State U., 1988. Cert. cash mgr. Tax acct. IRS, Ogden, Utah, 1967-69; staff acct. DelMonte Corp., San Francisco, 1969-71; fin. asst. to pres. Universal Distbg. Co., Sandy, Utah, 1971-72; staff acct. Hans Nievaard, CPA, Salt Lake City, Utah, 1972-73; contr. Master Lease, Inc., Salt Lake City, 1973-74; asst. treas. N.W. Energy Co., Salt Lake City, 1974-86; mgr. fin. resources Iomega Corp., Roy, Utah, 1986-87; asst. v.p. Key Bank of Utah, Salt Lake City, 1988; treas. Price Savers Wholesale Inc., Salt Lake City, 1989-91; pvt. practice fin. mgmt. cons. Kaysville, Utah, 1992—; exec. v.p., CFO VesCor Capital Corp., Ogden, Utah, 1992—. Aux. officer Utah Hwy. Patrol, Ogden, 1964-69; vol. fireman North Ogen Fire Dept., 1966-67; troop com. Boy Scouts of Am., Kaysville, 1978-88, explorer com. chmn., 1988-90. Mem. Treasury Mgmt. Assn. (bd. dirs. 1986-89, certification com. 1980-89), Treasury Mgmt. Assn. Utah (founder, pres. 1984-86), Nat. Risk and Ins. Mgmt. Soc., Risk and Ins. Mgmt. Soc. Utah. Republican. Mormon. Home: 293 Mourning Dove Cir Kaysville UT 84037

COTTRELL, JANET ANN, controller; b. Berea, Ohio, Dec. 2, 1943; d. Carmen and Hazel (French) Volpe; m. Melvin M. Cottrell, Mar. 2, 1963; children: Lori A., Gregory C. Student, Los Angeles State Coll., 1961-63. Lic. ins. agt., Calif. Loan processing Eastern Lenders, Covina, 1962-64; asst. bookkeeper Golden Rule Discount Stores, Rosemead, Calif., 1964-66; acctg. supr. Walter Carpet Mills, Industry, Calif., 1967-69; co-owner Motorcycle Specialties Co., Industry, 1969-78, Covina (Calif.) Kawasaki, 1978-84; v.p., contr. M.C. Specialties Inc., Covina, 1984—; v.p., controller Aviation Communications Inc., Covina, 1992—; active various coms. relating to promotion, safety and advancement of the recreational vehicle and auto industry, So. Calif., 1981—. Mem. com. Miss Covina Pageant, 1986—, presdl. task force, nat., 1982—, Rep. nat. com., 1986—. Mem. Covina C. of C., Calif. Motorcycle Dealers Assn., Nat. Auto Dealers Assn., Internat. Jet Ski Boating Assn. Republican. Office: Aviation Comm Inc 1025 W San Bernardino Rd Covina CA 91722-4106

COTTRELL, ROBERT CHARLES, history educator; b. Denver, Colo., Nov. 1, 1950; s. Robert and Sylvia (light) C.; m. Isabel Dolores Domenech; m. Susan Lou Phillips Cottrell, Aug. 12, 1989; 1 child, Jordan Alexandra. BA with honors, U. Tex., 1973; MA, U. Tex., Arlington, 1977; PhD, U. Okla., 1983; JD, Calif. No. Sch. Law, Chico, 1995. Instr. U. Okla.,

Norman, 1983-84; asst. prof. Calif. State U., Chico, 1984-89, assoc. prof., 1989-94, prof. History and Am. Studies, 1994—; adj. prof. of History Okla. City. C. C., 1980-84. Author: Izzy: A Biography of I.F. Stone, 1993; contbr. articles to profl. jours., essays to books. Grantee Am. Philos. Soc., 1993; recipient Muriel H. Wright award Okla. State Hist. Soc., 1984, Calif. State U. profl. achievement award, 1994, rsch. award, 1994; NEH summer stipend. Mem. Ogrn. Am. Historians, Phi Alpha Theta. Democrat. Jewish. Office: Calif State U Dept of History Chico CA 95929-0735

COUCH, JOHN CHARLES, diversified company executive; b. Bremerton, Wash., May 10, 1939; s. Richard Bailey and Frances Harriet (Gilmore) C. BS in Engring., U. Mich., 1963, MS, 1964; MBA, Stanford U., 1976. With Ingalls Shipbldg. div. Litton Industries, 1967-74; asst. to sr. v.p. engring. and marine ops. Matson Navigation Co. subs. Alexander and Baldwin., San Francisco, 1976-78; v.p. Matson Navigation Co., 1978-84; exec. v.p., chief operating officer Matson Navigation Co. subs. Alexander and Baldwin., San Francisco, 1984; pres., chief operating officer Matson Navigation Co., 1985, Alexander and Baldwin Inc., Honolulu, 1991—; pres., chief exec. officer Alexander & Baldwin, Inc., Honolulu, 1992-95, chmn., pres., CEO, 1995—; bd. dirs. A&B Devel. Co., Calif., A&B Properties, Inc., East Maui Irrigation Co., Ltd., Kahului Trucking & Storage, Inc., McBryde Sugar Co., Ltd., Ohanui Corp., WDCI Inc., Calif. and Hawaiian Sugar Co., First Hawaiian Bank, First Hawaiian Inc., Hawaiian Sugar Transp. Co., Inc., A&B Hawaii, Inc., Alexander & Baldwin, Inc., McBryde Farms, Inc., Kauai Comml. Co., Inc., Kukuiula Devel. Co., Inc., Matson Navigation Co., Inc., South Shore Community Svcs., Inc., South Shore Resources, Inc. Mem. Maui Econ. Devel. Bd., 1986—; mem. exec. bd. Aloha coun. Boy Scouts Am., 1986—; bd. dirs., mem. exec. com. Aloha United Way, 1988, campaign chmn., 1988, chmn. bd. dirs. Mem. Hawaiian Sugar Planters' Assn. (bd. dirs.), C. of C. of Hawaii (bd. dirs. 1986—), Hawaii Maritime Ctr. (vice-chmn. 1988-89, chmn. 1990—), Honolulu Club, Oahu Country Club, Plaza Club. Office: Alexander & Baldwin Inc PO Box 3440 822 Bishop St Honolulu HI 96813-3925

COUGER, JAMES DANIEL, computer scientist, writer; b. Olney, Tex., Oct. 20, 1929; s. James Leroy R. and Faye S. (Saylors) C.; m. Shirley Anne Thomas, Mar. 4, 1951; children: Daniel Ray, Todd David, Timothy Lee, Julie Anne. BA, Phillips U., 1951, MA; PhD, U. Colo., 1964. Supr. indsl. engring. Hallmark Cards Inc., 1953-58; chief computer plans and controls Martin-Marietta Corp, 1958-65; disting. prof. computer and mgmt. sci. U. Colo., Colorado Springs, 1965—; dir. Ctr. for Rsch. on Creativity and Innovation, 1988—; cons. to IBM, Hewlett Packard Co.; mem. affiliate faculty Japan Am. Inst. Mgmt. Sci., 1973-83; lectr. U.S. and abroad. Author: Fortran IV: A Programmed Instruction Approach, 1968, System Analysis Techniques, 1974, Introduction to Computer-Based Information Systems, 1975, First Course in Data Processing, 1977, Guidelines for Small Business Computer Selection, 1978, Motivation and Management of Computer Personnel, 1980, Advanced System Development and Feasibility Techniques, 1982, Motivation of Maintenance Programmers, 1985, Creative Problem Solving and Opportunity Finding, 1995, Creativity/Innovation in I.S. Organizations, 1995; editor: Wiley Series on Business Data Processing, 1965-80, Computing Newsletter for Schools of Business, 1967-85; columnist Computerworld, 1970-80; contbr. articles to profl. jours. Cubmaster Denver area coun. Boy Scouts Am., 1965-66; chmn. new ch. devel. Christian Chs. of Colo. and Wyo., 1969-71; pres. Gethsemane Christian Ch., Colorado Springs, 1972-73. Lt. USAF, 1951-53. Recipient Disting. Faculty award U. Colo., 1976, 80, Chancellor's award U. Colo., 1977, Outstanding Individual Achievement award Colorado Springs C. of C., 1977. Fellow Am. Inst. Decision Scis. (v.p.); mem. Assn. for Computing Machinery (chmn. lectureship series), Assn. for Systems Mgmt. (mem. edn. com., Disting. Svc. award 1966), Soc. for Mgmt. Systems (sec.), Data Processing Mgmt. Assn. (U.S. Computer Sci. Man of Yr. award 1977, U.S. Info. Systems Educator of Yr. award 1993), Assn. Computer Programmers and Analysts (Disting. Svc. award 1979). Republican. Presbyterian. Home: 2611 Northridge Dr Colorado Springs CO 80918-4317 Office: U Colorado Austin Bluff Pky Colorado Springs CO 80933-7150

COUGHENOUR, JOHN CLARE, federal judge; b. Pittsburg, Kans., July 27, 1941; s. Owren M. and Margaret E. (Widner) C.; m. Gwendolyn A. Kieffaber, June 1, 1963; children: Jeffrey, Douglas, Marta. B.S., Kans. State Coll., 1963; J.D., U. Iowa, 1966. Bar: Iowa 1963, D.C. 1963, U.S. Dist. Ct. (we. dist.) Wash. 1966. Ptnr. Bogle & Gates, Seattle, 1966-81; vis. asst. prof. law U. Washington, Seattle, 1970-73; judge U.S. Dist. Ct. (we. dist.) Wash., Seattle, 1981—. Mem. Iowa State Bar Assn., Wash. State Bar Assn. Home: 4305 NE 38th St Seattle WA 98105-5403 Office: US Dist Ct 609 US Courthouse 1010 5th Ave Seattle WA 98104-1130*

COULTER, CHRISTOPHER HARVEY, physician, healthcare executive; b. Rahway, N.J., Feb. 23, 1952; s. Harvey Franklin and Doris Lilliam (Collins) C. BA, Yale U., 1974; MD, U. Va., 1978; MPH, Johns Hopkins U., 1988. Diplomate Am. Bd. Internal Medicine, Am. Bd. Geriatrics, Am. Bd. Med. Mgmt. Intern, resident Georgetown Univ. Hosp., Washington, 1978-81; attending physician Bon Secours Hosp., Balt., 1981-87; med. dir. Schick Shadel Hosp., Santa Barbara, Calif., 1987-89, FHP, Fountain Valley, Calif., 1989-91; chief med. officer UltraLink, Costa Mesa, Calif., 1991—; surveyor Nat. Com. for Quality Assurance, Washington, 1993—. Mem. editorial bd. Managed Care Medicine, 1994; contbr. articles to profl. jours. Fellow Am. Coll. Physician Execs. Democrat. Office: UltraLink 3515 Harbor Blvd Costa Mesa CA 92626-1437

COULTER, CLARK, company executive; b. Detroit, May 10, 1946; s. Damon Lewis and Elijah Williams Brown; m. Elaina Reese, Mar. 10, 1986; children: Rastus J., Moriah, Luke. BA, Mich. State U.; PhD (hon.), Bapt. Bible Coll., 1991. Pres., prin. N.W. Peterbilt, Billings, Mont. Author: How to Use Government to Your Advantage, 1991. Pres. Mont. NAACP, Billings, 1993. Office: NW Truck Trailer Sales PO Box 2511 Billings MT 59103-2511

COULTER, GEORGE PROTHRO, retired lawyer, real estate executive; b. El Dorado, Ark., June 8, 1930; s. Edward Herbert Sr. and Estella Martha (Prothro) C.; m. Gloria Phyllis Cohn, Dec. 28, 1952; children: Craig R., Christopher N., Cameron M. AB, UCLA, 1951; JD, George Washington U., 1957; postgrad., U. So. Calif., 1958-59. With Nat. Security Agy., Washington, 1955-57; assoc. Gordon & Weinberg, L.A., 1958-63; ptnr. Coulter & Coulter, L.A., 1963-68; prin. Coulter, Vernoff & Pearson, Pasadena, Calif., 1968-94, of counsel, 1982-94; CEO Parade Properties, Inc., L.A., 1965-84; gen. ptnr. Welsh Hill Orgn., Temecula Valley, 1980—; cons. CLE, State Bar of Calif., 1982-83;. Pres., trustee Neighborhood Improvement Assn., Altadena, Calif., 1980-82; trustee Westminster Ctr., Pasadena, 1982—, pres., 1992; bd. dirs. Altadena Heritage, 1992—; trustee House of Rest Found., 1992. Lt. USN, 1951-56, Korea. Mem. Nat. Genealogical Soc., Honourable Soc. Cymmrodorion, Assn. Profl. Genealogists, Soc. Genealogists. Presbyterian.

COUNELIS, JAMES STEVE, education educator; b. Streator, Ill., June 26, 1927; s. Steve and Mary (Drivas) C.; m. Anna Catherine Marakas, Nov. 25, 1962; children: Steven George, George James. AA, Chgo. City Jr. Coll., 1948; AM, U. Chgo., 1951, PhD, 1961. Cert. high sch., jr. coll. tchr., pub. sch. principal, Ill. High sch. tchr. Chgo. Pub. Schs., 1951-55; asst. prof. history and social scis. Chgo. City Jr. Coll., Woodrow Wilson br., 1955-62, dir. evening program, 1962-64; asst. prof. edn. Chgo Tchrs. Coll., 1964-66; assoc. prof. edn. Pa. State U., University Park, 1966-67; sr. adminstrv. analyst U. Calif., Berkeley, 1968-70; prof. edn. U. San Francisco, 1970—, dir. instl. studies and mgmt. info. systems, 1971-75, coord. evaluation Sch. Edn., 1986-90, chmn. orgn. and leadership program, 1989-91. Author, editor: To Be A Phoenix: The Education Professoriate, 1969; author: Higher Learning and Orthodox Christianity, 1990, Inheritance and Change in Orthodox Christianity, 1995; contbr. articles, revs. and papers to profl. publs. pres., trustee Greek Orthodox Cathedral of the Ascension, Oakland, Calif., 1973; pres. Hellenic Am. Profl. Soc., San Francisco, 1974, 75; trustee Hellenic Coll./Holy Cross, 1951-53, trustee, 1982-86; mem. Calif. Council on Criminal Justice, 1987; bd. dirs. Paul Wattson Lecture series, 1989. Served with Signal Corps, U.S. Army, 1946-47. Recipient Archon Chartoularius (honoris causa) award Ecumenical Patriarchate Constantinople and New Rome, 1976, Norbert Wiener award The World Orgn. Gen. Systems and Cybernetics, 1978, Scholar U. Chgo., 1951-52, 60-61, Pacific Sch. Religion, 1958; U. Calif. grantee, Berkeley, 1962; Coolidge Rsch. fellow Andover-Newton Theol. Sch., 1985, Wayne J. Doyle Rsch. award, 1986, Hellenic Coun. on Edn. award for scholarship and univ. teaching, 1991. Mem. AAAS, Am. Assn. Artificial Intelligence, Am. Assn. Higher Edn., Am. Assn. Instnl. Rsch., Am. Ednl. Rsch. Assn., Am. Ednl. Studies Assn., Internat. Soc. System Scis., Hellenic Am. Profl. Soc. (Axion award 1982), Hellenic Coun. on Edn. (award for Scholarship and University Teaching 1991), Orthodox Theol. Soc. Am., U. San Francisco Faculty Assn., Mensa, Gold Key, Phi Delta Kappa (U. San Francisco chpt. v.p. for programs 1990-91, pres. 1991-92). Office: U San Francisco Sch Edn San Francisco CA 94117-1080

COUNSELL, ANN BERNER, academic administrator; b. Chgo., Aug. 2, 1960; d. Carl Frederick and Rosemary (Davis) B.; m. Richard Clay Counsell, Sept. 7, 1992; 1 child, Alyson Rose. Student, U. London, 1981; BA, Whitman Coll., 1982; MS, U. Oreg., 1988. Chpt. cons. Kappa Alpha Theta, Indpls., 1982-83; resident counselor Kappa Alpha Theta, Providence, R.I., 1983-84; asst. to the dean of students U. Oreg., Eugene, 1984-88; acting dir. of devel. Eastside Cath. High Sch., Bellevue, Wash., 1988-89; dir. devel. Forest Ridge Sch., Bellevue, 1989-90; assoc. v.p. for devel. Whitman Coll., Walla Walla, Wash., 1990-92; dir. of devel. Villa Acad., Seattle, Wash., 1992—. Mem. PEO, Bellevue, 1981-85, Eugene, 1985-88; vol. Whitman Coll. Admissions, Redmond, Wash., 1988-90, Make-A-Wish Found., Seattle, 1991-92. Mem. Kappa Alpha Theta Seattle Alumnae Assn. (Ann D. Bern award 1984, adv. bd. 1989-90), N.W. Devel. Officers Assn. Home: 6019 143rd Ct NE Redmond WA 98052-4674 Office: Villa Acad 5001 NE 50th Seattle WA 98105

COUNSIL, WILLIAM GLENN, electric utility executive; b. Detroit, Dec. 13, 1937; s. Glenn Dempsey and Jean Beverly (Rzepecki) C.; m. Donna Elizabeth Robinson, Sept. 10, 1960; children: Glenn, Craig. Student, U. Mich., 1955-56; BS, U.S. Naval Acad., 1960; Advanced Mgmt. Program, Harvard U., 1991. Ops. supr., asst. plant supt.. sta. supt. N.E. Nuclear Energy Co., Waterford, Conn., 1967-76; project mgr., v.p. nuclear engring. and ops. N.E. Utilities, Hartford, Conn., 1976-80, sr. v.p. nuclear engring. and ops., 1980-85; exec. v.p. nuclear engring. and ops., electric-generating div. Tex. Utilities Generating Co., 1985-88; vice chmn. Tex. Utilities Electric Co., 1989-93; mng. dir. Wash. Pub. Power Supply System, Richland, 1993—. With USN, 1956-67. Recipient Outstanding Leadership award ASME, 1986. Republican. Presbyterian. Home: 3806 W 40th Pl Kennewick WA 99337-2603 Office: Wash Pub Power Supply System 3000 George Washington Way Richland WA 99352-1617

COURNOYEA, NELLIE J., Canadian government official; b. Aklavik, N.W.T., Canada, 1940; div.; 2 children: John, Maureen. Radio announcer, later regional mgr. CBC, Inuvik, N.W.T.; negotiator, Com. for Original People's Entitlement; mem. territorial legislature Yellowknife, 1984—; minister of renewable resources, and of culture and communications, 1983-85, minister various portfolios, from 1987, govt. leader, 1991—; now premier N.W.T. Yellowknife. Office: Office of the Premier, PO Box 1320, Yellowknife, NT Canada X1A 2L9*

COURT, ARNOLD, climatologist; b. Seattle, June 20, 1914; s. Nathan Altshiller and Sophie (Ravitch) C.; m. Corinne H. Feibelman, May 27, 1941 (dec. Feb. 1984); children: David, Lois, Ellen; m. Mildred Futor Berry, Apr. 6, 1988. BA, U. Okla., 1934; postgrad., U. Wash., 1938, MS, 1949; PhD, U. Calif., Berkeley, 1956. Reporter and city editor Duncan (Okla.) Banner, 1935-38; observer, meteorologist U.S. Weather Bur., Albuquerque, Washington, Little Am., Los Angeles, 1938-43; chief meteorologist U.S. Antarctic Service, 1939-41; climatologist office Q.M. Gen. U.S. Army, Washington, 1946-51; research meteorologist U. Calif., Berkeley, 1951-56; meteorologist U.S. Forest Service, Berkeley, 1956-60; chief applied climatology, Cambridge Research Labs. USAF, Bedford, Mass., 1960-62; sr. scientist Lockheed-Calif. Co., Burbank, 1962-65; prof. climatology San Fernando Valley State Coll. (now Calif. State U.), Northridge, 1962-85, chmn. dept. geography, 1970-72, prof. emeritus, 1985—; part-time prof. Calif. State U., Northridge, 1986-87, UCLA, 1987-90. Editor: Eclectic Climatology, 1968; assoc. editor Jour. Applied Meteorology, 1978-88; chmn. editorial bd. Jour. Weather Modification, 1978-86; contbr. articles and revs. to profl. jours. Served to 1st lt. USAAF, 1943-46. Recipient Spl. Congl. medal, 1944. Fellow AAAS, Am. Meteorol. Soc., Royal Meteorol. Soc.; mem. Am. Geophys. Union (life), Am. Statis. Assn., Assn. Am. Geographers, Assn. Pacific Coast Geographers (pres. 1978-79), Calif. Geog. Soc., Weather Modification Assn. (trustee 1973-76), Western Snow Conf., Sigma Xi, Phi Beta Kappa. Home: 17168 Septo St Northridge CA 91325-1672 Office: Calif State U Dept Geography Northridge CA 91330

COURTNEY, ANGELA, veterinarian, researcher; b. L.A., Jan. 25, 1963; d. Walter James and Betty Jean (Stout) C. AS, AS Pierce Coll., 1980; DVM, Miss. State U., 1992. Med. lic. Calif., Fla. Extern Johns Hopkins Sch. of Medicine, 1992; animal health tech. rsch. asst. Letterman Army Inst. of Rsch., San Francisco, 1983-85; emergency animal tech. Calif. Animal Hosp., L.A., 1986; sr. clinician Cen. Orange County Emergency Animal Clinic, Newport Beach, Calif., 1992—; veterinary cons. Healthy PetsInc., La Habra, Calif., 1993—. With U.S. Army, 1983-85. Mem. Am. Veternary Med. Assn., Am. Acad. Scis., N.Y. Acad. Scis. Home: 24 Balise Ln Foothill Ranch CA 92610 Office: Orange Canyon Pet Clinic Emergency Animal Clinic 7614 E Chapman Ave Orange CA 92669

COURTNEY, RICHARD HOWARD, economist; b. Marion, Ohio, Jan. 2, 1938; s. Lawrence Eugene and Lyda Mae (Long) C.; m. Nancy Williams (div.); children: David Howard, Richard Craig; m. Victoria Black, Nov. 28, 1987. BSc, Ohio State U., 1963, MSc, 1964; PhD, U. Calif., Berkeley, 1968. CFP. Agrl. economist U. Calif. Agrl. Experiment Sta., Berkeley, 1968-74; assoc. prof. econs. U. Fla., Gainesville, 1974-75; economist Bank of Am., San Francisco, 1975—; instr. St. Mary's Coll. of Calif., Moraga, 1991—. Mem. steering com. Bay Area Econ. Forum, San Francisco, 1990-93. Mem. Nat. Assn. Bus. Economists. Office: Bank of Am 555 California St San Francisco CA 94104-1502

COURTRIGHT, MORRIS, electrical engineer and educator; b. Saginaw, Mich., May 2, 1930; s. Morris Alexander and Helen Esther (Gould) C.; m. Phyllis Joanne Jones, Mar. 2, 1952 (div. Mar. 1988); children: Helen, Patricia, Pamela, Mike, Deborah, Elaine, Eileen, David, Kathy, Gregory, Brenda; m. Barbara Jean Grzeczka, Aug. 15, 1989. BSEE, U. Colo., 1963; MSEE, Columbia Pacific Coll., San Rafael, Calif., 1986, PhD, 1987. Registered profl. engr., Ariz., Calif., N.Mex. Commd. 2d lt. USAF, 1956, advanced through grades to maj., 1966; cons. engr. Phoenix, Ariz., 1970—; tchr. Gateway Cmty. Coll., Phoenix, 1983-94, Eastern Ariz. Coll., Payson, 1994-95. Author/editor Broadcast Engring., 1968-76. Rep. Ariz. State Legis., Phoenix, 1979-82. Decorated Air Force Commendation medal; recipient Dept. of Def. Commendation, 1965. Mem. Soc. Broadcast Engrs. (nat. dir.), Assn. Fed. Comms. Cons. Engrs., Nat. Assn. Elec. Inspectors, Elks (sec. 1986—), KC (state dep.). Republican. Roman Catholic. Home: HC 1 Box 226 Strawberry AZ 85544-9701 Office: Courtright Engring 132 E Criswold Rd Phoenix AZ 85020

COUSE, R. D., construction company executive; b. 1947. BSME, Wash. State U. With Bechtel Constrn. Co., San Francisco, 1969—, now pres. Office: Bechtel Construction Co 50 Beale St San Francisco CA 94105-1813*

COUSINS, RICHARD FRANCIS, diversified financial services company executive; b. Oceanside, N.Y., Feb. 11, 1955; s. Richard Felix and Hedwig (Kobierec) C.; m. Alice Annette Arant, Sept. 3, 1977; 1 child, Kathryn. BA, Georgetown U., 1977; MBA in Acctg., NYU, 1987. Project analyst European div. Citibank, N.Y.C., 1977-78, fin. analyst, 1978-79, fin. mgr., 1979-80, project leader, bus. mgr., 1980-83; dir. opns. Merrill Lynch Hubbard, N.Y.C., 1983-85; sr. grad. asst. NYU Grad. Sch. Bus., N.Y.C., 1985-86; sr. systems cons. Am. Express, N.Y.C., 1986-88; mgr. strategic opns. Am. Express, Phoenix, 1988-92, project advisor, 1992—. Home: PO Box 43438 Phoenix AZ 85080-3438 Office: Am Express 6225 N 24th St Phoenix AZ 85016-2034

COUTURE, RICHARD EDMUND, tax auditor; b. Bay City, Mich., Nov. 30, 1950; s. Alfred Daniel Sr. and Florence Elaine (Beaumont) C. Student, Northeastern Sch. Commerce, 1970; BS in Acctg., Ferris State U., 1972. Acct. Victor H. Arida & Co., Tucson, 1973-75; field auditor I City of Tucson, 1975-76, field auditor II, 1976-79, field auditor III, 1979-88, prin. auditor, 1988—. Mem. Am. Coaster Enthusiasts. Home: 1710 S Kevin Dr Tucson AZ 85748-7454 Office: City of Tucson 255 W Alameda St Tucson AZ 85701-1303

COVER, THOMAS M., statistician, electrical engineer, educator; b. San Bernardino, Calif., Aug. 7, 1938; s. William Llewellyn and Carolyn (Merrill) C.; m. Sandra Detert, June 8, 1968 (div. 1972); 1 child, William. BS in Physics, MIT, 1960; MS in EE, Stanford U., 1961, PhD in EE, 1964. Asst. prof. elec. engring. Stanford (Calif.) U., 1964-67, assoc. prof., 1967-71, assoc. prof. elec. engring. and statistics, 1972-73, prof., 1973—, lab. dir. info. systems elec. engring., 1989—, Kwoh-Ting Li Prof. Engring., 1994; vis. assoc. prof. elec. engring. MIT, Cambridge, 1971-72. Author: Elements of Information Theory, 1991; editor: Open Problems in Communication and Computation, 1987; contbr. over 100 articles to profl. jours. Vinton Hayes fellow Harvard U., 1971-72. Fellow AAAS, IEEE (pres. info. theory soc. 1972, Shannon lectr. 1990, Outstanding Paper prize 1972), Inst. Math. Stats.; mem. Soc. for Indsl. and Applied Math., Nat. Acad. Engring. Office: Stanford U Dept Elec Engring & Stats Durand # 121 Stanford CA 94305

COVINGTON, ROBERT EDWARD, mining executive, geologist; b. Waterloo, Iowa, Mar. 24, 1921; s. Rex and Jeanne Marie Stephens C. BA in Geology, U Colo., 1947. Geologist Phillips Petroleum Co., Alvin, Tex., 1947, Carter Oil Co., Vernal, Utah, 1948-49; cons. and ptnr. Caldwell & Covington, Vernal, 1949-64; sec.-treas., mgr. exploration Hiko Bell Mining & Oil Co., Vernal, 1964—. Contbr. articles to profl. jours. With USN, 1942-45. Fellow AAAS; mem. Am. Inst. Profl. Geologists, Am. Assn. Petroleum Geologists, Geol. Soc. Am., Sigma Gamma Epsilon. Office: Hiko Bell Mining & Oil Co PO Box 1845 Vernal UT 84078-5845

COVINGTON, STEPHANIE STEWART, psychotherapist, writer, educator; b. Whittier, Calif., Nov. 5, 1942; d. William and Bette (Robertson) Stewart; children: Richard, Kim. BA cum laude, U. So. Calif., 1963; MSW, Columbia U., 1970; PhD, Union Inst., 1982. Pvt. practice psychotherapy, co-dir. Inst. for Relational Devel., La Jolla, Calif., 1981—; instr. U. Calif., San Diego, 1981—, Calif. Sch. Profl. Psychology, San Diego, 1982-88, San Diego State U., 1982-84, Southwestern Sch. Behavioral Health Studies, 1982-84, Profl. Sch. Humanistic Psychology, San Diego, 1983-84, U.S. Internat. U., San Diego, 1983-84, UCLA, 1983-84, U. So. Calif., L.A., 1983-84, U. Utah, Salt Lake City, 1983-84; co-dir. Inst. Relational Devel.; cons. L.A. County Sch. Dist., N.C. Dept. Mental Health, Nat. Ctrs. Substance Abuse Treatment and Prevention, Nat. Inst. Corrections, others; designer women's treatment, cons. Betty Ford Ctr.; presenter at profl. meetings; lectr. in field; addiction cons. criminal justice sys. Author: Leaving the Enchanted Forest: The Path from Relationship Addiction to Intimacy, 1988, Awakening Your Sexuality: A Guide for Recovering Women and Their Partners, 1991, A Woman's Way Through the Twelve Steps, 1994; contbr. articles to profl. jours. Mem. NASW (diplomate), Am. Assn. Sex Educators, Counselors and Therapists, Am. Bd. Med. Psychotherapists (diplomate), Am. Bd. Sexology (diplomate), Am. Pub. Health Assn., Assn. Women in Psychology, Calif. Women's Commn. on Alcoholism (Achievement award), Ctr. for Study of the Person, Friends of Jung, Internat. Coun. on Alcoholism and Addictions (past chair women's com.), Kettil Brun Soc. (Finland), San Diego Soc. Sex Therapy and Edn., Soc. for Study of Addiction (Eng.). Office: 7946 Ivanhoe Ave Ste 201B La Jolla CA 92037-4517

COVITZ, CARL D., state official, real estate and investment executive; b. Boston, Mar. 31, 1939; s. Edward E. and Barbara (Matthews) C.; m. Aviva Habert, May 15, 1970; children: Philip, Marc. BS, Wharton Sch., U. Pa., 1960; MBA, Columbia U., 1962. Product mgr. Bristol-Myers Co., N.Y.C., 1962-66; dir. mktg. Rheingold Breweries, N.Y.C., 1966-68; nat. mktg. mgr. Can. Dry Corp., N.Y.C., 1968-70; v.p. mktg., dir. corp. devel. ITT/Levitt & Sons, Lake Success, N.Y., 1970-73; owner, pres. Landmark Communities, Inc., Beverly Hills, Calif., 1973-87, pres., 1989-91; undersec. HUD, Washington, 1987-89; sec. bus., transp. and housing State of Calif., Sacramento, 1991-93; pres. Landmark Capital, Inc. (formerly Landmark Communities, Inc.), 1993—; chmn. bd. Fed. Home Loan Bank, San Francisco, 1989-91. Exec. com. Presl. Commn. Cost Control and Efficiency (Grace Commn.); co-chmn. Dept. Def. Task Force; past chmn. ops. com. Mus. Contemporary Art Los Angeles; chmn. L.A. County Delinquency and Crime Commn.; dir. Columbia U. Grad. Bus. Sch. Alumni Assn. Mem. Young Pres. Orgn.; chmn. L.A. Housing Authority Commn., 1989-91. Home: 818 Malcolm Ave Los Angeles CA 90024-3104 Office: 9595 Wilshire Blvd Beverly Hills CA 90212

COWAN, GEORGE ARTHUR, chemist, bank executive, director; b. Worcester, Mass., Feb. 15, 1920; s. Louis Abraham and Anna (Listic) C.; m. Helen Dunham, Sept. 9, 1946. BS, Worcester Poly. Inst., 1941; DSc, Carnegie-Mellon U., 1950. Research asst. Princeton U., 1941-42, U. Chgo., 1942-45; mem. staff Columbia U., N.Y.C., 1945; mem. staff, dir. rsch. Los Alamos (N.Mex.) Sci. Lab., 1945-46, 49-88, sr. fellow emeritus, 1988—; teaching fellow Carnegie Mellon U., Pitts., 1946-49; chmn. bd. dirs. Trinity Capital Corp., Los Alamos, others; pres. Santa Fe Inst., 1984-91; mem. The White House Sci. Coun., Washington, 1982-85, cons. 1985-90, Air Force Tech. Applications Ctr., 1952-88; chmn. Los Alamos Nat. Bank, 1965-94; bd. dirs. Applied Tech. Assocs., Inc., Title Guaranty, Inc., Universal Properties, Inc. Contbr. sci. articles to profl. jours. Bd. dirs. Santa Fe Opera, 1964-79; treas. N.Mex. Opera Found., Santa Fe, 1970-79; regent N.Mex. Inst. Tech. Socorro, 1972-75; bd. dirs. N.Am. Inst., Santa Fe Inst., Coalition for Quality TV. Recipient E.O. Lawrence award, 1965, Disting. Scientist award N.Mex. Acad. Sci., 1975, Robert H. Goddard award Worcester Poly. Inst., 1984, Enrico Fermi award, Presdl. Citation, Dept. Energy, 1990. Fellow AAAS, Am. Phys. Soc.; mem. Am. chem. Soc., N.Mex. Acad. Sci., Sigma Xi. Home: 721 42nd St Los Alamos NM 87544-1804 Office: Santa Fe Inst 1399 Hyde Park Rd Santa Fe NM 87501-8943

COWAN, RICHARD JOHN, cattle rancher; b. Chgo., July 17, 1921; s. Percy and Jean (Feldman) C.; m. Helen Ann Cran, June 15, 1947; children: Cran, Clifford. AB, Princeton U., 1942. Freelance cattle buyer Phoenix, 1946-49; section boss Parker Ranch, Kamaela, Hawaii, 1949-50; owner, operator SunTex Ranch, Riley, Oreg., 1950—. Mem., chmn. Harney County Hosp. Bd., Burns, Oreg., 1963-74, Burns Union High Sch. Bd., 1974-83. Capt. USAF, 1942-46. Mem. Nat. Cattlemens Assn. (various coms. 1985-88, promotion and rsch. bd. 1986-89), Oreg. Cattlemens Assn. (v.p. 1977-79), Oreg. Beef Council (chmn. 1980-88). Republican. Christian Scientist. Home and Office: SunTex Ranch Riley OR 97758

COWAN, STUART MARSHALL, lawyer; b. Irvington, N.J., Mar. 20, 1932; s. Bernard Howard and Blanche (Hertz) C.; m. Marilyn R.C. Toepfer, Apr., 1961 (div. 1968); m. Jane Alison Averill, Feb. 24, 1974 (div. 1989); children: Fran Lori, Catherine R.L., Erika R.L., Bronwen P.; m. Victoria Yi, Nov. 11, 1989. BS in Econ., U. Pa., 1952; LLB, Rutgers U., 1955. Bar: N.J. 1957, Hawaii 1962, U.S. Supreme Ct., 1966. Atty., Greenstein & Cowan, Honolulu, 1961-70, Cowan & Frey, Honolulu, 1970-89, pvt. practice, 1989—; of counsel Price Okomoto Himeno & Lum, 1993—; arbitrator Fed. Mediation & Conciliation Svc., Honolulu, 1972—, Am. Arbitation Assn., Honolulu, 1978—, Hawaii Pub. Employee Rels. Bd., 1972—. Bd. dirs. Honolulu Symphony. Lt. USN, 1955-61. Mem. ABA, Hawaii Bar Assn., Am. Judicature Soc., Trial Lawyers Assn. of Am. (state committeeman for Hawaii 1965-69, bd. govs. 1972-75), Hawaii Trial Lawyers Assn. (v.p. 1972-78), Japan-Hawaii Lawyers Assn., Soc. Profls. in Dispute Resolution, Inter Pacific Bar Assn. Jewish. Clubs: Waikiki Yacht (Honolulu), Hawaii Yacht, San Francisco Comml., Plaza Club, Honolulu Club, Hawaii Scottish Assn. (chieftain 1983-88), St. Andrews Soc., Caledonian Soc. (vice chieftain 1983-85), St. Francis Yacht Club, Honolulu Pipes and Drums (sec.-treas. 1985-90), New Zealand Pipe Band. Lodges: Masons (York Rite, Scottish Rite, Grand Lodge Hawaii, grand orator 1992, sr. grand steward 1993, jr. grand warden 1994, sr.grand warden 1995), Pearl Harbor (master 1971, chaplain 1992-95), Masada, Hawaiian Koolau,Elks. Home: 47-339 Mapumapu Rd Kaneohe HI 96744-4922 Office: 707 Richards St Honolulu HI 96813-4623 also: 47-653 Kamehameha Hwy # 202 Kaneohe HI 96744

COWART, BILL F(RANK), academic administrator; b. San Benito, Tex., Aug. 5, 1932; m. Janet Marie Dube, Aug. 6, 1954; 1 child, Richard. BS, Tex. A&I U., 1954; MA, Stephen F. Austin State Coll., 1959; PhD, U. Tex.,

1963. Asst. mgr. Brownie Butane, Inc., McAllen, Tex., 1956-57; office mgr. Cowart Cattle Co., Henderson, Tex., 1957-59; tchr. Tivy Jr. High Sch., Kerrville, Tex., 1959-61; dir. secondary teaching Tex. A&I U., Kingsville, 1963-66, dir. project Upward Bound, 1966-69; pres. Laredo State U., Tex., 1969-84; provost Western Oreg. State Coll., Monmouth, 1984-94, pres., 1994-95; mem. exec. coun. Univ. System of South Tex., 1969-84; mem. Commrs. Adv. Com. on Bi-Lingual Edn., State of Tex., 1974. Pres. United Fund of Laredo, 1980; chmn. Laredo Coun. for the Arts, 1980-84, Borderfest Steering Com., Laredo, 1980-83. 1st lt. U.S. Army, 1954-56. Named Man of Yr., Laredo Times, 1979, Exec. of Yr., Coll. de Licenciados en Adminstrn. de Nuevo, 1981. Mem. S.W. Philosophy of Edn. Soc. (pres. 1970-71). Home: 2313 Swallow Ave McAllen TX 78504

COWART, JIM CASH, business executive; b. Hereford, Tex., July 1, 1951; s. Orville P. and Rosa Stratton (Cash) C.; m. Janet Carol Bergman, Aug. 24, 1973; 1 child, Jefferson Cash. BA in Computer Sci., Pomona Coll., 1973; MBA with honors, Harvard U., 1977. Computer analyst U.S. Ho. of Reps., Washington, 1973-74; asst. v.p. mktg. Amtrak, Washington, 1974-75; v.p. investment banking Kidder, Peabody & Co., N.Y.C., 1977-82; sr. v.p. investment banking Shearson Lehman, N.Y.C., 1982-87; pres. Shearson Venture Capital, N.Y.C., 1983-87; gen. ptnr. Capital Resource Ptnrs., Mission Viejo, Calif. and Boston, 1987-91, Aurora Ptnrs., Laguna Niguel, Calif., 1991—; chmn., CEO Aurora Electronics, Inc., Irvine, Calif., 1992—; bd. dirs. BE Aerospace, Inc., Wellington, Fla. Office: Aurora Electronics Inc 2030 Main St Ste # 1120 Irvine CA 92714

COWART, R. GREG, sales executive; b. Woodville, Mar. 4, 1956; s. Raymon O. and Frances (Gregory) C. BBA Mktg., Stephen F. Austin St. U., 1986, BA in Psychology, 1986. Mgr. Angelina Sports, Lufkin, Tex., 1980-83; sales mgr. Angelina Health Spa, Lufkin, Tex., 1983-86, Hoffman LaRoche Inc., Nutley, N.J., 1986—; cons. in field. Football ofcl. Southwest Football Ofcls. Assn., Nacogdoches, 1983-89. Republican. Home: 2640-B W 235th St Torrance CA 90505

COWDEN, LOUIS FREDRICK, electronics executive, engineer; b. Hayden, Ariz., Nov. 11, 1929; s. Millard Martin and Lenore Eletha (Hedgepeth) C.; m. Ruth Norine Buchanan, May 13, 1953 (div. Sept. 1975); children: Mary Marguerite, Michael Millard, Timothy John; m. Anabel Joyce Tarantino, Nov. 19, 1976. BSEE, U. Ariz., 1957. Div. dir. Collins Radio Co., Newport Beach, Calif., 1957-75; pvt. ventures, 1976-76; mgr. GS engring. TRW, Redondo Beach, Calif., 1976-78; divsn. mgr. Control Data Corp., Anaheim, Calif., 1979-80; site mgr. TDRSS TRW, Las Cruces, N.Mex., 1981-83; staff mgr. TRW, Redondo Beach, 1983-89; asst. v.p. engring. Verilink Corp., San Jose, Calif., 1989; regional mgr. WPL, Inc., 1989-90; program mgr. GTE, Las Cruces, 1990—. With U.S. Army, 1948-53. Mem. Am. Mgmt. Assn. Republican. Office: GTE Govt Systems Corp PO Box 235 Las Cruces NM 88004-0235

COWEE, JOHN WIDMER, JR., architecture company executive; b. Madison, Wis., Jan. 23, 1949; s. John Widmer Cowee, Sr. and Annette (Oetking) C.; m. Marion Emiko Hironaka, Mar. 21, 1971; 1 child, Misa Melina. AB in Architecture, U. Calif., Berkeley, 1971, MA in Architecture, 1973. Assoc. architect Kaiser Engrs., Oakland, Calif., 1974-82; prin. Lundy, Ng & Cowee, Architects, Oakland, Calif., 1975-79; project mgr. ED2 Architects, San Francisco, 1982-84; assoc. Leo A. Daly Co. Architects, San Francisco, 1984-91; prin. Tecta Assocs., San Francisco, 1986-88; prin./owner Architectural Concepts, Albany, Calif., 1991—. Active El Cerrito, Calif. Redevel. Com., 1974-75, chmn. El Cerrito Design Review Bd., vice chmn. El Cerrito Planning Commn., 1975-79. Mem. El Cerrito Aquatic Masters, Friends of El Cerrito Pool (co-chmn. 1992-94). Democrat.

COWELL, ERNEST SAUL, lighting designer, consultant; b. Hollywood, Calif., Jan. 27, 1927; s. Ernest S. and Bernice Michael (Waterman) C.; m. Beverly Sue Bloom, Apr. 15, 1950 (div. May 1960); children: Steven Richard, Craig Wesley, Marilyn Tobiann. BA, UCLA, 1950; student, Moorpark Coll., 1971, Cerritos Jr. Coll., 1979. Regional mgr. Prentice Hall Inc., San Francisco, 1954-59; pvt. practice indsl. and govtl. sales L.A., 1959-70; area mgr. Philips Lighting, L.A., 1970-79; v.p. Coons & Cowell Lighting Unltd., Thousand Oaks, Calif., 1979-83; pres. Lighting Designs, L.A., 1983—; cons. City of Thousand Oaks, 1970—; crime prevention specialist L.A. Police Dept., 1991—, adv. bd., 1994—. Mem. Rep. Presdl. Task Force, 1978—, Rep. Nat. Com., 1992—, gen. plan com. City of Thousand Oaks, 1967, gen. plan rev. com., 1984, 86, 88; commdg. officer U.S. Naval Sea Cadet Corps Betsy Ross Divsn., 1994—. Sgt. U.S. Army, 1943-46, PTO; with USNR, 1950-58, 70-90. Recipient Edison award Excellence in Lighting, Gen. Electric Corp., 1985, 86. Fellow Inst. Advancement Engring.; mem. Illuminating Engring. Soc. (bd. dirs. So. Calif. sect. 1977-85, nat. chmn. schs and colls. lighting standards com., residential lighting standards com., Internat. Illumination Design award 1983, 84, 85, 87, Disting. Svc. award), Internat. Assn. Lighting Designers, U.S. Nat. Com. to Internat. Commn. Illumination, Libr. Lighting Stds. (nat. chmn. 1988-90), Designers Lighting Forum (bd. dirs. 1988-95), Internat. Soc. Interior Designers (design affiliate), Navy League (pres. Hollywood/L.A. coun. 1993-94), Roadway Lighting Forum (bd. dirs. 1988-90), Kiwanis (pres. Westlake Village club 1977-79).

COWEN, DONALD EUGENE, retired physician; b. Ft. Morgan, Colo., Oct. 8, 1918; adopted s. Franklin and Mary Edith (Dalton) C.; BA, U. Denver, 1940; MD, U. Colo., 1943; m. Hulda Marie Helling, Dec. 24, 1942; children: David L., Marilyn Marie Cowen Dean, Theresa Kathleen Cowen Cunningham Byrd, Margaret Ann Cowen Koenigs. Intern, U.S. Naval Hosp., Oakland, Calif., 1944; gen. practice medicine, Ft. Morgan, 1947-52; resident internal medicine U. Colo. Med. Ctr., Denver, 1952-54; practice medicine specializing in allergy, Denver, 1954-90, ret.; mem. staff Presbyn. Med. Ctr., Denver, Porter, Swedish hosps., Englewood, Colo.; clin. asst. prof. medicine U. Colo. Med. Center, 1964-91, ret., 1991; postgrad. faculty U. Tenn. Coll. Medicine, Memphis, 1962-82; cons. Queen of Thailand, 1973, 75, 77. Pres. Community Arts Symphony Found., 1980-82. Served to lt. M.C., USN, 1943-47. Fellow ACP, Am. Coll. Chest Physicians (vice chmn. com. on allergy 1968-72, 75-87, sec.-treas. Colo. chpt. 1971-77, pres. 1978-80), Am. Coll. Allergy and Immunology, Acad. Internat. Medicine, West Coast Allergy Soc., Southwest Allergy Forum, Am. Acad. Otolaryngic Allergy, Colo. socs. internal medicine, Colo. Allergy Soc. (past pres.), Ill. Soc. Opthalmology and Otolaryngology (hon.), Denver Med. Soc. (chmn. library and bldg. com. 1963-73), Arapahoe Med. Soc. (life emeritus mem.). Presbyterian (ruling elder 1956—). Club: Lions. Contbr. numerous articles to profl. jours. Home: 18560 Polvera Dr San Diego CA 92128-1120

COWHEY, PETER FRANCIS, international relations educator, government official, consultant; b. Chgo., Sept. 28, 1948; s. Eugene F. and Vivien (High) C.; m. Mary Pat Williams, July 1973 (div. June 1978); m. M. Margaret McKeown, June 29, 1985; 1 child, Megan. BS in Fgn. Svc., Georgetown U., 1970; MA, PhD, U. Calif., Berkeley, 1976. Lectr. U. Calif., Berkeley, 1975-76; from asst. to assoc. prof. polit. sci. U. Calif. San Diego, La Jolla, 1976-88, prof. polit. sci. & internat. rels., 1989—; sr. adviser internat. policy FCC, Washington, 1994—; market planner AT&T Internat., Basking Ridge, N.J., 1985-86; advisor Telemation Assocs., Washington, 1987-88; mem. telecom. adv. bd. A.T. Kearney, Chgo., 1988-91; co-dir. project on internat. and security affairs U. Calif., San Diego, 1990-94; rsch. scholar Berkeley Roundtable on the Internat. Economy, 1992-94; vis. prof. Juan March Inst., Madrid, 1992; rsch. prof. Inst. of Oriental Culture, U. Tokyo, 1993; U.S. del. G-7 Ministerial, 1995, U.S. del. Asian Pacific Econ. Cmty. Ministerial, 1995. Author: Problems of Plenty, 1985; co-author: Profit and the Pursuit of Energy, 1983, When Countries Talk, 1988, Managing the World's Economy, 1993; co-editor: Structure and Policy in Japan and the United States, 1994; mem. editl. bd. Internat. Orgn., 1989-94. Mem. adv. bd. Project Promothee, Paris, 1985-94, Ctr. on Telecom. Mgmt., Lincoln, Nebr., 1988-92; com. mem. NRC, 1992-93. Rockefeller Found. internat. affairs fellow, 1984-87. Mem. Am. Polit. Sci. Assn., Coun. Fgn. Rels. (internat. affairs fellow 1985-86), Internat. Studies Assn. Democrat. Home: 2820 Albemarle St NW Washington DC 20008-1036 Office: U Calif San Diego Grad Sch Internat Rels & Pacific Studies La Jolla CA 92093 also: Internat Bur FCC 2000 M St NW 8th Fl Washington DC 20554

COWINGS, EVERETT ALVIN, entertainment manager, film/television producer; b. Fresno, Calif., Feb. 11, 1963; s. Everett Alvin Cowings Sr. and Thelma Anita (Williams) Ricks. AA in Drama, Fresno C.C., 1984, AS in Engring., 1985; BS in Law, Western State U., Fullerton, Calif., 1989, postgrad.; postgrad., Calif. Polytechnic U., Pomona. Owner, printing broker Agape Printing Brokerage, Pomona, 1986-88; mentor, pub. speaker, C.C. System Calif. Ednl. System, Glendorn, Calif., 1985-88; law clerk L.A. City Atty's Office, summer 1988; movie recruiter Nat. Rsch. Group, Hollywood, Calif., 1990-92; prin., entertainment mgr. The Everett Cowings Group, Burbank, Calif., 1992-95; owner Unsigned Prodns., Inc., 1995—. Author TV script Home Alone II, 1991; actor Sunday Comics, Mancuso FBI, Days of Our Lives, 1987—; prodr. Back and Roll, Reality Is, 1994; exec. prodr. TV pilot and show Unsigned. Fellow Nat. Soc. Black Engrs., Calif. Lawyers for the Arts, Black Law Students (pres.); mem. Alpha Phi Alpha. Democrat. Office: The Everett Cowings Group Empire Burbank Studios 1845 W Empire Ave Ste 115 Burbank CA 91504-3402

COWLEY, PAULA JEAN, computer scientist, consultant; b. Spokane, Wash., Nov. 1, 1946; d. Harold Robert and Pauline (Morasch) Keiser; m. William L. Cowley; children: David, Brian. BA in Math. summa cum laude, Gonzaga U., Spokane, 1970; MS in Computer Sci., Wash. State U., Pullman, 1977. With Pacific N.W. Lab./Battelle Meml. Inst., Richland, Wash., 1977—, staff scientist specializing in info. mgmt., 1990—, project mgr. Hanford Environ. Info. Sys., 1987-94; cons. U.S. Dept. Energy, 1993—; mem. HEIS Configuration Control Bd., 1990-94. Contbr. articles to profl. jours. Mem. Columbia Basin Concert Band, 1979-91; choir accompanist Ch. Choir, 1985—. Episcopalian. Office: Battelle NW Labs PO Box 999 MS K7-22 Richland WA 99352

COWSER, DANNY LEE, lawyer, mental health specialist; b. Peoria, Ill., July 7, 1948; s. Albert Paul Cowser and Shirley Mae (Donaldson) Chatten; m. Nancy Lynn Hatch, Nov. 11, 1976; children: Kimberly Catherine Hatch Cowser, Dustin Paul Hatch Cowser. BA, No. Ill. U., 1972, MS, 1975; JD, DePaul U., 1980. Bar: Ill. 1980, Wis. 1981, U.S. Dist. Ct. (no. dist.) Ill. 1981, U.S. Ct. Appeals (7th cir.) 1983, U.S. Dist. Ct. (ea. and we. dists.) Wis. 1984, U.S. Supreme Ct. 1984, Ariz. 1985, U.S. Ct. Appeals (9th cir.) 1987, U.S. Dist. Ct. Ariz. 1989, U.S. Tax Ct. 1990, U.S. Ct. Claims 1990. Adminstr. Ill. Dept. Mental Health, Elgin, 1972-76, psychotherapist, 1976-79; assoc. Slaby, Deda & Henderson, Phillips, Wis., 1982-83; ptnr. Slaby, Deda & Cowser, Phillips, 1983-86; asst. atty. City of Flagstaff, Ariz., 1986-88; pub. defender Coconino County, Flagstaff, 1988-89; pvt. practice Flagstaff, 1989—; atty. City Park Falls, Wis., 1983-86; spl. dep. Mohave County capital def., 1989-90; instr. speech comms. No. Ariz. U., 1992—. Bd. dirs. DeKalb County (Ill.) Drug Coun., 1973-75, Counseling and Personal Devel., Phillips, 1985-86, Northland YM-WYCA, 1990-91. Reginald Heber Smith fellow, 1980-81; C.J.S. legal scholar, 1979; recipient Am. Jur. award secured transactions, 1979, Am. Jr. award corps., 1979. Mem. ABA, Ill. Bar Assn., Ariz. Bar Asn., Nat. Assn. Criminal Def. Attys., Nat. Criminal Def. Coll., Lions, State Bar of Ariz. (cert. specialist in criminal law), State Bar of Wis. Democrat. Office: PO Box 22329 612 N Beaver St Flagstaff AZ 86002

COX, ARTHUR NELSON, astrophysicist, researcher; b. Van Nuys, Calif., Oct. 12, 1927; s. Arthur Hildreth and Sara (Nelson) C.; m. Clarice Wruck, Jan. 3, 1958 (div. 1973); children: Charles, Edward; m. Joan Frances Ellis, Oct.. 21, 1973; children: Bryan, Kay, Sally. BS, Calif. Inst. Tech., 1948; AM, Ind. U., 1952, PhD, 1953, DSc (hon.), 1973. Staff mem. Los Alamos Sci. Lab., 1947-49, 53-57, 75-83, group leader, 1957-75, lab. fellow, 1983—; cons. Avco-Everitt (Mass.) Rsch. Lab., 1960-61; vis. prof. UCLA, 1966; program advisor NSF, Washington, 1973-74. Sr. editor: The Solar Interior and Atmosphere, 1991. Fellow NSF, 1952-53, NATO, 1968; Fulbright scholar U. Liege, Belgium, 1968-69. Mem. AAAS, Am. Astron. Soc., Internat. Astron. Union (pres. com. 35, 1982-85), Sigma Xi. Office: Los Alamos Nat Lab PO Box 1663 Los Alamos NM 87544-0600

COX, CHRISTOPHER, congressman; b. St. Paul, Oct. 16, 1952; s. Charles C. and Marilyn A. (Miller) C.; m. Rebecca Gernhardt; children: Charles, Kathryn. BA, U. So. Calif., 1973; MBA, JD, Harvard U., 1977. Bar: Calif. 1978, D.C. 1980. Law clk. to judge U.S. Ct. Appeals (9th cir.), 1977-78; assoc. Latham & Watkins, Newport Beach, Calif., 1978-82; lectr. bus. adminstrn. Harvard U., 1982-83; ptnr. Latham & Watkins, Newport Beach, Calif., 1984-86; sr. assoc. counsel to the Pres. The White House, Washington, 1986-88; mem. 101st-104th Congresses from 40th (now 47th) dist. Calif., Washington, 1986-87; mem. budget com., joint econ. com., govt. ops. com. U.S. Ho. of Reps., Washington, ranking mem. subcom. on commerce, consumer & monetary affairs; mem. Bipartisan Commn. on Entitlement and Tax Reform, Washington, 1994—; chmn. Rep. policy com., mem. commerce com., 1995—; prin., founder Context Corp., St. Paul, 1984-88. Editor Harvard Law Rev., 1975-77. Roman Catholic. Office: E Tower Ste 430 4000 Macarthur Blvd Newport Beach CA 92660-2516 Office: US Ho of Reps 2402 Rayburn HOB Washington DC 20515

COX, GARY EVANS, aerospace company official, consultant; b. Ogden, Utah, July 4, 1937; s. Donald Evans and Maxine Louise (Altweis) C.; m. Carole Sue Brown, June 6, 1959; children: Theresa, Patrick, Colleen. BS in Indsl. Mgmt., U. Portland, 1961; MS in Pub. Adminstrn., Auburn UU., 1973. Commd. 2d lt. USAF, 1961, advanced through grades to col., 1982; pilot USAF, Europe, Korea, Vietnam, U.S., 1961-87; ret., 1987; program mgr. McDonnell Douglas Corp., Phoenix, 1987—; cons. McDonnell Douglas Corp., St. Louis, 1987. Pres. Holy Redeemer Sch. Bd., Tampa, Fla., 1976-78; scoutmaster Tampa coun. Boy Scouts Am., 1977-78; com. chmn. Hampton (Va.) Rep. Com., 1982. Decorated DFC, 20 Air medals; recipient Superior Svc. award Dept. Def., 1987. Mem. Air Force Assn., Ret. Officers Assn., Daedalian Soc. Roman Catholic. Home: 7733 W Villa Theresa Dr Glendale AZ 85308-8262 Office: McDonnell Douglas Tng Syst PO Box 218 Litchfield Park AZ 85340-0218

COX, GEORGE WYATT, biology educator; b. Williamson, W.Va., Feb. 10, 1935; s. Ira F. J. and Edna (Davis) C.; m. Carolyn Celena Kay, Dec. 21, 1958 (div. Apr. 1969); m. Darla Gail Bell, June 6, 1969; children: Daniel Robert, David William. BA, Ohio Wesleyan U., 1956; MS, U. Ill., 1958, PhD, 1960. Asst. prof. biology U. Alaska, Fairbanks, 1960-61, Calif. Western U., San Diego, 1961-62; from asst. prof. to prof. biology San Diego State U., 1962-69; vis. prof. biology Universidad Católica, Santiago, Chile, 1974; program dir. ecology NSF, Washington, 1978-79. Author: Laboratory Manual of General Ecology, 1967, Conservation Ecology: Biosphere and Biosurvival, 1992; co-author: Dynamic Ecology, 1973, Agricultural Ecology, 1979; editor: Readings in Conservation Ecology, 1969. Mem. Ecol. Soc. Am., Soc. Conservation Biology, Am. Soc. Mammologists, N.W. Sci. Assn., Am. Ornithologist's Union. Office: San Diego State U Dept Biology San Diego CA 92182

COX, JIM, petroleum geologist, technical writer; b. Tulsa, May 19, 1932; s. Leland W. and Evelyn (Bell) C.; m. Marcia Ann Dick, Oct. 15, 1960; children: Galen, Karsten, Cydney. BS in Geology, Okla. State U., Stillwater, 1955. Geologist Gulf Oil Corp., Casper, Wyo., 1959-60, Mule Creek Oil Co., Billings, Mont., 1960-66; geologist Jim Cox-Petroleum Geologist, Inc., Gillette, Wyo., 1966-79, Prescott, Ariz., 1979-81, Littleton, Colo., 1981-87, Idaho Falls, Idaho, 1987—; v.p. Wulf Oil Co., Gillette, 1979-81; exploration mgr. Aberdeen Resources, Denver, 1980-81, Quantum Resources, Denver, 1981-83. Contbr. articles to profl. jours. 1st lt. USAF, 1955-58. Mem. Am. Assn. Petroleum Geologists. Home and Office: 2002 Dalmation Dr Idaho Falls ID 83402-2466

COX, JOE HOWARD, JR., petroleum engineer; b. Denver, Oct. 3, 1952; s. Joe Howard and Elvira Marcille (Kulish) C.; m. Lu Ann Heward, Oct. 8, 1977 (div. Apr. 1979); m. Carol Joan Craig, June 9, 1984; 1 child, Kathleen Ray. BS in Geology, U. Wyo., 1975. Svc. supr. Dowell Divsn. Dow Chem., Denver, 1976-78, Mercury, Nev., 1976-78; engr. Gulf Rsch. and Devel. Co., Houston, 1978-80; staff engr. Juniper Petroleum Corp., Denver, 1980-86; v.p. ops. Mallon Oil Co., Denver, 1986-94; pres. Joe H. Cox Jr. Consulting, Denver, 1994—. Mem. Am. Assn. Petroleum Geologists, Soc. Petroleum Engrs., Rocky Mt. Assn. Geologists. Independent. Home: 7951 S Bemis Cir Littleton CO 80120-4381

COX, JOSEPH WILLIAM, academic administrator; b. Hagerstown, Md., May 26, 1937; s. Joseph F. and Ruth E. C.; m. Regina M. Bollinger, Aug. 17, 1963; children—Andrew, Matthew, Abigail. B.A., U. Md., 1959, Ph.D., 1967. Successively instr., asst. prof., assoc. prof., prof. history Towson (Md.) State U., 1964-81, dean evening, summer and minimester programs, 1972-75, acting pres., 1978-79, v.p. acad. affairs and dean of univ., 1979-81; prof. history, v.p. acad. affairs. No. Ariz. U.,, Flagstaff, 1981-87; pres. So. Oregon Coll., Ashland, 1987-94; chancellor Oreg. State Sys. Higher Edn., Eugene, 1994—; Bd. dirs. Western Bank. Author: Champion of Southern Federalism: Robert Goodloe Harper of South Carolina, 1972, The Early National Experience: The Army Corps of Engineers, 1783-1812, 1979; mem. bd. editors Med. Hist. Mag., 1979-89; columnist S. Oreg. Hist. Mag.; contbr. articles to profl. jours. Bd. dirs. So. Oreg. Econ. Devel. Bd. Mem. AAUP, Am. Assn. Higher Edn., Am. Assn. State Colls. and Univs., Phi Kappa Phi, Omicron Delta Kappa. Episcopalian. Home: 2237 Spring Blvd Eugene OR 97403-1897 Office: Oreg State Sys Higher Edn Office of Chancellor PO Box 3175 Eugene OR 97403

COX, MERIDITH BRITTAN, publishing executive, risk manager, consultant; b. Bklyn., Oct. 25, 1941; d. Vergil McLeod Cox and Elizabeth Joan (Maxey) Vautier. BA, Golden Gate U., 1974, MPA, 1975, postgrad., 1977-81. Exec. dir. Info. Ctr.-Hosp. Conf., San Francisco, 1967-69; rsch. adminstr. ASME, N.Y.C., 1970-72; field rep. Vis. Nurse Assn., San Francisco, 1972-73; cons. med. malpractice El Cerrito, Calif., 1973-76; adj. prof. Golden Gate U., San Francisco, 1977-89; risk mgmt. cons. Meridith B. Cox Assocs., El Cerrito, 1977-89, Billings, Mont., 1990-91; pres. Risk Mgmt. Resource Systems, Billings, 1992—; part-time instr. Sch. Mgmt., Ea. Mont. Coll., Billings, 1993—; pub., risk mgr. Cox Publications, El Cerrito, 1977-90; pres. Cox Info. Svcs., Billings, 1994—. Author: An Introduction to the Law, Legal System & Legal Liability, 1988, Safety and Equipment Risks, 1991, Prevent Lawsuits, 1992, Standards of Care, 1984, (textbook) Risk Management for Department Head, 1991 (Nat. Fedn. Press Women award 1992); author, pub. The Nurse, The Patient and The Law, 1977—. Commr. El Cerrito Appeals Bd., 1979-80, El Cerrito Parks and Recreation Commn., 1980-81, El Cerrito Safety Commn., 1981-82; mem. Subcom. on Cost Containment Health Care for Montanans, 1991-92. With USN, 1960-63, USNR, 1964-68. Recipient Teaching award JFK Univ., 1987. Mem. ASTD (Big Sky chpt.), Nat. League Nursing, Mont. League Nursing (chmn. legis. and pub. affairs 1991-93), Nat. Fedn. Press Women (Risk Mgmt. Textbook award 1992), Mont. Press Women (v.p. 1991-93, pres. 1993—), Mont. Assn. Female Execs. Episcopalian. Office: Cox Publs PO Box 20316 Billings MT 59104-0316

COX, PAUL ALAN, biologist, educator; b. Salt Lake City, Oct. 10, 1953; s. Leo A. and Rae (Gabbitas) C.; m. Barbara Ann Wilson, May 21, 1975; children: Emily Ann, Paul Matthew, Mary Elisabeth, Hillary Christine. BS, Brigham Young U., 1976; MSc, U. Wales, 1978; AM, Harvard U., 1978, PhD, 1981. Teaching fellow Harvard U., Cambridge, Mass., 1977-81; Miller research fellow Miller Inst. Basic Research in Sci., Berkeley, Calif., 1981-83; asst. prof. Brigham Young U., Provo, Utah, 1983-86, assoc. prof., 1986—; ecologist Utah Environ. Council, Salt Lake City, 1976; staff ecologist Utah MX Coordination Office, Salt Lake City, 1981. Mem. editorial bd. Pacific Studies. Recipient Bowdoin prize; Danforth Found. fellow, 1976-81, Fulbright fellow, 1976-77, NSF fellow, 1977-81, Melbourne Univ. fellow, 1985-86; named NSF Presdl. Young Investigator, 1985—. Mem. Brit. Ecol. Soc., N.Y. Acad. Scis., Am. Soc. Naturalists, Assn. for Tropical Biology, AAAS, New Eng. Bot. Club. Mormon. Office: Brigham Young U Dept Botany Provo UT 84602

COX, ROGER GORDON, educational software company executive; b. Nov. 18, 1947. BS in Elec. Engring., U. Wis., 1970. Devel. engr. Hewlett-Packard, 1970-80; prin. Roger Cox, Cons. Engr., 1983-89; prin. engr. United Techs. Microelectronic Ctr., 1987-89; owner, operator Save the Planet Software, 1989—. Co-author: Ozone, UV and Your Health, 1994; patentee in feild; author tech. articles. Office: Save the Planet Software PO Box 45 513 River St Pitkin CO 81241

COX, WHITSON WILLIAM, architect; b. Crawford, Nebr., May 13, 1921; s. William Noah and Esther Mable (Stickley) C.; m. Loreen Baker, Sept. 8, 1946; children: Marilyn Cox Gendron, Teresa Cox Balick. BS, U. Oreg., 1943, BArch, 1948. Registered architect, Calif. Prin. Cox, Liske, Lionakis & Beaumont, Architects & Engrs., Sacramento, 1953-83; dir. Dept. Architecture and Constrn. State of Calif., Sacramento, 1983-86; prin. Whitson W. Cox, Architect, Sacramento, 1986—; cons. architect Calif. State U., 1972-83, Meth. Hosp., Sacramento, 1987—; tech. cons. Capitol Area Plan, Sacramento, 1983-86. Prin. works include Mira Loma High Sch., Sacramento, 1964, Mather AFB Chapel, Sacramento, 1968, Chico (Calif.) State Health Ctr., 1969, Sacramento County Adminstrn. Ctr., 1977; paintings exhibited in one-man and group shows, 1960—. Bd. dirs., pres. Crocker Art Mus., 1964-84; commr. Sacramento Metro Arts Commn., 1982; bd. dirs. Boy Scouts Am. Golden Empire Coun., 1962—. Lt. USNR, 1943-46, PTO. Recipient Silver Beaver award Boy Scouts Am., 1964, Commendation award Calif. Arts Coun., 1986. Fellow AIA (chpt. pres. 1963, state pres. 1972, nat. bd. dirs., 1974-78, dist. svc. citation 1985); mem. Rotary Club, Arden Hills Club. Home: 4711 Marguerite Way Carmichael CA 95608-5816 Office: Whitson W Cox FAIA 10 Fullerton Ct Sacramento CA 95825

COX, WILLIAM VAUGHN, lawyer; b. Jersey City, N.J., Nov. 12, 1936; s. Walter Miles and Emily (McNenney); divorced; children: Millicent S., Jennifer V. BA, Princeton U., 1958; LLB, Yale U., 1964. Bar: Colo. 1965, Conn. 1972, N.Y. 1974. Law clk. Holland & Hart, Denver, 1963; atty. Conoco Inc., Denver, 1966-72; asst. to v.p., gen. counsel Conoco Inc., Stamford, Conn., 1972-73; v.p., gen. counsel Stromberg-Carlson Corp., Rochester, N.Y., 1974-78; mng. ptnr. Bader & Cox, Denver, 1979-86, of counsel, 1986-88; pres. William V. Cox, P.C., Denver, 1988—, also bd. dirs.; project and planning dir. Interwest Comms. Corp., 1995—; pres., bd. dirs. New West Indies Trading Co., Denver, 1984—; pres. Coll. Football Ltd., Denver, 1990—. Sportswriter/editor: Colorado Springs (Colo.) Free Press, 1960-61. Football coach Cheyenne Mountain H.S., Colorado Springs, 1961; founder, v.p., bd. dirs., com. chmn. editor Colo. chpt. Nat. Football Found., 1992—, v.p., 1995—; mem. adv. bd. Downtown Denver Dist., 1991-93; bd. dirs., com. chmn. Downtown Denver Residents, 1990-93; pres., bd. dirs. Barclay Towers Condominiums, Denver, 1990-92; dist. capt. Rep. party, Cherry Hills, Colo., 1980-85; bd. dirs. Monroe County Humane Soc., Rochester, 1975-78. With USAR, 1959-65. Mem ABA, Colo. Bar Assn., Denver Bar Assn. (awards com.), Denver Lower Downtown Bar Assn. (v.p. 1992-94), Am. Legion, Ancient Order Hibernians, Univ Club Denver (admissions com.), Yale Club N.Y., Genesee Valley Club (Rochester) Rocky Mountain Princeton Club (com. chmn. 1966-72), Law Club Denver (com. chmn. 1969-72), Phi Delta Phi. Roman Catholic. Office: 1625 Larimer St Apt 2707 Denver CO 80202-1538

COY, DAVID DALE, marketing professional; b. Provo, Utah, Apr. 9, 1959; s. Dale Vern and JoAnne Elizabeth (Silver) C. AA, Snow Coll., 1981; BA, Brigham Young U., 1990. Missionary LDS Ch., Cordoba, Argentina, 1978-80; regional mgr. WordPerfect Corp., Dallas, 1984, Houston, 1985, 87-90, Rochester, N.Y., 1986; cons. in microcomputer hardware and software Roy, Utah, 1990—. Varsity scout coach Boy Scouts Am., Roy, 1992-93. Republican. Home: 4746 S 2325 W Roy UT 84067-1810 Office: PO Box 694 Roy UT 84067-0694

COYLE, MARA GENEVIEVE, physician, pediatrician; b. Pompton Plains, N.J., Feb. 14, 1961; d. James Butler and Frances Genevieve (Senger) C.; m. William D. Brown, May 30, 1992; 1 child, Ryan Douglas. BS, Boston Coll., 1982; postgrad., Dartmouth Coll., 1982-84; D of Medicine, Brown U., 1986. Pediatric intern Children's Hosp. of Phila., 1986, pediatric resident, 1987-89; neonatology fellowship Womens & Infants Hosp., Providence, 1989-92; staff neonatalogist Huntington Meml. Hosp., Pasadena, Calif., 1992-94; staff neonatologist Calif. Critical Children's Care Med. Group, L.A., 1994—. Fellow Am. Acad. Pediatrics (bd. cert. pediatrics); mem. Sigma Xi, Sci. Rsch. Soc., Phi Beta Kappa. Roman Catholic. Home: 300 La Follette St Los Angeles CA 90042-3514

COYLE, ROBERT EVERETT, federal judge; b. Fresno, Calif., May 6, 1930; s. Everett LaJoya and Virginia Chandler C.; m. Faye Turnbaugh, June 11, 1953; children—Robert Allen, Richard Lee, Barbara Jean. B.A., Fresno State Coll., 1953; J.D., U. Calif., 1956. Bar: Calif. Ptnr. McCormick, Barstow, Sheppard, Coyle & Wayte, 1958-82; chief judge U.S. Dist. Ct. (ea. dist.) Calif., 1982—; mem. exec. com. jud. coun. 9th Cir., chair space & security com. Mem. Calif. Bar Assn. (exec. com. 1974-79, bd. govs. 1979-82, v.p. 1981), Fresno County Bar Assn. (pres. 1972), 9th Cir. Dist. Judges

Assn. (past v.p., pres.), 9th Cir. Conf. of Chief Dist. Judges. Office: US Dist Ct 5116 US Courthouse 1130 O St Fresno CA 93721-2201

COZAD, LYMAN HOWARD, city manager; b. Painesville, Ohio, May 22, 1914; s. William Howard and Ethyl (Phelps) C.; m. Arliss Smith, Sept. 6, 1978; children: Bradford, Roberta, Kimberly. BSBA, Ohio State U., 1935, BS in Pub. Adminstrn., 1936; postgrad., Yale U., 1936-37, USC, 1948-57. Dir. examinations City of L.A., 1939-42; personnel officer Nat. Housing Agy., Washington, 1942-43; personnel dir. UNRRA, Washington, 1944-47; So. Calif. mgr. Louis J. Kroeger & Assocs., L.A., 1947-56; city mgr. City of Colton, 1957-64; adminstrv. officer City of Beverly Hills, Calif., 1964-66; city mgr. City of Arcadia, Calif., 1966-77; So. Calif. mgr. League of Calif. Cities, 1977-84; ranger rider, 1985—; v.p., So. Calif. rep. Pub. Svc. Skills Inc., Sacramento, 1986—; instr. U. So. Calif., 1941-42, 48-58, U. Calif., Riverside, 1961-63, Calif. State U., Long Beach, 1974-77. Contbr. articles to profl. jours. With U.S. Army, 1943-44. Mem. ASPA, Internat. City Mgrs. Assn., City Mgrs. Dept. League of Calif. Cities (Sacramento pres. 1972, life), So. Calif. Pub. Pers. Assn. L.A. (pres. 1942), Rotary (Colton chpt. dir. 1961-62, Arcadia chpt. 1970-71). Home: 952 Canyon View Dr La Verne CA 91750-1811 Office: Pub Svc Skills Inc 1400 K St Ste 400 Sacramento CA 95814-3916

COZEN, LEWIS, orthopaedic surgeon; b. Montreal, Canada, Aug. 14, 1911; came to U.S. 1922; AB, U. Calif., San Francisco, 1929, MD, 1934. Diplomate Am. Bd. Orthopedic Surgery. Intern San Francisco Hosp., 1933-34; resident orthopedic surgeron U. Iowa, 1934-35; resident and fellow orthopedic surgery San Francisco County Hosp., 1935-36, Children's Hosp. and Mass. Gen. Hosp., Boston, 1936-39; pvt. practice orthopedic surgery L.A., 1939-40, 45—; clin. prof. orthopedic surgery UCLA, 1965-93; assoc. clin. prof. emeritus Loma Linda Med. Sch., 1963—; attending orthopedic surgeon, emeritus Cedars Sinai Med. Ctr., 1939—, Orthopaedic Hosp., 1939—; chief orthopedic surgery City of Hope, 1948-67; sr. attending orthopedic surgeons, emeritus Unit One L.A. County Hosp., 1950-63; vis. lectr. U. Santo Tomas, Manila; Far East Sch. of Medicine, Manila, 1994, Hadassah Med. Ctr., Jerusalem, 1994; lectr. in field. Author: Office Orthopedics, 1955, 4th edit. 1973, Operative Orthopedic Clinics (with Dr. Avia Brockway), 1960, Atlas of Orthopedic Surgery, 1966, Difficult Orthopedic Diagnosis, 1972, Plannings and Pitfalls in Orthopedic Surgery, Natural History of Orthopedic Disease, 1993; mem. editorial bd. Resident & Staff Physician; contbr. numerous articles to profl. jours. Vol. physician Internat. Children's Program, Orthopedic Hosp., Mexicali, Mexico. Lt. col. U.S. Army, 1940-45. Fellow ACS, Internat. Coll. Surgeons; mem. Am. Rheumatism Assn., Am. Coll. Rheumatism, Am. Acad. Orthopedic Surgeons, So. Calif. Rheumatism Assn. (pres. 1979), Western Orthopedic Assn., Phi Beta Kappa, Alpha Omega Alpha.

COZENS, RICHARD, small business owner; b. Killeen, Tex., Oct. 21, 1952; s. Orman Roy and Betty Sue (Ward) C.; m. Kera Lynn Anderson, Apr. 30, 1988 (div. 1990); 1 child, Devon Killeen. BA, N.Mex. Highland U., 1975, MA, 1977. Apprentice upholsterer Don's Interiors, Las Vegas, N.Mex., 1977-79; owner/operator Blue Dart Ent., Las Vegas, 1979—. Home: 1632 Eighth St Las Vegas NM 87701-5024 Office: Blue Dart Ent 423 Railroad Ave Las Vegas NM 87701-3858

CRABBS, ROGER ALAN, publisher, consultant, small business owner, educator; b. Cedar Rapids, Iowa, May 9, 1928; s. Winfred Wesley and Faye (Woodard) C.; m. Marilyn Lee Westcott, June 30, 1951; children: William Douglas, Janet Lee Crabbs Turner, Ann Lee Crabbs Menke. B.A. in Sci., State U. Iowa, 1954; M.B.A., George Washington U., 1965, D.B.A., 1973; M.Christian Leadership, Western Conservative Bapt. Sem., 1978. Commd. 2nd lt. USAF, 1950, advanced through grades to lt. col., 1968, Ret., 1972; prof. mgmt. U. Portland, Oreg., 1972-79; prof. bus. George Fox Coll., Newberg, Oreg., 1979-83; pres. Judson Bapt. Coll., The Dalles, Oreg., 1983-85; pres., assoc. pub. Host Pubs. Inc. doing bus. as Travelhost of Oreg. and S.W. Wash., 1985—; pres., chmn. various corps., 1974-86; bd. dirs., past chmn. nat. adv. bd. TRAVELHOST, Inc.; cons. to various orgns., corps. and agys. Author: The Infallible Foundation for Management-The Bible, 1978, The Secret of Success in Small Business Management-Is in the Short Range, 1983; co-author: The Storybook Primer on Managing, 1976. Bd. dir. English Speaking Union, pres. 1994—; bd. dirs. Christ Cmty Ch., Washington County Visitors Assn., Oakhills Townhouse Assn.; mem. Minority Conv. Tourism Adv. Coun., Oreg. Decorated Air Force Commendation medal with oak leaf cluster, Meritorious Service medal Dept. Def.; rated Command Air Force Missileman; recipient regional, dist. and nat. awards SBA. Mem. Acad. Mgmt., Am. Abitration Assn., Svc. Corps Ret. Execs./Active Corps of Execs., Air Force Assn., Portland Officers Club, Rotary (past pres.), Masons, Alpha Kappa Psi, Delta Epsilon Sigma, Phi Mu Alpha. Republican. Office: Host Publs Inc 1075 NW Murray Rd Ste 173 Portland OR 97229-5501

CRABS, DONALD BENJAMIN, scenic and lighting designer, theater consultant; b. Puyallup, Wash., Oct. 29, 1926; s. Raymond D. Crabs and Dulcie (Bogie) Fullager; m. Clara Jane Kelly, Jan. 31, 1949; children: Kevin D., Krissy Ann., Shannon Maria. BA, U. Puget Sound, 1950; MA, Northwestern U., 1951. Asst. prof. Rutgers U., New Brunswick, N.J., 1951-65; prof. emeritus dept. theatre UCLA, L.A., 1965-91; cons. in field. Scenic, lighting designer including The House of Blue Leaves, The Rimers of Eldrich, No Place to be Somebody, Sleight of Hand, Mademoiselle Colombe, He Who Says, Yes, He Who Says, No., The Physicists, A Chorus Line, Ondine, U.S.A., Skin of Our Teeth, Troilus and Cressida, Sergeant Musgrave's Dance, The Measures Taken, Baal, Winterset; editor: California Theatre Index 1971: College & University Facilities, 1971; designer computer storage system for theatre facilities. With USN, 1944-46. Lecture and rsch. grantee U. Calif. Edn. Abroad Program, China, 1990. Mem. U.S. Inst. for Theater Tech. Methodist.

CRABTREE, DAVIDA FOY, minister; b. Waterbury, Conn., June 7, 1944; d. Alfred and Davida (Blakeslee) Foy; m. David T. Hindinger Jr., Aug. 28, 1982; stepchildren: Elizabeth Anne, D. Todd. BS, Marietta Coll., 1967; MDiv, Andover Newton Theol. Sch., 1972; D of Ministry, Hartford Sem., 1989. Ordained to ministry United Ch. of Christ, 1972. Founder, exec. dir. Prudence Crandall Ctr. for Women, New Britain, Conn., 1973-76; min., dir. Greater Hartford (Conn.) Campus Ministry, 1976-80; sr. min. Colchester (Conn.) Federated Ch., 1980-91; bd. dirs. Conn. Conf. United Ch. of Christ, Hartford, 1982-90; conf. min. So. Calif. Conf., United Ch. of Christ, Pasadena, 1991—; rsch. assoc. Harvard Div. Sch., Cambridge, Mass., 1975-76. Author: The Empowering Church, 1989 (named one of Top Ten Books of Yr. 1990); editorial advisor Alban Inst., 1990—. Bd. dirs. Hartford region YWCA, 1979-82; trustee Cragin Meml. Libr., Colchester, 1980-91, Hartford Sem.,1983-91; founder Youth Svcs. Bur., Colchester, 1984-89; pres. Creative Devel. for Colchester Inc., 1989-91; coun. Religious Leaders of L.A.,1991—; v.p. Hope in Youth Campaign, 1992—; trustee Sch. of Theology at Claremont, 1993—; dir. UCC Ins. Adv. bd., 1993—. Recipient Antoinette Brown award Gen. Synod, United Ch. of Christ, 1977, Conf. Preacher award Conn. Conf., United Ch. of Christ, 1982, Woman in Leadership award Hartford region YWCA, 1987; named one of Outstanding Conn. Women, UN Assn., 1987. Mem. Nat. Coun. Chs. (bd. dirs. 1969-81), Christians for Justice Action (exec. com. 1981-91).

CRAFT, BRIAN THOMAS, stand up comedian, embetterment consultant; b. Long Beach, Calif., N.Y., Aug. 20, 1957; s. Frank Henry and Geraldine (Shannon) C.; m. Kelly Jones, Nov. 25, 1989. Stand-up comedian, 1979—; owner Comedy Land Inc., Anaheim, Calif., 1988-92; embetterment cons. and CFO Comedy Lifeline Internat., Costa Mesa, Calif., 1989—. Cons. editor Hemalog, 1993—; author prose Ways and Means, 1994. Bd. dirs. and mem. golf fund-raising com. Hemophilia Found. of So. Calif., Pasadena, 1993—. Recipient Spl. award Nat. Hemophilia Found., 1985, Cert. of Appreciation, 1993, Svc. award Camp Fire Coun. of O.C., Tustin, Calif., 1991-92, Award of Excellence, Step into the Future Archer Found., 1991. Mem. Network of Coaches Alliance. Ch. of Religious Sci.

CRAFT, JOHN EDWARD, communications educator, media consultant; b. Hopedale, Ohio, Mar. 30, 1943; s. Clyde Edward and Mignon (Work) C.; m. Elizabeth Ann Harris, Dec. 18, 1965; children: Lauren, Jennifer. BFA in Dramatic Arts, Ohio U., 1966, MA in Radio and TV, 1972, PhD in Mass Communications, 1975. Dir. staging and lighting Sta. WOUB-TV, Athens, Ohio, 1965-66; dir. instructional TV Hancock County Schs., Weirton, W.Va., 1966-70; instructional TV coord. Ohio U., Athens, 1971-72; prof. Ariz. State U., Tempe, 1973—; analyst, Data for the Future, Phoenix, 1983-84; dir. video svcs., Samaritan Health Svcs., Phoenix, 1980-81; co-owner, Rich/Craft Prodns., Phoenix, 1974-75; field coord. Ednl. TV for S.E. Ohio, Athens, 1971-72; media cons. J. Craft, Cons., Tempe, 1969—; tech. staff mem., Ohio U. Theatre, Athens, 1964-65. Producer TV, Arizona Crossroads--Along Old Route 66, Ride and Rope 'Em Cowboy, Beauty of Individual Differences, 1990, Intervention Facilitator, 1983; producer, dir. TV, Staying Alive, 1981, The Cub, 1980, Princess and Tailor, 1966; appeared in plays, Ohio Valley Summer Theatre, 1963-65; contbr. articles to profl. publs. Bd. dirs. PAL Found., Mesa, Ariz., 1977. Recipient Outstanding Program award, Ariz. Med. Assn., Phoenix, 1981, Superior Achievement award, Internat. Radio & TV Soc., N.Y.C., 1985, Outstanding Program award, Alpha Epsilon Rho, Athens, 1964. Mem. NATAS (bd. dirs. 1973-76, 86—, pres. 1992-93, trustee 1994—), AAUP, Internat. TV Assn. (pres. 1983-85), Broadcast Edn. Assn., Ariz. Cable TV Forum, Phi Kappa Phi. Democrat. Home: 218 E Carter Dr Tempe AZ 85282-6705 Office: Ariz State U Stauffer Hall Tempe AZ 85287

CRAFT, REBECCA MIRIAM, pharmacologist, educator; b. Arlington, Mass., July 27, 1959; d. Arnold Murray and Atsuko (Onda) C.; m. Joseph Kevin Vaughan, Sept. 18, 1988. BS in Animal Sci., U. Md., 1981; MS in Zoology, N.C. State U., 1984; PhD in Exptl. and Biol. Psychology, U. N.C., 1991. Rsch. scientist dept. pharmacology Burroughs Wellcome Co., Research Triangle Park, N.C., 1984-87; rsch. assoc. dept. pharmacology U. Ariz., Tucson, 1991-93; asst. prof. dept. psychology Wash. State U., Pullman, 1993—. Author rsch. articles; ad-hoc reviewer Jour. Pharmacology and Exptl. Therapeutics, Drug and Alcohol Dependence, European Jour. Pharmacology, Life Scis., 1990—. Recipient rsch. grants. Mem. Soc. for Neurosci., Am. Pain Soc., Coll. on Problems of Drug Dependence (Travel award 1991), Assn. for Women in Sci. (treas. chpt. 1989-90, program coord. 1991-92). Office: Wash State U Dept Psychology Pullman WA 99164-4820

CRAFT, ROBBIE WRIGHT, artist; b. St. Louis, Feb. 22, 1951; d. Robert Edward and Irene (Tosch) Wright; m. Joseph Walter Epply III (div. 1978); 1 child, Joseph Walter IV; m. Raymond Wood Craft II, Feb. 14, 1987. Student, Casper Jr. Coll., 1969-71. Mgr. restaurant and bar Widow Browns, Crofton, Md., 1978-84; adminstrv. asst. U.S. Dept. Def., Andrews AFB, Md., 1974-75; illustrator, supr. U.S. Dept. Def., Cheyenne, Wyo., 1985-88, EEO counselor, 1987—, chief visual info., 1988—; ind. artist Maryland, Wyo., 1974—; ind. interior designer Wyo., 1985—. Mem. Internat. Platform Assn., United We Stand. Lutheran. Home: 7223 Tumbleweed Dr Cheyenne WY 82009-1014 Office: Visual Info Bldg 242 Cheyenne WY 82005

CRAGUN, CALVIN, business owner; b. Salt Lake City, Nov. 14, 1940; s. Robert Wallace and Vivian (Parker) C.; m. Celestia Van Tussenbroek, Dec. 20, 1967; children: Marlayn, Caroline, David, Robert. BS, U. Utah, 1963, MS, 1966. Tchr. Utah Sch. for the Deaf, Ogden, 1966-72; from salesperson to mgmt. dept. Home Life of N.Y., Salt Lake City, 1972-82; with ins. sales dept. Standard of Oreg., Salt Lake City, 1982-84; owner Custom Benefits, Salt Lake City, 1984—, Rocky Mt. Brokerage, Salt Lake City, 1985-88, Ins. Designers, Salt Lake City, 1988—. Mem. Nat. Conf. for Autism, Salt Lake City, 1983; regional coord. Internat. Winter Spl. Olympics, Salt Lake City, 1985—; mem. Utah Gov.'s Com. for Handicapped, Salt Lake City, 1983-84, Family Support Adv. Coun., 1995—; vol. Jr. Achievement, 1991—; tchr. Life Underwriter Tng. Coun., 1992—; chmn. steering com. Adult Handicap Social Club, 1994-95. Mem. Utah Coun. for Handicapped (v.p. 1982-83), After Hours (chairperson 1993—). Home and Office: 2686 Towne Dr Salt Lake City UT 84121-5146

CRAIB, KENNETH BRYDEN, resource development executive, physicist, economist; b. Milford, Mass., Oct. 13, 1938; s. William Pirie and Virginia Louise (Bryden) C.; m. Gloria Faye Lisano, June 25, 1960; children—Kenneth Jr., Judith Diane, Lori Elaine, Melissa Suzanne. BS in Physics, U. Houston, 1967; MA in Econs., Calif. State U., 1982; postgrad. Harvard U., 1989. Aerospace technologist NASA, Houston, 1962-68; staff physicist Mark Systems, Inc., Cupertino, Calif., 1968-69; v.p. World Resources Corp., Cupertino, 1969-71; dir. resources devel. div. Aero Service Corp., Phila., 1971-72; dir. ops. Resources Devel. Assocs., Los Altos, Calif., 1972-80, pres., chief exec. officer, Diamond Springs, Calif., 1980-85; owner Sand Ridge Arabians, 1980—; chmn., dir. Resources Devel. Assocs., Inc., 1982—, Devel. Support Internat. Inc., Placerville, Calif., 1981—; pres., chmn., dir. RDA Internat., Inc., 1986—; dir. Sierra Gen. Investments, 1985—, Transatlantic Fisheries, Inc., 1995—. Contbr. articles to profl. jours. Served with USAF, 1957-61. Recipient Sustained Superior Performance award NASA, 1966. NASA grantee, 1968. Mem. Am. Soc. Photogrammetry, Soc. Internat. Devel., Agrl. Research Inst., Calif. Select Com. Remote Sensing, Internat. Assn. Natural Resources Pilots, Remote Sensing Soc. (council), Am. Soc. Oceanography (charter), Aircraft Owners and Pilots Assn., Gulf and Caribbean Fisheries Inst., Placerville C. of C., Harvard Alumni Assn. Republican. Universalist. Home: 6431 Mary Ann Ln Placerville CA 95667-8167 Office: RDA Internat Inc 801 Morey Dr Placerville CA 95667-4411

CRAIB, RALPH GRANT, reporter; b. Oakland, Calif., Jan. 31, 1925; s. Alexander Leslie and Martha O.C. (Clerk) C.; m. Karola Maria Saekel, Dec. 4, 1962; children: Lisa Maria, Anne. B.A. with honors, San Francisco State Coll., 1950. From copy person, reporter and feature writer Oakland Tribune, 1942-59; mem. staff San Francisco Chronicle, 1959-91, editorial writer, 1968-70, mem. editorial bd., 1978-91; ret., contbr., 1990—; information officer, mem. staff gov. Am. Samoa, Pago Pago, 1965-66. Bd. dirs. No. Calif. chpt. Americans for Democratic Action, 1967-68. Served with AUS, World War II, ETO. Decorated Combat Infantrymans Badge Bronze star; recipient Joseph R. Knowland newswriting award, 1952, 57, Edward McQuade journalism award, 1977, Lifetime Excellence in Journalism award No. Calif. chpt. Soc. Profl. Journalists, 1990; Reid Found. fellow, New Guinea, Australia, 1955. Mem. San Francisco-Oakland Newspaper Guild (exec. com. 1976-78), Explorers Club (N.Y.C.). Democrat. Home: 638 The Alameda Berkeley CA 94707-1602

CRAIG, AMELIA AUDREY, lawyer; b. San Rafael, Calif., Apr. 30, 1960; d. Stephen Wright Craig and Margaret May (Baker) Chrisman. Student, U. Calif., Berkeley, 1981, Univ. Coll., London, 1981-82; BA, Dartmouth Coll., 1982; JD, Stanford U., 1986. Bar: Md. 1987, D.C. 1988, Calif. 1989, U.S. Dist. Ct. Md. 1988, U.S. Dist. Ct. D.C. 1988, U.S. Dist. Ct. (no. dist.) Calif. 1989, U.S. Dist. Ct. (ea. dist.) Calif. 1991, U.S. Ct. Appeals (9th cir.) 1991, U.S. Dist. Ct. (ctrl. dist.) Calif. 1993. Rsch. asst. Ariz. State Legislature, Phoenix, 1979; intern reporter The Bull., Phila., 1980; spl. assignment reporter The Times, London, 1981; paralegal Esdaile, Barrett & Esdaile, Boston, 1982-83; reporter The Bus. Jour., San Jose, Calif., 1984; legal extern Amnesty Internat., Washington, 1985; assoc. Baker & Hostetler, Washington, 1986-88; assoc. in litigation Heller, Ehrman, White & McAuliffe, San Francisco, 1988-93; mng. atty. western regional office Lambda Legal Def. and Edn. Fund, L.A., 1993-94, mng. atty., 1995—; com. crime victims and corrections Calif. Bar, 1992-94, exec. com. on legal svcs., 1994—. Bd. dirs. Washington Area Assn. for Children of Alcoholism and Other Addictions, 1988; mem. Calif. Bar Commn. on Corrections, 1990-91; vol. San Francisco AIDS panel, 1990-92; bd. dirs. Dartmouth GALA, 1994—, Bay Area Career Women; mem. Glide Meml. United Meth. Ch. Mem. ABA, ACLU, Nat. Gay and Lesbian Lawyers Assn., Calif. Women Lawyers, Bar Assn. San Francisco (mem. com. on gay and lesbian issues 1993—), L.A. County Bar Assn. (sec. 1993—, mem. com. on sexual orientation bias 1993-94), Bay Area Lawyers for Individual Freedom (bd. dirs. 1993—, gay legal referral svc. cochair bd. dirs. 1993—), Lawyers for Human Rights (bd. dirs. 1994, chair jud. com. 1994, mem. adv. com. HIV legal svcs. delivery project for Greater L.A. 1994—), Dartmouth Lawyers Assn., Amnesty Internat., Barristers Club San Francisco (vice chair criminal law com. 1992-93), Harvey Milk Lesbian and Gay Dem. Club. Office: Lambda Legal Def and Edn Fund 6030 Wilshire Blvd Ste 200 Los Angeles CA 90036-3617

CRAIG, CAROL MILLS, marriage, family and child counselor; b. Berkeley, Calif., May 7, 1952. BA in Psychology with honors, U. Calif., Santa Cruz, 1974; MA in Counseling Psychology, John F. Kennedy U., 1980; doctoral student, Calif. Sch. Profl. Psychology, Berkeley, 1980-87, Columbia Pacific U., San Rafael, Calif., 1987—. Psychology intern Fed. Correction Inst., Pleasanton, Calif., 1979-81, Letterman Army Med. Ctr., San Francisco, 1980-82; psychology intern VA Mental Hygiene Clinic, Oakland, Calif., 1981-82, Martinez, Calif., 1982-83; instr. Martinez Adult Sch., 1983, Piedmont Adult Edn., Oakland, 1986; biofeedback and stress mgmt. cons. Oakland, 1986—; child counselor Buddies-A Nonprofit, Counseling Svc. for Persons in the Arts, Lafayette, Calif., 1993—; founder Chesley Sch., 1994; rsch. asst. Irvington Pubs., N.Y.C., 1979, Little, Brown and Co., Boston, 1983. Mem. Calif. Assn. Marriage and Family Therapists (clin.), Musicians Union Local 424, Calif. Scholarship Fedn. (life).

CRAIG, DALE ALLAN, insurance company researcher; b. Illiopolis, Ill., Dec. 19, 1939; s. Wayne Adair and Margaret Elizabeth (Buchhorn) C.; m. Fannie Wai Lai Cheng, June 9, 1962 (div. 1988); 1 child, Gordon Frederick Craig; m. Catherine Louise Whitman, Aug. 25, 1989. BM, Millikin U, 1961; MA, Cornell U., 1964; DMA, Stanford U., 1968. Lectr. Chinese U., Hong Kong, 1969-76, Queensland Conservatorium, Brisbane, Australia, 1977-84; researcher The Doctor's Co., Napa, Calif., 1986—. Contbr. 25 articles to profl. jours. Com. mem. Napa City-County Libr., Napa, 1994—, literacy tutor, 1994—. Andrew Mellow fellow U. Pitts., 1961-62, Leverhulme fellow U. Western Australia, Perth, 1976. Mem. Green Party. Unitarian Universalist. Home: 11 Davis Ave Napa CA 94559-3541 Office: The Doctor's Co 185 Greenwood Rd Napa CA 94558-6270

CRAIG, LARRY EDWIN, senator; b. Council, Idaho, July 20, 1945; s. Elvin and Dorothy Craig. B.A., U. Idaho; postgrad, George Washington U. Farmer, rancher Midvale area, Idaho; mem. Idaho Senate, 1974-80, 97th-101st Congresses from 1st Dist. Idaho, 1981-90; senator 102nd Congress from Idaho, 1990—, mem. com. agr., nutrition and forestry, com. energy and natural resources, spl. com. on aging, Sen. ethics com., ethics study commn., chmn. subcom. on forests and pub. land mgmt., chmn. subcom. forestry conservation and rural revitalization; chmn. Idaho Rep. State Senate Races, 1976-78, chmn. senate steering com.; mem. joint econ. com., com. veterans' affairs, subcom. energy R & D. Pres. Young Rep. League Idaho, 1976-77; mem. Idaho Rep. Exec. Com., 1976-78; chmn. Rep. Central Com. Washington County, 1971-72; advisor vocat. edn. in public schs. HEW, 1971-73; mem. Idaho Farm Bur., 1965-79. Served with U.S. Army N.G., 1970-74. Mem. NRA (bd. dirs. 1983—), Future Farmers of Am. (v.p. 1965). Methodist. Office: US Senate 313 Hart Bldg Washington DC 20510-0009

CRAIG, LEXIE FERRELL, career development specialist, guidance counselor, educator; b. Halls, Tenn., Dec. 12, 1921; d. Monroe Stancil and Hester May (Martin) Ferrell; m. Philip L. Craig, May 19, 1951; children: Douglas H., Laurie K., Barbara Craig Peterson. BS magna cum laude, George Peabody Coll., Vanderbilt U., 1944; MA with honors in Guidance Counseling Devel., Denver U., 1965; postgrad. Colo. U., 1972—, Colo. State U., 1964—, U. No. Colo., 1964—. Cert. vocat. adminstr., Colo., vocat. guidance specialist, vocat. bus. edn. specialist, vocat. home econs. specialist, reading specialist, nat. recreation dir. specialist. Danforth grad. fellow, counselor Mich. State U., East Lansing, 1944-46; nat. coll. counselor, field dir. dept. of univ. pastor and student work in the dept. of higher edn. Am. Bapt. Conv., summer svc. career projects dir. U.S. and Europe, 1946-51; coord. religious and career activities counselor, Colo. U., 1951-52; tchr. home econs., phys. edn., counseling, dist. 96, Riverside, Ill., 1952-54; substitute tchr., psychometrist, reading specialist part time, Deerfield, Ill., 1956-59; substitute tchr. Littleton (Colo.) Dist. VI, 1960-62, guidance and career devel. counselor Littleton Pub. Schs., 1961-86, career devel. specialist, guidance counselor spl. assignments state and nat., Gov.'s Youth 2000 Task Force Com., 1988—, also mem. vocat. needs and assessment com., 1988-89, chmn. retirement workshops for educators in Littleton Pub. Schs., 1990-93; chmn. leadership AARP Works Employment Planning Team, Colo., 1989-91, state coordr. employment planning, 1988-93, pres. Greater Littleton chartered chpt., Colo., 1990-93, pres. employment planning program, 1992-93; mem. Gov. of Colo. Older Workers Adv. Coun., 1989—; dir./counselor Job Corps, Denver area, 1967-68; dir./counselor YWCA Extension Program, Job Corps, Denver, 1967-68; tchr. adult edn. home econs., evening classes, 1963-66; chartered, pres., mem. Colo. State Career Task Force, 1973-77; cons. vol. home econ. cons. Colo. State U extension office, 1988-89. Lay conf. rep. pastor and parish commn. St. Andrews Meth. Ch., vol. sr. citizens programs, Colo. state coord. Littleton Cmty. Ctr., 1987-90, mem. nominating and pers. work area com., youth work area chmn. membership com., 1989-92, pres., 1990-92, v.p. Women's Assn., 1994-95, also greeter; mem. Greater Denver Friendship Force, 1972—; bd. dirs. Career Awareness Council Boy Scouts Am., Metro Denver, 1972—; also mem. Colo. Career Awareness Council, 1972—; mem. So. Suburban Recreation, Littleton Cmty. Arts Ctr., mem. lit. book club; mem. Friends of Littleton Libr. and Mus.; charter mem. Littleton Townhall Music and Drama Ctr.; adv. council Powell PTO, 1981-84; adv. council SEMBCS area vocat. schs., 1969—; mem. local caucus com. Rep. Party; mem. Dist. Environ. Sci. Council. Didcott scholar, Peabody/Vanderbilt Coll., 1942; mem. AVS adv. council Early Childhood Edn., Health Occupation, Restaurant Arts and Coop Career Devel., 1970—, Gov's. Older Workers Task Force, Pvt. Sector Adv. Coun., 1989—; Danforth home econs. and leadership scholar, 1943, Danforth fellow, 1944-45 Danforth Found.; Am. Leadership Camp Found. scholar, Shelby, Mich., 1942-45; Hildegarde Sweet Scholar, 1983; recipient Sullivan award and grant, named outstanding grad., Geo. Peabody Coll., 1944; named Littleton Mother of Year, 1977, Colo. Vocat. Counselor of Yr., 1978, Colo. Vocat. Guidance Assoc. Counselor of Yr., 1984; recipient plaque for recruiting and career guidance Navy and Air Force, 1980-86, Clifford G. Houston Colo. Counselor award, 1985, Outstanding award Boy Scouts of Am. Career Awareness Council (Denver area), 1986—, Recognition Gold Pin award United Meth. Ch. Women, 1988, Colo. Disting. Silver Svc. award, 1990, Gov.'s Silver Trophy award AARP, 1991, Nat. award, 1991, Gov.'s Plaque-Outstanding Vol. Svc. to Colo. Sr. Citizens award, 1991-92, Gov.'s Silver trophy for svc. and establishing AARP employment planning program for Colo., 1992. Mem. NEA, AAUW, ous Values Assn. (mem. chmn. 1989), Colo. Edn. Assn., Littleton Edn. Assn., Am. Vocat. Assn. (pres. 1991-93), Colo. Vocat. Assn., Am. Assn. Counseling and Devel. (pres. 1990-91), Colo. Assn. for Adult Devel. and Aging (exec. bd., pres. 1989-93), Nat. Career Devel. Assn. (membership chmn.), Colo. Career Devel. Assn. (pres. 1983-86, membership chmn. 1987-91), Nat. Vocat. Guidance Assn. (Colo. rep.), Am. Assn. Retired Persons (charter mem., Colo. state vol., coord. employment planning program 1989-91, v.p. Greater Littleton chpt. 1991-93, pres. 1990-93), Colo. Ret. Sch. Employees Assn. (pres. 1990-93), Colo. Sch. Counselors Assn., Am. Field Service (pres. Littleton chpt.), Home Economists in Homemaking (Littleton and Bega, Australia clubs 1989—), Colo. Gerontol. Soc., Colo. Home Econ. Assn., Phi Delta Kappa, Delta Kappa Gamma Alpha Delta (past chpt. pres., Omega State DKG, state com. chmn. personal growth and svcs.), Order Eastern Star, Countryn Western Dance Club, Delta Pi Epsilon (past pres.), Pi Omega Pi (past pres.), Pi Gamma Mu (past pres.), Kappa Delta Pi (past pres.). Office: 2655 S Sheridan Ct Denver CO 80227-4037

CRAIG, MICHAEL SCOTT, real estate executive, pharmacologist; b. Atlanta, Tex., Feb. 21, 1956; s. Hoyt Dean and Ellenda Claudia (Clements) C.; m. Angela Ruth Francisco, May 30, 1992. BS in Pharmacy, U. Tex., 1979, MBA in Real Estate/Fin., 1985. Registered pharmacist, Tex.; registered real estate broker, Calif. Pharmacist mgr. Script Shop Pharmacies, Austin, Tex., 1979-83; comml. loan credit mgr. Franklin Savs. & Loan, Austin, 1985-87; asset mgr. Continental Mgmt., Dallas, 1987-88; v.p. asset mgmt. Postal Mgmt. Svc. Corp., L.A., 1988-89; sr. v.p. asset mgmt. RRP Mgmt. Corp., L.A., 1989—; dir. Supermarket Video, Inc., L.A., 1988; cons. Assoc. U.S. Postal Svc. Lessors, L.A., 1989-93. Mem. Inst. Real Estate Mgmt., Beta Gamma Sigma.

CRAIG, ROBERT WALLACE, educational and policy center administrator; b. Long Beach, Calif., Sept. 16, 1924; s. Harold Fleming and Ellen Amelia (Stagg) C.; m. Carol Williams Gallun, Nov. 5, 1957; children: Kathleen Elizabeth, Jennifer Courtney, Michael Brian. BS, BA cum laude, U. Wash., 1949; MA, Columbia U., 1951. V.p., exec. dir. Aspen (Colo.) Inst. for Humanistic Studies, 1954-64; v.p. Unimark Internat. Design Inc., Aspen and Chgo., 1965-71; prin. Robert Craig & Assocs., 1965-73; ptnr. Genesis Inc., 1971-73, Rieben & Craig, Denver, 1973-75; pres., founder The Keystone (Colo.) Ctr., 1975—; mountain and cold weather tng. cons. U.S. Army, 1951-54; hon. trustee, co-founder Aspen Ctr. for Physics. Author: (with Charles Houston and Robert Bates) K-2, The Savage Mountain, 1954, Storm and Sorrow, 1978. Bd. dirs. Snake River Health Clinic, Keystone, Colo. Outward Bound, 1985, Santa Fe Inst., Jimmie Heuga Ctr., Vail Valley Inst.; leader Am. Pamirs Expedition, 1974, Am. Tibetan Everest Expedtion, 1983; active U.S. Antarctic Safety Rev. Panel NSF, Washington Inst. Fgn. Affairs. Lt. (j.g.) USNR, 1943-46, PTO. Democrat. Episcopalian. Clubs: Am.

Alpine (pres. 1983-86), Century (N.Y.C.), Cactus (Denver), Bohemian (San Francisco), Met. (Washington). Office: Keystone Ctr PO Box 8606 Keystone CO 80435-7998

CRAIG, STEPHEN WRIGHT, lawyer; b. N.Y.C., Aug. 28, 1932; s. Herbert Stanley and Dorothy (Simmons) C.; m. Margaret M. Baker, June 10, 1958 (div. 1984); children: Amelia Audrey, Janet Elizabeth, Peter Baker; m. Bette Piller, 1984. AB, Harvard U., 1954, JD, 1959. Bar: Maine 1959, Calif. 1960, Ariz. 1963. Reporter Daily Kennebec Jour., Augusta, Maine, 1956; with pub. rels. staff Am. Savoyards, 1957; atty. IRS, San Francisco, 1959-61; atty.-adviser U.S. Tax Ct., 1961-63; ptnr. Snell & Wilmer, Phoenix, 1963-78, Winston & Strawn (formerly Craig, Greenfield & Irwin), Phoenix, 1978-87, Brown & Bain, Phoenix and Palo Alto, Calif., 1989—; guest lectr. Amos Tuck Sch. Bus., Dartmouth U., 1962; lectr. Ariz. and N.Mex. Tax Insts., 1966-67; guest lectr. sch. law Ariz. State U., 1984, adj. prof. law, 1985-87. Chmn. Jane Wayland Child Guidance Ctr., 1968-70; mem. Maricopa County Health Planning Coun., chmn. mental health task force.; bd. dirs. Combined Met. Phoenix Arts, 1968, adv. bd., 1968-69; adv. bd. Ariz. State U. Tax Insts., 1968-70; bd. dirs. Phoenix Community Coun., 1970-73, Ariz. Acad. With AUS, 1954-56. Home: 5214 N 34th Pl Phoenix AZ 85018-1521 Office: Brown & Bain 2901 N Central Ave Ste 2000 Phoenix AZ 85012-2740

CRAIGIE, EARLE JAMES, manufacturing consultant; b. Cambridge, Mass., Feb. 5, 1944; s. James Alexander and Louisa Florence (Harwood) C.; children: Kenneth D., Wayne A. BS in Indsl. Mgmt., Northeastern U., Boston, 1973. Line mgr. Analog Devices Inc., Norwood, Mass., 1966-80; bus. materials mgr. Digital Equipment Corp., Natick, Mass., 1980-82; promotion and tng. mgr. Digital Equipment Corp., Marlboro, Mass., 1982-84; corp. materials tng. mgr. Digital Equipment Corp., Northboro, Mass., 1984-87, materials and fin. cons., 1987-89; sr. mfg. cons. Digital Equipment Corp., Santa Clara, Calif., 1989—. Mem. Am. Prodn. and Inventory Control Soc. (past pres. Boston chpt., active mem. Santa Clara chpt., CPIM cert. coun.). Office: Digital Equipment Corp 2525 Augustine Dr Santa Clara CA 95054-3097

CRAIGO, STEADE RICHARD, architect, preservationist; b. Canonsburg, Pa., Dec. 21, 1946; s. Richard Jerome and Mary Susan (Jack) C.; m. Gretchen Howell Belser, Sept. 16, 1970 (div.). BArch, Clemson U., 1969; M in Constrn., York U., Eng., 1976. Lic. architect. Architect Ehni Architects, Charleston, S.C., 1972-74; staff architect Med. Univ. S.C., Charleston, S.C., 1974-75; project mgr. Ellis Island, Nat. Park Svc., N.Y.C., 1977; restoration architect Calif. Offices of Hist. Preservation, Sacramento, 1977-88, sr. restoration architect, 1988-89, dep. state hist. preservation officer, 1989-92, acting state hist. preservation officer, 1992-94, dep. state hist. preservation officer, 1994-95; mem. Calif. State Hist. Bldg. Safety Bd., Sacramento, 1981-95; bd. dirs. Nat. Conf. State Hist. Preservation Officers, Washington, 1993-95. Trustee Hist. Charleston Found., 1971-74; com. mem. Vets. Meml. Auditorium Com., Sacramento, 1992-93. Mem. Am. Inst. Architects, Calif. Coun. Am. Inst. Achitects, Nat. Trust for Hist. Preservation, The Am. Rsch. Ctr. of Egypt, Vets. Office of Strategic Svcs. Home: 949 Fremont Way Sacramento CA 95818-2135

CRAIN, CHESTER RAY, statistician, consultant; b. St. Louis, Apr. 17, 1944; s. Chester Raymond and Mary Louise (Landers) C.; m. Barbara Hope Fagnan, Sept. 2, 1967; 1 child, Michelle Wigmore. AB, Knox Coll., 1965; MA, U. Calif., Riverside, 1967; PhD, U. N.Mex., 1974. Rsch. statistician Knoll Pharm. Co., Whippany, N.J., 1980; mgr. stats. McNeil Pharm., Spring House, Pa., 1980-81; sr. biostatistician Miles Pharms., West Haven, Conn., 1981-83; dir. statis. svcs. Boots Pharms., Shreveport, La., 1983-84; mgr. biometrics DuPont Co., Wilmington, Del., 1984-85, cons. dept. cen. R & D, 1985-90; dept. coord. Corp. Electronic Info. Security Com., 1987-90; sr. statistician Baxter Hyland Div., Glendale, Calif., 1990-91, Advanced Micro Devices, Sunnyvale, Calif., 1991-93; ind. cons., 1993—. Author: Scientific Computing Division's Enhanced Statistical Products Product Plan; contbr. articles to profl. jours. Mem. Am. Soc. Quality Control (cert. quality engr., reliability engr., chmn-elect local sect. 1995—), Am. Statis. Assn., Soc. Clin. Trials, Biometric Soc., Phi Beta Kappa, Sigma Xi. Democrat. Unitarian. Home: 1038 Sandalwood Ln Milpitas CA 95035-3232

CRAIN, WILLIAM EDWIN, oil company executive; b. Duluth, Minn., Aug. 27, 1929; s. John Francis and Hildur Christine (Alm) C.; m. Jean Alice Grandmaison, Sept. 19, 1953; children: Elizabeth, Laureen, Bradley, Janet, Jeanne, Cathleen, Charles. BS in Bus. Econs., U. Minn., Duluth, 1953; MS in Geology, U. Minn., Mpls., 1957. Asst. to v.p., gen. mgr. Western Ops., San Francisco, 1974-76; chief geologist Calif. Co., New Orleans, 1976-77; mgr. western region Alaska exploration Chevron USA, San Francisco, 1977-80; gen. mgr. exploration western region Chevron USA, Concord, Calif., 1980-85; v.p. exploration Chevron USA, San Francisco, 1985-86, v.p. Chevron Corp. and sr. v.p. exploration, land and prodn., 1986-88; v.p. exploration and prodn. Chevron Corp., San Francisco, 1988—, also bd. dirs. Sgt. USAF, 1947-50. Mem. Am. Assn. Petroleum Geologists (editor jour. 1976-77), Am. Geol. Inst. Found. (bd. dirs.), Nat. Ocean Industries Assn. (bd. dirs.), Soc. Exploration Geophysicists, Am. Petroleum Inst. (exec. com. exploration affairs 1988). Republican. Roman Catholic. Club: World Trade. Office: Chevron Corp 555 Market St San Francisco CA 94105-2801

CRALLEY, LESTER VINCENT, retired industrial hygienist, editor; b. Carmi, Ill., Mar. 27, 1911; s. John W. Cralley and Martha Jones; m. Gertrude E. Wilson, Aug. 24, 1940; 1 child, Agnes D. BS, McKendree Coll., 1933; PhD, U. Iowa, 1942. Res. officer USPHS, Bethesda, Md., 1941-45; chief indsl. hygienist Aluminum Co. of Am., Pitts., 1945-67, mgr. environ. health svcs., 1968-74; mem. Sec. of Labor's Nat. Safety Adv. Com., Washington, 1969-70. Co-editor: Theory and Rationale of Industrial Hygiene Practice, 1985, new edit., 1994, In Plant Practices for Job Related Health Hazards Control, 1989, Health and Safety Beyond the Workplace, 1990. Mem. Am. Indsl. Hygiene Assn. (hon., treas. 1953-56, pres. 1956-57, Cummings Meml. award 1971), Am. Acad. Indsl. Hygiene, Internat. Commn. on Occupational Health, Planetary Soc. Home: 1453 Banyan Dr Fallbrook CA 92028-1105

CRAM, DONALD JAMES, chemistry educator; b. Chester, Vt., Apr. 22, 1919; s. William Moffet and Joanna (Shelley) C.; m. Jane Maxwell, Nov. 25, 1969. BS, Rollins Coll., 1941; MS, U. Nebr., 1942; PhD, Harvard U., 1947; PhD (hon.), U. Uppsala, 1977; DSc (hon.), U. So. Calif., 1983, Rollins Coll., 1988, U. Nebr., 1989, U. Western Ontario, 1990, U. Sheffield, 1991. Rsch. chemist Merck & Co., 1942-45; asst. prof. chemistry UCLA, 1947-50, assoc. prof., 1950-56, prof., 1956-90, S. Winstein prof., 1985-95, univ. prof., 1988-90, univ. prof. emeritus, 1990—; chem. con. Upjohn Co., 1952-88, Union Carbide Co., 1960-81, Eastman Kodak Co., 1981-91, Technicon Co., 1984-92, Inst. Guido Donegani, Milan, 1988-91; State Dept. exch. fellow to Inst. de Quimica, Nat. U. Mex., 1956; guest prof. U. Heidelberg, Fed. Republic Germany, 1958; guest lectr. S. Africa, 1967; Centenary lectr. Chem. Soc. London, 1976. Author: From Design to Discovery, 1990, (with Pine, Hendrickson and Hammond) Organic Chemistry, 1960, 4th edit., 1980, Fundamentals of Carbanion Chemistry, 1965, (with Richards and Hammond) Elements of Organic Chemistry, 1967, (with Cram) Essence of Organic Chemistry, 1977, (with Cram) Container Molecules and Their Guests, 1994; contbr. chpts. to textbooks, articles in field of host-guest complexation chemistry, carbanions, stereochemistry, mold metabolites, large ring chemistry. Named Young Man of Yr. Calif. Jr. C. of C., 1954, Calif. Scientist of Yr., 1974, Nobel Laureate in Chemistry, 1987, UCLA medal, 1993; recipient award for creative work in synthetic organic chemistry Am. Chem. Soc., 1965, Arthur C. Cope award, 1974, Richard Tolman medal, 1985, Willard Gibbs award, 1985, Roger Adams award, 1985, Herbert Newby McCoy award, 1965, 75, Glenn Seaborg award, 1989, Nat. Medal of Science, Nat. Sci. Found., 1993; award for creative rsch. organic chemistry Synthetic Organic Chem. Mfrs. Assn., 1965; Nat. Rsch. fellow Harvard U., 1947, Am. Chem. Soc. fellow, 1947-48, Guggenheim fellow, 1954-55. Fellow Royal Soc. (hon. 1989); mem. NAS (award in chem. scis. 1992), Am. Acad. Arts and Scis., Am. Chem. Soc., Royal Soc. Chemistry, Surfers Med. Assn., San Onofre Surfing Club, Sigma Xi, Lambda Chi Alpha. Office: UCLA Dept Chemistry Los Angeles CA 90024

CRAMER, DOUGLAS SCHOOLFIELD, broadcasting executive; b. Louisville, Aug. 22; s. Douglas Schoolfield and Pauline (Compton) C.; m. Joyce Haber, Sept. 25, 1966 (div. 1973); children: Douglas Schoolfield, III, Courtney Sanford. Student, Northwestern U., 1949-50, Sorbonne, Paris, 1951; B.A., U. Cin., 1953; M.F.A., Columbia U., 1954. Prodn. asst. Radio City Music Hall, N.Y.C., 1950-51; with script dept. Metro-Goldwyn-Mayer, 1952; mng. dir. Cin. Playhouse, 1953-54; instr. Carnegie Inst. Tech., 1955-56; TV supr. Procter & Gamble, 1956-59; broadcast supr. Ogilvy, Benson & Mather, 1959-62; v.p. program devel. ABC, 1962-66, 20th Century-Fox-TV, Los Angeles, 1966-68; exec. v.p. in charge prodn. Paramount TV, 1968-71; ind. producer, pres. Douglas S. Cramer Co., 1971—; exec. v.p. Aaron Spelling Prodns., 1976-87, vice-chmn., 1988-90; bd. dirs. Spelling Entertainment, Inc. Exec. prodr.: Bridget Loves Bernie, CBS-TV, 1972-73, QB VII, 1973-74, Dawn: Portrait of a Teenage Runaway, NBC-TV, 1976, Danielle Steel's Fine Things, Kalediscope, 1990, Changes, Daddy, Palomino, 1990-91, Secrets, 1991, Heart Beat, 1992, Star, Message to Nam, 1993, Vanished, Family Album, 1994, Zoya, 1993, Perfect Strangers, No Greater Love, 1995; co-exec. prodr.: Love Boat, ABC, 1977-86, Vegas, ABC, 1978-81, Wonder Woman, ABC, 1975-77, CBS, 1977-78, Dynasty, 1981-89, Hotel, 1983-87, Trade Winds, 1993; prodr.: (feature film) Sleeping Together, 1995; author: (plays) Call of Duty, 1953, Love Is A Smoke, 1957, Whose Baby Are You, 1963, Last Great Dish, 1994, Lust For Murder, 1995. Pres., Mus. Contemporary Art, L.A., 1990-93, 1st vice-chair, 1993—; mem. bd. trustees and internat. Coun. Mus. Modern Art, N.Y.C.; pres. Douglas S. Cramer Found. With U.S. Army, 1954. Mem. Univ. Club of N.Y.C., Beta Theta Pi. Office: The Cramer Co 4605 Lankershim Blvd Ste 617 North Hollywood CA 91602-1818

CRAMER, EUGENE NORMAN, nuclear power engineer, computer educator; b. Arkansas City, Kans., Apr. 26, 1932; s. Norman Charles and Hulda Margaret (Maier) C.; m. Donna Marie Gagliardi, May 18, 1957 (dec. 1984); children: Lorene, Kristine, Eileen, Carla; m. Marlene McLean, Dec. 29, 1985. B.S. in Physics, Kans. State Coll., 1955, B.S. in Math., 1955; grad. Oak Ridge Sch. Reactor Tech., 1959; M.A. in Mgmt., Claremont Grad. Sch., 1976, M.B.A., 1985. Registered profl. engr., Calif. Jr. engr. Westinghouse Bettis, Pitts., 1955-57; devel. engr. Oak Ridge Nat. Lab., 1959-69; cons. examiner AEC, 1961-73; engr. advanced energy system So. Calif. Edison, Los Angeles, 1969-88, mgr. nuclear comm., 1988-95, pres., asst. to edn. 1995—; sec. task force on nuclear safety research Electric Research Council, 1969-74; chmn. Pub. Edn. Utility Nuclear Waste Mgmt. Group, 1978-81, Pub. Edn. Calif. Radioactive Waste Mgmt. Forum, 1982—. Sect. editor Nuclear Safety jour., 1964-69. Contbr. articles to profl. jours. Mem. Capistrano Unified Sch. Dist. Edn. Found., 1994—. Served as 1st lt. Signal Corps, U.S. Army, 1957-59. Fellow Inst. for Advancement Engrng.; mem. Am. Nuclear Soc. (bd. dirs. 1978-81, Meritorious Service award 1981, pub. info. com. 1983—), Health Physics Soc., Soc. for Risk Analysis. Republican. Roman Catholic. Club: Sierra.

CRAMER, FRANK BROWN, engineering executive, combustion engineer, systems consultant; b. Long Beach, Calif., Aug. 29, 1921; s. Frank Brown and Clara Bell (Ritzenthaler) C.; m. Hendrika Van der Hulst, 1948 (div. 1962); children: Frieda Hendrika, Eric Gustav, Lisa Monica, Christina Elena; m. Paula Gil, Aug. 3, 1973; children: Alfred Alexander, Consuelo F., Peter M. BA, U. So. Calif., 1942, postgrad., 1942-43, 46-51. Rsch. fellow U. So. Calif., L.A., 1946-51; supr. engrng. Rocketdyne, Canoga Park, Calif., 1953-63; pres. Multi-Tech, Inc., San Fernando, Calif., 1960-69; systems cons. Electro-Optical Systems, Pasadena, Calif., 1969-70, McDonnell-Douglas Astronautic, Huntington Beach, Calif., 1971-72; pres. Ergs Unltd. Inc., Mission Hills, Calif., 1973-89, Acquisition, Mission Hills, 1988—; instr. engrng. stats. U. So. Calif., L.A., 1955-57, systems cons. dept. medicine, 1959-68; systems cons. Jet Propulsion Lab., Pasadena, 1964-68. Author: Statistics for Medical Students, 1951, Combustion Processes/Liquid Rocket Engineering, 1968; contbr. articles to profl. jours. Committeeman Libertarian Party, San Fernando Valley, Calif., 1966, Rep. Party, Mission Hills, 1967-68; dir. realtor's com. on the air quality mgmt. plan, So. Calif. Air Quality Control Dist., treas. realtor com. for air quality; pres. San Fernando Rep. Club, 1967-68.

CRAMER, JAMES DALE, physicist, scientific company executive; b. Canton, Ohio, Aug. 4, 1937; s. Dale and Vera Arlene (Lindower) C.; B.S., Calif. State U. at Fresno, 1960; M.S., U. Oreg., 1962; Ph.D., U. N.Mex., 1969; m. Geraldine M. Bendoski, July 20, 1957; children—Karen Lynn, Eric James. Mem. tech. staff U. Calif., Los Alamos, 1962-70; v.p., Davis-Smith Corp., San Diego, 1970-73; mem. tech. staff Sci. Applications Inc., LaJolla, Calif., 1970-73, group v.p., Albuquerque, 1973-80, dir., 1974-80; pres. Sci. & Engrng. Assocs., Inc., Albuquerque, 1980—; cons. in field. Pres. Albuquerque Mus. Found., 1981-83. Mem. Am. Phys. Soc., IEEE, Contbr. articles to profl. publs. nuclear physics. Home: PO Box 30691 Albuquerque NM 87190-0691 Office: 2500 Louisiana Blvd NE Albuquerque NM 87110-4319*

CRAMER, MARK STEVEN, family physician; b. Bluffton, Ohio, Jan. 17, 1949; s. Marco James and Eleanor Mae (Herzig) C.; m. Patricia Lynn Worsham, 1972; children: James Mark Leland, Marcella Patricia. BA in Biology with high honors, U. Calif., San Diego, 1971, MD, 1975. Diplomate Nat. Bd. Med. Examiners, Am. Bd. Family Physicians. Intern and resident in family practice Oakwood Hosp., Dearborn, Mich., 1975-79; physician, owner family practice Mark Steven Cramer, M.D., San Diego, 1980-91; physician, cons., expert witness Calif. Med. Bd., San Diego, 1987-92; physician, cons., specialist San Diego Sheriff's Dept., 1984—; family practice physician San Diego, 1991—; preceptor U. Calif. Sch. Medicine, San Diego, 1983-87, U. Calif., Davis, 1986-87; sr. med. staff Scripps Hosp., La Jolla, Calif., 1981—, edn. com., 1985—, Calif. com., 1985—, family practice supervisory com., 1986—; med. staff Sharp Hosp., San Diego, 1981-85. Contbr. papers to profl. publs. Wroker, ship labor Esperance, Inc., San Diego, 1972' dir. railfan patrol Pacific S.W. R.R. Mus., San Diego, 1983-85; tracker, search and rescue dept. San Diego Sheriff Dept., 1984-88, specialist, 1988—. Recipient fellowship Am. Acad. Family Physicians, 1989. Fellow Am. Acad. Family Physicians; mem. AMA, Calif. Med. Soc., San Diego Med. Soc., Mich. Acad. Family Physicians, San Diego Acad. Family Physicians, Calif. Acad. Family Physicians. Home: 3581 Millikin Ave San Diego CA 92122-2926

CRAMER, OWEN CARVER, classics educator; b. Tampa, Fla., Dec. 1, 1941; s. Maurice Browning and Alice (Carver) C.; m. Rebecca Jane Lowrey, June 23, 1962; children—Alfred, Thomas, Ethan, Benjamin. A.B., Oberlin Coll., 1962; Ph.D., U. Tex., 1973. Spl. instr. U. Tex., Austin, 1964-65; instr. in classics Colo. Coll., Colorado Springs, 1965-69, asst. prof. classics, 1969-75, assoc. prof. classics, 1975-84, M.C. Gile prof. classics, 1984—, dir. comparative lit., 1993—; cons. humanist Colo. Humanities Program, Denver, 1982-83; vis. prof. U. Chgo., 1987-88. Editorial asst. Arion, 1964-65; contbr. papers, articles on Greek lang. and lit. to profl. publs., 1974—; contbr. classical music revs. to Colorado Springs Sun, 1984-86. Chorus tenor Colo. Opera Festival, Colorado Springs, 1976-82; mem. El Paso County Democratic Central Com., Colo., 1968-88; active ordained elder Presbyn. Ch., 1992. Hon. Woodrow Wilson fellow, 1962; univ. fellow U. Tex., Austin, 1962-64. Mem. Am. Philol. Assn. (campus adv. svc. 1989—, chmn. com. on smaller depts. 1979-80), Classical Assn. of Middle West and South, Modern Greek Studies Assn., Colo. Classics Assn., Phi Beta Kappa. Presbyterian. Club: Round Table (Colorado Springs). Home: 747 E Uintah St Colorado Springs CO 80903-2546 Office: Colo Coll Dept Classics Colorado Springs CO 80903

CRAMMER, TERRY LYNN, nursing educator; b. Reading, Pa., Feb. 26, 1963; s. Roy Vincent and Elaine Marie (Amos) C.; m. Mylene Dizon dela Llana, July 2, 1988; children: Michael, Travis. AA, N.Mex. Mil. Inst., 1983; BSN, Calif. State U., Long Beach, 1988. RN, Calif.; cert. ACLS instr., Am. Heart Assn.; cert. BTLS instr., Calif. Chpt. Am. Coll. Emergency Physicians; cert. BCLS instr., Am. Heart Assn. Clin. nurse Harbor UCLA Med. Ctr., Torrance, 1988-91; paramedic instr. Parmedic Tng. Inst., Commerce, Calif., 1991—; cons. Premier Med. Educators, Whittier, Calif., 1991-93. Lt. U.S. Army. Mem. Emergency Nurses Assn. (cert. TNCC provider). Republican. Roman Catholic. Home: 11324 Agnes St Cerritos CA 90703-6504 Office: Paramedic Tng Inst 5555 Ferguson Dr Ste 220 Los Angeles CA 90022-5152

CRAMPTON, ESTHER LARSON, sociology and political science educator; b. Plainview, Nebr., Apr. 14, 1915; d. Charles W. and Anna Margrethe (Staugaard) Larson; m. Francis Asbury Crampton, Jan. 19, 1949 (dec.); children: Jacqueline, Edith. AB, Colo. Coll. of Edn., 1935; MA, U. Wis., 1937; PhD, Am. U., 1972. Observer, writer U.S. Weather Bur., Washington, 1942-48; interpreter Portuguese RFC Rubber Devel. Corp., Manaos, Brasil, 1943; tchr. Latin Glenn County High Sch., Willows, Calif., 1954-57; tchr. Latin/German Scottsdale (Ariz.) High Sch., 1957-62; tchr. Latin Natrona County High Sch., Casper, Wyo., 1962-64; tchr. social studies Bourgade High Sch., Phoenix, 1964-65; substitute tchr. Phoenix High Sch., 1965-66; instr. supr. We. N.Mex. U. Lab. Sch., Silver City, 1966-67; prof. sociology and polit. sci. Cochise C.C., Douglas, Ariz., 1967-77; adj. instr. Calif. Poly. State U., San Luis Obispo, 1991—. Sec., v.p., bd. dirs. Easter Seal Soc. of Santa Cruz, 1979-81; active Nat. Women's Polit. Caucus Br., Santa Cruz, 1979; tutor reading Literacy Coun., San Luis Obispo, 1988. Grantee Amazonia Rsch. Orgn. of Am. States, 1970, Am. Coun. of Learned Socs., 1941. Mem. AAUW (chair 1977-81, internat. rels. group Santa Cruz br. mem.-at-large 1981—), Am. Assn. Women in Cmty. and Jr. Colls. (charter mem.), Acad. Polit. Sci., Wilson Ctr. Assocs., Rainforest Action Network.

CRAMPTON, GEORGE HARRIS, science educator, retired army officer; b. Spokane, Wash., Nov. 20, 1926. BS, Wash. State U., 1949, MS, 1950; PhD, U. Rochester, 1954. Enlisted U.S. Army Res., 1944; advanced through grades to col. U.S. Army M.S.C., 1969; ret. U.S. Army, 1971; prof. Wright State U., Dayton, Ohio, 1971-86, prof. emeritus, 1987—. Home: 1842 N Dawnview Ter Oak Harbor WA 98277-8116

CRANDALL, NELSON DAVID, III, lawyer; b. Auburn, Calif., Aug. 8, 1954; s. Nelson David and Alice (Reimer) C.; m. Elizabeth L. Donovan, Aug. 25, 1984; children: Darren J., Colin M. Student, U. Calif., Irvine, 1974-76; AB with high honors, U. Calif., Berkeley, 1976; JD, U. Calif., Davis, 1979. Bar: Calif. 1979, U.S. Dist. Ct. (no. dist.) Calif. 1979, U.S. Dist. Ct. (ea. dist.) Calif. 1980. Shareholder Hopkins & Carley Law Corp., San Jose, Calif., 1979-95; prin. Enterprise Law Group, Inc., Menlo Park, Calif., 1995—. Contbr. articles to profl. jours. Mediator, arbitrator Santa Clara County Neighborhood Small Claims Project, San Jose, 1980-92; bd. dirs. Ctrl. Calif. region ARC Blood Svcs., 1992-94, sec., 1992-94; active Santa Clara Valley chpt. ARC, San Jose, 1986-92, sec., 1987-90; trustee Jr. Statesman Found., 1987—; bd. dirs. Hope Rehab. Svcs., San Jose, 1985-88. Mem. ABA, Calif. Bar Assn., Santa Clara County Bar Assn., Phi Beta Kappa. Republican. Office: Enterprise Law Group Inc Ste 280 4400 Bohannon Dr Menlo Park CA 94025-1041

CRANDELL, WILLIAM DEAN, geologist; b. Washington, June 13, 1950; s. William Palmer and Martha Josephine (Green) C.; divorced; children: Kimberly S., Allison S. BS in Geology, Clemson U., 1972. Dist. geologist Bur. of Land Mgmt., Ely, Nev., 1976-78, Spokane, Wash., 1978-85; phys. scientist U.S. Bur. of Mines, Spokane, Wash., 1985—. Author: Availability of Federally Owned Minerals for Exploration: Development in Western States-Nevada 1985, 1989, Availability of Federally Owned Minerals for Exploration: California Desert Conservation Area-1989, 1992. Capt. USNR. Mem. N.W. Mining Assn., Benjamin B. French Masonic, Spokane Valley Kiwanis. Republican. Episcopalian. Home: 2202 S Calvin Rd Veradale WA 99037-9429 Office: US Bur of Mines 360 E 3d Ave Spokane WA 99202-1413

CRANE, STEVEN, financial company executive; b. Los Angeles, Jan. 21, 1959; s. Roger D. and Violet (Heard) C.; m. Peggy Anne Gilhooly, Apr. 25, 1987; 1 child Allison Nicole. Grad. high sch. With Mobar Inc., Torrance, Calif., 1976-78; v.p. internat. Fluid Control Internat., Marina del Rey, Calif., 1978-79; pres. Energy Devel. Internat., Torrance, 1979-85; pres., chief exec. officer Kaempen USA, Inc., Anaheim, Calif., 1985-91; founding ptnr., chmn. Western Fin. Group, Inc., Redondo Beach, Calif., 1991—; CEO Artist Network, Huntington Beach, Calif., 1993—; bd. dirs. Artist Network; chmn. bd. dirs. We. Finance Group, Inc. Mem. Office: Artist Network 20422 Beach Blvd Ste # 245 Huntington Beach CA 92648

CRANSTON, FREDERICK PITKIN, physics educator; b. Denver, Aug. 28, 1922; s. Frederick Pitkin and Alta (Kinney) C.; m. Bonnie Louise Debe, Apr. 17, 1947 (div. Mar. 1971); children: Carol, Frederick, Rodney, claudia; m. Jerneral Warran Johnson, Mar. 21, 1971; 1 child, Lawrence Duncan Crist. BA in Physics, Colgate U., 1943; MS in Physics, Stanford U., 1950, PhD in Physics, 1959. Instr. Denver U., 1946-47; staff physicist Los Alamos (N.Mex.) Nat. Lab., 1953-62; assoc. prof. Humboldt State U., Arcata, Calif., 1962-66, prof., 1966—, dept. chair, 1971-74; cons. Lawrence Livermore (Calif.) Lab., 1964-69, Lawrence Berkeley Lab., 1970; vis. prof. U. Calif., berkeley, 1974. Pres. Los Alamos Fedn. Am. Scientists. Maj. U.S. Army, 1942-66. Mem. Am. Phys. Soc., Am. Assn. Physics Tchrs. Democrat. Unitarian. Home: PO Box 767 Trinidad CA 95570-0767 Office: Humboldt State U Arcata CA 95521

CRANSTON, HOWARD STEPHEN, lawyer, management consultant; b. Hartford, Conn., Oct. 20, 1937; s. Howard Samuel and Agnes (Corvo) C.; m. Karen Youngman, June 16, 1962; children: Margaret, Susan. BA cum laude, Pomona Coll., 1959; LLB, Harvard U., 1962. Bar: Calif. 1963. Assoc. MacDonald & Halsted, L.A., 1964-68; ptnr. MacDonald, Halsted & Laybourne, L.A., 1968-82, of counsel, 1982-86; pres. Knapp Comm., L.A., 1982-87; pres. S.C. Cons. Corp., 1987—; bd. dirs. Boys Republic, Mental Health Assn. of L.A. 1st lt. U.S. Army, 1962-64. Mem. Assn. Corp. Growth, San Gabriel Country Club, Harvard Club (N.Y.). Republican. Episcopalian. Author Handbook for Creative Managers, 1987, Management Decision Mag., 1988—. Office: 1613 Chelsea Rd # 253 San Marino CA 91108-2419

CRAPO, MICHAEL DEAN, congressman, lawyer; b. Idaho Falls, Idaho, May 20, 1951; s. George Lavelle and Melba (Olsen) C.; m. Susan Diane Hasleton, June 22, 1974; children: Michelle, Brian, Stephanie, Lara, Paul. BA Polit. Sci. summa cum laude, Brigham Young U., 1973; postgrad., U. Utah, 1973-74; JD cum laude, Harvard U., 1977. Bar: Calif. 1977, Idaho 1979. Law clk. to Hon. James M. Carter U.S. Ct. Appeals (9th cir.), San Diego, 1977-78; assoc. atty. Gibson, Dunn & Crutcher, L.A., 1978-79; atty. Holden, Kidwell, Hahn & Crapo, Idaho Falls, 1979-92, ptnr., 1983-92; mem. Idaho State Senate from 32A Dist., 1984-93; asst. majority leader, 1987-88; pres. Pro Tempore, 1989-92; congressman U.S. House of Reps., 2d Idaho dist., Washington, 1992—; mem. commerce and agrl coms., new mem. leader 103rd Congress, sophomore class leader 104th Congress, co-chair Congl. Beef Caucus, dep. whip we. region U.S. House of Reps., Washington; precinct committeeman Dist. 29, 1980-85; vice chmn. Legislative Dist. 29, 1984-85; Mem. Health and Welfare Com., 1985-89, Resources and Environ. Com., 1985-90, State Affairs Com., 1987-92; Rep. Pres. Task Force, 1989. Leader Boy Scouts Am., Calif., Idaho, 1977-92; mem. Bar Exam Preparation, Bar Exam Grading; chmn. Law Day; Bonneville County chmn. Phil Batt gubernatorial campaign, 1982. Named one of Outstanding Young Men of Am., 1985; recipient Cert. of Merit Rep. Nat. Com., 1990, Guardian of Small Bus. award Nat. Fedn. of Ind. Bus., 1990, 94, Cert. of Recognition Am. Cancer Soc., 1990, Idaho Housing Agy., 1990, Idaho Lung Assn., 1985, 87, 89, Friend of Agr. award Idaho Farm Bur., 1989-90, medal of Merit Rep. Presdl. Task Force, 1989, Nat. Legislator of Yr. award Nat. Rep. Legislators Assn., 1991, Golden Bulldog award Watchdogs of the Treas., 1994, Thomas Jefferson award NAWGA-IFDA, 1994, Spirit of Enterprise award U.S. C. of C., 1993, 94. Mem. ABA (antitrust law sect.), Idaho Bar Assn., Rotary. Mormon. Office: US Ho of Reps 437 Cannon HOB Washington DC 20515

CRAVEN, JAMES MICHAEL, economist, educator; b. Seattle, Mar. 10, 1946; s. Homer Henry and Mary Kathleen Craven; m. Aleyamma P. Thomas, Aug. 27, 1977. Student, U. Minn., 1966-68; BA in Sociology, U. Manitoba, Winnipeg, Can., 1971, BA in Econs., 1971, MA in Econs., 1974. Lic. pilot; cert. ground instr. Instr. econ. and bus. Red River C.C., Winnipeg, 1974-76; lectr. rsch. methods of stats. U. Manitoba, Winnipeg, 1977-78; instr. econ. and bus. Big Bend C.C., Moses Lake, Wash., 1980-81; planning analyst Govt. P.R., San Juan, 1984; prof. econs. and bus. Interam. U. P.R., Bayamon, 1984-85; instr. econs., lectr. history Green River C.C., Auburn, Wash., 1988-92; prof. dept. chair econs. Clark Coll., Vancouver, Wash., 1992—; vis. prof. St. Berchman's U., Kerala, India, 1981, 83, 86, 91; instr. econs. Bellevue (Wash.) C.C., 1988-92; cons. Bellevue, 1988—. Inventor in field; contbr. articles to profl. jours. Platform com. mem. Wash. State Dem., Seattle, 1992; cons. Lowry for Gov. Campaign, Seattle, 1992; mem. (assoc.) Dem. Party Nat. Com., 1994—; mem. Nat. Steering Com. for Re-election of Pres. Clinton, 1995—. With U.S. Army, 1963-66. Recipient pilot wings FAA, 1988-92; Govt. Can. fellow, 1973-74. Mem. AAUP, Internat. Platform Assn., Assn. Northwest Econ. Educators, Wash. Edn. Assn. Syrian Orthodox. Home: 904 NE Minnehaha St Apt C9 Vancouver WA 98665-8732 Office: Clark Coll Dept Econs 1800 E McLoughlin Blvd Vancouver WA 98663-3598

CRAW, NICHOLAS WESSON, motor sports association executive; b. Governor's Island, N.Y., Nov. 14, 1936; s. Demas Thurlow Craw and Mary Victoria Wesson. BA, Princeton U., 1959; MBA, Harvard U., 1982. Dir. ops. Project Hope, Washington, 1960-68; pres., CEO Scorpio Racing, Washington, 1968-80, Sports Car Club Am., Englewood, Colo., 1983—; pres. Sports Car Club Am. Found, Englewood, 1986—; chmn. Nat. Motorsports Coun., 1992—. Dir. Manpower divsn. VISTA, Washington, 1970-72; assoc. dir. ACTION, Washington, 1972-73; dir. U.S. Peace Corps, Washington, 1973-74. Office: Sports Car Club Am 9033 E Easter Pl Englewood CO 80112-2105

CRAWFORD, CHARLOTTE JOANNE, psychologist, psychoanalyst, psychological anthropologist; b. Santiago, Chile, June 10, 1942; came to U.S., 1953; d. Randall LaVern and Florence Ahleen (Bamber) C.; m. José Maria Garcia-Diez, Dec. 28, 1969 (div. Sept. 1986); children: S. Amaya Garcia, Tamara S. Garcia. BA in Sociology, U. Wash., 1965; MA in Anthropology, Columbia U., 1969; Lic. Psychology, U. Barcelona, Spain, 1974, PhD in Psychology, 1982. From asst. prof. to assoc. prof. U. Basque Country, Bilbao, Spain, 1970-90; vis. scholar Harvard U., Cambridge, 1990-91; rsch. assoc. U. Calif., Berkeley, 1991-92; clinician Children's Health Coun., Palo Alto, Calif., 1992—; pvt. practice clinician Cupertino, Calif., 1991—; adj. faculty Wright Inst., Berkeley, 1991-93, Pacific Grad. Sch. Psychology, Palo Alto, 1991—, Saybrook Inst., San Francisco, 1992—; pvt. practice clinician, Bilbao, 1975-90. Author, editor: Indetidad: Norma y Diversidad, 1988; author: La Psicoterapia de Inspiración Psicoanalitica, 1989, Estudio Integral de la Personalidad, 1990. Study fellow for internat. devel. Ford Found., 1966-68, grad. fellow Govt. of Spain, 1975-77; Barandiaran grantee Soc. for Basque Studies, 1981-83, rsch. grantee U. Basque Country, 1987-88, 90-91, 91-92, grantee Govt. of Spain, 1988-90, 90-91. Mem. APA, Internat. Psychoanalytical Studies Orgn. (pres. 1983-85), Soc. Psychol. Anthropology, Am. Anthropol. Assn. Democrat. Home: 10254 Parkwood Dr # 1 Cupertino CA 95014 Office: Children's Health Coun 800 Sand Hill Rd Palo Alto CA 94304

CRAWFORD, CHRIS CHARLES, computer game designer; b. Houston, June 1, 1950; m. Kathleen Marie Crawford. BS in Physics, U. Calif., Davis, 1972; MS in Physics, U. Mo., 1975. Computer game design Atari, 1979; computer game design Atari Home Computer Sys., supr., programmers trainer, mgr. games rsch. group, to 1984; freelance computer game designer, 1984—. Author: Art of Computer Game Design, 1984, (computer games) Eastern Front 1941, 1981, Balance of Power, 1985, Trust & Betrayal, 1987; editor: Jour. of Computer Game Design. Founder Computer Game Developer's Conf., Santa Clara, Calif., 1988. Home: 5251 Sierra Rd San Jose CA 95132-3418

CRAWFORD, DALE LEE, architect; b. Raton, N. Mex., Dec. 29, 1933; s. William Pierce and Ruth Harriet (Nelson); m. Barbara Ann Mitchell Crawford, Aug. 25, 1955; children: Kelly Mitchell, Kevin Lee, Keith Nelson. BS in Archtl. Engring., U. N. Mex., 1956; student, U. Colo., 1955, USAF Inst. TEch., Wright Patterson AFB, 1957. Registered architect, N.Mex., La., interior designer, N.Mex. Draftsman Brittle & Ginner Architects, Albuquerque, 1956-57; designer, draftsman Brittle-Ginner & Decker Architects, Albuquerque, 1960-61, James Liberty Architect, Albuquerque, 1961; designer, architect Stanley & Assocs., Architects, Albuquerque, 1961-65; architect Stanley, Oravec & Crawford, Inc., Albuquerque, 1965-66, Crawford & Oravec, Architects, Albuquerque, 1966-71, Dale Crawford, Architect, Albuquerque, 1971-73; pres. Dale Crawford & Assocs., P.C., Albuquerque, 1973—. Adminstrn. bd. Cen. United Meth. Ch., Albuquerque, 1985-94, Mil-Gracias Soc. Scholarship, N. Mex. St. U., 1981-84, Presdl. Scholarship program U. N. Mex., 1977-80. Served to capt. USAF, 1957-60. Mem. N. Mex. Soc. Architects (sec., treas. 1980, pres. elect, 1981, pres. 1982, dir. 1979-84), AIA (Albuquerque chpt. pres. 1978), N. Mex. Architects P.A.C. (pres. 1985-90), Am. Arbitration Assn. Republican. Home: 8727 Aztec Rd NE Albuquerque NM 87111-4507 Office: Dale Crawford & Assocs 10701 Montgomery Blvd NE # F Albuquerque NM 87111-3800

CRAWFORD, GEORGE TRUETT, management systems company executive, consultant; b. Alcorn County, Miss., Mar. 13, 1936; s. Bascrum Claude and Louise K. (Killough) C. Grad., Northwest Christian Coll. Dir. food svcs. Food Dimensions, Inc., San Francisco, 1975-81; dir. food and nutrition Dominican Santa Cruz (Calif.) Hosp., 1981-90; pres. Diverse Mgmt. Systems, Half Moon Bay, Calif., 1990-94; cons. Diverse Mgmt. Systems, 1987-89; bd. dirs. food tech. adv. bd. Cabrillo Coll., Santa Cruz. Contbr. articles to profl. jours. Pres. Calif. Hosp. Food Svc. Adminstrn., San Francisco, 1979. Mem. Food Svc. Cons. Soc. Internat., Am. Soc. Hosp. Food Svc. Adminstrn. No Calif. (sec. 1975-77, pres.-elect 1978, pres. 1979), Nat. Inst. Off Primis Catering (faculty). Republican. Baptist. Home: 607 4th St Petaluma CA 94952

CRAWFORD, JOYCE CATHERINE HOLMES, retired psychologist; b. Kansas City, Mo., May 30, 1918; d. Morton Henry and Lillian Catharine (Burton) Holmes; student Kansas City Jr. Coll., 1934-36; BS in Edn., U. Mo., 1938; M.A. in Guidance and Counseling, No. Ariz. U., 1957; PhD in Ednl. Psychology, Ariz. State U., 1976; m. Merle Eugene Crawford, Dec. 18, 1938; children: Hal Wayne, Kent Holmes. Tchr., Sedona, Ariz., 1948-49, Verde Valley Sch., 1949-51, Cottonwood, Ariz., 1952-69; sch. psychologist, child study cons., Phoenix, 1971-75, Riverside Sch. Dist., 1972-74, Avondale Sch. Dist., 1971-83; ret., 1983. Ranger-naturalist Tuzigoot Nat. Monument, U.S. Park Service, summers 1959-66; mem. Ariz. Gov.'s Adv. Com. on Mental Health, 1964-65, Ariz. Hosp. Survey and Constrn. Adv. Council, 1965-68; head start chmn. Cottonwood Neighborhood Council, 1967-69; sec. Yavapai County Head Start Policy Adv. Com., 1968-71; bd. dirs. Yavapai County Econ. Opportunity Council, 1967-70, sec., 1968-69; bd. dirs. Ariz. Assn. Mental Health, 1955-67, sec., 1961-64, founder Verde Valley chpt., 1956, pres., 1959-61; incorporating com. Verde Valley Community Guidance Clinic, 1965, bd. dirs., 1965-70; bd. dirs. No. Ariz. Comprehensive Guidance Center, 1967-69; bd. dirs., recreation chmn. Ariz. Congress Parents and Tchrs., 1954-55; bd. dirs. Westside Mental Health Svcs., 1980-87, pres., 1980, v.p., 1980-81; chmn. profl. referral com. Westside Children's Mental Health Svc., 1983-87; bd. dirs. Southwest Cmty. Network, 1985-87; rep. Pima County Interfaith Coun., 1994—. Cert., lic. Ariz. Bd. Psychologist Examiners, sch. psychologist. Mem. Nat. Assn. Sch. Psychologists, Ariz. Assn. Sch. Psychologists (chmn. profl. standards com. 1980-81, pres. 1982-83, awards chmn. 1983-84, Keith Perkins Meml. award for Outstanding Achievement in Sch. Psychology 1988), Ariz. Psychol. Assn., Ariz. Edn. Assn. (mental health and spl. edn. com. 1961-67, chmn. 1964-65), Ariz. Assn. Children with Learning Disabilities, Psychologists for Social Responsibility, Planned Parenthood, Common Cause, ACLU, League of Women Voters of Tucson (edn. study com.). Democrat. Mem. Unitarian Universalist Ch. Home: 6770 E Carondelet Dr Apt 126 Tucson AZ 85710-2134

CRAWFORD, MARK SEYMOUR, biochemist, biologist; b. Boulder, Colo., Mar. 18, 1954; s. Richard Hazen and Margery Jean (Quistgard) C.; m. Jennifer Houghton Wrenn, June 15, 1974 (div. Oct. 1990); m. Lorilee Mathison, June 15, 1991; children: Forrest, Cameron. BS, Colo. State U., 1977; MS, U. Iowa, 1979, PhD, 1982; grad. Exec. Mgmt. Program, U. Wash., 1991. Teaching and rsch. asst. U. Iowa, Iowa City, 1977-82; consulting scientist Ponderosa Assocs., Louisville, Colo., 1982-85; postdoctoral rsch. assoc. U. Colo., Boulder, 1982-84; postdoctoral rsch. assoc. Wash. State U., Pullman, 1984-85, asst. scientist, 1985-87; sci. project mgr. Panlabs, Bothell, Wash., 1987-90, dir. drug discovery, 1990-93; v.p. Lasure and Crawford, Seattle, 1993—, Worldwide R&D, Seattle, 1993—; presenter in field. Contbr. articles to profl. jours.; patentee in field. Recipient Predoctoral traineeship NIH, 1979-82, Tuition scholarship U. Iowa, 1978. Mem. AAAS, Am. Soc. Pharmacology and Exptl. Therapeutics, Soc. Indsl. Microbiology, Phi Beta Kappa.

CRAWFORD, MURIEL LAURA, lawyer, author, educator; d. Mason Leland and Pauline Marie (DesIlets) Henderson; m. Barrett Matson Crawford, May 10, 1959; children: Laura Joanne, Janet Muriel, Barbara Elizabeth. Student, U. Calif., Berkeley, 1958-60, 67-69; B.A. with honors, U. Ill., 1973; J.D. with honors, Ill. Inst. Tech., 1977; cert. employee benefit specialist U. Pa., 1989. Bar: Ill. 1977, Calif. 1991, U.S. Dist. Ct. (no. dist.) Ill. 1977, U.S. Dist. Ct. (no. dist.) Calif. 1991, U.S. Ct. Appeals (7th cir.) 1977, U.S. Ct. Appeals (9th cir.) 1991; CLU; chartered fin. cons. Atty., Washington Nat. Ins. Co., Evanston, Ill., 1977-80, sr. atty., 1980-81, asst. counsel, 1982-83, asst. gen. counsel, 1984-87, assoc. gen. counsel, sec., 1987-89, cons. employee benefit specialist, 1989-91; assoc. Hancock, Rothert & Bunshoft, San Francisco, 1991-92. Author: (with Beadles) Law and the Life Insurance Contract, 1989, (sole author) 7th edit. 1994; co-author Legal Aspects of AIDS, 1990; contbr. articles to profl. jours. Recipient Am. Jurisprudence award Lawyer's Coop. Pub. Co., 1975, 2nd prize Internat. LeTourneau Student Med.-Legal Article contest, 1976, Bar and Gavel Soc. award Ill. Inst. Tech./Chgo.-Kent Student Bar Assn., 1977. Fellow Life Mgmt. Inst.; mem. Ill. Inst. Tech./Chgo.-Kent Alumni Assn. (bd. dir. 1983-89). Democrat. Congregationalist.

CRAWFORD, NATALIE WILSON, applied mathematician; b. Evansville, Ind., June 24, 1939; d. John Moore and Edna Dorothea (Huthsteiner) Wilson; BA in Math., U. Calif., L.A., 1961, postgrad., 1964-67; m. Robert Charles Crawford, Mar. 1, 1969. Programmer analyst N.Am. Aviation Corp., El Segundo, Calif., 1961-64; mem. tech. staff Rand Corp., Santa Monica, Calif., 1964—, project leader, engring. tech., theater conflict and force employment programs, 1975—; dir. Theater Forces Program, 1988-90, Theater Force Employment Program, 1990-92, Force Structure and Force Modernization Program, 1992-93, Force Modernization and Employment Program, 1993-95, assoc. dir. Project Air Force, 1995—; mem. Air Force Sci. Adv. Bd., 1988—, vice chmn., 1990-91; cons., joint tech. coordinating group munition effectiveness. Named YWCA Woman of Yr., 1983. Mem. Am. Def. Preparedness Assn., USAF Assn., IEEE. Republican. Home: 20940 Big Rock Dr Malibu CA 90265-5316

CRAWFORD, PHILIP STANLEY, bank executive; b. Wichita, Kans., Nov. 30, 1944; s. Carson Eugene and Elizabeth Ellen (Childs) C.; m. Carolyn Louise Stephenson, June 10, 1989. BA, Sterling Coll., 1967; MBA, Baruch Coll., 1973. Programmer, analyst City of N.Y., 1968-72; planning analyst Fed. Reserve Bank, Boston, 1972-74; cons. Index Systems, Cambridge, Mass., 1974-79; sr. cons. Ernst & Whinney, Los Angeles, 1979; v.p. Union Bank, Los Angeles, 1979—. Mem. Pres.'s Coun. Sterling Coll. Mem. Mgmt. Info. Continuing Seminar (pres. 1985), Assn. Computing Machinery, Ops. Research Soc. Am., Inst. Mgmt. Sci. Republican. Home: 3815 Olive Ave Long Beach CA 90807-3519 Office: Union Bank 445 S Figueroa St Los Angeles CA 90071-1602

CRAWFORD, RICHARD A., JR., corporate executive; b. Wagner, S.D., May 15, 1930; s. Clarence L. and Lillian S. (Schlentz) C.; m. Donna M. Schultz, Dec. 31, 1950; children: Nancy J., Lee L., Jennifer A., Sarah B. BA, Mankato State U., 1953; MBA, Ind. U., 1954. Mgr. fin. planning Westinghouse Electric Corp., Mansfield, Ohio, 1957-60, ass. to v.p., 1961; sec., treas. Josten's, Inc., Owatonna, Minn., 1962-66, v.p. corp devel., 1967-68; pres. The American Cos., Inc., Topeka, 1968—; bd. dirs. First Nat. Bank, Topeka, Adams Bus. Forms Co., Topeka, Marling Stores, Topeka. Served to 2d lt. U.S. Army, 1951-53. Republican. Lodge: Rotary (local pres. 1985-86). Office: Randonm Access Inc 8000 E Iliff Ave Denver CO 80231-5317

CRAWFORD, SARAH CARTER (SALLY CRAWFORD), broadcast executive; b. Glen Ridge, N.J., Oct. 3, 1938; d. Raymond Hitchings and Katherine Latta (Gribbel) Carter; m. Joseph Paul Crawford III, Sept. 10, 1960 (dec. 1966). BA, Smith Coll., 1960. Media dir. Kampmann & Bright, Phila., 1961-64; sr. media buyer Foote, Cone & Belding, N.Y.C., 1964-69; assoc. media dir. Grey Advt., Los Angeles, 1969-75; account exec., research dir. Sta. KHJ-TV, Los Angeles, 1975-76; mgr. local sales Sta. KCOP-TV, Los Angeles, 1977-82; gen. sales mgr. Sta. KTVF-TV, Fairbanks, Alaska, 1982—; bd. dirs. Vista Travel, Fairbanks; mem. adv. com. Golden Valley Electric Corp., Fairbanks, 1984-86; mem. coun. UAF Tanana County Campus, 1989—, chair mktg. com. Chmn. Fairbanks Health and Social Svc. Commn., 1986—; vice chmn. Fairbanks North Star Borough Health and Social Svc. Commn., 1993—; pres. Fairbanks Meml. Hosp. Aux., 1988-90, creator trust fund, chmn. fin. com., 1990—; bd. dirs. Fairbanks Downtown Assn., 1984-87; mem. FBKS Health Ctr. Coalition; mem. search com. UAF Tanana Valley Campus dir.; bd. dirs. Interior Regional Health Corp.; mem. Tesoro (Alaska) Citizens Adv. Coun. Mem. Fairbanks Women's Softball Assn., Fairbanks Women's Hockey Assn.. Episcopalian. Home: 518 Juneau Ave Fairbanks AK 99701-3771 Office: Sta KTVF-TV 3528 International St Fairbanks AK 99701-7382

CRAWSHAW, RALPH, psychiatrist; b. N.Y.C., July 3, 1921. A.B., Middlebury (Vt.) Coll., 1943; M.D., N.Y. U., 1947. Diplomate: Nat. Bd. Med. Examiners, Am. Bd. Psychiatry and Neurology. Intern Lenox Hill Hosp., N.Y.C., 1947-48; resident Menninger Sch. Psychiatry, Topeka, 1948-50, Oreg. State Hosp., Salem, 1950-51; practice medicine specializing in psychiatry Washington, 1954; staff psychiatrist C.F. Menninger Meml. Hosp., Topeka, 1954-57; asst. chief VA Mental Hygiene Clinic, Topeka, 1957-60; staff psychiatrist Community Child Guidance Clinic, Portland, Oreg., 1960-63; founder, clinic dir. Tualatin Valley Guidance Clinic, Beaverton, Oreg., 1961-67; pvt. practice medicine, specializing in psychiatry Portland, 1960—; mem. staff Holladay Park Hosp., 1961—; lectr. dept. child psychiatry Med. Sch. U. Oreg., 1961-63, clin. prof. dept. psychiatry, 1976; lectr. Sch. Social Work, Portland State U., 1964-67; founder Benjamin Rush Found., 1968, pres., 1968—; founder Friends of Medicine, 1969, Ct. of Man, 1970, Club of Kos, 1974, Oreg. Health Decisions, 1983, Am. Health Decisions, 1989, Health Vol. Overseas, 1984; Sonian Machanic vis. prof. South African Coll. Medicine, 1993. Contbr. editor: AMA Jour. of Socio-Econs, 1972-75; Columnist: Prism mag, 1972-76, The Pharos, 1972—, Portland Physician, 1975, Western Jour. Medicine, 1980—; Contbr. articles to med. jours. Cons. Bur. Hearings and Appeals, HEW, 1964-90; cons. Albina Child Devel. Center, Portland, 1965-75, HEW Region 8 Health Planning, 1979; mem. Inst. Medicine, Nat. Acad. Sci., 1978, Oreg. Health Coordinating Council, 1979; Mem. Gov.'s Adv. Com. on Mental Health, 1966-72; ad hoc com. Nat. Leadership Conf. on Am. Health Policy, 1976, Gov.'s Adv. Com. on Med. Care to Indigent, 1976—; trustee Millicent Found., 1964-67, Multnomah Found. for Med. Care, 1977; vis. scholar Center for Study Democratic Instns., 1969, Jack Murdock Charitable Trust, 1977, U.S.-USSR exchange scholar, 1973. Served with AUS, 1943-46; to lt., M.C. USN, 1951-54. Named Oreg. Dr./Citizen of Yr., 1978; U.S.-USSR rsch. scholar, 1973, 79; recipient I.N. Piragou medal for humanitarian Svcs., Russian Govt., 1992; Ralph Crawshaw Ann. Lectr. in Civic Medicine named in honor by Oreg. Found. for Med. Excellence, 1987. Fellow Am. Psychiat. Assn.; mem. AMA, APA, AAAS, Nat. Med. Assn., Oreg. Med. Assn. (trustee 1972—), Multnomah County Med. Soc. (pres. 1975), Royal Soc. Medicine, Inst. of Medicine of NAS, North Pacific Soc. Neurology and Psychiatry, Soc. for Psychol. Study Social Issues, Western European Assn. Aviation Psychology, Am. Med. Writers Assn., Portland Psychiatrists in Pvt. Practice (pres. 1971), Russian Acad. Natural Scis. (fgn. mem.), Alpha Omega. Address: 2525 NW Lovejoy St Ste 404 Portland OR 97210-2865

CRAY, ED, writer, educator; b. Cleve., July 3, 1933; s. Max and Sara (Negin) C.; m. Marjorie Lee, 1963 (div. 1967); 1 child, Jennifer; m. Diane Markson Kovacs, Apr. 21, 1985. BS, UCLA, 1957. Freelance writer L.A., 1957-60; assoc. editor Frontier Mag., L.A., 1961-64; dir pubs. ACLU of So. Calif., L.A., 1965-70; dir. publicity L.A. Philharmonic, 1970-71; freelance writer L.A., 1971—; sr. lectr. U. So. Calif., L.A., 1976-82, assoc. prof., 1982-91, prof., 1991—. Author: Big Blue Line, 1967, The Erotic Muse, 1969, 2nd edit., 1991, In Failing Health, 1970, Burden of Proof, 1973, Levis, 1979, Chrome Colossus, 1981, General of the Army, 1990, American Datelines (with Jon Kotler and Miles Beller), 1990. With U.S. Army, 1952-54. Mem. ACLU. Democrat. Jewish. Office: Univ So Calif Sch Journalism Los Angeles CA 90089-1695

CRAY, SEYMOUR R., computer designer; b. Chippewa Falls, Wis., 1925. BSEE, U. Minn., 1950, BS in Math., 1950. Computer scientist Engring. Research Assocs. (later Remington Rand, Sperry Rand Univac div.), St. Paul, until 1957; co-founder Control Data Corp., 1957, computer scientist, 1957-72; founder Cray Research Inc., Mendota Heights, Minn., 1972; chmn. Cray Computer Corp., Colorado Springs, Colo., 1989—. Designer first computer made with transistors, Cray-1, Cray-2, other computer systems. Address: care Cray Research Inc PO Box 154 Minneapolis MN 55440-0154 Office: Cray Computer Corp PO Box 17500 Colorado Springs CO 80935-7500

CRAYMER, LORING GODDARD, engineer; b. Oklahoma City, Feb. 17, 1950; s. Loring Gentry and Mary Frances (Morrison) C.; m. Susan Jane Eberlein, Aug. 7, 1982 (div. 1988); 1 child, Kenneth Loring. BS in Biology, Calif. Inst. Tech., 1972; PhD in Genetics, U. Wis., 1977. Rsch. fellow Calif. Inst. Tech., 1977-87; mem. tech. staff Jet Propulsion Lab., Pasadena, Calif., 1988—. Contbr. articles to profl. jours. Office: Jet Propulsion Lab 4800 Oak Grove Dr Pasadena CA 91109-8001

CRAYNE, ZONNA MARIE, information systems executive; b. Ephrata, Wash., June 6, 1958; d. Albert Jr. and Geraldine Jeanet (Kearney) C. BA in Math. and Computer Sci., Ea. Wash. U., 1984; MS in Computer Sci., Pacific Luth. U., 1991; DRM cert., U. Wash., 1992. Student instr. Ea. Wash. U., Cheney, 1983-84; sys. engr. Itron, Spokane, Wash., 1984-87; civil engr. USAR, Spokane, 1982-89; software engr. BDM Corp., Tacoma, 1987-91; comms. officer Air NG, Tacoma, 1989—; data resources mgr. City of Tacoma, 1991—. Developer: (computer application) Res. Office Automation, 1987 (MSM award 1988). With U.S. Army, 1976-80. Mem. Assn. for Computing Machinery, Air NG Assn., Data Resource Mgmt. Assn. Republican. Roman Catholic. Office: City of Tacoma 3628 S 35th St Tacoma WA 98409-3115

CREAN, JOHN C., housing and recreational vehicles manufacturing company executive; b. Bowden, N.D., 1925; married. Founder Fleetwood Enterprises, Inc., Riverside, Calif., 1950, pres., 1952-70, chmn., chief exec. officer, 1950—, also dir. Served with USN, 1942; with U.S. Mcht. Marines, 1944-45. Office: Fleetwood Enterprises Inc 3125 Myers St PO Box 7638 Riverside CA 92523

CREE, DEAN EDWARD, computer software consultant; b. Torrance, Calif., Dec. 30, 1949; s. Frank Edward and Wilma Mae Cree; m. Marta Jean Lopez, Aug. 25, 1973; 1 child, David. BA, UCLA, 1973; MA, Calif. State U., L.A., 1975. Quality assurance mgr. F.E. Olds & Son, Fullerton, Calif., 1975-80; sr. analyst, mgr. Apollo Data Sys., Fullerton, Calif., 1980-86; R & D mgr. Bluebird Sys., Carlsbad, Calif., 1986-88; computer cons. Red Deer Sys., San Diego, 1988—. Composer Sonatina for Brass, 1985. Mem. Am. Prodn. and Inventory Control Soc. (cert.).

CREECH, WILBUR LYMAN, air force officer; b. Argyle, Mo., Mar. 30, 1927; s. Paul and Marie (Maloney) C.; m. Carol Ann DiDomenico, Nov. 20, 1969; 1 son, William L. Student, U. Mo., 1946-48; B.S., U. Md., 1960; M.S., George Washington U., 1966; postgrad., Nat. War Coll., 1966. Commd. 2d lt. U.S. Air Force, 1949; advanced through grades to gen.; fighter pilot 103 combat missions USAF, North Korea, 1950-51; pilot USAF Thunderbirds, 1953-56; comdr., leader Skyblazers, Europe aerial demo team USAF, 1956-60; dir. Fighter Weapons Sch., Nellis AFB, Nev., 1960-61; advisor to comdr. Argentine Air Force, 1962; exec., aide to comdr. Tactical Air Command, 1962-65; dep. comdr. fighter wing, 177 combat missions in F-100 fighters and asst. dep. chief staff for ops. 7th Air Force, Vietnam, 1968-69; comdr. fighter wings USAF in Europe, Spain and W.Ger., 1969-71; dep. for ops. and intelligence Air Forces Europe, 1971-74; comdr. Electronic Systems Div., Hanscom AFB, Mass., 1974-77; asst. vice chief of staff HQS Air Force, Washington, 1977-78; comdr. Tactical Air Command, Langley AFB, Va., 1978—; lectr., internat. mgmt. expert. Author: The Five Pillars of TQM, 1994. Decorated D.S.M. with three oak leaf clusters, Silver Star medal, Legion of Merit with two oak leaf clusters, D.F.C. with three oak leaf clusters, Air medal with 14 oak leaf clusters, Air Force Commendation medal with two oak leaf clusters, Army Commendation medal; Spanish Grand Cross. Home and Office: 20 Quail Run Rd Henderson NV 89014-2147

CREEL, DONNELL JOSEPH, research scientist, educator; b. Kansas City, Mo., June 17, 1942; m. Jalna Rose Schultz, Nov. 10, 1977; 1 child, Molly Rose. BA, U. Mo., 1964, MA, 1966; PhD, U. Utah, 1969. Rsch. assoc. VA, Kansas City, Mo., 1969-71; chief neuropsychology rsch. VA, Phoenix, 1971-76; rsch. scientist VA, Salt Lake City, 1976-78, rsch. career scientist, 1979—; rsch. prof. ophthalmology U. Utah, Salt Lake City, 1982—. Author book chpts. Decision Making in Pediatric Opthalmology, 1993, Metabolic Basis of Inherited Disease, 1995, others; contbr. articles to profl. jours. Office: Moran Eye Ctr U Utah Salt Lake City UT 84132

CREER, JAMES READ, financial officer; b. Ogden, Utah, Oct. 26, 1942; s. Harold and Geraldine (Jacobson) C.; m. Ann L. Curran, Aug. 7, 1964 (div. Aug. 1974); children: Wendy, Kellie, Mark, Jennifer; m. Carolyn Rudd, Jan. 11, 1985. BS in Acctg., U. Utah, 1968. CPA. Staff acct. PMM & Co., L.A., 1968-71; sr. acct. PMM & Co., Salt Lake City, 1971-72, Haynie, Tebbs & Smith, Salt Lake City, 1972-73; ptnr. Roberts & Creer, Salt Lake City, 1973-74; pvt. practice Salt Lake City, 1974-81; v.p., chief financial officer Johnstone Supply, Salt Lake City, 1981—, ACW Enterprises Inc., Salt Lake City, 1989—; acctg. instr. Utah Tech. Coll., Stevens-Henegar Coll. Bus., 1973-76. With USMC, 1960-63. Mem. Children's Justice Ctr. (adv. bd.), Rotary (pres. so. Salt Lake City chpt. 1989-90, Paul Harris fellow 1988). Republican. Mem. LDS Ch. Office: Johnstone Supply 2940 S 300 W Salt Lake City UT 84115-3405

CREIGHTON, JOHN W., JR., forest products company executive; b. Pitts., Sept. 1, 1932; married; 3 children. BS, Ohio State U., 1954, JD, 1957; MBA, U. Miami, 1965. With Arthur Andersen and Co., 1957-59, Arvida Corp., 1959-66; exec. v.p. Mortgage Cons. Inc., 1966-70; gen. mgr. Shelter Group Weyerhaeuser Co., 1970, corp. v.p., 1970-85, exec. v.p., 1985-88, pres., dir., 1988—; pres., CEO Weyerhaeuser Real Estate Co.; chmn. bd. dirs. Fed. Home Loan Bank Seattle; bd. dirs. Nat. Corp. Housing Partnership, Puget Sound Bancorp, Mortgage Investments Plus, Inc., Am. Paper Inst. Trustee U. Puget Sound; bd. dirs. Chief Seattle Coun. Boy Scouts Am., King County United Way. With U.S. Army, 1954-56. Office: Weyerhaeuser Co 33663 Weyerhaeuser Way S Auburn WA 98001-9646*

CRESPIN, LESLIE ANN, artist; b. Cleve., Sept. 30, 1947; d. Edwin Creaver and Eunice Jane (Pierce) Ulrich; m. Raimondo J. Vinella; children: Greg, Chris, Tony. Student, Cleve. Art Inst., U. Capetown (S. Africa), Hiram (Ohio) U. Instr. Taos (N.Mex.) Sch. Fine Art; works in permanent collections at Johnson Humrick House Mus., Ohio, Harwood Found., Mus. Taos Art, Midland Savs. and Loan, Denver, Monsanto Internat., N.Y.C., St. Louis, Carlsbad Fine Art Mus., Tubac Ctr. for the Arts, Rolm Corp., Dallas, Wichita Art Assn., Kans. Exhibits include Cleve. Mus. Art, Jewish Community Ctr., Cleve., Hiram U., U. Capetown, N.Mex. State U., Peyton Wright Gallery, Santa Fe, Roanoke (Va.) Fine Arts Mus., The New Gallery, Taos, 1981-84, Amarillo Art Ctr., 1983, Carlsbad Fine Arts Mus., 1984, Beachwood Mus., Ohio, 1985, Tubac Ctr. for Arts, Ariz., 1985, Erie (Pa.) Art Mus., 1986, Albuquerque Mus., 1991, 92, 93, 94, Harwood Found. Mus. Taos Art, 1987, Fenix Gallery, N.Mex., 1990-91, 92, 93, J. Richards Gallery, Englewood, N.J., 1990-91, 92, 93, Sharon Blaustein, N.J. and N.Y., 1990, 91, 92, 93, Fenix Gallery, 1990, 91, 92, 93, Lumina Gallery, 1994, Albuquerque Mus., 1993-94, Upper Edge Gallery, 1994; represented in permanent collections Harwood Found., Maytag, Wichita Art Assn., Kans., Monsanto Internat., Carlsbad Fine Art Mus., Tubac Ctr. for the Arts, Bernard Ewell ASA, Rolm Corp., Johnson Humrick House Mus., N. Pajarola Museumstrasse, Switzerland, Carson County Square House Mus. Recipient numerous purchase awards; Masterfield award, North Coast Collage Soc., 1985, Grumbacher award, Beachwood Mus., Ohio, 1986, Master Field award, KennedyCtr. Gallery, 1987. Mem. Soc. Artists in Multi-Media, North Coast Collage Soc., Soc. Exptl. Artists, Contemporary Art Soc. N.Mex., Taos Art Assn. Home and Office: PO Box 1569 Taos NM 87571-1569

CRESS, CECILE COLLEEN, retired librarian; b. Colorado Springs, Colo., Feb. 26, 1914; d. John Leo and Elizabeth Veronica (Rouse) Haley; m. Arthur Henry Cress, May 8, 1937 (div. 1960); children: Ronnie Lou Kordick, Dan, Elaine. BA, Adams State Coll., 1936; MA in English, Colo. Coll., 1964; MLS, Denver U., 1970. 5th grade tchr. Westcliffe (Colo.) Elem., 1953-56; English tchr. Penrose (Colo.) High Sch., 1956-59; English-social studies tchr.

Excelsior Jr. High, Sch. Dist. 70, Pueblo, Colo., 1959-64; libr. Pueblo County High, Sch. Dist. 70, Pueblo, 1964-80, Nat. Coll./Pueblo Br., 1980-91; cataloger in library Pueblo C.C., 1992—. Tutor adult literacy program South Cen. Bd. Coop. Svcs., 1991. Recipient Ace of Clubs award Am. Contract Bridge League, 1988, 89. Mem. AAUW, Pueblo Ret. Sch. Employees (v.p. 1990-92, pres. 1982-84, state bd. 1982-86, sec. 1995—), Colo. Libr. Assn., Unit 369 Am. Contract Bridge Assn., Irish Club Pueblo (pres. 1995—), Welsh Terrier Club Colo., Alpha Delta Kappa (Pueblo chpt., pres. 1976-78, state historian 1980-82, state bd. 1980-82, rec. sec. 1994—). Democrat. Roman Catholic. Home: 901 Jackson St Pueblo CO 81004-2425

CRESS, CHARLES R., pharmacology educator; b. Glendale, Calif., July 29, 1942; s. Harry M. and Delphina Pearl (Wical) C.; m. Gail Shiela Cress, Feb. 13, 1983; children: Kenneth, Peter, Heather, Loren. BS, Pacific Union Coll., 1965; PhD, Oreg. State U., 1970; MPH, Loma Linda U., 1994. Instr. pharmacology Loma Linda (Calif.) U.; asst. prof. pharmacology Loma Linda U.; assoc. prof. pharmacology —; adj. assoc. prof. pharmacology So. Calif. Coll. Optometry. Mem. Western Pharmacology Soc., Sigma Xi. Home: PO Box 6725 Crestline CA 92325-6725 Office: Loma Linda U Loma Linda CA 92350

CRESWELL, DONALD CRESTON, management consultant; b. Balt.; s. Carroll Creston and Verna Moore (Taylor) C.; student Johns Hopkins U.; MBA, U. Dayton; postgrad. bus. Stanford U.; m. Terri Sue Tidwell; 1 child, Creston Lee. Cons. engr. A.D. Ring & Assocs., Washington; sales and mktg. mgr. Ampex Corp., Redwood City, Calif.; dir. mktg., magnetic products div. RCA Corp., N.Y.C.; staff v.p. sales and advt. Pan Am. World Airways, N.Y.C.; prin. mgmt. cons., dir. mktg. svcs. Stanford Rsch. Inst., Menlo Park, Calif.; v.p. and gen. mgr. Decisions Systems; dir. R & D Strategy Practice; gen. mgr. R & D Decision Quality Assocs.; with Strategic Decisions Group, Menlo Park, Calif., 1987—; bd. dirs. Rogerson Aircraft Controls, 1981-85; bd. dirs., mgmt. com. Jets Cybernetics, 1987-94; lectr. planning and mktg. mgmt. Am. Mgmt. Assn., 1968-69; program chmn. Grad. Bus. Assn., 1965; rep. to Electronics Industries Assn., 1968-71, to Internat. Air Transport Assn., 1971-74. Bd. dirs. Peninsula Youth Soccer Club, 1981-82; nat. dir. referee assessment, mem. referee com. U.S. Soccer Fedn., 1986-88; regional chief referee San Carlos Am. Youth Soccer Orgn., 1981-85; State dir. assessment Calif. Soccer Assn., 1982-85; mem. L.A. Olympics Organizing Com., 1983-84, nat. referee assessor, 1987—; ofcl. N. Am. Soccer League, 1983-84, World Cup, 1994. Mem. Am. Mktg. Assn. (exec. mem.), Am. Theatre Organ Assn. (bd. dirs. 1978-79), Nat. Intercollegiate Soccer Ofcls. Assn. (World cup video inspector, 1994), Charles Lindbergh Fund, U.S. Soccer Fedn. (cert. soccer referee, nat. assessor, USSF referee inspector), Wings Club, The Churchill Club, Stanford Jazz Com. Republican. Home: 8 Pyrola Ln San Carlos CA 94070-1532 Office: Strategic Decisions Group 2440 Sand Hill Rd Menlo Park CA 94025-6900

CREVELT, DWIGHT EUGENE, computer company executive; b. Kansas City, Mo., Jan. 16, 1957; s. James Robert and Louise Gwendolynn (Wolchek) C.; m. Jean Anne Cassens, Aug. 11, 1979; children: William Michael, Michelle Anne, Matthew Henry, Megan Louise. Student, U. Las Vegas, 1973-74, U.S. Naval Acad., 1975-77; BS in Computer Engring., Iowa State U., 1979. Computer engr., cons. Las Vegas, Nev., 1972-73; software engr. Gamex Industries, Las Vegas, 1973-74, United Audio Visual, Las Vegas, 1977; computer engr. Sircoma, Las Vegas, 1979-80; dir. research Mills-Jennings, Las Vegas, 1981; pres., chmn. Crevelt Computer, Las Vegas, 1977—; mgr. spl. projects Electronic Data Techs., 1988-91; dir. engring., quality assurance mgr. Internat. Game Techs., 1991—; lobbyist Nev. Legis. Author: (computer programs) CDC160/NCR310 Disassembler, 1971, Computer Networking, 1983, Telephone Access Control, 1984, Fiber Optic Network, 1984; co-author: Slot Machine Mania, 1987, Video Poker Mania, 1991; patentee on automated electronic casino gaming system. Former corr. sec. Clark County Rep. Cen. Com.; mem. U.S. Congl. Adv. Bd. Mem. Eagle Scout Assn., Soc. Naval Engrs., Sales Mktg. Execs. Assn., Am. Philatic Soc., U.S. Naval Acad. Alumni Assn. (sec.), USN League, U.S. Naval Inst., Las Vegas Exch. Club (bd. dirs.) NRA. Office: Crevelt Computer System Inc 5391 Aston Ave Las Vegas NV 89122-1818

CREW, AUBREY TORQUIL, aerospace inspector; b. London, May 9, 1926; came to U.S. 1968; s. Thomas Alfred and Phyllis Sibil (Ibbetson) C.; m. Sally-Marie Thompson, Dec. 22, 1979; children: Clare Violet, Mark Ernest, Karen Audrey. Student, London Tech. Coll., 1956, Oslo State U., Norway, 1965-67. Marine radio officer Marchessini & Co., London, N.Y.C., 1956-57; flight radio officer Hunting Clan Aircraft Co., London, 1957-59; radio and TV engr. Radionette, Oslo, 1960-68; avionics tech. flight Lockheed Aircraft Co., Palmdale, Calif., 1971-82; aerospace inspector Rockwell International., Palmdale, 1983—. Appeared in film The Sundowners, 1959. Vol. blood donor Viking Group Charities, Beverly Hills, Calif., 1969—; capt. USAF Civil Air Patrol, 1978—. With Royal Navy, 1941-56. Fellow Royal Soc. St. George; mem. Air Force Assn. Republican. Episcopalian. Home: 1274 W Avenue H4 Lancaster CA 93534-1488

CREWS, JAMES CECIL, hospital administrator; b. Marshalltown, Iowa, July 29, 1937; married. BA, U. Wis., 1959; MA, U. Iowa, 1964. Asst. adminstr. Meth. Asbury Hosps., Mpls., 1964, adminstrv. resident, 1963-64, adminstr., 1964-66; adminstr. Illini Hosp., Silvis, Ill., 1966-69, Charleston Gen. Hosp., W.Va., 1969-72; exec. v.p. Charleston Area Med. Ctr., Charleston, W.Va., 1972-81, pres., 1981-88; exec. v.p., COO VHA Enterprises Inc., Irving, Tex., 1988-89, acting pres., CEO, 1989-90; pres., CEO Samaritan Health Svcs., Phoenix, 1990, Samaritan Health System, Phoenix, 1991—. Mem. W.Va. Hosp. Assn. (bd. dirs., pres 1979—). Home: 5236 N 45th Pl Phoenix AZ 85018-1701 Office: Samaritan Health System 1441 N 12th St Phoenix AZ 85006-2837

CRICK, FRANCIS HARRY COMPTON, science educator, researcher; b. June 8, 1916; s. Harry and Annie Elizabeth (Wilkins) C.; m. Ruth Doreen Dodd, 1940 (div. 1947); 1 son; m. Odile Speed, 1949; 2 daus. B.Sc., Univ. Coll., London; PhD, Cambridge U., Eng. Scientist Brit. Admiralty, 1940-47, Strangeways Lab., Cambridge, Eng., 1947-49; with Med. Rsch. Coun. Lab. of Molecular Biology, Cambridge, 1949-77; Kieckhefer Disting. prof. Salk Inst. Biol. Studies, San Diego, 1977—, pres., 1994—, non-resident fellow, 1962-73; pres. Med. Rsch. Coun. Lab. of Molecular Biology, San Diego, 1994—, 1994—; adj. prof. psychology U. Calif., San Diego; vis. lectr. Rockefeller Inst., N.Y.C., 1959; vis. prof. chemistry dept. Harvard U., 1959, vis. prof. biophysics, 1962; fellow Churchill Coll., Cambridge, 1960-61; Korkes Meml. lectr. Duke U., 1960; Henry Sidgewick Meml. lectr., Cambridge U., 1963; Graham Young lectr., Glasgow, 1963; Robert Boyle lectr., Oxford U., 1963; Vanuxem lectr. Princeton U., 1964; William T. Sedgwick Meml. lectr. Oxford U., 1966; Shell lectr. Stanford U., 1969; Paul Lund lectr. Northwestern U., 1977; Dupont lectr. Harvard U., 1979, numerous other invited meml. lectrs. Author: Of Molecules and Men, 1966, Life Itself, 1981, What Mad Pursuit, 1988, The Astonishing Hypothesis: The Scientific Search for the Soul, 1994; contbr. papers and articles on molecular, cell biology and neurobiology to sci. jours. Recipient Prix Charles Leopold Mayer French Academies des Scis., 1961; (with J.D. Watson) Rsch. Corp. award, 1961, Warren Triennial prize, 1959, (with J.D. Watson & Maurice Wilkins) Lasker award, 1960, Nobel Prize for medicine, 1962; Gairdner Found. award, 1962, Royal Medal Royal Soc., 1972, Copley Medal, 1975, Michelson-Morley award, 1981, Benjamin P. Cheney medal, 1986, Golden Plate award, 1987, Albert medal Royal Soc. Arts, London, 1987, Wright Prize VIII Harvey Mudd Coll., 1988, Joseph Priestly award Dickinson Coll., 1988, Order of Merit, 1991, Disting. Achievement award Oreg. State U. Friends of Libr., 1995. Fellow AAAS, Univ. Coll. London Royal Soc.; mem. Acad. Arts and Scis. (fgn. hon.), Am. Soc. Biol. Chemistry (hon.), U.S. Nat. Acad. Scis. (fgn. assoc.), German Acad. Sci., Am. Philos. Soc. (fgn. mem.), French Acad. Scis. (assoc. fgn. mem.) , Indian Acad. Scis. (hon. fellow), Order of Merit. Office: Salk Inst Biol Studies PO Box 85800 San Diego CA 92186-5800

CRIEL, LAURA VICTORIA, public affairs officer, education coordinator; b. Detroit, Apr. 11, 1933; d. William Ray Weible and Frieda Preshia (Lashley) Bradley; m. Harry Eugene Criel, June 13, 1953; children: Vicki Criel Fuchs, Bruce Harry, Todd Martin. Taxpayer svc. rep. IRS, Buffalo, 1974-77; aide U.S. Senator Harrison Schmitt, Albuquerque, 1978-80, taxpayer svc. rep., 1980-81, problem resolutions officer, 1981-82, revenue officer, 1982-84, pub. affairs officer, taxpayer edn. coord., 1984—. Mem. N.Mex. Bus. Assistance Coun. (chair Albuquerque chpt. 1990-91), Pub. Rels. Soc. Am. (bd. dirs., profl. edn. coord. 1992-94), Albuquerque Press Club. Home: 326 Paint Brush Dr NE Albuquerque NM 87122-1415 Office: IRS 5338 Montgomery Blvd NE Albuquerque NM 87109-1311

CRILEY, RICHARD LAWRENCE, retired advocate; b. Paris, Oct. 20, 1911; came to U.S., 1913; s. Theodore Morrow and Mary Myrtle (Brotherton) C.; m. Florence Atkinson, Jan. 1942 (dec. May 1976); m. Jan Bounds Cords, Jan. 1977 (dec. Sept. 1988); 1 stepchild, Ann Edgerton-Smith; m. Jan Franklin Penney, Apr. 21, 1989; several stepchildren. Student, Stanford U., 1930-32; BA in History, U. Calif., Berkeley, 1934; postgrad., U. Calif., 1934-36. Exec. dir. Chgo. Com. to Defend the Bill of Rights, 1960-77; midwest dir. Nat. Com. to Abolish the Ho. UnAm. Activities Com., Chgo., 1960-77; No. Calif. dir. Nat. Com. Against Repressive Legis., 1975—; exec. dir. Monterey County (Calif.) chpt. ACLU, 1980—; mem. coord. com. Nat. Com. Against Repressive Legis., L.A., Washington, 1984—, adv. coun. S.W. Chgo. War on Poverty, 1973; bd. dirs. United Cmty. Coun. of S.W. Lawndale, Chgo., 1964-77, Greater Lawndale Conservation Commn. (sec. 1962-70). Author: The FBI vs. the 1st Amendment, 1991. Mem. adv. com. affirmative action program, Monterey Peninsula C.C., 1986-90; pres., mem. bd. dirs. Carmel Highlands Assn., Inc., 1983-90. Capt. U.S. Army, 1942-46, ETO. Recipient Francis Heisler award Monterey chpt. ACLU, 1984, Earl Warren award ACLU of No. Calif., 1985, Human Rights Day award Baha'i Faith of Monterey Peninsula, 1993, cert. of recognition Ill. Youth Commn., Chgo., 1963. Home: Rt 1 Box 67 Carmel CA 93923

CRILLY, EUGENE RICHARD, engineering consultant; b. Phila., Oct. 30, 1923; s. Eugene John and Mary Virginia (Harvey) C.; m. Alice Royal Roth, Feb. 16, 1952; ME, Stevens Inst. Tech., 1944, MS, 1949; MS, U. Pa., 1951; postgrad. UCLA, 1955-58. Sr. rsch. engr. N.Am. Aviation, L.A., 1954-57; sr. rsch. engr., Canoga Park and Downey, Calif., 1962-66; process engr. Northrop Aircraft Corp., Hawthorne, Calif., 1957-59; project engr., quality assurance mgr. HITCO, Gardena, Calif., 1959-62; sr. rsch. specialist Lockheed-Calif. Co., Burbank, 1966-74; engring. specialist N.Am. aircraft ops. Rockwell Internat., El Segundo, Calif., 1974-89. Author tech. papers. Mem. nat. com. 125th Anniversary Founding of Stevens Inst. Tech. in 1870. Served with USNR, 1943-46; comdr. Res. ret. Mem. Soc. for Advancement Material and Process Engring. (chmn. L.A. chpt. 1978-79, gen. chmn. 1981 symposium exhbn., nat. dir. 1979-86, treas. 1982-85, Award of Merit 1986), Naval Inst., ASM Internat., Naval Res. Assn., VFW, Mil. Order World Wars (adj. San Fernando Valley chpt. 1985, 2d vice comdr. 1986, commdr. 1987-89, vice comdr. West, Dept Cen. Calif., 1988-89, comdr. Cajon Valley-San Diego chpt. 1990-92, adj./ROTC chmn. region XIV 1990-91, comdr. Dept. So. Calif. 1991-93, vice comdr. region XIV, 1992-93, dep. comdr. Gen. Staff Officer region XIV 1993-94, comdr. region XIV, 1994-95, Disting. Chpt. Comdr. Region XIV 1990-91), Former Intelligence Officers Assn. (treas. San Diego chpt. one 1990-94), Ret. Officers Assn. (treas. Silver Strand chpt. 1992—), Navy League U.S., Naval Order U.S., Naval Intelligence Profls. Assn., Brit. United Svc. Club L.A., Marines' Meml. Club (San Francisco), Sigma Xi, Sigma Nu. Republican. Roman Catholic. Home and Office: 276 J Ave Coronado CA 92118-1138

CRIMINALE, WILLIAM OLIVER, JR., applied mathematics educator; b. Mobile, Ala., Nov. 29, 1933; s. William Oliver and Vivian Gertrude (Sketoe) C.; m. Ulrike Irmgard Wegner, June 7, 1962; children: Martin Oliver, Lucca. B.S., U. Ala., 1955; Ph.D., Johns Hopkins U., 1960. Asst. prof. Princeton (N.J.) U., 1962-68; assoc. prof. U. Wash., Seattle, 1968-73; prof. oceanography, geophysics, applied math. U. Wash., 1973—, chmn. dept. applied math., 1976-84; cons. Aerospace Corp., 1963-65, Boeing Corp., 1968-72, AGARD, 1967-68, Lenox Hill Hosp., 1967-68, NASA Langley, 1990—; guest prof., Can., 1965, France, 1967-68, Germany, 1973-74, Sweden, 1973-74, Scotland, 1985, 89, 91, Eng., 1990, 91, Stanford, 1990, Brazil, 1992; Nat. Acad. exch. scientist, USSR, 1969, 72. Author: Stability of Parallel Flows, 1967; Contbr. articles to profl. jours. Served with U.S. Army, 1961-62. Boris A. Bakmeteff Meml. fellow, 1957-58, NATO postdoctoral fellow, 1960-61, Alexander von Humboldt Sr. fellow, 1973-74, Royal Soc. fellow, 1990-91. Mem. AAAS, Am. Phys. Soc., Am. Geophys. Union, Fedn. Am. Scientists, Soc. Indsl. and Applied Math. Home: 1635 Peach Ct E Seattle WA 98112-3428 Office: U Wash Dept Applied Math Box 352420 Seattle WA 98195

CRINELLA, FRANCIS MICHAEL, neuropsychologist, science foundation director; b. Petaluma, Calif., Dec. 22, 1936; s. Marino Peter and Marian (Eleanor) C.; m. Terrie Kay Lynd, Sept. 19, 1959; children: Ramona, Gina, Peter, Andrew, Christina. BA, U. Notre Dame, 1958; MS, San Francisco State U., 1962; PhD, La. State U., 1969. Lic. clin. and exptl. psychologist, Calif. Psychology intern Alameda County (Calif.) Guidance Clinic, 1961-62, New Orleans, 1968-69; rsch. assoc. spl. edn. La. State U., Baton Rouge, 1966-69; staff psychologist Sonoma State Hosp., Eldridge, Calif., 1969-72, sr. psychologist, 1971-72, cons. program rev., 1972-77; research psychologist Brain Behavior Research Ctr., Eldridge, 1969-77; dir. Petaluma Hosp. Dist., 1971-76, treas., 1975; exec. dir. Fairview State Hosp., Costa Mesa, Calif., 1977-85; assoc. clin. prof. to clin. prof. psychiatry U. Calif., Irvine, 1977—, assoc. clin. prof. to clin. prof. phys. medicine, 1981—; dir. Devel. Research Insts., Costa Mesa, 1985—; pres. Rehab. Ctr. for Brain Dysfunction, Irvine, 1982—. Contbr. articles on neuropsychiatry to profl. jours. Bd. dirs. United Way Orange County, Calif., Orange County Epilepsy Soc., also pres., 1978—. Served to capt. USAF, 1962-66. Recipient Career Scientist award Rehab. Ctr. Brain Dysfunction Inc., 1983; grantee Nat. Inst. Child Health and Human Devel., 1972, Nat. Inst. Neurol. Diseases Communicative Disorders and Stroke, 1973, Nat. Inst. Aging, 1985, Nat. Inst. Mental Health, 1989. Mem. AAAS, Am. Psychol. Assn., Am. Acad. on Mental Retardation, Nat. Acad. Neuropsychologists, Western Psychol. Assn., Redwood Psychol. Assn. Republican. Roman Catholic. Club: Mesa Verde Country (Costa Mesa). Office: State Devel Rsch Insts 2501 Harbor Blvd Costa Mesa CA 92626-6143

CRIPPENS, DAVID LEE, broadcast executive; b. Nashville, Sept. 23, 1942; s. Nathaniel and Dorothy (Sharp) C.; m. Eloise Brown, Aug. 3, 1968; 1 child, Gerald Chinua. BA in Polit. Sci., Antioch U., 1964; MSW, San Diego State U., 1968. Assoc. dir. ednl. opportunities program San Diego State U., 1968-69; producer KPBS-TV, San Diego, 1969-71; staff producer, writer, newsperson WQED-TV, Pitts., 1971-73; dir. ednl. svc. KCET, L.A., 1973-77, v.p. ednl. svc., 1977-80, v.p., sta. mgr., 1980-83, v.p. nat. prodns., 1983-85, sr. v.p. ednl. enterprises, 1985—; Rufus Putnam vis. prof. Ohio U. Sch. Telecommunications, Athens, fall 1995. Exec. producer Count On Me, New American Work Force, Not the Way to Go/Get a Life, Begingin the Journey, Giving Care Taking Care, Community Under Siege, Mindworks; contbr. articles to profl. publs. Bd. trustees Antioch U., 1987—, Cmty. Coalition for Substance Abuse Prevention and Treatment; bd. councilors Sch. Social Wk., U. So. Calif.; mem. edn. week bd. Prenatal Diagnostic Rsch. Found.; vol. Peace Corps Nigeria, 1964-66. Recipient Excellence in Edn. Commendation award Calif. Poly. Black Faculty and Staff Assn., 1991, Prin.'s Orgn. award Sr. High Sch. Prins., 1991, honor Assn. Adminstrs. L.A., 1988, Calif. Coalition for Pub. Edn., 1987, Nat. Assn. Media Women, 1986, Calif. Assembly Legis. Com., 1971, San Diego State Black Student Coun., 1971, named One of Pitts.' Most Influential Blacks, Pitts. Post Gazette, 1973, Outstanding Ednl. Leadership award Phi Delta Kappa, 1992, Nat. Citation award, 1993, Positive Image Award Frank D. Parent PTA, 1992, John Senett award for outstanding coverage of educational concerns Calif. Tchrs. Assn., 1993. Home: 5252 W 64th St Inglewood CA 90302-1016 Office: KCET 4401 W Sunset Blvd Los Angeles CA 90027-6017

CRISCUOLO, WENDY LAURA, lawyer, interior design consultant; b. N.Y.C., Dec. 17, 1949; d. Joseph Andrew and Betty Jane (Jackson) C.; m. John Howard Price, Jr., Sept. 5, 1970 (div. Apr. 1981); m. Ross J. Turner, July 23, 1988. BA with honors in Design, U. Calif., Berkeley, 1973; JD, U. San Francisco, 1982. Space planner GSA, San Francisco, 1973-79; sr. interior designer E. Lew & Assocs., San Francisco, 1979-80; design dir. Beier & Gunderson, Inc., Oakland, Calif., 1980-81; sr. interior designer Environ. Planning and Rsch., San Francisco, 1981-82; interior design cons. Hillsborough, Calif., 1982—; law clk. to Judge Spencer Williams U.S. Dist. Ct., San Francisco, 1983-84; atty. Ciros Investments, Rancho Santa Fe, Calif., 1984—. Author: (with others) Guide to the Laws of Charitable Giving, 3d rev. edit., 1983; staff mem. U. San Francisco Law Rev., 1983. Bd. dirs., v.p. and treas. Marin Citizens for Energy Planning, 1986-89; bd. dirs., pres. Calif. Ctr. for Wildlife, 1987-90; trustee Cayote Point Mus. for Environ. Edn., 1990-93. Mem. ABA, State Bar Calif. Republican. Episcopalian.

CRISMAN, MARY FRANCES BORDEN, librarian; b. Tacoma, Nov. 23, 1919; d. Lindon A. and Mary Cecelia (Donnelly) Borden; m. Fredric Lee Crisman, Apr. 12, 1975 (dec. Dec. 1975). BA in History, U. Wash., 1943, BA in Librarianship, 1944. Asst. br. librarian in charge work with children Mottet br. Tacoma Pub. Libr., 1944-45, br. librarian, 1945-49, br. librarian Moore br., 1950-55, asst. dir., 1955-70, dir., 1970-74, dir. emeritus, 1975—; corp. libr. Frank Russell Co., 1985—; chmn. Wash. Community Library Council, 1970-72. Hostess program Your Library and You, Sta. KTPS-TV, 1969-71. Mem. Highland Homeowners League, Tacoma, 1980—, incorporating dir. 1980, sec. and registered agt., 1980-82. Mem. ALA (chmn. mem. com. Wash. 1957-60, mem. nat. library week com. 1965, chmn. library adminstrn. div. nominating com. 1971, mem. ins. for libraries com. 1970-74, vice chmn. library adminstrn. div. personnel adminstrn. sect. 1972-73, chmn. 1973-74, mem. com. policy implementation 1973-74, mem. library orgn. and mgmt. sect. budgeting acctg. and costs com. 1974-75), Am. Library Trustee Assn. (legis. com. 1975-78, conf. program com. 1978-80, action devel. com. 1978-80), Pacific N.W. (trustee div. nominating com 1976-77), Wash. Library Assn. (exec. bd. 1957-59, state exec., dir. Nat. Library Week 1965, treas., exec. bd. 1969-71, 71-73), Urban Libraries Council (editorial sec. Newsletter 1972-73, exec. com. 1974-75), Ladies Aux. to United Transp. Union (past pres. Tacoma), Friends Tacoma Pub. Library (registered agt. 1975-83, sec. 1975-78, pres. 1978-80, bd. dirs. 1980-83), Smithsonian Assocs., Nat. Railway Hist. Soc., U. Wash. Alumni Assn., U. Wash. Sch. Librarianship Alumni Assn. Roman Catholic. Club: Quota Internat. (sec. 1957-58, 1st v.p. 1960-61, pres. 1961-62, treas. 1975-76, pres. 1979-80) (Tacoma). Home: 6501 N Burning Tree Ln Tacoma WA 98406-2108 Office: Frank Russell Co Russell Bldg 909 A St Tacoma WA 98402-5111

CRISOSTOMO, MANNY, photographer. Grad., U of Mo. Former photographer Detroit Free Press; freelance photographer Guam. Recipient Pulitzer prize for feature photography, 1989. Office: care Pacific Daily News PO Box Dn Agana GU 96910-9017

CRISP, GEORGE ROBERT, pastor; b. Washington, Mar. 10, 1951; s. George Robert Sr. and Betty Margurite (Harpst) C.; m. Sandra Margaret Turner, Oct. 30, 1974 (div. Jan. 1982); m. Leona Sue Crisp, Nov. 3, 1984; stepchildren: Andrew Stough, Matthew Stough. BA, U. Redlands, 1974; MDiv, Claremont Sch. Theology, 1982, DMin, 1993. Ordained to ministry Meth. Ch., 1981. Choir dir. Colton (Calif.) First Bapt. Ch., 1972-74; dir. youth ministries St. Paul's United Meth. Ch., San Bernardino, Calif., 1975-80; founding pastor Hesperia (Calif.) United Meth. Ch., 1980-85; pastor Del Rosa United Meth. Ch., San Bernardino, 1985-90; dir. Wesley Found. Calif. Polytech. Inst., San Luis Obispo, 1990-93; sr. pastor San Luis Obispo United Meth. Ch., 1990-93; pastor Wahiawa (Hawaii) United Meth. CH., 1993—. Author numerous poems; composer musical scores. Mem. coun. on youth ministries United Meth. Ch., Pasadena, 1980-84, mem. com. on status and role of women, 1984-88, sec. com. on equitable compensation, 1988—. Mem. Sn Bernardino Ministerial Assn. (pres. 1987), San Luis Obispo Ministerial Assn. (v.p. San Luis Obispo chpt. 1992-93), Kiwanis (chaplain Hesperia club 1984), Order of St. Luke (west jurisdiction formation officer 1993—). Democrat. Home: 350 Iliwai Dr Wahiawa HI 96786-2209 Office: Wahiawa United Meth Ch 1445 California Ave Wahiawa HI 96786-2541

CRISPIN, JAMES HEWES, engineering and construction company executive; b. Rochester, Minn., July 23, 1915; s. Egerton Lafayette and Angela (Shipman) C.; m. Marjorie Holmes, Aug. 5, 1966. A.B. in Mech. Engring., Stanford U., 1938; M.B.A., Harvard U., 1941; grad., Army Command and Gen. Staff Sch., 1943. Registered profl. mech. engr., Calif. With C.F. Braun & Co. Alhambra, Calif., 1946-62; treas. Bechtel Corp., San Francisco, 1962-73, v.p., mem. fin. com., 1967-75, mgr. investment dept., 1973-75; retired, 1976; investment cons., Santa Barbara, Calif., 1978—. Lt. col. Ordnance Corps, AUS., 1941-46. Mem. Mil. Order World Wars, S.R., Soc. Colonial Wars, Colonial Wars Calif., Baronial Order Magna Carta, Mil. Order Crusades, Am. Def. Preparedness Assn., World Affairs Coun. No. Calif. (trustee 1968-75), Santa Barbara Mus. Art (trustee 1979-91, pres. 1986-88, life hon. trustee 1992—), Calif. Hist. Soc. (trustee 1979-86), Valley Club of Montecito (pres. 1987-90, bd. dirs. 1981-91), Calif. Club L.A., World Trade Club San Francisco (pres. 1977-78, bd. dirs. 1971-78), Santa Barbara Club (pres. 1995-96, bd. dirs. 1991-96), Pacific Union Club, San Francisco, Beta Theta Pi. Republican. Home: 1340 E Mountain Dr Santa Barbara CA 93108-1215 Office: La Arcada Bldg 1114 State St Ste 220 Santa Barbara CA 93101-2716

CRISPO, RICHARD CHARLES, artist, ethnologist, minister; b. Bklyn., Jan. 13, 1945; s. Frank C. and Irene M. (Lamont) C. M.F.A., Trinity Hall Coll., 1975; Ph.D., Collegii Romanii, Rome, 1976, Th.D., 1977. Instr. art Monterey Peninsula Coll., 1968-69, instr. ethnic studies, 1976; instr. art history Hartnell Coll.; coord. Arts in Corrections, Art Project, Soledad Prison, 1976-83; am. cultural specialist to Latin Am. for U.S.; vis. lectr. U. Calif., Santa Cruz, interdisciplinary studies dept. Porter Coll.; instr. pub. sch. art, Monterey, Calif., 1967-72; counselor Intrim, Inc., Monterey, 1976; founder Mus. on Wheels, 1973-74; founder World Folk Art Collection, Monterey, 1972; 53 murals and 63 one-man shows; executed half-mile-long mural at Soledad Prison; priest N. Am. Old Roman Catholic Ch. Recipient numerous awards including 1st prize Calif. State Fair, 1964; UNESCO award, 1971-73; Calif. Arts Council grantee. Mem. Artist Equity, Found. for the Community of Artists, Carmel Art Assn., Pacific Grove Art Center. Contbr. articles to art jours.

CRISTIANO, MARILYN JEAN, speech communication educator; b. New Haven, Jan. 10, 1954; d. Michael William Mary Rose (Porto) C. BA, Marquette U., 1975, MA, 1977; postgrad., Ariz. State U., 1977; EdD, Nova U., 1991. Speech comm. instr. Phoenix Coll., 1977-87, Paradise Valley C.C., Phoenix, 1987—; presenter at profl. confs., workshops and seminars. Author tng. manual on pub. speaking, 1991, 92, 95; contbr. articles to profl. publs. Mem. ASTD, Speech Comm. Assn., Western Speech Comm. Assn., Ariz. Comm. Assn. Office: Paradise Valley CC 18401 N 32nd St Phoenix AZ 85032-1210

CRISWELL, KIMBERLY ANN, public relations executive, dancer; b. L.A., Dec. 6, 1957; d. Robert Burton and Carolyn Joyce (Semko) C. BA with honors, U. Calif.-Santa Cruz, 1980; postgrad. Stanford U., 1993—. Instr., English Lang. Services, Oakland, Calif., 1980-81; freelance writer Verbum mag., San Diego, Gambit mag., New Orleans, 1981; instr. Tulane U., New Orleans, 1981; instr., editor Haitian-English Lang. Program, New Orleans, 1981-82; instr. Delgado Coll., New Orleans, 1982-83; instr., program coord. Vietnamese Youth Ctr., San Francisco, 1984; dancer Khadra Internat. Folk Ballet, San Francisco, 1984-89; dir. mktg. comm. Centram Systems West, Inc., Berkeley, Calif., 1984-87; comm. coord. Safeway Stores, Inc., Oakland, 1985; dir. corp. comm. TOPS, div. Sun Microsystems, Inc, 1987-88; pres. Criswell Comm., 1988—. Vol. coord. Friends of Haitians, 1981, editor, writer newsletter, 1981; dancer Komenka Ethnic Dance Ensemble, New Orleans, 1983; mem. Contemp. Art Ctr.'s Krewe of Clones, New Orleans, 1983, Americans for Nonsmokers Rights, Berkeley, 1985; active San Francisco Multimedia Developers Group, Artspan. Mem. Sci. Meets the Arts Soc. (founding), Oakland Mus. Assn., Mus. Soc. Democrat. Avocations: visual arts, travel, creative writing.

CRITES, RICHARD RAY, international franchising company executive; b. Rapid City, S.D., Aug. 29, 1952; s. Charles Dayton and Marcia Ann (Heil) C.; m. Randel E. Golobic, Dec. 27, 1980 (div. May 1988). B of Liberal Studies, U. Okla., 1975; MS, Stanford U., 1978; cert. sr. security checker, Advanced Orgn. L.A., 1987, cert. false purpose rundown auditor, 1988. Cert. staff status II, exec. status I, Am. St. Hill Orgn., exec. dir. full hat course Celebrity Ctr. Internat., 1992. Nat. sales trainer Continental Mktg. Corp., Detroit, 1975-76, regional sales mgr., 1976-80; pres., chief exec. officer Retail Packaging Specialists, Inc., San Mateo, Calif., 1982-86; owner, chief exec. officer Miracle Method of San Mateo, Inc., 1985-87, Miracle Method of Beverly Hills, Inc., L.A., 1987-90, Miracle Method of So. Calif., Inc., L.A., 1986-92, Miracle Method of No. Calif., Inc., L.A., 1988-89; v.p., treas., chmn. bd. Miracle Methods of the U.S., Inc., L.A., 1988-92; pres., chmn. bd. dirs. Miracle Method of the U.S., Inc., L.A., 1992—; pres., chmn. bd. Internat. Miracle Method Appearance Ctrs. Pacific, Inc., L.A., 1988-92, Internat. Miracle Method Ctrs. Equip. & Supply, Inc., L.A., 1989-92; gen. mgr. Stellar Mgmt. Co., L.A., 1993—. Mem. Citizen's Commn. on Human Rights, Citizens for an Alternative Tax System. Mem. Internat. Assn.

Scientologists (sponsor). Republican. Scientologist. Office: Miracle Method of the US Inc 2767 W Broadway Los Angeles CA 90041-1038

CROCKER, KENNETH FRANKLIN, data processing consultant; b. Centralia, Wash., July 29, 1950; s. Earl Thomas and Mary Jane (Hamil) C.; m. Mary Louise Underwood, June 15, 1974 (div. Dec. 1987); children: Matthew A., Benjamin F., Jonathan C.; m. Sally Marlene Gammelgard, Dec. 21, 1987 (div. 1992). AS in Computer Programming and System Design, Control Data Inst., Long Beach, Calif., 1972. Programmer City of Greenville, S.C., 1973; computer operator Winn Dixie Stores, Greer, S.C., 1973-75; programmer Piedmont Industries, Greenville, S.C., 1975-78; systems engr. Micro-Systems, Greenville, 1978; sr. programmer Reeves Bros., Lyman, S.C., 1978-80; systems analyst Cryovac div. W.R. Grace Co., Duncan, S.C., 1980-84; sr. cons. Cap Gemini Am., San Francisco, 1984-85; prin. mem. tech. staff Citibank-FSB Calif., Oakland, 1985-91; sr. software engr. Lucky Stores Inc., Dublin, Calif., 1991-94; tech. cons. Lawrence Berkeley Labs., Berkeley, Calif., 1994-95, Lawrence Berkley Labs., San Francisco, 1994; plan arch. Safeway, Oakland, Calif., 1995—. Umpire Contra Costa Umpires Assn., 1990—. Libertarian. Baptist. Home and Office: 301 Livorna Heights Rd Alamo CA 94507-1326

CROCKER, MYRON DONOVAN, federal judge; b. Pasadena, Calif., Sept. 4, 1915; s. Myron William and Ethel (Shoemaker) C.; m. Elaine Jensen, Apr. 26, 1941; children—Glenn, Holly. A.B., Fresno State Coll., 1937; LL.B., U. Calif. at Berkeley, 1940. Bar: Calif. bar 1940. Spl. agt. FBI, 1940-46; practiced law Chowchilla, Calif., 1946-58; asst. dist. atty. Madera County, Calif., 1946-51; judge Chowchilla Justice Ct., 1952-58, Superior Ct. Madera County, 1958-59; U.S. judge Eastern Dist. Calif., Sacramento, 1959—. Mem. Madera County Republican Central Com., 1950—. Named Outstanding Citizen Chowchilla, 1960. Mem. Chowchilla C. of C. (sec.). Lutheran. Club: Lion. Office: US Dist Ct US Dist Courthouse 1130 O St Fresno CA 93721-2201*

CROCKER, SYLVIA FLEMING, psychotherapist, writer; b. Live Oak, Fla., Apr. 10, 1933; d. Tom and Lydia (Compton) Fleming; divorced; children: Sarah Lydia, Trena Elizabeth. AA, Stephens Coll., 1951; BA, U. Mo., 1957, PhD, 1969; MA, Northwestern U., Evanston, Ill., 1958; MS, U. Wyo., 1987. Lic. prof. counselor, Wyo. Grad. asst. in philosophy U. Mo., Columbia, 1960-63; asst. prof. philosophy Marquette U., 1966-70; lectr. in philosophy Calif. State U., San Bernardino, 1972-75, U. Wyo., 1975-76; pvt. practice Laramie, Wyo., 1980—. Mem. Assn. Advancement of Gestalt Therapy (steering com., chair of com. for Gestalt rsch. and theoretical devel.). Episcopalian. Home and Office: 2115 E Hancock St Laramie WY 82070-2935

CROCKER, THOMAS DUNSTAN, economics educator; b. Bangor, Maine, July 22, 1936; s. Floyd M. and Gloria F. (Thomas) C.; m. Sylvia Fleming, Dec. 31, 1961 (div. Sept. 1986); children: Sarah Lydia, Trena Elizabeth; m. Judith Powell, Sept. 9, 1989. AB, Bowdoin Coll., 1959; PhD, U. Mo., 1967. Asst. prof. econs. U. Wis., Milw., 1963-70; assoc. prof. U. Calif., Riverside, 1970-75; prof. U. Wyo., Laramie, 1975—, chairperson dept. econs. and fin., 1991-93, dir. Sch. Environment and Natural Resources, 1993—; rsch. assoc. U. Calif., Berkeley, 1973, Pa. State U., 1974; cons. Asarco, Inc., 1985-89, Mathtech, Inc., Princeton, N.J., 1987-88, Mountain Bell, Denver, 1987, Shea and Gardner, Washington, 1989, Arco, Inc., 1992, A. Coors Co., 1992; mem. sci. adv. bd. EPA, Washington, 1973-76; mem. panel on long range transport issues U.S. Congress, Washington, 1981. Co-author: Environmental Economics, 1971; author, editor: Economic Perspectives on Acid Deposition Control, 1984; editorial coun. Jour. Environ. Econs. and Mgmt., 1973-88; contbr. articles to profl. jours. Mem. com. impacts pollution on agriculture Orgn. for Econ. Cooperation and Devel., Paris, 1987-88. Grantee NSF, 1968, 73, 81, EPA, 1971, 76-85. Mem. Am. Econ. Assn., Assn. Environ. Resource Econs. (mem. awards structure com. 1981-83, contributed papers com. 1989), The Nature Conservancy, Air Pollution Control Assn. Republican. Office: Univ Wyo Dept Econs Laramie WY 82071-3985

CROCKETT, DENNIS, art historian; b. N.Y.C., Mar. 12, 1958; s. Joseph and Priscilla (Champa) C.; m. Susan Babilon, Aug. 13, 1982; children: Max Babilon-Crockett, Tobas Babilon-Crockett. MA, CUNY, 1985, PhD, 1993. Adj. prof. Queens Coll., CUNY, N.Y.C., 1985-86; instr. Sch. of Visual Arts, N.Y.C., 1988-92; asst. prof. Whitman Coll., Walla Walla, Wash., 1992—. Mem. Coll. Art Assn. Office: Whitman Coll Olin Hall Walla Walla WA 99362

CROCKETT, ROBERT YORK, architect; b. West Covina, Calif., Nov. 27, 1962; s. Bob York and Carolyn Kathleen (McLellan) C. BArch, U. So. Calif., 1985; Masters, UCLA, 1994. Registered architect, Calif., Nev., Ariz., Miss., La. Designer TNT Architecture Internat., Malibu, Calif., 1983-85, Pace Group, L.A., 1985-87; architect in pvt. practice Marina Del Ray, Calif., 1988—; bd. dirs. Planning Architecture Consulting Engring., Phoenix. Home and Office: 123 Catamaran St Marina Del Rey CA 90292

CROCKETT, RONALD MICHAEL, chiropractor; b. Salem, Oreg., Nov. 6, 1951; s. Donald Floyd and Valena Jean (Garver) C.; m. Christine Bernadette Kelley, Feb. 16, 1974; children: Chereen N., Jamie Lynn. BS, Oreg. Coll. Edn., 1974; DC, Western States Chiropractic, Coll./Portland, Oreg., 1979. Fellow Internat. Acad. Clin. Acupuncture. Chiropractor Bourland Chiropracti Clinic, Hillsboro, Oreg., 1979-80, Crockett Chiropractic Ctr., Salem, 1980—. Mem. Internat. Chiropractic Assn., Oreg. Doctors of Chiropractic. Office: Crockett Chiropractic Ctr 862 Lancaster Dr SE Salem OR 97301-5831

CROFT, RICHARD T., psychotherapist; b. Idaho Falls, Idaho, Sept. 11, 1967; s. Richard Paul and Kathy (Perkins) C. BA in Am. Studies, Idaho State U., 1990, MA in Counseling, 1992. Lic. profl. counselor. Primary therapist Aspen Crest Hosp., Pocatello, Idaho, 1992-93, Eastern Idaho Regional Behavioral Health Ctr., Idaho Falls, 1993—. Mem. ACA, Internat. Assn. Marriage and Family Counseling. Office: Eastern Idaho Regional Behavioral Health Ctr PO Box 2077 Idaho Falls ID 83403-2077

CROFT, VICKI FAYE, librarian; b. St. Louis, Jan. 13, 1948; d. Floyd Merle Keating and Vivian W. Keating Sorensen; m. James Vernon Croft, June 1, 1971. BS, Dana Coll., 1970; MSL.S., U. Ill., 1971. Asst. sci. libr. U. Nebr., Lincoln, 1971-76; head vet. med./pharmacy libr. Wash. State U., Pullman, 1976—; chair First Internat. Conf. of Animal Health Info. Profls., Reading, Eng., 1992. Editor Pets sect. Mags. for Librs., 1982, 86, 89. Mem. Med. Library Assn. (cert., sec.-treas. vet. med. librs. sect. 1985-86, chmn. 1986-87, sect. coun. 1988-91, mem. Pacific N.W. chpt., treas. 1994—), Nebr. Libr. Assn. (sec.-treas. coll. and rsch. sect. 1973-74), Wash. Med. Librs. Assn. (exec. bd. 1984-85), Pacific N.W. Libraries Assn. (disting.), Acad. Health Info. Profls. (disting.). Lutheran. Home: 1840 NW Hall Dr Pullman WA 99163-3551 Office: Wash State U Vet/Med Pharmacy Library 170 Wegner Hall Pullman WA 99164

CROGAN, NEVA LYNNE, nursing consultant; b. Colfax, Wash., Feb. 22, 1957; d. George Conrad and Beverly June (Harris) Russell; m. Bill Loren Dyck, Apr. 24, 1976 (div. 1987); 1 child, David Loren; m. David Martin Crogan, June 20, 1987. AA, Big Bend Community Coll., Moses Lake, Wash., 1977, Columbia Basin Coll., Pasco, Wash., 1979; BSN, SUNY, Albany, 1984; BS, Ea. Wash. U., 1983, MN, 1992. RN, Wash.; cert. nursing adminstrn. ANA. Staff nurse Othello (Wash.) Cmty. Hosp., 1977-80, Whitman Cmty. Hosp., Colfax, Wash., 1980-81; charge nurse Ritzville (Wash.) Meml. Hosp., 1981; nursing instr. Big Bend C.C., 1981-87; edn. coord. Moses Lake Clinic, 1987-88; utilization coord. Med. Svc. Corp., Spokane, Wash., 1988-89; in-svc. dir. St. Brendan Nursing Home, Spokane, 1989-90; dir. nursing svc. Wash. Health Care Ctr.-Northcrest, Spokane, 1990-91; instnl. nurse cons. DSHS Nursing Home Svcs., 1991-94; nurse cons. Beverly Enterprises, Spokane, Wash., 1994—; cons. Moses Lake, 1985-86; educator local ch. groups, Moses Lake, 1987-88. Recipient Women of the Moose grant, 1979; grad. scholar Intercollegiate Ctr. Nursing Edn., 1992. Mem. Nat. Gerontol. Nursing Assn., Sigma Theta Tau. Home: 11421 N Morrill Dr Mead WA 99021-9677 Office: 3011 E Wellesley Ave Ste 100 Spokane WA 99207-5978

CROMBACH, DANITA LYNN, communications professional; b. Ventura, Calif., Dec. 12, 1962; d. Edwin Marvin and Patricia Anne (Robinson) Osborne; m. Timothy John Crombach, May 9, 1992; children: Christopher Pritchard, Brian Jeffrey, Amanda Christine. Cert. tchr. in comm. and radio tech. Police reserve officer Oxnard (Calif.) Police Dept., 1982-84; pub. safety dispatcher III Oxnard (Calif.) Police & Fire Depts., 1984-89; pub. safety comm. instr. San Jose (Calif.) Police Dept., 1989-92; dir. ops. A&R Fin. and Ins. Svcs., Agoura Hills, Calif., 1992-94; comm. mgr. Inglewood (Calif.) Police & Fire Depts., 1994—; instr. Ventura (Calif.) C.C., 1989, West Valley Coll., Saratoga, Calif., 1989-92; cons. Apple, Inc., Cupertino, Calif., 1991, Vallejo (Calif.) Police Dept., 1991. Recipient Commendation cert. State of Calif., 1987. Mem. Comm. Ops. Mgrs. Assn., Tri-Counties Comm. Assn. (founder, pres.), Assn. Pub. Safety Comm. Officers.

CROMLEY, BRENT REED, lawyer; b. Great Falls, June 12, 1941; s. Arthur and Louise Lilian (Hiebert) C.; m. Dorothea Mae Zamborini, Sept. 9, 1967; children: Brent Reed Jr., Giano Lorenzo, Taya Rose. AB, Dartmouth Coll., 1963; JD, U. Mont., 1968. Bar: Mont. 1968, U.S. Dist. Ct. Mont. 1968, U.S. Ct. Appeals (9th cir.) 1968, U.S. Supreme Ct. 1978, U.S. Ct. Claims 1988, U.S. Ct. Appeals (D.C. cir.) 1988. Law clk. to presiding justice U.S. Dist. Ct. Mont., Billings, 1968-69; assoc. Hutton & Sheehy and predecessor firms, Billings, 1969-77, ptnr., 1977-78; ptnr. Moulton, Bellingham, Longo & Mather, P.C., Billings, 1979—, also bd. dirs. Contbr. articles to profl. jours. Mem. Yellowstone Bd. Health, Billings, 1972—; chmn. Mont. Bd. Pers. Appeals, 1974-80; mem. Mont. Ho. of Reps., 1991-92. Mem. ABA, ACLU, Internat. Assn. Def. Counsel, Mont. Bar Assn., Mont. Def. Trial Lawyers Bd., Yellowstone County Bar Assn. (various offices), Christian Legal Soc., Internat. Brotherhood of Magicians, Kiwanis. Home: 235 Parkhill Dr Billings MT 59101-0660 Office: Moulton Bellingham Longo & Mather PC 1900 Sheraton Plz Billings MT 59101

CROMPTON, ARNOLD, minister, educator; b. Leeds, Yorkshire, Eng., Dec. 19, 1914; came to U.S., 1923; s. Harold and May Almyeria (Milward) C. BA, Case Western Res. U., 1936; MA, U. Chgo., 1939; BD, Meadville Theol. Sch., Chgo., 1939; ThD, Pacific Sch. of Religion, 1956; DD (hon.), Meadville-Lombard Theol. Sch., 1972. Ordained to ministry Unitarian Ch., 1939. Minister 1st Unitarian Ch. of Erie, Pa., 1939-45, 1st Unitarian Ch., Oakland, Calif., 1945-82; minister emeritus 1st Unitarian Ch. of Erie, Oakland, Calif., 1982—; lectr. ch. history Starr King Sch. for the Ministry, Berkeley, Calif., 1953-67; dir. Earl Morse Wilbur Library, Berkeley, 1961-67, tutor, 1990—; adj. prof. history Union Inst., Cin., 1993—; anniversary lectr. Taegu (Republic of Korea) U., 1986; Wilbur Meml. lectr. on religion on Pacific Rim, Berkeley, 1990; lectr. Free Religious Assn., Japan, 1992; bd. dirs., past pres. Oakland-Fukuoka Soc., Oakland, 1975—; pres. Rossmoor Religious Coun., Walnut Creek, Calif., 1989—. Author: Apostle of Liberty, 1950, Unitarianism on Pacific Coast, 1954, Aurelia H. Reinhardt, 1981; contbr. articles to profl. jours. Lectr. Ebell Soc., Oakland, 1982—; pres. Internat. Inst. of the East Bay, Oakland, 1981-82, Rossmoor Activities Coun., Walnut Creek, 1989—; chmn. Alameda County Crime Prevention Commn., Calif., 1978-80; bd. dirs. English summer sch. Bir Zeit Coll., Jordan, 1963-64, English Lang. Program-Komagane, Japan, 1967. Recipient Silver Beaver award Boy Scouts Am., 1966, citation Calif. State Assembly, 1970, Calif. State Senate, 1975, Ho. of Reps., 1990, Ohio Ho. of Reps., 1989, Disting. Alumnus award Case Western Res. U., 1989, Pub. Svc. citation U. Chgo., 1992, Thomas Starr King award Starr King Sch. for Ministry, Berkeley, 1993; named one of Outstanding Immigrants, Internat. Inst., 1976. Mem. Unitarian Universalist Ministers Assn. (pres. Pacific Coast chpt. 1970, spl. envoy to chs. of Japan 1989), Rotary (pres. Rossmoor chpt. 1986-87), Masons (grand chaplain 1979-80), Phi Alpha Theta (hon.), Phi Kappa Tau. Home: 1449 Skycrest Dr # 1 Walnut Creek CA 94595-1870 Office: 1st Unitarian Ch 685 14th St Oakland CA 94612-1242

CRONE, RICHARD ALLAN, cardiologist, educator; b. Tacoma, Nov. 26, 1947; s. Richard Irving and Alla Marguerite (Ernst) C.; m. Rita Louzetta Mitchell, June 9, 1972 (div. Oct. 1981); m. Mika Jane Hinkle, Feb. 12, 1983 (div. Aug. 1991); m. Becky Jo Zimmerman, Dec. 11, 1993. BA in Chemistry, U. Wash., 1969, MD, 1973. Intern Madigan Army Med. Ctr., Tacoma, 1973-74, resident in medicine, 1974-76, fellow in cardiology, 1977-79; commd. med. officer U.S. Army, Tacoma, Denver, San Francisco, 1972; advanced through grades to lt. col. U.S. Army, 1981; dir. coronary care unit Fitzsimons Army Med. Ctr., Denver, 1979-81; practice medicine specializing in cardiology Stevens Health Clinic, Edmonds, Wash., 1981—, also dir. coronary care unit, cardiac catheter lab, 1982—; clin. asst. prof. medicine U. Wash., Seattle, 1983—. Fellow Am. Coll. Angiology; mem. AMA, Am. Coll. Cardiology, Am. Heart Assn., Seattle Acad. Internal Medicine, Wash. State Soc. Internal Medicine, Wash. State Med. Assn. Republican. Roman Catholic. Home: 10325 66th Pl W Mukilteo WA 98275-4559 Office: 21701 76th Ave W Ste 100 Edmonds WA 98026-7536

CRONEBERGER, HARRY LEONARD, JR., controller; b. S.I., N.Y., Aug. 3, 1955; s. Harry Leonard and S. Yvonne (Welty) C.; m. Judy Lynne Harner, June 5, 1980; children: Ian Leonard, Staci Lynne. AS in Bus. Adminstrn., Mt. San Jacinto Coll., 1991; BS in Bus. and Mgmt., U. Redlands, 1993. EMT Hemet (Calif.) Valley Ambulance, 1975-77, paramedic, 1977-89, info. svcs. mgr., 1986-90, contr., 1990—; spl. res. police officer, SWAT team paramedic, Hemet Police Dept., 1984-89. Bd. dirs. Mid County Child Care Coun., Hemet, 1992—. Republican. Home: 1041 E Whittier Ave Hemet CA 92543-6161

CRONER, JOHN ALTON, journalist; b. Soldier, Idaho, Feb. 10, 1916; s. Frank and Louella Croner; m. Jennie Frederickson, May 20, 1939 (div. June 1977); children: Dennis, Charles, John, Carol, Kerry; m. June Pitkin Bates, Mar. 4, 1978. Columnist, feature writer Ontario (Oreg.) Argus Observer, 1973—. Author: The Basque and the Boy, 1975; contbr. 20 Years in the Making, 1976. With USN, 1934-38. Democrat. Nazarene. Home: 845 Ayers Ave # 576 Fruitland ID 83619-2534 Office: Ontario Argus Observer PO Box 130 Ontario OR 97914-0130

CRONIN, THOMAS EDWARD, academic administrator; b. Milton, Mass., Mar. 18, 1940; s. Joseph M. and Mary Jane Cronin; m. Tania Zaroodny, Nov. 26, 1966; 1 child, Alexander. AB, Holy Cross Coll., 1961; MA, Stanford U., 1964, PhD, 1968; LLD (hon.), Marietta Coll., 1987, Franklin Coll., 1993. Tchg. fellow Stanford (Calif.) U., 1962-64; staff mem. The White House, Washington, 1966-67; faculty mem. U. N.C., 1967-70; staff fellow Brookings Instn., 1970-72; faculty mem. Brandeis U., Waltham, Mass., 1975-77, U. Del., Newark, 1977-79; McHugh prof. of Am. instns. The Colo. Coll., Colorado Springs, 1985-93, acting pres., 1991-92; pres. Whitman Coll., Walla Walla, Wash., 1993—; moderator Aspen Inst. Exec. Seminars, 1975—; pres. CRC, Inc., 1980—, Presidency Rsch. Group, 1981-82; cons. in field; guest polit. analyst various tv programs. Author: The State of the Presidency, 1980, Direct Democracy, 1989, Colorado Politics and Government, 1993; co-author: Government By the People, 1995. Dir. Nat. Civic League, Denver, Inst. for Ednl. Leadership, Washington; adv. bd. mem. Leadership Am., Dallas. Mem. AAUP, Am. Polit. Sci. Assn. (exec. com. 1990-92), Western Polit. Sci. Assn. (pres. 1993-94), Urban League, C. of C. Office: Whitman Coll 345 Boyer Ave Walla Walla WA 99362-2067

CRONKLETON, THOMAS EUGENE, physician; b. Donahue, Iowa, July 22, 1928; s. Harry L. and Ursula Alice (Halligan) C.; BA in Biology, St. Ambrose Coll., 1954; MD, Iowa Coll. Medicine, 1958; m. Wilma Agnes Potter, June 6, 1953; children: Thomas Eugene, Kevin P., Margaret A., Catherine A., Richard A., Robert A., Susan A., Phillip A. Diplomate Am. Bd. Family Practice. Rotating intern St. Benedict's Hosp., Ogden, Utah, 1958-59; Donahue, Iowa, 1959-61, practice family medicine, Davenport, Iowa, 1961-66, Laramie, Wyo., 1966—; asso. The Davenport Clinic, 1961-63, partner, 1963-66; active staff St. Luke's Hosp., Mercy Hosp., Davenport; staff physician U. Wyo. Student Health Service, 1966-69, 70-71, 74-75, 76—, acting dir., 1988-89; staff physician outpatient dept. VA Hosp., Iowa City, 1969-70: staff physician outpatient dept. VA Hosp., Cheyenne, Wyo., 1971-74, chief outpatient dept., 1973-74; dir. Student Health Service Utah State U., Logan, 1975-76; physician (part-time) dept. medicine VA Hosp., Cheyenne, 1976-81. Active Long's Peak council Boy Scouts Am., 1970—, scout chaplain Diocese of Cheyenne, 1980—, mem. Diocesan Pastoral Council, 1982-85. Served with USMC, World War II, Korea. Recipient Dist. Scouter award Boy Scouts Am., 1974, St. George Emblem, Nat. Cath. Scouter award, 1981, Silver Beaver award Longs Peak Coun. Boy Scouts, 1995, Bronze Pelican award Diocese of Cheyenne Adult Scouts, 1995; also 5, 10, and 15-yr. service pins Boy Scouts Am. Fellow Am. Acad. Family Practice; mem. Wyo. State Med. Soc., Albany County (Wyo.) Med. Soc., Iowa Med. Soc., Johnson County (Iowa) Med. Soc. Democrat. Roman Catholic. Club: K.C. (4 deg.). Home: 6414 N Mokane Ct Kansas City MO 64151

CROOK, SEAN PAUL, aerospace systems engineering manager; b. Pawtucket, R.I., July 6, 1953; s. Ralph Frederick and Rosemary Rita (Dolan) C.; m. Mary Wickman, June 10, 1978; children: Kimberly Anne, Kelly Dolan, Erin Webster, Mary Katherine. BSME, U.S. Naval Acad., 1975; MBA, U. So. Calif., 1991. Commd. ensign USN, 1975, advanced through grades to lt., 1979, resigned, 1981; sr. systems engr. space div. Gen. Electric Co., Springfield, Va., 1982-84; sr. aerospace systems engr. Martin Marietta Aero. Def. Systems, Long Beach, Calif., 1984-87; sr. aerospace system engring. mgr. Martin Marietta Aero Def. Systems, Long Beach, Calif., 1987-93; chief engr. GDE Sys. Inc., A Tracor Co., San Diego, 1993—. Commdr. USNR, 1992—. Mem. Am. Mgmt. Assn. Home: 23565 Via Calzada Mission Viejo CA 92691-3625 Office: GDE Sys Inc PO Box 509008 MZ 6500E San Diego CA 92150-9008

CROOKE, STANLEY THOMAS, pharmaceutical company executive; b. Indpls., Mar. 28, 1945; m. Nancy Alder (dec.); 1 child, Evan; m. Rosanne M. Snyder. BS in Pharmacy, Butler U., 1966; PhD, Baylor Coll., 1971, MD, 1974. Asst. dir. med. rsch. Bristol Labs., N.Y.C., 1975-76, assoc. dir. med. rsch., 1976-77, assoc. dir. R&D, 1977-79, v.p. R&D, 1979-80; v.p. R&D Smith Kline & French Labs., Phila., 1980-82; pres. R&D Smith Kline Beckman, Phila., 1982-88; chmn. bd., chief exec. officer ISIS Pharms., Inc., Carlsbad, Calif., 1989; cons. Enzytech, Cambridge, Mass., 1988, Bachem Biosci., Phila., 1988, Centocor, Malvern, Pa., 1988, BCM Techs., Houston, 1988; chmn. bd. dirs. GES Pharms., Inc., Houston, 1989-91; adj. prof. Baylor Coll. Medicine, Houston, 1982, U. Pa., Phila., 1982-89; bd. dirs. Cytel Corp., San Diego, GeneMedicine, Houston, Biotech. Industry Orgn., Calif. Healthcare Inst., Indsl. Biotech. Assn., Washington, 1993; mem. sci. adv. bd. SIBIA, La Jolla, Calif.; adj. prof. pharmacology UCLA, 1991, U. Calif. San Diego, 1994. Editor: Anti Cancer Drug Design, 1984; mem. editorial adv. bd. Molecular Pharmacology, 1986-91, Jour. Drug Targeting, 1992; patentee in field. Trustee Franklin Inst., Phila., 1987-89; mem., editorial bd. Antisense Rsch. and Devel.; bd. dirs. Mann Music Ctr., Phila., 1987-89; children's com. Children's Svcs., Inc., Phila., 1983-84; adv. com. World Affairs Coun., Phila. Recipient Disting. Prof. award U. Ky., 1986, Julius Stermer award Phila. Coll. Pharmacy and Sci., 1981, Outstanding Lectr. award Baylor Coll. Medicine, 1984. Mem. AAAS, Am. Assn. for Cancer Rsch. (state legis. com.), Am. Soc. for Microbiology, Am. Soc. Pharmacology and Exptl. Therapeutics, Am. Soc. Clin. Pharmacology and Therapeutics, Am. Soc. Clin. Oncology, Indsl. Biotech. Assn. (bd. dirs. 1992-93). Office: ISIS Pharms Inc 2280 Faraday Ave Carlsbad CA 92008-7208

CROSBY, GLENN ARTHUR, chemistry educator; b. nr. Youngwood, Pa., July 30, 1928; s. Edwin Glenn and Bertha May (Ritchey) C.; m. Jane Lichtenfels, May 29, 1950; children: Brian, Alan, Karen. B.S., Waynesburg Coll., 1950; Ph.D., U. Wash., 1954. Research assoc. Fla. State U., Tallahassee, 1955-57; vis. asst. prof. physics Fla. State U., 1957; asst. prof. chemistry U. N. Mex., Albuquerque, 1957-62; assoc. prof. chemistry U. N. Mex., 1962-67; prof. chemistry and chem. physics Wash. State U., Pullman, 1967—; chmn. chem. physics program Wash. State U., 1977-84; mem. adv. com. Rsch. Corp., Tucson, 1981-88, 90-92; vis. prof. phys. chemistry U. Tübingen, Fed. Republic Germany, 1964; vis. prof. physics U. Canterbury, Christchurch, N.Z., 1974; Humboldt sr. scientist, vis. prof. phys. chemistry U. Hohenheim, Fed. Republic Germany, 1978-79; mem. commn. on life scis. NRC, 1991—. Author: Chemistry: Matter and Chemical change, 1962; also numerous sci. and sci.-related articles. Recipient U.S. Sr. Scientist award Humboldt Found., Fed. Republic Germany, 1978-79, Catalyst award Chem. Mfrs. Assn., 1979, Disting. Alumnus award Waynesburg Coll., 1982, Faculty Excellence award Wash. State U., 1984, Pub. Svc. award Wash. State U., 1989, Disting. Prof. award Wash. State U. Mortar Bd., 1990; named Prof. of Yr., U. N.Mex., 1967; NSF fellow U. Wash., Seattle, 1953-54; Research Corp. venture grantee, 1960; Fulbright fellow, 1964. Fellow AAAS; mem. Am. Chem. Soc. (numerous activities including chmn. div. chem. edn. 1982, chmn. com. on edn. 1990-91, We. Conn. sect. Vis. Scientist award 1981, nat. award in chem. edn. 1985, bd. dirs. 1994-96), Am. Phys. Soc., Inter-Am. Photochem. Soc., Nat. Sci. Tchrs. Assn., Wash. Sci. Tchrs. Assn. (Outstanding Coll. Sci. Tchr. award 1975), Sigma Xi, Phi Kappa Phi, Sigma Pi Sigma. Home: 1825 NE Valley Rd Pullman WA 99163-4628 Office: Wash State U Dept Chemistry Pullman WA 99164-4630

CROSBY, JOHN O'HEA, conductor, opera manager; b. N.Y.C., July 12, 1926; s. Laurence Alden and Aileen Mary (O'Hea) C. Grad., Hotchkiss Sch., 1944; BA, Yale U., 1950, DFA (hon.) 1991; LittD (hon.), U. N.Mex., 1967; MusD (hon.), Coll. of Santa Fe, 1968, Cleve. Inst. Music, 1974; LHD (hon.), U. Denver, 1977. pres. Manhattan Sch. Music, 1976-86. Accompanist, opera coach, condr., N.Y.C., 1951-56, gen. dir., mem. conducting staff, Santa Fe Opera, 1957—; guest condr. various opera cos. in, U.S. and Can., 1967—; condr.: U.S. stage premiere Daphne, 1964, Friedenstag, 1988; world premiere Wuthering Heights, 1958. Served with inf. AUS, 1945-46, ETO. Recipient Nat. Medal of Arts, 1991, Verdienstkreuz 1st klasse Bundesrepublik, Deutschland, 1992. Roman Catholic. Clubs: Metropolitan Opera (N.Y.C.), Century Assn. (N.Y.C.), University (N.Y.C.). Office: Santa Fe Opera PO Box 2408 Santa Fe NM 87504-2408*

CROSS, ALLAN JOSEPH, security software company co-owner, executive; b. Syracuse, N.Y., Mar. 6, 1944; s. Kenneth J. and Mary Ann (Polinski) C.; m. Martha Balon, Oct. 11, 1980; 1 child, Danielle. BA in Sociology/Criminology, Syracuse U., 1965; BA in Bus., U. Wyo., 1970, MBA, 1972; post-grad., Air Force Inst. Tech., 1972, Air Command and Staff Coll. Cert. protection profl. Commd. 2d lt. USAF, 1965, advanced through grades to maj.; comdr. minuteman missile crew, 90th SMW UTAPAO RTNAB, Security Police Squadron, Thailand, 1968-74; comdr. Rhein Main AFB Security Police Squadron, Frankfurt, Fed. Republic of Germany, 1975-78; regional dir. Def. Investigative Svc., Phila., 1978-82; dir. security joint cruise missiles project USAF, Washington, 1982-84; chief ops. USAF/Def. Nuclear Agy., Washington, 1984-85; ret. USAF, 1985; mgr. RCA/GE, Camden, N.J., 1985-87; dir. assets protection Wall to Wall Sound & Video, Inc., Cinnaminson, N.J., 1987-89; v.p. PPM 2000, Inc., Edmonton, 1989—; Merchantville, N.J., 1989—; instr., lectr. U. Md., various locations, 1974-78, U. Del., Wilmington, 1985-88. Contbr. articles to profl. jours. Mem. Merchantville Hist. Soc., Better Bus. Bur., South Jersey, 1987-88. Fellow Quintillion Group; mem. VFW, Phila. C. of C., Am. Soc. Indsl. Security, Internat. Assn. Chiefs of Police, Acad. Security Educators and Trainers, Police Chiefs Assn. of S.E. Pa., Beta Gamma Sigma. Home: 218 E Maple Ave Merchantville NJ 08109-2662 Office: PPM 2000 Inc, 201 10803-182 St, Edmonton, AB Canada T5S 1J5

CROSS, CHRISTOPHER CHARLES, lawyer; b. Morgantown, W.Va., Sept. 11, 1952; s. Aureal T. and Aleen (Teyssier) C.; children: Nicholas, Connor. BA, Denison U., Granville, Ohio, 1974; JD, U. Denver, 1979. Bar: Colo. 1979, U.S. Dist. Ct. Colo. 1979, U.S. Ct. Appeals (10th cir.) 1992. Dep. dist. atty. Denver Dist. Atty.'s Office, 1979-84; assoc. Roath & Brega, P.C., Denver, 1984-86; pvt. practice Denver, 1986—. Named Outstanding Young Man of Am., Outstanding Young Men of Am., 1989. Mem. Colo. Bar Assn. (bd. govs. 1989-91, 93—), Denver Bar Assn., Colo. Criminal Def. Bar, Assn. Trial Lawyers Am., Colo. Trial Lawyers Assn. Office: 2303 E Dartmouth Ave Englewood CO 80110-3079

CROSS, CHRISTOPHER S., fundraising executive; b. Lawrence, Mass., Oct. 11, 1943; s. Jerome Whitman and Margaret (Bain) C. BS, Boston U., 1967. Assoc. dir. Haney Assocs., Concord, Mass., 1969-71; nat. dir. devel. U.S. Ski Team, Denver, 1971-72; dir. mktg. Denver Merchandise Mart, 1972-76; v.p. Profl. Travel Advisors, Boulder, Colo., 1976-79, Animal Health Ins. Co., Danbury, Conn., 1985-91; nat. dir. devel. Am. Humane Assn., Denver, 1983-85; devel. officer Boulder County Hospice, Boulder, 1992—; bd. dirs. Cross Assocs., Boulder. Bd. dirs. Desiderata Sch., Berthoud, Colo., 1992—, Ednl. Films Inst., Albuquerque, 1989; hon. chair Colo. Contingent for U.S. Ski Team, Boulder, 1977; co-founder Colo. Trade Show Coun., Denver, 1975. Decorated Bronze Star, Air medal. Mem. Cmty. Shares of Colo. (bd. dirs. 1994—), Nat. Soc. Fundraising Execs., Planned Giving Roundtable,

Assn. for Health Care Philanthropy. Office: Boulder County Hospice 2825 Marine St Boulder CO 80303-1027 Home: PO Box 1075 Niwot CO 80544-1075

CROSS, DENNIS WARD, insurance company executive; b. Santa Barbara, Calif., Sept. 22, 1943; s. Ward H. and Durith Ann (Stonner) C.; BS, Ill. Wesleyan U., 1965; MBA, Ind. U., 1967; CLU, Am. Coll., 1972; m. Judith M. Marston, Feb. 5, 1967; 1 child, Kimberly. Dir. consultation projects Life Ins. Mktg. and Rsch. Assn., Hartford, Conn., 1970-75; asst. v.p. sales USAA Life Ins. Co., San Antonio, 1975-78, v.p. sales, 1978-80, sr. v.p. sales, 1980-81, sr. v.p. mktg., 1981-86, sr. v.p. mktg., fin. svcs. div., 1986-89, also dir.; sr. v.p. sales and svc. USAA Investment Mgmt. Co., 1989-90, sr. v.p. mktg. sales and svc., 1990-91, also bd. dirs.; pres. USAA Life Gen. Agy., 1984-89; v.p. USAA Life Series Fund; sr. v.p. USAA Retirement Communities, bd. dirs. USAA Life Ins. Co.; chief oper. officer Jackson Nat. Life Ins. Co., 1991-92, also bd. dirs.; pres. Jackson Nat. Fin. Svcs., Inc., 1992-93; mng. dir. De Hayes Consulting Group, 1993; instr., hon. faculty Army Logistics Mgmt. Center, Ft. Lee, Va., 1968-70; guest instr. U. Tex., San Antonio, 1976-91, San Antonio Coll., 1978-81, St. Mary's U., 1981-91. Mem. Cattle Barons' Steering com.; bd. dirs., pres. Am. Cancer Soc., chmn. exec. com.; chmn. Vol. Devel. Com., Westside Expansion Project Steering Com.; bd. dirs., past pres. Jr. Achievement of South Tex.; with mktg. task force, United Way of San Antonio; chmn. bd. trustees Humana Hosp., San Antonio; bd. dirs. SW Craft Ctr. Capt. U.S. Army, 1967-70. Fellow Life Office Mgmt. Assn.; mem. Am. Soc. CLUs, Life Advertisers Assn., Life Ins. Mktg. and Rsch. Assn. (former bd. dirs.), Direct Response Mktg. Ins. Council (Exec. of Yr. 1987), Am. Advt. Fedn., Army Res. Assn., Mutual Fund Ednl. Alliance (bd. govs. 1987-89, 90-91), Investment Co. Inst. (rsch. com. 1990-91, mktg. com. 1991). Office: De Hayes Consulting Group 3300 Douglas Blvd Roseville CA 95661-3829

CROSS, GLENN LABAN, engineering company executive, development planner; b. Mt. Vernon, Ill., Dec. 28, 1941; s. Kenneth Edward and Mildred Irene (Glenn) C.; m. Kim Lien Duong, Aug. 30, 1968 (div. Oct. 1975); m. Tran Tu Thach, Dec. 26, 1975; children: Cindy Sue, Cristy Luu, Crystal Tu, Cassandra Caitlynn; BA, Calif. Western U., 1981, MBA, 1982. Hosp. adminstr. pub. health div. USAID, Dept. State, Washington, 1966-68; pers. mgr. Pacific Architects and Engrs., Inc., L.A., 1968-70, contract adminstr., 1970-73, mgr. mgmt. svcs., 1973-75; contracts adminstr. Internat. Svcs. div., AVCO, Cin., 1975-77; sr. contract adminstr. Bechtel Group, Inc., San Francisco, 1977-80, Arabian Bechtel Co. Ltd.; contract adminstrv. supr. Bechtel Civil, Inc., Jubail Industrial City, Saudi Arabia, 1980-85; cons. Bechtel Western Power Corp., Jakarta, Indonesia, Pacific Engrs. and Constructors, 1985-90, prin. contract adminstr. Ralph M. Parsons Co., Pasadena, Calif., 1990-93, contract adminstr. Parsons-Brinckerhoff, Costa Mesa, Calif., 1993; project adminstr. Pacific Architects and Engrs., Inc., 1993—. Author: Living With a Matrix: A Conceptual Guide to Organizational Variation, 1983. Served as sgt. 1st spl. forces group, airborne, AUS, 1962-65; Okinawa, Vietnam. Decorated Combat Infantryman's Badge. Mem. Nat. Contract Mgmt. Assn., Construction Mgmt. Assn. Am., Internat. Pers. Mgmt. Assn., Assn. Human Resource Systems Profls., Human Resource Planning Soc., Assn. MBA Execs., Am. Mgmt. Assn., Am. Arbitration Assn., Internat. Records Mgmt. Coun., Adminstrv. Mgmt. Soc. Republican. Avocations: swimming, reading. Home: 25935 Faircourt Ln Laguna Hills CA 92653-7517 Office: Pacific Architects and Engrs Inc 1111 W 6th St Los Angeles CA 90017-1800

CROSS, KATHRYN PATRICIA, education educator; b. Normal, Ill., Mar. 17, 1926; d. Clarence L. and Katherine (Dague) C. BS, Ill. State U., 1948; MA, U. Ill., 1951, PhD, 1958; LLD (hon.), SUNY, 1988; DS (hon.), Loyola U., 1980, Northeastern U., 1975; DHL (hon.), De Paul U., 1986, Open U., The Netherlands, 1989. Math. tchr. Harvard (Ill.) Community High Sch., 1948-49; rsch. asst. dept. psychology U. Ill., Urbana, 1949-53, asst. dean of women, 1953-59; dean of women then dean of students Cornell U., Ithaca, N.Y., 1959-63; dir. coll. and univ. programs Ednl. Testing Svc., Princeton, N.J., 1963-66; vis. prof. U. Nebr., 1975-76; rsch. educator Ctr. Rsch. and Devel. in Higher Edn. U. Calif., Berkeley, 1966-77; rsch. scientist, sr. rsch. psychologist, dir. univ. programs Ednl. Testing Svc., Berkeley, 1966-80; prof. edn., chair dept. adminstrn., planning & social policy Harvard U., Cambridge, Mass., 1980-88; Elizabeth and Edward Conner prof. edn. U. Calif., Berkeley, 1988-94, David Pierpont Gardner prof. higher edn., 1994—; del. to Soviet Union, Seminar on Problems in Higher Edn., 1975; vis. scholar Miami-Dade Community Coll., 1987; mem. sec. adv. com. on automated personal data systems Dept. HEW, 1972-73; speaker, cons. in field. Author: Beyond the Open Door: New Students to Higher Education, 1971, (with S.B. Gould), Explorations in Non-Traditional Study, 1972, (with J.R. Valley and Assocs.) Planning Non-Traditional Programs: An Analysis of the Issues for Postsecondary Education, 1976, Adults as Learners, 1981, (with Thomas A. Angelo) Classroom Assessment Techniques, 1993; contbr. articles, monographs to profl. publs., chpts. to books; mem. editorial bd. to several ednl. jours.; cons. editor ednl. mag. Change, 1980—. Trustee Nat. Acad. Edn., 1975—, Coun. for Advancement of Exptl. Learning, 1982-85, Bradford Coll., Mass., 1986-88, Antioch Coll., Yellow Springs, Ohio, 1976-78; mem. nat. adv. bd. Nat.Ctr. of Study of Adult Learning, Empire State Coll.; mem. nat. adv. bd. Okla. Bd. Regents; mem. higher edn. rsch. program Pew Charitable Trusts. Mem. Am. Assn. Higher Edn. (bd. dirs. 1987—, chair 1989-90), Am. Assn. Community and Jr. Colls. (vice chair commn. of future of community colls.), Carnegie Found. Advancement of Teaching (adv. com. on classification of colls. and univs.), Nat. Ctr. for Devel. Edn. (adv. bd.), New Eng. Assn. Schs. and Colls. (commn. on instns. higher edn. 1982-86), Am. Coun. Edn. (commn. on higher edn. and adult learner 1986-88). Office: U Calif Sch Edn 3531 Tolman Hall Berkeley CA 94720

CROSS, ROBERT LOUIS, realtor, land use planner, writer; b. Alton, Ill., Aug. 9, 1937; s. Louis William and Marion (Hanna) C.; m. Paula Sutton, June 8, 1958 (div. June 1970); children: Britomart, Christopher, Amoret; m. Carolee Sharko, May 5, 1990. BA, U. Kans., 1959, MA, 1961; grad., UCLA, 1969, Realtors Inst., L.A., 1980. Lectr. English lang. U. Kans., Lawrence, 1959-60, Washburn U., Topeka, Kans., 1960-61; editorial-mktg. rep. Prentice-Hall, Inc., Englewood Cliffs, N.J., 1962-64; dir. pub. info. Forest Lawn Meml. Pk., Glendale, Calif., 1964-68; account exec. pub. rels. J. Walter Thompson, L.A., 1968-70; sr. account exec. pub. rels. Botsford Ketchum, L.A., 1970-71, Harsh, Rotman & Druck, L.A., 1971-72; pres. Crossroads Combined Communications, L.A., 1973-80; real estate agt. Carmel (Calif.) Bd. Realtors, 1979—; gen. ptnr. Crossroads Design Ltd., Big Sur, Calif., 1990—; cons. Watts Mfg. Corp., L.A., 1970-73, U.S. Office Edn., Washington, 1971, U.S. Dept. Interior, Washington, 1972, Calif. State Coastal Commn., San Francisco, 1980-85. Author: Henry Miller: The Paris Years, 1991; assoc. editor Calif. Life Mag., 1976; contbr. IN Monterey Mag., 1977; real estate editor Monterey Life Mag., 1978. Pres., dir. Big Sur Hist. Soc., 1980-90, Coastlands Mut. Water Co., Big Sur, 1984—; co-founder Dialogue for Big Sur, 1984; dir. Big Sur Natural History Assn., 1984-86; founding docent Dept. Pks. and Recreation, Pt. Sur Historic State Park, Big Sur, 1987; With U.S. Army, 1961-63. Mem. Archeol. Inst. Am., Nat. Assn. Realtors, Nat. Assn. Real Estate Appraisers (cert.), Calif. Assn. Realtors, Carmel Bd. Realtors (Multiple Listing Svc. Sales award 1980), Carmel Multiple Listing Svc., Big Sur Grange, Coast Property Owners Assn., Environ. Assessment Assn. (cert.). Home: PO Box 244 Big Sur CA 93920-0244 Office: Crossroads Design Ltd PO Box 244 Big Sur CA 93920-0244

CROSSON, JOHN ALBERT, advertising executive; b. L.A., Oct. 5, 1961; s. Albert J. and Virginia (Kienzle) C.; m. Carolyn Stevens, Oct. 3, 1992. BA, Loyola Marymount U., 1983; MBA, U. So. Calif., L.A., 1984. Sr. v.p., mgmt. supr. Dailey & Assocs. Advt., L.A., 1984—; lectr. Loyola Marymount U., L.A., 1986—.

CROSWELL, BEVERLY ANN, women's health nurse; b. Wilkes-Barre, Pa., Jan. 7, 1954; d. George and Mary (Cahoot) Margitish; m. David Cameron Croswell, Aug. 25, 1979; 1 child, Ryan Christopher. BSN, Wilkes U., 1976. RNC, NAACOG, Calif; cert. Lamaze instr. Staff nurse Sibley Meml. Hosp., Washington, 1976-77; staff nurse LAC-USC Med.-Ctr. Women's Hosp., L.A., 1977-83, perinatal nurse educator, 1977-83, perinatal clin. nurse specialist, 1977-83, birthing ctr. nurse mgr., 1977-83, perinatal staff nurse, 1985-86; ob-gyn dpet. dir. Calif. Hosp. Med. ctr., L.A., 1983-85; perinatal nurse educator Hollywood Presbyn. Med. Ctr., L.A., 1986-88; regional nurse coord. preterm birth prevention program Kaiser Permanente, So. Calif. Region, Pasadena, 1988—; lamaze instr. Calif. Hosp., L.A., 1983-94; perinatal nurse educator, L.A., 1990—; chairperson March of Dimes-Vis. Profls. in Nursing, L.A., 1991—; com. mem. state steering com. for pre-term birth, Calif., 1991-93. Mem. NAACOG, Perinatal Adv. Coun. Home: 27771 Desert Pl Castaic CA 91384-4511 Office: Kaiser Permanente 393 E Walnut St Pasadena CA 91188-0001

CROTTI, JOSEPH ROBERT, aviation executive; b. Azzio, Italy, June 11, 1923; came to U.S., 1924; s. John Roberto and Teresa (Tabacchini) C.; m. Beverly J.DeGraff; children: Dennis, Laura Ann Rosio. Student, U. Calif., Berkeley, 1960-91; grad., Delahanty Inst. Fire Adminstrn., 1953. Accredited airport executive 1964. Dep. chief Merced (Calif.) Fire Dept., 1946-59; airport mgr./city mgr. pro tem Merced, 1959-67; dir. aeronautics State of Calif., Sacramento, 1967-74; dep. dir. Calif. Dept. Transp., Sacramento, 1974-75; exec. dir. Calif. Air Tankers Assn., Sacramento, 1975-79; cons. Pan Am. World Svc., Teterboro, N.Y., 1979-80; western region rep. Aircraft Owners & Pilots Assn., Frederick, Md., 1981—; v.p. Calif. Fire Chief's Assn., Merced, 1958-59, Calif. Assn. Airport Execs., Merced, 1967; vice chmn. Gov.'s Aerospace-Aviation Task Force, Sacramento, 1970; pres. No. Calif. Div. of CD, Merced, 1963; accident prevention counselor FAA, Sacramento, 1980—; mem. Calif. Divsn. Aeronautics Advisory Coun., Sacramento, 1988—. Contbr. numerous manuals and plans for airport regulations and safety. Scout master Boy Scouts Am. Air Explorers, Merced, 1954-65; gen. chmn. Mercy Hosp. Bldg., Merced, 1959; bd. dirs. United Givers, Merced, 1962; chmn. County Heart Fund Drive, Merced, 1967; v.p. Sacramento Youth Band, 1969. Recipient Nat. Flight Safety award, Nat. Fire Protection Assn., 1957-58, Harris Aviation Safety award, We. States Assn. Sheriff's Air Squadron, 1970, Bronze medal, Am. Meteorol. Soc., 1972, CD Commendation, Office of Emergency Svcs., 1986, Paul Harris Fellow, Rotary Internat., 1990, Gen. Aviation Sharples award, 1988, Disting. Svc. award FAA, 1994. Mem. Am. Assn. Airport Execs. (Outstanding Svc. award 1994), Nat. Assn. State Aviation Ofcls. (pres. 1972), Profl. Helicopter Pilots Assn., Aircraft Owners and Pilots Assn. (Joe Crotti Perpetual Trophy 1994), Calif. Assn. Airport Execs. (Outstanding Svc. award 1994), Calif. State Sheriffs Assn., Am. Legion, Cameron Park Rotary Club (pres. 1980), Delta Marina Yacht Club (commodore 1989). Office: Joe R Crotti & Assocs PO Box 549 Shingle Springs CA 95682

CROUCH, PAUL FRANKLIN, minister, church official; b. St. Joseph, Mo., Mar. 30, 1934; s. Andrew Franklin and Sarah Matilda (Swingle) C.; m. Janice Wendell Bethany, Aug. 25, 1957; children—Paul F., Matthew W. B.Th., Central Bible Coll. and Sem., Springfield, Mo., 1955. Ordained to ministry, 1955; dir. fgn. missions film and audio visual dept. Assemblies of God, 1955-58; assoc. pastor 1st Assembly of God, Rapid City, S.D., 1958-60, Central Assembly of God, Muskegon, Mich., 1960-62; gen. mgr. TV and film prodn. center Assemblies of God, Burbank, Calif., 1962-65; gen. mgr. Sta. KREL, Cornona, Calif., 1965-71, Sta. KHOF, KHOF-TV, Glendale, Calif., 1971-73; founder, pres. Sta. KTBN-TV, Trinity Broadcasting Network, Los Angeles, 1973—. Recipient Best Religious film award Winona Lake Film Festival, 1956. Mem. Nat. Assn. Religious Broadcasters, Western Religious Broadcasters Assn., Assn. Christian TV Stas. (founder). Office: Trinity Broadcasting Network 2442 Michelle Dr Tustin CA 92680-7015

CROW, KENNETH ARTHUR, pathologist; b. Boise, Idaho, July 16, 1938; s. Arthur Holbeach and Blanche Aleen (Tate) C.; m. Roberta Monroe, June 12, 1965; children: Jonathan and Jason (twins), Justin. AA, Boise Jr. Coll., 1958; BS, U. Utah, 1960; MD, U. Wis., 1964. Diplomate Am. Bd. Pathology. Rotating intern Denver Gen. Hosp., 1964-65; pathologist Albany (Oreg.) Gen. Hosp., 1973—; resident in pathology U. Colo. Med. Ctr., 1969-73; chief of pathology, clin. lab. Albany (Oreg.) Gen. Hosp., 1991—. Lt. USN, 1965-67. Fellow Am. Soc. Clin. Pathologists, Coll. Am. Pathologists; mem. AMA, Oreg. Med. Assn., Oreg. Pathologists Assn. Home: 1500 12th Ave SW Albany OR 97321-2033 Office: Albany Gen Hosp 1046 6th Ave SW Albany OR 97321-1916

CROWE, EDITH LOUISE, librarian; b. Buffalo, N.Y., Nov. 12, 1947; d. Harold Peter and Edith Louise (Robinson) C. BA in Art History with honors, SUNY, Buffalo, 1970; MLS, SUNY, Geneseo, 1971; MA in Humanities, Calif. State U., Dominguez Hills, 1980. Libr. San Jose (Calif.) State U., 1971-75, 77—, Calif. State U., Hayward, 1976-77; book reviewer Art Documentation, 1988—. Mem. editl. bd. Art Ref. Quar., 1992—; contbr. articles to profl. jours. Mem. ALA, Nat. Women's Studies Assn., Art Librs. Soc. (chair No. Calif. chpt. 1982-83, 93), Mythopoeic Soc., Phi Beta Kappa. Democrat. Office: San Jose State U Clark Libr 1 Washington Sq San Jose CA 95112-3613

CROWE, JOHN T., lawyer; b. Cabin Cove, Calif., Aug. 14, 1938; s. J. Thomas and Wanda (Walston) C.; m. Marina Protopapa, Dec. 28, 1968; 1 child, Erin Aleka. BA, U. Santa Clara, 1960, JD, 1962. Bar: Calif. 1962, U.S. Dist. Ct. (no. dist.) Calif. 1964, U.S. Dist. Ct. (ea. dist.) Calif. 1967. Practiced in Visalia, Calif., 1964—; ptnr. firm Crowe, Mitchell & Crowe, 1971-85; referee State Bar Ct., 1976-82; comdr. U.S. Army, 1983—, cmdg. gen., 311th corps support command, 1995—; gen. counsel Sierra Wine, 1986—; bd. dirs. World Parts Industries, 1993—. Bd. dirs. Mt. Whitney Area Coun. Boy Scouts Am., 1966-85, pres., 1971, 72; bd. dirs. Visalia Associated In-Group Donors (AID), 1973-81, pres., 1978-79; mem. Visalia Airport Commn., 1982-90. 1st lt. U.S. Army, 1962-64; major gen. Res. Decorated Legion of Merit, Meritorious Svc. Medal with 3 oak leaf clusters, Army Commendation Medal; named Young Man of Yr., Visalia, 1973; Senator, Jr. Chamber Internat., 1970; recipient Silver Beaver award Boy Scouts Am., 1983. Mem. ABA, Tulare County Bar Assn., Nat. Assn. R.R. Trial Counsel, State Bar Calif., Visalia C. of C. (pres. 1979-80). Republican. Roman Catholic. Clubs: Rotary (pres. 1980-81); Downtown (Fresno, Calif.). Home: 3939 W School Ave Visalia CA 93291-5514

CROWELL, JOHN C(HAMBERS), geology educator, researcher; b. State College, Pa., May 12, 1917; s. James White and Helen Hunt (Chambers) C.; m. Betty Marie Bruner, Nov. 22, 1946; 1 child, Martha Lynn Crowell Bobroskie. BS in Geology, U. Tex., 1939; MA in Oceanographic meteorology, Scripps Inst. Oceanography UCLA, 1946; PhD in Geology, UCLA, 1947; DSc (hon.), U. Louvain, Belgium, 1966. Geologist Shell Oil Co., Inc., Ventura, Calif., 1941-42; from instr. to prof. geology UCLA, 1947-67, chmn. dept., 1957-60, 63-66; prof. geology U. Calif., Santa Barbara, 1967-87, prof. emeritus, 1987, rsch. geologist Inst. for Crustal Studies, 1987—; chmn. Office of Earth Scis., NRC, Nat. Acad. Scis., 1979-82. Served to capt. U.S. Army USAAF, 1942-46. Fellow Geol. Soc. Am., Am. Acad. Arts and Scis.; mem. Am. Assn. Petroleum Geologists, Am. Geophys. Union, AAAS, Am. Inst. Profl. Geologists, Nat. Acad. Scis. Home: 300 Hot Springs Rd Montecito CA 93108-2055 Office: U Calif Inst for Crustal Studies Santa Barbara CA 93106

CROWL, CHARLES V(ERNE), physician, surgeon; b. Mpls., Apr. 23, 1921; s. Verne Chase and Miriam Lucile (Rice) C.; m. Jane Victoria Cotone, 1946 (div. 1961); children: Charlotte, Thomas C., Christinea, Marianne V.; m. Patricia Mitchell, 1965 (div. 1969); 1 child, Charles V. Jr.; m. LaDonna Lee Forrest, 1969 (div. 1970); m. LaDonna Lee Forrest, 1971; 1 stepson, Scott. BA, Occidental Coll., 1943; MD, U. So. Calif., 1947. Med. officer AUS, El Paso, Tex., 1947-49; physician, surgeon Drs. Cowgill, Crowl, Crowl, Huntington Park, Calif., 1949-66; pvt. practice Huntington Beach, Calif., 1966-79, Newport Beach, Calif., 1979—. Capt. AUS, 1943-49. Republican.

CROWLEY, DANIEL JOHN, anthropologist; b. Peoria, Ill., Nov. 27, 1921; s. Michael Bartholomew and Elsie Magdalene (Schnebelin) C.; m. Pearl Rita Ramcharan, Feb. 4, 1958; children: Peter Mahendranath, Eve Lakshmi, Magdalene Lilawati. AB, Northwestern U., 1943, PhD, 1956; MA, Bradley U., 1948. Instr. art history Bradley U., Peoria, 1948-50; tutor in anthropology U. West Indies, St. Augustine, Trinidad, 1953-56; instr. in anthropology Northwestern U., Evanston, Ill., 1956-57; asst. prof. U. Notre Dame, Ind., 1958-59; from asst. prof. to prof. U. Calif., Davis, 1961-93 ret.; vis. rsch. prof. Inst. African Studies U. Ghana, Legon, 1969-71; vis. prof. U. West Indies, 1973-74, Latrobe U., Bundoora, Australia, 1990. Author: I Could Talk Old-Story Good, 1966; editor African Folklore in the New World, 1977; contbg. editor African Arts, 1966—, Research in African Lits., 1973-90, Jour. African Studies, 1976—; translator (book) Congolese Sculpture, 1982; contbr. articles to profl. jours. Active U.S. Nat. Commn. for UNESCO, Washington, 1972-78. Served to lt. (j.g.) USN, 1942-46, PTO. Fellow Ford Found., 1959-60, Fulbright, 1978-79; grantee Indo-U.S. Commn., 1985; recipient Centennial Citation U. Calif. Santa Cruz, 1968, Archer Taylor Meml. lectr. U. Calif. Folklore Soc., 1986. Fellow Am. Folklore Soc. (life, pres. 1969-71, Stafford prize 1952), Am. Anthropol. Assn., Calif. Folklore Soc. (pres. 1980), African Studies Assn.; mem. Southwestern Anthropol. Assn., Sigma Xi. Democrat. Roman Catholic. Home: 726 Peach Pl Davis CA 95616-3218 Office: U Calif Dept Anthropology Davis CA 95616*

CROWLEY, JEROME JOSEPH, JR., manufacturing company executive; b. South Bend, Ind., Sept. 18, 1939; s. Jerome J. and Rosaleen (Giblin) C.; m. Carol Ann Ellithorn, June 23, 1962; children: Michael, Karen, Brian, Colleen. B.S., U. Notre Dame, 1961; M.B.A., U. Chgo., 1967. With O'Brien Corp., South San Francisco, Calif., 1965—; now pres. O'Brien Corp. Served with USMC, 1961-65. Roman Catholic. Office: The O'Brien Corporation 395 Oyster Point Blvd Ste 350 South San Francisco CA 94080-1931 Also: O'Brien Powder Products Inc 9800 Genard Rd Houston TX 77041-7624

CROWLEY, JOHN CRANE, real estate developer; b. Detroit, June 29, 1919; s. Edward John and Leah Helen (Crane) C.; m. Barbara Wenzel Gilfillan, Jan. 12, 1945; children: F. Alexander, Leonard, Philip, Eliot, Louise, Sylvia. BA, Swarthmore Coll., 1941; MS, U. Denver, 1943. Asst. dir. Mcpl. Finance Officers Assn., Chgo., 1946-48; So. Calif. mgr. League Calif. Cities, Los Angeles, 1948-53; mgr. City of Monterey Park, Calif., 1953-56; founder, exec. v.p. Nat. Med. Enterprises, L.A., 1968; pres. Ventura Towne House (Calif.), 1963—; mem. faculty U. So. Calif. Sch. Pub. Adminstrn., 1950-53; bd. dirs. Regional Inst. of So. Calif., The L.A. Partnership 2000, Burbank-Glendale-Pasadena Airport Authority. Trustee Pacific Oaks Friends Sch. and Coll., Pasadena, 1954-57, 92—; bd. dirs. Pasadena Area Liberal Arts Ctr., 1962-72, pres., 1965-68; bd. dirs. Pacificulture Found. and Asia Mus., 1971-76, pres., 1972-74; bd. dirs. Nat. Mcpl. League, 1986-92; mem. State Adv. Coun. on Retirement Housing, 1965-68; chmn. Pasadena Cultural Heritage Commn., 1975-78; city dir. Pasadena, 1979-91; pres. Pasadena Civic Improvement Corp., 1985-89; mayor City of Pasadena, 1986-88; bd. dirs. Western Justice Ctr., 1992—, LA County Commn. on Efficiency and Economy, 1994—. Sloan Found. fellow, 1941-43. Mem. Internat. City Mgmt. Assn., Nat. Mcpl. League (nat. bd. 1980-92, Disting. Citizen award, 1984), Inst. Pub. Adminstrn. (sr. assoc.), Phi Delta Theta. Democrat. Unitarian. Home: 615 Linda Vista Ave Pasadena CA 91105-1122

CROWLEY, JOSEPH NEIL, academic administrator; b. Oelwein, Iowa, July 9, 1933; s. James Bernard and Nina Mary (Neil) C.; m. Johanna Lois Reitz, Sept. 9, 1961; children: Theresa, Neil, Margaret, Timothy. BA, U. Iowa, 1959; MA, Calif. State U., Fresno, 1963; PhD (Univ. fellow), U. Wash., 1967. Reporter Fresno Bee, 1961-62; asst. prof. polit. sci. U. Nev., Reno, 1966-71, asso. prof., 1971-79, prof., 1979—, chmn. dept. polit. sci., 1976-78, pres., 1978—; bd. dirs. Citibank Nev., Channel 5 Pub. TV; policy formulation officer EPA, Washington, 1973-74; dir. instl. studies Nat. Commn. on Water Quality, Washington, 1974-75; cons. in field. Author: Democrats, Delegates and Politics in Nevada: A Grassroots Chronicle of 1972, 1976, Notes From the President's Chair, 1988, No Equal in the World; An Interpretation of the Academic Presidency, 1994; editor: (with R. Roelofs and D. Hardesty) Environment and Society, 1973. Mem. Commn. on Colls., 1980-87; mem. adv. commn. on mining and minerals rsch. U.S. Dept. Interior, 1985-91; mem. coun. NCAA, 1987-92, mem. pres.' commn., 1991-92, pres., 1993-95; bd. dirs., campaign chmn. No. Nev. United Way, 1985-90. Recipient Thornton Peace Prize U. Nev., 1971, Humanitarian of Yr. award NCCJ, 1986, Alumnus of Yr. award Calif. State U., 1989, ADL Champion of Liberty award, 1993, Disting. Alumni award U. Iowa, 1994, Giant Step award Ctr. for Study of Sport in Soc., 1994; Nat. Assn. Schs. Pub. Affairs and Adminstrn. fellow, 1973-74. Roman Catholic. Home: 1265 Muir Dr Reno NV 89503-2629 Office: U Nev Office of Pres Reno NV 89557-0095

CROWTHER, RICHARD LAYTON, architect, consultant, researcher, author, lecturer; b. Newark, Dec. 16, 1910; s. William George and Grace (Layton) C.; m. Emma Jane Hubbard, 1935 (div. 1949); children: Bethe Crowther Allison, Warren Winfield, Vivian Crowther Tuggle; m. 2d Pearl Marie Tesch, Sept. 16, 1950. Student, Newark Sch. Fine and Indsl. Arts, 1928-31, San Diego State Coll., 1933, U. Colo., 1956. Registered architect, Colo. Prin. Crowther & Marshall, San Diego, 1946-50, Richard L. Crowther, Denver, 1951-66, Crowther, Kruse, Landin, Denver, 1966-70, Crowther, Kruse, McWilliams, Denver, 1970-75, Crowther Solar Group, Denver, 1975-82, Richard L. Crowther FAIA, Denver, 1982—; vis. critic, lectr. U. Nebr., 1981; holistic energy design process methodology energy cons. Holistic Health Ctr., 1982-83; adv. cons. interior and archtl. design class U. Colo., 1982-83, Cherry Creek, Denver redevel., 1984-88, Colo. smoking control legislation, 1985, interior solar concepts Colo. Inst. Art, 1986, Bio-Electro-Magnetics Inst., 1987-88; mentor U. Colo. Sch. Architecture, 1987-88. Author: Sun/Earth, 1975 (Progressive Architecture award 1975), rev. edit., 1983, reprint, 1995, Affordable Passive Solar Homes, 1983, Paradox of Smoking, 1983, Women/Nature/Destiny: Female/Male Equity for Global Survival, 1987, (monographs) Context in Art and Design, 1985, Existence, Design and Risk, 1986, Indoor Air: Risks and Remedies, 1986, Human Migration in Solar Homes for Seasonal Comfort and Energy Conservation, 1986, 88, Ecologic Architecture, 1992, Ecologic Digest, 1993, others. NSF grantee, 1974-75. Fellow AIA (commr. research, edn. and environ. Colo. Central chpt. 1972-75, bd. dirs. chpt. 1973-74 AIA Research Corp. Solar Monitoring Program contract award).

CRUE, BENJAMIN LANE, JR., neurosurgeon; b. Rahway, N.J., May 22, 1925; s. Benjamin Lane and Grace J. (Cornish) C.; m. Beverly Marie Malyon, Sept. 22, 1943; children: Benjamin III, Catherine, Elizabeth, B. Jane. BS, U. Chgo., 1946, MD, 1948. Diplomate Am. Bd. Neurological Surgery. Chmn. clin. neurology City of Hope Nat. Med. Ctr., Duarte, Calif., 1960-80; prof. nuerosurgery, co-chmn. Calif. Coll. Medicine, L.A., 1962-63; clin. prof. neurosurgery U. So. Calif. Sch. Medicine, L.A., 1985; ret., 1984; clin. prof. neurosurgery emeritus U. So. Calif. Sch. Medicine, L.A., 1985—; bd. trustees San Gabriel (Calif.) Community Hosp., 1977-80, chief med. staff, 1980; bd. trustees Albambia Community Hosp., 1983-84; chief med. staff LaPlata Community Hosp., Durango, Colo., 1987. Contbr. numerous articles to profl. jours. Capt. USNR, 1943-79. Grantee NIH, 1961. Fellow ACS; mem. AMA, So. Calif. Neurosurgery Soc. (pres. 1973), L.A. Soc. Neurology (pres. 1979), Am. Pain Soc. (pres. 1980), Am. Acad. Pain Medicine (pres. 1984). Republican. Mormon. Home: 580 Oakcrest Dr Durango CO 81301-6905

CRUES, JOHN VERNON, III, radiologist, educator; b. Lubbock, Tex., Nov. 21, 1949; s. John Vernon Jr. and Dorothy Katherine (Sievers) C.; m. Jayne Ausanka, Aug. 7, 1976; children: Drew, Ry, Melissa. AB, Harvard U., 1972; postgrad., U. Salzburg, Austria, 1972; MS, U. Ill., 1975; MD, Harvard U., 1979. Diplomate Am. Bd. Internal Medicine, Am. Bd. Radiology, Nat. Bd. Med. Examiners; lic. physician, Calif.; cert. drug enforcement adminstrn., basic life support in cardiopulmonary resuscitation; lic. amateur radio operator, sr. parachute rigger, single engine pvt. pilot. Intern. L.A. County-U. So. Calif. Med. Ctr., L.A., 1979-80; resident in internal medicine Cedars-Sinai Med. Ctr., L.A., 1980-82, resident in diagnostic radiology, 1982-85; rsch. engr. dept. elec. and computer engring. U. Calif., Santa Barbara; asst. clin. prof. radiology UCLA, 1987—; dir. magnetic resonance, musculoskeletal and emergency radiology Cedars-Sinai Med. Ctr., L.A., 1993—; med. cons. Future Diagnostics Inc., L.A.; bd. dirs. Future Diagnostics Inc.; mem. rsch. bd. F. I. Internat.; mem. adv. bd. Teleradiology Svcs. Inc., Boston. Assoc. editor: Jour. Magnetic Resonance Imaging, 1993-96; column editor: Applied Radiology; mem. editl. bd.: Magnetic Resonance Quar., 1990-95; manuscript reviewer; contbr. articles to med. jours.; editor book chpts. Recipient Crues and Kressel award for outstanding contbns. to edn. of magnetic resonance technologists Sect. for Magnetic Resonance Technologists, 1991; Schlumberger scholar Harvard U., 1968-72. Mem. Soc. Magnetic Resonance (pres.), Radiol. Soc. N.Am., Am. Coll. Radiology (commn. on neurology and magnetic resonance; com. stds. and accreditation 1991—, com. mktg. and pub. rels. 1991—, com. human resources 1991—, com. magnetic resonance biol. effects 1993—, com. rsch. and tech. assessment 1993—). Soc. for Magnetic Resonance Imaging (1st v.p., interim bd. dirs. 1993—), Am. Soc. Emergency Radiology (charter), Internat. Skeletal

Soc. Office: Cedars-Sinai Imaging 8708 Beverly Blvd Los Angeles CA 90048-1804

CRUICKSHANK, JAMES DAVID, bishop; b. Vancouver, B.C., Can., June 10, 1936; s. James Cruickshank and Florence Mary (Mitchell) Bell; m. Susanne Margrot Nickelson, May 17, 1989 (div.); children: Jason Robert, Anna Dorthy. BA, U. Minn., Duluth, 1959; LTh with distinction, Coll. Emmanuel and St. Chad, Saskatoon, Sask., Can., 1962; DRel, Chgo. Theol. Sem., 1970; DD (hon.), Coll. Emmanuel and St. Chad, 1994. Vicar Upper Fraser Mission Anglican Ch., Cariboo Diocese, 1962-65; dir. Sorrento (B.C.) Lay Tng. Ctr., 1965-73; vice prin., prof. pastoral theology Vancouver Sch. Theology, 1973-83; dean, rector Christ Ch. Cathedral, Vancouver, 1983-92; bishop Cariboo Diocese Anglican Ch. Can., Kamloops, B.C., 1992—; chancellor bd. govs. Vancouver Sch. Theol., 1989—; mem. nat. ministry com. Anglican Ch., 1981-83, doctrine and worship com., 1986-92, nat. exec. coun., 1992—. Chmn. trustees Richardson Found. Mem. Vancouver Club. Office: Cariboo Diocese, # 5 618 Tranquille Rd, Kamloops, BC Canada V2A 3H6

CRUM, ROBERT M., business management executive. AB in English with highest honors, U. Pitts., 1950, JD, 1953; postgrad., U. Mich., 1959-60. Clk., rschr. Lewis and Drew Law Office, Pitts., 1954-55; rsch. analyst Blue Cross of Western Pa., Pitts., 1955-56, planning asst. to pres., 1956-61, asst. legal counsel, 1958-61; adminstrv. asst. to pres. Capital Blue Cross, Harrisburg, Pa., 1961-68, project coordinator for Medicare, 1966-68; mgr. pub. rels. and advt. Calif. Blue Shield, San Francisco, 1968-70, dir. corp. planning and rsch., 1970-72; exec. dir. Am. Dietetic Assn., Chgo., 1972-74; mng. dir. Nat. Parent Tchrs. Assn., Chgo., 1974-76; pres. Assn. and Soc. Mgmt., San Francisco, 1976—. Pres. Ch. Bd., Employee Credit Union. Mem. Am. Soc. Assn. Execs., No. Calif. Soc. Assn. Execs., Lions Club (bd. dirs.), Chgo. Soc. Assn. Execs., C. of C.

CRUMP, JULIETTE TAFT, dance educator; b. N.Y.C., Nov. 22, 1941; d. Gardner and Juliette Caze Taft; m. William Wood Crump Jr., May 10, 1964 (div. May 1974); 1 child, Mary Catherine; m. William Wade Bevis, June 4, 1976. AB, Randolph-Macon Woman's Coll., 1963; MA, George Washington U., 1973. Cert. movement analyst. Instr. Va. Commonwealth U., Richmond, 1968-73; asst. prof., head of dance U. Mont. Dept. Drama/Dance, Missoula, 1974-84, prof. dance, 1984—. Contbr. articles to profl. jours. U.S. Dept. Edn. Title I grantee, 1981. Democrat. Home: 2500 Raymond Ave Missoula MT 59802-3220 Office: U Mont Dept Drama/Dance Missoula MT 59812

CRUMP, RENE, school counselor; b. Pocatello, Idaho, Apr. 21, 1961; d. Kenneth Elmer and Hermese (Hatch) C. AS, Snow Jr. Coll., Ephraim, Utah, 1981; BS cum laude, Utah State U., 1983; MEd, Pa. State U., 1985. Cert. counselor, Utah, Pa., spl. edn. generalist, Utah. Elem. counselor Weber County Sch. Dist., Ogden, Utah, 1985-88, Sand Ridge Jr. H.S. counselor, 1988-89, South Ogden Jr. H.S. counselor, 1992—, co-developer co-option at-risk program, 1993—; South Cache Mid. Sch. counselor Cache County Sch. Dist., Logan, Utah, 1989-92; field supr. univ. internships, 1993—; mem. Agree Task Force, 1994—. Group leader Toughlove, Ogden, 1985-89. Recipient Apple for the Tchr. award Std. Examiner, 1994. Mem. Am. Counseling Assn., Utah Counselor Assn. (newsletter editor 1990-91, recognition chair 1991-92), Utah Sch. Counselors Assn. (guidance assn. 1989—).

CRUSE, ALLAN BAIRD, mathematician, computer scientist, educator; b. Birmingham, Ala., Aug. 28, 1941; s. J. Clyde and Irma R. Cruse. AB, Emory U., 1962, PhD, 1974; postgrad. (Woodrow Wilson fellow) U. Calif.-Berkeley, 1962-63, MA, 1965; teaching fellow Dartmouth Coll., 1963-64. Instr., U. San Francisco, 1966-73, asst. prof. math., 1973-76, assoc. prof., 1976-79, prof., 1979—, chmn. math. dept. 1988-91; vis. instr. Stillman Coll., summer 1967; vis. assoc. prof. Emory U., spring 1978; prof. computer sci. Sonoma State U., 1983-85; cons. math edn. NSF fellow, 1972-73. Mem. Am. Math. Soc. (chmn. No. Calif. sect.), Math. Am. Math. Soc., Math. Assn. Am. (chmn. No. Calif. sect.), Assn. Computing Machinery, U. San Francisco Faculty Assn., Sigma Xi (Dissertation award 1974). Author: (with Millianne Granberg) Lectures on Freshman Calculus, 1971; research, publs. in field. Office: U San Francisco Harney Sci Ctr San Francisco CA 94117

CRUSE, C(LYDE) LANSFORD, III, manufacturing company marketing executive; b. Middletown, Ohio, June 20, 1956; s. Clyde Lansford and Ruth Marie (Gillespie) C.; m. Stephanie Ann Wedig, Oct. 25, 1980; children: Clyde Lansford IV, Holly Corrine, Reid August. BSME, U. Cin., 1979; MBA, U. Tex., 1980. Asst. to v.p. Armco Nat. Supply, Houston, 1980-83; corp. acquisitions The Coleman Co., Wichita, Kans., 1983-85; dir. engring. Soniform Inc., Coleman, San Diego, 1985-86, v.p. fin., 1986-87, gen. mgr., 1987-88; pres., gen. mgr. Coleman Spas Inc., Chandler, Ariz., 1988-90; gen. mgr. spl. products div. Sulzer Bingham Inc., Portland, Oreg., 1990-91, gen. mgr. mktg., 1991—. Bd. dirs., strategic planning United Way, Gulf Coast, 1982-83. Home: 31 Partridge Ln Lake Oswego OR 97035-1025 Office: Sulzer Bingham Pumps Inc 2800 NW Front Ave Portland OR 97210-1502

CRUSE, DENTON W., marketing and advertising executive, consultant; b. Washington, May 21, 1944; s. Denton W. Sr. and Frances Rankin (Moore) C.; m. Susan Costello, June 11, 1988; 1 child, Thomas Moore. BS, Va. Commonwealth U., 1966; MBA, So. Ill. U., 1977. Media supr. Procter & Gamble Co., Cin., 1967-73; assoc. media dir. Ralston Purina Co., St. Louis, 1973-78; dir. advt. Armour-Dial Co., Phoenix, 1978-81; mktg. dir. Valentine Greeting Inc., Phoenix, 1981-82; dir. mktg. svcs. J. Walter Thompson/USA, L.A., 1982-83; cons. L.A., 1983-86; dir. advt. svcs. Mattel Inc., L.A., 1986-88; cons. C and O Assocs., L.A., 1988—; instr. UCLA, L.A., 1986—. Editor-in-chief: Cobblestone, 1965. Marathon monitor L.A. Olympic Organizing Com., 1984; bd. dirs. Old Hometown Fair. Mem. Mktg. Club L.A., Beta Gamma Sigma, Pi Sigma Epsilon. Republican. Presbyterian.

CRUTHERS, EVAN DOUGLAS, architect; b. Victoria, B.C., Can., July 20, 1941; s. Eldred John Cruthers and Eda Claire (Avery) Olney; m. Anita Inez Wilcomb, June 3, 1962; children—Christine, Mark, Paul, Matthew; m. Shirley Lavina York, Apr. 23, 1977. B.Arch., U. Idaho, 1964; postgrad. U. Hawaii, 1983-84. Registered architect, Wash., Oreg., Hawaii. Assoc. firm W.P. McCue Architect, Richland, Wash., 1967-68, ptnr. firm McCue & Cruthers, Richland, 1968-71; project mgr. NBBJ Architects, Seattle and Honolulu, 1971-72; prin., project dir. Media Five Ltd., Honolulu, 1972-82, chief exec. officer, 1982—; prin. works include Frank Clinic, Honolulu Straub Clinic, Pearl Ridge, Hawaii (Merit award AIA 1978), Unaccompanied Enlisted Personnel Housing, Pearl Harbor Naval Base (Merit award AIA 1984). Chmn. profl. sect. Aloha United Way, Honolulu, 1981. Mem. AIA (treas. 1984), Profl. Services Mgmt. Assn. Office: Media 5 Ltd 345 Queen St Fl 9 Honolulu HI 96813-4727

CRUZ, ANTONIO JOSE, JR., engineer; b. L.A., Sept. 9, 1958; s. Antonio J. and Rosa (Cabrera) C.; m. Isabele Yvonne Merle, Jan. 4, 1982; children: Sean, Christina, Candice. AS in Metallurgy, Don Bosco Tech. Inst.; BS in Engring., U. Calif., Berkeley; MS in Material Sci., Stanford (Calif.) U. Rsch. engr. Varian Assocs., Palo Alto, Calif., 1981-83; process engr. TRW, Sunnyvale, Calif., 1983-84; quality engr. Signetics, Sunnyvale, 1984-86, 88-89; process engr. McDonnell Douglas, Huntington Beach, Calif., 1986-88; reliability mgr. Siliconix, Santa Clara, Calif., 1989-90, Integrated Device Tech., San Jose, 1990-94. Alumni scholarship U. Calif., 1981. Mem. IEEE, Am. Soc. Quality Control, ESD Assn., Am. Statis. Assn. Home: 1009 November Dr Cupertino CA 95014-4122 Office: Integrated Device Tech 2670 Seely Ave San Jose CA 95134-1929

CRUZE, DEBORAH KAYE, judge; b. Scottsbluff, Nebr., Aug. 5, 1957; d. Eugene Morgan and Caroline Mae (Hartwig) Hughes; m. Gary Lee Cruze, June 14, 1980; children: Melissa Anne, Aaron Griffith, Rebecca Danielle. BS, No. Ariz. U., 1978; postgrad., Washington & Lee U., 1978-79; JD, Ariz. State U., 1981. Bar: Ariz. 1981. Legis. intern Ariz. State Senate, Phoenix, 1978; asst. atty. gen. Ariz. Atty. Gen.'s Office, Phoenix, 1981-82; adj. faculty Rio Salado Community Coll., Phoenix, 1985, Glendale (Ariz.) Community Coll., 1986-90, Ariz. State U., 1991; judge pro tempore Magistrate Ct. City of Glendale, 1990-91, judge, 1991—; congl. intern U.S. Senate, Washington, summer 1978; law clk. Mangum, Wall, Stoops & Warden, Flagstaff, Ariz., summer 1979, Samaritan Health Svc., Phoenix, summer 1980; mem. jud. conf. planning com. Jud. Coll. Ariz., 1993-94, chair, 1994-95. Participant, coord. Glendale Leadership and Devel. Program, 1985-86; chairperson Housing Authority Commn., City of Glendale, 1985-91, Faith United Meth. Presch. Bd., 1987-92; speaker Law Day Drug Edn. Program, Phoenix, 1988; mem. Alternative Expenditure Limitation Com., Glendale, 1989, Campaign Com. to Re-elect Mayor Renner, Glendale, 1989, edn. com. Christ's Community Ch., 1982-83; chairperson Parent Enrichment Program, 1984-86; active Faith United Meth. Presch. Bd., 1987-92, chairperson, 1989-91, Community Ch. of Joy, 1993—; speaker in field. Recipient Disting. Citizen award No. Ariz. U., 1993. Mem. Ariz. Bar Assn., Ariz. Women Lawyer's Assn. (mem. mother's forum 1990—), Ariz. Magistrates Assn., Maricopa Bar Assn. (mem. bench/bar rels. com. 1992—), Nat. Assn. Women Judges, P.E.O., Alpha Delta Pi (Dorothy Shaw Leadership award 1978), Phi Alpha Delta, Phi Kappa Phi (v.p. 1977-78, grad. fellow 1978), Phi Kappa Phi. Democrat.

CRYER, LINDA BROOKS, women's health nurse; b. Denver, July 20, 1948; d. Thomas Joseph and Anne Veronica (O'Leary) Brooks; m. James Michael Cryer, July 5, 1969; children: Nicole Anne, Michael Brooks. AA, Clark C.C., 1980; BSN summa cum laude, Ariz. State U., 1987. Staff nurse labor and delivery Mesa (Ariz.) Luth. Hosp., Chandler (Ariz.) Regional Hosp., Good Samaritan Med. Ctr., Phoenix. Mem. ANA, Sigma Theta Tau, Phi Kappa Phi.

CRYER, RODGER EARL, educational administrator; b. Detroit, Apr. 2, 1940. AB in Fine Arts, San Diego State U., 1965; MA in Edn. Adminstrn., Stanford U., 1972; PhD in Psychol. Services Counseling, Columbia-Pacific U., 1985. Cert. tchr., N.J., Calif.; cert. gen. adminstrn., Calif. Spl. asst. to commissioner N.J. State Dept. Edn., Trenton, 1967-68; cons. N.J. Urban Sch. Devel., Trenton, 1969-70; mgmt. cons. Rodger E. Cryer, Co., Pinole, Calif., 1970-73; adminstrv. asst. Franklin McKinley Sch. Dist., San Jose, Calif., pres. Chief Exec. Tng. Corp., San Jose, 1981-82; prin. McKinley Sch., 1986-91, prin. Hellyer Sch., 1991—; ptnr. Guided Learning Enterprises; bd. dirs., Commonwealth Cen. Credit Union, 1989—, Our City Forest, Inc., 1994—, Bd. dirs. Friends of San Jose Beautiful, Inc., 1994—; adv. com. City of San Jose Bicycle, 1994—. Mem. Nat. Sch. Pub. Rels. Assn. (sec. 1975—), Calif. Sch. Pub. Rels. Assn. (pres.). Contbr. articles to profl. jours. Commr. Home: 3529 Milburn St San Jose CA 95148-2250 Office: Hellyer Sch 725 Hellyer Ave San Jose CA 95111-1523

CRYSTALL, JOSEPH N., communications company executive; b. Bklyn., Dec. 19, 1922; s. Samuel H. and Frances (Eiten) C.; m. Martha Jane Ladson, Feb. 23, 1957; 1 child, Bonnie Leigh. Student, Bklyn. Coll., 1939-42, U. Pitts., 1942-43. Radio performer Sta. KOPO, Tucson, 1951-54; advt. agy. exec. The Wiener Co., Tucson, 1955-59; sta. mgr., TV performer Sta. KOLD-AM-TV, Tucson, 1959-69; gen. mgr. Sta. KOPO, Tucson, 1969-73, Stas. KEVT, KWFM, Tucson, 1974-81; pres., gen. mgr. Sta. KGVY, Green Valley, Ariz., 1981—; pres. Crystal Sets, Inc., Tucson, 1981—; instr. U. Ariz., Tucson, 1968-69. Author two books; contbr. articles, TV scripts, short stories to various publs., 1955—. Pres. Better Bus. Bur. So. Ariz., Tucson, 1983. Served as 1st lt. USAF, 1943-45, ETO, MTO. Decorated DFC, Air medal with three clusters. Mem. Ariz. Broadcasters Assn. (pres. 1966-67), Tucson Broadcasters Assn. (pres. 1971-72), Nat. Assn. Broadcasters, Tucson Advt. Club (pres. 1968-69, 73-74, named to Advt. Hall of Fame 1987), Am. Advt. Fedn. (Silver medal 1989), Green Valley C. of C. (bd. dirs., v.p. 1988—), Tucson Press (pres. 1967, 71, 72, Broadcaster of Yr. 1981), Elks, Lions (pres. 1974-75), Rotary (pres. 1989-90), Sigma Delta Chi. Home: 3147 E Pima St Tucson AZ 85716-3131 Office: Sta KGVY PO Box 767 Green Valley AZ 85622-0767

CSENDES, ERNEST, chemist, corporate and financial executive; b. Satu-Mare, Romania, Mar. 2, 1926; came to U.S., 1951, naturalized, 1955; s. Edward O. and Sidonia (Littman) C. m. Catharine Vera Tolnai, Feb. 7, 1953; children: Audrey Carol, Robert Alexander Edward. BA, Protestant Coll., Hungary, 1944; BS, U. Heidelberg (Ger.), 1948, MS, 1950, PhD, 1951. Rsch. asst. chemistry U. Heidelberg, 1950-51; rsch. assoc. biochemistry Tulane U., New Orleans, 1952; rsch. fellow chemistry Harvard U., 1952-53; rsch. chemist organic chems. dept. E. I. Du Pont de Nemours and Co., Wilmington, Del., 1953-56, elastomer chems. dept., 1956-61; dir. rsch. and devel. agrl. chems. div. Armour & Co., Atlanta, 1961-63; v.p. corp. devel. Occidental Petroleum Corp., L.A., 1963-64, exec. v.p. rsch., engring. and devel., mem. exec. com., 1964-68; COO, exec. v.p., dir. Occidental Rsch. and Engring. Corp., L.A., London, Moscow, 1963-68; mng. dir. Occidental Rsch. and Engring. (U.K.) Ltd., London, 1964-68; pres., CEO TRI Group, London, Amsterdam, Rome and Bermuda, 1968-84; chmn., CEO Micronic Techs., Inc., L.A., 1981-85; mng. ptnr. Inter-Consult Ltd., Pacific Palisades, Calif.; internat. cons. on tech., econ. feasibility and mgmt., 1984—; pres., chief tech. officer Gen. Grinding Corp., L.A., 1991—; chmn., CEO Eden Mgmt. Ltd., L.A. and London, 1993—. Contbr. 250 articles to profl. and trade jours., studies and books; achievements include 29 patents; research in area of elastomers, rubber chemicals, adhesives, dyes and intermediates, organometallics, organic and biochemistry, high polymers, antioxidants, phosphates, plant nutrients, pesticides, process engineering, design of fertilizer plants, sulfur, potash and phosphate ore mining and metallurgy, coal burning and acid rain, coal utilization, advanced building materials, methods for aerodynamic grinding of solids, advanced building materials, particles technology, petrochemicals, biomed. engring., consumer products, also acquisitions, mergers, internat. fin. related to leasing investments and loans, trusts and ins.; regional devel. related to agr. and energy resources. Recipient Pro Mundi Beneficio gold medal Brazilian Acad. Humanities, 1975; Harvard U. fellow, 1953. Fellow AAAS, Am. Inst. Chemists, Royal Soc. Chemistry (London); mem. AIAA, IEEE, AIChE, SMME, ASM International, Am. Chem. Soc., German Chem. Soc., N.Y. Acad. Sci., Am. Concrete Inst., Acad. Polit. Sci., Am. Def. Preparedness Assn., Sigma Xi. Home: 514 N Marquette St Pacific Palisades CA 90272-3314

CUBBISON, CHRISTOPHER ALLEN, editor; b. Honolulu, Dec. 22, 1948; s. Donald Cameron and Mary (Pritchett) C.; m. Linda Cicero, Jan. 3, 1976; children: Genevieve, Cameron. BJ, U. Mo., 1971. Reporter N.Y. Daily News, N.Y.C., 1971-72; reporter St. Petersburg (Fla.) Times, 1972-76, asst. city editor, 1976-78; editor various locations including The Miami Herald, 1978-89; asst. mng. editor Rocky Mountain News, Denver, 1989-90, mng. editor projects, 1990—. Home: 11 Sycamore Ln Littleton CO 80127-3525 Office: Rocky Mountain News 400 W Colfax Ave Denver CO 80127

CUBIN, BARBARA LYNN, congresswoman, former state legislator, public relations consultant; b. Salinas, Calif., Nov. 30; d. Russell G. and Barbara Lee (Howard) Sage; m. Frederick William Cubin, Aug. 1; children: William Russell, Frederick William III. BS in Chemistry, Creighton U., 1969. Chemist Wyo. Machinery Co., Casper, Wyo., 1973-75; mem. Wyo. Ho. Reps., 1987-92, Wyo. Senate, 1993-94; pres. Spectrum Promotions and Mgmt., Casper, 1993-94; congresswoman, Wyom. U.S. House Reps., Washington, D.C., 1995—; mem com. Nat. Coun. State Legislators, San Francisco, 1987—, Lexington, Ky., 1990—. Mem. steering com. Exptl. Program to Stimulate Competitive Research (EPSCOR); mem. Coun. of State Govts.; active Gov.'s Com. on Preventive Medicine, 1992; vice chmn. Cleer Bd. Energy Coun., Irving, Tex., 1993—; chmn. Wyo. Senate Rep. Conf., Casper, 1993—; mem. Wyo. Rep. Party Exec. Com., 1993. Toll fellow Coun. State Govts., 1990. Mem. Am. Legis. Exch. Coun., Rep. Women. Episcopalian. Office: US House Reps Office House Mem Washington DC 20515*

CUBRILOVIC, VEL, pharmaceutical company executive; b. Yugoslavia, Nov. 30, 1929; came to the U.S., 1956; s. Branko and Paula (Cabiglio) C.; m. Martha Kaufman, June 9, 1962 (div. June 1987); children: Randy, Marisa; m. Loretta Robinson, April 16, 1992. BS in Chemistry, U. Belgrade, Yugoslavia, 1954. Pres. Pharmacia AB, Piscataway, N.J., 1971-73, Upsala, Sweden, 1973-76; group v.p. Millipore Corp., Bedford, Mass., 1976-85; CEO, pres., dir. Vega Biotechnologies, Tucson, Ariz., 1985-87; v.p. ICN Pharmaceuticals, Inc., Costa Mesa, Calif., 1987—. Democrat. Mem. Serbian Orthodox Ch. Home: 2820 San Juan Ln Costa Mesa CA 92626 Office: ICN Biomedicals Inc 3300 Hyland Ave Costa Mesa CA 92626-1503

CUCINA, VINCENT ROBERT, management and financial consultant, educator; b. Balt., Mar. 31, 1936; s. Anthony James and Josephine (Lazzaro) C.; m. Rosemary Warrington, Apr. 24, 1965; children: Victor, Gregory, Russell. BS in Acctg., Loyola Coll., Balt., 1958; MS in Fin. Mgmt., George Washington U., 1967. Cert. Profl. Cons. Auditor Haskins & Sells, CPAs, Balt., 1958, 61-63; acctg. mgr. books and reports Chesapeake & Potomac Telephone Co. (AT&T), Cockeysville, Md., 1964-68; mgr. fin. controls ITT, N.Y.C., 1968; contr. ITT World Directories, N.Y.C., 1969-70; v.p. fin. analysis and planning Dart Industries, Inc., L.A., 1970-82; v.p. fin., chief fin. officer Epson Am., Inc., Torrance, Calif., 1984-87; cons. Westlake Village, Calif., 1988—; v.p., CFO, cons. Phoenix Furniture Co., L.A., 1988-89; cons. Universal Studios Tours, L.A., 1988, FMS Prodns., Carpinteria, Calif., 1990, Video Lang. Products, L.A. and Seattle, 1991, Golden Power Sys., Simi Valley, Calif., 1992, Wambold Furniture, Simi Valley, 1993; lectr. planning and fin. Calif. Luth. U., 1991—. Capt. U.S. Army, 1959-60, USAR, 61-64. Mem. AICPA, Fin. Execs. Inst., Acad. Profl. Cons. and Advisors. Roman Catholic. Home and Office: 32305 Blue Rock Rdg Westlake Village CA 91361-3912

CUDMORE, WYNN WATSON, biologist, educator; b. Winchester, Mass., Sept. 12, 1955; s. Lemuel Ralph and Jane Ellen (Robinson) C.; m. Carla Jean Eaton, Dec. 22, 1984; children: Calin Elizabeth, Alyssa Anne, Rebecca Jean. BS in Biology, Northeastern U., 1978; PhD in Ecology, Ind. State U., 1983. Postdoctoral rsch. assoc. Wash. State U., Pullman, 1984-85; life sci. instr. Chemeketa CC, Salem, Oreg., 1985—; cons. U.S. Forest Svc., Blue River, Oreg., 1985. Contbr. articles to profl. jours. Invited speaker UN Assn., Salem, 1992, Native Plant Soc., Salem, 1992; bd. dirs. Earth Kids, Salem, 1991-92. Mem. Am. Soc. Mammalogists, Ind. Acad. Sci. (chair zoology 1984), N.W. Scientific Assn., Sigma Xi, Phi Kappa Phi. Home: 14860 Orchard Knob Rd Dallas OR 97338-9618 Office: Chemeketa CC Dept Life Sci PO Box 14007 Salem OR 97309-7070

CUFF, WILLIAM, IV, food company executive; b. Stamford, Conn., Mar. 31, 1942; s. William III and Jean (Grant) C.; m. Judith Ann Watkins, Aug. 29, 1964 (div. Nov. 1976); children: Lisa Ann Zoellin, William David; m. Erin Ann Quinn, Dec. 1, 1978. BA, Yale U., 1964; MBA, Columbia U., 1966. With mktg. mgmt. Gen. Foods, White Plains, N.Y., 1966-77; v.p. bus. devel. Standard Brands, N.Y.C., 1977-79; v.p. specialty foods Liddy subs. Nestle Co., Chgo., 1979-86; pres. The Bachman Co., Reading, Pa., 1986—. Republican. Office: Diamond Walnut Growers Inc 10560 Diamond St Stockton CA 95205*

CULBERTSON, CHERYL ANN, home health nurse, medical-surgical nurse; b. Dodge City, Kans., Oct. 7, 1943; d. John Lee and Enafae Georgina (Stark) Shipman; divorced; 1 child, Jennetta Marle Culbertson. Grad., Anchorage C.C., 1963. LPN, Alaska, Ariz. Charge nurse Alaska Psychiat. Hosp., Anchorage, 1963-68; floor nurse Valley Hosp., Las Vegas, 1972, pvt. duty nurse, 1972-77; nurse, instr. Red Cross, Kodiak, Alaska, 1977-80; pvt. duty nurse Kenai, Alaska, 1980-90; nurse Flagstaff (Ariz.) Med. Facility, 1991; home health nurse Home Works, Flagstaff, 1991—. Pres. Am. Cancer Soc., Kodiak, 1978; instr. ARC, Kodiak, 1975-90; leader 4-H, Kenai, 1984-87; den leader, coach Cub Scouts, Kenai, 1984-87. Recipient Outstanding Svc. award Cancer Soc., 1978. Mormon. Home: 721 N Main St Cottonwood AZ 86326-3641

CULL, CHRIS ALAN, operations executive; b. Las Cruces, N.Mex., Jan. 3, 1947; s. William Roy Cull and Doris Jean (Compton) Morgan; m. DuAnne Elizabeth Diers King, July 26, 1967 (div. 1979); children: Joey Lynn, Jamie Ayn, Brandon Alan. BS, N.Mex. State U., 1976. Lab./field technician N.Mex. State U., Las Cruces, 1973-76; research soil scientist Mont. State U., Bozeman, 1976-77; reclamation supr. Western Energy Co., Colstrip, Mont., 1977-80; mgr. ops. permitting Western Energy Co., Billings, Mont., 1980-85; asst. project mgr. En Tech Inc., Butte, Mont., 1985-86; mgr. ops. Spl. Resource Mgmt. Inc., Billings, 1986-87; owner EnviroChek Inc., Billings, 1987-88; dir. environ. svcs. Western Tech. Inc., Tucson, 1988-90; dir. regulatory affairs Western Tech. Inc., Golden, Colo., 1990-91; mgr. regulatory affairs Sergent, Hauskins & Beckwith, Lakewood, Colo., 1991-92; mgr. regulatory svcs. Morrison-Maierle Environ., Billings, Mont., 1992, Morrison-Maierle Environ. Corp., Billings, 1992—; v.p. regulatory svcs., 1994—. Contbr. articles to profl. jours. Mem. Am. Indsl. Hygiene Assn., Nat. Assn. Environ. Profls., Soil Conservation Soc. Am. (chmn. surface mine reclamation com. 1978-80, mem. univ. and coll. rels. com. 1977-78, spl. task force surface mine reclamation divsn. 1977-79, pres. Mont. chpt. 1980-82), Mont. Coal Coun. (co-chmn. environ./tech. com. 1983-85), Mining and Reclamation Coun. Am. (tech. com. 1983-85), Am. Coun on Sic. and Health, SME Inc., N.W. Mining Assn., Mont. Mining Assn. Home: 3295 E Granger Ave #18 Billings MT 59102-6900 Office: Morrison-Maierle Einviron Corp 2020 Grand Ave Billings MT 59102-2679

CULLEN, ROBERT JOHN, publishing executive, financial consultant; b. York, Pa., Feb. 14, 1949; s. John Joseph and Florence Susanne (Staab) C.; m. Elizabeth Maule, Oct. 20, 1984; 1 child, Michael Joseph. BA, Winona (Minn.) State U., 1972. CFP; registered investment advisor. Editor-in-chief Overseas Life, Leimen, Fed. Republic of Germany, 1978-80; feature editor L.A. Daily Commerce, 1980-83; pres. HighTech Editorial, L.A., 1983—; fin. planner Cullen Fin. Svcs., Rancho Cucamonga, Calif., 1989—; computer editor Plaza Communications, Irvine, Calif., 1984-91. With U.S. Army, 1974-78, ETO. Mem. Internat. Assn. Fin. Planners, Calif. Advs. Nursing Home Reform.

CULP, WINNIE ELAINE, marketing professional; b. Feb. 20, 1949; d. Joel Winfield and Wilma Buckman (Kearns) C.; children: Tara Bloyd, Tobias Bloyd, Hana Ransom. Grad., George Sch., Bucks County, Pa., 1967. Mktg. mgr. Omega Inst. for Holistic Studies, Rhinebeck, N.Y., 1986-89; mgr. mktg. and sales Red Crane Books, Santa Fe, 1990—. Office: Red Crane Books 2008 Rosina St Santa Fe NM 87505-3271

CULTON, PAUL MELVIN, counselor, educator, interpreter; b. Council Bluffs, Iowa, Feb. 12, 1932; s. Paul Roland and Hallie Ethel Emma (Paschal) C. BA, Minn. Bible Coll., 1955; BS, U. Nebr., 1965; MA, Calif. State U., Northridge, 1970; EdD, Brigham Young U., 1981. Cert. tchr., Iowa. Tchr. Iowa Sch. for Deaf, Council Bluffs, 1956-70; ednl. specialist Golden West Coll., Huntington Beach, Calif., 1970-71, dir. disabled students, 1971-82, instr., 1982-88; counselor El Camino Coll., Via Torrance, Calif., 1990-93, acting assoc. dean, 1993-94; counselor El Camino Coll., Via Torrance, Caif., 1994—; interpreter various state and fed. cts., Iowa, Calif., 1960-90; asst. prof. Calif. State U., Northridge, Fresno & Dominguez Hills, 1973, 76, 80, 87-90; vis. prof. U. Guam, Agana, 1977; mem. allocations task force, task force on deafness, trainer handicapped students Calif. Community Colls., 1971-81. Editor: Region IX Conf. for Coordinating Rehab. and Edn. Svcs. for Deaf proceedings, 1970, Toward Rehab. Involvement by Parents of Deaf conf. proceedings, 1971; composer Carry the Light, 1986. Bd. dirs. Iowa NAACP, 1966-68, Gay and Lesbian Community Svcs. Ctr., Orange County, Calif., 1975-77; founding sec. Dayle McIntosh Ctr. for Disabled, Anaheim and Garden Grove, Calif., 1974-80; active Dem. Cent. Com. Pottawattamie County, Council Bluffs, 1960-70. League for Innovation in Community Coll. fellow, 1974. Mem. Registry of Interpreters for Deaf, Congress Am. Instrs. Deaf, Am. Deafness and Rehab. Assn., Calif. Assn. Postsecondary Educators Disabled, Am. Fedn. Tchrs., Nat. Assn. Deaf. Home: 2567 Plaza Del Amo Apt 203 Torrance CA 90503-8962 Office: El Camino Coll Spl Resource Ctr 16007 Crenshaw Blvd Torrance CA 90506-0001

CULVER, LARRY G., medical research executive; b. 1949. MBA, U. Wis., 1977. Dir. fin. planning Marine Power Group Brunswick Corp., Fon du Lac, Wis., 1971-79; controller Eaton Corp., Milw., Salt Lake City, 1979-85; CFO Summation Inc., Kirkland, Wash., 1985-91; sr. v.p. Cellpro Inc., Bothell, Wash., 1991—. Office: Cellpro Inc 22322 20th Ave SE Ste 100 Bothell WA 98021-7426*

CULVER, WESLEY ELLSWORTH, relief and development organization executive; b. Seattle, Apr. 14, 1927; s. Charles Percy and Nina Virginia (Wilkinson) C.; m. Josephine Y. Yankowski, Nov. 27, 1967 (div. Dec. 1992); children: Scott Ellsworth, Shannon Louise, Tania Marie; m. Esme Josephine Rymer, Jan. 14, 1995. BA, Asbury Coll., 1949. Exec. v.p. World Vision, Pasadena, Calif., 1958-61; asst. gen. dir. Overseas Crusades, Palo Alto, Calif., 1962-64; pres. Stover & Assocs., San Francisco, 1965-66, Involvement, Inc., Palo Alto, 1967-76; exec. dir. Alliance for Volunteerism, Boulder, Colo., 1977-78; exec. v.p. Food for the Hungry Internat., Scottsdale, Ariz., 1979-81; pres. Culver Stowell, Inc., Portland, Oreg., 1982—; pres. Mercy Corps Internat., Portland, 1984-93, v.p., 1994—; v.p., bd. dirs. ARCA Found., Washington, 1974—; chmn., bd. dirs. Spafford Children's Ctr., Jerusalem, 1991-93; bd. regents Warner Pacific Coll., Portland, 1990-94; bd. dirs. Mercy Corps Europe, Swindon, Eng., bd. dirs., exec. com. InterAction, 1991-94; co-founder Sports Ambs. Internat. People-to-People Program. Episcopalian. Office: Mercy Corps Internat 3030 SW 1st Ave Portland OR 97201-4708

CULY, DOUGLAS GALE, engineering economist, consultant; b. Medford, Oreg. B.S. in Mech. Engring., Oreg. State U., 1960; M.S. in Indsl. Engring., Ariz. State U., 1971, M.B.A., 1974. Registered profl. engr., Wash. Exptl. test engr. Pratt & Whitney Aircraft Co., East Hartford, Conn., 1960-61; research engr. Turbine div. Boeing Co., Seattle, 1961-64; sr. devel. engr. Airesearch Mfg. Co., Phoenix, 1964-76; mgr. process engring. Airco Temescal, Berkeley, Calif., 1976-77; supr. engring. mgmt. sys. devel. Garrett Turbine Engine Co., Phoenix, 1977-93; dir. Engring. Aviation Consulting, 1993—. Author seminars on econs. of gas turbines and risk analysis. Contbr. tech. papers and articles to profl. jours. Cons. project bus. Jr. Achievement. Mem. Soc. Automotive Engrs. (chmn. Ariz. sect. 1980-81, mem. sects. bd. 1981-85, chmn. life cycle cost com. 1987-92, 1994—), ASME, AIAA. Club: Toastmasters (pres. Phoenix 1983, dist. treas. 1982-83). Office: Aviation Consulting 1408 E Whalers Way Tempe AZ 85283-5503

CUMELLA, STEPHEN PAUL, geologist; b. Colorado Springs, Colo., Aug. 19, 1955; s. Ronald and Claire Mabel (Person) C.; m. Cindy Kay Carothers, July 12, 1986; children: Nathan, Paul, Kimberly. BS in Geology, U. Tex., 1977, MA in Geology, 1981. cert. petroleum geologist. Geologist Chevron U.S.A., Denver, 1981-90, Chevron Overseas Petroluem, Inc., San Ramon, Colo., 1988-90; cons. geologist Cockrell Oil Corp., Grand Junction, Colo., 1990-92; project mgr. Rust Environ. & Infrastructure, Grand Junction, Colo., 1992—. Contbr. articles and abstracts to scientific jours. Vol. Meals-on-Wheels, Denver, 1984-88, Grand Junction, 1995—. Mem. Am. Assn. Petroleum Geologists, Nat. Ground Water Assn., Grand Junction Geol. Soc. (pres. 1993), Uncompahgre Plateau Paleontological Soc. Home: 645 Kayenta Ct Grand Junction CO 81503-9530

CUMMERTON, JOAN MARIE, social work educator; b. Batavia, N.Y., Jan. 11, 1931; d. John J. and Loretta E. (Geissler) C. BS in Social Sci., Carnegie Mellon U., 1953; MS in Social Adminstrn., Case-Western Reserve U., 1956; D in Social Work, Washington U., St. Louis, 1970. Cert. Acad. Cert. Social Workers. Group worker Ferry Rd. Playground, Phila., 1953-54; dist. dir. Girl Scouts, St. Louis, 1956-58, field staff supr., 1958-60; asst. prof. U. Iowa, Iowa City, 1963-70; assoc. prof. San Francisco State U., 1970-80, prof. social work edn., 1980—; cons. Family Svc. Assn., Des Moines, 1966-67, Women, Inc., San Francisco, 1988-89. Mem. NASW, Coun. on Social Work Edn., Women in Psychology, Nat. Women's Studies Assn. Office: San Francisco State U 1600 Holloway Ave San Francisco CA 94132-1722

CUMMING, JANICE DOROTHY, clinical psychologist; b. Berkeley, Calif., Nov. 20, 1953; d. Gordon Robertson and Helen (Stanford) Cumming; 1 child, Shauna Cumming Keddy. BA, U. Calif., Davis, 1975; MA, Calif. State U., Sacramento, 1980; PhD, Calif. Sch. Profl. Psychology, Berkeley, 1985. Lic. psychologist, Calif. Counselor and instr. Serendipity Diagnostic/Treatment, Citrus Hts., Calif., 1978-79; reg. psychologist asst. John Gibbins, PhD, Castro Valley, Calif., 1984-87, Enrico Jones, PhD, Berkeley, Calif., 1985-86; asst. rsch. specialist U. Calif., Berkeley, 1985-90; clin. cons. Family Guidance, Children's Hosp., Oakland, Calif., 1987-90; clin. supr. psychiat. svcs. Children's Hosp., San Francisco, 1987-90; pvt. practice psychology Castro Valley, 1987-90, San Francisco, 1987-90, Oakland, Calif., 1990—; mem. rschr. San Francisco Psychotherapy Rsch. Group, 1987—, instr., 1991, conf. chair, 1992-93; conv. chair Calif. State Psychol. Assn., Sacramento, 1985, 86; asst. clin. prof. U. Calif., San Francisco, 1992—. Mem. APA, Calif. Psychol. Assn. (continuing edn. com. chair 1986, co-chair 1987), Psychologists for Social Responsibility (bd. dirs. 1984-87, chair 1987-89), No. Calif. Soc. Psychoanalytic Psychology, Alameda County Psychol. Assn., Phi Beta Kappa. Office: 5835 College Ave Ste C Oakland CA 94618-1653

CUMMINGS, BARTON, musician; b. Newport, N.H., July 10, 1946; s. C. Barton and Ruth (Ricard) C.; m. Florecita L. Lim, July 23, 1983;. BS in Music Edn., U. N.H., 1968; MusM, Ball State U., Muncie, Ind., 1973. Dir. music Alton (N.H.) Pub. Sch., 1971-72; lectr. San Diego State U., 1974-79; instr. music Point Loma Coll., San Diego, 1976-79; instr. San Diego Community Coll. Dist., 1977-79, Delta State U., Cleveland, Miss., 1979-82; supr. Clarksdale Separate Sch. Dist., 1982-84; dir. music Walnut (Calif.) Creek Concert Band, 1985-, Richmond Unified Sch. Dist., 1988—, Golden Hills Concert Band, 1990—; condr. Devil Mountain Symphony, 1991—; tuba player Vallejo Symphony Orch., 1988—, Concord Pavilion Pops Orch., 1985—, Brassworks of San Francisco, 1985—, Solano Dixie Jubilee. Author: The Contemporary Tuba, 1984, The Tuba Guide, 1989, Teaching Techniques for Brass Instruments, 1989; composer over two dozen pub. compositions; recorded on Capra, Coronet and Crystal labels. Mem. ASCAP, NACUSA, T.U.B.A., Am. Fedn. of Musicians, Conductor's Guild, Phi Mu Alpha Sinfonia. Home: 550 Cambridge Dr Benicia CA 94510-1316

CUMMINGS, DAROLD BERNARD, aircraft engineer; b. Batavia, N.Y., June 27, 1944; s. Bernard Laverne and Doris Helen (Klotzbach) C.; children from a previous marriage: Carla, Bret; m. Karen Jean Cacciola, Dec. 19, 1992; 1 child, Kyle. BS in Indsl. Design, Calif. State U., Long Beach, 1967. Engr. aircraft design Rockwell Internat., Los Angeles, 1967-82; chief engr. trainer aircraft Rockwell Internat., El Segundo, Calif., 1988—; chief designer advanced design Northrop Corp., Hawthorne, Calif., 1982-88; lectr. Calif. State U., Long Beach, 1969-73; pres. Matrix Design, Hawthorne, 1967—. Author: What Not to Name Your Baby, 1982; cons., actor (movie) Search for Solutions, 1979. Mem. Air Force Assn. Republican. Home: 5320 W 124th Pl Hawthorne CA 90250-4154 Office: Rockwell Internat El Segundo CA 90245

CUMMINGS, D(ONALD) W(AYNE), English language educator, dean; b. Seattle, May 21, 1935; s. Oliver Warren Cummings and Mildred Marie (Thayer) Smith; m. Carol Frances Feuling, Aug. 10, 1956; children: Daniel, Lon, Jody. BA in English, U. Washington, 1958, MA in English, 1964, Phd in English, 1965. Instr. English Ctrl. Wash. U., Ellensburg, 1960-64; asst. prof. English Cen. Wash. U., Ellensburg, 1964-66, assoc. prof. English, 1966-71, prof. English, 1971—, dir. acad. skills ctr., 1966-90, chair English dept., 1984-87, dean coll. of letters, arts and scis., 1989-93; tchr. English Newport High Sch., Bellevue, Washington, 1971-72. Co-author: (with J. Herum) Writing, Plans, Drafts, Revisions, 1971; co-author, editor Tempo: Life, Work, and Leisure, 1973; author Basic Speller for Older Students, 1988, American English Spelling, 1988. Office: Ctrl Wash U Dept English Coll Letters Arts/Sci Ellensburg WA 98926

CUMMINGS, LESLIE EDWARDS, hospitality management educator; b. Modesto, Calif., Feb. 17, 1951; d. George Robert and Mary Lou (Bomberger) Edwards; m. William Theodore Cummings Sr., Mar. 12, 1977. BS in Home Econs., Ariz. State U., 1974, MS in Agr., 1977, D in Pub. Adminstrn., 1990. Intern General Mills, Inc., Golden Valley, Minn., summer 1968; diet technician Mesa (Ariz.) Luth. Hosp., 1972-73; salesperson Romney Products, Inc., 1974; pharm. ins. auditor Pharm. Card Sys., Inc., 1974-76; mem. chain hdqrs. staff Fry's Supermarkets, Inc., 1977; adj. instr. foodsvc. Auburn (Ala.) U., 1978-79, from asst. mgr. to mgr. Campus Ctr. Foodsvcs., 1979-80; customer support analyst WANG Labs., Inc., 1981-83; asst. prof. U. Nev., Coll. Hotel Adminstrn., Las Vegas, 1983-87, assoc. prof., 1987-93, prof., 1993—; papers presented at Hotel-Motel Expo, 1985, So. Nev. Dietetics Assn. and So. Nev. Home Econs. Assn., Las Vegas, 1986, Internat. Assn. of Hospitality Accts., Las Vegas, 1986, Inst. Food Technologists, Las Vegas, 1987, Tex. Assn. Hospitality Accts., Las Vegas, 1988, Foodsvc. and the Environment, Scottsdale, Ariz., 1990, State of Ariz. Dietetics Assn., Scottsdale, 1991, Assn. for the Study of Food and Soc., Tucson, 1991, ASPA, Las Vegas, 1991, Foodsvcs. Sys. Beyond 2000 Conf., Israel, 1992, others; panelist, spkr. in field. Author: (textbook) (with Lendal Kotschevar) Nutrition Management for Foodservices, 1989, Instructor's Manual for Nutrition Management for Foodservices, 1989; contbr. articles to profl. jours. Vol. Women's Resource Network Career Event, Annual Nev. Gov.'s Conf. for Women. Recipient Nat. Assn. Schs. Pub. Adminstrn. dissertation award, 1990; fellow Rotary Internat., 1978. Mem. ASPA, Am. Dietetic Assn. (treas. environ. nutrition dietetic practice group 1992—, registered dietitian), Inst. Internal Auditors (cert.), Coun. on Hotel, Restaurant, and Instnl. Edn., Rsch. and Devel. Assocs. for Mil. Food and Packaging Sys., Inc., Phi Beta Kappa, Phi Kappa Phi, Pi Alpha Alpha. Office: WF Harrah Coll Hotel Adminstrn Food & Beverage Mgmt Dept 4505 Maryland Pkwy Las Vegas NV 89154-6022

CUMMINGS, NICHOLAS ANDREW, psychologist; b. Salinas, Calif., July 25, 1924; s. Andrew and Urania (Sims) C.; m. Dorothy Mills, Feb. 5, 1948; children—Janet Lynn, Andrew Mark. AB, U. Calif., Berkeley, 1948; MA, Claremont Grad. Sch., 1954; PhD, Adelphi U., 1958. Chief psychologist Kaiser Permanente No. Calif., San Francisco, 1959-76; pres. Found Behavioral Health, San Francisco, 1976—; chmn., chief exec. officer Am. Biodyne, Inc., San Francisco, 1985-93; chmn., CEO Kendron Internat., Ltd., Reno, Nev., 1992—; chmn. Nicholas & Dorothy Cummings Found., Reno, 1994—; co-dir. South San Francisco Health Ctr., 1959-75; pres. Calif. Sch. Profl. Psychology, Los Angeles, San Francisco, San Diego, Fresno campuses, 1969-76; chmn. bd. Calif. Community Mental Health Ctrs., Inc., Los Angeles, San Diego, San Francisco, 1975-77; pres. Blue Psi, Inc., San Francisco, 1972-80, Inst. for Psychosocial Interaction, 1980-84; mem. mental health adv. bd. City and County San Francisco, 1968-75; bd. dirs. San Francisco Assn. Mental Health, 1965-75; pres., chmn. bd. Psycho-Social Inst., 1972-80; dir. Mental Rsch. Inst., Palo Alto, Calif., 1979-80; pres. Nat. Acads. of Practice, 1981-93. Served with U.S. Army, 1944-46. Fellow Am. Psychol. Assn. (dir. 1975-81, pres. 1979); mem. Calif. Psychol. Assn. (pres. 1968). Office: Nicholas & Dorothy Cummings Found 561 Keystone Ave Ste 212 Reno NV 89503-4304

CUMMINGS, RUSSELL MARK, aerospace engineer, educator; b. Santa Cruz, Calif., Oct. 3, 1955; s. Gilbert Warren and Anna Mae (Phillips) C.; m. Cherilyn Suzanne Parsons, Mar. 25, 1983 (div. 1990). BS, Calif. Poly. State U., 1977, MS, 1985; PhD, U. So. Calif., 1988. Mem. tech. staff Hughes Aircraft Co., Canoga Park, Calif., 1979-86; rsch. assoc. Nat. Rsch. Coun. at NASA Ames Rsch. Ctr., Moffett Field, Calif., 1988-90; prof. aerospace engring. Calif. Poly. State U., San Luis Obispo, Calif., 1986—; dept. chmn. aero. engring. dept. Calif. Poly. State U., 1992—; cons. Steiner and Assocs., San Luis Obispo, 1989-90; vis. acad. computing lab. Oxford U., 1995. Contbr. chpt. to book Numerical and Physical Aspects of Aerodynamic Flows, 1990; contbr. 15 articles to profl. jours., presented 30 tech. papers at sci. confs. and meetings. Asst. scoutmaster Boy Scouts Am., San Luis Obispo, 1978-79. Hughes Engring. fellow 1980, Howard Hughes fellow 1984; NASA grantee, 1986-95; recipient Group Achievement awards NASA, 1989, 90, AIAA Nat. Faculty Advisor award, 1994, Northrop Grumman Excellence in Teaching and Applied Rsch. award, 1995. Fellow AIAA (assoc.); mem. Am. Soc. Engring. Educators, Royal Aero. Soc., Sigma Xi, Sigma Gamma Tau. Republican. Mem. Evangelical Christian Ch. Office: Calif Poly State U Dept Aero Engring San Luis Obispo CA 93407

CUMMINS, CHARLES FITCH, JR., lawyer; b. Lansing, Mich., Aug. 19, 1939; s. Charles F. Sr. and Ruth M. Cummins; m. Anne Warner, Feb. 11, 1961; children: Michael, John, Mark. AB in Econs., U. Mich., 1961; LLB, U. Calif., Hastings, 1966. Bar: Calif. 1966, Mich. 1976. Assoc. Hall, Henry, Oliver & McReavy, San Francisco, 1966-70, 1971-75; ptnr. Cummins & Cummins, Lansing, Mich., 1976-82, Pitto & Ubhaus, San Jose, Calif., 1982-85; prin. Law Offices Charles F. Cummins Jr., San Jose, 1985-87; ptnr. Cummins & Chandler, San Jose, 1987-92; prin. Law Offices of Charles F. Cummins, Jr., San Jose, 1992—. Bd. dirs., officer various civic orgns., chs. and pvt. schs. Lt. USNR, 1961-63. Mem. Kiwanis. Office: Law Offices of Charles F Cummins Jr 4 N 2nd St Ste 1230 San Jose CA 95113-1307

CUMMINS, JOHN STEPHEN, bishop; b. Oakland, Calif., Mar. 3, 1928; s. Michael and Mary (Connolly) C. A.B., St. Patrick's Coll., 1949. Ordained priest Roman Catholic Ch., 1953; asst. pastor Mission Dolores Ch., San Francisco, 1953-57; mem. faculty Bishop O'Dowd High Sch., Oakland, 1957-62; chancellor Diocese of Oakland, 1962-71; rev. monsignor, 1962, domestic prelate, 1967; exec. dir. Calif. Cath. Conf., Sacramento, 1971-77; consecrated bishop, 1974; aux. bishop of Sacramento, 1974-77; bishop of Oakland, 1977—; Campus minister San Francisco State Coll., 1953-57, Mills Coll., Oakland, 1957-71; Trustee St. Mary's Coll., 1968-79. Home: 634 21st St Oakland CA 94612-1608 Office: Oakland Diocese 2900 Lakeshore Ave Oakland CA 94610-3614*

CUMMINS, JOHN THOMAS, JR., lobbyist, writer, speaker; b. Hamilton AFB, Calif., Nov. 9, 1946; s. John Thomas Cummins Sr. and Retha Ellen (Howard) Martinson; m. Janet Marie Kalus; children: Carrie Marie, Kalani Malia. BA in Psychology cum laude, Pepperdine U., 1976; postgrad., Webster U., 1978-79, Naval War Coll., 1981-82, U. Okla., 1985-86, U. Wyo., 1989-91. Cert. lobbyist, Mont. Enlisted USMC, 1964, advanced through grades to lt. col., 1982; platoon comdr. Third Battalion, Fourth Marines USMC, Vietnam, 1969; co. comdr. Third Marine Div. USMC, Hawaii and Okinawa, 1971-73, 74-75; asst. chief of staff of electronics, Marine Corps Air Sta. USMC, El Toro, Calif., 1976-79, squadron comdr., Third Marine Aircraft Wing, 1979-81; chief test ops. Jt. Command Control Commn. Agy. USMC, Ft. Monmouth, N.J., 1982-84; asst. chief of staff Fleet Marine Forces USMC, Hawaii, 1984-87; asst. chief of staff Marine Corps Bases Okinawa, Japan, 1988-89; ret. USMC, 1989; exec. v.p. Mont. Farm Bur. Fedn., Boseman, 1991—; bd. dirs. Mont. Hwy. Users Fedn., 1991—, Bozeman Kiwanis. Mng. editor Spokesman monthly newsletter, 1991—. Mem. Mont. Soc. Assn. Execs., Marine Corps Assn., Nat. Assn. Farm Broadcasters, The Retired Officers Assn., Riverside Country Club. Republican. Episcopalian. Office: Mont Farm Bur Fedn 502 S 19th Ave Ste 4 Bozeman MT 59715-6827

CUMMINS, NANCYELLEN HECKEROTH, electronics engineer; b. Long Beach, Calif., May 22, 1948; d. George and Ruth May (Anderson) Heckeroth; m. Weldon Jay, Sept. 15, 1987; stepchildren: Tracy Lynn, John Scott, Darren Elliott. Student avionics, USMC, Memphis, 1966-67. Tech. publ. engr. Missile and Space divsn. Lockheed Corp., Sunnyvale, Calif., 1973-76, engring. instr., 1977; test engr. Gen. Dynamics, Pomona, Calif., 1980-83; quality assurance test engr. Interstate Electronics Co., Anaheim, Calif., 1983-84; quality engr., certification engr. Rockwell Internat., Anaheim, 1985-86; sr. quality assurance programmer Point 4 Data, Tustin, Calif., 1986-87; software quality assurance specialist Lawrence Livermore Nat. Lab., Yucca Mountain Project, Livermore, Calif., 1987-89, software quality mgr., 1989-90; sr. constrn. insp. EG&G Rocky Flats, Inc., Golden, Colo., 1990, sr. quality assurance engr., 1991, engr. IV software quality assurance, 1991-92, instr., developer environ. law and compliance, 1992-93; software, computer cons. CRI, Dabois, Wyo., 1993—; customer engr. IBM Gen. Sys., Orange, Calif., 1979; electronics engr. Exhibits divsn. LDS Ch., Salt Lake City, 1978; electronics repair specialist Weber State Coll., 1977-78. Author: Package Area Test Set, 6 vols., 1975, Software Quality Assurance Plan, 1989. Vol., instr. San Fernando (Calif.) Search and Rescue Team, 1967-70; instr. emergency preparedness and survival, Clairmont, Calif., 1982-84, Modesto, Calif., 1989; mem. Lawrence Livermore Nat. Lab. Employees Emergency Vols., 1987-90, EG&G Rocky Flats Bldg. Emergency Support Team, 1990—. Mem. NAFE, NRA, Nat. Muzzle Loading Rifle Assn., Am. Soc. Quality Control, Job's Daus. (majority mem.). Republican. Mem. LDS Ch. Home: PO Box 398 Dubois WY 82513 Office: CRI PO Box 414 Dubois WY 82513-0414

CUNEO, DENNIS CLIFFORD, automotive company executive; b. Ridgway, Pa., Jan. 12, 1950; s. Clifford Francis and Erma Theresa (Nissel) C.; m. Bonnie Frances Mish, Aug. 18, 1972; children: Corinne, Kyle, James. BS, Gannon U., 1971; MBA, Kent State U., 1973; JD, Loyola U., New Orleans, 1976. Bar: D.C. 1977. Trial atty. U.S. Dept. Justice, Washington, 1976-80; assoc. Arent, Fox, Kintner, Plotkin & Kahn, Washington, 1980-84; gen. counsel New United Motor Mfg. Inc. joint venture GM-Toyota, Fremont, Calif., 1984-88, v.p. legal and govt. affairs, 1988-90, v.p. corp. planning and legal affairs, 1990-92, v.p. corp. planning and external affairs, corp. sec., 1992—; chmn. pub. policy com. New United Motors, Fremont, 1986—, chmn. strategic bus. com., 1988—; chmn. Calif. Workside Rsch. Com., Sacramento, 1988—; lectr. exec. program U. Calif., Davis, 1988—; mem. Gov. Pete Wilson Trade Mission to Asia, 1993. Campaign chmn. United Way, Alameda County, 1993-95; co-chmn. Blue Ribbon com. to Save the Oakland A's, 1994; vice chmn. Alameda County Econ. Devel. Bd., Oakland, 1990—; bd. visitors Loyola Law Sch., 1987—; mem. select com. on jud. retirement, 1993; mem. steering com. Bay Area Coun., San Francisco, 1990—; vice chmn. Team Calif., Sacramento, 1994; mem. steering com. Bay Area Dredging Coalition, San Francisco, 1991—; bd. vis. Loyola Law Sch., 1987—. Mem. ABA, Calif. Mfrs. Assn. (vice chmn. 1994). Office: New United Motor Mfg Inc 45500 Fremont Blvd Fremont CA 94538-6326

CUNNANE, PATRICIA S., medical facility administrator; b. Clinton, Iowa, Sept. 7, 1946; d. Cyril J. and Corinne Spain; m. Edward J. Cunnane, June 19, 1971. AA, Mt. St. Clare Coll., Clinton, Iowa, 1966. Mgr. Eye Med. Clinic of Santa Clara Valley, San Jose, Calif. Mem. Med. Adminstrs. Calif. Polit. Action Com., San Francisco, 1987. Mem. Med. Group Mgmt. Assn., Am. Coll. Med. Group Adminstrs. (nominee), Nat. Notary Assn., NAFE, Exec. Women Internat. (v.p. 1986-87, pres. 1987—), Profl. Secs. Internat. (sec. 1979-80), Am. Soc. Ophthalmic Adminstrs., Women Health Care Execs., Healthcare Human Resource Mgmt. Assn. Calif. Roman Catholic. Home: 232 Tolin Ct San Jose CA 95139-1445 Office: Eye Med Clinic of Santa Clara Valley 220 Meridian Ave San Jose CA 95126-2903

CUNNINGHAM, BRUCE ARTHUR, biochemist; b. Winnebago, Ill., Jan. 18, 1940; s. Wallace Calvin and Margaret Wright (Clinite) C.; m. Katrina Sue Susdorf, Feb. 27, 1965; children—Jennifer Ruth, Douglas James. B.S., U. Dubuque, 1962; Ph.D., Yale U., 1966. NSF postdoctoral fellow Rockefeller U., N.Y.C., 1966-68; asst. prof. biochemistry Rockefeller U., 1968-71, assoc. prof., 1971-77, prof. molecular and devel. biology, 1978-92; mem. dept. neurobiology Scripps Rsch. Inst., San Diego, 1992—. Editorial bd.: Jour. Biol. Chemistry, 1978-82, Jour. Cell Biology, 1992—. Camille and Henry Dreyfus Found. grantee, 1970-75; recipient Career Scientist award Irma T. Hirschl Trust, 1975-80. Mem. AAAS, Am. Soc. Biol. Chemists, Am. Soc. Cell Biology, Protein Soc., Am. Chem. Soc., Harvey Soc., Am. Gynecol. Obstet. Soc. (hon.), Sigma Xi. Office: Scripps Rsch Inst 10666 N Torrey Pines Rd La Jolla CA 92037-1027

CUNNINGHAM, ELEANOR ELIZABETH, nurse; b. Bklyn., Mar. 13, 1931; d. Arthur Christian and Alice (Brusack) Philipps; m. Joseph Lawrence Cunningham, Sept. 6, 1958; children: Michael, Kevin, Kathleen, Matthew. RN, Mt. Sinai Sch. Nursing, 1951; BA in Social Svcs., U. Nev., Las Vegas, 1981; MS in Health Adminstrn., St. Francis Coll., 1987. RN, Nev.; cert. diabetes educator, Nev. Staff nurse Mt. Sinai Hosp., N.Y.C., 1951-53, Cedars of Lebanon Hosp., L.A., 1953-55, Mt. Sinai Hosp., L.A., 1955-58; staff nurse St. Rose Dominican Hosp., Henderson, Nev., 1958-87, head nurse med./surg. unit, 1973-85, hosp. educator, 1987-92; cert. diabetes educator In-House Home Health Inc., Las Vegas, 1993—; cert. diabetes educator Henderson Home Health Inc., Diabetes Treatment Ctr. at Desert Springs Hosp.; CPR instr., Las Vegas, 1990—; mem. ethics com. St. Rose Dominican Hosp., 1992-94; I Can Cope cancer facilitator Am. Cancer Soc., Las Vegas, 1990. Active crisis intervention-sudden death E.A.S.E./Nathan Adelson Hospice, Las Vegas, 1992—; mem. women's aux. Boys and Girls Club Nev., Las Vegas, 1980-88; area capt. Am. Heart Assn., Las Vegas, 1977; vol. St. Rose Dominican Hosp., 1992—, mem. women's aux., 1960-94. Named Nurse of Yr. March of Dimes, 1990. Mem. Am. Hosp. Assn., Clark County Health Educators (pres. 1990-91), So. Nev. Soc. Health, Edn. Tng. (sec.-treas. 1991—), Phi Kappa Phi. Roman Catholic. Home: 3581 Cherokee Ave Las Vegas NV 89121

CUNNINGHAM, GILBERT EARL, owner florist and gift shop; b. Fort Worth, Tex., May 4, 1930; s. George Alvin and Lillian Louise (Fogg) C. Student, Benz-Floral Design, 1948. Designer Balche's Flowers, Ft. Worth, Tex., 1948-53; owner, tchr. Ft. Worth Sch. of Floral Design, 1953-61; mgr. Cheri's Flowers, Tucson, Ariz., 1961-68; owner Ariz. Sch. of Floral Design, Tucson, 1961-68, Buddy's Distinctive Flowers and Gifts, Mesa, Ariz., 1968—; pres. Ariz. unit Teleflora, Inc., Mesa, 1976-78; instr. western U.S.A. Teleflora Nat. Conf., Cleve., 1968; instr. Florists Transworld Del., Phoenix, 1982. With U.S. Army, 1953-56. Mem. Mesa Merchants Assn. Republican. Baptist. Home: 8508 E Orange Blossom Ln Scottsdale AZ 85250-7427

CUNNINGHAM, LARRIE JOHN, retired engineering executive, arbitrator; b. Peterborough, Ont., Can., Feb. 8, 1934; came to U.S., 1959; s. Lorne Bertram and Alberta Catherine (Throop) C.; m. Judy Ann Long, Jan. 30, 1966. Diploma in archl. and bldg. tech., Ryerson Poly. Inst., Toronto, 1956. Estimator, asst. supt. Grirenthwaite Constrn. Co., Hamilton, Ont., 1956-57; asst. supt., field engr. S. Crump Mech. Ctr., Toronto, 1957-58; chief bldg. inspector, asst. city engr. Can. Dept. Mcpl. Affairs, Elliott Lake, Ont., 1958-59; exec. v.p., dir. Spencer, White & Prentis, Inc., San Francisco, 1959-89; pvt. practice as arbitrator, cons. Scottsdale, Ariz., 1989—; cons. Fleming Corp., L.A., 1990—, Marc S. Caspe Co., L.A., 1993—. Named Lecture Honorarium Dept. Civil Engring. U. Calif., 1977. Mem. Am. Arbitration Assn., U.S. Arbitration & Mediation Assn. Home: 8664 E Corrine Dr Scottsdale AZ 85260-5305

CUNNINGHAM, RANDY, congressman; b. L.A., Dec. 8, 1941; m. Nancy Jones; 3 children. BA, U. Mo., MA; MBA, Nat. U. Mem. 102nd-104th Congresses from Calif. dist. 44 (now 51), 1991—; mem. nat. security com. 102nd-103rd Congresses from Calif. dist. 44 (now 51), mem. econ. and ednl. opportunity com., chmn. subcom. on early childhood, youth and families. Republican. Baptist. Office: US Ho of Reps 227 Cannon HOB Washington DC 20515

CUNNINGHAM, VERNON CARL, insurance company official; b. Portsmouth, Va., June 16, 1948; m. Marlene Hudson, Aug. 15, 1970; children: Colleen, Kathleen, Patricia. CLU. Profl. surfer Vern Cunningham Surfboards, Hermosa Beach, Calif., 1966-73; agt. N.Y. Life Ins. Co., Torrance, Calif., 1973-76; agt. N.Y. Life Ins. Co., Riverside, Calif., 1988-90, tng. supr., 1990—; tng. dir. Lincoln Nat. Life Ins. Co., L.A., 1976-79; ind. agt. The Cunningham Agy., Riverside, 1979-88. Contbr. articles to fin. svc. mags.; originator orgn. tool The Tng. Matrix. Mem. Class of 1990, Leadership Riverside, 1989-90. Recipient svc. award Riverside Citrus Heritage Parade, 1986. Mem. Nat. Assn. Life Underwriters (chmn. edn. com. Riverside 1989, health com. 1990-92, chmn. 1994-95, Svc. award 1990), Gen. Agts. and Mgrs. Assn. (sec.-treas. Riverside 1993-95), Riverside C. of C. (amb. chmn. 1989-90, chmn. membership 1990-91, golf com. 1990-91). Republican. Roman Catholic. Office: NY Life Ins Co 4361 Latham St Ste 200 Riverside CA 92501-1767

CUPERY, ROBERT RINK, manufacturing executive; b. Beaver Dam, Wis., Apr. 5, 1944; s. Rink Eli and Ruby Elizabeth (Haima) C.; m. Kathleen Gonzalez; children: Ryan Edward, Jennifer. Airframe and Powerplant, Northrop U., 1967; BSBA, U. Redlands, 1978. Aircraft mechanic Northwest Airlines, Mpls., 1968-69; corp. flight engr. Northrop Corp., Hawthorne, Calif., 1969-76, engr., 1976-79, sr. staff customer relations, 1979-82, internat. quality mgr., 1982-84; pres., chief exec. officer Aircraft Window Repairs, Torrance, Calif., 1984—, Cupery Corp., Torrance, Calif.; bd. advisers Northrop Rice Aviation Sch., 1992; lectr. throughout U.S. and Europe, 1986, 89, 90. Contbr. articles to profl. jours. Served as staff sgt. USAF, 1962-66. Mem. Profl. Aviation Maintenance Assn. (corp.), Can. Aviation Mech. Engring., Nat. Bus. Aircraft Assn., Aero Club So. Calif. (bd. dirs. 1992). Republican.

CURCIO, CHRISTOPHER FRANK, city official; b. Oakland, Calif., Feb. 3, 1950; s. Frank William and Virginie Theresa (Le Gris) C. BA in Speech/Drama, Calif. State U., Hayward, 1971; MBA in Arts Adminstrn., UCLA, 1974; MPA in Pub. Policy, Ariz. State U., 1982. Intern John F. Kennedy Ctr. for Arts, Washington, 1973; gen. mgr. Old Eagle Theatre, Sacramento, 1974-75; cultural arts supr. Fresno (Calif.) Parks and Recreation Dept., 1975-79; supr. cultural and spl. events Phoenix Parks, Recreation and Libr. Dept., 1979-87, budget analyst, 1987, mgmt. svcs. adminstr., 1987—; mgmt. and budget analyst City of Phoenix, 1985; grants panelist Phoenix Arts Commn., 1987, Ariz. Commn. on Arts, 1987-88; voter Zony Theatre Awards, 1991-92; freelance theater critic, 1987-89; theater critic Ariz. Republic, 1990—. Active Valley Leadership Program, Phoenix, 1987—, Valley Big Bros./Big Sisters, 1980-94; chair allocation panel United Way, 1990-92; sec. Los Olivos Townhome Assn., Phoenix, 1986-92. Mem. Am. Soc. Pub. Adminstrn., Nat. Recreation and Park Assn., Am. Theatre Critics Assn., Internat. Theater Critics Assn., Ariz. Park and Recreation Assn. Republican. Office: Phoenix Parks Recreation and Libr Dept 200 W Washington St 16th Fl Phoenix AZ 85003

CURD, JOHN GARY, physician, scientist; b. Grand Junction, Colo., July 2, 1945; s. H. Ronald and Edna (Hegested) C.; m. Karen Wendel, June 12, 1971; children: Alison, Jonathan, Edward, Bethany. BA, Princeton U., 1967; MD, Harvard U., 1971. Diplomate Am. Bd. Internal Medicine, Am. Bd. Rheumatology, Am. Bd. Allergy and Immunology. Rsch. assoc. NIH, Bethesda, Md., 1973-75; fellow in rheumatology U. Calif., San Diego, 1975-77; fellow in allergy-immunology Scripps Clinic, La Jolla, Calif., 1977-78, asst. mem. rsch. inst., 1978-81, mem. div. rheumatology, 1981-91, head div. rheumatology, vice chmn. dept. medicine, 1989-91; pres. med. staff Green Hosp., La Jolla, 1988-90; clin. dir. Genentech Inc., South San Francisco, Calif., 1991—. Author numerous. sci. papers in field. Med. dir. San Diego Scleroderma Found., 1983-91; sec. San Diego Arthritis Found., 1986-87. Lt. comdr. USPHS, 1973-75. Mem. Princeton Club No. Calif. Republican. Home: 128 Reservoir Rd Hillsborough CA 94010-6957 Office: Genentech Inc 460 Point San Bruno Blvd South San Francisco CA 94080-4918

CURE, DEANN KAY, medical facility executive; b. Colorado Springs, Jan. 18, 1955; d. Glenn F. and Leona Marie (Pickard) Edmunds; m. Robert G. Cure, May 1, 1976; children: R. Wesley, Stephen, Anthony. Student, Blair Bus. Coll., Colorado Springs, 1974, U. Minn. Sec. Thomas & Thomas, P.C., Burlington, Colo., 1974-76; land use planner Coun. of Govts., Stratton, Colo., 1976-77; ins. clk. Kit Carson County Meml. Hosp., Burlington, 1985—, bus. office mgr., 1986—, chief fin. officer, 1988—, asst. adminstr., 1990-93, CEO, 1993—; chmn., bd. dirs. High Plains Rural Health Network. Dist. chair Colo. Farm Bur., 1984—; sec. bd. dirs. Kit Carson County Farm Bur., 1982—; precinct chair Kit Carson County Republicans, 1982—, chair, 1990-94. Rep. Leadership Program scholar, 1989. Mem. Healthcare Fin. Mgmt. Assn., Colo. Patient Acctg. Assn. Roman Catholic. Office: Kit Carson County Meml Hosp 286 16th St Burlington CO 80807-1651

CURKENDALL, BRENDA IRENE, financial planner, business owner; b. Mesa, Ariz., Dec. 20, 1954; d. Arthur Blatt and Dorothy June Goodnight; m. James Patrick Monagle (div.); m. Christopher Lee Curkendall; children: Robert, Chad, Jeremy, Sean. Student, Edison Jr. Coll., 1971-72; BA in History, Fla. State U., 1976; postgrad., Coll. for Fin. Planning, 1992. CFP; registered investment advisor. Realtor Harold A. Allen Co. Realtors, Tacoma, 1983; salesperson Computerland, Bellevue, Wash., 1983-84; systems analyst Boeing Computer Svcs., Seattle, 1985; stock broker Shearson Lehman Bros., Tacoma, 1985-87; fin. planner Curkendall Fin. Programs, Inc., Puyallup, Wash., 1988—; instr. Pierce Coll., Tacoma. Contbr. articles to profl. jours. Capt. U.S. Army, 1976-82, Korea. Mem. Apt. Assn. Pierce County (pres. 1988), Ft. Hood Flying Club (pres. 1980). Office: 12012 98th Ave E Ste B Puyallup WA 98373-5027

CURL, JAMES MICHAEL, special event producer, manager; b. N.Y.C., Dec. 19, 1948; s. Joseph Nicholas and Ann Maria (Horris) C.; m. Nicole Susan Ballenger, Apr. 1, 1978 (div. Jan. 1981); m. Karen Lynn Nelson, July 22, 1984; children: Caitlin Linnea, Emily Jean. AA, Cabrillo Coll., 1973; BA, U. Calif., Santa Cruz, 1975; JD, U. Calif., Berkeley, 1978. Bar: Calif. 1979. Legal rschr. Continuing Edn. of Bar, Berkeley, 1976-77; law clk. Hon. Harry A. Ackley, Woodland, Calif., 1978-79; assoc. Weintraub, Genshlea, Giannoni & Sproul, Sacramento, 1979-80, Turner & Sullivan, Sacramento, 1980-81; pres. Endurance Sports Prodns., Davis, Calif., 1981-84, CAT Sports, Carlsbad, Calif., 1984-94, Event Media, Del Mar, Calif., 1993—; faculty, speaker Internat. Events Group, Chgo., 1992-94; founder Triathlon Fedn. U.S.A., L.A., 1982, v.p., Colorado Springs, Colo., 1984-86. Author: How to Organize a Triathlon, 1982; developer sports events NFL Quarterback Challenge, 1988—, Michelob Night Riders, 1988, Bud Light U.S. Triathlon Series, 1982-93; developer, prodr. Caribbean Sports & Spl. Events Conf., Kingston, Jamaica, 1994-95. Chmn. Parks and Recreation Com., Encinitas, Calif., 1989-92; founder Encinitas Sister City, 1988. Recipient Spl. Achievement award Triathlete Mag., 1990. Mem. Calif. State Bar. Office: Event Media 13765 Mira Montana Dr Del Mar CA 92014

CURLEY, ELMER FRANK, librarian; b. Florence, Pa., Jan. 13, 1929; s. Augustus Wolfe and Bessie (Andrews) C. BA, U. Pitts., 1961; MLS, Carnegie Mellon U., Pitts., 1962; Adv. Cert., U. Pitts., 1964. Ref. librarian U. Pitts., 1962-64; head ref. dept. SUNY-Stony Brook, 1964-67; head pub. svcs. U. Nev.-Las Vegas, 1967-76, asst. dir. libr. svcs., 1976-81, ref. bibliographer, 1981-94, ret., 1994.

CURLEY, JOHN PETER, sports editor; b. N.Y.C., Apr. 12, 1952; s. James J. and Jean (Lyons) C.; children: Jordan, Lindsay. Student, Fairfield U., 1970-72, Boston U., 1972-74. Reporter Ridgewood (N.J.) News, 1975-76; reporter Paterson (N.J.) News, 1976-78, columnist, 1978-79; news editor L.A. Herald Examiner, 1979-81; copy editor San Francisco Chronicle, 1981-87, sports editor, 1987—. Mem. AP, Sports Editors Assn. Roman Catholic. Office: San Francisco Chronicle 901 Mission St San Francisco CA 94103-2905

CUROTTO, MICHAEL LLOYD, professional musician, educator; b. San Mateo, Calif., Dec. 23, 1949; s. Lloyd John and Rena Rose (Canziani) C.; m. Nga Nguyen, Feb. 19, 1989; 1 child, Angela René. AA in Music, Coll. of San Mateo, 1970; BA in Instrumental Music Percussion, San Jose State U., 1973. Head drumset instr. Gelb Music Teaching Inst., Redwood City, 1963—, Michael Curotto Drumset and Percussion Studies, Redwood City, Calif., 1966—. Performed and recorded with numerous rock, jazz, funk, fusion, Latin, Top 40 and casual bands, San Francisco Bay area, now with Rich Martini Orch. and the Karen Drucker Band, others. Mem. Am. Fedn. Musicians. Scientologist. Home: 145 Exeter Ave San Carlos CA 94070-1668 Office: Michael Curotto Drumset and Percussion Studies 2726 Broadway Redwood City CA 94062-1324

CURRAN, JAN BARER, writer, editor, public relations consultant; b. Walla Walla, Wash., May 2, 1937; d. David and Dora (Copeland) Barer; m. Alan Goldberg, June 16, 1957 (div. 1974); children: Lee Goldberg, Karen Goldberg Dinino, Linda Goldberg, Tod Goldberg; m. Don Curran, Dec. 27, 1976 (div. 1978). Student, U. Wash., 1958. Soc. editor, feature writer Lesher Comms., Walnut Creek, Calif., 1976-81; freelance feature writer Oakland (Calif.) Tribune, San Francisco Chronicle, 1981-85; feature writer Diablo Valley Mag., San Francisco Bay area, Calif., 1982-83; author HBJ, N.Y.C., 1976-80; editor Santa Barbara Writer's Conf., 1980-95; pub. rels. cons. Jan Curran Pub. Rels., Walnut Creek/Palm Springs, Calif., 1974-95; soc. editor, columnist The Desert Sun, Palm Springs, 1987—; cons. Watts Industries, Oakland, Calif., 1983-84, San Ysidro Ranch, Santa Barbara, 1975-89, Bay Area Optometric Soc., San Francisco Bay area, 1980-84, Cancer Care Corp., Salt Lake City, 1985-87; mem. adv. bd. Open Space Found., Walnut Creek, 1983-85, Walnut Festival, Walnut Creek, 1984-85; speaker San Diego Writers Conf., 1984-87, Romance Writers of Am. Conv., San Diego, 1984, The Springs, Rancho Mirage, Calif., 1990, Lions Clubs, Kiwanis and Rotary, Palm Springs, 1992, 93, 94. Author: The Statue of Liberty is Cracking Up, 1978, 79 (Honorarium San Diego Writers Conf., Merit award Santa Barbara Writers Conf., Gov.'s award/State of Wash., Walla Walla Pub. Libr. award); columnist: (newspaper) The Contra Costa Times, 1977, 78 (Outstanding Achievement award, Oakland Airport Achievement award); author, feature writer book and mag. articles, 1979 (Merit award Santa Barbara Writers Conf.). Mem. adv. bd. Am. Heart Assn., Walnut Creek, 1974-76, Am. Cancer Soc., Walnut Creek, 1979-82; bd. dirs. Vision Coun. San Francisco Bay Area, 1980, Nat. Panhellenic Couns., San Francisco Bay area, 1974-77, West Coast Opera League, Palm Springs, 1994-95, Palm Springs Youth Ctr., 1993, 94, 95; vol. tchr. Mt. Diablo Sch. Dist., Walnut Creek, 1976, speaker, 1975-80; leader 4-H, Walnut Creek, 1974; ADL chmn. B'nai Brith, Oakland, 1965; founding mem. Lupus Support Group, San Francisco Bay area, 1976; mem. bd. dirs. pub. info. Contra Cost Unit Am. Cancer Soc.; model Fashion Show for Desert Hosp., Palm Springs, 1991; celebrity participant Cerebal Palsy Telethon, Palm Springs, 1989-92; interviewee radio and TV Lupus Pub. Info., Cathedral City, Rancho Mirage, Palm Desert, Palm Springs, 1992; speaker Children's Orthopedic Hosp., Palm Springs, 1994, Desert Hosp., 1993. Named Princess: Mardi Gras Ball, San Francisco Children's Hosp., 1974, Woman of Yr., San Francisco Panhellenic, 1975, 76, Woman of Distinction, Friends of Hebrew U., 1991; recipient Proclamation of Honor, Congressman Al McCandless, Riverside County, 1992; Jan Curran Day named in her honor City of Palm Springs, 1992, A Salute to Jan Curran, A Woman of Valour, Nat. Jewish Hosp., Denver, 1992. Mem. So. Calif. Book Publicists, Young Profls. (McCallum Theater, Bob Hope Cultural Ctr. Desert Hosp., Desert Mus.), U. So. Calif. Law League of the Desert, Santa Barbara Screenwriters Assn., U. Wash. Alums, Wash. State U. Alums (hon. cougar award), Desert Press Club, Womens Press Club (Press Woman of the Yr.). Home: 803 E El Conquistador Palm Springs CA 92262-3246 Office: The Desert Sun 750 N Gene Autry Trl Palm Springs CA 92262-5463

CURRAN, MARK ALBERT, investment banker; b. St. Louis, May 6, 1954; s. William Henry and Esther A. (Borgwald) C.; m. Kristine Charnowski, June 1, 1985. BA in Polit. Sci., U. Calif., Berkeley, 1976; M in Urban Planning, San Jose State U., 1979. Adminstrv. asst. to city mgr. City of Foster City (Calif.), 1977-78; sr. v.p. City Bond & Mortgage Corp., Oakland, Calif., 1978-85; sr. v.p. Sutro & Co., San Francisco, 1985-90, mng. dir. pub. fin., 1990—; lectr. pub. fin. San Jose State U., Berkeley, 1980—; dir. Calif. City Mgmt. Found., Sacramento, 1988—. Mem. Pacific Securities Assn., Calif. City Mgmt. Found. (dir., treas. 1988—), Calif. Mcpl. Forum, San Francisco Bond Club. Roman Catholic. Home: 1976 Manzanita Dr Oakland CA 94611-1138 Office: Sutro & Co 201 California St San Francisco CA 94111-5002

CURRAN, MICHAEL HARVEY, finance executive; b. Pasadena, Calif., Mar. 5, 1948; s. James Albert and Jane Eleanor (Harvey) C.; m. Vicki Ann Rowland, Apr. 22, 1978; children: Sean, Robert. BBA, Loyola U., 1970; MBA, U. So. Calif., 1971. Cert. real estate broker Calif. V.p. Wells Fargo Bank, L.A., 1971-79; exec. v.p., CFO Real Property Resources, Torrance, Calif., 1979-90, Doric Devel., Alameda, Calif., 1990-93; CFO, treas. Continental Devel., El Segundo, Calif., 1993—; dir. Datasystems, Encino, Calif., 1986, also pres.; dir. Harbor Bay Bus. Park Assn., Alameda, 1990-93. Project dir. Jr. C. of C., L.A., 1973-79; mem. Internat. Coun. Shopping Ctrs., L.A., 1983-90. Home: 2311 John St Manhattan Beach CA 90266-2615 Office: Continental Devel Corp 2041 Rosecrans Ave El Segundo CA 90245-4707

CURRAN, NEIL WILLIS, state police chief; b. Raton, N.Mex., June 12, 1936; s. Cornelius R. and Buelah (Gibson) C.; m. Beatrice J. Ginther, Apr. 27, 1957; children: Kathy Jean, Robert Neil, Larry Troy. B of Agriculture and Elec. Engring., N.Mex. State U., 1959. With uniform div. N.Mex. State Police, 1965-69, with criminal investigations div., 1969-82, spl. investigations and intelligence div., 1969-70, narcotics div., 1970-74, ops. sgt. and adminstrv. asst. to bur. comdr., 1975-79, ops. lt., air detail lt., 1979-82, asst. div. comdr., adminstrv. and operational supr., 1981-82, property bur. comdr., 1982-83, asst. div. comdr. criminal investigations div., 1983-86, acting comdr. criminal investigations div., 1986-87, acting chief, 1987, chief dept. pub. safety, 1987—; instr. N.Mex. Dept. Corrections, Santa Fe, 1975-81, Criminal Investigations Div. In-Svc. Tng. Sch., 1980-81, N.Mex. State Police Recruit Sch., 1973-82; N.Mex. rep. Southwest Border Initiative, 1986—, U.S. Customs Svc. Steering Com., 1987—, Nat. Narcotics Border Interdiction System Steering Com., 1987—; testified numerous spl. hearings. Mem. Gov.'s Red Ribbon Campaign, Santa Fe, 1988, Law Enforcement Acad. Bd., 1988, Safer N.Mex. Now, 1988, Office of Med. Investigators Bd., 1988; mem. exec. bd. Turn in a Pusher, Albuquerque, 1988. Mem. Internat. Assn. Chiefs of Police, Nat. Narcotics Officers' Assn., Nat. Drug Enforcement Officers Assn. (pres. 1984-85, 85-86), N.Mex. Sheriff's and Police Assn., Fraternal Order of Police. Democrat. Home: 2026 Calle Perdiz Santa Fe NM 87505-5432 Office: Dept Pub Safety N Mex State Police Div PO Box 1628 Santa Fe NM 87504-1628

CURRY, JANE KATHLEEN, theater educator; b. Rock Island, Ill., Nov. 29, 1964; d. Richard Alan and Barbara Jean (Smith) C. BFA in Theater, U. Ill., 1985; MA in Theater, Brown U., 1987; PhD in Theater, CUNY, 1991. Asst. prof. theater Hunter Coll.-CUNY; asst. prof. theater and speech Mont. State U., Havre, 1993—. Author: Nineteenth-Century American Women Theater Managers, 1994. Mem. Am. Soc. Theater Rsch., Assn. for Theater in Higher Edn.

CURRY, LANDON, political science educator; b. Corpus Christi, Tex., Jan. 22, 1955; s. Landon and Connie C. (Cacciola) C.; m. Ashley Christine Grosse, July 11, 1992. BA, U. Tex., Austin, 1976; MA, U. Calif., Berkeley, 1977, PhD, 1984. Prof. U. Calif., Berkeley, 1977-82, U. Ga., Athens, 1983-84, U. Tex., Austin, 1985-92, Southwest Tex. State U., San Marcos, 1986-91, U. Idaho, Moscow, 1992—; cons. in field. Author: Politics of Fiscal Stress, 1990; contbr. articles to profl. jours. Dir. State Govt. Internship Program, Austin, 1986-92, Moscow, 1992-94. Mem. Am. Polit. Sci. Assn., Southwest Polit. Sci. Assn., Pacific Northwest Polit. Sci. Assn., U.S. Handball Assn. Home: 503 E C St Moscow ID 83843-2729 Office: U Idaho Dept Polit Sci 205 Adminstrn Moscow ID 83844

CURRY, WILLIAM SIMS, procurement manager; b. Mt. Vernon, Washington, Feb. 6, 1938; s. Eli Herbert Curry and Winona Geraldine (Davis) Mickelson; m. Kirsten Ingeborg Arms, May 20, 1971; children: William II, Kevin, Randal, Kim Cannova, Derek. BS in Bus. Mgmt., Fla. State U., 1967; MBA, Ohio State U., 1968. Cert. profl. contracts mgr. Asst. purchasing officer Stanford (Calif.) Linear Accelerator Ctr., 1977-80; subcontract adminstr. Lockheed Missiles & Space Co., Sunnyvale, Calif., 1980-81; materials mgr. Altus Corp., San Jose, Calif., 1981-86; purchasing mgr. Litton Electron Devices, San Carlos, Calif., 1986—; bd. dirs. Industry Coun. for Small Bus. Devel., Sunnyvale, 1992—, v.p. programs, 1992-93, exec. v.p., 1994-95, pres., 1995—. Contbr. articles to profl. jours. Capt. USAF, 1955-77. Decorated Meritorious Svc. medal with one oak leaf cluster, USAF, 1977. Fellow Nat. Contract Mgmt. Assn.; mem. Am. Mensa, Ltd., Beta Gamma Sigma. Republican. Home: 8289 Del Monte Ave Newark CA 94560-2129 Office: Comm & Power Indus 811 Hansen Way PO Box 50750 Palo Alto CA 94303-0750

CURTIN, DAVID STEPHEN, newswriter; b. Kansas City, Mo., Dec. 18, 1955; s. Gerald and Nadine (Pemberton) C. BS in Journalism, U. Colo., 1978. Newswriter Littleton (Colo.) Independent, 1976-77, Boulder (Colo.) Daily Camera, 1978-79, Greeley (Colo.) Daily Tribune, 1979-84, Durango (Colo.) Herald, 1984-87, Colorado Springs (Colo.) Gazette Telegraph, 1987—; Pulitzer Prize juror, 1991-92. Recipient Pulitzer Prize for feature writing, 1990. Democrat. Methodist.

CURTIN, THOMAS LEE, ophthalmologist; b. Columbus, Ohio, Sept. 9, 1932; s. Leo Anthony and Mary Elizabeth (Burns) C.; m. Constance L. Sallman; children: Michael, Gregory, Thomas, Christopher. BS, Loyola U., L.A., 1954; MD, U. So. Calif., 1957; cert. navy flight surgeon U.S. Naval Sch. Aviation Medicine, 1959. Intern, Ohio State U. Hosp., 1957-58; resident in ophthalmology U.S. Naval Hosp., San Diego, 1961-64; practice medicine specializing in ophthalmology, Oceanside, Calif., 1967—; mem. staff Tri City, Palomar Meml., Scripps Meml. Mercy hosps.; sci. adv. bd. So. Calif. Soc. Prevention Blindness, 1973-76; bd. dirs. North Coast Surgery Ctr., Oceanside, 1987—; cons. in field. Trustee, Carlsbad (Calif.) Unified Sch. Dist., 1975-83, pres., 1979, 82, 83; trustee Carlsbad Libr., 1990—, pres, 1993. Served as officer M.C., USN, 1958-67. Diplomate Am. Bd. Ophthalmology. Mem. Am., Calif. med. assns., San Diego County Med. Soc., Am. Acad. Ophthalmology, Aerospace Med. Assn., San Diego Acad. Ophthalmology (pres. 1979), Calif. Assn. Ophthalmology (dir.), Carlsbad Rotary, El Camino Country Club. Republican. Roman Catholic. Office: 3231 Waring Ct Ste S Oceanside CA 92056-4510

CURTIS, FRANCINE MARCO, nurse; b. Can., Nov. 15, 1948; m. William M. Curtis, May 20, 1977. ADN, L.A. City Coll., 1971; BS in Health Sci., Calif. State U., 1985; MN in Med.-Surg. Nursing, UCLA, 1992. Cert. infection control practitioner, 1994. House supr. Valley Park Med. Ctr., Canoga Park, Calif., 1984-85; infection control coord. Midway Hosp., L.A., 1985; utilization mgmt. coord. Hosp. of Good Samaritan, L.A., 1985-86; quality rev. nurse St. Vincent Med. Ctr., L.A., 1986-88; nurse epidemiologist UCLA Med. Ctr., 1989-90, 93—, staff nurse med.-surg., 1990-93;, 1993—. Mem. ANA (cert. med.-surg. 1991—), Assn. Profls. in Infection Control & Epidemiology, Sigma Theta Tau (Gamma Tau chpt. 1992). Office: 10833 Le Conte Ave Los Angeles CA 90024

CURTIS, GARY LYNN, accountant; b. Castro Valley, Calif., Feb. 3, 1956; s. Bill J. and Rosemary (Endsley) C.; m. Joyce Ann Ruddock, Jan. 1, 1993; 1 stepchild, Melanie Ruddock. BS, Phillips U., Enid, Okla., 1980. CPA, Okla. Mgr. Ernst and Whinney, Oklahoma City, 1980-86; sr. mgr. Deloitte & Touche, Dallas and L.A., 1987—; instr. Deloitte & Touche Reorgn. Svcs. Group and Mergers and Acquisition Group. Mem. Assn. Insolvency Accts. Home: 4417 Candleberry Ave Seal Beach CA 90740-3024 Office: Deloitte & Touche 1000 Wilshire Blvd Los Angeles CA 90017-2457

CURTIS, GLEN RUSSELL, program manager; b. Ogden, Utah, Oct. 17, 1947; s. Von R. and Barbara (Fougler) C.; m. Nancy Norr, Dec. 1, 1971; children: Tamara, Brian, Cathy, Angie, Julie, Jared. BS in Journalism and Polit. Sci., Weber State Coll., Ogden, 1972; MBA, U. Phoenix, 1992. Bus. mgr. Signpost, Ogden, 1970-72; prin. various bus., Tremonton, Utah, 1975-87; pub. The Leader, Tremonton, 1976-87; proposal mgr. Thiokol Corp., Brigham City, Utah, 1987-90, project mgr., 1990-93, sr. product mgr., 1993—. Scoutmaster, commr. Silver Beaver Lake Bonneville coun. Boy Scouts Am., Ogden, 1976—; chmn. state rules com. Rep. County Com., Salt Lake City, 1976-86; bd. dirs. Headstart, Area Aging Coun., Alcohol and Drug Bd., Logan, Utah, 1983-87; campaign dir. Wolthius for Congress, Ogden, 1972; county commr. Box Elder County, Brigham City, 1983-87; mem. bd. dirs., vice chair Bear River Area Bd. of Health, Logan, 1983-87, 93—; mem. bd. dirs. Utah Assn. of Local Bds. of Health, 1993—. 1st lt. USAF, 1972-75. Decorated Commendation medal; recipient Outstanding Svc. to Mental Health award Intermountain Assn. Mental Health, 1985, Outstanding Svc. to Job Tng. Utah Assn. Pvt. Industry Couns., 1987, Andy Rytting Community Svc. award Bear River Valley C. of C. 1988. Mormon. Home: 564 S 600 W Tremonton UT 84337-1745 Office: Thiokol Corp Space Ops PO Box 707 Brigham City UT 84302-0707

CURTIS, JESSE WILLIAM, JR., retired federal judge; b. San Bernardino, Calif., Dec. 26, 1905; s. Jesse William and Ida L. (Seymour) C.; m. Mildred F. Mort, Aug. 24, 1930; children: Suzanne, Jesse W., Clyde Hamilton, Christopher Cowles. A.B., U. Redlands, 1928, LL.D., 1973; J.D., Harvard U., 1931. Bar: Calif. 1931. Pvt. practice, 1931-35; mem. firms Guthrie & Curtis, San Bernardino, 1935-40, Curtis & Curtis, 1946-50, Curtis, Knauf, Henry & Farrell, 1950-53; judge Superior Ct. of Calif., 1953-62; judge U.S. Dist. Ct. (cen. dist.) Calif., 1962-90, ret., 1990; with Jud. Arbitration and Mediations Svc., L.A., 1990—; rep. dist. ct. on Jud. Council U.S., 1972-74. Chmn. San Bernardino Sch. Bd., 1942-46, mem., 1946-49; mem. Del Rosa Bd. Edn., 1950-53; chmn. San Bernardino County Heart Fund; dir., past pres. YMCA; bd. dirs. GoodWill Industries, Crippled Children's Soc., Arrowhead United Fund; adv. bd. Community Hosp. Mem. ABA, Calif. State Bar, Orange County Bar Assn., Am. Judicature Soc., Am. Law Inst., Newport Harbor Yacht Club, Phi Delta Phi. Democrat. Congregationalist. Home: 305 Evening Star Ln Newport Beach CA 92660-5704

CURTIS, JOHN BARRY, bishop; b. June 19, 1933; s. Harold Boyd and Eva B. (Saunders) C.; m. Patricia Emily Simpson, 1959; four children. BA, U. Toronto, 1955, LTh, 1958; student, Theol. Coll., Chichester, Sussex, Eng.; DD (hon.), Trinity Coll., 1985, U. Toronto, 1985. Ordained to deacon The Anglican Ch. of Can., 1958, priest, 1959. Asst. curate Holy Trinity, Pembroke, Ont., 1958-61; rector Parish of March, Kanota, Ont., 1961-65, St. Stephen's Ch., Buckingham, Que., 1965-69, All Saints (Westboro), Ottawa, Ont., 1969-78; program dir. Diocese of Ottawa, 1978-80; rector Christ Ch., Elbow Park, Calgary, Alta., 1980-83; bishop Diocese of Calgary, 1983-94; archbishop Calgary-Met. of Rupert's Land, 1994—. Mem. Ranchmen's Club (Calgary). Office: Diocese Calgary, 3015 Glencoe Rd SW, Calgary, AB Canada T2S 2L9

CURTIS, LINDA JENARIE, genealogist; b. Bend, Oreg., June 4, 1941; d. Joel Howard and Elnora H. (Allgood) Clift; m. Robert P. Temple, Dec. 27, 1959 (div. 1968); children: Steven, Laura Mazzella; m. Roger Ward Curtis, Apr. 5, 1969; children: Benjamin, Brian. Grad. high sch., Pendleton, Oreg. 1st v.p. Colo. Coun. Geneal. Socs., Denver, 1988-89. Editor (jour.) Allgood Ancestry, 1988. Mem. Nat. Geneal. Soc., Assn. Profl. Genealogists, Colo. Assn. Profl. Genealogists, Colo. Geneal. Soc. (instr., edn. coord. 1992), Aurora Geneal. Soc. (pres. 1988, 89, instr., genealogist 1992—). Home: 3709 S Mission Pky Aurora CO 80013-2405

CURTIS, MARIE THERESE DODGE, executive assistant; b. Niagara Falls, N.Y., May 1, 1935; d. Edward Francis and Agnes Anne (Dell) Dodge; m. Charles R. Curtis, July 30, 1967 (div. 1979). Cert., Katharine Gibbs Sch., N.Y.C., 1956. Corp. sec., dir. Topa Equities, Ltd., L.A., 1964—; corp. sec., dir. Ace Beverage Co., L.A., 1964—, Paradise Beverages, Inc., Honolulu, 1980—, West Indies Corp., Saint Thomas, U.S. Virgin Islands, 1982—. Office: Topa Equities Ltd # 1400 1800 Avenue of the Stars Los Angeles CA 90067

CURTIS, MICHAEL, food products executive; b. 1922; s. Glen C. Real estate broker Yuma, Ariz., 1950-72; with Glen Curtis, Inc., Yuma, Ariz., 1971-72. Office: Glen Curtis Inc 4400 E Us Highway 80 Yuma AZ 85365-7518*

CURTIS, NANCY NELL, publisher, rancher; b. Duncan, Okla., June 6, 1947; d. William Herbert Jr. and Edwina (Crabtree) Johnson; m. Douglas J. Curtis, July 23, 1966; 1 child, Wendy J.J. AA, Casper Coll., 1967; BA, U. Wyo., 1969; grad. in pub., U. Denver, 1986. Tchr. English, Douglas and Glendo (Wyo.) Schs., 1969-79; advt. mgr. White's Marine Ctrs., Glendo, 1984-91; rancher, Glendo, 1969—; pub. High Plains Press, Glendo, 1984—. Author: Visions of Wyoming, 1994; contbr. articles to various publs. Mem., clk. Platte County (Wyo.) Sch. Dist. 1, 1980-84; bd. dirs. Wyo. Coun. on Arts, 1994—. Recipient Wrangler award Nat. Cowboy Hall of Fame, Oklahoma City, 1991, 94. Mem. Rocky Mountain Book Pubs. Assn., Western Writers Am., Wyo. Writers (pres., treas., Emmie award 1982). Office: High Plains Press 539 Cassa Rd Glendo WY 82213-9628

CURTIS, ROBERT ORIN, research forester; b. Portland, Maine, Oct. 17, 1927; s. Walter Edson and Ruby (Whitehouse) C.; m. Helen Locke Thompson, Aug. 16, 1952; children: Stephen, Anne, Ruth. BS in Plant Sci., Yale U., 1950, MF, 1951; PhD in Silviculture and Biometrics, U. Wash., 1965. Rsch. forester Northeastern Forest Experiment Sta., U.S. Forest Svc., various locations, 1951-62; mensurationist Pacific N.W. Rsch. Sta., Portland, Oreg., 1965-78; prin. mensurationist Pacific N.W. Rsch. Sta., Olympia, Wash., 1978—; affiliate prof. Coll. Forest Resources, U. Wash., Seattle, 1988—. Mem. editorial bd. Forest Sci., Washington, 1971-85; contbr. articles to profl. jours. Served with U.S. Army, 1946-47. Mem. Soc. Am. Foresters. Home: 2312 Killarney Ct NW Olympia WA 98502-3445 Office: Pacific NW Rsch Sta 3625 93d Ave SW Olympia WA 98512

CURTIS, SEAN PATRICK, physician; b. Boulder, Colo., Nov. 29, 1962; s. George William and Mary (Magrath) C.; m. Ngozi Babette Okezie, June 6, 1992;. BA in Physics cum laude, Colo. Coll., 1981-85; MD, MPH, Tufts U., 1986-90. Med. lic. Colo.; diplomate Am. Bd. Med. Examiners. Internal medicine intern U. Colo. Health Scis. Ctr., Denver, 1990-91; internal medicine resident U. Colo. Health Scis. Ctr., Colorado Springs, 1991-93; staff physician dept. internal medicine Kaiser Permanente, Denver, 1993—; inst. English as Second Lang. Program, Denver., 1985-86; emergency room vol. Penrose Community Hosp., Colorado Springs, 1984-85. Home: 937 15th St Boulder CO 80302

CURTIS, THOM, marriage and family therapist, educator; b. Seattle, July 6, 1953; s. Robert L. and Kathleen E. (Hughley) C.; m. Susan Ann Burnham, Febr. 13, 1976; children: Rebecca, Robert, Aaron, Shawn, Christopher. BFA in Comm., Pacific Lutheran U., 1978; MS in family and marriage therapy, Mont. State, 1992; Phd in Marriage and Family Sci., Utah State, 1995. Gen. mgr. R.M. Kulski Advtg., Federal Way, Wash., 1976-78; acct. exec. KTAC-Radio, Tacoma, 1978-79; gen. sales mgr. KLAY-FM, KQLA-AM, Tacoma, 1979; gen. mgr. KOUS-TV, Billings, Mont., 1980-83; v.p., gen. mgr. Big Horn Comms., Billings, 1983-87; pres. Curtis Broadcast Cons., Bozeman, Mont., 1987-92; instr. Utah State U., Logan, Utah, 1992—; family therapist Evergreen Family Therapy, Logan, 1993—; v.p., dir. Big Horn Comms., Billings, Mont., 1982-87; pres. Telecrafter Broadcasting, Bozeman, Mont., 1982—; v.p., dir. No. Plains Broadcasting, Dickinson, N.D., 1982-84. Author: (book) Comprehensive Concordance, 1973; contbr. chpt. to encyclopedia, numerous articles to journ. in field. Scout coach Boy Scouts of Am., Bozeman, Logan, 1987-94; county chmn. Am. Red Cross Disaster Svcs., Logan, 1992-95, state chmn., Salt Lake City, 1994-95; swimming official U.S. Swimming, 1993-95. Recipient Presdl. fellow Utah

State U., 1992-93, Grad. Sch. fellow, 1993-94. Mem. APA, ACA, Nat. Coun. Family Rels., Utah Assn. Marriage & Family Therapy, Utah Coun. for Family Rels. Reorganized Ch. of Jesus Christ of Latter-Day Saints. Home: 487 E 180 S Smithfield UT 84335 Office: Evergreen Family Therapy Ctr 167 E 200 N Logan UT 84321

CURTIS, WILLIAM SHEPLEY, radiologist; b. St. Louis, Sept. 11, 1915; s. Edward Glion and Isabel (Wallace) C.; m. Frances Lois Elmer, Jan. 3, 1942; children: William Shepley Jr., David Jennings, Anne Goodson Curtis Curfman. AB, Dartmouth Coll., 1936; MD, Washington U., St. Louis, 1940. Diplomate Am. Bd. Radiology. Intern St. Luke's Hosp., St. Louis, 1940-41; resident St. Louis Maternity Hosp., 1941, Mallinkrodt Inst. Radiology, 1945-48; radiologist Wasson and Bouslog, Denver, 1948-52; radiologist, ptnr. Boulder (Colo.) Med. Ctr., 1953-83; cons. Wardenburg Student Health Ctr. U. Colo., Boulder, 1953-91; past trustee Colo. Blue Shield, Denver, cons. Past chmn. Colo. Found. Med. Care, Denver, Boulder County Health Com.; mem. Colo. Health Occupations Adv. Com., Denver; bd. dirs. Boulder Day Nursery. Lt. col. M.C., U.S. Army, 1941-46. Recipient U. Colo. medal, 1992. Fellow Am. Coll. Radiology (emeritus, past councilor); mem. Radiol. Soc. N.Am., Colo. Radiol. Soc. (past pres.), Colo. Med. Soc. (past pres., del.), Boulder County Med. Soc. (past pres.), Boulder Town and Gown, Rotary (past pres. Boulder chpt.). Unitarian. Home and Office: 3151 6th St Boulder CO 80304-2507

CURTISS, ELDEN F., bishop; b. Baker, Oreg., June 16, 1932; s. Elden F. and Mary (Neiger) C. B.A., St. Edward Sem., Seattle, M.Div., 1958; M.A. in Ednl. Adminstrn, U. Portland, 1965; postgrad., Fordham U., U. Notre Dame. Ordained priest Roman Catholic Ch., 1958; campus chaplain, 1959-64, 65-68; supt. schs. Diocese of Baker (Oreg.), 1962-70; pastor, 1968-70; pres./rector Mt. Angel Sem., Benedict, Oreg., 1972-76; mem. bd. regents Mt. Angel Sem., Benedict, 1990—; bishop of Helena (Mont.), 1976—; mem. priests senate Archdiocese of Portland, 1974-76; mem. ecumenical ministries State of Oreg., 1972; mem. pastoral services com. Oreg. State Hosp., Salem, 1975-76; bishop Diocese Helena, Mont., 1976—; mem. adminstrv. bd. Nat. Conf. Cath. Bishops, 1976-80, 89—; mem. pro-life com., 1977-89, chmn. com. on vocations, 1989—, mem. com. on priestly formation, also mem. com.. Nat. Cath. News Svc., bd. dirs. Cath. Mut. Relief Soc., 1977—, Mont. Cath. Conf., 1976—, Mont. Cath. Social Svcs., Inc.; mem. N.W. Assn. Bishops and Major Religious Superiors, 1976—, Mont. Assn. Chs., 1976—, bd. regents U Portland, bishops and pres's com ednl. dept. U.S. Cath. Conf.; chancellor Carroll Coll., Helena. Mem. Nat. Cath. Ednl. Assn. (Outstanding Educator 1972, bishops and pres's com. coll. dept.). Office: Archdiocese of Omaha 100 N 62nd St Omaha NE 68132-2702*

CURY, IVAN N., producer, director, educator; b. N.Y.C., June 29, 1937; s. Joel and Anne (Lechowitz) C.; m. Lynda Ruth Stone, June 24, 1962 (div. June 1987); children: James, Peter; m. Barbara Harris, Feb. 16, 1992. BFA, Carnegie Tech., 1959; MFA, Boston U., 1960. Producer, dir. Sta. WNET, N.Y.C., 1963-71, CBS-TV, N.Y.C., 1971-73; freelance producer, dir. N.Y.C. and Los Angeles, 1973—; prof. TV directing, acting UCLA, 1979-91; Calif. State U., L.A., 1991—; radio, TV coms. Mens Wearhouse, 1985—. Writer, producer, narrator: (video) Belgrade Through Eyes of Americans, 1985; (film) Postcards from Yugoslavia, 1987; dir.: (TV series, spls.) The Young and the Restless, 1985-86, Nashville Remembers Elvis, Elvis Remembered, Soul!, Miss Black Teenage America, Camera Three, Woman!; producer, dir. various commls. Served with U.S. Army, 1960-61. Recipient Fulbright award Council for Internat. Exchange of Scholars, Yugoslavia, 1985. Mem. Dirs. Guild Am., Acad. TV Arts and Scis. Home: 15726 Milbank St Encino CA 91436-1637 Office: Calif State U 5151 State University Dr Los Angeles CA 90032-4221

CUSANOVICH, MICHAEL ANTHONY, biochemistry educator; b. Los Angeles, Mar. 2, 1942; s. Lucian Anthony and Ruth Elizabeth (McElroy) C.; m. Carol Owens, June 15, 1963 (div. May 1973); children: Kurt Michael, Carrie Elizabeth; m. Marilyn Jean Wainio, Mar. 31, 1980; 1 child, Darren Anthony. BS, U. Pacific, 1963; PhD, U. Calif., San Diego, 1967, postgrad., 1967-68; postgrad., Cornell U., 1968-69. Asst. prof. biochemistry U. Ariz., Tucson, 1969-74, assoc. prof., 1974-79, prof., 1979—, acting vice-dean grad. coll., 1987-88, v.p. rsch., dean grad. coll., 1988—, interim provost, 1992; program dir. NSF, Washington, 1981-82; cons. Univ. Patents, Inc., Westport, Conn., 1983-88. Contbr. articles to profl. jours. Fellow NIH, 1968-69; recipient Career Devel. award NIH, 1975-80. Mem. Am. Soc. Biol. Chemists, Am. Chem. Soc., Am. Photobiology Soc. Republican. Office: U Ariz Dept Biochemistry Tucson AZ 85721

CUSHING, JAMES BYERS, English language educator; b. Palo Alto, Calif., Aug. 1, 1953; s. Frederic Sanford and Jean Marie (Byers) C.; m. Beth Murray Wettergreen, June 16, 1979 (div. Apr. 1986); 1 child, Iris Marble; m. Karen Sue Christiansen, June 21, 1986; 1 child, Alexander Miles. BA with honors, U. Calif., Santa Cruz, 1975; MA, U. Calif., Irvine, 1977, PhD, 1983. Tchg. asst. English dept. U. Calif., Irvine, 1977-83; instr. English dept. Pasadena (Calif.) Coll., 1983; lectr. English dept. U. Calif., Davis, 1983-84; instr. English dept. Cuesta Coll., San Luis Obispo, Calif., 1985—, Allan Hancock Coll., Santa Maria, Calif., 1987-89; lectr. English dept. Calif. Poly., San Luis Obispo, 1989—. Author: You and the Night and the Music, 1991. Jazz deejay KCBX-FM, San Luis Obispo, 1986—. Named Warlord of the Subculture, Renegade Mag., Wis., 1994. Mem. MLA, Internat. Assn. for Philosophy and Lit., N.Am. Nietzsche Soc., Beyond Baroque. Home: 966 Mesa St Morro Bay CA 93442-2623 Office: English Dept Calif Poly State Univ San Luis Obispo CA 93407

CUSHING, RICHARD GOLLÉ, journalist; b. N.Y.C., Apr. 30, 1917; s. Melvin Abbott and Blanche (Goll) C.; m. Nancy Heizer, Mar. 23, 1940; children: Jeffrey, Martha, Lincoln. BA, San Francisco State Coll., 1945; PhD (hon.), U. Havana, Cuba, 1955. Reporter AP, San Francisco, 1935-42; war corr. AP, PTO, 1943-45; bur. chief AP, Shanghai, 1945-46; news editor AP, San Francisco, 1947-49; fgn. svc. officer USIA, Santiago, Chile, 1950-65, Cuba, Nairobi and Caracas, Venezuela, 1953-65; acting dir. Voice of Am., Washington, 1966-69; mem. Sr. Seminar on Fgn. Policy, Washington, 1970-71; San Francisco corr. Voice of Am. USIA, 1977—. Author: Too Pure for the Hyenas, 1976. Mem. grand jury Marin County, Calif., 1984. Mem. World Affairs Coun. (San Francisco chpt.), Commonwealth Club (San Francisco), Press Club San Francisco, Nat. Geog. Soc. Democrat. Home and Office: 389 Molino Ave Mill Valley CA 94941-3301

CUSHMAN, THOMAS HENRY, sports editor, columnist; b. St. Louis, June 13, 1934; s. Thomas H. and Martha E. (Phillips) C.; m. Lois Rae Jordanger, June 3, 1961; 1 child, Scott Thomas. AB, S.E. Mo. State U., 1956; BJ, U. Mo., 1959. Asst. sports editor Gazette Telegraph, Colorado Springs, Colo., 1959-66; reporter, columnist Phila. Daily News, 1966-82; sports editor, columnist San Diego Tribune, 1982-92, San Diego Union-Tribune, 1992—. Bd. dirs. High Five Am., San Diego, 1990—; sponsor Midnight Basketball, San Diego, 1993—. 1st lt. USMC, 1955-58. Recipient Sportswriter of Yr. award Nat. Sportswriters & Sportscasters Assn., 1965, 78, Internat. Fleischer award for boxing journalism excellence, 1981, Ring of Truth award Copley Press, 1982, 85. Mem. Basketball Writers Assn., Pro Football Writers, Boxing Writers Assn., Baseball Writers Assn. Am., Golf Writers Assn. Presbyterian. Home: 4888 Casals Pl San Diego CA 92124-1502 Office: San Diego Union-Tribune PO Box 191 San Diego CA 92112-4106

CUSICK, JOSEPH DAVID, science administrator, retired; b. Chgo., Oct. 18, 1929; s. Joseph M. and Rose (Gerrity) C.; m. Kathryn Vermilya Moore, Feb. 2, 1952; children: Stephen, Anne, Eileen, Michael, Joseph R., Mary, James, John. BA, Stanford U., 1951; postgrad. in Law, U. San Francisco, 1956-58, U. Santa Clara, 1956-58; MBA, U. Santa Clara, 1963; postgrad. fellow in Bus., Stanford U., 1972-73; MS in Cybernetic Systems, San Jose State U., 1976; postgrad., Def. Systems Mgmt. Coll., Air Force Inst. Tech. Tech. writer Magna Power Tool Corp., Menlo Park, Calif., 1956, McGraw-Hill Publishing Co., San Francisco, 1956-57; adminstrv. asst. Lockheed Missiles and Space Co., Sunnyvale, Calif., 1958-61; supr. Satellite Test Ctr., Sunnyvale, 1962-68; civilian mgr./exec. dep. dir. Air Force Consol. Space Test Ctr., Sunnyvale, 1968-91 (ret.). Editor Libr. Assocs. Newsletter, Stanford Assocs. Report; contbr. articles to Def. Mgmt. Jour., The Lamp. Bd. dirs. Los Gatos (Calif.) Mus. Assn.; Lector St. Mary's Ch., Los Gatos; vol. fundraiser Stanford U.; active Stanford Hist. Soc.; adv. coun. Stanford U. Librs., 1995—; sec. Los Gatos Mus. Assn., 1993-95. With USN, 1951-56, lt. commdr. Res. ret. Recipient Gold Spike award Stanford U., 1973, Stanford Assocs. award 1995, Block S pin 1986, 1991, Outstanding Civilian Svc. medal 1991. Mem. AIAA, VFW, Stanford Arms Control and Internat. Security Group, Stanford Alumni, Stanford and Santa Clara Bus. Sch. Alumni Assns., Stanford U. Librs. (bd. dirs. 1976-88, 1994-97, chmn. 1984-86, 1994-95, Stanford U. Librs. adv. coun. 1995-98), Stanford Music Guild, Commonwealth Club Calif., Saratoga Mens Club (sec./treas. 1995—), Stanford Block S. Soc. and Buck Club, Los Gatos Mus. Assn. (sec. 1993-95), Nat. Assn. Ret. Fed. Employees, No. Calif. Golf Assn., Sigma Delta Chi (past pres. local chpt.).

CUSUMANO, JAMES ANTHONY, chemical company executive, former recording artist; b. Elizabeth, N.J., Apr. 14, 1942; s. Charles Anthony and Carmella Madeline (Catalano) C.; m. Jane LaVerne Melvin, June 15, 1985; children: Doreen Ann, Polly Jean. BA, Rutgers U., 1964, PhD, 1967; grad. Exec. Mktg. Program, Stanford U., 1981, Harvard U., 1988. Mgr. catalyst rsch. Exxon Rsch. and Engring. Co., Linden, N.J., 1967-74; pres., chief exec. officer, founder Catalytica Inc., Mountain View, Calif., 1974-85, chmn., 1985—, also bd. dirs.; pres., CEO, Catalytica Fine Chems., Inc., Mountain View, Calif., 1993—; also bd. dirs.; lectr. chem. engring. Stanford U., 1978, Rutgers U., 1966-67, Charles D. Hurd lectr. Northwestern U., 1989-90; advisor Fulbright scholar program Inst. Internat. Edn.; spkr. to chem. and physics grads. U. Wis., 1992, Mankato U., 1994; mem. com. on catalysts and environ. NSF; exec. briefings with Pres. George Bush and Cabinet mems., 1990, 92; plenary lectr. in field. Author: Catalysis in Coal Conversion, 1978, (with others) Critical Materials Problems in Energy Production, 1976, Advanced Materials in Catalysis, 1977, Liquid Fuels from Coal, 1977, Kirk-Othmer Encyclopedia of Chemical Technology, 1979, Chemistry for the 21st Century, Perspectives in Catalysis, 1992, Science and Technology in Catalysis 1994, 1995; contbr. articles to profl. jours., chpts. to books; founding editor Jour. of Applied Catalysis, 1980; rec. artist with Royal Teens and Dino Take Five for ABC Paramount, Capitol and Jubilee Records, 1957-67; single records include Short Shorts, Short Shorts Twist, My Way, Hey Jude, Rosemarie, Please Say You Want Me, Lovers Never Say Goodbye; albums include The Best of the Royal Teens, Newies But Oldies; appeared in PBS TV prodn. on molecular engring., Little by Little, 1989. Recipient Surface Chemistry award Continental Oil Co., 1964; Henry Rutgers scholar, 1963, Lever Bros. fellow, 1965, Churchill Coll. fellow Cambridge Univ., 1992. Mem. AIChE, Am. Chem. Soc. (plenary lectr. to chem. educators nat. meeting 1994), Am. Phys. Soc., N.Y. Acad. Scis., Am. Mus. Natural History, Pres.'s Assn., Smithsonian Assocs., Sigma Psi, Phi Lambda Upsilon (hon.). Republican. Roman Catholic. Home: 1644 Candace Way Los Altos CA 94024-6242 Office: Catalytica Inc 430 Ferguson Dr Ste 3 Mountain View CA 94043-5215

CUTINO, BERT PAUL, chef, restaurant owner; b. Carmel, Calif., Aug. 7, 1939; m. Bella Manigiapane; children: Marc, Bart. AA in Bus., Monterey Peninsula Coll., 1964; D of Culinary Arts (hon.), Johnson and Wales Coll., 1988. Various restaurant positions Monterey, Calif.; owner Sardine Factory, Monterey, 1968—; co-founder Cannery Row Co., Monterey, 1976—; comml. real estate developer, Pacific Hospitality, Inc., 1983—; protocol chmn. 1992 USA Nat. Culinary Team; formation of Western Region Culinary Team to 1988 Culinary Olympics, Frankfurt; founder Culinary Arts Program at local community coll., 1981; hospitality amb. internat. teams to Am. Culinary Classic, 1991; speaker and lectr. in field. Contbr. articles for hospitality industry publs. and profl. jours.; featured in TV commls. for Am. Express and Duralon. Food chmn. Calif. Wine Festival, 1977—, March of Dimes, 1985-89; chmn. Taste of Monterey, 1987-89; co-chmn. Easter Week Brunch for Alliance on Aging, March of Dimes, Monterey County, 1987-89, Jumpin Pumpkins money raiser for local pub. schs., 1984-87, African Relief Fund, 1985; v.p. Monterey Peninsula C. of C., 1984-88; mem. Sheriff's Adv. Com., Monterey County; hon. judge March of Dimes Gourmet Gala, 1985-92; dir. Found. to Support Monterey Peninsula Schs., 1984-86. With USNR, 1959-67. Recipient numerous awards including Disting. Restaurants N.Am., Mobil Guide, Nat. Restaurant News Hall of Fame, Calif. Top 10 Restaurants, Town and Country; one of 50 restaurants in Am. selected to serve at Pres. Reagan's Inauguration, 1981, 85; recipient Alumni award Calif. C.C., 1982, Antonin Careme Soc. medal Chefs Assn. of Pacific Coast, 1987, Medal of Honor, Escoffier Soc., 1986, Presdl. Medallion, Les Toques Blanches Internat., 1989, 1st Soviet-Am. Culinary Exchange Medallion, 1988, Medallion of World Trade Ctr., Moscow, 1988; named Chef of Yr., Monterey Peninsula Chefs Assn., 1983; named to Les Toques Blanches Internat. Hall of Fame, 1993, named 1st nat. pres. U.S.A., 1994. Mem. Am. Culinary Fedn. (life, cert. exec. chef, western region v.p. 1985-89, bd. dirs. The Chef and the Child Found. 1989, nat. membership com. 1982, western regional coord. 1983, nat. accreditation team 1987, Nat. Chef of Yr. 1988, Pres.'s medal 1982, 89, Pres. Recognition award 1994), Am. Acad. Chefs, Am. Acad. of Restaurant Scis., Am. Inst. of Wine and Food (founding), Knights of Vine (master knight), Wine Inst., Soc. for Am. Cuisine (founding), Calif. Restaurant Assn. (Chef of Yr., 1984), Nat. Restaurant Assn., Guild of Sommeliers Eng., Am. Inst. Food and Wine, Les Amis d'Escoffier Soc. N.Y. (amb.-at-large), Internat. Assn. Cooking Profls., Soc. Advancement of Food Svc. Rsch., Italian Restaurant Soc., Calif. Culinary Acad. (adv. bd. 1990—), L'Ordre Mondial Des Gourmets Degustateurs (spl. medal of honor, 1991), Confrerie de la Chaine Des Rotisseurs (vice chancelier-argentie, Bronze medal, 1990), Assn. Des Maitres Conseils en Gastronomie Francaise (comdr.), Les Toques Blanches Internat. Club (founder Monterey chpt., mem. internat. bd., Presdl. Medallion), Les Toques Blanches (1st nat. pres. 1994), Calif. Travel Industry Assn. (F. Norman Clark Entrepreneur award 1992), Monterey Peninsula C. of C. (v.p.). Office: Restaurants Central 765 Wave St Monterey CA 93940-1016

CUTLER, CASSIUS CHAPIN, physicist, educator; b. Springfield, Mass., Dec. 16, 1914; s. Paul A. and Myra B. (Chapin) C.; m. Virginia Tyler, Sept. 27, 1941; children: (Cassius) Chapin, William (Urban) (dec.), Virginia Cutler Raymond. B.Sc., Worcester Poly. Inst., 1937, D.Eng. (hon.), 1975. With Bell Telephone Labs, 1937-78; asst. dir. electronics and radio research Bell Telephone Labs, Murray Hill, N.J., 1959-63; dir. electronic and computer systems research lab. Bell Telephone Labs, Holmdel, N.J., 1963-78; prof. applied physics Stanford U., 1979—. Contbr. articles to profl. jours. Mem. 1st Ch. of Christ Scientist, Keyport, N.J., 1966-78, Menlo Park, Calif., 1979—, reader, chmn. bd., Plainfield, N.J., 1946-66. Recipient Robert H. Goddard Disting. Alumni award Worcester Polytechnic Inst., 1982. Fellow IEEE (Edison medal 1981, Centennial medal 1984, Alexander Graham Bell medal 1991), AAAS; mem. Nat. Acad. Engring. Nat. Acad. Scis., Sigma Xi. Home: 106 Peter Coutts Cir Palo Alto CA 94305-2516 Office: Stanford U Ginzton Lab Stanford CA 94305

CUTLER, HOWARD ARMSTRONG, economics educator, chancellor; b. Webster City, Iowa, Apr. 27, 1918; s. Harry O. and Myrtle (Armstrong) C.; m. Enid Ellison, Jan. 2, 1943; children: Cheryl Varian, Kristen Ellison, Sherwood Thor. A.B., U. Iowa, 1940, M.A., 1941; grad. certificate, Harvard U., 1943; Ph.D., Columbia U., 1952. Instr. econs. U. Iowa, 1946; asst. to economist Irving Trust Co., N.Y.C., 1946-47; instr. econs. U. Ill., Urbana, 1948-50; asst. prof. U. Ill., 1950; asst. to dean U. Ill. (Coll. Commerce), 1949-51; asst. prof. econs. Pa. State U., 1951-53, assoc. prof., 1953-56, prof., 1956-62, head dept., 1953-58, dir. gen. edn., 1957-62, asst. to v.p. academic affairs, 1958-61, asst. to pres., 1961-62; acad. v.p., prof. econs. U. Alaska, 1962-66, chancellor, 1976-81, chancellor emeritus, 1983—, Regents' prof. econs., 1981-83, Regents' prof. emeritus, 1983—; exec. v.p. Inst. Internat. Edn., N.Y.C., 1966-76; vis. prof. U. Chgo., 1955-56. Editor: Jour. Gen. Edn, 1960-62. Mem. Martin Luther King, Jr., Fellowship Selection Com., 1968-70; mem. pub.-at-large Ednl. Commn. for Fgn. Med. Grads., 1970-85; mem. chancellor's panel on univ. purposes State U. N.Y., 1970-72; mem. Nat. Liaison Com. Fgn. Student Admissions, 1968-75; mem. adv. com. Carl Duisberg Soc., 1968-75; bd. dirs. Nat. Council for Community Services to Internat. Visitors, 1971-75, Internat. Schs. Services, 1971-75, Axe-Houghton Found., 1970-85, bd. dirs. Alaska Council on Economic Edn., 1977—. Served to lt. USNR, 1942-46. Recipient Disting. Alumnus Achievement award U. Iowa, 1989, Howard A. Cutler award for Oustanding Contbn. to Econ. Edn. in Alaska, 1987. Mem. Phi Beta Kappa, Beta Gamma Sigma, Pi Gamma Mu, Omicron Delta Epsilon. Office: U Alaska Dept Econs Fairbanks AK 99775

CUTLER, LORRAINE MASTERS, interior designer, facilities manager; b. Indpls., Oct. 19, 1943; d. James Mark and Dorothy Aileen (DeLawter) Masters; m. Albert B. Cutler III, June 3, 1965 (div.); children: Valina Dawn, Anthony Bret. BFA, Ariz. State U., 1974, BA, 1974; MA, U. Phoenix, 1989. Intern Walsh Bros., Phoenix, 1973, jr. designer, 1973-74, staff designer, 1978-80; dir. interior design Dick & Fritsche Design Group, Phoenix, 1980-84; dir. interior design and space planning HNC Inc., Phoenix, 1984-87; mgr. advanced facilities planning PCS, Inc., Scottsdale, Ariz., 1987-89; cons. Cons. Mgmt. Systems, 1989—; asst. prof. interior design and facility mgmt. Ariz. State U., Tempe, 1991—. Participant Interior Design Efforts for Ariz. Legis., Phoenix, 1986-87; bd. dirs. Southwest Builds, 1985-88, chmn. fin. com., 1987-88. Recipient Presdl. Citation Am. Soc. Interior Designers, 1984. Mem. Internat. Interior Design Assn. (profl., acad. liaison 1991-93, pres. 1985-87, v.p. programs 1983-85, sec. 1981-83, Cert. Appreciation 1981), Internat. Facility Mgmt. Assn. (profl., treas.). Home: 4034 E Yowy St Phoenix AZ 85044-1527 Office: Ariz State U Coll Architecture and Environ Design Tempe AZ 85287-2105

CUTRUBUS, CHRISTINA NINA, publisher; b. Ogden, Utah, Feb. 8, 1934; d. Gus James and Athanasia (Gogoras) C. Student, Weber State U., 1952-54, U. Utah, 1954-56. Publicist Metro Goldwyn Mayer, 1957-64; owner Phonic Arts Agy., 1962, Univ. Svcs. Corp., 1971; owner, pub./editor Utah Preservation/Restoration Mag., Salt Lake City; personal rep., press agt. His Eminence Archbishop Iakovos, primate of Greek Orthodox Archdiocese of N. and S. Am.; advisor, cons. Goya Nat. Conf. Editor/pub. Utah Ballet West Mag.; compiler, editor, pubr. book: The Salt Lake Temple: A Monument to a People (world award); compiler, author book: D. Alt: Impressions of an Impressionist (1989 Award of Merit, Rounce & Coffin Club). Recipient Power of the Pen honor award Nat. Trust For Hist. Preservations in U.S. Mem. Salt Lake Advt. Club, Salt Lake C. of C., Zeta Phi Eta. Address: 1159 2nd Ave Salt Lake City UT 84103-4115

CUTTEN, BETTY BANCROFT, lighting designer, interior designer; b. L.A., Dec. 29, 1925; d. Frederick H. Baruch and Mildred (Walter) Lawler; m. William Hazard Bancroft, Sept. 21, 1946 (div. Apr. 1955); children: William Hazard Jr., Antoinette Victoria, Mary Walter Bancroft Robins; m. Merritt Edward Cutten, Aug. 3, 1957. Student, Stanford U., 1943-44. Owner, interior designer Betty Cutten, Interior Design, various cities, Calif., 1970—; ptnr., lighting designer Cutten Assoc., Lighting Design, Tahoe City, 1990—. Bd. dirs. Calif. Legis. Conf. on Interior Design, Sacramento, 1986-90. Mem. Am. Soc. Interior Designers (profl. mem., com. chair 1987-93, Design Excellence Gold award Calif. Ctrl. chpt. 1988, Presdl. citation for disting. svc. to the soc. and profession Calif. Ctrl. Chpt. 1990), Calif. Coun. for Interior Design (cert.), North Lake Tahoe C. of C. (bd. dirs. 1993-95). Republican. Episcopalian. Office: Cutten Assocs Lighting PO Box 6926 Tahoe City CA 96145-6926

CUTTER, GARY RAYMOND, biostatistician, epidemiologist; b. St. Louis, Feb. 18, 1948; s. Daniel and Mildred (Mandel) C.; m. Sharon R. Gornek, Aug. 24, 1969; children: Corey N., Scott J., Todd J. BA in Math., U. Mo., 1970; MS in Biometry, U. Tex., Houston, 1971, PhD in Biometry, 1974. Asst. prof. biometry U. Tex. Sch. Pub. Health, Houston, 1974-78; expert, cons. Nat. Cancer Inst., Bethesda, Md., 1978-79; assoc. prof. biostats. U. Ala., Birmingham, 1979-894; prof. pub. health, chair biostats. and info. systems St. Jude Children's Rsch. Hosp., Memphis, 1989-91; pres. Pythagoras, Inc., Birmingham, 1991—; dir. biostats. AMC Cancer Rsch. Ctr., Denver, 1994—. Author: A Module of Math., 1972, (with others) Evaluation of Health Education and Promotion Programs: Principles, Guidelines and Methods for the Practitioner, 1984, 2d edit., 1994; contbr. numerous articles to profl. jours. Bd. dirs. Legal Environ. Assistance Found., Birmingham, 1986-89, Temple Emanu El, Birmingham, 1987-89, Jewish Cmty. Ctr., Birmingham, 1984-88, Fair Share for Health, Denver, 1994—. Recipient numerous grants from NIH, NHLBI, NIDDK, others. Mem. Am. Pub. Health Assn., Am. Statis. Assn., Biometric Soc., Soc. Clin. Trials, Mountain Brook Soccer Club (bd. dirs. 1983-94), Mountain Brook Athletic Assn. (bd. dirs. 1986-88). Office: AMC Cancer Rsch Ctr 1600 Pierce St Denver CO 80214-1433

CUTTS, JAMES ALFRED, aerospace scientist; b. Liverpool, Eng., Sept. 29, 1943; came to U.S., 1965; s. John George-Bilton and Vera (Hopkin) C.; m. Karen Daine Lemos, Apr. 22, 1967; children: Brianna Catherine, Dominique Caroline. BA in Natural Scis., Cambridge U., 1965; MS in Geophysics, Calif. Inst. Tech., 1967, PhD in Planetary Sci., 1971. Mem. tech. staff Jet Propulsion Lab., Pasadena, Calif., 1967-75; divsn. mgr. Sci. Applications Internat. Corp., San Diego, 1975-82; divsn. technologist Jet Propulsion Lab., Pasadena, Calif., 1982-89, program mgr., 1989—; mem. Viking imaging team NASA, Washington, 1975-81, chmn. sensor working group, 1987-88, mem. TOPS sci. working group, 1992-93. Pres. Pasadena Young Musicians Orch., Pasadena, 1987-88. Recipient Robert N. Goddard trophy Nat. Space Club, 1978. Mem. AAAS (Newcomb Cleve. prize 1976), AIAA, Internat. Soc. Optical Engring. Office: Jet Propulsion Lab 4800 Oak Grove Dr Pasadena CA 91109-8001

CUZELLA, JEROME J., geologist, environmental scientist; b. Chgo., Dec. 31, 1949; s. Jerry F. and Amelia A. (Dragash) C.; m. Virginia A. Gilson, Apr. 17, 1982; children: James M., Jeanette E. BS in Geology, St. Joseph Coll., 1971; MS in Geology, Bowling Green State U., 1973; prof. degree in hydrogeology, Colo. Sch. of Mines, 1993. Registered profl. geologist, Wyo. Geologist Sargent & Lundy, Engrs., Chgo., 1973-78, Amoco Internat. Oil Co., Houston, 1978-79, U.S. Dept. Interior, Office of Surface Mining, Denver, 1979-81; sr. exploration geologist Anabarko Prodn. Co., Denver, 1981-85; sr. staff geologist Nat. Coop. Refinery Assn., Denver, 1985-91; consulting geologist Denver, 1991-94; v.p. environ. solutions Internat., Inc., Evergreen, Colo., 1993—. Mem. Geol. Soc. Am., Am. Assn. Petroleum Geologists, Soc. for Sedimentary Geology, Assn. Engring. Geologists, Rocky Mtn. Assn. Geologists, Nat. Water Well Assn., KC (Lakewood, Colo. trustee, home assn. pres. 1993-94). Democrat. Roman Catholic. Home: 95 Yarrow St Lakewood CO 80226-1521

CYRUS, JUDITH LYNN, software engineer; b. Grand Junction, Colo., June 16, 1952; d. Lloyd E. and Patricia E. (Nelson) Johnson; m. Gene R. Cyrus, May 29, 1970; children: Juli, Jaimi, Jillian, Michael, Crystal, Wesley, Joseph, Doloras, Breanna. BS in Computer Sci., U. Mont., 1986; MS in Computer Sci., Calif. State U., Chico, 1994. Tech. support engr. Hewlett Packard, Böblingen, Germany, 1986-87; software engr. Hewlett Packard, Böblingen, 1987-89, McMinnville, Oreg., 1989-92; engring. productivity mgr. Hewlett Packard, McMinnville, 1992-93; software engr. Heartstream, Seattle, 1993—. Contbr. articles to profl. jours. Mont. Power Co. Computer Sci. scholar, 1983. Lutheran.

CZAPLEWSKI, RUSSELL ANTHONY, museum curator; b. Lexington, Nebr., July 17, 1963; s. James Robert and Arvada Lenora (Nida) C. BA in History, Geography summa cum laude, Kearney (Nebr.) State Coll., 1985; MA in Hist. Adminstrn., Mus. Studies, U. Kans., 1988. Rsch. hist. Dawson County Hist. Mus., Lexington, 1981-88; part-time asst. Watkins Community Mus., Lawrence, Kans., 1986-87; asst. dir. Dawson County Hist. Mus., Lexington, 1988-89, acting dir., 1989, dir., 1989-91; curator of collections Kern County Mus., Bakersfield, Calif., 1991—. Author: Plum Creek to Lexington, 1989, Captive of the Cheyenne, 1993; co-author: Battle of the Bridges: author numerous papers in field. Roman Catholic. Office: Kern County Museum 3801 Chester Ave Bakersfield CA 93301-1345

DACIUK, MYRON MICHAEL, bishop; b. Mundare, Alta., Can., Nov. 16, 1919; s. Lucas and Ksenia (Bruchkowsky) D. Student in philosophy and theology, Basilian Sem. Mundare, Grimsby, Ont., 1943-45. Ordained priest Ukrainian Catholic Ch., 1945. Priest Ukrainian Cath. Ch., Can., 1945-82; aux bishop Ukrainian Cath. Archeparchy, Winnepeg, Can., 1982-91; bishop Ukrainian Cath. Ch., Winnipeg, Man., Can., 1982-90, Edmonton Eparchy, 1992—; superior Basilian Fathers, Mundare, 1959-64; superior Basilian Fathers, Edmonton, Alta., 1976-79, provincial superior, 1964-70. Home: 4324 - 49A St, Edmonton, AB Canada T6L 6J5 Office: Chancery, 9645-108 Ave, Edmonton, AB Canada T5H 1A3

DACKAWICH, S. JOHN, sociology educator; b. Loch Gelley, W.Va., Jan. 31, 1926; s. Samuel and Estelle (Jablonski) D.; m. Shirley Jean McVay, May 20, 1950; children—Robert John, Nancy Joan. B.A., U. Md., 1955; Ph.D., U. Colo., 1958. Instr. U. Colo., 1955-57; instr. Colo. State U., 1957-59; prof., chmn. sociology Calif. State U., Long Beach, 1959-70; prof. sociology

Calif. State U., Fresno, 1970-94, chmn. dept., 1970-75, prof. sociology emeritus, 1994—; pvt. practice survey research, 1962—. Contbr. articles and rsch. papers to profl. publs. Mem. Calif. Dem. Ctrl. Com., 1960-62; co-dir. Long Beach Ctrl. Area Study, 1962-64, Citizen Participation Study, Fresno. With USMCR, 1943-46, U.S. Army, 1950-53. Mem. Am. Assn., Pacific sociol. assns. Home: 5841 W Judy Ct Visalia CA 93277-8601 Office: Calif State U Dept Sociology 5340 N Campus Dr Fresno CA 93740-8019

DACKOW, OREST TARAS, insurance company executive; b. Wynyard, Sask., Can., Sept. 17, 1936; s. Luke Dackow and Irene Stacheruk; m. Florence Dorothy Waples, Sept. 20, 1958; children: Trevor Wade, Heather Lynn, Donna Louise. B.Commerce with honors, U. Man., Winnipeg, Can., 1958; Grad. Advanced Mgmt. Program, Harvard U., 1976. Enrolled actuary. V.p. individual ops. Great-West Life Ins. Co., Winnipeg, Man., Can., 1976-78, sr. v.p. individual ops., 1978-79, sr. v.p. U.S., 1979-83; exec. v.p., chief operating officer U.S. Great-West Life Assurance Co., Denver, 1983-88; exec. v.p. corp. fin. and control Great-West Life Assurance Co., Winnipeg, 1988-90, pres., 1990-94, dir., 1992—; pres., CEO, dir. Great-West Lifeco Inc., 1992—. Bd. dirs. Met. YMCA, Winnipeg, 1971-80, pres., 1979-80; bd. dirs. Met. YMCA, Denver, 1981-84, Colo. Alliance of Bus., 1986-87, Nat. Jewish Ctr. for Immunology and Respiratory Medicine, 1985—, Health Scis. Centre Rsch. Found., 1990-94, Instrumental Diagnostics Devel. Office, 1992-94. Fellow Soc. Actuaries, Can. Inst. Actuaries; mem. Am. Acad. Actuaries.

DADO, ARNOLD EMMETT, financial and insurance consultant; b. Petaluma, Calif., Mar. 17, 1938; s. Emmett Stephen and Madeline Lenore (Ouzts) D.; m. Frances Clark, June 10, 1958 (div. June, 1970); children: Alan, Sharlyn, Melanie; m. Susan Carol Forbes, June 9, 1990. Student, U. San Francisco, 1956-61. CLU, chartered fin. cons. Sales rep. ins. industry, 1962-67; asst. mgr. Mut. of N.Y., Oakland, Calif., 1967-71; tng. asst. Mut. of N.Y., N.Y.C., 1971; mgr. Mut. of N.Y., San Rafael, Calif., 1971-73, field sales dir. western region, 1973; mgr. Mut. of N.Y., Santa Rosa, Calif., 1973-80; pvt. practice fin. planning Santa Rosa, 1980—; expert witness for Tech. Adv. Svc. for Attys., 1990—, U.S. Dept. Justice, 1991; lectr. in field. Organizer Spl. Olympics, Santa Rosa, 1975—; bd. mem. Petaluma Wildlife Mus., 1994—. Sgt. U.S. Army, 1960-64. Mem. Am. Soc. CLU and Chartered Fin. Cons. (past pres., chmn. continuing edn. com.), Redwood Empire Assn. Life Underwriters (chmn. ethics com., former bd. dirs.), Estate Planning Coun. (former bd. dirs.), Elks Club. Democrat. Roman Catholic. Office: 2300 Bethards Dr Ste J Santa Rosa CA 95405-9005

DAEHLING, WILLIAM A., academic administrator. Chancellor Mont. State U. No., Havre. Office: Mont State U No Office of Chancellor Havre MT 59501

DAEMEN, JAAK JOSEPH K., mining and geotechnical engineering educator; came to the U.S., 1967; Degree in mining engring., U. Leuven, Belgium, 1967; PhD in Geol. Engring., U. Minn., 1975. Registered profl. engr., Ariz. Rsch. asst., then rsch. assoc. U. Minn., Mpls., 1967-75; rsch. engr. explosives products divsn. E.I. DuPont de Nemours & Co., Martinsburg, W.Va., 1975-76; asst.prof. mining and geol. engring. U. Ariz., Tucson, 1976-83; assoc. prof. mining and geol. engring., 1983-90; prof., dept. chair U. Nev., Reno, 1990—. Mem. ASCE, AIME, Internat. Soc. for Rock Mechanics, Am. Underground Space Assn., Am. Geophys. Union, Internat. Soc. Explosives Engrs., Internat. Soc. for Soil Mechanics and Found. Engring., Royal Flemish Engring. Soc., Royal Belgium Assn. of Engrs. and Industrialists. Home: 2620 Pioneer Dr Reno NV 89509-7605 Office: U Nev Dept of Mining Engring Reno NV 89557-0139

DAFFORN, GEOFFREY ALAN, biochemist; b. Cunningham, Kans., Feb. 4, 1944; s. Francis Elston and Anna Elizabeth Dafforn; m. Gail McLaughlin, July 14, 1973; 1 child, Christine Elizabeth. BA cum laude, Harvard U., 1966; PhD, U. Calif., Berkeley, 1970. Postdoctoral fellow U. Calif., Berkeley, 1973; asst. prof. U. Tex., Austin, 1974; from asst. prof. to assoc. prof. Bowling Green (Ohio) State U., 1974-81; sr. chemist Syva Co., Palo Alto, Calif., 1982-87, rsch. fellow, 1987—. Author articles and abstracts; patentee in field. Grantee Army Rsch. Office, 1979-82, Am. Chem. Soc., 1975-80. Mem. AAAS, Am. Chem. Soc., Sierra Club. Office: Syva Co MS 2-218 900 Arastradero Rd Palo Alto CA 94304-1332

DAFOE, DONALD CAMERON, surgeon, educator; b. Appleton, Wis., Nov. 22, 1949. BS in Zoology, U. Wis., 1971, MD, 1975. Diplomate Am. Bd. Surgery. Intern Hosp. of U. of Pa., Phila., 1975-76, resident, 1976-80, Measey rsch. fellow, 1978-80, chief resident, 1980-81, clin. fellow, Culpeper Found. fellow, 1981-82; asst. prof. surgery U. Mich., Ann Arbor, 1982-87; dir. clin. pancreas transplantation program u. Mich., Ann Arbor, 1984-87; assoc. prof. surgery U. Mich., Ann Arbor, 1987; assoc. prof. surgery, chief divsn. transplantation Hosp. of U. of Pa., Phila., 1987-91, Stanford (Calif.) U. Med. Ctr., 1991—; cons., physician advisor Keystone Peer Rev. Orgn., Inc., 1990-91. Reviewer various publs.; mem. editorial bd. Transplantation Sci., 1992, The Chimera, 1993; contbr. over 100 articles to profl. jours; also numerous book chpts. Mem. ACS, Am. Diabetes Assn., Am. Soc. Transplant Surgeons (membership com. 1989-90, sci. studies com. 1991—, newsletter com. 1991—, program & publs. com. 1994—), Assn. for Acad. Surgery, Soc. Internat. de Chirurgie, The Transplantation Soc., Ctrl. Surg. Assn., Frederick A. Coller Surg. Soc., Soc. Univ. Surgeons, Surg. Biology Club II, Ravdin-Rhoads Surg. Soc., United Network for Organ Sharing, Calif. Transplant Donor Network, Western Assn. Transplant Surgeons. Office: Dept Surgery MSOB X-300 Stanford Univ Med Ctr Stanford CA 94305

DAGG, STEVEN GREGORY, accountant; b. Vancouver, B.C., Can., Feb. 20, 1959; s. Keith Earl Dagg and Judith Diane Sansom. BBA, U. Tex., 1983. CPA, Tex.; cert. fin. planner. Tax mgr. Ernst and Young, Houston, 1984-91; v.p., gen. mgr. Copeland Communication, Inc., Victoria, B.C., 1991—. Mem. AICPA, Houston Soc. CPAs. Republican. Lutheran. Office: Copeland Comms, 759 Courtney St, Victoria, BC Canada V8W 1C3

DAGGETT, ROBERT SHERMAN, lawyer; b. La Crosse, Wis., Sept. 16, 1930; s. Willard Manning and Vida Naomi (Sherman) D.; children: Ann Daggett McCluskey, John Sullivan; m. Helen Hosler Ackerman, July 20, 1976. A.B. with honors in Polit. Sci. and Journalism, U. Calif.-Berkeley, 1952, J.D., 1955. Bar: Calif. 1955, U.S. Supreme Ct. 1967. Assoc. firm Brobeck, Phleger & Harrison, San Francisco, 1958-66, ptnr., 1966—; counsel, Reapportionment Lit. Calif. Senate, 1972-73; adj. prof. evidence and advocacy Hastings Coll. Law, 1982—; instr. No. Dist. Fed. Practice Program, 1982—, mem. teaching com., 1983—; demonstrator-instr. Nat. Inst. for Trial Advocacy, 1981—, Stanford and U. San Francisco Law Schs., Hastings Ctr. for Trial and Appellate Advocacy, 1981-88, mem. adv. bd., 1983-88; vol. pro tem judge San Francisco Mcpl. Ct., 1981-88, San Francisco Superior Ct., 1990—; arbitrator and pvt. comml. arbitrator, 1984—; co-host Face to Face, Sta. KQED-TV; commentaries KQED-FM. Bd. editors Calif. Law Rev., 1953-55; contbr. articles and lectures to profl. jours. Bd. dirs. San Francisco Legal Aid Soc.; bd. visitors U. Calif., Santa Cruz. 1st lt. JAGC, U.S. Army, 1958-62. Walter Perry Johnson scholar, 1953. Fellow Am. Bar Found.; mem. ABA, FBA (pres. no. dist. Calif. chpt. 1992-95), AFTRA, State Bar Calif., San Francisco Bar Assn. (past bd. dirs.), Am. Judicature Soc., Am. Law Inst., Bohemian Club, Commonwealth Club, Comml. Club (bd. dirs. 1989—, pres. 1993), Order of Golden Bear, Phi Delta Phi, Theta Xi. Republican. Office: Brobeck Phleger & Harrison Tower 1 Market Plz Spear St San Francisco CA 94105-1019

DAHL, BREN BENNINGTON, screenwriter; b. Gary, Ind., Nov. 15, 1954; d. Paul Wayland and Shirley Ann (Havard) Bennington; m. Curtis Ray Dahl; children: Austin Brooks, Darren Curtis. Student Principia Coll., Elsah, Ill., 1972-74, Sch. of Art Inst. of Chgo., 1983; BA in English with honors, U. Hawaii, 1977. Tchr. English, Peace Corps, Mbuji-Mayi, Zaire, 1977-79, Asahi Cultural Ctr., Osaka, Japan, 1981-82, Osaka Inst. Fgn. Trade, Osaka, 1981-82, Kansai U. of Fgn. Studies, Osaka, 1980-82, Matsushita Electric, Osaka, 1982; pres., owner Video Enterprises, North Palm Beach, Fla., 1983-87; producer's asst. Casady Entertainment, Hollywood, Calif., 1989-91. Mem. Palm Beach Opera Chorus, 1984-85. Fred Waring Scholar, 1972. Mem. Exec. Women of Palm Beaches, Fla. Motion Picture and TV Assn., Am. Film Inst., No. Palm Beach County C. of C. (co-chmn. spl. events 1985-86), Better Bus. Bur. Scriptwriters Network, Tourette Syndrome Assn.. Republican. Avocation: calligraphy, singing, gourmet cooking, running.

DAHL, CHRISTIAN ADAM, engineer; b. Salt Lake City, Feb. 8, 1954; s. Harold Arthur and Josephine Helen (Andersen) D.; m. Ann Marie Yensen, Dec. 11, 1952; children: Mark Douglas, Madelyn Marie, Patrick Andrew. BS in Chem. Engring., U. Utah, 1976, MS in Chem. Engring., 1979. Rsch. engr. Lockheed Idaho Techs. Co. and predecessors, Idaho Falls, 1978—, process surveillance engr., 1982-84, sr. engr., 1984, mgr. process monitoring, 1984-90, mgr. process evaluation, 1990-92, acting mgr. model integration, 1992, mgr. systems modeling, 1992-94, adv. engr., 1994—. Contbr. articles to profl. jours. Office: Lockheed Idaho Techs Co PO Box 1625 MS 3422 Idaho Falls ID 83415-3422

DAHL, DONALD DOUGLAS, newswriter; b. Savage, Mont., Mar. 25, 1920; s. Alfred Kristian and Elsie (McDonell) D.; m. Helen Copeland, Oct. 6, 1946 (div. 1978); children: Christine Dahl, Karen McKenzie. BA, U. N.D., 1941; MS, Columbia U., 1950. Supr. Fed. Writers Project, Bismarck, N.D., 1941; extension editor U. N.H., Durham, 1946-49; reporter Journal Bulletin, Providence, 1950; correspondent United Press, Manila, The Philippines, 1951-53; copy editor, wire editor, news editor The Albuquerque Tribune, 1954-82. Lt. USNR, 1942-46, PTO. Mem. Beta Theta Pi. Presbyterian.

DAHL, GARDAR GODFREY, JR., geologist, consultant; b. Hood River, Oreg., May 27, 1946; s. Gardar Godfrey Sr. and Margaret Jean (North) D.; m. Margarette Yvonne Beryyman Goodwin. BS in Geol. Engring., Mont. Coll. Mineral Sci. and Tech., 1969, MS in Geol. Engring., 1971. Registered profl. geologist. Asst. geologist Burlington No., St. Paul, 1971-72; mining geologist Burlington No., Seattle, Wash. and Billings, Mont., 1972-75; mgr. coal exploration and devel. Burlington No., Billings, 1975-79; dir. resource devel. Peabody Coal Co., Flagstaff, Ariz., 1979-81; chief geologist Cyprus Coal Co., Englewood, Colo., 1981-85, mgr. geology, 1985-88; mgr. tech. services Cyprus Shoshone Coal Co., Hanna, Wyo., 1988-90; sr. cons. geologist Cyprus Coal Co., Englewood, Colo., 1990-92; contract geologist Dahl & Assocs., 1992—; mng. dir. MEC Resources, Ltd., 1993—; sec. KFT Explorations Ltd., 1994—, Ky. Favorite Ventures, Inc., 1994—; dir. mining ventures Chartwell Internat., Inc., 1995—; dir. Mining Ventures. Mem. AIME, AAAS, Internat. Assn. Math. Geology, Rocky Mountain Coal and Mining Inst., Am. Assn. Profl. Geologists, Mont. Mining Assn., Colo. Mining Assn., Wyo. Profl. Geologists, Denver Coal Club. Lutheran. Home: 8008 S Newport Ct Englewood CO 80112-3121 Office: 6860 S Yosemite Ct Englewood CO 80112

DAHL, LOREN SILVESTER, retired federal judge; b. East Fairview, N.D., Mar. 1, 1921; s. William T. and Maude (Silvester) D.; m. Pamela B., Mar. 16, 1995; children: Candy Dahl, Walter Ray. AA, Coll. of Pacific, 1940; LLB, JD, U. Calif., San Francisco, 1949. Bar: Calif., 1950, U.S. Supreme Ct., 1957. Pvt. practice law Sacramento, 1950; sr. ptnr. Dahl, Hefner, Stark & Marois, Sacramento, 1950-80; chief judge U.S. Bankruptcy Ct. (ea. dist.) Calif., Sacramento, 1980, 86-94; chief judge emeritus, 1994—; Chmn. Conf. Chief Judges, 9th Cir., 1992. Pres. Golden Empire Coun. Boy Scouts Am., Sacramento, 1955-56, chmn. bd. trustees, 1956, exec. com. region 12, 1958, regional chmn. 1968-70, nat. exec. bd. 1968-70; Sacramento County Juvenile Justice Commn.; mem. bd. visitors McGeorge sch. law U. Pacific, 1987—; bd. dirs. Salvation Army, Sacramento, 1954-57; Sacramento Symphony Assn., 1958-59, Sacramento Safety Coun. With USAAF, 1942-46. Recipient Disting. Svc. award Jaycees, 1957, Silver Beaver award, Boy Scouts Am., 1957, Silver Antelope award, Boy Scouts Am., 1963, Disting. Eagle Scout award, Boy Scouts Am., Judge of Yr. award Sacramento County Bar Assn., 1993. Mem. U. of Pacific Alumni Assn. (pres. 1974-78, bd. regents 1980—, Disting. Alumnus award 1979), ABA, Calif. Bar Assn. (lectr. bankruptcy, continuing edn.), Am. Judicature Soc., Phi Delta Phi. Club: Del Paso Country. Lodge: Masons, Shriners, Lions (dir. Sacramento club 1952-53). Home: 842 Lake Oak Ct Sacramento CA 95864-6154

DAHLBERG, THOMAS ROBERT, columnist, screenwriter, author, attorney; b. Pitts., Nov. 28, 1961; s. J. Robert and Patricia Ann (McSweeney) D.; m. Teresa Marie Dorr, Aug. 21, 1981 (div. 1989); 1 child, Mary Katherine; m. Jeanne Marie Henderson, July 19, 1992 (dec. 1994). BS, Pa. State U., 1984, postgrad, 1982-84; AM, Georgetown U., 1986; JD, U. Notre Dame, 1987. Legis. asst. U.S. Senate, Washington, 1985; dir. fin. Ctr. Judical Studies, Washington, 1986; fgn. svc. officer U.S. Dept. State, Reston, Va., 1987-88; assoc. various firms, 1988-90; columnist, screenwriter, author Sacramento, 1991—; postdoctoral fellow Stanford (Calif.) U. Grad. Sch. Bus., 1994. Author: Drug Crazy, 1993, Literary Transaction Guide, 1993, (screenplay) Sequential Monogamy, 1992, (screenplay) Spooks and Loggers, 1992, (screenplay) Whippers and Slippers, 1992, (screenplay) Trauma Drama, 1993; editor Benchmark, Washington, 1986-87; Notre Dame Law Sch. editorial group, Harvard Jour. Law & Public Policy, editor, 1985-86, sr. editor, 1986-87; contbr. articles to profl. jours. and mags. Bd. dirs., chair strategic planning com. Boulder Vol. Connection, 1994—, Rocky Mountain Wolf Sanctuary, 1994—; spkr. Sacramento AIDS Found., 1991-92. Capt. USAR, 1979-90, Ctrl. Am., Europe. Nominee Pulitzer Prize for Disting. Commentary, 1993. Mem. Federalist Soc. for Law and Pub. Policy Studies (past pres. Notre Dame chpt. 1985-87), Assn. Trial Lawyers Am., Nat. Assn. Criminal Defense Lawyers (com. on prosecutorial misconduct, com. to free the innocent imprisoned, death penalty project), Writers Guild Am. (west), Amnesty Internat. (lawyer's com.), Mensa. Office: 5960 S Land Park Dr Ste 109 Sacramento CA 95822-3313 also: 2150 W 10th Ave Apt 202 Broomfield CO 80020-1079

DAHLBURG, JOHN-THOR THEODORE, newspaper correspondent; b. Orange, N.J., Apr. 30, 1953; s. Donald Russell and Madeline (Blackadore) D.; m. Yvonne Michelle Bastien, Nov. 18, 1980; children: Cecile, Charlotte. BA summa cum laude, Washington and Lee U., 1975; LLD with highest honors, U. Toulouse, France, 1980. Reporter, pub. affairs dir. Sta. WLUR-FM, Lexington, Va., 1971-75; stringer Lynchburg (Va.) News, 1974-75; news clk., intern Time Mag., Paris, 1974; reporter, editor Boca Raton (Fla.) News, 1980-81; newsman AP, Miami, Paris, 1981-83; editor, fgn. desk AP, N.Y.C., 1984-86; corr. AP, Moscow, 1986-90, L.A. Times, Moscow, 1990-93; bur. chief L.A. Times, New Delhi, 1993—. Journalistes en Europe fellow, 1983-84; recipient George Polk award L.I. U., 1993, Excellence citation Overseas Press Club Am., 1993; named finalist Pulitzer Prize in internat. reporting, 1992, 93, Cert. of Merit, AP News Execs. Coun., 1993. Office: LA Times, F-160 Malcha Marg Ground Flr, Chanakyapuri New Delhi India Office: LA Times Care Foreign Desk Times Mirror Sq Los Angeles CA 90053

DAHLIN, DENNIS JOHN, landscape architect; b. Ft. Dodge, Iowa, June 12, 1947; s. Fred E. and Arlene (Olson) D.; m. Jeanne M. Larson, Mar. 2, 1969 (div. 1990); 1 child, Lisa. BA, Iowa State U., 1970; M in Landscape Architecture, U. Calif., Berkeley, 1975. Lic. landscape architect. Assoc. planner San Luis Obispo County, Calif., 1971-73; prin. Dennis Dahlin Assocs., Modesto, Calif., 1975-90; v.p. WPM Planning Team, Inc., Modesto, 1991—; v.p. El Porvenir Found., Sacramento, Calif., 1991—. Contbg. author: The Energy Primer, 1976. Bd. dirs. Ecology Action Ednl. Inst., Modesto, 1984-85, Econ. Conversion Coun., San Diego, 1988-89; pres. San Joaquin Habitat for Humanity, Stockton, Calif., 1986-87. Ferrand fellow U. Calif., 1974, Kearney fellow Harvard U., 1975. Mem. Am. Planning Assn., Am. soc. Landscape Architects (bd. dirs. Sierra chpt. 1993—). Congregationalist. Office: WPM 1200 G St # 1B 116 I St Sacramento CA 95814-2205

DAHLSTEN, DONALD LEE, enviromental biology and forest entomology educator; b. Clay Center, Nebr., Dec. 8, 1933; s. Leonard Harold and Shirley B. (Courtright) D.; m. Reva D. Wilson, Sept. 19, 1959 (div.); children: Dia Lee, Andrea; m. Janet Clair Winner, Aug. 7, 1965; stepchildren: Karen Rae, Michael Allen. BS, U. Calif., Davis, 1956; MS, U. Calif., Berkeley, 1960, PhD, 1963. Asst. prof. Los Angeles State Coll., 1962-63; asst. entomologist U. Calif., Berkeley, 1963-65, lectr., 1965-68, asst. prof., 1968-69, assoc. prof., 1969-74, prof. entomology, 1974—, chmn. div. Biol. Control, 1980-88;, 1990-91; chmn. dept. cons. and resource studies U. Calif., Berkeley, 1989-91, dir. lab. biol. control, 1992-94; vis. prof. Yale Sch. Forestry and Environ. Studies, 1980-81, Integrated Pest Mgmt. Team People's Republic China, 1980, 81.. Mem. AAAS, Am. Inst. Biol. Scis. (vis. prof., lectr. 1970-71), Entomol. Soc. Am., Entomol. Soc. Can., Soc. Am. Foresters. Office: U Calif Lab Biol Control Berkeley CA 94720

DAHLSTROM, GRANT RUSSELL, hotel management professional; b. Pocatello, Idaho, Mar. 2, 1954; s. Hubert Mark and Leota (Sorensen) D.; m. Luci Ribeiro Campanella, Mar. 3, 1976; children: Jenefer, Josiah, Andy, Tony, Luciana. Grad. high sch., Pocatello. Tchr. English Rio de Janeiro, 1976-78; sales rep. Mr. Mac Clothier, Pocatello, 1975; thin film technician Am. Microsystems, Inc., Pocatello, 1979; field underwriter Met. Life Ins., Pocatello, 1979; sales rep. Satterfield Realty, Pocatello, 1980-81; co-owner, mgr. Cordon's Pies, Pocatello, 1981-83; field underwriter N.Y. Life Ins. Co., Pocatello, 1983-85; mgmt. trainee Pizza Hut, Pocatello, 1985; from front desk clk. to gen. mgr. Best Western Cotton Tree Inn, Pocatello, 1985—. Bd. dirs. Pocatello Sports Com., 1987-93, Time Max Inc. (formerly Mind Masters Inst.), 1992; active Pocatello strategic planning for econs. devel., 1987—. Mem. Pocatello C. of C. (chmn. com. on travel and tourism 1986-91, bd. dirs. 1987-90, chamber pres. 1992-93). Mormon. Home: 1656 Shasta St Pocatello ID 83201-2276 Office: Best Western Cotton Tree Inn 1415 Bench Rd Pocatello ID 83201-2444

DAHLSTROM, NORMAN HERBERT, retired engineering executive; b. Chgo., Oct. 22, 1931; s. Herbert D. and Myrtle C. (Papenthein) D.; m. Salome B. Filipiak, Oct. 25, 1952; children: Kenneth F., Dennis J. Susan M. Diploma, Chgo. Vocat. Sch., 1950; student, Northwestern U., 1952-56. Registered profl. engr., cert. mfg. engr. Mech. draftsman Halicrafters, Zenith Corps., Chgo., 1950-52; designer Stewart Warner Corp., Chgo., 1952-56; sr. design engr. Cook Rsch. Lab., Chgo., 1956-59; chief prodn. engr. Gen. Am. Transp. Corp., Chgo., 1959-69; pres., owner KDK Corp., Chgo., 1969-70; v.p., gen. mgr. KDK Corp. div. Pam Am. Resources, N.Mex., 1970-71; indsl. engring. mgr. bus. machine div. The Singer Co., Albuquerque, 1971-76; bus. tech. cons. Albuquerque, 1976-80; mfg. engring. mgr. Boeing Mil./Comml. Airplane Co., Wichita (Kans.) divsn., 1980-88; ops. program mgr. Boeing Mil. Airplanes, Wichita, Kans., 1988-90, mgr. Work Transfer Mfg. Engring., 1990-93; engring. mgr. comml. spares prodn., 1993; cons. self-employed Las Cruces, N.Mex., 1993—; cons. in field, 1976-80, 93—; advisor Wichita State U., 1987-88; chmn. Wichita Indsl. Trade Show, 1988. Inventor three patents. Capt. Rep. party, Morton Grove, Ill. 1968; lectr., tchr. St. Mary's Ch., Derby 1988. Mem. Soc. Mfg. Engrs. (chmn. region 10 1996, past chmn. chpts 52, 93), KC (4th degree). Roman Catholic.

DAHMER, JOAN MARIE, physician; b. Kitchener, Ont., Can., June 18, 1959; came to U.S., 1992; d. John Aloysius and Marie Genevive (McDonald) Keating; m. Scott J. Dahmer, June 14, 1980; children: Leah, Trevor. Student, U. Western Ont., London, Can., 1977-78, MD, 1982. Diplomate Am. Bd. Internal Medicine. Intern McGill U., Montreal, Can., 1982-83; resident in internal medicine Dalhousie U., Halifax, N.S., Can., 1983-86, chief resident, 1986-87, resident in hematology, 1987-88; fellow in hematology McMaster U., Hamilton, Can., 1988-89; pvt. practice Sudbury, Ont., Can., 1989-92; chief medicine Laurentian U., 1990-92; med. dir. Sudbury Regional Hemophilia Clinic, 1990-92; pvt. practice Windsor, Calif., 1992—; med. cons. Med. Scis. Lab., 1992-93; cons. physician N.E. Ont. Cancer Ctr., Sudbury; med. dir. HAVEN Program N.E. Ont., 1989-92; active staff Healdsburg Gen. Hosp.; provisional staff Santa Rosa (Calif.) Meml. Hosp.; tchg. staff Cmty. Hosp., Santa Rosa; speaker various schs. and civic orgns.; bd. dirs. HIV Caregiver Network, Blood Bank of the Redwoods; editorial advisor Chareot-Marie Toober Newsletter, 1984-90. Contbr. articles to profl. jours. and newsletters. Fellow Royal Physicians and Surgeons Can. (cert.); mem. Calif. soc. Internal Medicine (CME com. 1993—, women in medicine com. 1993—, HIV/AIDS com. 1993—), Sonoma County Med. Soc., Calif. Med. Assn., Amnesty Internat. (med. network 1984—), Healdsburg C. of C. (roundtable participant 1993), Windsor C. of C., Santa Rosa C. of C., U. Western Ont. Alumni Assn., Dalhousie Med. Alumni, Sierra Club, Alliance Francaise de Santa Rosa, Luther Burbank Ctr. Arts. Office: 911 Medical Center Plz Ste 22 Windsor CA 95492-7817

DAIGON, RUTH, editor, poet; b. Winnipeg, Manitoba, Can., Mar. 3, 1923; came to U.S., 1947; d. Nathan and Rose (Levin) Popeski; m. Arthur daigon, Apr. 11, 1952; children: Tom, Glenn. BA, U. Manitoba, 1943; Diploma in Music, Royal Conservatory of Toronto, Can., 1946. Soprano soloist Vancouver Symphony, B.C., Can., 1946-48; soloist Temple Emanuel, N.Y.C., 1949-54; soprano soloist N.Y. Pro Musica, N.Y.C., 1950-54; recording artist Columbia Records, N.Y.C., 1950-56; recital and TV artist U. Conn., Storrs, 1963-70; soloist Great Neck (N.Y.) Community Ch., 1952-63; editor Poets On: (series), Mill Valley, Calif. and, Cahplin, Conn., 1976—. Author: (poetry books) Learning Not To Kill You, 1975, A Portable Past, 1986, Between One Future And The Next, 1995; editor: (books) Poets On:, 1976—. Organizer poetry/Hartford (Conn.) Festival of Arts, 1980, other poetry programs for PBS/Conn., 1984-86. Recipient The Eve of St. Agnes nat. award Negative Capability Press, Mobile, Ala., 1993; fellow Va. Ctr. for Arts, 1987. Mem. PEN, Poetry Soc. of Am., Poets and Writers, Acad. of Am. Writers. Home: 29 Loring Ave Mill Valley CA 94941

DAILEY, CHARLES ANDREW, museum director, educator; b. Denver, May 25, 1935; s. Avery Frederick and Lollie Leola (Johnson) D.; m. Carol Jo Kane, Jan. 30, 1959; children: Travis Ashkee, Buffy Jo. BFA, U. Colo., 1962. Exhibit specialist Mus. No. Ariz., Flagstaff, N.Mex., 1960-61; curator exhibits Mus. N.Mex., Santa Fe, 1962-71; mus. dir. Inst. Am. Indian Art, Santa Fe, 1971-89, 95—, chmn. mus. studies dept., 1989—; mus. cons. various Native Am. Indian Mus. in U.S., 1971—; directed installation and opened Mus. Am. S.W., Milan, Italy, 1994; judge Indian exhibits Southwestern Assn. Indian Affairs, Santa Fe, N.Mex., 1978, 84, 89, 90, 93, 95; judge No. Plains Indian Exhibit, Sioux Falls, S.D., 1988. Author: (booklets) Museum Theory, 1984, Museum Problems, 1990; contbr. articles to profl. jours.Represented in numerous permanent collections including Dept. of Interior, Vincent Price Collection, Mus. N. Mex., Gallery 5, Santa Fe, Jemison Gallery, Santa Fe. Sgt. USMC, 1954-56. Mem. Am. Assn. Mus., N.Mex. Assn. Mus. (membership chair). Home: 64 Apache Ridge Rd Santa Fe NM 87505-8906 Office: Inst Am Indian Art Cathedral Pl Santa Fe NM 87504

DAILEY, DAVID KEVIN, psychiatrist; b. Jacksonville, Ill., Aug. 9, 1947; s. Paul Anthony and Margaret Ellen (Eagen) D. BA, U. Notre Dame, 1969; MEd, Boston Coll., 1975; MD, Loyola U., Chgo., 1985. Diplomate Am. Bd. Psychiatry and Neurology. Intern, resident Psychiat. and Psychosomatic Inst. Michael Reese Hosp. and Med. Ctr.; staff psychiatrist VA Hosp., Seattle, 1986-87, Group Health Coop, Seattle, 1987-88; med. dir. N.W. Mental Health Svcs., Auburn, Wash., 1988-91, Mental Health North, Seattle, 1991-95; clin. asst. prof. dept. psychiatry U. Wash. Sch. Medicine, Seattle, 1986—; med. dir. Cmty. Psychiat. Clinic/Mental Health North, Seattle, 1995—. Mem. Am. Psychiat. Assn., Physicians for Social Responsibility, Am. Assn. Cmty. Psychiatrists, Wash. Psychiat. Assn. (exec. com. 1993-94), Wash. Assn. Cmty. Psychiatrists (pres. 1993-94, exec. coun. 1989-95). Democrat. Office: Cmty Psychiat Clinic Ste 400 401 2d Ave W Seattle WA 98119

DAILEY, GARRETT CLARK, publisher, lawyer; b. Bethesda, Md., Mar. 22, 1947; s. Garrett Hobart Valentine and Margaret (Clark) Dailey; m. Carolynn Farrar, June 21, 1969; children: Patrick, Steven. AB, UCLA, 1969; MA, Ariz. State U., 1974; JD, U. Calif., Davis, 1977. Bar: Calif. 1977, U.S. Dist. Ct. (no. dist.) Calif. 1969. Assoc. Stark, Stewart, Simon & Sparrowe, Oakland, Calif., 1977-80; ptnr. Davies & Dailey, Oakland, 1980-85, owner, 1986-90; ptnr. Blum, Davies & Dailey, Oakland, 1985-86; pres., pub. Attys. Briefcase, Inc., Oakland, 1989-94, pres., CEO, 1989—; lectr. U. Calif. Davis Sch. Law, 1988-90, Golden Gate U. Grad. Sch. Taxation, San Francisco, 1986—. Dir. Amigos Delas Americas, San Ramon Valley, Calif., 1980-85, Rotary 517 Found., Oakland, 1985. Capt. USAF, 1969-74. Fellow Am. Acad. Matrimonial Lawyers; mem. Assn. Cert. Family Law Specialists. Democrat. Congregationalist. Home: 1651 W Livorna Rd Alamo CA 94507-1018 Office: Attys Briefcase Inc 519 17th St Fl 7 Oakland CA 94612-1503

DAILEY, JOSEPH CHARLES, development executive; b. Sacramento, Calif., Nov. 6, 1930; s. Berdie Mae Dailey; m. Lois Jean Reyman, Aug. 17, 1950; children: Bonnie, Carol, Joy. BA in Sacred Lit., San Jose Christian Coll., 1951; MA in Religion, Liberty U., 1992. Min. Guide Rock (Nebr.) Ch. of Christ, 1951-52, Sutter (Calif.) Ch. of Christ, 1952-55, Minnehaha Ch. of Christ, Vancouver, Wash., 1955-90; dir. devel. N.W. Coll. Bible, Portland, Oreg., 1992—; planner growth clinics, Portland, 1975-94; mgr. Dudley Christian Camp, Nachez, Wash., 1975-85; min. McDowell Creek Ch. of Christ, Lebanon, Oreg., 1993—. Editor: The Pattern, 1958-80. Treas. Clark

County Rep. Ctrl. Com., Vancouver, 1988-91; bd. dirs. Ret. Sr. Vol. Project, Vancouver, 1978; mem. adv. com. U.S. Senator Slade Gorton, Vancouver, 1988-90; treas., founding mem. Minnehaha Bus. Assn., Vancouver, 1990. Mem. Am. Assn. Christian Counselors. Home: 3704 NE 45th St Vancouver WA 98661-2535 Office: NW Coll Bible 1844 SE 39th Ave Portland OR 97214-5216

DALAL, KANU B., scientist, researcher; b. Bombay, Jan. 1, 1939; came to U.S., 1961; s. Bhaidas and Lalita (Pathan) D.; m. Mayuri K. Dalal, Jan. 20, 1968; children: Manish, Jai. BSc and BSc (Tech.), Bombay U., 1956, 59; MS, Utah State U., 1962, PhD, 1967. Rsch. fellow Ctrl. S.I.R. Govt. of India, Bombay, 1960-61; NIH fellow in plant biochemistry Utah State U., Logan, 1962-67; chief chemist Vintners Inc., Asti, Calif., 1967-68; postdoctoral fellow dept. neurology U. Calif., San Francisco, 1968-72; rsch. scientist dept. physiology U. Calif., Berkeley, 1973-75; sr. rsch. scientist MRI lab., Presbyn. Med. Ctr., San Francisco, 1976-83; tech. cons. Western Regional Lab Albany, Calif., 1984-85; staff scientist dept. radiation medicine Lawrence Berkeley Lab., Berkeley, Calif., 1985—; cons. San Francisco Day Care Ctr., 1976-88. Contbr. numerous articles to sci. publs. Vol., ARC, San Francisco, 1983, Unwed Mothers' Clinic, San Francisco, 1976, St. Anthony Ch., San Francisco, 1990; vol. tchr. and coach St. Anne's Sch., San Francisco, 1980. Grantee Bombay U., 1957, others. Mem. Soc. Nuclear Medicine, Am. Chem. Soc., Sigma Xi. Home: 852 Pacheco St San Francisco CA 94116-1351 *Died Feb. 1, 1995.*

DALDER, EDWARD NEIL CLIFF, materials engineer; b. Bklyn., May 24, 1935; s. Edward Henry and Estelle (Cliff) D.; m. Dorothy Jeanne Crosby, Aug. 12, 1967 (div. Jan. 1978); children: Erin Jeanne, Edward Robert, Linda Megan; m. Barbara Jeanne Kennedy, Oct. 2, 1982; 1 child, Brian Henry. BS in Engring., Polytechnic U., Bklyn., 1956, MS in Engring., 1964; PhD in Engring., Ohio State U., 1973. Metallurgist Grimman Corp., Bethpage, N.Y., 1956-59, Rep. Aviation Corp., Farmingdale, N.Y., 1959-62, United Air Craft Corp., East Hartford, Conn., 1962-64; group leader U.S. Steel Corp., Monroeville, Pa., 1964-69; project adminstr. Dept. Energy, Germantown, Md., 1973-79; materials engr. Lawrence Livermore (Calif.) Labs., 1979-83, project engr., 1983—; adj. prof. U. Calif., Berkeley, 1983-88, George Washington U., Washington, 1976-79. Contbr. articles to profl. jours. Treas. Shadyside Young Rep. Club, Pitts., 1964-69. Recipient Lincoln medal Lincoln Co. Found., Cleve., 1980. Mem. Am. Soc. for Metals, The Metall. Soc., Am. Welding Soc., Am. Nuclear Soc., ASME. Office: Lawrence Livermore Lab 7000 E Ave Livermore CA 94551

DALE, LEON ANDREW, economist, educator; b. Paris, May 9, 1921; m. Arlene R. Dale, Mar. 18, 1975; children: Melinda Jennifer, David Benjamin. B.A., Tulane U., 1946; M.A., U. Wis., 1947, Ph.D., 1949. News announcer to Occupied France BBC, London, 1944; Grad. asst. in econs. U. Wis., 1946-48; Asst. prof. labor econs. U. Fla., 1949-50; internat. economist AFL, Paris, 1950-53; AFL rep. at nat. labor convs. Greece, 1951, Naples, Italy, 1951, Switzerland, Sweden, Norway, Belgium, Austria, Luxembourg, Gt. Britain, 1950-53; cons. U.S. Govt., 1954-56; internat. economist U.S. Dept. Labor, Washington, 1956-59; prof., chmn. dept. mgmt. and indsl. rels., dir. internat. ctr., coord. courses for fgn. students U. Bridgeport, Conn., 1960-69; chief union task force Coll. Bus. Admstrn. Calif. State Poly. U., Pomona, 1980, coord. internat. activities Sch. Bus. Adminstrn., 1969-77, prof. mgmt. and human resources, 1969-91, prof. emeritus, 1991—, also, acting chmn. bus. mgmt. dept., summer 1973; chief Coll. Bus. Adminstrn. Calif. State U., Pomona, 1981; lectr. Internat. Conf. Tree Trade Unions Summer Sch., Wörgl, Austria, 1951; lectr. on Am. labor UN, Stockholm, 1952; lectr. U. Wis., Milw., 1960; asst. rschr., asst. moderator Labor Mgmt. Roundtable, 1961; participant televised ednl. programs Sta. WNHC-TV, New Haven, Conn., 1963; seminar leader Mgmt. Ctr, Cambridge, 1962-63, Rey area Police Dept.; Columbia U., 1966, 67, Bernard Baruch Sch. Bus. and Pub. Adminstrn., 1966-69; corrd. adminstrv. ops. and pub. rels. Rey Area Police Pers., 1966; instr. Perkins-Elmer Corp., Wilton, Conn., 1966; cons., arbitrator, fact-finder State of Conn., 1964-69; Am. del., speaker 3d Internat. Symposium on Small Bus., Washington, 1976, 4th Internat. Symposium on Small Bus., Seoul, Korea, 1977, 5th Internat. Symposium on Small Bus., Anaheim, Calif., 1978, 6th Internat. Symposium on Small Bus., Berlin, 1979; also mem. U.S. steering com. Internat. Symposium on Small Bus.; chief union task force Coll. Bus. Adminstrn. Calif. State Poly. U., Pomona, 1980; sr. cons. Am. Grad. U., Covina, Calif., 1981-82; adj. prof. econs. Nat. U., San Diego, 1981-90, Pepperdine U., 1986; discussion leader Calif. Inst. Tech. Internat. Conf. on Combining Best of Japanese and U.S. Mgmt., Anaheim, 1981; lectr. on indsl. rels. to execs. Miller Brewing Co., Irwindale, Calif., 1983; cons. Agy. Internat. Devel., N'Djamena, Republic of Chad, 1987; cons. to Minister for Planning, Republic of Chad; cons., instr. behavior courses U. Chad.; instr. mgmt. French-speaking African Students internat. ctr. Calif. State Poly. U., 1988; participant Ea. Europe and the West: Implication for Africa, So. Calif. Consortium on Internat. Studies conf., Pomona, 1990; lectr. confs. on leadership in French, Dakar, Senegal, 1990; seminar tchr. on leadership and mgmt. Citibank of N.Y., Dakar, Senegal, 1991; presenter, speaker numerous seminars in field; adj. prof. mgmt. Chapman U., Orange, Calif., 1994. Author: Marxism and French Labor, 1956, A Bibliography of French Labor, 1969; (video tape) Industrial Relations and Human Resources, 1982, Labor Relations in Crisis, 1989; originator Liberté (first French newspaper published in liberated France, 1944); French news announcer to occupied France, BBC London; contbr. articles to profl. jours. Served with U.S. Army, 1942-45. Recipient U. Bridgeport Faculty rsch. grantee, 1962; U. Wis. fellow, 1949; named one of Outstanding Educators of Am., 1972, 73. Mem. Am. Arbitration Assn. (nat. labor panel 1967—), Am. Acad. Polit. and Social Sci. Home and Office: 30 S La Senda Dr Laguna Beach CA 92677-3342

DALE, MARTIN ALBERT, investment banking executive; b. Newark, Jan. 3, 1932; s. Philip D. and Lucie M. (Mintz) D.; m. Joan Clements, Apr. 3, 1954 (div. 1977); children: Charles, W. Gregory, Pamela, Eric; m. Berteline Baier, Nov. 21, 1980. BA cum laude, Princeton, 1953; postgrad. (Fulbright fellow) U. Strasbourg (France), 1953-54; MA in Internat. Econs. with honors, Tufts U., 1955. Fgn. svc. officer U.S. Dept. State, 1955-60; pvt. counsellor, econ. adviser Prince Rainier III of Monaco, 1960-64; v.p., exec. asst. to pres. Grand Bahama Port Authority Ltd., Freeport, 1965-67; sr. v.p. fin., adminstrn. and ops. Revlon Internat. Corp., N.Y.C., 1967-72; corporate sr. v.p., dir. office strategic projects W.R. Grace & Co., N.Y.C., 1972-82; strategic planning cons. to Henkel KGaA, Duesseldorf, Germany, 1983-93; vice chmn. Hill Thompson Capital Markets, N.Y.C., 1993—; trustee, chmn. emeritus Lycée Francais de N.Y. Mem. Princeton Club N.Y., Phi Beta Kappa. Republican. Home: PO Box 4564 1041 Apollo Ct Incline Village NV 89450

DALESIO, WESLEY CHARLES, former aerospace educator; b. Paterson, N.J., Mar. 26, 1930; s. William James and Sarah (Sheets) Delison; m. Dorothy May Zellers, Nov. 17, 1951; children: Michael Kerry, Debra Kaye Dalesio Weber. Student, Tex. Christian U., 1950, U. Tex., Arlington, 1957. Enlisted USAF, 1948, advanced through grades to sr. master sgt., 1968; aircraft engine mech., mgmt. analyst USAF, worldwide, 1948-70; ins. agt. John Hancock Ins., Denver, 1970-71; office mgr. Comml. Builder, Denver, 1972-73; aerospace educator Sch. Dist. 50, Westminster, Colo., 1973-93; dir. aerospace edn. CAP, Denver, 1982-86. Mem. Crimestoppers, Westminster, 1988-91, Police and Citizens Teamed Against Crime, Westminster, 1992-93. Lt. col. CAP, 1981—. Mem. Nat. Assn. Ret. Mil. Instrs. (charter mem.), Westminster Edn. Assn., 7th Bomb Wg. B-36 Assn., Internat. Platform Assn., Nat. Aeronautic Assn., Acad. of Model Aeronautics, Arvada Associated Modelers. Episcopalian. Home: 2537 W 104th Cir Westminster CO 80234-3507

D'ALESSANDRO, MARY PATRICIA, essayist, poet, photographer, retired; b. Washington, Pa., Apr. 7, 1924; d. Battista and Rosaria (Valitutti) D'A.; children: Christopher Lee, Timothy Evance, Daniel Peter. BS in Human Relations/Orgnl. Behavior, U. San Francisco, 1982. Sec. FBI, Washington, 1942-45; adminstrv. asst. to dist. sales mgr. Trans World Airlines, San Francisco, 1946-55; travel counselor Stanford and Bungey Travel, Palo Alto, Calif., 1963-66; adminstrv. asst. to psychologist Menlo Park (Calif.) Sch. Dist., 1966-68; adminstrv. asst. to dean residential edn. Stanford (Calif.) U., 1971-76; adminstrv. asst. to v.p., gen. mgr. Levi Strauss and Co., San Francisco, 1977-82; adminstrv. asst. Internat. Women's Health Coalition, N.Y.C., 1985—; poetry tchr. Wellspring Women's Ctr., Sacramento; dir. poetry series Barnes & Noble Bookstore. Campaigner Dem. Ctrl. Com., San Francisco, 1971-82; bd. dirs. Menlo-Atherton (Calif.) H.S., 1964-68, Coun. Arts Palo Alto, 1968-74; bd. dirs., sec. IDEA Art Space. Fellow Squaw Valley Cmty. of Writers, 1979, 92; recipient hon. mention award Allen Ginsberg Poetry Contest, 1994, 1st Pl. award for poetry Calif. Writers, 1975, Honors award U. San Francisco, 1983, Judges award for photography City of N.Y., 1988. Mem. Zica Creative Arts and Lit. Guild, Sacramento Poetry Ctr., Passaic County Cmty. Poetry Ctr., Kingsley Art Club and Crocker Mus.

DALEY, LAURENCE STEPHEN, plant physiologist, biochemist; b. Liverpool, Eng., Sept. 21, 1936; came to U.S., 1962; s. Leonard and Leonela Garcia-Iniguez D.; m. Natalie Sue Cohen, June 12, 1967; children: Kara Hope, Ethan Leonard Henry, Jillian Bena. BS in Agr., U. Fla., 1964, MS in Agr., 1965; PhD, U. Calif., Davis, 1975. Assoc. prof., dept. horticulture Oreg. State U., Corvallis, 1983—. Contbr. articles to profl. jours. Office: Oreg State U Dept Horticulture Agr and Life Sci 4017 Corvallis OR 97331-7304

DALEY, RICHARD HALBERT, foundation executive; b. Centralia, Ill., Oct. 8, 1948; s. Richard Glen D.; m. Lucy W. Costen, Nov. 27, 1976. Student, Lake Forest (Ill.) Coll., 1966-67; BS, Colo. State U., 1970, MS, 1972. Instr. Colo. State U., Ft. Collins, 1972; from dir. biol. svcs. to dir. programs Mo. Bot. Garden, St. Louis, 1973-84; exec. dir. Mass. Hort. Soc., Boston, 1984-91, Denver Botanic Gardens, 1991—; instr. Environ. Ethics Denver U., 1992—. Mem. editorial com. Am. Mus. Natural History, N.Y.C., 1983-92. Bd. trustees Ctr. for Plant Conservation, 1994—. Mem. Am. Assn. Bot. Gardens (bd. trustees), Hort. Club Boston, Rotary Club Denver. Office: Denver Botanic Gardens 909 York St Denver CO 80206-3751

DALIS, IRENE, mezzo-soprano, opera company administrator, music educator; b. San Jose, Calif., Oct. 8, 1925; d. Peter Nicholas and Mamie Rose (Boitano) D.; m. George Loinaz, July 16, 1957; 1 child, Alida Mercedes. AB, San Jose State Coll., 1946; MA in Teaching, Columbia U., 1947; MMus (hon.), MS (hon.), San Jose State Coll., 1957; studied voice with, Edyth Walker, N.Y.C., 1947-50, Paul Althouse, 1950-51, Dr. Otto Mueller, Milan, Italy, 1952-72; MusD (hon.), Santa Clara U., 1987. Prin. artist Berlin Opera, 1955-65, Met. Opera, N.Y.C., 1957-77, San Francisco Opera, 1958-73, Hamburg (Fed. Republic Germany) Staatsoper, 1966-71; prof. music San Jose State U., Calif., 1977—; founder, gen. dir. Opera San Jose, 1984—; dir. Met. Opera Nat. Auditions, San Jose dist., 1980-88. Operatic debut as dramatic mezzo-soprano Oldenburgisches Staatstheater, 1953, Berlin Staedtische Opera, 1955; debut Met. Opera, N.Y.C., 1957, 1st Am.-born singer, Kundry Bayreuth Festival, 1961, opened, Bayreuth Festival, Parsifal, 1963; commemorative Wagner 150th Birth Anniversary; opened 1963 Met. Opera Season in Aida; premiered: Dello Joio's Blood Moon, 1961, Henderson's Medea, 1972; rec. artist Parsifal, 1964 (Grand Prix du Disque award); contbg. editor Opera Quarterly, 1983. Recipient Fulbright award for study in Italy, 1951, Woman of Achievement award Commn. on Status of Women, 1983, Pres.'s award Nat. Italian Am. Found., 1985, award of merit People of San Francisco, 1985, San Jose Renaissance award for sustained and outstanding artistic contbn., 1987, Medal of Achievement Acad. Vocal Arts, 1988; named Honored Citizen City of San Jose, 1986; inducted into Calif. Pub. Edn. Hall of Fame, 1985, others. Mem. Beethoven Soc. (mem. adv. bd. 1985—), San Jose Arts Round Table, San Jose Opera Guild, Am. Soc. Univ. Women, Arts Edn. Week Consortium, Phi Kappa Phi, Mu Phi Epsilon. Office: Opera San Jose 2149 Paragon Dr San Jose CA 95131-1312

DALKE, JOHN DAVID, family therapist; b. Stafford, Kans., Apr. 23, 1937; s. Jacob Joseph and Katherine Elizabeth (Shaler) D.; m. Sheryl Ankerstar, Oct. 6, 1990; children: Julie, Mike, Mary Beth. BA in Psychology, Sociology, Friends U., 1959; MTh, Drew Theol. Sch., Madison, N.J., 1962; DMin, San Francisco Theol. Seminary, San Anselmo, Calif., 1977. Pastor, cons. United Meth. Ch., Pratt and Belle Plaine, Kans., 1962-70; adminstrv. asst. Kans. Children's Svc. League, Wichita, 1970-75; family therapist Wichita and Longmont, Colo., 1975—; human resources dir. Air Mid-West Airline, Wichita, 1982-84; trainer for pub. seminars Career Track, Boulder, Colo., 1988; cons. to pvt./pub. orgns., 1975—; tchr. Friends U., Wichita, 1975, Aims C.C., Greeley, Colo., 1985—. Author books and video/audio tapes in field. Recipient Disting. Svc. award Nat. C. of C., Pratt, 1968. Mem. Am. Counseling Assn., Assn. of Death Edn. Counseling, Ctr. for Dispute Resolution. Office: 2133 Meadow St Longmont CO 80501-1254

DALLAS, SANDRA, correspondent, writer; b. Washington, June 11, 1939; d. Forrest Everett and Harriett (Mavity) Dallas; m. Robert Thomas Atchison, Apr. 20, 1963; children: Dana Dallas, Kendal Dallas. BA, U. Denver, 1960. Asst. editor U. Denver Mag., 1965-66; editorial asst. Bus. Week, Denver, 1961-63, 67-69, bur. chief, 1969-85, 90-91, sr. corr., 1985-90; book reviewer Denver Post, 1961—, regional book columnist, 1980—. Author: Gaslights and Gingerbread, 1965, rev. edit., 84, Gold and Gothic, 1967, No More Than 5 in a Bed, 1967, Vail, 1969, Cherry Creek Gothic, 1971, Yesterday's Denver, 1974, Sacred Paint, 1980, Colorado Ghost Towns and Mining Camps, 1985, Colorado Homes, 1986, Buster Midnight's Cafe, 1990; contbr. articles to various mags. Bd. dirs. Vis. Nurse Assn., Denver, 1983-85, Hist. Denver, Inc., 1979-82, 84-87. Recipient Wrangler award Nat. Cowboy Hall of Fame, 1980; named Colo. Exceptional Chronicler of Western History by Women's Library Assn. and Denver Pub. Library Friends Found., 1986. Mem. Women's Forum Colo., Denver Woman's Press Club, Western Writers of Am. Democrat. Presbyterian. Home and Office: # 3 850 Humboldt St Denver CO 80218-3573

DALPATADU, ROHAN JAYANTHA, mathematician, educator; b. Moratuwa, Sri Lanka, May 29, 1951; came to the U.S., 1980; s. Kosmapatabendige Arthur and Nandawathie (Manawadu) D.; m. Sreeni Manohari Punchihewa, Jan. 18, 1979. BS in Math. with honors, U. Ceylon, 1974; MS, So. Ill. U., 1981, PhD, 1986. Asst. lectr. U. Sri Jayewardenepura, Nugegoda, Sri Lanka, 1975-80; teaching asst. So. Ill. U., Carbondale, 1980-85; instr. U. Nev., Las Vegas, 1985-86, asst. prof., 1986-91, assoc. prof., 1991—; dir. freshman math. U. Nev., 1993-95, assoc. chair, 1995—. Contbr. articles to profl. jours. Mem. Soc. Actuaries (assoc.), Am. Math. Soc., Math. Assn. Am., S.W. Actuarial Edn. and Rsch. Consortium (program chmn. 1993—). Buddhist. Office: U Nev 4505 S Maryland Pky Las Vegas NV 89154-9900

DALPINO, IDA JANE, secondary education educator; b. Newhall, Calif., Oct. 20, 1936; d. Bernhardt Arthur and Walneta May (Blyler) Melby; m. Gilbert Augustus, June 14, 1963 (div. 1976); 1 child, Nicolette Jane. BA, Calif. State U., Chico, 1960; postgrad., Sacramento State, 1961-65, Sonoma State, 1970-71; MA, U. San Francisco, 1978. Cert. community counselor, learning handicapped, community coll. instr., exceptional children, pupil pers. specialist, secondary tchr., resource specialist. Tchr. Chico High Sch., 1959-60; counselor Mira Loma High Sch., Sacramento, 1960-66; tchr. ESL Phoenix Ind. High Sch., 1968-69; resource specialist Yuba City (Calif.) High Sch., 1971—; English tchr. Rough Rock Demonstration Sch., summers, 1975, 76. Office sec. Job's Daus., North Bend, Oreg., 1953—; active Environ. Def. Fund, Centerville Hist. Assn., Chico, 1991—. Mem. NEA, Calif. Tchrs. Assn., Calif. State Alumni Assn., Sigma Kappa Alumni. Democrat. Mem. Science of the Mind Church. Home: 4676 Cable Bridge Dr Chico CA 95928-8840 Office: Yuba City Unified Sch Dist 850 B St Yuba City CA 95991-4926

DALRYMPLE, GARY BRENT, research geologist; b. Alhambra, Calif., May 9, 1937; s. Donald Inlow and Wynona Edith (Pierce) D.; m. Sharon Ann Tramel, June 28, 1959; children: Stacie Ann Murray, Robynne Ann Sisco, Melinda Ann Dalrymple McGurer. AB in Geology, Occidental Coll., 1959; PhD in Geology, U. Calif., Berkeley, 1963; DSc (hon.), Occidental Coll., Los Angeles, 1993. Registered geologist, Calif. Rsch. geologist U.S. Geol. Survey, Menlo Park, Calif., 1963-81, 84-94, asst. chief geologist we. region, 1981-84; dean coll. oceanic and atmospheric sci. Oregon State U., Corvallis, 1994—; vis. prof. sch. earth scis. Stanford U., 1969-72, cons. prof., 1983-85, 90—; disting. alumni centennial speaker Occidental Coll., 1986-87; expert witness ACLU/State of Calif. Author: Potassium-Argon Dating, 1969, Age of Earth, 1991; contbr. chpts. to books and articles to profl. jours. Fellow NSF, 1961-63; recipient Meritorious Svc. award U.S. Dept. Interior, 1984. Fellow Am. Geophys. Union (pres.-elect 1988-90, pres. 1990-92), Am. Acad. Arts and Scis., Geol. Soc. Am.; mem. AAAS, NAS, Am. Inst. Physics (bd. govs. 1991—). Home: 1847 NW Hillcrest Dr Corvallis OR 97330-1859 Office: Oregon State U Coll Oceanic and Atmospheric Sci Corvallis OR 97331-5503

DAL SANTO, DIANE, judge; b. East Chicago, Ind., Sept. 20, 1949; d. John Quentin Dal Santo and Helen (Koval) D.; m. Fred O'Cheskey, June 29, 1985. BA, U. N. Mex., 1971; cert. Inst. Internat. and Comparative Law, Guadalajara, Mex., 1978; JD, U. San Diego, 1980. Bar: N.Mex. 1980, U.S. Dist. Ct. N.Mex. 1980. Ct. planner Met. Criminal Justice Coordinating Coun., Albuquerque, 1973-75; planning coord. Dist. Atty.'s Office, Albuquerque, 1975-76, exec. asst. to dist. atty., 1976-77, asst dist. atty. for violent crimes, 1980-82; chief dep. city atty. City of Albuquerque, 1983; assoc. firm T.B. Keleher & Assocs., 1983-84; judge Met. Ct., 1985-89, chief judge, 1988-89; judge Dist. Ct., 1989—; mem. faculty Nat. Jud. Coll., 1990—, bd. trustees, 1995—. Bd. dirs. Nat. Coun. Alcoholism, 1984, S.W. Ballet Co., Albuquerque, 1982-83; mem. Mayor's Task Force on Alcoholism and Crime, 1987-88, N.Mex. Coun. Crime and Delinquency, 1987—, bd. dirs., 1992-94, Mayor's Task Force Domestic Violence, 1987—; pres. bench, bar, media com., 1992, rules of evidence com. Supreme Ct., 1993—. U. San Diego scholar, 1978-79; recipient Women on the Move award YWCA, 1989, Disting. Woman award U. N.Mex. Alumni Assn., 1994, Outstanding Alumnus Dept. Sociology U. N.Mex., 1995; named Woman of Yr. award Duke City Bus. and Profl. Women, 1985. Mem. ABA, LWV, AAUW, Am. Judicature Soc., N.Mex. Women's Found., N.Mex. Bar Assn., N.Mex. Women's Bar Assn. (bd. dirs. 1991-92), Albuquerque Bar Assn., Josephson Inst. Ethics, Nat. Assn. Women Judges, Greater Albuquerque C. of C. (steering com. 1989), N.Mex. Magistrate Judges Assn. (v.p. 1985-89), Dist. Judges Assn. (pres. 1994—), Inns Ct. (master bencher) Democrat. Office: Dist Ct 415 Tijeras Ave NW Albuquerque NM 87102-3233

DALTON, JAMES EDWARD, aerospace executive, retired air force officer; b. N.Y.C., Oct. 17, 1930; s. Edward A. and Marion (Conway) D.; m. Betty Jane Irwin, Nov. 28, 1958; children: Christopher, Stephanie, Todd. B.S., U.S. Mil. Acad., 1954; M.S.E. in Instrumentation Engring, U. Mich., 1960, M.S.E. in Aero./Astronautical Engring, 1960; grad. with distinction, Air Command and Staff Coll., 1965, Indsl. Coll. Armed Forces, 1970. Commd. 2d lt. U.S. Air Force, 1954, advanced through grades to gen., 1983; served in numerous operational and research assignments, 1954-73; comdr. 39th Aerospace Rescue and Recovery Wing, Eglin AFB, Fla., 1973-75, Air Res. Personnel Center, Denver, 1975-76; dep. dir. concepts Hdqrs. USAF, Washington, 1976-77; dep. dir. Force Devel. and Strategic Plans, Plans and Policy Directorate, Office Joint Chiefs of Staff, Washington, 1977-78; vice dir. Joint Staff, 1978-80; commandant Indsl. Coll. of Armed Forces, Washington, 1980-81; dir. Joint Staff, 1981-83; chief of staff SHAPE, 1983-85; pres. Logicon RDA, corp. v.p.; bd. dirs. The Presley Cos. Decorated Def. Disting. Service medal with two oak leaf clusters, Legion of Merit with 1 oak leaf cluster, D.F.C., Bronze Star, Air medal with 5 oak leaf clusters, Meritorious Service medal with 2 oak leaf clusters, Air Force Commendation medal. Mem. Air Force Assn., Assn. Grads. U.S. Mil. Acad., Council Fgn. Relations. Roman Catholic. Home: 61 Misty Acres Rd Palos Verdes Peninsula CA 90274-5749

DALTON, PHYLLIS IRENE, library consultant; b. Marietta, Kans., Sept. 25, 1909; d. Benjamin Reuben and Pearl (Travelute) Bull; m. Jack Mason Dalton, Feb. 13, 1950. BS, U. Nebr., 1931, MA, 1941; MA, U. Denver, 1942. Tchr. city schs., Marysville, Kans., 1931-40; reference libr. Lincoln Pub. Libr., Nebr.; libr. U. Nebr., Lincoln, 1941-48; libr. Calif. State Libr., Sacramento, 1948-57, asst. state libr., 1957-72; pvt. libr. cons., Scottsdale, Ariz., 1972—. Author: Library Services to the Deaf and Hearing Impaired Individuals, 1985, 91 (Pres.' Com. Employment of Handicapped award 1985); contbr. chpt., articles, reports to books and publs. in field. Mem. exec. bd. So. Nev. Hist. Soc., Las Vegas, 1983-84; mem. So. Nev. Com. on Employment of Handicapped, 1980-89, chairperson, 1988-89; mem. adv. com. Nat. Orgn. on Disability, 1982-94; mem., sec. resident coun. Forum Pueblo Norte Retirement Village, 1990-91, pres. resident coun., 1991-94; bd. dirs. Friends of So. Nev. Libraries; trustee Univ. Library Soc., U. Nev.-Las Vegas; mem. Allied Arts Council, Pres.' Com. on Employment of People with Disabilities, mem. emeritus 1989—, Ariz. Gov.'s Com. on Employment of People with Disabilities, 1990—, Scottsdale Mayor's Com. on Employment of People with Disabilities, 1990—, Scottsdale Pub. Libr. Ams. With Disabilities Com., 1994—. Recipient Libraria Sodalitas, U. So. Calif., 1972, Alumni Achievement award U. Denver, 1977, Alumni Achievement award U. Nebr., Lincoln, 1983; named Mover and Shaker Scottsdale Mag., 1994. Mem. LWV, ALA (councilor 1963-64, exceptional svc. award 1981, award com. O.C.L.C. Humphreys Forest Press award 1994), Am. Assn. U. Women, Assn. State Librs. (pres. 1964-65), Calif. Libr. Assn. (pres. 1969), Nev. Libr. Assn. (hon.), Internat. Fedn. Libr. Assns. and Instns. (chair working group on libr. svc. to prisons, mem. standing com. Sect. Librs. Serving Disadvantaged Persons 1981-95), Nat. League Am. Pen Women (Las Vegas chpt. 1988-94, mem. com. on qualifications for Letters membership 1994—, parliamentarian Scottsdale chpt. 1989-94, v.p. 1992-94), Am. Correctional Assn. (libr. svcs. instns. com. 1994—), Pilot Internat. (mem.-at-large). Republican. Presbyterian. Home: 7090 E Mescal St Apt 261 Scottsdale AZ 85254-6125

DALTON, THOMAS GEORGE, paralegal, social worker, legal consultant; b. Hoonah, Alaska, Mar. 13, 1940; s. George and Jessie K. (Starr) D.; m. Hazel Hope, Nov. 1960 (div. Sept. 1965); children: Roderick O., Rhoeda J. Garcia, Pamela Y. Masterman; m. Kathy Pelan, Sept. 1972 (div. Feb. 1980); children: Deirdra J. (dec.), Thomas L., Michael G. AAS, Shoreline Community Coll., Seattle, 1981; BA, Seattle Pacific U., 1984. Paralegal, social worker Pub. Defender's Assn., Seattle, 1983—; client advocate in criminal justice system Seattle, 1984—; legal cons., Seattle; tchr. Tlingit Culture and Lang., Northwest Indian Coll., Tacoma, Wash. Elder United Presbyn. Ch., Hoonah, 1973—; pres. Alaska Native Brotherhood, Seattle, 1984—, Nat. Am. Community Coun., Seattle, 1990—; mem. Seattle chpt. Tlinget and Haida Indians Alaska. Recipient Founder's award Alaska Native Brotherhood, 1989. Democrat. Home: 7009 10th Ave NW Seattle WA 98117-5242 Office: Ctrl Bldg 8th fl 810 3rd Ave Seattle WA 98104

DALY, CAROL LYNN, economic policy center executive; b. Evanston, Ill., Oct. 4, 1942; d. James Clark and Cornelia Bertha (Gore) King; m. Paul Lawrence Daly, Mar. 20, 1921; stepchildren: Janette, Jennifer, Paula, Camilla. BA, Bennington (Vt.) Coll., 1964. Field rep. U.S. Office of Econ. Opportunity, Washington, 1964-65, Kansas City and Missoula, 1965-69; co-owner, v.p. Exec. Air Corp., Spokane, Wash., 1969-77; econ. devel. specialist Mont. Dept. of Cmty. Affairs, Helena, 1978-80; exec. dir. Pvt. Industry Coun., Helena, 1980-82; co-owner, v.p. JBM Inc., Kalispell, Mont., 1983-94; adminstr., bus. asst. Mont. Dept. Commerce, Helena, 1986-88; exec. dir. Flathead Econ. Devel. Corp., Kalispell, Mont., 1988-95; pres., exec. dir. Flathead Econ. Policy Ctr., 1995—; co-owner, operator Cattle/Hay/Timber ranches, Ovando and Condon, Mont., 1969-93; bd. dirs. North Flathead Mfg. Network, Columbia Falls, Mont.; mem. leadership coun. N.W. Policy Ctr., Seattle, 1992—; mem. loan com. N.W. Mont. Microbus. Fin., Kalispell, 1992—, Mont. Cmty. Fin. Corp., Helena, 1993—. Author: Potential Uses/Coal Tax Trust, 1985, Which Way To Tomorrow?, 1992; contbr. articles to reports. Judge bus. plans competition U. Mont., Missoula, 1990-94; co-chair Coop. Planning Coalition, Kalispell, 1993-94. Recipient Woman of Distinction award Soroptimists Internat., 1992, Partnership award Glacier Nat. Park, 1994. Mem. Am. Soc. Quality Control, Soc. of Mfg. Engrs. Democrat. Episcopalian. Home: 921 Columbia Ave Whitefish MT 59937-2841 Office: Flathead Econ Policy Ctr 15 Depot Park Kalispell MT 59901

DALY, KELLY SUE, English language educator, medical technician; b. Van Nuys, Calif., Dec. 14, 1964; d. Thomas Clarence and Camille (Contino) D.; m. B.L. Moore, Jan. 23, 1986; 1 child, Thomas Vincent Daly Moore. AA in Liberal Studies, Coll. of the Desert, Palm Desert, Calif., 1990; BA in English, Calif. State U., San Bernandino, 1992. Calif. teaching credential. Lab. med. tech. Desert Hosp., Palm Springs, Calif., 1983-93; English as a second lang. Desert Springs (Calif.) Middle Sch., 1994; 9th grade English tchr. Cathedral City (Calif.) H.S., 1993—. Author various poems, 1994. Mem. Coll. of the Desert Alumni Assn., Palm Desert, Calif., 1994—. Democrat.

DALY, PAUL SYLVESTER, retired academic administrator; b. Belmont, Mass., Jan. 8, 1934; s. Matthew Joseph and Alice Mary (Hall) D.; m. Maureen Teresa Kenny, May 25, 1957; children: Judith Mary, Paul S. Jr., Susan Marie, John Joseph, Maureen H. BS in Engring. Sci., Naval Post-grad. Sch., 1968; MBA, U. W. Fla., 1971. Commd. ensign USN, 1955; coll. dean Embry-Riddle Aero. U., Daytona Beach, Fla., 1979-81; advanced through grades to capt. Embry-Riddle Aero. U., 1979, chancellor, 1981-95; lectr. seminars, 1977-85; cons. British Aerospace, 1979-84, McDonnell Douglas, 1979-84, IBM, 1983-84; sr. faculty U. Phoenix, 1983-86. Bd. dirs. Yavapai Regional Med. Ctr., Prescott, Ariz., 1983-86, Ariz. Hosp. Fedn., Prescott C. of C., 1982-84; chmn. Ariz. State Bd. Pvt. Postsecondary Edn., Phoenix, 1982—, Interactive Health Corp.; pres. Ind. Coll. and Univs. of Ariz., Phoenix, 1982—; pres., founder West Yavapai County Am. Heart Assn. Chpt., chmn. affiliate of Am. Heart Assn./Ariz. Decorated Legion of Merit. Mem. Ariz. Airport Assn., Retired Officers Assn., Ariz. Town Hall, USAF Assn. Republican. Roman Catholic. Office: Embry-Riddle Aero U 3200 Willow Creek Rd Prescott AZ 86301-3721

DALY, TOM, mayor; m. Debra Daly; children: Anna, Ryan. BA, Harvard U., 1976. Elected mem. City Council of Anaheim, 1988, elected mayor, 1992-94, 94—. mem. bd. trustees Anaheim Union Hish Sch. Dist., 1985—; active Anaheim Library Bd., 1985—; mem. adv. bd. Anaheim Boys and Girls Club; mem. bd. dirs. cmty. support group Anaheim Meml. Hosp.; mem. bd. dirs. Orange County Transp. Authority, Urban Water Inst.; mem. El Toro Citizens Adv. Commn.; chair regional adv. planning coun. Orange County, 1992—. Office: Office of the Mayor/City Council City Hall 200 S Anaheim Blvd Anaheim CA 92805-3820

DAMASCHINO, ANN TOOTHMAN, school development administrator; b. Oakland, Calif., Dec. 14, 1938; d. James Wesley and Aileen Elizabeth (Cox) Toothman; m. Douglas Alan Damaschino, Aug. 12, 1961; children: Lori Damaschino Berry, Ellen Damaschino Mellies, Gerald, Anthony. BA in English Lit. with honors, Holy Names Coll., 1962; MA in Philanthropy and Devel., St. Mary's Coll. Minn., 1994. Reader in English/social studies Acalanes Union High Sch. Dist., Lafayette, Calif., 1964-77; interior designer, ptnr. Damaschino/Thurling, Lafayette, Calif., 1973-81; tech. writer, editor Shell Oil Co., Martinez, Calif., 1981-85; dir. devel. St. Mary's Coll. High Sch., Berkeley, Calif., 1985—. Pres., sec., treas. Walnut Creek (Calif.) Gallery Guild, 1968-76; mem. Contra Costa County Bd. "Project Second Chance" Adult Literacy Program, 1986-88. Mem. AAUW, Coun. for Advancement and Support of Edn., East Bay Devel. Dirs., Diocese of Oakland Devel. Dirs. Democrat. Roman Catholic. Office: Saint Marys Coll High Sch Peralta Park Berkeley CA 94706

DAMBROSIO, ANNETTE, English language educator; b. San Francisco, Apr. 10, 1953; d. John L. and Viola Dambrosio. MA English, Chico State U., 1978; postgrad., U. Calif., Berkeley, 1989—. English tchr./reading dept. coord. Solano Community Coll., Suisun, Calif.; mem. Basic Skills adv. com. CCC Chancellors Office; lectr. in field. Contbr. articles to profl. jours. Recipient 1984 Outstanding Contbn. to Lit. award Calif. Reading Assn., Nat. Advisor award Women in Comm., 1985. Mem. Am. Ednl. Rsch. Assn., Coll. Reading/Learning Assn., Nat. Coun. Tchrs. English, Nat. Assn. Devel. Edn., Calif. Reading Assn., Faculty Assn. Calif. C.C. (bd. govs., v.p.). Office: Solano Coll 4000 Suisun Valley Rd Suisun City CA 94585

DAMÉ-SHEPP, DIANE, art management administrator; b. Berkeley, Calif., Nov. 1, 1946; d. Paul David and Eleanor June Ingraham; m. Michael Joseph Damé (div.); children: Josette Laura, Criselle Lynn; m. Alan Martin Shepp; children: Castiel Armanda, Zia Felice. BA, U. Calif., Berkeley, 1977, cert. Mus. Mgmt. Inst. Am. Fedn. Arts, 1982; cert., Grantsmanship Tng. Ctr., San Francisco, 1984; cert. Leadership Inst., Calif. Arts Coun., Sacramento, 1988. Teaching asst., video co-prodr., writer art dept. Los Medanos Coll., Pittsburg, Calif., 1974-78; asst. security supr., spl. events coord. Univ. Art Mus., Berkeley, Calif., 1976-82, exec. dir. Univ. Art Mus. Coun., 1982-83; asst. devel. dir. Univ. Art Mus., U. Calif., Berkeley, 1983-85; exec. dir. Napa (Calif.) County Arts Coun., 1985-88, Solano County Arts Alliance, Fairfield, Calif., 1993-95; founding bd. mem., past pres. Calif. Assembly Local Arts Agys., San Francisco, 1986-92; leadership com. Nat. Assembly Local Arts Agys., Washington, 1987-91; art mgmt. cons. Calif. Arts Coun., Mono County Arts, Nevada County Arts, Napa Landmarks, Calif., 1988—, Nat. Spks. Bur. Fly Fishing, Tulsa, 1994—. Artist/sculptor Sacramento Met. Arts Commn.-Light Rail Project Starfire Sta., 1984-87; exhibited in group shows at Weiss Gallery, San Francisco, 1984-85, Zaks Gallery,Chgo., 1982-87, San Francisco Airport, 1987-88, San Francisco Mus. Modern Art Coun. Auction, 1988, New Langston Arts, San Francisco, 1990, Headlands Art Coun., Marin, Calif., 1993, Clos Pegase Winery, St. Helena, Calif., 1994, Sonoma State U., 1986, 88, 89, 90, 91, 94, Oakland Mus. Collectors Gallery, 1994. Founding bd. dirs., v.p., fundraising sec./treas. Napa Valley Opera House, Inc., 1985—; mem. faculty Leadership Napa, 1986-90; founding bd. mem., sec. Napa Valley Film Festival; sight coord. Internat. Sculpture Conf., Oakland, 1982. Recipient Calif. State Scholarship, 1976, Scholarship AAUW, 1975-77, Mus.Mgmt. Inst. Scholarship Art Mus. Assn., Berkeley, 1982. Home and Office: PO Box 2398 Yountville CA 94599

D'AMICO, MICHAEL, architect, urban planner; b. Bklyn., Sept. 11, 1936; s. Michael and Rosalie (Vinciguerra) D.; BArch, U. Okla., 1961; postgrad. So. Meth. U. Sch. Law, 1962-63, Coll. Marin, 1988-89;, San Francisco Law Sch., 1994—; m. Joan Hand, Nov. 26, 1955; children: Michael III, Dion Charles. Supr. advanced planning sect. Dallas Dept. City Planning, 1961-63; designer, planner in charge Leo A. Daly Co., San Francisco, 1963-66; project planner Whisler, Patri Assos., San Francisco, 1966-67; architect, urban planner D'Amico & Assocs., San Francisco, N.Y., Guam, 1967-73, pres. D'Amico & Assocs., Inc., Mill Valley and San Francisco, Calif., and Guam, 1973—; pres. Jericho Alpha Inc., 1979-82; cons. architect, planner City of Seaside (Calif.), 1967-72, 79-81, 89—; cons. urban redevel. Eureka (Calif.), 1967-82; cons. planner, Lakewood, Calif.; redevel. cons. to Daly City (Calif.), 1975-77; redevel. adviser to Tamalpais Valley Bus. Assn., 1975-77; archtl. and hist. analyst to Calif. Dept. Transp., 1975-77; agt. for Eureka, Calif. Coastal Commn., 1977-79; devel. cons. City of Scotts Valley, 1988—, City of Suisun, 1988-89, City of Union City, 1989-91. Mem. steering com. San Francisco Joint Com. Urban Design, 1967-72. Recipient Community Design award AIA, 1970; First prize award Port Aransas (Tex.) Master Plan Competition, 1964; Design award Karachi Mcpl. Authority, 1987, Merit award St. Vincent's/Silveira. Mem. AIA (inactive), Am. Inst. Cons. Planners, Am. Planning Assn., Calif. Assn. Planning Cons. (sec., treas. 1970-72), World Future Soc., Solar Energy Soc. Am. Office: 525 Midvale Way Mill Valley CA 94941-3705

DAMON, JAMES CHRISTIAN, communications engineer; b. Ft. Belvoir, Va., Oct. 30, 1951; s. John Charles and Alice Darlene (Hays) D. ASET, Grantham Sch. Engring., Washington, 1972. Lic. FCC 1st class radiotelephone with radar endorsement. Sr. engring. asst. Lockheed Missiles and Space, San Diego, to 1986; owner and prin. Signal Scis., Flagstaff, Ariz., 1986—; licensee, prin. KMJ-TV 6, Flagstaff, Ariz., 1991—. Designer programmable channel deletion filter, designer, builder RRCS com. CATV system for Rough Rock, Ariz. Precinct committeeman, Coconino County Rep. Party, Flagstaff, 1987-89; speaker, Sunshine Rescue Mission, Flagstaff, 1988. Mem. IEEE, Soc. Cable TV Engrs., Soc. Broadcast Engrs. Republican. Home: PO Box 1890 Flagstaff AZ 86002-1890 Office: Signal Sciences PO Box 1890 Flagstaff AZ 86002-1890

DAMON, JAMES G., lawyer; b. L.A., Dec. 5, 1957; s. James G. and Tessie A. Damon; m. Jennifer A. Damon; children: Allison, Corinne. BA, Johns Hopkins U., 1980; JD, Loyola Law Sch. L.A., 1984. Clk. to hon. Warren Eginton U.S. Dist. Ct. Judge, Bridgeport, Conn., 1985-86; assoc. Loeb and Loeb, L.A., 1986-92; ptnr. Voss Cook & Thel, Newport Beach, Calif., 1992—. Mem. Orange County Bar Assn. Office: Voss Cook & Thal 840 Newport Center Dr Ste 700 Newport Beach CA 92660-6326

DAMON, MICHAEL, systems design and marketing executive; b. L.A., Oct. 29, 1962; s. Richard Allen and Gloria Elizabeth (Fox) Olson. Student, San Diego State U., 1986, Pacific Western U., 1988. Lic. real estate broker, Calif.; credentials of ministry, Calif. Ptnr. MDO Investments, San Diego, 1981-84; sales dir. Promotional Concept, Inc., San Diego, 1984-85; sr. acct. exec. T.J. Carr Investment Co., La Jolla, Calif., 1985-88; sales dir. Discover The Bahama's Ltd., San Diego, 1988-90, Creative Mktg. Systems, San Diego, 1990-92; pres. Live to Win, La Jolla, 1989—; dir. system design and mktg. Nat. Response Media, San Diego, 1992—. Republican. Home: 108 N Palm Dr Beverly Hills CA 90210 Office: Nat Response Media Beverly Hills CA 90210

DAMPHOUSSE, VINCENT, professional hockey player; b. Montreal, Ont., Can., Dec. 17, 1967. Left wing/center Edmonton (Can.) Oilers, 1991-93; left wing Montreal Canadiens, 1993—; mem. Stanley Cup championship team, 1993. Shares NHL All-Star single-game record for most goals (4), 1991. Office: Montreal Canadiens, 2313 St Catherine St W, Montreal, PQ Canada H3H 1N2*

DAMSBO, ANN MARIE, psychologist; b. Cortland, N.Y., July 7, 1931; d. Jorgen Einer and Agatha Irene (Schenck) D. B.S., San Diego State Coll., 1952; M.A., U.S. Internat. U., 1974, Ph.D., 1975. Diplomate Am. Acad. Pain Mgmt. Commd. 2d lt. U.S. Army, 1952, advanced through grades to capt., 1957; staff therapist Letterman Army Hosp., San Francisco, 1953-54, 56-58, 61-62, Ft. Devers, Ft. Devens, Mass., 1955-56, Walter Reed Army Hosp., Washington, 1958-59, Tripler Army Hosp., Hawaii, 1959-61, Ft. Benning, Ga., 1962-64; chief therapist U.S. Army Hosp., Ft. McPherson, Ga., 1964-67; ret. U.S. Army, 1967; med. missionary So. Presbyterian Ch., Taiwan, 1968-70; psychology intern So. Naval Hosp., San Diego, 1975; predoctoral intern Naval Regional Med. Ctr., San Diego, 1975-76, postdoctoral intern, 1975-76, chief, founder pain clinic, 1977-86; chief pain clinic, 1977-86; adj. tchr. U. Calif. Med. Sch., San Diego; lectr., U.S., Can., Eng., France, Australia; cons. forensic hypnosis to law enforcement agys.; approved cons. in hypnosis. Contbr. articles to profl. publs., chpt. to book. Tchr. Sunday sch. United Meth. Ch., 1945—; Rep. Nat. Candidate Trust Presdl. adv. com., platform planning commn. at-large-del. Fellow Am. Soc. Clin. Hypnosis (psychology mem.-at-large, exec. bd. 1989-90), San Diego Soc. Clin. Hypnosis (pres. 1980); mem. AAUW, Am. Phys. Therapy Assn., Calif. Soc. Clin. and Hypnosis (bd. govs.), Am. Soc. Clin. Hypnosis Edn. Rsch. Found. (trustee 1992-94), Internat. Platform Assn., Am. Soc. Clin. Hypnosis (exec. bd.), Ret. Officers Am., Ret. Officers Assn. (rep. presdl. task force, pres. adv. com.), Toastmasters (local pres.), Job's Daus. Republican. Home and Office: 1062 W 5th Ave Escondido CA 92025-3802

DAMSKY, ROBERT PHILIP, communications executive; b. Boston, May 19, 1921; s. Mark and Ann (Wisser) D.; m. Rose Hollender, Jan. 18, 1955 (div. 1985); children: Marla Markley, Lori Diana. Cert., MIT, 1939, Tex. A&M U., 1944; diploma, Spartan Sch. Aero., Tulsa, 1946. Indsl. editor Spartan Aircraft Co., Tulsa, 1946-47; with Transocean Airlines, Hartford, Conn., 1947; chief pilot MIT, Beverly, Mass., 1947-48; sr. check pilot Civil Air Patrol, Beverly, 1948; airport mgr. Hartport, Inc., Bellfontaine, Ohio, 1948-49; airline pilot Slick Airlines and U.S. Overseas Airlines, Burbank, Calif. and Wildwood, N.J., 1949-55; founder Flight Edn. Assn., Santa Ana, Calif., 1955-80; pub., editor, pres. Aeromedia Nat. Syndicate, L.A., 1980—. Aviation editor: Beverly News, Mass., Gen. Aviation News. With U.S. Army Air Corps, 1940-45. Decorated Purple Heart, 1941. Mem. Airline Pilots Assn., Aircraft Owners and Pilots Assn., Silver Wings, VFW, Am. Legion, Pearl Harbor Survivors Assn. Home: PO Box 2704 Costa Mesa CA 92628-2704

DAN, BARBARA GRIFFIN, publisher, editor, author; b. Glen Ridge, N.J., Apr. 10, 1934; d. Frank L. Jr. and Marjorie McDougal Griffin; m. John Dan, May 9, 1959; children: Georgia Lee, Carrie Joyce, Michael Casey, Peter John. BA in Theatre Arts, Thomas A. Edison State Coll., Trenton, N.J., 1986; MA in Humanities, Calif. State U-Dominguez Hills, 1988. Cert. couples comms. workshop instr. Editor LionHearted Pub., Zephyr Cove, Nev., 1993—; pub., owner Eden Pub., The Lakes, Nev., 1994—. Author 8 novels; co-author: Power to Choose, 1994; writer for numerous orgns., TV prodn. co., mags., others; author articles, adventure and children's fiction. Co-founder Las Vegas Writers Workshop, 1993. Mem. Silver State Fiction Writers (chmn. Las Vegas chpt. 1992-93), Romance Writers Am. Republican. Christian. Office: Eden Pub 8635 W Sahara Ave Ste 459 Las Vegas NV 89117-5858

DANA, CHARLES HAROLD, JR., computer science educator; b. San Jose, Calif., Oct. 13, 1950; s. Charles Harold and Delvina Anna (Malatesta) D. BA, U. Calif., Santa Barbara, 1972, MS, 1974, PhD, 1981. Assoc. prof. Calif. Poly. State U., San Luis Obispo, 1982-88, prof. computer sci., 1988—. Mem. IEEE, Assn. Computing Machinery. Roman Catholic. Home: 1609 Royal Way San Luis Obispo CA 93405-6333 Office: Calif Poly State U Computer Sci Dept San Luis Obispo CA 93407

DANA, GEORGE F. (PETE DANA), consulting geologist; b. Waynesboro, Va., Oct. 23, 1929; s. George William and Madalyn (Hollar) D.; m. Phyllis Whitford, Aug. 15, 1949 (div. Sept. 1959); children: George, Debra, Sandra; m. Joan Nelson, Aug. 13, 1960; children: Donald, Karin. BS, U. Okla., 1952, MS, 1954. Registered profl. geologist, Wyo. Geologist Marathon Oil Co., Cody, Wyo., 1954-59, Husky Oil Co., Cody, 1959-60; chief ground water devel. State of Wyo.-Natural Resources Bd., Cheyenne, Wyo., 1960-63; geologist U. Wyo.-Nat. Resources Rsch. Inst., Laramie, Wyo., 1963-65; rsch. geologist U.S. Bur. Mines, Laramie, 1965-74, sr. geologist, 1974-79; mgr. geology and geochemistry US DOE-Laramie (Wyo.) Rsch. Ctr., 1979-83, Western Rsch. Inst., Laramie, 1983-85; pres., owner Dana Cons., Laramie, 1985—. Contbr. articles to profl. jours. Mem. Am. Assn. Petroleum Geologists (asst. oil shale councillor 1975-85), Elks. Lutheran. Home and Office: 1719 Downey St Laramie WY 82070-1918

DANA, HUGH RICHARD, internist, educator; b. Balt., May 28, 1950; s. Edward Runkle and Lilian Lorraine (Kirschner) D. BS, U. N.C., 1973; MD, U. So. Calif., 1978. Diplomate Am. Bd. Internal Medicine. Intern in medicine St. Mary's Hosp.-UCLA, Long Beach, 1978-79; rsch. in hematology Mayo Clinic, Rochester, Minn., 1979-80; resident in internal medicine U. Calif.-Irvine program VA Hosp., Long Beach, 1980-82, physician ambulatory care clinic, 1983-89; staff physician Kaiser Permanente, Bellflower, Calif., 1989-91, Family Health Plan Inc., Long Beach, Calif., 1991—; asst. clin. prof. U. Calif.-Irvine Sch. Medicine, Orange, 1989—. Mem. ACP, AMA. Home and Office: 5595 E 7th St Apt 297 Long Beach CA 90804-4453

DANA, RICHARD E., oil industry executive; b. 1944. BA, Alma Coll. CPA Coopers & Lybrand, 1967-72; contr. Total Petroleum N.Am., Denver, 1972-80, treas., 1980-82, v.p., treas., 1982-85; dir. non engring. functions Total Compagnie Francaise des Petroles, 1985-89; sr. v.p., CFO Total Petroleum N.Am., Denver, 1989-92, sr. v.p. product supply, 1992—. Office: Total Petroleum N Am 999 19th St # 2201 Denver CO 80202-2507

DANCE, FRANCIS ESBURN XAVIER, communication educator; b. Bklyn., Nov. 9, 1929; s. Clifton Louis and Catherine (Tester) D.; m. Nora Alice Rush, May 1, 1954 (div. 1974); children: Clifton Louis III, Charles Daniel, Alison Catherine, Andrea Frances, Frances Sue, Brendan Rush; m. Carol Camille Zak, July 4, 1974; children: Zachary Esburn, Gabriel Joseph, Caleb Michael, Catherine Emily. BS, Fordham U., 1951; MA, Northwestern U., 1953, PhD, 1959. Instr. speech Bklyn. Adult Labor Schs., 1951; instr. humanities, coordinator radio and TV U. Ill. at Chgo., 1953-54; instr. Univ. Coll., U. Chgo., 1958; asst. prof. St. Joseph's (Ind.) Coll., 1958-60; asst. prof., then assoc. prof. U. Kans., 1960-63; mem. faculty U. Wis., Milw., 1963-71, prof. communication, 1965-71, dir. Speech Communication Center, 1963-70; prof. U. Denver, 1971—; content expert and mem. faculty adv. bd. to Univ. Coll. on Mind Ext. U., 1993—; cons. in field. Author: The Citizen Speaks, 1962, (with Harold P. Zelko) Business and Professional Speech Communication, 1965, 2d edit., 1978, Human Communication Theory, 1967, (with Carl E. Larson) Perspectives on Communication, 1970, Speech Communication: Concepts and Behavior, 1972, The Functions of Speech Communication: A Theoretical Approach, 1976, Human Communication Theory, 1982, (with Carol C. Zak-Dance) Public Speaking, 1986, Speaking Your Mind, 1994; editor: Jour. Communication, 1962-64, Speech Tchr, 1970-72; adv. bd.: Jour. Black Studies; editorial bd.: Jour. Psycholinguistic Research; Contbr. articles to profl. jours. Bd. dirs. Milw. Mental Health Assn., 1966-67. 2d lt. AUS, 1954-56. Knapp Univ. scholar in communication, 1967-68; recipient Outstanding Prof. award Standard Oil Found., 1967; Master Tchr. award U. Denver, 1985, University Lectr. award U. Denver, 1986. Fellow Internat. Communication Assn. (pres. 1967); mem. Speech Communication Assn. (pres. 1982), Psi Upsilon. Office: U Denver Dept Human Comm Studies Denver CO 80208

DANG, MARVIN S.C., lawyer; b. Honolulu, Feb. 11, 1954; s. Brian K.T. and Flora (Yuen) D. BA with distinction, U. Hawaii, 1974; JD, George Washington U., 1978. Bar: Hawaii 1978, U.S. Dist. Ct. Hawaii 1978, U.S. Ct. Appeals (9th cir.) 1979. Atty. Gerson, Steiner & Anderson and predecessor firms, Honolulu, 1978-81; owner, atty. Law Offices of Marvin S.C. Dang, Honolulu, 1981—; sr. v.p., bd. dirs. Rainbow Fin. Corp., Honolulu, 1984—; bd. dirs. Foster Equipment Co. Ltd., Honolulu, Hawaii Cmty. Reinvestment Corp., bd. dirs.; bd. dirs. Hawaii Fin. Svcs. Assn., 1990—, sec., 1991, treas., 1992, v.p. 1993, pres. 1994; vice chmn. Hawaii consumer Fin. PAC, 1988—; hearings officer (per diem) Adminstrv. Drivers Licence Revocation Office, Honolulu, 1991—. State rep., asst. minority floor leader Hawaii State Legislature, Honolulu, 1982-84; chmn., vice chmn., mem. Manoa Neighborhod Bd., Honolulu, 1979-82, 84-87; pres., v.p., mem. Hawaii Coun. on Legal Edn. for Youth, Honolulu, 1979-86; mem. Hawaii Bicentennial Commn. of U.S. Constn., Honolulu, 1986-88;. Recipient Cert. of Appreciation award Hawaii Speech-Lang.-Hearing Assn., Honolulu, 1984; named one of Ten Outstanding Young Persons of Hawaii, Hawaii State Jaycees, 1983. Mem. ABA (resource devel. coun. of fund for justice and edn. 1993—, standing com. on law and electoral process 1985-89, spl. com. on youth edn. for citizenship 1979-85, 89-92, Hawaii membership chmn. 1981-93, exec. coun. young lawyers div. 1986-88), Hawaii Bar (bd. dirs. young lawyers div. 1990), Hawaii Fin. Svcs. Assn. (bd. dirs. 1990—, sec. 1991, treas. 1992, v.p. 1993, pres. 1994), Plaza Club Hawaii. Republican. Office: PO Box 4109 Honolulu HI 96812-4109

DANG, NGON TRUNG, engineering executive; b. Saigon, Vietnam, May 5, 1949; came to U.S., 1979; s. Quyen Trung and Beo Thi (Nguyen) D.; m. Hue Kim Dinh, Feb. 6, 1977; children: Nghia Trung Dang, Nghi Trung Dang, Nghiep Trung Dang. BSEE, San Diego State U., 1973, postgrad., 1980; postgrad., Saigon U., 1975. Project engr. Vietnam Power Co., Saigon, 1973-74; lab. mgr. Vietnam Bur. of Stds., Saigon, 1974-79; project engr. Vernitron Corp., San Diego, 1979-85, sr. project engr., 1991-93, engring. mgr., 1993; project engr. Imo Industries Inc., San Dimas, Calif., 1985-91; pres. D&D Engring., Laverne, Calif., 1988-91. Pres. Quoc Gia Nghia Tu Alumi, Saigon, 1973-74. Mem. IEEE, Am. Inst. of Motion Engrs. (founder). Home: 11735 Kismet Rd San Diego CA 92128-5009 Office: Vernitron Corp Motion Control Group 1601 Precision Park Ln San Diego CA 92173-1345

DANGER, SUZAN ELIZABETH, elementary education educator; b. Ft. Dodge, Iowa, Apr. 27, 1966; d. Clarence Ira and Carol Kay (Ellis) D. BA in Edn., Mt. St. Mary's Coll., 1988; MS in Counseling, Calif. State U., San Bernardino, 1994. Cert. tchr., Calif., Ky. Tchr. Riverside (Calif.) Unified Sch. Dist., 1988—. Appeared in TV comml. IBM, 1992. Mem. ACA, NEA, Calif. Sch. Counselors Assn., Phi Delta Pi, Delta Epsilon Sigma, Kappa Delta Chi. Home: 8795 Kentville St Riverside CA 92508-3241

DANGLA, KRISTINE LINDSAY, marketing director, consultant; b. Toronto, Ont., Canada, June 8, 1965; came to U.S., 1969; d. John Rufus and Marjorie Clare (Dwyer) Lindsay; m. Mathias Daniel Dangla, Aug. 3, 1991. BS in Mktg., Ohio State U., 1987. Prodn. asst. MCA Records, Universal City, Calif., 1988-90; mktg. coord. Giant Records, Divsn. Warner Bros. Records, L.A., 1990; product mgr. Polygram Video/Island Visual Arts, Divsn. Island Records, L.A., 1990-92; mktg. dir. Bad Animals/Seattle-Lawson Prodns., Inc., Seattle, 1992—; cons. mktg. Leadership Inst. Seattle, 1994—. Mem. external com. Seattle-Nantes Sister City Assn., 1993-94. Mem. Internat. TV and Video Assn. (bd. dirs., mem. external com. 1993-94). Office: Lawson Prodns Inc 2212 4th Ave Seattle WA 98121-2025

DANIEL, BARBARA ANN, secondary education educator, English educator; b. LaCrosse, Wis., Mar. 22, 1938; d. Rudolph J. and Dorothy M. (Farnham) Beranek; m. David Daniel; children: Raychelle, Clarence, Bernadette, Brenda. BS in Edn. cum laude, Midwestern U., Wichita Falls, Tex., 1967; postgrad., U. Alaska, Fairbanks, Anchorage, Juneau, U. Alaska, Bethel. Cert. tchr., Alaska. Primary tchr. Bur. Indian Affairs, Nunapitchuk and Tuntutuliak, Alaska, 1967-70; tchr., generalist English lang. devel. and ESL grades 4-12 Lower Kuskokwim Sch. Dist., Tuntutuliak, 1981—; mem. lang. arts curriculum revision task force Lower Kuskokwim Sch. Dist.; mem. state bd. Academic Pentathlon, Alaska; acad. decathlon, pentathlon coach. Rsch. video recording of elders in Alaskan village. Mem. NEA, Lower Kuskokwin Edn. Assn., Nat. Coun. Tchrs. English, Alaska Coun. Tchrs. English, Alaska Assn. Bilingual Tchr. Home: 25 West Circle PO Box WTL Tuntutuliak AK 99680-9998

DANIEL, CHRISTINE STEWART, lawyer; b. Anaheim, Calif., Dec. 16, 1963; d. Richard and Mary Ellen (Stewart) D. BA, Mills Coll., 1986; JD, U. Calif., Davis, 1989. Assoc. Hardin Cook et al, Oakland, Calif., 1989-92; dep. city atty. City of Berkeley, Calif., 1992—. Tutor adult literacy Berkeley Reads, 1993—; driver Project Open Hand, San Francisco, 1993—. Mem. ABA, State Bar Calif., Alumnae Assn. Mills Coll. (v.p. 1991—). Office: City of Berkeley 2180 Milvia St 4th fl Berkeley CA 94704-1100

DANIEL, GARY WAYNE, communications and music industry executive; b. Wendall, Idaho, June 22, 1948; s. Milan Chauncey Daniel and Ila Fay (Cox) Harkins; m. Jeanne Laurane Blandford, July 1969 (div. Aug. 1972); 1 child, Kelly Jean; m. Sandra Kay Modey, July 26, 1974; 1 child, Marcus Chauncey. AA, Boise Bus. Coll., 1969; PhD in Psychology, West Brook U., 1994. Cert. master practitioner Neuro Linguistic Programming. Program dir. Sta. KSKI, Sun Valley, Idaho, 1967-68, Sta. KYME, Boise, Idaho, 1968-69; gen. mgr. Sta. KSPD, Boise, 1969-72; radio personality Sta. KBBK-FM, Boise, 1972-74; account exec. ABC-TV, Nampa, Idaho, 1974-77; nat. sales dir. Agri-Steel Corp., Boise, 1977-79; mgmt. ptnr. Agri. Devel. Corp., Caldwell, Idaho, 1979-82; owner, prin. Video Magic Amusement Co., Caldwell, 1982-85; pres., chief exec. officer Victory Media Group, Santa Rosa, Calif., 1985—; gen. mgr. Victory Record Label, 1986—, also bd. dirs.; bd. dirs. Bay City Records, San Francisco; pres. Lightforce Music Pub., Santa Rosa, 1987—; mktg. cons. Firenze Records, San Francisco, 1987—, Capital Bus. Systems, Napa, Calif., 1986-91, Plum, Inc., Napa, 1985-86. Author: Concert Operations Manual, 1987; devel. of the Neuro Achievement System. Recipient Most Humorous TV Comml. award Boise Advt. Club, 1975, Most Creative TV Comml. award Boise Advt. Club, 1976; named Top Radio Personality Idaho State Broadcasters Assn., 1971. Mem. ASCAP, NARAS, Ind. Record Mfg. and Distbrs., Am. Coun. of Hypnotist Examiners, Hypnotist Examiners Coun. Calif., Am. Assn. Behavioral Therapists, Internat. Assn. of NLP, Time Line Therapy Assn. Republican. Office: Neuro Achievement Ctr 55 Maria Dr Ste 844 Petaluma CA 94954-3563

DANIEL, HELEN ANDERSON, secondary education educator, psychotherapist, intern; b. San Francisco, Aug. 16, 1941; d. Wallace Robert and Etta Mignon (Stanton) Anderson; m. Bernard Bell Thornquist, Aug. 29, 1960 (div. Dec. 1972); children: Ingrid Anne, Carl Robert; m. Douglas Walker Daniel, Dec. 26, 1985; stepchildren: Jennifer Lynn, Laura Lee. BA, San Jose State Coll., 1963; MA, John F. Kennedy U., 1992. Std. secondary tchg. credential. Tchr. DeAnza H.S., El Sobrante, Calif., 1964-65, Fredriksen Sch., Dublin, Calif., 1966-67, Fresno (Calif.) County Youth Authority, 1972; tchr. Livermore (Calif.) H.S., 1972—, chair English dept., 1976-82, 88—; therapist Valley Cmty. Health Ctr., Pleasanton, Calif., 1994—; com. mem. Dist. Curriculum Devel. Com., Livermore, 1988-90, Dist. Tech. Com., Livermore, 1990-92, Gifted and Talented Com., Livermore, 1990-92, Dist. Mentor Selection Com., 1994—; mentor tchr., Livermore H.S., 1986, 87, 92, 93. Author: (booklet) Star Writer: The Empowered Student, 1992. Tech. grantee State of Calif., 1992, libr. grantee, 1995. Home: 1950 Neptune Rd Livermore CA 94550-6322 Office: Livermore HS 600 Maple St Livermore CA 94550-3242

DANIELIAN, ARTHUR CALVIN, architect; b. Pasadena, Calif., Jan. 18, 1935; s. Moses and Siranoush (Arsenian) D.; m. Martha Annette Landre, Feb. 19, 1966; 1 son, John. A.A., Pasadena City Co., 1954; B.Arch., U. So. Calif., 1963. Designer Edward Fickett, Architect, 1963-65, William Blurock & Ptnrs., Architect, 1965-68; pres. Danielian Assocs., Newport Beach, Calif., 1968—; mem. Inst. Residential Market; speaker in field. Served with U.S. Army, 1956-58. Recipient Gold Nugget, 1973-75, 77-79; recipient award for wood sculpture U. So. Calif., 1961. Mem. AIA (chmn. nat. housing com., pres. Orange County 1977-78 award Aquatic Village). Office: Danielian Assocs 24 Purple Sage Irvine CA 92715-3706

DANIELL, VALERIE JEAN, clinical therapist, counselor; b. Norman, Okla., Aug. 13, 1952; d. Carroll V. and Mary Ellen (Edwards) Glines; m. Tim C. Daniell, Mar. 24, 1984. BA in Performing Arts and Dance, Am. U., 1975; BA in Dance for Deaf, Goddard Coll., 1977; MA in Counseling for Deaf, Gallaudet U., 1990. Mainstream pub. sch. interpreter, tutor Cherry Creek Schs., Aurora, Colo., 1980-89, Jefferson County Schs., Denver, 1980-89; asst. to state coord. on deafness Ctr. on Deafness, Denver, 1989-90; clin. therapist Human Svcs. Inc., Deaf Svcs., Denver, 1990-93; pvt. practice Denver, 1993—; mem. adv. bd. Denver Ear Inst., 1990-91, HIS Internal Mktg., Denver, 1992; participant numerous conf. and workshops in field; spkr. Family Svcs. Am., Seattle, 1991, Drug Free Schs. Nat. Conf., Gallaudet U., Washington, 1992, Colo. State Symposium on Deafness, Breckenridge, Colo., 1992, numerous Denver area pub. schs. deaf edn. programs for tchrs., parents of deaf children, 1991—, Metro State Coll., Denver, 1993, 21st Ann. Child Abuse and Neglect Symposium, Keystone, Colo., 1993. Contbr. articles to profl. jours. Mem. Am. Counseling Assn., Am. Mental Health Assn., Assn. for Play Therapy, Colo. Mental Health Assn. for the Deaf and Hard of Hearing, Colo. Assn. of Play Therapy. Home: 607 Columbine St Denver CO 80206-3816 Office: 4280 Hale Pky Denver CO 80220-3724

DANIELS, ARLENE KAPLAN, sociology educator; b. N.Y.C., Dec. 10, 1930; d. Jacob and Elizabeth (Rathstein) Kaplan; m. Richard Rene Daniels, June 9, 1956. B.A. with honors in English, U. Calif., Berkeley, 1952; M.A. in Sociology, 1954, Ph.D. in Sociology, 1960. Instr. dept. speech U. Calif., Berkeley, 1959-61; rsch. assoc. Mental Rsch. Inst., Palo Alto, Calif., 1961-66; assoc. prof. sociology San Francisco State Coll., 1966-70; chief Center for Study Women in Soc., Inst. Sci. Analysis, San Francisco, 1970-80; mem. faculty Northwestern U., Evanston, Ill., 1975-95; prof. dept. sociology Northwestern U., 1975-95, dir. Women's Studies, 1992-94; cons. NIMH, 1971-73, NEH, 1975-80, Nat. Inst. Edn., 1978-82. Editor: (with Rachel Kahn-Hut) Academics on the Line, 1970; co-editor: (with Gaye Tuchman and James Benét) Hearth and Home: Images of Women in the Mass Media, 1978, (with James Benét) Education: Straightjacket or Opportunity?, 1979, (with Rachel Kahn-Hut and Richard Colvard) Women and Work, 1982, (with Alice Cook and Val Lorwin) Women and Trade Unions in Eleven Industrialized Countries, (with Teresa Odendahl and Elizabeth Boris) Working in Foundations, 1985, Invisible Careers, 1988, (with Alice Cook and Val Lorwin) The Most Difficult Revolution: Women in the Trade Union Movement, 1992; editor: Jour. Social Problems, 1974-78; assoc. editor: Contemporary Sociology, 1980-82, Symbolic Interaction, 1979-84, Am. Sociol. Rev., 1987-90. Trustee Bus. and Profl. Women's Rsch. Found. Bd., 1980-85, Women's Equity Action League Legal and Ednl. Def. Fund, 1979-81; mem. Chgo. Rsch. Assoc. Bd., 1981-87. Recipient Social Sci. Rsch. Council Faculty Rsch. award, 1970-71; Ford Found. Faculty fellow, 1975-76; grantee Nat. Inst. Edn., 1978-79, 1979-80, NSF, 1974-75, NIMH, 1973-74. Mem. Inst. Medicine NAS, Sociologists Women in Soc. (pres. 1975-76), Am. Sociology Assn. (coun. 1979-81, chmn. occupations and orgns. 1987, chmn. pubs. com. 1985-87, sec. 1992-95, Jessie Bernard award 1995), Soc. Study Social Problems (v.p. 1981-82, pres. 1987 Lee Founders award 1988), Soc. Study Symbolic Inter-Action.

DANIELS, BLAKE H., education counselor; b. Mount Pleasant, Utah, Jan. 28, 1958; s. John H. and Catherine R. (Peterson) D.; m. Eva L. Price, June 4, 1982; children: Kevin, Stacy, Cody, Jeb. AS, Snow Coll., 1980; BS, Utah State U., 1982; MEd, Brigham Young U., 1988. Tchr. social studies Dugway (Utah) H.S., 1983-87; counselor North Summit H.S., Coleville, Utah, 1988-89, Davis County Schs. Ctrl., Layton, Utah, 1989—; cons. Tough Love Internat., Clearfield, Utah, 1990-92; 3-6 alternative jr. co-dir. Davis County Schs., Layton, 1994—. City chair Republican Party, Dugway, 1988, state del., 1988, county del., 1994. Recipient scholarship Dugway Woman's Club, 1987; grantee Utah State Office Edn., 1993. Mem. Am. Sch. Counselors, Utah Sch. Counselors (bd. dirs. 1990—), Davis Sch. Counselors (treas. 1992, v.p. 1993, pres. 1994). Republican. LDS. Home: 1621 N Celia Way Layton UT 84041-1401 Office: Ctrl Davis Jr High 663 Church St Layton UT 84041-3113

DANIELS, GEORGE NELSON, architect; b. Salt Lake City, Sept. 2, 1927; m. Rhonda Wilcox; children: Kathleen Daniels Snow, Janet, Christine Daniels Platt, Christopher, Brandee. Student, U. Utah; BA, U. Calif., 1951, MA, 1952. Registered profl. architect, Utah, Nev., Ariz., Calif., Wyo., Mont., Idaho, Nebr., N.D., S.D.; cert. NCARB. Architect Edwards & Daniels, Salt Lake City, 1957—, sec., treas. Archtl. projects include Basic High Sch., Las Vegas, Salt Lake City Pub. Libr., Ensign Elem. Sch., Salt Lake City, Robert Frost Elem. Sch., Salt Lake City, Cottonwood High Sch., Murray, Utah, Clark County Libr., Las Vegas, Humboldt County Libr., Winnemucca, Nev., U. Utah Med. Ctr. Libr., Salt Lake City, Utah Air N.G. Dining and Med. Facility, Kennecott Copper Co. Mine Adminstrn. Bldg. Mem. U. Utah Rsch. Park Adv. Bd., 1970—; mem. Civic Music Bd., 1967-72; bd. dirsYMCA, 1977-83, Westminster Found., U. Utah Mus. Natural History Bd. With U.S. Mcht. Marine/USN, 1944-45, 52-55. Fellow AIA (editor Utah Architecture 1961-62, chmn. aesthetics and environ. design com. 1971, exec. com. 1980-82), Rotary, Utah Watercolor Soc. Address: 111 E Broadway Ste 200 Salt Lake City UT 84111-5240

DANIELS, JAMES ARTHUR, electronics sales company executive; b. Indpls., Feb. 1, 1937; s. Arthur Weldon and Helen Marie (Collins) D.; m. Beverly Ann Monfreda, Aug. 25, 1956; children: Kristina, Rebecca, Kevin, Caroline, Bryan, Bret, Susan, Erica. AB in Sociology, U. Notre Dame, 1958; MBA, U. So. Calif., 1966. Engr. Ralph M. Parsons, Pasadena, Calif., 1960-61; sales engr. Dressen Barnes, Pasadena, Calif., 1961-64; sales mgr. Burton Mfg., Van Nuys, Calif., 1964-66; productmgr. Leach Relay, L.A., 1966-67; sales mgr. Bourns Trimpot Products, Riverside, Calif., 1967-74; pres. D2 Sales Inc., Solana Beach, Calif., 1974—; bd. dirs. San Diego Elec. Shows & Meeting Inc., 1985—. Mem. Elec. Rep. Assn. (pres. 1974, 75, dir. 1981-84, white pin 1983), Elec. VIPs, KC. Roman Catholic. Home: 662 S Nardo Ave Solana Beach CA 92075-2308 Office: D2 Sales Inc PO Box 1311 Solana Beach CA 92075-7311

DANIELS, JONATHAN PEARSON, obstetrician-gynecologist; b. Salt Lake City, Mar. 20, 1951; s. Courtney Robert and Marian Fay (Bolin) D.; m. Jacqueline Joy Marugg, Mar. 21, 1977; children: Jonathan P. Jr., Jeanette F., Natalie J. BS in Bus. Mgmt., U. Utah, 1975; student, U. Tex., Arlington, 1983; MD, U. Tex., Houston, 1989. Sys. analyst engring. dept. Gen. Dynamics Corp., Ft. Worth, 1984-85; intern, resident St. Joseph Hosp., Houston, 1989-91; ob-gyn. resident Franklin Square Hosp., Balt., 1991-93; ob-gyn. Mt. Home (Idaho) AFB Hosp., 1993—. With USAF, 1976-82. Mormon. Home: 1 Elm St # B Mountain Home A F B ID 83648-1156 Office: 366th Med Group 90 Hope Dr Home AFB ID 83648

DANIELS, LYDIA M., health care administrator; b. Louisville, Dec. 21, 1932; d. Effort and Gladys T. (Turner) Williams; student Calif. State U., Hayward, 1967, 69-72; BA, Golden Gate U., 1992, MS, 1993; cert. Samuel Merritt Hosp. Sch. Med. Record Adminstrs., 1959; student Cen. State Coll., Ohio, 1950-52; children by previous marriage: Danny Winston, Jeffrey Bruce, Anthony Wayne. Sec. chemistry dept. Cen. State Coll., Wilberforce, Ohio, 1950-52; co-dir. Indian Workcamp, Pala Indian Reservation, Pala, Calif., 1956-58; clk.-typist Camarillo (Calif.) State Hosp., 1956-58; student med. record adminstr. Samuel Merritt Hosp., Oakland, Calif., 1958-59, asst. med. record adminstr., 1962-63, asst. chief med. record adminstr., 1965, chief med. record adminstr., 1965-72; med. record adminstr. Albany (Calif.) Hosp., 1964-65; asst. med. record adminstr. Children's Hosp., San Francisco, 1960; co-dir. interns in community svc. Am. Friends Svc. Com., San Francisco, 1960-61; med. record adminstr. Pacific Hosp., Oakland, Calif., 1963-64; med. record cons. Tahoe Forest Hosp., Truckee, Calif., 1969-73; chief med. record adminstr. Highland Gen. Hosp., Oakland, 1972-74; dir. med. record svcs. U. Calif. San Francisco Hosps. and Clinics, 1975-82; mgr. patient appointments, reception and registration Kaiser-Permanente Med. Ctr., 1982-88; dir. ambulatory adminstrv. svcs., 1988-94, asst. dir. human resources, 1994—; adj. prof. mgmt., labor mgmt. rels. Golden Gate U., 1978—; pres. Daniels Consultation Svcs., 1988—. Leader Girl Scouts Am. Oakland area council, 1960-62; sunday sch. tchr. Soc. of Friends, Berkeley, Calif., 1961-63, mem. edn. com., 1965-68; mem. policy and adv. bd. Far West Lab. Demonstration Sch., Oakland, 1973-75. Recipient Mgmt. Fellowship award U. Calif., San Francisco, 1979-80. Mem. Am. Med. Record Assn., Calif. Med. Record Assn. (editorial bd. 1976-77, pres. 1974-75), East Bay Med. Record Assn. (chmn. edn. com. 1971-72, pres. 1969-70), Assn. Systems Mgmt., Am. Mgmt. Assn., San Francisco Med. Records Assn. (pres.-elect 1982-83, pres. 1983-84), Am. Assn. Tng. and Devel. (Golden Gate chpt., v.p. prof. devel. 1994—). Author: Health Record Documentation: A Look at Cost, 1981; Inservice Training as a Tool in Managing the Changing Environment in the Medical Record Department, 1983; the Budget as a Management Tool, 1983. Issues editor Topics in Health Record Management, Parts I and II, 1983. Home: 545 Pierce St Apt 1105 Albany CA 94706-1048 Office: Kaiser-Permanente Med Ctr 280 W Macarthur Blvd Piedmont CA 94611-5642

DANIELS, MADELINE MARIE, psychotherapist, author; b. Newark, Oct. 14, 1948; d. William and Dorothy Barlow; BA cum laude, CCNY, 1971; PhD, Union Grad. Sch., Yellow Springs, Ohio, 1975, PhD, Union Grad. Sch., Cin., 1988; m. Peter W. Daniels, Oct. 18, 1976; children: Jonathan, Jedediah, Jeremiah. Lectr., Westchester Community Coll., also Bronx Community Coll., 1973-74; mem. adj. faculty SUNY, Purchase, 1974-76; data processing coordinator GTE Internat., 1976-78; lectr. div. continuing edn. U. N.H., 1979-87; exec. dir. Crossroads Center Human Integration, East Kingston, N.H., 1979-88; administrator Spectrum Cross-Cultural Inst. Youth Inc., East Kingston, 1988-93; rsch./comm. cons. North Bay, Calif., 1994—; rsch./comm. cons. Metis Assocs., Santa Rosa, Calif., 1994—. psychotherapist, lectr., cons. in field. Cert. ind. biofeedback practitioner, clin. mental health counselor. Mem. APA, Internat. council Psychologists (area chair 1988), Biofeedback Soc. Am., Soc. Psychol. Athropology, N.H. Psychol. Orgn., Phi Beta Kappa. Author: Realistic Leadership, 1983, Living Your Religion in the Real World, 1985, A Culturally Different Perspective on Psychology, 1989, (video) The Rainbow Classroom, 1991. Office: Metis Assocs 368 Westbrook Dr Santa Rosa CA 95401

DANIELS, PHILIP BLISS, psychology educator; b. Annabella, Utah, Nov. 9, 1928; s. William Bliss and Lavern (Hawley) D.; m. Patsy Unger, July 3, 1951; children: Matt, Darsi, Jamie, Drew, Patrick. BS, Brigham Young U., 1954, MS, 1957; PhD, Harvard U., 1962. Prof. Brigham Young U., Provo, Utah, 1961-92; assoc. Nat. Tng. Lab., Washington, 1965-75; CEO Behavioral Sci. Resources, Provo, 1972-95; cons. pvt. practice, Provo, 1965—. Co-author: manual Management Profiling, 1975, 4 mgmt. profiling instruments, 1972, 1981, 1985, 1986. Capt. USAF, 1954-56. Recipient rsch. grant U.S. Office of Edn., 1964. Mormon. Home: 1814 N 1500 E Provo UT 84604-5750 Office: BSR PO Box 411 Provo UT 84603-0411

DANIELS, RICHARD MARTIN, public relations executive; b. Delano, Calif., Feb. 24, 1942; s. Edward Martin and Philida Rose (Peterson) D.; m. Kathryn Ellen Knight, Feb. 28, 1976; children: Robert Martin, Michael Edward. A.A., Foothill Coll., 1965; B.A., San Jose State U., 1967; M.A., U. Mo., 1971. News reporter Imperial Valley Press, El Centro, Calif., summers 1963-66, San Diego (Calif.) Evening Tribune, 1967-68, Columbia Daily Tribune (Mo.), 1969-70; nat. news copy editor Los Angeles Times, 1966-67; staff writer San Diego Union, 1971-74, real estate editor, 1974-77; v.p. pub. relations Hubbert Advt. & Pub. Relations, Costa Mesa, Calif., 1977-78; ptnr. Berkman & Daniels Mktg. Comm., San Diego, 1979-91; prin. Nuffer, Smith, Tucker, Inc., 1991-94; prin. Richard M. Daniels Comm., 1994—; lectr. various bus. groups and colls.. Chmn. bd. dirs. March of Dimes San Diego County, 1984-87; bd. dirs. Nat. Coun. Vols., 1983—. Served with USN, 1959-62. Mem. Pub. Rels. Soc. Am., Counselors Acad. (accredited). Republican. Office: 2261 Ritter Pl Escondido CA 92029-5608

DANIELSON, CRAIG, wholesale grocery corporation executive. Chmn. United Grocers Inc., Portland, Oreg. Office: United Grocers Inc 6433 SE Lake Rd Portland OR 97222-2136

DANIELSON, GORDON DOUGLAS, dentist; b. Everett, Wash., Nov. 11, 1942; s. Marvin and Elanor (Weers) D.; m. Jamie Lynn Waters, Jan. 9, 1977. BS with honors, U. Oreg., 1968; postgrad., MIT, 1968-69; MA in Molecular Biology, U. Calif., 1974, BS in Med. Sci., DDS, 1975. DDS. Pvt. practice Larkspur, Calif., 1975—; exec. v.p. Atmospheric Rsch. Tech., Sacramento, Calif., 1984-85; cons. Freeport Fin. Svcs., Denver, 1985-87; pres. Lynmar Enterprises Inc., Rno, 1987—; bd. dirs. Freeport Venture Fund. MIT fellow, 1968-69; U. Calif., Berkeley fellow, 1969-71; U. Calif., San Francisco fellow, 1973-75, pres. fellow, 1973-75. Mem. U. Calif. Dental Alumni Assn., U. Oreg. Alumni Assn., Marin County Dental Soc. (chmn. emergency care 1975-81), St. Francis Yacht Club (mem. com. 1973—), Aircraft Owners and Pilots Assn., Omicron Kappa Upsilon. Republican. Office: 5 Bon Air Rd Ste 114 Larkspur CA 94939-1127

DANIELSON, LUKE JEFFRIES, lawyer; b. Boulder, Colo., Aug. 8, 1948; s. Philip A. and Mildred S. (Page) D.; m. Rosa Venezia, Aug. 9, 1975. BA in Econ., Antioch Coll., 1971; JD, U. Calif.-Berkeley, 1975. Bar: Colo. 1975, U.S. Dist. Ct. Colo. 1975, U.S. Ct. Appeals (10th cir.) 1975, U.S. Dist. Ct. Nebr. 1984. Assoc. Holland & Hart, Denver, 1975-78; editor-in-chief Solar Law Reporter, Golden, Colo., 1978-79; counsel Nat. Wildlife Fedn., Boulder, Colo., 1979-81; ptnr. Danielson & Euser, Denver, 1982-85; Gersh & Danielson, Denver, 1985—; adj. asst. prof. U. Denver Coll. of Law, 1978, 85, 87, U. Denver, 1994, U. Colo. Sch. Law, Boulder, 1979-81, 82, 84, 94; arbitrator Am. Arbitration Assn., other orgns. Author articles on solar energy and law, energy policy, mediation and mediation of environ. disputes. Chmn. bd. dirs. Eco-Cycle, Inc., Boulder, 1985-86, bd. dirs., mem. 1983-86; bd. dirs. Colo. Conservation Found., Denver, 1985-94, Global Response, 1991—; vice chmn., mem. Nat. Wildlif Fedn. Action, Inc., 1992—; mem. Mined Land Reclamation Bd., 1987—, chair 1989, 91, 94; counsel Univ. Corp. Atmospheric Rsch. Found., 1987-89. Mem. ABA (sect. natural resources, energy and environ. law, vice chair internat. resources com. 1994—), Colo. Bar Assn. (bd. govs. 1992-94), Denver Bar Assn., Boulder Bar Assn., Wyo. Wildlife Fedn. (life), Colo. Wildlife Fedn., AAAS, Am. Solar Energy Soc. Office: Gersh & Danielson 4747 Table Mesa Dr Boulder CO 80303-5573

DANIHER, JOHN M., retired engineer; b. LaJunta, Colo., Aug. 2, 1926; s. Gerald and Mary Isabelle (Manly) D.; m. Edna Erle Hoshall, Sept. 4, 1948; children: Lyn Mari, Suzanne Laurie, Patricia Gail, Jerome Matthew, Michael Kevin. AB, Western State Coll., Gunnison, Colo., 1948; postgrad. Idaho State U., 1957-74, U. Idaho, 1974-76. High sch. tchr., Grand Junction, Colo., 1948-52; salesman Century Metalcraft, Denver, 1952-53; chem. plant supr. U.S. Chem. Corps., Denver, 1953-56; sr. engr. instrument and controls Phillips Petroleum Co., Idaho Falls, 1956-76; project engr. E G & G Idaho, Idaho Falls, 1976-85, engring. specialist, 1985-91; adv. Eastern Idaho Vocat. Tech. Sch., 1975-80. Cubmaster, Boy Scouts Am., 1970-75, asst. scoutmaster, 1975-80; v.p. Bonneville Unit Am. Cancer Soc., 1994, pres., v.p., 1995—. Recipient Cub Man of Yr., Boy Scouts Am., 1973. Mem. Am. Nuclear Soc. Roman Catholic. Club: K.C. (state dep. 1979-81, Supreme council 1979-84, 94) Home: 250 12th St Idaho Falls ID 83404-5370

DANILOV, VICTOR JOSEPH, museum management program director, consultant, writer, educator; b. Farrell, Pa., Dec. 30, 1924; s. Joseph M. and Ella (Tominovich) D.; m. Toni Dewey, Sept. 6, 1980; children: Thomas J., Duane P., Denise S. BA in Journalism, Pa. State U., 1945; MS in Journalism, Northwestern U., 1946; EdD in Higher Edn., U. Colo., 1964. With Sharon Herald, Pa., 1942, Youngstown Vindicator, 1945, Pitts. Sun-Telegraph, 1946-47, Chgo. Daily News, 1947-50; instr. journalism U. Colo., 1950-51; asst. prof. journalism U. Kans., 1951-53; with Kansas City Star, 1953; mgr. pub. relations Ill. Inst. Tech. and IIT Research Inst., 1953-57; dir. univ. relations and pub. info. U. Colo., 1957-60; pres. Profile Co., Boulder, Colo., 1960-62; exec. editor, exec. v.p. Indsl. Research Inc., Beverly Shores, Ind., 1962-69; pub., exec. v.p. Indsl. Research Inc., 1969-71; dir., v.p. Mus. Sci. and Industry, Chgo., 1971-77; pres., dir. Mus. Sci. and Industry, 1978-87, pres. emeritus, 1987—; dir. mus. mgmt. program, adj. prof. U. Colo., 1987—; mem. rural industrialization adv. group Dept. Agr., 1967; mem. panel internat. transfer tech. Dept. Commerce, 1968; mem. sci. info. coun. NSF, 1969-72; chmn. Conf. on Implications Metric Change, 1972, Nat. Conf. Indsl. Rsch., 1966-70; chmn. observance Nat. Indsl. Rsch. Week, 1967-70; chmn. Midwest White House Conf. on Indsl. World Ahead, 1972, Internat. Conf. Sci. and Tech. Museums, 1976, 82; mem. task force on fin. acctg. and reporting by non bus. orgns., others. Author: Public Affairs Reporting, 1955, Starting a Science Center, 1977, Science and Technology Centers, 1982, Science Center Planning Guide, 1985, Chicago's Museums, 1987, rev. edit., 1991, America's Science Museums, 1990, Corporate Museums, Galleries, and Visitor Centers: A Directory, 1991, A Planning Guide for Corporate Museums, Galleries, and Visitor Centers, 1992, Museum Careers and Training: A Professional Guide, 1994; also articles; editor: Crucial Issues in Public Relations, 1960, Corporate Research and Profitability, 1966, Innovation and Profitability, 1967, Research Decision-Making in New Product Development, 1968, New Products—and Profits, 1969, Applying Emerging Technologies, 1970, Nuclear Power in the South, 1970, The Future of Science and Technology, 1975, Museum Accounting Guidelines, 1976, Traveling Exhibitions, 1978, Towards the Year 2000, 1981; editor profl. procs. V.p., trustee Women of the West Mus., 1991—; trustee La Rabida Childrens Hosp. and Rsch. Ctr., 1973-83; mem. U. Chgo. Citizens Bd., 1978-87. Mem. Am. Assn. Mus. (exec. com. 1976-77, bd. dirs. 1985-88, chmn. mus. studies task force 1988-89), AAAS, Assn. Sci.-Tech. Ctrs. (bd. dirs. 1973-84, sec.-treas. 1973-74, pres. 1975-76), Internat. Coun. Mus. (com. on sci. and tech. mus. 1972—, vice chmn. 1977-87, chmn. 1982-83, bd. dirs. 1985-88), Chgo. Coun. on Fine Arts (chmn. 1976-84), Ill. Arts Alliance (bd. dirs. 1983-86), Sci. Mus. Exhibit Collaborative (pres. 1983-86), Mus. Film Network (pres. 1984-86). Home: 250 Bristlecone Way Boulder CO 80304-0413 Office: Univ Colo Mus Mgmt Program Univ Mus Boulder CO 80309

DANNER, PAUL KRUGER, III, telecommunications executive; b. Cin., Aug. 20, 1957; s. Paul Kruger Jr. and Phyllis Jean (Speak) D.; m. Cynthia Lee Hurst, May 5, 1984; children: Catherine Hurst, Elizabeth Speak, Caroline Tyree. BS, Colo. State U., 1979; MBA, Old Dominion U., 1986. Mktg. rep. Control Data Corp., Denver, 1985-86; dist. mgr. NEC Home Electronics (U.S.A.), Inc., Denver, 1987-88; regional mgr. NEC Home Electronics, Inc. subs. NEC Corp. (Tokyo), L.A., 1988-89, v.p. NEC Techs., Inc. subs., 1989-91; v.p. sales and mktg. Command Communications, Aurora, Colo., 1991—. Lt. USN, 1979-85; comdr. USNR, 1985—. Mem. Navy League of U.S., U.S. Naval Inst., NRA, Ducks Unltd., Met. Club, Castle Pines Country Club. Republican. Home: 503 Providence Dr Castle Rock CO 80104-9018

DANOFF, DUDLEY SETH, surgeon, urologist; b. N.Y.C., June 10, 1937; s. Alfred and Ruth (Kauffman) D.; m. Hevda Amrani, July 1, 1971; children: Aurele Alfie, Doran. BA summa cum laude, Princeton U., 1959; MD, Yale U., 1963. Diplomate Am. Bd. Urology. Surg. intern Columbia-Presbyn. Med. Ctr., N.Y.C., 1963-64; resident in surgery Yale New Haven Med. Ctr., 1964-65; resident in urologic surgery Squier Urologic Clinic, Columbia-Presbyn. Med. Ctr., 1965-69; NIH trainee Francis Delafield Hosp., N.Y.C., 1969; asst. in urology Columbia U..Columbia-Presbyn. Hosp., N.Y.C., 1969; cons., surgeon New Orleans VA Hosp., 1970; asst. surgeon Tulane U., New Orleans, 1970; pvt. practice urologic surgery L.A., 1971—; attending urologic surgeon Cedars-Sinai Med. Ctr., L.A., Midway Hosp., L.A., Century City Hosp., L.A., VA Hosp., L.A., Beverly Hills Med. Ctr., L.A.; attending urologic surgeon, clin. faculty UCLA. Author: Superpotency, 1993, Research: Laparoscopic Urologic Procedures; contbr. articles to profl. jours. Bd. dirs. Tel-Hashomer Hosp., Israel, Christian Children's Fund, Beverly Hills Edn. Found.; trustee Anti-Defamation League; mem. profl. adv. bd. The Wellness Cmty.; mem. nat. exec. bd. Gesher Found.; mem. adv. com., past pres. Med. divsn. L.A. Jewish Fedn. Coun.; mem. nat. leadership cabinet United Jewish Appeal; chmn. Am. Friends of Assaf Harofeh Med. Ctr., Israel; pres., western states region and internat. bd. govs. Am. Friends Hebrew U. Jerusalem; pres.-elect western region Am. Commn. for Shaare Zedek Med. Ctr. Jewusalem. Fellow ACS; mem. AMA, Internat. Coll. Surgeons, Israeli Med. Assn., Am. Fertility Soc., Soc. Air Force Clin. Surgeons, Am. Urologic Assn., Societe International d'Urologie, Transplant Soc. So. Calif., Los Angeles County Med. Assn., Soc. for Minimally Invasive Surgery, Am. Technion Soc., Profl. Men's Club of L.A. (past pres.), Princeton Club So. Calif., Yale Club So. Calif., Hillcrest Country Club, Phi Beta Kappa, Sigma Xi, Alpha Omega Alpha, Phi Delta Epsilon (past pres., mem. exec. com.). Jewish. Office: Cedars-Sinai Med Ctr Towers 8631 W 3rd St Ste 915E Los Angeles CA 90048-5912

DANSER, BONITA KAY, legal administrator, consultant; b. Altadena, Calif., Mar. 26, 1949; d. Earl Peter sna Sara Grace (Myer) Nisssley; m. Robin Danser, Aug. 28, 1971 (div. Feb. 1978); m. John Hullett, June 3, 1989. AA, Pasadena City Coll., 1969; student, San Diego State U., 1970-76; BSBA, U. Redlands, 1988. Legal adminstr. Rhodes, Kendall & Harrington, Newport Beach, Calif., 1978-86, Gardner and Martin, Newport Beach, 1986, Martin and Wilson, Santa Ana, Calif., 1987-89; freelance contract legal adminstr. Irvine, Calif., 1986-88; legal administrator, cons. Parilla, Militzok & Shedden, Irvine, 1989—. Citizen ambassador to China, People-to-People Internat., 1988. Mem. Assn. Legal Adminstrs. (treas. 1983, 85, sec. 1984, 2d v.p. 1990, 1st v.p. 1991, pres. 1992, region 6 comm. officer 1993, 94, 95), Theta Chi Epsilon (nat. bd. dirs. 1984-94, 95, Achievement award 1979, 94). Office: Parilla Militzok & Shedden 1 Park Plz Ste 1250 Irvine CA 92714-8509

DANTON, JOSEPH PERIAM, librarian, educator; b. Palo Alto, Calif., July 5, 1908; s. George Henry and Annina (Periam) D.; m. Lois King, Dec. 25, 1948 (div.); children—Jennifer, Joseph Periam. Ed., U. Leipzig, Germany, 1925-26; A.B. magna cum laude, Oberlin Coll., 1928; B.S., Columbia, 1929; A.M., Williams Coll., 1930; Ph.D., U. Chgo., 1935, (Carnegie fellow, 1933-35). With N.Y. Pub. Libr., Williams Coll. Libr. and ALA, 1928-33; librarian, assoc. prof. bibliography Colby Coll., Waterville, Maine, 1935-36, Temple U., Phila., 1936-46; dean Sch. Librarianship, U. Calif.-Berkeley, 1946-61, assoc. prof., 1946-47, prof., 1947-76, prof. emeritus, 1976—; vis. prof. Grad. Library Sch., U. Chgo., 1942, Columbia, 1946; vis. lectr. U. Toronto, 1963, Univs. of Belgrade, Ljubljana, Novi Sad, Zagreb, 1965, U. B.C., 1968, 79, McGill U., 1969, U. P.R., 1970, U. Md., 1977, U. N.C., 1977, U. Tex., 1979, Hebrew U., Jerusalem, 1965, 85; Fulbright research scholar, Germany, 1960-61, Austria, 1964-65; surveyor and cons. numerous libraries; UNESCO Library Cons., Jamaica, 1968; del. Internat. Fedn. Library Assns. meeting, 1939-1972; Ford Found. cons. on libraries in SE Asia (with R. C. Swank), 1963; hon. research fellow U. London, 1974-75. Author: Education for Librarianship, 1946, Education for Librarianship, Paris, 1950, United States Influence on Norwegian Librarianship, 1890-1940, 1957, Book Selection and Collections: A Comparison of German and American University Libraries, 1963, Index to Festschriften in Librarianship, 1970, (with Jane F. Pulis) vol. 2, 1967-1975, 1979, Between M.L.S. and Ph.D, 1970, The Dimensions of Comparative Librarianship, 1973; editor: The Climate of Book Selection; Social Influences on Sch. and Pub. Libraries, 1959; mem. editorial bd. Coll. and Research Libraries Monograph Series, 1966-69, Library Quar., 1968-89, Internat. Library Rev, 1968-77. Served as lt. USNR, 1942-45, PTO. Recipient Coll. and Research Libraries grant, 1960-61, Council on Library Resources grant, 1967-69, Berkeley citation, 1976, Beta Phi Mu award, 1983; Guggenheim fellow, 1971. Mem. ALA, Assn. Coll. and Ref. Librs. (treas. 1938-40), Calif. Libr. Assn., Assn. Am. Libr. Schs. (pres. 1949-50), Internat. Fedn. Libr. Assns. (chmn. com. libr. edn. 1967-72), Faculty Club. Democrat. Home: 500 Vernon St Apt 402 Oakland CA 94610-1403 Office: U Calif Sch Libr and Info Studies Berkeley CA 94720

D'ANTONIO, JAMES JOSEPH, lawyer; b. Tucson, Jan. 13, 1959; s. Lawrence Patrick and Rosemary Catherine (Kane) D'A. Student, Tufts U., 1978-79; BA, U. Ariz., 1981, JD, 1984. Bar: Ariz. 1984, U.S. Dist. Ct. Ariz. 1984. Ptnr. Law Office of D'Antonio and D'Antonio, Tucson, 1984-93; pvt. practice law Law Offices of James J. D'Antonio, Tucson, 1993—. Chmn. bd. govs. U. Ariz. Coll. Law, 1983-84. Named Outstanding Pro Bono Lawyer Pima County Vol. Lawyers Program. Fellow Ariz. Bar Found.; mem. ABA, Assn. Trial Lawyers Am., Ariz. Bar Assn., Ariz. Trial Lawyers Assn., Pima County Bar Assn. Office: 70 W Cushing St Tucson AZ 85701-2218

D'ANZA, LAWRENCE MARTIN, marketing educator; b. Hindsdale, Ill., June 20, 1953; s. Joseph James and Evelyn (Martinek) D'A.; m. Teresa D'Anza, June 14, 1980. BBEd, Eastern N.Mex. U., 1975; MA, U. N.Mex., 1984. Instr. cashiering Albuquerque Tech. Vocat. Inst., 1975-85; mktg. edn. tchr. coord. Eldorado High Sch., 1975-95; enrollment program coord. Del Norte High Sch., 1983-93; tchr. bus. mktg. Albuquerque Pub. Schs., 1984-85; bd. govs. N.Mex. DECA, 1988-90, chmn., 1983-84, 89-91, conf. cons., 1978—, secondary adv. coun. Nat. DECA, 1992-93, nat. bd. dirs., 1993—, conf. coord. western region, 1992, western region bd. dirs., 1993—. Mem. N.Mex. Mktg. Edn. Assn., Am. Vocat. Assn. (Region IV Mktg. Edn. Tchr.

of Yr. 1994-95, Vocat. Tchr. of Yr. 1994-95), N.Mex. Vocat. Assn. (pres. 1995—, N.Mex. Mitg. Tchr. of Yr. 1981-82, 87-88, 92-93, 93-94). Home: 5341 Revi Don Dr NE Albuquerque NM 87111-1928 Office: Eldorado High Sch 11300 Montgomery Blvd NE Albuquerque NM 87111-2602

DANZIGER, JERRY, broadcasting executive; b. N.Y.C., Jan. 23, 1924; s. Harry and Lillie (Lacher) D.; m. Zelda Bloom, Dec. 26, 1948; children: Sydney, Alan, Lee. Grad. high sch. With Sta. WTTV, Bloomington, Ind., 1950-53; ops. mgr. Sta. WTTV, Indpls., 1953-57; program mgr. Sta. WTSK-TV, Knoxville, Tenn., 1953; pres. Sta. KOB-TV, Albuquerque, 1957-88, v.p., 1983-88, pres., 1988-93, vice-chmn., 1993—; mem. Gov. N.Mex. Commn. for Film Entertainment, 1970-71. Bd. dirs. KIPC All Indian Pueblo Coun., 1975-88, Albuquerque Little Theatre, Albuquerque Pub. Broadcast, Albuquerque Jewish Welfare Fund, Albuquerque Econ. Devel. 1989—, Albuquerque Conv. and Visitors Bur., 1990-93, Great Southwest Coun. Boy Scouts Am., 1994—; v.p. for TV AP Broadcasting, 1980-88, Goodwill Industries N.Mex., 1980, bd. dirs., 1991—; mem. Albuquerque Econ. Forum. Recipient Compadre award Am. Women in Radio and TV, 1978, 80, Silver Medal award N.Mex. Advt. Fedn., 1990. Mem. N.Mex. Broadcasters Assn. (pres. 1972-73, Broadcaster of Yr. award , 1976, 78), Press Club, Advt. Club, Albuquerque Country Club. Office: Sta KOB-TV PO Box 1351 Albuquerque NM 87103-1351

DANZIGER, LOUIS, graphic designer, educator; b. N.Y.C., Nov. 17, 1923; s. Harry and Dora (Scheck) D.; m. Dorothy Patricia Smith, Apr. 10, 1954. Student, Art Ctr. Sch., Los Angeles, 1946-47, New Sch., N.Y.C., 1947-48. Asst. art dir. War Assets Adminstrn., Los Angeles, 1946-47; designer Esquire mag., N.Y.C., 1948; freelance designer, cons. Los Angeles, 1949—; instr. graphic design Art Ctr. Coll. Design, Los Angeles, 1952-60, 86—, Chouinard Art Inst., Los Angeles, 1960-72; instr. Calif. Inst. Arts, 1972-88, head graphic design program, 1972-82; vis. prof. Harvard U., Cambridge, Mass., summers 1978-80, 83, 84, 86-88; instr. Art Ctr. Coll. Design; mem. graphic evaluation panel Fed. Design Program, Nat. Endowment Arts, 1975—; design cons. Los Angeles County Mus. Art, 1957—. Served with cav. U.S. Army, 1943-45; PTO. Recipient numerous awards and medals, art dirs. show; Disting. Achievement award Contemporary Art Council, Los Angeles County Mus. Art, 1982; Disting. Designer award NEA, 1985. Mem. Alliance Graphique Internationale, Am. Inst. Graphic Arts, Art Dirs. Club Los Angeles, Am. Ctr. for Design (hon.). Home: 7001 Melrose Ave Los Angeles CA 90038-3307

DAO, TOM TRINH, electrical engineer; b. Saigon, Vietnam, Nov. 4, 1963; s. Chi Thai Dao and Loi Thi Nguyen; m. Anh Thi Phuong Doan, July 17, 1993. BSEE, U. Iowa, 1986, MS in Elec. and Computer Engring., 1990. Elec. engr. Francais Engring., Co., Cypress, Calif., 1987-88, Nyden Corp., Santa Clara, Calif., 1991-92, GE Nuclear Energy, San Jose, Calif., 1992—. Mem. Eta Kappa Nu. Avocations: soccer, volleyball. Office: GE Nuclear Energy 175 Curtner Ave # 334 San Jose CA 95125-1014

DAPPLES, EDWARD CHARLES, geologist, educator; b. Chgo., Dec. 13, 1906; s. Edward C. and Victoria (Gazzolo) D.; m. Marion Virginia Sprague, Sept. 2, 1931; children—Marianne Helena, Charles Christian. B.S., Northwestern U., 1928, M.S., 1934; M.A., Harvard, 1935; Ph.D., U. Wis., 1938. Geologist Ziegler Coal Co., 1928; geologist Truax-Traer Coal Co., 1928-32, mine supt., 1932; instr. Northwestern U., 1936-41, asst. prof., 1941, asso. prof., 1942-50, prof. geol. scis., 1950-75, prof. emeritus, 1975—; geologist Ill. Geol. Survey, 1939, Sinclair Oil Co., 1945-50, Pure Oil Co., 1950; dir. Evanston Exploration Corp., 1954-84; sr. vis. scientist U. Lausanne, Switzerland, 1960-61; vis. prof. U. Geneva, Switzerland, 1970. Author: Basic Geology for Science and Engineering, 1959, Atlas of Lithofacies Maps, 1960. Fellow Geol. Soc. Am., Soc. Econ. Geologist; mem. Am. Inst. Mining Engrs. (Legion of Honor), Assn. Petroleum Geologists, Internat. Assn. Sedimentologists, Soc. Econ. Paleontologists and Mineralogists (pres. 1970, hon. mem. 1974), Am. Inst. Profl. Geologists (pres. Ill.-Ind. sect. 1979, pres. Ariz. 1982, hon. mem. 1986), Assn. Engring. Geologists. Home: 2800 N Saddleback Way Unit 10 Flagstaff AZ 86004-7447

DARANY, MICHAEL ANTHONY, financial executive; b. Detroit, Sept. 10, 1946; s. Sam and Betty Darany; m. Deborah Collins; 1 child, Danielle. Cert. fin. planner. Debit agt. Met. Life Ins. Co., Coral Gables, Fla., 1968-71; pres. Darany, Malagon & Assocs. Ins. Agy., Miami, Fla., 1970-71; loan appraiser Mortgage Corp. Am., Miami, Fla., 1971-72; loan officer J.I. Kislak Mortgage Co., Miami, Fla., 1973-74, Midwest Mortgage Co., Miami, Fla., 1973-74; pres. Consortium Group (subs. D&R Internat.), Miami, Fla., 1974-76; staff mgr. Peninsular Life Ins. Co., Miami, Fla., 1976-78; asst. to mgr. Sun Life Can., Miami, Fla., 1978-82; pres. Consortium Group(subs. D&R Internat.), Miami, Fla., 1982—. Co-author: The Expert's Guide, 1988; contbr. articles to profl. pubs. First v.p. Unico Nat., Coral Gables, 1975-76, sec. 1978-79, pres., 1980-81. Served with USN, 1963-67, Vietnam. Recipient Man of Yr. award Sun Life Can., 1978-81. Mem. Inst. Cert. Fin. Planners, Internat. Assn. Fin. Planners, Nat. Assn. Life Underwriters, Registry Fin. Planning, Nat. Fin. Adv. Panel, Internat. Bd. Standards and Practices. Republican. Episcopalian.

DARBY, JOANNE TYNDALE (JAYE DARBY), arts and humanities educator; b. Tucson, Sept. 22, 1948; d. Robert Porter Smith and Joanne Inloes Snow-Smith; stepchildren: Margaret Loutrel, David Michael. BA, U. Ariz., 1972; MEd, U. Calif., L.A., 1986, postgrad. Cert. secondary tchr., gifted and talented tchr., Calif. Tchr. English, chmn. dept. Las Virgenes Unified Sch. Dist., Calabasas, Calif., 1979-82; tchr. English and gifted and talented edn. Las Virgenes Unified Sch.Dist., Calabasas, Calif., 1983-84; sch. improvement coord./lang. arts/social studies/drama tchr Las Virgenes Unified Sch. Dist., Calabasas, Calif., 1991-92; tchr. English and gifted and talented edn. Beverly Hills (Calif.) Unified Sch. Dist., 1982-83, 84-89, English and drama tchr., 1994; tchr., cons. Calif. Lit. Project, San Diego, 1985-87; cons., free lance editor L.A., 1977—; dir. Shakespeare edn. and festivals project Folger Libr., Washington, 1990-91; field work supr. tchr. edn. program Grad. Sch. Edn. and Info. Studies, UCLA, 1992—; cons. arts and edn., L.A., 1991—. Contbr. articles to profl. publs. Mem. Am. Alliance for Theatre and Edn., Am. Ednl. Rsch. Assn., Nat. Coun. Tchrs. English, Phi Beta Kappa, Phi Beta Phi, Alpha Lambda Delta. Home: 972 Hilgard Ave Apt 310 Los Angeles CA 90024-3066

DARBY, MICHAEL RUCKER, economist, educator; b. Dallas, Nov. 24, 1945; s. Joseph Jasper and Frances Adah (Rucker) D.; children: Margaret Loutrel, David Michael; Lynne Ann Zucker-Darby, 1992; stepchildren: Joshua R. Zucker, Danielle T. Zucker. A.B. summa cum laude, Dartmouth Coll., 1967; M.A., U. Chgo., 1968, Ph.D., 1970. Asst. prof. econs. Ohio State U., 1970-73; vis. asst. prof. econs. UCLA, 1972-73, assoc. prof., 1973-78, prof., 1978-87, prof. Anderson grad. sch. mgmt., 1987-94, Warren C. Cordner prof. money and fin. mkts., 1995—; vice chmn., 1992-93; dir. John M. Olin Ctr. for Policy, 1993—; research assoc. Nat. Bur. Econ. Research, 1976-86, 92—; asst. sec. for economic policy Treasury Dept., Washington, 1986-89; mem. Nat. Commn. on Superconductivity, 1988-89; under sec. for econ. affairs Commerce Dept., Washington, 1989-92; adminstr. Econs. and Stats. Adminstrn., 1990-92; v.p., dir. Paragon Industries, Inc., Dallas, 1964-83; mem. exec. com. Western Econ. Assn., 1987-90; chmn. The Dumbarton Group, 1992—; adj. scholar Am. Ent. Inst. for Pub. Policy Rsch., 1992—; economist stats. income divsn. IRS, 1992-94; mem. Regulatory Coordination Adv. Com. of the Commodity Futures Trading Commn., 1992—. Author: Macroeconomics, 1976, Have Controls Ever Worked: The Post-War Record, 1976, Intermediate Macroeconomics, 1979, 2d edit., 1986, The Effects of Social Security on Income and the Capital Stock, 1979, The International Transmission of Inflation, 1981, Labor Force, Employment, and Productivity in Historical Perspective, 1984, Reducing Poverty in America: Views and Approaches, 1995; editor Jour. Internat. Money and Fin., 1981-86, mem. editl. bd., 1986—; mem. editl. bd. Am. Econ. Rev., 1983-86, Contemporary Policy Issues, 1990-93, Contemporary Econ. Policy, 1994—, Internat. Reports, 1992-95. Bd. dirs. The Opera Assoc., 1992—; mem. acad. adv. bd. Ctr. Regulation and Econ. Growth of the Alexis de Tocqueville Instn., 1993—. Recipient Alexander Hamilton award U.S. Treasury Dept., 1989; sr. fellow Dartmouth Coll., 1966-67, Woodrow Wilson fellow, 1967-68, NSF grad. fellow, 1967-69, FDIC grad. fellow, 1969-70, Harry Scherman rsch. fellow Nat. Bur. Econ. Research, 1974-75, vis. fellow Hoover Instn., Stanford U., 1977-78. Mem. Acad. Polit. Sci., Am. Econ. Assn., Am. Fin. Assn., Am. Statis. Assn., Nat. Assn. Bus. Economists, Mont Pelerin Soc., Royal Econ. Soc., So. Econ. Assn., Western Econ. Assn. Episcopalian. Home: 3937 Purdue Ave Dallas TX 75225-7115 Office: UCLA Anderson Grad Sch Mgmt Los Angeles CA 90095-1481

DARBY, WESLEY ANDREW, minister, educator; b. Glendale, Ariz., Sept. 19, 1928; s. Albert Leslie and Beulah E. (Lamb) D.; student Bible Inst. L.A., 1946, No. Ariz. U., 1946-47, Rockmont Coll., Denver, 1948-50, Ariz. State U., 1965, St. Anne's Coll., Oxford (Eng.) U., 1978; m. Donna Maye Bice, May 29, 1947; children: Carolyn Darby Eymann, Lorna Dale, Elizabeth Darby Bass, Andrea Darby Perdue. Ordained to ministry Bapt. Ch., 1950; pastor Sunnyside Bapt. Ch., Flagstaff, Ariz., 1947-48, First Bapt. Ch. of Clifton, Ariz., 1950-55, West High Bapt. Ch., Phoenix, 1955-90; pastor emeritus, 1990—; dep. assessor Greenlee County, 1951-55; instr. English lit. and pastoral subjects Southwestern Conservative Bapt. Bible Coll., Phoenix, 1961-87. Chmn. bd. Conservative Bapt. Found. Ariz., 1974-83, Gospel Wings, 1960-88; v.p. Ariz. Bapt. Conf., 1976-83; pres. Ariz. Alcohol-Narcotic Edn. Assn., 1968—. Recipient God, Family and Country award Freeman Inst., 1981. Mem. Evang. Philos. Soc., Greater Phoenix Assn. Evangelicals (pres. 1960-63, 91—), Ariz. Breakfast Club, (chaplain 1969—). Contbr. articles to profl. jours. Republican. Home: 5628 N 11th Dr Phoenix AZ 85013-1714 Office: 3301 N 19th Ave Phoenix AZ 85015-5761

DARDEN, EDWIN SPEIGHT, SR., architect; b. Stantonsburg, N.C., Oct. 14, 1920; s. Edwin Speight and Sallie (Jordan) D.; m. s. Pauline K. Bartlett, Feb. 26, 1944; children: Edwin Speight III, Judith Ann, Diane Russell. BS in Archtl. Engring., Kans. State U., 1947. Registered architect, Calif. Assoc., Fred L. Swartz and William G. Hyberg, Fresno, Calif., 1949-59; ptnr. Nargis and Darden (Architects), Fresno, 1959-69; pres. Edwin S. Darden Assocs., Inc., Fresno, 1969-85, cons., 1985—; mem. state adv. bd. Office of Architecture and Constrn., 1970-78; cons. ednl. facilities, 1975—. Prin. works include Clovis (Calif.) High Sch., 1969, Clovis W. High Sch., 1976, Ahwahnee Jr. High Sch., Fresno, 1966, Tehipite Jr. High Sch., Fresno, 1973, Fresno County Dept. Health, 1978, Floyd B. Buchanan Edn. Ctr., Clovis, 1990. Served to 1st lt. C.E., AUS, 1942-46. Fellow AIA; mem. Sigma Phi Epsilon, Alpha Kappa Psi; bd. Sierra Thrift, Fresno, 1985—. Presbyterian. Club: Fresno Rotary. Office: Edwin S Darden Assocs Inc 1177 W Shaw Ave Fresno CA 93711-3704

DARGIS, JEAN ANTHONY, retired voluntary health agency executive; b. Mpls., Mar. 9, 1931; s. Henry Joseph and Josephine Marie (Violette) D.; m. Mary Ruth Buschman, July 2, 1956; 1 child, Melissa Jeanne Dargis Herzog. BA, St. Paul (Minn.) Sem., 1952; MusB, Universite Laval, Quebec, Can., 1954. Tchr. St. Anthony Acad., Mpls., 1954-59, Holy Childhood Sch., St. Paul, 1955-57; various positions March of Dimes Birth Defects Found., White Plains, N.Y., 1959-92; v.p., dir. nat. office of vols. March of Dimes Birth Defects Found., White Plains, 1989-92. Author: (handbook) Manual for Chapters, 1990; editor: (handbook) Volunteer Development Guide, 1991, (booklet) Basic Principles of Volunteer Developement, 1989. Mem. Diocesan Commn./Devel., San Jose, Calif., 1983-90; dir. Diocesan Choir, San Jose, 1983-90, St. Victor's Parish Choir, San Jose, 1971—. Mem. Mensa, Latin Liturgy Assn. Republican. Roman Catholic. Home: 3479 Grossmont Dr San Jose CA 95132-3120

DARKE, CHARLES BRUCE, academic administrator, dentist; b. Chgo., Sept. 22, 1937; s. Paul Olden and Annie Wanlene (Tennin) D.; m. Annetta McRae-Darke, Aug. 15, 1965 (div. 1982); 1 child, Charles B. II; m. Judith Anne Chew, Dec. 15, 1990. AA, Wilson Jr. Coll., Chgo., 1960; DDS, Meharry Med. Coll., 1964; MPH, U. Calif., Berkeley, 1972. Staff dentist Children's Hosp., Oakland, Calif., 1967-68, Mt. Zion Hosp., San Francisco, 1967-71; pvt. practice in dentistry San Francisco, 1967—; dir. dental svcs. San Francisco Gen. Hosp., 1973-80; asst. adminstr. outpatient svcs. San Francisco Med. Ctr., 1980-88; ops. officer primary care network San Francisco Dept. Health, 1988-89; dir. student health Calif. State U., Fullerton, 1989—; dental cons. Dept. Labor Job Corps, Washington, 1973-88; chief examiner state dental bd. Calif. State Bd. Dental Examiners, Sacramento, 1976-89; surveyor ambulatory care Joint Commn. on Accreditation of Health, Oakbrook, Ill., 1986—; bd. dirs. Yorba Hills Med. Ctr., Yorba Linda, Calif., 1993—. Found Tooth Trip-Free Dental Care, San Francisco, 1969. Capt. USAF, 1965-67. Mem. ADA, Am. Endodontic Soc., Nat. Dental Assn., Am. Coll. Health Assn., Pacific Coast Coll. Health Assn. (bd. dirs. 1993), Nat. Dental Soc. Bay Area (past pres.).

DARKEY, KERMIT LOUIS, association executive, lawyer; b. Berea, Ohio, Oct. 11, 1930; s. Louise Anna (Watts) D.; m. Barbara Jean Rufer, Aug. 17, 1957; children: Kathryn Ann, Susan Lynn, Scott Rufer. AB, Ohio Wesleyan U., 1952; JD, U. Colo., 1957. Bar: Colo. 1957. Mem. labor rels. staff Mountain States Employers Coun., Denver, 1957-64, dir. labor rels., 1964-70, v.p., 1970-80, pres., 1980—; bd. dirs. Norwest Colo., Inc., Archway Cookies, Inc., Battle Creek, Mich., RMO, Denver. Past chmn. Winter Park (Colo.) Recreation Assn., 1978-95, St. Joseph Hosp., Denver, 1984-86, R.M.O., Denver, Mile Hi chpt. ARC, Metro Denver Boys & Girls Clubs, Colo. Safety Assn., 1993-95. Capt. USAF, 1952-54. Mem. Colo. Bar Assn., Denver Bar Assn., Denver Mt. Exec. Club (pres. 1980), Univ. Club Denver (pres. 1995). Office: Mountain States Employers PO Box 539 Denver CO 80201-0539

DARLING, SCOTT EDWARD, lawyer; b. Los Angeles, Dec. 31, 1949; s. Dick R. and Marjorie Helen (Otto) D.; m. Cynthia Diane Harrah, June 1970 (div.); 1 child, Smokie; m. Deborah Lee Cochran, Aug. 22, 1981; children: Ryan, Jacob. BA, U. Redlands, 1972; JD, U.S.C., 1975. Bar: Calif. 1976, U.S. Dist. Ct. (cen. dist.) Calif. 1976. Assoc. atty. Elver, Falsetti, Boone & Crafts, Riverside, 1976-78; ptnr. Falsetti, Crafts, Pritchard & Darling, Riverside, 1978-84; pres. Scott Edward Darling, A Profl. Corp., Riverside, 1984—; grant reviewer HHS, Washington, 1982-88; judge pro tem Riverside County Mcpl. Ct., 1980, Riverside County Superior Ct., 1987-88; bd. dirs. Tel Law Nat. Legal Pub. Info. System, Riverside, 1978-80. Author, editor: Small Law Office Computer Legal System, 1984. Bd. dirs. Youth Adv. Com. to Selective Svc., 1968-70, Am. Heart Assn. Riverside County, 1978-82, Survival Ministries, 1986-89; atty. panel Calif. Assn. Realtors, L.A., 1980—; pres. Calif. Young Reps., 1978-80; mem. GI Forum, Riverside, 1970-88; presdl. del. Nat. Rep. Party, 1980-84; asst. treas. Calif. Rep. Party, 1981-83; Rep. Congl. candidate, Riverside, 1982; treas. Riverside Sickle Cell Found., 1980-82, recipient Eddie D. Smith award; pres. Calif. Rep. Youth Caucus, 1980-82; v.p. Riverside County Red Cross, 1982-84; mem. Citizen's Univ. Com., Riverside, 1978-84, World Affairs Council, 1978-82, Urban League, Riverside, 1980-82. Calif. Scholarship Fedn. (life). Named one of Outstanding Young Men in Am., U.S. Jaycees, 1979-86. Mem. ABA, Riverside County Bar Assn., Speaker's Bur. Riverside County Bar Assn., Riverside Jaycees, Riverside C. of C. Lodge: Native Sons of Golden West. Office: 3697 Arlington Ave Riverside CA 92506-3938

DARMSTAETTER, JAY EUGENE, secondary education educator; b. Altadena, Calif., Nov. 30, 1937; s. Eugene Jamison and Virginia (Fagans) D. AA, L.A. City Coll., 1958; BA, L.A. State Coll., 1960, MA, 1962; postgrad., U. So. Calif., 1962-65. Cert. secondary edn. tchr., secondary adminstr. Tchr. L.A. Unified Schs., 1960—, athletic dir., 1965-83; tng. tchr. UCLA, Calif. State U., Whittier Coll., L.A., 1966—; master tchr. L.A. Unified Schs., 1983-84; announcer L.A. Unified Schs., 1970—, CIF/So. Section, Artesia, Calif., 1964-85, State CIF, Fullerton, Calif., 1970-85. Soloist Christian Sci. Chs., L.A., 1958—; mem. Citizens Community Planning Coun., L.A. County, 1989—. Recipient Nat. Def. Edn. Assn. award Dept. of Edn., L.A., 1968. Mem. NEA, Calif. Tchrs. Assn., United Tchrs. L.A., Phi Mu Alpha Sinfonia. Republican. Office: Wilson High/LA Schools 4500 Multnomah St Los Angeles CA 90032-3703

DARNALL, ROBERTA MORROW, academic administrator; b. Kemmerer, Wyo., May 18, 1949; d. C. Dale and Eugenia Stayner (Christmas) Morrow; m. Leslie A. Darnall, Sept. 3, 1977; children: Kimberly Gene, Leslie Nicole. BS, U. Wyo., Laramie, 1972. Tariff sec., ins. adminstr. Wyo. Trucking Assn., Casper, 1973-75; asst. clerical supr. Wyo. Legislature, Cheyenne, 1972-77; congl. campaign press aide, 1974; pub. relations dir. in Casper, Wyo. Republican Central Com., 1976-77; asst. dir. alumni relations U. Wyo., 1977-81, dir. of alumni, 1981—; bd. dir. Ivinson Meml. Hosp. Found. Mem. Higher Edn. Assn. Rockies, Am. Soc. Assn. Execs., Laramie C. of C. (edn. com.), PEO (former courtesy com., officer), Zonta Internat. Republican. Episcopalian. Home: 15 Snowy View Ct Laramie WY 82070-5358 Office: PO Box 3137 Laramie WY 82071-3137

DARNELL, LARRY, plant manager; b. Aurora, Ill., Dec. 27, 1940; s. Norman F. and Arlene G. (Gee) D.; m. Francis Kaye Hill, July 3, 1959; children—Darren A., Dawn M. Student Aurora Coll., 1959-61. Draftsman, Aurora Pump Co., Ill., 1959-64; applications engr., 1964-70; regional sales mgr. Thrush Products, Inc., Peru, Ind., 1970-72, engring. mgr., 1972-80, mktg. mgr., 1976-80; plant mgr. Amtrol, Inc., Peru, 1980—. Exec. dir. St. John's Lutheran Ch., Peru, 1974-78. Mem. Am. Soc. San. Engrs., Phi Delta Kappa. Avocations: golf; hunting; fishing. Home: 529 Longview Dr Peru IN 46970-1563 Office: Lakeside Industries 7735 178th Pl NE Redmond WA 98052-4954

DARNEY, PHILIP DEMPSEY, gynecologist, educator; b. Granite, Okla., Feb. 27, 1943; s. Walter Preston and Corene (Barton) D.; m. Virginia Grant (div. 1981); children: Blair, Barton; m. Uta Landy, Oct. 13, 1984; 1 child, Undine. AB, U. Calif., Berkeley, 1964; MD, U. Calif., San Francisco, 1968; MSc, London Sch. Hygiene, 1972. Diplomate Am. Bd. Preventive Medicine, Am. Bd. Ob-Gyn. Intern USPHS Hosp., San Francisco, 1968-69; resident in ob-gyn Brigham and Women's Hosp., Boston, 1973-76; dep. dir. div. reproductive health Ctrs. Disease Control, Atlanta, 1971-73; asst. prof. ob-gyn Harvard Med. Sch., Boston, 1976-78; assoc. prof. ob-gyn U. Oreg. Med. Sch., Portland, 1978-80; prof. ob-gyn U. Calif. Sch. Medicine, San Francisco, 1981—; cons. AID, Washington, 1971-74, Pathfinder Internat., Boston, 1973-83, The Population Coun., Family Health Internat., Internat. Projects Assistance Svc., Family Planning Internat. Assistance, Johns Hopkins U., 30 countries;lectr., writer in field. Author: Ambulatory and Office Gynecologic Surgery, 1987, Clinical Guide for Contraception, 1992; contbr. over 100 articles on contraception, abortion and sterilization to med. jours., chpts. to books. Bd. dirs. Assn. for Vol. Surg. Contraception, Planned Parenthood Fedn. Am., N.Y.C., Alan Guttmacher Inst. Named Outstanding Young Profl. Am. Pub. Health Assn., 1984. Fellow Am. Coll. Obstetricians and Gynecologists, Am. Coll. Preventive Medicine. Democrat. Office: San Francisco Gen Hosp Dept Ob-Gyn San Francisco CA 94110

DA ROZA, VICTORIA CECILIA, human resources administrator; b. East Orange, N.J., Aug. 30, 1945; d. Victor and Cynthia Helen (Krupa) Hawkins; m. Thomas Howard Kaminski, Aug. 28, 1971 (div. 1977); 1 child, Sarah Hawkins; m. Robert Anthony da Roza, Nov. 25, 1983. BA, U. Mich., 1967; MA, U. Mo., 1968. Contract compliance mgr. City of San Diego, 1972-75; v.p. personnel Bank of Calif., San Francisco, 1975-77; with human resources Lawrence Livermore (Calif.) Nat. Lab., 1978-86; pvt. cons. Victoria Kaminski-da Roza & Assocs., 1986—; lectr. in field; videotape workshop program on mid-career planning used by IEEE. Contbr. numerous articles to profl. jours. Mem. social policy com. City of Livermore, 1982. Mem. Am. Soc. Tng. and Devel., Western Gerontol. Soc. (planning com. Older Worker Track 1983), Gerontol. Soc. Am. Home and Office: 385 Borica Dr Danville CA 94526-5457

DARRAH, JOAN, mayor. Mayor City of Stockton, Calif. Office: City of Stockton 425 N El Dorado St Stockton CA 95202-1951*

D'ARRIGO, STEPHEN, JR., agricultural company executive; b. Stockton, Cal., Mar. 8, 1922; s. Stephen and Constance (Picciotto) D'A.; B.S., U. Santa Clara, 1943; m. Rosemary Anne Murphy, Aug. 20, 1949; children—Stephen III, Kathleen Anne, Joanne Marie, Michael Andrew, Dennis Patrick, Patrick Shane. Sec.-treas., D'Arrigo Bros. Co. of Calif., San Jose, 1946-62, Salinas, 1962-83, ret., 1983; sec.-treas. Santa Cruz Farms (co. merged with D'Arrigo Bros. 1970), Eloy, Ariz., 1947-52, pres., gen. mgr. 1952-70, dir. 1947-70. Mem. Nat. Def. Exec. Res. Served from pvt. to 2d lt., AUS, 1943-46. Decorated Bronze Star, Combat Inf. Badge, Belgian Fouragere; recipient Distinguished Service award Santa Clara Heart Assn. Mem. Nat. Rifle Assn. (life), Springfield Armory Mus. (life), Smithsonian Assos. (nat. charter), Mil. Order World Wars, Assn. U.S. Army, Co. Mil. Historians, Am. Soc. Arms Collectors, Tex. Gun Collectors Assn. Home: 2241 Dry Creek Rd San Jose CA 95124-1216

DARRINGTON, DENTON, state senator. Mem. Idaho Senate from Dist. 24A. Office: Office of State Senate State Capitol Boise ID 83720 Home: RR 1 Declo ID 83323-9801

DARRINGTON, JOHN CHARLES, city administrator; b. Burley, Idaho, July 29, 1946; s. John Harry and Gladys (Tennant) D.; m. Susan Gayle Turner, Jan. 27, 1969; children: Melissa, John Scott, Spencer Bruce, Marcus Turner, Rebecca, Stephanie, Kimberly. BA, Brigham Young U., 1970, MPA, 1972; Cert., Harvard U., 1988. Manpower dir. Utah County Cmty. Action, Provo, 1972; dir. adminstrv. svcs. Mountainland Assn. of Govts., Provo, 1972-77; city adminstr. City of Soda Springs, Idaho, 1977-81; city mgr. City of Rawlins, Wyo., 1981-85; city adminstr. City of Gillette, Wyo., 1985—; mem. Environ. Quality Coun., State of Wyo., Cheyenne, 1988—, chmn., 1992-94. Author: Goal Setting-Steps To Progress, 1992. Mem. Ctrl. Wyo. Coun. Boy Scouts of Am. (pres. 1994), Rotary Internat. (pres. 1991). Republican. LDS. Home: 1310 Overdale Dr Gillette WY 82718-7545 Office: City of Gillette PO Box 3003 Gillette WY 82717

DARROW, GEORGE F., natural resources company owner, consultant; b. Osage, Wyo., Aug. 13, 1924; s. George Washington and Marjorie (Ord) D.; m. Elna Tannehill, Oct. 23, 1976; children by previous marriage: Roy Stuart, Karen Josanne, Reed Crandall, John Robin. AB in Econs., U. Mich., 1945, BS in Geology, 1949. Geologist Amerada Petroleum Corp., Billings, Mont., 1949-50; v.p. Northwest Petroleum Co., 1951-58; prin. Resource Consultants, Billings, 1959-76; pres., CEO Crossbow Corp., Billings, 1962—; v.p. Kootenai Galleries, Bigfork, Mont., 1976—; sr. ptnr. Crossbow Assocs., resource mgrs., Bigfork, 1976—; chmn. Mont. Environ. Quality Coun., Helena, 1971-73; bd. dirs. Ord Ranch Corp., Lusk, Wyo., Mont. Pvt. Capital Network; apptd. faculty affiliate U. Mont., 1995—. Contbr. articles on resource mgmt. and econs. to various publs. Elected mem. Mont. Ho. of Reps., 1967-69, 71-73, Mont. Senate, 1973-75; bd. dirs. Bigfork Ctr. Performing Arts, 1980—; apptd. mem. Mont. Ambs., 1994—. Lt. (j.g.) USNR, 1943-46, PTO. Mem. Internat. Soc. Ecol. Econs., Am. Assn. Petroleum Geologists (past pres. Rocky Mountain sect.), Am. Inst. Profl. Geologists (charter), Mont. Geol. Soc. (founder, charter), Billings Petroleum Club. Home and Office: Crossbow Corp 2014 Beverly Hill Blvd Billings MT 59102-2314 also: Paladin Farms 924 Chapman Hill Dr Bigfork MT 59911-6215

DARROW, PAUL GARDNER, painter, printmaker, cartoonist, illustrator; b. Pasadena, Calif., Oct. 31, 1921; s. Frank Richard and Ruth Anne (Coutant) D.; m. Nadine Gunderson, June 13, 1944 (div. 1963); children: Christopher, Joan, Elizabeth, Eric; m. Suzanne Standlee Smith, June 8, 1965 (dec. Nov. 1985). AA, Pasadena Jr. Coll., 1939; student, Art Ctr. Sch. Fine Arts, Pasadena, Calif., 1940-41, Colorado Springs Fine Arts Ctr., 1944-45, Claremont Grad. Sch., 1945-49. Prof. art Otis Art Inst., L.A., 1962-68; instr. Calif. Inst. Tech., Pasadena, 1979-72; prof. art Claremont (Calif.) Grad. Sch., 1955-92; prof. Scripps Coll., Claremont, 1955-92, prof. emeritus, 1992—; artist-corr. Vietnam war on ships at sea, Japan, Okinawa, Taiwan, 1964. 35 one-man shows, including mus in Phila., Denver, Museo del Arte Moderne, Brazil, La Mus., Newport Mus., Laguna Mus., Portland Mus.; retrospective show Lang Galleries, Claremont Colls., 1992; murals executed Air France, P & O SS, Wells Fargo Bank, Monsanto; illustrator N.Y. Times, Partisan Rev., Saturdy Rev; illustrator books Academic Bestiary (Richard Armour), 1973, Concrete Jungle (Couffer), 1963, Guide for the Married Man, 1967. Grantee NEH, 1972; Ford rsch. grantee, 1978. Mem. Calif. Watercolor Soc. (v.p. 1962-63), L.A. Printmaking Soc. (co-founder). Home and Studio: 690 Cuprien Way Laguna Beach CA 92651-2563

DARVAS, ENDRE PETER, artist; b. Kisvadra, Sz-Szatmar, Hungary, July 18, 1946; came to U.S., in 1957; s. Bela and Maria (Filtczer) Darvas. BFA, U. Tex., 1969. Pres. Studio Arts and Frames, Inc., South Lake Tahoe, Calif., 1974-78; owner Darvas Studio, South Lake Tahoe, 1969—. One-man shows include San Angelo, Tex., 1963, Taox, N.Mex., 1971, Carmel, Calif., 1975, San Carlos, Mex., 1987, Galerias del Pacifico, Sonora, Mex., 1989, Studio Retrospective, Lake Tahoe, 1990, Sierra Galleries, Lake Tahoe, 1991-94; represented in permanent collections Sierra Gallery, Sierra Galleries, Rosequist Gallery, Tucson. Recipient numerous awards from art exhibits. Mem. Soc. Am. Impressionists, Southwestern Watercolor Soc. Office: Darvas Studio PO Box 711 South Lake Tahoe CA 96156-0711

DAS, SUBHENDU, electrical engineer; b. Burnpur, India, Nov. 17, 1944; came to U.S., 1981; s. Satya Kinkar and Chandra Bali (Mohanta) D.; m. Swarna Rani Ghish, Mar. 6, 1981; children: Tania Debbie, Pamela Renee. BSEE, Jadavpur U., India, 1967; MSEE, Indian Inst. Tech., India, 1969; PhD of Elec. Engring., Indian Inst. Tech., 1972. Lectr. Jadavpur U., Calcutta, 1972-76; asst. prof. Indian Inst. Mgmt., Calcutta, 1976-81; engring. specialist Litton Guidance and Control, Woodland Hills, Calif., 1989-92; cons. L.A. AFB, 1993—; faculty mem. Calif. State U., Northridge, Ponoma, 1983-92; nat. assoc. Govt. India, 1975-80. Patentee in field; contbr. articles to profl. jours. Home: 9732 Kessler Ave Chatsworth CA 91311-5503 Office: Amcomp Corp 3525 Lonita Blvd # 102 Torrance CA 90505

DATSKO, TINA MICHELLE, writer, producer; b. Ann Arbor, Mich., Jan. 23, 1960; d. Joseph and Doris Mae (Ross) D. BA, U. Mich., 1983, MFA in Creative Writing, 1985; MFA in Profl. Writing, U. So. Calif., 1989. Film/video cons., 1986; story analyst Too Magic, Inc., Columbia Pictures, Burbank, Calif., 1987-88; scriptwriter Women in Film Festival, 1988; writer/producer Gypsycat Prodns., L.A., 1990—; writing, film/video cons., 1992—; lectr. radio/TV/film dept. Calif. State U., Long Beach, 1990—. Contbr. numerous articles to profl. publs. Recipient 14 Hopwood awards, 1978-85, L.A. Arts Coun. Assocs. award, 1988-89. Mem. Phi Kappa Phi. Home: 550 Orange Ave Unit 339 Long Beach CA 90802-7011 Office: Calif State U 1250 N Bellflower Blvd Long Beach CA 90840-0006

DATTA, ARUN KUMAR, molecular biologist; b. Calcutta, India, July 25, 1954; came to U.S., 1987; s. Sachi K. and Rekha (Roy) D.; m. Purabi Dhar Datta, Dec. 4, 1984; children: Shantanu, Sudipa. MS in Biochemistry, Calcutta U., India, 1978; PhD in Biochemistry, 1987. Lectr. Sch. Tropical Medicine, Calcutta, India, 1978-80; vis. scientist U. Newcastle Upon Tyne, U.K., 1986; scientific staff Ctrl. JALMA Inst., India, 1980-87; rsch. assoc. Dept. Bacteriology U. Wis., Madison, 1987-90; jr. faculty instr. Dept. Pharm. U. Tex. Southwestern Med. Ctr., Dallas, 1990-93; assoc. scientist Cytel Corp. and dept. Molecular Biology, Scripps Rsch. Inst., San Diego, 1993—; invited speaker Internat. Symposium on Biology of Actinomycetes, Madison, Wis., 1991; co-investigator on the D.S.T.; vis. fellow British Coun. Contbr. numerous articles and papers to profl. jours. Organized Internat. Festival UT Southwestern Med. Ctr., Dallas, 1991, 92. Mem. AAAS, Am. Soc. for Microbiology, Am. Soc. Biochemistry and Molecular Biology. Home: 13754 Mango Dr DelMar CA 92014-3432 Office: Cytel Corp 3525 John Hopkins Ct San Diego CA 92121-1121

DATTA, PURNA CHANDRA, clinical psychologist, educator; b. Barisal, India, Jan. 1, 1943; came to U.S., 1980; s. Jogendra Kumar and Kanak (Ghosh) D.; m. Anita Rani, Feb. 7, 1969; children: Partha Michael, Aparna Kara. BA in Philosophy with honors, Dacca (Bangladesh) U., 1963, MA in Philosophy, 1964, MA in Psychology, 1967; PhD in Clin. Psychology, Newcastle U., NSW, Australia, 1979, M in Clin. Psychology, 1982. Lic. psychologist, Ga., Calif.; cert. eye movement desensitization reprocessing. Psychologist Morisset (NSW) Hosp., 1974-80, clin. psychologist, 1983-84; psychologist Fairview State Hosp., Costa Mesa, Calif., 1980-83; psychologist Ctrl. State Hosp., Milledgeville, Ga., 1985-86, sr. psychologist, 1989-90; program dir. Gladesville (NSW) Hosp., 1984-85, So. Met. Devel. Disabilities Svc., Gladesville, 1986-88; staff psychologist Stockton (Calif.) Devel. Ctr., 1990-94, O.H. Close Sch. (Calif. Youth Advisory), Stockton, 1994—; lectr. psychology Dacca Coll., 1968-69, Dacca U., 1969-73; tutor, demonstrator Newcastle U., 1973-74; lectr. psychiat. nursing Newcastle Tech. Coll., 1974-80; clin. instr. psychiatry U. Calif., Irvine, 1981-83; adj. prof. psychology U. Pacific, Stockton, 1992—; clin. psychologist mental health svcs. Perry Street Cmty. Ctr., Newcastle, 1976-77, 77; clin. psychologist pediatric unit Royal Newcastle Hosp., 1977-78; psychol. asst. Dr. F.M. Crinella, Costa Mesa. 1982-83; presenter in field. Contbr. articles to profl. jours. Talent scholar Commonwealth U. Dacca, 1960-64. Mem. APA, Calif. Psychol. Assn., Am. Assn. Mental Retardation, Assn. for Behavior Analysis, Am. Assn. Clin. Hypnosis (cert. in hypnotherapy), Am. Coll. Forensic Psychology. Home: 7221 Shoreham Pl Stockton CA 95207-1224 Office: O.H. Close Sch Calif Youth Authority 7650 S Newcastle Rd Stockton CA 95213

DAUBEN, WILLIAM GARFIELD, chemist, educator; b. Columbus, Ohio, Nov. 6, 1919; s. Hyp J. and Leilah (Stump) D.; m. Carol Hyatt, Aug. 8, 1947; children: Barbara, Ann. AB, Ohio State U., 1941; AM, Harvard U., 1942, PhD, 1944; PhD (hon.), U. Bordeaux, France, 1980. Edward Austin fellow Harvard U., 1941-42, teaching fellow, 1942-43, research asst., 1943-45; instr. U. Calif. at Berkeley, 1945-47, asst. prof. chemistry, 1947-52, assoc. prof., 1952-57, prof., 1957—; lectr. Am.-Swiss Found., 1962; mem. med. chem. study sect. USPHS, 1959-64; mem. chemistry panel NSF, 1964-67; mem. Am.-Sino Sci. Cooperation Com., 1973-76; NRC, 1977-80. Mem. bd. editors Jour. of Organic Chemistry, 1957-62; mem. bd. editors Organic Syntheses, 1959-67, bd. dirs., 1971—; editor in chief Organic Reactions, 1967-83, pres., 1967-84, bd. dirs. 1967—; mem. edit. bd. Steroids, 1989—; contbr. articles profl. jours. Recipient citation U. Calif., Berkeley, 1990; Guggenheim fellow, 1951, 66, sr. fellow NSF, 1957-58, Alexander von Humboldt Found. fellow, 1980. Fellow Royal Soc. Chemistry, Swiss Chem. Soc.; mem. NAS (chmn. chemistry sect. 1977-80), Am. Chem. Soc. (chmn. div. organic chemistry 1962-63, councilor organic div. 1964-70, mem. coun. publ. com. 1965-70, mem. adv. com. Petroleum Research Fund 1974-77, award Calif. sect. 1959, Ernest Guenther award 1973, Arthur C. Cope scholar 1990), Am. Acad. Arts and Scis., Pharm. Soc. Japan (hon.), Phi Beta Kappa, Sigma Xi, Phi Lambda Upsilon, Phi Eta Sigma, Sigma Chi. Club: Bohemian. Home: 20 Eagle Hall Kensington CA 94707-1408 Office: U Calif Dept Chemistry Berkeley CA 94720-1460

DAUGHADAY, DOUGLAS ROBERT, computer engineer; b. Highland Park, N.J., Mar. 13, 1954; s. Robert Owings and Mary (Kirkpatrick) D.; m. Ilene D. Eichel, Feb. 14, 1987; 1 child, Brian Douglas. BSEE cum laude, W.Va. Inst. Tech., 1976; MSEE, U. So. Calif., 1979. Mem. tech. staff Hughes Aircraft Co., Culver City, Calif., 1977-79; sr. engr. Litton G&CS, Woodland Hills, Calif., 1979-80; lab. engr. Garrett Airesearch, Torrance, Calif., 1980-84; mem. tech. staff The Aerospace Corp., El Segundo, Calif., 1984-87, mgr., 1987-93; project engr., 1993—. Mem. IEEE, ACM, Soc. Am. Magicians (pres. assembly #22), Nat. Assn. Underwater Instrs. (instr.), U. S.C. Alumni Assn. (life), Eta Kappa Nu (life). Democrat. Home: 27910 Ridgebrook Ct Rancho Palos CA 90275-3300 Office: The Aerospace Corp 2350 E El Segundo Blvd El Segundo CA 90245-4609

DAUGHENBAUGH, MARY JANE, foundation administrator; b. Tiffin, Ohio, Sept. 8, 1941; d. Thomas Franklin and Imogene Dent (Updike) Boyd; m. LeRoy Edward Daughenbaugh, Aug. 2, 1958; children: LeRoy Edward, Mark Thomas, David Michael. BA in Psychology, Bowling Green State U., 1978; MA in Applied Behavioral Sci., Wright State U., 1979. Behavioral analyst Woodlane Sch. for Mentally Retarded, Bowling Green, Ohio, 1978; grad. teaching asst. Wright State U., Dayton, Ohio, 1979; rsch. analyst Green-Clinton County Mental Health/Mental Retardation Bd., Xenia, Ohio, 1979; exec. dir. Miami County Mental Health Ctr., Troy, Ohio, 1979-85; assoc. dir., then interim exec. dir. Behavioral Health Svcs., Inc., Yuma, Ariz., 1985-88; account exec. Toluca Pacific Securities Corp., Santa Barbara, Calif., 1988-89; nursing svcs. mgr. Cottage Care Ctr., Santa Barbara, Calif., 1990; exec. dir. Spl. Children's Found., Oxnard, Calif., 1990—. Mem. Camarillo Women's Day Com.; mem. Ventura County Vol. Coord. Coun.; mem. Area Bd. IX Legis. Com.; mem. vendor's adv. com., bd. dirs. Tri County Regional Ctr.; mem. Ventura County Vol. Coord. Coun. Recipient Key to City, Mayor of Troy, Ohio, 1984, Recognition award Big Bros./Big Sisters, 1987, Outstanding Svc. award Behavioral Health Svcs. Bd. Dirs., 1988; pub. rels. event held in her honor Dettmer Hosp., 1985. Mem. Employee Adv. Coun., Ventura County Pers. Assn., Oxnard C. of C., Ojai C. of C., Camarillo C. of C. (diplomat com.), Cmty. Residential Care Assn. Calif. Home: 3844-243 Channel Island Blvd Oxnard CA 93035

DAUGHERTY, LEO, literature and language educator; b. Louisville, May 16, 1939; s. F.S. and Mollie Repass (Brown) D.; m. Virginia Upton; 1 child, Mollie Virginia; m. Lee Graham. AB in Fine Arts and Lit., Western Ky. U., 1961; MA in English, U. Ark., 1963; PhD in Am. Lit., East Tex. State U., 1970; postgrad., Harvard U., 1970-71. Cert. fine arts tchr. Asst. prof. lit. U. Wis., Superior, 1962-63; teaching fellow East Tex. State U., Commerce, 1963-65; asst. prof. lit. Frederick Coll., Portsmouth, Va., 1965-66, Va. State U., Norfolk, 1966-68; prof. lit. and linguistics Evergreen State Coll., Olympia, Wash., 1972—; acad. dean Evergreen State Coll., Olympia, 1975-76, dir. Ctr. Study of Sci. and Human Values, 1990—; past grant evaluator NEH. Author: The Teaching of Writing at Evergreen, 1984; contbr. short stories, articles to profl. and literary jours. Active Friends of Bodleian Libr., Oxford, Eng., 1983—. Recipient NEH award, 1973. Mem. MLA, Internat. Assn. Fantasy in Arts, Shakespeare Assn. Am., Soc. Lit. and Sci. Office: Evergreen State Coll Olympia WA 98505

DAUGHERTY, SHARON, mental health counselor; b. Denver, June 26, 1960; life partner: Maureen Daugherty, July 3, 1993; 1 child, Kennedy Smith-Fliesher. BS, SUNY, Albany, 1990; MA, Century U., 1993; postgrad., Southwest U., 1994—, Kensington U., 1994—. Cert. Am. Counseling Assn., Am. Hypnosis Assn. TV ops. KMGH-TV7 McGraw-Hill, Denver, 1976-81; TV master control U.S. Army, Aberdeen, Md., 1982-86; broadcast supervisor Colo. Army Nat. Guard, Englewood, 1986—; TV master control Jones Spacelink, Englewood, 1994—; psychotherapist Daugherty & Assocs. Psychotherapy, Aurora, Colo., 1993—; founder Nat. Harry Benjamin Gender Dysphoric Assn., Aurora, 1994—, Nat. Gay & Lesbian Domestic Violence Victims Network, Aurora, 1991—. Author: Closeted Screams: A Service Provider Handbook for Same-Sex Domestic Violence Issues, 1992. Intake domestic vol. Legal Aid Soc. Met. Denver, 1993; bd. dirs. Gay and Lesbian Cmty. Ctr. of Colo., 1989. Roman Catholic. Office: Daughtery & Assocs Aurora CO 80013

DAVAGNINO, JUAN V., scientist; b. Santiago, Chile, July 14, 1952; came to U.S., 1985; s. Juan A. and Vicenta (Gilabert) D.; m. Judith M. Salinas, Mar. 8, 1956; 1 child, Andres. BS in Biology, U. Chile, Santiago, 1976, MS in Biology, 1978, PhD in Biochemistry, 1985. Postdoctoral fellow Harvard Med. Sch., Boston, 1985-90, Calif. Inst. Tech., Pasadena, 1990-92; scientist IV Baxter Healthcare Co., Duarte, Calif., 1992-94, scientist V, 1994-95, group leader formulation, 1995—. Contbr. articles to profl. jours. Nat. rsch. fellow Nat. Commn. for Rsch., Santiago, 1979-81, Harvard U. fellow, 1985, Cancer Rsch. Campaign Internat. fellow, 1986, Charles A. King Trust fellow Med. Found. Boston, 1987-89. Mem. AAAS. Office: Baxter Healthcare Co Hyland Divsn 1720 Flower Ave Duarte CA 91010-2923

DAVENPORT, ALFRED LARUE, JR., manufacturing company executive; b. Upland, Calif., May 6, 1921; s. Alfred Larue and Nettie (Blocker) D.; m. Darrow Ormsbee Beazlie, May 16, 1950 (div. 1953); m. Jean Ann Given, June 21, 1957 (wid. Apr. 1990); children: Lawrence, Terisa, Lisa, Nancy; m. Inez Bothwell, Aug. 8, 1993. Student, Chaffey Jr. Coll., Ontario, Calif., 1940; BE in Indsl. Engring., U. So. Calif., 1943. Weight engring. Lockheed Aircraft, Burbank, Calif., 1940-41; ptnr. Pacific Traders, L.A., 1946-48; founder, pres. Pactra Industries, Inc., L.A., 1947-79; owner Davenport Internat., Ltd., Van Nuys, Calif., 1979—; pres., founder Trans Container, Inc., Upland, Calif., 1970-79; pres., owner Pactra Hobby, Inc., Encino, Calif., 1983—, Davenport Export-Import, Inc., Encino, Calif., 1982-93; cons. Plasti-Kote, Inc., Medina, Ohio, 1985-87; pres. Pactra Coatings Inc., Hobby Div., Upland, 1985-89; mgr. craft div. Plasti-Kote Inc., Medina, Ohio, 1989-92; bd. dirs. R.C. Dudek, Inc., Westlake, Calif., 1978—, Aerosol Info. Assn., L.A., 1974-79; stockholder, mktg. dir. Enviroman Inc., 1994—. Lt. USN, 1943-46. Recipient Blue Key, U. So. Calif., L.A., 1942. Mem. So. Calif. Hobby Industry Assn. (sec. 1959-62), Hobby Industry Assn. Am. (dir. 1961-64), Young Pres. Orgn. (L.A. chpt.), World Bus. Coun., Woodland Hills Country Club (treas. 1981-83), Sigma Phi Epsilon (v.p. 1954-81, alumni bd. dirs. 1955-75, Disting. Bro. award 1979, Alumni of Yr. award 1975), Babboa Basin Yacht Club. Republican. Presbyterian. Home: 5330 Dubois Ave Woodland Hills CA 91367-6017 Office: Davenport Internat-Pactra Inc Enviroman Internat 18075 Ventura Blvd Encino CA 91316-3517

DAVENPORT, JANET LEE, real estate saleswomen, small business owner; b. Napa, Calif., Dec. 10, 1938; d. George Perry and Stella Dolores (Ramalho) Gomez; m. Bingo George Wesner, Aug. 4, 1957 (July 1978); children: Bing George, Diane Estelle; m. Marvin Eugene Davenport, Jan. 13, 1979. Student, U. Calif., Davis, 1956-57, Nat. Jud. Coll., 1975-79. Co-owner, operator Bar JB Ranch, Benicia, Calif., 1960-71, Lovelock, Nev., 1971-78; owner, mgr. Wesner Bookkeeping Svc., Lovelock, 1973-78; chief tribal judge Ct. Indian Offenses, Lovelock, 1975-79; justice of peace, coroner County of Pershing, Lovelock, 1975-79; paralegal, legal sec. Samuel S. Wardle, Carson City, Nev., 1979; dep. ct. adminstr. Reno Mcpl. Ct., Reno, 1979-81; co-owner horse farm Reno, 1979—, freelance real estate investor, 1979—; real estate saleswoman Merrill Lynch Realtors, Sparks, Nev., 1981-82; realtor, farm and ranch div. mgr. Copple and Assocs., Realtors, Sparks, 1982-91; real estate saleswoman Vail and Assocs. Realty, Reno, Nev., 1991—; co-owner, operator Lovelock (Nev.) Merc. Co., 1988—; sec. Nev. Judges Assn., 1977-78. Dir. Pershing County Drug and Alcohol Abuse Council, Lovelock, 1976-78. Mem. Reno/Sparks Bd. Realtors, Nat. Assn. Realtors, Nev. Assn. Realtors, Am. Quarter Horse Assn. Republican. Roman Catholic. Home: 4805 Sinelio Dr Reno NV 89502-9510 Office: Vail and Assocs Realty 1700 S Virginia St Reno NV 89502-2811

DAVENPORT, ROGER LEE, research engineer; b. Sacramento, Calif., Oct. 27, 1955; s. Lee Edwin and Ada Fern (Henderson) D.; m. Becky Alice Youtz, Dec. 31, 1977 (div. Apr. 1992). AB Physics, U. Calif., Berkeley, 1977; MSME, U. Ariz., 1979. Assoc. engr. Solar Energy Rsch. Inst., Golden, Colo., 1979-82; cons. Darmstadt, Fed. Republic Germany, 1982-84; missionary Eastern European Sem., Vienna, Austria, 1984-87; staff researcher Sci. Applications Internat. Corp., San Diego, 1987—. Mem. Am. Solar Energy Soc., Wycliffe Assocs., Sierra Club, Colo. Mountain Club, Phi Beta Kappa. Home: 19076 W 59th Dr Golden CO 80403-1057 Office: SAIC 15000 W 6th Ave Golden CO 80401-5047

DAVIAU, DONALD GEORGE, foreign language educator; b. West Medway, Mass., Sept. 30, 1927; s. George and Jenny (Burbank) D.; m. Patricia E. Mara, Aug. 20, 1950; children: Katherine Anne, Robert Laurence, Thomas George, Julie Marie. BA, Clark U., 1950; MA, U. Calif., Berkeley, 1952, PhD, 1955. From asst. prof. to prof. German U. Calif., Riverside, 1955—. Author: Hermann Bahr: The Catalyst of Modernity, 1986, The Major Figures of Austrian Literature, vol. 1, 1988, vol. 2, 1990, vol. 3, 1992, vol. 4, 1995; contbr. articles to profl. jours. With USN, 1945-46. Recipient Cross of Honor for Art and Sci. Austrian Govt., 1978. Mem. MLA, Am. Assn. Tchrs. German, Philol. Assn. the Pacific Coast, Internat. Arthur Schnitzler Assn. (pres.), Am. Coun. for the Study Austrian Lit. (pres.), Jura Soyfer Soc. Office: Univ Calif Dept Literatures Riverside CA 92521

DAVIDSON, ALAN CHARLES, insurance executive; b. L.A., Nov. 8, 1937; s. Charles Evans and Anna Louise (Wilson) D.; m. Gail Louise Ziebarth, June 17, 1961 (dec.); children: Karen Ashley, Douglas McPhail. BA, Whittier Coll., 1962. CLU, ChFC. Pres. Davidson & Pierson Ins., Whittier, Calif., 1967-71, Davidson, Pierson & Roth Inc., Whittier, 1971-81; ptnr. Davidson & Poyner, Whittier, 1978-79; pres. Davidson Co., Whittier, 1961-67, 79—. Producer, host Cable TV show Financial Sense, 1990—. Bd. dirs. Whittier Hist. Soc., 1989-91, Oralingua Sch. for Hearing Impaired, Whittier, 1991—. Recipient numerous awards Provident Mut. Mem. Am. Soc. CLU, Am. Soc. Pension Actuaries, Nat. Assn. Life Underwriters, Calif. Assn. Life Underwriters, Million Dollar Round Table, Life Leaders Round Table (pres.), Life Underwriters of L.A. (pres.), Life Underwriters of Whittier (pres.), Whittier Area C. of C. Republican. Quaker. Home: 6278 Southwind Dr Whittier CA 90601-3840 Office: The Davidson Co 7007 Washington Ave Ste 321 Whittier CA 90602-1486

DAVIDSON, ARLENE MARIE, product manager; b. Chicago Heights, Ill., Oct. 23, 1956; d. Lloyd George and Adeline Louise (Fehlner) Briggs; m. Howard Alexander Davidson III, May 27, 1978 (div. Mar. 1982). BS, Scottdale C.C., 1978; BS in Bus., Ariz. State U., 1988; M in Health Svcs. Adminstrn., U. Mich., 1991. RN, Ariz. RN ICU Santa Clara Valley Med. Ctr., San Jose, Calif., 1978; ICU nurse, head nurse, dept. mgr. St. Joseph's Hosp. and Med. Ctr., Phoenix, 1979-89; adminstrv. intern Scottsdale (Ariz.) Meml. Hosp., 1990; sr. analyst, quality coord., product mgr. Samaritan Group, Inc., Phoenix, 1991—; bd. dirs. Scott Engring., Inc., Phoenix, 1978-87; health adv. com. Ariz. State U., Tempe, 1988. Vol. St. Vincent de Paul Soc., Phoenix, 1993, Phoenix Art Mus., 1993. Mem. AACN (chpt. pres. 1978-88), APHA, Healthcare Adminstrs. Forum, Am. Coll. Healthcare Execs. Democrat. Office: Samaritan Group Inc 3141 N 3rd Ave Phoenix AZ 85013

DAVIDSON, BILL (WILLIAM JOHN DAVIDSON), entertainment journalist, author; b. Jersey City, Mar. 4, 1918; s. Louis J. and Gertrude (Platt) D.; m. Muriel Roberts, May 21, 1960 (dec. Sept. 1983); 1 child, Carol; m. Maralynne Beth Nitz, July 27, 1986. BA, NYU, 1939. Assoc. editor Collier's mag., N.Y.C., 1946-56; contbg. editor Look mag., N.Y.C., 1956-61; editor-at-large Saturday Evening Post, N.Y.C., 1961-69; radio commentator NBC, N.Y.C., 1968-71; TV writer Universal Studios, Universal City, Calif., 1971-76; contbg. editor TV Guide, Radnor, Pa., 1971-90, L.A. Mag., 1992-95; chmn. alumni communications com. NYU, 1959-64. Author: The Real and the Unreal, Six Brave Presidents, 1962, Indict and Convict, 1971, (with Sid Caesar) Where Have I Been?, 1982, Spencer Tracy: Tragic Idol, 1988, Jane Fonda: An Intimate Biography, 1990, (with Danny Thomas) Make Room for Daddy, 1991. Mem. N.Y. County Dem. com., N.Y.C., 1948-50. Served as sgt. U.S. Army, 1941-45, ETO. Recipient Disting. Reporting award Sigma Delta Chi, 1951, 53, Albert Lasker Med. Journalism award, 1953, Disting. Journalism award Family Service Assn. Am., 1963. Mem. Writers Guild Am. West. Democrat. Home: 13225 Morrison St Sherman Oaks CA 91423-2156

DAVIDSON, DAVID NEAL, securities sales executive; b. Pasadena, Calif., Jan. 20, 1956; s. Harold Wilson and Irene Francis (Muninger) D.; m. Constance Elizabeth Wagner, Apr. 25, 1987. BA, U. So. Calif., 1978; MBA, Nat. U., San Diego, 1992. Cert. fin. planner. Traffic mgr. Bozell & Jacobs, Newport Beach, Calif., 1978-80, Dasso & Assocs., Newport Beach, 1980-81; mgmt. cons. Lorenz Internat., Newport Beach, 1981-83; v.p. Municicorp of Calif., Newport Beach, 1983-88; sr. account exec. Smith Barney, Harris Upham & Co. Inc., 1988—. Mem. 552 Club, Hoag Meml. Hosp. Cancer Ctr., Newport Beach, 1987—. Mem. Am. Inst. for Econ. Rsch., Toastmasters (sec. 1986), Univ. Athletic Club, Monarch Bay Beach Club, Commerce Assocs. of U. So. Calif., U. So. Calif. Orange County Trojan Club, Center Club, Racquet Club of Irvine, Phi Delta Theta. Office: Smith Barney 660 Newport Center Dr Ste 1100 Newport Beach CA 92660-6406

DAVIDSON, DAVID SCOTT, architect; b. Great Falls, Mont., Dec. 17, 1925; s. David Adams and Florence Mae (Scott) D.; m. Marjorie Luella Huffman, Sept. 10, 1949; children: Carol M., Marilyn S., Scott L., Bruce F., Craig S. Student, U. Utah, 1943, Pasadena City Coll., 1944; B.S. in Architecture, Mont. State U., 1950. Registered architect, Mont. Architect in tng. Shanley & Shanley Architects, Great Falls, 1950-52; architect van Teylingen, Knight, van Teylingen, Great Falls, 1952-54; prin. David S. Davidson, Architect, Great Falls, 1954-56; ptnr. Davidson & Kuhr Architects, Great Falls, 1956-75; pres. Davidson & Kuhr Architects, P.C., Great Falls, 1975—; dir., pres. Great Falls Arts Assn., 1980-83; dir., pres. Mont. Inst. Arts, 1981—; mem. state constrn. adv. council State of Mont., 1983-84; dir., v.p. Paris Gibson Square, Great Falls, 1982—. Mem. Great Falls Zoning Bd., 1972-75; mem. rehab. com. Great Falls Housing Task Force, 1975-78; chmn. architecture div. United Way, 1975-78; dir. Great Falls Symphony Assn., 1992-93. Served with U.S. Army, 1943-46. Recipient 1st honor Mont. chpt. AIA, 1973, 75; recipient honor award in architecture Mont. chpt. AIA, 1973, 74, 78, 83, merit in architecture Mont. chpt. AIA, 1965, 2 awards U.S. Dept. Energy, 1986, Interior Design award Arch. Record, 1976, Internat. Union Bricklayers and Allied Crafts award, 1986, 87, 92. Fellow AIA (chpt. pres. 1965-66, dir. 1962-66), Great Falls Soc. Architects (pres. 1958-59), Jr. C. of C. (dir. 1956-60). Home: 1212 Buena Dr Great Falls MT 59404-3750 Office: Davidson and Kuhr Architects PC 401 Division Rd Great Falls MT 59404-1409

DAVIDSON, ERIC HARRIS, molecular and developmental biologist, educator; b. N.Y.C., Apr. 13, 1937; s. Morris and Anne D. B.A., U. Pa., 1958; Ph.D., Rockefeller U., 1963. Research asso. Rockefeller U., 1963-65, asst. prof., 1965-71; asso. prof. devel. molecular biology Calif. Inst. Tech., Pasadena, 1971-74; prof. Calif. Inst. Tech., 1974—, Norman Chandler prof. cell biology, 1981—. Author: Gene Activity in Early Development, 3d edit, 1986. NIH grantee, 1965—; NSF grantee, 1972—. Mem. Nat. Acad. Scis. Office: Calif Inst Tech Div Biology Mail Code 156 29 Pasadena CA 91125

DAVIDSON, GORDON, theatrical producer, director; b. Bklyn., May 7, 1933; s. Joseph H. and Alice (Gordon) D.; m. Judith Swiller, Sept. 21, 1958; children: Adam, Rachel. B.A., Cornell U.; M.A., Case Western Res. U.; L.H.D. (hon.), Bklyn. Coll.; D. Performing Arts (hon.), Calif. Inst. Arts; D.F.A. (hon.), Claremont U. Ctr. Stage mgr. Phoenix Theatre Co., 1958-60, Am. Shakespeare Festival Theatre, 1958-60, Dallas Civic Opera, 1960-61, Martha Graham Dance Co., 1962; mng. dir. Theatre Group at UCLA, 1965-67; artistic dir., producer Center Theatre Group Mark Taper Forum, 1967—; co-founder New Theatre For Now, Mark Taper Forum, 1970; Past mem. theatre panel Nat. Endowment for Arts; past pres. Theatre Communications Group; mem. adv. council Internat. Theatre Inst.; mem. adv. com. Cornell Ctr. for Performing Arts; cons. Denver Center for the Performing Arts; bd. dirs. several arts orgns. including Am. Arts Alliance. Producer, dir. over 150 major theatrical prodns. including The Deputy, 1965, Candide, 1966, The Devils, 1967, Who's Happy Now, 1967, In the Matter of J. Robert Oppenheimer, 1968 (N.Y. Drama Desk award), Sew, Murderous Angels, 1970, Rosebloom, 1970, The Trial of the Catonsville Nine, 1971 (Obie award, Tony award nomination), Henry IV, Part I, 1972, Mass, 1973, Hamlet, 1974, Savages, 1974 (Obie award), Too Much Johnson, 1975, The Shadow Box, 1975 (Tony award, Outer Critics Circle Best Dir. award), And Where She Stops Nobody Knows, 1976, Getting Out, 1977, Black Angel, 1978, Terra Nova, 1979, Children of a Lesser God, 1979, The Lady and the Clarinet, 1980, Chekhov in Yalta, 1981, Tales from Hollywood, 1982, The American Clock, 1984, The Hands of Its Enemy, 1984, Traveler in the Dark, 1985, The Real Thing, 1986, Ghetto, 1986, A Lie of the Mind, 1988; dir. operas including Cosi Fan Tutte, Otello, Beatrice and Benedick, Carmen, La Boheme, Il Trovatore, Harriet, A Woman Called Moses, A Midsummer Night's Dream, 1988; TV film The Trial of the Catonsville Nine, 1971; exec. producer Zoot Suit, 1981; producer for TV It's the Willingness, PBS Visions Series, 1979, Who's Happy Now?, NET Theatre in Am. Series; dir. A Little Night Music, 1990. Trustee Ctr. for Music, Drama and Art; past pres. League Resident Theatres; past v.p. Am. Nat. Theatre Acad; advisor Fund for New Am. Plays. Recipient N.Y. Drama Desk award for direction, 1969; recipient Los Angeles Drama Critics Circle awards for direction, 1971, 74, 75, Margo Jones award New Theatre for Now, 1970, 76, Obie award, 1971, 77, Outer Critics Circle award, 1977, Tony award for direction, 1977, award John Harvard, award Nat. Acad. TV Arts and Scis., award Nosotros Golden Eagle, award N.Y. League for Hard of Hearing, award N.Y. Speech and Hearing Assn., award Am. Theatre Assn., award Los Angeles Human Relations Commn.; Guggenheim fellow, 1983. Mem. League Resident Theatres (past pres.), ANTA (v.p. 1975). Office: Ctr Theatre Group Mark Taper Forum 135 N Grand Ave Los Angeles CA 90012-3013

DAVIDSON, HERBERT ALAN, Near Eastern languages and cultures educator; b. Boston, May 25, 1932; s. Louis Nathan and Ettabelle (Baker) D.; m. Kinneret Bernstein; children: Rachel and Jessica. BA, Harvard U., 1953, MA, 1955, PhD, 1959. Lectr. Harvard U., Cambridge, Mass., 1960-61; asst. prof. UCLA, 1961-66, assoc. prof., 1966-72, prof., 1972—, chmn. dept. near eastern langs. and cultures, 1984-91. Author: The Philosophy of Abraham Shalom, 1964, medieval Hebrew transls. of Averroes' Middle Commentary on the Isagoge and Categories, 1969, English transl., 1969, Proofs for Eternity, Creation, and the Existence of God in Medieval Islamic and Jewish Philosophy, 1987, Alfarabi, Avicenna, and Averroes on Intellect, 1992; contbr. articles and book revs. to profl. jours. Office: UCLA Dept Near Ea Langs and Cultures 405 Hilgard Ave Los Angeles CA 90024-1301

DAVIDSON, JOHN ROBERT JAY, banking executive; b. L.A., Mar. 30, 1950; s. John Robert Davidson and Carolyn Rose Monson Wiederanders; m. Kristina Maria Jonson, Dec. 29, 1978; children: Joshua Kingseley, Michelle Maria. BSME, U. N.D., 1972; postgrad., AMP Corp. Leadership Coll., 1990. Engr. Dow Chem. Co., Pauls Valley, Okla., 1972-74; investor Mpls., 1974-77; account exec. AMP Inc., Boulder, Colo., 1977-83; mkt. mgr. AMP Inc., Harrisburg, Pa., 1983-86; dist. mgr. AMP Inc., Denver, 1986-90, nat. mgr., 1990-95; chmn. of bd. 1st Am. State Bank of Denver, 1995—; dir./cons. Am. State Bank, Williston, N.D., 1988—, dir. funds mgmt. com., 1994—; chmn. bd. First Am. State Bank, Denver, 1995—; personal fin.

cons./investor, 1988—. Supporter Jr. League of Denver, Kempe Found., Am. Heart Assn., Arthritis Found., Cancer League, Children's Hosp.; mem. Rep. Nat. Com. Recipient Presdl. Legion of Merit, Colo. Rep. Party. Mem. Masons, Presdl. Legion of Merit. Home: 4845 S Dillon Way Aurora CO 80015-1267 Office: 1st Am State Bank 8101 E Belleview Ave Denver CO 80237

DAVIDSON, JULI, writer, entrepreneur; b. Houston, Aug. 23, 1960; d. Martin J. Davidson and Ruth Marder. Diploma, Park Sch., Brooklandville, Md., 1978; Cert., Richmond Coll., Surrey, Eng., 1978; student, Austin Coll., U. N.Mex, others, 1978-84. Cert. med. terminology and transcription, 1981. Pres. mail order co. Surrenderings, Inc., Albuquerque, 1989-93; owner, artist Juli Davidson Studio Gallery, Albuquerque, 1987-89; freelance writer, editor, photographer Albuquerque, 1985-86; pres., paper artist, writer SI: A Paperworks Gallery, Sante Fe, 1993; exec. adminstr. Albuquerque Art Bus. Assn., 1989; bd. sec. Albuquerque United Artists, 1988. Editor, pub. 2C3P ZN, 1995—; contbr. to various publs. and is subject of varous art revs.; writer, pub. mail-order publs., 1995—. Recipient 2d and 3d place photography awards Churches in N.Mex. Exhibit, 4th place Colorfest Human Interest Category, Colo. Mem. Garden Writers Assn. Am. (award for handmade booklet on dividing and multiplying potted plants), N.Mex. Organic Growers and Assocs., Comedy Writers Assn., Cassell Network of Writers. Studio: PO Box 21669-WW Albuquerque NM 87154-1669

DAVIDSON, MARIE DIANE, publisher; b. Los Angeles, Mar. 6, 1924; d. Charles Casper and Stella Ruth (Bateman) Winnia; divorced, 1953; children: David William, Ronald Mark. AB, U. Calif., Berkeley, 1943; MA, Calif. State U., Sacramento, 1959. cert. secondary tchr., 1944. Tchr. Campbell (Calif.) High Sch., 1944-45; actress Pasadena (Calif.) Playhouse, 1945, U.S.O. Camp Shows, N.Y.C., 1946-47; tchr. El Camino High Sch., Sacramento, 1954-85; publisher, editor Swan Books, Fair Oaks, Calif., 1979—; actress, cons. Valley Inst. TV Assn, Sacramento, 1971; writer Crown Pubs., N.Y.C., 1969. Author: Feversham, 1969; illustrator, editor: (book series) Shakespeare on Stage, vols. 1-8, 1979, Shakespeare for Young People, vols. 1-8, 1986. Mem. NEA, PEN, Authors Guild, Calif. Writers Club, Calif. Tchrs. Assn., Phi Beta Kappa, Pi Lambda Theta. Democrat. Episcopalian. Office: Swan Books PO Box 2498 Fair Oaks CA 95628-2498

DAVIDSON, MARK, writer, educator; b. N.Y.C., Sept. 25, 1938; m. Elizabeth Browne, May 29, 1989. BA in Polit. Sci., UCLA, 1958; MS in Journalism, Columbia U., 1960. Sci. writer U. So. Calif., L.A., 1980-90; prof. comm. Calif. State U., Dominguez Hills, Carson, 1985—; freelance writer, tenured, 1994; TV documentary juror NEH; faculty adviser Soc. Profl. Journalists, 1993—; lectr. in field. Author: Thought Control, rev., 1995 (Nat. Emmy for Writing Acad. TV Arts and Scis.), Watchwords: A Dictionary of American English Usage, 1995. Sackett scholar Columbia U. Mem. Am. Soc. Journalists and Authors, Nat. Assn. Sci. Writers, Am. Med. Writers Assn., Authors Guild, Writers Guild Am., Calif. Faculty Assn. (v.p. Dominguez Hills chpt. 1992—). Home: 195 Malcolm Dr Pasadena CA 91105-1309 Office: Calif State U 1000 E Victoria St Carson CA 90747-0001

DAVIDSON, ROBERT LEE, III, retired lawyer, author, consultant; b. Nevada, Mo., May 10, 1923; s. Robert Lee and Nancy Helen (Manker) D.; m. Lorena Elizabeth Turner, children: Roberta Anne, Curtis Lee. BSChemE, U. Mo., 1944, MSChemE, 1947; JD, Fordham U., 1978. Bar: N.J. 1980. Editor in chief Petro/Chem. Engring., Dallas, 1964-66; mng. editor Chem. Engring., N.Y.C., 1966-75; editor-in-chief McGraw Hill Book Co., N.Y.C., 1975-80, dir. book pub. ctr., 1980-82; pvt. practice, Princeton, N.J., 1980-93; ret., 1993; editor Attys. Computer Report, 1984-85, cons. on publs., 1982—. Author: Successful Process Plant Practices, 1958. Author: Contracting Your Services, 1990; editor: Petroleum Processing Handbook, 1967, Handbook of Water Soluble Gums and Resins, 1980, Contracting Your Services, 1990, Small Business Incorporation Kit, 1993, Small Business Partnership Kit, 1993, Small Business Bankruptcy Kit, 1993. 1st lt. U.S. Army, 1942-46. Mem. AIChE, Sigma Xi, Tau Beta Pi. Home: 18404 N Laurel Dr Sun City AZ 85373-1755 Office: PO Box 2286 Sun City AZ 85372-2286

DAVIDSON, ROBERT WILLIAM, merchant banker; b. Colfax, Wash., Sept. 18, 1949; s. William Martin and Lena (Soli) D.; m. Molly Evoy, Apr. 16, 1977; children: Ford Patrick, Matthew Harpur, Marshall Andrew. AB, Harvard U., 1971. Exec. dir. Sabre Found., Cambridge, Mass., 1971-72; adminstrv. asst. Congressman Joel Pritchard, Washington, 1973-79; asst. sec. state State of Wash., Olympia, 1979-80; pres. Frayn Fin. Printing, Seattle, 1982-87, Frayn Printing Co., Seattle, 1985-87; exec. dir. Woodland Park Zool. Soc., Seattle, 1987-93, pres., 1993-94; sr. v.p. Alistar Group, Bellevue, Wash., 1994—; mem. adv. com. Wash. State Software Ind. Devel. Bd., 1984-85. Chmn. pub. funding com. Mayor's Zoo Commn., Seattle, 1984-85; pres. Sacred Heart Sch. Bd., 1988-91; dir. Discovery Inst., 1992—, Internat. Snow Leopard Trust, 1994—; mem. sch. bd. Cath. Archdiocese of Seattle, 1995—; mem. Seattle U. Exec. Masters in Not-for-Profit Mgmt. vis. com., 1995—; mem. King County Bond Oversight Com., 1986-93. Mem. N.W. Devel. Officers Assn. (pres. 1994—), Roundtable Club, Downtown Rotary Club, Wash. Athletic Club. Republican. Roman Catholic. Office: Alistar Group 600 108th NE # 1014 Bellevue WA 98004

DAVIDSON, TERENCE MARK, surgery educator, otolaryngologist; b. Chgo., July 7, 1945. MD, UCLA, 1971. Diplomate Am. Bd. Otolaryngology. Intern UCLA, 1971-72; fellow Am. Acad. Facial Plastic and Reconstructive Surgery, Brookline, Mass., 1976; resident in surgery and otolaryngology U. Calif., San Diego, 1972-75; attending staff physician U. Calif. Med. Ctr., San Diego, 1976—, assoc. dean continuing med. edn., 1982—, asst. prof., 1976-82, assoc. prof., 1982-86, prof., 1986—, acting chief div. head and neck surgery, 1984-85; dir. Nasal Disfunction Clinic U. Calif., San Diego, 1985—; staff surgeon VA Med. Ctr., San Diego, 176—, sect. chief head and neck surgery, 1978-90, sect. chief, 1993—; courtesy staff physician Pomerado Hosp., Poway, Calif., 1981—, cons. staff physician, 1990—; clin. researcher in smell, taste, and nasal dysfunction, 1987—. Med. TV producer, 1976—. Grantee NIH, 1991-96. Fellow ACS, Skin Cancer Found. (hon.); mem. AMA, Am. Acad. Facial Plastic and Reconstructive Surgeons (John Dickinson Tchr. of Yr. award 1985), Am. Acad. Otolaryngology-Head and Neck Surgeons, Am. Rhinologic Soc., Calif. Med. Assn. Office: U Calif Med Ctr 200 W Arbor Dr Bldg 8895 San Diego CA 92103-1911

DAVIDSON, THOMAS FERGUSON, chemical engineer; b. N.Y.C., N.Y., Jan. 5, 1930; s. Lorimer Arthur and Elizabeth (Valentine) D.; m. Nancy Lee Selecman, Nov. 10, 1951; children: Thomas Ferguson, Richard Alan, Gwyn Ann. BS in Engring., U. Md., 1951. Sr. project engr. Wright Air Devel. Ctr., Dayton, Ohio, 1951-58; dep. dir. Solid Systems Div., Edwards, Calif., 1959-60; mgr. govt. ops. Thiokol Chem. Corp., Ogden, Utah, 1960-64; dir. aerospace mktg. Thiokol Chem. Corp., Bristol, Pa., 1965-67; dir. tech. mgmt. Thiokol Chem. Corp., Ogden, 1968-82; v.p. tech. Morton Thiokol Inc., Chgo., 1983-88, Thiokol Corp., Ogden, 1989-90; cons. Ogden, 1990—; mem. subcom. lubrications and wear NACA, Washington, 1955-57; chmn. Joint Army, Navy, NASA, Air Force exec. com., 1959-60. Editor: National Rocket Strategic Plan, 1990; contbr. articles to profl. jours. Chmn. bd. Wesley Acad., Ogden, 1990-94; trustee Family Counseling Svc., Ogden, 1991—; bd. dirs. Habitat for Humanit Internat., 1991-93; mem. Rep. Presdl. Task Force, Washington, 1987-92, Am. Security Coun., Washington, 1976—; vice moderator SHARED Ministry Utah, 1993-94; mem. Utah Bd. Edn., 1993-95, Utah Space Ctr. Authority Bd., 1993-95. Lt. USAF, 1951-53. Fellow AIAA (assoc., sect. chmn. 1979-80, chmn. AIA rocket propulsion com. 1987-90, mem. AIA aerospace tech. coun. 1987-90, Wyld Propulsion award 1991); mem. Am. Newcomen Soc., Smithsonian Instn., Exch. Club, Ogden Golf and Country Club. Republican. Methodist. Home: 4755 Banbury Ln Ogden UT 84403-4484

DAVIES, GREGORY LANE, lawyer; b. Seattle, Aug. 21, 1951; s. Cynric C. Davies and Marilyn R. (Baker) Amdal; m. Julia M. Dent, Apr., 1973 (div. 1975); m. Barbara A. Hess, Sept. 2, 1978; children: Andrea M., Susan E. AA, Edmonds Community Coll., 1975; BA, Cen. Wash. State U., 1977; JD, U. Puget Sound, 1980. Bar: Wash. 1980, U.S. Dist. Ct. (we. dist.) Wash. 1980, U.S. Tax Ct. 1981, U.S. Ct. Appeals (9th cir.) 1988, U.S. Supreme Ct. 1988. Legal intern Thurston County, Olympia, Wash., 1979-80; assoc. Rudolf Mueller, Everett, Wash., 1980-81; pvt. practice Everett, 1981-84; ptnr. Cooper, Lyderson, Cooper & Davies, Everett, 1984-87, Lyderson & Davies, Everett, 1987-91; pvt. practice law Everett, Wash., 1991—; arbitrator, ct. commr., arbitrator Snohomish County Superior Ct., Everett, 1987—. Tchr. community schs., Everett, 1981—; bd. dirs. Mental Health Snohomish County, 1987—; mem. Everett Citizen's Adv. Bd., 1988; treas. Arden Bedle for judge, Everett, 1988. With U.S. Army, 1971-73. Dean's scholar Cen. Wash. State U., 1977. Mem. Wash. State Bar Assn., Snohomish County Bar Assn. (bd. trustees), Phi Theta Kappa. Democrat. Office: 3721 Colby Ave Everett WA 98201-4910

DAVIES, HARRIETT MARIE (LOLLY DAVIES), home economist, educator; b. Chgo., July 2, 1942; d. Howard Jack and Mamie Marie (Harriett) Cox; m. Ronald Lee Davies, Mar. 22, 1975. BS in Home Econs., So. Ill. U., 1965, MS in Edn., 1973. Tchg. cert. in home econs., bus., mktg., Coop. Office Edn., Ariz. Home econs. tchr. Hanover (Ill.) H.S., 1965; home econs., health tchr., home econ. dept. head Scholes Jr. H.S., Milw., 1965-67; vocat. home econs., consumer edn. tchr. Roxana (Ill.) H.S., 1967-78; bus. instr. Lamson Bus. Coll., Tucson, Ariz., 1981-83; legal secretarial instr. Tucson Coll. Bus., 1983-84; instr. Project Portable Practical Edn. Preparation, Casa Grande, Ariz., 1984-85; tchr. bus., home econ. Casa Grande Union High Sch., 1985—; conv. coord. Ill. Consumer Edn. Assn., Springfield, Ill., 1973-75, v.p., 1975; spl. consumer cons. Ill. Office Edn., Springfield, 1975-78; mem. family fin. regional coun. Ind. State U., Terre Haute, Ind., 1973-75; coord. Sch.-Within-a-Sch., 1989-90. Food coord. C. of C. Golf Tourney, Casa Grande, 1993. Mem. NEA (life), Ariz. Edn. Assn., Ariz. Vocat. Assn., Casa Grande Edn. Assn. Avocations: reading, hunting, golf, travel. Home: 339 E Orange Dr Casa Grande AZ 85222-4043 Office: Casa Grande Union HS 420 E Florence Blvd Casa Grande AZ 85222-4140

DAVIES, HUGH MARLAIS, museum director; b. Grahamstown, South Africa, Feb. 12, 1948; came to U.S., 1956; s. Horton Marlais and Brenda M. (Deakin) D.; children: Alexandra, Dorian; m. Lynda Forsha; 1 stepdaughter, Mackenzie Forsha Fuller. AB summa cum laude, Princeton U., 1970, M.F.A., 1972, PhD, 1976. Dir., Univ. Gallery, U. Mass., Amherst, 1975-83, Mus. of Contemporary Art, San Diego (formerly La Jolla Mus. Contemporary Art,) Calif., 1983—; vis. prof. fine arts Amherst Coll., 1980-83; mem. mus. com. Rose Art Mus., Brandeis U., 1981-83; mem. adv. coun. dept. art and archeology Princeton U., 1989, panel mem. fed. adv. com. internat. exhbns., 1990-94; mem. Art in Public Places Profl. Adv. Com., Met. Dade County, 1980—; panel mem. Mass. Bay Transit Authority, Artist Selection Panel, 1990. Author: Francis Bacon: The Early and Middle Years: 1928-58; co-author: Sacred Art in a Secular Century: 20th Century Religious Art, 1978, Francis Bacon (Abbeville), 1986. Nat. Endowment Arts fellow, 1982. Mem. Am. Assn. Mus., Coll. Art Assn., Assn. Art Mus. Dirs. (trustee), Am. Fedn. Arts. Office: Mus Contemporary Art San Diego 700 Prospect St La Jolla CA 92037-4228

DAVIES, JACK LLOYD, vintner, consultant; b. Cin., June 19, 1923; s. John Lloyd and Celia (Davis) D.; m. Jamie Peterman; children: Bill, John, Hugh. Student, Northwestern U., 1942, Stanford U., 1946-68; MBA, Harvard U., 1950. Prodn. mgr. Avalon Desk Mfg., L.A., 1950-52; planning analyst Kaiser Aluminum, Oakland, Calif., 1952-55; assoc. McKinsey & Co., San Francisco, 1955-60; v.p. mktg. Fibreboard Corp., San Francisco, 1960-63; v.p. devel. Ducommun Inc., L.A., 1963-65; pres. Schramsberg Vineyards, Calistoga, Calif., 1965—, Schramsberg Assocs. Internat., Calistoga, 1989—, Caves Transmontanas LDA, Alijo, Portugal, 1989—. Sgt. USAF, 1942-46, ETO. Mem. Bohemian Club, Knights of St. John. Office: Schramsberg Vineyards Calistoga CA 94515

DAVIES, JOHN G., federal judge; b. 1929. BA, U. Mich., 1953; postgrad., U. Sydney, 1956-57; LLB, UCLA, 1959. Assoc. Hagenbaugh, Murphy & Davies, L.A., 1961-72, Rosenfeld, Meyer & Susman, Beverly Hills, Calif., 1972-86; dist. judge U.S. Dist. Ct., L.A., 1986—; L.A. Ct. Arbitrator; Inns of Ct. Winner Gold medal in swimming 1952 Olympic Games, Helsinki, Finland. Mem. ABA, Internat. Acad. Trial Lawyers,Am. COll. Trial Lawyers, Am. Bd. Trial Advocates. Office: US Dist Ct US Courthouse Rm 1006 Los Angeles CA 90012*

DAVIES, JOHN TUDOR, physicist; b. Pontypridd, Wales, Eng., May 9, 1937; s. Herbert John and Catherine Mary Davies; m. Kay Dierst, Aug. 4, 1964; children: Gwen, Ceri, Rhodri. BA, Oxford (Eng.) U., 1959, MA, 1963, DPhil, 1963. Rsch. assoc. U. Pitts., 1962-65; lectr. U. Wales, Swansea, 1965-78; tech. devel. mgr. Gasonics/IPC, San Jose, Calif., 1978—. Mem. Am. Vacuum Soc., Semicondr. Equipment and Materials Inst. Methodist.

DAVIES, MERTON EDWARD, planetary scientist; b. St. Paul, Sept. 13, 1917; s. Albert Daniel and Lucile (McCabe) D.; AB, Stanford, 1938, postgrad., 1938-39; m. Margaret Louise Darling, Feb. 10, 1946; children: Deidra Louise Stauff, Albert Karl, Merton Randel. Instr. math. U. Nev., 1939-40; group leader Math. Lofting, Douglas Aircraft Co., El Segundo, Calif., 1940-48; sr. staff Rand Corp., Santa Monica, Calif., 1948-59, 62—, liaison USAF, Washington, 1959-62. U.S. observer inspected stas. under terms Antarctic Treaty, 1967; TV co-investigator Mariner Mars, 1969, 71, Mariner Venus/Mercury 1973 Mission, Voyager Mission, Galileo Mission, Magellan Mission, Mars Observer Mission, Clementine Mission. Fellow AIAA (assoc.); mem. AAAS, Am. Soc. Photogrammetry. Author: (with Bruce Murray) The View from Space, 1971; (with others) Atlas of Mercury, 1978. Patentee in field. Home: 1414 San Remo Dr Pacific Palisades CA 90272-2737 Office: RAND 1700 Main St Santa Monica CA 90401-3208

DAVIES, PAUL LEWIS, JR., retired lawyer; b. San Jose, Calif., July 21, 1930; s. Paul Lewis and Faith (Crummey) D.; m. Barbara Bechtel, Dec. 22, 1955; children: Laura (Mrs. Segundo Mateo), Paul Lewis III. AB, Stanford U., 1952; JD, Harvard U., 1957. Bar: Calif. 1957. Assoc. Pillsbury, Madison & Sutro, San Francisco, 1957-63, ptnr., 1963-89; gen. counsel Chevron Corp., 1984-89; bd. dirs. FMC Corp., FMC Gold Co. Hon. trustee Calif. Acad. Scis., trustee, 1970-83, chmn., 1973-80; pres. Herbert Hoover Found.; bd. overseers Hoover Instn., chmn., 1976-82, 91-93; hon. regent U. of Pacific, regent, 1959-90. Lt. U.S. Army, 1952-54. Mem. Bohemian Club, Pacific-Union Club, Villa Taverna, World Trade Club (San Francisco), Claremont Country Club, Lakeview (Oakland, Calif.), Cypress Point (Pebble Beach, Calif.), Sainte Claire (San Jose, Calif.), Collectors, Explorers, Links (N.Y.C.), Met. Club, 1925 F St. (Washington), Chgo. Club, Phi Beta Kappa, Pi Sigma Alpha. Republican. Office: 50 Fremont St Ste 3520 San Francisco CA 94105-2239

DAVIES, ROBERT ABEL, III, consumer products company executive; b. Englewood, N.J., Sept. 10, 1935; s. Robert Abel Jr. and Lillian Louise (Vila) D.; m. Marilyn Jean Doering, June 16, 1957; children: Bruce Gregory, Mark Richard, Eric Doering, Nancy Louise. A.B., Colgate U., 1957; M.B.A., Columbia U., 1963. Salesman Proctor & Gamble Co., Cin., 1960-61; product mgr. Colgate Palmolive Co., N.Y.C., 1963-66; group product mgr. Boyle-Midway div. Am. Home Products, N.Y.C., 1966-69; v.p. mktg. Church & Dwight Co. Inc., Princeton, N.J., 1969-76, v.p., gen. mgr., 1976-81, pres., chief oper. officer, 1981-84, also dir., 1981-84; pres., chief exec. officer Calif. Home Brands Inc., Terminal Island, Calif., 1985-89; prin. Gold Coast Calamari Inc., Oxnard, Calif., 1990-94; pres. Arm & Hammer divsn. Church & Dwight Co., Inc., Princeton, N.J., 1995—. Served to lt. (j.g.) USNR, 1957-60. Office: 469 N Harrison St Princeton NJ 08543-5299

DAVIES, ROBERT OAKLEY, university program director; b. Flagstaff, Ariz., Feb. 8, 1967; s. Richard Oakley and Sharon Kay (Dye) D.; m. Sylvia Maria Walker, Aug. 11, 1990. BS in Mgmt., U. Nev., 1989; MBA, U. Oreg., 1991. Mktg. intern Big Sky Mktg., Twin Falls, Idaho, summer 1991; bus. analyst Dun & Bradstreet, Sacramento, Calif., 1991-92; dir. ann. fund U. Nev., Reno, 1992—. Mem. Coun. for Advancement and Support of Edn., Nat. Soc. Fund Raising Execs., Kiwanis. Home: 1495 Marne Dr Reno NV 89503-2033

DAVIES, WILLIAM RALPH, service executive; b. Santa Barbara, Calif., Aug. 17, 1955; s. Ralph Emmett and Georgann Marie (Cordingly) D.; m. Karen L. Blake, May 12, 1984. AA in Real Estate, Am. River Coll., 1978; BS in Fin., Ins. and Real Estate, Calif. State U., Sacramento, 1980; postgrad. in Internat. Bus., Golden Gate U., 1982-84. Real estate assoc. Kiernan Realtors, Sacramento, 1975-77; co-owner real estate firm Sacramento, 1977, pvt. practice real estate cons., property mgr., 1978-80; broker assoc. MBA Bus. Brokers, Sacramento, 1980-85, pres., 1985—; pres. WRD Cons. Group, Sacramento, 1984—; bd. dirs. WRD, Inc., Sacramento. Mem. Assn. Bus. Brokers and Intermediaries (bd. dirs.), Assisted Living Facilities Assn. Am., Calif. Assisted Living Facilities Assn. (bd. dirs.), Calif. Assn. Health Facilities, River City C. of C. Republican. Office: 1555 River Park Dr Ste 206 Sacramento CA 95815-4604

DAVIS, ALLEN, professional football team executive; b. Brockton, Mass., July 4, 1929; s. Louis and Rose (Kirschenbaum) D.; m. Carol Segall, July 11, 1954; 1 son, Mark. Student, Wittenberg Coll., 1947; A.B., Syracuse U., 1950. Asst. football coach Adelphi Coll., 1950-51; head football coach Ft. Belvoir, Va., 1952-53; player-personnel scout Baltimore Colts, 1954; line coach The Citadel, 1955-56, U. So. Calif., 1957-59; asst. coach San Diego Chargers, 1960-62; gen. mgr., head coach Oakland Raiders (now Los Angeles Raiders), 1963-66, owner, mng. gen. ptnr., 1966—, now pres., gen. ptnr.; former mem. mgmt. council and competition com. Nat. Football League. Served with AUS, 1952-53. Named Profl. Coach of Year A.P., Profl. Coach of Year U.P.I., Profl. Coach of Year Sporting News, Profl. Coach of Year Pro-Football Illustrated, 1963; Young Man of Yr. Oakland, 1963; only individual in history to be an asst. coach, head coach, gen. mgr., league commr. and owner. Mem. Am. Football Coaches Assn. Office: LA Raiders 332 Center St El Segundo CA 90245-4098*

DAVIS, ANTHONY J., journalist; b. L.A., Nov. 19, 1951; s. Fred W. and Meredith M. (Trahant) D.; m. Miriam D. Weber, Mar. 28, 1987. BS in Journalism, Northwestern U., 1973, MS in Journalism, 1974. Reporter Tucson Citizen, 1976-85, Valley Daily News, Kent, Wash., 1985-87, Albuquerque Tribune, 1987—. Contbr. numerous articles to High Country News, 1985—, Tucson Weekly, 1992—. Office: Albuquerque Tribune PO Drawer T Albuquerque NM 87103

DAVIS, ARTHUR DAVID, psychology educator, musician; m. Gladys Lesley Joyce, Dec. 29, 1965; children: Kimaili, Mureithi, Taisha. Student, Manhattan Sch. Music, 1953-56, Juilliard Sch. Music, 1953-56; BA suma cum laude, CUNY, 1973; MA, City Coll., N.Y.C., 1976, NYU, 1976; PhD with distinction, NYU, 1982. Lic. sch. psychologist. Musician various worldwide tours, 1962—, NBC-TV Staff Orch., N.Y.C., 1962-63, Westinghouse TV Staff Orch., N.Y.C., 1964-68, CBS-TV Staff Orch., N.Y.C., 1969-71; prof. Manhattan Community Coll., N.Y.C., 1971-86, U. Bridgeport, Conn., 1978-82; psychologist Lincoln Med. and Mental Health Ctr., Bronx, 1982-85; sch. psychologist, cons. Lakeside Union Free Sch. Dist., Spring Valley, N.Y., 1985-86; psychologist, tchr. N.Y. Med. Coll., Valhalla, 1982-87; prof. Orange Coast Coll., Costa Mesa, Calif., 1987—, Calif. State U., Fullerton, 1988-90, U. Calif.-Irvine, 1993-94; psychologist Cross Cultural Ctr., San Diego, 1986-91; cons. Head Start, Bklyn., 1981-82, Orange County Minority AIDS, Santa Ana, Calif., 1987-88, Orange County Fair Housing, Costa Mesa, 1988, Sickle Cell Anemia Assn., Santa Ana, Calif., 1987-88, Human Rels. Orange County City, Costa Mesa, 1988-89, William Grant Still Mus., L.A., 1988—; musician various symphonies Radio City Music Hall Orch. Nat. Symphony, Symphony of the Air, N.Y. Philharmonic, Met. Opera Orch., John Coltrane, others, 1960—. Author: The Arthur Davis System for Double Bass, 1976, 93; record composer Interplay, 1980, ARKIMU, 1985, Soulnote, 1987, A Time Remembered, 1995. Composer, condr., mem. coun. Diaglogue, Costa Mesa, 1988; mgr. Little League of Cortlandt, N.Y., 1979-82; pack master Cub Scouts Am., Cortlandt and Croton, N.Y., 1979-80, dist. chmn., 1980-81; bd. dirs. Local 47 Musicians' Union, Hollywood, Calif., 1993—, Orange County Urban League, Inc., 1992-95; chmn. Better Advantages for Students and Soc., Corona del Mar, Calif., 1993; adv. bd. dirs. John W. Cultrane Cultural Soc., Inc. NIMH grantee, 1976-77; named World's Foremost Double Bassist IBA, 1969—; recipient Lion award Black MBA Assn., 1985, Chancellor's Disting. Lectr.'s award U. Calif., Irvine, 1991-92, Exemplary Standards in Music Edn. award Orange County Urban League, 1993; Ann. Dr. Art Davis Scholarships established in his honor Dr. Art Davis Fan Club. Mem. APA, ASCAP, Am. Soc. Music Arrangers & Composers, Chamber Music Am., N.Y. Acad. Scis., Astron. Soc. of the Pacific (charter), Orange County Psychol. Assn., Assn. of Black Psychologists, Planetary Soc. (charter), Am. Hort. Soc., Nat Trust for Hist. Preservation Soc., Rec. Musicians Assn., Stanford U. Alumni Assn., NYU Alumni Assn., CCNY Alumni Assn., Sierra Club. Office: ARKIMU 3535 E Coast Hwy Ste 50 Corona Del Mar CA 92625-2404

DAVIS, BARBARA JOYCE WIENER, accountant, investment manager, consultant; b. Berkeley, Calif., Aug. 28, 1947; d. Milton and Kathryn Gertrude (Weiss) Wiener; 1 child, Scott Evan. BA in Psychology, U. Calif., Davis, 1970; MA in Psychology, San Jose State U., 1986; cert. lifetime teaching credential, U. Calif., Riverside, 1971. Investment mgr. Cupertino, Calif., 1968—; tchr. elem. edn. Santa Clara (Calif.) Unified Sch. Dist., 1971-83; acct. Owl Land Co., Inc., San Leandro, Calif., 1981—, pres.; rsch. and stats. cons. Cupertino, 1984—; tchr. Chabot Coll., Hayward, Calif., 1990-91; tutor stats. San Jose (Calif.) U., 1984-86. Mem. AAUW, APA, Women's Am. Overseas Rehab. Tng., Calif. Psychol. Assn., Santa Clara Psychol. Assn., Mensa, Pacific Grad. Sch. Psychology Round Table. Office: 7608 Erin Way Cupertino CA 95014-4343

DAVIS, BETTY JEAN BOURBONIA, real estate investment executive; b. Ft. Bayard, N.Mex., Mar. 12, 1931; d. John Alexander and Ora M. (Caudill) Bourbonia; BS in Elem. Edn., U. N.Mex., 1954; children: Janice Cox Anderson, Elizabeth Ora Cox. Gen. ptnr. BJD Realty Co., Albuquerque, 1977—. Bd. dirs. Albuquerque Opera Guild, 1977-79, 81-83, 85-86, 86-87, membership co-chmn., 1977-79; mem. Friends of Art, 1978-85, Friends of Little Theatre, 1973-85, Mus. N.Mex. Found.; mem. grand exec. com. N.Mex. Internat. Order of Rainbow for Girls; mem. Hodgin Hall Preservation com. U. N.Mex. Recipient Matrix award for journalism Jr. League. Mem. Albuquerque Mus. Assn., N.M. Hist. Soc., N.Mex. Symphony Guild, Jr. League Albuquerque, Alumni Assn. U. N.Mex. (dir. 1973-76), Mus. N.Mex. Found., Alpha Chi Omega (Beta Gamma Beta chpt., adv., bldg. corp. 1962-77), Tanoan Country Club, Order Eastern Star, Order Rainbow for Girls (past grand worthy adv. N.Mex., past mother adv. Friendship Assembly 50, state exec. com. N.Mex. Order 1989, chair pub. rels. com., co-chair gen. arrangements com. 1990-93). Republican. Methodist. Home: 9505 Augusta Ave NE Albuquerque NM 87111-5820

DAVIS, BETTYE JEAN, academic administrator, state official; b. Homer, La., May 17, 1938; d. Dan and Rosylind (Daniel) Ivory; m. Troy J. Davis, Jan. 21, 1959; children: Anthony Benard, Sonja Davis Wade. Cert. nursing, St. Anthony's, 1961; BSW, Grambling State U., 1971; postgrad., U. Alaska, 1972. Psychiat. nurse Alaska Psychiat. Inst., 1967-70; asst. dir. San Bernardino (Calif.) YWCA, 1971-72; child care specialist DFYS Anchorage, 1975-80, soc. worker, 1980-82, foster care coordinator, 1982-87; dir. Alaska Black Leadership Edn. Program, 1979-82; exec. dir. Anchorage Sch. Bd., 1982-89; mem. Alaska Legislature, 1990—; chair Children's Caucus Alaska Legis., 1992—. Pres. Anchorage Sch. Bd., 1986-87; bd. dirs. Blacks in Govt., 1980-82, March of Dimes, 1983-85, Anchorage chpt. YWCA, 1989-90, Winning with Stronger Edn. Com., 1991, Alaska 2000, Anchorage Ctr. for Families, 1992—, active Anchorage chpt. of NAACP, bd. dirs. 1978-82. Toll fellow Henry Toll Fellowship Program, 1992; named Woman of Yr., Alaska Colored Women's Club, 1981, Child Care Worker of Yr., Alaska Foster Parent Assn., 1983, Social Worker of Yr., Nat. Foster Parents Assn., 1983, Outstanding Bd. Mem, Assn. Alaska Sch. Bds., 1990,; recipient Outstanding Achievement in Edn. award Alaska Colored Women's Club, 1985, Outstanding Women in Edn. award Zeta Phi Beta, 1985, Boardsmanship award Assn. Alaska Sch. Bds., 1989, Woman of Achievement award YWCA, 1991, Outstanding Leadership award Calif. Assembly, 1992. Mem. LWV, Nat. Sch. Bd. Assn., Nat. Caucus of Black Sch. Bd. Mems. (bd. dirs. 1986-87), Alaska Black Caucus (chair 1984—), Alaska Women's Polit. Caucus, Alaska Black Leadership Conf. (pres. 1976-80), Alaska Women Lobby (treas.), Nat. Caucus of Black State Legis. (chair region 12, 1994—), Women Legislators Lobby, Women's Action for New Directions, North to Future Bus. and Prof. Women (pres. 1978-79, 83), Delta Sigma Theta (Alaska chpt. pres. 1978-80). Democrat. Baptist. Club: North to Future Bus. and Profl. Women (past pres.). Home: 2240 Foxhall Dr Anchorage AK 99504-3350

DAVIS, BRUCE WARREN, architect; b. Chgo., Oct. 27, 1947; s. Howard Warren and Elizabeth Florence (Barber) D. BArch., U. Ill., 1970. Registered architect, N.Mex. Jr. architect Skidmore, Owings & Merrill, Chgo.,

1969-73; pvt. practice, Santa Fe, Albuquerque, 1973—. Home and Office: 526 Wellesley Dr SE Albuquerque NM 87106-2318

DAVIS, CHARLES ARTHUR, psychiatrist; b. Greensboro, N.C., Nov. 14, 1921; s. Charles Arthur and Ann Ethel D. BS, Columbia Union Coll., Takoma Park, Md., 1950; MD, Loma Linda U., 1953. Diplomate Am. Bd. Psychiatry and Neurology, Am. Bd. Forensic Psychiatry. Chief addiction svc. USPHS Hosp., Ft. Worth, Tex., 1956-58; med. dir. Kings View Hosp., Reedley, Calif., 1958-73; clin. dir. Kings View Corp., Fresno, Calif., 1970-75; exec. dir. Kings County Mental Health, Hanford, Calif., 1975-91; lectr. U. Calif., San Francisco, 1980—; program adminstr. Calif. State Prison, Corcoran, 1992—; ct.'s examiner Superior Cts. of Fresno, Madera, Tulare & King Counties, 1960—; vis. prof. U. Guadalajara, Mexico, 1979-81. Pres. Fresno County Mental Health Adv. Bd., 1986-88. Lt. comdr. USPHS, 1955-58. Fellow Am. Psychiat. Assn. (life, Gold award 1970); mem. AMA, Cen. Calif., Psychiat. Soc. (pres. 1970), Calif. Med. Assn. (del. 1985-86), Kings County Med. Soc. (governing bd. 1981-87, pres. 1985), Calif. Conf. Local Mental Health Dirs., Am. Acad., Psychiatry and Law. Home and Office: 4400 Avenue 428 Reedley CA 93654-9150

DAVIS, CHARLES LEE, fire marshal; b. Anchorage, July 24, 1940; s. Edward V. and De Ette C. (Scholberg) D.; m. Mary Margaret Walker, Aug. 24, 1963; 1 child, Edward Charles. LLB, U. Idaho, 1966; grad. 28th Recruit Acad., Alaska Dept. Pub. Safety, 1977. Bar: Alaska; cert. firefighter, Alaska, fire svc. instr., Alaska, uniform fire code, plans examiner, mech. inspector, Nat. Fire Acad., safety and security dir., safety mgr., safety specialist, level II fire extinguisher permit, Alaska. Law clk., atty. Hughes, Thorsness, Lowe, Gantz & Clark, Anchorage, 1966-68; adjustor, appraiser Gen. Adjustment Bur., Alaska, 1968-73; adjuster, damage appraiser Alaska Adjusting Co., Fairbanks, 1974-75; dep. fire marshal State of Alaska, Fairbanks, 1975—. Contbr. posters, cards and photographs to numerous publs. Mem., past vestry mem., jr. warden St. Matthew's Episcopal Ch., Fairbanks, chmn. endowment bd., 1991—. Recipient prize Joint Pubs. of Am. Jurisprudence-Bancroft Whitney Co., 1966; scholar Rocky Mountain Mineral Law Inst., 1966. Mem. NRA, Internat. Conf. Bldg. Ofcls. (founder no. chpt., dir., v.p., pres.), Alaska Bar Assn., Pioneers of Alaska (life, igloo # 4), Moose (life lodge 1392), World Safety Orgn. Episcopalian. Home: 1359 Great View Ln Fairbanks AK 99712-2136 Office: Alaska Dept Pub Safety Divsn Fire Prevention 1979 Peger Rd Fairbanks AK 99709-5257

DAVIS, CLYDE WAYNE, engineering technician; b. Dallas, Nov. 21, 1947; s. Benjamin Franklin and Edna Geraldine (Lee) D.; m. Faye Dean Sandefer, Sept. 11, 1964; children: Clyde Alton, Kelvin Wayne, Carla Faye, Aaron Dell. Grad., Locksmithing Inst., N.J., 1972, Hotel Motel Mgmt. Sch., Dallas, 1973; AS, Eastern N.Mex. U., Portales, 1979. Farm worker Portales, 1957-64; truck driver Raymond Lightfoot, Portales, 1963-65; foreman Ellison Constrn., Houston, 1964-65; sta. attendant Phillips 66, Portales, 1965-66; broommaker P&M Broom Shop, Portales, 1966-69; night mgr. Stemmens Inn, Dallas, 1972-74; engring. R & D technician Sperry Flight Sys., Phoenix, 1979-85; sr. engring. R & D technician Burrows, Phoenix, 1985-87; sr. engring. devel. technician Honeywell Inc., Glendale, Ariz., 1987—; cons. Sperry Flight Sys., Phoenix, 1979-85, Honeywell, Inc., Phoenix, 1987-94. Scoutmaster Boy Scouts Am., Portales, N.Mex., 1973-79; dep. Sheriff's Office, Wittmann, Ariz., 1980-90. Mem. NRA. Republican.

DAVIS, COLEEN COCKERILL, home economist, educator, small business owner; b. Pampa, Tex., Sept. 20, 1930; d. Charles Clifford and Myrtle Edith (Harris) Cockerill; m. Richard Harding Davis, June 22, 1952 (div. Dec. 1984); children: David Christopher, Denis Benjamin (dec. 1979). BS, U. Okla., 1951; MS, UCLA, 1952; postgrad. U. So. Calif., Whittier Coll., UCLA. Cert. tchr., Calif. Chmn. dept. home econs., tchr. Whittier Union High Sch. Dist., Calif., 1952-85; substitute tchr., 1985—; home tchr., 1985—, cons. 1986—; owner CoHost Am.'s Bed & Breakfast, Whittier, 1983—, also founder, pres., exec. dir. Contbr. articles to newspapers. Founder Children of Murdered Parents, Whittier, 1984, Whistle Ltd., Whittier, 1984, Coalition of Orgns. and People, Whittier, 1984, chpt. leader Parents of Murdered Children, Whittier, 1984, Southeast/Long Beach: mem. citizens' adv. bd. Fred C. Nelles Sch. Mem. NAFE, NEA, Calif. Tchrs. Assn., Internat. Tour Mgmt. Inst., Whittier C. of C. (ambassador). Republican. Episcopalian. Avocation: volunteer worker. Office: CoHost Am's Bed & Breakfast PO Box 9302 Whittier CA 90608-9302

DAVIS, DANIEL EDWARD, museum director; b. Creston, Iowa, July 3, 1922; s. Fred M. and Myrtle A. D.; m. Mary Joan Kelly, July 15, 1947; children: Daniel B., Nancy, Terry, Barbara, Michelle. Student, U. Iowa, Nat. U. Mex., U. N.Mex., U. Mont. With Nat. Park Service, 1948-77; asso. regional dir. Nat. Park Service, Omaha, 1973-77; dir. Ariz.-Sonora Desert Mus., Tucson, 1977-90; adv. bd. Sch. Renewable Natural Resources, U. Ariz., 1980-81; adv. Arab Center Studies Arid Zones, Kouf Nat. Park, Libya.; cons. Egyptian Wildlife Service, Nat. Parks, Netherlands West Indies, Saudi Arabia Nat. Park Service, Thumamah Nat. Park, Kuwait Inst. Sci. Research; adj. prof. Sch. Renewable Natural Resources, U. Ariz., 1986—. Author: Hikers Guide to Grand Canyon, 1956, Boatman's Guide to the Colorado River, 1957, The Little Colorado, 1958, Backcountry Travel, Sequoia National Park, 1961. Bd. dirs. Tucson Coun. for Internat. Visitors (U.S.I.A.), S.W. Mission Rsch. Ctr. With AUS, 1943-46. Recipient Meritorious Service award Dept. Interior, 1956, Environ. Leadership medal UN, 1982. Mem. Coun. on Fgn. Rels., Nature Conservancy, Sierra Club. Office: 5732 E Finisterra Dr Tucson AZ 85715

DAVIS, DARRELL L., automotive executive; b. Sharon, Pa., Aug. 8, 1939; s. Paul Darrell and Dorothy Jane (Snyder) D.; m. Jacqueline Donna Pain, July 18, 1986; children: Paul Darrell II, Robert Tod. BS, Youngstown State U., 1963; cert. Stanford Exec. Program, Stanford U., 1987; cert. Global Leadership Program, U. Mich., 1993. Svc. rep., warranty mgr., dist. mgr., asst. zone mgr. Chrysler Motors Corp., Orlando, Fla., 1966-77; zone mgr. Chrysler Motors Corp., Omaha, 1977-78, Troy, Mich., 1978-79; nat. distbn. mgr., regional mgr., gen. mgr. import export ops., gen. sales mgr. Chrysler Motors Corp., Detroit, 1979-88; pres., chief exec. officer Alfa Romeo Distbrs. N. Am., Orlando, 1988-91; gen. sales mgr. Chrysler Corp., Orange, Calif., 1991-93; v.p. Chrysler Internat. Corp., Detroit, 1993-95; gen. mgr. Europe Chrysler Corp., Detroit, 1993-95; pres., COO Chrysler Fin. Corp., Detroit, 1995—. Lt. U.S. Army, 1963-65. Republican.

DAVIS, DENNIS ALBERT, college president; b. Westport, Oreg., Jan. 4, 1934; s. George J. and Gertrude C. (Hibbard) D.; m. Nancy Ree Friend, July 20, 1956; 1 child, Jeffrey Dennis. BA, N.W. Coll., Kirkland, Wash., 1956. Pastor Assembly of God, Rainier, Oreg., 1956-57; evangelist Assemblies of God, over 200 crusades, 1957-61; pastor First Assembly of God, Pacific Grove, Calif., 1961-67, The People's Ch., Salem, Oreg., 1967-87; state supt. Oreg. Dist. Assemblies of God, Salem, 1987-90; pres. N.W. Coll., 1990—. Bd. dirs. ARC Polk, Marion Counties, 1980-86; mem. Salem Meml. Hosp. Instl. Review Com., Salem, 1984-87. Mem. Salem Ministerial Assn., Rotary (pres. East Salem Club 1976-77, recipient Paul Harris award 1980), Delta Epsilon Chi. Republican. Office: NW Coll 5520 108th Ave NE Kirkland WA 98033-7523

DAVIS, DONALD ALAN, author, news correspondent, lecturer; b. Savannah, Ga., Oct. 5, 1939; s. Oden Harry and Irma Artice (Gay) D.; m. Robin Murphy, Mar. 17, 1983; children by previous marriage—Russell Glenn, Randall Scott. B.A. in Journalism, U. Ga., 1962. Reporter Athens (Ga.) Banner-Herald, 1961-62, Savannah Morning News, 1962; with UPI, 1963-65; reporter, editor St. Petersburg (Fla.) Times, 1965-66; with UPI, 1967-83, Vietnam corr., 1971-73, New Eng. editor, 1977-80, White House corr., 1981-83; polit. reporter, columnist San Diego Union, 1983-91; pub. Pacific Rim Report newsletter, 1985-88; instr. journalism Boston U., 1979; lectr. U.S. Naval War Coll., 1983, Queen Elizabeth 2, 1991, Vistafjord, 1992; bd. dirs. Fgn. Corr. Club, Hong Kong, 1974. Author: The Milwaukee Murders, 1991, The Nanny Murder Trial, 1992, Bad Blood, 1994, Death of an Angel, 1994, Fallen Hero, 1994, Appointment with the Squire, 1995. Fellow Keizai Koho Ctr., Tokyo, 1985. Presbyterian. Office: 1630 30th St # 141 Boulder CO 80301-1014

DAVIS, ERIC KEITH, former professional baseball player; b. L.A., May 29, 1962; m. Erica D. Baseball player Cin. Reds, 1980-91, L.A. Dodgers, 1991-93, Detroit Tigers, 1993-94. Mem. Nat. League All-Star Team, 1987, 89, Nat. League Silver Slugger team, 1987,89, NL Gold Glove 1987-89; named to Sporting News Nat. League. All-Star team, 1987, 89. Office: Detroit Tigers Tiger Stadium Detroit MI 48216*

DAVIS, FRANK GRODAVENT FOY, computer consultant; b. St. Joseph, Mich., Mar. 27, 1943; s. Frank Foy and Marjorie (Fickinger) D.; m. Julianne King, Jan. 23, 1971; 1 child, Elinor Jane Foy. BS in Psychology, U. Wyo., 1967, BA in Anthropology, 1972, MA in Anthropology, 1974, MS in Computer Sci., 1989. Cert. EMT. Rsch. asst., statis. cons. dept. psychology U. Wyo., Laramie, 1966-74, rsch. aide dept. atmosphere sci., 1974-77; computer specialist U.S. Dept. Energy, Laramie, 1977-83; sr. programmer analyst Western Rsch. Inst., Laramie, 1983-85; cons. computer sci. Laramie, 1990—. Contbr. articles to profl. jours. Instr. ARC, Laramie, 1964—, divsn. rep., chpt. chmn., 1979-82; nat. patroller Nat. Ski Patrol, Laramie, 1968—, patrol dir. 1979-83, sect. chief, 1983-91, ea. region winter emergency care adv. 1994-95, Rocky Mtn. divsn. outdoor emergency care adminstr. 1995—; winter emergency care instr. trainer, 1989—, Rocky Mtn. Divsn. ea. region winter emergency care adminstr., 1994—. Named Nat. Runner-up Outstanding Instr., Nat. Ski Patrol, 1993, Rocky Mountain Divsn. Outstanding Instr., Nat. Ski Patrol, 1993. Mem. IEEE Computer Soc., Assn. for Computing Machinery, Am. Assn. Avalanche Profls. Home and Office: Box 3192 University Sta Laramie WY 82071

DAVIS, GENE, public relations professional, state legislator; b. Salt Lake City, July 2, 1945; s. John Albert and Glenna Rachel (Cameron) D.; m. Penny Lou Hansen, Mar. 9, 1971; children: James, Pamela. Cert. electronic engring., Radio Operational Engring., Burbank, Calif., 1963; LLB, LaSalle Ext. U., Chgo., 1974. Announcer KNAK Radio, Salt Lake City, 1965-75; prodn. continuity dir. KALL Radio AM/FM, Salt Lake City, 1976-86; owner G. Davis Advt., Pub. Rels., Salt Lake City, 1986-91; pub. rels. profl. Valley Mental Health, Salt Lake City, 1990—; treas. Comm. Fed. Credit Union, Salt Lake City, 1981-86. Chmn. Sugar House Cmty. Coun., Salt Lake City, 1984-85; mem. Sugar House Park Authority, 1994—; vice chair East County Recreation Bd., Salt Lake City, 1991—; rep. Utah State Ho. Reps., health and environ. com., state and local com., health and human svcs. appropriations sub com., Salt Lake City, 1986—. Mem. Sugar House Rotary Club, Sugar House Park Authority. Democrat. Mem. LDS Ch. Home: 865 Parkway Ave Salt Lake City UT 84106-1704 Office: Valley Mental Health 5965 S 900 E Salt Lake City UT 84121-1720

DAVIS, GRAY, state controller; b. N.Y.C., Dec. 26, 1942; m. Sharon Ryer, Feb. 20, 1983. BA cum laude, Stanford U., 1964; JD, Columbia U., 1967. Chief of staff to Gov. Edmund G. Brown State of Calif., 1974-81, state rep., 1982-86, state contr., 1986—; chmn. Housing and Community Devel. Com., Calif. Coun. on Criminal Justice, Franchise Tax Bd., State Lands Commn.; mem. Bd. Equalization, State Tchrs. Retirement System, Pub. Employees Retirement System, Nat. Coun. Institutional Investors. Founder Calif. Found. for the Protection of Children. Office: Office of Lieutenant Governor 5777 W Century Blvd 1650 Los Angeles CA 90045-5631

DAVIS, J. ALAN, lawyer, producer, writer; b. N.Y.C., Nov. 7, 1961. Student, Marlborough Coll., Eng., 1979; BA, So. Meth. U., 1983; JD with honors, U. Tex., 1987. Bar: Calif. 1988. Assoc. O'Melveny & Myers, L.A., 1987-89, Rosenfeld, Meyer & Susman, Beverly Hills, Calif., 1989-90; pvt. practice L.A., 1990-94; ptnr. Davis & Benjamin, L.A., 1995—. Mem. Calif. Bar Assn., Beverly Hills Bar Assn. (entertainment law sect. exec. com.), Brit. Acad. Film and TV Arts. Office: Davis & Benjamin Ste 2580 2049 Century Park E Los Angeles CA 90067

DAVIS, JACK, securities dealer; b. 1938. With Harris Corp., Melbourne, Fla., 1962-86, Dataproducts Corp., Woodland Hills, Calif., 1986—; chmn. Morgan Wedbush Securities. Office: Morgan Wedbush Securities 1000 Wilshire Blvd Los Angeles CA 90017-2457*

DAVIS, JAMES ALLAN, gerontologist, educator; b. Portland, Oreg., May 20, 1953; s. Alfred Jack and Anne (Dickson) D.; m. Lois Carol Lindsay, Dec. 17, 1978; children: Sarah Elizabeth, Matthew Simon. BS, U. Oreg., 1975, MS, 1976, EdD, 1980. State mental health gerontologist Oreg. Mental Health Div., Salem, 1978-80; project dir. Oreg. Long Term Care Tng. Project, Salem, 1979-80; tng. specialist Nat. Assn. Area Agys. on Aging., Washington, 1981; asst. dir. for internships and vol. svc. exptl. learning programs U. Md., 1981-86, mem. rsch. and instructional faculty, 1982-86; com. adminstr. Oreg. State Resources Com., Salem, 1987; exec. dir. Oreg. State Coun. Sr. Citizens, Salem, 1987-90; program coord. for sr. mental health care Oreg. Sr. and Disabled Svcs. Div., Salem, 1989—; pres. James A. Davis and Assocs. Inc., Portland, 1991—; vis. asst. prof. Ctr. for Gerontology, U. Oreg., 1990-92; co-chair Audio-Visual Program, Internat. Congress Gerontology, 1985; nat. gerontology acad. adv. panel, Nat. Hosp. Satellite Network, 1983-85; presenter nat. confs. on aging, health care, exptl. edn., age stereotyping; lobbyist United Srs. Oreg., Oreg. State Coun. Sr. Citizens, 1987—, Oreg. State Denturist Assn., Oreg. State Pharmacist Assn., Oreg. Soc. Physician Assts., Oreg. Legal Techs. Assn., Oreg. Dental Lab. Assn., Wash. Denturist Assn., Nat. Denturist Assn., 1991—. Co-author: TV's Image of the Elderly, 1985; contbg. editor Retirement Life News, 1988-92; sr. issues editor Sr. News, 1989—; contbr. articles to profl. jours.; producer, host approximately 400 TV and radio programs. Founding pres. Oreg. Alliance for Progressive Policy, 1988-89; co-chair mental health com., vice chair legis. com., Gov.'s Commn. on Sr. Svcs., 1988-89; exec. coun., media chair Human Svcs. Coalition Oreg., 1988-89; bd. dirs. Oreg. Health Action Campaign, 1988-92; 2d v.p., bd. dirs. Oreg. State Coun. for Sr. Citizens, 1977-80, 90-92; mem. Gov.'s Task Force for Volunteerism, State of Md., 1983-84, State Legis. Income Tax Task Force, 1990; vice chair Oreg. State Bd. Denture Technology, 1991—; mem. com. for assessment on needs for volunteerism, Gov.'s Vol. Coun., State of Md., 1984-86; others. Recipient Disting. Svc. award City of Salem, 1980, Spl. Human Rights award, 1981, Svc. award U. Md., 1984, Hometown U.S.A. award Community Cable TV Producers, 1988, Disting. Svc. award Oreg. State Coun. Sr. Citizens, 1991. Mem. Nat. Assn. State Mental Health Dirs. (nat. exec. com. 1978-80, vice chmn. 1979-80, mem. aging div., spl. cons. 1981-82), Gerontol. Soc. Am. (mental health task force 1982-84, co-chmn. 1983-84), Nat. Gray Panthers (nat. bd. dirs. 1984-92, nat. exec. com. 1984-87, co-chmn. nat. program com. 1984-87, nat. media chair 1985-92, program co-chmn. nat. biennial conv. 1986, nat. health task force 1981—, co-chmn. 1983-84, chmn. mental health subcom. 1981-86, editor Health Watch, 1982-84, state program developer Oreg. chpt. 1979-80, 89, lobbyist 1987—). Democrat. Office: James A Davis and Assocs Inc 1750 SW Skyline Blvd Ste 10 Portland OR 97221-2543

DAVIS, JAMES IVEY, company president, laboratory associate; b. Repton, Ala., Apr. 9, 1937; s. James Ivey and Jewel Francis (Straughn) D.; m. Susan Elizabeth Endres, June 15, 1965 (div. Dec. 1980); 1 child, Melinda Cynthia; m. Roberta Claire Venerdi, Mar. 9, 1990. BS, Calif. Inst. Tech., 1962; MS, UCLA, 1965, PhD, 1969. Staff physicist Hughes Aircraft Co., Culver City, Calif., 1962-66; lectr. U. Ghana, Kumasi, 1966-67; dept. mgr. Hughes Aircraft Co., Culver City, Calif., 1970-74; assoc. dir. Lawrence Livermore (Calif.) Nat. Lab., 1974-93; cons., investor JIDCO, Danville, Calif., 1985-93; pres. Ivey Enterprises, Danville, 1993—; lab. assoc. Lawrence Livermore (Calif.) Nat. Lab., 1993—. Mem. The Commonwealth Club, San Francisco, 1987. With U.S. Army, 1953-56. Fellowship, Hughes Aircraft, 1963, NSF, 1969. Mem. AAAS, Am. Phys. Soc. Home and Office: 4114 Sugar Maple Dr Danville CA 94506-4639 Office: Lawrence Livermore Nat Lab PO Box 808 Livermore CA 94551-0808

DAVIS, JAMES LUTHER, retired utilities executive, lawyer; b. Memphis, May 8, 1924; s. Luther and Sarah (Carter) D.; m. Natalie Young, Jan. 26, 1947; children: James Luther, Fred C., Peggy E. BBA, U. Ariz., 1946, LLB, 1949. Bar: Ariz. 1949. Sole practice Tucson, 1949-52, asst. city atty., 1952-53, city mgr., 1953-55; with Tucson Gas & Electric Co. (now Tucson Electric Power Co.), 1955—; exec. v.p., 1958-59, pres., 1959-76, also bd. dirs., 1961-89, emeritus, 1989—, chmn. bd., 1967-88; bd. dirs. El Paso br. Fed. Res. Bd., Dallas, 1974-77, chmn. 1976-77. Mem. charter rev. com. City of Tucson, 1965-71; bd. dirs. Tucson Airport Authority, 1957-62, 64-70, pres., 1965; bd. dirs. Tucson Med. Ctr., 1955-58, 59-65, pres., 1957-58; mem. Tucson Indsl. Devel. Bd., 1959-64; bd. dirs. Ariz. Town Hall, 1962-74, 78-82, Health Planning Coun. Tucson, 1964-71, Tucson Regional Plan, 1966-89, United Way, 1985-88; bd. dirs. Green Fields Sch., 1964-69, chmn. bd., 1964-66; bd. dirs. U. Ariz. Found., 1985-92, dir. emeritus, 1992—. Mem. Nat. Assn. Mfrs. (bd. dirs. 1960-62), Tex. Bar Assn., Ariz. Bar Assn., Pacific Coast Gas Assn. (bd. dirs. 1958-60), Pacific Coast Elect. Assn. (bd. dirs. 1972-86, pres. 1978-79), Western Energy and Supply Assn. (bd. dirs. 1964-76), Tucson C. of C. (bd. dirs. 1958-60, 64-66, 80-90, chmn. 1987-88), So. Ariz. Water Resources Assn. (bd. dirs. 1982-88, pres. 1987), Blue Key, Phi Gamma Delta, Alpha Kappa Psi, Phi Delta Phi, Tucson Country Club. Home: 6781 N Altos Primero Tucson AZ 85718-2054

DAVIS, JAMES MCCOY, real estate executive; b. Columbus, Ohio, Oct. 19, 1914; s. James McCoy and Laura Victoria (Smith) D.; m. Phyllis Ruth Rowe, Jan. 24, 1948; children: Perine Davis Ceperley, Linda Davis Bryson, Carol, Paul, Jamie Davis Micalizzi. BBA, Ohio State U., 1937; postgrad., Union Theol. Sem., N.Y.C., 1937-39; BD, Oberlin Grad. Sch. Theol., 1942; MA, Columbia U., 1947, EdD, 1952; MDiv (hon.), Vanderbilt U., 1973. Lic. real estate broker, Calif. Minister First Congl. Ch., Ravenna, Ohio, 1939-42; field exec. Congl. Christian Com. War Victims and Services, N.Y.C., 1942-43; counselor for internat. services U. Wash., Seattle, 1948-54; dir., assoc. prof. U. Mich., Ann Arbor, 1954-64; v.p. Inst. Internat. Edn., N.Y.C., 1964-67; provost U.S. Internat. U., San Diego, 1967-70; pres. Northwestern Mich. Coll., Traverse City, 1970-73; realtor assoc. Klaus Radelow Realtor, San Diego, 1973-74; realtor James M. Davis, San Diego, 1974-77; pres. James M. Davis Inc. & Assocs., San Diego, 1977—. Contbr. articles to profl. jours. Pres. World Affairs Coun., San Diego, 1981-83; chmn. bd. Consumer Credit Counselors, San Diego, 1988-89; mem. San Diego County Grand Jury, 1990-91. Capt. U.S. Army, 1943-46. Decorated Bronze Star with oak leaf cluster. Mem. Nat. Assn. Fgn. Student Affairs (life, pres. 1959-60), Calif. Assn. Realtors (bd. dirs. 1978-79, 88), San Diego Assn. Realtors (com. chmn. 1978-79, 88), Self Svc. Storage Assn., Rotary. Republican. Presbyterian. Home: 4906 Pacifica Dr San Diego CA 92109-2311

DAVIS, JEREMY MATTHEW, chemist; b. Bakersfield, Calif., Aug. 5, 1953; s. Joseph Hyman and Mary (Pavetto) D.; m. Bernadette Sobkiewicz, Aug. 28, 1976; children: Andrew Jeremy, Christopher Peter. BS in Biol. Scis., U. Calif., Irvine, 1974; M in Pub. Adminstrn., Calif. State U., Long Beach, 1983. Chemist I, II, Orange County Water Dist., Fountain Valley, Calif., 1977-84, chemist supr., 1984—. Papers in field. Adult leader Boy Scouts Am.; lay Eucharistic minister St. Margaret of Scotland Episcopal Ch., San Juan Capistrano, Calif. Named Lab. Person of Yr., Calif. Water Environment Assn., Santa Ana River Basin, 1984. Mem. Am. Chem. Soc., Am. Water Works Assn., Calif. Water Environment Assn. (bd. dirs. Santa Ana River Basin chpt. 1984), Toastmasters Internat. (v.p. edn. 1995). Office: Orange County Water Dist PO Box 8300 Santa Ana CA 92728-8300

DAVIS, JOEL STEPHEN, systems engineer, scientist; b. Pitts., June 12, 1948; s. Emanuel and Dorothy Lewise (Winans) D.; m. Cornelia Wells Lange, Aug. 7, 1983. BS in Polit. Sci. and Physics, MIT, 1970; MS in Astro-Geophysics, U. Colo., 1976. Sci. analyst Sci. Applications, Inc., Arlington, Va., 1976-79; tech. mgr. Sci. Applications, Inc., Dayton, Ohio, 1979-83; sr. scientist Sci. Applications, Inc., Albuquerque, 1983-84; dept. mgr. Verac, Inc., Albuquerque, 1985-87; mgr. electro optics programs Ball Sys. Engring. Divsn., Albuquerque, 1987-92; chief engr./scientist Ball Corp. Sys. Engring. Ops., Albuquerque, 1992—; mem. strategic tech. panel Ball Aerospace, Boulder, 1991-93. Author: Climatological Cross-Correlation Analysis, 1980, (computer models) Fire Control Sensor Simulator, 1986, Night Vision Device Model, 1993. Vol. Children's Med. Ctr., Dayton, 1979-83; mem. Albuquerque Breakfast Club chpt. Civitans Internat., Albuquerque, 1990—. Recipient Disting. Svc. award Wright chpt. Am. Meteorol. Soc., 1982. Republican. Conservative Jewish. Home: 1310 Constitution Ct NE Albuquerque NM 87112-4601 Office: Ball Corp Sys Engring Ops 2901 Juan Tabo NE # 235 Albuquerque NM 87112

DAVIS, JOHN ALBERT, lawyer; b. Seattle, July 29, 1940; s. Carl Lee and Helen Irene (Corner) D.; m. Judith Ann colvin, June 21, 1959 (div. 1978); children: John Albert, James Colvin, Jennifer Lynn. Student, U. Calif., Berkeley, 1957-58; postgrad., Diablo Valley Coll., 1962; JD, Golden Gate U., 1970. Bar: Calif. 1971, U.S. Dist. Ct. (no. dist.) Calif. 1971, U.S. Ct. Appeals (9th cir.) 1971, U.S. Supreme Ct. 1986. Pres. Cal-State Distbrs., Oakland, Calif., 1959-78; pvt. practice Oakland, 1978-81, San Ramon, 1985—; v.p., chief operating officer Madre Mining, Ltd., Sacramento, 1981-85; pres., bd. dirs. O'Hara Resources, Ltd., Vancouver, B.C., Can., 1989—; bd. dirs. Troy Gold Industries, Ltd., Calgary, Alta., Can. Mem. Calif. Bar Assn., Commwealth Club Calif., Sequoia Woods Country Club. Republican. Presbyterian. Office: PO Box 2096 2 Annabel Ln Ste 200 San Ramon CA 94583-1659

DAVIS, JOHN JEFFREY, musician; b. Chgo., Aug. 15, 1944; s. John Ross Davis and Edith Elizabeth (Gogerty) Stephens. BA, Dallas Bapt. Coll., 1969; MMus, U. S.C., 1974. Factotum and carillonist U. Calif., Berkeley, 1983—; adjudicator Guild of Carillonneurs in N.Am., 1989—. Composer: Betsy Ross and the Red White and Blue, 1976, Three Liturgical Dances, 1974, Passion, 1993, Symphony for Orchestra, 1994. Pres. pastoral coun. Most Holy Redeemer Ch., San Francisco, 1989-90. Named Disting. Alumnus Nat. Music Camp, Interlochen, Mich., 1974, Berkeley medal U. Calif., 1993. Mem. Guild of Carillonneurs in N.Am., ASCAP. Home: 396 Diamond St San Francisco CA 94114-2821

DAVIS, KINGSLEY, sociologist, educator, researcher; b. Tuxedo, Tex., Aug. 20, 1908; s. Joseph Dyer and Winifred (Kingsley) D.; m. Jane Quinn, Aug. 20, 1936 (div.); children: Jo Ann Daily, Jefferson K.; m. Judith Blake, Nov. 3, 1954 (div. 1977); 1 dau., Laura Isabelle; m. Marta H. Seoane, 1985; 1 child, Austin Alexander Seoane. A.B. in English, U. Tex., 1930; M.A. in Philosophy, 1932; M.A. in Sociology, Harvard U., 1933; Ph.D. in Sociology, 1936. Instr. in sociology Smith Coll., 1934-36; asst. prof. sociology Clark U., 1936-37; assoc. prof., chmn. dept. Pa. State U., University Park, 1937-42, prof., chmn., 1942-44; vis. research assoc. Office Population Research, Princeton U., 1942-44; research assoc. Princeton U., 1944-48, assoc. prof. pub. affairs, 1944-45, assoc. prof. anthropology and sociology, 1945-48; prof. sociology grad. faculty Columbia U., N.Y.C., 1948-55; prof. sociology U. Calif.-Berkeley, 1955-70, chmn. internat. population and urban research, 1956-77, chmn. dept. sociology, 1961-63, Ford prof. sociology and comparative studies, 1970-76, Ford prof. emeritus, recalled, 1976-77; disting. prof. sociology U. So. Calif., Los Angeles, 1977-92; sr. research fellow Hoover Instn., Stanford U., Calif., 1981-92, emeritus sr. rsch. fellow, 1992—; U.S. rep. Population Commn., UN, N.Y.C., 1954-61; mem. NASA Adv. Council, Washington, 1977-82, Adv. Council Sci. and Tech., Legis Assembly, Sacramento, 1970-71; disting. lectr. SUNY-Stony Brook, 1983. Author: Human Society, 1949, The Population of India and Pakistan, 1951, World Urbanization, 1972; editor: Cities, 1973. Recipient Irene Taeuber award for disting. research in demography, 1979; recipient Common Wealth award for research in sociology, 1979; Oldright fellow, 1931-32; Henry Bromfield Rogers Meml. fellow, 1932-33; Social Sci. Research Council postdoctoral fellow, 1940-41; Carnegie Corp. traveling fellow, 1952; Ctr. Advanced Study Behavioral Scis. fellow, 1956-57, 80-81; NSF sr. postdoctoral fellow, 1964-65. Fellow AAAS (chmn. sect. 1963, 81, v.p. 1963), Am. Sociol. Assn. (pres. 1959 Disting. Career award), Am. Statis. Assn. (liaison mem. council 1968-69); mem. Population Assn. Am. (pres. 1962-63), Sociol. Research Assn. (pres. 1960), AAUP (mem. council 1962-65), Am. Eugenics Soc. (bd. dirs. 1953-55), Internat. Union Sci. Study Population (chmn. Am. com. 1967-68), Nat. Acad. Scis., Am. Acad. Arts and Scis., Am. Philos. Soc., World Acad. Art and Sci., Phi Beta Kappa (vis. scholar 1976-77). Home: 975 Wing Pl Stanford CA 94305-1028

DAVIS, LINDA JACOBS, public affairs development professional; b. Miami, July 10, 1955; d. Martin Jacque and Doris Harriet (Stucker) Jacobs; m. John Joseph Mantos, Jan. 1, 1984 (dec. 1988); m. Perry Davis, June 4, 1989; children: Aaron, Jacob. Student, U. South Fla., 1977. Mgr., cons. Werner Erhard & Assocs., San Francisco, 1978-82, program leader, 1979-90; asst. exec. dir. The Breakthrough Found., San Francisco, 1982-88; owner Mantagaris Galleries, San Francisco, 1988-92; dir. mktg. devel. Marin Child Care Coun., San Rafael, Calif., 1992-94; dir. devel. and pub. affairs Planned Parenthood of Marin, Sonoma and Menodcino, Calif., 1994—; ptnr. Women's Initiative for Leadership Devel., 1994—; profl. fund-raiser. Vol. The Hunger Project, Fla., 1977-78; bd. dirs. Marin Child Care Coun.; appointed commr. Marin Commn. on Women, 1994—. Recipient Outstanding

Young Women Am. Mem. NOW (pres. local chpt.), Marin Women's Coalition. Democrat. Jewish. Home: 419 Karla Ct Novato CA 94949 Office: Planned Parenthood 2 H St San Rafael CA 94901-1700

DAVIS, MARGARET ANNE, dietitian and educator; b. San Diego, Aug. 24, 1954; d. John Rondeau and Catherine Lee (Greene) D. BS in Dietetics, U. Calif., Davis, 1976; MBA, Calif. State U., Sacramento, 1982. Cert. nutrition support dietetitian; registered dietitian. Clin. dietitian Sutter Cmty. Hosps., Sacramento, 1977-84; dist. mgr. sales and mktg. Home Infusion Therapy Industry, Sacramento/San Francisco, 1984-90; adminstrv. dir. nutrition sci. ctr. Hermann Hosp., Houston, 1991; dietitian educator/nutrition cons. The Cutting Edge, Fremont, Calif., 1992—; bd. dirs. Nat. HIV Nutrition Team, Berkeley, Calif., 1994—; guest lectr. San Jose State U., 1993-94, U. Calif., Berkeley, 1994; lectr. in field. Co-author (booklet): Living Well with HIV/AIDS, 1993; editor-in-chief Baviews, 1988-89; reviewer (book): Clinical Nutrition, 1978; reviewer (periodical): HIV/AIDS Nutrition: Standards of Care Guidelines, 1992. Bd. dirs. Sacramento AIDS Walk, 1989. State of Calif. Gov.'s scholar, 1972. Mem. Am. Dietetic Assn., Am. Soc. for Parenteral and Enteral Nutrition, Nat. Assn. Vascular Access Networks (bd. dirs. 1993-95), Bay Area Vascualr Access Network (bd. dirs. 1988-90), Sacramento Valley Renal Dietitians (co-founder 1979-80). Home: 1674 Parkside Dr Walnut Creek CA 94596 Office: The Cutting Edge PO Box 14194 Fremont CA 94539-1394

DAVIS, NATHAN CHILTON, federal agency administrator; b. St. Albans, N.Y., May 2, 1954; s. Nathan Chilton Davis and Ferne Irene Snyder; m. Deborah Laurie Nygaard, Apr. 15, 1973; children: Nathan Chilton III and Richard Randall (twins), Jaime Rae, Evan Michael. AS, U. Calif., San Diego, 1979; BS, Kensington U., 1994. Cert. emergency paramedic, arson investigator, auditor. Fire chief, paramedic Salton City Svcs., Salton Sea, Calif., 1975-78; emergency paramedic City of San Bernardino/Riverside, Calif., 1978-79; detention officer U.S. Immigration, El Centro, Calif., 1981-83, physician asst., 1983-85; tng. administrator U.S. Immigration, Laguna Niguel, Calif., 1985-87, dep. asst. regional commr., 1987-88; officer in charge U.S. Immigration, El Centro, 1988—; instr. Fed. Law Enforcement Tng. Ctr., U.S. Dept. Justice, 1985, course developer U.S. Immigration Svc., 1986; arson investigator Riverside (Calif.) County Fire, 1976; chair Career Opportunity Program Adv. Coun., 1993. Author: Executive Protection, 1984, revised, 1994, Detention Operations, 1985, Corporate Violence, 1993, Leader's Guide to Office Management, 1994; numerous tng. programs. Capt. U.S. Army, 1980-88. Recipient Life Saving medal Salton Cmty. Svcs., 1980, Army Commendation award Dept. Def., 1987, Performance award Nat. Performance Rev.-V.P. Al Gore, 1994. Mem. Am. Correctional Assn. (gold), Am. Assn. Correctional Psychology. Home: 392 W B St Brawley CA 92227-1412 Office: US Immigration 1115 N Imperial Ave El Centro CA 92243-1739

DAVIS, NATHANIEL, humanities educator; b. Boston, Mass., Apr. 12, 1925; s. Harvey Nathaniel and Alice Marion (Rohde) D.; m. Elizabeth Kirkbride Creese, Nov. 24, 1956; children: Margaret Morton Davis Mainardi, Helen Miller Davis Presley, James Creese, Thomas Rohde. Grad., Phillips Exeter Acad., 1942; A.B., Brown U., 1944, LL.D., 1970; M.A., Fletcher Sch. Law and Diplomacy, 1947, Ph.D., 1960; postgrad. Russian lang. and area, Columbia, Cornell U., Middlebury Coll., 1953-54, U. Central de Venezuela, 1961-62; Norwich U., 1989. Asst. history Tufts Coll., 1947; joined U.S. Fgn. Service, 1947; 3d sec. Prague, Czechoslovakia, 1947-49; vice consul Florence, Italy, 1949-52; 2d sec. Rome, Italy, 1952-53, Moscow, USSR, 1954-56; Soviet desk officer State Dept., 1956-60; 1st sec. Caracas, Venezuela, 1960-62; acting Peace Corps dir. Chile, 1962; spl. asst. to dir. Peace Corps, 1962-63, dept. asso. dir., 1963-65; U.S. minister to Bulgaria, 1965-66; sr. staff Nat. Security Council (White House), 1966-68; U.S. ambassador to Guatemala, 1968-71; to Chile, 1971-73; dir. gen. Fgn. Service, 1973-75, asst. sec. of state for African affairs, 1975; U.S. ambassador to Switzerland, 1975-77; State Dept advisor and Chester Nimitz prof. Naval War Coll., 1977-83; Alexander and Adelaide Hixon prof. humanities Harvey Mudd Coll., Claremont, Calif., 1983—; faculty exec. com. Harvey Mudd Coll., 1986-89, acting dean of faculty, 1990; lectr. U.S. history Centro Venezolano-Americano, 1961; lectr. Russian, Soviet history Howard U., 1962-65, 66-68, lectr. constnl. law and social problems Salve Regina Coll., 1981-83. Author: The Last Two Years of Salvador Allende, 1985, Equality and Equal Security in Soviet Foreign Policy, 1986, A Long Walk to Church: A Contemporary History of Russian Orthodoxy, 1995. Mem. ctrl. com. Calif. Dem. Party, 1987-90, 91—, exec. bd., 1993—, L.A. County Ctrl. Com., 1988-90, 92—, regional vice chair, 1994—, del. Dem. Nat. Conv., 1988, 92, del. So. Calif. Conf. United Ch. of Christ, 1986-87. Lt. (j.g.) USNR, 1944-46. Recipient Cinco Aguilas Blancas Alpinism award Venezuelan Andean Club, 1962; Disting. Pub. Service award U.S. Navy, 1983. Mem. AAUP (pres. Claremont Coll. chpt. 1992—), Am. Fgn. Svc. Assn. (bd. dirs., vice chmn. 1964), Coun. on Fgn. Rels., Am. Acad. Diplomacy, Phi Beta Kappa. Club: Cosmos. Home: 1783 Longwood Ave Claremont CA 91711 Office: Harvey Mudd Coll 301 East 12th St Claremont CA 91711-3129

DAVIS, PAUL KENSIL, research manager, strategic analyst; b. Youngstown, Ohio, Dec. 20, 1943; s. Paul K. Davis and Ruth A. Gladhill; m. Joyce E. Lindstrom, Sept. 30, 1966; 1 child, Elise. BS in Chemistry, U. Mich., 1965; MIT, James Frank Inst., U. Chgo., 1971. Postdoctoral fellow James Franck Inst., Chgo., 1970-71; sr. staff mem. Inst. for Def. Analysis, Alexandria, Va., 1971-75; analyst U. S. Arms Control Agy., Washington, 1975-77; analyst Office of Sec. of Def., Washington, 1977-79, sr. exec., 1979-81; program dir. Rand, Santa Monica, Calif., 1982-90, corp. rsch. mgr. for def. and tech. planning, 1990—; mem. faculty Rand Grad. Sch. Policy Studies, Santa Monica, 1982—. Author: Deterring or Coercing Opponents in Crisis: The Case of Saddam Hussein, 1991, Defense Planning in the Past Cold War Era, 1993, editor, author: New Challenges for Defense Planning, 1994. Mem. Internat. Inst. of Strategic Studies, Sigma Xi. Home: 3243 Fermi Dr Topanga CA 90290-4432 Office: Rand 1700 Main St Santa Monica CA 90401-3208

DAVIS, RANDALL SCOTT, public relations executive; b. Ottumwa, Iowa, July 26, 1952; s. Donald Dale and Marguaritte Louise (Maier) D.; m. Ruthe Eugena Forbriger, Nov. 21, 1976; 1 child, Ryan Scott. BA, Calif. State U., L.A., 1974. Dir. merchandising and advt. Capitol Records, Hollywood, Calif., 1975-82; mktg. svcs. mgr. Walt Disney Home Video, Burbank, Calif., 1982-83; account exec. Berkhemer & Kline Pub. Rels., L.A., 1983-85; v.p. ops. Jensen Communications, Burbank, 1985-86; pres. The Creative Svc. Co., Colorado Springs, Colo., 1986—. Freelance writer various mags., newspapers and pub. rels. agys., L.A., 1970—. Recipient CLIO, N.Y.C., 1981. Mem. The Hemingway Found.

DAVIS, RANDY L., soil scientist; b. L.A., Nov. 23, 1950; s. Willie Vernon and Joyce Catherine (Manes) D. AA, Yuba Community Coll., 1972; BS in Soils and Plant Nutrition, U. Calif., Berkeley, 1976. Vol. soil scientist U.S. Peace Corps, Maseru, Lesotho, 1976-79; soil scientist Hiawatha Nat. Forest, Sault Saint Marie, Mich., 1979-86; forest soil scientist Bridger-Teton Nat. Forest, Jackson, Wyo., 1986—; detailed soil scientist Boise (Idaho) Nat. Forest, 1989, 92. Editor Soil Classifiers newsletter; contbr. articles to profl. jours. Pres. Sault Community Theater, Sault Saint Marie, 1984-86. Mem. Am. Chem. Soc., Soil Sci. Soc. Am., Soil and Water Conservation Soc. (bd. dirs. 1991-92, chpt. pres. 1993-95), Am. Water Resources Assn., Internat. Soc. Soil Sci., Soc. for Range Mgmt. Methodist. Home: PO Box 7795 Jackson WY 83001-7795 Office: Bridger-Teton Nat Forest PO Box 1888 Jackson WY 83001-1888

DAVIS, RICHARD CALHOUN, dentist; b. Manhattan, Kans., Jan. 4, 1945; s. William Calhoun and Alison Rae (Wyland) D.; Danna Ruth Ritchel, June 13, 1968; 1 child, Darin Calhoun. Student, Ariz. State U., 1963-65, BA, 1978; BA, U. Ariz., 1966; DDS, U. of Pacific, 1981. Retail dept. head Walgreens, Tucson, 1965-66; mgmt. trainee Walgreens, Tucson, San Antonio, 1967-70; asst. store mgr. Walgreens, Baton Rouge, 1970-72; field rep. Am. Cancer Soc., Phoenix, 1972-74; dept. head Lucky Stores, Inc., Tempe, Ariz., 1976-78; practice dentistry specializing in gen. dentistry Tucson, 1981—; bd. dirs. Home Again, Inc. Chmn. bd. Capilla Del Sol Christian Ch., Tucson, 1984. Mem. ADA, Acad. Gen. Dentists, Am. Straight Wire Orthodontic Assn., Tucson Bus. Network Internat., N.W. Dental Study Club, Optimists (past pres. N.W. club), Elks. Republican. Mem. Disciples of Christ Ch. Office: 2777 N Campbell Ave Tucson AZ 85719-3101

DAVIS, RICHARD ERNEST, engineer; b. San Francisco, Nov. 20, 1936; 1 child, Richard Jr.; m. Sharon L. Buss, Aug. 26, 1961; children: Dawn, Michelle. BS in Engring., Calif. State Poly. U., San Luis Obispo, 1967. Facilities engr., energy conservation engr. Naval Weapons Ctr., China Lake, Calif., 1967-77; solar program coordinator U.S. Dept. Energy, Oakland, Calif., 1977-78; program mgr. Solar Energy Research Inst., Golden, Colo., 1978-80; engring. specialist Holmes & Narver, Mercury, Nev., 1980-90; engring. specialist nuclear waste Nev./Yucca Mountain Project Raytheon Svcs., Mercury, 1990-93; sr. project engr. Fluor Daniel, Inc., Las Vegas, 1993—; constrn. coord. Constrn. Mgmt. Orgn. Yucca Mountain Project. Contbr. articles to profl. jours. Served with USAF, 1954-62. Home: HC 69 Box 495 Amargosa Valley NV 89020-9801 Office: Fluor Daniel Inc 101 Convention Center Dr Las Vegas NV 89109-2001

DAVIS, RICK JEFFREY, psychotherapist, educator; b. Salt Lake City, Dec. 7, 1948; s. Richard James and Constance Marie (Rosenthal) D.; m. Sharon Marie Confray, Aug. 17, 1989; 1 child, Jeffery; stepchildren: Stacey Alarotu, Cory Alarotu. BS in Psychology, Westminster Coll. Salt Lake City, 1986; MA in Marriage, Family and Child Therapy, Calif. Family Study Ctr., 1988. Cert. marriage, family and child therapist. Addictive behaviors program mgr. AIDS Project L.A., 1987-91; exec. dir. Ariz. AIDS Project, Phoenix, 1991; social work therapist Desert Vista Hosp., Mesa, Ariz., 1992—; HIV ednl. cons. Ariz. Dept. Edn., Phoenix, 1991-92. Recipient Humanitarian award Odyssey House of Utah, 1986, Humanitarian award for pub. svc. CBS Affiliate-Sta. KSL Radio, 1986. Home: 15628 E Thistle Dr Fountain Hls AZ 85268-4343 Office: Desert Vista Hosp 570 W Brown Rd Mesa AZ 85201-3227

DAVIS, ROBERT BRUCE, metallurgical engineer, consultant; b. Seattle, Dec. 14, 1952; s. Bruce Arthur and Gloria (Brooks) D.; 1 child, Charlotte Lynn. BS in Phys. Metallurgy, Wash. State U., 1975, MS. Rschr. Wash. State U., Pullman, 1976; rsch. sci. Westinghouse, Richland, Wash., 1976-79; rsch. engr. Exxon, Idaho Falls, Idaho, 1979-81; prin. metall. engr. Wash. Pub. Power Supply Sys., Richland, 1981—; cons. Tech. Seminars, N.Y.C., 1986-88, Apollo Associated Svcs., Richland, 1987-89, Vantage Tng., New Rochelle, N.Y., 1988—. Author: (tng. text) Power Plant Erosion/Corrosion, 1986, Corrosion of Power Plant Materials, 1987. Vol. Dial Help, Richland, 1977-79; leader Boy Scouts Am., Richland, 1982-88; chmn. fund raisier Spl. Olympics, Richland, 1994. Mem. ASTM, Am. Soc. Materials (sci. fair coord. 1988-91), Nat. Assn. Corrosion Engrs. (chpt. pres. 1987-89). Home: 3011 Lindemein Ct Pasco WA 99301-6525 Office: Wash Pub Power Supply Sys 3000 George Washington Way Richland WA 99352-1617

DAVIS, ROBERT H., controller, financial executive; b. Phila., Mar. 26, 1943; student Los Angeles Valley Coll., 1965-67, Alexander Hamilton Inst., 1965-68, Grad. Sch. of Credit and Fin. Mgmt., Stanford U., 1977-80, Pepperdine U., 1981; 1 dau., Michelle R. Internat. arbitrator, mediator, counselor Am. Arbitration Assn. Asst. controller, credit mgr. Wyo. Machinery Co., Casper, 1978-83; controller/sec.-treas., dir. John E. Burns Drilling Co., Casper, 1979—; comptroller, v.p. Philip Crosby Assocs., Inc., Winter Park, Fla., 1984—; v.p., treas. Crosby Assocs. Internat., Inc., Winter Park, Fla.; pres., CEO Davis, Keller & Davis, New Orleans, Oreg. and Wash., 1989—; mgmt/ cons. and legal internat. arbitrator/mediator, author, lectr. Am. Arbitration Assn., Singapore Arbitration Ctr., Langley, Wash., fin. cons. Western Energy Co., Huey's Smoked Meats, Nashville, Trans-Equip., Casper, Three Percent, Inc., Riverton, Wyo., 1979-80; mem. subcom. USA/NAFTA, Washington. Adv. bd. dirs. Highland Park Community Ch., 1980—. Served with USNR, 1961-63. Mem. Nat. Assn. Credit Mgmt. (state rep. 1979, 80, founder, chmn. Casper Credit Group), Credit Mgrs. Assn. So. Calif. (dir. bus. re-orgn. and bankruptcy 1973-74), Credit Research Found., Am. Mgmt. Assn., Practicing Law Inst. (assoc.), Wash. Export Coun., La. Export Coun., U.S. Dept. Commerce Industry Consultation Program, Stanford U. Alumni Assn., Internat. Platform Assn.; cons. U.S.A./NAPTA nat. com. mem. Alliance for GATT Pres's. Export Coun. Club: Order of Demolay (sr. award 1960). Author: Charting Your Businesses Practices-U.S. Small Business Adminstrn., Transnational Arbitration as a Means of Managing Corporate Risks, International Risk Management for U.S. Small Businesses, Leasing as a Secondary Source of Financing in the Heavy Equipment Industry.

DAVIS, RODERICK WILLIAM, retail executive; b. Borrolly, Calif., Sept. 14, 1936; s. Reginald William and Mary (Donnawit) D.; m. Judith Anne Hay, Dec. 31, 1937; children: Lori Lynn, Bradley William. BEE, Calif. Polytech. Inst., 1959; MEE, Ariz. State U., 1963; MBA, Chgo. State U., 1972. Dept. mgr. Gen. Electric, Phoenix, 1959-64; dir. Dart Industries, Los Angeles, 1964-66, Motorola, Chgo., 1966-72; v.p. Kimberly Clark Corp., Neenah, Wis., 1972-76, SuperUnlo Stores, Inc., Eden Prairie, Minn., 1976-84; sr. v.p. Safeway Stores, Inc., Oakland, Calif., 1984—. Home: 2339 W Johnston Ave Olathe KS 66061-6828 Office: Safeway Stores Inc 201 4th St Oakland CA 94607-4311

DAVIS, ROLAND CHENOWETH, lawyer; b. San Diego, Jan. 5, 1911; s. Percy Roland and Herta (Curme) D.; m. Harriet Allen, Oct. 24, 1934; children: Carolyn, Alan, Mary Anne, Roland Francis. BA, Stanford U., Palo Alto, 1932, JD, 1936. Bar: Calif. 1937, U.S. Dist. Ct. Calif. 1937, U.S. Ct. Appeals (9th cir.) 1937, U.S. Supreme Ct. 1954. Atty. Nat. Labor Bur., San Francisco, 1938-42; sect. head War Shipping Adminstrn., Washington, 1942-43; dir. Nat. Labor Bur., San Francisco, 1944-46; ptnr. Carroll, Davis & Freidenrich, San Francisco, 1947-58; sr. ptnr. Davis, Cowell & Bowe, San Francisco, 1958-87; of counsel Davis, Reno & Courtney, San Francisco, 1987—; counsel San Francisco Labor Coun. and State Coun. of Retail Clks. Unions, 1946-65; lectr. labor law Stanford U., 1950's and 60's; chmn. labor law com. San Francisco Bar Assn., 1956; chmn. labor rels. com. San Francisco Commonwealth Club, 1974-75; tchr. labor law City Coll. San Francisco, 1974-75. Parliamentarian Calif. Delegation, Nat. Dem. Conv., Phila., 1948; chmn. Dem. County Com, Santa Clara County, 1948-52; sec. state com. Dem. Party, Calif., 1952. Mem. ABA, Am. Arbitration Assn., Calif. State Bar Assn., De Anza Country Club (pres. 1976-79), Los Altos Golf and Country Club (pres. 1966), Calif. Conciliation Svc. (panel of arbitrators 1984—). Home: 1620 Cowper St Palo Alto CA 94301-3619 Office: Davis Reno and Courtney 90 New Montgomery St San Francisco CA 94105-4501

DAVIS, RON LEE, clergyman, author; b. Carroll, Iowa, Oct. 17, 1947; s. David Clarence and Elizabeth Regina (Thompson) D.; m. Shirley Louise O'Connor, Aug. 31, 1973; children: Rachael LeeAnn, Nathan Paul. BA cum laude, Tarkio (Mo.) Coll., 1969; MDiv cum laude, Dubuque (Iowa) Theol. Sem., 1971; DDiv, Bethel Theol. Sem., St. Paul, 1977. Ordained to ministry Presbyn. Ch., 1971. Chaplain Minn. Vikings, Mpls., 1975-80; assoc. pastor Hope Presbyn. Ch., Mpls., 1971-80; sr. pastor First Presbyn. Ch., Fresno, Calif., 1981-86, Community Presbyn. Ch., Danville, Calif., 1986-91; tchr. Bible Oakland (Calif.) A's, 1990-91; writer, 1983—; real estate loan cons. Danville Fin. Group, Calif., 1992—; invited speaker at gen. sessions and confs. and on TV. Author: Gold in the Making, 1983, A Forgiving God in an Unforgiving World, 1984, Healing Life's Hurts, 1986, A Time for Compassion, 1986, Courage to Begin Again, 1988, Mistreated, 1989, Becoming a Whole Person in a Broken World, 1990, Mentoring, 1990. Mem. pres.'s adv. coun. Fellowship of Christian Athletes; bd. dirs. Youth for Christ, cen. Calif., 1982-85, Fresno Pacific Coll., 1983-84. Recipient award for outstanding leadership State Bar; named to Outstanding Young Men of Am. Home: 3513 Canfield Dr Danville CA 94526-5507

DAVIS, SCOTT MILTON, information systems professional; b. Cin., Dec. 6, 1952; s. Robert Milton and Marjorie Alma Martha (Hecker) D. BA in Sociology, U. Cin., 1978; MA in Environ. Planning, Ariz. State U., 1986. From cons. to asst. to pres. Cosanti Found., Scottsdale, Cordes Jct., Ariz., 1981-84, 89—. Co-author: Paolo Soleri's Earth Casting, 1984. Vol. Yellowstone Nat. Park, 1978. Home and Office: Cosanti Found HC Box 4136 Mayer AZ 86333

DAVIS, STANFORD EVOL, civil engineer; b. Oakland, Calif., Jan. 31, 1937; s. Stanford Leroy and Leona (Parsons) D.; m. Carole Ann McCrindle, Mar. 26, 1960; children: Glen Leroy, Linda Carole. BS in Engring., San Jose State Coll., 1960; pub. adminstrn. cert., Calif. State U., Hayward, 1974; transp. cert., Calif. State U. Registered profl. civil engr., Calif.; registered traffic engr. Jr. and asst. engr. Contra Costa County, Martinez, Calif., 1960-64; asst. city engr. City of Antioch, Calif., 1964-69, city engr., 1969-73, dir. cmty. devel., city engr., 1973-78, dir. pub. works, city engr., 1978—; chair Contra Costa County Transp. Adv. Com., 1988-91; mem. City-County Engring. Adv. Com., Contra Costa County, 1969—; mem. Mcpl. Pub. Works Officers Conf., Bay Area, 1969—. Sgt. 1st class Calif. Army N.G. Mem. ASCE, NSPE, Am. Water Works Assn., Am. Pub. Works Assn., Calif. Soc. Profl. Engrs. (chpt. officer). Democrat. Home: 1409 Saint Francis Dr Antioch CA 94509-4629 Office: City of Antioch PO Box 130 Antioch CA 94509-0504

DAVIS, STANFORD MELVIN, engineering executive, publishing consultant; b. Camden, N.J., June 12, 1941; s. Winford and Rose Marie (Rich) D.; m. Pamela Davis, Nov. 25, 1967 (div. 1980); children: Peter, Shawna; m. Laura A. Rudolph, Feb. 21, 1987. AB, BSEE, Rutgers U., 1964; postgrad., UCLA, 1967; MBA, U. Portland, 1974. Elec. engr. RCA, Van Nuys, Calif., 1966-68; project engr. Tek, Wilsonville, Oreg., 1968-79; S/W mgr. Tektronix, Wilsonville, 1979-81, mgr. mktg., 1981-83; founder, v.p. engring. Concept Technologies, Portland, 1983-86; mgr. engring. program INTEL, Hillsboro, Oreg., 1986-87; product line mgr. INTEL, Hillsboro, 1987-88; engring. mgr. Graphic Printing div. Textronix, Wilsonville, Oreg., 1989-95; pres. Straight-on Industries, Beaverton, Oreg., 1995—; worldwide Web, Internet, software cons. Patentee in field. Served to capt. U.S. Army, 1964-66. Recipient Outstanding Product award Datapro, Delran, N.J., 1985. Mem. Assn. of Computing Machinery, IEEE. Home: 7320 SW 103rd Ave Beaverton OR 97008-6048

DAVIS, STEVEN ARTHUR, photographer, educator; b. July 12, 1957; s. James Robert and Ann Elizabeth (LaGrone) D.; m. Monique Anderson, Dec. 8, 1985. BS in Comms.-Photo/Film, U. Idaho, 1979, MFA, 1983. Photographer Evergreen State Coll., Olympia, Wash., 1986—, adj. faculty, 1987—, vis. faculty, 1993-94; vis. prof. U. Idaho, Moscow, 1989. Exhibited in one-person shows at Univ. Gallery, U. Idaho, 1978, Donnally/Hayes, Seattle, 1985, Prichard Gallery, Moscow, 1988, So. Light Gallery of Amarillo (Tex.) Coll., 1989; in group shows at Notre Dame U., 1992, Evergreen State Coll., 1993, L.A. Conv. Ctr., 1993, Pacific Luth. U., Tacoma, 1993, CyberSpace Gallery, West Hollywood, Calif., 1993, Holter Mus. Art, Helena, Mont., 1994, Krannert Mus., Champaign, Ill., 1995; in collections at Musee de la Photographie, Charleroi, Belgium, Bethel Sch. Dist., Pierce County, Wash., EZTV, Hollywood, Calif. Recipient Silver award Seattle Design and Advt. Show, 1981, award of merit Calif. Works, Sacramento, 1986, Award of Excellence Univ. and Coll. Designers Assn., 1990, others; artist fellowship Wash. State Arts Commn., 1989. Mem. Soc. for Photog. Edn. (chair regional conf. 1992), Coll. Art Assn., N.W. Comms. Assn. Office: Evergreen State Coll L 1302 Olympia WA 98505

DAVIS, WANDA ROSE, lawyer; b. Lampasas, Tex., Oct. 4, 1937; d. Ellis DeWitt and Julia Doris (Rose) Cockrell; m. Richard Andrew Fulcher, May 9, 1959 (div. 1969); 1 child, Greg Ellis; m. Edwin Leon Davis, Jan. 14, 1973 (div. 1985). BBA, U. Tex., 1959, JD, 1971. Bar: Tex. 1971, Colo. 1981, U.S. Dist. Ct. (no. dist.) Tex. 1972, U.S. Dist. Ct. Colo. 1981, U.S. Ct. Appeals (10th cir. 1981, U.S. Supreme Ct. 1976. Atty. Atlantic Richfield Co., Dallas, 1971; assoc. firm Crocker & Murphy, Dallas, 1971-72; prin. Wanda Davis, Atty. at Law, Dallas, 1972-73; ptnr. firm Davis & Davis Inc., Dallas, 1973-75; atty. adviser HUD, Dallas, 1974-75, Air Force Acctg. and Fin. Ctr., Denver, 1976-92; co-chmn. regional Profl. Devel. Inst., Am. Soc. Mil. Comptrollers, Colorado Springs, Colo., 1982; chmn. Lowry AFB Noontime Edn. Program, Exercise Program, Denver, 1977-83; mem. speakers bur. Colo. Women's Bar, 1995—, Lowry AFB, 1981-83; mem. fed. ct. liaison com. U.S. Dist. Ct. Colo., 1983; mem. Leaders of the Fed. Bar Assn. People to People Del. to China, USSR and Finland, 1986. Contbr. numerous articles to profl. jours. Bd. dirs. Pres.'s Coun. Met. Denver, 1981-83; mem. Lowry AFB Alcohol Abuse Exec. Com., 1981-84. Recipient Spl. Achievement award USAF, 1978; Upward Mobility award Fed. Profl. and Adminstrv. Women, Denver, 1979, Internat. Humanitarian award CARE, 1994. Mem. Fed. Bar Assn. (pres. Colo. 1982-83, mem. nat. coun. 1984—, Earl W. Kintner Disting. Svc. award 1983, 1st v.p. 10th cir. 1986—, Internat. Humanitarian award CARE, 1994), Zach Found. for Burned Children (award 1995), Colo. Trial Lawyers Assn., Bus. and Profl. Women's Club (dist. IV East dir. 1983-84, Colo. pres. 1988-89), Am. Soc. Mil. Comptrollers (pres. 1984-85), Denver South Met. Bus. and Profl. Women's Club (pres. 1982-83), Denver Silver Spruce Am. Bus. Women's Assn. (pres. 1981-82; Woman of Yr. award 1982), Colo. Jud. Inst., Colo. Concerned Lawyers, Profl. Mgrs. Assn., Fed. Women's Program (v.p. Denver 1980), Colo. Woman News Community adv. bd., 1988—, Dallas Bar Assn., Tex. Bar Assn., Denver Bar Assn., Altrusa, Zonta, Denver Nancy Langhorn Federally Employed Women. (pres. 1979-80). Christian.

DAVISON, HELEN IRENE, secondary education educator, counselor; b. Oskaloosa, Iowa, Dec. 19, 1926; d. Grover C. and Beulah (Williams) Hawk; m. Walter Francis Davison, June 20, 1953 (div.); 1 child, Linda Ellen. BS in Zoology, Iowa State U., 1948; MS in Biol. Sci., U. Chgo., 1951; MA in Ednl. Psychology and Counseling, Calif. State U., Northridge, 1985. Med. rsch. technician U. Chgo. Med. Sch., 1951-53; tchr. sci. Lane High Sch., Charlottesville, Va., 1953-55; med. rsch. asst. U. Va. Med. Sch., Charlottesville, 1955-56, U. Mich., Ann Arbor, 1956-60; tchr. sci. Monroe High Sch., Sepulveda, Calif., 1966—, chmn. sci. dept., 1990-91, sch. site coun., 1993-94; rsch. technician Los Alamos Sci. Labs., summer 1954; part-time counselor psychotherapy Forte Found., Encino, Calif., 1987-92, Tarzana, Calif., 1993—; mem. site coun. Monroe H.S., 1993-94. V.p. San Fernando Valley chpt. Am. Field Svc., 1980-81; vol. counselor Planned Parenthood Am., L.A., 1982-88. NSF fellow, 1985-86. Mem. Calif. Tchrs. Assn., Calif. Assn. Marriage and Family Therapists, Iowa Acad. Sci. (assoc.), AAUW. Home: 17425 Vintage St Northridge CA 91325-1538 Office: James Monroe High Sch 9229 Haskell Ave Sepulveda CA 91343-3114

DAVISON, JEAN DAVIS, anthropologist; b. Upland, Calif., Mar. 8, 1937; d. Madison Thenton and Elizabeth Virginia (Reynolds) Davis; m. William VanDyke Glascock, Sept. 6, 1959 (div. June 1976); children: Stephen L., William R., Ann. BA in Internat. Rels., Scripps Coll., 1959; MA in Edn., St. Mary's Coll., Moraga, Calif., 1980; MA in Anthropology, Stanford U., 1983, PhD in Internat. Devel. Edn., 1985. Std. teaching credential life. Multi-ethnic curriculum coord. Kentfield (Calif.) Sch. Dist., 1968-70; secondary sch. tchr. Tamalpais Union H.S., Larkspur, Calif., 1972-81; founder, 1st dir. Internat. Devel. Edn. Assn., San Anselmo, Calif., 1986-89; coord. MA program, sr. lectr. U. Malawi, Zomba, South Africa, 1989-92; vis. scholar Inst. for Rsch. on Women and Gender, Stanford U., 1992-93; rsch. dir. Ethiopia Edn. Demand Study Acad. Edn. Devel., Washington, 1993—; mem. adv. bd. Aid to Families with Dependent Children, Marin County, Calif., 1967-69; bd. mem. Soc. Internat. Devel., San Francisco, 1988-89, 92-94; mem. Marin County Grand Jury, 1995; prin. rschr. projects U.S. AID, World Bank, Harvard, Washington, Cambridge, Mass., Acad. for Ednl. Devel., UN World Food Program, 1990—. Editor: Agriculture, Woman and Land, 1988; author: Voices From Mutira: Lives of Rural Gikuyu Women, 1989. Mem. Human Rights Commn. County of Marin, San Rafael, 1966-67; co-chair Forum for Internat. Devel. Orgns., San Francisco, 1988-89. NSF grantee, Washington, 1980, rsch. grantee Stanford Internat. Ctr./Hewlett Found., Palo Alto, Calif., 1983. Mem. Internat. Devel. Edn. Assn. (pres. 1986, treas. 1992, award 1989), Am. Anthropol. Soc., African Studies Assn., Comparative and Internat. Edn. Soc. (award 1993), Internat. Diplomacy Coun., LWV (v.p. Ctrl. Marin County 1968-70, bd. dirs. 1966-70). Home: 120 Woodland Ave San Anselmo CA 94960-2732 Office: Internat Devel & Edn Assn 120 Woodland Ave Ste 2 San Anselmo CA 94960-2732

DAWDY, DORIS OSTRANDER, writer; d. Archie and Lydia (Matz) Ostrander; m. David R. Dawdy, Feb. 21, 1951; 1 child, Barbara Dahl. Student music, MacPhail Sch. Music, Mpls. cons. in field of writing. Composer: I Keep Telling Myself, 1947; author: Artists of the American West, vols. I, II, III, reprinted 1987, Congress in its Wisdom: The Bureau of Reclamation and the Public Interest, 1989, George Montague Wheeler: The Man and the Myth, 1993; editor: A Voice in Her Tribe, 1980, 3d edit. 1984, The Wyant Diary/An Artist with the Wheeler Survey, 1980, others. Mem. Western History Assn., The Westerners, Mus. Soc. San Francisco.

DAWDY, FAYE MARIE CATANIA, photographer, lecturer; b. San Mateo, Calif., Sept. 15, 1954; d. Frank Benjamin and Melba Rita (Arata) Catania; m. John Thomas Dawdy, May 5, 1974; children: Tracy Marie, John Franco. AA, Coll. of San Mateo, 1979; student, San Francisco State U., 1979—. With Proctor & Gamble Distbg. Co., San Mateo, 1973-78; ptnr. Dawdy Photography, Millbrae, Calif., 1978—; dir., sec.-treas. Millbrae Stamp Co., 1980—; instr. Winona Sch. Profl. Photography, Mt. Prospect, Ill.; lectr. to high schs., various clubs, photography convs. including Goteborg, Sweden, Idaho, Oreg., Colo., Tex., Ill., Fla., Mo., Kans., Nev., Iowa, N.J. Contbr. articles to profl. jours. Area chmn. Millbrae Am. Heart Assn. Ann. Fund Dr., 1977-82; mem. fund raising and nutrition coms. San Mateo County chpt. Am. Heart Assn., 1980-88; co-chmn. Miss Millbrae Pageant, 1981, Queen Isabella Columbus Day Festival, 1981; judge arts and crafts exhbns. Millbrae Art and Wine Festival; judge photography competition Marin County Fair Photography Exhibit; vol. photographer Rotoplast, La Serena, Chile, 1994; mem. sister city com. City of Millbrae; trustee Golden Gate Sch. Profl. Photographers, 1985-90. Recipient awards No. Calif. Coun. Camera Clubs, 1979, 81, Mktg. Contest award Mktg. Today mag., 1988. Mem. Profl. Photographers Am. (photog. craftsman degree), Profl. Photographers Greater Bay Area, Profl. Photographers No. Calif., Profl. Photographers Calif., Wedding Photographers Assn., NAFE, Millbrae C. of C. (sec. women's div. 1979, bd. dirs. 1991), Millbrae Art Assn. (pres. 1979-80), Portola Camera Club (nature chmn. 1978—), Millbrae Hist. Assn., Friends Millbrae Libr., Italian Cath. Fedn., Calif. Women in Profl. Photography, Fedn. Ind. Bus., St. Dunstan Women's Club, Soroptimist (sec. 1981-82). Democrat. Roman Catholic. Office: 449 Broadway Millbrae CA 94030-1905

DAWES, DOUGLAS CHARLES, retired military officer; b. Detroit, Nov. 24, 1952; s. Carl Joseph and Margaret Elisabeth (Ingalls) D.; m. Belle Ann Black, May 22, 1978 (div. Feb. 1986); m. Theresa Neel, June 9, 1990. BBA in Mgmt., Loyola U., New Orleans, 1974; grad. with honors, Command and Gen. Staff Coll., 1987; MA in Procurement and Acquisition Mgmt., Webster U., St. Louis, 1990. Field artillery officer U.S. Army, various locations, 1974-80; asst. fin. officer U.S. Army, Ft. Sill, Okla., 1980-82; deputy fin. and acctg. officer U.S. Army, Fed. Republic of Germany, 1982-86, Ft. Carson, Colo., 1986-87; comdr. and fin. officer U.S. Army, Ft. Carson, 1987-88, budget officer, asst. div. comptr., 1988-90, div. comptr., 1990-91; chief joint pay operation Joint Svc. Software, Def. Fin. and Acctg. Svc., Denver, 1991-94; ret., 1994; payroll analyst Neo Data Svcs., Inc., Louisville, Colo., 1995—. Vol., water safety instr. trainer ARC. Mem. Disabled Am. Vets. (life), Delta Sigma Pi (life, chancellor Delta Nu chpt. 1973, 1st v.p. 1974). Republican. Home: 17523 E Caspian Pl Aurora CO 80013-4172

DAWES, WALLACE ERNEST, paper specialist, small business owner; b. Grafton, Mass., Oct. 9, 1927; s. Wallace and Marion (Storey) D.; m. Marie (Furillo) Dawes, 1950 (div. Oct. 1970); children: Jane, Nancy; m. RoseMarie (Fusillo) Dawes, June 15, 1972. BA, CUNY (Bklyn. Coll.). Salesman F.W. Anderson Co., N.Y.C., 1952-59, Blake, Moffitt & Towne, L.A., 1973-75, Kirk Paper, L.A., 1975-77, Andrews/Nelson/Whitehead, N.Y.C., 1960-72; tech. mgr., product mgr. Paper Mill & Paper Source, L.A., 1977—; tchr., presenter numerous seminars on history, making and conservation of paper; guest lectr. Columbia U., N.Y.C., NYU, N.Y.C., Paper Historians Conf., Fabriano, Italy, 1976, UCLA, 1980, Internat. Conf. on Paper for Arts, Kyoto, Japan, 1983; instr. on paper Printing Industries Assn.; tchr., presenter papermaking workshop Internat. Conf. for Calligraphy, Claremont, Calif., 1985. Lt. USNR. Recipient award Printing Craftsmens Assn., 1993. Mem. Am. Inst. for Conservation, Western Assn. Art Conservation, Soc. for Calligraphy, Internat. Printing Mus., Printing House Craftman Assn. Home: 2349 Vestal Ave Los Angeles CA 90026

DAWRANT, STACEY BETH, dietitian; b. Elmhurst, Ill., June 9, 1968; d. Stanley Robert and Carole Susan (Prochazka) Rachesky; m. Andrew Charles Dawrant, July 5, 1991. BS, U. Ill., 1990; MS in Nutritional Sci., Hampton U., 1993; registered dietitian, Med. Coll. Va., 1994. Registered dietitian; cert. in food sanitation, Ill. Nutritional specialist Nutri Sys., Hampton, Va., 1991-93; cardiac dietitian U. Ill., Chgo., 1994; pvt. practice cons. dietitian Denver, 1994—; med. sales rep. Penny Saver Med. Supply, Denver, 1994—; sales rep. Stan's Frozen Foods, Inc., 1995—. Contbr. articles to profl. jours. Mem. Am. Dietetic Assn., Am. Diabetes Assn., N.Am. Assn. for the Study Obesity, Wellness Coun. Am. Home: 4431 S Independence Trail Evergreen CO 80439 Office: 12445 E 39th # 314 Denver CO 80239

DAWSON, FRANCES EMILY, poet, nurse; b. Augsburg, Germany, Dec. 7, 1952; d. Emmett C. Jr. and B. Louise (Boddie) D. BS in Nursing, Pa. State U., 1974. RN, D.C. Staff nurse Howard U. Med. Ctr., Washington, 1974-75, charge nurse, 1975-77. Author: Live for Today, 1986, With You in Mind, 1987, Reflections, 1988, (poetry cassette rec.) Soul Connection, 1992. Active Disabled Resource Ctr., Lupus Found. Am., Calif. Assn. Physically Handicapped; model Operation Confidence Program for the Disabled, 1985-86, head cheerleader drill team, 1985-86; mem. Long Beach Task Force for the Ams. with Disabilities Act, 1994—; active Christ 2d Baptist Ch., 1985—. Recipient Golden Poetry award, 1985-92, excellence in lit. award Pinewood Poetry, 1987-89. Mem. BMI, Walt Whitman Guild, Internat. Soc. Poets (hon. charter), Pa. State U. Alumni Assn., Detroit Black Poets Guild. Democrat. Baptist.

DAWSON, GILBERT EDWARD, II, systems engineer; b. New Orleans, July 15, 1945; s. Gilbert Edward and Helen Mabel (Fisher) D. BA, Rice U., 1968; MS in Computer Sci., U. So. Calif., 1973. Sr. systems analyst Telos Computing, Santa Monica, Calif., 1974-78, mktg. mgr., 1978-80; cognizant design engr. Jet Propulsion Lab., Pasadena, Calif., 1980-85; telemetry systems supr. Jet Propulsion Lab., Pasadena, 1985-87, sr. systems engr., 1987—. Sec. Great Am. Yankee Freedom Band, West Hollywood, Calif., 1980. Capt. USAF, 1968-72. Democrat. Home: 3828 Toland Way Los Angeles CA 90065-3644 Office: Jet Propulsion Lab 4800 Oak Grove Dr Pasadena CA 91109-8001

DAWSON, JOHN ALAN, artist; b. Joliet, Ill., Sept. 12, 1946; s. Thomas Allan and Margaret C. (McRoberts) D.; m. Linda Kay Williams, June 2, 1947 (div. 1989); m. Shirley Ann Bader, Mar. 1993. BFA, No. Ill. U., 1969; MFA, Ariz. State U., 1973. works in permanent collections at Western N.Mex. U., Ariz. State U., El Paso Mus. Art, Phoenix Art Mus., Scottsdale Ctr. for the Arts, Okla. Art Ctr., Ark. Art Center, Little Rock, U. P.R., Sheldon Meml. Art Gallery, Lincoln, Nebr., Ulrich Mus. Art, Wichita, Kans., Tucson Mus. Art, others. One man shows at Meml. Union Gallery, Tempe, Ariz., 1973, Del Mar Coll., 1974, Elaine Horwitch Gallery, Scottsdale, 1975, 76, 78, 80, 82, 84, Segal Gallery, N.Y.C., 1986, Ratliff-Williams Gallery, Sedona, Ariz., 1989, 91, 92, Benjamin Mangel Gallery, Phila., 1982, 85, 90, C.G. Rein Gallery, Santa Fe. 1988, 89, 90, many others; group shows include McCray Gallery, N.Mex., 1974, Phoenix Art Mus., 1975, Huntsville (Ala.) Mus. Art, 1981, Fine Arts Ctr. Tempe, 1984, others. Democrat. Home and Office: 10246 E Brown Rd Mesa AZ 85207-4516

DAWSON, LELAND BRADLEY, dentist; b. Princeton, Ill., Jan. 30, 1950; s. Harold Bradley and Frances Emilia (Strandholm) D.; m. Debra Hjort. BA, Pacific Luth. U., 1972; DDS, U. Ill., Chgo., 1976. Dentist Group Health Dental, Burien, Wash., 1976-78; pvt. practice dentistry Kent, Wash., 1978—; clin. instr. dental asst. program Highline Community Coll., Kent, 1978-85. Deacon Kent Covenant Ch., 1983-94. Mem. ADA, Pacific Luth. U. Alumni Assn., Seattle-King County Dental Soc., Q Club of Pacific Luth. U. Mem. Evang. Covenant. Home: 14224 SE 270th Pl Kent WA 98042-8001 Office: 13210 SE 240th St Ste 1B Kent WA 98042-5182

DAWSON, ROBERT CHARLES, educational and health care consultant; b. Washington, July 22, 1943; m. Ande Kormanyos, Dec. 31, 1966; children: Ange Marie Brickman, Robert Charles Jr. BS in Law Enforcement Adminstrn., Fla. State U., 1965, PhD in Adminstrn. of Higher Edn., 1975; MEd in Ednl. Adminstrn., Fla. Atlantic U., 1966. Program dir. J. Wayne Reitz Union U. Fla., Gainesville, 1967-70; dean. student activities Western Carolina U., Cullowhee, N.C., 1970-73; dir. Leisure Program Office, asst. prof. higher edn. Fla. State U., Tallahassee, 1973-76; dean of students, dir. aux. svcs. U. Ctrl. Ark., Conway, 1976-80; exec. asst. to pres. Slippery Rock (Pa.) U., 1980-84, exec. asst. to pres. univ. rels., 1984-85, exec. dir. univ. advancement, Slippery Rock Found., Inc., 1985-90; v.p. devel. and instl. advancement Eastern N.Mex. U., Portales, 1990-91; prin. R. C. Dawson and Assocs., Portales, 1991—; cons. ednl. and health care philanthropy Sr. Counsel, Hosp. Devel., Inc., Bozeman, Mont.; instr. U. South Fla., Tampa, 1966, Western Carolina U., Cullowhee, 1970-73, Nova U., Fort Lauderdale, Fla., 1975-76, U. Ctrl. Ark., Conway, 1976-80, Clovis (N.Mex.) C.C., 1992. Editor: Skylines, 1986-91. Mem. task force on founds., mem. legis. finance com. N.Mex. Legislature, 1990; active Curry County Maternal and Child Health Coun., N.Mex., 1992. Mem. Coun. Advancement and Support of Edn., Nat. Soc. Fund Raising Execs., Nat. Assn. Student Pers. Adminstrs., Am. Coll. Pers. Assn., Am. Assn. Higher Edn., MENSA Internat., Omicron Delta Kappa, Phi Delta Kappa. Home: PO Box 15421 Winston Salem NC 27113-0421 Office: Hosp Devel Inc 17 W Kagy Blvd Bozeman MT 59715-6052

DAY, ANTHONY, newspaper correspondent; b. Miami, Fla., May 12, 1933; s. Price and Alice (Alexander) D.; m. Lynn Ward, June 25, 1960; children—John, Julia (dec.). A.B. cum laude, Harvard U., 1955, postgrad. (Nieman fellow), 1966-67; L.H.D. (hon.), Pepperdine U., 1974. Reporter Phila. Bull., 1957-60, Washington, 1960-69; chief Washington bur. Phila. Bull., 1969; chief editorial writer L.A. Times, 1969-71, editor editorial pages, 1971-89, sr. corr., 1989—. Mem. nat. coun. Met. Opera. Served with AUS, 1955-57. Mem. Am. Soc. Newspaper Editors, Signet Soc. Harvard, Asia Soc., Inter Am. Press Assn., Coun. Fgn. Rels. Office: Los Angeles Times Times Mirror Sq Los Angeles CA 90012-3816

DAY, GERALD W., wholesale grocery company executive. With Albertson's, Heber City, Utah, 1945-72; operator Days Markets, from 1972; now chmn., bd. dirs. Associated Food Stores Inc. Office: Associated Food Stores Inc Box 30430 1812 Empire Rd Salt Lake City UT 84104-3809

DAY, JANICE ELDREDGE, cosmetic company executive; b. New Bedford, Mass., Sept. 26, 1919; d. Wendell Tripp and Lucy Forbush (Houghton) Eldredge; m. Frank Perrett, Apr. 22, 1949; 1 child, Janna. BA in English, Middlebury Coll., 1941, LittD (hon.), 1990. Publicity writer A.H. Handley, Boston, 1941-42; sec. media Ladies Home Jour., Boston, 1942-45, McCann, Erickson, N.Y.C., 1945; sec. Cambridge U. Press, MacMillan Co., N.Y.C., 1945-46; exec. sec. Fort Monroe, Va., 1946-47, Stone & Webster Engring., 1947-49; mgr. sales Collier Co., San Francisco, 1947-48; unit mgr. Stanley Home Products, L.A., 1949-51; dist. sales mgr. Beauty Creators Cosmetics, L.A., 1951-56; co-founder, v.p. sales and mktg. Jafra Cosmetics, Inc., Malibu, Calif., 1956-76, chmn. bd., 1976-87, pres. Jan and Frank Day Scholarship Fund, 1978. Recipient Alumni Achievement award Middlebury Coll., 1983. Mem. Direct Selling Assn. (dir.), DAR. Republican. Episcopalian. Office: Jafra Cosmetics Inc Westlake Village CA 91361

DAY, JOHN DENTON, retired company executive, cattle and horse rancher, trainer, wrangler, actor; b. Salt Lake City, Jan. 20, 1942; s. George W. and Grace (Denton) Jenkins; m. Susan Hansen, June 20, 1971; children: Tammy Denton Wadsworth, Jeanett B. Lloyd. Student, U. Utah, 1964-65; BA in Econs. and Bus. Adminstrn. with high honors, Westminster Coll., 1971. Riding instr., wrangler Uinta wilderness area U-Ranch, Neola, Utah, 1955-58; stock handler, driver, ruffstock rider Earl Hutchinson Rodeo Contractor, Idaho, 1959; wrangler, riding instr. YMCA Camp Rodger, Kamas, Utah; with Mil. Data Cons., Inc., L.A., 1961-62, Carlseon Credit Corp., Salt Lake City, 1962-65; sales mgr. sporting goods Western Enterprises, Salt Lake City, 1965-69; founder Rockin d Ranch, Millcreek, Utah, 1969; Western rep. PBR Co., Cleve., 1969-71; dist. sales rep. Crown Zellerbach Corp., Seattle and L.A., 1971-73; pres., founder Dapco paper, chem., instl. food and janitorial supplies, Salt Lake City, 1973-79, John D Day Greeting Cards, 1990—; owner, founder, pres. John D. Day, mfrs. reps., 1972—; dist. sales mgr. Surfonics Engrs., Inc., Woods Cross, Utah, 1976-78, Garland Co., Cleve., 1978-81; rancher Heber, Utah, 1976-90, horse tng. facility and ranch, Temecula, Calif., 1984-90, St. George, Utah, 1989—; sec. bd. Acquadyne, 1974, 75. Contbr. articles to jours. Group chmn. Tele-Dex fund raising project Westminster Coll.; vol. Dixie Nat. Forest, 1989-94, USDA Forest Svc.; U.S. wilderness ranger USDA, US Forest Svc., Dixie Nat. Forest, Pine Valley Ranger Dist., Pine Valley Mountain Wilderness, So. Utah, 1994—. With AUS, 1963-64. Recipient grand nat. award Internat. Custom Car Show, San Diego, 1962, Key to City, Louisville, 1964, Champion Bareback Riding award, 1957, Vol. award USDA Forest Svc., 1991, 92, 93; Dally team roping heading and heeling champion, 1982. Mem. Internat. Show Car Assn. (co-chmn. 1978-79), Am. Quarter Horse Assn. (high point reining champion 1981, qualified for world championship, Dodge, Toyota Fall Futurite Circuit Champion Working Cowhorse 1994, World Championship Show qualifier and participant Oklahoma City Sr. Cutting 1994), Intermountain Quarter Horse Assn. (sr. reining champion 1981, champion AMAT reining 1979-81), Utah Quarter Horse Assn. (champion AMAT reining 1979, 80, AMAT barrel racing 1980, working cowhorse champion 1982, trained working cowhorse and rider champion 1992, open cutting res. champion 1993, 94, open cutting champion 1994, Menlove Dodge Toyota Fall Futurity circuit champion working cowhorse, 1994, bd. dirs. 1992-94), Profl. Cowhorseman's Assn. (world champion team roping, heeling 1986, 88, high point rider 1985, world champion stock horse rider 1985-86, 88, world champion working cowhorse 1985, PCA finals open cutting champion, 1985-88, PCA finals 1500 novice champion 1987, PCA finals all-around champion 1985-88, inducted into Hall of Fame 1988, first on record registered Tex. longhorn cutting contest, open champion, PCA founder, editor newsletter 1985-89, pres. 1984-88), World Rodeo Assn. Profls. (v.p. Western territory 1989—). Home and Office: PO Box 55 Saint George UT 84771-0055 also: 1876 E 2450 S Daylark Ln Saint George UT 84771

DAY, JOHN FRANCIS, city official, former savings and loan executive, former mayor; b. Cleve., Mar. 14, 1920; s. Frank S. and Susan Josephine (O'Brien) D.; m. Gertrude Jane Schmitt, Dec. 29, 1941 (dec.); children: Susan, Mary, Timothy, Gertrude, Kathryn, Patrick, Fanchon, Josephine; m. Charlene Ann Thee, Nov. 8, 1986. Ed., Western Res. U., Staunton (Va.) Mil. Acad. Formerly with Cosgrove & Co., Seaboard Fin.; former v.p. Calif. Fed. Savs. & Loan, Los Angeles; mayor Glendale, Calif., 1981-82, mem. city council, 1977-89. Mem. Small Wilderness Area Preservation. Served with AUS, 1941-45. Decorated knight Equestrian Order of Holy Sepulchre of Jerusalem. Mem. Am. Legion. Democrat. Roman Catholic. Club: K.C. Home: 1200 Imperial Dr Glendale CA 91207-1526 Office: 613 E Broadway St Glendale CA 91206-4308

DAY, JOSEPH DENNIS, librarian; b. Dayton, Ohio, Sept. 23, 1942; s. John Albert and Ruth (Pearson) D.; m. Mary Louise Herbert, Oct. 10, 1964; children: Cindy, Jeff, Chris, Steve, Tom. B.A., U. Dayton, 1966; M.L.S., Western Mich. U., 1967; degree in Libr. Mgmt., U. Miami, 1975. Community libr. Dayton-Montgomery Pub. Libr., 1967-70; dir. Troy-Miami County Pub. Libr., Troy, Ohio, 1970-76, Salt Lake City Pub. Libr., 1976—; chmn. Miami Valley Library Orgn., 1971-73; pres. Ohio Library Assn., 1975-76; project dir. planning and constrn. first solar powered library in world, 1973-76; exec. devel. program Miami, Ohio, libr., 1975. Pres. Troy Area Arts Coun., 1973-74; v.p. SLC Salvation Army Bd., 1986-91. Recipient Disting. Community Service award Troy C. of C., 1974; John Cotton Dana award, 1975, 77, 83, 85; AIA-ALA architecture award, 1977. Mem. ALA (chmn. intellectual freedom com. 1981-84, exec. bd. 1987-93, rep. to Internat. Fedn. Libr. Assn. 1989—), ASPA, Utah Libr. Assn. (pres. 1979-80, Disting. Svc. award 1985), Mountain Plains Libr. Assn. (pres. 1990-91, Disting. Svc. award 1993), Kiwanis Club (pres. Troy 1975-76, Disting. Svc. award Troy 1973, pres. Salt Lake-Foothil 79-80), Snowbird Leadership Dustinte (exec. dir. 1991—). Address: Salt Lake City Pub Libr 209 E 5th S Salt Lake City UT 84111-3203

DAY, KEVIN ROSS, pomologist, researcher, consultant, farmer; b. Dinuba, Calif., Aug. 2, 1960; s. Ronald Keith and Dolores Ione (Unruh) D. AA, Reedley (Calif.) Coll., 1980; BS magna cum laude, Calif. State U., Fresno, 1983, MS with honors, 1985. Cert. tchr., Calif. Lectr. Calif. State U., Fresno, 1984-85; postgrad. rschr. U. Calif., Davis, 1985-88, rsch. assoc., 1988-91; farm advisor U. Calif., Berkeley, 1991—; mng. ptnr. Day Orchards, Dinuba, 1981—; cons. K.R. Day Hort. Cons., Dinuba, 1988—. Editor, author newsletter Orchard Notes, 1991—; contbr. chpt. to book, articles to profl. jours. Announcer Dinuba High Sch. Football and Baseball, 1988—. Calif. Agrl. Tech. Inst. fellow, 1984. Mem. Am. Soc. for Hort. Sci., Am. Pomological Soc., Dinuba Lions Club (bd. dirs. 1992—, sec. 1993—), Phi Kappa Phi. Republican. Presbyterian. Home: 41139 Road 70 Dinuba CA 93618-9702 Office: U Calf Agrl Bldg Ag Bldg County Civic Ctr Visalia CA 93291-4584

DAY, L. B., management consultant; b. Walla Walla, Wash., Sept. 16, 1944; s. Frank Edmond and Geraldine Eloise (Binning) D. BS, Portland State Coll., 1966; MBA, George Washington U., 1971. Design mktg. cons. Leadership Resources Inc., Washington, 1971-76; faculty mem. USDA Grad. Sch. of Spl. Programs, Washington, 1971-76; mgr. Office of Employee Devel. Oreg. Dept. Transp., Salem, 1972-75; prin. Day-Henry Assoc. Inc., Portland, Oreg., 1975-78, Day-Floren Assocs. Inc., Portland, Oreg., 1978—; cons. Allergan (U.S., Italy), Am. Bankers Assn., Arthur Andersen & Co., AMD, John Fluke Mfg. Co. (U.S. and Holland), Intel Corp. (U.S., Eng., France, Malaysia, P.R.), Sequent Computer Systems, Inc., Vitesse Semiconductor, Sun Microsystems, VLSI Tech., Inc., U.S. Nat. Bank Oreg., U.S. Army Corps Engrs., others; faculty Am. Bankers Assn., Bank Trainers Sch., 1981-84, Grad. Personnel Sch., 1982; adj. prof. Willamette U. Grad. Sch. Adminstrn., Salem, 1978; mem. bd. dirs. Microchip Tech., Inc. Author: The Supervisory Training Program, 1977, Performance Management, 1981, Team-Oriented Management, 1989; contbr. articles to profl. jours. With U.S. Army, 1967-70. Scottish Rite fellow George Washington U., 1970. Mem. Am. Soc. Tng. and Devel. (chmn. Transp. Spl. Interest Group 1977, cert. of appreciation). Office: Day-Floren Assocs Inc 806 SW Broadway Fl 11 Portland OR 97205-3333

DAY, LUCILLE ELIZABETH, health facility administrator, educator, author; b. Oakland, Calif., Dec. 5, 1947; d. Richard Allen and Evelyn Marietta (Hazard) Lang; m. Frank Lawrence Day, Nov. 6, 1965; 1 child, Liana Sherrine; m. 2nd, Theodore Herman Fleischman, June 23, 1974; 1 child, Tamarind Channah. AB, U. Calif., Berkeley, 1971, MA, 1973, PhD, 1979. Teaching asst. U. Calif., Berkeley, 1971-72, 75-76, research asst., 1975, 77-78; tchr. sci. Magic Mountain Sch., Berkeley, 1977; specialist math. and sci. Novato (Calif.) Unified Sch. Dist., 1979-81; instr. sci. Project Bridge, Laney Coll., Oakland, Calif., 1984-86; sci. writer and mgr. precollege edn. programs, Lawrence Berkeley (Calif.) Lab., 1986-90, life scis. staff coord., 1990-92; mgr. Hall of Health, Berkeley, Calif., 1992—. Author numerous poems, articles and book reviews; author: (with Joan Skolnick and Carol Langbort) How to Encourage Girls in Math and Science: Strategies for Parents and Educators, 1982; Self-Portrait with Hand Microscope (poetry collection), 1982. NSF Grad. fellow, 1972-75; recipient Joseph Henry Jackson award in lit. San Francisco Found., 1982. Mem. AAAS, No. Calif. Sci. Writers Assn., Nat. Assn. Sci. Writers, Math/Sci. Network, Phi Beta Kappa, Iota Sigma Pi. Home: 1057 Walker Ave Oakland CA 94610-1511 Office: Hall of Health 2230 Shattuck Ave Berkeley CA 94704-1424

DAY, PIETRINA ANN, therapist; b. Milw., Oct. 29, 1943; d. Peter Bernard and Bernadina (Campanelli) Sara; m. Steven Homer Day, Sept. 13, 1971 (div. Feb. 1983); 1 child, Sara Lynn Hunt; m. Barry Carr Sanborn, Feb. 14, 1987. BS, Nat. U., 1983, M of Counseling Psychology, 1984. Intern Vol. of Am., San Diego, 1984, Dr. Anne Evans, San Diego, 1984-89; alcoholism specialist The Landing Zone Alcohol Recovery Ctr., San Diego, 1985-88; pvt. practice marriage and family therapy San Diego, 1989—. Mem. Calif. Assn. Marriage and Family Therapists, Nat. U. Alumni Assn. (life), Vietnam Vets. of S.D. (assoc., appreciation award 1988). Democrat. Roman Catholic. Office: 4024 Ibis St Apt B San Diego CA 92103-1840

DAY, RICHARD ELLEDGE, newspaper editor; b. Denver, June 27, 1939; s. Bartle Henry and Clara Violet (Smith) D.; student Mesa Jr. Coll., 1958-60; BA, Western State Coll. Colo., 1962. Reporter, Rock Springs (Wyo.) Daily Rocket and Sunday Miner, 1962-64, Casper (Wyo.) Star-Tribune, 1964-66; reporter Montrose (Colo.) Daily Press., 1967-68, mng. editor, 1968—. Mem. accountability adv. com. Montrose County Sch. Dist.; Rep. precinct committeeman, Montrose, 1968-90; mem. exec. com. Montrose County Rep. party; bd. dirs. Montrose County United Fund, 1972, Western Slope Tb and Respiratory Disease Assn., 1968-73; trustee Colo. Western Coll., 1971-72. Mem. Nat. Press Photographers Assn., AP Mng. Editors Assn., Montrose County C. of C., Sigma Delta Chi. Mem. Christian Ch. Club: Denver Press. Lodges: Masons, Elks, Kiwanis. Home: PO Box 957 844 N 5th St Montrose CO 81401-3206 Office: PO Box 850 535 S 1st St Montrose CO 81401-3910

DAY, RICHARD SOMERS, author, editorial consultant; b. Chgo., June 14, 1928; s. Milo Frank and Ethel Mae (Somers) D.; m. Lois Patricia Beggs, July 8, 1950; children: Russell Frank, Douglas Matthew, Gail Leslie. Student, Ill. Inst. Tech., 1946, U. Miami, 1947. Promotion writer, editor Portland Cement Assn., Chgo., 1958-62, promotion writer, 1963-66; editor Am. Inst. Laundering, Joliet, Ill., 1962-63; freelance writer, Monee, Ill., 1966-69, Palomar Mountain, Calif., 1969-87; cons. editor home and shop Popular Sci. mag., N.Y.C., 1966-89; editorial cons. St. Remy Press, Montreal, Que., Can., 1987—; pres., exec. producer Vi-Day-O Prodns., Inc., Palomar Mountain, Calif., 1991—. Author numerous home improvement & repair books including: Patios and Decks, 1976, Automechanics, 1982, Do-It-Yourself Plumbing--It's Easy with Genova, 1987, Building Decks, Patios, and Fences, 1992 (Nat. Assn. Home and Workshop Writers Stanley Tools Do-It-Yourself Writing award 1992); editor: (newspaper) Powderlines, 1958; (mag.) Concrete Hwys. and Pub. Improvements, 1958-62; (mag.) Soil-Cement News, 1960-62; (mag.) Fabric Care, 1962-63; prodr. videos: How to Cure Toilet Troubles, 1994, Mountain Man Horse Packing, 1994; contbr. chpts. to books. Bd. dirs. Palomar Mountain Planning Orgn., 1984-91. Mem. Nat. Assn. Home and Workshop Writers (mng. editor newsletter 1982—, bd. dirs. 1974—, pres. 1984-85). Home: PO Box 10 Palomar Mountain CA 92060-0010

DAY, ROBERT WINSOR, cancer research administrator; b. Framingham, Mass., Oct. 22, 1930; s. Raymond Albert and Mildred (Doty) D.; m. Jane Alice Boynton, Sept. 6, 1957 (div. Sept. 1977); m. Cynthia Taylor, Dec. 16, 1977; children: Christopher, Nathalia. Student, Harvard U., 1949-51; MD, U. Chgo., 1956; MPH, U. Calif., Berkeley, 1958, PhD, 1962. Intern USPHS, Balt., 1956-57; resident U. Calif., Berkeley, 1958-60; research specialist Calif. Dept. Mental Hygiene, 1960-64; asst. prof. sch. medicine UCLA, 1962-64; dep. dir. Calif. Dept. Pub. Health, Berkeley, 1965-67; prof., chmn. dept. health services Sch. Pub. Health and Community Medicine, U. Wash., Seattle, 1968-72, dean, 1972-82, prof., 1982—; dir. Fred Hutchinson Cancer Rsch. Ctr., Seattle, 1981-91, pres., 1991—; mem. Nat. Cancer Adv. Bd., 1992—; cons. in field. Pres. Seattle Planned Parenthood Ctr., 1970-72. Served with USPHS, 1956-57. Fellow Am. Pub. Health Assn., Am. Coll. Preventive Medicine; mem. Am. Soc. Clin. Oncology, Soc. Preventive Oncology, Assn. Schs. Pub. Health (pres. 1981-82), Am. Assn. Cancer Insts. (bd. dirs. 1983-88, v.p. 1984-85, pres. 1985-86, chmn. bd. dirs., 1986-87). Office: Fred Hutchinson Cancer Rsch Ctr LY-301 1124 Columbia St # Ly-301 Seattle WA 98104-2015

DAY, THOMAS BRENNOCK, university president; b. N.Y.C., Mar. 7, 1932; s. Frederick and Alice (Brennock) D.; m. Anne Kohlbrenner, Sept. 5, 1953; children: Erica, Monica, Mark, Kevin, Sara, Timothy, Jonathan, Patrick, Adam. B.S., U Notre Dame, 1953; Ph.D., Cornell U., 1957. Prof. U. Md., College Park, 1964-78, vice chancellor for acad. planning and policy, 1970-77, spl. asst. to pres., 1977-78, vice chancellor for acad. affairs Baltimore County, 1977-78; pres. San Diego State U., 1978—; cons. Bendix Corp., IBM Corp., Digital Equipment Corp.; vis. physicist Brookhaven Nat. Lab., 1963; cons. Argonne Nat. Lab., Ill., 1967; vice chair Nat. Sci. Bd.; bd. dirs. Scripps Clinic and Research Found. Contbr. articles to profl. jours. Mem. Am. Phys. Soc., Sigma Xi, Phi Kappa Phi. Republican. Roman Catholic. Lodge: Rotary. Office: San Diego State U Office of Pres San Diego CA 92182-1690 also: NSF Nat Sci Bd 4201 Wilson Blvd Rm 1225 Arlington VA 22230-0001

DAYALA, HAJI FAROOQ, real estate broker; b. Karachi, Pakistan, Dec. 1, 1948; came to U.S., 1969; s. Haji Razzak and Hamida H. (Bai) D.; m. Susanna WK. Cheung, Aug. 25, 1973; children: Sabrina R., Ryan M. BS in Indsl. Engring., Calif. Poly. State U., 1972; M in Sci. and Adminstrn., Calif. State U., Dominguez Hills, 1979. Cert. GRI Calif. Assn. Realtors. Mgr. plant Thomas & Betts Corp., L.A., 1977-82, 84-86; v.p. ops. Prime Cir. Tech., San Jose, Calif., 1982-84; real estate agt. Merrill Lynch Realty, Diamond Bar, Calif., 1987-88; broker, co-owner Realty World-Ampak, Diamond Bar, Calif., 1988-90; real estate broker, assoc. SNS Realtors, Diamond Bar, Calif., 1990—; with H&S Tax and Fin. Svcs., Diamond Bar, 1992—. Mem. Nat. Notary Assn., Diamond Bar Realtor Bd. Home: 24324

E Knoll Ct Diamond Bar CA 91765-4308 Office: H&S Tax and Fin Svcs 24324 Knoll Ct Diamond Bar CA 91765-4308

DAYDAY, HENRY, mayor. Formerly alderman City of Saskatoon, Sask., elected mayor, 1988. Office: Office of Mayor, City Hall 222 3 Ave N, Saskatoon, SK Canada S7K 0J5*

DAY-GOWDER, PATRICIA JOAN, association executive, consultant; b. Lansing, Mich., Apr. 9, 1936; d. Louis A. and Johanna (Feringa) Whipple; m. Duane Lee Day, Jan. 7, 1961 (div.); children: Kevin Duane, Patricia Kimberley; m. William A. Gowder, Nov. 30, 1986. BA, Mich. State U., 1958; MA, Lindenwood (Mo.) Coll., 1979; postgrad. U. So. Calif., 1982-83. Cert. secondary tchr., Calif. Health edn. asst. YWCA, Rochester, N.Y., 1958-59; tchr. jr. high schs., Flint, Mich., 1959-61; tchr. Brookside Acad., Montclair, N.J., 1963-68; adult program dir. YMCA, Long Beach, Calif., 1968-73; community edn. dir. Paramount (Calif) Unified Sch. Dist., 1973-78; exec. dir. counseling ctr., Arcadia, Calif., 1978-80; sr. citizens program dir. City of Burbank (Calif.), 1981-83; div. dir. Am. Heart Assn., L.A., 1983-87 ; exec. dir. Campfire Orgn., Pasadena, 1987-89; exec. dir. greater L.A. chpt. Nat. Found. of Ileitis and Colitis, 1989-90; mgr. sr. citizens mktg. dept. Meth. Hosp. So. Calif., 1989—; cons. community edn. State Dept. Edn., Fed. Office Community Edn., L.A. County Office Edn. Bd. dirs., v.p. Children's Creative Ctr., Long Beach, Calif., 1969-73, Traveler's Aid Soc., 1969-72; vice-chmn. Cerritos YMCA, 1968-73. Mott Found. fellow, 1977-78. Mem. AAUW, Western Gerontology Assn., Nat. Assn. Female Execs., Calif. Community Edn. Assn. (sec.-treas., 1974-77), LWV. Democrat. Congregationalist. Avocations: tennis, hiking, bicycling, painting, reading. Home: 170 Oak Forest Cir Glendora CA 91741 Office: Meth Hosp So Calif 300 W Huntington Dr Arcadia CA 91007-3402

DAYNES, BYRON WILFORD, political science educator; b. Salt Lake City, Oct. 26, 1937; s. Byron Woodruff and Maxine (Gaddie) D.; m. Kathryn Mickelsen, June 20, 1966; children: Austen Laurence, Elizabeth Marie, Warren Joseph. BS, Brigham Young U., 1963, MS, 1965; PhD, U. Chgo., 1971. Prof. polit. sci. De Pauw U., Greencastle, Ind., 1971-90, chair dept. polit. sci., 1979-88; prof. polit. sci. Brigham Young U., Provo, Utah, 1990—; rsch. asst. Am. Judicature Soc., Chgo., summers 1967-69; mem. rsch. staff Congressman Lee H. Hamilton (Dem.-Ind.), Washington, summer 1973; vis. instr. Butler U., Indpls., 1974; vis. prof. Brigham Young U., 1986-87; book reviewer. Co-author: Contemporary Readings in American Government, 1980, The Politics of Abortion, 1981, Presidential Power in the United States, 1984; co-editor: Social Regulatory Policy, 1988; contbr. articles to profl. jours.; presenter So. Regional Sci. Assn., New Orleans, 1973, Ind. Acad. Social Scis., Indpls., 1973, 75, Ind. Polit. Sci. Assn., Ball State U., Muncie, Ind., 1978, Acad. Criminal Justice Scis., Oklahoma City, 1980, Ind. U.-Purdue U., Ft. Wayne, 1980, Loyola U. Chgo., 1987, We. Polit. Sci. Assn., Newport Beach, Calif., 1990, Pasadena, Calif., 1993, Albuquerque, 1994, Ind. Polit. Sci. Assn., 1993, Am. Polit. Sci. Assn., Washington, 1993, So. Polit. Sci. Assn., Savannah, Ga., 1993, others. Rsch. grantee Divsn. Govtl. Studies, Wash. State U., 1989. Mem. Am. Polit. Sci. Assn., Ind. Polit. Sci. Assn. (v.p. 1985-86, pres. 1980-81), Western Polit. Sci. Assn. (membership com. 1993-94), Alpha Lambda Delta, Phi Eta Sigma. Democrat. Mem. LDS Ch. Office: Brigham Young U Dept Polit Sci Provo UT 84602

DAYTON, DOUGLAS EMORY, computer marketing consultant; b. Lakewood, N.J., Sept. 17, 1951; s. Samuel S. and Estelle Dayton. BA, San Diego State U., 1973; postgrad., U. Calif., San Diego, 1974-75, U. Wash., 1976. Mktg. rep. IBM, Seattle, 1981-82; mgr. original equipment mfr. sales and contract support Microsoft Corp., Seattle, 1982-85; founder, pres. Dayton Assocs., Seattle, 1985—, Client-Centered Tng., Inc., Seattle, 1991—. Author: Computer Solutions for Business, 1988; contbr. articles to profl. jours. Mem. Wash. State Software Assn. Office: Dayton Assocs 477 123rd Pl NE Bellevue WA 98005-4819

DAYTON, MERRIL TAYLOR, gastrointestinal surgeon; b. Salt Lake City, Feb. 16, 1948; s. Sharon Reed and Lois Whitaker (Taylor) D.; m. Susan Thompson, June 8, 1973; children: Cameron, Damian, Brandon, Adrian, Ethan. BS, Brigham Young U., 1972; MD, U. Utah, 1976. Diplomate Am. Bd. Surgery, Nat. Bd. Med. Examiners. Resident in surgery UCLA Med. Sch., 1976-82, rsch. fellow, 1982-83, adj. asst. prof., 1982-83; asst. prof. U. Iowa Med. Sch., Iowa City, 1983-86; asst. prof. U. Utah Med. Sch., Salt Lake City, 1986-91, assoc. prof., 1991—; chief gen. surgery Salt Lake City VA Med. Ctr., 1987—, acting chief surgery, 1989; asst. dean admissions U. Utah Med. Sch., Salt Lake City, 1990—; mem. sci. adv. bd. Nat. Assn. for Ileitis and Colitis, Iowa City, 1984-86, Ostomy Found., Salt Lake City, 1987—. Editor: Essentials in General Surgery, 1988, Essentials of the Surgery Specialties, 1993 (Best Health Sci. Book award 1993), Manual of Surgical Objectives, 1988. Pres. Canyon Cove Homeowners Assn., Salt Lake City, 1990; merit badge counselor Boy Scouts Am., Salt Lake City, 1989—. Fellow Am. Coll. Surgeons; mem. Soc. Univ. Surgeons (nominating com. 1992—), Assn. for Surg. Edn. (pres. 1993—), Salt Lake Surg. Soc. (pres. 1993-94), Assn. for Acad. Surgery (chmn. com. on issues 1989—), Soc. for Surgery of Alimentary Tract. Republican. Mormon. Office: Univ Utah Sch Medicine 50 N Medical Dr Salt Lake City UT 84131

D'COSTA, ANTHONY PROMOTHES, international development educator and researcher; b. Darjeeling, India, Mar. 3, 1957; came to U.S., 1982; s. Vincent and Celine D'Costa; m. Janette Rawlings, May 24, 1986. MA in Econs. with honors, Birla Inst. Tech. and Sci., Pilani, India, 1980; PhD in Devel. Studies, U. Pitts., 1989. Rsch. exec. Ops. Rsch. Group, Calcutta, India, 1980-82; rsch. assoc. Ind. Bus. Rsch. Ctr., Bloomington, 1986-87; asst. prof. internat. devel. U. Wash., Tacoma, 1990—; vis. lectr. econs. Ind. U., Bloomington, 1988. Coantbr. articles to profl. jours. Pres. Tacoma Film Soc., 1993-94. Fulbright fellow Dept. of Edn., Washington, 1991, Am. Inst. Indian Studies sr. fellow, 1992, Rotary fellow, 1982; Tinker Found. Travel grantee, 1987. Fellow Korea FOund., Seol, 1995, Social. Sci. Rsch. Coun., mem. Assn. for Asian Studies, Devel. Studies Assn., Can. Assn. for the Study of Internat. Devel. Office: Univ of Washington 1103 A St Tacoma WA 98402-5003

DEACON, MAXINE SHIRLEY, grant writer, fundraiser; b. Aberdeen, S.D., Nov. 14, 1934; d. Albert William and Doris Bertha (Homer) Hunter; m. James Everett Deacon, Aug. 15, 1956 (div. Feb. 1984); children: Cynthia Doris, David Everett. AA, Midwestern U., Wichita Falls, Tex., 1954; student, U. Nev., 1963-87, U. N.Mex., 1968. Math. rsch. asst. U. Kans., Lawrence, 1956-57; adminstrv. asst. Centron Corp., Lawrence, 1957-60; exec. sec. Edgerton, Germeshausen and Grier, Inc., Las Vegas, 1961-65; group leader, spokesperson, vocalist Young Audiences Opera Quartet, Las Vegas, 1963-73; dir. music First Christian Ch., Las Vegas, 1962-73; asst. to dir. Desert Rsch. Inst., Las Vegas, 1961-71; storeowner Custom Leather Tack, Inc., Las Vegas, 1971-87; music tchr. Temple Beth Shalom, Las Vegas, 1987-89; asst. dir. Leisure Worlds, Las Vegas, 1989-92; grants writer, devel. dir. Nev Dance Theatre Nutcracker HOLIDAY MARKET, Las Vegas, 1993—; owner Hunter-Elliott Distinctive Creations, 1995—; bd. dirs. Nev. Sch. of the Arts, Las Vegas. Co-author: (slides and text) The Galapagos Islands: General Setting, Sea Lions, Birds, Iguanas and Tortoises, Baja California: Coastal Inhabitants; author: Handling Grief. Past officer, bd. dirs. Las Vegas Symphony, 1960-65, Assistance League of Las Vegas, 1980-83; instr. music Salvation Army, Gene Eppley Camp. Nev. State Champion equestrian, 1981-82, 93. Mem. Interior Decorator and Designer, Nat. Soc. Fund Raising Execs. Home and Office: 4790 Woodridge Rd Las Vegas NV 89121-5814

DEAL, LYNN EATON HOFFMANN, interior designer; b. Atlantic City, N.J., Nov. 7, 1953; d. Ralph Eaton and Helen P. Hoffmann; m. James A. Deal, Sept. 19, 1981; 1 child, Katherine M. Diploma in environ. and interior design, U. Calif., Irvine, 1989. Prin. Lynn Deal and Assocs., Newport Beach, Calif., 1982—; mem. adv. bd. U. Calif., Irvine, 1984—. Chmn. Philharm. Showcase House, 1992; mem. Orange County Philharm. Soc. Mem. Am. Soc. Interior Designers (recipient Chpt. award 1991, Pres.'s award 1992, author introductory video Orange County chpt.), Internat. Furnishings and Design Assn., Interior Educators Coun., Internat. Platform Assn. Republican. Episcopalian. Home: 218 Via Palermo Newport Beach CA 92663-5502

DEAL, TERRY DEAN, marketing executive; b. Lyons, Kans., Sept. 27, 1948; s. Willis Clifton and Geneva G. (Gamble) D.; m. Diana Kathlene Gerstner, Feb. 14, 1970; 1 child, M. Shane. BS Agricultural Bus., Ft. Hays Kans. State U., 1971. Area sales mgr. Senvita Products Inc., Seneca, Kans., 1971-73, total sales mgr., 1973-74; unit sales mgr. Agri-Distbrs. and Leasing, Abilene, Kans., 1974-75; gen. mgr. Agri-Distbrs. and Leasing, Abilene, 1975-76; terr. mgr. Owatonna (Minn.) Mfg. Co., 1976-84, regional sales mgr., 1984-87; dir. mktg. Impulse Hydraulics Inc., San Diego, 1987-90; product specialist ESCO Corp., Portland, Oreg., 1990—; pres. Agri-Distbrs. and Leasing, 1974-85. Bd. dirs. Persimmon Homeowners Assn., 1989—, Owatonna Swimming Assn., 1985-86; mem. Owatonna Little Theatre, 1984-88. Mem. NRA (presdl. transition com. 1989), Sertoma (bd. dirs. 1982-83), Elks, Tau Kappa Epsilon. Republican. Methodist. Office: ESCO Corp 2141 NW 25th Ave Portland OR 97210-2578

DEAN, BRITTEN, history educator; b. Syracuse, N.Y., May 27, 1935; s. Phillips Vose and Emily Mae (Britten) Dean; children: Dana Adams Dean, Cecilia Gratian Dean; m. Kayoko Ishizaki, Apr. 8, 1977; 1 child, Sophia Emily Dean. BA, Brown U., 1957; MA, Columbia U., 1962, PhD, 1969. Asst. prof. Calif. State U. Stanislaus, Turlock, 1967-70, assoc. prof., 1970-75, prof., 1975—, chmn. history dept., 1976-78, 91-95; resident dir. Calif. State U. Internat. Program, Japan, 1975-76; exch. prof. Hangzhou U., China, 1984-85, 87-88. Author: China and Great Britain, 1974; contbr. articles to profl. jours.; translator: (Chinese fiction) The Piano Tuner, 1989, The Banker, 1992. Fgn. Lang. fellow U.S. Govt., Columbia U., 1961-62, Fulbright fellow U.S. Govt., Republic of China, 1966-67, Rsch. fellow Social Sci. Rsch. Coun., Republic of China, 1972, Profl. fellow Japan Found., 1980-81; sabbatical leave grantee Calif. State U. Stanislaus, 1973, 80-81, 89. Mem. Assn. for Asian Studies, AAUP, NEA, Calif. Faculty Assn. Office: Calif State U 801 W Monte Vista Ave Turlock CA 95382-0256

DEAN, CAROLYNN LESLIE, health science technological administrator; b. Oak Park, Ill., Mar. 30, 1952; d. Robert Lee and Jeane Kathleen (Kenitz) D. Student, U. Hawaii, 1970-73; BS, Solano County Regional, Occupational Program, 1983. Registered vascular technologist, Calif. Cardiopulmonary and multi-phasic technologist Family Doctor Med. Group, Vallejo, Calif., 1976-78; non-invasive vascular technologist Alta Bates Hosp., Berkeley, Calif., 1979-80; cardiovascular technologist Herrick Hosp. Health Ctr., Berkeley, Calif., 1978-81; supr., dir. non-invasive vascular lab. St. Mary's Hosp., San Francisco, 1981--; ptnr. Cardiovascular Lab. Assocs., San Francisco, 1983--; sr. ptnr. Vascular Imaging Svcs., Vallejo, 1983; RVT Children's Hosp., San Francisco, 1988—; cons. in field. Contbr. articles to profl. jours. Mem. Soc. Non-Invasive Vescular Tech., Am. Registry Diagnostic Med. Sonographers, Am. Inst. Ultrasound in Medicine. Home: 113 Compass Ct Vallejo CA 94590-4028 Office: Vascular Lab St Marys Hosp and Health Ctr 450 Stanyan St San Francisco CA 94117-1079

DEAN, CHARLES ALBERT, writer, educator, clergy member; b. Birchtree, Mo., Feb. 11, 1944; s. James William and Nellie Marie (Mitchell) D.; m. Athena Daphne, Feb. 14, 1981; children: Molly, Roby, Ailen, Garrett, Aaron. BA in Ministerial, Cascade Coll., Bellevue, Wash., 1992. Ordained minister. Exec. officer Point Man Internat., Seattle, 1986-92; writer, tchr., minister Cascade Coll., Bellevue, Wash., 1992—; counselor Point Man Internat., Seattle, 1986-92; pub., editor Wine Press Pub., Mountlake Terrace, Wash. Author: Nam Vet-Making Peace with Your Past, 1988-90, How Far's The Enemy, 1988, Book of Soldiers Journey From War to Peace, 1991, Running Back, 1993. Staff. sgt. U.S. Army, 1963069, Vietnam. Mem. Vietnam Vets. Am., 173d Airborne Soc.

DEAN, DEAREST (LORENE GLOSUP), songwriter; b. Volin, S.D., Oct. 4, 1911; d. John Henry and Bessie Marie Donnelly Peterson; m. Eddie Dean, Sept. 11, 1931; children: Donna Lee Knorr, Edgar Glosup II. Grad. high sch., Yankton, S.D. Bd. dirs. Acad. Country Music, Hollywood, 1960-62. Composer songs including: One Has My Name, 1948, The Lonely Hours, 1970, 1501 Miles of Heaven, 1970, Walk Beside Me, 1980. Sec. ARC, Burbank, Calif., 1943. Mem. ASCAP. Republican. Roman Catholic. Avocation: golf.

DEAN, DONNA MARGARET, psychotherapist, writer; b. Ross, Calif., Feb. 23, 1941; d. William Joseph and Ruth Alberta (Baxter) Madden; m. Marvin Earl Dean, Nov. 11, 1972. AA, Santa Rosa Coll., 1961; BA, Calif. State U., Sacramento, 1967; MSEd in Guidance and Counseling, Old Dominion U., 1981; PhD, Union Inst., 1994. Cert. mental health counselor, Wash. Enlisted USN, 1963, advanced through ranks to lt., 1970, resigned, 1981; pvt. practice psychotherapy Sedro Woolley, Wash., 1981—. Author: Warriors Without Weapons: The Victimization of Military Women, 1994; contbr. article and short story to profl. publs. (Best of Class, Best of Divsn. awards for short story Skagit Fair 1994). Bd. dirs. Vietnam Vets. Intertribal Assn., 1982-87; mem. adv. com. for women vets. Dept. Vets. Affairs, Seattle, 1993—; mem. crime victims comp adv. com. Dept. Labor and Industries, Seattle, 1989-91. Mem. Nat. Psychology Adv. Assn., N.W. Native Writers Cir., Wash. State Assn. Counseling and Devel. (mem. exec. bd. 1983-93, Mental Health Counselor of Yr. 1991), Wash. Mental Health Counselors Assn. (pres. 1990-91), Skagit Writers.

DEAN, JEFFREY STEWART, dendrochronologist, archaeologist; b. Lewiston, Idaho, Feb. 10, 1939; s. Kenneth Franklyn and Margaret Mary (Mitchell) D; children: Alison Elizabeth, Carrie Margaret. Student, U. Idaho, 1957-58; BA, U. Ariz., 1961, PhD, 1967. Instr. U. Ariz., Tucson, 1966-67, asst. prof., 1967-72, assoc. prof., 1972-77, prof., 1977—; sr. scientist So. Ill. U., Carbondale, 1985-86; cooperating scientist Black Mesa Archeol. Project, Carbondale, 1979-83; peer reviewer Ariz. State Mus., Tucson, 1981-85. Author: Chronological Analysis of Tsegi Phase Sites in Northeastern Arizona, 1969; (with others) SW Dendroclimate, 680-1970, 1977, Arroyo Hondo Paleoclimate, 1981; also numerous articles. Grantee U.S. Nat. Park Service, 1967-77, NSF, 1985—. Fellow Am. Anthrop. Assn., AAAS; mem. Soc. Am. Archaeology (treas. 1977-80), Tree-Ring Soc. (sec. 1974—), Sigma Xi. Office: U Ariz Lab Of Tree Ring Resea Tucson AZ 85721

DEAN, NAT, artist, educator; b. Redwood City, Calif., Jan. 13, 1956; d. Richard William and Marianne Ridley (Smith) D.; m. Paul Singdahlsen, May 24, 1987. Student, Calif. Inst. of Arts, 1972-76, Cooper Union Coll., 1975; BFA, San Francisco Art Inst., 1977. Freelance artist, educator Fla./Calif, 1978-95; annual workshop leader, lectr. Calif. Inst. of Arts, Valencia, 1985—; dir. career planning Calif. Inst. Arts, Valencia, 1986-89; dir. of career ctr. Ringling Sch. of Art and Design, Sarasota, Fla., 1989-92; conf. co-organizer Arts Placment Profls. Groups, 1989, 91, 92, 93; pres., owner Ruta Zinc Fine Arts Agy., San Francisco and L.A., 1980-89; freelance artist, educator N.Mex./Calif., 1995—; guest lectr. Iowa State U., Ames, 1992; adj. faculty Md. Inst., Balt.; lectr. L.A. Internat. Art Fair, 1988-94, numerous others. One-person shows and group exhbns. include Valencia C.C., Orlando, Fla., 1995, Durango (Colo.) Art Ctr., 1995, Manatee C.C., Bradenton, Fla., 1994, Ormond Beach (Fla.) Meml. Art Mus., 1994, Oreg. Sch. of Arts & Crafts, Portland, 1993, The Edn. Ctr. Gallery, Longboat Key, Fla., 1993, Nutaalite, Buena Park, Calif., 1993, Sarasota County (Fla.) Arts Coun., 1993, ARTarget, Sarasota, Fla., 1993, Selby Gallery, Sarasota, Fla., 1992, Ctr. Gallaery, Miami-Dade C.C., 1991, NCCA Gallery/New Ctr. for Creative Awareness, Sarasota, 1990, Scottsdale (Ariz.) Ctr. for Arts, 1992, 95, Boca Raton (Fla.) Mus. Art, 1991, Coll. Creative Studies, U. Calif., Santa Barbara, 1990, San Francisco Mus. Modern Art Rental Gallery, 1986, 89, Galerie Anton Meir, Geneva, 1988, Orange County Ctr. Contemporary Art, Santa Ana, Calif., 1990, The Fukuoka Mcpl. Mus., Japan, 1987, others; co-author: The Visual Artist's Business and Legal Guide, 1995. Chmn. visual artists task force Sarasota County Arts Coun., 1991-92; AIDS subcom. Planned Approach to Community Health, Sarasota, 1991-92; visual aids com., Visual Aids: Day Without Art, 1989—; program adv. Regional Occupational Program, Contra Costa Bd. Edn., 1986, numerous others. Recipient Residency award The Bemis Project, Omaha, 1986, Profl. Devel. grant Ringling Sch. of Art and Design, Sarasota, 1990, Merit award Calif. Inst. of Arts, Valencia, 1976, others. Mem. Coll. Art Assn. (speaker 1992, 93), Nat. Artists Equity (speaker 1992), Women's Caucus for Art (speaker 1993), Nat. Soc. Exptl. Learning (speaker 1988, 89, 92, 93), Nat. Art Edn. Assn. (speaker 1992), Nat. Assn. Artists Orgns., Coll. Placement Coun., others. Studio and Office: Sierra Azul Rt 10 Box 94ND Santa Fe NM 87501 also: c/o M.S. Dean 32679 Seagate Dr # 202 Rancho Palos Verdes CA 90275

DEAN, NORMAN EMERSON (NED DEAN), coffee company executive; b. Madison, Wis., July 1, 1943; s. Norman E. Dean and Ruth E. (Baker) Reimer; m. Kathy Elaine Sandrock, June 26, 1965; children—Daniel, Richard, Matthew. BS, San Francisco State U., 1967. C.P.A., Calif. Ptnr. Dean, Petrie & Haas, Novato, Calif., 1967-78; sr. v.p., chief fin. officer Hills Bros. Coffee, San Francisco, 1978-81, pres., dir., from 1983, now chmn.; pres. Round Table Pizza Inc., San Francisco, 1981-83; dir. Round Table Pizza, Inc., 1979—. Chmn. Marin County Aviation Land Use Commn., San Rafael, Calif., 1976; chmn. Novato Planning Commn., 1977-78; regent Calif. Luth. Univ., 1985—. Mem. Novato C. of C. (pres. 1972). Republican. Lutheran. Office: Hills Bros Coffee Inc 2 Harrison St San Francisco CA 94105-1672 Office: Nestle Beverage Co 345 Spear St San Francisco CA 94105-1673

DEAN, PAUL JOHN, magazine editor; b. Pitts., May 11, 1941; s. John Aloysius and Perle Elizabeth (Thompson) D.; m. Jo-ann Tillman, Aug. 19, 1972 (div. Mar. 1981); children: Jennifer Ann, Michael Paul. Student engring., Pa. State U., 1959-60. Gen. mgr. Civic Ctr. Honda Co., Pitts., 1965-68, Washington-Pitts. Cycle Co., Canonsburg, Pa., 1968-70; nat. svc. mgr. Yankee Motor Co., Schenectady, 1970-73; competition congressman Am. Motorcyclist Assn., 1971, 72, trustee, sec. bd., 1988-91, chmn., 1991—; adv. bd., guest speaker L.A. Trade Tech. Coll., 1974-90; trustee Am. Motorcyclist Heritage Found., 1990-91. Engring. editor Cycle Guide mag., Compton, Calif., 1973-74, editor-in-chief, 1974-80, editorial dir., 1980-84; editor-in-chief Cycle World mag., Newport Beach, Calif., 1984-88, editorial dir. Cycle and Cycle World mags., 1988-92; v.p., editorial dir. Cycle World Mag. Group, 1992—; author manuals. Served with AUS, 1964-65. Home: 5915 Arabella St Lakewood CA 90713-1203 Office: Hachette Filipacchi Mags 1499 Monrovia Ave Newport Beach CA 92663-2752

DEAN, RONALD GLENN, lawyer; b. Milw., Feb. 18, 1944; m. Mary Blumberg, Jan. 25, 1969; children: Elizabeth Lucile, Joshua Henry. BA, Antioch Coll., 1967; JD, U. Wis. 1970. Bar: Wis. 1970, Calif. 1971; assoc. Mink & Neiman, L.A., 1971; pvt. practice, L.A., 1971-74; ptnr. Margolis, McTernan, Scope & Sacks, Los Angeles, 1974-77; pvt. practice, Pacific Palisades, 1977—; mem. judge pro-tem program L.A. County Bar, 1978-91; judge pro tem Beverly Hills Mcpl. Ct., 1980-90; arbitrator L.A. Superior Ct., 1980—, L.A. County Fee Dispute Panel, 1979-86, 94—, Santa Monica Mcpl. Ct., 1980—; referee for disciplinary matters State Bar Ct., 1980-88, supervising referee, 1984-88, rev. dept. 1988-90, judge pro tem 1990-94. Bd. dirs. Pacific Palisades Residents Assn., 1983—, pres., 1985-88; counsel to Pacific Palisades Cmty. Coun., 1983-92; mem. Councilman's Citizen Adv. Com. to Develop Palisades Specific Plan, 1983-85; bd. govs. Pacific Palisades Civic League, 1987-89; exec. bd. Pacific Palisades Dem. Club, 1990—, pres., 1991. Mem. Am. Arbitration Assn. (panel 1974—), ABA (co-chmn. preemption subcom., employee benefits com, labor sect., bd. sr. editors Employee Benefits Law), BNA Pension and Benefits Reporter (adv. bd. 1995), Wis. Bar Assn., Calif. Bar Assn., Calif. State Bar (chmn. pension and trust benefits com. of labor sect. 1984), L.A. County Bar Assn. Antioch Alumni Assn. (dir. 1982-88). Office: 15135 W Sunset Blvd Ste 280 Pacific Palisades CA 90272-3724

DEAN, WALTER EDWARD, JR., research geologist; b. Wilkes-Barre, Pa., July 12, 1939; s. Walter Edward and Marion (Cassedy) D.; m. Beverly Ann Nenstiel, Dec. 30, 1961; children: Scott Alan, Kevin Neil. AB in Geology, Syracuse U., 1961; MS in Geology, U. N.Mex., 1964, PhD in Geology, 1967. Rsch. assoc. U. Minn., Mpls., 1967-68; asst. and assoc. prof. Syracuse (N.Y.) U., 1968-75; rsch. geologist U.S. Geol. Survey, Denver, 1975—. Contbr. articles to profl. jours. Fellow Geol. Soc. Am.; mem. AAAS, Am. Assn Petroleum Geologists, Am. Geophysical Union, Am. Soc. Limnology and Oceanography, Soc. Econ. Paleontologists. Office: US Geol Survey MS939 Federal Center Denver CO 80225

DEAN, WILLIAM EVANS, aerospace agency executive; b. Greenville, Miss., July 6, 1930; s. George Thomas Dean and Martha Myrtle (Evans) Carlton; m. Dorothy Sue Hamilton, Oct. 14, 1953; children—Janet Lea, Jody Anne, Justin H. B. Aero. Engring., Ga. Inst. Tech., 1952; M.B.A., Pepperdine U., 1970. FAA cert. airplane and instrument flight instr. Commd. officer U.S. Air Force, 1952, advanced through grades to maj., 1962; div. mgr., dir. Rockwell Internat. Corp., L.A., 1962-67, v.p., div. gen. mgr., 1967-80; exec. v.p. Acurex Corp., Mountain View, Calif., 1981-82; pres., chief operating officer Acurex Corp., Mountain View, 1982-83, pres., chief exec. officer, 1983-90, chmn., 1990-91; assoc. dir. Ames Rsch. Ctr. NASA, Moffett Field, Calif., 1991-93, dep. ctr. dir., 1994—; lectr. Calif. State U., Chico, Calif., 1988, Santa Clara U., 1993—. Contbr. articles on gen. mgmt. and aero. engrng. to profl. jours. Bd. dirs. NCCJ, San Jose, Calif., 1984—, co-chmn., 1988—; bd. dirs. Santa Clara County Mfg. Group, San Jose, 1984-91, vice-chmn., 1988-91; bd. dirs. Saddleback Community Coll., Mission Viejo, Calif., 1976-77, United Fund, Orange County, Calif., 1971; United Way, Santa Clara County, San Jose, 1985-91; vice-chmn., bd. advisors Leavey Sch. Bus., Santa Clara U., 1987—, vice chmn., 1989-91. Maj. USAF, 1952-62. Decorated Air Force Commendation medal with oak leaf cluster; recipient Spl. Svc. award United Way, San Jose, 1986, Astronaut Personal Achievement award NASA Astronaut Corps, Houston, 1972, 84, Outstanding Contbn. to Manned Exploration of the Moon award NASA, 1972, Medal for Outstanding Leadership, NASA, 1995, Group Achievement awards (2) NASA, 1995, Silver Knight of Mgmt. award Nat. Mgmt. Assn., 1978, Commendation cert. Calif. State Assembly, 1986, Pres.'s award Santa Clara U., 1993. Fellow AIAA (bd. dirs. 1979-86, 91—, Space Shuttle award 1984), Am. Astron. Soc.; mem. Am. Electronics Assn. (edn. found. 1982-88), Aircraft Owners and Pilots Assn., Air Force Assn., Armed Forces Communications and Electronics Assn. Republican. Baptist. Office: NASA Ames Rsch Ctr Mail Stop 200-1B Moffett Field CA 94035

DEANGELIS, DAN, transportation executive; b. Stockton, Calif., July 23, 1947; m. Shari Thornton, 1973; children: Ryan, Jamie. BA in Adminstrn. Justice, Delta Coll., 1967. Lic. comml. pilot; cert. airline transport pilot. Chief pilot, flight instr. Werner's Aero Svc. Stockton Metropolitan Airport; with City of Manteca, 1974-76; airport ops. dep. Dept. Aviation County of San Joaquin, 1976-85, asst. airport ops. mgr., 1985-87, dep. airport mgr. ops., 1987-90; airport mgr. Stockton Metropolitan Airport, 1990—. Office: Stockton Met Airport 5000 S Airport Way Ste 202 Stockton CA 95206-3911*

DE ANGELIS, DEBORAH ANN AYARS, university athletics official; b. San Diego, July 2, 1948; d. Charles Orvil and Janet Isabel (Glithero) Ayars; m. David C. De Angelis, Sept. 29, 1984. B.A., U. Calif.-Santa Barbara, 1970, Certificate in Social Services, 1972; M.S., U. Mass., 1979. Eligibility worker County Welfare Dept., Santa Barbara, Calif., 1970-73; women's crew coach, U. Mass., 1978-79, Northeastern U., Boston, 1979-83, bus. mgr. women's athletics, 1983-87, asst. dir. bus., 1987-89; mgr. athletics bus. Calif. State U., Northridge, 1989-93, assoc. dir., 1993—; com. mem. Women's Olympic Rowing Com., 1976-84; life trustee Nat. Rowing Found., 1984; life mem. selection com. Rowing Found. Hall of Fame, 1984—, bd. dirs., 1994—; rowing mgr. Women's Olympic Team, 1976, 80; head mgr. U.S. Olympic Festival, Syracuse, N.Y., 1981, coach, Indpls., 1982, Colorado Springs, Colo., 1983; mem. alcohol and drug awareness com. Northeastern U., 1983. Mem. Nat. Women's Rowing Assn. (pres. 1976-80, Woman of Yr. award 1983), Fedn. Sociétés d'Aviron (women's commn. 1978—, U.S. del. to ann. congress 1978, 80-88, 95), U.S. Rowing Assn. (del. 1988, bd. dirs. 1975-80, 85—, co-chmn. internat. div., co-chmn. events div. 1985-86, chmn. internat. div. 1986-88, women's v.p. 1985-88, mem. exec. com. 1985-89, exec. v.p. 1988-89, sec. 1995—), Calif. State U. Northridge Intercollegiate Athletics Oversight Adv. Bd., Tri C. of C. July 4th Spectacular Com. Club: ZLAC Rowing. Home: 430-A Jeremiah Dr Simi Valley CA 93065-1672

DEAR, RONALD BRUCE, social work educator; b. Phila., Sept. 23, 1933; s. John David and Margaret (McDade) D.; 1 child, Bruce. BA, Bucknell U., 1955; honors cert., U. Aberdeen, Scotland, 1955; MSW, U. Pitts., 1957; PhD in Social Work, Columbia U., 1972. Cert. social worker, N.Y., Wash. Residence dir. Horizon House, Inc., Phila., 1961-64; prof. U. Wash., Seattle, 1970—; vis. prof. U. Bergen, Norway, 1984. Editor: Poverty in Perspective, 1973; contbr. articles to profl. jours. and encys. 1st lt. U.S. Army, 1957-61. Mem. NASW (Social Worker of Yr. Wash. chpt. 1981), Acad. Cert. Social Workers, Coun. on Social Work Edn. Home: 7328 16th Ave NE Seattle WA 98115-5737 Office: Sch Social Work Jh # 30 Seattle WA 98195

DEASON, EDWARD JOSEPH, lawyer; b. Pasadena, Calif., July 5, 1955; s. Edward Patrick Deason and Marye Annette (Erramouspe) Kennedy; m. Charlotte Thunberg, Aug. 1, 1987; children: Keelin Marie, Erin Michelle. BA, Loyola Marymount U., 1977, JD, 1982. Bar: Calif. 1983, U.S. Dist. Ct. (ctrl. dist.) Calif. 1983, U.S. Dist. Ct. (no. dist.) Calif. 1987, U.S. Ct. Appeals (9th cir.) 1993, U.S. Supreme Ct. 1994. Assoc. Law Offices Edwin C. Martin, L.A., 1983-86; ptnr. Martin & Deason, L.A., 1986-94; pvt. practice L.A., 1994—. Mem. Calif. Trial Lawyers Assn., Assn. Trial Lawyers Am., L.A. Lawyers Club, Loyola Scott Moot Ct. Democrat. Roman Catholic. Office: Law Offices of Edward J Deason 501 Shatto Pl Ste 100 Los Angeles CA 90020-1713

DEASY, CORNELIUS MICHAEL, architect; b. Mineral Wells, Tex., July 19, 1918; s. Cornelius and Monetta (Palmo) D.; m. Lucille Laney, Sept. 14, 1941; children—Diana, Carol, Ann. B. Arch., U. So. Calif., 1941. Practice architecture, Los Angeles, 1946-76, partner, Robert D. Bolling, 1960-76; Prin. works include prin. offices student union, Calif. State U., Los Angeles.; Author: Design for Human Affairs, 1974, Designing Places for People, 1985. Vice pres. Los Angeles Beautiful; dir. Regional Plan Assn. Commr., Los Angeles Bd. Zoning Appeals, 1973—. Recipient numerous design awards, Nat. Endowment Arts award, 1983. Fellow AIA (past pres., dir. So. Calif. chpt., chmn. com. research). Home and Office: Davenport Creek Farm 4979 Davenport Creek Rd San Luis Obispo CA 93401-8109

DEASY, JOHN BERCHMANS, environmental health specialist; b. San Francisco, Mar. 7, 1911; s. Thomas A. and Katherine G. (Conway) D.; m. Minna Lou Cangelosi, Apr. 16, 1947, 1 child, Yvonne A. Deasy-Gowdey. BS, U. San Francisco, 1933; grad., U.S. Army Command and Gen. Staff Coll., 1964. Registered environ. health specialist; cert. tchr. Gen. clerk City and County of San Francisco, 1934-48; insp. San Francisco Tax Office, 1948-54; insp., sr. insp., and prin. insp. San Francisco Dept. Health, 1954-72; pres. John Mulhern Co., San Francisco, 1981-83; tchr. San Francisco Gen. Hosp., Laguna Honda Hosp., 1973-74. Scoutmaster Boy Scouts Am., 1930-34, dist. commr., 1954-56, troop committeeman and scouting coord., 1974—; bd. dirs. U. San Francisco Health Profl. Soc. Lt. Col. U.S. Army, 1942-64, ETO, Korea. Decorated Bronze Star; recipient Silver Beaver award Boy Scouts Am. Mem. Young Men's Inst. (Outstanding Mem. award 1970, various offices), Res. Officers Assn. chpt. 90 (Man of Yr. award 1984, various offices), Ret. Officers Assn., San Francisco Ret. City Employees Assn., Sons in Retirement (Big Sir 1978, various offices), 86th Chem. Mortar Bd. Assn. (founder, adj.), Vets. Battle of Bulge (treas.), U. San Francisco Alumni Assn. (past bd. govs.), Am. Legion (life). Democrat. Roman Catholic. Home: 1830 30th Ave San Francisco CA 94122-4227

DEATHERAGE, WILLIAM VERNON, lawyer; b. Drumright, Okla., Apr. 17, 1927; s. William Johnson and Pearl Mae (Watson) D.; m. Priscilla Ann Campbell, Sept. 16, 1932; children: Thomas William, Andrea Susan. BS, U. Oreg., 1952, LLB with honors, 1954. Bar: Oreg. 1954, U.S. Dist. Ct. Oreg. 1956. Ptnr. Frohnmayer, Deatherage, Pratt, Jamieson & Clarke, Medford, Oreg., 1954—; bd. dirs. Oreg. Law Inst., U. Oreg. Found. Served with USN, 1945-48. Mem. Am. Coll. Trial Lawyers, Internat. Acad. Trial Lawyers, Delta Theta Phi, Rogue Valley Country Club (pres. 1988), Rogue River Valley Univ. Club. Democrat. Episcopalian. Address: 2592 E Barnett Rd Medford OR 97504

DEAVER, PHILLIP LESTER, lawyer; b. Long Beach, Calif., July 21, 1952; s. Albert Lester and Eva Lucille (Welton) D. Student, USCG Acad., 1970-72; BA, UCLA, 1974; JD, U. So. Calif., 1977. Bar: Hawaii 1977, U.S. Dist. Ct. Hawaii 1977, U.S. Ct. Appeals (9th cir.) 1978, U.S. Supreme Ct. 1981. Assoc. Carlsmith, Wichman, Case, Mukai & Ichiki, Honolulu, 1977-83, ptnr., 1983-86; mng. ptnr. Bays, Deaver, Hiatt, Kawachika & Lezak, Honolulu, 1986. Contbr. articles to profl. jours. Dir. Parents and Children Together. Mem. ABA (forum com. on the Constrn. Industry), AIA (affiliate Hawaii chpt.), Am. Arbitration Assn. (arbitrator). Home: 2471 Pacific Heights Rd Honolulu HI 96813-1029 Office: Bays Deaver Hiatt Kawachika & Lezak PO Box 1760 Honolulu HI 96806-1760

DEBARD, ROGER, investment executive; b. Cleve., Nov. 10, 1941; d. Victor and Margaret Ann (Henderson) DeB.; m. Janet Marie Schulz, July 3, 1965; children: Eila Burns, Ryan Alexander. BS, Bowling Green State U., 1963; MBA, Case Western Res. U., 1968; MA, Claremont Grad. Sch., 1978, PhD, 1981. Asst. v.p. A.G. Becker & Co., L.A., 1972-76; sr. portfolio mgr. Scudder Stevens & Clark, L.A., 1976-81; v.p. Crocker Investment Mgmt., L.A., 1981-85; exec. v.p., CFO Hotchkis and Wiley Funds, L.A., 1985—; gen. ptnr. Hotchkis and Wiley, L.A., 1985—; adj. prof. fin. Pepperdine U., L.A., 1981-85. Mem. The Founders-Music Ctr. L.A., L.A. World Affairs Coun., 1988—, L.A. Libr. Assn., 1976—, pres. 1980-81. Recipient First Pl. Pub. award Investment Dealers Digest, 1971, Outstanding Svc. award City of L.A., 1980; grad. fellow Rand Grad. Inst., 1974-76. Mem. L.A. Bd. Bond Club (sec./dir. 1986-89), L.A. Soc. Fin. Analysts, Yosemite Assoc., California Club, Bel-Air Bay Club, Sigma Chi. Republican. Episcopalian. Home: 48 Haldeman Rd Santa Monica CA 90402-1004 Office: Hotchkis and Wiley 800 W 6th St Los Angeles CA 90017-2704

DEBARTOLO, EDWARD JOHN, JR., professional football team owner, real estate developer; b. Youngstown, Ohio, Nov. 6, 1946; s. Edward J. and Marie Patricia (Montani) DeB.; m. Cynthia Ruth Papalia, Nov. 27, 1968; children: Lisa Marie, Tiffanie Lynne, Nicole Anne. Student, U. Notre Dame, 1964-68. With Edward J. DeBartolo Corp., Youngstown, Ohio, 1960—, v.p., 1971-76, exec. v.p., 1976-79, pres., chief adminstrv. officer, 1979—; owner San Francisco 49ers, 1977—; bd. dirs. Ralphs Supermarkets, Inc. Trustee Youngstown State U., 1974-77; nat. adv. coun. St. Jude Children's Rsch. Hosp., 1978—, local chmn., 1979-80; chmn. local fund drive Am. Cancer Soc., 1975—; mem. Nat. Cambodia Crisis Com., 1980—; chmn. 19th Ann. Victor Warner award, 1985, City of Hope's Spirit of Life Banquet, 1986; apptd. adv. coun. Coll. Bus. Adminstrn. U Notre Dame, 1988; adv. coun. Nat. Assn. People with AIDS, 1992; bd. dirs. Cleve. Clinic Found., 1991; lifetime mem. Italian Scholarship League. With U.S. Army, 1969. Recipient Man of Yr. award St. Jude Children's Hosp., 1979, Boy's Town of Italy in San Francisco, 1985, Sportsman of Yr. award Nat. Italian Am. Sports Hall of Fame, 1991, Cert. of Merit, Salvation Army, 1982, Warner award, 1986, Silver Cable Car award San Francisco Conv. and Visitors Bur., 1988, Nat. Football League Man of Yr. award Football News, 1989, Svc. to Youth award Cath. Youth Orgn., 1990, Hall of Fame award Cardinal Mooney High Sch., 1993. Mem. Internat. Coun. Shopping Ctrs., Italian Scholarship League (life), Tippecanoe Country Club, Fonderlac Country Club, Dapper Dan Club (dir. 1980—). Office: Edward J DeBartolo Corp PO Box 3287 Youngstown OH 44513-3287 also: care San Francisco 49ers 4949 Centennial Blvd Santa Clara CA 95054-1229*

DEBARTOLO, JACK, JR., architect; b. Youngstown, Ohio, May 6, 1938; s. Jack and Virginia (Sassinelli) DeB.; m. Patsy McLamore, Aug. 15, 1958; children: Ava, Gina, Jack III. B.Arch., U. Houston, 1962; M.Arch., Columbia U., 1964. Sr. v.p., dir. design Caudill Rowell Scott, 1964-73; sr. v.p. William Wilde & Assocs., Tucson, 1973; pres. Anderson DeBartolo Pan Inc., Phoenix, 1975-85; dir. design, founding prin. Anderson DeBartolo Pan Inc., Tucson, 1973-95; prin. DeBartolo Archs. Ltd., Phoenix, 1995—; Fellow Am. Inst. of Archs., bd. dirs., U. of Ariz. Found., mem. of exec. comm. of AIA Col. of Fellows. Notable works include: (award winning project), CRS Office Bldg., Houston, Joilet Jr. Coll., Ill., Pima Community Coll., Tucson, West Campus & Life Sci. Bldg. of Ariz. State Coll. Elder Grace Chapel, Tucson; deacon Phoenix First Assembly Ch. Fellow AIA (past pres. Ariz., So. Ariz. chpt., chmn. jury of fellows 1987-90); mem. Tuscon Tomorrow, City of Tuscon Pres.'s Club, U. Ariz. Found. Bd., Ariz. State U. Coll. Architecture Coun. of Design Excellence. Republican. Club: Tucson Breakfast. Office: DeBartolo Archs Ltd Ste 120 4450 N 12th St Phoenix AZ 85014

DEBENHAM, RAY GENE, electric supply company executive; b. Salt Lake City, Oct. 1, 1935; s. Shirley R. and Lillian (Greguhn) D.; m. Rita J. Peterson, Aug. 14, 1959; children: Debra, Julie, Michael, Shaun. BS, Alaska Pacific U., 1972; OPM, Harvard U., 1987. CEO Debenham Alaska Investments, Anchorage, 1960—, Taku Enterprises, Anchorage, 1988—; pres. Debenham Electric Supply, Anchorage, 1968-91, CEO, 1968—; chmn. bd. dirs. Profl. Botanicals, Ogden, Utah, 1979-80; bd. advisers SBA, Washington, 1983-88, Philips Lighting, 1990-92, Cuttler Hammer, 1989-90. Mem. bd. trustees Alaska Pacific U., 1992—. Mem. Nat. Assn. Elec. Distbrs. (chmn. utility com. 1981-85), Nat. Assn. Disbtrs., Am. Legion. Mormon.

DEBOCK, RONALD GENE, real estate company executive, clergy member; b. Buckley, Wash., Sept. 12, 1928; m. Donna J. DeBock, Sept. 24, 1949; children: Beverly J. DeBock Satter, Gary, Janice. BA, N.W. Coll., Kirkland, Wash., 1953; MDiv., Western Evangelical Sem., Portland, Oreg., 1960; AA, Tacoma (Wash.) C.C., 1979; PhD, Calif. Grad. Sch. Theology, Glendale, 1979. Ordained minister Assemblies of God Ch., 1953. Commd. ensign USNR, 1957; advanced through grades to lt. comdr. USN, 1971, chaplain, 1958-71; founder, owner Rainier Rentals, Puyallup, Wash., 1975—, Fireball Publs., Puyallup, 1993—. Author: Practice What You Preached, 1993. Decorated Vietnam Cross of Gallantry with palm. Mem. Wash. Assn Realtors, Inc., Puyallup C. of C., Mil. Chaplains Assn. USA, VFW, DAV, Rotary Internat. Office: Fireball Pubs 422 W Main Ave Ste P Puyallup WA 98371

DE BODE, OLEG, information systems administrator; b. San Cristobal, Venezuela, Oct. 26, 1956; came to U.S., 1963; s. Konstantine de Bode and Olga (Zavadsky) Kennedy. BS in Math. and Computer Sci., UCLA, 1978. Programmer Electronic Data Systems, Torrance, Calif., 1979-80; programmer/analyst EDS, Torrance, Calif., 1980-85; data processing mgr. Dep Corp., Rancho Dominguez, Calif., 1985-90, dir. mgmt. info. systems, 1990—. Instr. St. George Pathfinders, L.A., 1975—. Mem. COMMON, Focus, Data Processing Mgrs. Assn., Assn. Systems Mgmt. Republican.

DEBON, GEORGE A., security services company executive. Chmn. Loomis Corp., Seattle, Mayne Nickless Inc., Seattle. Office: Mayne Nickless Inc 720 Olive Way Seattle WA 98101-1853 also: Loomis Armored Inc 4400 Us Highway 9 # 1000 Freehold NJ 07728-1383

DEBREU, GERARD, economics and mathematics educator; b. Calais, France, July 4, 1921; came to U.S., 1950, naturalized, 1975; s. Camille and Fernande (Decharne) D.; m. Françoise Bled, June 14, 1945; children: Chantal, Florence. Student, Ecole Normale Supérieure, Paris, 1941-44, Agrégé de l'Université, France, 1946; DSc, U. Paris, 1956; Dr. Rerum Politicarum honoris causa, U. Bonn, 1977; D. Scis. Economiques (hon.), U. Lausanne, 1980; DSc (hon.), Northwestern U., 1981; Dr. honoris causa, U. des Scis. Sociales de Toulouse, 1983, Yale U., 1987, U. Bordeaux I, 1988. Rsch. assoc. Centre Nat. De La Recherche Sci., Paris, 1946-48; Rockefeller fellow U.S., Sweden and Norway, 1948-50; rsch. assoc. Cowles Commn., U. Chgo., 1950-55; assoc. prof. econs. Cowles Found., Yale, 1955-61; fellow Ctr. Advanced Study Behavioral Scis., Stanford U., 1960-61; vis. prof. econs. Yale U., fall 1961; prof. econs. U. Calif., Berkeley, 1962—, prof. Miller Inst. Basic Rsch. in Sci., 1973-74, prof. math., 1975—, univ. prof., 1985—; Guggenheim fellow, vis. prof. Ctr. Ops. Rsch. and Econometrics, U. Louvain, 1968-69, vis. prof., 1971, 72, 88; Erskine fellow U. Canterbury, Christchurch, New Zealand, 1969, 87, vis. prof., 1973; Overseas fellow Churchill Coll., Cambridge, Eng., 1972; Plenary address Internat. Congress Mathematicians, Vancouver, 1974; vis. prof. Cowles Found. for Rsch. in Econs., Yale U., 1976; vis. prof. U. Bonn, 1977; rsch. assoc. Cepremap, Paris, 1980; faculty rsch. lectr. U. Calif., Berkeley, 1984-85, univ. prof., 1985—, Class of 1958 Chair, 1986—; vis. prof. U. Sydney, Australia, 1987; lectr. in field. Author: Theory of Value, 1959, Mathematical Economics: Twenty Papers of Gerard Debreu, 1983; assoc. editor Internat. Econ. Rev., 1959-69; mem. editorial bd. Jours. Econ. Theory, 1972—, SIAM Jours. on Applied Math., 1976-79, Jours. of Complexity, 1985—, Games and Econ. Behavior, 1989—, Econ. Theory, 1991; mem. adv. bd. Jours. Math. Econs., 1974—; correspondent Math. Intelligencer, 1983-84. Served with French Army, 1944-45. Decorated Chevalier de la Légion d'Honneur, Commandeur de l'Ordre National du Mérite, Officier Le Légion d'Honneur; recipient Nobel Prize in Econ. Scis., 1983, Berkeley Citation, 1991; sr. U.S. Sci. awardee Alexander von Humboldt Found., 1977. Fellow AAAS, Econometric Soc. (mem. coun. 1964-72, 78-85, Fisher-Schultz lectr. 1969, exec. com. 1969-72, 80-82, pres. 1971), Am. Econ. Assn. (disting. fellow 1982, pres.-elect 1989, pres. 1990); mem. NAS (chmn. sect. econ. scis. 1982-85, com. human rights 1984-90, chair class V behavioral and social scis. 1989-92, mem. Coun. of NAS of USA 1993—), Am. Philos. Soc., French Acad. Scis. (fgn. assoc.), Berkeley Fellows. Office: U Calif Dept Econs 787 Evans Hall Berkeley CA 94720

DEBRO, JULIUS, university dean, sociology educator; b. Jackson, Miss., Sept. 25, 1931; s. Joseph and Seleana (Gaylor) D.; m. Darlene Conley; children—Renee Denys, Blair. B.A. in Polit. Sci., U. San Francisco, 1953; M.A. in Sociology, San Jose State U., 1967; Ph.D., U. Calif.-Berkeley, 1975. Research asst. U. Calif. Sch. Criminology, Berkeley, 1964-68; instr. dept. sociology Laney Coll., Alameda, Calif., 1968-69, Alameda Coll., Oakland, Calif., 1971, U. Md., College Park, 1971-72; asst. prof. Inst. for Criminal Justice and Criminology U. Md., 1972-79; mem. faculty Atlanta U., 1979-91, prof. criminal justice, 1979-91, chmn. dept. pub. adminstrn., 1979-80, chmn. dept. Criminal Justice Inst., 1979-89, chmn. dept. sociology, 1985-86; assoc. dean Grad. Sch., acting asst. provost U. Wash., Seattle, 1991—, affiliate prof. society and justice program, 1991—; mem. adv. bd. dirs. Criminal Justice Rev., 1977-87; prin. investigator Joint Commn. on Criminology and Criminal Justice Edn. and Standards, 1978-79; v.p. Atlanta Met. Crime Commn., 1986, pres., 1987; mem. investigative bd. Ga. Bar Assn., 1987; editor Blacks in Criminal Justice quar. news mag., 1987—. Assoc. editor Criminal Justice Quar., 1989—. Chmn. program evaluation com. Boys and Girls Home, Montgomery County, Md., 1979; bd. dirs. YMCA, Bethesda, Md., 1979, Totem Coun. Girl Scouts. Served to col. USAR, 1953-84. NIMH fellow, 1969-70; Ford fellow, 1971; grantee NIMH, 1974, Law Enforcement Assistance Adminstrn., 1979-81; postdoctoral rsch. assoc. Narcotic and Drug Rsch. Inc., N.Y.C., 1989-90; Inter-Univ. Seminar on Armed Forces and Soc. fellow, 1989; Western Soc. Criminology fellow, 1989; recipient Herbert Bloch award for Outstanding Svcs. to Criminal Justice Criminology, svc. to Am. Soc. Criminology. Fellow Narcotic Drug Rsch.; mem. NAACP, Nat. Assn. Blacks in Criminal Justice (editor quar. news mag. 1987—), Nat. Assn. Black Sociologists, Am. Soc. Criminology (exec. bd.), Am. Sociol. Assn., Acad. Criminal Justice Sci., Urban League, Rotary. Democrat. Home: 11531 36th Ave NE Seattle WA 98125-5632 Office: U Wash 201 Adminstrn Bldg AG-10 Seattle WA 98195

DEBRUHL, RICHARD R., television reporter; b. Southgate, Calif., June 22, 1955; s. H.L. and Bessie (George) Hammond; m. Patricia Kimberly White DeBruhl, June 18, 1977; children: Gregory, Kyle. BA, Calif. Poly. Inst., 1977. News dir. Sta. KAXY-AM, San Luis Obispo, Calif., 1977; anchorperson Sta. KCOY-TV, Santa Maria, Calif., 1978; reporter Sta. KPNX-TV, Phoenix, 1978—; reporter auto racing ESPN, Bristol, Conn., 1988, ESPN-Speedweek, Indpls., 1986-88; freelance writer various mags. Active Big Bros. of Phoenix, 1978-88; mem. St. Paul's Parish Coun., Phoenix, 1986-88. Named Big Bro. of Yr., 1987; recipient various 1st Pl. awards Ariz. AP, 1981-87. Mem. Ariz. Press Club (various 1st pl. awards, 1978-87), Nat. Acad. TV Arts and Scis. (recipient 2 Emmy awards 1982, 87). Democrat. Roman Catholic. Office: Sta KPNX-TV 1101 N Central Ave Phoenix AZ 85004-1818

DE BRUYCKER, JANE CRYSTAL, state legislator; b. Gonvick, Md., Oct. 24, 1936; d. Carl J. and Clara G. (Florence) Clemenson; m. Lloyd H. DeBruycker, July 2, 1954; children: Tammy, Mark, Cathy, Jacque, Kelly, Brett, Jody. Grad. high sch., Dutton, Mont., 1954. Mem. Mont. Ho. of Reps., 1991-92. Leader 4-H, Teton County; supt. Bethany Luth. Ch., Dutton; sec. Mont. Charolias Assn. Mem. W.I.F.E. (pres.). Democrat. Avocations: sewing, horse racing. Home: Box 7700 Dutton MT 59433

DE BRUYCKER, LLOYD HENRY, rancher, feedlot operator; b. Great Falls, Mont., Dec. 1, 1933; s. Achiel Henry and Rose Presperine (Emperor) De B.; m. Jane Crystal, July 2, 1954; 7 children. Grad. high sch., Dutton, Mont. Grain elevator laborer, 1954-59, rancher, 1959—. Home: Box 7700 Dutton MT 59433 Office: North Mt Feeders Inc 7 Miles N Box 218 Choteau MT 59422

DEBUS, ELEANOR VIOLA, retired business management company executive; b. Buffalo, May 19, 1920; d. Arthur Adam and Viola Charlotte (Pohl) D.; student Chown Bus. Sch., 1939. Sec., Buffalo Wire Works, 1939-45; home talent producer Empire Producing Co., Kansas City, Mo., sec. Owens Corning Fiberglass, Buffalo; public relations and publicity Niagara Falls Theatre, Ont., Can.; pub. rels. dir. Woman's Internat. Bowling Congress, Columbus, Ohio, 1957-59; publicist, sec. Ice Capades, Hollywood, Calif., 1961-63; sec. to contr. Rexall Drug Co., L.A., 1963-67; bus. mgmt. acct. Samuel Berke & Co., Beverly Hills, Calif., 1967-75; Gadbois Mgmt. Co., Beverly Hills, 1975-76; sec., treas. Sasha Corp., L.A., 1976-92; former bus. mgr. Dean Martin. Mem. Am. Film Inst. Republican. Lodge: Order Ea. Star. Contbr. articles to various mags.

DECARLO, ANGELA ROCCO, writer, journalist; b. Chgo., Sept. 11, 1949; d. Peter J. And Della (Serritella) Rocco; m. Daniel G. DeCarlo; children: Mark, Michael, Daniel. BA in Communications and Edn., Ill. Benedictine Coll., 1976. Cert. K-12 tchr., Ill. Disney writer Chgo. Tribune; journalist, columnist The Bus. Traveler Las Vegas (Nev.) Rev. Jour., 1985. Mem. Am. Bus. Women's Assn., Opera Pacific Alliance. Home and Office: 2718 N Vista Knolls Rd Orange CA 92667-1750

DE CECCO, JOHN PAUL, psychology and human sexuality educator, author; b. Erie, Pa., Apr. 18, 1925; s. John and Rose Marie (Lombardozzi) De C. BS, Allegheny Coll., 1946; MA, U. Pa., 1949, PhD, 1953. Tchr. Erie (Pa.) Pub. High Schs., 1946-48; faculty U. Detroit, 1953-55, Mich. State U., East Lansing, 1955-60; prof. psychology San Francisco State U., 1960—, dir. human sexuality studies, 1981—; dir. Gay, Lesbian & Bisexual Studies, 1992—. Editor: Homophobia, 1987, Gay Relationships, 1990, If You Seduce a Straight Person, 1993, Biology of Sexual Preference, 1995; editor Jour. of Homosexuality, 1977—; editor-in-chief (book series) Haworth Press, 1985—. Recipient Magnus Hirschfeld medal Germany Sociol. Soc., Berlin, 1992, Evelyn Hooker Rsch. award Gay Acad. Union, L.A., 1978; NIMH grantee, 1974-80. Fellow Internat. Acad. Sex Relationships; mem. APA, Soc. for Sci. Study of Sex. Office: San Francisco State Univ Dept of Psychology San Francisco CA 94132

DECHARIO, TONY HOUSTON, symphony orchestra executive; b. Girard, Kans., Sept. 25, 1940; s. Tony and Enid Eulalia (Frogue) D.; m. Rachel Dennisse Kennedy, Apr. 12, 1963 (div. Dec. 1974); children: Samuel Paul, Rachel Christina, Mary Rebecca; m. Mary Gill Roby, Dec. 29, 1974; 1 child, Toni Elizabeth; stepchildren: Edmund Kidd II, Kenneth Hamilton Kidd, Todd Roby Kidd. Student, U. Wichita, 1958-61; MusB, performer's cert., Eastman Sch. Music, U. Rochester, 1962, MusM, 1963. 2d trombone Kansas City (Mo.) Philharm. Orch., 1963-64; prin. trombone Dallas Symphony Orch., 1964-65; 2d trombone Rochester (N.Y.) Philharm. Orch., 1965-75, personnel mgr., 1972-75, gen. mgr., 1975-84, exec. dir., 1984-85, pres., chief exec. officer, 1985-88. Exec. dir. Honolulu Symphony Soc., 1991-95. Mem. Am. Symphony Orch. League.

DECHERT, PETER, photographer, writer, foundation administrator; b. Phila., Dec. 17, 1924; s. Robert and Helen Hope (Wilson) D.; m. Phoebe Jane Booth; children: Sandra, Robin Booth, Caroline. BA, U. Pa., 1948, MA, 1950, Ph.D., 1955. Owner, Peter Dechert Assocs., Bryn Mawr, Pa., 1956-68; asst. dir. Sch. of Am. Rsch., Santa Fe, 1968-71; pres. Indian Arts Fund, Santa Fe, 1971-72; pres. Southwest Found. for Audio-Visual Resources, Santa Fe, 1973-77; self-employed writer, photographer, Santa Fe; tchr., cons. photog. communications, 1964—. Author: Canon Rangefinder Cameras, 1933-68, 1985, The Contax Connection, 1990, Olympus Pen SLR Cameras, 1989, Canon SLR Cameras, 1959-91, 1992, The Contax S Camera Family, 1991, Los Alamos Ranch Book of Rosters, 1991; former contbg. editor Shutterbug mag., other photographic periodicals; contbr. articles on history and design of miniature cameras and other photog. topics to profl. publs. Bd. dirs. St. Vincent Hosp. Found. (pres. 1981-83, v.p. 1983-84); pres. Indian Arts Fund, 1971-72. Served with AUS, 1943-46. Mem. N.Mex. Poetry Soc. (pres. 1969-74), Am. Soc. Mag. Photographers, SAR, Southwest Assn. Indian Affairs, N.Mex. Jazz Workshop, Don Quixote Club, Phi Beta Kappa, Delta Psi. Address: PO Box 636 Santa Fe NM 87504-0636

DECIUTIIS, ALFRED CHARLES MARIA, medical oncologist, television producer; b. N.Y.C., Oct. 16, 1945; s. Alfred Ralph and Theresa Elizabeth (Manko) de C.; m. Catherine L. Gohn. B.S. summa cum laude, Fordham U., 1967; M.D., Columbia U., 1971. Diplomate Am. Bd. Internal Medicine, Am. Bd. Med. Oncology. Intern N.Y. Hosp.-Cornell Med. Ctr., N.Y.C., 1971-72, resident, 1972-74; fellow in clin. immunology Meml. Hosp.-Sloan Kettering Cancer Ctr., N.Y.C., 1974-75, fellow in clin. oncology, 1975-76, spl. fellow in immunology, 1974-76; guest investigator, asst. physician exptl. hematology Rockefeller U., N.Y.C., 1975-76; practice medicine, specializing in med. oncology Los Angeles, 1977—; host cable TV shows, 1981—; med. editor Cable Health Network, 1983—, Lifetime Network, 1984—; mem. med. adv. com. 1984 Olympics; co-founder Meditrina Med. Ctr., free outpatient surg. ctr., Torrance, Calif. Syndicated columnist Coast Media News, 1980's; producer numerous med. TV shows; contbr. articles to profl. jours.; author first comprehensive clin. description of chronic fatique syndrome as a neuro-immunologic acquired disorder. Founder Italian-Am. Med. Assn., 1982; co-founder Italian-Am. Legal Alliance, L.A., 1982—; mem. gov. bd. med. coun. Italian-Am. Found.; mem. Italian-Am. Civic Com., L.A., 1983, UCLA Chancellor's Assocs., Cath. League for Civil and Rel. Liberty, World Affairs Coun., L.A., Boston Mus. Fine Arts, Met. Mus. Served to capt. M.C., U.S. Army, 1972-74. Leukemia Soc. Am. fellow, 1974-76. Fellow ACP, Internat. Coll. Physicians and Surgeons; mem. AMA (Physician's Recognition award 1978-80, 82-85, 86-89, 89-91, 91-94), Am. Soc. Clin. Oncology, N.Y. Acad. Sci. (life), Calif. Med. Assn., Los Angeles County Med. Assn., AAAS, Am. Union Physicians and Dentists, Internat. Health Soc., Am. Pub. Health Assn., Am. Geriatrics Soc., Chinese Med. Assn., Drug Info. Assn., Nat. Geographic Soc., Internat. Platform Assn., Am. Soc. Hematology (emeritus), Nature Conservancy, Nat. Wildlife Fedn., Mensa, Phi Beta Kappa, Alpha Omega Alpha, Sigma Xi. Address: PO Box 384 Agoura Hills CA 91376

DECK, ALLAN FIGUEROA, priest; b. L.A., Apr. 19, 1945; s. George W. and Amparo Armida (Figueroa) D. BA, St. Louis U., 1969, PhD, 1974; MDiv, Jesuit Sch. Theology, Berkeley, Calif., 1976; STD, Gregorian U., 1988. Joined S.J., 1963, ordained priest Roman Cath. Ch., 1976. Lectr. in Latin Am. Lit. Pontifical U. of Comillas, Madrid, 1972; lectr. in Brazilian lit. St. Louis U., 1972-73; lectr. in Mex. Am. history U. Santa Clara, Calif., 1973-75; lectr. in hispanic ministry Immaculate Heart Coll., L.A., 1976-77; dir. Centro Pastoral Guadalupe, Santa Ana, Calif., 1976-79; pastor Our Lady of Guadalupe Ch., Santa Ana, 1976-79; dir. Hispanic ministry Diocese of Orange, Calif., 1979-85, synodal judge diocesan tribunal, 1982-85; asst. prof. dir. Hispanic ministry programs Jesuit Sch. Theology, Berkeley, 1987-92; asst. prof. Loyola Marymount U., L.A., 1992—; dir. Project 50, U. Santa Clara, 1973-75; co-founder, pres. Acad. Cath. Hispanic Theologians of the U.S., 1988-90; vis. prof. Latin Am. studies Cath. U. of Portugal, Braga, 1990; vis. prof. Hispanic studies Luth. Sch. Theology, Chgo., 1991; vis. prof. pastoral studies Mundelein (Ill.) Sem., U. St. Mary of the Lake, 1992; assoc. pastor Igreja de Santa Clara, Campo Grande, Rio de Janeiro, 1981; superior Jesuit Community of Orange County, 1984-85; adv. bd. Fund for Theol. Edn., 1993—; bd. dirs. Jesuit Hispanic Ministry Conf., Washington, 1983—, chair, 1983-89; cons. USCC Bishop's Com., 1992—, Lilly Endowment, Inc., Indpls., 1992—, Pew Charitable Trusts on Grad. Edn. of Latinos, 1993—; lectr. Loyola Marymount U., 1992-93. Author: Francisco Javier Alegre: A Study of Mexican Literary Criticism, 1976, The Second Wave: Hispanic Ministry and the Evangelization of Cultures, 1989, Frontiers of Hispanic Theology in the United States, 1992; assoc. editor Jour. Mex. Am. History, 1974-76; mem. editorial bd. Migration World, 1991—, Being Right: Am. Cath. Conservatives, 1992—, Studies in the Spirituality of Jesuits, 1992—; co-editor Notre Dame History of Hispanic Cath. in the U.S., 1991-93; contbr. articles, revs. to profl. publs. Trustee U. San Francisco, 1974-77; mem. Orange County Task Force on Med. Svcs. and the Undocumented, 1977, Sponsoring Com., 1976-85; sec. Episcopal Commn., Alta and Baja, Calif., 1979-85; bd. dirs. Orange County Sponsoring Com., Anaheim, Calif., 1976-85. Recipient O'Grady award Nat. Conf. Cath. Charities, 1978, Serra Internat. award, 1987, Best Book in Profession award Cath. Press Assn., 1989, Virgilio Elizondo award Acad. Cath. Hispanic Theologians U.S., 1992. Mem. Nat. Cath. Coun. for Hispanic Ministry, Inc. (pres. 1991—), Jesuit Hispanic Ministry Conf. (pres. 1979—), Cath. Theol. Soc. Am., 1988—, Acad. Cath. Hispanic Theologians (pres. 1988-90). Home: 5322 Franklin Ave Los Angeles CA 90027-1655 Office: Loyola Marymount U Ctr Pastoral Studies 7101 W 80th St Los Angeles CA 90045-2659

DECKER, BO, artist; b. San Jose, Calif., Jan. 2, 1969; s. Jerry Alton Mattson and Gayle Louise (Decker) Van Osten. BA in Studio Art, Calif.

State U., Chico, 1993; postgrad., Sch. Visual Arts, N.Y.C. Asst. scenic artist theatre dept. Calif. State U., Chico, 1992-93; scenic artist Forest Theatre Guild, Carmel, Calif., 1993; gallery asst. Holmes Fine Art, San Jose, 1993-94; scenic artist San Jose Repertory Co., 1994; freelance illustrator, 1995—; illustrator The News and Review, Chico, 1992. Contbg. sculptor Burning Man, Nevada desert, 1995; contbr. poetry to publs. Disc jockey Sta. KCSC, Chico, 1991-93. Mem. AAM, Cacophany Soc. Home: 5425 Nicole Way Gilroy CA 95020-6810

DECKER, DAVID B., architect, educator; b. Flint, Mich., Dec. 30, 1938; s. Arthur W. and Russelle (Wininger) D.; m. Sadie C. Neef, June 5, 1964; children: Ian David Neef Decker, Colin Welwood Decker. BA, U. Colo., 1961; MArch, Yale U., 1969. Lic. architect, Colo., Wyo. Architect MLTW Moore/Turnbull, New Haven, Conn., 1968-70, Muchow Assocs., Architects, Denver, 1970-74; prin. Decker & Assocs., Architects, Denver, 1974-88, 91—; mng. assoc. TRA-Airport Consulting, Denver, 1988-91; adj. prof. archtl. design Coll. Architecture & Planning U. Colo., Denver, 1978-88. Pres., bd. dirs., dir. Rocky Mountain Planned Parenthood, Denver. Mem. AIA (com. on design 1980—, v.p. Denver chpt. 1979, 81, treas. AIA Colo. 1977, bd. dirs. Denver chpt. 1976-81, Design awards 1972, 76). Office: Decker & Assocs Archs 1600 Broadway Ste 1950 Denver CO 80202-4919

DECKER, DONALD DARYL, range conservationist; b. Phoenix, May 9, 1960; s. Gregory Royce and Violet (Kenniston) D.; m. Catalina Laborin Escalante, July 14, 1990; 1 child, Katherine Brisa. BS in Renewable Natural Resources, U. Ariz., 1985. Biol. technician U.S.D.A. Forest Svc., Springerville, Ariz., 1983-87; soil conservationist U.S.D.A. Soil Conservation Svc., Douglas, Ariz., 1988-89; range conservationist Natural Resources Conservation Svc., Willcox, Ariz., 1990—. Mem. Soc. for Range Mgmt. (county dir. info. and edn. dir. 1990—). Republican. Baptist. Home: PO Box 119 Willcox AZ 85644-0119 Office: Natural Resources Conservation Svcs 247 South Curtis Willcox AZ 85643

DECKER, PETER RANDOLPH, rancher, former state official; b. N.Y.C., Oct. 1, 1934; s. Frank Randolph and Marjorie (Marony) D.; m. Dorothy Morss, Sept. 24, 1972; children: Karen, Christopher, Hilary. BA, Middlebury Coll., Vt., 1957; MA, Syracuse U., 1961; PhD, Columbia U., 1974. Tchr. Cate Sch., Carpinteria, Calif., 1961-63; sr. writer Congl. Quar., Washington, 1963-64; asst. to pres. Middlebury (Vt.) Coll., 1964-67; staff asst. Sen. Robert Kennedy, Washington, 1967-68; instr./lectr. Columbia U., N.Y.C., 1972-74; asst. prof. Duke U., Durham, N.C., 1974-80; owner/operator Double D Ranch, Ridgway, Colo., 1980—; commr. agr. State of Colo., Denver, 1987-89; pres. Decker & Assocs., Denver, Colo., 1989—; dir. Inst. Am. West, Nat. Western Stock Show, Denver; bd. dirs. Bank of Telluride, Fed. Res. Bd., Kansas City, Denver br., Western Colo. Bank. Author: Fortunes and Failures, 1978; contbr. articles to profl. jours. Overseer Middlebury Coll., 1988—, Colo. Commn. on Higher Edn., 1985-93; chmn. Ouray County Dem. Party, 1982-85; chmn. Ouray County Planning Commn., 1981-85; chmn. Colo. Endowment Humanities, 1982-85. Capt. U.S. Army, 1957-60. English Speaking Union scholar, 1952-53; Nat. Endowment for Humanities fellow, 1977-78; Rockefeller Found. fellow, 1979-80. Mem. Nat. Cattlemen's Assn., Am. Hist. Assn., Colo. Cattle Feeders Assn., Denver Athletic Club, Elks. Democrat. Home: Double D Ranch 6748 Highway 62 Ridgway CO 81432-9796

DECKER, RICHARD JEFFREY, lawyer; b. Manhasset, N.Y., Aug. 26, 1959; s. Alan B. and Shelley T. (Belkin) D.; m. Carrie Ann Gordon, Aug. 13, 1989. BA, Union Coll., Schenectady, N.Y., 1981; JD, Boston U., 1984. Bar: N.Y. 1985, Calif. 1985, Mass. 1985, U.S. Dist. Ct. (cen. dist.) Calif. 1985. Assoc. Turner, Gesterfeld, Wilk & Tigerman, Beverly Hills, Calif., 1985-86, Shapiro, Posell & Close, L.A., 1986-90, Katten, Muchin, Zavis & Weitzman, L.A., 1990-93, Ginsburg, Stephan, Oringher & Richman, L.A., 1993—. Mem. Los Angeles County Bar Assn., Beverly Hills Bar Assn., Century City Bar Assn. Office: Ginsburg Stephan Oringher & Richman 10100 Santa Monica Blvd Ste 800 Los Angeles CA 90067-2901

DECKER, RICHARD KELSEY, equipment distribution company executive; b. Monrovia, Calif., Dec. 31, 1927; s. Raymond Grant and Dorothy Irene (Heady) D.; m. Barbara Carolyn Carlson, 1956; children—Richard Brian, Carolyn Ann Decker Johnson. B.S., U. So. Calif., 1952. Cost. acct. S.W. Products Co., Monrovia, 1953-55; controller Scotsman Refrigeration Inc., Monterey Park, Calif., 1955-64; with Scotsman Distbrs. of Los Angeles, Inc., La Verne, Calif., 1964—, retired, 1991; pres., chief exec. officer, 1976—. Served with USN, 1945-47. Mem. Alpha Kappa Psi (pres.), Beta Gamma Sigma.

DECKER SLANEY, MARY TERESA, Olympic athlete; b. Bunnvale, N.J., Aug. 4, 1958; d. John and Jacqueline Decker; m. Ron Tabb (div. 1983); m. Richard Slaney, June 1, 1985; 1 child, Ashley Lynn. Student, U. Colo., 1977-78. Amateur runner, 1969—, holder several world track and field records, 1980—; winner 2 gold medals at 1500 and 3000 meters World Track and Field Championship, Helsinki, Finland, 1983; mem. U.S. Olympic teams, 1980, 84; cons. to CBS Records, Timex, Eastman Kodak. Recipient Jesse Owens Internat. Amateur Athlete award, 1982, Sullivan award AAU, 1982; named Amateur Sportswoman of the Yr., Women's Sports Found., 1982, 83, Top Sportswoman A.P. Europe, 1985. Address: 2923 Flintlock St Eugene OR 97408-4660*

DECKERT, HARLAN KENNEDY, JR., manufacturing company official; b. Evanston, Ill., May 22, 1923; s. Harlan Kennedy Sr. and Lady Otey (Hutton) D.; BS, U. Calif., Berkeley, 1949; MBA, U. So. Calif., 1962; m. Mary Emma Eldredge, Nov. 27, 1971; children: Mary Adrienne, Christine Ann, Daniel Gregory, Deborah Alice. Systems analyst Northrop Corp., Hawthorne, Calif., 1949-53, supr. engring. adminstrv. svcs., 1953-57, adminstrv. systems engr., 1957-59; with AiResearch Indsl. div. Garrett Corp., Torrance, Calif., 1959-88, systems svc. adminstr., 1962-72, mgr. adminstrv. svcs., 1972-75, adminstr. internat. ops., 1975-80, sr. staff advisor Garrett Automotive Group Allied-Signal, Inc., 1980-88, ret., 1988. Active mem. L.A. County Mus. Art, Wild Beast Soc., docent; Greater L.A. Zoo Assn.; mem. L.A. County Mus. Natural History, San Luis Obispo zoological Soc., Exotic Cat Breeding Compound, African Wildlife Found., Friends Cabrillo Marine Aquarium, Assn. Zoo & Aquarium Docents; supporting mem. Living Desert. With USAAF, 1943-46, CBI, capt. USAFR, 1946-57. Mem. Am. Assn. Zoo Keepers, Am. Zoo and Aquarium Assn., Nat. Wildlife Fedn., Oreg. Wildlife Safari, San Diego Zool. Soc. (Diamond Club), World Wildlife Fund, Nature Conservancy, Wildlife Waystation, Jane Goodall Inst., Santa Monica Mus. Flying, Wildlife Conservation Soc., Internat. Wolf Ctr. Home: 2509 20th St Santa Monica CA 90405-2705

DE CONCINI, DENNIS, former senator, lawyer; b. Tucson, May 8, 1937; s. Evo and Ora (Webster) DeC.; m. Susan Margaret Hurley, June 6, 1959; children: Denise, Christina, Patrick Evo. B.A., U. Ariz., 1959, LL.B., 1963. Bar: Ariz., D.C., 1963. Mem. firm Evo DeConcini; ptnr. DeConcini & McDonald, Tucson, 1968-73; dep. Pima County atty. Sch. Dist. 1, 1971-72, county atty., 1972-76; U.S. Senator from Ariz., 1977-95; atty. Perry-Romani Assocs., Washington, 1995—, De Concini, McDonald, Bramer, Yetwin & Lacy, Tuscon, 1995—; mem. appropriations com., U.S. Senate, chmn. subcom. on Treasury, Postal Svc. and Gen. Govt.; mem. subcom. on Def., subcom. on Energy and Water Devel., subcom. on Fgn. Ops., subcom. on Interior Related Agys.; mem. Jud. com.; chmn. subcom. on Patents, Copyrights and Trademarks; mem. subcom. on Antitrust, Monopolies and Bus. Rights, subcom. on the Constitution, com. on Rules and Adminstrn., com. on Vets. Affairs; chmn. select com. on Intelligence; chmn. Commn. on Security and Cooperation in Europe; select com. Indian Affairs; mem. Internat. Narcotics Control Caucus, West Coalition of Senators; former pres., bd. dirs. Shopping Ctrs., Inc.; bd. dirs. Fed. Home Mortgage Corp. Chmn. legis. com. Tucson Cmty. Coun., 1966-67; mem. major gifts com., devel. fund drive St. Joseph's Hosp., 1970, mem. devel. coun., 1971-73; bd. dirs. Fed. Home Mortgage Corp., Nat. Ctr. for Missing and Exploited Children; mem. major gifts com. Tucson Mus. and Art Ctr. Bldg. Fund, 1971; adminstr. Ariz. Drug Control Dist., 1975-76; precinct committeeman Ariz. Dem. Ctrl. Com., 1958—; mem. Pima County Dem. Ctrl. Com., 1958-67, Dem. State Exec. Com., 1958-68; state vice chmn. Ariz. Dem. Com., 1964-66, 70-72; vice chmn. Pima County Dem. Com., 1970-73. Served to 2d lt. JAG U.S. Army, 1959-60. Named Outstanding Ariz. County Atty., 1975. Mem. Am., Ariz., Pima County bar assns., Nat. Dist. Attys. Assn., Ariz. Sheriffs and County Attys. Assn., Am. Judicature Soc., Ariz. Pioneer Hist. Soc., NAACP, U. Ariz. Alumni Assn., Tucson Fraternal Order Police, Phi Delta Theta, Delta Sigma Rho, Phi Alpha Delta. Roman Catholic. Clubs: Nucleus (Tucson), Pres.'s U. Ariz. (Tucson), Latin Am. (Tucson), Latin Am. Social (Tucson).

DE COTEAU, DENIS, music director, conductor; b. N.Y.C.. BA, MA in Music, NYU; studied, Mozarteum, Salzburg, Austria; MusD, Stanford U. Asst. condr. San Francisco Ballet, 1970-74, music dir., condr., 1974—; artistic advisor Stockton Symphony, 1994—; condr. Oakland Symphony Youth Orch., 1970-79, Aichii U. Orch., Nagoya, Japan, 1982—, Tokyo City Philarm. Orch., 1989, San Francisco Conservatory of Music; prin. guest condr. Deutches Jugendorchester, 1976, 78, 80; guest condr. Nat. Music Camp Assn. Australian Youth Orch., 1980—, Oreg. Mozart Players, 1989; assoc. condr. San Francisco Symphony, 1986; music dir., condr. Flagstaff (Ariz.) Festival of Arts, 1977-83. Guest appearances with numerous dance cos. including Kansas City Ballet, State of Ala. Ballet, San Diego Ballet, Ballet West, Honolulu Ballet, and Oakland Ballet; guest condr. BBC Scottish Symphony, St. Louis Symphony, New Orleans Philharm., Tokyo City Philharm, Radio Frei Orch. (Berlin), San Francisco Symphony, Seattle Symphony, Oakland Symphony, San Francisco Chamber Orch. and others; appeared with Yomiuri Orch., Tokyo; invited condr. (recs.) Nat. Philharm. London, (concerts) Australia's Bicentennial, World Expo, Brisbane; condr. opera premiere Song of Pegasus (Marin Theatre Playhouse). Recipient Pierre Monteux Conducting Prize, 1969, Adventuresome Programming award ASCAP, 1976. Office: Conservatory of Music Orch 1201 Ortega St San Francisco CA 94122-4411 also: San Francisco Ballet 455 Franklin St San Francisco CA 94102-4438

DECTER, BETTY EVA, artist; b. Birmingham, Ala., Apr. 22, 1927; d. Kara Miracle; m. William Fenske, May 14, 1943 (div.); children: William Jr., Karalee; m. Gerald A. Decter, July 9, 1961; 1 stepchild, Tom. Freelance fashion model, 1950s; designer, stylist Decter Mannikin Co., Inc., 1962-92; v.p. Bellagio Arabians, 1985—. One-woman shows at Roger Morrison Gallery, L.A., 1985, Brand Libr. Art Gallery, Glendale, Calif., 1988, Riverside County Mus./Edward-Dean Mus., 1989, San Francis Gallery, Crossroads Sch. for Arts and Scis., Santa Monica, Calif., 1992, Thinking Eye Gallery, L.A., 1986, 87, Absolute Gallery, L.A., 1986, Warner Ctr. Gallery, 1987, Otis Art Inst. of Parsons Sch. Design, 1988, J.C. Cooper Gallery, 1988, Mus. Without Walls, Bemus Point, N.Y., 1992; contbr. articles to profl. jours. and encys. Founding mem., co-chair Save the Santa Monica Mountains Com., 1970; founding mem., chair No on Nowell Com., 1973-74; mem. L.A. City Atty.'s Com. on Polit. Reform, 1973-74; founding mem., chair Com. for Enforcement of Campaign Laws, 1974-78; founding mem. bd. William O. Douglas Outdoor Classroom, 1980-90; helped establish Nat. Urban Park in Santa Monica Mountains, 1978-80; active local politics, 1969—; mem. The Group, 1984-93; mem. adv. bd. Woman's Bldg., L.A., 1988. Recipient award Assocs. of Brand Libr., 1991, Bronze award Calif. Discovery Awards, 1994. Studio: 5412 W Washington Blvd Los Angeles CA 90016-1113

DEDEAUX, PAUL J., orthodontist; b. Pass Christian, Miss., Feb. 22, 1937; s. Mack and Harriet D.; m. Janet Louise Harter, June 29, 1971; children: Michele, Kristen, Kelly. BA, Dillard U., 1959; DDS, Howard U., 1963; MS, Fairleigh Dickinson U., 1975. Pvt. practice, Washington, 1967-69, Santa Ana, Calif., 1976—; instr. Howard U., Washington, 1967-69; dental dir. Dr. Martin Luther King Health Ctr., Bronx, N.Y., 1969-70, dentist, 1970-76; chief dentist Calif. State Dept. Corrections, Calipatria, Calif., 1993—; instr. Howard U., Washington, 1967-69; cons. Hostos C.C., Bronx, 1971-76; mem. adv. panel Dental Econs. mag., 1976; adj. assoc. prof. Columbia U., N.Y.C., 1970-72. Contbr. articles to profl. jours. Capt. U.S. Army, 1963-67, comdr. USAR, 1975—. Mem. Am. Assn. Orthodontists, Pacific Coast Soc. Orthodontists, ADA, Calif. Dental Assn., Assn. Mil. Surgeons of U.S. Democrat. Methodist. Home: 12181 Anzio St Garden Grove CA 92640-4644 Office: Calif State Dept Corrections 7018 Blair Rd Calipatria CA 92233

DEDERER, MICHAEL EUGENE, public relations company executive; b. Seattle, Apr. 30, 1932; s. Michael and Clare (Collon) D.; separated; children—David M., Claire M. B.A. in Journalism, U. Wash., 1953. Account exec. Hugh A. Smith Mktg. & Pub. Relations Co., Seattle, 1956-59; account exec. Kraft, Smith & Ehrig, Inc., Seattle, 1959-63; account exec. Jay Rockey Pub. Relations and The Rockey Co., Inc., Seattle, 1963, v.p., 1970-78, exec. v.p., 1978-86, pres., 1986-94, vice chmn., 1994—. Served to 1st lt. U.S. Army, 1953-55. Mem. Pub. Relations Soc. Am. (pres. Wash. chpt. 1970), Soc. Profl. Journalists. Roman Catholic. Office: Rockey Co Inc 2121 5th Ave Seattle WA 98121-2510

DEDES, GEORGE PANAYOTIS, direct marketing executive; b. Athens, Greece, Feb. 22, 1962; came to U.S., 1969; s. Panayotis G. and Panayota P. (Oikonomou) D. BA in internat. rels., Univ. Southern Calif., 1984, BS in aerospace engring., 1984. Ops. supr. United Airlines Mileage Plus, Long Beach, Calif., 1983-89; ops. mgr. Fukutake Publ. Co., Torrance, Calif., 1989-92, The Walt Disney Co., Burbank, Calif., 1992-94. Recipient Outstanding Student award Calif. Savings & Loan Assn., 1979, Outstanding Achievement award Bank of Am., 1979. Mem. Direct Mktg. Assn. Democrat. Home: 636 Alexander St Unit A Glendale CA 91203-1622

DEDINI, ELDON LAWRENCE, cartoonist; b. King City, Calif., June 29, 1921; s. Grutly Stefano and Oleta Regina (Loeber) D.; m. Virginia DeSales Conroy, July 15,1944; 1 son, Giulio. A.A., Hartnell Coll., Salinas, Calif., 1942; grad., Chouinard Art Inst., Los Angeles, 1942-44. Staff cartoonist: Salinas Morning Post, 1940-41; staff story dept., Walt Disney Studios, Burbank, Calif., 1944-46; staff cartoonist: Esquire mag, Chho., 1946-50, New Yorker mag, N.Y.C., 1950—, Playboy mag, Chgo., 1960—; Author: cartoon album The Dedini Gallery, 1961, A Much, Much Better World, 1985; anthologies of New Yorker, Playboy cartoons. Recipient ann. award for best color Cartoon Playboy, 1978. Mem. Nat. Cartoonists Soc. (Best Mag. Cartoonist award 1958, 61, 64, 89), Cartoonists Guild Inc (2d v.p. N.Y.C. 1970). Office: PO Box 1630 Monterey CA 93942-1630

DEE, ANTHONY JAMES, psychiatrist; b. Manila, Philippines, Feb. 15, 1940; s. Charles and Diana (Schmidt) D.; m. Mary Dee; children: Jocelyn Suzette, Anthony Mark. BS in Physics, U. Philippines, 1961; MD, U. of the East, Philippines, 1966; MBA, U. Hawaii, 1979. Diplomate Am. Bd. Psychiatry and Neurology. Asst. prof. Yale U., New Haven, 1970-75; dir. Diamond Head Health Ctr., Honolulu, 1975-82; chief of dept. VA Hosp., Erie, Pa., 1982-87; med. dir. West L.A. VA Hosp., 1987-89; pres. Pragma Tech., Manila, 1990—, Macani Enterprises, L.A., 1989—; assoc. prof. U. Hawaii, Honolulu, 1975-82, SUNY, Buffalo, 1982-87; assoc. clin. prof. UCLA, 1987-89. Contbr. articles to profl. jours. Mem. allocations com. United Way, L.A., 1993—; bd. dirs. ARC, L.A., 1993—, vice chmn., Erie, 1982-87; pres. Internat. Inst., Erie, 1985-87. Capt. USN, 1987. Office: 1606 S Barrington Ave Ste 1 Los Angeles CA 90025-4041

DEEMS, ANDREW WILLIAM, health facility administrator; b. Corpus Christi, Tex., Sept. 19, 1946; s. Ralph Francis and Ruth Frances (Pfister) D.; m. Glenda Jean Wyma, Apr. 6, 1968; children: Leslie, Matthew. BA with honors, Occidental Coll., 1968; MPH, U. Calif., Berkeley, 1972. Asst. adminstr. Merle West Med. Ctr., Klamath Falls, Oreg., 1972-77, Alta Bates Hosp., Berkeley, 1977-79; exec. v.p. Mt. Zion Hosp. and Med. Ctr., San Francisco, 1979-84; exec. v.p. St. Mary's Hosp. and Med. Ctr., San Francisco, 1984-88, pres., chief exec. officer, 1988-92; pres., CEO Palomar Pomerado Health System, Escondido, Calif., 1992—; pres. San Francisco Sect. Hosp. Coun., 1990-92, West Bay Hosp. Conf., 1990-92; bd. dir. Hosp. Coun. No. and Cen. Calif., 1990-92. Bd. dirs. United Way, 1993—, Hosp. Coun. San Diego and Imperial Counties, 1993—. Lt. (j.g.) USN, 1968-69. Recipient W. Glenn Ebersole award Hosp. Forum Mag., 1972. Fellow Am. Coll. Healthcare Execs.; mem. Calif. Assn. Hospsp. and Health Systems (bd. dirs.), West Bay Hosp. Conf. (pres., bd. dirs. 1990-92), Hosp. Coun. No. and Ctrl. Calif. (bd. dirs. 1990-92), Hosp. Coun. San Diego and Imperial Counties (bd. dirs. 1993—). Democrat. Presbyterian.

DEERING, FRED ARTHUR, insurance company executive; b. Winfield, Kans., Jan. 12, 1928; s. Frederick A. and Lucile (Phillips) D.; m. Isabell Staufenberg, June 14, 1949; m. Elizabeth Kimball MacMillan, Apr. 12, 1979; children: Anne Deering Buchanan, Kate. BS, U. Colo., 1951, LLB, 1951; LHD (hon.), Loretto Heights Coll., 1984. Bar: Colo. 1951. Assoc. firm Gorsuch, Kingis, Campbell, Walker & Grover, Denver, Denver, 1951-54; ptnr. Gorsuch, Kingis, Campbell, Walker & Grover, Denver, 1954-62; v.p., gen. counsel Security Life of Denver, 1962-66, pres., CEO, 1966-82, chmn., CEO, 1982-89, chmn., 1989-93; chmn. exec. com., 1994-95; bd. dirs. ING Am. Life Co.; chmn., CEO, dir. Midwestern United Life Ins. Co., 1983-89, Halifax Life Ins. Co., Toronto, 1985-88; vice chmn. bd. Invesco Funds Group, chmn., 1968-90; instr. Am. Inst. Banking, 1953-57; guest lectr. Colo. Sch. Law, 1958-59. Editor-in-chief Rocky Mountain Law Rev. Trustee Loretto Heights Coll., 1968-88, chmn. bd. dirs., 1968-84, chmn. emeritus, 1984-88; bd. dirs. Wallace Village for Children, 1968-78, Met. United Fund, 1969-71, Porter Hosp., 1970-79, U. Colo. Found., 1972-75; mem. adv. com. Met. Assn. for Retarded Children, Denver, 1970-71, Denver Rsch. Inst., 1972-76; trustee Huebner Found., 1980-85, St. Mary's Acad., Denver, 1989—; bd. dirs. Inst. Internat. Edn., Denver, 1986-92, Nat. Western Stock Show, 1990—, Global Health Scis. Fund. With U.S. Army, 1946-47. Named Colo. Businessman of Yr. Alpha Kappa Psi, 1977, Disting. Law Alumnus, U. Colo., 1982. Mem. ABA, Colo. Bar Assn., Denver Bar Assn., Am. Judicature Soc., Colo. Life Conf., Life Office Mgmt. Assn. (bd. dirs. 1977-81, 82-85, chmn. 1983-84), Denver C. of C., Met. Denver Execs. Club (pres. 1970-71), Old Baldy Club, Cherry Hills Country Club (bd. dirs. 1973-76, pres. 1975-76), Wigwam Club, Bang-a-Way Club, Mission Valley Country Club, Univ. Club, Order of Coif, Sigma Alpha Epsilon. also: 88 N Casey Key Rd Osprey FL 34229-9704

DEFAZIO, LYNETTE STEVENS, dancer, choreographer, educator, chiropractor, author, actress; b. Berkeley, Calif., Sept. 29; d. Honore and Mabel J. (Estavan) Stevens; children: J.H. Panganiban, Joanna Pang. student U. Calif., Berkeley, 1950-55, San Francisco State Coll., 1950-51; D. Chiropractic, Life-West Chiropractic Coll., San Lorenzo, Calif., 1983, cert. Techniques of Teaching U. Calif., 1985, BA in Humanities, New Coll. Calif., 1986; Lic. Chiropracter, Mich. Diplomate Nat. Sci. Bd.; eminence in dance edn., Calif. Community Colls. dance specialist, standard services, childrens ctrs. credentials Calif. Dept. Edn., 1986. Contract child dancer Monogram Movie Studio, Hollywood, Calif., 1938-40; dance instr. San Francisco Ballet, 1953-64; performer San Francisco Opera Ring, 1960-67; performer, choreographer Oakland (Calif.) Civic Light Opera, 1963-70; dir. Ballet Arts Studio, Oakland, Calif., 1960; teaching specialist Oakland Unified Sch. Dist., 1965-80; fgn. exchange dance dir. Academie de Danses-Salle Pleyel, Paris, France, 1966; instr. Peralta Community Coll. Dist., Oakland, 1971—, chmn. dance dept., 1985—; cons., instr. extension courses UCLA, Dirs. and Suprs. Assn., Pittsburg Unified Sch. Dist., 1971-73, Tulare (Calif.) Sch. Dist., 1971-73; researcher Ednl. Testing Services, HEW, Berkeley, 1974; resident choreographer San Francisco Childrens Opera, 1970—, Oakland Civic Theater; ballet mistress Dimensions Dance Theater, Oakland, 1977-80; cons. Gianchetta Sch. Dance, San Francisco, Robicheau Boston Ballet, TV series Patchwork Family, CBS, N.Y.C.; choreographer Ravel's Valses Nobles et Sentimentales, 1976. Recipient Foremost Women of 20th Century, 1985, Merit award San Francisco Children's Opera, 1985, 90. Author: Basic Music Outlines for Dance Classes, 1960, rev., 1968, Teaching Techniques and Choreography for Advanced Dancers, 1965, Basic Music Outlines for Dance Classes, 1965, Goals and Objectives in Improving Physical Capabilities, 1970, A Teacher's Guide for Ballet Techniques, 1970, Principle Procedures in Basic Curriculum, 1974, Objectives and Standards of Performance for Physical Development, 1975, Techniques of the Ballet School, 1970, rev., 1974, The Opera Ballets: A Choreographic Manual Vols. I-V, 1986. Assoc. music arranger Le Ballet du Cirque, 1964; assoc. composer, lyricist The Ballet of Mother Goose, 1968; choreographer: Valses Nobles Et Sentimentales (Ravel), Transitions (Kashevaroff), 1991, The New Wizard of Oz, 1991, San Francisco Children's Opera (Gingold); Canon in D for Strings and Continuo (Pachelbel), 1979; appeared in Flower Drum Song, 1993, Gigi, 1994. Mem. Calif. State Teacher Assn., Bay Area Chiropractic Research Soc., Profl. Dance Teacher Assn., Home and Office: 4923 Harbord Dr Oakland CA 94618-2506

DEFAZIO, PETER A., congressman; b. Needham, Mass., May 27, 1947; m. Myrnie Daut. BA in Econs. and Polit. Sci., Tufts U., 1969; postgrad., U. Oreg., 1969-71, MS in Pub. Adminstrn./Gerontology, 1977. Aide to U.S. Rep. Jim Weaver, 1977-82; sr. issues specialist, caseworker, dist. field office U.S. rep. Jim Weaver, 1977-78, legis. asst. Washington office, 1978-80, dir. constituent services, 1980-82; mem. commn. representing Springfield Lane County (Oreg.) Commn., 1982-86; mem. 100-103rd Congresses from 4th Oreg. dist., Washington, D.C., 1987—; ranking minority mem. resources com., mem. transp. and infrastructure com. Mem. Lane County Econ. Devel. com., Ingergovtl. Relations com.; bd. dirs. Eugene-Springfield Met. Partnership; Lane County Dem. precinct person, 1982—. Served with USAFR. Mem. Assn. of Oreg. Counties (legis. com.), Nat. Assn. of Counties (tax and fin. com.). Office: US Ho of Reps 2134 Rayburn Washington DC 20515*

DEFEO, SISTER THERESA F. MARIE, health facility administrator, educator; b. Bklyn., June 25, 1950; d. Joseph Francis and Rosalie Louise (Bizazza) DeF. AA, U. N.Mex., 1983, BS, 1987; MHA, Chapman U., 1992. Joined Sisters of Felician-Franciscans, Roman Cath. Ch., 1978, first vows, 1981, perpetual vows, 1987. Adminstrv. asst., dir. nursing svcs. Beckman Downtown Hosp., N.Y.C., 1973-75; exec. sec. to pres. Hinkle Corp., Albuquerque, N.Mex., 1975-76; adminstrv. asst., med. dir. St. Joseph Hosp., Albuquerque, N.Mex., 1976-79, rehab. clin. intern, 1981-82; adminstrv. asst., prin. Queen of Heaven Sch., Albuquerque, N.Mex., 1983-86; spl. edn. clin. intern Carrie Tingley Hosp., Albuquerque, N.Mex., 1983, N.Mex. Youth Diagnosis and Devel. Ctr., Albuquerque, N.Mex., 1986; adminstr. Good Shepherd Manor, Albuquerque, N.Mex., 1987—; part-time prof. Chapman U., Albuquerque, 1992—. Mem. Am. Soc. Aging, Am. Coll. Health Care Adminstrn., Cath. Health Assn., Am. Health Care Assn. Home and Office: PO Box 15092 Rio Rancho NM 87174

DEFFENBAUGH, KAY ANNE, secondary education art educator; b. Kennewick, Wash., Aug. 9, 1956; d. Robert Zwanzig and Frances Carma (Sloan) D.; m. David Roger Thiede, Oct. 22, 1988; 1 child, Shannon. AA, Columbia Basin Coll., 1976; BA in Fine Arts, Washington State U., 1980; cert. in edn., Ea. Wash. U., 1986, MEd, 1991. Cert. tchr., Wash. Wholesale rep. Armstrongs Gallery, Pomona, Calif., 1981-84; tchr. art Prosser (Wash.) Sch. Dist., 1986—; mem. arts adv. com. Comm. on Student Learning, 1994; fellow Summer Rsch. Internship Program for Tchrs., Battelle, Richland, 1994—. Mem. Wash. Art Edn. Assn., Nat. Art Edn. Assn., Southeast Wash. Amiga Users Group (pres. 1989-92, fair publicity coord. 1989-90), Arts Coun. Mid-Columbia (bd. dirs. 1992-95). Home: 1412 Cimarron Ave Richland WA 99352-9441 Office: Prosser Sch Dist PO Box 430 Prosser WA 99350-0430

DE FONVILLE, PAUL BLISS, historic organization administrator; b. Oakland, Calif., Mar. 3, 1923; s. Marion Yancey and Charlotte (Bliss) de F.; m. Virginia Harpell, June 17, 1967. Student, Calif. Poly. U., 1942-44, Michael Chekhov Group, 1947-52. Founder, pres. Cowboy Meml. and Libr., Caliente, Calif., 1969—; tchr. outdoor edn. Calif. State U., Bakersfield, 1980. Life mem. Presdl. Task Force, Washington, 1984—, Rep. Senatorial inner circle, Washington, 1989—, Nat. Rep. Congl. Com., Washington, 1990—, Rep. Nat. Com., 1987—, U.S. Senatorial Club, 1988—, Rep. Senatorial Commn., 1991, Presdl. Election Registry, 1992; del. Presdl. Trust, 1992; mem. Presdl. Commn. Am. Agenda; affiliate Lake Isabella Bd. Realtors, 1993; hon. marshall Lake Isabella, Kern County Christmas Parade, 1993. Recipient Slim Pickens award Calif. State Horsemen, 1980, Marshall-Working Western award Rose Parade, Pasadena, 1980, recognition Kern County, 1984, proclamations Mayor of Bakersfield, 1984, 85, Govt. of Calif., 1984, resolution Calif. Senate, 1988, Calif. Assembly, 1990, Presdl. Order of Merit, 1991, Congl. Cert. of Merit, 1992, Rep. Presdl. Legion of Merit award, 1992, Rep. Presdl. Legion of Merit award, 1992, document Gov. of Calif., 1993, Rep. Nat. Com. Cert. Recognition, 1992, Rep. Presdl. adv. Commn. Cert. award, 1993, Congl. Cert. Appreciation, 1993, Cert. Commendation Washington Legal Found., 1993, Rep. Presdl. award, 1994, Rep. Congl. Order of Liberty, 1993, Internat. Order of Merit medal, 1993, 20th Century award for achievement, 1993, Rep. Senatorial Medal of Freedom, 1994, Ronald Reagan Eternal Flame of Freedom medal and cert., 1995, Cmty. Svc. and Profl. Achievement medal, 1995. Mem. SAG, NRA, Calif. State Horsemen (life), Equestrian Trails (life), Forty Niners (life), Calif. Rep. Assembly, Heritage Found., Cowboy Turtles Assn. (life), Rodeo Cowboys Assn. (life), Pro Rodeo Cowboys Assn. (life), Internat. Platform Assn., Lake

Isabella C. of C., Kern County C. of C. Baptist. Home: 40371 Cowboy Ln Caliente CA 93518-1405

DE FOREST, EDGAR LESTER, actor, poet, educator; b. Hull, Mass.; s. Edgar Leonard and Ellen Marian (Huntington) De F.; m. Beulah Mary Ingalls, Nov. 21, 1940; children: Peter, Stephen, David, Richard. Diploma, Leland Powers Sch. of Theatre, Boston, 1937; BS, Boston U., 1940; MA, U. So. Calif., 1941; EdD, Columbia U., 1954. Cert. elem. tchr., Calif. (life); cert. secondary tchr., Calif. (life); cert. sch. adminstr., Calif. Dir. reading Mich. State U. (formerly Mich. State Coll.), East Lansing, 1945-48, asst. dir. summer program, 1954-57; dir. students Suffolk U., Boston, 1948-52; assoc. survey research Columbia U., N.Y.C., 1952-53; acting dean instruction Ventura (Calif.) Coll., 1957-60; prof. Coll. Desert, Palm Desert, Calif., 1962-78, prof. emeritus, 1979—; dean of ship U. Seven Seas, Whittier, Calif., 1964-65. Author various poems; appeared in plays Man of La Mancha, 1982, Death of a Salesman, 1983, Homage to Dali, 1988, Becket, The Fantastiks, Booth Majority of One, The King and I. Mem. Mayor's cultural planning 2000 com., Palm Desert, 1985-86; pres. Friends of the Library Coll. of the Desert, Palm Desert, 1983-85. Named Ideal Citizen of the Age of Enlightenment, World Govt. for the Age of Enlightenment, 1971. Mem. Mich. Reading Assn. (founder, pres. 1954-55), Lambda Chi Alpha. Democrat. Home: 220 Pinyon Crest Mountain Center CA 92561-9756

DEFREESE, VERNON LEE, JR., air force officer; b. Kittery, Maine, Sept. 29, 1962; s. Vernon Lee Sr. and Velma Jean (Glover) DeF.; m. Karen Lee Nagle, Feb. 14, 1987; children: Adrianna Corrin, Danielle Lee, Alexis Maria. BS in Bus. Adminstrn., Norwich U., Northfield, Vt., 1984; MS in Adminstrn., Ctrl. Mich. U., Mt. Pleasant, 1992. Commd. 2d lt. U.S. Air Force, 1984, advanced through grades to capt., 1988; with 91 Ops. Group U.S. Air Force, Minot AFB, 1985-90; missile staff officer Hdqrs. 15th Air Force U.S. Air Force, March AFB, Calif., 1990-91; missile staff officer 20th Air Force Hdqrs. U.S. Air Force, Vandenberg AFB, Calif., 1991-93, ops. flight comdr. for the 490 MS, 1993-94, dep. chief missile control flight, 1994—. Decorated Air Force Commendation medal (2). Mem. Missile Boosters Assn. (chmn. philanthropy 1992-94), Air Force Assn. (life), Kuk Sool Won Assn., San Diego Zool. Soc. Republican. Lutheran. Home: 6 Cedar St Great Falls MT 59405-6808 Office: 341 OSS/DO9 6932 Goddard Dr Bldg 165 Great Falls MT 59405

DEFTOS, LEONARD JOHN, medical scientist and educator; b. Brockton, Mass., 1937. B.A. cum honoribus, Brown U., 1959; M.D. cum laude, U. Vt., 1964. Diplomate: Am. Bd. Internal Medicine; subsplty. cert. endocrinology and metabolism. Intern in medicine Columbia U. Med. Ctr., N.Y.C., 1964-65; resident in medicine Columbia-Presbyn. Med. Center, N.Y.C., 1965-66; staff assoc., attending physician Clin. Center NIH, Bethesda, Md., 1966-68; instr. medicine Harvard Med. Sch., 1968-70, asst. prof., 1970-71; clin. and research fellow Mass. Gen. Hosp., Boston, 1968-70; assoc. prof. medicine U. Calif., San Diego, 1972-76; prof. U. Calif., 1976—; chief endocrine research lab. VA Med. Ctr., San Diego, 1972—; cons. U.S. Naval Hosp., San Diego, 1973—, Naval Regional Med. Ctr., Camp Pendleton, Cal., 1975—; clin. investigator VA, 1974-77; mem. study sect. NIH, 1975-79, 85-89; mem. sci. adv. bd. Osteoporosis Found., 1986—. Mem. editorial bd., reviewer, contbr. numerous articles to books and profl. jours. Served to lt. comdr. USPHS, 1966-68. Am. Cancer Soc. Research scholar, 1971. Mem. Am. Fedn. Clin. Research, Am. Soc. Clin. Investigation, Endocrine Soc., Am. Soc. Bone and Mineral Research, Western Assn. Physicians, Assn. Am. Physicians, Alpha Omega Alpha. Address: 3350 La Jolla Village Dr San Diego CA 92161-0002

DE GARCIA, LUCIA, marketing professional; b. Medellin, Colombia, June 26, 1942; came to the U.S., 1962; d. Enrique Giraldo Botero and Carolina (Vega) Estrada; m. Alvaro Garcia Osorio, July 30, 1962; children: Carolina Alexandra, Claudia Maria. BS, Nat. U., 1962. Engring. arch. designer Vorhees, Trindle & Nelson, Newport Beach, Calif., 1974-78; pres., CEO Elan Internat., Newport Beach, 1984—; speaker, lectr. on success, protocol in bus. with Latin Am., free trade agreement between U.S. and Mexico. Editor: Elan mag., 1988-90. Trustee Nat. U., Calif., 1989-93; area campaign mgr. Bush for Pres., Orange County, Calif., 1988, Christopher Cox for Congress, 1988, Pete Wilson for Gov., 1990, People to Watch, 1994; bd. dirs. ARC, 1985-90, Am. Cancer Rsch. Ctr., 1986—; active South Coast Repertory Theater, 1982—. Named Dama de Distincion U.S./Mexico Found., 1991, Hispanic Woman of Yr. LULAC, 1986, One on the 10 Most Influential Women in Orange County, Orange County Metropolitan, 1994, One of the Hispanic 100 Most Influential in the U.S., Hispanics Bus. Mag., 1994; recipient Internat. award U.S. Hispanic C. of C., 1992. Mem. U.S./Mexico Found. (trustee 1990—), Latin Bus. Assn. (bd. dirs. 1992-93), World Trade Ctr. Assn. Republican. Roman Catholic. Home: 30 Via Lucca Irvine CA 92715-0610 Office: Elan Internat 620 Newport Center Dr Fl 11 Newport Beach CA 92660-6420

DE GOFF, VICTORIA JOAN, lawyer; b. San Francisco, Mar. 2, 1945; d. Sidney Francis and Jean Frances (Alexander) De G.; m. Peter D. Coppelman, May 2, 1971 (div. Dec. 1978); m. Richard Sherman, June 16, 1980. BA in Math. with great distinction, U. Calif., Berkeley, 1967, JD, 1972. Bar: Calif. 1972, U.S. Dist. Ct. (no. dist.) Calif. 1972, U.S. Ct. Appeals 1972, U.S. Supreme Ct. 1989. Rsch. atty. Calif. Ct. Appeal, San Francisco, 1972-73; Reginald Heber Smith Found. fellow San Francisco Neighborhood Legal Assistance Found., 1973-74; assoc. Field, De Goff, Huppert & McGowan, San Francisco, 1974-77; pvt. practice Berkeley, Calif., 1977-80; ptnr. De Goff and Sherman, Berkeley, 1980—; lectr. continuing edn. of bar, Calif., 1987, 90-92, U. Calif. Boalt Hall Sch. Law, Berkeley, 1981-85, dir. appellate advocacy, 1992; cons. Calif. Civil Practice: Procedure, Bancroft Whitney, 1992; mem. Appellate Law Adv. Commn., 1995; apptd. applicant evaluation and nomination com. Calif. Supreme Ct., 1995. Author: (with others) Matthew Bender's Treatise on California Torts, 1985. Apptd. to adv. com. Calif. Jud. Coun. on Implementing Proposition 32, 1984-85; mem. adv. bd. Hastings Coll. Trial and Appellate Adv., 1984-91; expert 20/20 vision project, commn. on future cts. Jud. Coun. Calif., 1993, apptd. to appellate standing adv. com., 1993; bd. dirs. Calif. Supreme Ct. Hist. Soc., State Bar Calif. Appellate Law Cons. Group, 1994-95. Fellow Woodrow Wilson Found., 1967-68. Mem. Calif. Trial Lawyers Assn. (bd. govs. 1980-88, amicus-curiae com. 1981-87, editor-in-chief assn. mag. 1980-81, Presdl. award of merit 1980, 81), Calif. Acad. Appellate Lawyers (sec.-treas. 1989-90, 2d v.p. 1990-91, 1st v.p. 1991-92, pres. 1992-93), Am. Acad. Appellate Lawyers, Edward J. McFetridge Am. Inn of Cts. (counsellor 1990-91, edn. chmn. 1991-92, social chmn. 1992-93, v.p. 1993-94, pres. 1994—), Boalt Hall Sch. Law U. Calif. Alumni Assn. (bd. dirs. 1989-92), Order of Coif. Jewish. Office: 1916 Los Angeles Ave Berkeley CA 94707-2419

DEGRASSI, LEONARD RENE, art historian, educator; b. East Orange, N.J., Mar. 2, 1928; s. Romulus-William and Anna Sophia (Sannicolo) DeG.; m. Dolores Marie Welgoss, June 24, 1961; children: Maria Christina, Paul. BA, U. So. Calif., 1950, BFA, 1951, MA, 1956; postgrad., Harvard U., 1953, Istituto Centrale del Restauro di Roma, 1959-60, U. Rome, 1959-60, UCLA, 1970-73. Tchr. art Redlands (Calif.) Jr. High Sch., 1951-53, Toll Jr. High Sch., Glendale, Calif., 1953-61, Wilson Jr. High Sch., Glendale, 1961; mem. faculty Glendale Coll., 1962—, prof. art history, 1974-92, chmn. dept., 1972, 89, prof. emeritus, 1992—. Prin. works include: (paintings) high altar at Ch. St. Mary, Cook, Minn., altar screen at Ch. St. Andrew, El Segundo, Calif., 1965-71, 14 Stas. of the Cross Ch. St. Mary, Cook, Minn., altar screen at Ch. of the Descent of the Holy Spirit, Glendale, 14 Stas. of the Cross at Ch. of St. Benedict, Duluth, Minn; also research, artwork and dramatic work for Spaceship Earth exhbn. at Disney World, Orlando, Fla., 1980. Decorated knight Grand Cross Holy Sepulchre, 1974, knight St. John of Jerusalem, 1976, knight Order of Merit of Republic of Italy, 1973, Cross of Merit, 1984, 89; named First Disting. Faculty, 1987. Mem. Art Educators Assn., Am. Rsch. Ct. Egypt, Tau Kappa Alpha, Kappa Pi, Delta Sigma Rho. Office: 1500 N Verdugo Rd Glendale CA 91208-2809

DEGRAW, STEPHEN TODD, marketing executive; b. Long Beach, Calif., Apr. 14, 1956; s. Fredrick and Roseanne (Bertleshofer) DeG.; m. Juli Sage McGee, Feb. 23, 1991; children: Devin Sage, Cooper Stephen. BS in Pharmacology, U. Calif., Santa Barbara, 1979; MBA in Mktg., San Diego State U., 1988. Investigator, sr. rsch. assoc. Am. McGaw, Irvine, Calif., 1980-84; rsch. assoc. molecular biology dept. Scripps Clinic and Rsch. Found., La Jolla, Calif., 1984-87; grad. rsch. asst. San Liego State U., 1987-88; mktg. mgmt. cons. Am. Innovision, San Diego, 1988-89, biomed. product mgr., nat. sales mgr., 1989-92; product mgr. ONCOR, 1992-95, dir. sales and mktg., 1995—. Contbr. articles to profl. jours.; co-patentee cooled low light color video camera. Recipient silver medal Osaka (Japan) Dragon Boat Championship, 1989, Penang (Malaysia) Dragon Boat Championship, 1990, gold medal World Invitational Dragon Boat Championship, Singapore, 1990. Mem. San Diego Internat. Dragonboat Racing Assn. (pres. 1991—), Hano Hano Outrigger Canoe Club. Office: ONCOR 200 Perry Pky Gaithersburg MD 20877

DE GROAT, JAY R., human resource development specialist; b. Crownpoint, N.Mex., May 16, 1948; s. Harry and Hazel (Charles) De G.; m. Ethelyn M. De Groat, Jan. 4, 1969; children: DeJong, Jeremy, Jarrell, D'Ayn, Jermayne. BS, U. N.Mex., 1984. Agy. dir. Navajo Child Devel. Program, Crownpoint, 1969-79; exec. dir. Native Am. Materials Devel. Ctr., Albuquerque, 1979-83; agy. dir. Navajo Dept. of Employment and Tng., Crownpoint, 1984-88; program dir. Navajo Dept. of Employment and Tng., Window Rock, Ariz., 1988-90; exec. dir. Divsn. of Human Resources, Window Rock, 1990-91; asst. dir. Navajo Area Sch. Bd. Assn., Window Rock, 1991-92; pers. officer Crownpoint Inst. of Tech., 1992—; edn. cons. Jicarilla Tribe, Dulce, N.Mex., 1982-83; human resource devel. cons. Whiteriver Apache Tribe, 1983; Crown cultural cons. N.Mex. Libr. Assn., Las Vegas, 1993. Author: (poetry) Whimpering Chant, 1980. Bd. pres. T'iists'oozi Action for Youth, Crownpoint, 1994; coun. mem. N.Mex. Navajo Pvt. Industry Coun., Crownpoint, 1994; bd. vice-chmn. Navajo Bd. of Election Supr., 1994. Recipient Outstanding Svc. award N.Mex. Sec. of State, 1993, Inst. for Tomorrow's Generation of Leaders, 1993, Whitehouse Conf. on Indian Edn., 1992. Mem. Nat. Indian Edn. Assn. Democrat. Home: Lower West Mesa #01 PO Box 1414 Crownpoint NM 87313

DEHAAS, JOHN NEFF, JR., retired architecture educator; b. Phila., July 4, 1926; s. John Neff and Sadie Lavinia (Hagel) DeH.; m. C. Bernice Wallace, Dec. 27, 1950; children: Kenneth Eric, Jocelyn Hilda. BArch, Tex. A&M U., 1948, MArch, 1950. Registered architect, Mont. Instr. Tex. A&M U., College Station, 1948-50, U. Tex., Austin, 1950-51; successively instr. to prof. Mont. State U., Bozeman, 1951-80; supervisory architect Historic Am. Bldgs. Survey, summers San Francisco, 1962, Bozeman, 1963, 65, Milw., 1969; cons. Mont. Historic Preservation Office, Helena, 1977-78, mem. rev. bd., 1968-79. Author: Montana's Historic Structures, Vol. 1, 1864, Vol. 2, 1969, Historic Uptown Butte, 1977; editor quar. newsletter Mont. Ghost Town Preservation Soc., 1972—. Bd. dirs. Mont. Assn. for Blind, Kalispell, 1984—, pres. 1991-93. Recipient Centennial Preservation award Mont. Historic Preservation Office, 1989, Dorothy Bridgman award for Outstanding Svc. to the Blind Montana Assn. for the Blind, 1990. Fellow AIA (com. on historic resources 1974—); mem. Mont. Hist. Soc. (trustee's award 1989). Republican. Methodist. Home: 1021 S Tracy Ave Bozeman MT 59715-5329

DEHAVEN, KENNETH LE MOYNE, retired physician; b. The Dalles, Oreg., Mar. 28, 1913; s. Luther John and Dora (Beeks) DeH.; m. Ledith Mary Ewing, Jan. 11, 1937; children: Marya LeMoyne DeHaven Keeth, Lisa Marguerite DeHaven Jordan, Camille Suzanne DeHaven. BS, North Pacific Coll. Oreg., 1935; MD, U. Mich., 1946. Intern USPHS Hosp., St. Louis, 1947; intern Franklin Hosp., San Francisco, 1947-48, resident, 1949; clinician Dept. Pub. Health, City San Francisco, Dept. V.D., 1949-51; practice gen. medicine, Sunnyvale, Calif., 1955-87; mem. staff El Camino Hosp., Mt. View, Calif., San Jose (Calif.) Hosp. Pres. Los Altos Hills Assn. Served to capt., USAF, 1952-55. Fellow Am. Acad. Family Practice; mem. AMA, Ariz. Med. Assn., Calif. Med. Assn., N.Y. Acad. Scis., Santa Clara County Med. Soc., Astron. Soc. Pacific, Sunnyvale C. of C. (bd. dirs. 1955-56), Book Club (San Francisco), Masons, Alpha Kappa Kappa. Republican. Home: 9348 E Casitas Del Rio Dr Scottsdale AZ 85255-4313

DEHMELT, HANS GEORG, physicist; b. Germany, Sept. 9, 1922; came to U.S., 1952, naturalized, 1962; s. Georg Karl and Asta Ella (Klemmt) D.; 1 child from previous marriage, Gerd; m. Diana Elaine Dundore, Nov. 18, 1989. Grad., Graues Kloster, Berlin, Abitur, 1940; D Rerum Naturalium, U. Goettingen, 1950; D Rerum Naturalium (hon.), Ruprecht Karl-Universitat, Heidelberg, 1986; DSc (hon.), U. Chgo., 1987. Postdoctoral fellow U. Goettingen, Germany, 1950-52, Duke U., Durham, N.C., 1952-55; vis. asst. prof. U. Wash., Seattle, 1955; asst. prof. physics U. Wash., 1956, asso. prof., 1957-61, prof., rsch. physicist, 1961—; cons. Varian Assocs., Palo Alto, Calif., 1956-76. Contbr. articles to profl. jours. Recipient Humboldt prize, 1974, award in basic research Internat. Soc. Magnetic Resonance, 1980, Rumford prize Am. Acad. Arts and Scis., 1985, Nobel prize in Physics, 1989; NSF grantee, 1958—. Fellow Am. Phys. Soc. (Davisson-Germer prize 1970); mem. Am. Acad. Arts and Scis., Am. Optical Soc., Nat. Acad. Scis., Sigma Xi. Home: 1600 43rd Ave E Seattle WA 98112-3245 Office: U Wash Physics Dept FM 15 Seattle WA 98195*

DEIBEL, FARRELL LEE, aerospace engineer; b. Paris, Sept. 22, 1959; came to U.S., 1962; s. Karl Edward and Sandra Sue (Jackson) D.; m. Karlyn Marie Szabo, June 23, 1984; children: Taylor, Brent, Riley. BSME, Calif. Poly. State U., 1981; MSME, U. So. Calif., L.A., 1990. Registered profl. engr., Calif. Mem. tech. staff Hughes Aircraft Co., Torrance, Calif., 1981-85, staff engr., 1985-90, sr. staff engr., 1990—. Co-inventor hermetic seal, 1990. Recipient Golden State award Who's Who Hist. Soc., 1991. Mem. Tau Beta Pi, Phi Kappa Phi. Office: Hughes Aircraft Co 3100 Lomita Blvd Torrance CA 90505-5104

DEIKMAN, ARTHUR J., psychiatrist; b. N.Y.C., Sept. 24, 1929. AB, Harvard Coll., 1951; MD, Harvard Med. Sch., 1955. Assoc. prof. U. Colo. Med. Ctr., Denver, 1968-71; supr. psychiatrist Bur. of Alcoholism, San Francisco, 1971-76; assoc. clin. prof. U. Calif., San Francisco, 1972-85, clin. prof., 1985—. Author: Personal Freedom, 1976, The Observing Self, 1982, The Wrong Way Home, 1990. Capt. USAF, 1956-59. Mem. Am. Psychiat. Assn. (life). Office: 10 Millwood St Mill Valley CA 94941-2066

DEIKMAN, EUGENE LAWRENCE, lawyer; b. Denver, Nov. 27, 1927; s. Herman and Eva (Lader) D.; m. Dolores Korosec, 1952 (div. 1964); children: Diana Wong, Jill, Alan; m. Doris A. Walker, Sept. 2, 1967 (div. May 1984); 1 child, Jane. LLB, U. Colo., 1951. Bar: Colo. 1953, U.S. Dist. Ct. Colo. 1955, U.S. Ct. Appeals (10th cir.) 1956. Ptnr. Menin & Deikman, Denver, 1954-59, Montfort, Wilson & Deikman, Denver, 1959-62; sole practice Denver, 1962-79; pres. Eugene Deikman, P.C., Denver, 1979—; cons. Crusade for Justice, Denver, 1972-79. Mem. Colo. Bar Assn., Colo. Trial Lawyers Assn., Nat. Lawyers Guild (founder Denver chpt., Founder cert. 1987). Democrat. Office: 1700 Broadway Ste 1200 Denver CO 80290-1201

DEIOTTE, CHARLES EDWARD, computer software company executive; b. Gary, Ind., Jan. 31, 1946; s. Raymond Louis and Dorothy Jane (Paulson) D.; A.A., Skagit Valley Jr. Coll., 1966; student Wash. State U., 1970; m. Margaret Williams Tukey, Sept. 11, 1971; children—Raymond, Karl, Ronald. Programmer, Wash. State U., Pullman, 1969-70; project dir. AGT Mgmt. Systems, Renton, Wash., sr. tech. cons., sect. mgr. McDonnell-Douglas Automation, Bellevue, Wash., 1972-73; sr. engr. Boeing Computer Services, Seattle, 1973-75, computer based instrn. specialist, Tng. div., 1975-79; mgr. microprocessor design support center Boeing Aerospace Co., Kent, Wash., 1979-80; mgr. concept research Federal Express Corp., Colorado Springs, Colo., 1980-81, mgr. microprocessor support group, 1981-82; pres. Deitron Systems, Inc., Auburn, Wash., 1976-81; pres., chmn. bd. Logical Systems Inc., Colorado Springs, 1981-87; chmn., CEO Cedsys Inc., 1987-91, sr. software engr., cons. LinCom Corp., 1992-93; software systems specialist, MCI Corp., 1993—; chmn. bd. Summit Med. Systems, Inc., 1985-86 . Neighborhood commr. Chief Seattle council Boy Scouts Am., 1971-72; v.p. REACT alert, Seattle, 1974; advisor Jr. Achievement, Colorado Springs, 1980; coach Odyssey of the Mind, 1991-92. Recipient Boeing Aerospace Co. Cert. of Achievement, 1979. Mem. Assn. Computing Machinery, IEEE, AAAS, Data Processing Mgmt. Assn., Am. Mgmt. Assn., Gamma Sigma Epsilon. Home: 16955 Vollmer Rd Colorado Springs CO 80908-1622 Office: 4678 Alpine Meadows Ln Colorado Springs CO 80919-3159

DEIOTTE, MARGARET WILLIAMS TUKEY, nonprofit consultant, grants writer; b. Lafayette, Ind., Mar. 6, 1952; d. Ronald B. and Elizabeth A. (Williams) Tukey; m. Charles E. Deiotte, Sept. 11, 1971; children: Raymond, Karl, Ronald. Student, U. Wash., 1969-72, 77-79. V.p., treas. Logical Systems, Inc., Colorado Springs, 1982-86; v.p. CEDSYS, Inc., Colorado Springs, 1987-92; pres. Penrose Enrichment Program Found., Colorado Springs, Colo., 1988-89; free lance tech. and grant proposal writer, 1990-94; dir. Rexall Showcase Internat., 1994—; conf. coord. Colo. Assn. Ptnrs. in Edn., 1994; presenter seminar Pikes Peace Pace Conf., 1991, 92. Mem. adv. bd. gifted and talented Sch. Dist. 11, 1989—, mem. grant writing team; pres. Penrose Elem. PTA, 1989-91; 1st v.p. El Paso Coun. PTA, 1990-91, treas., 1991-92; mem. grants commn. Colo. State PTA, 1990-91; coach Odyssey of the Mind, 1990, 91-92; bd. dirs. YMCA Youth Leadership Inst., 1990-92, 92—; mem. dist. accountability com. Sch. Dist. 38, 1993-94; bd. dirs. Sch. Dist. 38 Found., 1994—; accountability chmn. Lewis-Palmer Mid. Sch. Mem. NAFE. Home and Office: 16955 Vollmer Rd Colorado Springs CO 80908-1622

DEISENROTH, CLINTON WILBUR, electrical engineer; b. Louisville, Aug. 9, 1941; s. Clifton Earl and Nell (Pierce) D.; m. Lisbeth D. Isaacs, May 10, 1974; 1 dau., Susan Michelle. BEE, Ga. Inst. Tech., 1965. With Raytheon Co., 1966-81, div. mgr. Addington Labs., Inc., solid state products div., Santa Clara, Calif., 1975-77, program mgr. electromagnetic systems div., Goleta, Calif., 1977-79, dir. surface navy electronic warfare systems, 1979-81; sr. v.p. systems div. Teledyne-MEC, 1981-84; pres. Teledyne CME, 1984-90; exec. v.p., gen. mgr. Aerospace Products div. G&H Tech., Inc., 1990-92; v.p. bus. devel. Whittaker Electronic Systems, 1992-94, v.p., gen. mgr., 1994, pres., 1994—. Mem. IEEE, Am. Mgmt. Assn., Am. Def. Preparedness Assn., Navy League. Home: 518 Oakhampton St Thousand Oaks CA 91361-1344 Office: Whittaker Electronic Systems 1785 Voyager Ave Simi Valley CA 93063-3349

DEITER, NEWTON ELLIOTT, clinical psychologist; b. N.Y.C., Dec. 12, 1931; s. Benjamin and Anna (Leibowitz) D. BS, UCLA, 1957; MS, Leland Stanford, 1960; PhD in Clin. Psychology, U. Chgo., 1965. Cert. in clin. psychology. Pvt. practice clin. psychology L.A., 1965-90; exec. dir. Nat. Family Planning Coun., L.A., 1965-76, Gay Media Task Force, L.A., 1976—; staff cons. Aaron Spelling Prodns., L.A., 1980-90, spl. cons. NBC, L.A., 1970-79, cons. broadcast standards dept. CBS, L.A., 1968-82, cons. City Coun., City of L.A., 1975-85. Columnist Bottomline Mag., 1992—. Mem. Dem. Ctrl. Com., L.A., 1972-76; bd. dirs. Gay Cmty. Svcs. Ctr., L.A., 1970-75, Am. Cancer Soc., L.A., 1972-77, Palm Springs Gay Tourism Coun., 1993-95; commr. L.A. Probation Commn., 1977-85; bd. advisors San Francisco Sheriffs Dept., 1969-79; pres. Internat. Gay Travel Assn., 1991-92. Lt. col. USAFR, 1950-75. Inductee Internat. Gay Travel Assn. Hall of Fame, 1994. Mem. Acad. TV and Scis., Press Club L.A., Internat. Gay Travel Assn. (bd. dirs. 1986-93, pres. 1991-92), Desert Bus. Assn. (v.p. 1993, bd. dirs. 1992), Internat. Food, Wine and Travel Writers Assn. (bd. dirs. 1995, sec./treas. 1995), Air Force Assn., Am. Mensa, Masons. Home: 71426 Estellita Dr Rancho Mirage CA 92270-4215 Office: Rancho Mirage Travel 71-428 Us Highway 111 Rancho Mirage CA 92270-4130

DEITRICH, RICHARD ADAM, pharmacology educator; b. Monte Vista, Colo., Apr. 22, 1931; s. Robert Adam and Freda Leona (Scott) D.; m. Mary Margaret Burkholder, Jan. 29, 1954; children: Vivian Gay, Leslie Lynn, Lori Christine. BS, U. Colo., 1953, MS, 1954, PhD, 1959. Postdoctoral fellow, then instr. Johns Hopkins U., Balt., 1959-63; asst. prof., then assoc. prof. U. Colo., Denver, 1963-76, prof. pharmacology, 1976—, sci. dir. Alcohol Rsch. Ctr., 1977—; vis. prof. U. Berne, Switzerland, 1973-74. Editor: Development of Animal Models, 1981, Initial Sensitivity to Alcohol, 1990; contbr. over 100 articles to sci. publs. Pres. Mile High Coun. on Alcoholism, Denver, 1972-73; moderator 1st Universalist Ch., Denver, 1979. With U.S. Army, 1954-56. Grantee Nat. Inst. Alcoholism, 1977—, Nat. Inst. Communicative Disease and Stroke, 1963, numerous others. Mem. Rsch. Soc. on Alcoholism (pres. 1981-83), Internat. Soc. Biomed. Rsch. on Alcoholism (treas. 1986-94), Am. Soc. Pharmacology, Am. Soc. Biol. Chemistry. Office: Univ Colo 4200 E 9th Ave Denver CO 80220-3706

DEJARNATT, GEORGE LEE, financial executive, business owner; b. Owensboro, Ky., Feb. 22, 1948; s. Benjamin Marshall and Mildred Ernestine (Fox) D.; m. Dana Haviland Meade, Sept. 1, 1974; 1 child, Dashiell Haviland. BA, Vanderbilt U., 1971; postgrad., U. Wash., 1973-74; MBA, U. Puget Sound, 1980. CPA, Wash.; cert. mgmt. acct. Rschr. Ctr. for Health Care Rsch., Nashville, 1970-73; office mgr. Timeline, Inc., Seattle, 1976-78; acct. Callahan, Reed, Gunn & Thomas, CPAs, Seattle, 1978-82; cons., owner Dash Mgmt., Seattle, 1980—; CEO Haviland Winery, Lynnwood, Wash., 1982-87; CFO Am. Communications, Seattle, 1987-92, Watchdog, Inc., Seattle, 1990—; instr. City U., Bellevue, Wash., 1988—. Vol. Boy Scouts Am., Seattle, 1988—, Lake Forest Park Montessori, Seattle, 1992—. Mem. AICPA, Wash. Soc. CPAs, Inst. Mgmt. Accts., Inst. Cert. Mgmt. Accts., Controllers' Roundtable, Hi-Tech Roundtable. Home: 18984 Forest Park Dr NE Seattle WA 98155-2436 Office: Watchdog Inc 3417 S 150th St Seattle WA 98188-2110

DEJU, RAUL ANTONIO, environmental company executive; b. Havana, Cuba, Mar. 14, 1946; came to the U.S., 1961; s. Jose M. and Olga (Nunez) D.; m. Leticia M. Deju, Dec. 20, 1968 (div. June 1974); m. Shari M. Moore, Mar. 10, 1979; children: Raul Jr., Michael Andrew. Cert. completion, Columbia U., 1965; BS in Math. and Physics, N.Mex. Inst. Mining & Tech., 1966, PhD in Geol. Scis., 1969. Vis. prof. U. Nat. Mexico, Mexico City, 1969-70; exploration geologist Gulf Oil Co., Pitts., 1970-71; assoc. prof. dept. geology Wright State U., Dayton, Ohio, 1971-73; dir. Rockwell Hanford Ops., Richland, Wash., 1973-82; sr. v.p. Internat. Tech. Corp., Pitts. and L.A., 1982-88; CEO URS, Inc., Consulting Engrs., San Francisco, 1988; pres. Chem. Waste, Inc., Western Region, Fremont, Calif., 1988-95; pres, CEO Deju, Dory & Langowski Internat., Inc., Moraga, Calif., 1995—; chmn. U.S.-Mexico Binational Environ. Bus. Com., La Jolla, Calif., 1991—; mem. U.S. EPA Adminstrs. Nat. Adv. Com., Washington, 1994—; mem. Pres.'s Adv. Com. on Environ. Tech. and Commerce, Washington, 1994. Author: The Environment and It's Resources, 1973, The Zeta Conspiracy, 1982; contbr. 150 articles to profl. jours. Recipient Symposium award ASME, Egypt, 1983. Mem. Am. Assn. Petroleum Geologists, Calif. Engring. Found. (bd. dirs. 1988—). Office: 5 Hastings Ct Moraga CA 94556

DE LA CRUZ, JENNIFER LYN, marketing executive; b. Long Beach, Calif., June 3, 1960; d. Reuben and Patricia Ann (Morris) De La Cruz; m. Jeffrey Alan Upton, Dec. 29, 1981. BSChemE cum laude, U. Mich., 1981; MSChemE, Stanford U., 1984; MBA, U. Pa., 1990. Summer intern GM Corp., Warren Mich., 1980, assoc. project engr., 1981-84, project engr., 1984-86, sr. process engr., 1986-89; mktg. assoc. Rohm and Haas Co., Phila., 1989-90; bus. mgr. Protogenesis, Inc., Carlsbad, Calif., 1990—. Mem. Soc. Mfg. Engrs. Home: 826 S Rancho Santa Fe Rd Apt F San Marcos CA 92069-4668 Office: Protogenesis Inc 2722 Loker Ave W Ste E Carlsbad CA 92008-6607

DELA CRUZ, JOSE SANTOS, retired state supreme court chief justice; b. Saipan, Commonwealth No. Mariana Islands, July 18, 1948; s. Thomas Castro and Remedio Sablan (Santos) Dela C.; m. Rita Tenorio Sablan, Nov 12, 1977; children: Roxanne, Renee, Rica Ann. BA, U. Guam, 1971; JD, U. Calif., Berkeley, 1974; cert., Nat. Jud. Coll., Reno, 1985. Bar: No. Mariana Islands, 1974, U.S. Dist. Ct. No. Mariana Islands 1978. Staff atty. Micro. Legal Svcs. Corp., Saipan, 1974-79; gen. counsel Marianas Pub. Land Corp., Saipan, 1979-81; liaison atty. CNMI Fed. Laws Commn., Saipan, 1981-83; ptnr. Borja & Dela Cruz, Saipan, 1983-85; assoc. judge Commonwealth Trial Ct., Saipan, 1985-89; chief justice Supreme Ct. No. Mariana Islands, 1989-95; ret.; mem. Conf. of Chief Justices, 1989-95, Adv. Commn. on Judiciary, Saipan, 1980-82; chmn. Criminal Justice Planning Agy., Saipan, 1985-95. Mem. Coun. for Arts, Saipan, 1982-83; chmn. Bd. of Elections, Saipan, 1977-82; pres. Cath. Social Svcs., Saipan, 1982-85. Mem. No. Marianas Bar Assn. (pres. 1984-85). Roman Catholic. Office: Commonwealth Supreme Ct Civic Ctr Saipan MP 96950

DELANEY, MARION PATRICIA, advertising agency executive; b. Hartford, Conn., May 20, 1952; d. William Pride Delaney Jr. and Marian Patricia (Utley) Murphy. BA, Union Coll., Schenectady, N.Y., 1973. Adminstrv. asst. N.Y. State Assembly, Albany, 1973-74; account exec. Foote, Cone & Belding, N.Y.C., 1974-78; sr. account exec. Dailey & Assocs., L.A., 1978-81; pub. rels. cons. NOW, Washington, 1981-83; account supr. BBDO/West, L.A., 1983-85; v.p. Grey Advt., L.A., 1985-87, San Francisco, 1987-89; sr. v.p. McCann-Erickson, San Francisco, 1989—. Del. Dem. Nat.

Conv., San Francisco, 1984; bd. dirs. JED Found., Hartford, Conn., 1989—, Easter Seals Soc., Bay Area, 1995—. Mem. NOW (v.p. L.A. chpt. 1980-83, pres. 1984, advisor 1985-87). Congregationalist. Home: 11 Gary Way Fairfax CA 94930-1002

DELANEY, MATTHEW SYLVESTER, educator, academic administrator; b. Ireland, Nov. 26, 1927; s. Joseph C. and Elizabeth M. (Berrigan) D.; came to U.S., 1947, naturalized, 1952; student St. John's Coll., 1947-51; BA, Immaculate Heart Coll., L.A., 1958; MS, Notre Dame U., 1960; PhD, Ohio State U., 1971. Ordained priest Roman Cath. Ch., 1951; assoc. pastor L.A. Cath. Diocese, 1951-55; instr. math., physics Pius X High Sch., Downey, Calif., 1955-58, vice prin., 1960-62; instr. math. Immaculate Heart Coll., L.A., 1962-65, asst. prof., 1965-72, assoc. prof., 1972-76, prof., 1976—; asst. acad. dean, 1973-78; dean acad. devel. Mt. St. Mary's Coll., L.A., 1978-82, acad. dean, 1978-91; prof. mathematics, 1991—. NSF grantee, 1959-60, 61. Mem. Am. Math. Soc., Math. Assn. Am., Am. Conf. Acad. Deans, N.Y. Acad. Scis.. Democrat. Contbr. articles to math. publs. Home: 13700 El Dorado Dr Apt 32C Seal Beach CA 90740-3843 Office: Mt St Mary's Coll 12001 Chalon Rd Los Angeles CA 90049-1526

DE LA PAVA, DANIEL, plastic surgeon; b. Bogota, Colombia, Oct. 30, 1942; came to U.S., 1969; s. Daniel and Maria Mercedes (Orrego) D.; m. Vianney Perdoma, Apr. 26, 1969; 1 child, Daniel Francisco. MD, U. Nat. de Colombia, 1967. Diplomate Am. Bd. Plastic Surgery. Intern Drs. Hosp., Washington, 1969-70; resident in gen. surgery Providence Hosp., Washington, 1970-73; resident in plastic surgery Christ's Hosp., Cin., 1973-75; fellow, clin. instr. Inst. Reconstructive and Plastic Surgery, NYU Med. Ctr., N.Y.C., 1975-76; pvt. practice Augusta, Maine, 1976-77, Sun City, Ariz., 1980—; Australia rsch. fellow, clin. asst. St. Vincent's Hosp., Melbourne, 1977-78; bd. dirs. Thunderbird Samaritan Hosp. Burn Svc.; asst. prof. Maricopa County Hosp. Plastic Surgery Residency Program, Ariz., 1980-87; organized micro-surgery unit, Taipei, Taiwan, 1978; spkr. in field; vol. surgery Yerevan, Armenia, 1993, Ctrl. and S.Am., 1970-90, Kuwait, 1991. Recipient Spl. Recognition award 10 yr. anny. celebration Taiwan Micro-Surgery Unit, 1988, Vol. Svc. award for Kuwait surgery, 1991. Mem. Am. Soc. Plastic Reconstructive Surgeons, Lipolysis Soc. N.Am., Ariz. Plastic Surgery Soc., U.S. Colombian Med. Assn., U.S. Mex. Soc., Maricopa County Plastic Surgeon Soc. (sec./treas. 1994—). Roman Catholic. Office: 1300 N 103rd Ave # 54 Sun City AZ 85351

DELAQUIS, NOEL, bishop; b. Notre-Dame de Lourdes, Man., Can., Dec. 25, 1934; s. Louis and Therese (Hebert) D. B.A., U. Man., 1954; B.Th., U. Laval, 1958; J.C.L., Latran, Rome, 1962. Ordained priest Roman Catholic Ch., 1958; asst. priest Christ the King Parish, St. Vital, Man., 1958-60; prof. canon law St. Boniface Sem., Man., 1962-68; chancellor Archdiocese of St. Boniface, Man., 1965-73; bishop of Gravelbourg, Sask., Can., 1974—. Address: CP 690, Gravelbourg, SK Canada S0H 1X0*

DE LA VEGA, DIANNE WINIFRED DEMARINIS (MRS. JORGE DE LA VEGA), government official; b. Cleve.; d. Gerald M. and Dorothy (Philp) DeMarinis; student Case Western Res. U., 1948-50, MA, 1969; BA, U. Am., 1952; PhD in Psychology, Internat. Coll., Los Angeles, 1977; MA, Goddard Coll., 1978; m. Jorge Alejandro de la Vega, July 19, 1952; children: Constance, Francisco Javier, Alexandra. Faculty, Western Res. U., Cleve., 1961-62; instr. Instituto Mexicano-Norteamericano de Relaciones Culturales, Mexico, 1967; supr. fgn. press Mexican Olympic Organizing Com., Mexico, 1968; asst. to producer Producciones Ojo, Canal 8 TV, Mexico, 1969; exec. asst. Internat. Exec. Service Corps, Mexico City, 1969-70; asst. to dir. U.S. Internat. U. Mexico, Mexico City, 1970-75; family planning evaluator for Latin Am., AID, 1976; with dept. spl. edn. region IX Nat. Ctr. on Child Abuse and Neglect, Children's Bur., Office Child Devel., HEW, Calif. State U., 1977—. Chmn. Puppet's Jr. League, Mexico City, 1967, chmn. ways and means, 1968; sec. Tlaxcala-Okla. Partner's of Alliance for Progress, 1967—; pres. acculturating hispanic refugee children Los Angeles Unified Sch. Dist.; bd. dirs. Hot Line of Mexico City; mem. Los Angeles adv. com. 1984 Olympics. Lic. marriage and family counselor. Mem. Los Angeles chpt. Calif. Marriage and Family Therapists Assn., Flying Samaritans, Pro Salud Maternal, Transactional Analysis Assn. Club: Jr. League (Los Angeles). Home: 130 Alta Ave Apt D Santa Monica CA 90402-2737

DELAWIE, HOMER TORRENCE, architect; b. Santa Barbara, Calif., Sept. 24, 1927; s. Fred Ely and Gertrude (Torrence) D.; m. Billie Carol Sparlin (div. 1969); m. Ethel Ann Mallinger, Sept. 3, 1973; children: Gregory, Claire, Shandell, Tracy, Stephanie, Scott. BS in Archtl. Engring., Calif. Poly. State U., San Luis Obispo, 1951. Registered architect, Calif. Pvt. practice architecture San Diego, 1958-61; founder, chief exec. officer Delawie Wilkes Rodrigues Barker & Bretton Assocs., San Diego, 1961—. Mem. Planning Commn., City of San Diego, 1969-82; adv. bd. KPBS Pub. TV. Recipient Award of Merit Calif. chpt. Am. Inst. Planners, Lay Citizens award Phi Delta Kappa, 1975, award Calif chpt. Am. Planning Assn., 1982; named Disting. Alumnus, Calif. Poly. State U., 1972. Fellow AIA (over 60 design awards 1973—, Architects Svc. award Calif. coun. 1973, spl. award San Diego chpt. 1978, Pub. Svc. award Calif. coun. 1981, Outstanding Firm award San Diego chpt. 1986). Democrat. Home: 2749 Azalea Dr San Diego CA 92106-1132 Office: Delawie Wilkes Rodriques Barker & Bretton Assocs 2827 Presidio Dr San Diego CA 92110-2722

DELAY, EUGENE RAYMOND, psychologist, educator, researcher; b. Coeur d'Alene, Idaho, Dec. 24, 1948; s. Raymond Joseph and Fairy Louise (Fisher) D.; m. Rona Jane Moore, Sept. 12, 1971; 1 child, Shawn Patrick. BS in Psychology, U. Idaho, 1972; MS in Biopsychology, U. Ga., 1977, PhD in Biopsychology, 1979. Asst. prof. Regis Coll., Denver, 1979-84, assoc. prof., 1984-90, prof., 1990—; provisional clin. cons. Denver VA Hosp., 1981-87; rsch. cons. Brenau Coll., Gainesville, Ga., 1978, Colo. State U., Ft. Collins, 1987—, rsch. assoc., 1993—. Contbr. articles to profl. jours. Served with U.S. Army, 1973-75. NSF grantee, 1989, NIH sr. fellow, 1995. Mem. APA, Southeastern Psychol. Assn., N.Y. Acad. Sci., Rocky Mountain Neurosci. Group, Rocky Mountain Psychol. Assn., Soc. Behavioral Medicine, Soc. Neurosci., Am. Psychol. Soc., Internat. Behavioral Neurosci. Soc. Home: 2819 Dundee Ct Fort Collins CO 80525-2208 Office: Regis U Dept Psychology 3333 Regis Blvd Denver CO 80221-1099

DEL CAMPO, MARTIN BERNARDELLI, architect; b. Guadalajara, Mexico, Nov. 27, 1922; came to U.S., 1949; s. Salvador and Margarita (Bernardelli) Del C.; BA, Colegio Frances Morelos, Mexico City, 1941; Archtl. degree Escuela Nacional de Arquitectura, Mexico City, 1948; m. Laura Zaikowska, May 25, 1945; children: Felicia (dec.), Margarita, Mario. Ptnr., Del Campo & Fruiht, architects, Santa Rosa, Cal., 1955-56, Del Campo & Clark, San Francisco, 1957-63; mgr. Hotel Victoria, Oaxaca, Mexico, 1964-67; pres. Gulli-Del Campo, architects, San Francisco, 1968-70; ptnr. Del Campo Assocs., San Francisco, 1977-81. Lectr. archtl. design Coll. Environmental Design, U. Calif., Berkeley, 1973-74. Mem. AIA. Archtl. works include: Calif. Med. Facility South, Vacaville, Phillip Burton Fed. Bldg. remodeling, San Francisco, Hall of Justice, San Francisco, San Francisco Airport Internat. Terminal. Address: Del Campo & Maru Architects Inc 45 Lansing St San Francisco CA 94105-2611

DELEAR, RICHARD HENRY, personnel consultant; b. Wichita, Kans., Dec. 19, 1927; s. Ernest C. Delear and Clara M. Boberg; m. Helen J. Clark (dec. Mar. 1994); children: Cherie, Cindy, Kimberly, Kirkland, Dianne, Michelle. Student, Hiedleburg U., Germany, 1946-47, San Jose St. U., 1959-60. Cert. hypnotheropist. Enlisted U.S. Army, 1944, advanced through grades to m/sgt., 1952, ret., 1959; entrepreneur Calif., 1960-74; human resources cons. Success Thru Humaneering, Scotts Valley, Calif., 1974—. Author: Leadership Strategies, 1988. Pres. Exchange club, Scotts Valley, 1978-79. Decorated two Bronze Stars, two Purple Hearts, Silver Star. Republican. Roman Catholic. Office: Success Thru Humaneering 202 Burlwood Dr Scotts Valley CA 95066-3704

DE LESPINAY, PHILIPPE, auto racing safety industry consultant, small business owner; b. Biarritz, France, May 8, 1945; came to U.S., 1970; s. Jacques Marquis de Lespinay de Pancy and Mary Magdalen (Hawke) de Lespinay; m. Kathryn Kathleen Walwick, July 1, 1977. Superior diploma, Ecole Superieure des Arts Mod, Paris, 1969; BEPC, Brevet Elem. d'Etudes Super, France, 1967. Cert. design engr./stylist. Project engr. Heller Mfg., Paris, 1966-70; cons. Riggen Mfg. Riggen Manuf., Innova Inc., L.A., 1970-73; mgr. rsch./devel. Cox Hobbies, Santa Ana, Calif., 1973-77; pres. Topline Inc., Tustin, Calif., 1978—; adviser Stand 21 Racewear, Dijon, France, 1982-94. Contbr. articles to profl. jours. Mem. Hist. Motorsports Assn. (Pebble Beach cup 1991), Mercedes Benz Club N.Am. Office: Topline/Electric Dreams 1121-M-Wakeham Ave Santa Ana CA 92705

DELEUR, ROBBIE LYNN, university program director; b. Ada, Okla., Oct. 14, 1956; d. Ralph Owren and Beverly Jane (Ferguson) Randles; children: Raymond A. Jr., John Robert. A of Bus. Adminstrn., Casper Coll., 1986; BS in Gen. Bus. Mgmt., U. Wyo., 1989. Sec., adminstr. Equipment Renewal Co., Rock Springs, Wyo., 1979-80; sr. clk. Brown & Root, Rock Springs and Green River, Wyo., 1980-82; unemployment eligibility reviewer Wyo. Employment Security Commn., Evanston and Rock Springs, Wyo., 1983-84; asst. money room mgr. Cent. Wyo. Fair and Rodeo, Casper, 1983-92; fin. aid specialist Casper Coll., 1986-89; dir. fin. aid. Western Wyo. Community Coll., Rock Springs, 1989—. Sec.-treas., bd. dirs. YWCA, Rock Springs, 1990. Mem. Nat. Assn. Student Fin. Aid Adminstrs., Wyo. State Assn. Student Fin. Aid (sec., treas. 1990-92, Disting. Svc. award 1992-93), Rocky Mountain Assn. Student Fin. Aid Adminstrs. (profl. devel. com. 1992-94, chmn. legis. response com. 1992-93, sec. 1994-95), Bus. and Profl. Women's Club Sweetwater County (chmn. scholarship com. 1988—, pres. 1991-92, chmn. Wyo. young career women 1992-93, Wyo. dir. dist. IV 1993-94, 1st v.p. Wyo. fedn. 1994-95, pres.-elect 1995—, Sweetwater County Young Careerist 1991). Democrat. Baptist. Home: 960 Hillside Dr Green River WY 82935-5014 Office: Western Wyo Community Coll 2500 College Dr Rock Springs WY 82901-5802

DELFFS, DUDLEY J., writer, educator; b. Sewanee, Tenn., Nov. 27, 1964; s. Dudley Julian and Norma (Thompson) D.; m. Dorothy Kilpatrick Scruggs, May 14, 1989; 1 child, Mary Elise. BA in English, U. Tenn., 1987, MA in English, 1989; MA in Counseling, Colo. Christian U., 1992. Tech. writer, rschr. Energy, Environ. Resource Ctr., Knoxville, Tenn., 1990-91; instr. English U. Tenn., Knoxville, Tenn., 1988-91, Met. State Coll., Denver, 1991—; counseling intern Colo. Christian U., Morrison, 1993-94. Author: (novel) Forgiving August, 1993; (non-fiction) Repentant Heart, 1995; contbr. poetry and short stories to lit. mags. Recipient Scholastic Press Poetry award Columbia U., 1986. Mem. Nat. Coun. Tchrs. English, Am. Counseling Assn., Assembly on Lit. for Adolescents, Colo. Lang. Arts Soc.

D'ELIA, WILLIAM VINCENT, film director; b. N.Y.C., Mar. 23, 1948; s. Vincent Peter and Dorothy (McGlynn) D'E.; m. Eleanor Ann Dombrowski, Apr. 8, 1972; children: Christopher, Matthew. BS in Communication, Ithaca Coll., 1969; MA in Communication, William Paterson Coll., 1975. Film dir. D'Elia, Uricola & Platt, N.Y.C., 1979-88, Fifth Ave. Films, N.Y.C., 1989-90. Writer, prodr., dir. feature film The Feud, 1990; dir. Northern Exposure CBS-TV, 1990-94, Doogie Howser, M.D. ABC-TV, 1990-92, Civil Wars, 1991-92, Reasonable Doubt NBC-TV, 1991-93, Beverly Hills 90210 Fox-TV, 1991-93, Harts of the West CBS-TV, 1993, Picket Fences CBS-TV, 1993-94, Lois and Clark ABC-TV, 1993-94, Time Well Spent ABC-TV, 1994, The Dottie West Story CBS-TV, 1995, Chicago Hope CBS-TV, 1994-95, The Tomorrow Man CBS-TV, 1995, After Laurette Fox-TV movie, 1995; consulting prodr., dir. Courthouse CBS-TV, 1995. With U.S. Army, 1970-71. Mem. Acad. TV Arts and Scis., Dirs. Guild Am., Montclair Golf Club. Roman Catholic.

DELISI, DONALD PAUL, fluid mechanician, geophysicist; b. Pitts., Nov. 15, 1944; s. Samuel P. and Jennie (Moffie) D.; m. Adele Pedicord Orr, Aug. 7, 1971; 1 child, Bergen Orr Delisi. B.S.E. magna cum laude, Princeton U., 1966; MS, U. Calif., Berkeley, 1967, PhD, 1972. Resident rsch. assoc. Geophys. Fluid Dynamics Lab./NOAA, Princeton, N.J., 1972-74; sr. rsch. scientist Flow Rsch., Inc., Kent, Wash., 1974-77; staff scientist Phys. Dynamics Inc., Bellevue, Wash., 1977-86; v.p., treas., sr. rsch. scientist N.W. Rsch. Assocs., Inc., Bellevue, 1986—. Contbr. articles to Jour. Geophys. Rsch., Jour. of the Atmospheric Scis., Pure and Applied Geophysics, AIAA Jour., Jour. of Aircraft. Mem. Am. Meteorol. Soc., Am. Geophys. Union, AIAA, Am. Inst. Physics. Office: NW Rsch Assocs Inc 300 120th Ave NE Bldg 7 Bellevue WA 98005-3020

DELK, RICHARD ALLEN, accountant, consultant; b. Joliet, Ill., Aug. 5, 1958; s. Franklin D. and Lois M. Delk. BA, Luther Coll., 1980; MBA, U. Phoenix, 1986; JD, U. Denver, 1994. Bar: Colo. 1994; CPA, Colo., Iowa. Asst. state auditor Office of Auditor of State of Iowa, Des Moines, 1980-81; state audit supr. Office of Auditor of State of Iowa, Ames, Iowa, 1981-84; internal auditor U.S. West, Inc., Englewood, Colo., 1984-87; gen. ledger mgr. U.S. West Info. Sys., Englewood, 1987-88; fin. analyst U.S. West Comms., Inc., Denver, 1988-93, sr. ops. cons., 1993—. Office: US West Comms Inc 1801 California St Ste 4920 Denver CO 80202-2658

DELL, KENNETH CHARLES, city planner and urban designer; b. Billings, Mo., Mar. 18, 1938; s. Charles Albert and Lollomary (O'Mallory) Dell; m. Sally Ann Henderson, Feb. 28, 1969; children: Tana, Tiffany. BS in Architecture, Mont. State U., 1963; postgrad., U. Colo., U. No. Colo. Cert. urban planning. Draftsman, jr. designer Harmon, O'Donnell and Henninger, Assocs., Inc., Denver, 1963-67; planner planning office divsn. neighborhood studies City of Denver, Colo., 1967; sr. planner planning dept. City of Boulder, Colo., 1967-72; planning dir. City of Longmont, Colo., 1972-77; assoc. Moberg and Assocs., Boulder, 1977-79; prin. Kenneth C. Dell and Assocs., Boulder, 1979-83; planner Rocky Mountain Cons., Inc., Longmont, 1983—. Mem. Bd. Environ. Affairs, Longmont, Colo., 1994. Mem. Am. Planning Assn. (charter mem.), Am. Inst. Cert. Planners (charter mem.), Sertoma (treas. 1987-94). Home: 1107 Purdue Dr Longmont CO 80503-3634 Office: Rocky Mountain Cons 700 Florida Ave Longmont CO 80501-6452

DELLAMAS, LLOYD RICHARD, government financial consultant; b. Santa Maria, Calif., Aug. 4, 1940; s. Victor Lloyd and Delya Eleanore (Freeman) deL.; m. Caroline Ruth Cox, Nov. 12, 1967; children: Ingrid Dionne, Chelsea Denise. BS, Calif. State U., San Diego, 1963. Analyst City of San Diego, 1963-66; asst. to city mgr. City of Torrance, Calif., 1966-68; city mgr. City of Woodlake, Calif., 1968-71, City of Lawndale, Calif., 1971-76, City of Monterey Park, Calif., 1976-87; pres. Hinderliter, deLlamas and Assocs., Diamond Bar, Calif., 1987—; also dir. HdL Coren & Cone, Diamond Bar. Active L.A. Com. on Sch. Orgn., Downey, Calif., 1989—. Mem. Calif. Mcpl. Fin. Officers Assn., Urban Land Inst., San Gabriel Valley City Mgrs. Assn. (pres. 1986), Calif. Redevel. Agencies Assn. (dir. 1981-87), Internat. City Mgmt. Assn. Office: HdL Cos 1340 Valley Vista Dr Diamond Bar CA 91765-3910

DELLAS, ROBERT DENNIS, investment banker; b. Detroit, July 4, 1944; s. Eugene D. and Maxine (Rudell) D.; m. Shila L. Clement, Mar. 27, 1976; children—Emily Allison, Lindsay Michelle. B.A. in Econs., U. Mich., Ann Arbor, 1966; M.B.A., Harvard U., Cambridge, 1970. Analyst Burroughs Corp., Detroit, 1966-67, Pasadena, Calif., 1967-68; mgr. U.S. Leasing, San Francisco, 1970-76; pres., dir. Energetics Mktg. & Mgmt. Assn., San Francisco, 1978-80; sr. v.p. E.F. Hutton & Co., San Francisco, 1981-85; prin. founder Capital Exchange Internat., San Francisco, 1976-94; CFO Big Top Prodns., San Francisco, 1994—; gen. ptnr. Kanland Assocs., Tex., 1982, Claremont Assocs., Calif., 1983, Lakeland Assocs., Ga., 1983, Americal Assocs., Calif., 1983, Chatsworth Assocs., Calif., 1983, Walnut Grove Assocs., Calif., 1983, Somerset Assocs., N.J., 1983, One San Diego Assocs., Calif., 1984, Big Top Prodns., L.P., Calif., 1994. Bd. dirs., treas. Found. San Francisco's Archtl. Heritage. Mem. U.S. Trotting Assn., Calif. Harness Horse Breeders Assn. (Breeders award for Filly of Yr. 1986, Aged Pacing Mare, 1987, 88, Colt of Yr. 1990), Calif. Golf Club San Francisco. Home: 1911 Sacramento St San Francisco CA 94109-3419 Office: Big Top Prodns 548 4th St San Francisco CA 94107

DELLIS, DEBORAH RUTH, assistant corporate secretary; b. Phoenix, Aug. 29, 1960; d. Horace Alan and Eleanor Ann (Ellison) D.; m. Michael Patrick Feeley, Oct. 13, 1984 (div. Apr. 1987); m. Rusty Dean Austerman, Oct. 22, 1994. BS in Journalism, Ariz. State U., 1982; MA in Orgnl. Mgmt., U. Phoenix, 1995. Pub. rels. intern Phoenix Suns Profl. Basketball Club, 1982-83; promotion asst. Sta. KPNX-TV/Gannett Co. Inc., Phoenix, 1983; community rels. rep. Salt River Project, Phoenix, 1983-91, asst. corp. sec., 1991—. Contbr. articles to profl. jours. Chmn. environ. expo com. Valley Forward Assn., Phoenix, 1990-92; mem. comm. com. Am. Cancer Soc., Phoenix, 1990-92; environ. com. Valley Citizens League. Mem. Meeting Planners Internat. (co-chair comm. com. 1988-89, co-chmn. program com., bd. dirs. 1989-90, sec. 1990-91), Friends of COMPAS. Congregationalist. Office: Salt River Project PO Box 52025 Phoenix AZ 85072-2025

DELLUMS, RONALD V., congressman; b. Oakland, Calif., Nov. 24, 1935; m. Leola Roscoe Higgs; 3 children. A.A., Oakland City Coll., 1958; B.A., San Francisco State Coll., 1960; M.S.W., U. Calif., 1962. Psychiat. social worker Calif. Dept. Mental Hygiene, 1962-64; program dir. Bayview Community Ctr., San Francisco, 1964-65; from assoc. dir. to dir. Hunters Point Youth Opportunity Ctr., 1965-66; planning cons. Bay Area Social Planning Coun., 1966-67; dir. concentrated employment program San Francisco Econ. Opportunity Coun., 1967-68; sr. cons. Social Dynamics, Inc., 1968-70; mem. 92nd-103rd Congresses from 9th Calif. Dist., 1971—; former chmn. house com. on D.C., former mem. permanent select com. on intelligence, chmn. house armed svcs. com., 1993; lectr. San Francisco State Coll., U. Calif., Berkeley; mem. U.S. del. North Atlantic Assembly, ranking minority mem. Nat. Security Com.; former chmn. Congl. Black Caucus, Calif. Dem. Congl. Del., Dem. Study Group. Author: Defense Sense: The Search For A Rational Military Policy, 1983. Mem. Berkeley City Coun., 1967-71. With USMCR, 1954-56. Democrat. Office: US Ho of Reps 2108 Rayburn Bldg Ofc Washington DC 20515-0005 also: 1301 Clay St Ste 1000 N Oakland CA 94612-5217*

DELLWO, DENNIS A., state legislator; b. Washington, Aug. 31, 1945; s. Robert D. and Madeline (Maguire) D.; m. Jeannine Dellwo; children: Allison, Julia. BA, Gonzaga U., 1967; JD, Ariz. State U., 1971. Bar: Wash. 1971, U.S. Dist. Ct. Wash. 1973. With Winston & Cashatt Law Offices, Spokane, Wash.; mem. Wash. State Ho. Reps., Olympia, 1983—. Home: 2636 W Riverview Dr Spokane WA 99205-3878 Office: Winston & Cashatt 1900 Seafirst Financial Ctr Spokane WA 99201

DELMERICO, GEORGE ANTHONY, publications executive; b. Dobbs Ferry, N.Y., Aug. 23, 1945; s. Patrick A. and Helen (Jordan) D. BFA in Visual Comm., Pratt Inst., 1967. Asst. art dir. N.Y. mag., N.Y.C., 1968-70; art dir. The Herald, N.Y.C., 1971, Newsday, Garden City, N.Y., 1972-74, N.Y. Times, N.Y.C., 1974-76; design dir. Village Voice, N.Y.C., 1976-85; assocl pub. design Santa Barbara (Calif.) News and Rev., 1986; creative dir. Santa Barbara Ind., 1986-90; dir. publs. U. Calif., Santa Barbara, 1990—; instr. Sch. Visual Arts, N.Y.C., 1972-85, Santa Barbara City Coll., 1987-90, U. Calif., Santa Barbara Extension, 1989—; cons. N.Y. Times Co., Santa Rosa, Calif., 1986. Recipient Bronze medal Coun. for Advancement and Support of Edn., 1992. Home: 1625 Laguna St #21 Santa Barbara CA 93101 Office: U Calif Publs Santa Barbara CA 93106

DELOACH, ROBERT EDGAR, corporate executive; b. Daytona Beach, Fla., Jan. 6, 1939; s. Ollie Newman and Sally Gertrude (Schrowder) DeL. Student U. Alaska-Anchorage, 1967-69, Alaska Meth. U., 1970, Pacific Luth. U., 1972. Lic. elec. engr. and adminstr., Alaska, 1979; lic. pvt. pilot, real estate broker, ins. agt. Former chmn. bd. Alaska Stagecraft, Inc., Anchorage; pres. BG Systems Co., BG Tax & Acctg., Inc., The Electric Doctor, Inc., Apollo Travel, Inc.; former pres. Coastal Electronics, Inc.; former owner-mgr. Bargain Towne, Anchorage. Active Anchorage Community Theatre, Anchorage Theater Guild. Mem. Assn. Ind. Accts., Internat. Assn. Theatrical Stage Employees and Moving Picture Machine Operators U.S. (pres. local 770), Ind. Elec. Contractors Assn., Internat. Assn. Elec. Insps. Home: 1207 W 47th Ave Anchorage AK 99503-6917 Office: 7910 King St Anchorage AK 99518-3058

DEL OLMO, FRANK, newspaper editor; b. L.A., May 18, 1948; s. Francisco and Margaret Rosalie (Mosqueda) D.; m. Karen Margaret King, Feb. 6, 1970 (div. Sept. 1982); 1 child, Valentina Marisol; m. Magdalena Beltran-Hernandez, Nov. 10, 1991; 1 child, Francisco Manuel. Student, UCLA, 1966-68; BS magna cum laude in Journalism, Calif. State U., Northridge, 1970. Reporter-intern L.A. Times, 1970-71, gen. assignment reporter, 1971-80, columnist, editorial bd., 1980-90, deputy editor, 1990—; instr. Chicano Studies, Calif. State U., 1970-71; contbg. editor Race Relations Reporter, Nashville, 1973-75; on-air host, writer "Ahora" Sta. KCET-TV, L.A., 1974; chief writer, rschr. KNBC, 1975; bd. contbrs., freelance reporter Nuestro Mag., 1976-81; program co-dir. Summer Program Minority Journalists, 1990, faculty mem. 1979, vis. faculty mem. 1978, 80-83, 85, 89; vis. profl. Dow-Jones Newspaper Fund U. So. Calif. Sch. Journalism, 1975, bd. dirs. Numerous lectrs., presentations at colls., univs. Named Senior Faculty of Summer Program Minority Journalists Inst. Journalism Edn.; recipient Emmy award, 1976, Sigma Delta Chi Achievement award, 1982, Profl. Achievement award UCLA Alumni, 1990, Pulitzer Prize, 1984; Neiman fellowship Harvard U., 1987-88. Office: Los Angeles Times 202 W 1st St Los Angeles CA 90012-4105

DELONEY, CINDY RAE, biologist; b. Spokane, Wash., Dec. 28, 1966; d. William Charles and Marlene Jewel (Schofield) DeL. BS in Biology cum laude, Gonzaga U., 1993; postgrad., Ea. Wash. U., 1994—. Sales clk. Jafco/Best Products, Spokane, 1986-87; file clk., receptionist Lukins & Annis, P.S. Law Firm, Spokane, 1987-89; computer lab asst. Gonzaga U., Spokane, 1990-91; pharmacy technician "A" Sacred Heart Med. Ctr., Spokane, 1991—. Copy editor Gonzaga Univ. Bul. 1989-90. Campaign coord. Jim McClure campaign, Post Falls, Idaho, 1984; pres. Jr. Statesman, Post Falls, 1984-85, del., Boise, 1984; del. Girls State U., Boise, 1984. Mem. Am. Mus. of Natural History, Wash. Pharmacy Asst. Assn., Am. Soc. Microbiology.

DELONG, JAMES CLIFFORD, air transportation executive; b. N.Y.C., Jan. 29, 1940; s. Mary (Oles) DeL.; m. Nancy L. Hill; children: Andrew Hill, Theodore James. BS, Colgate U.; MA, U. Calif. Asst. mgr. Wichita Mid-continent Airport, 1970, airport mgr., 1971-74; asst. mgr. Houston Inter-Continent Airport, 1975-77, airport mgr., 1980-85; airport mgr. Houston Hobby Airport, 1978-79; dep. dir. dept. aviation Houston Dept. Aviation, 1986-87; dir. aviation Phila. Divsn. Aviation, 1987-93, Denver Divsn. Aviation, 1993—. Bd. dirs. Phila. Conv. and Vis. Bur., 1992-93. Pilot, USAF, 1963-70. Mem. Am. Assn. Airport Execs. (bd. dirs. 1989), Internat. Civil Aviation Orgn. (helicopters panel 1985—), Airport Operators Internat. (bd. dirs. 1990, info. sys. com. 1988, chmn. tech. com. 1979), Airport Coun. Internat. (bd. dirs., 1st v.p. 1993—), Nat. Transp. Rsch. Bd. (exec. bd. dirs. 1992—), Variety Club Internat. (bd. dirs. 1992-93). Office: Denver Internat Airport Airforce Office Bldg 8500 Peña Blvd Denver CO 80239-6340*

DE LONG, KATHARINE, retired secondary education educator; b. Germantown, Pa., Aug. 31, 1927; d. Melvin Clinton and Katherine Frances (Brunner) Barr; m. Alfred Alvin De Long, June 21, 1947; children: Renée, Claudia, Jane. AA, Mesa Jr. Coll., Grand Junction, Colo., 1962; BA, Western State Coll., Gunnison, Colo., 1964; MA, Colo. State U., 1972. Camp dir. Kannah Creek Girl Scout Camp, 1960-64; tchr. Mesa County Valley Sch. Dist. #51, Grand Junction, 1964-84, dept. chmn., 1970-79; ret., 1984; tour coord., escort Mesa Travel, 1990—; substitute instr. Mesa State Coll., 1986-90; student council sponsor Mesa County Valley Sch., 1976-80; mem. bd. dirs. Am. Red Cross, 1995—. Bd. dirs. Chipeta Girl Scout Coun., Grand Junction, 1960-66; pct. committeewoman Mesa County Dem. Party; mem., vice-chmn. Profl. Rights and Responsibilities Commn. for Dist. #51 Schs., Grand Junction, 1978-84; trustee Western Colo. Ctr. for the Arts, Grand Junction, 1987-88; mem. Mesa County Hist. Soc. Mem. AAUW (pres. local chpt. 1979-81, chmn. state cultural interest), AARP (Colo. legis. com. area I, asst. state dir., transp. task force, dist. dir. dist. 1, del. to nat. conv., dir. state conv. 1991), LWV (Grand Jct Area, sec. bd. dirs. 1995—), Pub. Employers Retirement Assn. (legis. adv. com. 1990-91), Colo. Ret. Sch. Employees Assn., Phi Theta Kappa. Congregationalist.

DELONG, R. SCOTT, telecommunications executive; b. Long Beach, Calif., Dec. 9, 1959; s. James Robert and Patricia Joan (Ryan) DeL.; m. Terri Ann DeLong, Nov. 22, 1980 (div. May 1988); children: Shawna Marie, Douglas James; m. Cheryl Ann Higgins, Apr. 29, 1995; stepchildren: Eric Ryan Higgins, Erica Christeen Higgins, Evan Patrick Higgins. AA in Liberal Arts, Santa Ana Coll., 1980; BA in History, Brigham Young U., 1982. Mktg. mgr. USCP WESCO, L.A., 1982-87; v.p. sales and mktg. Whitney Prodns., Newark, 1987-90; gen. mgr. Rage Sports, Oceanside, Calif., 1991; CEO Pub. Access Comms. Inc., Fountain Valley, Calif., 1991—. Author, columnist: (trade publ.) On the Line Mag., 1992, 93. Mem. Calif. Payphone Assn. (chmn. GTE com. 1994—, regulatory com., bd. dirs. 1992—, chmn.),

Am. Pub. Comm. Coun. (bd. dirs.). Republican. Office: Pub Access Telephone 17150 New Hope 401 Fountain Valley CA 92708

DE LORCA, LUIS E., educational administrator, educator, speaker; b. L.A., Oct. 18, 1959; s. Patricia Jean Clougher Harvey; m. Lori Ann Vanzant, Mar. 23, 1991. AA, Rio Hondo Jr. Coll., Whittier, Calif., 1983; BA, Calif. State Poly. U., 1989. High sch. football coach various high schs., So. Calif., 1980; pub. rels. dir. Calif. Poly Pomona Music Dept., 1987-89; pres. Exclusive Concepts, L.A., 1987-89; lifeguard L.A. City Recreation Dept., 1980-87; tchr. English Cathedral High Sch., L.A., 1989-90; tchr., rsch. specialist Whittier (Calif.) Union High Sch., 1990; founder, dir. The Learning Advantage Ctr., Whittier, 1991—; elem. tchr. St. Paul of the Cross Sch., La Mirada, Calif., 1993-95; CEO New Ednl. Wave Inc., Whittier, 1994—. Active Big Bros. of Am., Fair Housing, Greenpeace. Mem. Whittier C. of C., Cousteau Soc. Democrat. Unity Ch. Home: 2010 Madonna Ln La Habra CA 90631-3344 Office: The Learning Advantage Ctr 13710 Whittier Blvd Ste 206 Whittier CA 90605-1994

DELORENZO, DAVID A., food products executive; b. 1947. Colgate U.; MBA, U. Pa. With Dole Food Co., Inc., Thousand Oaks, Calif., 1970—, exec. v.p., 1990-91, 93—, pres., 1991-93; pres. Dole Food Co., Internat., 1993—. Office: Dole Food Co Inc 31355 Oak Crest Dr Thousand Oaks CA 91361-4633*

DEL PAPA, FRANKIE SUE, state attorney general; b. 1949. BA, U. Nev.; JD, George Washington U., 1974. Bar: Nev. 1974. Staff asst. U.S. Senator Alan Bible, Washington, 1971-74; assoc. Law Office of Leslie B. Grey, Reno, Nev., 1975-78; legis. asst. to U.S. Senator Howard Cannon, Washington, 1978-79; ptnr. Thornton & Del Papa, 1979-84; pvt. practice Reno, 1984-87; sec. of state State of Nev., Carson City, 1987-91; atty. gen. State of Nev., 1991—. Mem. Sierra Arts Found. (bd. dirs.), Trust for Pub. Land (adv. com.), Nev. Women's Fund. Democrat. Office: Office of Atty Gen Capitol Complex Carson City NV 89710

DELUCCHI, GEORGE PAUL, accountant; b. Richmond, Calif., Apr. 20, 1938; s. George Carl and Rose Caroline (Golino) D. BA, San Jose State U., 1959. CPA, Calif. Ptnr. Delucchi, Swanson & Co., Santa Clara, Calif., 1968-74, Delucchi, Swanson & Sandival, Santa Clara, 1974-76, Delucchi, Sandoval & Co., Santa Clara, 1976-77, Wolf & Co., San Jose, Calif., 1977-78; v.p. Lautze & Lautze, San Jose, 1978-82, also bd. dirs.; sr. ptnr. G.P. Delucchi & Assocs. (name changed to Delucchi, Robinson, Streit & Co., Santa Clara, 1982—. Treas. Crippled Children Soc., San Jose, 1967-71, San Jose Cath. Charities, 1984—, F. Schmidt Found. for Youth; bd. dirs. Serra Med. Found., Mission City Cmty. Fund, Bill Wilson Marriage and Family Counseling Ctr.; pres. Santa Clara Police Activity League, 1977-78; bd. fellows Santa Clara U., 1975—; chair pioneer dist. Santa Clara coun. Boy Scouts Am. Lt. U.S. Army, 1959-62. Mem. AICPA, Calif. Soc. CPA's (dir. 1993-95), Silicon Valley Capital Club, Serra Club, Elks (Santa Clara exalted ruler 1969-70), Rotary (pres. 1993-94, bd. dirs. 1986-89), Knights of Malta (invested, Knight of Magistral Grace). Republican. Roman Catholic. Home: 774 Circle Dr Santa Clara CA 95050-5927 Office: 2075 De La Cruz Blvd Santa Clara CA 95050-3035

DELUGACH, ALBERT LAWRENCE, journalist; b. Memphis, Oct. 27, 1925; s. Gilbert and Edna (Short) D.; m. Bernice Goldstein, June 11, 1950; children: Joy, David, Daniel, Sharon. B.J., U. Mo., 1951. Reporter Kansas City (Mo.) Star, 1951-60, St. Louis Globe Democrat, 1960-69, St. Louis Post Dispatch, 1969-70; investigative reporter Los Angeles Times, 1970-89. Served with USNR, 1943-46. Recipient Pultizer prize for spl. local reporting, 1969, Gerald Loeb award for disting. bus. and fin. journalism, 1984. Mem. Sigma Delta Chi. Home: 4313 Price St Los Angeles CA 90027-2815

DELUZE, JAMES ROBERT, physician; b. L.A., Sept. 14, 1948; s. James Vierea and Jean Ruth (Hanna) DeL. BA, U. Hawaii, 1974; student, Andrews U., 1980-82; DO, U. Health Scis., Kansas City, 1987. Product specialist Hanna Enterprise, Kailua, Hawaii, 1972-74; pres. Ecol. Engring., Honolulu, 1976-79; intern Kirksville (Mo.) Osteo. Med. Ctr., 1987-88; pvt. practice medicine Kailua, 1988-89; physician Mental Health Systems, San Diego, 1989-90; pvt. practice Waialua, Hawaii, 1991—. Rep. candidate U.S. Ho. of Reps., 1992, U.S. Senate, 1994; pres. Waialua Rep. Precinct, 1992; del. Rep. State Conv., Honolulu, 1992. Mem. Am. Assn. Clin. Anatomists, Am. Coll. Occupational and Environ. Medicine, Am. Osteo. Assn. (del. 1992), Hawaii Assn. Osteo. Physicians and Surgeons (v.p. 1991-92, pres. 1992-93), Nat. Space Soc., U.S. C. of C. Republican. Seventh Day Adventist. Home and Office: PO Box 541 Waialua HI 96791-0541

DEL VECCHIO, DAWN MARIE, theatre manager; b. Phila., Mar. 16, 1957; d. Alfred Frederick and Edna Florence (McCoy) Del V. BS in Bus. Adminstrn., U. La Verne, Calif., 1994. Theatre mgr. Cinamerica Theatres, L.P., Encino, Calif., 1978—. Office: 1321 S Grand Ave Glendora CA 91740

DEMAISON, GERARD JEAN, petroleum exploration consultant, geology and geochemistry educator; b. Meudon, France, Sept. 9, 1927; naturalized citizen, 1977; s. Andre and Jeanne (Duvernet) D.; m. Shirley W. Wells, Aug. 9, 1971. BS, U. Paris, 1949; MS, Colo. Sch. Mines, 1954. British Petroleum, London, Paris, 1954-66, Chevron, San Ramon, Calif., 1971-90; internat. cons., prof. geology Stanford (Calif.) U., 1988—. Editor: Petroleum Geochemistry and Basin Evaluation, 1985; contbr. numerous articles to profl. jours. Mem. Am. Assn. Petroleum Geologists (Pres.'s award 1986, Wallace Pratt award 1993, Hon. Mem. award 1994). Republican. Office: PO Box 1877 Capitola CA 95010-1877

DE MARANVILLE, NANCY JOAN, secondary education educator; b. Sioux City, Iowa, Jan. 20, 1932; d. Harry Thurl and Esther Sophia (Dobbert) De M.; m. Edward Feigenbaum, Oct. 4, 1958 (div. 1974); children: Janet Denise Feigenbaum, Carol Leonora Feigenbaum. BS, UCLA, 1956, MEd, 1962. Tchr. Coll. San Mateo, Calif., 1974-78, San Francisco C.C., 1980-81, OICW Job Tng. Program, Menlo Park, Calif., 1984-86, John Swett High Sch., Crockett, Calif., 1986—. Mem. Calif. Tchrs. Assn., Berkeley Watercolor Soc. Democrat. Home: 401 Monte Vista Ave Apt 206 Oakland CA 94611-4509 Office: John Swett High Sch 1098 Pomona Ave Crockett CA 94525-1426

DEMARCHI, ERNEST NICHOLAS, aerospace engineering administrator; b. Lafferty, Ohio, May 31, 1939; s. Ernest Costante and Lena Marie (Cireddu) D.; B.M.E., Ohio State U., 1962; M.S. in Engring., UCLA, 1969; m. Carolyn Marie Tracz, Sept. 17, 1960; children—Daniel Ernest, John David, Deborah Marie. Registered profl. cert. mgr. With Space div. Rockwell Internat., Downey, Calif., 1962—, mem. Apollo, Skylab and Apollo-Soyuz missions design team in electronic and elec. systems, mem. mission support team for all Apollo and Skylab manned missions, 1962-74, mem. Space Shuttle design team charge elec. systems equipment, 1974-77, in charge Orbiter Data Processing System, 1977-81, in charge Orbiter Ku Band Communication and Radar System, 1981-85, in charge orbitor elec. power distbr., displays, controls, data processing, 1984-87, in charge space based interceptor flt. exper., 1987-88, kinetic energy systems, 1988-90, ground based interceptor program, 1990—. Recipient Apollo Achievement award NASA, 1969, Apollo 13 Sustained Excellent Performance award, 1970, Astronaut Personal Achievement Snoopy award, 1971; Exceptional Service award Rockwell Internat., 1972, Outstanding Contbn. award, 1976; NASA ALT award, 1979; Shuttle Astronaut Snoopy award, 1982; Pub. Service Group Achievement award NASA, 1982; Rockwell Pres.'s award, 1983, 87; registered profl. engr., Ohio. Mem. AIAA, ASME, Nat. Mgmt. Assn., Varsity O Alumni Assn. Home: 25311 Maximus St Mission Viejo CA 92691-4517 Office: 12214 Lakewood Blvd Downey CA 90242-2655

DEMARCO, RALPH JOHN, real estate developer; b. N.Y.C., Mar. 22, 1924; s. Frank and Mary (Castriota) DeM.; m. Arlene Gilbert, July 1, 1945; children: Sheryl DeMarco Grahn, Stephen, Laura DeMarco Wilson. BA, Claremont Men's Coll., 1956. Assoc. John B. Kilroy Co., Riverside, Calif., 1960-64, also mgr. ops. Riverside, San Bernardino counties, 1960-64; v.p. Marcus W. Meairs Co., 1964-67; pres. Diversified Properties, Inc., Riverside, 1967-72; v.p. Downey Savs. & Loan Assn. (Calif.), 1972-75; exec. v.p. DSL Svc. Co., 1972-75; pres. Interstate Shopping Ctrs., Inc., Santa Ana, Calif., 1975-87; exec. dir. comml. devel. Lewis Homes Mgmt. Corp., Upland, Calif., 1987-89; pvt. practice, San Diego, Calif., 1989—. Mem. City of Riverside Planning Commn., 1955-59, Airport Commn., 1960-70; mem. Urban Land Inst. 1st lt. USAF, 1942-45. Mem. Internat. Coun. Shopping Ctrs. Home: 44-489 Town Center Way # D 273 Palm Desert CA 92260-2723 Office: 1403 Scott St Ste 201 San Diego CA 92106-2728

DE MASSA, JESSIE G., media specialist. BJ, Temple U.; MLS, San Jose State U., 1967; postgrad., U. Okla., U. So. Calif. Tchr. Palo Alto (Calif.) Unified Sch. Dist., 1966; librarian Antelope Valley Joint Union High Sch. Dist., Lancaster, Calif., 1966-68, ABC Unified Sch. Dist., Artesia, Calif., 1968-72; dist. librarian Tehachapi (Calif.) Unified Sch. Dist., 1972-81; also media specialist, free lance writer, 1981—. Contbr. articles to profl. jours. Mem. Statue of Liberty Ellis Island Found., Inc.; charter supporter U.S. Holocaust Meml. Mus., Washington; supporting mem. U.S. Holocaust Meml. Coun., Washington. Fellow Internat. Biog. Assn.; mem. Calif. Media and Libr. Educators Assn., Calif Assn. Sch. Librs. (exec. coun.) AAUW (bull. editor chpt., assoc. editor state bull., chmn. publicity, 1955-68), Nat. Mus. Women in Arts. (charter), Hon. Fellows John F. Kennedy Libr. (founding mem.), Women's Roundtable of Orange County, Nat. Writer's Club. Home: 9951 Garrett Cir Huntington Beach CA 92646-3604

DEMELLO, AUSTIN EASTWOOD, astrophysicist, concert artist, poet, writer; b. New Bedford, Mass., Oct. 15, 1939; s. Manuel and Dora (Eastwood) De M; 1 child, Adragon Eastwood De Mello. BA in English, UCLA, 1974; MSc in Physics and Astronomy, Met. Coll. Inst., London, 1977, DSc in Theoretical Astrophysics, 1981. Engring. writer Raytheon Co., Santa Barbara, Calif., 1982; dir. research and sci. publs. Cosmosci. Research Inst., Sunnyvale, Calif., 1983—. Author: Black Night Poetry, 1960, Tangu, 1962, (record) El Duende Flamenco, 1965, The Metagalactic System, 1969, The Four States of Man, 1971, Early Development of the Scientific Mind, 1981, Theory of Cosmodynamics, 1983, The Cosmotorsion Effect, 1984, James Bay Missionaries, 1986, The Origin and Influence of Flamenco Music on the Classics, 1992, Offenbach and the Can-Can Dance, 1993, Adragon: The Youngest Scholar, 1993, Legacy of Poetry and Philosophy, 1993, The Magic Formula, 1993, Views of Chaos, 1993. Acad. Merit scholar UCLA, 1972-74. Mem. AIAA, AAAS, N.Y. Acad. Sci., Am. Astronautical Soc., Mensa Internat. Home: PO Box 461 Moss Landing CA 95039-0461 Office: CSR Inst 663 S Bernardo Ave Sunnyvale CA 94087-1020

DEMEREE, GLORIA See LENNOX, GLORIA

DEMERSMAN, JAMES RICHARD, museum director; b. Rochester, N.Y., July 31, 1957; s. Richard Oscar and Carolyn Ruth (Morse) DeM.; m. Pricilla Ann McClellan Hill, Nov. 29, 1980 (div. Dec. 1987); 1 child, Andrew Joseph; m. Richard Erland Patenaude, Oct. 9, 1993. BA in History and Bus. Adminstrn., Houghton Coll., 1980. Asst. to dir. edn. Genesee Country Mus., Mumford, N.Y., 1980; dir. edn. Hist. Speedwell Village, Morristown, N.J., 1980-83; dir. edn. Rosemount Victorian House Mus., Pueblo, Colo., 1983-85, exec. dir., 1985-87; asst. dir. Nat. Trust for Hist. Preservation, Washington, 1987-91; dir. Molly Brown House Mus., Denver, 1991-93; dir., curator Hi-Desert Nature Mus., Yucca Valley, Calif., 1993—; peer reviewer Inst. Mus. Svcs., Washington, 1985—. Editor: (newsletter) Integrity of the Desert, Palm Springs, Calif., 1994—. Male co-chmn. Alliance for Lesbian and Gay Concerns, Washington, 1993-95. Preservation Leadership tng. Nat. Trust for Hist. Preservation, 1993. Mem. Am. Assn. Museums (vis. cons. 1991—), Western Mus. Assn., Calif. Assn. Museums, Calif. Preservation Found., Registrar's Coun., Nat. Trust for Hist. Preservation. Democrat. Episcopalian. Home: 2050 Jason Ct Palm Springs CA 92262-4033 Office: Hi-Desert Nature Mus 57116 Twenty Nine Palms Hwy Yucca Valley CA 92284

DEMETER, STEVEN, neurologist, publishing company executive; b. Budapest, Hungary, Jan. 12, 1947; came to U.S., 1957; s. Arpad and Ilona (Wiesner) D.; m. Diane Simkin, Jan. 8, 1984; children: Sara, Nikki. BS, CUNY, 1969; MD, N.Y. Med. Coll., 1973. Diplomate Am. Bd. Psychiatry and Neurology. Intern Beth Israel Med. Ctr., N.Y.C., 1973-74; neurology resident Albert Einstein Coll. Medicine, Bronx, N.Y., 1974-77; inst. neurology N.Y. Med. Coll., N.Y.C., 1977-79; fellow in behavioral neurology U. Iowa Coll. Medicine, Iowa City, 1979-81; fellow Ctr. for Brain Rsch., U. Rochester (N.Y.) Sch. Medicine, 1981-84, instr. neurology, 1982-84, asst. prof. Ctr. for Brain Rsch., 1984-87, asst. prof. neurology, 1987-89, clin. asst. prof., 1989-91, clin. assoc. prof., 1991-93; pres. electronic pub. Arbor Pub. Corp., La Jolla, Calif., 1990—; assoc.clin. prof. neurosci. U. Calif., San Diego, 1995—; neurology cons. Rochester Psychiat. Ctr., 1985-91. Contbr. numerous articles to med. jours. Grantee Scottish Rite Schizophrenia Rsch. Found., 1987-90, Whitehall Found., 1990-93, NIH, 1991-94. Fellow Am. Acad. Neurology, Royal Soc. Medicine (London); mem. AAAS, Soc. for Neurosci., Tourette Syndrome Assn. (med. com. 1985-93, bd. dirs. 1987-93). Office: Arbor Pub Corp 4275 Executive Sq Ste 305 La Jolla CA 92037-1476

DEMETREON, DAIBOUNE ELAYNE, minister; b. Brunswick, Maine, Aug. 5, 1945; d. James Demetreon and Grace Lewis; m. James Allison Devine, Mar. 3, 1986; children from previous marriage: William Anthony Decker, James Steven Decker. Degree, Unity Sch. Practical Christianity & Ordination, 1975; postgrad., Rio Salado Coll., 1992; BA in Psychology, Ottawa U., 1994. Ordained min. Unity Ch., 1975; cert. practitioner Neuro-Linguistic Program. Sr. min. Unity of Ann Arbor, Mich., 1975-77, Unity of Boulder, Colo., 1977-78, Unity of Colorado Springs, 1980-86, Unity of Scottsdale, Ariz., 1989—; chmn. World of One Fellowship, Colorado Springs, 1986—, pastoral counselor, Scottsdale, 1989—; adv. bd. dirs. Boulder (Colo.) Psychiat. Inst., 1977-78; campus min. U. Mich., Ypsilanti, 1975-77; conductor workshops chaplains program U.S. Army, Ft. Carson. Author, narrator audio tape Transformations, 1985; host talk show God and You, 1983; contbr. articles to profl. publs. Chem. dependency counselor St. Luke's Hosp., 1993—. Office: World of One Fellowship 8556 E Via De Risa Scottsdale AZ 85258-3931

DEMETRESCU, MIHAI CONSTANTIN, computer company executive, scientist; b. Bucharest, Romania, May 23, 1929; s. Dan and Alina (Dragosescu) D.; M.E.E., Poly. Inst. of U. Bucharest, 1954; Ph.D., Romanian Acad. Sci., 1957; m. Agnes Halas, May 25, 1969; 1 child, Stefan. Came to U.S., 1966. Prin. investigator Research Inst. Endocrinology Romanian Acad. Sci., Bucharest, 1958-66; research fellow dept. anatomy UCLA, 1966-67; faculty U. Calif.-Irvine, 1967-83, asst. prof. dept. physiology, 1971-78, assoc. researcher, 1978-79, assoc. clin. prof., 1979-83; v.p. Resonance Motors, Inc., Monrovia, Calif., 1972-85; pres. Neurometrics, Inc., Irvine, Calif., 1978-82; pres. Lasergraphics Inc., Irvine, 1982-84, chmn., chief exec. officer, 1984—. Mem. com. on hon. degrees U. Calif.-Irvine, 1970-72. Postdoctoral fellow UCLA, 1966. Mem. Internat. Platform Assn., Am. Physiol. Soc., IEEE (sr.). Republican. Contbr. articles to profl. jours. Patentee in field. Home: 20 Palmento Way Irvine CA 92715-2109 Office: 20 Ada Irvine CA 92718-2303

DEMICHELE, BARBARA JOAN, public relations executive; b. Phoenix, Sept. 28, 1953; d. Glenn Vernon and Diana Jean (Warford) Stanley; m. O. Mark DeMichele, May 22, 1982; 1 child, Angela Marie. BA, U. Ariz., 1975. Editor Tombstone (Ariz.) Epitaph, 1974-75; reporter Herald Dispatch, Sierra Vista, Ariz., 1975-76; cmty. rels. Caithness Corp., Tucson, 1976-78; writer Ariz. Pub. Svc. Co., Phoenix, 1978-79; pub. rels. officer Valley Nat. Bank, Phoenix, 1979-81, United Bank of Ariz., Phoenix, 1981-83; pres. BJ Comms., Inc., Phoenix, 1984—. Chmn. Phoenix/Valley of the Sun Visitors and Conv. Bur., 1994-95; dir. Herberger Theater Ctr., Phoenix, 1994—; chmn. Phoenix Little Theater Co., 1985-86; bd. dirs. Phoenix Symphony, 1988-94; chmn. Symphony Ball, 1987, Herberger Headlines, 1995. Mem. Pub. Rels. Soc. Am., Phoenix C. of C. (vice chmn. 1994—). Republican. Episcopal. Office: BJ Comms Inc 3101 N Central Ave Ste 870 Phoenix AZ 85012-2640

DEMILLE, LESLIE BENJAMIN, artist; b. Hamilton, Ont., Can., Apr. 24, 1927; came to U.S., 1958; s. Warren Clarence and Nora Lillian (Connor) DeM.; m. H. Isobel Don, Sept. 6, 1947; children: Dianne Lynne, Leslie Dane, Malcolm Don, Richard Ian, Mark Cameron. Student, Art Students League, N.Y.C., 1945-47. Tchr. portraiture, 1960—. Portraits commd. by numerous people and orgns., including Pres. Richard M. Nixon and Pres. Ronald Reagan; bronze sculptures including "Peacemakers" presented to Pres. Reagan, 1988, now on permanent exhibit at Reagan Libr., Simi, Calif.; painter protraits of Arnold Palmer, Jack Nicklaus, others; monumental bronze sculpture of 3 Native Am. Indians, Sedona, Ariz., 1991. Home and Studio: 50 Cathedral Ln Sedona AZ 86336

DEMILLION, JULIANNE, health and fitness specialist and personal trainer, rehabilitation consultant; b. Monessen, Pa., Dec. 20, 1955; d. William Vincent and Enise Mary (Tocci) DeM. BA, BS, U. Pitts., 1977; cert. massage therapist Phoenix Therapeutic Massage Coll., 1985. Mgr. program devel. Exclusively Women Spas, Scottsdale, 1977-81; pvt. exercise therapist, Scottsdale, 1981-83, ; cons. City of Phoenix, 1981-88; cons., pvt. personal trainer, Scottsdale, 1983—; instr. advanced techniques Phoenix Therapeutic Massage Coll., 1986-90. Mem. NAFE, Am. Massage Therapy Assn. (State Meritorious award 1989), Ariz. Massage Therapy Assn. (sec.-treas. 1986-90, Svc. award 1991), Internat. Dance and Exercise Assn., Circulo-Systems Ltd., Am. Coll. Sports Medicine.

DEMOFF, MARVIN ALAN, lawyer; b. L.A., Oct. 28, 1942; s. Max and Mildred (Tweer) D.; m. Patricia Caryn Abelov, June 16, 1968; children: Allison Leigh, Kevin Andrew. BA, UCLA, 1964; JD, Loyola U., L.A., 1967. Bar: Calif. 1969. Asst. pub. defender Los Angeles County, 1968-72; ptnr. Steinberg & Demoff, L.A., 1973-83, Craighill, Fentress & Demoff, L.A. and Washington, 1983-86; of counsel Mitchell, Silberberg & Knupp, L.A., 1987—. Mem. citizens adv. bd. Olympic Organizing Com., L.A., 1982-84; bd. trustees Curtis Sch., L.A., 1985-94, chmn. bd. trustees, 1988-93; sports adv. bd. Constitution Rights Found., L.A., 1986—; bd. dirs. 4A Found., 1988—. Mem. ABA (mem. forum com. on entertainment and sports), Calif. Bar Assn., UCLA Alumni Assn., Phi Delta Phi. Office: Mitchell Silberberg Kn Los Angeles CA 90061

DEMPSEY, BARBARA MATTHEA, medical/surgical and critical care nurse; b. The Netherlands, July 27, 1943; d. Petrus Antonius and Hendrika Petronella (Kemp) Petersen; m. James D. Dempsey, June 13, 1981; children: Jennifer, Daniel. AA, Santa Monica (Calif.) Coll., 1970; cert. lactation educator, UCLA, 1982. Staff nurse med./surg. Santa Monica Hosp., 1967-72; surg. intensive care nurse VA Wadsworth Hosp., L.A., 1973-77; staff nurse med./surg. Community Hosp., Santa Rosa, Calif., 1988-90; staff nurse Redwood Nurses Registry, Santa Rosa, 1990-93, Norrell Healthcare, Santa Rosa, Calif., 1990-93; charge nurse Creekside Convalescent Hosp., 1994; ret., 1994.

DEMPSTER, STUART ROSS, trombonist, composer, music educator; b. Berkeley, Calif., July 7, 1936; s. Fred Harper and Kathryn Emlyn (Shepardson) D.; m. Renko Carolyn Ishida, Dec. 19, 1964; children: Brian Komei, Loren Kiyoshi. BA in Performance, San Francisco State Coll., 1958, MA in Composition, 1967. Part-time instr. San Francisco Conservatory of Music, 1961-66; part-time asst. prof. Calif. State U., Hayward, 1963-66; prof. U. Wash., Seattle, 1968—; prin. trombone Oakland (Calif.) Symphony, 1962-66; performer in field. Author: The Modern Trombone, 1979. Bd. dirs. Artist Trust, Seattle, 1986-89. With U.S. Army, 1958-60. Recipient Performance award Martha Baird Rockefeller Fund for Music, 1971; U. Ill. fellow, 1971-72, Nat. Endowment for the Arts fellow, 1978, 79, Guggenheim Found. fellow, 1981; Fulbright-Hays grantee Govt. of Australia, 1973. Mem. Internat. Trombone Assn., ASCAP. Office: U Wash Sch of Music Seattle WA 98195

DEMUTH, ALAN CORNELIUS, lawyer; b. Boulder, Colo., Apr. 29, 1935; s. Laurence Wheeler and Eugenia Augusta (Roach) DeM.; m. Susan McDermott; children: Scott Lewis, Evan Dale, Joel Millard. BA in Econs. and Gen. Studies cum laude, U. Colo., 1958, LLB, 1961. Bar: Colo. 1961, U.S. Dist. Ct. Colo. 1961, U.S. Ct. Appeals (10th cir.) 1962. Assoc. Akolt, Turnquist, Shepherd & Dick, Denver, 1961-68; ptnr. DeMuth & DeMuth, 1968—. Conf. atty. Rocky Mountain Conf. United Ch. of Christ, 1970-94; bd. dirs. Friends of U. Colo. Library, 1978-86; bd. dirs., sponsor Denver Boys Inc., 1987-93, sec., 1988-89, v.p., 1989-90, pres. 1992-93; bd. dirs. Denver Kids, Inc., 1993—, Childrens Svcs. of Colo., 1994—; bd. advisors Metro Denver Salvation Army, 1988—, vice chmn. 1994—. Mem. ABA, Colo. Bar Assn., Denver Bar Assn., Am Judicature Soc., Rotary, Phi Beta Kappa, Sigma Alpha Epsilon, Phi Delta Phi. Republican. Mem. United Ch. of Christ. Office: DeMuth & DeMuth 1660 S Albion St Ste 222 Denver CO 80222

DENARDO, GERALD LOUIS, academic director; b. Aug. 24, 1932. BA in Medicine, U. Calif., Berkeley, 1954; MD in Medicine, U. Calif., San Francisco, 1957. Diplomate Am. Bd. Internal Medicine, Am. Bd. Nuclear Medicine. Intern Letterman Gen. Hosp., San Francisco, 1957-58; resident in internal medicine William Beaumont Gen. Hosp., El Paso, Tex., 1958-60, chief resident, 1960-61, fellow in radioisotope-endocrinology svc., 1960-61; dir. Fitzsimmons Gen. Hosp., Denver, 1961-65, VA Hosp., Palo Alto, Calif., 1965-67; mem. staff Stanford U. Med. Ctr., 1967-70; from assoc. prof. to prof. vet. medicine U. Calif., Davis, 1970-85, mem. prof. staff, 1982-87, dir. sch. medicine, 1987—; cons. Letterman Army Med. Ctr., 1985—, HHS, FDA, 1986-89, Dept. Energy, 1987-89; v.p. Am. bd. Nuclear Medicine, 1979-80. Contbr. articles to profl. jours.; patentee in field. Mem. AAAS, AMA, Am. Fedn. Clin. Rsch., Am. Heart Assn. (coun. cardiovascular radiology), Am. Coll. Nuclear Physicians (pres. 1975-76), Nat. Soc. Nuclear Medicine (Berson Yalow award 1978, 84), Calif. Med. Assn., Western Regional Soc. Nuclear Medicine (Disting. Scientist award 1992), Soc. Nuclear Medicine (pres. 1969-71, 81-82), Soc. Biol. Therapy, Alpha Sigma Nu. Home: 1508 Alhambra Blvd # 214 Sacramento CA 95816-6510

DENDO, ALBERT ULYSSES, electronics executive; b. N.Y.C., Aug. 29, 1923; s. Morris and Celia (Blittner) D.; m. Elizabeth Ann Terwillegar, June 6, 1950; children: Michael Robert, Sandra Stacy Dendo Miller. AB, Cornell U., 1949, postgrad., 1949-50; MA in Econs., Am. U., 1966, postgrad., 1967-69. From analyst to sr. inspector CIA, Washington, 1950-79; mgr. planning and requirements analysis and adminstrn. Gen. Dynamics Electronics Div., San Diego, 1979-83, dir. mktg., 1983-84, div. dir. mktg., 1984-85, div. v.p. mktg., 1985—. Mem. Tech. Mktg. Soc. Am., U.S. Strategic Inst., U.S. Naval Inst., Assn. U.S. Army, Air Force Assn., Navy League San Diego, Assn. Old Crows. Office: Gen Dynamics Electronics Div 5011 Kearny Villa Rd San Diego CA 92123-1407

DENIOUS, JON PARKS, publishing executive; b. Buffalo, Apr. 5, 1939; s. Wilbur Franklin Jr. and Nancy (Parks) D.; m. Sharon Marie Fee, June 17, 1963; children: Timothy, Elizabeth. Owner Durango (Colo.) Printing and Graphics, 1985-90; publ. Silverton (Colo.) Standard and The Miner, 1990—. Mem. Nat. Newspaper Assn., Colo. Press Assn. Office: The Silverton Standard The Miner 1257 Greene St Silverton CO 81433

DENIOUS, SHARON MARIE, publisher; b. Rulo, Nebr., Jan. 27, 1941; d. Thomas Wayne and Alma (Murphy) Fee; m. Jon Parks Denious, June 17, 1963; children: Timothy Scot, Elizabeth Denious Cessna. Grad. high sch. Operator N.W. Pipeline co., Ignacio, Colo., 1975-90; pub. Silverton (Colo.) Standard & Miner, 1990—. Mem. Colo. Press Assn., Nat. Newspaper Assn. Office: Silverton Standard & Miner 1257 Greene St Silverton CO 81433

DENISON, MICHAEL STEVEN, education educator; b. Shirley, Mass., Dec. 8, 1954; s. Alan Everet and Alma Rose D.; m. Grace Lynn Bedoian, Aug. 30, 1991. AA with hons., County Coll. of Morris, 1975; MS in Marine Biology magna cum laude, St. Francis Coll., 1977; MS in Animal Physiology, Miss. State U., 1980; PhD in Environ. Toxicology, Cornell U., 1983. Asst. prof. dept. biochemistry Mich. State U., East Lansing, 1988-92; asst. prof. dept. environ. toxicology U. Calif., Davis, 1992—; adj. asst. prof. Pesticide Rsdch. Ctr. Mich. State U., 1990-93, dept. biochemistry; postdoct. rsch. Hosp. for sick Children, Toronto, 1983-85, Stanford (Calif.) U., 1985-88; numerous faculty coms.; participant scientific rev. panel, Washington, 1992; invited lectr. seminars in field. Editorial bd. mem. Molecular Toxicology jour., 1991, Biochem. Toxicology, 1991—, European Jour. of Pharmacology, 1991—; referee numerous jours. in field; contbr. articles to profl. jours. Mem. Am. Soc. Biochemistry and Molecular Biology, Soc. Toxicology, Internat. Soc. Study of Xenobiotics. Office: Univ Calif Dept Environ Toxicology Meyer Hall Davis CA 95616

DENISON, WILLIAM CLARK, mycologist, educator; b. Rochester, N.Y., June 1, 1928; s. Glenn M. and Rhoda T. (Torrance) D.; m. Margaret R.

Mellinger, Sept. 11, 1948; children: Robert Ford, Thomas C., Glenn T., Rebecca S. Denison Johnston. BA, Oberlin (Ohio) Coll., 1950, MA, 1952; PhD, Cornell U., 1956. Apprentice millwright Eastman Kodak Co., Rochester, 1944-46; co-dir. Kanawauke Regional Mus., Bear Mtn. (N.Y.) Park, summer 1947; preparator Dept. Preserved Materials Gen. Biol. Supply House, Chgo., 1948-49; teaching asst. Dept. of Botany Oberlin Coll., 1950-52; teaching asst. Dept. of Plant Pathology Cornell U., 1952-55; asst. prof. Dept. of Biology Swarthmore (Pa.) Coll., 1955-66; assoc. prof. Dept. of Botany & Plant Pathology Oreg. State U., Corvallis, 1966—, curator, 1966—; vis. asst. prof. Dept. of Botany U. N.C., Chapel Hill, 1958-59; pres., sr. scientist Northwest Mycological Cons., Inc., Corvallis, 1985—; rsch. in field. Contbr. articles to numerous profl. jours. Co-organizer, counselor Corvallis Draft Info. Ctr., 1968-72; chmn. North Benton County Citizen's Adv. Com., 1974-78; charter mem., firefighter Adair Rural Fire Protection Dept., Adair Village, Oreg., 1975-83; foster parent Children's Svcs. Div. Oreg. Dept. HHS, 1976-79; citizen mem. representing Benton County Benton Govt. Com., 1978-80; pres. Friends of Benton County, 1978-88; founding mem. First Alternative Coop., Corvallis; bd. dirs. Willamette Inst. Biol. Control. Grantee NSF, Am. Philos. Assn. Mem. Internat. Lichenological Assn., AAUP, AAAS, Mycological Soc. Am., Oreg. Natural Resources Coun., Oreg. Pub. Employee Union (assoc.). Home: 37043 Beldon Creek Rd Corvallis OR 97330-9358 Office: Oreg State Univ Dept Botany Corvallis OR 97331

DENKE, PAUL HERMAN, aircraft engineer; b. San Francisco, Feb. 7, 1916; s. Edmund Herman and Ella Hermine (Riehl) D.; m. Beryl Ann Lincoln, Feb. 10, 1940; children: Karen Denke Mottaz, Claudia Denke Tesche, Marilyn Denke Dunn. BCE, U. Calif.-Berkeley, 1937, MCE, 1939. Registered profl. engr., Calif. Stress engr. Douglas Aircraft Co., Santa Monica, Calif., 1940-62, mgr. structural mechanics Long Beach, Calif., 1962-65, chief sci. computing, 1965-71, chief structures engr. methods and devel., 1972-78, chief scientist structural mechanics, 1979-84, staff mgr. MDC fellow, 1985—; mem. faculty dept engring. UCLA, 1941-50. Assoc. fellow AIAA; mem. Soc. Automotive Engrs. (Arch T. Colwell Merit award 1966, IAE Outstanding Engr. Merit award 1985), Sigma Xi, Chi Epsilon, Tau Beta Pi. Democrat. Pioneered and developed finite element method of structural analysis; author numerous technical papers. Home: 1800 Via Estudillo Palos Verdes Peninsula CA 90274-1908

DENKLER, KEITH ALAN, surgeon; b. Alton, Ill., Dec. 25, 1954. MD, Baylor U., 1979. Intern St. Joseph Hosp., Houston, 1979-80, surgeon, 1981-84, plastic surgeon, 1985-87; hand surgeon U. Calif., San Francisco, 1984-85; cranial surgeon Dr. Paul Tessier, Paris, 1987-88; now surgeon Marin Gen. Hosp., Greenbrae, Calif. Office: Ste 305 599 Sir Francis Drake Blvd Greenbrae CA 94904-1732*

DENLEA, LEO EDWARD, JR., insurance company executive; b. N.Y.C., Mar. 7, 1932; s. Leo Edward Sr. and Teresa (Carroll) D.; m. Nancy Burkley, Aug. 16, 1959; children: Leo Edward III, Thomas, Gregory, Kathryn, Nancy, Rita, Philip. B.S. in Econs., Villanova U., 1954; M.B.A., U. Pa., 1959. Group v.p. fin. services Internat. Basic Economy Corp., N.Y.C., 1966-74; v.p., treas. Pacific Lighting Corp., Los Angeles, 1974-81; sr. v.p. fin. Farmers Group, Inc., Los Angeles, 1981-85, pres., 1985—, chief operating officer, 1985-86, chief exec. officer, chmn. bd., 1986—, also bd. dirs.; Bd. dirs. Alexander and Baldwin, Inc., B.A.T. Industries PLC. Served to lt. (j.g.) USN, 1954-57. Club: California; Wilshire Country. Office: Farmers Group Inc 4680 Wilshire Blvd Los Angeles CA 90010-3807

DENNERY, PHYLLIS ARMELLE, pediatrician, educator; b. Port au Prince, Haiti, June 5, 1958; came to U.S., 1980; d. Jean-Maurice and Mona (Leroy) D.; m. Gregory Lyman Mundy, Aug. 8, 1987; children: Ariana Lillian, Miles Alexander. BS in Biology, McGill U., Montreal, Quebec, Can., 1980; MD, Howard U., 1984. Diplomate Am. Bd. Pediatrics with subspecialty in neonatology. Resident in pediatrics Children's Hosp., Washington, 1984-87; postdoctoral fellowship Case Western Reserve U., Cleve., 1987-90; asst. prof. pediatrics Stanford U., Palo Alto, Calif., 1990—. Author: (book chpt.) Workbook of Practical Neonatology, 1992, Neonatal Management of Hemolytic Hyperbilirubinemia in Diseases of the Fetus and Newborn: Genetics, Pathology, Imaging & Management, 1994. Health adv. bd. NAACP, Santa Clara chpt., 1994. Recipient Michael Oliver Dumas prize Alpha Omega Alpha, 1984, Janet Glascow award AMA, 1984, Drew-Syphax prize in Surgery, Howard U., 1984; named Andrew W. Mellon fellow Mellon Found., 1992, 93. Mem. Am. Thoracic Soc. (membership com. 1990—, sci. com. 1993—, nominating com. 1994, chair membership com. 1995), Nat. Med. Assn., Western Soc. for Pediatric Rsch., Oxygen Soc., Alpha Omega Alpha. Roman Catholic. Office: Stanford U Sch of Medicine 750 Welch Rd Ste 315 Palo Alto CA 94304-1510

DENNEY, DORIS ELAINE, pharmacist; b. Norwalk, Conn., Sept. 5, 1940; d. Harry Taylor and Mary Matilda (Lobeda) D. BS in Pharmacy, U. Conn., 1962; MBA, Boise State U., 1990. Registered pharmacist, Conn., Idaho, Mass. Retail pharmacist Gilbert Pharmacy, Noroton Heights, Conn., 1963-64; sr. pharmacist Children's Hosp. Med. Ctr., Boston, 1964-68; pharmacist Project Hope, Colombia, 1968-70; adminstrv. intern Denver Gen. Hosp., 1972; dir. pharmacy svcs. Terry Reilly Health Svcs., Nampa, Idaho, 1973—; cons. (Bolivia) Mgmt. Scis. for Health, Cambridge, Mass., 1976. Bd. dirs. Payada drug abuse orgn., Boise, 1983-88; mem. health adv. com. Idaho State U., Boise, 1988-89; bd. dirs., mem. Boise Master Chorale, pres., 1992-94. Named Preceptor of Yr. Syntex Labs., 1987; recipient McKesson Leadership award McKesson-Robbins, 1987, Pharmacy Leadership award Nat. Assn. Retail Druggists, 1987. Mem. Idaho State Pharm. Assn. (pres. 1987-88), Am. Pharm. Assn., Am. Pub. Health Assn. (cons. 1978), Am. Soc. of Hosp. Pharmacists, Boise City Arts Commn., Lambda Kappa Sigma. Democrat. Lutheran. Home: 1519 N 19th St Boise ID 83702-0702 Office: Terry Reilly Health Svcs 223 16th Ave N Nampa ID 83687-4058

DENNEY, TERESA MARIE, nonprofit association executive; b. Corvallis, Oreg., Oct. 12, 1963; m. Douglas J. Denney, May 22, 1993. BSBA, Oreg. State U., 1986; M in Mgmt., Willamette U., 1993. Mgmt. trainee Timberline (Oreg.) Lodge, 1986; mgr. restaurant Timberhive (Oreg.) Lodge, 1987, dir. guest svcs., 1988, mktg. rep., 1989; program dir. Bend (Oreg.) C. of C., 1994—. Mem. adv. coun. Leadership Bend; mem. Cmty. Skills Task Force; founder, mem. C.O. Sch. to Work Task Force; founding bd. dirs. Big Bros./Big Sisters, v.p., 1994—; founding bd. dirs. Bend Women's Scholarship Fund. Boweman Found. scholar, 1992, Atkinson Merit scholar, 1992. Mem. Nat. Assn. Cmty. Leadership, Network Entrepreneurial Women. Home: 947 SE Morton Ct Bend OR 97702-1401

DENNING, MICHAEL MARION, computer company executive; b. Durant, Okla., Dec. 22, 1943; s. Samuel M. and Lula Mae (Waitman) D.; m. Suzette Karin Wallance, Aug. 10, 1968 (div. 1979); children: Lila Monique, Tanya Kerstin, Charlton Derek; m. Donna Jean Hamel, Sept. 28, 1985; children: Caitlin Shannon, Meghan O'Donnell. Student, USAF Acad., 1963; BS, U. Tex., 1966, Fairleigh Dickinson U., 1971; MS, Columbia U., 1973. Mgr. systems IBM, White Plains, N.Y., 1978-79; mgr. svc. and mktg. IBM, San Jose, Calif., 1979-81; nat. market support mgr. Memorex Corp., Santa Clara, Calif., 1979-81, v.p. mktg., 1981-82; v.p. mktg. and sales Icot Corp., Mountain View, Calif., 1982-83; exec. v.p. Phase Info. Machines Corp., Scottsdale, Ariz., 1983-84, Tricom Automotive Dealer Systems Inc., Hayward, Calif., 1985-87; pres. ADS Computer Svcs., Inc., Toronto, Ont., Can., 1985-87, Denning Investments, Inc., Palo Alto, Calif., 1987—, Pers. Solutions Group, Inc., Menlo Park, Calif., 1990—. With USAF, 1962-66; Vietnam. Mem. Rotary, English Speaking Union, Phi Beta Kappa, Lambda Chi Alpha (pres. 1965-66). Republican. Methodist. Home: 55 Shearer Dr Atherton CA 94027 Office: Denning Investments Inc 2370 Watson Ct Ste 220 Palo Alto CA 94303-3214

DENNING, ROBERT MARK, agricultural aviation sciences research officer; b. Sherborne, Dorset, U.K., Mar. 15, 1961; s. Edgar Thomas and Blanche Ruby (Morgan) D. BSc, U. London, 1982; MSc, Cranfield Inst. Tech., U.K., 1988. Researcher N.E.L.P., London, 1983-85; rsch. officer U. Calif., Davis, 1988—; cons. Calif. AG Aircraft Assn., Sacramento, 1988—, U.S. Forest Svcs., Davis, 1989—. Recipient Phys. Chemistry prize, U. London, 1980. Me4m. Aircraft Owners and Pilots Assn. (rep. 1989—). Republican. Mem. First Baptist Ch. Home: 718 L St Davis CA 95616-3942 Office: University of California Bainer Hall Davis CA 95616

DENNIS, DAVID TAPPEN, epidemiologist; b. Portland, Oreg., Mar. 31, 1939; s. Walter James and Louise Aline (Labbe) D.; m. Elizabeth Alison Jones, Dec. 27, 1969; 1 child, Sutinah Louise. AB, Whitman Coll., 1961; MD, Cornell U., 1965; Diploma Clin. Medicine of Tropics, U. London, 1970; MPH, Harvard U., 1974. Diplomate Am. Coll. Preventive Medicine. Fellow infectious diseases N.Y. Hosp., Cornell U., N.Y.C., 1969-70; commd. 2d lt. USN, 1970, advanced through grades to capt., 1974; med. officer in charge provincial health assistance team USN, Quang Tri, Vietnam, 1970-71; med. officer in charge US Naval Med. Rsch. Detachment USN, Addis Ababa, Ethiopia, 1971-73; officer in charge US Naval Med. Rsch. Unit USN, Jakarta, Indonesia, 1974-79; ret. USN, 1979; head rsch. and tng. team in tropical diseases Fed. Ctrs. for Disease Control & Prevention, Kuala Lumaur, Malaysia, 1979-83; state epidemiologist, chief bur. disease control Fed. Ctrs. for Disease Control & Prevention, Concord, N.H., 1983-87; med. epidemiologist Fed. Ctrs. for Disease Control & Prevention, Harrisburg, Pa., 1987-90; chief bacterial zoonosis branch Fed. Ctrs for Disease Control and Prevention, Fort Collins, Colo., 1990—; cons. WHO, Geneva, India, Brazil, 1985-92, CDC, Bahrain, 1985, Sudan, 1985, United Arab Emirates, Saudia Arabia, 1986-87, India, 1994. Contbr. over 70 articles to profl. jours., chpts. to books. Office: Ctrs for Disease Control PO Box 2087 Fort Collins CO 80522-2087

DENNIS, EDWARD ALAN, chemistry educator; b. Chgo., Aug. 10, 1941; s. Sol E. and Ruth (Marks) D.; m. Martha S. Greenberg; Mar. 30, 1969; children: Jennifer, Evan, Andrew. BA, Yale U., 1963; MA, Harvard U., 1965, PhD, 1968. Research fellow Harvard Med. Sch., Boston, 1967-69, vis. prof., 1983-84; asst. prof. chemistry U. Calif.-San Diego, La Jolla, 1970-75, assoc. prof., 1975-81, prof., 1981—, vice chmn. dept. chemistry, 1984-87, 92—; mem. NSF adv. panels, 1981-85; chmn. Faculty Acad. Senate, 1987-88; vis. scientist Brandeis U., 1984; cons. to pharm. industry. Editor: Methods in Enzymology Cumulative Indexes, 1975-85; mem. editl. bd. Jour. Biol. Chemistry, 1988-93, Jour. Cellular Biochemistry, 1986; patentee in field; contbr. over 180 articles to profl. jours. Guggenheim fellow, 1983-84; grantee NSF, 1970—, NIH, 1970—. Fellow AAAS; mem. Biophys. Soc. (chmn. biopolymers subgroup 1981-82), Am. Chem. Soc., Am. Soc. Biol. Chemists (com. 1979-81, program chair 1996), N.Y. Acad. Sci., Sigma Xi, Alpha Chi Sigma Chem. Home: 1921 Hypatia Way La Jolla CA 92037-3322 Office: U Calif Dept Chemistry 0601 La Jolla CA 92093-0601

DENNIS, EVIE, retired school system administrator. BS, St. Louis U., 1953; MA, U. Colo., 1971; postgrad., U. Denver, 1964-66; EdD, Nova U., 1976. Hosp. attendant St. Louis City Infirmary Hosp., 1947-52; lab. technician hypertension divsn. dept. internal medicine Sch. Medicine Washington U., St. Louis, 1952-55, rsch. asst. hypertension divsn. dept. internat medicine Sch. Medicine, 1955-58; rsch. asst. allergy rsch. lab. Jewish Hosp., St. Louis, 1956-58; rsch. asst. children's asthma rsch. inst. and hosp. Jewish Nat. Home for Asthmatic Children, Denver, 1958-63, rsch. assoc. children's asthma rsch. inst. and hosp., 1963-66; counselor, tchr. Lake Jr. High Sch. Denver Pub. Schs., 1966-71, community specialist, 1971-76, adminstrv. asst. to supt., 1976-77, dir. office human rels. and student adv. svcs., 1977-80, exec. dir. dept. human rels. and student adv. svcs., 1980-84, exec, dir. II ednl. and profl. devel. and svcs., 1984-86, exec. dir. II sch./community affairs, 1986-88, dep. supt., 1988-90, supt., 1990-94, ret., 1994; vis. prof. Met. State Coll., 1974-75, We. State Coll., 1977, Atlanta U., 1978, lectr. U. Colo., Denver, 1990, 91, 92, U. Denver, 1993; cons. North Ctrl. Assn. Colls. and Secondary Schs., 1972, Denver Vocat. Guidance Inst., 1972, Vibrations for Understanding, Inc., 1973, Denver Pub. Schs. Human Rels. Workshops, 1974-93, Kent State U. KEDS, 1978, U. No. Colo., 1978; presenter Leadership Denver, 1971, 85; participant Colo. Human Rights Symposium, 1974, 82; advisor Colo. Women's Coll. Women and Bus. Conf., 1979; keynote speaker Utah Dept. Edn. Adminstrs. Seminar, 1984. Active Nat. Adv. Allergy and Infectious Diseases Coun., 1979-82, Denver Bd. Health and Hosps., 1981-91, chmn., 1984-87; bd. dirs. Lupus Found. Am., Inc., 1982-87, exec. v.p., 1985-86, pres., 1986-87; mem. Nat. Arthritis and Musculoskeletal and Skin Diseases Adv. Coun., 1987-91; mem. Joseph Robichaux Meml. Found. Com., 1972-75; mem. finance com. women's track and field, chmn. region 10 womens track and field Amateur Athletic Union U.S.A., 1970-75, team mgr. womens track and field, 1973, nat. chmn. womens track and field, 1976-79, mem. exec. com. 1976-82, 2nd v.p. 1979-80; chmn. girls and womens track and field Rocky Mountain Assn., Amateur Athletic Union, 1970-73, mem. exec. com., 1973-84, v.p., 1976-79, 92-93, pres., 1980-82; mem. U.S. Women's Track and Field Team Com., 1973-80, mgr., 1976, 80; mem. internat. sect. Women's Track and Field, 1973-79; interim pres. The Athletics Congress/U.S.A., 1978-79, acting pres., 1979, v.p., 1980, nat. chmn. women's track and field, 1979-84, bd. dirs. 1979-92; mem. Gov.'s Coun. on Phys. Fitness, 1975-78, 80-82; mem. exec. com. U.S. Olympic Com., 1976-92, v.p., 1981-88, spl. asst. to pres., 1989-93; chief del. U.S. Team World Cup II, 1979, U.S. Olympic Team, Seoul, Korea, 1988; San Juan women's adminstr. Pan. Am. Games, 1979, bd. dirs., 1985-87, chief. Cuba del., 1991; chief del. U.S. Nat. Track and Field Team, Tokyo, Peking, 1980; bd. dirs. L.A. Olympic Organizing Com., 1982-84; chief del. U.S. Pan Am. Team, Caracas, 1983; team leader U.S. Taekwondo Team, Seoul, 1985; bd. visitors U.S. Sports Acad., 1984-91, bd. trustees, 1992—; U.S. del. Internat. Amateur Athletic Fedn., 1980-84, 90—, alt. del., 1986—; U.S. Del. Pan. Am. Sports Orgn., 1982-89; mem. tech. commn. Assn. Nat. Olympic Coms., 1987-92; bd. dirs. Colo. Sports Coun., 1990—; bd. dirs., mem. exec. com. U.S.A. Track & Field, Inc., 1993—; mem. State Equal Ednl. Opportunity Com., 1972-75, vice chmn., 1973-74; mem. Dem. State Equal Rights Commn., 1973-74, Dept. Navy Recruiting Dist. Assistance Coun., 1974-78, Mayor's Commn. on Youth, 1977-79, Denver Clean Air Task Force, 1978-85, Denver Pvt. Industry Coun., 1978-88, Denver Community Devel. Adv. Com., 1980-83, Denver Child Car Adv. Com., 1986-87, Denver Area Schs. Supts. Coun., 1990—, U.S. Def. Adv. Com. on Svc. Acad. Athletic Programs, 1992—; mem.-at-large Assn. Ednl. Alumni and Friends, U. Colo. Boulder Sch. Edn., 19bd. dirs. Northeast Denver Youth Svcs. Bur., 1973-75, 79-82, Colo. Career Info. System, 1979-81, Denver Met. YMCA, 1981—, Pub. Edn. Coalition, 1990—, Metro Denver Gives, 1990-91; bd. dirs. Women's Forum Colo., 1978-80, sec., 1979; bd. mgrs. Colo. Congress Parents and Tchrs., Inc., 1974-75; mem. exec. bd. Coun. Great City Schs., 1992—; vice-chmn. Denver Pan Helenic Coun., 1959-60, chmn., 1961-63; chmn. State Guidance Liason Com, 1972-73; chmn. membership Colo. Pers. and Guidance Assn., 1971-73; chmn. schs. and solicitation United Negro Coll. Fund, 1971; v.p. North City Park Civic Assn., 1976-79; Dem. Precinct Committeewoman, 1971-82. Recipient award People Let's Unite for Schs., 1975, NOW, 1975, Northeast Denver Optimist, 1975, Oustanding Adminstr. award Black Educators, 1977, Community Svc. award VFW, Woman of Yr. award Delta Sigma Theta, 1978, Operation Push award, 1979, Edn. award S.Y.L. Found., 1979, Sportswomen Pioneer award, 1979, Disting. Svc. award Denver Regional Coun. Govts., 1979, Pres.'s award Athletics Congress U.S.A., 1980, Salute to Women Sports award Big Sisters Colo., 1980, Congl. Gold Medal award U.S. Olympic Team, 1980, Colo. Black Women for Polit. Action award, 1981, Appreciation award Mayor's Adv. Coun., 1982, 83, Joseph Robichaux Meml. award, 1983, Honor Fellow award Nat. Assn. for Girls and Women in Sports, 1983, Pres.'s award, 1987, Spl. award Denver Pub. Schs. Hall Fame, 1983, Denver Community Devel. Agy. award, 1983, Robert Giegengack award Athletic Congres, 1985, Oustanding Achievement and Svc. award Colo. Gospel Music Acad., 1986, Oustanding Community Svc. and Leadership award, 1991, Appreciation cert. Colo. Alliance Bus., 1987, U.S. Collegiate Sports Coun., 1987, Racial Justice award YWCA, 1988, Outstanding Alumni Yr. award Nova U., 1988, Outstanding Contbn. Am. and Israel award Am.-Israel Friendship League, 1989, Contbn. to Sports award Sportswomen Colo., 1989, Spl. citation Colo. Sports Hall Fame, 1989, Citizen of Yr. award Denver Alumni chpt. Kappa Alpha Psi, 1989, Woman That Has Made a Difference award Internat. Women's Forum, 1990, Image award Joint Effort Community Sports Program, 1991, Oustanding Humanitarian Svcs. award Denver NAACP, 1991, Olympic Order award Internat. Olympic Com., 1992, Daniel Payne award Shorter COmmunity African Meth. Episc. Ch., 1993, Achievement in Edn. award Optimists, 1993, Women in Action award Syrian Ct. # 40 Daus. Isis, 1993. Mem. Nat. Assn. Black Sch. Educators, Adminstrs. and Suprs. Assn., Black Adminstrs. and Suprs. Assn., Denver Area Sch. Supts. Coun., We. Athletic Conf. (charter 1983—, Stan Bates award), Nova U. Alumni Assn., Rocky Mountain Assn. (amateur athletic union), Denver Rotary, DenCo Track Club (pres. 1974-79), Mile High Denver Track Club (pres. 1972-73), Denver Allstars Track Club (pres. 1965-72), Alpha Kappa Alpha (pres. Epsilon Nu Omega chpt. 1962-65, 72-73). Address: 1313 Steele St #801 Denver CO 80206

DENNIS, KAREN MARIE, plastic surgeon; b. Cleve., Dec. 23, 1948; d. Chester and Adele (Wesley) Denwicz; m. Miles Auslander, June 21, 1974; 1 child, Kristin. BS, Ohio State U., 1971, MD, 1974. Diplomate Am. Bd. Plastic Surgery, Am. Bd. Otolaryngology. Intern Kaiser Permanente, L.A., 1974-75; resident in otolaryngology Roosevelt Hosp., N.Y.C., 1976-79; resident in plastic surgery Ohio State Univ. Hosps., Columbus, 1979-81; pvt. practice Beverly Hills, Calif., 1981—. Mem. Am. Soc. Reconstructive and Plastic Surgeons, Calif. County Med. Assn., L.A. County med. Assn., L.A. Soc. Plastic Srugeons (sec. 1993-94), Phi Beta Kappa. Office: 433 N Camden Dr Beverly Hills CA 90210-4426

DENNIS, MICHAEL T. B., plastic surgeon; b. Louisville, 1942. MD, U. Fla., 1968. Intern Stanford (Calif.) U. Hosps., 1968-69, surgeon, 1969-72, plastic surgeon, 1972-75; now plastic surgeon Santa Barbara (Calif.) Coll. Hosp. Office: 317 W Pueblo St Santa Barbara CA 93105-4355*

DENNIS, SONYA RENEÉ, television station official; b. Silver Springs, Md., May 9, 1965; d. James Richard and Sandra Diane (Lewis) D. BA, U. Nev., Las Vegas, 1989; cert. of completion, Inst. Children's Lit., Las Vegas, 1991. Master control prodn. and traffic coord. Sta. KBLR-TV, Las Vegas, 1989-91; traffic coord. and asst. Sta. KVBC-TV3, Las Vegas, 1991-94, client mktg. asst., 1994—. Recipient Brotherhood Week award K.O. Knudson Jr. High Sch., 1991. Office: Sta KVBC-TV 1500 Foremaster Ln Las Vegas NV 89101-1103

DENNISON, ELIZABETH JANE, history educator, researcher; b. Hampton, Va., June 20, 1960; d. John William and Bettye Louise (Duncan) D. BA, U. Colo., 1982, MA, 1986; PhD, U. Ill., 1993. Teaching asst. U. Colo., Boulder, 1984-86; teaching asst. U. Ill., Urbana, 1986-92, instr., 1992; asst. prof. history U. Alaska, Anchorage, 1992—; mem. Alaska Humanities Forum Com., Anchorage, 1993—; co-chair U. Alaska Anchorage Women's History Month Com., 1992—. U. Ill. grantee and fellow, 1991, 92. Mem. Am. Hist. Assn., Am. Assn. for Advancement of Slavic Studies, Anchorage Mus. Assn., Phi Kappa Phi. Office: U Alaska Anchorage Dept History 3211 Providence Dr Anchorage AK 99508-4614

DENNISON, JOHN ROBERT, physicist, educator; b. Madison, Wis., Oct. 22, 1957; s. John Manley Dennison and Wilma Kay Bailey; m. Marian Roberta Campbell, June 21, 1986; children: James Arlo, Sarah Samantha. BS in Physics, Appalachian State U., 1979; MS in Physics, Va. Tech., 1983, PhD in Physics, 1985. Teaching asst. to rsch. asst. Va. Tech. U., Blacksburg, 1980-85; rsch. assoc. U. Mo., Columbia, 1985-88; asst. prof. Utah State U., Logan, 1988-94, assoc. prof., 1994—; rsch. collaborator Brookhaven Nat. Lab., Upton, N.Y., 1985—; cons. Varian/Elamar, Salt Lake City, 1988-89, Thiohol Corp., Brigham City, Utah, 1991-92, Mathsoft, Inc., Cambridge, Mass., 1995—. Grantee Petroleum Rsch. Fund, 1991-93, NSF, 1991, NASA, 1995—, Dept. of Energy, 1995, Utah Higher Edn. Technology Initiative, 1995-97. Mem. Am. Assn. Physics Tchrs., Am. Physical Soc., Soc. Physics Students, Sigma Pi Sigma, Phi Kappa Phi. Presbyn. Office: Utah State U Physics Dept Logan UT 84322-4415

DENNISON, RONALD WALTON, engineer; b. San Francisco, Oct. 23, 1944; s. S. Mason and Elizabeth Louise (Hatcher) D.; children: Ronald, Frederick. BS in Physics and Math., San Jose State U., 1970, MS in Physics, 1972. Physicist, Memorex, Santa Clara, Calif., 1970-71; sr. engr. AVCO, San Jose, Calif., 1972-73; advanced devel. engr. Perkin Elmer, Palo Alto, Calif., 1973-75; staff engr. Hewlett-Packard, Santa Rosa, Calif., 1975-79; program gen. mgr. Burroughs, Westlake Village, Calif., 1979-82; dir. engring., founder EIKON, Simi Valley, Calif., 1982-85; sr. staff technologist Maxtor Corp., San Jose, 1987-90; dir. engring. Toshiba Am. Info. Systems, 1990-93, cons. engr., 1994—; materials. Author tech. publs. Served to sgt. USAF, 1963-67. Mem. IEEE, Am. Vacuum Soc., Internat. Soc. Hybrid Microelectronics, Internat. Disk Drive Equipment and Materials Assn. Republican. Methodist. Mem. Aircraft Owners and Pilots Assn., Internat. Comanche Soc. Home: 2217 Yosemite Dr Milpitas CA 95035-6649

DENNISTON, DOUGLAS, artist, educator; b. Cornwall-on-Hudson, N.Y., Nov. 19, 1921; s. Jesse and Edith (Buchenberger) D.; Patricia Davidson, Oct. 29, 1945; children: Denise, Abigail, Joshua. Two-year cert. Richmond Profl. Inst., Coll. William and Mary, 1942; BFA, U. N.Mex., 1945, MA, 1948. Instr. U. N.Mex., 1947-48, Tex. Western Coll., El Paso, summer 1949, Colo. Women's Coll., Denver, 1948-59; prof. U. Ariz., Tucson, 1959-83, prof. emeritus, 1983—; instr. U. Nev., Reno, summer 1967. Illustrator: Edward Hopper: an Appreciation, 1963, Calendar: A Cycle of Poems (Richard Shelton), 1972; one-man shows include N.Mex. State Mus., Santa Fe, 1946, Acad. Arts, Flint, Mich., 1953, Denver Art Mus., 1954, La Galeria Escondida, Taos, N.Mex., 1954, 55, Johnson Art Gallery, Albuquerque, 1954, Ajo, Ariz., 1958, Colo. Women's Coll., Denver, 1959, Tucson Art Ctr., 1963, Dakota Art Gallery, Rapid City, S.D., 1977, Internat. Mus., McAllen, Tex., 1977, Coll. William and Mary, Williamsburg, Va., 1976, Fine Arts Ctr., Prescott, Ariz., 1986, Local 803 Gallery, Tucson, Ariz., 1995, others; group exhbns. include Va. Mus. Fine Arts, Richmond, 1943, N.Mex. State Fair, Albuquerque, 1944-47 (various prizes), Met. Mus. Art, N.Y.C., 1952, MOMA, N.Y.C., 1953, Denver Arts Mus., 1950, 52 (purchase prize), Denver Art Mus., 1951, 52, 54, 55, 56, 58, 61, 71, Joslyn Art Mus., Omaha, 1952, 54, Butler Art Inst., Youngstown, Ohio, 1954, San Francisco Art Mus., 1954, Tucson Art Ctr., 1961 (award), 66 (purchase), 67, 68, 69, 71, 72, 74, Mus. Fine Arts, Sante Fe, 1962, 76, Phoenix Art Mus., 1962, 69, 70, 73, Wollheim's Rosequist Galleries, Tucson, 1973, Ctrl. Art Collective, 1991, numerous others; represented in permanent collections Va. Mus. Fine Arts, Denver Art Mus., Gilpin County Arts Assn., Ctrl. City, Colo., Jonson Gallery, Albuquerque, Yuma Art Ctr., U. Ariz. Mus. Art, Tucson Airport. Home: 1844 N Vine Ave Tucson AZ 85719

DENNISTON, MARTHA KENT, business owner, author; b. Phila., Feb. 8, 1920; d. Samuel Leonard and Elizabeth (Cryer) Kent; m. Edward Shippen Willing, May 14, 1942 (div. 1972); children: Peter, Matthew, Thomas, Stephen; m. George C. Denniston, July 5, 1974. BA, Bryn Mawr (Pa.) Coll., 1941; MA, U. Wash., Seattle, 1965. Clinic dir. Population Dynamics, Seattle, 1973-84; pvt. practice investor, 1950—; resort owner Ecologic Pl., Port Townsend, Wash., 1972—; sec. bd. dirs. Population Inst., Washington, 1980-83, Ctr. for Population Communications, N.Y.C., 1983-86. Author: Beyond Conception, Our Children's Children, 1971, (poems) The Bladed Quiet, 1994. Bd. dirs. Population Action Coun., Washington, 1977-80. Mem. Nat. Soc. Colonial Dames Am., Am. Farmlands Trust, Sigma Xi. Office: Population Dynamics 2442 NW Market St Seattle WA 98107-4137

DENNY, JAMES CLIFTON, tree farm administrator, forestry consultant; b. Palo Alto, Calif., Aug. 3, 1922; s. James Milton and Alma May (Siler) D.; m. Ann Elliott, Oct. 31, 1948; children: Christine, Stuart, James, Matthew, Katharine. BS, U. Calif., Berkeley, 1948. Registered profl. forester, Calif. Forest fire dispatcher Calif. Div. Forestry, Redding, 1948-50, asst. forest technician, 1950-53, forest technician, 1953-59, sr. forest techinician, 1959-62; asst. dep. state forester Calif. Div. Forestry, Sacramento, 1962-71, Santa Rosa, Calif., 1971-75; chief resource mgmt. Calif. Dept. Forestry, Sacramento, 1975-80; forestry cons., 1980—; bd. dirs., sec. Forest Landowners of Calif., Sacramento, 1989—. 1st lt. USAF, 1942-46, ETO. Mem. Soc. Am. Foresters. Republican. Presbyterian. Home and Office: 8996 Ritts Mill Rd Shingletown CA 96088-9556

DENNY, JOHN LEIGHTON, JR., mathematics educator; b. Birmingham, Ala., Oct. 11, 1931; s. John Leighton and Miriam Marie (Stamm) D.; m. Anne Temple Hood, Sept. 5, 1953. BA, Stanford U., 1953; PhD, U. Calif., 1962. Asst. prof. math. Ind. U., Bloomington, 1962-65, U. Calif., Riverside, 1965-67; assoc. prof. math. U. Ariz., Tucson, 1967-72, prof. math., 1972-93, head statistics dept., 1985-90, prof. math. emeritus, 1994—. Editor: Section on Ergodic Theory and Probability, 1990-93; contbr. articles to profl. jours. With U.S. Army, 1954-56, Korea. Mem. Am. Statistical Assn. (vis. lectr. 1978-82), Optical Soc. Am.

DENT, ERNEST DUBOSE, JR., pathologist; b. Columbia, S.C., May 3, 1927; s. E. Dubose and Grace (Lee) D.; m. Dorothy McCalman, June 16, 1949; children: Christopher, Pamela; m. 2d, Karin Frehse, Sept. 6, 1970. Student, Presbyn. Coll., 1944-45; M.D., Med. Coll. S.C., 1949. Diplomate clin. pathology and pathology anatomy Am. Bd. Pathology. Intern U.S. Naval Hosp., Phila., 1949-50; resident pathology USPHS Hosp., Balt., 1950-54; chief pathology USPHS Hosp., Norfolk, Va., 1954-56; assoc. pathology Columbia (S.C.) Hosp., 1956-59; pathologist, dir. labs. Columbia Hosp., S.C. Baptist Hosp., 1958-69; with Straus Clin. Labs., L.A., 1969-72; staff pathologist Hollywood (Calif.) Community Hosp, St. Joseph Hosp., Burbank, Calif., 1969-72; dir. labs. Glendale Meml. Hosp. and Health Ctr., 1972-94; ret.; bd. dirs. Glendale Meml. Hosp. and Health Ctr. Author papers nat. med. jours. Mem. Am. Cancer Soc., AMA, L.A. County Med. Assn. (pres. Glendale dist. 1980-81), Calif. Med. Assn. (councillor 1984-90), Am. Soc. Clin. Pathology, Coll. Am. Pathologists (assemblyman S.C. 1965-67; mem. publs. com. bull. 1968-70), L.A. Soc. Pathologists (trustee 1984-87), L.A. Acad. Medicine, S.C. Soc. Pathologists (pres. 1967-69). Lutheran. Home: PO Box 9 3005 Roadrunner Dr Borrego Springs CA 92004 Office: S Central and Los Feliz Aves Glendale CA 91225-7036

DENT, RICHARD LAMAR, professional football player; b. Atlanta, Dec. 13, 1960. Student, Tenn. State U. Defensive end Chicago Bears, 1983-94, San Francisco 49ers, 1994—; part-owner men's clothing store, Chgo. Mem. Pro-Bowl Team, 1984-85, 90, 93, recipient Jack Griffin Award, 1995. Office: San Francisco 49ers 4949 Centennial Blvd Santa Clara CA 95054-1229

DENTE, MICHAEL FLORIN, sculptor, art educator; b. San Jose, Calif., Sept. 25, 1948; s. Florin and Georgia Jean (Copsey) D.; m. Laurel Anne Cusick, Sept. 26, 1970; children: Nicholas Amedeo, Vincent Tamayo, Sarah Florin. AA, Clark Coll., 1970; BS, Portland State U., 1973, MFA, 1976. Arts and craft coord. Aramco, Saudia Arabia, 1981; prof. fine arts U. Portland, Oreg., 1981—; drawing instr. Portland C.C., 1984-85; represented by Sovereign Gallery Portland; painting, drawing and sculpture instr. summer sch. U. Portland, 1982-92, adj. instr. edn. dept. outreach program, 1990-93; art instr., muralist Hillcrest Girl's Reform Sch., Salem, 1976, McLaren Sch. for Boys, Woodburn, Oreg., 1976, numerous other schs.; art instr. Met. Art Commn., Portland, 1976; editl. adv. bd. Colgate Press, 1993; artist in residence Lewis & Clark Sch., Astoria, Oreg., 1991-92, Long Beach, Wash., 1991; muralist various pub. and pvt. schs.; presenter workshops in field; adj. instr. art U. Portland, 1981-89; instr. sculpture Ras Tanura, Saudi Arabia, 1981; courtroom drawings Sta. KATU News, Portland, 1981; instr. painting Oreg. State Penitentiary Oreg. Arts Commn., 1975-76; sulpture workshops Cleve. H.S., Portland, 1979, Ardenwald Grade Sch., Milw., Oreg., 1976, Franklin H.S., Portland, 1976, Wash. H.S., Portland, 1976. Prin. works include monuments at Oreg. Convention Ctr., Benicia Calif., The Grotto, Portland, U. Portland, Mt. Cavalry Cemetery, Portland Chief Joseph Sch., Portland; executed mural at St. Mary's Cathedral, Portland; one man show at Willamette U., Salem, Oreg., 1987, Interstate Firehouse Cultural Ctr., Portland, 1985, Interstate Fire House Cultural Ctr., Oreg., 1989; exhibited in group shows at Portland Art Mus., 1987-88, Cohler Art Ctr., Wis., 1990, Civil Rights Mus., 1990; represented in collections Met. Arts Commn., U. Portland, Corvallis City Hall, Portland State U., Skamania County Women's Shelter, Portland City Hall, pvt. collections. V.p. Oak Lodge Presch., 1986-87; basketball coach Golden Ball, Portland, 1990-94; vol. artists N.W. pub. and pvt. schs., 1976—. Recipient Al Guisti award for excellence in teaching Assoc. Students U. Portland, 1989, Best of Show award Martin Luther King Exhbn., 1992, 1st Place Art award U.S. Bank, Bicentennial Art Exhibit award Portland Art Mus., 1975, 78, 87. Roman Catholic. Home: 6626 N Curtis Ave Portland OR 97217-4062 Office: U Portland 5000 N Willamette Blvd Portland OR 97203-5743

DENTON, PATRY REDDING, artist, educator; b. Scottsbluff, Nev., July 20, 1943; d. Dale and Louise (Covington) Redding; m. Lawrence Edward Denton, Aug. 23, 1964; children: Robert, Christopher Lance, Heather Redding. Cert. in Art, Art Instr. Sch., Mpls., 1968; vocat. cert., Colo. State U., Ft. Collins, 1994. Instr. Colo. Inst. Art, Denver, 1983-86, Arapahoe C.C., Colo., 1994—. Contbr. articles to Best of Colored Pencil II, 1994, Creative Colored Pencil, 1995, other profl. jours. Numerous awards to include San Diego Internat. Watercolor award, Rocky Mountain Nat. watermedia award, Poudre Valley Nat. Meritorious award N.E. Watercolor Soc. Nat. Excellence award, 1992, Parkersburg Art Ctr. award, Spl. award, Tubac Ctr. for Arts, Nat. Smallworks Tech. Excellence award, 1993. Mem. Nat. Watercolor Soc. (Festival of Arts Laguna Beach award), Ga. Watercolor Soc., Colo. Watercolor Soc., Foothills Art Ctr. Home: 2948 Pierson Way Lakewood CO 80215-7136

DEPAOLIS, POTITO UMBERTO, food company executive; b. Mignano, Italy, Aug. 28, 1925; s. Giuseppe A. and Filomena (Macchiaverna) deP.; Vet. Dr., U. Naples, 1948; Libera Docenza, Ministero Pubblica Istruzione (Rome, Italy), 1955; m. Marie A. Caronna, Apr. 10, 1965. Came to U.S., 1966, naturalized, 1970. Prof. food service Vet. Sch., U. Naples, Italy, 1948-66; retired, 1966; asst. prof. A titre Benevole Ecole Veterinaire Alfort, Paris, France, 1956; vet. inspector U.S. Dept. Agr., Omaha, 1966-67; sr. research chemist Grain Processing Corp., Muscatine, Iowa, 1967-68; v.p., dir. product devel. Reddi Wip, Inc., Los Angeles, 1968-72; with Kubro Foods, Los Angeles, 1972-73, Shade Foods, Inc., 1975—; pres. Vegetable Protein Co., Riverside, Calif., 1973—, Tima Brand Food Co., 1975—, Dr. Tima Natural Foods, 1977—. Fulbright scholar Cornell U., Ithaca, N.Y., 1954; British Council scholar, U. Reading, Eng., 1959-60; postdoctoral research fellow NIH, Cornell U., 1963-64. Mem. Inst. Food Technologists, Italian Assn. Advancement Sci., AAAS, Vet. Med. Assn., Biol. Sci. Assn. Italy, Italian Press Assn., Greater Los Angeles Press Club. Contbr. articles in field to prol. jours. Patentee in field. Home: Bel Air 131 Groverton Pl Los Angeles CA 90077-3732 Office: 8570 Wilshire Blvd Beverly Hills CA 90211-3133 also: 6878 Beck Ave North Hollywood CA 91605-6205

DE PASSE, DERREL BLAUVELT, electronics industry executive; b. Bronxville, N.Y., Jan. 17, 1950; d. Alfred Bernard and Josephine Martha (Weyland) De P. BA, U. Tex., 1971, MPA, 1973. Mgr. pub. affairs Container Corp. Am., Chgo., 1974-75; regional mgr. pub. affairs Container Corp. Am., Phila., 1976-78; dir. fed. pub. affairs Container Corp. Am., Washington, 1979-83; spl. asst. to dir. U.S. Peace Corps, Washington, 1984-85; dir. govt. affairs Varian, Palo Alto, Calif., 1985-90, v.p. govt. rels., 1990-92; v.p. worldwide govt. rels. Varian, Palo Alto, 1992—; vice chmn. industry sector adv. com. on electronics and instrumentation U.S. Dept. Commerce, Washington, 1987—; commr. Calif. state World Trade Com., 1992—. Trustee San Jose/Cleve. Ballet. Mem. Pub. Affairs Coun. (exec. com. bd. dirs. 1990—), Calif. Coun. for Internat. Trade (exec. com., bd. dirs. 1989—), Lincoln Club No. Calif. (exec. com.), No. Calif. Dist. Export Coun. Office: Varian 3050 Hansen Way Palo Alto CA 94304-1000

DE PASSE, SUZANNE, record company executive; m. Paul Le Mat. Student, Manhattan Community Coll. Former talent coordinator Cheetah Disco, N.Y.C.; creative asst. to pres. Motown Prodns., Los Angeles, 1968-81, pres., from 1981; now c.e.o. de Passe Entertainment, L.A. Acts signed and developed for Motown include The Commodores, The Jackson Five, Frankie Valli and the Four Seasons, Lionel Richie, Thelma Houston, Billy Preston, Teena Marie, Rick James, Stephanie Mills; co-author screenplay for film Lady Sings the Blues (Acad. award nomination); exec. producer: (TV miniseries) Lonesome Dove, (TV series) Motown on Showtime, Nightlife starring David Brenner, Motown Revue starring Smokey Robinson, Motown Returns to the Apollo (Emmy award, NAACP Image award), (TV spl.) Motown 25: Yesterday, Today, Forever (Emmy award, NAACP Image award); writer: (TV spls.) Happy Endings, Jackson 5 Goin' Back to Indiana, Diana; creative cons: Git on Broadway-Diana Ross & The Supremes & Temptations, TCB-Diana Ross & The Supremes & Temptations. Office: de Passe Entertainment 5750 Wilshire Blvd Ste 610 Los Angeles CA 90036-3697*

DEPEW, MARIE KATHRYN, retired secondary educator; b. Sterling, Colo., Dec. 1, 1928; d. Amos Carl and Dorothy Emelyn (Whitney) Mehl; m. Emil Carlton DePew, Aug. 30, 1952 (dec. 1973). BA, U. Colo., 1950, MA, 1953. Post grad. Harvard U., Cambridge, Mass., 1962; tchr. Jefferson County Pub. Schs., Arvada, 1953-73; mgr. Colo. Accountability Program, Denver, 1973-83; sr. cons. Colo. Dept. Edn., Denver, 1973-85, ret., 1985. Author: (pamphlet) History of Hammil, Georgetown, Colorado, 1967; contbr. articles to profl. jours. Chmn. Colo. State Accountability Com., Denver, 1971-75. Fellow IDEA Programs, 1976-77, 79-81. Mem. Colo. Hist. Assn., Jefferson County Edn. Assn. (pres. 1963-64), Colo. Edn. Assn. (bd. dirs. 1965-70), Ky. Colonels (hon. mem.), Phi Beta Kappa. Republican. Methodist. Home: 920 Pennsylvania St Denver CO 80203-3157

DEPINTO, JOSEPH ANTHONY, social worker; b. N.Y.C., Sept. 5, 1951; s. Marco John and Frances Rose (Barbaro) DeP.; m. Judith Ann Paris, Apr. 30, 1976 (div. 1984); children: Marco. BA, Ariz. State U., 1973, MSW, 1978. Cert. ind. social worker, cert. addictions counselor. Counselor Jane Wayland Ctr., Phoenix, 1975-78; caseworker Valley Big Bros., Phoenix, 1978-79; social worker Child Protective Svcs., Phoenix, 1979, Bostrom Alternative Ctr., Phoenix, 1979—; therapist Treatment Assessment Screening Ctrs., Phoenix, 1985-90, Youth Evaluation Treatment Ctrs., Phoenix, 1990-91; instr. Rio Salado Community Coll., Phoenix, 1990—; faculty assoc. Sch. Social Work, Ariz. State U., 1980—; cons. DePinto & Assocs., Mesa, 1989—. Therapist Ariz. Addiction Treatment Programs, Mesa, 1995—. Mem. NEA, Ariz. Edn. Assn. Democrat. Office: Bostrom Alternative Ctr 3535 N 27th Ave Phoenix AZ 85017-5015

DEPLOIS, MOLLY, library director; b. Coos Bay, Oreg., July 12, 1956; d. John A. and Violette E. (Carrillo) Barrett; m. Jacques Philippe DePlois, Aug. 2, 1992; children: Emmeline Cosette Adele, Madeline Marie Violette. Libr. asst. Coquille (Oreg.) Pub. Libr., 1976-85, asst. libr., 1985-86, libr. dir., 1986—. Adv. coun. Southwestern Oreg. Cmty. Coll., Coos Bay, 1990-94; bd. dirs. Sawdust Theatre, Coquille, 1987-92, pres., 1991-92. Mem. ALA, LWV, Oreb. Libr. Assn. Democrat. Roman Catholic. Home: 577 N Dean St Coquille OR 97423-1671 Office: Coquille Public Library 105 N Birch St Coquille OR 97423-1223

DEPREIST, JAMES ANDERSON, conductor; b. Phila., Nov. 21, 1936; s. James Henry and Ethel (Anderson) De P.; m. Betty Louise Childress, Aug. 10, 1963; children: Tracy Elisabeth, Jennifer Anne; m. Ginette Grenier, July 19, 1980. Student, Phila. Conservatory Music, 1959-61; BS, U. Pa., 1958, MA, 1961, LHD (hon.), 1976; LHD (hon.), Reed Coll., 1990; MusD (hon.), Laval U., Quebec City, Can., 1980, Linfield Coll., 1986; DFA (hon.), U. Portland, 1983, Pacific U., 1985, Willamette U., 1987, Drexel U., 1989, Oreg. State U., 1990; Doctor of Arts and Letters (hon.), St. Mary's Coll., Moraga, Calif., 1985; HHD (hon.), Lewis and Clark U., 1986; DFA (hon.), Drexel U., 1989; LHD (hon.), Reed Coll., 1990; DFA (hon.), Oregon State U., 1990; MusD (hon.), Juilliard, 1993; LHG (hon.), Portland State U., 1993. Am. specialist music for State Dept., 1962-63; condr.-in-residence Bangkok, 1963-64; condr. various symphonies and orchs., 1964—. Condr.: Am. debut with N.Y. Philharm., 1964, asst. condr. to Leonard Bernstein, N.Y. Philharm. Orch., 1965-66, prin. guest condr. Symphony of New World, 1968-70, European debut with Rotterdam Philharm., 1969; Helsinki Philharm., 1993; assoc. condr. Nat. Symphony Orch., Washington, 1971-75, prin. guest condr. Nat. Symphony Orch., 1975-76; music dir. L'Orchestre Symphonique de Que., 1976-83, Oreg. Symphony, 1980—, prin. guest condr. Helsinki Philharmonic, 1993, Mus. Dir. Monte Carlo Philharm., 1994; appeared with Phila. Orch., 1972, 76, 84, 85, 87, 90, 92, 93, 94, Chgo. Symphony, 1973, 90, 92, 94, Boston Symphony, 1973, Cleve. Orch., 1974; condr.: Am. premiere of Dvorak's First Symphony, N.Y. Philharm., 1972; chief condr. Malmö Symphony, 1991-94; author: (poems) This Precipice Garden, 1987, The Distant Siren, 1989. Trustee Lewis and Clark Coll., 1983—. Recipient 1st prize gold medal Dimitri Mitropoulos Internat. Music Competition for Condrs., 1964, Merit citation City of Phila., 1969, medal of City of Que., 1983; grantee Martha Baird Rockefeller Fund for Music, 1969, Insignia of Comdr. of Order of Lion of Finland, 1992. Fellow Am. Acad. Arts and Scis.; mem. Royal Swedish Acad. Music. Office: Oreg Symphony Orch 711 SW Alder St Ste 200 Portland OR 97205

DEPREZ, DANIEL ROBERT, writer; b. Portland, Oreg., June 20, 1954; s. Robert Newton and Alice (Stellges) DeP. AA in Radio Prodn., Mt. Hood C.C., Gresham, Oreg., 1975; BA, Evergreen State Coll., Olympia, Wash., 1976. Freelance writer, disc jockey Portland, 1976-78; standup comedian, 1983-91; features writer Willamette Week, Portland, 1991—; columnist X Mag., Portland, 1994—; commentator Oreg. Pub. Broadcasting, Portland, 1994—; cons. in pub. rels. and spl. event planning for non-profits, 1992—. Author: 31 Days At A Time, 1993; author/performer recording: Love and Denial, 1992. Mem. Portland Alano Club (bd. dirs. 1994—). Office: Daymare Prodns 12311 NE Glisan St # 150 Portland OR 97230-2118

DEPUY, CHARLES HERBERT, chemist, educator; b. Detroit, Sept. 10, 1927; s. Carroll E. and Helen (Plehn) DeP.; m. Eleanor Burch, Dec. 21, 1949; children: David Gareth, Nancy Ellen, Stephen Baylie, Katherine Louise. B.S., U. Calif., Berkeley, 1948; A.M., Columbia U., 1952; Ph.D., Yale U., 1953. Asst. prof. chemistry Iowa State U., 1953-59, asso. prof., 1959-62, prof., 1962-63; prof. chemistry U. Colo., Boulder, 1963-92, prof. emeritus, 1992—; vis. prof. U. Ill., summer 1954, U. Calif., Berkeley, summer 1960; NIH sr. postdoctoral fellow U. Basel, Switzerland, 1969-70; cons. A.E. Staley Co., 1956-80, Marathon Oil Co., 1964-89. Author: (with Kenneth L. Rinehart) Introduction to Organic Chemistry, 1967, rev. edit., 1975, (with Orville L. Chapman) Molecular Reactions and Photochemistry, 1970, (with Robert H. Shapiro) Exercises in Organic Spectroscopy; contbr. articles profl. jours. Served wih AUS, 1946-47. John Simon Guggenheim fellow, 1977-78, 86-87; Alexander von Humboldt fellow, 1988-89. Fellow AAAS; mem. Am. Chem. Soc. (exec. com. organic div., chmn. Colo. sect., mem. adv. bd. jour. 1987-92, gold medal), Sigma Xi. Home: 1509 Cascade Ave Boulder CO 80302-7631 Office: U Colo Boulder Dept Chemistry & Biochemistry Campus Box 215 Boulder CO 80309

DERBES, DANIEL WILLIAM, manufacturing executive; b. Cin., Mar. 30, 1930; s. Earl Milton and Ruth Irene (Grauten) D.; m. Patricia Maloney, June 4, 1952; children: Donna Ann, Nancy Lynn (dec.), Stephen Paul. B.S., U.S. Mil. Acad., 1952; M.B.A., Xavier U., Cin., 1963. Devel. engr. AiResearch Mfg. Co., Phoenix, 1956-58; with Garrett Corp., 1958-80; v.p., gen. mgr., then exec. v.p. Garrett Corp., L.A., 1975-80; dir. Garrett Corp., 1976-87; pres. Signal Cos., Inc., 1980-82, La Jolla, Calif., 1982-83; pres. Signal Advanced Tech Group, 1983-85, Allied-Signal Internat. Inc., 1985-88; exec. v.p. Allied-Signal, Inc., Morristown, N.J., 1985-88; pres. Signal Ventures, 1990—; bd. dirs. San Diego Gas & Electric Co., Oak Industries, Inc., WD-40 Co., Pacific Diversified Capital Co. Exec. bd. nat. coun. Boy Scouts Am., 1981-85; trustee U. San Diego, 1981—, vice-chmn., bd. trustees, 1990-93, chmn., 1993—. With AUS, 1952-56. Republican. Roman Catholic.

DERDENGER, PATRICK, lawyer; b. L.A., June 29, 1946; s. Charles Patrick and Drucilla Marguerite (Lange) D.; m. Jo Lynn Dickins, Aug. 24, 1968; children: Kristin Lynn, Bryan Patrick, Timothy Patrick. BA, Loyola U., L.A., 1968; MBA, U. So. Calif., 1971, JD, 1974; LLM in Taxation, George Washington U., 1977. Bar: Calif. 1974, U.S. Ct. Claims 1975, Ariz. 1979, U.S. Ct. Appeals (9th cir.) 1979, U.S. Dist. Ct. Ariz. 1979, U.S. Tax Ct. 1979, U.S. Supreme Ct. 1979; cert. specialist in tax law. Trial atty. honors program U.S. Dept. Justice, Washington, 1974-78; ptnr. Lewis & Roca, Phoenix, 1978—; adj. prof. taxation Golden Gate U., Phoenix, 1983-87; mem. Ariz. State Tax Ct. Legis. Study Commn. Author: Arizona State and Local Taxation, Cases and Materials, 1983, Arizona Sales and Use Tax Guide, 1990, Advanced Arizona Sales and Use Tax, 1987, Arizona State and Local Taxation, 1989, Arizona Sales and Use Tax, 1988, Property Tax Procedures Handbook. Past pres., bd. dirs. North Scottsdale Little League. Served to capt. USAF, 1968-71. Recipient U.S. Law Week award Bur. Nat. Affairs, 1974. Mem. ABA (taxation sect., various coms.), Ariz. Bar Assn. (taxation sect., various coms., chair sect. taxation, former treas., chmn. state and local tax com., chmn. continuing legal edn. com.), Maricopa County Bar Assn., Inst. Property Taxation, Inst. Sales Taxation, Phoenix Met. C. of C. (Ariz. corr. state tax notes), Ariz. C. of C. (tax com.), U. So. Calif. Alumni Club (past pres., bd. dirs.), Phi Delta Phi. Home: 9501 N 49th Pl Paradise Vly AZ 85253-1503 Office: Lewis & Roca 2 Renaissance Plz 40 N Central Ave Phoenix AZ 85004-4424

DERELIAN, DORIS VIRGINIA, nutrition educator, consultant; b. Palo Alto, Calif., Aug. 8, 1945; d. Sarkis David and Susan (Karahadian) D.; m. James J. Sullivan, Sept. 4, 1976; 1 child, Stacy Anne. BS in Dietetics, Calif. State U., Fresno, 1969; MS in Nutrition, U. Calif., Davis, 1973; PhD in Edn., UCLA, 1993. Food supr. St. Agnes Hosp., Fresno, 1965-68; chief dietitian UCLA Unibelic Camps, 1969-79; program dir. Dairy Coun. of Calif., L.A., 1979-83; educator, cons. Health Professions Tng., Fallbrook, Calif., 1983—; exec. dir. Calif. Dietetic Assn., L.A., part-time, 1981-83; assoc. researcher 10X Objectives Exch., L.A., 1978-80. Co-author: Public Relations Writing, 1990; contbr. articles to profl. jours. Fellow Am. Dietetic Assn. (pres. 1994—); mem. Calif. Coun. on Nutrition, L.A. Metabolic Found. Democrat. Presbyterian. Home and Office: 3553 Rosa Way Fallbrook CA 92028-2663

DERKSEN, CHARLOTTE RUTH MEYNINK, librarian; b. Newberg, Oreg., Mar. 15, 1944; d. John Philip and Wanda Marie (Rohrbough) Meynink; m. Roy Arthur Derksen, Dec. 27, 1966; children: Kathryn Marie Lesedi, Elizabeth Charlotte. BS in Geology, Wheaton (Ill.) Coll., 1966; MA in Geology, U. Oreg., 1968, MLS, 1973. Faculty and librarian Moeding Coll., Ootse Botswana, 1968-70, head history dept., 1970-71; tchr. Jackson Pub. High Sch. (Minn.), 1975-77; sci. librarian U. Wis., Oshkosh, 1977-80; librarian and bibliographer Stanford (Calif.) U., 1980—, acting chief scis., 1985-86, head Sci. and Engring. Librs., 1992—. Contb. author: Union List of Geologic Field Trip Guidebooks of North America, contbr. articles to profl. publs. Mem. ALA (rep. 1983-85), Spl. Library Assn., Western Assn. Map Librarians, Geosci. Info. Soc. (rep. 1985), Cartographic Users Adv. Council (chair 1988-90). Republican. Lutheran. Home: 128 Mission Dr Palo Alto CA 94303-2753 Office: Stanford U Branner Earth Scis Library Stanford CA 94305

DERMANIS, PAUL RAYMOND, architect; b. Jelgava, Latvia, Aug. 2, 1932; came to U.S., 1949; s. Pauls and Milda (Argals) D. BArch, U. Wash., 1955; MArch, MIT, 1959. Registered architect, Wash. Architect John Morse & Assocs., Seattle, 1961-62; assoc. Fred Bassetti & Co., Seattle, 1963-70; ptnr. Streeter/Dermanis & Assocs., Seattle, 1973—. Designs include Sunset house (citation 1984), treatment plant, 1992. Mem. Phinney Ridge Neighborhood Assn., Seattle, 1985—. With USN, 1955-57. Mem. AIA, Apt. Assn. Seattle and King County, U. Wash. Alumni Assn., MIT Club of Puget Sound, Phi Beta Kappa, Tau Sigma Delta. Democrat. Lutheran. Office: Streeter/Dermanis & Assocs 185 University St Seattle WA 98101-2901

DERN, CHRISTOPHER M., construction executive; b. 1956. Grad., U. Wash., 1979. With Arthur Anderson, Seattle, 1979-82, Peat Marwick, Seattle, 1982-89, Fletcher Challenge Industries USA Ltd., Seattle, 1989—. Office: Fletcher Chllnge Inds USA LTD 155 NE 100th St Ste 410 Seattle WA 98125-8012*

DE ROES, NANDA YVONNE, banker; b. Rotterdam, The Netherlands, Apr. 12, 1945; m. Anthony G. De Roes, Jan. 27, 1973 (dec.). Kandidaats, U. Leiden, The Netherlands, 1972. Asst. sec. Mitsui Mfrs. Bank, Los Angeles, 1979-81, Am. Savs. and Loan, Beverly Hills, Calif., 1981-83; sec. First Charter Fin. Corp., Am. Savs. and Loan, Beverly Hills, 1983, Fin. Corp. Am., Los Angeles, 1983-85; v.p., sec. Am. Savs. and Loan, Los Angeles, 1985; sr. v.p., sec. Fin. Corp. Am., Am. Savs. and Loan, Irvine, 1985-88, Am. Savs. Bank F.A., Irvine, Calif., 1989-92, New West Fed. Savs. and Loan Assn., Irvine, Calif., 1992—. Mem. Am. Soc. Corp. Secs. Republican. Office: Financial Corp of America 18401 Von Karman Ave Irvine CA 92715-1542

DE ROO, REMI JOSEPH, bishop; b. Swan Lake, Man., Can., Feb. 24, 1924; s. Raymond and Josephine (De Pape) De R. Student, St. Boniface (Man.) Coll.; STD, Angelicum U., Rome, Italy.; LLD (hon.), U. Antigonish, N.S., 1983, U. Brandon, Man., 1987; DD (hon.), U. Winnipeg, Man., 1990; LLD (hon.), U. Victoria, B.C., 1991. Ordained priest Roman Catholic Ch., 1950; curate Holy Cross Parish, St. Boniface, 1952-53; sec. to archbishop of St. Boniface, 1954-56; diocesan dir. Cath. action Archdiocese St. Boniface, 1953-54; exec. sec. Man. Cath. Con., 1958; pastor Holy Cross Parish, 1960-62; bishop of Victoria, B.C., Can., 1962—; Canadian Episcopal rep. Internat. Secretariat Apostleship See, 1964-78, Pontifical Commn. Culture, 1984-87; chairperson Human Rights Commn. B.C., 1974-77; mem. social affairs commn. Can. Conf. Cath. Bishops, 1973-87, 91—; pres. Western Cath. Conf. Bishops, 1984-88; mem. theology commn. Can. Conf. Cath. Bishops, 1987-91; hon. pres. World Conf. for Religion and Peace for Can., 1994—. Hon. fellow Ryerson Poly. Inst., 1987. Address: 4044 Nelthorpe St #1, Victoria, BC Canada V8X 2A1

DE ROQUE, BARBARA PENBERTHY, special education educator, consultant; b. Alameda, Calif., July 20, 1927; d. Cecil Albert and Constance (Maimone) Penberthy; m. Earl H. de Roque, June 23, 1950 (dec. Mar. 1989); children: Kathleen Fowler, Michael, Lisa, Richard, Tom, Jim. BA in Speech, U. Calif., Berkeley, 1949; MEd in Spl. Edn., Coll. of the Holy Names, 1979; EdD in Spl. Edn., Lincoln U., 1986. Tchr. Alameda Unified Sch. Dist., 1949-51; tchr. Lafayette (Calif.) Sch. Dist., 1965-66, Sch. of Santa Maria, Orinda, Calif., 1966-74, St. Joseph's Sch., Fremont, Calif., 1974-79; reading cons. Ohlone Coll., Fremont, 1976-77, Coll. of the Holy Names, Oakland, 1979-80; spl. edn. tchr. Fremont Unified Sch. Dist., 1979-95; substitute asst. prin. Horner Jr. High Sch., Fremont, 1986—; mentor tchr. Fremont Unified Sch. Dist., 1992—, chmn. spl. edn. curriculum com.; bd. dirs. Holy Rosary Coll., 1974-78; chmn. spl. edn. dept. Horner Jr. H.S., 1981—; peer cons. San Jose State U., 1990-91; mem. Bay ARea Writing Project, U. Calif., Berkeley, 1989-91; mem. Spl. Edn. Task Force Program; quality rev. team Fremont Unified Sch. Dist., lead reviewer, 1991-92, site coun. cons., 1992—, trainer, 1993-94; cons. to Middle Schs. for Proglram Quality Rev. Team. Commr. Fremont Library, 1975-77; mem., v.p. St. Joseph's Sch. Bd., Fremont, 1979-82; chmn. Cedar Jr. Br. Children's Hosp., Oakland, 1969-71. Mem. NEA, ASCD, Calif. Tchrs. Assn., Coun. Exceptional Children, Assn. of Adults and Children with Learning Disabilities, Assn. Ednl. Therapists. Home: 1473 Lemos Ln Fremont CA 94539-3762 Office: Horner Jr High Sch 41365 Chapel Way Fremont CA 94538-4202

DEROSA, FRANCIS DOMINIC, chemical company executive; b. Seneca Falls, N.Y., Feb. 26, 1936; s. Frank and Frances (Bruno) DeR.; m. Vivian DeRosa, Oct. 24, 1959; children: Kevin, Marc, Terri. Student, Rochester Inst. Tech., 1959-61; BS, Chadwick U., MBA; PhD, City U. L.A. Cert. med. photographer. Chief exec. officer Advance Chem. & Equipment Co. Inc., Mesa, Ariz., 1974—, Pottery Plus Ltd., Mesa, 1984—, Advance Tool Supply Inc., Mesa, 1989—. Vice chmn. bd. adjustments City of Mesa, 1983-89, bd. dirs. dept. parks and recreation, 1983-86; pres. Christ the King Mens Club, 1983-84; bd. dirs. Mesa C. of C., 1983-88. Mem. Ariz. Sanitary Supply Assn. (pres. 1983-84), Internat. Sanitary Supply Assn. (Coordinator Ariz. chpt. 1987-89, dist. dir. 1989-91, sec. bd. dirs. 1994—), Gilbert, Ariz. C. of C. (bd. dirs., v.p. 1992—), Gilbert Heights Owners Assn. (pres. 1992-93), Mesa Country Club, Santa Monica (Calif.) Yacht Club, Rotary (pres. Mesa Sunrise chpt. 1987-88, Paul Harris fellow 1988), Masons (pres. 1973), Sons of Italy (pres. 1983-84). Home: 513 E Horseshoe Ave Gilbert AZ 85296-1705 Office: Advance Chem & Equipment Co Inc 33 W Broadway Mesa AZ 85210-1505

DEROSSETT, DEBORAH STANTON, food company executive; b. Maringa, Parana, Brazil, May 10, 1956; came to U.S., 1960; d. Edward Earl and Dorothy Van Meter (Stanton) H. BS, U. Fla., 1978; MBA, Pepperdine U., 1990. Calf raiser and milker Twin Acres Farm, Brooksville, Fla., 1978-79; chemist Fla. Dept. Agriculture, White Springs, 1979-80; mgr. quality control Kraft Dairy Group, Tampa, Fla. and Memphis, 1980-82; mgr. loss control, prodn. coordinator Kraft Dairy Group, Jacksonville, Fla., 1982-83; fats and oils formulation technologist, cheese products customer rep. Kraft Indsl. Foods, Memphis, 1983-86; mgr. food tech. Kraft Food Ingredients Corp., Anaheim, Calif., 1986—. Docent Memphis Zoo, 1982; vol. Memphis Hemophilia Soc., 1983. Recipient Fla. State Team award of Excellence, 1979. Mem. Inst. Food Technologists, Council for Agrl. Sci. and Tech., Am. Inst. Baking. Evang. Christian. Clubs: Jazz Heritage (Los Angeles); Nat. Geog. Soc. Office: Kraft Food Ingredients Corp 125 W Cerritos St 7151 Cate Dr Buena Park CA 90621-1881

DERR, JOHN SEBRING, geophysicist, seismologist; b. Boston, Nov. 12, 1941; s. Thomas Sieger and Mary Ferguson (Sebring) D.; children: Alex, Mary, Nathan. BA, Amherst Coll., 1963; MA, U. Calif., Berkeley, 1965, PhD, 1968. Geophysicist Pan Am. Petroleum Corp., Midland, Tex., 1964; research assoc. MIT, Cambridge, 1968-70; research scientist Martin-Marietta Aeorspace Corp., Denver, 1970-74; chief ops. Nat. Earthquake Info. Service U.S. Geol. Survey, Golden, Colo., 1974-79; chief tech. reports U.S. Geol. Survey, Menlo Park, Calif., 1980-83; chief spl. seismol. analysis project U.S. Geol. Survey, Golden, Colo., 1983-89; global seismological networks U.S. Geol. Survey, Albuquerque, N.Mex., 1989—. Contbr. articles to profl. jours. Mem. AAAS, Am. Geophys. Union, Seismol. Soc. Am., Soc. Sci. Exploration (councilor 1986-93), Sigma Xi. Office: Albuquerque Seismologi Albuquerque NM 87115

DERR, KENNETH T., oil company executive; b. 1936; m. Donna Mettler, Sept. 12, 1959; 3 children. BME, Cornell U., 1959, MBA, 1960. With Chevron Corp. (formerly Standard Oil Co. of Calif.), San Francisco, 1960—, v.p., 1972-85; pres. Chevron U.S.A., Inc. subs. Chevron Corp., San Francisco, 1978-84; head merger program Chevron Corp. and Gulf Oil Corp., San Francisco, 1984-85; vice-chmn. Chevron Corp., San Francisco, 1985-88, chmn., chief exec. officer, 1989—, also bd. dirs.; bd. dirs. Citicorp, Potlatch Corp. Trustee Cornell U., The Conf. Bd. Mem. The Bus. Coun., Calif. Bus. Roundtable, Am. Petroleum Inst. (dir., chmn.), Nat. Petroleum Coun., Bus. Roundtable, Bus. Coun. Sustainable Devel., San Francisco Golf Club, Orinda Country Club, Pacific Union Club. Office: Chevron Corp PO Box 7137 225 Bush St San Francisco CA 94104

DERROUGH, NEIL E., television executive; b. Milo, Iowa, Jan. 31, 1936; s. James L. and Nell (Donehue) D.; m. Lois Sharron Lovejoy, July 4, 1981; children: Carolyn, Rebecca Gene, Althea. B.A., San Jose State U. With CBS, 1962-86; v.p., gen. mgr. KCBS Radio CBS, San Francisco, 1967-71; v.p., gen. mgr. WCBS Radio CBS, N.Y.C., 1971-73, WBBM-TV, Chgo., 1974-77, WCBS-TV, N.Y.C., 1978-80; pres. CBS TV Stas., N.Y.C., 1981-86; pres., gen. mgr. Sta. KSBY-TV, San Luis Obispo, Calif., 1986-88; v.p. broadcasting West Coast region, Gillett Group, 1988—; pres. New World Comm. of San Diego and gen. mgr. Sta. KNSD-TV, San Diego, 1988—; bd. dirs. TV Bur. of Advt., N.Y.C. Mem. broadcast adv. com. Congl. Subcom. on Communications, 1977-78; mem. San Diego Communications Coun., 1988—; bd. dirs. Ronald McDonald House, N.Y.C., Old Globe Theatre, 1988—, San Diego Consortium and Pvt. Industry Coun.; bd. dirs. San Diego chpt. Am. Cancer Soc., 1988—, pres., 1992; vice chair San Diego Hospice, 1993—; mem. exec. com. Sch.-to-Career, 1994—. Mem. Nat. Assn. Industry-Edn. Cooperation (bd. dirs.), N.Y. State Broadcasters Assn. (past pres.), San Diego C. of C. (bd. dirs., chmn. bus. roundtable edn.). Home & Office: Sta KNSD-TV 8330 Engineer Rd San Diego CA 92111-2413

DERVAN, PETER BRENDAN, chemistry educator; b. Boston, July 28, 1945; s. Peter Brendan and Ellen (Comer) D.; m. Jacqueline K. Barton; children: Andrew, Elizabeth. BS, Boston Coll., 1967; PhD, Yale U., 1972. Asst. prof. Calif. Inst. Tech., Pasadena, 1973-79, assoc. prof., 1979-82, prof. chemistry, 1982-88, Bren prof. chemistry, 1988—; chmn. div. chemistry & chem. engring., 1994—; adv. bd. ACS Monographs, Washington, 1979-81. Mem. adv. bd. Jour. Organic Chemistry, Washington, 1981—; mem. editorial bd. Bioorganic Chemistry, 1983—, Chem. Rev. Jour., 1984—, Nucleic Acids Res., 1986—, Jour. Am. Chem. Soc., 1986—, Acct. Chem. Res., 1988—, Bioorganic Chem. Rev., 1988—, Bioconjugate Chemistry, 1989—, Jour. Med. Chemistry, 1991—, Tetrahedron, 1992—, Bioorganic and Med. Chemistry, 1993—, Chemical and Engineering News, 1992—; contbr. articles to profl. jours. A.P. Sloan Rsch. fellow, 1977; Camille and Henry Dreyfus scholar, 1978; Guggenheim fellow, 1983; Arthur C. Cope Scholar award 1986. Fellow Am. Acad. Scis.; mem. NAS, Am. Chem. Soc. (Nobel Laureate Signature award 1985, Harrison Howe award 1988, Arthur C. Cope award, 1993, Willard Gibbs medal, 1993, Rolf Sammet prize, 1993, Nichols medal 1994). Office: Calif Inst Tech 1201 E California Blvd Pasadena CA 91125-0001

DE SÁ E SILVA, ELIZABETH ANNE, secondary education educator; b. Edmonds, Wash., Mar. 17, 1931; d. Sven Yngve and Anna Laura Elizabeth (Dahlin) Erlandson; m. Claudio de Sá e Silva, Sept. 12, 1955 (div. July 1977); children: Lydia, Marco, Nelson. BA, U. Oreg., 1953; postgrad., Columbia U., 1954-56, Calif. State U., Fresno, 1990, U. No. Iowa, 1993; MEd, Mont. State U., 1978. Cert. tchr., Oreg., Mont. Med. sec., 1947-49; sec. Merced (Calif.) Sch. Dist., 1950-51; sec., asst. Simon and Schuster, Inc., N.Y.C., 1954-56; tchr. Casa Roosevelt-União Cultural, São Paulo, Brazil, 1957-59, Coquille (Oreg.) Sch. Dist., 1978—; tchr. piano, 1967-78; instr. Spanish, Southwestern Oreg. C.C., Coos Bay, 1991-94. Chmn. publicity Music in Our Schs. Month, Oreg. Dist. VII, 1980-85; sec. Newcomers' Club, Bozeman, Mont., 1971. Quincentennial fellow U. Minn. and Found. José Ortega y Gasset, Madrid, 1991. Mem. AAUW (sec., scholarship chmn., co-pres.), Nat. Trust Hist. Preservation, Am. Coun. on Teaching Fgn. Langs., Am. Assn. Tchrs. Spanish and Portuguese, Nat. Coun. Tchrs. English, Music Educators Nat. Conf., Oreg. Music Educators Assn., Oreg. Coun. Tchrs. English, Confedn. Oreg. Fgn. Lang. Tchrs., VoiceCare Network. Republican. Home: 3486 Spruce St North Bend OR 97459-1130 Office: Coquille Sch Dist 140 E 10th St Coquille OR 97423-1370

DESAI, ASHA, allergist; b. Surat, India, 1950. MD, Gujarat U., Surat, India, 1973. Intern Phila. Gen. Hosp., 1974-75; pediatrician Mercy Cath. Med. Ctr., Phila., 1975-76, Coll. Medicine & Dentistry, Newark, 1976-77; allergist and immunologist Mt. Sinai Med. Sch., N.Y.C., 1981-83; now allergist Mercy Gen. Hosp., Sacramento. Office: 1995 Zinfandel Dr Ste 204 Rancho Cordova CA 95670-2862*

DESAI, CHANDRAKANT S., civil engineering and engineering mechanics educator; b. Nadisar, Gujarat, India, Nov. 24, 1936; came to U.S., 1964, naturalized, 1973; s. Sankalchand P. and Kamala M. (Kothari) D.; m. Patricia L. Porter, Apr. 28, 1969; children: Maya C., Sanjay C. B.Engring., U. Bombay, 1959; M.S. (Ideal Cement Co. fellow 1964), Rice U., Houston, 1966; Ph.D. (Am. Petroleum Inst. fellow 1966), U. Tex., Austin, 1968. Registered profl. engr., Miss. Civil engr. govt. and pvt. agencies India, 1959-64; research civil engr. USAE Wayerways Expt. Sta., Vicksburg, Miss., 1968-74; prof. civil engring., dir. computational methods group Va. Poly. Inst. and State U., Blacksburg, 1974-81; prof., dir. engring. mechanics, geomech. and structural mechanics program dept. civil engring. and engring. mechanics U. Ariz., Tucson, 1981-87, prof. civil engring. and engring. mechanics, 1987-89, Regent's prof., 1989—, head dept., 1987-91; Erskine prof. U. Canterbury, Christchurch, N.Z., 1980, 91. Author: Elementary Finite Element Method, 1979; co-author: Introduction to Finite Element Method, 1972, Constitutive Laws of Engineering Materials, 1983; co-editor, co-author: Numerical Methods in Geotechnical Engineering, 1977; Mechanics of Engineering Materials, 1984; gen. editor: Internat. Jour. Numerical and Analytical Methods in Geomechs; mem. editorial bds. profl. jours. Trustee Deep Founds. Inst., 1978-80; chmn./vice chmn. 1st, 2d, 4th, 5th, 6th, 7th Internat. Conf. Numerical Methods Geomechanics. Recipient Meritorious Civilian Svc. award C.E., U.S. Army, 1972, Alexander von Humboldt award German Govt., 1976, Theodore Cooke Meml. prize U. Bombay, 1958, Meritorious Contbns. medal Czech Acad. Scis., 1992; grantee NSF, Dept. Transp., C.E., El Paso Gas Found. Faculty Teaching Achievement award, 1995. Fellow ASCE (chmn. computer and numerical methods com. GT div. 1976-81); mem. ASTM, Inst. Structural Engrs. (Wallace Premium prize 1963), Internat. Soc. Soil Mechanics and Found. Engring., Earthquake Rsch. Inst., Am. Acad. Mechanics, Am. Soc. Engring. Edn., Internat. Assn. Computer Methods and Advances in Geomechanics (pres. 1991—, Outstanding Contbns. medal 1991). Home: 5110 N Calle La Cima Tucson AZ 85718-5815 Office: U Ariz Dept Civil Engring and Engring Mechanics Tucson AZ 85721

DE SANTIS, MARK EDWARD, anatomist, neuroscientist and educator; b. Vineland, N.J., May 9, 1942; s. Orazio James and Ellice Cecelia (Baier) De S.; m. Gail Marie Chambers, July 5, 1969; 1 child, Michael Kevin. BS, Villanova (Pa.) U., 1963; MS, Creighton U., Omaha, Nebr., 1966; PhD, UCLA, 1970. Rsch. assoc. Naval Aerospace Med. Rsch. Lab., Pensacola, Fla., 1970-71; instr. to assoc. prof. Georgetown U., Washington, 1971-78; assoc. prof. to prof. anatomy and neurosci. U. Idaho, Moscow, 1978—; cons. in neurobiology Dr. E.N. Albert, George Washington U., 1973-78; guest lectr. Walter Reed Army Med. Ctr., Washington, 1972-78, Madigan Army Med. Hosp., Tacoma, Wash., 1979-82; textbook reviewer Scott Foresman Little Brown & Co., Chgo., 1987-88. Contbr. articles to profl. jours. Scoutmaster Troop 344, Boy Scouts Am., Moscow, 1982-85. Recipient Golden Apple Teaching award Med. Class of 1980, Georgetown U., 1977, Excellence in Teaching award Med. Class of 1997, WAMI Program, 1994; Fulbright scholar, Egypt, 1994-95; NASA rsch. grantee, 1994—. Mem. Soc. for Neurosci., Am. Assn. Anatomists, Microscopy Soc. Am., Phi Sigma (faculty advisor 1987-93), Sigm Xi (chpt. pres. 1985). Office: Univ of Idaho Dept Biol Scis and WAMI Program Moscow ID 83844-3051

DESAUTEL, JAMES MICHAEL, public relations executive, writer; b. Nespelem, Wash., Dec. 27, 1948; s. Clarence Marcel Desautel and Julia J. (Carson) Woodward; m. Janice, May 10, 1969 (div. 1971); 1 child, Stacey Lynn; m. Cheryl Lynne, Feb. 13, 1982; 1 child, Sara Kay. Liberal studies, Ea. Wash. U., 1967-71. Photographer KREM-TV, Spokane, Wash., 1970-72; photographer, producer KING-TV, Seattle, 1972-74; reporter, anchor KREM-TV, Spokane, Wash., 1974-76; reporter, anchor, producer KOMO-TV, Seattle, 1976-79; pres. Desautel & Long, Inc., Spokane, Wash., 1979-84; pub. affairs mgr. USDA-Soil Conservation Svc., Spokane, 1984—; chmn. SCS Equal Opportunity Adv. Coun., Spokane, 1991-93; mem. SCS Employee Devel. Com., Spokane, Wash., 1991-93. Writer, prodr.: Washington Conservation Commission, 1991, The Secret, 1992, Emergency Watershed Program-SCS, 1993; author: Cannibals, 1994. Recipient News Photography Reporting awards (10) Sigma Delta Chi, Seattle, Spokane, 1970-78, CBS/NBC Fellowship award Michelle Clark Fellowship, N.Y., 1973, Emmy Nomination Acad. TV Arts and Scis., Seattle, 1978, Spokane MAX awards (22) Spokane Ad Fedn., 1979-84. Mem. Pub. Rels. Soc. Am. (cert.). Democrat. Roman Catholic. Home: 7614 N Audubon St Spokane WA 99208-8817 Office: USDA Soil Conservation Svc 316 W Boone Ave Ste 450 Spokane WA 99201-2346

DE SEIGNE, PASCAL (LAWRENCE), author, art appraiser; b. Paris, France; came to U.S., 1981; s. Antoine and Jeanne (de Fumel) de S. MPhil, Sorbonne U., Paris, 1967, M in Ethnology, 1970, cert. art appraisal, 1972. Pres. Gallery de Thezan, Nice, France, 1976-84; mgr. Gallery de Thezan, Beverly Hills, Calif., 1985-88. Author: Sculptures of Buddahs, 1975, Martial Arts, 1980, Au Nom de Ma Horde, 1992 (European bestseller 1992). Maj. comdg. officer spl. forces Airborne, 1967-76, comdr. Biafra, Laos. Republican. Roman Catholic. Home and Office: 6410 Green Valley Cir Apt 322 Culver City CA 90230-8007

DE SHAZO, BILLY W., physician, plastic surgeon; b. Ashford, Ala., Jan. 10, 1931; s. Neal C. and Woodie Lee (Harrison) De S.; m. Charlotte Jean McKay, Aug. 21, 1954; children: Jean, William, Edwin, John, Thomas. BS, So. Meth. U., 1952; MD, Southwestern Med. Sch., 1956. Diplomate Am. Bd. Plastic Surgery. Resident gen. surgery Calif. Hosp., L.A., 1959-62; resident plastic surgery U. Wis., Madison, 1962-64; chief plastic surgery Good Samaritan Hosp., St. Vincent's Hosp. Office: 1245 Wilshire Blvd Los Angeles CA 90017-4810

DESILVA, JOSEPH J., hospital administrator; b. Lowell, Mass., Dec. 10, 1940; married. BA, St. Anselm Coll., 1962, Boston Coll., 1974; MA, Babson Coll., 1980. Mgr. lab. svcs. Nashua (N.H.) Meml. Hosp., 1965-77; dir. lab. svcs. Burbank Hosp., Fitchburg, Mass., 1977-78; asst. adminstr. Harrington Meml. Hosp., Southbridge, Mass., 1978-80; dir. profl. svcs. Beverly (Mass.) Hosp., 1980-82, exec. v.p., 1982-85; sr. v.p., COO Univ. Hosps. Cleve., 1985-88; pres., CEO St. Joseph's Hosp., Phoenix, 1989—. Office: St Joseph's Hosp & Med Ctr PO Box 2071 Phoenix AZ 85001-2071

DESILVA, RANJIT NIHAL, leadership training consultant; b. Colombo, Sri Lanka, Apr. 10, 1943; came to U.S., 1988; s. Kenneth and Joyce (Jayawardene) D.; m. Iona Salome Pillai, Mar. 10, 1981; children: Nirmali, Dinesh, Sharon. BA in Practical Theology, Life Bible Coll., L.A., 1978; MA in Missiology, Fuller Theol. Sem., Pasadena, 1980, PhD in Leadership, 1994. Acad. dean Lanka Bible Coll., Sri Lanka, 1972-75, pres., 1980-88; dir. Lanka Village Ministries, Sri Lanka, 1984-88; dean Ministry Tng. Inst., L.A., 1990-93; leadership tng. cons. Pasadena, 1994—; spkr. WEGO, Dallas, 1977-94. Author: Discipling the Cities, 1980, Growing Church, 1982, Rejoicing Church, 1984; editor Ministry Today, 1984-88; contbr. articles to profl. jours. Recipient Leadership award Fuller Theol. Sem., 1994. Home and Office: 1245 Bedford Rd Bedford TX 76021

DE SMEDT, PHILIPPE, research scientist, technologist; b. Duffel, Belgium, Dec. 14, 1957; came to U.S., 1980; s. Albert and Louisa-Maria (De Meyer) De S. BA in Bus. Adminstrn., Cath. U. Leuven, 1980; MS in Computer Sci., U. Calif., Berkeley, 1982; MS in Engring. and Bus. and Tech., Stanford U., 1989. Intern internat. divsn. Chem. Bank, N.Y.C., 1980-81; sr. software engr. Digital Equipment Corp., Marlboro, Mass., 1984-85; rsch. scientist Hewlett-Packard Labs., Palo Alto, Calif., 1985—; grad. lectr. Santa Clara (Calif.) U., 1993-94; conf. com. treas. Assn. Computing Machinery-Sigmetrics, 1989, 91, 92. Contbr. articles to profl. jours. 1st vice chancelor San Francisco chpt. Confrerie des Vignerons de St. Vincent de Bourgogne et Macon, 1992—. Mem. IEEE, Soc. Computer Applications in Med. Care. Office: Hewlett-Packard Labs 1501 Page Mill Rd # 4 Palo Alto CA 94304-1126

DESOER, CHARLES AUGUSTE, electrical engineer; b. Ixelles, Belgium, Jan. 11, 1926; came to U.S., 1949, naturalized, 1958; s. Jean Charles and Yvonne Louise (Peltzer) D.; m. Jacqueline K. Johnson, July 21, 1966; children: Marc J., Michele M., Craig M. Ingenieur Radio-Electricien, U. Liege, Belgium, 1949, DSc (hon.), 1976; ScD in Elec. Engring, MIT, 1953. Rsch. asst. M.I.T., 1951-53; mem. tech. staff Bell Telephone Labs., Murray Hill, N.J., 1953-58; assoc. prof. elec. engring. and computer scis. U. Calif., Berkeley, 1958-62; prof. U. Calif., 1962-91, prof. emeritus, 1991—, Miller research prof., 1970-71. Author: (with L. A. Zadeh) Linear System Theory, 1963, (with E. S. Kuh) Basic Circuit Theory, 1969, (with M. Vidyasagar) Feedback Systems: Input Output Properties, 1973, Notes for a Second Course on Linear Systems, 1970, (with F. M. Callier) Multivariable Feedback Systems, 1982, (with L.O. Chua and E.S. Kuh) Linear and Nonlinear Circuits, 1987, (with A.N. Gündes) Alegebraic Theory of Linear Feedback Systems with Full and Decentralized Compensation, 1990, (with F.M. Callier) Linear System Theory, 1991; contbr. numerous articles on systems and circuits to profl. jours. Served with Belgian Arty., 1944-45. Decorated Vol.'s medal; recipient Best Paper prize 2d Joint Automatic Control Conf., 1962, Univ. medal U. Liège, 1976, Disting. Teaching award U. Calif., Berkeley, 1971, Prix Montefiore Inst. Montefiore, 1975; award for outstanding paper IEEE, 1979, Field award in control sci. and engring., 1986, Am. Automatic Control Council Edn. award, 1983, Berkeley Citation, 1992; Guggenheim fellow, 1970-71. Fellow IEEE (Edn. medal 1975), AAAS; mem. Nat. Acad. Engring., Am. Math. Soc., Math. Assn. Am., Soc. Indsl. and Applied Math. Office: U Calif Dept Elec Engring and Computer Sci Berkeley CA 94720

DESOTO, LEWIS DAMIEN, art educator; b. San Bernardino, Calif., Jan. 3, 1954; s. Lewis Dan and Albertina (Quiroz) DeS. BA, U. Calif., Riverside, 1978; MFA, Claremont Grad. Sch., 1981. Tchr. Otis Parsons, L.A., 1982-85; chmn. art dept. Cornish Coll. of Arts, Seattle, 1985-88; assoc. prof. art San Francisco State U., 1988—; dir. grad. studies Calif. Coll. Arts and Crafts, Oakland, 1993-95. Exhibited at New Mus., N.Y.C., 1992, Centro Cultural De La Raza, San Diego, 1993, Christopher Grimes Gallery, Santa Monica, Calif., 1994, Denver Art Mus., 1994, Columbus Mus. Art, 1994, Des Moines Art Ctr., 1995, Serralves Found., Oporto, Portugal, 1995. Mem. photo coun. Seattle Art Mus., 1987-88. Recipient New Genres award Calif. Arts Coun., 1992. Mem. L.A. Ctr. for Photographic Studies (bd. dirs. 1983-85), CameraWork (exec. bd. dirs. 1991-93), Ctr. for Arts (adv. bd. 1993—), Friends of Photography (peer award bd. 1991—). Office: San Francisco State U Art Dept 1600 Holloway Ave San Francisco CA 94132

DESPRES, DENISE ANN, veterinarian; b. Worcester, Mass., Dec. 19, 1953; d. Louis Victor and Rosemary (Thompson) D.; m. Richard Llyod Hueschen, June 15, 1980. BS, Purdue U., 1973, DVM, 1977. Owner, veterinarian Mountain Vet. Clin., Cedar Crest, N.Mex., 1978—. Mem. Albuquerque Aerostate Ascention Assn. Republican. Roman Catholic. Home: 2 Corte De Canoncito Cedar Crest NM 87008-9420

DESROCHERS, JERI KILZER, artist; b. Lincoln, Nebr., Sept. 24, 1957. BS in Bus. Adminstrn., Colo. State U., 1985. Works exhibited Greeley Stampede Art Show, 1992, NPVAG Nat. Juried Art Show, 1993, Boulder Open Juried Show, 1994, Glenwood Springs Fall Arts Festival, 1991, 92, 93, 94, Evergreen Fine Arts Fair, 1992, 93, 94, Phi Theta Kappa Six-State Art Competitive, 1993, Thompson Valley Regional Art Show, 1993, Colo. Watercolor Soc. Statewide Exhbn., 1993, 94, 95. Mem. Signature Colo. Watercolor Soc., Evergreen Artists Assn. (membership dir. 1989-95), Colorado Springs Art Guild, Foothills Art Ctr. Office: Studio Jeri Desrochers 27222 Hilltop Dr Evergreen CO 80439-9217

DESROCHES, BRIAN, psychotherapist, organizational systems consultant; b. Windsor, Ont., Can., Aug. 22, 1946; came to U.S., 1971; s. Henry and Mary (Zola) DesR.; m. Mara Pauli, June 9, 1971 (div. May 1978); m. Patricia I. DesRoches, Dec. 30, 1987; children: David Joseph, Christine Carmen. B in Comm. (hon.), U. Windsor, 1969; MHA, U. Ottawa, 1973; MS in Counseling, Ea. Mont. Coll., 1976; MBA, U. Puget Sound, 1980; PhD, N.W. Theol. Union, 1993. Mgr. computer ops. Henry Ford Hosp., Detroit, 1967-69; project mgr. NNE Regional Med. Program, Burlington, Vt., 1971; assoc. adminstr. Billings (Mont.) Deaconess Hosp., 1973-77; asst. adminstr. Providence Med. Ctr., Seattle, 1977-80; v.p. planning and devel.-health and hosp. svcs. Sister of St. Joseph, Bellevue, Wash., 1977-80; mgmt. cons. Seattle, 1981-83; exec. dir. Faulkner Treatment Ctr., Austin, Tex., 1983-84; psychotherapist, cons. Seattle, 1985—. Author: Reclaiming Yourself, 1990, Faces of Recovery, 1991, Your Boss Is Not Your Mother, 1995; contbg. author: Talk, Trust, Feel, 1992. Mem. bd. Mad-Jac Econ. Devel. Coun., Seattle, 1980-81, Cath. Community Svcs., Seattle, 1981. Mem. Am. Assn. Marriage and Family Therapists (clin.). Office: 2800 E Madison St # 302 Seattle WA 98112-4859

DEST, LEONARD RALPH, aerospace engineer, telecommunications specialist; b. Northampton, Pa., Oct. 31, 1949; s. Philip P. and Pauline (Michalgyk) D.; m. Beverly J. Teel, May 12, 1979. BS, Lehigh U., 1971, MS, 1973. With Fairchild Space/Electronics, Germantown, Md., 1973-74; engr. RCA Global Comm., Princeton, N.J., 1974-75; analyst COMSAT, Washington, 1975-78; sr. engr., supr. INTELSAT, Washington, 1978-82; mgr. spacecraft engring. INTELSAT, El Segundo, Calif., 1982-91; chief scientist Hughes Aircraft Co., El Segundo, Calif., 1991-93; v.p. mktg. Hughes Space and Communications Internat., L.A., 1994—. Mem. AIAA. Republican. Lutheran. Home: 1709 Club View Dr Los Angeles CA 90024-5311 Office: Hughes Space and Communications Internat PO Box 92919 Los Angeles CA 90009-2919

DETEMPLE, WILLIAM CHARLES, technology executive; b. Vancouver, B.C., Can., Sept. 4, 1953; s. James Clemmens and Mary Clare (Lipp) DeT.; m. Ethel Eileen Congdon, Aug. 30, 1975 (div. 1987); children: Renee Lynn, Ryan William; m. Wendy Rae Duggan, Nov. 19, 1988; 1 child, Joshua Donn Kelley. Grad. high sch., Port Coquitlam, B.C. Technician Can. Telephone and Supplies, Burnaby, B.C., 1973-75; sales mgr. Internat. Promotions, Inc., Edmonton, Alta., Can., 1975-78; pres. Aggressive Mktg., Inc., Coquitlam, B.C., 1978-84, Spectra Automotive Supplies, Rancho Cucamonga, Calif., 1985-87, Rest Mfg., Inc., Rancho Cucamonga, 1987-89, Pine Ridge Consulting, Upland, Calif., 1989-94; v.p. mktg./sales Gen. Power Corp., Anaheim, Calif., 1991-93; pres. WCD Assocs., Rancho Cucamonga, Calif., 1994—. Patentee remote electronic shelf edge label. Mem. North Vancouver Jaycees, 1977-80; active Vancouver Big Bros., New Westminister, B.C., 1979-83; sec.-treas. Coquitlam Kiwanis, 1984. Mem. So. Calif. Tech. Exec. Network, Orange County Venture Group. Home and Office: 10855 Terra Vista Pky Apt 119 Rancho Cucamonga CA 91730-6391

DETLEFSEN, WILLIAM DAVID, JR., chemist; b. Scottsbluff, Nebr., Nov. 14, 1946; s. William David Sr. and Janette Fern (Tuttle) D.; m. Melba Kay Cunningham, Nov. 12, 1982; children: Michael David, Erika Lee, Whitney Anne. BS in Forestry, U. Idaho, 1970; PhD in Chemistry, U. Oreg., 1993. Chemist, applications technologist Borden, Adhesives and Resins, Springfield, Oreg., 1972-76, coord. tech. svc., 1976-78, supr. phenolic resins devel., 1983-87, mgr. rsch. and devel., 1987—; sr. devel. chemist Ga.-Pacific Resins, Crossett, Ark., 1978-83. Contbr. articles to sci. jours. 1st. lt. U.S. Army, 1970-72, Germany. Mem. AAAS, Am. Chem. Soc., Forest Products Rsch. Soc. Republican. Office: Borden Inc Adhesives & Resins Divsn 610 S 2nd St Springfield OR 97477-5312

DETLOR, JOHN SYDNEY, security executive; b. Summerside, P.E.I., Can., Sept. 1, 1940; came to U.S., 1952; s. W. Lyall and Margaret A. (Baxter) D.; m. Cecile A. Foy, June 9, 1962 (dec. Jan. 1968); m. Jeanette L. Duncan, Apr. 26, 1969; children: William, Susan. BA, Whitworth Coll., 1962; JD, Willamette U., 1964. Spl. agt. FBI, Albuquerque, 1964-65, L.A., 1965-68, Seattle, 1968-89; dir. security Costco Wholesale, Kirkland, Wash., 1989-93; asst. v.p., ops. adminstr. Price Costco, Kirkland, Wash., 1993—. Elder Rose Hill Presby. Ch., 1991-94. Mem. Am. soc. Indsl. Security, Soc. for Former Spl. Agts. of the FBI (sec. 1992-93, treas. 1991-92, chmn. 1994-95). Home: 21837 NE 69th St Redmond WA 98053 Office: Price Costco 10809 120th Ave NE Kirkland WA 98033-5024

DETTERMAN, ROBERT LINWOOD, financial planner; b. Norfolk, Va., May 1, 1931; s. George William and Jeanneille (Watson) D.; m. Virginia Armstrong; children: Janine, Patricia, William Arthur. BS in Engring., Va. Poly. Inst., 1953; PhD in Nuclear Engring., Oak Ridge Sch. Reactor Tech., 1954, postgrad., 1954; cert. in fin. planning, Coll. Fin. Planning, Denver, 1986. Registered investment advisor, Calif. Engring. test dir. Foster Wheeler Co., N.Y.C., 1954-59; sr. research engr. Atomics Internat. Co., Canoga Park, Calif., 1959-62; chief project engr. Rockwell Internat. Co., Canoga Park, Calif., 1962-68, dir. bus. devel., 1968-84, mgr. internat. program, 1984-87; pres. Bo-Gin Fin., Inc., Thousand Oaks, Calif., 1987—; owner Bo-Gin Arabians, Thousand Oaks, 1963—; nuclear cons. Danish Govt., 1960, Lawrence Livermore Lab., Calif., 1959. Trustee, mem. exec. com. Morris Animal Found., Denver, 1984—, chmn., 1984-88, now trustee emeritus; treas., trustee Arabian Horse Trust, Denver, 1979-94, now trustee emeritus; pres. Rolling Oaks Homes Assn., Thousand Oaks, Calif., 1980-82; chmn. Cal Bred Futurity. Mem. Nat. Assn. Personal Fin. Advisers, Internat. Assn. Fin. Planners, Inst. Cert. Fin. Planners, Am. Nuclear Soc., Acad. Magical Arts, Am. Horse Shows Assn., Am. Horse Coun., Magic Castle Club, Internat. Arabian Horse Assn. Club, Tau Beta Phi, Eta Kappa Nu, Phi Kappa Phi. Republican. Office: Bo-Gin Fin Inc 3625 E Thousand Oaks Blvd Ste 220 Thousand Oaks CA 91362-3652

DETTMAN-MARSHALL, GERALDINE LOUISE, biologist; b. Evanston, Ill., Aug. 28, 1943; d. Walter Fred and Almyra Emelia (Hasse) D.; m. John E. Marshall, Oct. 25, 1993. BS in Biology, No. Ill. U.; PhD in Biology, U. Calif., Irvine, 1972. Asst. rsch. biologist U. Calif., Irvine, 1972-73, asst. adj. prof., 1973-79; asst. prof. med. scis. Brown U., Providence, R.I., 1980-83, radiation safety officer, 1980-85, biosafety officer, 1983-85; founder, pres. Viro Rsch. Internat., Inc., Durango, Colo., 1985—. Contbr. articles to profl. jours. NSF fellow, 1968-72. Office: 178 Bodo Dr Ste C Durango CO 81301-6506

DETWEILER, ROBERT CHESTER, university president, historian; b. French Camp, Calif., Dec. 8, 1938; s. Chester and Alice Mae (Gallagher) D.; m. Susan Jan Krudwig, Nov. 22, 1978; 1 dau., Lara Anne. B.A., Humboldt State U., 1960; M.A., San Francisco State U., 1965; Ph.D., U. Wash., 1968. Asst. prof. history San Diego State U., 1968-71, assoc. prof., 1971-74, prof., 1974-78, chmn. dept. history, 1977-78, assoc. dean Coll. Arts and Letters, 1978-80, dean coll., 1980-85; v.p. Calif. State U., San Bernardino, 1985-89; pres. Calif. State U., Dominguez Hills, 1989—; now pres./chancellor. Author: Richard Bland and the Origins of the Virginia Revolt, 1982; editor: Environmental Decay in Its Historial Context, 1973, Race, Prejudice and the Origins of Salvery in America, 1975, Liberation in the Americas,, 1978. Served to col. USMCR, 1960-89. Mem. Orgn. Am. Historians, Am. Hist. Assn., USMCR Officers Assn. (pres. chpt. 1977-79). Home: 1500 E Roosevelt Rd Long Beach CA 90807-3723 Office: Calif State U Dominguez Hills Office of President 1000 E Victoria St Carson CA 90747-0001*

DETWILER, PETER MURRAY, legislative consultant, educator; b. Visalia, Calif., Nov. 5, 1949; s. Donald M. and Mary Alice (Murray) D.; m. Caroline Margaret Cain, Sept. 2, 1972; children: Stephen C., Eric J. BA in Govt., St. Mary's Coll. Calif., 1971; MA in Pub. Policy and Adminstrn., U. Wis., 1972. Asst. exec. officer Local Agy. Formation Commn., San Diego, 1972-75; dir. local govt. unit Gov.'s Office Planning and Rsch., Sacramento, 1975-81; staff dir. Senate Local Govt. Com., Sacramento, 1982-95; cons. Senate Housing and Land Use Com., Sacramento, 1995—; instr. Calif. State U., Sacramento, 1991—. Author: (chpt.) Calif. Environ. Law, 1989, State & Regional Initiatives for Managing Development, 1992; mem. bd. exec. editors, contbr. articles Land Use & Environment Forum, 1991—. Leader Boy Scouts Am., Sacramento, 1984—. Recipient commendation for legis. League Calif. Cities, 1984. Mem. ASPA, Western Govtl. Rsch. Assn. (Samuel C. May Rsch. Paper award 1980). Democrat. Roman Catholic.

Office: Senate Housing and Land Use State Capitol Rm 4030 Sacramento CA 95814

DEUBLE, JOHN L., JR., environmental science and engineering services consultant; b. N.Y.C., Oct. 2, 1932; s. John Lewis and Lucille (Klotzbach) D.; m. Thelma C. Honeychurch, Aug. 28, 1955; children: Deborah, Steven. AA, AS in Phys. Sci., Stockton Coll., 1957; BA, BS in Chemistry, U. Pacific, 1959. Cert. profl. chemist, profl. engr., environ. inspector; registered environ. profl., registered environ. assessor. Sr. chemist Aero-Gen Corp., Sacramento, Calif., 1959-67; asst. dir. rsch. Lockheed Propulsion Co., Redlands, Calif., 1968-73; asst. div. mgr. Systems, Sci. and Software, La Jolla, Calif., 1974-79; gen. mgr. Wright Energy Nev. Corp., Reno, Nev., 1980-81; v.p. Energy Resources Co., La Jolla, 1982-83; dir. hazardous waste Aerovironment Inc., Monrovia, Calif., 1984-85; environ. cons. Encinitas, Calif., 1986-88; sr. program mgr. Ogden Environ. and Energy Svcs., San Diego, 1989—. Contbr. articles profl. jours. With USAF, 1951-54. Recipient Tech. award Am. Ordnance Assn., 1969, Cert. of Achievement Am. Men and Women of Sci., 1986, Envrion. Registry, 1992. Fellow Am. Inst. Chemists; mem. ASTM, Am. Chem. Soc., AM. Inst. Chem. Engrs., Am. Meteorol. Soc., Am. Nuclear Soc., Am. Def. Preparedness Assn., Air and Waste Mgmt. Assn., Calif. Inst. Chemists, Hazardous Materials Control Rsch. Inst., N.Y. Acad. Scis., Environ. Assessors Assn. Republican. Lutheran. Home: 369 Cerro St Encinitas CA 92024-4805 Office: Ogden Environ & Energy Svcs 5510 Morehouse Dr San Diego CA 92121-3720

DE URIOSTE, GEORGE ADOLFO, IV, software company executive; b. San Francisco, June 25, 1955; s. George Adolfo Sr. and Janet Germaine (Bruzzone) de U. BS, U. So. Calif., L.A., 1978; MBA, U. Calif., Berkeley, 1980. CPA, Calif. Auditor, cons. Deloitte Haskins & Sells, San Francisco, 1980-83; sr. fin. analyst Genstar Corp., San Francisco, 1983-85, Rolm Mil-Spec Computers, Inc., San Jose, Calif., 1986-88; mgr. fin. planning and analysis Ask Computer Systems, Inc., Mountain View, Calif., 1988-90; CFO TeamOne Systems, Inc., Sunnyvale, Calif., 1990-92; v.p. of fin. Remedy Corp., Mountain View, Calif., 1992—. Pres. Commerce Assocs., San Francisco, 1988-89. Mem. AICPA, Calif. Soc. CPAs, Churchill Club (bd. dirs., vice chmn. Palo Alto, Calif. 1989-94). Home: 282 Walker Dr Mountain View CA 94043-2108 Office: Remedy Corp 1505 Salado Dr Mountain View CA 94043-2108

DEUTSCH, BARRY JOSEPH, management development company executive; b. Gary, Ind., Aug. 10, 1941; s. Jack Elias and Helen Louise (La Rue) D.; B.S., U. So. Calif., 1969, M.B.A. magna cum laude, 1970; m. Gina Krispinsky, Feb. 20, 1972. Lectr. mgmt. U. So. Calif., L.A., 1967-70; pres., founder The Deutsch Group, Inc., mgmt. cons. co. tng. upper and middle mgmt., L.A., 1970—, chmn. bd., 1975—; founder, chief exec. officer, chmn. bd. Investment Planning Network, Inc., 1988—; dir. Red Carpet Corp. Am., 1975-77, United Fin. Planners, 1984-86. Chmn. bd. govs. Am. Hist. Ctr., 1980—. With M.I., U.S. Army, 1964-66. Mem. Am. Mgmt. Assn., Am. Soc. Bus. and Mgmt. Cons.'s, Am. Soc. Tng. and Devel., Internat. Mgmt. by Objectives Inst. Author: Leadership Techniques, 1969, Recruiting Techniques, 1970, The Art of Selling, 1973, Professional Real Estate Management, 1975, Strategic Planning, 1976, Employer/Employee: Making the Transition, 1978, Managing by Objectives, 1980, Conducting Effective Performance Appraisal, 1982, Advanced Supervisory Development, 1984, Managing A Successful Financial Planning Business, 1988, How to Franchise Your Business, 1991. Home: 4509 Candleberry Ave Seal Beach CA 90740-3026

DEUTSCH, NICHOLAS ANDREW, medical educator; b. N.Y.C., Oct. 15, 1959; s. Morton and Lydia D.; m. Lisa Matzer, Sept. 5, 1993. BA, Columbia U., 1981, MD, 1985. Diplomate Nat. Med. Bd. Examiners, Am. Bd. Anesthesiology. Resident U. Mich., Ann Arbor, 1986-89; asst. prof. UCLA, 1991—. Contbr. articles to profl. jours. Fellow UCLA, 1987-90, Rsch. fellow Am. Heart Assn., L.A., 1990-91; Am. Heart Assn. grant-in-aid, 1993—; recipient Clinician Scientist award Am. Heart Assn., 1991-94, Young Investigators award Found. Anesthesia Rsch., 1994—. Mem. Am. SOc. Anesthesiologists, Soc. Cardiovascular Anesthesiologists, Calif. Soc. Anesthesiologists. Office: UCLA 10833 Le Conte Ave Los Angeles CA 90024

DEVANEY, DONALD EVERETT, law enforcement official; b. Providence, Nov. 21, 1936; s. William Francis and Elizabeth Florence (Hill) D.; m. Tokiko Yoshida, May 19, 1960; 1 child, George Y. AA in Edn., El Paso Community Coll., 1973; BA, SUNY, Albany, 1979. Cert. healthcare protection adminstr. Internat. Healthcare Safety and Security Found. Sgt. maj. U.S. Army, 1954-83; customs inspector U.S. Customs Svc., Honolulu, 1983-84; provost marshal Tripler Army Med. Ctr., Honolulu, 1984—; regional chair Europe and Asia, 1989—; Pacific rep. Chief of Staff Retiree Coun.; past dir. Kalihi-Palama Immigrant Svc. Ctr.; extraordinary min. of the eucharist Tripler Catholic Cmty. Fin. donor Okinawa Cultural Ctr., Waipahu, Hawaii, 1987-89; cmty. mem. cmty. based ednl. coun. Webling Elem. Sch. Recipient Disting Svc. award Hawaii Joint Police, 1977, 86, George Washington Honor medal Freedom's Found., 1973; decorated Legion of Merit. Mem. Hawaii Joint Police Assn. (pres. 1985), U.S. Army CID Command (assoc.), Nat. Assn. for Uniformed Svcs. (v.p. Hawaii chpt.), U.S. Army Retiree Coun. (U.S. Army Pacific rep., vice chmn.), Hawaii Law Enforcement and Pvt. Security (chmn. awards com.), Hawaii Joint Police Assn. (past pres.), Internat. Assn. for Healthcare Security and Safety (sec. Hawaii chpt.), Noncommissioned Officer Assn. (life mem.), The Retired Enlisted Assn. (life), Disabled Am. Veterans (life mem. chpt. 3), Rotary (pres. Pearl Harbor chpt. 1991-92, dir. community svc. dist. 5000, 1992-93), KC. Roman Catholic. Home: 98-911 Ainanui Loop Aiea HI 96701-2766 Office: Office Provost Marshal Tripler Army Med Ctr Honolulu HI 96859

DEVENOT, DAVID CHARLES, human resource executive; b. Indpls., May 27, 1939; s. Charles Joseph and Pearl (Geodfry) D.; m. Mary Jennifer Bateman, July 7, 1970; children: Daniel, Mark. BBA, U. Hawaii, 1962. Dir. indsl. rels. USP Corp subs. Consol. Foods, Sara Lee, San Jose, Calif., 1964-70; sr. human resource cons. Hawaii Employers Coun., Honolulu, 1970—. Bd. dirs. Hawn Humane Soc., Honolulu, 1975—, Lanikila Rehab. Ctr., Honolulu, 1985—, Am. Cancer Soc., 1989, v.p. Pacific divsn. Mem. Santa Clara Valley Pers. Assn. (pres. 1968-69), Soc. Human Resource Mgmt., Indsl. Rels. Rsch. Assn. Home: 46-141 Nahiku St Kaneohe HI 96744-3629 Office: Hawaii Employers Coun 2682 Waiwai Loop Honolulu HI 96819-1938

DEVENS, MICHAEL WILLIAM, construction, contract disputes consultant; b. Tacoma, Oct. 12, 1961; s. John Wellington and Carol Christine (Cambio) D.; m. Lorraine Downes Dunn, Apr. 8, 1989; children: Michael William Jr., John Wellington II. BCE, Va. Mil. Inst., Lexington, 1983. Lt., platoon leader U.S. Army Corps Engrs., Karlsruhe, Fed. Republic Germany, 1983-84, Lt., logistics officer, 1984-86; Capt., intelligence officer U.S. Army Corps Engrs., Ft. Carson, Colo., 1987-88; staff engr. William H. Gordon Assocs., Woodbridge, Va., 1988; contract adminstr. Excell Inc., Colorado Springs, Colo., 1988-89, sr. contract adminstr., 1989-91, program dir., 1991-92, v.p., 1993—. Capt. U.S. Army, 1983-88. Mem. Nat. Contract Mgmt. Assn., Soc. Am. Mil. Engrs. Republican. Roman Catholic. Home: 2555 Edenderry Dr Colorado Springs CO 80919 Office: Excell Inc 5475 Mark Dabling Blvd Ste 300 Colorado Springs CO 80918-3845

DEVGAN, ONKAR DAVE N., technologist, consultant; b. Lahore, Panjab, India, Oct. 11, 1941; came to U.S., 1967; s. Thakar Dass Devgan and Sohag Wati Sharma; m. Veena Devgan, July 20, 1969; children: Sanjay, Pooja. BS, Panjab U., 1960; MS, Vikham U., 1963, PhD, 1966; MBA, Temple U., 1975. Instr., rsch. assoc. U. Pa., Phila., 1970-73; scientist C.E. Glass, Pennsauken, N.J., 1973-76; cons., vis. prof. U. Tex., Dallas, 1976-78; mgr. material devel., sr. engr. Tex. Inst., Dallas, 1978-83; engrng. mgr. Fairchild Semiconductor, Palo Alto, Calif., 1983-84, 88; program mgr. Varian Assocs., Palo Alto, 1984-86; dir. microelectronics Northrup Corp., L.A., 1986-88; dir. tech. and ops. Polylithics Inc., Santa Clara, Calif., 1989-90; tech. and mgmt. cons. Devgan Assocs., Sunnyvale, Calif., 1991—; co-founder, pres. Paragon System Tech.; co-chmn. Semi GaAs Com., Mt. View, Calif., 1984-85; mem. Semi Automation Com., Mt. View, 1984-86; advisor Semi Equipment Uptime Com., Mt. View; chair session on process control and monitor Internat. Semiconductor Mfg. Sci. Symposium, San Francisco. Contbr. articles to tech. and bus. jours. PhD fellow Govt. of India, 1963-66, Coun. of Sci. and Indsl. Rsch. sr. fellow, 1966-67; NIH postdoctoral fellow, 1967-70. Mem. IEEE, Am. Chem. Soc. Home and Office: 161 Butano Ave Sunnyvale CA 94086-7025

DEVILBISS, JONATHAN FREDERICK, aircraft sales engineer; b. Saiburi, Pattani, Thailand, July 23, 1961; s. Frederick Henry and Iva Marie (Weidner) D.; m. Laura Anne Carr, June 4, 1994. BS in Aero. Engring., Purdue U., 1984; BA in Liberal Arts, Wheaton (Ill.) Coll., 1984. Sales engr. Brit. Aerospace Inc., Herndon, Va., 1985-88, tech. sales engr., 1988-89, sr. tech. sales engr., 1989-91, sr. product engr., 1991-92; mgr. product mktg. Jetstream Aircraft subs. Brit. Aerospace, Sterling, Va., 1993-94. Mem. AIAA, SAE (assoc.). Republican. Evangelical Christian. Home: 1651 S Riverstone Ln Apt 305 Boise ID 83706

DEVITO, CARL LOUIS, mathematics educator; b. N.Y.C., Oct. 21, 1937; s. Salvatore and Rose (Giossi) DeV.; m. Marilyn Jane Zink, Aug. 26, 1965; 1 child, Stephanie Lee. BS, CUNY, 1959; PhD, Northwestern U., 1967. Computer programmer North Hills Electronic Co., Garden City, N.Y., 1959-60; instr. in maths. DePaul U., Chgo., 1965-66, asst. prof. maths., 1966-67; asst. prof. maths. U. Ariz., Tucson, 1967-71, assoc. prof. maths., 1971-85, 1988—; invited speaker 41st Congress of Internat. Astronautical Fedn., Dresden, Germany, 1990; adj. prof. maths. Naval Postgrad. Sch., Monterey, Calif., 1985-87; cons. dept. elec. engring. U.Ariz., summer 1979, 1983; vis. scholar Calif. Inst. Tech., Pasadena, 1981. Author: Functional Analysis, 1979, Functional Analysis and Linear Operator Theory, 1990. NSF fellow, 1962, 64; Naval Postgrad. Sch. Found. Rsch. grantee, 1987-88, 88-89, Rsch. Corp. grantee, 1989-90. Mem. Am. Math. Soc., Math. Assn. Am. Office: U Ariz Dept Math Tucson AZ 85721

DEVITT-GRASSO, PAULINE VIRGINIA, civic volunteer, nurse; b. Salem, Mass., May 13, 1930; d. John M. and Mary Elizabeth (Cologey) Devitt; m. Frank Anthony Grasso, Oct. 26, 1968; 1 stepson, Christopher Anthony. BSN, Boston Coll., 1952; student, Boston U., 1954-55, Boston State Tchrs. Coll., 1953-54. RN. Staff nurse J.P. Kennedy Jr. Meml. Hosp., Brighton, Mass., 1952-53; head nurse, day supr. J.P. Kennedy Jr. Meml. Hosp., Brighton, 1953-54, day supr., 1955, clin. instr., 1955-58, adminstrv. asst., 1968, dir. nursing edn., 1958-68; vis. instr. Boston Coll., Mass. State Coll., Meml. Hosp. Sch. Nursing, Newton, Mass. Meml. Hosp. Sch. Nursing, 1955-68, CUA S of N, 1990; bd. dirs. Behavioral Health Svcs. Inc. Pres. Project H.O.P.E., Manhattan Beach, Calif., 1982; pres. adv. coun. Meals on Wheels, Salvation Army, 1989, 90, 91, bd. dirs. Redondo Beach, 1992—, sec. bd. dirs., 1994; cons. Manhattan Beach Housing Found., 1986—, Manhattan Beach Case Mgr., 1982—; mem. adv. coun. South Bay Sr. Svcs., Torrance, Calif., 1986—, pres., 1994; sr. advocate City of Manhattan Beach, 1982; bd. dirs. Ret. Sr. Vol. Program, Torrance, 1986-90, Behavioral Health Svcs., 1992—; neighborhood chair Girl Scouts U.S.; mem. Beach City Coun. on Aging, 1983-91; mem. Salvation Army Ladies Aux.; mem. adv. bd. Salvation Army Corps, Redondo Beach. Recipient Cert. of Appreciation, County of L.A., 1988, Vol. of the Yr. award City of Manhattan Beach, 1988, Award of Honor County of L.A., 1989, State of Calif. Senate Rules Com. Resolution Commendation, 1988; named Outstanding Vol. Cath. Daus. of Am., 1986, Vol. of Yr. City Manhattan Beach, 1986-87; Rose and Scroll award Manhattan Beach C. of C., 1989, Art Michel Meml. Community Svc. award Manhattan Beach Rotary Club, 1989, Cert. of Appreciation KC's Queen of Martyers Coun., 1989, Redondo Beach Lila Bell award Salvation Army, 1989, others, Manhattan Beach Vol. Appreciation award, 1982, 83, 84, 85, 86, 88, 90, 91, 92, 93, cert. South Bay Centinela Credit Union, 1990; nominated for Pres's. Vol. Action award Project H.O.P.E., 1987. Mem. AARP, Am. Martyrs Altar Soc. (pres. 1983, coun. mem.-at-large 1992), Cath. U. Am. Nat. Alumni Assn. (hon.), Cath. U. Am. Sch. Nursing Alumni Assn. (hon.), Boston Coll. Alumni Assn., Manhattan Beach Sr. Citizens Club (pres. 1985-86, 88-89), Lions (Citizen of Yr. award Manhattan Beach club 1986), DAV (comdr.'s club 1990, 91, 92), Equestrian Order of Holy Sepulchre of Jerusalem. Democrat. Roman Catholic. Home: 329 3rd St Manhattan Beach CA 90266-6410

DEVLIN, DAVID STUART, biology educator; b. Greensboro, N.C., Dec. 12, 1957; s. Joseph Stuart and Margaret Joan (Wright) D.; m. Marguerite Cochrane, Aug. 1, 1981 (div. July 1989); 1 child, Joshua Ryan; m. Sandra Escobar, June 21, 1991; stepchildren: Stephanie Grijalva, Crystal Grigalva, Kathleen Grijalva, Levi Grijalva, Victoria Grijalva. BA, Luther Coll., 1980; MA in Tchg., Western N.Mex. U., 1993. Cert. secondary sci. and biology tchr. H.s. sci. tchr. Deming (N.Mex.) Pub. Schs., 1983-84; jr. h.s. sci. tchr. Cobre Pub. Schs., Bayard, N.Mex., 1984-93, dept. chair, 1989-93; field supr. for edn. Western N.Mex. U., Silver City, 1993; h.s. biology tchr. Apollo H.S., Glendale, Ariz., 1993—. Editor of jr. div. papers N.Mex. Jour. of Sci., 1993. Mem. NEA (local pres.), AAAS, Nat. Sci. Tchrs. Assn., N.Mex. Acad. of Sci. (state dir. of jr. acad. of sci. 1992-93, bd. dirs. 1992-93), N.Mex. Sci. Tchrs. Assn. Democrat. Office: Apollo H S 8045 N 47th Ave Glendale AZ 85302-6402

DEVOE, KENNETH NICKOLAS, food service executive, mayor; b. Mineola, N.Y., Sept. 13, 1944; s. Kenneth Pettit and Wykiena (Bos) D.; m. Linda Faye Mizer, May 7, 1965; children: Andrea W., Christina L., Kenneth C., Paula A. Student, Merced Coll., 1970-75. Police sgt. Merced (Calif.) Police Dept., 1966-75; sheriff sgt. Mariposa (Calif.) County Sheriff, 1975-81; pk. mgr. Am. Campgrounds Inc., Bellevue, Wash., 1981-83; owner DeVoe Enterprises, Atwater, Calif., 1983—. Chmn. Merced County Assn. Govts., 1990—, Atwater 4th of July Com., 1983—; asst. mayor City of Atwater, 1987-94, mayor, 1994—. With USAF, 1962-66. Mem. Atwater C. of C. (dir. 1991, dir.-at-large 1983-86, Citizen of Yr. 1987), Merced Trade Club (dir. 1991—), Castle Air Force Base Cols. Club., Kiwanis, Masons. Republican. Home: 3302 Sextant Dr Atwater CA 95301-4725 Office: Devoe Enterprises 1898 Bellevue Rd Atwater CA 95301-2668

DEVON, GARY ALBERT, newspaper editor; b. Ellensburg, Wash., Apr. 9, 1961; s. Larry D. and Judith A. (Connot) DeV.; m. Anne F. Ringwood, Sept. 24, 1994; children: Segornae, Morgan. BA in Comm. and Journalism, Gonzaga U., 1983. Reporter, photographer Post Falls (Idaho) Tribune, 1982-83; freelaance journalist and photographer, Seattle, 1983-87; mng. editor Okanogan Valley Gazette-Tribune, weekly, Oroville, Wash., 1987—. Recipient 1st place award for comprehensive coverage of story and for news photograph Wash. Newspaper Pubs. Assn., 1990, 1st place award for news photograph and 2d place award for best article, 1991, 2d place award for best news article, 1992, 1st place award for best editorial, 1993. Mem. Soc. Profl. Journalists. Democrat. Roman Catholic. Home: PO Box 1144 Oroville WA 98844-1144 Office: Okanogan Valley Gazette- Tribune 813 Central Ave Oroville WA 98844

DE VONTINE, JULIE ELISABETH (THE MARCHIONESS DE ROE DEVON), writer, lawyer; b. Edmund, Wis., Jan. 7, 1934; d. Clyde Elroy and Matilda Evangeline Knapp; m. Roe (Don Davis) Devon Gerringer-Busenbark, Sept. 30, 1968 (dec. Dec. 1972); student Madison Bus. Coll., 1952, San Francisco State Coll., 1953-54, Vivian Rich Sch. Fashion Design, 1955, Dale Carnegie Sch., 1956, Arthur Murray Dance Studio, 1956, Biscayne Acad. Music, 1957, L.A. City Coll., 1960-62, Santa Monica (Calif.) Jr. Coll., 1963; JD U. Calif., San Francisco, 1973; postgrad. Wharton Sch., U. Pa., 1977, London Art Coll., 1979; Ph.D., 1979; attended Goethe Inst., 1985. Bar: Calif., 1965. Actress, Actors Workshop San Francisco, 1959, 65, Theatre of Arts Beverly Hills (Calif.), 1963, also radio; cons, and systems analyst for banks and pub. accounting agys.; artist, poet, singer, songwriter, playwright, dress designer. Pres., tchr. Environ Improvement, Originals by Elizabeth; atty. Dometrik's, JIT-MAP, San Francisco, 1973—; steering com. explorations in worship, ordained min. 1978. Author: The Cardinal, 1947, Explorations in Worship, 1965, The Magic of Scents, 1967, New Highways, 1967, The Grace of Romance, 1968, Happening - Impact-Mald, 1971, Seven Day Rainbow, 1972, Zachary's Adversaries, 1974, Fifteen from Iowa, 1977, Bart's White Elephant, 1978, Skid Row Minister, 1978, Points in Time, 1979, Special Appointment-A Clown in Town, 1979, Happenings, 1980, Candles, 1980, Votes from the Closet, 1984, Wait for Me, 1984, The Stairway, 1984, The River is a Rock, 1985, Happenings Revisited, 1986, Comparative Religion in the United States, 1986, Lumber in the Skies, 1986, The Fifth Season, 1987, Summer Thoughts, 1987, Crimes of the Heart, 1987, Toast Thoughts, 1988, The Contrast of Russian Literature Through the Eyes of Russian Authors, 1988, A Thousand Points of Light, 1989, The Face in the Mirror, 1989, Sea Gulls, 1990, Voices on the Hill, 1991, It's Tough to Get a Matched Set, 1991, Equality, 1991, Miss Geranium Speaks, 1991, Forest Voices, 1991, Golden Threads, 1991, Castles in the Air, 1991, The Cave, 1991, Angels, 1991, Real, 1991, An Appeal to Reason, 1992, We Knew, 1992, Like It Is, 1992, Politicians Anonymous, 1993, Wheels Within Wheels, 1994. Mem. Assn. of Trial Lawyers of Am. Address: 1500 W El Camino Ave # 382 Sacramento CA 95833-1945

DEVORE, JOHN PAUL, county official; b. Akron, Ohio, Nov. 24, 1943; s. Paul and Margareatha DeVore; married, June 12, 1965; children: John David, Wesley Anne. BS in Polit. Sci., Ariz. State U., 1972. Mgr. MasterCharge Great Western Bank & Trust Co., Phoenix, 1972-74; adminstrv. asst. Native Ams. Community Action, Flagstaff, Ariz., 1974-75; asst. dir. area agy. on aging No. Ariz. Coun. Govts., Flagstaff, 1975-76, acting dir. Headstart, 1976, sr. human resource planner, 1976-77, chief human resource div., 1977-79; grants officer Missoula (Mont.) County, 1979-81, interim dir. Five Valley Econ. Devel. Dist., 1980, ops. officer, 1981-87, adminstrv. officer, 1987—; cons. State of Utah., Ackco, Inc., Boulder, Colo., WASSKA Tech. Systems and Rsch. Co., San Diego, Tribal Am. Cons. Corp., Downey, Calif. Author: Resource Development Manual for Title VI Project Staff, 1981, Weatherization Management Manual for Region VIII Grantees, 1982, Management Training Manual for Confederated Tribes of the Umatilla Indian Reservation, 1982, Grants Administration Manual for Tribal Administrators, 1984. Mem. Mont. Rural Devel. Coun., Missoula Correctional Svcs., Inc., Dist. 11 Human Resource Coun., Missoula Aging Found.; bd. dirs. Larchmont Golf Course; chair Planning Policy Coord. Com. Office: Missoula County Courthouse Anx Missoula MT 59802

DEVORE, MARILYN RUTH, education educator, consultant; b. Torrance, Calif., Mar. 6, 1947; d. Floyd Raymond and MaryEllen (Jordon) DeVore; numerous foster children. BA in Edn., Ariz. State U., 1968; MA in Adminstrn., Columbia Pacific U., 1979, PhD in Curriculum Devel., 1981. Cert. elem. tchr., math., tchr., adminstr., Calif. Tchr. Ocean View Sch. Dist., Huntington Beach, Calif., 1968-77; tchr. San Juan Ridge Union Sch. Dist., North San Juan, Calif., 1977-79, prin./supt., 1979-83, hmesch. program devel., 1979-83; program dir. Butte County Office Edn., Oroville, Calif., 1983-88; tchr. homesch. program Marysville (Calif.) Joint Unified Sch. Dist., 1988—; man contbr./cons. Idea & Co., North San Juan, 1982-89; alternative edn. cons. Calif. State Dept. Edn., Sacramento, 1981—; feasibility and needs specialist to numerous pvt. and pub. schs.; presenter in field. Author: The Home School Parent Manual, 1985; co-author: books, manuals, and curricula. Officer, mem. PTA, Huntington Beach, 1968-77; bd. dirs. San Juan Vol. Fire Dept. North San Juan, 1978-82; treas. Forbestown (Calif.) Adv. Coun., 1990—; v.p., mem. Yuba Feather Hist. Assn. and Mus., Forbestown, 1989—; adult edn. and continuation tchr., Forbestown, 1989—. Recipient Tchr. of Yr. award San Juan Tchrs. Assn., 1981. Mem. NEA (nat. del. 1970-76), Calif. Tchrs. Assn. (rep., Golden Apple awrd 1975), Ocean View Tchrs. Assn. (pres. 1975-77), Marysville Unified Tchrs. Assn., Learning Alternatives Resources Network, Nat. Assn. Investors, Habitat for Humanity. Democrat. Christian. Office: Abraham Lincoln Sch 1919 B St Marysville CA 95901

DE VRIES, KENNETH LAWRENCE, mechanical engineer, educator; b. Ogden, Utah, Oct. 27, 1933; s. Sam and Fern (Slater) DeV.; m. Kay M. McGee, Mar. 1, 1959; children: Kenneth, Susan. AS in Civil Engring., Weber State Coll., 1953; BSME, U. Utah, 1959, PhD in Physics, Mech. Engring., 1962. Registered profl. engr., Utah. Rsch. engr. hydraulic group Convair Aircraft Corp., Fort Worth, 1957-58; prof. dept. mech. engring. U. Utah, Salt Lake City, 1962—, mem. faculty, 1969—; prof. dept. mech. and indsl. engring., 1976—; Disting. prof. U. Utah, Salt Lake City, 1991—, chmn. dept., 1970-81, assoc. dean rsch. Coll. Engring., 1983—; program dir. div. materials rsch. NSF, Washington, 1975-76; materials cons. Browning, Morgan, Utah, 1972—; cons. 3M Co., Mpls., 1985—; tech. adv. bd. Emerson Electric, St. Louis, 1978—; mem. Utah Coun. Sci. and Tech., 1973-77; trustee Gordon Rsch. Conf., 1989—, chair, 1992-93. Co-author: Analysis and Testing of Adhesive Bonds, 1978; contbr. chpts. to numerous books, articles and abstracts to profl. publs. Fellow ASME, Am. Phys. Soc.; mem. Am. Chem. Soc. (polymer div.), Soc. Engring. Scis. (nat. officer), Adhesion Soc. (nat. officer). Mem. LDS Ch. Office: U Utah Coll Engring 2220 Merrill Engring Bldg Salt Lake City UT 84112

DEVYLDER, EMIL RAYMOND, investment executive; b. Kamsack, Sask., Can., July 16, 1930; s. Raymond Adolph and Rose (Cleutinx) DeV.; m. Marjorie Skrepnechuk, June 30, 1956. Student, Vancouver (Can.) Vocat., 1952; AS, Community Coll. So. Nev., 1981. Cert. single engine land pilot, 1971. Offset press operator Capital News, Kelowna, B.C., Can., 1948-51; field engr. Finning Tractor, Vancouver, 1952-56; owner, operator Starview Motel, Boulder City, Nev., 1957-78, Stagecoach Saloon, Boulder City, 1975-78; pres. Star-D-Inc. Investments, Boulder City, 1973—; mgr. electronics Community Coll. Southern Nev. (formerly Clark County Community Coll.), Las Vegas, 1981-94; bd. dirs. PAI-D-Inc., Boulder City; band leader Country & Western Fiddler, Kelowna, B.C., 1948-51. Inventor pick-pocket proof wallet. Mem. Elks, Phi Lambda Alpha. Democrat. Episcopalian. Home: 1243 Tamarisk Ln Boulder City NV 89005-2629

DEW, THOMAS RODERICK, museum librarian; b. N.Y.C., Dec. 16, 1940; s. Thomas Roderick and Sarah Montague (Caperton) D. BA, Yale U., 1963; MA in Librarianship, U. Denver, 1970, MA in History of Art, 1976. Asst. libr. Colorado Springs (Colo.) Fine Arts Ctr., 1977-78, libr., 1979—. Editorial adv. bd. Native Peoples mag. With U.S. Army, 1965-67. Mem. Art Librs. Soc. N.Am., Descendents of the Signers of the Declaration of Independence. Home: 1124 N Hancock Ave Colorado Springs CO 80903-2760 Office: Colorado Springs Fine Arts Ctr 30 W Dale St Colorado Springs CO 80903-3210

DEWALL-OWENS, KAREN MARIE, marketing consultant; b. Phoenix, May 31, 1943; d. Merle C. and Agnes M. (Larson) Feller; m. Charles E. DeWall, Sept. 3, 1963 (div. Feb. 1988); 1 child, Leslie Karen; m. John Dailor Owens, Apr. 16, 1995. AA, Phoenix Coll., 1969. Media buyer Wade Advt., Sacramento, 1964-66; media dir., Harwood Advt., Phoenix, 1967-71; co-owner, account exec. DeWall & Assocs. Advt. Co., 1971-87; dir. advt. Auto Media, Inc./Automotive Investment Group, Phoenix, 1987-93; owner Karen & Co. Advt., Phoenix, 1993—. Bd. dirs. Bosom Buddies-Breast Cancer Orgn., Sunday on Ctrl. Festivals; sustaining mem. Jr. League of Phoenix; mem. Heritage Sq. Commn., City of Phoenix. Named Ad-2 Advt. Person of Yr., Phoenix, 1984. Mem. Am. Women in Radio and TV (achievement award 1986), Phoenix Union Alumni Assn. Republican. Home: 10847 N 11th St Phoenix AZ 85020-5836 Office: Karen & Co Advt 10847 N 11th St Phoenix AZ 85020-5836

DEWALT, BROOK, theater executive, public relations executive; b. Sept. 5, 1964; s. Frank Pascal and Sydney (Maranov) DeW. AA in Music Edn., Scottsdale (Ariz.) C.C., 1984; BA in Journalism, Pub. Rels., Ariz. State U., 1989. Cert. substitute tchr., Ariz. Office asst. Ariz. Interscholastic Press. Assn., Flagstaff, 1981-86; fine arts office asst. Scottsdale C.C., 1982-84; mgr. AMC Theatres, Mesa, Ariz., 1984-94; pub. rels. cons. Eagle Cons. Group, Glendale, Ariz., 1993—; mgr. Harkins Theatres, Scottsdale, 1994—; guest prof. Ariz. State U., 1991—; substitute tchr. Ariz. Dept. Edn., 1989-91. Exec. posse mem. Maricopa County Sheriffs Office, Ariz., 1993—; media liaison Nat. Charity Awards Dinner, 1992; spl. judicial officer Maricopa County Justice Cts., 1991—; fundraiser various area charitable orgn., Phoenix, 1986-91; active Ariz. Rep. Assembly, 1993—, founding pres., 1993, legislative dist. 29 fin. chmn., 1993—, sec., exec. bd., 1992—; founding ptnr. Competitiveness Ctr. Hudson Inst., 1993—; founding assoc. Empower Am., 1993—; cand. Ariz. Ho. of Reps., 1993-94. Recipient Svc. Commendation award Maricopa Coutny Justice Cts., 1994, Spl. Achievement award Eastman Kodak Co., 1992, Mkting. Concept award Hollywood Reporter, 1989, 91. Mem. Pub. Rels. Soc. Am. (profl. devel. com. Phoenix chpt. 1989—, chmn. 1993, cmty. rels. com. co-chmn. 1994), Ariz. State U. Alumni Assn., Lincoln Caucus, Phi Theta Kappa. Republican. Mem. LDS Ch. Home: 132 E Brown Rd Apt 3034 Mesa AZ 85201-3560

DE WEERDT, MARK MURRAY, judge; b. Cologne, Germany, May 6, 1928; arrived in Can., 1949.; s. Hendrik Eugen and Ina Dunbar (Murray) de W.; m. Linda Anne Alden Hadwen, Mar. 31, 1956; children: Simon André, Murray Hadwen, David Lockhart, Charles Dunbar. MA, Glasgow (Scotland) U., 1949; LLB, B.C. U., 1955. Cert. barrister and solicitor, B.C. 1956, N.W.T. 1958. Assoc. solicitor Cross & O'Grady, Victoria, B.C., 1956-

57; adv. coun. Can. Dept. Justice, Ottawa, 1957-58; Crown Atty. Yellowknife, N.W.T., 1958-63; sr. counsel Can. Dept. Justice, Vancouver, 1976-79, gen. counsel and dir., 1979-81; sr. ptnr. deWeerdt, Searle, Finall et al., Yellowknife, N.W.T., 1958-71; magistrate and juvenile ct. judge N.W.T. Magistrate's Ct., Yellowknife, N.W.T., 1971-73; gen. solicitor Ins. Corp. B.C., Vancouver, 1974-76; justice N.W.T and Yukon Supreme Cts., Yellowknife & Whitehorse, 1981—, N.W.T and Yukon Cts. of Appeal, 1981-; chairperson judicial coun. N.W.T., Yellowknife, 1981—; dir. Canadian Judges' Conf., 1982-89; alternating mem. Can. Judicial Coun., 1985-7, 89-91, 93-95. Author profl. papers. Vice-chmn. Yellowknife Sch. Dist. #1, 1964-68. Apptd. Queen's Coun., Can., 1968. Mem. Can. Bar Assn., Can. Inst. Administrn. Justice (life), N.W.T. Bar Assn. (pres. 1967-71), MacKenzie River and N.W.T. Progressive Conservation Assn. (pres. 1959-71). Office: Court House, PO Box 1439, Yellowknife, NT Canada X1A 2PI

DEWEY, DONALD ODELL, university dean; b. Portland, Oreg., July 9, 1930; s. Leslie Hamilton and Helen (Odell) D.; m. Charlotte Marion Neuber, Sept. 21, 1952; children—Leslie Helen, Catherine Dawn, Scott Hamilton. Student, Lewis and Clark Coll., 1948-49; B.A., U. Oreg., 1952; M.S., U. Utah, 1956; Ph.D., U. Chgo., 1960. Mng. editor Condon (Oreg.) Globe-Times, 1952-53; city editor Ashland (Oreg.) Daily Tidings, 1953-54; asst. editor, assoc. editor The Papers of James Madison, Chgo., 1957-62; instr. U. Chgo., 1960-62; asst. prof., assoc. prof., prof. Calif. State U.-Los Angeles, 1962—, dean Sch. Letters and Sci., 1970-84, dean Sch. Natural and Social Sci., 1984—. Author: The Continuing Dialogue, 2 Vols., 1964, Union and Liberty: Documents in American Constitutionalism, 1969, Marshall versus Jefferson: The Political Background of Marbury v. Madison, 1970, Becoming Informed Citizens: Lessons on the Constitution for Junior High School Students, 1988, Invitation to the Dance: An Introduction to Social Dance, 1991, Becoming Informed Citizens: The Bill of Rights and Limited Government, 1995. Recipient Outstanding Prof. award Calif. State U., 1976. Mem. Am. Hist. Assn. (exec. coun. Pacific Coast br. 1971-74), Orgn. Am. Historians, Am. Soc. Legal History (adv. bd. Pacific Coast br. 1972-75), Gold Key, Phi Alpha Theta, Pi Sigma Alpha, Phi Kappa Phi, Sigma Delta Chi. Office: Calif State U Dept History 5151 State University Dr Los Angeles CA 90032-4221

DEWEY, DONALD WILLIAM, magazine publisher, editor, writer; b. Honolulu, Sept. 30, 1933; s. Donald William and Theckla Jean (Engeborg) D.; m. Sally Rae Ryan, Aug. 7, 1961; children: Michael Kevin, Wendy Ann. Student, Pomona Coll., 1953-55. With Pascoe Steel Corp., Pomona, Calif., 1955-56, div. Reynolds Aluminum Co., Los Angeles, 1956-58, Switzer Panel Corp., Pasadena, Calif., 1958-60; sales and gen. mgr. Western Pre-Cast Concrete Corp., Ontario, Calif., 1960-62; editor, pub. R/C Modeler Mag., Sierra Madre, Calif., 1963—, Freshwater and Marine Aquarium Mag., Sierra Madre, 1978—; pres., chmn. bd. R/C Modeler Corp., Sierra Madre, 1963—. Author: Radio Control From the Ground Up, 1970, Flight Training Course, 1973, For What It's Worth, Vol. 1, 1973, Vol. 2, 1975; contbr. articles to profl. jours. Sustaining mem. Rep. Nat. Com., 1981—; charter mem. Nat. Congl. Club, 1981—; mem. Rep. Presdl. Task Force, 1981—, U.S. Senatorial Club, 1983—, 1984 Presdl. Trust, Conservative Caucus, Nat. Tax Limitation Com., Nat. Conservative Polit. Action Com., Ronald Reagan Presdl. Libr. Served with Hosp. Corps, USN, 1951-53. Mem. Acad. Model Aeronautics, Nat. Aeronautic Assn., Sport Flyers Assn., Exp. Aircraft Assn., Nat. Amateur Radio Assn., Am. Radio Relay League, APS Writers Unit 30, Am. First Day Cover Soc., Am. Philatelic Soc., Am. Tropical Assn., Am. Revenue Assn., Am. Air-Mail Soc., United Postal Stationery Soc., Confederate Stamp Alliance, Bur. Issues Assn., Precancel Stamp Soc., Pitcairn Island Study Group, Am. Ctr. Law & Justice; Claremont Inst., Found. Endowment, Rutherford Inst., Leadership Inst., Heritage Found, Calif. State Sheriff's Assn., Am. Dedn. Police, Ven Order Michael the Archangel (hon. knight.). Republican. Lutheran. Home: 410 W Montecito Ave Sierra Madre CA 91024-1716 Office: 144 W Sierra Madre Blvd Sierra Madre CA 91024-2435

DEWEY, MICHAEL LEE, wood technologist; b. Spokane, Wash., Nov. 9, 1944; s. Leland Sullivan and Lorraine Margaret (Kofmehl) D.; m. Beverly Jean Thompson, Dec. 30, 1967; children: Cheryl, Michelle, Marci, Monica. BS in Wood Tech., U. Idaho, 1968, BS in Chemistry, 1969; AA in Acctg., Mendocino Community Coll., 1980, AA in Bus. Adminstrn., 1980. Chemist, U.S. Plywood, Lebanon, Oreg., 1969-70; wood chemist Koppers Co., Orrville, Ohio, 1971-76; process engr. Masonite Co., Ukiah, Calif., 1976-79, sr. process engr., 1979-82, cost acct., fin. analyst, 1982-83, acctg. mgr., 1983-92, controller Retech Inc., 1992—. Served with USNR, 1966-70. Mem. Am. Chem. Soc., Am. Mgmt. Assn., Forest Products Research Soc., Soc. Wood Sci. and Tech., Am. Legion, Alpha Phi Omega. Republican. Lodges: Elks (officer 1985-90), Lions (Ukiah treas. 1986-88). Home: 25912 Hayward Blvd Apt 206 Hayward CA 94542-1645 Office: Retech Inc PO Box 997 Ukiah CA 95482-0997

DEWEY, RICHARD RYDER, retired internist, educator; b. Westfield, N.J., Feb. 7, 1929; s. Benjamin Harold and Julia (Donlan) D.; m. June Louise Schoknecht, June 2, 1956; children: Richard R. Jr., Valerie Margaret. BA, St. Vincent Coll., 1951; MD, Washington U., St. Louis, 1955. Diplomate Am. Bd. Internal Medicine. Intern Barnes Hosp., St. Louis, 1955-56, asst. resident, 1956-57, fellow in medicine, 1957-58; sr. assoc. resident Strong Meml. Hosp., Rochester, N.Y., 1958-59; clin. instr. Stanford Med. Ctr., Palo Alto, Calif., 1956-64, clin. asst. prof., 1964-74, clin. assoc. prof., 1974-84, clin. prof. Medicine, 1984-94; emeritus clin. prof. medicine, 1994—; pres. Welch Rd. Internal Med. Orgn., Palo Alto, 1985-94. Dir. health commn. Santa Clara County, San Jose, Calif., 1975-76. Sgt. U.S. Army, 1946-48, Korea. Mem. Am. Soc. Internal Medicine. Republican. Roman Catholic. Home: 4 Sunset Ct Menlo Park CA 94025-6730

DEWHURST, TIMOTHY ANDREW, clinical cardiologist, researcher; b. Farnborough, Kent, Eng., Dec. 24, 1961; arrived in Can., 1969; arrived in U.S., 1986; s. William George and Margaret (Dransfield) D.; m. Rebecca Dana Fox, Aug. 21, 1988. BSc in Chem. and Biology with honors, Stanford U., 1982; MD in Rsch. with honors, U. Alberta, Edmonton, Alberta, Can., 1986. Diplomate Am. Bd. Internal Medicine, Am. Bd. Cardiovascular Diseases. Resident internal medicine Emory U. Affiliated Hosps., Atlanta, 1986-89; cardiology fellow U. Washington, Seattle, 1989-91, chief cardiology fellow, 1991-92, interventional cardiology fellow, 1992-93; acting instr. U. Washington Med. Ctr., Seattle, 1992—; staff physician U. Washington Med. Ctr., Seattle VA Med. Ctr., 1992-94; cardiologist The Polyclinic, Seattle, 1994—. Author: (with others) The Practice of Interventional Cardiology, 1993, Nuclear Cardiology: State of the Art and Future Directions, 1993, Nuclear Cardiology, 1994; contbr. to profl. jours. Am. Heart Assn. grantee, 1992-93. Fellow Am. Coll. Cardiology; mem. Am. Heart Assn., Am. Coll. Physicians, Alpha Omega Alpha. Office: The Polyclinic 1145 Broadway Seattle WA 98122-4201

DEWHURST, WILLIAM GEORGE, physician, psychiatrist, educator, researcher; b. Frosterley, Durham, Eng., Nov. 21, 1926; came to Can., 1969; s. William and Elspeth Leslie (Begg) D.; m. Margaret Dransfield, Sept. 17, 1960; children—Timothy Andrew, Susan Jane. B.A., Oxford U., Eng., 1947, B.M., B.Ch., 1950; MA, Oxford U., 1961; D.P.M. with distinction, London U., 1961. House physician, surgeon London Hosp., 1950-52, jr. registrar, registrar, 1954-58; registrar, sr. registrar Maudsley Hosp., London, 1958-62, cons. physician, 1965-69; lectr. Inst. Psychiatry, London, 1962-64, sr. lectr., 1965-69; assoc. prof. psychiatry U. Alta., Edmonton, Can., 1969-72, prof., 1972-92, prof. emeritus, 1992—, Hon. prof. pharmacy and pharm. scis., 1979—, chmn. dept. psychiatry, 1975-90, dir. emeritus neurochem. rsch. unit, 1990—, hon. prof. oncology, 1983—, chmn. med. staff adv. bd., 1988-90; mem. Atty. Gen. Alta. Bd. Rev., 1991, N.W.T. Bd. Rev., 1992; pres.'s coun. U. Alta. Hosps., 1988-90, quality improvement coun., 1988-90, ethics consultative com., 1984-88, planning com. Vision 2000, 1985-87, hosps.' planning com. and joint conf. com., 1971, 80, 87-90; cons. psychiatrist Royal Alexandra Hosp., Edmonton, Edmonton Gen. Hosp., Alberta Hosp., Ponoka, Ponoka Gen. Hosp.; chmn. med. coun. Can. Test Com., 1977-79, Royal Coll. Text Com. in Psychiatry, 1971-80, examiner, 1975-83. Co-editor: Neurobiology of Trace Amines, 1984, Pharmacotherapy of Affective Disorders, 1985; also conf. procs. Referee Nature, Can. Psychiat. Assn. Jour., Brit. Jour. Psychiatry; mem. editorial bd. Neuropsychobiology, Psychiat. Jour. U. Ottawa. Contbr. articles to profl. jours. Chmn. Edmonton Psychiat. Svcs. Steering Com., 1977-80; chmn. Edmonton Psychiat. Svcs. Planning Com., 1985-90; mem. Provincial Mental Health Adv. Coun., 1973-79, Mental Health Rsch. Com., 1973, Edmonton Bd. Health, 1974-76; Can. Psychiat. Rsch. Found., 1985— (also bd. dirs.); bd. dirs. Friends of Schizophrenics, 1980—, Alta., 1988; grant referee Health & Welfare Can., Med. Rsch. Coun. Can., Ont. Mental Health Found., Man. Health Rsch. Coun., B.C. Health Rsch. Found. Capt. Royal Army M.C., 1952-54. Fellow Can. Coll. Neuropsychopharmacology (pres. 1982-84, Coll. medal 1993), Am. Psychopathol. Assn., Am. Coll. Psychiatrists, Am. Psychiat. Assn., Royal Coll. Psychiatrist; mem. AAAS, Alta. Psychiat. Assn. (pres. 1973-74), Can. Psychiat. Assn. (pres. 1983-84), Alta Coll. Physicians and Surgeons, Alta. Med. Assn., Child and Adolescent Assn. (bd. dirs., v.p. 1992), Assn. for Acad. Psychiatry, Brit. Med. Assn., Faculty Club. Anglican. Office: U Alta Dept Psychiatry, 1E1 01 Mackenzie Ctr, Edmonton, AB Canada T6G 2B7

DEWILDE, DAVID MICHAEL, executive search consultant, financial services executive, lawyer; b. Bridgeton, N.J., Aug. 11, 1940; s. Louis and Dorothea (Donnelly) deW.; m. Katherine August, Dec. 30, 1984; children: Holland Stockdale, Christian DuCroix, Nicholas Alexander, Lucas Barrymore. AB, Dartmouth Coll., 1962; LLB, U. Va., 1967; MS in Mgmt., Stanford U., 1984. Bar: N.Y. 1968, D.C. 1972. Assoc. Curtis, Mallet-Prevost, Colt & Mosle, N.Y.C., 1967-69; assoc. gen. counsel HUD, Washington, 1969-72; investment banker Lehman Bros., Washington, 1972-74; dep. commr. FHA, Washington, 1974-76; pres. Govt. Nat. Mortgage Assn., Washington, 1976-77; mng. dir. Lepercq DeNeuflize & Co., N.Y.C., 1977-81; exec. v.p. policy and planning Fed. Nat. Mortgage Assn., Washington, 1981-82; pres. deWilde & Assocs., Washington, 1982-84; mng. dir., dir. fin. svcs. Boyden Internat., San Francisco, 1984-88; chief exec. officer Chartwell Ptnrs. Internat., San Francisco, 1989—; bd. dirs. Strategic Mortgage Investors, Glendale, Calif., 1985-89, Berkshire Realty Investment Trust, 1993—, Fritzi of Claif., 1993—. Editor-in-chief Va. Jour. Internat. Law, 1966-67. Lt. USN, 1962-64. Mem. Metropolitan Club (Washington), Belvedere Tennis Club. Republican. Office: Chartwell Ptnrs Internat 275 Battery St Ste 2180 San Francisco CA 94111-3336

DEWITT, BARBARA JANE, journalist; b. Glendale, Calif., Aug. 5, 1947; d. Clarence James and Irene Lottie (Kieborz) Brezina; m. Don DeWitt, Apr. 21, 1974; children: Lisa, Scarlett. BA in Journalism, Calif. State U., Northridge, 1971. Features editor The Daily Ind. Newspaper, Ridgecrest, Calif., 1971-84; fashion editor The Daily Breeze, Torrance, Calif., 1984-89; fashion reporter The Seattle Times, 1990; fashion reporter, columnist The Daily News, L.A., 1990—; instr. fashion writing UCLA, 1988. Dir. Miss Indian Wells Valley Scholarship Pageant, 1980-84. Recipient 1st Pl. Best Youth Page, Calif. Newspaper Pubs. Assn., 1980, 1st Pl. Best Fashion, Wash. Press Assn., 1989. Republican. Lutheran. Office: The Daily News 21221 Oxnard St Woodland Hills CA 91367-5015

DEWITT, JOHN BELTON, retired conservation executive; b. Oakland, Calif., Jan. 13, 1937; s. Belton and Florence Jeffery D.; m. Karma Lee Sowers, Sept. 17, 1960. BA in Wildlife Conservation, U. Calif., Berkeley, 1959. With U.S. Forest Svc. El Dorado Nat. Forest, 1955-56; ranger naturalist Nat. Park Svc., Yosemite Nat. Park, 1957-58, Mt. Rainer Nat. Park, 1959, Death Valley Nat. Monument, 1960; land law examiner, info. officer, land appraiser Bur. of Land Mgmt., Sacramento, 1960-64; asst. sec. Save-the-Redwoods League, 1964-71; dir. No. Calif. chpt. Nature Conservancy, 1976-77; dir. Tuolumne River Preservation Trust, 1981-85; exec. dir., sec. Save-the-Redwoods League, 1971-95; adv. coun. Trust for Pub. Land, 1975-78, Anza Borrego Desert Com., 1983-93; advisor to U.S. Sec. Interior (4 adminstrns.). Author: California Redwood Parks and Preserves, 1982, 3d edit., 1993. Recipient Nat. Conservation award DAR, 1982, Golden Bear award Calif. State Park & Recreation Commn., 1982, Gulf Oil Conservation award, 1985, Calif. State Park Partnership award, 1995; named hon. Calif. Park Ranger, 1985, Nat. Park Ranger, 1995; hon. recognition Calif. State Assembly, 1995. Mem. Sierra Club (conservation com. 1953-63), Am. Forestry Assn., Nat. Parks Assn., Wilderness Soc., Nat. Audubon Soc. Office: Save the Redwoods League 114 Sansome St Ste 605 San Francisco CA 94104-3814

DEWOLFE, FRED STANLEY, social science educator, consultant; b. Seattle, Jan. 7, 1928; s. Tom E. and Mary (Chamberlain) DeW.; m. Brigitte Stolwitzer, Feb. 10, 1955; children: Andrew, Christopher. BA, Lewis & Clark Coll., 1954; MA, Portland U., 1960, Reed Coll., 1963. Mgr. speakers bur. Southwestern Oreg. Community Coll., Coos Bay, Oreg., 1962-63; chmn. faculty assn. Clackamas Community Coll., Oregon City, Oreg., 1968-70; film lectr., N.W. Film Studies Ctr. Clackamas Community Coll., Oregon City, 1970's, chmn. social sci. dept., 1967—; cons., discussant on war and architecture on various TV stas., Portland, 1970—: staff writer N.W. Examiner, Portland. Author: Impressions of Portland, 1970, Old Portland, 1973, Portland West, 1976, Portland Tradition Buildings and People, 1980, Heritage Lost: Two Portlaand Mansions through the Lens of Minorwhite, 1995; contbr. articles to profl. jours. Dir. S.W. Hills Residential League, 1989. With U.S. Army, 1951. Decorated Purple Heart. Mem. Oreg. Hist. Soc., Multnomah, Athletic Club. Home: 2752 SW Roswell Ave Portland OR 97201-1664 Office: Clackamas Community Coll 19600 S Molalla Ave Oregon City OR 97045-8980

DEWOOD, MARCUS ALBERT, nuclear cardiologist, researcher; b. Spokane, Wash., May 7, 1949; s. Edward A. and Eileen N. (Norton) DeW. BS in Biology, Gonzaga U., 1970; MD, Creighton U., 1974. Diplomate Am. Bd. Internal Medicine (internal medicine, cardiovascular disease). Intern Sacred Heart Med. Ctr., Spokane, 1976-77; resident dept. medicine Creighton U., 1977-78; fellow in cardiology Cedars Sinai Med. Ctr., L.A., 1978-79, U. Calif., Davis, 1979-80; staff cardiologist Sacred Heart Med. Ctr., Deaconess Med. Ctr., Spokane, 1981—, dir. cardiovascular rsch., 1983-93; dir. cardiovascular rsch. and nuclear cardiology The Heart Inst. of Spokane, 1990-93; dir. nuclear lab. Med. Ctr. Imaging, Spokane, 1994—; cons. Cardiorenal Adv. Bd., FDA, 1992—; pres. Spokane Heart Rsch. Found., 1983—; manuscript reviewer Am. Jour. Cardiology, Circulation, Can. Med. Assn., Jour. AMA, Annals of Internal Medicine, Am. Jour. Medicine, New Eng. Jour. Medicine, N.Y. State Jour. Medicine, Jour. Am. Coll. Cardiology; conf. speaker. Contbr. numerous articles, abstracts to profl. jours., chpts. to books. Fellow Am. Coll. Cardiology; mem. AAAS, N.Y. Acad. Scis., Am. Fedn. Clin. Rsch., Am. Heart Assn., Am. Soc. Nuclear Cardiology (founding mem.), Alpha Omega Alpha. Office: Med Ctr Cardiology 820 S Mcclellan St Ste 226 Spokane WA 99204-2446

DE WREEDE, CLARICE EVANS, retired special education educator; b. East St. Louis, Ill., July 12, 1928; d. Cecil Field and Clara Helen (Kindsvater) Evans; m. Harry Richard Schoen, June 21, 1947 (div. 1964); children: Richard Evans, Sara Diane, William Francis; m. John De Wreede, Mar. 29, 1967 (dec. 1986). BA cum laude, Mich. State U., 1964; postgrad., U. Mich., 1966-67, Santa Clara U., 1973. Tchr. Grand Rapids (Mich.) Sch. Dist., 1963-67; tchr. counselor for physically handicapped Kent County Edn. Dist., Grand Rapids, 1967-71; tchr. of deaf Union Sch. Dist., San Jose, Calif., 1971-88; home-tchr. of deaf East Side Union High Sch. Dist., San Jose, 1991. Mem. DAR (John Mitchell chpt. Anchorage), Daus. of Am. Colonists (Ala. chpt.), Am. Hist. Soc. of Germans from Russia (Golden Gate chpt. sec. 1990—), Calif. Assn for Tchrs. of Hearing-Impaired, Internat. Assn. Cancer Victors and Friends (nat. bd. govs. 1990—), South Bay Scottish Soc. Genealogy (chmn. 1991—), Santa Clara County Hist. and Geneal. Soc. (cons. in libr. genealogy room, chmn. family newsletter 1980—), Daus. of 1812 (David Farragut chpt. Santa Clara County, Calif.). Democrat. Lutheran. Home: 2296 Whitaker Dr Kearns UT 84118-1683

DEXTER, PETER WHITTEMORE, columnist, writer; b. Pontiac, Mich., July 22, 1943; m. Dian McDonough; 1 child, Casey. BA, U. S.D., 1969. Columnist Phila. Daily News, 1976-86, Esquire mag., N.Y.C., 1985-86, Sacramento Bee, 1986—. Author: (novels) God's Pocket, 1983, Dead Wood, 1986, Paris Trout, 1988 (Nat. Book award 1988), The Paperboy, 1994. Recipient Mark Twain award AP, Calif.-Nev., 1987, Penn West award, L.A., 1988, Bay Area Book Revs. award, 1988. Office: Sacramento Bee 21st & Q Sts Sacramento CA 95852

DEY, CAROL RUTH, secondary education educator; b. N.Y., Mar. 9, 1943; d. Robert Lewis Adelson and Anne Millman; m. John Peter Dey, Feb. 9, 1968 (div. Feb. 1978). AA, San Bernardino Valley Coll., 1965; BA, Calif. State U., Sacramento, 1969; MBA, Calif. State U., San Bernardino, 1983, postgrad., 1994—. Sec. U.S. Dept of Interior, USAF, Retail Industry, San Bernardino, Sacramento, Calif., 1960-80; logistics mgr. USAF, San Bernardino, 1980-94; substitute tchr. San Bernardino Unified Sch. Dist., 1994—. Dancer Coppélia, San Bernardino, Calif., 1984; mem. St. Anne's Ch., San Bernardino, 1978—. Mem. Am. Bus. Women's Assn. (Calif. State Coll. scholar), Smithsonian Inst., AF Assn., Alumni Assn. Calif. State U. San Bernardino. Republican. Roman Catholic.

DHADA, MUSTAFAH, political scientist, educator; b. Nova-Lusitania, Mozambique, Manica-E-Sofalia, Nov. 18, 1951; came to U.S., 1987; s. Dawood and Zubeda (Karatella) D.; m. Safiah Henrietta von Bissing, Aug. 7, 1981; children: Roxana von Bissing, Zubeda von Bissing. BA with honors, Sussex U., Falmer, Eng., 1977; PhD, U. Oxford, Eng., 1984. Legal drafter Subud Human Welfare Trust, U.K., 1978-79; lectr. Islamic Cultural Ctr., Eng., 1980-81, Keble Coll., Oxford, Eng., 1981-84; founder, dir. Oceans Internat. Svcs., Leeds, Eng., 1982-84; asst. prof. U.S. Internat. U., London, 1984-86; cons., assoc. prof. The Am. Coll., Leysin, Switzerland, 1987-89; tech. writer, cons. Software Helpline, London, 1989; assoc. prof. U. No. Colo., Greeley, 1990—; dir., gen. factotum The Gilt-Edge, Greeley, 1991—. Author: (book) Mustafah Dhada, Warriors At Work, 1993; contbr. articles to profl. jours. and chpts. to books. Seminar speaker in field for Greeley Cmty. Mem. Am. Polit. Sci. Assn., African Studies Assn., Internat. Studies Assn., Western Polit. Sci. Assn., Third World Studies Assn., Internat. Sculpture Ctr. Home: 4932 W 8th Street Rd Greeley CO 80634-1929 Office: U No Colo Smith House Greeley CO 80639

DHUEY, MICHAEL JOSEPH, computer engineer; b. Milw., July 20, 1958; s. Joseph Norbert and Anne King (Neinuber) D.; 1 child, Erica. BSEE, U. Wis., 1980. Computer programmer Northwest Mutal Life, Milw., 1974-80; computer engr. Apple Computer, Cupertino, Calif., 1980—. Designer Macintosh II Computer, 1987. Mem. IEEE, ACM. Office: Apple Computer 1 Infinite Loop Cupertino CA 95014-2083

DIAMOND, AVIVA, communications consultant; b. New York, May 14, 1953; d. Herbert and Lynne D. Student, Hebrew U., 1972-73; BA in French and English with honors, Wellesley Coll., 1974; MS in Journalism, Columbia U., 1976. Anchor, producer, reporter Sta. WAAB Radio, Worcester, Mass., 1974-75; staff reporter The Miami Herald, Fla., 1976-77; mgmt. trainee Westinghouse Broadcasting, Boston, 1977-78; reporter, anchor Sta. WRAL-TV, Raleigh, N.C., 1978-79; med. reporter Sta. KTVI, St. Louis, 1979-82; corr. ABC Network News, L.A., 1982-84; anchor, reporter Sta. KATV, Little Rock, 1985-87; v.p. Ready for Media, L.A., 1988-90; pres. Blue Streak A Communications Co., L.A., 1990—. Recipient Emmy award, 1980, Emmy nominations 1981, 82, Feature Reporting award Sigma Delta Chi, 1985, RTNDA Regional award Spot News, 1979; Wellesley Coll. scholar, 1974; Columbia U. Internat. fellow, 1975-76. Mem. Pub. Rels. Soc. Am. Office: Blue Streak A Communications Co 1817 Hillcrest Rd Ste 42 Los Angeles CA 90068-3150

DIAMOND, DAVID MARK, neurobiologist, educator; b. Newark, Aug. 14, 1957; s. Robert and Arlene (Cohen) D.; children: Elise, Matthew. BS in Biology, U. Calif., Irvine, 1980, PhD in Neurobiology, 1985. Postdoctoral fellow U. Calif., Irvine, 1985-86; postdoctoral fellow U. Colo. Health Sci. Ctr., Denver, 1986-90, instr. neurobiology, 1990-93, asst. prof., 1993—; rsch. biologist VA Med. Ctr., Denver, 1989—; grant/manuscript referee NSF Neurobiology Jours., 1990—. Contbr. articles to profl. jours. Office of Naval Rsch. grantee, 1991—, VA Med. Ctr. grantee, 1990—. Mem. Soc. for Neurosci., Internat. Brain Rsch. Orgn., Rocky Mountain Region Neurosci., N.Y. Acad. Scis., Toastmasters Orgn. (pres. Denver 1990). Home: 10150 E Harvard Ave Apt D532 Denver CO 80231-3928 Office: U Colo Health Sci Ctr Dept Pharmacology Campus Box C236 Denver CO 80262

DIAMOND, JEFFREY BRIAN, lawyer; b. N.Y.C., Sept. 17, 1950; s. Norman and Sylvia (Kurinsky) D.; m. Evalynn Joyce Stern, Apr. 15, 1977. BA, Dickinson Coll., 1972; JD, Pepperdine U., 1976. Bar: N.Mex. 1976, U.S. Dist. Ct. N.Mex. 1980, U.S. Ct. Appeals (10th cir.) 1985. Ptnr. Shuler & Diamond, Carlsbad, N.Mex., 1976-77, Paine, Blenden & Diamond, Carlsbad, N.Mex., 1977-92; prin. Jeffrey B. Diamond P.A., Carlsbad, N.Mex., 1992—; atty. Eddy County, Carlsbad, 1983-84. Chmn. Eddy County Dems., Carlsbad, 1981-85; pres. Carlsbad Jewish Congregation, 1979-81, Carlsbad Mental Health Assn., 1985-89, also founder Carlsbad Area Counselling and Resource Ctr., 1977-83, also bd. dirs.; sec. Eddy County Sheriff's Posse, 1987-90; pres. Carlsbad Mcpl. Schs. Bd. Edn., 1989-91; bd. dirs. Anti-Defamation League (B'nai Brith), 1990—, Boys and Girls Club of Carlsbad. Mem. ABA, ATLA, N.Mex. Bar Assn., Eddy County Bar Assn., N.Mex. Trial Lawyers Assn., Elks. Home: 1427 Verdel Ave Carlsbad NM 88220-9233 Office: Jeffrey B Diamond PA 323 W Mermod Carlsbad NM 88220

DIAMOND, JOSEF, lawyer; b. L.A., Mar. 6, 1907; s. Michael and Ruby (Shifrin) D.; m. Violett Diamond, Apr. 2, 1933 (dec. 1979); children: Joel, Diane Foreman; m. Ann Dulien, Jan. 12, 1981 (dec. 1984); m. Muriel Bach, 1986. B.B.A., U. Wash., 1929, J.D., 1931. Bar: Wash. 1931, U.S. Dist. Ct. (we. dist.) Wash. 1932, U.S. Ct. Appeals (9th cir.) 1934, U.S. Supreme Ct. 1944. Assoc. Caldwell & Lycette, Seattle, 1931-35; ptnr. Caldwell, Lycette & Diamond, 1935-45; ptnr. Lycette, Diamond & Sylvester, 1945-80, Diamond & Sylvester, 1980-82, of counsel, 1982-88; of counsel Short, Cressman & Burgess, 1988—; chmn. bd. Diamond Parking Inc., Seattle, 1945-70; cons. various businesses. Bd. dirs. Am. Heart Assn., 1960; chmn. Wash. Heart Assn., 1962. Col. JAGC U.S. Army, World War II. Decorated Legion of Merit. Mem. Assn. Trial Lawyers Wash., Wash. Bar Assn., Seattle Bar Assn., The Beavers, Mil. Engrs. Soc., Wash. Athletic Club, Bellevue Athletic Club, Harbor Club, Seattle Yacht Club, Rainier Club. Office: 3000 First Interstate Ctr 999 3rd Ave Seattle WA 98104-4001

DIAMOND, MILTON, anatomy and reproductive biology educator; b. N.Y.C., Mar. 6, 1934; s. Aaron and Jennie (Arbor) D.; m. Grace H. Whitney, Dec. 18, 1955 (dec. Sept. 1989); children: Hinda Louise, Irene Wanda, Sara Elizabeth, Leah Naiomi. BS, CCNY, 1955; PhD, U. Kans., 1962. Instr., asst. prof. anatomy U. Louisville, 1962-67; assoc. prof. anatomy U. Hawaii, 1967-71, prof. anatomy and reproductive biology, 1971—; rsch. prof. psychiatry SUNY, Stony Brook, 1976-78; dir. Pacific Ctr. for Sex and Soc., 1985—; dept. edn. State of Hawaii, 1971-88, NSF/NIH, 1973-88, others; prin. investigator various studies on abortion and contraception and sex. Author: Abortion Politics, 1976, Sexual Decision, 1980, Sex Watching, 1984, 2d edit., 1992, AIDS: Love, Sex, Disease, 1989; editor: Perspectives in Reproduction and Sexual Behavior, 1967; mem. editl. bd. Archives Sexual Behavior, Jour. Psychology and Human Sexuality, others. Chair Hawaii AIDS Task Group, 1985-92. 1st lt. U.S. Army, 1955-58. Fellow Soc. for Scientific Study of Sex (pres. western region 1987); mem. Am. Assn. Sex Educators, Counselors and Therapists (cert. educator, therapist), Animal Behavior Soc. (charter), Harry Benjamin Internat. Soc. for Gender Dysphoria, Internat. Acad. Sex Rsch. (charter), Soc. for Devel. Psychobiology, Soc. for Study of Reproduction (charter), Assn. Sexologists (charter), Polish Acad. Sexological Sci. (hon., Sodalem honoris causa). Office: U Hawaii Sch Medicine 1951 E West Rd Honolulu HI 96822-2321

DIAMOND, RICHARD, secondary education educator; b. N.Y.C., June 23, 1936; s. Oscar and Frieda (Rosenfeld) D.; m. Donna Jean Berkshire Wilson, June 14, 1961 (div. June 1974); m. Betty Ruth Jane Foster, Nov. 17, 1975; children: Thomas, Laura, Rick, Jeff. BA, U. Calif., Berkeley, 1958. Cert. tchr., Calif. Tchr. Riverside (Calif.) Unified Schs., 1959-67, 73—, coord. social studies, 1967-69, program dir., 1969-72, attendance officer, 1972-73. Contbr. articles and photographs to profl. and popular publs. Dem. party worker, 1964-72; Rep. party worker, 1992—. Named Social Studies Tchr. of Yr., Inland Empire Social Studies Assn., 1980, Tchr. of Yr., Arlington H.S., Riverside, 1992; recipient hon. svc. award Dist. Coun. PTA, Riverside, 1993. Mem. NEA, Calif. Tchrs. Assn., Riverside County Tchrs. Assn. Presbyterian. Office: Arlington HS 2951 Jackson St Riverside CA 92503-5732

DIAMOND, ROCHELLE ANNE, biologist; b. Phoenix, Aug. 9, 1951; d. Harold and Helen (Garfinkle) D.; m. Clifford L. Sailor Jr., July 6, 1976 (div. 1985). BA in Molecular Biology, U. Calif., Santa Barbara, 1974. Technician U. So. Calif., L.A., 1974-77; rsch. technician City of Hope Nat. Med. Ctr., Duarte, Calif., 1978-81; assoc. biologist UCLA, 1981-82; rsch. biologist

Calif. Inst. Tech., Pasadena, 1982-91, chief opr., tech. applications specialist cell sorting facility, 1984—, mem. profl. staff, 1991—. Guest editor Methods, 1991; contbr. articles to profl. jours. Com. mem. AIDS Project L.A. Med. Adv. Com., 1985-87; bd. dirs., v.p. Lesbian and Gay Health and Health Policy Found., 1994—. Mem. AAAS, Am. Chem. Soc., Nat. Orgn. Gay and Lesbian Scientists and Tech. Profls. (chmn. 1985—), N.Y. Acad. Sci., L.A. Gay and Lesbian Scientists (co-chmn. 1984—), Internat. Soc. Analytical Cytology, Athenaeum. Democrat.

DIAMOND, STANLEY JAY, lawyer; b. Los Angeles, Nov. 27, 1927; s. Philip Alfred and Florence (Fadem) D.; m. Lois Jane Broida, June 22, 1969; children: Caryn Elaine, Diana Beth. B.A., UCLA, 1949; J.D., U. So. Calif., 1952. Bar: Calif. 1953. Practiced law Los Angeles, 1953—; dep. Office of Calif. Atty. Gen., Los Angeles, 1953; ptnr. Diamond & Tilem, Los Angeles, 1957-60, Diamond, Tilem & Colden, Los Angeles, 1960-79, Diamond & Wilson, Los Angeles, 1979—; lectr. music and entertainment law UCLA; Mem. nat. panel arbitrators Am. Arbitration Assn. Bd. dirs. Los Angeles Suicide Prevention Center, 1971-76. Served with 349th Engr. Constrn. Bn. AUS, 1945-47. Mem. ABA, Calif. Bar Assn., Los Angeles County Bar Assn., Beverly Hills Bar Assn., Am. Judicature Soc., Calif. Copyright Conf., Nat. Acad. Rec. Arts and Scis., Zeta Beta Tau, Nu Beta Epsilon. Office: 12304 Santa Monica Blvd Fl 3 Los Angeles CA 90025-2551

DIAMOND, STEPHEN EARLE, investor, consultant, inventor; b. San Francisco, Dec. 2, 1944; s. Earl Conrad and Sally (Gonzales) D. Pvt. study music and drama, 1956-65; grad., Ft. Sam Houston Army Med. Sch., 1964; Cert. computer sci. programmer, Elkins Coll. Nat. Career Inst., 1969; PhD, World Acad. Assn., 1994; D Med. Sci., London Inst. Applied Rsch., 1994, LLD (hon.), 1995. Exec. dir. Gondia Corp., San Francisco, 1973-76, exec. chmn., 1976-78; chief exec. officer G.C.I. C'ies, San Francisco, 1978-80, chief adminstrv. officer, 1980-85; owner S.E. Diamond Founds., San Francisco, 1985-86, S.E. Diamond Assn., San Francisco, 1986—, The Dover Rd. Inn Group, 1990—; prof. neurophysics, life fellow Australian Inst. Coordinated Rsch., 1994. Discoverer in field, inventor; patentee in field; contbr articles to profl. jours.; assoc. prodr. Nat. Empowerment TV, 1992. Leader 5th Congl. dist. Strategic Def. Initiative, chmn. high frontier def. com. 5th-8th Congress dists. west region, 1989; active Am. Inst. Cancer Rsch., 1981—, Ronald Reagan Rep. Ctr., Washington, 1987, Stanford (Calif.) U. Libr., 1987; state advisor U.S. Congl. adv. bd., Washington and San Francisco, 1983-86; hon. charter mem. St. Mary's Hosp., San Francisco, 1988; friend San Francisco Symphony Orch., 1980—; founding mem. Am. Space Frontier Com., Falls Church, 1984-86, Challenger Space Ctr., 1987—, Am. Air Mus., Duxbury, Eng., 1994—; sponsor, prodr. Concerned Women for Am., 1984—; mem. world planning coun. WWII Victory 50th Anniversary Events, 1992—; charter mem. Citizens Against Govt. Waste, 1991—, mem. coun.; charter mem. Rep. Nat. Commn. on Am. Agenda; founding charter mem. Normandy D-Day Mus., Caen, France, 1990—; charter founding mem. USN Meml. U.S.A. Washington Dist., 1989; charter founder mem. Nat. Com. to Preserve Social Security; mem.nat. gov. bd. U.S. Olympic Com. Shooting Team, 1994. Recipient merit award Rep. Nat. Com., 1984, merit award Rep. Party, 1985, Achievement award United Inventors and Scientists, L.A., 1975. Mem. Nat. Small Bus. Assn., Nat. Taxpayers Union, Statue of Liberty and Ellis Island Found. (charter), Presdl. Task Force (charter), Clan Morrison Soc. (life active), North Shore Animal League, Internat. Affairs Inst. Paris, Internat. Cult. Corr. Inst. India, Academie Maison, Internat. Des Intellectuels, M.I.D.I., A.M.U., Munich, Germany, 1994. Republican. Home: Oxford St # 248 San Francisco CA 94134-1352 Office: PO Box 640238 San Francisco CA 94164-0238 also: PO Box 246 South Lake Tahoe CA 96156-0246

DÍAZ, ELENA R., community health nurse; b. Aubuquerque; d. María E. Lopez. BSN, U. Ariz., 1975. RNC, Ariz.; cert. community health nursing. Community health nurse Pima County Health Dept., Tucson, 1975—; mem. minority recruitment and retention community task force Coll. Nursing U. Ariz. Tucson. Recipient St. Cyril's Clair Dunn/Judith Lovchik award Peace and Justice Com., 1987, La Esperanza award, 1987. Mem. APHA, Am. Assn. Hispanic Nurses, Am. Heart Assn., Nat. Coalition Hispanic Health and Human Svcs. Orgns., Tucson Assn. Hispanic Nurses.

DIAZ, MICHAEL ANTHONY, electrical engineer, software engineer; b. West Point, N.Y., Aug. 26, 1957; s. Antonio and Gloria (Torado) D.; m. Yvonne Marie Martinez, Apr. 20, 1991. BSEE, MS in Computer Engring., Boston U., 1991. Softwre programmer IBM, Poughkeepsie, N.Y., 1978, Sandia Labs., Albuquerque, 1979, 80, Hewlett Packard, Cupertino, Calaif., 1981; sr. software engr. Motorola GSTG, Scottsdale, Ariz., 1982—. Contbr. articles to symposia. With USN, 1975-76. Recipient award for outstanding software Dept. Def., Nat. Security Agy., 1993. Mem. IEEE, Assn. for Computing Machinery. Home: 8244 E Appaloosa Trl Scottsdale AZ 85258-1305 Office: Motorola GSTG 8201 E Mcdowell Rd Scottsdale AZ 85257-3812

DIAZ, RAMON VALERO, retired judge; b. Manila, Oct. 13, 1918; came to Guam, 1951; s. Vicente and Bibiana (Valero) D.; m. Josefina Dela Concepcion, July 3, 1945; children: Carlos, Marilu, Mariles, Maribel, Marilen, Maryann, Anthony, Vincent, Ramon, Maricar. PhB, U. St. Tomas, Manila, 1940, LLB, 1941; grad. U.S. Army J.A.G. Sch., 1945; Diploma Jud. Skills, Am. Acad. Jud. Edn., 1984. Bar: Philippines 1941, Guam 1956, U.S. Ct. Appeals (9th cir.) 1966, High Ct. of Trust Territories 1977, No. Marianas 1985. Assoc. Diokno Law Office, Manila, 1943-44; pvt. practice, Guam, 1960-80; judge Superior Ct. of Guam, Agana, 1980-94; ret. 1994; mem. U.S. Selective Service Bd. Appeals, Guam, 1950-62. Permanent deacon Roman Catholic Ch. Judge Adv. Gen.'s Svc., Philippine Army, 1941-51. Mem. ABA, Am. Judges Assn., Nat. Council Juvenile and Family Ct. Judges, VFW II and POW. Survivor Bataan Death March, 1942. Home: 114 Manga Ct Dededo GU 96912-1451 Office: PO Box 22978 GMF Barrigada GU 96921-2978

DIAZ-BARRIOS, ANA PAULINA, manufacturing and marketing consultant; b. Guadalajara, Jal, Mex., Sept. 17, 1964; came to U.S., 1991; d. Javier and Ana Rosa (Barrios) D. BS in Indsl. Engring., Instituto Techologico de Estudios Superiores de Occidente, Guadalajara, 1986; diplomate in bus., Harvard U., 1988, MBA, 1993. Mktg. dir. Electrotec, Guadalajara, 1988-91; mng. assoc. Assemble in Mex., Inc., San Diego, 1993—; mem. duediligence activies com. Bristol Assocs., Del Mar, Calif., 1993—; fin. and feasability analyst Sovereign Capital, La Jolla, Calif., 1993—. Mem. San Diego-Tijuana Sisters Cities Assn. Mem. Nat. Assn. Pvt. Enterprises (sec. 1990), Nat. Assn. Women in Bus., Strategic Connections Group, N.Y. Harvard Bus. Club, San Diego Harvard Bus. Club. Democrat. Roman Catholic. Home: 8895 Towne Centre Dr Ste 105 San Diego CA 92122-5542 Office: Assemble in Mex 751 Design Ct Chula Vista CA 91911-6159

DIAZ-FLORES, HEBERT DE JESUS, scientist, engineer, consultant; b. Merida, Yucatan, Mexico, Jan. 11, 1960; came to U.S., 1982; s. Hebert De Jesus Diaz-Vazquez and Gloria (Flores-Cervera) Flores-Diaz; m. Suzanne Marie Britz, June 30, 1984; 1 child, Gloria Patricia. BS in Engring., Merida (Mex.) Inst. Tech., 1981; MS in Engring., Purdue U., 1984; PhD in Engring., U. Calif., Davis, 1991. Prof., rschr. Veracruz (Mex.) Inst. Tech., 1984-86, grad. coord., 1985-86; grad. rsch. asst. Calif. Energy Commn., Sacramento, 1986-89, energy analyst, 1989, assoc. energy specialist, 1989-92, energy commn. specialist, 1992; sr. engr., scientist Radian Corp., Sacramento, 1992-95; energy planning cons. Telos Corp., Sacramento, 1994-95; rsch. mgr. Calif. Energy Commn., Sacramento, 1995—. Contbr. articles to profl. jours.; editor (newsletter) Mex. Student Assn., U. Calif., Davis, 1988-90. V.p. Mex. Student Assn., U. Calif., Davis, 1988-89;. Recipient scholarship Coun. of Sci. and Tech., Mex., 1986; named nat. rschr. Coun. of Sci and Tech., Mex., 1984. Mem. IEEE, Air and Waste Mgmt. Assn., Assn. Computer Machinery, Sacramento Foxpro Users Group. Home: 1470 Springdale Dr Woodland CA 95776-5757 Office: Calif Energy Commn 1516 9th St Sacramento CA 95814

DIAZ-ZUBIETA, AGUSTIN, nuclear engineer, executive; b. Madrid, Spain, Mar. 24, 1936; came to U.S., 1953; s. Emilio Diaz Cabeza and Maria Teresa Zubieta Atucha; m. Beth Lee Fortune, Sept. 6, 1958; children: Walter Agustin, Michael Joel, Anthony John. B, U. Madrid, 1953; BSc in Physics, U. Tenn., 1958; MSc in Mech. Engring., Duke U., 1960; PhD in Nuclear Engring., U. Md., 1981. Nuclear engr. Combustion Engring., Tenn., 1954-58; instr. engring. Duke U., Durham, N.C., 1958-60; nuclear physicist Allis Chalmers Co., Washington, 1960-64; country mgr. South Africa Allis Chalmers Co., 1964-66; mgr. internat. power generation projects GE, N.Y.C., 1966-69, mgr. Europe and Middle East strategic planning, 1969-71; dir. internat. constrn. planning GE, Westport, Conn., 1971-75, dir. constrn., 1975-83; chief exec. officer GE Affiliate, Westport, 1983-87; v.p. internat. sales, devel. Internat. Tech. Corp., L.A., 1987-94; mng. dir. IT Italia S.P.A., IT Spain, S.A. Author: Measurement of Subcriticality of Nuclear Reactors by Stocastic Processes, 1981. Pres. Fairfield (Conn.) Assn. Condo Owners, 1983-87. Named Astronomer of Yr. Barnard Astronomical Soc., Chattanooga, 1957; fgn. exchange scholar U.S. Govt., 1953-58; grantee, NSF, 1958-60, U.S. Office of Ordinance Rsch. U.S. Army, 1958-60. Mem. Am. Nuclear Soc., Am. Soc. Mech. Engrs., Am. Soc. Profl. Engrs., Sigma Xi. Republican. Roman Catholic. Home: 47 Country Meadow Rd Rolling Hills Estates CA 90274

DIBARTOLOMEO, DENNIS, data acquisition and process control engineer; b. N.Y.C., Aug. 21, 1949; s. Carl and Leona (Spallone) DiB. BS in Astronomy, Calif. Inst. Tech., 1971; MA in Psychology, U. Calif., Berkeley, 1974; postgrad., City Coll. San Francisco, 1977-78. Rsch. technician Lawrence Berkeley Lab., 1978-84, sr. rsch. assoc., 1984-89, prin. rsch. assoc., 1989—. Contbr. articles to profl. jours. Mem. Internat. Soc. for Study Subtle Energies and Energy Medicine, Parapsychology Rsch. Group, Union Concerned Scientists, Inst. Noetic Scis., Assn. Transpersonal Psychology. Buddhist. Home: 747 Elm St El Cerrito CA 94530-3102 Office: Lawrence Berkeley Lab Bldg 90 Rm 3111 Berkeley CA 94720

DIBB, CHARLES ROBERT, physician, educator; b. Downey, Calif., July 21, 1959; s. Alfred Wallace and Betty Ann (Dayton) D.; m. Sandra Louise Hammons, Apr. 26, 1986; children: William Kenneth, James Thomas, Alexander Joseph. BS, U. Calif., Davis, 1981; MD, U. Health Sci. Chgo. Med. Sch., 1985. Diplomate Am. Bd. Internal Medicine, Am. Bd. Med. Oncology. Intern, resident U. Tex. Health Sci. Ctr., Houston, 1985-88; fellow U. Mich., Ann Arbor, 1989-92, lectr., 1992; staff physician Medford (Oreg.) Clinic, 1992—; med. dir. Rogue Valley Med. Ctr. Hospice, 1992—; investigator Nat. Sci. Adj. Breast and Bowel Project, 1992—. Author: (book chpt.) Yearbook of Head and Neck Cancer, 1994. Mem. AMA, Am. Coll. Physicians, Assn. Hospice Physicians, Oreg. Med. Assn., Jackson County Med. Soc., Sierra Club. Episcopalian. Home: 428 Silverado Cir Medford OR 97504-8167 Office: Medford Clinic PC 555 Black Oak Dr Medford OR 97504-8311

DIBB, ROGER ALAN, accountant; b. Salt Lake City, June 25, 1947; s. George and Marjorie G. (Dreier) D.; m. Ann Monson, Mar. 5, 1974; children: Sarah, Alan, Mark, Jeffrey. BS in Bus. Fin., Brigham Young U., 1972, MPA in Pub. Fin., 1974; BS in Acctg., U. Utah, 1976. CPA, Utah. From acct. to mgr. Deloitte, Hasking & Sells, Salt Lake City, 1976-84; mgr., tax acct. Coopers & Lybrand, Salt Lake City, 1984-92; prin. Roger A. Dibb, CPA, P.C., Salt Lake City, 1992—. Author computer program. Bishop Ch. of Jesus Christ of Latter Day Sts., Salt Lake City, 1995—. Mem. AICPA, Utah Assn. CPAs. Republican. Office: PO Box 17868 Salt Lake City UT 84117-0868

DIBBLE, DAVID VAN VLACK, visually impaired educator, lawyer; b. San Francisco, Feb. 5, 1928; s. Oliver and Isabelle (Bishop) D.; m. Frances Bauer, May 3, 1984; 1 child, T.C. Clark. AA, San Mateo Jr. Coll., 1948; BA, U. Calif., Berkeley, 1952; JD, U. Calif., San Francisco, 1962; grad. in Edn., Calif. State U., Hayward, 1969; MA, San Francisco State U., 1981. Bar: Calif., 1962; cert. elem. tchr., spl. edn. visually impaired, Calif. Tchr. Marine Corps Inst., Washington, D.C., 1953-54; purser Am. Pres. LInes, San Francisco, 1955; passenger agt. Am. Pres. LInes, Honolulu, 1956-58, San Francisco, 1958-60; trial lawyer Barfield, Barfield & Dryden, San Francisco, 1963-65; ptnr. Thorpe & Dibble, Hayward, Calif., 1966-69; part time tchr. various Calif. sch. dists., 1970-74; lawyer and vision tchr. pvt. practice, San Francisco, 1974-82; sec., dir. Original Sixteen to One Mine, Inc., Alleghany, Calif., 1978-81; vision tchr. Oakland (Calif.) Pub. Schs., 1982-89; cons. vision edn. pvt. practice, Oakland, 1989—. Contbr. articles on Art of Seeing to various pubs. Pub. defender Legal Aid Soc., San Francisco, 1965-66; bd. dirs. Healing Ctr., San Francisco, 1974-78; vol. Multiple Sclerosis Soc. No. Calif., Oakland, 1974-90; bd. dirs., v.p. Calif. Heritage Coun., 1970-92, Telegraph Hill Dwellers, 1979-88, pres., 1976, San Francisco; bd. dirs., v.p. Dimond Improvement Assn., Oakland, 1987-88; vestry and warden St. Paul's Episc. Ch., Oakland, 1989-92; docent Oakland Mus., 1992, Presdl. Yacht OSS Patomac, Jack London Mus.; dir. Fruitvale Cmty. Devel. Dist. Coun., Oakland, 1989-95. Recipient Cert. Appreciation, Calif. Heritage Coun., San Francisco, 1990. Mem. Bar Assn. Calif., Oakland Tchrs. Assn., Calif. Assn. Orientation and Mobility Specialists, Calif. Alumni Assn., Nat. Audubon Soc. San Francisco Boy Wildlife Soc., E.C.V. History, Bates-Corbett Tchr. Assn., St. Andrew's Soc. of San Francisco, SAR, Phi Gamma Delta. Republican. Episcopalian. Home: 2806 Bellaire Pl Oakland CA 94601-2010

DIBBLEE, THOMAS WILSON, JR., retired geologist; b. Santa Barbara, Calif., Oct. 11, 1911; s. Thomas Wilson and Anita Orena D.; m. Loretta Escabosa, Nov. 22, 1949. BA, Stamford U, 1936. Geologist Union Oil Co. of Calif., Lompoc, 1936, Richfield Oil Corp., Los Angeles, 1937-52, U.S. Geological Survey, Claremont and Menlo Park, Calif., 1952-77, U.S. Forest Svc., Santa Barbara, Calif., 1978-84; rsch. assoc. in geology U. Calif., Santa Barbara, 1972—. Home: 316 E Mission St Santa Barbara CA 93101

DIBLE, ROSE HARPE MCFEE, special education educator; b. Phoenix, Apr. 28, 1927; d. Ambrose Jefferson and Laurel Mabel (Harpe) McFee; m. James Henry Dible, June 23, 1951 (div. Jan. 1965); 1 child, Michael James. BA in Speech Edn., Ariz. State U., Tempe, 1949; MA in Speech and Drama, U. So. Calif., L.A., 1950; fellow, Calif. State U., Fullerton, 1967. Cert. secondary tchr., spl. edn. tchr. English and drama tchr. Lynwood (Calif.) Sr. High Sch., 1950-51, Montebello (Calif.) Sr. High Sch., 1952-58; tchr. English and Social Studies Pioneer High Sch., Whittier, Calif., 1964-65; spl. edn. tchr. Bell Gardens (Calif.) High Sch., 1967-85, spl. edn. cons., 1985-90. Mem. DAR, Daus. Am. Colonists, Whittier Christian Woman Assn., La Habra Womans Club, Eastern Star Lodge, Kappa Delts, Phi Delta Gamma. Republican. Presbyterian. Home: 1201 Russell St La Habra CA 90631-2530 Office: Montebello Unified Sch Dist 123 Montebello Blvd Montebello CA 90640

DICERO, SUZANNE JOAN, retail chain executive; b. New Haven, Feb. 21, 1963; d. Eugene and Joan Francis (Pietracatella) DiC. BA, Smith Coll., 1986. Catalog asst. supr. The Gap Inc., Hayward, Calif., 1986-87, ops. supr., 1987, 89, inventory supr., 1987-88, inventory mgr., 1989-92, fin. supr., 1992-94, corp. inventory control mgr., 1994—. Fundraiser, vol. coord., weekend mgr. Ronald McDonald House, Palo Alto, Calif., 1992—. Mem. Am. Prodn. and Inventory Control Soc. Office: The Gap Inc 1000 Cherry Ave San Bruno CA 94066-2303

DICK, BERTRAM GALE, JR., physics educator; b. Portland, Oreg., June 12, 1926; s. Bertram Gale and Helen (Meengs) D.; m. Ann Bradford Volkmann, June 23, 1956; children—Timothy Howe, Robin Louise, Stephen Gale. B.A., Reed Coll., 1950; B.A. (Rhodes scholar), Wadham Coll., Oxford (Eng.) U., 1953, M.A., 1958; Ph.D., Cornell U., 1958. Research assoc. U. Ill., 1957-59; mem. faculty U. Utah, 1959—, prof. physics, 1965—, Univ. prof., 1979-80, chmn. dept., 1964-67, dean grad. sch., 1987-93; cons. Minn. Mining and Mfg. Co., 1960-67; vis. prof. Technische Hochschule, Munich, 1967-68; vis. scientist Max Planck Institut für Festkörperforschung, Stuttgart, Fed. Republic Germany, 1976-77; faculty Semester at Sea, fall 1983, 86. Mem. Alta Planning and Zoning Commn., 1972-76; pres. Chamber Music Salt Lake City, 1974-76; bd. dirs. Citizen's Com. to Save Our Canyons, 1971 , Coalition for Utah's Future Project 2000, 1989 . Served with USNR, 1944-46. Fellow Am. Phys. Soc.; mem. AAAS, Am. Alpine Club, Sierra Club, Phi Beta Kappa, Sigma Xi. Home: 1377 Butler Ave Salt Lake City UT 84102-1803 Office: U Utah Dept Physics Salt Lake City UT 84112

DICK, HENRY HENRY, minister; b. Russia, June 1, 1922; s. Henry Henry and Mary (Unger) D.; m. Erica Penner, May 25, 1946; children—Janet (Mrs. Arthur Enns), Judith (Mrs. Ron Brown), James, Henry. Th.B., Mennonite Brethren Bible Coll., 1950. Ordained to ministry Mennonite Brethren Ch., 1950; pastor in Orillia, Ont., Can., 1950-54, Lodi, Calif., 1954-57, Shafter, Calif., 1958-69; faculty Tabor Coll., 1954-55; gen. sec. Mennonite Brethren Conf. of U.S.A., 1969-72; pres. Mennonite Brethren Bibl. Sem., Fresno, Calif., 1972-76; vice moderator Gen Conf. Mennonite Brethren Ch., 1975-78, moderator, 1979-84; pastor Reedley Mennonite Brethren Ch., 1976-88; ret., 1989; dir. ch. and constituency relations Mennonite Brethren Biblical Sem., 1987-89; moderator Pacific Dist. Conf., 1959-60, 61-63, 75-77; mem. exec. com. Mennonite Central Com. Internat., 1967-75, mem. bd. reference and counsel, 1966-69, 72-75, mem. bd. missions and services, 1969-72; exec. sec. Bd. Edn. Mennonite Brethren, 1969-72; chmn. Bd. Missions and Services, 1985-91; pastor emeritus Reedley Mennonite Brethren Ch., 1987. Columnist bi-weekly publ. Christian Leader, 1969-75. Bd. dirs. Bob Wilson Meml. Hosp., Ulysses, Kans., 1969-72; dist. minister Pacific Dist. Conf. Mennonite Brethren, 1989—. Recipient Humanitarian award Shafter C. of C., 1969, Citation bd. dirs. Bibl. Sem. Clubs: Kiwanis, Reedley Rotary. Home: 783 W Carpenter Ave Reedley CA 93654-3903 Office: 1632 L St Reedley CA 93654-3340

DICKASON, JAMES FRANK, land and farming company executive; b. San Francisco, July 5, 1922; s. James Frank and Jean Dempster (Humbird) D.; m. Linda Celeste Stewart, Dec. 9, 1961; children: James B., Thomas H., Margaret J., Bradford S. B.A., Harvard U., 1944; M.B.A., Stanford U., 1951. Successively asst. sec., sec., v.p., dir. White Investment Co., San Francisco, 1951-63; exec. v.p. Newhall Land & Farming Co., Valencia, Calif., 1963-71, pres., 1971-85, chief exec. officer, 1971-87, chmn. bd., 1979-87, dir., 1963—, chmn. exec. com., 1987—; dir. Wells Fargo & Co., Pacific Enterprises. V.p. bd. dirs. Calif. Mus. Sci. & Industry; trustee S.W. Mus.; vice chmn., bd. dirs. Automobile Club of So. Calif. With U.S. Army, 1943-46. Mem. Newcomen Soc. U.S., Calif. C. of C. (bd. dirs., chmn. So. Calif. chpt.), Lambda Alpha. Republican. Presbyterian. Clubs: California (Los Angeles); Pacific Union, Bohemian (San Francisco); Valley Hunt (Pasadena, Calif.). Home: 930 Rosalind Rd San Marino CA 91108-1124 Office: Newhall Land & Farming 550 S Hope St 23d Fl Los Angeles CA 90071-2627

DICKAU, KEITH MICHAEL, artist, secondary science educator; b. Monterey Park, Calif., Apr. 20, 1944; s. Keith Robert and Beaula May (Chamness) D.; m. Ramona Sue Wilson, May 6, 1967; children: Robert Michael, Ian Christopher; m. Carolyn Gloria Isaak, Dec. 22, 1973. BA in Zoology, U. Calif., Davis, 1966. Cert. secondary tchr., Calif. Tchr. math. L.A. City Sch. Dist., 1967-70; tchr. sci. and math. Grant Joint Union H.S. Dist., Sacramento and Rio Linda, Calif., 1970—. Exhibited in numerous shows including Anna Gardner Gallery, Stinson Beach, Calif., Artists' Collaborative Gallery, Sacramento, Fla. State U., Tallahassee, Crocker Art Mus. Sculpture Park, Sacramento, Whittier (Calif.) Mus., Gallery 25, Fresno, Calif., L.A. Artist Equity Assn., Sacramento Fine Arts Ctr., Mercer Gallery, Rochester, N.Y., The Artery, Davis, Archivio Artistico, Ravenna, Italy, Antic Ajuntament, Terragona, Spain, Santa Barbara (Calif.) Mus.; contbr. poetry and art to mags. Recipient Hon. Sci. award Bausch and Lomb, 1962, Sculpture award Calif. Art League, 1987, Artist of Month award No. Calif. Artists, numerous other awards; NSF grantee, 1972. Mem. NEA, Calif. Tchrs. Assn., Grant Dist. Edn. Assn. (bldg. co-pres. 1972-73), No. Calif. Artists, Inc. Democrat. Methodist.

DICKERSON, BARBARA ANN RANSOM, dean, education educator, consultant; b. Jackson, Miss., Apr. 18, 1952; d. Jimmie Lee and Marie Eunice (West) Ransom; m. Mark Steven Dickerson, Dec. 30, 1978; children: Amber Tiffany, Christopher Ryan. BS, Grand Canyon Coll., 1974; MA, Ariz. State U., 1976, PhD, 1987. Tchr. Pendergast Elem. Dist., Tolleson, Ariz., 1974-76; reading clin. S. Mountain High Sch. Dist., Phoenix, 1976-80; instr. High Sch. Drop Out Program, Phoenix, 1978, Mesa (Ariz.) Community Coll., 1978; reading specialist Deer Valley Sch. Dist., Phoenix, 1980-82; asst. dir. Honors Coll. Ariz. State U., Tempe, 1984-87, asst. prof. edn., 1988-89; faculty mem. Grand Canyon Coll., Phoenix, 1987-88; dean Coll. Arts and Sci. Grand Canyon U., 1991—, dean Coll. of Liberal Arts and Social Scis.; cons. Rising Star, Phoenix, 1987—. Pres. Valley Christian Ctrs., Phoenix, 1984-89; youth instr. First Bapt. Ch., Phoenix, 1987-88; active Foster Care Rev. Bd., Ariz., Ariz. Adoption Spl. Kids. Greater Phoenix Area Writing Project fellow, 1979. Mem. Ariz. Tchrs. of Reading, Ariz. English Tchrs. Assn., Assn. for Curriculum and Devel., Delta Sigma Theta (sec., v.p. 1977—). Democrat. Home: 8533 N 50th Pl Scottsdale AZ 85253 Office: Grand Canyon U 3300 W Camelback Rd Paradise Valley AZ 85253-2006

DICKERSON, COLLEEN BERNICE PATTON, artist, educator; b. Cleburne, Tex., Sept. 17, 1922; d. Jennings Bryan and Alma Bernice (Clark) Patton; m. Arthur F. Dickerson; children: Sherry M., Chrystal Charmine. BA, Calif. State U., Northridge, 1980; studied with John Pike. One woman shows include Solo Show, Morro Bay Comunity Bldg.; exhibited in group shows at Aquarius Watercolor Show, Brushstrokes Oil Show, Great Western Painting Show, Morro Bay Monthly Show; represented in permanent collections at Polk Ins. Co., San Luis Obispo, Med. Ctr. MDM Ins. Co., L.A.; demonstrations at Cayucos Art Assn., Morro Bay Art Assn., El Camino Real Art Assn. Mem. Cen. Coast Watercolor Soc. (pres. 1986-87), Art. Ctr., Oil Acrylic Pastel Group (chmn., co-chmn. 1989—), Morro Bay Art Assn., Les Arts, San Luis Obispo Art Ctr. Home and Studio: 245 Hacienda Ave San Luis Obispo CA 93401-7967

DICKERSON, CYNTHIA ROWE, marketing firm executive, consultant; b. Cin., Apr. 14, 1956; d. Richard Emmett and Frances Jeanette (Ellwanger) Rowe; m. Mark Alan Dickerson, Oct. 24, 1981; children: Shannon Gayle, Meredith Lynne. BSBA, U. So. Calif., 1979. Mgmt. asst. Computer Scis. Corp., Pasadena, Calif., 1974-78; rsch. asst. Dailey & Assocs., L.A., 1978-79; account exec. Young & Rubicam, L.A., 1979-81, Rowley & Linder Advt., Wichita, Kans., 1981-82, Chiat/Day Inc. Advt., San Francisco, 1983-85; product mgr. Sun-Diamond Growers of Calif., Pleasanton, 1985-88; mktg. cons. San Francisco, 1988-90; sr. bus. mgr. Del Monte Foods, San Francisco, 1990-93; dir. mktg. Yorkshire Dried Fruit & Nuts, INc., San Francisco, 1993-94, Potlatch Corp., 1995—. Named Outstanding Youth Women of Am., Jr. C. of C., 1985. Mem. Am. Rose Soc., Heritage Rose Group. Republican.

DICKERSON, TIM EDWARD, insurance executive; b. Park Rapids, Minn., Mar. 12, 1948; s. Ernest Walter and Mildred Imogene (Burton) D.; m. Darlene Leah Manchester, Aug. 19, 1967; children: Tamara Lynn, Shelley Kay. AA in Bus. Adminstrn., San Bernardino Valley Coll., 1969; BSBA in Mgmt., Calif. Polytech., 1971. Middle mgmt. Kaiser Steel Corp., Fontana, Calif., 1965-74; agt. N.Y. Life Ins. Co., San Bernardino, Calif., 1974-75, sales mgr., 1975-78; gen. mgr. N.Y. Life Ins. Co., Redding, Calif., 1978-83, Sacramento, 1983—. Mem. CLU, Nat. Assn. Life Underwriters, Gen. Agts. & Mgrs. Assn. Office: NY Life Ins Co 2999 Douglas Blvd Roseville CA 95661-3840

DICKERSON, WILLIAM ROY, lawyer; b. Uniontown, Ky., Feb. 15, 1928; s. Benjamin Franklin and Honor Mae (Staples) D. BA in Acctg., Calif. State U., 1952; JD, UCLA, 1958. Bar: Calif. 1959. Dep. atty., ex-officio city prosecutor City of Glendale, Calif., 1959-62; assoc. James Brewer, Los Angeles, 1962-68, LaFollette, Johnson, Schroeter & DeHaas, Los Angeles, 1968-73; sole practice, Los Angeles, 1973—; arbitrator Los Angeles Superior Ct.; judge pro tem Los Angeles Mcpl. Ct., judge pro tem Los Angeles Superior Ct., Small Claims Ct., Traffic Ct.; lectr. and speaker in field. Bd. dirs. LosFeliz Improvement Assn., 1986-88, Zoning Commn.; co-chmn. Streets and Hwys. Commn. Mem. ABA, Calif. Bar Assn., Los Angeles County Bar Assn., Soc. Calif. Accts., Fed. Bar Assn., Am. Film Inst., Internat. Platform Assn. Home and Office: 813 N Doheny Dr Beverly Hills CA 90210-3528

DICKEY, GARY ALAN, minister; b. Santa Monica, Calif., Jan. 25, 1946; s. Charles Harry and Audrey W. (White) D.; m. Tamara Jean Kimble, Jan. 11, 1976. BA, UCLA, 1968; MDiv, Fuller Theol. Sem., Pasadena, 1972; DMin, Sch. Theology, Claremont, Calif., 1974; PhD studies, Trinity Theol. Seminary, 1993—. Assoc. pastor Magnolia Pk. United Meth. Ch., Burbank, Calif., 1974-78; sr. pastor St. James United Meth. Ch., Pasadena, 1978-90, First United Meth. Ch. of Canoga Park, 1990—; exec. com. mem. Calif.-Pacific Ann. Conf. Bd. of Ordained Ministry, 1980-88; chmn. Pasadena Dist. Com. on Ordained Ministry, 1978-90; supervising pastor Bd. Higher Edn., Nashville, 1978—. Recipient Polonia Restituta, Polish Peoples Republic, 1990. Mem. Soc. Colonial Wars (mem. gentlemen of coun. 1993—), Soc.

War of 1812 (chaplain 1989—), Soc. of Sons of Am. Revolution (chaplain 1988—, pres. 1994, 95, Outstanding Citizenship award 1990, Meritorious Svc. award 1995), Soc. of Sons of the Revolution, Descendants of Soldiers of Valley Forge, Soc. Sons Am. Colonists, Soc. Sons. Vets. Civil War, Vet. Corps Artillery State N.Y., United Empire Loyalists Assn. (Can.), Royal Soc. St. George (Eng.), Rotary (pres. 1989-90, Paul Harris fellow 1986). Republican. Methodist. Home: 22167 Bryant St Canoga Park CA 91304-2306 Office: First United Meth Ch 22700 Sherman Way Canoga Park CA 91307-2332

DICKEY, PATRICIA ANN, dietitian; b. Bozeman, Mont., Mar. 16, 1952; d. Paul Wester and Bertha Francis (Sullivan) Eblen; m. David Bruce Dickey, July 14, 1973; children: Brian Scott, Clarke Matthew, Justin Bradley. BS, Mont. State U., 1974. Dietetic intern Vanderbilt U. Med. Ctr., Nashville, 1976; cons. dietitian Bakke Enterprises, Bozeman, 1976-77; W.I.C. program dir. Fltd. County Health Dept., Kalispell, Mont., 1977-78; nutrition cons. Fltd. Head Start Program, Kalispell, 1977-83, Area Agy. on Aging, Kalispell, 1979-81; program dir. Title III Nutrition Program, Kalispell, 1981-84; nutrition svcs. dir. Kalispell (Mont.) Regional Hosp., 1984—. Guest spkr. Am. Cancer Soc., Kalispell, 1989—; vol. bd. mem. Mont. Heart Assn., Kalispell, 1993—. Named Outstanding Young Career Woman, Bus. and Profl. Women's Assn., Kalispell, 1978. Mem. ASHFSA (pres.-elect Mont. chpt. 1993—), Am. Dietetic Assn. (CDHCF practice group area I regional nominating com. western region 1983-84), Mont. Dietetic Assn. (pres., pres-elect, coun. on practice, nominating com. 1978-91, Recognized Young Dietitian 1978, Mont. Recognized Dietitian 1984).

DICKEY, ROBERT MARVIN (RICK DICKEY), property manager; b. Charleston, S.C., Dec. 3, 1950; s. John Lincoln II and Ruth (Marvin) D.; m. Teresa Ann Curry, Dec. 19, 1969 (div. 1979); 1 child, Gena Lynette. A of Computer Sci., USMC Degree Program, Washington, 1975. Cert. apt. property supr. Nat. Apt. Assn., Wash., occupancy specialist Nat. Ctr.for Housing Mgmt., Wash. Enlisted USMC, 1968, advanced through grades to staff sgt., 1968-78; shop mgr., bookkeeper Amalgamated Plant Co., Las Vegas, Nev., 1978-79; supr. constrn. Joseph Yousem Co., Las Vegas, 1979-80; apt. mgr. Robert A. McNeil Corp., Las Vegas, 1980, comml. bldg. mgr., leasing agt., 1980-82; asst. v.p., regional property mgr. Westminster Co., Las Vegas, 1982-87, Weyerhaeuser Mortgage Co., Las Vegas, 1988-89; pres., ptnr. Equinox Devel., Inc., Las Vegas, 1989-91; residential dept. mgr. R.W. Robideaux & Co., Spokane, Wash., 1991—. Contbr. articles to profl. jours. Mem. Inst. Real Estate Mgmt. (accredited residential mgr., legis. chmn. 1987-88,Accredited Residential Mgr. award 1985, 86, 90), Nev. Apt. Assn. (v.p. 1985, pres. 1988—, bd. dirs.), So. Nev. Homebuilders Assn., Las Vegas Bd. Realtors (mgmt. legis com. 1988).

DICKEY, ROBERT PRESTON, author, educator, poet; b. Flat River, Mo., Sept. 24, 1936; s. Delno Miren D. and Naomi Valentine (Jackson) D.; children: Georgia Rae, Shannon Ezra, Rain Dancer. BA, U. Mo., 1968, MA, 1969; PhD, Walden U., 1975. Instr. U. Mo., 1967-69; asst. prof. English and creative writing U. So. Colo., 1969-73; assoc. mem. faculty Pima Coll., Tucson, 1975-78. Author: (with Donald Justice, Thomas McAfee, Donald Drummond) poetry Four Poets, 1967, Running Lucky, 1969, Acting Immortal, 1970; Concise Dictionary of Lead River, Mo., 1972, The Basic Stuff of Poetry, 1972, Life Cycle of Seven Songs, 1972, McCabe Wants Chimes, 1973, Admitting Complicity, 1973; opera librettos Minnequa, 1976, The Witch of Tucson, 1976; Jimmie Cotton!, 1979, Way Out West, 1979, The Poetica Erotica of R.P. Dickey, 1989, The Little Book on Racism and Politics, 1990, The Way of Eternal Recurrence, 1994; contbr. poetry to popular mags., Poetry, Saturday Rev., Commonweal, Prairie Schooner; founder, editor: The Poetry Bag quar., 1966-71; poetry editor: So. Colo. Standard, 1973-74. With USAF, 1955-57. Recipient Mahan award for poetry U. Mo., 1965-66. Home: PO Box 4072 Taos NM 87571

DICKINSON, ANN, fundraiser; b. Topeka, Sept. 12, 1961; d. Jacob Alan II and Ruth (Curd) D.; m. Michael James Mahoney, May 29, 1993. AB in History, Grinnell Coll., 1983; postgrad., McGill U., Montreal, Quebec, Can., 1985. Analyst, corp. fin. dept. E.F. Hutton & Co., Inc., N.Y.C., 1983-85; pres., owner The Dark Side, N.Y.C., 1985-87; asst. dir. individual giving Meml. Sloan-Kettering Cancer Ctr., N.Y.C., 1987-88, dir. spl. gifts, 1988-91; assoc. dir. devel. Sch. Humanities and Scis. Stanford (Calif.) U., 1991—; devel. asst. regional office Brandeis U., N.Y.C., 1987. Vol. interviewer Grinnell Coll., N.Y.C., San Francisco, 1983—; vol. Tom Huening for Congress, Palo Alto, Calif., 1992. Mem. Nat. Soc. Fund Raising Execs., Jr. League San Francisco, Hist. Topeka Assn., Friends of Filoli (Woodside, Calif.). Republican. Episcopalian. Office: Stanford U Bldg One Stanford CA 94305

DICKINSON, CHARLES TWEED, information science administrator, programmer; b. Oxnard, Calif., July 16, 1965; s. Eldon Charles and Betty Darlene (Logan) D.; m. Lisa Ann Kasper, Feb. 14, 1988; 1 child, Logan Charles. BBA in Mgmt., Loma Linda U., 1987. Acct. Data Exch. Corp., Camarillo, Calif., 1987-88, computer programmer, 1988-90, MIS mgr. ops., 1990-92, MIS dir., 1992—. Republican. Seventh-Day Adventist. Office: Data Exch 3600 Via Pescador Camarillo CA 93012-5051

DICKINSON, DAN CALVIN, medical librarian; b. Olden, Tex., Sept. 15, 1920; s. William Calvin and Flossie Stella (Pierce) D.; m. Suzanne Clubb, Feb. 20, 1959. Student, U. Okla., 1938-41, U. Ariz., 1944-45; BA, U. So. Calif., 1949, MS in Bacteriology, 1963. Bacteriology technician U. So. Calif., L.A., 1945-46; chemistry and microbiology instr. Calif. Coll. Mortuary Sci., L.A., 1946-74; substitute libr. Indio (Calif.) H.S., 1975-76; med. libr. John F. Kennedy Meml. Hosp., Indio, 1976—; libr. asst. Desert Hosp., Palm Springs, Calif., 1977-79; libr. tech. Eisenhower Med. Ctr., Rancho Mirage, Calif., 1978-86; microbiology chmn. Joint Com. Mortuary Edn., 1955-68; mem. question com. Conf. Funeral Svc. Exam. Bds., Washington, Ind., 1955-74. With U.S. Army, 1942-43. Mem. Med. Libr. Assn., Med. Libr. Group S. Calif. Democrat. Methodist. Office: John F Kennedy Meml Hosp 47-111 Monroe St Indio CA 92201-6739

DICKINSON, JAMES GORDON, editor; b. Melbourne, Australia, Nov. 13, 1940; came to U.S., 1974, naturalized, 1983; s. David Rushbrook and Lorna Aida (Anderson) D.; m. Carol Rosslyn McBurnie, Sept. 7, 1963; children: Craig, Peter (dec.), Samantha; m. Sheila Laraine Ferguson McManus, Aug. 20, 1982. Student Melbourne U., 1960-63. Cadet reporter Hobart Mercury, 1957-59, Melbourne Age, 1959-63; reporter Melbourne Herald, 1963-64, TV Channel O, Melbourne, 1964-66; cons. Internat. Public Relations Pty. Ltd., 1966-68; editor, pub. Australian Jour. Pharmacy, 1968-74; asst. exec. dir. Am. Pharm. Assn., Washington, 1975; sr. editor FDC Reports Inc., Washington, 1975-78; founder, editor Washington Drugwire, 1978-79; Washington bur. chief Drug Topics, Med. Econs. Co., 1978-83; Washington corr. Scrip, Clinica World Med. Device News, Animal Pharm World Vet. News (U.K.), 1978-85, Pharm. Tech., Pharm. Exec., 1977-89, N.Z. Pharmacy, Brit. Pharm. Jour., Drug News & Perspectives mag. (Spain), Med. Device and Diagnostic Industry mag., Med. Mktg. & Media, 1990—; pres., chief exec. officer Ferdic Inc., 1982—; editor, pub. Dickinson's FDA and Dickinson's PSAO industry newsletters, 1985-93, VixeNews, 1989-90, Dickinson's Pharmacy newsletter, 1989—, Dickinson's FDA Inspection newsletter, 1992-93, Dickinson's FDA Review, 1994—, Dickinson's FDA Update by Fax Weekly; columnist syndicated all state pharm. jours., 1986-94; cons. to drug industry; pres. Australian Monthly Newspapers and Periodicals Assn., 1972-74; founding sec. Melbourne Press Club, 1971-74. Editor: Weekly Pharmacy Reports, 1975-78. Mem. Australian Liberal Party, 1971-74; pres. Lee Forest Civic Assn., 1977-79. Mem. Periodical Corrs. Assn., Am. Pub. Health Assn. Club: Nat. Press (Washington). Office: PO Box 367 Las Cruces NM 88004-0367

DICKINSON, JANET MAE WEBSTER, relocation consulting executive; b. Cleve., Oct. 2, 1929; d. Richard and Gizella (Keplinger) Fisher; m. Rodney Earl Dickinson, June 18, 1965 (div. 1976); 1 child, Kimberly Cae. Grad., Larson Coll. for Women, New Haven; student, Portland State Coll. Lic. broker, Oreg. Pub. rels./promotion dir. KPTV-Channel 27, Portland, Oreg., 1951-54; exec. dir. Exposition-Recreation Commn., Portland, 1954-58; v.p. Art Lutz & Co., Realtors, Portland, 1975-79, Lutz Relocation Mgmt., Portland, 1977-79; corp. relocation mgr. Ga. Pacific Corp., Portland, 1979-82; pres., broker Ga. Pacific Fin. Co., Portland, 1980-82; pres., chief exec. officer The Dickinson Cons. Group, Portland, 1982—; pres. Wheatherstone Press, Lake Oswego, Oreg., 1983—, The Relocation Ctr., Portland, 1984—; cons. in field; lectr. in field; conductor workshops/seminars in field. Author: The Complete Guide to Family Relocation, The International Move, Building Your Dream House, Obtaining the Highest Price for Your Home, Have a Successful Garage Sale, Moving with Children, My Moving Coloring Book, The Group Move, Counseling the Transferee, Games to Play in the Car, Portland (Oreg.) Facts Book, Welcome to the United States, many others; contbr. articles to profl. jours. Mem. Pres.'s Com. to Employ Physically Handicapped, Oreg. Prison Assn.; established Women's Aux. for Waverly Baby Home; bd. dirs. Columbia River coun. Girl Scouts U.S.A., Salvation Army; active various polit. orgns.; chmn. ways and means com. Oreg. Symphony Soc., Portland Art Mus., Assistance League, Portland Jr. Symphony, March of Dimes, others. Mem. Employee Relocation Coun., City Club, Multnomah Athletic Club, Tualatin Valley Econ. Devel. Assn. (dir. 1988—). Republican. Episcopalian. Home: 20 Wheatherstone Lake Oswego OR 97035-1916 Office: The Dickinson Cons Group Lincoln Ctr 10250 SW Greenburg Rd Ste 125 Portland OR 97223-5460

DICKINSON, ROBERT EARL, atmospheric scientist, educator; b. Millersburg, Ohio, Mar. 26, 1940; s. Leonard Earl and Carmen L. (Ostby) D.; m. Nancy Mary Mielinis, Jan. 5, 1974. AB in Chemistry and Physics, Harvard U., 1961; MS in Meteorology, MIT, 1962, PhD in Meteorology, 1966. Rsch. assoc. MIT, Cambridge, 1966-68; scientist Nat. Ctr. Atmospheric Rsch., Boulder, Colo., 1968-73, sr. scientist, 1973-90, head climate sect., 1975-81, dep. dir. A.A.P. div., 1981-86, acting dir., 1986-87; prof. atmospheric physics U. Ariz., 1990-93; regents prof., 1993—; mem. climate rsch. com. NRC, Washington, 1985-90, chmn., 1987-90, com. earth sci., 1985-88, global change com., 1985-92; mem. WCRP sci. steering group GEWEX, 1988-92; UNU steering com. Climatic, Biotic and Human Interactions in Humid Tropics, 1984-88, steering com. Internat. Satellite Land Surface Climatology project, 1984-89. Editor: The Geophysiology of Amazonia, 1986; contbr. articles to profl. jours. Fellow AAAS, Am. Meteorol. Soc. (chmn. com. biometeorol. and aerobiol. 1987-89, Meisinger award 1973, Editors award 1976, Jule Charney award 1987, Walter Orr Roberts lectr. in interdisciplinary sci. 1995), Am. Geophys. Union (com. earth as a sys. 1986-88, pres.-elect 1988-90, pres. 1990-92); mem. NAS, Internat. Assn. Meteorol. and Atmospheric Physics (sec. climate commn. 1983-87). Democrat. Home: 9290 N Yorkshire Ct Tucson AZ 85741-9357 Office: U Ariz Inst Atmospheric Physi Tucson AZ 85721

DICKINSON, SCOTT WARD, printing company executive; b. Hartford, Conn., Sept. 20, 1960; s. Robert Carl and Sheila Vance (Lee) D.; m. Robin Lou Karras, Oct. 19, 1985; children: Katie Lee, Daniel Robert. Student, Harvard U., 1977, Rochester Inst. Tech., 1982-84. Butcher's apprentice Ye Olde Butcher Shoppe, Acton, Mass., 1976-78; estimator Polaris Printing, Las Vegas, Nev., 1978-82; mgr. The Print Shop, Las Vegas, 1984-86; v.p., gen. mgr. Dickinson Printers, Las Vegas, 1986—. Founder, editor: (newspaper) The Nev. Rep., 1990-91. Counselor Code Hotline, Acton, 1974-78; lobbyist Nev. Assoc. and Ind. Business, Carson City, Nev., 1991, 93, 95; mem. state cen. com. Nev. Rep. Party, Carson City, 1992-94; mem. county exec. bd. Clark County Rep. Party, Las Vegas, 1988-94; vice chmn. state party Ind. Am. Party of Nev., 1994-95; mem. Leadership Las Vegas, 1994-95. Recipient Pres.'s Legion of Merit, Rep. Nat. Com., Washington, 1993-94. Mem. Nat. Assn. Printers and Lithographers, Nev. Assn. Ind. Bus. (bd. trustees 1990-94, v.p. 1995), So. Nev. Graphic Arts Assn. (sec. 1992—), Printing Industries of Am., Las Vegas C. of C. (com. chair 1992—), Las Vegas S.W. Rotary, Las Vegas Fremont Rotary (bull. editor 1986-91), Citizens for Responsible Govt., Nev. Concerned Citizens (lobbyist, bd. dirs. 1994-95), Phi Kappa Tau (sgt. at arms Gamma Nu chpt. 1982), Gamma Epsilon Tau (hon.). Home: 3616 Fortune Ave Las Vegas NV 89107-2174 Office: Dickinson Printers 3131 Meade Ave Las Vegas NV 89102-7809

DICKS, NORMAN DE VALOIS, congressman; b. Bremerton, Wash., Dec. 16, 1940; s. Horace D. and Eileen Cora D.; m. Suzanne Callison, Aug. 25, 1967; children: David, Ryan. BA, U. Wash., 1963, JD, 1968; LLD (hon.), Gonzaga U., 1987. Bars: Wash. 1968, D.C., 1978. Salesman, Boise Cascade Corp., Seattle, 1963; labor negotiator Kaiser Gypsum Co., Seattle, 1964; legis. asst. to Senator Warren Magnuson of Wash., 1968-73, adminstrv. asst., 1973-76; mem. 95th-103rd Congresses from 6th Wash. dist., Washington, D.C., 1977—. Mem. U. Wash. Alumni Assn., Sigma Nu. Democrat. Lutheran. Office: US Ho Reps 2467 Rayburn House Office Bldg Washington DC 20515

DICKSON, DAVID DOUGLAS, humanities educator; b. Ogden, Utah, Sept. 2, 1939; s. Forde and Elma B. (Whitesides) D.; m. Eleanor Taylor Ridges, Aug. 31, 1964; children: Catherine Marie Dickson Sutherland, Johnathan David. AA, Weber Coll., 1959; BA, Weber State, 1964; MA, Brigham Young U., 1966. Laborer Reed Constrn. Co., Morgan, Utah, 1958-59; missionary, min. LDS Ch., various locations, Germany, 1959-63; documents-libr. asst. U. Utah, Salt Lake City, 1963-64; landscapist, gardener Portand Cement Co., Devils Slide, Utah, 1964-66; teaching asst. Brigham Young U., Provo, Utah, 1965-66; prof. humanities Sierra Coll., Rocklin, Calif., 1966—; cons. for German Geneal. Socs., Calif., 1986-93; chair LLRC Sierra Coll., 1992-95. Author: Great Germans, 2 vols., 1972, 84, Adolf Clarenbach, The Reformer, 1987, (with others) Philo Hodge, 1756-1842, 1992; co-author: Life Story of Elma B. Whitesides, 1987; author, prodr. (video and book) Berlin, 1986. Chair varsity scouts Boy Scouts Am., greater Auburn area, 1966-89; tour leader Greater Saeto Cultural Exch. Club, Europe, 1967—; club leader 4-H, Meadow Vista, Calif., 1979-89; coach Am. Fedn. Soccer Clubs, greater Auburn area, 1983-85; coord. name extraction Auburn Calif. LDS Stake, Grass Valley, Nevada City, others, 1986-93. Mem. Nat. Coun. Tchrs. English, Am. Assn. Tchrs. German, Modern Lang. Assn., Sierra Coll. Faculty Assn. Home: 800 Cole Rd Meadow Vista CA 95722 Office: Sierra Coll 5000 Rocklin Rd Rocklin CA 95677

DICKSON, EVA MAE, credit bureau executive; b. Clarion, Iowa, Jan. 16, 1922; d. James and Ivah Blanche (Breckenridge) D. Grad. Interstate Bus. Coll., Klamath Falls, Oreg., 1943. Reporter, Mchts. Credit Service, Klamath Falls, 1941; credit dept. Montgomery Ward, Klamath Falls, 1941-42; bookkeeper Heilbronner Fuel Co., Klamath Falls, 1942; stenographer City of Klamath Falls, 1943, bookkeeper, office mgr., 1943-52; owner, operator All Star Bus. Service, Klamath Falls, 1953-58, Ace Mimeo Service, Klamath Falls, 1958-73; mgr. Mchts. Credit Service, 1973-87; customer service rep. CBI/Credit N.W., 1987-91. Bd. dirs. United Way, Klamath Falls, 1980—; sec. Klamath Community Concert Assn., 1956—; treas., memls. chmn. Klamath County chpt. Am. Cancer Soc.; bd. dirs., treas. Hope in Crisis; mem. Klamath County Centennial Com., 1982, Unification for Progress Joint Planning Com., 1985; mem. nursing adv. com. Oreg. Inst. Tech., 1982—; mem. Klamath Employment Tng. Adv. Com., 1983-86; bd. dirs., sec., treas. Klamath Consumer Council; sec. Unified City for Progress Task Force, 1983-84, Snowflake Winter Festival, 1984—; sec. First Presbyn. Ch., 1992—. Recipient Bronze Leadership award Assoc. Credit Burs., Inc., 1976. Mem. Daughters of Am. Colonists (past regent local chpt.), Consumer Credit Assn. Oreg. (pres. 1984-85), Credit Profl. Internat. (treas. dist. 10 1984-85, 2d v.p. dist. 10 1987-88, 1st v.p. 1988-89, pres. 1989-90, internat. bull. chmn. 1990-91, 92—), Assoc. Credit Bur. Pacific N.W. (pres. 1981-82), Assoc. Credit Bur. Oreg. (pres. 1978-80), Klamath Basin Credit Women-Internat. (pres. 1976-78), Soc. Cert. Consumer Credit Exec., Internat. Consumer Credit Assn., Klamath County C. of C. (pres. 1979, ambs. com. 1980—, Nat. Fedn. Bus. and Profl. Women's Club (chmn. nat. fin. com. 1983-84, nat. fin. com. 1982-83), Oreg. Fedn. Bus. and Profl. Women's Club (state pres. 1971-72), Klamath Falls Bus. and Profl. Women's Club (pres. 1966-67, 76-77). Republican. Presbyterian. Club: Quota (pres. 1958-59, dist. gov. 1969-70). Avocations: painting, traveling.

DICKSON, FREDERIC HOWARD, financial executive; b. Balt., Jan. 6, 1946; s. Frederic Harold and Clio Edith (Russell) D.; m. Linda Elisabeth Makosky, Mar. 23, 1968; children: Katherine, Barbara. BS, Pa. State U., 1967; MBA, SUNY, Buffalo, 1973. Mktg. research supr. Gen. Foods Corp., White Plains, N.Y., 1970-73; v.p. research Goldman, Sachs & Co., N.Y.C., 1973-82; chief investment officer SHAREINVEST, Ridgefield, Conn., 1982-87; v.p., sr. portfolio mgr. Mgmt. Asset Corp., Westport, Conn., 1987-89; founder, mng. dir. TDA Capital Mgmt. Co., Westport, Conn., 1990-92; v.p., dir. rsch. D.A. Davidson & Co., Great Falls, Mont., 1993—; sr. lectr. N.Y. Inst. Fin., N.Y.C., 1978—. Contbr. articles to profl. jours. Named disting. educator N.Y. Inst. Fin., 1982, disting. alumni, Pa. State U. Coll. Bus. Adminstrn., University Park, 1983. Mem. Market Technicians Assn. (pres. 1983-84, v.p. 1982-83, treas. 1981-82). Presbyterian. Office: DA Davidson & Co PO Box 5015 Great Falls MT 59403-5015

DICKSON, ROBERT LEE, lawyer; b. Hot Springs, Ark., Sept. 3, 1932; s. Constantine John and Georgia Marie (Allen) D.; m. Christina Farrar, Oct. 29, 1978; children—Robert Lee, Geoffrey, Alexandra, Christopher, George, John. B.B.A., U. Tex., 1959, LL.B., 1960. Bar: Tex. 1960, Calif. 1965, U.S. Dist. Ct. (no. dist.) Tex. 1960, U.S. Dist. Ct. (ea. dist.) Wis. 1979, U.S. Supreme Ct. 1980, U.S. Dist. Ct. (ea. dist.) Calif. 1983, U.S. Ct. Appeals (7th cir.) 1983, U.S. Dist. Ct. (no. and so. dists.) Calif. 1984, U.S. Ct. Appeals (9th cir.) 1987, U.S. Ct. Appeals (1st and 10th cirs.) 1989. Assoc. to ptnr. Eplen, Daniel & Dickson, Abilene, Tex., 1960-65; assoc. to sr. ptnr. Haight, Dickson, Brown & Bonesteel, Santa Monica, Calif., 1965-88; sr. ptnr. Dickson, Carlson & Campillo, Santa Monica, 1988—; bd. advisors UCLA Sch Nursing. Contbr. articles to profl. jours. Fellow Am. Coll. Trial Lawyers; mem. Ind. Bar Com., Def. Rsch. Inst. (steering com. of drug and device litigation com.), Fedn. Ins. and Corp. Counsel (chmn. pharm. liability litigation sect. 1984-87, v.p. 1986-89, bd. dirs. 1989—, sec.-treas. 1991-92, pres.-elect 1992-93, pres. 1993-94, chmn. 1994-95), Am. Bd. Trial Advocates, Assn. So. Calif. Def. Counsel (pres. 1976). Republican. Roman Catholic. Club: Bel Air Bay (Pacific Palisades). Home: 14952 Alva Dr Pacific Palisades CA 90272-4401 Office: Dickson Carlson & Campillo 120 Broadway 3d Fl PO Box 2122 Santa Monica CA 90407-2122

DICOCCO, MARC, flight test engineer; b. Lackland AFB, Tex., Aug. 17, 1962; s. Severino and Anne Marie (Bopp) DiC. BS in Aerospace Engring., Va. Poly. Inst., 1985; MS in Aerospace Engring., U. Dayton, 1990. Commd. 2d lt. USAF, 1985; advanced through ranks to capt., 1989; technician Prophet 21 Systems Inc., Yardley, Pa., 1984-85; advance concepts design engr. USAF Aeronautical Systems Divsn., Wright-Patterson AFB, Ohio, 1985-88, acquisition officer in tng., 1985-88, test project mgr., 1988-90; F-15E flight test engr. USAF Weapons and Tactics Ctr., Nellis AFB, Nev., 1990-94; chief engring. ops. br. Centaur Upper Space Div Space and Missile Ctr, L.A. AFB, 1994—; pres. aeronautic systems divsn. company grade officers adv. coun. Wright-Patterson AFB, 1989-90. Min. to youth club Our Lady of Peace Cath. Ch., Wright-Patterson AFB, 1987-90; altar server trainer Lady of the Skies Cath. Ch., Nellis AFB, 1993-94. Mem. AIAA, Aircraft Owners & Pilots Assn., Air Force Assn. (life), Planetary Soc.

DICOCHEA, ALFRED QUIJADA, municipal executive; b. Tucson, Aug. 23, 1944; s. Luis Miranda and Frances (Quijada) D.; m. Mary Ann Gutierrez, Oct. 5, 1968; children: Alfred Jr., Elizabeth Ann, Catherine Ann. BA, U. Ariz., 1968, MPA, 1975. Asst. town mgr. Town of South Tucson, 1968-70; program mgr. Com. for Econ. Opportunity, Tucson, 1970-72; citizen participation adminstr. City of Tucson, 1972-74; interim dir. Tucson-Pima Drug Abuse Clinic, 1974; urban programs adminstr. City of Tucson, 1974-78, departmental adminstrv. mgr., 1978—; urban transp. internship Carnegie-Mellon U., Pitts., 1977. Mem. Town of South Tucson Health Community Retirement Assn., 1968-70, Mex.-Am. Forum, 1969-74, Liaison in Neighborhood Knowledge, 1969-70, Awareness House, 1971-72, Policy Bd. of Model Cities, 1971-72, Mex.-Am. Scholarship Found., 1973-80, Ctr. Econ. Devel., 1974, Accion 80's, 1982-85; chmn. leadership com. San Xavier dist. Boy Scouts Am., 1969-70, Model Cities, Unit 10, 1972; past pres. Mex.-Am. Unity Coun., 1971; alt. to Study Group Coun. of Model Cities, 1972; del. to Transp. Task Force, 1972; pres. IMAGE de Tucson, 1977-78; mem. Spanish speaking coun. Diocese of Tucson, 1978-81; dir. region IX Nat. IMAGE Inc., 1979-81; mem. govt. rels. com. United Way, 1989-90; bd. dirs. Pio Decimo Ctr., 1971-73, Local Alcoholism Reception Ctr., 1973-75, Nosotros, Inc., 1978-93. With Ariz. Army N.G., 1967-73. Recipient Image of Tucson Community award Hispanic Image Chpt., 1978, Hispanic Recognition award Hispanic Community, 1992. Mem. Am. Mgmt. Assn., Am. Pub. Works Assn., Nat. Hispanic Assn. Inc. (bd. dirs. 1981-86), League United Latin Am. Citizens (chpt. # 1046), Ariz. Mcpl. Mgmt. Asst. Assn. Democrat. Roman Catholic. Office: City of Tucson Dept Transp PO Box 27210 Tucson AZ 85726-7210

DIEDERICH, J(OHN) WILLIAM, financial consultant; b. Ladysmith, Wis., Aug. 30, 1929; s. Joseph Charles and Alice Florence (Yost) D.; m. Mary Theresa Klein, Nov. 25, 1950; children: Mary Theresa Diederich Evans, Robert Douglas, Charles Stuart, Michael Mark, Patricia Anne Diederich Irelan, Donna Maureen (dec.), Denise Brendan, Carol Lynn Diederich Weaver, Barbara Gail, Brian Donald, Tracy Maureen, Theodora Bernadette, Tamara Alice, Lorraine Angela. PhB, Marquette U., Milw., 1951; MBA with high distinction, Harvard U., 1955. With Landmark Comm., Inc., Norfolk, Va., 1955-90, v.p., treas., 1965-73, exec. v.p. fin., 1973-78, exec. v.p. community newspapers, 1978-82, exec. v.p., CFO, 1982-90, fin. cons., 1990—; chmn. bd. dirs. Landmark Cmty. Newspapers, Inc., 1977-88; pres. Exec. Productivity Sys., Inc., 1982-88, LCI Credit Corp., 1991-93, Landmark TV Inc., 1991—, LTM Investments, Inc., 1991—; v.p., treas. KLAS, Inc., 1994—; v.p. Internet Express, Inc., 1994—; instr. Boston U., 1954, Old Dominion U., 1955-59. Bd. dirs. Internet Express, Inc., Landmark TV, Inc., LTM Investments, Inc. Lt. Col. USMC, 1951-53, USMCR, 1953-71 (ret.). Baker scholar Harvard U., 1955. Mem. SAR, Nat. Assn. Accts., Am. Numismatic Assn., Nat. Geneal. Soc., Wis. Geneal. Soc., Pa. Geneal. Soc., Sigma Delta Chi. Roman Catholic. Home and Office: PO Box 7334 1466 Glarus Ct Incline Village NV 89452-7334

DIEDRICK, GERALDINE ROSE, retired nurse; b. Chgo.; d. Milton Edward and Rose Agnes (Michalski) Goodman; R.N., Mt. San Antonio Coll., Walnut, Calif., 1963; BS, Calif. State U., L.A., 1966; MS, UCLA, 1968; divorced; 1 son, Scott Wesley. Nurse, State of Calif., 1960-83, dir. nursing Met. State Hosp., Norwalk, 1977-83; cons. in mental health, devel. disabilities. Recipient Letter of Commendation, State of Calif., 1974-77. Mem. Am. Nurses Assn., Nat. League Nursing, Am. Assn. Devel. Disabilities, Calif. Nurses Assn. (svc. awards), Am. Hosp. Assn., World Future Soc., Town Hall Calif. Lutheran. Contbr. to profl. jours.

DIEHL, DIGBY ROBERT, journalist; b. Boonton, N.J., Nov. 14, 1940; s. Edwin Samuel and Mary Jane Shirley (Ellsworth) D.; m. Kay Beyer, June 6, 1981; 1 dau., Dylan Elizabeth. A.B. in Am. Studies (Henry Rutgers scholar), Rutgers U., 1962; M.A. in Theatre Arts, UCLA, 1966, postgrad., 1966-69. Editor Learning Center, Inc., Princeton, N.J., 1962-64; dir. research Creative Playthings, Los Angeles, 1964-66; editor Coast mag., Los Angeles, 1966-68, Show mag., Los Angeles, 1968-69; book editor Los Angeles Times, 1969-78; v.p., editor-in-chief Harry N. Abrams, Inc., N.Y.C., 1978-80; book editor LA. Herald Examiner, 1981-86; movie critic, entertainment editor Sta. KCBS TV, Los Angeles, 1986-88; book columnist Playboy mag., Pasadena, Calif., 1988—; lit. corr. ABC-TV Good Morning America, N.Y.C., 1989—; instr. journalism UCLA, 1969-78; jurist Nat. Book Awards, 1972, Internat. Imitation Hemingway Contest, 1978—; mem. nominating com. Nat. Medal for Lit., 1972-75; v.p. Nat. Book Critics Cir., 1975-78, bd. dirs., 1981-87; jurist Am. Book Awards, 1981-85, v.p. programming, 1984-86; lit. columnist IBM/Prodigy, 1987—; columnist Modern Maturity, Long Beach, Calif., 1987—. Author: Supertalk: Extraordinary Conversations, 1974, Front Page, 1981. Trustee KPFK-Pacifica Found. Recipient; Irita Van Doren award, 1977. Mem. AAUP, PEN (pres. L.A. Ctr. 1987, v.p. treas. 1988—), AFTRA, Am. Soc. Journalists and Authors, Writers Guild Am., Phi Beta Kappa, Phi Sigma Delta. Home: 788 S Lake Ave Pasadena CA 91106-3948

DIEKMANN, BARBARA BRANDENBURG, computer systems researcher; b. Chgo., Aug. 11, 1946; d. Warner Otto and Anne (Storm) Brandenburg; m. Jeffrey Craig Fowler; children: Megan Anne, Molly Jean; m. James Edward Diekmann; stepchildren: Joshua, Jessica, Jacob. BA in Philosophy, Colo. State U., 1968; MA in Linguistics, U. Colo., 1990, Cert. in Cognitive Sci., 1993, postgrad., 1995. U.S. West Advanced Technologies; Eng. tchr. U.S. Peace Corps, Tamil Nadu, India, 1968-69; planning and scheduling engr. Bechtel Corp., San Francisco, and Edmonton, Alberta, Can., 1970-75; office mgr. Idaho Conservation League, Boise, Idaho, 1976-77; software editor, writer, troubleshooter IBM, Boulder, Colo., 1985-87; program analyst, staff asst. Nuc. Ops. Pub. Svc. Co., Denver and Platteville, Colo., 1987-89; student assoc. U.S. West Techs., Boulder, 1992—. Editl. bd. Colo. Rsch. in Linguistics. Mem. Inst. Cognitive Sci., Linguistic Soc. Am., Cognitive Sci. Soc., Computer Human Interaction, Assn. Computing Machinery. Home: 11797 Flatiron Dr Lafayette CO 80026

DIELI, MARY ADELAIDE, software engineer consultant. BA in Am. Studies, SUNY, Binghamton, 1977; PhD in Rhetoric, Carnegie Mellon U., 1986. Rsch. asst. Comm. Design Ctr., Carnegie Mellon U., Pitts., 1981-82; product trainer Apple Computer, Inc., 1982, project supr., cons., 1983-84; sr. document designer AT&T, 1984-85; document design cons. Lasselle-Ramsay, Inc., 1986-88; usability mgr. Microsoft Corp., Redmond, Wash., 1988-93; user interface design, usability cons. Seattle, 1994—; tchg. asst. SUNY-Binghamton, 1978-79, instr., 1979, 80; instr. Broome C.C., BinADRmton, 1980, Carnegie Mellon, 1980-81, Jefferson C.C., Watertown, N.Y., 1986; vis. asst. prof. dept. English Santa Clara U., 1986-87; tech. publs. mgr. Adobe Sys., Inc., Mountain View, Calif., 1987-88; affiliate asst. prof. tech. comm. dept. U. Wash., Seattle, 1991-93; mem. usability adv. bd. PC/Computing, 1993—; presenter in field. Contbr. articles to profl. jours. Mem. IEEE (Profl. Comm. Soc.), Wash. Software Assn., Soc. for Tech. Comm., Nat. Coun. Tchrs. English, Human Factors Soc. (spl. interest groups on computer sys., personality and individual differences in human performance, test and evaluation, visual performance), Assn. Computing Machinery (spl. interest groups on computer human interaction and documentation). Home: 120 W Highland Dr #421 Seattle WA 98119 Office: 1509 Queen Anne Ave N # 270 Seattle WA 98109

DIEMER, WILLIAM DAVID, retired engineer, research analyst; b. Cleve., May 19, 1924; s. Clarence Peter and Eleanor Marie (Champion) D.; m. Doris Grover Mudgett, June 11, 1960; children: Diane Beatrice, Karen Lisa. BS in Civil Engring., Case Inst. Tech., 1945; AM in Edn., U. Chgo., 1952. Structural engr. Am. Rolling Mill Co., Middletown, Ohio, 1945-46; cadastral engr. F.A. Pease Engring. Co., Cleve., 1946-48; admissions counselor Case Inst. Tech., Cleve., 1948-50; structural engr. Chgo., 1952-53; instr. mechanics Ill. Inst. Tech., Chgo., 1953-59; structural engr. Bertrand Goldberg Assocs., Chgo., 1959-60; rsch. project dir. Coll. Engring., UCLA, 1960-67; simulation programmer McDonnell-Douglas Corp., Santa Monica, Calif., 1968-70; dir. Acad. Census Data Ctr., Pacific Palisades, Calif., 1971; programmer Jet Propulsion Lab., Pasadena, 1972-73; rsch. analyst City of L.A., 1973-86, liaison 1990 census, 1987-90; founder, dir. Nat. Housing Register, Davis, Calif., 1991—. Author: Los Angeles Street Address Directory, 1989-93, Catalog I: Academic Census Data Center, 1971. Bd. dirs., pres. Consumers Co-op, Santa Monica, 1965-70, Unitarian Soc. L.A. West, 1962-66; bd. dirs. UN Assn. U.S.A., Davis, Calif., 1992—, Davis Cmty. Network, 1993—. Recipient Commendation/Plaque/Cert., City of L.A., 1990. Mem. Urban and Regional Info. Systems Assn. Democrat. Unitarian. Home: 27239 Meadowbrook Dr Davis CA 95616-5049 Office: Nat Housing Register 1403 5th St Davis CA 95616

DIENER, ROYCE, corporate director, retired health care services company executive; b. Balt., Mar. 27, 1918; s. Louis and Lillian (Goodman) D.; m. Jennifer S. Flinton; children: Robert, Joan, Michael. BA, Harvard U.; LLD, Pepperdine U. Comml. lending officer, investment banker various locations to 1972; pres. Am. Med. Internat., Inc., Beverly Hills, Calif., 1972-75, pres., chief exec. officer, 1975-78, chmn., chief exec. officer, 1978-85, chmn. bd., 1986-88, chmn. exec. com., 1986-89; bd. dirs. Calif. Econ. Devel. Corp., Acuson, Inc., Advanced Tech. Venture Funds, Am. Health Properties, AMI Health Svcs., plc., Consortium 2000. Author: Financing a Growing Business, 1966, 3d edit., 1978. Bd. visitors Grad. Sch. Mgmt., UCLA; mem. governing bd., UCLA Med. Ctr.; mem. vis. com. Med. Sch. and Sch. Dental Medicine, Harvard U.; bd. dirs. L.A. Philharm. Assn., L.A. chpt. ARC, Heritage Sq. Mus., Santa Monica. Served to capt. USAF, 1942-46, PTO. Decorated D.F.C. with oak leaf cluster. Mem. L.A. C. of C. (bd. dirs.), Calif. C. of C. (bd. dirs.), Calif. Bus. Round Table (bd. dirs.), Harvard Club, Regency Club, Calif. Yacht Club, Riviera Country Club (L.A.), Marks Club (London).

DIEPHOLZ, DANIEL RAY, real estate consultant, accountant; b. Hemet, Calif., Aug. 25, 1964; s. Eugene L. and Ruby J. (Forsch) D. BSBA in Acctg., Valparaiso U., 1985; MS in Real Estate with acad. honors, NYU, 1990. CPA, Calif.; lic. real estate broker, Calif. Auditor Blue Cross Calif., Woodland Hills, 1986-87; corp. fin. assoc., v.p. Bateman Eichler, Hill Richards Inc., L.A., N.Y.C., 1987-89; real estate cons. Price Waterhouse, L.A., 1990—; chmn. bd. Taos Palms Inc., L.A., 1990—. Mem. Nat. Assn. Accts. (bd. dirs. 1990—). Republican. Mem. LDS Ch. Home: 270 N Canon Dr # 1140 Beverly Hills CA 90210-5323 Office: Price Waterhouse 1880 Century Park E Los Angeles CA 90067-1600

DIESTELKAMP, DAWN LEA, systems analyst; b. Fresno, Calif., Apr. 23, 1954; d. Don and Joy LaVaughn (Davis) Diestelkamp. BS in Microbiology, Calif. State U.-Fresno, 1976, MS in Pub. Adminstrn., 1983, MBA, 1995, cert. in tng. design & mgmt., 1992. Lic. clin. lab. technologist, Calif.; cert. clin. lab. dir. Clin. lab. technologist Valley Med. Ctr., Fresno, 1977-82, info. systems coord., 1983-84, quality control coord. Valley Med. Ctr., Fresno, 1984-90, systems & procedures analyst, 1990-91; systems & procedures analyst Mcpl. Ct. Consol. Fresno Jud. Dist., 1991—; instr. Fresno City Coll. Tng. Inst., 1993—; cons., instr. in field. Mem. ASTD (dir. info.), Assn. Mcpl. Ct. Clks. Calif. (edn. and tng. com.), Fresno Women's Network (chair scholarship com., chair newsletter com., bd. dirs.), Fresno Met. Mus. Soc. Democrat. Office: 1100 Van Ness Ave Rm 200 Fresno CA 93721-2012

DIETRICH, DAWN YVETTE, English language educator; b. Livonia, Mich., Dec. 10, 1960; d. Edward Donald and Darlene Yvette (Hamlin) D. BA in English Lang. and Lit., Ea. Mich. U., 1983; MA in English Lang. and Lit., U. Mich., 1987, PhD in English Lang. and Lit., 1992. Lectr. English Johannes Gutenberg U., Mainz, Germany, 1990-91; asst. prof. English Western Wash. U., Bellingham, 1992—; mem. women's studies com., 1992—. Contbr. scholarly essays to Word and Image, 1992, Contemporary Literature, 1994; asst. editor: Theatre Jour., 1989-90. Patrides fellow U. Mich., 1988; creative rsch. grantee Western Wash. U., 1993-95; recipient NEH award, 1995. Mem. MLA, Soc. for Lit. and Sci., Coll. Art Assn., N.W. Women's Studies Assn. Office: Western Wash U Dept English Bellingham WA 98225

DIETRICH, WILLIAM ALAN, reporter; b. Tacoma, Sept. 29, 1951; s. William Richard and Janice Lenore (Pooler) D.; m. Holly Susan Roberts, Dec. 19, 1970; children: Lisa, Heidi. BA, Western Wash. U., 1973. Reporter Bellingham (Wash.) Herald, 1973-76, Gannet News Svc., Washington, 1976-78, Vancouver (Wash.) Columbian, 1978-82, Seattle Times, 1982—. Author: The Final Forest, 1992, Northwest Passage, 1995. Recipient Paul Tobenkin award Columbia U., 1986, Pulitzer prize for nat. reporting, 1990; Nieman fellow Harvard U., 1987-88. Office: Seattle Times PO Box 70 Seattle WA 98111-0070

DIETTERT, GERALD ALLEN, cardiologist; b. Moscow, Idaho, Sept. 25, 1927; s. Reuben Arthur and Charlotte (Thompson) D.; m. Ethel P. Caras, June 12, 1949; children: Craig, Carol, Scott, Bruce. Student, U. Mont., 1945-46, 48-50, BA, 1984, MA, 1990; MD, Washington U., St. Louis, 1954. Diplomate Am. Bd. Internal Medicine. Intern medicine Barnes Hosp., St. Louis, 1954-55; resident in medicine Barnes Hosp., 1955-56; fellow in cardiology Washington U., St. Louis, 1956-58; internist, cardiologist Western Mont. Clinic, Missoula, 1960-90; assoc. prof. U. Wash., Seattle and Missoula, 1970-85; pres. med. staff St. Patrick Hosp., Missoula, 1976, governing bd., 1976-82; pres. bldg. corp. Western Mont. Clinic, Missoula, 1970-80; pres. Mont. Heart Assn., Great Falls, 1963-64. Author: Grinnell's Glacier, 1992; contbr. articles to profl. jours. Mem. bd. edn. Sch. Dist. #5, Missoula, 1960-66, Missoula County H.S., 1962-66, Sch. Dist. #1, Missoula, 1966-72. With U.S. Army, 1946-48. Mem. Missoula Exch. Club (pres. 1961, Man of Yr. 1970, 80). Republican. Congregationalist. Home and Office: 9505 Nevada Trl Missoula MT 59802-9335

DIETZ, DONALD ARTHUR, vocational education educator; b. Vacaville, Calif., July 11, 1939; s. Arthur H. and Dorothy V. (Donald) D.; widowed, Jan. 1991; children: James, Corine, Loretta. BA in Indsl. Arts, San Francisco State U., 1962, MA in Indsl. Arts and Counseling, 1966; cert. in vocat. edn., U. Calif., Berkeley, 1966; cert. in counseling and adminstrn., U. San Francisco, 1967. Cert. tchr., Calif. Tchr. San Francisco Unified Sch. Dist., 1963-69, Acalanes Union High Sch. Dist., Lafayette, Calif., 1969—; counselor Acalanes Union High Sch. Dist., Lafayette, La., 1973-76; guest panelist Internat. Graphic Arts Educator Conf., Calif. State Poly. Coll., 1967; presenter workshop on archtl. model making Calif. Indsl. Edn. Bay Sect., Antioch, 1974; presenter seminar on engring. and drafting orientation Advantage Pers. Svcs., 1991. Contbr. articles to profl. publs. Recipient Outstanding Leadership award Calif. State Dept. Edn., 1990, Program of Excellence award Contra County Sch. Adminstrn., 1992. Mem. Calif. Tchrs. Assn., Calif. Indsl. Tech. Edn. Assn. (past v.p., past bd. dirs. Contra Costa chpt.), Calif. Graphic Arts Educators Assn., Am. Vocalition Assn., Acalanes Edn. Assn. (pres. 1976), Internat. Club Printing House Craftsmen (bd. dirs. Diablo chpt.), Diablo Craftsmens Club (v.p., Outstanding Craftsman award 1992). Home: 52 Overhill Rd Orinda CA 94563-3131 Office: Acalanes High Sch 1200 Pleasant Hill Rd Lafayette CA 94549-2623

DIETZ, JANIS CAMILLE, sales executive; b. Washington, May 26, 1950; d. Albert and Joan Mildred (MacMullen) Weinstein; m. John William Dietz, Apr. 10, 1981. BA, U. R.I., 1971; MBA, Calif. Poly. U., Pomona, 1984; postgrad. Claremont McKenna Coll., 1991—. Customer svc. trainer People's Bank, Providence, 1974-76; salesman, food broker Bradshaw Co., L.A., 1976-78; salesman Johnson & Johnson, L.A., 1978-79, GE Co., L.A., 1979-82; regional sales mgr. Leviton Co., L.A., 1982-85; nat. sales mgr. Jensen Gen. div. Nortek Co., L.A., 1985-86; retail sales mgr. Norris div. Masco, L.A., 1986-88; nat. sales mgr. Thermador Waste King div. Masco, L.A., 1988-91; nat. accts. mgr. Universal Flooring div. Masco, 1991-92; western regional mgr. Peerless Faucet div. Masco, 1992-95; performance devel. cons., Delta Faucet, div. Masco, 1995—; sales trainer, Upland, Calif., 1985—; instr. Calif. Poly. U., 1988—; lectr. Whittier Coll., 1994. Dir. pub. rels. Jr. Achievement, Providence, 1975-76; bd. trustees Nat. Multiple Sclerosis Soc., So. Calif. chpt. Recipient Sector Svc. award GE Co., Fairfield, Conn., 1980, Outstanding Achievement award, 1988. Mem. NAFE, Sales Profls. L.A. (v.p. 1984-86), Toastmasters (adminstrv. v.p. 1985). Unitarian.

DIETZ, PATRICIA ANN, engineering administrator; b. L.A., Nov. 30, 1958; m. Frank Raymond Dietz, July 1, 1978; children: Lindy K., Frank R. Jr. BA in Polit. Sci., U. Colo., 1983; MA in Psychology, Pepperdine U., 1993; Paralegal Cert., U. San Diego, 1988. Investment broker 1st Investors Corp., Colorado Springs, Colo., 1986-88; paralegal Law Offices of Ben Williams, Santa Monica, Calif., 1988-89; mgmt. analyst Bur. of Engring., City of L.A., 1989—; camp commandant Operation Safe Harbor-Haitian Humanitarian Relief Effort, 1992. Mem. Parent Tchr. Student Assn., Rosamond, Calif., 1992. Capt. USAR, 1986—. Nat. Urban fellow, 1991. Mem. Civil Affairs Assn., Res. Officers Assn., Engrs. and Architects Assn. Republican.

DIETZ, RUSSELL SCOTT, communications company executive; b. Freeport, N.Y., Mar. 1, 1963; s. Russell N. and Mary E. (Sattler) D.; m. Carla R. Cadwell, June 4, 1983. BS in Computer Sci., SUNY, Stony Brook, 1985. Computer system mgr. Shoreham Wading River Schs., Shoreham, N.Y., 1979-81; sr. computer programming RMS Data Svcs., Hicksville, N.Y., 1981-83; bd. dirs. Technically Elite Concepts Inc., Hermosa Beach, Calif.; sr. systems programmer/analyst Bendix Field Engring. Corp., St. Inigoes, Md., 1983-84; system implementation specialist Magnavox Electronic Systems Co., Ashburn, Va., 1984-87; prin. software specialist Digital Equipment Corp., Landover, Md., 1987-88; v.p. systems devel. Technically Elite Concepts Inc., Hermosa Beach, Calif., 1988—; cons. Cedars-Sinai Med. Ctr., L.A., 1988-90. Contbr. articles to profl. jours. Mem. Digital Equipment Corp. User Soc., DC VAX Local Users Group (chmn. 1985-87). Republican. Lutheran. Office: Technically Elite Concepts Inc 2615 Pacific Coast Hwy Ste 322 Hermosa Beach CA 90254-2227

DIETZ, VIDA LEE, utility company executive; b. Brawley, Calif., July 2, 1952. BSBA, U. Nev., 1975. Spl. asst. Sierra Pacific Co., Reno, 1976-78, asst. analyst, 1978-79, adminstr. extension agreement, 1979-83, adminstr. speaker's bur. and sch. programs, 1983-85, rep. community info., 1985-87; dir. spl. events, adminstr. charitable foundation Sierra Pacific Power Co., Reno, 1988—. Bd. dirs., 1st v.p. Sierra Nev. coun. Girl Scouts U.S., Reno, 1984-90, mem. nominating com., 1991-93; chmn. pub. rels. com. Jr. League Reno, 1986, chmn. ways and means, trustee, 1990-91, 93-94; chmn. meetings and events com. United Way No. Nev., 1987, mem. pub. rels. and spl. events com., 1988—; mem. individual sessions com. Nev. Gov.'s Conf. Women, 1989; mem. Sierra Arts Found., Nev. Women's Fund Scholarship Selection Com., 1989; bd. dirs. Western Nev. Clean Communities, 1990—, Nev. Women's Fund, 1992—; vol. pub. TV Sta. KNPB. Mem. AAUW (program v.p. 1986), Reno Women in Advt. (ednl. chmn. 1986), Western Indsl. Nev., Reno-Sparks C. of C. (ednl. com. 1986-87), Leadership Reno Alumni Assn. (bd. dirs. 1995—), U. Nev. Coll. Bus. Alumni Assn. (bd. dirs., treas. 1989-90, pres.-elect 1993-94, 95—, Outstanding Alumnus award 1994), U. Nev. Reno Alumni Assn. (treas. 1992-93, pres. 1994), Meetings Profls. Internat. Office: Sierra Pacific Power Co PO Box 10100 6100 Neil Rd Reno NV 89520

DIFALCO, JOHN PATRICK, arbitrator, lawyer; b. Steubenville, Ohio, Nov. 24, 1943; s. Pat John and Antoinette (Ricci) DiF.; m. Carolyn L. Otten, June 11, 1977; children: Elizabeth Ann, Jennifer Ann, Kevin John. BA, Ohio State U.; MA, U. No. Colo.; JD, Ohio State U. Bar: Ohio 1968, Colo. 1972, U.S. Dist. Colo. 1972, U.S. Ct. Appeals Colo. 1972, U.S. Supreme Ct. 1972, U.S. Ct. Appeals (fed. cir.) 1986, D.C. 1989. Atty., hearing officer, dir. U.S. Postal Svc., Washington, 1970-77; labor rels. specialist City and County of Denver, 1977-80; city atty. City of Greeley, Colo., 1980-87; pvt. practice Greeley, 1987—; prin. John P. DiFalco & Assocs., P.C., Ft. Collins, Colo., 1987—; instr. Regis U., Denver, U. Phoenix, Denver, Aims Community Coll., Greeley, Arapahoe Community Coll., Littleton, Colo., Pikes Peak Community Coll., Colo. Springs, Tri-State Coll., Angola, Ind.; arbitrator, 1980—; speaker in field. Contbr. Postmaster Advocate mag., also articles to profl. jours. Named an Outstanding City Atty. Colo., 1986. Mem. ABA (com. on pub. employee bargaining), Colo. Bar Assn. (labor law sect., Spl. Achievement award 1987), Fed. Bar Assn. (coms. on pub. sector labor rels., arbitration and office mgmt.), Colo. Trial Lawyers Assn., Indsl. Rels. Rsch. Assn., Nat. Pub. Employer Labor Rels. Assn., Am. Arbitration Assn., Nat. Inst. Mcpl. Law Officers (com. on law office mgmt.), Larimer County Bar Assn., Colo. Mcpl. League (chmn. attys. sect., mcpl. govt. issues and open meeting coms.), Met. Denver City Attys. Assn. (pres.), Ohio State U. Pres.'s Club, Rotary. Republican. Roman Catholic. Office: 1136 E Stuart St Ste 4102 Fort Collins CO 80525-1173

DIGBY, JAMES FOSTER, research engineer; b. Farmerville, La., Aug. 11, 1921; s. Sebe Lee and Maud Eloise (McLees) D.; m. Mary Jane Bruck, Dec. 5, 1959; children: Ward McLees, Drew James, Leslie Jane. BS, La. Tech., 1941; MA, Stanford (Calif.) U., 1942. Editor Watson Labs., USAF, Eatontown, N.J., 1946-47, def. planner, 1947-49; rsch. engr. The Rand Corp., Santa Monica, Calif., 1949-55, dept. head, 1956-58, program mgr. internat. studies, project leader, 1959-86, cons., 1986—; exec. dir. Calif. Seminar, Santa Monica, 1976-90; cons. Pres.'s Sci. Adv. Com., Washington, 1959-73, Commn. on Long Term Strategy, Washington, 1986-88; vice dir. Pan Heuristics, Marina del Rey, Calif., 1986-88; v.p. Am. Inst. for Strategic Coop., L.A., 1986-90; bd. dirs. European Am. Inst. for Security Rsch., L.A., 1976—. Author: (monograph) Precision-Guided Weapons, 1976. 1st lt. USAF, 1942-46, ETO. Mem. Internat. Inst. for Strategic Studies. Democrat. Home: 20773 Big Rock Dr Malibu CA 90265-5311 Office: The Rand Corp 1700 Main St Santa Monica CA 90401-3208

DIGENOVA, SILVANO ANTONIO, rare coin and fine art dealer; b. Avellino, Italy, Mar. 20, 1962; came to U.S., 1964; s. Antonio and Maddallena (Moscarello) DeG.; m. Eve Remmer, Sept. 4, 1993. Student, U. Pa., 1980-84. Chmn., pres. Tangible Investments of Am., Phila. and Laguna Beach, Calif., 1984—. Mem. Am. Numismatic Assn., Profl. Numismatic Guild, Coin and Bullion Numismatic Accreditation Bd. (bd. dirs. 1986-89). Office: Tangible Investments of Am 2025 S Pacific Coast Hwy Laguna Beach CA 92651

DIGRE, KATHLEEN B., neurology and ophthalmology educator; b. Mpls., July 6, 1950; d. Clifford B. and E. Bernice (Hoversten) D.; children: Johanna Martha, Gita Elena Varner. BA, Augustana Coll., 1972; MA, U. Ark., 1975; MD, U. Iowa, 1981. Resident in neurology U. Iowa, Iowa City, 1982-85, fellow in neurology-ophthalmology, 1985-87; asst. prof. neurology and ophthalmology U. Utah, Salt Lake City, 1987-91, assoc. prof. neurology and ophthalmology, 1992—. Fellow Am. Acad. Neurology, N.Am. Neuro-Ophthal. Soc. (treas. 1994); mem. Phi Beta Kappa. Office: Univ Utah Dept Neurology-Ophthalmology 50 N Medical Dr Salt Lake City UT 84132-0001

DILBECK, CHARLES STEVENS, JR., real estate company executive; b. Dallas, Dec. 2, 1944; s. Charles Stevens Sr. and Betty Doris (Owens) D.; 1 child, Stephen Douglas; m. Carolyn Jane DeBoer, Sept. 4, 1994. BS, Wichita State U., 1968; MS, Stanford U., 1969, postgrad., 1970-71. Engr. United Tech. Ctr., Sunnyvale, Calif., 1971-72; cons. Diversicom, Inc., Santa Clara, Calif., 1972-73; engr. Anamet Labs., San Carlos, Calif., 1973-75; cons. real estate investment Cert. Capital Corp., San Jose, Calif., 1975-82; pvt. practice in real estate, San Jose, 1981—; prin. Am. Equity Investments, San Jose, 1982—; mem. Los Gatos (Calif.) Rent Adv. Com., 1988. Mem. Nat. Apt. Assn., San Jose Real Estate Bd., Tri-County Apt. Assn., Gold Key Club, Tau Beta Pi (pres. 1968), Sigma Gamma Tau. Republican. Home: 301 Alta Loma Ln Santa Cruz CA 95062-4620 Office: Am Equity Investments 301 Alta Loma Ln Santa Cruz CA 95062

DILIBERTO, HELEN BRATNEY, librarian, retired educator; b. Newark, June 9, 1920; d. Leon and Julia (Spilchak) Bratney; m. Stephen Peter Diliberto, June 29, 1943 (div. 1972); children: Nina Diliberto Marlowe, Stephen Paul, Michael Lucio, James J. BA, N.J. Coll. for Women, 1943, U. Calif., Berkeley, 1961. Cert. tchr., N.J., Calif. Libr. League of Nations, Princeton, N.J., 1943-45; tchr. elem. grades Berkeley (Calif.) Unified Sch. Dist., 1961-65, libr., media specialist, 1965-72; libr., media specialist U.S. Overseas Dependency Schs., Yokosuka, Japan, 1980-82; now ret.; chmn. Berkeley Libr. Adv. Com., 1969-70; bd. dirs. Berkeley Educator's Assn., 1974-75; mem. Berkeley Supt.'s Edn. and Grade Com., 1974-75; mem. membership com. Overseas Educators Assn., Yokosuka, 1981; developer playwriting and puppetry program for children, 1972-76; cons. on audio-visual and book materials. Actress, Oreg. Barnstormers, Grants Pass, 1979, Yokosuka Drama Group, 1980-82; docent Oakland (Calif.) Mus., 1988-91; mem. choir Unitarian Universalist Ch., Berkeley, 1977—. Mem. LWV, NEA, AAUW, El Cerrito Hist. Soc., Grey Panthers. Democrat. Unitarian. Home: 769 Balra Dr El Cerrito CA 94530-3302

DILL, JEFFREY, lawyer, environmental geologist; b. New Brunswick, N.J., May 7, 1961; s. Charles George and Rita (Birssner) D.; m. Cynthia Jean Nogues, Aug. 12, 1989; 1 child, Kevin William. BS in Geology, W.Va. U., 1983; MBA, Calif. State U., Fullerton, 1990; JD, Western State U., Fullerton, 1991. Bar: Calif. 1992. Exploration geologist intern Consolidated Natural Gas Co., Clarksburg, W.Va., 1982; tchg./rsch. asst. Tulane U., New Orleans, 1983; materials supr. Cosmair, Inc., Piscataway, N.J., 1984-85; regional supr. Nissan Motor Corp., Costa Mesa, Calif., 1985-87; law clk., geologist Meserve, Mumper & Hughes, Irvine, Calif., 1990-91; assoc. atty. Lane Powell Spears Lubersky, L.A., 1992-93, Meserve, Mumper & Hughes, Irvine, 1993—. Mem. Rep. Law Students Assn., Fullerton, 1989. Mem. ABA, L.A. County Bar Assn., Orange County Bar Assn. (environ. program coord. 1994—), Peter Elliot Inn of Ct. (assoc.), JD/MBA Assn., Beta Gamma Sigma. Lutheran. Office: Meserve Mumper & Hughes 18500 Von Karman Ave Ste 600 Irvine CA 92715-0504

DILL, KILIAN, research scientist; b. Obersinn, Germany, Jan. 11, 1948; came to U.S., 1954; s. Anton and Elizabeth (Koenig) D.; m. Linda Begina (div.); 1 chld, Eric; m. Drena Kay Baker; children: Franz, Autumn L., Sona E. AB in Chemistry, CUNY, 1971; PhD in Chemistry, Calif. Inst. Tech., 1976. Rsch. assoc. Ind. U., Bloomington, 1976-80; prof. chemistry Clemson (S.C.) U., 1980-92; sr. rsch. scientist Molecular Devices, Sunnyvale, Calif., 1992—; cons., mem. summer faculty Battelle Meml. Inst., Columbus, Ohio, 1985-90. Contbr. numerous articles to profl. jours., chpts. to books. Grantee NIH, S.C. Heart Assn., Cottrell, U.S. Army, 1978-92. Mem. AAAS, Am. Chem. Soc. Home: 7170 La Honda Rd PO Box 496 La Honda CA 94020

DILL, LADDIE JOHN, artist; b. Long Beach, Calif., Sept. 14, 1943; s. James Melvin and Virginia (Crane) D.; children: Ariel, Jackson Caldwell. BFA, Chouinard Art Inst., 1968. lectr. painting and drawing UCLA, 1975-88. Exhbns. include: San Francisco Mus. Modern Art, 1977-78, Albright Knox Mus., Buffalo, 1978-79, Charles Cowles Gallery, N.Y.C., 1983-85, The First Show, Los Angeles; represented in permanent collections: Mus. Modern Art, N.Y.C., Laguna Mus. Art, Los Angeles County Mus., Mus. Contemporary Art, Los Angeles, Santa Barbara Mus., San Francisco Mus. Modern Art, Seattle Mus., Newport Harbor Art Mus., Oakland Mus., Smithsonian Instn., IBM, Nat. Mus., Seoul, Republic of Korea, San Diego Mus. Art, La. Mus., Denmark, Am. Embassy, Helsinki, Finland, Corcoran Gallery Art, Washington, Chgo Art Inst., Greenville County (S.C.) Mus., Palm Springs Desert Mus., Phoenix Art Mus., William Rockhill Nelsen Mus., Kansas City, Phillips Collection. Nat. Endowment Arts grantee, 1975, 82; Guggenheim Found. fellow, 1979-80; Calif. Arts Council Commn. grantee, 1983-84.

DILLARD, JOHN MARTIN, lawyer, pilot; b. Long Beach, Calif., Dec. 25, 1945; s. John Warren and Clara Leora (Livermore) D.; student U. Calif., Berkeley, 1963-67; BA, UCLA, 1968; JD, Pepperdine U., 1976; m. Patricia Anne Yeager, Aug. 10, 1968; children: Jason Robert, Jennifer Lee. Instr. pilot Norton AFB, Calif., 1973-77. Bar: Calif., 1976. Assoc. Magana, Cathcart & McCarthy, L.A., 1977-80, Lord, Bissell & Brook, L.A., 1980-85; of counsel Finley, Kumble, Wagner, 1985-86, Schell & Delamer, 1986-94, Law Offices of John M. Dillard, 1986—, v.p., gen. counsel, dir. Resort Aviation Svcs, Inc., Calif., 1988-93; mng. ptnr. Natkin & Weisbach, So. Calif., 1988-89. Active Am. Cancer Soc.; bd. dirs. Ednl. Found., Inc. Capt. USAF, 1968-73, Vietnam. Mem. ATLA (aviation litigation com.), Am. Bar Assn. (aviation com.), Orange County Bar Assn., Fed. Bar Assn., L.A. County Bar Assn. (aviation com.), Century City Bar Assn., Internat. Platform Assn., Res. Officers Assn., Orange County Com. of 100, Sigma Nu. Home: 19621 Verona Ln Yorba Linda CA 92686-2858 Office: 313 N Birch St Santa Ana CA 92701-5263

DILLARD, MARILYN DIANNE, property manager; b. Norfolk, Va., July 7, 1940; d. Thomas Ortman and Sally Ruth (Wallerich) D.; m. James Conner Coons, Nov. 6, 1965 (div. June 1988); 1 child, Adrienne Alexandra Coons (dec.). Studied with Russian prima ballerina, Alexandra Danilova, 1940's; student with honors at entrance, UCLA, 1958-59; BA in Bus. Adminstrn. with honors, U. Wash., 1962. Modeling-print work Harry Conover, N.Y.C., 1945; ballet instr. Ivan Novikoff Sch. Russian Ballet, 1955; model Elizabeth Leonard Agy., Seattle, 1955-68; mem. fashion bd., retail worker Frederick & Nelson, Seattle, 1962; retail worker I. Magnin & Co., Seattle, 1963-64; property mgr. Seattle, 1961—; antique and interior designer John J. Cunningham Antiques, Seattle, 1968-73; owner, interior designer Marilyn Dianne Dillard Interiors, 1973—; mem. rsch. bd. advisors Am. Biog. Inst., Inc., 1990—. Author: (poetry) Flutterby, 1951, Spring Flowers, 1951; contbr., asst. chmn. (with Jr. League of Seattle) Seattle Classic Cookbook, 1980-83. Charter mem., pres. Children's Med. Ctr., Maude Fox Guild, Seattle, 1965—, Jr. Women's Symphony Assn., 1967-73, Va. Mason Med. Ctr. Soc., 1990—, Nat. Mus. of the Am. Indian, Smithsonian Instn., Washington, 1992; mem. Seattle Jr. Club, 1962-65; bd. dirs. Patrons N.W. Civic, Cultural and Charitable Orgns. (chmn. various coms.), Seattle, 1976—, prodn. chmn., 1977-78, 84-85, auction party chmn., 1983-84, exec. com., 1984-85, chmn. bd. vols., 1990-91, adv. coun., 1991—; mem. U. Wash. Arboretum Found. Unit, 1966-73, pres., 1969; bd. dirs. Coun. for Prevention Child Abuse and Neglect, Seattle, 1974-75; v.p., mem. various coms. Seattle Children's Theatre, 1984-90, asst. in lighting main stage plays, 1987-93, mem. adv. coun., 1993—; asst. in lighting main stage plays Bathhouse Theatre, 1987-90; adv. bd. N.W. Asian Am. Theatre, 1987—, Co-Motion Dance Co., 1991—; organizer teen groups Episcopal Ch. of the Epiphany, 1965-67; provisional class pres. Jr. League Seattle, 1971-72, next to new shop asst. chmn., 1972-73, bd. dirs. admissions chmn., 1976-77, exec. v.p., exec. com., bd. dirs., 1978-79, sustaining mem., 1984—; charter mem. Jr. Women's Symphony Assn., 1967-73; mem. Seattle Art Mus., 1975-90, Landmark, 1990—, Corp. Coun. for the Arts, 1991—; founding dir. Adrienne Coons Meml. Fund, 1985, v.p., 1985-92, pres. 1992—; mem. steering com. Heart Ball Am. Heart Assn., 1986, 87, auction chmn., 1986; mem. steering com. Bellevue Sch. Dist. Children's Theatre, 1983-85, pub. rels. chair, 1984, asst. stage mgr., 1985. Named Miss Greater Seattle, 1964. Mem. AFTRA, Am. Biographical Inst., U. Wash. Alumnae Assn. (life), Pacific N.W. Ballet Assn. (charter), Progressive Animal Welfare Soc., Associated Women (student coun. U. Wash. 1962), Profl. Rodeo Cowboys Assn. (assoc.), Seattle Tennis Club. Republican. Episcopalian. Home and Office: 2053 Minor Ave E Seattle WA 98102-3513

DILLARD, MICHAEL L., food products company executive; b. 1942. BS in Acctg., Miss. Coll., 1964. Various acctg. positions Chrysler Corp., Cape Canaveral, Fla., 1964-66; divsn. acct. Blue Goose Growers, Vero Beach, Fla., 1966-76; CFO Pure Gold, Redlands, Calif., 1976-85, Saticoy Lemon Assocs., Inc., Santa Paula, Calif., 1985—. Office: Saticoy Lemon Assoc Inc 103 N Peck Rd Santa Paula CA 93060-3013*

DILLEY, WILLIAM GREGORY, aviation company executive; b. Sterling, Colo., June 6, 1922; s. William Gregory and Ethel Marie (Chandler) D.; m. M. Jean McCarthy, May 14, 1944; children: Gregory Dean, Karen Kay. BEng, U. Colo., 1951. Founder Spectra Sonics, Ogden, Utah, 1963—; cons., lectr. in field; investigator USAF Directorate of Flight Safety Rsch.. Contbr. over 300 articles to profl. jours.; patentee in field. Organizing mem. Minutemen. With USAF, Colo. Air N.G. Recipient Disting. Engring. Alumnus award U. Colo., 1977, Centennial medal; named one of prominent engrs. in U.S. Sci. and Tech. div. Libr. of Congress; fellow Audio Engring. Soc., 1970. Office: Spectra Sonics 3750 Airport Rd Ogden UT 84405-1531

DILLINGHAM, CHARLES, III, performing arts executive; b. Washington, Nov. 25, 1942; s. Charles and Barbara (Kibler) D.; m. Susan D. Clines, June 7, 1975; children: Jonathan Charles, Samantha Elizabeth. BA, Yale U., 1965, MFA, 1969. Gen. mgr. Am. Conservatory Theatre, San Francisco, 1969-78; free-lance producer, mgr. San Francisco, 1978-79; gen. mgr. Bklyn. Acad. Theatre Co., N.Y.C., 1979-81; gen. mgr. Am. Ballet Theatre, N.Y.C., 1981-84, exec. dir., 1984-89; pres., chief exec. officer The Entertainment Corp. U.S.A., N.Y.C., 1989-91; mng. dir. Center Theatre Group, L.A., 1991—; cons. Calif. Arts Coun.; co-founder, treas. Calif. Theatre Coun., co-founder, pres. Dance U.S.A. Democrat. Unitarian. Office: Center Theatre Group 13460 Bayliss Rd Los Angeles CA 90049-1833

DILLMAN, DONALD ANDREW, sociologist, educator; b. Chariton, Iowa, Oct. 24, 1941. BS, Iowa State U., 1964, MS, 1966, PhD, 1969. Rsch. assoc. Iowa State U., Ames, 1967-69; asst. prof. Wash. State U., Pullman, 1969-73, assoc. prof., dept. chair, 1973-81, prof., 1978—, dir. social and econ. scis. rsch. ctr., 1986—; guest prof. German Ctr. for Survey Methods Rsch., Mannheim, Fed. Republic of Germany, 1985, 87; sr. survey methodologist Office of Dir. U.S. Bur. Census, 1991-95; cons. and lectr. in field. Author: Mail and Telephone Surveys, 1978; co-author 5 books; contbr. articles to profl. jours. Kellogg fellow, 1981-83; grantee in field. Fellow AAAS, Am. Statis. Assn.; mem. Am. Sociology Assn., Rural Sociol. Soc. Am. (pres. 1983-84, Outstanding Svc. award 1983), Am. Assn. Pub. Opinion Rsch., World Future Soc. Home: 705 SW Mies St Pullman WA 99163-2056 Office: Wash State U Wilson Hall 133 Pullman WA 99164-4014

DILLON, CHARLES G., architect; b. Danville, Va., Oct. 31, 1940; s. Edward and Angline (Caporaso) D.; Dawn Mander Nov. 25, 1968; children: Kristen Marie, Lauren Marie, Kelsey Lynn. BArch, Pratt Inst., Bklyn., 1963, MArch, 1966. Registered architect, Ariz. Designer Hilltopp, Inc., Tucson, 1966-75, project designer, planner, 1975-89; v.p. Werik & Werik, Ltd., Las Vegas, 1989—. Fellow AIA; mem. Downtown Athletic Club, Kappa Alpha. Republican. Roman Catholic. Office: Werik & Werik Ltd 3305 Spring Mountain Rd Ste 60 Las Vegas NV 89102-8624

DILLON, FRANCIS PATRICK, human resources executive, management and personnel sales consultant; b. Long Beach, Calif., Mar. 15, 1937; s. Wallace Myron and Mary Elizabeth (Land) D.; B.A., U. Va., 1959; M.S., Def. Fgn. Affairs Sch., 1962; M.B.A., Pepperdine U., 1976; m. Vicki Lee Dillon, Oct. 1980; children: Cary Randolph, Francis Patrick Jr., Randee, Rick. Traffic mgr., mgr. pers. svcs. Pacific Telephone Co., Sacramento and Lakeport, Calif., 1966-69; asst. mgr. manpower planning and devel. Pan-Am. World Airways, N.Y.C., 1969-71; mgr. pers. and orgn. devel. Continental Airlines, L.A., 1971-74; dir. human resources Bourns, Inc., Riverside, Calif., 1974-80; v.p. employee and cmty. relations MSI Data Corp., 1980-83; pres. Pavi Enterprises, 1983—; cons. mgmt. Pers. Outplacement Counseling/Sales/Mgmt., fin. svcs./mortgage reductions 1983—; pres., CEO Pers. Products & Svcs., Inc., 1984-91; v.p. Exec. Horizons, Inc., 1988-94; sr. profl. svcs. cons. Right Assocs., 1994—; pres. Meditrans Inc. Bd. dirs. Health Svcs. Maintenance Orgn., Inc., Youth Svcs. Ctr., Inc.; vol. precinct worker. Served to lt. comdr. USN, 1959-66; asst. naval attaché, Brazil, 1963-65. Recipient Disting. Svc. award Jaycees, 1969; Jack Cates Meml. Vol. of Year award Youth Svc. Ctr., 1977. Mem. Assn. Internal Mgmt. Cons.'s, Am. Soc. Personnel Adminstrn., Personnel Indsl. Rels. Assn., Am. Soc. Tng. and Devel., Am. Electronics Assn. (human resources com., chmn. human resources symposium), Lake Mission Viejo Assn. (sec., bd. dirs. 1990-94). Republican. Episcopalian. Clubs: Mission Viejo Sailing, YMCA Bike, Mission Viejo Ski, Caving, Toastmasters (pres. 1966-67), Have Dirt Will Travel, Capo Valley 4 Wheelers. Office: Pavi Enterprises 27331 Via Amistoso Mission Viejo CA 92692-2410

DILLON, GEORGE CHAFFEE, manufacturing company executive; b. Kansas City, Mo., Oct. 29, 1922; s. Edward J. and Mary (Coon) D.; m. Joan Alamo Kent, Sept. 11, 1948; children: Kent, Courtney, Emily. BS, Harvard U., 1944, MBA, 1948. Adminstrv. asst. J. A. Bruening Co., Kansas City, Mo., 1948-51; with Butler Mfg. Co., Kansas City, Mo., 1951-86, treas., from 1960, v.p., 1961-63, exec. v.p., 1963-67, pres., 1967-78, chmn. bd., chief exec. officer, 1978-86; chmn. Manville Corp., Denver, 1986-91; bd. dirs. Johns Manville Corp., Phelps Dodge Corp., Newhall Land and Farming Co., Astec Industries, Chattanooga; chmn. oversight com. Nat. Renewable Energy Lab. Past. chmn. bd. trustees Midwest Research Inst., Kansas City, Mo.; trustee Mayo Found., Rochester, Minn., Children's Mercy Hosp., Kansas City, Mo.; bd. overseers Harvard U., 1980-86. Lt. USNR, 1943-46. Home and Office: 5049 Wornall Rd Kansas City MO 64112-2423

DILLON, MICHAEL EARL, engineering executive, mechanical engineer, educator; b. Lynwood, Calif., Mar. 4, 1946; s. Earl Edward and Sally Ann (Wallace) D.; m. Bernardine Jeanette Staples, June 10, 1967; children: Bryan Douglas, Nicole Marie, Brendon McMichael. BA in Math., Calif. State U., Long Beach, 1978, postgrad. Registered profl. engr. Calif., Colo., Tex., Nev., Utah, Ariz., Wyo., Pa., Hawaii, N.Y. Journeyman plumber Roy E. Dillon & Sons, Long Beach, 1967-69, ptnr., 1969-73; field supr. Dennis Mech., San Marino, 1973-74; chief mech. official City of Long Beach, 1974-79; mgr. engr. Southland Industries, Long Beach, 1979-83; v.p. Syska & Hennessy, L.A. and N.Y., 1983-87; prin. Robert M. Young & Assoc., Pasadena, Calif., 1987-89; pres. Dillon Cons. Engrs., Long Beach, 1989—; mech. cons. in field; instr. U. Calif., Irvine, San Diego and L.A., U. So. Calif., L.A., Calif. State U., Long Beach, U. Tex., Arlington; lectr. in field. Contbr. over 160 poems to various publs., 25 articles to profl. jours. Vice chair Mechanical, Plumbing, Elec. and Energy Code Adv. Commn. of Calif., Bldg. Stds. Commn.; bd. examiners Appeals and Condemnations, Long Beach; mem. State Fire Marshals Adv. Bd., Sacramento, Calif.; adv. bd. City of L.A.; mem. bus. adv. bd. City of Long Beach. Recipient Environ. Ozone Protection award U.S. EPA, 1993. Fellow ASHRAE (bd. dirs.), Inst. of Refrigeration Heating, Air Conditioning Engrs. of New Zealand, Inst. Advancement Engring.; mem. ASCE, NSPE, ASTM, ASME, Am. Cons. Engrs. Coun., Am. Soc. of Plumbing Engrs, Internat. Soc. Fire Safety Sci., Chartered Inst. Bldg. Svcs. Engrs. Great Britain and Ireland, Nat. Acad. of Forensic Engrs., Nat. Inst. for Engring. Ethics, Nat. Fire Protection Assn., Internat. Conf. Bldg. Officials, Internat. Platform Assn., Internat. Fire Code Inst., So. Bldg. Code Congress Internat. Inc., Bldg. Officials and Code Adminstrs. Internat., Cons. Engrs. and Land Surv. Calif., Soc. of Fire Protection Engrs., Tau Beta Pi, Pi Tau Sigma, Chi Epsilon, others. Office: Dillon Cons Engrs 1165 E San Antonio Dr Ste D Long Beach CA 90807-2374

DILLON, ROBERT MORTON, retired association executive, architectural consultant; b. Seattle, Oct. 27, 1923; s. James Richard and Lucille (Morton) D.; m. Mary Charlotte Beeson, Jan. 6, 1943; children: Robert Thomas, Colleen Marie Dillon Brown, Patrick Morton. Student, U. Ill., 1946-47; BArch., U. Wash., 1949; MA in Architecture, U. Fla., 1954. Registered architect, Fla. Designer-draftsman Williams and Longstreet (Architects), Greenville, S.C., 1949-50, William G. Lyles, Bissett, Carlisle & Wolff (Architects), Columbia, S.C., 1949-50, Robert M. Dillon and Wm. B. Eaton (Architects), Gainesville, Fla., 1952-55; staff architect Bldg. Rsch. Adv. Bd., Nat. Acad. Scis.-NRC, Washington, 1955-56, project dir., 1956-58, exec. dir., 1958-77; exec. sec. U.S. nat. com. for Conseil Internat. du Batiment, 1962-74; Sec. U.S. Planning Com. 2d Internat. Conf. on Permafrost, Yakutsk, USSR, 1972-74; exec. asst. to pres. Nat. Inst. Bldg. Scis., Washington, 1978-81, v.p., 1982-84, acting contr., 1983-84; exec. v.p. Am. Coun. Constrn. Edn., Washington, 1984-89, cons., 1989—; asst. prof. arch. Clemson Coll., 1949-50; instr., asst. prof. arch. U. Fla., 1950-55; lectr. structural theory and design Cath. U. Am., 1956-62; guest lectr. Air Force Inst. Tech., Wright-Patterson AFB, 1964-65; disting. faculty Acad. Code Adminstrn. and Enforcement U. Ill., 1972, professorial lectr. George Washington U., 1973-77, 81-82; vis. prof. Coll. Environ. Design U. Okla., 1984, adj. assoc. prof. bldg. sci., 1985-89. Author: (with S.W. Crawley) Steel Buildings: Analysis and Design, 1970, 4th edit., 1993 (also 3d edit. pub. in Spanish 1992); contbg. author: Funk and Wagnall's New Ency., 1972, Ency. of Architecture, 1989; editor-in-chief: Guide to the Use of NEHRP Provisions in Earthquake Resistant Design of Buildings, 1987, Building Seismic Safety Coun., Nat. Inst. Bldg. Scis. Cons. Ednl. Facilities Labs., N.Y.C., 1958-71; mem. adv. com. low-income housing demonstration program HUD, Washington, 1964-67; mem. working groups U.S.-USSR Agreement on Housing and Other Constrn., 1975-85; mem. sub-panel housing White House Panel on Civilian Tech., Washington, 1961-62; mem. advs. to F. Stuart Fitzpatrick Meml. Award Trustee, 1969-84, chmn., 1974-78; mem. adv. panel Basic Homes Program OEO and HUD, 1972-77; mem. Nat. Adv. Coun. Rsch. Energy Conservation, 1975-78; mem. adv. com. Coun. Am. Bldg. Ofcls., 1976-86; mem. tech. coun. on bldg. codes and standards; sec. Home and Land Owners Assn., Angel Fire, N.Mex., 1991-95; co-chmn. initial bd. dirs. Assn. Angel Fire Property Owners, 1995. Mem. AIA (com. rsch. for architecture 1962-67, chmn. 1969, chmn. com. archtl. barriers 1967-68, nat. housing com. 1970-72, 84-85, mem. emeritus 1990—), ASCE (task com. cold regions 1977-79, tech. coun. cold regions engring., exec. com. 1976-84, chmn. 1981, standards com. 1987-94), DAV (life), Nat. Acad. Code Adminstrn. (trustee 1976-80, exec. com. 1978-82, new bd. dirs. 1980-82, 83-84, sec.-treas. 1982-82, life), Am. Inst. Steel Constrn., Am. Inst. Constructors, Am. Coun. Constrn. Edn. (trustee), N.Mex. Soc. Architects, Nat. Inst. Bldg. Scis. (cons. coun. 1984-93). Home and Office: PO Box 193 Angel Fire NM 87710

DILORENZO, FRANCIS X., bishop; b. Philadelphia, PA, Apr. 15, 1942. ordained priest May 18, 1968. Titular bishop of Tigia, 1988; aux. bishop Diocese of Scranton, 1988; apostolic admin. Diocese of Honolulu, 1993-94, bishop, 1994—. Office: Chancery Office 1184 Bishop St Honolulu HI 96813-2838*

DILUIGI, RONALD RICHARD, health care agency executive; b. Vineland, N.J., Aug. 26, 1946; s. Dominick and Anna (Alzerano) DiL.; m. Paula Louise Pletcher, July 8, 1967; children: Jason Ronald, Marisa Nicole, Adrienne Christine. BA, Calif. State U., Fullerton, 1972, MPA, 1974; grad. exec. program, U. Calif., Irvine, 1984. Cert. community coll. instr., Calif. Adminstrv. intern City of Huntington Beach (Calif.) City Mgrs. Office, 1972-73; adminstrv. aide City of Huntington Beach Dept. of Fin., 1973-74; adminstrv. analyst Orange County Adminstrv. Office, Santa Ana, Calif., 1974-76; asst. chief mgmt., budget and legis. Orange County Adminstrv. Office, Santa Ana, 1976-82; dir. agy. adminstrn. Orange County Health Care Agy., Santa Ana, 1982-86, asst. agy. dir., 1986—; Bd. dirs. Maternal Outreach Mgmt. Sys., Santa Ana, St. Jude Med. Ctr. Meml. Found., 1989-93, St. Jude Heritage Health Found., Fullerton, Calif.; exec. coun. Am. Soc. Pub. Adminstrn., County of Orange, Calif., 1981-83; bd. trustees St. Jude Hosp., Yorba Linda, 1984-89. Chair planning commn. City of Yorba Linda, 1983—; mem. parks and recreation commn., 1983-89, mem. housing and cmty. devel. coun., 1983-89; mem. care for poor fund allocation com. St. Joseph Health Sys., Orange, Calif., 1991—. With USNR, 1966-68. Mem. Calif. State Fullerton Alumni Assn. Home: 20780 Paseo De La Rambla Yorba Linda CA 92687-2420 Office: Orange County Health Care 515 N Sycamore St Santa Ana CA 92701-4637

DIMARCHI, DAVID OSCAR, air force officer; b. Teaneck, N.J., Feb. 6, 1952; s. John Phillip and Ramona Elaina (Sather) DiM.; m. Nancy Louise Peterson, June 8, 1974; children: Lisa, Peter, Paul. BS in Engring. Mgmt., USAF Acad., 1974; MS in Mgmt., Webster U., 1983. Commd. 2d lt. USAF, 1974, advanced through grades to col.; B-52 pilot 320th Bomb Wing USAF, Mather AFB, Calif., 1976-78; chief T-38 acad. tng. 71st Flying Tng. Wing, Vance AFB, Okla., 1978-81; chief CAI br. HQ ATC, 3305 Sch. Sq., Randolph AFB, Tex., 1981-84; commandant of cadets AFROTC DET 206, SIUE, Edwardsville, Ill., 1984-86; rsch. fellow Ctr. for Aerospace Doctrine, Maxwell AFB, Ala., 1986-87; chief, trainer acquisition br. Asst. Sec. A.F./Acquisition, The Pentagon, Washington, 1987-90; chief mgmt. effectiveness & safety HQ 64th Flying Tng. Wing, Reese AFB, Tex., 1991-93; chief policy, plans & programs HQ USAF Acad., Colorado Springs, Colo., 1993—. Author: Managing the Career Trainer Force, 1987. Asst. scoutmaster Troops 157/79 Boy Scouts Am., Lubbock, Tex. & Colorado Springs, 1991—. Mem. Air Force Assn., USAF Acad. Assn. Grads. Republican. Roman Catholic. Home: 1165 Big Valley Dr Colorado Springs CO 80919-1032 Office: HQ USAFA/XPP 2304 Cadet Dr Ste 350 U S A F Academy CO 80840-5099

DI MASSA, ERNANI VINCENZO, JR., broadcast executive, television producer, writer; b. Phila., Sept. 12, 1947; s. Ernani Vincenzo and Rita C. (Iacovoni) Di M.; m. Karen Sue Bryant, July 10, 1976; 1 child, Michael Colin. BS, La Salle Coll., 1970; MS, Temple U., 1972. Producer, writer Mike Douglas Show, Phila. and L.A., 1969-81, Regis Philbin Show, L.A., 1981, Fantasy NBC-TV, L.A., 1981-83; exec. producer, writer Thicke of the Night, L.A., 1983-84, Tony Orlando Show, L.A., 1985-86; supervising producer Hollywood Squares, L.A., 1987-89; sr. v.p. programming and devel. King World Prodns., L.A., 1989—. Supervising producer Candid Camera; exec. in charge prodn. Rolonda. Recipient Emmy award NATAS, 1982. Mem. Producers Guild Am., Writers Guild Am. Roman Catholic. Office: King World Inc 115 E Broadway Apt G104 San Gabriel CA 91776-1893

DIMATTIO, TERRY, historic site administrator. Park supt. Cabrillo National Monument, San Diego, Calif. Office: Cabrillo Nat Monument PO Box 6670 San Diego CA 92166-0670

DIMITRIADIS, ANDRE C., health care executive; b. Istanbul, Turkey, Sept. 29, 1940; s. Constantine N. and Terry D. BS, Robert Coll., Istanbul, 1964; MS, Princeton U., 1965; MBA, NYU, 1967, PhD, 1970. Analyst Mobil Oil Internat., N.Y.C., 1965-67; mgr. TWA, N.Y.C., 1967-73; dir. Pan Am. Airways, N.Y.C., 1973-76; asst. treas. Pan Am. Airways, 1976-79; v.p., chief fin. officer Air Calif., Newport Beach, 1979-82; exec. v.p. fin. and adminstrn., chief fin. officer Western Airlines, Los Angeles, 1982-85; dir. Western Airlines; sr. v.p. (fin) Am. Med. Internat., from 1985, chief fin. officer, 1985-89, exec. v.p., 1988-89; dir., exec. v.p. fin., chief fin. officer Beverly Enterprises Inc., Ft. Smith, Ark., 1989-92; chmn., CEO LTC Properties, Inc., 1992—; bd. dirs. Charter Med. Group, Sunhealthcare Inc., Homecare Mgmt. Inc., Assisted Living Concepts, Inc. Democrat. Greek Orthodox. Home: 4470 Vista Del Preseas Malibu CA 90265-2540

DIMMICK, CAROLYN REABER, federal judge; b. Seattle, Oct. 24, 1929; d. Maurice C. and Margaret T. (Taylor) Reaber; m. Cyrus Allen Dimmick, Sept. 10, 1955; children: Taylor, Dana. BA, U. Wash., 1951, JD, 1963; LLD, Gonzaga U., 1982, CUNY, 1987. Bar: Wash. Asst. atty. gen. State of Wash., Seattle, 1953-55; pros. atty. King County, Wash., 1955-59, 60-62; sole practice Seattle, 1959-60, 62-65; judge N.E. Dist. Ct. Wash., 1965-75, King County Superior Ct., 1976-80; justice Wash. Supreme Ct., 1981-85; judge U.S. Dist. Ct. (we. dist.) Wash., Seattle, 1985-94, chief judge, 1994—; chmn. Jud. Resources Com., 1991—, active, 1987—. Recipient Matrix Table award, 1981, World Plan Execs. Council award, 1981, others. Mem. ABA, Am. Judges Assn. (gov.), Nat. Assn. Women Judges, World Assn. Judges, Wash. Bar Assn., Am. Judicature Soc., Order of Coif (Wash. chpt.), Wash. Athletic Club, Wingpoint Golf and Country Club, Harbor Club. Office: US Dist Ct 911 US Courthouse 1010 5th Ave Seattle WA 98104-1130

DIMSDALE, JOEL EDWARD, psychiatry educator; b. Sioux City, Iowa, Apr. 16, 1947; s. Lewis J. and Phyllis (Green) D.; m. Nancy Kleinman, Sept. 17, 1978; 1 child, Jonathan Jared. BA in Biology, Carleton Coll., 1968; MA in Sociology, Stanford U., 1970, MD, 1973. Diplomate Am. Bd. Psychiatry. Resident in psychiatry Mass. Gen. Hosp., Boston, 1973-76; instr. psychiatry Harvard U. Sch. Medicine, Boston, 1976-80, asst. prof., 1980-84, assoc. prof., 1984-85; assoc. prof., now prof. psychiatry U. Calif., San Diego, 1985—; cons. to Pres.'s Commn. on Mental Health, Washington, 1977-78, NIH, Washington, 1980—. Editor: Survivors, Victims and Perpetrators, 1980; editor-in-chief Psychosomatic Medicine, 1992—; mem. editorial bd. Internat. Jour. Behavioral Medicine, 1993—, Applied Biobehavioral Rsch., 1994—, Am. Jour. Human Biology, 1994—; contbr. articles to profl. jours. Fellow Am. Psychopathol. Assn., Am. Psychiat. Assn., Acad. Behavioral Med. Rsch. (coun. 1988-91, pres. 1991-92); mem. Am. Psychosomatic Soc. (coun. 1982-85), Sigma Xi. Home: 1684 Lugano Ln Del Mar CA 92014-4126 Office: U Calif Med Ctr 225 Dickinson St San Diego CA 92103-1910

DI MUCCIO, MARY JO, retired librarian; b. Hanford, Calif., June 16, 1930; d. Vincent and Theresa (Yovino) DiMuccio. B.A., Immaculate Heart Coll., 1953, M.A., 1960; Ph.D., U.S. Internat. U., 1970. Tchr. parochial schs. Los Angeles, 1949-54, San Francisco, 1954-58; tchr. Govt. of Can., Victoria, B.C., 1959-60; asst. librarian Immaculate Heart Coll. Library, Los Angeles, 1960-62; head librarian Immaculate Heart Coll. Library, 1962-72; adminstrv. librarian City of Sunnyvale, Calif., 1972-88; ret., 1988; part-time instr. Foothill C.C., 1977—. Exec. bd., past pres. Sunnyvale Community Services. Mem. ALA, ICF (past pres.), Spl. Libr. Assn., Cath. Libr. Assn. (past pres.), Calif. Libr. Assn., Sunnyvale Bus. and Profl. Women, Peninsula Dist. Bus. and Profl. Women (past pres.). Home: 736 Muir Dr Mountain View CA 94041-2509

DINEL, RICHARD HENRY, lawyer; b. L.A., Sept. 16, 1942; s. Edward Price and Edith Elizabeth (Rheinstein) D.; m. Joyce Ann Korsmeyer, Dec. 26, 1970; children: Edward, Alison. BA, Pomona Coll., 1964; JD, Stanford U., 1967. Bar: Calif. Owner Richard H. Dinel, A Profl. Law Corp., L.A., 1971-79; ptnr. Richards, Watson & Gershon, L.A., 1979-92, of counsel, 1992-93; pres. R. H. Dinel Investment Counsel, Inc., 1992—; bd. dirs. The Price Co., 1990-92. Chmn. bd. Pomona Coll. Assocs., 1987-89; ex-officio trustee Pomona Coll., 1987-89; arbitrator Chgo. Bd. Options Exch., 1978—, Pacific Stock Exch., 1979—; bd. govs. Western Los Angeles County counsel Boys Scouts Am., 1993—. Mem. Securities Ind. Assn. (speaker compliance and legal div. 1978-92), Pomona Coll. Alumni Assn. (chmn. alumni fund and continuing edn. com. 1972-73), Nat. Assn. Securities Dealers (mem. nat. bd. arbitrators 1978-90), City Club on Bunker Hill, Bond Club L.A. Office: 11661 San Vicente Blvd Ste 400 Los Angeles CA 90049-5112

DING, MAE LON, employee compensation consultant; b. Norwalk, Calif., May 7, 1954; d. Lock Gee and Ruth (Tang) D.; m. Stephen M. Batcheller, Nov. 30, 1985 (div. Mar. 1992). BA, UCLA, 1976; MBA, U. So. Calif., 1979. Cons. Forum Corp., Boston, 1978, Wyatt Co., Boston, 1978-81; sr. cons. R. A. Smith & Assoc., Mission Viejo, Calif., 1981-83; mgr. compensation Allergan Pharms., Irvine, Calif., 1983-85; pres. Pers. Systems Assoc., Tustin, Calif., 1985—; instr. U. Calif., Irvine, 1988-89, Calif. State U., Long Beach, 1988-90, Calif. State Coll., Pomona, 1987-88, Chapman Coll., Orange, Calif., 1991; speaker in field. Author: Survey Sources, 1991, 3rd rev. edit. 1993; contbr. articles to profl publs. Mem. Assn. Profl. Cons. (bd. dirs. 1989—, pres. 1993-94, 94-95), Am. Compensation Assn. (instr. 1984—), Orange County Compensation Assn., Orange County Forensic Cons. Assn. (bd. dirs. 1994, 95). Office: Pers Systems Assoc 2282 Aspen St Tustin CA 92680-8341

DINI, JOSEPH EDWARD, JR., state legislator; b. Yerington, Nev., Mar. 28, 1929; s. Joseph and Elvira (Castellani) D.; widowed; children: Joseph, George, David, Michael. BSBA, U. Nev., Reno, 1951. Mem. Nev. State Assembly, Carson City, 1967-93; majority leader Nev. State Assembly, 1975; speaker Nev. State Assembly, Carson City, 1977, 87, 89, 91, 93, 95; minority leader Nev. State Assembly, 1985; interim fin. com. mem., 1985-94, speaker pro tem, 1973, chmn. water policy com. Western Legis. Conf., 1993-94; pres. Dini's Lucky Club Casino, Yerington, Nev., 1972—. Recipient Outstanding Citizen award Nev. Edn. Assn., 1973, Friend of Edn. award Nev. State Edn. Assn., 1986, Citizen of Yr. award Nev. Judges Assn., 1987, Dedicated and Valued Leadership award Nat. Conf. State Legislatures, 1989, Excellence in Pub. Svc. award Nev. Trial Lawyers Assn., 1990, Silver Plow award Nev. Farm Bur., 1991; named Conservation Legislator of Yr. Nev. Wildlife Fedn., 1991. Mem. Mason Valley C. of C. (pres.), Rotary (pres. Yerington 1989), Lions (pres. Yerington chpt. 1975), Masons, Shriners, Gamma Sigma Delta. Home: 104 N Mountain View St Yerington NV 89447-2239 Office: Dini's Lucky Club Inc 45 N Main St Yerington NV 89447-2230

DINKEL, JOHN GEORGE, magazine editor; b. Bklyn., Aug. 1, 1944; s. Charles Ernest and Loretta Gertrude D.; m. Leslie Hawkins, Oct. 25, 1969; children: Meredith Anne, Kevin Carter. BS in Mech. Engring, U. Mich., 1967, MS in Mech. Engring, 1969. Staff engr. Chrysler Corp., Highland Park, Mich., 1967-69; engring. editor Car Life Mag., Newport Beach, Calif., 1969-70; engring. editor Road & Track Mag., Newport Beach, 1972-79, editor, 1979-88, editor in chief, 1988-91, editor at large, 1991-92; dir. product communications Hill-Holliday, 1991-92; pres. John Dinkel & Assocs., 1991—; editor-at-large Sports Car Internat., 1992—; organizer, chmn. sessions on fuel economy and small cars SAE, 1978-79; commencement speaker U. Mich., Dearborn, 1987; hon. judge Meadow Brook Hall Concourse D'Elegance, 1985-86, Hillsborough Concourse D'Elegance, 1989, Palo Alto Concours D'Elegance, 1990; v.p. editl. ops., Calcar, 1994—; spkr. Direct Mktg. Club So. Calif., 1992. Author: Road & Track Auto Dictionary, 1977; co-author: RX-7: Mazda's Legendary Sports Car, 1991; co-host daily radio show Auto Report, 1986-88; contbr. articles to profl. jours. Nat. chmn. U. Mich. Ann. Fund, 1988—; commr. Irvine (Calif.) Baseball Assn.; organizer clothing drive victims of Armenia earthquake, 1988; soccer coach AYSO, 1984-90, Irvine Soccer Club, 1991—; baseball coach Northwood Little League, 1994—; basketball coach Irvine Boys and Girls Club, 1993—. Honored by Colden Ctr. for the Performing Arts, Queens Coll., N.Y.C., 1990. Mem. Soc. Automotive Engrs. (panelist conf. on impacts of intelligent vehicle hwy. systems 1990), Am. Racing Press Assn., Internat. Motor Press Assn., Sports Car Club Am., Internat. Motor Sports Assn., Motor Press Guild (pres. 1991), Pi Tau Sigma.

DINKELSPIEL, PAUL GAINES, investment banking and public financial consultant; b. San Francisco, Feb. 12, 1935; s. Edward Gaines and Pauline (Watson) D. A.B., U. Calif., Berkeley, 1959. Gen. ptnr. Stone & Youngberg, San Francisco, 1961-71; 1st v.p. Shearson Lehman Hutton and predecessor firms, San Francisco, 1971-79; pres., chmn. bd. dirs. Dinkelspiel, Belmont & Co., Inc., San Francisco; investment banking and pub. fin. cons., 1979—; bd. dirs. Gemstone Investors Assurance Corp., N.Y.C. With AUS, 1959-60. Mem. Govt. Fin. Officers Assn., Am. Water Works Assn., San Francisco Mcpl. Forum, Calif. Pub. Securities Assn. (public fin. com.), San Francisco Comml. Club, Commonwealth Club of Calif., Mcpl. Bond Club, N.Y. World Trade Club, Calif. Waterfowl Assn., Ducks Unltd., Sigma Chi. Home: PO Box 727 Stinson Beach CA 94970-0727 Office: 101 California St Fl 37 San Francisco CA 94111-5802

DINNER, MARIE BERNICE, social services program administrator; b. Bolton, Eng., Mar. 3, 1947; came to U.S., 1958; d. Philip and Sarah (Reich) Myers; m. Bruce Jon Dinner, June 18, 1967; children: Alec W., Tara Lee. BA, U. Denver, 1971, MA, 1973; PhD, U. Colo., 1981. Cert. clin. competence-audiology. Audiologist Rose Med. Ctr., Denver, 1973-76; clin. supr. U. Colo. Comm. Disorders Clinic, Denver and Boulder, Colo., 1977-81; audiologist Pfenninger Inst., Wheat Ridge, Colo., 1982-84; dir. of cochlear implants Childrens Deafness Found., Denver, 1984-88, exec. dir., 1987-88; founder, pres. Hear Now, Denver, 1988—. Bd. dirs. Allied Jewish Fedn., Denver, 1990-94; pres. Beth Joseph Congregation, Denver, 1989-91. Mem. Sales Profls. Internat., Am. Speech, Hearing, Lang. Assn., Acad. of Audiology, Cochlear Implant Club Internat. (adv. bd. 1990-92, bd. dirs. 1992—). Democrat. Office: Hear Now 9745 E Hampden Ave Ste 300 Denver CO 80231-4923

DINSMORE, PHILIP WADE, architect; b. Gilroy, Calif., Nov. 4, 1942; s. Wilbur Allen and Elizabeth Eleanor (Hill) D.; m. Mary Kathryn Mead; children: Robert Allen, Kerry Philip. B.Arch., U. Ariz., 1965. Registered arch., Ariz., Calif., Nev., N.C., Nat. Coun. Archtl. Registration Bds. Designer, William L. Pereira & Assocs., L.A., 1965-67; assoc. CNWC Archs., Tucson, 1967-69; prin., ptnr. Architecture One Ltd., Tucson, 1970-90; pres. Durrant Roberts/Dinsmore Assoc., Phoenix and Tucson, 1995, bd. dir. Durrant Group, 1992—. Mem., chmn. Archtl. Approval Bd., City of Tucson, 1974-75, 77; bd. dir. Tucson Met. YMCA, 1993—. Fellow AIA (nat. bd. dirs. 1981-84, nat. sec. 1984-88, Ariz. Archs. medal 1985, Western Mountain Region Citation award 1973, 76, 78, Award of Honor 1983, Silver medal 1992); mem. Am. Archtl. Found. (bd. regents 1988-92), Constrn. Specifications Inst., Ariz Soc. Archs. (citation 1977-80, 89). Recipient Tucker award Bldg. Stone Inst., 1986. Republican. Presbyterian. Office: Durrant Roberts/Dinsmore Assoc 450 W Paseo Redondo Ste 130 Tucson AZ 85701-8275

DI PALMA, JOSEPH ALPHONSE, brokerage house executive, lawyer; b. N.Y.C., Jan. 17, 1931; s. Gaetano and Michela May (Ambrosio) Di P.; m. Joycelyn Ann Engle, Apr. 18, 1970; children: Joycelyn Joan, Julianne Michelle. BA, Columbia U., 1952; JD, Fordham U., 1958; LLM in Taxation, NYU, 1959. Bar: N.Y. 1959. Tax atty. CBS, N.Y.C., 1960-64; v.p. tax dept. TWA, N.Y.C., 1964-74; pvt. practice law N.Y.C., 1974-87; investor, exec. dir. Di Palma Family Holdings, Las Vegas and N.Y.C., 1987—; cons. in field; head study group Comprehensive Gaming Study, N.Y.C. and Washington, 1990—; think tank exec. dir. Di Palma Position Papers. Contbr. articles to profl. jours.; author: Di Palma Position Papers. Bd. dirs. Friends of the Henry St. Settlement, N.Y.C., 1961-63, Outdoor Cleanliness Assn., N.Y.C., 1961-65; chmn. Air Transport Assn. Taxation Com., 1974. With U.S. Army, 1953-54. Recipient Disting. Svc. and Valuable Counsel commendation award Air Transport Assn., 1974. Mem. Internat. Platform Assn., N.Y. State Bar Assn., N.Y. Athletic Club. Roman Catholic. Home: 3111 Bel Air Dr Apt 21B Las Vegas NV 89109-1506 Office: PO Box 72158 Las Vegas NV 89170-2158 also: 930 Fifth Ave # 4J New York NY 10021 also: 1600 Parker Ave Apt 19C Fort Lee NJ 07024-7006

DIRKS, JERALD FREDERICK, psychotherapist; b. Newton, Kans., Dec. 28, 1949; s. Fred and Hazel Marie (Mickelson) D.; m. Debra Lea Stucky, Sept. 14, 1969; 1 child, Sean. BA in Philosophy, Harvard U., 1971, MDiv, 1974; MA in Child Clin. Psychology, U. Denver, 1976, PsyD in Clin. Psychology, 1978. Chief clin. psychology Nat. Jewish Hosp., Denver, 1978-82; asst. prof. psychiatry U. Colo. Sch. Medicine, Denver, 1980-83; psychotherapist Nelson F. Jones & Assocs., Denver, 1978—; adj. asst. prof. U. Denver, 1978-82; dir., ptnr. Psychometric Designs, Denver, 1990—; ptnr. Nelson F. Jones & Assocs., Denver, 1978—; cons. Colo. Rehab. Inst., Denver, 1986—, Centennial Rehab. Assocs., Denver, 1982—. Contbr. numerous articles to profl. jours. Mem. adv. bd. Sch. Profl. Psychology, U. Denver, 1976, Bethesda Comty. Mental Health Ctr., Denver, 1976-77, Colo. Multiple Sclerosis Soc., Denver, 1981-82. Hollis scholar Harvard U., 1968. Fellow Am. Bd. Med. Psychotherapists (diplomate); mem. Am. Psychosomatic Soc., Soc. for Personality Assessment, Internat. Psychosomatic Inst., N.Y. Acad. Sci., Arabian Horse Historians Assn. (founding mem., sec.-treas. 1992-93). Islam. Office: Nelson F Jones & Assocs 2343 E Evans Ave Denver CO 80210-4709

DIRUSCIO, LAWRENCE WILLIAM, advertising executive; b. Buffalo, Jan. 2, 1941; s. Guido Carmen and Mabel Ella (Bach) DiR.; m. Gloria J. Edney, Aug. 19, 1972; children: Lawrence M., Lorie P., Darryl C., Teresa M., Jack D. With various broadcast stas. and instr., adminstr. Bill Wade Sch. Radio and TV, San Diego, San Francisco, Los Angeles, 1961-69; account exec. Sta. KGB Radio, San Diego, 1969, gen. sales mgr., 1970-72; pres. Free Apple Advt., San Diego, 1972-94, Fin. Mgmt. Assocs., Inc., San Diego, 1979-84, Self-Pub. Ptnrs., San Diego, 1981—, Media Mix Assocs. Enterprises, Inc., 1984-86; pres. Press-Courier Pub. Co., Inc., 1985-86; pres. Media Mix Advt. and Pub. Relations, 1985—, Taking Care of Bus. Pub. Co., 1990—; pres. Formula Mktg. Co., 1993. Chmn. bd. Quicksilver Enterprises, Inc., A Public Corp., 1992-93; lectr., writer on problems of small bus. survival. Served with USN, 1958-60. Five Emmy nominations for T.V. commercial writing and prodn. Mem. Nat. Acad. TV Arts and Scis. Democrat. Roman Catholic. Office: Media Mix Advt and Pub Rels 726 W Kalmia St San Diego CA 92101-1311

DISALLE, MICHAEL DANNY, secondary education educator; b. Denver, May 16, 1945; s. Michael and Agnes Marie (Kulik) DiS.; m. Marikaye Lucas, June 22, 1968; children: Katharine Marie, Kristin Jean, Michael Charles, Matthew Gregory. BA, Regis Coll., 1967; MEd, Lesley Coll., 1992. Cert. tchr., Colo. Tchr. Assumption Sch., Welby, Colo., 1968-74, Cherry Creek High Sch., Englewood, Colo., 1974-95. Author: (computer program/tchr.'s guide) Adventures of Tom Sawyer, 1983, One Day in the Life of Ivan Denisovich, 1984. Asst. den leader Boy Scouts Am., Aurora, Colo., 1988-89. Mem. ASCD, Nat. Coun. Tchrs. of English, Nat. Scholastic Press Assn., Journalism Edn. Assn., Colo. Lang. Arts Soc., Colo. State High Sch. Press Assn., Columbia Scholastic Press Assn.

DISMUKES, VALENA GRACE BROUSSARD, physical education educator; b. St. Louis, Feb. 22, 1938; d. Clobert Bernard and Mary Henrietta (Jones) Broussard; m. Martin Ramon Dismukes, June 26, 1965; 1 child, Michael Ramon. AA in Edn., Harris Tchrs. Coll., 1956; BS in Phys. Edn., Washington U., St. Louis, 1958; MA in Phys. Edn., Calif. State U., L.A., 1972; BA in TV and Film, Calif. State U., Northridge, 1981. Cert. phys. edn. tchr., standard svcs. supr. Phys. edn. tchr., coach St. Louis Pub. Schs., 1958-60; phys. edn. tchr., coach L.A. Unified Sch. Dist., 1960-84, health and sci. tchr., mentor tchr., 1984-93; coord. gifted and talented program 32d St./U.So. Calif. Magnet Sch., 1993-95, magnet coord., 1995; adminstrv. asst. Ednl. Consortium of Ctrl. L.A., Calif., 1993—; owner, bus. cons. Grace Enterprises, 1994—; coord. Chpt. I, 1989-93; mem. sch. based mgmt. team, 1990-93. Editor parent newsletter, 1975-80; photographs exhibited in one-woman shows include The Olympic Spirit, 1984, L.A.-The Ethnic Place, 1986; contbr. articles to profl. jours. Mem. adv. com. Visual Comm., L.A., 1980; bd. dirs. NACHES Found., Inc., L.A., 1985-86; mem. Cmty. Consortium, L.A., 1986-87; mem. adv. com. L.A. Edn. Partnership, 1986-87; mem. adv. bd. Expo Sports Club, L.A., 1994. Marine Educators fellow, 1992; photography grantee L.A. Olympic Organizing Com., 1984, Teaching grantee L.A. Edn. Partnership, 1987-89; recipient Honor award L.A.-Calif. Assn. Health, Phys. Edn. and Recreation, 1971. Mem. ACLU, NAACP, Am. Fedn. Tchrs., United Tchrs. of L.A., Am. Home Bus. Assn., Urban League, Sierra Club. Home: 3800 Stocker St Apt 1 Los Angeles CA 90008-5127

DISNEY, MICHAEL GEORGE, financial services executive; b. Harvey, Ill., Nov. 30, 1955. Grad. high sch., Harvey, Ill.; grad., Life Underwriters Tng. Coun. Sales mgr. Met. Life Ins. Co., Naperville, Ill., 1979-84; regional dir. Firemens Fund Ins. Co., San Diego, 1984-85; owner, mgr. Disney Fin., Inc., San Diego, Calif., 1985—; pres. Grossmont Letip, 1993—. Mem. Nat. Assn. Life Underwriters, Life Underwriters Tng. Council (moderator-cons. 1986-87), Million Dollar Round Table (coord., chmn. San Diego chpt 1987-89), La Mesa (Calif.) C. of C., San Diego C. of C., El Cajon C. of C., LaMesa C. of C., Toastmasters. Home: 3910 Dorsie Ln La Mesa CA 91941-7335 Office: 4420 Hotel Circle Ct # 205 San Diego CA 92108

DISRUD, CAROL ANN, interior designer; b. Rolla, N.D., Apr. 7, 1946; d. Oral Desmond and Vera Cecelia (Bisom) D.; m. James Kormier, June 28, 1990. BS in Interior Design, N.D. State U., 1968. Mgr. furniture showrooms AB Bacos and Berg, Halmstad, 1968-73; mgr. small shopping ctr. The Farm, Bruchuelbach, Germany, 1973-74; interior designer Design Collaborative/VVKR Architects, Alexandria, Va., 1970-79; v.p. Gensler and Assocs. Architects, San Francisco, 1980-92; owner, pres. Carol Disrud & Assocs., Healdsburg, Calif., 1992—; speaker in field. Recipient outstanding alumni award N.D. State U., 1993. Fellow Internat. Interior Design Assn. (nat. v.p. 1985-87, no. Calif. chpt. pres. 1982-85, disting. merit award 1991, Best Of competition award IBD/Interior Design mag. 1989, Top Ten award 1991, Interior Design award 1993); mem. Healdsburg C. of C. (bus. and econ. devel. com. 1991—). Democrat. Office: Carol Disrud & Assocs 1207 Vine St Healdsburg CA 95448-4824

DISTECHE, CHRISTINE M., geneticist; b. Liege, Belgium, July 22, 1949. PhD, U. Liege, Belgium, 1976. Genetics fellow Harvard U., Boston, 1977-80; now med. geneticist U. Wash. Hosp., Seattle; prof. pathology U. Wash., Seattle. Office: U Wash Hosp Dept Pathology SM 30 Seattle WA 98195*

DISTEFANO, JOSEPH JOHN, III, bioengineering and biocybernetics educator, consultant; b. Bklyn., Apr. 30, 1938; s. Joseph and Angelina DiStefano; children: Joseph, Allegra. BEE, CCNY, 1961; MS, UCLA, 1964, PhD, 1966. Registered profl. engr., Calif. Research engr. Autonetics, Anaheim, Calif., 1961-63; asst. prof. UCLA, 1966-72, assoc. prof., 1972-76, prof. dept. computer sci., dept. medicine, 1976—, chair interdepartmental cybernetics major, 1982—. Mem. editl. bd.: Optimal Control Applications and Methods, 1983—; editor Modeling Methodology Forum, Am. Jour. Physiology, Jour. Applied Physiology; mem. editl. bd.: Annals of Biomed. Engring., 1971-93; author: Feedback and Control Systems, 1967, 2d edit., 1990. Recipient Dist. Teaching award Engring. Systems, UCLA, 1971; Fulbright Hays sr. scholar, 1979. Mem. Endocrine Soc., Am. Thyroid Assn., Control Systems Soc. Office: 4532 Boelter Hall UCLA Los Angeles CA 90024-1596

DITCHIK, ROBERT ANDREW, biochemist, consultant, small business owner; b. N.Y.C., Mar. 29, 1958; s. Philip M. Ditchik and Harriet A. (Lane) Shpiner. BS in Biochemistry, Calif. Polytech. U., 1980; MBA, Ariz. State U., 1982. Bus. analyst, purchasing agt. TRW, Inc, Redondo Beach, Calif., 1982-84; sr. price/cost analyst TRW, Inc, Redondo Beach, 1984-87; div. bus. mgr. PRC, Inc., Camarillo, Calif., 1987-92; owner, mgr. DNA Bus. Ops. Consulting Svcs., Encino, Calif., 1992—. Mem. Rep. Nat. Com. Recipient scholarship Ariz. State U., Tempe, 1981-82. Office: DNA Bus Ops Consulting Svcs 16000 Ventura Blvd Ste 500 Encino CA 91436-2730

DITTMAN, DEBORAH RUTH, real estate broker; b. Sacramento, Apr. 15, 1932; d. Charles Harwood and Ruth (Potter) Kinsley; m. John Alvin Cardoza, Sept. 1950 (div. 1964); children: Harold Cardoza, Nancy Jongeward, John Allan Cardoza, Gregory Cardoza, Janice Boswell; m. Edgar Marshall Dittman, Jan. 22, 1967 (dec. Jan. 6 1982); m. Philip George Vrieling, July 7, 1990. Student Humprey's Coll., Stockton, Calif., 1966; grad. real estate sales Anthony Schs., 1978; cert. in real estate San Joaquin Delta Coll., 1977. Lic. real estate broker, Calif., 1978, real estate sales assoc., 1974-78; cert. residential specialist. Sec. Calif. Dept. Water Resources, Patterson and Tracy, 1966-72; hostess Welcome Wagon, Tracy, 1973-74; assoc. realtor Reeve Assocs., Tracy, 1975-80; broker Allied Brokers, Tracy, 1980-83; ptnr. real estate Putt, Fallavena, Willbanks & Dittman, Tracy, 1983—; mem. adv. bd. Tracy Fed. Bank(formerly Tracy Savings & Loan), 1989—, Women's Coun. Realtors, 1990—. Mem. Residential Sales Coun., 1989, Women's Coun. Realtors, 1990. Mem. Tracy Bd. Realtors (pres. 1981, 85, dir. 1976, 77, 80-83, 85-86), Calif. Assn. Realtors (dir. 1980-81, 85), Cert. Real Estate Specialists (v.p. no. Calif. chpt. 1990, pres. 1991), Nat. Assn. Realtors, Cen. Valley Assn. Realtors, So. Alameda Assn. Realtors, Tracy C. of C. (bd. dirs. 1988-90). Home: 12134 Midway Dr Tracy CA 95376-9113 Office: 1045 Tracy Blvd Tracy CA 95376-3726

DITTMAN, WILLIAM ALBERT, hematologist; b. La Crosse, Wis., July 31, 1926; s. Albert L. and Kathleen (Kennedy) D.; m. Catherine Harris, Dec. 19, 1950; children: William A. Jr., John C., Andrew H. BA, U. Wis., 1949, MD, 1953. Diplomate Am. Bd. Internal Medicine, Am. Bd. Hematology. Intern Salt Lake County Gen. Hosp., Salt Lake City, 1953-54; resident in internal medicine U. Utah, Salt Lake City, 1954-56, fellow in hematology, 1956-58; staff physician VA Hosp., Albuquerque, 1958-59; pvt. practice, Spokane, Wash., 1959-77; dir. hematology Sacred Heart Med. Ctr., Spokane, 1961—; chmn. Inland N.W. Blood Ctr., 1992-93. Sgt. U.S. Army. Fellow ACP; mem. Am. Soc. Hematology. Office: Sacred Heart Med Ctr 101 W 8th Ave Spokane WA 99220-2555

DITZLER, ANN MARIE, nutritionist; b. Flint, Mich., June 4, 1947; d. James Alfred and Elsie (McDowell) Herrick; m. Thomas F. Ditzler, Feb. 20, 1971; children: Benjamin T.E., Nathan J.M. BS, Mich. State U., 1969; MS, Case Western Res. U., 1971. Registered dietitian. Chief/clin. dietitian Flint (Mich.) Osteo. Hosp., 1971-79; clin. dietitian Honolulu Area Hosps., 1979-83; supr., staff asst. Hawaii Med. Svc. Assn., Honolulu, 1983-91, trainer, analyst long range system planning, 1992-95, sys. tester, 1995. Chair Windward subarea coun. State Health Planning and Devel. Agy., Honolulu, 1990-95; chair troop com. Aloha coun. Boy Scouts Am., Honolulu, 1993—; mem. Gov.'s Conf. on Health Care in the 1990s, Honolulu, 1985-86; loaned exec. Aloha Pacesetter campaignn United Way, 1995. Recipient Borden award Mich. State U., 1969, DuBois award, 1969. Mem. Am. Dietetic Assn. (Recognized Young Dietitian 1977), Jr. League of Honolulu (sustaining mem.), Profl. Women's Network, Internat. Baseball Goodwill Assn. of Hawaii (v.p. 1991—). Home: 112-4 Puwa Pl Kailua HI 96734

DIVELY, DWIGHT DOUGLAS, finance director; b. Spokane, Wash., Sept. 24, 1958; s. Richard Lorraine and Marie Eleanor (Barnes) D.; m. Susan Lorraine Soderstrom, June 13, 1987; children: Nathan Douglas, Natalie Lorraine. BSChemE, Rose-Hulman Inst. Tech., 1980; MPA of Pub. Affairs, Princeton U., 1982; PhC in Civil Engring., U. Wash., 1986. Rsch. scientist Battelle, Seattle, 1982-84; policy analyst, staff dir. Wash. High Tech. Coord. Bd., Seattle, 1984-86; cons. Bellevue, Wash., 1986-87; legis. analyst Seattle City Coun., 1987-90, supervising analyst, 1990-92, staff dir., 1992-94; dir. Seattle Fin. Dept., 1994—; cons. We. Interstate Commn. on Higher Edn., Boulder, Colo., 1986-91; affiliate prof. U. Wash., 1989—; instr. South Seattle C.C., 1992—; mem. faculty Cascade Ctr., Seattle, 1992—. Co-author: Benefit-Cost Analysis in Theory and Practice, 1994. Chmn. interview panel Truman Scholarship Found., Washington, 1989—. Recipient Elmer B. Staats award Truman Scholarship Found., 1994. Mem. Govt. Fin. Officers Assn. Lutheran. Office: Fin Dept Rm 103 600 4th Ave Ste 103 Seattle WA 98104-1826

DIVINE, THEODORE EMRY, electrical engineer; b. Hailey, Idaho, May 27, 1943; s. Theodore Clyde and Muriel Juanita (Kirtley) D.; BSEE, U. Wash., Seattle, 1966, MBA, 1970; m. Roberta Louise Erickson, Mar. 19, 1966; children: Timothy Shannon, Brianna Kristine, Rachel Melissa. Engr., Gen. Telephone Co. of N.W., 1968-69; mem. tech. staff NW ops. Computer Scis. Corp., 1970-72; research engr. Battelle Pacific N.W. Labs., Richland, Wash., 1973—, research sect. mgr., 1978, staff engr., def. programs, 1980-89; program mgr., special programs Idaho Nat. Engr. Lab., 1989—, mgr. Nat. Security Programs Office, 1992-93, spl. programs mgr., 1993—. Pres., Mid-Columbia Sci. Fair Assn., 1975-76; ruling elder First Presbyn. Ch., Prosser, Wash., 1982-84. Served as officer Signal Corps, USAR, 1966-84; Vietnam, 1967. Decorated Bronze Star. Mem. IEEE, Am. Def. Preparedness Assn., Assn. of U.S. Army, Am. Soc. Agrl. Engrs. (com. chmn. 1977-78, 82-83, chmn. nat. conf. on electronics in agr. 1983), Beta Gamma Sigma. Mem. editorial adv. bd. Internat. Jours. Computers & Electronics in Agr., Elsevier, The Netherlands, 1983—.

DIVITO, ANTONIO MORENO, company executive, consultant; b. Detroit, Oct. 25, 1952; s. John William and Dolly Ann (Martin) DiV.; 1 child, Antonio M. II. BA, Wayne State U., 1973; MA, U. Hawaii, 1993. Prof. planner, dec. Can. Spec., L.A., 1975-85; entrepreneur, cons. Hawaii Plus, Honolulu, 1985-94. Vol. Hawaii Plus, 1985-94. Mem. Am. Legion. Home: PO Box 4728 Honolulu HI 96812-4728

DIVOLA, JOHN, artist; b. Santa Monica, Calif., June 6, 1949; s. John M. and Marion (Foster) D. BA, Calif. State U., Northridge, 1971; MA, UCLA, 1973, MFA, 1974. Instr. Calif. Inst. of the Arts, Valencia, 1978-88; prof. U. Calif., Riverside, 1988—. Fellowship John Simon Guggenheim, 1987, Nat. Endowment for the Arts, 1973, 76, 79, 90. Home: 245 Ruth Ave Venice CA 90291-2711 Office: U Calif Art Dept 1107 Olmstead Hall Riverside CA 92521

DIXIT, VIVEK, medical educator; b. Bombay, India, Nov. 7, 1954; came to U.S., 1988; s. Mahesh Chandra and Kaushal (Tiwari) Dikshit; m. Neeta Awasthi, Dec. 27, 1987; children: Vineet Aditya, Ram Anand. BSc in Biology magna cum laude with honors, Concordia U., Montreal, Que., Can., 1978; MSc in Physiology, McGill U., Montreal, Que., Can., 1980, PhD in Physiology, 1986. Postdoctoral fellow Sunnybrook Med. Ctr./U. Toronto, Can., 1986-88; vis. asst. rschr. UCLA, 1988-91, asst. researcher, 1991-93, assoc. prof., 1993—; dir. rsch., liver bio-support, hepatitis rsch. lab., 1990—, co-dir. basic sci. tng. program divsn. digestive diseases, 1993—; liver disease program steering com. mem. Sunnybrook Med. Ctr., Toronto, 1986-87; lectr. and presenter in field. Manuscript reviewer Artificial Organs, ASAIO Jour., Cell Transplantation, Gastroenterology, Hepatology, Jour. of Artificial Cells, Blood Substitutes and Immobilization Biotech. and Jour. Hepatology. Sunnybrook Fund fellow U. Toronto, 1987, McGill U. fellow, 1981, 85, Ministry Edn. Que. fellow, 1981-83, 86-87; grantee UCLA, 1994, United Liver Assn., 1988, 90-92, Physicians Svcs. Inc. Found., 1987-89. Mem. Internat. Soc. for Artificial Cells, Blood Substitutes and Immobilization Biotech. (internat. program com., editl. bd. jour.), Internat. Assn. Study of Liver, Am. Soc. for Artifical Internal Organs (program com., editl. bd. jour.), Cell Transplant Soc. (editl. bd. jours.), Gastroenterology Rsch. Group, Am. Gastroenterol. Assn., Am. Assn. for Study Liver Diseases. Hindu. Home: 5522 Babcock Ave North Hollywood CA 91607-1531 Office: UCLA Sch Medicine 675 Circle Dr S # 1240 Los Angeles CA 90024-8322

DIXON, DIANE BROOKS, communications executive; b. Evanston, Ill., Nov. 11, 1951; d. James Read and Helen (Green) Brooks; m. Patrick Richard Dixon, Sept. 6, 1975; 1 child, Colleen Brooks. BA in Polit. Sci. with honors, U. So. Calif., 1973, postgrad. Asst. mgr. govt. rels. L.A. Area C. of C., 1973-77; mgr. govtl. affairs programs GTE-Calif., Thousand Oaks, 1977-79; account exec. Deaver & Hannaford, Inc., L.A., 1979-81; princ. Diane Dixon and Assocs., L.A., 1981-82; dir. corp. comm. Avery Dennison Corp., Pasadena, Calif., 1982-85; v.p. corp. comm. Avery Dennison Corp., Pasadena, 1985—. Past chair L.A. Pub. Affairs Officers' Assn.; dir. Five Acres Children's Agy., trustee Polytechnic Sch., Pasadena; co-founder Women in Pub. Affairs, L.A. Mem. Nat. Investor Rels. Inst., Pub. Rels. Soc. Am., Pasadena C. of C. (dir.), Calif. Bus. Roundtable (dep.), Pasadena C. of C. (dir.). Office: Avery Dennison Corp 150 N Orange Grove Blvd Pasadena CA 91103-3534

DIXON, JULIAN CAREY, congressman; b. Washington, Aug. 8, 1934; m. Betty Lee; 1 son, Cary Gordon. B.S., Calif. State U., Los Angeles, 1962; LL.B., Southwestern U., Los Angeles, 1967. Mem. Calif. State Assembly, 1972-78; mem. 96th-104th Congresses from Calif. 28th (now 32nd) Dist.; mem. House Appropriations Com. 96th-102nd Congresses from Calif. 32d Dist.; ranking mem. subcom. of D.C.; mem. subcom. Commerce, Justice, State and Judiciary; mem. select com. on intelligence, mem. intelligence select com., mem. house Democrats steering and policy com.; Pres. CBC Found., Inc., 1986-90. Served with U.S. Army, 1957-60. Mem. NAACP, Urban League, Calif. Arts Commn. Democrat. Office: House of Representatives 2252 Rayburn Washington DC 20515*

DIXON, KATIE LOOSLE, county official; b. Clarkston, Utah, Oct. 10, 1925; d. Reuben O. and Sylvia (Griffiths) Loosle; divorced; children: Jerry, Michael, Keven Todd, Darcy. BS, Utah State U., 1945; LDH, Salt Lake C.C., 1993. Recorder Salt Lake County, Salt Lake City, 1975-94; trainer, facilitator workshops and seminars; mem. panel to evaluate U.S. std. lics. and certs. Nat. Ctr. Stats., USPHS, 1984-85; mem. State of Utah adv. bd. Nat. Hist. Publs. and Records Commn., 1979-91, chmn. local govt. records task force, 1983-84. Contbr. articles to profl. publs. Bd. dirs., mem. strategic planning com. Leadership Am., Fairfax, Va., 1991—; mem. Concord Coalition Adv. Bd., 1993—; mem. alumni recognition adv. com. Utah State U., 1991; nat. adv. bd. U. Utah Children's Dance Theater, Salt Lake City, 1990-91; adv. bd. Utah Women's Arts Project, Salt Lake City, 1989—; mem. Salt Lake C.C. Devel. Bd., Salt Lake City, 1989-91; chmn. Utah Columbus Quincentenary Commn., 1988-92; mem. celebrity roast com. Am. Lung Assn. of Utah, 1988; bd. dirs. Women's Fedn. Utah Reps., 1968-69; active Salt Lake County Rep. Party, 1960-89, Utah State Rep. Party, 1966-84; campaign co-mgr. Sherman P. Lloyd Congl. campaigns, 1964, 66, 68, 70; mem. adv. bd. Utah Citizens for Arts, 1981-89, Utah Assn. Retarded Citizens, 1982-89; mem. Utah com. Fifty States Project on Discrimination Against Women in the Law, 1982-83; mem. art adv. bd. Salt Lake County, 1982, mem. bicentennial community com. on U.S. Constitution, 1986-87; mem. funding study com. Utah State Bd. Edn., 1984; mem. adv. com. Utah Women's Conf., 1984—; chmn. child care task force Salt Lake County, 1985; mem. dean's adv. coun. Coll. Bus. Utah State U., Logan, 1986-89; chair membership com., chair govt. com. Utah Women's Forum, Salt Lake City, 1987; bd. dirs. Utah Opera Guild, Salt Lake City, 1987-94, Westminster Coll. Found., Salt Lake City, 1987-89; mem. adv. bd. U. Utah Grad. Sch. Social Work, 1987-93, vice chair, 1989, chair, 1990-93; mem. policy coun. on strengthening the family Nat. Policy Form, Washington, 1994. Katie Dixon scholar, 1993, scholar Nat. Dem. and Rep. Coms., 1986; recipient Cert. of Honor, Soroptimist Internat. of Salt Lake, 1990, Alumnus of Yr. award Utah State U., 1978, Disting. Svc. award Utah Tech. Coll., 1979, Susa Young Gates award Utah Women's Polit. Caucus, 1980; named Hon. Chmn. Ann. Banquet, NAACP, 1977. Mem. ASPA (chmn. state conf. 1977), Nat. Assn. Counties (bd. dirs. 1980-81, 83-5, 87—, mem. various coms., mem. NACoNet 1992-93, chmn. bd. event 1991, Salt Lake County com. for ann. conf. 1991), Nat. Assn. County Recorders and Clks. (bd. dirs. 1976-78, 79—, sec./treas. 1979-80, chmn. convention com. 1976-77, v.p. 1982-83, pres. 1983-84, mem. various coms.), Women Ofcls. of Nat. Assn. Counties (v.p. 1979-80, pres. 1980-81), Inst. for Land Info. (1st v.p. 1986, 87, pres. 1988-90), Utah Women's Internat. Connection, Internat. Women's Forum, Utah Assn. Counties (bd. dirs. 1976-77), Salt Lake Area C. of C. (civic responsibility com. 1987, state legis. action com. 1987—, WIBCO program planning com. 1987), Utah Key Rep. Club (bd. dirs. 1985—), Pi Alpha Alpha. Mem. LDS Ch. Home: 3781 Lois Ln Salt Lake City UT 84124-2309 Office: Salt Lake County Recorder 2001 S State St # 1600 Salt Lake City UT 84190-0001

DIXON, MICHAEL WAYNE, designer, writer; b. Honolulu, Hawaii, May 3, 1942; s. Gordon Alvin and Terry (Mendes) D.; m. Janis Marie Travis, Jan. 4, 1963 (div. 1977); children: Kimberlee Ann, Gregory Page, Morgan Ashley. Tech. illustrator Rockwell Internat., Anaheim, Calif., 1962-66, Western Gear Corp., Lynwood, Calif., 1966-69; owner Unisex Clothing Store, Norwalk, Calif., 1969-71; mgr. Am. Health Industries, Downey, Calif., 1971-72; police officer Vernon Police Dept., L.A. Police Dept., 1972-81; designer, pres. Dornaus and Dixon Enterprises, Inc., Huntington Beach, Calif., 1979-88; freelance writer Huntington Beach, 1986—. Inventor firearm safety devices; 10mm auto cartridge; Just'n Case police holster; MAWB cutter police bullet; BodyHugger holsters and ammunition holders; author: Bren Ten Owner's Manual, 1982, BodyShaping, 1985, BodyQuest, 1993, BodySense, 1993, BodyLanguage, 1993, Courtroom Rapport, 1993. Founder, dir. Street Smart Pepper Spray Hdqs. of Calif., 1994—. With USN, 1959-62. Mem. N.Y. Acad. Scis., Am. Film Inst., Rsch. Coun. Scripps Clinic and Rsch. Found., Smithsonian Instn., L.A. County Mus. Art, Linus Pauling Inst. Sci. and Medicine.

DIXON, MICHEL LAVON, educational administrator; b. Norman, Okla., Oct. 2, 1945; s. Gerald R. and Erma M. (Fischer) D.; m. Mary Dee Brown, July 12, 1970 (div. 1994); children: Terri, Kelly, Kristi, Johanna. BA, Athens Coll., 1968, BE, 1972; MEd, U. Ala., 1976. Ins. adjustor Gen. Adjustment Bur., Birmingham, Ala., 1968-71; tchr. Adamsburg Sch., DeKalb County, Ala., 1971-72, Decatur (Ala.) City Schs., 1972-80; pubs. rep. Economy Pub. Co., Oklahoma City, 1980-82, Jostens Printing & Pub. Div., Mpls., 1982-84; course dir. AS100 Air Force ROTC, Maxwell AFB, Ala., 1984-85; pub. Civil Air Patrol News Aux. USAF, Maxwell AFB, 1985-86; tng. specialist, course mgr. Corps Engrs. Tng. div. U.S. Army, Huntsville, Ala., 1986-89; adminstr. Lawrence County High Sch., Moulton, Ala., 1989-90, Dept. Defense Dependent Sch., Nuernburg, Fed. Repub. Germany, 1990-91; dir. edn. programs in all western states U.S. Army 6th Recruiting BDE, Ft. Baker, Calif., 1991-94; prin. Round Valley H.S., Covelo, Calif., 1994—; test proctor Am. Mensa Soc. Author: textbook AS 100, 1984; editor The Air Force Today, 1985; author, editor 3 slide briefings Aircraft and Weapons of AF, Vietnam, Korea, 1984-85; pub. Civil Air Patrol News, 1985-86. Presbyterian. Home: PO Box 366 Covelo CA 95428-0366 Office: Round Valley H S PO Box 276 Covelo CA 95428-0276

DIXON, PAUL WILLIAM, psychology educator; b. N.Y.C., Aug. 1, 1936; s. Edward Everet and Esther (McCracken) D.; children: Michael H., Theodore K., Eleanor T., Aaron T. BA in English, Blackburn Coll., 1960; MA in Gen. Exptl. Psychology, U. Hawaii, 1963, PhD in Gen. Exptl. Psychology, 1966. Cert. tchr., Ill. Prof. psychology Coll. Arts and Scis. U. Hawaii, Hilo, 1965—, chmn. dept. liberal studies Coll. Arts and Scis., 1972-82, chmn. dept. psychology Coll. Arts and Scis., 1972-75; vis. assoc. prof. psychology internat. divsn. Sophia U., Tokyo, 1971-72; vis. prof. dept. microbiology and immunology, UCLA, 1978-79; all-campus faculty pers. com. U. Hilo, 1967-68, pers. com. social scis. and edn. divsn., 1968-69, faculty senate, 1970-71, libr. com., 1970-71, acad. freedom, privilege and tenure com., 1973-74, dissertation com. dept. polit. sci., 1974-78, Rsch. Coun., 1977-78, chmn. all-coll. faculty pers. com., 1970, libr. com., 1973-74, liberal studies com., 1973-82. Contbr. numerous articles to psychol. and ednl. jours. Presenter, demonstrator Frequency Transfer Hearing Aid to Action Group for the Hearing Impaired, Honolulu, 1980, also to State Hearing and Visual Handicapped Svc., Hilo, Hawaii, 1980. Nominee Nobel prize in physics, 1986; NDEA fellow, 1963-66; aid grantee U. Hawaii Rsch. Coun., 1965-70, U. Hawaii

Hilo Fund, 1970. Fellow Am. Anthrop. Assn., Soc. for Applied Anthropology; mem. AAAS, APA (travel grantee 1972), Internat. Congress of Anthrop. and Ethnographic Scis. Home: PO Box 244 Volcano HI 96785-0244 Office: U Hawaii Coll Arts and Scis 200 W Kawili St Hilo HI 96720-4075

DIXON, RICHARD ERWIN, physician, medical director; b. Nashville, Sept. 15, 1942; s. Erwin and Lucile (Grimsley) D.; m. Sarah Lee Dawson, Aug. 26, 1967; children: Rebecca Reilly, Ashley Elizabeth. AB in History, Princeton U., 1964; MD, Vanderbilt U., 1969. Diplomate Nat. Bd. Med. Examiners, Am. Bd. Internal Medicine (subsplty. infectious disease). Intern U. Wash. Affiliated Hosps., Seattle, 1969-70, jr. resident in internal medicine, 1970-71; sr. resident in internal medicine Mass. Gen. Hosp., Boston, 1974-75, fellow in infectious diseases, 1975-76; epidemic intelligence svc. officer, med. epidemiologist Ctr. Disease Control, Atlanta, 1971-73, chief hosp. infections br., 1973-74, 76-80; co-dir. med. residency tng. program Trenton (N.J.) Affiliated Hosps., 1980-90; dir. dept. medicine Helene Fuld Med. Ctr., Trenton, 1980-89, hosp. epidemiologist, dir. dept. clin. epidemiology, 1986-93, med. dir., 1989-93; med. dir. Alta Bates Med. Resources, Berkeley, Calif., 1993—; clin. asst. prof. medicine Emory U. Sch. Medicine, Atlanta, 1976-80; clin. assoc. prof. medicine Hahnemann U., Phila., 1980-82, assoc. prof. medicine, 1982-91, assoc. clin. prof. medicine, 1992; lectr. Grad. Sch. Edn., U. Pa., Phila., 1983-84; cons. NIH, Bethesda, Md., 1978-80, WHO, 1977-80; attending physician Grady Meml. Hosp., Atlanta, 1976-80, Helene Fuld Med. Ctr., Trenton, 1980-93, St. Francis Med. Ctr., Trenton, 1980-89, Mercer Med. Ctr., Trenton, 1982-93; mem. working group Ctrs. for Disease Control, 1982-83, infectious diseases adv. com. U.S. VA, 1976-80; lectr. various hosps., med. schs. and other orgns. in 23 states and 9 fgn. countries. Editor: Nosocomial Infections, 1982; co-editor: Isolation Techniques for Use in Hospitals, 1975; editorial dir.: (video program) Nosocomial Infections, 1981-85; mem. editorial bd. Infection Control and Hosp. Epidemiology, 1981—, Jour. Clin.Microbiology, 1979-81, Manual Clin. Microbiology, 3d edit., 1979; contbr. numerous articles to profl. jours. Med. dir. USPHS, 1971-80, res., 1980—. Recipient 1st place award John Muir Med. Film Festival, 1984, Silver medal Internat. Film and TV Festival of N.Y., 1984. Fellow Infectious Diseases Soc. Am., ACP (N.J. chpt. coun. mem. 1984-87); mem. Am. Soc. Microbiology, Assn. Practitioners in Infection Control, Assn. Program Dirs. in Internal Medicine, N.J. Acad. Medicine (chmn. com. edn. 1989-92, dir. med. edn., bd. dirs. 1989-92, sec. 1991-92, 2d v.p. 1992-93), Soc. Hosp. Epidemiologists Am. (v.p. 1982, pres.-elect 1983, pres. 1984). Home: 291 Monte Vista Ridge Rd Orinda CA 94563-1627 Office: Alta Bates Med Group 2000 Powell St Emeryville CA 94608 also: PO Box 5039 Berkeley CA 94705-0039

DIXON, WILLIAM CORNELIUS, lawyer; b. Dexter, N.Y., July 1, 1904; s. Frank and Celia (Potter) D.; m. Arvilla Pratt, Nov. 20, 1934; children—Anne Arvilla, Nancy Cornelia. A.B., U. Mich., 1926, J.D., 1928. Bar: Ohio 1928, Calif. 1948, Supreme Ct. U.S 1948. Asso. Holliday-Grossman-McAfee, Cleve., 1928-32; asst. dir. law Cleve., 1932-33, practiced law, 1933-38; justice Supreme Ct. Ohio, 1938; spl. asst. in anti-trust div. to atty. gen. U.S. Dept. Justice, 1944-54, chief asst. trial sect. anti-trust div., 1945, apptd. chief West Coast offices Anti-trust div., 1946, chief trial counsel for Govt. U.S. versus Standard Oil Co. Calif. et al, 1948, chief Los Angeles Office, 1948-54; pvt. law practice Los Angeles, 1954-59; asst. atty. gen. in charge state anti-trust enforcement Calif., 1959-63; legal adviser and mem. Joint War and State Depts., Zaibatsu Mission to Japan, 1946. Dir. relief for Ohio under Emergency Relief Act, 1938-39; moderator Los Angeles Assn. Congl. Chs., 1957; moderator Congl. Conf. So. Calif. and S.W., 1960; mem. constn. commn. United Ch. of Christ; mem. United Ch. Bd. for Homeland Ministries, 1962-65. Papers included in Truman Library, Library of Contemporary History, U. Wyo., Ohio State U. and UCLA libraries. Mem. Calif., Los Angeles bar assns., Delta Sigma Rho, Pi Kappa Alpha. Democrat. Home: 1590 W San Marcos Blvd #168 San Marcos CA 92069

DJALATTA, LORETTA JEAN, securities company executive, real estate broker; b. Columbus, Ohio, June 16, 1943; d. Charles Edward and Vivian Edwards (Burton) Rose; m. James Peterson, Dec. 3, 1957 (div. 1963); children: James, Carlos, Shelley Foster, George Carr. Student, Long Beach (Calif.) City Coll., 1976-79. Real estate agt. Century-21 A Marketplace, Long Beach, 1985-86, Wagner-Jacobson Brokerage, L.A., 1986-87, Exclusive Realtors, L.A., 1987-89; real estate broker Long Beach, 1989—; registered rep. NAP Fin. Corp., Santa Ana, Calif., 1989-91, registered prin., 1991—; arbitrator Better Bus. Bur., Cypress, Calif., 1989—; mem. State Panel Consumer Arbitrators, Nat. Panel Consumer Arbitrators. chief exec. officer Youth Devel. Agy., Long Beach. Mem. Long Beach Area C. of C. Office: Aragon Fin Svcs 555 Pointe Dr Bldg 3 # 204 Brea CA 92621

D'JAVID, ISMAIL FARIDOON, surgeon; b. Rasht, Iran, Apr. 10, 1908; arrived in Germany, 1926; came to U.S. 1946; s. Youssef and Khadidja D'Javid. Grad. high sch., Iran; MD, Friedrich Wilhelm U., Berlin, 1937, PhD, 1941. Diplomate Bd. Surgery. Intern and resident Urban-Krankenhous, Robert-Koch Krankenhous and Charite, Berlin, 1938-41; physician Imperial Iranian Embassy, Berlin, 1938-41; appointed by Shah as surgeon 500-bed hosp. Mash-had, Iran, 1941; chief surgeon Army Hdqrs., Tehran, 1941-43; surgeon-in-chief Iranian 4th Army, Kordestan, Iran; pvt. practice surgery Tehran, 1941-46; intern, resident various hosps. in U.S., 1947-49, chief resident in thoracic and abdominal surgery, 1950-63; major, surgeon U.S. Army M.C., 1953-55; pvt. practice specializing in surgery N.Y.C., 1957-78. Contbr. numerous articles to profl. jours.; patentee in field. Recipient Physician's Recognition award, AMA, 1977-80, 83. Sr. life fellow Am. Coll. Gastroenterology, Deutsche Gesellschraft fur Chrirurgie (Surg. Soc. Greater Germany); life fellow Am. Coll. Surgery, Acad. Sci., Assn. Mil. Surgeons of U.S., Am. Soc. Abdominal Surgeons, Am. Physician's Art Assn., Assn. Am. Physicians and Surgeons; mem. AMA, Coll. Surgeons, German Plastic Surg. Soc., Pan-Am. Med. Assn., Med. Soc. D.C., Calif. Med. Soc., World Med. Assn., N.Y. County Med. Soc., N.Y. State Med. Soc., Rudolf-Wirchow Med. Soc. Home: 230 Fairway Oaks Dr VOC Sedona AZ 86351-8823

DJAWAD, SAID TAYEB See JAWAD, SAID TAYEB

DJUJICH, DAVID B., computer software company executive; b. Redondo Beach, Calif., Jan. 14, 1964; s. Bosko and Mirjana Djujich. BS in Info. and Computer Sci., U. Calif., Irvine, 1987. Programmer Lakeshore Toys, Carson, Calif., 1987-88; mng. cons., head of programming Prounis Cons. Group, N.Y.C., 1989-92; pres. Info. Mgmt. Solutions, Torrance, Calif., 1992—. Mem. IEEE Computer Soc., Assn. for Computing Machinery, Young Execs. of Am. Office: Info Mgmt Solutions 24807 Glencoe Way 2d Fl Torrance CA 90505-6608

DMYTRYSHYN, BASIL, historian, educator; b. Poland, Jan. 14, 1925; came to U.S., 1947, naturalized, 1951; s. Frank and Euphrosinia (Senchak) Dmytryshyn; m. Virginia Roehl, July 16, 1949; children: Sonia, Tania. BA, U. Ark., 1950; MA, U. Ark, 1951; PhD, U. Calif.-Berkeley, 1955; hon. diploma, U. Kiev-Mohyla Acad., 1993. Asst. prof. history Portland State U., Oreg., 1956-59; assoc. prof. Portland State U., 1959-64, prof., 1964-89, prof. emeritus, 1989—, assoc. dir. Internat. Trade and Commerce Inst., 1984-89; vis. prof. U. Ill., 1964-65, Harvard U., 1971, U. Hawaii, 1976, Hokkaido U., Sapporo, Japan, 1978-79; adviser U. Kiev-Mohyla Acad., 1993. Author books including: Moscow and the Ukraine, 1918-1953, 1956, Medieval Russia, 900-1700, 3d edit., 1990, Imperial Russia, 1700-1917, 3d edit., 1990, Modernization of Russia Under Peter I and Catherine II, 1974, Colonial Russian America 1817-1832, 1976, A History of Russia, 1977, U.S.S.R.: A Concise History, 4th edit., 1984, The End of Russian America, 1979, Civil and Savage Encounters, 1983, Russian Statecraft, 1985, Russian Conquest of Siberia 1558-1700, 1985, Russian Penetration of the North Pacific Archipelago, 1700-1799, 1987, The Soviet Union and the Middle East, 1917-1985, 1987, Russia's Colonies in North America, 1799-1867, 1988, The Soviet Union and the Arab World of the Fertile Crescent, 1918-1985, 1994; contbr. articles to profl. jours. U.S., Can., Yugoslavia, Italy, South Korea, Fed. Republic Germany, France, Eng., Japan, Russia, Ukraine. State bd. dirs. PTA, Oreg., 1963-64; mem. World Affairs Council, 1965-92. Named Hon. Rsch. Prof. Emeritus, Kyungnam U., 1989—; Fulbright-Hays fellow W. Germany, 1967-68; fellow Kennan Inst. Advanced Russian Studies, Washington, 1978; recipient John Mosser award Oreg. State Bd. Higher Edn., 1966, 67; Branford P. Millar award for faculty excellence Portland State U., 1985, Outstanding Retired Faculty award, 1994; Hillard scholar in the humanities U. Nev., Reno, 1992. Mem. Am. Assn. Advancement Slavic Studies (dir. 1972-75), Am. Hist. Assn., Western Slavic Assn. (pres. 1990-92), Can. Assn. Slavists, Oreg. Hist. Soc., Nat. Geog. Soc., Conf. Slavic and East European History (nat. sec. 1972-75), Am. Assn. for Ukrainian Studies (pres. 1991-93), Ctr. Study of Russian Am. (hon.), Assn. Study Nationalities (bd. mem.-at-large USSR & Ea. Europe 1993—), Czechoslovak Soc. Arts and Scis., Soc. Jewish-Ukraine Contacts, Assn. Home: 2745 S Via Del Bac Green Valley AZ 85614-1071

DO, TAI HUU, mechanical engineer; b. Quang Binh, Vietnam, May 31, 1942; came to U.S., 1975; s. Mau Do and Thi Hai Nguyen; 1 child, Frederick Quan. BSME, U. Paris, 1970, MS, 1971. Rsch. engr. Soc. Automobile Engrs., Paris, 1970-71; test engr. Yanmar Diesel Co., Ltd., Osaka, Japan, 1971-72; prodn. mgr. Vietnam Products Co., Ltd., Saigon, Vietnam, 1972-75; chief engr. European Parts Exchange, Irvine, Calif., 1975-77; project mgr. Fairchild Aerospace Div., Santa Ana, Calif., 1977—. Co-author: Literary Dissident Movement in Vietnam; editor: Khai Phong Mag.; patentee in field; contbr. articles to profl. jours. Mem. Soc. Automotive Engrs., Soc. Mfg. Engrs. Buddhist. Office: Fairchild Aerospace Div 3130 W Harvard St Santa Ana CA 92704-3937

DOAK, ROBERT A., JR., geologist; b. Canyon, Tex., Feb. 5, 1928; s. R.A. and Thelma C. (Crawford) D.; m. Frances L. Doak. BS in Geology, U. Oreg., 1952, MS in Geology, 1953. Geologist Texaco, Wichita Falls, Tex., 1953-55, Vandyke Oil Co., Wichita Falls, Tex., 1955-57, Denver, 1958-79; pres. Mountains West Exploration, Inc., Albuquerque, 1979—. Served to sgt., U.S. Army, 1946-48. Mem. Am. Assn. Petroleum Geologists. Office: Mountains West Exploration 616 Central Ave SE Ste 230 Albuquerque NM 87102-3656

DOAN, XUYEN VAN, lawyer; b. Hadong, Vietnam, Apr. 1, 1949; came to U.S., 1975; s. Quyet V. Doan and Binh T. Kieu; m. Binh Thanh Tran, 1980; children: Quy-Bao, Ky-Nam. Licence en droit, U. Saigon Law Sch., Vietnam, 1971; MBA, U. Ark., 1977; JD, U. Calif., Hastings, 1982. Bar: Saigon 1972, Calif. 1982. Sole practice Costa Mesa and San Jose, Calif., 1982-84; ptnr. Doan & Vu, San Jose, 1984-90; prin. Doan & Tran, San Jose, 1995—; prin. Law Offices of Xuyen V. Doan, 1990-95. Author: Of the Seas and Men, 1985. Named Ark. Traveler Ambassador of Good Will, State of Ark., 1975. Office: 210 N 4th St # 101 San Jose CA 95112-5569

DOANE, SAMUEL WALLACE, sales executive; b. Fort Polk, La., Sept. 14, 1956; s. Neal Byron and Lynell (Firesheets) D.; children: Andrea Morgan, Samantha Paige. AA, Tallahassee Community Coll., 1978; BFA, Fla. State U., 1980. Asst. prodn. mgr. Alley Theatre, Houston, 1981; prodn. mgr. Stages Theatre, Houston, 1981; audio visual technician AVW Audio Visual Inc., Houston, 1981-82; dir. audio visual svcs. Westin Galleria, Houston, 1982-83; rental mgr. AVW Audio Visual Inc., New Orleans, 1983-84, sales mgr., 1984-87, nat. sales mgr., 1987-91; creative dir. Kipling Rock Prodns., 1991—; audio visual cons. Nat. Assn. TV Program Execs., L.A., 1985—; media cons. Rep. Nat. Conv., New Orleans, 1988; internat. audio visual cons. Gardiner-Caldwell Med. Symposium, 1989-90, others. Cons. various polit. campaigns. Mem. Sales and Mktg. Execs. (Dist. Sales award 1989), Hotel Sales and Mktg. Assn., healthcare Exhibn. and Conv. Assn., Internat. Comm. Industry Assn. (audio visual trainer 1989), Profl. Conv. Mgmt. Assn.

DOBBEL, RODGER FRANCIS, interior designer; b. Hayward, Calif., Mar. 11, 1934; s. John Leo and Edna Frances (Young) D.; m. Joyce Elaine Schnoor, Aug. 1, 1959; 1½ child, Carrie Lynn. Student, San Jose State U., 1952-55, Chouinard Art Inst., L.A., 1955-57. Asst. designer Monroe Interiors, Oakland, Calif., 1957-66; owner, designer Rodger Dobbel Interiors, Piedmont, Calif., 1966—. Pub. in Showcase of Interior Design, Pacific edit., 1992, 100 Designers' Favorite Rooms, 1993; contbr. articles to mags. and newspapers. Decorations chmn. Trans. Pacific Ctr. Bldg Opening, benefit Oakland Ballet, and various other benefits and openings, 1982—; chmn. Symphonic Magic, Lake Marritt Plaza., Opening of Oakland Symphony Orch. Season and various others, 1985—; cons. An Evening of Magic, Oakland Hilton Hotel, benefit Providence Hosp. Foudn., bd. dirs., 1991. Recipient Cert. of Svc., Nat. Soc. Interior Designers, 1972, 74; recipient Outstanding Contbn. award, Oakland Symphony, 1986, Nat. Philanthropy Day Disting. Vol. award, 1991. Mem. Nat. Soc. Interior Designers (profl. mem. 1960-75, v.p. Calif. chpt. 1965, edn. found. mem. 1966—, nat. conf. chmn. 1966), Am. Soc. Interior Designers , Claremont Country, Diabetic Youth Found. Democrat. Roman Catholic.

DOBBS, GREGORY ALLAN, journalist; b. San Francisco, Oct. 9, 1946; s. Harold Stanley and Annette Rae (Lehrer) D.; m. Carol Lynn Walker, Nov. 25, 1973; children: Jason Walker, Alexander Adair. B.A., U. Calif., Berkeley, 1968; M.S.J., Northwestern U., 1969. Assignment editor, reporter Sta. KGO-TV, San Francisco, 1966-68; news dir. San Francisco Tourist Info. Program Service, 1968; editor ABC Radio, Chgo., 1969-71; producer ABC News, Chgo., 1971-73; corr. ABC News, 1973-77, London, 1977-82, Paris, 1982-86, Denver, 1986-92; host The Greg Dobbs Show/Sta. KOA Radio, 1992—; lectr. Northwestern U. Sch. Journalism, 1975, 76. Recipient Sigma Delta Chi Disting. Svc. award for TV reporting Soc. Profl. Journalists, 1980, Emmy award for outstanding documentary, 1989, award of excellence Colo. Broadcasters Assn., 1993, 94, award for best talk show Colo. Soc. Profl. Journalists, 1994; Lippmann fellow Ford Found., 1975. Office: 1380 Lawrence St Denver CO 80204-2054

DOBEL, J. PATRICK, graduate studies director, educator; b. Kansas City, Mo., Sept. 15, 1948; s. Jerome Patrick Jr. and Joan (Woehler) D.; m. Lea Vaughn, June 12, 1978; children: Hilary Vaughn, Matthew Patrick. AB in Polit. Sci., Boston Coll., 1970; PhD, Princeton U., 1976. Lectr. Univ. Mich., Dearborn, 1974-76, asst. prof., 1976-80, assoc. prof., 1980-84; assoc. prof. Univ. Wash., Seattle, 1984—; dir., grad. studies, Sch. Pub. Affairs, Univ. Wash., Seattle, 1988—. Author: Compromise and Political Action: Political Morality in Liberal and Democratic Life, 1991; contbr. articles to profl. jours. Chair Seattle Overflight Com., 1985-86, King County (Wash.) Ethics Bd., 1987—, cons. on polit. ethics. With USAR, 1970-76. Recipient Nat. Endowment of Humanities fellowship to Inst., Chgo., Nat. Endowment of Humanities fellowship for Coll. Tchrs., Washington. Mem. Am. Polit. Sci. Assn., Am. Soc. Pub. Adminstrn., Assn. for Policy Analysis and Mgmt., Soc. for Legal and Polit. Philosophy. Roman Catholic. Office: Univ Wash Grad Sch Pub Affairs PO Box 353055 Seattle WA 98195

DOBELIS, GEORGE, manufacturing company executive; b. July 31, 1940; s. John and Dorothy Dobelis; m. Dolores Ann Nagle, Dec. 2, 1972; children: Sally Ann Berg, Christian Eric Berg, Kurt Conrad Berg. AA in Engring., Santa Monica Coll., 1963; student, Control Data Inst., 1970. Engring. Masterite Ind., Torrance, Calif., 1969-70; engring. mgr. Elco Corp., El Segundo, Calif., 1964-76, mgr. new products, 1976-77; pres. Connector Tech. Inc., Anaheim, Calif., 1977—. Patentee in field; contbr. articles to profl. jours. Served as sgt. N.G., 1963-69. Mem. IEEE. Republican.

DOBKIN, DAVID SHABSI, science administrator, ecologist, zoology educator; b. Washington, May 17, 1950; s. Harry Israel and Gertrude Madeline (Rosengarten) D.; m. Donna Rose Latzko, Apr. 24, 1980; children: Gabriel, Adria, Elliot. BA, George Washington U., 1972; MS, Colo. State U., 1975; PhD, U. Calif., Berkeley, 1983. Grad. rsch. asst. Internat. Biol. Program, Ft. Collins, Colo., 1974-75; lectr. biol. sta. U. Mich., Pellston, 1975; ornithology curatorial asst. Mus. Vertebrate Zoology U. Calif., Berkeley, 1976; grad. rsch. asst. U. Calif., Berkeley, 1978-81; instr. Coyote Point Natural History Mus., San Mateo, Calif., 1982-83; postdoctoral rsch. fellow dept. biol. scis., sr. ecologist, acting asst. prof. Stanford (Calif.) U., 1983-86; asst. prof. zoology Rutgers U., Camden, N.J., 1986-92; founder, exec. dir. High Desert Ecol. Rsch. Inst., Bend, Oreg., 1993—; master bander U.S. Fish and Wildlife Svc. Author: The Birder's Handbook, 1988, Birds in Jeopardy, 1992, Birdwatcher's Handbook, 1994, Conservation and Management of Neotropical Migrant Landbirds in the Northern Rockies and Great Plains, 1994; also chpts. in books. Mem. endangered and nongame species adv. com. State of N.J., 1988-91, nongame wildlife task force State of Oreg., 1991—. Recipient Luis Agassiz Fuertes award Wilson Ornithol. Soc., 1974; U. Calif. Regents fellow, 1977-78, NSF fellow, 1983-84, Henry Rutgers Rsch. fellow, 1986-88. Mem. AAAS, Am. Ornithologists Union, Am. Soc. Naturalists, Ecol. Soc. Am., Soc. for Conservation Biology, Cooper Ornithological Soc. Office: High Desert Ecological Rsch Inst 15 SW Colorado Ave Ste 300 Bend OR 97702-1149

DOBLER, DAVID LEE, pastor; b. Yankton, S.D., Sept. 30, 1949; s. Walter Emmanuel and Pauline Marie (Schillereff) D.; m. Laura Mary Ellithorpe, Sept. 15, 1979; 1 child, Isaac Emmanuel; children from previous marriage: Catherine Therese, David Christian. Student, Reed Coll., 1969-71; MDiv, San Francisco Theol. Sem., 1980; DD (hon.), U. Dubuque Theol. Sem., 1994. Ordained pastor Presbyn. Ch. Buyer, mgr. Wood Bros. Lumber Co., Tucson, Ariz., 1972-77; pastor Yakutat (Alaska) Presbyn. Ch., 1980-85, Jewel Lake Parish, Anchorage, 1985-95; exec. presbyter Yukon Presbytery PC (USA), Anchorage, 1995—; moderator 205th gen. assembly Presbyn. Ch. USA, Louisville, Ky., 1993-94. Bd. dirs. Alaska Refugee Outreach, Anchorage, 1989—, United Campus Ministry, Anchorage, 1991—; trustee Sheldon Jackson Coll., Sitka, Alaska, 1995—. Home: 2930 Lexington Cr Anchorage AK 99502 Office: Presbytery of Yukon 616 W 10th Anchorage AK 99501

DOBSON, L. KRISTINE, career counselor, counselor educator; b. Tooele, Utah, Jan. 31, 1953; d. William R. and LaFair (Jensen) D.; 1 child, Shelby. BS, Utah State U., 1974; MS, U. Utah, 1980. Cert. tchr., counselor, ednl. adminstr., Utah; nat. cert. vocat. evaluator. Tchr. Granite Sch. Dist., Salt Lake City, 1974-84, ednl. coord., 1984—; edn. specialist Utah Bd. Regents, Salt Lake City, 1981-82; editl. cons. UTAh SOICC, Salt Lake City, 1982—; instr. U. Phoenix, Salt Lake City, 1991—; tng. cons. Careerware, Ogdensburg, N.Y., 1991—; exec. mem. State Coun. on Applied Tech. Edn., Salt Lake City, 1990—; v.p. bd. trustees Children at Risk Found., Salt Lake City, 1992—; mem. Utah Edn. Strategic Planning Com., Salt Lake City, 1990-91. Editor: Utah's Career Guide, 1982—; co-editor: (newsletter) Utah Counseling Today, 1986-87; contbr. articles to profl. jours. Mem. Utah Foster Parents Assn. Recipient Svc. award Utah State Office Edn., 1990. Mem. Am. Vocat. Assn. (pub. info. com. 1991—, co-editor newsletter 1991—), Utah Vocat. Assn. (Counselor of the Yr. award 1988), Utah Sch. Counselor/Vocat. Guidance Assn. (exec. bd. 1988-89), NEA (del. 1992), Utah Edn. Assn. (del.), Utah Vocat. Assessment Assn. (pres. 1986-87, Svc. award 1990). Democrat. Office: Careerware PO Box 18 834 W 8300 S Paradise UT 84328

DOBY, KAREN ELAINE, data processing company executive; b. Amarillo, Tex., Nov. 1, 1955; d. Laurance Lee and Helen Marie (Davis) D. AS, Belleville (Ill.) Area Coll., 1976; BS, So. Ill. U., Edwardsville, Ill., 1977; MS, Georgetown U., 1978; MBA, Loyola U., New Orleans, 1984. Ops. researcher Dept. of Energy, Washington, 1977-78; geophysicist Naval Oceanographic Office, Bay St. Louis, Miss., 1978-82; engring. analyst Middle S. Utilities System, New Orleans, 1982; sr. systems analyst, mgr. Exploration and Devel. Systems CNG Producing Co., New Orleans, 1982—; cons. Macrobiotic Inst., New Orleans, 1987—. Mem. Nat. Computer Graphics Assn., IEEE Computer Soc., Am. Assn. Petroleum Geologists. Democrat. Home: 4546 B-10 El Camino Real # 360 Los Altos CA 94022-1041

DOBYNS, ZIPPORAH POTTENGER, minister, educator, writer; b. Chgo., Aug. 26, 1921; d. William Albert and Martha Cobb (Livingston) Pottenger; m. Henry F. Dobyns (div. Aug. 1958); children: Rique, William, Maritha, Mark. BA in anthropology, U. Chgo., 1944; MA in psychology, U. Ariz., 1966, PhD in psychology, 1969. Minister and dir. psychology svcs. L.A. Cmty. Ch. of Religious Sci., 1969—. Author: God's World, 1957, Expanding Astrology's Universe, 1983, Progressions, Divs. and Rect., 1974, Paths to Understanding, 1987, Finding the Person in the Horoscope, 1973, (with Maritha Pottenger) Planets in the Move, 1994; contbr. articles to profl. jours. Recipient Outstanding Contb. award Profl. Astrologers Inc., 1975, Regulas award United Astrology Congress, 1992. Mem. Am. Psychological Assn., Assn. Humanistic Psychology, Transpersonal Psychological Assn., Internat. Soc. Astrological Rsch. (dir. 1969—), Nat. Coun. Geocasmic Rsch. (adv. bd. 1975—), Assn. for Astrological Networking (adv. bd. 1986—). Home: 2036 Honey Springs Rd Jamul CA 91935-7506

DOCKSON, ROBERT RAY, savings and loan executive; b. Quincy, Ill., Oct. 6, 1917; s. Marshall Ray and Letah (Edmondson) D.; m. Katheryn Virginia Allison, Mar. 4, 1944; 1 child, Kathy Kimberlee. A.B., Springfield Jr. Coll., 1937; B.S., U. Ill., 1939; M.S. in Fgn. Service, U. So. Calif., 1940, Ph.D., 1946. Lectr. U. So. Calif., 1940-41, 45-46, prof., head dept. mktg., 1953-59; dean U. So. Calif. (Sch. Bus. Adminstrn.); and prof. bus. econs., 1959-69; vice chmn. bd. Calif. Fed. Savs. & Loan Assn., Los Angeles, 1969-70; pres. Calif. Fed. Savs. & Loan Assn., 1970-77, chmn., 1977-88, chief exec. officer, 1973-83; chmn. CalFed Inc., 1984-88, chief exec. officer, 1984-85, also dir.; instr. Rutgers U., 1946-47, asst. prof., 1947-48; dir. Bur. Bus. and Econ. Research, 1947-48; economist Western home office Prudential Ins. Co., 1948-52, Bank of Am., San Francisco, 1952-53; econ. cons., 1953-57; bd. dirs. IT Corp., Computer Scis. Corp. Am. specialist for U.S. Dept. State; mem. Town Hall, 1954—, bd. govs., 1963-65, hon. bd. govs., 1965—, pres., 1961-62; trustee John Randolph Haynes and Dora Haynes Found., Com. for Econ. Devel., Calif. Council for Econ. Edn.; chmn. bd. Rose Hills Meml. Park Assn., 1990-92; trustee, pres. Orthopedic Hosp.; bd. councilors Grad. Sch. Bus. Adminstrn., U. So. Calif.; bd. regents, chmn. univ. bd. Pepperdine U.; chmn. housing task force Calif. Roundtable, Commn. on the Future of the Calif. Cts., 1991-93. Served from ensign to lt. USNR, 1942-44. Decorated Star of Solidarity Govt. of Italy.; Recipient Asa V. Call Achievement award; Disting. Community Service award Brandeis U.; Whitney M. Young Jr. award Urban League, 1981, Albert Schweitzer Leadership award; Man of Yr. award Nat. Housing Conf., 1981; Industrialist of Yr. award Calif. Mus. Sci. and Industry, 1984. Mem. Am. Arbitration Assn., Newcomen Soc. N.Am., Hugh O'Brian Youth Found., Calif. C. of C. (pres. 1980, bd. dirs. 1981-86), L.A. C. of C. (bd. dirs.), Phi Kappa Phi (Diploma of Honor award 1984), Beta Gamma Sigma, Bohemian Club, Calif. Club, L.A. Country Club, One Hundred Club, Birnam Wood Golf Club, Thunderbird Country Club. Office: 6310 San Vicente Blvd Ste 402 Los Angeles CA 90048-5426

DOCKSTADER, JACK LEE, retired electronics executive; b. Los Angeles, Dec. 14, 1936; s. George Earl and Grace Orine (Travers) D.;m. Kerry Jo King, Oct. 24, 1987; children: Travis Adam Mayer, Bridget Olivia Mayer. student UCLA, 1960-70. Rate analyst Rate Bur., So. Pacific Co., Los Angeles, 1954-57; traffic analyst traffic dept. Hughes Aircraft Co., Fullerton, Calif., 1957-58, Culver City, Calif., 1958-59, traffic mgr. Hughes Research Labs., Malibu, Calif., 1959-70, material mgr., 1970-75; material mgr. Hughes Aircraft Co., Culver City, 1975-80, prodn. material mgr. Electro-Optical and Data Systems Group, El Segundo, Calif., 1980-84, mgr. material total quality 1984-85, mgr. cen. material ops. and property mgmt. 1987-88, mgr. group property mgmt., 1988-93, mgr. electro optical systems, property mgmt., aerospace and def. sector, 1993; ret., 1993. Mem. adv. council transp. mgmt. profl. designation program UCLA, 1966-80, mem. Design for Sharing Com., 1977-82; adv. com. transp. program Los Angeles Trade Tech. Coll., 1970-80. Served with USNR, 1954-76. Mem. Nat. Property Mgmt. Assn. (pres. L.A. chpt. 1992, 93), UCLA Alumni Assn., Nat. Contracts Mgmt. Assn., Naval Enlisted Res. Assn., Hughes Aircraft Co. Mgmt. Club, Delta Nu Alpha (pres. San Fernando Valley chpt. 1965-66, v.p. Pacific S.W. region 1969-71, region man of year 1971). Presbyterian. Home: PO Box 3156 Redondo Beach CA 90277-1156

DOCKTOR, WILLIAM JAY, pharmacist, educator; b. Jamestown, N.D., Apr. 19, 1951; s. Alvin M. and Grace K. (Ellis) D.; m. Paulette K. Reuther, Aug. 26, 1972; children: Lisa Ann, Paul Jay. BS, N.D. State U., 1974; D in Pharmacy, U. Mich., 1977. Cert. pharmacotherapy specialist. Intern pharmacist Osco Drug, Elkhart, Ind., 1974-75; pharmacist Osco Drug, Grand Forks, N.D., 1975; assoc. in clin. pharmacy Wash. State U., Pullman, 1975-76; asst. prof. U. Mont., Missoula, 1977-83, assoc. prof., 1983—; cons. Mont. Mental Disablities Bd. Visitors, Helena, 1977—; U.S. Forest Svc., Missoula, Mont., 1980—; clin. cons. St. Patrick Hosp., Missoula, 1988—, acting clin. coord. pharmacy, 1991-92; presenter continuing edn. programs, 1977—. Author: (with others) various books and manuals; editor drug info. column. Mont. Pharmacist, 1989-94; also articles. Soccer coach YMCA, Missoula, Mont., 1979-82; judge Mont. State Sci. Fair, Missoula, 1979-86, 90—; sec.-treas. Lorraine South County Water Dist., Missoula, 1985—; pres. ch. coun. Atonement Luth. Ch., Missoula, 1986-89. Named one of Outstanding Young Men Am., U.S.Jaycees, 1982. Mem. Am. Coll. Clin. Pharmacy, Am. Soc. Hosp. Pharmacists, Am. Assn. Colls. of Pharmacy,

Mont. Soc. Hosp. Pharmacists (continuing edn. and publicity chair 1982-83, program chair 1983-84, 88-89, pres. 1984-85, bd. dirs. 1983-86), Mont. State Pharm. Assn. Lutheran.

DODD, DARLENE MAE, nurse, air force officer; b. Dowagiac, Mich., Oct. 11, 1935; d. Charles B. and Lila H. D.; diploma in nursing Borgess Hosp. Sch. Nursing, Kalamazoo, 1957; grad. U.S. Air Force Flight Nurse Course, 1959, U.S. Air Force Squadron Officers Sch., 1963, Air Command and Staff Coll., 1973; BS in Psychology and Gen. Studies, So. Oreg. State Coll., 1987, postgrad., 1987; Commd. 2d lt. U.S. Air Force, 1959, advanced through grades to lt. col., 1975; staff nurse, Randolph AFB, Tex., 1959-60, Ladd AFB, Alaska, 1960-62, Selfridge AFB, Mich., 1962-63; Cam Rahn Bay Air Base, Vietnam, 1966-67, Seymour Johnson AFB, N.C., 1967-69, Air Force Acad., 1971-72; flight nurse 22d Aeromed. Evacuation, Tex., 1963-66; chief nurse Danang AFB, Vietnam, 1967; flight nurse Yokotu AFB, Japan, 1969-71; clin. coordinator ob/gyn and flight nurse, Elmendorf AFB, Alaska, 1973-76; clin. nurse coordinator obstetrics-gynecology and pediatric services USAF Med. Center, Keesler AFB, Miss., 1976-79, ret., 1979. Decorated Bronze Star, Meritorious Service medal, Air Force Commendation medal (3). Mem. Soc. of Ret. Air Force Nurses, DAV, Ret. Officers Assn., Vietnam Vets. Am., VFW, Uniformed Services Disabled Retirees, Air Force Assn., Psy Chi, Phi Kappa Phi. Club: Women of Moose. Home: 712 1st St Phoenix OR 97535-9787

DODD, JOE DAVID, safety engineer, consultant, administrator; b. Walnut Grove, Mo., Jan. 22, 1920; s. Marshall Hill and Pearl (Combs) D.; m. Nona Bell Junkins, Sept. 17, 1939; 1 dau. Linda Kay Dodd Craig. Student S.W. Mo. State U., 1937-39, Wash. U., 1947-33. Cert. profl. safety engr. Calif. Office asst. retail credit co., Kansas City, Mo., 1939-42; bus driver City of Springfield (Mo.), 1945-47; ops., engring., and personnel positions Shell Oil Co., Wood River (Ill.) Refinery, 1947-66; health and safety dept. mgr. Martinez Mfg. Complex, Calif., 1966-83, retired 1983; exec. dir. Fire Protection Tng. Acad., U. Nev.-Reno; rep. Shell Oil Co., Western Oil and Gas Assn., 1970-81. Mem. Republican Presdl. Task Force. Served with USMC, 1942-45. Decorated Presdl. Citation. Mem. Western Oil and Gas Assn. (Hose Handler award 1972-81, Outstanding mem. award), Am. Soc. Safety Engrs., Veterans Safety, State and County Fire Chiefs Assn., Peace Officers Assn., Nat. Fire Protection Assn. Presbyterian (elder). Established Fire Protection Tng. Acad., U. Nev.-Reno, Stead Campus.

DODDS, DALE IRVIN, chemicals executive; b. Los Angeles, May 3, 1915; s. Nathan Thomas and Mary Amanda (Latham) D.; m. Phyllis Doreen Kirchmayer, Dec. 20, 1941; children: Nathan E., Allan I., Dale I. Jr., Charles A. AB in Chemistry, Stanford U., 1937. Chem. engr. trainee The Texas Co., Long Beach, Calif., 1937-39; chemist Standard Oil of Calif., Richmond, 1939-41; chief chemist Scriver and Quinn Interchem., L.A., 1941-46; salesman E.B. Taylor and Co. Mfg. Rep., L.A., 1947-53, Burbank (Calif.) Chem. Co., 1953-57, Chem. Mfg. Co./ICI, L.A., 1957-68; pres., gen. mgr. J.J. Mauget Co., L.A., 1969—. Inventor: Systemic Fungicide, 1976; patentee in field; contributed to devel. Microinjection for Trees. Fellow Am. Inst. Chemists; mem. Am. Chem. Soc., L.A. Athletic Club, Sigma Alpha Epsilon Alumni (pres. Pasadena, Calif. chpt. 1973, 90). Republican. Christian Scientist. Office: JJ Mauget Co 2810 N Figueroa St Los Angeles CA 90065-1524

DODGE, DOUGLAS STUART, federal agency administrator; b. Van Nuys, Calif., May 26, 1951; s. John Marvin and Barbara Jean (McMillan) D.; m. Leslie Ann Condron, Apr. 24, 1982; children: Sarah Elizabeth, Gwendolyn Marie. BA in History, U. Calif., Davis, 1975. Outdoor recreation planner Bur. Land Mgmt., U.S. Dept. Interior, Yuma, Ariz., 1976-80, Salt Lake City, 1980-83; dist. archeologist Bur. Land Mgmt., U.S. Dept. Interior, Salt Lake City, Utah, 1983-88; supervisory resource mgmt. specialist Bur. Land Mgmt., U.S. Dept. Interior, Bishop, Calif., 1989—. Softball umpire Am. Softball Assn., U.S. Slow-pitch Softball Assn., So. Calif., Mcpl. Athletic Fedn., Calif., Ariz., Utah, 1976—. Mem. Utah Profl. Archeologist Coun., Roundalab Internat. Tchrs. Assn. (ednl. com. 1987-88), Utah Round Dance Assn. (pres. 1988-89), Utah Round Dance Tchrs. Assn. (chmn. 1983-85), Lions. Home: 131 Mountain Rd Big Pine CA 93513-2005 Office: Bur Land Mgmt 785 N Main St Ste E Bishop CA 93514-2430

DODGE, PETER HAMPTON, architect; b. Pasadena, Calif., July 1, 1929; s. Irving C. and Edna D. (Allison) D.; m. Janice Coor-Pender, Aug. 30, 1952; children: Susan Julia, Sarah Caroline. Student, Art Center Sch., Calif., 1947-49; A.B. with honors in Architecture, U. Calif., Berkeley, 1956. Cert. architect, Calif., Hawaii, Nev., Idaho, Colo., The Nat. Coun. of Archtl. Registration Bds., (NCARB). Apprentice Alvin Lustig (designer), Los Angeles, 1949-50; draftsman Joseph Esherick (AIA), 1956, architect, 1959-63; asso. architect Joseph Esherick and Assos. (architects), San Francisco, 1963-72; prin. Esherick, Homsey, Dodge and Davis (architects and planners, P.C.), San Francisco, 1972—; pres. Esherick, Homsey, Dodge and Davis (architects and planners, P.C.), 1979-85; lectr. dept. architecture U. Calif., Berkeley, 1961-64, 71; vis. lectr. dept. design San Francisco Art Inst., 1965. Prin. archtl. works include grad. residence facility U. Calif.-Davis, 1970, Shortstop Inc. markets, office and warehouse, Benicia, Calif., 1976, Ekahi Village (297 condominium units) Wailea, Hawaii, 1976, TWA and Western Airlines at San Francisco Internat. Airport, 1977, Citizens Utility Ctr., Susanville, Calif., 1983, various projects Golden Gate U., San Francisco, 1984—, additions and renovation Forest Hill Mcpl. R.R. Sta., San Francisco, 1985, Life Sci. Bldg. Mills Coll., Oakland, Calif., 1986, showroom R.A.B. Motors Mercedes-Benz , San Rafael, Calif., 1986, U.S. Embassy, La Paz, Bolivia, 1979-87, boarding area "B" expansion San Francisco Internat. Airport, 1987, additions and renovations Mills. Coll. Art Ctr., Oakland, 1987, F.W. Olin Libr. Mills Coll., Oakland, 1989, Calif. State U. at Bakersfield Walter Stiern Libr., 1993, Mills Hall restoration, Olney Hall rehab. Mills Coll., 1994 ; mem. editorial bd. Architecture Calif. mag., 1984-88, chmn. bd., 1985-88, Landscape mag., 1986—. Mem. Rockridge Community Planning Council, Oakland, Calif., 1971. Served with C.E., U.S. Army, 1957-58. Firm recipient of highest nat. honor for archtl. firm. AIA, 1986. Fellow AIA (dir. Calif. council 1979-81, dir. San Francisco chpt. 1977-78, sec. 1979, v.p. 1980, pres. San Francisco chpt. 1981, Honor award 1970, Bartlett award 1970); mem. U. Calif. at Berkeley Coll. Environ. Design Alumni Assn. (mem. founding steering com., pres. 1990-91). Office: c/o Esherick Homsey Dodge & Davis 2789 25th St San Francisco CA 94110-3516

DODS, WALTER ARTHUR, JR., bank executive; b. Honolulu, May 26, 1941; s. Walter Arthur Sr. and Mildred (Phillips) D.; m. Diane Lauren Nosse, Sept. 18, 1971; children: Walter A. III, Christopher L., Peter D., Lauren S. BBA, U. Hawaii, 1967. Mktg. officer 1st Hawaiian Bank, Honolulu, 1969, asst. v.p. mktg. div., 1969-71, v.p., chmn. mktg. and rsch. group, 1971-73, sr. v.p. mktg. and rsch. group, 1973-76, exec. v.p. retail banking group, 1976-78, exec. v.p. gen. banking group, 1978-84, pres., 1984-89, chmn., ceo, 1989—; chmn., pres., CEO First Hawaiian, Inc., 1989-90, chmn., CEO, 1989—; chmn., CEO First Hawaiian Creditcorp., 1989-92; bd. dirs. First Hawaiian Inc., 1st Hawaiian Bank, First Hawaiian Creditcorp Inc., First Hawaiian Leading, Inc., Alexander & Baldwin Inc., A&B-Hawaii Inc., Duty Free Shoppers Adv. Bd., Matson Navigation Co. Inc., 1st Ins. Co. Hawaii Ltd., GTE Calif., GTE Hawaiian Telephone Co., GTE Northwest, Grace Pacific Corp., Oceanic Cablevision Inc., Pacific Guardian Life Ins. Co., Princeville Adv. Group, RHP, Inc., Restaurant Suntory USA, Inc., Suntory Resorts, Inc. Bd. dirs. Ahahui Koa Anuenue, East-West Ctr. Found.; past sec., treas. The Rehab. Hosp. of the Pacific; exec. bd. mem. Aloha Coun., Boy Scouts Am.; trustee, past chmn., trustee Blood Bank Hawaii; past chmn. bd. Aloha United Way; past chmn. Bd. Water Supply; bd. govs., v.p. fin. Ctr. for Internat. Comml. Dispute Resolution; bd. dirs., treas. Coalition for Drug-Free Hawaii; trustee Contemporary Mus. co-chmn. corp. campaign com.; mem. Duty Free Shoppers Adv. Bd.; past chmn. Gubernatorial Inauguration, 1974, 82; bd. govs. Hawaii Employers Coun.; trustee Hawaii Maritime Ctr; mem. Gov.'s Adv. Bd. Geothermal/Inter-Island Cable Project, Gov.'s Blue Ribbon Panel on the Future of Healthcare in Hawaii; dir., past chmn. Hawaii Visitors Bur.; exec. com. Hawaiian Open; past spl. dir. Homeless Kokua Week; bd. gov. Honolulu Country Club, Japanese Cultural Ctr. Hawaii, Pacific Peace Found.; trustee Japan-Am. Inst. Mgmt. Sci., The Nature Conservancy Hawaii, Punahou Sch.; Hawaii chmn. Japan-Hawaii Econ. Coun.; chmn., dir. Pacific Internat. Ctr. for High Tech. Rsch.; past co-chmn., chmn. bldg. fund St. Louis High Sch.; treas. The 200 Club; dir. World Cup Honolulu 1994. Named Outstanding Jaycee in Nation, 1963, Outstanding Young Man Am. from Hawaii, 1972, Marketer of Yr., Am. Mktg. Assn., 1987; recipient Riley Allen Individual Devel. award, 1964, Hawaii State Jaycees 3 Outstanding Young Men award, 1971, Am. Advt. Fedn. Silver medal, 1977, St. Louis High Sch.'s Outstanding Alumnus award, 1980. Mem. Am. Bankers Assn., Bank Mktg. Assn., Hawaii Bankers Assn., Hawaii Bus. Roundtable, C. of C. of Hawaii, Honolulu Press Club. Office: 1st Hawaiian Bank PO Box 3200 Honolulu HI 96847*

DOELGER, NANCY MICKLICH, geologist, resource advisor; b. Lawrence, Kans., Oct. 11, 1949; d. John Robert and Katherine Louise (Ewing) Micklich; m. Mark Jonathan Doelger, July 2, 1978; children: Peter Jonathan, Gwendolyn Marie. BS in Geology and Chemistry, No. Ariz. U., 1972; MS in Geology, U. Wyo., 1981. Registered profl. geologist, Wyo. Geol. engr. Shell Oil Co., Midland/Houston, 1972-74; coal geologist U.S. Geol. Survey, Casper, Wyo., 1974-78; exploration geologist Gulf Oil Corp., Casper, Wyo., 1980-83; consulting geologist Clark and George, Casper, Wyo., 1983-86; geologist, engr., environ. specialist, resource advisor Bur. of Land Mgmt., Casper, Wyo., 1987—; pres. Wyo. State Geol. Survey Bd., Laramie, 1993, sec., 1994. Mem. Am. Assn. Petroleum Geolgists, Rocky Mtn. Assn. Geologists, Wyo. Geol. Assn. (sec. 1983, 1st v.p. 1984, pres. 1992, Frank Morgan award 1987), Five Trails Rotary. Home: 3331 Carmel Dr Casper WY 82604-4992

DOERFLING, HANK, aerospace engineer; b. San Pedro, Calif., Nov. 3, 1936; s. Laurence Howard and Julia Margret (Rusbarsky) D.; B.S. in Physics, Oreg. State U., 1958, M.S., 1963; M.Pub. Adminstrn., Pepperdine U., 1975; m. Elaine Carole; children: Howard, Carrie, Cassie, Tony, Evon. Analyst, No. Am. Aviation Co., Downey, Calif., 1963-64; mem. tech. staff TRW Systems Redondo Beach, Calif., 1964-66, adminstrv. and project mgr. Logicon, San Pedro, Calif., 1966-77; sr. scientist, engr. advanced digital communication program systems sector Hughes Aircraft Co., El Segundo, Calif., 1977—, with Hughes Aircraft, London, Eng. 1994—. Mem. Hermosa Beach Improvement Commn., 1970-72, chmn., 1971-72; mem. City of Hermosa Beach City Coun., 1972-80, mayor, 1973-74, 79-80; pres. South Bay Cities Assn., 1975-76; commr. South Coast (Calif.) Regional Coastal Commn., 1977-80, Calif. Coastal Commn., 1978-80. With USN, 1958-61. Mem. Hermosa Beach C. of C. (bd. dirs. 1970-71), League Calif. Cities, Sigma Pi Sigma. Home: 1011 2nd St Hermosa Beach CA 90254-5334 Office: Directorate Gen Military Survey, Charting & Mapping Elmwood Ave, Feltham Middlesex TW13 7AE, England also: 1 Riverway Barry Ave, Windsor Berkshire 5L4 55A, England

DOERPER, JOHN ERWIN, publisher, editor; b. Wuerzburg, Fed. Republic of Germany, Sept. 17, 1943; came to U.S., 1963, permanent resident, 1973; s. Werner and Theresia (Wolf) D.; m. Victoria McCulloch, Dec. 2, 1970. BA, Calif. State U., Fullerton, 1968; MA/ABD, U. Calif., Davis, 1972. Food writer/author Seattle, 1984—; food columnist Washington, Seattle, 1985-88, Seattle Times, 1985-88; food editor Wash.-The Evergreen State Mag., Seattle, 1989-94, Pacific Northwest mag., 1989-94, Seattle Home and Garden, 1989-91; pub., editor, founder Pacific Epicure, Quarterly Jour. Gastronomy, Bellingham, Wash., 1988—; dir. Annual N.W. Invitational Chef's Symposium. Author: Eating Well: A Guide to Foods of the Pacific Northwest, 1984, The Eating Well Cookbook, 1984, Shellfish Cookery: Absolutely Delicious Recipes from the Wst Coast, 1985; author, illustrator: The Blue Carp, 1994; contbr. articles to profl. jours., intro. and chpts. to books; co-author: Washington: A Compass Guide, 1995. Recipient Silver medal, White award for city and regional mags. William Allen White Sch. Journalism, U. Kans. Mem. Oxford Symposium Food and Cookery (speaker 26th Ann. Pacific Northwest Writer's Conf. 1982, 92). Home: 610 Donovan Ave Bellingham WA 98225-7315

DOERR, STEPHEN EUGENE, research engineer; b. Myrtle Beach, S.C., July 30, 1959; s. Eugene Joseph and Eva Mary (Highlander) D.; m. Lisa Lynn Glazener, July 24, 1982; children: Kelsey Ann, Emily Christine. MS, U. Ill., 1984; PhD, U. Tex., 1990. Tech. staff Sandia Nat. Labs., Albuquerque, 1984-87; rsch. engr. U. Tex., Austin, 1987-90, Ktech Corp., Albuquerque, 1990-93; sr. engr. Sci. Applications Internat. Corp., Albuquerque, 1993—; invited lectr., conf. chair. Contbr. articles to profl. jours. Fellow U. Tex., 1987. Mem. AIAA (sr., sect. chmn., aerospace measurement tech. com.), Soc. Photo-Optical Engrs. Office: Sci Applications Internat Corp 2109 Airpark Rd SE Albuquerque NM 87106-3258

DOGLIONE, ARTHUR GEORGE, data processing executive; b. Bklyn., May 24, 1938; s. Francis and Georgia (Smith) D.; m. Maryann Laurette Bonfanti, Sept. 3, 1960; children: Dana Ann, Arthur Todd, Lora Michele. AA, Scottsdale (Ariz.) Community, 1978; AAS, Maricopa Tech. Coll., Phoenix, 1984; BS, Ariz. State U., 1985. Salesman Columbus Realty Co., Trenton, N.J., 1962-65; appraiser J.H. Martin Appraisal Co., Trenton, 1965-68; office mgr. Mcpl. Revaluations, Avon-by-the-Sea, N.J., 1968-69; pres., broker Area Real Estate Agy., Wall, N.J., 1969-76; property appraiser Ariz. Dept. Revenue, Phoenix, 1976-78; investment appraiser Continental Bank, Phoenix, 1978-79; appraisal systems specialist Ariz. Dept. Revenue, Phoenix, 1979-80; project dir. Ariz. Dept. Adminstrn., 1980-83; pres. Logical Models, Scottsdale, Ariz., 1983-95; founder Genus Tech., Scottsdale, 1989—; tax assessor Upper Freehold Twp., N.J., 1974-75, Borough of Bradley Beach, N.J., 1975; lectr. in field. Author various software. Counselor SCORE, SBA, Mesa, Ariz., 1986-90. Mem. Phi Theta Kappa. Republican. Roman Catholic. Office: Genus Technology PO Box 725 Scottsdale AZ 85252-0725

DOHERTY, DENNIS EDWIN, immunologist, educator; b. Cin., Dec. 11, 1955; s. John Irwin and Gloria Anne (DiVirgilio) D.; m. Kimberlee Ann Surface, May 18, 1985; children: Erin Elizabeth, Collin Patrick. BA in Sci., Johns Hopkins U., 1977; MD, Ohio State Coll. Medicine, 1980. Intern/resident in Internal Medicine Ohio State U. Hosps., Columbus, 1980-83; fellow pulmonary/critical care medicine Health Sci. Ctr. U. Colo., Denver, 1983-86; asst. prof. Medicine dept. Internal Medicine U. Colo., Nat. Jewish Ctr. for Immunology, VA Med. Ctr., Denver, 1986-92, assoc. prof. of Medicine, 1992—; prin. investigator NIH, Denver, 1986—; reviewer Jour. Clin. Investigation, 1989—, Jour. Applied Physiology, 1990—, Exptl. Lung Rsch., 1989—, Am. Jour. Respiratory and Critical Care Medicine, 1988—, Am. Jour. Respiratory Cell and Molecular Biology, 1991—, Am. Jour. Pathology, 1991—. Contbr. articles to profl. jours. VA Merit Rev. grantee, 1989—, Clin. Investigator grantee, 1992—, NIH grantee, 1986—. Mem. ACP, AAAS, Am. Thoracic Soc., Am. Coll. Chest Physicians, Colo. Trudeau Soc., Am. Soc. Cell Biology, Western Soc. Clin. Investigation. Roman Catholic. Office: Nat Jewish Ctr Immunology & Respiratory Medicine 1400 Jackson St Rm D508 Denver CO 80206-2761

DOHERTY, FRED VINCENT, advertising executive; b. Jamaica Long Island, N.Y., Jan. 2, 1948; s. Frederick Vincent Sr. and Betty Louise (Williams) D.; m. Vicky Ann Haas Horn, Sept. 1, 1967 (div. June 1973); children: Sean Michael, Michelle Louise. BA, U. Minn., 1969. Sales rep. Washington Nat. Life Ins., Mpls., 1969-70; distbr. Vanguard Fire Alarms, Harrisburg, Pa., 1970-75; v.p. sales Interstate Engring. Corp., Anaheim, Calif., 1975-79; v.p. The Party Givers, Menlo Park, Calif., 1979-83; pres. V.I.P. Gourmets, Inc., Foster City, Calif., 1983-86; v.p. BPS Mortgage Bankers, San Francisco, 1986-88; v.p. mktg. Calif. Ctrl. Mktg. Corp., Costa Mesa, 1988-93; CEO Pinnacle Interest Group, Ltd., Huntington Beach, 1993—; assoc. dir. Calif. Spring Classic, Garden Grove, 1993-94. Baseball commr. Foster City (Calif.) Youth Sports, 1980-86, supr. parks and recreation, 1983-84. Democrat. Roman Catholic. Home: 17530 Santa Domingo Cir Fountain Vly CA 92708-4314 Office: Pinnacle Interest Group Ltd 2973 Harbor Blvd # 348 Costa Mesa CA 92626-3912

DOHERTY, PATRICK FRANCIS, communications executive, educator; b. Phila., Aug. 3, 1942; s. Patrick Francis and Nancy (White) D.; children: Patrick James, Norine Ann. BS, St. Joseph's U., 1965; MBA, U. Tampa, 1978; postgrad., GTE's Mgmt. Devel. Ctr., Norwalk, Conn., 1979-92. Rsch. assoc. Phila. Bull., 1970-72; product mgr. GTE, Tampa, 1972-78; regional mgr. GTE, Dallas, 1979-83; corp. mgr. GTE, Stamford, Conn., 1983-88; mgr. west area GTE, Thousand Oaks, Calif., 1988—; adj. prof., lectr. U. La Verne, Thousand Oaks, 1991-92. Author, editor (periodical) Winning in Competitive Markets, 1989. Pres. Homeowners Assn., 1972-78, v.p. 1995-96; mem. Nat. Property Owners Assn., Tampa, 1978, Nat. Graffiti, L.A., 1991-92, Info. Network, L.A. Capt. USAF, 1965-69. Recipient Leadership award United Way, 1988, Disting. Svc. award U.S. Olympic Festival, 1991. Home: 5735 Tanner Ridge Ave Westlake Village CA 91362-5238

DOI, LOIS, psychiatric social worker; b. Honolulu, Oct. 24, 1951; d. James Masato and Thelma Kimiko Miyamoto; m. Brian Doi, May 26, 1972; children: Michael, Lorian. BS, U. Hawaii, 1974, MSW, 1978. Lic. clin. social worker, Calif. Psychiat. social worker, child specialist Desert Community Mental Health Ctr., Indio, Calif., 1979-92, coordinator children's day treatment program, 1982-91; pvt. practice psychiat. social worker 1-2-1 Counseling, Palm Springs, Calif., 1992—; psychiat. social worker, adult case mgr. Desert Community Mental Health Ctr., Palm Springs, Calif., 1992-93; expert examiner, Bd. of Behavioral Sci. Examiners, 1987—. Vol. advisor Community Recreation Ctr. Youth Group, Hawaii, 1967-69; vol. interviewer ARC Food Stamp Program, Hawaii, 1973; vol. asst. YWCA Programs Young Mothers and Teens, Hawaii, 1973; vol. group leader YWCA Juvenile Delinquent Program, Hawaii, 1973; placement counselor Vols. In Service to Am., L.A., 1975; VISTA counselor L.A. Urban League, 1975-76. Mem. Nat. Assn. Social Workers. Office: 1-2-1 Counseling 400 S Farrell Dr Ste B116 Palm Springs CA 92262-7964

DOI, ROY HIROSHI, biochemist, educator; b. Sacramento, Mar. 26, 1933; s. Thomas Toshiteru and Ima (Sato) D.; m. Joyce Takahashi, Aug. 30, 1958 (div. 1992); children: Kathryn E., Douglas A.; m. Joan M. Saul, Feb. 14, 1992. AB in Physiology, U. Calif., Berkeley, 1953, AB in Bacteriology, 1957; MS in Bacteriology, U. Wis., 1958, PhD in Bacteriology, 1960. NIH postdoctoral fellow U. Ill., Urbana, 1960-63; asst. prof. Syracuse (N.Y.) U., 1963-65; asst. prof. U. Calif., Davis, 1965-66, assoc. prof., 1966-69, prof. biochemistry, 1969—, chmn. dept. biochemistry and biophysics, 1974-77, coord. for biotech., 1989-92; cons. NIH, Bethesda, Md., 1975-79, 82-84, Syntro Corp., San Diego, 1983-88; treas. Internat. Spores Conf., Boston, 1980-89; mem. recombinant DNA adv. com. NIH, 1990-95. With U.S. Army, 1953-55. Fellow NSF, 1971-72; recipient Sr. Scientist award, von Humboldt Found, Munich, 1978-79, vis. scholar award Naito Found, Tokyo. Fellow AAAS; mem. AAUP, Am. Soc. Biochem. Molecular Biology, Am. Soc. Microbiology, Sigma Xi. Democrat. Unitarian. Office: U Calif Sect Molecular & Cellular Biology Davis CA 95616

DOIDA, STANLEY Y., dentist; b. Kalamath Falls, Calif., Dec. 15, 1944; s. Sam S. and Mae M. (Nakao) D.; m. Eileen M. Crilly; children: Stanley Jr., Scott Samuel. Student, Knox Coll., 1965-67; DDS, Northwestern U., 1970. Asst. prof. Sch. Dentistry Northwestern U., Chgo., 1970-71; pres. Midtown Dental, Denver, 1971—; instr. U. Colo. Dental Sch., Denver, 1972-74. Mem. ADA, Acad. Operative Dentistry, Acad. Gold Foil Operators, Glenmoor Country Club. Home: 9638 E Maplewood Cir Englewood CO 80111-7016 Office: Midtown Dental 1800 Vine St Denver CO 80206-1122

DOIG, BEVERLY IRENE, systems specialist; b. Bozeman, Mont., Oct. 21, 1936; d. James Stuart Doig and Elsie Florence (Andes) Doig Townsend. AA, Graceland Coll., 1956; BA, U. Kans., 1958; MS, U. Wis., 1970; cert. in Interior Design, UCLA, 1993. Aerodynamic technician II Ames Labs.-NACA, Moffett Field, Calif., 1957; real time systems specialist Dept. of Army, White Sands Missile Range, N.Mex., 1958-66; large systems specialist computing ctr. U. Wis., Madison, 1966-70; sr. systems analyst Burroughs, Ltd., Canberra, Australia, 1970-72; systems specialist Tech. Info. Office Burroughs Corp., Detroit, 1973-78; sr. systems specialist Burroughs Gmbh, Munich, 1978-79, Burroughs AB, Stockholm, 1979-80; networking cons. Midland Bank, Ltd., Sheffield, Eng., 1980-83; networking specialist Burroughs Corp. (now UNISYS), Mission Viejo, Calif., 1983—; teaching asst. Canberra (Australia) Coll., 1972; tchr. Wayne State U. Ext., Detroit, 1976-77; freelance interior designer, 1992—. Vol. youth groups and camps Reorganized LDS Ch., N.Mex., Wis., Australia, Mich., Calif., Germany, U.K.; inner youth worker, Detroit. Scholar Mitchell Math., 1956-58, Watkins Residential, 1956-58. Mem. Assn. Computing Machinery (local chpt. chmn. membership 1969), Lambda Delta Sigma. Republican. Office: UNISYS 25725 Jeronimo Rd Mission Viejo CA 92691-2711

DOIG, IVAN, writer; b. White Sulphur Springs, Mont., June 27, 1939; s. Charles Campbell and Berneta (Ringer) D.; m. Carol Dean Muller, Apr. 17, 1965. BJ, Northwestern U., 1961, MS in Journalism, 1962; PhD in History, U. Wash., 1969; LittD (hon.), Montana State U., 1984, Lewis and Clark Coll., 1987. Editorial writer Lindsay-Schaub Newspapers, Decatur, Ill., 1963-64; asst. editor The Rotarian, Evanston, Ill., 1964-66. Author: (memoir) This House of Sky, 1978; (non-fiction) Winter Brothers, 1980; (novels) The Sea Runners, 1982, English Creek, 1984, Dancing at the Rascal Fair, 1987, Ride With Me, Mariah Montana, 1990, Heart Earth, 1993. Sgt. USAFR, 1962-69. Recipient Gov.'s Writers Day award, 1979, 81, 85, 88, award for lit. excellence Pacific N.W. Booksellers, 1979, 81, 83, 85, 88, 94, Disting. Achievement award Western Lit. Assn., 1989, Evans Biography award, 1992; fellow Nat. Endowment for Arts, 1985. Mem. Authors Guild, PEN Am. Ctr.

DOLAN, ANDREW KEVIN, lawyer; b. Chgo., Dec. 7, 1945; s. Andrew O. and Elsie (Grafner) D.; children: Andrew, Francesca, Melinda. BA, U. Ill., Chgo., 1967; JD, Columbia U., 1970, MPH, 1976, DPH, 1980. Bar: Wash. 1980. Asst. prof. law Rutgers-Camden Law Sch., N.J., 1970-72; assoc. prof. law U. So. Calif., L.A., 1972-75; assoc. prof. pub. health U. Wash., Seattle, 1977-81; ptnr. Bogle & Gates, Seattle, 1988-93; pvt. practice law, 1993—. Commr. Civil Svc. Commn., Lake Forest Park, Wash., 1981; mcpl. judge City of Lake Forest Park, 1982—. Russell Sage fellow, 1975. Mem. Order of Coif, Rainier Club, Washington Athletic Club. Office: 2200 Columbia Ctr 701 5th Ave Seattle WA 98104-7016

DOLAN, GRACE FRANCES, elementary education educator; b. Nevada City, Calif., Apr. 16, 1939; d. Harold Still and Frances Gwendolen (Bigelow) Anderson; m. Edward Henry Beck, June 6, 1959 (div. 1971); children: Laura Frances Beck Whitacre, Reid Edward Beck, Connie Leigh Beck Hanle; m. Robert Michael Fitzpatrick, June 17, 1973 (dec. June 1986); m. Kenneth Burton Dolan, Jan. 20, 1992. BA in Edn., Chico (Calif.) State Coll., 1971; MS in Marriage, Family, and Child Counseling, Calif. State U., Sacramento, 1994. Cert. elem. tchr., sch. counselor, Calif.; registered marriage, family and child counselor-intern, Calif. Title I reading tchr. Hennessy Sch., Grass Valley, Calif., 1971-74; tchr. 3d grade Grass Valley Sch. Dist., 1974—, mentor tchr. in sci., 1985-88, also summer sch. tchr.; drama coach Children's Theater Co., Grass Valley, 1990; Odyssey of the Mind coach Hennessy Sch., 1986-94. Grant writer. Recipient Disting. Svc. in Edn. award Ptnrs. in Edn., Nevada County, 1990. Mem. NEA, ASCD, Calif. Tchrs. Assn., Grass Valley Tchrs. Assn. (pres. 1988-90), Calif. Sci. Tchr. Assn., Calif. Assn. Marriage and Family Therapists, Phi Kappa Phi. Episcopalian. Home: 101 Fiddick Ln Grass Valley CA 95945-7337 Office: Hennessy Sch 225 S Auburn St Grass Valley CA 95945-7229

DOLAN, JAMES MICHAEL, JR., zoological society executive; b. N.Y.C., Feb. 27, 1937; s. James Michael and Emily Catherine (Wackerbauer) D. BS, Mt. St. Mary's Coll., Emmitsburg, Md., 1959; PhD, Inst. fur Haustierkunde, U. Kiel, Fed. Republic Germany, 1963. Asst. curator birds San Diego Zoo, 1963-64, assoc. curator birds, 1964-73, dir. animal sci., 1973-74; gen. curator San Diego Wild Animal Pk., 1974-81; gen. curator mammals Zool. Soc. San Diego, 1982-85, dir. collections, 1986—; advisor Econ. Rsch. Assocs.; adj. prof. zoology San Diego State U.; tech. asst. UN in Malaysia, 1970, Indian Zool. Gardens, 1976, Kuwait Zool. Garden, 1978, Seoul (Korea) Zool. Garden; mem. Survival Svc. Commn., Faro, Portugal, 1978; zoo advisory for U.S. Fish & Wildlife Svc. to India, 1980; del. internat. confs. including Conv. on Internat. Trade in Endangered Species Wild Fauna and Flora, Buenos Aires, 1985, Internat. Conf. Rupricaprines, Japan, 1987. Collecting expdns. to Cen. Am. countries, 1965, Australia, 1966, Papua-New Guinea, 1966, Java and Borneo, 1969, Fiji, 1970, Costa Rica, 1976; participant giant eland capture expdn. Senegal and Mali, 1979; mem. adv. bd. Internat. Zoo Yearbook, London. Fellow Am. Assn. Zool. Pks. and Aquariums (coordinator Arabian oryx group species survival plan); mem. Internat. Union Dirs. Zool. Gardens, Internat. Union for Conservation of Nature & Natural Resources (active several species survival comm. specialist groups, del. meetings and confs. Eng., Australia, Czechoslovakia, Hong Kong 1980-84, Fed. Republic Germany, 1987, reintroduction program Przewalski's horse Republic of China and Tibet, 1987, conf. Arabian oryx Saudi Arabia, 1987, com. to review new Taipei Zoo 1987), Am. Pheasant and Waterfowl Assn., African Lovebird Soc., Avicultural Soc., Explorer's Club, Fauna Preservation

Soc., Found. Protection and Preservation of Przewalski Horse, Internat. Crane Found., World Pheasant Assn., Zooculturists, German Soc. Mammalogists. Home: 18836 Paradise Mountain Rd Valley Center CA 92082-7430 Office: San Diego Wild Animal Park PO Box 551 San Diego CA 92112-0551

DOLAN, MARY ANNE, journalist, columnist; b. Washington, May 1, 1947; d. William David and Christine (Shea) D.; B.A., Marymount Coll., Tarrytown, N.Y., 1968, H.H.D. (hon.), 1984; student Queen Mary, Royal Holloway colls. U. London, London Sch. Econs., also Kings Coll., Cambridge U., 1966-68. Reporter, editor Washington Star, 1969-77, asst. mng. editor, 1976-77; mng. editor Los Angeles Herald Examiner, 1978-81, editor, 1981—; speaker Internat. Soc. Appraisers conv., San Francisco. Author: Commonsense Collecting, 1991. Recipient Golden Flame award Calif. Press Women, 1980, Woman Achiever award Calif. Fed. Bus. and Profl. Women's Clubs, 1981; bd. selectors for Neiman Fellows Harvard U.; mem. Pulitzer Prize Journalism Jury, 1981, 82. Mem. Am. Soc. Newspaper Editors, NOW. Club: Los Angeles Athletic. Office: M.A.D. Inc. 1033 Gayley Ave Ste 205 Los Angeles CA 90024-3417

DOLAN, MARYANNE MCLORN, small business owner, writer, educator, lecturer; b. N.Y.C., July 14, 1924; d. Frederick Joseph and Kathryn Cecilia (Carroll) McLorn; m. John Francis Dolan, Oct. 6, 1951 (dec.); children: John Carroll, James Francis McLorn, William Brennan. B.A., San Francisco State U., 1978, M.A., 1981. Tchr. classes and seminars in antiques and collectibles U. Calif., Berkeley, Davis, Santa Cruz, Coll. of Marin, Kentfield, Calif., Mills Coll., Oakland, St. Mary's Coll., Moraga, 1969-90, Solano C.C., 1990—; tch. writing Dolan Sch., 1969-90; owner antique shop, Benicia, Calif., 1970—; lectr. Nat. Assn. Jewelry Appraisers Symposium, Tucson; lectr. Vintage Fashion Expo., Oakland, Coll. for Appraisers, Placentia, Calif. Author: Vintage Clothing, 1880-1980, 3d edit., 1983, Collecting Rhinestone Jewelry, 1984, Old Lace and Linens, 1989, Commonsense Collecting, 1991, 300 Years of American Sterling Silver Flatware, 1992; weekly columnist The Collector, 1979-88; contbr. articles to profl. jours. Mem. AAUW, Antique Appraisal Assn. Am. Inc., Costume Soc. Am., New Eng. Appraisers Assn., Questers, Women's Nat. Book Assn. Inc., Nat. Assn. Jewelry Appraisers, Internat. Soc. Appraisers (lectr. ann. meeting), Internat. Platform Assn. Republican. Roman Catholic. Home: 138 Belle Ave Pleasant Hill CA 94523-4640 Office: 138 Belle Ave Pleasant Hill CA 94523-4640

DOLBERG, DAVID SPENCER, business executive, lawyer, scientist; b. L.A., Nov. 28, 1945; s. Samuel and Kitty (Snyder) D.; m. Katherine Blumberg, Feb. 22, 1974 (div. 1979); 1 child, Max; m. Sarah Carnochan, May 23, 1992. BA in Biology with honors, U. Calif., Berkeley, 1974; PhD in Molecular Biology, U. Calif., San Diego, 1980; JD, U. Calif., Berkeley, 1989. Bar: Calif. 1989, U.S. Dist. Ct. (no. dist.) Calif. 1989, U.S. Patent and Trademark Office, 1990. Staff biologist, postdoctoral fellow Lawrence Berkeley Lab. U. Calif., 1980-85; assoc. Irell & Manella, Menlo Park, Calif., 1989-91; v.p. EROX Corp., Menlo Park, Calif., 1991-92; v.p. sci. and patents Pherin Corp., Menlo Park, Calif., 1992-94; pvt. practice Berkeley, 1994—; speaker in field. Contbr. articles to Jour. Gen. Virology, Jour. Virology, Nature, Science, Psychoneuroendocrinology. Home: 1322 Santa Fe Ave Berkeley CA 94702-1047 Office: 1322 Santa Fe Ave Berkeley CA 94702-1047

DOLCOURT, JOYCE LINDA, social service administrator; b. Denver, Sept. 24, 1949; d. David I. and Rose (Kraut) Papper; m. John Lawrence Dolcourt, Sept. 3, 1972; children: Bram Austin, Cameron Grant. BA, Temple Buell, 1971; MA, U. Denver, 1974. Dir. Freeman-Sheldon Parent Support Group, Salt Lake City, 1981—; Consumer Mountain States Regional Genetic Svcs. Network, 1985—. Adv. bd. mem. Fedn. Reconstructionist Congregations and Havurot Com. on Inclusion for People with Disabilities, 1994—. Mem. Nat. Orgn. for Rare Disorders, Alliance of Genetic Support Groups. Office: Freeman-Sheldon Parent Support Group 509 Northmont Way Salt Lake City UT 84103-3324

DOLENC, MAX RUDOLPH, geologist, researcher; b. Rock Springs, Wyo., Jan. 15, 1943; s. Max Jack and Elsie Rose (Yardas) D.; m. Jeanne Marie Greenhalgh, June 22, 1963 (div. Aug. 1973); children—Patrick Vincent, Paige Marie; m. 2d, Louise Edna Peterson, Nov. 8, 1980; stepchildren—Theresa Satoyo Togo, Tami Kyoko Togo. BS in Chemistry, U. Wyo.-Laramie, 1966, BSBA, 1969; MS in geology, U. Idaho-Moscow, 1988; MS in Geology, 1988. Radiation specialist Wyo. Health Dept., Cheyenne, 1967-69; field mgr. ATCOR, Inc., Denver, 1969-70; research physicist El Paso Natural Gas, 1970-76; environ. geosci. mgr. EG&G Idaho, Inc., Idaho Falls, 1976-78, sr. geosci. engr., 1978-83, sr. project engr., 1983-89; sr. radioactive waste mgmt. specialist Reynolds Elec. & Engring. Co., Las Vegas, 1989—. Contbr. articles in field. Mem. Am. Assn. Petroleum Geologists, Am. Assn. Individual Investors, Geol. Soc. Nev., Phi Epsilon Phi. Roman Catholic. Home: 2732 Tidewater Ct Las Vegas NV 89117-2447 Office: Reynolds Elec & Engring Co Inc PO Box 98521 Las Vegas NV 89193-8521

DOLGOW, ALLAN BENTLEY, consulting company executive; b. N.Y.C.; BIE, NYU, 1959, MBA, 1972; postgrad. Hunter Coll., 1976, U. Calif., 1991; m. Nina Kim; children: Nicole, Marc, Ginger, Kimbie. with, Republic Aviation Corp., Farmingdale, N.Y., 1959-60; mgr. Internat. Paper Co., N.Y.C., 1960-73; project mgr. J.C. Penney Co. Inc., N.Y.C., 1973-76; dir. mfg. and planning Morse Electro Products, N.Y.C., 1976-77, exec. mgr. Morse Electrophonic Hong Kong Ltd., 1976-77; internat. project mgr. Revlon Inc., Edison, N.J., 1977-79; cons. SRI Internat., Menlo Park, Calif., 1979—. With U.S. Army, 1954-56, Germany. Office: 333 Ravenswood Ave Menlo Park CA 94025-3453

DOLIBER, DARREL LEE, design engineer, consultant, laboratory manager; b. Mpls., June 19, 1940; s. Russell Clifford Doliber and Helen Carol (Homa) Price; m. Ethel Lorraine Dzivi, June 17, 1962; children: Wendy Lorraine, Heather Leigh; m. Helga Renate Miggo, Oct. 31, 1986. AA, Palomar Coll., 1973. Prodn. engr. Hughes Aircraft Co., Carlsbad, Calif., 1969-74; sr. engr. I.T.T., Roanoke, Va., 1974-77; dir. mfg. Gainsboro Elec. Mfg. Co., Inc., Roanoke, Va., 1977-78; mfg. engr. Litton Industries, Tempe, Ariz., 1978-82; sr. engr. Datagraphix, Inc., San Diego, 1982-84; lab. mgr. S.A.I.C., San Diego, 1984—. Contbr. articles in field; patentee in field. Mem. Soc. Photo-Optical and Instrumentation Engrs. Roman Catholic. Home: 2952 N Victoria Dr Alpine CA 91901-3673 Office: Sci Applications Internat Corp 4161 Campus Point Ct San Diego CA 92121-1513

DOLICH, ANDREW BRUCE, professional basketball team executive; b. Bklyn., Feb. 18, 1947; s. Mac and Yetta (Weiselter) D.; m. Ellen Andrea Fass, June 11, 1972; children: Lindsey, Caryn, Cory. BA, Am. U., 1969; MEd, Ohio U., 1971. Adminstrv. asst. to gen. mgr. Phila. 76ers, NBA, 1971-74; v.p. Md. Arrows Lacrosse, Landover, 1974-76; mktg. dir. Washington Capitals, NHL, Landover, 1976-78; exec. v.p., gen. mgr. Washington Diplomats Soccer, 1978-80; v.p. bus. ops. Oakland A's Baseball, Calif., 1980-92, exec. v.p., 1993-95; pres., COO Golden State Warriors NBA, Oakland, Calif., 1995—; nat. fundraising chmn. sports adminstrs. program Ohio U., Athens, dir., 1978-82; lectr. sports mktg. U. Calif. Ext. Bd. dirs. Bay Area Sports Hall of Fame, 1982—, Celebrate Oakland Com., Internat. Sports Mktg. Coun., Oakland Zoo Adv. Coun. Recipient Alumni of Yr. award Ohio U. Sports Adminstrs. Program, Athens, 1982; recipient Clio award Am. Advt. Fedn., 1982. Office: Golden St Warriors Oakland Coliseum Blvd Oakland CA 94621

DOLL, LINDA A., artist, educator; b. Bklyn., May 5, 1942; d. William James Harrington and Ann B. (Casey) Cook; m. William John Doll, Feb. 4, 1962; children: Patricia, William Jr. AA, Palomar Coll., 1974; BA, San Diego State U., 1976. chairperson Arts Adv. Com. to Congressman Jim Bates, 1983-84; U.S. Coast Guard Artist, 1985—. Exhibited in group shows with Am. Watercolor Soc., 1985-91 (selected for one yr. nat. travel show, Elsie and David Ject-key award 1988) N.Y.C., 1986, 87, 88, Canton, Ohio, 1985, Nat. Watercolor Soc., Brea, Calif., 1984-89, Watercolor West Annual, Riverside, Calif., 1982, 84-88 (E. Gene Crain Purchase Selection award 1985, Second Place Jurors award 1982), Rocky Mountain Nat., Golden, Colo., 1984-85, Midwest Annual, Davenport, Iowa, 1983, 85, Nat. Watercolor Soc., Riverside, 1985 (selected for one yr. nat. travel show) 88, Canton Ohio, 1985, Watercolor Internat., San Diego, 1978-79, 82-88 (selected for one yr. nat. travel show 1983-84), Watercolor Okla., 1982-84 (Harry Hulett Jr. award 1984), Pa. Soc. Watercolor Painters, Harrisburg, 1988, 1982 (hon. mention); represented in permanent collections including E. Gene Crain Collection, Scripps Hosp., La Jolla, Calif., Redlands Community Hosp., Riverside, Campbell River Community Art Council, Can., Simpact Assocs. Inc., San Diego. Mem. San Diego Watercolor Soc. (past pres., life), Nat. Watercolor Soc. (past pres., life), Knickerbocker Artists, Am. Watercolors Soc. (past juror, bd. dirs.). Office: PO Box 160729 Big Sky MT 59716

DOLL, NANCY MARIE, arts administrator and curator; b. Chgo., Nov. 14, 1947; d. Lawrence Anthony and Mary (Trexler) D. BFA, Mundelein Coll., Chgo., 1969; MA in Art History, U. Iowa, 1971. Registrar/adminstrv. asst. Krannert Art Mus., Champaign-Urbana, Ill., 1971-72; instr. U. Tenn., Chattanooga, 1973-75; adminstrv. asst. Ctr. for Advanced Visual Studies, MIT, Cambridge, Mass., 1975-77; dir. Thorne Art Gallery, Keene, N.H., 1977-80, Gallery Eleven, Tufts U., Medford, Mass., 1980-86; curator 20th Century art and contemporary art Santa Barbara (Calif.) Mus. Art, 1986-92; dir. Contemporary Arts Forum, Santa Barbara, 1992—. Author exhbn. catalogs: Figurative Impulses, 1988, Inner Natures, 1990, Currents, 1989, Matt Mullican: The Spectrum of Knowledge, 1992. Mem. Visual Arts in Pub. Places, Santa Barbara, 1988-94, Arts Adv. Com., Santa Barbara, 1994—; bd. dirs. The Arts Fund, Santa Barbara, 1993—, The Downtown Orgn., Santa Barbara, 1992—. Mem. ArtTable, Am. Assn. Mus., MS Group. Office: Contemporary Arts Forum 653 Paseo Nuevo Santa Barbara CA 93101-3392

DOLL, WILLIAM, computer company executive; b. 1939. BA in Math., Rutgers U., 1964. Programmer Bell Telephone Labs., Whippany, N.J., 1960-66; sr. sys. programmer Foxboro (Mass.) Co., 1966-68; sr. sys. analyst GE, Mountainside, N.J., 1968-69; dir. programming Sys. Engring. Labs., Ft. Lauderdale, Fla., 1969-73; various positions Simpact Assocs., Inc., San Diego, 1973—, now pres., chmn. bd. dirs. Office: Simpact Assoc Inc 9210 Sky Park Ct San Diego CA 92123-4302*

DOLLINGER, MALIN ROY, physician, author; b. San Francisco, Oct. 7, 1935; s. Mel King and Marilyn Hinda (Rosenbloom) D.; m. Lenore Carole Levy, June 5, 1960; children: Jeffrey, Marc, Deborah, Cynthia. AB in Biology, Stanford U., 1956; MD, Yale U., 1960. Diplomate Am. Bd. Internal Medicine, Am. Bd. Med. Oncology, Am. Bd. Quality Assurance and Utilization Rev. Physicians. Intern UCLA, 1960; resident in internal medicine U. Calif. Hosps., San Francisco, 1961, 63-65; USPHS fellow in oncology Meml./Sloan Kettering Inst., N.Y.C., 1965-68; clin. asst. physician Meml. Hosp., N.Y.C., 1969; assoc. Pasadena (Calif.) Tumor Inst., 1970-71; dir. oncology svc. UCLA-Harbor Med. Ctr., Torrance, Calif., 1971-72; ptnr. Cancer Care Assocs., Torrance, 1972-95; v.p. for med. affairs John Wayne Cancer Inst., Santa Monica, Calif., 1995—; Mellor vis. scholar Meml. Hosp., N.Y.C., 1973; clin. prof. medicine U. So. Calif., L.A., 1991—. Author: Everyone's Guide to Cancer Therapy, 1991; assoc. editor poetry Mediphors, 1992—. Mem. physician's adv. coun. Wellness Cmty., L.A., 1991—; poet-at-large L.A. County Med. Assn., L.A., 1993—. Lt. USN, 1961-63. Fellow ACP, Am. Coll. Clin. Pharmacology; mem. Am. Cancer Soc. (pres. 1990-93, Achievement awards 1975-94), Am. Bd. Forensic Examiners. Office: John Wayne Cancer Inst 2200 Santa Monica Blvd Santa Monica CA 90404-2301

DOLLIVER, JAMES MORGAN, state supreme court justice; b. Ft. Dodge, Iowa, Oct. 13, 1924; s. James Isaac and Margaret Elizabeth (Morgan) D.; m. Barbara Babcock, Dec. 18, 1948; children: Elizabeth, James, Peter, Keith, Jennifer, Nancy. BA in Polit. Sci. with high honors, Swarthmore Coll., 1949; LLB, U. Wash., 1952; D in Liberal Arts (hon.), U. Puget Sound, 1981. Bar: Wash. 1952. Clk. to presiding justice Wash. Supreme Ct., 1952-53; sole practice Port Angeles, Wash., 1953-54, Everett, Wash., 1961-64; adminstrv. asst. to Congressman Jack Westland, 1955-61, Gov. Daniel J. Evans, 1965-76; justice Supreme Ct. State of Wash., 1976—, chief justice, 1985-87; adj. prof. U. Puget Sound Sch. Law, 1988-92. Chmn. United Way Campaign Thurston County, 1975; chmn. Wash. chpt. Nature Conservancy, 1981-83; pres. exec. bd. Tumwater Area coun. Boy Scouts Am., 1972-73, Wash. State Capital Hist. Assn., 1976-80, 85—, also trustee, 1983-84; trustee Deaconess Children's Home, Everett, 1963-65, U. Puget Sound, 1969—, chair exec. com., 1990-93, Wash. 4-H Found., 1977-93, Claremont (Calif.) Theol. Sem., assoc. mem., Community Mental Health Ctr., 1977-84; bd. mgrs. Swarthmore Coll., 1980-84; bd. dirs. Thurston Mason Community Health Ctr., 1977-84, Thurston Youth Svcs. Soc., 1969-84, also pres., 1983, mem. exec com. 1970-84, Wash. Women's Employment and Edn., 1982-84; mem. jud. coun. United Meth. Ch., 1984-92, gen. cong., 1970-72, 80—, gen. bd. ch. and soc., 1976-84; adv. coun. Ret. Sr. Vol. program, 1979-83; pres. Wash. Ctr. Law-related Edn., 1987-89, bd. dirs. 1987—; bd. dirs. World Assn. for Children and Parents, 1987-93; trustee U. Wash. Law Sch. Found., 1982-90, Olympic Park Inst., 1988-94; mem. bd. visitors U. Wash. Sch. Social Work, 1987-93; chair bd. visitors U. Puget Sound Sch. Law, 1988-90, bd. visitors, 1988-93; chmn. bd. dirs. Pub. Lands Employee Recognition Fund, 1994—; mem. bd. dirs. St. Peter Hosp. Med. Rehab. Community Adv. Bd., 1993—. With USN, 1943-45; ensign USCG, 1945-46. Recipient award Nat. Council Japanese Am. Citizens League, 1976; Silver Beaver award, 1971; Silver Antelope award, 1976. Mem. ABA, Wash. Bar Assn., Am. Judges Assn., Am. Judicature Soc., Pub. Broadcast Found. (bd. dirs. 1982-94), Masons, Rotary, Phi Delta Theta, Delta Theta Phi. Office: Wash Supreme Ct PO Box 40929 Temple of Justice (AV-11) Olympia WA 98504

DOLOWITZ, DAVID AUGUSTUS, otolaryngologist, educator; b. N.Y.C., Nov. 3, 1913; s. Alexander and Florence Reda (Levine) D.; m. Frances Marie Fleisher, May 6, 1937 (dec. 1967); children: David S., Julia Louise, Wilma Florence, Susan Reda, Fridolyn Gimble; m. Emma Ruth Halvorsen, June 11, 1968. AB, Johns Hopkins U., 1933; MD, Yale U., 1937; MA, U. Utah, 1951, ScD (hon.), 1978.Intern, Morristown (N.J.) Meml. Hosp., 1937-38, Albany (N.Y.) Hosp., 1938-39; resident Johns Hopkins Hosp., Balt., 1939-43; practice medicine, specializing in otolaryngology, Salt Lake City, 1946-78; asst. otolaryngology Johns Hopkins U., Balt., 1938-39, instr., 1942-43; instr. U. Utah, Salt Lake City, 1943-48, assoc. clin. prof., 1948-58, assoc. prof., chief otolaryngology, 1958-67, clin. prof. otolaryngology, 1967-83, emeritus prof., 1983—; instr. biology Dixie Coll., St. George, Utah, 1987-93; staff Holy Cross Hosp., VA Hosp., Salt Lake City, U. Utah Med. Hosp., Primary Children's Hosp., Salt Lake City, all 1946-78; councilman, treas. Town of Toquerville (Utah), 1982-87, mayor, 1987-90. Chmn. bd. Pioneer Craft House, Salt Lake City, 1965-84; mem. gov.'s com. study exceptional children, Utah, 1967; mem. Com. for Endowment of the Humanities, 1988-94; mem. otolaryngologic del. to China, People to People, 1986. Served with M.C., U.S. Army, 1943-46. NIH fellow, U. Lund, Sweden, 1959-60; Merit of Honor award Emeritus Alumni Assn. Univ. Utah, 1993. Fellow ACS; mem. AMA, Utah Med. Assn. (editorial bd. 1991—), Am. Bd. Otolaryngology, Am. Acad. Otolaryngology, Am. Bd. Clin. Allergy, Am. Otol. Soc., Deafness Research Found., Soc. Univ. Otolaryngologists (adv. com. pulmonary-allergy drugs 1973-78), Am. Laryngology, Rhinology and Otolaryngology Soc., Barany Soc., C. of C. Democrat. Jewish. Author: Basic Otolaryngology, 1964; editor: Allergy in Otolaryngologic Practice: The Otolaryngologic Clinics of North America, 1971; Transactions of Am. Soc. Ophthalmologic and Otolaryngologic Allergy, 1973-78; contbr. articles to profl. jours. Home: 1715 Cannes Way Salt Lake City UT 84121-2144

DOLSEN, DAVID HORTON, mortician; b. Durango, Colo., Feb. 27, 1940; s. Donald B. and Florence I. (Maxey) D.; BA, Southwestern Coll., 1962; Mortuary Sci. Degree, Dallas-Jones Coll. Mortuary Sci., 1963; m. Jo Patricia Johnson, Dec. 23, 1962; children: Wendy, Douglas. Apprentice, Davis Mortuary, Pueblo, Colo., 1963-64; bus. mgr. George F. McCarty Funeral Home, Pueblo, 1964-65; owner Dolsen Mortuary, Lamar, Colo., 1965-72; pres., gen. mgr., dir. Almont, Inc., Pueblo, 1972-92; sec. Dolsen, Inc., 1967—; pres. Wilson Funeral Dirs. Inc., 1972-92, Carlson Travel Network/Let's Talk Travel, Inc., Pueblo/Denver. Mem. Lamar City Council, 1969-73; mayor City of Lamar, 1971-73. Bd. dirs. Lamar Community Coll., 1967-73, Prowers County Hist. Soc., 1966—, San De Cristo Arts and Conf. Center, 1979-85; bd. dirs., sec. Pueblo Met. Mus. Assn., 1975-79; chmn. council on fin. and adminstrn. Rocky Mountain Conf. United Meth. Ch., 1976-94, del. Gen. Conf., 1980, 84, 88, 92, dir. adminstrv. svcs., treas., 1994—; mem. Pres.'s Council Nat. Meth. Found., 1978-90, Iliff Sch. Theology, 1986-88; trustee, mem. exec. com. Southwestern Coll., Winfield, Kans., 1979—; dist. chmn. Boy Scouts Am., 1981-88; treas., mem. exec. com. Girl Scouts USA, 1981-88; mem. council on fin. and adminstrn. Western Jurisdiction, United Meth. Ch., 1980-88; trustee, gen. council on fin. and adminstrn. United Meth. Ch., 1980-88, gen. coun. on mininstries, mem. gen. bd. of higher edn. and ministries; trustee Meth. Corp., 1988—, United Meth. Ch. Ins. Trust, 1982-88, Iliff Sch. Theology, 1992—; mem. Assn. United Meth. Conf. Pension and Benefit Officers, 1994—, Assn. United Meth. Treas., 1994—; mem. World Service Commn., Meth. Episcopal Ch., 1980-88; mem. gen. council on adminstrn., bd. adminstrn. Ch. of United Brethren in Christ, 1980-88; trustee Sunny Acres Retirement Community, 1986, bd. dirs.; trustee Africa U., Mutare, Zimbabwe. Mem. Am. Soc. Travel Assn. Execs., Nat. Funeral Dirs. Assn., Nat. Selected Morticians, Cremation Assn. Am., Monument Builders N.Am., Colo. Funeral Dirs. Assn., Internat. Assn. Travel Agts., Masons, Shriners, Elks, Rotary (bd. dirs., pres. 1990—, Paul Harris fellow), Pi Sigma Eta, Pi Kappa Delta, Pi Gamma Mu. Home: 3503 Morris Ave Pueblo CO 81008-1345 Office: 2200 S University Blvd Denver CO 80210-4708

DOMAN, MARGARET HORN, land use planner consultant, civic official; b. Portland, Oreg., July 28, 1946; d. Richard Carl and Dorothy May (Teepe) Horn; m. Steve Hamilton Doman, July 12, 1969; children: Jennifer, Kristina, Kathryn. BA, Willamette U., 1968; postgrad., U. Wash., 1968-69, 72. Cert. tchr. Tchr. jr. high Bellevue (Wash.) Sch. Dist., 1969-70, subs. tchr., 1990-91; tchr. jr. high University City (Mo.) Sch. Dist., 1970-71; employment counselor employment security dept. State of Wash., Seattle, 1971; planning commn. mem. City of Redmond, Wash., 1980-83, chmn., 1982-83; city coun. mem. City of Redmond, 1983-91, pres., 1990-91; exec. dir. Eastside Human Svcs. Coun., Redmond, Wash., 1992; employment specialist Wash. State Dept. Employment Security, 1993; cons. land use planning & govt. process Redmond, 1993—; Redmond rep. Puget Sound. Coun. of Govt., Seattle, 1984-91, vice chmn., 1988, 90, chmn. transp., 1986-88, exec. bd., 1987, mem. standing com. on transp., 1986-91; bd. dirs., pres. Eastside Human Svcs. Coun., Bellevue, 1983-91, pres., 1990. Bd. dirs. Redmond YMCA, 1985-86; mem. state exec. com. Nat. History Day, Olympia, Wash., 1986; vol. Bellevue Sch. Dist., 1977—; bd. dirs. Eastside br. Camp Fire, Bellevue, 1992-94. Mem. Redmond C. of C. (land use and transp. com. 1994—). Republican. Unitarian. Home: 2104 180th Ct NE Redmond WA 98052-6032

DOMANTAY, NORLITO VALDEZ (LITO DOMANTAY), communications executive; b. Manila, Oct. 28, 1946; came to U.S. 1970.; s. Juan and Felicidad (Valdez) D.; m. Deborah Anne Huffman, Aug. 25, 1980; 1 child, Devon James. BSC, AB, De La Salle U., Manila, 1968; MBA, Columbia U., 1971. Brand mgr. Procter & Gamble, Cin., 1971-80; v.p. mktg. Fed. Express Corp., Memphis, 1980-82; v.p. brand mgmt. Brown & Williamson Tobacco, Louisville, 1982-84; exec. v.p. Simon Mktg., Inc., L.A., 1984-94; pres. Peninsula Communications, L.A., 1990—; CEO Vision Express (Asia), Manila, 1994—; chmn. Marketvision, L.A., 1994—; bd. dirs. Express Data Svcs., Anaheim, Nobel Med. Ctr., L.A. Contbr. articles to profl. jours. Cons. Skid Row Devel., L.A., 1987, Cultural Found., L.A., 1986. Anheuser-Busch fellow, 1971. Mem. Promotion Mktg. Assn. Am. Republican. Home: 9420 Eden Dr Beverly Hills CA 90210-1309 Office: Marketvision 3921 Wilshire Blvd Ste 500 Los Angeles CA 90010

DOMARADZKI, JULIAN ANDRZEJ, physics educator; b. Szczecin, Poland, June 7, 1951; came to U.S., 1981; s. Julian Domaradzki and Zofia Wukowicz; m. Anna Teresa Kulesza, Feb. 11, 1979; children: Mateusz Barnaba, Julia Jagna. MS, U. Warsaw, Poland, 1974; PhD, U. Warsaw, 1978. Asst. prof. U. Warsaw, 1978-80; von Humboldt fellow Essen (Germany) U., 1980-81; rsch. staff Princeton (N.J.) U., 1981-83; rsch. assoc. MIT, Cambridge, Mass., 1983-84; rsch. scientist Flow Industries, Inc., Kent, Wash., 1984-87; asst. prof. U. So. Calif., L.A., 1987-91, assoc. prof. aerospace engring., 1991—. Recipient Sr. Rsch. award Alexander von Humboldt Found., Bonn, Germany, 1992. Mem. AIAA, Am. Phys. Soc., Soc. Indsl. and Applied Math. Office: U So Calif Aerospace Engring Los Angeles CA 90089-1191

DOMENICI, PETE (VICHI DOMENICI), senator; b. Albuquerque, May 7, 1932; s. Cherubino and Alda (Vichi) D.; m. Nancy Burk, Jan. 15, 1958; children: Lisa, Peter, Nella, Clare, David, Nanette, Helen, Paula. Student, U. Albuquerque, 1950-52; BS, U. N.Mex., 1954, LLD (hon.); LLB, Denver U., 1958; LLD (hon.), Georgetown U. Sch. Medicine; HHD (hon.), N.Mex. State U. Bar: N.Mex. 1958. Tchr. math. pub. schs. Albuquerque, 1954-55; ptnr. firm Domenici & Bonham, Albuquerque, 1958-72; chmn., ex-officio mayor Albuquerque, 1967; mem. U.S. Senate from N.Mex., 1972—; city commr. Albuquerque, 1966-68; mem. energy and natural resources com., chmn. subcom. on energy rsch. and devel.; mem. com. on environ. and public works, chmn. budget com.; mem. Presdl. Adv. Com. on Federalism. Mem. Gov.'s Policy Bd. for Law Enforcement, 1967-68; chmn. Model Cities Joint Adv. Com., 1967-68. Recipient Nat. League of Cities award Outstanding Performance in Congress; Disting. Svc. award Tax Found., 1986, Legislator of Yr. award Nat. Mental Health Assn., 1987. Mem. Nat. League Cities, Middle Rio Grande Council Govts. Office: US Senate 328 Hart Senate Office Bldg Washington DC 20510-0001

DOMHOFF, GEORGE WILLIAM, psychology and sociology educator; b. Youngstown, Ohio, Aug. 6, 1936; s. George William and Helen Susanne (Cornett) D.; m. Judith Clare Boman, Aug. 20, 1961 (div. July 1975); children: Lynne Starr, Lori Susanne, William Packard, Joel James. BA, Duke U., 1958; MA, Kent State U., 1959; PhD, U. Miami, 1962. Asst. prof. psychology L.A. State U., 1962-65; from asst. prof. to prof. psychology and sociology U. Calif., Santa Cruz, 1965—. Author: Who Rules America?, 1967, The Higher Circles, 1970, Fat Cats and Democrats, 1972, The Bohemian Grove and Other Retreats, 1974, Who Really Rules in New Haven?, 1978, The Powers That Be, 1979, Who Rules America Now?, 1983, The Mystique Dreams, 1985, The Power Elite and the State, 1990; co-author: Jews in the Protestant Establishment, 1982, Blacks in the White Establishment, 1991. Harbor commr. Santa Cruz Port Dist., 1977-78. Office: U Calif Dept Psychology Santa Cruz CA 95064

DOMINGO, ESTRELLA TINA, fashion designer, consultant, paralegal; b. Bacarra, The Philippines, Sept. 26, 1965; came to U.S., 1969; d. Jaime Madrid and Estrella (Taganas) D. AA in Fashion Design, Brooks Coll., Long Beach, Calif., 1986; BA in Psychology, San Francisco State U., 1989; postgrad, Sawyer Coll., 1994. Diploma paralegal. Sales assoc. J.C. Penney Co., Salinas, Calif., 1984; clk.-typist VA Med. Ctr., Palo Alto, Calif., 1987, sec. to chief anesthesiology svc., 1987-88; clk.-typist VA Med. Ctr., Menlo Park, Calif.; adminstr. dept. anesthesia Stanford (Calif.) U. Sch. Medicine, 1988-92; adminstrv. asst. Western Digital, 1992-93; from exec. asst. to v.p., sec., gen. counsel Robert Half Internat., Inc., Menlo Park, Calif., 1993—. Mem. rsch. adv. bd., editorial bd., dep. gov. ABI, adv. coun. IBC. Recipient Commemorative Medal of Honor, N.C. & Women of the Yr. award, 1991, Spl. Contbn. award VA Med. ctr., 1987, Superior Performance award, 1989; scholar Calif. Scholarship Assn., 1984. Mem. NAFE (hon. advisor, dep. gov. ABIRA & Women's Inner Circle of Achievement, The World Found. Successful Women, fellowship), Smithsonian Assocs., Calif. Honor Soc. Roman Catholic. Office: Robert Half Internat Inc 2884 Sand Hill Rd Ste 200 Menlo Park CA 94025

DOMINICK, PETER HOYT, JR., architect; b. N.Y.C., June 9, 1941; s. Peter Hoyt and Nancy Parks D.; m. Philae M. Carver, Dec. 9, 1978; children—Philae M., James W. B.A., Yale U., 1963; M.Arch., U. Pa., 1967. Registered architect, Colo. Project designer John R. Wild, Pty., Ltd., Papau, New Guinea, 1968-69, Spence Robinson, Hong Kong, 1969-71, W.C. Muchow & Ptnrs., Denver, 1971-74; pres. Wazee Design/Devel., Denver, 1973-75; prin. Dominick Architects, Denver, 1975-88; prin. Urban Design Group, Inc., 1988—. Trustee Downtown Denver, Inc., Civic Ventures, 1984-94 , Met. Denver Arts Alliance, 1983-84; mem. Mayor's Commn. on the Arts, 1983; juror Gov.'s awards, Denver, 1982. Fellow AIA (nat. com. on design, bd. dirs.); mem. Colo. Soc. Architects. Republican. Episcopalian. Club: Cactus, Arapahoe Tennis. Office: Urban Design Group Inc 1621 18th St Ste 200 Denver CO 80202-1267

DOMINIK, JANE KATHRYN, English language educator, writer; b. Madison, Wis., Sept. 18, 1957; d. William Carl and Shirley Anne (Crisman) D. BA, U. of Pacific, 1980; MA, U. Chgo., 1981; MFA, Rutgers U., 1985. Editorial asst. St. Martin's Press, N.Y.C., 1985-86; editorial svcs. specialist Ginn Press, Lexington, Mass., 1986-87; tchr. Tabor Academy, Marion, Mass., 1987-90; English instr. San Joaquin Delta Coll., Stockton, Calif., 1990—. Mem. MLA, Nat. Coun. Tchrs. English, English Coll. Coun. Two-Yr. Colls. (membership chair, regional dir., 1993—). Home: 1528 Stanton

Way Stockton CA 95207 Office: San Joaquin Delta Coll 5151 Pacific Ave Stockton CA 95207

DOMINITZ, SIDNEY, editor, journalist; b. N.Y.C., Sept. 4, 1941; s. William and Blanca (Hitner) D.; m. Sydelle Lapidus, June 7, 1964 (div. 1982); 1 child, Zachary William. BA, CCNY, 1963. Reporter UPI, Newark, 1966-67; chief copy editor Reuters, Ltd., London, 1969-75; journalism instr. Coll. of Redwoods, Eureka, Calif., 1980-84; devel. dir. North Country Clinic, Arcata, Calif., 1987-92; editor of ECONEWS Northcoast Environ. Ctr., Arcata, 1976—; journalism instr. Humboldt State U., Arcata, 1978, 80, 85, 86. Home: PO Box 541 Trinidad CA 95570-0541 Office: Northcoast Environ Ctr 879 9th St Arcata CA 95521-6229

DOMINO, KAREN BARBARA, anesthesiology educator; b. Chgo., Oct. 21, 1951; d. Edward F. and Antoinette (Kaczorowski) D.; m. Gene L. Brenowitz, June 7, 1975; children: Willa Domino Brenowitz, Noah Domino Brenowitz. BA, Vassar Coll., 1973; MA in Psychology, U. N.Mex., 1974; MD, U. Mich., 1978. Diplomate Am. Bd. Anesthesiology. Asst. prof. anesthesiology U. Pa., Phila., 1982-83, U. Pitts., 1983-86; asst. prof. anesthesiology U. Wash., Seattle, 1986-91, assoc. prof. anesthesiology, 1991—; adj. assoc. prof. neurologic surgery U. Wash., Seattle, 1991—. Contbr. articles to med. jours. Recipient B.B. Sankey Anesthesia Advancement award, 1990, Clin. Investigator award Nat. Heart, Lung, and Blood Inst., 1990-95. Mem. Internat. Anesthesia Rsch. Soc., Soc. Neurosurg. Anesthesia and Critical Care, Assn. Univ. Anesthesiologists (sci. adv. bd., councillor-at-large), Am. Soc. Anesthesiologists (respiration subcom.), Phi Beta Kappa, Alpha Omega Alpha. Office: Harborview Med Ctr Dept Anesthesiology 325 9th Ave Seattle WA 98104-2420

DOMMISSE, JOHN VLOK, nutritional-metabolic physician, psychiatrist; b. Worcester, South Africa, Oct. 19, 1940; arrived in Can., 1967; came to U.S., 1976; s. John Herbert and Louise Adriana (Vlok) D.; m. Marion Linsingen, Apr. 2, 1965 (div. Feb. 1972); m. Bettina Dignas, Oct. 21, 1972; children: Liesl Angelique, Janneke Andria. MBChB, U. Capetown Med. Sch., 1965. Rotating intern in medicine, pediat., obstetrics, gynecology, psychiatry, emergency medicine # 2 Mil. Hosp., CapeTown, South Africa, 1966; gen. practice resident Bridgeport (Conn.) Hosp., 1967; clin. med. officer of health Worcester, South Africa, 1971-73; sr. med. officer Eben Donges Gen. Hosp., Worcester, 1974; demonstrator in psychiatry U. Toronto, 1975-76; dir. out-patient svcs. Maryview Psychiat. Hosp., Cmty. Mental Health Ctr., Portsmouth, Va., 1976-78; pvt. practice psychiatry and nutritional medicine Portsmouth, 1978-94, pvt. practice metabolic medicine, 1988-94; pvt. practice psychiatry and nutritional medicine and metabolic medicine Tucson, 1994—; pvt. gen. practice, Worcester, 1967, Toronto, 1971. Contbr. articles to profl. jours. Recipient Benjamin Rush award Benjamin Rush Soc., 1985, Book award Coalition Against Racism & Apartheid, 1985. Fellow Royal Coll. Physicians of Can. (cert. in psychiatry); mem. Can. Psychiat. Assn., Physicians for Nat. Health Program, African Nat. Congress of South Africa (health dept. 1978—), Com. Health in So. Africa, Nat./Va./Portsmouth Alliance for the Mentally Ill, Tidewater Acad. Psychiatry, Portsmouth Acad. Medicine, Tidewater Nutrition Coun., Complementary Med. Assn., Am. Preventive Med. Assn. Democrat. Unitarian. Office: Nutrnl-Mtblc Med & Psych Ste 210 1840 E River Rd & Campbell Ave Tucson AZ 85718-5892

DOMNIE, SCOTT HAROLD, real estate investor, country club operator; b. Milw., Jan. 19, 1954; s. Harold G. and Pearl (Watters) D.; m. Robin Castle, Sept. 27, 1986; 1 child, Adam Scott, Katherine Alyce. Student, U. Wis., Menomonie, 1972-74. V.p. ops. Breakers Restaurants, Inc., Calif., 1975-80; with real estate devel. dept. Calif. Brokers, 1981-84; investment broker Fed. Investors Corp., Fla., 1984-88; gen. mgr. Belmont Country Club, Fresno, Calif., 1988—; cons. to country clubs, Tampa, Fla., 1985-88; seminar presenter, Fla., 1986. Contbr. articles to profl. jours. Mem. Calif. Wine Soc. (bd. dirs. 1990—), Club Mgrs. Assn. Am., Nat. Restaurant Assn., Internat. Wine Soc., Sonoma County Enology Assn. Republican. Lutheran. Home: PO Box 644 Pebble Beach CA 93953-0644

DOMONDON, OSCAR, dentist; b. Cebu City, Philippines, July 4, 1924; Came to U.S., 1954, naturalized, 1956.; s. Antero B. and Ursula (Maglasang) D. ; m. Vicky Domondon. children—Reinelda, Carolyn, Catherine, Oscar. DMD, Philippine Dental Coll., 1951; DDS, Loma Linda U., 1964. Dentist Manila Sanitarium and Hosp., 1952, U.S. Embassy, Manila, 1952-54; pvt. practice dentistry Long Beach, Calif., 1964—; Dentist, Children's Dental Health Center, Long Beach, part-time, 1964-68; past mem. Calif. State Bd. Dental Examiners. Past pres., Filipino Community Action Services, Inc. With AUS, 1946-49, U.S. Army, 1954-60. Fellow Acad. Dentistry International, Acad. Gen. Dentistry, Internat. Inst. Community Service, Acad. Internat. Dental Studies, Internat. Coll. Dentists, Am. Coll. Dentists (life), Acad. Continuing Edn.; mem. ADA (life), Am. Soc. Dentistry Children, Am. Acad. Oral Radiology (award 1964), Internat. Acad. Orthodontists, Am. Soc. Clin. Hypnosis, Am. Endodontic Soc., Western Conf. Dental Examiners and Dental Sch. Deans, Fedn. of Assns. of Health Regulatory Bds., Calif. Assn. Fgn. Dental Grads. (past pres.), Filipino Dental Soc. (past pres.), Philippine Tech. and Profl. Soc. (v.p.), Am. Acad. Dentistry for Handicapped, Am. Assn. Dental Examiners (life), Nat. Assn. Filipino Dentists in Am. (past pres.), Pierre Fauchard Acad., Knights of Rizal (comdr.), Lions (past pres.), Elks (past chmn. rangers), Masons, Shrine Noble. Republican. Home: 3570 Aster St Seal Beach CA 90740-2801 Office: 3714 Atlantic Ave Long Beach CA 90807-3409

DONAHOO, STANLEY ELLSWORTH, orthopaedic surgeon; b. St. Joseph, Mo., Dec. 3, 1933; s. Charles Ellsworth and Opal (Cole) D.; m. Cheryl R. Donahoo; children: Shan Maureen, Brian Patrick, Mary Kathleen, Jane Eileen; stepchildren: Trina Person, Kevin. MD, U. Wash., 1963. Resident, Duke U., Durham, N.C., 1967-68, U.S. Naval Hosp., Oakland, Calif., 1963-67; commd. lt., U.S. Navy, 1963 advanced through grades to lt. comdr. (orthopaedic surgeon), 1971; practice medicine, specializing in orthopaedic surgery, Roseburg, Oreg., 1971—; chief surgery Mercy Hosp., Roseburg, 1973-74; chief surgery Douglas Community Hosp., Roseburg, 1973, chief of staff, 1974—; cons. Guam Meml. Hosp., co-dir. rehab. unit, 1970-71; cons. orthopaedic surgery VA Hosp., Roseburg, 1971—; chmn. Douglas County (Oreg.) Emergency Med. Services Com., 1973-74. Trustee Douglas Community Hosp., 1975. Served with AUS, 1952-55. Diplomate Am. Bd. Orthopaedic Surgery. Fellow Am. Acad. Orthopaedic Surgeons (admissions com. region 14), North Pacific Orthopaedic Assn. (v.p. 1984-85, trustee 1991—); mem. Piedmont Orthopaedic Soc., Oreg. Med. Assn. (mem. sports medicine com., med. rev. com. 1981), Guam Med. Soc. (pres. 1970), Am. Trauma Soc. (founding mem.), Roseburg C. of C. (bd. govs. 1978—). Home: 173 Songbird Ct Roseburg OR 97470-9400 Office: 1813 W Harvard Blvd Ste 100 Roseburg OR 97470-2753

DONAHUE, DENNIS DONALD, foreign service officer; b. Indpls., May 31, 1940; s. George Robert and Lucille Kathryn (Tanrath) D.; m. Gretchen Jane Siedling, Sept. 21, 1963 (dec. 1987); children: Mauree Denise, Megan Jane, Benjamin Josef; m. Diane Burdette Obenchain, Mar. 25, 1990. BA, Marian Coll., 1962; student, Ind. U., 1962-63; MA, Am. U., 1980, postgrad., 1981—. With USIA, 1967—; asst. cultural officer Am. Consultate Gen., Calcutta, India, 1969-70; asst. publs. officer Am. Embassy, New Delhi, 1970-72; publs. officer Am. Embassy, Saigon, Republic of Vietnam, 1973-75; cultural affairs officer Am. Embassy, Wellington, New Zealand, 1975-78; country/program officer East Asia/Pacific Office, Washington, 1979-81, 83-84; East Asia policy officer Voice of Am., Washington, 1982-83; program chief Am. Embassy, Tokyo, 1984-88; advisor U.S. Pacific Command, Honolulu, 1988-90; counselor for pub. affairs Am. Embassy, Singapore, 1990-94; cultural affairs officer Am. Embassy, Brasilia, Brazil, 1995—; adj. lectr. polit. sci. Temple U. Japan, Tokyo, 1986. Mem. Am. Fgn. Svc. Assn., Assn. Mass. Comm. Rsch. and Info. Ctr., Internat. Comm. Assn., Internat. House Japan, Phi Kappa Phi. Roman Catholic.

DONAHUE, EDWARD JOSEPH, surgeon; b. Phila., Jan. 30, 1949; children: Christopher, Brian. BS in Chemistry, Villanova U., 1970; MD, Temple U., 1979; MS in Surgery, U. Ill., 1982. Diplomate Am. Bd. Med. Examiners, Am. Bd. Surgery. Intern, resident Rush Presbyn./St. Luke's Hosp., Chgo.; staff surgeon St. Joseph's Hosp., Phoenix, 1984—. Lt. USN, 1970-75, Vietnam. Fellow ACS; mem. AMA, Ariz. Med. Assn. Home: 6529 N Central Ave Phoenix AZ 85012-1139 Office: Saint Josephs Hosp 333 W Thomas Ste 203 Phoenix AZ 85013

DONAHUE, JAMES J., JR., retired corporate executive, consultant; b. Pueblo, Colo., Dec. 16, 1919; s. James John and Sarah Evelyn (Bryden) D.; m. Laura L. Sherman, Sept. 7, 1968 (div. 1981); m. Priscilla Arlene Mourning, Apr. 11, 1982; children: James J. III, Thomas M. Donahue, David, Paul, Lisa, Nancy Berg. Student, Lawrence U., 1938-40, U. Minn., 1940-41, U. Md., Am. U., George Washington U., 1957-63; AA, Nat. Def. U. Salesman Am. Brass Co., Mpls., 1938-40; sales and advt. mgr. United Van Lines, Skellet Van & Storage Co., Mpls., 1947-50; dir. rsch., devel. Conwed Corp., St. Paul, 1967-71; v.p., gen. mgr. Anderson Machine Co., Inc., Chaska, Minn., 1971-73; exec. v.p., treas., dir. U.S. Bedding Co., St Paul, 1973-80; bus. cons., realtor Calhoun Realty Co., Edina, Minn., 1980-82; faculty mem. Command & Gen. Staff Coll., Ft. Leavenworth, KS., 1953-57; nuclear specialist, Dept. of Army Staff, SHAPE (NATO), Joint Chiefs of Staff, 1958-66. Contbr. articles to profl. jours. Bd. dirs. 7 cos.; dir. Jr. C. of C., Rotary Internat., United Fund, ARC. Col. U.S. Army, 1942-46, 51-66. Decorated Legion of Merit, Joint Services Commendation medal, Bronze Star with three oak leaf clusters, Air medal. Mem. Nat. Def. Exec. Reserve Retired Officers Assn., Advt. Club, Traffic Club, Nat. Treas. Assn., Mason (32 degree), Cottonwood Golf Club. Republican. Home: 26221 S Howard Dr Sun Lakes AZ 85248-7231

DONAHUE, PHILIP RICHARD, artist, educator; b. Detroit, Apr. 1, 1943; s. Theodore R. and Margaret M. (Schneider) D. BA, St. Peter's Coll., Jersey City, 1969; MA, Spring Hill Coll., Mobil, Ala., 1974, Jesuit Sch. Theology, Berkeley, Calif., 1977; PhD, U. Calif., Berkeley, 1985. Joined S.J., Roman Cath. Ch., 1964, ordained priest, 1976. Artist, educator, adminstr., priest S.J., Rome, 1964-82; v.p. Link Art Internat., San Francisco, 1982-86; owner, adminstr., educator, artist Donahue Studios, Oakland, Calif., 1986—. Author: Visual Hermeneutics, 1985, Meaning in Visual Art, 1992; exhibited in groups shows at AT Gallery, Tokyo, 1982-91, Hunger Project, San Francisco, 1982-85, Farralon Co., San Francisco, 1991-94, Link Art Internat. Ltd., San Francisco, 1982-94, others; represented in permanent collections including City Hall, Jersey City, Gov.'s Mansion, Birmingham, St. Peter's Coll., Jersey City, Farralon Co., San Francisco, Grace Cathedral, San Francisco. Recipient award U.S. dir. fine arts Hakuhodo, Tokyo, 1991-83, Oscar d'Italia Acad. Italia, Calvatone, 1985. Mem. Internat. Soc. Artists (bd. dirs. No. Hemisphere 1977—). Studio: 3700 Virden Ave Oakland CA 94619-1537

DONAHUE, RICHARD KING, athletic apparel executive, lawyer; b. Lowell, Mass., July 20, 1927; s. Joseph P. and Dorothy F. (Riordan) D.; m. Nancy Lawson, Sept. 19, 1953; children: Gail M., Timothy J., Michael R., Nancy C., Richard K., Daniel J., Alicia A., Stephen J., Christopher P., Tara E., Philip A. A.B., Dartmouth Coll., 1948; J.D., Boston U., 1951. Bar: Mass. 1951. Ptnr. Donahue & Donahue, Attys., P.C., Lowell, Mass., 1951-60, 63-90; v.p., chmn. bd., Nike, Inc., 1990— ; asst. to Pres. Kennedy, Washington, 1960-63. Served with USNR. Recipient Herbert Harley award Am. Judicature Soc., 1981. Mem. Am. Bd. Trial Advs., ABA (gov., ho. of dels. 1972—), Am. Coll. Trial Lawyers, Mass. Bar Assn. (past pres., Gold medal 1979), New Eng. Bar Assn. (past pres.). Clubs: Union League (Boston); Vesper Country (Tyngsboro, Mass.); Fed. City (Washington); Yorick (Lowell). Office: Nike Inc 1 Bowerman Dr Beaverton OR 97005-0979*

DONALDSON, GEORGE BURNEY, chemical company executive; b. Oakland, Calif., Mar. 16, 1945; s. George T. and L.M. (Burney) D.; m. Jennifer L. Bishop, Feb. 16, 1974; children: Dawn Marie, Matthew George. AS in Criminology, Porterville Coll., 1972. Registered environ. assessor, Calif.; cert. transp. specialist. Police officer City of Lindsay (Calif.), 1966-67; distbn. mgr. Ortho div. Chevron Chem. Co., Lindsay, 1967-73; safety specialist Wilbur-Ellis Co. Fresno, Calif., 1973-77, safety dir., 1977-79, dir. corporate regulatory affairs, 1979—; industry rep. to White House Inter-Govtl. Sci. Engring., and Tech. Adv. Panel, Task Force on Transp. of Non-Nuclear Hazardous Materials, 1980; industry rep. Transp. Rsch. Bd.'s Nat. Strategies Conf. on Transp. of Hazardous Materials and Wastes in the 1980's, NAS, 1981, Hazardous Materials Transp. Conf., Nat. Conf. of State Legislatures, 1982. speaker and moderator in field; dir. Western Fertilizer and Pesticide Safety seminar, Sacramento, 1979; speaker Southeastern Agrl. Chem. Safety seminar, Winston-Salem, N.C., 1986. Chmn. industry/govt. task force for unique on-site hazardous waste recycling, devel. task force for computerized regulatory software and data base system, devel. task force modifying high expansion foam tech. for fire suppression; hazardous materials adviser, motor carrier rating com. Calif. Hwy. Patrol, 1978-79. With U.S. Army, 1962-65. Mem. Western Agrl. Chems. Assn. (past chmn. transp., distbn. and safety com., outstanding mem. of year 1981, govtl. affairs com., trustee polit. action com.), Nat. Agrl. Chems. Assn. (past chmn. transp. and distbn. com., occupational safety and health com., environ. mgmt. com., state affairs com., moderator spring conf. 1989), Am. Soc. Safety Engrs., Calif. Fertilizer Assn. (transp. and distbn. com., environ. com.), Fresno City and County C. of C. (agrl. steering com., govt. affairs com.), Calif. C. of C. (environ. policy com.), Am. Legion, Elks. Republican. Office: 191 W Shaw Ave Ste 107 Fresno CA 93704-2826

DONALDSON, JOHN RILEY, physics educator; b. Dallas, Nov. 24, 1925; s. John Riley and Marguerette Hoover (Atkinson) D.; m. Shirley Jean Brown, June 30, 1951; children: Nancy Gullett, Dorothy Chaffee, Jack Donaldson, Jane Hollingsworth. BS, Rice U., 1945, MA, 1947; MS, Yale U, 1949, PhD, 1951. Physicist Calif. R & D, Livermore, 1950-53; assoc. prof. U. Ariz., 1953-54; physicist U.S. Army, Frederick, Md., 1954-56; asst. prof. then assoc. prof. Calif. State U., Fresno, 1956-67, prof., 1967-91, chmn. dept. physics, 1983-91, prof. emeritus, 1991—; vis. prof. Swiss Fed. Inst. Tech., Zurich, 1967-68, 82-83. Choir dir. Coll. Community Congl. Ch., Fresno, 1956—, moderator, 1960-61; elected supr. Fresno County, 1973-80. Mem. AAAS, Am. Phys. Soc., Am. Assn. Physics Tchrs. Democrat. Mem. United Church of Christ. Home: 4559 N Dewitt Ave Fresno CA 93727-7160 Office: Calif State U Fresno Shaw And Cedar Ave Fresno CA 93740

DONALDSON, MARY KENDRICK, nurse; b. Tifton, Ga., June 25, 1937; d. Howard Story and Trudy (Donalson) Marlin; m. Harvey Kendrick Sr., Apr. 13, 1953 (dec. 1965); children: Jerome, Micheal, Harvey Jr., Merry, Sheila, Larry; m. Isaac Hargett, Feb. 16, 1985. AA, Compton (Calif.) Coll., 1969; BS, Pepperdine U., 1972, MA, 1976; diploma in nursing, SW Coll., Los Angeles, 1984. Staff nurse St. Francis Hosp., Lynwood, Calif., 1965-67; pvt. duty nurse Profl. Nurse's Registry, Los Angeles, 1967-82; elem. tchr. Compton Sch. Dist., Calif., 1975-80; caseworker, clk. Los Angeles County Probation Dept., 1980-90, dep. probation officer, 1990—; pediatric, nurse companion Personal Care Health Service, Torrance, Calif., 1984—; home economist Dept. Welfare, Compton, 1970-72; asst. dir. Century Plaza Hotel, Century City, Calif., 1971-72. Chairperson Com. To Elect Garland Hardeman For Councilman, Inglewood, Calif., 1987. Exec. Housekeeping scholarship Century Plaza Hotel, Los Angeles, 1971. Mem. Fellow Am. Home Econs. Assn., Pepperdine Alumni Assn., Pepperdine's Kappa Kappa Sorority, Am. Nurse's Assn. Democrat. Home: 4730 Falcon Ave Long Beach CA 90807-2377 Office: L A County Probation Dept 1601 Eastlake Ave Los Angeles CA 90033-1009

DONALDSON, MICHAEL CLEAVES, lawyer; b. Montclair, N.J., Oct. 13, 1939; s. Wyman C. and Ernestine (Greenwood) D.; m. Diana D., Sept. 12, 1969 (div. 1979); children: Michelle, Amy, Wendy; m. Mimi Schwied, Sept. 14, 1991. BS, U. Fla., 1961; JD, U. Calif., Berkeley, 1967. Bar: Calif. 1967, U.S. Dist. Ct. (cen. dist.) Calif. 1967, U.S. Ct. Appeals (9th cir.) 1967. Assoc. Harris & Hollingsworth, L.A., 1969-72; ptnr. McCabe & Donaldson, L.A., 1972-79; pvt. practice Law Office of M.C. Donaldson, L.A., 1979-90; ptnr. Dern & Donaldson, L.A., 1990-94, Berton and Donaldson, Beverly Hills, Calif., 1994—; lectr. in field; judge, preliminary and finalist judge Internat. Emmys; preliminary judge Night Time Emmys; gen. counsel Ind. Feature Project West, Internat. Documentary Assn. Author: Honey, Plase Put the Seat Down-How to Negotiate Anything You Want in Life, EZ Legal Guide to Copyright and Trademark, 1995, (booklet) Something Funny Happened on the Way to Dinner, 1976; contbg. author: Conversations with Michael Landon, 1992. Bd. dirs. Calif. Theatre Coun., L.A. 1st lt. USMC, 1951-64. Mem. ABA (entertainment and sports sect.), NATAS, Nat. Acad. Cable Broadcasting, Beverly Hills Bar Assn. (chmn. entertainment sect.), Century City Bar Assn. (entertainment sect.), L.S. Copyright Soc. Republican. Home: 2074 Benedict Canyon Dr Beverly Hills CA 90210-1404 Office: Donaldson & Berton 9595 Wilshire Blvd Ste 711 Beverly Hills CA 90212-2507

DONALDSON, MILFORD WAYNE, architect, educator; b. Jacksonville, N.C., Aug. 13, 1943; s. Milford Wayne and Jean (Mingus) D.; m. Nancy Ann Schever, Sept. 5, 1964; 1 child, Erica Lynn. BA, Uppsala U., Sweden, 1966; BArch, Calif. Poly. U., 1967; MS, U. Strathclyde, Glasgow, Scotland, 1970; postgrad., U. Stuttgart, Fed. Republic Germany, 1972. Lic. architect, Calif.; cert. community coll. tchr., contractor. Design fabricator Polytecture Inc./GRP Housing, Pitts., 1971-72; project architect Mosher/Drew/Watson, San Diego, 1972-77; pres. Sixteen Penny Constrn., San Diego, 1979—; pvt. practice in architecture San Diego, 1978—; instr. Calif. Poly. U., 1969-70, U. Strathclyde, 1970-72, Southwestern Community Coll., Chula Vista, Calif., 1972—; chmn. task force study San Diego Downtown Redevel., 1982-83; bd. dirs. San Diego Hist. Sites, 1982—; speaker various hist. preservation ctrs. Mem. curriculum com. SDSU, San Diego, 1981-86; commr. State Hist. Resources Bd., 1986—; trustee Calif. Preservation Found., 1985—; bd. dirs. Ilan Leal Found., 1983—, San Diego Hist. Gaslamp Quarter Council, 1981-87, chmn., 1982-83; bd. dirs. Save Our Heritage Orgn., 1985—, chmn., 1980, preservationist for San Diego Hardware Bldg., 1985. Named Preservationist of Yr. Save Our Heritage Orgn., 1986. Mem. AIA (design chmn. San Diego chpt. 1982-83, Orchid award 1984, numerous others), San Diego Hist. Soc., San Diego Track and Field Assn., U.S. Hang Gliding Assn., Scarab (pres.), The Inst. for Hist. Study, Calif. Preservation Found. (pres. 1985—). Republican. Home: 1845 W Montecito Way San Diego CA 92103-1229 Office: 846 5th Ave Ste 300 San Diego CA 92101-6105

DONALDSON, NIKKI A., physician, executive; b. Concord, Calif., May 31, 1951; d. James M. and Pauline L. (Stice) Clark; m. David P. Donaldson, Nov. 29, 1980; children: Ryan C., Samantha T. BS magna cum laude, Calif. State U., Fresno, 1974, MA magna cum laude, 1978; DO, Coll. Osteo Medicine Pacific, 1994. Clin. supr. phys. therapy Leon S. Peters Rehab. Ctr., 1976-78; pres., chief exec. officer Sports & Orthopedic Phys. Therapy Clinic, Fresno, Calif., 1978—; intern, resident Downey (Calif.) Community Hosp., 1994—, U. Calif. Davis Med. Ctr., Sacramento, 1994—; cons. cardiac rehab. YMCA, Fresno, 1982-84, cons. post mastectomy patients, 1978-82. V.p. Coll. Osteo. Medicine of the Pacific, Pomona, Calif., 1991; vice chair Santa Workshop, 1990, 91. Recipient William G. Stahl D.O. Meml. award, 1991, Muriel Chapman D.O. Meml. award, 1992; named to Nat. Deans List, 1991, 92, 93. Mem. Am. Phys. Therapy Assn., Am. Family Practice Assn., Am. Coll. Gen. Practitioners, Am. Med. Women's Assn., Sigma Sigma Phi (treas.), Phi Kappa Phi. Republican. Roman Catholic. Home: 16644 E Goodfellow Ave Sanger CA 93657-9545

DONALDSON, WILBURN LESTER, property management corporation executive; b. St. Augustine, Fla., Mar. 2, 1938; s. Chester Campbell and Dovie (Pratt) D.; m. Patricia Lilias Babcock, Sept. 11, 1956; children: John Randolph, David Chester, James Robert. BA, San Francisco State U., 1968, MBA, 1971. Transp. clk. Armour Food Co., San Francisco, 1958-60, transp. mgr., 1960-65, product mgr., 1965-70; So. Calif. sales mgr. Armour Food Co., L.A., 1970-73; tng. mgr. Armour Food Co., Phoenix, 1973-77, nat. mktg. mgr., 1977-80; region sales mgr. Armour Food Co., Pitts., 1980-83; nat. tng. mgr. Armour Food Co., Phoenix, 1983-84; pres. Allied Investment Mgrs., Inc., Phoenix, 1984—. Author: How To Use Psychological Leverage, 1978, Conversational Magic, 1978, Behavioral Supervision, 1980, Human Resource Development, 1986. Mem. Nat. Real Estate Assn. Republican. Home: 350 E Deepdale Rd Phoenix AZ 85022-4229 Office: Allied Investment Inc 1121 E Missouri Ave Ste 123 Phoenix AZ 85014-2711

DONATH, THERESE, artist, author; b. Hammond, Ind.; m. Jefferson Richardson Scoville, 1986; student Monticello Coll., 1946-47; BFA, St. Joseph's Coll., 1975; additional study Oxbow Summer Sch. Painting, Immaculate Heart Coll., Hollywood, Calif., Penland, N.C., Haystack, Maine; radio/TV personality, 1978-92. Interviewer, producer Viewpoint, Sta. WLNR-FM, Lansing, Ill., 1963-64; reporter, columnist N.W. Ind. Sentinel, 1965; freelance writer Monterey Peninsula Herald, 1981-85; contbg. author Monterey Life mag. 1981-85; asst. dir. Michael Karolyi Meml. Found., Vence, France, 1979; one-woman shows include: Ill. Inst. Tech., Chgo., 1971; group shows include: Palos Verdes (Calif.) Mus., 1974, L.A. Inst. Contemporary Art, 1978, Mus. Contemporary Art, Chgo., 1975, Calif. State U., Fullerton, 1973, No. Ill. U., DeKalb, 1971, Bellevue (Wash.) Mus. Art, 1986-87; represented in permanent collections including Kennedy Gallery, N.Y.C., also pvt. collections; creative cons. Aslan Tours and Travel, 1983-85; instr., lectr. Penland, N.C., 1970, Haystack Mountain Sch., Deer Isle, Maine, 1974, Sheffield Poly., Eng., 1978. Bd. dirs., sec. Mental Health Soc. Greater Chgo., 1963-64; exec. dir. Lansing (Ill.) Mental Health Soc., 1963-64. Recipient awards No. Ind. Art Mus., 1966, 70, 71, 73; grantee Ragdale Found., Lake Forest, Ill., 1982. Represented in The Mirror Book, 1978; author: Screams and Laughter, 1992; author, illustrator: Before I Die, A Creative Legacy, 1989; contbr. articles to profl. jours., newspapers; illustrator: Run Computer Run, 1983.

DONATI, DANIEL EDWARD, marketing professional; b. Lombard, Ill., Nov. 6, 1968; s. Daniel Frederick Donati and Caroline Jean (Lansing) Lange; m. Liane Jean Keith, May 23, 1993. BABA, Calif. State U., San Bernardino, 1991. Acctg. mgr. Siltron Illumination, Rancho Cucamonga, Calif., 1987-91; sales coord. Walter Fletcher Inc., Santa Monica, Calif., 1991—. Mem. adv. coun. Vol. Ctr. West, L.A., 1993-94, vol., advisor, 1993—; vol. Neighborhood Youth Assn., 1993—. Republican. Mem. 7th Day Adventist Ch. Office: Walter Fletcher Inc 2525 Ocean Park Blvd Santa Monica CA 90405-5201

DONATONI, PAUL J., pharmacist; b. L.A., Dec. 4, 1957; s. Jerry and Stella D. BA in Biology, UCLA, 1980; PharmD, U. Calif., San Francisco, 1986. Pharmacy resident NIH, Bethesda, Md., 1986-87; pharmacist UCLA Med. Ctr., 1987—. Mem. Am. Soc. Hosp. Pharmacists, So. Calif. Soc. Hosp. Pharmacists (com. mem.), Phi Delta Chi. Office: UCLA Med Ctr 10833 Le Conte Ave Los Angeles CA 90024

DONAVIN, GEORGIANA, English language educator; b. Fresno, Calif., Nov. 21, 1958; d. Rodney Keith and Gail Lee (Patnott) Sutton; m. Kirkwood William Donavin, June 13, 1989 (div. July 1992); 1 child, Kirkwood Paul. BA, Calif. State U., Sacramento, 1983, MA, 1985; PhD, U. Oreg., 1992. Teaching asst. Calif. State U., Sacramento, 1984-85; grad. teaching fellow U. Oreg., Eugene, 1987-92; asst. prof. English Westminster Coll., Salt Lake City, 1992—. Author: Incest Narratives and the Structure of Gower's Confessio Amantis, 1993 (Manford A. Shaw award 1994); editor: (textbook) Webfoot Reader, 1990. Gore Rsch. and Writing grantee Gore Industry, 1993, 94. Mem. Nat. Coun. Tchrs. English, Medieval Assn. of Pacific, Medieval Acad., Rocky Mount Medieval and Renaissance Assn. Methodist. Home: 622 Milton Ave Salt Lake City UT 84105-2113 Office: Westminster Coll 1840 S 1300 E Salt Lake City UT 84105-3617

DONE, ROBERT STACY, criminal investigation specialist, consultant; b. Tucson, Apr. 7, 1965; s. Richard Avon Done and Nancy Jane (Meeks) Burks; m. Michele Renae Barwick, May 17, 1987 (div. Mar. 1990); m. Elizabeth Evans Robinson, Feb. 20, 1993. AS in Law Enforcement, Mo. So. State Coll., 1987, BS in Criminal Justice Adminstrn., 1987; MPA, U. Ariz., 1992. Lic. realtor, Ariz., pvt. investigator, Ariz. Criminal investigator Pima County, Tucson, 1988—; pres. Data Methods Corp., Tucson, 1984—. Mem. Am. Soc. for Pub. Adminstrn., Ariz. Mcpl. Mgmt. Assts. Assn. Republican. Home: PO Box 64967 Tucson AZ 85728-4967 Office: Pima County Pub Defender 2225 E Ajo Way Tucson AZ 85713-6201

DONEGAN, ELIZABETH ANN, anesthesiologist; b. Springfield, Mo., Dec. 6, 1946; d. George Joseph and Elizabeth (Shepard) D. BS in Biology, Webster Coll., 1968; MS in Microbiology, U. Mo., 1972, MD, 1975. Diplomate Am. Bd. Anatomic and Clinical Pathology. Intern in medicine U.S. Pub. Health Hosp., San Francisco, 1975-76; resident lab. medicine, anatomic pathology U. Calif., San Francisco, 1976-80; asst. rsch. physician, adj. lectr. U. Calif., 1980-81, asst. clin. prof., 1981-89, assoc. prof., 1989-93, resident in anesthesia, 1993—; pathologist Good Samaritan Hosp., San Jose, Calif., 1981-82, Naval Hosp., Oakland, Calif., 1982-85; med. dir. blood bank Moffitt-Long Hosps., chief blood bank and donor ctr., U. Calif., San Francisco,

1985-91. Served to cmdr. U.S. Navy, 1985—. Office: Dept Anesthesia Box 6048 U Calif San Francisco CA 94143

DONELSON, IRENE W., property manager; b. Placerville, Calif., Mar. 5, 1913; d. John H. and Emma Marie (Frechette) Witmer; m. Kenneth Wilber, July 25, 1937; children: Carol Korb, Richard Kenneth. AA, U. Calif., Berkeley, 1932; postgrad., Sacramento City Coll., 1934, U. of the Pacific, 1951. Advt. copywriter Hale's Dept. Store, Sacramento, 1934-37, Breuner's Home Furnishings, Sacramento, 1939-41; law office mgr., legal asst. Kenneth W. Donelson, Sacramento, 1951—; property mgr. The Law Bldg., Sacramento, 1986—. Co-author: (with Kenneth Donelson) When You Need a Lawyer, 1964, How to Handle Your Legal Problems, 1965, revised edits., 1968, 71, Married Today, Single Tomorrow: Marriage Breakup and the Law, 1969; contbr. articles to nat. mags. Recipient Woman With a View award Sacramento Union, 1972. Mem. NAFE, Calif. Writers Club (pres. 1962-63, 76-77, dir. 1978-79, Jack London award 1979). Republican. Office: 708 10th St Ste 150 Sacramento CA 95814-1806

DONELSON, KENNETH LAVERN, English language educator; b. Holdrege, Nebr., June 16, 1927; s. Lester Homer Irving and Minnie Irene (Lyons) D.; m. Virginia Juanita Watts (div. 1970); children: Sheryl Lynette George, Kurt Allen; m. Marie Elizabeth Smith, May 30, 1983; 1 child, Jeanette. BA, U. Iowa, 1950, MA, 1951, PhD, 1963. English tchr. Glidden (Iowa) High Sch., 1951-56, Thomas Jefferson High Sch., Cedar Rapids, Iowa, 1956-63; asst. prof. English Edn. Kans. State U., Manhattan, 1963-65; asst. prof. English Ariz. State U., Tempe, 1965-67, assoc. prof. English, 1967-71, prof. English, 1971—. Co-author: Literature for Today's Young Adults, 1980, 4th edit., 1993, Inspiring Literacy, 1993; author: The Student's Right to Read, 1972. With USN, 1945-46. Mem. Nat. Coun. Tchrs. English (chmn. conf. on English edn. 1974-76, Award for Outstanding Contbn. to the Field of Adolescent Lit. 1983, pres. adolescent lit. assembly 1980-81, co-editor English Jour. 1980-87). Democrat. Episcopalian.

DONER, JOHN ROLAND, hospital administrator; b. Ontario, Oreg., May 6, 1949; s. L. L. and Majorie R. (Robinson) D.; m. Kathleen M. Lang, Mar. 6, 1970; children: J. R., Erica C. BA in Bus. Adminstrn., Boise (Idaho) State U., 1971. Lic. nursing home adminstr., Idaho. Disability claims adjucator Idaho Disability Determinators Unit, Boise, 1972-74, quality assurance specialist, 1974-76, unit mgr., 1976-78; mgmt. and fin. cons. Idaho Dept. Health & Welfare, Boise, 1978-81; asst. adminstr. Idaho State Sch. & Hosp., Nampa, 1981-92, adminstrv. dir., 1993—. Sec., treas. bd. dirs. Idaho Spl. Olympics, Boise, 1985-92; vice chmn. Nampa Cmty. Work Release Ctr. Bd., 1987—; mem. adv. bd. Bogus Basin Recreation Assn. Inc., Boise, 1987—; mem., v.p., bd. dirs. Archie B. Teater Fund for Hanidcapped, Inc., 1991—. Mem. Profl. Ski Instrs. Am. (cert.). Home: 10341 Shiloh Dr Boise ID 83704-2736 Office: Idaho State Sch & Hosp 3100 11th Ave N Ext Nampa ID 83687-3188

DONG, ALVIN LIM, law librarian, lawyer; b. Seattle, Dec. 11, 1955; s. Hep Tai Dong. BA, U. Wash., 1978, MLS with distinction, 1981; JD, SUNY, Buffalo, 1988. Life cert. profl. libr., Wash. Law libr. Norfolk Law Libr., Dedham, Mass., 1985-86; staff atty. Criminals Appeals Bur. Legal Aid Soc., N.Y.C., 1988-89; lawyer, libr. New York Law Sch. Libr. N.Y.C., 1989-92; reference libr. Westminster Law Libr. U. Denver, 1993—; part-time faculty legal asst. program Edmonds C.C., Lynnwood, Wash., 1992. Student editor Law and Policy, 1987-88. Co-dir. Buffalo Pub. Interest Law Program, 1984-85; vol. Internat. Dist. Community Health Clinic, 1993. Recipient Cert. of Disting. Svc. Asian-Am. Student Counseling Svics (U. Wash.)-Cmty. Advising Bd., 1983-84; U.S. Dept. Edn. Title II-B fellow, 1979-80. Mem. ABA, Am. Assn. Law Librs., Southwestern Assn. Law Librs., Colo. Assn. Law Librs. Democrat. Office: Univ Denver Coll Law Westminster Law Libr 1900 Olive St Denver CO 80220-1857

DONGES, SAMUEL ARNOLD, process control engineer; b. Ashland, Ohio, Oct. 9, 1958; s. George H. and Cathleen (Vanosdal) D. BSEE, Metro State U., 1971. Quality control Martin Co., Denver, 1960-61; water commr. City of Frisco (Colo.), 1961-65; contract adminstr. MSI of Tenn., Huntsville, Ala., 1966-68; svc. mgr. BCS Assocs., Orlando, Fla., 1968-69; prodn. supr. Honeywell, Denver, 1969-70; process control engr. Denver Autometrics Inc., Boulder, Colo., 1970—. Designer several process control sys. for So. Peru Copper, Indpls. Light & Power, CODELCO, Chile. With USN, 1956-60. Mem. Instrument Soc. Am., Elks, Masons, Scotish Rite, York Rite. Office: Denver Autometrics Inc 6235 Lookout Rd Boulder CO 80301-3335

DONKER, RICHARD BRUCE, health care administrator; b. Modesto, Calif., Sept. 29, 1950; s. Luverne Peter and Ruth Bernice (Hoskenga) D.; m. Elizabeth Gail Content, May 3, 1986; children: Elizabeth Anne, Danica Ruth. AA, Modesto Jr. Coll., 1970; BS, Calvin Coll., Grand Rapids, Mich., 1972; MA, Calif. State Coll., Turlock, 1978; EdD, U. Pacific, 1980. Grant dir. Yosemite Community Coll. Dist., Modesto, 1975-77; dir. flight ops. Meml. Hosps. Assn., Modesto, 1980-85, adminstrv. coord., 1985-87, v.p. bus. systems, 1987-89; v.p. clin. svcs. Meml. Hosp. Assn., Modesto, 1989-92; prin. Global Bus. Network, Emeryville, Calif., 1992—; divisional pres. Coastal Health Care Group, Inc., Durham, N.C., 1993—; exec. dir. MediPLUS Health Plans, Inc., Modesto, 1986-92; pres. Calif. Aeromed. Rescue and Evacuation, Inc., Modesto, 1985—; lectr. Am. Hosp. Assn., Chgo., 1984—; bd. dirs. Synergistic Sys., Inc.; cons. in field, 1984—. Author: Emergency Medical Technician Outreach Training, 1977, (with others) The Hospital Emergency Department: Returning to Financial Viability, 1987, Restructuring Ambulatory Care, A Guide to Reorganization, 1990, The Hospital Emergency Department, 1992. Bd. dirs. Stanislaus Paramedic Assn., Modesto, 1978-82, Head Rest, Inc., Modesto, 1980; bd. dirs. regional occupational program Stanislau County Dept. Edn., 1980; del. People-to-People Citizen Amb. Program, People's Republic of China, 1988. Mem. Am. Acad. Med. Adminstrs., Nat. Acad. Scis. Inst. Medicine (com. pediatric emergency med. svcs. 1991-92), Phi Delta Kappa, Commonwealth Club. Presbyterian. Home: 1322 Edgebrook Dr Modesto CA 95354-1537 Office: 1 Kaiser Plz Ste 1700 Oakland CA 94612-3612

DONLON, TIMOTHY A., cytogeneticist; b. Pasadena, Calif., Apr. 16, 1952. PhD, U. Oreg., 1984. Med. genetics fellow Children's Hosp., Boston, 1984-86; chief molecular clin. cytogenetics Kapiolani Med. Ctr., Honolulu, 1992—; assoc. prof. U. Hawaii Burns Sch. Medicine, Honolulu, 1992—. Office: Kapiolani Med Ctr Dept Molecular & Clin Cytogenetics 1946 Young St Ste 400 Honolulu HI 96826*

DONLON, WILLIAM CHRISTOPHER, maxillofacial surgeon, educator, author, editor; b. N.Y.C., Oct. 17, 1952; s. William Aloyisius and Margaret Mary (O'Donovan) D.; m. Marianne Patricia Truta, May 28, 1983; 1 child, Sean Liam Riobard. BA, Hofstra U., 1974, MA, 1975; DMD, Tufts U., 1979. Diplomate Am. Bd. Oral Maxillofacial Surgery (examining com. 1993—). Resident Mt. Sinai Med. Ctr., N.Y.C., 1979-81, chief resident, 1981-82; asst. clin. prof. U. Pacific, San Francisco, 1982-88, assoc. clin. prof., 1988—; prin. surgeon Peninsula Maxillofacial Surgery, South San Francisco, Calif., 1982—, Burlingame, Calif., 1988—, Redwood City, Calif., 1990-95, Menlo Park, Calif., 1990-95, San Carlos, Calif., 1995—; dir. Facial Pain Rsch. Ctr., San Francisco, 1986-93; lectr. in field; vis. faculty dept. maxillofacial surgery U. Mich., 1994—; vis. prof. dept. maxillofacial, head, neck and facial plastic surgery U. Chile, 1993—; mem. hosp. staff Mills-Peninsula Hosps., 1984—, chief svc., 1992—; mem. hosp. staff Sequoia Hosp., 1990—, San Mateo County Gen. Hosp., 1992—; mem. courtesy staff Seton Med. Ctr., 1984—, Kaiser Hosps., San Francisco and Redwood City, 1984—. Editor: Headache and Facial Pain, 1990; reviewer Cleft Craniofacial jour.; contbr. articles to profl. jours. Fellow Am. Dental Soc. Anesthesiology, Am. Assn. Oral Maxillofacial Surgeons (chmn. com. on hosp. affairs 1992-95, chmn. reference com., House of Dels., 1992—, Committeeman of Yr. 1994), Am. Coll. Oral Maxillofacial Surgeons; mem. AMA, ADA, Am. Soc. TMJ Surgeons, Am. Cleft Palate-Craniofacial Assn., North American Skull Base Soc., Western Soc. Oral Maxillofacial Surgeons (bd. dirs. 1993—), European Assn. Craniomaxillofaicial Surgery, Internat. Assn. Maxillofacial Surgery, Calif. Dental Assn., No. Calif. Oral Maxillofacial Surgeons (bd. dirs. 1986-88, sec.-treas. 1990-91, pres. 1992-93), Calif. Assn. Oral Maxillofacial Surgeons (bd. dirs. 1991-94, pres.-elect 1993-94, pres. 1994-95), Soc. of Med. Friends Wine, Tufts Dental Alumni Assn. (v.p. Calif. chpt. 1984—, pres. 1986-94). Office: Peninsula Maxillofacial Surgery 1860 El Camino Real Ste 300 Burlingame CA 94010-3114

DONNALLY, PATRICIA BRODERICK, fashion editor; b. Cheverly, Md., Mar. 11, 1955; d. James Duane and Olga Frances (Duenas) Broderick; m. Robert Andrew Donnally, Dec. 30, 1977. B.S., U. Md., 1977. Fashion editor The Washington Times (D.C.), 1983-85, The San Francisco Chronicle, 1985—. Recipient Atrium award, 1984, 87, 88, 89, 90, 95, Lulu award, 1985, 87, award Am. Cancer Soc., 1991, Aldo award, 1994. Avocation: travel. Office: Chronicle Pub Co 901 Mission St San Francisco CA 94103-2905

DONNALLY, PATRICK ANDREW, quality management consultant; b. South Charleston, W.Va., Sept. 7, 1932; s. Charles Lewis and Gladys Olean (Bright) D.; m. Bonnie Lou Blosser, Nov. 29, 1963; children: Shea Lynn, Melissa Ann, Kevin Patrick. BS in Indsl. Engring., W.Va. U., 1959, MS in Indsl. Engring., 1963; MBA, Rollins Coll., 1985. Registered profl. engr., Calif. Quality systems cons. Gen. Systems Co., Pittsfield, Mass., 1976-79; dir. corp. quality Storage Tech. Corp., Louisville, Colo., 1979-81, MagneTek, Inc., L.A., 1990-92; v.p. Stromberg Carlson, Lake Mary, Fla., 1981-84; sr. v.p. Philip Crosby Assocs., Winter Park, Fla., 1984-89; sr. cons. Ernst & Young, San Jose, Calif., 1989-90; pres., CEO Jones Reilly, Milpitas, Calif., 1992-93, Patrick Donnally Assocs., San Ramon, Calif., 1993—; speaker in field. Mem. patient care com. San Jose Med. Ctr., 1987-90. With U.S. Army, 1953-55. Mem. Am. Soc. Quality Control (sr.), Alpha Pi Mu. Democrat. Baptist. Office: Patrick Donnally Assocs 11 Crow Canyon Ct Ste 109 San Ramon CA 94583-1619

DONNELLY, DONALD FRANK, mathematics educator, computer consultant; b. San Diego, Nov. 23, 1928; s. George Dewey and Helen Mabel (Jones) D.; m. Barbara Gay Moore, Nov. 22, 1952 (div. Aug. 1964); m. Mary Ruth Hutchinson, June 1, 1974; children: Kathleen Alice, Michael Patrick, Christiane, Kelley Ann, Kerry Colleen. BA, San Diego State Coll., 1954; MA, Calif. Western U., 1964; EdS, Point Loma Coll., 1983; EdD, No. Ariz. U., 1986. Tchr., coach William S. Hart Sch. Dist., Newhall, Calif., 1955-56, San Diego City Schs., 1956-72; instr. health edn. and math. San Diego City Coll., 1957-69; tchr., coach Grossmont Union High Sch. Dist., El Cajon, Calif., 1972-88; instr. math. Grossmont C.C., El Cajon, 1988—; part-time health edn. and math. instr. San Diego City Coll., 1957-69. Actor Old Globe Theatre, San Diego, 1966-76, San Diego Opera Co., 1973-81, SAG, San Diego, 1981—. Warrant officer USNG, 1948-50, 57-64, with U.S. Army, 1950-52, Korea. Inductee Herbert Hoover High Sch. Athletic Hall of Fame. Mem. AFTRA, VFW, Am. Legion, Old Mission Beach Athletic Club, San Deigo Aerospace Mus., San Diego State U. Aztec Varsity Club (membership chair 1991—), Aztec Athletic Found., Friendly Sons of St. Patrick of San Diego, Elks, Phi Delta Kappa (historian 1984-86). Democrat. Roman Catholic. Office: Grossmont CC 8800 Grossmont College Dr El Cajon CA 92020-1765

DONNELLY, JOHN, philosophy educator; b. Worcester, Mass., Mar. 30, 1941; s. Donald Smith and Viola Frances (Norton) D.; m. Joyce Marie Mattress, June 10, 1967; children: Colin, Maria. BS, Holy Cross Coll., 1963; MA, Boston Coll., 1965; AM, Brown U., 1967, PhD, 1969. Prof. U. San Diego, 1976—. Editor: Suicide: Right or Wrong, 1990, Reflective Wisdom, 1989, Language, Metaphysics and Death, 1978, 94, Logical Analysis and Contemporary Theism, 1972, Conscience, 1973; mem. editl. bd.: Internat. Philos. Quar., N.Y.C., 1972-76. Recipient award NEH, 1980. Mem. Am. Philos. Assn., Soc. Christian Philosophers, Am. Acad. Religion, Soren Kierkegaard Soc. (v.p. 1988, pres. 1989). Democrat. Roman Catholic. Home: 7890 Hummingbird Ln San Diego CA 92123-2720 Office: U San Diego Alcala Park San Diego CA 92110

DONNELLY, MARGARITA PATRICIA, editor; b. Caracas, Venezuela, Mar. 9, 1942; came to U.S., 1957; d. Harry Francis X. and Mary Catherine (Donnelly) D.; 1 child, Angelique Xochime Brady. BA, San Francisco State U., 1967; MEd, Oreg. State U., 1972. Founder, mng. editor Calyx Inc., Corvallis, Oreg., 1976%; editor U. Oreg. ERIC Clearinghouse, Eugene, 1983-88. Editor: Women and Aging, 1986, The Forbidden Stitch, 1989 (Am. Book award 1990); editor Calyx, A Jour. of Art and Lit. by Women. Office: Calyx PO Box B 216 SW Madison # 7 Corvallis OR 97339

D'ONOFRIO, MARY ANN, medical transcription company executive; b. Detroit, Jan. 24, 1933; d. Charles Henry and Cecilia Rose (Levan) Clifford; m. Dominic Armando D'Onofrio, Apr. 19, 1958; children: Margaret Clement, Anthony, Elizabeth, Maria Spurgeon. BA, Marygrove Coll., 1954; MLS, U. Mich., 1955. Cert. med. transcriptionist. Reader's advisor Detroit Pub. Libr., 1955-58; cataloger Willow Run (Mich.) Pub. Libr., 1959-61, St. Thomas Grade and High Sch., Ann Arbor, Mich., 1968-72; med. record analyst Chelsea (Mich.) Community Hosp., 1972-79; pres. Meditranscript Svc., Ann Arbor, 1979-81; asst. office mgr. Dr. Maxfield, D.O., Tucson, 1981-82; quality assurance analyst, utilization rev. Tucson (Ariz.) Gen. Hosp., 1983-86; exec. asst. Dr. McEldoon M.D., Tucson, 1986-88; pres. Meditranscript Svc., Tucson, 1986-88; co-owner Med-Comm Assocs., Tucson, 1989—; co-owner, assoc. designer EMA of Tucson custom apparel and jewelry design co. Co-author: Psychiatric Words & Phrases, 1990; contbr. articles to profl. jours; co-developer Cross-Search. Block leader Infantile Paralysis Assn., Ann Arbor, 1975-80, Easter Seal Assn., Tucson, 1983-86, Am. Heart Assn., 1994; capt. Tucson chpt. Am. Cancer Soc., 1992. Mem. Am. Assn. for Med. Transcription (parliamentarian Sonora Desert chpt. 1984-86, 90-93, 95—, compiler/editor AAMT Annotated Bibliography 1981, Named Disting. Mem. 1984, treas. Sonora Desert chpt. 1987, jour. columnist 1982-86, by-laws com. 1995), Ednl. Honor Soc., Pi Lambda Theta (life).

DONOHUGH, DONALD LEE, physician; b. Los Angeles, Apr. 12, 1924; s. William Noble and Florence Virginia (Shelton) D.; m. Virginia Eskew McGregor, Sept. 12, 1950 (div. 1971); children: Ruth, Laurel, Marilee, Carol, Greg; m. Beatrice Ivany Redick, Dec. 3, 1976; stepchildren: Leslie Ann, Andrea Jean. BS, U.S. Naval Acad., 1946; MD, U. Calif., San Francisco, 1956; MPH and Tropical Medicine, Tulane U., 1961. Diplomate AM. Bd. Internal Medicine. Intern U. Hosp., San Diego, 1956-57; resident Monterey County Hosp., 1957-58; dir. of med. svcs. U.S. Depart. Interior, Am. Samoa, 1958-60; instr. Tulane U. Med. Sch., New Orleans, 1960-63; resident Tulane Svcs. V.A. and Charity Hosp., New Orleans, 1961-63; cons. Internat. Ctr. for Rsch and Tng., Costa Rica, 1961-63; asst. prof. medicine & preventive medicine La. State U. Sch. Medicine, 1962-63; assoc. prof., 1963-65; vis. prof. U. Costa Rica, 1963-65; faculty advisor, head of Agy. Internat. Devel. program U. Costa Rica Med. Sch., 1965-67; dir. med. svcs. Med. Ctr. U. Calif. (formerly Orange County Hosp.), Irvine, 1967-69; assoc. clin. prof. U. Calif., Irvine, 1967-79, clin. prof., 1980-85; pvt. practice Tustin, Calif., 1970-80; with Joint Commn. on Accreditation of Hosps., 1981; cons. Kauai, Hawaii, 1981—. Author: The Middle Years, 1981, Practice Management, 1986, Kauai, 1988, 3d edit., 1990; co-translator; Rashomon (Ryonosuke Akutagawa), 1950; also numerous articles. Lt. USN, 1946-52, capt. USNR, 1966-84. Fellow Am. Coll. Physicians (life); mem. Delta Omega. Republican. Episcopalian. Home: 4890 Lawai Beach Rd Koloa HI 96756-9675

DONOVAN, DENNIS, agricultural products executive; b. 1951. With family farm, Salinas, Calif., 1972-76, Pismo-Oceanao (Calif.) Vegetable Exch., 1976—. Office: Pismo-Oceanao Vegetable Exch 1731 Railroad St Oceano CA 93445-9510*

DONOVAN, WALTER EDGAR, retired mayor; b. Santa Ana, Calif., Mar. 7, 1926; s. Walter Raymond and Pretoria (Garver) D.; m. Diane Gertrude Mead, Mar. 28, 1948; children: Walter M., Thomas J., Victoria. Student, U. Oreg., 1945-47. Sales rep. So. Calif. Edison Co., Long Beach, Calif., 1950-55; mayor City of Garden Grove, Garden Grove, Calif., 1988-92; area mgr. So. Calif. Edison Co., Garden Grove, Calif., 1965-80, Cypress and Garden Grove, Calif., 1980-86; councilman City of Garden Grove, 1972-80, 1984-88, mayor, 1988-92.; bd. dirs. Garden Grove Hosp.-Med. Ctr., 1982-90; commr. Orange County (Calif.) Waste Mgmt. Commn., 1984-92. Recipient Community Americana Garden Grove award Cypress Coll., 1980. Mem. Rotary (pres. 1962-63), Masons, Shriners, Elks. Republican.

DONOVAN, WILLARD PATRICK, retired elementary education educator; b. Grand Rapids, Mich., Sept. 1, 1930; s. Willard Andrew and Thelma Alfreda (Davis) D.; m. Dorothy Jane Nester, Nov. 27, 1954 (dec. May 1981); children: Cindy Jane, Kimberly Sue. BS, Ea. Mich. U., 1965, MA, 1969. Cert. grades K-8, Mich. Enlisted U.S. Army, 1947, advanced through grades to master sgt., 1953, platoon sgt. Korean War, ret., 1964; pharm. sales Nat. Drug Co., Detroit, 1964-66; tchr. Cromie Elem. Sch. Warren (Mich.) Consol. Schs., 1966-95, ret., 1995; reading textbook and curriculum devel. com. Warren (Mich.) Consol. Schs., 1969-73, sci. com., 1970-95; curriculum and textbook com. Macomb County Christian Schs., Warren, 1982-95. Decorated Combat Infantry badge U.S. Army, Korea, 1950, Purple heart with three clusters U.S. Army, Korea, 1950-51, Korea-Japan Svc. medal, 1951, Presdl. citation, 1951, Korean medal with three campaign clusters, 1951, Nat. Def. Svc. medal, 1951, Bronze star, Silver star. Mem. NRA, Am. Quarterhouse Assn., Assn. U.S. Army, Detroit Area Coun. Tchrs. Math., Met. Detroit Sci. Tchrs. Assn., The Chosin Few, Nat. Edn. Assn., Mich. Edn. Assn., Warren (Mich.) Edn. Assn. Home: PO Box 563 8440 Mission Hills Arizona City AZ 85223

DONOVAN-JOHNSON, D.J., artist, educator; b. Thayer, Kans., June 14, 1940; d. Lawrence R. and Pauline Rosilind (Shearer) Hague; m. John Thomas Donovan, June 4, 1960 (dec. 1969); 1 child, Erik; m. Gregory B. Johnson, Dec. 29, 1972; children: Ruthie, Julie. BS, Western Mich. U., 1962; MA, Wash. State U., 1965. Instr. pub. schs., Mont., Mich. and Wash.; juror for art shows; workshop instr. One woman and group shows include Salmagundi Club, State of the Art, N.Y.C., Water Media U.S., Open, Facet, Taos, N.Mex., Gallery of Interior, Washington, Thorsten Gallery, Jewish Cmty. Ctr., Art Mart, U. Denver, Colorado Springs Art Ctr., Coyote Woman Gallery, Harbor Springs, Mich., Art Expo/Calif., L.A., Miriam Pearlman Gallery, Chgo. Bd. dirs., founding pres. Flatirons Ctr. for Arts, Boulder, 1986-89;ch. sch. tchr. First Presbyn. Ch., Boulder, 1980—. Recipient Best of Boulder, Artist Choice award Daily Camera, 1992, Wash. State W.S. award, 1994, Kans. State W.S. award, 1994, Red River W.S. Silver medal award, 1994. Mem. Nat. Painters in Casein and Acrylic, Nat. League Am. Pen Women, Studio Six Artists Coop. (founding mem.). Home and Studio: 225 Bristlecone Way Boulder CO 80304-0467

DONTIGNY, RICHARD LOUIS, physical therapist; b. Havre, Mont., Aug. 9, 1931; s. Theodore Emil and Helen Estelle (Halverson) D.; m. Josephine Virginia Faltrino, June 15, 1957; children: Debra Jo, Laura Jean, Richard Emil, Julie Ann. BS, Mont. State Coll., 1954; cert. in phys. therapy, U. Iowa, 1958. Staff therapist St. Francis Hosp., Colorado Springs, Colo., 1958-60, chief therapist, 1960-61; staff therapist No. Pacific Beneficial Assn., Missoula, Mont., 1961-63; chief therapist Sacred Heart Hosp., Havre, Mont., 1963-74, Deaconess Hosp., Havre, 1963-74, No. Mont. Hosp., Havre, 1974-83; staff therapist Havre Clinic, 1983-86; pvt. practice DonTigny Phys. Therapy, Havre, 1986—; mem. Mont. Bd. Phys. Therapy Examiners, 1984-87; book, manuscript reviewer Jours. Phys. Therapy, Arlington, Va., 1978—. Contbr. articles to profl. publs., chpt. to book. With U.S. Army, 1954-56. Mem. Am. Phys. Therapy Assn. (pres. Mont. chpt. 1970-74, subject matter expert orthopedic specialty coun. 1987). Home: 66 15th St W Havre MT 59501-5274 Office: DonTigny Phys Therapy 115 2nd St W Havre MT 59501-3435

DONZE, JERRY LYNN, electrical engineer; b. Wauneta, Nebr., June 12, 1943; s. John Henry and Virgina May (Francis) D.; m. Marilyn Grace Bascue, Feb. 22, 1964 (div. May. 1980); children: Scott. L., Michele A.; m. Sandra Kay Morris, July 25, 1981. Cert. technician, Denver Inst. Tech., 1964; BSEE, U. Colo., 1972; postgrad., Advanced Metaphysics Inst. Religios Sci., 1986. Electronic technician A.B.M. Co., Lakewood, Colo., 1964-71; computer programmer Nat. Bur. Standards, Boulder, Colo., 1971-72; electronic engr. Autometrics Co., Boulder, Colo., 1972-76, Gates Research and Devel., Denver, 1976-77; devel. engr. Emerson Electric Co., Lakewood, 1977; engring. mgr. Storage Tech., Louisville, Colo., 1977—; cons. Sun Co., Arvada, Colo., 1974-75. Patentee in field. Mem. IEEE Student Soc. (treas. 1971-72), Eta Kappa Nu. Republican. Religious Scientist. Home: 12021 W 54th Ave Arvada CO 80002-1907 Office: Storage Tech 2270 S 88th St Louisville CO 80028-0001

DOOLAN, MARIAH, lawyer; b. Tempe, Ariz., Apr. 19, 1940; d. Leonard and Karen Barker; m. Kevin M. Reisinger; children: Jennifer Lynn, Jeffrey Michael. BS magna cum laude, Tufts U., 1962; MS summa cum laude, U. Ariz., 1964; JD, U. Pa., 1966. Bar: Ariz., 1966, U.S. Dist. Ct. Ariz., 1966, U.S. Supreme Ct., 1978. Assoc. Rubinstein, Dunne, White, Krawiecki & Budka, Phoenix, 1966-72, ptnr., 1973-82; ptnr. Winnie, Cox, White, Krawiecki, Budka & Doolan, Phoenix, 1983-89; pvt. practice Tucson, 1990—. Contbr. articles to profl. jours. Mem. ABA, Ariz. Bar Assn. Republican. Methodist. Home: Werik Gardens 5399 E 29th St Tucson AZ 85711

DOOLEY, CALVIN MILLARD, congressman; b. Visalia, Calif., Jan. 11, 1954. BS, U. Calif., Davis; MA, Stanford U. Mem. 102nd-103rd Congresses from Calif. Dist. 17(now 20th), 1991—; mem. agriculture com., mem. natural resources com. Democrat. Methodist. Office: House of Representatives 1227 Longworth Bldg Washington DC 20515-0004*

DOOLEY, MICHAEL P., economist, educator; b. Euclid, Ohio, Nov. 11, 1944; s. Richard Almon and Edna Ruth (Sweetnam) D.; m. Grace Elizabeth Noa, June 10, 1967; children: Matthew, Jill. BS in Econs., Duquesne U., 1966; MA in Econs., U. Del., 1968; PhD in Econs., Pa. State U., 1971. Economist divsn. internat. fin. Bd. of Govs. FRS, 1971-83, asst. dir. divsn. internat. fin., 1982-83; asst. dir. rsch. dept. Internat. Monetary Fund, 1983-91; prof. econs. U. Calif., Santa Cruz, Calif., 1992—; part time instr. econs. Pa. State U., 1969-70; vis. asst. prof. econs. Bucknell U., 1971; vis. lectr. George Washington U., 1973-84, U. Tex., Austin, 1974-75; vis. asst. prof. Econs. and Internat. Bus. U. Chgo., 1976-77; asst. divsn. chief. Internat. Monetary Fund, 1981-82; rsch. assoc. Nat. Bureau Econ. Rsch., 1992—; lectr. World Bank Conf., Kiel Inst., Ctrl. European U., Prague, Fed. Reserve Bd., U. Calif., Davis, Princeton U., Japanese Ministry of Fin. Conf., Tokyo, Bank of Japan, Tokyo, Christian Albrechts U. zu Kiel, Germany, Am. Express Bank, London, and many others. Author: The Political Economy of Policy Making, 1979, Analytical Issues in Debt, 1989; author (with others) Revista De Analisis Economico, 1989, Finance and the International Economy, 1993, Internat Savings and Investment Balances, 1993; contbr. numerous articles to profl. jours. Office: U Calif Dept Econs Santa Cruz CA 95064

DOOLIN, JAMES LAWRENCE, artist, educator; b. Hartford, Conn., June 28, 1932; s. Lawrence J. and Ruth Jennie (Blodgett) D.; m. Leslie E. Edwards, June 28, 1962 (div. Mar. 1984); children: Matthew James, Paul Lawrence; m. Lauren J. Richardson, Mar. 30, 1985; 1 child, Eve Eleanor. BFA, Phila. U. of Arts, 1954; MFA, UCLA, 1971. Instr. adult edn. Union Carbide Corp., N.Y.C., 1964-65; lectr. Prahran Coll. Advanced Edn., Melbourne, Australia, 1965-66; lectr. dept. art UCLA, 1972-80; instr. Otis Art Inst., L.A., 1977, 79-80, Cerro Coso Coll., Ridgecrest, Calif., 1982-83, Santa Monica (Calif.) Coll., 1984-86, Art Inst. So. Calif., Laguna Beach, 1992, 93; vis. artist Victorian Coll. of Arts, Melbourne, 1978, Claremont (Calif.) Grad. Sch., 1985, 87, U. Nev., Las Vegas, 1988; artist L.A. County Transp. Authority, 1993, 94, lead artist, 1994. One man shows include Gallery A, Melbourne, 1966, Ctrl. St. Gallery, Sydney, Australia, 1967, 70, Boise (Idaho) State U., 1974, L.A. Mcpl. Gallery, 1977, Victorian Coll. of Arts, Australia, 1978-79, Cerro Coso Coll., 1982, Koplin Gallery, Santa Monica, Calif., 1984, 86, 92, U. So. Calif. Atelier Gallery, Santa Monica, 1985, U. Wis., Oshkosh, 1993; exhibited in group shows at Victorian Nat. Gallery, Melbourne, Australia, 1968, Art Gallery N.S.W., Sydney, Australia, 1968, Long Beach (Calif.) Mus. Art, 1971, Palos Verdes (Calif.) Mus. Art, 1972, DeYoung Mus. Downtown Ctr., San Francisco, 1977, Australian Nat. Gallery, Canberra, 1983, Acad. Fine Arts, N.Y.C., 1986, Laguna Art Mus., Laguna Beach, Calif., 1986, Power Gallery Contemporary Art, Sydney, 1987, San Diego Mus. Art, 1991, Santa Barbara Contemporary Arts Forum, 1991, L.A. Mcpl. Art Gallery, 1991, El Camino Coll., Torrance, Calif., 1991, Security Pacific Gallery, San Francisco, 1991, Oakland (Calif.) Mus., 1992, Nev. Mus. Art, Reno, 1992, Fresno (Calif.) Met. Mus., 1992, Stremmel Gallery, Reno, Nev., 1993, Riverside (Calif.) Art Mus., 1993; represented in permanent collections Art Gallery N.S.W., Sydney, Australian Nat. Gallery, Canberra, Australian Nat. U., Canberra, Bank of Am., L.A., Contemporary Art Mus., Honolulu, Homart Devel. Co., L.A., Jonathan Club, L.A., Long Beach Mus. Art, Loyola Law Sch., L.A., Mus. Contemporary Art, Sydney, Nat. Gallery Victoria, Melbourne, Nestle U.S.A., Inc., Glendale, Calif., Newcastle Art Mus., N.S.W., State Gallery Queensland, Brisbane, Australia, U. Vt., Burlington. With U.S. Army, 1955-57. Painting fellow Guggenheim

Found., 1980, Nat. Endowment for Arts, 1981, 85, 91. Home: 2619 Cardiff Ave Los Angeles CA 90034-1842

DOOLITTLE, JOHN TAYLOR, congressman; b. Glendale, Calif., Oct. 30, 1950; s. Merrill T. and Dorothy Doolittle; B.A. in History with honors, U. Calif., Santa Cruz, 1972; J.D., McGeorge Sch. Law, U. Pacific, 1978; m. Julia Harlow, Feb. 17, 1979; children: John Taylor Jr., Courtney A. Bar: Calif. 1978. Mem. Calif. State Senate, 1980-90; mem. 102nd-103rd Congresses from Calif. 4th dist., 1991—; mem. agriculture com., natural resources com. Republican. Mem. LDS Ch. Office: House of Representatives 1526 Longworth Bldg Washington DC 20515-0004

DOOLITTLE, MICHAEL JIM, lawyer; b. Boise, Idaho, Feb. 29, 1956; s. Wallace Gale and Jean Mary (Fisher) D.; m. Jeanette Lynn Johnson, Aug. 16, 1980; children: Bradford Nicholas, Holly Anne, Nicole Jeanette. BBA, Boise State U., 1979; JD, U. Idaho, 1982. Bar: Idaho 1982, U.S. Dist. Ct. Idaho 1982, U.S. Ct. Appeals (fed. cir.) 1987, U.S. Ct. Appeals (9th cir.) 1988. Pvt. practice legal researcher Boise, 1982-83; assoc. Dennis J. Sallaz, Boise, 1983-87; ptnr. Sallaz and Doolittle, Boise, 1988-89, Sallaz, Doolittle & Gordon, Chtd., Boise, 1989-94; atty. Ringert Clark Chartered, Boise, 1994—. Recipient Am. Jurisprudence award Lawyers Coop. Pub., Moscow, Idaho, 1981, Outstanding Adv. award Idaho Assn. Def. Counsel, 1982, Pro Bono Svc. award Idaho State Bar, 1989. Mem. Idaho Bar Assn., Boise Bar Assn., Assn. Trial Lawyers Am., Idaho Trial Lawyers Assn., Idaho Attys. for Criminal Justice. Roman Catholic. Office: Ringert Clark Chartered PO Box 2773 455 S 32d St Boise ID 83701-2773

DOOLITTLE, ROBERT FREDERICK, II, high energy astrophysicist; b. Chgo., Dec. 21, 1925; s. Arthur K. and Dortha (Bailey) D.; m. Mary Agnes Parker, Apr. 30, 1955 (dec. Dec. 1972); children: Robert Arthur, Nancy Elizabeth; m. Karen K. Kruse, Dec. 28, 1978. AB, Oberlin Coll., 1948; MS, U. Mich., 1950, PhD, 1958. Asst. prof. physics San Diego State U., 1958-60; sr. scientist TRW Space and Def., Redondo Beach, Calif., 1960-83; various computer programming positions, 1983—; cons. Space Tech. Labs., L.A., 1959, 3D Graphics, Pacific Palisades, Calif., 1993, Magnesys, Santa Clara, Calif., 1987. Lt. comdr. USNR, 1944-46, 52-54. Mem. Am. Astron. Soc., Assn. for Computing Machinery. Home: 1290 Monument St Pacific Palisades CA 90272-2541

DORAN, VINCENT JAMES, steel fabricating company consultant; b. Ephrata, Wash., June 13, 1917; s. Samuel Vincent and Sarah Anastasia (Fitzpatrick) D.; B. Phil., Gonzaga U., Spokane, 1946; m. Jean Arlene Birrer, Jan. 15, 1949; children: Vincent James, Mollie Jean, Michele Lee, Patrick Michael. Mgr., Flying Service, Coulee Dam, Wash., 1947-48; mgr. constrn. Morrison-Knudsen Co., Wash. and Alaska, 1953-60; co-owner C.R. Foss Inc., constrn., Anchorage, 1961-64; mgr. Steel Fabricators, Anchorage, 1965-86. Inventor method of reducing and dewatering sewage sludge. Active Boy Scouts Am.; co-founder, pres. Chugach Rehab. Assn., 1962; mem. Alaska Gov.'s Rehab. Adv. Bd., 1962-63; mem. CAP. Served with USAAF, 1943-45, USAF, 1949-50. Decorated Air medal with 4 clusters. Mem. Welding Inst. Alaska (co-organizer, dir. 1977-78), 34th Bomb Group Assn., Am. Arbitration Assn. Roman Catholic. Club: Toastmasters. Compiler, pub. home owners' and builders' guide to sun's positions in N.Am. during solstices and equinoxes, designer packaged water, sewage treatment plants and water collection systems Arctic communities. Home: 3811 Knik Ave Anchorage AK 99517-1061 Office: 3243 Commercial Dr Anchorage AK 99501-3020

DORATO, PETER, electrical and computer engineering educator; b. N.Y.C., Dec. 17, 1932; s. Fioretto and Rosina (Lachello) D.; m. Marie Madeleine Turlan, June 2, 1956; children: Christopher, Alexander, Sylvia, Veronica. BEE, CCNY, 1955; MSEE, Columbia U., 1956; DEE, Poly. Inst. N.Y., 1961. Registered profl. engr., Colo. Lectr. elec. engring. dept. CCNY, 1956-57; instr. elec. engring. Poly. Inst. N.Y., Bklyn., 1957-61, prof., 1961-72; prof. elec. engring., dir. Resource System Analysis U. Colo., Colorado Springs, 1972-76; prof. elec. and computer engring. U. N.Mex., Albuquerque, 1984—, chmn. dept., 1976-84; hon. chaired prof. Nanjing Aero. Inst., 1989. Co-author Linear Quadratic Control, 1995, Robust Control for Unstructured Perturbations, 1992; editor: Robust Control, Recent Results in Robust Control and Advances in Adaptive Control, reprint vols., 1987, 90, 91, IEEE Press Reprint Vol. Series, 1989-90; assoc. editor Automatica Jour., 1969-83, 89-92, editor rapid publs., 1994—; assoc. editor IEEE Trans on Edn., 1989-91; contbr. articles on control systems theory to profl. jours. Fellow IEEE; mem. Am. Soc. for Engring. Edn., IEEE Control Systems Soc. (Disting. Mem. award). Democrat. Home: 1514 Roma Ave NE Albuquerque NM 87106-4513 Office: U NMex Dept Elec Computer Eng Albuquerque NM 87131

DORAY, ANDREA WESLEY, advertising administrator, writer; b. Monte Vista, Colo., Oct. 4, 1956; d. Dant Bell and Rosemary Ann (Kassap) D. BA, U. No. Colo., 1977, postgrad., 1994—. Cert. post secondary tchr. Asst. advt. mgr. San Luis Valley Publ. Co., Monte Vista, 1977-78; mktg. dir. Stuart Scott & Assocs. (formerly Philip Winn & Assocs.), Colorado Springs, Colo., 1978-80; sr. v.p. Heisley Design & Advt., Colorado Springs, Colo., 1980-85; pres., creative dir. Doray Doray, Monument, Colo., 1985—; account svcs. dir. Praco Ltd., Advt., Colorado Springs, 1987-88; dir. corp. community rels. Current, Inc., Colorado Springs, 1988-90; creative writer greeting cards, children's books, 1990-93; copy mgr. Cheeks Advt., 1993—; artist in residence The Childrens Mus., Colorado Springs, Colo.; part-time instr. Pikes Peak C.C., Colorado Springs, 1983-86, 92, 95, mem. mktg. adv. coun., 1985-93, chair, 1994-95, chair mktg. mgmt. com.; guest lectr. Colo. Mountain Coll., 1982-84, U. So. Colo., 1983, Pikes Peak C.C., 1983-87, U. Colo., Colorado Springs, 1988—. Author: The Other Fish, 1976, Oil Painting Lessons, 1986, Coming to Terms, 1986, Roger Douglas, 1987, Sunshine and the Very First Christmas, 1991, The Wonderful Birthday Star, 1991, Too-Late Tiffany and the Little Shepherd, 1991, If Only It Would Snow, 1992, The Year There Could Be No Christmas, 1992, Boris Bear Remembers His Manners, 1992, The Day Daisy Found Christmas, 1992, Friends, 1993, What Do We Want for Christmas, 1994; editor: Current Impressions, 1988-90; contbg. editor Colorado Springs Bus. Mag., 1984-86; creative writer World Cycling Fedn. Championships, 1986; speaker in field. Chmn. Colorado Springs Local Advt. Rev. Program, 1985; chmn., mem. exec. com. advt. and pub. rels. task force U.S. Olympic Hall of Fame, 1986; mem. State Legis. Alert and Action Coalition, 1985-87; mem. project bus. cons. Jr. Achievement, Colorado Springs, 1985-87; trustee Citizen's Goals Colorado Springs, 1988-89; speaker Nat. Coun. Community Rels., Orlando, Fla., 1988; grad. Leadership 2000, 1988; commencement speaker Yuma (Colo.) High Sch., 1987; social styles trainer Producing Results with Others; mem. adv. bd. El Paso County Ptnrs. Program, 1995. Named One of Colorado Springs Leading Women, Colorado Springs Gazette Telegraph, 1984, One of Women of 90s, 1989; Outstanding Young Alumna, U. No. Colo., 1987. Mem. Am. Advt. Fedn. (chmn. dist. 12 legis. com. 1985-87, pub. rels. com. 1986, Silver medal award 1986), Pikes Peak Advt. Fedn. (pres. 1984-86, Advt. Person of Yr. award), Colorado Springs C. of C. (advt. roundtable, spkr. small bus. coun. 1986—, comm. task force 1989-90, spkr. woman in bus. conf.). Office: Current Inc PO Box 2559 Colorado Springs CO 80901-2559

DORE, BONNY ELLEN, film and television production company executive; b. Cleve., Aug. 16, 1947; d. Reber Hutson and Ellen Elizabeth (McNamara) Barnes; m. Sanford Astor, May 22, 1987. BA, U. Mich., 1969, MA, 1975. Cert. tchr., Mich. Dir., tchr. Plymouth (Mich.) Community Schs., 1969-72; gen. mgr. Sta. WSDP-FM, Plymouth, 1970-72; prodn. supr. pub. TV N.Y. State Dept. Edn., 1972-74; producer TV series Hot Fudge Sta. WXYZ-TV, Detroit, 1974-75; mgr. children's programs ABC TV Network, L.A., 1975, dir. children's programs, 1975-76, dir. prime time variety programs, 1976-77; dir. devel. Hanna-Barbera, L.A., 1977; v.p. devel. and prodn. Krofft Entertainment, L.A., 1977-81, Centerpoint Prodn., L.A., 1981-82; pres., owner in assn. with Orion TV The Greif-Dore Co., L.A., 1983-87, Bonny Dore Prodns. Inc., L.A., 1988—; mem. Caucus of Writers, Producers and Dirs., 1989—; Marsh speaker Pres. Fund for Pres. Weekend U. Mich., 1989. Producer TV series The Krofft Superstar Hour, ABC, 1978 (2 Emmy awards 1979), comedy series The 1/2 Hour Comedy Hour (starring Arsenio Hall and Victoria Jackson), ABC, 1983-84, mini-series Sins (starring Joan Collins), CBS, 1986, comedy series First Impressions, CBS, 1987-88, mini-series Glory! Glory! (starring Ellen Greene, Richard Thomas and James Whitmore; 2 Ace cable awards), HBO, 1988-89, NBC movie Reason for Living, The Jill Ireland Story, 1990-91, ABC movie Captive!, 1991, The Sinking of the Rainbow Warrior, 1993, numerous others. Mem. fundraising com. U. Mich., 1990—; assoc. mem. Nat. Trust for Hist. Preservation, 1988—. Named Outstanding Young Tchr. of Yr., Cen. States Speech Assn., 1973; Cert. of Appreciation, Gov. of Mich., 1985, City of Beverly Hills, Calif., 1985, Coun. on Social Work Edn., 1990; recipient Action for Children's TV award, 1975, Gold medal Best TV Mini-series, Best TV Screenplay Silver medal Houston Internat. Film Festival, 1990, Best. TV Actress award, 1990, Best TV Supporting Actor, 1990, Best Music, 1990, Winner Best Mini Series Houston Film Festival, 1990. Mem. NATAS, Am. Film Inst. (corr. sec.), Women in Film (v.p. 1978-81, pres. 1980-81), Women in Film Found. (trustee 1981—, exec. prodr. The Signature Series, co-chair 1994—), Nat. Cable TV Assn., Beverly Hills C. of C. (cons. 1985), Exec. Roundtable L.A. (trustee 1987—), Hollywood Radio and TV Soc., Acad. TV Arts and Scis. (mem. caucus of writers, prodrs., dirs. 1991—, co-chair caucus writers, prodrs. and dir.).

DORER, FRED HAROLD, chemistry educator; b. Auburn, Calif., May 3, 1936; s. Fred H. and Mary E. (Fisher) D.; m. Marilyn Pearl Young, Sept. 6, 1958; children: Garrett Michael, Russell Kenneth. B.S., Calif. State U.-Long Beach, 1961; Ph.D., U. Wash., 1965; postgrad., U. Freiburg, (Germany), 1965-66. Rsch. chemist Shell Devel. Co., Emeryville, Calif., 1966-67; prof. chemistry Calif. State U., Fullerton, 1967-75; assoc. program dir. chem. dynamics NSF, Washington, 1974-75; chmn., prof. chemistry San Francisco State U., 1975-81; dean natural sci. Sonoma State U., Rohnert Park, Calif., 1981-82, provost, v.p., 1982-84; acad. v.p. Calif. State U., Bakersfield, 1984—. Contbr. articles to profl. jours. Served with USMC, 1954-57. Grantee Research Corp., 1968; grantee NSF, 1969-73, Petroleum Research Fund, 1978, 80; fellow NSF, 1965. Mem. AAAS, Am. Assn. Higher Edn., Am. Chem. Soc. Home: 2809 English Oak Dr Bakersfield CA 93311-1729 Office: Calif State U 9001 Stockdale Hwy Bakersfield CA 93311-1022

DORF, RICHARD CARL, electrical engineering and management educator; b. N.Y.C., Dec. 27, 1933; s. William Carl and Marion (Fraser) D.; m. Joy H. MacDonald, June 15, 1957; children: Christine, Renée. BS, Clarkson U., 1955; MS, U. Colo., 1957; PhD, U.S. Naval Postgrad. Sch., 1961. Registered profl. engr., Calif. Instr. Clarkson U., Potsdam, N.Y., 1956-58; instr., asst. prof. U.S. Naval Postgrad. Sch., Monterey, Calif., 1958-63; prof., chmn. U. Santa Clara, Calif., 1963-69; v.p. Ohio U., Athens, 1969-72; dean of extended learning U. Calif., Davis, 1972-81, prof. in mgmt. and elec. engring., 1972—; lectr. U. Edinburgh, Scotland, 1961-62; cons. Lawrence Livermore (Calif.) Nat. Lab., 1981—; chmn. Sacramento Valley Venture Capital Forum, 1985-90. Author: The Mutual Fund Portfolio Planner, 1988, The New Mutual Fund Advisor, 1988, Electric Circuits, 2d edit., 1993, Modern Control Systems, 7th edit., 1995; editor: Ency. of Robotics, 1987, Circuits, Devices and Systems, 1991, Handbook of Electrical Engineering, 1993, Handbook of Manufacturing and Automation, 1994. Bd. dirs. Sta. KVIE, PBS, Sacramento, 1976-79; ruling elder Davis Cmty. Ch., 1973-76; chmn. Sonoma Valley Econ. Devel. Assn., 1993—; mem. City Coun., City of Sonoma, 1995—; vice mayor City of Sonoma, 1994—. With U.S. Army, 1956. Recipient Alumni award Clarkson U., 1979. Fellow IEEE; mem. Am. Soc. Engring. Edn. (sr., chmn. div. 1980—), University Club (bd. dirs. 1988-91), Rotary (bd. dirs. 1978-80). Presbyterian. Office: U Calif Elec Engring Dept Davis CA 95616

DORFMAN, RACHELLE A., social sciences educator, writer; b. Phila., July 24, 1945; d. Frank and Frances (Handelman) Abramson; m. K. Dorfman, Feb. 8, 1961 (div. Apr. 1994); children: Holly Sue, Jeffrey Adam. BS, Hahnemann U., 1981; MSS, Bryn Mawr Coll., 1983; PhD, Temple U., 1990. Lic. clin. social worker, Calif. Asst. prof. Hahnemann U., Phila., 1984-88, UCLA, 1989—; dep. dir. Calif. Geriatric Edn. Ctr., 1989-92; psychotherapist, Phila., 1983-88; vis. prof. U. Hong Kong, 1994. Author: Aging Into the 21st Century, 1994; editor: Paradigms of Clinical Social Work, 1988; contbr. articles to profl. jours. Mem. NASW, Am. Soc. Aging, Geriat. Soc. Am., Acad. Cert. Social Workers. Home: 20224 Sherman Way Apt 46 Canoga Park CA 91306-3229 Office: UCLA Sch Pub Policy/Social Rsch 405 Hilgard Ave Los Angeles CA 90024-1301

DORFMAN, STEVEN DAVID, electronics company executive; b. Bklyn., Sept. 26, 1935; s. Murray Dorfman and Eleanor Judith (Blitzer) Pisani; m. Georgina Breckenridge (divorced): 1 child, Jennifer; m. Beverly Joan Pain, Dec. 28, 1965; children: Lorraine, Gene, Lynn. BSEE, U. Fla., 1957; MSEE, U. So. Calif., 1959. With Hughes Cos., 1957—; mgr. adv. programs Hughes Aircraft Co., El Segundo, Calif., 1967-72, mgr. Pioneer Venus, 1972-78, assoc. mgr. NASA Systems Div., 1978-82, mgr. NASA Systems Div., 1983; pres., chief exec. officer Hughes Communications Inc. subs. Hughes Aircraft Co., L.A., 1983-86; corp. v.p., pres. space and communications group, mem. policy bd. Hughes Aircraft Co., L.A., 1986-92; pres., CEO Hughes Space & Comm. Co., L.A., 1992-93; pres. telecomms. and space, sr. v.p., mem. office of chmn. GM Hughes Electronics Corp., L.A., 1993—; chmn. comml. space transp. adv. com. (COMSTAC) Washington Dept. Transp., 1987—; mem. space systems tech. adv. com. NASA, Washington, 1982—; mem. U.S. Info. Agy. TV/Telecom Adv. Coun., Washington, 1985-90; mem. Nat. Rsch. Coun. Aeronautics and Space Engring. Bd., 1992—. Contbr. articles to profl. jours.; patentee in field. State Senate scholar, Fla., 1955-56; recipient Disting. Pub. Svc. medal NASA, 1980. Mem. NEA, Nat. Rsch. Coun. Home: 517 Veteran Ave Los Angeles CA 90024-1915 Office: GM Hughes Electronics PO Box 80028 Los Angeles CA 90080-0028

DORIUS, EARL FREDRIC, lawyer; b. Salt Lake City, Mar. 26, 1947; s. Earl Nelson and Ruth Lapriel (Damron) D.; m. Katherine Bean, Sept. 4, 1968; children: Jennifer, Dawn, Ashley, Amanda, Joshua, Adam. BS, U. Utah, 1971, JD, 1973. Bar: Utah 1973, U.S. Supreme Ct. 1976. Asst. atty. gen. Utah Atty. Gen., Salt Lake City, 1973-89; legal counsel Utah Alcoholic Beverage Control, Salt Lake City, 1989—; chief govt. affairs Utah Atty. Gen., Salt Lake City, 1983-89, chief criminal appeals, 1982-89; legal counsel U. Utah/Weber State, Salt Lake City, 1981; extradition counsel Gov. of Utah, Salt Lake City, 1973-89. Author: Utah Extradition Manual, 1990, Capital Punishment, 1980, Utah Justice of Peace, 1976. Mem. Alcoholic Beverage Control Task Force, Salt Lake City, 1988-89, Gov.'s Task Force on Corrections, Salt Lake City, 1974-76, Utah Task Force on Insanity Def., Salt Lake City, 1982-83; instr. Utah Corrections Acad., Salt Lake City, 1974-80; mem. Adv. Bd. on Criminology, U. Utah, 1975. Mem. Assn. Govt. Attys. in Capital Litigation (pres. 1980-81), Nat. Assn. Extradition Ofcls. (pres. 1988-89), Nat. Assn. Attys. Gen. Commn. on Habeas Corpus, Utah Supreme Ct. Adv. Commn. on Criminal Procedure, Utah Peace Officer Standards & Tng. Coun. LDS. Office: Utah Alcohol Beverage 1625 S 900 W Salt Lake City UT 84104-1630

DORIUS, KERMIT PARRISH, architect; b. Salt Lake City, Aug. 2, 1926; s. Raymond E. and Claire Ford (Parrish) D.; m. Arlene Roehm, June 15, 1979; children: Lynn, Kristin, Mark. Student, U. Utah, 1943-44; B.Arch., U. Calif., Berkeley, 1950. Project architect Frederick Hodgdon (AIA), Newport Beach, Calif., 1954-57; prin. Brownell & Dorius, Corona Del Mar, Calif., 1957-59; pres. Kermit Dorius & Assocs., Corona Del Mar, 1960—. Recipient numerous awards Nat. Assn. Homebuilders/Pacific Coast Builders Conf., Orange County chpt. AIA, Better Homes & Gardens, 1975—. Fellow AIA (pres. Orange County chpt. 1966, v.p. Calif. coun. 1976-77); mem. Architects, Designers, Planners for Social Responsibility (chair Orange County chpt. 1987—), Orange County Bldg. Industry Assn. (HomeAid exec. com. 1991—). Office: JBZ Dorius 2415 Campus Dr Ste 200 Irvine CA 92715

DORLAND, FRANK NORTON, art conservator, educator; b. Peru, Nebr., Oct. 11, 1914; s. Frank Norton and Marion Hope (Abbot) D.; m. Mabel Vyvyan Jolliffe, July 29, 1938 (dec. Mar. 1991); m. Vandria Rayner, Apr. 7, 1995. Student Calif. Christian Coll., 1931-33; San Diego State Coll., 1933-38. Artist preliminary design engring. Convair Co., San Diego, Calif., 1938-49; pvt. practice as art conservator, La Jolla, Calif., 1949-59, San Francisco, 1959-63, Mill Valley, Calif., 1963-73, Santa Barbara, Calif., 1973-85; head art dept. The Quaderia Inst., San Luis Obispo, Calif., 1994—; formerly engaged in authentication and classification art objects; cons. art assns. galleries, mus., collectors, chs. Author: Holy Ice: The Story of Electronic Quartz Crystal, 1992; autheticated original Our Lady of Kazan (The Black Virgin of Kazan) Russian Icon, 1963. Mem. Internat. Inst. for Conservation, Internat. Coun. Museums, Am. Mus. Assn. Pioneer in use of spl. waxes in painting; inventor oil and water mix wax mediums, first scientifically compounded fine arts wax; invented first scientifically formulated fine arts wax (1948), engaged in research and devel. waxes and resins and properties and usage of electronic quartz crystals, also pioneer biocrystallographer, researcher on crystals, the human mind and the evolution of human consciousness. Home: PO Box 6233 Los Osos CA 93412-6233

DORMAN, GARY JAY, consulting economist; b. Queens, N.Y., Aug. 22, 1950; s. Elliott N. and Molly (Weiss) D.; m. Linda Sue Gibson, July 14, 1973; children: Monica, Rachael, Michelle. BA with high distinction, high hons. in econ., U. Mich., 1972; PhD in Econs., U. Calif., Berkeley, 1976. Asst. prof. econs. U. Md., College Park, 1976-79; sr. economist U.S. Dept. Energy, Washington, 1978-79, Nat. Telecommunications and Info. Adminstrn., Dept. Commerce, Washington, 1979-80; sr. v.p., dir. Nat. Econ. Rsch. Assocs., Inc., L.A., 1980—; cons. in field; expert witness various U.S. cts. and regulatory agencies; lectr. in field. Editorial cons. The Am. Econ. Rev., 1977-81; contbr. articles to profl. jours. Sims Sr. Hons. scholar in econs., U. Mich., 1972; Probert scholar, U. Calif., 1972; Sloan Transp. fellow, 1975; U. Md. Faculty Rsch. awardee, 1977. Mem. ABA, Am. Econ. Assn., Phi Beta Kappa. Home: 2226 Canyonback Rd Los Angeles CA 90049-1177 Office: National Econ Rsch Assocs 555 S Flower St Ste 4100 Los Angeles CA 90071-2417

DORMAN, REX LEE, forest products executive; b. Wendell, Idaho, Jan. 13, 1934; s. Lee Roy and Leona Rose (Dillie) D.; m. Marilyn Jane Frazier, May 6, 1956; children; Donald, Michael, Diane. AA, Boise Jr. Coll., 1954; BS in Acctg./Econs., U. Idaho, 1961; postgrad., Stanford U., 1975. CPA, Idaho. Acct. Low, Viehweg, Hill and Grow, Boise, Idaho, 1961-66; supr., internal auditor Boise Cascade Corp., 1966-69, mgr. internal audit, 1969-73, asst. controller, 1973-75, controller, 1975-84, v.p. planning and control, 1984-86, v.p. control and info. services, 1986-90, sr. v.p., chief fin. officer, 1990—; bd. dirs. Boise Cascade Can., Ltd., Toronto, Ont. Mem. adv. bd. U. Idaho, Moscow, 1968—; treas. Boise Philharm. Assn., 1969-72, Boise Civic Opera, Inc., 1977-80; chmn. Associated Taxpayers Idaho, Boise, 1982. Lt. (j.g.) USN, 1954-58. Mem. AICPA (internal control com. 1978-79), Idaho Soc. CPAs (pres. 1976-77), Am. Paper Inst., Fin. Acctg. Standards Bd. (task force 1979-86, cert. internal auditor 1962—). Republican. Clubs: Arid (Boise), Crane Creek Country. Office: Boise Cascade Corp 1 Jefferson Sq Boise ID 83728-0001

DORN, EDWARD MERTON, poet, educator; b. Villa Grove, Ill., Apr. 2, 1929. Student, U. Ill., Black Mountain Coll. Vis. prof. Am. lit., Fulbright lectr. U. Essex, 1965-68; vis. poet U. Kans., 1968-69; mem. faculty Idaho State U., Northeastern Ill. U., U. Colo., 1977—; sr. editor Rolling Stock mag., Boulder, Colo., 1981—. Author: What I See in the Maximus Poems, 1960, The Newly Fallen: Poems, 1961, Hands Up!, 1964, From Gloucester Out, 1964, (with M. Rumaker and W. Tallman) Prose I, 1964, The Rites of Passage: A Brief History, 1965, rev. edit. as By the Sound, 1971, Idaho Out, 1965, Geography, 1965, The Shoshoneans: The People of the Basin-Plateau, 1966, North Atlantic Turbine, 1967, Gunslinger Book I, 1968, Gunslinger Book II, 1969, Twenty Four Love Songs, 1969, The Midwest is That Space Between the Buffalo Statler and the Lawrence Eldridge, 1969, The Cosmology of Finding Your Spot, 1969, Songs: Set Two, A Short Count, 1970, Spectrum Breakdown: A Microbook, 1971, A Poem Called Alexander Hamilton, 1971, The Cycle, 1971, Some Business Recently Transacted in the White World, 1971, The Hamadryas Baboon at the Lincoln Park Zoo, 1972, Gunslinger Book II: The Winterbook Prologue to the Great Book IV Kornerstone, 1972, Recollections of Gran Apacheria, 1973, Gunslinger, Books I, II, III, IV, 1975, Collected Poems of Edward Dorn, 1975, 1984, Hello, La Jolla, 1978, Views, Interviews, 1978, Selected Poems, 1978, Yellow Lola, 1981, Captain Jack's Chaps, 1983, Abhorrences, 1990; By the Sound, 1991, Way West, 1993, The Denver Landing, 1994; translator Image of the New World, 1979, (with G. Brotherston) Tree Between the Two Walls, 1969, Our World: Guerilla Poems from Latin America, 1968, Selected Poems by Vallejo, 1976, (with Jennifer Dunbar) Manchester Square, 1975. Nat. Endowment for Arts grantee, 1966, 68; D.H. Lawrence fellow, 1969. Office: U Colo Campus Box 226 Boulder CO 80309*

DORN, JAMES MARTIN, police sergeant; b. Poughkeepsie, N.Y., May 30, 1961; s. William Henry Sr. and Anne E. Elizabeth (Mooney) D.; m. Irene Nemec, Sept. 17, 1983; children: Cristina Elizabeth, Katherine Marie. AAS, Albuquerque Tech. Vocat. Inst., 1990; BA in Polit. Sci., U. N.Mex., 1992, MPA, 1995. Police officer Albuquerque Pub. Sch. Police Dept., 1982-83, police sgt., 1985—; police officer Rio Rancho (N.Mex.) Police Dept., 1983-85; mem. bd. dirs. So. Sandoval County Arroyo Flood Control Authority, 1995—. Mem., vice chair Rio Rancho Parks and Recreation Commn., 1993—; bd. dirs. Southern Sandoval County Arroyo Flood Control Authority, 1995—. Donald C. Rider Meml. scholar N.Mex. Mcpl. League, 1993, 94; U.S. Army ROTC scholar, 1979. Mem. Nat. Assn. Sch. Safety and Law Enforcement Officers. Republican. Roman Catholic. Office: Albuquerque Pub Schs PO Box 25704 Albuquerque NM 87125-0704

DORN, MARIAN MARGARET, educator, sports management administrator; b. North Chicago, Ill., Sept. 25, 1931; d. John and Marian (Petkovsek) Jelovsek; m. Eugene G. Dorn, Aug. 2, 1952 (div. 1975); 1 child, Bradford Jay. B.S., U. Ill., 1953; M.S., U. So. Calif., 1961. Tchr., North Chicago Community High Sch., 1954-56; tchr., advisor activities, high sch., Pico-Rivera, Calif., 1956-62; tchr., coach Calif. High Sch., Whittier, 1962-65; prof. phys. edn., chmn. dept., coach, asst. chmn. div. women's athletic dir. Cypress (Calif.) Coll., 1966—; men's, women's golf coach; mgr. Billie Jean King Tennis Ctr., Long Beach, Calif., 1982-86; founder King-Dorn Golf Schs., Long Beach, 1984; pres. So. Calif. Athletic Conf., 1981; curriculum cons. Calif. Dept. Edn., 1989-92. Recipient cert. of merit Cypress Elem. Sch. Dist., 1976; Outstanding Service award Cypress Coll., 1986. Mem. Calif. (v.p. So. dist.), San Gabriel Valley (pres.) assns. health, phys. edn. and recreation, So. Calif. Community Coll. Athletic Council (sec., dir. pub. relations), NEA, Calif. Tchrs. Assn., AAHPERD, Ladies Profl. Golf Assn. Republican. Conglist. Author: Bowling Manual, 1974. Office: 9200 Valley View St Cypress CA 90630-5805

DORN, ROOSEVELT F., judge; b. Checotah, Okla., Oct. 29, 1935; s. William M. and Nettie (Brinkley) D.; m. Joyce Evelyn Glosson, July 10, 1965; children: Bryan Keith, Renee Felicia, Rochelle Francine. JD, Whittier Coll., 1969. Bar: Calif. 1970. Dep. sheriff L.A. County, Calif., 1961-69; asst. city atty. L.A. City Atty.'s Office, 1970-79; mcpl. ct. judge Inglewood (Calif.) Jud. Dist., 1979-80; superior ct. judge Los Angeles County and State of Calif., L.A., 1980—. Founder Project Hope, Multi-Orgn. to Fight Truancy, Inglewood, 1983—, RDM Scholarship Fund, Inglewood, 1983; pres., bd. dirs. 100 Black Men, Inc., L.A., 1983-93; mem., bible tchr., local elder 1st AME Meth. Ch., L.A., mem. man-child mentoring program; past chmn. bd. L.A. Community Sports and Arts Found. for At Risk Youth. With USAF, 1954-58. Recipient Nat. Top Ladies of Distinction Humanitarian award, 1984, Meritorious Svc. Youth award Inglewood Tchrs. Assn., 1985, Outstanding Community Svc. award Harmony Missionary Bapt. Ch., 1985, Pub. Svc. award Probation Dept. City of Inglewood, 1987, Christ's Caring Presence award L.A. Baptist Mission Soc., 1988, Spl. Vol. award Young Black Scholars, 1988, Outstanding Svc. to Edn. and Welfare of Youth award Prairie View A&M U. Alumni Assn., 1989, Spl. Svc. award Martin Luther King Com., Inglewood, 1989, Profl. Svc. award People Who Care Ctr., Inc., 1990, Cert. of Spl. Congl. Recognition Congressman Julian Dixon, 1990, Cert. of Commendation Mayor of L.A., 1990, Letter of Commendation Pres. Bush and Gov. Deukmejian for being recipient of L.A. Area Boy Scouts of Am. Centinela Dist. Good Scout award, numerous others. Mem. ABA, NAACP (Legacy award 1995), Nat. Bar Assn., L.A. County Bar Assn., L.A. Trial Lawyers Assn., Calif. Dist. Attys. Assn., Calif. Judges Assn., Calif. Black Lawyers and Judges Assn., John M. Langston Bar Assn. (judges' divsn.), Young Black Scholars (bd. dirs.), Masons (33d degree Prince Hall, Disting. Svc. award 1995). Office: Superior Ct Dept 240 110 Regent St Inglewood CA 90301-9999

DORNAN, ROBERT KENNETH, congressman; b. N.Y.C., Apr. 3, 1933; s. Harry Joseph and Gertrude Consuelo (McFadden) D.; m. Sallie Hansen, Apr. 16, 1955; children: Robin Marie, Robert Kenneth II, Theresa Ann, Mark Douglas, Kathleen Regina. Student, Loyola U., Westchester, Calif., 1950-53. Nat. spokesman Citizens for Decency Through Law, 1973-76;

mem. 95th-97th Congresses from 27th Calif. dist., 1977-83, 99th-103rd Congresses from 38th (now 46th) Calif. dist., 1985—; vice chmn. Ho. Rep. Study Commn. 99th-102d Congresses from 38th Calif. dist., 1989-91; mem. 103d Congress from 46th Calif. dist.; chmn. Nat. Sec. Subcom. on Military Personnel, chmn. Tech. and Tactical Intelligence. Host TV polit. talk shows in Los Angeles, 1965-73; host, producer: Robert K. Dornan Show, Los Angeles, 1970-73; combat photographer/broadcast journalist assigned 8 times to Laos-Cambodia-Vietnam, 1965-74; originator POW/MIA bracelet. Served to capt. as fighter pilot USAF, 1953-58, as fighter pilot, amphibian rescue pilot and intelligence officer USAFR, 1958-75. Mem. Am. Legion, Navy League, Air Force Assn., Res. Officers Assn., AMVETA, Assn. Former Intelligence Officers, Am. Helicopter Soc., AFTRA. Republican. Roman Catholic. Lodge: K.C. Office: 1201 Longworth Washington DC 20515-0564

DORNBLASER, DAVID W., marketing professional; b. La Mesa, Calif., Sept. 22, 1958; s. Stanley P. and Ellen M. (Fredrickson) D. BS, Harvey Mudd Coll., 1980; MBA, Fla. Atlantic U., 1986. Flight test engr. Boeing, Seattle, 1980-84; sales rep. AMD, Dallas, 1984-87; regional sales mgr. NCR, Dallas, 1987-90; sr. mgr. tech. devel. SGS-Thomson, San Jose, Calif., 1990-93; dir. mktg. Integrated Circuit Systems, San Jose, Calif., 1993-95; v.p. mktg. and sales Ark Logic, 1995—. Mem. Video Electronics Standards Assn., San Jose, 1980—, Am. Electronics Assn. Office: Integrated Circuit Systems 1271 Parkmoor Ave San Jose CA 95126-3448

DORNEMAN, ROBERT WAYNE, manufacturing engineer; b. Oaklawn, Ill., Nov. 13, 1949; s. Robert John and Julia (Vorchenia) D.; M. Katrina Holland, July 30, 1977; children: Tamara, Tiana. BA in Biol. Sci., Calif. State U., Fullerton, 1974. Mfg. engr. Gen. Telephone Co., Anaheim, Calif., 1974-77, Xerox/Century Data, Anaheim, 1977-80; advance mfg. engr. MSI Data, Costa Mesa, Calif., 1980-83; sr. mfg. engr. Parker Hannifin, Irvine, Calif., 1983-86; sr. advanced mfr. engr. Western Digital, Irvine, 1986-89, mgr. advanced mfg. engring., 1989-91; mfg. engr. Pairgain Tech., Cerritos, Calif., 1991-93, mgr. mfg. engring., 1993-94; mgr. engring. svcs. Pairgain Tech., Tustino, Calif., 1994—; specialist automated assembly of circuits; cons. Base 2, Fullerton, 1980; developer surface mount tech. for computer mfg. industry; set up computer assemble plants internat. Devel. and implimented environ. safe mfg. process for computer bd. industry; contbr. articles in 3M-Alert to profl. jours. Mem. Nat. Assn. Realtors (broker), N. Orange County Bd. Realtors (broker), Calif. Assn. Realtors, Internat. Platform Assn., Internat. Soc. Hybrid Mfg., Phillips Ranch Assn., Tau Kappa Epsilon. Republican. Home: 21 Fair Elms Laguna Niguel CA 92677-5908 Office: Pairgain Tech 14402 Franklin Ave Tustin CA 92680-7013

DORNETTE, RALPH MEREDITH, church organization executive, educator, minister; b. Cin., Aug. 31, 1927; s. Paul A. and Lillian (Bauer) D.; m. Betty Jean Pierce, May 11, 1948; 1 child, Cynthia Anne Dornette Orndorff. AB, Cin. Bible Coll., 1948; DD, Pacific Christian Coll., 1994. Ordained to ministry Christian Ch., 1947. Min. Indian Creek Christian Ch., Cynthiana, Ky., 1946-51; assoc. prof. Cin. Bible Coll., 1948-51; sr. min. First Christian Ch., Muskogee, Okla., 1951-57; founding min. Bellaire Christian Ch., Tulsa, 1957-59; exec. dir. So. Calif. Evangelistic Assn., Torrance, Calif., 1959-62, 68-77; sr. min. Eastside Christian Ch., Fullerton, Calif., 1962-68; dir. devel., prof. ministries Cin. Bible Coll. & Sem., 1977-79; exec. dir. Ch. Devel. Fund, Inc., Fullerton, 1968-77, CEO, 1979-94; sr. preaching minister 1st Christian Ch., Downey, Calif., 1971, 91; preaching minister Hemet (Calif.) Valley Christian Ch., 1992—; pres. So. Calif. Christian Mins. Assn., Fullerton, 1975. Author: Bible Answers to Popular Questions, 1954, Walking With Our Wonderful Lord, 1955, Bible Answers to Popular Questions II, 1964. Pres. Homeowners Assn., Anaheim, Calif., 1980-81. Named Churchman of Yr. Pacific Christian Coll., Fullerton, 1973; recipient Disting. Alumni award Cin. Bible Coll. and Seminary, 1994. Mem. N.Am. Christian Conv. (conv. com. Cin. chpt. 1963, chair nat. registration 1963, v.p. 1972, exec. com. 1963, 70-72, 80-82).

DORNHELM, MARILYN CELIA, computer consultant, owner; b. Bklyn., Dec. 20, 1945; d. Jacob and Ella Landau; m. Richard Baruch Dornhelm, Dec. 31, 1969; children: Rachel, Ethan. BS in Math., SUNY, Binghamton, N.Y., 1966. Trainee, programmer AT&T, N.Y.C., 1966-67; programmer, systems analyst Fireman's Fund, San Francisco, 1967-69, ZIM, Haifa, Israel, 1970-72, UCLA, 1973-75; computer cons. self-employed Eureka, Calif., 1984-85; owner Dornhelm Consulting, Walnut Creek, Calif., 1986—. Bd. dirs. Temple Beth El, Eureka, 1980-84, Hebrew sch. prin., 1978-84; exec. bd. mem. B'nai Shalom Sisterhood, Walnut Creek, 1987—; steering com. mem. San Francisco Youth Orch., 1980-92; bd. dirs. Friends of the Oakland (Calif.) Youth Orch., 1988-89. Mem. Assn. Database Developers. Office: Dornhelm Consultants 975 Tumwater Ct Walnut Creek CA 94598-4441

DORRELL, TORRIE ANN, recording industry executive; b. Van Nuys, Calif., Mar. 17, 1960; d. Donald Evans and Patricia Jane (McNulty) D.; m. Eric Andrew Junker, Sept. 30, 1989. BA in Journalism with honors, Pepperdine U., 1982. Asst. to publ. JM Enterprises Pub., Santa Barbara, Calif., 1982-84; assoc. editor Santa Barbara News & Rev., 1984-86, City Sports Mag., Marina del Rey, Calif., 1986-88; sr. editor publ. UCLA Med. Ctr., Westwood, 1988-90; mgr. live artist series Walt Disney Records, Burbank, Calif., 1990-94; dir. kid rhino entertainment Rhino Entertainment, Inc., Burbank, Calif., 1994—; speaker, panelist Childrens Music Seminar, N.Y.C., 1992—. Editor: Brindlefish, 1993—. Cmty. vol. Doing Something, L.A., 1994—; team leader AIDS Walk L.A., 1994. Recipient Gold Record award Recording Industry Am., 1991-92; named Best Paddler of Yr. Marina del Rey Outrigger Canoe Club, 1991. Mem. Children's Entertainment Assn., Am. Acad. Childrens Entertainment, Women in Music. Office: Rhino Entertainment 10635 Santa Monica Blvd Los Angeles CA 90025-4900

DORRENBACHER, CARL JAMES, aerospace transportation executive; b. Mishawaka, Ind., Jan. 6, 1928; s. Carl and Carla Valborg (Carlsen) D.; m. Beverly Bushnell, Feb. 3, 1949 (div. Aug. 1991); children: Steffany Joan Dorrenbacher-Prall, John Mark, Jan Ann, Randi Lynn, Teri Lea Koger; m. Judith Ann Reith, Aug. 31, 1991; stepchildren: Sarah Ann Hahn, Mark Edward Hahn, Timothy Carl Hahn. BSEE, Purdue U., 1949, PhD in Engring., 1989; MSEE, U. Ill., 1950. Teaching asst. U. Ill., Urbana, Ill., 1949-50; field group engr. Douglas Aircraft Co., White Sands, N.Mex., 1950-53, design group engr., 1953-58, design selection chief, 1958-60, chief design engr., 1960-61, chief engr. space systems, 1961-62, dir. manned spacecraft programs, 1962-65, v.p. advanced systems and tech., 1965-68; v.p. advanced systems and tech. McDonnell Douglas Astronautics, Huntington Beach, Calif., 1968-73, v.p. product devel., 1973-75, v.p. engring., 1975-78; v.p. Monrovia McDonnell Douglas Astronautics, Monrovia, Calif., 1978-79; v.p. gen. mgr. McDonnell Douglas Astronautics, Huntington Beach, Calif., 1979-81, exec. v.p., 1987-88; pres. McDonnell Douglas Space Systems Co., Huntington Beach, Calif., 1988-90; corp. v.p. McDonnell Douglas Corp., Huntington Beach, Calif., 1981-87; sr. v.p. group exec. McDonnell Douglas Corp., Long Beach, Calif., 1990—. Author technical papers and reports on space station and aerospace electronics. Campaign chmn. Discovery Sci. Ctr. Space and Flight Pavilion, Santa Ana, Calif., 1991—; restructuring chmn. L.A. Ednl. Partnership, 1991—. Named Engr. of Yr. Orange County Engring. Coun., Huntington Beach, 1990. Fellow AIAA; mem. Nat. Space Club (bd. govs. pres.). Office: McDonnell Douglas Corp 4060 N Lakewood Blvd Long Beach CA 90808-1700

DORWARD, DAVID WILLIAM, microbiologist, consultant; b. Columbus, Ohio, June 5, 1956; s. Donald Lyle and Helen Ruth (Birkett) D.; m. Margaret Lynn Brockhaus, Apr. 23, 1983 (div. Sept. 1987); 1 child, Lori Marie Dorward. BS in Botany, Miami U., Oxford, Ohio, 1979; MS in Botany, Miami U., 1981; PhD in Microbiology, U. Mont., 1987. Instr. Botany dept. U. Mont., Missoula, 1985, 88; instr. Microbiology dept. U. Mont., 1987; staff fellow NIH Rocky Mt. Labs., Hamilton, Mont., 1988-92; sr. staff fellow NIH Rocky Mt. Labs., Hamilton, 1992—; owner Infectious Disease Consulting, Hamilton, 1991—. Contbr. articles, editorials, rsch. proceedings to profl. jours. Patentee in field. Vol. Nat. Ski Patrol, Missoula, 1981-85. Recipient Sigma Xi rsch. grant Miami U., 1980, Bertha Morton scholarship U. Mont., 1987. Mem. AAAS, Am. Soc. for Microbiology, Microscopy Soc. Am. Home: PO Box 1623 Hamilton MT 59840-1623 Office: NIH Rocky Mt Labs 903 S 4th St Hamilton MT 59840-2932

DORY, GERRY R. "RUDY", food products executive; b. Oakland, Calif., Nov. 25, 1946; s. Habert Loren and Ida Helen (Ballenger) D.; m. Deborah G. Yaw, Feb. 21, 1986; children: Gary, Lauren. Asst. mgr. Albertsons, Eugene/Salem, Oreg., 1968-70; store mgr. Nameless Market, Salem, 1970-74; gen. mgr., ptnr. Oreg. Grocery Stores, Bend and Eugene, Oreg., 1974-91; pres., owner Rudy's Markets, Inc., Bend, 1991—. With USN, 1964-67. Named an Outstanding Ind. Operator, Progressive Grocers, IGA Internat. Retailer of the Yr., Chgo., 1994. Mem. Nat. Carrousel Assn., Classic Thunderbird Club, Oreg. Food Industries (bd. dirs. 1985-88). Home: 704 NW Harmon Blvd Bend OR 97701-2413 Office: Rudys Markets Inc 1121 NW Newport Ave Bend OR 97701-1619

DOSCHER, RICHARD JOHN, police captain, division commander; b. Livermore, Calif., Aug. 31, 1952; s. Henry John and Violet Mary (Sutton) D.; m. Kathryn Laura Vierria, May 5, 1979; children: Cameron, Shannon. AS in Adminstrn. Justice, Yuba C.C., Maryville, Calif., 1987; BPA, U. San Francisco, 1991, MPA, 1993. From police officer to sgt. Yuba City (Calif.) Police Dept., 1977-85, sgt., watch commander, 1985-86, lt., divsn. commdr., 1986-89, lt., divsn. cmmdr. tech. svcs. and support, 1989-91, capt., divsn. cmmdr. field ops, 2d in command agy., 1991-93, capt., divsn. cmmdr. investigation, 2d in commd. agy.; many ancillary positions within the Yuba Police Orgn. including valedictorian in Police Basic Acad., dignitary protection coord., project mgr. city-wide safety com. chmn. Bd. dirs. Yuba/Sutter Easter Seal Soc., 1988—; vol. Calif. Prune Festival, 1988—, Spl. Olympics, 1987—, Bok Kai Chinese Cultural Festival, 1993—, Yuba City Cmty. Theater, 1992—; adv. com. Adminstrn. of Justice Yuba Coll., 1993—; eucharistic min. St. Isidore's Cath. Ch., 1984—. With USAF, 1972-76. Mem. Calif. Peace Offiers Assn., Peace Officers' Rsch. Assn. of Calif., Yuba City Police Officers Assn. (past officer 1978-80), Am. Soc. for Pub. Adminstrn., Calif. Assn. Police Tng. Officers, Kiwanis Club (bd. dirs., 2d v.p. Yuba City), Yuba City Health and Racquet Club. Office: Yuba City Police Dept 1545 Poole Blvd Yuba City CA 95993-2615

DOSS, JAMES DANIEL, electrical engineer, writer; b. Reading, Pa., Mar. 9, 1939. BS in Maths., Ky. Wesleyan Coll., 1964; MSEE, U. N.Mex., Albuquerque, 1969. Mem. staff Los Alamos (N.Mex.) Nat. Lab., 1964—; adj. instr. in radiology and surgery U. N.Mex. Sch. of Medicine. Author: Engineer's Guide to High Temperature Superconductivity, 1989, (novel) The Shaman Sings, 1993; contbr. numerous articles to profl. jours. Mem. Mystery Writers Am. Episcopalian. Office: Los Alamos Nat Lab NIS-8 # B230 Los Alamos NM 87545

DOSSETT, LAWRENCE SHERMAN, professional services company official; b. Santa Ana, Calif., May 11, 1936; s. Wheeler Sherman and Eunice Elizabeth (Bright) D.; student U. Ariz., 1957-58, U. Calif., Irvine, 1973-75, Loyola Marymount Coll., 1974; m. Joanne Kallisch; children: Todd Sherman, Garrick Robert (dec.), Dana Shelene, Ryan William. Engring. draftsman Hughes Aircraft Co., Tucson, 1955-57, John J. Foster Mfg. Co., Costa Mesa, Calif., 1958, Standard Elec. Products, Costa Mesa, 1959; engring. mgr. Electronic Engring. Co., Santa Ana, 1959-79; product quality mgr. Farwest Data Systems, Irvine, Calif., 1979-82; dist. mgr. profl. svcs., nat. cons. mgr., sr. industry cons. Comserv/MSA/DBSoftware, 1982-92, sr. manufacturing industry cons., 1992-93; mfg. cons. Marcam Corp., 1993-94; sr. industry cons. Cincom Sys., 1994—. Mem. Western Electronic Mfrs. Assn., Am. Prodn. and Inventory Control Soc., Computer Mfrs. Conf., Cert. in mgmt. Am. Mgmt. Assn. Author: MRPXXI Asset/Liability Management System, 1993; co-author patent reel spindle, 1972.

DOSTOURIAN, DICK, computer systems executive; b. L.A., Oct. 30, 1948; s. John and Elizabeth (Cholakian) D.; m. Jeanette Adrienne Torigian; children: Leslie Ann, Christopher Scott. AA in Engring., East L.A. Coll., 1968; BS in Math., Calif. State U., L.A., 1970, MS in Math., 1972. Computer engr. McDonnell Douglas, L.A., 1973-76, prin. computing specialist, 1976-80, sect. mgr. engring. sys., 1980-83, mgr. product definition sys., 1983-89, mgr. info. tech., 1989-94; sr. mgr. software devel. Keane, Inc., L.A., 1994—. Mem. St. James Armenian Ch., L.A., 1989-94. Mem. IEEE, Assn. for Computing Machinery, Nat. Computer Graphics Soc., Data Processing Mgmt. Assn., Calif. State U. Alumni Assn. Home: 10781 Via Jacara Stanton CA 90680-1926 Office: Keane Inc 6701 Center Dr Ste 400 Los Angeles CA 90067

DOTO, IRENE LOUISE, statistician; b. Wilmington, Del., May 7, 1922; d. Antonio and Teresa (Tabasso) D. BA, U. Pa., 1943; MA, Temple U., 1948, Columbia U., 1954. Engring. asst. RCA-Victor, 1943-44; research asst. U. Pa., 1944; actuarial clk. Penn Mut. Life Ins. Co., 1944-46; instr. math. Temple U., 1946-53; commd. lt. sgt. health services officer USPHS, 1954, advanced through grades to capt., 1963; statistician Communicable Disease Ctr., Atlanta, 1954-55, Kansas City, Kans., 1955-67; chief statis. and publ. services, ecol. investigations program Ctr. for Disease Control, Kansas City, 1967-73, chief statis. services, div. hepatitis and viral enteritis, Phoenix, 1973-83; statis. cons., 1984—; mem. adj. faculty Phoenix Ctr., Ottawa U., 1982—. Mem. Am. Statis. Assn., Biometrics Soc., Am. Pub. Health Assn., Ariz. Pub. Health Assn., Ariz. Council Engring. and Sci. Assn. (officer 1982-90, pres. 1988-89), Primate Found. Ariz. (mem. animal care and use com. 1986—), Bus. and Profl. Women's Club Phoenix, The Retired Officers Assn. (state sec., treas.), 1995—, Sigma Xi, Pi Mu Epsilon. Office: PO Box 22197 Phoenix AZ 85028-0197

DOTSON, GERALD RICHARD, biology educator; b. Brownsville, Tex., Sept. 8, 1937; s. Jasper William and Mary Agnes (Courtney) D.; m. Rose Delores Gonzales; children: Roberta, Anna. BS, Coll. Santa Fe (N.Mex.), 1960; MS, U. Miss., 1966; PhD, U. Colo., 1974; postgrad., U. Tex., Loyola U. New Orleans, El Paso, 1960-61, Loyola U., New Orleans, 1962-63. Sci. tchr. Cathedral High Sch., El Paso, Tex., 1959-61; sci./math./music tchr. St. Paul's High Sch., Covington, La., 1961-62; sci./math./Spanish tchr. Christian Bros. Sch., New Orleans, 1962-63; sci. tchr., chmn. Hanson High Sch., Franklin, La., 1963-67; biology instr. Coll. Santa Fe (N.Mex.), 1967-69, U. Colo., Boulder, 1969-70, Community Coll. Denver, 1970-77; prof. biology and chmn. sci. Front Range Community Coll., Westminster, Colo., 1977—; mem. com. for teaching excellence FRCC in Westminster, 1988—, mem. curriculum devel. com., 1980—, mem. acad. standards com., 1980—. Reviewer biology text books, 1970—; contbr. articles to profl. jours. Mem. recreation dept. City of Westminster, 1971—. Avocations: fishing, hunting, camping, golf, bowling, walking, fly tying. Mem. Am. Microscopical Soc., Am. Soc. Limnology and Oceanography, Nat. Assn. Biology Tchrs., Nat. Sci. Tchrs. Assn. (regional sec. 1985), Human Anatomy and Physiology Soc., Eagles, KC (3rd and 4th deg.), Elks, Sigma Xi, Phi Sigma. Roman Catholic. Home: 8469 Otis Dr Arvada CO 80003-1241 Office: Front Range Community Coll 3645 W 112th Ave Westminster CO 80030-2105

DOTSON, KEVIN D., minister; b. Oakland, Calif., Oct. 18, 1956; s. Bernerd and Oneda (Kosack) D.; m. Dareathia Brothers, May 15, 1976; children: Brenda, Dwayne. Attended, Dallas Christian Coll., Eastern N.Mex. State U. Ordained to Gospel Ministry, 1986. Supr. beef packing plants Hereford and Amarillo, Tex.; parts mgr. Clovis, N.Mex.; pastor/tchr. Community Bapt. Ch., San Antonio, N.Mex.; pastor Washington Ave. Bapt. Ch., Roswell, N.Mex., Calvary Bapt. Ch., Raton, N.Mex. Recipient Enchantment award N.Mex. Women's Missionary Union, 1991. Office: 2401 N Main Clovis NM 88101

DOTY, EVERETT, food products executive; b. 1929. With Inland Fruit & Produce Co., Wapato, Wash., 1964—, v.p., 1992—. Office: Inland Fruit & Produce Co Frontage Rd Wapato WA 98951*

DOTY, HORACE JAY, JR., theater administrator, arts consultant; b. St. Petersburg, Fla., May 25, 1924; s. Horace Herndon and Mabel (Bruce) D.; student Sherwood Music Sch., Chgo., 1942-43; BA in Music, Pomona Coll., 1950; cert. La Verne Coll., 1969; MA in Edn., Claremont Grad. Sch., 1972; cert. in Bus. Adminstrn., 1984; m. Wanda L. Flory, Dec. 27, 1947; 1 child, Janet. Propr. Jay Doty's Inc., Claremont, 1960-68; concert mgr. Claremont Colls., 1968-73, supr. Garrison Theater, U. Ctr. Box Office, dir. Auditorium, theater events, coordinator programs, 1973-79, 81-90; exec. dir. Flint Ctr. for Performing Arts, Cupertino, Calif., 1979-81. Mem. blue ribbon com. Fox Theater Restoration, Pomona, Calif., 1982; mem. Claremont Bicentennial Com. for Performing Arts, 1975-76; mem. touring adv. panel, cons. and site visitor Calif. Arts Council; mem. exec. bd., Calif. Presenters. Served with inf. AUS, 1943-46. NEA fellow, 1986. Mem. Assn. Coll., Univ. and Community Arts Adminstrs. (dir. 1983-86), Western Alliance Arts Adminstrs. (pres. 1975-77), Internat. Assn. Auditorium Mgrs., Claremont C. of C. (pres. 1965-66). Office: Jay Doty Arts Cons 4145 Oak Hollow Rd Claremont CA 91711-2329

DOTY, KATHLEEN LEILANI, English and linguistics educator; b. Little Rock, Aug. 15, 1951; d. Dorothy Clay (Thornton) D.; m. Hugh Charles Jenkins, June 16, 1984. BA, Portland State U., 1973; MA, U. Wash., 1979, PhD, 1984. Grad. tchg. asst. U. Wash., Seattle, 1978-83; asst. prof. U. Wis., Whitewater, 1986-89, Humboldt State U., Arcata, Calif., 1989-93; assoc. prof. Humboldt State U., Arcata, 1993—; advisor grad. student newsletter Humboldt State U., Arcata, 1991-94, dir. composition, 1993-95. Contbr. essays and articles to profl. publs. Fulbright fellow William J. Fulbright Commn., U.S. Info. Agy., U. Turku, Finland, 1995. Mem. MLA (exec. com. gen. linguistics group 1987-91), Internat. Pragmatics Assn., Nat. Coun. Tchrs. English, Linguistic Soc. Am. Office: Humboldt State Univ Dept English Arcata CA 95521

DOUBLEDEE, DEANNA GAIL, software engineer, consultant; b. Akron, Ohio, July 29, 1958; d. John Wesley and Elizabeth (Nellis) Doubledee; m. Philip Henry Simons, Jan. 1, 1986. BSc in Computer Sci., Ohio State U., 1981; MSc in Software Engring., Nat. U., Inglewood, Calif., 1988. Cons. Ohio State U., Columbus, 1980-81; engr. Ocean Systems div. Gould, Inc., Cleve., 1981-82, Aircraft div. Northrop Corp., Hawthorne, Calif., 1982-83; tech. staff SEDD, TRW, Inc., Redondo Beach, Calif., 1983-85; staff engr. MEAD, TRW, Inc., Redondo Beach, Calif., 1985-88, subproject mgr., 1988-89; project engr. SDD, TRW, Inc., Redondo Beach, Calif., 1989-91; CEO, pres. Innovatice Concepts Continuum, Redondo Beach, Calif., 1993—; dir. software engring. TWI Engring., Inglewood, Calif., 1991-92; cons. Microcosm, Inc., Torrance, Calif., 1990-91; sr. computer scientist IIT Rsch. Inst., 1993-94; cons. JAPA Sys. Engring.; judge state sci. fair Ohio Acad. Sci., Columbus, 1988; active Orange County Venture forum, 1992, MIT Enterprise forum, Chgo., 1992-93. Chmn. bd. dirs. Fedn. of Presch. and Community Edn. Svcs. (Headstart), Carson, Calif., 1988-90, bd. dirs. 1990-91. Recipient award for outstanding vol. svc. Fedn. of Presch. and Community Edn. Ctrs., 1987; Exemplar Ohio Acad. Sci., 1987, 89, 90. Mem. IEEE, ACM, IEEE Computer Soc., Soc. Women Engrs. (awards chair 1987), Am. Astron. Soc.

DOUDNA, MARTIN KIRK, English language educator; b. Louisville, June 4, 1930; s. Arthur Bundy and Ruth Edson (Dewey) D.; m. Dorothy Jane Williams, Sept. 15, 1962; children: Jennifer Anne, Ellen Ruth, Sarah Corinne. AB in English, Oberlin (Ohio) Coll., 1952; postgrad., Princeton (N.J.) U., 1952-53; MA in English, U. Louisville, 1959; PhD in Am. Culture, U. Mich., 1971. Writer USAF, Washington, 1959-66; asst. prof. English Mackinac Island (Mich.) Coll., 1966-69; assoc. prof. English U. Hawaii, Hilo, 1971-78, prof. English, 1978—; sec. Hawaii Com. for the Humanities, Honolulu, 1986-88. Author: Concerned About the Planet, 1977; editor: Greene, Transcendentalism (1849), 1981; author: (play) Have You Any Room for Us?, 1975; contbr. articles to profl. jours. With U.S. Army, 1953-55. Rackham fellow U. Mich., 1970; Nat. Endowment for the Humanities, 1976, 83, 88. Mem. Modern Lang. Assn., Thoreau Soc., Phi Beta Kappa. Home: 181 S Wilder Rd Hilo HI 96720-1443 Office: U Hawaii Hilo HI 96720-4091

DOUGHERTY, BETSEY OLENICK, architect; b. Guanatamo Bay, Cuba, Oct. 25, 1950; (parents Am. citizens); d. Everett and Charlotte (Kristal) Olenick; m. Brian Paul Dougherty, Aug. 25, 1974; children: Gray Brenner, Megan Victoria. AB in Architecture, U. Calif., Berkeley, 1972, MArch, 1975. Registered architect, Calif.; cert. Nat. Coun. Archtl. Registration Bds. Designer, drafter Maxwell Starkman, L.A., 1972-73, HO & K, San Francisco, 1975-76; job capt. Wm. Blurock & Ptnrs., Newport Beach, Calif., 1976-78; assoc. architect U. Calif., Irvine, 1978-79; architect Dougherty & Dougherty, Newport Beach, 1979—. Mem. Newport Beach Specific Area Plan Com., 1985, Career Edn. Adv. Com., Newport Beach, 1986; leader Boy Scout Am., Girl Scouts U.S.A. Recipient Gold Nugget grand award Pacific Coast Builders Conf., 1989, Coalition for Adequate Sch. Housing award of excellence, 1992, 94, Calif. Masonry award, 1992, So. Calif. Edison award of excellence, 1994. Fellow AIA (pres. Orange County chpt. 1984, Calif. chpt. 1988, nat. bd. dirs. 1989-91, nat. sec. 1993-95, design awards Orange County chpt. 1981-86, 89-90). Office: Dougherty & Dougherty 3 Civic Plz Ste 230 Newport Beach CA 92660-5923

DOUGHERTY, CHARLENE, legislative staff member; b. Great Falls, Mont., Nov. 13, 1941; d. Arthur Holland and Marjorie (Rustad) Weinland; married Alfred F. Dougherty Jr., Feb. 8, 1964 (div. 1979). BA in Polit. Sci., George Washington U., 1963, MA in Polit. Sci., 1970. Program officer Office of Emergency Preparedness now FEMA, Washington, 1970-73; dir. comm. Environ. Defense Fund., Washington, 1974-76, legis. dir., 1977-79; asst. Washington rep. Tenn. Valley Authority, Washington, 1979-80; dir. environ. liaison divsn. Dept. Energy, Washington, 1980-81; dir. legis. Nat. Audubon Soc., Washington, 1981-87; profl. staff Nat. Resources Com., U.S. Ho. Representatives, Washington, 1987—. Recipient Conservation award Chevron, 1987. Home: 760 Northstar Ct Boulder CO 80304 Office: 1328 Longworth House Office Bldg Washington DC 20515

DOUGHERTY, DENNIS A., chemistry educator; b. Harrisburg, Pa., Dec. 4, 1952; s. John E. and Colleen (Canning) D.; m. Ellen M. Donnelly, June 3, 1973; children: Meghan, Kayla. BS, MS, Bucknell U., 1974; PhD, Princeton U., 1978. Postdoctoral fellow Yale U., New Haven, 1978-79; asst. prof. Calif. Inst. Tech., Pasadena, 1979-85, assoc. prof. chemistry, 1985-89, prof., 1989—. Contbr. articles to sci. jours. Recipient ICI Pharms. award for excellence in chemistry, 1991, Arthur C. Cope Scholar award, 1992; Alfred P. Sloan Found. fellow, 1983; Camille and Henry Dreyfus Tchr. scholar, 1984. Fellow AAAS; mem. Am. Chem. Soc., Phi Beta Kappa. Home: 1817 Bushnell Ave South Pasadena CA 91030-4905 Office: Calif Inst Tech Div Chemistry & Chem Engring Calif Inst Tech # 164-30 Pasadena CA 91125

DOUGHERTY, MICHAEL, writer, filmmaker; b. Hammond, Ind., Dec. 28, 1924; s. Edward Daniel and Mary Estelle (Race) D.; divorced; 1 child, Race. BS, U. So. Calif., 1950. From press agt. to dir. spl. projects CBS TV, 1950-60; motion picture producer in South and S.E. Asia U.S. Fgn. Svc., Pakistan and India, 1960-62; electronic media cons. U.S. Dept. State, Washington, 1967; freelance writer, ind. documentary film producer, 1963—. Author: To Steal A Kingdom, 1994; writer or dir. (films) Colette, A Bridge to Space, Building the New Hawaii, others; scriptwriter No Free Lunch, Cross Roads, No Best Culture, Our Children's Children, The Big Island, Da Kine Sandbox, Rivers of Fire, others. Served with USMC, 1942-45, PTO. Hawaii State Found. of Culture and Arts grantee, 1978. Home: 41-020 Alaihi St Waimanalo HI 96795-1601

DOUGHERTY, MICHAEL JOSEPH, oil company executive; b. Olympia, Wash., May 17, 1949; s. Joseph John and Thelma Christine (Holthusen) D.; m. Paula Marie Fournier, June 26, 1971; children: Ronald C., Brian A., Jennifer A. BS in Chemistry, Oreg. State U., 1971; MS in Environ. Sci., Calif. State U., Fullerton, 1977; postgrad., Harvard U., 1989. Rsch. chemist Union Oil, Brea, Calif., 1971-77; coord. environ. control Union Oil, L.A., 1977-80, mgr. environ. control, 1980-86; mgr. state govt. rels. Unocal, L.A., 1986—. Chmn. petroleum com. Air Pollution Control Assn., Pitts., 1978-81; chmn. air pollution rsch. adv. com. Coord. Rsch. Coun., Atlanta, 1985-86; leader Boy Scouts Am., Placentia, Calif., 1989—; mem. Orange (Calif.) Diocese Cath. Com. on Scouting. 1990—. Mem. Am. Petroleum Inst., Western States Petroleum Assn. Republican. Roman Catholic. Home: 668 Highlander Ave Placentia CA 92670-3229 Office: Unocal 1201 W 5th St Los Angeles CA 90017-1461

DOUGHERTY, (MARY) PATRICIA, history educator; b. Monterey, Calif., Dec. 7, 1944; d. John Francis Dougherty and Clotilde (Quarelli) Hoefle. BA, Dominican Coll., 1967; MA, Georgetown U., 1979, PhD, 1984. Tchr. grades 4-8, 1967-77; teaching asst. dept. history Georgetown U., Washington, 1978-81, 82-83; chmn. dept. history Dominican Coll., San Rafael, Calif., 1984—. Contbr. articles and revs. to profl. jours. Fulbright fellow, Paris, 1981-82, Georgetown U. fellow, Washington, 1978-81, 82-83. Mem. Am. Hist. Assn., Am. Cath. Hist. Assn., Soc. French Hist. Studies. Office: Dominican Coll 50 Acacia Ave San Rafael CA 94901-2230

DOUGHERTY, RAE ANN, semiconductor manufacturing company executive; b. Palo Alto, Calif., Feb. 26, 1955; d. Russell A. and Ilse D. (Dittman) E.; m. Richard Edward Dougherty, Aug. 24, 1979. BS in Environ. Sci., Rutgers U., 1977; MS in Engring., Colo. State U., 1979; MBA in Engring. Mgmt., U. Dallas, 1993. Rsch. asst. Colo. State U., Ft. Collins, 1977; meteorologist NOAA, Environ. Rsch. Lab., Boulder, Colo., 1979; project engr. TRC Environ. Cons., Denver, 1979-81; conservation engr. to dir. safety, health, environ. svcs. Arco Oil and Gas Co., Dallas, 1981-93; worldwide mgr. environ., health and safety Intel Corp., Rio Rancho, N. Mex., 1993—. Contbr. articles to profl. jours. Active Girl Scouts U.S.A., 1973—, bd. dirs. Tejas coun. 1992-94, Chapparell coun., 1994—, World Assn. Girl Guides and Girl Scouts Com., 1994—. Recipient Tejas Continuing Svcs. award Tejas Girl Scout Coun., Inc., 1989, Green Angel award, 1988. Mem. Soc. Petroleum Engrs., Soc. Women Engrs., Am. Meteorol. Soc. (sec. 1979-81, Howard H. Hanks Jr. award 1979), Bus. and Profl. Womans Club (1st v.p. 1989-92), Leadership Tex., DAR (treas. 1988), Zonta (Amelia Earhart fellow 1977-79). Home: 10405 Prestwick NE Albuquerque NM 87111-6554 Office: Intel Corp 4100 Sara Rd SE # F954 Tr Rio Rancho NM 87124-1025

DOUGHERTY, RALEIGH GORDON, manufacturer's representative; b. Saginaw, Mich., Aug. 19, 1928; s. Raleigh Gordon and Helen Jean (McCrum) D.; 1 child, Karen Kealani. Salesman, H.D. Hudson Mfg. Co., Chgo., 1946-48; field sales rep. Jensen Mfg. Co., Chgo., 1948-50; field sales mgr. Regency Idea, Indpls., 1950-54; mgr. Brenna & Browne, Honolulu, 1954-56; owner, pres. Dougherty Enterprises, Honolulu, 1956—. With U.S. Army, 1950-52. Mem. Hawaii Hotel Assn., Internat. Home Furnishings Reps. Assn., Air Force Assn., D.A.V. (life), Am. Soc. Interior Designers (industry found.), Navy League U.S., Am. Legion, Hawaii Restaurant Assn., Nat. Fedn. Ind. Bus., Korean Vet. Small Bus. of Hawaii, Historic Hawaii Found., Hawaii Visitors Bur., Elks (past trustee Hawaii), Kani Ka Pila Golf Club. Republican. Methodist. Home and Office: 1326 Lunalilo Home Rd Honolulu HI 96825

DOUGHTY, JOHN ROBERT, mechanical engineer, college president; b. Clarksburg, W.Va., July 30, 1936; s. Merrill Newton and Margaret Clara (Watson) D.; m. Betty Jeanette Smith, June 5, 1970; children: Donna, Marc, John, Denise, James, Dawn. BSME, U. N.Mex., 1958; PhD, U. Ariz., 1971. Registered profl. engr., Calif., N.Mex. Commd. 2d lt. USAF, 1958, advanced through grades to lt. col., 1975; sect. head Air Force Weapons Lab., Kirtland AFB, N.Mex., 1970-75; div. chief Air Force Space Div., L.A. Air Force Sta., 1975-79; ret., 1979; mem. tech. staff Gen. Rsch. Corp., El Segundo, Calif., 1979-80; sect. head space and tech. group TRW, Redondo Beach, Calif., 1980-85; vis. lectr., researcher Ben Gurion U., Beersheva, Israel, 1985-86; cons. engr. Doughty Rsch. Engring., Huntington Beach, Calif., 1986-88, Albuquerque, 1988-94; adj. prof. Embry-Riddle Aero. U., Kirtland AFB Ext., 1990-94. Contbr. articles to profl. jours. Mem. exec. com. Am. Assocs. Ben Gurion U., Orange County, Calif., 1984-88; sec. Christian Missionary Pilots, Newport Beach, Calif., 1983-85; v.p. Albuquerque Bible Coll., 1989-91, pres., 1991—; sec.-treas. Creation Sci. Fellowship N.Mex., Albuquerque, 1990—; pilot N.Mex. Wing, CAP, 1991—. Mem. AIAA, ASME. Republican. Home and Office: 532 Calle De Los Hijos NW Albuquerque NM 87114-2039

DOUGLAS, DIANE MIRIAM, museum director; b. Harrisburg, Pa., Mar. 25, 1957; d. David C. and Anna (Barron) D.; m. Steve I. Perlmutter, Jan. 23, 1983; 1 child, David Simon. BA, Brown U., 1979; MA, U. Del., 1982. Oral history editor Former Members of Congress, Washington, 1979-80; assoc. curator exhibitions John Michael Kohler Arts Ctr., Sheboygan, Wis., 1982-83; dir. arts ctr. Lill Street Gallery, Chgo., 1984-88; exec. dir. David Adler Cultural Ctr., Libertyville, Ill., 1988-91; dir., chief curator Bellevue (Wash.) Art Mus., 1992—; program chair, exec. bd. nat. Coun. for Edn. in Ceramic Arts, Bandon, Oreg., 1990-93; nat. adv. bd. Friends of Fiber Art, 1992; artists adv. com. Pilchuck Glass Sch., 1993—; mem. bd. dirs. Archie Bray Found., Helena, Mont., 1995—. Bd. dirs. Archie Bray Found., Helena, Mont., 1995. Office: Bellevue Art Mus 301 Bellevue Sq Bellevue WA 98004-5000

DOUGLAS, DONALD WILLS, JR., energy executive; b. Washington, July 3, 1917; s. Donald Wills and Charlotte Marguerita (Ogg) D.; m. Molly McIntosh, May 1, 1939 (dec.); children: Victoria Thoreson, Holly Douglas Adams; m. Jean Cooper, Aug. 17, 1950 (dec.); m. Linda Alstead, Nov. 16, 1986. Student, Stanford U., 1934-38, Curtiss-Wright Tech. Inst., Glendale, Calif., 1939. With engring. Douglas Aircraft Co., 1939-43, dir. testing divsn., 1943-51, dir. contract adminstrn., 1948-51, dir. rsch. labs., 1949-51, v.p., 1951-57, pres., 1957-67, also bd. dirs.; corp. v.p. adminstrn. McDonnell Douglas Corp., 1967-71, corp. sr. v.p. adminstrn., 1971-72, pres. Douglas Devel. Corp., 1972-74; sr. ptnr. Ptnrs. Real Estate, Inc., 1978-80; pres. Douglas Energy Co., Placentia, Calif., 1981-86, chmn., CEO, 1986—; Chmn. Group IX Aerospace Systems, 1984—; chmn. Douglas Internat. Group, 1989—; mem. Nat. Export Expansion Coun., U.S. Dept. Commerce, 1964-73, exec. com., 1965-73, com. econ. devel., 1970-73, coun. fgn. rels., 1970-73; sr. cons. McDonnell Douglas Corp., 1974-75; bus. cons., 1974—; sr. cons. market devel. Biphase Energy Systems, joint venture Rsch.-Cottrell and Transamerica Delaval, 1981-82, Biphase Energy Systems, subs. Transamerica Delaval, 1982-86; chmn., CEO DCOR Ptnrs., Inc., 1979-80; dir., chmn. bd. Aerotech Cons., Inc., 1982-84; dir. Reno Airline. Mem. Pres. Com. on Youth Fitness, 1958-59; coun. v.p. fin. Boy Scouts Am., 1981-86, chmn. adv. com. Gt. Western Coun., 1978-80, hon. pres., 1968, bd. mem. St. Louis area coun., 1970-72; hon. pres. Crescent Bay Coun., 1967, pres., 1955-67, mem.-at-large nat. coun., 1951—; chmn. trustees Donald Douglas Mus. & Libr., 1975-89, Mus. of Flying, 1989—. Recipient Officiale of Order of Merit Republic of Italy, 1962, Chevalier, French Legion of Honor award, 1961, Silver Antelope award Boy Scouts Am., western region, 1983. Assoc. fellow AIAA; mem. Aerospace Industries Assn. (chmn. bd. govs. 1964), Air Force Assn., Air Force Mus. Assn., Assn. U.S. Army (adv. bd. 1966-67), Conquistadores del Cielo (pres. 1965-66, chmn. bd. 1966-67, sports chmn. 1965—, sec.-treas. 1971—), Nat. Def. Transp. Assn. (life, nat. v.p. 1958-63, gen. chmn. 22nd Forum La. 1967), Naval Aviation Mus. Assn., Inc. (dir. 1971—), Navy League U.S. (life), Transpacific Yacht Club, L.A. Yacht Club, Rancheros Visitadores, Phi Gamma Delta. Home: Skycrest Farm 38851 Avenida La Cresta Murrieta CA 92562 Office: Douglas Energy Co 181 W Orangethorpe Ave Ste D Placentia CA 92870-6931

DOUGLAS, EVERETT LAWRENCE, physicist, environmental engineer; b. St. Louis, May 24, 1939; s. Curtis Albert and Alice Rose (Elsie) D. BA in Zoology, U. Mo., 1961; PhD in Marine Biology/Animal Physiology, U. Calif. San Diego, 1967. Prof. U. Mo., Columbia, 1967-73; sr. postdoctoral assoc. Case We. Res. U., Cleve., 1974-75; physicist U.S. Navy, San Diego, 1977—; br. head Aircraft Environ. Support Office, USN, San Diego, 1991—. Contbr. articles to profl. jours. Lectr. on preservation of wilderness areas San Diego City Schs., 1965—. Recipient Antarctica Svc. medal U.S. Govt., 1965-74; Sverdrup fellow Scripps Instn. Oceanography, 1962-67. Mem. Soc. Aerospace Engrs. (vice chair E-31 com.), Phi Beta Kappa, Sigma Xi. Home: 4310 Piedmont Dr San Diego CA 92107-4135

DOUGLAS, LEE WAYLAND, association executive; b. Spokane, Wash., Dec. 9, 1931; s. Theodore Wayland and Lee Paynter (Bohan) D.; m. Patricia Murphy; 1 child, Elizabeth Lee Douglas Bell; m. Simone Carlier. AB, Harvard U., 1953. U.S. govt. messenger Hoof & Mouth Disease Commn., Mexico City, 1948-49; gen. mgr. Cromo y Terminados, S.A., Mexico City, 1956-57; exec. v.p. Chem. Linings de Mexico, Mexico City, 1957-59; gen. mgr. The Dorsey Co., Mathews, La., 1972-73; sys./program analyst U.S. Dept. Energy, Washington, 1973-82; recorder gen. Naval Order of the U.S., Washington, 1983—. Author: The Log of Naval Reserve Association, 1984, revised, 1995. Past nat. historian Naval Res. Assn., 1979-93. Lt. comdr. USN, 1953-56, 60-71, Korea, Vietnam. Recipient Nat. award of merit Naval Res. Assn., 1976, 79. Mem. Harvard Club San Diego. Democrat. Episcopal. Home: 5251 Glasgow Dr San Diego CA 92117-1037

DOUGLAS, MARION JOAN, labor negotiator; b. Jersey City, May 29, 1940; d. Walter Stanley and Sophie Frances (Zysk) Binaski; children: Jane Dee, Alex Jay. BA, Mich. State U., 1962; MSW, Sacramento State Coll., 1971; MPA, Calif. State U.-Sacramento, 1981. Owner, mgr. Linkletter-Totten Dance Studios, Sacramento, 1962-68, Young World of Discovery, Sacramento, 1965-68; welfare worker Sacramento County, 1964-67, welfare supr., 1968-72, child welfare supr., 1972-75, sr. personnel analyst, 1976-78, personnel program mgr., 1978-81, labor relations rep., 1981-89; cons. State Dept. Health, Sacramento, 1975-76; cons. in field. Author/editor: (newsletter) Thursday's Child, 1972-74. Presiding officer Community Resource Orgn., Fair Oaks, Calif., 1970-72; exec. bd. Foster Parent's Assn., Sacramento, 1972-75; organizer Foster Care Sch. Dist. liaison programs, 1973-75; active Am. Lung Assn., 1983-87, 93-94; rep. Calif. Welfare Dirs. Assn., 1975-76; county staff advisor Joint Powers Authority, Sacramento, 1978-81; mem. Mgmt. Devel. Com., Sacramento, 1979-80; vol., auctioneer sta. KVIE Pub. TV, Sacramento, 1970-84, 88-90; adv. bd. Job and Info. Resource Ctr., 1976-77; spl. adv. task force coordinator Sacramento Employment and Tng. Adv. Council, 1980-81; vol. leader Am. Lung Assn., Sacramento, 1983-86, 94—, Calif. Dept. Social Welfare ednl. stipend, 1967-68, County of Sacramento ednl. stipend, 1969-70. Recipient Achievement award Nat. Assn. Counties, 1981. Mem. Mgmt. Women's Forum, Indsl. Relations Assn. No. Calif., Indsl. Relations Research Assn., Nat. Assn. Female Execs., Mensa. Republican. Avocations: real estate, nutrition. Home: 7812 Palmyra Dr Fair Oaks CA 95628-3423

DOUGLAS, STEPHEN, publishing company executive; b. Glendale, Calif., Apr. 20, 1954. Founder, pres. Redheads Internat., Corona del Mar, Calif., 1981—; exec. dir., prodr. USA Petites, Prodns., Inc. Author: The Redhead Dynasty, 1986. Democrat. Office: 537 Newport Center Dr Newport Beach CA 92660-6937 also: Redheads Internat PO Box 2000 Corona Del Mar CA 92625-0020

DOUGLASS, AMY ANITA, museum director; b. Rio de Janeiro, Feb. 9, 1955; d. Ralph Julius and Juanita Ruth (Walls) D.; m. Bradley Nelson Lichtenstein, July 17, 1993. BA, Wellesley (Mass.) Coll., 1976; MA, Syracuse (N.Y.) U., 1980; PhD, Ariz. State U., 1987. Curatorial asst. Mus. of the Am. Indian, Heye Found., N.Y.C., 1976-78; crew chief archaeology Ariz. State U., Tempe, 1983, U. N.Mex., Albuquerque, 1983-84; exhibit coord. Ariz. State U., Tempe, 1987; pub. liaison Northland Rsch. Inc., Tempe, 1987; mus. dir. Tempe Hist. Mus., Tempe, 1988—. Author: Prehistoric Exchange and Sociopolitical Development, 1991. Mem. Soc. for Am. Archaeology, Ariz. Archaeol. Coun., Mus. Assn. of Ariz. (meeting co-chair), Ctrl. Ariz. Mus. Assn., Phi Kappa Phi, Phi Beta Kappa.

DOUGLASS, CRAIG BRUCE, computer technology executive; b. Santa Monica, Calif., July 3, 1956; s. W. Bruce and Frances A. (Ellingwood) D. AB, Dartmouth Coll., 1978; MBA, U. Chgo., 1980. Sr. bus. devel. analyst Bell & Howell Co., Chgo., 1980-82, product mgr., 1982-83, sr. product mgr., 1983, mgr. product and market devel., 1983-86; v.p. product and market devel. Bell & Howell Co., Torrance, Calif., 1986-89, Bell & Howell Quintar Co., 1989-94; v.p. mktg. & product devel. Quintar Co., Torrance, Calif., 1994—. Inventor digital film recording. Mem. Nat. Computer Graphics Assn. (pres. Ill. chpt. 1985-86, v.p. Los Angeles Orange County chpt. 1986—, nat. com. 1986—). Club: Dartmouth (Chgo.) (v.p. 1984-85), Los Angeles (bd. dirs. 1986-95 pres. 1993-95). Office: Quintar Co 370 Amapola Ave Ste 106 Torrance CA 90501-1475

DOUGLASS, DONALD ROBERT, banker; b. Evanston, Ill., Oct. 7, 1934; s. Robert William and Dorothy (Gibson) D.; m. Susan Douglass. BBA, U. N.Mex., 1959, MBA, 1966. With Security Pacific Nat. Bank, Los Angeles, 1961—, mgmt. trainee, 1962-63, asst. mgr. Vernon (Calif.) br., 1963-64, asst. mgr. Whittier (Calif.), 1964, asst. v.p., 1965, asst. v.p., credit officer regional adminstrn., Los Angeles, 1966-69, v.p., San Francisco, 1969-74, mgr. corp. accounts credit adminstrn. No. Calif. Corp. Banking, 1974-77; group v.p. Annco Properties, Burlingame, Calif., 1977-79; v.p., sr. loan officer Borel Bank and Trust Co., San Mateo, Calif., 1979-83, sr. v.p., 1983-84, exec. v.p. mortgage banking div. comml. property sales, Los Altos, 1984-87 ; ptnr. Key Equities, Inc., San Mateo, 1987—; ptnr., broker Centre Fin. Group, Inc., San Mateo, 1987—, Centre Fin. Group South Inc., Menlo Park, 1987—; instr. Am. Inst. Banking, 1963, Coll. San Mateo, 1982—. Served with AUS, 1954-56. Mem. U. N.Mex. Alumni Assn., Sigma Alpha Epsilon, Delta Sigma Phi. Republican. Presbyterian. Home: 745 Celestial Ln San Mateo CA 94404-2771

DOUGLASS, ENID HART, educational program director; b. L.A., Oct. 23, 1926; d. Frank Roland and Enid Yandell (Lewis) Hart; m. Malcolm P. Douglass, Aug. 28, 1948; children: Malcolm Paul Jr., John Aubrey, Susan Enid. BA, Pomona Coll., 1948; MA, Claremont (Calif.) Grad. Sch., 1959. Research asst. World Book Ency., Palo Alto, Calif., 1953-54; exec. sec., asst. dir. oral history program Claremont Grad. Sch., 1963-71, dir. oral history program, 1971—, history lectr., 1977—; mem. Calif. Heritage Preservation Commn., 1977-85, chmn. 1983-85. Contbr. articles to hist. jours. Mayor pro tem City of Claremont, 1980-82, mayor, 1982-86; mem. planning and rsch. adv. coun. State of Calif.; mem. city coun. City of Claremont, 1978-86; founder Claremont Heritage, Inc., 1977-80, bd. dirs., 1986-95; bd. dirs. Pilgrim Pla., Claremont; founder, steering com., founding bd. Claremont Cmty. Found., 1989—, pres., 1990-94. Mem. Oral History Assn. (pres. 1979-80), Southwest Oral History Assn. (founding steering com. 1981, J.V. Mink award 1984), Nat. Council Pub. History, LWV (bd. dirs. 1957-59, Outstanding Svc. to Community award, 1986). Democrat. Home: 1195 N Berkeley Ave Claremont CA 91711-3842 Office: Claremont Grad Sch Oral History Program 710 N College Ave Claremont CA 91711-5530

DOUGLASS, JOHN MICHAEL, internist; b. Takoma Park, Md., Apr. 13, 1939; s. Jones All and Helen Louise D.; BA, Columbia Union Coll., Takoma Park, 1959; MD (Salutatorian), U. So. Calif., 1964; DPH Pacific West U., 1986; PhD Clayton U., 1987. m. Sue Nan Peters, May 15, 1962; children: Dina Lynn, Lisa Michele. Rotating intern Los Angeles County, U. So. Calif. Med. Ctr., 1964-65, resident internal medicine, 1965-67, home care physician, 1965-68; practice medicine specializing in internal medicine, Cin., 1968-70, L.A., 1970-91; physician Pasadena Emergency Ctr., 1965-68, Deaconess Hosp., 1968-70; postdoctoral fellow automobile safety and trauma rsch. UCLA, 1967-68, med. cons. Emergency Med. Svcs. Project, 1970-71; commd. officer USPHS, 1968, advanced through grades to comdr., sr. surgeon USPHS Res. 1982—, asst. sci. adviser injury control program ECA, Cin., 1968-69, med. specialities cons. Office Product Safety, FDA, 1969-70; internal medicine cons. East End Neighborhood Community Health Ctr. Cin., 1968-70, Hollywood Sunset Free Clinic, 1971-72; sr. med. cons. multidisciplinary hwy. accident investigation unit U. So. Calif., 1971-73; staff internist, coordinator health improvement service Kaiser Found. Hosp., L.A., 1970-92; instr. biomedical engring. course UCLA, 1968, sr. med. cons., assoc. sci. advisors, 1970—, instr. internal medicine, 1971-74; instr. internal medicine U. Cin. Sch. Medicine, 1968-70; instr. kinesthesiology, traumatic anatomy and head injury U. So. Calif., 1971-74, instr. foodstyle and lifestyle, 1977—; mem. med. adv. bd. Dominican Sisters of Sick Poor, 1969; traffic safety cons. Countywide Conf. on Emergency Med. Svcs., 1972; mem. nutrition council Las Virgenes Sch. Dist., 1977; coord. K-PMG Health Svc.; CFO Prepared Gormet, Inc.; engring. biomed. cons; tchr. anatomy and physiology. Active mgmt devel program Boy Scouts Am. Execs., 1966; bd. dirs. Calif. Assn. Pvt. Schs. and Colls., 1967, Coronary Club (adult jogging program), 1967-68; co-organizer Oriental rug exhibit Pacificulture Mus., Pasadena, Calif., 1973; v.p. L.A. Med. Milk Commn. Diplomate Nat. Bd. Med. Examiners, Am. Bd. Internal Medicine. Fellow ACP; mem. AMA, Am. Acad. Body Sculpting, Calif. Med. Assn., L.A. County Med. Assn., Am. Soc. Internal Medicine, Calif. Soc. Internal Medicine, L.A. Soc. Internal Medicine, Am. Assn. Automotive Medicine (exec. com. Western chpt. 1977-82), Am. Cancer Soc. (profl. edn. com., nutrition subcom.), Internat. Hajji Baba Soc., Decorative Arts Council, L.A. Mus. Art, Sierra Club, Phi Delta Epsilon, Alpha Omega Alpha, Phi Kappa Phi. Author: The Lost Language; contbr. over 100 articles to profl. jours.

DOUKE, DANIEL WAYNE, art educator, artist; b. L.A., Sept. 18, 1943; s. Edward Joseph and Geraldine Lucille (Williams) D.; m. Nadine Margret Foreman, June 18, 1979; 1 child, Samantha Suzanne Sisk. AA, Pasadena City Coll., 1965; BA, Calif. State U., L.A., 1969, MA, 1971. Prof. art Calif. State U., L.A., 1975—; guest lectr. Pitzer Coll., Claremont, Calif., 1984-91; guest artist Art Ctr. Coll. Design, Pasadena, Calif., 1986. Exhibited in group shows at L.A. County Mus. of Art, 1991; one-man shows include O.K. Harris, N.Y.C., 1993, Tortue Gallery, Santa Monica, Calif., 1994, Las Vegas Cultural Ctr., 1994. With USNR, 1966-69, Vietnam. Recipient Phelan award San Francisco Found., 1973. Home: 2481 Arabian Trl Fallbrook CA 92028-9267 Office: Calif State Univ LA 5151 State University Dr Los Angeles CA 90032-4221

DOVE, DONALD AUGUSTINE, city planner, educator; b. Waco, Tex., Aug. 7, 1930; s. Sebert Constantine and Amy Delmena (Stern) D.; m. Cecelia Mae White, Feb. 9, 1957; children: Angela Dove Gaddy, Donald, Monica, Celine, Austin, Cathlyn, Dianna, Jennifer. BA, Calif. State U.-L.A., 1951; MA in Pub. Adminstrn., U. So. Calif., 1966. Planning and devel. cons. D. Dove Assocs., L.A., 1959-60; supr. demographic rsch. Calif. Dept. Pub. Works, L.A., 1960-66, environ. coordinator, Sacramento, 1971-75; dir. transp. employment project State of Calif., L.A., 1966-71, chief Los Angeles Region transp. study, 1975-84; chief environ. planning Calif. Dept. Transp., L.A., 1972-75; dir. U. So. Calif. Praetors, L.A., 1984-87; panelist, advisor Pres. Conf. on Aging, Washington, 1970—, Internat. Conf. on Energy Use Mgmt., 1981; guest lectr. univs. western U.S., 1969—. Author: Preserving Urban Environment, 1976; Small Area Population Forecasts, 1966. Chmn. Lynwood City Planning Commn., Calif., 1982—; pres. Area Pastoral Coun., L.A., 1982-83; mem., del. Archdiocesan Pastoral Council, L.A., 1979-86, Compton Community Devel. Bd., Calif., 1967-71; pres. Neighborhood Esteem/Enrichment Techniques Inst., 1992-93. Served to cpl. U.S. Army, 1952-54. Mem. Am. Planning Assn., Am. Inst. Planners (transp. chmn. 1972-73), Calif. Assn. of Mgmt. (pres. 1987-88), Am. Inst. Cert. Planners, Assn. Environ. Profls. (co-founder 1973), Optimists (sec. 1978-79). Democrat. Roman Catholic. Home and Office: 11356 Ernestine Ave Lynwood CA 90262-3711

DOVE, MICHAEL ROGER, anthropology researcher; b. Dec. 26, 1949; m. Carol Carpenter. BA, Northwestern U., 1971, MA, Stanford U., 1972, PhD, 1981. Postdoctoral fellow, rsch. fellow Rockefeller Found., Java, 1979-83; project coord. East-West Ctr. Ford Found., Java, 1984-85; sr. project anthropologist Winrock Internat. Inst. Agr. Devel., Pakistan, 1985-89; fellow East-West Ctr., 1989-91; sr. fellow East-West Ctr., mem. grad. faculty anthropology U. Hawaii, Honolulu, 1991—; tchg. asst. Stanford U., 1972, instr., 1978; vis. prof. Gadjah Mada U., 1979-85; vis. fellow Yale U., 1991-92; cons., lectr. in field. Author: Nelayan dan Kemiskinan, 1984, Swidden Agriculture in Indonesia, 1985, The Real and Imagined Role of Culture in Development, 1988, The Sociology of Natural Resources in Pakistan, 1992; contbr. chpts. to books and articles to profl. jours. Fellow Borneo Rsch. Coun.; mem. Am. Anthropol. Assn., Am. Ethnological Soc., Assn. Asian Studies, Wash. Assn. Profl. Antrhopologists, Royal Asiatic Soc., Koninklijk Inst. voor Taal-Land en Volkenkunde, Soc. Applied Anthropology, Soc. Econ. Botany. Office: East West Ctr (ENV) 1777 East-West Rd Honolulu HI 96848

DOW, MARY ALEXIS, auditor; b. South Amboy, N.J., Feb. 19, 1949; d. Alexander and Elizabeth Anne (Reilly) Pawlowski; m. Russell Alfred Dow, June 19, 1971. BS with honors, U. R.I., 1971. CPA, Oreg. Staff acct. Deloitte & Touche, Boston, 1971-74; sr. acct. Price Waterhouse, Portland, Oreg., 1974-77, mgr., 1977-81, sr. mgr., 1981-84; CFO Copeland Lumber Yards Inc., Portland, 1984-86; ind. cons. in field, 1986-94; elected auditor Metro, Portland, 1995—; bd. dirs. Longview Fibre Co. Bd. dirs., past treas. Oreg. Mus. Sci. and Industry; past chmn. bd., mem. exec. com. Oreg. Trails chpt. N.W. Regional Blood Svcs. ARC; pres. Portland chpt. Fin. Execs. Inst. Mem. AICPA, Am. Woman's Soc. CPAs, Oreg. Soc. CPAs (bd. dirs. ednl. found.), Fin. Execs. Inst. Roman Catholic. Clubs: City (bd. govs.), Multnomah Athletic. Contbr. articles to profl. publs. Office: Office of Auditor Metro 600 NE Grand Ave Portland OR 97232-2736

DOWDLE, PATRICK DENNIS, lawyer; b. Denver, Dec. 8, 1948; s. William Robert and Helen (Schraeder) D.; m. Eleanor Pryor, Mar. 8, 1975; children: Jeffery William, Andrew Peter. BA, Cornell Coll., Mt. Vernon, Iowa, 1971; JD, Boston U., 1975. Bar: Colo. 1975, U.S. Dist. Ct. Colo. 1975, U.S. Ct. Appeals (10th cir.) 1976, U.S. Supreme Ct. 1978. Acad. dir. in Japan Sch. Internat. Tng., Putney, Vt., 1974; assoc. Decker & Miller, Denver, 1975-77; ptnr. Miller, Makkai & Dowdle, Denver, 1977—; designated counsel criminal appeals Colo. Atty. Gens. Office, Denver, 1980-81; guardian ad litem Adams County Dist. Ct., Brighton, Colo., 1980-83; affiliated counsel ACLU, Denver, 1980—. Mem. Colo. Bar Assn., Denver Bar Assn. (various coms.), Porsche Club of Am. Democrat. Home: 3254 Tabor Ct Wheat Ridge CO 80033-5367 Office: Miller Makkai & Dowdle 2325 W 72nd Ave Denver CO 80221-3101

DOWELL, DAVID RAY, library administrator; b. Trenton, Mo., Nov. 14, 1942; s. Clarence Ray and Ruth Lucille (Adams) D.; m. Arlene Grace Taylor, May 9, 1964 (div. 1983); children: Deborah Ruth, Jonathan Ray; m. Denise Jaye Christie, Aug. 19, 1983; stepchildren: David Lee Smithey, Jason Alan Smithey. BA in History, Okla. Bapt. U., 1964; AM in History, U. Ill., 1966, MLS, 1972; PhD, U. N.C., 1986. Tchr. Wilson Jr. High Sch., Tulsa, 1964-65; head library adminstrv. services Iowa State U., Ames, 1972-75; asst. univ. librarian Duke U., Durham, N.C., 1975-81; dir. libraries Ill. Inst. Tech., Chgo., 1981—; cons. County Commr.'s Library Planning Com., Durham, 1976, Gov.'s Conf. on Libraries and Info. Services, Raleigh, N.C., 1978, Biblioteca do Centro Batista, Goiania, Brazil, 1978. Contbr. articles to profl. jours. Trustee Glenwood-Lynwood Pub. Library Dist., Ill., 1985-87. Served to capt. USAF, 1967-71. Mem. ALA (chmn. profl. ethics com. 1977-78, chmn. election com. 1982-83, chmn. library personnel adv. com. 1979-80), Assn. Coll. and Research Libraries (nominating com. 1979-80), Library Adminstrn. and Mgmt. Assn. (bd. dirs. 1981-83, chmn. personnel adminstrn. sect. 1982-83, exec. com. library orgn. sect. 1979-81), Met. Chgo. Library Assembly (bd. dirs. 1981-82), Chgo. Acad. Library Council (treas. 1981—), Chgo. Library System Affiliates Council (chair 1987-88), Internat. Fedn. Library Assns. (chmn. registration com. 1984-85), Kappa Delta Pi, Phi Alpha Theta, Beta Phi Mu. Democrat. Baptist. Home: 372 N Canyon Blvd Monrovia CA 91016-2361 Office: Pasadena City College 1570 E Colorado Blvd Pasadena CA 91106-2003

DOWLIN, CHARLES EDWIN, librarian; b. Laird, Colo., June 3, 1933; s. Ross Everett and Fern May (Peterson) D.; m. May Nichol, Sept. 5, 1960; children: Patrick Edwin, Kerry Anne. BS in Bus., U. Colo., 1955, MPS, 1956; MA, U. Denver, 1963; PhD, U. Pitts., 1980. Quality control clk. Sunstrand Aviation, Denver, 1960-62; city librarian Provo (Utah) City Corp., 1963-67; head libr. devel. State Libr. of Ohio, Columbus, 1967-70; state librarian N.Mex. State Libr., Santa Fe, 1970-77; sr. rsch. scientist Applied Mgmt. Scis., Inc., Silver Spring, Md., 1978-80; dir. sch. libr. sci. Sam Houston State U., Huntsville, Tex., 1980-85; dir. Golden Libr., Ea. N.Mex. U., Portales, 1985—. Bd. dirs. N.Mex. Outdoor Drama Assn., 1989-92. With U.S. Army, 1956-59. Mem. ALA, Sci. Fiction Rsch. Assn., N.Mex. Libr. Assn. (Librarian of the Yr. 1977), N.Mex. Coun. of Acad. Libraries (bd. dirs. 1989-91), Rotarian. Presbyterian. Home: 508 E 17th Ln Portales NM 88130-9291 Office: Eastern New Mexico Univ Golden Library Station #32 Portales NM 88130

DOWLIN, JANICE MARIE, science administrator; b. Hugo, Colo., June 11, 1940; d. James W. and Helen Ann (Brandt) Simmons; m. Kenneth Everett Dowlin, Mar. 11, 1961; children: Kevin E., Kristopher E. BS in Med. Tech., U. Colo., 1962. Nat. cert. lab. dir.; lic. med. technologist, Calif.; nat. cert. Assn. Clin. Lab. Scientists, Med. Technologists, Am. Soc. Clin. Pathologists. Intern in med. tech. U. Colo., Denver, 1962; chief med. technologist Physicians-Surgeons Med. Lab., Denver, 1962-64; med. technologist Natrona County Meml. Hosp., Casper, Wyo., 1969-71; sr. biochem. technologist Meml. Hosp., Colorado Springs, Colo., 1977-82; med. technologist Nat. Health Labs., Colorado Springs, 1984-87; lab. mgr. Physicians Med. Clinic Labs., Daly City, Calif., 1987—; clin. labs. improvement amendments insp. Health Care Fin. Adminstrn. Fed. Govt., San Francisco, 1994—; mem. adv. panel Med. Lab. Observer, 1990—. Mem. Calif. Assn. Med. Lab. Tech., Clin. Lab. Mgmt. Assn. Home: 359 Melrose Ave San Francisco CA 94127 Office: PMC Labs 901 Campus Dr # 103 Daly City CA 94015

DOWLIN, KENNETH EVERETT, librarian; b. Wray, Colo., Mar. 11, 1941; s. Ross Everett and Fern Mae (Peterson) D.; m. Janice Marie Simmons, Mar. 11, 1961; children: Kevin Everett, Kristopher Everett. BA, U. Colo., 1963, MPA, 1981; MA, U. Denver, 1966. Bookmobile libr., libr. asst. Adams County Public Libr., Westminster, Colo., 1961-63; libr. asst. II Denver Pub. Libr., 1962-64; head libr. Arvada Public Libr., Colo., 1964-68; adminstrv. asst. Jefferson County Pub. Libr., Colo., 1969; dir. Natrona

County Pub. Libr., Casper, Wyo., 1969-75, Pikes Peak Regional Libr. Dist., Colorado Springs, Colo., 1975-87; city libr. San Francisco Pub. Libr., 1987—; instr. Casper Coll., 1971-73; chmn. Colo. Librs. in Coop., 1975-76, Colo. Ad-hoc Com. Networking, 1976; libr. City of San Francisco, 1987; mem. Western Interstate Commn. Higher Edn. Libr. Network Task Force; past trustee Wyo. Dept. Libr., Archives and History; mem. Libr. of Congress Commn. on Book of Future; bd. dirs. Satellite Libr. Info. Network; bd. mem. Libr. Found. of San Francisco, 1987—, Friends of the Libr., 1987—, Bay Area Book Festival, 1988-90; mem. Calif. State Libr. Task Force on Networking, 1988—, Calif. State Libr. of Tomorrow Task Force, 1995; founding mem. Greater Bay Area Libr. Coun., 1994—; vis. instr. U. Denver, 1980, 81; vis. faculty U. Calif., Berkeley, 1993; cons. in cable TV. Editorial bd. Microcomputers for Info. Mgmt., Libr. Hi Tech., Elec. Libr. Mem. adv. bd. for series on tech. WNET, N.Y.C., 1981-83; active San Francisco Mayor's com. on Juveniles in Detention; bd. dirs. Citizens Goals for Colorado Springs, 1981-85; bd. govs. Colo. Tech. Coll., 1982-85. With USMCR, 1959-65. Recipient Disting. Alumni award U. Denver Grad. Sch. for Libr. and Info. Mgmt. Mem. ALA (coun. mem. 1985-89, commn. on equality and freedom access to info. 1984-85, chmn. awards com. 1985-86, pres.'s com. on preservation 1990—, ad hoc com. on MARC licensing, chair local arrangements com. for 1992, 1989-92, pres.'s com. on preservation policy 1989-90, Hammond Inc. Libr. Award Jury 1968), ALA Libr. and Info. Tech. Assn. (long range planning com. 1981-82, pres. 1983-84, com. mem. Gaylord Awards), Mountain Plains Libr. Assn., Calif. Libr. Assn. (fin. com., coun. mem. 1989—), Colo. Libr. Assn. (pres. 1968-69), Denver Coun. Govts. (chmn. librs. com. 1966), Colo. Mcpl. League (chmn. librs. sect. 1967), Bibliog. Ctr. Rocky Mountains (pres. 1972-74), Pikes Peak Area C. of C. (chmn. cultural affairs com. 1976-77). Office: San Francisco Pub Libr Civic Ctr San Francisco CA 94102

DOWNER, SPELMAN EVANS, artist, consultant; b. Pasadena, Calif., Aug. 25, 1954; s. George Spelman Downer and Agnes (Evans) Kalb; m. Nancy Marie Dobrydnio, May 20, 1995. BA in Environ. Design, Stanford U., 1977; MA, San Francisco State U., 1982. Mem. artist Visual Arts Ctr. of Alaska, Anchorage, 1985-92; adj. faculty U. Alaska, Soldotna, 1990-94; owner Impeccable Prodns., Cooper Landing, Alaska, 1984-94, Tri-Coastal Consulting, Cooper Landing, 1994—. Works exhibited at Dru Arstark Gallery, N.Y.C., 1995, The Hudson River Mus. of Westchester, Yonkers, 1995, Fairbanks Art Assn., Alaska, 1995, Art Think Tank Gallery, N.Y.C., 1994, Pratt Mus., Homer, Alaska, 1992, U.S. Geol. Survey, Reston, Va., 1991, Visual Arts Ctr. of Alaska, Anchorage, 1989. Paintings purchased by Libr. of Congress, Washington, 1992, Nat. Pk. Svc., Bettles, Alaska, 1991, U. Alaska, Fairbanks, 1989, AAAS, Washington, 1994. Muralist Downtown Bus. Assn., Anchorage, 1989; mem. Kenai River Sport Fishing, Inc., Soldotna, 1992—. Mem. Alaska Photographic Ctr., Flusing Coun. on Culture and the Arts. Home and Office: PO Box 825 Cooper Landing AK 99572-0825

DOWNEY, DANIEL LEE, plastic surgeon; b. Sacramento, 1956. MD, U. Wash., 1983. Intern Virginia Mason Hosp., Seattle, 1983-84, surgeon, 1984-88, now plastic surgeon; plastic surgeon U. Rochester, N.Y., 1988-90. Office: Virginia Mason Hosp 1100 9th Ave X-11 Seattle WA 98101-2799*

DOWNEY, JAMES EDGAR, manufacturing executive; b. Spartanburg, S.C., Sept. 29, 1950; s. Vernon P. and Lu Vera (McGraw) D.; m. Jean Lucille Gallo, May 24, 1980; 1 child, Jeana Marie. BBA, U. Phoenix, 1987; postgrad., Golden Gate U., 1992—. Draftsman Pacific Rolling Door Co., San Lorenzo, Calif., 1970-74; prodn. mgr. Pacific Rolling Door Co., San Lorenzo, 1975-87, v.p. mfr., 1988—. Instr. ARC, Hayward, Calif., 1968-80, bd. dirs., 1983-87, vice chmn. disaster svcs., Solano County, Calif., 1980-90. With USAFR, 1970-91. Republican. Presbyterian. Office: Pacific Rolling Door Co 15900 Worthley Dr San Lorenzo CA 94580-1844

DOWNEY, MICHAEL DEAN, publicist, grantsmanship consultant; b. Sidney, Nebr., Feb. 16, 1951. AA, SUNY, Albany, 1973; BSW, U.Nev., Las Vegas, 1979; MPA, U. Nev., 1981; PhD, Columbia Pacific U., San Rafael, Calif., 1987. Instr. polit. sci. and history Western Nev. C.C., Carson City; health planner, statistician State of Nev., Carson City; social worker State of Nev., Las Vegas; health resources analyst State of Nev., Carson City. With USN, 1972-78. Mem. ASPA, NASW, Am. Statis. Assn., Nat. Assn. Health Data Orgns. (founder), Alliance for Cmty. Media. Home: 610 E Proctor St Apt 5 Carson City NV 89701-4282 Office: Carson Access TV 934 Corbett St Carson City NV 89706-3103

DOWNIE, PAMELA, psychologist; b. Chester, Calif., Dec. 1, 1954; d. William John and June (De La Mont) D. BA, Widener U., 1980; MS, Villanova U., 1985; postgrad., U. So. Calif., 1987—. Counselor, trainer Del. County C.C., Media, Pa., 1985-87; counselor, instr. New Beginnings, Media, 1984-87; tchg. asst. U. So. Calif., 1989-91, instr. practicum, 1991, psychol. intern., 1991-93; staff psychologist U. San Diego, 1994—. Mem. APA (student), NAFE, AACD, Am. Mental Health Coun. Assn., Assn. for Multicultural Counseling, Pa. Counselors Assn., Assn. for Specialists in Group Work, Assn. for Coun. Edn. and Supervision. Home: PO Box 660582 Arcadia CA 91066-0582 Office: U San Diego Student Counseling Svcs Linda Vista Ave San Diego CA 92110

DOWNING, DAVID CHARLES, minister; b. South Gate, Calif., June 24, 1938; s. Kenneth Oliver and Edna Yesobel (Casaday) D.; m. Tommye Catherine Tew, July 11, 1959 (dec. Dec. 11, 1985); children: Sheri Lynn, Teresa Kay, Carla Jeane, Michael David. BA, N.W. Christian Coll., 1961; B in Divinity, Tex. Christian U., 1966, M in Theology, 1973; DMin, San Francisco Theol. Sem., 1987. Ordained to ministry Christian Ch., 1961. Min. Marcola (Oreg.) Ch. of Christ, 1958-59; assoc. min. First Christian Ch., Lebanon, Oreg., 1960-63; min. First Christian Ch., Ranger, Tex., 1963-65, Knox City, Tex., 1966-68, Fredonia, Kans., 1968-74; min. Ctrl. Christian Ch., Huntington, Ind., 1974-77; regional min., pres. Christian Ch. Greater Kansas City, Mo., 1978-94; sr. minister Univ. Christian Ch., San Diego, 1994—; trustee Phillips Grad. Sem., Enid, Okla., 1988-94; bd. dirs. Ch. Fin. Coun., Indpls., Midwest Career Devel. Svc., Chgo.; v.p. bd. dirs. Midwest Christian Counseling Ctr., Kansas City. Author: A Contrast and Comparison of Pastoral Counseling in Rural and Urban Christian Churches, 1972, A Design for Enabling Urban Congregations to Cope with Their Fear of Displacement When Faced with Communities in Transition, 1987. Pres. Kansas City Interfaith Peace Alliance, 1980-82. Democrat. Home: 4460 Caminito Fuente San Diego CA 92116-1003 Office: Univ Christian Ch 3700 Cleveland Ave San Diego CA 92103

DOWNING, DOUGLAS ALLAN, economics educator, writer; b. Seattle, Oct. 11, 1957; s. Robert Allan and Marguerite Louise (Hayland) D.; m. Lori Rosenau, 1994. BS, Yale U., 1979, MPhil, 1982, PhD in Econs., 1987. Acting instr. Yale U., New Haven, Conn., 1981-83; asst. prof. Seattle Pacific U., 1983-91, assoc. prof., 1991—. Author: Calculus the Easy Way, 1982, Algebra the Easy Way, 1983, Trigonometry the Easy Way, 1984; co-author: Dictionary of Computer Terms, 1986, and 8 others. Mem. State Com. on Teenage Parents, Olympia, Wash., 1986-88; witness Wash. State Legis., Olympia, 1991-94; vol. legis. compaign, Wenatchee, Wash., 1992. Austin Howard grad. fellow Yale U., 1979. Mem. Am. Econ. Assn., Seattle Economist Club, Yale Assn. Western Wash. (treas. 1987—), Phi Beta Kappa. Presbyterian. Home: 18539 NE 184th St Woodinville WA 98072-8228 Office: Seattle Pacific U McKenna Hall Seattle WA 98119

DOWNING, JAMES CHRISTIE, lawyer; b. Los Angeles, Dec. 17, 1924; s. Dorman Perkins and Merle Grace (Christie) D.; m. Betty Griggs, Dec. 23, 1949; children: Colleen, James, Kimberly, Kelly, Kathleen. BS, U. Calif., 1949; LLB, U. Calif.-San Francisco, 1952. Bar: Calif. 1953, U.S. Dist. Ct. (no. dist.) Calif. 1953, U.S. Dist. Ct. (ea. dist.) Calif. 1975, U.S. Ct. Appeals (9th dir.) 1953. Assoc. Walkup, Downing, Shelby, Bastian, Melodia, Kelly & O'Reilly, and predecessors, San Francisco, 1954-59, ptnr., 1959-70, exec. v.p., 1970-84; ptnr. Downing & Downing, 1985—; lectr. Calif. Continuing Edn. of Bar Program. Served in AC, U.S. Army, 1943-45. Decorated Air medal with 5 oak leaf clusters. Fellow Am. Coll. Trial Lawyers; mem. ABA, State Bar Calif., Bar Assn. San Francisco (vice chmn. trial practice com. 1970), San Francisco Trial Lawyers Assn. (pres. 1972), Am. Bd. Trial Advs. (nat. exec. com. 1970-73, nat. sec. 1971, nat. chmn. membership 1972-73, 76-77, nat. pres. 1974, pres. San Francisco chpt. 1974, Calif. Trial Lawyer of Yr. 1978), Internat. Soc. Barristers, Internat. Acad. Trial Lawyers, Trader Brown Soc. Republican. Office: Downing & Downing PO Box 398 Middletown CA 95461-0398

DOWNS, FLORELLA MCINTYRE, civic worker, pilot; b. Selmer, Tenn., Sept. 19, 1921; d. Edward N. and Ella Pearle (Byrd) McIntyre; m. James Harold Downs, May 27, 1946; children: Linda Downs Ulner, William Edward, James Patrick. BA, LaVerne U., 1969. Flight instr., comml. pilot FAA, Memphis, 1945-46; pilot flight examiner CAA, 1946; owner, mgr. Basic Tutoring Svc., Ventura, Calif., 1982-86; civil air patrol pilot, 1956-57. Pres. Naval Officer's Wives, Patuxent River, Md., 1957; active charitable orgns., Md., Italy, Ventura, Calif., 1946—; vol. Children's Home Soc., Ventura and Carpenteria, Calif., 1962-70. Ferry pilot WASP, USAF, 1943-44, 1st lt. USAFR, 1952-56. Mem. AAUW (area rep. community issues VTA 1980-82), Women's Air Force Svc. Pilots, Toastmistress (pres. Ventura 1982-83). Democrat. Home: 751 Montgomery Pl Ventura CA 93004-2169

DOWNS, KATHLEEN ANNE, healthcare operations director; b. Toledo, Sept. 20, 1951; d. Keith Landis and Cecelia Josephine (Wood) Babcock; m. Michael Brian Thomas, July 17, 1971 (dec. Oct. 1973); m. David Michael Downs, Aug. 8, 1981. Student, San Diego Mesa Coll., 1968-70; BS, Union Inst., 1989. Cert. med. staff coordinator. Sec. Travelodge Internat., Inc., El Cajon, Calif., 1970-73; intermediate stenographer City of El Cajon, 1973-77; adminstrv. asst. MacLellan & Assocs., El Cajon, 1977-78; sr. sec. WESTEC Services, Inc., San Diego, 1978; adminstrv. sec. El Cajon Valley Hosp., 1978-80; asst. med. staff Grossmont Dist. Hosp., La Mesa, Calif., 1980-83, coordinator med. staff, 1983-87, mgr., 1987-94; mgr. med. staff Sharp Meml. Hosp., San Diego, 1994; dir. med. staff svcs. Sharp HealthCare, San Diego, 1994—; tchr. The Vogel Inst., San Diego, 1986; mem. med. staff svcs. adv. com. San Diego Community Dist.; adj. faculty Union Inst., 1991—, Chemeketa Community Coll., 1991—. Mem. Nat. Assn. Med. Staff Svcs. (edn. coun. 1989-93, chmn. 1991-93, mem. editl. bd. Over View 1993—, lectr., speaker), Calif. Assn. Med. Staff Svcs. (treas. San Diego chpt. 1984-86, pres. 1986-87). Office: Sharp Healthcare Crowder Grove 7901 Frost St San Diego CA 92123-2701

DOWNS, KATHLEEN JOAN, purchasing supervisor; b. Chgo., Aug. 16, 1950; d. Joseph C. and Joan Ida (Godfrey) D.; div.; 1 child, Marsha Leigh Hill. BBA, Nat. U., 1987, MBA in Fin., 1989. Buyer Rush-Presbyn. St. Luke's Med. Ctr., Chgo., 1972-74, Loyola U. Med. Ctr., Maywood, Ill., 1979-85; adminstrv. asst. U. Calif. San Diego Med. Ctr., 1986-91; purchasing supr. San Diego C.C. Dist., 1991—. Bd. dirs. Loyola U. Employees' Fed. Credit Union, Maywood, 1983-85. Mem. Parents Without Ptnrs. (1st v.p. San Diego chpt. 1989, pres. 1990), San Diego Writers/Editors Guild (mem. bd.). Unitarian. Office: San Diego CC Dist 3375 Camino Del Rio S San Diego CA 92108-3807

DOWNS, KEITH DAVID, county official; b. Hollywood, Calif., June 25, 1944; s. Vern and Ella (Davidson) D.; m. Linda Lou Dilday, Aug. 22, 1981; 1 son, Erik. B.A., Calif. State U.-Los Angeles, 1967; postgrad. U. Calif.-Riverside, 1975; M.A., Calif. State U.-San Diego, 1977. Intern planner Port Authority, San Diego, 1972; planner II, Riverside County, Calif., 1973-74; assoc. planner Planning Dept., Riverside, Calif., 1974-79, supervising planner, 1979-81, dep. dir., 1981-89, asst. dir., 1990-92, interim dir., 1992, aviation dir., 1994; project mgr. Joint Environ. Document Wind Energy, Riverside, 1981-82; county project mgr. Habitat Conservation Plan, Coachella Valley, Calif., 1983-86. Bd. dirs., officer Riverside County Employees Credit Union, 1978—, chmn. 1986-88. Served with U.S. Army, 1967-69. Decorated Bronze Star. Mem. Am. Assn. Geography, Am. Planning Assn. (dir.). Republican. Office: Riverside County Planning Dept Box 1409 4080 Lemon St 9th Fl Riverside CA 92502-1409

DOWNS, WILLIAM FREDRICK, geochemist; b. Santa Maria, Calif., Aug. 4, 1942; s. William Nielson and Lotus (Mankins) D.; m. Karen Mona Farnsworth, July 15, 1967; 1 child, William Ross. BA, U. Colo., 1965, MS, 1974; PhD, Pa. State U., 1977. Registered geologist, Calif., Idaho. Reseach assoc. Pa. State U., University Park, Pa., 1974-77; scientist Idaho Nat. Engring. Lab., Idaho Falls, Idaho, 1977-88; geochemist Jacobs Engring. Group, Albuquerque, 1988-92; sr. assoc. Hart Crowser Inc., Seattle, 1992-94; sr. geochemist Jacobs Engring. Group, Denver, 1994—; adj. prof. U. Idaho, Idaho Falls, 1979-90, Idaho State U., Idaho Falls, 1984-90. Mem. tech. adv. bd. N.Mex. Waste Edn. & Rsch. Consortium; mem. dept. adv. bd. dept. geoscis. U. Colo., 1991—. Lt. USNR, 1966-69, Vietnam. Mem. Geochem. Soc., Geol. Soc. Am., Civitan (pres. Idaho Falls chpt. 1986-87), Am. Legion (commander Idaho Falls 1980-81). Home: 15415 E Dorado Ave Aurora CO 80015-4247

DOXEY, GORDON EARL, physical therapist; b. Ogden, Utah, July 5, 1954; s. George Rhodes and R'Lene (Paul) D.; m. Nina Droubay, July 8, 1977; children: Rebecca, Rachael, Lindsay. BS in Zoology, Weber State U., 1973; BS in Phys. Therapy, U. Utah, 1981, MS in Exercise Physiology, 1986. Lic. phys. therapist, Utah. Staff phys. therapist St. Benedict's Hosp., Ogden, Utah, 1981-86; indsl. phys. therapist McKay Dee Hosp., Ogden, Utah, 1986-87; asst. mgr. phys. therapy St. Benedict's Hosp., Ogden, Utah, 1988-90, mgr. phys. therapy, 1990-91, mgr. rehab. svcs., 1991-94, instr. quality mgmt., 1993-94; mgr. rehab. svcs. Ogden Regional Med. Ctr., 1994—; exercise cons. Weber State U. Ogden, 1983-86; pres. Utah chpt. Allied Arthritis Health Profls., Salt Lake City, 1985; health cons. Newgate Mall Walkers Club, Ogden, 1981-92; team mem. Holy Cross Rehab. Svcs. Line Quality and Strategic Planning Teams, 1993-94. Contbr. articles to profl. jours. Instr. adult Sunday sch. LDS Ch., Clinton, Utah, 1981-87, pres. elders quorum, Roy, Utah, 1992-93, bishop Roy 20th ward, 1994, vol. missionary in Eng., 1973-75; leader Boy Scouts Am., 1994. Mem. Am. Phys. Therapy Assn. LDS. Office: Ogden Regional Med Ctr 5475 S 500 E Ogden UT 84405-6978

DOYEL, DAVID ELMOND, archaeologist, museum director; b. Lindsay, Calif., Aug. 24, 1946; s. Lester Levi Doyel and Jewell Mae (Hill) Burney; m. Sharon S. Debowski, Apr. 23, 1983. BA, Calif. State U., Chico, 1969, secondary teaching credential, 1971, MA, 1972; PhD, U. Ariz., 1977. Archaeologist Ariz. State Mus., Tucson, 1972-79; dir. Archaeology and Mus. Div., Window Rock, Ariz., 1979-82; mgr. Soil Systems, Inc., Phoenix, 1982-83; dir. Pueblo Grande Mus., City of Phoenix, 1984-89; cons. Estrella Cultural Rsch., Phoenix, 1990—; dir., cons. rsch. projects for govt. agys., Indian tribes, others. Contbr. articles to profl. publs. Bd. dirs. San Juan County Mus., Farmington, N.Mex., 1993. Named Outstanding Supr., Navajo Nation, Window Rock, 1980. Mem. Soc. Am. Archaeology, Ariz. Archaeol. and Hist. Soc. (exec. coun. 1976), Mus. Assn. Ariz., Planetary Soc., Ariz. Archaeol. Coun. (pres. 1982), Sigma Xi. Office: PO Box 60474 Phoenix AZ 85082-0474

DOYLE, ALFREDA CARROL, publisher, writer; b. Houston, Feb. 1, 1953; d. Spencer A. and Ruby L. (Tatum) D. Pres., founder Update Publicare Co., Denver, 1982—; pres., CEO Story Time Stories That Rhyme, Denver, 1989—. Author: Fish Convention, 1994, (newsletter) Stories That Rhyme Every Time Kids Pages, 1992, (cassette tape) Story Time Stories That Rhyme, 1993. Mem. ASCD, COSMEP, Nat. Assn. for Preservation and Perpetuation of Storytelling, Assn. Booksellers for Children, Multicultural Pubs. Exch., Nat. Mid. Sch. Assn. Office: Story Time Stories That Rhyme PO Box 416 Denver CO 80201-0416

DOYLE, HARLEY JOSEPH, laboratory technician; b. Springfield, Ohio, Oct. 10, 1942; s. William Cecil and Norma Louise Doyle. Grad. high sch., Shawnee H.S., Springfield, Ohio. With Quick Mfg., Springfield, Ohio, 1963-64, Hugo Bosco, Springfield, 1964-65, Boise Cascade, Springfield, 1965-68, Robbins & Myers, Springfield, 1968-70, Wm. Bayley Co., Springfield, 1970-73, Frigidaire, Dayton, Ohio, 1973-78; sr. lab. prep. specialist Alpha Therapeutics, L.A., 1979—. With Air Nat. Guard, 1963-68. Mem. Mamie Van Doren Fan Club (pres. 1986—). Avocations: reading, collecting movie memoribilia, autographed biographies of actors and actresses. Home: 8340 Rush St Rosemead CA 91770-3617

DOYLE, MICHAEL JAMES, educational administrator, organist; b. Bell, Calif., Aug. 24, 1939; s. Joseph Edward and Irma Louise (Smith) D.; m. Mina Katherine Martensen, Feb. 8, 1964; children: Michael James II, Mary Katherine, Matthew John. BA, Whittier Coll., 1961, MEd, 1971. Tchr. El Rancho Unified Sch. Dist., Pico Rivera, Calif., 1961-79, dept. chmn., 1967-74, acting prin., 1979; tchr., asst. prin. Alta Loma (Calif.) Sch. Dist., 1979-86, summer sch. prin., 1985, prin., 1986—; organist, dir. various Luth. chs. in So. Calif., 1955-86; organist St. Paul's Luth. Ch., Pomona, Calif., 1986—; mem. Calif. State Program Rev., 1982-83; assoc. mem. Calif. Sch. Leadership Acad., Ontario, 1986—; v.p. So. Calif. Luth. Music Clinic, 1978-81. Clk. Zion Luth. Sch. Bd. Edn., Maywood, Calif., 1962-64, chmn., 1966-67; mem. Downey (Calif.) City Water Bd., 1977-78; mem. Luth. High Personnel Commn., La Verne, Calif., 1988-92. Named Outstanding Tchr. of Yr., Burke Jr. High Sch. PTA, Pico Rivera, 1973; recipient hon. svc. award Jasper Sch. PTA, Alta Loma, 1983, continuing svc. award, 1988; employee recognition award Alta Loma Sch. Dist., 1985. Mem. Assn. Calif. Sch. Adminstrs., Assn. West End Sch. Adminstrs., Calif. Tchrs. Assn., Am. Guild Organists, Downey Hist. Soc., Cucamonga Hist. Soc., Casa de Rancho (Cucamonga, Calif.), Phi Delta Kappa (pres. Mt. Baldy chpt. 1993—, found. chmn. 1991-93). Democrat. Lutheran. Home: 2085 N Palm Ave Upland CA 91784-1476 Office: Jasper Sch 6881 Jasper St Alta Loma CA 91701-4521

DOYLE, PETER THOMAS, accountant, realtor; b. Chgo., Nov. 22, 1928; s. Peter Vincent and Elizabeth Mary (Maguire) D.; m. Mary Leontina Ulrath, Jan. 17, 1953. BA in Acctg. cum laude, Claremont McKenna Coll., 1955; postgrad., UCLA, 1962-63. CPA, Calif.; realtor, Calif. Staff auditor Price Waterhouse & Co., L.A., 1955-59; asst. treas. Pardee Contrn. Co., L.A., 1959-64; treas. Provident Mortgage Corp., Pasadena, Calif., 1964-67; contr. William L. Pereira Assocs., L.A., 1967-72, Hosp. of Good Saaritan, L.A., 1972-73; contr., treas. ArchiSystems Internat., Van Nuys, Calif., 1973-79; v.p., fin., dir. McClellan/Cruz/Gaylord & Assocs., Inc., Pasadena, 1979-85; v.p., sec. dir. Doyle Properties, Inc., 1975—; dir. Brandeis Constrn., Inc., Brandeis Property and Facilities Mgmt. Co., Inc., The Bannister Group, Romaine Devel. Corp. Bd. dirs. Sunset Mesa Property Owners Assn., 1973-75; mem. Town Hall Calif. With U.S. Army, 1946-48. Mem. AICPA, Calif. Soc. CPAs, Inst. Mgmt. Accts. Republican. Home: 3430 Cloudcroft Dr Malibu CA 90265-5632 Office: 10345 W Olympic Blvd Los Angeles CA 90064-2524

DOYLE, RICHARD JAMES, photojournalist, photo software developer; b. Lynwood, Calif., Feb. 19, 1954; s. James Thomas and Marie Elizabeth (Dobb) D. BA, San Diego State U., 1981. Asst. pro Stephen McCarroll Photography, San Diego, 1980; photojournalism intern Surfer Mag., Dana Point, Calif., 1980; pub. rels. intern Pacific S.W. Airlines, San Diego, 1981; prin. Rick Doyle, Action Photography, Solana Beach, Calif., 1982—; freelance photojournalist AP, Sports Illustrated, NFL Properties, Inc., N.Y. Times, San Diego Union, San Diego Chargers, Nissan, Kodak, Chevron USA, CBS-TV, ESPN Sports, OceanPacific, Foodmaker Inc., Focus On Sports, Inc., N.Y., Black Star Inc., Chart House Inc., Leukemia Soc. Am., Surfer Mag., Action Sports Retailer, WaterSki Mag., Windsurf Mag., Outside Mag., San Diego Mag., Travel & Leisure, Sportfishing Mag., and others, 1982—. Producer, dir. Riding a New Wave, Windsurfer Internat. Corp. Inc., 1981; photographer Sonny Boy, Trans World Entertainment, 1987, Out of the Blue, McFadden Films, 1989; photo software developer (CD ROM) Ocean Imagery, 1989, Rick Doyle Digital Imagery Vol. 1, 1990, Vol. 2, 1993. Supporter Surfrider Found., 1988—. With USN, 1972-77. Mem. Nat. Press Photographers Assn. (assoc. mem.), Kodak Pro Passport. Office: Rick Doyle Digital Imagery PO Box 599 Solana Beach CA 92075-0599

DOYLE, THERESA LIPARI, real estate and marketing executive; b. Long Beach, Calif., Aug. 27, 1957; d. Joseph and Joyce Lorraine (Wagle) Lipari; m. Timothy Xavier Doyle, June 26, 1982. BA, Calif. State U., Fullerton, 1980. Fundraising asst. Am. Heart Assn., Santa Ana, Calif., 1980; account exec. Kerr & Assocs. Pub. Rels., Huntington Beach, Calif., 1980-83; dir. mktg. Covington Homes, Fullerton, Calif., 1983-86; dir. sales and mktg., Covington Homes, Orange County, Calif., 1986, v.p. sales and mktg., 1986-88; v.p. sales and mktg. Covington Homes, So. Calif., 1988-92, ind. mktg. cons., 1992—; pub. rels. cons. Am. Heart Assn., 1980-84, Family Crisis Ctr., Orange County, 1980-83. Recipient Outstanding Pub. Rels. award Publicity Club L.A., 1980, 3 Mem. Inst. Residential Mktg. awards Nat. Assn. Home Builders, 1986. Mem. Women in Communications, Inc. (Outstanding Mag. Article award 1980, Outstanding Pub. Rels. award 1980), Bldg. Industry Assn. (bd. dir. sales and mktg. coun. 1984-86, 9 Major Achievment in Merchandising Excellence awards, 1984-88), So. Calif. Women in Advertising, Calif. State U., Fullerton Alumni Assn. Republican. Roman Catholic.

DOYLE, WILFRED EMMETT, retired bishop; b. Calgary, Alta., Can., Feb. 18, 1913; s. John Joseph and Mary (O'Neill) D. B.A., U. Alta, 1935; D.C.L., U. Ottawa, Ont., Can., 1949. Ordained priest Roman Cath. Ch., 1938; chancellor Archdiocese Edmonton, Alta., Can., 1949-58; bishop Nelson, B.C., Can., 1958-89, bishop emeritus, 1989—; Chmn. bd. govs. Notre Dame U., Nelson, 1963-74. Address: 10661-82 Ave, Edmonton, AB Canada T6E 2A6

DOYLE, WILLIAM THOMAS, retired newspaper editor; b. Oakland, Calif., May 22, 1925; s. Albert Norman and Catherine (Stein) D.; m. Claire Louise Wogan, Sept. 1, 1946 (dec. Nov. 10, 1984); children: Patrick, Lawrence, Brian, Carrie; m. Mary M. Doren, May 3, 1986. B.Journalism, U. Nev., 1950. Reporter Richmond (Calif.) Independent, 1950-53; reporter Oakland Tribune, 1953-62, asst. state editor, 1962-64, telegraph editor, 1964-67, fin. editor, 1967-79; editor San Francisco Bus. Jour., 1979-81; news dir. Fireman's Fund Ins. Cos., Novato, Calif., 1981-84; mng. editor West County Times, Pinole, Calif., 1984-88. Mem. editorial adv. bd.: Catholic Voice. Pres. Richmond Jr. C. of C., 1957-58; bd. dirs. Cath. Social Svc. Contra Costa County, Calif., 1959-62, Bay Area Coop. Edn. Clearing House, 1977-88, Contra Costa Coll. Found., 1984-88, Richmond Unified Edn. Fund, 1984, Am. Cancer Soc.-WCC, 1986—; mem. Richmond Schs. Citizens Adv. Com., 1969. Served with USAAF, 1943-45. Recipient award for best financial sect. daily newspaper Calif., Calif. Newspaper Pubs. Assn., 1968, 70, 72, 74, Knowland award for outstanding performance, 1972, Gen. Excellence award Nat. Newspaper Assn., 1987, Outstanding Editorial Writing award Suburban Newspapers Assn., 1989, 90, 1st Place award for editorial writing Nat. Newspaper Assn., 1992; Hughes fellow Rutgers U., 1969. Mem. Soc. Am. Bus. Writers, Marine Exchange San Francisco Bay Area, Sigma Delta Chi. Clubs: Contra Costa (Calif.); Press (Best News Story award 1965) (pres. 1956), Serra of West Contra Costa. Home: 2727 Del Monte Ave El Cerrito CA 94530-1507 Office: West County Times 4301 Lakeside Dr Richmond CA 94806-5281

DOZIER, FLORA GRACE, civil and human rights activist, entrepreneur; b. Pineland, Tex., Apr. 5, 1937; d. Whitto G. and Agatha (Price) Grace; m. Robert Alan Dozier, Dec. 16 1962 (div. Jan. 1967); 1 child, Martine Denise. AA in Real Estate, 1979; BA in Polit. Sci., Calif. State U., 1985; cert., Golden Gate U., 1993. Various positions Fed. Civil Svc., 1964-84; real estate saleswoman, 1971-77. Author poems. Mem. Merritt Coll. Community Ctr. Literacy Task Force; bd. dirs. Black Cowboys Assn.; advisory bd. Nat. Youth Sports Program. Recipient Parade Trophy Black Cowboy Assn., 1992, Golden Poet award, 1993, Golden Poet award World of Poetry, 1992, Franam Scholarship for Black Women San Francisco State U., 1992-93, Presidl. award Ctr. Black Concerns, 1994. Mem. NAACP, NAFE, NCNW, IPA, NCNW (life), Internat. Black Writers Assn., Ctr. for Black Concerns, Internat. Platform Assn., Oakland Black Writers Guild, Black United Front for Edn. Reform, Nat. Assn. of Black Reading and Lang. Educators (membership sec. Bay Area chpt.), Bay Area Black Journalists Assn., Help Abolish Legal Tyranny. Baptist. Address: 408-13th St Ste 437 Oakland CA 94612

DRACHNIK, CATHERINE MELDYN, art therapist, artist; b. Kansas City, Mo., June 7, 1924; d. Gerald Willis and Edith (Gray) Weston; m. Joseph Brennan Drachnik, Oct. 6, 1946; children: Denise Elaine, Kenneth John. BS, U. Md., 1945; MA, Calif. State U., Sacramento, 1975. Lic. family and child counselor; registered art therapist. Art therapist Vincent Hall Retirement Home, McLean, Va., Fairfax Mental Health Day Treatment Ctr., McLean, Arlington (Va.) Mental Health Day Treatment Ctr., 1971-72, Hope for Retarded, San Jose, Calif., Sequoia Hosp., Redwood City, Calif., 1972-73; supervising tchr. adult edn. Sacramento Soc. Blind, 1975-77; ptnr. Sacramento Div. Mediation Svcs., 1981-82; instr. Calif. State U., Sacramento, 1975-82, 92-93, Coll. Notre Dame, Belmont, Calif., 1975—; art therapist, mental health counselor Psych West Counseling Ctr. (formerly Eskaton Am. River Mental Health Clinic), Carmichael, Calif., 1975-93; instr. U. Utah, Salt Lake City, 1988-92; lectr. in field. One woman shows throughout Calif.,

East Coast and abroad; group juried shows in Calif. and Orient. Active various charitable orgns. Mem. Art Therapy Assn. (hon. life, pres. 1987-89), No. Calif. Art Therapy Assn. (hon. life), Calif. Coalition Rehab. Therapists, Nat. Art Edn. Assn., Am. Assn. Marriage and Family Therapists, Kappa Kappa Gamma Alumnae Assn. (pres. Sacramento Valley chpt. 1991-92), Alpha Psi Omega, Omicron Nu. Republican. Home and Office: 4124 American River Dr Sacramento CA 95864-6025

DRAGE, STARLA RAE, fashion designer; b. Santaquin, Utah, Oct. 1, 1932; d. Andrew William and Vera Mae (Chatwin) Larsen; m. James Don Drage, Feb. 3, 1951; children: William Joe, Julia Ann, Callene, Darrell Edward. Seamstress Jolene Co., Provo, Utah, 1959, fore-lady, 1960-61, pattern grader, 1963-82, purchasing and prodn. coord., 1978-83, designer 1st patterns, 1984-90; designer, pattern grader Little Gems, Provo, 1961-63; v.p., designer Weinland Mktg. Corp. div. Roanna Togs, N.Y.C., 1990-93; designer, pattern maker Mini World, Provo, 1993—.

DRAGOON, KENNETH MYER, electric utility engineer; b. Vancouver, Wash., Sept. 30, 1956; s. Morrie Dragoon and Belle (Hochberg) Canon; m. Darlene Gay Teters; children: Lindsay, Stephanie. BS in Physics, Western Wash. U., 1978; MS in Physics, U. N.H., 1982. Field engr. Schlumberger Well Svcs., Mt. Pleasant, Mich., 1978-79; elec. engr. Bonneville Power Adminstrn., Portland, Oreg., 1982—. Vol., co-dir. Bonneville Power Adminstrn. Summer Sci. Camp, Portland, 1992-93, Hands On Sci. Program, 191-93; mem. physics adv. coun. Portland State U., 1993-94. Mem. Am. Assn. Physics Tchrs., Planetary Soc. Home: 6321 NE 22nd Ave Portland OR 97211-5482 Office: Bonneville Power Adminstrn PO Box 3621 Portland OR 97208-3621

DRAKE, E MAYLON, academic administrator; b. Nampa, Idaho, Feb. 8, 1920; s. Austin Henry and Daisy Naomi (Smith) D.; m. Lois Elloise Noble, Oct. 12, 1940; children: E. Christopher, Cameron Lee. BS, U. So. Calif., Los Angeles, 1951, MS, 1954, EdD, 1963. Mgr. Frederick Post Co., San Francisco, 1943-47; asst. supt. Baldwin Park (Calif.) Schs., 1947-51; supt. Duarte (Calif.) Schs., 1951-64, Alhambra (Calif.) City Schs., 1964-70; dep. supt. Los Angeles County Schs., 1970-78; dir. Acad. Ednl. Mgmt., Los Angeles, 1978-80; pres. L.A. Coll. Chiropractic, Whittier, 1980-90, chancellor, 1990-93, chancellor emeritus, 1993—; adj. prof. U. So. Calif., 1964-90, bd. councilors, 1991—. Author Attaining Accountability in Schools, 1972; contbr. articles to profl. jours. Pres. Industry-Ednl. Council So. Calif., 1978; dir. United Way 1970; dir. Greater Los Angeles Zoo Bd., 1970. Recipient Am. Educator's medal Freedom Found.; named Educator of Yr. Los Angeles Chiropratic Soc., 1981. Mem. Coun. on Chiropractic Edn. (pres. 1988-90), Rotary (pres. Duarte 1954-56, bd. dirs. Alhambra 1964-70). Republican. Presbyterian. Home: Casa de Ville 206 445 S Los Robles Ave Pasadena CA 91101 Office: LA Coll Chiropractic 16200 E Amber Valley Dr Box 1166 Whittier CA 90609-1166

DRAKE, HUDSON BILLINGS, aerospace and electronics company executive; b. L.A., Mar. 3, 1935; s. Hudson C. and Blossom (Billings) D.; m. Joan M. Johnson, Feb. 9, 1957; children: Howard Billings, Paul Marvin. BA in Econs., UCLA, 1957, postgrad., 1990; MBA, Pepperdine U., 1976. Mgr. Autonetics div. Rockwell Inc., Anaheim, Calif., 1958-68; exec. dir. Pres.'s Commn. White House Fellows, Washington, 1969-70; dep. under sec. U.S. Dept. Commerce, Washington, 1970-72; v.p., gen. mgr. Teledyne Ryan Electronics, San Diego, 1972-80, pres., 1980-84; pres., group exec. Teledyne Ryan Aero., San Diego, 1984-88; v.p., group exec. Teledyne Inc., L.A., 1987-88, sr. v.p., group exec., 1988-89, sr. v.p., pres. aerospace and electronics segment, 1989—; mem. Def. Procurement Adv. Com. on Trade, Washington, 1988-93. Contbr. articles to profl. jours. trustee Children's Hosp., San Diego, 1981-86, chmn. rsch. corp., 1983-86; mem. Pres.'s Coun. San Diego (Calif.) State U., 1984-90; mem. bd. overseers U. Calif., San Diego, 1985-88. With USNR, 1953-61. Decorated Silver Knight of Mgmt., Nat. Mgmt. Assn., 1975, Gold Knight of Mgmt., 1986; San Diego Bd. Suprs. resolution, 1988; White House fellow, 1968. Mem. IEEE, AIAA, Navy League (life), Inst. Navigation, Georgetown Club, Stone Ridge Country Club, San Diego C. of C. (bd. dirs.). Republican. Episcopalian. Home: 18047 Sencillo Dr San Diego CA 92128-1322 Office: Teledyne Inc 2049 Century Park E Fl 15 Los Angeles CA 90067-3101

DRAKE, JESSICA, dialect and speech coach; b. L.A., Apr. 25, 1956; d. Kenneth and Sylvie D. BA, Julliard Sch. Drama, 1981. Accent reduction/ speech and dialect coach UCLA, 1988—; faculty, dialect coach L.A. City Coll., 1988-90; faculty, speech/dialect Am. Acad. Dramatic Art, Pasadena, Calif., 1986-88, Calif. inst. for Arts, Valencia, 1989-90. Dialect coach: (films) Virtuosity, 1995, Don Juan de Marco, 1995, The Centerfold, 1995, Geronimo, 1994, I'll Do Anything, 1994, Forrest Gump, 1994, Ed Wood, 1994, What's Love Got To Do With It, 1993, Bram Stoker's Dracula, 1992, Ruby, 1992, Hot Shots, 1991, Indian Runner, 1991, Shattered, 1991, (TV shows) Truman, 1995, A Woman of Independent Means, 1995, A Streetcar Named Desire, 1995, Return to Lonesome Dove, 1993, Murder Between Friends, 1993, Brooklyn Bridge, 1991-93, An Inconvenient Woman, 1991, The Broken Chain, 1993; actress: (TV shows) A Woman of Independent Means, 1995, Return to Lonesome Dove, 1993, thirtysomething, 1989, Highway to Heaven, 1988, 87, Return of Dennis the Menace, 1987, others; extensive stage work in regional theatre. Recipient Edith Skinner Speech award Julliard Sch. Drama, N.Y.C., 1979. Office: c/o Diane Kamp PO Box 1185 Big Timber MT 59011-1185

DRAKE, LUCIUS CHARLES, JR., school administrator, university consultant; b. Tacloban, The Philippines, June 29, 1946; s. Lucius Charles and Victoria (Badiles) D. BA, Fisk U., 1968; EdM, Temple U., 1970. Cert. sch. adminstr.; cert. guidance counselor. Math. tchr. Sch. Dist. of Phila., 1968-70, Gary (Ind.) City Schs., 1970-72, Dept. Defense Dependents Sch., Fed. Republic Germany and Okinawa, 1972-77; elemtary tchr. Dept. Defense Dependents Sch., Philippines, 1977-79; guidance counselor Dept. Defense Dependents Sch., Japan and Korea, 1979-83; asst. prin. Dept. Defense Dependents Sch., Seoul and Taegu, Korea, 1983-886; univ. cons. U. No. Colo., 1988-89; employment counselor Ft. Collins, Colo., 1989-90; asst. prin. Misawa, Japan, 1990-91, Philippines, 1991-92; chmn. math dept. Sayre Jr. High Sch., Phila., 1969-70; math. curriculum rev. com., Dept. Defense Dependents Schs., Karlsruhe, Fed. Republic Germany, 1972-73; dir. Far East Basketball Tourney, Taegu, Korea, 1984-86; mem. regional mgmt. council, Dept. Defense Dependents Schs., Okinawa, 1985-86. Chairperson human rels. commn. Ft. Collins City Coun., 1990. Recipient Disting. Educator award IDEA Acad. Fellows, Denver, 1985. Fellow Am. Bd. Master Educators (disting.); mem. ASCD, Assn. Am. Sch. Adminstrs., Nat. Assn. Secondary Sch. Prins., Nat. Assn. Elem. Sch. Prins., Internat. Educator's Inst., Phi Delta Kappa, Alpha Phi Alpha (edn. sec. Seoul chpt. 1984-85). Democrat. Baptist. Home: 3318 Hickok Dr Unit B Fort Collins CO 80526-2502 Office: U N Colo Tchr Edn Ctr McKee Hall Greeley CO 80639

DRAKE, PATRICIA EVELYN, psychologist; b. Lewiston, Maine, Feb. 9, 1946; d. Lewis and Anita (Bilodeau) D.; m. Colin Matthew Fuller, May 13, 1973 (div. Aug. 1983); children: R. Matthew, Meaghan Merry. Diploma, St. Mary's Sch. Nursing, 1967; BS, U. Nev., 1985; MA, Calif. Sch. Profl. Psychology, 1987, PhD, 1989. RN. Nurse Maine Med. Ctr., Portland, 1967-73, U. Calif. Sacramento Med. Ctr., 1973-78, Ben Taub Hosp., Houston, 1978-79; psychology intern Shasta County Mental Health Ctr., Redding, Calif., 1988-89, clin. psychologist, 1989-91, tng. dir., chief psychology, 1991—; psychologist pvt. practice, Redding, Calif., 1991—. Mem. AAUW, APA, Calif. Psychol. Assn., Shasta County Psychol. Assn., Phi Kappa Phi. Democrat. Roman Catholic. Office: Shasta County Mental Health 2640 Breslauer Way Redding CA 96001-4246 also: 2464 Old Eureka Way Redding CA 96001-0380

DRAKE, RICHARD PAUL, physicist, educator; b. Washington, Oct. 25, 1954; s. Hugh Hess and Florence Jean (Steele) D.; m. Joyce Elaine Penner, Aug. 30, 1980; children: Katherine Anne, David Alexander. BA in Philosophy and Physics magna cum laude, Vanderbilt U., 1975; PhD in Physics, Johns Hopkins U., 1979. Physicist Lawrence Livermore (Calif.) Lab., 1979-89; assoc. prof. dept. applied sci. U. Calif., Davis, 1990-91, prof., 1991-93; dir. Plasma Physics Rsch. Inst. Lawrence Livermore Nat. Lab., 1990—; ski instr. Squaw Valley (Calif.) USA, 1985-92; chair Anomalous Absorption Conf., Tahoe City, Calif., 1987; referee NSF, Nature, Phys. Rev. Letters, other jours. Contbr. 100 articles to sci. publs. Mem. Fellow Am. Phys. Soc.; mem. AAAS, Am. Vacuum Soc., Phi Beta Kappa. Home: 2463 Covey Way Livermore CA 94550-6804 Office: Plasma Physics Rsch Inst L 418 PO Box 808 Livermore CA 94551-0808

DRAKE, STANLEY JOSEPH, association executive; b. New Britain, Conn., Mar. 8, 1916; s. Joseph Nicholas and Alice (Tokarzewska) D.; m. Virginia Allen Drake, Oct. 6, 1940 (dec. Apr. 1993); children: Alice Drake Berg, Janet Drake Gardner, Jane Drake Dover; m. Elsie York, May 18, 1994. BS in Bus. Edn., Bryant Coll., Smithfield, R.I., 1937; MS, Temple Bar Coll., Mpls., 1944; PhD, McKinley Roosevelt Inst, Chgo., 1948; D. Pedagogy (hon.), Bryant Coll., 1963; DBA (hon.), Ind. No. U., 1966; Dr.Bus.Adminstrn., Cleary Coll., 1967; LHD, Internat. Fine Arts Coll., 1968; EdD, Ft. Lauderdale U., 1973. Instr. Mt. Vernon (Ohio) Coll., 1945-48, Broward Coll., Ft. Lauderdale, Fla., 1948-56; pres. Ft. Lauderdale Coll., 1956-76; adj. prof. Tampa (Fla.) Coll., 1977-78, Orlando Coll., 1978-81, Gaston Coll., Dallas, N.C., 1981-94. Author: Thoughts from the Bible, 1991, The Essentials of Esperanto, 1993. Mem. Am. Assn. of Pres. of Ind. Colls. and Univs. (pres. 1967-68, sec. 1969-70), Am. Assn. Specialized Colls. (pres. 1965-67), UN Assn. of U.S.A., Internat. Soc. Friendsihp and Good Will (pres. 1982—, sec. gen. 1978-82). Republican. Home: 9538 Summerfield St Spring Valley CA 91977-2852 Office: Internat Soc Friendship 9538 Summerfield St Spring Valley CA 91977-2852

DRAZNIN, JULES NATHAN, journalism and public relations educator, consultant; b. Chgo., May 14, 1923; s. Charles G. and Goldie (Malach) D.; m. Shirley Bernstein, Apr. 9, 1950; children: Dean, Jody, Michael. Student, Wright City Coll., Chgo., 1941; BA in Journalism, Calif. State U., Northridge, 1978, MA in Higher Edn., 1984. Various journalism positions City News Bur., Chgo., 1941; promotions and publicity Balaban & Katz Theaters, Chgo., 1942-43; asst. dir pub. rels. Combined Jewish Appeal, Chgo., 1944; prin. J.N. Draznin Assocs., Chgo., 1945-50; account supr. Olian & Bronner Advt. Agy., Chgo., 1951-53; dir. advt. Chgo. Defender Robert S. Abbott Pub. Co., 1953-55; freelance cons. Chgo., 1955-60; v.p. pub. rels. Harshe-Rotman, Chgo., 1956; pub. rels. dir. Abel and Lamensdorf Properties, Chgo., 1960-62; editor-in-chief, assoc. pub. Indsl. News Bender Publs., Calif., 1962-64; labor editor, spl. features writer Valley News, Calif., 1964; ind. ins. agt. Calif., 1965-74; tch. pub. rels. UCLA and Calif. State U., L.A.; prof. journalism and pub. rels. L.A. Trade Tech. Coll., 1975-95, chmn. lang. arts dept., 1984-90; ret., 1995; prof. journalism and pub. rels. L.A. City Coll., L.A. Pierce Coll., L.A. Southwest Coll., East L.A. Coll., L.A. Mission Coll.; guest lectr. Calif. State U., Northridge. Mem. Assn. for Edn. in Journalism and Mass Communication, Soc. Profl. Journalists, Greater L.A. Press Club.

DRECHSEL, EDWIN JARED, retired magazine editor; b. Bremen, Germany, Apr. 17, 1914; came to U.S., 1924, naturalized, 1935; s. William A. and Estelle Laura D.; m. Ilona Bolya, Aug. 12, 1972; children: John M., Barbara A. Grad., Dartmouth Coll., Amos Tuck Sch. Bus. Adminstrn., 1936. With Standard Oil Co., N.J., 1936-43; with U.S. News and World Report, 1943-79; regional editor, editorial ombudsman U.S. News and World Report, San Francisco, 1976-79. Author shipping company histories and fleet lists, catalogs of ship mail postal markings, including A Century of German Ship Posts, 1886-1986, 1987, Norddeutscher Lloyd, Bremen 1857-1970, vol. 1, 1994, vol. 2, 1995. Former chmn. Reed Sch. Bd., Marin County, Calif.; lay reader, former vestryman St. Stephen's Episcopal Ch., Belvedere, Calif., former mayor, City of Belvedere. Club: San Francisco Press. Home: 170 Hillcrest Rd Berkeley CA 94705-2846

DREIER, DAVID TIMOTHY, congressman; b. Kansas City, Mo., July 5, 1952; s. H. Edward and Joyce (Yeomans) D. BA cum laude, Claremont McKenna Coll., 1975; MA in Am. Govt., Claremont Grad. Sch., 1976. Dir. corp. rels. Claremont McKenna Coll., 1975-78; dir. mktg. and govt. rels. Indsl. Hydrocarbons, San Dimas, Calif., 1978-80; mem 97th-103rd Congresses from 35th (now 28th) Calif. dist., 1980—; v.p. Dreier Devel. Co., Kansas City, Mo., 1985—; vice chmn. rules com., 1995—, chmn. rules of the house subcom., chmn. task force on fgn. policy, speaker's task force on Calif., mem. task force on POW/MIAs; mem. spl. task force on the devel. of parliamentary instns.; mem. U.S.-Mex. Interparliamentary Caucus; bd. dirs. Internat. Rep. Inst.; vice co-chmn. joint com. on orgn. of Congress; vice chmn. GOP Calif. Congl. Del.; regional whip; mem. task force on fed. mandates; chmn. Calif. Task Force; mem. spkrs. steering com. Recipient Golden Bulldog award Watchdogs of the Treasury, 1981-94, Taxpayers Friends award Nat. Taxpayers Union, 1981-94, Clean Air Champion award Sierra Club, 1988. Office: 411 Cannon HOB Washington DC 20515

DREIER, PETER, politics and public policy educator, journalist; b. Plainfield, N.J., July 12, 1948; s. Theodore and Beatrice (Braveman) D.; m. Catherine Theresa Meng, July 5, 1992. BA, Syracuse U., 1970; MA, U. Chgo., 1972, PhD, 1977. Asst. prof. sociology Tufts U., Medford, Mass., 1977-83; dir. housing Boston Redevel. Authority, 1984-92; E.P. Clapp Disting. prof. politics Occidential Coll., L.A., 1992—, dir. pub. policy program, 1994—; bd. dirs. Nat. Housing Inst., Orange, N.J., Nat. Low-Income Housing Coalition, Washington; cons. MacArthur Found., Chgo., 1992, U.S. Dept. HUD, Washington, 1993—; mem. adv. bd. Resolution Trust Corp., Washington, 1993—, Right-to-Know Project, Washington, 1995—. Editor: Jewish Radicalism, 1973; contbr. articles to numerous publs.; mem. editorial bd. Urban Affairs Quar., 1992—. Founder Mass. Tenants Orgn., Boston, 1981. Pub. Svc. Sci. resident NSF, 1981-82; rsch. grantee U.S. Dept. HUD, 1993, Social Sci. Rsch. grantee, 1993, Haynes Found., 1994. Sr. fellow Internat. and Pub. Affairs Ctr.; mem. Am. Sociol. Assn. (chair Spivack program on applied pub. policy), Am. Planning Assn. Democrat. Jewish. Office: Occidental Coll Internat and Pub Affairs Ctr Los Angeles CA 90041

DREIFUSS-KATTAN, ESTHER, psychoanalyst, art therapy educator; b. Zurich, Switzerland, June 3, 1949; came to U.S., 1989; d. Max and Suzanne (Levy) Dreifuss; m. Shlomo Kattan, Dec. 29, 1983; children: Sarit Jolanda, Gabriela Caroline. Diploma in fashion design, Fashion Sch., Zurich; MA in Art Therapy, Goddart Coll., 1976; PhD in Art Therapy, Union Grad. Inst., 1990; PhD in Rsch. Psychoanalysis, So. Calif. Psychoanalytic Inst, 1994. Art therapist C. Jung Clinic & Rsch. Ctr., Zurich, 1972-74; art therapist, dir. Chestnut Lodge Hosp., Rockville, Md., 1974-78; art therapy cons., psychooncologist Univ. Hosp. Dept. Internal Medicine, Zurich, 1978-83; psychooncologist, cons. Tel-Hashomer U., Tel Aviv, 1983-86; lectr. art therapy U. Tel Aviv, 1984-89; lectr. art history, art therapy and health scis. UCLA Extension, L.A., 1990—; pvt. practice psychoanalysis, art therapy Beverly Hills, Calif., 1992—. Author: Clinical Introduction to Art Therapy, 1986, Cancer Stories, Creativity and Self Repair, 1989, 94; contbr. numerous sci. articles to med. jours., chpts. to books. Mem. APA (divsn. psychoanalysis), Am. Psychoanalytic Assn., Am. Art Therapy Assn. (registered). Jewish. Office: 9437 Santa Monica Blvd Beverly Hills CA 90210-4604

DREISBACH, JOHN GUSTAVE, investment banker; b. Paterson, N.J., Apr. 24, 1939; s. Gustave John and Rose Catherine (Koehler) D.; m. Janice Lynn Petitjean; children: John Gustave Jr., Cassandra Michelle, Niklas Philip, Christopher Erik. BA, NYU, 1963. With Dreyfus & Co., 1959-62, with Shields & Co., Inc., 1965-68, Model, Roland & Co., Inc., N.Y.C., 1968-72, F. Eberstadt & Co., Inc., N.Y.C., 1972-74; v.p. Bessemer Trust Co., 1974-78; pres. Community Housing Capital, Inc., 1978-80; chmn., pres. John G. Dreisbach, Inc., Santa Fe, N.Mex., 1980—; JGD Housing Corp., 1982—; gen. ptnr. numerous real estate ltd. partnerships; bd. dirs., pres. The Santa Fe Investment Conf., 1986—; assoc. Sta. KNME-TV. Mem. Santa Fe Community Devel. Commn. Served with USAFR, 1964. Mem. Internat. Assn. for Fin. Planning, Nat. Assn. Securities Dealers, Inc., NYU Alumni Assn., N.Mex. First, Friends of Vieilles Maisons Francaises Inc., Mensa, Santa Fe C. of C., Augustan Soc. Republican. Mem. Episcopalian Ch. and Lutheran Ch. Clubs: St. Bartholomew's Community, Essex, Hartford, Amigos del Alcalde. Avocations: travel, art, arch-design appreciation, classical music, long distance running. Home: 730 Camino Cabra Santa Fe NM 87501-5924

DRENNAN, MICHAEL ELDON, banker; b. Yakima, Wash., June 24, 1946; s. George Eldon and Jane (Nilsson) D.; m. Alice Marie Seabolt, May 13, 1972; children: Brian, David. BS in Fin., U. Oreg., 1968; grad., Pacific Coast Banking Sch. U. Wash., 1981. Ops. officer First State Bank, Aloha, Oreg., 1972-73; ops., loan officer First State Bank, Portland, Oreg., 1973-74; asst. mgr. First State Bank, Milwaukie, Oreg., 1974-76; asst. v.p. Citizens Bank, Corvallis, Oreg., 1976-80, v.p., 1980-81; pres., chief exec. officer Bank of Corvallis, 1981-87; v.p. dist. mgr. U.S. Bank, Corvallis, Oreg., 1987; sr. v.p. market area mgr. U.S. Bank, Bend, Oreg., 1988-94; sr. v.p., dist. mgr. U.S. Bank, Eugene, Oreg., 1994—; bd. dirs. Cascades W. Fin. Svcs. Bd. dirs. United Way Benton County, 1984-88; trustee Good Samaritan Hosp. Found., 1984-88; bd. dirs. Jr. Achievement of Benton County, 1983-85, treas. 1984-85, mem. exec. bd., 1984-85; mem. budget comm. Corvallis Sch. Dist., 1987; bd. dirs. Benton County Family YMCA, 1978-80, sec. 1979, mem. fin. com., 1978-80, mem. personnel com. 1979, active sustaining membership dr.; bd. dirs. Cmty. Club, 1978-83, pres., 1978, treas. 1979-80; active Corvallis Ambassadors, 1976-88; mem. mgmt. com. Corvallis Conv. and Vis. Bur., 1982-85; fund. raising chmn. Com. City Improvemnt Levy, 1980; mem. exec. com. Pack 17 Boy Scouts Am., 1984-87, treas. 1984-87; mem. adv. bd. Cen. Oreg. Econ. Devel. Corp., 1988-90, bd. dirs., exec. bd., treas., 1991-93, v.p., 1993, pres., 1994—; bd. dirs. Regional Arts Coun. of Cen. Oreg., treas. 1989-92; bd. dirs. Cen. Oreg. Air Svc. Task Force, 1989-94, chmn. airline rels. com., 1990; mem. Bend Bus. Assistance Team, 1989-90, United Way Deschutes county, chmn. Loaned exec. recruitment, 1992; mem. planning com. St. Charles Med. Ctr. Found., 1993, dir. adminstrn. capital fund drive, 1993; mem. adv. bd. Deschutes County Fair, 1993-94; bd. dirs. Birth to Three, Eugene, 1994—, Lane Arts Coun., 1995—, Convention & Visitor Assn. Lane County, 1995—. Lt. USN, 1968-71. Named Jr. First Citizen, Corvallis, 1980. Mem. Bend C. of C. (chmn. mem. dir. task force 1988, chmn. mem. svcs. coun. 1989, chmn. chamber forums com. 1990, Outstanding Leadership award 1989), Corvallis C. of C. (v.p. fin. 1980-83, pres. 1985-86, chmn. bd. dirs. 1986-87, Econ. Devel. award 1978, Chmn. of Bd. award 1979, George award 1980-81, Devel. award 1983), Am. Inst. Banking (cert.), Rotary (bd. dirs. Corvallis club 1981-87, Bend 1988-94, Eugene, 1994—), Chi Phi, Alpha Kappa Psi, Beta Gamma Sigma. Home: 2574 W 20th Ave Eugene OR 97405-1456 Office: US Bank PO Box 10308 Eugene OR 97440-2308

DRESP, DONALD FRANCIS, library director; b. Omaha, Feb. 17, 1936; s. John Joseph and Helen Marjorie (Babbitt) D.; m. Winifred Adams, Jan. 24, 1970; children: David Joseph, Jeanne Angela. AB in Philosophy and History, Immaculate Conception Coll., 1958; postgrad., Creighton U., 1958-60; MA in LS, U. Denver, 1965; postgrad., Ariz. State U., 1970. Libr. Loveland (Colo.) H.S., 1962-65; edn. libr. Ariz. State U., Tempe, 1965-67; asst. libr. dir. Scottsdale (Ariz.) Pub. Libr., 1967-71; libr. dir. Thomas Branigan Meml. Libr., Las Cruces, N.Mex., 1971—; host weekly radio program KOBE-1450 AM, 1988-91; del. to White House Conf. on Librs. and Info. Scis., Washington, 1991; col. aide-de-camp Staff of Gov. of N.Mex., 1974. Bd. dirs. ARC, 1977-83, Dona Ana Arts Coun., 1976-81, Head Start, Dona Ana County, 1973-75, Las Cruces Meml. Med. Ctr. Found., 1990—; pres. Las Cruces Crime and Drug Commn., 1980—, pres., 1983-84; campaign divsn. dir. United Way, 1972, 83, 84, exec. bd., 1985-87; City of Las Cruces rep. to Cmty. Action Agy. of Dona Ana County, 1972-80. Recipient Libr. of Yr. award Border Regional Libr. Assn., 1975, Regular Guy award Las Cruces Cable TV, 1986; named Employee of Yr., City of Las Cruces, 1987. Mem. ALA, N.Mex. Libr. Assn. (v.p. 1972-73, pres. 1973-74, pres. pub. libr. divsn. 1984-85, libr. devel. com. 1974-77, 82-84, Libr. of Yr. 1991), N.Mex. Mcpl. Librs. (pres. 1976-77, 86-87), Dona Ana County Hist. Soc., Rotary (Paul Harris fellow 1992, bd. dirs. 1987-89). Roman Catholic. Home: 1845 Las Tunas Dr Las Cruces NM 88011-4956 Office: Thomas Branigan Meml Libr 200 E Picacho Ave Las Cruces NM 88001-3457

DRESSER, JACK WILLIAM, research psychologist; b. Fullerton, Calif., June 1, 1936; s. Jack William and Florence Ruth (Chaffee) D.; children: Jon A., Tascha L., Tobin B., Lara V. BA, Pomona Coll., 1958; MA, La. State U., 1962, PhD, 1966. Sales agt. Streitfeld Realty, L.A., 1954-58; child psychologist Kennedy Child Study Ctr., Santa Monica, Calif., 1966-72; pvt. practice Affiliated Psychol. Cons., Downey, Calif., 1972-80; program dir. Open Door Clinics, Alhambra, Calif., 1981-86; prevention cons. Alhambra Sch. Dist., 1987-88; sr. rsch. scientist Integrated Rsch. Svcs., Eugene, Oreg., 1988—. Contbg. editor (newsletter) Prevention Rschr., 1994; contbr. articles to profl. publs.; artist (cartoons) Internat. Gymnast, 1984. UN cons. drug demand reduction Asia-Pacific region, 1987; cons. sch. and cmty. prevention locations including San Mateo County, Calif., Linn, Benton, Douglas and Deschutes counties, Oreg., 1989—. Recipient stipend USPHS, La. State U., 1959; rsch. grantee Nat. Hwy. Traffic Safety Adminstrsn., N.Y. and Minn., 1992, 93, U.S. Dept. Edn., Oreg. and Calif., (5), 1989-95, Nat. Inst. on Alcohol Abuse and Alcoholism, 1995-2000. Mem. APA (health psychology divsn., cmty. psychology divsn.), Lane County Psychol. Assn. Office: Integrated Rsch Svcs 66 Club Rd Ste 370 Eugene OR 97401-2459

DRESSER, JESSE DALE, real estate investor; b. San Diego, May 5, 1906; s. Charlwood Fessenden and Ora (Evans) D.; m. Mary A. Goldsworthy, June 9, 1934; children: Dennis T., Brian D., Linda A. Ed. pub. schs. Trainee Union Title Ins. Co., San Diego, 1926; sr. title examiner, chief title officer, v.p. So. Title & Trust Co., San Diego, 1937-51; v.p., chief title officer Security Title Ins. Co., San Diego, 1951-54; asst. to pres. San Diego Fed. Savs. & Loan Assn., 1954-55, v.p., sec., 1955-56, exec. v.p., dir., 1956-70; v.p., dir. Calif. Gen. Mortgage Service, Inc., 1967-70, San Diego Federated Ins. Agy., Inc., 1967-70; real estate investments La Mesa, Calif., 1970-86; ret., 1986. Home: 3833 Acacia Ave Bonita CA 91902-2523

DRESSLER, ALAN MICHAEL, astronomer; b. Cin., Mar. 23, 1948; s. Charles and Gay (Stein) Dressler. BA in Physics, U. Calif., Berkeley, 1970; PhD in Astronomy, U. Calif., Santa Cruz, 1976. Carnegie Instn. of Washington fellow Hale Obs., Pasadena, Calif., 1976-78, Las Campanas fellow, 1978-81; sci. staff Carnegie Obs. (formerly Mt. Wilson and Las Campanas Obs., formerly Hale Obs.), Pasadena, 1981—, acting assoc. dir., 1988-89. Contbr. to sci. jours. Fellow Am. Acad. Arts and Scis.; mem. Am. Astron. Soc. (councilor 1989-91, Pierce prize 1983), Internat. Astron. Union. Office: Carnegie Obs 813 Santa Barbara St Pasadena CA 91101-1232

DRESSLER, JOSHUA, lawyer, educator; b. N.Y.C., Mar. 30, 1947; s. David and Belle (Jaffe) D.; m. Dorothy Ann Kridler, Nov. 26, 1969; 1 child, David Bethune. BA, UCLA, 1968, JD, 1973. Bar: Calif. 1973, U.S. Supreme Ct. 1973. Asst. prof. law San Fernando Valley Coll. Law, L.A., 1975-77; assoc. prof. Sch. Law, Hamline U., St. Paul, 1977-82; vis. prof. Sch. Law, UCLA, 1983-84, Law Sch., U. Mich., Ann Arbor, 1991; prof. Law Sch., Wayne State U., Detroit, 1982-83, 84-93. Author: Understanding Criminal Law, 1987, Understanding Criminal Procedure, 1991, Cases and Materials on the Criminal Law, 1994; contbr. articles to profl. publs. Mem. Am. Law Inst., Assn. Am. Law Schs. (chairperson sect. in criminal justice 1991), Am. Soc. for Polit. and Legal Philosophy, Reform of Criminal Law, Order of Coif, Phi Beta Kappa. Jewish. Office: McGeorge Sch Law 3200 5th Ave Sacramento CA 95817-2705

DREUSIKE, DONALD, construction executive; b. 1946. BArch., Calif. Poly Tech. Inst., 1970. With Dinwiddie Constrn. Co., San Francisco, 1970—, pres. Office: Dinwiddie Constrn Co 275 Battery St Ste 300 San Francisco CA 94111-3330*

DREVER, MARK, food products executive; b. 1956. BA, U. the Pacific; JD, Loyola U. Atty. Fresh Express Inc., Salinas, Calif., 1988—, pres. Office: Fresh Express Inc 1020 Merrill St Salinas CA 93901-4409*

DREW, CHARLES MILTON, chemist; b. McKinney, Tex., Feb. 13, 1921; s. Andrew Everett and Lutie Lella (Weger) D.; divorced; children: Darrell Everett, Donna Lee, Lynn Milton, Carl Allen. BS, U. N. Tex., 1943. Supr. chemist Columbia Southern, Corpus Christi, Tex., 1943-47; research scientist Naval Weapons Ctr., China Lake, Calif., 1947-70; cons. U. Ariz., Tucson, 1980—. Author: Principles of Gas Chromatography, 1959; contbr. articles to profl. jours.; patentee in field. Mem. Rsch. Soc. Am., Soaring Soc. Am., Colo. West Soaring Club, Glider Club (pres. China Lake, Calif. chpt. 1967-70), Rockhounds Club (pres. local chpt. 1949-50), Sigma Xi. Home: 1420 Walker View Rd Wellington NV 89444-9326

DREW, SHARON LEE, sociologist; b. L.A., Aug. 11, 1946; d. Hal Bernard and Helen Elizabeth (Hammond) D.; children: Keith, Charmagne. BA, Calif. State U., Long Beach, 1983; postgrad., Calif. State U., Dominguez Hills, 1988—. Clerical support Compton (Calif.) Unified Sch. Dist., 1967-78; case worker L.A. County Dept. Pub. Social Svcs., 1978—. Den mother Boy Scouts Am., Compton, 1971-72; employee vol. Dominguez Sr. H.S., Comptn, 1972-73; project coord. Calif. Tomorrow's Parent Edn. Leadership Devel.

Project, 1990; mem. L.A. Caregiver's Network, 1993—; vol. Calif. State Univ., Dominguez Hill's Older Adult Ctr., 1994. Recipient cert. Calif. Tomorrow-Parent Edn. Leadership Devel. Project, 1990. Mem. Am. Statis. Assn. (so. Calif. chpt.), Internat. Soc. for Exploratoin of Teaching Alternatives, Calif. Sociol. Assn. (1st gov. at large grad. student 1990-91), Dominguez Hills Gerontology Assn. (chairperson 1990-91), Sociology of Edn. Assn., Alpha Kappa Delta (Xi chpt. treas. 1992—). Home: 927 N Chester Ave Compton CA 90221-2105

DREWS, CARL, software engineer; b. Summit, N.J., Aug. 11, 1960; s. William Paul and Lois Edel (Brandt) D. BSEE, Stanford U., 1982. Software engr. Storage Tech. Corp., Louisville, Colo., 1982-84; software developer Micro Analysis & Design, Boulder, Colo., 1984—. Author computer program Micro Saint, 1986. Vol., speaker Habitat for Humanity, Boulder, 1988—; chmn. youth com. Atonement Luth. Ch., Boulder, 1990-93. Home: 5640 Pennsylvania Ave Boulder CO 80303-2943 Office: Micro Analysis & Design 4900 Pearl East Cir Ste 201E Boulder CO 80301-6108

DREXLER, KENNETH, lawyer; b. San Francisco, Aug. 2, 1941; s. Fred and Martha Jane (Cunningham) D.; BA, Stanford U., 1963; JD, UCLA, 1969. Bar: Calif. 1970. Assoc., David S. Smith, Beverly Hills, Calif., 1970, McCutchen, Doyle, Brown and Enersen, San Francisco, 1970-77; assoc. Chickering & Gregory, San Francisco, 1977-80, ptnr., 1980-82; ptnr. Drexler & Leach, San Rafael, Calif., 1982—. Served with AUS, 1964-66. Mem. Calif. State Bar (resolutions com. conf. of dels. 1979-83, chmn. 1982-83, adminstrn. justice com. 1983-89, chmn. 1987-88), Marin County Bar Assn. (bd. dirs. 1985-87), Bar Assn. San Francisco (dir. 1980-81), San Francisco Barristers Club (pres. 1976, dir. 1975-76), Marin Conservation League (bd. dirs. 1985—). Office: 1330 Lincoln Ave Ste 300 San Rafael CA 94901-2143

DREXLER, KIM ERIC, researcher, author; b. Oakland, Calif., Apr. 25, 1955; s. Allan Barry and Hazel Edna (Gassmann) D.; m. Christine Louise Peterson, June 18, 1981. BS in Interdisciplinary Sci., MIT, 1977, MS in Engring., 1979, PhD in Molecular Nanotech., 1991. Researcher, author, lectr., inventor Cambridge, Mass., 1980-85; researcher, author, lectr., cons. Palo Alto, Calif., 1985—; rsch. affiliate MIT Space Lab, Cambridge, 1980-86, MIT Artificial Intelligence Lab, Cambridge, 1986-87; sr. rsch. fellow Inst. for Molecular Mfg., 1991—; vis. scholar Stanford (Calif.) U. Computer Sci. Dept., 1986-92; bd. dirs., chmn. The Foresight Inst., Palo Alto, 1986—. Author: Engines of Creation, 1986, Nanosystems, 1992 (Assn. Am. Pubs. Best Computer Science Book, 1992); co-author: Unbounding the Future, 1991; contbr. articles to profl. jours.; inventor high performance solar sail, method for processing and fabricating metals in space. Sec. bd. dirs. L5 Soc., Tucson, 1981, bd. dirs., 1979-86, advisor, 1979-86, co-editor jour., 1983-84; bd. dirs. Nat. Space Soc., 1986—. Grad. fellow NSF, MIT, 1977; recipient Space Pioneer award for Scientist/Engr., Nat. Space Soc., 1991, Kilby Young Innovator award Kilby Found., Dallas, 1993. Mem. AAAS, Am. Vacuum Soc., Am. Chemistry Soc. Office: The Foresight Inst PO Box 61058 Palo Alto CA 94306-6058

DREXLER, MILLARD S., retail executive; b. 1944; married. Exec. v.p. merchandising, pres. Gap Stores div. Gap Inc., San Bruno, Calif., from 1983; now pres., bd. dirs. The Gap Inc., San Bruno; pres., chief exec. officer Ann Taylor Co. Office: The Gap Inc 1 Harrison St San Francisco CA 94105-1602

DREYER, THOMAS MORGAN, plastic surgeon; b. Phoenix, 1947. MD, U. Ill., 1972. Resident Duke U. Med. Ctr., Durham, N.C., 1972-74; otolaryngologist U. Iowa, Iowa City, 1975-79; plastic surgeon U. N.C., Chapel Hill, 1979-81; now plastic surgeon Sacred Heart Gen. Hosp., Eugene, Oreg. Office: 2995 Capital Dr Eugene OR 97403-1886*

DREYFUSS, JOHN ALAN, journalist; b. N.Y.C., Dec. 1, 1933; s. Henry and Doris (Marks) D.; m. Katharine Elizabeth Rich, June 28, 1958; children: Karen Elizabeth, James Henry, Kimberly Anne, Katharine Marks. BS in Biology, Boston U., 1959. Tchr. schs. in Montclair, Pebble Beach and Los Olivos, Calif., 1959-63; reporter, editor San Luis Obispo (Calif.) Telegram Tribune, 1963-64; advt. salesman Ventura County (Calif.) Star-Free Press, 1964-66; gen. assignment writer Los Angeles Times, 1966-69, 73-75, higher edn. writer, 1969-72, environment writer, 1972-73, architecture and design critic, 1975-84, feature writer View sect., 1984-87, graphics editor View sect., 1987-89, asst. to assoc. editor, 1989-93; v.p., CFO, sec. J. Dreyfuss & Assocs., Santa Monica, Calif., 1993-94; newswriter Sta. KTLA-TV, L.A., 1994—. Served with AUS, 1953-55. Office: Sta KTLA-TV 5800 W Sunset Blvd Los Angeles CA 90028-6600

DRIEVER, LOUIS MILTON, JR., airline executive; b. Troy, Ohio, Oct. 5, 1957; s. Louis Milton and Betty Jean (Pooler) D.; children: Megan Rene, Morgan Louis. BA in Psychology, Pitzer Coll., 1981. Regional dir. Europe Worldwide Cargo Inc., Florence, Italy, 1985-87; mng. ptnr. Westcom Tech. Svcs., Roy, Wash., 1987-89; regional dir. Asia/Pacific Evergreen Internat. Airlines, McMinnville, Oreg., 1989-91, dir. sta. ops., 1991—; mem. airport affairs com. LAX, L.A., 1991-94; mem. planning com. Denver Airport, 1990-94. Sgt. U.S. Army, 1981-85. Mem. Air Transport Assn. (mem. facilitation com. 1990-94). Republican. Home: 4155 Three Mile Ln # 39 Mcminnville OR 97128 Office: Evergreen Internat Airlines 3850 Three Mile Ln Mcminnville OR 97128-9402

DRINKARD, TERRELL DEWAYNE, aeronautical engineer; b. Mobile, Ala., Apr. 7, 1957; s. William Woodrow and Susan Drinkard. BS in Aero. Engring., Calif. Poly. State U., 1991. Numerically controlled mill operator Mainland Machine, San Luis Obispo, Calif., 1987-88; computer tester Tandon Computers, San Luis Obispo, 1988-89; liaison engr. Boeing Comml. Airplane Group, Seattle, 1990-91, configuration analyst, 1992-95; mktg. product analyst Boeing Comml. Airplane Group, 1995—; pvt. practice computer cons., San Luis Obispo, 1987-90. Inventor in field. Conv. del. King County (Wash.) Dems., 1992. Sgt. U.S. Army, 1975-81. Mem. AIAA (young mems. com. Pacific N.W. chpt. 1990-92, facilities dir. 1992-93, dir. pub. rels. 1994-95). Home: 22104 39th Ave W Mountlake Terrace WA 98043-4241 Office: Boeing Comml Airplane Group PO Box 3707 Seattle WA 98124-2207

DRINKWATER, HERBERT R., mayor; m. Jackie Drinkwater; 2 children. Asst. bus. mgr. Phoenix Union High Sch. and Jr. Coll. System; owner, oper. ind. bus., 1964; mem. Scottsdale (Ariz.) City Coun., 1970-78, chmn. fin. com.; mem. Design Rev. Bd. City of Scottsdale, vice mayor, 1972-73, 76, mayor, 1980—; apptd. to Phoenix adv. coun. U.S. Bur. Land Mgmt.; chmn. Regional Pub. Transit Authority; ex-officio mem. Fiesta Bowl Com.; bd. dirs. No. Trust Co. of Ariz., Mayor's Com. on Employment of Persons with Disabilities. Bd. dirs. Ariz. Heart Inst., Lucky 13 Edn. and Rehab. Ctr., Scottsdale Boys Club, Found. for Handicapped, Ch. of the Beatitudes, Scottsdale Symphony Orch.; co-vice chmn. govt. div. Valley of the Sun campaign United Way; past mem. Scottsdale Adv. Bd., Hospice of the Valley; active Ariz. Acad., Ariz. Sr. Olympics Gold Medal Adv. Group, Camelback Mental Health Found., Scottsdale Sister Cities. Named Nationwide Retailer of Yr., 1968; named Outstanding Young Man, City of Scottsdale, 1972; recipient Disting. Achievement award Ariz. State U. Coll. Pub. Programs, 1986, Disting. Citizen award Boy Scouts Am. Mem. U.S. Conf. Mayors (arts, culture and recreation, energy and environ. standing coms.), League Ariz. Cities and Towns (treas., exec., resolution coms.), Ariz. Mcpl. Water Users Assn., Scottsdale Charros, Ariz. Wildlife Fedn., Paralyzed Vets. Assn. (life mem. Ariz. chpt.), Jaycees (pres. and exec. bd. Scottsdale chpt., internat. senate, adv. bd. Parada Del Sol 1970-74), Lions, Rotary (hon.). Office: 3939 N Civic Center Blvd Scottsdale AZ 85251-4433*

DRISCOLL, CHARLES F., research physicist; b. Tucson, Feb. 28, 1950; s. John Raymond Gozzi and Barbara Jean (Hamilton) Driscoll; m. Susan C. Bain, Dec. 30, 1972; children: Thomas A., Robert A. BA in Physics summa cum laude, Cornell U., 1969; MS, U. Calif. San Diego, La Jolla, 1972, PhD, 1976. Staff scientist Gen. Atomics, San Diego, 1969; rsch. asst. U. Calif. San Diego, La Jolla, 1971-76, rsch. physicist, sr. lectr., 1976—; staff physicist, cons. Molecular Biosystems, Inc., San Diego, 1981-82; assoc. dir. Inst. for Pure and Applied Scis., La Jolla, 1991—; cons. Sci. Applications, Inc., 1980-81. Editor: Non-Neutral Plasma Physics, 1988; contbr. 30 articles to sci. jours. Fellow NSF, 1969-71. Fellow Am. Phys. Soc. (Excellence in Plasma Physics Rsch. award 1991); mem. AAAS, Math. Assn. Am., Phi Beta Kappa. Office: U Calif San Diego Dept Physics 0319 9500 Gilman Dr La Jolla CA 92093-5003

DRISCOLL, MICHAEL P., bishop; b. Long Beach, Calif., Aug. 8, 1939. MSW, St. John's Sem., Camarillo, Calif.; student, U. So. Calif. Ordained priest Roman Cath. Ch., 1965, titular bishop of Massita. Aux. bishop Orange, Calif., 1990—. Office: Chancery Office 2811 E Villa Real Dr Orange CA 92667-1932

DROHOJOWSKA-PHILP, HUNTER, author, critic; b. Schenectady, N.Y., Sept. 5, 1952; d. Richard Arlington and Carol Creps Gleason. BFA, Inst. San Miguel de Allende, Guanajuato, Mex., 1976. Film critic Japan Times, Tokyo, 1978; art editor L.A. Weekly, 1981-84; art and architecture editor L.A. Style, 1984-86; arts reporter L.A. Herald Examiner, 1984-87; chair dept. liberal arts and scis. Otis Sch. Art and Design, L.A., 1987-95; pvt. practice-writer Beverly Hills, Calif., 1995—; west coast corr. Art News Mag. Author: Peter Shire-Rizzoli, 1990; contbr. Art Issues Mag. Mem. Internat. Assn. Art Critics, Coll. Art Assn., Found. Advanced Critical Studies (bd. dirs.).

DROWN, EUGENE ARDENT, federal agency administrator; b. Ellenburg, N.Y., Apr. 25, 1915; s. Frank Arthur and Jessie Kate D.; BS, Utah State U., 1938; postgrad. Mont. State U., 1939-40; PhD in Pub. Adminstrn., U. Beverly Hills, 1979; m. Florence Marian Munroe, Mar. 5, 1938; children: Linda Harriett Oneto, Margaret Ruth Lunn. Park ranger Nat. Park Svc., Yosemite Nat. Park, 1940-47; forest ranger U.S. Forest Svc., Calif. Region, 1948-56; forest mgr. and devel. specialist U.S. Bur. Land Mgmt., Calif., 1956—; forest engring. cons., 1970—; R&D coord. U.S. Army at U. Calif., Davis., 1961-65. Mem. adv. bd. Sierra Coll., Rocklin, Calif., 1962—; active Boy Scouts Am.; instr. ARC, 1954—. With AUS, 1941-45. Decorated Bronze Star, Silver Star; registered profl. engr., profl. land surveyor, profl. forester, Calif. Recipient Nat. Svc. medal ARC, 1964. Mem. Nat. Soc. Profl. Engrs., Soc. Am. Foresters, Am. Inst. Biol. Scientists, Ecol. Soc. Am., Res. Officers Assn. U.S., NRA, Internat. Rescue and First Aid Assn., Internat. Platform Assn., Bulldog Sentinels of Superior Calif., Masons, Shriners. Methodist. Home: 5624 Bonniemae Way Sacramento CA 95824-1402

DROZD, LEON FRANK, JR., lawyer; b. Victoria, Tex., Sept. 11, 1948; s. Leon Frank and Dorothy Lucille (Smith) D.; BBA, Tex. A&M U., 1971; J.D., U. Denver, 1979. Bar: Colo., Calif., U.S. Dist. Ct. Colo. U.S. Dist. Ct. (no. dist.) Calif., U.S. Ct. Appeals (9th and 10th cirs.). Legis. asst. U.S. Ho. of Reps., also Dem. Caucus, Washington, 1971-74, chief clk. com. on sci. and tech., 1974-75; asst. to dean for devel. Coll. Law, U. Denver, 1975-79; v.p. Braddock Publs., Inc., Washington, 1975-79; land and legal counsel Chevron Shale Oil Co., Chevron Resources Co., 1980-87, ins. div., 1987-88; sr. counsel Chevron Corp. Law Dept. 1987—, Chevron Overseas Petroleum and White Nile Petroleum Co. Ltd. (Sudan), 1983, Colo. elector Anderson/Lucey Nat. Unity Campaign, 1980. Mem. ABA, Colo. Bar. Assn., San Francisco Bar Assn., Fed. Bar Assn., Am. Trial Lawyers Assn., Denver C. of C. (steering com. 1981-82). Office: Chevron Corp Law Dept PO Box 7141 555 Market St San Francisco CA 94105-2801

DRUBKA, ROBERT EDWARD, aerospace executive; b. Chgo., June 24, 1953; s. Edward Louis and Victoria Ann (Malec) D.; m. Barbara Chyra, Oct. 23, 1982; children: Christopher, Gregory. BS in Mech. and Aerospace Engring., Ill. Inst. Tech., 1975, MS in Mech. and Aerospace Engring., 1977, PhD in Mech. Engring., 1981; MBA, U. Calif., Irvine, 1993. Asst. prof. SUNY, Stony Brook, 1982-87; rsch. engr. McDonnell Douglas, Huntington Beach, Calif., 1987-92, sr. mgr., 1992—. Patentee in field; contbr. articles to profl. publs. Inst. Gas Tech. scholar, 1975; Ill. Inst. Tech. fellow, 1977-80. Mem. AIAA, Am. Phys. Soc., Beta Gamma Sigma. Home: 6801 Gas Light Dr Huntington Beach CA 92647-2927 Office: McDonnell Douglas Aerospace 5301 Bolsa Ave # 11/3 Huntington Beach CA 92647-2048

DRUFFEL, ANN BERNICE, psychic researcher, writer; b. Riverside, Calif., Aug. 12, 1926; d. William and Aileen (Walsh) McElroy; m. Charles K. Druffel, Jan. 24, 1953; children: Ellen, Diana, Carolyn, Charlotte, Allis Ann. BA in Sociology, Immaculate Heart Coll.; postgrad., Cath. U. Registered social case worker, Calif. Family and child welfare worker Cath. Welfare Bur., L.A. and Long Beach, Calif., 1948-53; researcher Nat. Investigations Com. for Aerial Phenomena, Washington, 1957-73, Ctr. for UFO Studies, Chgo., 1975—; rschr., cons. Mutual UFO Network, Seguin, Tex., 1973—; asst. researcher Mobius Soc., L.A., 1980-92. Co-author: (with D. Scott Rogo) The Tujunga Canyon Contacts, 1980, paperback edit., 1989, The Psychic and the Detective, 1983, 2d edit., 1995, (with Armand Marcotte) Past Lives: Future Growth, 1986, 2d edit., 1994; contbr. to Ency. of UFOs; (anthology) UFO Abductions, also contbr. over 100 articles to profl. publs.; cons. Flying Saucer Rev., London, 1980—; contbg. editor Mufon UFO Jour., Seguin, Tex., 1980—, assoc. editor, 1978-84; author: (filmscript) Dixie North; (TV) Psychic Detectives 1989, Report from Unknown, 1990. Recipient cert. of appreciation AIAA-IEEE/Harvard-Radcliffe Club, 1989. Mem. Mutual UFO Network (investigator), Ctr. for UFO Studies (assoc.).

DRUMHELLER, GEORGE JESSE, motel and hotel chain owner; b. Walla Walla, Wash., Jan. 30, 1933; s. Allen and Ila Margaret (Croxdale) D.; student Wash. State U., 1951-52, Whittier Coll., 1955-58; m. Carla Rene Cunha, May 4, 1965 (div. 1985). Asst. mgr. Olympic Hotel, Seattle, 1959; jr. exec. Westin Hotels, Seattle, 1959-63; founder, pres. George Drumheller Properties, Inc., motel holding co., Pendleton, Oreg., 1963—; founder, chmn. bd. Dalles Tapadera, Inc., motel and hotel holding co., The Dalles, Oreg., 1964-77; founder, pres. Lewiston Tapadera, Inc. (Idaho), motel holding co., 1970-77; founder, pres. Yakima Tapadera, Inc. (Wash.), 1971-77; founding ptnr. Drumheller & Titcomb (Tapadera Motor Inn), Ontario, Oreg., 1972-84; merger with Tapadera motel holding cos. and George Drumheller Properties, Inc., 1978—, founder Tapadera Budget Inns, Kennewick and Walla Walla, Wash., 1981-85, also merged with George Drumheller Properties, Inc., 1986; engaged in farming, eastern Wash., 1958-80; bd. dirs. Privacy Fund Wash. State PAC, 1991-92. With USCG, 1952-55. Mem. Am. Hotel and Motel Assn. (nat. dir. 1980-84, pres.'s exec. com. 1983-84), Oreg. Hotel Motel Assn. (dir. 1974-78), Wash. State Lodging Assn. (dir., v.p. 1976-84), Spokane Club, Walla Walla Country Club, Washington Athletic Club, J.D. Shea Club, LaJolla Beach and Tennis Club. Home: 244 Marcus St Walla Walla WA 99362-2028 also: 7960 Sunset Dr Neahkahnie OR 97131-9235 Office: George Drumheller Properties Inc PO Box 1234 Walla Walla WA 99362-0023

DRUMMER, DONALD RAYMOND, financial services executive; b. Binghamton, N.Y., Oct. 10, 1941; s. Donald Joseph and Louise Frances (Campbell) D.; AS, Broome C.C., 1962; BS, U. Colo., 1972; MBA, Regis U., 1981; m. Rita Kovac, May 22, 1965; children: Shelley Rita, Adam Donn. With, Lincoln First Bank, Binghamton, N.Y., 1962-69; asst. comptr. Adams & Horne, Denver, 1969; with Colo. State Bank, Denver, 1969-87, v.p., 1972-81, comptr., 1972-87, sr. v.p., 1981-87; sr. v.p., CFO Wyo. Nat. Bancorp. (formerly Affiliated Bank Corp. of Wyo.), Casper, 1987-91; v.p., contr. Crop Hail Mgmt., Kalispell, Mont., 1991-92, sr. v.p., CFO, 1992; treas. Rural Community Ins, 1992; sr. v.p., CFO Wyo. Nat. Bank, Casper, Cheyenne, 1987-91; bd. dirs. Wyo. Nat. Bank, Lovell and Kemmerer, 1987-88; corp. sec. Wyo. Nat. Bancorp. (formerly Affiliated Bank Corp. of Wyo.), 1987-91; sr. v.p. finance Am. Nat. Bank, Cheyenne, 1993—; v.p. Cmty. First Bancorp, Inc., 1994—; bd. dirs. Wheatland Ins. Agency, 1989-91; CFO, exec. com. Am. Bankers Assn., 1989-91; adj. faculty Regis U., mem. grad. edn. task force, 1986-87. Editor: Chronicle, 1980-81. Bd. dirs. Girl's Club of Casper, 1988. Mem. Inst. Mgmt. Accts. (dir. 1975-79, v.p. 1977-79), Am. Acctg. Assn., Am. Taxation Assn., Denver Sertoma Club (past pres.), City Club (v.p., dir. 1979-83). Office: 1912 Capitol Ave Cheyenne WY 82001-3650

DRUMMOND, GERARD KASPER, lawyer, retired minerals company executive; b. N.Y.C., Oct. 9, 1937; s. John Landells and Margaret Louise (Kasper) D.; m. Donna J. Mason, Sept. 14, 1957 (div. 1976); children: Alexander, Jane, Edmund; m. Sandra Hamilton, Aug. 31, 1985. B.S., Cornell U., 1959, LL.B. with distinction, 1963. Bar: Oreg. 1963. Assoc. Davies, Biggs, Strayer, Stoel & Boley, Portland, Oreg., 1963-64; assoc., ptnr. Rives, Bonyhadi, Drummond & Smith, Portland, 1964-77; pres. Nerco, Inc., Portland, from 1977-87, chmn. bd. dirs., 1987-93; mem. corp. policy group PacifiCorp, 1979-93, exec. v.p., 1987-93, also bd. dirs.; bd. dirs. Willamette Industries Inc., 1991—; of counsel Stoel Rives, Portland, 1993—. Pres., bd. dirs. Tri-County Met. Transit Dist., Portland, 1974-85; Oreg. Investment Coun., 1987—, chmn., 1990—; bd. dirs., exec. com. Oreg. Bus. Coun., 1987—; trustee Reed Coll., 1982—; bd. dirs. Oreg. Symphony, 1987-93, pres., 1990-92; cmty. bd. dirs. Providence Hosp., 1986—, chmn., 1993; mem. adv. coun. Cornell U. Law Sch., 1991—; bd. dirs. Oreg. Shakespeare Festival Assn., 1992—, Oreg. chpt. Nature Conservancy, 1992-93; chmn. bd. dirs. N.W. Bus. Commn. for Arts, 1992-94. 1st lt. USAR, 1959-67. Mem. ABA, Oreg. Bar Assn., Am. Mining Congress (bd. dirs. 1986-92), Arlington Club, Univ. Club. Home: 28815 S Needy Rd Canby OR 97013-9570 Office: Stoel Rives Boley Et Al 900 SW 5th Ste 2300 Portland OR 97204

DRUMMOND, HAROLD DEAN, education educator; b. Bettsville, Ohio, June 8, 1916; s. Ray W. and Velma T. (Foor) D.; m. Erma Catherine Street, Aug. 30, 1939 (dec. Aug. 1986); 1 child, Harold Evan; m. E. Josephine (Stanley) Raths, Nov. 23, 1988. Student, Westminster Coll., 1933-35; AB, Colo. State Coll., 1937, MA, 1940; EdD, Stanford U., 1948. Prin., tchr. White Deer (Tex.) Ind. Sch. Dist., 1938-42; prof. elem. edn. George Peabody Coll. for Tchrs., Nashville, 1947-60; acting prof. tchr. edn. assigned to U. Philippines, Stanford (Calif.) U., 1954-55; prof. elem. edn. U. N.Mex., Albuquerque, 1960-79, emeritus prof., 1979—; adv. bd. Childcraft, 1957-60, 67-80. Author: (with Charles R. Spain and John I. Goodlad) Educational Leadership and the Elementary School Principal, 1956; Our World Today series, A Journey Through Many Lands, Journeys Through the Americas, The Eastern Hemisphere, The Western Hemisphere, 1960-83. Lt. USNR, 1942-45, PTO. Laureate mem. Kappa Delta Pi, 1984; laureate counselor, 1984-88, 89-90. Mem. ASCD (pres. 1964-65), NEA, Nat. Assn. Elem. Sch. Prins., Nat. Coun. Social Studies, Nat. Coun. Geog. Edn., Nat. Soc. Study Edn., Profs. Curriculum. Home: 536 Graceland Dr SE Albuquerque NM 87108-3333

DRUMMOND, MARSHALL EDWARD, business educator, university administrator; b. Stanford, Calif., Sept. 14, 1941; s. Kirk Isaac and Fern Venice (McDeritt) D. BS, San Jose State U., 1964, MBA, 1969; EdD, U. San Francisco, 1979. Adj. prof. bus. and edn. U. San Francisco, 1975-81; adj. prof. bus. and info. systems San Francisco State U., 1981-82; prof. MIS, Ea. Wash. U., Cheney, 1985—, exec. dir. info. resources, 1988, assoc. v.p. adminstrv. svcs., chief info. officer, 1988-89, v.p. adminstrv. svcs., 1989-90, exec. v.p., 1990, pres., 1990—; cons. Sch. Bus., Harvard Coll., U. Ariz. Contbg. editor Diebold Series; contbr. articles to profl. jours. Democrat. Home: PO Box 187 Cheney WA 99004-0187 Office: Ea Wash U Mail Stop 130 Cheney WA 99004*

DRURY, DORIS MARIE, economics educator, consultant, researcher; b. Louisville, Nov. 18, 1926; d. Coleman F. and Ursula P. (Darst) D. B.S., U. Louisville, 1955, M.B.A., 1957; M.A., Ind. U., Bloomington, 1962, Ph.D., 1964; postgrad., U. Denver Coll. Law, 1973-74. Asst. prof. econs. U. Wyo., Laramie, 1962-63; assoc. prof. La. State U., 1963-65; prof. econs. U. Denver, 1965-90, chmn. div. research, 1968-71, chmn. econs., 1972-79; John Sullivan prof., exec. dir. MBA programs Regis U., 1990—; dir. Fed. Res. Bank, Kansas City, 1980-84, chmn. bd., 1985, chmn. audit, 1980-83; dir., chmn. audit com. Pub. Service Co., Denver, 1979—; dir., founder Women's Bank, Denver, 1977-78; dir. Colo. Nat. Bankshares, Equitable of Iowa; pres., chief exec. officer Ctr. for Bus. and Econ. Forecasting, Inc. Author: Accidents in Coal Producing Countries, 1964, Phase II Economic Controls, 1972, Key Public Economic Issues, 1971, Construction Industry in Colorado, 1969, 83—; editor quarterly rev. Colo. economy and econs. perspective. Mem. Gov.'s Blue Ribbon Panel on Econ. Planning, Colo., 1979-81; bd. dirs. YWCA, Denver, 1979-81. Recipient Disting. Teaching Specialist Commendation, U. Denver, 1973; Resources of the Future, Inc. fellow, 1961-62. Mem. Nat. Assn. Bus. Economists, Am. Econ. Assn., Denver C. of C. Home: 10879 E Powers Dr Englewood CO 80111-3959 Office: Regis U 3333 Regis Blvd Denver CO 80221-1099

DRUTCHAS, GERRICK GILBERT, publishing executive; b. Detroit, Sept. 23, 1953; s. Gilbert Henry and Elaine Marie (Rutkowski) D.; 1 child, Gilbert Henry II. BA, Mich. State U., 1975; postgrad., U. Redlands, 1983-85. Pres. Argentum Publs., L.A., 1986—; pres. Silver Shield Info. Svcs., Pasadena, Calif.; bd. dirs. Le Baron Investigations, Pasadena. Dir. Childrens Welfare Found. Sgt. USAR, 1981-85. Named Baron, Royal House of Alabona-Ostrogojsk, 1992. Mem. Order of the Swan (chevalier), Order of St. Angilbert (chevalier), K. of P. (past chancellor 1983, 84), Delta Sigma Phi. Unitarian. Home: 601 E California Blvd Pasadena CA 91106-3852 Office: Le Baron Investigations Pasadena CA 91106

DRYDEN, ROBERT EUGENE, lawyer; b. Chanute, Kans., Aug. 20, 1927; s. Calvin William and Mary Alfreda (Foley) D.; m. Jetta Rae Burger, Dec. 19, 1953; children: Lynn Marie, Thomas Calvin. AA, City Coll., San Francisco, 1947; BS, U. San Francisco, 1951, JD, 1954. Bar: Calif. 1955; diplomate Am. Bd. Trial Advocates. Assoc. Barfield, Dryden & Ruane (and predecessor firm), San Francisco, 1954-60, jr. ptnr., 1960-65, gen. ptnr., 1965-89; sr. ptnr. Dryden, Margoles, Schimaneck, Hartman & Kelly, San Francisco, 1989—; lectr. continuing edn. of the bar, 1971-77; evaluator U.S. Dist. Ct. (no. dist.) Calif. Early Neutral Evaluation Program; master atty. San Francisco Am. Inn of Ct.; mem. Product Liability Adv. Coun. Mem. bd. counsellors U. San Francisco, 1993—. With USMCR, 1945-46. Fellow Am. Coll. Trial Lawyers, Am. Bar Found., Internat. Acad. Trial Lawyers; mem. ABA (mem. product liability adv. coun.), San Francisco Bar Assn., Assn. Def. Counsel (bd. dirs. 1968-71), Def. Rsch. Inst., Internat. Assn. Ins. Counsel, Fedn. Ins. Counsel, Am. Arbitration Assn., U. San Francisco Law Soc. (mem. exec. com. 1970-72), U. San Francisco Alumni Assn. (mem. bd. govs. 1977), Phi Alpha Delta. Home: 1320 Lasuen Dr Millbrae CA 94030-2846 Office: Dryden Margoles Schimaneck Hartman & Kelly 1 California St Ste 3100 San Francisco CA 94111-5432

DRYE, ROBERT CALDWELL, psychiatrist; b. N.Y.C., Oct. 1, 1927; s. John Wilson R. Jr. and Loraine Livingston (Caldwell) D.; m. Vivian Nevue, Sept. 10, 1955 (dec. Sept. 1979); children: Richard, David, Barbara, Robert Caldwell Jr., Caroline, Elizabeth, Loraine. BS, MIT, 1947; MD, NYU, 1951. Intern Lenox Hill Hosp., N.Y.C., 1951-53; resident in psychiatry Army Med. Svc. Sch., Ft. Sam Houston, Tex., 1953, Ill. Rsch. and Edn. Hosp., Chgo., 1955-56, Michael Reese Hosp., Chgo., 1956-58; psychiatrist in student health U. Chgo., 1958-59; pvt. practice River Forest, Ill., 1959-70; chief Michael Reese Svc. Ill. State Psychiat. Inst., Chgo., 1959-61, asst. clin. dir., 1969-70; dir. edn. Ill. Dept. Mental Health, Chgo., 1961-69, dir. div. prof. svcs., 1964-65; mem. staff Western Inst. Group/Family Therapy, Watsonville, Calif., 1970-86; pvt. practice Carmel and Seaside, Calif., 1970-87; clin. dir. psychiatry dept. Oil City (Pa.) Area Health Ctr., 1987-90; pvt. practice Oil City, Pa., 1987-93; mem. adv. bd. Venango County Mental Health/Mental Retardation Svcs., Franklin, Pa., 1988—; med. dir. partial hosp. Venango County Counseling Ctr., Oil City, 1988-90; mem. NIMH psychiatry tng. com., 1967-71; lectr. dept. psychiatry Stanford U., 1970-87; clin. instr. Dept. of Psychiatry, U. Ariz., 1994—. Author: The Borderline Syndrome, 1968; contbr. articles to profl. jours. Pres. Oak Park and River Forest Com. for Human Rights, 1966—. 1st lt. USAR, 1953-55. Life fellow Am. Psychiat. Assn.; mem. Internat. Transactional Analysis (bd. dirs. 1970-85), Sigma Chi. Democrat. Presbyterian.

DRYSDALE, GEORGE MARSMAN, lawyer, venture capitalist; b. Manila, Sept. 16, 1954; (parents Am. citizens); s. George Williams and Anne (Marsman) D.; m. Diane Elizabeth Rogers, Aug. 17, 1991; children: Catherine Elizabeth, Jennifer Alexandra. BS in Engring., Harvey Mudd Coll., 1976; MBA, Stanford U., 1980, JD, 1980. Bar: N.Y., Calif. Cons. Braxton Assocs., Boston, 1980; lawyer Davis Polk & Wardwell, N.Y.C., 1981-83; gen. ptnr. Hambrecht & Quist Venture Ptnrs., San Francisco, 1983-87; asst. to sec. USDA, Washington, 1987-88; mng. gen. ptnr. Westar Capital, Costa Mesa, Calif., 1988-91; pres. Drysdale Enterprises, Newport

Beach, Calif., 1991—; vice chmn. Marsman-Drysdale Group, Manila, Philippines, 1992—; bd. dirs. H&Q Ventures, Marsman Group Plantations, Skyvision, Pepsi Mktg., Upside Pub., Internat. Wireless Comm., Philippine Wireless. Mem. Guardsmen, San Francisco, 1985; exec. dir. Nat. Adv. Coun. Small Bus., 1991; trustee Harvey Mudd Coll. Mem. Western Assn. Venture Capitalists (bd. dirs.), Pacific Club, N.Y. Athletic Club, Bahia Corinthian Yacht Club. Republican. Office: Drysdale Enterprises 177 Bovet Rd Ste 600 San Mateo CA 94402-3122

DRYSDALE, VALERIE MICOLE, elementary education educator; b. Yuma, Ariz., Aug. 11, 1941; d. Maurice Bennett McCullough and Natalie Azalia (Diemoz) Hulsey; m. Raymond R. Drysdale, Feb. 14, 1964; children: Valerie, Debra, Carmen. BFA, U. Ariz., 1969. Cert. art specialist. Art tchr., part-time painting instr. Ariz. Western Coll., Yuma, 1970-71; art specialist Yuma Sch. Dist., 1969—. Mem. Ariz. Art Edn. Assn. (bd. dirs. S.W. region coun. 1994-96, Ariz. Art Educator for Elem. Schs. 1993), Yuma Area Art Educators (chmn. 1971), Yuma Fine Arts Assn. (bd. dirs. 1969-70), Nat. Art Edn. Assn., Yuma Strategic Planning Com., Yuma Golf and Country Club. Democrat. Episcopalian. Home: 3011 S Arizona Ave Yuma AZ 85364-8230

D'SILVA, AECIO MOURA, aquaculture scientist; b. Belo Jardim, Brazil, Jan. 30, 1951; came to U.S., 1989; s. Francisco Frade and Clotildes Moura (Brasil) D'S.; m. Marilene da Fonseca, Apr. 4, 1970. Degree aquaculture engr., U. Fed. Rural of PE, Recife-Pernambuco, 1974; MS, Okla. State U., 1983; PhD, U. Ariz., 1993, postdoctorate, 1993—. Extension agt. Brazilian Extension Svc., Florianopolis, S.C., 1975; head of fishery affairs office Ministry of Agriculture, Brasilia, 1976-79; sr. adviser Prodecor-Ministry-Agriculture, Brasilia, 1980-83; cons. CODEVASF Ministry-Interior, Brasilia, 1983-84; pvt. cons. various cos., Brazil, USA, Can., 1985-87; head Brazilian Fishery Inst., Brazilia, 1987-88; exec. head State EPA, Joao Pessoa, 1989; prof. UN-FAO, Brazil, 1987-89; rschr. U. Ariz., Tucson, 1990—; cons. Concept. Can., Quebec, 1987, Sunwest Internat., Tucson, 1991—, World Bank, 1992—; software co. exec. NID Technologies, Tucson, 1991—. Author: Fishing Project Methodology, 1976, Mercury in the Environment, 1988, Environment Impact Assessment, 1989; inventor neurocomputing integration design software technology. Del. Internat. Labor Orgn., Geneva, 1988. Mem. World Aquaculture Soc., Am. Fishery Soc., Aquacultural Engring. Soc. Office: U Ariz 104 Bioeast Tucson AZ 85741

DUBES, MICHAEL J., insurance company executive; b. Dubuque, Iowa, Oct. 19, 1942; s. Wilmar C. and Cleo (Lenz) D.; m. Glenda Ra. Ackerlund, July 31, 1965; children: Scot (dec.), Heather. BS, Iowa State U., 1966; MS, Am. Coll., Bryn Mawr, Pa., 1981; postgrad., Harvard U., 1987, 90, LIMRA Strategies Inst., 1990. CLU, LLIF; cert. fin. planner; chartered fin. cons. Agt. Northwestern Nat. Life Ins. Co., Des Moines, Iowa, 1967-68, staff asst., Mpls., 1968-70, tng. mgr., St. Paul, 1970-72, supt. agys., Mpls., 1972-73, asst. mgr., Des Moines, 1973-78, br. mgr., 1978-83, regional mgr., 1983-84, 2d v.p. individual ins. sales, Mpls., 1984-85, v.p. indiv. ins. sales, 1985-87, sr. v.p. individual ins., 1987—; exec. v.p. Northwestern Nat. Life Ins. Sales Co., Mpls., 1984-85, pres., 1985-87; vice chmn., CEO Washington Square Securities, Inc., Mpls., 1984-87; chmn. Washington Sq. Securities, Mpls., 1987—; bd. dirs. Mpls., NWNL Found.; mem. NWNL Cos. Enterprise Coun., mgmt. com.; bd. dirs. Northern Life Ins. Co. (an NWNL co.), Seattle, CEO, pres. Amb. Iowa State U.; mem. MBA Inst. Mgmt. adv. com. U. St. Thomas. With USAR, 1967. Recipient Gene Helton award Des Moines Life Underwriters, 1982. Mem. Nat. Assn. Life Underwriters (bd. dirs. 1983-84), Am. Soc. CLUs, Life Ins. Mktg. and Rsch. Assn. (exec. devel. com. 1985-91, ops. com. 1989—, bd. dirs. 1991-93, chmn. membership com.), Agy. Officer Round Table (meeting chmn. 1994), Gen. Agts. and Mgrs. Assn. (pres. 1983-84), Cert. Fine. Planners, MBA Ins. Mgmt. Adv., U. St. Thomas, Met. Breakfast Club (bd. dirs. 1988-94), Interlachen Country Club (bd. govs.), Desert Mountain Country Club, Rainier Club, Amb. Club (Iowa State U.), Variety Club of Iowa (bd. dirs. 1983-84), Sahalee Country Club, Harvard Bus. Sch. Club Minn., Mpls. Club, Boys and Girls Club Mpls. (bd. dirs., exec. com., devel. com.), Rotary (Paul Harris fellow 1988, bd. dirs.). Home: 3529 264th Ave SE Issaquah WA 98027-9138 Office: Northern Life Ins Co 1110 3rd Ave Seattle WA 98101-2930

DUBESA, ELAINE J., biotechnology company executive; b. Alton, Ill., July 26, 1943; m. Michael Dubesa, Oct. 28, 1967. BS in Med. Tech., Loyola U., New Orleans, 1966. Rsch. assoc. pesticides project U. Hawaii, Honolulu, 1968-69; field rep., pesticides project La. State U., New Orleans, 1970-71; lab. supr. Beaufort (S.C.) County Meml. Hosp., 1971-72; asst. supr. hematology Mayo Clinic, Rochester, Minn., 1973-75; edn. coord. Sherman Hosp., Elgin, Ill., 1975-78; sect. chief PCL (now Nichols Inst.), Portland, Oreg., 1978-80; quality control supr. PCL-RIA, Inc., Portland, 1980-82; quality control mgr. Am. Bioclinical Inc., Portland, 1982-87; quality assurance mgr., regulatory affairs mgr. Epitope, Inc., Beaverton, Oreg., 1987-91, v.p. regulatory affairs, 1991—. Active Troutdale (Oreg.) Hist. Soc. Mem. Am. Soc. Quality Control, Regulatory Affairs Profl. Soc., Am. Soc. Clinical Pathologists, Beta Epsilon Upsilon.

DUBOFF, LEONARD DAVID, lawyer, educator; b. Bklyn., Oct. 3, 1941; s. Rubin Robert and Millicent Barbara (Pollach) DuB.; m. Mary Ann Crawford, June 4, 1967; children: Colleen Rose, Robert Courtney, Sabrina Ashley. JD summa cum laude, Bklyn. Law Sch., 1971. Bars: N.Y. 1974, Oreg. 1977, U.S. Dist. Cts. (so. and ea. dists.) N.Y. 1974, U.S. Ct. Appeals (2d cir.) 1974, U.S. Ct. Appeals (9th cir.) 1990, U.S. Customs Ct. 1975, U.S. Supreme Ct. 1977, U.S. Fed. Dist. Ct. 1990. Teaching fellow Stanford (Calif.) U. Law Sch., 1971-72; mem. faculty Lewis & Clark Coll. Northwestern Sch. Law, Portland, Oreg., 1972-94, prof. law, 1977-94; ptnr. DuBoff & Assocs., Portland, 1994—; instr. Hastings Coll. Law Coll. Civil Advocacy, San Francisco, summers 1978, 79. Founder, past pres. Oreg. Vol. Lawyers for Arts; mem. lawyers' com. ACLU, 1973-78, bd. dirs. Oreg., 1974-76; mem. Mayor's Adv. Com. Security and Privacy, 1974; bd. dirs. Portland Art Mus. Asian Art Council, 1976-77, Internat. Assn. Art Security, N.Y.C., 1976-80; pres. Arts Commn. of Tigard Tualatin and Sherwood, 1990-92; Gov. Oreg. Com. Employment of Handicapped, 1978-81; cons., panelist spl. projects Nat. Endowment for Arts, 1978-79; mem. Mayor's Adv. Com. on Handicapped, 1979-81; mem. Wash. State Atty. Gen's. Com. to Reorganize Maryhill Mus.; Oreg. Commn. for Blind, 1987-93; Oreg. Com. for Humanities, 1981-87. Recipient Bklyn. Law Sch. Stuart Hirschman Property, Jerome Prince Evidence, Donald W. Matheson Meml. awards, 1st scholarship prize; Hofstra U. Lighthouse scholar 1965-71; recipient Hauser award, 1967, Howard Brown Pickard award, 1967-69, Oreg. Govs. Arts award, 1990. Mem. Am. Soc. Internat. Law, Assn. Alumni and Attenders of Hague Acad. Internat. Law, Assn. Am. Law Schs. (standing com. sect. activities 1975, chmn. sect. law and arts 1974-80, 91-93, spl. com. on disabilities 1989-91), ABA, N.Y. State Bar Assn., Oreg. Bar Assn., Delta Kappa Phi, Sigma Pi Sigma, Sigma Alpha. Spl. columnist on craft law, The Crafts Report, 1973-77; editor, contbr. materials to legal and art textbooks; author textbooks and articles for legal and art jours. Office: DuBoff & Assocs 9320 SW Barbur Blvd Ste 340 Portland OR 97219-5404

DU BOIS, DAVID D., plastic surgeon; b. Story City, Iowa, 1940. MD, U. Iowa, 1965. Instr. Phila. Gen. Hosp., 1965-66; resident surgeon Mayo Clinic, Rochester, N.Y., 1968-72, plastic surgeon, 1972-74; now plastic surgeon Penrose Hosp., Colorado Springs, Colo. Office: 2727 N Tejon St Colorado Springs CO 80907-6231*

DUBOIS, MARK, environmental activist; b. Sacramento, Calif., Feb. 24, 1949; s. Noel A. and Connie C. McGuire D.; m. Sharon A. Negri; 1 child, Tevon. Co-founder, river guide, educator "etc" (Environ. Traveling Companions), 1972-74; co-founder, dir. Friends of the River, 1973—, Internat. Rivers Network, 1984-89; founder grassroots campaign for internat. bank reform WorldWise, 1991—; strategist, lobbyist World Bank, Inter-Am. Devel. Bank, Asian Devel. Bank annual mtgs., 1986-95; internat. coord. Earth Day, 1990; advisor Together Found., 1991-93; outreach coord. Resource Renewal Inst., 1993; bd. mem. Friends of the River (emeritus), Friends of the Ganges, Tuolumne River Preservation Trust; adv. bd. Solar Cooker Internat., Rivers Network, Shomrei Adamah, Galupga; spkr., advisor, activist confs., tours, explorations. Co-publisher: International Directory of Non-Governmental Organizations. Co-initiator, dir. Proposition 13, Water Conservation and Efficiency Act, Calif., 1981-82. Recipient Burt Chapell award, 1967, Giraffe award, 1981, Global 500 award U.S. Friends of UN Environ. Programme, 1988; co-recipient Beyond War award Earth Day 1990; named River Conservationist of the Yr., Sierra Club, 1981, Am. Wilderness Alliance, 1982, Perception, 1988. Address: 401 San Miguel Way Sacramento CA 95819-2717

DUBOIS, PATRICIA LAVONNE, retail mobile electronics company executive; b. Spokane, Wash., July 20, 1963; d. Richard Allen and Charlotte LaVerne (Kleweno) DuB. BA, Gonzaga U., 1985. Exec. asst. N.W. Sound, Inc., Seattle, 1985-87; office mgr. N.W. Yeshiva High Sch., Seattle, 1987-88; exec. asst. Car Toys, Seattle, 1988-90, corp. ops. mgr., 1990-92, gen. mgr., 1992—; cons., sec.-treas. Omniscient Prodn., Seattle, 1993—. Vol. Oil Spill Clean Up, State of Wash., Ocean Shores, 1989. Roman Catholic. Office: Car Toys 4516 S W Holgate Seattle WA 98116

DUBOSE, FRANCIS MARQUIS, clergyman; b. Elba, Ala., Feb. 27, 1922; s. Hansford Arthur and Mayde Frances (Owen) DuB.; BA cum laude, Baylor U., 1947; MA, U. Houston, 1958; BD, Southwestern Bapt. Sem., 1957, ThD, 1961; postgrad. Oxford (Eng.) U., 1972; m. Dorothy Anne Sessums, Aug. 28, 1940; children: Elizabeth Anne Parnell, Frances Jeannine Huffman, Jonathan Michael, Celia Danielle. Pastor Bapt. chs., Tex., Ark., 1939-61; supt. missions. So. Bapt. Conv., Detroit, 1961-66; prof. missions Golden Gate Bapt. Sem., 1966—, dir. World Mission Ctr., 1979—, sr. prof., 1992; lectr., cons. in 115 cities outside U.S., 1969-82; v.p. Conf. City Mission Supts., So. Bapt. Conv., 1964-66; trustee Mich. Bapt. Inst., 1963-66; mem. San Francisco Inter-Faith Task Force on Homelessness. Mem. Internat. Assn. Mission Study, Am. Soc. Missiology, Assn. Mission Profs. Co-editor: The Mission of the Church in the Racially Changing Community, 1969; author: How Churches Grow in an Urban World, 1978, Classics of Christian Missions, 1979, God Who Sends: A Fresh Quest for Biblical Mission, 1983, Home Cell Groups and House Churches, 1987, Mystic on Main Street, 1994; contbr. to Toward Creative Urban Strategy; Vol. III Ency. of So. Baptists, also articles to profl. jours. Home: 2 Carpenter Ct San Francisco CA 94124-4429 Office: Golden Gate Bapt Sem Mill Valley CA 94941

DUBOW, SUSAN DIANE, financial consultant; b. Phila., June 13, 1948; d. Milton and Esther (Kalish) D.; m. Thomas J. Volgy, Feb. 8, 1987. BArch with distinction, U. Ariz., 1974-78, postgrad., 1988-. Architect in tng. Macneil Riedel Architects,, Tucson, 1977-79; constrn. coordinator Empire West Cos., Tucson, 1979-81; investment broker A.G. Edwards, Tucson, 1982-85, Merrill Lynch, Tucson, 1985-86, Rauscher Pierce Refsnes, Inc., Tucson, 1986-94, Smith Barney Inc., Tucson, 1994—; owner Sparky's Tailwaggers, Pet Products for Pet Lovers, 1991—; nat. speaker on investment planning, 1989—; investment broker Women's Investment Network, Tucson, 1982-89, Red Herring, Tucson, 1986-88, Health Investment Profile, Tucson, 1987-89, Great Expectations, Tucson, 1988. Mem. Tucson Women's Commn., 1983-84; coord. Cigna/Michael Landon Celebrity Tennis Classic, Tucson, 1987-88; bd. dirs. Comstock Children's Found., 1985-88; steering com., chair speakers bd. Tucson First, 1987-89; vol. Primavera Found., 1990—, bd. dirs., 1991-93, So. Ariz. Women's Fund, 1993—. Mem. Nat. Assn. Security Dealers, Pres.'s Club of Rauscher Pierce Refsnes, Inc. Democrat. Office: Smith Barney 5285 E Williams Cir # 5500 Tucson AZ 85711-4485

DUBROFF, HENRY ALLEN, journalist; b. Neptune, N.J., Nov. 28, 1950; s. Sol and Gilda (Burdman) D.; married, 1980 (div. 1986). AB in History and Lit., Lafayette Coll., 1972; MS in Journalism, Columbia U., 1982. Staff writer Dept. Health and Human Svcs., Washington, 1972-73; tchr. English Holyoke (Mass.) St. Sch., 1974-78; employment & tng. program mgr. Knoxville (Tenn.)-Knox CY Community Action, 1978-81; bus. writer, columnist Springfield (Mass.) Newspapers, 1982-85; bus. writer, columnist The Denver Post, 1985-88, bus. editor, 1988—; contbg. writer CFO Mag., Boston, 1985-90. Contbr. articles to N.Y. Times, 1982-89. Vol. Russian Resettlement Program Jewish Family & Children's Svcs., Denver, 1989-90. Recipient N.Y. Fin. Writers Assn. scholarship, 1982, Morton Margolin prize U. Denver, 1988, Bus. Story of Yr. award AP, 1989. Mem. Soc. Am. Bus. Editors and Writers. Office: The Denver Post 1560 Broadway Denver CO 80202-5133

DUCA, FRANK A., software engineer, researcher; b. Tulsa, Sept. 9, 1956; s. Joe W. and Joyce Ann (Moore) D. BSEE in Physics, Rice U., 1978; MS in Computer Sci., U. Colo., 1995. Devel. engr. Storage Tech. Corp., Louisville, 1978-80; geophys. sys. devel. mgr. Occidental Oil and Gas, Tulsa, 1980-86; tech. mktg. cons. Unisys Corp., St. Louis, 1986-90; adv. engr. Storage Tech. Corp., Louisville, 1990-95; instr. U. Colo., 1995—; principle cons. Network Solutions Inc., Houston, 1989-90. Recipient Tech. Excellence award Storage Tech. Corp., 1992, 94. Mem. Assn. for Computing Machinery, IEEE Computer Soc. Home: 2795 Darley Ave Boulder CO 80303-6305 Office: Dept Computer Sci & Engring U Colo 1200 Larimer Denver CO 80204

DUCETTE, SHERYL JANE, counselor, educator, therapist; b. Kearny, N.J., Aug. 16, 1952; d. Earl Stuart Whitaker and Virginia Jane (Messerschmidt) Fowler. BA magna cum laude, Drew U., 1974; MEd in Counseling, Fla. Atlantic U., 1981; MS in Pub. Mgmt., Nova U., 1981. Rehab. specialist, adminstr. various orgns., Mich., Fla., and Oreg., 1974-82; ednl. dir., therapist various orgns., Fla. and Oreg., 1974—; dir. social svcs., vol. svcs. various orgns., Portland, Oreg., 1984—; counselor Crossroad Resources/Wellspring Counseling, Portland, Oreg., 1986—; instr., pub. spkr. various orgns., Portland, 1982—; cons., Portland, 1986—. Vol. Meridian Park Hosp., St. Vincent's Hosp., Kiwanis, Portland, 1989-92; bd. dirs. Small Change, 1995—. Grantee Lake Worth Cmty. Edn., 1978, various social svcs. grants, 1979-93. Mem. Am. Counseling Assn., Oreg. Assn. of Dirs. of Vols. in Health Care Orgns., N.W. Oreg. Vol. Adminstrs. Assn., Sigma Phi. Office: Kaiser Permanente 3414 N Kaiser Center Dr Portland OR 97227 also: Wellspring Counseling 12525 SW 68th Tigard OR 97068

DUCKER, JAMES HOWARD, historian, writer; b. Rochester, N.Y., July 24, 1950; m. Brenda A. Theyers; 1 child, Allison Marie. BA, Villanova U., 1972; PhD, U. Ill., 1980. Author: Men of the Steel Rails: Workers on AT&SF Railroad, 1983; editor Alaska History, 1985—. Recipient Cert. commendation Am. Assn. for State and Local History, 1989. Mem. Orgn. Am. Historians, Western Hist. Assn., Alaska Hist. Soc. (bd. dirs. 1988-91), Cook Inlet Hist. Soc.

DUCKWORTH, GUY, musician, educator; b. L.A., Dec. 19, 1923; s. Glenn M. and Laura (Lysle) D.; m. Ballerina Maria Farra, May 23, 1948. BA, UCLA, 1951; MusM, Columbia U., 1953, PhD, 1969. Piano soloist Metro Goldwyn Mayer Studios, 1936-41, Warner Bros. Studios, 1936-41, Sta. KFI, L.A., 1938, Sta. KNX, L.A., 1939, Sta. KHJ, L.A., 1940; artist Columbia Artists, 1942-49; asst. prof. music. U. Minn., Mpls., 1955-60, assoc. prof., 1960-62; prof. piano, fellow Northwestern U., Evanston, Ill., 1962-70; chmn. dept. preparatory piano Northwestern U., 1962-70; prof. music U. Colo., Boulder, 1970-88; prof. emeritus U. Colo., 1988, originator, coordinator masters and doctoral programs in mus. arts; piano concert tours in U.S., Can., Mexico, 1947-49; condr. various music festivals, U.S., 1956—; dir. Walker Art Children's Concerts, Mpls., 1957-62; nat. piano chmn. Music Educators Nat. Conf., 1965-71; vis. lectr., scholar 96 univs., colls. and conservatories, U.S. and Can., 1964—; cons. to Ill. State Dept. Program Devel. for Gifted Children, 1968-69; vis. prof. U. Colo., 1988-90. Author: Keyboard Explorer, 1963, Keyboard Discoverer, 1963, Keyboard Builder, 1964, Keyboard Musician, 1964, Keyboard Performer, 1966, Keyboard Musicianship, 1970, Guy Duckworth Piano Library, 1974, Guy Duckworth Musicianship Series, 1975, Keyboard Musician: The Symmetrical Keyboard, 2 vols., 1987-88, Keyboard Musician: The Symmetrical Keyboard, 1988, rev. edit., 1990; contbr. to over 6 books, 23 articles on pedagogy of music to various jours.; producer, performer video tapes on piano teaching; producer, writer (film) The Person First: A Different Kind of Teaching, 1984. Nominator Irving S. Gilmore Internat. Keyboard Festival, Gilmore Artist and Young Artist Awards. With U.S. Army, 1943-46. Recipient All-Univ. Teaching award for excellence, U. Colo., 1981, Pedagogy Honors award Nat. Conf. Piano Pedagogy, Chgo., 1994; named Pioneer Pedagogue Nat. Corp. Piano Pedagogy, Princeton U. Retrospective, 1992. Mem. Music Tchrs. Nat. Assn., Colo. State Music Tchrs. Assn., Coll. Music Soc., Music Educators Nat. Conf., Music Teachers Assn. Calif., Phi Mu Alpha, Pi Kappa Lambda. Home: Condo # 311 720 Camino De La Reina San Diego CA 92108-3225 Office: U Colo Boulder CO 80302

DUCKWORTH, TARA ANN, insurance company executive; b. Seattle, June 7, 1956; d. Leonard Douglas and Audrey Lee (Limbeck) Hill; m. Mark L. Duckworth, May 16, 1981; children: Harrison Lee III, Andrew James, Kathryn Anne. AAS, Highline Community Coll., Seattle, 1976. Acctg. clk. SAFECO Inc. Co., Seattle, programmer analyst, 1977-80, programming supr., 1980-85, info. systems supr., 1985-90; rate systems mgr. mut. funds SAFECO Credit, SAFECO Trust, PNMR, Seattle, 1990-94, sys. mgr., 1994—; mem. tech adv. com. for the computer info. svcs. program North Seattle Community Coll., 1984—, chairperson tech. adv. com., 1988-90. Mem. STar Lake Improvement Club, 1988-94, St. Lukes Luth. Ch., 1986—, fellowship com. Mem. NAFE, Nat. Assn. for Ins. Women, Soc. for State Filers, Nat. PTA. Office: SAFECO Ins Co SAFECO Plz Seattle WA 98185

DUDA, LUTHER, food products executive; b. 1939. Sec. Gene Jackson Farms Inc., Oxnard, Calif. Office: Gene Jackson Farms Inc 195 Victoria Ave Oxnard CA 93030-8796*

DUDAS, THOMAS M., marketing company executive; b. St. Louis, Jan. 17, 1951; s. Michael and Jane Dudas; m. Dawn Dudas, Dec. 30, 1981; children: Tamara, Michael, Daniel. BA, Ft. Lewis Coll., Durango, Colo., 1975; student, U. Nev., Las Vegas, 1988-89, Inst. Real Estate Mgmt., Las Vegas, 1993. Notary pub., Stae of Nev. Dist. mgr. mktg. Ford Steel Co., St. Louis, 1978-83; hotel dir. Landmark Hotel & Casino, Las Vegas, 1983-90; realtor Western Properties, Las Vegas, 1990-93; pres. Dudas Mktg. Inc., Las Vegas, 1989—. Candidate for mayor City of Las Vegas, 1991; founder, pres. Art League, Durango, Colo., 1975. Mem. Breakfast Club of Las Vegas (pres. 1990). Republican. Office: Dudas Mktg Inc 1917 Verdinal Dr Las Vegas NV 89102-3048

DUDDLES, CHARLES WELLER, food company executive; b. Cadillac, Mich., Mar. 31, 1940; s. Dwight Irving and Bertha (Taylor) D.; m. Judith Marie Robinson, June 23, 1962; children: Paul, Steven, Lisa. B.S., Ferris State U., 1961. C.P.A. Mich., Mo. Audit mgr. Price Waterhouse & Co., Battle Creek, Mich., 1961-72; mgr. gen. acctg. Ralston Purina Co., St. Louis, 1973-77, dir. spl. acctg. services, 1977-79; v.p., controller Foodmaker, Inc., San Diego, 1979-81, sr. v.p. fin. and adminstrn., chief fin. officer, 1981-87, sr. v.p., chief fin. officer, 1988, exec. v.p., chief fin. officer, chief adminstrv. officer, dir., 1988—; dir. Family Restaurants, Inc., 1994. Mem. Fin. Execs. Inst., Nat. Assn. Accts., Am. Inst. C.P.A.s. Republican. Presbyterian. Lodge: Rotary (San Diego). Home: 4804 Mount Helix Dr La Mesa CA 91941-4395 Office: Foodmaker Inc PO Box 783 San Diego CA 92112-4126

DUDEK, F. EDWARD, educator; b. Columbus, Nebr., Sept. 12, 1947; married; children: Sara, Amanda. BS in Biol. Sci., U. Calif., Irvine, 1969, PhD in Physiology, 1973. Trainee dept. ophthalmology rsch. Columbia U., Coll. Physicians, N.Y.C., 1973-74; rsch. assoc. dept. psychobiology U. Calif., Irvine, 1974; rsch. assoc. biomed. inst. dept. physiology & biophysics U. Tex. Med. Br., Galveston, 1974-75; asst. prof. dept. zoology U. Toronto (Ont., Can.), 1975-80; assoc. prof. dept. physiology Tulane U. Sch. Medicine, New Orleans, 1980-84, prof., 1984-87; prof. mental retardation rsch. ctr. U. Calif, L.A., 1987-92, assoc. dir., 1989-91; prof., chmn. dept. anatomy and neurobiology Colo. State U., Ft. Collins, 1992—. Contbr. chpts. to books and articles to profl. jours. Isaad and Clara Jacobs scholar, 1969-70, Brython Davis scholar, 1969-70; NSF Undergrad. Rsch. fellow, 1968; recipient NIH Javits Neurosci. Investigator award, 1987-94, Behavioral and Neuriscis. Study sect. award, 1985-88, Tulane Owl Club Teaching award, 1984Edward Steinhaus Outstanding Teaching award, 1972. Mem. AAAS, Am. Physiological Soc., Am. Epilepsy Soc., Soc. Neurosci. Office: Colo State U Dept Anatomy & Neurobiology Fort Collins CO 80523

DUDIS, JOHN BETZ, lawyer; b. Chgo., Nov. 6, 1946; s. John A. and Dorothy (Geiger) D.; m. Rhonda Marie Pettinato, July 30, 1977; children: Amanda Robin, Allison JoHanna. BA in Bus., Econs. summa cum laude, Rocky Mountain Coll., 1969; JD, U. Mont., 1972; LLM in Taxation, U. Mo., 1974. Law clk. to chief justice Mont. Supreme Ct., Helena, 1972-73; assoc. law Murphy, Robinson, Heckathorn & Phillips, P.C., Kalispell, Mont., 1974—; bd. mem. Mont. Bd. Realty Regulation, Dept. of Commerce, State of Mont., 1983-86, chmn., 1986-91; speaker tax and estate planning continuing edn. ins. licensees, real estate licensees, bankers, ABA, gen. pub., Mont., 1974—. Assoc. editor, contbr. Mont. Law Rev., 1970-72. Mem. Mont. Arts Coun., Helena, 1991; chmn. Flathead County Red Cross Chpt., Kalispell, Mont., 1981; mem. adv. bd. State of Mont. Blood Svcs. ARC, Gt. Falls, 1983-90; bd. dirs. Salvation Army, Kalispell, 1991, United Way, Flathead County, Kalispell, 1982-91; pres. Kalispell Tastmasters Club, 1979; com. chmn. Job Svc. Employers com., Kalispell, 1989-91; sec., bd. mem. Bigfork (Mont.) Ctr. for Performing Arts, 1981—; fin. chmn. Glacier dist. Boy Scouts Am., Kalispell, 1992, Eagle Scout, 1963. Recipient Testimonial of Appreciation, Mont. Assn. Realtors, 1991; named Boss of Yr., Flathead Valley Legal Secs. Assn., Kalispell, 1985; Phi Delta Phi scholar U. Mont. Law Sch., 1971-72. Mem. ABA, Mont. Bar Assn., NW Mont. Bar Assn., Elks. Republican. Roman Catholic. Office: Murphy Robinson et al 431 1st Ave NW Kalispell MT 59901-3908

DUELL, PAUL BARTON, internist, endocrinologist; b. May 22, 1956. BS cum laude, Willamette U., Salem, Oreg., 1978; MD, Oreg. Health Scis. U., 1983. Diplomate Am. Bd. Internal Medicine, Am. Bd. Endocrinology, Metabolism and Nutrition; lic. physicia, Oreg., Wash. Intern U. Chgo., 1983-84; resident in medicine Oreg. Health Scis. U., Portland, 1984-86; fellow in endocrinology, metabolism U. Wash., Seattle, 1986-89, acting instr., 1989-90; asst. prof. medicine Oreg. Health Scis. U., Portland, 1990—, attending physician, 1990—; attending physician Portland VA Hosp., 1990—; med. scientist; lectr. in field. Contbr. articles to profl. jours., chpts. to books. Named Disting. Citizen, State of Wash., 1988; Tartar Trust Rsch. fellow, 1980, Oreg. Heart Assn. rsch. fellow, 1980; Oreg. scholar, 1974, Mary L. Collins scholar, 1976, 77. Fellow Arteriosclerosis Coun. Am. Heart Assn.; mem. ACP, Am. Fedn. for Clin. Rsch., Am. Inst. Nutrition, Am. Soc. for Clin. Nutrition, Am. Diabetes Assn., Juvenile Diabetes Found. Internat., Phi Eta Sigma, Alpha Kappa Nu, Mortar Bd. (v.p. 1977). Office: Oreg Health Scis Univ Divsn of Endocrinology Diabetes/Nutrition L465 Portland OR 97201-3098

DUERNBERGER, PAUL M., computer services director, computer and electrical engineering educator. BS in Meteorology and Oceanography, SUNY, 1968; postgrad., U. Miami, 1975-76, Armes Forces Staff Coll., 1982; MS in Applied Sci., Naval Postgrad. Sch., 1986. With U.S. Dept. Commerce, NOAA, 1968-89; cons. King County Superior Ct., Seattle, 1989-90; dir. computer svcs. Found. Ednl. Achievement, San Diego, 1990—; prof. computer sci. and elec. engring. Cogswell Coll. North, Kirkland, Wash., 1990—. Pres. Boradview Community Coun., Seattle, 1991-92. Mem. IEEE, Am. Cetecean Soc. (bd. dirs Pacific Northwest chpt.), Wash. Software Assn., Assn. Computing Machinery, Soc. Am. Mil. Engrs., Digital Equipment Corp. User's Soc., Lions. Office: Cogswell Coll N 10626 NE 37th Cir Kirkland WA 98033-7921

DUERR, ALFRED, mayor. Formerly alderman City of Calgary, Alta., Can., elected mayor, 1989. Office: City of Calgary, PO Box 2100 Stn M, Calgary, AB Canada T2P 2M5*

DUERR, NAOMI SMITH, state agency administrator, geologist; b. Champaign-Urbana, Ill., May 4, 1956; d. Aaron and Joan G. (Gertsacov) Smith; m. Herb Duerr, Oct. 24, 1993. BS in Geology, U. Nev., Reno, 1979, M of Pub. Adminstrn. and Policy, 1983. Registered profl. geologist, Fla. Contract field geologist Phillips Uranium Corp., Conoco, Inc., others, 1977-80; geologist, resource analyst Geothermal Devel. Assocs., Reno, 1980-81; project mgr. Noranda Exploration, Inc., Reno, 1981; Congl. aide Mines and Mining Subcom., U.S. Congress, Washington, 1982; grad. asst. dept. polit. sci. U. Nev., Reno, 1981-83; asst. dir. Dept. Resource Mgmt./St. Johns River Water Mgmt. Dist., Palatka, Fla., 1986-93; adminstr. Nev. Div. Water Planning, Carson City, 1993—; mem. Adv. Coun. on Water Resources Rsch., Reno, 1993—; mem. local govt. adv. coun. U. North Fla., Jacksonville, 1991-93. Author articles. Chmn. Mug Race, Jacksonville, Fla., 1993; coord., fundraiser United Way, no. Nev., 1994. Named Fla. Regulatory Person of Yr., Fla. Rural Water Assn., 1990. Mem. Am. Water Resources Assn., Nev. Water Resources Assn., Nat. Water Works Assn. Home: 12475 Overbrook Dr Reno NV 89511-7724 Office: Nev Div Water Planning 1550 East Coll Pky Carson City NV 89710

DUESTER, KAREN CHRISTENSEN, nutritionist, food industry executive; b. Minden, Nebr., June 7, 1958; d. Edwin LeRoy and Maxine Carol (Sorensen) Christensen; m. Gregg Lee Duester, Sept. 21, 1992. BS, U. Nebr., 1980; MS, Tex. Woman's U., 1981. Registered dietitian. Intern Houston VA Med. Ctr., 1980-81; clin. dietitian Iowa Meth. Med. Ctr., Des Moines, 1982-83; chief clin. nutritionist Cleveland Meml. Hosp., Shelby, N.C., 1983-85; regional sales mgr. Practorcare, Inc., Denver, 1985-88, sales mgr. western divsn., 1988-92; v.p. healthcare Practorcare, Inc., San Diego, 1992-93; owner Food Consulting Co., San Diego, 1993—; cons. in field, 1983—; speaker profl. confs., 1982—. Contbr. articles to profl. jours., reviewer jours. Mem. Am. Dietetic Assn. (Recognized Young Dietitian of Yr. award 1987), So. Calif. Culinary Guild, Dietitians in Bus. and Comm. Republican. Office: The Food Consulting Co 12966 Carmel Creek Rd Apt 142 San Diego CA 92130-2131

DUFF, JAMES GEORGE, financial services executive; b. Pittsburg, Kans., Jan. 27, 1938; s. James George and Camilla (Vinardi) D.; m. Linda Louise Beeman, June 24, 1961 (div.); children: Michele, Mark, Melissa; m. Beverly L. Pool, Nov. 16, 1984. B.S. with distinction (Sunray Mid-Continent Scholar; Bankers Scholar), U. Kans., 1960, M.B.A., 1961. With Ford Motor Co., Dearborn, Mich., 1962—; various positions fin. staff Ford Motor Co., 1962-71; dir. product, profit, price, warranty Ford of Europe, 1972-74; controller Ford Div., 1974-76, controller car ops., 1976, controller car product devel., 1976-80; exec. v.p. Ford Motor Credit Co., 1980-88, bd. dirs.; pres., COO U.S. Leasing Internat. Inc. (now USL Capital), San Francisco, 1988-89, pres., CEO, 1990-91; chmn., CEO USL Capital, San Francisco, 1991—, also bd. dirs.; bd. dirs. Airlease Mgmt. Svcs.; mem. Conf. Bd., 1990—. Mem. adv. bd. U. Kans. Sch. Bus., 1980—; bd. dirs. Bay Area Coun., 1990—; trustee San Francisco Mus. Modern Art, 1990—; chmn. bus. devel. unit Detroit United Fund, 1980-85, chmn. edn. and local govt. unit Detroit United Fund, 1986-88. Mem. San Francisco C. of C. (bd. dirs. 1990-91). Home: 7 Russian Hill Pl San Francisco CA 94133-3605 Office: USL Capital 733 Front St San Francisco CA 94111-1909

DUFFY, BARBARA JEAN, county official, librarian, education consultant, publisher; b. Colorado Springs, Colo., Dec. 13, 1938; d. Eugene Hagaman and Ruth Mae (Sills) Vannest; m. William M. Campbell (div.); children: Holli Denise Campbell Dowell, Heidi Diane Campbell; m. Donald D. Duffy (div.). BS, Cen. State U., Edmond, Okla., 1972; MEd, U. Okla., 1974, EdD, 1983. From clk. to acctg. dept. Continental Oil Co., Ponca City, Okla., 1959-65; sec. Apco Oil Co, Oklahoma City, 1966-70; libr. media specialist Putnam City West High Sch., Oklahoma City, 1973-80; curriculum coord. Okla. State Dept. Edn., Oklahoma City, 1980-89; cons./publisher Bayview Assocs., San Mateo, Calif., 1989-90; grants dir., profl. svcs. assoc. Assn. Calif. Sch. Adminstrs., Burlingame, Calif., 1992; program dir. libr. media and prodn. resources Sonoma County Office Edn., Santa Rosa, Calif, 1992—; ind. cons., advisor, 1992—. Editor: One of a Kind, 1983, 86; author, producer: video tape Magical Mix, 1985. Mem. Edmond Women's Polit. Caucus, 1980; chair Gov.'s Speak-out on Librs. 1977; chair North Bay Video Consortium, 1994-95; adv. com. v.p. KQED; pres. Gateway Reading Coun. Mem. Ednl. Media Assn. (sec. 1995), ASCD (dir. clearinghouse on learning teaching styles and brain behavior 1986-90), Assn. for Edn. Communications and Tech. (pres. divsn. ednl. media mgmt. 1990-91, chair long-range planning com. 1986-88), Internat. Visual Literacy Assn. (bd. dirs. 1987-89), Okla. Libr. Assn. (chair libr. devel. com. 1975-76). Democrat. Mem. Unity Ch. Home: 112 Airport Blvd E Santa Rosa CA 95403-8007 Office: Sonoma County Office Edn 5340 Skylane Blvd Santa Rosa CA 95403-1082

DUFFY, BERNARD KARL, educator; b. Bremen, Fed. Republic Germany, Apr. 27, 1948; came to U.S., 1953; s. Bernard E. and Elfriede G. (Loenenecker) D.; m. Susan Jacobelli, Aug. 14, 1976; 1 child, Elizabeth. BA with great distinction, San Jose State Coll., 1970, MA, 1971; PhD, U. Pitts., 1976. Asst. prof. Hiram (Ohio) Coll., 1976-79; asst. prof. Clemson (S.C.) U., 1979-84, assoc. prof., 1984-87, prof., 1987-88; prof. Calif. Poly. State U., San Luis Obispo, 1988—, dept. chair, 1988-91. Author: (with Martin Jacobi) The Politics of Rhetoric: Richard M. Weaver and the Conservative Tradition, 1993; editor: (with Halford Ryan) American Orators of the Twentieth Century, 1987, American Orators Before 1900, 1987; series advisor Great American Orators, 1989—; contbr. articles to profl. jours. NEH Summer Seminar grantee, 1981, 84. Mem. Speech Communication Assn., Western Speech Communication Assn., Phi Kappa Phi. Democrat. Episcopalian. Office: Calif Poly State U Speech Communication Dept San Luis Obispo CA 93407

DUFFY, LAWRENCE KEVIN, biochemist, educator; b. Bklyn., Feb. 1, 1948; s. Michael and Anne (Browne) D.; m. Geraldine Antoinette Sheridan, Nov. 10, 1972; children: Anne Marie, Kevin Michael, Ryan Sheridan. BS, Fordham U., 1969; MS, U. Alaska, 1972, PhD, 1977. Teaching asst. dept. chemistry U. Alaska, 1969-71, rsch. asst. Inst. Arctic Biology, 1974-77; postdoctoral fellow Boston U., 1977-78, Roche Inst. Molecular Biology, 1978-80; rsch. asst. prof. U. Tex. Med. Br., Galveston, 1980-82; asst. prof. neurology (biol. chemistry) Med. Sch. Harvard U., Boston, Mass., 1982-87, adv. biochemistry instr. Med. Sch., 1983-87; instr. gen. and organic chemistry Roxbury Community Coll., Boston, 1984-87; prof. chemistry and biochem. U. Alaska, Fairbanks, 1992—, coord. program biochem and molecular biology, summer undergrad. res. in chemistry and biochem., 1987-93, head dept. chemistry and biochemistry, 1994—. Pres., bd. dirs. Alzheimer Disease Assn. of Alaska, 1988—; mem. instnl. rev. bd. Fairbanks Meml. Hosp., 1990. Lt. USNR, 1971-73. NSF trainee, 1971; J.W. McLaughlin fellow, 1981; W.F. Milton scholar, 1983; recipient Alzheimers Disease and Related Disorders Assoc. Faculty Scholar award, 1987. Mem. Am. Soc. Neurochemists, Am. Soc. Biol. Chemists, N.Y. Acad. Sci., Am. Chem. Soc. (Analytical Chemistry award 1969), Internat. Soc. Toxicologists, Sigma Xi (pres. 1991 Alaska club), Phi Lambda Upsilon. Roman Catholic. Office: U Alaska Fairbanks Inst Arctic Biology Fairbanks AK 99775

DUFFY, MICHAEL LEE, marketing professional, engineer; b. Safford, Ariz., Aug. 2, 1970; s. John Taylor and Katherine Ann (Pierce) D.; m. Michele Lynn Dugas, July 11, 1992. BSEE, Colo. U., 1993, postgrad., 1994—. Registered engr.-in-tng., Colo. Gas transp. analyst Western Natural Gas & Transmission, Denver, 1990-93; gas transp. analyst Gerrity Oil & Gas Corp., Denver, 1993, mktg. rep., 1993-94; sr. gas marketer Energy West, Inc., Denver, 1974—. Mem. IEEE, Assn. Energy Engrs., Rocky Mountain Natural Gas Assn., Ind. Petroleum Assn. Mountain States (mem. natural gas com. 1993—), U.S. Tae Kwon Do Assn. (instr. 1994—). Home: 10828 Milliken St Parker CO 80134-7619 Office: Energy West Inc 621 17th St #2640 Denver CO 80293

DUFFY, PATRICK SEAN, marketing research executive; b. Long Beach, Calif., Sept. 16, 1964; s. Thomas Peter Duffy and Maureen Lucille (McNerney) Habel. BA in Econs., U. Calif., San Diego, 1986. Asst. to v.p. and gen. mgr. Kaiser Devel. Co., Carlsbad, Calif., 1986; treasury adminstrn. specialist Imperial Corp. Am., San Diego, 1986-87; v.p. Market Profiles San Diego, 1987-93; owner, mgr. Cmty. Info. Systems, San Diego, 1992-93; corp. mktg. rsch. mgr. INCO Homes Corp., Upland, Calif., 1993—. Contbr. articles to profl. publs. Bd. dirs., treas. San Diego Uptown Cmty. Planning Com., 1991-93; bd. dirs. ReVisions Resources, 19916; mem. host com. AIDS Found. San Diego, 1993; grad. L.E.A.D. San Diego, 1994. Mem. Constrn. Industry Fedn. San Diego (alt. mem. polit. policies com. 1993, mem., co-chmn. fund raising subcom. 1993), Bldg. Industry Assn. San Diego (mem., column editor real estate fin. com. 1990-91, planning retreat com. 1992, co-chmn. SAM awards com. 1993), Toastmasters (v.p. pub. rels. 1992). Home: 1070 W Arrow Hwy # D Upland CA 91786-4459 Office: INCO Homes Corp 1282 W Arrow Hwy Upland CA 91786-5024

DUFFY, WAYNE EDWARD, lawyer; b. Boise, Idaho, Dec. 28, 1920; s. Charles Edward and Lorena Essie (Buxton) D.; m. Florence A. Reichel, Apr. 27, 1951 (div. Apr. 1968); 1 stepchild, James Michael Moore; m. Ruth Seville Leonard, Sept. 3, 1983; stepchildren: Deborah, Diane. BA, Coll. of Idaho, 1947; MS, U. Idaho, 1948; postgrad., N.Y. Coll. of Forestry, 1950; JD, Lincoln U., 1972. Bar: Calif. 1973, U.S. Patent Office 1981. Supr. mass spectrom Am. Cyanamid, Phillips Petroleum, NRTS (name now INEL), Idaho Falls, Idaho, 1951-55; sr. engr., lab. supr. Westinghouse-Bettis, Pitts., 1956; sr. rsch. engr. Atomics Internat., Canoga Park, Calif., 1956-59; mgr. mass Spectrom Gen. Electric, Pleasanton, Calif., 1959-68; sr. staff engr. Martin-Marietta, Denver, 1969-70; pvt. practice law Fresno, Calif., 1976-82; dep. county coun. Fresno County Coun., Fresno, 1974-76; pvt. practice law Santa Ana, Calif., 1982-83; pvt. practice patent atty., chem. cons. Nampa, Idaho, 1983—; cons. EG&G, San Ramon, Calif., 1969, Denver Rsch. Inst. U. Denver, 1970, Nyssa-Nampa Beet Growers Assn., Nyssa, Oreg., 1988—. Inventor patented Chem. Process; asst. editor Lincoln Law Rev., 1971, 72; contbr. articles to profl. jours. 1st sgt. U.S. Army, 1942-46. Fellow Am. Inst. Chemists; mem. U.S. Patent Bar. Republican. Home and Office: 107 Central Kings Rd Nampa ID 83687-3653

DUFOUR, FRANK DENNIS, plastic surgeon; b. Peoria, Ill., 1947. MD, UCLA, 1973. Intern UCLA Med. Ctr., 1973-75, surgeon, 1977-80, plastic surgeon, 1980-82; now plastic surgeon St. John's Hosp. Health Ctr., Santa Monica, Calif.; prin. Dufour Surg. Assocs., Sylmar, Calif. Office: Dufour Surg Assoc PO Box 921447 Sylmar CA 91392-1447*

DUFOUR, KIM, university official; b. San Jose, Calif., Sept. 29, 1959; d. Philip L. and Bonnie R. (Bodie) Morris; m. Jeff T. DuFour, Oct. 3, 1987; children: Kristen, Jennifer. BA in Social Work and Corrections, Calif. State U., Chico, 1981, MPA, 1989. Intern memte County Mental Health, 1980; exec. asst. to contr. Calif. State U., Chico, 1980-81, dir. cmty. action vols. in edn., 1981-83, program coord. student activities, 1983-88; devel. officer Sutter Hosps. Found., 1988-93; devel. officer Coll. Engring. Computer Sci. and Technology Calif. State U., Chico, 1993—. Treas. far west region Nat. Assn. for Campus Activities, 1984-86, chair far west regional conf., 1986, mem. leadership staff, 1985; bd. dirs. Cmty. Action Agy., 1981-82, Rape Crisis Intervention, 1983-84, Assoc. Students Children's Ctr., 1983-88; mem. agy. rep. United Way, 1981-83; bd. dirs., ann. events chair Project Child, 1987-88; chair bd. dirs. Chico Runaway Youth Program, 1984-85; mem. adv. bd., mem. grant writing com. Butte County Homeless and emergency Runaway Effort, 1984; founding sponsor Chico State Leaders, 1992—; mem. gala ball com. Sacramento Camellia Festival, 1992, 93; alumni bd. dirs. Calif. State U., Chico, 1991—. Mem. Assn. for Healthcare Philanthropy, Campus Opportunity Outreach League. Office: Calif State U Coll Engring/Computer Sci Chico CA 95929-0003

DUFRESNE, ARMAND FREDERICK, management and engineering consultant; b. Manila, Aug. 10, 1917; s. Ernest Faustine and Maude (McClellan) DuF.; m. Theo Rutledge Schaefer, Aug. 24, 1940 (dec. Oct. 1986); children: Lorna DuFresne Turnier, Peter, m. Lois Burrell Klosterman, Feb. 21, 1987. BS, Calif. Inst. Tech., 1938. Dir. quality control, chief product engr. Consol. Electrodynamics Corp., Pasadena, Calif., 1945-61; pres., dir. DUPACO, Inc., Arcadia, Calif., 1961-68; v.p., dir. ORMCO Corp., Glendora, Calif., 1966-68; mgmt., engring. cons., Duarte and Cambria, Calif., 1968—; dir., v.p., sec. Tavis Corp., Mariposa, Calif., 1968-79; dir. Denram Corp., Monrovia, Calif., 1968-70, interim pres., 1970; dir., chmn. bd. RCV Corp., El Monte, Calif., 1968-70; owner DUFCO, Cambria, 1971-82; pres. DUFCO Electronics, Inc., Cambria, Calif., 1982-86, chmn. bd. 1982-92; pres. Freedom Designs, Inc., Simi Valley, Calif., 1982-86, chmn. bd. dirs., 1982—; owner DuFresne Consulting, 1992—; chmn. bd., pres. DUMEDCO,Inc., 1993-95. Patentee in field. Bd. dirs. Arcadia Bus. Assn., 1965-69; bd. dirs. Cambria Community Services Dist., 1976, pres., 1977-80; mem., chmn. San Luis Obispo County Airport Land Use Commn., 1972-75. Served to capt. Signal Corps, AUS, 1942-45. Decorated Bronze Star. Mem. Instrument Soc. Am. (life), Arcadia (dir. 1965-69), Cambria (dir. 1974-75) C. of C., Tau Beta Pi. Home: 901 Iva Ct Cambria CA 93428-2913

DUGAN, MARIANNE GUENEVERE, lawyer; b. N.Y.C., Nov. 20, 1959; d. Kieran T.R. and Sheila M. (Johnson) D.; m. Michael S. Fields, July 14, 1984; 1 child, Selena Dugan-Fields. BA, U. Colo., 1980; JD, U. Oreg., 1993. Bar: Oreg. 1993, U.S. Dist. Ct. Oreg. 1993, U.S. Ct. Appeals (2d cir.) 1993, (9th cir.) 1994. Housing coord. Karok Tribe of Calif., Happy Camp, 1980-81; shipping clk. Feminist Press, Old Westbury, N.Y., 1981-83; delivery subcontractor Product Devel. Corp., Portland, Oreg., 1983-86; sr. coord. Gleaning Network, Medford, Oreg., 1987-88; patients accounts mgr. Ashland (Oreg.) Cmty. Hosp., 1988-90; staff atty. Western Environ. Ctr., Eugene, Oreg., 1993—; freelance writer N.Y.C., 1986—; grantwriter, sec. So. Oreg. Gleaning Network, Central Point, Oreg., 1988-90; peer reviewer Tech. Studies, Lethbridge, Can., 1994; treas. The Seamless Web, Eugene, 1992-93. Editor, writer (newsletter) Report on So. Oreg. Economy, So. Oreg. Fair Share, 1987-89; mem. editl. bd. Jour. Environ. Law and Litigation, 1992-93; contbr. articles to profl. jours. Mem. steering com. So. Oreg. Women's History Month, Ashland, 1988, 89. Recipient Am. Jurisprudence award, Lawyer's Coop. Pub., 1993. Mem. Nat. Lawyers Guild, Oreg. Trial Lawyers Assn., Oreg. Women Lawyers, Oreg. State Bar Assn., Lane County Bar Assn., Order of Coif. Democrat. Office: Western Environ Law Ctr 1216 Lincoln St Eugene OR 97401

DUH, QUAN-YANG, surgeon; b. Taipei, Taiwan, Dec. 21, 1954; came to U.S., 1970; s. Dong Liang and Lee Shiow (lee) D.; m. Ann Marie Comer, May 8, 1983; children: Katherine Lenna, Emily Ann. BS summa cum laude, Yale U., 1977; MD, U. Calif., San Francisco, 1981. Diplomate Am. Bd. Surgery. Intern U. Calif., San Francisco, 1981-82, resident in gen. surgery, 1982-88; attending surgeon surg. scv. Vet. Affairs Med. Ctr., San Francisco, 1988—, asst. chief surg. svc., 1991—; asst. prof. dept. surgery U. Calif., San Francisco, 1988-94, assoc. prof. dept. surgery, 1994—. Inventor laparoscopic tube placement; contbr. articles to profl. jours. Recipient Nusz award for outstanding rsch. U. Calif. Dept. Surgery, 1988, Student award for excellence in teaching, 1991. Fellow ACS. Democrat. Office: VA Med Ctr 4150 Clement St San Francisco CA 94121-1545

DUHNKE, ROBERT EMMET, JR., aerospace engineer; b. Manitowoc, Wis., Jan. 28, 1935; s. Robert Emmet and Vivian Dorothy (Abel) D.; m. Patricia R. Ebben, 1956 (div. 1972); children: Kim Marie, Lori Ann, Dawn Diane, Robert III, Mary Lynn; m. Judy Anne Lind, Feb. 14, 1978. B of Aero. Engring., Purdue U., 1957. Engr. Convair/Aerodyns. Group, Pomona, Calif., 1957-58; engr., instr. Boeing Co., Seattle, 1964-66, 72-84, engr. instr., 1990—, engr., analyst mil. div., 1984-90; flight navigator Flying Tigers, San Francisco, 1966-68; salesman various real estate and ins. cos., Seattle, 1968-72. Author poems in English, German and Spanish. Sponsor World Vision, Pasadena, Calif.; mem. Citizens Against Govt. Waste. Capt. USAF, 1958-64. Recipient Hon. Freedom Fighter award Afghan Mercy Fund, 1987. Mem. Inst. Navigation, Air Force Assn., Wild Goose Assn. Home: 1219 30th St NE Auburn WA 98002-2471

DUKE, DONALD NORMAN, publisher; b. L.A., Apr. 1, 1929; s. Roger V. and Mabel (Weineger) D. BA in Ednl. Psychology, Colo. Coll., 1951. Comml. photographer Colorado Springs, Colo., 1951-53; pub. rels. Gen. Petroleum, L.A., 1954-55; agt. Gen. S.S. Corp., Ltd., 1956-57; asst. mgr. retail advt., sales promotion Mobil Oil Co., 1958-63; pub. Golden West Books, Alhambra, Calif., 1964—; dir. Pacific R.R. Publs., Inc., Athletic Press; pub. relations cons. Santa Fe Ry., 1960-70. Author: The Pacific Electric--A History of Southern California Railroading, 1958, Southern Pacific Steam Locomotives, 1962, Santa Fe...Steel Rails to California, 1963, Night Train, 1961, American Narrow Gauge, 1978, RDC: The Budd Rail Diesel Car, 1989, The Brown Derby, 1990, Camp Cajon, 1991, Fred Harvey: Civilizer of the American West, 1995; editor: Water Trails West, 1977, Branding Iron, 1988-91. Recipient Spur award for Trails of the Iron Horse Western Writers Am., 1975. Mem. Ry. and Locomotive Hist. Soc. (dir. 1944—), Western History Assn., Newcomen Soc., Lexington Group of Transp. History, Western Writers Am., P.E.N. Internat. (v.p. 1975-77), Authors Guild Am., Book Pubs. Assn. So. Calif. (dir. 1968-77), Cal. Writers Guild (dir. 1976-77), Calif. Book Pubs. Assn. (dir. 1976-77), Westerners Internat. (hon., editor Branding Iron 1971-80, 88-91), Hist. Soc. So. Calif. (dir. 1972-75), Henry E./Arabella Huntington Soc., Kappa Sigma (lit. editor Caduceus 1968-80). Home: PO Box 80250 San Marino CA 91118-8250 Office: Golden West Books 525 N Electric Ave Alhambra CA 91801-2032

DUKE, ELLEN KAY, mortgage company professional, community activist; b. Indpls., June 7, 1952; d. Richard Thomas and Ruby Mae (Wright) D. Student Chapman Coll., Orange, Calif., 1972; BS in Pub. Affairs, Ind. U.-Bloomington, 1975; postgrad. Portland State U., 1980-81. Cert. Dale Carnegie Pub. Speaking Instr., 1987-93; News reporter, Salem Statesman, Corvallis, Oreg., 1976-78; com. adminstr. Oreg. State Legislature, Salem, 1979-80; pub. involvement coordinator Met. Regional Service Dist., Portland, 1981-82; account mgr. Thunder & Visions, Portland, 1982-83; project asst. Amdahl Corp., Sunnyvale, Calif., 1983-84; spl. project coordinator Computerland Corp., Hayward, Calif., 1984-89; prodr., lead facilitator Sage, Inc., Walnut Creek, Calif., 1982—; loan broker Capital Trust Mortgage, Campbell, Calif., 1994—; pub. rels. dir. local YMCA. Co-author: (ednl. film) Communication Skills, 1975. Chairperson Corvallis Budget Commn., Oreg., 1978; commr. Hayward Library, Calif., 1985—, Alameda County Consumer Affairs, Oakland, 1985; rep. Nat. Democratic Conv., N.Y.C., 1982. Named Able Toastmaster Toastmasters Internat., 1981; grad. Leadership Oakland, 1991. Mem. NAFE, Pub. Rels. Soc. Am., Sierra Club (San Francisco). Office: Capital Trust Mortgage 155 E Campbell Ave Ste 101 Campbell CA 95008-2046

DUKE, HAROLD BENJAMIN, JR., retired holding company executive; b. Washington, Iowa, Jan. 11, 1922; s. Harold Benjamin and Nordica (Wells) D.; m. Maud Bernard Banks, June 11, 1949; children: James Lenox, Harold Benjamin III, Lester Perrin, Charles Banks. B.A., Williams Coll., 1943. With Gates Corp., Denver, 1946-87, mem. exec. com., 1959—, v.p., 1960-73, exec. v.p., 1973-83, pres., 1983-89, vice-chmn., 1987-94, also dir.; ret.; bd. dirs. subs. cos. Gates Corp., A-Bar-A Ranches, Gates Land Co. Mem. Denver Com. on Fgn. Rels., 1967-85; bd. dirs. Boys Clubs Denver, 1960-89; pres., trustee Denver Country Day Sch., Englewood, Colo., 1958-71; trustee Social Sci. Found., U. Denver, 1967-75, pres., 1972-75; trustee Denver Pub. Libr. Friends Found., 1974—, pres., 1976-79, 90-92; nat. bd. dirs. Jr. Achievement, 1986-89; trustee Colo. Nature Conservancy, 1984—, Vail Valley Found., 1983—. With U.S. Army, 1943-45. Decorated Bronze Star medal, Purple Heart. Mem. Nat. Assn. Mfrs. (nat. dir. 1986-88). Republican. Clubs: University, Mile High, Denver Country, Country of Colo, Castle Pines. Office: The Gates Corp PO Box 5887 900 S Broadway Denver CO 80209-4010

DUKE, MELISSA ANN, nurse; b. Indio, Calif., Mar. 23, 1966; d. Eugene Edward and Francis Juanita (Yakley) D.; m. Daniel E. Thompson, June 13, 1994; 1 child, Jennifer Ann Duke Thompson. Diploma, Concorde Career Coll. Nursing, San Bernardino, Calif., 1989; postgrad., San Bernardino Valley Coll., 1992—. Lic. vocat. nurse, Calif. Staff nurse Loma Linda (Calif.) U. Med. Ctr., 1990-91; medication nurse Loma Linda Behavioral Medicine, Redlands, Calif., 1991-93. Vol. San Bernardino County Med. Ctr., 1988; ind. cons. pro-life and other issues to area teens, San BErnardino, 1985. With U.S. Army, 1986-88. Republican. Baptist.

DUKE, PAMELA RUTH, reading specialist; b. Salt Lake City, Feb. 14, 1945; d. Carson Bailey Duke and Ruth (Jones) Stafford. BA, Calif. State U., Chico, 1966; MA, Chapman U., 1973. Tchr. Murray Sch. Dist., Dublin, Calif., 1967-69; tchr. Lompoc (Calif.) Unified Schs., 1969-72, math specialist, 1972-86, reading specialist, 1986—; math fellow Tri-County Math. Project, Santa Barbara, 1985; fellow Impact II, Santa Barbara, 1987—. Grantee Impact II Santa Barbara, 1988, 90; recipient PTA scholarships, Calif. State PTA, L.A., 1966—. Mem. PTA, Santa Maria Kennel Club, Calif. Tchrs. Assn., Reading Specialists Calif., Internat. Reading Assn., Calif. Reading Assn., Atari Fed. Office: Fillmore Elementary School 1211 E Pine Ave Lompoc CA 93436-4238

DUKE, WILLIAM EDWARD, public affairs executive; b. Bklyn., July 18, 1932; m. Leilani Kamp Lattin. BS, Fordham U., 1954. City editor Middletown (N.Y.) Record, 1956-60; asst. state editor Washington Star, 1961-63; exec. asst. to U.S. Senator from N.Y. State, Jacob K. Javits, Washington, 1963-69; dir. pub. affairs Corp. Pub. Broadcasting, Washington, 1969-72; dir. fed. govt. rels. Atlantic Richfield Co., Washington, 1973-78, mgr. pub. affairs, L.A., 1978-90; mgr. external affairs We. States Petroleum Assn., 1993-95; coun. Pacific Visions Comm., 1995—; lectr. U. So. Calif. Grad. Sch. Journalism, 1988—; cons. in field. Fellow Pub. Rels. Soc. Am., Nat. Press Club, Capitol Hill Club, L.A. Athletic Club. Office: Pacific Visions Com 9000 Sunset Blvd Los Angeles CA 90069

DUKES, LAJENNE MARIE, chiropractic physician; b. Chadron, Nebr., Sept. 12, 1931; d. James Ellsworth and LuRena Mary (Malsi) Phillips; m. Henry Benard Dukes, May 19, 1951 (div. Apr. 1985); children: Christine Dukes Creigh, Catherine Dukes Lucchesi, Craig, Cheryl. AAS in Retail/Mktg., Bus./Midmgmt., AA, Clark County Community Coll., 1980; D of Chiropractic, Western States Chiropractic, Portland, Oreg., 1983. Diplomate Nat. Bd. Chiropractic Examiners. Dictaphone sec. Las Vegas Conv. Bur., 1963-64, part-time registration convs. and housing, 1963-76; typist-clk. housing bur. Las Vegas Conv. Visitors Authority, 1976-78; svc. rep. Cen. Telephone Co., Las Vegas, 1978-80; casino security guard Stardust Hotel and Casino, Las Vegas, 1981; intern/preceptorship Chiropractic Physicians Ctr., Las Vegas, 1983-85; owner Spring Valley Chiropractic Ctr., Las Vegas, 1985—; prof., lectr. Americana Leadership Coll., Inc. Contbr. articles to mags. Mem. Am. Chiropractic Assn., Nev. State Chiropractic Assn., Oreg. Chiropractic Physicians Assn., Parker Chiropractic Rsch. Found., Toastmasters Internat., Women's Coun. C. of C., Coop. Assn. Chiropractic Physicians, Calif. Chiropractic Assn., David Singer Enterprises (chiropractic cons.), Found. Chiropractic Edn. and Rsch., Las Vegas Success Network, Las Vegas C. of C., Clark County Women's Dem. Club, Beta Sigma Phi. Democrat. Roman Catholic. Office: Spring Valley Chiropractic 3233 W Charleston Blvd # 109 Las Vegas NV 89102-1923

DUKICH, THOMAS DANIEL, utility executive; b. Grand Rapids, Minn., Apr. 29, 1945; s. Daniel and Violet Amelia (Katalinich) D.; m. Marlene Rea Allen, Oct. 30, 1964 (div. Nov. 1981); children: Cynthia, Steven; m. Carolyn Sue Schmitz, Apr. 10, 1987. BA in Psychology, U. Minn., 1967; Ma in Psychology, U. Mont., 1970, PhD in Exptl. Psychology, 1972. Assoc. prof. Conzaga U., Spokane, 1971-78; forecasting & rsch. supr. Wash. Water Power, Spokane, 1978-81, rates mgr., 1981—; adj. prof. Eastern Wash. U., Cheney, 1989; pub. art juries City of Spokane, 1988-93. Chair Spokane Arts Commn., 1988-93; bd. dirs. Artist Trust Wash., 1990-92, Spokane ACLU chpt., 1992-94; mem. CCMM Art Com., 1988-92; pres. Bead Lake Clean Water Assn., 1994—. NDEA Grad. fellow, U. Mont., 1967-70. Home and Office: E 3123 Hills Ct Spokane WA 99202

DULANEY, ANDREW G., lawyer; b. San Francisco, June 13, 1963; s. William Dykes Dulaney and Bruni Ohlhauser Henerlau. BA magna cum laude, San Francisco State U., 1988; JD, U. Calif., Berkeley, 1991. Bar: Calif., 1991. Assoc. Robins, Kaplan, Miller & Ciresi, San Francisco, 1991—; bd. dirs. Bay Concert Arts, Watsonville, Calif. Author: Resolving Claims of Self-Determination: A Proposal for Integrating Principles of International Law with Specific Application to the Tibetan People, 1993. Mem. ABA, Calif. Bar Assn., Bar Assn. San Francisco, Internat. Com. Lawyers Tibet. Office: Robins Kaplan Miller & Ciresi 444 Market St Ste 2700 San Francisco CA 94111-5332

DULBECCO, RENATO, biologist, educator; b. Catanzaro, Italy, Feb. 22, 1914; came to U.S., 1947, naturalized, 1953; s. Leonardo and Maria (Virdia) D.; m. Gulseppina Salvo, June 1, 1940 (div. 1963); children: Peter Leonard (dec.), Maria Vittoria; m. Maureen Muir; 1 dau., Fiona Linsey. M.D., U. Torino, Italy, 1936; D.Sc. (hon.), Yale U., 1968, Vrije Universiteit, Brussels, 1978; LL.D., U. Glasgow, Scotland, 1970. Asst. U. Torino, 1940-47; research asso. Ind. U., 1947-49; sr. research fellow Calif. Inst. Tech., 1949-52, asso. prof., then prof. biology, 1952-63; sr. fellow Salk Inst. Biol. Studies, San Diego, 1963-71; asst. dir. research Imperial Cancer Research Fund, London, 1971-74; dep. dir. research Imperial Cancer Research Fund, 1974-77; disting. research prof. Salk Inst., La Jolla, Calif., 1977—, pres., 1989-92; pres. emeritus Salk Inst., La Jolla, 1993—; prof. pathology and medicine U. Calif. at San Diego Med. Sch., La Jolla, 1977-81, mem. Cancer Ctr.,; vis. prof. Royal Soc. G.B., 1963-64, Leeuwenhoek lectr., 1974; Clowes Meml. lectr. Atlantic City, 1961; Harvey lectr. Harvey Soc., 1967; Dunham lectr. Harvard U., 1972; 11th Marjory Stephenson Meml. lectr., London, 1973, Harden lectr., Wye, Eng., 1973, Am. Soc. for Microbiology lectr., L.A., 1979; mem. Calif. Cancer Adv. Coun., 1963-67; mem. vis. com. Case Western Res. Sch. Medicine; adv. bd. Roche Inst., 1968-71, Inst. Immunology, Basel, Switzerland, others; esperto Italian Nat. Rsch. Coun.; trustee Am.-Italian Fedn. for Cancer Rsch.; mem. bd. dirs. Scientific Counselors Dept. Etiology NCI; cons. Nat. Rsch. Coun. ESPERTO, 1994—. Trustee La Jolla Country Day Sch., Am.-Italian Fedn. for Cancer Rsch.; bd. mem. sci. counselors dept. etiology NCI. Recipient John Scott award City Phila., 1958; Kimball award Conf. Pub. Health Lab. Dirs., 1959; Albert and Mary Lasker Basic Med. Research award, 1964; Howard Taylor Ricketts award, 1965; Paul Ehrlich-Ludwig Darmstaedter prize, 1967; Horwitz prize Columbia U., 1973; (with David Baltimore and Howard Martin Temin) Nobel prize in medicine,

1975; Targa d'oro Villa San Giovanni, 1978; Mandel Gold medal Czechoslovak Acad. Scis., 1982, Via de Condotti prize, 1990; Cavaliere di Gran Croce Italian Rep., 1991, Natale Di Roma prize, 1993, Columbus prize, 1993; named Man of Yr. London, 1975; Italian Am. of Yr. San Diego County, Calif., 1978; hon. citizen City of Imperia (Italy), 1983, City of Arezzo, City of Sommariva Perno, City of Catanzaro; Guggenheim and Fulbright fellow, 1957-58; decorated grand ufficiale Italian Republic, 1981; hon. founder Hebrew U., 1981. Mem. NAS (Selman A. Waksman award 1974, com. on human rights), Am. Assn. Cancer Rsch., Internat. Physicians for Prevention Nuclear War, Am. Philos. Assn., Academia Nazionale del Lincel (fgn.), Academia Ligure di Scienze e Lettre (hon.), Royal Soc. (fgn.), Fedn. Am. Scientists, Am. Acad. Arts and Scis., Comitato di Collaborazione Culturale (hon. mem.), Alpha Omega Alpha. Home: 7525 Hillside Dr La Jolla CA 92037-3941

DULEY, CHARLOTTE DUDLEY, vocational counselor; b. Lincoln, Nebr., Oct. 2, 1920; d. Millard Eugene and Inez Kathryn (Miller) Dudley; student U. Nebr., 1938-41; M.A. in Guidance Counseling, U. Idaho, 1977; B.S., Lewis and Clark State Coll., 1973; m. Phillip D. Duley, Mar. 28, 1942; (dec. Sept. 1984); children: Michael Dudley (dec.), Patricia Kaye; m. P. Fredrik Nordgaard, Sep.1, 1990. Tchr., Nebr. schs., 1951-56; with Dept. of Employment, Lewiston, Idaho, 1958-81, local office counselor handling fed. tng. programs, 1958-81; ind. job cons.; counselor; rep. Avon, Lewiston; part-time counselor, tester, 1981—. Pres., bd. dirs. Civic Arts, Inc., 1972-81; mem. women's svc. league Wash.-Idaho Symphony Orch., 1972—; bd. dirs. YWCA, 1980-88, treas., 1981-88; mem. adv. bd. Salvation Army, 1980-94; dir. artist series Lewis and Clark State Coll., 1984-90. Recipient Altrusa Woman of Achievement award, 1984. Mem. Am., Idaho pers. guidance Assns., Idaho State Employees Assn., Internat. Assn. Employees in Employment Security, Am. Assn. Counseling & Devel., Idaho State Employment Counselors Assn. (pres. 1979-80), Stateline Guidance and Counseling Assn. (sec.-treas. 1964, 76-77), Lewiston Cmty. Concert Assn. (bd. dirs., 1980—, pres. 1980-94), Greater Lewiston C. of C. (chmn. conv. and tourism com. 1984—), Altrusa (bd. dirs.), Elks (pres. 1986-87, exec. bd. 1985-88, election bd. chmn. 1986-94, 1st v.p., 1993-95, ladies of elks pres. 1995—). Baptist. Home: 1819 Ridgeway Dr Lewiston ID 83501-3890

DULIN, JACQUES M. (JAMES DULIN), lawyer, consultant, pollution control company executive; b. Toledo; s. James and Renee Dulin. BS in Biochemistry, U. Chgo.; M in Acctg.; JD with honors, George Washington U. Bar: Va., Ill., Calif., U.S. Dist. Ct. (no. dist.) Ill. Patent examiner U.S. Patent Office, Washington; law clk., tech. advisor U.S. Patent Ct., Washington; pres., chmn. exec. com., bd. dirs. Indsl. Resources Inc., Chgo., 1972-89; with Pillsbury Madison & Sutro, San Jose, Calif., 1989—; adj. prof. intellectual property div. John Marshall Law Sch., Chgo., Santa Clara U. Law Sch.; speaker in field. Contbr. articles to newspapers and profl. jours. including S.J. Mercury News, The Bus. Jour.; inventor, patentee in air, hazardous wastes, water pollution control. Recipient Nathan Burkan Meml. Copyright award ASCAP, Van Vleck Moot Ct. award; du Pont fellow U. Chgo. Mem. Calif. Bar Assn., Va. Bar Assn., Ill. Bar Assn., Peninsula Intellectual Property Law Assn. (pres. 1992-93), Santa Clara County Bar Assn. (chair high tech. law sect. 1995), Am. Arbitration Assn. (nat. panel patent arbitrators), Order of Coif. Office: Pillsbury Madison & Sutro 10 Almaden Blvd Ste 800 San Jose CA 95113

DULUDE, GARY JOSEPH, copywriter; b. Abilene, Tex., June 29, 1966; s. Ronald Joseph and Patricia Lillian (Earle) D. BA, Angelo State U., 1987. Copywriter Mark Anderson Assocs., Scottsdale, Ariz., 1988-92; account exec. Allred Mktg., Phoenix, 1992-93; copywriter, pub. rels. mgr. TRACER Design Inc., Phoenix, 1993—. Author: Becoming A Computer Artist, 1994; contbr. articles to profl. jours. Mem. Internat. Assn. Bus. Communicators. Baptist. Office: TRACER Design Inc 4206 N Central Ave Phoenix AZ 85012-1812

DUMAINE, R. PIERRE, bishop; b. Paducah, Ky., Aug. 2, 1931; student St. Joseph Coll., Mountain View, Calif., 1945-51, St. Patrick Sem., Menlo Park, Calif., 1951-57; Ph.D., Cath. U. Am., 1962. Ordained priest Roman Cath. Ch., 1957; asst. pastor Immaculate Heart Ch., Belmont, Calif., 1957-58; mem. faculty dept. edn. Cath. U. Am., 1961-63; tchr. Serra High Sch., San Mateo, Calif., 1963-65; asst. supt. Cath. schs., Archdiocese of San Francisco, 1965-74, supt., 1974-78; ordained bishop, 1978, bishop of San Jose, Santa Clara, Calif., 1981—; dir. Archdiocesan Ednl. TV Ctr., Menlo Park, Calif., 1968-81. Mem. Pres.'s Nat. Adv. Council on Edn. of Disadvantaged Children, 1970-72; bd. dirs. Cath. TV Network, 1968-81, pres., 1975-77; bd. dirs. Pub. Service Satellite Consortium, 1975-81. Mem. Nat. Cath. Edn. Assn., Assn. Cath. Broadcasters and Allied Communicators, Internat. Inst. Communications, Assn. Calif. Sch. Adminstrs. Office: Diocese of San Jose 900 Lafayette St Ste 301 Santa Clara CA 95050-4966*

DUMARS, KENNETH W., medical geneticist educator, pediatrician; b. Denver, Sept. 28, 1921; s. Kenneth W. Sr. and Annie (Wright) D.; m. Barbara Lou Belcher Dumars, Sept. 17, 1942 (dec. Sept. 1967); children: Stephen Craig, David Bruce, Peter Kent, Janet Rae, Leslie Marie; m. Gayle E. Fialko Dumars, Jan. 17, 1976. BA in Zoology, U. Denver, 1942; MD, U. Colo. Sch. Medicine, 1945. Diplomate Am. Bd. Pediatrics, Am. Bd. Med. Genetics in Clin. Genetics and Clin. Cytogenetics. Intern Mpls. Gen. Hosp., 1945-46; residency U. Colo. Sch. Medicine Pediatrics, 1948-50; pvt. practice Gt. Falls, Mont., 1950-51, Colo. Springs, 1951-61; attending physician Neurology Clinic U. Colo. Med. Ctr., 1955-61; med. dir. Cardinal Hill Convalescent Hosp., Lexington, Ky., 1961-62; dir. Chromosome Laboratory Penrose Cancer Hosp., Colo. Springs, Colo., 1963-65; pediatrician Rancho Los Amigos Hosp., Downey, Calif., 1965-68; attending physician White Meml. Hosp. Med. Ctr., L.A., 1965-68, L.A. County Gen. Hosp., 1965-68, Children Hosp. Orange County, 1965-95, U. Calif. Irvine Med. Ctr., 1968—; clin. instr. pediatrics U. Colo. Med. Ctr., 1955-61; asst. prof. pediatrics U. Ky. Sch. Medicine, 1961-62, U. Colo. Med. Ctr., 1962-63; asst. clin. prof. pediatrics U. Colo. Med. Ctr., 1963-65; assoc. prof. pediatrics U. Calif. Irvine Coll. Medicine, 1971-79; vis. prof. Dept. Child Health Welsh Nat. Sch. Medicine, Cardiff, Wales, 1976-77; prof. pediatrics U. Calif. Irvine Coll. Medicine, 1979-91; prof. obstetrics and gynecology, U. Calif. Irvine Coll. Medicine, 1982-91; prof. pediatrics emeritus U. Calif. Irvine Coll. Medicine, 1991—; cons. Colo. State Health Dept. for Traveling Epilepsy Clinic State of Colo., 1958-65, Fort Carson Hosp., Colo., 1958-65, Penrose Cancer Hosp., Colo. Springs, Colo., 1958-65, Divsn. of Adoptions Orange County Dept. Pub. Welfare, 1968-82, Easter Seal Rehabilitation Ctr. Orange County, 1968-71, Genetic Disease Branch Calif. State Health Dept., Berkeley, 1974-92 (numerous grants), Adminstrn. Devel. Disabilities, Sacramento, Calif., 1972-88, Washington, 1978-84 (numerous grants), Nat. Fdn. March of Dimes, Orange County, Calif., 1974-89 (numerous grants, disting. svc. award, 1976, 79, 89, med. adv. com. Orange chpt. 1974-89, exec. com. Orange chpt. 1987-89), Nat. Tuberous Sclerosis Assn., Landover, Md., 1983-91 (commendation and award 1986, med. adv. bd. 1983-91, med. rsch. com. 1983-91), Huntington Disease Fdn., L.A. chpt., 1988— (med. advisor 1988—); med. dir. Med. Genetics Fountain Valley a MediGene Facility, 1991-93; dir. Southeast Asian Genetic Program, 1984-91, U. Calif. Irvine U. Affiliated Program, 1972-86, Cytogenetics Laboratory Dept. Pediatrics, 1965-86, Divsn. of Clin. Genetics and Devel. Disabilities Dept. Pediatrics, 1972-86; dir. cytogenetic laboratory U. Calif. Irvine Coll. Medicine, 1965-86; mem. Coun. Regional Network for Genetic Diseases, Atlanta, 1988— (chair thalassemia com. 1988—, mem. sickle cell, thalassemia, other hemoglobin variants com., 1988—) and numerous others. Contbr. articles to profl. jours.; speaker in field. Cons. Rehabilitation Inst. Orange, Orange County, Calif., 1968-71, Navajo Nation, Gallup, N.M., 1980-82. Capt. AUS, 1946-48. Continuing Edn. award AMA, 1982, 90, 93, Continuing Edn. award Calif. Med. Assn., 1986-88, 89-92. Founding Fellow Am. Coll. Med. Genetics, fellow Am Bd. Paediatrics, Am. Bd. Med. Genetics; mem. AAAS, Am. Soc. Human Genetics, Am. Assn. Mental Deficiency, Am. Eugenics Soc., Environmental Mutagen Soc., Western Soc. Paediatric Rsch., European Soc. for Human Genetics, Royal Photographic Soc. of Great Britain Med. Section. Office: U Calif Irvine Med Ctr 101 City Dr S Orange CA 92660

DUMAS, JEFFREY MACK, lawyer; b. Corpus Christi, Tex., Sept. 29, 1945; s. Glenn Irven and Virginia (Jones) D.; m. Penny Mary Walter, June 5, 1971; children: Todd Glenn, Rebecca Hope. BS, U.S. Naval Acad., 1968; MSEE, Stanford U., 1969; JD, Harvard U., 1978; registered profl. engr., Colo., Wash., Mont., Calif. Bar: Wash. 1979, U.S. Ct. Appeals (9th cir.) 1979, Mont. 1981, Calif. 1983, U.S. Supreme Ct., 1984, U.S. Patent and Trademark Office, 1990. Fellow, UN, N.Y.C., 1978; corp. counsel Boeing Co., Seattle, 1978-80; atty. McClelland Law Office, Missoula, Mont., 1980-82; gen. counsel Briton-Lee, Inc., Los Gatos, Calif., 1982-83; sr. counsel Nat. Semicondr. Corp., Singapore, 1983-87; gen. counsel, sec. Cypress Semiconductor Corp., Santa Clara, Calif., 1987-91; assoc. gen. counsel Silicon Graphics, Inc. Santa Clara, Calif., 1991—. Author: (with Richard Gowan) Signals and Systems, 1975; contbr. articles to profl. jours. Chmn. Common Cause, Mont., 1982, Vietnam Vets. of Mont., 1982; chmn. Pikes Peak chpt. Sierra Club, 1975, treas. Cascade chpt., Seattle, 1980. Served with USN, 1968-75, aviator Southeast Asia, 1970-73. Decorated Dist. Flying Cross, Air medals, Bronze Star; recipient George Washington medal Freedoms Found., 1975. Mem. IEEE, AIAA, Council on Fgn. Relations, U.S. Naval Inst., Sigma Xi. Address: 121 Albert Ct Los Gatos CA 95032-5509

DUMAS, LOUISE ISABELLE, elementary school educator; b. Greensboro, Ala.; d. Walter James and Alise (Collins) Outland; m. Andrew Alexander Dumas, July 8, 1962; children: Andrew A. Jr., Cassandra Alise. BS, Ala. State U., 1956; Hon. PhD, Faith Coll., Birmingham, Ala., 1993. Tchr. Hale Country Elem. Sch., Greensboro, Ala., 1956-66, Muroc Unified Sch. Dist., Edwards, Calif., 1967—. Mem. Antelope Valley Alpha Charter Guild of Antelope Valley Hosp.; v.p. A.V. Juliettes, Lancaster, Calif., 1986-89. Mem. NEA, AAUW (scholarship com.), Muroc Edn. Assn. (bldg. rep. 1971-73), Calif. Elem. Edn. Assn., Calif. Tchrs. Assn., Delta Sigma Theta, Delta Kappa Gamma. Republican. Methodist. Home: 43636 Devyn Ln Lancaster CA 93535-5804

DUMAS, WILLIAM JOSEPH, filmmaker; b. Landstuhl, Fed. Republic of Germany, July 24, 1956, came to U.S., 1959; s. William Fred and Erika (Besslich) D. AA, Mohegan C.C., 1976; BA, Calif. State U., Long Beach, 1978; MFA, Am. Film Inst., 1992. Owner, exec. prodr. Vinyl Siding Records, Jewett City, Conn., 1982-90; sr. configuration mgmt. analyst Gen. Dynamics, Groton, Conn., 1982-90; devel. intern Marvin Worth Prodns., Hollywood, Calif., 1990-91; prodn. intern Propaganda Films, Hollywood, Calif., 1991; dir. devel. SPI Entertainment, L.A., 1991-94; vis. instr. film. Conn. Coll., 1995. Writer, prodr., dir. Boston Film and Video Found., 1987-90, Bill Dumas Prodns., L.A., 1992-94, (film) Through the Walls, 1993 (finalist USA Film Festival 1993-94); prodr. Pacifica Films (feature film) The Barrow Gang; exec. prodr. (feature film) Together & Alone; film series coord. Hygienic Art Show, New London, Conn., 1994-95; camera operator, sound engr. AFI Women's Directing Program, L.A., 1991. Mem. Am. Film Inst. Alumni Assn. Home: 375 Taylor Hill Rd Jewett City CT 06351-2514 Office: Bill Dumas Prodns 1973 N Van Ness Ave Los Angeles CA 90068-3624

DUMITRESCU, DOMNITA, Spanish language educator, researcher; b. Bucharest, Romania; came to U.S., 1984; d. Ion and Angela (Barzotescu) D. Diploma, U. Bucharest, 1966; MA, U. So. Calif., L.A., 1987, PhD, 1990. Asst. prof. U. Bucharest, 1966-74, assoc. prof., 1974-84; asst. prof. Spanish, U. So. Calif., 1985-89; assoc. prof. Calif. State U., L.A., 1990-94, prof., 1995—. Author: Gramatica Limbii Spaniole, 1976, Indreptar Pentru Traducerea Din Limba Romana in Limba Spaniola, 1980; translator from Spanish lit. to Romanian; contbr. articles to profl. jours. Fulbright scholar, 1993—. Mem. MLA, Am.-Romanian Acad. Arts and Scis., Linguistic Soc. Am., Internat. Assn. Hispanists, Assn. Linguistics and Philology L.Am., Am. Assn. Tchrs. Spanish and Portuguese (past pres. So. Calif. chpt.). Office: Calif State U 5151 State University Dr Los Angeles CA 90032-4221

DUMOULIN, DIANA CRISTAUDO, marketing professional; b. Washington, Jan. 5, 1939; d. Emanuel A. and Angela E. (Cogliano) Cristaudo; m. Philip DuMoulin, May 30, 1964; children: Joanmarie Patricia, John Philip. MA, U. Wis., 1967; BA, Rosary Coll., 1961. Project mgr. IDC Cons. Group, Framingham, Mass., 1982-84; sr. market analyst Cullinet, Inc., Westwood, Mass., 1984-86; prof. assoc. Ledgeway Group, Lexington, Mass., 1987-89; prin. Customer Mktg. Specialist, Brookline, Mass., 1989-93; pres. Customer Solutions Int., Phoenix, 1994—; adj. faculty Ulster Count Community Coll., Stone Ridge, N.Y., 1967-74, Mass. Bay Community Coll., Wellesley Hills, Mass., 1983; lectr. Boston Coll., Chestnut Hill, Mass., 1976. Contbr. articles to profl. jours. Pres. League Women Voters, Kingston, N.Y., 1973-74. Recipient Svc. to Young Adults award 70001 Career Assn., 1977; faculty fellow U. Wis., 1964-66. Mem. Am. Field Svc. Mgrs. Internat. (software support spl. interest group, chmn. minuteman chpt. 1991-92). Home: 8441 N 1st Dr Phoenix AZ 85021-5515 Office: Customer Solutions Internat 8441 N 1st Dr Phoenix AZ 85021-5515

DUNAWAY, MARGARET ANN (MAGGIE DUNAWAY), state agency administrator, consultant; b. Fresno, Calif., Feb. 10, 1943; d. Joseph John and Anna Frances (Dice) Cumero; children from previous marriage: Christian Anthony Freitag, Erika Lynn Bullard; m. Michael Earl Babcoke, Oct. 6, 1990; 1 stepchild, Jason Ethan Babcoke. Student, U. Calif., Davis, 1960-62, U. Calif., Berkeley, 1962-63. Supr. Gov's Office, Sacramento, 1969-72; office mgr. State Health and Welfare Agy., Sacramento, 1972-73; analyst regulations devel. Calif. State Depts. Health and Social Svcs., Sacramento, 1974-84, cons. adult and children's svcs., 1984-90, rep. adult svcs., 1984-90, with food drive com., 1987-88, rep. ind. living program com., 1989-90; community program specialist Calif. State Dept. Devel. Svcs., Sacramento, 1990—; project coord. SDSS study L.A. County Children's Svcs. Caseload, 1989-90. Active Southpark Homeowner's Assn., Sacramento, 1974-78; presenter Adult Svcs. Ann. Asilomar Conf., 1987. Office: Calif Dept Devel Svcs 1600 9th St Rm 340 Sacramento CA 95814-6404

DUNAWAY, PHILLIP LEE, JR., secondary school education educator; b. Asher, Okla., Jan. 29, 1936; s. Phillip L. and Jannie (Smith) D.; m. Marlene Ann Dunaway, Nov. 19, 1960; children: Russell Phillip, Curtis Lee. MusB, BA, U. Pacific, 1958; postgrad., San Francisco State U., Sonoma State U. Cert. gen. elem., gen. secondary, spl. secondary music, Calif. Tchr. Benicia (Calif.) Unified Sch. Dist., 1958-66, Mt. Diablo Unified Sch. Dist., Concord, Calif., 1966—; chair social studies dept. Foothill Mid. Sch., 1978-93; gospel singer, rec. artist, 8 albums, 1966—; min. music various chs., 1961-87; pres. Philmar Ministries, Inc., Benicia, 1971—, active fgn. missions ministry, 1976—; music dir. Celebration of Life weekly TV show, San Francisco, 1975-77; mem. dist. social studies com. Mt. Diablo Unified Sch. Dist., 1978-93; tour dir. 8th grade trip to Washington Foothill Mid. Sch., 1980—. Arranger, composer: (records) Songweaver on the Move, 1967-68, Paul Weaver Chorale On Stage, Young Life Songs; arranger, composer Sacred Concert Pub., 1965-70, Lillenas Pub. Co., 1971. Counselor Am. Heritage Merit badge Boy Scouts Am., 1986-87. Recipient Nat. Evangel. Film Found. award, 1968; scholar Am. Legion Freedom Found., 1979. Mem. NEA, Mt. Diablo Edn. Assn., No. Calif./Nev. Assemblies of God, Calif. Tchrs. Assn., Phi Mu Alpha Sinfonia. Home: 2257 First St Benicia CA 94510

DUNAWAY, ROBERT LEE, sales and marketing executive; b. Indpls., Sept. 26, 1942; s. Robert Lee and Rosemary Ellen (McInturf) D.; children: Robert III, Kirk E., Darcy L. BS in Mech. Engring., Purdue U., 1966; student, U. Utah, 1993—. Sales engr. Fisher Controls Co., Marshalltown, Iowa, 1966-73; sales mgr., owner, pres. Controls, Valves, Instrumentation Inc., Salt Lake City, 1973-87; regional sales and application mgr. Circle Seal Controls Co., Anaheim, Calif., 1989-91; sales and mktg. mgr. Crane Aerospace Corp., Burbank, Calif., 1991-92; mgr. sales western region Crane Ferguson Co., 1993-94. Bd. dirs. Marshalltown Community Theatre. Recipient Martha Ellen Tye award, 1970. Mem. Instrument Soc. Am. (sr. mem., sect. pres. 1975-76), Kappa Kappa Psi (hon.). Republican. Episcopalian. Home: PO Box 6543 Thousand Oaks CA 91359-6543

DUNAYEVA, DINA GAVRIILOVNA, cross-cultural training program administrator; b. Cheznobayevka, Ukraine, Jan. 5, 1952; came to U.S., 1992; d. Gavriil Mitrofanovich Martinenko and Yevdokia Tzybulska; m. Dunayev Igor Grigorievich, Mar. 10, 1974; children: Dunayeva Tanya. BA in Fgn. Langs., Pedagogic and Methods, Moscow Pedagogical Inst., 1976; student, Inst. Mgmt., Moscow, 1980-82; MA, Moscow Inst. Youth, 1987. Tchr. mgmt. English State Acad. Mgmt., Moscow, 1976-91, head Econika bus. sch., 1989-91; dir. lang. tng. ctr. UNICON Consulting Group, Moscow, 1991-92; dir. ctr. cross-cultural programs GAMMA Russian Joint Stock Co., Kent, Wash. and Moscow, 1992; dir. cross-cultural tng. program, sr. internat. cons. edn. and tng. ctr. Green River C.C., Kent, 1992—; presenter in field. Author: Professional English for Managers, 1992, other publs. in field. Mem. Ukrainian Acad. Nat. Progress (corr.). Home: 2205 S 312th St # 32 Federal Way WA 98003 Office: Green River CC Edn & Tng Ctr 841 N Central Ave # 106 Kent WA 98032

DUNBAR, FRANK ROLLIN, landscape architect; b. Alhambra, Calif., Mar. 18, 1953; s. Warren Marvin and Valerie (Hill) D.; m. Linda Reighley, July 2, 1951; 1 child, Tenaya Alexandria. BS in Landscape architecture, Calif State Poly. U., Pomona, 1976. Registered landscape architect, Calif. Assoc. J. Charles Hoffman & Assocs., Pasadena, Calif., 1976-81, Eriksson, Peters, Thoms, Pasadena, 1981-84; instr. design, faculty chmn. UCLA, 1981-85; chief landscape architect Holmes & Narver, Engrs., Orange, Calif., 1983-84; prin. Berry & Dunbar, San Juan Capistrano, Calif., 1984-85, Cardoza Dilallo Harrington, Pleasanton, Calif., 1985—; oral commr. Calif. State Bd. of Landscape Architects, Sacramento, 1984—. Editor: U.N.E. Workbook, 1978. bd. dirs. Pasadena chpt. ARC, 1982-84; bd. dirs., v.p. Pasadena Jaycees, 1980-84. Recipient Jack Evans Meml. award for design Calif. Poly. State U., 1975; named Outstanding Tchr. in landscape architecture, UCLA, 1983. Mem. Am. Soc. Landscape Architects (pres. So. Calif. chpt. 1983, trustee 1985-88, nat. v.p. 1988-90). Democrat. Presbyterian. Office: Cardoza Dilallo Harrington 450 Main St Ste 212 Pleasanton CA 94566-7364

DUNBAR, MAURICE VICTOR, English language educator; b. Banner, Okla., May 24, 1928; s. Moyer Haywood and Louise Edna (Curry) D.; m. Carol Ann Cline, July 28, 1948 (div. 1963); children: Kurt, Karl, Karla, Karen, Kristen. AA, Compton Jr. Coll., 1948; BA, U. Calif., Berkeley, 1952; MA, Calif. State U., Sacramento, 1965. Tchr. elem. sch. Lone Tree Sch., Beale AFB, Calif., 1962-64; tchr. jr. high sch. Anna McKenney, Marysville, Calif., 1964-66; tchr. high sch. Yuba City (Calif.) High Sch., 1966-67; instr. jr. coll. Foothill Coll., Los Altos Hills, Calif., 1967-82; prof. English De Anza Coll., Cupertino, Calif., 1982—. Author: Fundamentals of Book Collecting, 1976, Books and Collectors, 1980, Collecting Steinbeck, 1983, Books and Bibliophiles, 1995; contbr. articles to profl. jours. With U.S. Army, 1948-58, PTO. Mem. Masons, Shriners (orator, librarian San Jose Scottish Rite Temple, 1982—). Republican. Office: De Anza Coll Cupertino CA 95014-5797

DUNBAR, PATRICIA LYNN, new product development consultant; b. St. Louis, Feb. 11, 1953; d. William R. and Beryl Ione Noland (Ferrand) Dunbar; m. Michael R. Jeffrey, Oct. 2, 1950. BS, Northwestern U., 1973, MFA, 1975. With NBC-TV, Chgo., 1975-79; regional sales/mktg. mgr. HBO, Chgo., 1979-81; sr. product mgr. Bank of Am., San Francisco, 1981-82, v.p., 1982-84; interactive comm. svcs. prodr. and cons., 1984—; bd. dirs. Sci. and Tech. Enrichment Program, 1982—, pres., 1993-94. Mem. Women in Cable (1st pres. Chgo. chpt. 1981), Jr. League Seattle. Episcopalian. Patentee on child's chair, 1973.

DUNBAR, RICHARD PAUL, sales manager; b. Watertown, S.D., Aug. 28, 1951; s. Earl Paul and Leona Matilda (Clausen) D. Student, S.D. State U., 1969-71; BSBA, U. Ariz., 1981. Account mgr. bus. forms and supplies div. Nat. Cash Register, Phoenix, 1981-83; sales cons. Compugraphic Corp., Phoenix, 1983-84; sales rep. constrn. products div. W.R. Grace and Co., Phoenix and Tucson, 1985-87; sales rep. constrn. products div. for Ariz., so. Nev., N.Mex., El Paso (Tex.) region Pleko SW, Inc., Tempe, Ariz., 1987-92, S.W. regional sales mgr., 1992—. Mem. Jaycees (treas. 1977-78, recipient Outstanding Jaycee award, Pres.'s award, Jaycee of Month award), Constrn. Specifications Inst. (constrn. documents technologist, chmn. tech. documents com. Tucson chpt. 1987, program chmn. Phoenix chpt. 1988-89, Chpt. Pres.' Cert. award 1988, 90, 91, 92, dir. Phoenix chpt. 1989-90, Outstanding Indsl. award 1989, editor monthly newsletter Phoenix chpt. 1990-91, Inst. Publs. Commendation award 1990, 91, Gem award 1990, 1st v.p. Phoenix chpt. 1991, rep. Ariz. Constrn. Industries Coalition 1991-93, chmn. S.W. region publs. 1992, pres.-elect Phoenix chpt. 1992, chmn. nominating com. 1992, CCPR inst. rev. com. 1992, past pres. Phoenix chpt. 1994, planning chmn. 1994, S.W. region membership chmn. 1994, mem. inst. awards com. 1994, inst. dir.-elect S.W. region 1994, inst. dir. 1995—, region dir. citation 1992, S.W. region cert. thanks 1992, pres. Phoenix chpt., 1993, Individual Appreciation award 1991, Inst. Cert. Appreciation 1993, 94, Region Publ. award S.W. region 1994, Pres.'s citation Phoenix chpt. 1994, cert. thanks S.W. region 1994), Constrn. Products Mfrs. Coun. (treas. 1986), Alpha Mu Alpha. Republican. Congregational. Office: Pleko SW Inc 1824 E 6th St Tempe AZ 85281-2950

DUNCAN, DORIS GOTTSCHALK, information systems educator; b. Seattle, Nov. 19, 1944, d. Raymond Robert and Marian (Onstad) D.; m. Robert George Gottschalk, Sept. 12, 1971 (div. Dec. 1983). BA, U. Wash., Seattle, 1967, MBA, 1968; PhD, Golden Gate U., 1978. Cert. data processor, systems profl., computer profl., data educator. Comm. cons. Pacific NW Bell Telephone Co., Seattle, 1968-71; mktg. supr. AT&T, San Francisco, 1971-73; sr. cons., project leader Quantum Sci. Corp., Palo Alto, Calif., 1973-75; dir. co. analysis program Input Inc., Palo Alto, 1975-76; dir. info. sci. dept. Golden Gate U., San Francisco, 1982-83, mem. info. systems adv. bd., 1983-85; lectr. acctg. and info. systems Calif. State U., Hayward, 1976-78, assoc. prof., 1978-85, prof., 1985-94, coord. computer info. sys., prof., 1994—; cons. pvt. cos., 1975—; speaker profl. groups and confs. Author: Computers and Remote Computing Services, 1983; contbr. articles to profl. jours. Loaned exec. United Good Neighbors, Seattle, 1969; nat. committeewoman, bd. dirs. Young Reps., Wash., 1970-71; adv. Jr. Achievement, San Francisco, 1971-72; mem. nat. bd. Inst. for Certification of Computer Profls. Edn. Found., 1990-93; mem. Editorial Rev. bd. Journal Info. Systems Edn., 1992—; bd. dirs. Computer Repair Svcs., 1992-94. Mem. Data Processing Mgmt. Assn. (Meritorious Svc. award, Bronze award 1984, Silver award 1986, Gold Award 1988, Emerald award 1992, Diamond award 1994, Nat. grantee, 1984. dir., edn. chmn. San Francisco chpt. 1984-85, sec. and v.p. 1985, pres. 1986, assn. dir. 1987, by-laws chmn. 1987, chair awards com., 1992-95, nat. bd. dirs. spl. interest group in edn. 1985-87), Am. Inst. Decision Scis., 1982-83, Western Assn. Schs. and Colls. (accreditation evaluation team, 1984-85), Assn. Computing Machinery, 1984—. Club: Junior (Seattle, Beautiful Home award 1994, 95). Subspecialties: Information systems (information science). Current work: curriculum development, professionalism in data processing field, professional certification, industry standards, computer literacy and user education, sys. analysis and design, design of data bases and data banks. Office: Calif State U Sch of Bus and Econs Hayward CA 94542

DUNCAN, ELIZABETH CHARLOTTE, marriage and family therapist, educational therapist, educator; b. L.A., Mar. 10, 1919; d. Frederick John de St. Vrain and Nellie Mae (Goucher) Schwankovsky; m. William McConnell Duncan, Oct. 12, 1941 (div. 1949); 1 child, Susan Elizabeth Duncan St. Vrain. BA, Calif. U., Long Beach, 1953; MA, UCLA, 1962; PhD, Internat. Coll., 1984. Cert. marriage and family therapist, Wash. Dir. gifted program Palos Verdes Sch. Dist., Calif., 1958-64; TV tchr., participant ednl. films L.A. County, 1961-64; dir. U. So. Calif. Presch., L.A., 1965-69, Abraham Maslow rsch. assoc., 1962-69; pvt. practice family counselor, Malibu and Ventura, Calif., Eastsound, Wash., 1979—, also, Seattle, pvt. practice in psychotherapy, Renton, Wash., 1994—; pub. spkr., lectr. comm.; cons. in field; psychotherapist Mentor Program Eastsound, 1992; bd. dirs. Children's Program North Sound Regional Support Network, 1992; resident psychologist for film series Something Personal, 1987—; mem. Rsch. Inst. of Scripps Clinic, La Jolla, Calif.; charter mem. Inst. Behav. Med., Santa Barbara, Calif.; TV performer: (documentary) The Other Side, 1985. Creator: Persephone's Child, 1988; author: Do Hearts Really Break? 1990. Active Chrysalis Ctr., L.A., 1984-86, Ventura County Mental Health Adv. Bd., Calif., 1985-86, United Way, L.A., 1985-92; mem. Menninger Found. San Juan County, Wash., 1992; adv. bd. North Sound Regional Support Network, 1992. Recipient Emmy award for best documentary Am. TV Arts and Scis., 1976, Child Adv. of Yr. Calif. Mental Health Adv. Bd., 1987. Mem. AACD (Disting. Svc. award 1990), Transpersonal Psychol. Assn., Calif. State Orgn. Gifted Edn. (sec. 1962-64), Internat. Platform Assn., Am. Assn. for Marriages and Family Therapy. Democrat. Avocations: swimming, plays, concerts, boating, political issues, especially women and child abuse. Office: 4505 44th Ave SW Seattle WA 98116

DUNCAN, ELMORE EDWARD, psychiatrist; b. Chehalis, Wash., May 2, 1932; s. Lewis Edward and Mildred Lucille (Tucker) D.; m. Elizabeth Sylvia Wassenaar, June 20, 1958; children: Steven Lewis, Susan Mae, Kathleen Joan. BS, Pacific Luth. U., 1954; MD, U. Wash., 1958. Intern USN, Great

Lakes, Ill., 1958-59; resident Monterey County Hosp., Salinas, Calif., 1962-63; family practitioner Carlisle Med. Group, El Cajon, Calif., 1963-68; resident psychiatry U. Oreg. Health Sci. Ctr., Portland, 1968-71; med. dir. Delaunay Inst., Portland, 1971-73, Woodland Park Health Unit, Portland, 1973-75; acting med. dir. St. Vincent Psychiatric Unit, Portland, 1983-84; med. dir. Caremark Behavioral Health Svcs., Portland, 1993-94; assoc. bd. dirs. Portland Access Mental Health Inc., 1995—; asst. clin. prof. U. Oreg. Health Scis. Ctr., 1972—. Lt. USN, 1957-62. Mem. AMA, Am., Psychiat. Assn., Oreg. Psychiat. Assn. (pres. 1994-95), Oreg. Med. Assn., Mult County Med. Soc., Christian Med.-Dental Soc. Baptist. Office: Northwest Resource Group 700 NE Multnomah # 560 Portland OR 97232

DUNCAN, JAMES RICHARD, broadcast engineer; b. Little Rock, June 3, 1948; s. James Richard and Mary (Bond) D. BA in Geography, U. Calif., Berkeley, 1969; postgrad. in mass comms., Denver U., 1970. Cons. self-employed San Jose, Calif., 1972-90; broadcast engr. Nationwide Comms., San Jose, Calif., 1985-90; corp. engr. Kool Comms., San Jose, Calif., 1990—; cons. Ohlone Community Coll., Fremont, Calif., 1990—. Mem. Soc. Broadcast Engrs. (cert.), Am. Coun. for Arts, Ariel Dance Co., Santa Clara Ballet, No. Calif. Frequency Coord. Commn. Home: 380 Blossom Way Scotts Valley CA 95066 Office: Sta KBAY Radio 399 N 3d St Campbell CA 95008

DUNCAN, JOHN WILEY, mathematics and computer educator, retired air force officer; b. San Francisco, Aug. 8, 1947; s. Vernon Alexander and Nellie May (Shaw) D.; m. Trudy Rae Hirsch, Feb. 25, 1967; children: Amber Rose, John Anthony. BS in Math. and Physics, N.W. Mo. State U., 1969; MBA, So. Ill. U., 1973; MS in Computer Sci., U. Tex., San Antonio, 1982. Tchr. Savannah (Mo.) High Sch., 1969; enlisted USAF, 1969, advanced through grades to maj.; aeromed. officer 9AES USAF, Clark Air Base, The Philippines, 1978-80; student UTSA, San Antonio, 1981-82; systems implementation team leader Sch. of Health Care Scics., Sheppard AFB, Tex., 1982-83; asst. chief med. systems Hdqrs. Air Tng. Command, Randolph AFB, Tex., 1983-86; chief med. systems Hdqrs. Pacific AF, Hickham AFB, Hawaii, 1986-89, 15 Med. Group, Hickham AFB, Hawaii, 1989; instr. Kapiolani C.C., Honolulu, 1989-94; sys. mgr. Hawaii Correctional Industries, Aiea, 1994—; computer cons., 1983—; instr. Tex. Luth. Coll., Seguin, 1984-86, Hawaii Pacific Coll., Honolulu, 1987-89, Leeward Community Coll., 1989-91. Cons. Ronald McDonald House, San Antonio, 1986. Presbyterian. Home: 2114 Aluka Loop Pearl City HI 96782-1317

DUNCAN, REGINALD WALLACE, clergyman, former municipal judge and educator; b. Wichita Falls, Tex., May 20, 1925; s. Howell Cobb and Eva Lois (Kelley) D.; m. Patsy Jean Gunnell, Nov. 1, 1946; children: Ralph, Barbara, Reginald, Lydia, Beth, Clydene. BS with honors, Ea. N.Mex. U., 1976; MA in Rels., Pepperdine U., 1979. Cert. tchr. N.Mex. Enlisted man USN, 1943, advanced through grades to chief electronic technician, 1956; assigned to Yokosuka, Japan, 1955-57; instr. U.S. Naval Electronic Sch., Treasure Island, Calif., 1957-62; ret., USN, 1962; tchr. Pacific Christian Acad., Graton, Calif., 1962-63; svc. tech. and mgr. Sears Roebuck, various cities Calif., N.Mex., 1963-72; tchr. electronics Clovis (N.Mex.) High Sch., 1972-76; asst. supr. trades and indsl. edn. Santa Fe, N.Mex., 1976-78; dir. indsl. edn. Lubbock (Tex.) Christian Coll., 1978-80; min. Church of Christ, Appleton, Wis., 1980-84; tchr. indsl. arts Gadsden H.S., Anthony, N.Mex., 1984-90; mcpl. judge Town of Anthony, Tex., 1991-93; mem. N.Mex. State Vica Adv. Com., 1985-90; mem. adv. com. vocat. elec. Dona Ana C.C., Las Cruces, 1988-90. Mem. Fleet Reserve Assn., Am. Radio Relay League, Am. Vocat. Assn. (life mem.). Home: 54 Dry Canyon Ct Cloudcroft NM 88317

DUNCAN, RICHARD FREDRICK, JR., secondary education educator, travel consultant; b. Millry, Ala., July 12, 1947; s. Richard F. and Claire Louise (Wood) D.; m. Rebecca Susan Davis, July 14, 1973. AA, Okaloosa-Walton Jr. Coll., 1967; BS, Fla. State U., 1969, MS, 1971; postgrad., Ore. State U., 1981-82. Tchr. Gadsden County Sch. Bd., Quincy, Fla., 1970-71, Leon County Sch. Bd., Tallahassee, Fla., 1972-73, Beaverton (Oreg.) Sch. Dist. No. 48, Ore., 1973—; microbiologist Washington County, Hillsboro, Ore., 1971-72; cons. on sci. edn. Northwest Regional Ednl. Lab., Portland, Ore., 1978-79; cons. on marine edn. Ore. Dept. Edn., Salem, 1980-81. Recipient award for excellence in sci. teaching Ore. Mus. Sci. and Industry, Portland, 1984, Psdl. award, 1984. Mem. Assn. Presdl. Awardees in Sci. Teaching (nat. pres. 1987-88), Nat. Assn.Biology Tchrs. (Ore. Biology Tchr. of Year award 1981), Nat. Sci. Tchrs. Assn. (Presdl. award for excellence in sci. teaching, 1983), Oreg. Sci. Tchrs. Assn. (pres. 1980-81, Oreg. Jr. High Tchr. of Yr. award 1982), North Assn. Marine Educators (state dir. 1978-80), Masons, Shriners. Democrat. Home: 13240 SW Juanita Pl Beaverton OR 97008-6831 Office: Beaverton Sch Dist # 48 PO Box 200 Beaverton OR 97075-0200

DUNCKER, MICHAEL CHARLES, dentist; b. Montebello, Calif., Dec. 30, 1950; s. Charles Montiel and Helen (Hunick) D.; m. Marie DeLeon, 1975 (div. 1985); 1 child, Vanessa Leann. BA, U. So. Calif., L.A., 1976; DDS, UCLA, 1980. Sr. staff dentist Community Health Found., East L.A., 1980-86; dentist/owner Cali Family Dental Ctr., Huntington Park, Calif., 1986—; pvt. practice Downey, Calif., 1993—. With U.S. Army, 1970-72. Mem. Latin Am. Dental Assn. (pres. 1991-92), Kiwanis (bd. dirs. 1991-92). Office: 11411 Brookshire Ave Ste 405 Downey CA 90241-5006

DUNDAS, DENNIS FRANKLIN, plastic surgeon; b. L.A., Oct. 12, 1942; s. John Arthur and Wanda (Yoakum) D.; m. Zoe Lynn Anderson, Feb. 9, 1969; children: Gregory, Denise. BA, Johns Hopkins U., 1964; MD, U. So. Calif., 1968. Diplomate Am. Bd Plastic Surgery. Pvt. practice Kirkland, Wash., 1978—. Lt. comdr. USN, 1978—. Fellow ACS; mem. Am. Soc. Plastic Surgeons. Office: 13114 120th Ave NE Kirkland WA 98034

DUNDON, BRIAN R., motor company executive; b. 1946. With Century Electric, 1976-86; exec. v.p. motor and generators Magnetek Inc., L.A., 1986—. Office: MagneTek Inc 11150 Santa Monica Blvd Los Angeles CA 90025-3386

DUNFORD, MAX PATTERSON, biology educator; b. Bloomington, Idaho, June 17, 1930; s. George Osmond and Venna (Patterson) D.; m. Katie Pearl Thornhill, Sept. 1, 1954; children: Mark L., Steven O., Keith M., Thomas M., Karen, Allen R. A.S., Snow Coll., 1950; B.S., Brigham Young U., 1954, M.S., 1958; Ph.D., U. Calif., Davis, 1962. Faculty U. Calif., Santa Barbara, 1961-62, Mills Coll., Oakland, Calif., 1962-63; faculty biology dept. N.Mex. State U., Las Cruces, 1963—, asst. chmn. dept. biology, 1992—. Contbr. articles to profl. jours. Served with U.S. Army, 1954-56. NSF grantee, 1966-68, 75, 77, 78, 79, 81. Fellow AAAS (exec. officer Southwestern and Rocky Mountain div. 1973-78, pres. SWARM 1981-82, mem. council, com. for council affairs 1973-79); mem. Bot. Soc. Am., Am. Genetic Assn. Mem. Ch. of Jesus Christ of Latter-day Saints. Home: 905 Conway Ave Apt 49 Las Cruces NM 88005-7706

DUNGAN, GLORIA KRONBECK, critical care nurse; b. Little Falls, Minn., July 4, 1938; d. Hans Emil and Marie (Hahn) Kronbeck; divorced; 1 child, Kirk. Diploma, Abbott Hosp. Sch. Nursing, Mpls., 1958; BS in Nursing, U. Alaska, 1978. CCRN. Nurse at hosps. Mpls., Anchorage, 1958-63; staff nurse, charge nurse Narrabri (Australia) Hosp., 1963-64; night supr., staff nurse, charge nurse Providence Hosp., Anchorage, 1964-65; night supr., staff nurse Anchorage Community Hosp., 1966-67, Greater Juneau Borough Hosp., Juneau, Alaska, 1968-69; asst. head nurse nights intensive care unit Providence Hosp., Anchorage, 1970-77; staff nurse Alaska Nurses Registry, Anchorage, 1977-78; from nurse mgr. to staff nurse intensive care unit Providence Hosp., Anchorage, 1978-83; staff nurse intensive care unit King Fahd Mil. Hosp., Jeddah, Saudi Arabia, 1983-84; staff nurse intensive care Providence Hosp., Anchorage, 1984-90; staff nurse critical care Am. Critical Care Svcs., Anchorage, 1990-92, Humana Hosp. Alaska, Anchorage, 1992, Alaska Native Med. Ctr., 1992—. Mem. Am. Assn. Critical Care Nurses (pres. Anchorage chpt. 1980-81, presenter ednl. programs), Sigma Theta Tau.

DUNGWORTH, DONALD L., veterinary educator, consultant; b. Hathersage, Derbyshire, Eng., July 16, 1931; came to U.S., 1957; s. Lawrence and Alice (Dearnaley) D.; m. Margaret Alice Begg, July 28, 1961; children: Dawn Lesley, Duncan Lawrence. BVSc, Liverpool U., Eng., 1956; PhD, U. Calif., Davis, 1961. Lectr. U. Bristol, Eng., 1961-62; from asst. prof. to prof., dept. veterinary med. pathology U. Calif., Davis, 1962-93, prof. emeritus, 1993—, chmn., 1969-93; cons. pulmonary path and inhalation toxicology, Internat. Agy. for Rsch. on Cancer and various nat. and internat. insts., 1980—. Author, editor books. Lt. Brit. Army, 1949-51. Recipient Sr. award Von Humboldt Found., 1990-91; WHO fellow, 1968-69, Fulbright fellow Fulbright-Hays Program, 1976-77. Mem. Royal Coll. of Vet. Surgeons, Am. Assn. Pathologists, Am. Coll. Toxicology, Internat. Acad. Pathology, Am. Coll. Vet. Pathologists (diplomate, pres. 1977-78).

DUNIGAN, PAUL FRANCIS XAVIER, JR., federal agency administrator; b. Richland, Wash., June 22, 1948; s. Paul Frances Xavier Sr. and Eva Lucille (Reckley) D.; m. Elizabeth Anne Henricks, Apr. 8, 1978; children: Katherine Anne, Theresa Anne. BS in Biology, Gonzaga U., 1970; MS in Environ. Sci., Washington State U., 1973. Tech. program mgr. ERDA, AEC, Richland, 1972-75; environ. biologist U.S. Dept. Energy, ERDA, Richland, 1975-81; waste mgmt. engr. U.S. Dept. Energy Waste Mgmt., Richland, 1981-84; civilian program mgr. Surplus Facilities Mgmt. Program U.S. Dept. Energy, Richland, 1984-87, environ. biologist, 1987—; also compliance officer Nat. Environ. Policy Act. Contbr. articles to profl. jours. Mem. AAAS, Water Pollution Control Fedn., Pacific Northwest Pollution Control Fedn. Roman Catholic. Home: 1612 Judson Ave Richland WA 99352-2944 Office: US Dept Energy PO Box 550 Richland WA 99352-0550

DUNIPACE, IAN DOUGLAS, lawyer; b. Tucson, Dec. 18, 1939; s. William Smith and Esther Morvyth (McGeorge) D.; m. Janet Mae Dailey, June 9, 1963; children: Kenneth Mark, Leslie Amanda. BA magna cum laude, U. Ariz., 1961, JD cum laude, 1966 Bar: Ariz. 1966, U.S. Supreme Ct. 1972, Nev. 1994. Reporter, critic Long Branch (N.J.) Daily Record, 1963; assoc. firm Jennings, Strouss, Salmon & Trask, Phoenix, 1966-69; assoc. Jennings, Strouss & Salmon, PLC, Phoenix, 1969-70, ptnr., 1971-93, mem., 1993—. Reporter Phoenix Forward Edn. Com., 1969-70; mem. Phoenix Arts Commn., 1990-93, chmn., 1992-93; bd. mgmt. Downtown Phoenix YMCA, 1973-80, chmn., 1977-78; bd. dirs. Phoenix Met. YMCA, 1976-87, 88—, chmn., 1984-85; bd. mgmt. Paradise Valley YMCA, 1979-82, chmn., 1980-81; bd. mgmt. Scottsdale/Paradise Valley YMCA, 1983, mem. legal affairs com. Pacific Region YMCA, 1978-81; chmn. YMCA Ariz. State Youth and Govt. Com., 1989—; bd. dirs. The Schoolhouse Found., 1990—, pres., 1990-94, Kids Voting, 1990-94, Beaver Valley Improvement Assn., 1977-79, Pi Kappa Alpha Holding Corp., 1968-72, The Heard Mus. 1993-94; trustee Paradise Valley Unified Sch. Dist. Employee Benefit Trust, 1980-93, chmn., 1987-93, Sch. Theology, Claremont, Calif., 1994—; trustee First Meth. Found. of Phoenix, 1984-93; mem. Greater Paradise Valley Community Coun., 1985-87; bd. dirs. Heard Mus. Coun., 1990—, pres. 1993-94; mem. Ariz. Venture Capital Conf. Planning Com., 1994—, Assn. for Corp. Growth, 1995—. Capt. AUS, 1961-63. Mem. State Bar Ariz. (securities regulation sect. 1970—, chmn., 1991-92, mem. com. unauthorized practice of law 1972-84, chmn. 1975-83, mem. bus. law sect. 1981—, chmn., 1984-85), State Bar Nev., Am., Fed. (pres. Ariz. chpt. 1980-81), Maricopa County bar assns., Ariz. Zool. Soc., U. Ariz. Law Coll. Assn. (bd. dirs. 1983-90, pres. 1985-86), Smithsonian Assn., U. Ariz. Alumni Assn. (bd. dirs. 1985-86), Phi Beta Kappa, Phi Kappa Phi, Phi Delta Phi, Phi Alpha Theta, Sigma Delta Pi, Phi Eta Sigma, Pi Kappa Alpha (nat. counsel 1968-72). Democrat. Methodist (mem. met. Phoenix commn. 1968-71, lay leader 1975-78, trustee 1979-81, pres. 1981; mem. Pacific S.W. ann. conf. 1969-79, lawyer commn. 1980-85, chancellor Desert S.W. ann. conf. 1985—). Clubs: Renaissance. Lodges: Masons, Kiwanis (pres. Phoenix 1984-85, disting. lt. gov. 1986-87, SW dist. community service chmn. 1987-88, dist. activity com. coord. 1988-89, dist. laws and regulation chmn. 1989-90, 92-93, 95—, asst. to dist. gov. for club svcs. 1990-91, field dir. 1991-92, dist. conv. chmn., 1993-94, mem. internat. com. on Project 39, 1988-89, internat. com. On to Anaheim 1990-91, internat. com. on leadership tng. and devel. 1991-92, 93-94, trustee SW dist. found. 1987-92, 1st v.p. 1990-92). Comments editor Ariz. Law Rev., 1965-66. Home: 4147 E Desert Cove Ave Phoenix AZ 85028-3514 Office: Jennings Strouss & Salmon PLC 2 N Central Ave Phoenix AZ 85004-2393

DUNKEL, FLORENCE VACCARELLO, entomologist; b. Kenosha, Wis., Oct. 10, 1942; d. Vincent James and Mildred (Behr-Naegeli) Vaccarello; m. Thomas Beatty Dunkel, Dec. 27, 1964 (div. 1982); children: Anne-Marie C., Alexander J., Marylynn S.; m. Robert Eller Diggs, June 20, 1987. Student, Lawrence U., 1960-62; BS in Zoology, U. Wis., 1964, MS in Zoology, 1966, PhD in Entomology, 1969; postgrad. studies, U. Minn., 1973-75. Rsch. fellow dept. entomology U. Minn., St. Paul, 1975-84; team leader USDA Office Internat. Cooperation, People's Republic China, 1982; project dir. internat agrl. programs U. Minn., 1983-87; pres., cons. Internat. Postharvest Systems, Inc., Minnetonka, Minn., 1985—; head Mont. State U., Bozeman, 1988-92, assoc. prof. dept. entomology, 1988—. Patentee in field. Vis. scholar Nat. Acad. Scis. Zhongshan U., 1981; recipient Disting. Achievement award Lawrence U., 1989; AAUW Marie Curie fellow, 1975-76; C.A. Lindbergh grantee in anthropology, 1992, numerous grants for rsch., 1977—. Mem. AAAS, Entomol. Soc. Am. (Pacific br. Teaching award 1994), Am. Soc. Mammalogists, Sigma Xi, Gamma Sigma Delta. Home: 8118 Indian Paint Brush Dr Bozeman MT 59715-9529 Office: Mont State U 324 Leon Johnson Hall Bozeman MT 59717

DUNKEL, PETER CARL, university administrator; b. New Britain, Conn., Aug. 12, 1962; s. William Carl and Dorothy Signe (Peterson) D.; m. Kristina Delmy Beatriz Rivera, Dec. 14, 1985; children: Peter Wesley, Stephen Christopher, Elizabeth Samantha. BA, Wesleyan U., Middletown, Conn., 1984; MA, Fuller Theol. Sem., Pasadena, Calif., 1988; postgrad., UCLA. Corp. fin. analyst Merrill Lynch Capital Markets, N.Y.C., 1984-86; dir. capital programs Biola U., La Mirada, Calif., 1989-91; dir. capital programs Calif. Luth. U., Thousand Oaks, 1992-93, dir. devel., 1994—; sec.-treas. bd dirs. China Ministry Internat., Pasadena, 1993—. Vol. L.A. Mission, 1991—. Mem. Nat. Soc. Fundraising Execs., Coun. for Advancement and Support of Edn. Republican. Evangelical. Home: 2321 Goldsmith Ave Thousand Oaks CA 91360-3131 Office: Calif Luth U 60 Olsen Rd Thousand Oaks CA 91360-2700

DUNLAP, F. THOMAS, JR., electronics company executive, engineer, lawyer; b. Pitts., Feb. 7, 1951; s. Francis Thomas and Margaret (Hubert) D.; married; children: Bridgette, Katie. B.S.E.E., U. Cin., 1974; J.D., U. Santa Clara, Calif., 1979. Bar: Calif., 1979, U.S. Dist. Ct. (no. dist.) Calif. 1979. Mgr. engring. Intel Corp, Santa Clara, Calif., 1974-78, adminstr. tech. exchange, 1978-80, European counsel, 1980-81, sr. atty., 1981-83, gen. counsel, sec., 1983-87, v.p., gen. counsel, sec., 1987—. drafter, lobbyist Semiconductor Chip Protection Act, 1984. Republican. Roman Catholic. Office: Intel Corp 2200 Mission College Blvd # 4- Santa Clara CA 95054-1537

DUNLAP, JACK STUART, financial investigator; b. Mullens, W.Va., Jan. 6, 1930; s. James Edward and Mary Katherine (Carpenter) D.; m. Harriett June Foglesong, Sept. 27, 1952 (div. Apr. 1977); children: Katherine Gaye, James Edward, Jack Carter; m. Linda Sue Hayes, May 1, 1978. BSBA, Concord Coll., 1958; postgrad., Saddleback Coll., 1985-90. Lic. pvt. investigator, Calif. Spl. agt. U.S. Treasury Dept., IRS, Toledo, 1959-64, 65-67, Charleston, W.Va., 1964-65, San Diego, 1967-72, 77-80, L.A., 1972-75, Santa Ana, Calif., 1975-77; pvt. practice Dunlap Investigations, El Cajon, Calif., 1980-84, San Clemente, Calif., 1984—; pres. Intelligence Investigations, Inc., San Diego, 1982-85; expert witness, 1980—; mem. Am. Bd. Forensic Examiners. Coach Singing Hills Little League, El Cajon, 1969-72; asst. scoutmaster Boy Scouts Am., Mullens, 1950-59. Sgt. U.S. Army, 1951-53. Mem. Assn. Cert. Fraud Examiners (cert., bd. dirs. San Diego chpt.). Democrat. Baptist. Home: 2985 Calle Frontera San Clemente CA 92673-3051 Office: Dunlap Investigations PO Box 4328 San Clemente CA 92674-4328

DUNLAP, JAMES RILEY, SR., former financial executive, credit manager; b. Portland, Oreg., May 21, 1925; s. William Gates and Laura (Riley) D.; m. Betty Towe; children: James R. Jr., Brian Jay, William David. BSBA, U. Oreg., 1950; postgrad., Portland State Coll., 1963-65. Sales rep. Hyster Co., Portland, 1950-61; br. asst. mgr. Reynolds Metals Co., Portland, 1961-71; corp. credit mgr. Burns Bros. Inc., Portland, 1971-79, sec.-treas., 1979-89. Contbr. articles on credit and fin. mgmt. to profl. jours. With USAAF, 1943-46. Mem. Nat. Assn. Credit Mgmt. (past pres., bd. dirs.), Internat. Assn. Credit Mgmt. (past pres., bd. dirs., Disting. Svc. award 1985, Herb Barnes Meml. award 1987), Portland Retail Credit Assn. (past pres., bd. dirs.), Oreg. State Cons. Credit Assn. (past pres., lifetime bd. dirs.), Portland J. C. of C., Oreg. Motor Supply Credit Assn. (past pres., bd. dirs.), Consumer Counseling Svc. Oreg. (exec. com. 1979—), Am. Contract Bridge League (past pres. Portland chpt., life master), Lions (past pres. local club), Masons, Elks, Delta Tau Delta Alumni Assn. (past pres.).

DUNLAP, RON, investment securities executive; b. South Bend, Ind., Oct. 31, 1937; s. Claude Delbert and Thelma Marie (Sanner) D.; m. Allison Marie Dale, Oct. 12, 1966; children: Marcia Marie, Lynne Marie. BS, Purdue U., 1959, MS, 1961. Engr. Boeing Co., Seattle, 1962-74, fin. analyst, 1974-80; exec. King Co., Seattle, 1981-82; resident mgr. Dain Bosworth, Bellevue, Wash., 1982--. State rep. U.S. Ho. of Reps., Olympia, 1974-80; candidate U.S. Congress, Washington, 1980. Mem. Rotary. Republican. Office: Dain Bosworth 10900 NE 4th St Ste 1400 Bellevue WA 98004-5841

DUNLAP, SCOTT HOWARD, systems integration consultant, music producer; b. Chgo., Apr. 29, 1969; m. Christen Drue, July 24, 1993. BS in Fin. and Mktg., U. Oreg., 1992. Prodr. Surreal Sounds, Portland, Oreg., 1992—; sr. cons. Andersen Consulting, Portland, 1992—. Active Children First Oreg., Portland, 1994. Mem. Oreg. Young Entrepreneurs Assn., Portland Music Assn., Assn. Systems Mgmt., City Club Portland. Office: Andersen Consulting 111 SW Columbia St Ste 1400 Portland OR 97201-5846

DUNLAVEY, DEAN CARL, lawyer; b. Waterloo, Iowa, Oct. 31, 1925; s. Ralph Ernest and Lou Emma (Caffall) D.; m. Dorian Brown, Sept. 8, 1948; children: Dudley Ralph, Dean Geoffrey, Dana Charles. B.S., Harvard U., 1949, LL.M., 1956; Ph.D., U. Calif., Berkeley, 1952, LL.B., 1955. Bar: Calif. 1956. Assoc. firm Gibson, Dunn & Crutcher, Los Angeles, 1956-61; partner Gibson, Dunn & Crutcher, 1962—. Served to capt. AUS, 1943-45. Mem. Calif. State Bar, Am. Coll. Trial Lawyers. Republican. Home: 3255 Parkhurst Dr Rancho Palos Verdes CA 90275-6389 Office: Gibson Dunn & Crutcher 333 S Grand Ave Los Angeles CA 90071-1504

DUNLOP, LAURENCE JAMES, religious studies educator; b. Adelaide, Australia, Jan. 7, 1939; came to U.S., 1980; s. Walter James and Jean Wilson (Eardley) D. Licentiate in Theology, Gregorian U., Rome, 1966; Licentiate in Scripture, Pontifical Bibl. Inst., Rome, 1967, Doctorate in Scripture, 1970. Lectr. Sacred Heart Monastery, Canberra, Act, Australia, 1964-65; lectr. St. Paul's Nat. Sem., Sydney, N.S.W., Australia, 1970-79, rector, 1975-79; asst. prof. Loyola U., Chgo., 1981-83; assoc. prof. Marymount Coll., Rancho Palos Verdes, Calif., 1983—. Author: The Happy Poor, 1975, Patterns of Prayer in the Psalms, 1981; contbr. articles to profl. jours. Roman Catholic. Office: Marymount College 30800 Palos Verdes Dr E Rancho Palos Verdes CA 90274

DUNMEYER, SARAH LOUISE FISHER, health care consultant; b. Ft. Wayne, Ind., Apr. 13, 1935; d. Frederick Law and Jeanette Blose (Stults) Fisher; m. Herbert W. Dunmeyer, Sept. 9, 1967; children: Jodi, Lisa. BS, U. Mich., 1957; MS, Temple U., 1966; EdD, U. San Francisco, 1983. Lic. clin. lab. technologist, Calif. Instr. med. tech. U. Vt., Burlington, 1966-67; instr. med. tech. Northeastern U., Boston, 1967-68, instr. lab. asst. program, 1968-70; educator, coord. sch. med. tech. Children's Hosp., San Francisco, 1970-73; dir. continuing edn. program Pacific Presbyn. Med. Ctr., San Francisco, 1974-82; project mgr., cons. Peabody Mktg. Decisions, San Francisco, 1983-87; sr. rsch. assoc. Inst. for Health and Aging, U. Calif., San Francisco, 1986-89; external cons. Health Care Consulting Svcs., San Francisco, 1986-95; rsch. analyst student acad. svcs. U. Calif., San Francisco, 1991-94; seminar presenter Am. Assn. Blood Banks, San Francisco, 1976, Am. Soc. Clin. Pathologists, Miami Beach, Fla., 1977, Ann. Meeting of Am. Soc. Med. Technology, Atlanta, 1977; site surveyor Nat. Accrediting Agy. for Clin. Lab. Scis., Chgo., 1974-80. Contbr. articles to profl. jours.

DUNN, DAVID CAMERON, entrepreneur, business executive; b. Juneau, Alaska, Dec. 8, 1941; s. Robert Charles and Kay (Watson) D.; m. Karen Ann Leonard, Jan. 17, 1970 (div. 1990); children: David Cameron Jr., Paige. BA, Stanford U., 1963; MBA, U. Pa., 1968. Account exec. J. Walter Thompson, N.Y.C., 1968-70; product mgr. Gen. Foods, White Plains, N.Y., 1970-73; dir. mktg. Heublein, San Francisco, 1973-77; exec. v.p. Perelli-Minetti Winery, San Francisco, 1977-79; sr. v.p., bd. dirs. Valchris Farms, Modesto, Calif., 1980-84, DFS Advt., San Francisco, 1984-87; pres. Thomas-Rahm Advt., Oakland, Calif., 1987-89, Mktg. Comms. Assocs., Oakland, 1990—; co-founder Re-Con Systems (OTC) 1968; bd. dirs. PC Guardian, San Rafael, Calif. Trustee Oakland Symphony, 1989-90, Orinda (Calif.) Edn. Found., 1986-87. 1st lt. U.S. Army, 1964-66, Germany. Mem. Lakeview Club, Oakland Athletic Club, Oakland C. of C. (Small Bus. of Yr. 1991), Commonwealth Club. Republican. Roman Catholic. Office: Mktg Communs Assocs 40 Jack London Sq Oakland CA 94607-3700

DUNN, DAVID JOSEPH, financial executive; b. Bklyn., July 30, 1930; s. David Joseph and Rose Marie (McLaughlon) D.; BS, U.S. Naval Acad., 1955; MBA, Harvard U., 1961; m. Marilyn Percaccia, June 1955 (div.); children: Susan, Steven, Linda; m. Marilyn LaMarsh, June, 1976 (div.); m. Kathryn Alari, Apr. 1986 (div.); m. Marilyn Bell, Apr. 1994. Investment banker G.H. Walker & Co., N.Y.C., 1961-62; ptnr. J.H. Whitney & Co., N.Y.C., 1962-70; mng. ptnr. Idanta Ptnrs., San Diego, 1971—; chmn. bd. Iomega Corp., Ogden, Utah, Munchkin Bottling, Inc., Van Nuys, Calif.; bd. dirs. Visionary Design Systems, Inc., Mountain View, Calif. Mem. Univ. Club (N.Y.C.), San Diego Yacht Club, LaJolla (Calif.) Country Club, Pauma Valley Country Club. With USMC, 1950-51, 55-59. Home: 9776 La Jolla Farms Rd La Jolla CA 92037-1133

DUNN, JENNIFER BLACKBURN, congresswoman; b. Seattle, Wash., July 29, 1941; d. John Charles and Helen (Gorton) Blackburn; div.; children: Bryant, Reagan. Student, U. Wash., 1960-62; BA, Stanford U., 1963. Former chmn. Rep. Party State of Wash.; now mem. 103rd Congress from 8th Wash. dist., Washington, D.C., 1993—; mem. house oversight com., mem. Ways and Means Com. Del. Rep. Nat. Conv., 1980, 84, 88; presdl. apptd. adv. coun. Historic Preservation; presdl. apptd. adv. coun. volunteerism SBA. Mem. Gamma Phi Beta. Office: 432 Cannon Washington DC 20515-4708*

DUNN, JUDITH LOUISE, secondary school educator; b. L.A., Jan. 6, 1945; d. Arthur B. and Lillian M. (Eyrich) D. BA, U. Calif., Santa Barbara, 1966; MA Edn., Pepperdine U., 1978; postgrad., U. Calif., Santa Barbara, 1967. Cert. secondary tchr., adminstr., Calif; cert. lay speaker United Meth. Ch. English tchr. Santa Maria (Calif.) Joint Union High Sch. Dist., mentor tchr., chmn. dept. English, 1991-94; mem. adv. coun. Student Age Parenting and Infant Devel. Program; dist. tchr. rep. Impact II Adv. Coun.; dist. rep. Ctrl. Coast Literacy Coun.; mem. del. tchrs. of English of People to People Citizen Amb. Program visitation to Gt. Britain, 1995. Assoc. lay leader Santa Barbara dist. Calif.-Pacific Annual Conf., 1986-89, United Meth. Ch., bd. Higher Edn. and Campus Ministry, 1982-90; English tchr. del. citizen amb. program People to People to Gt. Britain, 1995. Fellow South Coast Writing Project; Disseminator grantee, 1988, 89. 91. Mem. CTA, NEA, Nat. Coun. Tchrs. English, Local Faculty Assn. (profl. rels. chair 1986-88), Delta Kappa Gamma (immediate past pres. Eta Lambda chpt.). Office: Santa Maria High Sch 901 S Broadway Santa Maria CA 93454-6603

DUNN, KAREN K., mental health center executive, psychotherapist; b. Clovis, N.Mex., Dec. 10, 1944; d. Kent King II and Regina Catherine (Seitz) Chesney; m. Thurman Stanley Dunn, Mar. 31, 1969; children: Michell, Stan II. BS, Ea. N.Mex. U., 1966; MA, U. N.Mex., 1968; postgrad., U. Ariz., 1973-76, Denver Sem., 1995—. Employment counselor Ariz. State Employment Svc., Tucson, 1970-73; counselor, faculty mem. Pima C.C., Tucson, 1975-76; instr. psychology Cochise Coll., Sierra Vista, Ariz., 1976-78; pvt. practice Denver, 1979-81; pres., CEO Discovery Learning Ctr., Parker, Colo., 1981-85; mental health therapist Prince William County, Manassas, Va., 1988; substance abuse specialist Prince William County Schs., Manassas, Va., 1989; exec. dir., CEO KM Counseling and Resource Ctr., Parker, Colo., 1990—. Contbr. articles to profl. jours. Active Mile High United Way; v.p., pres. Parker Newcomers Club; health com. Douglas County Commnrs., Castle Rock, Colo., 1994-95; bd. dirs. Human Resource Coun., 1993-95, Douglas County Com. Youth and Families, 1995. Mem. Colo. Assn. Non-

Profit Execs., Parker C. of C., Douglas County Srs. Home: 6281 S Netherland Way Aurora CO 80016

DUNN, KIMBERLY ANN, state agency administrator, archaeologist; b. Salem, Oreg., Nov. 25, 1947; d. Forrest Reid and Doris Wynona (Gubser) Gish; m. Robert Lee Shaw, Feb. 11, 1967 (div. June 1974); 1 child, Megan Alyson. BA, U. Oreg., 1973, postgrad., 1974; postgrad., U. Wis., 1974-75. Intern in archaeology Bonneville Power Adminstrn., Portland, Oreg., 1973; planner S.W. Wis. Cmty. Action Program, Dodgeville, 1977-80; regional housing coord. Wis. Rural Housing Found., Madison, 1980-82; econ. devel. dir. S.W. Wis. Community Action Program, Dodgeville, 1982-84; planner Mid Willamette Jobs Coun., Salem, Oreg., 1985-88; grants coord., marketer State Job Tng. Partnership Act Adminstrn., Salem, 1988-91; grants coord. State Hist. Preservation Office, Salem, 1991—; nat. mem. Bus. Enterprise Devel. Corp., Denver, 1982-84; mem. Oreg. Occupl./Info. Adv. Com., Salem, 1985-88. Co-author: Field Guide to Archaeology, 1973, Guide to Archaeology for Managers, 1973, Evaluation of Housing Programs in Midwest, 1982, Guide to Older Worker Programs, 1983. Active Oreg. Ocean Policy Adv. Coun., Portland, 1993—. Mem. Hist. Preservation League Oreg., Assn. Oreg. Archaeologists. Home: 4505 E Portland Rd Newberg OR 97132-6963 Office: State Hist Preservation Office 1115 Commercial St NE Salem OR 97310-1000

DUNN, PAUL JAMES, lawyer; b. Tiffin, Ohio, Sept. 23, 1939; s. James Marion and Elenora Rosina (Theis) D.; m. Carolyn Ann Bittner, Mar. 20, 1965; children: Cheryl Ann, Brian James. BA, Cath. U., 1962; JD, Ohio State U., 1964. Bar: Ohio 1965, Ariz. 1981. Pvt. practice Tiffin, 1965-84, Prescott, Ariz., 1982—. Law dir. City of Tiffin, 1972-73; mem. Prescott St. Commn., 1983-87; bd. dirs. Tiffin C. of C., 1975-78; trustee Yavapai Regional Med. Ctr., Prescott, 1986. Named Boss of Yr., Seneca County, Ohio Legal Secs., 1983. Mem. ABA (taxation, real property, probate and trust sects.), Ariz. Bar Assn. (exec. com. probate and trust law sect. 1986-90, chmn. 1988, editor newsletter 1986-88), Seneca County Bar Assn. (pres. 1975), Kiwanis (pres. Tiffin 1981), Elks. Home and Office: 2155 Nolte Dr Prescott AZ 86301-5328

DUNN, RANDY EDWIN, lawyer; b. Hutchinson, Kans., Oct. 8, 1954; s. Roy Edwin and Joan Irene (Farney) D.; m. Michelle Renee Sandwith, Dec. 18, 1976 (div. Aug. 1979); 1 child, Brandi Dawn Sandwith; m. Rosalind O'Nita Heiman, Dec. 22, 1990. BA magna cum laude, Wichita State U., 1977; JD, U. Colo., 1983. Bar: Colo. 1983, U.S. Dist. Ct. Colo. 1986. Store and sales mgr. Pop Shoppe, Inc., Wichita, Kans., 1976-77; sales rep. Lifesavers, Inc., Wichita, 1977-80; asst. mgr. Quik Trip, Inc., Wichita, 1980; assoc. McIntyre & Varallo, P.C., Greeley, Colo., 1983-85; pvt. practice law Denver, 1985-87; ptnr. Dean & Dunn, P.C., Denver, 1987-89; assoc. Lau & Choi, P.C., Denver, 1989-90, Baker & Hostetler, Denver, 1991, Hopper & Kanouff, P.C., Denver, 1991—. Mem. ABA, Colo. Bar Assn., Denver Bar Assn., Masons. Democrat. Office: Hopper & Kanouff PC Ste 200 1610 Wynkoop St Denver CO 80202

DUNN, RICHARD JOSEPH, investment counselor; b. Chgo., Apr. 5, 1924; s. Richard Joseph and Margaret Mary (Jennett) D.; AB, Yale U., 1948; LLB, Harvard U., 1951; MBA, Stanford U., 1956; m. Marygrace Calhoun, Oct. 13, 1951; children: Richard, Marianne, Anthony, Gregory, Noelle. Admitted to Tex. bar, 1952; mem. firm Carrington, Gowan, Johnson & Walker, Dallas, 1951-54; investment counselor Scudder, Stevens & Clark, San Francisco, 1956-84, v.p., 1965-77, sr. v.p., 1977-84, gen. ptnr., 1974-84; ret. Served with AUS, 1943-46. Decorated Combat Infantry Badge, Bronze Star, Purple Heart; Knight of the Sovereign Mil. Hospitaller Order of St. John of Jerusalem of Rhodes and of Malta, Western Assn., 1978—, chancellor 1987-93, pres. 1993—, knight of obedience, 1990, comdr. Cross of Merit, 1989. Roman Catholic. Home: 530 Junipero Serra Blvd San Francisco CA 94127-2727

DUNN, ROBERT PAUL, English language educator; b. Rockford, Ill., Nov. 18, 1941; s. Marion Francis and Catherine Helene (Silvers) D.; m. Kathleen Elisabeth Kelpien, Aug. 6, 1963; children: Deborah Dunn Ferreira, Clark Robert. BA, Pacific Union Coll., 1963; PhD, U. Wis., 1970; M Religion, Sch. Theology, Claremont, Calif., 1977. Asst. prof. English La Sierra U., Riverside, Calif., 1970-73, assoc. prof. English, 1973-79, prof. English, 1979—, chair dept. English, 1977-81, 87-90, assoc. dean Coll. Arts and Scis., 1990-94. Mem. Studia Mystica (editorial bd. 1986—). Home: 5566 Peacock Ln Riverside CA 92505-3168

DUNN, STEVEN ALLEN, chemist; b. Laurens, Iowa, May 1, 1948; s. Lloyd and Avis (Nelson) D.; m. Diana R. Epply, Jan. 11, 1986; children: Mark William, Jeffrey Allen. BS in Phys. Sci., Peru (Nebr.) State Coll., 1980. Electronics technician Gen. Communications Co., Omaha, 1971-76; math. tutor, maintenance worker Peru State Coll., 1976-80; chemist power generation sect. Colo.-Ute Electric Assn., Hayden, 1980-92; sr. chemist power generation sec. Pub. Svc. Co. Colo., Hayden, 1992—. With USCG, 1967-71. Mem. Lions (sec. Hayden club 1986-87, pres. 1988). Democrat. Office: Pub Svc Co of Colo PO Box C Hayden CO 81639-0108

DUNNE, THOMAS, geology educator; b. Prestbury, U.K., Apr. 21, 1943; came to U.S., 1964; s. Thomas and Monica Mary (Whitter) D. BA with honors, Cambridge (Eng.) U., 1964; PhD, Johns Hopkins U., 1969. Research assoc. USDA-Agrl. Research Service, Danville, Vt., 1966-68; research hydrologist U.S. Geol. Survey, Washington, 1969; asst. prof. McGill U., Montreal, Que., Can., 1969-73; from asst. prof. to prof. U. Wash., Seattle, 1973—, chmn. dept., 1984-89; vis. prof. U. Nairobi, Kenya, 1969-71; cons. in field, 1970—. Author (with L.B. Leopold) Water in Environmental Planning. Fulbright scholar 1984; grantee NSF, NASA, Rockefeller Found., 1969—; named to NAS. 1988, Guggenheim fellow, 1989-90. Fellow Am. Geophys. Union, Am. Acad. Arts and Scis.; mem. AAAS, NAS, Geol. Soc. Am., Brit. Geomorphol. Rsch. Group, Sigma Xi. Office: U Cal Sch Enviro Scis & Mgmt 4670 Physical Sciences N Santa Barbara CA 93106

DUNNER, DAVID LOUIS, medicine educator; b. Bklyn., May 27, 1940; s. Edward and Reichel (Connor) D.; m. Peggy Jane Zolbert, Dec. 27, 1964; children: Laura Louise, Jonathan Michael. AA, George Washington U., 1960; MD, Washington U., St. Louis, 1965. Diplomate Am. Bd. Psychiatry and Neurology. Intern Phila. Gen. Hosp., 1965-66; resident in psychiatry Barnes Renard Hosp. of Washington U., St. Louis, 1966-69; research psychiatrist N.Y. State Psychiat. Inst., N.Y.C., 1971-79; from asst. prof. to assoc. prof. clin. psychiatry Columbia U., N.Y.C., 1972-79; chief psychiatry Harborview Med. Ctr., Seattle, 1979-89, dir. outpatient psychiatry, 1989—; prof. psychiatry and behavioral scis. U. Wash., Seattle, 1979—, vice chmn. clin. svcs., 1989—; cons. Found. for Depression and Manic Depression, N.Y.C., 1974-94. Contbr. articles to profl. jours. Served to lt. comdr. USPHS, 1969-71. Fellow Am. Psychiat. Assn., Am. Psychopathol. Assn. (pres. 1986), Am. Coll. Neuropsychopharmacology, West Coast Coll. Biol. Psychiatry (charter, pres. 1987); mem. Psychiat. Research Soc. (pres. 1984). Office: U Wash Med Ctr 4225 Roosevelt Way NE Ste 306 Seattle WA 98105-6099

DUNNETT, DENNIS GEORGE, state official; b. Auburn, Calif., Aug. 5, 1939; s. George DeHaven and Elizabeth Grace (Sullivan) D. AA in Elec. Engring., Sierra Coll., 1959; AB in Econs., Sacramento State Coll., 1966. Engring. technician State of Calif., Marysville, 1961-62; data processing technician State of Calif., Sacramento, 1962-67, EDP programmer and analyst, 1967-74, staff services mgr. and contract adminstr., 1974-76, hardware acquisition mgr., 1976-86, support services br. mgr., information security officer, 1986-90, chief Office Security and Operational Recovery, 1990-92, spl. projects mgr., 1992-93, customer support ctr. mgr., 1994, procurement mgr., 1994—. Mem. AARP, IEEE Computer Soc., Data Processing Mgmt. Assn., Assn. Inst. Cert. of Computers Profls. (certs.), Intergovtl. Coun. on Tech. of Info. Processing, Data Processing Mgmt. Assn., The Mus. Soc., Crocker Art Mus., San Francisco Opera Guild. Home: 729 Blackmer Cir Sacramento CA 95825-4704 Office: Teale Data Ctr 2005 Evergreen St Sacramento CA 95815-3831

DUNNIGAN, MARY ANN, former educational administrator; b. St. Maries, Idaho, Sept. 7, 1915; d. William Henry and Mary Ellen (Kelly) D.; BA, Holy Names Coll., Spokane, 1942; MA, Gonzaga U., Spokane, 1957; postgrad. U. Idaho, UCLA. Tchr. rural schs. Bonner County, 1936-41, elem. schs., 1941, 45-59, high sch., 1942, 45, coordinator elem. edn., 1959-78; prin. kindergarten Sch. Dist. 271, Coeur d'Alene, Idaho, 1978-81; tchr. extension classes U. Idaho; curriculum chmn. Gov.'s Conf. on Edn.; adv. council Head Start. Mem. adv. coun. Coun. for Aging; mem. N. Idaho Mus., Community Council, Community Concerts, Community Theater, N. Idaho Booster Club, Mayor's Com. on Handicapped; mem. task force and diocesan bd. Cath. Edn. of Idaho, 1969-74; mem. Coeur d'Alene U.S. Constn. Bicentennial Com., 1986-91. Bd. dirs. Coeur d'Alene Tchrs. Credit Union, 1958-87, pres., treas., 1976-89; hist. chmn. Coeur d'Alene Centennial, 1986-89, chmn. hist. com., 1988, mem. state centennial com. for Koetenai county, 1990; parliamentarian Idaho Coun. Catholic Women State Conv., 1993, Idaho Cath. Daus. of Am. State Conv., 1994, sterring com. New Holy Famliy Cath. Sch. in Koatenai County Idaho, 1994, Parliomentation fo Idaho Coun. of Cath. Women, 1992. Named Citizen of Yr. N. Idaho Coll., 1974, Idaho Cath. Dau. of Year, 1968; named to Idaho Retired Tchr.'s Hall of Fame, 1987; recipient Hon. Alumnus award N. Idaho Coll., 1987, Nat. Community Svc. award AARP/NRTA, 1989. Mem. Idaho Edn. Assn., NEA, Idaho Ret. Tchrs. Assn. (state chmn. pre-retirement 1985-92), Kootenai County Ret. Tchrs. Assn. (pres. 1983-87), Delta Kappa Gamma (charter, past pres Zeta chpt 1947-92). Club: Cath. Daus. Am. (state regent 1956-62). Home: 720 N 9th St Coeur D Alene ID 83814-4259

DUNNING, KENNETH LAVERNE, research physicist; b. Yale, Iowa, Sept. 24, 1914; s. Howard Grant and Gertrude Estelle (Dygert) D.; m. Ruth Ellen Pyle, Sept. 2, 1941; children: David M., Jane B., John K., Marion Leigh. BEE, U. Minn., 1938; MS in Physics, U. Md., 1950; PhD in Physics, Cath. U. Am., 1968. Engr. Western Union, N.Y.C., 1938-41; physicist U.S. Naval Research Lab., Washington, 1945-80; cons. Port Ludlow, Wash., 1981—. Contbr. articles to profl. jours. Pres. Highland Greens Condominium Assn., Port Ludlow, 1983-84, v.p. 1984-85. Served to maj. U.S. Army, 1941-45. Recipient Research Pub. award Naval Research Lab., 1971. Mem. IEEE, Am. Phys. Soc., Coll. Club Seattle, Sigma Xi, Tau Beta Pi, Eta Kappa Nu. Home and Office: 10 Foster Ln Port Ludlow WA 98365-9611

DUNNING, WILLIAM VANCE, fine arts educator; b. Glendale, Calif., Oct. 29, 1933; s. Judge B. and Billy Jolly Dunning; m. Sandra Jane Springer, Apr. 6, 1963; children: Stacy Rain, Amy Snow, Judge Blue. AA in Arch., El Camino C.C., 1954; BFA, U. So. Calif., L.A., 1958, MFA in Sculpture, 1961; MFA in Painting, U. Ill., 1964. Art instr. Imperial Valley Coll., Imperial, Calif., 1957-59, Phoenix (Ariz.) Coll., 1960-62; sr. preceptor Parsons Coll., Fairfield, Iowa, 1966-67; prof. fine arts Cen. Wash. U., Ellensburg, 1964—. Author: Changing Images of Pictorial Space: A History of Spatial Illusion in Painting, 1992 (One of Outstanding Acad. Books Choice mag. 1992), Roots of Postmodernism, 1994; contbr. articles to prof. jours. including Jour. Aesthetics and Art Criticism, Brit. Jour. Aesthetics, also books; exhibited sculpture and paintings throughout Midwest and Western U.S. Home: 806 W 15th Ave Ellensburg WA 98926-9467 Office: Cen Wash U Ellensburg WA 98926-7564

DUNSTAN, LARRY KENNETH, insurance company executive; b. Payson, Utah, May 26, 1948; s. Kenneth Leroy Dunstan and Verna Matilda (Carter) Taylor; m. Betty K. Limb, Sept. 23, 1966 (div. June 1975); children: Tamara, Thane; m. Jacqueline Lee Darron, Oct. 7, 1975; children: Tessa, Matthew, Bennett, Spencer, Adam. CLU, CPCU, chartered fin. cons., registered health underwriter, life underwriter tng. council fellow. Mgr. Diamond Bar Inn Ranch, Jackson, Mont., 1972-73; agt. Prudential Ins. Co., Missoula, Mont., 1973-77; devel. mgr. Prudential Ins. Co., Billings, Mont., 1977-78; div. mgr. Prudential Ins. Co., Gt. Falls, Mont., 1978-83; pres. Multi-Tech Ins. Services, Inc., West Linn, Oreg., 1983—; agy. mgr. Beneficial Life Ins. Co., Portland, Oreg., 1983-88. Mem. planning commn. City of West Linn, Oreg., 1986; mem. bishopric Ch. Jesus Christ of Latter Day Sts., West Linn, 1984-86, exec. sec. Lake Oswego Oreg. Stake, 1987-89; scouting coordinator Boy Scouts Am., West Linn, 1984-86, scoutmaster various troops; pres. West Linn Youth Basketball Assn., 1991—, West Linn/Wilsonville Youth Track Club, 1993—. Named Eagle Scout Boy Scouts Am., 1965, recipient Heroism award 1965. Fellow Life Underwriter Tng. Coun. (bd. dirs. 1980-81); mem. Gen. Agts. and Mgrs. Assn. (bd. dirs. 1981-82), Am. Soc. CLU (pres. 1982-83). Republican. Home: 19443 Wilderness Dr West Linn OR 97068-2005 Office: Multi-Tech Ins Svcs 19125 Willamette Dr West Linn OR 97068-2019

DUONG, NGHIEM DUC, estate planner; b. Saigon, Vietnam, Dec. 2, 1946; came to the U.S., 1975; s. Trac Duc and Thom Thi (Nguyen) D.; m. Vuong Thi; children: Hong-Thy, Thuy-Tien, Phoi-Thien. BA in Oriental Philosophy, Saigon U., 1974. Cert. estate planner. Pres., CEO Unipoint Corp., Costa Mesa, Calif., 1985—; ins. agt., broker, mgr. Metlife Ins. Co., Torrance, Calif., 1979—; registered rep. Metlife Securities, Inc., Del., 1985—. Promoter, fundraiser for lepers in Vietnam, 1991-92. Fellow Life Underwriter Tng. Coun., 1985. Home: 28401 Via Alfonse Aliso Viejo CA 92656-4576

DU PEN, EVERETT GEORGE, sculptor, educator; b. San Francisco, June 12, 1912; s. George E. and Novelle (Freeman) DuP.; m. Charlotte Canada Nicks, July 1, 1939; children: Stuart, Destia, Novelle, William, Ninia, Marguerite. Student, U. So. Calif., 1931-33, Chouinard Art Sch., Los Angeles, summer 1932, Harvard Sch. Architecture, summer 1933; B.F.A. (scholar), Yale, 1937; B.F.A. European traveling fellow, 1937-38. Teaching fellow Carnegie Inst. Tech. Sch. Art, 1939-39; teaching asst. sculpture Washington U. Sch. Art, St. Louis, 1939-42; marine draftsman and loftsman Sausalito Shipbldg. Corp., Calif., 1942-45; instr. sculpture U. Wash. Sch. Art, Seattle, 1945-47; asst. prof. U. Wash. Sch. Art, 1947-54, assoc. prof. sculpture, 1954-60, prof. art, 1960-82, prof. emeritus, 1982—, chmn. sculpture div. One-man shows include Seattle Art Mus., 1950, Bon Marche Nat. Gallery, Seattle, 1970, Fred Cole Gallery, Seattle, 1973, Pacific Luth. U., Tacoma, 1975, Wash. Mut. Savs. Bank, Seattle, 1979-80, Frye Art Mus., Seattle, Martin and Zambito Gallery, Seattle; exhibited Prix de Rome Exhbn., Grand Central Gallery, N.Y.C., 1935-37, 39, St. Louis Mus. Ann., 1939-42, Nat. Acad. Design, N.Y.C., 1943, 49, 53-55, 57-58, Seattle Art Mus. Ann., 1945-59, Pa. Acad. Art, Phila., 1950-52, 55-58, Ecclesiastical Sculpture competition, 1950, Sculpture Ctr., N.Y.C., 1951, 53, 54, Pa. Acad. Fine Arts, 1954-58, Detroit Mus. Art, 1958, N.W. Inst. Sculpture, San Francisco Art Assn., 1959, Mainstreams, 1972, Marietta Coll., 1972, Holt Galleries, Olympia, Wash., 1980, Martin & Zambotti Gallery, Seattle, 1991-92, Freemont Art Gallery, Seattle, 1991-92, Ellensburg, Wash. Community Art Gallery, 1988, Bellevue, Wash. Invitational, Bellevue Art Mus., 1988, NAD, 1989, Wash. State Art Centennial Exhbn., Tacoma Art Mus., 1990; retrospective exhibits at Martin & Zambet Gallery, Seattle, 1994, Firye Art Mus., Seattle, 1994; represented in permanent collections Wash. Mut. Savs. Bank, Seattle, Bell Telephone Co., Seattle, Nat. Acad. Design, N.Y.C. (Saltus medal 1954), Seattle Art Mus., Safeco Ins. Co., U. Wash.; also sculptures in pvt. collections; creator garden figures and portrait heads, small bronze, terra cotta, hardwood sculptures, archtl. medallions, sculpture panels for comml. bldgs. and theatres, figures and wood carvings various chs., relief panels U. Wash. campus, 1946, 83, bronze fountain Wash. State Library, Olympia, 1959, Du Pen Fountain, bronze fountain Coliseum Century 21, Seattle World's Fair, 2 walnut screens Mcpl. Bldg., Seattle, 8 large sculpture commns. Seattle chs., 1957-64, wood carving Risen Christ, St. Pius X Cath. Ch., Montlake Terrace, Wash., 1983, 3-foot wood carving St. Joseph and Mary, 1985, 6-foot wood carving Ascension, St. Elizabeth Seton Ch., Bothell, Wash., 1986, Elizabeth and Mary, 5-foot mahogany for Visitation Ctr., Fed. Way, Wash., 1990, 2-figure group for Dallas, 1982, bronze figure Edmonds, Wash., 1983-84, bronze sculpture of Charles Odegaard, pres. U. Wash., 1973, pvt. commns. Mem. U. Wash. Senate, 1952-55, exec. com., 1954-55; v.p. Allied Arts Movement for Seattle; mem. Seattle Municipal Art Commn., 1958-63. Recipient Saltus gold medal NAD, 1954, 1st prize for sculpture Bellevue (Washington) Arts and Crafts Fair, 1957; U. Wash. research grantee for creative sculpture, 1953-54. Fellow Nat. Sculpture Soc. (hon. mention Henry Herring competition); mem. Artists Equity Assn. (bd. Seattle chpt.), Nat. Acad. Design, Puget Sound N.W. Painters Group (bd.), N.W. Inst. Sculpture (pres. 1957), Allied Artists Am., U. Wash. Research Soc., Northwest Stone Sculptors, Seattle (bd. dirs. 1989—). Home: 1231 20th Ave E Seattle WA 98112-3530

DUPONT, COLYER LEE, television and film producer, video and film distributing company executive; b. Golden, Colo., Oct. 23, 1957; s. Alfred Lee and Frances Dudley (Smith) D. BA, More U., 1980. Advt. mgr. Magical Blend mag., San Francisco, 1981-83; owner, mgr. Newave Co., San Francisco, 1983; mktg. dir. Venture Rsch., Inc., San Francisco, 1983-84; assoc. producer Left Coast Prodns., San Francisco, 1984-86; owner, mgr. Cinemagic Prodns., San Francisco, 1986—. Writer, producer, dir. TV spl. Computer Magic, 1987; videoworks exhibited Mus. Modern Art, N.Y.C., Nat. Mus. Natural History, Smithsonian Inst., Washington, N.Y. Hall of Sci., Corona, Fine Arts Mus. L.I., Hempstead, N.Y.; inventor belt-attached carrier. Recipient Chris award 34th Columbus (Ohio) Internat. Film and Video Festival, 1986, Silver medal Internat. Film and TV Festival N.Y., 1986, Joey award of merit Profl. Media Network, 1986, Golden Eagle award Coun. for Internat. Non-theatrical Events, 1987, Gold Electra award Birmingham (Ala.) Internat. Edn. Film Fetival, 1987, Silver plaque Chgo. Internat. Film Festival, 1987. Mem. Bay Area Video Coalition, Ind. Filmmakers No. Calif. (founder), Film Arts Found., Visual Communicators Calif., San Francisco Advt. Club (Excellence award 1987). Office: Cinemagic Prodns 537 Jones St Ste 898 San Francisco CA 94102-2007

DUPPER, FRANK FLOYD, health care facility executive; b. La Salle, Colo., Jan. 20, 1933; s. Henry and Caroline (Beierle) D.; m. Norma Jean Eder, June 24, 1956; children: Debbie, Brent. BA, Union Coll., 1954. Treas. Newbury Park (Calif.) Acad., 1959-64; controller Glendale (Calif.) Sanitarium, 1964-68; asst. adminstr. Glendale Adventist Hosp., 1968-72; v.p. fin. Glendale Adventist Med. Ctr., 1972-74; v.p. Adventist Health Service, Glendale, 1974-79; pres. Adventist Health System/West, Roseville, Calif., 1980—; cons. Loma Linda (Calif.) U., 1981-82. Bd. dirs. United Way, Glendale, 1986. Recipient William G. Follmer award Fin. Mgmt. Assn., 1975, Robert H. Reeves award Fin. Mgmt. Assn., 1979. Fellow Hosp. Fin. Mgmt. Assn. (Fredrich Muncie award 1985); mem. Am Acad. Med. Adminstrs., Am. Coll. Hosp. Execs., Am. Hosp. Assn., Am. Protestant Hosp. Assn., Ariz. Assn. Homes for Aging, Assn. Western Hosps., Calif. Hosp. Assn., Hosp. Council So. Calif. (Outstanding Service to Hosps. award 1979), Pres.' Assn.,. Home: 6305 Oak Hill Dr Roseville CA 95746-8908 Office: Adventist Health System-W PO Box 619002 Roseville CA 95661-9002

DUPPONG, MARGIE ANN CLAUS, retired law enforcement official; b. St. John, Kans., Dec. 8, 1939; d. Fredrick Snowden and Esther Jeannette (Beers) Claus; m. Jack Ruhl Griffin, Nov. 13, 1958 (div. 1960); 1 child, Jack Ruhl Jr.; m. Richard Bendtsen, July 12, 1965 (div. June 1968); m. Edwin Joseph Duppong, Dec. 31, 1971. Student, U. Nebr., 1969-72, Lincoln U., 1982-83. Various positions in law enforcement, 1959-84; election judge City of New Town, N.D., 1988-91, Lamar, Colo., 1994. Leader Boy Scouts Am., 1968—, commr., 1975-79, asst. dist. commr., 1979-88, 90, 93-94, 95—, dist. commr., 1988, 89, 91, 92, coun. commr., 1988, 92; pub. rels. chmn. St. Frances DeSales Ch., 1991-92, R.M. coun. tng. chmn. 1995—; judge New Town Art Show, 1988. Named Unicameral scholar U. Nebr., 1971, 1st Columbine Queen State of Colo., 1962; recipient Dist. Award of Merit Boy Scouts. Am., 1982, Wood Badge NC-122 award, 1979, St. George award, 1995. Mem. Mo. Correctional Officers Assn., AFL-CIO, Am. Legion Aux., Zonta Internat., Brush & Pallet Art Club, Southeast Colo. Art Guild, Head Injury Assn. N.D., Univ. High Sch. Alumni (sec. 1990—), Beta Sigma Phi (Laureate Rho chpt., chpt. sec. 1993-95). Democrat. Roman Catholic.

DUPRAT, JO ANN, pediatric rehabilitation nurse, consultant; b. Vallejo, Calif., May 21, 1948; d. Albert John Chester Jr. and Dorothy Marie (Anderson) Smith; m. Dennis Albert Duprat, May 14, 1966; children: Dana Marie, Daniel Gordon. ASN, Contra Costa Coll., San Pablo, Calif., 1982; BS in Health and Human Svcs., Columbia Pacific U., San Rafael, Calif., 1991, MS in Health and Human Svcs., 1992, postgrad., 1994—. RN, Calif.; CRRN, cert. rehab. nursing, UR/QA/discharge planning/risk mgmt. Learning Tree Univ. Staff nurse, adolescent Children's Hosp., Oakland, Calif., 1982-83, staff nurse med./surg. pediatric, 1983-84, pediatric rehab. nurse specialist, 1984—; nursing supr. Adult Care Svcs., Walnut Creek, Calif., 1992-93; nurse cons. in pvt. practice, San Pablo, 1984—; nurse cons. Regional Ctr. of East Bay, Emeryville, Calif., 1985—; panel nurse Calif. Children's Svcs., Sacramento, 1985—. Author: Spina Bifida, Current Trends, 1991; Historical Perspectives and Attitudes Towards Women, Sexuality, Childbirth and Parenting, 1993. Supporting mem. San Pablo Little League, 1991-92. Mem. Spina Bifida of Calif., Assn. Rehab. Nurses, Children's Orthotics/Prosthetics Clinics, Nat. Neurofibramatosis Soc., Assn. for Syringomyelia, Alpha Gamma Sigma. Office: Children's Hosp 747 52nd St Oakland CA 94609-1809

DUPRIEST, DOUGLAS MILLHOLLEN, lawyer; b. Ft. Riley, Kans., Dec. 28, 1951; s. Robert White and Barbara Nadine (Millhollen) DuP. AB in Philosophy with high honors, Oberlin Coll., 1974; JD, U. Oreg., 1977. Bar: Oreg. 1977, U.S. Dist. Ct. Oreg. 1977, U.S. Ct. Appeals (9th cir.) 1977. Assoc. Coons & Anderson and predecessors, Eugene, Oreg., 1977-81, Hutchinson, Harrell et al, 1981; ptnr. Hutchinson, Anderson, Cox & Coons and predecessors, 1982—; adj. prof. sch. law U. Oreg., 1986; mem. task forces Wetlands Mgmt., 1988-89, 92-93. Author: (with others) Land Use, 1982, Administrative Law, 1985; contbg. editor Real Estate & Land Use Digest, 1983-86; articles editor, mng. bd. mem. U. Oreg. Law Rev., 1976-77. Bd. dirs. Home Health Agy., Eugene, 1977-79, pres., 1978-79; bd. dirs. Oreg. Environ. Coun., Portland, 1979-84, pres., 1980-81; mem. Lane Econ. Com., 1989-91; chair voters pamphlet com. Eugene City Club, 1993. Recipient Disting. Svc. award Oreg. Environ. Coun., 1988. Mem. Oreg. Bar Assn. (exec. com. real estate and land use sect. 1978-81). Home: 225 Dartmoor Dr Eugene OR 97401-6620 Office: Hutchinson Anderson Cox & Coons PC 777 High St Ste 200 Eugene OR 97401-2750

DUQUETTE, DIANE RHEA, library director; b. Springfield, Mass., Dec. 15, 1951; d. Gerard Lawrence and Helen Yvette (St. Marie) Morneau; m. Thomas Frederick Duquette Jr., Mar. 17, 1973. BS in Sociology, Springfield Coll., 1975; MLS, Simmons Coll., 1978. Libr. asst. Springfield City Libr., 1975-78; reference libr. U. Mass., Amherst, 1978-81; head libr. Hopkins Acad., Hadley, Mass., 1980; instr. Colo. Mountain Coll., Steamboat Springs, 1981-83; libr. dir. East Routt Libr. Dist., Steamboat Springs, 1981-84; agy. head Solono County Libr., Vallejo, Calif., 1984; dir. libr. svcs. Shasta County Libr., Redding, Calif., 1984-87; dir. librs. Kern County Libr., Bakersfield, Calif., 1987—; chmn. San Joaquin Valley Libr. System, 1988. Contbr. articles to profl. jours. Recipient John Cotton Dana Spl. Pub. Rels. award, H.W. Wilson and ALA, 1989. Mem. ALA, Calif. Libr. Assn. (mem. coun. 1987—), Calif. County Librs. Assn. (pres. 1990). Democrat. Roman Catholic. Home: PO Box 6595 Pine Mountain Club Frazier Park CA 93222 Office: Kern County Libr 701 Truxtun Ave Bakersfield CA 93301-4816

DURAN, MICHAEL CARL, bank executive; b. Colorado Springs, Colo., Aug. 27, 1953; s. Lawrence Herman and Jacqueline Carol (Ward) D. BS magna cum laude, Ariz. State U., 1980. With Valley Nat. Bank (name now Bank One, Ariz., N.A.), Phoenix, 1976—; corp. credit trainee Bank One Ariz. (formerly Valley Nat. Bank Ariz.), Phoenix, 1984-85; comml. loan officer Valley Nat. Bank Ariz. (name now Bankone, Ariz.), Phoenix, 1985-86, br. mgr., asst. v.p., 1986-90, comml. banking officer, asst. v.p., 1990-93, credit mgr., v.p., 1993—; cons. various schs. and orgns., 1986—; incorporator Avondale Neighborhood Housing Svcs., 1988. Mem. Cen. Bus. Dist. Revitalization Com., Avondale, Ariz., 1987-88, Ad-Hoc Econ. Devel. Com., 1988; coord. Avondale Litter Lifters, 1987-88; vol. United Way, Phoenix, 1984; bd. dirs. Jr. Achievement, Yuma, Ariz., 1989-91, vol., Phoenix, 1993—; yokefellow 1st So. Bapt. Ch. of Yuma, 1990-91. Recipient Outstanding Community Svc. award City of Avondale, 1988. Mem. Robert Morris Assocs., Ariz. State U. Alumni Assn. (life), Toastmasters, Kiwanis (local bd. dirs. 1986-88), Beta Gamma Sigma, Phi Kappa Phi, Phi Theta Kappa, Sigma Iota Epsilon. Democrat. Baptist. Home: 925 N Quartz St Gilbert AZ 85234-3661

DURHAM, BARBARA, state supreme court justice; b. 1942. BSBA, Georgetown U.; JD, Stanford U. Bar: Wash. 1968. Former judge Wash. Superior Ct., King County; judge Wash. Ct. Appeals; assoc. justice Wash. Supreme Ct., 1985—, chief justice, 1995—. Office: Wash Supreme Ct Temple of Justice PO Box 40929 Olympia WA 98504-0929

DURHAM, HARRY BLAINE, III, lawyer; b. Denver, Sept. 16, 1946; s. Harry Blaine and Mary Frances (Oliver) D.; m. Lynda L. Durham, Aug. 4, 1973; children: Christopher B., Laurel A. BA cum laude, Colo. Coll., 1969; JD, U. Colo., 1973. Bar: Wyo. 1973, U.S. Tax Ct. 1974, U.S. Ct. Appeals (10th cir.) 1976. Assoc., Brown, Drew, Apostolos, Massey & Sullivan,

Casper, Wyo., 1973-77; ptnr. Brown & Drew, 1977—. Permanent class pres. Class of 1969, Colo. Coll., Nat. Alumni Coun. Colo. Coll., 1995—; bd. dirs. Casper Amateur Hockey Club, 1970-77, sec. 1974-77; bd. dirs. Casper Symphony Assn., 1974-88, v.p., 1979-82, pres., 1983-87; bd. dirs., sec. Wyo. Amateur Hockey Assn., 1974-85, pres., 1985-88; bd. dirs. Natrona County United Way, 1974-76, pres., 1975-76; mem. City of Casper Parks and Recreation Commn., 1985-94, vice chmn., 1987-94, Nat. Alumni Coun. of The Colo. Coll., 1995—. Mem. ABA, Wyo. Bar Assn., Natrona County Bar Assn., Nat. Assn. Railroad Trial Counsel, Phi Beta Kappa. Republican. Articles editor U. Colo. Law Rev., 1972-73. Home: 3101 Hawthorne Ave Casper WY 82604-4975 Office: 123 W 1st St Ste 800 Casper WY 82601-2486

DURHAM, ROBERT LEWIS, architect; b. Seattle, Apr. 28, 1912; s. William Worth and Abbie May (McNett) D.; m. Dorothy Evelyn Wyatt, May 14, 1935 (dec. Nov. 1935); m. Marjorie Ruth Moser, Sept. 19, 1936; children: David Robert, Gail Maureen Durham Philippson, Catherine Louise Durham Gunstone, Jennifer Ann Durham Jerde. Student, Coll. Puget Sound, 1930-31; B.Arch. cum laude, U. Wash., 1936. Draftsman B. Dudley Stuart (Architect), Seattle, 1936-38; cost engr. FHA, 1938-41; partner Stuart & Durham (Architects), Seattle, 1941-51, Robert L. Durham & Assos., Seattle, 1951-54, Durham, Anderson & Freed (Architects), Seattle, 1954-74; pres. Durham, Anderson & Freed (Architects), 1974-77; cons. HDR Inc. (Architects), 1977-84; mem. Bldg. Code Adv. Commn. City Seattle, Seattle Planning Commn., 1969-75; mem. Seattle Municipal Art Commn., 1955-65, chmn., 1957-59; chmn. cultural arts com. Century 21 Expn., Seattle, 1958-62; speaker art, architecture. Prin. works include Constrn. Center, Seattle, Downtown YWCA, student union Seattle Pacific Coll, Evergreen State Coll. Library, Fidelity Savs. & Loan Assn. Recipient honor award for various chs. Ch. Archtl. Guild Am., 1952, 55, 57, 59, 60, 64; honor awards Wash. chpt. AIA, 52, 59, 54, 56; award for S.W. Br. Library Seattle; award for S.W. Br. Library AIA-ALA, 1964. Fellow AIA (past pres. Washington, nat. pres. 1967-68, bursar Coll. Fellows 1976-78, vice chancellor Coll. Fellows 1978-79, chancellor 1979-80, Kemper award 1981); hon. fellow Royal Archtl. Inst. Can., Mexican Soc. Architects, Peruvian Soc. Architects; mem. Ch. Archtl. Guild Am. (v.p. 1963-65, dir), Tau Sigma Delta. Congregationalist. Club: Seattle Engrs. Home: 900 University St Apt 3V Seattle WA 98101-2727

DURINGER, JACOB CLYDE, project engineer, researcher; b. Calexico, Calif., Oct. 18, 1956; s. Jacob Clyde Sr. and Stella Marie (Pippin) D.; m. Catherine Ann Grecich, Sept. 20, 1986 (div. Feb. 1988); 1 child, Irena Mauve; m. Mary Helen Montes, May 27, 1989; 1 child, Trint Jacob. AA in Electronics, Electronic Tech. Inst., 1978. Staff engr. Mitsubishi Electronics, Santa Ana, Calif., 1978-81; sr. technician Efratom, Irvine, Calif., 1981-82, MCT Electronics, Carpinteria, Calif., 1982-83; project engr. Parker Bertea Aerospace, Irvine, 1985—. Inventor monolithic two dimensional keyboard. Mem. Nat. Assn. Music Mchts. Mem. Christian Ch. Home: 23341 La Glorieta Apt E Mission Viejo CA 92691-2869

DURST, ERIC, television and commercial director. BFA in Film, Calif. Inst. Arts. Dir. TV documentaries, creator short films PBS, N.Y.C.; founder, dir. commls. Eric Durst Films, N.Y.C.; dir. commls. Dream Quest Images, Simi Valley, Calif., 1984—; Dir. nat. comml. campaigns for various companies, including Volkswagen, Polaroid, Texaco, Dodge, Johson and Johnson, PepsiCo, Converse, Nintendo, Motorcraft. Office: Dream Quest Images 2635 Park Center Dr Simi Valley CA 93065-6212

DURYEE, DAVID ANTHONY, management consultant; b. Tacoma, Wash., July 29, 1938; s. Schuyler L. and Edna R. (Muzzy) D.; m. Anne Getchell Peterson, Nov. 26, 1966; children: Tracy Anne, Tricia Marie. BA in Bus., U. Wash., 1961, MBA, 1969; diploma, Pacific Coast Banking Schs., Seattle, 1973. Cert. fin. planner. Lending officer Seattle 1st Nat. Bank, 1964-68, v.p., trust officer, 1970-80; cons., chmn. Mgmt. Adv. Svcs., Inc., Seattle, 1980-93; mng. prin. Mgmt. Adv. Svcs. divsn. Moss Adams, 1994—; bd. dirs. Laframboise Newspapers, Inc., Seattle; lectr. in field; expert witness Wash., N.Y., Md., Calif., Mass., Ind., Fla. Author: The Business Owners Guide to Achieving Financial Success, 1994; contbr. articles to profl. jours. Capt. U.S. Army, 1962-64. Mem. Am. Soc. Appraisers, Internat. Assn. Fin. Planners, Inst. for Cert. Planners, Inst. Bus. Appraisers (speaker), Am. Bankers Assn., Nat. Retail Jewelers, Nat. Moving and Storage assn., Pacific N.W. Bankers Assn., Internat. Assn. for Fin. Planning, Estate Planning Coun. Seattle, Washington Bar Assn., Wash. State Trial Lawyers Assn., Wash. State Automobile Dealers Assn., Ky./Mo. Auto Dealers Assn., Motor Dealers Assn. B.C., Nat. Office Products Assn., Mayflower Warehousemen's Assn., Can. Movers Assn., Fedn. of Automobile Dealer Assns. of Can., Seattle Tennis Club, Seattle Yacht Club, Rotary. Home: 3305 E John St Seattle WA 98112-4938 Office: Mgmt Adv Svcs 1001 4th Ave Ste 2700 Seattle WA 98154-1199

DUSANIC, LINDA NELSON, bank executive; b. Sioux City, Iowa, May 22, 1959; d. C. Howard and Mary Joyce (Forney) Nelson; m. Matthew J. Dusanic. BA in Bus., U. Wash., 1981; MBA, Boston Coll., 1987. Loan officer Wash. Mut. Savs. Bank, Seattle, 1981-83; ins. rep./agt. Wash. Mut. Service Corp., Seattle, 1983-85; teaching asst. Boston Coll., Chestnut Hill, Mass., 1985-87; bank examiner Fed. Res. Bank Boston, 1987-89, Fed. Res. Bank, San Francisco, 1989—; cons. Manassa Systems Inc., Boston, 1986, Welling & Woodard, 1990. Mem. Nat Assn. Bus. Econs. (v.p. San Francisco chpt. 1993). Office: Fed Res Bank 101 Market St San Francisco CA 94105-1530

DUSCHA, JULIUS CARL, journalist; b. St. Paul, Nov. 4, 1924; s. Julius William and Anna (Perlowski) D.; m. Priscilla Ann McBride, Aug. 17, 1946 (dec. Sept. 1992); children: Fred C., Steve D., Suzanne, Sally Jean. Student, U. Minn., 1943-47; AB, Am. U., 1951; postgrad., Harvard Coll., 1955-56. Reporter St. Paul Pioneer Press, 1943-47; publicist Dem. Nat. Com., 1948, 52; writer Labor's League for Polit. Edn., AFL, 1949-52, Internat. Assn. Machinist, 1952-53; editorial writer Lindsay-Schaub Newspapers, Ill., 1954-58; nat. affairs reporter Washington Post, 1958-66; assoc. dir. profl. journalism fellowships program Stanford (Calif.) U., 1966-68; dir. Washington Journalism Ctr., 1968-90; columnist, freelance journalist, West Coast corr. Presstime mag., San Francisco, 1990—. Author: Taxpayer's Hayride: The Farm Problem from the New Deal to the Billie Sol Estes Case, 1964, Arms, Money and Politics, 1965, The Campus Press, 1973; editor: Defense Conversion Advisory; contbr. articles to mags., including Washingtonian, N.Y. Times Mag., Changing Times. Recipient award for distinguished Washington corr. Sigma Delta Chi, 1961. Mem. Cosmos Club (Washington), Kappa Sigma. Home: 2200 Pacific Ave Apt 7D San Francisco CA 94115-1412

DUSHANE, PHYLLIS MILLER, nurse; b. Portland, Oreg., June 3, 1924; d. Joseph Anton and Josephine Florence (Eicholtz) Miller; m. Frank Maurice Jacobson, Mar. 13, 1945 (dec. 1975); children: Karl, Kathleen, Kraig, Kirk, Karen, Kent, Krista, Kandis, Kris, Karlyn; m. Donald McLelland DuShane, July 21, 1979 (dec. 1989); stepchildren: Diane DuShane Bishop, Donald III. BS in Biology, U. Oreg., 1948; BS in Nursing, Oreg. Health Scis. U., 1968. R.N., Oreg. Pub. health nurse Marion County Health Dept., Salem, Oreg., 1968-77; pediatric nurse practitioner Marion County Health Dept., Salem, 1977-91, Allergy Assocs., Eugene, Oreg., 1979-89; mem. allied profl. staff Sacred Heart Gen. Hosp., Eugene, 1979—. Named Oreg. Pediatric Nurse Practitioner of Yr., 1991. Mem. P.E.O., Oreg. Pediatric Nurse Practitioners Assn. (v.p. Salem chpt. 1977-78), Am. Nurses Assn., Oreg. Nurses Assn., Nat. Assn. Pediatric Nurse Assocs. and Practitoners, Am. Acad. Nurse Practitioners, Nurse Practitioners Spl. Interest Group, Salem Med. Aux. (sec. 1968), Oreg. Republican Women, Delta Gamma Alumni (v.p. 1979), Rep. Rubicon Soc. Presbyterian. Home: 965 E 23rd Ave Eugene OR 97405-3074 Office: Clinic For Children & Young Adults 755 E 11th Ave Eugene OR 97401-3702 also: Oakway Pediatrics P C 465 Oakway Rd Eugene OR 97401-5405 also: Eugene Pediatric Assocs 1680 Chambers St Eugene OR 97402-3655

DUSSERRE, MICHELLE, dietitian, gymnastics coach; b. Long Beach, Calif., Dec. 26, 1968; d. Martin Burdette and Kerry Elizabeth (Eckholdt) D. BS, Ariz. State U., 1992; postgrad., Colo. U. Asst. coach women's gymnastics Ariz. State U., Tempe, 1987-92; sports rschr. Olympic Games NBC TV, Barcelona, Spain, summer 1992; dietetic intern Calif. State U., Long Beach, 1992-93; gymnastics coach Aerials Gymnastics, Colorado Springs; mem. U.S. Olympic Com. Athletes Coun., Colorado Springs, 1994—. Full acad. scholar Ariz. State Women's Gymnastics Coach, 1987-91; Fitch Craig scholardept. home econs. Ariz. State U., 1991; 5-time Nat. Team, mem. 1984 Olympic Gymnastics Team. Mem. Am. Dietetic Assn., USA Gymnastics (mem. athletes coun. 1990-94, mem. women's selection com. ad hoc com. 1992-94, mem. exec. com. 1992-94.

DUSTER, TROY, sociology educator; b. Chgo., July 11, 1936; s. Benjamin Cecil and Alfred Margarita (Barnett) D.; m. Ellen Marie Johansson, May 16, 1964 (div. 1974). B.S., Northwestern U., 1957, Ph.D., 1962; M.A., UCLA, 1959. Asst. prof. sociology U. Calif., Riverside, 1963-65; asst. research sociologist U. Calif., Berkeley, 1965-69, assoc. prof. sociology, 1970-78, prof., 1979—; chmn. dept. U. Calif., 1986—; dir. Inst. for the Study of Social Change, U. Calif., 1976—; Bernhard prof. anthropology and sociology Williams Coll., 1985. Author: Legislation of Morality, 1970, (monograph) Aims and Control of the Universities, 1972, Backdoor to Eugenics, 1990; co-editor: Cultural Perspectives on Biological Knowledge, 1984. Mem. assembly of behavioral and social scis. Nat. Acad. Scis., Washington, 1973-78; mem. research panel Pres.'s Commn. on Mental Health, Washington, 1977-78; cons., advisor Pres.'s Commn. for Study of Ethical Problems in Medicine, Washington, 1980; mem. bio-tech. adv. council State of Calif.; mem. Ethical, Legal, and Social Issues Commn. Nat. Ctr. Human Genome Rsch., Washington, 1995—, Nat. Panel of the Am. Commitments Initiative Assn. Am. Colls. and Univs., Washington, 1993—, Com. Social and Ethical Impact of Advances in Biomedicine Inst. of Medicine, Nat. Acad. Scis., Washington, 1991-94, Spl. Commn. Meeting the Challenge of Diversity in an Acad. Democracy Assn. Am. Law Schs., Washington, 1991-95, Subcom. Protection of Human Subjects, Health and Environ. Rsch. Adv. Com. Dept. Energy, 1994; adv. bd. Ctr. for Study of Race, Crime, and Social Policy. Swedish Govt. fellow Uppsala U., 1962-63; Guggenheim Found. fellow London Sch. Econs., 1971-72; Ford Found. fellow, 1978-79. Mem. Am. Sociol. Assn. (mem. exec. office of the budget coun. 1991-94). Home: 3031 Benvenue Ave Berkeley CA 94705-2509 Office: U Calif-Berkeley Dept Sociology Berkeley CA 94720

DUTT, BIRENDRA, research specialist; b. 1950. Cons. L.A.; with R & DLabs., Culver City, Calif., 1983—, now pres. Office: Research & Development Labs 5800 Uplander Way Culver City CA 90230-6608*

DUTTON, PAULINE MAE, fine arts librarian; b. Detroit, July 15; d. Thoralf Andreas and Esther Ruth (Clyde) Tandberg; B.A. in Art, Calif. State U., Fullerton, 1967; M.S. in Library Sci., U. So. Calif., 1971; m. Richard Hawkins Dutton, June 21, 1969. Elem. tchr., Anaheim, Calif., 1967-68, Corona, Calif., 1968-69; fine arts librarian Pasadena (Calif.) Public Library, 1971-80; art cons., researcher, 1981—. Mem. Pasadena Librarians Assn. (sec. 1978, treas. 1979-80), Calif. Library Assn., Calif. Soc. Librarians, Art Librarians N.Am., Nat. Assn. Female Execs., Am. Film Inst., Am. Entrepreneurs Assn., Gilbert and Sullivan Soc., Alpha Sigma Phi. Club: Toastmistress (local pres. 1974).

DUUS, PETER, history educator; b. Wilmington, Del., Dec. 27, 1933; s. Hans Christian and Mary Anita (Pennypacker) D.; m. Masayo Umezawa, Nov. 25, 1964; 1 child, Erik. AB magna cum laude, Harvard U., 1955, PhD, 1965; MA, U. Mich., 1959. Asst. prof. history Washington U., St. Louis, 1964-66, Harvard U., Cambridge, Mass., 1966-70; assoc. prof. history Claremont (Calif.) Grad. Sch., 1970-73; assoc. prof. history Stanford (Calif.) U., 1973-78, prof., 1978—. Author: Party Rivalry and Political Change in Taishô Japan, 1968, Feudalism in Japan, 1969, The Rise of Modern Japan, 1976, The Cambridge History of Japan, Vol. 6: The Twentieth Century, 1989, The Japanese Informal Empire in China, 1989, The Abacus and the Sword: The Japanese Penetration of Korea, 1995. Exec. sec. Inter-Univ. for Japanese Lang. Studies, Tokyo, 1974-90; bd. dirs. Com. for Internat. Exchange of Scholars, Washington, 1987-91. Served with U.S. Army, 1955-57. NEH sr. fellow, 1972-73, Japan Found. postdoctoral fellow, 1976-77, Fulbright rsch. fellow, 1981-82, 94-95, Japan Found. rsch. fellow, 1986-87. Fellow AAAS, mem. Assn. for Asian Studies (bd. dirs. 1972-75, nominating com. 1983), Am. Hist. Assn. (bd. editors 1984-87). Home: 818 Esplanada Way Palo Alto CA 94305-1015 Office: Stanford U Dept of History Stanford CA 94305

DUVIVIER, KATHARINE KEYES, lawyer; b. Alton, Ill., Jan. 1, 1953; d. Edward Keyes and Marjorie (Attebery) DuV.; m. James Wesley Perl, Mar. 30, 1985; 2 children: Alice Katharine Perl, Emmett Edward Perl. BA in Geology and English cum laude, Williams Coll., 1975; JD, U. Denver, 1982. Bar: Colo. 1982, U.S. Dist. Ct. Colo. 1982, U.S. Ct. Appeals (10th cir.) 1982. Intern-curator Hudson River Mus., Yonkers, N.Y., 1975; geologist French Am. Metals Corp., Lakewood, Colo., 1976-79; assoc. Sherman & Howard, Denver, 1982-84, Arnold & Porter, Denver, 1984-87; atty. Office of City Atty., Denver, 1987-90; instr. sch. law Univ. Colo., 1990—. Contbr. articles to profl. jours. Mem. Denver Botanic Garden, 1981-88; vol. Outdoor Colo., Denver, 1985-87. Mem. ABA (vice chmn. subcom. 1985-91), Colo. Bar Assn., Boulder Bar Assn., Boulder Women's Bar Assn. (pres. 1991-93), Alliance Profl. Women (bd. dirs. 1985-90, pres. 1988-89), Work and Family Consortium (bd. dirs. 1988-90), St. Ives, William Coll. Alumni Assn. (co-pres. Colo. chpt. 1984-86), Phi Beta Kappa. Home: 4761 Mckinley Dr Boulder CO 80303-1142 Office: U Colo Sch Law PO Box 401 Boulder CO 80303

DUZY, MERRILYN JEANNE, artist, educator; b. L.A., Mar. 29, 1946; d. Berton John and Marva Lorinne (Barrow) D.; m. Howard Bentkower, Sept. 28, 1974. BA, Calif. State U., Northridge, 1974; MFA, Otis Art Inst., L.A., 1988. Tchr. L.A. H.S. for Arts, 1988-90; freelance comml. artist, West Hills, Calif., 1988—; pvt. tchr., lectr., West Hills, 1991-93; instr. Calif. State U., 1994; lectr., creator slide lecture Walking through History: Women Artists Past and Present, 1982—; curator Autobiographies, 1977, Erotica '88, 1988, Angeles, Ancestors and Spirit Guides, 1994, Closure invitational Artspace Gallery, 1994. Founder Artists Networking, Woodland Hills, Calif., 1992-93. Mem. Coll. Art Assn., Women's Caucus for Art (pres. So. Calif. chpt. 1980-82, founder, pres. Fla. West Coast chpt. 1983-84, mem. nat. adv. bd.), Artists Alliance. Home and Studio: 8356 Capistrano Ave Canoga Park CA 91304-3319

DVORAK, RAY P., insurance company official; b. Center, N.D., Sept. 24, 1931; s. Stanley Joseph and Katherine (Schimpf) D.; m. Deanna Ellen Kern, June 1961 (div. 1974); children: Mitchell Scott, Lara Suzanne; m. Delores Marie Davis, Mar. 12, 1975 (dec. Jan. 1990). BS, U. Oreg., 1953; LLB, LaSalle Extension U., Chgo., 1964. CLU; CPCU; charter fin. cons. Claim rep. State Farm Ins. Co., Salem, Oreg., 1957-67; claim supt. State Farm Ins. Co., Medford, Oreg., 1967—. With USAF, 1953-55, lt. col. Res. ret. Mem. Soc. CPCU, Am. Soc. CLU's. Republican. Methodist. Home: PO Box 188 840 S Oregon St Jacksonville OR 97530 Office: State Farm Ins Co PO Box 790 Medford OR 97501-0055

DWIGHT, DONALD STEARNS, artist, retired military officer; b. Cin., Aug. 25, 1921; s. Harold Stearns and Rosalind Dell (Vail) D.; m. Nancy Bartron, Oct. 22, 1949; 1 child, Jennifer. Grad., Cen. Acad. Comm. Art, Cin., 1942. Commd. 2d lt. U.S. Army Air Corps, 1943; advanced through grades to lt. col. USAF, ret., 1966; dist. sales mgr. L.L. Sams & Sons, Waco, Tex., 1966-76; ind. artist Colorado Springs, Colo., 1977—. Exhbns. of watercolors include Rocky Mountain Nat. Watermedia, Golden, Colo., 1980, 81, 86, Watercolor West, Redlands, Calif., 1986, 87, 88, Madison (Wis.) Nat., 1986, 87, 88, Southwestern Watercolor Soc., Dallas, 1987, 92, Georgia Watercolor Soc., Atlanta, 1988, 89, 92, Tex. Watercolor Soc., San Antonio, 1988, Ky. Watercolor Soc., Louisville, 1988, Kans. Watercolor Soc., Wichita, 1989, 91, Nat. Watercolor Soc., Fullerton, Calif., 1990, Midwest. Recipient Grumbacker Gold Medal for Color, 1987, Betsy Crooks award North Fla. Watercolor Soc., 1990, George Sponable award Adirondacks Nat., 1992. Mem. Watercolor West, Ga. Watercolor Soc. (Atlanta Artists Club award 1992), Tex. Watercolor Soc., Am. Watercolor Soc. (Bronze medal 1992). Home: 46 Upland Rd Colorado Springs CO 80906-4246

DWYER, DARRELL JAMES, financial executive; b. Vermillion, S.D., Nov. 27, 1946; s. Michael Leroy and Faye Awilda (Hansen) D.; m. Helen K. Howard, 1989; 1 child, Sean Patrick. BS, Mankato State U., 1977; MBA, U. Calif., Berkeley, 1978. CPA; Cert. Mgmt. Acct., Internal Auditor; cert. data processor. Acct. Touche Ross & Co., Salem, Oreg., 1978-79; cons. Arthur, Persons Co., Salem, 1980-82; v.p. fin. Evergreen Internat. Airlines Inc, McMinnville, Oreg., 1982-87; chief fin. officer The Erickson Group Ltd., Medford, Oreg., 1987-89; sr. v.p., corp. sec. Evergreen Internat. Aviation, Inc., McMinnville, Oreg., 1989-90; pres., chief exec. officer The Dwyer Group, Ltd., Sacramento, Calif., 1990—. Calif. State scholar; recipient award of merit Evergreen Internat. Aviation, McMinnville, Oreg., 1984. Mem. AICPA, Calif. Soc. CPA, Inst. Cert. Mgmt. Accts. Republican. Episcopalian. Office: The Dwyer Group Ltd 5175 Meyers St Rocklin CA 95677-2813

DWYER, WILLIAM L., federal judge; b. Olympia, Wash., Mar. 26, 1929; s. William E. and Ila (Williams) D.; m. Vasiliki Asimakopulos, Oct. 5, 1952; chldren: Joanna, Anthony, Charles. BS in Law, U. Wash., 1951; JD, NYU, 1953; LLD (hon.), Gonzaga U., 1994. Bar: Wash. 1953, U.S. Ct. Appeals (9th cir.) 1959, U.S. Supreme Ct. 1968. Law clk. Supreme Ct. Wash., Olympia, 1957; ptnr. Culp, Dwyer, Guterson & Grader, Seattle, 1957-87; judge U.S. Dist. Ct. (we. dist.) Wash., Seattle, 1987—. Author: The Goldmark Case, 1984 (Gavel award ABA 1985, Gov.'s award Wash. 1985). 1st lt. U.S. Army, 1953-56. Recipient Outstanding Svc. award U. Wash. Law Rev., 1985, Helen Geisness disting. Svc. award Seattle-King County Bar Assn., 1985, Disting. Alumnus award U. Wash. Sch. of Law, 1994, W.G. Magnuson award King County Mcpl. League, 1994, Judge of Yr. Wash. State Trial Lawyers, 1994. Fellow Am. Coll. Trial Lawyers, Am. Bar Found., Hon. Order of Coif; mem. ABA, Inter-Am. Bar Assn., Am. Judicature Soc., Supreme Ct. Hist. Soc., 9th Cir. Hist. Assn. Office: US Dist Ct 502 US Courthouse 1010 5th Ave Seattle WA 98104-1130

DWYRE, WILLIAM PATRICK, journalist, public speaker; b. Sheboygan, Wis., Apr. 7, 1944; s. George Leo and Mary Veronica (O'Brien) D.; m. Jill Ethlyn Jarvis, July 30, 1966; children—Amy, Patrick. B.A., U. Notre Dame, Ind. Sports copy editor Des Moines Register, 1966-68; sports writer, asst. sports editor, sports editor Milw. Jour., 1968-81; asst. sports editor, sports editor Los Angeles Times, 1981—; speaker Mark Reede's Sportstars, Los Angeles, 1986; columnist Referee Mag., 1977—; voting mem., bd. dirs. Amateur Athletic Found. Nat. Sports Hall of Fame, 1981—. Named Sportswriter of Yr., Wis. Nat. Sportscasters, Sportswriters Assn., 1980; Nat. Editor of Yr., Nat. Press Found., 1985, award for Sustained Excellence by Individual, Los Angeles Times, 1985. Mem. Assoc. Press Sports Editors (pres. 1989), Nat. Baseball, Pro Basketball and Football Writers Assn. Club: Milw. Pen and Mike. Office: Los Angeles Times Times Mirror Sq Los Angeles CA 90012

DYBOWSKI, DOUGLAS EUGENE, education educator, economist; b. Wiesbaden Air Base, Germany, Dec. 7, 1946; s. Eugene L. and Margaret Alma (Hart) D.; m. Deborah Jane Dalpiaz, Dec. 27, 1986; children: Noelle C., Eric W. BA in Govt. and Politics, U. Md., College Park, 1969; grad. edn. econ., Trinity U., San Antonio, 1971; Calif. teaching credential, Calif. State U., San Bernardino, 1975; AS in Computer Sci., San Bernardino Valley Coll., 1982. Legis. aide to hon. Michael Feighan U.S. Congress, Washington, 1969; econ. Bur. Labor Statistics Dept. Labor, Dallas, 1971-73; fine jewelry salesman May Co., San Bernardino, Calif., 1974-78; tchr. Rialto and San Bernardino Sch. Dists., 1973-85; realtor Gallery of Homes, San Bernardino, Calif., 1979; tchr. Diocese of San Bernardino, Calif., 1985-87; instr. computer sci. San Bernardino Valley Coll., Calif., 1983-84; tchr. Colton (Calif.) Joint Unified Sch. Dist., 1987—; art ctr. cons. Bud Rickert's Art Ctr., San Bernardino, Calif., 1989—. Artist (painting) San Bernardino County Mus., 1994. Recipient Lounsbury Svc. award San Bernardino Valley Coll., 1982. Mem. Sigma Chi. Republican, Presbyterian. Office: Colton Joint Unified Sch Dist 1212 Valencia St Colton CA 92324

DYCK, ANDREW ROY, philologist; b. Chgo., May 24, 1947; s. Roy H. and Elizabeth (Beck) D.; m. Janis Mieko Fukuhara, Aug. 20, 1978. BA, U. Wisc., 1969; PhD, U. Chgo., 1975. Sessional lectr. U. Alberta, Edmonton, Can., 1975-76; vis. asst. prof. UCLA, 1976-77, asst. prof., 1978-82, assoc. prof., 1982-87, prof., 1987—, chair dept. classics, 1988-91; asst. prof. U. Minn., Mpls., 1977-78. Editor: Epimerismi Homerici (2 vols.), 1983-95, Essays on Euripides and George of Pisidia and on Heliodorus and Achilles Tatius (Michael Psellus), 1986. Alexander von Humboldt-Stiftung fellow, Bonn, Fed. Republic of Germany, 1980-89; NEH fellow, 1991-92. Mem. Am. Philol. Assn., Calif. Classical Assn., Byzantine Studies Conf., Soc. for Promotion of Byzantine Studies, U.S. Nat. Com. on Byzantine Studies. Office: UCLA Classics Dept 405 Hilgard Ave Los Angeles CA 90024-1301

DYER, ALICE MILDRED, psychotherapist; b. San Diego, July 4, 1929; d. William Silas Cann and Louise Lair (Addenbrooke) Vaile; divorced; children: Alexis Dyer Guagnano, Bryan, Christine Dyer Morales; m. James Vawter, Dec. 26, 1972. BA, Calif. State U., Fullerton, 1965, MA, 1967; PhD, U.S. Internat. U., 1980. Coord., counselor Brea (Calif.)-Olinda High Sch., 1968-72; sch. psychologist Cypress (Calif.) Sch. Dist., 1972-86; instr. North Orange County Community Coll., Fullerton, 1975-77; pvt. practice ednl. psychology Long Beach and Fountain Valley, Calif., 1978—; pvt. practice marriage and family therapy Fullerton and Brea, Calif., 1979—; psychologist, cons. Multiple Sclerosis Soc. Orange County, 1986-95; facilitator adult mental health La Habra (Calif.) Comty. Hosp., 1988-89. Bd. dirs., officer, pres. Friends of Fullerton Arboretum, 1994—; pres., bd. dirs. Fullerton Beautiful..., 1987-88, Brea Ednl. Found., 1988-89; therapist Orange County Juvenile Connection Project, 1988—. Recipient Appreciation award Gary Ctr., La Habra, 1975, Multiple Sclerosis Soc. Orange County, 1987. Mem. Calif. Assn. Marriage and Family Therapists, Assn. for Children and Adults with Learning Disabilities (cons. 1970—, bd. dirs., facilitator), AAUW, Am. Bus. Women's Assn., Soroptomists (health chmn. Brea chpt. 1987-88). Republican. Unitarian. Office: Brea Mental Health Assocs PO Box 1688 Brea CA 92622-1688

DYER, ARLENE THELMA, retail company owner; b. Chgo., Oct. 23, 1942; d. Samuel Leo Sr. and Thelma Arlene (Israel) Lewis; m. Don Engle Dyer, July 3, 1965 (div. 1970); 1 child, Artel Terren. Cert. in mgmt. effectiveness, U. So. Calif., 1987. Community resource rep. Calif. State Employment Devel. Dept., Los Angeles, 1975-76, spl. projects rep., 1976; employment services rep. Culver City, Calif., 1977; contract writer Los Angeles, 1976-80, employment program rep., 1980—; pres. Yabba and Co., Los Angeles, 1981-83; pres., designer, cons. Spiritual Ties Custom Neckwear, Los Angeles, 1985—; pres. Dyer Custom Shirts, Blouses and Suits, Beverly Hills, Calif., 1988—; founder self-evaluation seminar. Author: Who Are You and What Are You All About?, 1994; exhibited in fashion shows, Calif., 1984—; radio personality. Vol. Big Sister Gwen Bolden Found., L.A., 1986; mem. Operation PUSH, Chgo., 1983, Mahogany Cowgirls & Co.; program chair Black Advs. in State Svc., 1987—; leader Girl Scouts U.S., L.A., 1982, L.A. Urban League; spirit team leader Calif. Special Olympics. Mem. Nat. Alliance Homebased Businesswomen (v.p., program chair 1987), Nat. Assn. Female Execs., Calif. State Employees Assn., U. So. Calif. Alumni Assn., L.A. Urban League, Black Women's Forum, NAACP (Beverly Hills-Hollywood chpt.). Democrat. Club: 92d St Block.

DYER, CAROLYN PRICE, artist, writer; b. Seattle, Dec. 19, 1931; d. Herbert Frederick and Evelyn Ida (Nelson) Price; m. M. Clark Dyer, Sept. 7, 1954; children: Philip Nelson, Paul Clark, Andrew Mark Price. Student, U. Wash., 1949-50; BA, Mills Coll., Oakland, Calif., 1953; MA, Mills Coll., 1955. Coll. level teaching credential, Calif. Owner Stone Ct. Gallery Contemporary Art, Yakima, Wash., 1958-65; prin. Carolyn Dyer Textiles, Pasadena, Calif., 1965-93, Tacoma, 1993—; mem. faculty L.A. C.C., 1970-78, Pasadena Art Mus. Art Workshops, 1971-73; owner Carolyn Price Dyer Gallery, Tacoma, 1994—; freelance writer art and travel publs., 1976—; juror N.W. Craftsmen's Exhbn., Seattle, 1964, Fiber Structure Nat., Downey, Calif., 1983; curator So. Calif. Galleries, 1974, Blue Heron Ctr. for Arts, Vashon, Wash., 1991. One-woman shows include The Kennedy-Douglass Ctr. for the Arts, Florence, Ala., 1992, Commencement Gallery, Tacoma, 1995; two-woman shows include Monrovia (Calif.) Arts Ctr., 1985, Blue Heron Ctr. for Arts, 1988; major exhibitions in group shows include Fullerton (Calif.) Mus. Ctr., 1985, Cortland (N.Y.) Arts Coun. Gallery, 1985, Brea (Calif.) Mcpl. Art Gallery, 1987, Mills Coll., 1987, Laguna Art Mus., Laguna Beach, Calif., 1988, Oreg. Sch. Arts and Crafts, Portland, 1985, 89, 90, Mariposa Gallery, Santa Fe, 1990, Frye Art Mus., Seattle, 1991, Wignall Mus. and Gallery, Rancho Cucamonga, Calif., 1991, Maude Kerns Art Ctr., Eugene, Oreg., 1991, Blue Heron Ctr. for Arts, 1991, Anchorage (Alaska) Mus. Art and History, 1994-95; represented in numerous pvt. and corp. collections; contbg. editor Fiberarts mag., 1978—;

editor (newsletter) Lineup, 1978—. Bd. dirs. Pasadena Art Alliance, 1981-87, Pasadena Arts Coun., 1977-79. Recipient Gold Crown award Pasadena Arts Coun., 1982; Trustee scholar Mills Coll., 1950-53, Grad. fellow, 1953-55. Mem. Am. Craft Coun., Northwest Designer Craftsmen, Tapestry Artists of Puget Sound, Calif. Fibers, Tacoma Art Mus. (mem. docent coun.). Address: PO Box 1962 Vashon WA 98070-1962

DYER, KECIA CAROLE, interior project designer; b. Dallas, Mar. 27, 1965; d. Eldon Royce and Carole Lynn (Wade) D. BS in Interior Design, U. Tex., 1989. Cert. interior designer. Designer Reese Design, Austin, Tex., 1989-90; project designer Space Designs, Inc., Mountainview, Calif., 1990-95; assoc. Reel Grobman and Assocs., Interior Architecture, San Jose, Calif., 1995—. Vol. Design Response, bd. dirs.; task force mem. Palo Alto (Calif.) Task Force for Disability Awareness, 1993-94. Recipient C.J. Davidson scholarship U. Tex., Austin, 1989. Mem. Internat. Interior Design Assn. (bd. dirs. No. Calif. chpt. 1993—). Republican. Office: Reel Grobman and Assocs 38 W Santa Clara St San Jose CA 95113

DYER, RICHARD HUTCHINS, risk management executive; b. Washington, Jan. 11, 1931; s. Robert Francis and Sarah Antoinette (Worley) D. BA, Yale U., 1953; JD, George Washington U., 1956. Legal liaison U. Calif. Lawrence Berkeley Lab., Berkeley, 1960-64; risk mgr. U. Calif. Lawrence Livermore Lab., Livermore, 1964-94; cons. Teknokron Inc., Berkeley, Calif., 1967; mem. Legis. Com. Calif. Self Insurer Assn., 1981-94; pres. Golden Gate Risk Mgmt. Soc., San Francisco, 1985—, legis. dir., 1986-93. Pres. PTA, Lafayette, Calif., 1970-71; bd. dirs. Berkeley Missionary Home, 1985-90; mem. Calif. Gov's Toxic Task Force, Sacramento, 1985-86; v.p. Diablo View Wellness Coun., Livermore, 1985-94, Friends Outside, 1992-94; mem. fin. com. Danville (Calif.) Sch. Dist., 1974-75; mem. Contra Costa County Rep. Ctrl. Com., Danville, 1970-82; ruling elder Danville Presbyn. Ch., 1984-93; mem. com. on preparation for ministry San Francisco Presbytery, 1993—; treas. Spinnaker Clipper Couples Club, 1993-95; docent Mus. at Blackhawk Guild, 1995. Lt. USNR, 1959-63. Recipient citation Gov.'s Toxic Task Force, 1987. Mem. Commonwealth Club San Francisco, Yale Club No. Calif., Masons, Pi Sigma Alpha,, Phi Alpha Delta. Home: 1360 Brookside Dr Danville CA 94526 Office: U Calif Lawrence Livermore Lab Box 808 L-708 Livermore CA 94551

DYER-RAFFLER, JOY ANN, special education diagnostician, educator; b. Stiltner, W.Va., Aug. 10, 1935; d. Ralph William and Hazel (Terry) Dyer; m. John William Raffler, Sr., Jan. 1, 1993; 1 child from a previous marriage, Keith Brian DeArmond. BA, U. N.C., 1969; MEd in Secondary Edn., U. Ariz., 1974, MEd in Spl. Edn., 1976. Cert. spl. edn.-learning disabilities, art edn., spl. edn.-emotionally handicapped. Art educator Tucson Unified Sch. Dist., Tucson, 1970-75, spl. edn. educator, 1975-89, spl. edn. diagnostician, 1989—. Den mother Cub Scouts Am., Raleigh, N.C., 1968-69. Recipient grant Tucson Unified Sch. Dist., 1977. Mem. NEA, Tucson Edn. Assn., Learning Disabilities Assn., Coun. Exceptional Children, Coun. Ednl. Diagnostic Svcs. Home: 4081 N Kolb Rd Tucson AZ 85715-6127 Office: AJO Svc Ctr 2201 W 44th St Tucson AZ 85710-6127

DYESS, EDWIN EARL, academic administrator; b. Roswell, N.Mex., Apr. 23, 1949; s. Marion and Johnnie Lorea (Murray) D.; m. Delila Ann Frazier, May 12, 1973; 1 child, Tyler Christopher. BBA, Ea. N.Mex. U., 1971. Supt. grounds Ea. N.Mex. U., Roswell, 1972-78, N.Mex. Mil. Inst., Roswell, 1978—; sec. S.W. Phys. Plant Suprs. Assn., Albuquerque, N.Mex., 1980-81. Named Outstanding Young Man of Am., 1982. Mem. N.Mex. Irrigation Assn., Delta Sigma Pi. Republican. Baptist. Home: 1005 Hamilton Dr Roswell NM 88201-1132 Office: NMex Mil Inst 101 W College Blvd Roswell NM 88201-5174

DYGERT, HAROLD PAUL, JR., cardiologist; b. Rochester, N.Y., June 21, 1919; s. Harold Paul and Elsie Viola (Howe) D.; m. Helen Adelaine Nelson, Apr. 22, 1944; children: Harold Paul III, William Nelson, Peter Howe. BA, U. Rochester, 1941; postgrad., Alfred U., 1942-43; MD, Syracuse U., 1950. Diplomate Am. Bd. Internal Medicine. Intern Receiving Hosp., Detroit, 1950-51, resident internal medicine, 1951-53, chief resident, 1953-54; instr. medicine Wayne State U., Detroit, 1954-55; mem. staff VA Hosp., Vancouver, Wash., 1955-59; practice medicine specializing in cardiology and internal medicine Vancouver, 1959—; chmn. Health Care Consortium, 1974-87. Pres. Wash. State Med., Ednl. and Research Found., 1971-73; bd. dirs. Wash.-Alaska Regional Med. Program, 1966-72; participant Manhattan Project, 1943-46. Served with AUS, 1943. Fellow ACP, Am. Coll. Cardiology; mem. AMA (del. 1976-77), Am. Fedn. Clin. Research, Wash. State Med. Assn. (pres. 1973-74), Portland Heart Club (pres. 1975-77), Wash. State Soc. Internal Medicine (trustee 1976-80). Home: 8407 SE Evergreen Hwy Vancouver WA 98664-2335 Office: 2101 E Mcloughlin Blvd Vancouver WA 98661

DYKK, LLOYD HENRY, journalist; b. Vita, Man., Can., Oct. 15, 1944; s. Henry and Mary D. BA, U. Sask., 1966. Writer, rschr. Sask. Rsch. Coun., Saskatoon, 1966; reporter Star-Phoenix, Saskatoon, 1967-68; arts critic Vancouver (B.C.) Sun, 1968-92, columnist, features writer, 1992—. Recipient Nat. Newspaper award for critical writing Nat. Newspaper Awards, 1993. Mem. New Democratic Party. Office: The Vancouver Sun, 2250 Granville St, Vancouver, BC Canada V6H 3G2

DYKSTRA, DAVID CHARLES, management executive, accountant, consultant, author, educator; b. Des Moines, July 10, 1941; s. Orville Linden and Ermina (Dunn) D.; m. Ello Paimre, Nov. 20, 1971; children: Suzanne, Karin, David S. BSChemE, U. Calif., Berkeley, 1963; MBA, Harvard U., 1966. CPA, Calif. Corp. contr. Recreation Environs., Newport Beach, Calif., 1970-71, Hydro Conduit Corp., Newport Beach., 1971-78; v.p. fin. and adminstrn. Tree-Sweet Products, Santa Ana, Calif., 1978-80; pres., owner Dykstra Cons., Irvine, Calif., 1980-88, Newport Beach, 1991-94; exec. v.p. Northstar Svcs., Bellevue, Wash., 1994—; pres. Easy Data Corp., 1981-88; pub. Easy Data Computer Comparisons, 1982-87; sr. mgr. Deloitt & Touche, Costa Mesa, Calif., 1988-90; prof. mgmt. info. systems Nat. U., Irvine, 1984—; pub. Dykstra's Computer Digest, 1984—; pres., owner Golden West Pers., Long Beach, 1992-93; exec. v.p. Northstar Svcs., Inc., Bellevue, Wash., 1994—. Author: Manager's Guide to Business Computer Terms, 1981, Computers for Profit, 1983; contbr. articles to profl. jours. Chmn. 40th Congl. Dist. Tax Reform Immediately, 1977-80; mem. nat. com. Rep. Com.; vice-chmn. Orange County Calif. Rep. Assembly, 1979-80; bd. dir. Corona Del Mar Rep. Assembly, 1980—, v.p., 1980-87, pres. 1987-89. Mem. AICPA, Am. Mgmt. Assn., Calif. Soc. CPA's, Data Processing Mgmt. Assn., Am. Prodn. and Inventory Control Soc., Ind. Computer Cons. Assn., Internat. Platform Assn., Data Processing Mgmt. Assn., Orange County C. of C., Newport Beach C. of C., Harvard U. Bus. Sch. Assn. Orange County (bd. dir. 1984—, v.p 1984-86, 87-88, pres. 1986-87, 91-92, chmn. 1993-94), Harvard U. Bus. Sch. Assn. So. Calif. (bd. dirs. 1986-87, 91-92, v.p. 1992-93), Harvard U. Bus. Sch. Assn. Puget Sound, Town Hall, John Wayne Tennis Club, Lido Sailing Club, Rotary (bd. dirs. 1984-86). Home: 2500 81st Ave SE Apt 307 Mercer Island WA 98040-2253 Office: 14205 SE 36th St Ste 100 Bellevue WA 98006-1553

DYKSTRA, EDIE M., human resource director; b. Gary, Ind., Nov. 9, 1954; d. Wayne H. and Edith P. (Christoff) D. BA in History, Ind. U., 1976; MPA in Urban, State, Fed. Gov. and Human Resources, Golden Gate U., 1986. Supr. internal acctg. KPMG Peat Marwick, San Francisco, 1980-87; asst. to dir. fin. City of Oakland, Calif., 1987; compensation and benefits analyst The Harper Group, San Francisco, 1987-89; mgr. internal svcs. Watson Wyatt Worldwide (formerly The Wyatt Co.), San Francisco, 1989-92; mgr. human resources The Wyatt Co., San Francisco, 1992-94, dir. human resources, 1994—. Vol. Raphael House Shelter for Homeless Families, San Francisco, 1988—, vol., crisis counselor Woman Inc., 1988—. Mem. ASTD, Soc. for Human Resource Mgmt., Bay Area Personnel Assn. (pres. 1990-91), Bay Area Orgnl. Devel. Network, No. Calif. Human Resource Coun. Democrat. Office: The Wyatt Co 345 California St San Francisco CA 94104-2635

DYKSTRA, RONALD JOSEPH, military officer; b. Savannah, Ga., Mar. 17, 1960; s. Joseph Henry and Barbara Eden (Holm) D.; m. Michele Marie Maestaz, Dec. 27, 1984; 1 child, Grant Michael. BS in Engring., U.S. Mil. Acad., 1982. Commd. 2d lt. U.S. Army, 1983, advanced through grades to major, 1988, various positions, 1983-88; asst. ops. officer 2nd brigade, 4th infantry divsn. U.S. ANG, Colorado Springs, 1986-88; co. comdr. A co./1-82 cavalry U.S. ANG, Fallon, Nev., 1988-90; asst. bn. ops. officer troop command U.S. ANG, 1990; asst. tng. officer HQ STARC U.S. ANG, Carson City, Nev., 1990-91; reading officer U.S. ANG, 1991-92, chief mobilization readiness br., 1992—. Cubmaster pack 100 Pinenut dist. Nev. area coun. Boy Scouts Am., 1992—; admissions rep. U.S. Mil. Acad., 1991—; mem. U.S. Acads. Selection Bd., 1991—; rep. Vucanovich's Def. Adv. Bd., 1992—. Mem. Nat. Guard Assn. U.S. (life), U.S. Biathlon Assn. Home: 18 Yhvona Dr Carson City NV 98706 Office: Office of Mil 2525 S Carson St Carson City NV 89701-5502

DYM, CLIVE LIONEL, engineering educator; b. Leeds, England, July 15, 1942; came to U.S., 1949, naturalized, 1954; s. Isaac and Anna (Hochmann) D.; children: Jordana, Miriam. BCE, Cooper Union, 1962; MS, Poly. Inst. Bklyn., 1964; PhD, Stanford U., 1967. Asst. prof. SUNY, Buffalo, 1966-69; assoc. professorial lectr. George Washington U., Washington, 1969; research staff Inst. Def. Analyses, Arlington, Va., 1969-70; assoc. prof. Carnegie-Mellon U., Pitts., 1970-74; vis. assoc. prof. TECHNION, Israel, 1971; sr. scientist Bolt Beranek and Newman, Inc., Cambridge, Mass., 1974-77; prof. U. Mass., Amherst, 1977-91, head dept. civil engring., 1977-85; Fletcher Jones prof. engring. design Harvey Mudd Coll., Claremont, Calif., 1991—; vis. sr. rsch. fellow Inst. Sound and Vibration Rsch., U. Southampton, Eng., 1973; vis. scientist Xerox PARC, 1983-84; vis. prof. civil engring. Stanford U., 1983-84, Carnegie Mellon U., 1990; cons. Bell Aerospace Co., 1967-69, Dravo Corp., 1970-71, Salem Corp., 1972, Gen. Analytics Inc., 1972, ORI, Inc., 1979, BBN Inc., 1979, Avco, 1981-83, 85-86, TASC, 1985-86; vice chmn. adv. bd. Amerinex Artificial Intelligence, 1986-88. Author: (with I.H. Shames) Solid Mechanics: A Variational Approach, 1973, Introduction to the Theory of Shells, rev. edit. 1990, Stability Theory and Its Applications to Structural Mechanics, 1974, (with E.S. Ivey) Principles of Mathematical Modeling, 1980, (with I.H. Shames) Energy and Finite Element Methods in Structural Mechanics, 1985, (with R.E. Levitt) Knowledge-Based Systems in Engineering, 1990, Engineering Design: A Synthesis of Views, 1994; editor: (with A. Kalnins) Vibration: Beams, Plates, and Shells, 1977, Applications of Knowledge-Based Systems to Engineering Analysis and Design, 1985, Artificial Intelligence for Engring. Design Analysis and Mfg., 1986—; contbr. articles and tech. reports to profl. publs. NATO sr. fellow in sci., 1973. Fellow Acoustical Soc. Am., ASME, ASCE (Walter L. Huber research prize 1980); mem. AAAS, Am. Assn. for Artificial Intelligence, Computer Soc. of IEEE, ASEE (Western Electric Fund award 1983). Jewish. Office: Harvey Mudd Coll Engr Dept 301 E 12th St Claremont CA 91711-5901

DYRNESS, WILLIAM ARTHUR, religion educator, dean; b. Geneva, Ill., Jan. 23, 1943; s. Enock Christian and Grace (Williams) D.; m. Grace Strachan Roberts, Mar. 16, 1968; children: Michelle Lynn, Andrea Elisabeth, Jonathan Roberts. BA, Wheaton (Ill.) Coll., 1965; BD, Fuller Theol. Sem., Pasadena, Calif., 1968; ThD, U. Strasbourg, France, 1970; Doctorandus, Free U., Amsterdam, The Netherlands, 1975. Prof. theology Asian Theol. Sem., Manila, 1974-82; prof. theology New Coll. Berkeley, Calif., 1982-90, pres., 1982-86; dean, prof. theology and culture Fuller Theol. Sem., 1990—. Author: Themes in Old Testament Theology, 1979, Christian Apologetics in a World Community, 1983, How Does America Hear the Gospel?, 1989, Learning About Theology from the Third World, 1990. Democrat. Presbyterian. Office: Fuller Theol Sem 135 N Oakland Ave Pasadena CA 91182-0001

DYSON, ALLAN JUDGE, librarian; b. Lawrence, Mass., Mar. 28, 1942; s. Raymond Magan and Hilda D.; m. Susan Cooper, 1987; 1 child, Brenna Ruth. BA in Govt., Harvard U., 1964; MSLS, Simmons Coll., 1968. Asst. to dir. Columbia U. Librs., N.Y.C., 1968-71; head Moffitt Undergrad. Libr. U. Calif., Berkeley, 1971-79; univ. libr. U. Calif., Santa Cruz, 1979—. Editor Coll. and Rsch. Librs. News, 1973-74; chmn. editl. bd. Choice mag., 1978-80, Am. Librs., 1986-89. CFO Cabrillo (Calif.) Music Festival, 1985-86; chmn. No. Calif. Regional Libr. Bd., 1986-88, 94—. Lt. U.S. Army, 1964-66. Decorated Army Commendation medal; Coun. on Libr. Resources fellow, 1973-74. Mem. ALA, ACLU, Assn. Coll. and Rsch. Librs., Librs. Assn. U. Calif. (pres. 1976), Sierra Club. Home: 775 Toll House Gulch Rd Felton CA 95018-9661 Office: U Calif McHenry Libr Santa Cruz CA 95064

DZIEWANOWSKA,ZOFIAELIZABETH,neuropsychiatrist, pharmaceutical executive, physician; b. Warsaw, Poland, Nov. 17, 1939; came to U.S. 1972; d. Stanislaw Kazimierz Dziewanowski and Zofia Danuta (Mieczkowska) Rudowska; m. Krzysztof A. Kunert, Sept. 1, 1961 (div. 1971); 1 child, Martin. MD, U. Warsaw, 1963; PhD, Polish Acad. Sci., 1970. MD recert. U.K., 1972, U.S., 1973. Asst. prof. of psychiatry U. Warsaw Med. Sch., 1969-71; sr. house officer St. George's Hosp., U. London, 1971-72; assoc. dir. Merck Sharp & Dohme, Rahway, N.J., 1972-76; vis. assoc. physician Rockefeller U. Hosp., N.Y.C., 1975-76; adj. asst. prof. of psychiatry Cornell U. Med. Ctr., N.Y.C., 1978—; v.p., global med. dir. Hoffmann-La Roche, Inc., Nutley, N.J., 1976-94; sr. v.p. and dir. global med. affairs Genta Inc., San Diego, 1994—; lectr. in field. Contbr. articles to profl. publs. Bd. dirs. Royal Soc. of Medicine Found., U.K. Recipient TWIN Honoree award for Outstanding Women in Mgmt., Ridgewood (N.J.) YWCA, 1984. Mem. AMA, AAAS, Am. Soc. Pharmacology and Therapeutics, Am. Coll. Neuropsychopharmacology, N.Y. Acad. Sci., Pharm. Rsch. and Mfrs. Assn. of Am. (vice chmn. steering com. med. sect.), Royal Soc. Medicine (U.K.), Drug Info. Assn. (Women of the Yr. award 1994, Most Admired Women of the Decade from Am. Biog. Inst. 1994), Alumni Coun. Cornell Med. Ctr., Am. Assn. Pharm. Physicians. Roman Catholic. Office: Genta Inc 3550 General Atomics Ct San Diego CA 92121

EADINGTON, WILLIAM RICHARD, economist, educator; b. Fullerton, Calif., Jan. 1, 1946; s. Thomas James and Mary Elizabeth (Bastanchury) E.; m. Margaret Ann Dean, Feb. 3, 1968; children: Diana, Michael. BS, Santa Clara U., 1967; MA, Claremont Grad. Sch., 1970, PhD, 1973. Asst. prof. econs. U. Nev., Reno, 1969-74, assoc. prof., 1974-81, prof. econs., 1981—, U. Nev. Reno Found. prof., 1990-91; dir. Inst. for Study of Gambling and Comml. Gaming, Reno, 1989—; vis. prof. U. Utah, Germany, 1977-78; vis. prof. Ctr. Addiction Studies, Harvard U., Cambridge, Mass., 1989-90, lectr. Kennedy Sch. Govt., 1990; acad. visitor London Sch. Econs., 1978, 87. Editor: Gambling and Society, 1976, Annals Am. Acad. Soc. and Polit. Sci., 1984, Gambling Resarch, 1988, Indian Gaming and the Law, 1990, Gambling and Public Policy, 1991, Gambling and Commercial Gaming, 1992, Tourism Alternatives, 1992, Gambling Behavior and Problem Gambling, 1993, Jour. Gambling Studies, 1989; assoc. editor Annals Tourism Rsch., 1983-89. Named Outstanding Rschr./Educator Nat. Coun. Compulsive Gambling, 1989. Fellow Internat. Acad. Study of Tourism; mem. Am. Econ. Assn. Republican. Roman Catholic. Home: 25 Somers Loop Crystal Bay NV 89402 Office: U Nev Dept Econs Reno NV 89557

EAGEN, ISAAC BRENT, priest, academic administrator; b. Upland, Calif., Dec. 14, 1929; s. James O. and Stella E. (Powell) E. BA, St. Francis Sem., 1951; MA, Loyola-Marymount U., 1961; DHL (hon.), U. San Diego, 1980. Ordained priest Roman Catholic Ch., 1956, rev. monsignor, 1969; assoc. pastor St. Joseph Cathedral, 1956; assoc. pastor Holy Rosary Ch., 1956-59; asst. prof. U. San Diego, 1960-65; prof. Mercy Coll. Nursing, San Diego, 1962-64, dir. sch. rels., 1965-67; chancellor Diocese of San Diego, 1968-89; pastor Mission San Diego de Alcala, 1971-93; pres. Cathedral Plaza Corp., San Diego, 1971-93; bd. dirs. Diocese San Diego Edn. and Welfare Corp., 1968-89; pres. Guadalupe Plaza Corp., San Diego, 1979-93; v.p. U. San Diego, 1993—. Trustee, U. San Diego, 1968-93; pres. Community Welfare Council, 1970; mem. Mayor's Crime Control Commn., 1981. Named Headliner of Year, San Diego Press Club, 1975; named Man for All Seasons, St. Vincent de Paul, 1989; recipient Daughter of the Am. Revolution medal of Honor, 1993, Unity award Diocese of San Diego, 1993, Unity award Ecumenical Coun. of San Diego County, 1995. Mem. NCCJ (nat. trustee, Brotherhood award 1971), Canon Law Soc. Am., Navy League U.S., Scholia, Phi Kappa Theta. Clubs: La Jolla Beach and Tennis. Home: 7962 Caminito Del Cid La Jolla CA 92037-3405 Office: U San Diego 5998 Alcala Park San Diego CA 92110-2429

EAKIN, MARGARETTA MORGAN, lawyer; b. Ft. Smith, Ark., Aug. 27, 1941; d. Ariel Thomas and Oma (Thomas) Morgan; m. Harry D. Eakin, June 7, 1959; 1 dau., Margaretta E. B.A. with honors, U. Oreg., 1969, J.D., 1971. Bar: Oreg. 1971, U.S. Dist. Ct. Oreg. 1973, U.S. Ct. Appeals (9th cir.) 1977. Law clk. to chief justice Oreg. Supreme Ct., 1971-72; Reginald Heber Smith Law Reform fellow, 1972-73; house counsel Hyster Co., 1973-75; assoc. N. Robert Stoll, 1975-77; mem. firm Margaretta Eakin, P.C., Portland, Oreg., 1977—; tchr. bus. law Portland State U., 1979-80; speaker; mem. state bd. profl. responsibility Oreg. State Bar, 1979-82. Mem. bd. visitors U. Oreg. Sch. of Law, 1986-93, vice chair, 1989-91, chair, 1992-93; mem. ann. fund com. Oreg. Episc. Sch., 1981, chmn. subcom. country fair, 1981; sec. Parent Club Bd., St. Mary's Acad., 1987; mem. Oreg. State. Bar Com. on Uniform State Laws, 1989-93. Paul Patterson fellow. Mem. ABA, Assn. Trial Lawyers Am., Oreg. Trial Lawyers Assn., Oreg. Bar Assn., Multnomah County Bar Assn. (jud. selection com. 1992-94), 1000 Friends of Oreg., City Club. Office: 30th Fl Pacwest Ctr 1211 SW 5th Ave Portland OR 97204-3713

EAKLE, ARLENE HASLAM, genealogist; b. Salt Lake City, July 19, 1937; d. Thomas E. and margaret (Mitchell) Haslam; m. Alma D. Eakle, Jr., Feb. 8, 1957; children: JoAnn, Richard, Linda, John. ADN, Weber State U.; MA in English history, U. Utah, PhD of English history. Co-author: Family History for Fun and Profit, 1972, (with Johni Cerny) The Source: A Guidebook for American Genealogy, 1984, (with Johni Cerny) Ancestry's Guide to Research, 1985; editor: Research News, Immigration Digest; contbg. editor: Geneal. Jour.; adv. bd. mem. Utah Hist. Quar. Fellow Utah Geneal. Assn., 1987; recipient Award of Merit Fedn. Geneal. Soc., 1984. Mem. Am. Family Records Assn., Assn. Profl. Genealogists (pres. 1980-82, Grahame Thomas Smallwood Jr. Award of Merit 1984), Md. Geneal. Soc., Utah Geneal. Assn., West Fla. Geneal. Soc. Home: 875 N 300 E Tremonton UT 84337-1010 Office: Genealogical Inst PO Box 22045 Salt Lake City UT 84122

EAMER, RICHARD KEITH, health care company executive, lawyer; b. Long Beach, Calif., Feb. 13, 1928; s. George Pierce and Lillian (Newell) E.; m. Eileen Laughlin, Sept. 1, 1951; children: Brian Keith, Erin Maureen. B.S. in Acctg., U. So. Calif., 1955, LL.B., 1959. Bar: Calif. 1960; C.P.A., Calif. Acct. L. H. Penney & Co. (C.P.A.s), 1956-59; asso. firm Ervin, Cohen & Jessup, Beverly Hills, Calif., 1959-63; partner firm Eamer, Bell and Bedrosian, Beverly Hills, 1963-69; chmn. bd., chief exec. officer Nat. Med. Enterprises, Inc., Los Angeles, 1969—; also dir. Nat. Med. Enterprises, Inc.; dir. Union Oil Co. Calif., Imperial Bank. Mem. Am. Bar Assn., Am. Inst. C.P.A.s, Calif. Bar Assn., Los Angeles County Bar Assn. Republican. Clubs: Bel Air Country, Bel Air Bay; California. Office: Nat Med Enterprises Inc 11620 Wilshire Blvd Los Angeles CA 90025-1706

EARL, WILLIAM JOHN, software engineer; b. East Stroudsburg, Pa., July 5, 1950; s. Lawrence William and Helen Olga (Gaisler) E.; m. Marion Helen Kaufman, Feb. 11, 1977; children: John William, Lesley Ann. BS, Calif. Inst. Tech., 1972; postgrad., U. Calif., Irvine, 1972-77. Sr. programmer Varian Data Machines, Irvine, 1976-77; supervising programmer Sperry Univac, Irvine, 1977-80; software designer Tandem Computers, Cupertino, Calif., 1980-84; software engr. Daisy Systems, Mountain View, Calif., 1984-86; mgr. operating systems group Am. Info. Tech., Cupertino, 1986-87; prin. engr. MIPS Computer Systems Inc., Sunnyvale, Calif., 1987-92, Silicon Graphics, Inc., Mountain View, Calif., 1992—. Mem. Assn. Computing Machinery. Republican. Presbyterian. Office: Silicon Graphics Inc 2011 N Shoreline Blvd Mountain View CA 94043-1321

EARLE, TIMOTHY, anthropology educator; b. New Bedford, Mass., Aug. 10, 1946; s. Osborne and Eleanor (Clark) E.; m. Eliza Howe, June 14, 1969; children: Caroline, Hester. BA summa cum laude, Harvard U., 1969; MA, U. Mich., 1971, PhD, 1973. Rsch. archaeologist Bishop Mus., Honolulu, 1971-72; prof. anthropology UCLA, 1973-95, dir. Inst. of Archaeology, 1987-92; prof. anthropology Northwestern U., Evanston, Ill., 1995—, chair dept., 1995—. Co-author: Evolution of Human Society, 1987; editor: Exchange Systems in Prehistory, 1977, Contexts for Prehistoric Exchange, 1982, Chiefdoms, 1991. Mem. Am. Anthrop. Assn. (pres.-elect archaeology divsn. 1993—), Soc. Am. Archaeology, Soc. Economic Anthrop., Phi Beta Kappa. Office: Northwestern U Dept Anthropology Los Angeles CA 60208

EARLEY, SCOTT, microbiologist; b. Dover-Foxcroft, Maine, Apr. 5, 1963; s. Drummond Jr. and Joy Lee (Crafts) E. BSEE, U. Maine, 1986, MS in Microbiology, 1988. Rsch. asst. U. Maine, Orono, 1982-88; sr. rsch. asst. McLaughlin Rsch. Inst., Great Falls, Mont., 1988-89; lab. mgr. InterMountain Labs., Inc., Bozeman, Mont., 1990-93; pres., co-founder TransGenic Sys., Inc., Bozeman, 1993—; cons. Agrl. Bioengring., Inc., Bozeman, 1992-94. Author article, book chpts. in field. Mem. AAAS, Am. Soc. Microbiology, Am. Homebrewers Assn. Democrat. Home: PO Box 6461 Bozeman MT 59771-6461

EARLY, JAMES MICHAEL, electronics research consultant; b. Syracuse, N.Y., July 25, 1922; s. Frank J. and Rhoda Gray E.; m. Mary Agnes Valentine, Dec. 28, 1948; children: Mary Beth Early Dehler, Kathleen, Joan Early Farrell, Rhoda Early Alexander, Maureen Early Mathews, Rosemary Early North, James, Margaret Mary Early Staton. B.S., N.Y. Coll. Forestry, Syracuse, N.Y., 1943; M.S., Ohio State U., 1948, Ph.D., 1951. Instr., research assoc. Ohio State U., Columbus, 1946-51; dir. lab. Bell Telephone Labs., Murray Hill, N.J., 1951-64, Allentown, Pa., 1964-69; dir. research and devel. Fairchild Semicondr. Corp., Palo Alto, Calif., 1969-83, sci. advisor, 1983-86; research cons., 1987—. Contbr. over 20 papers to profl. jours. Served with U.S. Army, 1943-45. Fellow AAAS, IEEE (numerous coms., John Fritz Medal bd. of award); mem. IEEE Electron Device Soc. (J.J. Ebers award 1979), Am. Phys. Soc., Internat. Platform Assn. Roman Catholic. Home and Office: 708 Holly Oak Dr Palo Alto CA 94303-4142

EARLY, ROBERT JOSEPH, magazine editor; b. Indpls., Sept. 22, 1936; s. Robert Paul and Helen Theresa (Schluttenhofer) E.; m. Gail Louise Horvath, Sept. 6, 1958; children: Mary Jane, Joseph Robert, Jill Ann. BA, U. Notre Dame, 1958. Reporter Indpls. Star, 1958-61; reporter The Ariz. Republic, Phoenix, 1961-66, asst. city editor, 1966-69, city editor, 1969-77, asst. mng. editor, 1977-78, mng. editor, 1978-82; pres. Telesource Communication Svcs. Inc., Phoenix, 1982-90; editor Phoenix Mag., 1985-89, Ariz. Hwys., Phoenix, 1990—; lectr. Ariz. State U., 1992, 94; editor in residence No. Ariz. U., 1992, 93, 94.. Chmn. Victims Bill of Rights Task Force, Phoenix, 1989. Recipient Virg Hill Newsman of Yr. award Ariz. Press Club, 1976. Mem. Soc. Profl. Journalists. Republican. Roman Catholic. Office: Ariz Hwys 2039 W Lewis Ave Phoenix AZ 85009-2819

EARNER, WILLIAM ANTHONY, JR., naval officer; b. Pitts., Nov. 2, 1941; s. William Anthony and Marie Veronica (Ward) E.; m. Jennifer Elizabeth Laurence, Dec. 11, 1971; children: William Andrew, John Laurence. BS, U.S. Naval Acad., 1963; MS, U.S. Naval Postgrad. Sch., 1969; DBA, Harvard U., 1973. Commd. ensign USN, 1963, advanced through grades to vice adm., 1994; 1st lt. USS Blue USN, Yokosuka, Japan, 1963-65; weapons officer USS Black USN, San Diego, 1965-67; ops. officer River Sect. 534 USN, Vietnam, 1967-68; weapons officer USS Dale USN, Mayport, Fla., 1973-75, exec. officer USS Luce, 1975-77; prof. Naval War Coll. USN, Newport, R.I., 1977-78, fellow strategic studies group, 1987-88; with Office Chief Naval Ops. USN, Washington, 1978-81; comdg. officer USS Deyo USN, 1981-83; mil. asst. to dir. NET assesment Office of Sec. Def. USN, Washington, 1983-85, comptr. naval air systems, 1988-90; comdr. Destroyer Squadron Four USN, Charleston, S.C., 1985-87; comdr. naval Surface Group Mid-Pacific USN, Pearl Harbor, Hawaii, 1990-92; budget officer Dept. Navy, 1992-94, dep. chief naval ops. (logistics), 1994—; instr. Harvard Grad. Sch. Edn., Cambridge, Mass., 1972-73; adj. prof. Bryant Coll., Smithfield, R.I., 1977-78. Decorated Legion of Merit, Bronze Star with V device. Mem. U.S. Naval Inst., Am. Soc. Mil. Comptrs., U.S. Naval Acad. Alumni Assn. Office: DCNO (Logistics) Office of the CNO Washington DC 20350

EASLEY, GEORGE WASHINGTON, construction executive; b. Williamson, W.Va., Mar. 14, 1933; s. George Washington and Isabel Ritchie (Saville) E.; student U. Richmond, 1952-56; children: Bridget Bland, Kathy Clark, Saville Woodson, Marie Alexis, Isabell Roxanne, George Washington, Laura Dean, Dorothy Elizabeth, Isabel Louiza. m. Bettyrae Fedje Hanner, Sep. 15, 1990. Hwy. engr. Va. Dept. Hwys., Richmond, 1956-62; dep. city mgr. City of Anchorage, 1962-68; prin. assoc. Wilbur Smith & Assos., Los Angeles, 1969-70; commr. pub. works State of Alaska, Juneau, 1971-74; exec. v.p. Burgess Internat. Constrn. Co., Anchorage, 1974, pres., 1975; pres., chmn. bd. George W. Easley Co., Anchorage, 1976-86 ; pres. Alaska Aggregate Corp., Fairbanks Sand & Gravel Co., 1986-90; constrn. mgr. Alyeska Pipeline Svc. Co., 1990—; bd. dirs. Totem Ocean Trailer Express, Inc. Recipient commendations City of Anchorage, 1966, Greater Anchorage, Inc., 1969, Ketchikan C. of C., 1973, Alaska State Legis., 1974, Gov. of Alaska, 1974; named one of Outstanding Young Men, Anchorage Jaycees, 1964. Registered profl. engr., Calif. Mem. U.S. C. of C. (nat. com. on small bus.), Alaska C. of C. (dir. 1978—, chmn. 1982-83), Anchorage C. of C. (sec.-treas. 1976, v.p. 1977, pres.-elect 1978, pres. 1979-80, dir. 1982-88, Gold Pan award 1969, 77), Hwy. Users Fedn. Alaska (dir. 1972—, treas. 1974—), Orgn. Mgmt. of Alaska's Resources (past dir.), Am. Pub. Works Assn., Anchorage Transp. Commn. (past chmn.), Associated Gen. Contractors (dir. Alaska chpt. 1978—, chpt. treas. 1980-81, sec. 1981, pres. 1984, nat. com. labor relations, Hard Hat award, 1985), Am. Mil. Engrs. (v.p. Alaska chpt. 1978), Alaska Trucking Assn. (bd. dirs. 1986—), Inst. Mcpl. Engrs., Inst. Traffic Engrs., Internat. Orgn. Masters, Mates and Pilots (hon.), Common Sense for Alaska (past pres.), Commonwealth North (charter). Democrat. Presbyterian. Club: San Francisco Tennis. Lodge: Rotary. Home: 4921 Sportsman Dr Anchorage AK 99502-4193 Office: 3601 C St # 4035 Anchorage AK 99503-5925

EASLEY, LOYCE ANNA, painter; b. Weatherford, Okla., June 28, 1918; d. Thomas Webster and Anna Laura (Sanders) Rogers; m. Mack Easley, Nov. 17, 1939; children: June Elizabeth, Roger. BFA, U. Okla., 1943; postgrad., 1947-49; student, Art Students League, N.Y.C., 1977; postgrad., Santa Fe Inst. Fine Arts, 1985. Tchr. Pub. Sch., Okmulgee, Okla., 1946-47, Hobbs, N.Mex., 1947-49; tchr. painting N.Mex. Jr. Coll., Hobbs, 1965-80; tchr. Art Workshops in N.Mex., Okla., Wyoming. Numerous one-woman shows and group exhbns. in mus., univs. and galleries, including Gov.'s Gallery, Santa Fe, Selected Artists, N.Y.C., Roswell (N.Mex.) Mus., N.Mex. State U., Las Cruces, West Tex. Mus., Tex. Tech U., Lubbock; represented in permanent collections USAF Acad., Colorado Springs, Colo., Roswell Mus., Carlsbad (N.Mex.) Mus., Coll. Santa Fe, N.Mex. Supreme Ct, also other pvt. and pub. collections; featured in S.W. Art and Santa Fe mag., 1981, 82. Named Disting. Former Student, U. Okla. Art Sch., 1963; nominated for Gov's. award in Art, N.Mex., 1988. Mem. N.Mex. Artists Equity (lifetime mem. 1963). Democrat. Presbyterian. Home: 10909 Country Club Dr NE Albuquerque NM 87111-6548

EASTER, DAVID WAYNE, surgery educator; b. Phila., Oct. 4, 1955; m. Klansee Clark, Aug. 1977. BS magna cum laude, Graceland Coll., 1977; MD cum laude, Yale U., 1983. Intern U. Calif., San Diego, 1983-84, resident, 1984-88, 88-89, asst. prof. surgery, 1990—. Author: New Applications of Laparoscopy, 1993; contbr. 41 articles to profl. jours.; mem. edit. bd. Jour. Surg. Techniques, 1993—. Fellow Ninewells Hosp. and Med. Sch. Dept. Surgery, Dundee, Scotland, 1989-90, Student Rsch. fellow Am. Liver Found., 1980; Graceland Acad. scholar, 1974-77; Graceland Leadership grantee, 1976-77; recipient U. Calif. Found. Student Teachng award, 1988, Spl. Area Contbn. award, 1977. Mem. AMA, Assn. Acad. Surgery, Am. Coll. Surgeons, San Diego Soc. Gen. Surgeons, Internat. Hepato-biliary Pancreatic Assn., Assn. Surg. Edn., Soc. Am. Gastrointestinal Endoscopic Surgeons, Lambda Delta Sigma. Office: USCD Med Ctr 220 W Arbor Dr San Diego CA 92103-1911

EASTER, GAYL ALMA, nutritionist; b. Wilkes Barre, Pa., Aug. 10, 1953; d. Elmore Worth and Leeta Elma (Sachs) E. BS in Nutritional Scis., U. Conn., 1976. Clin. dietitian St. Mary-Corwin Hosp., Pueblo, Colo., 1976-82; nutritionist, counselor Family Athletic Club, Pueblo, Colo., 1982-83; renal nutritionist Presbyn.-St. Lukes Med. Ctr., Denver, 1983-94; cons. dietitian Mediplex Rehab. Hosp., Thornton, Colo., 1994—; rep. end-stage renal bd. Rocky Mountain Coun. on Renal Nutrition, Colo., 1970s. Author: Guidelines for the Nutritional Intervention of the Adult Dialysis Patient, 1990; author pamphlet: Not Eating Well? Let's Explore the Reasons, 1993; contbr. articles to profl. jours. Cons. Nat. Kidney Found., Denver, 1970-80. Mem. Am. Soc. for Parenteral and Enteral Nutrition, Denver Dietetic Assn. Lutheran.

EASTHAM, THOMAS, foundation administrator; b. Attelboro, Mass., Aug. 21, 1923; s. John M. and Margaret (Marsden) E.; m. Berenice J. Hirsch, Oct. 12, 1946; children: Scott Thomas, Todd Robert. Student English, Northwestern U., 1946-52. With Chgo. American, 1945-56, asst. Sunday editor, 1953-54, feature writer, 1954-56; news editor San Francisco Call Bull., 1956-62, exec. editor, 1962-65; exec. editor, then D.C. bur. chief San Francisco Examiner, 1965-82; press sec. to mayor of San Francisco, 1982-88; v.p., western dir. William Randolph Hearst Founds., 1988—. Served with USMC, 1941-45. Pulitzer prize nominee, 1955. Mem. Am. Soc. Newspaper Editors, Inter-Am. Press Assn., Am., Internat. press insts., White House Corrs. Assn., Nat. Press Club, Ind. Sector, Coun. on Foundations, Commonwealth Club, Sigma Delta Chi. Home: 1473 Bernal Ave Burlingame CA 94010-5559 Office: Hearst Found 90 New Montgomery St Ste 1212 San Francisco CA 94105-4504

EASTIN, KEITH E., lawyer; b. Lorain, Ohio, Jan. 16, 1940; s. Keith Ernest and Jane E. (Heimer) E. A.B., U. Cin., 1963, M.B.A., 1964; J.D., U. Chgo., 1967. Bar: Ill. 1967, Tex. 1974, Calif. 1975, U.S. Supreme Ct. 1975, D.C. 1983. Atty. Vedder, Price, Kaufman & Kammholz, Chgo., 1967-73; v.p., sec., gen. counsel Nat. Convenience Stores, Inc., Houston, 1973-79; ptnr. Payne, Eastin & Widmer, Houston, 1977-83; dep. under sec. U.S. Dept. Interior, 1983-86; prin. dep. asst. sec. USN, 1986-88; ptnr. Hopkins & Sutter, Washington, 1989-91; sr. v.p. Guy F. Atkinson Co., San Francisco, 1991-92; pres. Infrastructure Group, Incline Village, Nev., 1992—; sr. v.p., gen. counsel Guy F. Atkinson Co., 1991-92; dir. Nat. Money Orders Inc., Feast & Co., Inc., Kempco Petroleum Co., Bertman Drilling Co., Pacific Options, Inc., Del Rey Food Svcs., Inc., Stratford Feedyards, Inc.; prin. Westec Environ., Inc., Reno, 1993—. Bd. dirs. Theatre Under the Stars, Houston, Statue of Liberty-Ellis Island Found.; mem. exec. com. Harris County Republican Party, 1976-83. Mem. ABA, Ill. Bar Assn., Tex. Bar Assn., D.C. Bar Assn., State Bar Calif., Beta Gamma Sigma, Phi Delta Phi, Beta Theta Pi. Clubs: University (Houston); Capitol Hill (Washington).

EASTMAN, MICHAEL PAUL, chemistry educator; b. Wis., Apr. 14, 1941; s. Leroy Irons and Virginia Marie (Anderson) E.; m. Frances Lyle, Oct. 23, 1963 (div. Jan. 1976); children: Nathan, Eli; m. Carol Kennedy, Aug. 23, 1980. BA, Carleton Coll., 1963; PhD, Cornell U., 1968. Postdoctoral Los Alamos (N.Mex.) Nat. Lab., 1968-70; asst. prof. chemistry U. Tex., El Paso, 1970-74, assoc. prof. chemistry, 1974-80, prof. chemistry, 1980-88, asst. dean of sci., 1981-84, asst. v.p. acad. affairs, 1984-85; prof. chemistry No. Ariz. U., Flagstaff, 1988—, chmn. dept. chemistry, 1988—, interim dir. environ. sci., 1990-91; elected mem. Assn. Western Univs., Utah, 1990-93; com. chmn. Edn. and Rsch. Coun., 1993; mem. com. on lab. sci. admission requirements Ariz. Bd. Regents, Flagstaff, 1992. Contbr. articles to profl. jours. mem. environ. task force Flagstaff C. of C., 1992—, chmn., 1993. Mem. Sigma Xi, Phi Beta Kappa. Home: 853 Parker Dr Flagstaff AZ 86001-8958 Office: No Ariz U Dept Chemistry PO Box 5698 Flagstaff AZ 86011

EASTMAN, RICHARD PHILLIP, marketing executive; b. Whittier, Calif., Dec. 15, 1938; s. Samuel C. and Virginia E. (Phillips) E.; children: Stephen, Jay. BS, Calif. Polytech. U., 1962; MBA, Pepperdine U., 1979. Cert. flight instr. Prin., owner The Eastman Group, Inc., Newport Beach, Calif., 1968—; contracted through Eastman Group, Inc. v.p. info. svcs. Assoc. Travel, Santa Ana, Calif., 1985-93, chief mktg. officer Air Lanka Ltd., Colombo, Sri Lanka, 1980-85, pres. Polymorphic Sys., Santa Barbara, Calif., 1979-80. Lt. USNR, 1964-66. Republican. Office: The Eastman Group Inc 20321 SW Birch St Ste 201 Newport Beach CA 92660-1756

EASTMOND, DAVID ALBERT, environmental toxicology educator; b. Logan, Utah, Mar. 23, 1956; s. Jefferson Nicholls and Alberta (Van Wagoner) E.; m. Elizabeth Sessions, Aug. 11, 1989; stepchildren: C. Chad Anselmo, Matthew J. Anselmo, Barbara T. Anselmo, Peter R. Anselmo. BS in Zoology, Brigham Young U., 1980, MS in Entomology, 1983; PhD in Environ. Health Scis., U. Calif., Berkeley, 1987. Field technician Brigham Young U., Raft River, Idaho, 1978; field supr. Utah State U., Delta, 1979; rsch. asst. in environ. toxicology Brigham Young U., Provo, 1979-83; intern with Environ. Effects Br., Office Toxic Substances EPA, Washington, 1983; rsch. asst. biochem. toxicology U. Calif., Berkeley, 1983-87; Alexander Hollaender Disting. postdoctoral fellow Livermore Nat. Lab., Livermore, 1987-89; asst. rsch. toxicologist biomed. and environ. health scis. U. Calif., Berkeley, 1989; asst. prof. environ. toxicology dept. entomology U. Calif., Riverside, 1990—; participant internat. program on chem. safety task group WHO, Carshalton Surrey, Eng., 1993; manuscript reviewer Environ. and Molecular Mutagenesis, Mutation Rsch., Mutagenesis, Toxicology and Applied Pharmacology, Chemico-Biol. Interactions, Internat. Jour. Radiation Biology, Cytometry, Cancer Rsch., Am. Jour. Human Genetics, 1987—; cons. on projects assessing potential of projects assessing the potential from human exposure to solvents and groundwater contaminants, 1985—. Contbr. articles to profl. jours.;, chpts. for conf. proceedings; mem. editl. bd. Mutation Rsch., 1994—. Recipient outstanding postdoctoral rsch. presentation award Genetic and Environ. Toxicology Assn. No. Calif., 1988; Alvin S. Barrett scholar Brigham Young U., 1974-75, 77-80. Mem. AAAS, Soc. Toxicology (new investigator 1987), Environ. Mutagen Soc., Sigma Xi, Phi Kappa Phi. Office: U Calif Dept Entomology Riverside CA 92521

EASTON, ROBERT (OLNEY), author, environmentalist; b. July 4, 1915; s. Robert Eastman and Ethel (Olney) E.; m. Jane Faust, Sept. 24, 1940; children: Joan Easton Lentz, Katherine Easton Renga (dec.), Ellen Easton Brumfiel, Jane. Student, Stanford U., 1933-34, postgrad., 1938-39; B.S., Harvard U., 1938; M.A., U. Calif., Santa Barbara, 1960. Ranch hand, day laborer, mag. editor, 1939-42; co-pub., editor Lampasas (Tex.) Dispatch, 1946-50; instr. English Santa Barbara City Coll., 1959-65; writing and pub. cons. U.S. Naval Civil Engring. Lab., Port Hueneme, Calif., 1961-69. Author: The Happy Man, 1943, (with Mackenzie Brown) Lord of Beasts, 1961, (with Jay Monaghan and others) The Book of the American West, 1963, The Hearing, 1964, (with Dick Smith) California Condor: Vanishing American, 1964, Max Brand: The Big Westerner, 1970, Black Tide: The Santa Barbara Oil Spill and Its Consequences, 1972, Guns, Gold and Caravans, 1978, China Caravans: An American Adventurer in Old China, 1982, This Promised Land, 1982, Life and Work, 1988, Power and Glory, 1989, (with Jane Faust Easton) Love and War, 1991; editor: Max Brand's Best Stories, 1967, (with Mackenzie Brown) Bullying the Moqui, 1968, (with Jane Faust Easton) Max Brand's Best Poems, 1992, (with Jane Faust Easton) Max Brand: Collected Stories, 1994; contbr. to numerous mags. including Atlantic and N.Y. Times mag.; also anthologies including Great Tales of the American West. Co-chmn. Com. for Santa Barbara, 1973-81; trustee Santa Barbara Mus. Natural History, 1975-78, rsch. assoc., 1980-83; trustee Santa Barbara Community Environ. Coun., 1974-79; co-founder Sisquoc Sanctuary for Calif. Condor, 1937, also first wilderness area established under Nat. Wilderness Act, Los Padres Nat. Forest, Calif., 1968. Served to 1st lt. inf. U.S. Army, World War II. Recipient Honor award Calif. Conservation Coun., 1975. Home: 2222 Las Canoas Rd Santa Barbara CA 93105-2113

EASTON, ROGER DAVID, art history educator; b. Douglaston, N.Y., Jan. 4, 1923; s. Spencer Garnet and Ruth Natalie (Albright) E.; m. June Marcella Healy, Dec. 21, 1953. BS, SUNY, 1949; MA, State U. Iowa, 1951; EdD, U. Denver, 1958; postgrad., U. Rochester, Fogg Mus., Harvard U. Cert. tchr., N.Y., Colo. Fellow U. Iowa, Iowa City, 1950-51; instr. to assoc. prof. SUNY, Cortland, 1951-58; prof. Ball State U., Muncie, Ind., 1958-85, ret., 1985. One-man shows include S.W. Savs. and Loan, Green Valley, Ariz., 1989; exhibited in group shows at Smithsonian Instn. Crafts Invitational Nat. Traveling Exhibit, 1960-62, Ball State U. Art Gallery, 1977-80, 80-81, Sheldon Swope Art Gallery, Terre Haute, Ind., 1979-80, 83, Ft. Wayne Mus. Art, 1981-82, Tubac Ctr. of the Arts, 1989, 90, Santa Cruz Valley Art Assn., Tubac, Ariz., 1990, 93-95, Kessel-Long Gallery, Scottsdale, Ariz., 1990, So. Ariz. Watercolor Guild, 1991, 92-95, Ariz. Aqueous, 1992, 95, So. Ariz. Art Guild, 1993, 95, Canoa Ctr. Exhbns., 1994-95, Ariz. Watercolor Assn. Phoenix Exhbn., 1990-91, 94-95, and numerous others; contbr. articles to profl. jours. Mem. Nat. Watercolor Soc., So. Ariz. Watercolor Guild, Santa Cruz Valley Art Assn., Ariz. Watercolor Assn., Nat. Art Edn. Assn., Ariz. Art Edn. Assn. Home: 3371 Placita Esconces Green Valley AZ 85614

EATON, DAVID E., city administrator; b. Laconia, N.H., July 15, 1959; s. David Elwell and Doris Aileen (VanBlaricum) E.; m. Judy Kuen Toy, Nov. 21, 1980; children; Meagan Mei-Lai, Nathaniel David. BA, Sangamon State U., 1982; MA, Claremont Coll., 1986. Ordained priest Soto-Zen Buddhist Ch.; lic. real estate broker, Calif. Cmty. outreach worker, caseworker Salvation Army and United Meth. Ministries, Chgo., 1977-82; youth edn. dir. Presbyn. Ch. USA, L.A., 1983-87; mil. intelligence specialist U.S. Dept. Def., 1987; mktg. rep. Anheuser Busch & Adolph Coors, L.A., 1988-90; acctg. tech. Fed. Civil Svc., DOD, L.A., 1990-93; priest, psychotherapist Shoshinkai Fellowship, Phoenix, 1993; job developer, caseworker II dislocated workers program dept. human svcs. City of Phoenix, 1994—. Contbr. articles to profl. jours. Active Chinatown 10k Com., L.A., 1992, Chinese-Am. Citizen's League, Phoenix, 1993-94, Japan-Am. Citizens League, Phoenix, 1993. Recipient Citizens Svc. to Local Cmty. award Castelar Elem. Sch., 1991. Mem. ACA, Am. Mental-Health Counseling Assn., Nat. Employment Counselor Assn., Nat. Employment and Tng. Profl. Assn., Constructive Living Assn. Democrat. Home: 18836 N 15th St Phoenix AZ 85024-8200 Office: City of Phoenix Dislocated Workers Program 1145 E Washington St Phoenix AZ 85034-1009

EATON, GARETH RICHARD, chemistry educator, university dean; b. Lockport, N.Y., Nov. 3, 1940; s. Mark Dutcher and Ruth Emma (Ruston) E.; m. Sandra Shaw, Mar. 29, 1969. BA, Harvard U., 1962; PhD, MIT, 1972. Asst. prof. chemistry U. Denver, 1972-76, assoc. prof., 1976-80, prof., 1980—, dean natural scis., 1984-88, vice provost for rsch., 1988-89; organizer annual Internat. Electron-Paramagnetic Resonance Symposium. Author, editor 2 books; mem. editorial bd. 4 jours.; contbr. articles to profl. jours. Served to lt. USN, 1962-67. Mem. AAAS, Am. Chem. Soc., Royal Soc. Chemistry (London), Internat. Soc. Magnetic Resonance, Soc. Applied Spectroscopy, Am. Phys. Soc., Internat. Electron Paramagnetic Resonance Soc. Office: U Denver Denver CO 80208

EATON, GEORGE WESLEY, JR., petroleum engineer, oil company executive; b. Searcy, Ark., Aug. 3, 1924; s. George Wesley and Inez (Roberson) E.; m. Adriana Amin, Oct. 28, 1971; 1 child, Andrew. BS in Petroleum Engring., U. Okla., 1948. Registered profl. engr. Tex., N.Mex. Petroleum engr. Amoco, Longview, Ft. Worth, Tex., 1948-54; engring. supr. Amoco, Roswell, N.Mex., 1954-59; dist. engr. Amoco, Farmington, N.Mex., 1959-70; constrn. mgr. Amoco Egypt Oil Co., Cairo, 1970-81; ops. mgr. Amoco Norway Oil Co., Stavanger, 1981-84; petroleum cons. G.W. Eaton Cons., Albuquerque, 1984-94; adj. prof. San Juan Coll., Farmington, 1968-70. Bd. dirs. Paradise Hills Civic Assn., Albuquerque, 1986-89; elder Rio Grande Presbyn. Ch., Albuquerque, 1987-90; mem. Rep. Nat. Com., Washington, 1986-92. Mem. N.Mex. Soc. Profl. Engrs. (bd. dirs. 1967-70), Soc. Petroleum Engr. (sr.), Egyptian Soc. Petroleum Engrs. (chmn. 1980-81). Home: 5116 Russell Dr NW Albuquerque NM 87114-4325

EATON, HENRY TAFT, forest products executive, consultant; b. N.Y.C., Aug. 29, 1918; s. Henry Taft and Ina (Kissel) E.; m. Gladys Foote, June 12, 1938 (dec.); children: Penelope, Wendy; m. Phyllis Elaine Thompson, Oct. 13, 1989; stepchildren: Vaile, Danny, Terry, Theresa. Student, Harvard U., 1941. Pres. Eaton-Young Lumber Co., Eugene, Oreg., 1948-68, Henry Eaton & Co., Eugene, 1969-78; owner Henry Eaton & Co., Bend, Oreg., 1979—; pres. Veneer Products Singapore-U.S.A. div., Eugene, 1969-74; v.p. Persis Corp, Honolulu, 1977-79; cons. Bunnings Bros. Pty. Lty., Perth, West Australia, 1982-90, Persis Corp., 1980—. Author: (tech. manual) Tropical Hardwood Plywood, 1972; inventor The Time Wheel. Chmn. Eugene Airport Commn., 1960-67; comdr. CAP, Eugene, 1964-66; mem. mktg. adv. coun. U. Oreg., Eugene, 1965-67. 1st lt. inf. U.S. Army, World War II, ETO. Decorated Purple Heart. Mem. Bend Golf Country Club, South Cowichan Lawn Tennis Club. Republican. Home and Office: 4441 Captains Way Fernandina Beach FL 32034-4351

EATON, JULIA H., counselor; b. N.Y.C., Apr. 13, 1964; d. Gerald Godfrey and Patricia (Vollmer) Hotchkiss; m. David Reed Eaton, Sept. 15, 1990. BA, Denison U., 1986; MA, Mont. State U., 1994. Tchr. asst. The Learning Ctr., Waltham, Mass., 1986-88, leisure and recreation specialist, 1988-90; group home specialist Counterpoint Inc., Livingston, Mont., 1990-93, group home mgr., 1993-95; counselor crisis intervention specialist Mental Health Svcs., Livingston, Mont., 1995—; intern Livingston Mental Health, 1994—. Mem. Am. Counseling Assn. Democrat. Home: 208 SD Livingston MT 59047 Office: Mental Health Svcs Livingston MT 59047

EATON, PAULINE, artist; b. Neptune, N.J., Mar. 20, 1935; d. Paul A. and Florence Elizabeth (Rogers) Friedrich; m. Charles Adams Eaton, June 15, 1957; children: Gregory, Eric, Paul, Joy. BA, Dickinson Coll., 1957; MA, Northwestern U., 1958. Lic. instr., Calif. Instr., Mira Costa Coll., Oceanside, Calif., 1980-82, Idyllwild Sch. Music and Arts, Calif., 1983—; juror, demonstrator numerous art socs. Recipient award Haywood (Calif.) Area Forum for the Arts, 1986. Exhibited one-woman shows Nat. Arts Club, N.Y.C., 1977, Designs Recycled Gallery, Fullerton, Calif., 1978, 80, 84, San Diego Art Inst., 1980, Spectrum Gallery, San Diego, 1981, San Diego Jung Ctr., 1983, Marin Civic Ctr. Gallery, 1984, R. Mondavi Winery, 1987; group shows include Am. Watercolor Soc., 1975, 77, Butler Inst. Am. Art, Youngstown, Ohio, 1977, 78, 79, 81, NAD, 1978, N.Mex. Arts and Crafts Fair, (Best in Show award) 1994, Corrales Bosque Gallery; represented in permanent collections including Butler Inst. Am. Art, St. Mary's Coll., Md., Mercy Hosp., San Diego, Sharp Hosp., San Diego, Redlands Hosp., Riverside, 1986; work featured in books: Watercolor, The Creative Experience, 1978, Creative Seascape Painting, 1980, Painting the Spirit in Nature, 1984, Exploring Painting (Gerald Brommer); author: Crawling to the Light, An Artist in Transition, 1987. Trustee San Diego Art Inst., 1977-78, San Diego Mus. Art, 1982-83. Recipient Best of Show award N.Mex. Arts and Crafts Fair, 1994. Mem. Nat. Watercolor Soc. (exhibited traveling shows 1978, 79, 83, 85), Rocky Mountain Watermedia Soc. (Golden award 1979, Mustard Seed award 1983), Nat. Soc. Painters in Acrylic and Casein (hon.), Watercolor West (Strathmore award 1979, Purchase award 1986), Soc. Experimental Artists (pres. 1989-92, Nautilus Merit award 1992), Marin Arts Guild (instr. 1984-87), San Diego Watercolor Soc. (pres. 1976-77, workshop dir. 1977-80), Artists Equity (v.p. San Diego 1979-81), San Diego Artists Guild (pres. 1982-83), N.Mes. Watercolor Soc. (Grumbacher award), Western Fedn. Watercolor Socs. (chmn. 1983, 3d prize 1982, Grumbacher Gold medal 1983), West Coast Watercolor Soc. (exhbns. chmn. 1983-86, pres. 1989-92), Eastbay Watercolor Soc. (v.p. 1988-90), Soc. Layerists in Multi-Media (bd. dirs. 1992—), Corrales Bosque Gallery (charter mem.). Democrat. Home: 68 Hop Tree Trl Corrales NM 87048-9613

EATON, RICHARD MAXWELL, history educator; b. Grand Rapids, Mich., Dec. 8, 1940; s. Robert Menzo and Miriam (Adams) E. BA, Coll. Wooster, 1962; MA, U. Va., 1967, U. Wis., 1968; PhD, U. Wis., 1972. Asst. prof. history U. Ariz., Tucson, 1972-78, assoc. prof., 1978-94, prof., 1994—. Author: Sufis of Bijapur, 1978, The Rise of Islam and The Bengal Frontier, 1993. Mem. Assn. Asian Studies, Mid. East Studies Assn. Office: Univ Ariz Dept History Tucson AZ 85721

EATON, THOMAS CLARK, insurance and financial consultant; b. Fresno, Calif., Nov. 24, 1952; s. Robert Louis and Polly (Gregory) E.; m. Deborah Thomason, Nov. 19, 1983; children: Jonathan, Elisabeth. BA, Pacific U., 1976. Salesman Fred S. James & Co., Portland, Oreg., 1974-75; v.p., treas. Eaton & Eaton Ins. Brokers, Fresno, 1976-84; mgr. truck ins. divsn. Marsh & McLennan, San Francisco, 1984-85; chmn., pres. Wyndham Ins. Svcs. Ltd., Burlingame, Calif., 1985-91; ind. cons. Fresno, Calif., 1991—; chmn. bd. Wyndham Cons. Svcs., Burlingame, Calif., 1985-91. Dir. San Mateo (Calif.) County Vol. Ctr., 1987—. Mem. Ind. Ins. Agts. and Brokers, Fedn. Afro Asian Insurors and Reinsurors, Sunnyside Country Club, Green Hills Country Club. Republican. Office: 287 W Vartikian Ave Fresno CA 93704-1547

EATON, WILLIAM LEE, lawyer; b. Effingham, Ill., Mar. 14, 1947; s. Harold William and Mary Ellen (Reaugh) E.; m. Mary Ellen Nicholson, Nov. 9, 1968; children: Jason Hale, Joshua Garth, Meghan Ellen. BA in History, U. Ill., 1969; JD with distinction, U. Ariz., 1972. Bar: Ariz. 1973, U.S. Dist. Ct. Ariz. 1973. Ptnr. Boyle, Brown & Eaton, Prescott, Ariz., 1973-81, Boyle, Eaton & Pecharich, Prescott, 1981-85; pvt. practice law Prescott, 1985-86, 87—; ptnr. Eaton & Furlong, Prescott, 1986-87; instr. Yavapai Coll., Prescott, 1976-86, Embry Riddle U., Prescott, 1984—; juvenile commr. Yavapai County Superior Ct., Prescott, 1983-86. Chmn. mayor's ad hoc com., Prescott, 1981; regional commr. Ariz. Youth Soccer Assn., Prescott, 1976-81. Recipient Disting. Svc. award Ariz. Ct. Appeals, 1984. Mem. Ariz. Bar Assn. (chmn. 1985, disting. svc. cert. 1985), Bd. Legal Specialization. Democrat. Home: 1976 Shadow Valley Dr Prescott AZ 86301-3931 Office: PO Box 2695 Prescott AZ 86302-2695

EAVES, STEPHEN DOUGLAS, vocational administrator, educator; b. Honolulu, Aug. 30, 1944; s. Alfred Aldee and Phyllis Clarissa (Esty) E.; m. Sally Ann Winslow, Apr. 27, 1974; children: Trevor Bernard, Lindsay Douglas, Christian Francis. BA in Polit. Sci., U. Hawaii, 1967; MS in Bus. Mgmt., U. Ark., 1974; postgrad., Colo. State U. Cert. secondary tchr., prin., vocat. dir., post secondary bus. tchr., Colo. Commd. 2d lt. USAF, 1967, advanced through grades to lt. col., ret., 1989; aerospace sci. tchr. Adams County Sch. Dist. 50, Westminster, Colo., 1989-94, vocat. dir./asst. prin., 1994—; cons. Dept. of Edn., Colo., 1993—. Eucharistic min. Spirit of Christ Cath. Ch., Arvada, Colo., 1989—. Decorated Silver Star, Disting. Flying Cross, Air medals, Commendation medals, Air Force Achievement medal. Mem. ASCD, Coun. for Exceptional Children, Am. Vocat. Assn., Colo. Vocat. Assn., Colo. Assn. Vocat. Adminstrs., Colo. Assn. Sch. Execs., Am. Nat. Rose Soc., Royal Nat. Rose Soc., Lions (sec. Adams Centennial chpt. 1991-92, Lion of Yr. 1992), Elks, Phi Delta Kappa, Omicron Tau Delta. Home: 8708 Independence Way Arvada CO 80005-1247 Office: Career Enrichment Park 7300 Lowell Blvd Westminster CO 80030-4821

EBBINGA, CRYSTALLE YVONNE, social services administrator; b. Wall, S.D., Jan. 23, 1936; d. Earl Benjamin and Josie Amanda (Lee) Adamson; m. Gerald Richard Ebbinga, June 3, 1961; children: Kurtis Herm, Spencer Kirk, Brittanee Leigh. MusB, MacPhail Coll. Music, Mpls., 1960. Tchr. elem. music Boyceville (Wis.) Consol., 1960-61; tchr. and music supr. St. Louis Park (Minn.) Elem. Sch., 1961-63, St. Crois Consol. Sch. Dist., Hammond and Roberts, Wis., 1963-66; substitute tchr. Prince Albert (Sask., Can.) Pub. Schs., 1979-80; parish asst. First Luth. Ch., Pomona, Calif., 1981-86; adminstrv. asst. LaVerne (Calif.) U., 1986-87; asst. to gen. dir. YMCA, Pomona, 1988-89; dir. Hill and Dale Child Devel. Ctr., Las Vegas, Nev., 1989-90; pres., CEO St. Thomas Child and Family Ctr., Great Falls, Mont., 1990—. Editor The Supporter newsletter, 1992-94. Chmn. agy. dirs. United Way, Great Falls, Mont., 1992-94; bd. dirs. Families Count, Great Falls, 1992—; adv. bd. Families Self-Sufficiency (Great Falls Housing Authority), 1993—; lobbyist Mont. Child Care Assn., Helena, 1992; asst. chmn. Great Falls Community Needs Assessment Com.; mem. steering com. Dept. Family Svcs. Parnership Project. Mem. NAFE, Soc. for Non-Profit Orgn., Nat. Parent Aide, Mont. Coun. for Families, Healthy Mothers Healthy Babies, C.M. Russell Mus., Great Falls Ad Club, Great Falls C. of C. (Leadership Great Falls 1991). Home: 6 Meadowlark Rdg Rd Great Falls MT 59405-5532 Office: St Thomas Child & Family Ct 416 23rd St N Great Falls MT 59401-2847

EBBS, GEORGE HEBERLING, JR., management consulting company executive; b. Sewickley, Pa., Sept. 20, 1942; s. George Heberling and Mae Isabelle (Miller) E.; m. Agnes Rak, 1989; children: Stacey Kirsten, Cynthia Lynn. BS in Engring., Purdue U., 1964; MBA, U. Wash., 1966; PhD in Bus., Columbia U., 1970. Sr. engr. Boeing Co., Seattle, 1966; assoc. Booz Allen & Hamilton, N.Y.C., 1969-72, sr. v.p., 1974-86; v.p. Fry Cons., N.Y.C., 1973; chmn., pres. The Canaan Group, Park City, Utah, 1986—; adj. prof. Columbia U., N.Y.C., 1978-80. Trustee Utah Opera. Bronfman fellow, Columbia U., N.Y.C., 1967; Purdue Old Master. Mem. Met. Opera Club, Wings Club, Iron Key, Omicron Delta Kappa, Beta Gamma Sigma. Presbyterian. Home: 2565 Fairway Village Dr Park City UT 84060-7023 Office: The Canaan Group Ltd PO Box 680580 2052 Prospector Ave Park City UT 84068

EBEL, DAVID M., federal judge; b. 1940. BA, Northwestern U., 1962; JD, U. Mich., 1965. Law clk. assoc. justice Byron White U.S. Supreme Ct., 1965-66; pvt. practice Davis, Graham & Stubbs, Denver, 1966-88; judge U.S. Ct. Appeals (10th cir.), Denver, 1988—; adj. prof. law U. Denver Law Sch., 1987-89; sr. lectr. fellow Duke U. Sch. Law, 1992-94. Mem. Am. Coll. Trial Lawyers, Colo. Bar Assn. (v.p. 1982), Jud. Conf. U.S. (com. on codes of conduct 1991—, co-chair 10th cir. gender bias task force 1994—). Office: US Ct Appeals 1823 Stout St Rm 109L Denver CO 80257-0001

EBERL, PATRICIA JO, professional society administrator, editor; b. Cleve., May 26, 1947; d. David Reidinger and Peggy L. (Laughlin)

Buschman; m. Dennis D. Eberl, Mar. 7, 1970; children: Karuna Sky, Lucas Elliot. Student, Conn. Coll. for Women, 1965-67; BA, Case Western Reserve U., 1970; postgrad., U. Colo., Denver, 1983, U. Colo., Boulder, 1993-94. ESL tchr. Jefferson County Sch. Dist., Evergreen, Lakewood, Colo., 1983-85; free lance editor Evergreen, 1986-89; mgr./editor Clay Minerals Soc., Boulder, Colo., 1989—; editl. intern Human Rights Info. Ctr. of Coun. of Europe, Strasbourg, France, 1992. Editor: The Third Sector, 1982-83, The Hardware's Mountain Handbook, 1989, (quar. publ.) CMS News, 1989—. County coord. fgn. langs. in elem. schs., Jefferson County Schs., Lakewood, 1982-85; with edn./publicity divsn. Global Response, Boulder, 1991-93; prodn. editor, advocate Boulder Action for Soviet Jewry, 1991—; vol. Am. Indian Sci. & Engring. Soc., Boulder, 1993; mem./sponsor Colo. Friends of Tibet; mem. Native Am. Rights Fund. Office: Clay Minerals Soc PO Box 4416 Boulder CO 80306

EBERLE, MICHAEL LEE, air force officer; b. Evanston, Ill., Sept. 24, 1955; s. Marcus Herbert and E. Louise (Wilkins) E.; m. Karen Ann Straight, Aug. 12, 1978; children: Ernest James, Matthew Jonathan, Janet Christine. BS in Aero. Engring., USAF Acad., 1977; MS in Aero. and Astronautics, U. Wash., 1978. Registered profl. engr., Va.; lic. single and multi engine comml. pilot. Commd. 2d lt. USAF, 1977—, advanced through grades to lt. col., 1993; student pilot 82d Flying Tng. Wing, Williams AFB, Ariz., 1978-79, T-38 instr. pilot/acad. instr., 1979-82; instructional program developer 3305 Sch. Squadron, Randolph AFB, Tex., 1982-84; asst. prof. dept. mechanics U.S. Mil. Acad., West Point, N.Y., 1984-87; flight comdr./chief acads. 47th Flying Tng. Wing, Laughlin AFB, Tex., 1987-89; comdr. companion trainer program detachment 43d Air Refueling Wing, Malmstrom, Mont., 1989-92; chief companion trainer program sect. 15th Air Force, Travis AFB, Calif., 1992—. Contbr. articles to profl. jours. Coach N.E. Youth Soccer Assn., San Antonio, 1983; referee Laughlin-Del Rio Soccer Assn., 1987-88; mem. Civairs, Great Falls, Mont., 1989-92. NSF fellow, 1977-78. Mem. AIAA (sr.), Air Force Assn., USAF Acad. Assn. Grads., Order of Daedalians. Home: 101 Freedom Ct Vacaville CA 95687-6778

EBERSOLE, MARTHA C., writer and producer; b. San Antonio, Aug. 13, 1942; d. Herman McQuin and Mary Katherine (Santos Coy) Holland; children: Jennifer Ebersole Lawson, Joshua. Feature/staff writer Pacific Art and Travel, 1988, Maui Inc. Mag., 1989; reporter/feature writer Garden Island Newspaper, 1990-93; pres. Shared Vision Prodns., Hanapepe, Hawaii, 1993—; script writer and artistic dir. Ho'olokahi Arts and Cultural Troup at Children's Internat. Arts Festival, Guiyang, China, 1993. Producer, dir., writer Martha's Friends-PBS Doeumentary; author plays and screenplays: The Legend of Kama Pua'a, Out of Montgomery, Law Abiding Citizens, texas Tacky, 1984, The 12 Marias, 1991, The Houston Mutiny, 1992 (winner screenwriting competition Hawaii Internat. Film Festival); author books: Triumph in the Face of Disaster, 1993; contbr. articles to profl. jours. Sec. Spiritual Assembly of the Baha'is of Waimea. Hawaii State Commn. on Status of Women grantee, 1993. Mem. Kauai Prodrs. Assn., Kauai Soc. Latino's (charter mem. Kauai chpt.).

EBERWEIN, BARTON DOUGLAS, construction company executive, consultant; b. Balt., Aug. 19, 1951; s. Bruce George and Thelma Joyce (Cox) E. BS, U. Oreg., 1974, MBA, 1988. Sales mgr. Teleprompter of Oreg., Eugene, 1974-75; pres., owner Oreg. Images, Eugene, 1975-80; mktg. mgr. Clearwater Prodns., Eugene, 1980-82; sales mgr. Western Wood Structures, Portland, Oreg., 1982-84, mktg. coordinator, 1984-85, mktg. dir., 1985-89; dir. bus. devel. Hoffman Constrn. Co., Portland, 1989-93, v.p., 1993—. Bd. dirs. N.W. Youth Corps, Eugene, 1984—, Police Activity League, 1991, Portland Arts and Lectrs., 1994—; vol. bd. dirs. Goodwill, Oreg. Symphony. Mem. Soc. Mktg. Profl. Svcs., Am. Mktg. Assn., Univ. Club, Founders Club, Riverside Athletic Club. Democrat. Presbyterian. Home: 5639 SW Menefee Dr Portland OR 97201-2781 Office: Hoffman Constrn Co 1300 SW 6th Ave Portland OR 97201-3464

EBI, KRISTIE LEE, epidemiologist, consultant; b. Detroit, Nov. 17, 1950; d. Albert R. and Dorothy (Wicen) Ebi; 1 child, Katherine M. Kryston. MS, MIT, 1977; MPH, U. Mich., 1983, PhD, 1985. Biochem. rsch. asst. Upjohn Co., Kalamazoo, 1973-74; toxicologist Equitable Environ. Health, Inc., Rockville, Md., 1977-78; indsl. toxicologist GM, Detroit, 1978-81; rsch. fellow London Sch. Hygiene and Tropical Medicine, 1985-87; rsch. asst. Med. Coll. of St. Bartholomew's Hosp., London, 1988-90; sr. scientist Failure Analysis Assocs., Inc., Menlo Park, Calif., 1990-93; mgr. Electric Power Rsch. Inst., Palo Alto, Calif., 1993—. Contbr. articles to sci. jours. Mem. Am. Coll. Epidemiology, Soc. for Epidemiologic Rsch., Internat. Epidemiologic Assn., Soc. Toxicology (assoc.), Mortar Bd. Office: EMF Health Studies Program Electric Power Rsch Inst 3412 Hillview Ave Palo Alto CA 94304-1395

EBIE, WILLIAM D., museum director; b. Akron, Ohio, Feb. 7, 1942; s. William P. and Mary Louise (Karam) E.; m. Gwyn Anne Schumacher, Apr. 11, 1968 (div. Jan. 1988); children: Jason William, Alexandra Anne; m. Mary Teresa Hayes, June 10, 1989. BFA, Akron Art Inst., 1964; MFA, Calif. Coll. of Arts and Crafts, 1968. Graphic artist Alameda County Health Dept., Oakland, Calif., 1967-68; instr. painting Fla. A&M U., Tallahassee, 1968-69; instr. photography Lawrence (Kans.) Adult Edn. Program, 1969-70; asst. dir. Roswell (N.Mex.) Mus. & Art Ctr., 1971-87, dir., 1987—; juror various art exhbns., 1971—; panelist N.Mex. Arts Divsn., Santa Fe, 1983-87; field reviewer Inst. for Mus. Svcs., 1988-90; mem. State Capitol Renovation Art Selection Com., Santa Fe, 1991-92; bd. dirs. State Capitol Found., Santa Fe. Chmn. Roswell Cultural Arts Com. Mem. Am. Assn. of Mus., Mountain Plains Mus. Assn., N.Mex. Assn. of Mus. Democrat. Office: Roswell Mus & Art Ctr 100 W 11th St Roswell NM 88201-4910

EBLING, FANNY MARMOL, microbiologist, medical educator; b. Guayaquil, Ecuador, Oct. 23, 1933; d. Enrique J. and Isabel A. (Cevallos) Marmol; divorced; children: Tanya, Alan. BS, Coll. of Guayaquil, 1954, PhD in Chemistry and Natural Sci., 1959. Tech. asst. Nat. Inst. Health, Guayaquil, 1958-59, head virology sect., 1959-64; Fulbright fellow U. Pitts., 1961-62; cancer rsch. scientist in virology Roswell Park Meml. Inst., Buffalo, 1964-69, cancer rsch. scientist in biol. resources, 1972-73; rsch. scientist, dept. supt. preventive medicine SUNY, Buffalo, 1969-70; rsch. asst. rheumatology Washington U., St. Louis, 1978-83; asst. prof. medicine/rheumatology UCLA, 1983-89, assoc. prof., 1989—. Contbr. articles to profl. jours., chpt. to book. Mem. AAAS, N.Y. Acad. Scis. Republican. Roman Catholic. Office: UCLA Sch Medicine Divsn Rheumatology 1000 Veteran Ave Rm 32-48 Los Angeles CA 90095-1670

EBNER, REINHARD, cell biologist; b. Kötzting, Germany, Feb. 11, 1957; came to U.S., 1989; s. Anton and Maria (Probst) E. Diploma in Biology, U. Regensburg, Germany, 1982; PhD, U. Osnabrück, Germany, 1987. Asst. prof. U. Osnabrück, Germany, 1987-89; postdoctoral fellow Genentech, Inc., South San Francisco, 1989-91; vis. scientist U. Calif., San Francisco, 1991—. Contbr. articles to profl. jours. Recipient Postdoctoral Rsch. fellowship U. Calif., 1992—; grantee in field. Office: U Calif Growth and Development San Francisco CA 94143-0640

EBY, MICHAEL JOHN, marketing research and technology consultant; b. South Bend, Ind., Aug. 3, 1949; s. Robert T. and Eileen Patricia (Holmes) E.; m. Judith Alyson Gaskell, May 17, 1980; children: Elizabeth, Katherine. Student, Harvey Mudd Coll., 1969-70; BS in Biochemistry with high honors, U. Md., 1972, MS in Chemistry, 1977; postgrad., IMEDE, Lausanne, Switzerland, 1984. Product mgr. LKB Instruments Inc., Rockville, Md., 1976-79; mktg. mgr. LKB-Produkter AB, Bromma, Sweden, 1979-87; strategic planning mgr. Pharmacia LKB Biotech. AB, Bromma, 1987-88; dir. mktg. Am. Bionetics, Hayward, Calif., 1988-89; pres. PhorTech Internat., Belmont, Calif., 1989—. Author: The Electrophoresis Explosion, 1988, Electrophoresis in the Nineties, 1990, DNA Amplification, 1993, DNA Sequencing, 1993, Blotting and Hybridization, 1993, Densitometers and Image Analysis, 1993, Capillary Electrophoresis, 1993, HPLC in the Life Sciences, 1994, Molecular Biology Reagent Systems, 1994, Global Laboratory Product Usage, 1994, DIJA Diagnostics, 1995, Microplate Equipment, 1995, Synthetic Oligonucleotides, 1995, Electrophoretic Gel Media, 1995, Visualization Reagents, 1995; contbr. articles to profl. jours. Mem. AAAS, Am. Chem. Soc., Am. Soc. CellBiology, Am. Electrophoresis Soc., Internat. Electrophoresis Soc., Spirit of LKB Internat. Assn., U. Md. Alumni Assn., San Carlos C. of C. Episcopalian. Office: PhorTech Internat 238 Crestview Dr San Carlos CA 94070

ECCLES, MATTHEW ALAN, golf course and landscape architect; b. Ft. Dodge, Iowa, Apr. 19, 1956; s. Guy Eldon Jr. and Mary Ellen (Baldwin) E.; m. Debra Kay Sorenson, Mar. 19, 1983; children: Stephanie Ann, Jason Alan. BS in Landscape Architecture, Iowa State U., 1978. Registered landscape architect, Kans., Minn. From project mgr. to dir. golf course design THK Assocs., Inc., Greenwood Village, Colo., 1980-94; pres. Eccles Design Inc., Englewood, Colo., 1994—. Mem. Am. Soc. Landscape Architects, U.S. Golf Assn., Golf Course Supts. Assn. Am., Nat. Golf Found., Nat. Ski Patrol, Tau Sigma Delta. Home: 8120 S Monaco Cir Englewood CO 80112-3022 Office: Eccles Design Inc 8120 S Monaco Cir Englewood CO 80112-3022

ECCLES, SPENCER FOX, banker; b. Ogden, Utah, Aug. 24, 1934; s. Spencer Stoddard and Hope (Fox) E.; m. Cleone Emily Peterson, July 21, 1958; children: Clista Hope, Lisa Ellen, Katherine Ann, Spencer Peterson. B.S., U. Utah, 1956; M.A., Columbia U., 1959; degree in Bus. (hon.), So. Utah State Coll., 1982; LLB (hon.), Westminster Coll., Salt Lake City, 1986. Trainee First Nat. City Bank, N.Y.C., 1959-60; with First Security Bank of Utah, Salt Lake City, 1960-61, First Security Bank of Idaho, Boise, 1961-70; exec. v.p. First Security Corp. Salt Lake City, 1970-75, pres., 1975-86, chief operating officer, 1980-82, chmn. bd. dirs., chief exec. officer, 1982—; dir. Union Pacific Corp., Anderson Lumber Co., Zions Corp., Merc. Instn.; mem. adv. council U. Utah Bus. Coll. Served to 1st lt. U.S. Army. Recipient Pres.'s Circle award Presdl. Commn., 1984, Minuteman award Utah N.G., 1988; Named Disting. Alumni U. Utah, 1988. Mem. Am. Bankers Assn., Assn. Bank Holding Cos., Assn. Res. City Bankers, Salt Lake Country Club, Alta Club. Office: 1st Security Corp PO Box 30006 79 S Main St Salt Lake City UT 84130*

ECHEVESTE, JOHN ANTHONY, public relations consultant; b. Compton, Calif., Dec. 14, 1949; s. John Robert and Margaret (Suarez) E.; m. Patrician Ann Griffin, Sept. 28, 1985; childen: John Matthew, Michael Anthony. BA in Comm., Calif. State U., Fullerton, 1973. Reporter San Gabriel Valley Daily Tribune, West Covina, Calif., 1976; dir. comm. TELACU, L.A., 1977-82, v.p. comm., 1985-88; adminstrv. asst. Rep. Matthew Martinez, Rosemead, Calif., 1982; mgr. pub. com. So. Calif. Assn. Govts., L.A., 1982-85; ptnr. Valencia, Maldonado & Echeveste, Pasadena, Calif., 1988—. Chmn. East L.A. YMCA, 1993-94; mem. Calif. com. comms. Am. Cancer Soc., 1991; mem. cultural adv. bd. L.A. County Mus. Art, 1988; mem. L.A. Regional Family Planning Coun., 1990; chmn. comm. San Gabriel Valley chpt. United Way, 1991. Mem. Hispanic Pub. Rels. Assn. (founder, pres., bd. dirs. 1982—). Democrat. Office: 117 E Colorado Blvd Ste 510 Pasadena CA 91105-1954

ECK, DENNIS K., supermarket chain executive; b. 1942. Exec. v.p. Am. Stores Co., 1983-90, COO, chmn. bd., 1988-90; past pres., COO, vice chmn. bd. Vons Cos. Inc., now dir. Office: Vons Cos Inc PO Box 3338 618 Michillinda Ave Arcadia CA 91007-6300*

ECKARD, ROY CONRAD (CONNIE ECKARD), communications consultant, writer, editor; b. Fulton, N.Y., Dec. 25, 1933; s. Frank Brewer and Rachel Hester (Warner) E.; m. Betty Joyce Deaux, May 29, 1975 (div. 1974); children: Andrea Lea, Charles Kevin, Steven Deaux; m. Patricia Harold Brown, Apr. 21, 1975 (div. 1986); m. Donna Irene Wolf, Aug. 8, 1988; children: Shirley Ann Wolf, Debra Sue Wolf. BA in English and Journalism, A&M Coll. Tex., 1957; postgrad., Tex. A&M U., 1968-70; PhD in Comm. Mgmt., Pacific Western U., L.A., 1985; PhD (hon.), Clayton U., 1983; LLD (hon.), Pacific States U., 1986. Internal comm. mgr. Tex. Instruments Inc., Dallas, 1963-68; dir. publs. Assn. Former Students, College Station, Tex., 1968-71; publs. coord. Skelly Oil Co., Tulsa, 1971-77; publs. editor Getty Refining and Mktg. Co., Tulsa, 1977-80; spl. comm. mgr. Atlantic Richfield Co., L.A., 1980-84; exec. prin. The Communicationist, L.A., 1984-85; employee comm. specialist Aircraft divsn. Northrop Corp., Hawthorne, Calif., 1985-86; sr. mgmt. systems analyst Electro-Mech. divsn. Northrop Corp., Anaheim, Calif., 1986-88; mgr. employee comm. LTV Corp., Dallas, 1988-91; v.p. Editorial Svcs., Dallas, 1991-92; mgmt. comm. specialist Westinghouse Hanford Co., Richland, Wash., 1992-93; sr. staff asst. ICF Kaiser Hanford Co., Richland, 1993—; mng. editor Homesick Texan, 1991-93. Contbr. articles to profl. publs.; contbg. editor Comm. Illustrated, 1984-86. Mem. pub. rels. com. Hanford 50th Anniversary, Richland, 1993-94; mem. corps. devel. coun. Tex. A&M U., College Station, 1989—; chair ROTC adv. coun. Calif. State U.-Long Beach, 1986-88; mem. admissions adv. panel USAF Acad., Colorado Springs, 1984-87; singer gospel, recovery No Half Measures, Richland, 1993—; performer Richard Players, 1994—; softball player Columbia Basin A&M Club, Richland, 1992—; allocation rev. team Tri-Cities Corp. Coun. for Arts, Richland, 1995—. Col. USAFR, 1957-89. Named Admissions Liaison Officer of Yr., USAF Acad./Air Force ROTC, Colorado Springs, 1987; recipient Dist. Tech. Comm. award Soc. Tech. Comm., Dallas, 1992, Matrix award Women in Comm., Inc., Dallas, 1992. Mem. Internat. Assn. Bus. Communicators (acredited, v.p. fin. 1973-75, dist.-at-large rep. 1994—, Gold Quill award 1972, 75, 79, 81, 82, Chmn.'s award 1990), Tulsa/Dallas chpt. Internat. Assn. Bus. Communicators (life, treas. Dallas 1966, pres. Tulsa 1979, numerous awards 1965-93), Soc. Profl. Journalists (chair various coms. 1967, 83), Women in Comm., Inc., Air Force Assn. (life, v.p. edn. L.A. chpt. 1984-88, Merit award 1985), Res. Officers Assn. (life, v.p. Air Force Tulsa 1979-80). Republican. Mem. Christian Ch. Home: 1321 Perkins Ave Richland WA 99352-3106 Office: ICF Kaiser Hanford Co PO Box 888 Richland WA 99352-0888

ECKARDT, CHARLES LINCOLN, university official, accountant; b. Phila., Feb. 2, 1930; s. George Herbert and Lillian Louisa (Marsden) E.; m. Eillean Jeannie Young, Mar. 16, 1957. BA in Bus. Adminstrn., Franklin & Marshall, 1977; MDiv., Phila. Theol. Sem., 1977. Pastor Third Reformed Presbyn. Ch., Phila., 1956-65; contr. Quarryville (Pa.) Presbyn. Home Inc., 1965-74; fin. dir. World Presbyn. Missions, Inc., Wilmington, Del., 1974-83; contr. Tri Mark, Inc., New Castle, Del., 1983-91, Medco Rsch., Inc., L.A., 1992-93; controller Pacific Oaks Coll., Pasadena, Calif., 1993—. Mem. Inst. Mgmt. Accts. (bd. dirs. West Los Angeles chpt. 1991-92, San Fernando Valley chpt. 1994—). Republican. Mem. Reformed Church in America.

ECKBO, GARRETT, landscape architect, urban designer; b. Cooperstown, N.Y., Nov. 28, 1910; s. Axel and Theodora (Munn) E.; m. Arline Williams, Sept. 17, 1937; children: Marilyn Kweskin, Alison Peper. B.S., U. Calif., Berkeley, 1935; M. Landscape Architecture, Harvard U., 1938; DFA honoris causa, U. N. Mex., 1992. Landscape architect Armstrong Nurseries, Ontario, Calif., 1935-36, Farm Security Adminstrn., U.S. Dept. Agr., San Francisco, 1939-42; pvt. practice landscape architecture San Francisco Bay Area, 1942-46, 65—, L.A., 1946-65; vis. lectr. landscape architecture U. So. Calif., 1948-56; prof. landscape architecture U. Calif., Berkeley, 1965-78; chmn. dept. landscape architecture U. Calif., 1965-69. Author: Landscape for Living, 1950, The Art of Home Landscaping, 1956, Urban Landscape Design, 1965, The Landscape We See, 1969, Home Landscape, 1978, Public Landscape, 1978; spl. issue Philosophy of Landscape, Process: Architecture 90 Tokyo Japan. Recipient numerous awards including; Calif. Gov.'s award for Union Bank Sq. Los Angeles, 1966; AIA citation for excellence in community architecture for Fresno (Calif.) Mall, 1965; Am. Soc. Landscape Architects medal, 1975; merit award for Shelby Farms, Memphis, 1976; spl. award for U. N.Mex., 1978; honor award for Tucson Community Center, 1978; certificate of achievement in publ. and writing Harvard U. Dept. Landscape Architecture, 1976. Fellow Am. Soc. Landscape Architects; mem. Internat. Fedn. Landscape Architects, World Soc. for Ekistics. Home and Office: 1006 Cragmont Ave Berkeley CA 94708-1412

ECKEL, JAMES ROBERT, JR., financial planner; b. Morley, Tenn., Nov. 3, 1927; s. James Robert and Jane Scott (Seymour) E. BS magna cum laude, U. Tenn., 1953, MS, 1957; JD, U. West L.A., 1974. CFP; enrolled agt.; registered patent agt. Instr. elec. engring. U. Tenn., 1953-57, U. Wis., 1957-62; sr. engr. Northrop Corp., L.A., 1962-66; staff engr. TRW Systems, L.A., 1966-69; sr. project engr. Hughes Aircraft Co., Culver City, Calif., 1969-89; fin. planner Culver City, 1989—; real estate broker, Calif. With USN, 1946-49. Mem. IEEE, Am. Inst. Aeros. and Astronautics, Am. Soc. for Engring. Edn., Sigma Xi, Kappa Sigma, Omicron Delta Kappa, Phi Kappa Phi, Tau Beta Pi, Eta Kappa Nu, Phi Eta Sigma. Episcopalian. Home and Office: 5104 Copperfield Ln Culver City CA 90230-7501

ECKELMAN, RICHARD JOEL, engineering specialist; b. Bklyn., Mar. 25, 1951; s. Leon and Muriel (Brietbart) E.; m. Janet Louise Fenton, Mar. 21, 1978; children: Christie, Melanie, Erin Leigh. Student, Ariz. State U., 1988-91. Sr. engr., group leader nondestructive testing Engring. Fluor Corp., Irvine, Calif., 1979-83; sr. engr. nondestructive testing McDonnell Douglas Helicopter Co., Mesa, Ariz., 1983-91; engring. specialist Convair div. Gen. Dynamics, San Diego, 1991-94; sr. tech. specialist McDonnell Douglas Techs., Inc., San Diego, 1994—. Mem. Am. Soc. Nondestructive Testing (nat. aerospace com. 1987—, sec. Ariz. chpt. 1987-88, treas. 1988—, sect. chmn. 1989—, sect. bd. dirs. 1990-91), Am. Soc. Quality Control, Soc. Mfg. Engrs., Porsche Owners Club Am., Lindbergh Yacht Club. Home: 12408 Carmel Cape San Diego CA 92130

ECKERMAN, ROY EMMANUEL, clergyman; b. Grantsburg, Wis., July 12, 1921; s. Carl Adolph and Esther (Carlson) E.; m. Evelyn Mae Tarasenko, Nov. 1, 1944; children: Arva Dell Mae Eckerman Seltzer, Ginger Sue Eckerman Kent. BA, Union Coll., 1944; MEd, Ind. U., 1965. Ordained clergyman, Adventist Ch., 1948. Clegyman Iowa Conf., Spencer, 1944-49, S.D. Conf., Aberdeen, 1949-51, Mich. Conf., Pt. Huron, Escanaba, 1951-56, Ind. Conf., Bloomington, 1956-63, Upper Columbia Conf., Coeur d'Alene, Idaho, 1963-68; dir. pub. rels. Upper Columbia Conf., Spokane, Wash., 1968-73; dir. found. and corp. rels. Loma Linda (Calif.) U., 1973-84; pres., trustee Opportunity With Legacy Found., Salinas, Calif., 1977—. State conf. exec. com. Lansing, Mich., 1952-55, Spokane, 1964-69; treas. Ministeral Assn., Coeur d'Alene, 1966-67. Republican. Home: 25199 Casiano Dr Salinas CA 93908-8956 Office: Opportunity With Legacy Found 25199 Casiano Dr Salinas CA 93908-8956

ECKERMANN, GERALD CARLTON, writer, corporate executive; b. Covina, Calif., Feb. 10, 1934; s. Carlton Herman and Ethel Marie (Argue) E.; m. Gwendolyn Wegeforth, Feb. 10, 1990; children: G. Kevin, Darci Lee, Darin Allen. BBA, UCLA, 1956. Personnel specialist Gen. Dymanics/Astronautics, San Diego, Calif., 1960-65; dir. personnel Computer Scis. Corp., El Segundo, Calif., 1965-66; internal cons. ITT, N.Y.C., 1966-71; v.p. personnel Kaiser Industries, Oakland, Calif., 1971-75; cons. prin. Exec. Mgmt. Cons., Walnut Creek, Calif., 1975-77; dir. personnel Lawrence Livermore Labs., Livermore, Calif., 1977; dir. regional practice compensation A.S. Hensen, L.A., 1978-81; gen. mgr. Security Corp. of Am., Westlake Village, Calif., 1981-82; mgmt. cons. Coopers & Lybrand CPAs, L.A., 1982-83, Grant-Thorton CPAs, L.A., 1983-86, Legal Info. Tech. Group, L.A., 1986-90; pres. Marina Bus. Svcs., 1990-92; CFO LaserCare, 1992—; dir. Transp. Scis. Corp., L.A., 1979—. Author: Price of Ambition, 1986, Forgotten Man, 1988, Amethyst Idol, 1989, Echos from the Past, 1990, Women Ask...Men Answer, 1991. Vice chmn. bd. trustees West Coast U., L.A., 1979-89; nat. rep. Boy Scouts Am., 1973; v.p. Mt. Diablo Coun., 1974-75; bd. dirs. Mt. Diablo Rehab. Ctr., Alameda County Counseling Ctr., 1973-76. With USN, 1956-62; commdr. USNR. Mem. Am. Compensation Assn., Am. Soc. Pers. Adminstrs., Res. Officers Assn., Naval Res. Assn. (v.p. Jack London chpt. 1976), Jonathan Club, Calif. Yacht Club (chmn. yachting luncheons 1989, pub., editor in chief Breeze 1990, 91). Republican. Home: 13908 Fiji Way Apt 357 Marina Del Rey CA 90292

ECKERSLEY, DENNIS LEE, professional baseball player; b. Oakland, Calif., Oct. 3, 1954; m. Nancy O'Neill; 1 child, Mandee. Baseball player Cleve. Indians, 1972-78, Boston Red Sox, 1978-84, Chgo. Cubs, 1984-87, Oakland A's, 1987—. Recipient Cy Young award Baseball Writers Assn. Am., 1992, named MVP, 1992; mem. Am. League All-Star Team, 1977, 82, 88, 90-92; named A.L. Fireman of Yr. The Sporting News, 1988, 91, 92, Am. League Rookie Pitcher of Yr., 1975; pitched no-hit game, 1977. Office: Oakland Athletics PO Box 2220 Oakland CA 94621-0120*

ECKERSLEY, JOHN ALAN, mining company executive; b. Vancouver, B.C., Can., Feb. 14, 1945; s. Gilbert and Rosa (Württemburger)E.; m. Debbie Tjoei, May 12, 1971; children: Rica, Olivia. BSc, U. B.C., Vancouver, 1965, LLB, 1970. Bar: B.C. 1971. Lawyer Worrall, Page & Co., Vancouver, 1971-73; asst. sec. subs. Placer Devel. Ltd., Vancouver, 1973-75, solicitor legal dept., 1975-80, sec., 1984-87; sec. Placer U.S., Inc., San Francisco, 1980-84; gen. mgr. corp. adminstrn. Placer Pacific Ltd., Sydney, Australia, 1987-88; sec. Placer Dome, Inc., Vancouver, 1988-91, v.p., sec., gen. counsel, 1991—. Mem. Law Soc. B.C. Office: Placer Dome Inc, Bentall Postal Sta PO Box 49330, Vancouver, BC Canada V7X 1P1

ECKERSLEY, NORMAN CHADWICK, banker; b. Glasgow, Scotland, June 18, 1924; came to U.S., 1969; s. James Norman and Beatrice (Chadwick) E.; m. Rosemary J. Peters, May 23, 1986, 1 child, Anne. D Laws Strathclyde U., Scotland. With Chartered Bank, London and Manchester, 1947-48; acct., Bombay, 1948-52, Singapore, 1952-54, Sarawak, 1954-56, Pakistan, 1956-58, Calcutta, 1958-59, Hong Kong, 1959-60, asst. mgr. Hamburg, 1960-62, mgr. Calcutta, 1962-67, Thailand, 1967-69; pres. Chartered Bank London, San Francisco, 1964-74, chmn., chief exec., 1974-79; chmn. Standard Chartered Bancorp, 1978-81; dep. chmn. Union Bank, L.A., 1979-82; chmn., CEO The Pacific Bank, San Francisco, 1982-93, chmn. emeritus, 1993; chmn. Diners Club (Asia), 1967-69, Devel. Bank Thailand, 1967-69, Scottish Am. Investment Com., U. Strathclyde Found.; chmn., CEO Balmoral Capital Corp., 1994; chmn. Balmoral Fin. Corp., 1995—. With RAF, 1940-46. Decorated D.F.C.; comdr. Order Brit. Empire. Mem. Overseas Banks Assn. Calif. (chmn. 1972-74), Calif. Coun. Internat. Trade, San Francisco C. of C., World Trade Assn., Royal and Ancient Club, Royal Troon Golf Club (Scotland), World Trade Club, San Francisco Golf Club, Pacific Union Club (San Francisco). Mem. Ch. of Scotland. Home: 401 El Cerrito Ave Hillsborough CA 94010-6819 Office: 340 Pine St Ste 402 San Francisco CA 94104-3221

ECKERT, GERALDINE GONZALES, language professional, educator, entrepreneur; b. N.Y.C., Aug. 5, 1948; d. Albert and Mercedes (Martinez) Gonzales; m. Robert Alan Eckert, Apr. 1, 1972; children: Lauren Elaine, Alison Elizabeth. BA, Ladycliff Coll., Highland Falls, N.Y., 1970; student, U. Valencia, Spain, 1968; MA, N.Y.U., 1971; student, Instituto de Cultura Hispanica, Madrid, 1970-71. Tchr. Spanish Clarkstown High Sch. N. (N.Y.), 1971-73, Rambam Torah Inst., Beverly Hills, Calif., 1973-75; translator City of Beverly Hills, 1976-83; edn. cons. Los Angeles County of Calif. Dept. Forestry, Capistrano Beach, 1982-84; lang. services and protocol Los Angeles Olympic Organizing Com., 1983-84; pension adminstr. Pension Architects, Inc., Los Angeles, 1984-87; instr. El Camino Coll., Torrance, Calif., 1987-88, Santa Monica (Calif.) Coll., 1975—; owner, pres. Bilingual Pension Cons., L.A., 1987-89; bd. dirs. Institute for Hispanic Cultural Studies, Los Angeles; spl. asst. to Internat. Olympic Com., Lausanne, Switzerland, 1983—. V.p. Notre Dame Acad. Assoc., West L. A., 1987—; mem. L.A. March of Dimes Ambassadors Group, 1987; co-founder, pres. Blind Cleaning Express, L.A., 1989—; bd. dirs. Inst. Hispanic Cultural Studies, L.A., 1984-89; spl. asst. to pres. Internat. Olympic Com. Lausanne, Switzerland, 1983—. Democrat. Roman Catholic. Clubs: Five Ring, Los Angeles, Friends of Sport, Amateur Athletic Found., Los Angeles. Office: 8885 Venice Blvd Ste 103 Los Angeles CA 90034-3242

ECKERT, STEVEN PAUL, social services administrator; b. Boston, July 4, 1955; s. Arthur Frederick John and Audrey (Hill) E.; m. Janaki Elizabeth Tompkins, Aug. 30, 1987 (div. 1992). BA in Psychology, Lynchburg Coll., 1978; MSW, San Francisco State U., 1984. Lic. clin. social worker, Calif. Program specialist Youth Family Assistance, Redwood City, Calif., 1980-82; counseling intern Family Svc. Agy. San Francisco, 1983-84; family therapist North Peninsula Family Alternatives, South San Francisco, Calif., 1984—, JSO program coord., 1988-90, clin. coord., 1990-92, dir., 1992—; pvt. practice, San Bruno, Calif., 1988—; cons. San Quentin Prison, San Francisco, 1990—; traffic violators instr. Pacific Seminars, 1986-88. Mem. NASW, Calif. Assn. Marriage and Family Therapists. Democrat. Office: 883 Sneath Ln # 117 San Bruno CA 94066-2413

ECKHERT, CURTIS DALE, environmental health sciences educator; b. Buffalo, N.Y., Mar. 31, 1944; s. Kenneth Harry and Marjorie Marie Eckhert; m. 1988; children: Marc, Robert, Erik. BS, Westminster Coll., 1966; MS, U. Ariz., 1971; PhD, Cornell U., 1974. Postdoctoral scholar Cornell U., Ithaca, N.Y., 1974-75; NIH postdoctoral fellow U. Calif., Davis, 1975-77; NIH fellow vision rsch. Stanford (Calif.) U., 1977-79; asst. prof. environ. health sci. UCLA, 1979-83, assoc. prof., 1983-91, prof., 1991—. Contbr. more than 70 articles to profl. jours. With USMC, 1967-69. Office: UCLA Dept Environ Health Sci Los Angeles CA 90024

ECKLES, PAUL DAVID, city manager; b. Whittier, Calif., Aug. 19, 1940; s. Paul Newton and Loretta May (Madison) E.; m. Donna Maria Arrigone, July 24, 1966; children: Paul Madison, Janice Marie. BA in Econs., Stanford U., 1962; MPA, Ill. Inst. Tech., 1970. Adminstrv. trainee Calif. Dept. Employment, Sacramento, 1963; adminstrv. analyst Calif. Dept. Gen. Svcs., Sacramento, 1964-66; mgmt. cons. Pub. Adminstrn. Svc., Chgo., 1966-73; asst. city mgr. City of Inglewood, Calif., 1973-75; city mgr. City of Inglewood, 1975—. Bd. dirs. Cities in Schs., Inglewood, 1988—, St. Mary's Acad., Inglewood, 1989—; pres. Centinela Valley YMCA, Inglewood, 1984-85. Mem. Internat. City Mgmt. Assn.

ECKLEY, ALICIA KATHRYN, editor, writer, public relations specialist; b. Columbus, Ohio, Mar. 31, 1959; d. Richard McCoy and Helen Louise (Martin) E. BA in Journalism, Ohio State U., 1981. Editorial asst. Diagnostic Imaging Mag., Miller Freeman Publs., San Francisco, 1982-83, asst. editor, 1983-84; pub. affairs mgr. Squibb Corp., Princeton, N.J., 1984-87; pub. relations mgr., Diasonics, Inc., South San Francisco, Calif., 1987-89; prin. Communication Essentials, San Francisco, 1989—; mng. editor Forbes ASAP, Redwood City, Calif., 1992-94; mng. editor Upside Mag., Foster City, Calif., 1991-92. Mem. Media Alliance, Soc. Profl. Journalists.

EDBLOM, DALE CLARENCE, city official; b. Belle Plaine, Minn., Aug. 25, 1934; s. Clarence Edwin and Emma Bertha (Leikam) E.; m. Leona Mae Evenson, July 6, 1957; children: Terri, Todd. AA, San Diego Jr. Coll., 1960. Apprentice carpenter City of San Diego, 1952-54, 56-58, carpenter, 1958-60, carpenter supr., 1960-62, bldg. maintenance supr., 1962-70, sr. bldg. maintenance supr., 1970-90. With USMC, 1954-56. Mem. Eagles, Am. Legion. Republican. Home: 5745 Lodi St San Diego CA 92117-1143

EDDY, DAVID MAXON, health policy and management educator. BA, Stanford (Calif.) U., 1964, PhD with great distinction, 1978; MD, U. Va., 1968. Intern in gen. surgery Stanford U. Med. Ctr., 1968-69, resident, postdoct. fellow cardiovascular surgery, 1969-71, acting asst. prof., 1976-78; dir. program for the analysis of clin. policies Dept. Engring.-Econ. Systems, Stanford U., 1978-81, assoc. prof., 1978-80, prof., 1980-81; dir. Ctr. for Health Policy Rsch. and Edn., Duke U., 1981-88; J. Alexander McMahon prof. health policy and mgmt. Duke U., 1986-90, prof. health policy and mgmt., 1990—; dir. WHO Collaborating Ctr. for Rsch. in Cancer Policy, 1984—; sr. advisor health policy mgmt. Kaiser Permanente So. Calif. Region, 1991—; columnist Jour. of the AMA, 1990—; spl. govt. employee Hillary Rodham Clinton's Health Care Task Force, 1993; assoc. prof. by courtesy Sch. of Medicine, Stanford U., 1978-81; expert adv. panel on cancer WHO, 1981—; adv. coun. World Orgn. for Sci. and Health, 1985—; mem. internat. commn. Centre Oncologique et Biologique de Recherche Appliquee, 1987—; cons. numerous cos., orgns. and assns. Author: A Manual for Assessing Health Practices and Designing Practice Policies, 1992, FAST*PRO: Software for Meta-Analysis by the Confidence Profile Method, 1992, The Statistics Synthesis of Evidence: meta-Analysis by the Confidence Profile Method, 1992, Common Screening Test, 1991, Screening for Cancer: Theory, Analysis and Design (Lanchester Prize, 1981); Editl. bd. Jour. Ctr. for the Future of Children, 1990—, Report Med. Guidelines and Outcomes Rsch., 1990—; contbr. articles to profl. jours. Fellowship NIH, 1970-71, Bay Area Heart Assn., 1969-70; rsch. Scientific and Technol. Achievement award EPA, 1993, FHP Prize Internat. Soc. of Tech. Assessment in Health Care, 1991. Home: PO Box 32 Jackson WY 83001-0032

EDDY, ROBERT PHILLIP, retired mathematician; b. Indpls., Nov. 19, 1919; s. Myron Elmer and Hazel Marguerite (Merrill) E. m. Consuelo Sanz, June 26, 1948; children: Robert A., James M. BS, Beloit Coll., 1941; postgrad., U. Wis., 1941-42; MS, Brown U., 1948. Staff mathematician aeroballistic div. Naval Ordnance Lab., White Oak, Md., 1948-52; head engring. applications br. Applied Math. Lab. David Taylor Model Basin, Carderock, Md., 1953-57; staff mathematician, analyst Computation and Math. Dept. Naval Ship Rsch. and Devel. Ctr., Bethesda, Md., 1958-80; ret. Naval Ship Rsch. and Devel. Ctr., Bethesda, 1980. With AUS, 1943-46. Mem. Am. Math. Soc., Soc. Indsl. and Applied Math., Phi Beta Kappa. Home: 2902 Flintridge Sq Colorado Springs CO 80918-4202

EDEL, (JOSEPH) LEON, biographer, educator; b. Pitts., Sept. 9, 1907; s. Simon and Fannie (Malamud) E.; m. Roberta Roberts, Dec. 2, 1950 (div. 1979); m. Marjorie P. Sinclair, May 30, 1980. MA, McGill U., 1928, LittD, 1963; D.és.L., U. Paris, 1932; DLitt, Union Coll., 1963; D.Litt., U. Sask., 1982; DLitt, Hawaii Loa Coll., 1988. Writer, journalist, 1932-43; vis. prof. N.Y. U., 1950-52, assoc. prof. English, 1953-54, prof. English, 1955-66, Henry James prof. English and Am. letters, 1966-73, emeritus, 1973; citizens prof. humanities U. Hawaii, 1971-78, emeritus, 1978—; mem. faculty Harvard U., summer 1952, vis. prof., 1959-60; Centenary vis. prof. U. Toronto, 1967; Gauss seminar lectr. Princeton U., 1952-53; vis. prof. Ind. U., 1954-55, U. Hawaii, summer 1955, 69-70, Purdue U., 1970; Alexander lectr. U. Toronto, 1956; Westminster Abbey address Henry James Meml., 1976; vis. prof. Center Advanced Study, Wesleyan U., 1965; vis. fellow Humanities Rsch. Ctr., Canberra, Australia, 1976; Vernon prof. biography Dartmouth Coll., 1977; Bollingen Found. fellow, 1958-61. Author: Henry James: Les années dramatiques, 1932, The Prefaces of Henry James, 1932, James Joyce: The Last Journey, 1947, The Life of Henry James, 5 vols. (The Untried Years, 1953, The Conquest of London and The Middle Years, 1962, The Treacherous Years, 1969, The Master, 1972), Henry James, A Life, 1985; (with E.K. Brown) Willa Cather, A Critical Biography, 1953; The Psychological Novel, 1955, revised, 1959, Literary Biography, 1957; (with Dan H. Laurence) A Bibliography of Henry James, 1957, revised edit., 1985; Henry D. Thoreau, 1970, Henry James in The Abbey, The Address, 1976, Bloomsbury, A House of Lions, 1979, Stuff of Sleep and Dreams, Experiments in Literary Psychology, 1982, Writing Lives, Principia Biographica, 1984, Some Memories of Edith Wharton, 1993. Editor: (writings of Henry James) The Complete Plays, 1949, revised edit., 1990, Ghostly Tales (reissued as Tales of the Supernatural, 1970), rev. edit., 1990, Selected Fiction, 1954, Selected Letters, 1955, American Essays, 1956, revised edit., 1990, The Future of the Novel: Critical Papers, 1956; (with Gordon N. Ray) James and H.G. Wells, Letters, 1958; Complete Tales, 12 vols., 1962-64, HJ: Letters, 4 vols., 1974-84; (with Mark Wilson) Complete Criticism, 2 vols., 1984; (with Lyall H. Powers) The Complete Notebooks, 1987; Henry James Reader, 1965, Selected Letters, 1987. Editor (other authors) Edmund Wilson Papers, 4 vols., 1972-86, Literary History and Literary Criticism, 1965, The Diary of Alice James, 1964. Mem. adv. com. edn. Met. Mus. Centenary, 1969-70; mem. ednl. adv. com. Guggenheim Found., 1967-80. Served as 1st lt. AUS, World War II, 1945; dir. Press Agy. 1945-46, U.S. zone Germany. Decorated Bronze Star; recipient Pulitzer prize in biography, 1963; Nat. Book award for non-fiction, 1963; Nat. Book Critics Circle award for biography, 1985; medal of lit. Nat. Arts Club, 1981; Nat. Inst. Arts and Letters grantee, 1959; elected to Am. Acad. Arts and Letters, 1972; Gold medal for biography Acad.-Inst., 1976; Hawaii Writers award, 1977; Guggenheim fellow, 1936-38, 65-66; Nat. Endowment for Humanities grantee, 1974-77. Fellow Am. Acad. Arts and Scis., Royal Soc. Lit. (Eng.); mem. Nat. Inst. Arts and Letters (sec. 1965-67), W.A. White Psychoanalytic Soc. (hon.), Am. Acad. Psychoanalysis (hon.), Soc. Authors (Eng.), Authors Guild (mem. council, pres. 1969-71), P.E.N. (pres. Am. Center 1957-59), Hawaii Lit. Arts Council (pres. 1978-79), Century Club (N.Y.C.). Address: 3817 Lurline Dr Honolulu HI 96816-4003

EDELHERTZ, HERBERT, criminologist; b. N.Y., Jan. 7, 1922; s. Isidore and Bessie (Shabman) E.; m. Ruth Weiss; children: Jean, Paul. AB, U. Mich., 1943; JD, Harvard Law Sch., 1948. Lawyer Tompkins, Lauren & Edelhertz, N.Y., 1949-58, ptnr., 1958-62; chief and deputy chief fraud sec. crim. div. Dept. Justice, Washington, 1962-69; acting center chief Nat. Inst. Justice, Washington, 1969-71; ctr. dir. and staff scientist Battelle Meml. Inst., Seattle, 1971-84; counsel Appel & Glueck, Seattle, 1984-92; pres. Northwest Policy Studies Ctr., Kirkland, Wash., 1984-95. Co-author: Public Compensation to Victims of Crime, 1974, The White-Collar Challenge to Nuclear Safeguards, 1978, A National Strategy for Containing White-Collar Crime, 1980, White-Collar Crime: An Agenda for Research, 1982, The Containment of Organized Crime, 1983, The Business of Organized Crime, 1993. Recipient Spl. Commendation award U.S. Dept. Justice, Washington, 1968, Superior Performance award, 1965. Home and Office: 4509-102nd Ln NE Kirkland WA 98033

EDELMAN, GERALD MAURICE, biochemist, educator; b. N.Y.C., N.Y., July 1, 1929; s. Edward and Anna (Freedman) E.; m. Maxine Morrison, June 11, 1950; children: Eric, David, Judith. B.S., Ursinus Coll., 1950, Sc.D., 1974; M.D., U. Pa., 1954, D.Sc., 1973; Ph.D., Rockefeller U., 1960; M.D. (hon.), U. Siena, Italy, 1974; DSc (hon.), Gustavus Adolphus Coll., 1975, Williams Coll., 1976; DSc Honoris Causa, U. Paris, 1989; LSc Honoris Causa, U. Cagliari, 1989; DSc Honoris Causa, U. degli Studi di Napoli, 1990, Tulane U., 1991, U. Miami, 1995, Adelphi U., 1995. Med. house officer Mass. Gen. Hosp., 1954-55; asst. physician hosp. of Rockefeller U., 1957-60, mem. faculty, 1960-92, assoc. dean grad. studies, 1963-66, prof., 1966-74, Vincent Astor disting. prof., 1974-92; mem. faculty and chmn. dept. neurobiology Scripps Rsch. Inst., La Jolla, Calif., 1992—; mem. biophysics and biophys. chemistry study sect. NIH, 1964-67; mem. Sci. Council, Ctr. for Theoretical Studies, 1970-72; assoc., sci. chmn. Neurosciences Research Program, 1980—, dir. Neurosci. Inst., 1981—; mem. adv. bd. Basel Inst. Immunology, 1970-77, chmn., 1975-77; non-resident fellow, trustee Salk Inst., 1973-85; bd. overseers Faculty Arts and Scis., U. Pa., 1976-83; trustee, mem. adv. com. Carnegie Inst., Washington, 1980-87; bd. govs. Weizman Inst. Sci., 1971-87, mem. emeritus; researcher structure of antibodies, molecular and devel. biology. Author: Neural Darwinism, 1987, Topobiology, 1988, The Remembered Present, 1989, Bright Air, Brilliant Fire, 1992. Trustee Rockefeller Bros. Fund., 1972-82. Served to capt. M.C. AUS, 1955-57. Recipient Spencer Morris award U. Pa., 1954, Ann. Alumni award Ursinus Coll., 1969, Nobel prize for physiology or medicine, 1972, Albert Einstein Commemorative award Yeshiva U., 1974, Buchman Meml. award Calif. Inst. Tech., 1975, Rabbi Shai Shacknai meml. prize Hebrew U.-Hadassah Med. Sch., Jerusalem, 1977, Regents medal Excellence, N.Y. State, 1984, Hans Neurath prize, U. Washington, 1986, Sesquicentennial Commemorative award Nat. Libr. Medicine, 1986, Cécile and Oskar Vogt award U. Dusseldorf, 1988, Disting. Grad. award U. Pa., 1990, Personnalité de l'année, Paris, 1990, Warren Triennial Prize award Mass. Gen. Hosp., 1992. Fellow AAAS, N.Y. Acad. Scis., N.Y. Acad. Medicine; mem. Am. Philos. Soc., Am. Soc. Biol. Chemists, Am. Assn. Immunologists, Genetics Soc. Am., Harvey Soc. (pres. 1975-76, Am. Chem. Soc., Eli Lilly award biol. chemistry 1965), Am. Acad. Arts and Scis., Nat. Acad. Sci., Am. Soc. Cell Biology, Acad. Scis. of Inst. France (fgn.), Japanese Biochem. Soc. (hon.), Pharm. Soc. Japan (hon.), Soc. Developmental Biology, Council Fgn. Relations, Sigma Xi, Alpha Omega Alpha. Office: Scripps Rsch Inst Dept Neurobiol SBR-14 10666 N Torrey Pines Rd La Jolla CA 92037-1027

EDELMAN, JOEL, medical center executive; b. Chgo., Mar. 24, 1931; s. Maurice B. and Ethel J. (Newman) E.; m. Beth L. Sommers, July 31, 1955; children: Peter J., Ann Elizabeth, Deborah S. B.A. in Spl. Edn., U. Mich., 1952; J.D., DePaul U., 1960. Bar: Ill. 1961. Program dir. Chgo. Heart Assn., 1955-61; staff atty. Michael Reese Hosp. and Med. Center, Chgo., 1961-70; exec. v.p. Michael Reese Hosp. and Med. Center, 1971-73; dir. Ill. Dept. Pub. Aid, 1973-74; exec. dir. Ill. Legis. Adv. Com. on Pub. Aid, 1974-77; pres. Rose Med. Ctr., Denver, 1979-95; prin., sr. v.p. Frontier Holdings, Inc., Englewood, Colo., 1995—; asst. prof. dept. preventive medicine U. Colo.; U.; dir. office legal affairs Am. Hosp. Assn., 1970. Contbr. articles to profl. jours. Served with AUS, 1955. Mem. Soc. Hosp. Attys. (charter). Home: 3156 S Hills Ct Denver CO 80210-6830 Office: Frontier Holdings Inc 6312 S Fiddler's Green Cir Englewood CO 80111

EDEN, RALPH MOSELEY, aeronautical engineer; b. Balt., July 15, 1933; s. Ralph Moseley and Anita Freda (Turk) E.; m. Patricia Anne Parker, Sept. 18, 1954 (div. Nov. 1979); children: April Diane, Valerie Patrice (dec.); m. Jean Jaffray Penrose-Simmons, Apr. 25, 1981. B of Aero. Engring., Ga. Inst. of Tech., 1956; MS in Mgmt., U. La Verne, 1982; MS in Engring., Calif. Poly. U., 1993. Svc. manuals engr. Lockheed Ga. Co., Marietta, 1960-61, sr. aerodynamicist, 1961-67; lead aerodynamicist Ling-Temco-Vought, Dallas, 1967-69; sr. design engr. Lockheed Calif. Co., Burbank, 1969-73; mem. tech. staff Rockwell Internat. Space Divsn., Downey, Calif., 1973-74, 77-84, Rockwell Internat. B-1 Divsn., El Segundo, Calif., 1975-77; engring. specialist Northrop B-2 Divsn., Pico Rivera, Calif., 1984—. Artist (book) Northrop P-61 Black Widow, 1991. 1st lt. USAF, 1956-60, capt. res. Mem. AIAA (sr., treas. Atlanta sect., sec. L.A. sect., vice chmn. membership), Royal Aero. Soc. (Gt. Britain), Am. Aviation Hist. Soc., Sigma Alpha Epsilon, Phi Kappa Phi (scholastic mem.). Republican. Episcopalian. Home: 1061 Sandlewood Ave La Habra CA 90631-6908

EDENFIELD, T(HOMAS) KEEN, JR., real estate developer; b. Chattanooga, May 8, 1943; s. Thomas Keen Sr. and Francis (Love) E.; m. Ann Louise Goodney, Jan. 24, 1976; children: Thomas Keen III, Andrew Ward, Stuart Douglas, Curtis Arthur. BS in Econs., Emory U., 1967; MBA, Oxford Sch. Econs., London, 1969. Capt. Saudi Arabian Airlines, 1976-78, Air Jamaica, 1978-80; owner, pres. Mountain Hospitality, Inc., Albuquerque, 1982-86, Lamb Realty & Investment, Albuquerque, 1980—; pres. Seeganex Internat. Ltd., London, 1984—; chmn. Seeganex N.Am., Albuquerque; pres. Vidsonic Corp., Santa Fe, 1993—; CIA aviation operative, Washington, 1974-85. Contbr. articles to profl. jours. Decorated Turkish Civilian Wings award, 1976; recipient Jamaican Disting. Citizen Humanitarian award, 1978, Nicaraguan Civilian Humanitarian award, 1984. Mem. Albuquerque Country Club, Wings Club of Arabia (pres. 1978-79). Office: Lamb Realty & Investment PO Box 26026 Albuquerque NM 87125-6026

EDENS, GARY DENTON, broadcasting executive; b. Asheville, N.C., Jan. 6, 1942; s. James Edwin and Pauline Amanda (New) E.; m. Hannah Suellen Walter, Aug. 21, 1965; children: Ashley Elizabeth, Emily Blair. BS, U. N.C., 1964. Account exec. PAMS Prodns., Dallas, 1965-67; account exec. Sta. WKIX, Raleigh, N.C., 1967-69; gen. mgr. Sta. KOY, Phoenix, 1970-81; sr. v.p. Harte-Hanks Radio, Inc., Phoenix, 1978-81, pres., chief exec. officer, 1981-84; chmn., chief exec. officer Edens Broadcasting, Inc., 1984—; dir. Gt. Western Bank & Trust Ariz., 1975-86, Citibank Ariz., 1986—, Inter-Tel, Inc., 1994—; chmn. The Hanover Cos., Inc., 1995—. Bd. dirs. Valley Big Bros., 1972-80, Ariz. State U. Found., 1979—, COMPAS, 1979—, Men's Arts Coun., 1975-78. Named One of Three Outstanding Young Men, Phoenix Jaycees, 1973; entrepreneurial fellow U. Ariz., 1989. Mem. Phoenix Execs. Club (pres. 1976), Nat. Radio Broadcasters Assn. (dir. 1981-86), Radio Advt. Bur. (dir. 1981—), Young Pres. Orgn. (chmn. Ariz. chpt. 1989-90), Chief Execs. Orgn., Ariz. Pres. Orgn., Phoenix Country Club, Univ. Phoenix Club. Republican. Methodist. Office: Ste 1400 2400 E Arizona Biltmore Cir Phoenix AZ 85016-2107

EDER, JAMES ALVIN, artist, educator; b. Buffalo, Jan. 9, 1942. BS in Phys. Edn., SUNY, Buffalo, 1963; MS in PHysics, U. Nebr., 1966; MA in Art Edn., No. Ariz. U., 1975. Past nuclear physicist Germany. One-man shows at Yavapai Coll., Prescott, Ariz., 1985, Grand Canyon (Ariz.) Visitor Ctr., 1986, U. Ariz., Tucson, 1980, 86, Phoenix Coll., 1979, 88, Scottsdale Coll., 1981, 90, 91, 1st Interstate Bank, Phoenix, 1989, Ariz. State Capitol, Phoenix, 1987, 90, Suzanne Brown Gallery, Scottsdale, Ariz., 1990, Riggins Gallery, Scottsdale, 1991, Sedona (Ariz.) Arts Ctr., 1991, Showcase, Telequepaque, Sedona, 1992, Tucson Jewish Cmty. Ctr., 1994; group exhbns. include Merrill Chase Galleries, Chgo., 1982, DeCordova Mus., Boston, 1982, Marilyn Butler Galleries, Scottsdale, 1983, No. Ariz. U., 1987, Yuma Arts Ctr., 1985, 87, Tuscon Art Mus., 1991, Miriam Perlman Gallery, Chgo., 1993, Mus. No. Ariz., 1994, Wave Hill, N.Y.C., 1994, others; permanent collections include Albuquerque Mus., Hunt Inst. Bot. Documentation, Pitts., Nelson Art Ctr., Tempe, IBM, Honeywell, Del Webb Corp., No. Ariz. U., City of Tempe, others; executed mural Tempe (Ariz.) Arts Ctr., 1994.

EDGAR, HERMAN BURTON, aerospace engineer, managment and tax consultant; b. Memphis, Tex., Dec. 27, 1928; s. Everett Burton and Willie Mae (Loftin) E.; m. Eura Dell Clark, Nov. 5, 1957 (div. May. 1970); children: Stephany, John, George; m. Rose Iva Chatman, Nov. 21, 1970; children: Keith, Jacques, Herman Burton, Marlene. BSME in Machine Design, Healds Coll., 1955; BSEE in Feedback Control Systems, West Coast U., 1967, MSSE in Systems Mgmt., 1969; postgrad., U.S. Internat. U., San Diego, 1981-86. Engr. Rockwell Internat. (N.R.) Corp., Downey, Calif., 1955-89; mgr., owner Burton's Profl. Svcs., Altadena, Calif., 1971—; systems design engr. Apollo, GAM 77, N.Am./Rockwell Internat., Downey and Seal Bech, Calif., 1964-72; supr. hydraulics analysis and test Space Shuttle, Rockwell Internat., Downey, 1973-78, mgr. hydraulics system, 1979-84, project mgr. mech. fluid systems, 1985-89. Co-Author: WCU Systems Anal Jour., 1969, Servo Control VLVS Design, 1959. Cons. engr. Altadena Town Coun., 1992—; deacon, pres. long-range planning com. Lincoln Ave Bapt. Ch., Pasadena, 1974. Served with U.S. Army, 1950-52, Korea. Selected to 1st flight team Apollo, NASA-Johnson Space Ctr., Clearlake, Tex., 1969; recipient Excellence in Leadership award NASA-Johnson Space Ctr. and Rockwell Internat. Corp., Clearlake, 1980, Group Achievement award for first space shuttle flight Johnson Space Ctr., 1983; Cert. of Honor, Glorious Praise Christian Acad., Pasadena, Calif., 1992. Fellow Rockwell Mgmt. Club; mem. Altadena Srs. Golf Club (pres. 1992—), Altadena Optimist Club (v.p. 1993). Democrat. Home: 1701 Skyview Dr Altadena CA 91001-2143

EDGAR, JAMES MACMILLAN, JR., management consultant; b. N.Y.C., Nov. 7, 1936; s. James Macmillan Edgar and Lilyan (McCann) E.; B in Chem. Engring., Cornell U., 1959, MBA with distinction, 1960; m. Judith Frances Storey, June 28, 1958; children: Suzanne Lynn, James Macmillan, Gordon Stuart. New product rep. E.I. duPont Nemours, Wilmington, Del., 1960-63, mktg. services rep., 1963-64; with Touche Ross & Co., 1964-78, mgr., Detroit, 1966-68, ptnr., 1968-71, ptnr. in charge, mgmt. services ops. for No. Calif. and Hawaii, San Francisco, 1971-78, ptnr. Western regional mgmt. services, 1978; sr. ptnr. Edgar, Dunn & Co., San Francisco, 1978—; bd. dirs. Associated Oreg. Industries Svcs. Corp., 1991—. Active San Francisco Mayor's Fin. Adv. Com., 1976—, mem. exec. com., 1978—, Blue Ribbon com. for Bus., 1987-88, Alumnae Resources adv. bd., 1986-94, San Francisco Planning and Urban Rsch. Bd., 1986-89, mem. adv. bd., 1989-93; mem. alumni exec. council Johnson Grad. Sch. Mgmt. Cornell U., Cornell Coun., 1970-73; mem. steering com. Bay Area Coun., 1989—; chmn. San Francisco Libr. Found., 1989—. Recipient Award of Merit for outstanding pub. svc. City and County of San Francisco, 1978; Honor award for outstanding contbns. to profl. mgmt. Johnson Grad. Sch. Mgmt., Cornell U., 1978. CPA, cert. mgmt. cons. Mem. Assn. Corp. Growth (v.p. membership San Francisco chpt. 1979-81, v.p. programs 1981-82, pres. 1982-83, nat. bd. dirs. 1983-86), AICPA, Calif. Soc. CPAs, Inst. Mgmt. Cons. (regional v.p. 1973-80, dir. 1975-77, bd. v.p. 1977-80), Profl. Services Mgmt. Assn., San Francisco C. of C. (bd. dirs. 1987-89, 91—, mem. exec. com. 1988-89, 91—, chmn. mktg. San Francisco program 1991-92, membership devel. 1993, chmn. bd. dirs. 1994), Tau Beta Pi. Clubs: Pacific Union, Commonwealth of San Francisco, Marin Rod and Gun. Patentee nonwoven fabrics. Home: 10 Buckeye Way San Rafael CA 94904-2602 Office: Edgar Dunn & Co Inc 847 Sansome St San Francisco CA 94111-1529

EDGEMAN, RICK LEE, statistics educator, consultant; b. Pueblo, Colo., Nov. 28, 1954; s. Howard Curtis and Eunice Marie (Stucker) E.; m. Lisa Anne Allen, Aug. 12, 1978; children: Emily, Grant, Stephen. BS in Exptl. Psychology, U. So. Colo., 1977; MS in Rsch. and Statis. Methodology, U. No. Colo., 1979; PhD in Stats., U. Wyo., 1983. Lectr. in stats. U. Wyo., Laramie, 1981-83; asst. prof. bus. Bradley U., Peoria, Ill., 1983-85; study design and analysis mgr. Bausch and Lomb, Rochester, N.Y., 1985; asst. prof. stats. Rochester (N.Y.) Inst. Tech., 1985-86; asst. prof. mgmt. sci. U. North Tex., Denton, 1986-88; assoc. prof. computer info. sys. Colo. State U., Ft. Collins, 1988-93, prof. computer ino. sys., 1993—, dir. Ctr. for Quality and Productivity Improvement, 1988—; statis. cons. Eastman-Kodak, Rochester, 1985-86, Mobil Chem., Macedon, N.Y., 1985-86, Hewlett-Packard, Ft. Collins, 1988-89, Colo. Dept. Social Svcs., Denver. Contbr. some 70 articles to profl. jours. Pres. Colo. Citizens for Decency, Ft. Collins, 1989-91; dir. Jesus Video Project Ft. Collins (Colo.), Campus Crusade for Christ, 1993-94. Caterpillar Tractor Co. Rsch. fellow Caterpiller Rsch. Found., Peoria, 1983-84. Mem. IEEE (mem. reliability soc., higher edn. com.), Internat. Assn. for Sci. and Tech. in Econ. Devel., Am. Soc. for Quality Control (editor Quality Progress 1991-94), Am. Statis. Assn. (pres. Rochester N.Y. chpt. 1985-86), Sigma Xi. Republican. Home: 4010 Highlands West Dr Fort Collins CO 80526-5394 Office: Colo State U Computer Info Sys Dept C115 Clark Bldg Coll Bus Fort Collins CO 80523

EDGERTON, BRADFORD WHEATLY, plastic surgeon; b. Phila., May 8, 1947; s. Milton Thomas and Patricia Jane (Jones) E.; children: Bradford Wheatly Jr., Lauren Harrington. BA in Chemistry, Vanderbilt U., 1969, MD, 1973. Diplomate Am. Bd. Plastic Surgery, Am. Bd. Hand Surgery. Intern in surgery U. Calif., San Francisco, 1973-74; resident U. Va., Charlottesville, 1974-78; resident in plastic surgery Columbia-Presbyn., N.Y., 1979-81; fellow in hand surgery NYU, 1981-82, clin. instr. plastic surgery, 1981-89; ptnr. So. Calif. Permanente Med. Group, L.A., 1989—; assoc. prof. clin. plastic surgery U. So. Calif., L.A., 1989—, dir. hand surgery fellowship. v.p., trustee W. Alton Jones Found., Charlottesville, Va., 1978—. Mem. Am. Assn. Hand Surgery, Am. Soc. Plastic and Reconstructive Surgery, Am. Soc. Surgery of Hand, L.A. Tennis Club, Iron City Fishing Club. Republican. Episcopal. Home: 400 S Plymouth Blvd Los Angeles CA 90020-4708 Office: 6041 Cadillac Ave Los Angeles CA 90034-1702

EDGETT, STEVEN DENNIS, transportation consultant; b. Indpls., June 3, 1948; s. Robert Neil and Elizabeth Catherine (Hatch) E.; m. Catherine Ann Bartel, June 19, 1971; children: Jeffrey Steven, Christopher Steven. Student, N. Mex. State U., 1965-67, U. Cin., 1967-68, Grossmont Coll., 1971-72, San Diego State U., 1974-75. Lead designer U.S. Elevator Corp., San Diego, 1970-76; safety engr. State Calif., San Diego, 1976-78; assoc. Skidmore, Owings & Merrill, San Francisco, 1978-86; pres. Edgett Williams Cons. Group, Inc., Mill Valley, Calif., 1986—; mgr. bldg. transp. dept. Jaros, Baum & Bolles Consulting Engrs., N.Y.C., 1995—. Mem. Constrn. Specifications Inst., ASCE Coun. Tall Bldgs. Home: 541 Shasta Way Mill Valley CA 94941-3726 Office: Edgett Williams Cons Group Inc 102 E Blithedale Ave # 1 Mill Valley CA 94941-2024

EDMISTON, JOSEPH TASKER, state official; b. Monterey Park, Calif., Oct. 27, 1948; s. Tasker Lee and Beula Viola (Bates) E.; m. Pepper Salter Abrams, 1985; children: William Tasker, Charles Henry. AA, East L.A. Coll., 1968; AB, U. So. Calif., 1970. Mgr. of ct. process Roy Rottner & Associates, Hollywood, Calif., 1970-73; So. Calif Coastal coord. Sierra Club, L.A., 1973-76, energy coord., Sacramento, Calif., 1976-77; dir. State of Calif. Santa Monica Mountains Land Acquisition Program, 1979-80; exec. dir. Santa Monica Mountains Comprehensive Planning Commn., L.A., 1977-79; exec. dir. Santa Monica Mountains Conservancy, State of Calif., 1980—; regents lectr. Coll. Environ. Design U. Calif., Berkeley, 1995—. Pres. Associated Students, East L.A. Coll., 1968. Recipient Weldon Heald Conservation award Sierra Club, 1970; Hollywood Heritage, Inc. (bd. dirs.). Mem. Marine Tech. Soc. (dir. L.A. region sect. 1975-77), Coastal Soc., Am. Planning Assn. (vice dir. policy L.A. Sect. 1989-90), Phi Rho Pi, Delta Sigma Rho, Tau Kappa Alpha. Democrat. Office: 3700 Solstice Canyon Rd Malibu CA 90265-2901

EDMONDS, CHARLES HENRY, publisher; b. Lakewood, Ohio, Sept. 4, 1919; s. Howard H. and Mary Frances (Galena) E.; student Woodbury Bus. Coll., 1939-40; m. Ruth Audrey Windfelder, Nov. 4, 1938; children: Joan Dickey, Charles Henry, Carolyn Anne, Dianne Marie. Owner, Shoreline Transp. Co., L.A., 1946-58; mgr. transp. Purity Food Stores, Burlingame, Calif., 1958-61; supr. Calif. Motor Express, San Jose, 1961-64; account exec. Don Wright Assos., Oakland, Calif., 1964-65; sales mgr. Western U.S., Shippers Guide Co., Chgo., 1965-70; pub. No. Calif. Retailer, San Jose, 1970-83; v.p. Kasmar Publs., 1983-88; pub. Retail Observer, 1990—. Recipient journalism awards various orgns. Republican. Roman Catholic. Contbr. articles to profl. jours. Home: 1442 Sierra Creek Way San Jose CA 95132-3618

EDMONDS, IVY GORDON, writer; b. Frost, Tex., Feb. 15, 1917; s. Ivy Gordon and Delia Louella (Shumate) E.; student pub. schs.; m. Reiko Mimura, July 12, 1956; 1 dau., Annette. Freelance writer; author books including: Solomon In Kimono, 1957; Ooka the Wise, 1961; The Bounty's Boy, 1963; Hollywood RIP, 1963; Joel of the Hanging Gardens, 1966; Trickster Tales, 1966; Taiwan—the Other China, 1971; The Possible Impossibles of Ikkyo The Wise, 1971; The Magic Man, 1972; Mao's Long March, 1973; Motorcycling for Beginners, 1973; Micronesia, 1974; Pakistan, Land of Mystery, Tragedy and Courage, 1974; Automotive Tuneups for Beginners, 1974; Ethiopia, 1975; The Magic Makers, 1976; The Shah of Iran, 1976; Allah's Oil: Mid-East Petroleum, 1976; Second Sight, 1977; Motorcycle Racing for Beginners, 1977; Islam, 1977; Buddhism, 1978; The Mysteries of Troy, 1977; Big U Universal in the Silent Days, 1977; D.D. Home, 1978;

Bicycle Motocross, 1979; Hinduism, 1979; Girls Who Talked to Ghosts, 1979; The Magic Brothers, 1979; (with William H. Gebhardt) Broadcasting for Beginners, 1980; (with Reiko Mimura) The Oscar Directors, 1980; The Mysteries of Homer's Greeks, 1981; The Kings of Black Magic, 1981; Funny Car Racing for Beginners, 1982; The Magic Dog, 1982; author textbooks: (with Ronald Gonzales) Understanding Your Car, 1975, Introduction to Welding, 1975; also author pulp and soft cover fiction and nonfiction under names of Gene Cross and Gary Gordon and publishers house names; pub. relations mgr. Northrop Corp., Anaheim, Calif., 1968-79, indsl. editor, Hawthorne, Calif., 1979-86. Served with USAAF, 1940-45, USAF, 1946-63. Decorated D.F.C., Air medals, Bronze Star. Home: 5801 Shirl St Cypress CA 90630-3326

EDMONDS, ROBERT LESLIE, forestry educator; b. Sydney, NSW, Australia, May 6, 1943; came to the U.S., 1966; s. Harold M. and Elizabeth (Osborne) E.; m. Victory C. Lesher, Apr. 25, 1969; children: Nicole T., Stephen R. BS, Sydney (Australia) U., 1964; MS, U. Wash., 1968, PhD, 1971. Rsch. forestry officer Forest Rsch. Inst., Canberra, Australia, 1964-65; rsch. asst. dept. forestry Australian Nat. U., Canberra, 1965-66; rsch. asst. Coll. for Rsch., U. Wash., Seattle, 1966-70, rsch. asst. prof., 1973-76, asst. prof., 1976-79, assoc. prof., 1979-82, prof., 1982—, chair ecosystem sci. and conservation divsn., 1993—; program coord. to dir. U.S.-internat. biol. program aerobiology program botany dept. U. Mich., Ann Arbor, 1971-73. Author, editor: Aerobiology: The Ecological System Approach, 1979, Analysis of Coniferous Forest Ecosystems in the Western United States, 1982; assoc. editor: Northwest Sci. Jour.; contbr. articles to profl. jours. Mem. U.S. Nat. Com. for the Internat. Biol. Program, NRC, Washington, 1973-74, chmn. aerobiology com., 1976-80; mem. mayor's com. Secondary Use Com. for the Cedar River Watershed, Seattle, 1987-88. Rsch. grantee NSF. Mem. Am. Phytopathol. Soc., Internat. Assn. for Aerobiology, Soil Sci. Soc. Am., Soc. Am. Foresters, Ecol. Soc. Am. Office: Univ Wash Coll Forest Resources Seattle WA 98195

EDMONDSON, FRANK KELLEY, JR., lawyer, legal administrator; b. Newport, R.I., Aug. 27, 1936; s. Frank Kelley Sr. and Margaret (Russell) E.; m. Christiane Semirot, Mar. 5, 1959 (div. Sept. 1969); children: Mylene Anne, Yvonne Marie, Catherine May; m. Elaine Sueko Kaneshiro, Aug. 17, 1970 (div. June 1992); m. Karen Louise Bishop, Feb. 27, 1993. BBA, Ind. U., 1958; MBA, So. Ill. U., 1978; JD, U. Puget Sound, 1982. Bar: Wash. 1982, U.S. Dist. Ct. (we. dist.) Wash. 1983. Commd. 2d lt. USAF, 1959, advanced through grades to maj., 1969, ret., 1979; contracts specialist Wash. State Lottery, Olympia, 1982-85, asst. contracts adminstr., 1985-87; contracts officer 1989 Washington Centennial Commn., 1987-90; fin. svc. officer Office of the Adminstr. for the Cts., 1990-92; contracts officer, office of adminstr. for the cts. State of Wash. Supreme Ct., Olympia, 1992—. Bd. dirs. Friends of Chambers Creek, Tacoma, 1981-90; mem. pro bono panel Puget Sound Legal Assistance Found., Olympia, 1985-90. Mem. ABA, Wash. State Bar Assn. (spl. dist. counsel 1993-95), Thurston County Bar Assn., Govt. Lawyers Bar Assn. (sec. 1985-86, 1st v.p. 1986-87, pres. 1987-89, liaison to Wash. State Bar Assn. 1989-93), Beta Gamma Sigma, Coll. Club. Home: 908 Bates St SE Olympia WA 98501-4118 Office: State of Wash Supreme Ct Office of Adminstr for Cts 1206 Quince St Olympia WA 98504-1170

EDMUNDS, HOLLY BROOK, market research consultant; b. Lansing, Mich., May 27, 1960; d. Gary Lee Twichell and Heather Kay (Powell) Farrant; m. David James Edmunds, Sept. 25, 1988; children: James Easley IV, Rebecca Lynn. BA in Econs. and Mgmt. and French, Albion Coll., 1982; postgrad., Ea. Mich. U., 1984-87. Internat. mem. svc. rep. FTD, Southfield, Mich., 1982-83, rsch. analyst, 1983-84; rsch. coord. FTD, Southfield, 5, 1984-88; sr. project mgr. Market Trends Rsch., Bellevue, Wash., 1988-90; R&D devel. officer Puget Sound Bancorp, Tacoma, 1990-92; pres. Edmunds Rsch. Svcs., Redmond, Wash., 1991—; instr. U. Wash. Ext., Seattle, 1991. Bd. dirs. Puget Sound Rsch. Forum; mem. mktg. com., cons. Bathhouse Theatre, 1993-94. Mem. Am. Mktg. Assn., U. Wash. Speakers' Bur., Greater Seattle C. of C. Home and Office: Edmunds Rsch Svcs 1120 E Bishop Dr Tempe AZ 85282

EDMUNDS, JOHN SANFORD, lawyer; b. L.A., Jan. 3, 1943; s. Arthur Edmunds and Sarah Bernadine (Miles) E.; m. Virginia Maejan Ching, Nov. 10; children: Laura, Shauna. AB, Stanford U., 1964; JD, U. So. Calif., 1967. Bar: Hawaii 1972, U.S. Dist. Ct. Hawaii, U.S. Ct. Appeals (9th cir.), U.S. Supreme Ct. Chief dep. pub. defender State of Hawaii, 1970-72, spl. dep. atty. gen., 1974-75; acting chief justice Supreme Ct., Republic of Marshall Islands, 1980-81; ptnr. Edmunds & Verga, Honolulu, 1981—; adj. prof. law U. Hawaii, 1976-77, 85-89; counsel Hemmeter Investment Co., Obayashi Corp., Shell Oil Co. Bd. dirs. Legal Aid Soc. Hawaii, 1974-75. Fellow Internat. Acad. Trial Lawyers, Am. Coll. Trial Lawyers (state chmn. 1991-92), Internat. Soc. Barristers, Am. Bar Found.; mem. ABA, ACLU (bd. dirs. 1969-73, pres. 1971-73, adv. counsel 1974-75), Hawaii Bar Assn., Assn. Trial Lawyers Am., Hawaii Acad. Plaintiffs Attys (bd. govs. 1995—), Master of Bench, Am. Inns. of Ct. Office: Edmunds & Verga 841 Bishop St Ste 2104 Honolulu HI 96813-3921

EDSALL, RONALD SCOTT, electrical engineer; b. Billings, Mont., Mar. 22, 1962; s. Grant Edgar and Jean Margaret (Davis) Edsall; m. Kandy Kay Gosage, Dec. 31, 1988; children: Tanya Kay, Tiffany Rianna, Tina Pearl. BSEE, U. Colo., 1986. Digital designer Chalfant R&D, Colorado Springs, Colo., 1978-80; engring. student, site mgr. Mission Rsch. Corp., Colorado Springs, 1982-87; software engr. Computer Scis. Corp., Colorado Springs, 1987-88; logic design and test engr. Cray Computer Corp., Colorado Springs, 1988-93; sr. systems engr. Ncube, Beaverton, Oreg., 1993—. Office: Ncube 1825 NW 167th Pl Beaverton OR 97006-4828

EDSON, WILLIAM ALDEN, electrical engineer; b. Burchard, Nebr., Oct. 30, 1912; s. William Henry and Pearl (Montgomery) E.; m. Saralou Peterson, Aug. 23, 1942; children: Judith Lynne, Margaret Jane, Carolyn Louise. B.S. (Summerfield scholar), U. Kans., 1934, M.S., 1935; D.Sc. (Gordon McKay scholar), Harvard U., 1937. Mem. tech. staff Bell Telephone Labs., Inc., N.Y.C., 1937-41; supr. Bell Telephone Labs., Inc., 1943-45; asst. prof. elec. engring. Ill. Inst. Tech., Chgo., 1941-43; prof. physics Ga. Inst. Tech., Atlanta, 1945-46; prof. elec. engring. Ga. Inst. Tech., 1946-51, dir. sch. elec. engring., 1951-52; vis. prof., research asso. Stanford U., 1952-56, cons. prof., 1956; mgr. Klystron sub-sect. Gen. Electric Microwave Lab., Palo Alto, Calif., 1955-61; v.p., dir. research Electromagnetic Tech. Corp., Palo Alto, 1961-62; pres. Electromagnetic Tech. Corp., 1962-70; sr. scientist Vidar Corp., Mountain View, Calif., 1970—71; asst. dir. Radio Physics Lab., SRI Internat., Menlo Park, Calif., 1971-77; sr. prin. engr. Geosci. and Engring. Ctr., SRI Internat., 1977—; cons. high frequency sect. Nat. Bur. Standards, 1951-64; dir. Western Electronic Show and Conv., 1975-79. Author: (with Robert I. Sarbacher) Hyper and Ultra-High Frequency Engineering, 1943, Vacuum-Tube Oscillators, 1953. Life fellow IEEE (chmn. San Francisco sect. 1963-64, com. standards piezoelectricity 1950-67); mem. Am. Phys. Soc., Sigma Xi, Tau Beta Pi, Sigma Tau, Phi Kappa Phi, Eta Kappa Nu, Pi Mu Epsilon. Home: 23350 Sereno Ct Unit 29 Cupertino CA 95014-6543 Office: SRI Internat 333 Ravenswood Ave Menlo Park CA 94025-3453

EDSTROM, ERIC DONALD, chemistry educator; b. Aspen, Colo., Sept. 22, 1959; s. Neil Arthur and Karen Oliva (Synder). BS, Ft. Lewis Coll., Durango, Colo., 1983; PhD, U. Minn., 1987. Postdoctoral assoc. Stanford (Calif.) U., 1987-89; asst. prof. chemistry Utah State U., Logan, 1989—. Contbr. chpts. to books, articles to profl. jours. Am. Cancer Soc. jr. faculty rsch. awardee, 1992-95. Mem. Am. Chem. Soc., Internat. Soc. Heterocyclic Chemistry. Office: Utah State U Dept Chemistry/Biochemistry Logan UT 84322-0300

EDSTROM, PAM, public relations executive; b. 1954. Pvt. practice, 1968-74; with Fred Meyer Savings and Loan, Portland, Oreg., 1974-77, Tektronix, Inc., Beaverton, Oreg., 1977-81, Micro Soft, Redmond, Wash., 1981-83; sr. v.p. Waggener Edstrom, Inc., Portland, 1983—. Office: Waggener Edstrom Inc 6915 SW Macadam Ave Portland OR 97219-2398*

EDWARDS, ANDREW, arts administrator; b. N.Y.C., Sept. 19, 1952; s. Jack Edwards and Lois Rea; m. Valarie Lynn Grudier, Sept. 15, 1979; children: Pierce Andrew Carl, Caitlin Rea. BA, Dickinson Coll., 1974; MFA, U. Portland, 1981. Theatre mgr. Lake Oswego (Oreg.) Cmty. Theatre, 1977-79; exec. dir. Lakewood Theatre Co., Lake Oswego, 1979—, Lakewood Ctr. for Arts, Lake Oswego, 1980—; bd. dirs. Portland (Oreg.) Area Theatre Alliance, 1987-90, pres., 1990-92, active, 1987—. Recipient Vocat. Svc. award Lake Oswego Rotary, 1994. Mem. Lake Oswego C. of C., Lake Oswego Rotary Club (pres. 1988-89). Roman Catholic. Office: Lakewood Ctr for Arts 368 S State St Lake Oswego OR 97034-3936

EDWARDS, ANNETTE WINFREY, nurse; b. Richmond, Va., June 25, 1963; d. William Elisha and Addie Nell (Price) Winfrey; m. David Scott Edwards, Dec. 28, 1957. BSN, Oral Roberts U., 1985; MSN, Marymount U., 1988. Cert. ACLS instr., PALS instr. Clin. nurse in med./surg. area Malcolm Grow USAF Med. Ctr., Andrews AFB, Md., 1985-88; clin. nurse in emergency rm. Malcolm Grow USAF Med. Ctr., Andrews AFB, 1988-90; charge nurse in outpatient clinics 63D Med. Group, Norton AFB, Calif., 1990-93; nurse mgr. in pediatric clinic 722D Med. Group, March AFB, Calif., 1994—. Mem. Air Force Assn., Emergency Nurses Assn. (cert.), Sigma Theta Tau Internat. Soc. of Nursing. Republican. Baptist. Home: 28227 Cherokee Rose Dr Highland CA 92346 Office: USAF 722D Med Group SGHMC March AFB CA 92518

EDWARDS, ARDIS LAVONNE QUAM, retired elementary education educator; b. Sioux Falls, S.D., July 30, 1930; d. Norman and Dorothy (Cade) Quam; m. Paul Edwards, Apr. 18, 1953 (dec. Sept. 1988); children: Kevin (dec. 1980), Kendall, Erin, Sally, Kristin, Keely. Teaching credentials, Augustana Luth. Coll., Sioux Falls, 1949; provisional teaching credentials, San Jose State Coll., 1953. Lic. pvt. pilot, FAA, 1984. Mgr. The Cottage Restaurant, Sioux Falls, 1943-50; one-room sch. tchr. Whaley Sch., Colman, S.D., 1949-50, East Sioux Sch., Sioux Falls, 1950-51; recreation dir. City of Albany, Calif., 1951-52; first grade tchr. Decoto (Calif.) Sch. Dist., 1952-58. Author Health Instrn. Unit Study Packet for Tchrs. Bible sch. tchr. East Side Luth. Ch., Sioux Falls, S.D., 1945-51, Sun. sch. tchr., 1945-51; charter mem. Our Savior Luth. Ch., Fremont, Calif., 1964—, mem. choir; Christian Week Day Sch. tchr., 1970, 87, ch. historian, 1986—, other offices; treas. PTA, Hayward, Calif., 1959, mem., 1959-76; pres. Luth. Women's Missionary League, 1976; chmn. OSLC Blood Bank, 1968—; edn. officer, fraternal communicator Luth. Brotherhood, respected officer. Recipient Spl. Svc. award Girl Scouts U.S., 1971, Arthritis Found., Fremont, 1974, 75, Spl. Commendation March Fong Eu, 1954. Mem. NAFE, AARP, Republic Airlines Ret. Pilots Assn., Ret. Airline Pilots Assn., N.W. Airlines Ret. Pilots Assn., Aircraft Owners and Pilots Assn., S.W. Airways Pilots Wives Assn., Concerned Women for Am., Am. Heart Assn., Am. Cancer Soc., Arthritis Found., March of Dimes, World Affairs Coun. Republican.

EDWARDS, BRUCE GEORGE, ophthalmologist, naval officer; b. Idaho Springs, Colo., Apr. 6, 1942; s. Bruce Norwood and Evelyn Alice (Kohut) Edwards. BA, U. Colo., 1964; MD, U. Colo., Denver, 1968. Diplomate Am. Acad. Ophthalmology. Commd. ensign USN, 1964; advanced through grades to capt. U.S. Naval Hosp., 1980; intern U.S. Naval Hosp., San Diego, 1968-69; USN med. officer USS Long Beach (CGN-9), 1969-70; gen. med. officer U.S. Naval Hosp., Taipei, Taiwan, 1970-72, U.S. Naval Dispensary Treasure Island, San Francisco, 1972-73; resident in ophthalmology U.S. Naval Hosp., Oakland, Calif., 1973-76, U. Calif., San Francisco, 1973-76; mem. opthalmologist staff Naval Hosp., Camp Pendleton, Calif., 1976-83; ophthalmologist, chief of med. staff Naval Hosp., Naples, Italy, 1983-85; ophthalmology head Camp Pendleton Naval Hosp., Camp Pendleton, 1985—; dir. surg. svcs. Camp Pendleton Naval Hosp., 1990-92, dir. physician advisor quality assurance, 1985-86; vol. Internat. Eye Found., Harar, Ethiopia, 1975. Fellow Am. Acad. Ophthalmology; mem. AMA, Calif. Med. Assn., Calif. Assn. Ophthalmologists, Am. Soc. Contemporary Ophthalmologists, Assn. U.S. Mil. Surgeons, Pan Am. Assn. Ophthalmology, Order of DeMolay (Colo. DeMolay of Yr. 1961, Idaho Springs Chevalier, Colo. State sec. 1961-62). Republican. Methodist. Office: US Naval Hosp Ophthalmology Dept Camp Pendleton CA 92055

EDWARDS, CHARLES GARLAND, minister, counselor, health educator; b. Muncie, Ind., Sept. 25, 1926; s. Lowell Adelbert and Josephine Thelma (Cunnington) E.; m. June Elizabeth Day, Aug. 4, 1946; children: James Joseph, Robert Jan. BA, Andrews U., 1946; MS in Pub. Health, Loma Linda (Calif.) U., 1975; PhD, Newport (Calif.) U., 1981. Pastor, evangelist Ind. Conf. of Seventh Day Adventists, 1946-54, Ky., Tenn. Seventh Day Adventists, 1954-63, So. New England Seventh Day Adventists, 1963-64; evnagelist, youth and public rels. dir. Upper Columbia Seventh Day Adventists, Spokane, Wash., 1964-68; youth dir. Northern Calif. Seventh Day Adventists, Oakland, 1968-71; health and pub. rels. Northern Calif. Seventh Day Adventists, Pleasant Hills, 1971-85; pastor Upper Columbia Seventh Day Adventists, Wentachee, Wash., 1985—. Author: A Bold One for God., 1978, Stress, 1980, Wacifundo and the Whirlwind, 1994. Bd. mem. Friendship Ctr., Wenatchee, 1985—, Habitat for Humanity, 1992—; pres. Cooperating Christian Chs. of the Wenatchee Valley, 1990-94. Mem. Riverview Kiwanis (pres. 1971-72, award 1972). Home and Office: 818 Lambert St Wenatchee WA 98801

EDWARDS, CHARLES RICHARD, retired printing equipment and supplies company executive; b. South Bend, Ind., July 16, 1931; s. Bernard Stuart and Mary Irene (Chamberlaine) E.; student pub. schs.; m. Joanne Wood, Dec. 15, 1950; children: Timothy Stuart, Terry Lynne, David Bryan. Pressman, Toastmasters Internat., Santa Ana, Calif., 1954-60; with 3M Co., 1960-69, Salesman, Western U.S. tech. service and nat. market mgr., St. Paul, 1966-69; CEO, sec., CFO, co-owner Graphic Arts Supplies, Inc., Orange, Calif., 1969-86; owner, operator Edwards Bus. Svcs., 1987-91; bus. and trade cons., 1986-91; instr., cons. in field. Bd. dirs., treas. #1 Network, Inc., Chgo., 1982-86. Served with USAF, 1950-54; Korea. Mem. Nat. Assn. Lithographic Clubs (chpt. co-founder, officer, dir.), Nat. Assn. Printing House Craftsmen (past chpt. pres., regional officer), Toastmasters, Hobo Golf Assn. (pres. 1985—). Republican. Home: 7221 Judson Ave Westminster CA 92683-6163

EDWARDS, DALE LEON, library director; b. Nampa, Idaho; s. Wayne Martin and Thelma Lucile Edwards; m. Julie Ann Rosa, Aug. 19, 1975; children: David, Corey, Stephen, Lisa, Russell. BA, Brigham Young U., 1980, M of Libr. and Info. Sci., 1990. Program dir., announcer Sta. KSUB, Cedar City, Utah, 1977-80; news dir. Sta. KRPX, Price, Utah, 1980-84; news writer Sun Advocate Newspaper, Price, 1984-86; dir. Learning Resource Ctr., Price Libr., Price, 1986-90; dir. libr. svcs. Treasure Valley Community Coll., Ontario, Oreg., 1990—; legis. com. mem. Utah Libr. Assn., Salt Lake City, 1986-90. Recipient Excellence in Reporting award Utah Sch. Bds. Assn., 1985. Mem. ALA, Oreg. Libr. Assn., Oreg. C.C. Libr. Assn. (pres. 1993-94), Oreg. Edn. Assn. (legis. com. 1990—), Pacific N.W. Libr. Assn., Treasure Valley Chorale (pres. 1991-93), Beta Phi Mu. Mormon. Office: Treasure Valley CC Libr 650 College Blvd Ontario OR 97914-3423

EDWARDS, DANIEL WALDEN, lawyer; b. Vancouver, Wash., Aug. 7, 1950; s. Chester W. Edwards and Marilyn E. Russell; m. Joan S. Heller, Oct. 18, 1987; children: Nathaniel, Matthew, Stephen, Alexander. BA in Psychology magna cum laude, Met. State Coll., Denver, 1973, BA in Philosophy, 1974; JD, U. Colo., 1976. Bar: Colo. 1977, U.S. Dist. Ct. Colo. 1977. Dep. pub. defender State of Colo., Denver, 1977-79, Littleton, 1979-81, Pueblo, 1981-86; head office pub. defender State of Colo., Brighton, 1987-89; mem. jud. faculty State of Colo., 1988-91; sole practitioner Denver, 1991-93; magistrate Denver Juvenile Ct., 1993—; instr. sch. of law U. Denver, 1988-91, adj. prof., 1991—, coach appellate advocacy team, 1991—; adv. coun. Colo. Legal Svcs., 1989—; adj. mem. Colo. Supreme Ct. Grievance Com., 1991—. Author: Basic Trial Practice: An Introduction to Persuasive Trial Techniques, 1995. Mem. visual arts com. City Arts III, 1989-90, com. chmn., mem. adv. coun., 1991; bd. dirs. Metropolitan State Coll. Alumni Assn., 1991-92; vol. lectr. CSE Thursday Night Bar Pro Se Divorce Clinic, 1991—. Named Pub. Defender of Yr. Colo. State Pub. Defender's Office, 1985, Outstanding Colo. Criminal Def. Atty., 1989. Mem. ABA, Assn. Trial Lawyers Am., Colo. Bar Assn., Adams County Bar Assn., Denver Bar Assn., Met. State Coll. Alumni Assn. (bd. dirs. 1991—). Home: 2335 Clermont St Denver CO 80207-3134 Office: Denver Juvenile Ct Divsn 6 City and County Bldg Denver CO 80202

EDWARDS, DAWN ANN, marketing professional; b. Valley Forge, Pa., Jan. 13, 1956; d. George Francis and Severina (Bacer) E. BS, Syracuse U., 1978, MS, 1979. Account mgmt. staff asst. Ted Bates Worldwide, Inc., N.Y.C., 1980-83; asst. account exec. Backer & Spielvogel, Inc., N.Y.C., 1983-85; asst. product mgr. Am. Home Products Corp., N.Y.C., 1985-86, Carter-Wallace, Inc., N.Y.C., 1986-89; product mgr. L&F Products Inc. subs. Eastman Kodak, Montvale, N.J., 1989-91; bus. devel. mgr. Pfizer, Inc., N.Y.C., 1991-93; worldwide mktg. sr. product mgr. Oral-B Labs. divsn. The Gillette Co., Redwood City, Calif., 1993—. Mem. Healthcare Bus. Womens Assn., Am. Mktg. Assn., Soc. Childrens Book Writers and Illustrators, Syracuse U. Alumni Assn., Delta Gamma Alumnae. Home: 751 Laurel St # 424 San Carlos CA 94070-3113 Office: The Gillette Co Oral-B Labs Divsn 1 Lagoon Dr Redwood City CA 94065-1562

EDWARDS, DON, congressman; b. San Jose, Calif., Jan. 6, 1915; s. Leonard P. and Clara (Donlon) E.; m. Edith B. Wilkie; children—Leonard P., Samuel D., Bruce H., Thomas C., William D. A.B., Stanford, 1936; student, Law Sch., 1936-38. Bar: Calif. Agt. FBI, 1940-41; mem. 88th-93d Congresses from 9th Calif. Dist., 94th-102nd Congresses from 10th Calif. Dist., 103rd Congress from 16th Calif. Dist., 1963—; Nat. chmn. Americans for Democratic Action, from 1965. Served to lt. USNR, 1941-45. Democrat. Unitarian. Office: US Ho of Reps 2307 Rayburn Bldg Ofc Washington DC 20515-0005

EDWARDS, EDITH LOUISE, principal; b. Margarita Canal Zone, Panama, Sept. 7, 1944; came to the U.S., 1960; d. Donald D. and Edith C. (Sumrall) E. BTh, Life Bible Coll., 1966; M in Theol. Studies, Harvard U., 1981; MS in Ednl. Adminstrn., Nat. U., 1990. Calif. adminstrv. svcs. credential; Calif. tchg. credentials. Tchr. L.A. (Calif.) Unified Sch. Dist., 1968-84; coord. spl. projects Watsonville (Calif.)/Aptos Adult Edn., 1984-88; exec. dir., grant writer Ventura (Calif.) Unified Sch. Dist. Edn. Found., 1988-89; prin. Coachella (Calif.) Valley Cmty. Adult Sch., 1989-92, Weed (Calif.) H.S., 1992—; part time instr. Am. Inst. Banking, L.A., 1969-71, L.A. (Calif.) C.C., 1969-83, Glendale (Calif.) C.C., 1969-83, Cabrillo C.C., 1984-85; part time tchr. Beverly Hills (Calif.) Adult Sch., 1981-84; part time lectr. Calif. State U., L.A., 1981-83; pvt. practice word processing cons., Beverly Hills, 1983-84; guest spkr. in field. Mem. Assn. Calif. Sch. Adminstrs. Office: Weed High Sch 909 Hillside Dr Weed CA 96094-2415

EDWARDS, F(LOYD) KENNETH, journalist, educator, management consultant, marketing executive; b. Salina, Kans., Sept. 29, 1917; s. Floyd Altamus and Grace Frances (Miller) E.; AB, Fort Hays State U., 1940; MS, 1970; m. Virginia Marie Lewark, Sept. 10, 1970; children: Elaine Patricia, Diana, Kenneth, John Michael, Melody, Daniel J. Ins. sales exec., Denver, 1947-50; reporter Sterling (Colo.) Daily Jour., 1950, editor, 1950-52; editor Waverly (Iowa) Newspapers, 1953-55; editor, pub. Edina (Minn.) Courier Newspapers, 1955-56; v.p., editor Mpls. Suburban Newspapers, Hopkins, Minn., 1956-65; editor, gen. mgr. Valley of the Sun Newspapers, Tempe, Ariz., 1968; instr. Mankato (Minn.) State U., 1970-72, asst. prof., 1972-73; assoc. prof. U. Ala., 1973-80, prof., 1980, prof. emeritus, 1981—; vis. prof. communications U. Portland (Oreg.), 1981-83, Western Wash. U., 1987-88; mktg. and sales dir. C.C. Publs., Tualatin, Oreg., 1983-86; pres. GoodLife Publs., Bellingham, Wash., 1988-93; cons. on newspaper mgmt., mktg., pub. rels. Pres. Calhoun-Harriet Home Owners Assn., Mpls., 1958-60; bd. dirs. Hennepin County Assn. for Mental Health, 1959-60, S.W. Activities Council, 1960-61, S.W. High Sch. PTA, Mpls., 1960-61. With USN, World War II. Grantee Ford Found., 1976, U. Ala., 1977. Recipient awards for community svc. and editorial writing. Mem. VFW, Nat. Conf. of Editorial Writers, X-Press. Republican. Contbr. articles to profl. jours., chpts. to books; author newspaper profit planning and management manual. Home: 15709 W Sentinel Dr Sun City West AZ 85375-6685

EDWARDS, GERALD ELMO, botany educator; b. Mt. Airy, Va., Sept. 17, 1942; s. Thomas George and Ruth (Inge) E.; m.Sandra Ann Gee, July 3, 1969; children: Christopher, Sara. BS in Agrl. Edn., Va. Poly. Inst., 1965; MS in Agronomy, U. Ill., 1966; PhD in Plant Sci./Plant Physiology, U. Calif., Riverside, 1969. NIH postdoctoral fellow biochemistry dept. U. Ga., Athens, 1969-71; asst. prof. horticulture dept. U. Wis., Madison, 1971-75, assoc. prof., 1975-78, prof., 1978-81; prof., chmn. botany dept. Wash. State U., Pullman, 1981-86, fellow Inst. Biol. Chemistry, 1983—, prof. botany dept., 1986—; cons. Calgene, Inc., Davis, Calif., 1984-85, Phytogen, Inc., Pasadena, Calif., 1985, 89-91. Co-author: C3, C4: Photosynthesis, 1984; assoc. editor Photosynthesis Rsch., 1988—; mem. editorial bd. Archives of Biochemistry and Biophysics, 1985—; past mem. editorial bd. Plant Physiology, Plant and Cell Physiology; contbr. articles to profl. jours., chpts. to books. Guggenheim fellow Simon Guggenheim Found., Eng., 1977-78, Fulbright fellow Fulbright Found., Eng., 1992-93; grantee USDA, NSF, EPA, others. Mem. Am. Soc. Plant Physiologists, Japanese Soc. Plant Physiologists, Scandinavian Soc. Plant Physiology, Am. Soc. Biochemistry and Molecular Biology, Sigma Xi (pres. Wash. State U. chpt. 1995—), Alpha Zeta, Phi Kappa Phi. Democrat. Methodist. Office: Wash State U Botany Dept Pullman WA 99164-4238

EDWARDS, H. BOYD, air transportation executive; b. 1956. Grad., Western State Coll., 1979. Prin. Aspen (Colo.) Aviation, 1980-84; v.p. Aspen (Colo.) Base Ops., Inc., 1984—. Office: Aspen Base Ops Inc 198 W Airport Rd Aspen CO 81611*

EDWARDS, JOHN DAVID, artist; b. Pitts., Aug. 15, 1952; s. John Rex and Winifred (Beattie) E.; m. Brenda L. Duchemin, Jan. 12, 1974 (div. Feb. 1981); 1 child, John David Duchemin; m. Eunice Ying Zhou, June 10, 1987. AA in Fine Art, City Coll. San Francisco, 1976; BA in Studio Art and Art History, U. Calif., Berkeley, 1979. Ellen Battell Stoeckel fellow Summer Sch. Music and Art Yale U., New Haven, 1978; asst. in mural painting U. Calif., 1977-79; instr. color etching Associated Students of Univ. of Calif. Studio, Berkeley, 1981-82; master printer Vorpal Gallery, San Francisco, 1985—; workshop mgr. Kala Inst., Berkeley, 1988—. Exhibited in group shows at Summer Sch. Music and Art Yale U., 1978, Crocker Art Mus., Sacramento, 1982, 93, San Francisco Arts Festival, 1984, Bannam Pl., San Francisco, 1985, 86, Weir Gallery, Berkeley, 1987, 93, Rolando Castellon Art Gallery, San Francisco, 1987, Kala Inst., Berkeley, Calif., 1988, 90, 92, Juniper Gallery, Napa, Calif., 1991, Pyramid Atlantic, Washington, 1992, L.A. Printmaking Soc., 1992, Manhattan Graphics, N.Y., 1993, others. Mem. L.A. Printmaking Soc., Kala Inst. (ed. various workshops 1988—). Roman Catholic. Office: PO Box 621 Berkeley CA 94701-0621

EDWARDS, JOHN STUART, zoology educator, researcher; b. Auckland, N.Z., Nov. 25, 1931; came to U.S., 1962; s. Charles Stuart Marten and Mavis Margaret (Wells) E.; m. Ola Margery Shreeves, June 21, 1957; children—Richard Charles, Duncan Roy, Marten John, Andrew Zachary. B.Sc., U. Auckland, 1954, M.Sc. with 1st class honors, 1956; Ph.D., U. Cambridge, Eng., 1960. Asst. prof. biology Western Res. U., 1963-67, assoc. prof., 1967; assoc. prof. zoology U. Wash., Seattle, 1967-70, prof., 1970—, dir. biology program, 1982-88, dir. univ. honors program, 1994—. Recipient Alexander von Humboldt award, 1981; Guggenheim fellow, 1972-73; vis. fellow Gonville and Caius Coll., Cambridge U., Eng., 1989-90, Fellow Royal Entomol. Soc., AAAS; mem. Soc. Neurosci., Am. Soc. Zoologists, Western Apicultural Soc. (v.p. 1983). Home: 5747 60th Ave NE Seattle WA 98105-2035 Office: U Wash Dept Zoology NJ15 Seattle WA 98195

EDWARDS, JOHN WESLEY, JR., urologist; b. Ferndale, Mich., Apr. 9, 1933; s. John W. and Josephine (Wood) E.; m. Ella Marie Law, Dec. 25, 1954; children: Joella, John III. Student, Alma Coll., 1949-50; BS, U. Mich., 1954; postgrad., Wayne State U., 1954-56; MD, Howard U., 1960. Internship Walter Reed Gen. Hosp., 1960-61, surg. resident, 1962-63, urol. resident, 1963-66; asst. chief urology Tripler Army Med. Ctr., 1966-69; comdr. 4th Med. Battalion, 4th Infantry Div., Vietnam, 1969; chief profl. svcs., urology 91st Evacuation Hosp., Vietnam, 1969-70; urologist Straub Clinic, Inc., 1970-74; pvt. practice, 1974—; v.p. med. staff. svcs. Queen's Med. Ctr., Honolulu, 1993-94; v.p. physician rels. Queen's Health Sys., Honolulu, 1994—; chief Dept. Surgery, Straub Clinic and Hosp., 1973; asst. chief Dept. Surgery Queen's Med. Ctr., 1977-79, chief, 1989-93; cons. in urology; chief Dept. Clin. Svcs., Kapiolani Women's and Children's Med. Ctr., 1981-83; clin. assoc. prof. U. Hawaii Sch. of Medicine; chmn. task force on phys. hosp. collaboration The Queens Health System, 1993—. Contbr. articles to profl. jours. Bd. dirs. Am. Cancer Soc., Honolulu unit, 1977-79, Hawaii Med. Svc. Assn., 1979-85, Hawaii Heart Assn., 1977-79, Hawaii Assn. for Physicians Indemnification, 1980-86; commr. City and County of Honolulu

Liquor Commn., 1986-89; mem. reorgn. commn. City and County of Honolulu, 1990-91; mem. med. adv. bd. Nat. Kidney Found., Hawaii, 1994—; mem. adv. bd. MADD, Hawaii, 1992—. Recipient Howard O. Gray award for Professionalism, 1988, Leaders of Hawaii award, 1983; named Hawaii African-Am. Humanitarian of the Yr. by Hawaii chpt. Links, Inc., 1991. Fellow ACS (sec.-treas. Hawaii chpt. 1980-81, gov.-at-large 1986-92); mem. AMA, NAACP, Am. Urol. Assn. (alt. del. Western sect. 1991-92, gen. chmn. Western sect. 56th ann. meeting 1980, exec. com. 1983-84, del. dist. 1 1985-86, gen. chmn. 63d ann. meeting 1987, pres. 1989-90, nom. com. 1990-93, chmn. nom. 1992-93), Am. Coll. Physician Execs., Nat. Med. Assn., Hawaii Urol. Assn., Hawaii Med. Assn., Surgicare of Hawaii (v.p. 1983-86), Alpha Phi Alpha, Chi Delta Mu, Alpha Omega Alpha. Office: The Queen's Health Sys 201 Merchant St Ste 2220 Honolulu HI 96813-2929

EDWARDS, KENNETH NEIL, chemist, consultant; b. Hollywood, Calif., June 8, 1932; s. Arthur Carl and Ann Vera (Gomez) E.; children: Neil James, Peter Graham, John Evan. BA in Chemistry, Occidental Coll., 1954; MS in Chem. and Metall. Engring., U. Mich., 1955. Prin. chemist Battelle Meml. Inst., Columbus, Ohio, 1955-58; dir. new products rsch. and devel. Dunn-Edwards Corp., L.A., 1958-72; sr. lectr. organic coatings and pigments dept. chem. engring. U. So. Calif., L.A., 1976-80; bd. dirs. Dunn-Edwards Corp., L.A.; cons. Coatings & Plastics Tech., L.A., 1972—. Contbr. articles to sci. jours. Mem. Am. Chem. Soc. (chmn. divisional activities 1988-89, exec. com. div. polymeric materials sci. and engring. 1963—), Alpha Chi Sigma (chmn. LA.A profl. chpt., 1962, pacific dist. counselor 1967-70, grand profl. alchemist nat. v.p. 1970-76, grand master alchemist nat. pres. 1976-78, nat. adv. com. 1978—). Home: 2926 Graceland Way Glendale CA 91206-1331 Office: Dunn Edwards Corp 4885 E 52d Pl Los Angeles CA 90040

EDWARDS, KIRK LEWIS, real estate company executive; b. Berkeley, Calif., July 30, 1950; s. Austin Lewis and Betty (Drury) E.; m. Barbara Lee Preston, Oct. 21, 1983; children: Elliott Tyler, Jonathan Bentley. BA in Rhetoric and Pub. Address, U. Wash., Seattle, 1972; postgrad., Shoreline Coll., 1976. Cert. bus. broker. From salesperson to mgr. Rede Realty, Lynnwood, Wash., 1973-77; br. mgr. Century 21/North Homes Realty, Lynnwood, Wash., 1977-79, Snohomish, Wash., 1979-81; pres., owner Century 21/Champion Realty, Everett, Wash., 1981-82, Champion Computers, Walker/Edwards Investments, Everett, 1981-82; br. mgr. Advance Properties, Everett, 1982-87; exec. v.p. Bruch & Vedrich Better Homes & Garden, Everett, 1987-88, dir. career devel., 1988-90; pres., chief exec. officer Century 21/Champion Realty, Everett, 1991—. Mem. Snohomish County Camano Bd. Realtors (chmn. 1987-88), Snohomish County C. of C., Hidden Harbor Yacht Club. Republican. Home: 20210 107th Ave NE Bothell WA 98011-2464 Office: Century 21/Champion Realty 12811 8th Ave W Ste 201C Everett WA 98204-6300

EDWARDS, MARIE BABARE, psychologist; b. Tacoma; d. Nick and Mary (Mardesich) Babare; B.A., Stanford, 1948, M.A., 1949; m. Tilden Hampton Edwards (div.); 1 son, Tilden Hampton Edwards Jr. Counselor guidance center U. So. Calif., Los Angeles, 1950-52; project coordinator So. Calif. Soc. Mental Hygiene, 1952-54; pub. speaker Welfare Fedn. Los Angeles, 1953-57; field rep. Los Angeles County Assn. Mental Health, 1957-58; intern psychologist UCLA, 1958-60; pvt. practice, human rels. tng., counselor tng. Mem. Calif., Am., Western, Los Angeles psychol. assns., AAAS, So. Calif. Soc. Clin. Hypnosis, Internat. Platform Assn. Author: (with Eleanor Hoover) The Challenge of Being Single, 1974, paperback edit., 1975. Office: 6100 Buckingham Pky Culver City CA 90230-7237

EDWARDS, PATRICIA BURR, small business owner, counselor, consultant; b. Oakland, Calif., Feb. 19, 1918; d. Myron Carlos and Claire Idelle (Laingor) Burr; m. Jackson Edwards, Nov. 14, 1942; children: Jill Forman-Young, Jan Kurzweil. AB, U. So. Calif., 1939, MSEd, 1981. Prin. Constructive Leisure, L.A., 1968—; speaker, lectr. in field; writer, prodr. counseling materials for career, leisure and life planning including computer software, audio cassettes and assessment surveys. Author: You've Got to Find Happiness: It Won't Find You, 1971, Leisure Counseling Techniques: Individual and Group Counseling Step-by-Step, 1975, 3d edit., 1980, Leisure PREF, 1986, Adapting to Change: The NVAB Attitude Modification Program, 1995; contbr. articles to profl. jours., mags. and books. Chmn. L.A. County Foster Families 50th Anniversary, 1962-64, Hollywood Bowl Vols., L.A., 1952—. Mem. Am. Counseling Assn., Calif. Assn. for Counseling and Devel., Nat. Recreation and Park Assn., Assn. for Adult Devel. and Aging, Trojan League, Travellers Aid Soc., Jr. League L.A., First Century Families of L.A., Delta Gamma. Republican. Episcopalian.

EDWARDS, PATRICK MICHAEL, sales consultant; b. Burbank, Calif., Sept. 20, 1947; s. Kenneth Charles and Thelma Kay (Allen) E.; m. Sherry Johnson, Aug. 5, 1995. BS, Calif. Poly State U., 1975. Med. salesperson Burroughs Wellcome Co., Research Triangle Park, N.C., 1975-79; sr. cons. G.D. Searle & Co., Chgo., 1979—. Author photo essay in Ford Times mag., 1989. With USCG, 1968-72. Mem. Assn. of Pharm. Reps. (pres. 1986). Republican. Home and Office: 244 Houston Way Pismo Beach CA 93449

EDWARDS, PETER JOHN, secondary education educator, historic preservation consultant, coach; b. Seattle, Oct. 16, 1965; s. Harry Brad Edwards and Linda Ellen (Griep) Ottmar. BA in History, Internat. Affairs, Lewis and Clark Coll., Portland, Oreg., 1988; MA in Social Studies, Lewis and Clark Coll. 1992. Archeol. technician USDI Bur. Land Mgmt., Oreg., 1988; social studies tchr. Beaverton (Oreg.) H.S., 1993—; head rowing coach Lewis and Clark Coll., Portland, Oreg., 1988-94; historic resources cons. Columbia Hist. Rsch., Portland, Oreg., 1990—. Contbr. articles to profl. jours. dir. Lewis and Clark Alumni Assn., Portland, Oreg., 1989-91. Mem. Hist. Preservation League of Oreg., 1000 Friends of Oreg., Nat. Trust for Hist. Preservation, Nat. Coun. for Pub. History, U.S. Rowing Assn., Station L Rowing Club (pres.). Democrat. Home and Office: 6128 SW Corbett Ave Portland OR 97201-3602

EDWARDS, PHYLLIS MAE, accountant, graphologist; b. Wichita, Kans., June 25, 1921; d. William Noble and Nettie Mae (Riggs) Merry; m. Joseph Andrew Edwards, Sept. 19, 1945 (dec.); children: Joseph Noble (dec.), James Richard, Robert Andrew (dec.), Jacqueline Merry. Student, Bus. Preparatory Sch., Wichita, Kans., 1939; BA in Journalism, Wichita State U., 1944; grad. advanced graphologist, Sampson Inst. Graphology, 1967; cert. of proficiency, Tao Acupuncture, 1975; D of Graphology Sci., Rocky Mountain Graphology, 1978. Cert. profl. graphologist. Sec., bookkeeper Healy & Co., Wichita, 1939-42, Wichita State U., 1942-43; acct. Moberly & West, Pub. Accts., Wichita, 1943-45, McQuain, Edwards, & Teffs, Oakland, Calif., 1952-55; acct., graphologist Rocky Mountain Graphology Sch., Denver, 1972-81; prin. Multi-Pro Svcs., Denver, 1976—; acct. Indsl. Hard Chrome Plating Co., Denver, 1957-94; expert witness for all levels of ct., Colo., Wyo., 1976—; pub. and pvt. speaker Colo., Wyo., 1976—; sec., treas. Indsl. Hard Chrome Plating Co., Denver, 1990-94. Den mother Aurora (Colo.) Cub Scout Troop, 1956-59; asst. troop leader Girl Scouts U.S., Denver, 1960-64; charity fund raiser various churches, schs., and non-profit orgns., 1967—. Mem. AAUW (Denver br. treas. 1975-77, bull. editor 1980-81, 92-93, sec. 1986-88, roster/circulation editor, pres.-elect 1988-90, pres. 1990-92, chair interbr. coun. 1991-92), Am. Handwriting Analysts Found. (Rocky Mountain chpt.), Am. Assn. Handwriting Analysts, Coun. Graphological Socs., Rocky Mountain Graphology Assn. (treas. 1972-81), U. Denver Women's Libr. Assn. Home: 2986 S Fairfax St Denver CO 80222-6841 Office: Indsl Hard Chrome Plating 2986 S Fairfax St Denver CO 80222-6841

EDWARDS, RALPH M., librarian; b. Shelley, Idaho, Apr. 17, 1933; s. Edward William and Maude Estella (Munsee) E.; m. Winifred Wylie, Dec. 25, 1969; children: Dylan, Nathan, Stephen. B.A., U. Wash., 1957, M.Library, 1960; D.L.S., U. Calif.-Berkeley, 1971. Libr. N.Y. Pub. Libr., N.Y.C., 1960-61; catalog libr. U. Ill. Libr., Urbana, 1961-62; br. libr. Multnomah County Libr., Portland, Oreg., 1964-67; asst. prof. Western Mich. U., Kalamazoo, 1970-74; chief of the Central Libr. Dallas Pub. Libr., 1975-81; city librarian Phoenix Pub. Libr., 1981—. Author: Role of the Beginning Librarian in University Libraries, 1975. U. Calif. doctoral fellow, 1967-70; library mgmt. internship Council on Library Resources, 1974-75. Mem. ALA, Ariz. Library Assn., Pub. Library Assn. Democrat. Home: 4839 E Mulberry Dr Phoenix AZ 85018-6520 Office: Phoenix Pub Libr 1221 N Central Ave Phoenix AZ 85004

EDWARDS, RAPHA OLGA JONES, social worker; b. Paris, Ark., Aug. 23, 1903; d. James William and Mary (Wear) Jones; mn. James Franklin Trail, Oct. 5, 1921 (div. Aug. 8, 1950); 1 child, Gloria Olga Trail Holman; m. Oliver Thomas Edwards, Oct. 2, 1953 (dec. Feb. 19, 1984). BS in Edn., U. Ark., 1939, MS, 1947. Cert. social worker. Case worker ARC, Kansas City, Mo., 1947-48, Vets. Hosp., Tacoma, 1952-65; geneaologist self-employed Tacoma and Puyallup, Wash., 1962-94. Author: Genealogy of a Jones Family of Arkansas and Missouri, 1957, Descendants of East Tennessee Pioneers, 1963, The Connection of West Tennessee, 1969, From Here and There to the White House, 1990. Mem. East Tenn. Hist. Soc. Home: 15820 81st St E Puyallup WA 98372-3900

EDWARDS, SARAH ANNE, radio, cable television personality, clinical social worker; b. Tulsa, Jan. 7, 1943; d. Clyde Elton and Virginia Elizabeth Glandon; B.A. with distinction, U. Mo., Kansas City, 1965; M.S.W., U. Kans., 1974; m. Paul Robert Edwards, Apr. 24, 1965; 1 son, Jon Scott. Cmty. rep. OEO, Kansas City Regional Office, 1966-68; social service/parent involvement specialist, program rev. and resource specialist Office Child Devel., HEW, Kansas City, Kans., 1968-73; dir. tng. social services dept., children's rehab. unit U. Affiliated Facility, U. Kans. Med. Ctr., Kansas City, 1975-76; co-dir. Cathexis Inst. S., Glendale, Calif., 1976-77; pvt. practice psychotherapy, tng. and cons. personal, interpersonal, organizational behavior, Sierra Madre, Calif, 1973-80; systems operator working from home CompuServe Info. Svc., 1983—; prodr., co-host radio show Working From Home on the Business Radio Network, 1988—; co-host cable show Working From Home Scripp's Howard Home and Garden Cable TV Network, 1995—. Columnist for Home Office Computing Mag., 1988—; co-author: How to Make Money with Your Personal Computer, 1984, Getting Business to Come to You, 1991, Working From Home, rev. edit. 1994, Making it on Your Own, 1994. Address: 2607 2nd St Apt 3 Santa Monica CA 90405-4123

EDWARDS, THOMAS ALUN, physician; b. Rhymney, Wales, U.K., Jan. 17, 1922; came to U.S., 1926; s. Charles and Annie Rosina (Jones) E.; m. Dorothea Irion, June 26, 1948; children: Anne Kathleen, Elizabeth Helen, Thomas Irion, David Charles, Richard Albert, Margaret Dorothea. BA, Colo. Coll., 1943; MD, U. Colo., 1951. Sec., mem. med. staff Good Samaritan Hosp., Phoenix, 1958-60; chief of medicine St. Luke's Hosp., Phoenix, 1965-68, chief of med. staff, 1968-70; med. cons. Ariz. State Bd. Med. Examiners, Phoenix, 1988—. Trustee St. Lukes Hosp. & Med. Ctr., Phoenix, 1979-83, Combined Health Resources, Phoenix, 1980-83, Vis. Nurses Assn., Phoenix, 1963; vestry & sr. warden Christ Church, Episc., Paradise Valley, Ariz., 1972-80. 1st lt. USMC, 1943-46, PTO. Mem. Maricopa County Med. Soc. (sec. 1969-71). Home: 7033 N 13th St Phoenix AZ 85020-5433 Office: Ariz State Bd Med Examiners 1641 E Morten Ave Phoenix AZ 85020-4610

EDWARDS, WAYNE A., school administrator, religious studies educator; b. Putnam, Conn., Dec. 26, 1934; s. Dorian Arthur and Celia Evangeline (Gallup) E.; m. Esther Sylvia Balwit, June 4, 1955; children: Valerie, Kevin, Karen, Lynette. BA in Psychology and Sociology, Ea. Nazarene Coll., 1959; MEd in Edn. and Reading, Holy Names Coll., 1974; postgrad., Western Evang. Sem., 1995—. Teaching asst. Ea. Nazarene Coll., Wollaston, Mass., 1957-59; educator Oakland (Calif.) Pub. Schs., 1959-76; cons. NEA, Burlingamee, Calif., 1976-77; exec. v.p. Ednl. Svcs., Inc., Oakland, 1965-72; owner, adminstr. Wayne Edwards Learning Ctrs., Walnut Creek, Calif., 1972-92; Bibl. counselor trainer McMinnville, 1992—; adminstr. Valley Christian Sch., McMinnville, 1995—; vice chmn. retirement com. Calif. Tchrs. Assn., Oakland, 1975-77; ednl. cons., 1993—. Author: (seminar program) Learning for Keeps, 1987. Dir. West Contra Costa PTA Coun., Richmond, Calif., 1968-72; dir., v.p., pres. Pinole (Calif.) C. of C., 1977-85; founding dir., counselor, educator Shepherd's Way Drug Rehab., San Pablo, Calif., 1989-91. Scholar Calif. Assn. Neurologically Handicapped Children, 1974. Mem. Nat. Released Time Edn. Assn. (western dir. 1988—, pres. 1993-94), Calif. Released Time Edn. Assn. (founding pres. 1982-89, bd. dirs., tchr. trainer 1989-92), Coun. Exceptional Children, El Sobrante C. of C., Gideons Internat. (various offices 1960-67). Home: 531 Westvale St Mcminnville OR 97128-7123 Office: Biblical Counseling Tng PO Box 456 Mcminnville OR 97128-0456

EDWARDS, WILLIAM H., SR., retired hotel corporation executive; b. Muskegon, Mich., May 25, 1917; s. William H. and Ruby A. (Tipson) E.; m. Ruth Ann Nolan, May 16, 1942; children: William H., Bradley N. BA, U. Mich., 1939; LLD, Northwood U., Midland, Mich., 1982. Cert. hotel adminstr. V.p., mng. dir. Palmer House Hilton, Chgo., 1966-68; v.p. Chgo. div. Hilton Hotels Corp., Chgo., 1968-70, sr. v.p., 1970-71, exec. v.p. ops., 1971-78; pres. Hilton Hotel div. Hilton Hotels Corp., Beverly Hills, Calif., 1978-89, vice chmn., 1985-89, bd. dirs., mem. exec. com., 1971-89, vice chmn. and dir. emeritus, 1989—; bd. dirs. Conrad Hilton Found., L.A., 1989—; bd. dirs. Travel and Tourism adv. bd. Dept. Commerce, Washington, 1983-88. Trustee, treas. Radiol. Soc. N.Am./Rsch. and Edn. Fund, Oak Brook, Ill., 1988-93; trustee, v.p. So. Calif. chpt. Nat. Multiple Sclerosis Soc., 1984—. Lt. USNR, 1942-45, ETO. Recipient Cmty. Svc. award Brandeis U., 1975, Am. Tourism award New Sch. for Social Rsch., 1983, Amb. of Hospitality award Nat. Restaurant Assn. Ednl. Found., 1990, Convention Liaison Coun.-Hall of Leaders award, 1985. Mem. L.A. Country Club. Republican. Roman Catholic. Home: 10350 Wilshire Blvd Los Angeles CA 90024-4700

EEN, MIRIAM BLACKHAM, dietitian; b. Murray, Utah, May 23, 1963; d. VerNon T. and Lorene (Burton) Blackham; m. Kim Perry Een, June 30, 1990; children: Aria, Alayna. BS in Med. Dietetics, Brigham Young U., 1985; MS in Nutrition, U. Calif., Berkeley, 1991. Registered dietitian. Lab. asst. Benson Inst. Lab., Provo, Utah, 1983-85; therapeutic dietitian Valley Hosp., Las Vegas, Nev., 1985-86; cons. dietitian Beverly Manor, Las Vegas, 1985-86; nutrition cons. Sunnyvale (Calif.) Med. Clinic, 1987-88; rsch./tchg. asst. in nutrition sci. U. Calif., Berkeley, 1988-90; dietary svc. cons. Horizon Healthcare Corp., Las Vegas, 1990-93; asst. prof. U. Nev. Sch. Medicine, Las Vegas, 1991—; adj. faculty mem. U. Nev., Las Vegas, 1990-91, C.C. So. Nev., Las Vegas, 1994—. Contbr. rsch. papers, abstracts to profl. jours. Recipient Hope of Am., Kiwanis, 1975. Mem. Am. Dietetic Assn. (mem. abstract rev. team 1994—), So. Nev. Dietetic Assn. (schair nominating com. 1990-94), Nev. Dietetic Assn. (pres.-elect, pres. 1994—), Nutrition Educators of Health Profls., Soc. Tchrs. of Family Medicine, Omicron Nu, Alpha Zeta. Republican. Mem. LDS Ch. Office: U Nev Sch Medicine 2040 W Charleston Blvd Ste 200 Las Vegas NV 89102-2206

EFFORD, MICHAEL ROBERT, police administrator, educator; b. L.A., July 22, 1950; s. Robert Victor and Mary (Athens) E.; m. Jolene Lynn Buttner, Mar. 20, 1976 (dec. Jan. 1980); m. Patricia Ann Jones, Feb. 2, 1985; children: Stacy Anne, Ashley Elizabeth. AA in Criminal Justice, Western Nev. Community Coll., 1976; BA in Bus., Calif. Coast U., 1990, MBA, 1992. Trooper Nev. Hwy. Patrol, Las Vegas, 1976-80; law instr. Western Nev. Community Coll., Carson City, 1980—; adminstrv. lt. Carson City Sheriff's Dept., 1972—, in charge of planning & tng., 1993—; sheriff Carson City, 1980-94; chief of police Sonora, Calif., 1994—; instr. Reno Police Acad., 1980—, Nev. Hwy Patrol Acad., Carson City, 1980—, Nev. Peace Officer Stds. and Tng. Acad. Editor Carson City Sheriff's Supervisory Assn. newsletter, 1989—. Pres. Carson City Labor Coalition, 1992—, planning commr. Regional Planning Commn., Carson City, 1989—; mem. Mainstreet/Redevel. Authority Carson City, 1991—; mem. Nev. Day com., Carson City, 1985—, 4th of July com., 1985—, Gov.'s Ball com., 1985—; apptd. to criminal justice tech. skills com. Western Nev. C.C., 1994. Sgt. U.S. Army, 1970-73. Recipient Svc. award Carson City Bd. Suprs., 1984. Mem. AFL-CIO Police Assn. (pres. 1989—), Kiwanis. Republican. Roman Catholic. Home: 542 Stockton Rd Sonora CA 95370

EGAN, TALMAGE D., physician, educator; b. Salt Lake City, Nov. 25, 1959; s. Merritt H. and Marcia (White) E.; m. Julie Cook, July 15, 1984; children: James, Adam, Zeke, Sara Jane. BA, Brigham Young U., 1982; MD, U. Utah, 1986. Intern U. Utah Med. Ctr., Salt Lake CIty, 1986-87, resident, 1987-88, 88-90; resident Stanford U., Palo Alto, Calif., 1990-91, instr. anesthesia, 1991-92, asst. prof. anesthesia, 1992-93; asst. prof. anesthesia U. Utah Med. Ctr., 1993—. Stanford U. fellow, 1991-92. Mem. AMA, Am. Soc. Anesthesiology, Am. Soc. Clin. Pharmacology, Internat. Anesthesia Rsch. Soc. Office: U Utah Med Ctr Dept Anesthesia 5 N Med Dr Salt Lake City UT 84132

EGER, DENISE LEESE, rabbi; b. New Kensington, Pa., Mar. 14, 1960; d. Bernard D. and Estelle (Leese) E. BA in Religion, U. So. Calif., 1982; MA in Hebrew Letters, Hebrew Union Coll., L.A., 1985; Rabbi, Hebrew Union Coll., N.Y.C., 1988. Ordained rabbi, 1988. Rabbi Temple Beth Ora, Edmonton, Alta., Can., 1983-85; chaplain Isabella Geriatric Ctr., N.Y.C., 1986-88; Rabbi Beth Chayim Chadashim, L.A., 1988—. Contbr. articles to religious publs., chpt. to anthology. Bd. dirs. Pacific Area Reform Rabbis, Nechama: A Jewish Response to AIDS; mem. AIDS task force S.W. Coun. Union Am. Hebrew Congregations; vice chmn. spiritual Adv. com. AIDS Project L.A.; mem. community adv. bd. Shanti Found.; instl. rev. bd. co-chair Search Alliance. Mem. Cen. Conf. Am. Rabbis. Office: Beth Chayim Chadashim 6000 W Pico Blvd Los Angeles CA 90035-2625

EGER, MARILYN RAE, artist; b. Offett A.F.B., Nebr., Jan. 2, 1953; d. John W. and Joyce Faye (Carpenter) Shaver, stepmother Myrle I. MAsoner; m. Darrell W. Masoner, Feb. 28, 1971 (div. Sept. 1977); children: William Matthew, Melissa Rae; m. Gerard J. Eger, Jan. 30, 1982. BA, Calif. State U., Turlock, 1987. Cert. art tchr. 1990, Calif., lang. devel. specialist, 1993. Freelance artist oil painting Gibson Greetings Inc., Cin.; tchr. art, A.P. art, sculpture and ceramics Bear Creek High Sch., Stockton, Calif.; tchr. art privately. One-woman shows include Stockton Fine Arts Gallery, 1984-88, Accurate Art Gallery, Sacramento, 1989-90, Sharon Gile Gallery, Isleton, Calif., 1988-91, Le Galerie, Stockton, 1989-91, Masterpiece Gallery, Carmel, Calif., 1991-95, Alan Short Gallery, Stockton, 1991; represented by Iona's Gallery, Stockton, 1995—; represented in permanent collections Gulf Oil Chems., Kaiser Permanente, Masterpiece Gallery; prints pub. in Mus. Edits. West. Bd. dirs. Lodi Art Ctr., 1988-91, chmn. 1989. Recipient Award of Excellence Unitarian Fall Art Festival, 1990, Award of Excellence in Oils, 1992, Ben Day Meml. award, 1993, Bank Stockton award and H.M. Haggin Mus., 1989, U.S. Nat. Collegiate Art Merit award, 1988, Lodi 31st Ann., 1st Oils, 1988, Award of Excellence in Pastel Haggin Mus., 1992, 1st Oils and Don Morrell Meml. award CCAL Gallo Show, 1993, Art of Calif. Bronze Discovery award, 1993, 1st pastel Lodi Art Ann., 1995; Mellon grantee, 1994. Mem. C.A.E.A., Stockton Art League, Nat. League Am. Pen. Women, West Coast Pastel Soc., Calif. Art League, Ctrl. Calif. Art League. Republican. Methodist. Home: 1295 E Peltier Rd Acampo CA 95220-9652 Office: Gallery III Art Studio 104 N School St Ste 306 Lodi CA 95240-2120

EGERTER, JOHN T., computer services consultant; b. Wilmington, Del.; s. George and Harumi Egerter. BS in Computer Sci., U. Wash., 1989. Database cons. King County Med. Examiner, Seattle, 1988-89; client svcs. cons. SoundTel, Inc., Woodinville, Wash., 1990—; vol. database cons. Seattle Police Dept. Cmty. Svc. Officers Divsn., 1987-88, Fremont Pub. Assn., Seattle, 1988-89. Mem. Assn. for Computing Machinery. Home: PO Box 3168 Lynnwood WA 98046-3168 Office: SoundTel Inc 19501 144th Ave NE Ste D-700 Woodinville WA 98072

EGGAN, PETER CORNELIUS, mathematician; b. Eugene, Oreg., Mar. 19, 1958; s. Lawrence Carl Eggan and Janet Francis (Windecker) Glubrecht; m. Madeline Faith Greenberg, Sept. 14, 1986; 1 child, Elliott Reuben. BA in Math. and Physics, U. Ill., 1981; MA in Math., UCLA, 1983, PhD of Math., 1985. Staff engr. Hughes Aircraft Co., El Segundo, Calif., 1985-90; sr. mem. tech. staff Aerospace Corp., El Segundo, 1990—. Contbr. articles to profl. jours. Mem. IEEE, AIAA (Artificial Intelligence Tech. com.), Internat. Neural Networks Soc., Math. Assn. Am., Assn. Computer Machinery. Office: Aerospace Corp PO Box 92957 Los Angeles CA 90009-2957

EGGER, ERNEST ALOIS, urban planner; b. San Diego, Dec. 21, 1956; s. Ivo and Ernestine Gertrude (Stockalper) E.; m. Corinne Mary Chavez, Mar. 12, 1983; children: Ryan Alfred, Hollyann Corinne. BS, Calif. State Poly. U., Pomona, 1979. Registered environ. assessor, Calif. Asst. planner City of Brea, Calif., 1979-80; assoc. planner County of Riverside, Calif., 1980-81; prin. planner Willdan Assocs., Industry, Calif., 1981-89; dir. planning Trans-Pacific Cons., Temecula, Calif., 1989-93; prin./v.p. Urban Logic Cons., Temecula, 1993—. Dir. Hillcrest Carden Sch., Temecula, 1993—, Cherry Festival Assn., Beaumont, Calif., 1994—. Mem. Am. Planning Assn. (vice dir. profl. devel. 1991-93, newsletter editor 1989-91, Meritorious Planning award 1990), Am. Inst. Cert. Planners, Beaumont C. of C. Republican. Roman Catholic. Office: Urban Logic Consultants 43517 Ridge Park Dr Ste 200 Temecula CA 92590-3602

EGGERS, ALFRED JOHN, JR., research corporation executive; b. Omaha, June 24, 1922; s. Alfred John and Golden May (Meyers) E.; m. Elizabeth Ann Hills, Sept. 9, 1950; children—Alfred John III, Philip Norman. B.A., U. Nebr.-Omaha, 1945; M.S., Stanford U., 1951, Ph.D., 1957. Aerospace scientist, asst. dir. NASA Ames Research Ctr., Mountain View, Calif., 1944-64; dep. assoc. adminstr., asst. adminstr. for policy NASA, Washington, 1964-71; Hunsaker prof. MIT, Cambridge, 1969-71; asst. dir. NSF, Washington, 1971-77; dir. Lockheed Research Lab., Palo Alto, Calif., 1977-79; chmn. bd., chief exec. officer RANN, Inc., Palo Alto, Calif., 1979—; mem. sci. adv. bd. USAF, Washington, 1958-72, Aerospace Engring. Bd., NAE, Washington, 1973-77; mem. adv. bd. Solar Energy Rsch. Inst., Golden, Colo., 1985-89; chmn. A.J. Eggers & Co., Atherton, Calif., 1981—. Author: Hypersonic Flow, 1962; contbr. articles to profl. jours.; patentee in field. Vice chmn. Sch. Community Devel. Com., Los Altos Hills, Calif., 1963-64; mem., chmn. troop com. Boy Scouts Am., Arlington, Va., 1968-75; mem. safety com. ARC, Arlington, 1975-77. Served to lt. (j.g.) USN, 1943-46. Recipient Arthur S. Flemming award USJCC, 1956, TOYM award USJCC, 1957, Exceptional Svc. medal NASA, 1971, Disting. Svc. medal NSF, 1975, Disting. Svc. medal Pres. of U.S., 1977, commendation Nat. Sci. Bd., 1977. Fellow AAAS, AIAA (founder, bd. dirs. 1962-66, Sylvanus Albert Reed award 1961), Am. Astron. Soc.; mem. NAE (long-range planning and devel. com. 1983-85), Am. Wind Energy Assn., Washington Golf and Country Club, Sigma Xi, Tau Beta Pi. Republican. Home: 23 Fair Oaks Ln Atherton CA 94027-3808 Office: RANN Inc 260 Sheridan Ave Ste 414 Palo Alto CA 94306-2011

EGGERT, ROBERT JOHN, SR., economist; b. Little Rock, Dec. 11, 1913; s. John and Eleanora (Fritz) Lapp; m. Elizabeth Bauer, Nov. 28, 1935 (dec. Dec. 1991); children: Robert John, Richard F., James E.; m. Annamarie Hayes, Mar. 19, 1994. BS, U. Ill., 1935, MS, 1936; candidate in philosophy, U. Minn., 1938; LHD (hon.), Ariz. State U., 1988. Research analyst Bur. Agrl. Econs., U.S. Dept. Agr., Urbana, Ill., 1935; prin. marketing specialist War Meat Bd., Chgo., 1943; research analyst U. Ill., 1935-36; rsch. analyst U. Minn., 1936-38; asst. prof. econs. Kans. State Coll., 1938-41; asst. dir. marketing Am. Meat Inst., Chgo., 1941-43; economist, assoc. dir. Am. Meat Inst., 1943-50; mgr. dept. marketing research Ford div. Ford Motor Co., Dearborn, Mich., 1951-53; mgr. program planning Ford div. Ford Motor Co., 1953-54, mgr. bus. research, 1954-57, mgr. marketing research marketing staff, 1957-61; mgr. marketing research Ford div. Ford Motor Co. (Ford div.), 1961-64, mgr. internat. marketing research marketing staff, 1964-65, mgr. overseas marketing research planning, 1965-66; mgr. marketing research Ford div. Ford Motor Co. (Lincoln-Mercury div.), 1966-67; dir. agribus. programs Mich. State U., 1967-68; staff v.p. econ. and marketing research RCA Corp., N.Y.C., 1968-76; pres., chief economist Eggert Econ. Enterprises, Inc., Sedona, Ariz., 1976—; lectr. mktg. U. Chgo., 1947-49; adj. prof. bus. forecasting No. Ariz. U., 1976—; mem. econ. adv. bd. U.S. Dept. Commerce, 1969-71, mem. census adv. com., 1975-78; mem. panel econ. advisers Congl. Budget Office, 1975-76; interim dir. Econ. Outlook Ctr. Coll. Bus. Adminstrn. Ariz. State U., Tempe, 1985-86, cons., 1985—; mem. Econ. Estimates Commn. Ariz., 1979—; apptd. Ariz. Gov.'s Commn. Econ. Devel., 1991—, Investment Adv. Coun. Ariz. State Retirement System, 1993—; bd. trustees Marcus J. Lawrence Med. Ctr. Found., 1992—. Contbr. articles to profl. lit.; editor: monthly Blue Chip Econ. Indicators, 1976—; exec. editor Ariz. Blue Chip, 1984—, Western Blue Chip Econ. Forecast, 1986—, Blue Chip Job Growth Update, 1990—, Mexico Consensus Econ. Forecast, 1993—. Elder Ch. of Red Rocks. Recipient Econ. Forecast award Chgo. chpt. Am. Statis. Assn., 1950, 60, 68; Seer of Yr. award Harvard Bus. Sch. Indsl. Econs., 1973. Fellow Am. Statis. Assn. (chmn. bus. and econ. stats. sect. 1957—, pres. Chgo. chpt. 1948-49), Nat. Assn. Bus. Economists (council 1969-72); mem. Coun. Internat. Mktg. Rsch. and Planning Dirs. (chmn. 1965-66), Am. Mkting. Assn. (dir., v.p. mktg. mgmt. divsn. 1972-73, nat. pres. 1974-75), Fed. Stats. Users Conf. (chmn. trustees 1960-61), Conf. Bus Economists (chmn. 1973-74), Am. Quarter Horse Assn. (dir. 1966-73), Ariz. Econ. Roundtable, Am. Econs. Asssn., Phoenix Econ. Club (hon.), Ariz. C.

of C. (bd. dirs.), Plaza Club (Phoenix), Alpha Zeta. Republican. Office: Eggert Econ Enterprises Inc PO Box 2243 Sedona AZ 86339-2243

EGGERTSEN, FRANK THOMAS, research chemist; b. Provo, Utah, Mar. 26, 1913; s. Burton Simon and Anne (Thomas) E.; m. Beth Marie Krueger, Dec. 29, 1939; children: Karl F., Thomas K., Grace Ann. BA, U. Utah, 1934; PhD, U. Minn., 1939. Rsch. chemist Sherwin-Williams Co., Chgo., 1939-43, Shell Devel. Co., Emeryville, Calif., 1943-72; prin. rsch. scientist Calif. Ink Co. div. Flint Ink Corp., Berkeley, Calif., 1973-90; cons. Flint Ink Corp., Berkeley, 1990-91; ret., 1992. Contbr. articles to profl. jours.; patentee in field. Shevlin fellow U. Minn., 1938-39. Mem. Am. Chem. Soc., Sigma Xi, Phi Lambda Upsilon, Phi Kappa Phi. Democrat. Mormon. Home: 3710 W 6800 S Spanish Fork UT 84660-4124

EGGLESTON, ROSE MARY LEWIS QUARRELS, elementary education educator, clergywoman; b. Muskogee, Okla., Aug. 28, 1938; d. Euclid William and Willa Mae (McCollum) E.; m. Rayford B. Hairrington Sr., July 13, 1961 (div. June 1973); children: Rayford B. Hairrington Jr., Lisa Lynn Hairrington. BS in Elem. Edn., Langston U., 1960; MS in Sch. Mgmt., U. LaVerne, 1982. Ordained to ministry, 1993; notary pub. Childcare tchr. 6th Avenue Sch., L.A., 1959; tchr., homebound tchr., libr. Okla. City Schs., Oklahoma City, 1960-62; tchr. Compton (Calif.) Unified Schs., 1962-87, Pasadena (Calif.) Unified Schs., 1987; tchr., vice prin. L.A. Unified Schs., 1987-91; spl. edn. tchr. Pasadena Unified Schs., 1993—. Author: Baby Cheerfully Pottie Trained at Nine Months, 1992. Vol. Superior Ct. Probate Visitation Alliance, L.A., 1990—, Nissan Open, Spl. Olympics; tutor L.A. Jr. C. ov C.; reader Braille Inst.-City of Hope, 1990—. Mem. NEA, Calif. Tchrs. Assn., Compton Tchrs. Assn. (Disting. Svc. award 1985), Okla. Tchrs. Assn., Langston U. Club, Delta Sigma Theta. Home: 10107 E Avenue R14 Littlerock CA 93543-1526

EGLEY, THOMAS ARTHUR, computer services executive, accountant; b. Aberdeen, S.D., June 23, 1945; s. Ralph Joseph and Cora Ellen (Wade) E.; m. Cecelia K. Kuskie, Feb. 22, 1985. BBA, U. Mont., 1967, postgrad., 1973-75. CPA, Mont. Programmer, analyst Comml. Data, Missoula, Mont., 1973-77; data processing mgr. John R. Daily, Inc., Missoula, 1977-78; ptnr. Egley & White CPA's, Missoula, 1978-84, Egley & White Computer Services, Missoula, 1978-85; pres. Able Fin., Inc., Missoula, 1984—, PC Software, Inc., 1987—, E & W Computer Services, Inc., 1983—; lectr., Missoula, 1973—. Bd. dirs. Missoula Children's Theater, 1975-82. Served to sgt. U.S. Army, 1968-71. Mem. Am. Inst. CPAs, Mont. Soc. CPAs, Inst. Mgmt. Accts., Phi Sigma Kappa Alumni Club (pres. 1973—). Republican. Lutheran. Lodge: Elks. Home and Office: E&W Computer Svcs Inc PO Box 2729 Missoula MT 59806-2729

EGLINTON, WILLIAM MATTHEW, utility company executive; m. Paula Eglinton; children: Amy, Carrie. BSME, U. N.Mex., 1970. Various positions Pub. Svc. Co. N.Mex., Albuquerque, 1970-1983, v.p. planning and regulation, 1983-84, sr. v.p. retail customer svc. sector, 1988, exec. v.p., chief operating officer, 1988—. Trustee U. Albuquerque; bd. dirs., mem. fin. com. St. Joseph Health Care Corp., Greater Albuquerque C. of C. Exec. Com., vice chairperson ednl. affairs div.; bd. dirs. United Way Exec. Com., vice chairperson resource devel. com.; chairperson Albuquerque Bus. Edn. Compact.

EGUCHI, YASU, artist; b. Japan, Nov. 30, 1938; came to U.S., 1967; s. Chihaku and Kiku (Koga) E.; m. Anita Phillips, Feb. 24, 1968. Student, Horie Art Acad., Japan, 1958-65. Exhibited exhbns., Tokyo Mus. Art, 1963, 66, Santa Barbara Mus. Art, Calif., 1972, 73, 74, 85, Everson Mus. Art, Syracuse, N.Y., 1980, Nat. Acad. Design, N.Y.C., 1980—, one-man shows, Austin Gallery, Scottsdale, Ariz., 1968-87, Joy Tash Gallery, Scottsdale, 1989—, Greyston Galleries, Cambria, Calif., 1969, 70, 72, Copenhagen Galleries, Calif., 1970-78, Charles and Emma Frye Art Mus., Seattle, 1974, 84, Hammer Galleries, N.Y.C., 1977, 79, 81, 93, City of Heidenheim, W. Ger., 1980, Artique Ltd., Anchorage, 1981—; pub. and pvt. collections, Voith Gmbh, W. Ger., City of Giengen and City of Heidenheim, Fed. Republic Germany, represented, Deer Valley, Utah, Hunter Resources, Santa Barbara, Am. Embassy, Paris, Charles and Emma Frye Art Mus., Seattle, Nat. Acad. Design, N.Y.C.; author: Der Brenz Entlang, 1980; contbr. to jours in field. Active Guide Dogs for the Blind, San Raphael, Calif., 1976; active City of Santa Barbara Arts Council, 1979, The Eye Bank for Sight Restoration, N.Y., 1981, Anchorage Arts Council, 1981, Santa Barbara Mus. Natural History, 1989. Recipient Selective artist award Yokohama Citizen Gallery, 1965; recipient Artist of Yr. award Santa Barbara Arts Council, 1979, Hon. Citizen award City of Heidenheim, 1980, The Adolph and Clara Obrig prize NAD, 1983, Cert. of Merit NAD, 1985, 87. Home: PO Box 30206 Santa Barbara CA 93130-0206*

EHLER, LESTER ERVIN, entomology educator; b. Slaton, Tex., Jan. 3, 1946. BS, Tex. Tech U., 1968; PhD, U. Calif., Berkeley, 1972. Asst. prof. Tex. A&M U., College Station, 1972-73; asst. prof. U. Calif., Davis, 1973-79, assoc. prof., 1979-85, prof., 1985—. Office: U Calif Dept Entomology Davis CA 95616

EHLER, RICHARD LEE, advertising executive, publisher, consultant; b. Holywood, Kans., July 11, 1930; s. John and Katie Anna (Schmidt) E.; m. Sharon K. DePue, 1959 (div. Apr. 1981); 1 child, Quinton John; m. Barbara J. Decker (div. May 1984). BS in Tech. Journalism, Kans. State U., 1952. Mgr. tech. communications GE, 1955-63; supr. tech. communications Motorola, Phoenix, 1963-64; account exec. Lennen & Newell Inc., San Francisco, 1964-65; v.p. Chace Co. Advt. Inc, Santa Barbara, Calif., 1965-72; account exec. Larson/Bateman Inc., Santa Barbara, 1972-79; owner Richler & Co., Santa Barbara, 1979—. Author: The Print Media Planning Manual, 1991, Directory of Print Media Advertising Resources, Print Media Analysis Tools, Checklists for Print Media Advertising Planning and Buying, 1991. Staff sgt. U.S. Army, 1952-54. Mem. Internat. Assn. of Ind. Pubs., Pubs. Mktg. Assn., Santa Barbara Advt. Club (bd. dir. 1970), Soc. of Tech. Communications (sr., nat. 1963-72), Screenwriters Assn. of Santa Barbara, Toastmasters Internat. (ATM cert. 1984), Elks. Republican. Mem. Unity Ch.

EHLERS, ELEANOR MAY COLLIER (MRS. FREDERICK BURTON EHLERS), civic worker; b. Klamath Falls, Oreg., Apr. 23, 1920; d. Alfred Douglas and Ethel (Foster) Collier; BA, U. Oreg., 1941; secondary tchrs. credentials Stanford, 1942, master gardener cert. Oreg. State U., 1993; m. Frederick Burton Ehlers, June 26, 1943; children: Frederick Douglas, Charles Collier. Tchr., Salinas Union High Sch., 1942-43; piano tchr. pvt. lessons, Klamath Falls, 1958—. Mem. Child Guidance Adv. Coun., 1956-60; mem. adv. com. Boys and Girls Aid Soc., 1965-67; mem. Gov.'s Adv. Com. Arts and Hunanities, 1966-67; bd. mem. PBS TV Sta. KSYS, 1988-92, Friends of Mus. U. Oreg., 1966-69, Arts in Oreg., 1966-68, Klamath County Colls. for Oreg.'s Future, 1968—; co-chmn. Friends of Collier Park, Collier Park Logging Mus., 1986-88, sec. 1988—; chpt. pres. Am. Field Svc., 1962-63; mem. Gov.'s Com. Governance of Community Colls., 1967; bd. dirs. Favell Mus. Western Art and Artifacts, 1971-80, Community Concert Assn., 1950—, pres., 1966-74; established Women's Guild at Merle West Med. Ctr., 1965, sec. bd. dirs, 1962-65, 76-90, bd. dirs., 1962—, mem. bldg. com. 1962-67, mem. planning com., chmn. edn. and rsch. com. hosp. bd., 1967—; pres., bd. dirs. Merle West Med. Ctr., 1990-92, vice chmn., 1992—. Named Woman of Month Klamath Herald News, 1965; named grant to Oreg. Endowed Fellowship Fund, AAUW, 1971; recipient greatest Svc. award Oreg. Tech. Inst., 1970-71, Internat. Woman of Achievement award Quota Club, 1981, U. Oreg. Pioneer award, 1981. Mem. AAUW (local pres. 1955-56), Oreg. Music Tchrs. Assn. (pres. Klamath Basin dist. 1979-81), P.E.O. (Oreg. dir. 1968-75, state pres. 1974-75, trustee internat. Continuing Edn. Fund 1977-83, chmn. 1981-83), Pi Beta Phi, Mu Phi Epsilon, Pi Lambda Theta. Presbyterian. Home: 1338 Pacific Ter Klamath Falls OR 97601-1833

EHMAN, MICHAEL FREDERICK, electronics executive; b. Springfield, Ohio, Aug. 14, 1945; s. Burnell Frederick and Doris (Daugherty) E.; m. Carol Gampher; children: Heather Lyn, Matthew Frederick. BA in Mineralogy, Miami U., Oxford, Ohio, 1967; PhD in Solid State Sci., Pa. State U., 1970; MBA, So. Meth. U., 1982. With tech. staff Rockwell Internat., Anaheim, Calif., 1970-74; mgr. engrng. Rockwell Internat., Chgo., 1975, Newport Beach, Calif., 1976; dir. engring. Rockwell Internat., Dallas, 1977-80; v.p. advt. tech. optoelectronics TRW, Carrolton, Tex., 1980-81; pres. Morgan Semiconductor Inc., Garland, Tex., 1982-85; gen. mgr. elect. materials Ethyl Corp., Garland, 1985-89; mktg. mgr. Alcoa Electronic Packaging, 1989-92, Splty. Metals div. Alcoa, New Kensington, Pa., 1992-93; gen. mgr. integrated tech. div. Bourns, Inc., Logan, Utah, 1994—; bd. dirs. ESS Technologies, San Francisco. Contbr. 22 articles to profl. jours.; patentee in field. Mem. IEEE, Am. Soc. Metals, Electrochem. Soc., Am. Assn. Crystal Growth. Republican. Methodist. Office: Bourns Inc Integrated Tech Div 1400 N 1000 W Logan UT 84321-1900

EHMANN, ANTHONY VALENTINE, lawyer; b. Chgo., Sept. 5, 1935; s. Anthony E. and Frances (Verweil) E.; m. Alice A. Avina, Nov. 27, 1959; children: Ann, Thomas, Jerome, Gregory, Rose, Robert. BS, Ariz. State U., 1957; JD, U. Ariz., 1960. Bar: Ariz. 1960, U.S. Tax Ct. 1960, U.S. Sup. Ct. 1968; CPA, Ariz.; cert. tax specialist. Spl. asst. atty. gen., 1961-68; mem. Ehmann and Hiller, Phoenix, 1969—. Republican dist. chmn. Ariz., 1964; pres. Grand Canyon council Boy Scouts Am., 1987-89, mem. exec. com., 1981—; v.p. western region Boy Scouts Am., 1991—. Recipient Silver Beaver award Boy Scouts Am., 1982, Bronze Pelican award Cath. Com. on Scouting, 1981, Silver Antelope award Boy Scouts Am., 1994. Mem. State Bar Ariz. (chmn. tax sect. 1968, 69), Central Ariz. Estate Planning Council (pres. 1968, 69). Republican. Roman Catholic. Clubs: KC (grand knight 1964, 65) (Glendale, Ariz.), Serra Internat. (pres. Phoenix club 1992-93, dist. gov. Ariz. 1993-95), Knight of Holy Sepulchre, Knight of Malta. Office: Ehmann & Hiller 2525 E Camelback Rd Ste 720 Phoenix AZ 85016-4229

EHRESMAN, PAULA SUZETTE, information manager, researcher; b. Bloomington, Ill., Mar. 5, 1951; d. Earl Loyd and Betty Adiene (Diggle) E. BA, Western State Coll., 1974; MLS, Emporia State U., 1992; cert. in computer mgmt., U. Colo., 1993. Edn. specialist Dickson Mounds State Mus., Lewistown, Ill., 1978-80; med. asst. Western Neurol. Group, Denver, 1980-82; rsch. historian Roxborough State Pk., Littleton, Colo., 1982-83, Chatfield State Recreation Area, Littleton, Colo., 1983-86, Denver Botanic Gardens, Denver, 1984; rsch. specialist KRMA-TV, Denver, 1984-85; co-producer cablevision program Littleton Pub. Schs., 1985-86; edn. asst. internship Littleton Hist. Mus., 1986; rschr., info. mgmt. Internat. Broadcasting Network, Denver, 1986-93; photo libr. Rocky Mountain News, Denver, 1994—; cons. Chatfield State Recreation Area, Littleton, 1990-91; mem. Chatfield Hist. Restoration Subcom., Littleton, 1985—, chairperson, 1991—. Mem. Colo. Women's C. of C., Denver, 1990-93, Coun. of Homeowner's for a Planned Environment, Denver, 1985-90, pres., 1987-88, adv. coun. Arapahoe C.C., Littleton, 1988. Named one of Outstanding Young Women of Am., 1984. Mem. ALA, Spl. Libr. Assn. (bd. dirs. 1994—), Denver Art Mus.

EHRET, CHRISTOPHER PAUL, history and linguistics educator; b. San Francisco, July 27, 1941; s. Robert Ashworth and Margaret (Scott) Fish; m. Patricia Louise Clemmer; children: Susannah Marie, Seth John, Allan Thomas Gulledge, Jana Chrystene Gulledge. BA, U. Redlands, 1963; MA, Northwestern U., 1966, PhD, 1968. Asst. prof. U. Calif., L.A., 1968-72, assoc. prof., 1972-78, prof., 1978-94, disting. (step VI) prof., 1994—; chair undergrad. program in African studies U. Calif., L.A., 1976—; lectr. in field. Author: Southern Nilotic History: Linguistic Approaches to the Study of the Past, 1971, The Historical Reconstruction of Southern Cushitic Phonology and Vocabulary, 1980, Reconstructing Proto-Afroasiatic: Vowels, Tone, Consonants and Vocabulary, 1995; author, editor: The Archaeological and Linguistic Reconstruction of African History, 1982; editl. bd. Sprache und Geschichte in Africa, 1975—; contbr. articles to profl. jours. Coach Am. Youth Soccer, Calif., 1983-90. Grantee Ford Found., U.S., Kenya, Tanzania, 1971-76; Nat. Merit scholar Caltech, U. Redlands, 1959-63; Fgn. Area fellow Social Sci. Rsch. Coun., Kenya, Tanzania, Uganda, 1966-68; Fulbright Rsch. fellow, Somalia, 1982. Mem. African Studies Assn. (life). Office: Univ Calif Los Angeles CA 90024

EHRHORN, RICHARD WILLIAM, electronics company executive; b. Marshalltown, Iowa, Jan. 21, 1934; s. Theodore Raymond and Zelda Elizabeth (Axtell) E.; BSEE, U. Minn., 1955; MSEE, Calif. Inst. Tech., 1958; m. Marilyn Patrick, Aug. 1, 1959; children: Scott Patrick, Kimberlee Dawn. Sr. engr. Gen. Dynamics Corp., Pomona, Calif., 1956-60; sr. rsch. engr. Calif. Inst. Tech. Jet Propulsion Lab., Pasadena, 1960-63; mgr. advanced devel. lab. Electronic Communications Inc., St. Petersburg, Fla., 1963-68; gen. mgr. Signal/One div., 1968-70; chmn. bd. dirs., CEO Ehrhorn Tech. Ops., Inc., Colorado Springs, Colo., 1970—. Bd. dirs. Fremont County (Colo.) Econ. Devel. Council, 1978-84; trustee, bd. dirs. St. Thomas More Hosp., Canon City, 1981-88; trustee First United Meth. Ch., Canon City, 1980-85; mem. Fremont Re-1 Dist. Bd. Edn., 1983-88, pres., 1985-88; regent Liberty U., 1995—. Mem. IEEE (sr., chmn. sect. 1967-68), Armed Forces Communications and Electronics Assn., Am. Radio Relay League, Radio Club Am., Quar. Century Wireless Assn. Author: (with others) Principles of Electronic Warfare, 1959; patentee in field. Home: 3060 Sheiks Pl Colorado Springs CO 80904-1138 Office: 4975 N 30th St Colorado Springs CO 80919-4101

EHRHORN, THOMAS FREDERICK, electronics engineer; b. Lebanon, Pa., Nov. 12, 1946; s. Frederick William and Evelyn Matilda (Daullary) E.; m. Elaine Mae Thernlund, Feb. 16, 1974; 1 child, Susan Marie. BA in Computer Sci., SUNY, Albany, 1981; AS in Tng. Devices Technology, C.C. of the Air Force, Maxwell AFB, Ala., 1986; MA in Edn., Chapman U., 1992. Cert. tchr. computer sci., Calif. Enlisted USAF, 1966, advanced through ranks to chief master sgt.; electronics tech. USAF, various, 1966-86; ret. USAF, 1986; electronics tech. Systems Rsch. Labs, Castle AFB, Calif., 1986-89; computer sci. USAF, Castle AFB, 1989-93; electronics engr. USAF, Kirtland AFB, N.Mex., 1994—. Registrar Atwater (Calif.) Youth Soccer League, 1990-93; mem./pres. Winton (Calif.) Sch. Bd., 1987-91; exec. bd. Yosemite Area Coun., Boy Scouts Am., modesto, Calif., 1985-87; chmn. Fresno (Calif.) Diocese Youth Ministry Bd., 1985-86. Mem. IEEE, Assn. Old Crows, Mensa, K.C. Democrat. Roman Catholic. Office: OO-ALC/LIRAC 4249 Hercules Way SE Kirtland AFB NM 87117

EHRLICH, ALAN M., marketing company executive; b. N.Y.C., Oct. 3, 1963; s. Jerrold I. and Elaine J. Ehrlich. BA in Econs. and Polit. Sci., U. Rochester, 1985; MBA in Mktg., Loyola Marymount U., L.A., 1993. With customer rels. dept. Marine Midland Bank, Rochester, N.Y., 1983-85; staff auditor Marine Midland Bank, N.Y.C., 1985-86; budget coord., fin. analyst, sr. project acct. Simon Mktg. Inc., L.A., from 1986, mgr. project acctg. Vol. ARC, L.A., 1994. Mem. Platinum Users Group, L.A. Jr. C. of C. Office: Simon Mktg Inc 1900 Avenue Of The Stars Los Angeles CA 90067-4301

EHRLICH, STEPHEN RICHARD, lawyer; b. Rockville Centre, N.Y., Dec. 28, 1949; s. Harry Simon and Ida G. (Lable) E. BA, U. Pa., 1971; JD, U. Denver, 1977. Bar: Colo. 1977, U.S. Dist. Ct. Colo. 1977. Pvt. practice Denver, 1977—. Mem. Assn. Trial Lawyers Am., Colo. Bar Assn., Colo. Trial Lawyers Assn., Denver Bar Assn. Home: 534 E 7th Ave Denver CO 80203-3883 Office: 847 Sherman St Denver CO 80203-2913

EHRLICH, STEVEN DAVID, architect; b. N.Y.C., June 12, 1946; s. Samuel J. and Betty Ehrlich; m. Marlo Lani, Jan. 3, 1981; children: Vanessa, Sarah, Julia, Bebecca. BS, Rensselaer Poly. Inst., 1968, BArch., 1969. Registered architect, Calif. Architect Peace Corps, Morocco, 1969-71; tchr. Ahmadu Bello U., Nigeria, 1974-77; pvt. practice architecture, Venice, Calif., 1978—; tchr. U. So. Calif., L.A., 1982-83, Sci.-Arch, Santa Monica, Calif., 1983, UCLA, 1985. Recipient Builders Choice Grand award Builders Mag., 1983, 85. Mem. AIA (Design awards Los Angeles chpt. 1981, 82, 83, 87 Calif. chpt. 1983-84, 88 Sunset chpt. 1983). Office: Ehrlich Architects 75 Market St Venice CA 90291-3603

EHRSAM, ELDON EDWARD, operations research analyst, real estate broker; b. Bern, Kans., July 8, 1936; s. Loyd and Elma Elizabeth (Bauman) E.; m. Clara Louise Schwartz, Nov. 20, 1957; children: Elizabeth Sue, Jeffrey Edward, John Eldon, Brian Loyd. BS, Washburn U., Topeka, 1962; MS, U. So. Calif., 1969; cert. computer tech., U. Calif., Santa Barbara, 1972. Lic. real estate broker, Calif. Physicist Naval Ordnance Lab., Corona, Calif., 1962-65; electronic engr. Hdqs. Space and Missile Test Ctr., Vandenberg AFB, 1968-73, telemetry sys. mgr., 1973-76, ops. rsch. analyst, 1976—; broker assoc. Real Properties Investments, Solvang, Calif., 1981-89; securities rep. Vestcap Securities Corp., Solvang, 1982-89; broker Hunter Prudential Realty, Lompoc, Calif., 1990—. Co-contbr. articles to profl. jours. Asst. scoutmaster Boy Scouts Am. Mem. AIAA, Internat. Platform Assn., Nat. Assn. Securities Dealers, Nat. Assn. Realtors, Real Estate Securities and Syndication Inst., Sigma Pi Sigma, Masons, Elks. Office: Space and Missile Sys Ctr Detachment 9 Vandenberg AFB CA 93437-5320

EICHINGER, MARILYNNE H., museum administrator; m. Martin Eichinger; children: Ryan, Kara, Julia, Jessica, Talik. BA in Anthropology and Sociology magna cum laude, Boston U., 1965; MA, Mich. State U., 1971. With emergency and outpatient staff Ingham County Mental Health Ctr., 1972; founder, pres., exec. dir. Impression 5 Sci. and Art Mus., Lansing, Mich., 1973-85; pres. Oreg. Mus. Sci. and Industry, Portland, 1985-95; bd. dirs. Portland Visitors Assn., 1994—; pres. Informal Edn. Products Ltd., Portland, 1995—; bd. dirs. Portland Visitors Assn., 1994—, NW Regional Edn. Labs., 1991—; instr. Lansing (Mich.) C.C., 1978; ptnr. Eyrie Studio, 1982-85; bd. dirs. Assn. Sci. Tech. Ctrs., 1980-84, 88-93; mem. adv. bd. Portland State U.; condr. numerous workshops in interactive exhibit design, adminstrn. and fund devel. for schs., orgns., profl. socs. Author: (with Jane Mack) Lexington Montessori School Survey, 1969, Manual on the Five Senses, 1974; pub. Mich. edit. Boing mag. Founder Cambridge Montessori Sch., 1964; bd. dirs. Lexington Montessori Sch., 1969, Mid-Mich. South Health Sys. Agy., 1978-81, Cmty. Referral Ctr., 1981-85, Sta. WKAR-Radio, 1981-85; active Lansing "Riverfest" Lighted Boat Parade, 1980; mem. state Health Coordinating Coun., 1980-82; mem. pres.'s adv. coun. Portland State U., 1986—; mem. pres.' adv. bd. Portland State U., 1987-91. Recipient Diana Cert. Leadership, YWCA, 1976-77, Woman of Achievement award, 1991, Community Svc. award Portland State U., 1992. Mem. Am. Assn. Mus., Oreg. Mus. Assn., Assn. Sci. and Tech. Ctrs., Zonta Lodge (founder, bd. dirs. East Lansing club 1978), Internat. Women's Forum, Rotary Club Portland, City Club Portland, Portland C. of C. Office: Oreg Mus Sci and Industry 1945 SE Water Ave Portland OR 97214-3356

EICHMAN, PATRICIA FRANCES, interior designer; b. Hamtramck, Mich., Dec. 12, 1938; d. Stanley Z. Pasierbek and Annette T. (Rogusz) Spindler; m. Richard R. Bourassa, Mar. 1, 1957 (div. Nov. 1978); children: Robert, Jeffrey, Lori; m. John W. Eichman Jr., Sept. 30, 1983 (div.). Grad. H.S., Detroit. Cert. interior designer, Calif. Sales designer Ethan Allen Store, Phoenix, 1974-79; interior designer Lou Regester Furniture, Phoenix, 1979-84, VJ Lloyds Furniture, San Diego, 1985-94; pvt. practice San Diego, 1994—. Treas. Friends of Downtown, San Diego, 1993, bd. dirs., 1993-94, co-chair charities, 1994, 2d v.p., 1995; bd. dirs. Design Alliance to Combat Areas, San Diego, 1990-91. Recipient Sam award Bldg. Industry Assn., San Diego, 1993, Grand Orchid award Orchid & Onions, San Diego, 1993, Best Master Bedroom Suite award Street of Dreams, San Diego, 1991. Mem. Internat. Soc. Interior Designers (pres. San Diego chpt. 1992, treas. 1987-89, bd. dirs. 1989-93), Am. Soc. Interior Designers, Internat. Interior Design Assn. Home: 6321 Caminito del Cervato San Diego CA 92111 Office: P Eichman Interior Design 6321 Caminito Del Cervato San Diego CA 92111-6854

EIFLER, CARL FREDERICK, retired psychologist; b. Los Angeles, June 27, 1906; s. Carl Frederick and Pauline (Engelbert) E.; m. Margaret Christine Aaberg, June 30, 1963; 1 son, Carl Henry; 1 adopted son, Byron Hisey. BD, Jackson Coll., 1956; Ph.D., Ill. Inst. Tech., 1962. Insp. U.S. Bur. Customs, 1928-35, chief insp., 1936-37, dep. collector, 1937-56; bus. mgr. Jackson Coll., Honolulu, 1954-56, instr., 1955-56; grad. asst. instr., research asst. Ill. Inst. Tech., Chgo., 1959-62; psychologist Monterey County Mental Health Services, Salinas, Calif., 1964-73; ret., 1973. Contbg. author Psychon. Sci., vol. 20, 1970; co-author: The Deadliest Colonel; author, pub.: Jesus Said. Served with U.S. Army, 1922-23, 40-47; col. ret. Decorated Combat Infantryman's Badge, Legion of Merit with 2 oak leaf clusters, Bronze Star medal, Air medal, Purple Heart; named to Military Intelligence Corps Hall of Fame, 1988; recipient Albert Gallatin award U.S. Treas. Dept., 1963, Gen. William J. Donovan award, 1993. Mem. AAUP, Am. Psychol. Assn., Western States Psychol. Assn., Calif. Psychol. Assn., Res. Officers Assn. (Hawaii pres. 1947), Assn. Former Intelligence Officers (bd. govs., Western coord.), Pearl Harbor Survivors, 101 Assn., Assn. U.S. Army Vets. of OSS (past bd. govs., Western coord., v.p.), Ret. Officers Assn., Masons, KT, Shriners, Elks, Nat. Sojourners, Psi Chi. Home: 22700 Picador Dr Salinas CA 93908-1116

EIGLER, DONALD MARK, physicist; b. L.A., Mar. 23, 1953; s. Irving Baer and Evelin Muriel (Baker) E.; m. Roslyn Winifred Rubesin, Nov. 2, 1986. BA, U. Calif., San Diego, 1975, PhD in Physics, 1984. Rsch. assoc. U. Köln (Fed. Republic Germany), 1975-76; rsch. assoc. U. Calif., San Diego, 1977-84, postdoctoral rsch. assoc., 1984, assoc. rsch. physicist dept. physics, 1986; postdoctoral mem. tech. staff AT&T Bell Labs., Murray Hill, N.J., 1984-86; rsch. staff mem. IBM, San Jose, Calif., 1986-93, IBM fellow, 1993—; Alexander M. Cruickshank lectr., 1994; 1994 Alexander M. Cruickshank lectr. in physical sci. (Gordon Rsch. Confs.). Co-winner Newcomb Cleve. prize AAAS, 1993-94. Office: IBM Almaden Rsch Ctr 650 Harry Rd San Jose CA 95120-6001

EIGSTI, ROGER HARRY, insurance company executive; b. Vancouver, Wash., Apr. 17, 1942; s. Harry A. and Alice E. (Huber) E.; m. Mary Lou Nelson, June 8, 1963; children: Gregory, Ann. BS, Linfield Coll., 1964. CPA, Oreg., Wash. Staff CPA Touche Ross and Co., Portland, Oreg., 1964-72; asst. to controller Safeco Corp., Seattle, 1972-78, controller, 1980; controller Safeco Life Ins. Co., Seattle, 1978-80; pres. Safeco Credit Co., Seattle, 1980-81, Safeco Life Ins. Co., Seattle, 1981-85; exec. v.p., CFO Safeco Corp., Seattle, 1985—, chmn., pres., CEO. bd. dirs. Ind. Colls. of Wash., Seattle, 1981-87, bus. dir. Seattle Repertory Theatre, 1981—, bd. dirs. 1981—. Mem. Am. Inst. CPA's, Life Office Mgmt. Assn. (bd. dirs. 1983—), Seattle C. of C. (chmn. metro budget rev. com. 1984—). Republican. Clubs: Mercer Island (Wash.) Country (treas., bd. dirs. 1981-84); Central Park Tennis. Home: 11701 NE 36th Pl Bellevue WA 98005-1234*

EIKENBERRY, ARTHUR RAYMOND, writer, service executive, researcher; b. Sebring, Fla., June 5, 1920; s. Leroy Albertus and Vernie Cordelia (Griffin) E.; m. Carol Jean Parrott, June 10, 1955; children: Robin Rene, Shari LaVon, Jan Rochelle, Karyn LaRae, Kelli Yvette. Student, Pasadena (Calif.) Jr. Coll., 1939, Kunming U., China, 1944-45. MSgt. Army Air Corps, 1941-45, re-enlisted in grade of TSgt., 1947; advanced through grades to SMSgt. USAF, 1968; ret., 1973, mgmt., pers., adminstrv. and security insp.; mgr. inventory control TR Devel. Co., Englewood, Colo., 1973-74; real estate agt. The Pinery, Parker, Colo., 1974-75; mgr., patient acctg. dept. Univ. Colo. Health Scis. Ctr., Denver, 1975-89. Author: Investment Strategies for the Clever Investor, 1989, LOTTO GURU (Omni-Personal Selection Systems & Strategies), 1989. Charter mem. U.S. Congl. Adv. Bd. Fellow Internat. Biog. Ctr. (hon. life patron, dep. dir. gen.); mem. Am. Biog. Inst. (life, dep. gov., nat. adviser), World Inst. of Achievement (disting.), Masons, Royal Order of the Amaranth. Address: The Lakes 8524 W Sahara Ave # 174 Las Vegas NV 89117-1818

EILBER, FREDERICK RICHARD, surgeon; b. Detroit, Aug. 17, 1940; s. Frederick Benjamin and Margaret (Patterson) E.; m. Harriet Harris Comstock, Dec. 2, 1964; children: Frederick C., Gregory K., Timothy B., Matthew C. MD, U. Mich., 1965. Intern U. Md., 1965-66; surg. resident U. Md., Balt., 1965-72; clin. assoc. NIH Surgery, Bethesda, Md., 1967-71; sr. fellow M.D. Anderson, Houston, 1972-73; asst. prof. dept. surgery UCLA, 1973-75, assoc. prof., 1975-79, prof., 1979-91, prof., chief surgery/oncology, 1991—. Recipient Disting. Alumni award M.D. Anderson, 1985. Fellow ACS, Am. Surg. Assn., Soc. Univ. Surgeons, Soc. Head and Neck Surgeons, Soc. Surg. Oncology (James Ewing Resident award 1970); mem. Am. Radium Soc. (pres. 1986). Office: UCLA Divsn Surg Oncology 54-140 CHS 10833 Le Conte Ave Los Angeles CA 90024

EILENBERG, LAWRENCE IRA, theater educator, artistic director; b. Bklyn., May 26, 1947; s. Jerome and Dorothy Vera (Natleson) E.; m. Diane Marie Eliasof, Nov. 25, 1973 (dec. Dec. 1984); children: David Joseph, Benjamin Alan; m. Judith Heiner, Nov. 10, 1990 (dec. Nov. 1994). BA, Cornell U., 1968; MPhil, Yale U., 1971, PhD, 1975. Jr. fellow Davenport Coll., Yale U., New Haven, 1971-72; asst. prof. theatre dept. Cornell U., Ithaca, N.Y., 1972-75; vis. asst. prof. in theatre U. Mich., Ann Arbor, 1975-77; asst. prof., then assoc. prof. U. Denver, 1977-82, 83; prof. San Francisco State U., 1983—, chmn. theatre arts dept., 1984-92; artistic dir. Magic Theatre, San Francisco, 1992-93; theatre corr. Sta. KCFR (NPR), Denver, 1979-82; literary mgr. Denver Ctr. Theatre Co., 1981-83; artistic dir. San

Francisco New Vaudeville Festival, 1985-89; dramaturg One Act Theatre Co., San Francisco, 1986-88; bd. dirs. Theatre Bay Area, San Francisco, 1985-90, pres., 1987-89; co-dir. Congress of Clowns, 1994; speaker, lectr. in field. Editor Stage/Space mag., 1981-83; contbr. articles, book and theater revs. to profl. publs. U.S. del. Podium Festival of USSR, Moscow, 1989. Grantee Lilly Found., 1981, Idaho Humanities Assn., 1983, 84, 85, NEA, 1986, 92, Calif. Arts Coun., 1987, 88, 92; recipient Best Broadcast award Colo. Broadcasters Assn., 1982. Mem. Literary Mgrs. and Dramaturgs Am. (v.p. 1989-90), Nat. Assn. Schs. of Theatre (bd. accreditation, 1990-91, evaluator 1986—). Home: 1568 Columbus Ave Burlingame CA 94010-5512 Office: San Francisco State U Theatre Arts Dept 1600 Holloway Ave San Francisco CA 94132-1722

EILERMAN, BETTY JEAN, marriage and family counselor; b. Phila., Nov. 1, 1942; d. Frank Irving and Elizabeth Marquerite (Lennon) Gunsauls; m. Jerome Louis Eilerman, Dec. 15, 1969. BA, Rosemont Coll., 1964; M.Rel.Ed., Loyola U., Chgo., 1970; PhD, Calif. Pacific U., 1980; MA, U. San Francisco, 1984. Lic. marriage and family therapist, Calif., Minn. Instr. Maria Goretti High Sch., Phila., 1964-66, Bishop McDevitt High Sch., Wyncote, Pa., 1966-68; assoc. editor George A. Pflaum Pub., Dayton, Ohio, 1968-69; instr. Acad. of Our Lady of Peace, San Diego, 1970, The Bishop's Schs., LaJolla, Calif., 1970-80; ptnr. Write Right!, LaJolla, 1979-81; counselor Ctr. Creative Consciousness, Santa Rosa, Calif., 1982; intern Clin. Cognitive Inst., Santa Rosa, 1982-83; counselor Cath. Community Svc., Santa Rosa, 1983-84; pvt. practice Santa Rosa, 1988-92, Fargo, N.D., 1988-92; bereavement counselor Home Hospice, Santa Rosa, 1983-85; hypnotherapist, Santa Rosa and Fargo, 1985—; co-facilitator Rebuilding: Divorce Workshops, Santa Rosa, 1986-88; co-dir. Reconnections, Santa Rosa, 1987-88, Counselor Employee Support Systems, Santa Rosa, 1987-88; founder Crossing, Fargo, 1988-92, Bridge House, Santa Rosa, 1993—. Pres. Profl. Women's Group, Phila., 1966=67, Newcomers Club, Santa Rosa, 1982; dir. Svc. League, LaJolla, 1970-80. Honoree Nat. Disting. Svc. Registry for Counseling and Devel., 1990. Mem. Am. Assn. Marriage & Family Therapy, Calif. Assn. Marriage & Family Therapy, Assn. Humanistic Psychology, Assn. Transpersonal Psychology, Am. Mental Health Counselors Assn., Am. Assn. Counseling and Devel., Am. Assn. Pastoral Counselors, Nat. Honor Soc., Delta Epsilon Sigma. Office: 1211 Pacific Ave Santa Rosa CA 95404-3401

EINSTEIN, STEPHEN JAN, rabbi; b. L.A., Nov. 15, 1945; s. Syd C. and Selma (Rothenberg) E.; m. Robin Susan Kessler, Sept. 9, 1967; children: Rebecca Yael, Jennifer Melissa, Heath Isaac, Zachary Shane. AB, UCLA, 1967; B.H.L., Hebrew Union Coll., L.A., 1968; M.A.H.L., Hebrew Union Coll., Cin., 1971; D.H.L., Hebrew Union Coll., L.A., 1995. Ordained rabbi. Rabbi Temple Beth Am, Parsippany, N.J., 1971-74; rabbi Temple Beth David, Westminster, Calif., 1974-76, Congregation B'nai Tzedek, Fountain Valley, Calif., 1976—; bd. dirs. Heritage Pointe. Co-author: Every Person's Guide to Judaism, 1989; co-editor: Introduction to Judaism, 1983. Pres., trustee Fountain Valley (Calif.) Sch. Bd., 1984-90; mem. Personnel Commn. Fountain Valley Sch. Dist., 1991—; chaplain Fountain Valley Police Dept. Honored for Maj. Contributions to Jewish Learning, Orange County (Calif.) Bur. Jewish Edn., 1986; recipient Micah Award for Interfaith Activities, Am. Jewish Com., 1988. Mem. Ctrl. Conf. Am. Rabbis (exec. bd. 1989-91, ethics com. 1993—), Pacific Assn. Reform Rabbis (exec. bd. 1987-91), Orange County Bd. Rabbis (pres., sec.-treas. 1974-79), Jewish Educators Assn. Orange County (pres. 1979-81), Orange County Bur. Jewish Edn. (v.p. 1982-84, 92-94, pres. 1994—), Am. Cancer Soc. (v.p. West Orange County dist. 1994—). Democrat. Office: Congregation Bnai Tzedek 9669 Talbert Ave Fountain Valley CA 92708-5146

EIRMAN, THOMAS FREDRICK, music festival manager; b. N.Y.C., July 8, 1947; s. Fredrick Joseph E. AA, Queensborough Coll., 1972; postgrad., SUNY, Queens, 1972-75. Tech. dir. Western Opera Theatre, San Francisco, 1982-83; asst. lighting designer Portland (Oreg.) Opera, 1985-87; prodn. mgr. Pacific Ballet Theater, Portland, 1985-87; gen. mgr. Aspen Music Festival, N.Y.C. Office: Music Assocs Aspen PO Box AA Aspen CO 81612

EISCHEN, JAMES J., JR., lawyer; b. Great Lakes, Ill., July 30, 1962; s. James J. and Nada M. (Tangway) E.; m. Cyndi J. Dillon, Dec. 27, 1986; children: James J. III, Faith Elizabeth. BA in English, Creighton U., 1984; JD, U. Calif., Davis, 1987. Bar: Calif. 1987, U.S. Dist. Ct. (so. dist.) Calif. 1987, U.S. Ct. Appeals (9th cir.) 1987. Assoc. Higgs, Fletcher & Mack, San Diego, 1987-89, Lillick & McHose, San Diego, 1989-90; sole practitioner San Diego, 1990-91; prin. Shannahan, Smith & Dailey, La Jolla, Calif., 1991-92; mng. prin. Smith, Dailey & Eischen, La Jolla, 1992—. Contbr. articles to profl. jours. Bd. dirs. Visual Arts Found., La Jolla, 1989-91, La Jolla Cmty. Theater, 1990. Mem. ABA (real property, probate and trust law com.), San Diego Bar Assn. (eminent domain, bus./corp. and real property sects.), San Diego Yacht Club (flag mem. 1990—), San Diego Host Lions Club (chair 1992, chair sight impaired com., chair youth activities com., bd. dirs. 1993—). Republican. Roman Catholic. Office: Atty at Law 836 Prospect St Ste 1 La Jolla CA 92037-4206

EISEL, GUNNAR GEORG, music educator; b. Mannheim, Germany, Sept. 22, 1949; came to U.S., 1958; m. Roberta Lee Sackett, Apr. 15, 1973; children: Heather, Alison. MusB, Calif. State U., Long Beach, 1973; MA in Music, Calif. State U., Fullerton, 1980. Cert. community coll. instr., Calif. Artist-in-residence Whittier (Calif.) Coll., 1980-88; music instr. Citrus Coll., Glendora, Calif., 1974—; asst. prof. music Calif. State U., L.A., 1974—; gen. mgr. Guitar Found. Am., Claremont, Calif., 1987—. Mem. Am. String Tchrs. Assn. (chair guitar div. 1987-89). Home: 2723 Monticello Rd Claremont CA 91711-1816 Office: Guitar Found Am PO Box 1240 Claremont CA 91711-1240

EISELE, MILTON DOUGLAS, viticulturist; b. N.Y.C., Apr. 2, 1910; s. Charles Francis and Helen Agnes (Dolan) E.; B.A., U. Calif.-Berkeley, 1933; grad. San Francisco Stock Exch. Inst., 1938; m. Barbara Lois Morgan, July 26, 1941; children: Helen Frances Eisele Osthimer, Barbara Glennis, William Douglas. Investment cashier Wells Fargo Bank, San Francisco, 1934-39; coordinator cement sales Permanente Corp., 1940-41, constrn. supt., 1941-43; mgr. refractory div. Kaiser Aluminum, 1943-47, mgr. regional sales, Chgo., 1947-50, mgr. foil div., 1950-55, mgr. prodn., 1955-60, mgr. market and prodn. devel., 1960-65, mgr. investments, 1966-71; ret., 1971; former owner, operator Eisele Vineyards, Napa Valley, Calif., 1969-89. Dir., former pres. Napa Valley Found., 1981-85; bd. dirs., past chmn. Vintage Hall, Inc., 1973-85; bd. dirs., pres. Napa Valley Heritage Fund, 1973—; past pres., bd. dirs. Upper Napa Valley Assocs., 1976-80; mem. adv. coun. Napa County Land Trust, 1976-79; mem. Napa County Grand Jury, 1988-89, hon. co-chmn. 150th anny. planting first grapes. Mem. Am. Soc. Enologists, Napa Valley Grape Growers Assn. (dir.), Calif. Assn. Wine Grape Growers (dir., former sec., chmn. 1986-87), Calif. Vintage Wine Soc. (bd. dirs., pres. 1994—), Agrl. Coun. of Napa County, Wine and Winegrape Mktg. Order State of Calif. (dir. 1984), Napa Valley Growers and Vinters (chmn. bd. dirs., mktg. and promotion com. 1985—), Marin County Wine & Food Soc., Kappa Alpha Order. Republican. Episcopalian (vestryman, sr. warden 1966-69). Home and Office: PO Box 687 1865 St Helen Hwy Rutherford CA 94573

EISEMANN, KURT, director computer center, mathematics educator; b. Nuremberg, Germany, June 22, 1923; came to U.S., 1948; s. Lazarus and Lina (Bacharach) E.; m. Marlene K. Cross, June 22, 1969 (div. Oct. 1988); children: Jamin, Caroline. BA in Math., Yeshiva U., 1950; MS in Applied Math., MIT, 1952; PhD in Applied Math., Harvard U., 1962. Sr. mathematician IBM, N.Y.C., 1952-56; rsch. mathematician IBM, 1956-61; mgr. math. rsch. Univac Div. Sperry Rand Corp., Washington, 1961-63; dir. computer ctr., assoc. prof. Sch. Engring. Cath. U. Am., Washington, 1963-66; tech. dir. Comput. Usage Devel. Corp., Boston, 1966-68; dir. acad. computer svc., prof. computer sci. Northeastern U., Boston, 1968-74; dir. computer svc., prof. math and computer sci. U. Mo. Kansas City, Kansas City, 1974-82; dir. univ. computer ctr., prof. math. and computer sci. San Diego State U., 1982-92, prof. emeritus, 1992—; lectr. Yeshiva U., 1953-55, Cath. U. Am., 1962-63. Office: San Diego State U Math Dept San Diego CA 92182

EISENBERG, GEORGE HENRY GILBERT, JR., retired army officer; b. St. Louis, Mar. 4, 1940; s. George Henry Gilbert and Camille Fredericka (Kuhne) E.; m. Nancy Anderson, Aug. 14, 1965; children: Lani Brooke. BS, MIT, 1962; PhD, U. Md., 1971. Commd. U.S. Army, 1965, advanced through grades to lt. col., to present; microbiologist Brooke Army Med. Ctr., Ft. Sam Houston, Tex., 1971-72, Walter Reed Army Inst. of Rsch., Washington, 1972-74; chief microbiology sect. USAMRU-BELEM (Transamazon), Belem, Brazil, 1974; microbiologist Walter Reed Army Inst. Rsch., 1974-78; chief div. cutaneous hazards Letterman Army Inst. Rsch., San Francisco, 1979-82; chief microbiology div. 10th Med. Lab., Landstuhl, Germany, 1984-87; microbiologist U.S. Army Inst. Dental Rsch., Washington, 1987-91, chief microbiology br., 1991-93. Contbr. articles to profl. jours. Mem. AAAS, Assn. U.S. Army. Republican. Methodist.

EISENBERG, RONALD LEE, radiologist; b. Phila., July 11, 1945; s. Milton and Betty (Klein) E.; m. Zina Leah Schiff; 2 children. AB, U. Pa., 1965, MD, 1969. Diplomate Am. Bd. Radiology. Staff radiologist VA Med. Ctr., San Francisco, 1975-80; prof. and chmn. dept. radiology La. State U., Shreveport, 1980-91; chmn. dept. radiology Highland Hosp., Oakland, Calif., 1991—. Author: Gastrointestinal Radiology, 1982, Diagnostic Imaging in Internal Medicine, 1985, Diagnostic Imaging in Surgery, 1986, Atlas of Differential Diagnoses, 1988, Radiology: An Illustrated History, 1992, others; contbr. over 70 articles to profl. jours. Maj. U.S. Army, 1971-73. Named Man of the Yr., Am. Physicians Fellowship, Boston, 1987. Mem. Radiol. Soc. N.Am., Am. Roentgen Ray Soc., Assn. of Univ. Radiologists, Soc. for Gastrointestinal Radiology, So. Med. Assn., Am. Coll. Radiology, Ark-La-Tex Radiol. Soc. Office: Highland Hosp Dept Radiology 1411 E 31st St Oakland CA 94602-1018

EISENHUT, DONNA PARSON, community library manager; b. Valley, Nebr., Aug. 28, 1920; d. Reuben Walter and Alice Victoria (Wicklund) Parson; m. Dale Duane Eisenhut, June 30, 1946 (dec. Sept. 1981); children: Alice Marie, Donna Lynn, Jani Sue. AA, Wayne (Nebr.) State Coll., 1941; student, Creighton U., summer 1943, Sacramento State Coll., summer 1959, 60. Emergency Calif. teaching credential, Nebr. teaching credential. Pub. sch. tchr. Pershing Sch., Omaha, 1941-44; substitute sch. tchr. Avalon (Calif.) Pub. Schs., 1950-80; libr. asst. L.A. County Pub. Libr., Avalon, 1967-80, mgr. L.A. County Cmty. Libr., 1980—; libr. chmn. Santa Catalina Woman's Club, Avalon, 1980—. Sunday sch. supt. Avalon Cmty. Ch., Avalon, 1952-71; leader Girl Scouts Am., Avalon, 1956-69, Avalon coord., 1969-80; grand marshal 4th of July Parade City of Avalon, 1989. Mem. PTA (hon. life). Office: County of LA Pub Libr PO Box 585 Avalon CA 90704-0585

EISNER, MICHAEL DAMMANN, entertainment company executive; b. Mt. Kisco, N.Y., Mar. 7, 1942; s. Lester and Margaret (Dammann) E.; m. Jane Breckenridge; children: Breck, Eric, Anders. BA, Denison U., 1964. Began career in programming dept. CBS; asst. to nat. programming dir. ABC, 1966-68, mgr. spls. and talent, dir. program devel.-East Coast, 1968-71, v.p. daytime programming, 1971-75, v.p. program planning and devel., 1975-76, sr. v.p. prime time prodn. and devel., 1976; pres., chief operating officer Paramount Pictures, 1976-84; chmn., chief exec. officer Walt Disney Co., Burbank, Calif., 1984—. Bd. dirs. Denison U., Calif. Inst. Arts, Am. Hosp. of Paris Found., Environ. Media Assn. Mem. Environ. Media Assn. Office: Walt Disney Co 500 S Buena Vista St Burbank CA 91521-0001

EISSLER, FREDERICK, environmentalist, retired educator; b. Phila., May 19, 1922; s. Frederick and Anne (Stonesifer) E.; m. Anne Parker, Apr. 14, 1952; children: Margaret, Christine. BA in Lit., U. N.C., 1943. Cert. elem.-secondary tchr., Calif. Primary, secondary tchr. Santa Barbara (Calif.) Sch. Dist., 1958-81; exec. dir. Scenic Shoreline Preservation Conf., Santa Barbara, 1968—; exec. dir. Scenic Shoreline Def. Fund., Santa Barbara, 1981—. Mem. nat. bd. dirs. Sierra Club, San Francisco, 1963-69, sec., 1969. Civilian pub. svc. with Am. Friends Svc. Com., 1942-46. Mem. Phi Beta Kappa. Home: 4623 More Mesa Dr Santa Barbara CA 93110-2028

EISSMANN, WALTER JAMES, consulting company executive; b. Newark, N.J., Apr. 20, 1939; s. Walter Curt Eissmann and Alice Delice (Irving) Clark; m. Dorothea Ann Donaldson, June 1, 1963; children: Patricia Helene Ridenhour, Walter William. B.S. in Indsl. Engring., Rutgers U., 1962. Account mgr. Gen. Electric, Engelwood Cliffs, N.J., 1962-67; regional sales mgr. Tymshare, Engelwood Cliffs, 1968-71, Buffalo, N.Y., 1971-73, Washington, 1973-74, v.p. mktg. service div., Cupertino, Calif., 1974-79, div. v.p., Cupertino, 1980-84; sr. v.p. McDonnell Douglas Corp., Cupertino, 1984-86; gen. ptnr. Archer Assocs., 1985-92; pres., chmn. bd. Walter J. Eissmann, Inc., Saratoga, 1989—; bd. dirs. NSF Corp., Nutri/System Franchisee Corp., 1986-90; chmn. bd. Businesswise, Inc., 1992-93. Bd. dirs. Saratoga Little League, Calif., 1976-81, Saratoga Boosters, 1981-84; active Vienna Theatre Players, Va., 1973; mem. Church Men's Choir, Saratoga, 1980-82. Named to President's Club Tymshare, Golden Circle, Nutri/System Master of the Keys. Mem. Pi Tau Sigma. Republican. Office: PO Box 3425 Saratoga CA 95070-1425

EITEL, KARL EMIL, hotel executive; b. Chgo., Dec. 26, 1928; s. Karl F. and Suzanne (Schmidt) E.; m. Mary Ann Lease, June 16, 1951; children: Richard, Susan, Janet. Student, Trinity Coll., 1946-48; BS, Mich. State U., 1951. Room clk. St. Anthony Hotel, San Antonio, 1951-52; with Cosmopolitan Hotel, Denver, 1952-58, exec. asst. mgr., 1954-58; exec. asst. mgr. Sir Francis Drake Hotel, San Francisco, 1958-61; mgr. Broadmoor Hotel, Colorado Springs, Colo., 1961-66, exec. v.p., mng. dir., 1966-81; exec. v.p., then pres. Broadmoor Hotel Inc., 1981-90, ret., 1990; bd. dirs. Bank One Colorado Springs, Garden City Co., Manitou and Pikes Peak Ry. Co. Trustee El Pomar Found. (chmn. exec. com.). Mem. Am. Hotel and Motel Assn., Colo.-Wyo. Hotel And Motel Assn., Hotel Greeters Am., Colorado Springs C. of C., Hotel Sales Mgmt. Assn., Inter-Am. Hotel Assn., Nat. Assn. Travel Orgns. Clubs, U.S. Tennis Lawn Assn., Navy League U.S., Assn. U.S. Army, Colo.-Wyo. Restaurant Assn., Broadmoor Golf Club (pres., bd. dirs.), Cheyenne Mountain Country Club, Rio Verde (Ariz.) Country Club, Sigma Nu. Home: 15 Thayer Rd Colorado Springs CO 80906-4220 Office: El Pomar Found 10 Lake Cir Colorado Springs CO 80906-4201

EITELBERG, MARK JAN, public administration educator, consultant; b. Jan. 5, 1948; s. Alfred Jack and Olga Barbara (Lipski) E.; m. Deborah Jean Brant, July 20, 1982; children: Matthew Jan, Andrew James. AB in Govt., Franklin and Marshall Coll., 1970; MPA, NYU, 1973, PhD, 1979. Pers. analyst State of N.J., 1975; mem., contbg. author mil. svc. working group Atlantic Coun. U.S., Washington, 1980-81; assoc. staff fgn. policies studies program Brookings Instn., Washington, 1980-82; rsch. asst. Human Resources Rsch. Orgn., Alexandria, Va., 1975—, rsch. assoc., 1975-76, rsch. scientist, 1976-79, sr. scientist, 1979-82; adj. rsch. prof. pub. adminstrn. U.S. Naval Postgrad. Sch., Monterey, Calif., 1982-89, assoc. prof. pub. adminstrn., 1989—; assoc. chmn. dept. sys. mgmt. U.S. Naval Postgrad. Sch., 1995—; mem. tech. coop. program, Dept. Def., Washington, 1990—; cons. global demographic trends group, Pres.'s Commn. on Integrated Long-Term Strategy, Nat. Def. U., Washington, 1987-88, Nat. Commn. on Testing and Pub. Policy, U. Calif., Berkeley, 1988-89; presenter papers in field. Author: Military Representation, 1979, Blacks and the Military, 1982, Screening for Service, 1984, Manpower for Military Occupations, 1988, Becoming Brass, 1991, Marching Toward the 21st Century, 1994, America's All-Volunteer Force, 1995; contbr. articles to profl. jours. and govt. docs. With U.S. Army Res. and N.G., 1970-76. Fellow Inter-Univ. Seminar on Armed Forces and Soc. (assoc. chmn.); mem. APA, ASPA, Mil. Testing Assn., Am. Edni. Rsch. Assn. Office: US Naval Postgrad Sch Dept Sys Mgmt Monterey CA 93943

EIZENBERG, JULIE, architect. BArch, U. Melbourne, Australia, 1978; MArch II, UCLA, 1981. Lic. architect, Calif., reg. architect, Australia. Principal, architect Koning Eizenberg Architecture, Santa Monica, Calif., 1981—; instr. various courses UCLA, MIT, Harvard U.; lectr. in field; jury member P/A awards. Exhbns. incl. "House Rules" Wexner Ctr., 1994, "The Architect's Dream: Houses for the Next Millenium" The Contemporary Arts Ctr., 1993, "Angels & Franciscans" Gagosian Gallery, 1992, Santa Monica Mus. Art, 1993, "Broadening the Discourse" Calif. Women in Environmental Design, 1992, "Conceptional Drawings by Architects" Bannatyne Gallery, 1991, Exhbn. Koning Eizenberg Projects Grad. Sch. Architecture & Urban Planning UCLA, 1990; prin. works include Digital Domain Renovation and Screening Room, Santa Monica, Lightstorm Entertainment Office Renovation and Screening Room, Santa Monica, Gilmore Bank Addition and Remodel, L.A., 1548-1550 Studios, Santa Monica, (with RTA) Materials Rsch. Lab. at U. Calif., Santa Barbara, Ken Edwards Ctr. Community Svcs., Santa Monica, Sepulveda Recreation Ctr., L.A., PS # 1 Elem. Sch., Santa Monica, A.L.A. Sr. Svc. Ctr., West Hollywood, Vitalize Fairfax Project, L.A., Farmers Market, L.A. Additions (Westside Urban Forum prize 1991), Stage Deli, L.A., Simone Hotel, L.A. (Nat. Honor award AIA 1994), Boyd Hotel, L.A., Community Corp. Santa Monica Housing Projects, St. John's Hosp. Replacement Housing Program, Santa Monica, Liffman Ho., Santa Monica, (with Glenn Erikson) Electric Artblock, Venice (Beautification award L.A. Bus. Coun. 1993), 6th St. Condominiums, Santa Monica, Hollywood Duplex, Hollywood Hills (Record Houses Archtl. Record 1988), California Ave. Duplex, Santa Monica, Millen Apts., Santa Monica, Tarzana Ho. (Award of Merit L.A. chpt. AIA 1992, Sunset Western home Awards citation 1993-94), 909 Ho., Santa Monica (Award of Merit L.A. chpt. AIA 1991), 31st St. Ho., Santa Monica (Honor award AIACC 1994), others. Recipient 1st award Progressive Architecture, 1987; named one of Domino's Top 30 Architects, 1989. Mem. L.A. County Mus. Art, Westside Urban Forum, Urban Land Inst., Architects and Designers for Social Responsibility, Mus. Contemporary Art, The Nature Conservancy, Sierra Club. Office: Koning Eizenberg Architecture 1548 18th St Santa Monica CA 90404-3404

EKDALE, ALLAN ANTON, geology educator, paleontology researcher; b. Burlington, Iowa, Aug. 30, 1946; s. Warren E. and Marian L. (Nielsen) E.; m. Susan Faust Rostberg, July 5, 1969; children: Joan Diane, Eric Gregory. BA, Augustana Coll., Rock Island, Ill., 1968; MA, Rice U., 1973, PhD, 1974. Prof. geology U. Utah, Salt Lake City, 1974—. Fellow AAAS; mem. Geol. soc. Am., Internat. Assn. Sedimentologists, Nat. Assn. Geology Tchrs., Paleontol. Soc., Soc. Econ. Paleontologists and Mineralogists. Office: U Utah Dept Geology and Geophysics Salt Lake City UT 84112

EKSTROM, WALTER F., utility company executive; b. 1927; married. AA, Phoenix Coll., 1957; BS, U. Ariz., 1960. With Ariz. Pub. Svc. Co., Phoenix, 1960—, v.p., 1982-88, exec. v.p., 1988—. Office: Ariz Pub Svc Co PO Box 53999 Mail Sta 9080 Phoenix AZ 85072

ELA, PATRICK HOBSON, museum director, consultant, educator; b. Oakland, Calif., June 20, 1948; s. Benjamin W., Jr., and Jeanette (Lamoreau) E. B.A., Occidental Coll., 1970; postgrad. in Art History, UCLA, 1970-71, M.B.A., 1973. Curator Gemini Graphics Edits., Ltd., Los Angeles, 1970-71; edn. intern Alta Pinakothek, Munich, W.Ger., 1972; asst. dir. Kohler Arts Ctr., Sheboygan, Wis., 1973-74; edn. specialist Los Angeles County Mus. Art, 1974-75; adminstrv. dir. Craft and Folk Art Mus., Los Angeles, 1975-82, exec. dir., 1982—; prin. Crown Internat. Travel Inc.; mgmt. cons.; instr. Occidental Coll., Calif. State U.-Fullerton; mem. faculty mus. studies program John F. Kennedy U. Vice pres., pres. alumni bd. govs. Occidental Coll., 1979-80; bd. dirs. R.M. Schindler House, Scott Newman Ctr., 1986-91, 94—, Plaza de la Raza, 1995—. Mem. Calif. Assn. Mus. (founding bd. 1980-81), Millicent Rogers Mus., 1993—. Office: Craft and Folk Art Mus 6067 Wilshire Blvd # 5 Los Angeles CA 90036-3604

ELAINE, KAREN, musician, educator; b. San Jose, Calif., Nov. 6, 1965; d. Gaston Ortega and Alice Lee (Ray) Sanders, III. Diploma in music, Curtis Inst. of Music, Phila., 1987; studies with Karen Tuttle, Michael Tree, Curtis Inst. Music, 1987; studies with Louis Kievman, L.A., 1988-90. Solo viola New Am. Chamber Orch., Detroit, 1986-87; prin. viola San Diego Symphony Orch., 1987-90; string specialist Sch. Creative & Performing Arts, San Diego, 1987-90; pvt. instr. Studio of Karen Elaine, San Diego, 1987—; violist Rinaldi String Quartet, San Diego, 1988-91; prin. viola Internat. Symphony Orch. Tijuana, Mex., 1988—; viola prof. Chanterelle Music Festival, Pouidoux, Switzerland, 1989—; solo and prin. viola Sun Valley Summer Symphony (formerly Elkhorn Music Festival), 1991—; adj. prof. viola San Diego State U., 1989—; featured on TV program Reflections in Music, San Diego, El Cajon, Calif., 1990; solo viola Delos Internat. Records, Paraiba Symphony Orch., Brazil, 1988, Laurel Records, London Symphony Orch., 1990, Harmonia Mundi, City of London Sinfonia, 1990; guest soloist and lectr. 19th Internat. Viola Congress, 1991, solo recitalist throughout U.S.; guest speaker Sta. KFSD-FM, Sta. KPBS-FM; with San Diego Civic Youth Orch., 1994 under sponsorship of Australian Broadcast Co. and Australian Arts Coun. Commissions include Concert Piece for Viola, David Baker, 1989, Cinnabar Concerto for Viola and Strings, David Ward-Steinman, 1991, Concerto for Viola and Orch., Gordon Kerry, 1993, Sounds for Solo Viola, John Naples, 1992, Li'l Phrygian Rondo for Karen, Katrina Wreede, 1992; contbg. editor Mythos to Melos; Greek Tragedy in Opera, 1992-93; contbr. articles to Jour. of Internat. Viola Soc. Donor World Wildlife Fund, Washington, 1989—. Recipient 1st Pl. award Bruno Giurana Internat. Viola Competition, Brazil, 1988; winner numerous solo competitions Musical Merit of San Diego, 1988, 89, Rio Hondo Symphony Young Artists' Solo Competition, 1989, S.E. L.A. Young Artists Solo Competition, 1990, Nat. Assn. Negro Musicians Young Artists Solo Competition, 1992. Mem. Am. Viola Soc., Musicians Union Locals 325 (San Diego) and 47 (L.A.). Democrat. Home: 208 Welling Way San Diego CA 92114-5947

EL-BAYOUMY, LOTFI E., engineering executive; b. Fayoum, Arab Republic of Egypt, Jan. 18, 1942; came to U.S., 1966; s. El-Sayed Ibrahim and Nageyya F. (El-Zainy) El-B.; m. Shahira A. El-Masry, Aug. 17, 1973; children: Sharif, Khalid, Dena. BS with honors, Cairo U., 1964, MS, 1966; PhD with honors, NYU, 1970. Asst. prof. NYU, 1969-70; prin. engr. Dathar Corp., Ramsey, N.J., 1970-72; advanced vibrations analyst Pratt & Whitney, East Hartford, Conn., 1972-74; group engr. Sundstrand Corp., Rockford, Ill., 1975-80; mgr. engring. tech. Western Gear Corp. (now Lucas Western Inc.), Park City, Utah, 1980—; engring. cons. NASA Lewis, Cleve., 1981—; assoc. prof. mech. engring. Calif. State U., Long Beach, 1981—, No. Ill. U., Dekalb, 1979-80. Contbr. articles to profl. jours. Mem. Am. Acad. Mechanics (founding), AIAA, ASME (Power Transmision and Gearing com. 1983—), Assn. Egyptian-Am. Scholars, Nat. Mgmt. Assn., Soc. Automotive Engrs. (G-5 com. 1984—). Home: 5105 Vista Montana Yorba Linda CA 92686-4505 Office: Lucas Aerospace 6125 Silver Creek Dr Park City UT 84060

ELDER, CURTIS HAROLD, geologist; b. Laramie, Wyo., Mar. 30, 1921; s. Cecil and Agnes Christine (Miller) E.; m. Wiese Wild, Jan. 2, 1948; children: George W., Christian N., Robin T., Melody C. Student, U. Mo., 1939-43, BS in Geology, 1951, postgrad., 1951-52. Grad. asst. U. Mo., Columbia, 1950-52; jr. rsch. engr. Pan Am. Petroleum Corp., Tulsa, 1952-56; intermediate geologist Pan Am. Petroleum Corp., Salt Lake City, 1956-59; geologist Pan Am. Petroleum Corp., Denver, 1959-63; ind. cons. geologist pvt. practice, Denver, 1963-65; geologist U.S. Bur. Mines, Pitts., 1965-82, U.S. Dept. Interior, Pitts., 1982-88; pvt. practice Evergreen, Colo., 1988—; docen Hiwan Mus., Jefferson County, 1989—. Conservation chmn. Denver Area coun. Boy Scouts Am.; assoc. dir. Allegheny Soil and Water Conservation Dist., 1966-81. Recipient Silver Beaver award Allegheny Trails coun. Boy Scouts Am. Fellow Geol. Soc. Am. (sr.); mem. Am. Inst. Profl. Geologists (cert.), Soc. Econ. Paleontologists and Mineralogists, Mineralogical Soc. Am., Nat. Audubon Soc., Jefferson County Hist. Soc., Rocky Mountain Assn. Geologists, Tulsa Geol. Soc., Pitts. Geol. Soc., Kappa Sigma. Republican. Presbyterian. Home: 33172 Lynx Ln Evergreen CO 80439-6823

ELDER, ROBERT LAURIE, newspaper editor; b. Nashville, June 23, 1938; s. Charles Jerome and Dorothea Eloise (Calhoun) E.; m. Betty Ann Doak, Sept. 1, 1958 (div. May 1969); children—Mark Christopher, Jeffrey Cathcart. B.A., Washington and Lee U., 1960; M.A., Vanderbilt U., 1966; postgrad., Stanford U., 1976-77. Reporter Nashville Tennessean, 1964-68; asst. dir. So. Newspaper Pubs. Assn. Found., Atlanta, 1969; reporter The Miami Herald, Fla., 1970-76; editor San Jose (Calif.) Mercury News, 1978—, v.p., 1987—. Author: Crash, 1977. Bd. dirs. Santa Clara U. Ctr. for Applied Ethics, 1987—. 1st lt. U.S. Army, 1960-62. Recipient Disting. Achievement award Fla. Soc. Newspaper Editors, 1973, White House Conf. on Librs. Pub. award, 1994. Episcopalian. Office: San Jose Mercury News 750 Ridder Park Dr San Jose CA 95131-2432

ELDREDGE, JEFFREY ROBERT CARLETON, librarian; b. St. Albnas, Vt., Jan. 17, 1951; s. Carleton and Faith E. BA, U. N.H., 1973; MLS, U. R.I., 1982. Libr. asst. U. N.H., Durham, 1973-83; libr. Hawaii State Pub. Libr. System, Honolulu, 1984-90; dist. adminstr. Hawaii State Pub. Libr. System, Lihue, 1990-92, Pearl City, 1993—. Adv. bd. Retired Srs. Vol.

Program, Lihue, 1990-92; mem. Friends of the Libr. of Hawaii, Honolulu, 1991—. Mem. ALA, Hawaii Libr. Assn. (treas. 1988-90), Kauai Libr. Assn. (v.p. 1991-92). Republican. Office: West Oahu Libr Dist 1138 Waimano Home Rd Pearl City HI 96782-2647

ELDRIDGE, MAXINE JEW, flower grower, shipper, wholesaler; b. San Francisco, June 7, 1941; d. She Sun and Duck Fong (Chiang) Jew; m. Philip D. Eldridge, Feb. 12, 1961 (div. June 1986); children: Vernon Lee, Katherine Louise, David Scott. Student, U. Calif., San Jose, 1960-61. Owner, operator Eldridge Nursery, Morgan Hill, Calif., 1986-94. Worker bee S.C. County Farm Bur., San Jose, 1978-80.

ELDRIDGE, ROGER GILBERT, JR., education educator; b. Middleborough, Mass., Apr. 19, 1946; s. Roger G. and Carolyn M. (Nason) E.; m. Polly G. Sherman, June 24, 1967 (div. Sept. 1980); children: Jeffrey, Jana, Myles; m. Patricia A. Heino. BA, U. Mass., 1969; PhD, U. Wis., 1981. Cert. elem. tchr., reading specialist. Elem. tchr. Mattapoisett (Mass.) Schs., 1969-73; reading specialist Barnstable (Mass.) Schs., 1973-78; rsch. asst., reading lectr. U. Wis., Madison, 1978-81; asst. prof., assoc. prof. East Carolina U., Greenville, N.C., 1981-89; assoc. prof., prof. U. No. Colo., Greeley, 1989—. Contbr. chpts. in books and articles to profl. jours. Office: Univ No Colo Greeley CO 80639

ELDRIDGE, TERRANCE FOY, avionics engineer; b. Phoenix, Nov. 28, 1957; s. Robert Vincent Sr. and Ruth Loretta (Foy) E.; m. Kristen Marie Marut, July 19, 1985; children: Katelyn Marie, Erin Lindsey. BS in Physics, Harvey Mudd Coll., 1980; PhD in Physics, MIT, 1985. Rsch. asst. Los Alamos (N.Mex.) Nat. Lab., 1981, 1967-69, 1980, Livermore (Calif.) Nat. Lab., 1981, MIT, Cambridge, Mass., 1981-85; software engr. Hughes Aircraft Co., El Segundo, Calif., 1985-87; avionics engr. McDonnell Douglas, Mesa, Ariz., 1987—; rsch. scientist Ariz. State U., Tempe, 1994—. Contbr. articles to profl. jours. Mem. IEEE, Am. Phys. Soc. Home: 5940 E Fountain Cir Mesa AZ 85205-5513 Office: McDonnell Douglas 5000 E Mcdowell Rd Mesa AZ 85215-9797

ELECCION, MARCELINO, marketing executive, editor, writer, lecturer, artist; b. N.Y.C., Aug. 22, 1936; s. Marcelino G. and Margaret J. (Krcha) E.; m. Marcia L. Smith, June 6, 1962; 1 child, Mark Eaton; m. Naomi E. Kor, Jan. 5, 1978; 1 child, Jordan Kai. BA, NYU, 1961; postgrad. Courant Inst. Math. Scis., 1962-64; AS, Coll. San Mateo, 1988; postgrad. San Jose State U., 1988-91. Electromech. draftsman Coll. Engring., NYU, Bronx, 1954-57, chief designer dept. elec. engring., 1957-60, tech. editor lab. for electrosci. research, 1960-62, editor publs. Sch. Engring. and Scis., 1962-67; asst. editor IEEE Spectrum, N.Y.C., 1967-69, assoc. editor, 1969-70, staff writer, 1970-76, contbg. editor, 1976—; dir. adminstrn. Internat. Bur. Protection and Investigation, Ltd., N.Y.C., 1976-78; account exec. Paul Purdom & Co., pub. relations, San Francisco, 1978-81, creative dir., 1981-83; dir. mktg. communications Am. Info. Systems, Palo Alto, 1983-85; dir. engring. Tech. Cons., Palo Alto, 1986—; cons. tech. artist, 1953—; music orchestration cons., 1956-70; cons. Ency. Britannica, 1969-70, Time-Life Books, 1973; spl. guest lectr. Napa Coll., 1979—. Aux. police officer, N.Y.C. Police Dept., 1964-70, aux. sgt., 1970-73, aux. lt., 1973-76, aux. capt., 1976-78. Recipient Mayor's commendation award N.Y.C., 1971. Mem. IEEE (sr.), N.Y. Acad. Scis., Am. Math. Soc., AAAS, Optical Soc. Am., Smithsonian Assocs., Am. Numis. Assn., Nat. Geog. Soc., U.S. Judo Fedn., Athletic Congress, AAU. Fedn. Home: 3790 El Camino Real # 2004 Palo Alto CA 94306-3314

ELFVING, DON C., horticulturist, administrator; b. Albany, Calif., June 20, 1941; m. Beverley Brown, Dec. 27, 1985. BS in Botany, U. Calif., Davis, 1964, MS in Horticulture, 1966; PhD in Plant Physiology, U. Calif., Riverside, 1971. From asst. prof. to assoc. prof. pomology Cornell U., Ithaca, N.Y., 1972-79; rsch. scientist Hort. Rsch. Inst. Ontario, Simcoe, Can., 1979-91; mgr. rsch. programs Hort. Rsch. Inst. Ontario, Vineland, Can., 1991-93; supt. Tree Fruit Rsch. and Extension Ctr. Wash. State U., Wenatchee, 1993—; cons. U.S. AID, 1977; cons. Internat. Agrl. Devel. Svc., Ark., 1981-82. Author: Training and Pruning of Apple and Pear Trees, 1992. Recipient U.P. Hedrick 1st Pl. award Am. Pomological Soc., 1992. Mem. Am. Soc. for Hort. Sci. (bd. dirs. 1993-95, chair publs. com. 1993-95), Internat. Dwarf Fruit Tree Assn. (R.F. Carlson Disting. lectr. 1993). Office: Tree Fruit Rsch and Ext Ctr 1100 N Western Ave Wenatchee WA 98801-1230

ELGIN, GITA, psychologist; b. Santiago, Chile; came to U.S., 1968, naturalized 1987; d. Serafin and Regina (Urízar) Elguin; BS in biology summa cum laude, U. Chile, Santiago, DPs, 1964; PhD in Counseling Psychology, U. Calif., Berkeley, 1976; m. Bart Bödy, Oct. 23, 1971; children: Dio Christopher Károly, Alma Ilona Raia Julia. Clin. psychologist Barros Luco-Trudeau Gen. Hosp., Santiago, 1964-65; co-founder, co-dir. Lab. for Parapsychol. Rsch., Psychiat. Clinic, U. Chile, Santiago, 1965-68; rsch. fellow Found. Rsch. on Nature of Man, Durham, N.C., 1968; researcher psychol. correlates of EEG-Alpha waves U. Calif., Berkeley, 1972-76; originator holistic method of psychotherapy Psychotherapy for a Crowd of One, 1978; co-founder, clin. dir. Holistic Health Assos., Oakland, Calif., 1979—, Montclair Mediation Group, Oakland, 1994; lectr. holistic health Piedmont (Calif.) Adult Sch., 1979-80; hostess Holistic Perspective, Sta. KALW-FM, Nat. Public Radio, 1980. Author: (video documentary) Taking the Risk: Sharing the Trauma of Sexual & Ritualistic Abuse in Group Therapy, 1992. Lic. psychologist, Chile, Calif. Chancellor's Patent Fund grantee U. Calif., 1976, NIMH fellow, 1976. Mem. APA, Am. Holistic Psychol. Assn. (founder 1995—), Alameda County Psychol. Assn., Calif. State Psychol. Assn., Montclair Health Profls. Assn. (co-founder, pres. 1983-85), Sierra Club, U. Calif. Alumni Assn. Contbr. articles in clin. psychology and holistic health to profl. jours. and local periodicals. Presenter Whole Life Expo, 1986. Office: Montclair Profl Bldg 2080 Mountain Blvd Ste 203 Oakland CA 94611-2817

ELGIN, RON ALAN, advertising executive; b. Milw., Sept. 15, 1941; s. Carl John and Vivian Elaine (Phillips) E.; m. Bonnie Kay Visintainer, Dec. 3, 1968; 1 child, Alison. BA in Advt., U. Wash., 1965. With Cole & Weber, Seattle, 1965-81; pres. Elgin Syferd, Seattle, 1981—; chmn. Elgin Syferd, Boise, Idaho, 1987—; pres. DDB Needham Retail, 1990-93; chmn. Hornall Anderson Design Works, Seattle, 1982-91; ptnr. Christiansen & Fritsch Direct, Seattle, 1988—. Bd. dirs. Ronald McDonald House, Seattle, 1984—, Big Bros., Seattle, 1986—, Spl. Olympics, Seattle, 1987-90, Pacific N.W. Ballet, Seattle, 1988—, Poncho, Seattle, 1991—, Oddysee, 1993—; mem. adv. bd. U. Wash., Wash. State U. Ltd. U.S. Army, 1965-69. Mem. Am. Assn. Advt. Agencies, Am. Mktg. Assn., Mktg. Comm. Execs. Internat. Office: DDB Needham Worldwide Inc Elgin Syferd/DDB Needham 1008 Western Ave Seattle WA 98104-1032

ELIAS, SHEILA, artist; b. Chgo., June 30. MA, Calif. State U., Northridge, 1975; BFA, Columbus Coll. Art & Design, 1973; student, Art Inst. of Chgo., 1963-73. One-woman shows include Alex Rosenberg, N.Y.C., 1987, U. N.C., Chapel Hill, 1987, Gallery 99, Bay Harbor, Fla., 1988, Paula Allan Gallery, N.Y.C., 1987-89, Ratner Gallery, Chgo., 1990, others: group exhbns. include Louvre, Paris, 1987, Valerie Miller Fine Arts, Palm Springs, Calif., 1988, Otis Parsons Sch. of Design, L.A., 1988, Anne Jaffe Gallery, Bay Harbor, 1989, Santa Monica (Calif.) Heritage Mus., 1991, Ft. Lauderdale Mus., 1991, New England Mus. of Contemporary Art, 1993, Art and Cultural Ctr. of Hollywood, 1993; pub. collections include Bklyn. Mus. Art, Chase Manhattan Bank, N.Y.C., First L.A. Bank, Exec. Life Ins., L.A., Security Pacific Bank, L.A., Paramount Pictures, L.A., Laguna Beach Mus. Art, Kinsan Contemporary Mus., Korea. Address: 1800 S Robertson Blvd Ste 6 Los Angeles CA 90035-4352 Also: 510 Broome St Apt 7W New York NY 10012

ELIAS, THOMAS SAM, botanist, author; b. Cairo, Ill., Dec. 30, 1942; s. George Sam (dec.) and Anna (Clanton) E.; m. Barbara Ana Boyd (dec.); children: Stephen, Brian. BA in Botany, So. Ill. U., 1964, MA in Botany, 1966; PhD in Biology, St. Louis U., 1969. Asst. curator Arnold Arboretum of Harvard U., Cambridge, Mass., 1969-71; adminstr., dendrologist Cary Arboretum, N.Y. Botanical Garden, Millbrook, 1971-73, asst. dir., 1973-84; dir., CEO Rancho Santa Ana Bot. Garden, Claremont, Calif., 1984-93; chmn., prof. dept. botany Claremont Grad. Sch., 1984-93; dir. U.S. Nat. Arboretum, Washington, 1993—; lectr. in extension Harvard U., 1971; adj. prof. Coll. Environ. Science and Forestry, Syracuse, N.Y., 1977-80; coord. U.S.A/U.S.S.R. Botanical Exch., Program for U.S. Dept. of Interior, Washington, 1976—, U.S.A./China Botanical Exch., Program for U.S. Dept. of Interior, 1988—. Editor: Extinction is Forever, 1977 (one of 100 Best Books in Sci. and Tech. ALA 1977), Conservation and Management of Rare and Endangered Plants, 1987; author: Complete Trees of North America, 1980 (one of 100 Best Books in Sci. and Tech. ALA 1980), Field Guide to Edible Wild Plants of North America (one of 100 Best Books in Sci. and Tech. ALA 1983). Recipient Cooley award Am. Soc. Plant Taxonomist, 1970, Disting. Alumni award So. Ill. U., 1989. Home: 2447 San Mateo Ct Claremont CA 91711-1652 Office: US Nat Arboretum 3501 New York Ave NE Washington DC 20002-1958

ELIASON, LESLIE CAROL, comparative public policy educator; b. Portland, Oreg., Aug. 12, 1959; d. William Alexander and Nancy Carol (Kirchner) E. BA, U. Va., 1981; MA, Stanford U., 1985, PhD, 1988. Asst. prof. Scandinavian studies U. Wash., Seattle, 1988-92, asst. prof. Pub. Affairs, 1992—; lectr. U.S. Fulbright Found., Aarhus, Denmark, 1990; term mem. Coun. Fgn. Rels., 1994—. Contbr. articles to profl. publs. Coord. Hubert H. Humphrey fellowship program, U. Wash., mem. grad. sch. coun., 1993—. Swedish Inst. grantee, 1989. Mem. Assn. Pub. Policy and Mgmt., Am. Polit. Sci. Assn., Western Polit. Sci. Assn., Soc. for Advancement of Scandinavian Studies (co-editor women's caucus newsletter 1989—, adv. com. 1993—), European Cmty. Studies Assn., Coun. European Studies, Coun. Fgn. Rels. (team mem. 1994—). Office: U Wash Grad Sch Pub Affairs Box 353055 Seattle WA 98195-4900

ELIEN, MONA MARIE, air transportation professional; b. Atwood, Kans., June 13, 1932; d. Lawrence Wallace Berry and Adele Rosina (Gulzow) Wright; m. R.J. Wright, Jan. 1952 (div. 1957); m. J.P. Kobus, Nov. 1968 (div. 1991); m. Robert Louis Tour, Oct. 3, 1992. BS, U. Ariz., 1961; grad., Swiss Mountain Climbing Inst., Rosenlaui, 1963; postgrad., No. Ariz. U., 1966-67, Ariz. State U., 1967-69, 86-87; MPA, Ariz. State U., 1981. Customer rels. rep. Ariz. Pub. Svc. Co., Casa Grande, Flagstaff, Ariz., 1961-67; owner/operator Mona's Clipping Svc., Phoenix, 1969-74; various positions City of Phoenix, 1974—; contract mgr. Phoenix CETA/PSE/PNP, 1978-81; planning and devel. asst. Phoenix Sky Harbor Internat. Airport, 1986—; staff asst. 1988 Citizens Bond Com. for Aviation, Phoenix, 1987-88. Compiler, editor: Aviation Acronyms and Abbreviations, 1987, 2d rev. edit., 1992; editor, writer (newsletter) Rapsheet, 1972-75; author profl. columns, 1961-67. Pres. state home econs. occupations adv. bd. Ariz. State U., 1983-84; mem. Phoenix City Mgr.'s Women's Issues Com., 1989-91; pres. elect Tri-City (Ariz.) Zonta Internat., 1964-65; vol. speaker's bur. Phoenix Cmty. Alliance and Prep. Acad. Partnership, 1992—; mem. exec. com. Svc. Fund Drive, Phoenix, 1984-86; mem. precinct com. Yuma County Dem. Com., 1958; mem. employee-of-yr. com. Phoenix Aviation Dept., 1993, co-chmn., 1994. Recipient recognition pub. svc. award Ariz. Dept. Econ. Security, 1975, Heart and Soul award Barry M. Goldwater Terminal 4, 1990, PHXcellence awards, 1993, 94, Art Hero award Phoenix Sky Harbor Internat. Airport, 1993; named one of outstanding young women of Am., 1966. Mem. ASPA (life; Phoenix chpt. awards banquet com. 1991, 92, nat. com. 1990-91), Am. Home Econs. Assn. (life), Ariz. Home Econs. Assn. (pres. no. region 1965-67), Sinagua Soc. Museum No. Ariz., Satisfied Frog Gold Mountain Club, Flagstaff C. of C. (chmn. Indian princesses, retail mchts. sect. 1965-67), So. Ariz. Hiking Club, Desert Bot. Gardens, Swinging Stars Square Dance Club, Delta Delta Delta. Republican. Lutheran. Home: 2201 E Palmaire Ave Phoenix AZ 85020-5633 Office: Phoenix Sky Harbor Internat Airport 3400 E Sky Harbor Blvd Phoenix AZ 85034-4403

ELIKANN, LAWRENCE S. (LARRY ELIKANN), television and film director; b. N.Y.C., July 4, 1923; s. Harry and Sadye (Trause) E.; m. Corinne Schuman; Dec. 6, 1947; children—JoAnne Jarrin, Jill Barad. B.A., Bklyn. Coll., 1943; E.E., Walter Harvey Coll., 1948. Tech. dir. NBC-TV, N.Y.C., 1948-64; comml. dir. VPI-TV, N.Y.C., 1964-66, Filmex-TV, N.Y.C., 1966-68, Plus two TV, N.Y.C., 1968-70. Dir. mini-series Last Flight Out, The Great L.A. Earthquake, The Big One, The Inconvenient Woman, cable TV, Fever, Story Lady, One Against the Wind, Bonds of Love, I Know My First Name is Steven, Hands of a Stranger, Kiss of a Killer, God Bless the Child, Out of Darkness, Menendez-A Killing in Beverly Hills, Tecumseh-The Last Warrior, A Mother's Prayer. Mem. Mus. Contemporary Art of L.A., L.A. County Mus.; mem. rsch. coun. Scripps Clinic and Rsch. Found. With Signal Corps, U.S. Army, 1943-46. Recipient Emmy award, 1978-79, 89, Golden Globe award, 1989, 91, Christopher award 1973-76, 77, 78-79, 91, Chgo. Internat. Film Festival award 1977, Internat. Film and TV Festival of N.Y. award, 1977, Dir. of Yr. award Am. Ctrs. for Children, 1978; Humanitas prize, 1988, 94. Mem. NATAS (gov. 1961-63), Dirs. Guild Am., Am. film Inst., Nat. Hist. Preservation Soc., Smithsonian Inst., Scripps Inst. (bd. dirs.), Acad. TV Arts and Scis.

ELINSON, HENRY DAVID, artist, language educator; b. Leningrad, USSR, Dec. 14, 1935; came to U.S., 1973; s. David Moses and Frida Zelma (Ufa) E.; m. Ludmila Nicholas Tepina, Oct. 7, 1955; 1 child, Maria Henry. Student, Herzen State Pedagogical U., Leningrad, 1954-57; BA, Pedagogical Inst., Novgorod, USSR, 1958; MA, Pedagogical Inst., Moscow, 1963. Cert. educator. Spl. edn. tchr. Leningrad Sch. Spl. Edn., 1961-64; supr. dept. speech therapy Psychoneurological Dispensary, Leningrad, 1964-73; instr. Russian lang. Yale U., New Haven, Conn., 1975-76, Def. Lang. Inst., Presidio of Monterey, Calif., 1976—. One-man shows include The Light and Motion Transmutation Galleries, N.Y.C., 1974, Thor Gallery, Louisville, 1974, Monterey (Calif.) Peninsula Art Mus., 1977, U. Calif. Nelson Gallery, Davis, 1978, Nahamkin Gallery, N.Y.C., 1978, Nahamkin Fine Arts, N.Y.C., 1980, Gallery Paule Anglim, 1981, 85, 87, Gallery Paule Anglim, San Francisco, 1991, 93, Dostoevsky's Mus., St. Petersburg, Russia, 1992, Mus. Art, Santa Cruz, Calif., 1994; exhibited in group shows at Bklyn. Coll. Art Ctr., 1974, CUNY, 1974, Galleria II Punto, Genoa, Italy, 1975, New Art From the Soviet Union, Washington, 1977, Gallery Hardy, Paris, 1978, Mus. of Fine Art, San Francisco, 1979, Santa Cruz Mus. Fine Arts, 1994, and numerous others; represented in permanent collections Mus. Fine Arts, San Francisco, Yale U. Art Gallery, Monterey Mus. Art, U. Calif. Art Mus., Berkeley, Bochum Mus., West Germany, Check Point Charlie Mus., West Berlin, State Russian Mus., Leningrad, Zimmerly Art Mus., Rutgers U., N.J.; participant Nonconformist Art Exhbns., St. Petersburg, 1960; contbr. articles to profl. jours. Mem. Underground Anti-Soviet Govt. Students' Orgn., 1957. Recipient Gold medal Art Achievement City of Milan, 1975. Home: 997 Benito Ct Pacific Grove CA 93950-5333

ELIOT, THEODORE LYMAN, JR., international consultant; b. N.Y.C., Apr. 14, 1951; m. Patricia F. Peters. B.A., Harvard U., 1948, M.P.A., 1956; LL.D., U. Nebr., Omaha, 1975. With U.S. Fgn. Svc., 1949-78; spl. asst. to under sec. of state, to sec. treasury; country dir. for Iran Dept. State; exec. sec. State Dept.; also spl. asst. to sec. of state Dept. State; ambassador to Afghanistan; insp. gen. Dept. State, Washington; dean Fletcher Sch. Law and Diplomacy, Tufts U., 1979-85; exec. dir. Ctr. for Asian Pacific Affairs Asia Found., San Francisco, 1985-87; bd. dirs. Raytheon Co., Neurobiol. Tech., Fiberstars. Trustee Asia found. Pt. Reyes Bird Observatory, pres., 1990-92. Mem. Am. Acad. Diplomacy, Somerset Club, Univ. Club (San Francisco).

ELKAN, CHARLES PETER, engineer educator; b. Wellington, New Zealand, Mar. 17, 1963; came to U.S., 1984; s. Peter Gabriel and Anne Mildred (Marsh) E. BA, U. Cambridge, Eng., 1984; PhD, Cornell U., 1990. Postdoctoral assoc. U. Toronto, Ont., Can., 1989-90; asst. prof. U. Calif., San Diego, 1990—. Contbr. articles to profl. jours. Mem. IEEE Computer Soc., Am. Assn. Artificial Intelligence. Office: U Calif Dept Computer Sci & Engring La Jolla CA 92109-0114

ELKINS, CARL, food products executive; b. 1932. Attended, Taft Coll., 1955-57. Potato broker Higby & Sons, Bakersfield, Calif., 1957-60; office mgr. Sycamore Farms, Arvin, Calif., 1960-63; salesman, office and packing house mgr. Miller & Lux Corp., Bakersfield, 1963-72; pvt. practice, 1972-74; salesman Demont Packing Co., Victor, Calif., 1974-76; various positions Delta Packing Co., Lodi, Calif., 1976—, now pres. With USAF, 1951-55. Office: Delta Packing Co 5950 E Kettleman Ln Lodi CA 95240*

ELKUS, JONATHAN BRITTON, music publisher, music educator; b. San Francisco, Aug. 8, 1931; m. Marilyn McCormick, July 30, 1966; 1 child, Ian. BA, U. Calif., Berkeley, 1953; MA, Stanford U., 1954. Prof. music Lehigh U., Bethlehem, Pa., 1957-73; dir. music Cape Cod Acad., Osterville, Mass., 1979-85, chmn. dept. humanities, 1985-89; founder J.B. Elkus & Son, Music Publs., Laureate Music Press, Overland Music Distbrs., East Bay Books, Berkeley, 1984—; chmn. dep. history Stuart Hall, Staunton, Va., 1989-92; lectr. music U. Calif., Davis, 1992—; editorial assoc. Charles Ives Soc., N.Y.C., 1977—. Composer: (opera) The Mandarin, 1968, (plays) Tom Sawyer, 1952, Act Your Age, 1983; contbr. profl. mags. and jours. Ford Found. fellow, 1962. Mem. ASCAP. Office: Overland Music Distbrs PO Box 9526 Berkeley CA 94709-0526

ELLEGOOD, DONALD RUSSELL, publishing executive; b. Lawton, Okla., June 21, 1924; s. Claude Jennings and Iva Claire (Richards) E.; m. Bettie Jane Dixon, Dec. 11, 1947; children—Elizabeth Nemi, Francis Hunter, Kyle Richards, Sarah Helen. B.A., U. Okla., 1948, M.A., 1950. Asst. editor U. Okla. Press, 1950-51; editor Johns Hopkins Press, 1951-54; dir. La. State U. Press, 1954-63, U. Wash. Press, Seattle, 1963—. Contbr. articles to profl. jours. Served to 1st lt. USAAF, 1943-46. Decorated Air medal, D.F.C. Mem. Am. Univ. Pubs. Group London (dir.), Am. Assn. Univ. Presses (pres.), Phi Beta Kappa. Home: 17852 49th Pl NE Seattle WA 98155-4312 Office: U Wash Press PO Box 50096 Seattle WA 98145-5096

ELLER, DEBRA, management consultant; b. Port Hueneme, Calif., Dec. 11, 1955; d. Johnny Howard Godfrey and Patsy Lee (Gossett) Webb; m. William Reed Eller, Apr. 7, 1991; 1 child, Brian Reed. BA in Liberal Arts, Ariz. State U., 1977. Buyer, group sales mgr., dept. mgr. Dayton Hudson Corp., Mpls., 1977-79, mgr. recruiting and pers., 1979-82, mgr. tng. and exec. devel., 1982-84; sales rep. Bellia & Assocs., Calif., 1979-81; tng. mgr. semicondr. products sector Motorola, Inc., Ariz., 1984-89; mgr. tng. and orgn. devel. VLSI Tech., Calif., 1989-91; pres. Stuxor, Inc., Scottsdale, Ariz., U.K., Belgium, 1991—. Mem. Coun. for Continuous Improvement (bd. dirs. 1990-91). Home: Blvd Louis Schmidt 119, 1040 Brussels Belgium Office: Stuxor Inc 10105 E Via Linda # 103-237 Scottsdale AZ 85258-5311

ELLERBROEK, DAVID ANDREW, hydrologist; b. Cedar Falls, Iowa, Nov. 9, 1961; s. Lee Tripp and Elizabeth Ann (Meinen) E.; m. Marilyn Sue Jensen, May 27, 1989. BS in Geophys., U. Colo., 1985; MS in Environ. Sci., Colo. Sch. Mines, 1989; PhD in Environ. Engring., Colo. State U., 1993. Hydrologist Bur. of Land Mgmt., Denver, 1987-89; rsch. assoc. Colo. State U., Ft. Collins, 1989-91; sr. hydrologist Advanced Aquatic Tech., Ft. Collins, 1991-93, S.M. Stoller Corp., Boulder, Colo., 1993—. Home: 903 W Mountain Ave Fort Collins CO 80521-2509 Office: S M Stoller Corp 5700 Flatiron Pky Boulder CO 80301-5718

ELLINGBOE, BRADLEY ROSS, musician, educator; b. Farmington, Min., Apr. 16, 1958; s. Oscar Glenn and Veola Yvonne (Soberg) E.; m. Karen Lee Hersey, July 18, 1981; children: Peter, Alexander, Kristen. BA, Saint Olaf Coll., 1980; M in Music, Eastman Sch. Music, 1983. Assoc. prof. music U. N.Mex., Albuquerque, 1985—; bass soloist with numerous orchestras U.S., Germany, Scandinavia, Japan, Korea, Mex., 1980—. Editor: A Grieg Song Anthology, 1990, 45 Songs Edvard Grieg, 1988; composer choral music; contbr. articles to profl. jours. Recipient Medal of St. Olav, King Harald of Norway, 1994. Lutheran. Office: U New Mex Dept of Music Albuquerque NM 87131

ELLINGS, RICHARD JAMES, political research institution executive; b. Santa Barbara, Calif., Jan. 7, 1950; s. George MacMachan and Barbara Marie (Kollin) E.; m. Marta Anna Korduba; children: Katherine Nicole, John William, Julia Nicole. AB, U. Calif., Berkeley, 1973; MA, U. Wash., 1976, PhD, 1983. Lectr. Calif. Poly. State U., San Luis Obispo, 1980-81; lectr. U. Wash., Seattle, 1982-83, assoc. dir. Henry M. Jackson Sch. Internat. Studies, 1986-89; legis. asst. U.S. Senate, Washington, 1984-85; exec. dir. Nat. Bur. Asian Rsch., Seattle, 1989—; also bd. dirs.; participant Continuing N.W. Regional Colloquim on Internat. Security, 1982—; dir. George E. Taylor Fgn. Affairs Inst., Seattle, 1986-89; lectr. USIA, 1992; cons. in field. Author: Embargoes and World Power, 1985; co-author: Private Property and National Security, 1991, (monograph) Asia's Challenge to American Strategy, 1992; editor: Americans Speak to APEC: Building a New Order with Asia, 1993, MFN Status, Human Rights and U.S.-China Relations, 1994, NBR Analysis, 1990—. Del. Rep. Party State Conv., Tacoma, 1988; advisor Explorers, Seattle, 1992—. Grantee Dept. Def., 1990—, Dept. State, 1994. Mem. Am. Polit. Sci. Assn., Western Polit. Sci. Assn., Internat. Studies Assn. Home: PO Box 95673 Seattle WA 98145-2673 Office: Nat Bur Asian Rsch 715 Safeco Plz Seattle WA 98185

ELLINGTON, JAMES WILLARD, mechanical design engineer; b. Richmond, Ind., May 26, 1927; s. Oscar Willard and Leola Lenora (Sanderson) E.; m. Sondra Elaine Darnell, Dec. 6, 1952; children: Ronald, Roxanna. BSME summa cum laude, West Coast U., L.A., 1978. Designer NATCO, Richmond, Ind., 1954-67; design engr. Burgmaster, Gardena, Calif., 1967-69; sr. mfg. engr. Xerox Co., El Segundo, Calif., 1969-84; cons. mem. engring. staff Xerox Co., Monrovia, 1984-87; staff engr. Photonic Automation, Santa Ana, Calif., 1987-88; sr. mech. engr. Optical Radiation Co., Azusa, Calif., 1988; sr. staff engr. Omnichrome, Chino, Calif., 1988—. With USN, 1945-52. Mem. Soc. Mfg. Engrs. (sec. 1984), West Coast U. Alumni Assn. (bd. dirs. 1988—, v.p. budget and fin.). Republican. Baptist. Office: Omnichrome 13580 5th St Chino CA 91710-5113

ELLINGTON, WILL BOYD, forester, consultant; b. Palo Alto, Calif., Dec. 10, 1930; s. Will Boyd and Elsie Vivian (Prosser) E.; m. Janet Anne Chipman, June 9, 1956; children: Mark William, Lynn Rose Ellington Reese. BS, U. Calif., Berkeley, 1952. Registered profl. forester, Calif. Summer forestry aide Castle Creek Lumber Co., Castella, Calif., 1948-51; engr. officer U.S. Army, Korea, 1952-54; main logging road engr. Wildwood (Calif.) Lumber Co., 1955-58; operation forester Ralph L. Smith Lumber Co., Castella, 1958-61; forestry & logging mgr. Ralph L. Smith Lumber Co., Mt. Shasta, Calif., 1961-67; field forestry rep. Western Wood Products Assn., 1967-71; chief forester Associated Oreg. Loggers, 1971-73; project forestry cons. H.C. Mason & Assocs., 1973-77; pres. Lava Nursery, Inc., Parkdale, Oreg., 1977-93, chmn. bd. dirs., 1993—. 1st lt. U.S. Army Corps of Engrs., 1952-54. Mem. Soc. Am. Foresters, Assn. Consulting Foresters, Calif. Lic. Foresters Assn., Oreg. Small Woodlands Assn. Republican. Home: 1161 Sunningdale Rd Lake Oswego OR 97034-1736

ELLION, M. EDMUND, engineering executive; b. Boston, Jan. 20, 1923; s. Michael N. and Beatrice Elizabeth (Patterson) E.; m. Dolores Diana Rolph, July 3, 1954; children: Laurie Ann, Thomas Michael. BS, Northeastern U., 1943, Tufts U., 1944; MS, Harvard U./MIT, 1947; PhD in Engring. Physics, Calif. Inst. Tech., 1953. Exec. dir. Nat. Engring. Sci. Corp., Pasadena, Calif., 1955-60; pres. Dynamic Sci. Corp., Pasadena, 1960-64; dir. tech. GM Hughes Electronics, L.A., 1964-88; pres. Sci. Industries Inc., Santa Ynez, Calif., 1988—; lectr. Stanford U and Calif. Inst. of Tech., 1970—; lectr. Stanford U., Calif. Inst. Technology, UCLA, 1957-87. Contbr. articles to profl. jours.; holder 28 patents in field. Served to lt. USNR, 1943-46, PTO. Inst. scholar Calif. Inst. Tech., 1953. Fellow Am. Inst. Aeros. (assoc.), IEEE (assoc.). Republican. Home: 3660 Woodstock Rd Santa Ynez CA 93460-9718 Office: PO Box 645 Santa Ynez CA 93460-0645

ELLIOTT, BRUCE DAVID, rehabilitation counselor; b. Detroit, Sept. 12, 1961; s. George Thomas and Rita Virginia (Cook) E. Grad. high sch., Harper Woods, Mich. Prodn. supr. Asian Rehab. Svcs., L.A., 1988-91, employment trainer, 1991-94, rehab. counselor, 1994—. Author and actor plays Tabu Island, 1993, Last Night at the Cattle Call, 1994. Mem. Nat. Uniform Assn. (local chief 1993), LAPD Hist. Soc. Republican. Buddhist. Office: Nat Assn For Advancement of Time 6201 Sunset Ste 114 Hollywood CA 90028

ELLIOTT, CORINNE ADELAIDE, retired copywriter; b. Chgo., Nov. 20, 1927; d. Bertram Otto and Lylia Arletta (Mansfield) Briscoe; m. William S. Elliott, June 18, 1947 (div. Nov. 1985); children: Patricia Frances, Christine Grace, Annie Lou. Cert., Famous Artists Schs., Conn., 1959; BA in English maxima cum laude, Carroll Coll., 1975. Advt. writer Sandy McPherson, Realtor, Helena, Mont., 1975-79; advt. copywriter KCAP Radio, Helena, 1979-83; Helena corr. Great Falls (Mont.) Tribune, 1981-83; radio copywriter Sta. KMTX-AM-FM, Helena, 1986-93; writer in field, 1994—; pres., owner The Funding Edge, Helena, 1991—, Elliott Impress Silk Screen Works, Whitefish, Mont., 1960-70, Lotus Light Designs, Helena, 1988—; contbr. Salem Press, Pasadena, Calif. One-person show at Mont. Hist. Soc.,

1956-59, Deer Lodge, Mont., 1994; exhibited in group shows at Electrum Fine Arts Show (Merit award), Hockaday Art Gallery, Kalispell, Mont., Ball State U., Mont. Inst. Arts, 1992, Art Chateau, Butte, Mont., 1992, New Eng. Fine Arts Inst., Boston, 1993, Mont. Interpretations, Butte, 1994 (Honorable mention); works represented in permanent collections Cason Gallery, Helena, also Utick and Grosfled Collection, Helena; contbr. articles to mags. Leader 5-8th grades Girl Scouts U.S., Stanford, Mont., 1955-59; tchr. Happy Medium Art Group, Whitefish, 1959-68; violinist Waukegan Philharm., 1945-47, Billings Symphony, 1951-55; donated art works for benefit auctions to Hockaday Gallery, 1970, Kalispell, 1971, Mont. Food Bank, 1991, 92, 93, Aids Found., 1990, Helena Area Habitat for Humanity, 1993. Mem. Mont. Inst. Arts, Mont. Watercolor Soc. (bd. mem. 1983), Nat. Writers Club.

ELLIOTT, EDWARD PROCTER, architect; b. Warrington, Eng., 1916; came to U.S., 1939, naturalized, 1951; s. Arthur Spencer and Ethel Gertrude (Musket) E.; m. Cynthia Jean Heideman, June 7, 1958; children by former marriage: Stewart, Edward, Lauren, Eleanor. B.Arch. with honors, Liverpool U., Eng., 1939; fellow in City Planning, Cranbrook Acad. Art, Mich., 1939-40. Chief designer Eero Saarinen & Assocs. (architects), Bloomfield Hills, Mich., 1945-50; partner Elliott & Dworski, Birmingham, Mich., 1950-57; planning supr. Knoll Assocs., Inc., 1951-57; partner Knorr-Elliott & Assocs., San Francisco, 1957-74, Lane-Knorr-Elliott, Anchorage, Alaska, 1972-74; supervising architect Bechtel Power Corp., Gaithersburg, Md., and San Francisco,, 1974-87; cons. architect Bechtel Power Corp., San Francisco, 1987-90; mem. Nat. Council Archtl. Registration Bds.; assoc. Mich. Acad. Sci. Arts and Letters, 1957; arbitrator Am. Arbitration Assn., 1990-95. Planning and constrn. projects completed in Alaska, Ariz., Calif., Mich., Miss., N.Y. and Saudi Arabia; completed works include comml. projects, indsl. projects, fed. and state projects, univ. projects. Served to lt. comdr. Royal Canadian Navy, 1940-45. Recipient AIA awards, 1953, 56, 59, 63, Nat. Gold medal Exhbn. N.Y., 1962, award of excellence Am. Inst. Steel, 1963, Nat. award U. Alaska, 1967, Top Ten awards Comml. Indsl. Bldgs., 1968, Environmental award San Francisco, 1972. Mem. Royal Inst. Brit. Architects, Archtl. Rsch. Group of Ottawa, Can., Am. Arbitration Assn. Home: 22 Newport Way San Rafael CA 94901-4411

ELLIOTT, GORDON JEFFERSON, English language educator; b. Aberdeen, Wash., Nov. 13, 1928; s. Harry Cecil and Helga May (Kennedy) E.; m. Suzanne Tsugiko Urakawa, Apr. 2, 1957; children: Meiko Ann, Kenneth Gordon, Nancy Lee, Matthew Kennedy. AA, Grays Harbor Coll., 1948; BA, U. Wash., 1950; Cert. Russian, Army Lang. Sch., Monterey, Calif., 1952; MA, U. Hawaii, 1968. Lifetime credential, Calif. Community Coll. System. English prof. Buddhist U., Ministry of Cults, The Asia Found., Phnom Penh, Cambodia, 1956-62; English instr. U. Hawaii, Honolulu, 1962-68; dir., orientation English Coll. Petroleum and Minerals, Dhahran, Saudi Arabia, 1968-70; asst. prof., English/linguistics U. Guam, Mangilao, 1970-76; tchr., French/English Medford (Oreg.) Mid High Sch., 1976-77; instr., English Merced (Calif.) Coll., 1977—; cons. on Buddhist Edn., The Asia Found., San Francisco, Phnom Penh, Cambodia, 1956-62; cons. on English Edn., Hawaii State Adult Edn. Dept., Honolulu, 1966-68; conf. on English Edn. in Middle East, Am. U., Cairo, Egypt, 1969; vis. prof. of English, Shandong Tchrs. U., Jinan, China, 1984-85. Co-author: (textbooks, bilingual Cambodian-English) English Composition, 1962, Writing English, 1966, (test) Standard English Recognition Test, 1976; contbr. articles to profl. jours. Mem. Statue of Liberty Centennial Commn., Washington, 1980-86, Heritage Found., Washington, Lincoln Inst., Am. Near East Refugee Aid, Washington, Sgt. U.S. Army Security Agy., 1951-55. Tchr. Fellowship, U. Mich., Ann Arbor, 1956; recipient summer seminar stipend, Nat. Endowment For Humanities, U. Wash., Seattle, 1976, travel grants, People's Rep. of China, Beijing, 1984-85. Mem. NRA, Collegiate Press (editorial adv. bd.), Merced Coll. Found., Am. Assn. Woodturners, Elks. Republican. Home: 680 Dennis Ct Merced CA 95340-2410 Office: Merced Coll 3600 M St Merced CA 95348-2806

ELLIOTT, JAMES HEYER, retired university art museum curator, fine arts consultant; b. Medford, Oreg., Feb. 19, 1924; s. Bert R. and Marguerite E. (Heyer) E.; m. Judith Ann Algar, Apr. 23, 1966 (div.); children: Arabel Joan, Jakob Maxwell. BA, Willamette U., Salem, Oreg., 1947, DFA (hon.), 1978; AM, Harvard U., 1949; DFA (hon.), San Francisco Art Inst., 1991. James Rogers Rich fellow Harvard U., 1949-50; Fulbright grantee Paris, 1951-52; art critic European edit. N.Y. Herald-Tribune, 1952-53; curator, acting dir. Walker Art Center, Mpls., 1953-56; asst. chief curator, curator modern art Los Angeles County Mus. Art, 1956-63, chief curator, 1964-66; dir. Wadsworth Atheneum, Hartford, Conn., 1966-76; dir. Univ. Art Mus., Berkeley, Calif., 1976-88, chancellor's curator, 1989-90, dir. emeritus, 1990—; adj. prof. Hunter Coll., N.Y.C., 1968, U. Calif., Berkeley, 1976-90; commr. Conn. Commn. Arts, 1970-76; fellow Trumbull Coll., Yale U., 1971-75; mem. mus. arts panel Nat. Endowment Arts, 1974-77; bd. dirs. San Francisco Art Inst., 1980-90; art adv. com. Exploratorium, 1982-91; adv. com. Artists TV Access, 1987-90. Author: Bonnard and His Environment, 1964, James Lee Byars: Notes Towards a Biography, 1990. Trustee Marcia Simon Weisman Found., 1991—, 23--5 Found., San Francisco, 1993—; mem. adv. bd. Artspace San Francisco, 1989—. With USNR, 1943-46. Mem. Internat. Coun. Mus., Am. Assn. Mus., Coll. Art Assn., Assn. Art Mus. Dirs. (sec., trustee 1980-81), Artists Space N.Y. (bd. dirs. 1980-84), Arts Club (Berkeley). Club: Arts (Berkeley). Home: 13 Yellow Ferry Harbor Sausalito CA 94965-1327

ELLIOTT, JEANNE MARIE KORELTZ, transportation executive; b. Virginia, Minn., Mar. 9, 1943; d. John Andrew and Johanna Mae (Tehovnik) Koreltz; m. David Michael Elliott, Apr. 30, 1983. Student, Ariz. State U., 1967, U. So. Calif. Cert. aviation safety inspector. Tech. asst. Ariz. State U., Tempe, 1966-68; from supr. to mgr. inflight tng./in-svc. programs Northwest Airlines Inc. (formerly Republic Airlines, Hughes Airwest, Air West Inc.), Seattle, 1968—; air carrier cabin safety specialist Flight Standards Service, FAA, Washington, 1975-76; cons. Interaction Research Corp., Olympia, Wash., 1982—. Contbg. editor Cabin Crew Safety Bull., Flight Safety Found., 1978—. Recipient Annual Air Safety award Air Line Pilots Assn., Washington, 1971, Annual Safety award Ariz. Safety Council, Phoenix, 1972; first female to hold FAA cabin safety inspector's credential, 1976. Mem. Soc. Air Safety Investigators Internat., Survival and Flight Equipment Assn., Assn. Flight Attendants (tech. chmn. 1968-85), Soc. Automotive Engrs. (chmn. cabin safety provisions com. 1971—), Teamsters Local 2000 (chair nat. safety and health). Republican. Roman Catholic. Home: 16215 SE 31st St Bellevue WA 98008-5704 Office: NW Airlines Inc Inflight Svcs Dept Seattle-Tacoma Internat Airport Seattle WA 98158

ELLIOTT, JOHN ED, economics educator; b. Los Angeles, Oct. 22, 1931; s. James Edgar and Jessie Fisher (Metcalf) E.; m. Elda Rose Wilson, Dec. 22, 1975; children: John David, Richard Lee, Elizabeth Ann, James Hall. BA in Econs., Occidental Coll., 1952; MA in Polit. Sci., Harvard U., 1956, PhD in Econs., 1956. Instr. U. So. Calif., Los Angeles, 1956-59, asst. prof. econs., 1959-61, assoc. prof., 1961-66, prof., 1966—; dir. faculty seminar NEH, 1980, 82, 84, 86, 88, 93, 95. Author: Comparative Economic Systems, 1985, Marx and Engels Economics Politics Society, 1981, Competing Philosophies American Political Economics, 1975; contbr. articles to profl. jours. Mem. AAUP (nat. council 1985—, pres. Calif. conf. 1985—), Hist. Econs. Soc. (v.p. 1988), Assn. Social Econs. (exec. council. 1985—, v.p. 1988, pres. 1989), Am. Econ. Assn., Western Econ. Assn., Assn. for Evolutionary Econ., Atlantic Econ. Soc., Union Radical Polit. Econs. Democrat. Office: U So Calif Dept Econs University Park Los Angeles CA 90089

ELLIOTT, JOHN GREGORY, aerospace design engineer; b. Surabaya, Dutch East Indies, Nov. 9, 1948; came to U.S., 1956; s. Frans Jan and Charlotte Clara (Rosel) E.; m. Jennifer Lee Austin, May 7, 1988. AA, Cerritos Coll., 1974; BS, Calif. State U., Long Beach, 1978. Design engr. Douglas Aircraft Co., Long Beach, 1978-82, lead engr., 1983-89, sect. mgr. elect. installations group, 1989—. With USN, 1969-73. Mem. So. Calif. Profl. Engring. Assn., Douglas Aircraft Co. Tennis Club, Douglas Aircraft Co. Surf Club, Douglas Aircraft Co. Mgmt. Club. Republican. Presbyterian. Office: Douglas Aircraft Co Internal Mail Code 800-53 3855 N Lakewood Blvd Long Beach CA 90846-0003

ELLIOTT, JON FREDERICK, environmental consultant, educator, lawyer; b. Atlanta, Sept. 30, 1956; m. Elizabeth Lees Taggart; 1 child, Martin Alexander. BSE in Mech. Engring., Princeton U., 1977; M of Pub. Policy, U. Calif., Berkeley, 1980, JD, 1981. Bar: Calif.; registered environ. assesor, Calif. Advisor to pres. Calif. Pub. Utility Commn., San Francisco, 1981-83; staff atty. Toward Utility Rate Normalization, San Francisco, 1983-87; program mgr., regulatory info. Exceltech, Inc., Fremont, Calif., 1987-89; prin., v.p. EPICS Internat., Oakland, Calif., 1989-92; pres. Touchstone Environ., Inc., Oakland, 1992—; mem. exec. com. Environ. Law sect. State Bar Calif., San Francisco, 1992—, chair legis. com., 1993—; bd. dirs. Santa Fe Coun. for Environ. Excellence, 1991—. Prin. author: Hazardous Materials Program Commentary, 1988; contbg. editor: The Complete Guide to Hazardous Materials Enforcement and Liability, 1990, Environmental Compliance--A Simplified National Guide, 1992, others. Mem. adv. com. No. Calif. Bus. Environ. Assistance Ctr., Santa Clara, 1994—. Democrat. Office: Touchstone Environ Inc 449 15th St Ste 301 Oakland CA 94612-2821

ELLIOTT, RICHARD L., school administrator; b. Colorado Springs, Colo., Apr. 6, 1943; s. Harry Raymond Elliott and Georgia Louise (McCarty) Coston; m. Erlene Frances Oxtoby, June 11, 1977; children: Shane Maurice, Tiffany Louise. BA, No. Colo. U., 1966; MEd, Ea. N.Mex. U., 1986. Cert. tchr., adminstr., N.Mex., Colo. Tchr., football coach St. Mary's High Sch., Colorado Springs, 1967-69, Palmer High Sch., Colorado Springs, 1969-73, Mitchell High Sch., Colorado Springs, 1973-76, Fruita Monument High Sch., Grand Junction, Colo., 1976-77; custom home builder Bump Elliott Constrn., Colorado Springs, 1977-80; tchr., football coach Air Acad. High Sch., Colorado Springs, 1980-81; asst. athletic dir., football coach N.Mex. Mil. Inst., Roswell, 1981-88; athletic dir. Las Cruces (N.Mex.) Pub. Schs., 1988—. Bd. dirs. Bantam Weight Youth Sports Assn., Las Cruces, 1989—, United Way Dona Ana County, Las Cruces, 1990—, March of Dimes, Las Cruces, 1994—. Named Region 8 Athletic Dir. of Yr., Nat. High Sch. Athletic Coaches Assn., 1992. Mem. AAHPERD, N.Mex. Athletic Dirs. Assn. (pres. 1990-91), Nat. Fedn. Interscholastic Coaches, Nat. Interscholastic Athletic Adminstrs., Nat. Coun. Secondary Schs. Athletic Dirs. (Western Regional Athletic Dir. of Yr. 1992), N.Mex. H.S. Coaches Assn. (Athletic Dir. of Yr. 1990), N.Mex. Activities Assn. (exec. com. 1989—, Adult Sportsman of Yr. 1990), K.C., Lions, Elks. Roman Catholic. Home: 797 Frank Maes Ave Las Cruces NM 88005-1230 Office: Las Cruces Pub Schs Loretto Towne Ctr 505 S Main St Las Cruces NM 88001-1245

ELLIOTT, ROBERT JAMES, mathematician; b. Swanwick, Derby, Eng., June 12, 1940; s. James Alfred and Marjorie Jane (Hilditch) E.; m. Ann Beardsley, Aug. 29, 1962; children—Jane Ann, Catherine Louise. B.A., Oxford U., 1961, M.A., 1964; Ph.D., Cambridge U., 1965, Sc.D., 1983. Lectr. U. Newcastle, Eng., 1964-65; instr. Yale U., 1965-66; fellow, lectr. Oriel Coll. and Oxford U., 1966-69; sr. research fellow Warwick U., England, 1969-72; prof. Hull U., Eng., 1973-76, G.F. Grant prof., 1976-86; prof. U. Alberta, Can., 1986—; vis. prof. Northwestern U., 1972-73, U. Toronto, 1972, U. Alberta, 1985-86, Australian Nat. U., 1983; disting. vis. prof. U. Alta., 1984-85. Author: Stochastic Calculus, 1982. Co-author: Values in Differential Games, 1972, Hidden Markov Models, 1994, also articles. Mem. Am. Math. Soc., Soc. for Indsl. and Applied Math., Math. Assn. Am. Avocation: music. Office: U Alberta Dept Math Scis, 434 CAB, Edmonton, AB Canada T6G 2G1

ELLIOTT, ROSS COX, insurance company executive; b. Orem, Utah, June 9, 1948; s. Grant Hansen and Pauline (Cox) E.; m. Mynon Hayes, Apr. 23, 1970; children: Edgar M., James W., Rosann. BS in Bus. Mgmt., Brigham Young U., 1972. Regional sales mgr. ADP Dealer Svcs., Denver, 1975-76, regional customer svc. mgr., 1976-78; dir. tng. Automatic Data Processing-Dealer Svcs., Portland, Oreg., 1979-85; dir. ins. svcs. Larry H. Miller Group, Murray, Utah, 1986—; chief oper. officer Landcar Life Ins. Co., Murray, 1986—, Landcar Agy., Murray, 1986—, Landcar Ins. Co. Colo., Murray, 1990—. Chmn. Murray City Gang Task Force, 1992-93. Mem. Ins. Acctg. and Systems Adminstrn., Utah Life and Disability Ins. Guaranty Assn. (bd. dirs. 1990—, Murray City C. of C. (bd. dirs. 1992). Republican. Mem. LDS Ch. Home: 5865 Holstein Way Murray UT 84107-6541 Office: Landcar Insurance Svcs 5650 S State St Salt Lake City UT 84107-6131

ELLIOTT, SCOTT OLLER, lawyer; b. San Jose, July 26, 1957; s. Roland Meredith and Sandra Gale (Deem) E.; m. Nancy Marie Oller, Apr. 6, 1979; children: Tristan Robin, Jordan Brook, Robin Sage, Forest Dream. BA in Drama magna cum laude, Calif. State Univ. Stanislaus, Turlock, 1979; JD, U. Oreg., 1987. Bar: Oreg. 1987, U.S. Ct. Appeals (9th cir.) 1992, U.S. Dist. Ct. Oreg. 1988. Assoc. Larry O. Gildea, Eugene, Oreg., 1987-88, Thorp, Dennet, Purdy & Golden, 1988; law clk. U.S. Dist. Ct., Las Vegas, Nev., 1988-89; ptnr. Green, Elliott & Posen, Lincoln City, Oreg., 1989—. Precinct com. Lincoln County Dems., Newport, 1990-94, orgnl. chair, 1992, bylaws chair, 1993, 94. U. Oreg. Theatre grad. teaching fellow, 1979-80. Mem. ABA, Assn. Trial Lawyers Am., Oreg. Trial Lawyers Assn., Oreg. Bar (procedure and practice com.), Lincoln County Bar. Office: Green Elliott & Posen Green & Elliott 2137NW Hwy 101 Lincoln City OR 97367

ELLIS, CARLTON CASE, managed futures trading specialist; b. Chgo., May 18, 1954; s. John Ogborn and Amanda Sophronia (Rogers) E.; m. Donna Lynn Sirjord, Oct. 12, 1985; children: Arthur John, Michael Stewart. AAS, Paul Smiths Coll., 1974; BS, Cornell U., 1976; M. Forestry, Oreg. State U., 1979. Cons. forester Sanders Cronk & Holmes, Portland, Oreg., 1979-81; mgmt. trainee Holman Transfer, Portland, 1981-82; pres. Mescan, Inc., Seattle, 1982-84; assoc. v.p. Prudential Securities, Seattle, 1984—. Mem. Managed Futures Assn., Cornell Club of Western Wash. (treas. 1990—, membership dir. 1989—, pres. 1992—), Wash. Athletic Club.

ELLIS, DEBORAH LYNN, horticulturist, arborist, consultant; b. Cleve., Mar. 28, 1958; d. Edward Joseph and Frances V. (Warren) Dobbs; m. Timothy E. Ellis, Aug. 13, 1983; 1 child, Sara Marie. AS in Ornamental Horticulture, Foothill Jr. Coll., Los Altos Hills, Calif., 1978; BS in Ornamental Horticulture, Calif. Poly State U., San Luis Obispo, 1981; MS in Plant Protection & Pest Mgmt., U. Calif., Davis, 1983. Ind. horticultural cons. San Jose, Calif., 1984—. Leopold Edwards Wrasse Agrl. scholar Calif. Poly. U., 1978-79; Calif. Assn. Nurserymen scholar Calif. Poly. U., 1980-81. Mem. Am. Soc. Consulting Arborists, Calif. Native Plant Soc., Calif. Oak Found., Calif. Native Grass Assn., Internat. Soc. Arboriculture, No. Calif. Turfgrass Coun., Saratoga Horticultural Found., San Jose Cactus and Succulent Soc., Pi Alpha Xi. Office: PO Box 10013 San Jose CA 95157-1013

ELLIS, ELDON EUGENE, surgeon; b. Washington, Ind., July 2, 1922; s. Osman Polson and Ina Lucretia (Cochran) E.; BA, U. Rochester, 1946, MD, 1949; m. Irene Clay, June 26, 1948 (dec. 1968); m. Priscilla Dean Strong, Sept. 20, 1969 (dec. Feb. 1990); children: Paul Addison, Kathe Lynn, Jonathan Clay, Sharon Anne, Eldon Eugene, Rebecca Deborah; m. Virginia Michael Ellis, Aug. 22, 1992. Intern in surgery Stanford U. Hosp., San Francisco, 1949-50, resident and fellow in surgery, 1950-52, 55; Schilling fellow in pathology San Francisco Gen. Hosp., 1955; ptnr. Redwood Med. Clinic, Redwood City, Calif., 1955-87, med. dir., 1984-87; semi-ret. physician, 1987—; med. dir. Peninsula Occupl. Health Assocs. (now Peninsula Indsl. Med. Clinic), San Carlos, Calif., 1991-93, part-time with, 1995—; dir. Sequoia Hosp., Redwood City, 1974-82; asst. clin. prof. surgery Stanford U., 1970-80. Pres. Sequoia Hosp. Found., 1983-92, bd. dirs.; pres., chmn. bd. dirs. Bay Chamber Symphony Orch., San Mateo, Calif., 1988-91; mem. Nat. Bd. of Benevolence Evang. Covenant Ch., Chgo., 1988-93; mem. mgmt. com. The Samarkand Retirement Community, Santa Barbara, Calif.; past pres. Project Hope Nat. Alumni Assn., 1992-94, bd. dirs., 1994—; med. advisor Project Hope, Russia Commonwealth Ind. States, 1992. Served with USNR, 1942-46, 50-52. Named Outstanding Citizen of Yr., Redwood City, 1987. Mem. San Mateo County (pres. 1961-63), Calif. (pres. 1965-66), Am. (v.p. 1974-75) heart assns., San Mateo Med. Soc. (pres. 1969-70), San Mateo County Comprehensive Health Planning Coun. (v.p. 1969-70), Calif., Am. med. assns., San Mateo, Stanford surg. socs., Am. Coll. Chest Physicians, Calif. Thoracic Soc., Cardiovascular Council. Republican. Mem. Peninsula Covenant Ch. Club: Commonwealth. Home: 3621 Farm Hill Blvd Redwood City CA 94061-1230 Office: Peninsula Indsl Med Clinic 1581 Industrial Rd San Carlos CA 94070-4111

ELLIS, EUGENE JOSEPH, cardiologist; b. Rochester, N.Y., Feb. 23, 1919; s. Eugene Joseph and Violet (Anderson) E.; m. Ruth Nugent, July 31, 1943; children: Eugene J., Susan Ellis Renwick, Amy Ellis Miller. AB, U. So. Calif., L.A., 1941; MD, U. So. Calif., 1944; MS in medicine, U. Minn., 1950. Diplomate Am. Bd. Internal Medicine and Cardiovascular Diseases. Intern L.A. County Hosp., 1944, resident, 1946; fellowship Mayo Clinic, Rochester, Minn., 1947-51; dir. dept. cardiology St. Vincent's Hosp., L.A., 1953-55; dir. dept. cardiology Good Samaritan Hosp., L.A., 1955-84; ret., ret., 1984; prof. emeritus medicine U. So. Calif., 1984—; Mem. Med. Bd. of Calif., 1984-91; pres., 1988; pres. Div. of Med. Quality, State of Calif., 1985-89; exec. com. trustees U. Redlands, 1976-86. Lt. USN, 1944-46. Contbr. articles to profl. jours. Lt. USN, 1944-46. Mem. L.A. Country Club, Pauma Valley Country Club (dir. 1980-83), Birnfim Wood Country Club, Valley Club of Montecito. Republican. Home: 450 Eastgate Ln Santa Barbara CA 93108-2248

ELLIS, GEORGE EDWIN, JR., chemical engineer; b. Beaumont, Tex., Apr. 14, 1921; s. George Edwin and Julia (Ryan) E.; B.S. in Chem. Engring., U. Tex., 1948; M.S., U. So. Calif., 1958, M.B.A., 1965, M.S. in Mech. Engring., 1968, M.S. in Mgmt. Sci., 1971, Engr. in Indsl. and Systems Engring., 1979. Research chem. engr. Tex. Co., Port Arthur, Tex., 1948-51, Long Beach, Calif., Houston, 1952-53, Space and Information div. N.Am. Aviation Co., Downey, Calif., 1959-61, Magna Corp., Anaheim, Calif., 1961-62; chem. process engr. AiResearch Mfg. Co., Los Angeles, 1953-57, 57-59; chem. engr. Petroleum Combustion & Engring. Co., Santa Monica, Calif., 1957, Jacobs Engring. Co., Pasadena, Calif., 1957, Sesler & Assos., Los Angeles, 1959; research specialist Marquardt Corp., Van Nuys, Calif., 1962-67; sr. project engr. Conductron Corp., Northridge, 1967-68; information systems asst. Los Angeles Dept. Water and Power, 1969-92. Instr. thermodynamics U. So. Calif., Los Angeles, 1957. Served with USAAF, 1943-45. Mem. ASTM, ASME, Nat. Assn. Purchasing Mgmt., Nat. Contract Mgmt. Assn., Am. Inst. Profl. Bookkeepers, Am. Soc. Safety Engrs., Am. Chem. Soc., Am. Soc. Materials, Am. Electroplaters and Surface Finishers Soc., Am. Inst. Chem. Engrs., Inst. Indsl. Engrs., Am. Prodn. and Inventory Control Soc., Am. Soc. Quality Control, Am. Inst. Plant Engrs., Am. Indsl. Hygenists Assn., Steel Structure Painting Coun., Inst. Mgmt. Accts., Soc. Mfg. Engrs., L.A. Soc. Coating Tech., Assn. Finishing Processes, Pi Tau Sigma, Phi Lambda Upsilon, Alpha Pi Mu. Home: 1344 W 20th St San Pedro CA 90732-4408

ELLIS, GEORGE RICHARD, museum administrator; b. Birmingham, Ala., Dec. 9, 1937; s. Richard Paul and Dorsie (Gibbs) E.; m. Sherroll Edwards, June 20, 1961 (dec. 1973); m. Nancy Enderson, Aug. 27, 1975; 1 son, Joshua. BA, U. Chgo., 1959, MFA, 1961; postgrad., UCLA, 1971. Art supr. Jefferson County Schs., Birmingham, 1962-64; asst. dir. Birmingham Mus. Art, 1964-66; asst. dir. UCLA Mus. Cultural History, 1971-81, assoc. dir., 1981-82; dir. Honolulu Acad. Arts, 1981—. Author various works on non-western art, 1971—. Recipient Ralph Altman award UCLA, 1968; recipient Outstanding Achievement award UCLA, 1980; fellow Kress Found., 1971. Mem. Pacific Arts Assn. (v.p. 1985-89, exec. bd. 1989—), Hawaii Mus. Assn. (v.p. 1986-87, pres. 1987-88), Assn. Art Mus. Dirs., Am. Assn. Mus., L.A. Ethnic Arts Coun. (hon.), Friends of Iolani Palace (bd. dirs. 1989—), Pacific Club. Office: Honolulu Academy of Arts 900 S Beretania St Honolulu HI 96814-1429

ELLIS, HARLAN FRED, obstetrician and gynecologist; b. Vallejo, Calif., Aug. 5, 1925; s. Claud Maurice and Edna Bess E.; m. Betty LeVonne Zuiderweg, Aug. 3, 1947 (div. Apr. 1972); children: Robert, Jane, Chuck, Susan, Cathy; m. Joan Hayden Heisler, Sept. 25, 1978. BA, U. Calif., Berkeley, 1948; DO, Calif. Coll. Osteo. Physicians, 1952; MD, U. Calif., Irvine, 1962. Diplomate Am. Bd. Obstetrics and Gynecology. Resident L.A. County Hosp./Burbank Cmty. Hosp., 1955-58; asst. clin. prof. ob-gyn. U. Calif., Irvine, 1958-68; pvt. practice Kaweah Sierra Med. Group, Visalia, Calif., 1968—; chmn. dept. ob-gyn. Cmty. Hosp. L.A., 1960-68, also cons. staff; cons. staff Burbank Cmty. Hosp., 1958-68, L.A. County Hosp., 1958-68; chmn. dept. ob-gyn. Visalia Cmty. Hosp., 1968—; cons. State of Calif. for Maternal Mortality, 1965-72; organizer, lectr. on natural childbirth and newborn bonding, 1959—. Co-editor: Ghildbirth Without Fear, 1972, 5th edit. 1994. Pres. Valley Birthing Network. Fellow ACOG; mem. AMA, Calif. Med. Assn., Tulare County Med. Assn., Calif. Assn. Ob-Gyn., Pacific Coast Infertility Soc., Am. Assn. Gynecologic Laparoscopists, Internat. Soc. for Study of Reprodn., Am. Infertility Soc.

ELLIS, JAMES REED, lawyer; b. Oakland, Calif., Aug. 5, 1921; s. Floyd E. and Hazel (Reed) E.; m. Mary Lou Earling, Nov. 18, 1944 (dec.); children: Robert Lee, Judith Ann (dec.), Lynn Earling, Steven Reed. B.S., Yale, 1942; J.D., U. Wash., 1948; LL.D., Lewis and Clark U., 1968, Seattle U., 1981, Whitman Coll., 1992. Bar: Wash. 1949, D.C. 1971. Ptnr. Preston, Thorgrimson, Horowitz, Starin & Ellis, Seattle, 1952-69, Preston, Thorgrimson, Starin, Ellis & Holman, Seattle, 1969-72, Preston, Thorgrimson, Ellis, Holman & Fletcher, Seattle, 1972-79; sr. ptnr. Preston, Thorgrimson, Ellis & Holman, Seattle, 1979-90, Preston, Thorgrimson, Shidler, Gates & Ellis, Seattle, 1990-92; ret., of counsel Preston, Gates & Ellis, Seattle, 1992—; chmn., CEO Wash. State Convention and Trade Ctr., Seattle, 1986—; dep. pros. atty. King County, 1952; gen. counsel Municipality of Met. Seattle, 1958-79; dir., mem. exec. com. Key Bank of Wash., 1969-94, Kiro, Inc., 1965-95; dir. Blue Cross of Wash. and Alaska, 1989—. Mem. Nat. Water Commn., 1970-73; mem. urban transp. adv. council U.S. Dept. Transp., 1970-71; mem. Wash. Planning Adv. Council, 1965-72; mem. Washington State Growth Strategies Commn., 1989-90; pres. Forward Thrust Inc., 1966-73; chmn. Mayors Com. on Rapid Transit, 1964-65; trustee Ford Found., 1970-82, mem. exec. com., 1978-82; bd. regents U. Wash., 1965-77, pres., 1972-73; trustee Resources for the Future, 1983-92; mem. council Nat. Mcpl. League, 1968-76, v.p., 1972-76; chmn. Save our Local Farmlands Com., 1978-79, King County Farmlands Adv. Commn., 1980-82; pres. Friends of Freeway Park, 1976—; bd. dirs. Nat. Park and Recreation Assn., 1979-82; trustee Lewis and Clark U., 1988-94; pres. Mountains to Sound Greenway Trust, Inc., 1991—; trustee Henry M. Jackson Found., 1992—. 1st lt. USAAF, 1943-46. Recipient Bellevue First Citizen award, 1968, Seattle First Citizen award, 1968, Nat. Conservation award Am. Motors, 1968, Distinguished Service award Wash. State Dept. Parks and Recreation, 1968, Distinguished Citizen award Nat. Municipal League, 1969, King County Distinguished Citizen award, 1970, La Guardia award Center N.Y.C. Affairs, 1975, Environ. Quality award EPA, 1977, Am. Inst. for Public Service Nat. Jefferson award, 1974, U. Wash. Recognition award, 1981, State Merit medal State of Wash., 1990, Nat. Founders award Local Initiatives Support Corp., 1992. Fellow Am. Bar Found.; mem. ABA (ho. dels. 1978-82, past chmn. urban, state and local govt. law sect.), Nat. Assn. Bond Lawyers (com. standards of practice), Wash. Bar Assn., Seattle Bar Assn. (Pres.'s award 1993), D.C. Bar Assn., Am. Judicature Soc., Acad. Pub. Adminstrn., Coun. on Fgn. Rels., Mcpl. League Seattle and King County (past pres.), Order of Hosp. of St. John of Jerusalem, AIA (hon.), Order of Coif (hon.), Phi Delta Phi, Phi Gamma Delta, Rainier Club (Seattle). Home: 903 Shoreland Dr SE Bellevue WA 98004-6738 Office: 5000 Columbia Seafirst Ctr 701 5th Ave Seattle WA 98104-7016

ELLIS, JOHN W., professional baseball team executive, utility company executive; b. Seattle, Sept. 14, 1928; s. Floyd E. and Hazel (Reed) R.; m. Doris Stearns, Sept. 1, 1953; children: Thomas R., John, Barbara, Jim. B.S., U. Wash., 1952, J.D., 1953. Bar: Wash. State bar 1953. Ptnr. Perkins, Coie, Stone, Olsen & Williams, Seattle, 1953-70; with Puget Sound Power & Light Co., Bellevue, Wash., 1970—, exec. v.p., 1973-76, pres., CEO, 1976-87, also dir., chmn., CEO, 1987-92, chmn. bd., 1992—; dir., chmn. Seattle br. Fed. Res. Bank of San Francisco, 1982-88; chief exec. officer Seattle Mariners, 1992—; mem. Wash. Gov.'s Spl. Com. Energy Curtailment, 1973-74; mem. Wash. Gov.'s Coun. on Edn., 1991—; chmn. Pacific N.W. Utilities Coordinating Com., 1976-82; bd. dirs. Wash. Mut. Savs. Bank, Seattle, SAFECO Corp., Nat. Energy Found., 1985-87, FlowMole Corp., Assoc. Electric & Gas Ins. Svcs. Ltd.; chmn. Electric Power Rsch. Inst., 1984—; chmn., CEO, The Baseball Club of Seattle, L.P.; regent Wash. State U., 1992—. Pres. Bellevue Boys and Girls Club, 1969-71, Seattle/King County Econ. Devel. Council, 1984—; mem. exec. dirs. Seattle/King County Boys and Girls Club, 1972-75; bd. dirs. Overlake Hosp., Bellevue, 1974—, United Way King County, 1977—, Seattle Sci. Found., 1977—, Seattle Sailing Found., Evergreen Safety Council, 1981, Assn. Wash. Bus., 1980-81, Govs. Adv. Council on Econ. Devel., 1984—; chmn. bd. Wash. State Bus. Round Table, 1983; pres. United for Washington; adv. bd. Grad. Sch. Bus. Adminstrn. U. Wash., 1982—, Wash. State Econ. Ptnrship., 1984—; chmn. Seattle Regional Panel White Ho. Fellows, 1985—; trustee Seattle U., 1986—. Mem. ABA, Wash. Bar Assn., King County Bar Assn., Nat. Assn. Elec. Cos. (dir. 1977-79), Edison Electric Inst. (dir. 1978-80, exec. com. 1982, 2d vice chmn. 1987, 1st vice chmn. 1988, now chmn.), Assn. Edison Illuminating Cos. (exec. com. 1979-81), Seattle C. of C. (dir. 1980—, 1st vice chmn. 1987-88, chmn. 1988—), Phi Gamma Delta, Phi Delta Phi. Clubs: Rainier (Seattle) (sec. 1972, v.p. 1984, pres. 1985), Seattle Yacht (Seattle), Corinthian Yacht (Seattle); Meydenbauer Bay Yacht (Bellevue), Bellevue Athletic. Lodge: Rotary (Seattle). Home: 901 Shoreland Dr SE Bellevue WA 98004-6738 Office: Seattle Mariners PO Box 4100 83 King St Seattle WA 98104-2860 also: Puget Sound Power & Light Co PO Box 97034 Bldg Bellevue WA 98009-9734*

ELLIS, LEE, publisher, editor; b. Medford, Mass., Mar. 12, 1924; s. Lewis Leeds and Charlotte Frances (Brough) E.; m. Sharon Kay Barnhouse, Aug. 19, 1972. Child actor, dancer, stage, radio, movies, Keith-Albee Cir., Ea. U.S., 1927-37; announcer, producer, writer, various radio stas. and CBS, Boston and Miami, Fla., 1946-50; TV dir. ABC; mem. TV faculty Sch. Journalism U. Mo., Columbia, 1950-55; mgr. Sta. KFSD/KFSD-TV, San Diego, 1955-60, GM Imperial Broadcasting System, 1960-62; v.p., dir. advt., Media-Agencies-Clients, Los Angeles, 1962-66; v.p., dir. newspaper relations Family Weekly (name now USA Weekend), N.Y.C., 1966-89; pres., owner, editor Sharlee Publs., 1989—; voice of Nat. Date Festival, 1990-93; lectr. gen. semantics and communications Idaho State U., Utah State U., San Diego State U. Served with USN, 1941-44, PTO. Mem. San Diego Press Club, Indio C. of C. Republican. Methodist. Home and Office: 47-800 Madison St Spc 53 Indio CA 92201-6673

ELLIS, NORMAN DERL, air force chaplain; b. Lansing, Mich., Nov. 9, 1953; s. Roy Balos and Lillian Virginia (Talley) E.; m. Molly Patricia Gill, July 20, 1979; children: Ryan Jay (dec.), Tyler Jay, Jase Gill, Sunni Melissa. BS in Psychology, McNeese State U., 1982; MDiv, New Orleans Bapt. Theol. Sem., 1985. Ordained minister Bapt. Ch., 1985. Enlisted USAF, 1971—, commd., 1985, advanced through grades to capt., 1983, commd. chaplain, 1986, air freight/supply specialist, 1971-75, artillery computer specialist, 1976-79; res. chaplain 23 TFW Eng. AFB, Alexandria, La., 1986-91, 926 FG New Orleans Naval Air Sta., 1991-93; wing chaplain 58th Spl. Ops. Wing, Kirtland Force Base, N.Mex., 1993—; pastor Magnolia Bapt. Ch., Ragley, La., 1986-93; vis. lectr. psychology McNeese State U., Lake Charles, La., 1986-93. Mem. Res. Officer Assn. Republican. Office: 1377 ABW/HC 1950 2nd St SE Albuquerque NM 87117-5520

ELLIS, ROBERT HARRY, retired television executive, university administrator; b. Cleve., Mar. 2, 1928; s. John George Ellis and Grace Bernice (Lewis) Ellis Kline; m. Frankie Jo Lanter, Aug. 7, 1954; children: Robert Harry Jr., Kimberley Kay Ellis Murphy, Shana Lee. BA, Ariz. State U., 1953; MA, Case Western Res. U., 1962. Newswriter, announcer Sta. KOY, Phoenix, 1953-55, continuity dir., 1955-61; dir., radio ops. Ariz. State U., Tempe, 1959-61; gen. mgr. Sta. KAET-TV, Tempe, 1961-87; assoc. v.p. Ariz. State U., Tempe, 1986-90; exec. com. bd. dirs. Pub. Broadcasting Svc., Washington, 1972-77, 80-86; founder Pacific Mountain Network, Denver, 1972, pres., 1973-75; mem. ednl. telecomm. com. Nat. Assn. Ednl. Broadcasters, Washington, 1973-77, 80-86. Mem. Sister City, Tempe, Tempe Ctr. For the Handicapped, East Valley Mental Health Alliance, Mesa, Ariz., Ariz. Acad., State Ariz. Behavior Health Bd. of Examiners, 1991-92. Bd. Govs. award Pacific Mountain Network, 1987. Mem. Nat. Assn. TV Arts and Scis. (life, v.p., bd. trustees 1969-70, bd. dirs. Phoenix chpt. 1986, silver circle award 1992), Nat. Assn. Pub. TV Stas. (bd. dirs. 1988-94), Tempe C. of C. (diplomate, bd. dirs. 1987-90), Sundome Performing Arts Assn. (bd. dirs. 1986-90), Ariz. Zool. Soc. (bd. dirs., sec. 1984-90), Ariz. State U. Alumni Assn. (life), Ariz. State U. Retirees Assn. (founder, pres. 1991-92), Tempe Conv. and Visitors Bur. (founder, sec./treas. 1988-93), Tempe Sports Authority (founder 1989-95), ASU Faculty Emeritus Orgn. (pres. 1992-93). Methodist.

ELLIS, ROBERT RICHMOND, Spanish language educator; b. L.A.. BA, Pomona Coll., 1977; MA, UCLA, 1979, PhD, 1984. Asst. prof. Spanish Occidental Coll., L.A., 1984-90, assoc. prof. Spanish, 1990—, chair dept. Spanish and French lit. studies, 1995—. Author: The Tragic Pursuit of Being: Unamuno and Sartre, 1988, San Juan de la Cruz: Mysticism and Sartrean Existentialism, 1992. Home: 4951 Wawona St Los Angeles CA 90041-1832 Office: Occidental Coll 1600 Campus Rd Los Angeles CA 90041-3384

ELLIS, TED ELLSWORTH, banker; b. Rexburg, Idaho, Aug. 1, 1927; s. Ted R. and Zella (Ellsworth) E.; m. Margaret Lewis, Oct. 8, 1947; children—Nancy C. Ellis Chopko, Jolynn Woodworth, Patricia Ann. Student, Ricks Coll., 1947, U. Wash., 1963. With First Security Bank of Idaho, 1947-77, sr. v.p., dir., 1972-77; exec. v.p., chief adminstrv. officer Idaho Bank and Trust Co., Pocatello, 1977—; pres., chief exec. officer Idaho Bank and Trust Co., 1981-88; chmn. Key Bank of Idaho, 1988-92. Bd. dirs. Bannock County ARC, 1965, Salvation Army, 1973—, Boy Scouts Am., 1976—, Jr. Achievement, 1977—, Idaho State Civic Symphony, 1977-78, YMCA, 1974—; pres. Pocatello Downtown Devel. Corp., 1970—. Served with USNR, 1945-46. Mem. Pocatello C. of C. (pres. 1969-70). Club: Pocatello Rotary (pres. 1973-74). Home: 9410 N Winterwood Ln Boise ID 83703-1776 Office: Key Bank of Idaho 702 W Idaho St Boise ID 83702-8901

ELLISON, CYRIL LEE, publisher; b. N.Y.C., Dec. 11, 1916; s. John and Rose (Ellison) E.; m. Anne N. Nottonson, June 4, 1942. With Watson-Guptill Publs., 1939-69, v.p., advt. dir., 1939-69, assoc. pub. Am. Artist mag.; exec. v.p. Communication Channels, Inc., N.Y.C., 1969-88; pub. emeritus Fence Industry, Access Control, Pension World, Trusts and Estates, Nat. Real Estate Investor, Shopping Center World; pres. Lee Comms., 1980—; assoc. Kids Countrywide, Inc.; pub. cons., book rep., advt. and mktg. cons.; cons. Mark Clements Rsch. N.Y., Inc., 1994—; pub. cons. Mag. Rsch. Mktg. Co., 1994—. Pres. Westbury Hebrew Congregation, 1954, chmn. bd. trustees, 1955. Served with USAAF, 1942-46, PTO. Named Gray-Russo Advt. Man of Year Ad Men's Post Am. Legion, 1954; recipient Hall of Fame award Internat. Fence Industry Assn., 1985. Mem. Am. Legion (life, comdr. advt. men's post 1954, 64). Home: 6839 N 29th Ave Phoenix AZ 85017-1213 Office: Lee Communications 5060 N 19th Ave Phoenix AZ 85015-3210

ELLISON, LAWRENCE J., computer software company executive; b. 1944. BS. With Amdahl, Inc., Santa Clara, Calif., 1967-71; systems architect Amdahl, Inc.; pres. systems div. Omex Corp., 1972-77; with Oracle Corp., Redwood, Calif., 1977—, pres., chief exec. officer, 1978—, also bd. dirs. Office: Oracle Corp 500 Oracle Pky Redwood City CA 94065-1600

ELLIS-VANT, KAREN MCGEE, elementary and special education educator, consultant; b. La Grande, Oreg., May 10, 1950; d. Ellis Eddington and Gladys Vera (Smith) McGee; m. Lynn F. Ellis, June 14, 1975 (div. Sept. 1983); children: Megan Marie, Matthew David; m. Jack Scott Vant, Sept. 6, 1986; children: Kathleen Erin, Kelli Christine (dec.). BA in Elem. Edn., Boise State U., 1972, MA in Spl. Edn., 1979; postgrad. studies in curriculum and instruction, U. Minn., 1985—. Tchr. learning disabilities resource room New Plymouth Joint Sch. Dist., 1972-73, Payette Joint Sch. Dist., 1973, diagnostician project SELECT, 1974-75; cons. tchr. in spl. edn. Boise Sch. Dist., 1975-90; tchr. 1-2 combination, 1990-91, team tchr. 1st grade, 1991-92, 95—, chpt. 1 program cons., 1992-95; mem. profl. Standards Commn., 1983-86. Bd. dirs. Hotline, Inc., 1979-82; mem. Idaho Coop. Manpower Commn., 1984-85. Recipient Disting. Young Woman of Yr. award Boise Jaycettes, 1982, Idaho Jaycettes, 1983; Coffman Alumni scholar U. Minn., 1985-86. Mem. NEA (mem. civil rights com. 1983-85, state contact for peace caucus 1981-85, del. assembly rep., 1981-85), NSTA, ASCD, Internat. Reading Assn., NCTE, Internat. Coop. Learning Assn., Idaho Edn. Assn. (bd. dirs. region VII 1981-85, pres. region VII 1981-82), Boise Edn. Assn. (v.p. 1981-82, 84-85, pres. 1982-83), Nat. Council Urban Edn. Assn., World Future Soc., Council for Exceptional Children (pres. chpt. 1978-79), Nat. Coun. Tchrs. English, Minn. Coun. for Social Studies, Calif. Assn. for Gifted, Assn. for Grad. Edn. Students, Phi Delta Kappa. Contbr. articles to profl. jours.; editor, author ednl. texts and communiques; conductor of workshops, leadership tng. coop. learning. and frameworks. Office: Highlands Elem 3434 Bogus Basin Rd Boise ID 83702

ELLSAESSER, HUGH WALTER, retired atmospheric scientist; b. Chillicothe, Mo., June 1, 1920; s. Charles Theobald and Louise Minerva (Bancroft) E.; m. Lois Merle McCaw, June 21, 1946; children: Corbin Donald, Adrienne Sue. AA, Bakersfield (Calif.) Jr. Coll., 1941; SB, U. Chgo., 1943, PhD, 1964; MA, UCLA, 1947. Commd. 2d lt. USAF, 1943, advanced through grades to lt. col., 1960; weather officer USAF, Washington, Fla., Eng., 1942-63; ret., 1963; physicist Lawrence Livermore (Calif.) Nat. Lab., 1963-86, guest scientist, 1986—. Editor: Global 2000 Revisited, 1992; contbr. numerous articles to profl. jours. Mem. Am. Meteorol. Soc., Am. Geophysics Union. Republican. Presbyterian. Home: 4293 Stanford Way Livermore CA 94550-3463 Office: Lawrence Livermore Nat Lab PO Box 808 L-262 Livermore CA 94551-0808

ELLSWORTH, RICHARD GERMAN, psychologist; b. Provo, Utah, June 23, 1950; s. Richard Grant and Betty Lola (Midgley) E.; BS, Brigham Young U., 1974, MA, 1975; PhD, U. Rochester (N.Y.), 1979; postgrad. UCLA, 1980-84; PhD, Internat. Coll., 1983; m. Carol Emily Osborne, May 23, 1970; children: Rebecca Ruth, Spencer German, Rachel Priscilla, Melanie Star, Richard Grant, David Jedediah. Cert. Am. Bd. Med. Psychotherapy, (fellow), Am. Bd. Sexology. Instr. U. Rochester, 1976-77, Chapman U., 1995—; rsch. assoc. Nat. Tech. Inst. for Deaf, Rochester, 1977; instr. West Valley Coll., Saratoga, Calif., 1979-80, San Jose (Calif.) City Coll., 1980; psycholinquist UCLA, 1980-81; rsch. assoc. UCLA, 1982-85; psychologist Daniel Freeman Meml. Hosp., Inglewood, Calif., 1981-84, Broderick, Langlois & Assocs., San Gabriel, Calif., 1982-86, Beck Psychiat. Med. Group, Lancaster, Calif., 1984-87, Angeles Counseling Ctr., Arcadia, Calif., 1986-89, Assoc. Med. Psychotherapists, Palmdale, Calif., 1988—; cons. LDS Social Svcs. Calif. Agy., 1981—, Antelope Valley Hosp. Med. Ctr., 1984—, Palmdale Hosp. Med. Ctr., 1984—, Treatment Ctrs. of Am. Psychiat. Hosps., 1985-86, Hollywood Cmty. Hosp., 1994—. Scoutmaster, Boy Scouts Am., 1976-79. UCLA Med. Sch. fellow in psychiatry, 1980-81. Mem. Am. Psychol. Assn., Am. Assn. Sex Educators, Counselors and Therapists, Assn. Mormon Counselors and Psychotherapists, Am. Soc. Clin. Hypnosis, Psi Chi. Contbr. articles to profl. jours. Office: 1220 East Ave S Ste A Palmdale CA 93550

ELMORE, JAMES WALTER, architect, retired university dean; b. Lincoln, Nebr., Sept. 5, 1917; s. Harry Douglas and Marie Clare (Minor) E.; m. Mary Ann Davidson, Sept. 6, 1947; children: James Davidson, Margaret Kay. A.B., U. Nebr., 1938; M.S. in Architecture, Columbia U., 1948. Mem. faculty Ariz. State U., 1949-86, prof. architecture, 1959-86, founding dean Coll. of Architecture,, 1964-74; cons. architect, 1956—. Trustee Heard Museum, Phoenix, 1968-79; bd. dirs. Valley Forward Assn., 1969-89 , pres., 1985; bd. dirs. Central Ariz. chpt. Ariz. Hist. Soc., 1973-89; bd. dirs. Ariz. Architects Found., 1978-86, Rio Salado Devel. Dist., 1980-87. Served to col., C.E. U.S. Army, 1940-46. Decorated Bronze Star. Fellow AIA; mem. Ariz. Acad. Home: 6229 N 29th Pl Phoenix AZ 85016-2251

ELMQUIST, DONNA LOIS, educator, consultant, writer, researcher; b. Sturgis, S.D., July 4, 1948; d. Donald Phillip Hines and Lois Elaine (Morrill) Watson. BA in English, Augustana Coll., 1970; MS in Spl. Edn., U. Utah, 1977; PhD in Behavioral Disorders, Utah State U., 1992. Cert. edn. adminstrn. and supervision, learning disabled and behavioral disorders tchr., spl. edn. resource tchr., secondary English and speech tchr., Utah. Rsch. asst. U. Utah, Salt Lake City, 1975-77; tchr. Granite Sch. Dist., Salt Lake City, 1977-87; rsch. assoc. Utah State U., Logan, 1987-91; sr. ptnr., co-founder Terrel Bell and Assocs., Salt Lake City, 1991—; cons. Swiss Fed. Inst. Tech., Zurich, 1992, United Arab Emirates U., Al Ain, 1990-91, Office for Substance Abuse Prevention, Balt., 1990; founder, nat. commr. Nat. Acad. League; presenter in field. Author: How To Shape Up Our Nation's Schools, 1991; contbr. articles to profl. jours. Mem. Utah State Course of Study, Utah State Textbook Commn. in Lang. Arts and Spl. Edn., Coun. for Exceptional Children. Office: Terrel Bell and Assocs 9 Exchange Pl Ste 417 Salt Lake City UT 84111

ELMSTROM, GEORGE P., optometrist, writer; b. Salem, Mass., Dec. 11, 1925; s. George and Emily Irene (Wedgwood) E.; grad. So. Calif. Coll. Optometry, 1951; m. Nancy DePaul, Apr. 29, 1973; children—Pamela, Beverly, Robert. Pvt. practice optometry, El Segundo, Calif., 1951—; mem. staff So. Calif. Coll. Optometry, 1951—; book cons. Med. Econs. Books, 1970—; instrument and forensic editor Jour. Am. Optical Assn.; comml. airplane and balloon pilot, 1968—. Served with U.S. Army, World War II. Decorated Silver Star; named Writer of Year, Calif. Optometric Assn., 1957, Man of Year, El Segundo, 1956; recipient spl. citation Nat. Eye Found., 1955. Fellow Am. Acad. Optometry, AAAS, Southwest Contact Lens Soc., Disting. Service Found. of Optometry, Internat. Acad. Preventive Medicine; mem. Am. Optometric Assn., Assn. for Research in Vision, Am. Soc. Ultrasonography, Am. Pub. Health Assn., Optometric Editors Assn., Assn. Research in Vision, Internat. Soc. Ophthalmic Ultrasound, Profl. Airshow Pilots Assn., Flying Optometrists Assn. Am., Beta Sigma Kappa, So. Calif. Coll. Optometry Alumni (pres. 1955-56). Author: Optometric Practice Management, 1963; Legal Aspects of Contact Lens Practice, 1966; Advanced Management for Optometrists, 1974; Modernized Management, 1982; mgmt. editor Optometric Monthly, 1973. Home: 484B Washington St Monterey CA 93940-3030 Office: PO Box S-3061 Carmel CA 93921-3061

ELPERS, JOHN RICHARD, psychiatrist, educator; b. Hammond, Ind., Jan. 8, 1938; m. Beverly K. Abbott; children: Steven W., Mark R. BA in Med. Sci., Ind. U., 1960; MD, Ind. U., Indpls., 1963; MS in Adminstrv. Medicine, Columbia U., 1968. Diplomate Am. Bd. Psychiatry and Neurology; lic. Ind., Calif., N.Y., N.J., Md. Intern Orange County (Calif.) Med. Ctr., 1963-64; asst. resident and resident in psychiatry N.Y. State Psychiatric Inst. and Presbyn. Hosp., N.Y.C., 1964-67; instr. occupational and physical therapy Columbia U., N.Y.C., 1965-67; pvt. practice, 1967-85, 88—; staff psychiatrist dir. mental health svc. programs Nat. Inst. Mental Health, 1968-70; asst. clin. prof. psychiatry and human behavior U. Calif., Irvine, 1970-74, assoc. clin. prof., 1974-78, clin. prof., 1978-85; assoc. prof. U. So. Calif., 1979-84; adj. prof. psychiatry UCLA, 1984—; dir. cons./liaison svcs. L.A. County-Harbor-UCLA Med. Ctr., 1984—, vice chmn. planning and devel., 1993—, dir. ISP/ABLE, 1990—; chief ambulatory care svcs. L.A. County-Harbor-UCLA Med. Ctr., ((#—; cons. in field 1966-68; planner and first dir. Heights House, 1966-68; dir. Mt. Carmel Guild Guidance Ctr., Union City, N.J., 1967-68; instr. Columbia U., 1967-68, Wash. Sch. Psychiatry, 1969-70, deputy dir. community mental health Orange County, Calif., 1970-78, cons. and community edn., 1970-72, dep. dir. dept. mental health for rsch. evaluation and program planning, 1971-72; clin. dir. program chief Dept. Mental Health, 1972-77, dir. health agy. and pub. health officer Emergency Med. Svcs., 1976-77; chief alcoholism, drug abuse and mental health svcs., Human Svcs. Agy., 1977-78; commr. L.A. Health Planning & Devel. Agy, 1980-83; del. Calif. Assn. Health Sys. Agencies, 1980-83; dir. L.A. County Dept. Mental Health, 1978-84; examiner Am. Bd. Psychiatry and Neurology, 1979-93; grant reviewer; expert witness in field; lectr. in field; cons. Calif. County Mental Health Programs, 1984—. Tech. cons. (NBC movie) Strange Voices, 1987; editorial bd. mem. Jour. of Mental Health Adminstrn., 1988—; contbr. articles to profl. jours. bd. dirs. Merit Hall Apartments, 1989—; adv. bd. Village Integrated Svcs. Agy., 1993—. Recipient Ravdin medal, 1963; numerous honors, awards and citations in field. Fellow Am. Psychiat. Assn. (com. on membership 1973-81, chair 1976-79, coun. on psychiat. svcs. 1982-87); mem. Am. Coll. Mental Health Adminstrn. (exec. bd. mem. 1988-91), Nat. Mental Health Assn. (bd. dirs. 1993—), Orange County Psychiat. Assn., Mental Health Assn. L.A. County (v.p. pub. affairs 1985-90, v.p. clin. svcs. 1993—), L.A. Advocates for Mentally Ill. Office: Harbor UCLA Med Ctr Bldg D-2 Box 444 1001 W Carson St Torrance CA 90509

ELRICK, BILLY LEE, English language educator; b. Jackson, Miss., May 21, 1941; d. William Robert and Wesley James (Hall) Chambers; m. Donald Lee Elrick, June 29, 1965; children: Laura Katherine, John William. BA, Millsaps Coll., 1963; MA in Edn., U. Phoenix, 1992. Tchr. lang. arts North Arvada (Colo.) Jr. High, 1963-92, dept. chair, 1984-92; dean Wheat Ridge (Colo.) High Sch., 1993; tchr. English Arvada (Colo.) H.S., 1993-94, 95—, asst. prin., 1994-95; tchr. English Arvada H.S., 1995—; mentor tchr. Jefferson County Schs.-North; workshop presenter in field. Mem. ASCD, Phi Delta Kappa, Delta Kappa Gamma (sec. 1990-94, 2d v.p. 1994—), Sigma Lambda, Kappa Delta Epsilon. Democrat. Methodist. Home: 10615 Irving Ct Westminster CO 80030-2238 Office: Arvada High Sch 7951 W 65th Ave Arvada CO 80004-3300

ELROD, JERRY DAVID, clergyman; b. Palestine, Tex., Dec. 31, 1938; s. Joe Regester and Hazel Louise (Fitzgerald) E.; m. Jerry Jo McNeely, Aug. 4, 1963 (div. 1971); 1 child, Joel David; m. Sharon Ann Shaw, Aug. 31, 1975. BA, Southwestern U., 1960; MDiv, So. Meth. U., 1963; DD (hon.), Nebr. Wesleyan U., 1984. Ordained to ministry Meth. Ch., 1963. Assoc. editor Tex. Meth., Dallas, 1960-62; exec. dir. United Meth. Ministries, Omaha, 1966-82; dist. supt. Omaha Dist. United Meth. Ch., 1982-85; exec. dir. Tucson Met. Ministry, 1985-88; sr. pastor Desert Skies United Meth. Ch., Tucson, 1988—; del. South Cen. Jurisdictional Conf., 1972, 80, 84; vice chmn. Conf. Coun. on Ministries Desert SW Conf., 1988—; chmn. Bd. of Communications Desert SW Conf., 1988—; del. World Meth. Conf., 1991. Producer, host TV talk show Point of View, Omaha and Tucson, 1975-87. Bd. dirs. Joint Action in Community Svcs., Washington, 1971—, mem. exec. com., 1991—; bd. dirs. Nebr. Meth. Hosp., 1982-85. Named Outstanding Citizen City of Omaha, 1976. Democrat. Home: 12802 W La Terraza Dr Sun City West AZ 85375-3248 Office: Desert Skies United Meth Ch 3255 N Houghton Rd Tucson AZ 85749-9561

ELROD, RICHARD BRYAN, lawyer; b. Denver, July 14, 1949; s. Walter Frank and Doris Beach (Kinnison) E.; m. Martha Jane Riddell, June 8, 1974; children: Jacob Jonathan, Kenin Casey. BS, U. No. Colo., 1971; JD, U. Denver, 1975. Bar: Colo. 1975, U.S. Dist. Ct. Colo., U.S. Tax Ct. U.S. Ct. Appeals (10th cir.). Assoc. Thomas & Esperti P.C., Denver, 1975-78; ptnr., founder Esperti, Elrod, Katz, Peterson, Schmit and Preeo, Denver, 1978-80, Esperti, Elrod and Wills, Denver, 1980-82, Schmidt, Elrod and Wills, Denver, 1982-85, Elrod, Katz, Preeo, Look, Moison & Silverman, Denver, 1985—; tchr. advanced CLU course on taxation, Denver, 1981, Coll. Fin. Planning, 1990-91. Contbr. articles to profl. jours., chpts. to books. Mem. Fellowship of Christian Fin. Advisors, Denver, 1984— (lectr.), exec. council St. Joseph's Hosp., Denver, 1985—; elder Cherry Hills Community Ch., Denver, 1984—. Mem. ABA (tax div. 1975—), Colo. Bar Assn., Denver Estate Planning Council (lectr. 1980—). Office: Elrod Katz Preeo Look Moison & Silverman PC 1120 Lincoln St Ste 1100 Denver CO 80203-2139

ELSBERRY, SUSAN DAVISE, computer-aided manufacturing engineer; b. Lincoln, Nebr., Oct. 27, 1953; d. Leo Herbert and Genevieve (Richards) Bischof; m. Terence Ray Elsbberry, Aug. 9, 1986; 1 child, Colin Ray. BS, Brigham Young U., 1985, MS, 1992. Computer-aided mfg. engr. Northrop, Hawthorne, Calif., 1986-91; owner, tng. instr. mine safety Safety First, 1993—; ptnr. Elsberry Enterprises, 1994—; software trainer ExecuTrain, 1994—. Mem. Westec Adv. Com., 1987-90. named Whirlpool Corp. fellow, 1984-86. Fellow Inst. for Advancement of Engring.; mem. Soc. Mfg. Engrs. (officer chpt. 106 1993-94). Democrat. Roman Catholic. Home: 1555 W Highsmith Dr Tucson AZ 85746-3308

ELSBREE, LANGDON, English language educator; b. Trenton, N.J., June 23, 1929; s. Wayland Hoyt and Miriam (Jenkins) E.; m. Aimee Desiree Wildman, June 9, 1952; 1 child, Anita. BA, Earlham Coll., 1952; MA, Cornell U., 1954; PhD, Claremont Grad. Sch., 1963. Instr. in English Miami U., Oxford, Ohio, 1954-57, Harvey Mudd Coll., Claremont, Calif., 1958-59; instr. humanities Scripps Coll., Claremont, Calif., 1959-60; instr., prof. Claremont McKenna Coll., 1960—; mem. grad. faculty Claremont Grad. Sch., 1965—; part-time lectr. Calif. State U., L.A., 1968-70; vis. prof. Carleton Coll., 1987. Author: The Rituals of Life, 1982, Ritual Passages and Narrative Structures, 1991; co-author: Heath College Handbook, 6th-12th edits., 1967-90; guest editor D.H. Lawrence Rev., 1975, 87. Bd. dirs. Claremont Civic Assn., 1964-66; mem. founding com. Quaker Studies in Human Betterment, Greensboro, N.C., 1987. Fulbright Commn. lectr., 1966-67; grantee NEH, 1975, Claremont McKenna Coll., 1980, 82, 87. Mem. AAUP, MLA, Friends Assn. Higher Edn., D.H. Lawrence Soc. (exec. bd. 1990), Virginia Woolf Soc., Coll. English Assn., Sci. Fiction Rsch. Assn., Phi Beta Kappa. Democrat. Mem. Soc. of Friends. Office: Claremont McKenna Coll Bauer Ctr 890 Columbia Ave Claremont CA 91711-3901

ELSER, DANNY RAY, financial planner; b. Butte, Mont., June 22, 1953; s. Duane Donald and Edith N.H. (Tam) E.; m. Janet L. Bottom, Dec. 1, 1974; children: Sara E., Katie V., Andrew J., Patrick M. BS, Colo. St. U., 1976. CLU. Mgr. Coll. Life, Bloomington, Ind., 1976-82, Prin. Fin. Group, Bloomington, 1982-86; prin. Fin. Strategies Corp., Bloomington, 1986-88; mgr. No. Colo. Prin. Fin. Group, 1988-89, Prin. Fin. Group, Billings, Mont., 1989—. Bd. dirs. Cmty. Svc. Coun., Bloomington, 1982-85; mem. Young Reps., Bloomington, 1982-86; mission chmn. Evang. Cmty. Ch., Bloomington, 1985-86, missions com. Faith Evang. Ch., Ft. Collins, Colo., 1987-88, 91—, mem. ch. coun., 1991—; ch. lay leader, coun. mem., missions com. Faith Evang. Ch., Billings; bd. dirs. working com. Mont. Food. Consumer Ins. Edn. Bd. Mem. Nat. Assn. Life Underwriters (Nat. Quality and Sales Achievement award 1980-88, Outstanding Young Man of Am., 1983-85), Ind. State Assn. Life Underwriters (Bloomington chpt. bd. dirs. 1980-84, state bd. dirs. 1985-86), S.E. Mont. Assn. Life Underwriters (sec., prog. chmn., v.p. 1989-92, pres. 1992-93), Internat. Assn. Fin. Planning, Nat. Assn. Security Dealers (registered rep.), So. Ind. Estate Planning Forum, Million Dollar Round Table, Bloomington C. of C. (chmn. leadership Bloomington 1982-86), Ft. Collins C. of C. (bus. excellence com.), No. Rocky Mountain Chpt. CLU (sec., treas. 1988, bd. dirs. chartered fin. cons. 1988), Mont. Gen. Agts.-Mgrs. Assn. (bd. dirs. 1989—, Nat. Mgmt. award 1989, 90, 91, 92, 93, pres. 1992-94, past pres. 1991-92), Mont. Soc. CLU and Chartered Fin. Cons., Bloomington Jaycees (pres. 1982-86), ECC Club (mission chmn. 1985-86). Republican. Office: Prin Fin Group 401 N 31st St Ste 950 Billings MT 59101-1200

EL SHAMI, AHMED SAÏD, company executive; b. Alexandria, Egypt, Aug. 10, 1942; came to U.S., 1969; s. Ahmed Mohamed and Sekina (Gonneid) El S.; m. Patricia Ann Williams, May 26, 1973; children: Nadeam A., Omar Saïd, Amir Saïd. BSc in Chemistry, Am. U., Cairo, 1965, MSc in Phys. Scis., 1965, PhD Program in Biochemistry, 1968-69. Rsch. assoc. U.S. Naval Med. Rsch. Unit #3, Cairo, 1965-69; chief chemist Clin. Labs. Nashville, 1969-74, St. Mary's Hosp., Rochester, N.Y., 1974-78; sr. v.p. rsch. and devel. Diagnostic Products Corp., L.A., 1978—. Editor: Allergy and Molecular Biology, 1989; 7 inventions measurement of biol. ligands, 1984-88; contbr. articles to profl. jours. Home: 11016 Red Barn Rd Camarillo CA 93012-9268 Office: Diagnostic Products Corp 5700 W 96th St Los Angeles CA 90045-5544

ELSORADY, ALEXA MARIE, secondary education educator; b. San Francisco, Jan. 4, 1946; d. Willard John and Helen Mary (Bardmess) Saunders; m. R.M. Elsorady, Nov. 24, 1972; children: Tarik, Alexander. BA, San Jose State U., 1967, MA, 1976. Cert. secondary and community coll. tchr. Tchr. biology, integrated sci. and English, Fremont Union High Sch. Dist., San Jose, Calif., 1970—. Named Mentor Tchr., State of Calif., 1987-88, Mentor, 1993-94; grantee Superschs. Found. Sci.-Math.; fellow NSF, 1992, Evolution and Nature of Sci. Inst., San Jose State U., 1993, Mayor Susan Hammer's San Jose Edn. Network Tech. Inst., summer 1994. Mem. ASCD, nat. Sci. Tchrs. Assn., Nat. Assn. Biology Tchrs., Santa Clara County Sci. Tchrs. Assn., San Jose State U. Alumni Assn. (life), Kappa Alpha Theta (life), Phi Kappa Phi (life), Phi Alpha Theta (life). Home: 1233 Redmond Ave San Jose CA 95120-2745 Office: Lynbrook High Sch 1280 Johnson Ave San Jose CA 95129-4172

ELSTON, LESTER CHARLES, management consultant; b. Flint, Mich., Sept. 22, 1929; s. Alfred Samuel and Elizabeth Catherine (Nankervis) E.; m. Marilyn Joyce Anderson, July 12, 1952; children: David, Arthur, Nancy, Karen. Student, U. Mich., Flint, 1947-48, So. Ill. U., 1948-49; profl. cert., Ariz. State U., 1972, degree in mgmt., 1976. Cert. profl. contract mgr. Design engr. Bendix Aviation, South Bend, Ind., 1949-55; sr. design engr. Electric Boat div. Gen. Dynamics, Groton, Conn., 1955-59; sr. devel. engr. AiResearch Mfg. Co. of Ariz., Phoenix, 1959-68; mgr. of contracts Garrett Turbine Engine co., Phoenix, 1968-88; dir. contracts and quotations Allied Signal Aerospace Co., Phoenix, 1988-90; cons. in domestic and internat. contracting affairs, 1990. Cpl. U.S. Army, 1951-53. Mem. Machinery and Allied Products Inst., Nat. Contract Mgmt. Assn., El Zariba Shrine, Vasa (master Ariz. dist. 1988-90). Republican. Lutheran. Home: PO Box 358 Rimrock AZ 86335-0358

ELSTON, WOLFGANG EUGENE, geology educator, researcher; b. Berlin, Germany, Aug. 13, 1928; came to U.S., 1945; s. Frederick Gustave and Anny (Halpert) E.; m. Lorraine Hind, Dec. 26, 1952; children: Stephen,

Richard. BS, CCNY, 1949; MA, PhD, Columbia U., 1953. Geologist N.Mex. Bur. Mines, Socorro, summers 1950-64; asst. prof. Tex. Technol. Coll., Lubbock, 1955-57; asst. prof. U. N.Mex., Albuquerque, 1957-63, assoc. prof., 1963-67, prof. geology, 1967—, acting chmn. dept. geology, 1982, dir. volcanology program, 1991—, sr. rsch. prof., 1992—; lectr. Columbia U., N.Y.C., 1951-52; cons. Govt. Agys. Industry, Albuquerque, 1957—; prin. investigator NASA, 1964-91, NSF, 1978—, U.S. Geol. Survey, 1975-81, N.Mex. Energy Inst., 1975-81; Univ. Found. visitor U. Auckland, N.Z., 1985-86; exchange scientist NSF, 1979, 85-86. Author, editor: Volcanism in Southwest New Mexico, 1976; co-editor: Cauldrons and Ore Deposits, 1978, Ash-Flow Tuffs, 1979; prin. editor, lead author: Volcanic Centers as Guides to Mineral Exploration, 1994; contbr. articles to profl. jours. Served with U.S. Army, 1953-55. Rsch. fellow Royal Soc. Great Britain, 1986. Fellow AAAS, Geol. Soc. Am. (v.p. Rocky Mountain sect. 1990-91); mem. Nat. Assn. Geology Tchrs. (pres. S.W. sect. 75-76), Am. Inst. Profl. Geologists (cert., pres. N.Mex. sect. 1982, 90) Internat. Assn. Volcanology and Chemistry of Earth's Interior (sec. working group on explosive volcanism 1983-86), N.Mex. Geol. Soc. (hon. life). Home: 1023 Columbia Dr NE Albuquerque NM 87106-2626 Office: U NMex Dept Earth/Planetary Scis Albuquerque NM 87131

ELTRINGHAM, THOMAS JAMES GYGER, telecommunications professional; b. Riverside, Calif., Nov. 4, 1943; s. Thomas Lamar and May Kathryn (Gyger) E.; m. Hana Libuse Strachen, Jan. 21, 1966 (Feb. 1978); m. Lydia Rose Boss, Oct. 4, 1980; children: Glenn Alexander, Eric Douglas. HSST, Hubbard Coll., Copenhagen, 1969. Ordained to ministry. Minister Ch. of Scientology, L.A. and Clearwater, Fla., 1961-83; installations mgrs. Am. Sun, Inc., Commerce, Calif., 1984-86; v.p. ops. Power Ins. Inc., Santa Fe Springs, Calif., 1986-90; dir. L.D. Svcs., Inc., Santa Fe Springs, Calif., 1990—. Contbr. articles to profl. jours.; developer drug rehab. program, L.A., 1966. Mem. Internat. Assn. Scientologists. Republican.

ELWAY, JOHN ALBERT, professional football player; b. Port Angeles, Wash., June 28, 1960; s. Jack Elway; m. Janet Elway; 2 daughters: Jessica Gwen, Jordan Marie. BA in Econs., Stanford U., 1983. Quarterback Denver Broncos, 1983—. Mem. Mayor's Council on Phys. Fitness, City of Denver; chmn. Rocky Mountain region Nat. Kidney Found. Played Super Bowl XXI, 1986, XXII, 1987, XXIV, 1989; named to Sporting News Coll. All-Am. team, 1980, 82, Sporting News NFL All-Pro team, 1987, Pro Bowl team, 1986, 87, 89, 91, 93. Office: Denver Broncos 13655 Broncos Pky Englewood CO 80112-4150*

ELWOOD, JAMES PETER, air transportation executive; b. Columbus, Nebr., Nov. 13, 1958; s. Dick E. and Ruth Janice (DeSmidt) E.; m. Hille Anne Johnson, Sept. 18, 1982; children: Kelsey, Chloe. BS in Aviation Mgmt., Met. State Coll., 1982. Accredited airport exec. Supr. Combs-Gates Aviation, Englewood, Colo., 1979-82; sales exec. Ken Lowe Aircraft, Englewood, 1982-85; mktg. exec. Jeppesen Sanderson, Englewood, 1985-86; prin. In-Touch, Inc., Englewood, 1986-88; asst. airport mgr. Cheyenne (Wyo.) Airport Bd., 1988-92; dir. aviation Pueblo (Colo.) Meml. Airport, 1992—. Bd. dirs. Pueblo chpt. ARC, 1993; com. mem. Pueblo 2010 Strategic Planning, 1994. Recipient Leadership Pueblo award Pueblo C. of C., 1994. Mem. Internat. N.W. Aviation Coun. (bd. dirs. 1994—), Am. Assn. Airport Execs. (vice-chmn. internat. airport facilities conf. N.W. chpt. 1993-94, chmn. 1995), Colo. Airport Ops. Assn. (sec./treas. bd. dirs. 1993—), Rotary.

ELY, MARICA MCCANN, interior designer; b. Pachuca, Mex., May 2, 1907 (parents Am. citizens); d. Warner and Mary Evans (Cook) McCann; m. Northcutt Ely, Dec. 2, 1931; children: Michael and Craig (twins), Parry Haines. B.A., U. Calif.-Berkeley, 1929; diploma Pratt Inst. of Art, N.Y.C., 1931. Free-lance interior designer, Washington and Redlands, Calif., 1931—; lectr. on flower arranging and fgn. travel, 1931—; prof. Sogetsu Ikebana Sch., Tokyo, 1972. Art editor (calendar) Nat. Capital Garden Club League, 1957-58. Pres. Kenwood Garden Club, Md.; bd. dirs. Nat. Libr. Blind, Washington; mem. adv. bd. George C. Marshall Home Preservation Fund, Inc. Leesburg, Va.; v.p. bd. dirs. Washington Hearing and Speech Soc., 1969; co-founder Delta Gamma Found. Pre-Sch. Blind Children, Order of Delta Gamma Rose. Finalist Nat. Silver Bowl Competition, Jackson-Perkins Co., 1966; garden shown on nat. tour Am. Hort. Soc., 1985. Mem. Calif. Arboretum Found., Redlands Hort. and Improvement Soc. (bd. dirs. 1982-94), Redlands Panhellenic Soc., Redlands Country Club, Chevy Chase Club (D.C.), Delta Gamma.

ELY, NORTHCUTT, lawyer; b. Phoenix, Sept. 14, 1903; s. Sims and Elizabeth (Northcutt) E.; m. Marica McCann, Dec. 2, 1931; children: Michael and Craig (twins), Parry Haines. A.B., Stanford U., 1924, J.D., 1926. Bar: Calif. 1926, N.Y. 1928, D.C. 1932, U.S. Supreme Ct. 1932. Practice law N.Y., 1926-29, D.C. and Calif., 1933—; exec. asst. to Sec. Interior, Washington, 1929-33; chmn. tech. adv. com. Fed. Oil Cons. Bd., Washington, 1931-33; represented Sec. Interior in negotiation of Hoover Dam power and water contracts, 1930-33; counsel to Gov. of Okla. in negotiating Interstate Oil Compact, 1934-35; co-executor of estate of ex-Pres. Herbert Hoover, 1964-68; spl. counsel Colo. River Bd. of Calif., 1946-76 and various Calif. water and power entities; spl. Asst. Atty. Gen. State of Calif., 1953-64 in Ariz. v. Calif.; mem. nat. Petroleum Council, 1968-76; counsel in 7 U.S. Supreme Ct cases involving rights in Colo., Columbia, Cowlitz, Niagara Rivers and fed. natural resource statutes; legal advisor to Ruler of Sharjah in boundary disputes with Iran, Umm al Qawain, and internat. arbitration of boundary with Dubai; counsel to Swaziland in internat. river dispute with Republic of South Africa and to Mekong Commn. (U.N.) in settling principles for devel. of Mekong Basin; counsel to govts. and cos. in determination of seabed boundaries in Gulf of Thailand, Mediterranean, East China, South China, Caribbean seas, Persian Gulf; represented U.S. Mining cos. in enactment of Deepsea Hard Minerals Act, & subsequent reciprocal internat. recognition of mining leases; gen. counsel Am. Pub. Power Assn., 1941-81; counsel L.A., So. Calif. Edison Co. in renewal of Hoover Power contracts, 1980—; counsel from time to time to Govts. of Saudi Arabia, Turkey, Republic of China, Algeria, Malagasy Republic, Ethiopia, Grenada, Thailand on mining and petroleum legis.; mem. U.S. del. to UN Conf. on application of Sci. and Tech. for Benefit Less Developed Areas, 1963, UN Conf. on mineral legislation, Manila, 1969, Bangkok, 1973; mem. bd. overseers Hoover Instn.; trustee Herbert Hoover Found., Hoover Presdl. Libr. Assn. Author: Summary of Mining & Petroleum Laws of the World, Oil Conservation Through Interstate Agreement, Authorization of Federal Water Projects, The Hoover Dam Documents; co-author Law of International Drainage Basins, Economics of the Mineral Industries. Mem. bd. visitors Stanford Law Sch., 1978-79. Fellow Am. Bar Found. (life); mem. ABA (chmn. natural resource sect. 1973-74, ho. dels. 1974-80, regulatory reform com.), Calif. State Bar Assn., D.C. Bar Assn., Am. Law Inst. (life), Internat. Law Assn. (chmn. Am. br. com. on deep sea mineral resources 1970-79), Internat. Bar Assn., Sigma Nu, Phi Delta Phi, Sigma Delta Chi. Republican. Clubs: Bohemian (San Francisco); California (Los Angeles); Metropolitan, Chevy Chase, University (Washington); Fortnightly (Redlands, pres. 1989); Redlands Country. Home: 222 Escondido Dr Redlands CA 92373-7215 Office: 300 E State St Redlands CA 92373-5235

EMBLETON, TOM WILLIAM, horticultural science educator; b. Guthrie, Okla., Jan. 3, 1918; s. Harry and Katherine (Smith) E.; m. Lorraine Marie Davidson, Jan. 22, 1943; children: Harry Raymond (dec.), Gary Thomas, Wayne Allen, Terry Scott, Paul Henry. BS, U. Ariz., 1941; PhD, Cornell U., 1949; Diploma de Honor al Ingeniero Agronomo, Coll. Engring. Agronomy, Santiago, Chile, 1991. Jr. sci. aide Bureau Plant Industry USDA, Indio, Calif., 1942, horticulturist Bureau Plant Industry, 1942, 1946; asst. horticulturist Wash. State Coll., Prosser, 1949-50; asst. horticulturist to prof. hort. sci. U. Calif., Riverside, 1950-86, prof. hort. sci. emeritus, 1987—; cons. in field, 1973—. Contbr. numerous articles to profl. jours. Scoutmaster, coun. committeeman, pack com. Riverside Boy Scouts of Am., 1952-74. Recipient Citrograph rsch. award Citrograph mag., 1965, Chancellor's Founders' award U. Calif., 1990. Fellow AAAS, Am. Soc. Hort. Sci. (Wilson Popenoe award 1985, chmn. western region 1958-59); mem. Internat. Soc. Horticultural Sci., Internat. Soc. Citriculture (mem. exec. bd. 1984—), Am. Soc. Agronomy (mem. nat. and Calif. chpt., Honor award 1993), Soil Sci. Soc. Am., Western Soc. Soil Sci., Calif. Avocado Soc. (Honor award 1987, life), Coun. Soil Testing and Plant Analysis, Coun. Agrl. Sci. and Tech., Lemon Men's Club (Honor award 1987, life), U. Calif. Riverside Faculty Club (pres. 1958), Sigma Xi (pres. Riverside chpt. 1981-82), others. Home: 796 Spruce St Riverside CA 92507-3039 Office: U Calif Dept Botany Plant Scis Riverside CA 92521-0124

EMBURG, KATHRYN MARIA, social worker, writer; b. Nurnburg, Republic of Germany, Oct. 13, 1959; d. Richard Maximillian and Carol Ann (Duvall) Hohenberger; m. Edwin Kenneth Emburg, Feb. 14, 1987; children: Leann Maria, Kaitlyn Ashley. BA in English, Rutgers U., 1981. Office mgr. IHI, Inc., N.Y.C., 1985-87; bookseller Waldenbooks, Sacramento, 1987-90; eligibility worker Sacramento County, 1990-93, social worker, 1993—; child protective svc. liaison Sacramento County, 1991-93; foster parent Sacramento County, 1988-93, Families First, Davis, Calif., 1993—. Author: The Whispering Belltower, 1993, Recipe for Love, 1995; co-author: The Adventures of Susan Slut, 1990, vol. 2, 1991, vol. 3, 1993, The Girls' Series Companion, 1990, 2d edit., 1994; editor The Whispered Watchword mag., 1985—. Mem. Soc. Phantom Friends (pres. 1985—), Doll Exch. United Meth. Home: 4100 Cornelia Way North Highlands CA 95660-4426 Office: Sacramento County DHHS 4875 Broadway Sacramento CA 95820-1500

EMENHISER, JEDON ALLEN, political science educator, academic administrator; b. Clovis, N.Mex., May 19, 1933; s. Glen Allen and Mary Opal (Sasser); m. Patricia Ellen Burke, Jan. 27, 1954; 1 child, Melissa Mary Emenhiser Westerfield. Student, Am. U., 1954; BA, U. Redlands, 1955; PhD, U. Minn., 1962. Cert. community coll. adminstr., Calif. Instr. to prof. polit. sci. Utah State U., Logan, 1960-77, acting dean, 1973-74; prof. Humboldt State U., Arcata, Calif., 1977—, dean, 1977-86; acting v.p. Humboldt State U., Arcata, 1984; chair Social Sci. Rsch. and Instrnl. Coun. Calif. State U., 1994-95; prof. Jr. Statesmen Summer Sch., Stanford U., 1989—; vis. instr. U. Redlands, Calif., 1959-60; vis. prof. U. Saigon, Vietnam, 1964-65; asst. dean. Colgate U., Hamilton, N.Y., 1972-73; staff dir. Utah Legislature, Salt Lake City, 1967, cons., 1968-77; dir. Bur. Govt. and Opinion Rsch., Logan, 1965-70; cons. USCG, McKinleyville, Calif., 1982; v.p. Exch. Bank, New Franklin, Mo., 1970-76; reader advanced placement exam. U.S. Govt. Coll. Bd., 1990—. Author: Utah's Governments, 1964, Freedom and Power in California, 1987; editor, contbr. Dragon on the Hill, 1970, Rocky Mountain Urban Politics, 1971; producer, dir. TV broadcasts The Hawks and the Doves, 1965-66; contbr. articles to profl. jours. Sec. Cache County Dem. Party, Logan, 1962-63; chmn. Mayor's Commn. on Govt. Orgn., Logan, 1973-74; campaign mgr. various candidates and issues, Logan, 1965-75; bd. dirs. Humboldt Connections, Eureka, Calif., 1986—, pres., 1989-92; elder Presbyn. ch. Sr. Fulbright-Hays lectr. Com. Internat. Exch. of Persons, Vietnam, 1964-65; Adminstrv. fellow Am. Coun. Edn., Colgate U., 1972-73; Paul Harris fellow Rotary Internat. Mem. Am. Polit. Sci. Assn., Western Polit. Sci. Assn., Am. Studies Assn., Phi Beta Kappa, Omicron Delta Kappa. Presbyterian. Home: PO Box 250 Bayside CA 95524-0250 Office: Humboldt State U Dept Polit Sci Arcata CA 95521

EMERINE, STEPHEN EDWARD, communications executive; b. Scottsbluff, Nebr., May 4, 1935; s. Edward and Mary Lou (Stephenson) E. BA, U. Idaho, 1956; postgrad., U. Ariz., 1973. Reporter, editor Twin Falls Times-News, Idaho, 1956-57; info. officer USAF, Little Rock, 1957-60; reporter, editor Tucson Daily Citizen, 1960-67; asst. prof. journalism Univ. Ariz., 1967-70; pres., editor, pub. The Green Valley News, Ariz., 1967-71; pres. Steve Emerine & Assocs., Tucson, 1971-73; county assessor Pima County, Tucson, 1973-80; editor, columnist The Ariz. Daily Star, Tucson, 1980-87; assoc. dir. pub. info. The U. Ariz., 1987-94; owner Steve Emerine Pub. Rels., Tucson, 1994—. Co-author, editor: (book) Jack Sheaffer's Tucson, 1985. Vice chmn. Tucson Commn. Human Rels., 1968-71; bd. dirs. Ariz. Families Children, Tucson, 1986—; pres. Tucson Jazz Soc., 1993—. Named Newspaper Reporter of the Year Tucson Press Club 1967. Mem. Pub. Rels. Soc. Am., Tucson Press Club (pres. 1965). Democrat. Home: 4973 E Silver St Tucson AZ 85712-5726 Office: PO Box 41824 Tucson AZ 85717-1824

EMERSON, ALTON CALVIN, physical therapist; b. Webster, N.Y., Sept. 29, 1934; s. Homer Douglas and Pluma (Babcock) E.; m. Nancy Ann Poarch, Dec. 20, 1955 (div. 1972); children: Marcia Ann, Mark Alton; m. Barbara Irene Stewart, Oct. 6, 1972. BS in Vertibrate Zoology, U. Utah, 1957; cert. phys. therapy, U. So. Calif., 1959. Staff phys. therapist Los Angeles County Crippled Children's Services, 1958-65; pvt. practice phys. therapy Los Angeles, 1966—; cons. City of Hope, Duarte, Calif., 1962-72; trustee Wolcott Found. Inc., St. Louis, 1972-86, chmn. bd. trustees, 1980-85. Recipient Cert. of Achievement, George Washington U., Washington, 1986. Mem. Aston Martin Owners Club, Masons (pres. Temple City High Twelve Club 1971, master Camellia 1973, pres. Calif. Assn. High Twelve Clubs 1986, internat. pres. High Twelve 1990-91, mem. High Twelve Internat., Pasadena Scottish Rite Bodies, Legion Merit), Royal Order Scotland, Al Malaikah Temple, Ancient Arabic Order Nobles Mystic Shrine, DeMolay Legion of Honor, Order of DeMolay (hon. internat. supreme coun.). Home and Office: 287 W Avenida De Las Flores Thousand Oaks CA 91360-1808

EMERSON, FREDERICK GEORGE, transportation company executive; b. Quincy, Mass., Dec. 6, 1933; s. George Bliss and Mildred Louella (Hynes) E.; m. Marion Orr Stewart, June 10, 1961; children: Elizabeth Lynn, David George. B.A. with honors in Philosophy, U. Va., 1955, J.D., 1960. Sec., counsel Commonwealth Gas Corp., N.Y.C., 1960-67; asst. sec. The Dial Corp. (and subs. cos.), Phoenix, 1967-77, sec., 1977-88, v.p., sec., 1988—. Bd. dirs. Inst. Cultural Affairs Ariz., 1971-80, Lupus Found., Phoenix, 1980—, Tchr. Venture Inc., 1982-88, Friendly House, Inc., 1974-78; pres., dir. Crisis Nursery, 1988—. 1st lt. Transp. Corps, U.S. Army, 1955-57. Mem. Am. Soc. Corp. Secs. (sec., dir., exec. com.). Office: Dial Corp Dial Towers Phoenix AZ 85077

EMERSON, R. CLARK, priest, business administrator; b. L.A., Mar. 9, 1945; s. George Heins and Irma Furney (Sorter) E.; m. Katharine Ann Lawrence, June 27, 1980; children: Cynthia, Holly, Angela, William, Richard. BA, San Jose State U., 1966; MDiv, Ch. Div. Sch. of Pacific, 1972. Ordained deacon Episcopala Ch., 1972, ordained priest, 1973; cert. secondary tchr., Calif. Comml. tchr. Middletown (Calif.) High Sch., 1967-69; asst. to rector St. Francis Ch., Palos Verdes, Calif., 1972-76; adminstr. Power Transistor Co., Torrance, Calif., 1977-85; priest assoc. St. John's Ch., L.A., 1976-85; adminstr. Richard B. Belli Accountancy, San Jose, Calif., 1988—; priest assoc. St. Luke's Ch., Los Gatos, Calif., 1985—. Contr. St. John's Well Child Ctr., L.A., 1985. Republican. Episcopalian.

EMERSON, SHIRLEY, counseling educator; b. Houston, Dec. 29, 1930; d. Riley C. and Neola (Pinckney) Armstrong; m. David W. Emerson, Sept. 4, 1954; children: Richard, Eric, Ellen. BA, Rice U., 1953; MA, U. Mich., 1966, PhD, 1977. Lic. marriage and family therapist, Nev. Prof. counseling U. Nev., Las Vegas, 1984—. Contbr. articles to profl. jours. Pres. Nev. State Bd. Marriage and Family Therapist Examiners, 1989—. Mem. Am. Assn. Marriage and Family Therapists (clin. mem., approved supr.). Home: 4240 Woodcrest Rd Las Vegas NV 89121-4942 Office: Univ Nev Las Vegas 4505 S Maryland Pky Las Vegas NV 89154-9900

EMERSON, THOMAS JAMES, mathematician, software engineer; b. St. Paul, Sept. 4, 1947; s. Harold Thomas and Marion Deloras (McGuire) E.; children: Kerstin, Michael. BS, U. Minn., 1979; MS, NYU, 1988, PhD, 1995. Mem. tech. staff AT&T Bell Labs., Summit, N.J., 1980-91; staff software engr. Amdahl Corp., Sunnyvale, Calif., 1991-93, Sun Microsystems Inc., Mountain View, Calif., 1993—. Contbr. articles to profl. jours. Mem. IEEE Computer Soc. (referee), ACM (referee), Am. Math. Soc. Office: Sun Microsystems Inc 2550 Garcia MTV12-33 Mountain View CA 94043

EMERSON, VIRGIL LEON, lawyer, retired judge; b. Atwood, Okla., Apr. 14, 1925; s. William Harry and Ella Rea (Pegg) E.; m. Lee Kessler Emerson, Apr. 5, 1975; children: Donald Leon, David Paul, Julia Ellen; stepchildren: Darylle Lynn Goodfield, Randall Ryan Bruno. AA, Compton C.C., 1948; JD, Southwestern U., 1951. Pvt. practice in law Downey, Calif., 1952-61; judge Downey Mcpl. Ct., 1961-85; atty., arbitrator; chmn. So. Calif. Coun. Alcohol and Drugs, Downey, 1972-74, Downey Area Counseling Ctr., 1968-71, Mcpl. Judges Cmty. Conf., Downey, 1967. Scoutmaster Troop 807, Downey, 1963-70. Named Man of Yr., Downey Coord. Coun. and N.Am. Mgmt. ASsn. Mem. Masons, Kiwanis, S.E. Bar Assn., L.A. Trial Lawyers Assn., L.A. Bar Assn., Calif. State Bar Assn., Calif. Trial Lawyers. Home: 7607 Yankey St Downey CA 90242-2237

EMERT, GEORGE HENRY, biochemist, academic administrator; b. Tenn., Dec. 15, 1938; s. Victor K. Emert and Hazel G. (Shultz) Ridley; m. Billie M. Bush, June 10, 1967; children: Debra Lea Lipp, Ann Lanie Taylor, Laurie Elizabeth, Jamie Marie. BA, U. Colo., 1962; MA, Colo. State U., 1970; PhD, Va. Tech. U., 1973. Registered profl. chem. engr. Microbiologist Colo. Dept. Pub. Health, Denver, 1967-70; post doctoral fellow U. Colo., Boulder, 1973-74; dir. biochem. tech. Gulf Oil Corp., Merriam, Kans., 1974-79; prof. biochemistry, dir. biomass rsch. ctr. U. Ark., Fayetteville, 1979-84; exec. v.p. Auburn (Ala.) U., 1984-92; pres. Utah State U., Logan, 1992—; adj. prof. microbiology U. Kans., Lawrence, 1975-79. Editor, author: Fuels from Biomass and Wastes, 1981; author book chpt.; contbr. articles to profl. jours. Mem. So. Tech. Coun., Raleigh, N.C., 1985-92; dir. Ala. Supercomputer Authority, Montgomery, 1987-92. Capt. U.S. Army, 1963-66, Vietnam. Named to Educators Hall of Fame, Lincoln Meml. U., 1988. Fellow Am. Inst. Chemists; mem. Auburn Arts Assn., Rotary (Paul Harris fellow, pres., v.p. 1989-90). Republican. Office: Utah State U Old Main Logan UT 84322-1400

EMERY, EARL EUGENE, steel company executive; b. Youngstown, Ohio, Apr. 1, 1931; s. Earl Eugene and Florence (Machin) E.; m. Mary Therese Orton, June 4, 1955; children—Maria, Catherine, Erin, Kevin, Martin, Sheila, Noreen, Terrence, Earl Eugene III, Mary. Met.E., Youngstown State U. Cert. purchasing mgr. Buyer, Youngstown Sheet & Tube Co., Ohio, 1959-71, mgr. purchasing, 1971-75, gen. mgr. purchasing, 1975-78; dir. purchases CF&I Steel Corp., Pueblo, Colo., 1978-83, dir. purchases and traffic, 1983-93; mgr. materials and transp. CF&I Steel, L.P., 1993—. Mem. exec. com. Mahoning County Rep. Com., Youngstown, 1973-76; bd. dirs. John Neuman Cath. Sch., Pueblo, 1981-85, Goodwill Industries, Pueblo, 1982-93; v.p. United Way of Pueblo, 1982-86 . Purchasing Mgmt. Assn. So. Colo. (pres. 1982-83, dir. nat. affairs 1983-84, 87-91), Assn. Iron and Steel Engrs. (chpt. chmn. 1983-84, nat. bd. dirs. 1985-86), Am. Iron and Steel Inst., Elks, KC. Home: 7 Kingsbridge Pl Pueblo CO 81001-1435 Office: 1612 E Abriendo Ave Pueblo CO 81004-3406

EMERY, SUSAN WOODRUFF, investment trust official; b. Salt Lake City, Jan. 13, 1923; d. Russell Kimball and Margaret Anglin (McIntyre) Woodruff; m. Terrence John Osborn, May 30, 1959 (div. Dec. 1963); 1 child, John Russell; m. Stephen Earnest Emery, Apr. 7, 1972 (dec. Apr. 1977). BA, U. Utah, 1944. Cashier Merrill Lynch, Pierce, Fenner & Beane, Portland, 1946-51; personal sec. to parents, Portland, 1951-71; co-trustee R.K.-M.M. Woodruff Trust, Portland, 1971—. Vol. driver ARC, Portland, 35 yrs.; mem. Rep. Nat. Com., 1944—, Oreg. Rep. Com., 1944—. Mem. AAUW (life), U. Utah Alumni Assn. (life), Univ. Club, Alpha Delta Pi. Episcopalian. Home and Office: 255 SW Harrison St Portland OR 97201-5338

EMIGH, MIKE, agricultural products company executive; b. 1948. BA in Acctg., U. Nev., 1973. Plant contr. Johns Manville, Fresno, Calif., 1973-79; asst. contr. Sun Maid Growers of Calif., Inc., Kingsburg, Calif., 1979-84; sec., v.p., treas. Valley Fig Growers, Inc., Fresno, Calif., 1984—. Office: Valley Fig Growers Inc 2028 S 3rd St Fresno CA 93702-4156*

EMIGH, ROGER ALAN, materials scientist; b. Pullman, Wash., May 24, 1961; s. Stuart Grant and Carla Evelyn (Troeh) E.; m. Rachelle Marie Farman, June 25, 1983; children: Paul, Will. BS in Materials Sci., Wash. State U., 1983; MS in Materials Sci., U. Calif., Berkeley, 1985, PhD in Materials Sci., 1990. Metallurgist Precision Castparts, Portland, Oreg., 1990-93; group leader electronic packaging rsch. Johnson Matthey, Spokane, Wash., 1993—. Mem. Am. Soc. Metals (chmn. Inland Empire chpt. 1993-94), The Minerals, Metals and Materials Soc. Home: 6051 Frazier St Post Falls ID 83854-8897

EMMANOUILIDES, GEORGE CHRISTOS, physician, educator; b. Drama, Greece, Dec. 17, 1926; came to U.S., 1955; s. Christos Nicholas and Vassiliki (Jordanopoulos) E.; married; children: Nicholas, Elizabeth, Christopher, Martha, Sophia. MD, Aristotelion U., 1951; MS in Physiology, UCLA, 1963. Diplomate Am. Bd. Pediatrics (pediatric cardiology and neonatal-perinatal medicine). Asst. prof. UCLA, 1963-69, assoc. prof., 1969-73, prof., 1973-95, prof. emeritus, 1995—; chief divsn. pediatric cardiology Harbor UCLA Med. Ctr., Torrance, Calif., 1963-69. Co-author: Practical Pediatric Electrocardiography, 1973; co-editor: Heart Disease in Infants, Children and Adolescents, 2d edit., 1977, Moss' Heart Disease in Infants, Children and Adolescents, 3d edit., 1983, 4th edit., 1989, 5th edit., 1995, Neonatal Cardiopulmonary Distress, 1988; contbr. more than 70 articles in field to profl. jours. Served as 2d lt. M.C., Greek Army, 1953-55. Recipient Sherman Mellincoff award UCLA Sch. Medicine, 1982, several rsch. awards Am. Heart Assn., 1965-83. Fellow Am. Acad. Pediatrics (cardiology sect. chmn. 1978-80), Am. Coll. Cardiology; mem. Am. Pediatric Soc., Soc. for Pediatric Rsch., Hellenic-Am. Med. Soc. (pres.), Acad. Athens (corr.). Democrat. Greek Orthodox. Clubs: Hellenic Univ. (Los Angeles) (bd. dirs.). Home: 4619 Browndeer Ln Rllng Hls Est CA 90275-3911 Office: Harbor-UCLA Med Ctr 1000 W Carson St Torrance CA 90502-2004

EMMANUEL, JORGE AGUSTIN, chemical engineer, environmental consultant; b. Manila, Aug. 28, 1954; came to U.S., 1970; s. Benjamin Elmido and Lourdes (Orozco) E.; 1 child, Andres Layanglawin. BS in Chemistry, N.C. State U., 1976, MSChemE, 1978; PhD in Chem. Engring., U. Mich., 1988. Registered profl. engr., Calif., environ. profl.; cert. hazardous materials mgr. Process engr. Perry Electronics, Raleigh, N.C., 1973-74; rsch. asst. N.C. State U., Raleigh, 1977-78; rsch. chem. engr. GE Corp. R & D Ctr., Schenectady, N.Y., 1978-81; Amoco rsch. fellow U. Mich., Ann Arbor, 1981-84; sr. environ. analyst TEM Assocs., Inc., Emeryville, Calif., 1988-91; pres. Environ. & Engring. Rsch. Group, Hercules, Calif., 1991—; environ. cons. to the Philippines, UN Devel. Program, 1992, 94; rsch. assoc. U. Calif., Berkeley, 1988-90. Contbr. articles to profl. jours. Mem. Assn. for Asian Studies, Ann Arbor, 1982-88; sec. Alliance for Philippine Concerns, L.A., 1983-91; assoc. Philippine Resource Ctr., Berkeley, 1988-92; bd. dirs. Arms Control Rsch. Ctr., San Francisco, 1990—. N.C. State U. grantee, 1976, Phoenix grantee U. Mich., 1982. Mem. NSPE, AAAS, Air and Waste Mgmt. Assn., Calif. Acad. Scis., N.Y. Acad. Sci., Filipino-Am. Soc. Architects and Engrs. (exec. sec. 1989-90, Svc. award 1990). Office: The Environ & Engring Rsch Group PO Box 5544 Hercules CA 94547-5544

EMMELUTH, BRUCE PALMER, investment banker, venture capitalist; b. Los Angeles, Nov. 30, 1940; s. William J. and Elizabeth L. (Palmer) E.; children: William J. II (dec.), Bruce Palmer Jr., Carrie E.; m. Canda E. Samuels, Mar. 29, 1987. Sr. investment analyst, corp. fin. dept. Prudential Ins. Co. Am., L.A., 1965-70; with Seidler Amdec Securities, Inc., 1970-90, sr. v.p., mgr. corp. fin. dept., 1974-90, also bd. dirs.; pres., bd. dirs. SAS Capital Corp., venture capital subs. Seidler Amdec Securities, 1977-90; mng. dir. corp. fin., mgr. corp. fin. dept., mem. exec. com. Van Kasper & Co., L.A., 1990—, also bd. dirs.; bd. dirs. Denar Corp.; bd. advisors Entrepreneurial Studies Program, Grad. Sch. Mgmt. UCLA, 1985—, past. bd. dirs. With Army NG, 1965-71. Mem. Assn. for Corp. Growth (pres. L.A. chpt. 1979-80), Los Angeles Venture Assn., Beta Gamma Sigma. Republican. Presbyterian. Club: Jonathan. Home: 17146 Palisades Cir Pacific Palisades CA 90272-2141 Office: Van Kasper & Co 11661 San Vicente Blvd Ste 709 Los Angeles CA 90049-5115

EMMERT, RUSSELL LEROY, interior designer; b. Honolulu, Jan. 4, 1932; s. Russell Edwin and Marguerite Lee (Halm) E. Student, Red Oak Jr. Coll., 1950-51, Kansas City Art Inst., 1951-52, Art Ctr. Coll., L.A., 1955-56. Art dir. Butler Publs., Inc., L.A., 1960-65, Vertu Designers, L.A., 1965-75; interior designer Emmert & Assocs., Inc., Portland, Oreg., 1981-86; furniture designer Eurasia, Inc., Portland, 1986-88; design cons. Luxor, Ltd., Scappoose, Oreg., 1988—. Paintings, interior residence designs appeared in various publs., including Archtl. Digest, Oregonian newspaper, Oreg. Mag., Designers West, Better Homes & Gardens. Bd. dirs. Area Agy. for Aging, Columbia County, Oreg., 1994-95. Sgt. U.S. Army, 1952-54. Recipient award for sculpture Seventh Day Adventist Ch., 1974, award for paintings Oreg. Pub. Broadcasting, 1977. Mem. Am. Soc. Interior Designers (pres. Oreg. chpt. 1981-82, nat. bd. dirs. 1983), Scappoose Sr. Citizens, Inc. (pres.

1994-94). Mem. First Christian Ch. Office: Luxor Ltd 33470 SW Chinook Plz Ste 199 Scappoose OR 97056-3726

EMMONS, DONN, architect; b. Olean, N.Y., Oct. 4, 1910; s. Frederick E. and Mary (Fogarty) E.; m. Nancy Pierson, Apr. 4, 1942; children—Zette, Luli, Andrew; m. Audrey Durland, Oct. 29, 1960. Student, Cornell U., 1928-33, U. So. Calif., 1934; LLD (hon.), U. Victoria, B.C., Can., 1988. With office William W. Wurster, architect, San Francisco, 1938-42; ptnr. Wurster, Bernardi & Emmons, San Francisco, 1945-63; prin. Wurster, Bernardi & Emmons, Inc., 1963—, pres., 1969; cons. architect Bay Area Rapid Transit, 1964-67, U. Calif.-Berkeley, 1968—, U. Victoria, B.C., Can., 1974—, Office Fgn. Bldgs., U.S. Dept. State, 1979-82; speaker Symposium on Waterfront Planning, Yokohama, 1986. Prin. works include Golden Gateway Redevel. Project, San Francisco, Ghirardelli Sq., San Francisco, Capitol Towers Redevel. Project, Sacramento, Bank of Am. world hdqrs., San Francisco, Merritt Coll., Oakland, Woodlake and Oakcreek Apt. Projects, master plan for San Francisco Civic Ctr., master plan for South Miami Beach bus. dist. Mem. Potomac River Task Force for Rehab. of River. Served to lt. comdr. USNR, 1942-45. Recipient over 100 awards for excellence in design. Fellow AIA (pres. No. Calif. chpt. 1953-54). Home: 18 Girard Ave Sausalito CA 94965-1845 Office: Wurster Bernardi & Emmons Inc 40 Gold St San Francisco CA 94133-5110

EMMONS, ROBERT JOHN, corporate executive; b. Trenton, N.J., Sept. 18, 1934; s. Charles John and Ruth Marie (Heilhecker) E.; m. Christine Young Bebb, July 13, 1980; children: Bradley Thomas, Cathy Lynne, Christopher Robert, Ryan Hunter. A.B. in Econs, U. Mich., 1956, M.B.A., 1960, J.D., 1964. V.p. Baskin-Robbins Co., Burbank, Calif., 1964-68; pres. United Rent-All, Los Angeles, 1968-69, Master Host Internat., Los Angeles, 1969-71; prof. Grad. Sch. Bus., U. So. Calif., 1971-82; pres. LTI Corp., Monterey, Calif., 1982-84; chmn., chief exec. officer, dir. Casino USA/SFI Corp., from 1984; chmn. Casino USA/Smart & Final Inc., Santa Barbara, Calif. Author: The American Franchise Revolution, 1970, The American Marketing Revolution, 1980; poetry Other Places, Other Times, 1974, Love and Other Minor Tragedies, 1980. Mem. AAUP, Am. Mktg. Assn., European Mktg. Assn., Am. Econ. Assn., Calif. Yacht Club (Honolulu), The Valley Club of Montecito (Calif.), Useppa Island Club (Fla.), Santa Barbara Club, Beta Gamma Sigma, Pi Kappa Alpha. Office: Casino USA/Smart & Final Inc 524 Chapala St Santa Barbara CA 93101

EMPEY, GENE F., real estate executive; b. Hood River, Oreg., July 13, 1923; BS in Animal Husbandry, Oreg. State U., 1949; M. of Tech. Journalism Iowa State U., 1950; m. Janet Halladay, Dec. 27, 1950; children: Stephen Bruce, Michael Guy. Publs. dir. U. Nev., Reno, 1950-55; mgr. Zephyr Cove Lodge Hotel, Lake Tahoe, Nev., 1955-65; owner Empey Co., real estate agy., Carson City and Tahoe, Nev., 1964—; land developer, owner investment and brokerage firm. Mem. Nev. Planning Bd., 1959-72, chmn., 1961-66; mem. Nev. Tax Commn., 1982—. Capt., inf. U.S. Army, 1943-47; PTO. Grad. Realtors Inst. Mem. Nat. Assn. Realtors, (cert. comml. investment mem.; pres. Nev. chpt. 3 terms), Tahoe Douglas C. of C. (pres. 1962, dir.), Carson City C. of C., Carson-Tahoe-Douglas Bd. Realtors, Capital City Club, Rotary, Heavenly Valley Ski (pres. 1968) Club, The Prospector's Club. Republican. Home: PO Box 707 Zephyr Cove NV 89448-0707 Office: 512 S Curry St Carson City NV 89703-4614

EMPEY, MICHAEL D., protective services official; b. Hurricane, Utah, Sept. 17, 1947; s. Henry W. and Melba (Eagar) E.; m. Colleen Garrett, Dec. 1, 1978. AA, Dixie Jr. Coll., 1969; BS, Brigham Young U., 1971. From police officer to police lt. Ogden (Utah) Police, 1971-91, police chief, 1991—; instr. Weber State Acad., Ogden, 1983—; v.p. Utah SWAT Assn., 1990-91; mem. Utah Chiefs of Police, 1991—; mem. Utah Children's Justice Adv. Bd., 1993—. mem. bd. dirs. Youe Cmty. Connection, Ogden, 1993—; co-chair Safe At Home Com., 1994—; mem. steering com. Utah Conf. on Violence, 1992-94; mem. cmty. ptnr. Hill Air Force Base, Ogden, 1994. Named Police Officer of the Yr. Exchange Club, 1983. Mem. Internat. Assn. Chiefs of Police, Footprinters Internat., Downtown Ogden Inc. (ad hoc mem. 1993-95), Weber Area Chief/Sheriffs Assn., Cmty. Anti-Gang Coalition (project dir. 1992-95), Lions Club (mem. bd. dirs. 1991-95). Office: Ogden City Police 2549 Washington Blvd Ogden UT 84401

EMSLIE, WILLIAM ARTHUR, electrical engineer; b. Denver, Oct. 30, 1947; s. William Albert and Hazel Esther (Niles) E.; m. Tracey Jane Palmer, Feb 22, 1975; children: David Barrett, Andrew Niles, Charles William, Alexis Claire. BSEE, U.S. Naval Acad., 1971; MSEE, Mich. State U., 1972. Registered profl. engr., Colo. Commd. ensign USN, 1971, advanced through grades to lt., 1975; with USNR, 1978—, advanced through grades to cmdr., 1992; energy conversion engr. Pub. Svc. Co. of N.Mex., Albuquerque, 1978-79; mgr. engr. Horizon Tech., Ft. Collins, Colo., 1979-80; staff engr. Platte River Power Authority, Ft. Collins, 1980-85, planning supr., 1985-89, mgr. quality improvement, 1989-92, exec. engr., 1992—; mem. renewable task force Electric Power Rsch. Inst., Palo Alto, Calif., 1982-85, mgt. com. Western Energy Supply and Transmission Assocs., Albuquerque, 1991—, vice chair., 1994-95; chmn. Am. Pub. Power Assn. Demonstration of Energy Efficient Devels. Bd., Washington, 1992-94. Chmn. campaign Ft. Collins Area United Way, 1986, pres. bd. dirs., 1988; chmn. Sch. Mill Levy Tax Com., Ft. Collins, 1988. Grantee State of Colo., Am. Public Power Assn./ Demonstration of Energy Efficient Devels., Western Energy Supply and Transmission Assocs., U.S. Dept. Energy, City of Colorado Springs, 1986-90. Mem. IEEE, Foothills Rotary of Ft. Collins (pres.-elect 1994, pres. 1995). Home: 825 E Pitkin St Fort Collins CO 80524-3839 Office: Platte River Power Authority 2000 E Horsetooth Rd Fort Collins CO 80525-2942

ENDEMAN, RONALD LEE, lawyer; b. Riverside, Calif., May 13, 1936; s. Walter Metsger and May Florence (Higdon) E.; m. Judith Lynn Sherman, May 27, 1959; children—Michael Scott, Melissa May. B.A., U. Calif.-Riverside, 1959; J.D., U. So. Calif., 1966. Bar: Calif. 1967, U.S. Dist. Ct. (so. dist.) Calif. 1967, U.S. Ct. Claims 1972, U.S. Ct. Appeals (9th cir.) 1973, U.S. Supreme Ct. 1972. Trial atty. Calif. Legal Div., San Diego, 1967-71; ptnr. Jackson, Turner, Endeman & Mulcare, Burlingame, Calif., 1971-73; ptnr. Jennings, Engstrand & Henrikson, San Diego, 1973-87; ptnr. Endeman, Lincoln, Turek & Heater, 1987—. Mem. State Bar Com. on Condemnation, 1987-89. Mem. ABA, Calif. Bar Assn., San Diego County Bar Assn., Assn. Trial Lawyers Am., Calif. Trial Lawyers Assn., San Diego County Trial Lawyers Assn., Am. Arbitration Assn., Internat. Right of Way Assn., Guild of Real Estate Appraisers (Man of Yr. 1971). Republican. Home: 10602 Noakes Rd La Mesa CA 91941-5776 Office: 600 B St Ste 2400 San Diego CA 92101-4508

ENDICOTT, WILLIAM F., journalist; b. Harrodsburg, Ky., Aug. 26, 1935; s. William O. and Evelyn E.; m. Mary Frances Thomas, Dec. 27, 1956; children: Gene, Fran, Greg. Student, Am. U., 1955; B.A. in Polit. Sci., Transylvania U., 1957. With Lexington (Ky.) Leader, 1957; sports writer Louisville Courier-Jour., 1958-62; reporter Tulare (Calif.) Advance-Register, 1963; reporter, city editor Modesto (Calif.) Bee, 1963-66; city editor Sacramento Union, 1966-67; with Los Angeles Times, 1968-85; Capitol bur. chief Sacramento Bee, 1985—; Hearst vis. profl. U. Tex., 1993. Served with USMCR, 1957-58. Recipient various journalism awards Dixing. Alumnus award Transylvania U., 1980. Episcopalian. Office: 925 L St Ste 1404 Sacramento CA 95814-3704

ENDLER, JOHN ARTHUR, biology educator, researcher; b. Montreal, Quebec, Canada, Oct. 8, 1947; s. Herman George and Fruma E. BA in Zoology, U. Calif., Berkeley, 1969; PhD in Zoology, U. Edinburgh, 1973. Lectr. and postdoctoral fellow Princeton (N.J.) U., 1972-73, asst. prof., 1973-79; assoc. prof. U. Utah, Salt Lake City, 1979-84, prof., 1984-86; prof. U. Calif., Santa Barbara, 1986—. Assoc. editor Evolution, 1986-89; editor Evolution, 1990-92; author: Geographic Variation, Speciation, and Clines, 1977, Natural Selection in the Wild, 1986; editor: Alternative Hypotheses in Biogeography, 1982, Sensory Drive, 1992; co-editor: Speciation and Its Consequences. Recipient Guggenheim fellowship, 1988. Fellow Linnean Soc. London, Animal Behavior Soc.; mem. Soc. for the Study of Evolution (pres. 1994—), Ecol. Soc. Am., Assn. for Tropical Biology, Am. Soc. Naturalists (v.p. 1990). Office: U Calif Dept Biol Scis Santa Barbara CA 93106

ENERSEN, BURNHAM, lawyer; b. Lamberton, Minn., Nov. 17, 1905; s. Albert H. and Ethel (Rice) E.; m. Nina H. Wallace, July 21, 1935; children: Richard W., Elizabeth. A.B., Carleton Coll., 1927, L.H.D., 1974; LL.B., Harvard U., 1930. Bar: Calif. 1931. Assoc. McCutchen, Doyle, Brown & Enersen, San Francisco, 1930-43, ptnr., 1943-78, counsel, 1978—; dir. Pomfret Estates, Inc., Calif. Student Loan Fin. Corp., 1981-90; chmn. Gov.'s Com. Water Lawyers, 1957; mem. Calif. Jud. Coun., 1960-64; vice chmn. Calif. Constn. Revision Commn., 1964-75; mem. com. to rev. Calif. Master Plan for Higher Edn., 1971-72. Mem. Calif. Citizens Commn. for Tort Reform, 1976-77; bd. dirs. Assn. Calif. Tort Reform, 1979-93, chmn. 1979-80; mem. Calif. Postsecondary Edn. Com., 1974-78; bd. dirs. Criminal Justice Legal Found., 1982-94, chmn. bd. trustees, 1985-86; bd. dirs. Fine Arts Mus. Found., 1983-94, pres. bd. trustees, 1987-92; pres. United Bay Area Crusade, 1962, United Crusades of Calif., 1969-71; trustee Mills Coll., 1972-82, chmn., 1976-80. Fellow Am. Bar Found.; mem. ABA (ho. of dels. 1970-76), State Bar Calif. (pres. 1960), Bar Assn. San Francisco (pres. 1955), Assn. of Bar of City of N.Y., Am. Judicature Soc., Am. Law Inst., Calif. C. of C. (dir. 1962-78, pres. 1971), Calif. Hist. Soc. (bd. trustees 1976-78, 83-89), Bohemian Club, Pacific-Union Club, Commercial Club (pres. 1966), Commonwealth Club Calif., San Francisco Golf Club, Cypress Point Club. Home: 40 Arguello Blvd San Francisco CA 94118-1403 Office: 3 Embarcadero Ctr San Francisco CA 94111-4003

ENFIELD, D(ONALD) MICHAEL, insurance executive; b. L.A., Jan. 24, 1945; s. Fred Donald Jr. and Suzanne Arden (Hinkle) E.; m. Roseanne Burke, Dec. 29, 1978; children: Susan Ann, Michael David, Peter Christian. BA in Polit. Sci., U. San Francisco, 1967. Mgmt. trainee Marsh & McLennan, Inc., San Francisco, 1967-70, acct. exec., 1970-77, asst. v.p., 1977-79, v.p., 1979-81, sr. v.p., 1981-82, mng. dir., 1982-89; chmn., CEO Frank B. Hall & Co. of No. Calif., San Francisco, 1989-92; founder, chmn., CEO Metro/Risk, Inc., San Francisco, 1992—; cons. in field. Contbr. articles to profl. publs. Bd. dirs. Ronald McDonald House, San Francisco, 1989-92; chmn. bd. dirs. Midsummer Mozart Festival, San Francisco, 1985. Mem. San Francisco C. of C. (dir. bus./arts coun. 1987-93), Soc. Calif. Pioneers (county v.p. 1974—), Lotos Club of N.Y., City Club of San Francisco, Olympic Club of San Francisco. Office: Metro/Risk Inc 505 Montgomery St Ste 1600 San Francisco CA 94111-2552

ENG, CATHERINE, health care facility administrator, physician, medical educator; b. Hong Kong, May 20, 1950; came to U.S., 1953; d. Doi Kwong and Alice (Yee) E.; m. Daniel Charles Chan; 1 child, Michael B. BA, Wellesley Coll., 1972; MD, Columbia U., 1976. Diplomate Am. Bd. Internal Medicine, Am. Bd. Gastroenterology; cert. added qualifications geriatrics. Intern in internal medicine Presbyterian Hosp./Columbia, Presbyterian Med. Ctr., 1976-77, resident in internal medicine, 1977-79; fellow in gastroenterology/hepatology N.Y. Hosp./Cornell U. Med. Coll., 1979-81; instr. medicine Cornell U. Coll. Medicine, N.Y.C., 1980-81; staff physician On Lok Sr. Health Svcs., San Francisco, 1981-86, supervising physician, 1986-91, med. dir., 1992—; asst. clin. prof. dept. family and cmty. medicine U. Calif., San Francisco, 1986—, asst. clin. prof. dept. medicine, 1992—; primary care specialist Program of All-inclusive Care for the Elderly, San Francisco, 1987-94; asst. chief dept. medicine Chinese Hosp., San Francisco, 1993-94. Instr. BLS Am. Heart Assn., San Francisco, 1988-92; mem. nominating com. YWCA of Marin, San Francisco, San Mateo, 1991—; mem. mgmt. com. YWCA-Chinatown/North Beach, San Francisco, 1989—; bd. dirs. Chinatown Cmty. Children's Ctr., San Francisco, 1987-90. Durant scholar Wellesley Coll., 1972. Mem. ACP, Am. Geriatrics Soc., Am. Soc. Aging, Am. Gastroent. Assn., Calif. Med. Assn. (assoc.), San Francisco Med. Soc. (assoc.), Sigma Xi, Alpha Omega Alpha. Office: On Lok Sr Health Services 1333 Bush St San Francisco CA 94109-5611

ENG, CHRISTOPHER KAMUELA, minister, educator; b. Honolulu, Mar. 13, 1949; s. Frank Harold and Joan (Mung) E.; m. Cheri M. Shimose, Feb. 14, 1988; children: Skye S. T., Joy S. K. BA cum laude, U. Hawaii, 1971, MA with honors, 1973; MDiv, Fuller Theol. Sem., 1977; D of Ministry, San Francisco Theol. Sem., 1985. Ordained to Am. Bapt. Ch., 1979. Campus min. Hawaii Conf. United Ch. Christ to U. Hawaii, Honolulu, 1975; asst. pastor Chinese United Meth. Ch., L.A., 1975-77; assoc. min. Japanese Bapt. Ch., Seattle, 1978-81, Nuuanu Congl. Ch. United Ch. Christ, Honolulu, 1981-85; sr. pastor Walpahu United (Hawaii) Ch. Christ, 1985—; instr. T'ai-Chi Ch'uan U. Hawaii, Leeward Community Coll., 1987—, Wahiawa Gen. Hosp., 1995—; bd. dirs. Hawaii Conf. United Ch. Christ, Honolulu, 1984—; vol. chaplain Kuakini Med. Ctr. Oncology Team, Honolulu, 1986—; pres. Oahu Assn. United Ch. Christ Mokupuni, Honolulu, 1989-90; trainer curriculum United Ch. of Christ. Contbr. articles to profl. jours. Bd. mgrs. Nuuanu YMCA, Honolulu, 1981-91, Leeward YMCA, Waipahu, 1991—; vol. Honolulu Jaycees and Jaycettes, 1982; mem. Hawaii's Plantation Village, Min.'s Coun. Masland fellow Union Theol. Sem. N.Y., 1990; recipient Pro Deo et Patria God and Country award Boy Scouts Am., 1967, Svc. award YMCA, 1987; named legis. intern Ctr. Govtl. Devel., 1971. Mem. AAUP, Nat. Assn. Underwater Instrs., Hawaii Sociological Assn., Waipahu Community Assn. Democrat. Office: Waipahu United Ch Christ 94-330 Mokuola St Waipahu HI 96797-3313

ENG, HOWARD, airport administrator; b. Hong Kong, Nov. 26, 1952; married; 2 children. BSc, U. Alta., Can., 1979, BComm, 1980. Adminstrv. trainee western region Transport Can., 1981-82, planning officer western region, 1982-84, project devel. mgr. western region, 1984-85; mgr. airport devel. Edmonton (Alta.) Internat. Airport, Can., 1985-88, mgr. terminal and indsl., 1988-92, airport gen. mgr., v.p. ops., 1992-95; gen. mgr. aviation support svcs. Hong Kong Provisional Airport Authority, 1995—. Office: Edmonton Internat Airport, Box 9860, Edmonton, AB Canada T5J 2T2

ENG, JAMIE PEARL, statistics educator; b. N.Y.C.; d. Jim and Juanita E.; m. John Jin Lee. BS, MIT, 1973; MS, Harvard U., 1975, DSc, 1977. Asst. prof. NYU, 1977-81; assoc. prof. San Francisco State U., 1981-85, prof., 1985—. Contbr. articles to profl. jours. Ednl. counselor MIT, 1985—; vice chair Bay Area Ednl. Coun., MIT, 1986—. Mem. Am. Statistical Assn., Asian Bus. League of San Francisco. Office: San Francisco State U 1600 Holloway Ave San Francisco CA 94132

ENG, LAWRENCE FOOK, biochemistry educator, neurochemist; b. Spokane, Wash., Feb. 19, 1931; s. On Kee and Shee (Hue) E.; m. Jeanne Leong, Aug. 30, 1957; children: Douglas, Alice, Steven, Shirley. BS in Chemistry, Wash. State U., 1952; MS in Chemistry, Stanford U., 1954, PhD in Chemistry, 1962. Chief chemistry sect. lab. svc. VA Med. Ctr., Palo Alto, Calif., 1961—; rsch. assoc. dept. pathology Sch. Medicine Stanford (Calif.) U., 1966-70, sr. scientist dept. pathology Sch. of Medicine, 1970-75, adj. prof., 1975-82, prof. dept. pathology Sch. of Medicine, 1982—; mem. ad hoc neurol. sci. study sect. and neurology B study sect. NIH, 1976-79, mem. neurol. sci. study sect., 1978-83; mem. adv. bd. VA Office of Regeneration Rsch. Program, 1985-89; mem. VA Merit Rev. Bd. for Neurobiology, 1987-90; mem. Nat. Adv. Neurol. Disorders and Stroke Coun., 1991-94. Mem. editorial bd. Neurobiology, 1970-75, Jour. of Neurochemistry, 1978-85, Jour. of Neuroimmunology, 1980-83, Molecular and Chem. Neuropathology, 1982—, Glia, 1987—, Jour. for Neurosci. Rsch., 1991—, Neurochemical Rsch., 1993—. Capt. USAF, 1952-57. Mem. Am. Soc. for Neurochemistry (coun. 1979-83, 85-87, 93—, sec. 1987-93), Am. Soc. Biochemistry and Molecular Biology, Internat. Soc. for Neurochemistry, Soc. for Neurosci. Office: VA Med Ctr Lab Svc 3801 Miranda Ave Palo Alto CA 94304-1207

ENG, ROGER S.C., dentist, educator; b. Seattle; m. Sylvia Diane Chow; four children. BS in Chemistry, U. Wash., 1958; DDS, U. Calif., San Francisco, 1966. Analytical chemist The Dow Chem. Co., 1959-62; dental staff San Francisco (Calif.) County Pub. Health Dept., 1966, Santa Clara (Calif.) County Pub. Health Dept., 1968-73; pvt. practice dentistry Calif., 1966—; asst. clin. prof. U. Calif. Sch. Dentistry, San Francisco, 1990—; coun. mem. Nat. Adv. Dental Rsch. Coun., Nat. Inst. Dental Rsch., 1990-94. Bd. dirs. Sunnyvale (Calif.) Chpt. United Way, 1979—, Orgn. Chinese Ams.-Silicon Valley chpt., 1991—; councilman City of Los Altos, Calif., 1980-88, mayor pro tem, 1980, 85, mayor, 1981-86, mem. former mayors com., 1988—, chmn. mayor's blue ribblon com. for affordable housing, 1992; auditor, bd. dirs. Chinese-Am. Citizen Alliance-Peninsula Chpt., 1989—; mem. exec. coun. Stanford Area Coun., Boy Scouts Am., 1991—; v.p. Shih Lin subcom. Los Altos Sister Cities, Inc., 1992—; mem. planning and allocations coun. United Way, Santa Clara County, 1979-87; del. Assn. Bay Area Govts., 1982-87; mem. Santa Clara County intercity coun., 1980-87, transp. commn., 1985-87, Intergovtl. Coun., 1981, planning policy com., 1974, social concerns subcom., 1974, airport land use com., 1972-73, drug abuse coun., 1983; mem. nat. adv. coun. East Asian and Pacific Affairs, 1979; chmn. Santa Clara County Dentists for Bush, 1988; mem. North Santa Clara County Solid Waste Mgmt. Authority, 1980-84; mem. planning commn. City of Los Altos, 1972-80, chmn., 1976-77, mem. bd. adjustments, 1972-80, chmn., 1974, 79, mem. beautification com., 1972-73; bd. dirs. Sunnyvale Cmty. Svcs., 1978-82; pres. Peninsula Lodge Chinese-Am. Citizens Alliance, 1976-77, grand lodge rep., 1978-79; treas. Troop #30 Boy Scouts Am., 1979-84, mem. parents com., 1979-84; bd. dirs. Asian Bus. League Silicon Valley, 1988-91; mem. Calif. State Rep. Ctrl. Com., 1982-89. Recipient Profile in Excellence award Peninsula Chinese Am. Club/Stanford Area Chinese Am. Club, 1986; fellow Internat. Coll. Craniomandibular Orthopedics, 1986, Paul Harris fellow The Rotary Found. Rotary Internat. Mem. ADA, Calif. Dental Assn., Mid-Peninsula Dental Assn., Santa Clara County Dental Soc. (pres. 1991, legis. com. 1982-89, sec. 1989), Univ. Calif. Dental Alumni Assn., U. Wash. Alumni Assn. (life), Stanford Area Chinese Club, Palo Alto Masons, Chinese-Am. C. of C. of Santa Clara County (bd. dirs., organizer, chmn. bd. 1988-89, pres. 1990—), Los Altos Rotary Club, Sunnyvale Met. Lions Club. Office: Wrightmont Profl Ctr 990 W Fremont Ave Ste Q Sunnyvale CA 94087

ENGAR, ANN WILLARDSON, humanities educator; b. Columbus, Ohio, Sept. 7, 1954; d. Robert Kent and Beth Marie (Bennett) Willardson; m. Richard Engar, June 21, 1977; children: Robert, Thomas, Julia. BA, Stanford U., 1975; MA, U. Wash., 1977, PhD, 1981. Instr. U. Wash., Seattle, Brigham Young U., Salt Lake City, Wayne State U., Detroit; assoc. instr. U. Utah, Salt Lake City, 1982—, disting. honors prof., 1992-93, presdl. teaching scholar, 1995—. Co-author: Approaches to Teaching Candide, 1987, Dictionary of Literary Biography: American Literary Biographers, 1991, Beacham's Guide to Literature for Young Adults, 1991, Encyclopedia of Romanticism, 1992, Dictionary of Literary Biography: British Romantic Novelists, 1992, Encyclopedia of Mormonism, 1992, Approaches to Teaching Samuel Johnson, 1993, Dictionary of Literary Biography: Nineteenth-Century British Literary Biographers, 1994, Utah History Encyclopedia, 1994; bibliographer MLA International Bibliography. Mem. MLA, Nat. Coun. Tchrs. Eng., Am. Assn. for 18th Century Studies. Home: 1806 Glenbrook Cir Salt Lake City UT 84121-1213 Office: U Utah 101 Carlson Hall Salt Lake City UT 84112

ENGAR, RICHARD CHARLES, insurance executive, dentist, educator; b. Salt Lake City, Apr. 2, 1953; s. Keith Maurice and Amy Kathryn (Lyman) E.; m. Elizabeth Ann Willardson, June 21, 1977; children: Robert Keith, Thomas William, Julia Elizabeth. BA in Psychology, U. Utah, 1976; DDS, U. Wash., 1980. Resident gen. practice Sinai Hosp., Detroit, 1980-81; pvt. practice Salt Lake City, 1981-91; cons. Profl. Ins. Exch., Salt Lake City, 1990-91, atty.-in-fact, 1991—; clin. instr. dept. pathology, dental gen. practice residency program U. Utah Med. Ctr., Salt Lake City, 1988—. Author: Dental Treatment of the Sensory Impaired Patient, 1977. Dist. trainer Spring Creek Dist., Great Salt Lake coun. Boy Scouts Am., 1989-92. Fellow Acad. Gen. Dentistry (regional dir. 1991—, regional dir. chmn. 1995—), Pierre Fauchard Acad., Utah Acad. Gen. Dentistry (pres. 1987); mem. ADA, Salt Lake Dist. Dental Soc. (treas. 1986-88), Utah Dental Assn. (editor 1985-88), Sugar House Rotary (bull. chair 1992-93, 94-95), No. Utah Plastic Modelers Assn. (v.p. 1992, 94), Phi Beta Kappa, Phi Kappa Phi. Mem. LDS Ch. Home: 1806 Glenbrook Cir Salt Lake City UT 84121-1213 Office: 445 E 4500 S Salt Lake City UT 84107-3101

ENGDAHL, TODD PHILIP, newspaper editor; b. Jamestown, N.Y., Feb. 8, 1950; s. George Philip and Janice Marie (Wallin) E.; m. Caroline C.N. Schomp, Dec. 29 , 1973; children: Anders Justus Schomp, Mats Philip Schomp. BA, Pomona Coll., 1971; MS, Northwestern U., 1972. Reporter Oregonian, Portland, 1972-75; reporter Denver Post, 1975-80, asst. city editor, 1980-83, night city editor, 1983-85, Sunday editor, 1985-86, city editor, 1986-90, exec. city editor, 1990-95, editor, 1995—; lectr. journalism Portland State U., 1974; bd. dirs. Augsburg Fortress Pubs. Democrat. Lutheran. Office: Denver Post PO Box 1709 Denver CO 80201

ENGEL, EMILY FLACHMEIER, school administrator; b. Columbus, Tex., Sept. 15, 1938; d. William August and Jeanette D. (Hastedt) F.; m. Lars N. Engel, Dec. 28, 1957; children: Jan Kristin, Karen Gale. BSEd, U. Tex., 1959, MEd, 1966. Cert. tchr., counselor, adminstr., N.Mex. Sch. counselor, guidance team leader Los Alamos (N.Mex.) Pub. Schs., 1967-85, coord., fed. projects, 1985-87; asst. prin. Los Alamos Mid. Sch., 1987-89; prin. Mountain Elem. Sch., Los Alamos, 1989—; presentor nat. confs. and convs. Bd. dirs. Los Alamos Family Coun., 1985-91, Family Strengths Network, 1994—, Self-Help, Inc., 1993—; mem. adv. com. Sci.-at-Home, 1994—. Mem. ASCD, NDEA (mem. counseling and guidance inst. U. Tex. Austin 1962-63), Nat. Assn. Elem. Sch. Prins., N.Mex. Assn. Elem. Sch. Prins. (pres.-elect 1992-93, pres. 1993-94), N.Mex. Assn. Sch. Adminstrs., Los Alamos Assn. Sch. Adminstrs. (pres. 1991-92), Delta Kappa Gamma (Rho chpt. sec.), Pi Lambda Theta. Methodist. Home: 192 Loma Del Escolar Los Alamos NM 87544-2525

ENGEL, GENEVIEVE, library system analyst; b. San Francisco, Jan. 28, 1957; d. Benjamin Rush Payne and Karen Engel. BA in Sociology, U. Calif., Berkeley, 1982, MLIS, 1994. Legal asst. Reavis & McGrath, San Francisco, 1981; sales staff 800-Software, Berkeley, 1982-83; computer operator U. Calif., Libr. Automation, Oakland, Calif., 1983-85; sr. computer operator U. Calif., Libr. Automation, Oakland, 1985-88, computer ops. supr., 1988, user svcs. asst., 1988-94, user svcs. analyst, 1994—. Co-author: Internet Connections, 1993, 2d edit., 1995; contbr. chpts. to books. Vol. driver Project Open Hand, Oakland, 1993—; vol. libr. worker World Affairs Coun. of No. Calif., San Francisco, 1993-94. Mem. ALA, Libr. and Info. Tech. Assn. (internet rm. steering com. 1994—, chair HM11G 1995—), Assn. for Computing Machinery (spl. interest group in computer human interaction). Office: U Calif 300 Lakeside Dr 8th Fl Oakland CA 94612-3550

ENGEL, LINDA JEANNE, mining executive; b. Denver, Aug. 24, 1949; d. Thomas Mintor and Irene Evelyn (Esbenson) Kelley; m. William Stephen Engel, May 6, 1972; children: Kacey, Ryan. BA in Polit. Sci., U. Colo., 1975. Statis. researcher Martin Marietta, Waterton, Colo., 1971; asst. dir. Fed. Drug Abuse Program, Denver, 1972-74; corp. sec./treas. Grayhill Exploration Co., Arvada, Colo., 1981-84; controller Western Internat. Gold-Silver, Westminster, Colo., 1985-86; investor rels. dir. and corp. sec. Canyon Resources Corp., Golden, Colo., 1986-94. Dem. campaign mgr., Mayor of Boulder, Colo., 1970. Mem. NAFE, Am. Soc. Corp. Secs., Nat. Investor Rels. Inst., Fellowship Christian Athletes, Delta Delta Delta. Republican.

ENGEL, RICHARD L., career officer; b. L.A., July 2, 1946; s. Richard Leroy and Margret Ellen (Wilson) E.; m. Connie Jean Ricks, Sept. 8, 1973; children: Lindsey, Jennifer, Shelly. BS in Mech. Engring., Tex. A&M U., 1968; MS in Indsl. and Sys. Mgmt. Engring., Ariz. State U., Tucson, 1975; student, Air Force Test Pilot Sch., 1976-77, Armed Forces Staff Coll., 1981; M in Nat. Security Strategic Studies, Naval War Coll., 1988. Commd. 2d lt. USAF, 1968, advanced through grades to brig. gen., 1993; pilot spl. ops. USAF, South Vietnam, 1970-71; instr. pilot USAF, Williams AFB, Ariz., 1971-74; air staff officer Hdqs. Air Tng. Command, Randolph AFB, Tex., 1974-76; advanced simulator rsch. flight test officer Air Force Human Resources Lab., Williams AFB, 1978-81; chief of acads. Air Force Test Pilot Sch., Edwards AFB, Calif., 1981-83; dep. dir. F-16 LANTIRN Test Program, Edwards AFB, 1983-85; comdr. F-16 and LANTIRN Combined Test Forces, Edwards AFB, 1985-87; divsn. chief weapons sys. divsn. Office of Legis. Liaison for Sec. of Air Force, Washington, 1988-89; comdr. 3246th Test Wing, Air Force Devel. Test Ctr., Eglin AFB, Fla., 1989-92, 412th Test Wing, Edwards AFB, 1992-93, Air Force Flight Test Ctr., Edwards AFB, 1993—. Decorated Legion of Merit, D.F.C. with two oak leaf clusters, Air medal with nine oak leaf clusters, Air Force Commendation medal. Mem. AIAA, Soc. Exptl. Test Pilots. Home: 5308 Palo Verde Dr Edwards CA 93523 Office: Air Force Flight Test Ctr 1 S Rosamond Blvd Edwards CA 93524-1000

ENGEL, THOMAS P., airport executive. Dir. Sacramento Met. Airport, Calif.; dir. of airports Sacramento County Dept. of Airports, Calif. Office: Sacramento County Calif Dept of Airports 6900 Airport Blvd Sacramento CA 95837-1109*

ENGELBACH, DAVID CHARLES, scriptwriter, television producer; b. Phila., Sept. 20, 1946; s. Charles David and Perle (Dogole) E.; m. Kathryn Joan Beatie, Oct. 21, 1983 (div. Aug. 1987); m. Annalisa Marta Fields, Oct. 13, 1990. BS, Fairleigh Dickinson U., L.A., 1968; postgrad., U. So. Calif., 1968-70. Motion picture scriptwriter Write Ink-Direct, Inc., L.A., 1983—, motion picture dir., 1985—; TV producer Orion Prodns., L.A., 1984-85. Writer/dir.: (motion picture) America 3000, 1986; scriptwriter (motion pictures) Over the Top, 1987, Death Wish II, 1981; creator: (TV series) Lottery, 1982. Bd. dirs. Valley Village (Calif.) Assn., 1992-94. Mem. Dirs. Guild of Am., Writers Guild of Am./West. Office: c/o Above the Line 9200 W Sunset Blvd Ste 401 Los Angeles CA 90069-3506

ENGELHARDT, BARBARA ANN, nutritionist and registered dietitian; b. Moses Lake, Wash.; d. Franklin Andrew and Beverly Ann (Bidwell) Engelhardt; 1 child, Maryrose Azalea. BS in Nutrition Sci., U. Calif., Davis, 1980; MA in Counseling Psychology, Pacific Grad. Inst., Carpinteria, Calif., 1993. Nutritionist Elderly Nutrition Program Yolo and Placer Counties, Calif., 1981-84; nutrition asst. Kaiser Permanente, Sacramento, 1985-87, clin. dietitian, 1987-93; eating disorder specialist Nutrition Alternatives, Sacramento, 1989—; cons. dietitian/MFCC intern Sacramento County Mental Health Treatment Ctr., Sacramento, 1992—; instr. Cosumnes C.C., Sacramento, 1987-89; nutrition counselor Am. Heart Assn. Health Fair, Sacramento, 1988-90. Chair Sacramento County Libertarian Party, 1994, supper club organizer, 1989—; spkr. Sacramento Arthritis Assn., 1989-90. Mem. Am. Dietetic Assn. (registered), Calif. Dietetic Assn., Golden Empire Dist. Dietetic Assn. Office: Nutrition Alternatives 2011 P St Ste 103 Sacramento CA 95814-5225

ENGELKING, PAUL CRAIG, chemistry educator; b. Glendale, Calif., May 11, 1948; s. Fred Carl and Gladys M. (Nicol) E.; m. Patricia Donaldson, Aug. 2, 1975; children: Kirstin, Gwynne. BS, Calif. Inst. Tech., 1971; MPhil, Yale U., 1974, Ph.D., 1976. Rsch. asst. Joint Inst. Lab. Astrophysics, Boulder, Colo., 1976-78; asst. prof. chemistry U. Oreg., Eugene, 1978-84, assoc. prof., 1984-91, prof., 1991—; vis. fellow Joint Inst. Lab. Astrophysics, Boulder, 1985-86. Contbr. articles to profl. jours. Mem. city coun., Lowell, Oreg., 1983-84. Alfred P. Sloan fellow, 1982. Mem. Am. Chem. Soc., Am. Phys. Soc. Democrat. Home: PO Box 236 Lowell OR 97452-0236 Office: U Oreg Dept Chemistry Eugene OR 97403

ENGFER, SUSAN MARVEL, zoological park executive; b. Mpls., Dec. 6, 1943; d. Frederick Paul and Dorothy M. Engfer. BS, Albion Coll., 1965; MS, U. Wyo., 1968; postgrad., U. Calif., Santa Barbara, 1975-76; dipl., Sch. Profl. Mgmt. Devel. for Zoo and Aquarium Pers., 1981. Ranger, naturalist Grand Teton Nat. Park, Moose, Wyo., 1967; cancer rsch. technician U. Calif., Santa Barbara, 1967-68; zoo keeper Santa Barbara Zool. Gardens, 1968-70, edn. curator, 1970-72, asst. dir., 1972-88; pres., CEO Cheyenne Mountain Zool. Park, Colorado Springs, Colo., 1988—; cons. oiled bird rehab. Union Oil and Standard Oil Co., 1968-70; master plan cons. Moorpark (Calif.) Coll., 1986-88; instr., bd. regents Sch. Profl. Mgmt. Devel. Zoo and Aquarium Pers., Wheeling, W.V., 1984-87. Author: North American Regional Studbook, Asian Small-Clawed Otter (Aonyx cinerea), 1987—. Fellow Am. Assn. Zool. Pks. and Aquariums (profl., bd. dirs. 1987-90, mem. accreditation commn. 1990—, chmn. accreditation commn. 1994-95); mem. Internat. Union Dirs. Zool. Gardens, Internat. Union Conservation of Nature and Natural Resources (mem. otter specialist group), Soc. Conservation Biology, Colo. Women's Forum, Rotary. Office: Cheyenne Mountain Zool Pk 4250 Cheyenne Mountain Zoo Rd Colorado Springs CO 80906-5728

ENGLADE, KENNETH FRANCIS, writer; b. Memphis, Oct. 7, 1938; s. Joseph George and Sara (Schneider) E.; m. Sharon Flynn, Nov. 27, 1960 (div. Feb. 1971); children: Dennis Alan, Michelle Suzanne, Mark Andrew; m. Sara Elizabeth Crews, Feb. 29, 1980 (div. Sept. 1991). BA in Journalism, La. State U., 1960. Reporter LaFourche Comet, Thibodaux, La., 1960-63; reporter, bur. mgr., corr. UP Internat., Baton Rouge, 1963-64, New Orleans, 1964-67, Edinburgh, Tex., 1967-68, Albuquerque, 1968-71, N.Y.C., 1971-72, Saigon, Vietnam, 1972-73, Hong Kong, 1973-75, Dallas, 1975-77; freelance writer, 1977-79, 81—. Author: (non-fiction) Cellar of Horror, 1989, Murder in Boston, 1990, Beyond Reason, 1990, Deadly Lessons, 1991, A Family Business, 1992; (fiction) Hoffa 1992, To Hatred Turned, 1993, Blood Sister, 1994. Mem. Am. Soc. Journalists and Authors, Mystery Writers of Am. Democrat. Roman Catholic. Office: PO Box 3148 Corrales NM 87048

ENGLE, CINDY, medical transcriptionist; b. Denver, Aug. 12, 1958; d. Wallace Clyde and Mary Margaret (Ingram) E. AA, Arapahoe C.C., 1979; BA in Kinesiology, U. No. Colo., 1992. Cert. paralegal; cert. paramedic, Colo. EMT/paramedic Ambulance Svc. Co., Denver, 1978-80; pers. asst. payroll Burns Security Svc., Denver, 1980-82; part-time asst. mgr. Tokoyo Bowl Restaurant, Denver, 1982-85; paramedic Platte Valley Ambulance, 1982-85; part-time flight paramedic for Air Life North Colo. Med. Ctr., Greeley, Colo., 1986-91; paramedic Weld County Ambulance, Greeley, 1985-92; intern exercise svcs. Greeley (Colo.) Med. Clinic, 1992, med. transcriptionist, 1993-94; med. transcriptionist North Colo. Med. Ctr., Greeley, 1994—; part-time EMS/criminal justice instr. Aims C.C., Greeley, 1987—; founder The Human Factor, 1992—. Author ednl. game: The Reality Game, 1993. Office: The Human Factor 2626 23d Ave Greeley CO 80631

ENGLE, ROBERT IRWIN, music educator, musician, composer, writer; b. New Kensington, Pa., Feb. 11, 1945; s. Dale Clair Engle and Rosalyn Imogene (Timblin) Erickson. BS in Music Edn., U. Cin., 1967; postgrad., Stanford U., 1967-68, Ind. U., 1969, U. So. Calif., 1969-71; MA in Music, U. Hawaii, 1973; PhD in Music Edn., U. Wash., 1994. Cert. tchr. music grades K-12, Calif., Wash. Choral instr. Terminal Island Prison, San Pedro, Calif., 1969-71; choral music tchr. Palos Verdes (Calif.) High Sch., 1968-72; dir. music Makiki Christian Ch., Honolulu, 1978-84, 1st United Meth. Ch., Honolulu, 1986-88; tchr. music and French Redemption Acad., Kailua, Hawaii, 1988-91; dir. music Kapiolani Community Coll., Honolulu, 1975-95; dir. choral activities U. Hawaii, Hilo, 1995—; cons. Performing Arts Abroad, Kalamazoo, 1979—, Pacific Basin Choral Festival in Hawaii, Berkeley, Calif., 1989—; tchr. music theory, piano S. Seattle C.C., 1993-94; choral music tchr. Inglemoor H.S., Bothell, Wash., 1994; speaker Internat. Soc. Music Edn Convention, Tampa, Fla., 1994. Author: Taking Note of Music, 1988, Piano Is My Forte, 1989; composer: Tatalo A Le Alii, 1984 (3d pl. state competition); composer, recording artist: Pese Pa'ia, 1988; profl. recording Christmas Aloha; contbr. articles to profl. jours. Founder E Himeni Kakou Colls. Choral Festival, Honolulu, 1976—; founder, dir. Maile Aloha Singers, Honolulu, 1973-92, Carols at the Centerstage Festival, Honolulu, 1989—, Lokahi Choral Festival, Honolulu, 1989—, Aloha, America! Invitational Choral Festival, Honolulu, 1995—. Dir. mus. group representing Hawaii, Cultural Office for Territorial Activity, Papeete, Tahiti, 1982, World U. Games, 1983, Casa De La Cultura, Southeastern Mex., 1984, La. World EXPO, 1984, EXPO '86, Vancouver, Hawaiian Airlines, 1987, Goodwill Tour Am. Samoa, 1989, Artists in the Schs. Auckland, N.Z., 1991; dir. mus. group representing U.S.A., U.S. Dept. State, EXPO '85, Tsukuba, Japan, 1985; Dir. award 2d pl. group Collegiate Showcase, Chgo., 1988, Dir. award 1st place Choral Groups All Am. Festival, Orlando, Fla., 1994. Mem. AAUP, Am. Choral Dirs. Assn. (Hawaii chpt. 1978—, editor newsletter 1987-89, state pres. 1989-91), U. Hawaii Profl. Assembly, Samoa Fealofani Club, Delta Tau Delta (life). Republican. Mem. Pentecostal Ch. Office: Kapiolani Community Coll 4303 Diamond Head Rd Honolulu HI 96816-4421

ENGLE, STEPHEN EUGENE, artist; b. Honolulu, Dec. 27, 1950; s. Peter King and Barbara Jean (Akesson) E. BFA in Sculpture, Santa Barbara Art Inst., 1973; MFA, Ind. U., 1980; postgrad. studies in figure painting, Pa. Acad Fine Art, 1982-84. presenter woodcarving sculpture workshop Sonoma State U., Rohnert Park, Calif., 1993. Solo exhibitions Lisa Harris Gallery, Seattle, 1990, 92; group exhibitions include: Contemporary Art Ctr., Honolulu, 1981, Shreveport (La.) Art Guild, 1982, Roger LaPelle Gallery, Phila., 1987, Phila. City Hall, 1988, Seattle Ctr. Modern Art Pavilion, 1990, 93, Alternative Mus., N.Y.C., 1991, Bellevue (Wash.) Art Mus., 1992 (Juror award), Security Pacific Gallery, Seattle, 1992, Paris Gibson Sq. Mus. of Art, Great Falls, Mont., 1993 (Best of Category); included in private, corp. collections. Recipient Tuition scholarship Santa Barbara Art Inst., 1972-73, Ford grant N.Y. Sch. Painting and Drawing, 1979, Betty Bowen Meml. Recognition award, Seattle Art Mus., 1989, NEA fellowship, 1990, Seattle Arts Commn. grant, 1990, included in Wash. State Arts Commn. Slide registry.

ENGLEMAN, DAVID S., diversified financial services executive; b. 1937. CFO, exec. v.p. Mortgage Guarantee & Ins. Corp., Milw., 1962-74; mgmt. cons., 1962-79; founder, pres. Fin. Am. Network, San Diego, 1983-87; dir. Comml. Fed. Savings & Loan, Omaha, 1979—; chmn. bd., pres., CEO Union Fed. Savings Bank, 1991—, Unionfed Fin. Corp., Brea, Calif. Office: Unionfed Fin Corp 330 Lambert Rd Brea CA 92621-4112*

ENGLER, MARY B., physiologist, educator, nurse, researcher; b. Washington. AAS, Marymount U., 1975; BS, Am. U., 1978, MS, 1981; PhD in Physiology, Georgetown U., 1988. RN, Calif., Md. Critical care nurse Suburban Hosp., Bethesda, Md., 1975-80; clin. nurse cardiovascular NIH, Nat. Heart, Lung and Blood Inst., Bethesda, 1980-88; assoc. prof. physiol. nursing, dir. cardiovascular program U. Calif., San Francisco, 1988—; cons., educator in field. Contbr. rsch. papers to profl. jours. Recipient Clin. Nursing Rsch. award Am. Heart Assn., 1989-90. Mem. Am. Physiol. Soc., N.Y. Acad. Scis., Fedn. Am. Soc. Exptl. Biology, AACN, Am. Heart Assn. (coun. basic sci. circulation, nursing arteriosclerosis), Sigma Theta Tau. Office: U Calif 3d and Parnassus N # 611Y San Francisco CA 94143

ENGLISH, DONALD MARVIN, loss control representative; b. Raleigh, N.C., July 31, 1951; s. Marvin Lee and Lois (Woodard) E.; m. Rebecca Pritchard, Sept. 3, 1970 (div. 1977); m. Kathryn A. Sumner, July 3, 1993. Student, Miami U., Oxford, Ohio, 1969-70, 73-74, U. Cin., 1977-78, Calif. State U., Fresno, 1980—; AA, Fresno City Coll., 1991. Ins. inspector Comml. Services, Cin., 1974-78, Ohio Casualty Ins. Co., Fresno, 1978-93; owner Loss Control Systems, Renton, Wash., 1993; sr. loss control specialist Scott Wetzel Svcs., Inc., Federal Way, Wash., 1993—. Served with U.S. Army, 1970-73. Mem. Am. Soc. Safety Engrs., Soc. CPCU (cert.), Ins. Inst. Am. (assoc. in loss control mgmt. 1990—), East Fresno Exch. Club (pres. 1984-85). Home: 16116 SE 175th St Renton WA 98058-9113 Office: Scott Wetzel Svcs Inc 33801 1st Way S Ste 351 Federal Way WA 98003-6219

ENGLISH, GERALD MARION, otolaryngologist; b. Caldwell, Idaho, Feb. 14, 1931; s. Marion L. and Opal V. (Sackett) E.; m. Carol Katherine Baker, Aug. 23, 1953; children: Elizabeth Katherine, Margaret Susan, Gerald Marion Jr. Student, Coll. of Idaho, 1949-52; MD, Tulane U., New Orleans, 1956. Diplomate Am. Bd. of Otolaryngology. Intern, resident in pathology The Charity Hosp. of La., New Orleans, 1956-58; resident in gen. surgery, otolaryngology U. Colo. Med. Ctr., Denver, 1965-66, 66-69; staff Pathology Health Rsch. Lab., Los Alamos Sci. Lab., 1958-59; pvt. gen. practice medicine Denver, 1960-65, pvt. practice otolaryngology, 1974—; asst. prof. div. otolaryngology dept. gen. surgery U. Colo., Denver, 1969-73; assoc. prof. otolaryngology U. Colo., 1973-74, clin. assoc. prof. otolaryngology, 1974-79, clin. prof. otolaryngology, 1979—; cons. otolaryngology Nat. Jewish Hosp., Denver, 1969-82, VA Hosp., Denver, 1969-76, Fitzsimons Army Med Ctr., 1977—; attending physician Gen. Rose Meml. Hosp., St. Luke's Hosp., St. Anthony's Hosp., Luth. Med. Ctr., Presbyn. Med. Ctr., Swedish Med. Ctr./Porter Meml. Hosp.; attending physician Denver Children's Hosp., bd. dirs., 1985-86; bd. med. advisers Listen Found., Denver, 1977-81; bd. dirs. Ctr. Hearing, Speech and Lang., Denver, 1989—; lectr. in field. Author: Otolaryngology-A Textbook, 1976; editor-in-chief Otolaryngology, 1974—; editorial bd. Outpatient Surgery, 1985—; contbr. numerous articles to profl. jours., chpts. to books. Pres., bd. dirs. Ctr. Speech, Lang., and Hearing, Denver, 1974—; vestry St. Johns Episcopal Cathedral, Denver, 1987-90, mem. forward planning com., 1985-90, chmn. organ com., 1987-90. Comdr. USPHS, 1958-60. Fellow Am. Acad. Otolaryngology, ACS; mem. AMA, Am. Soc. Head and Neck Surgery, Am. Coun. Otolaryngology, Am. Bd. Otolaryngology, Colo. Med. Soc., Clear Creek Valley Med. Soc., Arapahoe County Med. Soc., Colo. Otolaryngology Maxillo Facial Soc., Soc. Univ. Otolaryngologists, Physicians of Am., Triologic Soc., Orders and Medal Soc. Am., U.S. Naval Inst., Korean Vets. Assn., Am. Soc. Mil. Insignia Collectors, Alpha Omega Alpha. Republican. Episcopalian. Home: 2649 S Tennyson Way Denver CO 80219-5706 Office: 601 E Hampden Ave Ste 390 Englewood CO 80110-2769

ENGLISH, JOAN PATRICIA, municipal official; b. Newark, N.J., Feb. 11, 1944; d. John Patrick Sr. and Mary Joan (McGrail) E. BA, U. W.Va., 1966; MPA, U. So. Calif., 1968. Community svc. officer State of N.J. Dept. Community Affairs, 1968-69; dep. dir. Hoboken (N.J.) Model Cities Agy., 1969-73; fin. mgmt. system project mgr. Office Mgmt. Svcs., Portland, Oreg., 1973-74; asst. pub. works adminstr. City of Portland, 1974-79, exec. asst. to mayor, 1980, dir. traffic mgmt. Office Transp., 1985-89, pub. works system mgr., 1989-90; mgmt. cons., interim mgr. Washington County Washington County Oreg. and Portland Bur. Transp., 1980-85; dir. transp. and pub. works City fo West Hollywood, Calif., 1990—. Mem. ASPA, Am. Pub. Works Assn., Internat. City Mgmt. Assn., League Calif. Cities (com. transp. and pub. works), Womens Transp. Seminar. Home: 999 N Doheny Dr West Hollywood CA 90069-3146 Office: City of West Hollywood 8611 Santa Monica Blvd West Hollywood CA 90069-4109

ENGLISH, PHILIP STEPHEN, account manager, consultant; b. Accrington, Eng., Feb. 21, 1946; s. Arthur and Anne (Hargreaves) E.; m. Victoria Kucyn English, May 12, 1979. BS in Physics, London U., 1967; MS in Math., Cambridge U., Eng., 1968; PhD in Physics, U. Waterloo, Can., 1972; MBA in Internat. Bus., U. Miami, 1993. Asst. prof. St. Frances Xavier U., Antigonish, Can., 1973-79; gen. mgr. Chocolate Cove Players, Deer Island, Can., 1979-84; acct. exec. Satellite Comm., Ft. Lauderdale, Fla., 1984-86; acct. exec. Executone Inc., Miami, Fla., 1986-87, sales mgr., 1987-88; acct. exec. AT&T, Miami, Fla., 1988-90, sys. cons., 1990-92, acct. mgr., 1992-93; nat. acct. mgr. AT&T, Phoenix, 1993—; mem. AT&T Leaders Coun., 1995. Contbr. articles to profl. jours. Chmn. Kinsmen Club, Antigonish, Can., 1977. Named Valedictorian MBA Class U. Miami, Fla., 1993. Mem. Phoenix Jaycees. Office: AT&T 2800 N Central Ave Ste 1000 Phoenix AZ 85004-1007

ENGLUND, LORI JEAN, financial products company executive; b. Omaha, Sept. 20, 1961; d. Earl Winston and Barbara Jean (Van Wie) McClellan; m. Leslie Donald Englund, Feb. 12, 1960; 1 child, Jessica Marie. BS, Ariz. State U., 1983. Mktg. rep. GNA, Austin, Tex., 1983-84, sr. mktg. rep., 1985-86; regional acct. exec. GNA, Austin and Long Beach, Calif., 1987; regional mktg. dir. GNA, Long Beach, 1988—. Mem. Nat. Assn. Female Execs., Fin. Inst. Mktg. Assn. Republican. Roman Catholic. Office: GNA 3780 Kilroy Airport Way Ste 200 Long Beach CA 90806-2459

ENGORON, EDWARD DAVID, food service consultant, television and radio broadcaster; b. Los Angeles, Feb. 19, 1946; s. Leo and Claire (Gray) E.; m. Charlene Scott, Oct. 7, 1970 (div. July 1982). BArch., U. So. Calif., 1969, MBA, 1973, PhD, 1974; MA, Cordon Bleu, Paris, 1975. Art dir. ABC, L.A., 1964-67, Paramount Pictures, L.A., 1967-68, Warner Bros. Pictures, Burbank, Calif., 1968-69; mktg. dir. Lawry's Foods Inc., Burbank, 1969-74; v.p. Warehouse Restaurants, Marina del Rey, Calif., 1968-72; pres. Perspectives, San Francisco, 1974-82, Perspectives Comm. Syndicated Talk Shows, L.A., 1986—, China Rose Inc., Dallas, 1982-86; exec. v.p. T.G.I. Fridays Inc., Dallas, 1986-87; pres., chief exec. officer, bd. dirs. Guilt Free Goodies, Ltd., Vancouver, B.C., Can., 1986-90, Sugarless Co., L.A., 1986-90; cons. Southland Corp., Dallas, 1982-86, Pizza Hut Inc., Wichita, Kans., 1975-87, Frank L. Carney Enterprises, Wichita, 1982-87, Safeway Stores, Inc., Freemont, Calif., Romacorp, Dallas, Bel-Air Hotel Co., L.A., Capital Cities-ABC, Hollywood, Nestle Foods, White Plains, Screiber Foods, Green Bay, Rich's Food Products, Buffalo, Arby's Inc., Ft. Lauderdale, Fla., Sizzler Internat., L.A., ednl. found. Nat. Restaurant Assn., Taco Bell, Inc., Irvine, Calif., Basic Am., Inc. San Francisco, Nat. Super Markets, St. Louis, Wok Fast, Inc., L.A., The Vons Cos., L.A., 1989—; pres. Sweet Deceit, Inc., Guilt-Free Goodies, Ltd.; co-host nationally syndicated radio talk show The Super Foodies, ABC. Author: (cookbook) Stolen Secrets, 1980; patentee pasta cooking sta., 1981, micro-wave controller, 1982. Bd. govs. Los Angeles Parks, 1971-74; mem. Fine Arts Commn., Tiburon, Calif., 1974-76. Mem. Foodsvc. Cons. Soc. Internat., Soc. Motion Picture Art Dirs., Food, Wine and Travel Writers Assn., Internat. Assn. Culinary Profls., Masons. Republican. Office: 11030 Santa Monica Blvd Ste 301 Los Angeles CA 90025-7514

ENGRAV, LOREN HENRY, plastic surgeon; b. LaCrosse, Wis., Oct. 24, 1941; s. Henry Johannes and Ruby Martha (Olsen) E.; m. Candace Joan Gowan, July 24, 1965; children: Peter, Rebecca. BS, U. Calif., Davis, 1965; MD, UCLA, L.A., 1969. Resident in surgery St. Paul(Minn.)-Ramsey, 1975; resident plastic surgery U. Kans., Kansas City, 1977; faculty divsn. plastic surgery U. Wash. Sch. Medicine, Seattle, 1977—. Author: (book) Surgical Management of the Burn Wound, 1984; contbr. articles to profl. jours. Recipient Burn Rehab. Model System Grant Nat. Inst. on Disability & Rehab. Rsch., Washington, 1993. Fellow: Am. Assn. Plastic Surgeons, Am. Burn Assn., Am. Coll. Surgeons, Am. Soc. Plastic & Reconstructive Surgeons, Plastic Surgery Rsch. Coun.; mem. Alpha Omega Alpha. Office: Harborview Med Ctr 325 9th Ave Box 359796 Seattle WA 98104

ENGSTROM, ERIKA JULIE, communications educator; b. Tokyo, Japan, Sept. 20, 1964; d. Alex Joseph and Margaret Mary (Mizukami) E. BA in Radio/TV, U. Ctrl. Fla., 1984, MA in Comm., 1986; PhD in Mass Comm., U. Fla., 1991. News anchor, producer, asst. news dir. WUCF-FM, Orlando, Fla., 1984-85; tv newswriter WCPX-TV, Orlando, 1985; news anchor, producer WUFT-FM, Gainesville, Fla., 1987; grad. tchg. asst. U. Fla., Gainesville, 1986-91; asst. prof. U. Nev., Las Vegas, 1991—. Mem. Assn. for Edn. in Journalism and Mass Comm., Speech Comm. Assn., Broadcast Edn. Assn., Las Vegas Women in Comm. Home: 1851 N Green Valley Pkwy 2323 Henderson NV 89014 Office: Univ Nev 4505 S Maryland Pky Las Vegas NV 89154-9900

ENGSTROM, SALLEE FOX, retired English and elementary music educator; b. Petoskey, Mich., May 13, 1931; d. Herschel C. and Cleora M. (Beach) Fox; m. Keith D. Engstrom, June 19, 1954; children: John, Peter, Susanna. BA, Mich. State U., 1953; MA, Alfred U., 1972; PhD, U. Denver, 1994. Cert. secondary and elem. tchr., Mich., N.Y. Tchr. Enlgish, Am. govt., speech and drama DeWitt (Mich.) and Albion (Mich.) high schs., 1954-56; tchr. music Corning (N.Y.) Pub. Schs., 1968-72; elem. tchr. Green Acres Sch., Rockville, Md., 1973-76; instr. English, Corning C.C., 1977-79; lectr. comm. arts Cornell U., Ithaca, N.Y., 1981-86; tchg. asst. freshman English, U. Denver, 1988-91. Mem. AAUW. Home: 2917 S Hiwan Dr Evergreen CO 80439-8951

ENLOW, CLAIR LOU, newspaper editor, journalist; b. Woodward, Okla., Nov. 2, 1952; d. Louis Russell and Mary Lou (Williams) E.; m. Ralph Hetrick Emerson III, Oct. 3, 1976 (div. Aug. 1985); m. Donald Eugene Comstock, May 27, 1987; children: William Cropper Comstock, August Russell Comstock. BA in English, Whitman Coll., 1975; postgrad., Parsons Inst., 1980. Reporter Desert Star, Desert Sentinel, Yucca Valley, Calif., 1978-79; archtl. designer John Hueser Assocs., Kansas City, Mo., 1983-85; marketer of profl. svcs. Stafford Architects and W.H. Pacific, Seattle, 1986-90; architecture and engring. editor Seattle Daily Jour. of Commerce, Seattle, 1990—; speaker Am. Pub. Works Assn., Olympia, Wash., 1994; guest lectr. Evergreen State Coll., Olympia, 1991. Editor ann. spl. edit. newspaper Landscape, 1994; contbr. Observer Observed, 1993; editl. bd. Arcade Mag., 1993-94; contbr. over 300 articles to profl. jours. Recipient 3d place award for best bus. story Wash. Newspaper Pub.'s Assn., 1993, ASCE Chpt. Award for Excellence in Journalism, 1994. Mem. AIA (juror Tacoma chpt. design awards program 1994, profl. affiliate, hon. Seattle 1995), Soc. Mktg. Profl. Svcs. (spkr. 1994), Soc. Profl. Journalists. Democrat. Home: 3245 37th Ave S Seattle WA 98144-7013

ENNIS, KENT TAYLOR, economist; b. Dallas, June 27, 1953; s. Donald Taylor and Geneva Lee (Carpenter) E.; m. Terry Suzanne Shelby, Aug. 10, 1975 (div. Dec. 1984); m. Muriel Irma Dreyfus, Mar. 10, 1985. BA in Econ., U. Tex., 1975; MSC in Econ., London Sch. Econ., 1977. Banking officer, asst. v.p. Capital Bank, Houston, 1978-79; asst. v.p. Mercantile Nat. Bank, Dallas, 1979, v.p., 1980-85; v.p. Banque Paribas, Dallas, 1985-86; economist Comptroller of Pub. Accts., Austin, Tex., 1986-88; sr. economist Joint Budget Com, Phoenix, 1988—. Republican. Home: 7706 Via Camello del Sur Scottsdale AZ 85258 Office: 1716 W Adams St Phoenix AZ 85007-2602

ENNIS, THOMAS MICHAEL, health foundation executive; b. Morgantown, W.Va., Mar. 7, 1931; s. Thomas Edson and Violet Ruth (Nugent) E.; m. Julia Marie Dorety, June 30, 1956; children: Thomas John, Robert Griswold (dec.). Student, W.Va. U., 1949-52; AB, George Washington U., 1954; JD, Georgetown U., 1960. With Gov. Employees Ins. Co., Washington, 1956, 59, Air Transport Assn. Am., Washington, 1959-60; dir. ann. support program George Washington U., 1960-63; nat. dir. devel. Project HOPE, People to People Health Found., Inc., Washington, 1963-66; nat. exec. dir. Epilepsy Found. Am., Washington, 1966-74; exec. dir. Clinton, Eaton, Ingham Community Mental Health Bd., Lansing, Mich., 1974-83; nat. exec. dir. Alzheimer's Disease and Related Disorders Assn., Inc., Chgo., 1983-86; exec. dir., pres. French Found. for Alzheimer Rsch., Los Angeles, 1986—; clin. instr. dept. cmty. medicine and internat. health Georgetown U., 1967-74; adj. assoc. prof. dept. psychiatry Mich. State U., 1975-84; lectr. Univ. Ctr. for Internat. Rehab., 1977; cons. health and med. founds., related orgns.; cons. Am. Health Found., 1967-69, Reston, Va.-Georgetown U. Health Planning Project, 1967-70. Contbr. articles on devel. disabilities, mental health and health care to profl. jours. Mem. adv. bd. Nat. Center for the Law and the Handicapped, 1971-74; advisor Nat. Reye's Syndrome Found.; mem. Nat. Com. for Research in Neurol. Disorders, 1967-72; mem. nat. adv. bd. Developmental Disabilities/Tech. Assistance System, U. N.C., 1971-78; nat. trustee Nat. Kidney Found., 1970-74, mem. exec. com. and bd. Nat. Capitol Area chpt., pres., 1972-74; bd. dirs. Nat. Assn. Pvt. Residential Facilities for Mentally Retarded, 1970-74; bd. dirs., mem. exec. com. Epilepsy Found. Am., 1977-84, Epilepsy Center Mich., 1974-83; nat. bd. dirs. Western Inst. on Epilepsy, 1969-72; bd. dirs., pres. Mich. Mid-South Health Systems Agy., 1975-78; sec. gen. Internat. Fedn. Alzheimer's Disease and Related Disorders, 1984-86; mem. panel mem. Alzheimer's Disease Edn. and Referral Ctr., 1990—. World Rehab. Fund fellow Norway, 1980. Mem. Nat. Epilepsy League (bd. dirs. 1977-78), Mich. Assn. Cmty. Mental Health (pres. 1977-79), Nat. Coalition Rsch. Neurol. Disorders (dir. at-large 1991—), Scan Health Plan (bd. govs.), Phi Alpha Theta, Phi Kappa Psi. Office: French Found Alzheimer Rsch 11620 Wilshire Blvd Ste 820 Los Angeles CA 90025-1793

ENNIS, WILLIAM LEE, physics educator; b. Houston, Aug. 10, 1949; s. Arthur Lee and Helen Ruth Ennis; m. Constance Elizabeth Livsey, July 20, 1991. BS, Auburn (Ala.) U., 1974, BA, 1978. Rsch. tech. Nat. Tillage Lab., Auburn, Ala., 1974-76; tchr. Stanford Jr. High Sch., Hillsborough, N.C., 1979-81; physics tchr., chmn. sci. dept. East H.S., Anchorage, 1981—; chair Anchorage Sch. Dist. Physics Tchrs.; curriculum devel. sci. cons. Copper River Schs., Anchorage, 1991; sci. cons. Imaginarium, Anchorage, 1987—. Named Tandy Tech. Outstanding Tchr., 1989-90; Fermi Lab. scholar U.S. Dept. Energy, 1991. Fellow N.Y. Acad. Scis.; mem. AAAS, Am. Assn. Physics Tchrs., Am. Phys. Soc., Nat. Sci. Tchrs. Assn., Alaska Sci. Tchrs. (life). Office: East High Sch 4025 E Northern Lights Blvd Anchorage AK 99508-3588

ENNISS, LEONARD FRANKLIN, religious educator; b. Kankakee, Ill., Oct. 30, 1955; s. Leonard Franklin and Elsie Irene (Lamb) E.; m. Sharon Diane Stanfield, July 17, 1976; 1 child, Clairessa Mary Fern. ThB, Western Evang. Sch. Theology, Phoenix, 1980, MEd, 1981, PhD, 1984; BA in Religion magna cum laude, Ottawa U., Phoenix, 1992. Pres. Western Evang. Sch. Theology, Phoenix, 1981-90; provost and master regent S.W. Christian U., Phoenix, 1990-94; assoc. Nat. Inst. for Certification of Engring. Tech., Alexandria, Va., 1986—. Contbr. articles to profl. jours. Mem. Soc. of Christian Philosophers. Libertarian. Mem. Charismatic Episcopal Ch. Home: 5807 W Osborn Rd Phoenix AZ 85031-3241 Office: Southwest Christian Univ 5807 W Osborn Rd Phoenix AZ 85031-3241

ENOCH, CHARLES JOHNSON, raisin packing company executive; b. Fresno, Calif., Feb. 19, 1917, s. Charles Johnson and Mary B (Bosmajian) E.; m. Mary K. Tateosian, May 10, 1941; children—Judith (Mrs. Lee Yeramian), Charlene, Janice Enoch Wahlen. B.A., Fresno State Coll., 1939. Gen. mgr. Enoch Packing Co., Inc., Del Rey, Calif., 1939-57, pres., 1957—. Served with U.S. Army, 1944-45. Mem. Dried Fruit and Tree Nut Assn. (bd. dirs. 1976—, chmn. bd. 1985-87), Raisin Adminstrv. Commn., Calif. Raisin Adv. Bd. Presbyterian. Lodges: Elks, Lions (pres. Del Rey Club 1965).

Home: 5399 S Mccall Ave Del Rey CA 93616-9702 Office: Enoch Packing Co Inc PO Box 339 Del Rey CA 93616-0339*

ENOCH, JAY MARTIN, vision scientist, educator; b. N.Y.C., Apr. 20, 1929; s. Jerome Dee and Stella Sarah (Nathan) E.; m. Rebekah Ann Feiss, June 24, 1951; children: Harold Owen, Barbara Diane, Ann Allison. BS in Optics and Optometry, Columbia U., 1950; postgrad., Inst. Optics U. Rochester, 1953; Ph.D. in Physiol. Optics, Ohio State U., 1956; DSc honoris causa, SUNY, 1993. Asst. prof. physiol. optics Ohio State U., Columbus, 1956-58; assoc. supr. Ohio State U. (Mapping and Charting Rsch. Lab.), 1957-58; fellow Nat. Phys. Lab., Teddington, Eng., 1959-60; rsch. instr. dept. ophthalmology Washington U. Sch. Medicine, St. Louis, 1958-59, rsch. asst. prof., 1959-64, rsch. assoc. prof., 1965-70, rsch. prof., 1970-74; fellow Barnes Hosp., St. Louis, 1960-64, cons. ophthalmology, 1964-74; rsch. prof. dept. psychology Washington U., St. Louis, 1970-74; grad. rsch. prof. ophthalmology and psychology Coll. Medicine U. Fla., Gainesville, 1974-80, grad. rsch. prof. physics, 1979-80; dir. Ctr. for Sensory Studies, 1976-80; dean Sch. Optometry, chmn. Grad. Group in Vision Sci. U. Calif., Berkeley, 1980-92, prof. optometry and vision sci., mem. grad. group, 1980-94, prof. of Grad. Sch., 1994—; prof. physiol. optics in ophthalmology U. Calif., San Francisco, 1980—; chmn. subcom. contact lens stds. Am. Nat. Stds. Inst., 1970-77; mem. nat. adv. eye coun. Nat. Eye Inst., NIH, 1975-77, 80-84; exec. com., com. on vision NAS-NRC, 1973-76; mem. U.S. Nat. Com. Internat. Commn. Optics, 1976-79, health scis. com. systemwide adminstrn. U. Calif., 1989-93, co-chmn., 1993-94; mem. scientific adv. bd. Fight-for-Sight, 1988-92, scientific adv. bd. Allergan Corp., 1991-93; mem. Lighthouse for Blind, N.Y., 1989—, chair, 1995, Pisart medal com. Contbr. numerous chpts. and articles on visual sci., receptor optics, perimetry, contact lenses and infant vision to sci. jours.; contbr. chpts. in field to med. books; assoc. editor: Investigative Ophthamology, 1965-75, 83-88, Sight-Saving Rev., 1974-84, Sensory Processes, 1974-80; mem. editl. bd. Vision Rsch., 1974-80, Internat. Ophthamology, 1977-93, Binocular Vision, 1984—, Clin. Vision Sci., 1986-93, Biomed. Optics, 1988-90; mem. editl. bd. optical scis Springer-Verlag, Heidelberg, 1978-87, biomed. scis., 1988-95. Mem. nat. sci. adv. bd. Retinitis Pogmentosa Found., 1977-95; U.S. rep. Internat. Perimetric Soc., 1974-90; also exec. com., chmn. Rsch. Group Stds.; bd. dirs. Friends of Eye Rsch., 1977-88; trustee Illuminating Engring. Rsch. Inst., 1977-81; bd. dirs. Lighting Rsch. Bd., 1988—, 2d lt. U.S. Army, 1951-52. Recipient Career Devel. award NIH, 1963-73, Everett Kinsey award Contact Lens Assn. Ophthalmologists, 1991. Fellow AAAS, Am. Acad. Optometry (Glenn A. Fry award 1972, Charles F. Prentice medal award 1974), Optical Soc. Am. (chmn. vision tech. sect. 1974-76), Am. Acad. Ophthalmology (honor award 1985); mem. Assn. for Research in Vision and Ophthalmology (trustee 1967-73, pres. 1972-73, Francis I. Proctor medal 1977), Concilium Ophthalmologicum Universale (chmn. visual functions com. 1982-86), Am. Optometric Assn. (low vision sect., Vision Care award 1987), Sigma Xi. Home: 54 Shuey Dr Moraga CA 94556-2621 Office: U Calif Sch of Optometry Berkeley CA 94720-2020

ENOS, THERESA, English educator, editor; b. Arlington, Tex.; d. Russell Hascal Jarnagin and Edna Leta (Blackburn) King; m. Arthur G. Enos, June 25, 1964 (div. Aug. 1987); children: Mark Young, Michele Rayburn, Brennan. BA, Tex. Christian U., 1973, PhD, 1980; MA, Baylor U., 1975. Asst. prof. So. Meth. U., Dallas, 1980-87; assoc. prof. U. Ariz., Tucson, 1987—. Editor: (book) Sourcebook for Basic Writing Teachers, 1987, Defining the New Rhetorics, 1992, Professing the New Rhetorics, 1993; founder, editor Rhetoric Rev., 1982— (Best Jour. Design award 1985). Grantee So. Meth. U., 1983, Exxon Edn., 1986, Coun. Writing Program Adminstrn., 1991, U. Ariz., 1990. Mem. Nat. Coun. Tchrs. English (coll. sect. officer 1993-97, rep. Conf. Coll. Composition and Comm. 1993-97), Conf. Coll. Composition and Comm. (exec. com. 1990-93), Coun. Writing Program Adminstrn. (bd. dirs. 1992-95, publicity chair 1992-95, bd. cons./evaluators 1989—), Rhetoric Soc. Am. Episcopalian. Office: Univ of Arizona Dept of English Tucson AZ 85721

ENRIGHT, CYNTHIA LEE, illustrator; b. Denver, July 6, 1950; d. Darrel Lee and Iris Arlene (Flodquist) E. BA in Elem. Edn., U. No. Colo., 1972; student, Minn. Sch. Art and Design, Mpls., 1975-76. Tchr. 3d grade Littleton (Colo.) Sch. Dist., 1972-75; graphics artist Sta. KCNC TV, Denver, 1978-79; illustrator No Coast Graphics, Denver, 1979-87; editorial artist The Denver Post, 1987—. Illustrator (mag.) Sesame St., 1984, 95; illustrator, editor "Tiny Tales" The Denver Post, 1991-94. Recipient Print mag. Regional Design Ann. awards, 1984, 85, 87, Phoenix Art Mus. Biannual award, 1979. Mem. Mensa. Democrat. Home: 1210 Ivanhoe St Denver CO 80220-2640 Office: The Denver Post 1560 Broadway Denver CO 80202-5133

ENRIQUEZ, CAROLA RUPERT, museum director; b. Washington, Jan. 2, 1954; d. Jack Burns and Shirley Ann (Orcutt) Rupert; m. John Enriquez, Jr., Dec. 30, 1989. BA in history cum laude, Bryn Mawr Coll., 1976; MA, U. Del., 1978, cert. in mus. studies, 1978. Personnel mgmt. trainee Naval Material Command, Arlington, Va., 1972-76; teaching asst. dept. history, U. Del., Newark, 1976-77; asst. curator/exhibit specialist Hist. Soc. Del., Wilmington, 1977-78; dir. Macon County Mus. Complex, Decatur, Ill., 1978-81; dir. Kern County Mus., Bakersfield, Calif., 1981—; pres. Kern County Mus. Found., 1991—; advisor Kern County Heritage Commn., 1981-88; chmn. Historic Records Commn., 1981-88; sec.-treas. Arts Council of Kern, 1984-86, pres. 1986-88; county co-chmn. United Way, 1981, 82; chmn. steering com. Calif. State Bakersfield Co-op Program, 1982-83; mem. Community Adv. Bd. Calif. State Bakersfield, Anthrop. Soc., 1986-88; bd. dirs. Mgmt. Council, 1983-86, v.p., 1987, pres. 1988; bd. dirs. Calif. Council for Promotion of History, 1984-86, v.p., 1987-88. pres., 1988-90; mem. community adv. bd. Calif. State U.-Bakersfield Sociology Dept., 1986-88; mem. women's adv. com. Girl Scouts U.S., 1989-91; bd. dirs. Greater Bakersfield Conv. and Visitors Bur., 1993—; co-chair 34th St. Neighborhood Partnership, 1994—. Hagley fellow Eleutherian Mills-Hagley Found., 1977-78; Bryn Mawr alumnae regional scholar, 1972-76. Mem. Calif. Assn. Mus. (regional rep. 1991—, v.p. legis. affairs 1992—), Am. Assn. for State and Local History (chair awards com. Calif. chpt. 1990—), Exces. Assn. Kern County. Unitarian Universalist. Office: Kern County Museum 3801 Chester Ave Bakersfield CA 93301-1345

ENSIGN, DONALD DALE, art director; b. Bellingham, Wash., May 26, 1948; s. William Russell and Lucille Winifred (Holden) E. BA in Art, Western Wash. U., 1970. Assoc. art dir. Campus Crusade for Christ Internat., San Bernardino, Calif., 1976-80, art dir., 1980-82; art dir. Naramore Christian Found., Rosemead, Calif., 1982—; chmn. bd. dirs. Christian Comic Arts Soc., South Pasadena, Calif., 1984-94; founder Good Name Enterprises, 1994. Editor: (newsletter) Valiant, 1984; pub. (book) Emerald Light, 1995. Campaign worker John Paul Stark for Congress, San Bernardino, 1978, 80, 82, Reagan for Pres., San Bernardino, 1976, Bill Hoge for State Assembly, Pasadena, Calif., 1992. Mem. New Eng. Hist. Genealogical Soc., British Isle Family History Soc. L.A., San Gabriel Valley MacIntosh Users Group, Alpha Omega (founder 1985). Republican. Congregationalist. Home: 1120 Buena Vista St South Pasadena CA 91030-1708 Office: Narramore Christian Found 1409 Walnut Grove Ave Rosemead CA 91770-3709

ENSIGN, DONALD H., landscape architect; b. Salt Lake City, Sept. 5, 1936; s. C. Wesley and Mildred (Harker) E.; m. Kay Bateman, Sept. 9, 1959 (div. 1970); m. Nancy Ensign; children: Philip Wesley, Craig Allen, Michael Donald. B in Landscape Architecture, Utah State U., 1963; M in Landscape Architecture, U. Mich., 1968. Registered landscape architect, Mich., N.C. Landscape architect Frehner and Assocs., Salt Lake City, 1961-62; planner Roswell/Ensign and Assocs., Salt Lake City, 1962-66; instr. dept. landscape architecture and environ. planning Utah State U., Logan, 1963-66; planner Richard B. Wilkinson and Assocs., Ann Arbor, Mich., 1966-68; prin. Design Workshop, Inc., Aspen, Colo., 1970—; assoc. prof. sch. design N.C. State U., 1968-74, dir. basic design program, 1971-73. Prin. works include Aspen Inst., Grand Valley High Sch., Marolt Ranch, U. Mich., Utah State U., Estrella Lake Parks, Goodyear, Ariz., Fox River, Geneva, Ill., Lauder Residence, Aspen, Resort at Squaw Creek, Squaw Valley, Calif., 700 East Main, Aspen, Snowmass (Colo.) Club, Blackcomb Resort, Whistler, British Columbia, Early Winters Resort, Mazama, Wash., Grand Champions Resort, Aspen, many others. Office: Design Workshop 120 E Main St Aspen CO 81611-1714

ENSLOW, MEL DENNIS, fire chief; b. St. Joseph, Mo., Oct. 7, 1941; s. Earl Ernest and Daisy Evelyn (Lanning) E.; m. Valerie J. Maclean, Mar. 2, 1962; children: Katherine, Karen, Kenneth. Cert. tchr. fire tactics and strategy, arson investigation. Millwright Kaiser Steel Plant, Fontana, Calif., 1960-63; firefighter Fontana Fire Dept., 1963-68, engr., 1968-73, capt., 1973-78; battalion chief/fire marshall San Bernardino County, Fontana, 1978-86, asst. fire chief, 1986-88, dep. fire chief, 1988-91; fire chief Redlands (Calif.) Fire Dept., 1991—; pres. San Bernardino (Calif.) County Arson Investigator, 1975-76; chmn. Confire Joint Powers Authority, San Bernardino County, 1991—. Author: (working program) Citation Program for Fire Inspectors, 1974, Cost Recovery of Fire Suppression, 1993, Civic Leader Tour of Working Fire Stations, 1994; co-author: (working program) Juvenile Firesetter Counseling Program, 1979. Bd. dirs. Redlands Cmty. Music Assn., 1995. Mem. Rotary. Office: Redlands Fire Dept 2 E Cajon Ave Redlands CA 92373

ENTRIKEN, ROBERT KERSEY, management educator; b. McPherson, Kans., Jan. 15, 1913; s. Frederick Kersey and Opal (Birch) E.; m. Elizabeth Freeman, May 26, 1940 (div. Nov. 1951); children—Robert Kersey, Jr., Edward Livingston Freeman, Richard Davis; m. Jean Finch, June 5, 1954; 1 child, Birch Nelson. B.A., U. Kans. 1934; M.B.A., Golden Gate U., 1961; postgrad. City Univ. Grad. Bus. Sch., London, 1971-73. C.P.C.U. Ins. broker, Houston, Tex. and McPherson, Kans., 1935-39; asst. mgr. Cravens, Dargan & Co., Houston, 1939-42; br. mgr. Nat. Surety Corp., Memphis and San Francisco, 1942-54; v.p. Fireman's Fund Ins. Co., San Francisco. 1954-73; adj. prof. Golden Gate U., San Francisco, 1953-73, prof. mgmt., 1974-89; resident dean Asia Programs, Singapore, 1987-88; prof. emeritus 1989—, underwriting mem. Lloyd's of London, 1985—. Contbr. articles to trade and profl. jours. Bd. dirs., sec., treas. Northstar Property Owners Assn., Calif., 1982-86. Served to capt. USNR, 1941-73, ret., 1973. Mem. Ins. Forum San Francisco (pres. 1965, trustee 1975-78, 84-88), Surety Underwriters Assn. No. Calif. (pres. 1956), CPCU Soc. (pres. No. Calif. chpt. 1957, Ins. Profl. of Yr., San Francisco chpt. 1981, bd. dirs., 1989-93), Chartered Ins. Inst., Ins. Inst. London, Musicians' Union Local No. 6 (life), U.S. Naval Inst., Assn. Naval Aviation, Phi Delta Theta. Episcopalian. Clubs: University, Marines' Meml. (San Francisco); Commonwealth. Lodge: Naval Order U.S. Office: 109 Minna St Ste 525 San Francisco CA 94105-3728

ENYART, GREGORY LEONARD, art dealer; b. Hollywood, Calif., June 21, 1960; s. Jack Warren and Mary Elizabeth (Leonard) E.; m. Diana Lynn Carr, Nov. 4, 1984. AA, Monterey Peninsula Coll., 1991. Cert. yoga instr., Calif. Tchr. various schs., Carmel, Calif., 1987—; art gallery owner Carmel, 1993—; lectr. Ctr. for Photography, Carmel, 1994. Dir., writer: (film) A Cowboy's Guide to Foreign Films, 1991 (award 1993). Vol. Planned Parenthood, Monterey, 1994. Winner Best Art Gallery award Coast Weekly News, Monterey, 1994.

ENZI, MICHAEL BRADLEY, accountant, state legislator; b. Bremerton, Wash., Feb. 1, 1944; s. Elmer Jacob and Dorothy (Bradley) E.; m. Diana Buckley, June 7, 1969; children: Amy, Bradley, Emily. BBA, George Wash. U., 1966; MBA, Denver U., 1968. Cert. profl. human resources, 1994. Pres. NZ Shoes, Inc., Gillette, Wyo., 1969—, NZ Shoes of Sheridan, Inc., Wyo., 1983-91; acctg. mgr. Dunbar Well Svc., Inc., Gillette, 1985—; mem. Wyo. Ho. of Reps., Cheyenne, 1987-91, Wyo. State Senate, Cheyenne, 1991—; chmn. bd. dirs. 1st Wyo. Bank, Gillette, 1978-88; bd. dirs. Black Hills Corp., chmn. Senate Revenue Com., 1992—. Mayor City of Gillette, 1975-82; pres. Wyo. Assn. Mcpls., Cheyenne, 1980-82. Sgt. Wyo. Air NG, 1967-73. Mem. Wyo. Order of DeMolay (state master councilor 1963-64), Wyo. Jaycees (state pres. 1973-74), Masons (Sheridan and Gillette lodges), Scottish Rite, Shriners, Lions. Republican. Presbyterian. Home: 431 Circle Dr Gillette WY 82716 Office: Dunbar Well Svc Inc PO Box 1209 Gillette WY 82717-1209

EPCAR, RICHARD MICHAEL, actor, writer, director; b. Denver, Apr. 29, 1955; s. George Buck and Shirley (Learner) E.; m. Ellyn Jane Stern, Aug. 15, 1982; children: Jonathan Alexander, Jacqueline Elizabeth. BFA in Performing Arts, U. Ariz., 1978; postgrad., U. So. Calif., L.A., 1980, U. Calif., L.A., 1981, Am. Film Inst., 1982. Pres. Trouble Shooter Prodns., L.A., 1986—. Actor (films) including Memoirs of an Invisible Man, D.C. Collins, Incident of War, Street Hawk, Escape to Love, Not of This World, (TV series) Beverly Hills 90210, Cheers, General Hospital, Guns of Paradise, Matlock, Who's the Boss?, Sonny Spoons, Moonlighting, Highway to Heaven, Amazing Stories, Fast Times, Crazy Like a Fox, Hell Town, Stir Crazy, Santa Barbara, (on stage) Why a Hero, Dracula, An Evening With Lincoln, Real Inspector Hound, Richard II; actor, writer (play) (on stage) Take My Wife...Please!, 1980; wrote and directed English adaptation of Acad. award winning Cinema Paradiso, Women on the Verge of a Nervous Breakdown (Acad. award nomination); dir. (for TV) A Cowboy Christmas. Mem. L.A. Zoo Assn., 1983-90, 91, 94, Natural History Mus., L.A., 1989-91, Earth Save, L.A., 1990, L.A. Mus. Art, 1991; host fall festival Sta. KCET-Pub. TV, L.A., 1980; active Am. Cancer Soc. Recipient Haldeman Found. scholarship, U. Ariz., 1973-78; named Nat. Best Actor of Yr., Nat. Players, 1977, CPC Repertory Group, 1980; recipient Irene Ryan Soloist award, 1978. Office: Trouble Shooter Prodns PO Box 5429 North Hollywood CA 91616-5429

EPPELE, DAVID LOUIS, columnist, author; b. Jersey City, Apr. 4, 1939; s. Joseph Anton and Lena Marie (Tadlock) E.; m. Gladys Emily Padilla (div. 1975); children: David D., Joseph E.; m. Geneva Mae Kirsch, July 7, 1977. Student, N.Mex. State U., 1958, U. N.Mex., 1966, U. Portland, 1972. Field botanist SW Deserts and Mex., 1947-95, N.Mex. Cactus Rsch., Belen, 1953-62; dir. Ariz. Cactus and Succulent Rsch., Bisbee, 1984—; editor Ariz. Cactus News, 1984—; columnist Western Newspapers, 1987—. Author (newspaper column) On the Desert, 1986—; author: On the Desert, 1991; editor: Index of Cactus Illustrations, 1990, Desert in Bloom, 1989. Mem. Mule Mountain Dem. Party, Bisbee, 1978—. With USN, 1958-59. Mem. AAAS, Cactus and Succulent Soc. Am., N.Mex. Acad. Sci., Bisbee C. of C., Cochise County Hist. and Archaeology Soc. Home and Office: Ariz Cactus 8 Cactus Ln Bisbee AZ 85603-9754

EPPERSON, ERIC ROBERT, financial executive, film producer; b. Oregon City, Oreg., Dec. 10, 1949; s. Robert Max and Margaret Joan (Crawford) E.; m. Lyla Gene Harris, Aug. 21, 1969; 1 child, Marcie. B.S., Brigham Young U., 1973, M.Acctg., 1974; M.B.A., Golden Gate U., 1977, J.D., 1981. Instr. acctg. Brigham Young U., Provo, Utah, 1973-74; supr. domestic taxation Bechtel Corp., San Francisco, 1974-78; supr. internat. taxation Bechtel Power Corp., San Francisco, 1978-80; mgr. internat. tax planning Del Monte Corp., San Francisco, 1980-82, mgr. internat. taxes, 1982-85; internat. tax specialist Touche Ross & Co., San Francisco, 1985-87; dir. internat. tax Coopers & Lybrand, Portland, 1987-89; exec. v.p., chief fin. officer Epperson Dayton Sorenson Prodns., Inc., Salt Lake City, 1989-90, Epperson Prodns., 1990-92; exec. dir. The Oreg. Trail Found., Inc., Oregon City, 1992-93; pres. MFD Ltd., Portland, Oreg., 1993—. Author: (with T. Gilbert) Interfacing of the Securities and Exchange Commission with the Accounting Profession: 1968 to 1973, 1974; producer (motion picture) Gathering Evidence, 1995; exec. producer (motion picture) Dream Machine, 1989. Scoutmaster, Boy Scouts Am., Provo, 1971-73, troop committeeman, 1973-74, 83—; mem. IRS Vol. Income Tax Assistance Program, 1972-75; pres. Mut. Improvement Assn., Ch. Jesus Christ of Latter-day Saints, 1972-74, pres. Sunday sch., 1977-79, tchr., 1974-80, ward clk., 1980-83, bishopric, 1983-87; bd. dirs. Oreg. Art Inst. Film Ctr., Oreg. Trail Coordinating Coun., Hist. Preservation League of Oreg.; vice chmn. ranch devel. com. Boy Scouts Am., Butte Creek. Mem. World Affairs Coun., Japan/Am. Soc., Internat. Tax Planning Assn., Internat. Fiscal Assn., Oreg. Trail Coordinating Coun. (exec. bd.), Oreg. Hist. Soc., U.S. Rowing Assn., Oreg. Calif. Trail Assn., Commonwealth Club. Republican. Office: 25-6 NW 23rd Ave # 180 Portland OR 97210-3518

EPPERSON, VAUGHN ELMO, civil engineer; b. Provo, Utah, July 20, 1917; s. Lawrence Theophilus and Mary Loretta (Pritchett) E.; m. Margaret Ann Stewart Hewlett, Mar. 4, 1946; children: Margaret Ann Epperson Hill, Vaughn Hewlett, David Hewlett, Katherine (Mrs. Franz S. Amussen), Lawrence Stewart. BS, U. Utah, 1953. With Pritchett Bros. Constrn. Co., Provo, 1949-50; road design engr. Utah State Road Commn., Salt Lake City, 1951-53, bridge design engr., 1953-54; design engr. Kennecott Copper Corp., Salt Lake City, 1954-60, office engr., 1960-62, sr. engr., 1962, assigned concentrator plant engr., 1969-73, assigned concentrator project engr., 1973-78; cons. engr. Vaughn Epperson Engring. Service, Salt Lake City, 1978-87; project engr. Newbery-State Inc., Salt Lake City, 1980, geneal. computerized research programs, 1983-88, ancestral file programs family history dept. Ch. Jesus Christ of Latter-Day Saints, 1989—. Scoutmaster Troop 190, Salt Lake City, 1949-51. Served to capt. AUS, 1941-45; maj. N.G., 1951; col. Utah State Guard, 1952-70. Decorated Army Commendation medal; recipient Service award Boy Scouts Am., 1949, Community Service award United Fund, 1961, Service award VA Hosp., Salt Lake City, 1977. Mem. ASCE, Am. Soc. Mil. Engrs., Sons of Utah Pioneers. Republican. Mormon. Home: 1537 Laird Ave Salt Lake City UT 84105-1729

EPSTEIN, MELVIN, engineering educator; b. N.Y.C., July 17, 1930; s. Paul and Rose Diana (Korenman) E.; m. Marie Wallner, Dec. 22, 1951 (div. 1974); children: David Sidney, Nancy Epstein; m. Joyce Brenner, Apr. 29, 1979 (div. 1984); m. Golda Freedman, July 17, 1990. BS, NYU, 1951; MS, MIT, 1953; PhD, Poly. Inst. Bklyn., 1959. Sr. aerodynamicist Rep. Aviation Corp., Farmingdale, N.Y., 1955-56; rsch. scientist Gen. Applied Sci. Labs., Hempstead, N.Y., 1956-59, U. So. Calif., L.A., 1959-61; sr. staff scientist Aerospace Corp., El Segundo, Calif., 1961-81; prof. Calif. State U., Northridge, 1981—; chair Pen-X Com., Washington, 1963; mem. adv. com. Instnl. Media Ctr., Northridge, 1985-92. Prodr., dir. documentary film The Spark, 1975. 1st lt. USAF, 1953-55. Fellow AIAA (assoc.); mem. Internat. Interactive Comms. Soc., Am. Phys. Soc. Office: Calif State U 18111 Nordhoff St Northridge CA 91330-0001

EPSTEIN, NORMAN RICHARD, internist; b. N.Y.C., May 2, 1947; s. Benjamin and Ann (Stevens) E.; m. Margaret Mary Ann Pope, Sept. 23, 1980; 1 child, Evan David. BA, N.Y.U., 1960, MD, SUNY Downstate Med Ctr., Bklyn., 1972. cert. Internal Medicine. Internist El Rio Neighborhood Health Ctr., Tucson, 1975-89; med. dir. CIGNA Healthcare of Ariz., Tucson, 1980-87, v.p., 1984-87, internist, 1980—. Bd. dirs. Tucson Loan Chest, 1992-95. Recipient Physicians Recognition award AMA, 1979, 82, 87, 90, 93. Mem. Am. Coll. Physicians, Am. Coll. Physician Execs., Am. Soc. Clin. Hypnosis, Physicians for Social Responsibility, Sierra Club, Nature Conservancy. Office: CIGNA Healthcare of Ariz 535 N Wilmot Tucson AZ 85711

EPSTEIN, WILLIAM LOUIS, dermatologist, educator; b. Cleve., Sept. 6, 1925; s. Norman N. and Gertrude (Hirsch) E.; m. Joan Goldman, Jan. 29, 1954; children—Wendy, Steven. A.B., U. Calif., Berkeley, 1949, M.D., 1952. Mem. faculty U. Calif., San Francisco, 1957—; assoc. prof. div. dermatology U. Calif., 1963-69, prof. div. dermatology, 1969—, dir. dermatol. rsch., 1957-70, acting chmn. div. dermatology, 1966-69, chmn. dept. dermatology, 1970-85; cons. dermatology Outpatient Dept.; cons. various hosps. Calif. Dept. Public Health; cons. Food and Drug Adminstrn., Washington, 1972—, Dept. Agriculture, 1979; dir. div. research Nat. Program Dermatology, 1970-73; Dohi lectr., Tokyo, 1982; Beecham lectr., 1988-89; Nippon Boehringer Ingelheim lectr. 18th Hakone Symposium on Respiration, Japan, 1990. Mem. AAAS, AMA, Am. Soc. Cell Biology, Am. Acad. Dermatology and Syphlology (nominating com. 1984), Pacific Dermatologic Assn., Am. Fedn. Clin. Rsch., Soc. Investigative Dermatology (bd. dirs., pres. 1985), Am. Dermatol. Assn., Assn. Profs. Dermatology (sr. mem.), Dermatology Found. (pres. 1986-87), Phi Beta Kappa, Sigma Xi. Home: 267 Golden Hinde Passage Corte Madera CA 94925-1953

ERB, RICHARD LOUIS LUNDIN, resort and hotel executive; b. Chgo., Dec. 23, 1929; s. Louis Henry and Miriam (Lundin) E.; m. Jean Elizabeth Easton, Mar. 14, 1959; children: John Richard, Elizabeth Anne, James Easton, Richard Louis. BA, U. Calif.-Berkeley, 1951, postgrad., 1952; student, San Francisco Art Inst., 1956. Cert. hotel adminstr. Asst. gen. mgr. Grand Teton Lodge Co., Jackson Hole, Wyo., 1954-62; mgr. Mauna Kea Beach Hotel, Hawaii, 1964-66; v.p., gen. mgr. Caneel Bay Plantation, Inc., St. John, V.I., 1966-75; gen. mgr. Williamsburg (Va.) Inn, 1975-78; exec. v.p., gen. mgr. Seabrook Island Co., Johns Island, S.C., 1978-80; v.p., dir. hotels Sands Hotel and Casino, Inc., Atlantic City, 1980-81; v.p., gen. mgr. Disneyland Hotel, Anaheim, Calif., 1981-82; COO Grand Traverse Resort, Grand Traverse Village, Mich., 1982-93; gen. mgr. Stein Eriksen Lodge, Deer Valley, Utah, 1993—; pres. Spruce-Park Mgmt. Co., 1989; mem. adv. bd. travel and tourism Mich. State U., 1992—; vice chmn. Charleston (S.C.) Tourism Coun., 1979-81; bd. dirs. Anaheim Visitors and Conv. Bur., 1981-82, Grand Traverse Conv. and Visitors Bur., 1985-90, U.S. 131 Area Devel. Assn., 1983-93; assoc. Cayuga Hospitality Advisers, 1993—; hosp. adv. bd. Utah Valley State U. Contbr. articles to trade jours. Vice-pres. V.I. Montessori Sch., 1969-71, bd. dirs., 1968-76; bd. dirs. Coll. of V.I., 1976-79; adv. bd. U. S.C., 1978-82, Calif. State Poly. Inst., 1981-82, Orange Coast C.C., 1981-82, Northwestern Mich. Coll., 1983-93; adv. bd. hospitality mgmt. program Ea. Mich. U., 1989-93; trustee Munson Med. Ctr., Traverse City, 1985-93; bd. dirs. Traverse Symphony Orch., 1984-88, N.A. Vasa, 1987-89; adv. panel Mich. Communities of Econ. Excellence Program, 1984-88; mem. hospitality adv. bd. Utah Valley State Coll., 1994—. Lt. arty. U.S. Army, 1952-54. Named hon. prof. Mich. State U. Hotel Sch., 1992—. Fellow Edn. Inst. (trustee 1988-92); mem. Am. Hotel and Motel Assn. (dir. 1975-77, , 90-94, exec. bd. 1991-94, Service Merit award 1976, Lawson Odde award 1993, Gold Medalist Membership award 1993, trustee Ednl. Inst. 1977-83, mktg. com., exec. com. 1978-83, chmn. projects and programs com. 1982-83, AH&MA resort com. 1986—, AH&MA condominium com. 1985—, chmn. ratings com. 1988—, Ambassador award 1986, Blue Ribbon task force 1988-89, Resort Exec. of Yr. 1988, Hotelier of Yr., 1991, Lawson Odde award 1993), Caribbean Hotel Assn. (1st v.p. 1972-74, dir. 1970-76, hon. life mem., Extraordinary Service Merit award 1974), V.I. Hotel Assn. (pres. chmn. bd. 1971-76, Merit award 1973), Calif. Hotel Assn. (dir. 1981-82), Caribbean Travel Assn. (dir. 1972-74), Internat. Hotel Assn. (dir. 1971-73), S.C. Hotel Assn. (dir. 1978-82), Am. Hotel Assn. Edn. Inst., (Lamp of Knowledge award 1988), Va. Hotel Assn., Williamsburg Hotel Assn. (bd. dirs. 1975-78), Atlantic City Hotel Assn. (v.p. 1981-82), Cornell Soc. Hotelmen, Mich. Travel and Tourist Assn. (bd. dirs. 1983-94, treas. 1986, sec. 1987, v.p. 1988, mktg. com. 1986-93, govtl. affairs com. 1986-93, chmn. edn. com. 1983-84, chmn. bd. 1989-90, Mich. Hotelier of Yr. 1991), Mich. Restaurant Assn. (bd. dirs. 1989-91, chmn. adminstrv. com. 1989-90), Mich. Gov.'s Task Force on Tourism, 1986-87, Grand Island Adv. Commn., Grand Traverse C. of C. (bd. dirs. 1984-89), Nat. Restaurant Assn., Mich. Restaurant Assn. (bd. dirs. 1989-90), Utah Hotel and Motel Assn. (bd. dirs. 1994—), Leadership Grand Traverse (exec. com. 1984-92, fellow 1992), Park City Lodging Assn. (bd. dirs. 1993—), Park City C. of C. (bd. dirs. 1994—), Tavern Club, Golden Horseshoe Club, German Club, Greate Bay Club, Seabrook Island Club, Kiawah Island Club, Grand Traverse Resort Club, Rotary (Paul Harris fellow 1990), Beta Theta Pi. Congregationalist.

ERBURU, ROBERT F., media and information company executive; b. Ventura, Calif., Sept. 27, 1930. BA, U. So. Calif., 1952; JD, Harvard U. Law Sch., 1955. Chmn. bd., CEO, pres. Times Mirror Co., L.A., also bd. dirs.; bd. dirs. Tejon Ranch Co., Cox Comm., Inc. Trustee Nat. Gallery of Art; chmn. bd. trustees J. Paul Getty Trust, Huntington Library, Art Collections and Bot. Gardens, trustee, 1981—; dir. Tomas Rivera Ctr.; mem. Villa I Tatti Coun.-Harvard U. Ctr. Italian Renaissance Studies, Florence, Italy; hon. trustee Brookings Instn., past trustee; bd. dirs. LA. World Affairs Coun.; dir. Fed. Reserve Bank of San Francisco (chmn. 1989-91), life dir. Ind. Colls. Southern Calif.; dir. YMCA Met. L.A., 1973-91; mem. archdiocesan fin. coun. Cath. Archdiocese L.A.; bd. dirs. Flora and William Hewlett Found., 1980—, Carrie Estelle Doheny Found., Fletcher Jones Found., 1982—, Ralph M. Parsons Found., 1985—, Times Mirror Found., Pfaffinger Found., 1974—; Ahmanson Found. Mem. Newspaper Assn. Am. (bd. govs., exec. bd., exec. com., bd. dirs. 1980-92, officer 1988-92, chmn. 1991-92), Coun. Fgn. Rels. (bd. dirs.), Calif. Bus. Roundtable, Bus. Coun., past dir. C of C of U.S., L.A. Area C of C. Home: 1518 Blue Jay Way Los Angeles CA 90069-1215 Office: Times Mirror Co Times Mirror Sq Los Angeles CA 90053*

ERDEN, SYBIL ISOLDE, artist; b. N.Y.C., Nov. 30, 1950; d. Mark and Annelise (Stautner) E.; m. Philip M. Freund, July 7, 1970 (div. 1978); m. Jerry Buley, June 15, 1991. Student, Acad. of Art, San Francisco, 1970-71, San Francisco Art Inst., 1971-73, Ariz. State U., 1992-93. lectr. Calif. Coll. Arts and Crafts, 1978, Tempe Fine Art Ctr., 1985, Collins Gallery, San Francisco, 1986, Collage Art Appreciation Group, Colorado Springs, Colo., 1987, South Park Sch. Dist., Fairplay, Colo., 1987, Al Collins Sch. Graphic Design, 1989-90, Cerro Coso C.C., Calif., 1991, Chico State U., 1991; tchr.

workshops City of Phoenix, 1991, Cerro Coso C.C., 1991, Phoenix Coll., 1992—, Cochise Coll., 1993; guest speaker 6th ann. Tempe Art Ctr. Seminar for Artists, 1993, Mesa C.C., 1994—, Gilbert/Chandler C.C., 1995. Shows include San Francisco Art Inst., 1973, The Bush Street Gallery, San Francisco, 1977, The Top Floor Gallery, San Francisco, 1979, I-Beam, San Francisco, 1980, Diablo Valley Coll., Walnut Creek, Calif., 1980, The Stable, San Francisco, 1982, Tempe Fine Arts Ctr., 1985, Collins Gallery, San Francisco, 1986, 89, 90—, Berkeley (Calif.) Art Ctr., 1986, The Cave, San Francisco, 1981, Alwun House, Phoenix, 1985, 87-93 (award 1989), Grand Canyon Coll., Phoenix, 1988, N.Mex. Jr. Coll., 1988, 90 (award 1990), San Francisco State U., 1988, Pa. State U., 1989, Ohio State U., 1989, Mendocino Art Ctr., 1990, Jewish Cmty. Ctr., Denver, 1990, Cerro Coso Cmty. Coll., Kern County, Calif., 1990-91, Chico State U., 1991, Sierra Arts Found., 1991, Ea. N.Mex. U., 1992, Shemer Art Ctr., Phoenix, 1991, Chico (Calif.) State U., 1992, Sierra Arts Found., Reno, Nev., 1992, Movemiento Artistico del Rio Salado Artspace, 1993—, IOA Artspace, Oklahoma City, Okla., 1995; executed mural office of Dr. Peter Eckman, San Francisco, 1977, HandBall Express, San Francsico, 1981; archived by Smithsonian Mus. Archive Am. Art, Washington. Mem. Am. Surrealist Initiative, Ariz. Visionary Alternative (founder, dir. 1984-85, 87—), Movemiento Artistico del Rio Salado Artspace (artist mem.). Democrat. Jewish.

ERDMANN, JOACHIM CHRISTIAN, physicist; b. Danzig, June 5, 1928; s. Franz Werner and Maria Magdalena (Schreiber) E.; doctorate Tech. U. Braunschweig (Germany), 1958; m. Ursula Maria Wedemeyer, Aug. 24, 1957; children—Michael Andreas, Thomas Christian, Maria Martha Dorothea. Physicist, Osram Labs., Augsburg, Germany, 1954-60; sr. research scientist Boeing Sci. Research Labs., Seattle, 1960-72; sr. research scientist Boeing Aerospace Co., Seattle, 1972-73; prin. engr. Boeing Comml. Airplane Co., Seattle, 1973-81, sr. prin. engr., 1981-84; sr. prin. engr. Boeing Aerospace, Seattle, 1984—; vis. prof. Max Planck Inst. for Metals Research, Stuttgart, Germany, 1968-69; lectr. Tech. U. Stuttgart, 1968-69; pres. Optologics Inc., Seattle, 1973—. Mem. Am. Phys. Soc., Optical Soc. Am., Soc. Photo Optical Instrumentation Engrs. Author: Heat Conduction in Crystals, 1969. Contbr. articles to profl. jours. Research in cryogenics, statis. physics and opto electronics. Home: 14300 Trillium Blvd SE Apt 8 Bothell WA 98012-1313 Office: Boeing Def and Space Group PO Box 3999 Seattle WA 98124-2499

EREKSON, LAURIE IDA, school administrator; b. San Jose, Calif., Jan. 10, 1957; d. Harry and Geraldine Anne (Caliri) Copelan; m. Scott Erekson; children: Scott R., Nicholas J., Daniel R. BS in History with honors, Portland State U., 1982; MPA, Lewis & Clark Coll., 1993, cert. in ednl. adminstrn., 1993. Math. and sci. team leader, math. tchr. Parrish Mid. Sch.-Salem (Oreg.) Sch. Dist., 1984-91, math. counts coach, 1986-91; math. tchr. Mountain View Intermediate Sch.-Beaverton (Oreg.) Sch. Dist., 1983-84; sch. adminstr. Richmond Elem. Sch., 1993-94, Waldo Mid. Sch., 1994—; del. Oreg. Math. Leaders, 1990; com. mem. Mid. Sch. Improvement Process and implementation, Salem, 1990-94; mem. task force gifted and talented, 1994; trainer and presenter in field. Author: Mathematics Laboratory, 1985, The Seeds of Change: An Interdisciplinary Unit on the Cultural Encounter of 1492, 1992, Interdisciplinary Teaming: A Guide for Teachers and Principals, 1992, Interdisciplinary Teaming: The Centerpiece for Middle School Restructuring, 1993. Mem. Boys and Girls Aid Soc., Salem, 1991-94; planner, trainer, presenter Expanding Your Horizons Conf., 1987-95. Mem. ASCD, AAUW, N.W. Women in Adminstrn., Confedn. Oreg. Sch. Adminstrs., Oreg. Mid. Level Assn., Nat. Mid. Sch. Assn. Home: 5056 Cindy Pl SE Salem OR 97306-1709

EREM, SIMON SHIMON, economist, researcher; b. Kaunas, Lithuania, Feb. 27, 1922; came to U.S., 1970; s. Moshe and Riva (Regensberg) E.; m. May Zerubavel, Mar. 31, 1949 (div. 1969); children: Tsabar, Iris; m. Danielle Nelson Lederberg, Nov. 13, 1970; children: Roy Jordan, Vivian, Sharon. MSc, Hebrew U., Jerusalem, 1947; diploma, Coll. of Polit. Sci., 1956. Gen. mgr. TNUFA, Tel-Aviv, 1956-60, Dizengoff West Africa, Ibadan, Nigeria, 1960-64, Mesurado Fishing Co., Lagos, Nigeria, 1964-66; pres. Hotels & Vacation Ctrs., Tel-Aviv, 1966-70; sec., treas. AMI, L.A., 1971-73; pres. Strategic Studies West, L.A., 1973—; chmn. Ctr. for Strategic Studies West, L.A., 1973-90, bd. dirs., Washington Inst. for Near East, Ctr. for Strategic Studies, Tel Aviv Univ. Author: Silence...Eight Grade Tests, 1946, National Security Israel, 1968. Pres. Zionist Orgn. of Am., Pacific, 1984-86, B'nai B'rith Western U.S., 1988-90; chmn. State of Israli Bonds Israel Task Force, 1980-84, Assn. for Soldiers, L.A., 1980-84. Col. Inf., Israeli Army, 1967-73. Recipient Leadership and Svc. award Friends of Israel Def., 1986, Israel Bonds Negev award, 1982, Presdl. award B'nai B'rith, 1986. Mem. World Alliance of Christian and Jews (co-chmn. 1989-90, Excellence and Svc. award 1990), Anti-Defamation League, Soc. of Fellows, World War II Avengers (hon. pres. 1946-69, Svc. Leadership award 1969), Shalom Lodge (pres. 1978-81). Republican. Office: World Alliance Christians & Jews 930 Westbourne Dr Apt 100 West Hollywood CA 90069-4129

ERIACHO, BELINDA PEARL, environmental scientist; b. Ft. Defiance, Ariz., May 28, 1963; d. Tony Leopoldo Eriacho Sr. and Irene Rosalyn Lewis. BS, Ariz. State U., 1986; postgrad., U. N.Mex., 1988-89; MPH, U. Hawaii, 1990; postgrad., U. Mich., 1992, Ariz. State U., 1993—. Adminstrv. asst. health educator Maricopa County Health Svcs., Phoenix, 1986-87; health educator Navajo Nation Dept. Health, Window Rock, Ariz., 1987-88; tng. coord. Navajo Nation Family Planning Corp., Window Rock, Ariz., 1988-89; extern Navajo Area Indian Health Svc., Window Rock, Ariz., 1989-90, jr. health adminstrv. officer, 1990; sr. environ. sci. Ariz. Pub. Svc. Co., Phoenix, 1991—; speaker No. Ariz. U., Flagstaff, 1994; speaker math., engring., sci. achievement, Phoenix, 1992, Window Rock H.S., 1992, NTUA, Ft. Defense, Ariz., 1994—. Environ. cons. Navajo Tribal Utility Authority, 1993—; pre-med. intern Scottsdale Meml. Hosp., 1986; health assoc. Phoenix Indian Med. Ctr., 1985; Phys., Intellectual, Emotional and Spiritual vol. Ariz. State U. Health Svcs., Tempe, 1984-85; EMT asst. Navajo Emergency Med. Svcs., Ft. Defiance Indian Health, 1983; bd. dirs. Indian Comty. Health Inc., 1994. Recipient scholarship Navajo Nation, 1990, Nat. Action Coun. for Minorities in Engring., 1981-82; named one of Outstanding Young Women of Am., 1994-95. Mem. APHA, Am. Indian Sci. and Engring. Soc., Am. Indsl. Hygiene Assn., Ariz. Indsl. Hygiene Assn., Ariz. State U. Alumni, Ariz. State Native Am. Alumni Assn. (bd. dirs. 1988-89), Ariz. State U. Indian Grad. Assn., Environ. Auditing Roundtable, U. Hawaii Pub. Health Alumni Assn., Delta Omega. Office: Ariz Pub Svc Co PO Box 53999 Sta 9366 Phoenix AZ 85072-3999

ERICKSEN, KENNETH JERROLD, English literature educator; b. Everett, Wash., June 7, 1939; s. Frank Ludwig and Evelyn Elvera (Carlson) E.; m. Donna Gayle Clodfelter, Jan. 1, 1976; children: Richard Harland, Douglas Craig, Hillary Janette, Adam Jerrold. BA, Pacific Luth. U., Tacoma, 1961; MA, Rice U., 1963, PhD, 1967. Prof. English Linfield Coll., McMinnville, Oreg., 1965—. Mem. MLA, Jane Austen Soc. N.Am., Am. Soc. for Eighteenth Century Studies, N.W. Soc. for Eighteenth Century Studies (pres. 1992-93, co-editor Transactions 1991-93). Lutheran. Home: 3321 Lavina Dr Forest Grove OR 97116-1041 Office: Linfield Coll Mcminnville OR 97128

ERICKSON, ARTHUR CHARLES, architect; b. Vancouver, B.C., Can., June 14, 1924; s. Oscar and Myrtle (Chatterson) E. Student, U. B.C., Vancouver, 1942-44; B.Arch., McGill U., Montreal, Que., Can., 1950; LL.D. (hon.), Simon Fraser U., Vancouver, 1973, U. Man., Winnipeg, Can., 1978, Lethbridge U., 1981; D.Eng. (hon.), Nova Scotia Tech. Coll., McGill U., 1971; Litt.D. (hon.), U. B.C., 1985. Asst. prof. U. Oreg., Eugene, 1955-56; assoc. prof. U. B.C., 1956-63; ptnr. Erickson-Massey Architects, Vancouver, 1963-72; prin. Arthur Erickson Architects, Vancouver, 1972-91, Toronto, Ont., Can., 1981-91, Los Angeles, 1981-91; prin. Arthur Erickson Archtl. Corp., Vancouver, 1991—. Prin. works include Can. Pavilion at Expo '70, Osaka (recipient first prize in nat. competition, Archtl. Inst. of Japan award for best pavilion), Robson Square/The Law Courts (honor award), Mus. of Anthropology (honor award), Eppich Residence (honor award), Habitat Pavilion (honor award), Sikh Temple (award of merit), Champlain Heights Community Sch. (award of merit), San Diego Convention Ctr., Calif. Plz., L.A., Fresno City Hall; subject of Time mag. cover article and New Yorker profile; contbr. articles to profl. publs. Mem. com. on urban devel. Coun. of Can., 1971; bd. dirs. Can. Conf. of Arts, 1972; mem. design adv. coun. Portland Devel. Commn., Can. Coun. Urban Rsch.; trustee Inst. Rsch. on Pub. Policy. Capt. Can. Intelligence Corps., 1945-46. Recipient Molson prize Can. Coun. Arts, 1967, Triangle award Nat. Soc. Interior Design, Royal Bank Can. award, 1971, Gold medal Tau Sigma Delta, 1973, residential design award Can. Housing Coun., 1975, August Perret award Internat. Union Archiects Congress, 1975, Chgo. Architecture award, 1984, Gold medals Royal Archtl. Inst. Can., 1984, French Acad. Architecture, 1984, Pres. award excellence Am. Soc. Landscape Architects, 1979; named Officer, Order of Can., 1973, Companion Order of Can., 1981. Fellow AIA (hon., Pan Pacific citation Hawaiian chpt. 1963, gold medal 1986), Royal Archtl. Inst. Can. (recipient award 1980); mem. Royal Inst. Brit. Archs., Archtl. Inst. B.C., Royal Inst. Scottish Archs. (hon.), Coll. d'arquitectos de España (hon.), Coll. d'architectos de Mex. (hon.), Royal Can. Acad. Arts (academician), Heritage Can., U. B.C. Faculty Club. Office: Arthur Erickson Archtl Corp, 1672 W 1st Ave, Vancouver, BC Canada V6J 1G1

ERICKSON, CALVIN HOWARD, computer systems engineer; b. Worcester, Mass., June 18, 1946; s. Stanley Howard and Mae Harriet (Wivagg) E.; m. Radmila Frencic, June 5, 1970; children: Jennifer Joy, Melissa Mae. Student, Clark U., 1975-77; ABS in Computer Sci., Quinsigamond Community Coll., Worcester, 1971; cert. Unix System Mgmt. and Adminstrn., U. Calif., Santa Cruz, 1991. Sr. systems programmer Datatrol Inc., Hudson, Mass., 1972-76; tech. support mgr. Keane Inc., Wellesley, Mass., 1976-81; software support specialist Data Gen. Corp., Westboro, Mass., 1981-87; computer systems engr. Loral Rolm-Mil Spec Computers, San Jose, Calif., 1987-92; co devel. support engr., cons. engr. Adobe Systems, Mountain View, Calif., 1992—. Author: AOS/VS Internals Manual, 1986. With USN, 1965-71. Mem. Nat. Geog. Soc., San Francisco Zool. Soc., Golden Gate Nat. Park Assn., The Friends of Photography (sustaining), Smithsonian (assoc.), Alpha Nu Omega. Home: 34786 Comstock Common Fremont CA 94555-2820 Office: Adobe Systems 1585 Charleston Rd Mountain View CA 94043-1225

ERICKSON, CHERYL ANN, librarian; b. Renton, Wash., Apr. 20, 1944; d. Cy L. and Doris M. (Hedlund) Swanson; 1 child, Ben. BA, U. Minn., 1966, MA, 1967. Ref. libr. U. Minn., Mpls., 1967-68; children's libr. Fairfax County, Alexandria, Va., 1968-69; serials libr. Calif. State U., Long Beach, 1969-70; br. libr. San Bernardino County, 29 Palms, Calif., 1970-94, Yucaipa, Calif., 1994—. Founding mem. 29 Palms Hist. Soc., 1983; organist Little Ch. of the Desert, 29 Palms, 1979-94. Named County Libr. Employee of Yr., 1991. Mem. Calif. Libr. Assn., 29 Palms Artists Guild. Home: PO Box 403 Yucaipa CA 92399-0403

ERICKSON, CHRISTOPHER ANDREW, economics educator; b. St. Helens, Oreg., Oct. 18, 1957; s. Kenneth S. and Valerie I. (Williams) E.; children: Andrew S., Mischelle I. BA, Willamette U., 1980; PhD, Ariz. State U., Tempe, 1989. Bus. analyst Dun & Bradstreet, Seattle, 1981-83; analyst Criterion Inc., Phoenix, 1985-86; asst. prof. econs. N.Mex. State U., Las Cruces, 1987—. Precinct committeeman Dem. Party, Warren, Oreg., 1978-80; chmn. Sykes for County Commr. campaign, Columbia County, Oreg., 1980. Mem. Am. Econ. Assn., Western Econ. Assn., So. Econ. Assn., Assn. Borderland Scholars. Democrat. Home: 4908 Chagar St Las Cruces NM 88005 Office: NMex State U Dept Econs 30001 3d CG Las Cruces NM 88003

ERICKSON, DAVID BELNAP, lawyer; b. Ogden, Utah, Oct. 13, 1951; s. Eldred H. and Lois (Belnap) E.; m. Julie Ann Hill, Apr. 19, 1974; children: Rachel, John, Michael, Jared, Emily, Steven, Katherine, Daniel, Elizabeth. BA, Brigham Young U., 1975; MEd, Utah State U., 1979; JD, Gonzaga Sch. Law, 1982. Bar: Utah 1982, U.S. Claims Ct. 1990, U.S. Dist. Ct. Utah 1982, U.S. Ct. Appeals (10th cir.) 1984, U.S. Ct. Appeals (9th cir.) 1987, U.S. Supreme Ct. 1987. English tchr., debate coach Bonneville High Sch., Ogden, 1976-79; law clk. U.S. Atty.'s Office, Spokane, Washington, 1980-81; law clk. to judge U.S. Dist. Ct., Salt Lake City, 1982-83; with Kirton, McConkie & Poelman, Salt Lake City, 1983-92; sr. counsel Intermountain Health Care, Salt Lake City, 1992—. Co-author: Utah Appellate Practice Manual, 1986, Utah Sr. Citizen's Handbook, 1987; editor-in-chief Gonzaga Law Rev., 1981-82; assoc. editor: Utah Barrister, 1986-87, Utah Bar Jour., 1988—. Mem. LDS Hosp. Bioethics Com.; mem. planning and zoning commn. Pleasant View City, 1991-95, chmn., 1994-95; chmn. Weber View Dist. Boy Scouts Am., 1993—; trustee Utah Alliance for Health Care, 1994—. Mem. ABA (litigation sect.), Fed. Bar Assn., Utah Bar Assn. (law jour. com., bridging the gap com., needs of the elderly com., legal and med. com., examiner constl. law bar, assoc. editor Utah Bar jour.), Salt Lake County Bar Assn., Weber County Bar Assn., Am. Acad. Hosp. Attys. (Utah state law devel. rep.), Nat. Health Lawyers Assn., Phi Delta Phi. Mem. LDS Ch.

ERICKSON, DENNIS, professional football coach, former university football coach. Head coach U. Miami Hurricanes, 1989-95, Seattle Seahawks, 1995—. Office: Seattle Seahawks 11220 NE 53rd St Kirkland WA 98033

ERICKSON, EDWARD LEONARD, biotechnology company executive; b. Chgo., Dec. 7, 1946; s. Leonard Gerald and Eleanore Antoinette (Picek) E.; m. Helen Leonora Masten, Dec. 29, 1979. BS in Math. and Physics, Ill. Inst. Tech., 1968, MS in Math., 1970; MBA in Gen. Mgmt., Harvard U., 1980. Mktg. rep. IBM, Miami, Fla., 1975-76; sr. systems engr. Advanced Tech., Inc., McLean, Va., 1976-78; cons. Bain & Co., Boston, 1979-80; sr. assoc. Resource Planning Assocs., Washington, 1980-82; dir. mgmt. com. Resource Planning Assocs., London, 1982-83; dir. corp. devel. Amersham Internat. plc., Little Chalfont, Eng., 1983-86, gen. mgr. internat. ops., 1986-88; v.p. fin. ops. The Ares-Serono Group, Boston, 1988-90; pres. Serono-Baker Diagnostics (The Ares-Serono Group), Allentown, Pa., 1990-91; pres., chief exec. officer, dir. Cholestech Corp., Hayward, Calif., 1991-93; pres., CEO, DepoTech Corp., La Jolla, Calif., 1993—; also bd. dirs. Depo Tech Corp., La Jolla, Calif. Contbr. articles to profl. jours. Mem. Rep. Nat. Com., Washington, 1990—, The 1992 Presdl. Trust, Washington, 1991; charter mem. Rep. Campaign Coun., Washington, 1991; precinct chmn. Va. Rep. Party, Aldie, 1977. Lt. USN, 1970-75. John L. Loeb fellow Harvard U., 1980, George F. Baker scholar, 1980, NASA fellow, 1968-70. Mem. Sigma Pi Sigma. Republican. Home: 6887 Tohickon Hill Rd Pipersville PA 18947-1415

ERICKSON, ELIZABETH ANN (LISA ERICKSON), mental health counselor, educator, consultant; b. Vermillion, S.D.; d. James Lee and Marian Elizabeth (Guitteau) E. BA, U. Kans., 1976, MS, 1983. Cert. mental health counselor, Wash. Rsch. asst. Dept. Psychology U. Kans., Lawrence, 1974-76; counselor, rsch. asst. Achievement Place, Lawrence, 1976-79; program dir. Battered Women's Task Force, Topeka, 1979-80; psychotherapist Drug Abuse Coun., Everett, Wash., 1980-84; program coord. Ctr. for Human Svcs.-Adult Drug, Seattle, 1984-85; program dir. Ctr. for Human Svcs., Seattle, 1985-87; pvt. practice Seattle, 1986—; adj. faculty grad. psychology Antioch U., Seattle, 1985—. Columnist (monthly newspaper) Journey, 1990-92. Bd. dirs. Stop Abuse, Everett, 1982-84, N.W. Family Tng. Inst., Seattle, 1989-90; founding mem., sec., exec. bd. dirs. Kans. Assn. Domestic Violence Programs, 1979-80. Mem. Am. Counseling Assn., Nat. Assn. Alcohol and Drug Abuse Counselors, Wash. Mental Health Counselors Assn., Seattle Counselor's Assn. (pres. 1995-96). Office: 2611 NE 125th St Ste 245 Seattle WA 98125-4357

ERICKSON, ERIC DOUGLAS, chemist; b. Astoria, Oreg., July 31, 1955; s. Douglas Leon and Patricia (Thiebes) E.; m. Barbara Marie Davenport, Sept. 3, 1977; children: Ivy Marie, Benjamin Clark. BS in Chemistry, Oreg. State U., 1977; Cert. of Proficiency Indsl. Hygiene, San Diego City Coll., 1980; PhD in Chemistry, Mich. State U., 1989. Chemist AMTECH Labs., San Diego, 1977-80, Naval Weapons Ctr., China Lake, Calif., 1980-84; teaching/rsch. asst. Mich. State U., East Lansing, 1984-89; chemist Naval Weapons Ctr., China Lake, 1989-92; chemist weapons div. Naval Air Warfare Ctr., China Lake, 1992—. Contbr. articles to profl. jours. Scout leader Cub Scouts/Boy Scouts Am., Ridgecrest, Calif., 1990-93, sci. explorer, post advisor, 1992—. Mem. Am. Chem. Soc. (treas. 1990-92), Sigma Xi (v.p. 1990, pres. 1991). Office: Naval Air Warfare Ctr Mail Stop 218D Weapons Divsn Code 474230D China Lake CA 93555

ERICKSON, GARY MICHAEL, business and management educator; b. Anacortes, Wash., July 7, 1945; s. Leroy Alexander and Ruby Lucille Erstrom; m. Jane Abad Sabado, June 29, 1968; children: Alvaro Sabado, Aurora Abad. BS, U. Wash., 1967; MBA, Stanford U., 1973, PhD, 1978. Asst. prof. Bus. and Mgmt. U. Pa., Phila., 1978-80; asst. prof. Bus. and Mgmt. U. Wash., Seattle, 1980-86, assoc. prof. Bus. and Mgmt., 1986-94, prof. Bus. and Mgmt., 1994—. With U.S. Army, 1969-71. Mem. Am. Mktg. Assn., The Inst. Mgmt. Scis. (assoc. editor Management Science 1978—). Office: Dept Mktg & Internat Bus Wash DJ-10 Seattle WA 98195

ERICKSON, JOYCE LILLIAN, telephone services company executive; b. Palo Alto, Calif., May 13, 1940; d. Rodney Lyle Erickson and Doris Lillian Serva Correa; m. Sam Y. Ghulam, July 20, 1959 (div. Dec. 15, 1970); children: Roxanne Santiago, Laith, Lance. Student, Acad. of Bus., San Jose, 1957. Fgn. student specialist U. Calif., Berkeley; officer worker Oakland (Calif.) Kelly Svcs.; adminstrv. asst. Ins. Adjusters, Oakland, 1986-92; appointment setter Advanced Tele-Svcs., Canoga Park, Calif., 1993—; editorial asst. Scarlet St. Mag., 1993—; adminstrv. editorial asst., movie star interviewer Outré Mag.; stand-up comedienne Curtain call, San Fancisco, Regis Hotel, San Franciso, Bottome Line, Danville, Calif., Stripes, Fremont, Calif., others; lectr. in field. Songwriter: Higher Recycling, 1991, Forever Maybe, 1991, Hollywood and Plum, 1991; contbr. articles to profl. jours. commentaries to newspaper, poetry pub. (8 poetry awards). Recipient 2d prize Rumple Minze Peppermint Schnapps Myth-Defy-Us Contest for Writing, 1991; Hollywood Scriptwriting Inst. scholar, 1992. Democrat.

ERICKSON, RALPH D., retired physical education educator, small business owner, consultant; b. Beresford, S.D., June 25, 1922; s. John Henning and Ester Christina (Lofgren) E.; m. Nancy Erickson, Sept. 1949 (div. 1961); m. Patricia Erickson, Apr. 1973 (div. 1975); m. Karen Ann Erickson, June 1, 1989; 1 child, Karina Ann. BS in Phys. Edn., Northwestern U., 1949, MA in Edn., 1953. Swim instr., coach Chgo. Park Dist., 1946-54; social studies tchr., swim coach Elmwood Park (Ill.) High Sch., 1954-65; swimming, water polo coach Loyola Univ., Chgo., 1965-87, assoc. prof. phys. edn., 1971-87; salesman Alexander Hamilton Inst., Chgo., 1966-69; tchr. Chgo. Bd. Edn., 1969-70; bd. dirs. Capital Investments & Ventures Corp., Santa Ana, Calif., 1983-93, Cosmopolitan Comm., Santa Ana, 1991-93; vice chmn. Internat. Profl. Assn. Diving Inst., Santa Ana, 1966-93. Author: Under Pressure, 1961, Discover the Under Water World, 1971, V/W Navigation, 1972, Search and Recovery, 1973. Sgt US Army, 1942-45. Recipient Reach Out award Diving Equipment Mfg. Assn.; named to Athletic Hall of Fame Loyola U. Chgo., 1986. Mem. Profl. Assn. Diving Instrs. (co-founder). Home and Office: 17307 Whippoorwill Trl Leander TX 78645-9734

ERICKSON, RICHARD BEAU, life insurance company executive; b. Chgo., May 14, 1952; s. Charles Arthur and Carole Annette (Beaumont) E.; m. Pamela J. Sievers, Aug. 20, 1977. BS, U. Ky., 1974, MBA, 1975. CLU. Sales rep. Met. Life and affiliated cos., Chgo. Hgts., Ill., 1975-78; sales mgr. Met. Life and affiliated cos., Flossmoor, Ill., 1978-80; mktg. specialist Met. Life and affiliated cos., Aurora, Ill., 1980-81; branch mgr. Met. Life and affiliated cos., Orland Park, Ill., 1981-84; corp. dir. Met. Life Gen. Ins. Agy. Inc., N.Y.C., 1984-86; regional sales mgr. Met. Life Gen. Ins. Agy. Inc., L.A., 1986-89, agy. v.p., sr. mktg. and sales exec., 1989—, agy. v.p., 1989; rep. (Midwest) Sales Mgr. Adv., N.Y.C., 1979; dir. South Cook County Assn. Life Underwriters, Chgo., 1983. Author: Met. Manpower Development, 1981, Met. Manpower Development: A Guideline for Success, 1986. Sponsor UCLA Soccer, 1986—. Mem. NRA, Nat. Assn. Securities Dealers, Life Underwriters Tng. Counsel, Chartered Life Underwriters, U. Ky. Alumni Assn., Nat. Assn. Life Underwriters, Gen. Agts. & Mgrs. Assn., Sierra Club, Sigma Nu. Republican. Office: Met Life 801 N Brand Blvd Ste 245 Glendale CA 91203-1243

ERICKSON, ROBERT PORTER, genetics researcher, educator, clinician; b. Portland, Oreg., June 27, 1939; s. Harold M. and Marjorie S. (Porter) E.; m. Sandra De'Ath, June 20, 1964; children—Andrew Ian, Colin De'Ath, Tanya Nadene, Tracy Lynn, Michelle Lee, Christof Phillipe. B.A., Reed Coll., 1960; M.D., Stanford U., 1965. Diplomate Am. Bd. Pediatrics. Asst. prof. pediatrics U. Calif.-San Francisco Med. Sch., 1970-75; vis. scientist Institut Pasteur, Paris, 1975-76; assoc. prof. human genetics and pediatrics U. Mich., Ann Arbor, 1976-80, prof., 1980—, dir. div. pediatric genetics, 1985—; vis. scientist Imperial Cancer Research Fund, London, 1983-84. Editorial bd. Jour. Reproductive Immunology, 1978—, Dictionary of Laboratory Technology, 1983. Contbr. articles to sci. jours. Served with USPHS, 1967-69. Guggenheim fellow, Paris, 1975; Eleanor Roosevelt fellow, London, 1983; Fulbright grantee, London, 1983; NIH grantee, 1971—. Mem. Am. Soc. Human Genetics, Soc. Pediatric Research, Am. Soc. Cell Biology. Avocations: skiing; backpacking. Home: 5200 N Camino Real Tucson AZ 85718-5029 Office: U Mich Ann Arbor MI 48109

ERICKSON, RUSSELL JOHN, pediatrician; b. Sauk Center, Minn.; s. Russell John and Valerie Jeanette (Rose) E.; m. Patricia Ann Parker, June 22, 1958; children: Karen Michelle, Kevin David, Keith Lawrence. AB in Chemistry cum laude, Occidental Coll., 1957; MD, U. Calif., San Francisco, 1961; cert. in acupuncture, UCLA, 1990. Intern, resident and fellow in Pediatrics U. Calif., San Francisco, 1961-63; resident and fellow U. Wash., Seattle, 1963-65; pediatrician, asst. chief pediatrics Kaiser-Permanente, Oakland, Calif., 1965-66, 68-72; chief pediatrics Kaiser-Permanente, Richmond, Calif., 1972-88, chief quality assurance, 1978-84, chief med. edn., 1980-82, sr. cons., 1988—; clin. instr. U. Calif. Med. Sch., San Francisco, 1965-66, 68-72; chair manpower com. No. Calif. Acad. Pediatrics, 1976-78; mem. State Pediatric Healthplan Com., Calif., 1979. Editor AFMA Ann. Acupunture Lit. Rev., 1994-95; contbr. articles to med. jours. Founder, bd. dirs. Moraga (Calif.) Park and Recreation Dept., 1968-76; bd. dirs. Moraga Community Assn., 1970-74; pres. Saddleridge Homeowners, Pleasant Hill, Calif., 1990-93; sec. Sunrise Hills II Homeowners, Calif., 1993; trustee Am. Found. Med. Acupuncture, 1993—. Capt. U.S. Army, 1966-68. Fellow Am. Acad. Pediatrics; mem. Am. Acad. Med. Acupuncture, Sierra Club (life). Office: Kaiser-Permanente Med 901 Nevin Ave Richmond CA 94801-3143

ERICKSON, VIRGINIA BEMMELS, chemical engineer; b. Sleepy Eye, Minn., June 19, 1948; d. Gordon Boothe and Marion Mae (Rieke) Bemmels; m. Larry Douglas Erickson, Sept. 6, 1969; children: Kirsten Danielle, Dean Michael. Diploma in Nursing, Swedish Hosp. Sch. Nursing, 1969; BSChemE, U. Wash., 1983, MChemE, 1985. RN. Asst. head nurse N. Meml. Hosp., Mpls., 1970-73; intensive care RN Swedish Med. Ctr., Seattle, 1973-83; research asst. U. Wash., Seattle, 1983-85; instrumentation and control engr. CH2M Hill, Bellevue, Wash., 1985—, mgr. dept., 1988-93, mgr. info. mgmr., 1994—, v.p., 1995—; cons. instrumentation and control engr. Mem. editorial adv. bd. Control. Leader Girl Scouts U.S., Seattle, 1985; supt. Seattle Ch. Sch., 1983; rep. United Way, 1986—. Recipient Cert. Achievement, Soc. Women Engrs., 1983, Teenfeed, 1990. Mem. AICE, NAFE, Instrument Soc. Am., Tau Beta Pi. Democrat. Mem. United Methodist Ch. Home: 6026 24th Ave NE Seattle WA 98115-7009 Office: CH2M Hill PO Box 91500 777 108th Ave NE Bellevue WA 98009-2050

ERICKSON, WILLIAM HURT, state supreme court justice; b. Denver, May 11, 1924; s. Arthur Xavier and Virginia (Hurt) E.; m. Doris Rogers, Dec. 24, 1953; children: Barbara Ann, Virginia Lee, Stephen Arthur, William Taylor. Degree in petroleum engring., Colo. Sch. Mines, 1947; student, U. Mich., 1949; LLB, U. Va., 1950. Bar: Colo. 1951. Pvt. practice law Denver; justice Colo. Supreme Ct., 1971—, chief justice, 1983-85; faculty NYU Appellate Judges Sch., 1972-85; mem. exec. Commn. on Accreditation of Law Enforcement Agys., 1980-83; chmn. Pres.'s Nat. Commn. for Rev. of Fed. and State Laws Relating to Wiretapping and Electronic Surveillance, 1976. With USAAF, 1943. Recipient Disting. Achievement medal Colo. Sch. Mines, 1990. Fellow Internat. Acad. Trial Lawyers (former sec.), Am. Coll. Trial Lawyers, Am. Bar Found. (chmn. 1985), Internat. Soc. Barristers (pres. 1971); mem. ABA, (bd. govs. 1975-79, former chmn. com. on standards criminal justice, former chmn. coun. criminal law sect., former chmn. com. to implement standards criminal justice, mem. long-range planning com., action com. to reduce ct. cost and delay), Colo. Bar Assn. (award of merit 1989), Denver Bar Assn. (past pres., trustee), Am. Law Inst. (coun.), Practising Law Inst. (nat. adv. coun., bd. govs. Colo.), Freedoms Found. at Valley Forge (nat. coun. trustees, 1986—), Order of Coif, Scribes (pres. 1978). Home: 10 Martin Ln Englewood CO 80110-4820 Office: Colo Supreme Ct 2 E 14th Ave Denver CO 80203-2115

ERICSON, JONATHON EDWARD, environmental health science educator, researcher; b. Bronx, N.Y., May 22, 1942; s. Erling and Ruth Cecila E.; m. Glenda Prince Ericson, Dec. 19, 1987; 1 child, Hana Christine; 1 child from previous marriage, Burke Evan. AB in Exploration Geophysics, UCLA, 1970, MA in Anthropology, 1973, PhD in Anthropology, 1977. Conservation chemist L.A. County Mus. Art, 1976-78; assoc. prof. dept. anthropology Harvard U., Cambridge, Mass., 1978-83; asst. prof. program in social ecology U. Calif., Irvine, 1983-85, assoc. prof. Dept. Environ. analysis and Design, 1985-91, assoc. prof. dept. anthropology, 1987-91, prof. depts. environ analysis and design, anthropology, 1991—; chair Irvine divsn. edn. aboard com. U. Calif., Irvine, 1991-94; cons. NASA-Ames, Moffett Field, Calif., 1983, Keith Co./Irvine Co., 1988-93; designer Ctr. for Archaeol. Rsch. and Devel., Harvard U., 1978-80. Co-editor: Exchange Systems in Prehistory, 1977, Contexts of Prehistorical Exchange, 1982, Prehistoric Quarries and Lithic Production, 1984 , American Southwest and Mesoamerica: Systems of Prehistoric Exchange, 1993, Prehistoric Exchange Systems in North America, 1994. Mem. Orange County Quincentenary Com., 1988-93; v.p. Mus. Natural History and Sci., Aliso Viejo, Calif., 1988-91; asst. scout master Boy Scouts Am., Dana Point, Calif., 1990-95. Fulbright Hayes scholar, 1980, 91; NASA fellow, 1983; NSF grantee, 1984-86. Fellow Sigma Xi (pres. U. Calif. at Irvine chpt. 1995—); mem. AAAS, Soc. Am. Archaeology, U.S. Systems in Space (regent), Soc. Archaeol. Scis. (pres. 1981-82). Episcopalian. Office: U Calif Dept Environ Analysis Irvine CA 92717

ERICSON, MARK FREDERICK, investment analyst; b. Colorado Springs, Colo., June 28, 1957; s. Frederick Walter and Eleanor Joan (Juraska) E. BS in Civil Engring., U. Colo., 1979, MBA, 1986. Registered profl. engr., Colo. Project mgr. JR Engring. Ltd., Englewood, Colo., 1982-86; cons. Kirkham Michael & Assocs., Greenwood Village, Colo., 1988-89, Merrick & Co., Aurora, Colo., 1989—; pres. Ericson Investors, Aurora, 1986—. Author: Follow the Crowd and Be Contrary, 1991, You Can Have Eternal Life for Certain, 1994; contbr. (book) Salvador Dali-A Retrospective of Master Films, 1992; co-producer God's News Behind the News, 1994. Elder, lay pastor Calvary Temple, Disciple of Jesus Christ. Mem. ASCE, Am. Assn. Individual Investors, Chi Epsilon. Office: 2068 S Pitkin St Aurora CO 80013-1263

ERICSON, RICHARD VICTOR, social science and law educator, university administrator; b. Montreal, Que., Sept. 20, 1948; s. John William and Elizabeth Mary (Hinkley) E.; m. Diana Lea McMillan, May 31, 1969; 1 child, Matthew Simon. BA, U. Guelph, Ont., 1969; MA, U. Toronto, 1971; PhD, Cambridge U., Eng., 1974, LittD, 1991. Asst. prof. U. Toronto, 1974-79, assoc. prof., 1979-82, prof. sociology, prof. criminology, 1982-93, dir. Ctr. of Criminology, 1992-93; prof. sociology, prof. law U. B.C., Vancouver, 1993—, prin. Green Coll., 1993—; vis. rsch. prof. Coll. Pub. Programs Ariz. State U., Tempe, 1991; vis. fellow Inst. Criminology Cambridge U., 1979, 84-85, Churchill Coll. Cambridge U., 1979, 84-85. Author: Making Crime (2d edit.), 1993; co-author: Negotiating Control, 1989, Representing Order, 1991, The Culture and Power of Knowledge, 1992. Hon. vis. fellow Green Coll., Oxford, 1993—. Fellow Royal Soc. Can. Home: Principal's Residence, Green College at U BC, Vancouver, BC Canada V6T 1Z1 Office: Green College at U BC, 6201 Cecil Green Park Rd, Vancouver, BC Canada V6T 1Z1

ERIKSSON, ANNE-MARIE, social services executive, educator; b. Dunkirk, N.Y., Mar. 30, 1932; d. J. Kenneth and Kate Findley; m. Erik A. Eriksson, Jan. 1, 1984; 3 children from prior marriage. BS, SUNY, Fredonia, 1955; postgrad., Hunter Coll. CUNY, 1960. Probation officer N.Y., 1972-84; social worker N.Y. State Dept. Social Welfare, N.Y.C., 1960-64; founder, pres. 1st Incest Survivors Resource Network Internat., N.Y.C., 1983; a Quaker witness ednl. resource participant Com. Internat. Orgns., 1983—; cons. mental health needs UN Hdqs., 1987; presenter 1st and 3d Internat. Conf. Incest and Related Problems, Zurich, 1987, London, 1989; founder first internat. incest tel. helpline, 1983. Mem. Quaker Studies Human Betterment, Internat. Soc. Traumatic Stress Studies (founding co-chair bldg. bridges between profls. and self-help interest area), World Fedn. Mental Health, others. Office: Incest Survivors Resource Network Internat PO Box 7375 Las Cruces NM 88006-7375

ERMSHAR, LINDA CHARLINE, health services school director; b. L.A., Apr. 29, 1943; d. Herman Jerry and Fern Dorothy (Haynes) Mayer; m. Marvin Carl Ermshar, Dec. 16, 1962; children: Kurt Jerry Douglas, Kimberly Renee, Victoria Rochelle. AA, El Camino Coll., 1964; teaching cert., UCLA, 1973. RN; ltd. x-ray tech., std. designated teaching credential and cmty. coll. credential, Calif. Allied health dir. Southland Career Inst., Montebello, Calif., 1969-88; ednl. dir., assoc. dir. Modern Tech. Sch. X-Ray, Anaheim, Calif., 1988—. RN in charge of students ARC Health Fairs, Whittier, Calif., 1980-87. Recipient Cert. of Recognition Nat. Assn. Trade and Tech. Schs., Washington, 1991. Mem. Am. Assn. Med. Transcription. Republican. Seventh Day Adventists. Office: Modern Tech Sch X-Ray 1232 E Katella Ave Anaheim CA 92805-6623

ERNEST, DOROTHETTA P., health facility administrator, critical care nurse; b. San Angelo, Tex., Aug. 20, 1939; d. Japson and Dorothy Naomi (McWilliams) Pettit; m. Henry Mason Ernest, Aug. 9, 1958; children: Robert Henry, Mason Luin, Margret Ruth, James Benjamin. Diploma, Meth. Hosp., Lubbock, Tex., 1960; AS, Cypress (Calif.) Jr. Coll., 1976; BSN, Mesa State Coll., 1989. Cert. ACLS, CCRN, CPR/First Aid instr. Head nurse Cerritos Gardens Hosp., Hawiian Gardens, Calif., 1972-73; dir. of nursing svc. Citrus Care Convalescent Hosp., Fontana, Calif., 1981-82; staff/head nurse, spl. care unit Orange Grove Community Hosp., Pomona, Calif., 1983-85; staff nurse, ICCU Southwest Meml. Hosp., Cortez, Colo., 1985-93; staff nurse ICU Lincoln County Med. Ctr., Ruidsoso, N.Mex., 1994-95; quality assurance/edn. specialist Chaves County Home Health Agy., Roswell, N.Mex., 1995—. Mem. AACN, ADA. Home: PO Box 4825 108 Paradise Canyon Dr Ruidoso NM 88345

ERNST, CHADWICK ELLSWORTH, fastener company executive; b. Oakland, Calif., Mar. 19, 1933; s. Archibald Ellsworth and Beatrice Jessie (Ort) E. B.A., U. Calif., Berkeley, 1958. Gen. mgr. Cee Mdse. Co., Oakland, Calif., 1948-67; v.p. F.W. Aurich & Co., Inc., Seattle, 1967-68; exec. v.p. Aimsco Inc., Seattle, 1969-75; pres., dir. Cheler Corp., Seattle, 1976—; dir. Beacon Wholesale, Chgo., Amalgamated Counseling Services, Inc., N.Y.C.; dir., chmn. bd., pres. Aurich, Inc., Aimsco, Inc.; owner Cee Mdse. Co., Everett Typesetting Co., C.W. Warren Co., City Comml. Printing Co., Nat. Eyelet & Mfg. Co., Ernst Sales Bor., Ernst Publ. Co.; pub. Mail Order World, Prog. Mail Trade, Mail Factory, Mail Order Roundup, Swing Your Ptnr., Where?, The Schemer, Mail Order Bull., Cen. Mail Advertiser, Can. Mail Advertiser, Popular Advertiser, The Guide, The Fireside Shopper, Mail Sale Advertiser. Active CD, Berkeley, 1955-62; elder, commr. Presby. Ch. Fellow Internat. Biographers Assn.; mem. Internat. Mail Dealers Assn., Mfrs. Agts. Nat. Assn., Nat. Assn. Credit Mgmt., Gideons Internat., Nat. Assn. Notaries (life), Am. Philatelic Soc., Seattle Opera Assn., Seattle Symphony Assn., Swedish Club, Lake of the Woods Country Club. Home: 6411 23rd Ave S Seattle WA 98108-3603 Office: 5705 Airport Way S Seattle WA 98108-2712

ERNST, DONALD WILLIAM, producer; b. L.A., Jan. 25, 1934; s. William McKinley and Dorothy Elizabeth (Hast) E.; m. Janice Elaine Barber, Apr. 16, 1966; children: Stacey Dawn, Darci Lynn. BS in Civil Engring., UCLA, 1956. Apprentice editor Telemat, L.A., 1956-61; asst. editor Columbia Pictures, L.A., 1961-62, Metro-Goldwyn-Mayer, Culver City, Calif., 1962-64; film editor CBS, Studio City, Calif., 1964-72, Bakshi Prodns., L.A., 1972-79; sound editor Echo Films, L.A., 1979-82, Horta Editorial, Burbank, Calif., 1982-88; film editor Walt Disney Pictures, Glendale, Calif., 1988-89; prodr. Walt Disney Pictures, Glendale, 1989—. Prodr.: (animated film) Roller Coaster Rabbit, 1990; co-prodr.: (animated film) Aladdin, 1992; exec. prodr.: (live action film) Homeward Bound: The Incredible Journey, 1993. Recipient Emmy awards TV Acad. Arts and Scis., 1977, 82. Mem. Am. Cinema Editors, Acad. Motion Picture Arts and Scis. Home: 26026 Trana Cir Calabasas CA 91302-1054 Office: Walt Disney Feature Animation 1420 Flower St Glendale CA 91201

ERNST, ELDON GILBERT, religion educator, seminary dean; b. Seattle, Jan. 27, 1939; s. Kenneth G. and Bydell N. (Painter) E.; m. Joy S. Skoglund, June 12, 1959; children: Michael P., David G., Peter J., Samuel F., Rachel J. BA, Linfield Coll., 1961; BD, Colgate Rochester Divinity Sch, 1964; MA, Yale U., 1965, PhD, 1968. Prof. Am. Bapt. Sem. of the West, Berkeley, Calif., 1967-82, Grad. Theol. Union, Berkeley, 1983-90; prof., dean Am. Bapt. Sem. of the West, Berkeley, 1990—; rep. No. Calif. Ecumenical Coun., 1985-88; mem. Bapt. Peace Fellowship of North Am., 1970—. Author: Moment of Truth for Protestant America, 1974, Without Help or Hindrance, 1977, 87, Pilgrim Progression 1993; author: (with others) religion and Society in the American West, 1987; contbr. articles to profl. jours. Rsch. grantee Lilly Endowment, U. Calif., Santa Barbara, 1989-92. Mem. Am. Acad. Religion (pres. West regional chpt. 1985-86), Am. Soc. Ch. History, Am. Hist. Assn., Calif. Hist. Soc., Pacific Coast Theol. Soc., Sierra Club. Democrat. Home: 1855 San Antonio Ave Berkeley CA 94707-1617 Office: Am Bapt Sem of the West 2606 Dwight Way Berkeley CA 94704-3029

ERSKINE, JOHN MORSE, surgeon; b. San Francisco, Sept. 10, 1920; s. Morse and Dorothy (Ward) E. BS, Harvard U., 1942, MD, 1945. Diplomate Am. Bd. Surgery. Surg. intern U. Calif. Hosp., San Francisco, 1945-46; surg. researcher Mass. Gen. Hosp., Boston, 1948; resident in surgery Peter Bent Brigham Hosp., Boston, 1948-53; George Gorham Peters fellow St. Mary's Hosp., London, 1952; pvt. practice in medicine specializing in surgery San Francisco, 1954—; asst. clin. prof. Stanford Med. Sch., San Francisco, 1956-59; asst., assoc. clin. prof. U. Calif. Med. Sch., San Francisco, 1959—; surg. cons. San Francisco Vets. Hosp., 1959-73. Contbr. articles to profl. jours., chpts. to books. Founder No. Calif. Artery Bank, 1954-58, Irwin Meml. Blood Bank, San Francisco, commr., pres., 1969-74; bd. dirs. People for Open Space-Greenbelt Alliance, 1984—; chmn. adv. coun. Dorothy Enskine Open Space Fund. Capt. with U.S. Army, 1946-48. Fellow ACS; mem. San Francisco Med. Soc. (bd. dirs. 1968-72), San Francisco Surg. Soc. (v.p. 1984), Pacific Coast Surg. Soc., Am. Cancer Soc. (bd. dirs. San Francisco br. 1965-75), Calif. Med. Assn., Olympic Club, Sierra Club. Democrat. Unitarian. Home: 233 Chestnut St San Francisco CA 94133-2452 Office: 2340 Clay St San Francisco CA 94115-1932

ERSLEV, ERIC ALLAN, geologist, educator; b. Harvard, Mass., Jan. 30, 1954; s. Allan Jacob and Betsy (Lewis) E.; m. Kathryn Tweedie, June 19, 1976; children: Peter Tweedie, Brett Covey. BS, Wesleyan U., 1976; AM, Harvard U., 1978, PhD, 1981. Asst. prof. Lafayette Coll., Easton, Pa., 1981-83; asst. prof. Colo. State U., Fort Collins, 1983-89, assoc. prof., 1989-95; prof., 1995—. Editor: Laramide Basement Deformation, 1993; contbr. articles to profl. jours. Mem. Am. Assn. Petroleum Geologists, Geol. Soc. Am., Colo. Sci. Soc. (councilor 1992-94), Rocky Mountain Assn. Geologists (structure series editor 1988—). Unitarian. Office: Colo State Univ Dept Earth Resources Fort Collins CO 80523

ERVIN, ARDITH ANN, psychiatric social worker; b. St. Charles, Ill., June 13, 1935; d. Arden J. and Helen Mildred (Carlson) Zollers; m. Don L. Ervin, Sept. 25, 1954 (div. Mar. 1975); children: Ann Lee, Mark Richard, Daniel Arden; m. Bill D. Toland, Dec. 31, 1983 (div. Aug. 1987). Student, Presbyn. Hosp. Sch. Nursing., 1953-54; RN, Community Coll. of Denver, 1973; BSW magna cum laude, Met. State Coll., 1974; MSW magna cum laude, U. Denver, 1984. With Jefferson County Dept. Social Services, Lakewood, Colo., 1972-75, Larimer County Dept. Social Services, Ft. Collins, Colo., 1975-83; pvt. practice social work Colo., 1976-78; psychiat. social worker S.E. Wyo. Mental Health Ctr., Cheyenne, 1984-87; founder with others The Jacob Center, Inc., 1988. Organizer Parents Anonymous Groups, Ind., 1975, leader; v.p. Child Protective Service Workers, 1979-80; bd. dirs. United Day Care Ctr., Ft. Collins., 1978-79, Larico Youth Home, Ft. Collins., 1978-80, Youth Shelter Care, Ft. Collins, 1980-82. Vol. Service award, Jefferson County; named one of Agency of Yr., 1992. Mem. Nat. Assn. Social Workers. Lutheran. Home: 1217 Village Ln Fort Collins CO 80521-4232

ERVIN, MARGARET HOWIE, elementary educator, special education educator; b. L.A., May 13, 1924; d. James Stanley and Margaret (Goff) H.; m. E. Frank Ervin, Mar. 22, 1947 (div. 1957); children: Frank, Daniel, Charles. BA, Fresno (Calif.) State U., 1958; grad. student, Purdue U., 1965-66, San Francisco State U., 1974-75. Cert. elem. and spl. edn. tchr. Elem. tchr. Clovis (Calif.) Schs., 1958-60, Fremont (Calif.) Unified Schs., 1960-83; spl. tchr. in summers Dominican Coll., San Rafael, Calif., 1972-78; asst. dir., cons. Arena Sch. and Learning Ctr., San Rafael, 1974-75; dir. Ervin Sch. and Learning Ctr., San Rafael, 1983-88; researcher, tchr. Primaria Sch. #110 PRI9745, Celaya, Mex., 1988; elem., spl. tchr. Napa (Calif.) City/County Schs., 1989—; diagnosis cons. Ervin Learning Ctr., Napa, 1989—; spl. edn. guest speaker various cities, U.S., Can., 1974—; learning seminar Parents and Tchrs., Mexico, summer 1992, Psycho-motor Tgn. Don Bosco Home for Girls, Mexico, summer 1993. Vol. Option Inst. and Fellowship, "Sonrise" autism/devel. disabilities, Sheffield, Mass., summer 1994; pres. Children Handicapped Learning Devel., Calif., 1971-72, tchr. parents, 1970-80, 94—; bay area rep. Calif. Tchrs. Assn., Burlingame, 1970-74. Recipient cert. of merit Calif. Tchrs. Assn., Burlingame, 1974, $5,000 gift to Ervin Sch. Calif. Assn. Neurol. Handicapped Children, Fremont, 1984. Mem. AAUW, NOW, Assn. Children With Learning Disabilities (trustee). Democrat. Unitarian. Home and Office: Ervin Learning Ctr 1695 Pine St # 9 Napa CA 94559-3852

ERVIN, PATRICK FRANKLIN, nuclear engineer; b. Kansas City, Kans., Aug. 4, 1946; s. James Franklin and Irma Lee (Arnett) E.; m. Rita Jeanne Kimsey, Aug. 12, 1967; children: James, Kevin, Amber. BS in Nuclear Engring., Kans. State U., 1969, MS in Nuclear Engring., 1971; postgrad., Northeastern U., 1988. Registered profl. engr., Ill., Colo., Calif., Idaho, Wash.; cert. paleontology paraprofl., Colo. Reactor health physicist Dept. Nuclear Engring. Kans. State U., Manhattan, 1968-69, rsch. asst. Dept. Nuclear Engring., 1969-72, sr. reactor operator, temp. facility dir. Dept. Nuclear Engring., 1970-72; system test engr. Commonwealth Edison Co., Zion, Ill., 1972-73, 73-74; shift foreman Commonwealth Edison Co., Zion, 1973, shift foreman with sr. reactor operator lic., 1974-76, prin. engr., 1976-77, acting operating engr., 1977; tech. staff supr. Commonwealth Edison Co., Byron, Ill., 1977-81; lead test engr. Stone & Webster Engring. Corp., Denver, 1982-83, project mgr., 1982—, ops. svcs. supr., 1982-86, asst. engring. mgr., 1986-89, consulting engr., 1989-94; sr. cons., 1994—. Contbr. articles to profl. jours. Served with U.S. Army N.G., 1971-77. Mem. Am. Nuclear Soc. (Nat. and Colo. chpts.), Am. Nat. Standards Inst. (working group on containment leakage testing). Republican. Roman Catholic. Home: 2978 S Bahama St Aurora CO 80013-2340 Office: Stone & Webster Engring PO Box 5406 Denver CO 80217-5406

ERVING, CLAUDE MOORE, JR., military career officer, pilot; b. St. John's, N.F., Can., Sept. 10, 1952; s. Claude Moore Sr. and Ingeborg (Mauss) E.; m. Donna Lee Mathis, June 17, 1978; children: Zachary C., Allyson B., Michael J. M. BS in Geography, USAF Acad., 1975. Commd. 2d lt. USAF, 1975, advanced through grades to lt. col., 1979; check pilot, instr. 85th Flying Tng. Squadron, Laughlin AFB, Tex., 1976-80; flight examiner, instr. pilot, flight comdr. 460th Fighter Interceptor Tng. Squadron, Peterson AFB, Colo., 1980-82; flight comdr. 49th Fighter Interceptor Squadron, Griffiss AFB, N.Y., 1982-85; chief of tng. 18th Tactical Fighter Squadron, Eielson AFB, Alaska, 1985-86; chief of flight safety, asst. chief of safety 343d Tactical Fighter Wing, Eielson AFB, Alsaka, 1986-88; chief ops. plans div. and exec. officer to dep. comdr. ops. for 11th Air Force and Alaskan NORAD region Hdqrs. Alaskan Air Command, Elmendorf AFB, 1988-92; comdr. 94th airmanship tng. squadron USAF Acad., Colo., 1992-94, dep. dir. pub. affairs, 1994—; aircraft accident investigator USAF, worldwide, 1986—. Mem. CAP (flight comdr. 1990-93). Republican. Home: 1049 Golden Pine Ln Monument CO 80132-9345

ERWIN, DONALD CARROLL, plant pathology educator; b. Concord, Nebr., Nov. 24, 1920; s. Robert James and Carol (Sexson) E.; m. Veora Marie Endres, Aug. 15, 1948; children: Daniel Erwin, Myriam Erwin Casey. Student, Wayne State (Nebr.) Tchrs.Coll, 1938-39; BSc, U. Nebr., 1949, MA, 1950; PhD, U. Calif.-Davis, 1953. Jr. plant pathologist U. Calif., Riverside, 1953-54; asst. plant pathologist U. Calif., 1954-60, assoc. plant pathologist, 1960-66, prof. plant pathology, 1966—, emeritus prof., 1991. Editor: Phytophthora: Its Biology, Taxonomy, Ecology and Pathology, 1983; contbr. articles to profl. jours. With U.S. Army, 1942-46; ETO. Nathan Gold fellow, 1949, Guggenheim fellow, 1959. Fellow Am. Phytopathol. Soc., Sigma Xi. Democrat. Roman Catholic. Office: U Calif Dept Plant Pathology Riverside CA 92521

ERWIN, ELMER LOUIS, vintager, cement consultant; b. Visalia, Calif., Oct. 6, 1926; s. Louis Nelson and Myra Erla (Hector) E.; m. Jeanne Prothero, Feb. 27, 1954; children: Catherine Lynn, Christopher Lawrence. B.S., U. Calif.-Berkeley, 1950. Registered profl. engr., Calif. With Kaiser Cement Corp., Oakland, Calif., 1957-80, v.p. mfg. and distbn., 1980-87; freelance vintager; cons. internat. cement plant projects.

ESCAMILLA, RICHARD, farm labor contracting executive; b. 1985. Field supr. Bud Antle, Salinas, Calif., 1962-85; with Escamilla & Sons, Inc., Salinas, Calif., 1985—, pres.; v.p. Tara Packing Co., Salinas, Calif. Office: Tara Packing Co 320 W Market St Salinas CA 93901-1420*

ESCHENBACH, RICHARD COREY, mechanical engineer; b. Williamsport, Pa., Apr. 9, 1927; s. A. Edgar and C. Vivian (Corey) E.; m. Mary Margaret Graham, Dec. 24, 1948 (div. Aug. 1965); children: Theodore G., Sherry E.; m. Julia Faulkner Hull, Dec. 27, 1966; 1 child, Allen Edgar. BS in Physics, Carnegie-Mellon U., 1948, MS in Physics, 1949; PhD in Mech. Engring., Purdue U., 1957. Rsch. engr. Union Carbide Corp., Tonawanda, N.Y., 1948-54; supr. Union Carbide Corp., Speedway, Ind., 1954-69; mgr. adminstrn. and svcs. Union Carbide Corp., Tarrytown, N.Y., 1969-83; tech. mgr. Retech Inc., Ukiah, Calif., 1983—; mem. evaluation com. NCEE, NSF, Washington, 1988. Author: (with others) Metallurgical Applications of Plasma Technology, 1987; patentee (13) in field. Chmn. parks and recreation Town of Somers, N.Y., 1973-83; dir. choir Good Shepherd Episcopal Ch., Granite Springs, N.Y., 1975-83. George Westinghouse scholar, 1944; Shell Oil Co. fellow, 1957. Mem. AAAS (life), Am. Contract Bridge Club, Mining Met. and Materials Soc. Republican. Lutheran. Home: 2181 Fawn Pl Ukiah CA 95482-3623 Office: Retech Inc 100 Henry Station Rd Ukiah CA 95482-9601

ESFORMES, JOSEPH, agricultural products company executive; b. 1934. Graduate, U. Miami, 1957. V.p. Jack Esformes Corp., Miami, Fla., 1950—, Triple E Produces Corp., Tracy, Calif., 1965—; with Esformes Properties, Tracy, Calif., 1985—. Office: Triple E Produces Corp 8690 W Linne Rd Tracy CA 95376-9137*

ESFORMES, NATHAN, food products executive; b. 1936. BS, U. Miami, 1953. Pres. Jack Esformes Corp., 1950—, Triple E Produce Corp., 1953—. Office: Triple E Produce Corp 8690 W Linne Rd Tracy CA 95376

ESHELMAN, ENOS GRANT, JR., prosthodontist; b. Birmingham, Ala., Oct. 18, 1943; s. Enos Grant and Kathleen Marie (Lokey) E.; m. Mary Darlene Duncan, Nov. 22, 1975; children: Duncan Grant, Hunter Nicholas, Parker Jacob. AB, Franklin and Marshall Coll., Lancaster, Pa., 1965; DDS, Columbia U., 1969; MS, U. Mo., 1980. Commd. 2d lt. USAF, advanced through grades to col., 1969-86; gen. dental officer USAF, Lackland AFB, Tex., 1969-72; asst. base dental surgeon, oral surgeon, dental officer USAF, Korat Air Base, Thailand, 1972-73; asst. base dental surgeon, prosthodontics and lab. officer USAF, Sembach Air Base, Germany, 1973-78; chief prosthodontics USAF, Norton AFB, Calif., 1980-83; prosthodontics tng. officer USAF Hosp., Davis Monthan AFB, Ariz., 1983-89; chief prosthodontics, dental lab. officer 36 TFW Hosp., Bitburg Air Base, Germany, 1989-93; tng. offcr. prosthodontics USAF Hosp., Langley AFB, Va., 1993—; asst. prof. Loma Linda (Calif.) U. Sch. Dentistry, 1981-83; prosthodontics cons. Jerry Pettis Vets. Hosp., Loma Linda, 1982-83, Vets. Affairs Med. Ctr., Tucson, 1983-89; pres. Fed. Svcs. Regional Dental Conf., Davis Monthan AFB, Ariz., 1983-85. Pres. Jr. Officers Coun., Korat Air Base, Thailand, 1973; asst. coach Sabino Little League Baseball, Tucson, 1988-89; pres. Cmty. Summer Swim Team. Rinehart Found. rsch. grantee U. Mo. Sch. Dentistry, 1978; decorated Meritorious Svc. medal. Mem. ADA, Am. Coll. Prosthodontics, Fedn. Prosthodontic Orgns., Internat. Coll. Dentists, Air Force Assn., Psi Omega. Home: 7141 E River Canyon Rd Tucson AZ 85715-2111

ESHELMAN, WILLIAM ROBERT, librarian, editor; b. Oklahoma City, Aug. 23, 1921; s. Cyrus Lenhert and Fern (Reed) E.; m. Mimi Blau, July 3, 1952 (div. Aug. 1956); m. Eve Kendall, June 21, 1957 (div. Apr. 1975); children: Ann, Benjamin, Zachary; m. Pat Rom, Dec. 29, 1977. BA, Chapman Coll., Los Angeles, 1943; MA, U. Calif. at Los Angeles, 1950; BLS, U. Calif. at Berkeley, 1951. Conscripted in civilian pub. service Waldport, Oreg., 1943-46; asst. dir., 1944-45; ptnr. Untide Press, Pasadena, Calif., 1946-65; teaching asst. UCLA, 1949-50, library asst., 1950; faculty Los Angeles State Coll., 1951-65, asst. librarian, 1954-59, coll. librarian, 1959-65; librarian, prof. bibliography Bucknell U., 1965-68; editor Wilson Library Bull., 1968-78; pres. Scarecrow Press, Metuchen, N.J., 1979-86; proprietor The Press at the Camperdown Elm, Wooster, Ohio, 1987-93. Editor: Take Hold Upon the Future: Letters on Writers and Writing by William Everson and Lawrence Clark Powell, 1938-1946, 1994; contbg. author: Perspectives on William Everson, 1992; mem. editl. bd. Choice, 1966-71. Bd. dirs. Grolier Edn. Corp., 1979-86; mem. adv. council edn. for librarianship U. Calif., 1961-64; mem. acad. senate Calif. State Colls., 1964-65. Mem. AAUP (v.p. L.A. State Coll. 1958-59, pres. 1964-65), ALA (winner Libr. Periodicals award 1960, editorial com. 1964-66, mem. coun. 1972-76, com. accreditation 1977-79), Calif. Libr. Assn. (chmn. intellectual freedom com., pres. so. dist. 1965, editor Calif. Libr. jour. 1960-63), Assn. Coll. and Rsch. Librs. (publs. com.), Assn. Calif. State Coll. Profs., ACLU, Friends Com. Legis., N.J. Libr. Assn. (hon.), Rounce and Coffin Club (L.A.; sec.-treas. 1953-56), Typophiles CLub (N.Y.C.). Home and Office: 950 SW 21st Ave Apt 912 Portland OR 97205-1518

ESHOO, ANNA GEORGES, congresswoman; b. New Britain, Conn., Dec. 13, 1942; d. Fred and Alice Alexandre Georges; children: Karen Elizabeth, Paul Frederick. AA with honors, Canada Coll., 1975. Chmn. San Mateo County Dem. Ctrl. Com., Calif., 1978-82; chair Human Rels. Com., 79-82; mem. Congress from 14th Dist. Calif., 1993—; mem. com. on commerce Congress from 14th Calif. dist., 1995—; regional minority whip 5; chief of staff Calif. Assembly Spkr. Leo McCarthy, 1981; regional majority whip No. Calif., 1993-94. Co-founder Women's Hall of Fame; chair San Mateo County (Calif.) Dem. Party, 1980; active San Mateo County Bd. Suprs., 1982-92, pres., 1986; pres. Bay Area Air Quality Mgmt. Dist., 1982-92; mem. San Francisco Bay Conservation Devel. Commn., 1982-92; chair San Mateo County Gen. Hosp. Bd. Dirs. Roman Catholic. Office: US Ho of Reps Office Of House Mems Washington DC 20515

ESKEW, CATHLEEN CHEEK, social services administrator; b. Oklahoma City, Oct. 20, 1953; d. John Dasherman and Nancy Lucile (Gray) Cheek; m. Bruce Lynn Eskew, Aug. 23, 1986; children : William Michael amd Matthew James (twins), Anna Elaine. BA in Math., Whitworth Coll., 1976; MST, Fuller Sem., Pasadena, Calif., 1984; postgrad., U. Colo., Colorado Springs, Inst. Children's Lit., 1989-91. Cert. secondary tchr., Colo. Tchr., adminstrv. asst. The Colorado Springs Sch., 1976-78; recruiter, trainer Young Life, Colorado Springs, 1978-82; mem. publs. and stats. staff Young Life Internat., Port-au-Prince, Haiti, 1982-83; documentation specialist Compassion Internat., Colorado Springs, 1984-85, program adminstr., 1986-88; secondary edn. math. tutor, 1994. Elder Presbyn. Ch., 1992-94, growth commn., 1993-94. Named Outstanding Young Woman in Am., 1981. Mem. Assn. Evang. Relief and Devel. Orgn., Whitworth Coll. Alumni Assn. (coun. person 1978-81). Democrat. Home: 1365 Oak Hills Dr Colorado Springs CO 80919-1425

ESKIN, BARRY SANFORD, court investigator; b. Pitts., Mar. 6, 1943; s. Saul and Dorothy (Zaron) E.; m. M. Joyce Rosalind, Sept. 12, 1965; 1 child, David. AA, Los Angeles City Coll., 1963; BA, Calif. State U., Los Angeles, 1965; JD, Citrus Belt Law Sch., 1976. Bar: Calif. 1976. Social service worker San Bernardino (Calif.) Dept. Pub. Social Services, 1965-77; assoc. Law Office of Lawrence Novack, San Bernardino, 1978; ct. investigator San Bernardino Superior Ct., 1978, supervising investigator, 1978—; pro bono atty. Mex. Am. Commn., 1977-78. Mem. ARC Svc. Ctr. Advising Bd., San Bernardino, 1980-82; bd. dirs. Golden Valley Civ. Assn., San Bernardino, 1978-81, Congregation Emanuel, San Bernardino, 1984-87, bd. dirs. 1994—. Mem. ABA, Calif. Assn. of Superior Ct. Investigators (pres. 1980-81, treas. 1984-85, bd. dirs.), San Bernardino County Bar Assn., Alpha Phi Omega. Democrat. Jewish. Office: San Bernardino Superior Ct 351 N Arrowhead Ave Rm 200 San Bernardino CA 92401-1605

ESKRIDGE, JAMES ARTHUR, toy company executive; b. San Diego, Dec. 25, 1942; s. Arthur Walker and Evelyn Louise (Meyers) E.; m. Sharen Elaine Creamer, Mar. 14, 1962; children: Jennifer, Mark. BA, U. Calif., Riverside, 1968; MBA, Harvard U., 1975. Acct. Gen. Motors Corp., L.A., 1968-70; dir. treasury Gen. Motors Corp., N.Y.C., 1970-77; exec. asst. pres. Gen. Motors Corp., Detroit, 1977-82; v.p. control and adminstrn. Gen. Mills Non Foods, Mpls. and N.Y.C., 1982-86; exec. v.p. fin. and adminstrn. Cooper Communities, Inc., Bentonville, Ark., 1986-88; exec. v.p., chief fin. officer Mattel Inc., Hawthorne, Calif., 1989—. Pres. adv. bd. First Meth. Ch., Bentonville; bd. dirs. YMCA, Minnetonka, Minn., 1984; mem. N.W. Ark. Symphony Guild. Baker scholar Harvard U., 1975; Gen. Motors fellow, N.Y.C., 1973-75. Mem. Harvard Club, Palos Verdes Golf Club. Republican. Office: Mattel Inc 333 Continental Blvd El Segundo CA 90245-5032

ESLER, JOHN KENNETH, artist; b. Pilot Mound, Man., Can., Jan. 11, 1933; s. William John and Jennie Mae (Thompson) E.; m. Annemarie Schmid, June 26, 1964; children—William Sean, John Derek. B.F.A., U. Man., B.Ed., 1962. Mem. faculty dept. art Alta. Coll. Art, 1964-68; mem. faculty U. Calgary, Alta., Can., 1968-80; chmn. Print and Drawing Council Can., 1976-78. One-man exhbn., Gallery Moos, Toronto, Ont., 1978, Past and Present: One-Man Exhbn. Painting. Triangle Gallery, Calgary, Alberta, 1994, Retrospective/35 Years Printmaking, U. of C. Nickle Arts Mus., Calgary, Travelling exhbn., Sept. 1994; represented in permanent collections, Victoria and Albert Mus., London, Eng., Albright Knox Gallery, Buffalo, N.Y., Mus. Modern Art, N.Y.C., Nat. Gallery Can., Ottawa, Ont.; Author: Printing in Alberta. Life mem. Print and Drawing Coun. Can. Address: Box 2 Site 7, SS 1, Calgary, AB Canada T2M 4N3

ESLINGER, MICHAEL RONALD, nurse anesthetist; b. Newport, Tenn., Apr. 1, 1948; s. Mike Little and Vivian Ruth (Ray) E.; m. Karen Elaine Brooks, Feb. 13, 1976. Diploma, St. Mary's Nursing Sch., Knoxville, Tenn., 1970; diploma in anesthesia, U. Tenn., Knoxville, Tenn., 1974; BS in Health Care Adminstrn., St. Joseph's Coll., Windham, Maine, 1989; MA in Nat. Security & Strategic Studies, U.S. Naval War Coll., Newport, R.I., 1994. RN, Tenn., Fla. Pediatric nurse practitioner U.S. Army pediatric clinic, 1970-73; staff nurse anesthetist Knoxville Anesthesia Group, 1975-85; commd. lt. USN, 1969, advanced through grades to comdr., 1994; served with nurse corps Naval Hosp., Long Beach, Calif., 1985-88; nurse anesthetist USS Forrestal USN, 1989-90; staff nurse anesthetist Naval Hosp., Jacksonville, Fla., 1990-93, USNS Mercy, Oakland, Calif., 1994—; pres. Pro-Ed Seminars, Knoxville, 1978-84, Mika Health Care, Orange Park, Fla., 1991-92. Author, editor First Aid Book, 1989; contbr. to profl. publs. Pvt. USMC, 1966-67. Mem. Am. Assn. Nurse Anesthetists (cert.), Hypnosis Guild, Calif. Assn. Nurse Anesthetists, Assn. Mil. Surgeons of U.S. Office: US Navy USNS Mercy T-AH 19 Naval Supply Ctr Oakland CA 94625

ESPEY, WILLIAM MALLONEÉ, psychiatrist; b. Trinidad, Colo, June 3, 1938; s. James Gill Jr. and Virginia (Mallonee) E. BA, U. Colo., 1960, MD, 1964. Diplomate Am. Bd. Psychiatry and Neurology. Resident in psychiatry U. Colo. Sch. Medicine, 1968-72; staff psychiatrist Colo. State Hosp., 1970-71, teaching fellow, 1971-72; pvt. practice Denver, 1972—; asst. clin. instr. psychiatry U. Colo., Denver, 1972-80, asst. clin. prof. psychiatry, 1980—; staff psychiatrist Denver VA Hosp., 1972-77, 90—; cons. United Airlines, 1989-90; therapist HIV support group Denver Nursing Project in Human Caring, 1990—; mem. mental health clinic staff VA Hosp., 1972-77, 90—; cons. to dept. pastoral counseling Presbyn. Med. Ctr., 1976-80; mem. partial hospitalization com. Mount Airy Psychiat. Hosp., 1975-79, chmn., 1977-78, med. exec. com., 1981-82; mem. med. necessities com. Bethesda Psychiat. Hosp., 1977-81, 85-86, adolescent adv. com., 1978-80, patient care evaluation com., 1981-84, med. records com., 1987-90; staff psychiatrist Fitzsimmons Army Hosp., 1990-92. Mem. Gov.'s AIDS Coun., 1992—, vice chairperson, 1993—, chairperson HIV testing issues policy com. Fellow Am. Psychiat. Assn.; mem. Colo. Psychiat. Soc. (program com. 1986-87, AIDS edn. com. 1988—, exec. coun. 1989-91, sr. trustee area VII 1990-91), Colo. Med. Soc., Denver Med. Soc. Office: 4495 Hale Pky Ste 350 Denver CO 80220-6204

ESQUER, DEBORAH ANNE, elementary education educator; b. Omaha, Oct. 28, 1950; d. Thomas Ross and Carolyn Mae (Wright) Woods; m. Mario H. Esquer, Aug. 21, 1971 (div. Apr. 1991); children: Mario, Michael. BA, Ariz. State U., 1972, MA in Edn., 1972, 78; postgrad., Ottawa U., Phoenix, 1990-92. Cert. elem. tchr., spl. edn. Tchr. Paradise Valley Sch. Dist., Phoenix, 1972—. Dem. precinct com. person; state Dem. com. person. Tchr. venture grantee, Phoenix, 1988. Mem. NEA, Ariz. Edn. Assn., Paradise Valley Edn. Assn., Paradise Valley Reading Coun., Phoenix Art Mus., Ariz. Hist. Soc., Paradise Valley Jr. Women's Club (corr. sec. 1991-92), Alpha Delta Kappa (pres. 1986-88, ctrl. dist. treas. 1986-88, corr. sec. 1992-94, treas. 1994—), Alpha Phi. Democrat. Methodist. Office: Desert Springs 6010 E Acoma Dr Scottsdale AZ 85254-2521

ESQUIVEL, JOE G., food products executive; b. 1938. With Hanson Farms, Salinas, Calif., 1967-83; pres. Adobe Packing Co., Salinas, Calif., 1983—. Office: Adobe Packing Co 373 W Market St Salinas CA 93901-1423*

ESQUIVEL, MARY, agricultural products company executive; b. 1945. Homemaker, 1976; ct. interpreter State of Calif., Salinas, 1976-83; sec., treas. Adobe Packing Co., Salinas, 1983—. Office: Adobe Packing Co 373 W Market St Salinas CA 93901-1423*

ESRALIAN, MICHAEL JIM, process engineer; b. Pontiac, Mich., Jan. 16, 1951; s. Charles Jim and Sarah Whit (Loftice) E.; m. Shirley C., Aug. 5, 1983; 1 child, Jonathan Scott Cruse. BS in Chemistry, Oakland U., 1973; MS in Chemistry, U. Wyo., 1976. Process engr. Tex. Instruments, Sherman, Tex., 1976-79, Mostek Corp., Carrollton, Tex., 1979-81; sr. process engr. Teccor Semiconductor, Irving, Tex., 1981-85, Tektronix, Beaverton, Oreg., 1985-93; diffusion engr. Intel Corp., Aloha, Oreg., 1993—. Elder Presbyn. Ch., Pontiac, Mich., 1973-74. Presbyterian. Home: 2400 SW 204th Ave Aloha OR 97006-1873 Office: Intel Corp Aloha OR 97006

ESSA, LISA BETH, elementary education educator; b. Modesto, Calif., Nov. 19, 1955; d. Mark Newyia and Elizabeth (Warda) E. BA, U. Pacific-Stockton, 1977, MA in Curriculum and Instrn. Reading, 1980. Cert. tchr. elem., multiple subject and reading specialist, Calif. Tchr. primary grades Delhi (Calif.) Elem. Sch. Dist., 1978-80; reading clinic tutor San Joaquin Delta Community Coll., Stockton, Calif., 1980; tchr. primary grades Hayward (Calif.) Unified Sch. Dist., Supr., San Francisco host com. Dem. Nat. Conv., 1984. Femmes Club scholar, 1973; U. Calif. Optometry Alumni Assn. scholar, 1973; Jobs Daughters scholar, 1974. Mem. Internat. Reading Assn., Calif. Tchrs. Assn., Hayward Unified Tchrs. Assn., San Francisco Jr. C. of C., Jr. League San Francisco. Democrat. Episcopalian. Home: 1960 Clay St Apt 109 San Francisco CA 94109-3435

ES-SAID, OMAR SALIM, metallurgy educator; b. Cairo, Egypt, Apr. 3, 1952; came to U.S., 1981; s. Salim Asim and Haifa Aref (El-Imam) E. BS, Am. U., Cairo, 1976, MS, 1979; PhD, U. Ky., 1985. Bilingual tng. tchr Arabian Am. Oil Co., Dharan, Saudi Arabia, 1979-81; grad. rsch. asst. U. Ky., Lexington, 1981-85; asst. prof. mech. engring. Loyola Marymount U., L.A., 1985-92, assoc. prof., 1992—, dir. mech. engring. grad. program, 1986-90. Contbr. articles to profl. jours. Mem. Islamic Catholic Com., L.A., 1986—. Grantee NSF, 1986, Soc. Mech. Engrs., 1987, Dept. of Engery, 1988. Mem. AAUP, ASME, AIME, Am. Soc. Metals, Internat. Assn. Sci. and Tech. for Devel., Am. Soc. Engring. Edn., Alpha Sigma Mu. Home: 8155 Manitoba St Apt 9 Playa Del Rey CA 90293-8671 Office: Loyola Marymount U Loyola Blvd at W 80th St Los Angeles CA 90045

ESSICK, RAYMOND BROOKE, III, amateur sports administrator; b. Murphysboro, Ill., Sept. 18, 1933; s. Raymond Brooke Jr. and Ida Mae (Bailey) E.; m. Frances Antoinette Stewart, June 14, 1958; children: Raymond Brooke IV, Anne, Bradley, Katherine. BS in Phys. Edn., U. Ill., 1955, MS in Phys. Edn., 1958. Swimming tchr., coach New Trier Twp. High Sch., Winnetka, Ill., 1958-66, So. Ill. U., Carbondale, 1966-73; swimming coach Harvard U., Cambridge, Mass., 1973-76; swimming adminstr. Nat. Amateur Athletic Union, Indpls., 1976-78; exec. dir. U.S. Swimming, Inc., Colorado Springs, Colo., 1978—. Contbr. articles to profl. jours. With USN, 1955-57. John Newman award Ill. Swimming Assn., 1977; named Coach of Yr., Coll. Swimming Coaches Assn., 1971. Mem. Am. Swimming Coaches Assn., Nat. Interscholastic Swim Coach Assn., U. Ill. Lettermans Club, Colo. Springs Sports Corp., Ind. Amateur Sports Corp., Broadmoor Golf Club, Country Club Colo., U.S. Olympic Com. (chmn. coaches edn. com., athlete performance com., substance abuse com., TV com.). Office: US Swimming Inc One Olympic Plz Colorado Springs CO 80909

ESSLINGER, ANNA MAE LINTHICUM, realtor; b. Clifton, Tenn., May 29, 1912; d. Wallace Prather and Minnie P. (Bates) Linthicum; student Miss. State Coll. Women, La. State U.; m. William Francis Esslinger, Sept. 29, 1932; children—Ann Lynn (Mrs. James C. Wilcox), Susan Angie (Mrs. Heinz J. Selig). Founder, Esslinger-Wooten-Maxwell Inc., real estate, Coral Gables, Fla., 1968-85 . Pres. Coral Gables Bd. Realtors, 1975. Mem. Fla. (dir.) Assn. Realtors, Nat. Assn. Realtors, DAR, Assistance League of Eugene, Am. Contract Bridge League, Eugene Country Club, Eugene Symphony Guild, Chi Omega. Christian Scientist. Home: 759 Fairoaks Dr Eugene OR 97401-2392 Office: 1360 S Dixie Hwy Miami FL 33146-2904

ESTEBAN, MANUEL ANTONIO, university administrator, educator; b. Barcelona, Spain, June 20, 1940; came to U.S., 1970; s. Manuel and Julia Esteban; m. Gloria Ribas, July 7, 1962; 1 child, Jacqueline. BA with 1st class honors in French, U. Calgary, Can., 1969, MA in Romance Studies, 1970; PhD in French, U. Calif., Santa Barbara, 1976. From asst. prof. to prof. French and Spanish langs. and lit. U. Mich., Dearborn, 1973-87, assoc. dean, 1984-86, acting dean coll. arts, scis., and letters, 1986-87; dean arts and scis. Calif. State U., Bakersfield, 1987-90; provost, v.p. acad. affairs Humboldt State U., Arcata, Calif., 1990-93; pres., prof. French and Spanish Calif. State U., Chico, 1993—; mem. Calif.-Catalonia Sister State Task Force, Sacramento, 1988-92; mem. Joint Policy Coun. on Agr. and Higher Edn., 1995—. Author: Georges Feydeau, 1983; contbr. books revs. and articles to profl. publs. Bd. dirs. Mercy Hosp., Bakersfield, 1989-90, U.S. Distance Learning Assn., 1994—. Woodrow Wilson fellow, 1969, doctoral fellow U. Calif., Santa Barbara, 1970-73, Can. Coun doctoral fellow, Govt. Can., 1970-73; Rackham grantee U. Mich., 1979, fellow, 1982-83. Mem. Coun. Colls. Arts and Scis. (bd. dirs. 1988-90), N.Am. Catalan Soc. (bd. dirs. 1984-93), Calif. State U. Inst. Tech. and Learning, U.S. Distance Learning Assn. Office: Calif State U Chico CA 95929-0150

ESTES, ANGELA M., English language educator; b. Washington, Dec. 12, 1950; d. John Douglas and Jane A. Estes. BS in Psychology, Washington State U., 1972, BA in English, 1973; MA in English, U. Ore., 1978, PhD in English, 1985. Asst. prof. dept. English Calif. Poly. State U., San Luis Obispo, 1987-92; assoc. prof. Calif. Poly. State U., 1992—; writing cons. Office Pers. Mgmt. Western Regional Tng. Ctr. U.S. Govt., 1983-84; faculty-artist-in-residence Calif. State U. Faculty Arts Inst., Kirkwood, Calif., 1989. Author: Boarding Pass, 1990, The Uses of Passion, 1995; contbr. articles, poems to profl. jours. Calif. Coun. Arts fellow, 1993, Children's Lit. Assn. rsch. fellow, 1992; Woodrow Wilson grantee, 1983; winner Peregrine Smith Poetry Competition, 1994. Mem. MLA, Philological Assn. Pacific Coast, Rocky Mountain MLA, Phi Beta Kappa, Phi Kappa Phi, Alpha Lambda Delta. Office: Calif Poly State U English Dept. San Luis Obispo CA 93407

ESTRIN, GERALD, computer scientist, engineering educator, academic administrator; b. N.Y.C., Sept. 9, 1921; married; 3 children. B.S., U. Wis., 1948, M.S., 1949, Ph.D. in Elec. Engring., 1951. Research engr. Inst. Advanced Study, Princeton U., 1950-53, 55-56; dir. electronic computing project Weizmann Inst. Sci., Israel, 1953-55; assoc. prof. engring. UCLA, 1956-58, prof., 1958-91, prof. emeritus, 1991—, chmn. dept. computer sci., 1979-82, 85-88; mem. adv. bd. applied math. div. Argonne Nat. Lab., 1966-68, mem. assoc. univs. rev. com. for chmn., 1976-77, mem. adv. bd. applied math. div., 1974-80, adv. com. NASA space Applications, 1983-86; dir. Computer Communications, Inc., 1966-67, Systems Engring. Labs., 1977-80; mem. internat. program com. Internat. Fedn. Info. Processing Congress, 1968; internat. program chmn. Jerusalem Conf. Info. Tech., 1971; mem. math. and computer sci. research adv. com. AEC; mem. sci. com., operating bd. Gould, Inc., Rolling Meadows, Ill., 1981-86; bd. govs. Weizmann Inst. Sci., 1971—. Lipsky fellow, 1954, Guggenheim fellow, 1963, 67; recipient Disting. Svc. award U. Wis., 1975, Jerusalem Conf. on Info. Tech. Spl. Recognition award, 1978, NASA Commendation, 1986. Fellow AAAS, IEEE (disting. spkr. 1980), Assn. Computing Machinery (nat. lectr. 1966-67). Office: UCLA Dept Computer Sci Los Angeles CA 90024-1596

ESTRUTH, JERRY THOMAS, financial professional; b. San Jose, Calif., Feb. 6, 1943; s. Thomas and Thelma Jeannette (Harter) E.; m. Margo Linn Spencer, Jan. 1, 1990; children: Jeannette Alden, Molly Kristen, Thomas Douglas. BA, Stanford U., 1964; CFP, Coll. Fin. Planning, Denver, 1985; cert., Dean Witter Mgmt. Tng., N.Y.C., 1985. Account exec., v.p. Dean Witter Reynolds, San Jose, 1969—; computer cons. Dean Witter Reynolds, 1982—, asst. mgr., 1986—. Columnist Sr. Times, 1987-88. Vol. Peace Corps, Colombia, 1964-67, mem. staff, 1967-69; mem. city coun. City of San Jose, 1979-84, vice-mayor, 1980; reader for Spanish-speaking blind Variety Audio and Peninsula Blind Ctr., San Jose and Palo Alto, Calif., 1974, 84; pres. Santa Clara unit Am. Cancer Soc., 1988; chair Open Space Com., Santa Clara County, 1988-90, Yes on Tobacco Tax com. Santa Clara County, 1990. Recipient Am. Field Svc. scholarship, 1959. Mem. Silicon Valley Capital Club (founder, mem. exec. com. 1990—), Masons (lodge trustee, Hiram award 1988). Democrat. Episcopalian. Home: 1254 University Ave San Jose CA 95126-1738 Office: Dean Witter Reynolds PO Box 1239 San Jose CA 95108-1239

ETCHART, FERDINAND J., food products executive. Mgr. Admiral Packing Co., Glendale, Ariz., 1964-72; now pres. Everkrisp Vegetables, Inc. Office: Everkrisp Vegetables Inc 9202 W Harrison St Tolleson AZ 85353*

ETCHART, MIKE, agricultural products company executive; b. 1961. V.p. Everkrisp Vegetables, Inc., Tolleson, Ariz. Office: Everkrisp Vegetables Inc 9202 W Harrison St Tolleson AZ 85353*

ETH, SPENCER, medical educator, psychiatrist; b. N.Y.C., May 16, 1950; s. William and Roslyn (Gable) E.; m. Cheryl D. Miller, Jan. 21, 1978; children: Warren S., Simon R., Marni L., A.B., NYU, 1971; postgrad. Oxford U., 1973-75; M.D., UCLA, 1976. Diplomate Am. Bd. Psychiatry and Neurology. Resident in psychiatry N.Y. Hosp-Cornell Med. Ctr., N.Y.C., 1976-79; fellow in child psychiatry Cedars-Sinai Med. Ctr., Los Angeles, 1979-81; asst. prof. psychiatry Los Angeles County-U. So. Calif. Med. Ctr., Los Angeles, 1981-84; clin. assoc. prof. psychiatry, U. So. Calif., 1987-93; asst. prof. psychiatry UCLA, 1984-93; clin. prof. psychiatry W. So. Calif., 1993—; assoc. prof. clin. psychiatry UCLA, 1992—; cons. in field. Editor monograph: Post-Traumatic Stress Disorder in Children, 1985; contbr. articles to profl. jours. Rhodes scholar, 1973. Fellow Am. Psychiat. Assn., Am. Acad. Child Psychiatry (J.F. Robinson award 1982), Am. Acad. Psychiatry and Law (M.S. Guttmacher award 1986). Office: W LA VA Med Ctr Los Angeles CA 90073

ETHRIDGE, FRANK GULDE, geology educator, consultant; b. Meridian, Miss., Dec. 21, 1938. BS, Miss. State U., 1960; MS, La. State U., 1966; PhD, Tex. A&M U., 1970. Prodn. geologist Chevron Oil Co., New Orleans, 1965-67; asst. prof. So. Ill. U., Carbondale, 1970-74, assoc. prof., 1974-75; assoc. prof. Colo. State U., Ft. Collins, 1975-81, prof., 1981—, acting head dept. earth resources, 1989, 95; cons. in field, Ft. Collins, 1977—. Co-editor: Recent and Ancient Nonmarine Depositional Environments: Medals for Exploration, 1981, Fluvial Sedimentology, 1987. 1st Lt. U.S. Army, 1960-63. Fellow Tex. A&M U., 1967, 68, grad. fellow 1970, Halbouty scholar, 1969; faculty devel. grantee Colo. State U., 1986; recipient Achievement award for outstanding performance in grad. edn. Burlington No., 1993. Mem. Internat. Assn. Sedimentologists, Am. Assn. Petroleum Geologists (assoc. editor 1983-94), Soc. Sedimentary Geologists (Rocky Mtn. sect. sec. 1977-78, v.p. 1978-79, pres. 1983-84), Rocky Mtn. Assn. Geologists, Sigma Xi. Roman Catholic. Office: Colo State U Dept Earth Resources Fort Collins CO 80523

ETT, ALAN PAUL, composer; b. Detroit, Mar. 2, 1952; s. Seymour and Florence (Lesan) E. BA in Psychology, U. N.C., 1972; MM, New Eng. Conservatory, 1978. Faculty Berklee Coll. Music, Boston, 1976-79; internat. concert performer W. Europe, North Am., 1979-83; composer, producer various groups, L.A., 1983—; musical dir. in field; master classes W. German Kulturamt, 1979-83. Composer music for TV shows including 227, Who's the Boss, 1987-89, Unsolved Mysteries, 1989-91, Wild & Crazy Kids, Why Didn't I Think of That, 1992, TV's Funniest Commercials, 1992, Shame on You, 1993, How'd They Do That, 1993, Behind the Scenes with Joan Lunden, 1994; films including Fourth War, Cold Feet, Mob Boss, Madhouse, 1988-90, Pacific Heights, Thelma & Louise, Madonna-Truth or Dare; videos including Kareem-Reflections, 1989 (Golden Globe award); advt. campaigns including MCI, GM, Mazda, MCA Universal. Mem. Broadcast Music Inc., Am. Fedn. Musicians. Home: 11542 Decente Dr Studio City CA 91604-3868 Office: Alan Ett Music 3500 W Olive Ave Ste 1470 Burbank CA 91505-4628

ETTENBERG, FRANK JOSEPH, artist; b. Bklyn., May 7, 1945; s. Manuel David and Rose (Edelman) E.; m. Silvia Stenitzer, Dec. 16, 1990. BS in Design, U. Mich., 1966; MA in Painting, U. N.Mex., 1971. Cert. in graphoanalysis Internat. Graphoanalysis Soc., Chgo., 1977. Gallery preparator Hills Gallery, Santa Fe, 1975-77; slipcaster Animals and Co., La Cienega, N.Mex., 1982-84; picture framer Gavin Collier & Co., Santa Fe, 1990-91; preparator, registrar Erdman Designs, Santa Fe, 1991-93; exhibiting artist Galerie Cosmos, Vienna, Austria, 1994—, Okum Gallery, Santa Fe, N. Mex., 1995—; handwriting analyst pvt. practice, Santa Fe, 1972—; crater, shipper, Santa Fe, 1972—; art restorer Santa Fe, 1976—. Paintings include Deep Sea Falls, 1989; represented in Albuquerque Internat. Airport Collection. Steering com. Advocates for Contemporary Art, Santa Fe, 1974-76, 77-78. Recipient Artists-in-Residence scholarship Tamarind Inst., Albuquerque, 1987; Artist-in-Residence grantee Roswell Mus. and Art Ctr., 1971-72.

ETTINGER, JOSEPH ALAN, lawyer; b. N.Y.C., July 21, 1931; s. Max and Frances E.; children: Amy Beth, Ellen Jane. BA, Tulane U., 1954, JD with honors, 1956. Bar: La. 1956, Ill. 1959. Asst. corp. counsel City of Chgo., 1959-62; pvt. practice Chgo., 1962-73, 76—; sr. ptnr. firm Ettinger & Schoenfield, Chgo., 1980-92; sole practice Chgo., 1993—; assoc. prof. law Chgo.-Kent Coll., 1973-76; chmn. Village of Olympia Fields (Ill.) Zoning Bd. Appeals, 1969-76; chmn. panel on corrections Welfare Coun. Met. Chgo., 1969-76. Capt., Judge Adv. Gen. Corps, U.S. Army, 1956-59. Contbr. articles to profl. publs. Recipient Svc. award Village of Olympia Fields, 1976. Mem. Chgo. Bar Assn., Assn. Criminal Def. Lawyers (gov. 1970-72). Office: 33 N LaSalle St Ste 2119 Chicago IL 60602-2606

ETTLICH, ERNEST EARL, communications educator; b. Spokane, Wash., Nov. 9, 1937; s. Fred Ernest and Dorothy Sue (Olney) E.; m. Shiela Marie Ruppel, Aug. 7, 1958; children—Sherry Anne, Stephen Andrew. B.A., Los Angeles State U., 1959; M.S., U. Oreg., 1960, Ph.D., 1964. Asst. prof. U. Idaho, Moscow, 1961-65; prof. Wash. State U., Pullman, 1965-75; v.p., acad. dean Westmont Coll., Santa Barbara, Calif., 1975-78; dean acad. affairs So. Oreg. State Coll., Ashland, 1978-89, prof. comm. and honors, 1989—; pres. Assn. Communications Adminstrn., Falls Church, Va., 1975-76; assoc. Resource Ctr. Planned Change, Washington, 1979—; trustee Western Sem., 1990—. Mem. Rhetoric Soc. Am., Western States Communication Assn., Am. Polit. Sci. Assn., Speech Comm. Assn., Internat. Soc. History Rhetoric, Ctr. Study of Presidency, Phi Kappa Phi, Alpha Lambda Delta, Delta Sigma Rho-Tau Kappa Alpha, Phi Delta Kappa. Republican. Baptist. Home: 1055 Beswick Way Ashland OR 97520-3575 Office: So Oreg State Coll Ashland OR 97520

ETZLER, MARILYNN EDITH, biochemist, educator; b. Detroit, Oct. 30, 1940; d. Elmer Ellsworth and Doris (Tegge) E. BS, BA, Otterbein Coll., Westerville, Ohio, 1962; PhD, Washington U., St. Louis, 1967. Asst. prof. biochemistry U. Calif., Davis, 1969-75, assoc. prof. biochemistry, 1975-79, prof. biochemistry, 1979—. Contbr. articles to sci. publs. Grantee NIH, 1970—, NSF, 1981-92. Mem. Am. Soc. Biochemistry and Molecular Biology, Am. Soc. Cell Biology, Complex Carbohydrate Soc., Am. Soc. Plant Physiology, Protein Soc. Office: U Calif Dept Biochemistry Biop Davis CA 95616

EU, MARCH FONG, United States ambassador, former state official; b. Oakdale, Calif., Mar. 29, 1929; d. Yuen and Shiu (Shee) Kong; children by previous marriage: Matthew Kipling Fong, Marchesa Suyin Fong; m. Henry Eu, Aug. 31, 1973; stepchildren: Henry, Adelina, Yvonne, Conroy, Alaric. Student, Salinas Jr. Coll.; BS, U. Calif.-Berkeley, 1943; MEd, Mills Coll., 1947; EdD, Stanford U., 1956; postgrad., Columbia U., Calif. State Coll.-Hayward; LLD, Lincoln U., 1984; LLB (hon.), Western U., 1985, Pepperdine U., 1993. Chmn. div. dental hygiene U. Calif. Med. Center, San Francisco, 1948-56; dental hygienist Oakland (Calif.) Pub. Schs., 1948-56; supr. dental health edn. Alameda County (Calif.) Schs.; lectr. health edn. Mills Coll., Oakland; mem. Calif. Legislature, 1966-74, chmn. select com. on agr., foods and nutrition, 1973-74; mem. com. natural resources and conservation, com. commerce and pub. utilities, select com. med. malpractice; sec. state State of Calif., 1975-95, chief of protocol, 1975-83, sec. of state, 1975-94; Ambassador to Federated States of Micronesia U.S. Dept. of State, Washington, 1994—; chmn. Calif. State World Trade Commn., 1983-87; ex officio mem. Calif. State World Trade Commn., 1987—; spl. cons. Bur. Intergroup Relations, Calif. Dept. Edn.; ednl., legis. cons. Sausalito (Calif.) Pub. Schs., Santa Clara County Office Edn., Jefferson Elementary Union Sch. Dist., Santa Clara High Sch. Dist., Santa Clara Elementary Sch. Dist., Live Oak Union High Sch. Dist.; mem. Alameda County Bd. Edn., 1956-66, pres., 1961-62, legis. adv., 1963, Assembly Retirement Com., Assembly Com. on Govtl. Quality Com., Assembly Com. on Pub. Health; pres. Alameda County Sch. Bds. Assn., others. Mem. budget panel Bay Area United Fund Crusade; mem. Oakland Econ. Devel. Council; mem. tourism devel. com. Calif. Econ. Devel. Commn.; mem. citizens com. on housing Council Social Planning; mem. Calif. Interagy. Council Family Planning; edn. chmn., mem. council social planning, dir. Oakland Area Baymont Dist. Community Council; charter pres., hon. life mem. Howard Elementary Sch. PTA; charter pres. Chinese Young Ladies Soc., Oakland; mem., vice chmn. adv. com. Youth Study Centers and Ford Found. Interagy. Project, 1962-63; chmn. Alameda County Mothers' March, 1971-72; bd. councillors U. So. Calif. Sch. Dentistry, 1976; mem. exec. com. Calif. Democratic Central Com., mem. central com., 1963-70, asst. sec.; del. Dem. Nat. Conv., 1968; dir. 8th Congl. Dist. Dem. Council, 1963; v.p. Dems. of 8th Congl. Dist., 1963; dir. Key Women for Kennedy, 1963; women's vice chmn. No. Calif. Johnson for Pres., 1964; bd. dirs. Oakland YWCA, 1965. Recipient ann. award for outstanding achievement Eastbay Intercultural Fellowship, 1959; Phoebe Apperson Hearst Disting. Bay Area Woman of Yr. award; Honor award Sacramento Dist. Dental Soc., award of Merit Calif. Chiropractic Assn. legis. dept., Lamplighter award for Outstanding Achievement in Crime Prevention Oakland Real Estate Bd. Lite-the-Night Com., Loyalty Day award VFW of U.S., Woman of Achievement award Golden Gate Chpt. Bus. and Profl. Women's Club, Woman of Yr. award Calif. Retail Liquor Dealers Inst., 1969; Merit citation Calif. Assn. Adult Edn. Adminstrs., 1970; Art Edn. award; Outstanding Woman award Nat. Women's Polit. Caucus, 1980; Person of Yr. award Miracle Mile Lions Club, 1980; Humanitarian award Milton Strong Hall of Fame, 1981; Outstanding Leadership award Ventura Young Dems., 1983; Woman of Achievement award Los Angeles Hadassah, 1983, Outstanding Leadership award Filipino-Am. C. of C., 1985, CARE award, 1985, Disting. Svc. award Republic of Honduras, 1987, Polit. Achievement award Calif Dem. Party Black Caucus, 1988, JFK Am. Leadership award Santa Ana Dem. Club, 1989, L.A. County Good Scout award, Boy Scouts Am., 1989; named Woman of Yr., Dems. United, San Bernadino, 1989, Woman of Distinction, Soroptimist Internat., Monterey Park, 1987, Woman of Achievement, Santa Barbara Legal Secs. Assn. and County Bar Assn.,987, one of Am.'s 100 Most Important Women, Ladies Home Jour., 1988; recipient Community Leadership award Torat-Haijun Hebrew Acad., 1990, Special Appreciation U. Vietnamese Student Assns. So. Calif., 1990, Nat. Assn. Chinese-Am. Bankers, 1990, Orange County Buddhist Assn., 1990, Internat. Bus. award, West Coast U., 1992, others. Mem. Navy League (life), Am. Dental Hygienists Assn. (pres. 1956-57), No. Calif. Dental Hygienists Assn., Oakland LWV, AAUW (area rep. in edn. Oakland br.), Calif. Tchrs. Assn., Calif. Agrl. Aircraft Assn. (hon.), Calif. Sch. Bd. Assn., Alameda County Sch. Bd. Assn. (pres. 1965), Alameda County Mental Health Assn., Calif. Pub. Health Assn. Northern Divsn. (hon.), So. Calif. Dental Assn. (hon.), Bus. and Profl. Women's Club, Soroptimist (hon.), Hadassah (life), Ebell Club (L.A.), Chinese Retail Food Markets Assn. (hon.), Delta Kappa Gamma, Phi Alpha Delta (hon.), Phi Delta

Gamma (hon.), others. Office: American Embassy PO Box 1286 Kolonia, Pohnpei FM 96941*

EUSTER, JOANNE REED, librarian; b. Grants Pass, Oreg., Apr. 7, 1936; d. Robert Lewis and Mabel Louise (Jones) Reed; m. Stephen L. Gerhardt, May 14, 1977; children: Sharon L., Carol L., Lisa J. Student, Lewis and Clark Coll., 1953-56; B.A., Portland State Coll., 1965; M.Librarianship, U. Wash., 1968, M.B.A., 1977; Ph.D., U. Calif.-Berkeley, 1986. Asst. libr. Edmonds Community Coll., Lynnwood, Wash., 1968-73, dir. libr.-media ctr., 1973-77; univ. libr. Loyola U. of New Orleans, 1977-80; libr. dir. J. Paul Leonard Libr., San Francisco State U., 1980-86; univ. libr. Rutgers State U. N.J., New Brunswick, 1986-89, v.p. info. svcs., 1989-91, v.p. univ. librs., 1991-92; univ. libr. U. Calif., Irvine, 1992—; cons. Coll. S.I., Union Ejidal, La Penita, Nayarit, Mexico, 1973, Univ. D.C., 1988; co-cons. Office of Mgmt. Svcs. Assn. of Rsch. Librs., 1979—; bd. regents, Kansas; mem. adv. coun. Hong Kong U. Sci. and Tech. Librs., 1988—, Princeton U. Libr., 1988-92, U. B.C., Can., 1991—. Author: Changing Patterns of Internal Communication in Large Academic Libraries, 1981, The Academic Library Director, Management Activities and Effectiveness, 1987; columnist Wilson Libr. Bull., 1993—; contbr. articles to profl. jours. Mem. ALA, Calif. Libr. Assn., Assn. Coll. and Rsch. Librs. (pres. 1987-88), Am. Assn. for Higher Edn., Rsch. Librs. Group (chmn., bd. dirs. 1991-92). Office: Univ Calif Main Libr PO Box 19557 Irvine CA 92713-9557

EVANKOVICH, GEORGE JOSEPH, labor union administrator; b. Butte, Mont., Jan. 27, 1930; s. Joseph and Lubja (Broze) E.; m. Nevada Murray, Aug. 16, 1969; children: Karen, Lucy, Joseph, Janna. Student, U. Mont., 1954-57; BA, U. San Francisco, 1958. Miner Anaconda Co., Butte, 1946-50, Ind. Lease Mining, Helena, Mont., 1957-60; sec., treas. local 261 Laborers Internat. Union, San Francisco, 1960-68, bus. mgr., 1968-87, pres., 1987—; mem. bd. govs. dept. indsl. rels. Occupational Safety and Health Standards Bd. State of Calif., Sacramento, 1990—; pres. calif. region Pub. Employee Coun. AFL-CIO, 1973—; pres. No. Dist. Coun. of Laborers, 1977—; bd. dirs., trustee Laborer's Trust Funds, Inc., San Francisco; mem. adv. bd. NET, 1994, Lincoln Inst. Dir. labor studies program San Francisco City Coll., 1978—; chmn. San Francisco Housing Authority, 1972-76; advisor various senatorial, congl. and mayoral campaigns, 1966—; sustained mem. Rep. Nat. Com., 1980—. With inf. U.S. Army, 1951-54, Korea. Mem. Laborers Polit. Action Com. (bd. dirs.), Heritage Found., Commonwealth Club of San Francisco. Roman Catholic. Office: Laborers Union Local #261 3271 18th St San Francisco CA 94110-1920

EVANOFF, MARK EVAN, advocate; b. San Diego, Nov. 19, 1955; s. Evan and Louise Alda (Wire) E. AA, Citrus Coll., 1974; BA, Sonoma State U., 1976; MPA, Calif. State U., Hayward, 1977. Organizer, writer Abalone Alliance, San Francisco, 1978-81; writer Friends of the Earth, San Francisco, 1981-84; field dir. Greenbelt Alliance, San Francisco, 1984-94; adminstrv. asst. Assembly Mem. Michael Sweeney, 1994—; rsch. historian Calif. Pub. Utilities Com., San Francisco, 1985-86. Author various newspaper articles. founder Bay Area Ridge Trail Coun., 1986, dir., 1992—; organizer Measure AA East Bay Regional Dist., 1988, Ridelands Agreement, Pleasanton, 1993, East County Area Plan, Livermore Valley, 1994. Recipient Pioneer award Bay Area Ridge Trail Coun., San Francisco, 1990. Mem. Earth Island Inst., Sierra Club. Home: 29851 Clearbrook Cir # 85 Hayward CA 94544 Office: Assemblymember Michael Sweeney 22320 Foothill Blvd Ste 130 Hayward CA 94541

EVANS, ANTHONY HOWARD, university president; b. Clay County, Ark., Sept. 24, 1936; s. William Raymond and Thelma Fay (Crews) E.; m. Lois Fay Kirkham, Aug. 29, 1959. BA, East Tex. Bapt. Coll., Marshall, 1959; MA, U. Hawaii, 1961; PhD, U. Calif.-Berkeley, 1966. Program officer Peace Corps, Seoul, Korea, 1970-72; chief program planning Peace Corps, Washington, 1972-73, dir. planning office, 1973-75; asst. to pres. Eastern Mich. U., Ypsilanti, 1975-76, exec. v.p., 1976-79, acting pres., 1978-79, provost, v.p. acad. affairs, 1979-82; pres. Calif. State U., San Bernardino, 1982—. Mem. Orgn. Am. Historians, Phi Kappa Phi. Home: 664 E Parkdale Dr San Bernardino CA 92404-1731

EVANS, BERNARD WILLIAM, geologist, educator; b. London, July 16, 1934; came to U.S., 1961, naturalized, 1977; s. Albert Edward and Marjorie (Jordan) E.; m. Sheila Campbell Nolan, Nov. 19, 1962. B.Sc., U. London, 1955; D.Phil., Oxford U., 1959. Asst. U. Glasgow, Scotland, 1958-59; departmental demonstrator U. Oxford, 1959-61; asst. research prof. U. Calif., Berkeley, 1961-65; asst. prof. U. Calif., 1965-66, assoc. prof., 1966-69; prof. geology U. Wash., Seattle, 1969—; chmn. dept. geol. scis. U. Wash., 1974-79. Contbr. articles to profl. jours. Recipient U.S. Sr. Scientist award Humboldt Found., Fed. Republic Germany, 1988-89. Fellow Geol. Soc. Am., Mineral Soc. Am. (pres. 1993-94, award 1970), Geochem. Soc., Geol. Soc. London, Mineral. Soc. Gt. Britain, Swiss Mineral. Soc. Home: 8001 Sand Point Way NE Apt 55C Seattle WA 98115-6356 Office: U Wash Dept Geol Scis AJ-20 Seattle WA 98195

EVANS, BERNE, III, food products company executive; b. 1936. Student, 1968. With Ernst & Ernst, Denver, 1972-75; sec., treas. Exeter (Calif.) Packers, Inc., Consolidated Growers, Inc., 1986—. With U.S. armed forces, 1968-72. Office: 7th Standard Ranch Co 33374 Lerdo Hwy Bakersfield CA 93308-9782*

EVANS, BRADLEY DENNIS, psychiatrist, industrial consultant; b. Phila., June 17, 1950; s. Herman Harry Evans and Ida Evans-Swersky; m. Kristin Marie Updegrove, June 3, 1989; children: Jennifer, Katlyn. BS, Phila. Coll. Pharmacy and Sci., 1971; MD, Thomas Jefferson U., Phila., 1975. Diplomate Am. Bd. Psychiatry and Neurology; cert. Am. Soc. of Addiction Medicine, 1988; lic. psychiatrist, Ariz., Pa., N.J. Resident in psychiatry Thomas Jefferson U. Hosp., Phila., 1975-79, asst. prof. psychiatry, 1979-80; clin. asst. and prof. psychiatry U. Pa., Phila., 1982-84; staff physician Phila. VA Med. Ctr., 1981-84; staff psychiatrist Carrier Found., Belle-Mead, N.J., 1984-90, dir. Addiction Recovery Svc. div., 1987-90; clin. asst. prof. psychiatry Rutgers Coll. Medicine, U. Medicine and Dentistry N.J., 1985-91; pvt. practice Tucson, 1991—; vis. faculty Ctr. for Alcohol Studies Rutgers U., Piscataway, N.J., 1989-91; cons. Thomas Jefferson U. Hosp. Drug and Alcohol Outreach Program, Phila., 1979-81. Contbr. numerous articles profl. jours. Recipient Earl D. Bond award dept. of psychaitry U. Pa., 1983. Fellow Am. Coll. Psychiatrists (Laughlin fellow); mem. AMA, Am. Psychiat. Assn.,Am. Soc. Addiction Medicine (cert.), Ariz. Med. Assn., PimaCounty Med. Soc., Ariz. Psychiat. Soc., Acad. of Organl. and Occupl. Psychiatry. Office: 2920 N Swan Rd Ste 206 Tucson AZ 85712-1255

EVANS, CHRISTOPHER PAUL, urologist; b. Madison, Wis., Sept. 3, 1958; s. Alfred Spring and Brigitte (Kluge) E.; m. Karen Lisa Crow, July 11, 1987. BA, U. Vt., 1981; MD, Dartmouth Coll., 1986. Diplomate Nat. Bd. Med. Examiners. Intern in surgery Madigan Army Med. Ctr., Tacoma, 1986-87; resident in surgery U. Calif., San Francisco, 1990-91, resident urology, 1991-94, chief resident urology, 1994-95; fellow urologic oncology M.D. Anderson Cancer Ctr., Houston, 1995—. Author: Therapeutic Strategies in Prostate Cancer, 1993; contbr. articles to profl. jours. Capt. U.S. Army, 1986-90. Nat. Kidney Found. Rsch. fellow, 1993-94. Mem. ACS, Am. Assn. for Cancer Rsch., Am. Urology Assn., Assn. of Mil. Surgeons of the U.S., Uniformed Svcs. Univ. Surg. Assocs. Home: 3412 Albans St Houston TX 77005

EVANS, DARRELL J., secondary education educator; b. Pocatello, Idaho, Dec. 3, 1937; s. Cedric Coffin and Elsie Christine (Jensen) E.; m. Laurel Bradley, June 13, 1955 (div. Apr. 1962); children: Mark Bradley, Athena Denice; m. Penny L. Deay, Aug. 1963 (div. June 1980); 1 child, Dana Jacqueline; m. Judith Claire Peterson, Feb. 10, 1984 (div. Apr. 1993). AA, San Diego Jr. Coll., 1967; BA, San Diego State Coll., 1969; MA, UCLA, 1970; postgrad., U. Idaho, 1986—. Cert. tchr. art advanced secondary, Idaho, advanced secondary vocat. specialist, Idaho, C.C. cert., Calif. Asst. art instr. Chula Vista (Calif.) Sch. Dist., summer 1968; dir. arts and crafts Camp Roosevelt, Mountain Center, Calif., summer 1970; art tchr., intern Blackfoot (Idaho) High Sch., 1971-72; chief illustrator-draftsman USN, 1972-84; tech. and art tchr. McCall (Idaho)-Donnelly High Sch., 1984—; art tchr. Fairfield (Calif.) Suisun Evening Sch., 1973-74; art instr. U. Md.-Naples, Italy, 1975-76; mem. panel Idaho Commn. on Arts, Boise, 1990, 91, 94; owner Evans Design Inc., McCall, Idaho; mem. fine arts framework writing com. Schs. 2000, Idaho State Dept. Edn., 1994; co-chair art 5-12 curriculum writing com. Idaho State Dept. Edn. With USN, 1954-84, ret. 1984. Art Coun. scholar UCLA Art Coun., 1969-70. Mem. Idaho Art Edn. Assn. (pres. 1993-95), Nat. Art Edn. Assn. (chair tech. com. dels. assembly 1995—). Home: 935 Lick Creek Rd Mc Call ID 83638-3302 Office: McCall-Donnelly H S PO Box 967 Mc Call ID 83638-0967

EVANS, DEBORAH LYNNE, private investigator, writer; b. Alhambra, Calif., Oct. 6, 1956; d. Richard Alan and Dianne (Herring) Evans; m. Eric Roger Warkentien, Nov. 20, 1993; children: Hunter Evan, Cole Evan. Student, Coastline Jr. Coll., 1977-80, Saddleback Coll., Mission Viejo, Calif., 1982-86. Lic. pvt. investigator, Calif. Investigator Block Investigations, Newport Beach, Calif., 1976-85; owner The Information Source, Newport Beach, 1985—; cons. Block Investigations, Newport Beach, 1985—. Contbr. articles to profl. jours. Mem. Newport Beach Bus. Club (v.p. 1986-92), DAR. Republican. Office: The Information Source 280 Newport Center Dr Newport Beach CA 92660-7526

EVANS, HANDEL E., marketing professional; b. 1935. Exec. v.p. IMS Internat. Inc., 1965-81; mng. dir., co-founder SMS Internat., 1981-86; pres., CEO Walsh Internat., Inc., 1988—; chmn. bd. Pharm. Mktg. Svcs., Inc., Phoenix. Office: Walsh Internat 2394 E Camelback Rd Phoenix AZ 85016-3429*

EVANS, HIRAM KRAIG, forensic chemist; b. Chula Vista, Calif., July 8, 1953. BA in Chemistry, Ctrl. Coll., Pella, Iowa, 1975; AS in Criminal Justice, Southwestern Coll., Chula Vista, 1976; MS in Criminalistics, Calif. State U., Los Angeles, 1982. Cert. criminalist, lead auditor, controlled substance analyst. Tech. asst. Harris & Harris, Los Angeles, 1977; criminalist I Ventura County (Calif.) Sheriff's Dept., 1978-79; criminalist San Diego County Sheriff's Dept., 1979-81; supervising criminalist, dep. sheriff San Bernardino County (Calif.) Sheriff's Dept. Forensic Sci. Lab., 1982—; adj. prof. forensic sci. Nat. U., San Diego, 1980-83; instr. Regional Criminal Justice Tng. Ctr., San Bernardino, 1983—; prof. criminalistics Calif. State U., L.A., 1992—. Contbr. articles to profl. jours, chpt. to book. Fellow Am. Bd. Criminalistics, Am. Acad. Forensic Scis. (criminalistics sect.); mem. Am. Chem. Soc., Calif. Assn. Criminalists (sec. 1986-92), Calif. Assn. Crime Lab. Dirs., Ctrl. Coll. Alumni Assn., Internat. Assn. Forensic Scis., Midwestern Assn. Forensic Scientists (ASTM com. E-30 on forensic sci.), Assn. Ofcl. Analytical Chemists, Pacific S.W. Ry. Mus. Assn., Masons. Republican. Home: PO Box 782 Highland CA 92346-0782 Office: San Bernardino County Sheriff's Dept PO Box 569 San Bernardino CA 92402-0569

EVANS, JAMES HANDEL, university administrator, architect, educator; b. Bolton, Eng., June 14, 1938; came to U.S., 1965.; s. Arthur Handel and Ellen Bowen (Ramsden) E.; m. Carol L. Mulligan, Sept. 10, 1966; children: Jonathan, Sarah. Diploma of Architecture, U. Manchester, Eng., 1965; MA in Architecture, U. Oreg., 1967; postgrad., Cambridge (Eng.) U., 1969-70. Registered architect, Calif., U.K.; cert. NCARB. Assoc. dean. prof. architecture Calif. Poly. State U., San Luis Obispo, 1967-78; prof. art and design San Jose (Calif.) State U., 1979—, assoc. exec. v.p., 1978-81, interim exec. v.p., 1981-82, exec. v.p., 1982-91, interim pres., 1991-92, pres., 1992-95; vice chancellor Calif. State U System, Long Beach, CA, 1995—; cons. Ibiza Nueva, Ibiza, Spain, 1977-80; vis. prof. Ciudad Universitaria, Madrid, 1977; vis. lectr. Herriott Watt U., Edinburgh, 1970; mem. adv. com. Army Command Staff Coll., Ft. Leavenworth, Kans., 1988. Trustee Good Samaritan Hosp., San Jose, 1987-90; bd. dirs. San Jose Shelter, 1988-90; dir. San Jose C. of C., 1991-94. Sci. Rsch. Coun. fellow Cambridge U., 1969-70. Fellow AIA; mem. Royal Inst. Brit. Architects, Assn. Univ. Architects. Office: Office of the Vice Chancellor Calif State U 915 L St Ste 1160 Sacramento CA 95814-3705

EVANS, JOHN JOSEPH, management consultant; b. St. Louis, Mar. 1, 1940; s. Roy Joseph and Henrietta Frances (Schweizer) E.; BA, Centenary Coll., 1962; postgrad. Syracuse U., 1969, U. Wis., 1971, Harvard Bus. Sch., 1971-73; MBA, Pepperdine U., 1972; children—Todd, Karlyn, Jane, Mark. Pres. Evans & Co., 1966—; adj. prof. Centenary Coll. Bd. dirs. ARC, Mental Health Assn.; trustee Grad. Sch. Sales Mgmt. and Mktg.; pres. La. Real Estate Investment Trust; pres. N. La. Mental Health Hosp. Bd. Recipient awards United Way, 1965-69, ITVA awards, 1987-88. Mem. Nat. Beer Wholesalers Assn. (adv. dir.), Sales and Mktg. Execs. of Shreveport (pres.), S.W. Sales and Mktg. Execs. Council (pres.), Young Pres. Orgn., Conf. Bd., Aspen Inst., Sales and Mktg. Execs. Internat., Am. Soc. Tng. and Devel., Am. Soc. Personnel Adminstrn., Syracuse U. Grad. Sch. Sales Mgmt. and Mktg. Alumni Assn. (past pres., past trustee), Westlake Village C. of C. (past v.p., bd. dirs.), Personnel and Indsl. Relations Assn. (vice chmn., bd. dirs.), Harvard Club of San Diego. Home and Office: 9974 Scripps Ranch Blvd # 175 San Diego CA 92131-1825

EVANS, LAWRENCE JACK, JR., lawyer; b. Oakland, Calif., Apr. 4, 1921; s. Lawrence Jack and Eva May (Dickinson) E.; m. Marjorie Hisken, Dec. 23, 1944; children: Daryl S. Kleweno, Richard L., Shirley J. Coursey, Donald B. Diplomate Near East Sch. Theology, Beirut, 1951; MA, Am. U. Beirut, 1951; grad. Command and Gen. Staff Coll., 1960; PhD, Brantridge Forest Sch., Sussex, Eng., 1968; JD, Ariz. State U., 1971; grad. Nat. Jud. Coll., 1974. Bar: Ariz. 1971, U.S. Dist. Ct. Ariz. 1971, U.S. Ct. Claims 1972, U.S. Customs Ct., 1972, U.S. Tax Ct. 1972, U.S. Ct. Customs and Patent Appeals 1972, U.S. Ct. Appeals (9th cir.) 1972, U.S. Supreme Ct. 1975. Enlisted U.S. Navy, 1938-41, U.S. Army, 1942-44, commd. 2d lt. U.S. Army, 1944, advanced through ranks to lt. col., 1962; war plans officer, G-3 Seventh Army, 1960-62, chief, field ops. and tactics div., U.S. Army Spl. Forces, 1963, chief spl. techniques div., U.S. Army Spl. Forces, 1964, unconventional warfare monitor, U.S. Army Spl. Forces, 1964-65; ops. staff officer J-3 USEUCOM, 1965-68; mem. Airborne Command Post Study Group, Joint Chiefs of Staff, 1967; ret., 1968; mem. faculty Ariz. State U., 1968; sole practice law, cons. on Near and Middle Eastern affairs, Tempe, Ariz., 1971-72, 76—; v.p., dir. Trojan Investment & Devel. Co., Inc., 1972-75; active Ariz. Tax Conf., 1971-75; mem. adminstrv. law com., labor mgmt. relations com., unauthorized practice of law com. Ariz. State Bar. Author: Legal Aspects of Land Tenure in the Republic of Lebanon, 1951, International Constitutional Law, (with Helen Miller Davis) Electoral Laws and Treaties of the Near and Middle East, 1951; contbr. articles to mags., chpts. to books. Chmn. legal and legis. com. Phoenix Mayor's Com. To Employ Handicapped, 1971-75; active Tempe Leadership Conf., 1971-75; chmn. Citizens Against Corruption in Govt., 1976-95; mem. Princeton Council on Fgn. and Internat. Studies, 1968; comdr. Ranger Area-Ariz., Ranger Region-West, 1993—. Decorated Silver Star, Legion of Merit, Bronze Star, Purple Heart, Combat Infantryman badge, Master Parachutist badge, Aircrewman badge; named Outstanding Adminstrv. Law Judge for State Service for U.S., 1974; named to U.S. Army Ranger Hall of Fame, 1981. Fellow Coll. of Rites of U.S.A.; mem. UA Local # 469 (life), Ranger Bns. Assn. World War II (life), Tempe Rep. Mens Club (v.p., bd. dirs. 1971-72), U.S. Army Airborne Ranger Assn. (life), Mil. Order Purple Heart (life), NRA (official referee, life), Masons, Masonic Order of the Bath, Royal Order of Scotland, BL (twice past master Thunderbird Lodge # 48 Phoenix, past master Ariz. Rsch. Lodge # 1), Order Ky. Colonels, Sovereign Mil. Order of Temple of Jerusalem (grand avocat pro tem 1993, grand officier 1993), Fraternal Order of Medieval Knighthood, Internat. (sovereign venerable master Ariz. Coll. 1988-93, supreme sovereign grand master 1991), YR (past high priest, past thrice illustrious master, twice eminent past comdr., Knight Templar Cross of Honor, 1988, Orator Order of High Priesthood, Grand Chpt. YRM 1989, York Rite Mason of Decade, Scottsdale YRB 1989), SR (32, ritual dir.), Chief Adept Ariz. Coll. Socs. Rosicruceana In Civitatibus Foederatis VIII Degree, Grand Commandery of Knights Templar of Ariz. (grand insp. gen. 1990-91), Masons (knight U.S.A., Chevalier and Ami du Patriarchate, KCM Ordo Sancti Constantini Magni), Order of Secret Monitor, So. Calif. Rsch. Lodge, Royal Order of Scotland (Comdr. Ranger Area-Ariz., Ranger Region- West Red 1993), United Assn. (local #469 Phoenix), Phi Delta Phi, Delta Theta Phi. Episcopalian. Home: 539 E Erie Dr Tempe AZ 85282-3712

EVANS, LOUISE, psychologist, investor, philanthropist; b. San Antonio; d. Henry Daniel and Adela (Pariser) E.; m. Thomas Ross Gambrell, Feb. 23, 1960. BS, Northwestern U., 1949; MS in Clin. Psychology, Purdue U., 1952, PhD in Clin. Psychology, 1955. Lic. Marriage, Family and Child Counselor Calif., Nat. Register of Health Svc. Providers in Psychology; lic. psychologist N.Y. (inactive), Calif.; diplomate Clin. Psychology, Am. Bd. Profl. Psychology (fellow). Intern clin. psychology Menninger Found.-Topeka (Kans.) State Hosp., 1952-53, USPHS-Menninger Found. postdoctoral fellow clin. child psychology, 1955-56; staff psychologist Kankakee (Ill.) State Hosp., 1954; head staff psychologist child guidance clinic Kings County Hosp., Bklyn., 1957-58; dir. psychology clinic Barnes-Renard Hosp., instr. med. psychology Washington U. Sch. Medicine, 1959; clin. rsch. cons. Episc. City Diocese, St. Louis, 1959; pvt. practice clin. psychology, 1960-92; approved fellow Internat. Coun. Sex Edn. and Parenthood, 1984; psychol. cons. Fullerton (Calif.) Community Hosp., 1961-81; staff cons. clin. psychology Martin Luther Hosp., Anaheim, Calif., 1963-70; nat., internat. lectr. clin. psychology schs. and profl. groups, 1950—; chairperson, participant psychol. symposiums, 1956—; guest speaker clin. psychology civic and cmty. orgns., 1950—. Elected to Hall of Fame, Central H.S., Evansville, Ind., 1966; recipient Svc. award Yuma County Head Start Program, 1972, Statue of Victory Personality of the Yr. award Centro Studi E. Ricerche Delle Nazioni, Italy, 1985; named Miss Heritage, Heritage Publs., 1965. Fellow APA (clin. divsn., psychology of women divsn., divsn. psychotherapy, cons. divsn., dir. exec. bd. 1976-79), Acad. Clin. Psychology, Am. Assn. Applied and Preventative Psychology (charter), Royal Soc. Health England (emeritus), Internat. Council of Psychologists (dir. 1977-79, sec. 1962-64, 73-76), AAAS (emeritus), Am. Orthopsychiat. Assn. (life), World Wide Acad. of Scholars of N.Z. (life), Am. Psychol. Soc. (charter); mem. AAUP (emeritus), Nat. Register Health Svc. Providers in Psychology, L.A. Soc. Clin. Psychologists (exec. bd. 1966-67), Calif. State Psychol. Assn. (life, ins. com. 1961-65), L.A. County Psychol. Assn. (emeritus), Orange County Psychol. Assn. (charter founding mem., exec. bd. 1961-62), Orange County Soc. Clin. Psychologists (founder, exec. bd. 1963-65, pres. 1964-65), Am. Public Health Assn. (emeritus), Internat. Platform Assn., N.Y. Acad. Scis. (emeritus), Purdue U. Alumni Assn. (life, mem. pres. coun., dean's club pacesetters, Citizenship award 1975, Disting. Alumni award 1993, Old Master 1993), Center for Study of Presidency, Soc. Jewelry Historians USA (charter), Alumni Assn. Menninger Sch. Psychiatry, Soc. Sigma Xi Nat. Rsch. Hon. (emeritus), Pi Sigma Pi (pres. 1947-48, sec. 1946-47). Contbr. articles on clin. psychology to profl. publs. Achievements include development of innovative theories and techniques of clinical practice; acknowledged pioneer in devel. psychology as sci. and profession both nat. and internat., and pioneer in marital and family therapy. Office: PO Box 6067 Beverly Hills CA 90212-1067

EVANS, MAX ALLEN, writer, artist; b. Ropes, Tex., Aug. 29, 1924; s. W. B. and Hazel (Swafford) E.; m. Helene Caterlin, June 10, 1942 (divorced); 1 child, Sharon; m. Patsy Jo James, Aug. 4, 1949; children: Charlotte and Sheryl (twins.). Student pub. schs., N.Mex., Tex. Pres. Solar Metals, Inc., Taos, N.Mex., 1954-59; v.p. Evans Minerals, Inc., Taos, 1955-57; dir. Taos Minerals, Inc.; v.p. Taos Rodeo Assn., 1955-57; founding dir. N.Mex. State Film Commn., Santa Fe, 1969-73; hon. lifetime mem. bd. chancellors U. Tex. System, 1969—; founding dir. N.M. Farm and Ranching Inst. N.Mex. State U., Las Cruces, 1986—; bd. dirs. Cowboy Culture Inst. Tex. Tech. U., 1989—; mem. Gov.'s 1st N.M. Film Commn., 1967. Author: Southwest Wind, 1958, Long John Dunn of Taos, 1959, The Rounders, 1960, The Hi Lo Country, 1961, The One-Eyed Sky, 1963, The Mountain of Gold, 1965, The Shadow of Thunder, 1969, My Pardner, 1972 (L.A. Commendation award 1975), Sam Peckinpah - Master of Violence, 1972, Bobby Jack Smith You Dirty Coward, 1974, The White Shadow, 1977, The Great Wedding, 1984, Xavier's Folly and Other Stories, 1984, Super Bull and Other True Escapades, 1986, Rounders 3 - A Trilogy, 1990; (novellas) The Orange County Cowboys, 1987 (Golden Spur award for best short fiction 1988), Candles in the Bottom of the Pool, 1988, The Wild One -- The New Frontier Anthology, 1989, Old Bum, 1993, Bluefeather Fellini, 1993, Bluefeather Fellini in the Sacred Realm, 1994, Spinning Sun, Grinning Moon, 1995, Broken Bones, Broken Hearts, 1995; (artist) produced over 300 water color and oil for public and private collections, shown in juried shows inluding The Harwood Found., Taos, Mus. of N.Mex., Sante Fe; (films) The Rounders (also TV series), 1965, The Ballad of Cable Hogue, 1972, The Wheel, 1973, documentaries include Every Man's Mountain, Fred Martin-Out of the West, Rio Grande-River of Legends. With U.S. Army, 1942-45, ETO. Recipient Golden Spur award Western Writers of Am., Inc., 1983, 87, Nat. Cowboy Hall of Fame Wrangler award, 1984, Levi Straus Golden Saddleman award for Lifetime Achievement, 1990, State of N.Mex.'s Ann. Rounders' award Gov. N.Mex. and Sec. Agr., Lifetime Achievement Culture award Nat. Cowboy Symposium, 1993, N.Mex. Gov.'s award for excellence in arts, 1993, Wrangler Best Novel award Western Heritage, 1994; Max Evans Day named in his honor, Hobbs, N.Mex., 1968, Albuquerque, 1985, Excellence and Achievement in the Arts award Gov. N.Mex., 1993; named to Nat. Cowboy Hall of Fame. Home: 1111 Ridgecrest Dr SE Albuquerque NM 87108-3457

EVANS, MAX JAY, historical society administrator; b. Lehi, Utah, May 11, 1943; s. Karl Robinson and Lucile (Johnson) E.; m. Mary Wheatley, June 16, 1967; children: David Max, Joseph Michael, Katherine Anne, Laura, Emily. BS, U. Utah, 1968; MS, Utah State U., 1971. Archivist Mormon Ch. Hist. Dept., Salt Lake City, 1971-75, asst. ch. librarian, archivist, 1975-77; dep. state archivist State Hist. Soc. Wis., Madison, 1977-86, library dir., 1986; dir. Utah State Hist. Soc., Salt Lake City, 1986—; acting dir. Utah State Archives, Salt Lake City, 1986-88; archival cons. N.Y. State Archives, Albany, 1981, Wyo Dept. Archives and Hist., Cheyenne, 1982. Co-author: MARC for Archives and Manuscripts: A Compendium of Practice, 1985 (SAA Coker award 1986); articles in field. Trustee Middleton (Wis.) Pub. Libr., 1974-86, Am. West Heritage Found., 1995—; bd. dirs. Rsch. Librs. Group, 1991-92. Fellow Soc. Am. Archivists; mem. Utah State Hist. Soc. Mem. LDS Ch. Office: Utah State Hist Soc 300 Rio Grande St Salt Lake City UT 84101-1106

EVANS, NEIL, retired secondary school science educator; b. Santa Rosa, Calif., July 31, 1939; s. Alan Earl and Catherine Evans; m. Carolyn Alice Bibler, Sept., 1960 (div. May, 1975); children: Philip, Paul, Karen; m. Shirley Ann Bihn, June 15, 1975; stepchildren: Debbie, Dana. BA, Humboldt State Coll., 1961; MS, U. Calif., Berkeley, 1969. Cert. gen. secondary tchr. (life), Calif., gifted and talented specialist. Sci. tchr. Calistoga (Calif.) Joint Union H.S., 1963-64; sci. tchr. Mission San Jose (Calif.) H.S., 1964-95, head sci. dept., 1989-95; adj. biology instr. Ohlone C.C., 1969, 72; mentor tchr. Fremont Unified Sch. Dist., 1989—, mem. instrn. com., 1983-94, critical thinking task force, 1988-90, tech. com., 1992—. Elected elder Centerville Presbyn. Ch., Fremont, 1987-89; elected rep. at large , exec. bd. Tri-City Ecology, Fremont, Calif., 1972-78; mem. com. for Sch. Bond Proposal, Fremont Unified Schs., 199o-91. Recipient Outstanding Educator award, Live Oak Family Svc., Fremont, 1990; named Tchr. of Yr. Fremont Unified Sch. Dist., 1993-94, Tandy Tech. Scholar, Tandy Corp., 1993. Mem. NEA, Fremont Unified Dist. Tchrs. Assn. (exec. com. 1978-80), Calif. Tchrs. Assn., Nat. Sci. Tchrs. Assn., Nat. Biology Tchrs. Assn., Calif. Biology Educators, Calif. Sci. Tchrs. Democrat.

EVANS, PAULINE D., physicist, educator; b. Bklyn., Mar. 24, 1922; d. John A. and Hannah (Brandt) Davidson; m. Melbourne Griffith Evans, Sept. 6, 1950; children: Lynn Janet Evans Hannemann, Brian Griffith. BA, Hofstra Coll., 1942; postgrad., NYU, 1943, 46-47, Cornell U., 1946, Syracuse U., 1947-50. Jr. physicist Signal Corps Ground Signal Svc., Eatontown, N.J., 1942-43; physicist Kellex Corp. (Manhattan Project), N.Y.C., 1944; faculty dept. physics Queens Coll., N.Y.C., 1944-47; teaching asst. Syracuse U., 1947-50; instr. Wheaton Coll., Norton, Mass., 1952; physicist Nat. Bur. Standards, Washington, 1954-55; instr. physics U. Ala., 1955, U. N.Mex., 1955, 57-58; staff mem. Sandia Corp., Albuquerque, 1956-57; physicist Naval Nuclear Ordnance Evaluation Unit, Kirtland AFB, N.Mex., 1958-60; programmer Teaching Machines, Inc., Albuquerque, 1961; mem. faculty dept. physics Coll. St. Joseph on the Rio Grande (name changed to U. Albuquerque 1966), 1961—, assoc. prof., 1965—, chmn. dept., 1961—. Mem. AAUP, Am. Phys. Soc., Am. Assn. Physics Tchrs., Fedn. Am. Scientists, Sigma Pi Sigma, Sigma Delta Epsilon. Achievements include patents on mechanical method of conical scanning (radar), fluorine trap and primary standard for humidity measurement Home: 730 Loma Alta Ct NW Albuquerque NM 87105-1220 Office: U Albuquerque Dept Physics Albuquerque NM 87140

EVANS, RICHARD LLOYD, financial services company executive; b. Seattle, Oct. 16, 1935; s. Lloyd Herman and Dorleska L. (Rotta) E.; m. Judith Anne Sahlberg, Dec. 20, 1958; children: Dallas J., Douglas L., Daniel A., Marjorie A., Rebecca M. BA in Bus. Adminstrn., U. Wash., 1957. CLU; chartered fin. cons. Agt. Phoenix Mut. Life Ins. Co., Seattle, 1960-69; pres. R.L. Evans Co. Inc., Seattle, 1969—; mng. prin. Evans Capital Mgmt. Assocs., Seattle; speaker on ins. and fin. planning to numerous orgns., 1975—. Mem. exec. bd. Chief Seattle coun. Boy Scouts Am., 1976—; chmn. N.W. Theol. Union, Seattle, 1984-88. Lt. USN, 1957-59. Recipient award of merit Chief Seattle coun. Boy Scouts Am., 1984. Mem. Am. Soc. CLU, Am. Soc. Chartered Fin. Cons., Nat. Assn. Life Underwriters, Wash. State Assn. Life Underwriters (bd. dirs. 1973-79, pres. 1977-78), Seattle Assn. Life Underwriters (v.p. 1972-73), Assn. Advanced Underwriting, Million Dollar Round Table, Estate Planning Coun. Seattle, Rainier Club, Masons, Rotary (dir.). Republican. Presbyterian. Home: HC1 Box 37 Olga WA 98279 Office: 1210 Plz 600 Bldg Seattle WA 98101

EVANS, RICHARD MARLOWE, educational psychologist; b. Mason City, Iowa; s. Marlowe Rufus and Dorthy Marie (Toft) E.; m. Marilee Irma Haddock, June 1, 1958 (dec. Dec. 1978); children: Jay Bruce, Gwendolyn Lee. EdD, No. Ill. U., 1969. Pilot Chgo. Helicopter Airways, 1959-62; tchr. Cook County Sch. Dist. 160, Country Club Hills, Ill., 1962-65; asst. prof. U. Houston, 1969-71; assoc. prof. Morningside Coll., Sioux City, Iowa, 1971-79; comdr. USMC, 29 Palms, Calif., 1979-81; psychologist Tng. Analysis and Evaluation Group, Orlando, Fla., 1981-85, Naval Tng. Sys. Ctr., Orlando, 1985-87; analyst Def. Tng. and Performance Data Ctr., Orlando, 1987-92; sr. scientist BDM Internat., Monterey, Calif., 1992-93; analyst Def. Inst. for Tng. Resource Analysis, Monterey, 1993—. Contbr. articles to profl. jours. Col. USMC, 1955-84. Mem. Am. Edn. Rsch. Assn., Assn. Computing Machinery. Home: 84321 San Juan Carmel CA 93921 Office: Def Inst Tng Resource Anal Fort Ord CA 93941

EVANS, ROBERT JAMES, architect; b. Alameda, Calif., Apr. 15, 1914; s. Edwin Florence and Idella Mary (Cranna) E.; m. Carol Ann Benton, Sept. 11, 1937; children: Joan Carlson, Ann Lockey, Marcia Mothorn. A.B., U. Calif., Berkeley, 1935. Registered architect, Calif. Draftsman Wm. C. Hays Architect, San Francisco, 1935-37; draftsman U. Calif., 1937-41, architect, 1941-45, univ. architect, 1945-72, asst. v.p., 1971-72; cons. architect Marshall, Calif., 1973—; asst. to chancellor U. Mich.-Flint, 1972-73; supervising architect U. Calif., Davis, 1942-45, Berkeley, 1948-55; cons. architect campus plan U. Ryukus, Okinawa, 1969; cons. architect campus paln U. N.C., Greensboro, 1979-82; cons. architect campus plan Kabul U., Afghanistan, 1955, U. Hawaii, 1960-62, Salk Inst., San Diego, 1983-84. Founder Tomales Bay Assn., Marshall Calif., 1964. Fellow AIA (emeritus), Assn. Univ. Architects (pres. 1955-57). Clubs: Richmond Yacht (treas.) (1961); Inverness Yacht. Address: 18545 Hwy 1 PO Box 788 Marshall CA 94940

EVANS, ROBERT JOHN, retired biochemistry educator, researcher; b. Logan, UT, Mar. 18, 1909; s. Robert James and Alice Hazel (Stallings) E.; m. Alice Pugmire, Aug. 14, 1941 (dec.); children: Patricia Alice Evans Leavitt, Robert P. Student, Brigham Young U., 1929; BS, Utah State U., 1934, MS, 1936; PhD, U. Wisc., 1939. Instr. Carbon Coll., Price, UT, 1939-40; assoc. chemist Washington Agrl. Expt. Sta., Pullman, Wash., 1940-47; prof. Biochemistry Mich. State U., East Lansing, Mich., 1947-77; prof. emeritus Mich. State U., East Lansing, 1977—; vis. prof. Cambridge U., England, 1963-64, U. Edinburgh, Scotland, U. Coll. London, England, 1971, Rowett Rsch. Inst., Aberdeen, Scotland, 1971, Cambridge U., 1971. Contbr. articles to profl. jours. Active Boy Scouts Am., East Lansing, PTA, Lansing, Mich., Citizens Mich., Lansing. Recipient Rsch. Achievement award Poultry and Egg Nat. Bd., 1958, rsch. grants Nat. Inst. Health, 1963-75. Fellow AAAS; mem Am. Chem. Soc., Am. Inst. Nutrition., Poultry Sci. Assn. Mem. LDS Ch. Home: 760 Polk Ave Ogden UT 84404-5255

EVANS, ROBERT VINCENT, engineering executive; b. Mobile, Ala., Sept. 21, 1958; s. William Alexander Evans and Katherine Barbara (Doerr) Davidson; m. Debra Marie Winters, July 27, 1984; children: James Vernon, Chelsea Marie. BS in Computer Info. Systems, Regis U., Denver, 1987, BS in Tech. Mgmt., 1987. Electrician Climax (Colo.) Molybdenum Co., 1978-82; applications engr. Honeywell, Inc., Englewood, Colo., 1982-83, sales engr., 1983-87; systems engr. Apple Computer, Inc., Seattle, 1987-88; regional systems engring. mgr. Apple Computer, Inc., Portland, Oreg., 1988—. Author: Anthology of American Poets, 1981. Dir. Operation Lookout, Seattle, 1989; mem. Rep. Nat. Com. Recipient USMC Blues award, Marine Corps Assn. Leatheanger award, 1977, Denver Post Outstanding Svc. award, 1983, N.Y. Zool. Soc. Hon. medal. Mem. Am. Mgmt. Assn., Mensa. Republican. Mem. Vineyard Ch. Office: Apple Computer Inc 10210 NE Points Dr Ste 310 Kirkland WA 98033-7872

EVANS, RONALD ALLEN, lodging chain executive; b. Louisville, Apr. 5, 1940; s. William Francis and Helen Maxine (Hart) E.; m. Lynne Anne Ingraham, Aug. 25, 1979; children: Nicole Louise, Michele Lynne, Christopher Hart. B.S. in Mgmt., Ariz. State U., 1963. Vice pres. Electronic Data Systems, Dallas, 1969-73; vice pres. First Fed. Savs., Phoenix, 1973-77, Community Fin. Corp., Scottsdale, Ariz., 1977-78; pres. Evans Mgmt. Services, Inc., Phoenix, 1978-84; pres., CEO Best Western Internat., Inc., Phoenix, 1979—. Served to lt. USNR, 1963-66. Decorated Bronze Star. Republican. Episcopalian. Lodges: Masons (32 deg.), KT, Shriner. Office: Best Western Internat Inc PO Box 10203 Phoenix AZ 85064-0203*

EVANS, THOMAS EDGAR, JR., title insurance agency executive; b. Toronto, Ohio, Apr. 17, 1940; s. Thomas Edgar and Sarah Ellen (Bauer) E.; BA, Mt. Union Coll., 1963; m. Cynthia Lee Johnson, Feb. 23; children: Thomas Edgar, Douglas, Melinda, Jennifer. Tchr. Lodi, Ohio, 1963-64; salesman Simpson-Evans Realty, Steubenville, Ohio, 1964-65, Shadron Realty, Tucson, 1965-67; real estate broker, co-owner Double E Realty, Tucson, 1967-69; escrow officer, br. mgr., asst. county mgr., v.p. Ariz. Title Ins., Tucson, 1969-80; pres. Commonwealth Land Title Agy., Tucson, 1980-82, also dir.; pres. Fidelity Nat. Title Agy., 1982-90; bd. govs. Calif. Land Title Assn., 1990—; exec. v.p. Fidelity Nat. Title Ins. Co., 1990-92; v.p. Inland Empire Divsn. Fidelity Nat. Title, 1991-93, v.p. Orange County Divsn., 1993—; bd. dirs. Western Fin. Trust Co., Fidelity Nat. Fin. Inc., Fidelity Nat. Title Ins. Co., Fidelity Nat. Title Agy. Pinal, The Griffin Co., Computer Market Place, Inc.; bd. dirs., chmn. bd. Cochise Title Agy., TIPCO; v.p., dir. A.P.C. Corp. Named Boss of Year, El Chaparral chpt. Am. Bus. Women's Assn., 1977. Mem. Calif. Land Title Assn. (pres. 1995—), So. Ariz. Escrow Assn., So. Ariz. Mortgage Bankers Assn. (bd. dirs. 1982-85), Ariz. Mktg. Bankers Assn., Old Pueblo Businessmen's Assn. Tucson, Tucson Bd. Realtors, Ariz. Assn. Real Estate Exchangors (bd. dirs. 1968-69), Land Title Assn. Ariz. (pres. 1984), So. Ariz. Homebuilders Assn., Blue Key, Sigma Nu. Republican. Methodist. Clubs: Old Pueblo Courthouse, La Paloma, Ventana Country, Centre Court, Elks, Pima Jaycees (dir. 1966), Sertoma (charter pres., chmn. bd. Midtown sect. 1968-70); Tucson Real Estate Exchangors (pres. 1968); Sunrise Rotary; Old Pueblo. Home: 28861 Glen Rdg Mission Viejo CA 92692-4301 Office: 2100 Main St Ste 400 Irvine CA 92714-6240

EVANS, VICTORIA LYNN, publishing executive; b. Portland, Oreg., Oct. 27, 1951; d. Lyle B. and Lela Nina (Davis) E.; m. William G. Sturgill, Mar. 8, 1980 (div. 1991). Student, Portland State U., 1969-70; degree in computers, C.E.I., 1986. Exec. sec. Liberty House/Amfac Co., Portland, 1974-75; various positions Nordstrom, Portland, 1975-76; co-owner Texaco Sta. Car Wash, Clackamas, Oreg., 1977-80; owner, operator Kalligraphia, Etc., Beaverton, Oreg., 1981-87, Kalligraphia Pub., Inc., Beaverton, Oreg., 1987-94; sr. loan closer Old Stone Mortgage, Lake Oswego, Oreg., 1986-88; cons. various orgns., Portland, 1983-94. Author: Guide to Oregon Craft Sales, 1992, Guide to NW Craft Sales and Events, 1994, Guide to NW Bed and Breakfasts, 1994, Guide to NW Antiques, 1994; editor: Victoria's Gazette, 1991-93. Fundraiser Candlelighters, Portland, 1985-86. Mem. Girls League Oreg. (1st v.p. 1968-69, sec. 1967). Democrat. Office: Kalligraphia PO Box 581 Tualatin OR 97062-0581

EVANS, WILLIAM THOMAS, physician; b. Denver, Aug. 21, 1941; s. Alfred Lincoln and Marian Audrey (Biggs) E.; m. Lucy Fales. BA, U. Colo., 1963; MD, Baylor U., 1967; grad., Chinese Coll. U.K.; Licentiate Acupuncture, Oxford, Eng., 1976. Intern Mary Fletcher Hosp., Burlington, Vt., 1967; physician Villages of Kodiak Island and Lake Iliamna, 1968-70; founder, dir. emergency dept. St. Elizabeth Hosp., Yakima, Wash., 1970-75; practice medicine specializing prevention and conservative treatment of spine injuries Denver; founder, dir. Colo. Back Sch., Denver, 1979-89; assoc. med. dir. Ctr. for Spine Rehab., 1989—; mem. edn. coun. Colo. Neurol. Inst. Contbr. articles on prevention and edn. mgmt. of low back pain. Dir. Colo. Think First Program for Prevention of Head and Spinal Cord Injuries; Friends of Earth del. Limits to Medicine Congress, 1975; initiator Colo. Sun Day, 1978. Lt. comdr. Indian Health Svc., USPHS, 1968-70. Mem. AMA, Rocky Mountain Traumatological Soc. (pres.), Arapahoe County Med. Soc., Colo. Med. Soc. (workmen's compensation com.), N.Am. Spine Soc. (mem. ednl. coun.), Am. Coll. Occupational Medicine Assns., Rocky Mountain Acad. Occupational Medicine (pres.), Am. Coll. Sports Medicine, Traditional Acupuncture Soc. Home: PO Box 174 Littleton CO 80160-0174 Office: 125 E Hampden Ave Englewood CO 80110-2546

EVEN, JAN, newspaper editor; b. Oak Park, Ill., Apr. 18, 1950; d. Francis A. and Margaret Hope (Herrick) E.; m. Thomas E. Osborne, Feb. 13, 1988. BS in Edn., Northwestern U., 1972, MSJ, 1978; MA in Eng., U. Ill., 1973; postgrad., Oxford U., 1972, U. Cin., 1973. Tchr., 1973-76; editorial asst. Rand McNally Pub. Co., 1976-77; freelance reporter Lerner Newspapers, Chgo., 1977-78; reporter The Herald, Arlington Hgts., Ill., 1978-79; reporter newsfeatures dept. Seattle Times, 1980-81; reporter, copyeditor Tacoma News Tribune, 1981-83; copy editor, editorial dept. Seattle Times, 1984-86, copy editor, news desk, 1986-87, zone news editor, 1987, night news editor, 1987-90, arts and entertainment editor, 1990—; secondary sch. tchr., 1973-76; instr. Pacific Luth. U., Tacoma, Wash., 1985-86. Office: The Seattle Times PO Box 70 Fairview Ave N & John St Seattle WA 98111

EVENSON, S. JEANNE, small business owner; b. Wheeler County, Tex., Oct. 17, 1938; d. Glynn Edward and LaVerne (Bailey) Pugh; m. A. Berniel Evenson, May 31, 1957; children: Tara Jean Harper, Troy Berniel. BA in Secondary Edn., Coll. Great Falls, 1972. Tchr. East Jr. High Sch., Great Falls, 1972-78; owner, operator Cattail Lawn Svc., Great Falls, 1976-80, B-J Pac-A-Part, Great Falls, 1976—. Methodist. Home: 410-25 Avenue S Great Falls MT 59405

EVERETT, CARL NICHOLAS, management consulting executive; b. Ardmore, Okla., June 4, 1926; s. Elmer Edwards and Cecile (Jones) E.; B.S., Columbia U., 1948; M.B.A. with distinction, Harvard U., 1951; m. Susan Blessing Lindstrom, Oct., 1975; children by previous marriages—Carl N., Karen Lee, E. Anthony. With Benton and Bowles, N.Y.C., 1951-54, asso. account exec. Gen. Foods Corp., asst. account exec. Hellmanns and Best Foods Mayonnaise; with Campbell Mithun, Mpls., 1954-56, sr. account exec. Pillsbury Mills, account exec. Pillsbury Refrigerated Products; with McCann Erickson, N.Y.C., 1956-62, bottle sales account exec. Coca Cola Co., sr. account exec. Esso. Standard Oil, accounts supr. Westinghouse Electric Corp., account dir. Liggett and Myers Tobacco, mem. marketing plans bd. and marketing and advt. cons. Coca Cola Co.; sr. v.p., dir. Western region operations Barrington & Co., N.Y.C., 1962-64; founder, pres. Everett Assos., Inc., marketing and mgmt. consultants, N.Y.C., 1964-74; founder, pres. Everett Corp., Scottsdale, Ariz., 1974—; cons. Chrysler Corp., Pepsico Inc., Michelin Tire Corp., Gen. Electric Corp., Can. Dry Corp., Allied Van Lines, Continental Airlines; co-founder, dir. Precision Investment Co., Denver, 1977—; founder, mng. partner Wilmot Properties, Scottsdale, Ariz., 1979-90; prof. of Bus. Northwest Nazarene Coll. 1992—. Chmn. bd. dirs. Phoenix Meml. Hosp. Primary Care; bd. dirs. Phoenix Meml. Health Resources, Inc.; chmn. bd. adjustment Town of Paradise Valley, Ariz.; chmn. Commn. on Salaries for Elective Officers; mem. Ariz. Cost Efficiency Commn. Served with USNR, 1944-46. Mem. Am. Mgmt. Assn., Sigma Alpha Epsilon. Unitarian. Clubs: Harvard Bus. Sch. (bd. dirs. Ariz.), Harvard (bd. dirs.), Harvard Club of ID. (pres.), Campfire. Patentee in field. Home: 525 Lawrence Ave Boise ID 83709-0826 Office: Northwest Nazarene Coll Nampa ID 83686

EVERETT, HOBART RAY, JR., engineer, naval officer, consultant, researcher, inventor; b. Charleston, S.C., Nov. 29, 1949; s. Hobart Ray and Ruth (Humphreys) E.; m. Rachael Patricia Lewis, Dec. 30, 1971; children: Todd Ashley, Rebecca Nicole. BEE, Ga. Inst. Tech., 1973; MS in Mech. Engring., Naval Postgrad. Sch., 1982. Commd. ensign U.S. Navy, 1973, advanced through grades to comdr., 1988; asst. engr. USS Nitro, 1975-77; engring. recruiter for officer programs, Montgomery, Ala., 1977-80; robotics coordinator Naval Sea Systems Command, Washington, 1983-84, dir. Office of Robotics and Autonomous Systems, 1984-86; autonomous systems project officer Naval Ocean Systems Ctr., San Diego, 1986-88, chief engr. USMC teleoperated vehicle program, 1988-89, assoc. div. head advanced systems div., 1988-93; cons. to Computer Scis. Corp., Falls Church, Va., 1993-94; assoc. divsn. head robotics Naval Command, Control and Ocean Surveillance Ctr., San Diego, 1994—; founder DoD Robotics and Artificial Intelligence Database, 1983; Navy rep. to tri-svc. Joint Tech. Panel for Robotics, 1984-86; guest lectr. in robotics U. Md., U. Pa., 1983-86, U. Calif., San Diego, 1988; robotics researcher Naval Ocean Systems Ctr., prin. tech. cons. U.S. Army Mobile Detection Assessment and Response System interior program, 1990-93; tech. dir. Joint Army-Navy Mobile Detection Assessment and Response System interior and exterior program, 1993—. Author: Sensors for Mobile Robots; contbg. author Robotics Age mag., 1982-86, Sensors mag., 1987—; mem. editorial bd., contbg. author Robotics and Autonomous Systems mag.; contbr. 60 tech. publs.; inventor 1st autonomous sentry robot; patentee in field. Decorated Navy Commendation,1981, 86; recipient Naval Sea Systems Command award for Acad. Excellence, 1982, Woelful award for Acad. Excellence, Naval Sea Systems Command, 1983, Gen. Dynamics award for Acad. and Mil. Accomplishment, 1973. Mem. IEEE, Soc. Mfg. Engrs. (sr.), Robotics Inst. Am., Nat. Svc. Robot Assn. (bd. dirs. 1991—), Sigma Xi. Office: Naval Command Control & Ocean Surveillance Ctr RDT & E Divsn Code 5303 53400 Woodward Rd San Diego CA 92152-7308

EVERETT, PAMELA IRENE, legal management company executive, educator; b. L.A., Dec. 31, 1947; d. Richard Weldon and Alta Irene (Tuttle) Bunnell; m. James E. Everett, Sept. 2, 1967 (div. 1973); 1 child, Richard Earl. Cert. Paralegal, Rancho Santago Coll., Santa Ana, Calif., 1977; BA, Calif. State U.-Long Beach, 1985; MA, U. Redlands, 1988. Owner, mgr. Orange County Paralegal Svc., Santa Ana, 1979-85; pres. Gem Legal Mgmt. Inc., Fullerton, Calif., 1986—; co-owner Bunnell Publs., Fullerton, Calif., 1992—; instr. Rancho Santiago Coll., 1979—, chmn. adv. bd., 1980-85; instr. Fullerton Coll., 1989—, Rio Hondo Coll., Whittier, Calif., 1992-94; advisor Nat. Paralegal Assn., 1982—, Saddleback Coll., 1985—, North Orange County Regional Occupational Program, Fullerton, 1986—, Fullerton Coll. So. Calif. Coll. Bus. and Law; bd. dirs. Nat. Profl. Legal Assts. Inc., editor PLA News. Author: Legal Secretary Federal Litigation, 1986, Bankruptcy Courts and Procedure, 1987, Going Independent--Business Planning Guide, Fundamentals of Law Office Management, 1994. Republican. Office: 406 N Adams Ave Fullerton CA 92632-1605

EVERETT, STEPHEN EDWARD, advertising and communications educator, researcher; b. Tulsa, Feb. 5, 1958; s. George A. and Sandra J. (Stephens) E.; m. Shu-Ling Chen, Apr. 7, 1988. PhD, U. Tenn., 1989. Announcer Sta. KWHO, Salt Lake City, 1977-78, Sta. WUOT U. Tenn., Knoxville, 1978-85; disk jockey Sta. WOKI, Oak Ridge, Tenn., 1978-82; program dir. Sta. WUAL, U. Ala., Tuscaloosa, 1983-84; account exec. Sta. WBMK, Knoxville, 1985; adminstrv. asst. U. Tenn., 1985-88; asst. prof. U. Colo., Boulder, 1988—; rsch. cons., Denver, 1988—, Colo. Dept. Revenue, 1992, office of comm. United Ch. of Christ, Colo. Springs Gazette Telegraph opinion polls. Contbr. articles to profl. jours. Vol. rsch. cons. Mile High United Way, Denver, 1988, Colo. Alliance for Mentally Ill, 1990. Mem. Am. Acad. Advt., Assn. Edn. Journalism & Mass Communication, Am. Assn. Pub. Opinion Rsch., Midwest Assn. Pub. Opinion Rsch. (exec. bd.). Home: 7441 Old Mill Trl Boulder CO 80301-3909 Offce: U Colo Journalism Mass Communication CB 287 Boulder CO 80309-0287

EVERETTE, MABLE LOUISE, nutrition educator; b. Morrilton, Ark., Feb. 6, 1947; d. James Arthur and Mable (Brown) E. BS, Tuskegee U., 1969; MPH, U. Mich., 1971. Registered dietitian. Nutritionist City of Houston Health Dept., 1971-75, State of Calif. Health Dept., Sacramento, 1975-78; cons. sr. nutrition programs L.A., Orange and Ventura counties, 1978-91; dir. nutrition programs Charles Drew U., L.A., 1991—; mem. adv. bd. African-Am. nutrition programs Nat. Coun. Negro Women, 1991—. Editor: (video) Careers in Dietetics, 1991. Recipient Outstanding Svc. award Am. Dietetic Assn., 1988, Vol. Svc. award Eternal Promise Bapt. Ch., 1992, Continuing Svc. award Am. Heart Assn., 1991. Mem. Calif. Dietetic Assn. (chair, legis. com. 1993—, Legis. Contact award L.A. dist. 1990-91). Office: Charles Drew U MP # 22 1621 E 120th St Los Angeles CA 90059-3025

EVERHART, LEON EUGENE, retired air force officer; b. Abilene, Kans., Jan. 14, 1928; s. Charles Francis and Florence Etta (Amess) E. BS with distinction, Ariz. State U., 1957; postgrad., U. Tenn., 1965. Commd. 2d lt. USAF, 1952, advanced through grades to col., 1970, ops. officer Berlin Air Safety Ctr., 1961-63; project officer Missile Devel. Ctr. USAF, Holloman AFB, N.Mex., 1963-65, chief spl. projects div. Missile Devel. Ctr., 1965-66; tactical fighter pilot, flight commander USAF, South Vietnam, 1967-68; system program dir. Aero. Systems Div. USAF, Wright Patterson AFB, Ohio, 1968-72; dir. test engring. Devel. and Test Ctr. USAF, Eglin AFB, Fla., 1973-78; comdr. Air Force Western Test Range USAF, Vandenberg AFB, Calif., 1978-82; ret. USAF, 1982; cons. in field. Speaker on big-game hunting in Africa and wildlife conservation for various civic and ednl. orgns. Mem. Amateur Trapshooting Assn. Ohio, NRA. Home: 1285 Oak Knolls Rd Santa Maria CA 93455-4302

EVERHART, THOMAS EUGENE, academic administrator, engineering educator; b. Kansas City, Mo., Feb. 15, 1932; s. William Elliott and Elizabeth Ann (West) E.; m. Doris Arleen Wentz, June 21, 1953; children—Janet Sue, Nancy Jean, David William, John Thomas. A.B. in Physics magna cum laude, Harvard, 1953; M.Sc., UCLA, 1955; Ph.D. in Engring., Cambridge U., Eng., 1958. Mem. tech. staff Hughes Research Labs., Culver City, Calif., 1953-55; mem. faculty U. Calif., Berkeley, 1958-78, prof. elec. engring. and computer scis., 1967-78, Miller research prof., 1969-70, chmn. dept., 1972-77; prof. elec. engring., Joseph Silbert dean engring. Cornell U., Ithaca, N.Y., 1979-84; prof. elec. and computer engring., chancellor U. Ill., Urbana-Champaign, 1984-87; prof. elec. engring. and applied physics, pres. Calif. Inst. Tech., Pasadena, 1987—; fellow scientist Westinghouse Rsch. Labs., Pitts., 1962-63; guest prof. Inst. Applied Physics, U. Tuebingen, Germany, 1966-67, Waseda U., Tokyo, Osaka U., 1974; vis. fellow Clare Hall, Cambridge, U., 1975; chmn. Electron, Ion and Photon Beam Symposium, 1977; cons. in field; mem. sci. and ednl. adv. com. Lawrence Berkeley Lab., 1978-85, chmn., 1980-85; mem. sci. adv. com. GM, 1980-89, chmn., 1984-89, bd. dirs., 1989—; bd. dirs. Hewlett Packard Corp., 1991—; tech. adv. com. R.R. Donnelly & Sons, 1981-89. Chmn. Sec. of Energy Adv. Bd., 1990-93; bd. dirs. KCET, 1989—, Corp. for Nat. Rsch. Initiatives, 1990—. NSF sr. fellow, 1966-67, Guggenheim fellow, 1974-75. Fellow IEEE, AAAS, ASEE, Royal Acad. Engring.; mem. NAE (ednl. adv. bd. 1984-88, mem. com. 1984-89, chmn. 1988, coun. 1988-94), Microbeam Analysis Soc. Am., Electron Microscopy Soc. Am. (coun. 1970-72, pres. 1977), Coun. on Competitiveness (vice-chmn. 1990—), Assn. Marshall Scholars and Alumni (pres. 1965-68), Athenaeum Club, Sigma Xi, Eta Kappa Nu. Home: 415 S Hill Ave Pasadena CA 91106-3407 Office: Calif Inst Tech Office of Pres 1201 E California Blvd Pasadena CA 91125-0001

EVERINGHAM, HARRY TOWNER, editor, publisher; b. Memphis, Aug. 14, 1908; s. William Kirby and Ida Pauline (Towner) E.; m. Margaret Sophia Johnson, May 1, 1934; children: Martha Meister, Barbara Miller, Richard Kirby. Student, Northwestern U., Evanston, Ill., 1936-39, U. Chgo., 1940. Radio writer, producer Miles Lab., Chgo., 1934-35, Wade Advt. Agy., Chgo., 1934-35; v.p. Sehl Advt. Agy., Chgo., 1936-41; broadcasting Henry C. Lytton & Co., Chgo., 1936-41; film producer, lectr. Employers Assn., Chgo., 1942; pub. rels. dir. Ingalls-Shepard Div. Wyman Gordon Co., Harvey, Ill., 1943-45; editor, pub. The Fact Finder, Chgo., 1942-65, Phoenix, 1965-89, Scottsdale, Ariz., 1989—; Founder, pres. We, The People, 1955-68, We, the People - United, 1978—. Editor, pub. U.S.A.-Beyond the Crossroads, Chgo., 1952, The Am. Patriot, 1959—; syndicated newspaper columnist, 1960-63. Vice pres. Greater Chgo. Churchmen, 1946-47. Mem. Publicity Club Chgo. (founder 1942), Ariz. Breakfast Club (pres., founder Phoenix 1969—). Republican. Office: We the People UNITED Box A Scottsdale AZ 85252

EVERS, LAWRENCE JOSEPH, English language educator; b. Grand Island, Nebr., Aug. 15, 1946; s. Lawrence C. and Lois (Schwenk) E.; m. Barbara Zion Grygutis, Dec. 20, 1982; children: Noah Zion, Elly. BA, U. Nebr., 1968, MA, 1969, PhD, 1972. Asst. prof. English U. Ariz., Tucson, 1974-80, assoc. prof., 1981-86, prof., 1987—. Co-author: Yaqui Deer Songs, 1987; editor: The South Corner of Time, 1980, Home Places, 1995; producer (video series) Words and Place, 1979. Bd. dirs. El Presidio Hist. Dist. Adv. Bd., Tucson, 1986—. Recipient 1st prize Chgo. Folklore prize U. Chgo., 1988; U. Chgo. postdoctoral fellow, 1972-73. Mem. MLA, Assn. Study Am. Indian Lit. Office: U Ariz Dept English Tucson AZ 85721

EVERS, MARK, media research firm executive; b. Monterey, Calif., Sept. 14, 1956; s. Richard Edgar and Nancy Lee (Nelsen) E.; m. Mindy Kay Trustman, Aug. 21, 1982; 1 child, Grant Wallace. BS in Bus./Mktg., U. Ariz., 1978. Mktg. dir. Am. Savs., Tucson, 1978-80; asst. advt. mgr. Home Fed. Savs., Tucson, 1980-82; account supr. Grey Advt., San Francisco, 1982-85; v.p. mktg. Great Am. Bank, Tucson, 1985-87; pres. Voice Trak Inc., Tucson, 1987—. Office: Voicetrak Inc 6420 E Tanque Verde Rd Tucson AZ 85715-3826

EVERSLEY, FREDERICK JOHN, sculptor, engineer; b. Bklyn., Aug. 28, 1941; s. Frederick William and Beatrice Agnes (Syphax) E. B.S.E.E., Carnegie-Mellon U., 1963. One-man shows include Whitney Mus. Am. Art, N.Y.C., 1970, Nat. Acad. Sci., Washington, 1976, 81, L.A. Inst. Contemporary Art, 1976, Santa Barbara Mus., 1976, Newport Harbor Art Mus., 1976, Oakland Mus. Art, 1977, Palm Springs (Calif.) Desert Mus., 1978, AIA, 1981, Va. Mus., 1981, Bacardi Art Gallery, Miami, 1984, Laband Art Gallery, 1985, Loyola Marymount U., L.A., Hokin Gallery, Palm Beach, Fla., 1988, Juda Gallery, London, 1988, Eva Cohen Gallery, Chgo., 1991, Lorenzelli Arte, Milan, 1992, Pavilion of Saudi Arabia, Expo 92, Seville, Spain, 1992; represented in permanent collections Smithsonian Instn., Washington, Calif. State Coll., L.A., Oakland (Calif.) Art Mus., Milw. Art Center, Whitney Mus. Am. Art, N.Y.C., John Marin Meml. Collection, N.Y.C., U., Kans. Art Gallery, Lawrence, Long Beach (Calif.) Mus. Art, Currier Gallery Art, Manchester, N.H., Taft Mus. Art, Cin., Cranbrook Art Gallery, Bloomfield Hills, Mich., Nat. Acad. Sci., Washington, Nat. Collection Fine Arts, Washington, MIT, Cambridge, Neuberger Mus. Art, Purchase, N.Y., Newport Harbor Art Mus., Newport Beach, Calif., Guggenheim Mus., N.Y.C., Smith Coll. Mus. Art, Northhampton, Mass., Nat. Air and Space Mus., Mus. Contemporary Art, L.A., Palm Springs Desert Mus., Rose Mus. of Art, Brandis U., Boston, Sammlung Goetz, Munich Germany; artist in residence Nat. Air and Space Mus., Washington, 1977-80. Nat. Endowment Arts grantee, 1972. Mem. L.A. Inst. Contemporary Art, Artworkers Coalition. Address: 1110 Abbot Kinney Blvd Venice CA 90291

EVERSON, STEVEN LEE, lawyer, real estate executive; b. Philippi, W.Va., June 16, 1950; s. Billie Lee and Mildred Ann (Hill) E.; m. Donna Janine Chmielarz, May 29, 1976; 1 child, Michael. BA in Math. magna cum laude, W. Va. U., 1972; JD, Northwestern U., 1979. Bar: Colo. 1979; CPA, Colo. Tax sr. acct. Deloitte, Haskins & Sells, Colorado Springs, Colo., 1979-82; v.p., chief fin. officer Schuck Communities, Inc., Colorado Springs, 1982—; instr. real estate U. Colo. Bd. dirs., treas., past chmn. Pikes Peak Found. for Mental Health, Colorado Springs, 1986—, Boys and Girls Club of Pikes Peak Region, Colorado Springs, 1987-90; mem. UCCS Exec. Club, Colorado Springs, 1988-90; treas. Steve Schuck for Gov. Com., 1988—; project bus. instr. Jr. Achievement, 1985-87. Capt. USAF, 1972-76. Mem. Phi Beta Kappa, Colo. Soc. CPAs. Republican. Mem. Ch. of Christ. Home: 1450 Lone Scout Lookout Monument CO 80132-8036 Office: Schuck Communities Inc 2 N Cascade Ave Ste 1280 Colorado Springs CO 80903-1631

EVERT, JOHN ANDREW, JR., surgeon; b. Brainerd, Minn., Oct. 31, 1917; s. John A. and Pearl Alma (Nash) E.; m. Nora Staael, May 10, 1980. BS, Haverford (Pa.) Coll., 1938; MD, Harvard U., 1942; MS in Surgery, U. Minn., 1946. Diplomate Am. Bd. Surgery. Pvt. practice surgery St. Paul, 1947-53, Missoula, Mont., 1955—; dir. Health Svc. Assn., St. Paul, 1975-90. Chmn. Montpac, Mont., 1962-64.Capt. U.S. Army 1953-55. Fellow in Surgery Mayo Found., Rochester, N.Y., 1943-46. Fellow ACS; mem. Am. Soc. Colon and Rectal Surgeons (assoc. fellow), Western Mont. Med. Soc. Home: 1925 Alvina Dr Missoula MT 59802-3660 Office: 900 N Orange St Missoula MT 59802-2998

EVERTON, MARTA VE, ophthalmologist; b. Luling, Tex., Nov. 12, 1926; d. T.W. and Nora E. (Eckols) O'Leavy; B.A., Hardin-Simmons U., 1945; M.A., Stanford U., 1947; M.D., Baylor U., 1955; postgrad. N.Y.U.-Bellevue Hosp., 1956-57; m. Robert K. Graham, Oct. 15, 1960; children: Marcia, Christie, Leslie Fox. Intern, Meth. Hosp., Houston, 1955-56; resident in ophthalmology Baylor Affiliated Hosps., Houston, 1957-59; clin. instr. ophthalmology Baylor U., 1959-60; asst. clin. prof. ophthalmology Loma Linda U., 1962-73; practice medicine specializing in ophthalmology, Houston, 1959-60, Pasadena, Calif., 1961-74, Escondido, Calif., 1974—. Mem. Calif. Med. Assn., Am. Acad. Ophthalmology, Alpha Omega Alpha. Home: 3024 Sycamore Ln Escondido CA 92025-7433 Office: 820 E Ohio Ave Escondido CA 92025-3421

EVES, JEFFREY P., entertainment industry executive; b. Omaha, Nov. 3, 1946; s. Wayne P. Eves and Laurette (Marcotte) Naylor. BS, U. Nebr., 1968; MA, U. Calif., Berkeley, 1969. Sales rep. Crown Zellerbach Corn, San Francisco, 1969-71; chief spokesman The U.S. Price Commn., Washington, 1971-73; spl. asst. to pres. White House, Washington, 1973-76; mgr. govt. affairs Potlatch Corp., San Francisco, 1976-79; dir. govt. affairs, internat trade Scott. Paper Co., Phila., 1979-86; v.p. Ft. Howard Corp., Green Bay, Wis., 1986-94; pres. Video Software Dealers Assn. (Home Video Entertainment), Encino, Calif., 1994—; bd. dirs. Nat. Recycling Coalition, Washington, St. Vincent Hosp., Green Bay. Lt. USAR, 1968-74. Mem. Am. Forest and Paper Assn., U.S. Conf. of Mayors. Republican. Roman Catholic. Home: 12647 Promontory Rd Los Angeles CA 90049 Office: Video Software Dealers Assn 16530 Ventura Blvd Ste 400 Encino CA 91436-4551

EVETT, MALCOLM, educator; b. Chgo., June 20, 1942; s. Arthur Floyd and Esther (Mann) E. BS, U. Ill., 1964; PhD, U. Calif., Berkeley, 1968. Postdoctoral fellow U. Alta., Can., 1968-70; chemistry researcher U. Calif., 1971-76; cons. Airesearch, 1976—; instr. San Jose (Calif.) City Coll., 1991—. Mem. AAAS, ASHRAE, Phi Beta Kappa, Phi Kappa Phi.

EVRIGENIS, JOHN BASIL, obstetrician-gynecologist; b. Athens, Greece, Feb. 23, 1929; came to U.S., 1951; s. Basil I. and Maria (Soteriou) E.; m. Sophia M. Goritsan, June 22, 1952; children: Maryellen, E. Debbie, W. Gregory, John Jr. BA, U. Athens, 1947, MD, 1951. Diplomate Am. Bd. Ob-Gyn. Intern Providence Hosp., Portland, Oreg., 1951-52, resident in gen. practice medicine, 1952-53; resident in ob-gyn Emanuel Hosp. and U. Oreg. Med. Sch., Portland, 1953-56; pvt. practice specializing in ob-gyn Sacramento, 1956—; assoc. clin. prof. ob-gyn Med. Sch., U. Calif., Davis, 1975—; chief ob-gyn dept. Mercy Hosp., Sacramento, 1972-73. Mem. AMA, Am. Fertility Soc., Pan-Am. Med. Soc., Royal Soc. Medicine, Royal Soc. Health, Sacramento County Med. Soc., Calif. Med. Assn., So. Calif. Ob-Gyn. Assembly, Am. Soc. Gynecol. Laproscopists, Am. Soc. Abdominal Surgeons, No. Calif. Ob-Gyn. Soc. (pres. 1975-76), Dynamis Club, Ahepa, Del Paso Country Club, Northridge Country Club, Sutter Club, Sacramento Club, Lions, Elks, Masons, Rotary Club. Eastern Orthodox. Home: 3615 Winding Creek Rd Sacramento CA 95864-1530 Office: 3939 J St Ste 360 Sacramento CA 95819-3631

EWELL, A. BEN, JR., lawyer, businessman; b. Elyria, Ohio, Sept. 10, 1941; s. Austin Bert and Mary Rebecca (Thompson) E.; m. Suzanne E.; children: Austin Bert III, Brice Ballantyne. BA, Miami U., Oxford, Ohio, 1963; JD, Hasting Coll. Law, U. Calif.-San Francisco, 1966. Bar: Calif. 1966, U.S. Dist. Ct. (ea. dist.) Calif. 1967, U.S. Supreme Ct. 1982, U.S. Ct. Appeals (9th cir.) 1967. Pres. A. B. Ewell, Jr., A. Profl. Corp., Fresno, 1984—; formerly gen. counsel to various water dists. and assns.; gen. counsel, chmn. San Joaquin River Flood Control Assn., 1984-88; CEO Millerton New Town Devel. Co., 1988-94, chmn., 1994—; pres. Brighton Crest Country Club Inc., 1989—; mem. task force on prosecution, cts. and law reform Calif. Coun. Criminal Justice, 1971-74; mem. Fresno Bulldog Found., Calif. State U.; mem. San Joaquin Valley Agrl. Water commn., 1979-88; co-chmn. nat. adv. coun. SBA, 1981, 82, mem. 1981-87; bd. dirs. Fresno East Cmty. Ctr., 1971-73; mem. Fresno County Water Adv. Com., 1989, Fresno Cmty. Coun., 1972-73; chmn. various area polit. campaigns and orgns., including Reagan/Bush, 1984, Deukmejian for Gov., 1986; mem. adv. com. St. Agnes Med. Ctr. Found., 1983-89; trustee U. Calif. Med. Edn. Found., 1989-90, Fresno Met. Mus. Art, History and Sci., active, 1989—, mem. adv. coun., 1993—; bd. dirs. Citizens for Cmty. Enrichment, Fresno, 1990—, Police Activities League, 1995—; mem. Hist. Preservation Commn., City of Fresno. Mem. Phi Alpha Delta, Sigma Nu. Congregationalist. Office: 516 W Shaw Ave Ste 200 Fresno CA 93704-2515

EWELL, P. LAMONT, fire department chief. Fire chief Oakland (Calif.) Fire Dept. Office: Oakland Fire Dept 1605 Martin Luther King Jr Way Oakland CA 94612-1328*

EWER, DAVID, state legislator, bond program officer; b. Bourne, Mass., July 29, 1954; m. Gail Speck; children: Meredith, Mallory. BA, Northeastern U.; MCRP, Harvard U. State rep. Mont. Ho. of Reps., Helena, 1992—; bond program officer Mont. Bd. Investments, Helena. Home: 1016 5th Ave Helena MT 59601-4444 Office: Board of Investments Capitol Station Helena MT 59620

EWERS, ANNE, opera company director. Gen. dir. Boston Lyric Opera, 1984-89, Utah Opera, Salt Lake City, 1990—; panelist Nat. Endowment for Arts; freelance stage dir. San Francisco Opera, N.Y.C. Opera, Can. Opera Co., Minn. Opera, Vancouver Opera, numerous others. Dir. nearly fifty opera prodns. including La Giaconda, Un Ballo in Maschera, La Rondine, The Merry Widow, Ring Cycle, Salome, Dialogues des Carmelites, Eugene Onegin; dir. Dame Joan Sutherland's North American Farewell, Dallas Opera. Bd. dirs. Opera Am., 1993—. Office: Utah Opera 50 W 2d South Salt Lake City UT 84101

EWING, DENNIS D., county clerk, realtor; b. Murray, Utah, Mar. 17, 1941; s. Deane James and Margaret (Rigby) E.; m. Zelda Marie Schorzman, Jan. 25, 1963 (div. Jan. 1988); children: Dennis Deane, Denise Marie, Deborah Ann, DeDee Kae; m. Carma Burr, Sept. 23, 1989; stepchildren: R. Brad Shafter, Sandy Shafter, Carolyn Andreasen, Marcy Andreasen, Wendy Andreasen. Student, Yuba State Coll., 1962, Weber State Coll., 1971-73. Cert. pub. ofcl. Patrolman Tooele (Utah) City Police Dept., 1966-68; dep. sheriff Tooele County Sheriff Dept., 1968-73; county clk. Tooele County Corp., 1973—; co-host summer workshops; mem. tech. publs. com. Nat. Assn. Govt. Archives and Records Adminstrs., 1990-91. Past mem. adv. bd. KUED-TV and KUER-FM Radio; mem. Tooele Vol. Fire Dept., 1970—, past fire insp.; neighborhood chair Easter Seals Fund Raiser. Served with USAF, 1961-65. Mem. Utah Assn. Counties (pres. 1992-94, intergovtl. rels. steering com., legis. com., rep. to state retirement adv. coun., rep. to Salt Lake City Olympic bid com. bd. trustees, bd. dirs. Ins. Mut., bd. dirs., chmn. by-laws com. 1993), Nat. Assn. Counties (bd. dirs. 1991-92), Nat. Assn. County Recorders and Clks. (resolutions and budget coms., pres. 1990-91, past chair elections com., chair com. future, past parliamentarian, bd. dirs.), Utah Assn. County Clks. and Auditors (past pres.), Eagles. Democrat. Mem. LDS Ch. Home: 620 Kingston Dr Tooele UT 84074-2833 Office: Tooele County Corp 47 S Main St Tooele UT 84074-2131

EWING, EDGAR LOUIS, artist, educator; b. Hartington, Nebr., Jan. 17, 1913; s. David E. and Laura (Buckendorf) E.; m. Suzanna Peter Giovan, Feb. 12, 1941. Grad., Art Inst. Chgo., 1935; studied in France, Eng., Italy, 1935-37. Mem. faculty Art Inst. Chgo., 1937-43, U. Mich., Ann Arbor, 1946; asst. prof. fine arts U. So. Calif., 1946-54, assoc. prof., 1954-59, prof., 1959-78, Disting. prof. emeritus, 1978—; Mellon prof. Carnegie-Mellon U., Pitts., 1968-69. One-man shows M.H. DeYoung Meml. Mus. Art, San Francisco, 1948,, Long Beach Mus. Art, 1955, Dalzell Hatfield Galleries, Los Angeles, 1954, 56, 58, 61, 63, 65, Hewlett Gallery-Carnegie Mellon U., Pitts., 1969, Nat. Gallery, Athens, Greece, 1973, Los Angeles Mcpl. Art Gallery, 1974, Palm Springs (Calif.) Desert Mus., 1976-77, Fisher Gallery U. So. Calif., 1978; group exhbns. Cin Art Mus., Corcoran Gallery Art, Washington, Denver Art Mus., Dallas Mus. Fine Arts, Fort Worth Art Ctr., Met. Mus., N.Y.C.; represented: San Francisco Mus. Art, Dallas Mus. Fine Arts, Ft. Worth Art Ctr., Met. Mus., N.Y.C., Sao Paulo (Brazil) Mus. Art, Wichita Art Mus., Fisher Gallery, U. So. Calif., 1994. Served with C.E., U.S. Army, 1943-46, PTO. Recipient Aberle Florscheim Meml. prize for Oil Painting, Art Inst. Chgo., 1943, Purchase award for oil painting Los Angeles County Mus. Art, 1952, Samuel Goldwyn award, 1957, Ahmanson Purchase award City of Los Angeles Exhbn., 1962, Disting. Prof. Emeritus award U. So. Calif., 1987; Edward L. Ryerson fellow, 1935; Louis Comfort Tiffany grantee, 1948-49, Jose Drudis Fund grantee, Greece, 1967; named one of 100 Artists-100 Yrs., Art Inst. Chgo., 1980. Mem. AAUP, Nat. Watercolor Soc. (v.p. 1952, pres. 1953). Democrat. Home: 4226 Sea View Ln Los Angeles CA 90065-3350

EWING, JACK ROBERT, accountant; b. San Francisco, Feb. 14, 1947; s. Robert Maxwell and Blanche Julia (Diak) E.; m. Joan Marie Coughlin Ewing, Nov. 25, 1967; children: Theresa Marie Ewing, Christina Ann Ewing. BS, U. Mo., 1969. CPA. Staff acct. Fox & Co., St. Louis, 1969-70; radio station opr. USAF, Mountain Home, Idaho, 1970-72; internal auditor Air Force Audit Agy., Warren, Wyo., 1972-74; supr. auditor Fox & Co., St. Louis, 1974-79; audit mgr. Erickson, Hunt & Spillman, P.C., Ft. Collins, Colo., 1979-82; stockholder, owner Hunt, Spillman & Ewing, P.C., Ft. Collins, Colo., 1982-93; owner Jack R. Ewing, CPA, 1993—. Mem., pres. Parent Adv. Bd., Beattie Elem. Sch., 1982-83, 86-87; mem. Entrepreneur of Yr. Selection Com., Ft. Collins, Colo., 1989-92, Suicide Resource Ctr. of Larimer County, Ft. Collins, Colo., 1992—, bd. dirs.; mem. Leadership Ft. Collins-Class of 1992, State of Colo. Mental Health Planning Coun., 1993—; dir. treas. One West Contemporary Art Ctr., 1989—, Ctr. for Diversity in Work Place, 1991—; pres., adv. bd. Larimer County Mental Health Ctr., 1992—. Mem. Am. Inst. CPAs, Colo. Soc. CPAs, Eye Openers Kiwanis Club. Office: 3112 Meadowlark Ave Fort Collins CO 80526-2843

EWING, RUSSELL CHARLES, II, physician; b. Tucson, Aug. 16, 1941; s. Russell Charles and Sue M. (Sawyer) E.; m. Louise Anne Wendt, Jan. 29, 1977; children: John Charles, Susan Lenore. BS, U. Ariz., 1963; MD, George Washington U., 1967. Intern, Los Angeles County-U. So. Calif. Med. Ctr., Los Angeles, 1967-68; gen practice medicine and surgery, Yorba Linda, Calif. and Placentia, Calif., 1970—; mem. staff St. Judes Hosp., Fullerton, Calif., 1970—; mem. staff Placentia Linda Community Hosp., 1972—, vice chief staff, 1977-78, chief staff, 1978-80; sec., dir. Yorba Linda Med. Group, Inc., 1974-90; dir. Western Empire Savs. & Loan Assn. (Calif.). Bd. dirs. Yorba Linda YMCA, 1973-88, pres., 1973-74, 81; bd. dirs. Placentia Linda Community Hosp., 1974-81. Served with USN, 1968-70. Diplomate Am. Bd. Family Practice. Fellow Am. Acad. Family Practice; mem. AMA, Calif. Med. Assn. (house of del. 1978-90, 92—, trustee 1990-92), Orange County Med. Assn. (bd. dirs. 1983-90, pres. 1988-89). Republican. Episcopalian. Home: 9212 Smoketree Ln Villa Park CA 92667-2219 Office: 603 Valencia Ave Ste 204 Brea CA 92621-6346

EXNER, ADAM, archbishop; b. Killaly, Sask., Can., Dec. 24, 1928. Ordained priest Roman Catholic Ch., 1957, consecrated bishop, 1974. Bishop of Kamloops B.C., Can., 1974-82; archbishop of Winnipeg Man., Can., 1982-91; archbishop of Vancouver B.C., Can., 1991—. Office: Archdiocese of Vancouver, 150 Robson St, Vancouver, BC Canada V6B 2A7

EYER, BRUCE JARRETT, school district administrator; b. Kelso, Wash., Oct. 29, 1941; s. Carman James and Thelma Laura (West) E.; m. Martha Patricia Ann Husa, Feb. 9, 1962; children: Allison, Angela. AA, Lower Columbia Coll., 1961; BA, Wash. State U., 1964; MEd, Cen. Wash U., 1969. High sch. tchr. math. Yakima (Wash.) Pub. Schs., 1964-69, dir. learning resources, 1969—. Contbr. articles to Medium mag. Pres. Sta. KYVE-TV, Yakima, 1975-78; bd. dirs. Yakima Valley Mus., 1985-90, pres. 1988-90, 91-92. Recipient Disting. Svc. award Yakima Edn. Assn., 1977. Mem. ALA, Assn. for Ednl. Comms. and Tech., Wash. Libr. Media Assn. (treas. 1976-83, Pres.'s award 1989, Supr. of Yr. 1994), Optimist Club (pres. Yakima chpt. 1980-81, named Disting. Pres. 1981), Phi Delta Kappa (Outstanding Educator award Yakima club 1977). Methodist. Office: Yakima Pub Schs 104 N 4th Ave Yakima WA 98902-2636

EYRING, HENRY BENNION, bishop; b. Princeton, N.J., May 31, 1933; s. Henry and Mildred (Bennion) E.; m. Kathleen Johnson, July 27, 1962; children: Henry J., Stuart J., Matthew J., John B., Elizabeth, Mary Kathleen. BS, U. Utah, 1955; MBA, Harvard U., 1959, PhD, 1963; D of Humanities (hon.), Brigham Young U., 1985. Asst., then assoc. prof. Stanford U., Palo Alto, Calif., 1962-71; pres. Ricks Coll., Rexburg, Idaho, 1972-77; dep. commr. edn., then commr. LDS Ch., Salt Lake City, 1977-85, presiding bishopric, 1985—. Co-author: The Organizational World, 1973. With USAF, 1955-57. Sloan faculty fellow MIT, 1963-64. Office: LDS Ch Presiding Bishopric 50 E North Temple Fl 18 Salt Lake City UT 84150

EZAKI-YAMAGUCHI, JOYCE YAYOI, renal dietitian; b. Kingsburg, Calif., Mar. 18, 1947; d. Toshikatsu and Aiko (Ogata) Ezaki; m. Kent Takao Yamaguchi, Oct. 28, 1972; children: Kent Takao, Jr., Toshia Ann. AA, Reedley Coll., 1967; BS in Foods and Nutrition, U. Calif., Davis, 1969. Dietetic intern Henry Ford Hosp., Detroit, 1969-70, staff dietitian, 1970-71; renal dietitian Sutter Meml. Hosp., Sacramento, 1971-72; therapeutic dietitian Mt. Sinai Hosp., Beverly Hills, Calif., 1972-73; clin. dietitian Pacific Hosp., Long Beach, Calif., 1973-77; consulting dietitian Doctor's Hosp., Lakewood, Calif., 1976-77; clin. dietitian Mass. Gen. Hosp., Boston, 1977-78, Winona Meml. Hosp., Indpls., 1978-80; renal dietitian Fresno (Calif.) Community Hosp., 1980—. Author: (computer program) Dialysis Tracker, 1987; author: (with others) Cultural Foods and Renal Diets for the Dietitian, 1988, Standards of Practice Guidlines for the Practice of Clinical Dietetics, 1991. Mem. Nat. Kidney Found. (exec. com. coun. renal nutrition 1992—, region I rep. 1992-93, chair elect 1994-95, chair 1995—), Am. Dietetic Assn. (bd. cert. renal nutrition specialist, renal practice group 1993—), No. Calif./No. Nev. chpt. Nat. Kidney Found. (disting. achievement award coun. on renal nutrition 1993, co-chair-elect 1993, co-chair 1994, treas., corr. sec.). Buddhist. Office: Cmty Hosps Ctrl Calif Fresno & R Sts Fresno CA 93715-2094

EZRA, DAVID A., federal judge; b. 1947. BBA magna cum laude, St. Mary's U., 1969, JD, 1972. Law clk. Office of Corp. Counsel City and County Honolulu, 1972; mem. firm Greenstein, Cowen & Frey, 1972-73, Anthony, Hoddick, Reinwald & O'Connor, 1973-80, Ezra, O'Connor, Moon & Tam, 1980-88; dist. judge U.S. Dist. Ct., Hawaii, 1988—; adj. prof. law Wm. S. Richardson Sch. Law, 1978—. Co-editor, author: Hwaii Construction Law - What to Do and When, 1987; editor: Hawaii Collection Practices Manual. 1st lt. USAR 1971-77. Daugherty Fund scholar, 1971, San Antonio Bar Assn. Aux. scholar, 1972. Mem. ABA, Hawaii State Bar, Am. Arbitration Assn., Delta Epsilon Sigma, Phi Delta Phi. Office: US Dist Ct PO Box 50128 Honolulu HI 96850*

FAATZ, JEANNE RYAN, state legislator; b. Cumberland, Md., July 30, 1941; d. Charles Keith and Myrtle Elizabeth (McIntyre) Ryan; B.S., U. Ill., 1962; postgrad. (Gates fellow) Harvard U. Program Sr. Execs. in state and local Govt., 1984; M.A., U. Colo.-Denver, 1985. children: Kristin, Susan. Instr. Speech Dept., Met. State Coll., Denver, 1985—; sec. to majority leader Colo. Senate, 1976-78; mem. Colo. Ho. Reps. from Dist. 1, 1978—, asst. majority leader. Past pres. Harvey Park (Colo.) Homeowners Assn., Southwest Denver YWCA Adult Edn. Club; Southwest met. coord. UN Children's Fund, 1969-74; mem. citizens adv. coun. Ft. Logan Mental Health Center; bd. mgrs. Southwest Denver YMCA. Mem. Bear Creek Rep. Women's Club. Home: 2903 S Quitman St Denver CO 80236-2208 Office: State Capitol Denver CO 80203

FACELLI, JULIO CESAR, physics researcher, university administrator; b. Buenos Aires, Feb. 9, 1953; came to U.S., 1983; s. Julio César and Elva Nelida (Morato) F.; m. Ana Maria Elena Ferreyro, Oct. 18, 1980; children: Julie Anna, Maria Elizabeth. Licenciado in Physics, U. Buenos Aires, 1977, PhD, 1981. Undergrad. asst. dept. physics U. Buenos Aires, 1976, grad. asst. dept. physics, 1977-82; dir. Instituto de Fisica de la Atmósfera Servicio Meteorologico Nacional, Buenos Aires, 1979; rsch. assoc. dept. chemistry U. Ariz., Tucson, 1983; rsch. assoc. dept. chemistry U. Utah, Salt Lake City, 1984-86, rsch. asst. prof. dept. chemistry, 1986-90, assoc. dir. acad. supercomputing Utah Supercomputing Inst., 1989—, acting dir. Utah Supercomputing Inst., 1992—; assoc. prof. ad honorem dept. physics, U. Buenos Aires, 1987—, vis. prof., 1992; adj. assoc. prof. dept. chemistry, U. Utah, Salt Lake City, 1990—; reviewer Jour. Am. Chem. Soc., Jour. Phys. Chemistry, Chem. Revs., Jour. Computational Chemistry, Theoretica Chimica Acta, Magnetic Resonance in Chemistry; invited speaker various univs., rsch. ctrs. and confs.; steering com. Supercomputing by Univ. People for Edn. and Rsch., 1989-92, chmn., 1990-91; insts. and confs. adv. bd. U. Utah, 1991—; smart node adv. bd. Cornell Nat. Supercomputing Facility, 1991—, steering com. SUP'EUR European user's group, 1990-91; libr. and data comm. com., Utah Edn. Network, 1993—. Contbr. numerous articles in sci. jours. 1st lt. Argentinian Air Force, 1978-80. Mem. Am. Chem. Soc., IEEE (Computer Soc.). Roman Catholic. Home: 1847 S 2600 E Salt Lake City UT 84108-3369 Office: Utah Supercomputing Inst Univ Utah 85 SSB Salt Lake City UT 84112

FACTOR, MAX, III, lawyer, investment advisor; b. L.A., Sept. 25, 1945; s. Sidney B. and Dorothy (Levinson) F.; BA in Econs. magna cum laude, Harvard Coll., 1966; JD, Yale U., 1969. Bar: Calif. 1970, U.S. Ct. Appeals (6th cir.) 1971, U.S. Dist. Ct. (cen. dist.) Calif. 1971. Law clk. U.S. Ct. Appeals (6th cir.), 1969-71; exec. dir. Calif. Law Ctr., Los Angeles, 1973-74; dir. Consumer Protection Sect., Los Angeles City Atty., 1974-77; pvt. practice Factor & Agay, Beverly Hills, Calif, 1978—. expert witness numerous state and fed. bds., 1974-78; guest lectr. UCLA, U. So. Calif., Los Angeles County Bar Assn., Calif. Dept. Consumer Affairs, 1974-76; hearing examiner City of Los Angeles, 1975. Contbr. articles to profl. jours. Bd. dirs. Western Law Ctr. for the Handicapped, Los Angeles, 1977-79, Beverly Hills Unified Sch. Dist., 1979-83; pres. Beverly Hills Bd. Edn., 1983; bd. councilors U. So. Calif. Law Ctr., Los Angeles, 1983—; chmn. Beverly Hills Visitors Bur., 1989-90. Recipient scholarship award Harvard Coll., 1965; Max Factor III Day proclaimed in his honor Beverly Hills City Council, 1979; recipient Disting. Service to Pub. Edn. award Beverly Hills Bd. Edn., 1979. Mem. Los Angeles County Bar Assn. (chmn. various coms. 1976-78), Beverly Hills C. of C. (pres. 1987-88), Beverly Hills Edn. Found. (pres. 1977-79).

FADDEN, DELMAR MCLEAN, electrical engineer; b. Seattle, Nov. 10, 1941; s. Gene Scott and Alice Elizabeth (McLean) F.; m. Sandra Myrene Callahan, June 22, 1963; children: Donna McLean, Lawrence Gene. BSEE, U. Wash., 1963, MSEE, 1975. Lic. comml. pilot, Wash. With Boeing Comml. Airplane Co., Seattle, 1969—, chief engr. 737/757 avionics/flight systems, 1990—. Contbr. articles to IEEE Proceedings. Capt. USAF, 1963-69. Mem. AIAA, IEEE, Human Factors Soc., Soc. Automotive Engrs. (vice chmn. G-10 com. 1981-91, chmn. systems integration task group 1990—), Mountaineers (pres. 1984-85). Home: 5011 298th Ave SE Preston WA 98050 Office: Boeing Comml Airplane Co PO Box 3707 M Seattle WA 98124

FADELEY, EDWARD NORMAN, state supreme court justice; b. Williamsville, Mo., Dec. 13, 1929; m. Darian Cyr, Sept. 12, 1993; children: Chuck, Shira. A.B., U. Mo., 1951; J.D. cum laude, U. Oreg., 1957. Bar: Oreg. 1957, U.S. Supreme Ct. 1968. Practice law Eugene, Oreg., 1957-88; mem. Oreg. Ho. of Reps., 1961-63; mem. Oreg. Senate, 1963-87, pres., 1983-85; justice Oregon Supreme Ct., 1989—; mem. jud. working group Internat. Water Tribunal, Amsterdam, The Netherlands; invitee Rio Environ. Conf., 1992, Indigenous Peoples of World Conf., New Zealand, 1993; adj. prof. law U. Oreg. Chmn. Oreg. Dem. party, 1966-68; chmn. law and justice com. Nat. Conf. Legislators, 1977-78; adv. com. to State and Local Law Ctr., Washington; participants com. Washington Pub. Power Supply System, 1984-88; candidate for nomination for gov., 1986; bd. dirs. Wayne Morse Hist. Park. Lt. USNR, 1951-54. Recipient First Pioneer award U. Oreg., 1980, Assn. Oreg. Counties award for reform of state ct. system, 1982. Mem. ABA (internat. law, pub. utility law, judicial adminstrn.), Oreg. State Bar Assn. (chmn. uniform laws com. 1962-64), Order of Coif, Alpha Pi Zeta, Phi Alpha Delta. Democrat. Methodist. Office: Oreg Supreme Ct Supreme Ct Bldg Salem OR 97310

FAGELSON, HARVEY J., emergency physician, dermatologist, educator; b. Chgo., June 19, 1938; s. Lawrence Larry and Eva (Stein) F.; m. Rosalie Schwartz, July 12, 1964; children: James E., Nancy E., Robert E. Student, U. Ill., Chgo., 1958, MD, 1962. Diplomate Am. Bd. Dermatology. Intern St. Francis Hosp., Evanston, Ill., 1962-63; resident in dermatology U. Ill. Rsch. and Ednl. Hosps., Chgo., 1963-66; med. dir. emergency clinic L.A. County-U. So. Calif. Med. Ctr., L.A., 1969—; asst. prof. emergency medicine U. So. Calif., L.A., 1973—. Capt. USAF, 1966-68. Fellow Am. Acad. Dermatology. Office: LAC-USC Med Ctr 1200 N State St # 211 Los Angeles CA 90033-4525

FAGERBERG, DIXON, JR., retired accountant, weather observer; b. Prescott, Ariz., Mar. 20, 1909; s. Dixon and Amy (Nelson) F.; m. Mary Jergens, June 21, 1933 (div. Aug. 1980); children: Dick, Mary, Nelson; m. Lorraine Brenn, Sept. 22, 1980. AB in Econs. summa cum laude, Stanford U., 1931. CPA, Ariz. Valuation engr. Calif. R.R. Commn., San Francisco, 1931-32; acct. Harmon Audit Co., Prescott, 1933-34; owner, mgr. Dixon Fagerberg, Jr., CPA, Flagstaff, Kingman, Phoenix, Ariz., 1935-57; ptnr.-in-charge Peat, Marwick, Mitchell & Co., Phoenix, 1957-71; ret., 1971; vol. cons. Internat. Exec. Svc. Corps, Guatemala City, Guatemala, 1975. Co-author: 108 Sedona Westerner Trail Walks, 1979; author: Boyhood Recollections of Prescott, Arizona, 1983, Dix's Almanac of Weather and Climate, 1989; columnist Practitioner's Forum, 1954-56. Bd. dirs. Phoenix Libr., 1960-65; mem. Coconino County Planning and Zoning Commn., Flagstaff, 1973-76; councilman City of Sedona, 1988. Lt. USNR, 1944-46. Recipient medal of merit U. Ariz., 1960, Outstanding CPA award Mountain States Acctg. Conf., 1966. Mem. AICPA (nat. v.p. 1955-56), Ariz. Soc. CPA's (pres. 1938-39, columnist The Oasis 1972—), Am. Soc. Mining Engrs., Assn. Am. Weather Observers, Sedona Westerners (trail boss 1973-74), Pinewood Country Club, Masons.

FAGG, RUSSELL, judge, lawyer; b. Billings, Mont., June 26, 1960; s. Harrison Grover and Darlene (Bohling) F.; m. Karen Barclay, Feb. 15, 1992. BA, Whitman Coll., 1983; JD, U. Mont., 1986. Law clerk Mont. Supreme Ct., Helena, Mont., 1986-87; atty. Sandall Law Firm, Billings, Mont., 1987-89; city prosecutor City of Billings, Mont., 1989-91; dep. atty. Yellowstone County, Billings, Mont., 1991-94; mem. Montana State Legislator, Helena, 1991-94; judge State Dist. Ct. (13th dist.) Mont., Billings, 1995—; dir. Midland Empire Pachyderm Club, 1988-94, pres. 1990-91; chmn. judiciary com. House of Reps., 1993-94. Named Outstanding Young Montanan, Mont. Jaycees, 1994. Home: 3031 Rimview Dr Billings MT 59102-0955 Office: PO Box 35027 Billings MT 59107

FAGNANI, MICHELE ANN, production supervisor; b. San Francisco, July 15, 1945; d. Melvin ANthony and Ann (Garetti) F.; children: Tamera Ann, Troy James. Student, San Mateo (Calif.) Bus. Coll., 1964, John Roberts Powers Coll., 1968. Draftsman Ampex, Redwood City, Calif., 1965-68; profl. model, 1967-69; draftsman Numetrics, Palo Alto, Calif., 1968-70; electronic assembler Westvalley Engrng., Palo Alto, 1970-72; prodn. control planner Fairchild, San Jose, Calif., 1972-78; prodn. supr. Intel, Sunnyvale, Calif., 1978-80; prodn. mgr. Robinton Product, Inc., Sunnyvale, 1980-83, Optical Coating Labs., Santa Rosa, Calif., 1983-85, Weightronix, Santa Rosa, 1986-91; ret., 1991; landlord rentals, San Jose and Santa Rosa, 1978; rancher, Santa Rosa, 1982-85. Democrat. Roman Catholic.

FAHLMAN, BETSY LEE, American art history educator; b. Wolfeboro, N.H., July 18, 1951. BA in Art History magna cum laude, Mount Holyoke Coll., 1973; Ma, U. Del., 1977, PhD, 1981. Instr., catalogue, curator, rsch. asst. Slide Libr. Mount Holyoke Coll., South Hadley, Mass., 1972-77; resident fellow, lectr. in art history Franklin and Marshall Coll., Lancaster, Pa., 1977-79; guest curator Corcoran Gallery of Art, Washington, 1979-80; asst. prof. dept. art Old Dominion U., Norfolk, Va., 1980-88; assoc. prof. art history Sch. of Art Ariz. State U., Tempe, 1988—; vis. scholar Nat. Collection of Fine Arts, Smithsonian Instn., Washington, summer 1978; adv. bd. Northlight Gallery, 1991—, U. Art Mus., 1989—, faculty senator, 1992—; lectr. in field. Contbg. editor Latin American Art, 1989-91; guest editor Indsl. Archeology, vol. 12, 1986; book reviewer; contbr. articles to profl. jours. Mem. speakers bur. Ariz. Humanities Coun., 1992-94; mem. visual arts com. Scottsdale Cultural Coun., 1989-93, bd. dirs. 1993-94, pub. art and collections com., 1991-94. Unidel fellow U. Del., 1973-77, Rockefeller fellow U. Del., 1979, Smithsonian Postdoctoral fellow Nat. Mus. Am. Art, 1983-84; Summer Rsch. grantee Old Dominion U. Rsch. Found., 1982, 83, Am. Philos. Soc. grantee, 1983, , NEH grantee, 1985, Old Dominion U. grantee, 1986, 87, 88, Coll. of Fine Arts Rsch. grantee Ariz. State U., 1992, Study grantee Ariz. Humanities Coun., 1993, Short Term Visitor grantee Smithsonian Instn., 1993. Mem. AAUW (postdoctoral fellowship 1985-86), Am. Assn. Mus., Am. Studies Assn., Ariz. Hist. Soc., Assn. Historians of Am.

Art, Coll. Art Assn., Maine Citizens for Hist. Preservation, Mount Holyoke Club of No. and Ctrl. Ariz., Nat. Trust for Hist. Preservation, Phoenix Art Mus., Soc. Indsl. Archeology, Soc. Archtl. Historians, Southeastern Coll. Art Conf., Victorian Soc. Am., Phi Beta Kappa. Office: Ariz State Univ School of Art Tempe AZ 85287-1505

FAIN, GORDON LEE, physiology educator; b. Washington, Nov. 24, 1946; s. Robert Forbes and Margaret (Smith) F.; m. Margery Jones, June 22, 1968; 2 children. Student, U. Chgo., 1964-65; BA in Biology, Stanford U., 1968; PhD in Biophysics, Johns Hopkins U., 1973. NIH predoctoral fellow Johns Hopkins U., Balt., 1968-73; NIH postdoctoral fellow Biol. Labs. Harvard U., Cambridge, Mass., 1973-74; Grass fellow Marine Biol. Labs., Woods Hole, Mass., 1974; exchange fellow Harvard U. Med. Sch. and Inst. Nat. de la Sante et de la Recherche Med., Lab. de Neurobiologie, Paris, 1974-75; asst. prof. ophthalmology UCLA Sch. Medicine, Jules Stein Eye Inst., 1975-78, assoc. prof., 1978-82, prof. ophthalmology, 1982—; assoc. dir. Jules Stein Eye Inst., Los Angeles, 1985-94; prof. physiol. sci., 1991—, vice-chair dept. physiol. sci., 1994—; vice chair Physiol. Sci. Dept.; speaker in field. Contbr. numerous articles to profl. jours. Recipient NIH Merit award, 1989—; NIH grantee, 1980-85, 84-88, 85—, 88—, NSF travel grantee, 1985-87. Mem. Assn. for Rsch. in Vision and Ophthalmology, Biophys. Soc., Soc. Neurosci., Am. Physiological Soc., English Physiological Soc. (fgn. mem.), Phi Beta Kappa. Office: UCLA Physiol Sci Dept Life Scis Bldg 3836 Los Angeles CA 90095-1527

FAIN, KAREN KELLOGG, history and geography educator; b. Pueblo, Colo., Oct. 10, 1940; d. Howard Davis and Mary Lucille (Cole) Kellogg; m. Sept. 1, 1961; divorced; 1 child, Kristopher. Student, U. Ariz., 1958-61; BA, U. So. Colo., 1967; MA, U. No. Colo., 1977; postgrad., U. Denver, 1968, 72-93, Colo. State U., 1975, 91, U. No. Ill., 1977, 83, Ft. Hayes State Coll., 1979, U. Colo., 1979, 86-87, 92, Ind. U., 1988. Cert. secondary tchr., Colo. Tchr. history and geography Denver Pub. Schs., 1967—; tchr. West H.S., Denver, 1992—; area adminstr., tchr. coord. Close Up program, Washington, 1982-84; reviewer, cons. for book Geography, Our Changing World, 1990. Vol., chmn. young profls. Inst. Internat. Edn. and World Affairs Coun., Denver, 1980—; mem. state selection com. U.S. Senate and Japan Scholarship Com., Denver, 1981-89, Youth for Understanding, Denver; mem. Denver Art Mus., 1970—; vol. Denver Mus. Natural History, 1989—; bd. overseas Dept. Def. Dependents Sch., Guantanamo Bay, Cuba, 1990-91. Fulbright scholar Chadron State Coll., Pakistan, 1975; Geog. Soc. grantee U. Colo., 1986; recipient award for Project Prince, Colo. U./Denver Pub. Schs./Denver Police Dept., 1992. Mem. Colo. Coun. Social Studies (sec. 1984-86), Nat. Coun. Social Studies (del. 1984), World History Assn., Fulbright Assn., Am. Forum for Global Edn., Rocky Mountain Regional World History Assn. (steering com. 1984-87), Colo. Geographic Alliance (steering com. 1986), Gamma Phi Beta, Kappa Kappa Iota. Democrat. Episcopalian. Home: 12643 E Bates Cir Aurora CO 80014-3315 Office: West High Sch 951 Elati St Denver CO 80204-3939

FAIR, ANNIE MAY, computer specialist; b. Coolidge, Ariz., Sept. 21, 1939; d. Jack C. and Birdie Geneva (Strickland) Cullins; m. Charles Leroy Fair, Sept. 12, 1964; children: Rex Lee Myers, Kathleen Ann, Rebecca Elizabeth. Student, Wichita State U., 1979-81, U. Colo., 1982-84, 94—, Met. State U., Denver, 1983-84. Cert. geol. engr. Pres., bd. dirs. Fresnal Minerals, Inc., Tucson, 1975-80; geol. technician Foxfire Exploration, Inc., Wichita, Kans., 1980-81, Coastal Oil & Gas Corp., Denver, 1981-93; insp. fluid minerals U.S. Dept. Interior Bur. Land Mgmt., Canon City, Colo., 1993—; geol. cons. C.L. Fair & Assocs., Littleton, Colo., 1984-93. Active adv. bd. Masonic-Rainbow Girls-Grand Cross of Color, Denver, 1983-84; vol.- helper United Way Campaign, Denver, 1990, 91; vol. Am. Cancer Soc., Littleton, 1991, 92; art judge Reflections Nat. Art Contest, Denver, 1992, 93, Skyline Elem. Sch., Canon City, 1993. Recipient Grand Cross of Color, Masons-Order Rainbow/Girls, 1957; Music scholar U. No. Ariz., 1957. Mem. Am. Assn. Petroleum Geologists, Geol. Soc. Am., Rocky Mountain Assn. Geologists, Computer Oriented Geol. Soc., Alpha Lambda Delta. Home: 2853 Melvina Canon City CO 81212

FAIR, JAMES STANLEY, hospital administrator; b. Delisle, Sask., Can., May 21, 1933; married. Bachelors degree, U. Sask., 1955; masters degree, U. Toronto, Ont., Can., 1968. Adminstrv. rschr. Toronto Gen. Hosp., 1967-68; asst. adminstr. Mckellar Gen. Hosp., Ft. William, Ont., 1968-72; dir. diagnostic svcs. Vancouver Gen. Hosp., B.C., Can., 1972-73; acting exec. dir. Gorge Road Hosp., Victoria, B.C., 1984, pub. adminstr., 1984-85; exec. dir. Victoria Gen. Hosp., 1973-84, Guelph (Ont.) Gen. Hosp., 1985-88; pres., CEO Fraser-Burrard Hosp., New Westminster, B.C., 1989—; CEO Simon Fraser Health Region, New Westminster, B.C., 1995. Contbr. articles to profl. jours. Office: Fraser-Burrard Hosp Soc, 260 Sherbrooke St, New Westminster, BC Canada V3L 3M2

FAIR, MARY LOUISE, retired elementary school educator; b. Emporia, Kans., July 16, 1931; d. Dale Franklin Fair and Beulah Fair (Emma) Martin. BA, Marymount Coll., 1953. Bus. edn. tchr. Geneseo (Kans.) High Sch., 1953-55, St. John (Kans.) High Sch., 1955-56; sec. YMCA, Salina, Kans., 1956-57; alumna sec. Marymount Coll., Salina, Kans., 1957-58; bus. edn. tchr. Hayden High Sch., Topeka, Kans., 1958-59; sec. Mental Health Assn., Denver, 1959-60; sec., substitute tchr. Denver Pub. Schs., 1960-62, elem. tchr., 1962-86. 1st v.p. AARP, Heather Gardens, Aurora, Colo., 1988-90, pres. 1991, parliamentarian 1994, active with publication com. 1994—; tutor Aurora and Cherry Creek elem. schs., 1987—. Mem. AAUW (Aurora br., historian 1993-94), Marymount Coll. Alumnae Assn. (pres. 1956-58), Alpha Delta Kappa (state sgt.-at-arms 1982-84, state pres. 1986-88, S.W. regional sgt.-at-arms 1989-91, internat. chmn. living meml. scholarship com. 1991-93, chpt. pres. 1994-96, chpt. pres. coun. (pres. 1994-96). Republican. Baptist. Home: 3022 S Wheeling Way Apt 311 Aurora CO 80014-5607

FAIRBANKS, MARY KATHLEEN, data analyst, researcher; b. Manhattan, Kans., June 4, 1948; d. Everitt Edsel and Mary Catherine (Moran) F. BS, St. Norbert Coll., 1970; postgrad., Calif. Family Study Ctr., 1981-82. Neuropsychology researcher U.S. VA Hosp., Sepulveda, Calif., 1970-76; mgr. print shop Charisma In Missions, City of Industry, Calif., 1976-77; neuropsychology researcher L.A. County Women's Hosp., 1977-79; mem. tech. staff Computer Scis. Corp., Ridgecrest, Calif., 1979-81; systems programmer Calif. State U., Northridge, 1982-84; bus. systems analyst World Vision, Monrovia, Calif., 1984-86; configuration analyst Teledyne System Co., Northridge, 1986-87; applications system analyst Internat. Telephone and Telegraph/Fed. Electric Corp., Altadena, Calif., 1987-88; supr. data analysts OAO Corp., Altadena, 1988—. Co-author, contbr.: Serotonin and Behavior, 1973, Advances in Sleep Research, vol. 1, 1974. Mem. OAO Mgmt. Assn., So. Calif. Application System Users Group, Digital Equipment Computer Users Soc. Roman Catholic. Home: 37607 Lasker Ave Palmdale CA 93550-7721 Office: OAO Corp 787 W Woodbury Rd Ste 2 Altadena CA 91001-5368

FAIRBROTHER, KATHRYN LOUISE, customer relations executive; b. Inglewood, Calif., Jan. 8, 1957; d. Edward McCullough Fairbrother and Carolyn (Howe) Stevens. BA in English Lit., UCLA, 1979; MBA, Calif. State U., Dominguez Hills, 1994. Asst. dept. mgr. Broadway, Westchester, Calif., 1978-79; customer svc. rep. Grand Rent A Car subs. First Gray Line Corp., L.A., 1979-82, supr. customer svc., 1982-84, mgr. charter sales, 1984-87, security investigator, 1987-88; mgr. charter sales Gray Line Tours subs. First Gray Line Corp., L.A., 1984-87; sr. supr. customer rels. Toyota Motor Sales, USA, Inc., Torrance, Calif., 1988—. Mem. AIDS project L.A. Mem. NAFE, Soc. Consumer Affairs Profls., Delta Mu Delta. Democrat. Presbyterian. Home: 5301 Knowlton St Apt B Los Angeles CA 90045-2041

FAIRECHILD, DIANA, aviation health analyst, author, speaker; b. Bklyn., Feb. 6, 1944; d. Franklin and Pearl (Kaufman) Elias; m. J.G. Ruggles, 1969 (div. 1977); m. JG Alfer, 1981 (div. 1983). BA in French Lit., Boston U., 1965. Internat. flight attendant Pan Am World Airways, Miami, L.A., San Francisco, Honolulu, 1966-86, United Airlines, Honolulu, 1986-87; writer, pub., lectr. Maui, Hawaii, 1992—. Author, pub.: Jet Smart, 1992; author Healthy Flying, a cyberspace column on Internet. Address: Flyana Rhyme Inc PO Box 300 Makawao HI 96768-0300

FAIRHURST, JEFFREY THOMAS, software consultant; b. Tacoma, Wash., May 10, 1955; s. Cyrel Jackson and Evelyn Marie Fairhurst; m. Irene Johanna Moser, Sept. 22, 1976 (div. Dec. 1982); children: Johanna Evelyn, Jeffrey Jackson. Student, Ctrl. Tex. Coll. Analyst Barclay's Bank, San Jose, Calif., 1984; ind. cons. San Jose, 1984-85; analyst GE Nuclear Energy Bus., San Jose, 1985; software developer CSC, San Diego, 1986-87; analyst Lorimar, Culver City, Calif., 1987-88, Decom Sys. Inc., San Marcos, Calif., 1988, Profl. Computer Resources, Inc., Cypress, Calif., 1989, Psicor Inc., San Diego, 1990; ind. cons. Carlsbad, Calif., 1990-92, Midcom Corp., Cypress, 1992-93, Logicorp Inc., Bingham Farms, Mich., 1994; cons. Air Touch, Irvine, Calif. With U.S. Army, 1973-84. Home: 3990 Scott Dr Carlsbad CA 92008-3625

FAIRLEY RANEY, REBECCA, journalist; b. Columbia, Mo., Sept. 7, 1965; d. James Lewis Raney and Phyllis Gail Fairley. BJ magna cum laude, U. Mo., 1987. Intern San Bernardino (Calif.) County Sun, summer 1987, reporter/computer-assisted projects, 1990—; reporter The Hemet (Calif.) News, 1987-88; gen. assignment reporter Inland Valley Daily Bulletin, Ontario, Calif., 1988-90. First violinist The Claremont (Calif.) Symphony Orchestra, 1988—; classroom vol. Citrus Elem. Sch., Upland, Calif., 1991-92. Recipient Celebrate Literacy award Arrowhead Reading Coun., San Bernardino, 1993, 1st pl. award Calif. Newspaper Pubs. Assn., 1993, various awards Gannett; recipient various univ. scholarships, 1st pl. award investigative reporting Best of Gannett, 1994, 1st pl. award Calif. Newspaper Pub. Assn. Pub. Svc., 1994, finalist for Livingston award. Mem. Investigative Reporters and Editors, Press Club of So. Calif. (former bd. dirs., 1st pl. investigative reporting, 1993, others 1988—), Soc. Profl. Journalists (1st pl. awards in health, polit. and minority affairs writing 1988—), Scholarship Soc., Kappa Tau Alpha. Office: San Bernardino County Sun 399 N D St San Bernardino CA 92401-1518

FAIRWEATHER, EDWIN ARTHUR, electronics company executive; b. London, July 21, 1916; came to U.S., 1967; s. Arthur Henry and Elizabeth (Dawson) F.; m. Joan Barbara Branson, Sept. 14, 1946; children: David Martin, Janet Elizabeth Fairweather Nelson. BSME, London Poly., 1940. Quality engr. Lucas-Rotex, Toronto (Ont., Can.) and Birmingham (Eng.), 1951-58; mfg. engr. Flight Refuelling Co., Dorset, Eng., 1958-62, Spar Aerospace, Toronto, 1962-67, Sperry Flight Systems, Phoenix, 1967-71; engr. research and devel. Ford Aerospace Co., Palo Alto, Calif., 1971-85; founder, pres., chief engr. Fairweather & Co., Sunnyvale, Calif., 1980—. Patentee in field. Served with RAF, 1940-46. Home and Office: 1442 S Wolfe Rd Sunnyvale CA 94087-3669

FALBAUM, BERTRAM SEYMOUR, investigator; b. N.Y.C., July 28, 1934; s. Abraham and Shari (Greenfield) F.; m. Roberta Jessie Oberstone, Sept. 1, 1957; children: Vance Leonard, Stacy Lynn. AA, L.A. City Coll., 1961; BS with honors, Calif., State U.-L.A., 1962; postgrad. George Washington U., 1966-68; MPA, Syracuse U., 1972. Agt., U.S. Customs Service, Los Angeles and Nogales, Ariz., 1961-66; instr. Treasury Law Enforcement Sch., Washington, 1966-69; spl. agt. U.S. Customs Service, Washington, 1969-73; dep. chief law enforcement U.S. Fish & Wildlife Service, Washington, 1973-78, spl. projects officer, Washington, 1978-79; sr. criminal investigator U.S. Dept. Justice (office spl. investigations), Washington, 1979-86; v.p. The Investigative Group, Inc., Washington, 1986-92; pres. Investigative Dynamics, Inc., Tucson, 1992—; adj. prof. Am. U., 1977-78, 1990-91. Author: Basic Investigative Photography, 1967; Marksmanship, 1969. Contbr. articles to profl. jours. Chmn. troop com. Nat. Capital Area council Boy Scouts Am., Centreville, Va., 1974-77. Served with USAF, 1953-57. Recipient commendations U.S. Customs Svc., U.S. Dept. Justice. Mem. Am. Criminal Justice Assn. (chpt. pres. 1959-61), Assn. Fed. Investigators (bd. dirs. 1979-86 , cert. profl. investigator), Am. Judicature Soc., Fed. Investigators Assn., Am. Fedn. Police, Am. Law Enforcement Officers Assn., Internat. Assn. Chiefs of Police, Assn. Cert. Fraud Examiners (cert. fraud examiner), Am. Soc. Indsl. Security (cert. protection profl.), Nat. Dist. Attys. Assn., Coun. Internat. Investigators, World Assn. Detectives, Assn. Legal Investigators, Internat. Narcotic Enforcement Officers Assn., Assn. of Former Intelligence Officers, Nat. Coun. Investigation and Security Svcs., Ariz. Assn. of Lic. Pvt. Investigators (bd. dirs. 1994-95), Fed. Law Enforcement Officers Assn., Fraternal Order of Border Agents, Fraternal Order of Police, Nat. Assn. Chiefs of Police, Pvt. Investigators and Security Assn., Pvt. Investigators Assn. of Va., Customs Special Agent Assn. (pres. 1994-95), Vidocq Soc., Sunrise Territory Village Homeowners Assn. (v.p. 1994, pres. 1995), Lambda Alpha Epsilon. Jewish. Clubs: Chantilly Country (v.p. for golf 1978, 80, 81, 83, bd. dirs. 1984, chmn. bd. 1985-89), La Paloma Country (golf com. and handicap chmn. 1994-95). Home: 4921 N Ft Verde Trail Tucson AZ 85715-5903

FALBO, NADINE LOIS, contractor; b. Swickley, Pa., Feb. 16, 1949; d. John Joseph and Bernadine (Juracko) F. Student, Riverside (Calif.) C.C., 1986-89, UCLA, 1987-88, Loyola Marymount U., 1987-89, Harvard U., 1993. Lic. gen. contractor, Calif.; cert. Calif. Coun. for Interior Design. Constrn. worker Calif., 1973-83; interior designer Nadine's Enterprises, Riverside, 1984—, gen. contractor, 1989—; thoroughbred horse trainer, Calif., N.Mex., 1973-83; mem. adv. bd. Serra Retreat, Malibu, Calif., 1994. Roman Catholic. Office: Nadines Enterprises 5590 46th St Riverside CA 92509-6578

FALCO, CHARLES MAURICE, physicist, educator; b. Fort Dodge, Iowa, Aug. 17, 1948; s. Joe and Mavis Margaret (Mickelson) F.; m. Dale Wendy Miller, May 5, 1973; children: Lia Denise, Amelia Claire. BA, U. Calif., Irvine, 1970, MA, 1971, PhD, 1974. Trainee NSF, 1970-74; asst. physicist Argonne (Ill.) Nat. Lab., 1974-77, physicist, 1977-82, group leader superconductivity and novel materials, 1978-82; prof. physics and optical scis., research prof. U. Ariz., Tucson, 1982—, dir. lab. x-ray optics, 1986—; vis. prof. U. Paris Sud, 1979, 86, U. Aachen, 1989; lectr., 1974—; mem. panel on artificially structured materials NRC, 1984-85; co-organizer numerous internat. confs. in field, 1978—; mem. spl. rev. panel on high temperature superconductivity Applied Physics Letters, 1987—; mem. panel on superconductivity Inst. Def. Analysis, 1988—; researcher on artificial metallic superlattices, X-ray optics, asuperconductivity, condensed matter physics, electronic materials. Editor: Future Trends in Superconductive Electronics, 1978, Materials for Magneto-Optic Data Storage, 1989; contbr. articles to profl. jours.; patentee in field. Mem. divsn. condensed matter physics Exec. Com. Arts, 1992—. Alexander vo Humboldt Found. sr. disting. grantee, 1989. Fellow Am. Phys. Soc. (counselor 1992-94, exec. com. div. condensed matter physics 1992-94, exec. com. div. internat. physics 1994—); mem. IEEE (sr.), Am. Vacuum Soc., Materials Rsch. Soc., Sigma Xi. Home: 6301 N Caravan Ln Tucson AZ 85704-2802 Office: U Ariz Dept Physics 1118 E 4th St Tucson AZ 85721

FALEY, ROBERT LAWRENCE, instruments company executive; b. Bklyn., Oct. 13, 1927; s. Eric Lawrence and Anna (Makahon) F.; B.S. cum laude in Chemistry, St. Mary's U., San Antonio, 1956; postgrad. U. Del., 1958-59; m. Mary Virginia Mumme, May 12, 1950; children: Robert Wayne, Nancy Diane. Chemist, E.I. Dupont de Nemours & Co., Inc., Wilmington, Del., 1956-60; sales mgr. F&M Sci., Houston, 1960-62; pres. Faley Assos., Houston, 1962-65; sales mgr. Tech. Inc., Dayton, Ohio, 1965-70; biomed. mkt. mgr. Perkin-Elmer Co., Norwalk, Conn., 1967-69; mktg. dir. Cahn Instruments, Los Angeles, 1970-72; pres. Faley Internat., El Toro, Calif., 1972-93; pres. Status Internat., Las Vegas, Nev., 1993—. Internat. speaker in field; dir. Whatman Lab. Products Inc., 1981-82, Status Instrument Corp., 1985-87; tech. mktg. cons. Whatman Ltd., Abbott Labs., OCG Tech., Inc., Pacific Biochem., Baker Commodities, Bausch & Lomb Co., Motorola Inc., Whatman Inc., Filtration Scis. Corp., PMC Industries, UVP, Inc., Ericomp, Inc., Data I/O. Mem. adv. com. on Sci., tech., energy and water U.S. 43d Congl. Dist., 1985-87. With USMS, 1944-47, 1st lt. USAF, 1948-53. Charter mem. Aviation Hall Fame. Fellow Am. Inst. Chemists, AAAS; mem. ASTM, Am. Chem. Soc. (sr.), Instrument Soc. Am. (sr.), Inst. Environ. Scis. (sr.), Aircraft Owners and Pilots Assn., U.S. Power Squadrons, Delta Epsilon Sigma. Club: Masons. Contbr. articles on technique of gas chromatography to profl. jours. Home: 27850 Espinoza San Juan Capistrano CA 92692-2156 Office: 1800 E Sahara Ave Ste 107 Las Vegas NV 89104-3732

FALGIANO, VICTOR JOSEPH, electrical engineer, consultant; b. San Francisco, Nov. 25, 1957; s. Victor Anthony and Frances Mary Falgiano; m. Linda Maxine Owens, July 24, 1982; children: Gregory Joseph, Nicholas Rexford. BS in Elec. Engring. Tech. magna cum laude, Cogswell Coll., 1989, BS in Computer Engring. magna cum laude, 1989. Sr. design engr. Amdahl Corp., Sunnyvale, Calif., 1978-93; staff system devel. engr. Nat. Semiconductor Corp., Santa Clara, Calif., 1993—; mem. steering com. System Design and Integration Conf., Santa Clara, Calif.; mem. acad. adv. com. Cogswell Coll., Cupertino, Calif., 1991; evaluator Accrediting Bd. Engring. and Tech., 1995—. Contbr. articles to profl. publs. Advisor to high sch. students Jr. Achievement. Mem. IEEE (sr.), Assn. Computing Machinery, Internat. Soc. Hybrid Microelectronics. Office: Nat Semicondr MCM Bus Unit PO Box 58090 M/S 10-225 2900 Semiconductor Dr Santa Clara CA 95052

FALICK, ABRAHAM JOHNSON, printing company executive; b. Chgo., Oct. 11, 1920; s. Simon Falick and Ellen Martina (Johnson) Sherwood; m. Carolyn Weber, Dec. 11, 1947; 1 child, Leslie Carol Falick Koplof. BA, Ind. U., 1947; MBA, U. Chgo., 1951; MA, UCLA, 1967, PhD, 1970. Cert. pub. planner. Commd. ensign USNR, 1941, advanced through grades to lt. comdr., 1941-46, ret., 1967; mgr. sales/mktg. Webb-Linn Printing Co., Chgo., 1948-56; pres., chief exec. officer Murray and Gee, Inc., Culver City, Calif., 1956-60; planning economist City of Los Angeles, 1967-75; pres., chief exec. officer AJ Falick Assocs., Los Angeles, 1960-67, Navigator Press, Inc., Los Angeles, 1975—. Contbr. transp. research articles to profl. jours. Chmn. Coalition Rapid Transit, Los Angeles, 1978—, Friends of Geography UCLA, 1989—; v.p. Westwood Dem. Club, 1988—; chair L.A. Bus./Profl. Dem. Club, 1992—. Mem. Am. Econ. Assn., Am. Planning Assn., Am. Inst. Cert. Planners (counselor 1972-74). Democrat. Jewish. Office: Navigator Press Inc 516 N Fair Oaks Ave Pasadena CA 91103-3304

FALK, CANDACE SERENA, historian, biographer, documentary editor; b. N.Y.C., July 30, 1947; m. Lowell Stewart Finley, Oct. 23, 1977; two children. BA, U. Chgo., 1969, MA, 1971; PhD, U. Calif., Santa Cruz, 1984. Author: (biography) Love, Anarchy and Emma Goldman, 1984; editor: (documentary, microfilm edit.) The Emma Goldman Papers, 1991, (source book) Emma Goldman: A Guide to Her Life and Documentary Sources, 1995. Woodrow Wilson Women's Studies grantee, 1979; grantee Nat. Hist. Publ. Records Commn., 1980-94, Nat. Endowment for Humanities, Ford Found., The Rockefeller Found., others. Mem. Am. Coun. of Learned Socs., Orgn. of Am. Historians (com. on archives and historians), Am. Hist. Assn. (Joan Kelly prize in feminist history 1991), Assn. Documentary Editors. Democrat. Jewish. Office: Emma Goldman Papers Univ Calif/Berkeley 2372 Ellsworth St Berkeley CA 94704-1550

FALKENBERG, WILLIAM STEVENS, architect, contractor; b. Kansas City, Mo., July 21, 1927; s. John Joseph and Maraba Elizabeth (Stevens) F.; m. Janis Patton Hubner, Apr. 13, 1951; children: Ruth Elizabeth, Christopher Joseph, Charles Stevens. BS in Archtl. Engring., U. Colo., 1949. Pres. Falkenberg Constrn. Co., Denver, 1951-71, 74-84, devel. cons., 1984—; broker Hogan & Stevenson Realty, Denver, 1971-74. Chmn. constrn. Archdiocesan Housing Com., Inc.; chmn. restoration 9th Street Hist. Park; chmn. bldg. comm. Four Mile House Hist. Park; chmn. Housing Trust Coun., Denver, 1986-90; chmn. Rocky Mountain Better Bus. Bur., 1965-67; pres. Denver Friends Folk Music, 1966. Lt. (j.g.) USNR, 1945-51. Mem. AIA (bd. dirs. Denver chpt. 1978-81, treas. 1981), Home Builder Assn. Met. Denver, Colo. Hist. Soc. Found. (trustee, sec. 1987—), Serra Internat. (pres. 1971, dist. gov. 1973), Nat. Assn. Atomic Vets., Colo. Archeol. Soc., Denver Athletic Club, Equestrian Order of Holy Sepulchre, Cactus Club (pres. 1995—). Home and Office: 430 Marion St Denver CO 80218-3930

FALKNER, JAMES GEORGE, foundation executive; b. Spokane, Wash., Dec. 24, 1952; s. Albert Andrew and Amanda Rosalia (Reisinger) F.; m. Joleen Rae Ann Brown, June 22, 1974; children: James Jr., Jayson, Jerin, Jarret. BS in Acctg., U. Wash., 1975. CPA, Wash. CPA LeMaster & Daniels, Spokane, 1975-80; treas. Dominican Sisters Spokane, 1980-95; pres. Dominican Outreach Found., Spokane, 1995—; bd. dirs. Dominican Network, Spokane, Dominican Health Svcs., Providence Svcs., Spokane; mem. Bishop's Fin. Coun. Spokane Diocese, 1990—. Bd. dirs. sch. bd. St. Mary's Ch., Veradale, Wash., 1986-89, 90—, sch. found., 1987—; active acctg. adv. com. Spokane Falls Community Coll., 1989—. Mem. Healthcare Fin. Mgmt. Assn. (bd. dirs. 1982-85), AICPA, Wash. State Soc. CPAs, Conf. Religious Treas., Nat. Assn. Treas. Religious Insts., Nat. Notary Assn. Office: Dominican Outreach Found 3102 W Fort George Wright Dr Spokane WA 99204-5203

FALKOW, STANLEY, microbiologist, educator; b. Albany, N.Y., Jan. 24, 1934; s. Jacob and Mollie (Gingold) F.; children from previous marriage: Lynn Beth, Jill Stuart; m. Lucy Stuart Tompkins, Dec. 3, 1983. BS in Bacteriology cum laude, U. Maine, 1955, DSc (hon), 1979; MS in Biology, Brown U., 1960, PhD, 1961; MD (hon.), U. Umea, Sweden, 1989. Asst. chief dept. bacterial immunity Walter Reed Army Inst. Rsch., Washington, 1963-66; prof. microbiology Med. Sch. Georgetown U., 1966-72; prof. microbiology and medicine U. Wash., Seattle, 1972-81; prof., chmn. dept. med. microbiology Stanford (Calif.) U., 1981-85; prof. microbiology, immunology & medicine, 1981—; Karl H. Beyer vis. prof. U. Wis., 1978-79; Sommer lectr. U. Oreg. Sch. Medicine, 1979, Kinyoun lectr. NIH, 1980; Rubbro orator Australian Soc. Microbiology, 1981; Stanhope Bayne-Jones lectr. Johns Hopkins U., 1982; mem. Recombinant DNA Molecule Com, task force on antibiotics in animal feeds FDA, microbiology test com. Nat. Bd. Med. Examiners. Author: Infectious Multiple Drug Resistance, 1975; editor: Jour. Infection and Immunity, Jour. Infectious Agents and Diseases. Recipient Ehrlich prize, 1981, Becton-Dickinson award in Clin. Microbiology, ASM, 1986, Altemeier medal Surg. Infectious Diseases Soc., 1990; Bristol-Myers Squibb unrestricted infectious disease grantee. Fellow Am. Acad. Microbiology; mem. AAAS, Infectious Disease Soc. Am. (Squibb award 1979), Am. Soc. Microbiology, Genetics Soc. Am., Nat. Acad. Sci., Sigma Xi. Home: 8 Long Spur St Portola Vally CA 94028-8038 Office: Stanford U Dept Med Microbiology Stanford CA 94305

FALL, TIMOTHY LEE, lawyer; b. San Francisco, Jan. 27, 1960; s. Robert J. and Dorothy Phyllis (Faubion) F.; m. Elizabeth Hom, Sept. 6, 1987; children: Kyle Matthew, Jenna Lee. AA, Skyline Coll., San Bruno, Calif., 1981; postgrad., Sussex U., Falmer, Eng., 1983-84; BA, U. Calif., Santa Barbara, 1984; JD, U. Calif., Davis, 1987. Bar: Calif. 1987, U.S. Dist. Ct. (ea. dist.) Calif. 1987, U.S. Dist. Ct. (no. and cen. dist.) Calif. 1987, U.S. Ct. Appeals (9th cir.) 1987. Research asst. U. Calif. Sch. Law, Davis, 1985; jud. extern to Chief Judge U.S. Dist. Ct. (ea. dist.), Sacramento, Calif., 1986; ptnr. Bolling, Walter & Gawthrop, Sacramento, 1987—. Youth min. 1st Bapt. Ch., Davis, 1986-88, elder 1989-92, worship leader, 1992—; min. Young Life, Davis, 1987-88. Mem. ABA, Sacramento County Bar Assn., Yolo County Bar Assn. Home: 4115 Vista Way Davis CA 95616-4938 Office: Bolling Walter & Gawthrop 8880 Cal Center Dr Ste 400 Sacramento CA 95826-3266

FALLIN, WILLIAM L., computer manufacturing company official; b. Norfolk, Va., Aug. 17, 1940; s. John Hugh and Virginia Ethel (Slade) F.; m. Joyce Elaine Clark, July 31, 1947; children: Alyssa, Erica B., Ian Slade. Student, Old Dominion U., 1959-61. Support specialist Unisys Corp., McLean, Va., 1972-83; support specialist Tandem Computers Inc., Reston, Va., 1983-86, mgr. comm. sect., 1986-88; mgr. sys. support for Cupertino Tandem Computers Inc., Cupertino, Calif., 1988-93, mgr. sys. support Ams., 1993—. Mem. Software Support Profls. Assn., Nat. Space Soc., Nat. Geog. Soc., Guitar Fedn. Ams. Home: 111 Brian Ln Santa Clara CA 95051-6703 Office: Tandem Computers Inc 10400 Ridgeview Ct Cupertino CA 95014-0704

FALTIN, BRUCE CHARLES, hotel executive; b. Cin., Mar. 7, 1947; s. Charles F. and Meryl (Gunther) F.; m. H. Ann Walker: children: Sharon, Laura, John. BS, Cornell U., 1969. Mgr. Winegardner & Hammons Inc., Cin., 1969-78; ptnr. Idahotels Ltd., Boise, Idaho, 1978—; pres. Mountain States Mgmt. Inc., Boise, 1978—, also bd. dirs; trustee Rodeway Inns Advt. Fund, Phoenix, 1985-94; chmn. Rodeway Inns Owner's Coun., Phoenix, 1986-88. Co-founder, dir., pres. Idaho Hospitality Edn. Found., 1990-91. Mem. Am. Hotel and Motel Assn. (state dir. 1983-84), Nat. Restaurant Assn., Idaho Innkeepers Assn. (bd. dirs. 1974-86, 88-94, pres. 1979, treas. 1988-91), Greater Boise C. of C. (bd. dirs. 1987), Choice Hotels Brands Adv. Coun., Idaho Hospitality Edn. Found. (pres. 1990-91), Idaho Hospitality and Travel Assn. (pres. 1994-95). Home: 2423 Hillway Dr Boise ID 83702-0933 Office: Rodeway Inn of Boise 1115 N Curtis Rd Boise ID 83706-1233

FALUDI, SUSAN C., journalist, scholarly writer. Formerly with West Mag., San Jose, Calif., Mercury News; with San Francisco Bur., Wall St. Jour.; spkr. in field. Author: Backlash: The Undeclared War Against American Women, 1991 (National Book Critics Circle award for general nonfiction 1992); contbr. articles to mags. Recipient Pulitzer Prize for explanatory journalism, 1991. Office: care Sandra Dijkstra Sandra Dijkstra Literary Agency 1155 Camino Del Mar Ste 515 Del Mar CA 92014-2605

FANCHER, MICHAEL REILLY, newspaper editor, newspaper publishing executive; b. Long Beach, Calif., July 13, 1946; s. Eugene Arthur and Ruth Leone (Dickson) F.; m. Nancy Helen Edens, Nov. 3, 1967 (div. 1982); children: Jason Michael, Patrick Reilly; m. 2d Carolyn Elaine Bowers, Mar. 25, 1983; Katherine Claire, Elizabeth Lynn. BA, U. Oreg., 1968; MS, Kans. State U., 1971; MBA, U. Wash., 1986. Reporter, asst. city editor Kansas City Star, Mo., 1970-76, city editor, 1976-78; reporter Seattle Times, 1978-79, night city editor, 1979-80, asst. mng. editor, 1980-81, mng. editor, 1981-86, exec. editor, 1986—, now vice pres., exec. editor, 1989-95; sr. v.p., 1995—; bd. dirs. Walla Walla Union-Bulletin, Yakima Herald Rep. Ruhl fellow U. Oreg., 1983. Mem. Am. Soc. Newspaper Editors. 1985-91), Soc. Profl. Journalists, Nat. Press Photographers Assn. (Editor of Yr. 1986). Office: Seattle Times Fairview Ave N & John St PO Box 70 Seattle WA 98111-0070

FANG, CHUNCHANG, physical chemist, chemical engineer; b. Taiwan, Republic of China, July 9, 1955; came to U.S., 1980; s. Chuan Jyue and Chuen Huei (Lin) F.; m. Inghwa Suen, Jan. 24, 1986; children: Phyllis, Miranda, Stella. BS in Chemistry, Tung Hai U., Taichung, Taiwan, 1978; MS in Petroleum Engring., U. Houston, 1982; MS in Chem. Engring., Ohio State U., 1985, PhD in Phys. Chemistry, 1989. Rsch. asst. environ. engring. program U. Houston, 1982-83; rsch. assoc. dept. chem. engring. Ohio State U., Columbus, 1984-85, rsch. assoc. dept. chemistry, 1986-89; process rsch. chemist QO Chems., Inc., Belle Glade, Fla., 1989-91; process devel. engr. QO Chems., Inc., Belle Glade, also Memphis, 1991-94; engring. cons. for furfural and thermoplastic polyurethane elastomer industries. 2d lt. Taiwan Army, 1978-80. Mem. Am. Chem. Soc., Am. Inst. Chem. Engrs. Home: 1796 Country Oaks Ln Thousand Oaks CA 91362-1900 Office: Chem Rite Cons Group 1796 Country Oaks Ln Thousand Oaks CA 91362

FANGEROW, KAY ELIZABETH, nurse; b. Thomas, Okla., June 27, 1952; d. Byron Frederick and Wilma Jean (Bickford) Mayfield; children: David Andrew, Sarah Elizabeth; m. Stephen Fangerow. Student Oral Roberts U., 1970-71; BS in Nursing magna cum laude, Calif. State U.-Long Beach, 1975; MS in Health Care Adminstrn., U. LaVerne, 1991. RN, Calif.; cert. pub. health nurse. Staff nurse pediatrics service Long Beach Meml. Hosp., 1974-75, Riverside (Calif.) Community Hosp., 1975-76, Parkview Community Hosp., Riverside, 1982-84; supervising pub. health nurse County Health Dept., San Bernardino, Calif., 1976—; cons. Am. Home Health, Santa Ana, Calif., 1986—. Instr. Inland Counties chpt. Am. Cancer Soc., Riverside, 1977—, also mem. pub. and profl. edn. coms. Mem. Am. Pub. Health Assn. (co-author abstract 1986, 87, 89, coordinator hypertension worksite project, diabetes control project, pub. health nursing homeless project, presenter ann. meeting 1986, 87, 89), Pub. Health Nurse Group (chmn. 1977-78, vice chmn. profl. preformance com. 1978, sec. peer rev. com. 1978), So. Calif. Pub. Health Assn., Pub. Health Advs., Vis. Nurse Assn. Pomona (West End utilization rev. com.). Democrat. Home: PO Box 3308 Running Springs CA 92382-3308

FANGOR, VOY, painter; b. Warsaw, Poland, Nov. 15, 1922; came to U.S., 1966; s. Konrad and Wanda Fangor; m. Magdalena Shummer. MFA, Acad. of Fine Arts, Warsaw, 1946. Asst. prof. Warsaw Acad. Art, 1953-61; tchr. Fairleigh Dickinson U., Madison, N.J., 1966-83; participant internat. artist seminar Fairleigh Dickinson U., Madison, 1965; vis. lectr. Bath Acad. Art Corsham, Wiltshire, Eng., 1965-66; vis. critic arch. Grad. Sch. Design, Harvard U., Cambridge, Mass., 1967-68; set designer Martha Graham Dance Co., 1970. One-man shows include Inst. Contemporary Art, Washington, 1962, Galerie Lambert, Paris, 1963, Galerie Falazik, Bochum, Germany, 1964, Dom Galerie, Cologne, Germany, 1966, Galerie Chalette, N.Y.C., 1967, 69, 70, Solomon R. Guggenheim Mus., N.Y.C., 1970, Univ. Art Mus., Berkeley, Calif., 1971, Fort Worth Art Mus., Tex., 1971, Hokin Gallery, Chgo., 1974, Walter Kelly Gallery, Chgo., 1978, Bodley Gallery, N.Y.C., 1983, Zacheta Gallery, Warsaw, 1990, Mitchell Algus Gallery, N.Y.C., 1993; group shows include Stedlijk Mus., Amsterdam, 1959, Mus. Modern Art, N.Y.C., 1961, 65, Guggenheim Mus., N.Y.C., 1964, 67, 80, Riverside Mus., N.Y.C., 1965, Carnegie Inst., Pitts., 1967, 70, Newark Mus., 1969, Cin. Art Mus., 1969, Thorp Gallery, N.Y.C., 1980, Harm Bouckaert Gallery, N.Y.C., 1984, Gallery 53, Cooperstown, N.Y., 1988; represented in permanent collections Guggenheim Mus., N.Y.C., Mus. Modern Art, N.Y.C., San Antonio Mus. Art, Phillips Collection, Washington, Newark Mus., State Mus., Trenton, N.J., Aldrich Mus. Contemporary Art, Ridgefield, Conn., Rose Art Mus., Waltham, Mass., Carnegie Mus. Art, Pitts., Hirshhorn Mus., Smithsonian Inst., Washington, Power Gallery Art, Sidney, Australia, Muzeum Sztuki, Lodz, Poland, Muzuem Narodowe, Poznan and Warsaw, Poland, Stedelijk Mus., Amsterdam, Schloss Morsbroich Mus., Leverkusen, Germany, Mus. des XX Jahrhunderts, Berlin, Aachen (Germany) Mus. Art, Mus. Art, Munich, Milw. Mus. Art, Harlem Mus., N.Y.C. Recipient Alfred Jurzykowski Found. award, 1978; fellow Inst. Contemporary Art, 1962; Ford Found. grantee, 1964-65. Home: 2006 Conejo Dr Santa Fe NM 87505-6109

FANN, JAMES ILIN, cardiothoracic surgeon; b. Taipei, Taiwan, May 4, 1961; came to U.S., 1968; s. Charles C.P. and Nancy C.L. (Lee) F.; m. Andrea Hutchinson. BS, Northwestern U., 1983, MD with distinction, 1985. Diplomate Am. Bd. Surgery. Resident Stanford (Calif.) U. Med. Ctr., 1985-92; rsch. fellow Stanford U., 1987-89; vascular surgery fellow Stanford U. Med. Ctr., 1992-93, cardiothoracic surgery fellow, 1993—; rsch. asst. Northwestern U., Chgo., 1982-84. Contbr. articles to profl. jours. Nat. Merit scholar, 1979; Carl and Leah McConnell Cardiovascular Rsch. fellow, 1987-89. Mem. AMA, Am. Heart Assn., Am. Coll. Cardiology, Calif. Med. Assn., Alpha Omega Alpha. Roman Catholic. Home: 1098 S Springer Rd Los Altos CA 94024-4930 Office: Stanford U Med Ctr 300 Pasteur Dr Palo Alto CA 94304-2203

FANN, MARGARET ANN, counselor; b. Pasco, Wash., July 16, 1942; d. Joseph Albert David and Clarice Mable (Deaver) Rivard; m. Jerry Lee Fann, June 13, 1986; children: Brenda Heupel, Scott Sherman, Kristin Johnson, Robert Lack III. AA, Big Bend C.C., Moses Lake, Wash., 1976; BA in Applied Psychology magna cum laude, Ea. Wash. U., 1977, MS in Psychology, 1978. Cert. mental health counselor, Wash. Cert. chem. dependency counselor II, nat. cert. addictions counselor II. Intern counselor Linker House Drug Rehab., Spokane, Wash., 1976-78; drug counselor The House drug program, Tacoma, Wash., 1978-80; exec. dir. Walla Walla (Wash.) Commn. Alcohol, 1980-82; dir. Cmty. Alcohol Svcs. Assn., Kennewick, Wash., 1982-86; primary care coord. Carondelet Psychiat. Care Ctr., Richland, Wash., 1986-90; part-time instr. Ea. Wash. U., Cheney, 1981-88; instr. Columbia Basin Coll., Pasco, 1990-93; adminstr. Action Chem. Dependency Ctr., Kennewick, 1993—; bd. dirs. Benton-Franklin County Substance Abuse Coalition, Pasco, Kennewick, Richland, 1990—. Vol. Pat Hale for Senator, Kennewick, 1994. Mem. Am. Counselors Assn., Nat. Mental Health Counselors Assn., Wash. State Mental Health Counselors Assn., Tri-Cities Counselors Assn., Phi Theta Kappa. Office: Action Chem Dependency Ctr 552 N Colorado Ste 5525 Kennewick WA 99336

FANNING, DON BRIAN, poet, computer services consultant; b. Burbank, Calif., Feb. 10, 1957; s. Donald Floyd and Lorraine Gwendolyn (Smith) F. BS in Physics cum laude, UCLA, 1979. With Hughes Aircraft Co., El Segundo, Calif., 1981-84; programmer UCLA, Westwood, 1985-86; computer svcs. cons. L.A., 1986-94; founder, facilitator Iguana Poets' Circle, North Hollywood, Calif., 1989-92, Barnsdall Arts Park Poets' Circle, Hollywood, Calif., 1992—; dir. poet "lariat" Iguanaland Poetry Reading, North Hollywood, 1989-92. Author/co-author: Spaghetti and Rice, 1990, Woodlands and Waterways, 1994; editor: Tail of the Iguana, 1991, Of the People, 1994—. Outreach person Out Loud Poets Calendar, L.A., 1990-92, Poetry Flash, L.A., 1992-94; non-violent protestor Nev. Nuclear Weapons Test Site, Las Vegas, 1990-92, Desert Storm/Gulf War, L.A., 1991. Mem. Algonquin Tribe, Sigma Pi Sigma. Office: Valley Poets Co-op PO Box 7667 Van Nuys CA 91409-7667

FARACH FARACH, JOSE EDUARDO, energy executive; b. Tegucigalpa, Francisco Morazan, Honduras, Apr. 25, 1963; came to U.S., 1981; s. Issa and Jeanette Miriam (Farach) Farach. BSEE, U. Tex. Austin, 1985, MSE, 1987, PhD, 1993. Programming asst. Empresa Nacional de Energia Electrica, Tegucigalpa, Honduras, 1985; ops. and svc. chief engr. Empresa Nacional de Energia Electrica, Tegucigalpa, 1988; grad. rsch. asst. Ctr. for Energy Studies, Austin, Tex., 1985-87, 89-92; power sys. analyst Landis and Gyr Energy Mgmt. Inc., San Jose, Calif., 1993—; cons. Inesscon, Inc., Concord, Calif., 1993—. Contbr. articles to profl. jours. Mem. IEEE, Eta Kappa Nu, Tau Beta Pi, Phi Eta Sigma. Roman Catholic. Home: 330 Elan Village Ln Unit 225 San Jose CA 95134-2553 Office: Landis & Gyr Energy Mgmt 1730 Technology Dr San Jose CA 95110-1303

FARAH, JOSEPH FRANCIS, newspaper editor, writer; b. Paterson, N.J., July 6, 1954; s. John Joseph and Loretta Gertrude (Comeau) F.; m. Judith Gale Smagula, Apr. 16, 1983; children: Alana Jihan, Alyssa Alexandra. BA, William Paterson Coll., 1977. Reporter Paterson News, 1978, news editor, 1978; asst. news editor Herald Examiner, Los Angeles, 1979-80, news editor, 1980-82, exec. news editor, 1982-87; exec. editor The Leader Newspapers, Glendale, Calif., 1987-88, columnist, 1989-90; editor Sacramento Union, 1990-91, New Dimensions Mag., 1992, Capitol Pub. Co., 1993—; prin. Farah & Assocs., Fair Oaks, Calif., 1993—; instr. UCLA, 1982.

FARAH, TAWFIC ELIAS, political scientist; b. Nazareth, Palestine, Aug. 12, 1946; s. Elias Tawfic and Itaf Fahim F.; BA, Calif. State U., Fresno, 1970, MA, 1971; PhD, U. Nebr., 1975; m. Linda Maxwell, Apr. 24, 1969; children—Omar Lee, Aliya Jane. Market researcher Xerox Corp., Lincoln, Nebr., 1974-75; asst. prof. polit. sci. Kuwait U., 1975-79; pres. Merg Analityca, 1979—; vis. assoc. prof. UCLA, summers 1978-83, fellow Center for Internat. and Strategic Affairs, 1980-81, Ctr. for Near Eastern Studies, 1986; Fulbright scholar, 1983. Toyota Found. grantee, 1985. Mem. Am. Polit. Sci. Assn., Middle East Studies Assn. Greek Orthodox. Author: Reinventing Palestinian Politics: A New Order in the Middle East, 1995; co-author: Research Methods in the Social Sciences, 1977; A Dictionary of Social Analysis, 1980; author: Aspects of Modernization and Consociationalism: Lebanon as an Exploratory Test Case, 1975, 77; co-editor: Palestinians Without Palestine: Socialization of Palestinian Children, 1979; Learning to Become Palestinians, 1985; editor Political Behavior in the Arab States, 1983; Pan Arabism and Arab Nationalism: The Continuing Debate, 1986, Political Socialization in the Arab States, 1987, Survey Research in the Arab World, 1987; editor Jour. Arab Affairs, 1981—.

FARANDA, JOHN PAUL, college administrator; b. Orange, Calif., Feb. 21, 1957; s. Paul L. and Kay S. (Wilson) F. BA cum laude, Claremont McKenna Coll., 1979. Staff liaison L.A. County Bar Assn., 1979-80; spl. programs adminstr. L.A. County Med. Assn., 1980-85; dir. corp. rels. Claremont (Calif.) McKenna Coll., 1985-87, dir. campaign and devel. svcs., 1987-89, dir. devel., 1989—. Contbr. articles to profl. jours. Campaign chmn. United Way, Mt. Baldy Region, Ontario, Calif., 1987-90; bd. govs. Faculty Ho. of the Claremont Colls., pres., 1993—. Recipient Gold award Mt. Baldy United Way, 1988, 91. Mem. L.A. County Bar Assn. (com. on arbitration), Coun. for Advancement and Support of Edn. (USX award 1986), Athletic Club L.A. Office: Claremont McKenna Coll Bauer Ctr #320 500 E 9th St Claremont CA 91711-5903

FARBER, BERNARD, sociologist, educator; b. Chgo., Feb. 11, 1922; s. Benjamin and Esther (Axelrod) F.; m. Annette Ruth Shugan, Dec. 21, 1947 (div. 1970); children—Daniel, Michael, Lisa, Jacqueline; m. Rosanna Bodanis, June 10, 1971 (dec. June 1988); 1 dau., Tanya. A.B., Roosevelt U., Chgo., 1943; A.M., U. Chgo., 1949, Ph.D., 1953. Research asso. U. Chgo., 1951-53; asst. prof. Henderson State Tchr. Coll., Arkadelphia, Ark., 1953-54; mem. faculty U. I., 1954-71, prof. sociology, 1964-71; asso. dir. Inst. Research Exceptional Children, 1967-69; prof. Ariz. State U., 1971-92, prof. emeritus, 1992—, chmn. dept. sociology, 1971-75, 90-92; vis. prof. U. Tex., Austin, 1974-75, U. Ill., Chgo., 1988—; cons. in field, 1957—. Author: Family: Organization and Interaction, 1964, Mental Retardation: Its Social Context and Social Consequences, 1968, Kinship and Class, 1971, Guardians of Virtue, 1972, Family and Kinship in Modern Society, 1973, Conceptions of Kinship, 1981; editor Sociol. Perspectives, 1985-89. Mem. mental retardation research com. Nat. Inst. Child Health and Human Devel., 1971-75. Served with AUS, 1943-46. Recipient E.W. Burgess award Nat. Council on Family Relations, 1975; Disting. Research award Ariz. State U., 1980. Mem. Am. Sociol. Assn. (coun. mem. family sect. 1966-69), Ill. Sociol. Assn. (founding pres. 1965-66), Pacific Sociol. Assn. (pres. 1986-87). Jewish. Home: 7949 E Montebello Ave Scottsdale AZ 85250-6108 Office: Ariz State U Dept Sociology Tempe AZ 85287

FARHAT, CAROL S., motion picture company executive; b. Santa Monica, Calif.; d. Annis Abraham and Jacklin (Thomas) F.; divorced; 1 child, Michael. AA, Santa Monica Coll., 1967; student, Inst. Audio Rsch., 1976-78, Otis Parsons Inst., 1980-84, UCLA, 1984-90; BA in Bus., Music, Antioch U., 1992. Recording studio mgr. The Village Recorder, L.A., 1972-78; audio engr. The Village Recorder Studio, L.A., 1978-79; music adminstr. 20th Century Fox Film Corp., Beverly Hills, Calif., 1980-82, music supr., 1983-86, music dir., 1986-92; supr. internat. music 20th Century Fox Film Corp., Tokyo, 1993; music prodr. Scopus Films, England, 1987-89; songwriter Music Experts Ltd., Santa Monica, Calif., 1989-90; v.p. music 20th Century Fox Film Corp., 1994—. Author: China Diary, 1992; composer (music book) Children's Songbook, 1991; songwriter (for film) Rockin' Reindeer, 1990. Mem. BMI, NATAs, NARAS, Women in Film, Am. Film Inst., Pacific Composers Forum, Entertainment Industry Counsel. Office: 20th Century Fox Film Corp PO Box 900 Beverly Hills CA 90213-0900

FARIAS, JAMES ARTHUR, resource development planner, writer; b. Raynham, Mass., May 23, 1943; s. Arthur James and Evelyn May (Lima) F. Student, U. Ariz., 1961-63; BA, L.I. U., 1980. Resource devel. planner III PPEP & Affiliates, Tucson, 1985-94; cons. Assn. Ariz. Food Banks, Phoenix, 1990, Ariz. Rural Human Svcs. Network, Tucson, 1990-94, People with AIDS Coalition, Tucson, 1992-94, City of Eloy, Ariz., 1994. Playwright: The Messiah of Mickle Street, 1982; producer: Arizona Gay, 1984-85. Facilitator, bus., devel. forum HandsNet, San Jose, 1993-94; bd. mem. Bank One Citizens Adv. Commn., Tucson, 1994. Mem. Nat. Cmty. Reinvestment Corp., Alliance for Pub. Tech., Dramatists Guild, Poets and Writers. Democrat. Home: 2937 W Pepper Dr Tucson AZ 85741-3639 Office: PPEP & Affiliates 802 E 46th St Tucson AZ 85713-5006

FARIDANY, NANCY LOFTON, cultural organization executive; b. Winston-Salem, N.C., Sept. 4, 1941; s. Richard Morrison Lofton and Nancy Elizabeth Schallert Morrow Burkett; m. Edward Kay Mars Faridany, June 12, 1964 (div. July 1, 1985); children: Francesca, Lucy. BA in English, U. Calif., Berkeley, 1963; MEd in English/Edn., State Coll. of Boston, 1965; Licentiate, London Coll. Music, 1978. Adminstr. Carmel (Calif.) Bach Festival, 1984-91, exec. dir., 1992—. Office: Carmel Bach Festival PO Box 575 Rm 11 San Carlos and 9th Carmel CA 93921

FARIS, CHARLES OREN, civil engineer; b. Plymouth, Idaho, Sept. 8, 1924; s. Brady V. and Ellen (Alta) F.; m. Dorothy Phillips, Dec. 21, 1979; children from a previous marriage: Ellen Eileen, Nancy Claire. BS in Civil Engring., Oregon State U., 1949. Registered profl. engr., Idaho, Oreg., Wash., Calif., Ariz., Colo., Kans., S.C., Va., Mont., Mo., Ark. Engr. Consolidated Builders Inc., Mill City, Oreg., 1949-52; asst. supr. plant design State of Punjab, Nangal, India, 1952-54; office engr. dam divnsn. Morrison-Knudsen Inc., Ione, Wash., 1954-55; chief plant engr. Morrison-Knudsen Inc., Strawberry, Calif., 1955; plant engr. divsn. constrn. Morrison-Knudsen Inc., Boise, Idaho, 1955-57, plant mgr. divsn. constrn., 1957-64; plant mgr. we. divsn. constrn. Dravo Corp., Bellevue, Wash., 1964-66, asst. mgr. we constr. divsn., 1966-67, dist. mgr. Seattle, 1967-71; ptnr. Hamlin-Faris Co., Bellevue, 1971-73; pres. Hamlin-Faris Internat. Inc., Bellevue, 1973-91, Faris Assocs. Inc., Bellevue, 1973—; cons. in field to Am. and fgn. contractors and govtl. orgns. With U.S. Army, 1943-46, PTO. Fellow ASCE; mem. NSPE, Am. Concrete Inst., U.S. Com. Large Dams, Wash. Athletic Club. Republican. Mem. First Ch. Christ. Home: 9949 Lake Washington Blvd NE Bellevue WA 98004-6068 Office: Faris Assocs 1750 112th Ave NE Ste C-234 Bellevue WA 98004-3727

FARIS-STOCKEM, DEBBIE ANNE, architectural sheet metal executive; b. Portland, Oreg., Jan. 6, 1955; d. Ernest Duane and Elizabeth Anne (McCullough) Faris; m. Robert A. Stockem, Oct. 18, 1975 (div.); children: Melissa Gene, Cassandra Lynn. Office mgr. Faris Sheet Metal, Inc., Portland, 1975-84, v.p., 1984-88, pres., 1988—. Mem. Nat. Assn. Women in Constrn. (bd. dirs. Portland chpt. 1987—, pres. 1990-91). Republican. Office: Faris Sheet Metal Inc 102 SE 99th Ave Portland OR 97216-2304

FARKAS, ABRAHAM KRAKAUER, urban developer, educator; b. Dunkirk, N.Y., Oct. 31, 1947; s. Louis Ari and Hedy (Krakauer) F.; m. Pamela Ann Price, June 15, 1970; children: Madeleine, Uri, Jacob. BA in Polit. Sci., Purdue U., 1969, MA in Am. Studies, 1971; PhD in Am. Studies, U. Minn., 1976. Asst. prof. housing and pub. policy U. Tenn., Knoxville, 1976-80; dir. community devel. and planning City of Ft. Wayne, Ind., 1980-83; mgr. econ. devel. City of Seattle, 1983-85; exec. dir. planning and devel. City of Eugene, Oreg., 1985—; mem. bd. advisors for housing and mktg. Oreg. State U., Corvallis, 1990-94. Editor Housing and Society, 1980; contbr. articles to profl. jours. Bd. dirs. Temple Beth Israel, Eugene, 1990-91, Networking for Youth, Inc., 1993—, Eugene YMCA, 1993—. Lilly fellow, 1979; Tenn. Endowment for Humanities grantee, 1978. Mem. Urban Land Inst., Nat. Community Devel. Assn. (bd. dirs. 1982), Coun. for Urban Econ. Devel. (treas. N.W. chpt. 1986-87). Jewish. Office: City of Eugene 99 W 10th Ave Eugene OR 97401

FARLAND, EUGENE HECTOR, retired educational consultant; b. Woonsocket, R.I., Aug. 20, 1918; s. Joseph and Alma (Cayer) F.; m. Felice Ursala Paquin, Dec. 20, 1944 (div. 1967); children: Julien H., Linda F. Student, U. Calif., 1976-78. Cert. edn.-aeronautics. Mcpl. field engr. Woonsocket, 1939-40; ind. ins. broker R.I., Mass., 1946-55; ins. claims br. mgr. Portland, Maine, 1955-57; bush pilot Nome, Alaska, 1961-66; flight instr. Alaska, 1964-66; instr. flight and aircraft mechanics Community Coll., San Francisco, 1966-79; cons. edn. sch. system San Francisco, 1979-84; geol. studies and field trips with local coll. Arbiter Better Bus. Bur., Phoenix, 1987-90; chair UN Children Crusade Drive, Woonsocket, 1948; asst. chair Red Cross Drive, Woonsocket, 1948; pres. Kiwanis Club, Woonsocket, 1948; counselor YMCA, Woonsocket, 1951. 1st lt. USAAF, 1941-46, ETO. Recipient Presdl. citation USAAF, 1945; decorated Air medal with 1 star. Mem. Explorers Club, OXS Aviation Pioneers. Office: PO Box 6519 Yuma AZ 85366-6519

FARLEY, BARBARA SUZANNE, lawyer; b. Salt Lake City, Dec. 13, 1949; d. Ross Edward Farley and Barbara Ann (Edwards) Farley Swanson; m. Arthur Hoffman Ferris, Apr. 9, 1982 (div. 1995); children: Barbara Whitney, Taylor Edwards. BA with honors, Mills Coll., 1972; JD, U. Calif.-San Francisco, 1976. Bar: Calif. 1976. Extern law clk. to justice Calif. Supreme Ct., San Francisco, 1975; assoc. Pillsbury, Madison & Sutro, San Francisco, 1976-78, Bronson, Bronson & McKinnon, San Francisco, 1978-80, Goldstein & Phillips, San Francisco, 1980-84; ptnr., head litigation, Rosen, Wachtell & Gilbert, San Francisco, 1984-89; of counsel Lempres & Wulfsberg, Oakland, Calif., 1989—; arbitrator U.S. Dist. Ct. (no. dist.) Calif., San Francisco, 1981—, Calif. Superior Ct., San Francisco, 1984-89; judge pro tem San Francisco Mcpl. Ct., 1983—; probation monitor Calif. State Bar, 1990—; speaker Nat. Bus. Inst. Estate Adminstrn. Contbg. author Calif. Continuing Edn. of the Bar; mng. editor U. Calif.-San Francisco Constl. Law Quarterly, 1975-76; civil litigation reporter. Mills Coll. scholar, 1970-72, U. Calif.-San Francisco scholar, 1973-76. Mem. ATLA, San Francisco Bar Assn., Calif. Trial Lawyers Assn., San Francisco Trial Lawyers Assn., Alameda Bar Assn. Office: Lempres & Wulfsberg 300 Lakeside Dr Ste 2400 Oakland CA 94612-3539

FARLEY, BILL THOMAS, entertainment industry executive; b. Yonkers, N.Y., July 11, 1944; s. William Thomas and Flora May (Rae) F. BA, Cornell U., 1966. Reporter White Plains (N.Y.) Reporter Dispatch, 1966-67; news dir. WVOX-AM/FM, New Rochelle, N.Y., 1967-69; writer/publicist Am. Broadcasting Cos., N.Y.C. and L.A., 1969-79; creative dir. BGPR Agy., L.A., 1979-83; info. mgr. 1984 Summer Olympic Games, L.A., 1984; pub. rels. mgr. Playboy Enterprises, Inc., L.A., 1985-87, dir. comm., 1987-89, nat. dir. comm., 1989—; pres. WordSmith Comm., Hollywood, Calif., 1985—. Author/editor: Apollo II: Man's Greatest Adventure, 1969; author: My Other Car Is A Porsche, 1994; author mag. Unofficial Guide to the 1984 Lia Games, 1984. Libertarian. Office: Playboy Enterprises Inc 9242 Beverly Blvd Beverly Hills CA 90210-3710

FARLEY, FRANK FREDERIC, retired oil industry executive; b. Perrysburg, Ohio, Oct. 9, 1912; s. Frank Eugene and Mary Teresa (Shiple) Farley; m. Maureen Alice O'Neil, Aug. 28, 1941 (dec. 1988); children: Jeanne Alice, George Francis, Anne Maureen. AB, St. John U., Toledo, Ohio, 1934; MS, U. Detroit, 1936; PhD, Iowa State U., 1941. Chemistry instr. U. Detroit, 1941-42; sr. rsch. chemist Shell Oil Co., Wood River, Ill., 1942-43, rsch. supr., 1943-46, chief rsch. chemist, 1946-53; chief rsch. chemist Shell Oil Co., Martinez, Calif., 1953-61, rsch. dir., 1961-64; environ. affairs rep. Shell Oil Co., San Francisco, 1972-77; rsch. mgr. Shell Devel. Co., Emeryville, Calif., 1964-72; cons. Environ. Affairs, Inc., Oakland, Calif., 1977-85, ret., 1985. Contbr. articles to profl. jours.; patentee in rust preventive and chemical manufacture. mem. Am. Chem. Soc., Nat. Soc. Graphology, Serra Club, Rotary. Republican. Roman Catholic.

FARLEY, GEORGE FRANCIS, veterinarian; b. St. Louis, July 15, 1947; s. Francis Frederick and Maureen Alice (O'Neil) F.; m. Georgia Lee Anderson, July 18, 1970; children: Wendy Lynn, Brett Christopher. BS in Animal Sci., U. Calif., Davis, 1969, DVM, 1973. Lic. vet., Calif., Wash. Assoc. vet. Noble Vet. Clinic, Hayward, Calif., 1973-87; hosp. dir. Hayward (Calif.) Vet. Clinic, 1987—; med. dir. Alameda County Animal Control, San Leandro, Calif., 1974-75, Hayward (Calif.) County Animal Control, 1975-76, 80-82; career speaker Moreau High Sch., Hayward, 1984—. Nat. bd. Presbyn. Marriage Encounter, 1985-86. Recipient Cert. USDA, 1973, Calif. State Pers. Bd., 1973. Mem. Am. Vet. Med. Assn., Am. Animal Hosp. Assn., Calif. Vet. Med. Assn., Alameda County Vet. Assn. (dir. 1980-82). Office: Hayward Vet Clinic 605 Greeley Ct Hayward CA 94544-6112

FARLEY, LAWRENCE, clergyman; b. Toronto, Mar. 19, 1954; s. Rheal and Vera Thelma (Cade) F.; m. Donna Anne Knight, May 8, 1976; children: Rhiannon, Magdalen. BA, Trinity Coll., U. Toronto, Canada, 1976; MDiv, Wycliffe Coll., Canada, 1979; diploma orthodox studies, St. Tikhon's Sem., Pa. Parish priest Anglican Ch., Canada, 1979-85; converted to Orthodox Ch., 1985; parish priest St. Herman's Orthodox Mission, Archdiocese of Can., 1987—. Recipient Gold Cross award Holy Bishops Orthodox Ch. in Am., 1992. Address: 9642 139 St, Surrey, BC Canada V3T 5H3

FARLEY, ROBERT DAY, metropolitan planning official; b. Jackson, Mich., Feb. 15, 1936. AA, Jackson C.C., 1956; BA in Polit. Sci., Mich. State U., 1958; MPA, U. Colo., 1981. Asst. city assessor City of East Lansing (Mich.), 1958; city mgr. Corunna, Mich., 1958-59, Hudson, Mich., 1959-62; asst. dir. Suprs. for Inter-County Com., Detroit, 1962-66; dir. intergovtl. rels. Met. Fund, Inc., Detroit, 1966-68; dep. exec. dir. S.E. Mich. Coun. of Govts., Detroit, 1968-70; exec. dir. Denver Regional Coun. Govts., 1970—, mem. transp. com., 1977—; disting. pub. exec. in residence, U. Denver, 1978; vis. lectr. U. Tex., Austin, 1978; mem. adv. coun. Grad. Sch. Pub. Affairs, U. Colo., 1978-81; mem. intergovernmental adv. com. State of Colo., 1977-81. Ex-officio mem. Denver Olympic Com. Planning Bd., 1971-72; mem. capital improvements adv. com. Denver Water Bd., 1973; mem. solid waste adv. com. Nat. League of Cities and U.S. Conf. Mayors, 1973; mem. mayor's com. on the Platte Valley, City and County of Denver, 1971-73, mayor's com. on youth problems, 1973, mayor's manpower com., 1971-73; mem. policy com. Regional Emergency Med. Care, 1973; mem. Mayor's Com. to Keep Denver a Great City, 1975-76; mem. adv. com. dept. social planning Mile High United Way, 1971-73, sect. leader campaign, 1981, 92; mem. met. community svc. bd. Colo. Coun. Chs., 1973-79, vice chmn., mem. exec. com., 1974-76, 78-79; mem. adv. panel on urban impacts Charles F. Kettering Found., Dayton, Ohio, 1980; mem. community adv. com. Jr. League Denver., 1979-84. mem. policy bd. Urban Obs. Denver, 1971-83; bd. govs. Metro Denver Urban Coalition, 1971-79, chair nominating com. 1973, exec. com., 1976; mem. adv. com. Denver Met. Area leadership Devel. and Advocacy Program, Mex. Am. Legal Def. and Edn. Fund, 1982; bd. dirs. Colo. Assn. Regional Couns., 1977—; mem. Adv. Com. Hispanic Agenda, Latin Am. Rsch. and Svc. Agy., 1988-92; chmn. transp. and parking task team. Mayor's Denver Downtown Agenda, 1992-93. Recipient Outstanding Contbn. in Meeting Urban Problems award, Denver Fed. Exec. Bd., 1987, Walter A. Scheiber Regional Leadership award Nat. Assn. Regional Coun., 1978, L.P. Cookingham award for Career Devel. Internat. City Mgmt. Assn., 1978, award Commn. on Cmty. Rels., 1976. Mem. ASPA, Nat. Assn. Regional Coun. (bd. dirs. 1972-75, 93—, exec. dirs. adv. com. 1972-79, 81-85, 88—, chmn. 1993—, coord. U.S. presentations at 5th Internat. Conf. on regionalism 1982, mem. tng. adv. com. 1978, chmn. ann. dir.'s conf. planning com. 1977, among others), Internat. City Mgmt. Assn. (COG adv. com. 1973-80, com. on regionalism policy 1973-74, com. on growth mgmt. 1973-76, conf. planning com. 1973, 77, 83, acad. for profl. devel. 1976, metro city mgrs. assn. 1982—). Office: 2480 W 26th Ave Ste 200-b Denver CO 80211-5503

FARLEY, THOMAS T., lawyer; b. Pueblo, Colo., Nov. 10, 1934; s. John Baron and Mary (Tancred) F.; m. Kathleen Maybelle Murphy, May 14, 1960; children: John, Michael, Kelly, Anne. BS, U. Santa Clara, 1956; LLB, U. Colo., 1959. Bar: Colo. 1959, U.S. Dist. Ct. Colo. 1959, U.S. Ct. Appeals (10th cir.) 1988. Dep. dist. atty. County of Pueblo, 1960-62; pvt. practice Pueblo, 1963-69; ptnr. Phelps, Fonda & Hays, Pueblo, 1970-75, Petersen & Fonda, P.C., Pueblo, 1975—; bd. dirs. Pub. Svc. Co. Colo., Denver, Norwest Pueblo, Norwest Sunset, Health Systems Internat., Inc. Minority leader Colo. Ho. of Reps., 1967-75; chmn. Colo. Wildlife Commn., 1975-79, Colo. Bd. Agr., 1979-87; bd. regents Santa Clara U., 1987—; commr. Colo. State Fair; trustee Colo. Wildlife Heritage Found., Great Outdoors Colo. Trust Fund. Recipient Disting. Svc. award U. So. Colo., 1987, 93, Bd. of Regents, U. Colo., 1993. Mem. ABA, Colo. Bar Assn., Pueblo C. of C. (bd. dirs. 1991-93), Rotary. Democrat. Roman Catholic. Office: Petersen & Fonda PC 650 Thatcher Bldg Pueblo CO 81003

FARMER, GEORGE THOMAS, JR., environmental scientist, consultant; b. Pulaski, Va., May 26, 1937; s. George Thomas and Eulalia Helen Farmer; m. Donna Wellen, Dec. 29, 1984. BA, U. Va., 1958, MS, 1960; PhD, U. Cin., 1968. Assoc. prof. geology James Madison U., Harrisonburg, Va., 1965-79; sr. hydrogeologist JRB/SAIC, McLean, Va., 1979-82; sr. hydrogeologist, chief geologist Versar, Inc., Springfield, Va., 1982-84; sr. hydrogeologist Uranium Mill Tailings Remedial Action Project, Albuquerque, 1984-86; sr. hydrogeologist, prin. Ecology and Environment, Inc., L.A., 1986-87; sr. hydrogeologist, quality assurance officer Brown and Caldwell Engrs. and Geologists, Pasadena, Calif., 1987-89; regional office mgr. Applied Geosys., Inc., Culver City, Calif., 1989-90; programmatic project leader Los Alamos (N.Mex.) Nat. Lab., 1990—; cons. hydrogeologist, Kleinfelder, Compton, Calif., 1986. Co-author: Earth Materials: Earth Processes, 1992. Mem. Am. Geol. Inst., Am. Assn. Profl. Geologists (cert.), Sigma Xi, Sigma Gamma Epsilon. Home: 8 Los Arboles Dr Los Alamos NM 87544-3081 Office: Los Alamos Nat Lab ER Program MS M 992 Los Alamos NM 87545

FARMER, JAMES DAVID, journalist; b. Quincy, Ohio, June 16, 1938; s. James Harvey and Claire Gertrude (Paulson) F.; m. Hinda Schorr, July 23, 1960; children: Melissa, Richard James. BA in Journalism, U. So. Calif., L.A., 1961. Reporter The AP, L.A. and Las Vegas, 1961-63; reporter, asst. city editor The San Diego (Calif.) Union, 1963-68; prodr. KNXT-TV (now KCBS-TV), L.A., 1968-71; exec. prodr. WCBS-TV, N.Y.C., 1971-79; prodr. CBS News, N.Y.C., 1979-83; supervising prodr. Cable News Network, Atlanta, 1984-87; bur. chief Cable News Network, L.A., 1987-88; v.p., bur. chief Cable News Network, N.Y.C., 1988-90, L.A., 1990—. Recipient Emmy award Acad. TV Arts and Scis., N.Y.C., 1976, Cable Ace award Nat. Cable TV Acad., 1994; named Outstanding Alumnus, U. So. Calif. Sch. Journalism, 1994. Mem. Radio and TV News Assn. (bd. dirs. 1994—, Golden Mike award 1969, 90). Office: Cable News Network 6430 W Sunset Blvd Ste 300 Los Angeles CA 90028-7901

FARMER, JAMES DOUGLAS, park manager; b. Mount Vernon, Wash., Sept. 23, 1947; s. Bascom Coleman and Inez Clare (Calkins) F.; m. Denise Anne O'Hara, Feb. 16, 1968; 1 child, Christopher Dean. Student, Skagit Valley Coll., 1971. Park ranger Wash. State Parks, Oak Harbor, 1971-73, Wenberg State Park, Stanwood, Wash., 1973-74, Deception Pass State Park, Oak Harbor, 1975-79, Larrabee State Park, Bellingham, Wash., 1979-90, Moran State Park, Eastsound, Wash., 1990-91, Fort Worden State Park, Port Townsend, Wash., 1991—. Mem. parks commn. Port Townsend City Parks, 1994—; adv. com. Skagit Valley Coll., Mt. Vernon, 1972-82. Recipient Dirs. award Wash. State Parks, 1994. Mem. Wash. Recreation and Parks Assn. (bd. dirs. 1992-93), Port Townsend Rotary. Office: Fort Warden State Park 200 Battery Way Port Townsend WA 98368-3699

FARMER, JANENE ELIZABETH, artist, educator; b. Albuquerque, Oct. 16, 1946; d. Charles John Watt and Regina M. (Brown) Kruger; m. Michael Hugh Bolton, Apr. 1965 (div.); m. Frank Urban Farmer, May, 1972 (div.). BA in Art, San Diego State U., 1969. Owner, operator Iron Walrus Pottery, 1972-79; designer ceramic and fabric murals, Coronado, Calif., 1979-82; executed commns. for clients in U.S.A., Can., Japan and Mex., 1972—; designer fabric murals and bldg. interiors; painter rare and endangered animals, Coronado and La Jolla, Calif., 1982—; tchr. Catholic schs., San Diego, 1982-87, Ramona Unified Sch. Dist., 1988—, mentor tchr.; instr. U. Calif., San Diego, 1979-83, 92—, resident artist. Mem. Coronado Arts and Humanities Coun., 1979-81. Grantee Calif. Arts Coun., 1980-81; U. San Diego grad. fellow dept. edn., 1984. Mem. Am. Soc. Interior Designers (affiliate). Roman Catholic. Home: 4435 Nobel Dr Apt 35 San Diego CA 92122-1559

FARMWALD, PAUL MICHAEL, inventor, engineer; b. Anderson, Ind., May 30, 1954; s. Oliver Eugene and Viola Elizabeth (Glick) F. BS, Purdue U., 1974; PhD, Stanford U., 1981. Project scientist S-1 project Lawrence Livermore Nat. Lab., Livermore, Calif., 1976-86; chief scientist, bipolar MIP Computer Systems, Sunnyvale, Calif., 1986-89; assoc. dir. EECS, assoc.prof. U. Ill., Champaign-Urbana, 1989-90; founder Rambus, Inc., Mountain View, Calif., 1990—, Xenon Microsystems, Inc., Mountain View, 1993—. Patentee in field. Home: 190 Golden Oak Dr Portola Vally CA 94028-7912 Office: Rambus Inc 2465 Latham St Mountain View CA 94040-1419

FARNHAM, MARY GLADE SIEMER, artist; b. Ross, Calif., Nov. 1, 1924; d. Albert Henry and Mabel Meta (Jones) Siemer; children: Thomas Ross, Evan Neil, Gwen Marie, William Blair, Hugh Porter. Student Marin Jr. Coll., 1942-43, Goucher Coll., 1943-44; B.A., U. Calif.-Berkeley, 1947. Profl. athlete, Curry Co., Yosemite, Calif., 1945; advt. prodn. mgr. City of Paris/Hale's, San Francisco, 1947; advt. artist Lipman Wolfe, Portland, Oreg., 1947-48; advt. layout artist Meier & Frank, Portland, 1948; art dir. Olds & King, Portland, 1948-50; free lance comml. artist, Portland, 1950-56; pres. Marin County Devel. Co., San Anselmo, Calif., 1963-78; pres., designer Mary Farnham Designs, Inc., Portland, 1983-89. Exhibited in 14 one woman shows and numerous group shows, U.S. & abroad. Mem. pub. art selection panel II, Met. Arts Commn., Portland, 1982-83; bd. dirs. N.W. Artists Workshop, Portland, 1977-78; sec. Artist Membership, Portland Art Assn., 1973-74. Episcopalian. Club: Multnomah Athletic. Avocations: swimming; diving.

FARNUM, NANCY ALYSON, communications executive; b. Birmingham, Ala., Mar. 2, 1949; d. Leon Vernon and Martha Reeves (McGahee) F. BA, Rockford Coll., 1971; MSLS, Case We. Reserve U., 1972. cert. health information profl. Information specialist Merrell-Nat. Lab. Pharm. Co., Cin., 1973-78; U.S. adminstr. Applied Human Cybernetics, London, 1975-78; asst. prof. and online search analyst Coll. Medicine E. Tenn. State U., Johnson City, Tenn., 1982-84; assoc. dir. N.W. Area Health Edn. Ctr., Salisbury, N.C., 1984-88; asst. prof. Bowman Gray Sch. Medicine, Winston Salem, 1984-88; coord. multimedia svcs. U. Ala., Birmingham, 1989-92; cons. MRM Communications, Claremont, Calif., 1988—; cons. St. George's (Grenada) U. Sch. Medicine, 1989; chair K-12 com. U. of the World, La Jolla, Calif., 1989—; mem. Gov.'s Tech. Task Force on Edn. Reform, Montgomery, Ala., 1993—. Coord. Global Awareness Seminar Birmingham Pub. Schs., 1988-93, World Peace Day Friends of the City of Birmingham, 1988—. Recipient Grad. endowment Nat. Inst. Health, Bethesda, Md., 1971-72; scholarship Sch. Theology at Claremont (Calif.), 1993. Mem. NAFE, Med. Libr. Assn., Network Birmingham, Acad. Health Informational Profls. Methodist. Home: 1325 N College Ave Claremont CA 91711-3154

FARQUHAR, MARILYN GIST, cell biology and pathology educator; b. Tulare, Calif., July 11, 1928; d. Brooks DeWitt and Alta (Green) Gist; m. John W. Farquhar, June 4, 1952; children: Bruce, Douglas (div. 1968); m. George Palade, June 7, 1970. AB, U. Calif., Berkeley, 1949, MA, 1952, PhD, 1955. Asst. rsch. pathologist Sch. Medicine U. Calif., San Francisco, 1956-58, assoc. rsch. pathologist, 1962-64, assoc. prof., 1964-68, prof. pathology, 1968-70; rsch. assoc. Rockefeller U., N.Y.C., 1958-62, prof. cell biology, 1970-73; prof. cell biology Sch. Medicine Yale U., New Haven, 1973-87, Sterling prof. cell biology and pathology, 1987-90; prof. pathology div. cell molecular medicine U. Calif., San Diego, 1990—, coord. div. cellular and molecular medicine, 1991—. Mem. editorial bd. numerous sci. jours.; contbr. articles to profl. jours. Recipient Career Devel. award NIH, 1968-73, Disting. Sci. medal Electron Microscope Soc., 1987. Mem. NAS, Am. Acad. Arts and Scis., Am. Soc. Cell Biology (pres. 1981-82, E.B. Wilson medal 1987), Am. Assn. Investigative Pathology, Am. Soc. Nephrology (Homer Smith award 1988). Home: 12894 Via Latina Del Mar CA 92014-3730

FARQUHAR, PETER HENRY, management educator, research director; b. Boston, May 7, 1947; s. Henry Adamson Farquhar Jr. and Alice Mai (Grant) Kearney; m. Andrea Pyne, Apr. 12, 1949; children: Thomas Henry, Michelle Denise, David Charles. BS magna cum laude, Tufts U., 1969; MS, Cornell U., 1972, PhD, 1974. Assoc. mathematician The Rand Corp., Santa Monica, Calif., 1974-75; asst. prof. Northwestern U., Evanston, Ill., 1975-78, Harvard Bus. Sch., Boston, 1978-80; assoc. prof. U. Calif., Davis, 1980-84; assoc. prof. mktg. Carnegie-Mellon U., Pitts., 1984-92; dir. Ctr. for Product Rsch., Pitts., 1987-92; prof. mgmt. Claremont (Calif.) Grad. Sch., 1992—; dir. Product Strategy Inst., Claremont, Calif., 1992—; mgmt. cons., Pitts. and Claremont, 1984—; adv. bd. NPD Group, 1991—. Contbr. articles to profl. jours. Bd. mem. Sch. Dist. 67, Morton Grove, Ill., 1977-78. Recipient award of merit Ill. Assn. Sch. Bds., 1978; rsch. grantee Office Naval Rsch., 1978-89, NSF, 1988-91, Mktg. Sci. Inst., 1988-93, Carnegie Bosch Inst., 1990-92. Mem. Product Devel. and Mgmt. Assn. (v.p. 1989, bd. dirs. 1990-93), Ops. Rsch. Soc. Am. (area editor 1989-94), Inst. Mgmt. Sci. (publs. com. 1987-93), Am. Mktg. Assn. Office: Claremont Grad Sch Drucker Grad Mgmt Ctr 165 E 10th St Claremont CA 91711-3945

FARQUHARSON, WALTER HENRY, minister, church official; b. Zealandia, Sask., Can., May 30, 1936; s. James and Jessie Ann (Muirhead) F.; m. Patricia Joan Casswell, Sept. 16, 1958; children: Scott, Michael, Catherine, Stephen. BA, U. Sask., Saskatoon, 1957, Diploma in Edn., 1969; BD, St. Andrew's Coll., Saskatoon, 1961, DD (hon.), 1975. Ordained to ministry United Ch. of Can., 1961. Min. Saltcoats-Bredenbury-Churchbridge Pastoral Charge, Sask., 1961—; moderator United Ch. of Can., 1990-92; exec. gen. coun., pres. Sask. Conf. Contbr. numerous hymns and religious songs; retreat leader. Recipient Commemorative medal 125th anniversary Confedn. Can. Home: PO Box 126, Saltcoats, SK Canada S0A 3R0 Office: United Ch of Can, PO Box 58, Saltcoats, SK Canada S0A 3R0

FARR, DAVID DONALD, musician, educator, administrator; b. Coquille, Oreg., Feb. 28, 1942; s. Donald Haines and Emma Frances (Mulkey) F.; m. Kathleen McIntosh, June 19, 1968 (div. 1975). BA, U. Oreg., 1965, MusM, 1966; PhD in Theology and the Arts, Grad. Theol. Union, 1986; ed. various mus. seminars. Tchg. asst. U. Oreg., Eugene, 1965-66; fellow Coll. Ch. Musicians, Wash. Nat. Cathedral, 1968; choirmaster/organist St. Mark's Episcopal Ch., Berkeley, Calif., 1968-72; music master Coll. Prep. Sch., Oakland, Calif., 1970-72; choirmaster/organist All Sts. Episcopal Ch., Pasadena, Calif., 1972-78, St. Mary Magdalen Ch., Berkeley, 1979-85; dir. music, liturgical cons. to campus ministry St. Mary's Coll., Moraga, Calif., 1981-83; mus. dir. St. Luke's Episcopal Ch., San Francisco, 1986-94; exec. dir. San Anselmo (Calif.) Organ Festival, 1992—; pvt. instr. organ, piano and voice, 1960—; organist St. Ignatius Ch., U. San Francisco, 1994—; condr. seminars in field; mus. dir. Jr. Bach Festival Assn., Inc., Berkeley, 1983-85; founder 1st Am. br. Royal Sch. Ch. Music, 1977; cons. mem. Standing Commn. on Ch. Music of Episcopal Ch., 1977-79; cons. design of liturgical space/acoustical and mus. parameters St. Andrew's Newman Student Ctr., Riverside, Calif., 1985-89; cons. organ selection, design, installation All Soul's Episcopal Ch., San Diego, 1978-86. Author: A Guide to Anthems for the Lectionary, 1994; co-contbr. chpt. to: Clergy and Church Musicians, 1980; contbr. articles to profl. pubs. Choral clinician to conf. on liturgy and music Diocese Miss; chmn. commn. on liturgy and ch. music Episcopal Diocese L.A., 1976-78; planner ann. conf. Chmn. of Diocesan Liturgical Commns., Santa Barbara, Calif., 1976, Albuquerque, 1979; mem. liturgical renewal commn. Diocese Calif. Mem. Am. Musicological Soc., Assn. Anglican Musicians (pres. 1974-75, chmn. membership com. 1976-77, chmn. profl. standards, status and compensation com. 1977-79, planner conf. 1975), Am. Guild Organists (dean San Francisco chpt. 1988-92, planner mid-winter conclave 1976, cons. to Western Regional Conv. 1993), Organ Hist. Soc. Democrat. Home: 500 Plymouth Ave San Francisco CA 94112-2914 Office: San Anselmo Organ Festival 2 Kensington Rd San Anselmo CA 94960-2905

FARR, DONALD EUGENE, engineering scientist; b. Clinton, Iowa, July 1, 1933; s. Kenneth Elroy and Nellie Irene (Bailey) F.; m. Sally Joyce Braver, Mar. 8, 1954; children: Erika Lyn Farr Leventis, Jolene Karyn Farr. BA in Engring. Psychology, San Diego State U., 1961; MT with honors, Nat. U., 1974; postgrad., Calif. Pacific U., 1976-80. Human factors specialist Bunker Ramo Corp., Canoga Park, Calif., 1964-69; sr. design specialist Gen. Dynamics, San Diego, 1955-63, 69-76; tech. staff Sandia Nat. Labs., Albuquerque, 1977-80; group supr., sr. tech. advisor The Babcock and Wilcox Co., Lynchburg, Va., 1980-82; dir. human factors sys. Sci. Applications, Inc., Lynchburg, 1982-83; human engring. scientist Lockheed Calif. Co., Burbank, 1983-91; MANPRINT mgr. Teledyne Electronic Sys., Northridge, Calif., 1991-94; human engring. scientist Symvionics, Inc., Pasadena, Calif., 1994—; ergonomics safety cons. govt., industry and academia, 1977—. Contbr. articles to profl. jours. Precinct capt., voter registration vol. Rep. Party, 1963—; lectr., support group Am. Diabetes Assn., L.A., 1993—. With USN, 1952-53. Scholarship USN, 1953; recipient N.S.I.A., 1963. Mem. Human Factors and Ergonomics Soc. (pres. San Diego, L.A. chpt.), Internat. Numismatic Soc. (pres. 1973-75), Am. Nuclear Soc. (human factors chair 1980-82), Am. Legion, NRA Golden Eagles (honor role). Lutheran. Home: 13100 Bromont Ave Apt 36 Sylmar CA 91342-7437 Office: Ergonomics Cons PO Box 921952 Sylmar CA 91392-1952

FARR, G(ARDNER) NEIL, lawyer; b. L.A., Jan. 9, 1932; s. Gardner and Elsie M. (Schuster) F.; m. Lorna Jean, Oct. 26, 1957; children: Marshall Clay, Jennifer T., Thomas M. BA, U. Calif., Berkeley, 1957, JD, U. Calif., San Francisco, 1960. Bar: Calif. 1961, U.S. Supreme Ct. 1977. Cert specialist family law Calif. Bd. Specialization, 1980. Dep. dist. atty. Solano County, 1961-66; recreation commr. City of Fairfield, 1964-66; dep. dist. atty. Kern County, 1966-69; ptnr. Young, Wooldridge, Paulden, Self, Farr & Hugie (now Law Offices of Young Wooldridge), Bakersfield, Calif., 1969—; dir. Cen. Calif. Appellate Program, Inc.; judge protem Kern County Superior Ct. Chmn. Kern County Juvenile Justice Commn. With USNR, 1949-53. Mem. ABA, Calif. Bar Assn., Kern County Bar Assn. (pres. 1984, past pres. family law sect.), Calif. Trial Lawyers Assn. Office: Young Wooldridge 1800 30th St Fl 4 Bakersfield CA 93301

FARR, JOHN KEVIN, social sciences educator; b. Riverside, Calif., Apr. 30, 1957; s. Conrad Landis and Mary Jean (Reilly) F.; m. Jane Margaret Petrilli, July 25, 1981; children: Kevin Landis, Margaret Elizabeth, William Conrad. BA in History and European Studies, U. San Diego, 1979; MA in Edn., San Diego State U., 1984. Cert. tchr. and adminstr., Calif. Tchr. jr. h.s. and h.s. Damascus (Syria) Cmty. Sch., 1988-89; tchr. h.s. Corona-Norco Unified Schs., Corona, Calif., 1984-88, tchr. jr. h.s., 1989—; presenter Near East South Asia Ednl. Conf., Athens, Greece, 1988, Calif. Assn. for Gifted, Long Beach, 1991. Co-author: Corona: Citrus, Races and More. . ., 1993. Bd. dirs., past pres. Corona Hist. Preservation Soc., 1991—; pres. sch. bd. St. Edward Sch., Corona, 1992—; chmn. Riverside County Libertarian Party, 1991, 92; active Riverside County Hist. Commn., 1993—, Mission Inn Found., 1984—; mem., pres. Corona Civic Concert Band, 1993-94. Recipient Spl. award for rescuing drowning child City of Corona, 1970. Mem. NEA, Calif. Tchrs. Assn. (site rep. 1990, 91), Cath. League for Religious and Civil Rights. Office: Corona Fundamental Intermediate Schs 1230 S Main St Corona CA 91720-4464

FARR, LEE EDWARD, physician; b. Albuquerque, Oct. 13, 1907; s. Edward and Mabel (Heyn) F.; m. Anne Ritter, Dec. 28, 1936 (dec.); children: Charles E., Susan A., Frances A.; m. Miriam Kirk, Jan. 22, 1985. BS, Yale U., 1929, MD, 1933. Asst. pediatrics Sch. Medicine, Yale U., 1933-34; asst. medicine Hosp. of Rockefeller Inst. Med. Research, 1934-37, assoc. medicine, 1937-40; dir. research Alfred I. duPont Inst. of Nemours Found., Wilmington, Del., 1940-49; vis. assoc. prof. pediatrics Sch. Medicine, U. Pa., 1940-49; med. dir. Brookhaven Nat. Lab., 1948-62; prof. nuclear medicine U. Tex. Postgrad. Med. Sch., 1962-64, prof. nuclear and environ. medicine Grad. Sch. Bio-Med. Scis., U. Tex. at Houston, 1965-68; chief sect. nuclear medicine U. Tex.-M.D. Anderson Hosp. and Tumor Inst., 1962-67, prof. environ. health U. Tex. Sch. Pub. Health, Houston, 1967-68; head disaster health services Calif. Dept. Health, 1968, chief emergency health services unit, 1968-70, 1st chief bur. emergency med. services, 1970-73; Lippitt lectr. Marquette U., 1941; Sommers Meml. lectr. U. Oreg. Sch. Med., Portland, 1960; Gordon Wilson lectr. Am. Clin. and Climatol. Assn., 1956; Sigma Xi nat. lectr., 1952-53; guest scientist Institut fur Medizinder Kernforschungsanlage, Julich, Germany, 1966; Brookhaven Nat. Lab. lectr., 1990. Mem. NRC adv. com. Naval Med. Res., 1953-68; chmn. NRC adv. com. Atomic Bomb Casualty Commn., 1953-68; mem. adv. com. Naval Res. to Sec. of Navy and CNO, 1968-72; NRC adv. com. on medicine and surgery, 1965-66, exec. com., 1962-65; Naval Research Mission to Formosa, 1953; tech. adviser U.S. delegation to Geneva Internat. Conf. for Peaceful Uses Atomic Energy, 1955; mem. N.Y. Adv. Com. Atomic Energy, 1956-59; mem. cholera commn. SEATO Conf., Bangkok, 1960; mem. AMA Com. Nuclear Medicine, 1963-66; mem. com. med. isotopes NASA Manned Spacecraft Ctr., 1966-68; mem. expert adv. panel radiation WHO, 1957-79; mem. Calif. Gov.'s Ad Hoc Com. Emergency Health Service, 1968-69; mem. sci. adv. bd. Gorgas Meml. Inst., 1967-72; numerous other sci. adv. bds., panels; cons. TRW Systems, Inc., 1966-70, Consol. Petroleum Co., Beverly Hills, Calif., 1946-70. Mem. alumni bd. Yale, 1962-65, mem. alumni fund, 1966-76, agent alumni fund 1994—. With USNR, 1942-46; capt. (M.C.) USNR, ret. Recipient Mead Johnson award for pediatric research, 1940, Gold Cross Order of Phoenix, Greece, 1960, Verdienstkreuz 1st class Fed. Republic Germany, 1963; named Community Leader in Am., 1969, Disting. Alumni Yale U. Med. Sch., 1989. Diplomate Nat. Bd. Med. Examiners, Am. Bd. Pediatrics. Fellow AAAS, Royal Soc. Arts, Am. Acad. Pediatrics, N.Y. Acad. Scis., Royal Soc. Health, Am. Coll. Nuclear Medicine (disting. fellow); mem. Soc. Pediatric Research, Soc. Exptl. Biology, Harvey Soc., Am. Pediatric Soc., Soc. Exptl. Pathology, Am. Soc. Clin. Investigation, Radiation Research Soc., AMA (mem. council on sci. assembly 1960-70, chmn. 1968-70), Med. Soc. Athens (hon. mem.), Alameda County Med. Assn., Sigma Xi, Alpha Omega Alpha, Phi Sigma Kappa, Nu Sigma Nu, Alpha Chi Sigma. Club: Commonwealth (San Francisco). Author articles on nuclear medicine, protein metabolism, emergency med. services, radioactive and chem. environ. contaminants, environ. noise. Home: 2502 Saklan Indian Dr Apt 2 Walnut Creek CA 94595-3001

FARR, LEONARD ALFRED, hospital administrator; b. Pleasant Hill, La., Mar. 19, 1947. BA, La. State U., 1969; MA, Washington U., 1974. Adminstr. resident HCA Wesley Med. Ctr., Wichita, Kans., 1973-74, night adminstr., 1974-75; asst. adminstr. Physicians & Surgeons Hosp., Shreveport, La., 1975, exec. v.p., 1975-76; adminstr. Colo. Springs. (Colo.) Community Hosp., 1976-78; pres., CEO St. Francis Hosp. Systems, Colo. Springs, Colo., 1978-87; COO Penrose-St. Francis Hosp., Colo. Springs, 1987-91, pres., CEO, 1991—. Mem. Am. Hosp. Assn. (alternate del., del.), Colo. Hosp. Assn. (chmn. bd.). Office: Penrose-St Francis Healthcare System PO Box 7021 Colorado Springs CO 80933

FARR, SAM SHARON, congressman; b. Calif., July 4, 1941; m. Shary Baldwin; 1 child, Jessica. BSc Biology, Willamette U., 1963; student, Monterey Inst. Internat. Studies, U. Santa Clara. Vol. Peace Corps, 1963-65; budget analyst, cons. Assembly com. Constl. Amendments; bd. suprs. Monterey (Calif.) County; rep. Calif. State Assembly, 1980-93; mem. 103d U.S. Congress from 17th Calif. dist., 1993—; agrl. com. mem., natural resources com. mem., 103d U.S. Congress from 17th Calif. dist. Named Legislator of Yr. Calif. 9 times. Democrat. Office: House of Representatives 1117 Longworth House Office Bl Washington DC 20515

FARRAR, ELAINE WILLARDSON, artist; b. L.A.; d. Eldon and Gladys Elsie (Larsen) Willardson; BA, Ariz. State U., 1967, MA, 1969, PhD, 1990; children: Steve, Mark, Gregory, JanLeslie, Monty, Susan. Tchr., Camelback Desert Sch., Paradise Valley, Ariz., 1966-69; mem. faculty Yavapai Coll., Prescott, Ariz., 1970-92, chmn. dept. art, 1973-78, instr. art in watercolor and oil and acrylic painting, intaglio, relief and monoprints, 1971-92; grad. advisor Prescott Coll. Master of Arts Program, 1993—. One-man shows include: R.P. Moffat's, Scottsdale, Ariz., 1969, Art Center, Battle Creek, Mich., 1969, The Woodpeddler, Costa Mesa, Calif., 1979; group show Prescott (Ariz.) Fine Arts Assn., 1982, 84, 86, 89, 90-95, N.Y. Nat. Am. Watercolorists, 1982; Ariz. State U. Women Images Now, 1986, 87, 89, 90, 91, 92; works rep. local and state exhibits, pvt. collections; supt. fine arts dept. County Fair; com. mem., hanging chmn. Scholastic Art Awards; owner studio/gallery Willis Street Artists, Prescott. Mem. AAUW, Mountain Artists Guild (past pres.), Ariz. Art Edn. Assn., Nat. Art Edn. Assn., Ariz. Coll. and Univ. Faculty Assn., Ariz. Women's Caucus for Art, Women's Nat. Mus. (charter Washington chpt.), Kappa Delta Pi, Phi Delta Kappa (Yavapai chpt. v.p. mem., 1994-95). Republican. Mormon. Home: 535 Copper Basin Rd Prescott AZ 86303-4601

FARRAR, LUCY ELLEN, real estate broker; b. Knoxville, Tenn., Oct. 5, 1936; d. Raymond Leon and Mable Glen (Crass) Hatmaker; m. Robert David Proffitt, Oct. 5, 1956 (div. Aug. 1974); children: Robert David Jr., Karen Lelia, Stephen Keith, Kevin Scott; m. Charles Richard Farrar, Sr., Oct. 19, 1983. BA, U. Tenn., 1963, MA, 1967. Lic. real estate broker, Colo. Instr. Maryville (Tenn.) Coll., 1967-72; prodr./hostess talk show WSJK TV (PBS), Knoxville, Tenn., 1972-74; dir. devel. Barter Found., Abingdon, Va., 1974-78; tng. coord. gas ops. Aramco, Abqaiq, Saudi Arabia, 1979-83; planning analyst fin. and acctg. Aramco, Dhahran, Saudi Arabia, 1984-85; broker, owner Pinnacle Properties, Monument, Colo., 1989-93; broker, ptnr. Tri-Lakes Realty, Inc., Monument, 1993—; dir. Realtor Svc. Corp., Colorado Springs, 1993—. Recipient nat. awards Operation Healthy Babies March of Dimes/Nat. Coun. Women's Club, Chgo., 1963, Project Concern/Jim Turpin, Nashville, 1964. Mem. Women's Coun. Realtors, Pikes Peak Assn. Realtors (chmn. tech. rev. and adv. 1992—, dir. 1994—), Tri-Lakes C. of C., Woodmoor Country Club (dir., sec., registered agt. 1988-90), Pi Beta Phi Alumni Club. Home: PO Box 9 Monument CO 80132-0009

FARRELL, DENNIS, sports association executive; b. Orange, Calif., Feb. 23, 1951; s. Fred Bernard and Janet Louise (Crawford) F.; m. Charlene Louise Cassingham, Jan. 11, 1975; Timothy William, Michael Ted. AA in Liberal Arts, Santa Ana Coll., 1971; BA in Journalism, San Diego State U., 1973. Sports editor Saddleback Valley News, Mission Viejo, Calif., 1974-77; sports info. dir. Saddleback Coll., Mission Viejo, Calif., 1977-80; asst. commr. Pacific Coast Athletic Assn., Santa Ana, Calif., 1980-88; assoc. commr. Big West Conf., Santa Ana, Calif., 1988-92; commr. Big West Conf., Irvine, Calif., 1992—. Mem. Collegiate Commrs. Assn. Office: Big West Conf 2 Corporate Park Ste 206 Irvine CA 92714-5128

FARRELL, EDWARD JOSEPH, retired mathematics educator; b. San Francisco, Mar. 28, 1917; s. Christopher Patrick and Ethel Ann (Chesterman) F.; m. Pearl Philomena Rongone, Aug. 21, 1954; children: Paul, Paula. B.Sc., U. San Francisco, 1939; M.A., Stanford U., 1942. Mem. faculty U. San Francisco, 1941—, prof. math., 1968-82, prof. emeritus, lectr., 1982-93; Guest lectr. regional and nat. meetings Nat. Council Tchrs. Math., 1966, 67, 69; cons. math. text pubs. Mem. adv. panels NSF, 1966—, dir. summer and in-service insts., 1960-75, dir. confs. geometry, 1967, 68, 70-75; mem. rev. panel Sci. Books. Author math. reports; editor studies teaching contemporary geometry. Served with AUS, 1944-46. NSF faculty fellow, 1956-57. Mem. AAAS, Am. Assn. Physics Tchrs., Nat. Council Tchrs. Math., Sch. Sci. and Math. Assn. Republican. Roman Catholic. Home: 2526 Gough St San Francisco CA 94123-5013

FARRELL, FRANCINE ANNETTE, psychotherapist, educator; b. Long Beach, Calif., Mar. 26, 1948; d. Thomas and Evelyn Marie (Lucente) F.; m. James Thomas Hanley, Dec. 5, 1968 (div. Dec. 1988); children: Melinda Lee Hanley, James Thomas Hanley Jr. BA in Psychology with honors, Calif.

State U., Sacramento, 1985, MS in Counseling, 1986. Lic. marriage, family and child counselor, Calif.; nat. cert. addiction counselor. Marriage, family and child counselor intern Fulton Ct. Counseling, Sacramento, 1987-88; pvt. practice psychotherapist Sacramento, 1988—; instr. chem. dependency studies program, Calif. State U., Sacramento, 1985-94, acad. coord. chem. dependency studies program, 1988-90; trainee Sobriety Brings a Change, Sacramento, 1986-87; assoc. investigator, curriculum coord. Project S.A.F.E., Sacramento, 1990-91; presenter Sacramento Conf., ACA, 1986, 88, 89, 91, 92, Ann. Symposium on Chem. Dependency, 1993. Presenter (cable TV series) Trouble in River City: Charting a Course for Change, 1991. Mem. Nat. Coun. on Alcoholism, Calif. Assn. Marriage and Family Therapists, Calif. Assn. Alcoholism and Drug Abuse Counselors (bd. dirs. region 5, 1988-90), Phi Kappa Phi. Roman Catholic. Office: 2740 Fulton Ave # 100 Sacramento CA 95821-5108

FARRELL, JOHN STANISLAUS, manufacturing company executive; b. County Down, No. Ireland, May 19, 1931; arrived in Can., 1931, naturalized, 1931; s. George Stanislaus and Agnes Anna (McCartney) F.; m. Vyra June white, Aug. 7, 1959; children—John McCartney, Lizanne Jennifer. B.A.Sc. in Elec. Engring., U. Toronto, 1956. Registered profl. engr., Can. With ITT Can., Ltd., Montreal, Que., Can., 1962-69; dir. avionics and transmission ITT Can., Ltd., 1968-69; mktg. dir. Leigh Instruments, Ltd., Carleton Place, Ont., 1969-70; gen. mgr. Leigh Instruments, Ltd., 1970-73; pres., chief exec. officer Gestalt Internat. Ltd., Vancouver, B.C., Can., 1973-76; v.p. Cornat Industries, Ltd., Vancouver, 1976-78; sr. v.p. Versatile Corp., Vancouver, 1978-86; exec. dir. Rimquest Internat., Vancouver, 1986-88; pres. Versatech Trading and Devel. Corp., Vancouver, 1988—, also bd. dirs.; chmn., dir. Auspulp Pty. Ltd., Australia, Jara Mgmt. Inc., U.S.; bd. dirs. Versatech Trading and Devel. Corp., Vancouver, Brigdon Resources, Inc., Calgary, Alta., Can., Napier Internat. Techs. Inc., Vancouver, Resource Svcs. Australia, Sydney. Bd. dirs. Resource Svcs. Australia, Sydney. With RCAF, 1950-59. Mem. Profl. Engrs. of Ont. Club: Vancouver Lawn Tennis and Badminton.

FARRELL, KEVIN, architect; b. Pontiac, Mich., Dec. 6, 1956; s. Thomas Patrick and Shirley Ann (Thrasher) F.; 1 child, Elle Andrea. BArch, So. Calif. Inst. Architects. Registered architect, Calif. Designer SGPA Arch., San Diego, 1982; worked with Grondona Arch., San Diego, 1982; apprentice Morphosis, L.A., 1983; prin. Farrell Design Assoc., Inc., San Diego, 1984—; furniture designer Nicholas Applegate, San Diego, 1994. Recipient Interior Design Mag. award, N.Y., 1989, World Space Design award, Tokyo, 1989, San Diego Home Garden award, 1987, 90, 92, 94. Mem. AIA (award 1986), Calif. Inst. Arch., NCARB. Office: Farrell Design Assoc Inc 2211 Cambridge Ave Cardiff By The Sea CA 92007-1901

FARRELL, LARRY DON, microbiology educator; b. Woodward, Okla., Nov. 5, 1942; s. Donal Mervin and Frieda Marie (Rector) F.; m. Julia Ann Robinson, Aug. 8, 1965; children: Denise Eileen, Meghan Kathleen. BS, U. Okla., 1964, MS, 1966; PhD, UCLA, 1970. Postdoctoral and instr. Coll. Medicine U. Ill., Chgo., 1970-72; asst. prof. microbiology Idaho State U., Pocatello, 1972-78, chmn. microbiology dept., 1977-84, assoc. prof., 1978-89, prof., 1989—, asst. chmn. dept. biol. scis., 1988-90. Contbr. articles to profl. jours. Mem. exec. bd. Idaho AIDS Found., former co-dir. edn. task force. Mem. AAAS, Am. Soc. Microbiology, Idaho Acad. Scis., Idaho Com. Correspondence (liaison/pres. 1982-89), Internat. Soc. for AIDS Edn., S.E. Idaho AIDS Coalition, Sigma Xi. Democrat. Home: 843 N 10th Ave Pocatello ID 83201-5249 Office: Idaho State U Dept Biol Scis Pocatello ID 83209

FARRELL, PATRICK JOSEPH, lawyer; b. Tucson, Sept. 25, 1951; s. Charles Henry and Mary Agnes (Harrington) F.; m. Catherine Cullen Brophy, Sept. 30, 1978 (div. Mar. 1983); m. Karen Ann Ruby, Oct. 13, 1984; children: Tara Kelly, Kevin Patrick, Kelly Colleen. BS, U. Ariz., 1973, JD, 1976. Bar: Ariz. 1976. Atty. Law Office of Jay S. Kittle, Tucson, 1976-78; assoc. Corey, Farrell, Kime & Bromiel, P.C., Tucson, 1978—. Bd. dirs. The Blake Found. (formerly Cerebral Palsy Found. So. Ariz.), 1985—, Tucson St. Patrick's Day Parade Com., 1987-91; bd. dirs. Downtown Bus. Assn., 1986—, pres., 1991; bd. mgrs. Lohse Family br. YMCA, 1993—; officer Exch. Club Downtown Tucson, 1978-84. Mem. ABA (bus. law, real property, probate and trust, law practice mgmt. sects.), Pima County Bar Assn., Assn. Trial Lawyers Am., So. Ariz. Estate Planning Coun. Republican. Roman Catholic. Home: 2612 E 8th St Tucson AZ 85716-4710 Office: Corey Farrell Kime & Bromiel PC 1 S Church Ave Ste 830 Tucson AZ 85701-1620

FARRELL, THOMAS DINAN, lawyer; b. Chgo., Feb. 14, 1948; s. Francis George and Marian F.; m. Elizabeth Ann McElyea, Apr. 26, 1975; children: Brian, Timothy. AB in Politics, Princeton U., 1970; JD, U. Calif., Berkeley, 1973. Bar: N.J. 1974, Calif. 1977, N.Y. 1987. Asst. counsel Nat. Gambling Commn., Washington, 1974-76; asst. U.S. atty. U.S. Dept. Justice, L.A., 1976-78; assoc. Pitney, Hardin & Kipp, Morristown, N.J., 1978-80; v.p. Hilton Hotels Corp., Beverly Hills, Calif., 1980-82, Harrah's, Atlantic City, 1982-85; sr. v.p., gen. counsel Trusthouse Forte, Inc., N.Y.C., 1985-90; sr. v.p. devel. Hilton Hotels, 1990-94; exec. v.p. devel. Airport Group Internat., Glendale, Calif., 1994—. Commr. Alcoholic Beverage Study Commn., Trenton, N.J., 1983-85. Served to capt. USAR, 1972-80. Nat. Merit Scholar 1966. Mem. N.J. Bar Assn. (chmn. casino law com. 1984-85). Episcopalian. Home: 1100 Palos Verdes Dr W Pls Vrds Est CA 90274-1870 Office: Airport Group Internat 330 N Brand Blvd Glendale CA 91203

FARRELL, THOMAS JOSEPH, insurance company executive, consultant; b. Butte, Mont., June 10, 1926; s. Bartholomew J. and Lavina H. (Collins) F.; m. Evelyn Irene Southam, July 29, 1951; children: Brien J., Susan M., Leslie A., Jerome T. Student U. San Francisco, 1949. CLU. Ptnr. Affiliated-Gen. Ins. Adjusters, Santa Rosa, Calif., 1949-54; agt. Lincoln Nat. Life Ins. Co., Santa Rosa, 1954-57, supr., 1957-59, gen. agt., 1959-74; pres. Thomas J. Farrell & Assos., 1974-76, 7 Flags Ins. Mktg. Corp., 1976-81, Farrell-Dranginis & Assocs., 1981-88; pres., bd. dirs. Lincoln Nat. Bank, Santa Rosa, San Rafael. Pres. Redwood Empire Estate Planning Council, 1981-82, Sonoma County Council for Retarded Children, 1956-59, Sonoma County Assn. for Retarded Citizens, City Santa Rosa Traffic and Parking Commn., 1963; specialist State of Calif. Dept. Devel. Svcs., 1990—. del. Calif. State Conf. Small Bus., 1980; mem. Santa Rosa City Schs. Compensatory Edn. Adv. Bd.; bd. dirs. Santa Rosa City Schs. Consumer Edn. Adv. Bd.; pres., nat. dir. United Cerebral Palsy Assn., 1954-55; nat. coord. C. of C.-Rotary Symposia on Employment of People with Disabilities, 1985-87; v.p. Vigil Light, Inc.; chmn. bd. dirs. Nat. Barrier Awareness for People with Disabilities Found., Inc.; pres. Commn. on Emoloyment of People with Disabilities, 1986-92; mem. Pres.'s Com. on Mental Retardation, 1982-86; chmn. Santa Rosa Community Relations Com., 1973-76; pres. Sonoma County Young Reps., 1953; past bd. dirs. Sonoma County Fair and Expn., Inc.; bd. dirs. Sonoma County Family Service Agy., Eldridge Found., North Bay Regional Ctr. for Developmentally Disabled; trustee Sonoma State Hosp. for Mentally Retarded. Recipient cert. Nat. Assn. Retarded Children, 1962, Region 9 U.S. HHS Community Service award, 1985, Sonoma County Vendor's Human Service award, 1986, Individual Achievement award Community Affirmative Action Forum of Sonoma County, 1986. Mem. Nat. Assn. Life Underwriters, Redwood Empire Assn. CLU's (pres. 1974—), Japanese-Am. Citizens League, Jaycees (Outstanding Young Man of Year 1961, v.p. 1955), Santa Rosa C. of C. (bd. dirs. 1974-75), Calif. PTA (hon. life). Lodge: Rotary. Home: 963 Wyoming Dr Santa Rosa CA 95405-7342

FARRELL, WILLIAM EDGAR, sales executive, infosystems specialist, management consultant; b. Jeanette, Pa., Mar. 13, 1937; s. Arthur Richard and Lelia (Ryder) F.; m. Sara Lynnette Swing, Aug. 20, 1960, children: Wendy J., Tracy L., Rebecca J. BS in Edn., Pa. State U., 1959. Location mgr. IBM Corp., Dover, Del., 1969-72; corp. lobbyist IBM Corp., Washington, 1972-74, planning cons., 1974-78, nat. mktg. mgr., 1978-80, exec. asst., 1980-81; account exec. IBM Corp., Denver, 1981-87, policy exec., 1987-91; pres., CEO Weatherall Co., Inc., Englewood, Colo., 1993—; CFO Wide Horizon, Inc., Denver, 1987-92, chmn. bd. trustees, 1989-92; pres. Exec. Mgmt. Cons., 1987—; sec.-treas., bd. dirs. Electronic Shoe Enterprises Inc., 1991—; apptd. by gov. Colo. Info. Mgmt. Commn., 1992—; bd. dirs. Energaire Corp. Founding mem. River Falls Community Assn., Potomac, Md., 1975; first reader First Ch. of Christ Scientist, Chevy Chase, Md., 1976-80; chmn. Amigo's De Ser; bd. dirs. Rocky Mountain Ser, 1991-92. Recipient Outstanding Contbn. award IBM Corp., 1968. Republican.

FARRER, CLAIRE ANNE RAFFERTY, anthropologist, folklorist, educator; b. N.Y.C., Dec. 26, 1936; d. Francis Michael and Clara Anna (Guerra) Rafferty; 1 child, Suzanne Claire. BA in Anthropology, U. Calif., Berkeley, 1970; MA in Anthropology and Folklore, U. Tex., 1974, PhD in Anthropology and Folklore, 1977. Various positions, 1953-73; fellow Whitney M. Young Jr. Meml. Found., N.Y.C., 1974-75; arts specialist, grant adminstr. Nat. Endowment for Arts, Washington, 1976-77; Weatherhead resident fellow Sch. Am. Research, Santa Fe, 1977-78; asst. prof. anthropology U. Ill., Urbana, 1978-85; assoc. prof., coord. applied anthropology Calif. State U., Chico, 1985-89, prof., 1989—; dir. Multicultural and Gender Studies, 1994; cons. in field, 1974—; mem. film and video adv. panel Ill. Arts Coun., 1980-82; mem. Ill. Humanities Coun., 1980-82; vis. prof. U. Ghent, Belgium, spring 1990. Author: Living Life's Circle: Mescalero Apache Cosmovision, 1991, Play and Inter-Ethnic Communication, 1991, Thunder Rides a Black Horse: Mescalero Apaches and the Mythic Present, 1994; co-founder, co-editor Folklore Women's Communication, 1972; editor spl. issue Jour. Am. Folklore, 1975, 1st rev. edit., 1986; co-editor: Forms of Play of Native North Americans, 1979, Earth and Sky: Visions of the Cosmos in Native North American Folklore, 1991; contbr. numerous articles to profl. jours., mags. and newspapers, chpts. to books. Recipient numerous awards, fellowships and grants. Fellow Am. Anthrop. Assn., Royal Anthrop. Inst. (U.K.), Am. Astronomy Assn. (History divsn.); mem. Am. Ethnol. Soc., Am. Folklore Soc., Am. Soc. Ethnohistory. Mem. Soc. of Friends. Office: Calif State U Dept Anthropology Butte 311 Chico CA 95929-0400

FARRIMOND, GEORGE FRANCIS, JR., management educator; b. Peerless, Utah, Sept. 23, 1932; s. George Francis Sr. and Ruth (Howard) F.; m. Polly Ann Fowler, Mar. 21, 1988; children: George Kenneth, Ronald Kay, Carrie Frances, Holly Jean. BS, U. Utah, 1955; MBA, U. Mo., 1968; PhD, Portland State U., 1989. Cert. profl. contracts mgr. Enlisted USAF, 1955, advanced through grades to lt. col., 1971; master navigator USAF, various locations, 1955-71; flight commdr. 360th tactical elec. war squadron USAF, Saigon, Socialist Republic of Vietnam, 1971-72; chief procurement ops. USAF, Wright-Patterson AFB, Ohio, 1972-73, chief pricing ops. div., 1973-76; ret. USAF, 1976; asst. prof. bus. So. Oreg. State Coll., Ashland, 1976-82, assoc. prof., 1982-89, prof., 1989—; cons. small bus., Jackson County, Oreg., 1976-95; cons. Japanese mgmt., Jackson County, 1981-94; facilitated decision making body for econ. devel. in So. Oreg., 1995. Author: (computer program) Spanish Verb Conjugation, 1980, (workbook) Pricing Techniques, 1983. Chmn. Wright-Patterson AFB div United Fund, 1973-76; little league coach various teams, Ark. and Mo., 1963-71; Sunday Sch. tchr. Ch. of Latter-day Saints, various states. Decorated Disting. Flying Cross, 5 Air medals; Minuteman Ednl. scholar Air Force Inst. Tech., 1964, Education with Industry scholar Air Force Inst. Tech., 1970. Mem. Am. Prodn. and Inventory Control Soc. (v.p. edn. com. 1982-84), Prodn. Ops. Mgmt. Soc., Cascade Systems Soc., Air Force Soc., Soc. Japanese Studies, Beta Gamma Sigma. Republican. Home: 550 Carmen Rd Talent OR 97540-9708 Office: So Oreg State Coll Sch Bus 1250 Siskiyou Blvd Ashland OR 97520-5010

FARRIS, JEROME, federal judge; b. Birmingham, Ala., Mar. 4, 1930; s. William J. and Elizabeth (White) F.; widower; children: Juli Elizabeth, Janelle Marie. B.S., Morehouse Coll., 1951, LL.D., 1978; M.S.W., Atlanta U., 1955; J.D., U. Wash., 1958. Bar: Wash. 1958. Mem. firm Weyer, Roderick, Schroeter and Sterne, Seattle, 1958-59; ptnr. Weyer, Schroeter, Sterne & Farris and successor firms, Seattle, 1959-61, Schroeter & Farris, Seattle, 1961-63, Schroeter, Farris, Bangs & Horowitz, Seattle, 1963-65, Farris, Bangs & Horowitz, Seattle, 1965-69; judge Wash. State Ct. of Appeals, Seattle, 1969-79, U.S. Ct. of Appeals (9th cir.), Seattle, 1979—; lectr. U. Wash. Law Sch. and Sch. of Social Work, 1976—; mem. faculty Nat. Coll. State Judiciary, U. Nev., 1973; adv. bd. Nat. Ctr. for State Cts. Appellate Justice Project, 1978-81; founder First Union Nat. Bank, Seattle, 1965, dir., 1965-69. Del. The White House Conf. on Children and Youth, 1970; mem. King County (Wash.) Youth Commn., 1969-70; vis. com. U. Wash. Sch. Social Work, 1977-90; mem. King County Mental Health-Mental Retardation Bd., 1967-69; past bd. dirs. Seattle United Way; mem. Tyee Bd. Advisers, U. Wash., 1984—, bd. regents, 1985—, pres., 1990-91; trustee U. Law Sch. Found., 1978-84. With Signal Corps, U.S. Army, 1952-53. Recipient Disting. Service award Seattle Jaycees, 1965, Clayton Frost award, 1966. Fellow Am. Bar Found.; mem. ABA (exec. com. appellate judges conf. 1978-84, 87—, chmn. conf. 1982-83, del. jud. adminstrn. coun. 1987-88), Wash. Council on Crime and Delinquency (chmn. 1970-72), Am. Bar Found. (bd. dirs. 1987, exec. com. 1989—), State-Fed. Jud. Council of State of Wash. (vice chmn. 1977-78, chmn. 1983-87), Order of Coif (mem. law rev.), U. Wash. Law Sch. Office: US Ct Appeals 9th Cir 1030 US Courthouse 1010 5th Ave Seattle WA 98104-1130

FARRIS, LARRY DEAN, financial planner; b. Eugene, Oreg., Sept. 29, 1964; s. Grady Washington Jr. and Ardell Anna (Towne) F.; m. Brenda Lee Robison, Dec. 7, 1985; children: Spencer W., Benson V.R. BS in Mgmt., Linfield Coll., 1989. Co-owner, mgr. G & A Trucking, Springfield, Oreg., 1985-87; exec. v.p. Ardell, Inc., Springfield, 1987; exchange officer Banco Continental, Guayaquile, Ecuador, 1987; prin. Advantage Svcs., Springfield, 1989-94; sr. assoc. World Mktg. Alliance, Eugene, Oreg., 1993—. Missionary LDS Ch., Recife, Brazil, 1984-85; Republican candidate for Oreg. Ho. of Reps., 1988; precinct person Lane County Rep. Ctrl. Com., 1987-94; del. to Rep. Nat. Conv., 1988; chmn. Oregonians Against Crime for Lane County. Home: 3424 Virginia Ave Springfield OR 97478-6368

FARRIS, MARTIN THEODORE, economist, educator; b. Spokane, Wash., Nov. 5, 1925; s. Jacob B. and Edith S. (Gunderson) F.; m. Rhoda H. Harrington, Aug. 20, 1948 (dec. 1992); m. Marian B. Bolton, July 2, 1994; children: Christine A. Farris Zenobi, Diana Lynn, Elizabeth M. Theodore II. BA, U. Mont., 1949, MA, 1950; PhD, Ohio State U., 1957. Grad. asst. U. Mont., 1949-50; asst. in econs. Ohio State U., Columbus, 1950-51, asst. instr., 1953-55, instr., 1955-57; asst. prof. Ariz. State U., Tempe, 1957-59, assoc. prof., 1959-62, chmn. dept. econs., 1967-69, prof. transp. and pub. utility econs., 1962-72, prof. transp., 1972-88, Regents' prof., 1988-92, prof. emeritus, 1992—; vis. prof. U. Hawaii, 1969-70, vis. scholar, 1979. Author: (with Roy Sampson and David Shrock) Domestic Transportation: Practice, Theory and Policy, 6th edit., 1990; (with Roy Sampson) Public Utilities: Regulation, Management and Ownership, 1973; (with Paul McElhiney) Modern Transportation, 2nd edit., 1973; (with Grant Davis and Jack Holder) Management of Transportation Carriers, 1975; (with Forrest Harding) Passenger Transportation, 1976; (with Dave Bess) U.S. Maritime: History and Prospects, 1981, (with Stephen Happel) Modern Managerial Economics, 1987; contbr. articles to profl. jours. Served with U.S. Army, 1944-46, PTO. Decorated Philippine Liberation medal with bronze star; recipient Outstanding Faculty Achievement award Ariz. State U. Alumni Assn., 1978, Outstanding Faculty Researcher award Coll. Bus. Ariz. State U., 1982, Transp. and Logistics Educator of Yr. award Colo. Transp. Forum, 1991. Mem. Am. Econ. Assn. (Outstanding Contbn. to Transp. and Pub. Utilities award 1984), Western Econ. Assn. (bd. dirs. 1966-67), Assn. Transp. Practitioners, Transp. Rsch. Forum (Disting. Transp. Rschr. of Yr. award, 1994), Am. Soc. Transp. and Logistics (chief examiner 1961-73, Joseph C. Schleen award 1988), Coun. Logistics Mgmt., Traffic Clubs Internat., Traffic Club Phoenix (pres. 1960, Ariz. Transp. Man of Yr. 1992), Phi Kappa Phi, Omicron Delta Epsilon, Sigma Phi Epsilon, Delta Nu Alpha (Transp. Man of Yr. 1972), Beta Gamma Sigma. Episcopalian. Club: Traffic (Phoenix) (pres. 1960). Home: 9475 N 115th Pl Scottsdale AZ 85259-5855 Office: Ariz State U Coll Bud Adminstrn Tempe AZ 85287-4706

FARVER, ED, vintner; b. 1947. Engr. RCA, Cherry Hill, N.J., 1968-70; with Touche Ross, San Francisco, 1970-77; various positions Domaine Chandon, Inc., Yountville, Calif., 1977-92, pres., 1992—. Office: Domaine Chandon Inc 1 California Dr Yountville CA 94599*

FARWELL, HERMON WALDO, JR., parliamentarian, educator, former speech communication educator; b. Englewood, N.J., Oct. 24, 1918; s. Hermon Waldo and Elizabeth (Whitcomb) F.; A.B., Columbia, 1940; M.A., Pa. State U., 1964; m. Martha Carey Matthews, Jan. 3, 1942; children—Gardner Whitcomb, Linda Margaret (Mrs. Richard Hammer). Commd. USAF, 1940, advanced through grades to maj., various positions, 1940-66, ret., 1966; instr. aerial photography Escola Tecnica de Aviação, Brazil, 1946-48; faculty U. So. Colo., Pueblo, 1966-84, prof. emeritus speech communication, 1984—; cons., tchr. parliamentary procedure. Mem. Am. Inst. Parliamentarians (nat. dir. 1977-87), Commn. on Am. Parliamentary Practice (chmn. 1976), Ret. Officers Assn., Nat. Assn. Parliamentarians, Am. Legion, VFW. Author: The Majority Rules-A Manual of Procedure for Most Groups; Parliamentary Motions; Majority Motions; editor The Parliamentary Jour., 1981-87, 91-93. Home and Office: 65 Macalester Rd Pueblo CO 81001-2052

FASI, FRANK FRANCIS, state senator; b. East Hartford, Conn., Aug. 27, 1920. B.S., Trinity Coll., Hartford, 1942. Mem. Hawaii Senate, 1959—; Dem. mayor City and County of Honolulu, 1969-81, Rep. mayor, 1985-94; resigned, 1994. Mem. Dem. Nat. Com. for Hawaii, 1952-56; del. 2d Constl. Conv., 1968; mem.-at-large Honolulu City Coun., 1965-69. Served to capt. USMCR. Mem. Pacific-Asian Congress Municipalities (founder, past pres., exec. dir.), VFW (former comdr. Hawaii dept.), AFTRA (past v.p.). Office: 100 N Beretania St Ste 203 Honolulu HI 96817-4709

FATEMAN, RICHARD J., computer science educator, researcher; b. N.Y.C., Nov. 4, 1946; s. Sol C. and Adelaide (Lapidus) F.; m. Martha A. Nelson, June 15, 1968; children: Abigail, Johanna. BS in Physics, Union Coll., 1966; PhD in Applied Math., Harvard U., 1971. Instr., lectr. math. dept. MIT, Cambridge, Mass., 1971-74; scientist Lawrence Livermore/Berkeley (Calif.) Lab., summer 1974, 78; prof. U. Calif., Berkeley, 1974—, chair, prof., 1987-90; bd. dirs. Computing Rsch. Assn. Inc., Washington, Franz, Inc., Berkeley; bd. dirs., treas. Internat. Computer Sci. Inst., Berkeley, 1987-90. Contbr. numerous articles to profl. jours. Bd. dirs. Claremont/Elmwood Neighborhood Assn., Berkeley, 1990—. NSF grantee, and many others. Mem. Assn. for Computing Machinery (chair SIGSAM, 1983-85), Soc. for Indsl. and Applied Math. Home: 2965 Magnolia St Berkeley CA 94705-2329 Office: U Calif Computer Sci Divsn EECS Dept Berkeley CA 94720

FATHAUER, THEODORE FREDERICK, meteorologist; b. Oak Park, Ill., June 5, 1946; s. Arthur Theodore and Helen Ann (Mashek) F.; m. Mary Ann Neesan, Aug. 8, 1981. BA, U. Chgo., 1968. Cert. cons. meteorologist. Rsch. aide USDA No. Dev. Labs., Peoria, Ill., 1966, Cloud Physics Lab., Chgo., 1967; meteorologist Sta. WLW Radio/TV, Cin., 1967-68, Nat. Meteorol. Ctr., Washington, 1968-70, Nat. Weather Svc., Anchorage, 1970-80; meteorologist-in-charge Nat. Weather Svc., Fairbanks, Alaska, 1980—; instr. U. Alaska, Fairbanks, 1975-76, USCG aux., Fairbanks and Anchorage, 1974—. Contbr. articles to weather mags. and jours. Bd. dirs. Fairbanks Concert Assn., 1988—; bd. dirs., sec. Fairbanks Symphony Assn., 1994—; pres., bd. dirs. Friends U. Alaska Mus., 1993—. Recipient Outstanding Performance award Nat. Weather Service, 1972, 76, 83, 85, 86, 89, Fed. Employee of Yr. award, Fed. Exec. Assn., Anchorage, 1978. Fellow Am. Meterol. Soc. (TV and radio seals of approval), Royal Meteorol. Soc.; mem. AAAS, Am. Geophys. Union, Western Snow Conf., Arctic Inst., N.Am. Oceanography Soc., Coll. Fellows U. Alaska. Republican. Lutheran. Home: 1738 Chena Ridge Rd Fairbanks AK 99709-2612 Office: Nat Weather Svc Forecast Office 101 12th Ave Fairbanks AK 99701-6236

FAUCHIER, DAN R(AY), project management executive; b. Blackwell, Okla., Sept. 27, 1946; s. Wallace Munroe and Betty Lou F.; m. Sylvia Stephanie Chan Fauchier, Mar. 15, 1969; 1 child, Angele Calista Fauchier. BA cum laude, Southwestern Coll., 1964-68; student, Sch. Theology, Claremont, Calif., 1968-69, Claremont Grad. Sch., 1969-70. Lic. Bldg. Contractor, Calif., Coll. Pub. Adminstrn. life credential. Adminstr. Calif. Youth Authority, Paso Robles, Calif., 1969-76; tchr. Chaffey Coll., Rancho Cucamonga, Calif., 1971-74, Pacific Fin. Svcs., Beverly Hills, Calif., 1977-81; pres. Littlefields Corp., Corona del Mar, Calif., 1978-81; systems designer Teltrans Corp., L.A., 1982-85; project mgr. Pacific Sunset Builders, L.A., 1985-87, DW Devel., Fontana, Calif., 1987-90; owner Fauchier Group Builders, San Diego, Calif., 1988—; pres. Empire Bay Devel. Corp., San Bernardino, Calif., 1991-92; project mgr. White Systems L.A. Cen. Libr., L.A., 1993; dir. project mgmt. White Systems Divsn. Pinnacle Automation, Inc., San Diego, 1993—; founding dir. Neighborhood Restoration Project, San Bernardino, Calif., 1991-92. Contbr. cons.: President's Commission on Criminal Justice, 1972; co-author: Consumer Credit, 1984. Deputy Registrar Voters San Bernardino, Calif., 1975; mem. Skid Row Mental Health Adv. Bd., L.A., 1986, Chaffey Coll. Adv. Bd. Rancho Cucamonga, Calif., 1991-95, chmn. Bus. Security Alliance, San Bernardino, Calif., 1992. Named Nat. fellow Woodrow Wilson Fellowship, Princeton, N.J., 1968-69; recipient Full Grad. scholarship State of Calif., Claremont, 1969. Mem. Self-Realization Fellowship, Habitat for Humanity, Internat. Platform Assn., Inst. for Comty. Econ., Homeless Coalition, People for Ethical Treatment of Animals, Rainforest Alliance. Home: 9921 Carmel Mountain Rd San Diego CA 92129-2813 Office: 30 Boright Ave Kenilworth NJ 07033-1015 also: 4104 Sorrento Valley Blvd San Diego CA 92121-1407

FAULCONER, KAY ANNE, communications executive, dean; b. Shelbyville, Ind., Aug. 19, 1945; d. Clark Jacks and Charlotte (Tindall) Keenan; children: Kevin Lee, Melissa Lynne. BA in English, Calif. State U., Northridge, 1968; MBA, Pepperdine U., 1975, MA in Comm., 1976; EdD in Higher Edn., U. So. Calif., 1993. Pres., Kay Faulconer & Assocs., Oxnard, Calif., 1977—; instr. Oxnard Coll., U. LaVerne; dean, econ. and cmty. devel., Ventura (Calif.) Coll., 1994—. Former pres., founder Oxnard Friends of Libr.; former exec. bd. Ventura County March of Dimes; mem. PTA; officer, bd. dirs. Oxnard Girls Club. Named Businesswoman of Yr., Ventura Bus. and Profl. Women's Club, 1976; Woman of Achievement, Oxnard Bus. and Profl. Women's Club, 1973, recipient Career Woman award, 1974.Mem. Am. Soc. Tng. and Devel., Am. Assn. Women in Community and Jr. Colls. (Leaders for 80's program), Ventura County Profl. Women's Network. Club: Oxnard Jr. Monday (past pres., hon. life). Home and Office: PO Box 5643 Oxnard CA 93031-5643

FAULCONER, THOMAS PLEASANT, aircraft and small ships consultant, retired engineering executive; b. San Diego, Apr. 7, 1912; s. Thomas Nichols and Margaret (Adams) F.; B.S. in M.E., U. Calif., 1940; m. Barbara Dauchy, May 1, 1936 (dec.); m. Lillian Mathis, Feb. 14, 1965; children: Marion Dauchy, Katharine, Ann. Engr., Consol. Aircraft Corp., San Diego, 1936-38, engr. charge landing gear design, 1940-41, dir. edn., 1941-43, asst. dir. indsl. relations, 1943-46, asst. chief engr. flying automobile, 1946-49; mgr. indsl. relations Solar Aircraft Corp., San Diego, 1949-53; pres. Jet Air Engring. Corp., San Diego, 1953-55; mil. relations rep. Convair div. Gen. Dynamics Corp., 1958-59; pres Rick-Faulconer Engring. Corp., 1957-59, Thomas Faulconer Co., Inc., 1959-71, Geo. E. Barney Co., Inc., San Diego, 1959-62; Faulconer Bros. Inc., 1962-69; owner, licensor Caliputer Engring. & Sci. Instruments Co., 1962-69; cons. on aircraft and small ships, 1984—. Mem. engring. adv. council U. Calif., 1946-70. Served as lt. USCGR, 1943-45. Asso. fellow AIAA; mem. San Diego C. of C. (edn. and aviation com. 1946-47), San Diego County Industries Assn. (dir. 1946-48), San Diego Maritime Mus., U.S. Naval Inst., Mensa. Clubs: San Diego Yacht, Rotary of Point Loma (dir. 1946-56, pres. 1954). Author: Introduction to Aircraft Design; How to Make Money in California Real Estate, 1962; A New Concept of the Theory of Virtual Mass; High Altitude, High Speed Interceptor Study; FLAUNT—Fleet Air Ultra Naval Transport Harrier Carrier, 1984; editor, illustrator: Preparing for Aviation; prodr. of various videotapes; contbr. to tech. mags., profl. jours.; patentee sliderule, caliper, traffic folding barrier system, sailing yacht leeway reducing keel. Home and Office: 1354 Clove St San Diego CA 92106-2560

FAULKNER, DEXTER HAROLD, magazine publishing executive, editor; b. Grand Island, Nebr., Sept. 10, 1937; s. Jack L. and Wanetta May (Howland) F.; student U. Calif.-Fresno, 1956-58, Ambassador Coll., 1958-60; m. Shirley Ann Hume, Jan. 11, 1959; children: Nathan Timothy, Matthew Benjamin. Ordained minister Worldwide Ch. of God. European Bur. chief, 1990-93; exec. editor Plain Truth Mag; editor Good News mag., Youth/90 mag. and Worldwide News-Tabloid. Internat. div. Ambassador Coll., Sydney, Australia, 1960-66, news rsch. asst. dir. Ambassador Coll. Editorial, Pasadena, Calif., 1966-71, regional editor Plain Truth mag., Washington, 1971-75, asst. mng. editor, Pasadena, 1975-78, mng. editor, 1980-82, exec. editor, 1982-90, mng. editor Good News mag., Worldwide News-Tabloid, 1978-85, editor, 1986-90; mng. editor Youth/90 mag., 1981-85, editor, 1986-90; assoc. pastor Kansas City, Topeka, Kans.; instr. mass communications Ambassador Coll., 1980-90; columnist Just One More Thing . . . Mem. Inst.

Journalists (London), Profl. Photographers Am. Inc., Bur. Freelance Photographers (London), Nat. Press Club, World Affairs Council (Los Angeles), The Fgn. Press Assn. (London), Internat. Assn. Bus. Communicators, Nat. Press Photographers Assn., Am. Mgmt. Assn., Sigma Delta Chi, Rotary Internat. Mem. Worldwide Ch. God. Contbr. articles, photos on internat. relations, social issues to Plain Truth mag., Good News mag., Worldwide News Publs. Club: Commonwealth of Calif. Home: 7859 Wentworth St Sunland CA 91040-2201 Office: Plain Truth Mag 300 W Green St Pasadena CA 91129-0001

FAULKNER, SEWELL FORD, real estate executive; b. Keene, N.H., Sept. 25, 1924; s. John Charles and Hazel Helen (Ford) F.; AB, Harvard, 1949; MBA, 1951; m. June Dayton Finn, Jan. 10, 1951 (div.); children: Patricia Anne, Bradford William, Sandra Ford, Jonathan Dayton, Winthrop Sewell; m. Constance Mae Durvin, Mar. 15, 1969 (div.); children: Sarah Elizabeth, Elizabeth Jane. Product mgr. Congoleum Nairn, Inc., Kearny, N.J., 1951-55; salesman, broker, chmn., pres. Jack White Co. real estate, Anchorage, 1956-86; chmn. Faulkner, Inc.; chmn. Mem. Anchorage City Council, 1962-65, Greater Anchorage Area Borough Assembly, 1964-65, Anchorage Area Charter Commn., 1969-70. Pres., Alaska World Affairs Council, 1967-68; treas. Alyeska Property Owners, Inc., 1973-75, pres., 1977-78; pres. Downtown Anchorage Assn., 1974-75; mem. Girdwood Bd. Suprs. Served with USAAF, 1943-45. Mem. Anchorage Area C. of C. (dir. 1973-74), Alaska Notch Club. Office: Faulkner Real Estate 604 K St Anchorage AK 99501-3329

FAULSTICH, PAUL EVAN, environmental studies educator, researcher; b. Arcadia, Calif., Aug. 11, 1957; s. Raymond E. and Genevieve (Wozniak) F.; m. Maslin Susanne Faulstich, Jul. 14, 1986; children: Hanna Justine, Karina Genevieve. BA, Pitzer Coll., 1979; MA, Stanford U., 1982; PhD, U. Hawaii, 1990. Instr. Claremont (Calif.) Collegiate Sch., 1981; tchr. Alhambra (Calif.) Sch. Dist., 1982-83; asst. curator anthropology Southwest Mus., L.A., 1984-86; degree assoc. East-West Cen., Honolulu, 1987-90; asst. prof. Pitzer Coll., Claremont, 1991; adj. prof. Lindfield Coll., McMinnville, Oreg., 1991-92; curator of Native Am. Art Portland Art Mus., Portland, 1992-93; prof. Pitzer Coll., Claremont, 1993—; cons. Eco-Ethos Consulting, Honolulu, 1989-90; correspondent Wild Earth Jour., Richmond, Vt., 1990—; editorial bd. Rock Art Rsch., Melbourne, Australia, 1986—, com. mem. Unesco Internat. Coun. on Mus., Washington, 1986—. Author: Time and Space: Dating and Spatial Considerating in Rock Art Research, 1993, Spirits on the Rock, 1986, A Guide to Claremont Architecture, 1977. Steering com. Aloha Aina Action Congress, Honolulu, 1990; con. Hawaii Cmty. Found., 1990; grassroots orgn. O'Ahu Rainforest Action Group, Honolulu, 1988-91; conservation com. rep. Am. Rock Art Research Assn., 1992-93. Thomas J. Watson fellowship Thomas J. Watson Found., Providence, R.I., 1979-80; Rsch. award Kampulan Kebudayaan Malaysia, Kuala Lumpur, Malaysia, 1984; Am. Cultural Specialist U.S. Info. Agency, Washington, 1992. Mem. Australian Rock Art Rsch. Assn. (founding, grant 1988), Am. Rock Art Rsch. Assn. (Essay award 1983), Am. Anthropological Assn., Am. Assn. Mus., Coun. on Mus. Anthropology, Coll. Art Assn. Office: Pitzer Coll 1070 N Mills Ave Claremont CA 91711-3908

FAUS, RICHARD DUANE, lawyer; b. July 18, 1947; s. Reo Rae and Mildred Jerauld Faus; m. Linda Westlund, Nov. 25, 1976; children: Evert Arthur, Matthew Reo, Robert Richard. BA, Calif. State Coll., Fullerton, 1969; postgrad., U. Hawaii, 1969-70; JD, Willamette U., 1974. Bar: Oreg., U.S. Supreme Ct., U.S. Dist. Ct. Oreg., Supreme Ct. of Fed. States of Micronesia, High Ct. the Trust Territory of the Pacific Islands. Legal rschr., 1971-74; staff atty., dir. litigation 6th Jud. Dist. Legal Aide Soc., Pendleton, Oreg., 1975; legal counsel, criminal justice planner East Ctrl. Oreg. Assn. Counties, 1976-77; pvt. practice law Sutherlin, Oreg., 1977-78; intake counselor, atty. Dougals County Juvenile Dept., Roseburg, Oreg., 1978-80; city atty. City of Newberg, Oreg., 1980-86; atty. gen., chief divsn. law, asst. atty. gen. Nat. Govt. Federated States of Micronesia, Truk and Pohnpei, 1986-89; legal counsel Bd. Edn. Pub. Sch. System Commonwealth North Mariana Islands, Saipan, 1989-90; county counsel, planning dir. Baker County, Oreg., 1990-91; asst. city atty. City of Gresham, Oreg., 1991—. Served with U.S. Army, 1970-71. Mem. Oreg. State Bar Assn., Oreg. City Attys. Assn. Office: City of Gresham 515 NE Roberts Ave Gresham OR 97030-7336

FAUSCH, KURT DANIEL, fisheries ecology educator; b. Crookston, Minn., Jan. 17, 1955; s. Homer David and Guinevere Jean (Smythe) F.; m. Deborah Anne Eisenhauer, Dec. 20, 1975; children: Emily Rebecca, Benjamin Thomas. BS in Zoology, U. Minn., Duluth, 1976; MS in Fisheries and Wildlife, Mich. State U., 1978, PhD in Fisheries and Wildlife, 1981. Postdoctoral fellow U. Ill., Champaign, 1981-82; asst. prof. fisheries biology Colo. State U., Ft. Collins, 1982-87, assoc. prof., 1987-92; prof. Colo. State U., 1992—, chmn. fishery biology major, 1991-93, 95—; vis. assoc. prof. U. B.C., 1990; vis. rsch. fellow Japanese Soc. for Promotion of Sci., 1994. Contbr. articles to profl. jours. Mem. AAAS, Am. Fisheries Soc. (assoc. editor 1988-90, Albert S. Hazzard award 1982), Ecol. Soc. Am., Soc. Conservation Biology, Am. Soc. Ichthyologists and Herpetologists, Japanese Soc. Ichthyology, Sigma Xi, Gamma Sigma Delta. Office: Colo State U Dept Fishery & Wildlife Biology Fort Collins CO 80523

FAUSKIN, GARY NEALE, pediatrician; b. Fargo, N.D., Dec. 11, 1931; s. Arthur Oliver and Laurette Aretta (Kruger) F.; m. Elizabeth Nevedo (div.); children: Michael, James, Laura, Jean Eric; m. Lana Lea Halstead; 1 child, Jeffrey Jon. BS in Chemistry, N.D. State Coll., 1952; BS in Medicine, U. N.D., 1958; MD, U. Tex., 1960. Control chemist Montrose Chem. Corp., Torrance, Calif., 1953-54; intern Rotating Gen. Cedars Lebanon Hosp., L.A., 1960-61; pediatric resident Cedars of Lebanon Hosp., L.A., 1961-63; pvt. practice pediatrics El Cajon, Calif., 1963—; chmn. infection control com. Valley Med. Ctr., El Cajon; mem. dept. pediatrics, spkrs. bur. Grossmont Dist. Hosp., La Mesa, Calif.; mem. dept. pediatrics, pharmacy and therapeutics com. Alvarado Hosp. Med. Ctr., San Diego; clin. asst. prof. internal medicine and pediatrics Coll. Osteo. Medicine of the Pacific, Pomona, Calif.; asst. clin. prof. dept. pediatrics Harbor UCLA Med. Ctr., Torrance, 1966-85, U. Calif. San Diego; presenter and cons. in field; others. Contbr. articles to profl. jours. With USAF, 1954-56. Mem. Mem. Am. Acad. Pediatrics (chairperson com. on hosp. care dist. 9 Calif. chpt. 3), Soc. for Ear, Nose and Throat Advances in Children, Calif. Med. Soc., L.A. Pediatric Soc., San Diego County Med. Soc., German Am. Soc. San Diego (sec. fin. com. 1988—). Office: 1662 E Main Street 319 El Cajon CA 92021

FAUTSKO, TIMOTHY F., national court management consultant; b. Canton, Ohio, Dec. 27, 1945; s. Frank F. and Helen E. (Gozdan) F.; m. Marianne O'Carroll; children: T. Matthew, David F. BA in English and Bus. Adminstrn., Walsh Coll., 1967; MA in Human Services Adminstrn., U. Colo., 1972. Nat. Vista Programs, Washington, 1967-70; nat. tng. cons. Nat. Info. Ctr. on Volunteerism, Boulder, Colo., 1972-76; judicial dist. adminstr. State of Colo., 1976-92; sr. staff Nat. Ctr. for State Cts., 1993—, mediator, 1993—; instr. Colo. Mountain Coll., Regis Univ., Glenwood Springs, Aspen, Colo., 1980—. Co-author: Volunteer Programs in Prevention/Diversion, 1973, 2d rev. edit., 1978, Solving Problems in Meetings, 1981, QUID-How You Can Make the Best Decisions of Your Life, 1978, Como Tomar las Mejores Deciones de Su Vida, 1985. HEW scholar, U. Colo., Boulder, 1971-72; recipient Cert. Appreciation Office of Mayor, Denver, 1978, Outstanding Alumni award Walsh Coll., 1987, Hon. Svc. award Colo. Supreme Ct., 1990. Mem. Nat. Assn. Ct. Mgmt. Office: Nat Ctr for State Cts 1331 E 17th Ave Ste 402 Denver CO 80218-1526

FAVELL, GENE HUNTER, museum director; b. May 2, 1926; s. Eugene George and Ruth (Bernard) F.; m. Winifred Carol Lamm, June 19, 1949; children: Alice, Janet, Doug, Carol, Ann, Mark. BA in Econs., Stanford U.; postgrad., U. Ore. Owner Favell Mus. of Western Art & Indian Artifacts, Klamath Falls, Ore., 1972—. Co-founder Little League Baseball, Klamath Falls, pres. 1958-59; trustee Freedo s Found.; bd. dirs. Ore. Advocates for the Arts, 1988-89. Served in U.S. Navy, 1944-47. Recipient disting. svc. award, young man of yr. award Klamath Falls Jr. C. of C., 1960, Klamath County Retailer of Yr. Klamath Falls C. of C., 1990. Mem. Kiwanis Internat. (club pres. 1960, lt. gov. 1962, dist. com. chmn., gov. Pacific Northwest Dist. 1966, chmn. Internat. com. on resolutions 1967, internat. trustee 1967, internat. found. trustee 1969-71, 73-77), Elks, Masons, Shriners. Office: Favell Mus 125 W Main St Klamath Falls OR 97601-4287

FAVRE, JUNE MARIE, actress, singer; b. Clay County, Kans., June 14, 1937; d. Riley Otto and Edythe May (Constable) Woellhof; m. Joseph Jean Favre, Jan. 16, 1957 (dec. Jan. 1988). Cert. respiratory therapist. Owner N.Y. Connection, Denver, 1979-92; event coord. Colo. Contemporary Dance, Denver, 1993; exec. dir. Joey Favre Humanities Ctr., Denver, 1988—; guest artist Met. State Coll., Denver, 1977, N.Mex. State Theatre, Raton, 1974; founder, actor The Third Eye Theatre, Denver, 1966-78; cons. First Night Colo., Denver, 1994; publicist Gypsy Prodns., Denver, 1992, 93. Author (children's theatre) A Christmas Carol, 1994. Recipient Writing award Fla. Citrus Dept., 1991, associateship Rocky Mountain Women's Inst., 1995. Recipient Writing award Fla. Citrus Dept., 1991, Rocky Mountain Women's Inst. Associateship award, 1995. Mem. AFTRA, The Friday Club.

FAW, DUANE LESLIE, retired military officer, law educator, lay worker, author; b. Loraine, Tex., July 7, 1920; s. Alfred Leslie and Noma Leigh (Elliott) F.; m. Lucile Elizabeth Craps, Feb. 20, 1943; children: Cheryl Leigh, Bruce Duane, Debra Leoma, Melanie Loraine. Student, N. Tex. State Coll., 1937-41; J.D., Columbia U., 1947. Bar: Tex. 1948, D.C. 1969, U.S. Supreme Ct. 1969. Commd. 2d lt. USMC, 1942, advanced through grades to brig. gen., 1969, bn. comdr., 1959-61, staff judge adv., 1961-64, policy analyst Marine Hdqrs., 1964-67, dep. chief of staff III Marine Amphibious Force, 1967-68, judge Navy Ct. Mil. Rev., 1968-69; dir. Judge Ad. Div. Marine Hdqrs. USMC, Washington, 1969-71; ret. USMC, 1971; prof. law Pepperdine U. Sch. Law, Malibu, Calif., 1971-85; Bible tchr. So. Presbyn. Ch., Denton, Tex., 1948-50, Camp Pendleton, N.C., 1959-61, Quantico. Va., 1962-63, United Meth. Ch., Arlington, Va., 1963-71; Bible tchr. , elder Presbyn. Ch., Van Horn, Tex., 1950-52; lay speaker, Bible tchr. United Meth. Ch., Tustin, Malibu, and Laguna Hills, Calif., 1972—, lay mem. ann. conf., 1974-81, 91, 95. Author: The Paramony, 1986, The Joy of Spiritual Discovery, 1995; co-author: The Military in American Society, 1978. Gen. councilor URANTIA Brotherhood, 1979-88, gen. councilor of FELLOWSHIP, 1991-94; bd. dirs. Jesusonian Found., Boulder, 1988—, Touch for Health Found., Pasadena, Calif., 1988-94. Decorated Air medal with gold star, Navy Commendation medal with gold star, Legion of Merit with combat V with gold star; UN Cross of Gallantry with gold star; VN Honor medal 1st class. Mem. ABA (adv. com. mil. justice 1969-71, adv. com. lawyers in Armed Forces 1969-71), Fed. Bar Assn. (council), Judge Advs. Assn., Am. Acad. Religion, Soc. Bibl. Lit. Club: Masons. Home: 2399-3A Via Mariposa West Laguna Hills CA 92653

FAWCETT, CHARLES WINTON, lawyer; b. Long Beach, Calif., May 26, 1946; s. Phillip Nimmons and Beatrice Stricker (Winton) F.; m. Kathleen Gloria Mayes, Dec. 15, 1975; children: Reid Charles, Tracie Diane, Ryan Mayes, Marni Taylor. BA, U. Calif., Santa Barbara, 1968; JD, U. Calif., Berkeley, 1971. Bar: Idaho 1971, Wash. 1975, U.S. Tax Ct. 1982. Staff atty. Idaho Legal Aid Services, Lewiston, 1971-73, Caldwell, 1973-74; adminstrv. law judge State of Wash., Seattle, 1974-76; asst. atty. gen. State of Idaho, Boise, 1976-77; sr. ptnr. Skinner, Fawcett and Mauk, Boise, 1977—. Contbr. articles to law jour. Mem. Idaho Bar Assn., Boise Bar Assn., Nat. Assn. Bond Lawyers, Comml. Law League Am. Office: Skinner Fawcett and Mauk PO Box 700 Boise ID 83701-0700

FAXON, THOMAS BAKER, lawyer; b. Des Moines, Oct. 15, 1924; s. Ralph Henry and Prue (Baker) F.; m. Virginia Webb Johnson, Sept. 8, 1949; children: Rebecca Webb Osgood, Thomas Baker Jr. BA, Princeton U., 1949; LLB, Harvard U., 1952. Bar: Colo. 1953. Asst. prof., asst. dir. Inst. Govt. U. N.C., Chapel Hill, 1952-53; assoc. Pershing, Bosworth, Dick & Dawson, Denver, 1953-57; ptnr. Dawson, Nagel, Sherman & Howard, Denver, 1957-84; of counsel Sherman & Howard, Denver, 1984-92; bd. trustees Colo. Legal Aid Found., Denver, 1984-91. Bd. dirs. Urban League Colo., Denver, 1964-67, Colo. chpt. UN Assn. of U.S.A., 1980-81, Recording for the Blind Colo., 1988-94; pres. bd. trustees 1st Unitarian Ch., Denver, 1960; mem. Denver Equality of Edn. Com., 1969. USAAF, 1943-46. Mem. Rocky Mountain Princeton Club, Harvard Law Sch. Assn. Colo. (pres. 1968), Cactus Club Denver. Democrat. Address: 830 Race St Denver CO 80206-3734

FAY, ABBOTT EASTMAN, history educator; b. Scottsbluff, Nebr., July 19, 1926; s. Abbott Eastman and Ethel (Lambert) F.; m. Joan D. Richardson, Nov. 26, 1953; children: Rand, Diana, Collin. BA, Colo. State Coll., 1949, MA, 1953; postgrad., U. Denver, 1961-63, Western State U., 1963. Tchr. Leadville (Colo.) Pub. Schs., 1950-52, elem. prin., 1952-54; prin. Leadville Jr. High Sch., 1954-55; pub. info. dir., instr. history Mesa Coll., Grand Junction, Colo., 1955-64; asst. prof. history Western State Coll., Gunnison, Colo., 1964-76, assoc. prof. history, 1976-82, assoc. prof. emeritus, 1982—; adj. faculty Adams State Coll., Alamosa, Colo., Mesa State Coll., Grand Junction, Colo., 1989—; propr. Mountaintop Books, Paonia, Colo.; bd. dirs. Colo. Assoc. Univ. Press; profl. spkr. in field; dir. hist. tours; columnist Valley Chronicle, Paonia, Best Times Beacon, Grand Junction, Colo., Guidelines, Denver. Author: Mountain Academia, 1968, Writing Good History Research Papers, 1980, Ski Tracks in the Rockies, 1984, Famous Coloradans, 1990, I Never Knew That About Colorado, 1993; playwright: Thunder Mountain Lives Tonight!; contbr. articles to profl. jours.; freelance writer popular mags. Founder, coordinator Nat. Energy Conservation Challenge; project reviewer NEH, Colo. Hist. Soc. Served with AUS, 1944-46. Named Top Prof. Western State Coll., 1969, 70, 71; fellow Hamline U. Inst. Asian Studies, 1975, 79. Mem. Western Writers Am., Rocky Mountain Social Sci. Assn. (sec. 1961-63), Am. Hist. Assn., Assn. Asian Studies, Western History Assn., Western State Coll. Alumni Assn. (pres. 1971-73), Internat. Platform Assn. Profl. Guides Assn. Am. (cert.), Rocky Mountain Guides Assn., Colo. Antiquarian Booksellers Assn., Am. Legion (Outstanding Historian award 1981), Phi Alpha Theta, Phi Kappa Delta, Delta Kappa Pi. Home: 1750 Hwy 133 Paonia CO 81428-9709

FAY, RICHARD JAMES, mechanical engineer, executive, educator; b. St. Joseph, Mo., Apr. 26, 1935; s. Frank James and Marie Jewell (Senger) F.; m. Marilyn Louise Kelsey, Dec. 22, 1962; BSME, U. Denver, 1959, MSME, 1970. Registered profl. engr., Colo., Nebr. Design engr. Denver Fire Clay Co., 1957-60; design, project engr. Silver Engring. Works, 1960-63; research engr., lectr. mech. engring. U. Denver, 1963-74, asst. prof. Colo. Sch. of Mines, 1974-75, founder, pres. Fay Engring. Corp., 1971—. Served with Colo. N.G., 1962. Mem. Soc. Automotive Engrs. (past chmn. Colo. sect.), ASME (past chmn. Colo. sect., past regional v.p.), La Societe des Ingenieurs de L'Automobile (France). Contbr. articles to profl. jours.; patentee in field. Office: 5201 E 48th Ave Denver CO 80216-5316

FAYAD, MIKE SAMIH, financial analyst; b. Sidon, Lebanon, Feb. 7, 1953; came to U.S., 1974; s. Samih Ali and Samia Abdul (Shuayb) F.; m. Maria Teresa Mojica, July 25, 1987. B of Elec. Engring., Am. U., 1974; M of Elec. Engring., U. So. Calif., 1976, MBA, 1984. Bus. adminstrn. trainee Elec. Constrn. Co., Wolver Hampton, England, 1973; trainer Westinghouse Corp., Jubail, Saudi Arabia, 1977; systems analyst IBM Corp., Riyadh, Saudi Arabia, 1978-81; product mktg. engr. Intel Corp., Santa Clara, Calif., 1983; mktg. mgr. SEAM Internat., Palos Verdes, Calif., 1985-86; coord. data entry dept. Webster Coll., L.A., 1988-89; mainframe specialist Andrew Corp., Torrance, 1990; sr. fin. analyst City of Hope, Duarte, 1990—; adj. faculty Nat. U., L.A., 1993-94; fin. cons. LifeCare Corp., Whittier, Calif., 1987; dir. Trader's Internat., L.A., 1991. Author of poems. Mem. Cedars, Agoura Hills, Calif., 1991, Internat. Bus. Assn., L.A., 1982; v.p. Gen. Knowledge Com., Beirut, 1974, HopeMasters, Durate, Calif., 1995. Mem. HBOC Users Group (speaker). Home: 3175 S Hoover St # 571 Los Angeles CA 90007-5320 Office: City of Hope 1500 E Duarte Rd Duarte CA 91010

FAY-SCHMIDT, PATRICIA ANN, paralegal; b. Waukegan, Ill., Dec. 25, 1941; d. John William and Agnes Alice (Semerad) Fay; m. Dennis A. Schmidt, Nov. 3, 1962 (div. Dec. 1987); children: Kristin Fay Schmidt, John Andrew Schmidt. Student, L.A. Pierce Coll., 1959-60, U. San Jose, 1960-62, Western State U. of Law, Fullerton, Calif., 1991-92. Cert. legal asst., Calif. Paralegal Rasner & Rasner, Costa Mesa, Calif., 1979-82; paralegal, adminstr. Law Offices of Manuel Ortega, Santa Ana, Calif., 1982-92; sabbatical, 1992-94; mem. editorial adv. bd. James Pub. Co., Costa Mesa, 1984-88. Contbg. author: Journal of the Citizen Ambassador Paralegal Delegation to the Soviet Union, 1990. Treas., Republican Women, Tustin, Calif., 1990-91; past regent, 1st vice regent, 2d vice regent NSDAR, Tustin, 1967—; docent Richard M. Nixon Libr. and Birthplace, 1993—, bd. dirs. Docent Guild, 1994—; docent Orange County Courthouse Mus., 1992-94. Mem. Orange County Paralegal Assn. (hospitality chair 1985-87). Roman Catholic. Home: 13571 Hewes Ave Santa Ana CA 92705-2215

FAZIO, VIC, congressman; b. Winchester, Mass., Oct. 11, 1942; m. Judy Kern; children: Dana Fazio, Anne Fazio, Kevin Kern, Kristie Kern. BA, Union Coll., Schenectady, 1965; postgrad., Calif. State U., Sacramento. Journalist, founder Calif. Jour.; congl. and legis. cons., 1966-75; mem. Calif. State Assembly, 1975-78; mem. 96th -103rd Congresses from Calif. 3rd Dist., 1979—; former chmn. Dem. Congl. Campaign Com.; chmn. Dem. caucus, house steering policy com.; ranking mem. House Oversight Com.; former chmn. Dem. Congl. Campaign Com.; ranking mem. legis. br. appropriations subcom., mem. appropriations subcom. energy and water; majority whip-at-large 96th-103rd Congress; also co-chmn. Fed. Govt. Svcs. Task Force 96th-101st Congresses, former chmn. bipartisan com. on ethics; former mem. Sacramento County Charter and Planning Commns. Bd. dirs. Asthma Allergy Found., Jr. Statesman, Nat. Italian-Am. Found. Coro Found. fellow; named Solar Congressman of Yr. Mem. Air Force Assn. Office: House Of Representatives Washington DC 20515*

FEARN, DEAN HENRY, statistics educator; b. Portland, Oreg., June 8, 1943; s. Clyde Henry Fearn and Sylvia Adele (Dahl) Christensen; m. Gloria June Wilber, Oct. 1, 1966; children: Neal, Justin. BS in Math., U. Wash., 1965; MA in Math., Western Wash. State U., 1967; PhD in Math., U. Calif., Davis, 1971. Teaching asst. U. Calif., Davis, 1967-71; sr. mathematician Aerojet-Gen., Rancho Cordova, Calif., 1969-70; prof. of stats. Calif. State U., Hayward, 1971—. Contbr. articles to profl. jours. Mem. Am. Statis. Assn. (pres. Calif. chpt. 1991-92), Inst. Math. Stats., Math. Assn. Am., Pi Mu Epsilon. Democrat. Lutheran. Home: 3255 Sunnybrook Ct Hayward CA 94541-3535 Office: Calif State U Dept Stats Hayward CA 94542

FEARON, LEE CHARLES, chemist; b. Tulsa, Nov. 22, 1938; s. Robert Earl and Ruth Belle (Strothers) F.; m. Wanda Sue Williams, Nov. 30, 1971. Student, Rensselaer Polytech. Inst., 1957-59; BS in Physics, Okla. State U., Stillwater, 1961, BA in Chemistry, 1962, MS in Analytical Chemistry, 1969. Rsch. chemist Houston process lab. Shell Oil Co., Deer Park, Tex., 1968-70; chief chemist Pollution Engring. Internat., Inc., Houston, 1970-76; rsch. chemist M-I Drilling Fluids Co., Houston, 1976-83; cons. chemist Profl. Engr. Assocs., Inc., Tulsa, 1983-84; chemist Anacon, Inc., Houston, 1984-85; scientist III Bionetics Corp., Rockville, Md., 1985-86; sr. chemist L.A. County Sanitation Dist., Whittier, Calif., 1986; chemist Quanterra-Sacramento, West Sacramento, Calif., 1986-87; consulting chemist Branham Industries, Inc., Conroe, Tex., 1987-89; adv. laboratorian EILS, QA sect. Wash. State Dept. Ecology, Manchester, 1989—; cons. chemist Terra-Kleen, Okmulgee, Okla., 1988-94, Excel Pacific, Inc., Camarillo, Calif., 1993—, U.S. Patent for Environ. Soil Remediation Tech., 1994. Patentee for environ. soil remediation tech., 1994. With U.S. Army, 1962-65. Fellow Am. Inst. Chemists; mem. AAAS, Am. Chem. Soc. Home: PO Box 514 Manchester WA 98353-0514 Office: PO Box 488 Manchester WA 98353-0488

FEAVER, GEORGE A., political science educator; b. Hamilton, Ont., Canada, May 12, 1937; came to U.S., July 4, 1967; s. Harold Lorne and Doris Davies (Senior) F.; m. Nancy Alice Poynter, June 12, 1963 (div. 1978); m. Ruth Helene Tubbesing, Mar. 8, 1986 (div. 1991); children: Catherine Fergusson, Noah George. B.A. with Honors, U. B.C., 1959; Ph.D., London Sch. of Econs., 1962. Asst. prof. Mt. Holyoke Coll., South Hadley, Mass., 1962-65; lectr., research assoc. London Sch. Econs. and Univ. Coll., London, 1965-67; assoc. prof. Georgetown U., Washington, 1967-68, Emory U., Atlanta, 1968-71; assoc. prof. U.B.C., Vancouver, B.C., Canada, 1971-74, prof., 1974—; vis. fellow Australian Nat. U., Canberra, 1987. Author: From Status to Contract, 1969; editor: Beatrice Webb's Our Partnership, 1975; editor: The Webbs in Asia: The 1911-12 Travel Diary, 1992; co-editor: Lives, Liberties and the Public Good, 1987; contbr. articles to profl. jours., books. Fellow Canada Council, 1970-71, 74-75, Am. Council Learned Socs., 1974-75, Social Scis. and Humanities Research Council of Canada, 1981-82, 86-91. Mem. Can. Polit. Sci. Assn., Am. Polit. Sci. Assn., Am. Soc. for Polit. and Legal Philosophy, Conf. for Study of Polit. Thought, Inst. Internat. de philosophie politique. Club: Travellers' (London). Home: 4776 W 7th Ave, Vancouver, BC Canada V6T 1C6 Office: Univ British Columbia, Dept Polit Sci, Vancouver, BC Canada V6T 1Z1

FEDAK, BARBARA KINGRY, technical center administrator; b. Hazleton, Pa., Feb. 7, 1939; d. Marvin Frederick and Ruth Anna (Wheeler) Siebel; m. Raymond F. Fedak, Mar. 27, 1993; children: Sean M., James Goldey. BA, Trenton State Coll., 1961; MEd, Lesley Coll., Cambridge, Mass., 1986. Registered respiratory therapist. Dept. dir. North Platte (Nebr.) Community Hosp., 1974-75; newborn coord. Children's Hosp., Denver, 1975-79; edn. coord. Rose Med. Ctr., Denver, 1979-81; program dir. respiratory tech. program Pickens Tech., Aurora, Colo., 1981-86; mktg. rep. Foster Med. Corp., Denver, 1986-87; staff therapist Porter Meml. Hosp., Denver, 1987-88; dir., br. mgr. Pediatric Svcs. Am., Denver, 1988-90; dir. clin. edn. Pickens Tech., Aurora, Colo., 1991, divsn. chair health occupations, 1991—; site evaluator Joint Rev. Com. for Respiratory Therapy Edn., Euless, Tex. Met. coun. mem. Am. Lung Assn., 1987-91. Mem. Am. Assn. Respiratory Care (edn. sect. program com. 1992-95, mem. abstract rev. com. 1993-95), Colo. Soc. Respiratory Care (dir. at large 1983-86, 90-92, sec. 1980-81, program com. 1982-92), Colo. Assn. Respiratory Educators (chair 1991—). Methodist. Home: 11478 S Marlborough St Parker CO 80134-7318 Office: Pickens Tech 500 Airport Blvd Aurora CO 80011

FEDERICI, TONY, state legislator, small business owner; b. St. Helens, Oreg., Mar. 21, 1937; s. Nickolas and Rose (Albrizio) F.; m. Nancy Alice Weeks, July 10, 1965; children: Nick, Catherine. BA, U. Oreg., 1963. Science instr. Salem Pub. Schs., Oreg., 1963-65; owner Tony's Shoes, St. Helens, 1965—; mem. Oreg. State Legislature, 1993—. City councilman City of St. Helens, 1980-88; port commr. Port of St. Helens, 1988-92. With U.S. Army, 1960-62. Mem. Western Ind. Shoe Enterprises (pres. 1979, chmn. 1980), St. Helens Lion Club (pres. 1972—). Democrat. Roman Catholic. Home: 59945 Sunrise Dr Saint Helens OR 97051-1163 Office: Tony's Shoes 1620 Columbia Blvd Saint Helens OR 97051-1729

FEDJE, LAURIE ANNE, special education educator; b. Grand Forks, N.D., July 30, 1955; d. Arthur Magel and Leila Eileen (Schmitt) Lund; m. Robert Olaf Fedje, Jan. 6, 1984; 1 child, James Leif. BS in Elem./Spl. Edn., U. N.D., 1977, MEd in Learning Disabilities, 1984. Spl. edn. tchr. Smith Lake (N.Mex.) Elem. Sch., 1977-78; resource tchr. Kasson-Mantorville High Sch., Kasson, Minn., 1978-80; spl. edn. tchr. Tse Bonito (N.Mex.) Elem. Sch., 1980-82; resource tchr. Gallup (N.Mex.) Middle Sch., 1982-83, Natrona County High Sch., Casper, Wyo., 1984-88; vocat. facilitator Gallup-McKinley County Schs., 1988-89; work study supr. Vocat. Learning Ctr., Casper, 1989-90; tchr. for emotionally disturbed Natrona County High Sch., Casper, 1990-91; resource tchr. Sagewood Elem. Sch., Casper, 1991—; lectr. in field; cons. Converse County Sch. Dist. #2, Glenrock, Wyo., 1990. Adv. bd. at-risk and spl. needs edn. com. U. N.Mex., Gallup br., 1988-89. Office: Sagewood Elementary Sch 2451 Shattuck Ave Casper WY 82601-5059

FEDJE, LORREEN ANN, dietitian; b. Minot, N.D., July 24, 1952; d. Henry and Thelma L. (Sivertson) F.; m. Ralf W. Palin, Dec. 27, 1975 (div. Oct. 1981). BS in Nutrition, N.D. State U., 1974. Intern U. Calif. Hosp., San Francisco, 1975; clin. dietitian Oreg. Health Sci. U., Portland, 1975-79; renal dietitian Good Samaritan Hosp., Portland, 1979-83, clin. dietitian mgr., 1983-84, asst. dir., 1984-87; renal dietitian mgr. Good Samaritan Dialysis Unit, Portland, 1987—. Co-author: Pocket Guide to Nutritional Assessment, 1993, Oregon Diabetic Exchange Booklet, 1994; nutrition editor (newspaper) Family Focus, 1990-92; co-editor Living Well on Dialysis. Mem. Oreg. Dietetic Assn. (chair quality assurance 1986), Oreg. Coun. Renal Nutrition (co-founder, sec., chair 1977), Portland Dietetic Assn. (treas. 1985), Coun. Renal Nutrition/Nat. Kidney Found. (rep. 1990-92, sec./treas. 1992-94, chair-elect 1994, chair 1995), Nat. Kidney Found. (pub. edn. com. chair 1993-95, bd. dirs. 1993-95). Office: Good Samaritan Dialysis Ctr 1015 NW 22nd Ave Portland OR 97210-3025

FEDORCHAK, TIMOTHY HILL, facility planning and program consulting executive; b. Lodi, Calif., Jan. 15, 1958; s. John and Betty Francis (Daugherty) F. Student, San Joaquin Delta Coll., 1976-77, U. Utah, 1977-78; BS in Urban Planning, Calif. State Poly. U., 1981. Pub. works technician

City of Lodi, Calif., 1979-80, planner, 1980-81; assoc. Steinmann, Grayson, Smylie, L.A., 1981-87; dir. Steinmann, Grayson, Smylie, Sacramento, 1987-89; prin. Daniel C. Smith & Assocs., Sacramento, 1989—; project mgr., cons. Facilities Master Plan, Maricopa County, Ariz., 1982, Corp. Yard Relocation Plan, Scottsdale, Ariz., 1983, Marin County Civic Ctr. Master Plan, San Rafael, Calif., 1984, San Joaquin Human Svcs. Facility Program, Stockton, Calif., 1985-86, over 50 other facility plans and program projects. Pres. Lodi History Hunters, 1972; univ. rep. Calif. State Poly. Univ., 1980-81. Mem. Am. Planning Assn. (charter), Am. Pub. Works Assn., Am. Jail Assn., Calif. State Poly. U. Planning Alumni Assn. (treas. 1986-88), Phi Eta Sigma. Democrat. Home: PO Box 1444 Sacramento CA 95812-1444 Office: Daniel C Smith & Assocs 2150 Capitol Ave Ste 210 Sacramento CA 95816-5721

FEDORE, RONALD J., telecommunications company executive; b. Bklyn., Feb. 19, 1948; s. Francis G. and Sylvia C. (Hornack) F.; m. Dorothy J. Cooke, Sept. 18, 1971; children: Craig, Carolyn, Christopher. BS in Physics, Drexel U., 1971. Sr. systems analyst Cir. F Industries, Trenton, N.J., 1971-74, Gould Inc., Langhorn, Pa., 1974-75; project analyst Catalytic Inc., Phila., 1975-79; mgr. mgmt. info. systems Siemens Info. System, Boca Raton, Fla., 1979-82, mgr. mgmt. info. system devel., 1982-86; project mgr. methods/procedures Tel Plus Comms. Co. div. Siemens, Boca Raton, Fla., 1986-91, mgr. bus. adminstrn., 1991-93; project mgr. Bus. Solutions Rolm, A Siemens Co., Santa Clara, Calif., 1993—; spl. events v.p. Employee Club, 1993—; mgr. comms. programs Siemens Rolm Communications, Inc., 1995—; export compliance ofcl. Siemens/Tel Plus, Boca Raton, 1986-93, mem. svc. com., 1984-93; rep. to various local charities. Creator, dir. Flamingo Strut parade, 1987-89. Mem. Boca Raton Cmty. Rels. Bd., 1989-91; candidate for Boca Raton City Coun., 1991; mem. site coun. Dublin (Calif.) H.S., 1993—; mem. parish coun. St. Raymond Ch., 1994—. Recipient Outstanding Leadership award, Boca Raton C. of C., 1989, Spl. Svc. cert. U.S. Atomic Energy Commn., 1968; named Person of Yr., Boca Raton C. of C., 1988. Home: 11897 W Vomac Rd Dublin CA 94568-1048 Office: ROLM 4900 Old Ironsides Dr Santa Clara CA 95054-1811

FEDRICK, C. RICHARD, food products executive; b. 1925. Chmn. Fedrick CR, Inc., Novato, Calif., 1960—; vice chmn. Synatt Corp., Tucson, Ariz., 1980—. Office: Sundt Corp 4101 E Irving Rd Tucson AZ 85726*

FEE, WILLARD EDWARD, JR., otolaryngologist; b. Portchester, N.Y., June 10, 1943; s. Willard E. and Jane Frances (Cromwell) F.; m. Caroline Fee, June 13, 1965; children: Heather, Adam. BS cum laude, U. San Francisco, 1965; MD magna cum laude, U. Colo., 1969. Intern Harbor Gen. Hosp., Torrance, Calif., 1969-70; resident in gen. surgery Wadsworth VA Hosp., L.A., 1970-71; resident in head and neck surgery UCLA Sch. Medicine, 1971-74; asst. prof. Stanford (Calif.) U. Med. Ctr., 1974-80, assoc. prof., chmn., 1980-86, prof., chmn. in otolaryngology, 1986—; dir. Am. Bd. of Otolaryngology, Houston, 1985—; chmn. med. sch. faculty senate Stanford U., 1992-94. Editl. bd. Archives in Otolaryngology, Chgo., 1984—; contbr. numerous articles to profl. jours. Mem. Collegium ORLAS-US (sec. 1994—), Paul H. Ward Soc., Inc. (pres. 1988-89), Am. Soc. for Head and Neck Surgery, Am. Acad. of Otolaryngology Head and Neck Surgery, Alpha Omega Alpha. Home: 27299 Ursula Ln Los Altos CA 94022-3222 Office: Stanford Univ Med Ctr Divn Otolaryngology Edwards R135 300 Pasteur Stanford CA 94305-5328

FEER, CHARLES LEWIS, lawyer, consultant; b. Bakersfield, Calif., Aug. 3, 1960; s. Kenneth L. and Ruth G. (Gilbreath) F.; m. Teri Lea Thorpe, Sept. 27, 1980 (dec. May 1993); 1 child, Candyce Anne. AA, Bakersfield Coll., 1981; BS, Western State U., 1987, JD, 1988; MPA, Calif. State U., Bakersfield, 1992. Bar: Calif. 1994. Asst. mgr. Thrifty Drug Corp., Bakersfield, 1980-82; counselor Kern County Probation Dept., Bakersfield, 1982-83; dep. sheriff Kern County Sheriff's Dept., Bakersfield, 1983-84; pvt. investigator S.W. Investigations, Bakersfield, 1984-88; law clk. Noriega & Alexander, Bakersfield, 1988, Rawson & Tafoya, Bakersfield, 1989; owner Pretrial Svcs., Bakersfield, 1989—; mng. ptnr. Strategic Planning Assocs., Bakersfield, 1990—; instr. Watterson Bus. Coll., Bakersfield, 1988-89. Candidate Kern High Sch. Dist. Trustees, Bakersfield, 1989. Recipient Am. Jurisprudence award, 1986, 87; named Outstanding Young Men of Am., 1988. Mem. Calif. Attys. for Criminal Justice, Nat. Assn. Criminal Def. Lawyers, Wilson Inst., U.S. Naval Inst. Republican. Methodist. Home: 4909 Stockdale Hwy # 227 Bakersfield CA 93309-2637

FEES, NANCY FARDELIUS, special education educator; b. Santa Monica, Calif., Mar. 25, 1950; d. Carl August and Dodi Emma (Hedenschau) Fardelius; m. Paul Rodger Fees, June 4, 1971; children: Evelyn Wyoming, Nelson August. BS, Mills Coll., 1971; MA in Edn., Idaho State U., 1975. Cert. tchr., Calif., Idaho, Wyo., R.I. Specialist curriculum mgmt. Barrington (R.I.) High Sch., 1975-81; coordinator learning skills ctr. Northwest Community Coll., Powell, Wyo., 1982-84, instr., 1985—; pres. Children's Resource Ctr., 1985-89, bd. dirs., 1983-89, 91—. Editor (with others) The Great Entertainer, 1984. Vol. Buffalo Bill Hist. Ctr., Cody, Wyo., 1981—; mem. Centennial Com., Cody, 1983; mem. parent's adv. com. Livingston Sch., 1989-92, chmn., 1991-92. Mem. Council Exceptional Children, Assn. Children with Learning Disabilities, Council Adminstrs. of Spl. Edn. Democrat. Episcopalian. Home: 1718 Wyoming Ave Cody WY 82414-3320

FEHLBERG, ROBERT ERICK, architect; b. Kalispell, Mont., Apr. 28, 1926; s. Otto Albert Erick and Mary Grace (Nelson) F.; m. LaDonna Karen Rognlie, May 31, 1953; children: Kolby J., Kenje A., Kurt E., Klee J. B.S. in Architecture, Mont. State U., 1951. Architect in tng. with Gehres D. Weed Architect, Kalispell, 1952-55; partner Weed & Fehlberg Architects, Kalispell, 1955-57; pvt. practice Kalispell, 1957-58; with Cushing Terrell Assos., Billings, Mont., 1958-72; partner Cushing Terrell Assos., 1960-72; v.p. CTA Architects Engrs., Inc., Billings, 1973-87; ptnr. Collaborative Design Architects, Oakland, Calif., 1987-91, Robert Fehlberg Architects, Pleasanton, Calif., 1991—. Bd. dirs. Yellowstone Art Center Found., 1965-84, 1st pres., 1965; bd. dirs. Mont. Inst. Arts Found., 1976-86, pres., 1976-80, treas., 1980-86. Served with AUS, 1944-46. Recipient (with wife) Gov.'s award for arts, 1983. Fellow AIA (pres. Mont. 1965, nat. dir. 1971-74), Mont. Inst. Arts (pres. 1963-64); mem. Prodn. Systems for Architects and Engrs. (dir. 1971-74, chmn. 1974), East Bay AIA. Home: 7566 Rosedale Ct Pleasanton CA 94588-3762 Office: Robert Fehlberg Architect 7566 Rosedale Ct Pleasanton CA 94588-3762 also: PO Box 2431 Sitka AK 99835-2431

FEHR, J. WILL, newspaper editor; b. Long Beach, Calif., Mar. 8, 1926; s. John and Evelyn (James) F.; m. Cynthia Moore, Sept. 4, 1951; children—Michael John, Martha Ann. B.A. in English, U. Utah, 1951. City editor Salt Lake City Tribune, 1964-80, mng. editor, 1980-81, editor, 1981-91. Served to 1st lt. USAF, 1951-53. Mem. Am. Soc. Newspaper Editors, Sigma Chi. Clubs: Hidden Valley, Fort Douglas (Salt Lake City). Home: 468 13th Ave Salt Lake City UT 84103-3229 Office: Salt Lake City Tribune 143 S Main St Salt Lake City UT 84111-1917

FEHR, LARRY MICHAEL, state agency administrator, educator; b. Ellensburg, Wash., Oct. 14, 1952; s. James Thomas and Edna May (Burgess) F.; m. Gina Lynn Ringstad, July 24, 1976; children: Lindsey Brooke, Megan Elizabeth. BA in Sociology and Polit. Sci., Wash. State U., Pullman, 1974; student, U. Wales, Cardiff, Eng., 1972-73; MPA, U. Wash., Seattle, 1983. Teaching asst. Cen. Wash. U., Ellensburg, 1974-75, U. Wash., Seattle, 1975-76; rsch. analyst Inst. for Govtl. Rsch., Seattle, 1975-76; law and justice planner N.W. Regional Coun. of Govts., Bellingham, Wash., 1976-78, planning coord., 1978-81; lectr. in criminal justice & pub. adminstrn. Seattle U., 1987—; exec. dir. Wash. Coun. on Crime & Delinquency, 1981—; founding mem. Wash. Coalition of Crime Victim Advocacy, Seattle, 1986—, N.W. Youth Svcs., Bellingham, 1977-80. Founding mem. Wash. Pub. Interest Rsch. Group, Seattle, 1975-76; pres. Leadership Tomorrow Alumni Assn., Seattle, 1988-89; chmn. youth panel United Way, Bellingham, 1980-81; trustee Internat. Festival of the Arts, Bellingham, 1979-80; mem. vis. com. dept. sociology U. Wash., 1989—; mem. planning com. Seattle Pvt. Industry Coun., 1983-89; mem. Regional Law, Safety and Justice Com., 1990—, Kids Count Adv. Bd., 1992—, State Children's Adminstrn. Adv. Com., 1992—; regional trustee Group Health Coop., 1987-88. Recipient Spl. Achievement award United Way of Whatcom County, 1981, Profl. award Wash. Correctional Assn., 1987, Exceptional Svc. award Cath. Archdiocese, 1987. Mem. Am. Correctional Assn. (mem. task force on violence 1994—), Wash. Law and Justice Planning Assn. (pres. 1978-80), Wash. Ctr. for Law Related Edn. (trustee, past pres.), Exec. Dirs. Coalition, Phi Beta Kappa. Office: Wash Coun Crime Delinquency 1305 4th Ave Ste 602 Seattle WA 98101-2401

FEHR, LOLA MAE, nursing association director; b. Hastings, Nebr., Sept. 29, 1936; d. Leland R. and Edith (Wunderlich) Gaymon; m. Harry E. Fehr, Aug. 15, 1972; children: Dawn, Cheryl, Michael. RN, St. Luke's Hosp., Denver, 1958; BSN magna cum laude, U. Denver, 1959; MS, U. Colo., Boulder, 1975. Dir. staff devel. Weld County Gen. Hosp., Greeley, Colo., 1972-76; dir. nursing Weld County Gen. Hosp., 1976-80; exec. dir. Colo. Nurses Assn., Denver, 1980-89; dir. membership Assn. Oper. Rm. Nurses, Inc., Denver, 1989-90, exec. dir., 1990—. Editor Colo. Nurse, 1980-89. Recipient U. Colo. Alumni award, Colo. Nurses Assn. Profl. Nurse of the Yr. award. Mem. Nat. Assn. Parliamentarians, Am. Soc. Assn. Execs., Colo. Nurses Assn., Sigma Theta Tau.

FEHRIBACH, RONALD STEVEN, investment executive; b. Huntingburg, Ind., Nov. 2, 1949; s. Edwin Joseph and Stella Ann (Edele) F. BS in Polit. Sci., Ind. State U., 1974; postgrad., Rose Hulman Inst. Tech., 1974, Ind. U., 1977; MA, Eastern Ky. U., Richmond, 1980. Crew supr. Ahrens and Son's Nursery, Huntingburg, Ind., 1966-70; constrn. worker Nailer Constrn. Co., Huntingburg, 1971; fin. and program analyst HEW, Chgo., Washington, 1972; investment exec. Moseley, Hallgarten, Estabrook & Weeden Inc., Chgo., 1980-87, LaSalle St. Securities, Inc., Chgo., 1987-93, F.J. Garber & Co., Mesa, Ariz., 1993-95; pres. Fehribach Investments Inc., Chgo., 1986—; owner Mama's Place - The Legend Continues, Mesa, 1991—; corp. comdr. Res. Officer Tng. Program, Terre Haute, 1973-74. Capt. U.S. Army, 1975-77, Korea; with Ind. Nat. Guard, 1977-79. Named Rookie of Yr., Moseley Assocs., Boston, 1983; recipient Outstanding Sales award Am. Fin. Group, Boston, 1986.

FEIG, STEPHEN ARTHUR, pediatrics educator, hematologist, oncologist; b. N.Y.C., Dec. 24, 1937; s. Irving L. and Janet (Oppenheimer) F.; m. Judith Bergman, Aug. 28, 1960; children: Laura, Daniel, Andrew. AB in Biology, Princeton U., 1959; MD, Columbia U., 1963. Diplomate Am. Bd. Pediatrics, Am. Bd. Hematology-Oncology. Intern Mt. Sinai Hosp., N.Y.C., 1963-64, resident in pediatrics, 1964-66; hematology fellow Children's Hosp. Med. Ctr., Boston, 1968-71, assoc. in medicine, 1971-72; asst. prof. pediatrics UCLA, 1972-77, chief div. hematology and oncology, sch. medicine, 1977—, assoc. prof., 1977-82, prof., 1982—, exec. vice chmn. dept. pediatrics sch. mediicne, 1994—; cons. Olive View Med. Ctr., Van Nuys, Calif., 1973—, Valley Med. Ctr., Fresno, Calif., 1973—, Sunrise Hosp. dept. pediatrics, Las Vegas, Nev., 1980—; med. advisory com. Los Angeles chpt. Leukemia Soc. Am., 1978—; bd. trustees, 1984—; bd. dirs. Camp Ronald McDonald for Good Times; active numerous other pediatric hosp. and med. sch. coms. Reviewer Am. Jour. Pediatric Hematology/Oncology, Blood, Jour. Clin. Investigation, Pediatrics, Pediatric Rsch., Am. Jour. Diseases of Children, Jour. Pediatrics; contbr. articles to profl. jours. Served with USNR, 1966-68. Mem. Am. Soc. Hematology, Soc. Pediatric Research, Am. Pediatric Soc., Internat. Soc. Exptl. Hematology, Am. Assn. Cancer Research. Jewish. Office: UCLA Sch Medicine Dept Pediatrics 10833 Le Conte Ave Los Angeles CA 90024

FEIGENBAUM, CLIFFORD SCOTT, newsletter editor, financial consultant; b. Cin., Nov. 9, 1961; s. Phillip Stanley and Helen Lee (Potts) F.; m. Mardelle Ceaser, March 1995; 1 child, Candice M. Payne-Feigenbaum. BA in Bus. Mgmt., Whitworth Coll., 1986. Retail mgmt. asst. Squire Shop/Kinney Shoes, Spokane, Wash., 1979-82; treas., bookkeeper Discovery Sch., Spokane, 1986-87; bus. and account asst. Sta. KAYU-TV, Spokane, 1987-89; payroll specialist II, Empire Health Svcs., Spokane, 1989-91; creator, pub., co-editor The GreenMoney Jour. Socially Responsible business investing & consumer Resources Newsletter, Spokane, 1992—; co-creator The GreenMoney Online Guide-Worldwide, 1995—; guest on socially responsible ethical investing various radio stas., Spokane, also Peace and Justice Action League Seminar, Spokane, 1992. Contbr. articles to profl. jours. Vol. Habitat for Humanity, Spokane Food Bank, also others, 1984—, Oil Smart, alternative transp. programs, Spokane, 1992; vol., bd. dirs. Discovery Sch., 1984-87; bd. mem. Citizens for Clean Air, 1993—. Recipient Recycling Leadership award Spokane City and County Solid Waste Disposal Project, 1991. Mem. Whitworth Coll. Alumni Assn., A Spokane Men's Group, various health clubs. Home and Office: 608 W Glass Ave Spokane WA 99205-2961 Home and Office: 1003 Linwood Ave Saint Paul MN 55105

FEIL, LINDA MAE, tax preparer; b. Dallas, Oreg., Apr. 9, 1948; d. Fred Henry and Ruth Irene (Hoffman) F. AA, West Valley Community Coll., 1975; student, Golden Gate U. Ctr. for Tax Studies, 1975, Menlo Coll. Sch. Bus. Adminstrn., 1978. Enrolled agt. IRS; cert. in fed. taxation. Income tax preparer, office mgr. H & R Block, Inc., Santa Clara, Calif., 1972-74, asst. area mgr., 1974-76; propr. L.M. Feil Tax Service, Santa Clara, 1976-80; ptnr. Tennyson Tax Service, Santa Clara, 1980-81; owner McKeany-Feil Tax Service, San Jose, Calif., 1981-83; owner Feil Tax Service, San Jose, 1983-90, Richmond, Calif., 1990—. Mem. Nat. Soc. Pub. Accts., Nat. Assn. Enrolled Agts. (chpt. sec. 1981-83, chpt. v.p. 1983-84), Mission Soc. Enrolled Agts. (pres. 1984-85, Enrolled Agt. of Yr. 1985), Calif. Soc. Enrolled Agts. (bd. dirs. 1985-86). Home: 4843 Silver Creek Rd Fairfield CA 94533 Office: Feil Tax Svc 3065 Richmond Pky # 108 Richmond CA 94806-1904

FEIN, RONALD LAWRENCE, lawyer; b. Detroit, Aug. 26, 1943; s. Lee Allen and Billie Doreen (Thomas) F.; m. Rosemary Heath, Sept. 2, 1966; children: Samantha, Mark. AB with honors, UCLA, 1966; JD with honors, U. San Diego, 1969. Bar: Calif. 1970, U.S. Dist. Ct. (cen. dist.) Calif. 1970. Assoc. Gibson, Dunn & Crutcher, Los Angeles, 1969-75; chief dep. commr. of corps. State of Calif., Los Angeles, 1975-78; ptnr., mem. adv. com., chmn. corp. fin./mergers and acquisitions sect. Jones, Day, Reavis & Pogue, Los Angeles, 1978-87; ptnr., mem. exec. com., chmn. gen. bus. dept. Wyman, Bautzer, Kuchel & Silbert, L.A., 1987-91; of counsel Stutman, Treister & Glatt, 1991—; bd. dirs. Executours, Inc., Los Angeles, Lottery Info., North Hollywood, Calif., Malibu Grand Prix, Woodland Hills, Calif.; adj. prof. law Loyola U., Los Angeles, 1978—; mem. Commr.'s Circle Adv. Com. to the Calif. Commr. of Corps., Fin. Lawyers Conf. Articles editor San Diego Law Rev., 1969; contbr. articles to profl. jours. Co-dir. protocol for boxing Los Angeles Olympic Organizing Com., 1984. Lt. USAF, to 1966-69. Mem. ABA (corp., banking and bus. law sect., mem. ad hoc com. on merit regulation, mem. fed. regulation of securities com., mem. ad hoc com. on the Uniform Limited Offering Exemption, com. on Counsel Responsibility, mem. ad hoc com. on Regulation D, mem. subcom. on Registration Statements—1933 Act, vice chmn. state regulation securities com., chmn. pvt. offering exemption and simplification of capital formation subcom.), Calif. Bar Assn. (bus. law sect.), Los Angeles County Bar Assn. (mem. exec. com. bus. and corps. law sect.), Nat. Assn. of Securities Dealers, Inc. (mem. subcom. on indemnification, mem. arbitration panel). Club: Regency. Home: 10983 Wellworth Ave Apt 310 Los Angeles CA 90024-6255 Office: Stutman Treister & Glatt 3699 Wilshire Blvd Ste 900 Los Angeles CA 90010-2766

FEIN, WILLIAM, ophthalmologist; b. N.Y.C., Nov. 27, 1933; s. Samuel and Beatrice (Lipschitz) F.; m. Bonnie Fern Aaronson, Dec. 15, 1963; children: Stephanie Paula, Adam Irving, Gregory Andrew. BS, CCNY, 1954; MD, U. Calif., Irvine, 1962. Diplomate Am. Bd. Ophthalmology. Intern L.A. County Gen. Hosp., 1962-63, resident in ophthalmology, 1963-66; instr. U. Calif. Med. Sch., Irvine, 1966-69; mem. faculty U. So. Calif. Med. Sch., 1969—, assoc. clin. prof. ophthalmology, 1979—; attending physician Cedars-Sinai Med. Ctr., L.A., 1966—, chief ophthalmology clinic svc., 1979-81, chmn. div. ophthalmology, 1981-85; attending physician Los Angeles County-U. So. Calif. Med. Ctr., 1969—; chmn. dept. ophthalmology Midway Hosp., 1975-78; dir. Ellis Eye Ctr., L.A., 1984—. Mem. editorial bd. CATARACT, Internat. Jour. of Cataract and Ocular Surgery, 1992—; contbr. articles to med. publs. Chmn. ophthalmology adv. com. Jewish Home for Aging of Greater L.A., 1993—. Fellow Internat. Coll. Surgeons, Am. Coll. Surgeons; mem. Am. Acad. Ophthalmology, Am. Soc. Ophthalmic Plastic and Reconstructive Surgery, Royal Soc. Medicine, AMA, Calif. Med. Assn., L.A. Med. Assn. Home: 718 N Camden Dr Beverly Hills CA 90210-3205 Office: 415 N Crescent Dr Beverly Hills CA 90210-4860

FEINBERG, DAVID ALLEN, computer software executive; b. Seattle, Feb. 17, 1947; s. Herman Stanford and Zelda (Hindin) F.; m. Lynne Brechner, Jan. 21, 1978; children: Kerri Jeanne, Todd Breck, Jamie Leigh, Megan Dawn, Eric Anthony. BS, Stanford U., 1968; MS in Adminstrn., George Washington U., 1972. Cert. data processor. Systems programmer Stanford (Calif.) Computer Ctr., 1966-68, NCR Corp., Los Angeles, 1968-69; systems analyst System Devel. Corp., Washington, 1971-75; mgr. Boeing Co., Seattle, 1975-87; tech. dir. Spacelabs, Inc., Redmond, 1987-90; dir. R&D Revelation Techs. Inc., Bellevue, Wash., 1990-91; founder, mng. prin. M.T. Writings. Co., Seattle, 1983—; mgr. networking and interfacing PHAMIS Inc., Seattle, 1992—; lectr. various orgs., Seattle, 1983—. Contbr. articles to profl. jours. Pres. Rainier Beach High Sch. PTSA, Seattle, 1981; advisor Seattle Recreation Dept., 1983—; official Seattle Metro League, 1980—, Seattle Recreation Dept., 1990—; tournament umpire Pony Baseball, 1990—; founder, treas. Montgomery Savoyards, Rockville, Md., 1973-75. Served to 1st. lt. Signal Corps, U.S. Army, 1969-71. Mem. Computer Soc. IEEE (affiliate), Data Processing Mgmt. Assn., Assn. Computing Machinery, Am. Arbitration Assn. (arbitrator, panelist). Home: 3662 SW Othello St Seattle WA 98126-3246 Office: PHAMIS Inc Ste 200 401 2d Ave S Seattle WA 98104-2837

FEINBERG, RICHARD ALAN, clinical psychologist; b. Oakland, Calif., Aug. 12, 1947; s. Jack and Raechel Sacks (Hoff) F. BA, Calif. State U.-Hayward, 1969; MA in Clin. Psychology, Mich. State U., 1972, PhD, 1979; Nat. Register of Health Service Providers in Psychology, 1980. Instr., Merritt Coll., Oakland, 1975-76; clin. psychologist Highland Gen. Hosp., Oakland, 1976-79; asso. Lafayette Center Counseling and Edn., 1978-79; clin. psychologist Tri-City Mental Health Center, Fremont, Calif., 1979-81, dir., 1981-86; pvt. practice clin. psychology, 1976—; participant profl. conf. USPHS fellow, 1969-71. Mem. Am. Psychol. Assn., Calif. Psychol. Assn. Jewish. Office: 38950 Blaco Rd Ste D Fremont CA 94536

FEINHANDLER, EDWARD SANFORD, writer, photographer, art dealer, sports mentor, consultant, educator; b. Elko, Nev., Jan. 13, 1948; s. Samuel and Sylvia (Manus) F. BA, U. Nev., Reno, 1972. Supr. underpriveledged Washoe County Extension Program, Reno, 1970-71; sports editor, writer Sagebrush Campus newspaper, Reno, 1971-72; internal salesman, mgr. Trigon Corp., Sparks, Nev., 1975-88; owner, operator Art Internat. Gallery Extraordinaire, Reno, 1981—; tennis dir. City of Sparks, 1991-93, Cmty. Edn. Program, Sparks, 1994, Sparks YMCA, 1995; with nat. news Top Ten radio interviews, U.S. and Can., 1978-79; freelance writer and photographer. Contbr. articles to newspapers; extra in various movies; TV interviewee AM Chgo., AM L.A., 1979, Afternoon Exchange, Cleve., 1979, To Tell the Truth, 1975, Reno Tonight TV show, 1989, Fox Across America TV show, 1989. Player, coach Summer Volleyball League, Reno, 1982-85; tennis coach Cmty. Svc. Ctr., Reno, 1986-88; participant Make-A-Wish Found., Reno, 1985-995, U. Nev. Journalism Dept., 1985-93, UNR Children's Svcs., Reno, 1986-88; coach Cath. Basketball, 1987-89 (2d pl.); head coach girls Varsity Tennis Bishop Manogue H.S., 1989-91; coach boys varsity tennis Sparks H.S., 1993-95; spl. olympics, 1989, girls Jr. Varsity Basketball, 1989; active Ptnrs. in Edn., 1988-90, Jr. Achievement, 1989-94, Animal Welfare Inst., Statue of Liberty Found., 1984-91, No. Nev. Cancer Coun., United Blood Svcs., Arthritis Found., Cancer Soc., Sta. KNPB, Ret. Sr. Citizens; Sierra Arts Found. Sgt. U.S. Army, 1968-69, Vietnam. Winner Ugley Man contest U. Reno, 1967, 70-72, No. Nev. Bone Marrow Program, 1991-95; winner ind. category Ugly Bartender contest Multiple Sclerosis, 1989-90; Sparks Tennis Club singles, doubles, and mixed doubles, Champion B/C divsn., 1994; recipient numerous tennis, billiards, volleyball and bowling awards including 1st pl. C divsn. NNCC Tennis Tournament, 1991, Mixed Doubles Champ., 1992, finalist Sr. Open Singles, Sparks City, 1993, Open Doubles Champ., 1993; world record holder nosedarts and squint, 1972—. Mem. DAV, Orthodox Jewish Union. Democrat. Office: Art Internat Gallery Extraordinaire PO Box 13405 Reno NV 89507-3405

FEINSTEIN, BEVERLY, psychiatrist, psychoanalyst; b. N.Y.C., Dec. 11, 1943. BA, Barnard Coll., 1964; MD, NYU, 1968; PhD in Psychoanalysis, So.Calif. Psychoanalytic Inst., 1988. Diplomate in psychiatry Am. Bd. Psychiatry and Neurology; lic. physician, Calif. Intern Bellevue Hosp, N.Y.C., 1968-69; resident in psychiatry UCLA Neuropsychiat. Inst., 1969-72; fellow UCLA Brain Rsch. Inst., 1971-72; staff psychiatrist, biofeedback and insomnia rsch. Sepulveda (Calif.) VA Hosp., 1972-76; asst. clin. prof. UCLA, 1972—; assoc. staff St. John's Hosp., Santa Monica, Calif., 1976—, Westwood Hosp., L.A., 1976-93. Contbr. articles to profl. jours.; presenter in field. Co-originator, co-dir. UCLA Methadone Maintenance Clinic, 1970-72; cons. Am. Inst. Family Resl., 1977-78, Jewish Family Svc., 1984-85. So. Calif. Psychoanalytic Soc. grantee to lecture in Israel, 1983. Mem. Am. Psychiat. Assn., Am. Psychoanalytic Assn., So. Calif. Psychoanalytic Inst. and Soc. (chmn. ethics com. 1991-92), So. Calif. Psychiat. Soc. (councillor 1990-92, sec. 1992-93, pres. 1995—). Address: 586 E Channel Rd Santa Monica CA 90402-1344

FEINSTEIN, (ALLAN) DAVID, psychologist, author; b. Bklyn., Dec. 22, 1946; s. Sol and Edith (Fuhrman) F.; m. Donna Colleen Eden, Oct. 7, 1984. BA, Whittier (Calif.) Coll., 1968; MA, U.S. Internat. U., 1970; PhD, Union Inst., 1973. Lic. psychologist, Oreg., Calif. Youth dir. San Diego YMCA, 1968-70; instr. Sch. of Medicine Johns Hopkin's U., Balt., 1970-75; sr. clin. psychologist San Diego County Mental Health Svcs., 1975-83; exec. dir. Innersource, Ashland, Oreg., 1983—. Co-author: Personal Mythology, 1988, Rituals for Living & Dying, 1990, Mortal Acts, 1993; contbr. articles to profl. jours. Mem. APA, Assn. for Humanistic Psychology. Office: Innersource 777 E Main St Ashland OR 97520-2117

FEINSTEIN, DIANNE, senator; b. San Francisco, June 22, 1933; d. Leon and Betty (Rosenburg) Goldman; m. Bertram Feinstein, Nov. 11, 1962 (dec.); 1 child, Katherine Anne; m. Richard C. Blum, Jan. 20, 1980. BA History, Stanford U., 1955; LLB (hon.), Golden Gate U., 1977; D Pub. Adminstrn. (hon.), U. Manila, 1981; D Pub. Service (hon.), U. Santa Clara, 1981; JD (hon.), Antioch U., 1983, Mills Coll., 1985; LHD (hon.), U. San Francisco, 1988. Fellow Coro Found., San Francisco, 1955-56; with Calif. Women's Bd. Terms and Parole, 1960-66; mem. Mayor's com. on crime, chmn. adv. com. Adult Detention, 1967-69; mem. Bd. of Suprs., San Francisco, 1970-78, pres., 1970-71, 74-75, 78; mayor of San Francisco, 1978-88, U.S. senator from Calif., 1992—; mem. exec. com. U.S. Conf. of Mayors, 1983-88; Dem. nominee for Gov. of Calif., 1990; mem. Nat. Com. on U.S.-China Rels., mem. Judiciary Comm., Rukes & Adminstrn., Senate Dem. Policy Com. Mem. Bay Area Conservation and Devel. Commn., 1973-78. Recipient Woman of Achievement award Bus. and Profl. Women's Clubs San Francisco, 1970, Disting. Woman award San Francisco Examiner, 1970, Coro Found. award, 1979, Coro Leadership award, 1988, Pres. medal U. Calif., San Francisco, 1988, Scopus award Am. Friends Hebrew U., 1981, Brotherhood/Sisterhood award NCCJ, 1986, Comdr.'s award U.S. Army, 1986, French Legion of Honor, 1984, Disting. Civilian award USN, 1987; named Number One Mayor All-Pro City Mgmt. Team City and State Mag., 1987. Mem. Trilateral Commn., Japan Soc. of No. Calif. (pres. 1988-89), Inter-Am. Dialogue, Nat. Com. on U.S.-China Rels. Office: US Senate 331 Senate Hart Office Bld Washington DC 20510*

FEIR, JOHN DOUGLAS, geologist; b. Winnipeg, Man., Can., Oct. 19, 1930; came to U.S., 1981; s. John Thomas and Octavia Marie (Cinq Mars) F.; m. Ann Shwetz, June 28, 1957; children: Lesley Dawn, John David. BSc in Geology with honors, U. Man., 1952. Geologist to sr. staff geologist Shell Can. Ltd., Calgary, Alta., Can., 1952-80; sr. staff geologist Shell Oil Co. (Pecten Internat. Co.), Houston, 1981-91; ret., 1991. Home: 22828 N 91st Way Scottsdale AZ 85255-4396

FEIR, SCOTT EUGENE, minister; b. Tacoma, Wash., Sept. 30, 1964; s. Larry E. and Mellodean (Barnes) F.; m. Kimberly Teel, June 23, 1990. AA, Ft. Steilacoom Community Coll., 1985; BA, Seattle Pacific U., 1987; MDiv, Golden Gate Bapt. Sem., 1991, MA, 1992. Ordained to ministry Meth. Ch., 1992. Assoc. min. Richmond Highlands Bapt. Ch., Seattle, 1985-88, Lucas Valley Community Ch., Mill Valley, Calif., 1990-92; sr. min. Fed. Way (Wash.) Free Meth., 1992—; speaker Calif. State Youth Retreat, 1990. Mem. Pacific N.W. Conf. of Free Meths. Home and Office: 32644 49th Pl SW Federal Way WA 98023-1927

FEISS, GEORGE JAMES, III, financial services company executive; b. Cleve., June 24, 1950; s. George James Jr. and Bettie (Kalish) F.; m. Susan Margaret Cassel, May 30, 1981; children: Kalish Ilana Cassel-Feiss, Nika Catherine Cassel-Feiss. BA in Social Studies, Antioch Coll., 1973; MBA in Internat. Fin., Am. Grad. Sch. Internat. Mgmt., Phoenix, 1975. Registered investment advisor; CFP. Ptnr. Healthcare Cons., Seattle, 1976-80; pres. M2 Inc., Seattle, 1980—; cons. Sta. KRAB, Seattle, 1988-89, Zion Christian Acad., Seattle, 1990—. Author: Mind Therapies/Body Therapies, 1979, Hope & Death in Exile - The Economics and Politics of Cancer in the United States, 1981. Bd. dirs. B'nai Brith, Seattle, 1988-91; mem. fin. com. Univ. Child Devel. Sch., Seattle, 1989—; mem. social action com. Am. Jewish Com., Seattle, 1992. Mem. Eastside Estate Planning Coun., Inst. for CFPs, Social Investment Forum, TOES (The Other Econ. Summit). Home: 603 38th Ave Seattle WA 98122-6423 Office: M2 Inc 1932 1st Ave Ste 614 Seattle WA 98101

FEIST-FITE, BERNADETTE, international and business education consultant; b. Linton, N.D., Sept. 28, 1945; d. John K. and Cecilia (Nagel) F.; m. William H. Fite. BS in Dietetics, U. N.D., Grand Forks, 1967; MS in Edn., Troy (Ala.) State U., 1973; EdD U. So. Calif. Commd. officer USAF, 1965, advanced through grades to maj., 1983; prof. health and fitness Nat. Def. U., Ft. McNair, Washington, 1989—; pres. Feist Assocs., 1989—; instr. seminars, workshops, researcher on internat. bus. and edn. issues; mgr. Coffeehouse Unitarian Ch. Mem. Alexandria Little Theatre. Decorated Air Force Commendation medal, Dept. Def. Meritorious Svc. medal. Mem. NAFE, VFW, Soc. Internat. Edn., Tng. and Rsch., Am. Dietetic Assn., Nat. Assn. Women Bus. Owners, Women in Defense, Japan-Am. Soc. Washington, Dietitians in Bus. and Industry, Sports and Cardiovascular Nutritionists, Andrews Officers Club. Home: 2442 Cerrillos Rd Ste 312 Santa Fe NM 87505-3262 Office: Feist Assocs PO Box 7105 Alexandria VA 22307-0105

FEISTHAMEL, JUDY, language educator, interpreter, translator; b. Prague, Czechoslovakia, Oct. 25, 1944; came to U.S., Feb. 1959; d. Ladislav Kratky and Jitka Kadlec Elton; m. John Feisthamel, May 27, 1972; children: Mark, Matthew. BA with honors, UCLA, 1966, MA, 1967, PhD, 1972; MA in Edn., Calif. State U., San Jose, 1993. Cert. ct. interpreter, Calif. Asst. prof. U. Hawaii, 1970-73; instr. Defense Lang. Inst., Monterey, Calif., 1974-76; ESL cons. Pacific Grove (Calif.) Sch. Dist., 1980-82; bilingual resource tchr. Salinas (Calif.) Sch. Dist., 1982—; instr. Monterey (Calif.) PeninsulaColl., 1982—; interpreter, translator Cortes Translation, Carmel, Calif., 1982-95. Author: Spanish Basic Course, 1976, Mil Maravillas Workbook, 1986, Campanitas de Oro, 1987. Tchg. fellow UCLA, 1968-70. Mem. Am. Assn. Tchrs. of Spanish, Am. Translators Assn., Calif. Ct. Interpreters Assn. (sec. 1980), Calif. Assn. Bilingual Edn., Modern Lang. Assn. Home: 8325 E Camino Estrada Carmel CA 93923

FEIT, MICHAEL DENNIS, physicist; b. Easton, Pa., Nov. 15, 1942; s. Joel E. and Kathryn T. (Bracken) F.; m. Lorraine R. Mauriel, Dec. 30, 1967; children: Sean M., Kathryn R. BA, Lehigh U., 1964; PhD, Rensselaer Poly. Inst., 1970. Rsch. asst. Rensselaer Poly. Inst., Troy, N.Y., 1964-69; rsch. assoc. U. Ill., Urbana, 1969-72; physicist Lawrence Livermore (Calif.) Nat. Lab., 1972—, leader theoretical optical physics group, 1992—; adj. faculty dept. applied sci. U. Calif., Davis, 1985—. Contbr. numerous articles to profl. jours. Fellow Am. Phys. Soc., Optical Soc. Am.; mem. AAAS, Phi Beta Kappa, Sigma Xi. Office: Lawrence Livermore Nat Lab Mail Stop L-438 PO Box 808 Livermore CA 94550

FELCHLIN, MARY KATHLEEN CONROY, financial executive; b. Cleve., Feb. 16, 1951; d. Ernest J. and Margaret Jane Conroy; B.A., U. Calif., Berkeley, 1973; M.B.A., U. So. Calif., 1977. Adminstrv. asst. Mason McDuffie Investment Co., Berkeley, 1974-75; mortage mktg. staff Gibraltar Savs. & Loan, Beverly Hills, summer 1976; account officer Wells Fargo Bank, Los Angeles, 1977-79; sr. account officer Citicorp Real Estate, Inc., Los Angeles, 1979-80, asst. v.p., 1981-82, v.p., 1982—; v.p. Citicorp Real Estate Capital, 1985—; v.p. Citicorp Investment Bank, L.A., 1988-90, Citicorp Investment Mgmt., 1990—. Wittenberg fellow, 1975-76; Commerce Assos. fellow, 1976-77. Home: 8960 Wonderland Ave West Hollywood CA 90046-1854

FELDAVERD, NICHOLAS EDWARD, III, music educator, musician; b. Sigourney, Iowa, Jan. 3, 1949; s. Nicholas Edward and Nellie Jeanette (Greenlee) F.; m. Joyce Diane Furnas, Dec. 15, 1973; children: Andrea Michelle, Nicholas Edward IV. BS in Edn., S.W. Mo. State U., 1972; M of Music Edn., So. Ill. U., 1978; postgrad., Ariz. State U., 1980—, Phoenix Coll., 1985-87. Band dir. Normandy (Mo.) Pub. Schs., 1973-78, Mesa (Ariz.) Pub. Schs., 1978—; prin. trombonist Mesa Symphony Orch., 1978—; wind coach Met. Youth Orch., Mesa, 1980—; adj./clinician and pvt. instr., 1978—. Mem. Am. Fedn. Musicians, Nat. Assn. Jazz Educators, Ariz. Bd. and Orch. Dirs., Music Educators Nat. Conf. Republican. Office: Taylor Jr High Sch 705 S 32nd St Mesa AZ 85204-3943

FELDMAN, ANNETTE YOUNG, civic worker; b. Hoopeston, Ill., July 23, 1916; d. Reuben and Ida (Horvitz) Yonkelowitz; m. Jerome Feldman, Oct. 19, 1941 (dec. 1986); children: Jill Feldman Crane, Robert. Student, Northwestern U., 1934-36; BS, U. Chgo., 1938, MS, 1940. Nutritionist ARC, Chgo., 1940-41; nutrition cons. Med. Coll. Va., Richmond, 1941-42; specialist food and nutrition U. Ill. Extension Svc., Champaign, 1943-45; tutor East Bay Literacy Coun., 1990—; historian Alameda Contra Costa Med. Aux. Dist. II, 1990—. Editor cookbooks for philanthropic orgns. Chmn. fund drives and disaster food ARC, Hayward, Calif., 1948, bd. dirs., 1954-58; chmn. bldg. fund St. Rose Hosp., Hayward, 1956; chmn. heart fund drive Am. Heart Assn., Hayward, 1958; mem. adult edn. com. Congregation Beth Jacob, Oakland, Calif., 1965; chmn. fund-raising events Scholarships, Inc., Hayward, 1969; pres. Alameda-Contra Costa Med. Aux., 1961-62, condr. nutritional symposium, 1975; charter assoc. Children's Hosp. Found. Circle of Friends, 1985—; life mem. Hayward Sch. Dist. PTA, Hayward Forum Arts; mem. Friends of Hayward Edn. Fund, World Affairs Coun., Women's Am. Orgn. for Rehab. Through Tng., Judah Magnes Mus.; mem. Tamarack br. Children's Med. Ctr. No. Calif.; tutor Inter Bay Literacy Coun., 1990. Recipient Appreciation award Alameda-Contra Costa Med. Aux., 1962. Mem. Am. Dietetic Assn. (life; registered), Bay Area Dietetic Assn., Eden Hosp. Found., AAUW, Chgo. Alumni Assn., Hill and Valley Club, Order of Ea. Star, Hadassah (life mem. Eden chpt., Svc. award 1960). Home: 22119 Prospect St Hayward CA 94541-2627

FELDMAN, FREDRIC JOEL, health products executive; b. N.Y.C., Feb. 9, 1940; s. Morris M. and Minnie (Gesse) F.; m. Claire Judith Gershen, July 8, 1962; children: Eric, Julie. BS in Chemistry, Bklyn. Coll., 1960; MS in Organic Chemistry, U. Md., 1964, PhD in Analytical Chemistry, 1967. Prin. investigator Walter Reed Inst. Rsch., Washington, 1964-68; dir. atomic absorption R&D Instrumentation Lab., Lexington, Mass., 1968-70, v.p. biomed., 1984-86, pres., 1986-88; program mgr. Beckman Instruments, Fullerton, Calif., 1970-77; dir. European ops. Beckman Instruments, Geneva, Switzerland, 1977-81; div. mgr. Beckman Instruments, Brea, Calif., 1981-84; pres. Microgenics, Concord, Calif., 1988-92; CEO, chmn. Oncogenetics, Phoenix, 1992—; chmn. Blex, Inc., Denver, 1992—. Author: Atomic Absorption Spectroscopy, 1970; contbr. numerous articles to scientific jours. Office: Oncogenetics 1275 Pacific Ave Laguna Beach CA 92651-1918

FELDMAN, GERALD DONALD, history educator; b. N.Y.C., Apr. 24, 1937; s. Isadore and Lillian (Cohen) F.; m. Philippa Blume, June 22, 1958 (div. Feb. 31, 1982); children: Deborah, Aaron; m. Norma von Ragenfeld, Nov. 30, 1983. BA in History, Columbia U., 1958; MA in History, Harvard U., 1959, PhD in History, 1964. Asst. prof. U. Calif., Berkeley, 1963-68, assoc. prof., 1968-70, prof. history, 1970—; dir. Ctr. for German and European Studies, U. Calif., Berkeley, 1994—. Author: (book) Army Industry and Labor in Germany, 1914-1918, 1966, Iron and Steel in the German Inflation, 1916-1923, 1985, Von Weltkrieg zur Weltwirtschaftskrise, 1985, The Great Disorder: Politics, Economics and Society in the German Inflation, 1914-1924, 1993. Guggenheim fellow, 1973-74, German Marshall Fund fellow, 1981-82, fellow Historisches Kolleg, Munich, 1982-83, fellow Inst. for Advanced Study, Berlin, 1987-88, Woodrow Wilson fellow, 1991-92. Office: U of Calif Dept of History Berkeley CA 94720

FELDMAN, JEFFREY MICHAEL, software developer, music educator; b. Bklyn., Dec. 27, 1947; s. Harold and Lee (Charm) F. AB, U. Calif., Berkeley, 1969; MA, U. Mich., 1973, PhD, 1975. Lectr. Calif. State U., Dominguez Hills, 1977-90, L.A., 1981-82; dir. computer ops. CBS/Program Analysis, L.A., 1981—; owner Digitala, Venice, Calif., 1986—. Author: The Tabla Legacy of Taranath Rao, 1994, (book and audio cassette) Learning Tabla with Alla Rakha, 1986; inventor Vidigraph. Am. Inst. Indian Studies granty, Bombay, 1980-81. Jewish. Office: Digitala PO Box 96 Venice CA 90294-0096

FELDMAN, LEONARD, family practitioner; b. N.Y.C., Oct. 25, 1948; s. Herman and Sonia (Factor) F.; m. Laura Gene Lovell, June 21, 19790 (div. 1981); 1 child, Hannah Carrington; m. Ellene Lee Frances Roberts, May 27, 1988; children: Benjamin Carl, Sharon Rae Olivia. MD, Johns Hopkins U., 1976. Diplomate Am. Bd. Family Medicine. Resident in family practice Conemaugh Valley Meml. Hosp., Johnstown, Pa., 1976-79; family physician Group Health Corp. of Puget Sound, Renton, Wash., 1979-81, Dr. Stan Jones' Clinic, Haines, Alaska, 1982-86, Craig (Alaska) Family Clinic, 1986-87, Langley (Wash.) Med. Clinic, 1987-88, various locations, Wash. and Alaska, 1988-89; med. dir. Lynn Canal Med. Group, Haines, 1990—; physician boat-based family medicine practice, visiting remote locations in S.E. Alaska, 1982-87. Fellow Am. Acad. Family Physicians. Home: PO Box 697 Haines AK 99827-0697

FELDMAN, ROGER LAWRENCE, artist, educator; b. Spokane, Wash., Nov. 19, 1949; s. Marvin Lawrence and Mary Elizabeth (Shafer) F.; m. Astrid Lunde, Dec. 16, 1972; children: Kirsten B., Kyle Lawrence. BA in Art Edn., U. Wash., 1972; postgrad., Fuller Theol. Sem., Pasadena, Calif., 1972-73, Regent Coll., Vancouver, B.C., 1974; MFA in Sculpture, Claremont Grad. Sch., 1977. Teaching asst. Claremont (Calif.) Grad. Sch.; assoc. prof. art Biola U., La Mirada, Calif., 1989—; adj. instr. Seattle Pacific U., 1979, 80, 82, 83, Linfield Coll., 1978, Edmonds C.C., 1978-80, Shoreline C.C., 1978; one person shows include Art Ctr. Gallery of Seattle Pacific U., 1977, 83, 84, Linfield Coll., McMinnville, Oreg., 1979, Blackfish Gallery, Portland, 1982, Lynn McAllister Gallery, Seattle, 1986, Biola U., 1989, Coll. Gallery, La. Coll., Pineville, 1990, Gallery W., Sacramento, 1991, Aughinbaugh Gallery, Grantham, Pa., 1992, Biola U., 1993, Riverside Art Mus., 1994, Azusa Pacific U., 1995; guest artist and lectr. Group shows include Pasadena Artist's Concern Gallery, 1976, Libra Gallery, Claremont, 1977, Renshaw Gallery, McMinnville, 1978, Cheney Cowles Mus., Spokane, 1979, 80, 83, Lynn McAllister Gallery, Seattle, 1985, Bumbershoot, Seattle, 1985, 86, West Bend (Wis.) Gallery, 1992, L.A. Mcpl. Satellite Gallery, 1993, Greenbelt 93, Northamptonshire, Eng., 1993, Claremont Sch. Theology, 1994, Queens Coll. Cambridge U., Eng., 1994, Jr. Arts Ctr. Gallery, Barnsdale Park, L.A., 1994, Cen. Arts Collective, Tucson, 1995; comms. include Renton Vocat. Tech. Inst., 1987-89, East Hill Cmty. Ctr., Gresham, Oreg., 1979; contbr. articles to profl. jours. Recipient King County Arts Commn. Individual Artist Project award, Seattle, 1988, David Gaiser award for sculpture Cheney Cowles Mus., 1980, Disting. Award for Harborview Med. Ctr. "Viewpoint", Soc. for Tech. Comm., 1987, Design award for "Seafirst News", Internat. Assn. Bus. Comm., 1987, Pace Setter award, 1987, others; grantee Nat. Endowment for Arts, 1986, Connemara Sculpture grante, 1990, Biola U., 1991. Office: Biola Univ 13800 Biola Ave La Mirada CA 90639-0002

FELDMAN, STANLEY GEORGE, state supreme court chief justice; b. N.Y.C., N.Y., Mar. 9, 1933; s. Meyer and Esther Betty (Golden) F.; m. Norma Arambula; 1 dau., Elizabeth L. Student, U. Calif., Los Angeles, 1950-51; LL.B., U. Ariz., 1956. Bar: Ariz. 1956. Practiced in Tucson, 1956-81; ptnr. Miller, Pitt & Feldman, 1968-81; justice Ariz. Supreme Ct., Phoenix, 1982, chief justice, 1992—; lectr. Coll. Law, U. Ariz., 1965-76, adj. prof., 1976-81. Bd. dirs. Tucson Jewish Community Council. Mem. ABA, Am. Bd. Trial Advocates (past pres. So. Ariz. chpt.), Ariz. Bar Assn. (pres. 1974-75, bd. govs. 1967-76), Pima County Bar Assn. (past pres.), Am. Trial Lawyers Assn. (dir. chpt. 1967-76), Conf. of Chief Justices (bd. dirs.). Democrat. Jewish. Office: Ariz Supreme Ct 1501 W Washington St Phoenix AZ 85007-3231

FELDSTEIN, PAUL JOSEPH, management educator; b. N.Y.C., Oct. 4, 1933; s. Nathan and Sarah (Solomon) F.; m. Anna Martha Lee, Dec. 24, 1968; children: Julie, Jennifer. BA, CCNY, 1955; MBA, U. Chgo., 1957, PhD, 1961. Dir. div. of rsch. Am. Hosp. Assn., Chgo., 1961-64; prof. Sch. Pub. Health U. Mich., Ann Arbor, 1964-87; prof. Grad. Sch. Mgmt. U. Calif., Irvine, 1987—; trustee Sutter Health, Sacramento, 1988—. Author: Health Care Economics, 4th rev. 1993, Health Policy Issues: An Economic Perspective, 1994; contbr. articles to profl. jours. 1st lt. inf. U.S. Army, 1955-57. Mem. Am. Econs. Assn. Office: U Calif Grad Sch Mgmt Irvine CA 92717

FELISKY, BARBARA ROSBE, artist; b. Chgo., Mar. 24, 1938; d. Robert Lee and Margaret (Black) Rosbe; m. Timothy Felisky, Oct. 6, 1962; children: Kendra, Marc, Kyra. Student, U. Mich. Tchr. Peekskill (N.Y.) Sch. Dist., 1960-63; asst. to edn. dir. Simplicity Pattern Co., N.Y.C.; tchr. Anaheim (Calif.) Sch. Dist. Bd. guilds Orange County Performing Arts Ctr., Costa Mesa, Calif., 1983-85. Mem. Laguna Beach Art Mus., L.A. County Mus. Art, Gamma Phi Beta. Home and Studio: 2942 E Lake Hill Dr Orange CA 92667-1910

FELL, FRASER M., mining executive; b. Toronto, Ont., June 17, 1928; s. Charles P.F. and Grace Elizabeth (Matthews) F. BA, LLD, McMaster U. Bar: Ont., 1953; named Queen's Counsel, 1965. With Fasken, Robertson, Aitchison, Pickup and Calvin, 1953-63; ptnr. Fasken and Calvin, 1963; chmn. Placer Dome Inc., 1987—, Aetna Life Ins. Co. of Can., from 1988; bd. trustees The Toronto Hosp., Toronto Western Hosp. Mem. Can. Bar Assn., Delta Chi. Office: Placer Dome Inc, Box 49330/Bantall Postal Sta, Vancouver, BC Canada V7X 1P1

FELLER, DANIEL M., history educator; b. Washington, Oct. 19, 1950; s. David E. and Gilda (Halpern) F.; m. Claudia Dean, Aug. 29, 1992; 1 child, Deborah Elizabeth. BA, Reed Coll., 1972; MA, U. Wis., 1974, PhD, 1981. Asst. prof. Northland Coll., Ashland, Wis., 1980-83; asst. editor The Papers of Andrew Jackson, Nashville, 1983-86; asst. prof. U. N.Mex., Albuquerque, 1986-91, assoc. prof., 1991—. Author: The Public Lands in Jacksonian Politics, 1984, The Jacksonian Promise, 1995; co-editor: The Papers of Andrew Jackson, 1987; contbr. chpt. to book, articles to profl. jours. Mem. Am. Hist. Assn., So. Hist. Assn., Orgn. Am. Historians, Assn. Documentary Editing (membership chair 1987-89), Soc. Historians of Early Am. Republic (edtl. bd. 1990-94, conv. coord. 1990-95). Democrat. Office: Dept History U NMex Albuquerque NM 87131-1181

FELLER, WILFORD CARTER, jewelry retailer, manufacturing company executive; b. St. George, Utah, June 9, 1953; s. George Russell and Mary Luella (Carter) F.; m. Deborah Lee Oxspring, Aug. 26, 1977; children: Tate, Trevor, Chelan, Christin. AA with honors, Dixie Coll., St. George, 1975; BA magna cum laude, Brigham Young U., 1977. Owner, mgr. WD Ltd., Provo, Utah, 1975—; ptnr. Amgold Corp. (doing bus. as Goldsmith Co. Jewelers), Provo, 1980-92, owner, mgr., 1992—; ptnr. John Beesley Goldsmith Co., Provo, 1979-80. Former neighborhood chmn. City of Provo. Mem. Jewelers Am. (Gemological Inst. Am. scholar), Ind. Jewelers Orgn., Intermountain Jewelers Am., Provo-Orem C. of C. (past bd. dirs.), Downtown Mchts. Assn. (past pres.). Republican. Mem. LDS Ch. Home: 1179 E 40 N Orem UT 84057-8224 Office: Goldsmith Co Jewelers 100 N University Ave Provo UT 84601-2820

FELLIN, OCTAVIA ANTOINETTE, retired librarian; b. Santa Monica, Calif.; d. Otto P. and Librada (Montoya) F. Student U. N.Mex., 1937-39; BA, U. Denver, 1941; BA in L.S., Rosary Coll., 1942. Asst. libr., instr. libr. sci. St. Mary-of-Woods Coll., Terre Haute, Ind., 1942-44; libr. U.S. Army, Bruns Gen. Hosp., Santa Fe, 1944-46, Gallup (N.Mex.) Pub. Libr., 1947-90; post libr. Camp McQuaide, Calif., 1947; freelance writer mags., newspapers, 1950—; libr. cons.; N.Mex. del. White House Pre-Conf. on Librs. & Info. Svcs., 1978; dir. Nat. Libr. Week for N.Mex., 1959. Chmn. Red Mesa Art Ctr., 1984-88; pres. Gallup Area Arts Coun., 1988; mem. Western Health Found. Century Com., 1988, Gallup Multi-Model Cultural Com., 1988—; v.p., publicity dir. Gallup Community Concerts Assn., 1957-78, 85—; organizer Gt. Decision Discussion groups, 1963-85; co-organizer, v.p. chair fund raising com. Gallup Pub. Radio Com., 1989—; mem. McKinley County Recycling Com., 1990—; mem. local art selection com. N.Mex. Art Dirs., 1990; mem. Gallup St. Naming Com., 1958-59, Aging Com., 1964-68; chmn. Gallup Mus. Indian Arts and Crafts, 1964-78; mem. Eccles. Conciliation and Arbitration Bd., Province of Santa Fe, 1974; mem. publicity com. Gallup Inter-Tribal Indian Ceremonial Assn., 1966-68; mem. Gov's. Com. 100 on Aging, 1967-70; mem. U. N.Mex.-Gallup Campus Community Edn. Adv. Coun., 1981-82; N.Mex. organizing chmn. Rehoboth McKinley Christian Hosp. Aux., pres., 1983, chmn. aux. scholarship com., 1989—, chmn. cmty. edn. loan selection com. 1990—, bd. dirs., corr. sec., 1991—; mem. N.Mex. Libr. Adv. Coun., 1971-75, vice chmn., 1974-75; chmn. adv. com. Gallup Sr. Citizens, 1971-73; mem. steering com. Gallup Diocese Bicentennial, 1975-78, chmn. hist. com., 1975; chmn. Trick or Treat for UNICEF, Gallup, 1972-77, Artists Coop, 1985-89; chmn. pledge campaign Rancho del Nino San Huberto, Empalme, Mex.; active Nat. Cath. Social Justice Lobby; bd. dirs. Gallup Opera Guild, 1970-74; bd. dirs., sec., organizer Gallup Area Arts Council, 1970-78; mem. N.Mex. Humanities Council, 1979, Gallup Centennial Com., 1980-81; mem. Cathedral Parish Council, 1980-83, v.p., 1981, century com. Western Health Found., 1988-89; active N.Mex. Diamond Jubilee/U.S. Constn. Bicentennial Gallup Com., 1986-87, N.Mex. Gallup Campus 25 Silver Anniversary Com., 1994. Recipient Dorothy Canfield Fisher $1,000 Libr. award, 1961, Outstanding Community Service award for mus. service Gallup C. of C., 1969, 70, Outstanding Citizen award, 1974, Benemerenti medal Pope Paul VI, 1977, Celebrate Literary award Gallup Internat. Reading 8 Assn., 1983-84, Woman of Distinction award Soroptimists, 1985, N.Mex. Disting. Pub. Svc. award, 1987, finalist Gov's award Outstanding N.Mex. Women, 1988, Edgar L. Hewett award Hist. Soc. N.Mex., 1992; Octavia Fellin Pub. Libr. named in her honor, 1990. Mem. ALA, N.Mex. Library Assn. (hon. life, v.p., sec., chmn. hist. materials com. 1964-66, salary and tenure com., nat. coordinator N.Mex. legislative com., chmn. com. to extend library services 1969-73, Librar. of Yr. award 1975, chmn. local and regional history roundtable 1978, Community Achievement award 1983, Membership award 1994), AAUW (v.p., co-organizer Gallup br., N.Mex. nominating com. 1967-68, chmn. fellowships and centennial fund Gallup br., chmn. com. on women), Plateau Scis. Soc., N.Mex. Folklore Soc. (v.p. 1964-65, pres. 1965-66), N.Mex. Hist. Soc. (dir. 1979-85), Gallup Hist. Soc., Gallup Film Soc. (co-organizer, v.p. 1950-58), LWV (v.p. 1953-56), NAACP, Pax Christi U.S.A., Women's Ordination Conf. Network, Gallup C. of C. (organizing chmn. women's div. 1972, v.p. 1972-73), N.Mex. Women's Polit. Caucus, N.Mex. Mcpl. League (pres. libr.'s div. 1979—), Alpha Delta Kappa (hon.). Roman Catholic (Cathedral Guild, Confraternity Christian Doctrine Bd. 1962-64, Cursillo in Christianity Movement, mem. of U.S. Cath. Bishop's Adv. Council 1969-74; corr. sec. Latin Am. Mission Program 1972-75, sec. Diocese of Gallup Pastoral Council 1972-73, c. liturgical commn. Diocese of Gallup 1977). Author: Yahweh The Voice that Beautifies The Land, A Chronicle of Mileposts: A Brief History of the University of New Mexico Gallup Campus. Home and Office: 513 E Mesa Ave Gallup NM 87301-6021

FELLMAN, JOHN KEEGAN, physiology educator, biochemist; b. St. Louis, Nov. 26, 1952; m. Harriet L. Hughes, Oct. 16, 1976; children: Mary Alice, John Murray. BS, Clemson (S.C.) U., 1974; PhD, U. Idaho, 1982. Postdoctoral fellow U. Idaho, Moscow, 1981-82, 1983; postdoctoral fellow Wash. State U., Pullman, 1983-86; rsch. chemist USDA/ARS, Wenatchee, Wash., 1987-88; asst. prof. U. Idaho, Moscow, 1988-93, assoc. prof., 1993-95; assoc. prof. Wash. State U., 1995—; pvt. practice post-harvest biochemist cons., pacific n.w., 1988—. Contbr. articles to profl. jours. Mem. AAAS, Am. Soc. Plant Physiologists, Am. Soc.for Horticultural Sci., Internat. Dwarf Fruit Tree Assn., Am. Chem. Soc., Sigma Xi (v.p. 1989-90, pres. 1990-92, U. Idaho chpt.). Office: U Idaho Dept Plant Soil Entomol Moscow ID 83843

FELLOWS, ALICE COMBS, artist; b. Atlanta, Sept. 14, 1935; d. Andrew Grafton III and Wilhelmina Drummond (Jackson) Combs; m. Robert Ellis Fellows Jr., Aug. 20, 1957 (div. 1978); children: Ariadne Elisabeth, Kara Suzanne. BFA, Syracuse U., 1957; M in Clin. Psychology, Antioch U., 1992. instr. Santa Monica Emeritus Coll., L.A., 1981; guest artist Yaddo, Saratoga Springs, N.Y., 1991; artist-in-residence Dorland Colony, Temecula, Calif., 1983. Exhibited works in numerous group and one-woman shows including Claremont Grad. Sch. Gallery, 1991, Saxon-Lee Gallery, L.A., 1989, Santa Monica Coll. Gallery Art, 1988, J. Rosenthal Gallery, Chgo., 1986, The Biennial Hirshhorn Mus. and Sculpture Garden, Washington, 1986, Kirk de Gooyer Gallery, L.A., 1984, 85, many others; works represented in numerous collections including The Norton, Santa Monica, Broad Found., Santa Monica, Mint Mus., Charlotte N.C., N.C. Mus. Raleigh, N.C., Security Pacific Corp., L.A., others. Grants selection juror Santa Monica Arts Coun., 1993. Nat. Endowment for Arts Painting fellow, 1991, Getty Trust Painting fellow, 1990, Western States Arts Fedn. Painting fellow, 1990. Home and Studio: 656 Copeland Ct Santa Monica CA 90405-4416

FELLOWS, DONALD MATTHEW, university official; b. Palo Alto, Calif., Dec. 7, 1955; s. Wilbur Lombard and Coralie Irene (Hill) F.; m. Jill Anne Fisher, Jan. 19, 1985; children: Lauren Catherine, Ryan Matthew, Austin Michael. BA in Pub. Adminstrn., San Diego State U., 1980; MEd in Edn. Leadership, U. San Diego, 1994. Asst. v.p. Gt. Am. Bank, San Diego, 1976-82; asst. dir. alumni and devel. San Diego State U., 1982-85; dir. corp. rels. Stanford (Calif.) U., 1985-90; dir. devel. U. San Diego, 1990—; cons. on fundraising. Bd. dirs. Burn Inst., San Diego, 1983-85. Mem. Nat. Soc. Fund Raising Execs., Coun. for Advancement and Support Edn., Rotary. Republican. Roman Catholic. Home: 8896 Calle Tragar San Diego CA 92129-2155 Office: U San Diego Alcala Pk San Diego CA 92110

FELT, JAMES PATTERSON, computer programmer; b. Ogden, Utah, June 13, 1950; s. John Gillingham and Claramay (Patterson) F. BA, Weber State Coll., Ogden, 1974, Weber State Coll., Ogden, 1980; MA, U. Ariz., 1978. Programmer 1st Security Bank, Salt Lake City, 1980-84, sr. programmer, 1984-92; v.p. Felt Auto Parts Co.; newsletter editor Salt Lake City, 1988-90, 92—. Organist, Salt Lake Liberty Stake LDS Ch., 1989—, clk., 1991—. Mem. Am. Guild Organists (Salt Lake chpt. newsletter editor 1988-90, 91—, publicity com. 1991—). Home: 48 W 300 S Apt 801 Salt Lake City UT 84101-2010

FELTER, EDWIN LESTER, JR., lawyer, agency administrator; b. Washington, Aug. 11, 1941; s. Edwin L. Felter and Bertha (Peters) Brekke; m. Yoko Yamauchi-Koito, Dec. 26, 1969. B.A., U. Tex., 1964; J.D., Cath. U. of Am., 1967. Bar: Colo. 1970, U.S. Dist. Ct. Colo. 1970, U.S. Ct. Appeals (10th cir.) 1971, U.S. Supreme Ct. 1973, U.S. Tax Ct. 1979, U.S. Ct. Claims 1979, U.S. Ct. Internat. Trade 1979; Dep. pub. defender State of Colo., Ft. Collins, 1971-75; asst. atty. gen. Office of the Atty. Gen., Denver, 1975-80; state adminstrv. law judge Colo. Div. of Adminstrv. Hearings, Denver, 1980-83, chief adminstrv. law judge, dir., 1983—; disciplinary prosecutor Supreme Ct. Grievance Com., 1975-78. Contbg. editor Internat. Franchising, 1970. Mem. Colo. State Mgmt. Cert. Steering com., 1983-86; No. Colo. Criminal Justice Planning council, Ft. Collins, 1973-75; bd. dirs., vice chmn. The Point Community Crisis Ctr., Ft. Collins, 1971-73; mem. Denver County Dem. Party Steering Com., 1978-79; chmn. 12th legis. dist., 1978-79, bd. dirs., pres. Denver Internat. Program, 1989-90. Mem. ABA, Nat. Conf. Adminstrv. Law Judges, Colo. Bar Assn. (chmn. grievance policy com. 1991-94), Arapahoe County Bar Assn., Nat. Assn. of Adminstrv. Law Judges (pres. Colo. chpt. 1982-84, Nat. Fellowship winner 1994). Office: Colo Divsn Adminstrv Hearings 1120 Lincoln St Ste 1400 Denver CO 80203-1718

FELTER, JUNE MARIE, artist; b. Oakland, Calif., Oct. 19, 1919; m. Richard Henry Felter, Feb. 7, 1943; children: Susan, Tom. Student, San Francisco Art Inst., 1960, 61, Oakland Art Inst., 1937-40. Instr. San Francisco Mus. Art, 1965-78, San Francisco State U., 1970-78, U. Calif., 1979-80, Santa Rosa (Calif.) Jr. Coll., 1981, Elaine Badgley-Arnoux Sch. Art, San Francisco, 1982, 83, U. Calif., San Francisco, 1979-80, 84-85. One-woman shows include Gumps Gallery, San Francisco, 1965-66, Linda Ferris Gallery, Seattle, 1971, Richmond Art Gallery, 1971-74, Dana Reich Gallery, San Francisco, 1978, 80-81, New Work, June Felter and Adelie Landis, 1992; exhibited in group shows at San Francisco Mus. Art., 1960-79, Civic Arts Gallery, Walnut Creek, Calif., 1983, U.S. Art, San Francisco, 1990, Oakland Art Mus., 1991, Wiegand Gallery, 1992, Jack London Square Oakland, 1993 and numerous others. Home and Office: 1046 Amito Dr Berkeley CA 94705-1502

FELTON, SAMUEL PAGE, biochemist; b. Petersburg, Va., Sept. 7, 1919; s. Samuel S. and Pearl (Williams) F.; m. Helen Florence Martin, Dec. 31, 1955; 1 child, Samuel Page. Degree in pharmacy, U.S. Army, San Francisco, 1942; BS in Chemistry, U. Wash., 1951, postgrad., 1954. Chief technician U.

Wash., Seattle, 1952-59, research assoc., 1959-62, sr. research assoc., 1976—, dir. cen. facilities lab. anesthesiology, 1969-73, dir. water quality lab., 1976-83, dir. biochem. lab. sch. of Fisheries, 1983-85; emeritus Sch. Fisheries, U. Wash., Seattle, 1985; asst. mem., asst. to dir. div. biochemistry Scripps Clinic and Research Found., La Jolla, Calif., 1962-66; asst. biochemist Children's Orthopedic Hosp., Seattle, 1966-68; vis. scientist Va. Inst. Marine Scis. at Coll. William and Mary, Williamsburg, 1985. Mem. bd. of adjustments City of Edmonds, Wash. Served to sgt. MC, U.S. Army 1941-45. Fellow Am. Inst. Chemists; mem. Am. Chem. Soc., Am. Inst. Fishery Research Biologists, N.Y. Acad. of Scis., Soc. Exptl. Biology and Medicine. Office: U Wash Fisheries Rsch & Teaching HF-15 Seattle WA 98195

FENG, JOSEPH SHAO-YING, physicist, electrical engineer; b. Peiping, China, June 21, 1948; came to U.S., 1950; s. Paul Yen Hsiung and Mary (Pai) F. BS in Physics, Calif. Inst. Tech., Pasadena, 1969; MS in Physics, Northwestern U., 1970, MSEE, 1971; PhD in Elec. Engring., Calif. Inst. Tech., 1975. Mem. rsch. staff T. J. Watson Rsch. Lab. IBM, Yorktown Heights, N.Y., 1974-77; scientist, engr. IBM Gen. Products Div., San Jose, Calif., 1977—. Inventor in field; contbr. articles to profl. jours. Incorporation chmn. Banner Run, San Jose, 1989. Mem. ASCIT (treas. Pasadena, Calif. chpt. 1968-69), IEEE, Am. Phys. Soc., Mediaeval Acad. of Am., Greenburgh (N.Y.) Karate Club (treas. 1977), Chi Ski (officer 1980-84), Nisei Ski (officer 1986-88).

FENNELL, DIANE MARIE, marketing executive, process engineer; b. Panama, Iowa, Dec. 11, 1944; d. Urban William and Marcella Mae (Leytham) Schechinger; m. Leonard E. Fennell, Aug. 19, 1967; children: David, Denise, Mark. BS, Creighton U., Omaha, 1966. Process engr. Tex. Instruments, Richardson, 1974-79; sr. process engr. Signetics Corp., Santa Clara, Calif., 1979-82; demo lab. mgr. Airco Temescal, Berkeley, Calif., 1982-84; field process engr. Applied Materials, Santa Clara, 1984-87; mgr. product mktg. Lam Rsch., Fremont, Calif., 1987-90; dir. sales and mktg. Ion & Plasma Equipment, Fremont, Calif., 1990-91; pres. FAI, Half Moon Bay, Calif., 1991—; founder, coord. chmn. Plasma Etch User's Group, Santa Clara, 1986-88; tchr. computer course Adult Edn., Half Moon Bay, Calif., 1982-83. Founder, bd. dirs. Birth to Three program Mental Retardation Ctr., Denison, Tex., 1974-75; fund raiser local sch. band, Half Moon Bay, 1981-89; community rep. local sch. bd., Half Moon Bay, 1982-83. Mem. Am. Vacuum Soc., Soc. Photo Instrumnentation Engrs., Soc. Women Engrs., Material Rsch. Soc. Home: 441 Alameda Ave Half Moon Bay CA 94019-1365

FENNING, LISA HILL, federal judge; b. Chgo., Feb. 22, 1952; d. Ivan Byron and Joan (Hennigar) Hill; m. Alan Mark Fenning, Apr. 3, 1977; 4 children. BA with honors, Wellesley Coll., 1971; JD, Yale U., 1974. Bar: Ill. 1975, Calif. 1979, U.S. Dist. Ct. (no. dist.) Ill., U.S. Dist. Ct. (no., ea., so. & cen. dists.) Calif., U.S. Ct. Appeals (6th, 7th & 9th cirs.), U.S. Supreme Ct. 1989. Law clk. U.S. Ct. Appeals 7th cir., Chgo., 1974-75; assoc. Jenner and Block, Chgo., 1975-77, O'Melveny and Myers, Los Angeles, 1977-85; judge U.S. Bankruptcy Ct. Cen. Dist. Calif., Los Angeles, 1985—; bd. govs. Nat. Conf. Bankruptcy Judges, 1989-92; pres. Nat. Conf. of Women's Bar Assns., N.C., 1987-88, pres.-elect, 1986-87, v.p., 1985-86, bd. dirs.; lectr., program coord. in field; bd. govs. Nat. Conf. Bankruptcy Judges Endowment for Edn., 1992—, Am. Bankruptcy Inst., 1994—. Mem., bd. advisors: Lawyer Hiring & Training Report, 1985-87; contbr. articles to profl. jours. Durant scholar Wellesley Coll., 1971; named one of Am's. 100 Most Important Women Ladies Home Jour., 1988. Fellow Am. Bar Found., Am. Coll. Bankruptcy; mem. ABA (mem. commn. on women in the profession 1987-91, Women's Caucus 1987—, Individual Rights and Responsibilities sect. 1984—, Bus. Law sect. 1986—, Bus. Bankruptcy com.), Nat. Assn. Women Judges (Nat. Task Force Gender Bias in the Cts. 1986-87, 93-94), Nat. Conf. Bankruptcy Judges (mem. endowment edn. bd.), Am. Bankruptcy Inst. (nominating com. 1994-95, bd. steering com. statis. project 1994—), Calif. State Bar Assn. (chair com. on women in law 1986-87), Women Lawyers' Assn. L.A. (ex officio mem., bd. dirs., chmn., founder com. on status of women lawyers 1984-85, officer nominating com. 1986, founder, mem. Do-It Yourself Mentor Network 1986—), Phi Beta Kappa. Democrat. Office: US Bankruptcy Ct 255 E Temple St Rm 1682 Los Angeles CA 90012-3334

FENTON, DONALD MASON, retired oil company executive; b. L.A., May 23, 1929; s. Charles Youdan and Dorothy (Mason) F.; m. Margaret M. Keehler, Apr. 24, 1953; children: James Michael, Douglas Charles. BS, U. Calif., L.A., 1952, PhD, 1958. Chemist Rohm and Haas Co., Phila., 1958-61; sr. rsch. chemist Union Oil Co., Brea, Calif., 1962-67, rsch. assoc., 1967-72, sr. rsch. assoc., 1972-82, mgr. planning and devel., 1982-85; mgr. new tech. devel. Unocal, Brea, 1985-92; cons. AMSCO, 1967-73; co-founder, 1st chmn. Petroleum Environ. Rsch. Forum; chmn. bd. dirs. Calif. Engring. Found., 1991-92. With U.S. Army, 1953-55. Fellow Am. Inst. Chemists, Alpha Chi Sigma; mem. Am. Chem. Soc. Home: 2861 E Alden Pl Anaheim CA 92806-4401

FENTON, TERRY LYNN, author, artist, consultant; b. Regina, Sask., Can., July 1, 1940; s. John Albert and Gertrude (Hirons) F.; m. Sheila Ann Cowie, Dec. 1, 1962; 1 son, Mark. B.A. in English Lit., U. Sask., 1962. Social worker Province of Alta., Edmonton, 1962-65; asst. to dir. Mackenzie Gallery, Regina, 1965-71; dir. Edmonton Art Gallery, 1972-87; artistic dir. Leighton Found., Calgary, 1988—. Author: Anthony Caro, 1986; co-author: Modern Painting in Canada, 1978; author books and catalogues on contemporary art; painter landscapes; co-founder Triangle Artists Workshop, NY, 1982. Home: 15713-89A Avenue, Edmonton, AB Canada T5R 4T1 Office: Edmonton Art Gallery, 2 Sir Winston Churchill Sq, Edmonton, AB Canada TSJ2C1

FENWICK, JAMES H(ENRY), editor; b. South Shields, Eng., Mar. 17, 1937; came to U.S., 1965; s. James Henry and Ellen (Tinmouth) F.; m. Suzanne Helene Hatch, Jan. 27, 1968. BA, Oxford U., Eng., 1960. Freelance lectr., writer, 1960-65; assoc. editor Playboy mag., Chgo., 1965-71; planning and features editor Radio Times, BBC, London, 1971-77; U.S. rep. Radio Times, BBC, N.Y.C., 1978-87; sr. editor Modern Maturity mag., Lakewood, Calif., 1987-90, exec. editor, 1990-91, editor, 1991—. Office: Am Assn Ret Persons 3200 Carson St Lakewood CA 90712-4038

FERBER, NORMAN ALAN, retail executive; b. N.Y.C., Aug. 25, 1948; m. Rosine Ferber; children: Robert, Lauren, Richard. Student, L.I. U. Buyer, mdse. mgr. Atherton Industries, N.Y.C., 1976-79; v.p., mdse. mgr. Raxton Corp., N.Y.C., 1979-82; v.p. Fashion World, N.Y.C., 1982; v.p merchandising, mktg. and distbn. Ross Stores Inc., Newark, Calif., 1982-87, pres., chief operating officer, 1987-88, pres., chief exec. officer, 1988—. Home: 1455 Edgewood Dr Palo Alto CA 94301-3118 Office: Ross Stores Inc PO Box 728 8333 Central Ave Newark CA 94560

FERBER, ROBERT RUDOLF, physics researcher, educator; b. New Eagle, Pa., June 11, 1935; s. Rudolf F. and Elizabeth J. (Robertson) F.; m. Eileen Merhaut, July 25, 1964; children: Robert Rudolf, Lynne C. BSEE, U. Pitts., 1958; MSEE, Carnegie-Mellon U., 1966, Ph.D. in Semiconductor Physics, 1967. Registered profl. engr., Pa. Mgr. engring. dept. WRS Motion Picture Labs., Pitts., 1954-58, sec., 1959-76, v.p., 1976-79; sr. engr. Westinghouse Rsch. Labs., Pitts., 1956-67; mgr. nuclear effects group Westinghouse Elec. Corp., Pitts., 1967-71, mgr. adv. engr. energy projects, East Pittsburgh, 1971-77; photovoltaic materials and collector rsch. mgr. Jet Propulsion Lab., Pasadena, Calif. 1977-85, SP100 Project contract tech. mgr., 1985-90, asst. project mgr. Spaceborne Imaging Radar, 1990—; v.p. Executaire Inc., Pitts., 1960-64; pres. Tele-Cam Inc., Pitts., 1960-78. Editor: Transactions of the 9th World Energy Conf. 1974, Digest of the 9th World Energy Conf., 1974. Contbr. articles to profl. jours. Patentee in field. Mem. Franklin Regional Sch. Dist. Bd., Murrysville, Pa., 1975-77. Fellow Buhl Found., 1965-66, NDEA, 1976-77. Mem. IEEE (sr.), ASME (chmn. 1986 Solar Energy Div. Conf.). Republican. Lutheran. Home: 5314 Alta Canyada Rd La Canada Flintridge CA 91011-1606 Office: Jet Propulsion Lab 4800 Oak Grove Dr Pasadena CA 91109-8001

FERDON, EDWIN NELSON, JR., ethnologist; b. St. Paul, June 14, 1913; s. Edwin Nelson and Julie Beatha (O'Meyer) F.; m. Constance Potter Etz, Oct. 14, 1939 (dec. Jan., 1969); children: Richard, Derre, Julie; m. Lola Vearl Baker, June 18, 1972. BA, U. N.Mex., Albuquerque, 1937; MA, U. So. Calif., L.A., 1942. Curator br. mus. Mus. of N.Mex., Santa Fe, 1937-38, curator Mid. Am. archaeology, 1938-40; rsch. assoc. Hispanic studies Mus. N.Mex./Sch. Am. Rsch., Santa Fe, 1940-45, rsch. assoc. in charge Hispanice studies, 1945-57; assoc. dir. in charge Mus. Internat. Folk Art Mus. N.Mex., Santa Fe, 1958-60, coord. interpretation div. dept. anthropology, 1960-61; assoc. dir. Ariz. State Mus. U. Ariz., Tucson, 1961-78, ethnologist Ariz. State Mus., 1978-83, ret., 1983. Author: One Man's Log, 1966, Early Tahiti as the Explorers Saw It, 1981, Early Tonga as the Explorers Saw It, 1987, Early Observations of Marquesan Culture, 1993, (monograph) Studies in Ecuadorian Geography, 1950. Fellow AAAS; mem. Sigma Xi. Home: 2141 E Juanita St Tucson AZ 85719-3818

FERDON, RICHARD PAUL, nutritionist, consultant; b. Arcadia, Calif., June 29, 1965; s. Robert Bruce and Rose Ann (Morelli) F. AA, L.A. Harbor Coll., 1985; BS, Calif. State U., 1988. Clinic supr. Dept. Pub. Health, Orange, Calif., 1990-91; nutrition support dietitian Saddleback Medical Ctr., Laguna Hills, Calif., 1991-92; medical sales Sherwood Medical, 1992-94; acct. mgr. Alcon Surgical, Laguna Niguel, Calif., 1994—; pres. Student Dietetic Assn., 1988, v.p., 1987. Recipient scholarship 1987-88. Mem. Aircraft Owners/Pilots Assn., Civil Air Patrol (sr.), Profl. Assn. Diving Instrs., Am. Dietetic Assn. Office: Alcon Surgical 6201 South Fwy Fort Worth TX 76134-2001

FERENCE, HELEN MARIE, nursing consultant; b. Ohio, Sept. 1, 1946; d. Emery and Josephine Leona (Terlecki) F.; m. William Verill Nick. Diploma, Youngstown (Ohio) Hosp. Assn., 1967; BS, Youngstown U., 1970; MS, Ohio State U., 1972; PhD, NYU, N.Y.C., 1979. Cert. advanced cardiac life support; cert. nursing sci. Cons., pres. Nursing Cons. and Rsch., Pebble Beach, Calif., 1972—; dir. rsch. and programs Sigma Theta Tau, Indpls., 1986-88; dir. clin. evaluation, rsch. and nursing standards Mt. Sinai Hosp., N.Y.C., 1986-88; asst. prof. Ohio State U., Columbus, 1972-80; cons. Battelle Meml. Inst., Columbus, 1972-81, VA, Chillicothe, Ohio, 1975-80; asst. prof. NYU, 1979-80; cons. McGraw-Hill, Monterey, Calif., 1981-85; bd. dirs. Mt. Sinai Hosp., N.Y., 1986-88. Editor Notes on Nursing Sci., 1986—. Bd. dirs. Monterey Health Inst. Recipient Laureate: Nightingale Prize, 1991. Fellow Nightingale Soc. (bd. dirs.); mem. Sigma Theta Tau. Home: PO Box 862 Pebble Beach CA 93953-0862

FERGUS, GARY SCOTT, lawyer; b. Racine, Wis., Apr. 20, 1954; s. Russell Malcolm and Phyl Rose (Muratore) F.; m. Isabelle Sabina Beekman, Sept. 28, 1985; children: Mary Marckwald Beekman Fergus, Kirkpatrick Russell Beekman Fergus. SB, Stanford U., 1976; JD, U. Wis., 1979; LLM, NYU, 1981. Bar: Wis. 1979, Calif. 1980. Assoc. Brobeck, Phleger & Harrison, San Francisco, 1980-86, ptnr., 1986—. Author, inventor (software) Nat. Case Mgmt. for Asbestos Litigation. Mem. ABA. Home: 3024 Washington St San Francisco CA 94115-1618 Office: Brobeck Phleger & Harrison 1 Market Plz San Francisco CA 94105

FERGUSON, BILLY COKER, civil engineer; b. Birmingham, Ala., Aug. 24, 1936; s. Clyde William and Julia Edna (Coker) F.; m. Barbara Mae Keller, Jan. 30, 1959; 1 child, Mark Anthony; m. Minerva Ruth Victoria Deveyra Allado, June 8, 1973; children: Shawn Wilson, Jamie Dee, Laren Dael. BSCE, U. Mich., 1961, MSCE, 1962; postgrad., U. Calif., Davis, 1965. Registered profl. engr., Calif. Assoc. engr. Calif. Dept. of Water Resources, Sacramento, 1962-67; civil engr. Devel. and Resources Corp., Sacramento, 1967-70, resident mgr. Iran, 1973-78; civil engr. Sacramento, 1970-73, 78-79, Coeur D'Alene, Idaho, 1985-86; resident mgr. Indonesia Internat. Engring., San Francisco, 1979-85; supervising engr. Calif. Dept. Water Resources, Sacramento, 1986—; cons. civil engring. R.W. Beck & Assocs., Seattle, 1991—; mem. Prestressed Concrete Cylinder Pipe Users Group, 1990—. Contbr. tech. papers to profl. publs. With U.S. Army, 1955-58, ETO. Libertarian. Office: Calif Dept Water Resources 1416 9th St Sacramento CA 95814-5511

FERGUSON, BRUCE A., construction executive, contractor; b. 1944. BA, Colo. State U. With Gerald H. Phillips Co., Denver, 1966—, now pres. Office: Gerald H. Phillips Inc 1530 W 13th Ave Denver CO 80204*

FERGUSON, E. ROBERT, construction and engineering company executive; b. Phila., Mar. 26, 1932; s. John Harold and Vivian (Livingston) F.; m. Patricia Ann Heckman, Feb. 5, 1955; children: Robin, Sandra, Erin. BSCE, U. Mich., 1955. V.p. Dillingham Corp. & Gordon H. Ball Inc., Danville, Calif., 1958-75, Pacific Constrn. Co., Honolulu, 1975-76; mgr. ops. Rigging Internat., Oakland, Calif., 1976-81; sr. v.p. ASI Bldg. Systems Inc., Dallas, 1982-85; pres., chmn. bd. dirs., CEO, COO Kasler Corp., San Bernardino, Calif., 1985-92; pres. North Pacific Morrison Knudsen, Honolulu, 1992; v.p. internat. ops. Morrison Knudsen, Boise, 1993-95. Served as 1st lt. USMC, 1955-58. Office: Morrison Knudsen Plz PO Box 22 Boise ID 83707-0022

FERGUSON, JACK LEE, lawyer; b. Richmond, Kans., Sept. 24, 1931; s. Oliver Lee and Mary Marjorie (Knittles) F.; m. Brent Anne Berry, Dec. 16, 1951 (div. June 1969); children: Seana Dawnelle, Robin Leigh, Valerie Lynn, Scott Wesley, Grant Angus; m. Madeleine Ruth Cash, May 19, 1976. Student, Calif. State U., 1950-52; JD, LaSalle U., 1957. Ins. investigator Equifax, Sacramento, Calif., 1954-59; right of way agt. Caltrans, Fresno, Calif., 1959-62; pvt. practice law Napa, Calif., 1962—. Supervisor County of Napa, 1965-69, asst. dist. atty., 1963-64, vice chmn. bd. edn., 1956-59. Cpl. USMCR, 1948-52. Named oustanding young man of Am. Jaycees, 1966; recipient Man-Boy award Boys & Girls Clubs of Am., 1969. Mem. Napa County Bar Assn. (chmn. fee arbitration com. 1980-95), 25th Dist. Agrl. Assn. (dir. 1985-93), Am. Legion, Masons, Shriners, Elks, U.S. Navy League (v.p. Napa chtp. 1994), Sons of Italy in Am., Marines Meml. Assn.

FERGUSON, LARRY EMMETT, educational administrator; b. Coolridge, W.Va., Oct. 19, 1934; s. Clarence Emmett and Marjorie Evelyn (Ransom) F.; m. Lynne Alice Jackson, May 17, 1957 (div. May 1975); children: David (dec.), Karen J. Ramsey; m. Alma Jeanette (Jeanne) Mitchell, Oct. 24, 1975; stepchildren: Dona Williamson, Patti Rae, Terri Musa-Jones, Ron Musa. AAS, Clark Coll., Vancouver, Wash., 1977; BS in Psychology and Elem. Edn., Portland State U., 1979, postgrad., 1979-91. Cert. continuing tchr., Wash. Customer engr. RCA Svc. Co., Portland, Oreg., 1975-77; tchr. Ft. Simcoe Job Corps, White Swan, Wash., 1982-89; mgr. Life Skills Tng. Inst., Vancouver, Wash., 1990—. Bd. dirs. Slocum Theatre Group, Vancouver, Wash., 1982; loaned exec. Consolidated Fed. Campaign, Yakima, Wash., 1988. Master sgt. USAF, 1954-75. Mem. Internat. Order Foresters, Non-Commd. Officers Assn., Am. Legion. Mem. Disciples of Christ. Office: Life Skills Tng Inst 1920 Broadway Vancouver WA 98663

FERGUSON, LLOYD ELBERT, manufacturing engineer; b. Denver, Mar. 5, 1942; s. Lloyd Elbert Ferguson and Ellen Jane (Schneider) Romero; m. Patricia Valine Hughes, May 25, 1963; children: Theresa Renee, Edwin Bateman. BS in Engring., Nova Internat. Coll., 1983. Cert. hypnotherapist, geometric tolerance instr. Crew leader FTS Corp., Denver, 1968-72; program engr. Sundstrand Corp., Denver, 1972-87, sr. assoc. project engr., 1987-90, sr. liaison engr., 1990-93, sr. planning engr., 1993—; v.p. Valine Corp. Lic. practitioner of religious sci. United Ch. of Religious Sci., L.A.; team capt. March of Dimes Team Walk, Danver, 1987; mem. AT&T Telephone Pioneer Clowns for Charity. Recipient recognition award AT&T Telephone Pioneers, 1990. Mem. Soc. Mfg. Engrs. (chmn. local chpt. 1988, zone chmn. 1989, achievement award 1984, 86, recognition award 1986, 90, appreciation award 1988), Nat. Mgmt. Assn. (cert., program instr. 1982—, honor award 1987, 90), Am. Indian Sci. and Engring. Soc., Colo. Clowns. Mem. United Ch. of Religious Sci. Home: 10983 W 76th Dr Arvada CO 80005-3481 Office: Sundstrand Corp 2480 W 70th Ave Denver CO 80221-2501

FERGUSON, WARREN JOHN, federal judge; b. Eureka, Nev., Oct. 31, 1920; s. Ralph and Marian (Damele) F.; m. E. Laura Keyes, June 5, 1948; children: Faye F., Warren John, Teresa M., Peter J. B.A., U. Nev., 1942; LL.B., U. So. Calif., 1949; LL.D. (hon.), Western State U., San Fernando Valley Coll. Law. Bar: Calif. 1950. Mem. firm Ferguson & Judge, Fullerton, Calif., 1950-59; city atty. for cities of Buena Park, Placentia, La Puente, Baldwin Park, Santa Fe Springs, Walnut and Rosemead, Calif., 1953-59; mcpl. ct. judge Anaheim, Calif., 1959-60; judge Superior Ct., Santa Ana, Calif., 1961-66, Juvenile Ct., 1963-64, Appellate Dept., 1965-66; U.S. dist. judge Los Angeles, 1966-79; judge U.S. Circuit Ct. (9th cir.), Los Angeles, 1979-86; sr. judge U.S. Ct. Appeals (9th cir.), Santa Ana, 1986—; faculty Fed. Jud. Ctr., Practising Law Inst., U. Iowa Coll. Law, N.Y. Law Jour.; assoc. prof. psychiatry (law) Sch. Medicine, U. So. Calif.; assoc. prof. Loyola Law Sch. Served with AUS, 1942-46. Decorated Bronze Star. Mem. Phi Kappa Phi, Theta Chi. Democrat. Roman Catholic. Office: US Circuit Ct 9th Cir 500 Fed Bldg 34 Civic Center Plz Santa Ana CA 92701-4025

FERGUSON-HUNTINGTON, KATHLEEN ELIZABETH, artist, educator; b. Chgo., Jan. 31, 1945; d. Paul and Catherine A. (Graham) Wurtz; m. Stuart Ferguson, Sept. 26, 1964 (div. 1968); m. Hugh H. Huntington, Oct. 10, 1992. BFA with honors, Layton Sch. Art, 1969; MFA, RISD, 1971. Exhibit coord. Smithsonian Instn., Washington, 1973; asst. prof. L.I. U., Greenvale, N.Y., 1973-75, Nassau C.C., Garden City, N.Y., 1976; lectr. Gallery Passport, N.Y.C., 1978; vis. artist Conn. Coll., New London, 1979, U. Ky., Lexington, 1980-82, Transylvania U., Lexington, 1985; dir. Art Acumen Ednl. Systems, N.Mex., 1983—; creativity cons. K.F.C. Corp., Louisville, 1986, GE Co., Daytona Beach, Fla., 1987, E.I. DuPont deNemours, Wilmington, Del., 1988, Honeywell Corp., Mpls., 1994—; lectr. in field. One women shows at Smithsonian Instn., 1972, Conn. Coll., 1975, U. R.I., Kingston, 1975, Nobe Gallery, N.Y.C., 1977, 79, Jan Cicero Gallery, Chgo., 1979, 84, R. H. Oosterom Gallery, N.Y.C., 1980, Ctr. for Contemporary Art, U. Ky., 1980, U. Cin., 1982, Graham Modern, N.Y.C., 1985, High Mus. Art, Atlanta, 1986, Southeastern Ctr. for Contemporary Art, Winston-Salem, N.C., 1987, J.B. Speed Mus., Louisville, 1987, Sun Cities (Ariz.) Art Mus., Angels Gate Art Ctr., L.A., others; group exhbns. include Hundred Acres Gallery, N.Y.C., 1971, 73, Virginia Mus., Richmond, 1973, 112 Green St., N.Y.C., 1975, Artists Space, N.Y.C., 1975, Whitney Mus., N.Y.C., 1975, Mus. Modern Art, N.Y.C., 1976, Ginza Nissan Gallery, Tokyo, 1976, Queens Mus., Flushing, N.Y., 1978, 55 Mercer Gallery, N.Y.C., 1978, Washington Sq. Gallery, N.Y.C., 1979, Betty Parsons Gallery, N.Y.C., 1979, R. H. Oosterom Gallery, N.Y.C., 1979, Indpls. Mus. Art, 1980, Jan Cicero Gallery, Chgo., 1980, Jacksonville (Fla.) Mus. Arts, 1983, McNay Art Inst., San Antonio, 1984, Owensboro (Ky.) Mus., 1987, 88, Gallery for Contemporary Art, Raleigh, N.C., 1987, Mus. N.Mex., 1993, others; contbr. articles to profl. publs.; sculpture Honeywell Corp. Fellow Provincetown Fine Arts Work Ctr., 1971, MacDowell Colony, 1973, Helene Wurlitzer Found., 1985, 89; grantee Ky. Found. for Women, 1985, Ky. Arts Coun./Nat. Endowment for Arts, 1985, Gloval Village, N.Y.C., 1975, travel grantee Provincetown Fine Arts Work Ctr., 1971-72; named to Hon. Order of Ky. Cols., 1986—. Mem. Nat. Artists Equity Assn., Permacultural Drylands (mem. ecology teaching team 1992-94), Taos Art Assn., Angels Gate Cultural Ctr. Home and Studio: PO Box 316 Arroyo Hondo NM 87513-0316

FERGUSSON, ROBERT GEORGE, retired army officer; b. Chgo., May 20, 1911; s. Archibald Campbell and Anne (Sheehan) F.; m. Charlotte Lawrence, Nov. 18, 1937; 1 son, Robert Lawrence (dec.). Student, Beloit Coll., 1929-32; BS, U.S. Mil. Acad., 1936; MA in Internat. Rels., Boston U., 1959. Commd. 2d lt. U.S. Army, 1936, advanced through grades to maj. gen., 1962; comdg. officer 14th Inf. Regt., Hawaii, 1955-57; chief army adv. group Naval War Coll., Newport, R.I., 1957-61; asst. divsn. comdr. 24th Inf. Divsn., Augsburg, Ger., 1961-62; chief staff Hdqrs. Central Army Group (NATO), Heidelberg, Ger., 1962-65; comdg. gen. U.S. Army Tng. Center, Inf., Ft. Ord, 1965-67; comdr. U.S. Forces, Berlin, 1967-70; ret., 1970; corp. group v.p. manpower planning Dart Industries, Inc., Los Angeles, 1970-78; cons., 1978-82, ret., 1982. Decorated D.S.M., Legion of Merit with oak leaf cluster, Bronze Star with 3 oak leaf clusters, Purple Heart (U.S.); knight comdr. Cross with badge and star Order of Merit (W.Ger.); officer Legion of Honor (France). Mem. Clan Fergusson Soc. (Scotland), Beta Theta Pi. Clubs: Cypress Point (Pebble Beach); Old Capitol (Monterey, Calif.). Home: PO Box 1515 Pebble Beach CA 93953-1515

FERINI, ROBERT PAT, agricultural products company executive; b. 1963. With Betteravia Farms, Santa Maria, Calif.; now ptnr. Office: Betteravia Farms PO Box 5845 Santa Maria CA 93456-5845*

FERKEL, RICHARD DENNIS, orthopedic surgeon, educator; b. Rockford, Ill., May 4, 1951; s. Louis Robert and Eve Rebecca Ferkel; m. Michelle Lynn Herman, July 20, 1974; children: Eric Ian, Megan Lisa. Student, UCLA, 1969-72; AB in Biochemistry, U. Calif., Berkeley, 1973; MD, Northwestern U., 1977. Diplomate Am. Bd. Orthopedic Surgery, Nat. Bd. Med. Examiners. Intern in surgery UCLA Med. Ctr., 1977-78, resident in orthopaedic surgery, 1978-82; resident in orthopaedic surgery Wadsworth VA Med. Ctr., L.A., 1978-82, chief arthroscopy, attending surgeon, 1983—; chief resident Harbor Gen. Hosp.-UCLA Med. Ctr., 1980; fellow in sports medicine and knee reconstructive surgery So. Calif. Sports Medicine and Orthopedic Med. Group, Van Nuys, Calif., 1982-83; resident in children's orthopaedics L.A. unit Shriner's Hosp. for Crippled Children, 198l, asst. surgeon, 1983—; pvt. practice So. Calif. Orthop. Inst., Van Nuys, 1983—, dir. sports medicine fellowship program; clin. instr. orthopaedic surgery UCLA Sch. Medicine, 1983—; attending surgeon Sepulveda VA Hosp., 1985—; presenter in field; orthopaedic cons. local high schs., Pierce Coll.; vol. physician Calif. Spl. Olympics, 1978—; team physician Crespi High Sch., Encino, Calif., L.A. Valley Coll., Van Nuys; cons. NFL; physician specialist L.A. XXIII Olympiad. Editor: (with M.J. Friedman) Prosthetic Ligament Reconstruction of the Knee, 1988; contbr. articles to med. jours., chpts. to books; reviewer Am. Jour. Sports Medicine, Arthroscopy Jour., Clin. Orthopedic Related Rsch. Gore Corp. grantee, 1985-86. Mem. AMA (physician recognition award 1986—), Calif. Med. Assn., L.A. Med. Assn., Am. Acad. Orthopedic Surgeons, Arthroscopy Assn. N.Am., Internat. Arthroscopy Assn., Am. Orthopedic Soc. for Sports Medicine, Orthopedic Rsch. Soc., Western Orthopedic Assn. (best paper award 1986), Am. Coll. Sports Medicine, Arthroscopic Surgeons Shoulder Study Group, Bay Area Knee Soc., Northwestern U. Med. Sch. Alumni Assn., U. Calif. Alumni Assn., UCLA Athletic Fund, City of Hope, L.A. Found. Med. Care. Office: So Calif Orthopedic Inst 6815 Noble Ave Van Nuys CA 91405-3729

FERM, BRITA ELLEN, public health administrator-educator, researcher; b. Kansas City, Mo., May 21, 1951; d. Carl Axel and Barbara Marie (Reagan) F.; m. Richard Lee Schneider, May 28, 1990; children: Rebecca Anne David, Barbara Kathleen David, Carl Werner Schwenk, Erich Burkhardt Schwenk. BS in Health Sci. summa cum laude, San Diego State U., 1990; MA in Edn., U.S. Internat. U., 1991. Cert. community coll. instr., Calif. Facilitator Navy Alcohol & Drug Safety Action Program, San Diego, 1988-91; community educaotr Chemically Dependent Mothers Project, San Diego, 1990-91; program mgr. South Bay Drug Abuse Svcs., Chula Vista, Calif., 1991; dir. Happy Child, Inc., San Diego, 1986—; bd. dirs. Adult Children of Alcoholics, San Diego, 1984-85, Early Childhood Parenting Inst., San Diego, 1987—. Author: Secret Families/Problem Families, 1988, Secret Families/Problem Families curricula, 1990, Happy Child, 1990. Performer piano with Radio City Music Hall Rockettes, Super Bowl XXII, San Diego, 1988. Recipient TAP award Soroptimist Internat., 1988, San Diego County Outstanding Citizen award, 1994; scholar Bus. and Profl. Women's Assn., 1989; named Outstanding Alumnus San Diego Mesa Coll., 1989, Outstanding Grad. Dept. Health Scis., San Diego State U., 1990; High Risk Youth grantee Office of Substance Abuse Prevention, Washington, 1991. Mem. Soc. Pub. Health Edn., Nat. Coun. on Alcoholism, Calif. Women's Commn. on Alcohol and Drug Dependencies, Nat. Assn. Prevention Profls., Women's Action Com. on Alcohol, Nat. Parenting Assn., Eta Sigma Gamma. Office: Happy Child Inc 4420 Rainier Ave Ste 304 San Diego CA 92120-3329

FERNANDES, DIONISIO A., physician; b. Goa, India, Oct. 3, 1945; s. Joao Andre and Carmina F.; m. Fiola C. Rebello, May 28, 1976; children: Chris, Jason, Melissa. BS with honors, St. Xaviers Coll., Bombay, 1963; MD, Armed Forces Med., India, 1969. cert. Calif. Med. Bd. Intern pediatrics Jewish Hosp., Bklyn., 1970-71; resident pediatrics Baylor Coll. Medicine, Houston, 1971-72; chief pediatrician J.N. Health Ctr., Buffalo, N.Y., 1972-74, C.S.Y. Project, Dayton, Ohio, 1974-75; fellow allergy & immunology La. State U., New Orleans, 1977—; pvt. practice Castro Valley, Calif., 1977—; asst. clin. prof. U. Calif., San Francisco, 1982—. Fellow Am. Acad. Pediatrics, Am. Acad. Allergy, Am. Coll Allergy, Am. Coll. Chest Physicians; mem. Calif. Med. Assn., No. Calif. Allergy Soc. Roman Catholic. Office: 20055 Lake Chabot Rd Castro Valley CA 94546-5331

FERNANDES, WINSTON JEROME, computer scientist; b. Kuwait City, Kuwait, Sept. 5, 1972; came to U.S., 1982; s. Henry and Regina (Lasrado) F. Degree in computer sci., U. Calif., Berkeley, 1990. CEO OCO-Office Computer Ops., Santa Monica, Calif., 1990—; cons. George Iny Enterprises, Venice, Calif., 1987—, Gold Coast Properties, Venice, 1987—, K.L. Omni Internat., Venice, 1987—, Henry's Market, Venice, 1987—. Office: OCO-Office Computer Ops 9 Dudley Ave Venice CA 90291-2405

FERNANDES SALLING, LEHUA, state senator, lawyer; b. Lihue, Hawaii, Dec. 6, 1949; d. William Ernest Fernandes and Evelyn (Ohai) Fernandes; m. Michael Ray Salling, Aug. 14, 1971; 1 child. BS, Colo. State U., 1971; JD, Cleveland Marshall Coll., 1975. Ptnr. Fernandes Salling & Salling, Kapaa Kauai, Hawaii, 1976—; mem. Hawaii Senate, 1982—. Mem. Hawaii State Bar Assn., Maile Bus. and Profl. Women's Club, Kamokila Canoe Club, Zonta. Office: Hawaii State Capitol Honolulu HI 96813

FERNANDEZ, CLEMENTE GUAJARDO, environmental specialist; b. Devine, Tex., Nov. 5, 1940; m. Carmen Sanchez, Jan. 23, 1966; children: David A., Adria L. AAS in Police Sci., C.C. USAF, 1984; A in Gen. Studies, Pima C.C., 1987; BS in Mgmt., Park Coll., 1989. Enlisted USAF, 1960, advanced through grades to sr. master sgt., retired, 1987; air quality enforcement officer Dept. environ. Quality, Tucson, Ariz., 1987-90, environ. specialist, 1990—; asbestos bldg. insp. Dept. Environ. Quality, Tucson, 1990—, asbestos contract supr., 1990—, visible emissions evaluator, 1987—; hostage negotiator USAF, 1981-87. Author: (dept. manuals) Field Service Training Manual, 1993, Field Inspection Protocol, 1994, Inspection Safety Manual, 1994, Respiratory Protection Program, 1994. Admission rep. Park Coll., Davis-Monthan AFB, Ariz., 1994—; v.p. parish coun. Christ the King Cath. Ch., Davis-Monthan AFB, 1982-83, fund coun. mem., 1982-87. Decorated Meritorious Svc. medals (3), Commendation Svc. medals (4). Democrat. Office: Pima County Dept Environn Quality 130 W Congress St Tucson AZ 85701-1332

FERNANDEZ, FERDINAND FRANCIS, federal judge; b. 1937. BS, U. So. Calif., 1958, JD, 1963; LLM, Harvard U., 1963. Bar: Calif. 1963, U.S. Dist. Ct. (cen. dist.) Calif. 1963, U.S. Ct. Appeals (9th cir.) 1963, U.S. Supreme Ct. 1967. Elec. engr. Hughes Aircraft Co., Culver City, Calif., 1958-62; law clk. to dist. judge U.S. Dist. Ct. (cen. dist.) Calif., 1963-64; pvt. practice law Allard, Shelton & O'Connor, Pomona, Calif., 1964-80; judge Calif. Superior Ct. San Bernardino County, Calif., 1980-85, U.S. Dist. Ct. (cen. dist.) Calif., L.A., 1985-89, U.S. Ct. Appeals (9th cir.), L.A., 1989—; Lester Roth lectr. U. So. Calif. Law Sch., 1992. Contbr. articles to profl. jours. Vice chmn. City of La Verne Commn. on Environ. Quality, 1971-73; chmn. City of Claremont Environ. Quality Bd., 1972-73; bd. trustees Pomona Coll., 1990—. Fellow Am. Coll. Trust and Estate Counsel; mem. ABA, State Bar of Calif. (fed. cts. com. 1966-69, ad hoc com. on attachments 1971-85, chmn. com. on adminstrn. of justice 1976-77, exec. com. taxation sect. 1977-80, spl. com. on mandatory fee arbitration 1978-79), Calif. Judges Assn. (chmn. juvenile cts. com. 1983-84, faculty mem. Calif. Jud. Coll. 1982-83, faculty mem. jurisprudence and humanities course 1983-85), Hispanic Nat. Bar Assn., L.A. County Bar Assn. (bull. com. 1974-75), San Bernardino County Bar Assn., Pomona Valley Bar Assn. (co-editor Newsletter 1970-72, trustee 1971-78, sec.-treas. 1973-74, 2d v.p. 1974-75, 1st v.p. 1975-76, pres. 1976-77), Estate Planning Coun. Pomona Valley (sec. 1966-76), Order of Coif, Phi Kappa Phi, Tau Beta Pi. Office: US Ct Appeals 9th Cir 125 S Grand Ave Ste 602 Pasadena CA 91105-1621*

FERNANDEZ, FERNANDO LAWRENCE, research company executive, aeronautical engineer; b. N.Y.C., Dec. 31, 1938; s. Fernando and Luz Esther (Fortuno) F.; m. Carmen Dorothy Mays, Aug. 26, 1962; children: Lisa Marie, Christopher John. BSME, Stevens Inst. Tech., 1960, MS in Applied Mechanics, 1961; PhD in Aeronautics, Calif. Inst. Tech., 1969. Engr. Lockheed Missiles & Space Co., Sunnyvale, Calif., 1961-63; div. mgr. The Aerospace Corp., El Segundo, Calif., 1963-72; program mgr. R & D Assocs., Santa Monica, Calif., 1972-75; v.p. Phys. Dynamics, Inc., San Diego, 1975-76; pres. Arete Assocs., San Diego, 1976-93, Arete Engring. Tech. Corp., San Diego, 1994—; mem. Chief Naval Ops. Exec. Panel, Washington, 1983—. Editor Jour. AIAA, 1970; contbr. articles to Fluid Mechanics. Office: Arete Engring Tech Corp 10975 Torreyana Rd San Diego CA 92121-1111

FERNANDEZ, LINDA FLAWN, entrepreneur, social worker; b. Tampa, Fla., Sept. 14, 1943; d. Frank and Rose (D'Amico) F.; 1 child, Marci. B.S., U. South Fla., 1965; M.S., U. Nev., 1976. Social worker Hillsborough County, Tampa, Fla., 1965-67; parole officer adult div. Fla. Parole Commn., Tampa, 1967-69; dir. social services Sunrise Hosp., Las Vegas, Nev., 1969-78; ind. real estate investor, Fla. and Nev., 1965—; pres. Las Vegas Color Separations, Inc., 1978—, Las Vegas Typesetting, Inc., 1983—; LMR Enterprises, Inc., Las Vegas, 1984—; sec.-treas. Sierra Color Graphics, Inc., Las Vegas, 1983—. Founder, organizer Human Relations, pet mascots for elderly; team ofcl. girls' softball, 1985; mem. Clark County Citizens Com. Efficiency and Cost Reduction, 1991; vice-chmn. Citizens Com. Efficiency and Cost Reduction, 1992. Recipient numerous awards Ad Club Fedn. Mem. Las Vegas C. of C. (congl. com.) Women's Las Vegas C. of C., Ad Club Fedn., Citizens for Pvt. Enterprise, U.S. C. of C. Avocations: tennis; water skiing. Office: 3351 S Highland Dr Ste 210 Las Vegas NV 89109-3430

FERRAIUOLO, PERUCCI DIANDREA, journalist; b. Denver, Nov. 20, 1946; s. Francesco and Carolyn (Andrew) F.; m. Barbara Nesland, Mar. 21, 1992; children: Lisa, Megan, Benjamin. AA, Saddleback Coll., 1972; BS, Calif. State Coll., 1974. Reporter, columnist Capo Valley News, San Juan Capistrano, Calif., 1981-82; editor, syndicated writer Lifestyle Mag., Orange County, Calif., 1982-84; syndicated interviewer Intro Mag., L.A., 1983-84; syndicated feature writer O.C. Mag., Orange County, 1984-86; nat. syndicated columnist N.W. Christian Jour., Seattle, 1983—; reporter N.Y. Times Syndicated/Religious News Svc., 1980-95, Daily Jour. Am., 1995—; biography writer Sparrow Records, Nashville, 1993—, StarSong Records, Nashville, 1993—, Benson Records, Nashville, 1993—, Broken Records, Nashville, 1993—; scriptwriter Parade Pictures Corp., Hollywood, Calif., 1973-80. Author: Laughing Your Way to God, 1995; frequent guest radio talk shows. With USMC, 1965-71. Decorated Purple Heart (2). Mem. Soc. Profl. Journalists, Investigative Reporters and Editors, Nat. Assn. Evang., Evang. Press Assn., Gospel Music Assn. Republican. Home: 8252 126th Ave NE Kirkland WA 98033-8075

FERRANG, ANTOINETTE M., dietitian educator; b. Charleston, W.Va., Apr. 17, 1966; d. James Peter and Dorothy Marie (Fink) F. BS, Ohio U., 1988; MS, Pa. State U., State Coll., 1990. Registered dietitian, 1990. Owner, nutrition cons. Food for Thought Nutrition Consulting, San Mateo, Calif., 1991—; instr. Coll. of San Mateo, Calif., 1991—, De Anza Cmty. Coll., Cupertino, Calif., 1993—. Author: Seminars to Go!, 1994; contbr. to profl. jours. Mem. Am. Dietetic Assn., Soc. for Nutrition Edn., Consulting Nutritionists (mentor coord. 1994—, sec. treas. 1994—), Sports and Cardiovascular Nutritionists. Republican. Roman Catholic. Office: Food For Thought Nutrition Cons 1670 S Amphlett Blvd Ste 214 San Mateo CA 94402-2511

FERRANTE, JOHN ANTHONY, engineering consultant; b. Maple Heights, Ohio, Nov. 23, 1932; s. John and Mary Louise (Feast) F.; m. Doris Ann Kniley, Mar. 19, 1955; children: John, Traci Ann, William. BS in Metall. Engring., Lafayette Coll., 1954; MS in Physics, St. Mary's Coll., 1967. Registered prof. engr., Minn. Metall. engr. Nat. Screw & Mfg., Cleve., L.A., 1954-59, Perry Kislby, Inc., L.A., 1959-60; sales engr. Wallingford Steel, Burbank, Calif., 1960-61; from metall. engr. to disk quality engr. IBM, various locations, 1961-92; ind. contractor Nashua Computer Products, Stor Media Corp., Santa Clara, Calif., 1992—. Holder patent in field. Fellow Am. Soc. Quality Control (treas. San Francisco sect. 1991-93); mem. Am. Soc. Metals (chair Minn. chpt. 1968), Soc. Mfg. Engrs. (chair region 13 1993-94). Home and Office: 194 French Ct San Jose CA 95139-1418

FERRARI, DAVID GUY, auditor; b. Scottsbluff, Nebr., Jan. 12, 1944; s. Guy C. and Waunita E. (Bailey) F.; m. Kay Cooper, May 29, 1966; children: Brian S., Justin D. BSBA, U. Wyo., 1966, MS in Bus. Adminstrn., 1971. Fin. dir. Wyo. Dept. Edn., Cheyenne, 1967-71; budget analyst State of Wyo., Cheyenne, 1971-73, state budge dir., 1973-75, dep. state auditor, 1975-87; cons. Cheyenne, 1987-90; state auditor State of Wyo., Cheyenne, 1991—. Author, cons.: Wyoming 1988-A Study of Revenues and Expenditures, 1988, A Study in State Government Efficiency, 1989, Accountability and Efficiency in State Government, 1990, The Final Report on Accountability and Efficiency in State Government, 1991. Elected state ofcl. Rep. Party, Cheyenne, 1991—. Mem. Rotary (hon.). Office: State Auditors Office Rm 114 Capitol Bldg Cheyenne WY 82002

FERRARI, DOMENICO, computer science educator; b. Gragnano, Piacenza, Italy, Aug. 31, 1940; came to U.S., 1970; s. Giacomo and Erina (Fracchioni) F.; m. Alessandra Ferrari Cella-Malugani, Apr. 16, 1966; children: Giuliarachele, Ludovica. Dr. Ing., Politecnico di Milano, Italy, 1963. Asst. Milano Politecnico di Milano, 1964-67, asst. prof. computer sci., 1967-70, prof., 1976-77; asst. prof. U. Calif., Berkeley, 1970-75, assoc. prof., 1975-79, prof. dept. elec. engring. and computer sci., 1979—, dep. vice chmn. dept. elec. engring. and computer sci., 1977-79, chmn. computer sci., 1983-87; dep. dir. Internat. Computer Sci. Inst., 1988-90; cons. in field. Author: Computer Systems Performance Evaluation, 19787; (with Serazzi and Zeigner) Measurement and Tuning of Computer Systems, 1983; editor: Performance of Computer Installations, 1978, Experimental Computer Performance Evaluation, 1981, Theory and Practice of Software Technology, 1983, Performance Evaluation, 1979-90, Jour. Multimedia Systems, 1993—; contbr. articles to profl. jours. Recipient Libera Docenza, Italian Govt., 1969; O. Bonazzi award Associaz Elettrotecnica Italiana, 1970. Grantee NSF, 1974—, Univ. Calif., 1982—, Def. Advanced Research Projects Agy., 1983—; Commander Order of Merit of the Republic of Italy, 1992. Fellow IEEE (editor Transactions on Software Engring. 1984-87, Trans Parallel and Distributed Systems, 1989-90); mem. Computer Measurement Group (A.A. Michelson award 1987), Assn. Computing Machinery, Univ. Calif. Faculty Club, Kosmos Club (Berkeley). Office: U Calif Computer Sci Divsn Dept Eecs Berkeley CA 94720

FERRARI, DONNA MAE, autobody and mechanical shop owner; b. Grants Pass, Oreg., Oct. 21, 1931; d. Clyde Willis and Lorene Margaret (Hart) Brewer; m. William Dominic Ferrari, June 2, 1956 (div. May 1977), remarried Nov. 24, 1977 (div. June 1987); children: Julie Ann Calleja, Jennifer Lynn Tuomi. Student, Humboldt State Coll., 1949-50. Optician Dr. Ferdinand Shaw, San Francisco, 1951-57; co-owner Superb Auto Reconstrn., San Francisco, 1966-77; optician Dr. Donald Schulz, San Francisco, 1977-84; owner Superb Auto Reconstrn., San Francisco, 1987—. Mem. Calif. Autobody Assn., Clement St. West Merchants, Better Bus. Bur., Women's Bus. Network. Presbyterian. Office: Superb Auto Reconstrn Co 2535 Clement St San Francisco CA 94121-1817

FERRARO, JOSEPH JAMES, architect; b. Albany, N.Y., June 10, 1949; s. Joseph James and Eleanor R. Ferraro; m. Nadine Jac Stern, Jan. 6, 1987; children: Aubrey A. Hawk, Amber T. Olson. BFA, Pratt Inst., Bklyn., 1971; postgrad., U. Hawaii, 1983-87. Registered architect, Hawaii. Interior designer Interior Design Assocs., N.Y.C., 1971-72; draftsman Marvin Hammerman, Inc., N.Y.C, 1972-76; interior designer McDonald Assocs., Architects, Whitestone, N.Y., 1976-77, Sheridan Assocs. Ltd., N.Y.C., 1977-82; architect/interior designer C.J.S. Group Architects, Honolulu, 1982-88; architect Ferraro Choi and Assocs., Honolulu, 1988—. Prin. works include Crary Lab. McMurdo Sta. Nat. Sci. Found., Amundsen-Scott South Pole Replacement Sta. Antarctica. Mem. AIA (Honolulu bd. dirs. 1992—, interiors com. 1986—, Design award of merit 1992, 94), NCARB, Nat. Trust for Hist. Preservation, Malama o Manoa (design com. 1993—), Rotary Club of Honolulu Sunrise (bd. dirs. 1991—). Office: Ferraro Choi & Assocs Ltd 707 Richards St Honolulu HI 96813-4623

FERREIRA, ARMANDO THOMAS, sculptor, educator; b. Charleston, W.Va., Jan. 8, 1932; s. Maximiliano and Placeres (Sanchez) F.; children—Lisa, Teresa. Student, Chouinard Art Inst., 1949-50, Long Beach City Coll., 1950-53; B.A., UCLA, 1954, M.A., 1956. Asst. prof. art Mt. St. Mary's Coll., 1956-57; mem. faculty dept. art Calif. State U., Long Beach, 1957—, prof., 1967—, chmn. dept. art, 1971-77, assoc. dean Sch. Fine Arts, acting dean Coll. Arts; lectr., cons. on art adminstrn. to art schs. and universities, Brazilian Ministry Edn. One man shows include, Pasadena Mus., 1959, Long Beach Mus., 1959, 69, Eccles Mus., 1967, Clay and Fiber Gallery, Taos, 1972, group shows include, Los Angeles County Art Mus., 1948, 66, Wichita Art Mus., 1959, Everson Mus., 1960, 66, San Diego Mus. Fine Arts, 1969, 73, Fairtree Gallery, N.Y.C., 1971, 74, Los Angeles Inst. Contemporary Art, 1977, Utah Art Mus., 1978, Bowers Mus., Santa Ana, Calif., 1980, No. Ill. U., 1986, Beckstrand Gallery, Palos Verdes (Calif.) Art Ctr., 1987, U. Madrid, 1993; permanent collections include Utah Mus. Art, Wichita Art Mus., State of Calif. Collection; vis. artist, U. N.D., 1974, exhibited widely abroad including, Poland, Portugal, Morocco, Spain, France. Fulbright lectr. Brazil, 1981. Fellow Nat. Assn. Schs. Art and Design (dir.); mem. Internat. Video Network (dir.), Assn. Calif. State Univ. Profs. Office: Calif State U 1250 N Bellflower Blvd Long Beach CA 90840-0006

FERRELL, YVONNE SIGNE, state recreation commission administrator; b. Centralia, Wash., Apr. 8, 1936; d. Clifford Francis and Lenora Matilda (Carlson) Battson; m. Richard L. Ferrell, Nov. 5, 1955; 1 child, Linnea Ferrell Bruns. Personnel mgr. Dept. Social and Health Services, Olympia, Wash.; chief personnel and tng. Wash. State Parks, Olympia, asst. dir., dep. dir. Appointed mem. Gov.'s Com. on Status of Women, Olympia, 1980-82; appointed by Sec. of Transp. to Nat. Boating Safety Council, 1986—; bd. dirs. Wash. State Employees Credit Union, Olympia, 1970-79, pres. 1976-77. Mem. Nat. Parks and Recreation Assn., Wash. Parks and Recreation Assn. Republican. Lutheran. Home: 2366 Seminary Hill Rd Centralia WA 98531-8971 Office: Parks & Rec Dept PO Box 83720 Boise ID 83720-0002

FERREY-LAUGHON, BARBARA ELOYCE, journalist, newspaper editor; b. Bishop, Calif., Oct. 28, 1964; d. Robert Hayes and Sandra Lee (Jensen) F.; m. Paul E. Laughon, May 16, 1992. BA, U. Nev., 1987. Staff writer Chalfant Press, Inc., Bishop, 1987-88, sr. staff writer, 1988-89, community news editor, editor spl. issue, 1989, city editor, 1989-90, news editor, 1990-92, editor, 1992—. Co-recipient 1st place award for recreation publs. Calif. Newspaper Advt. Execs. Assn., 1989, 93; recipient Altrusa Outstanding Svc. award, 1991-2. Mem. Soc. Profl. Journalists, Altrusa Internat. of the Eastern Sierra (rec. sec. 1993-94, 1st v.p. 1994-95, pres. 1995—, pub. rels. chair 1990-95, Altrusa Pres.'s award 1994-95, pub. rels. chair Altrusa Internat. Dist. 11 1995—), Calif. Soc. Newspaper Editors. Office: Chalfant Press Inc 450 E Line St Bishop CA 93514-3506

FERRIS, EVELYN SCOTT, lawyer; b. Detroit, d. Ross Ansel and Irene Mabel (Bowser) Nafus; m. Roy Shorey Ferris, May 21, 1969 (div. Sept. 1982); children: Judith Ilene, Roy Sidney, Lorene Marjorie. J.D., Willamette U., 1961. Bar: Oreg. 1962, U.S. Dist. Ct. Oreg. 1962. Law clk. Oreg. Tax Ct., Salem, 1961-62; dep. dist. atty. Marion County, Salem, 1962-65; judge Mcpl. Ct., Stayton, Oreg., 1965-76; ptnr. Brand, Lee, Ferris & Embick, Salem, 1965-82; chmn. Oreg. Workers' Compensation Bd., Salem, 1982-89. Bd. dirs. Friends of Deepwood, Salem, 1979-82, Salem City Club, 1972-75, Marion County Civil Svc. Commn., 1970-75; com. mem. Polk County Hist. Commn., Dallas, Oreg., 1976-79; mem. Oreg. legis. com. Bus. Climate, 1967-69, Govs. Task Force on Liability, 1986. Recipient Outstanding Hist. Restoration of Comml. Property award Marion County Hist. Soc., 1982. Mem. Oreg. Mcpl. Judges Assn. (pres. 1967-69), Altrusa, Internat., Mary Leonard Law Soc., Western Assn. Workers Compensation Bds. (pres. 1987-89), Capitol Club (pres. 1977-79), Internat. Assn. Indsl. Accident Bds. and Commns. (pres. 1992-93), Phi Delta Delta. Republican. Episcopalian. Home: 747 Church St SE Salem OR 97301-3715

FERRIS, RONALD CURRY, bishop; b. Toronto, Ont., Can., July 2, 1945; s. Harold Bland and Marjorie May (Curry) F.; m. Janet Agnes Waller, Aug. 14, 1965; children: Elisa, Jill, Matthew, Jenny, Rani, Jonathan. Grad., Toronto Tchrs. Coll., 1965; BA, U. Western Ont., London, 1970; MDiv, Huron Coll., London, 1973, DD hon., 1982; DMin, Pacific Sch. of Religion, Calif., 1995. Ordained to ministry Anglican Ch., 1970. Tchr. Pape Ave. Sch., Toronto, 1965-66; prin. Carcross Elem. Sch., Y.T., 1966-68; incumbent St. Luke's Ch., Old Crow, Y.T., 1970-72; rector St. Stephen's Ch., London, Ont., 1973-81; bishop Diocese of Yukon, Whitehorse, 1981-95, Diocese of Algoma, Sault Sainte Marie, Can., 1995—. Author: (poems) A Wing and a Prayer, 1990. Home: 134 Simpson St, Sault Sainte Marie, ON Canada P6A 3V4 Office: Diocese of Algoma, Box 1168, Sault Sainte Marie, ON Canada P6A 5N7

FERRIS, RUSSELL JAMES, II, freelance writer; b. Rochester, N.Y., June 11, 1938; s. Russell James and Phyllis Helen (Breheny) F.; m. Ilma Maria dos Santos, June 29, 1968. Student, St. Bonaventure U., 1956-59; BS, U. Rochester, 1967; MS, Emerson Coll., 1989; PhD, Universal Life Ch., 1983. Cert. social worker. Film inspector City of Rochester, 1962-67; social worker Tulare County, Visalia, Calif., 1967-69, Alameda County, Oakland, Calif., 1969-71; ghostwriter self-employed, San Francisco, 1971—. Author: Crescendo, 1972 and 9 other novels. With USAR, 1956-68. Recipient Botany fellowship Emerson Coll., 1989. Mem. Assn. U.S. Army, Air Force Assn., Navy League U.S., Ret. Officers Assn. (life), Res. Officers Assn. (life), Internat. Platform Assn., Am. Mensa Inc. Libertarian. Roman Catholic. Home and Office: 202 Font Blvd San Francisco CA 94132-2404

FERRO, JAMES MICHAEL, publishing executive; b. Honolulu, Nov. 19, 1940; s. James Michael Calhau (dec.), James Augustine (stepfather) and Helen Frances (Souza) Ferro; m. Darleen Nohea Kennedy, June 30, 1964 (div. Feb. 1978); children: Liticia Marie, Alyssa Michelle, Sean Michael (dec.); m. Jackie Helen Doke, Apr. 28, 1979; 1 child, Paige Noelani. AA, NYU, 1963. NASD rep. Oppenheimer Co., N.Y.C., 1960-64; fin. mgr. Budget Industries, L.A., 1964-69; founder, owner Calco Group, Fresno, Calif., 1969-82; dir., owner Mazzei Flying Svcs., Fresno, Calif., 1975-91; founder, dir. emeritus Golden Oak Bank, Oakhurst, Calif., 1977-94; pub. Family TV, Fresno, 1984-94; pub., cons. News Reporter, San Marcos, Calif., 1991-94; self-pub. Carlsbad, Calif., 1994—. Active Boys and Girls Club, San Marcos, 1991—. With USN, 1958-64. Named Citizen of Yr., City of San Francisco, 1964.

FERRO, ROBERT JOSEPH, electronics engineer, researcher; b. Middle Village, N.Y., May 15, 1952; s. Ernest Edward and Zita Ann (Parsons) F. BSEE, U. Notre Dame, 1974; MSEE, U. Vt., 1977, PhD, 1985. Assoc. engr. IBM, Essex Junction, Vt., 1977-86; engr. Hughes Rsch. Labs., Malibu, Calif., 1986-91, Aerospace Corp., L.A., 1991—. Contbr. articles to profl. jours. Mem. IEEE, Sigma Xi (chpt. v.p. 1990), Tau Beta Pi, Eta Kappa Nu. Republican. Roman Catholic. Office: Aerospace Corp Mail Sta M4 991 PO Box 92957 Los Angeles CA 90009-2957

FERRY, MILES YEOMAN, state official; b. Brigham City, Utah, Sept. 22, 1932; s. John Yeoman and Alta (Cheney) F.; m. Suzanne Call, May 19, 1952; children: John, Jane Ferry Stewart, Ben, Helen, Sue Ferry Thorpe. BS, Utah State U., 1954. Rancher Corinne, Utah, 1952; gen. mgr. J.Y. Ferry & Son, Inc.; mem. Utah Ho. of Reps., 1965-66; mem. Utah Senate, 1967-84, minority whip, 1975-76, minority leader, 1977-78, pres. senate, 1979-84; mem. presdl. advisor commn. on intergovtl. affairs, 1984; mem. governing bd. Council State Govts., 1983-84; v.p. Legis./Exec. Consulting Firm, 1994—. Pres. Brigham Jr. C. of C., 1956-61, Nat. Conf. of State Legislators, 1984, v.p., 1982, pres.-elect, 1983, pres., 1984; v.p. Utah Jr. C. of C., 1960-61; nat. dir. Utah Jaycees, 1961-62; pres. Farm Bur. Box Elder County, 1958-59; commr., bd. dirs., mem. council com. Lake Bonneville council Boy Scouts Am.; food and agr. commr. USDA, commr. agr. State of Utah, 1985-93. Recipient award of merit Boy Scouts Am., 1976, Alumnusi of Yr. award Utah State U., 1981, award of merit Utah Vocat. Assn., 1981, Friend of Agr. award Utah Farm Bur., 1988, Cert. Appreciation USDA, 1988, Contbn. to Agr. award Utah-Idaho Farmers Union, 1989, Disting. Svc. award Utah State U., 1993, 94; named Outstanding Young Man of Yr., Brigham City Jr. C. of C., 1957, Outstanding Nat. Dir. U.S. Jaycees, 1963, Outstanding Young Man in Utah, Utah Jr. C. of C., 1961, Outstanding Young Farmer, 1958, One of 3 Outstanding Young Men of Utah, 1962, Rep. Legislator of Yr., 1984, One of 10 Outstanding Legislators of Yr., 1984. Mem. SAR, Sons Utah Pioneers, Gov.'s Cabinet, Utah Commn. Agr., Fed. Rsch. Com., Nat. Assn. State Depts. Agr. (bd. dirs. 1989), Western Assn. of State Depts. of Agr. (v.p. 1990-91, pres. 1991-92), Western U.S. Agr. Trade Assn. (sec. treas- elect 1987-88, pres. 1989-90), Utah Cattlemen's Assn., Nat. Golden Spike Assn. (dir. 1958—), Phi Kappa Phi, Pi Kappa Alpha. Republican. Address: 815 N 6800 W Corinne UT 84307-9737

FERRY, RICHARD MICHAEL, executive search firm executive; b. Ravenna, Ohio, Sept. 26, 1937; s. John D. and Margaret M. (Jeney) F.; m. Maude M. Hillman, Apr. 14, 1956; children: Richard A., Margaret L., Charles Michael, David W., Dianne E., Ann Marie. BS, Kent State U., 1959. CPA. Cons. staff Peat, Marwick, Mitchell, Los Angeles, 1965-69, ptnr., 1969; chmn., pres., co-founder Korn/Ferry Internat., Los Angeles, 1969—; bd. dirs. 1st Bus. Bank, L.A., Avery Dennison, Pasadena, Calif., Dole Food Co., Calif., Pacific Mut. Life Ins. Co., Newport Beach, Calif. Trustee Calif. Inst. Tech., L.A., St. John's Hosp., Santa Monica, Calif.; bd. dirs. Cath. Charities, L.A. Republican. Roman Catholic. Office: Korn/Ferry Internat 1800 Century Park E Ste 900 Los Angeles CA 90067-1512

FERTIG, TED BRIAN O'DAY, producer, public relations and association executive; b. Miami, May 18, 1937; s. Peter John and Frances Marie (Aswell) F.; A.B., 1960; M.B.A., 1969. Mem. profl. staff Congress U.S., Washington, 1965; dir. mem. relations Nat. Bellas Hess, Inc., Kansas City, 1963-69; mgr. employment/manpower planning Capitol Industries, Inc., 1969-70; pres. Mgmt. Cons. Group, Hollywood, Calif., 1970—, Fertig, Toler & Dumond, Hollywood, 1973; sr. partner Nascency Prodns., Hollywood and Sacramento, 1971—; exec. dir. Soc. Calif. Accts., 1974-83, Ednl. Found., Inc., 1975-80. Pres., Hollywood Community Concert Assn., 1971-72; exec. dir. Hollywood Walk of Fame, 1971-74; sec.-treas. Save the Sign, 1972-73; producer, Santa Claus Lane Parade of Stars, Hollywood, 1971-73; dir. Old Eagle Theatre, Sacramento, Sacramento Film Festival. Trustee, finance chmn. Los Angeles Free Clinics, 1970-71; mem. Calif. Commn. on Personal Privacy. Served with AUS, 1960-62. Cert. assn. exec. Mem. Pub. Relations Soc. Am., Am. C. of C. Execs., Am. Soc. Assn. Execs., Calif. Soc. Assn. Execs. (pres. 1980). Author: A Family Night to Remember, 1971; Los Ninos Cantores de Mendoza, 1972; (with Paul Yoder) Salute to Milwaukee, 1965. Office: 715 Regatta Dr Sacramento CA 95833-1715

FERY, JOHN BRUCE, forest products company executive; b. Bellingham, Wash., Feb. 16, 1930; s. Carl Salvatore and Margaret Emily (Hauck) F.; m. Delores Lorraine Carlo, Aug. 22, 1953; children: John Brent, Bruce Todd, Michael Nicholas. BA, U. Wash., 1953; MBA, Stanford U., 1955; D of Law (hon.), Gonzaga U., 1982; D of Nat. Resources (hon.), U. Idaho, 1983. Asst. to pres. Western Kraft Corp., 1955-56; prodn. mgr., 1956-57; with Boise Cascade Corp., Idaho, 1957—, pres., CEO, 1972-78, chmn. bd., CEO, 1978-94; chmn. Boise Cascade Corp., Boise, Idaho, 1995—; bd. dirs. Albertsons, Inc., Hewlett-Packard Co., West One Bancorp, The Boeing Co.; active mem. Bus. Coun. Chmn. bd. Idaho Community Found.; mem. exec. com., bd. govs. Nat. Coun. Air and Stream Improvement. With USN, 1950-51. Named Most Outstanding Chief Exec. Officer Fin. World, 1977, 78, 79, 80. Mem. Am. Forest and Paper Assn. (exec. com., bd. dirs.), Arid Club, Hillcrest Country Club, Arlington Club, Links. Office: Boise Cascade Corp PO Box 50 Boise ID 83728-0050*

FERZIGER, JOEL HENRY, mechanical engineering educator, mathematician; b. Bklyn., Mar. 24, 1937; s. Moe L. and Bessie (Steinberg) F.; divorced; children: Ruth, Shoshanah Ferziger Cohen. B in Chem. Engring., Cooper Union, 1957; MS in Nuclear Engring., U. Mich., 1959, PhD in Nuclear Engring., 1962. Prof. dept. mech. engring. Stanford (Calif.) U., 1961—. Recipient Max Planck award, 1991; Fulbright fellow, 1978, Humboldt fellow, 1987. Fellow Am. Phys. Soc.; mem. AIAA, Am. Soc. Mech. Engrs., Soc. Indsl. and Applied Math. Jewish. Office: Stanford U Dept Mech Engring Stanford CA 94305

FESQ, LORRAINE MAE, aerospace and computer engineer; b. Pennsauken, N.J., June 26, 1957; d. John Fred Henry and Natalie Nicola (Nasuti) F.; m. Frank Tai, May 14, 1988. BA in Math., Rutgers U., 1979; MS in Computer Sci., UCLA, 1990, PhD in Computer Sci. and Astrophysics, 1993. Sci. programmer Systems and Applied Sci. Corp., Greenbelt, Md., 1979-81; computer engr./mgr. Ball Aerospace Systems Div., Boulder, Colo., 1981-86; systems engr. OAO, El Segundo, Calif., 1986-87; spacecraft systems engr. TRW, Redondo Beach, Calif., 1987—. Contbr. articles to IECEC Proceedings, AAS Proceedings, Diagnostic Workshop (DX-92) Proceedings, NASA Goddard Space Applications of Artificial Intelligence Proceedings. Mem. Playa Del Rey (Calif.) Network, 1988—. MS fellow TRW, 1988-89, PhD fellow, 1990-93. Mem. AIAA (sr., tech. com. mem. artificial intelligence tech. com. 1990—), Am. Astronautical Soc., Am. Assn. for Artificial Intelligence, Am. Astronomical Soc. Home: 6738 Esplanade St Playa Del Rey CA 90293-7525 Office: TRW 1 Space Park Blvd Redondo Beach CA 90278-1001

FESSLER, DIANE MARCIA, publisher; b. Chgo., Nov. 25, 1935; d. Frank P. and Katherine M. (Krause) Burke; m. George Robert Fessler Jr., Dec. 29, 1962; 1 child, William B. BA in Journalism, Ariz. State U., 1957. Owner, mgr. Many Feathers Book and Maps, Phoenix, 1981-88; owner, pub. Primer Publishers, Phoenix, 1980—. Mem. Ariz. Authors Assn., Ariz. Book Pub. Assn. (v.p. 1994-95). Roman Catholic. Office: Primer Pubs 5738 N Central Ave Phoenix AZ 85012-1316

FETTER, TREVOR, film executive; b. San Diego, Jan. 16, 1960; s. Thompson and Jane (Trevor) F.; m. Melissa Foster, July 9, 1983; 1 child, Holly Elizabeth. BA, Stanford U., 1982; MBA, Harvard U., 1986. Assoc. Merrill Lynch Capital Mktg., L.A., 1982-88; exec. v.p. Metro-Goldwyn-Mayer Inc., Culver City, Calif., 1988—; chief fin. officer Maple Drive Ptnrs., Beverly Hills, Calif., 1987—. Bd. dirs. Neighborhood Youth Assn., Venice, Calif., 1990—. Mem. Stanford Sailing Assn. (trustee 1986—), San Diego Yacht Club, Calif. Yacht Club. Republican. Episcopalian. Office: Metro-Goldwyn-Mayer Inc 10000 Washington Blvd Culver City CA 90232-2728

FETTERS, JOAN FRANCES, child care center administrator, educator; b. South Sioux City, Nebr., Apr. 4, 1939; d. Elmer David and Rose Viola (Leuenhagen) Owen; m. Harold Lee Fetters, June 9, 1958; children: Ricky Lee, Troy Dow, Mark Owen. BA, U. No. Colo., 1960; postgrad. Mesa Coll., 1975. Tchr. pub. schs., L.A., Oakland and Woodland, Calif., 1960-67, Ft. Collins, Colo., 1967-70, Crow Indian Reservation, Pryor, Mont., 1971-72; owner, mgr. Children's Workshops, Ft. Collins, 1983—, Learning Tree Children's Ctrs., Grand Junction, Colo., 1975—; dir., owner/founder Spring Creek Country Day Sch., 1990—; chmn. bd. Harold Lee Fetters, Inc., 1989—; founder Fun Learning Experiences Sch. Age Programs, 1991-94; sec., treas. Old Town Ale House, Inc. Mem. Mesa County Dirs. Orgn. (pres. 1978-79), Larimer County Assn. for Edn. of Young Children, Nat. Assn. for Edn. of Young Children. Avocations: piano, reading, biking. Home: 3206 Norwood Ct Fort Collins CO 80525-2919 Office: Spring Creek Country Day Sch 1900 Remington St Fort Collins CO 80525-1400

FEUERSTEIN, MARCY BERRY, employee benefits administrator; b. Wellsville, N.Y., June 18, 1950; d. Marshall Newton and Miriam May (Lingle) Jones; m. Ronald Glenn Berry, Aug. 7, 1967 (div.); 1 child, Angelia Lynn; m. Richard Alan Feuerstein, Jan. 8, 1984. Jr. clk. N.Y. Life Ins., L.A., 1970-73; jr. acct. FMC Corp., Pomona, Calif., 1973-78; sec. Gen. Med. Ctrs., Anaheim, Calif., 1978-79, svc. rep., 1979-80; dir. mktg. svcs. Protective Health Providers, San Diego, 1980-81, Dental Health Svcs., Long Beach, Calif., 1981-87; owner Mar-Rich Enterprises, 1985—; v.p. So. Calif. chpt. Healthdent of Calif., 1987-88; account exec. Oral Health Svcs., Inc., 1988-89; employee benefits adminstr. Imperial Irrigation Dist., El Centro, Calif., 1989—. Mem. NAFE. Republican. Home: 1531 S 19th St El Centro CA 92243-4102 Office: Imperial Irrigation Dist 1284 W Main St El Centro CA 92243-2817

FEVURLY, KEITH ROBERT, educational administrator; b. Leavenworth, Kans., Oct. 30, 1951; s. James R. Fevurly and Anne (McDade) Barrett; m. Peggy L. Vosburg, Aug. 4, 1978; children: Rebecca Dawn, Grant Robert. BA in Polit. Sci., U. Kans., 1973; JD, Washburn U. of Topeka Sch. Law, 1976; postgrad., U. Mo. Sch. Law, 1984; MBA, Regis U., 1988; LLM, U. Denver, 1992. Bar: Kans. 1977, Colo. 1986; cert. fin. planner. Sole practice Leavenworth, 1977; atty. estate and gift tax IRS, Wichita and Salina, Kans., Austin, Tex., 1977-83; atty., acad. assoc. Coll. for Fin. Planning, Denver, 1984-91, program dir., 1991-95, v.p. edn., 1995—; adj. prof. taxation Met. State Coll., Denver; adj. faculty in retirement planning and estate planning Coll. Fin. Planning. Contbg. author tng. modules, articles on tax mgmt., estate planning. Mem. Kans. Bar Assn., Colo. Bar Assn., Delta Theta Phi, Pi Sigma Alpha. Republican. Presbyterian. Club: Toastmasters Internat. (pres. Salina chpt. 1981-82). Home: 7761 S Columbine St Littleton CO 80122-3304 Office: Coll for Fin Planning 4695 S Monaco St Denver CO 80237-3403

FEY, RUSSELL CONWELL, urban and regional planning educator; b. Lincoln, Nebr., Mar. 12, 1926; s. Harold Edward and Golda Esper (Conwell) F.; m. Patricia Marian Baker, Aug. 23, 1952; children: Sarah, David, Ellen. AB, Hiram Coll., 1948; postgrad., U. Ill., 1951, 52; M of City Planning, U. Calif., Berkeley, 1958; MA, U. Calif., Riverside, 1982. Cert. Am. Inst. Cert. Planners. Assoc. planner planning dept. City Tacoma, Wash., 1954-55; assoc. redevel. planner Richmond (Calif.) Redevel. Agy., 1955-56; land use planner Fresno (Calif.)-Clovis Area Planning Commn., 1956, 57; sr. planner Planning Dept., Modesto, Calif., 1958-61; planning dir. Planning Dept., Modesto, 1962-69; prof. urban and regional planning Calif. State U., Fresno, 1969-94, chmn. dept. urban and regional planning, 1975-78, 82, emeritus, 1995—; cons. City of Sanger, Calif., 1958, City of Riverbank, Calif., 1960, City of Orange Grove, Calif., 1972; pres. planning dept. League Calif. Cities, 1968-69; cons. historic preservation inventory City of Reedley, Calif., 1984, City of Tulare, Calif., 1987, Calif. Dept. Transp., 1992. Exhibited photographs and watercolor paintings at various shows, 1969—. Moderator Coll. Cmty. Congregational Ch., 1976-78; mem. Planning Commn., 1977-79; chmn. Historic Preservation Commn., Fresno, 1990-91, 94—; bd. dirs. Calif. Preservation Found., 1988-89, Self Help Housing, Inc., Visalia, Calif., 1984-90, Habitat for Humanity, Fresno, 1985-87, Fresno City-County Hist. Soc., 1986-93; mem., vice chmn. Fresno County Hist. Landmarks Commn., 1986-94. Sgt. U.S. Army, 1944-46, ETO. Mem. Am. Planning Assn. (mem.-at-large Calif. chpt. 1962-63, v.p. Calif. chpt. 1964-65), Ctrl. Calif. Photographers Guild (pres. 1986-88). Democrat. Home: 2943 E Garland Ave Fresno CA 93726-6737 Office: Dept Geography Calif State Univ Fresno CA 93740

FFOLKES, MARCO RODGERS, security specialist, researcher, consultant; b. Victoria, Tex., Dec. 4, 1953; s. Robert Victor Rodgers and Lois Beryle (Wilcox) DeCarlo. PhD in Divinity, 1992. Bishop Worldwide Apostolic Brotherhood. Police officer Chaves County, N.Mex., 1972-73; intelligence officer SDI, 1973-78; investigator City of Albuquerque, N.Mex., 1978-79, Calif. and N.Mex., 1979-84; rev. Rev. Dr. Gene Scott, Glendale, Calif., 1984-85; cons. Rodgers Ffolkes Security Cons., Montclair, Calif., 1985-91; founder, dir. Security Intelligence Command, Claremont, Calif., 1991—; founder, dir. The Ffolkes Inst. for Security Studies, Claremont, 1993-95, Paso Robles, Calif., 1995—; mem. Bishopric of the Orthodox Eastern Ch. Pub. rels. officer ARC, Calif., N.Mex., 1980-88. Mem. Assn. Former Intelligence Officers, Law Enforcement Alliance Am., Internat. Platform Assn. Republican. Office: PO Box 584 Claremont CA 91711-0584

FIALKOW, PHILIP JACK, academic administrator, medical educator; b. N.Y.C., Aug. 20, 1934; s. Aaron and Sarah (Ratner) F.; m. Helen C. Dimitrakis, June 14, 1960; children: Michael, Deborah. BA, U. Pa., 1956; MD, Tufts U., 1960. Diplomate: Am. Bd. Internal Medicine, Am. Bd. Med. Genetics. Intern U. Calif., San Francisco, 1960-61, resident, 1961-62; resident U. Wash., Seattle, 1962-63, instr. medicine, 1965-66, asst. prof., 1966-69, assoc. prof., 1969-73, prof. medicine, 1973—, chmn. dept. medicine, 1980-90, dean Sch. Medicine, 1990—, v.p. for med. affairs, 1992—; chief med. svc. Seattle VA Ctr., 1974-81; physician-in-chief U. Wash. Med. Ctr., Seattle, 1980-90; attending physician Harborview Med. Ctr., Seattle, 1965—; cons. Children's Orthopedic Hosp., Seattle, 1964—. Contbr. articles to profl. jours.; mem. editorial bds. profl. jours. Trustee Fred Hutchinson Cancer Research Ctr., Seattle, 1982-90. NIH fellow, 1963-65; NIH grantee, 1965—. Fellow ACP; mem. AAAS (at large), Am. Soc. Clin. Investigation, Assn. Am. Physicians, Am. Soc. Human Genetics (bd. dirs. 1974-77), Assn. Am. Med. Colls. (at large, coun. deans 1993—), Am. Soc. Hematology, Inst. Medicine, Alpha Omega Alpha. Office: U Wash Box 356350 1959 NE Pacific Seattle WA 98195-6350

FICKETT, EDWARD HALE, architect, planner, arbitrator; b. L.A., May 19, 1918; s. George Edward and Marguerite (Hale) F.; m. Joyce Helen Steinberg, Apr. 8, 1982. BArch, U. So. Calif., grad. studies in engring. and archaelogy, 1942; M in City Planning, MIT, MArch. Registered architect, 50 states. Pvt. practice architecture L.A., 1950—; archtl. advisor to Pres. Dwight D. Eisenhower, 1957-60; archtl. commr. City of Beverly Hills, Calif., 1977-86, chmn. Archtl. Commn., 1979-82; guest lectr., vis. prof. UCLA, U. Calif., Berkeley, MIT, Stanford U., U. So. Calif., U. Fla., Calif. Poly. State U.-San Luis Obispo, Rensselaer Poly. Inst., N.Y., U. Chgo.; speaker in field; arbitrator Nat. Panel Arbitrators, 1961—, Am. Arbitration Assn., 1963—. Archtl. works include L.A. Harbor Cargo and Passenger Terminals, San Pedro, Sands Hotel, Las Vegas, Nev., La Costa Resort and Condominiums, Carlsbad, Calif., Las Cruces Resort Hotel, La Paz, Mex., Hacienda Hotel, Cabo San Lucas, Mex., Bistro Gardens Restaurant, Beverly Hills, Calif., Univ. High Sch., L.A., master plans for Edwards AFB, Calif., Norton AFB, Calif., Murphy Canyon Heights Naval Base, Calif., L.A. City Hall Seismic and Hist. Renovation, others; architect comml. devels., master planned communities, office bldgs., restaurants, resorts, hotels, homes, condominiums, shopping ctrs., air force bases, naval bases, schs., renovation of hist. bldgs., seismic rehab. ctrs., over 20,000 homes. Mem. Gov. Pat Brown's Housing Bd. for Calif. Lt. comdr. C.E., USN. Recipient Merit of Honor award Pres. of U.S., Progressive Archtecture Design awards, city beautification awards from L.A., Beverly Hills, Reno, Seattle, numerous Nat. Assn. Home Builders awards, Sunset Magazine and House and Home awards, Nat. Assn. Home Builders awards, others. Fellow AIA (First Honor award, numerous merit awards, nat. com. for bldg. industry, chmn. 1962-72, bd. dirs. So. Calif. chpt. 1958-62, pres. Calif. chpt. 1962, featured speaker nat. convs., lectr., developed and participated in AIA Univ. Lecture series), N.A.H.B. (speaker nat. convs.), Calif. Coun. Architecs (sec. 1960), Am. Archtl. Found. Octagon Soc., U. So. Calif. Archtl. Guild (charter). Office: 7421 Beverly Blvd Los Angeles CA 90036-2703

FIEDLER, BOBBI, community agency director, former congresswoman; b. Santa Monica, Calif., Apr. 22, 1937; d. Jack and Sylvia (Levin) Horowitz; m. Paul Clarke, Feb. 15, 1987; children: Lisa, Randy. LLD (hon.), West Coast Coll. Law, 1978. Gen. office duties Miller & Co., 1955-60; owner, ptnr. 2 pharmacies, 1969-77; founder, exec. dir. BUSTOP, 1976-77; mem., chmn. com. of whole, chmn. bus. ops. com., bldg. com. L.A. Bd. of Edn., 1977-81; mem., house budget com., joint econ. com. U.S. Congress, 1981-87; bd. dirs., chmn. nominations com., vice chmn. audit com. United Edn. and Software, 1987-93; bd. commrs. L.A. Comty. Redevel. Agy., 1993—; lottery commn. Calif., 1993-94; advt. artist; 1955-60, interior decorater, 1957-60; polit. commentator Sta. KABC-TV, 1986-87; bd. commrs. Calif. State Lottery, 1993-94; cons. in pub. rels. and govt., 1987—. Vol. various comty. activities; mem. notification com. Reagan and Bush nominations, 1984; co-chair Wilson for Gov., San Fernando Valley, 1990, 94; Calif. vice-chair Bush for Pres., 1992; Calif. co-chair Bush for Pres., 1988; Calif. del. Rep. Nat. Conv., 1980, 84, 88, 92; mem. L.A. Citizen's Com. on Transit Solutions, 1987, Calif. Space and Def. Coun., 1981-87, Hadassah; statewide spokesperson Proposition 13, 1978, Proposition 1 & 4, 1979. Recipient Golden Bulldog award Watchdogs of the Treasury, 1981-87, Guardian of Small Bus. award Nat. Fedn. Ind. Bus., 1981-87, Golden Age award Nat. Alliance of Sr. Citizens, 1981-87, numerous commendations from city couns.; named Newsmaker of Yr., L.A. Daily News, 1977, 80, 84, one of Outstanding Women of So. Calif., L.A. Herald Examiner, 1978, Legislator of Yr., VFW, 1985, Outstanding Legislator, L.A. Jewish Fedn. Coun., 1982. Mem. Bus. and Profl. Women's Assn. (Woman of Yr.), Nat. Sch. Bds. Assn., Calif. State Soc. (bd. dirs.), San Fernando Valley Bus. & Profl. Assn., B'nai Brith Youth Orgn. (sponsor's bd., Anita S. Perlman award 1982).

FIEDLER, JOHN AMBERG, marketing scientist; b. Evanston, Ill., Nov. 14, 1941; s. George and Agnes Zoe (Amberg) F.; m. Frances Eudora Murphy, June 18, 1966 (div. 1984); children: Margaret, Neil; m. Lesley A. Bahner, Dec. 28, 1986. BA, U. Wis., 1965; MBA, U. Chgo., 1969. V.p. Leo Burnett Co., Inc., Chgo., 1969-72, 74-79; mgr. decision systems Market Facts, Inc., Chgo., 1972-73; exec. v.p. Ted Bates Co., Inc., N.Y.C., 1980-84; prin., founder, chief exec. officer POPULUS, Inc., Boise, Idaho, 1985—. Co-author: (book) Psychological Effects of Advertising, 1985; contbr. articles to profl. jours. and confs.; inventor Ballot Box (TM) communication assessment system, 1985. Rsch. dir. Reagan-Bush '84, Wash., 1984, bd. dirs. Childreach, U.S.A., 1986—, mem. exec. com. Mem. Am. Mktg. Assn. Republican. Roman Catholic. Office: POPULUS Inc HC 33 Box 3270 Boise ID 83706-9701

FIELD, ALEXANDER JAMES, economics educator, dean; b. Boston, Apr. 17, 1949; s. Mark George and Anne (Murray) F.; m. Valerie Nan Wolk, Aug. 8, 1982; children: James Alexander, Emily Elena. AB, Harvard U., 1970; MS, London Sch. Econs., 1971; PhD, U. Calif., Berkeley, 1974. Asst. prof. econs. Stanford (Calif.) U., 1974-82; assoc. prof. Santa Clara (Calif.) U., 1982-88, acad. v.p., 1986-87, prof., chmn. dept. econs., 1988-93; assoc. dean Leavey Sch. Bus. and Adminstrn., 1993—; mem. bd. trustees Santa Clara U., 1988-91. Author: Educational Reform and Manufacturing Development in Mid-Nineteenth Century Massachusetts, 1989; author, editor: The Future of Economics, 1994; assoc. editor Jour. Econ. Lit., 1981—; editor: Research in Economic History, 1993—; mem. editl. bd. Explorations in Econ. History, 1983-89. Recipient Nevins prize Columbia U., 1975; NSF rsch. grantee, 1989. Mem. Phi Beta Kappa, Beta Gamma Sigma. Home: 3762 Redwood Cir Palo Alto CA 94306-4255 Office: Santa Clara Univ Dept Econs Santa Clara CA 95053

FIELD, CAROL HART, writer, journalist, foreign correspondent; b. San Francisco, Mar. 27, 1940; d. James D. and Ruth (Arnstein) Hart; m. John L. Field, July 23, 1961; children: Matthew, Alison. BA, Wellesley Coll., 1961. Contbg. editor, assoc. editor, asst. editor City Mag., San Francisco, 1974-76; contbg. editor New West/Calif. Mag., San Francisco, L.A., 1975-80, San Francisco Mag., 1980-82; fgn. corr. La Gola, Milan, Italy, 1990—; lectr. Smithsonian Inst., Washington, 1991, 95; bd. dirs. Bay Package Prodns. Author: The Hill Towns of Italy, 1983 (Commonwealth Club award 1984), The Italian Baker, 1985 (Internat. Assn. Culinary Profls. award 1986), Celebrating Italy, 1990 (Commonwealth Club award Internat. Assn. Culinary Profls. award 1991), Italy in Small Bites, 1993 (James Beard award), Focaccia: Simple Breads from the Italian Oven, 1994; contbr. articles to profl. jours. Mem. lit. jury Commonwealth Club Calif., San Francisco, 1987, 88, 92; bd. dirs. Women's Forum West, San Francisco, 1990-92, Bancroft Libr. U. Calif., Berkeley, 1991—, The Headlands Inst., San Francisco, 1992-93; bd. dirs. The Mechanics' Inst., San Francisco, 1987-92, pres., 1990-92; bd. dirs. Bay Package Prodns., 1994—. Recipient Internat. Journalism prize Maria Luigia Duchessa di Parma, Italy, 1987, Barbi Colombini prize Tuscany, 1991; named Alumna of Yr. Head Royce Sch, Oakland, Calif., 1991. Mem. Accademia Italia della Cucina, Authors Guild, Am. Inst. Wine and Food, Les Dames d'Escoffier, Internat. Assn. Culinary Profls. Home and Office: 2561 Washington St San Francisco CA 94115-1818

FIELD, CHARLES WILLIAM, metallurgical engineer, small business owner, consultant; b. Kankakee, Ill., Feb. 4, 1934; s. Euell Charles and Genevieve Thelma (Fletcher) F.; m. Barbara Sue Bird, Sept. 20, 1957; children: Charles Scott, Lynda Lois. BS in Metall. Engring., U. Ariz., 1960. Lic. real estate broker, Ariz. Research metallurgist Titanium Metals Corp. Am., Henderson, Nev., 1960-62; mgr. tech. service Titanium Metals Corp. Am., N.Y.C., 1962-67; with materials dept. for supersonic transport engine Large Jet Engine div. Gen. Electric Co., Cin., 1967-69; sr. engr. specialist, advanced tech. dept. Garrett Corp., Phoenix, 1969-76; real estate broker, prin. C.W. Field & Co., Scottsdale, 1985—; cons. titanium alloy applications, failure analysis; cons. to NASA, USAF, Secret Svc. Contbr. articles to profl. jours. Recipient commendation from U.S. Govt., 1964, Pres.'s Round Table award Phoneix Bd. Realtors, 1981, 84. Mem. AIAA, Am. Soc. Metals, Nat. Assn. Corrosion Engrs., Space Age Materials and Process Engrs., Scottsdale Realtors (Million Dollar Club), Rotary (bd. dirs. Scottsdale), Camelback Country Club.

FIELD, EARL LYLE, dean, education educator; b. Memphis, June 20, 1943; s. Earl Lyle and Bonnie Thelma (McMahan) F.; m. Barbara Elaine Tatham, Aug. 26, 1965; children: Bonnie Elaine, Brenda Eileen. BA, Biola Coll., La Mirada, Calif., 1966, MA, 1978; PhD, Grace Grad. Sch., Long Beach, Calif., 1984. Cert. tchr., Calif. Tchr. Whittier (Calif.) Christian Schs., 1973-77; tchr., adminstr. Pomona (Calif.) 1st Bapt. Sch., 1978-82; prof. edn., chmn. dept., dean Ariz. Coll. of Bible, Phoenix, 1982—; adj. prof. Columbia (S.C.) Bible Coll., 1987-90, Ottawa U., 1990—, Grand Canyon U., 1993—; ednl. cons. various sch. dists., Ariz., Calif., 1984—; seminar and conf. speaker, Ariz.; bd. dirs. Rutherford Inst. Am. Author: Christian Schools in Alien World, 1982, Audio Visual for Teachers, 1989; contbg. editor Coll. Press; contbr. articles to various publs. Chmn. USS Arizona Mast Com., 1989-91. Mem. ASCD, Assn. Christian Schs. Internat. (accreditation commn.), Ariz. Assn. for Supervision and Curriculum Devel., Christian Educators Assn., Western History Assn., Civil War Reenactment Assn. Republican. Baptist. Home: 5437 W Dahlia Dr Glendale AZ 85304-1935 Office: Ariz Coll of Bible 2045 W Northern Ave Phoenix AZ 85021-5157

FIELD, EDWARD C., research executive; b. 1936. BS, Lehigh U., 1958, MS in Physics, 1960; PhD in Physics, UCLA, 1964. Rsch. analyst Rand Corp, Santa Monica, Calif., 1960-72; with Pacific Sierra Rsch. Corp., Santa Monica, Calif., 1972—, now sr. v.p. Office: Pacific Sierra Research Corp 2901 28th St Santa Monica CA 90405-2938*

FIELD, JEFFREY FREDERIC, designer; b. Los Angeles, July 6, 1954; s. Norman and Gertrude Clara (Ellman) F.; m. Susan Marie Merrin, Jan. 8, 1978. BA in Art, Calif. State U., Northridge, 1977, MA in Art, 1980. Cert. indsl. plastics tchr., Calif. Designer Fundamental Products Co., N. Hollywood, Calif., 1972-82; designer/model maker The Stansbury Co., Beverly Hills, Calif., 1982-84; mech. engr. Vector Electronic Co., Sylmar, Calif., 1984-87; pres., prin. Jeffrey Field Design Assocs., Sepulveda, Calif., 1987—; cons. MiniMed Techs., Sylmar, 1987—, Best Time Inc., Leander, Tex., 1987—, Spectrum Design, Granada Hills, Calif., 1987—, Raycom Systems Inc., Boulder, Colo., 1988-89, Alfred E. Mann Found. for Sci. Rsch., Sylmar, 1988—, Atomic Elements, L.A., E-O Products, Laguna Hills, Calif., Autogenics, Newbury Park, Calif., 1990—, Pacesetter Systems, Sylmar, 1990—, Baxter Healthcare Corp., Pharmaseal Div., Valencia, Calif., 1990—, Surgidev Corp., Goleta, Calif., 1990—, Indsl. Strength Eyewear/Grafix Mktg. Group, Manhattan Beach & Campbell, Calif., 1991—. Democrat. Jewish. Home and Office: 16715 Vincennes St Sepulveda CA 91343-2711

FIELD, JOHN LOUIS, architect; b. Mpls., Jan. 18, 1930; s. Harold David and Gladys Ruth (Jacobs) F.; m. Carol Helen Hart, July 23, 1961; children: Matthew Hart, Alison Ellen. B.A., Yale, 1952; M. Arch., 1955. Individual practice architecture San Francisco, 1959-68; v.p. firm Bull, Field, Volkmann, Stockwell, Architects, San Francisco, 1968-83; ptnr. Field/Gruzen, Architects, San Francisco, 1983-86, Field Paoli Architects, San Francisco, 1986—; guest lectr. Stanford, 1970; chmn. archtl. council San Francisco Mus. Art, 1969-71; mem. San Francisco Bay Conservation and Devel. Commn., Design Rev. Bd., 1980-84; founding chmn. San Francisco Bay Architects Review, 1977-80. Co-author, producer, dir.: film Cities for People (Broadcast Media award 1975, Golden Gate award San Francisco Internat. Film Festival 1975, Ohio State award 1976); documentary film maker: film The Urban Preserve (Calif. Council AIA Commendation of excellence 1982); co-design architect: design for New Alaska Capital City (winner design competition). Recipient Archtl. Record award, 1961, 1972; AIA, Sunset mag. awards, 1962, 64, 69; No. Calif. AIA awards, 1967, 82; Calif. Council AIA award, 1982; certificate excellence Calif. Gov.'s Design awards, 1966; Homes for Better Living awards, 1962, 66, 69, 71, 77; Albert J. Evers award, 1974, Best Bldg. award Napa (Calif.) C. of C., 1987, Design award Internat. Council Shopping Ctrs., 1988, Stores of Excellence award Nat. Mall Monitor, 1989, 92, 93, Pacific Coast Builders Gold Nugget award, 1989, 91, Urban Design award Calif. Coun. AIA, 1991, 93. Fellow AIA (mem. com. on design); mem. Nat. Council Archtl. Registration Bds., Urban Land Inst., Lambda Alpha. Club: Yale (San Francisco). Address: Field Paoli Architects 57 Post St San Francisco CA 94104-5003

FIELD, MORTON RICHARD, lawyer; b. Chgo., July 28, 1923; s. Leo and Minnie (Rubin) F.; m. Gloria M. Krause, July 15, 1951; children: Bradley, Cathleen. BA, U. Ill., 1946; LLB, DePaul U., 1948. Bar: Ill. 1948, Calif. 1951, U.S. Ct. Mil. Appeals 1956, D.C. 1957, U.S. Supreme Ct., 1957. Atty.-advisor SEC, Chgo., 1948-50, L.A., 1950-52; ptnr. Wallenstein and Field, L.A., 1952-73, Jackson & Goodstein, L.A., 1973-79, Alschuler Grossman & Pines, L.A., 1979-88, Spensley Horn Jubas & Lubitz, L.A., 1988—; bd. dirs. Frederick's of Hollywood, Inc., L.A. Author: (audiocassette) Going Public, 1991. Capt. U.S. Army, 1942-54. Home: 306 Bronwood Ave Los Angeles CA 90049-3106 Office: Spensley Horn Jubas Lubitz 1880 Century Park E Fl 5 Los Angeles CA 90067-1600

FIELD, RAY ARVID, animal science educator; b. Ogden, Utah, Dec. 15, 1933; s. Vern James F.; children: Jim, Linda, David, Daniel, Mike. BS, Brigham Young U., 1958; MS, U. Ky., 1961, PhD, 1963. Prof. U. Wyo., Laramie, 1962—, dept. head animal sci., 1989—. Author: Sheep and Wool-Science, Production, Management, 1988. Recipient Good Tchg. award AMOCO Found., Inc., 1983, Sr. Fellowship award Nat. Rsch. Adv. Coun. New Zealand, 1983, Pres.'s award Wyo. Meat Processors, 1986, Albany County Stockgrowers and Cowbelles Friend of Agr. award, 1986, Achievement award For Efforts to Aid the Wyo. Economy, 1989, Burlington No. Found. Faculty Achievement award, 1990. Mem. Am. Meat Sci. Assn. (bd. dirs., pres.-elect, pres. 1978-81, Disting. Meat Rsch. award 1983, Signal Svc. award 1984), Am. Soc. Animal Sci. (editl. bd. 1970-72, 77-79, 85-87, pres. western sect. 1992-93, dir. 1991-93, award in meat rsch. 1975), Inst. Food Techs., Alpha Zeta (Outstanding Faculty award 1973), Gamma Sigma Delta (Sr. Faculty award of merit 1977, Faculty award of merit 1985), Sigma Xi, Phi Kappa Phi. Republican. Mormon. Home: 1625 Howe Rd Laramie WY 82070-6889 Office: Univ Wyo Animal Sci Dept Box 3684 Laramie WY 82071

FIELD, RICHARD CLARK, lawyer; b. Stanford, Calif., July 13, 1940; s. John and Sally Field; m. Barbara Faith Butler, May 22, 1967 (dec. Apr. 1984); 1 child, Amanda Katherine; m. Eva Sara Halbreich, Dec. 1, 1985. BA, U. Calif., Riverside, 1962; JD, Harvard U., 1965. Bar: Calif. 1966, U.S. Supreme Ct., 1971, U.S. Ct. Appeals (9th cir.) 1979. Assoc. Thompson & Colegate, Riverside, 1965-69; ptnr. Adams, Duque & Hazeltine, Los Angeles, 1970-89, mem. mgmt. com., 1981-84, chmn. litigation dept., 1985-89; ptnr. Cadwalader, Wickersham & Taft, Los Angeles, 1989—, chmn. West Coast litigation practice group. Contbr. articles to law jours. Bd. dirs. ARC Los Angeles chpt. Mem. ABA (litigation, torts and ins. practice sects., bus. torts com., products, gen. liability and consumer law com.), Los Angeles County Bar Assn. (trial lawyers sect.), Assn. Bus. Trial Lawyers (bd. govs. 1978-82), Am. Arbitration Assn. (comml. arbitration panel), So. Calif. Def. Counsel. Episcopalian. Office: Cadwalader Wickersham & Taft 660 S Figueroa St Los Angeles CA 90017-3452

FIELD, RICHARD JEFFREY, chemistry educator; b. Attleboro, Mass., Oct. 26, 1941; s. Jeffrey Hazard and Edna Catherine (Hawkins) F.; m. Judith Lauchaire, Sept. 5, 1966; children: Elijah, Sara. BS, U. Mass., 1963; MS, Holy Cross Coll., 1964; PhD, U. R.I., 1968. Rsch. assoc., vis. asst. prof. U. Oreg., Eugene, 1968-74; sr. rsch. chemist Carnegie-Mellon U., Pitts., 1974-75; asst. prof., then assoc. prof. dept. chemistry U. Mont., Missoula, 1975-83, prof. chemistry, 1984—, chmn. dept. chemistry, 1990—; vis. prof. U. Notre Dame, Ind., 1980, U. Würzburg, Fed. Republic Germany, 1985-86; referee various jours., granting agys., 1970—; mem. NSF panel on grad. fellowships, Washington, 1980-83; asst. dir. EPSCOR program in Mont., NSF, 1990—. Editor: Oscillations and Traveling Waves in Chemical Systems, 1985, Chaos in Chemistry and Biochemistry, 1993; contbr. rsch. articles to profl. publs. Grantee NSF, 1978—; recipient Burlington No. award for scholarship, 1990. Mem. Am. Chem. Soc. (tour spkr 1983, 85, 89, 91, 92, 94, 95, chair Mont. sect. 1979, editl. adv. bd. Jour. Phys. Chemistry 1988-94, Internat. Jour. Chem. Kin. 1995—). Roman Catholic. Home: 317 Livingston Ave Missoula MT 59801-8007 Office: U Mont Dept Chemistry Missoula MT 59812

FIELDEN, C. FRANKLIN, III, educational administrator; b. Gulfport, Miss., Aug. 4, 1946; s. C. Franklin and Georgia (Freeman) F.; children: Christopher Michaux (dec.), Robert Michaux, Jonathan Dutton. Student, Claremont Men's Coll., 1964-65; AB, Colo. Coll., 1970; MS, George Peabody Coll. Tchrs., 1976, EdS, 1979. Tutor Proyecto El Guacio, San Sebastian, P.R., 1967-68; asst. tchr. GET-SET Project, Colorado Springs, Colo., 1969-70, co-tchr., 1970-75, asst. dir., 1972-75; tutor Early Childhood Edn. Project, Nashville, 1975-76; pub. policy intern Donner-Belmont Child Care Ctr., Nashville, 1976-77; asst. to urban min. Nashville Presbytery, 1977; intern to prin. Steele Elem. Sch., Colorado Springs, 1977-78, tchr., 1978-86; resource person Office Gifted and Talented Edn. Colorado Springs Pub. Schs., 1986-87; tchr. Columbia Elem. Sch., Colorado Springs, 1987-92; tchr., pre-sch. team coord. Helen Hunt Elem. Sch., Colorado Springs, 1992-93; validator Nat. Acad. Early Childhood Programs, 1992—; mentor, 1994—;

cons. Colo. Dept. Edn., Denver, 1993—; lectr. Arapahoe C.C., Littleton, Colo., 1981-82; instr. Met. State Coll., Denver, 1981; cons. Jubail Human Resources Devel. Inst., Saudi Arabia, 1982; mem. governing bd. GET-SET Project, 1969-79, 91-93. Mem. ad hoc bd. trustees Tenn. United Meth. Agy. on Children and Youth, 1976-77; mem. So. Regional Edn. Bd. Task Force on Parent-Caregiver Relationships, 1976-77; mem. day care com. Colo. Commn. Children and Their Families, 1981-82; mem. Nashville Children's Issues Task Force, 1976-77, Tenn. United Meth. Task Force on Children and Youth, 1976-77, Citizens' Goals Leadership Tng., 1986-87, Child Abuse Task Force, 4th Jud. Dist., 1986-87, FIRST IMPRESSIONS-(Colo. Govs. Early Childhood Initiative) Task Force, 1987-88; mem. El Paso County Placement Alternatives Commn., 1990—; mem. proposal rev. team Colo. Dept. Edn., 1992—; co-chair City/County Child Care Task Force, 1991-92; mem. Colo. State Presch. Adv. Coun., 1992-93; charter mem. City/County Early Childhood Care and Edn. Commn., 1993—. Recipient Arts/Bus./Edn. award, 1983, Innovative Tchg. award 1984; fellow NIMH, 1976. Mem. ASCD, Nat. Assn. Edn. Young Children (founding mem. primary caucus 1992—, co-chair Western States Leadership Network 1993, Membership Action Group grantee 1993, mem. panel profl. ethics in early childhood edn. 1993—), Colo. Assn. Edn. Young Children (legis. com. 1979-84, governing bd. 1980-84, 85-86, 89-95, exec. com. 1980-84, 93, sec. 1980-84, rsch. conf. chmn. 1982, tuitions awards com. 1983-86, chmn. tuition awards com. 1985-86, pub. policy com. 1989—, treas. 1993, chmn. primary grades conf. 1994, primary grades conf. chmn. 1994), Pikes Peak Assn. Edn. Young Children, Am. Film Inst., Colorado Springs Fine Arts Ctr., Huguenot Soc. Great Britain and Ireland, Nat. Trust Hist. Preservation, Country Club Colo., Phi Delta Kappa. Presbyterian. Home: PO Box 7766 Colorado Springs CO 80933-7766 Office: 201 E Colfax Ave Denver CO 80203-1704

FIELDING, BRIAN J(ACKSON), lawyer; b. Powell, Wyo., Mar. 31, 1959; s. Marion Orlando and Faye (Jackson) F.; children: Jacqueline Baker, Chase Baker. BA in History, Brigham Young U., 1984; JD, Columbia U., 1987. Bar: Colo. 1987, Utah 1989. Assoc. Davis, Graham & Stubbs, Denver, 1987-88, Salt Lake City, 1988-91; atty. Kennecott Corp., Salt Lake City, 1991—, RTZ Corp plc, London, 1995—. Participant 1991 Leadership Utah Program; bd. trustees, chair spl. events com. Children's Mus. Utah. Mem. Salt Lake C. of C. (bus. of yr. award subcom. and bus. seminar subcom.). Office: RTZ Corp plc, 6 St James's Sq, London SW1Y 4LD, England

FIELDING, HAROLD PRESTON, bank executive; b. Roaring Springs, Tex., Oct. 18, 1930; s. Rennon Preston and Merle (Woods) F.; m. Ingrid Margarete Eva Ziegler, May 4, 1962; children: Terry Stephen, Harold Preston Jr., Rennon Preston II, Marcel Preston, Noël Preston. AA, Fresno City Coll., 1972; BA, Calif. State U., 1976. Enlisted U.S. Army, 1950, command sgt. major, 1950-72, retired, 1972; br. mgr. Bank of Am., Stockton, Calif., 1972-78; exec. v.p. Bank of Oreg., Woodburn, 1978-84; pres., chief exec. officer Calif. Valley Bank, Fresno, 1984-86; pres., chief exec. officer Am. Samoa Bank, Pago Pago, Am. Samoa, 1986—, bd. dirs. Bd. dirs. Am. Samoa Econ. Devel. Authority, Pago Pago, 1990, C. of C. of Am. Samoa, Pago Pago, 1987, Goodwill Industries of Am. Samoa, Pago Pago, 1988, Tony Solaita Scholarship Trust Fund, Pago Pago, 1990; treas. S. Pacific Mini-Games for 1997. Mem. Am. Bankers Assn., Western Ind. Bankers Assn., Calif. Bankers Assn., Oreg. Bankers Assn. Democrat. Roman Catholic.

FIELDS, ANTHONY LINDSAY AUSTIN, health facility administrator, oncologist, educator; b. St. Michael, Barbados, Oct. 21, 1943; arrived in Can., 1968; s. Vernon Bruce and Marjorie (Pilgrim) F.; m. Patricia Jane Stewart, Aug. 5, 1967. MA, U. Cambridge, 1969; MD, U. Alta., 1974. Diplomate: Am. Bd. Internal Medicine. Sr. specialist Cross Cancer Inst., Edmonton, Alta., Can., 1980-85, dir. dept. medicine, 1985-88, dir., 1988—; asst. prof. medicine U. Alta., Edmonton, 1980-84, assoc. prof., 1984—, dir. divsn. med. oncology, 1985-89, dir. divsn. oncology, 1988-93. Mem. adv. com. cancer control Nat. Cancer Inst. Can., Toronto, 1993—. Fellow ACP, Royal Coll. Physicians and Surgeons Can. (specialist cert. med. oncology, internal medicine); mem. Can. Soc. Med. Oncologists (pres. 1994—), Am. Soc. clin. Oncology, Am. Fedn. Clin. Rsch., Can. Soc. for Clin. Investigation, Can. Med. Assn. Office: Cross Cancer Inst, 11560 University Ave, Edmonton, AB Canada T6G 1Z2

FIELDS, MICHELLE RENEÉ, emergency nurse; b. Lynwood, Calif., Apr. 10, 1962; d. Homer Lee Fields and Phyllis Eloise (Powers) Hogadone. Cert. paramedic, Daniel Freeman Hosp., 1983; AA in Libr. Arts and Philosophy, Cerritos Coll., 1983, ADN, 1989. Cert. emergency nurse, BLS, ALS Am. Heart Assn., mobile intensive care nurse, Calif. EMT Assoc. Ambulance, Bell Garden, Calif., 1981, McCormicks Ambulance, Inglewood, Calif., 1983; paramedic Risher Ambulance, Montebello, Calif., 1984-86; med. examiner Am. Svcs. Beurau, L.A., 1986-87; paramedic Adams Ambulance, South Gate, Calif., 1986-87; emergency nurse Downey (Calif.) Community Hosp., 1990—. Mem. Calif. Nurses Assn. (Professionalism award 1989). Office: Downey Community Hosp 11500 Brookshire Ave Downey CA 90241-4917

FIELDS, R. WAYNE, business development executive, consultant; b. Tulsa, Feb. 1, 1941; s. Rance William and Mary Margaret (Bearden) F.; m. Lorraine Eleanor Boucher, Feb. 3, 1967; 1 child, Nicole Marie. BS, Oreg. State U., 1963; PhD, Oreg. Health Scis. U., 1969. Staff scientist NASA, Cambridge, Mass., 1969-70; dir. biophysics lab. Oreg. Health Scis. U., Portland, 1970-78; mgr. advanced devel. B-D Drake Willock, Portland, 1978-84; v.p. Premium Equity Corp., Vancouver, B.C., Can., 1984-87; pres., co-owner Venture Solutions Ltd., Lake Oswego, Oreg., 1987—; cons., Gladstone, Oreg., 1987—; mem. nat. adv. bd. One-Eighty Degrees, Portland, 1989—; bd. dirs. 5 ind. corps., Portland, 1989—. Patentee in field; contbr. articles to profl. jours. Mem. Elks. Home: 6490 Chessington Ln Gladstone OR 97027-1011 Office: Venture Solutions Ltd 4500 Kruse Way Ste 220 Lake Oswego OR 97035-2564

FIELDS, WILLIE, JR., social welfare administrator; b. Shelby, Miss., Sept. 21, 1952; children: Lazaka, Quisha. BA, M.I. Coll., 1976; postgrad., CUNY, 1979-80, Spalding U., 1981-82, Sierra Coll. of Bus., 1985. Cert. CNA. Sch. coord. Jefferson County Sch. Dist., Louisville, 1978-79; project dir. CUNY, Louisville, 1979-80; tchr. Broad St. High Sch., Shelby, Miss., 1983; social worker Convalescent Care Ctr., L.A., 1984-88; social worker, counselor Longwood Mgmt. Corp., 1988-91; case mgr., counselor Watts Health Found., L.A., 1992; substance abuse supr. Shields for Families, L.A., 1993; dir. L.A. I.P.S. Project, 1994—. Author: Living Among the Rich, 1990, Through the Eyes of a Child, 1993, (poetry) The Art of Living, 1988 (award 1988), Drugs Killing America, 1990 (award 1990). Home and Office: Ste 2 1316 W 110th St Apt 2 Los Angeles CA 90044-1451

FIFE, DENNIS JENSEN, military officer, chemistry educator; b. Brigham City, Utah, Feb. 10, 1945; s. Glen Shumway and June (Jenson) F.; m. Metta Marie Gunther, June 22, 1972; children: Kimball, Kellie, Keith, Kurt, Katie, Kenton. BS in Chemistry, Weber State U., Ogden, Utah, 1969; MBA, Inter-Am. U., San German, P.R., 1973; MS in Chemistry, Utah State U., 1978, PhD in Phsy. Chemistry, 1983. Assoc. chemist Thiokol Chem. Corp., Brigham City, 1969; commd. 2d lt. USAF, 1969, advanced through grades to lt. col.; pilot, instr., flight examiner Hurricane Hunters, Ramey AFB, P.R. and Keesler AFB, Miss., 1971-76; test project pilot 6514th Test Squadron, Ogden, Utah, 1979-81; instr. chemistry USAF Acad., Colorado Springs, Colo., 1977-79, asst. prof., 1983-85, assoc. prof., 1985-90; prof. USAF Acad., 1990; pres. Select Pubs., Inc., Colorado Springs 1985-90, also chmn. bd. dirs., 1990; mgr. analytical labs. dept. Thiokol Corp., Brigham City, Utah, 1990—. Author: How to Form a Colorado Corporation, 1986; contbr. articles to profl. jours. Active Boy Scouts Am., 1981—, sustaining mem. Rep. Nat. Com., Washington, 1983—. Decorated Air medal with oak leaf cluster; NSF research grantee, 1967-68. Mem. Internat. Union Pure and Applied Chemistry (affiliate), Am. Chem. Soc., Phi Kappa Phi. Republican. Mormon. Office: Thiokol Corp PO Box 707 M/S 245 Brigham City UT 84302-0707

FIFER, LINDA SUE, speech pathologist, interior designer; b. Mansfield, Ohio, Nov. 7, 1952; d. Joseph Stanley and Martha Eleanor (Weatherhead) F.; m. Raymond Lee Prill, Jan. 12, 1980 (div. Aug. 1987). BA, Kent State U., 1974, MS, 1975; cert., Sheffield Sch. Interior Design, 1993. Cert. clin. competence, Am. Speech Hearing Assn., speech and lang. pathologist, Mont. Teaching asst. Kent (Ohio) State U., 1974-75; speech/lang. pathologist Mont. Easter Seal Soc., Great Falls, 1975-79, Hellgate H.S., Missoula, Mont., 1980, Cmty. Med. Ctr., Missoula, Mont., 1980—; dir., founder Paws Abilities, Missoula, 1990-92; dir. speech/lang. dept. Cmty. Med. Ctr., Missoula, 1982-86; pres. Apple Hearth Interiors, Missoula, 1993—. Writer, lyricist (musical play) Eaton Street, 1986. Pres. Missoula chpt. Pilot Club, 1987-88; bd. dirs. Missoula chpt. Am. Cancer Soc., 1986-87. U.S. Dept. Edn. grantee, 1990-93.

FIGA, PHILLIP SAM, lawyer; b. Chgo., July 27, 1951; s. Leon and Sarah Figa; m. Candace Cole, Aug. 19, 1973; children: Benjamin Todd, Elizabeth Dawn. BA, Northwestern U., 1973; JD, Cornell U., 1976. Bar: Colo. 1976, U.S. Dist. Ct. Colo. 1976, U.S. Ct. Appeals (10th cir.) 1980, U.S. Supreme Ct. 1980. Assoc. Sherman & Howard, Denver, 1976-80; ptnr. Burns & Figa, P.C., Denver, 1980-90, pres. 1988-90; pres., shareholder Burns, Figa & Will, P.C., Englewood, Colo., 1991—; instr. U. Denver Law Sch., 1984, 86, Nat. Inst. Trial Advocacy, Rocky Mountain Region, 1992, 94; bd. dirs. Colo. Lawyers Com., Denver, 1984-89, vice chair 1987-88, treas. 1988-89; mem. com. on group legal svcs. and advt. Colo. Supreme Ct., 1982-86; mem. joint com. to study model rules of profl. conduct Colo. Supreme Ct./Colo. Bar, 1987-92; mem. adv. com. U.S. Dist. Ct. Civil Justice Reform Act., 1994—; active Colo. Commn. on Jud. Discipline, 1995—. Contbr. articles to legal jours.; articles editor Cornell Internat. Law Rev., 1975-76. Bd. trustees Rose Med. Ctr., 1987-95, exec. com. 1990-95, AMC Cancer Rsch. Ctr., 1993—; bd. dirs. B'nai B'rith Anti-Defamation League, 1984—; co-chmn. Civil Rights Com., 1988-90. Evans scholar, 1969-73. Mem. ABA, Colo. Bar Assn. (bd. ethics com. 1978-93, chair ethics com. 1984-85, bd. govs. 1986-88, 89-91, pres. 1995—), Denver Bar Assn., Am. Judicature Soc., Phi Beta Kappa, Phi Eta Sigma. Home: 9928 E Ida Ave Englewood CO 80111-3743 Office: Burns Figa & Will PC One DTC PH3 5251 DTC Pkwy Englewood CO 80111

FIGLIN, ROBERT ALAN, physician, hematologist, oncologist; b. Phila., June 22, 1949; s. Jack and Helen Figlin; m. Leslie Anne Figlin, 1 child, Jonathan B. BA in Chemistry, Temple U., 1970, postgrad., 1972; MD, Med. Coll. Pa., 1976. Diplomate Am. Bd. Internal Medicine, sub-bd. Med. Oncology; diplomate Nat. Bd. Med. Examiners; lic. physician, Calif. Med. intern, resident in medicine Cedars-Sinai Med. Ctr., L.A., 1976-79, chief resident in medicine, 1979-80; fellow in hematology-oncology UCLA, 1980-82; asst. prof. medicine UCLA Sch. Medicine, 1982-88, assoc. prof., 1988—; dir. Bowyer Oncology Ctr., dir. outpatient clin. rsch. unit Jonsson Comprehensive Cancer Ctr., 1990-92, dir. clin. rsch. unit, 1993—. Editor Interferons in Cytokines, 1988-90, Kidney Cancer Jour., 1993—; affiliate editor Current Clin. Trials, 1992—; mem. editorial bd. UCLA Cancer Trials Newsletter, 1990—; author articles and revs. Recipient numerous awards. Fellow ACP; mem. Am. Soc. Clin. Oncology, Am. Fedn. Clin. Rsch., Am. Assn. for Cancer Rsch., Soc. for Biologic Therapy, S.W. Oncology Group, Eastern Coop. Oncology Group. Office: Ste 510-13 200 UCLA Med Plz Los Angeles CA 90095

FIGUEIREDO, HUBERT FERNANDES, aerospace engineer; b. Elizabeth, N.J., Nov. 21, 1958; s. Fernando and Maria Alexandria F.; 1 child, Christine Alexis. BS in Aerospace Engring., Polytech. Inst. N.Y., 1980; postgrad. in systems mgmt., U. So. Calif., 1986—. Prodn. inspector Amax, Inc., Carteret, N.J., 1978; analytical engr. Pratt and Whitney Aircraft Corp., East Hartford, Conn., 1979; space shuttle mech. systems test engr. Rockwell Internat. Space Div., Palmdale, Calif., 1980-84, pub. rels. speaker, 1981-84; space shuttle mechanisms/structures engr. Lockheed Space Ops. Co., Vandenberg AFB, Calif. and Kennedy Space Ctr., Fla., 1984-87; with B-2 div. Northrop Grumman Corp., Palmdale, Calif., 1987-89; engring. specialist, lead structures design engr. Northrop Corp., Palmdale, Calif., 1990-91, group lead engr. B-2 structures design, 1990-94, engring. specialist B-2 flight line and delivery ops., 1994—; interviewed on progress of space shuttle Challenger on the Spanish Internat. Network, 1983. Mem. rsch. bd. adv. Am. Biog. Inst. Recipient Superior Achievement award Rockwell Internat. Space Div. Mem. AIAA, Northrop Grumman Mgmt. Club. Republican. Roman Catholic. Office: Northrop B-2 Divsn D/LW612-4F AF Plant 42 Site 4 Palmdale CA 93550 Address: 2557 Garnet Ln Lancaster CA 93535-5643

FILENER, MILLARD LEE, wholesale and retail distribution company executive; b. Delta, Colo., May 4, 1946; s. Millard Otis and Rosie Everetta F.; m. Connie Sue Einspahr; children: Kimberly, Weslee. BA in Acctg., Western State Coll., Gunnison, Colo., 1972. Mgmt. trainee Am. Parts Systems, Denver, 1972-76; ops. mgr. Am. Parts Systems, Portland, Oreg., 1976; sales mgr. Am. Parts Systems, Portland, 1977; corp. parts mgr. Howard-Cooper Corp., Portland, 1977-79; sales mgr. Mark VII Data Systems, Portland, 1980; dist. mgr. Valley Refuse Removal BFI, Grand Junction, Colo., 1981-82; co-owner, bd. dirs. Superior Trash Co., Montrose, Colo., 1981-84; distrbn. mgr. Meta Systems Inc, Gladstone, Oreg., 1984-87; pres. Meta Systems Inc, Gladstone, 1987-91, The Distribution Group, 1991—; bus. cons., 1991—, Resource Metabolics, 1993—; bd. dirs. The Distribution Group, 1991—, Resource Metabolics Inc., 1993—; computer cons. City of Palisade, Colo., 1981; pres. Resource Metabolics Inc., 1993—; mem. standards com. Natural Products Quality Assurance Alliance. Designed software various bus. applications, 1974—. Mem. West. Colo. Health Facilities Review Bd., Grand Junction, 1982; bd. dirs. Metabolic Health Orgn., Portland, Oreg., 1985-91. With U.S. Army, 1965-67. Office: The Distribution Group Inc PO Box 567 Beavercreek OR 97004-0567

FILES, GORDON LOUIS, lawyer, judge; b. Ft. Dodge, Iowa, Mar. 5, 1912; s. James Ray and Anna (Louis) F.; m. Kathryn Thrift, Nov. 24, 1942; children: Kathryn Lacey, James Gordon. A.B. in Polit. Sci. with honors, UCLA, 1934; LL.B., Yale U., 1937. Bar: Calif. 1937, U.S. Supreme Ct. 1957. Law clk. U.S. Ct. Appeals (8th cir.), 1937-38; enforcement atty. Office Price Adminstrn., 1942; ptnr. Freston & Files, Los Angeles, 1938-59; judge Los Angeles Superior Ct., 1959-62; assoc. justice 2d dist., div. 4 Calif. Ct. Appeal, 1962-64, presiding justice, 1964-82, adminstrv. presiding justice, 1970-82; arbitrator, referee and mediator, 1982-86; mem. Jud. Council Calif., 1964-71, 73-77; mem. governing com. Ctr. for Jud. Edn. and Research, 1981-82; mem. bd. govs. State Bar Calif., 1957-59. Mem. bd. editors Yale Law Jour., 1935-37. Served to lt. USN, 1942-45. Fellow Am. Bar Found.; mem. ABA, Am. Judicature Soc., Inst. Jud. Adminstrn., Los Angeles County Bar Assn. (trustee 1952-56), Calif. Judges Assn. (exec. com. 1971-72), Am. Legion, Order of Coif, Phi Beta Kappa, Phi Delta Phi. Democrat. Clubs: Chancery (pres. 1972-73) (L.A.); Valley Hunt (Pasadena). Home: 154 S Arroyo Blvd Pasadena CA 91105-1535

FILES, JAMES LINCOLN, editor; b. Barnhill, Ill., Sept. 18, 1946; s. James Vernon and Dorothy May (Atteberry) F.; m. Margaret Kay Bryan, Nov. 22, 1971; 1 child, Steven. BS, U. Ill., 1972. Editor Village Publ., Bourbonnais, Ill., 1975-76, The Weekly Newspaper, Glenwood Springs, Colo., 1976-83; gen. mgr. TV Guam Mag., Tamuning, Guam, 1983-86; news editor Mobridge (S.D.) Tribune, 1987; editor Apache Junction (Ariz.) Ind., 1987—. Contbr. articles, book revs., poems to numerous publs. Cpl. USMC, 1966-69. Recipient Fiction Writing award Nat. Endowment for Arts, 1983, Rocky Mountain Writers Forum, 1977, Mary Roberts Rinehart Found., 1972. Mem. Ariz. Press Assn., Colo. Press Assn. (chmn. ethics com. 1983), Nat. Newspaper Assn. Home: 11012 E Crescent Ave Apache Junction AZ 85220-5815 Office: Apache Junction Independent 201 W Apache Trl Ste 708 Apache Junction AZ 85220-3968

FILES, L(AWRENCE) BURKE, financial consultant; b. Chgo., Sept. 12, 1961; s. Eben Stuart and Rita (McGowan) F.; m. Laura Beatrice Ritter, Nov. 17, 1990. Fund mgr. Oppenheimer Rouse, Phoenix, 1982-85; fin. cons. Crystal Resources, Inc., Tempe, Ariz., 1985-87; dir. corp. fin. Am. Nat. Corp., Phoenix, 1987-88; pvt. practice fin. cons. Tempe, 1988—; chmn., pres., bd. dirs. Flexi Lease Ltd., Tempe, 1989—; dir. Tiberia Internat., Ltd.; mng. mem. Sonovan Venture Mgmt. L.L.C. Contbr. articles to profl. jours.; co-host radio show The Am. S.W. Found. Presents, 1988-89. Mem. adv. bd. Gov.'s Solid Waste Mgmt., Phoenix, 1987-88, Gov.'s Bd. Econ. Devel., 1987-88; mem. Mayor's Econ. Devel. Bd., Tempe, 1989; founding mem. Pres.'s Rep. Task Force, Washington, 1987—. Recipient Presdl. medal of merit Pres. of U.S.A. and Rep. Party, 1987. Fellow Am. S.W. Found. (sr.). Roman Catholic. Home and Office: 3422 S Lola Ln Tempe AZ 85282-5937

FILEVICH, BASIL, bishop; b. Jan. 13, 1918. Ord. priest, Roman Catholic church, 1942. Consecrated bishop Ukrainian Eparchy of Saskatoon, Sask., Can., 1984. Office: Bishop's Residence, 866 Saskatchewan Crescent E, Saskatoon, SK Canada S7N 0L4

FILIP, HENRY (HENRY PETRZILKA), physicist; b. Chgo., Mar. 29, 1920; s. Joseph and Aloisie (Filip) Petrzilka; m. Marie Louise Krajcovic, Sept. 17, 1957; children: Henry Jr., Frederick, Marie Louise; 1 stepchild, Jan Janecka. BS, Ill. Wesleyan U., 1944. Tech. asst. Fermi Pile, Manhattan Project U. Chgo., 1944; rsch. asst. atom bomb external trigger system Los Alamos (N.Mex.) Nat. Lab., 1944-49, rsch. asst. internal neutron source for atom bomb, 1949-56, exptl. researcher Rover program Flyable Nuclear Reactor, 1956-72, exptl. researcher isotope separation program, 1972-84, exptl. physicist x-ray analysis of atomic explosions, 1984-85; exptl. physicist Western Rsch. Corp., San Diego, 1985; exptl. physicist Star Wars Laser System Jan Bec Corp., San Diego, 1985-88; cons. x-ray analysis Los Alamos Nat. Lab., 1984-85, Western Rsch. Corp., San Diego, 1984-85. Mem. Pierottis Clowns. Mem. Palisade Lions (bd. mem. 1989-92), Los Alamos Rotary (pres. 1983-87), Los Alamos Kiwanis (hon.). Democrat. Home: 362 W 1st St Palisade CO 81526-8781

FILLER, GARY B., computer company executive. Past chmn. bd., past CEO Burke Industries; chmn. bd. Seagate Tech., Inc., 1991—. Office: Seagate Tech Inc 920 Disc Dr Bldg 1 Scotts Valley CA 95067-0360*

FILNER, BOB, congressman; b. 1942; m. Jane Merrill; children: Erin, Adam. BA in Chemistry, Cornell U.; MA in History, U. Del.; PhD in History, Cornell U. Prof. history San Diego State U., 1970-92; legis. asst. Senator Hubert Humphrey, 1974, Congressman Don Fraser, 1975; spl. asst. Congressman Jim Bates, 1984; city councilman 8th dist. City of San Diego, 1987-92, dep. mayor, 1992; mem. 103rd Congress from 50th Calif. dist., 1993—. Pres. San Diego Bd. Edn., 1982, mem.-elect 1979-83; chmn. San Diego Schs. of the Future Commn., 1986-87. Democrat. Office: US Ho of Reps 504 Cannon Bldg Washington DC 20515-0003

FINAN, ELLEN CRANSTON, secondary education educator, consultant; b. Worcester, Mass., June 26, 1951; d. Thomas Matthew and Maureen Ann (Moulton) F. BA, U. San Francisco, 1973; MA, U. Calif., Riverside, 1978. ESL specialist U.S. Peace Corps, Finote Selam, Ethiopia, 1974-75; English instr. U. Redlands, Calif., 1977-79; mentor tchr. Jurupa Unified Sch. Dist., Riverside, 1979—; teaching supr. U. Calif., Riverside, 1993—; tech. writer Callan Assocs., San Francisco, 1973-74, Wilshire Assocs., Santa Monica, Calif., 1976-77; English instr. U. Pa., Phila., 1979; writing cons. Inland Area Writing Project U. Calif., Riverside, 1980—; tchr., coordinator U. Calif., Riverside, 1982. Author: Prickley Pear, 1981, CAP Attack Handbook, 1987. NEH fellow, 1992; Squaw Valley Community of Writers scholar, 1981, Carnegie Mellon fellow, 1987, NEH Inst. fellow, 1993. Mem. Nat. Council English Tchrs., Assn. Supervision and Curriculum Devel., Alpha Sigma Nu, Phi Delta Kappa. Democrat. Home: 22440 Mountain View Rd Moreno Valley CA 92557-2655 Office: Jurupa Unified Schs 4250 Opal St Riverside CA 92509-7251

FINBERG, JAMES MICHAEL, lawyer; b. Balt., Sept. 6, 1958; s. Laurence and Harriet (Levinson) F.; m. Marian D. Keeler, June 28, 1986. BA, Brown U., 1980; JD, U. Chgo., 1983. Bar: Calif. 1984, U.S. Dist. Ct. (no. dist.) Calif. 1984, U.S. Dist. Ct. (ea. dist.) Calif. 1987, U.S. Ct. Appeals (9th and fed. cirs.) 1987, U.S. Dist. Ct. Hawaii, 1988, U.S. Supreme Ct. 1994. Law clk. to assoc. justice Mich. Supreme Ct., 1983-84; assoc. Feldman, Waldman and Kline, San Francisco, 1984-87, Morrison and Foerster, 1987-90; ptnr. Lieff, Cabraser & Heimann, San Francissco, 1991—. Exec. editor U. Chgo. Law Rev., 1982-83. Mem. ABA, ACLU (bd. dirs. No. Calif. chpt.), Bar Assn. San Francisco (jud. evaluation com.), Calif. Bar Assn. (vice chair standing com. on legal svcs. to poor 1993-94), Lawyers Com. for Civil Rights of San Francisco Bay Area (bd. dirs. fin. chair). Home: 286 Green St San Francisco CA 94133-4150 Office: Lieff Cabraser & Heimann 275 Battery St Fl 30 San Francisco CA 94111-3305

FINCH, THOMAS WESLEY, corrosion engineer; b. Alhambra, Calif., Dec. 17, 1946; s. Charles Phillip and Marian Louisa (Bushey) F.; m. Jinx L. Heath, Apr. 1979. Student Colo. Sch. Mines, 1964-68. Assayer, prospector Raymond P. Heon, Inc., Idaho Springs, Colo., 1968; corrosion engr. Cathodic Protection Service, Denver, 1973-80, area mgr., Lafayette, La., 1980-81; area mgr. Corrintec/USA, Farmington, N.Mex., 1981-83; dist. mgr. Cathodic Protection Services Co., Farmington, 1983—. Served with C.E., U.S. Army, 1968-72. Mem. Nat. Assn. Corrosion Engrs., Soc. Am. Mil. Engrs., U.S. Ski Assn., Am. Security Council (nat. adv. bd. 1978—), Kappa Sigma. Republican. Lutheran. Home: 1710 E 22nd St Farmington NM 87401-4363 Office: PO Box 388 Farmington NM 87499-0388

FINCHER, JOHN HENRY, artist; b. Hamilton, Tex., Aug. 4, 1941; s. Raymon Harold and Burta Christine (Ball) F. BA, Tex. Tech. Coll., 1964; MFA, The U. Okla., 1966. One-man exhbns. include J. Cacciola Gallery, N.Y.C., 1990, Elaine Horwitch Galleries, Scottsdale, Ariz., 1989, Nimbus Galler, Dallas, 1985, Rt 66 Gallery, Phila., 1984; exhbited in group shows at Old Pueblo Mus., Tucson, 1990, Albuquerque Mus. 1988, Haggar Gallery, 1988, Elaine Horwitch Galleries, 1987, Colo. Springs Fine Arts Ctr., 1986, Segal Gallery, N.Y.C., 1985, Munson Gallery, 1985, Mus. Modern Art Latin Am., 1984 and others; contbr. articles to profl. jours. Wurlitzer Found. grant, 1972. Democrat. Home: 610 Don Canuto St Santa Fe NM 87501-4269

FINDLAY, ROBERT B., paper manufacturing company executive. Pres., CEO MacMillan Bloedel Ltd., Vancouver, B.C., Can., 1990—. Office: MacMillan Bloedel Ltd, 925 W Georgia St, Vancouver, BC Canada V6C 3L2

FINDLAY, SUSAN HALTON, company executive; b. Pasadena, Calif., Apr. 27, 1943; d. Edward Herbert and Sarah Felithe (Dudley) Halton; m. William Sterling Findlay; children: Kathryn, Johnathan. BA, Colo. Coll., 1966; MA, Oreg. State U., 1969. Bookkeeper, clk. Halton Tractor Co., Portland, Oreg., 1966-67; tchr. Portland Sch. Dist. #1, 1967-70; mgr. Halton Found., Portland, 1971—; corp. sec., gen. mgr. material handling divsn. The Halton Co., Portland, 1976—; dir. Double T. Holding Co., Portland, 1979—. Mem. Child Abuse Domestic Violence Hotline Adv. Com. State of Oreg., 1981-87; mem. Jr. League Portland, 1966—, lobbyist, 1980-81; bd. dirs. Emanuel Med. Ctr. Found., 1991—. Named for Extraordinary Svc. Childrens Protective Svc., 1981. Mem. Grantmakers N.W. Oreg. and S.W. Wash., Town Club, Multnomah Athletic Club. Office: The Halton Co PO Box 3377 Portland OR 97208-3377

FINDLEY, PAUL RAJ, physicist; b. Kobe, Japan, Dec. 14, 1952; came to U.S., 1959; s. Paramajand Lugani and Sita Devi (Liu) Findley; m. Naomi Kotake, Aug. 29, 1982; 1 child, Nina Miyako. BS in Physics, U. Calif., Santa Barbara, 1975, PhD in Physics, 1983; MS in Physics, U. N.Mex., 1978. Sr. process devel. engr. Advanced Micro Devices, Sunnyvale, Calif., 1983-84, Integrated Device Tech., Santa Clara, Calif., 1984-87; mgr. BiCMOS Tech. Synergy Semiconductor, Santa Clara, 1987-90; sr. device physicist Meta-Software, Campbell, Calif., 1990-94; mgr. device modeling VLSI Tech., Inc., San Jose, Calif., 1994—. Contbr. articles to profl. jours. Regents scholar Regents of U. Calif., 1973-75, fellowship, 1978-82. Republican. Buddhist. Home: 22431 Carnoustie Ct Cupertino CA 95014-3949 Office: VLSI Tech Inc 1109 Mckay Dr San Jose CA 95131-1706

FINE, NIKKI PAIGE, acquisitions editor; b. Berkeley, Calif., Nov. 3, 1963; d. Arthur Barry and Marjorie (Blank) F. BA, U. Calif., Santa Barbara, 1985, MA, 1988. Asst. acquisitions editor Academic Press, San Diego, 1989-90, assoc. acquisitions editor, 1990-91, acquisitions editor, 1991—. Office: Academic Press 525 B St Ste 1900 San Diego CA 92101-4411

FINE, RICHARD ISAAC, lawyer; b. Milw., Jan. 22, 1940; s. Jack and Frieda F.; m. Maryellen Olman, Nov. 25, 1982; 1 child, Victoria Elizabeth. B.S., U. Wis., 1961; J.D., U. Chgo., 1964; Ph.D. in Internat. Law, U. London, 1967; cert., Hague (Netherlands) Acad. Internat. Law, 1965, 66; cert. comparative law, Internat. U. Comparative Sci., Luxembourg, 1966; diplôme supérieur, Faculté Internat. pour l'Enseignement du Droit Comparé, Strasbourg, France, 1967. Bar: Ill. 1964, D.C. 1972, Calif. 1973.

Trial atty. fgn. commerce sect. antitrust div. U.S. Dept. Justice, 1968-72; chief antitrust div. Los Angeles City Atty.'s Office, also spl. counsel gov. efficiency com., 1973-74; prof. internat., comparative and EEC antitrust law U. Syracuse (N.Y.) Law Sch. (overseas program), summers 1970-72; individual practice Richard I. Fine and Assocs., Los Angeles, 1974—; mem. antitrust adv. bd. Bur. Nat. Affairs, 1981—; bd. dirs. Citizens Island Bridge Co., Ltd.; chmn. L.A. adv. com. London Sch. Econs., 1992—; mem. vis. com. U. Chgo. Law Sch., 1992—. Contbr. articles to legal publs. Mem. ABA (chmn. subcom. internat. antitrust and trade regulations, internat. law sect. 1972-77, co-chmn. com. internat. econ. orgn. 1977-79), Am. Soc. Internat. Law (co-chmn. com. corp. membership 1978-83, mem. exec. council 1984-87, budget com. 1992—, regional coord. for L.A. 1994—, 1995 ann. program com. 1994—, corr. editor Internat. Legal Materials 1983—), Am. Fgn. Law Assn., Fed. Bar Assn., Internat. Law Assn., Brit. Inst. Internat. and Comparative Law, Am. Trial Lawyers Assn., State Bar Calif. (chmn. antitrust and trade regulation law sect. 1981-84, exec. com. 1981-87), Retinitis Pigmentosa Internat. (bd. dirs. 1985-90), Los Angeles County Bar Assn. (chmn. antitrust sect. 1977-78, mem. exec. com. sect. internat. law 1993—), Ill. Bar Assn., Am. Friends London Sch. Econs. (bd. dirs. 1984—, co-chmn. So. Calif. chpt. 1984—), L.A. World Affairs Coun. (internat. circle 1990—), Phi Delta Phi.

FINEMAN, JO ANN BOOZE, psychiatrist, psychoanalyst; b. Bloomington, Ind.; d. Herbert Henry and Nira Verne (Secrest) Booze; children: James Cameron Wilson, Neira Rebecca Fineman. Degree in Zoology, Ind. U. Lic. psychiatrist, Ind., Mass., Ariz., Calif., N.Mex. Intern New Eng. Hosp., Boston; resident in psychiatry Worcester (Mass.) State Hosp., Boston U. Med. Ctr.; fellow in child psychiatry Judge Baker Guidance Ctr. and Children's Hosp. Med. Ctr., Boston; asst. in psychiatry Harvard U. Med. Sch., Boston; pvt. practice child, adolescent and adult psychiatry, psychoanalysis Boston, 1960-83, Tucson, 1983-86, Santa Fe, Albuquerque, 1988—; mem. faculty, clin. staff Harbor-UCLA Med. Ctr., Torrance, Calif., 1986-88; asst. clin. prof. child psychiatry Boston U. Med. Sch., 1962-68, assoc. clin. prof. child psychiatry, 1968-78; assoc. clin. prof. psychiatry Tufts U. Med. Sch., Tufts New Eng. Med. Ctr., Boston, 1978-83; clin. assoc. prof. psychiatry and pediat. U. Ariz., Tucson, 1983; asst. clin. prof. Step III dept. psychiatry UCLA, 1987; lectr. psychiatry Harvard U. Med. Faculty, Boston, 1981-83; sr. lectr. psychiatry dept. psychiatry U. Ariz., 1988; assoc. attending psychiatry McLean Hosp., Belmont, Mass., 1970, assoc. attending child psychiatrist, 1977-80, assoc. child psychiatrist, 1978-83, dir. outpatient svcs. children's ctr., 1982-83; vis. staff dept. pediat. Boston City Hosp., 1972-78, dept. psychiatry Univ. Hosp., Boston, 1972-78; staff psychiatrist Union Hosp., Lynn, Mass., 1979-83, Tuscon, 1984; mem. faculty, staff U. Ariz. Health Scis. Ctr., Tucson, 1982; clin. dir. child and adolescent psychiatry divsn. Harbor-UCLA Med. Ctr., 1986-88, mem. med. staff, 1987; cons. in field; spkr., lectr., presenter, panelist, coord. numerous confs., meetings, symposia, workshops. Contbr. articles to profl. jours. Grantee U. Ariz. Med. Ctr., Dept. Edn., State of Ariz., 1985-86, 86-87. Fellow Am. Orthopsychiat. Assn.; mem. Am. Psychoanalytic Assn., Ariz. Psychoanalytic Study Group, Boston Psychoanalytic Soc. and Inst., New Eng. Coun. for Child Psychiatry, Am. Acad. Child Psychiatry, Assn. for Child Psychoanalysis, Am. Psychiat. Assn., So. Calif. Psychoanalytic Inst., So. Calif. Psychoanalytic Soc., N.Mex. Psychiat. Soc.

FINER, WILLIAM A., lawyer; b. Bklyn., Nov. 10, 1942; s. Samuel and Rachel Finer; 1 child, Jessica Rose. AB in Econs., Calif. State U., Long Beach, 1969; JD, Loyola U., L.A., 1972. Bar: Calif. 1972, U.S. Dist. Ct. (cen. dist.) Calif. 1972. Sole practitioner Palos Verdes Estates, Calif., 1973-76, Torrance, Calif., 1977-85; mng. dir. Bell, Fainsbert & Finer, El Segundo, Calif., 1985-87, Finer, Kim & Stearns, Torrance, 1988—; counsel Palos Verdes Art Ctr., Rolling Hills Estates, Calif., 1988-92, pres.-elect, 1992-94, pres. 1994-95; counsel, bd. dirs. Palos Verdes Beach and Athletic Club, Palos Verdes Estates, 1990-94, South Bay Svc. Ctr., Torrance, 1978-92. With USN, 1960-63. Mem. ABA, Los Angeles County Bar Assn., South Bay Bar Assn., Kiwanis (pres. 1988-90). Republican. Office: 3424 W Carson St Ste 500 Torrance CA 90503-5701

FINESILVER, JAY MARK, lawyer; b. Denver, June 10, 1955; s. Sherman G. and Annette (Warren) F.; m. Debra K. Wilcox, Apr. 6, 1979 (div.); children: Justin, Lauren. BA, Washington U., St. Louis, 1977; JD, U. Denver, 1980. Bar: Colo. 1981, U.S. Dist. Ct. Colo. 1980, U.S. Ct. Appeals (7th and 10th cirs.) 1981. Law clk. to judge U.S. Ct. Appeals (7th cir.), Chgo., 1980-81; assoc. Rothgerber, Appel & Powers, Denver, 1981-85, Elrod, Katz, Preeo & Look, Denver, 1985-86; pvt. practice Denver, 1986-90; v.p. corp. affairs Daniels Communications Inc., Denver, 1990—; instr. Denver Paralegal Inst., 1987-88. Author: Colorado Foreclosure and Bankruptcy, 1988; contbr. articles to profl. jours. Pres. Denver Citizenship Day Com., 1983-86, Mayfair Neighbors, Inc., Denver, 1984-87. Named Outstanding Neighbor Mayfair Neighbors Inc., 1988. Mem. ABA, Mortgage Bankers Assn. Am., Colo. Bar Assn., Denver Bar Assn., Colo. Mortgage Bankers Assn., Washington U. Alumni Assn. (Colo. chmn. 1982-87). Office: Ste 460 3200 Chevy Creek South Dr Denver CO 80209

FINESILVER, SHERMAN GLENN, retired federal judge; b. Denver, Oct. 1, 1927; s. Harry M. and Rebecca M. (Balaban) F.; m. Annette Warren, July 23, 1954; children: Jay Mark, Steven Brad, Susan Saunders. BA, U. Colo., 1949; LLB, U. Denver, 1952; cert., Northwestern U. Traffic Inst., 1956; LLD (hon.), Gallaudet Coll., Washington, 1970, Met. State Coll., Denver, 1981, N.Y. Law Sch., N.Y.C., 1983, U. Colo., 1988. Bar: Colo. 1952, U.S. Ct. of Appeals (10th cir.) 1952, U.S. Supreme Ct. 1952. Legal asst. Denver City Atty.'s Office, 1949-52; asst. Denver city atty., 1952-55; judge Denver County Ct., 1955-62; judge Denver Dist. Ct., 2d Jud. Dist., 1962-71, presiding judge domestic relations div., 1963, 67, 68; judge U.S. Dist. Ct., Denver, from 1971, elevated to chief judge, 1982-94; ret., 1995—; spl. counsel Popham Haik Schnobrich & Kaufman, Attys. at Law, Denver, 1995—; adj. prof. U. Denver Coll. Law and Arts and Sci. Sch., 1955—, Met. State Coll., 1989—; mem. faculty Nat. Coll. Judiciary, Reno, 1967-84, Atty. Gen.'s Advocacy Inst., Washington, 1974—, seminars for new fed. judges, 1974—; elected to Jud. Conf. U.S., 1985-88; mem. Jud. Conf. Com. on Rules for Admission to Practice in Fed. Cts., 1976-79, Com. on Adminstrn. Probation System, 1983-87, Adv. Com. on Criminal Rules, 1984-87, Com. on Bicentennial of Constn., 1985-87, Com. on Criminal Law and Probation Adminstrn., 1988—. Contbr. chpt. to Epilepsy Rehabilitation, 1974; contbr. articles and publs. on law, medicine, legal rights of deaf, aging, physically impaired and many others, 1974-94. Mem. task force White House Conf. on Aging, 1972, presdl. commn., 1980-84; mem. Probation Com., U.S. Cts., 1985-88, Nat. Com. to Study Qualifications to Practice in Fed. Cts., 1976-82, bd. visitors Brigham Young U., 1977-80, Nat. Commn. Against Drunk Driving, 1982-86. Decorated Inspector Gen. 33d degree; recipient numerous awards including medallion for outstanding service by a non-handicapped person to physically disabled Nat. Paraplegia Found., 1972, cert. of commendation Sec. Transp., 1974, Norlin award for outstanding alumni U. Colo., 1988, numerous others. Fellow Am. Coll. Legal Medicine (Chgo., hon. fellow); mem. ABA (nat. chmn. Am. citizenship com. 1968, award of merit Law Day 1968), Colo. Bar Assn. (chmn. Law Day 1964, chmn. Am. citizenship com. 1963, bd. govs. 1982-94), Denver Bar Assn. (chmn. Law Day 1964), Am. Judicature Soc., Am. Amateur Radio, B'nai B'rith, Masons, Shriners, Phi Sigma Delta (trustee 1960-66, Nat. Man of Yr. Zeta Beta Tau chpt. 1989). Office: 2400 One Tabor Ctr 1200 17th St Denver CO 80202*

FINK, JAMES BREWSTER, geophysicist, consultant; b. Los Angeles, Jan. 12, 1943; s. Odra J. and Gertrude (Sloot) F.; m. Georgeanne Emmerich, Aug. 24, 1970; 1 child, Jody Lynn. BS in Geophysics and Geochemistry, U. Ariz., 1969; MS in Geophysics cum laude, U. Witwatersrand, Johannesburg, Transvaal, Republic of South Africa, 1980; PhD in Geol. Engring., Geohydrology, U. Ariz, 1989. Registered profl. engr., Ariz., N.Mex.; registered land surveyor, Ariz.; registered profl. geologist, Wyo.; cert. environ. inspector. Geophysicist Geo-Comp Exploration, Inc., Tucson, 1969-70; geophys. cons. IFEX-Geotechnica, S.A., Hermosillo, Sonora, Mex., 1970; chief geophysicist Mining Geophys. Surveys, Tucson, 1971-72; research asst. U. Ariz., Tucson, 1973; cons. geophysics Tucson, 1974-76; sr. minerals geophysicist Esso Minerals Africa, Inc., Johannesburg, 1976-79; sr. research geophysicist Exxon Prodn. Research Co., Houston, 1979-80; pres. Geophynque Internat., Tucson, 1980-90, hydroGeophysics, Inc., Tucson, 1990—; cons. on NSF research U. Ariz., 1984-85, adj. lectr. geol. engring., 1985-86, assoc. instr. geophysics, 1986-87, supr. geophysicist, geohydrologist, 1986-88, bd. dirs. Lab. Advanced Subsurface Imaging, 1986—; v.p. R&D Alternative Energy Engring., Inc., Tucson, 1992—, also bd. dirs.; lectr. South African Atomic Energy Bd., Pelindaba, 1979; cons. Argonne Nat. Lab., 1992-93, Los Alamos Nat. Lab., 1987—. Contbr. articles to profl. jours. Served as sgt. U.S. Air NG, 1965-70. Named Airman of Yr., U.S. Air NG, 1967. Mem. Soc. Exploration Geophysicists (co-chair internat. meetings 1980, 81, 92, sr. editor monograph 1990, reviewer), Am. Geophys. Union (reviewer), European Assn. Exploration Geophysicists, South African Geophys. Assn., Assn. Ground Water Scientists, Nat. Water Well Assn. (reviewer), Mineral and Geotech. Explorationists, Ariz. Geol. Soc., Ariz. Water Well Assn., Environ. and Engring. Geophys. Soc., Pres.'s Club U. Ariz. Republican. Home and Office: Hydrogeophysics Inc 5865 S Old Spanish Trl Tucson AZ 85747-9487

FINK, KRISTIN DANIELSON, secondary education educator; b. Camden, N.J., Sept. 23, 1951; d. Ralph J. and Marguerite J. (Bickerstaff) Danielson; m. Garl L. Fink, Nov. 23, 1976; children; Karl Tony, Tracy Denise, Brittany Mar. BA in English, U. Utah, 1973, MA in Edn., 1979. Cert. secondary edn. tchr., Utah; endorsements in English, theatre, speech, reading, journalism and gifted/talented edn. Tchr., dept. chair performing arts Kearns (Utah) Jr. High, 1978-80, 83-85, Hunter Jr. High, West Valley City, Utah, 1986-93; tchr. English Olympus High Sch., Salt Lake City, 1993—; adj. instr. U. Utah, 1993-94; grad. com. adv. Westminster Coll., 1979; dir. Hunter Acting Co., 1985-93; presenter in field. Lead tchr. Cmty. of Caring; peer leadership team advisor. Named Tchr. of Yr., Hunter PTA, WVC, 1988; recipient Granite Dist. Employees Ptnrs. in Edn. Outstanding Svc. award, 1989-90, 1st Pl. award Best Jr. High Sch. Newspaper in the State of Utah, Utah Press Assn., 1990, Holladay Rotary Club Svc. award, 1994, Excel Outstanding Educator award, 1995. Mem. NEA, Utah Edn. Assn., Nat. Coun. Tchrs. English, Granite Edn. Assn. Home: 3179 Dunshill Cir Salt Lake City UT 84118-2274 Office: Olympus High Sch 4055 S 2300 E Salt Lake City UT 84124-1831

FINK, ROBERT MORGAN, biological chemistry educator; b. Greenville, Ill., Sept. 22, 1915; s. William Harvey and Pearl (Smith) F.; m. Kathryn L. Ferguson, Jan. 6, 1941; children—Patricia Kay, Suzanne Joyce. Student, Kans. State Coll., 1933-35; A.B., U. Ill., 1937; postgrad., Lehigh U., 1937-38; Ph.D., U. Rochester, 1942. Mem. faculty UCLA, 1947—, prof. biol. chemistry, 1963-78, prof. emeritus, 1978—; research biochemist VA, 1947-54; Mem. subcom. on internal dose, nat. com. radiation protection Nat. Bur. Standards, 1947-49. Author: Biological Studies with Polonium, Radium and Plutonium, 1950. Mem. Am. Soc. Biol. Chemists. Home: 17774 Tramonto Dr Pacific Palisades CA 90272-3131

FINK, ROBERT RUSSELL, music theorist, former university dean; b. Belding, Mich., Jan. 31, 1933; s. Russell Foster and Frances (Thornton) F.; m. Ruth Joan Bauerle, June 19, 1955; children: Denise Lyn, Daniel Robert. B.Mus., Mich. State U., 1955, M.Mus., 1956, Ph.D., 1965. Instr. music SUNY, Fredonia, 1956-57; instr. Western Mich. U., Kalamazoo, 1957-62, asst. prof., 1962-66, assoc. prof., 1966-71, prof., 1971-78, chmn. dept. music, 1972-78; dean Coll. Music U. Colo., Boulder, 1978-93; prin. horn Kalamazoo Symphony Orch., 1957-67; accreditation examiner Nat. Assn. Schs. Music, Reston, Va., 1973-92, grad. commr., 1981-89, chmn. grad. commn., 1987-89, assoc. chmn. accreditation commn., 1990-91, chmn., 1992. Author: Directory of Michigan Composers, 1972, The Language of 20th Century Music, 1975; composer: Modal Suite, 1959, Four Modes for Winds, 1967, Songs for High School Chorus, 1967; contbr. articles to profl. jours. Bd. dirs. Kalamazoo Symnphony Orch., 1974-78, Boulder Bach Festival, 1983-90. Mem. Coll. Music Soc., Soc. Music Theory, Mich. Orch. Assn. (pres.), Phi Mu Alpha Sinfonia (province gov.), Pi Kappa Lambda. Home: 643 Furman Way Boulder CO 80303-5614

FINK, STUART HOWARD, accountant; b. N.Y.C., Dec. 13, 1948; s. Arthur Milton and Mollie (Wrubel) F.; m. Robin Heather Heacock, Aug. 25, 1984; children: Laura, Allison. BA, Queens Coll., 1970; MBA, U. Rochester, 1972, Golden Gate U., 1986. CPA. Sr. acct. Brout and Co., N.Y.C., 1972-78; audit rev. mgr. Alexander Grant & Co., San Francisco, 1978-82; acctg. tax mgr. Jones, Schiller & Co., San Francisco, 1982-92; pvt. practice Castro Valley, Calif., 1992—. Pres. Stonegate Terrace Homeowners Assn., San Francisco, 1983-84; com. mem. Jewish Community Fedn. Young Adults, San Francisco, 1980-82; vol. San Francisco Fair, 1983, 85, March of Dimes, San Francisco, 1984. Mem. AICPA, Calif. Soc. CPAs (coop. credit grantors com.), Castro Valley Lions Breakfast Club (bull. editor 1990—, pres. 1991-92). Democrat. Home and Office: 19715 Michaels Ct Castro Valley CA 94546-4012

FINKELSTEIN, JAMES ARTHUR, management consultant; b. N.Y.C., Dec. 6, 1952; s. Harold Nathan and Lilyan (Crystal) F.; m. Lynn Marie Gould, Mar. 24, 1984; children: Matthew, Brett. BA, Trinity Coll., Hartford, Conn., 1974; MBA, U. Pa., 1976. Cons. Towers, Perrin, Forster & Crosby, Boston, 1976-78; mgr. compensation Pepsi-Cola Co., Purchase, N.Y., 1978-80; mgr. employee info. systems Am. Can. Co., Greenwich, Conn., 1980; mgr. bus. analysis Emery Airfreight, Wilton, Conn., 1980-81; v.p. Meidinger, Inc., Balt., 1981-83; prin. The Wyatt Co., San Diego, 1983-88; pres., chief exec. officer W. F. Corroon, San Francisco, 1988-95; chmn., CEO FutureSense, Inc., Larkspur, Calif., 1995—; mem. regional adv. bd. Mchts. and Mfrs. Assn., San Diego, 1986-88; instr. U. Calif., San Diego, 1984-88. Mem. camp com. State YMCA of Mass. and R.I., Framingham, 1982-86; pres. Torrey Pines Child Care Consortium, La Jolla, Calif., 1987-88; vice chmn. La Jolla YMCA, 1986-88; bd. dirs. YMCA, San Francisco, 1988—, chmn. fin. and audit com., 1986—, vice chmn.; bd. dris. San Domenico Sch., 1994—. Home: 17 Bracken Ct San Rafael CA 94901-1587 Office: FutureSense Inc Ste 116 101 Larkspur Landing Cir Larkspur CA 94939

FINLAY, AUDREY JOY, environmental educator, consultant, naturalist; b. Davidson, Sask., Can., Sept. 18, 1932; d. Leonard Noel and Vilhemine Marie (Rossander) Barton; m. James Campbell Finlay, June 18, 1955; children: Barton Brett, Warren Hugh, Rhonda Marie. BA, U. Man., Can., 1954; profl. diploma in edn., U. Alta., 1974, MEd, 1978. Social worker Children's Aid, Brandon, Man., 1954-55; foster home worker Social Services Province of Sask., Regina, 1955-56, City of Edmonton, Alta., 1956-59; naturalist City of Edmonton, 1965-74; tchr., cons., adminstr. Edmonton Pub. Bd., 1974-88; cons. edn., interpretation numerous projects, 1965—. Author: Winter Here and Now, 1982; co-author: Parks in Alberta, 1987, Ocean to Alpine, A British Columbia Nature Guide, 1992; contbr. nature articles to profl. jours. Chmn., chief exec. officer Wildlife '87: Canadian Centennial Wildlife Conservation, 1985-87. Named Ms. Chatelaine, Chatelaine mag., 1975; recipient Order of Bighorn award Alta Gov., Ralph D. Bird award, 1987, Can. Park Svc. Heritage award Environ. Can., 1990, Order of Can. award, 1990, Reeve's award of Distinction County of Strath, 1991, Douglas Pimlot award Can. Nat. Fedn., 1991. Fellow Alta. Tchrs. Assn. , Edmonton Outdoor Coun. (founder, 1st pres., disting. mem.); mem. Canadian Nature Fedn. (v.p. 1984-90), Edmonton Natural History Soc. (Loran Goulden award 1980), Am. Nature Study Soc. (bd. dirs. 1984-91, pres. 1991—), N.Am. Environ. Edn. Assn. (bd. dirs. 1983-89), Fedn. Alta Naturalists (bd. dirs. 1970s). Home and Office: 61 E Whitecroft, 52313 Rge Rd 232, Sherwood Park, AB Canada T8B 1B7

FINLAY, JAMES CAMPBELL, retired museum director; b. Russell, Man., Can., June 12, 1931; s. William Hugh and Grace Muriel F.; m. Audrey Joy Barton, June 18, 1955; children: Barton Brett, Warren Hugh, Rhonda Marie. BSc, Brandon U., 1952; MSc in Zoology, U. Alta., 1968. Geophysicist Frontier Geophys. Ltd., Alta., 1952-53; geologist, then dist. geologist Shell Can., Ltd., 1954-64; chief park naturalist and biologist Elk Island (Can.) Nat. Park, 1965-67; dir. hist. devel. and archives, dir. hist. and sci. service, dir. Nature Center, dir. interpretation and recreation City of Edmonton, Alta., 1967-92; founder Fedn. Alta. Naturalists, 1969. Author: A Nature Guide to Alberta, Bird Finding Guide to Canada; (with Joy Finlay) Ocean to Alpine-A British Columbia Nature Guide, A Guide to Alberta Parks. Recipient Order of the Bighorn Govt. of Atla., 1987, Heritage award Environment Can., 1990, Loran Goulden award Fedn. Alta Naturalists, 1991, Can. 125th Anniversary award, 1993; named to Edmonton Hist. Hall of Fame, 1976. Mem. Can. Mus. Assn. (pres. 1976-78), Alta. Mus. Assn. (founding mem., past pres.), Am. Mus. Assn. (past council), Am. Ornithol. Union. Home: 61 E Whitecroft, 52313 Age Rd 232, Sherwood Park, AB Canada T8B 1B7

FINLEY, JAMES DANIEL, physics educator; b. Louisville, Aug. 2, 1941; s. James Daniel and Lucile (Carter) F.; m. Nancy Carlisle Newton (div. 1982); children: Ian Brendan, Moira Lynn. BA in Math., BS in Physics, U. Tex., 1963; PhD in Physics, U. Calif., Berkeley, 1968. Rsch. scientist Tracor Inc., Austin, Tex., 1962-63; teaching/rsch. asst. U. Calif., Berkeley, 1963-68; asst. prof. physics U. N.Mex., Albuquerque, 1968-73; assoc. prof. physics U. N.Mex., 1973-78, prof. physics, 1978—, chmn. dept. physics, 1985-92; vis. prof. Centro de Inv. y Est. Avanz. del IPN, Mexico City, 1975, 82; vis. prof. U. Canterbury, Christchurch, New Zealand, 1990. Contbr. articles to profl. jours., chpts. to books. Mem. Am. Phys. Soc., Soc. for Gen. Rel. and Gravitation, Cactus and Succulent Soc. Am., Phi Beta Kappa, Sigma Xi. Office: U NMex Dept Physics and Astronomy Albuquerque NM 87131

FINLEY, LEWIS MERREN, financial planner; b. Reubens, Idaho, Nov. 29, 1929; s. John Emory and Charlotte (Priest) F.; student public schs., Spokane; m. Virginia Ruth Spousta, Feb. 23, 1957; children—Ellen Annette, Charlotte Louise. With Household Finance Co., Portland, Oreg. and Seattle, 1953-56; with Doug Gerow Fin., Portland, 1956-61; pres. Family Fin. Planners Inc., Portland, 1961—; assoc. broker Peoples Choice Realty, Inc., Milwaukie, Oreg., 1977-82, Lewis M. Finley, Real Estate Broker, Inc., 1982—. Standing trustee Chpt. 13, Fed. Bankruptcy Ct., Dist. of Oreg., 1979-80. Served with U.S. Army, 1951-53. Mem. Oreg. Assn. Credit Counselors (past pres.), Northwest Assn. Credit Counselors (past treas.), Am. Assn. Credit Counselors (v.p. 1982—), Authors Guild. Republican. Methodist. Clubs: Masons (past master), Shriners. Author: The Complete Guide to Getting Yourself Out of Debt, 1975. Home: 3015 SE Riviere Dr Portland OR 97267-5548 Office: 2154 NE Broadway St Ste 120 Portland OR 97232-1561

FINLEY, MITCHEL BRENT, writer; b. LaGrande, Oreg., Dec. 17, 1945; s. Ralph M. and Marjorie (Klinghammer) F.; m. Kathleen M. Hickey, Mar. 9, 1974; children: Sean, Patrick, Kevin. BA in Religious Studies, Santa Clara U., 1973; MA in Theology, Marquette U., 1976. Dir. Family Life Office, Cath. Diocese of Spokane, Wash., 1977-82; freelance writer Spokane, 1982—. Author: Christian Families in The Real World, 1984 (Thomas More Medal award 1984), Catholic Spiritual Classics, 1987, Your Family in Focus, 1993, Everybody Has a Guardian Angel, 1993 (Cath. Press Assn. Book award 1994), Catholic Is Wonderful!, 1994, Heavenly Helpers: St. Anthony and St. Jude, 1994, The Gospel Truth, 1995. Recipient Silver Medal award Coun. for Advancement & Support Edn., 1991. Mem. Am. Soc. Journalists & Authors (Excellence in Writing award 1992), Cath. Press Assn. U.S. and Can. Roman Catholic.

FINN, SARA SHIELS, public relations executive; b. Cin., July 12; d. Paul Vincent and Freda K. Shiels; m. Thomas Finn. BA in English, Maryville Coll., 1950. Reporter La Jolla (Calif.) Jour.; advt. and pub. rels. rep. San Diego Mag., 1964-71; dir. pub. rels. U. San Diego, 1971-87; owner Sara Finn Pub. Rels., San Diego, 1987—; pres. Finn/Hannaford (a divsn. of The Hannaford Co., Washington), San Diego, 1987—; lectr. and cons.; bd. dirs. Ptnrs. for Livable Places; active Internat. Affairs Bd. City of San Diego, San Diego Hist. Soc., All Hallows Cath. Ch., La Jolla, Calif., Sister City Assn. San Diego/Tiajuan; pres. Nat. Assn. Alumnae of Sacred Heart, 1979-81. Inducted into Equestrian Order Holy Sepulchre, Rome, 1982. Mem. Pub. Rels. Soc. Am. (accredited), Inst. Latin Profls., Pub. Rels. Soc. Am. Counselors Acad., San Diego Press Club (charter star), San Diego C. of C. Roman Catholic. Office: 7817 Ivanhoe Ave Ste 300 La Jolla CA 92037-4542

FINNANE, DANIEL F., professional basketball team executive; m. Carol Finnane; children: Cedric, Kelly, Dan, Ann, David. Grad. Univ. Wis., 1958. CPA. Registered rep. Robert W. Baird and Co., Wis., 1965-68; sr. v.p. Dain Bosworth and Co., Mpls.; pres. First Fin. Group, 1975-82; exec. v.p. TOTAL-TV Inc. cable television system, Janesville, Wis., 1980-85; co-owner, now also pres. Golden State Warriors (Nat. Basketball Assn.), Oakland, Calif.; mem. bd. dirs. Milw. Bucks (Nat. Basketball Assn.), 1978-85. Office: Golden State Warriors Oakland Coliseum Arena Oakland CA 94621-1918*

FINNBERG, ELAINE AGNES, psychologist, editor; b. Bklyn., Mar. 2, 1948; d. Benjamin and Agnes Montgomery (Evans) F.; m. Rodney Lee Herndon, Mar. 1, 1981; 1 child, Andrew Marshal. BA in Psychology, L.I. U., 1969; MA in Psychology, New Sch. for Social Rsch., 1973; PhD in Psychology, Calif. Sch. Profl. Psychology, 1981. Lic. psychologist, Calif. Rsch. asst. in med. sociology Med. Coll. Cornell U., N.Y.C., 1969-70; med. abstractor USV Pharm. Corp., Tuckahoe, N.Y., 1970-71, Coun. for Tobacco Rsch., N.Y.C., 1971-77; editor, writer Found. of Thanatology Columbia U., N.Y.C., 1971-76, cons. family studies program cancer ctr. Coll. Physicians &Surgeons, 1973-74; dir. grief psychology and bereavement counseling San Francisco Coll. Mortuary Scis., 1977-81; rsch. assoc. dept. epidemiology and internat. health U. Calif., San Francisco, 1979-81, asst. clin. prof. dept. family and community medicine, 1985-93, assoc. clin. prof., dept. family and community medicine, 1993—; chief psychologist Natividad Med. Ctr., Salinas, Calif., 1984—; asst. chief psychiatry svc. Natividad Med. Ctr., 1985—, acting chief psychiatry, 1988-89, vice chair medicine dept., 1991-93, sec.-treas. med. staff, 1992-94. Editor: (newspaper) The California Psychologist, 1988—; editor Jour. of Thanatology, 1972-76, Cathexis, 1976-81. Mem. gov.'s adv. bd. Agnews Devel. Ctr., San Jose, Calif., 1988—, chair, 1989-91, 94—. Mem. APA, Nat. Register Health Svc. Providers in Psychology, Calif. Psychol. Assn. (Disting. Svc. award 1989), Soc. Behavioral Medicine, Mid-Coast Psychol. Assn. (sec. 1985, treas. 1986, pres. 1987, Disting. Svc. to Psychology award 1993). Office: Natividad Med Ctr PO Box 81611 1330 Natividad Rd Salinas CA 93912-1611

FINNEGAN, DANIEL, statistician; b. Cleve., Mar. 23, 1949; s. Edward Francis and Mary Gail (Sheppard) F.; m. Patricia Ann Wright, Feb. 19, 1972 (div.); 1 child, Carolyn Beth. BA, U. Calif., Berkeley, 1974, MA, 1976, PhD, 1978. Cert. fraud examiner. Instr. U. Calif., Berkeley, 1978-80; divsn. dir. Applied Mgmt. Scis., Washington, 1980-84; pres. Quality Planning, Oakland, Calif., 1984—; sr. staff mem. U.S. Senate, Washington, 1989; cons. Office of Pres., U.S. Senate, Depts. of Commerce, Dept. Agr., Dept. Edn., NSF, Washington, 1980—. Author: Statistical Sampling for Non Statisticians, 1982, Statistics and Data Analysis, 1982. Cons. to Disability Rights Edn. and Def. Fund, Berkeley, 1984-90. Mem. Am. Statis. Assn. Office: Quality Planning 1999 Harrison St # 1420 Oakland CA 94612-3517

FINNEY, LINNEA RUTH, tailor, educator, accountant; b. Seattle, May 4, 1952; d. Donald Bruce and Ethel Ruth (Hagli) Deans; m. Raymond Howard Finney, Oct. 5, 1977; children: Sean Howard, Chelan Kimber. A of Arts and Scis., Shoreline C.C., Seattle, 1995, A of Applied Arts and Scis. in Acctg., 1995. Dental asst., technician Dr. Donald Bruce Deans, Seattle, 1966-74; dental technician Zundel Dental Lab., Seattle, 1976-79; tailor Carol McClellan Suedes & Leathers, Seattle, 1982, 84; wardrobe asst. Diana Ross on Tour, Seattle, 1982, Harry Belafonte on Tour, Seattle, 1987, Rod Stewart on Tour, Seattle, 1988, Dream Girls Nat. Tour, Seattle, 1988; home tchr. Mukilteo (Wash.) Sch. Dist., 1991-94; tailor Haute Couture, Bothell, Wash., 1964-74, 81-84, Seattle, 1977-80, Everett, Wash., 1984-95, Stanwood, Wash., 1995—. Vol. Habitat for Humanity, 1992. Home: 7719 274th St NW Stanwood WA 98292-5927 Office: Dr Donald Bruce Deans 6334 NE 157th St Bothell WA 98011-4345

FINNEY, RICHARD S., screenwriter; b. Honolulu, Feb. 15, 1961; s. Gerald Gordon and Celia (Chong) Finney; m. Noni Lynn Brown, Oct. 5, 1985 (div. 1989); m. Kelley Jo Nelms, Oct. 1, 1989; children: Rachel, Emily. BA in TV and Film, Calif. State U., Northridge, 1984. Editor FOX-TV, Hollywood, Calif., 1989-94; freelance screenwriter Disney, Warner Bros., Hollywood, 1990—. Mem. Writers Guild West. Home: 324 Via Colinas Thousand Oaks CA 91362-5018

FINNIE, C(LARENCE) HERBERT (HERB FINNIE), aerospace company executive; b. San Marcos, Tex., Feb. 22, 1930; s. Clarence Herbert and Robbie Mary (Hinkle) F.; B.S., S.W. Tex. State U., 1951; M.A., U. Calif.-Berkeley, 1955; M.B.A., U. Santa Clara, 1968; m. Bruna Rebecchi, June 28, 1955; children: Elisa Gene, John Herbert, Mary Lea, Ann Catherine. Bur. chief, disk jockey KCNY, 1950; with Lockheed Missiles & Space Co., Inc., Sunnyvale, Calif., 1958—, supr. computer programming, systems analyst, mgr. software design and devel., advanced systems staff engr. sr; free-lance writer, photographer; pres. Creative Imagineering, Sunnyvale, 1984—; cons. in field. Served to Capt. USAF, 1951-58. Mem. Assn. Computing Machinery,

Nat. Mgmt. Assn., Pentagon Players (charter), Photog. Soc. Am., Air Force Assn., Assn. Old Crows, Marquis Club, Alpha Chi, Beta Gamma Sigma, Phi Mu Alpha Sinfonia. Roman Catholic. Designed and developed first generally used compiler prepared for a digital electronic computer (Univac I), computer game package and a universally used tng. system, 1952; original documentation and reference materials deeded to the Smithsonian Institution. Home: 1582 Lewiston Dr Sunnyvale CA 94087-4148 Office: 1111 Lockheed Way Sunnyvale CA 94087-4148

FINNIGAN, DENNIS MICHAEL, management consultant; b. Buffalo, Aug. 10, 1928; s. Charles Marcellus and Marie Florence (Jacobs) F; m. Barbara Ann Pfeiffer, June 16, 1951; children: Cecilia, Eileen, Dennis Jr., Kathy, Margaret, Teresa, Timothy, Kevin, Marie. BA, Stanford U., 1953, postgrad., 1953-54. With IBM Corp., Buffalo, 1949; dept. mgr. Sunsweet Growers, San Jose, Calif., 1949-51; systems analyst Stanford U., Palo Alto, Calif., 1951-53; v.p. SRI Internat., Menlo Park, Calif., 1953-81; pres. D.M. Finnigan Assocs., Los Altos, Calif., 1981—; chmn. bd. dirs. ABB Flakt, Inc., Atlanta, Blenheim, N.V., Rotterdam, The Netherlands. Bd. dirs. Serene Lakes (Calif.) Property Assn., 1980-84. Staff sgt. USAF, 1946-49. Awarded Royal Order of North Star by His Majesty the King of Sweden, 1983. Mem. Swedish-Am. C. of C. (chmn. San Francisco chpt. 1986-88). Democrat. Roman Catholic.

FINSTAD, SUZANNE ELAINE, author, lawyer, producer; b. Mpls., Sept. 14, 1955; d. Harold Martin and Elaine Lois (Strom) F. Student, U. Tex., 1973-74; BA in French, U. Houston, 1976, JD, 1980; postgrad., London Sch. Econs., 1980, U. Grenoble, France, 1979. Bar: Tex. 1981. Legal asst. Butler & Binion, Houston, 1976-78, law clerk, 1978-81, assoc., 1982; spl. counsel Ad Litem in the Estate of Howard Hughes Jr., Houston, 1981; mng. ptnr. Finstad & Assoc., Houston, 1990—. Author: Heir Not Apparent, 1984 (Frank Wardlaw award 1984), Ulterior Motives, 1987, Sleeping With the Devil, 1991, Queen Noor: A Biography, 1995; prodr. Sleeping With the Devil, CBS, 1996; contbr. articles to various mags. Recipient Am. Jurisprudence award in climinal law U. Houston, 1979, named to Order of Barons, Bates Coll. Law, 1979-80. Democrat. Office: Joel Gotler Renaissance Agy 8523 W Sunset Blvd West Hollywood CA 90069-2309

FINTON, KENNETH HARPER, writer, publishing executive; b. Cleve., Sept. 21, 1942; s. William Kenneth and Doris Maxine (Harper) F.; m. Chaya Thompson, Sept. 22, 1986; stepchildren: Tasha, Robert. Grad., Bus. Sch. for Brokers, Denver, 1983. Staff writer Big Seven Music, N.Y.C., 1970-73; owner Heliotrope Music, Arvada, Colo., 1968—, HT Records, Arvada, 1980—. Author: From Tribes to Nations, 1992; editor, writer, pub. mag. The Plantagenet Connection, 1992—; pub. William Whitley Newsletter, 1992—; producer Atlantic Records, N.Y.C., 1970-73, Ghost Towns of Colo., 1991. Mem. Broadcast Music, Inc. Home and Office: 7060 Vrain St Westminster CO 80030-5863

FIOCK, SHARI LEE, design entrepreneur, researcher; b. Weed, Calif., Oct. 25, 1941; d. Webster Bruce and Olevia May (Pruett) F.; m. June 6, 1966 (div. 1974); children—Webster Clinton Pfingsten, Sterling Curtis. Cert. Art Instrn. Sch., Mpls., 1964; pvt. student. Copywriter Darron Assocs., Eugene, Oreg., 1964-66; staff artist Oreg. Holidays, Springfield, 1966-69, part-time 1971; co-owner, designer Artre Enterprises, Eugene, 1969-74; design entrepreneur Shari & Assocs., Yreka, Calif., 1974— (retained as cons., devel. sec. Cascade World Four Season Resort, Siskiyou County, Calif., 1980-86); part time administrv. asst., coord. of regional catalog Great Northern Corp./U.S. Dept. Commerce and Econ. Devel., 1994—; cons., pres. Reunions, Family, Yreka, 1984—. Designer 5 ton chain saw sculpture, Oreg. Beaver, 1967; author: Goose Gabble, 1992; illustrator: Holiday Fun Book, 1978; author, illustrator Blue Goose Legend, 1995; co-creator Klamath Nat. Forest Interpretive Mus., 1979-91; owner Coyote Pub. Author, illustrator Family Reunions and Clan Gatherings, 1991. Residential capt. United Way, Eugene, 1972; researcher Beaver Ofcl. State Animal, Eugene, 1965-71; counselor Boy Scouts, 1983-91. Mem. Nat. Writers Assn. (founder, pres. Siskiyou chpt., past v.p. State of Jefferson chpt., N.W. rep.). Avocations: family activities; outdoor recreation; travel; theater; music. Home: 406 Walters Ln # 1854 Yreka CA 96097-9704

FIORINO, JOHN WAYNE, podiatrist; b. Charleroi, Pa., Sept. 30, 1946; s. Anthony Raymond and Mary Louise (Caramela) F.; m. Susan K. Bonnett, May 2, 1984; children—Jennifer, Jessica, Lauren, Michael. Student Nassau Coll., 1969-70; B.A. in Biology, U. Buffalo, 1972; Dr. Podiatric Medicine, Ohio Coll. Podiatric Medicine, 1978. Salesman, E. J. Korvettes, Carle Place, N.Y., 1962-65; orderly Nassau Hosp., Mineola, N.Y., 1965-66; operating room technician-trainee heart-lung machine L.I. Jewish-Hillside Med. Center, New Hyde Park, N.Y., 1967-69; pharmacy technician Feinmel's Pharmacy, Roslyn Heights, N.Y., 1969-70; mgr., asst. buyer Fortunoffs, Westbury, N.Y., 1972-73; bd. certified perfusionist L.I. Jewish-Hillside Med. Center, New Hyde Park, N.Y., 1973-74; clin. instr. cardiopulmonary tech. Stony Brook (N.Y.) Univ., 1973-74; operating room technician Cleve. Met. Hosp., 1975; lab. technician Univ. Hosp., Cleve., 1976-78; surg. resident Mesa Gen. Hosp., 1978-79; staff podiatrist, 1979—; pvt. practice podiatry, Mesa, 1979—; staff podiatrist Sacaton (Ariz.) Hosp., 1979—, Mesa Gen. Hosp., 1979, Valley Luth. Hosp., Mesa, 1985, Chandler Community Hosp., 1985, Desert Samaritan Hosp., Mesa, 1986, podiatrist U.S. Govt. Nat. Inst., Sacaton, 1980-87, Indian Health Services, Sacaton, 1980-87; cons. staff Phoenix Indian Med. Ctr., 1985. Served with USN, 1966-67. Mem. Am. Podiatry Assn., Ariz. Podiatry Assn. (treas. 1984-86), Acad. Ambulatory Foot Surgery, Am. Coll. Foot Surgeons (assoc.), Mut. Assn. Profls., Am. Acad. Pain Mgmt. (cert.), Pi Delta, Alpha Gamma Kappa. Home: 2624 W Upland Dr Chandler AZ 85224-7870 Office: 5520 E Main St Mesa AZ 85205-8793

FIPPS, MICHAEL W., corporate executive; b. Tabor City, N.C., Aug. 24, 1942; s. David Earl and Ina (Etheridge) F.; m. Angelique Peggy Ryjkschroeff, July 15, 1972; 1 child, Sean, Brandon. B.A., U. N.C., Wilmington, 1968. C.P.A., Calif. Acct. Platt Warren & Swinson C.P.A.s, Wilmington, N.C., 1966-68; acct. Baxter Labs., Chgo., 1968-69; auditor Allstate Ins. Co., Chgo., 1969-71, Flying Tiger Line Inc., Los Angeles, 1971-73; treas. Bergen Brunswig Corp., Los Angeles, 1973—. Mem. Am. Inst. C.P.A.s, Am. Mgmt. Assn., Fin. Execs. Inst., Calif. Soc. C.P.A.s. Republican. Office: Bergen Brunswig Corp 4000 W Metropolitan Dr Orange CA 92668-3502

FIRESTONE, FREDERICK NORTON, surgeon, educator; b. San Francisco, Dec. 6, 1931; s. Fred and Adrienne Henrietta (Norton) F.; children: Julie Sarah, Laurie Lynn, Daniel Norton. AB in Biol. Sci., Stanford U., 1953, MD, 1956. Diplomate Am. Bd. Surgery, Am. Bd. Thoracic Surgery. Intern and resident Boston City Hosp., 1956-59, resident in thoracic surgery, 1964-66; resident pediat. surgery, sr. fellow cardiovascular surgery Childrens Hosp. Med. Ctr., Boston, 1962-63; asst. clin. prof. surgery U. Calif. Coll. Medicine, Irvine, 1970—; chmn. thoracic surgery Hoag Meml. Hosp. Presbyn., Newport Beach, Calif., 1986-89; chief surgery Coll. Hosp., Costa Mesa, Calif., 1984, vice chief staff, 1985, chief of staff, 1986; cons. vascular lab. Hoag Meml. Hosp., Presbyn., Newport Beach, 1982-90. Contbr. articles to profl. jours. Bd. dirs. Am. Cancer Soc., Orange County, Calif., 1977-90, pres., 1983-85; bd. dirs. Newport Found. for Study Major Econ. Issues, Newport Beach, 1986-90; founder paramedic program, Orange County, 1972-76; pres. Am. Heart Assn., Orange County, 1976-77. Capt. M.C., U.S. Army, 1960-66. Fellow ACS; mem. Am. Trauma Soc. (founding), Am. Numismatic Assn. (life), Soc. Thoracic Surgeons, Orange County Surg. Soc. (pres. 1992), Nature Conservancy (life), Nat. Audubon Soc. (life). Republican. Home: 245 Palmer St Costa Mesa CA 92627-3747

FIRMINGER, HARLAN IRWIN, pathologist, educator; b. Mpls., Dec. 31, 1918; s. Harry and Emily (Irwin) F.; m. Jane Ryder Hollings, Sept. 14, 1942; children: Ann Laura Firminger Howard, Carol Jean Firminger Feeney, Barbara Lynn. A.B., Washington U., St. Louis, 1939, M.D., 1943. Diplomate Am. Bd. Pathology. Intern Barnes Hosp., St. Louis, 1943; resident pathology Mass. Gen. Hosp., Boston, 1946-47; pathologist Nat. Cancer Inst., Bethesda, Md., 1948-51; practice medicine specializing in pathology Kansas City, Kans., 1951-57, Balt., 1957-75, Denver, 1975—; asst. prof., prof. pathology U. Kans., 1951-57; prof., chmn. dept. pathology U. Md., 1957-67, prof. pathology, 1967-75; dir. anatomic pathology Gen. Rose Meml. Hosp., Denver, 1975-76; prof. pathology U. Colo., 1975-89, prof. emeritus, 1989—; dir. Univs. Asso. for Research and Edn. in Pathology, 1964-71, scientist-asso., 1971-75; mem. sci. adv. bd. Armed Forces Inst. Pathology, 1965-70; mem. com. on pathology div. med. scis. Nat. Acad. Scis.-NRC, 1966-72. Editor Atlas of Tumor Pathology, 1966-75, mem. editorial adv. com., 1975-83; contbr. articles to profl. jours. Pres. Md. div. Am. Cancer Soc., 1967-68. Served to capt. M.C. AUS, 1943-46. Mem. Am. Soc. Investigative Pathology, Internat. Acad. Pathology, Am. Assn. Cancer Research, Soc. Mayflower Descs. (gov. Md. chpt. 1967-70), Md. Soc. Pathologists (pres. 1969-71), Colo. Soc. Clin. Pathology, Alpha Omega Alpha. Office: U Colo Health Scis Ctr 4200 E 9th Ave Denver CO 80220-3706

FISCHER, ALFRED GEORGE, geology educator; b. Rothenburg, Germany, Dec. 10, 1920; came to U.S., 1935; s. George Erwin and Thea (Freise) F.; m. Winnifred Varney, Sept. 26, 1939; children: Joseph Fred, George William, Lenore Ruth Fischer Walsh. Student, Northwestern Coll., Watertown, Wis., 1935-37; BA, U. Wis., 1939, MA, 1941; PhD, Columbia U., 1950. Instr. Va. Poly. Inst. and State U., Blacksburg, 1941-43; geologist Stanolind Oil & Gas Co., Kans. and Fla., 1943-46; instr. U. Rochester, N.Y., 1947-48; from instr. to asst. prof. U. Kans., Lawrence, 1948-51; sr. geologist Internat. Petroleum, Peru, 1951-56; prof. geology Princeton (N.J.) U., 1956-84, U. So. Calif., Los Angeles, 1984—. Co-Author: Invertebrate Fossils, 1952, The Permian Reef Complex, 1953, Electron Micrographs of Limestone, 1967; editor: Petroleum and Global Tectonics, 1975. Recipient Verrill medal Yale U., Geol. Soc. London (hon. Lyell medal) 1992. Fellow Geol. Soc. Am. (Penrose medal 1993), Ecol. Soc. London (hon., Lyell medal 1992), Soc. Econ. Paleontologists (hon., Twenhofel medal); mem. AAAS, NAS, Am. Assn. Petroleum Geologists, Paleontol. Soc., German Geol. Soc. (Leopold van Buch medal), Geol. Union (Gustav Steinmann medal 1992), Mainz Acad. Sci. Lit. (corr.) Lincei Acad. Rome (fgn.), Sigma Xi. Home: 1736 Perch St San Pedro CA 90732-4218 Office: U So Calif Dept Geol Scis Univ Park Dept Earth Scis Los Angeles CA 90089-0741

FISCHER, ALVIN EUGENE, JR., marketing executive; b. Glendale, Calif., July 31, 1942; s. Alvin Eugene Sr. and Roberta Maxine (Barker) F.; m. Michel Jane Gorham, Dec. 20, 1960 (div. Oct. 1982); children: Theresa Michele, Todd Alan, Alvin Eugene III; m. Laurie Ann Simpson, Aug. 22, 1986. Student, Orange Coast Coll., 1960-70, UCLA, 1967, U. Calif., Irvine, 1970. Lic. bldg. contractor, Calif. Supt. constrn. K.W. Koll Builders, Costa Mesa, Calif., 1960-65; gen. sales mgr. Mills Inc., Santa Ana, Calif., 1965-70; gen. mgr. Royal Interiors Inc., Santa Ana, 1970-72; v.p. nat. ops. Larwin Home Ctr., Beverly Hills, Calif., 1972-74; broker Village Real Estate, Huntington Beach, Calif., 1975-78; v.p. sales Phillips Floor Covering, Santa Ana, 1978-81; gen. sales mgr. G.A.F./Tarkett/Star Distbn., Commerce, Calif., 1981-83; v.p. sales and mktg. LaSalle-Deitch Co., Tustin, Calif., 1983-84; gen. sales mgr. LD Brinkman, Ontario, Calif., 1984-85; sales mgr. western region Nat. Floor Products Inc., Florence, Ala., 1986—; panelist Western Floor Covering Assn., 1979. Mgr. pubs. Newport Theatrical Arts, Newport Beach, Calif., 1983; mem. South Coast Community Ch., Irvine, Calif. Mem. Am. Mgmt. Assn., So. Calif. Floor Covering Club, Newport Sail Club. Office: Nat Floor Products Inc PO Box 354 Florence AL 35631-0354

FISCHER, DALE SUSAN, lawyer; b. East Orange, N.J., Oct. 17, 1951; d. Edward L. and Audrey (Tenner) F. Student Dickinson Coll., 1969-70; BA magna cum laude, U. So. Fla., 1977; JD, Harvard U., 1980. Bar: Calif. 1980. Ptnr. law firm Kindel & Anderson, L.A., 1986—; judge pro tem L.A. Mcpl. Ct.; faculty Nat. Inst. Trial Advocacy; lawyer in classroom Constl. Rights Found.; moderator, panelist How to Win Your Case with Depositions. Mem. ABA, Am. Arbitration Assn. (mem. panel arbitrators), L.A. County Bar Assn., L.A. Complex Litigation Inn of Ct. Home: 3695 Hampton Rd Pasadena CA 91107-3004 Office: Kindel and Anderson 555 S Flower St Los Angeles CA 90071-2300

FISCHER, DAVID JOSEPH, ambassador; b. Bridgeport, Conn., Feb. 18, 1939; s. Joseph D. and Jeanne (Brandt) F.; m. Pamela Popkin, Sept. 9, 1961; children: Keith, Mark, Anne. B.A., Brown U., 1960; postgrad., Harvard U., 1961. Joined U.S. Fgn. Service, 1961; served U.S. Fgn. Service, Ger., Poland, Bulgaria and Nepal, 1961-77; dir. Office Pub. Affairs U.S. Fgn. Service, Washington, 1977-79; dep. chief of mission Am. embassy, Dar es Salaam U.S. Fgn. Service, Tanzania, 1979-82; ambassador to Seychelles U.S. Fgn. Service, Victoria, 1982-85; dir. East Africa Dept. State, 1986—. Home: 955 Clayton St Apt 3 San Francisco CA 94117-4470 Office: World Affairs Coun 312 Sutter St San Francisco CA 94108-4305

FISCHER, EDMOND HENRI, biochemistry educator; b. Shanghai, Republic of China, Apr. 6, 1920; came to U.S., 1953; s. Oscar and Renée (Tapernoux) F.; m. Beverley B. Bullock. Lic. es Sciences Chimiques et Biologiques, U. Geneva, 1943, Diplome d'Ingenieur Chimiste, 1944, PhD, 1947; D (hon.), U. Montpellier, France, 1985, U. Basel, Switzerland, 1988, Med. Coll. of Ohio, 1993, Ind. U., 1993, U. Bochum, Germany, 1994. Pvt. docent biochemistry U. Geneva, 1950-53; research assoc. biology Calif. Inst. Tech., Pasadena, 1953; asst. prof. biochemistry U. Wash., Seattle, 1953-56, assoc. prof., 1956-61, prof., 1961-90, prof. emeritus, 1990—; mem. exec. com. Pacific Slope Biochem. Conf., 1958-59, pres. 1975; mem. biochemistry study sect. NIH, 1959-64; symposium co-chmn. Battelle Seattle Research Ctr., 1970, 73, 78; mem. sci. adv. bd. Biozentrum, U. Basel, Switzerland, 1982-86; sci. adv. bd. Friedrich Miescher Inst., Ciba-Geigy, Basel, 1976-84, chmn. 1981-84. Contbr. numerous articles to sci. jours. Mem. sci. council on basic sci. Am. Heart Assn., 1977-80, sci. adv. com. Muscular Dystrophy Assn., 1980-88. Recipient Lederle Med. Faculty award, 1956-59, Guggenheim Found. award, 1963-64, Disting. Lectr. award U. Wash., 1983, Laureate Passano Found. award, 1988, Steven C. Beering award, 1991, Nobel Prize in Physiology or Medicine, 1992; NIH spl. fellow, 1963-64. Fellow Am. Acad. Arts and Scis.; mem. NAS, AAAS, AAUP, Am. Soc. Biol. Chemists (coun. 1989-93), Am. Chem. Soc. (adv. bd. biochemistry divsn. 1962, exec. com. divsn. biology 1969-72, monograph adv. bd. 1971-73, editl. adv. bd. Biochemistry, 1961-66, assoc. editor 1966-91), Swiss Chem. Soc. (Werner medal), Spanish Royal Acad. Scis. (fgn. assoc.), Venice Inst. Sci., Arts and Letters (fgn. assoc.), Japanese Biochem. Soc. (hon.). Office: U Washington Med Sch Dept Biochemistry Sj # 70 Seattle WA 98195

FISCHER, JAMES ADRIAN, clergyman; b. St. Louis, Oct. 15, 1916; s. John and Agnes (Henke) F. A.B., St. Mary's Sem., Perryville, Mo., 1941; S.T.L., Cath. U. Am., 1949; S.S.L., Pontifical Bib. Inst., Rome, Italy, 1951; LL.D. (hon.), Niagara U., 1968. Joined Congregation of Mission, 1936; ordained priest Roman Cath. Ch., 1943; prof. sacred scripture St. John's Sem., San Antonio, 1943-45; prof. sacred scripture St. Mary's Sem., Houston, 1951-56, Perryville, 1958-62; provincial Western province Vincentian Fathers, 1962-71, De Andreis Sem., Lemont, Ill., 1971-81; pres. Kenrick Sem., St. Louis, 1981-86, St. Thomas Sem., Denver, 1986—. Author: The Psalms, 1974, God Created Woman, 1979, How to Read the Bible, 1981, Priests, 1987, Looking for Moral Guidance, 1993. Chmn. bd. trustees De Paul U., Chgo., 1962-71. Mem. Cath. Bibl. Assn. (pres. 1976-77). Address: St Thomas Sem 1300 S Steele St Denver CO 80210-2526

FISCHER, JAY EDWARD, consulting service company executive; b. S.I., N.Y., Mar. 6, 1956; s. Jacob Fredrick and Signa Joan (Hannaford) F.; m. Pamela Robinson, June 7, 1978 (div. Dec. 1981); m. Junko Suganuma, Dec. 30, 1989; children: Christine Kaede, Amy Miyako. BA in Edn., Auburn U., 1978, BSEE, 1982. Engr. Intergraph Corp., Huntsville, Ala., 1983-85; applications engr. HHB Systems, Mahwah, N.J., 1985-88; dir. of Far East Ikos Systems, Cupertino, Calif., 1988-93; ind. contractor Quorum Internat., Phoenix, 1993-94; owner Cons. Svcs., Los Gatos, Calif., 1994—. Home and Office: 216 Drakes Bay Ave Los Gatos CA 95032-2406 Office: Quorum 15732 Los Gatos Blvd Ste 100 Los Gatos CA 95032-2504

FISCHER, JOEL, social work educator; b. Chgo., Apr. 22, 1939; s. Sam and Ruth (Feiges) F.; m. Renee H. Furuyama; children: Lisa, Nicole. BS, U. Ill., 1961, MSW, 1964; D in Social Welfare, U. Calif., Berkeley, 1970. Prof. sch. social work U. Hawaii, Honolulu, 1970—; vis. prof. George Warren Brown Sch. Social Work, Washington U., St. Louis, 1977, U. Wis. Sch. Social Welfare, Milw., 1978-79, U. Natal, South Africa, 1982, U. Hong Kong, 1986; cons. various orgns. and univs. Author: (with Harvey L. Gochros) Planned Behavior Change: Behavior Modification in Social Work, 1973, Handbook of Behavior Therapy with Sexual Problems, Vol. I, 1977, Vol. II, 1977, Analyzing Research, 1975, Interpersonal Helping: Emerging Approaches for Social Work Practice, 1973, The Effectiveness of Social Casework, 1976, Fundamentals of Social Work Practice, 1982, Effective Casework Practice: An Eclectic Approach, 1978, Treat Yourself to a Better Sex Life, 1980, Helping the Sexually Oppressed, 1986; (with Martin Bloom) Evaluating Practice: Guidelines for the Helping Professional, 1982; (with Kevin Corcoran) Measures for Clinical Practice, 1987; (with Daniel Sanders) Visions for the Future: Social Work and Pacific-Asian Perspectives, 1988; (with Martin Bloom and John Orme) Evaluating Practice, 2d edit., 1995; (with Kevin Corcoran) Measures for Clinical Practice, 2d edit., Vol. 1, Couples, Families, Children, Vol. 2, Adults, 1994, East-West Connections: Social Work Practice Traditions and Change, 1992; mem. editl. bd. 12 profl. jours.; contbr. over 150 articles, revs., chpts. and papers to profl. pubs. With U.S. Army, 1958. Mem. Hawaii Com. for Africa, Nat. Assn. Social Workers, Coun. Social Work Edn., Acad. Cert. Social Workers, Nat. Conf. Social Welfare, AAUP, Unity Organizing Com., Hawaii People's Legis. Coalition, Bertha Reynold Soc. Democrat. Home: 1371-4 Hunakai St Honolulu HI 96816 Office: U Hawaii 2500 Campus Rd Honolulu HI 96822-2217

FISCHER, MICHAEL LUDWIG, environmental executive; b. Dubuque, Iowa, May 29, 1940; s. Carl Michael and Therese Marie (Stadler) F.; m. Jane Pughe Rogers; children: Christina Marie, Steven Michael. BA in Polit. Sci., Santa Clara U., 1964; M in City and Regional Planning, U. Calif., Berkeley, 1967; grad. exec. program in environ. mgmt., Harvard U., 1980. Planner City of Mountain View, Calif., 1960-65, County of San Mateo, Calif., 1967-69; assoc. dir. San Francisco Planning and Urban Rsch. Assn., nonprofit civc orgn., 1969-73; exec. dir. North Cen. region Calif. Coastal Zone Conservation Commn., San Rafael, 1973-76; chief dep. dir. Gov.'s Office Planning and Rsch., Sacramento, 1976-78; exec. dir. Calif. Coastal Commn., San Francisco, 1978-85; sr. assoc. Sedway Cooke Assocs., environ. cons., San Francisco, 1985-87; exec. dir. Sierra Club, San Francisco, 1987-93; resident fellow John F. Kennedy Sch. Govt., Inst. Politics, Harvard U., Cambridge, Mass., 1993; sr. cons. Natural Resources Def. Coun., San Francisco, 1993—; exec. officer Calif. Coastal Conservancy, Oakland, 1994—; chair environ. com. adv. coun. Calvert Social Investment Fund, 1989—; mem. Harvard Commn. Global Change Info. Policy; pres., chmn. bd. Yosemite Restoration Trust; mem. com. on impact of maritime facility devel. NAS/NRC, 1975-78. Co-author Calif. state plan, An Urban Strategy for Calif., 1978. Recipient Life Achievement award Assn. Environ. Profls., 1986, Disting. Leadership award. Am. Soc. Pub. Adminstrn., 1987, Outstanding Nat. Leadership award Coastal States Orgn., 1990. Mem. Wilderness Soc., Nat. Audubon soc., Nat. Resources Def. Coun., Marin Conservation League, E Clampus Vitus (New Helvetia, Yerba Buena chpts.), 1000 Friends of Fla., 1000 Friends of Kauai, Calif. Planning and Conservation League, Lambda Alpha. Office: Calif Coastal Conservancy 1330 Broadway Fl 11 Oakland CA 94612-2503

FISCHER, PETER HEINZ, public affairs and communications specialist; b. Nuremberg, Ger., Feb. 17, 1942; came to U.S., 1950, naturalized, 1956; s. Hans and Helen (Müller) F.; m. Marianne Dee, Apr. 22, 1964; children: Christopher, Melanie. BA in English and Journalism, Stephen F. Austin U., 1964. Cert. pub. relations, 1976. Editor, Shell Oil Co., Houston and Deer Park, Tex., 1964-69, regional editor, New Orleans, 1969-71, pub. relations rep., 1971-78, sr. pub. relations rep., 1978-81, mgr. community relations southeast, 1981-82, mgr. nat. news media relations, Houston, 1982-83, sr. staff environ. pub. affairs rep., Shell Products, 1983-87; mgr. community relations central/east region, 1987-90; projects mgr. mktg. and communications rsch. Shell Oil Co., Houston, 1990—93; mktg. and comm. cons., 1993—. Mem. East Harris County Mfrs. Assn. (past chmn. pub. rels. com.), Tex. Chem. Coun. (pub. affairs com., Disting. Svc. award 1988), Chem. Mfrs. Assn. (pub. opinion rsch. task group 1991), Pub. Rels. Soc. Am. (accredited, Colo. chpt.), Rocky Mt. Pub. Rels Assn., Evergreen C. of C. (dir.), Rocky Mtn. Pet Dealers Assn. (dir.). Republican. Contbr. articles to profl. jours. Home: 3578 S Saddle Rd Evergreen CO 80439-8508

FISCHER, ROBERT EDWARD, meterologist; b. Bethlehem, Pa., Aug. 4, 1943; s. Frederic Philip and Muriel Winifred (Johnson) F. BS cum laude, U. Utah, 1966; MS, Colo. State U., 1969. Meterologist Nat. Weather Service, Fairbanks, Alaska, 1973—. Contbr. articles to profl. jours. Vol. classical music program producer Sta. KUAC-FM, Fairbanks. Recipient Nat. Oceanic and Atmospheric Adminstrn. Unit citation, 1989. Fellow Royal Meteorol. Soc.; mem. Am. Meteorol. Soc. (Charles L. Mitchell award 1985), Nat. Weather Assn. (Outstanding Operational Performance award 1987), Assn. Lunar and Planetary Observers, Am. Assn. Variable Star Observers, Royal Astron. Soc. Can., Sigma Xi, Phi Kappa Phi. Home: PO Box 82210 Fairbanks AK 99708-2210 Office: Nat Weather Service Forecast Office 101 12th Ave Ste 12 Fairbanks AK 99701-6237

FISCHER, ZOE ANN, real estate and property marketing company executive, real estate consultant; b. L.A., Aug. 26, 1939; d. George and Marguerite (Carrasco) Routsos; m. Douglas Clare Fischer, Aug. 6, 1960 (div. 1970); children: Brent Sean Cecil, Tahlia Georgienne Marguerite Bianca. BFA in Design, UCLA, 1964. Pres. Zoe Antiques, Beverly Hills, Calif., 1973—; v.p. Harleigh Sandler Real Estate Corp. (now Prudential), 1980-81; exec. v.p. Coast to Coast Real Estate & Land Devel. Corp., Century City, Calif., 1981-83; pres. New Market Devel., Inc., Beverly Hills, 1983—; dir. mktg. Mirabella, L.A., 1983, Autumn Pointe, L.A., 1983-84, Desert Hills, Antelope Valley, Calif., 1984-85; cons. Lowe Corp., L.A., 1985. Designer interior and exterior archtl. enhancements and remodelling; designed album cover for Clare Fischer Orch. (Grammy award nomination 1962). Soprano Roger Wagner Choir, UCLA, 1963-64. Mem. UCLA Alumni Assn. Democrat. Roman Catholic. Avocations: skiing, designing jewelry, interior, landscape and new home design, antique collecting.

FISCHLE, DANIEL KARL, school system administrator; b. North Tonawanda, N.Y., May 24, 1944; s. Edward Karl and Jane (Kendall) F.; m. Linda Reh Owen, June 12, 1981 (dec.); children: Gretchen Danielle, Rebecca Reh. BA in History and Polit. Sci., Calif. State U.-Stanislaus, Turlock, 1966, MA in History, 1972. Cert. tchr., ednl. adminstr., Calif. Tchr. Turlock Union H.S. Dist., 1967-69; tchr. Selma (Calif.) Unified Sch. Dist., 1971-73, asst. H.S. prin., 1973-80; adminstrv. cons. Fresno (Calif.) County Office Edn., 1980-81; prin. Kerman (Calif.) Union H.S., 1981-83; asst. supt. Kerman Unified Sch. Dist., 1983-87, dep. supt., 1987—. Photographer: (book) Sentenial, 1966. Pres. Peace Luth. Ch., Fresno, 1982-85; bd. dirs. Calif. Assn. Dirs. of Activities, 1974-76, Fresno County Adminstrs. Assn., 1980-84, Region IX Assn. Calif. Adminstrs., 1988-93. Mem. Am.-Hellenic Edn. Progressive Assn., Kiwanis (pres. 1985-86). Republican. Office: Kerman Unified Sch Dist 151 S 1st St Kerman CA 93630-1029

FISCHLER, BRYANT, venture capital executive; b. Bklyn., Nov. 15, 1928; s. Alfred Louis and Fannie (Kluger) F.; m. Joyce Pepose (div. 1976); children: Diane, Scott, Deborah, Lisa, Aimee. BA, L.I. U., 1951; LLB, Bklyn. Law Sch., 1954. Bar: U.S. Dist. Ct. (so. and ea. dists.) N.Y. 1959, U.S. Tax Ct. Ins. agt. Occidental TransAm. Ins. Co., Phoenix, 1981, INA Life Ins. Co., Phoenix, 1981, State Mut. Life Ins. Co., Phoenix, 1981-82; prof. bus. law, mgmt., and bus. adminstrn. Western Internat. U., Phoenix, 1981—, Ottawa U., Phoenix, 1986—; prof. bus. law, mgmt. and bus. adminstrn. LaSalle U., 1995—; chmn. bd. Omni Fin. and Ins. Services Ltd., 1982-86; chmn., bd. dirs., pres. U.S. Capital Corp., Phoenix, 1983-90; sec. treas., owner White Eagle Travel, Inc., Peoria, Ariz., 1986—; chief exec. officer U.S. Venture Capital Fund, Inc., Phoenix, 1988—; mediator Ariz. Atty. Gen. Office, 1987—. Author: (poems) Feelings, 1980. Chmn. N.Y. State Selective Service Draft Bd., 1973-75; bd. dirs. Widow's Guild, Phoenix, 1980-84. Served as seaman 1st class USN, 1946-48. Recipient Robert Roesler de Villier's decoration Leukemia Soc. of Am., 1968, Community Leader of Am. award, 1969, Cert. Appreciation former U.S. Pres. Richard Nixon, 1973. Mem. Am. Arbitration Assn. Home and Office: US Venture Capital Fund Inc Exec Towers 207 W Clarendon Ave Apt 2G Phoenix AZ 85013-3400

FISETTE, SCOTT MICHAEL, golf course designer; b. Orange, Tex., May 17, 1963; s. Roderick John and Addie Faye (Byrnes) F.; divorced; 1 child, Shane Roderick. BS in Landscape Architecture, Tex. A&M U., 1985. Registered landscape architect, Tex., Hawaii, Commonwealth of No. Mariana Islands. Project architect Dick Nugent Assocs., Long Grove, Ill., 1985-90; prin., pres. Fisette Golf Designs, Kaneohe, Hawaii, 1991—. Mem. Golf Course Supts. Assn. Am., Am. Soc. Landscape Architects, Nat. Golf Found., Hawaii Turf Grass Assn. (bd. dirs. 1991—), Donald Ross Soc., Urban Land Inst. Office: Fisette Golf Designs PO Box 1433 Kaneohe HI 96744-1433

FISH, JAMES HENRY, library director; b. Leominster, Mass., Feb. 21, 1947; s. Danny Mack and Doris Grace (Harvey) F. BA, U. Mass., 1968; MLS, Ind. U., 1971; MBA, Anna Maria Coll., Paxton, Mass., 1979. Dir. libr. Levi Heywood Meml. Libr., Gardner, Mass., 1971-72; dir. Leominster Public Libr., 1972-77, Robbins Libr., Arlington, Mass., 1977-80; state librarian Mass. State Libr., Boston, 1980-82; dir. Springfield City Libr. (Mass.), 1982-90; city librarian San Jose (Calif.) Pub. Libr., 1990—. Author libr. reports and cons. projects, community analysis, planning and evaluation. Bd. dirs. United Fund Leominster, 1974-76, Vis. Nurses Assn. Leominster, 1974-76, Leominster chpt. ARC, 1975-77, Santa Clara Valley YMCA, 1991-94; chmn. Leominster Bicentennial Com., 1975-76. With U.S. Army, 1969-71. Decorated Commendation medal; recipient Disting. Service award Arlington C. of C., 1979. Mem. ALA, Pub. Libr. Assn. (New Standards Task Force 1986-87, adv. com. chmn. Pub. Libr. Data Svc., mem. conf. program com., 1988-90, 90-91, mem. nominating com. 1993, mem. common concerns com. 1994, mem. ptnrs. program 1994), Calif. Libr. Assn.(mem. com., 1993—, conf. planning com., 1994—, chair local arrangements com., 1994—), Urban Librs. Coun. (steering com., video tng. project, 1994—), Beta Phi Mu. Office: San Jose Pub Libr 180 W San Carlos St San Jose CA 95113-2005

FISH, RUBY MAE BERTRAM (MRS. FREDERICK GOODRICH FISH), civic worker; b. Sheridan, Wyo., July 24, 1918; d. Ryan Lawrence and Ruby (Beckwith) Bertram; R.N., St. Luke's Hosp., 1936; postgrad. Washington U., St. Louis, 1941; m. Frederick Goodrich Fish, Apr. 12, 1942; children: Bertram Frederick, Lisbeth Ann Fish Kalstein. Staff nurse Huntington Meml. Hosp., Pasadena, Calif., 1941-42; dr.'s office nurse, Denver, 1943-44; travel cons. Buckingham Travel Agy., Aurora, Colo., 1976—. Bd. dirs. Jefferson County Easter Seal Soc., 1949—, pres., 1952-53, 56-57, 66-67; pres. Colo. Easter Seal Soc., 1960-61; bd. dirs. Nat. Easter Seal Soc., 1968-69, sec. ho. of dels., 1976-77; bd. dirs. Assistance League Denver, 1968-70, 75-76, People to People for Handicapped, 1981— (Vol. of Yr. award 1991); mem. Pres.'s Com. on Employing Handicapped, 1976—; active Rehab. Internat. of U.S.A., 1972—, Rehab. Internat., 1960—. Mem. Dau. Nile-El Mejedel. Home: 6900 W Stetson Pl # 3 Littleton CO 80123-1331 Office: 13741 E Mississippi Ave Aurora CO 80012-3628

FISHBACK, PRICE VANMETER, economics educator; b. Louisville, July 8, 1955; s. William Vanmeter and Frances Henry (Taylor) F.; m Pamela Elaine Slaten, June 9, 1989. BA, Butler U., 1977; MA, U. Washington, 1979, PhD, 1983. Econ. cons. Weyerhaeuser Co., Federal Way, Wash., 1980-81; asst. prof. U. Ga., Athens, 1982-86, assoc. prof., 1987-90; assoc. prof. U. Ariz., Tucson, 1990-93; prof. U. Ariz., 1993—; rsch. assoc. Nat. Bur. Econ. Rsch., 1994—; vis. prof. U. Tex., Austin, 1987-89. Author: Soft Coal, Hard Choices: The Economic Welfare of Bituminous Coal Miners, 1890-1930, 1992; contbr. articles to profl. jours. Rsch. grantee U. Ga. Found., 1985, Earhart Found., 1988, 92, Bradley Found., 1989, NSF, 1993—. Office: U Ariz Econs Dept Tucson AZ 85721

FISHBEIN, MICHAEL CLAUDE, physician, pathologist; b. Brussels, May 25, 1946; came to U.S., 1949; s. Fred F. and Celia (Feldman) F.; m. Astrid Lorette du Mortier, Aug. 11, 1974; children: Danielle Renee, Gregory Andrew. BS, U. Ill., 1967; MD, U. Ill., Chgo., 1971. Diplomate Coll. Am. Pathologists; cert. anatomic and clin. pathology. Intern UCLA/Harbor Gen. Hosp., 1971-72, resident, 1972-75; asst. prof. pathology Harvard U. Sch. Medicine, Boston, 1975-78; assoc. pathologist Peter Bent Brigham Hosp., Boston, 1975-78, Cedars-Sinai Med. Ctr., Los Angeles, 1978—; cons. Beth Israel Hosp., Boston, 1975-78, mem. faculty Harvard U.-MIT program in health scis., Boston, 1975-78; prof. UCLA Sch. Medicine, 1978—. Achievements include research in heart disease; contbr. over 200 articles to profl. jours. and 6 chpts. to books. Mem. Phi Beta Kappa, Alpha Omega Alpha. Jewish. Office: Cedars-Sinai Med Ctr 8700 Beverly Blvd Los Angeles CA 90048-1804

FISHER, BART, agricultural products company executive; b. 1949. With Fisher Ranch Corp., Blythe, Calif., 1965—; now v.p.; with Fisher Comms., Blythe, Calif., 1983—, Fisher Ranch III, Blythe, Calif., 1982—. Office: Fisher Ranch Corp 10600 Ice Plant Rd Blythe CA 92225-2757*

FISHER, BRUCE DAVID, elementary educator; b. Long Beach, Calif., Dec. 24, 1949; s. Oran Wilfred and Irene (May) F.; m. Mindi Beth Evans, Aug. 15, 1976; 1 child, Jenny Allison Viola. BA, Humboldt State U., 1975, standard elem. credential, 1976, learning handicapped credential, 1977. Instrnl. svcs. specialist Blue Lake (Calif.) Elem. Sch.; resource specialist Fortuna (Calif.) Union Sch. Dist., tchr. 3d grade, tchr. 5th grade, 1988—; curriculum writer. Vice-chmn. Tchrs. Edn. and Cmty. Helpers, Arcata, Calif., 1990—; v.p. Sequoia Park Zool. Soc., Eureka, 1989-90, chmn. Whale Fair, 1989—; mem. selection com. Christa McAuliffe Fellowship; bd. dirs. Redwood Environ. Edn. Fair, Eureka, 1990—, Family Wellness Project, 1991; apptd. Calif. Curriculum and Supplemental Materials Commn.; commr. Calif. Curriculum Commn., 1992-95; chair math. assessment Calif. Dept. Edn., 1995; cons. PITSCO Sci., 1995, NASA/JPL, 1995. Named Calif. Tchr. of Yr. Dept. Edn., 1991, Favorite Tchrs. ABC-TV, 1991, Humboldt County Tchr. of Yr., 1991; recipient Leadership Excellence award Calif. Assn. Sci. Specialists, 1990, Masonic Meritorious Svc. award for Pub. Edn., 1991, Profl. Best Leadership award Learning Mag., Oldsmobile Corp., and Mich. State U., 1991, Nat. Educator award Milken Found. Calif. State Dept. Edn., 1991, NASA/NSTA Newest award, 1993, Newton's Apple Multimedia Inst., 1995. Mem. Calif. Tchrs. Assn., Calif. Sci. Tchrs. Assn., Calif. Assn. Health, Phys. Edn., Recreation, and Dance. Democrat. Home: 4810 14th St Arcata CA 95521-9778 Office: Fortuna Elem Sch 843 L St Fortuna CA 95540-1921

FISHER, DANA B., food product executive; b. 1918. With Fisher Ranch Corp., pres.; with Hi Value Proceesor, Inc., 1976—, pres., 1983—. Office: Fisher Ranch Corp 10600 Ice Plant Rd Blythe CA 92225-2757*

FISHER, DARRELL REED, medical physicist, researcher; b. Salt Lake City, Feb. 12, 1951; s. Wayne Ekman and Zina Vae (Moore) F.; m. Anna Jeanetta Thomas, June 23, 1988; children: Bryan, Jenny, Aaron, Brit, Jake, Kimberly. BA in Biology, U. Utah, 1975; MS, U. Fla., 1976, PhD in Nuclear Engring. Scis., 1978. Rsch. asst. Radiobiology Lab., U. Utah, Salt Lake City, 1973-75; grad. asst. Nuclear Engring, U. Fla., Gainesville, 1975-78; rsch. scientist Battelle, Pacific N.W. Labs., Richland, Wash., 1978-80; sr. rsch. scientist Battelle, Pacific N.W. Labs., Richland, 1980—, tech. group leader, 1991-93, staff scientist, 1993—; affiliate asst. prof. U. Wash. Sch. Medicine, Seattle, 1991—; adj. assoc. prof. Wash. State U., Richland, 1992—; affiliate investigator Fred Hutchinson Cancer Rsch. Ctr., Seattle, 1993—, cons., 1987—, Divsn. Nuclear Medicine U. Wash., Seattle, 1986—, NeoRx Corp., Seattle, 1987—. Editor: Current Concepts in Lung Dosimetry, 1983, Inhaled Particles VI, 1988, Population Exposure from the Nuclear Fuel Cycle, 1988; assoc. editor Jour. Health Physics, 1985-91, Antibody Immunoconjugates and Pharmaceuticals, 1991—. Cert. arbitrator Better Bus. Bur. Ea. Wash., Yakima, 1981—. Mem. Am. Assn. Physicists in Medicine, Health Physics Soc. (Elda E. Anderson award 1986, bd. dirs. 1988-93, pres. Columbia chpt. 1983-84), Radiation Rsch. Soc. Republican. Mem. LDS Ch. Home: 229 Saint St Richland WA 99352-2061 Office: Battelle Pacific NW Labs Health Physics Dept Battelle Blvd Richland WA 99352

FISHER, DAVID CLARENCE, optometrist; b. Detroit, Jan. 31, 1960; s. Edward Thomas and Bertha Lynn (Sanders) F. BS in Biol. Sci., U. Calif., Irvine, 1983; MPH in Epidemiology, UCLA, 1985; BS in Visual Sci., So. Calif. Coll. Optometry, Fullerton, 1987, OD, 1989. Lic. optometrist, Calif. Med. researcher U. Calif. Med. Ctr., Orange, 1982-83; epidemiologist Wadsworth VA Hosp., Brentwood, Calif., 1984-85; optometrist U.S. Indian Health Svc., Chinle, Ariz., 1988, Brentwood VA Hosp., 1989, Bellflower (Calif.) Med. Group, 1989-90, Rancho Calif. Vision Ctr., Temecula, Calif., 1990-93; optometrist Norton AFB, 1991-93, George AFB, 1991-93. Dep. sheriff Orange County Sheriff's Dept., Santa Ana, 1986—. Libert U. scholar, 1978-80, USPHS scholar UCLA, 1983-85. Mem. Am. Optometric Assn., Calif. Optometric Assn., Orange County Optometric Assn., Am. Pub. Health Assn., U. Calif.-Irvine Alumni Assn., So. Calif. Coll. of Optometry Alumni Assn., U. Calif.-L.A. Alumni Assn. Office: Whittier Contact Lens Ctr 13127 Philadelphia St Whittier CA 90601-4302

FISHER, DELBERT ARTHUR, physician, educator; b. Placerville, Calif., Aug. 12, 1928; s. Arthur Lloyd and Thelma (Johnson) F.; m. Beverly Carne Fisher, Jan. 28, 1951; children: David Arthur, Thomas Martin, Mary Kathryn. BA, U. Calif., Berkeley, 1950; MD, U. Calif., San Francisco, 1953. Diplomate Am. Bd. Pediatrics. Intern, resident in pediatrics U. Calif. Med. Center, San Francisco, 1953-55; resident in pediatrics U. Oreg. Hosp., Portland, 1957-58; from asst. prof. to assoc. prof. pediatrics Med. Sch. U. Ark., Little Rock, 1960-67, prof. pediatrics, 1967-68; prof. Med. Sch. UCLA, 1968-73; prof. pediatrics and medicine Med. Sch., UCLA, 1973-91, prof. emeritus, 1991—; chief, pediatric endocrinology Harbor-UCLA Med. Ctr., 1968-73, rsch. prof. devel. and perinatal biology, 1975-85, chmn. pediatrics, 1985-89, sr. scientist Rsch. and Edn. Inst., 1991—; dir. Walter Martin Rsch. Ctr., 1986-91; pres. Nichols Inst. Reference Labs, 1991-93; pres. Nichols Acad. Assocs., 1993-94, chief sci. officer, 1993-94; pres. acad. assocs., chief sci. officer Corning Nichols Inst., 1994—; cons. genetic disease sect. Calif. Dept. Health Svcs., 1978—; mem. organizing com. Internat. Conf. Newborn Thyroid Screening, 1977-88; examiner Am. Bd. Pediatrics, 1971-80, mem. subcom. on pediatric endocrinology, 1976-79. Co-editor: Pediatric Thyroidology, 1985, four other books; editor-in-chief Jour. Clin. Endocrinology and Metabolism, 1978-83, Pediatric Rsch., 1984-89; contbr. chpts. to numerous books; contbr. over 400 articles to profl. jours. Capt. M.C., USAF, 1955-57. Recipient Career Devel. award NIH, 1964-68. Mem. Inst. Medicine NAS, Am. Acad. Pediatrics (Borden award 1981), Soc. Pediatric Rsch. (v.p. 1973-74), Am. Pediatric Soc. (pres. 1992-93), Endocrine Soc. (pres. 1983-84), Am. Thyroid Assn. (pres. 1988-89), Am. Soc. Clin. Investigation, Assn. Am. Physicians, Lawson Wilkins Pediatric Endocrine Soc. (pres. 1982-83), Western Soc. Pediatric Rsch. (pres. 1983-84), Phi Beta Kappa, Alpha Omega Alpha. Home: 24582 Santa Clara Ave Dana Point CA 92629-3031 Office: Nichols Inst 33608 Ortega Hwy San Juan Capistrano CA 92690

FISHER, DENISE DANCHES, public relations executive, marketing consultant; b. Miami Beach, Fla.. AA, Miami Dade Coll., 1975; BA in Communcations, U. Miami, 1977. Mktg. dir. Dadeland Mall, Miami, 1978-83; advt. dir. Galleria Novita, Miami, 1983-84; freelance cons. Miami, 1984—; community relations dir. Am. Lung Assn., Miami, 1986-91; coord. community relations Hospice of Metro Denver, 1993-95; dir. mktg. Jewish Family Svc., Denver, 1995—. Tchr. Confrat. Christian Doctrine, St. Joseph's Ch., 1988—, Ch. of Risen Christ, 1991—. Recipient Addy awards, 1978, 80, Communications Excellence award Congress Lung Assn., 1989. Mem. Pub. Rels. Soc. Am. (accredited, chpt. bd. dirs.), Advt. Fedn. Republican. Office: Jewish Family Svc 1355 S Colorado Blvd Ste 400 Denver CO 80222

FISHER, DONALD G., casual apparel chain stores executive; b. 1928; married. B.S., U. Calif., 1950. With M. Fisher & Son, 1950-57; former ptnr. Fisher Property Investment Co.; co-founder, pres. The Gap Stores Inc., San Bruno, Calif., dir., now chmn., CEO. Office: Banana Republic Inc 1 Harrison St San Francisco CA 94105-1602*

FISHER, DONNE FRANCIS, telecommunications executive; b. Three Forks, Mont., May 24, 1938; s. Francis George and Dolreta (Chryst) F.; m. Sue Lynch Fisher, Sept. 10, 1960; children: William Kevin, Blake Francis, Scott Michael, Steven John. BS, Mont. State U., 1962. CPA, Alaska, Mont. Exec. v.p. Office of Chief Exec., CFO, Tele-Comm. Inc., Denver, also bd. dirs. Served with U.S. Army, 1956-58. Democrat. Roman Catholic. Home: Tele-Comm Inc 9513 Pinyon Trl Littleton CO 80124-3077 Office: Tele-Communications Inc 5619 Denver Tech Center Pky Englewood CO 80111-3017

FISHER, EARL MONTY, utilities executive; b. Chgo., June 26, 1938; s. Harry George and Fannie (Feinberg) F.; m. Joyce Leah Bender, Mar. 14, 1959 (div. Dec. 1978); children: Jan Carol, Wendy Robin; m. Teri Jean Janssen, Jan. 27, 1979. Student, La. Trade Tech. Coll., 1961. Apprentice and journeyman Comfort Air Refrigeration Corp., L.A., 1955-64; contractor Bonanza Air Conditioning and Refrigeration Corp., Van Nuys, Calif., 1964—. Bd. dirs. Hidden Hills (Calif.) Homeowners Assn., 1982-84, vice chmn.,, v.p., 1990; chmn. Hidden Hills Gate Ops. Commn., 1988-91; commr. emergency svcs. City of Hidden Hills, 1986—; pres. Hidden Hills Cmty. Assn., 1991-93; mem. Hidden Hills City Coun., 1994; elected mayor pro tempore Hidden Hills, 1995—. Mem. Air Conditioning Sheet Metal Assn. (vice chmn. 1994—). Democrat. Office: Bonanza Air Conditioning Heating & Refrigeration Corp 7653 Burnet Ave Van Nuys CA 91405-1006

FISHER, FREDERICK HENDRICK, oceanographer; b. Aberdeen, Wash., Dec. 30, 1926; s. Sam (Sverre) and Astrid (Kristoffersen) F.; m. Julie Gay Saund, June 17, 1955 (dec. 1993); children: Bruce Allen, Mark Edward, Keith Russell, Glen Michael; m. Shirley Mercedes Lippert, Oct. 10, 1994. BS, U. Wash., 1949, PhD, 1957. Rsch. fellow acoustics Harvard, 1957-58; rsch. physicist, rsch. oceanographer Marine Phys. Lab., Scripps Instn. Oceanography, La Jolla, Calif., 1958-91, assoc. dir., 1975-87, dep. dir., 1987-93, acting assoc. dir., 1993-94; dir. rsch. Havens Industries, San Diego, 1963-64; prof., chmn. dept. physics U. R.I., Kingston, 1970-71; mem. governing bd. Am. Inst. Physics, 1984-90. Editor IEEE Jour. Oceanic Engring., 1988-91. Mem. San Diego County Dem. Cen. Com., 1956-57, 60-62. NCAA nat. tennis doubles champion, 1949; named to U. Wash. Athletic Hall of Fame, 1989; recipient Disting. Svc. award IEEE Oceanic Engring. Soc., 1991. Midshipman U.S. Naval Acad., 1945-47; with USNR, 1945. Fellow Acoustical Soc. Am. (assoc. editor jour. 1969-76, v.p. 1980-81, pres. 1983-84); mem. IEEE (sr.), Marine Tech. Soc., Am. Geophys. Union, The Oceanographic Soc., Seattle Tennis Club. Co-designer research platform FLIP, 1960-62. Home: 5034 Park West Ave San Diego CA 92117 Office: U Calif Marine Phys Lab Scripps Inst Oceanography La Jolla CA 92093-0701

FISHER, GERALD SAUL, publisher, financial consultant, lawyer; b. Bronx, N.Y., Mar. 24, 1931; s. Abraham Samuel and Rose (Richards) F.; m. Sue L. Chidakel, Apr. 7, 1957; children: Stevan Laurence, Adrienne Jody, David Scot. B.B.A., Clark U., 1952; J.D., Boston U., 1955. Bar: Mass. 1955, D.C. 1962, U.S. Supreme Ct. 1962. Atty.-adviser div. corp. fin. SEC, 1956-58; with SBA, 1958-67, asst. dep. adminstr. investment, 1963-65, asst. dep. adminstr. procurement and mgmt. assistance, 1965-67; adminstrv. v.p. internat. foods div. Internat. Industries, 1967-68; pres. Copper Penny Family Restaurants (an Internat. Industries Co.), 1969-71; v.p. real estate Internat. Industries, 1971-72; pres. Triota Orgn., 1972—; pres., chmn. Sir Speedy, Inc., 1975-78; pub. Tile & Decorative Surfaces mag., Worldwide Meetings and Incentives mag., Contemporary Dialysis mag., Dimensional Stone mag., For Patients Only, Tile Italia, Ceramic World Rev., Designing with Tile, Woodland Hills, Calif., 1978—, Interactive Index Libr. of Stone on CD-ROM, Woodland Hills, Calif.; pres. Environ. Water Products, Inc., 1992-93, Perfect Pool Products, Inc., 1994—; lectr. franchising and small bus. financing Practising Law Inst. Author articles in field.; sr. editor Boston U. Law Rev. Recipient awards for outstanding service to govt. Mem. ABA, Fed. Bar Assn., Phi Theta Kappa. Home: 4450 Callada Pl Tarzana CA 91356-5105 Office: 6300 Variel Ave Ste I Woodland Hills CA 91367-2513

FISHER, JOSEPH STEWART, management consultant; b. Athens, Pa., Mar. 3, 1933; s. Samuel Royer and Agnes Corinne (Smith) F.; m. Anita Ann Coyle, May 15, 1954; 1 child, Samuel Royer. BS in Tech. Mgmt., Regis U., 1981; postgrad., U. Colo., 1986-87, Iliff Sch. Theology, 1988-89. Field engr. IBM Corp., Syracuse, N.Y., 1956-60; qualtiy analyst, engr. IBM Corp., Endicott, N.Y., 1960-68; systems support adminstr. IBM Corp., Boulder, Colo., 1968-72, field support adminstr., 1972-78, systems assurance adminstr., 1978-79, security adminstr., 1979-87; sec. cons. Fisher Enterprises, Boulder, 1975—; bd. dirs. Vervcraft Inc., Loveland, Colo.; dir. adminstrn. Lexicon Med. Tech., Inc., 1993-95. Leadership devel. Boy Scouts Am., 1975—, chmn. long range planning, 1982-86, chaplain, 1991—; bd. dirs. Longs Peak Coun., 1983-87, Colo. Crime Stoppers, 1983-88; exec. dir. Caring About People, Inc., Colo., 1990—; v.p. Helplink, Inc., Boulder, 1991—. With USN, 1952-56, Korea. Recipient Silver Beaver award Boy Scouts Am., Boulder, 1978, God and Svc. award Boy Scouts Am. and United Meth. Ch., 1991. Mem. Am. Soc. Indsl. Security (cert. CPP 1984, treas. 1985), Colo. Crime Prevention Assn., Mason (treas. Columbia lodge #14 1969-85, 90—), Royal Arch. Masons and Commandery Knights Templar of York Rite. Republican. Methodist. Home and Office: 4645 Bedford Ct Boulder CO 80301-4017

FISHER, LAWRENCE W., public relations company executive; b. L.A., June 5, 1938; s. Gilbert W. and Augusta (Gelsheimer) F.; AB magna cum laude, U. So. Calif., 1960; m. Elizabeth Sheridan Burke, July 16, 1966; children: Lawrence Timothy, Lara Elizabeth. Legislative asst. Speaker Assembly, Calif. Legislature, 1960-62; exec. dir. Democratic State Central Com., 1962-66; pres. Braun & Co., Los Angeles, 1966—, L.A. County Asset Leasing Corp., 1988—. Dir. Norris Cancer Hosp. and Rsch. Center. Mem. Town Hall, Phi Beta Kappa, Sigma Delta Chi. Home: 1350 Sugar Loaf Dr La Canada Flintridge CA 91011-3918 Office: Braun/ Ketchum PR 11755 Wilshire Blvd Los Angeles CA 90025-1506

FISHER, MARK JAY, neurologist; b. N.Y.C., Aug. 23, 1949; s. Ralph Aaron and Dorothy Ann (Weissman) F.; m. Janeth Godeau, Aug. 5, 1994. BA in Polit. Sci., UCLA, 1970; MA in Polit. Sci., U. S.D., 1972, BS in Medicine, 1973; MD, U. Cin., 1975. Diplomate Am. Bd. Psychiatry and Neurology. Intern UCLA Sepulveda VA Hosp., 1975-76; resident UCLA Wadsworth VA Hosp., 1976-79, chief resident, 1979-80; faculty mem. U. So. Calif. Sch. of Medicine, L.A., 1980—, assoc. prof. neurology, 1987—, dir. stroke rsch. program, 1980—, dir. residency tng. program, 1992—. Editor: Medical Therapy of Acute Stroke, 1989. Recipient Tchr. Investigator award NIH, Bethesda, Md., 1984-89, Program Project grantee, 1994—. Mem. Am. Acad. Neurology, Am. Neurol. Assn., Am. Heart Assn. (stroke coun.), Nat. Stroke Assn., Internat. Soc. for Thrombosis and Haemostasis. Office: U So Calif Sch Medicine Dept of Neurology 1333 San Pablo St MCH 246 Los Angeles CA 90033

FISHER, MARLA JO, newspaper reporter; b. Denver, May 24, 1956; d. James I. Fisher and Margaret I. Newbury. Student, U. Utah, 1974-77. Staff writer Glendale (Calif.) News Press, 1987-90, Pasadena (Calif.) Star-News, 1990-91, San Gabriel Valley Newspapers, Pasadena, 1991-94, Orange County Register, Santa Ana, 1994. Treas. Utah Equal Rights Coalition, Salt Lake City, 1982. Recipient Investigative Reporting award Greater L.A. Press Club, 1993, Pub. Svc. Writing award Calif. Newspapers Publ. Assn., 1990; named Best News Story Thomson Newspapers N. Am., 1994, Best News Story Internat. Spl. Libraries Assn., Washington, 1989, 1st Place Feature & Profile Southern Calif. Press Club, 1992. Mem. Calif. First Amendment Coalition, Soc. Profl. Journalists, Investigative Reporters and Editors. Home: 366 Y Pl # A Laguna Beach CA 92651-2326

FISHER, MARVIN MARK, English educator, author; b. Detroit, Nov. 19, 1927; s. Julius and Helen (Goldman) F.; m. Jill Ann Jones, Jan. 6, 1956; children: Ann Katherine, Sarah Alice, Laura Ann. AB, Wayne State U., Detroit, 1950, AM, 1952; PhD, U. Minn., 1958. Asst. prof. Ariz. State U., Tempe, 1958-60, assoc. prof., 1960-66, prof., 1966—, chmn. dept. English, 1977-83; vis. prof. Aristotle U., Thessaloniki, Greece, 1961–63, U. Oslo, Norway, 1966-67, U. Calif., Davis, 1969-70, U. Tubingen, Fed. Rep. of Germany, 1988-89; cons. Somerset Imports, L.A., 1977-79, NEH, Washington, 1978-80, Hiram Walker, Inc., Windsor, Ont., Can., 1982-84, Morrison Hecker Inc., 1993; mem. nat. screening com. Fulbright-Hays awards Inst. for Internat. Edn., 1977-80, 94—. Author: Workshops in the Wilderness, 1967, Going Under, 1977, Continuities, 1986, Herman Melville, 1988; editorial adv. bd. The Centennial Rev., 1990—; contbr. numerous articles to profl. jours. Precinct committeman Ariz. Dems., Tempe, 1986-88; staff mem. Task Force on Excellence, Efficiency and Competitiveness, Phoenix, 1987-88. With U.S. Army, 1946-47. Fulbright grantee Greece, 1961-63, Norway, 1966-67, Fed. Republic Germany, 1988-89. Mem. Nat. Coun. Tchrs. English, MLA, Western Res. Club, Melville Soc. Am. (pres. 1994-95), Phi Beta Kappa. Office: Ariz State U Dept English Tempe AZ 85287

FISHER, MYRON R., lawyer; b. Chgo., Aug. 13, 1935. B.A., Calif. State U., Long Beach, 1964; J.D., Southwestern U., 1969. Bar: Calif. 1970, U.S. Dist. Ct. (cen. dist.) Calif. 1970, U.S. Supreme Ct. 1974. Dep. pub. defender San Bernardino County (Calif.), 1970-71; assoc. Anderson, Adams & Bacon, Rosemead, Calif., 1971-74; sole practice, San Clemente, Calif., 1974—; judge pro tem South Orange County Mcpl. Ct., 1978—. Served with U.S. Army, 1955-57. Mem. State Bar Calif., South Orange County Bar Assn. (dir. 1978-83), Orange County Bar Assn., Los Angeles Trial Lawyers Assn., Orange County Trial Lawyers Assn., Calif. Trial Lawyers Assn., Assn. Trial Lawyers Am. Office: Fisher Profl Bldg 630 S El Camino Real San Clemente CA 92672-4200

FISHER, NANCY LOUISE, pediatrician, medical geneticist, former nurse; b. Cleve., July 4, 1944; d. Nelson Leopold and Catherine (Harris) F.; m. Larry William Larson, May 30, 1976; 1 child, Jonathan Raymond. Student, Notre Dame Coll., Cleve., 1962-64; BSN, Wayne State U., 1967; postgrad., Calif. State U., Hayward, 1971-72; MD, Baylor Coll. of Medicine, 1976; M in Pub. Health, U. Wash., 1982, certificate in ethics, 1993. Diplomate Am. Bd. Pediatrics, Am. Bd. Med. Genetics. RN coronary care unit and med. intensive care unit Highland Gen. Hosp., Oakland, Calif., 1970-72; RN coronary care unit Alameda (Calif.) Hosp., 1972-73; intern in pediatrics Baylor Coll. of Medicine, Houston, 1976-77, resident in pediatrics, 1977-78; attending physician, pediatric clinic Harborview Med. Ctr., Seattle, 1980-81; staff physician children and adolescent health care clinic Columbia Health Ctr., Seattle, 1981-87, founder, dir. of med. genetics clinic, 1984-89; maternal child health policy cons. King County div. Seattle King County Dept Pub. Health, 1983-85; dir. genetic svcs. Va. Mason Clinic, 1986-89; dir. med. genetic svcs. Swedish Hosp., 1989-94; nurses aide psychiatry Sinai Hosp., Detroit, 1966-67; charge nurse Women's Hosp., Cleve., 1967; research asst. to Dr. Shelly Liss, 1976; with Baylor Housestaff Assn., Baylor Coll. Medicine, 1980-81; clin. asst. prof. grad. sch. nursing, U. Wash., Seattle, 1981-85; clin. asst. prof. dept. pediatrics, U. Wash., Seattle, 1982—; com. appointments include Seattle CCS Cleft Palate Panel, 1984—; bd. dirs., first v.p. King County Assn. Sickle Cell Disease 1985-86, acting pres. 1986, pres. 1986-87; hosp. affiliation include Childrens Orthopedic Hosp. and Med. Ctr., Seattle, 1981-89, Virginia Mason Hosp., Seattle, 1985—, Harborview Hosp., Seattle, 1986—. Contbr. articles to profl. jours. Active Seattle Urban League, 1982—, 101 Black Women, 1986—; bd. dirs. Seattle Sickle Cell Affected Family Assn., 1984-85; mem. People to People Citizen Ambassador Group. Served to lt. USN Nurse Corps, 1966-70. Fellow Am. Coll. Medicine Genetics (founder); mem. Student Governing Body and Graduating Policy Com. Baylor Coll. Medicine (founding mem. 1973-76), Loans and Scholarship Com. Baylor Coll. Medicine (voting mem. 1973-76), Am. Med. Student Assn., Student Nat. Med. Assn., Admission Com. Baylor Coll. Medicine (voting mem. 1974-76), AMA, Am. Med. Women's Assn., Am. Acad. Pediatrics, Am. Pub. Health Assn. (co-chmn. genetic subsect. Mat. Child Health), Am. Soc. Human Genetics, Birth Defects and Clin. Genetics Soc., Wash. State Assn. Black Providers of Health Care, Northwest Chpt. Soc. Adolescent Medicine, Wash. State Soc. Pediatrics, Seattle C. of C. (mem. Leadership Tomorrow 1988—), Sigma Gamma Rho, Phi Delta Epsilon. Address: 600 Wellington Ave Seattle WA 98122-6470 Offfice: 4020 E Madison St Ste 327 Seattle WA 98112-3150

FISHER, ROBERT JOHN, business educator; b. North Battleford, Sask., Can., June 15, 1957; came to U.S., 1987; s. John Ingram and Shirley Anne (Aitken) F.; m. Fiona Ann Hare; children: Jane Ann, John Arthur, Amy Johnston. B Commerce, U. Sask., 1979; MBA, York U., Toronto, Ont., Can., 1984; PhD, U. Colo., 1990. Terr. mgr. Can. Packers, Edmonton, Alta., Can., 1979-81; rsch. analyst SGI, Regina, Sask., 1981-83; mktg. mgr. Beline Mfg., Kindersley, Sask., 1984-87; vis. asst. prof. U. Colo., Boulder, 1990-91; mem. faculty Sch. Bus. U. So. Calif., L.A., 1991—. Contbr. articles to profl. jours. Soccer coach Am. Youth Soccer Orgn., Hacienda Heights, Calif., 1994. Social Scis. and Humanities Rsch. Coun. grantee, 1989, 90; Gerald Hart fellow, 1988, doctoral consortium fellow U. Colo., 1989. Mem. Am. Mktg. Assn. (faculty advisor 1993-94), Assn. for Consumer Rsch. Home: 1536 Drumhill Dr Hacienda Hgts CA 91745-3353 Office: U So Calif Sch Bus Los Angeles CA 90089-1421

FISHER, ROBERT M., foundation administrator, university administrator; b. St. Paul, Minn., Oct. 15, 1938; s. S.S. and Jean Fisher; m. Elinor C. Schectman, June 19, 1960; children: Laurie, Jonathan. AB magna cum laude, Harvard Coll., 1960; JD, Harvard U., 1963; PhD, London Sch. Econs, Polit. Sci., 1967; LLD, West Coast U., L.A., 1981; DHL, Profl. Sch. Psychology, San Francisco, 1986; DPS, John F. Kennedy U., Orinda, Calif., 1988. Rsch. assoc. Mass. Mental Health Ctr., Cambridge, 1957-62; rsch. asst. Ctr. Study Juvenile Delinquency, Cambridge, 1961-63; spl. asst. to chief psychologist British Prison Dept. Home Office, London, 1963-67; prof. Sch.

Criminology U. Calif., Berkeley, 1965-71; profl. race car driver, 1972-77; pres. John F. Kennedy U., Orinda, Calif., 1974-85; exec. dir. 92d St. YMHA, N.Y.C., 1984-85; dir. The San Francisco Found., 1987—; mayor. councilman Lafayette, Calif., 1968-76; mem. Minn. and Calif. Bar Specialty: charitable gift planning. Scholar-in-medicine Rockefeller Found., 1994; Polit. Sci. vis. fellow, 1994. Home: 85 Southwood Dr Orinda CA 94563-3026 Office: The San Francisco Foundation 685 Market St Ste 910 San Francisco CA 94105-4200

FISHER, WESTON JOSEPH, economist; b. Glendale, Calif., Aug. 29; s. Edward Weston and Rosalie Eloise (Bailey) F. BS, U. So. Calif., 1962, MA, 1965, MS, 1971, PhD, 1989. Sr. mgr. Naval Undersea Ctr., Pasadena, Calif., 1964-69; chief exec. officer, prin. Ventura County, Ventura, Calif., 1969-73; So. Calif. dir. County Suprs. Assn., L.A., 1974-75; coord. govtl. rels. So. Calif. Assn. Govts., L.A., 1975-78; devel. dir. Walter H. Leimert Co., L.A., 1979-90; bd. dirs. Gray Energy Corp., L.A., Mission Inn Group, Riverside, Calif., Coun. of Leaders and Specialists - UN, Peterson Oil and Gas. Mem. Gov.'s Adv. Coun. for Econ. growth, Channel Islands Conservancy. Mem. Medieval Acad. Am., El Dorado Country Club, Univ. Club, South Coast Yacht Club, Cave Creek Club, Lambda Alpha. Republican. Home: 28261 Westover Way Sun City CA 92586-2525

FISHER, WILLIAM HENRY, education educator; b. York, Pa., July 4, 1912; s. Charles Henry and Mary Naomi (Light) F.; m. Christine Albers, June 25, 1938 (dec. Nov. 1959); 1 child, Charles Albers; m. Ruth Dyer, Dec. 27, 1962. BA in Sociology, Secondary Edn., U. Wash., 1935, MEd, 1943; DEd in Social Studies Edn., Columbia U., 1949. Tchr. social studies Wapato (Wash.) Sr. High Sch., 1936-39, Kirkland (Wash.) Sr. High Sch., 1939-44, Fieldston Sch. of The Ethical Culture Soc., N.Y.C., 1945-47; asst. prof. edn., sociology Eastern Wash. State U., Cheney, 1947-50; asst. prof., supr. student tchrs. U. Ariz., Tucson, 1950-51, Temple U., Phila., 1951-52, Wilkes Coll., Wilkes-Barre, Pa., 1952-53; curriculum dir. Las Vegas (N.Mex.) Pub. Schs., 1953-56, supt. schs., 1956-61; assoc. prof. edn. U. Tex., El Paso, 1961-67, assoc. prof., 1967-71; prof. U. Mont., Missoula, 1971—; vis. prof. (summers) Highlands U., Las Vegas, N.Mex., 1950-55, U. N.Mex., Albuquerque, 1961, Western State Coll., Gunnison, Colo. (summers) 1960, 63, 66, Eastern Ill. U., Charleston, 1967, U. Fla. Gainesville, 1971, U. Tenn., Knoxville, 1976; v.p. student council Tchrs. Coll., Columbia, 1946-47; appointed to commn. to revise the high sch. Phys. Edn. Curriculum, N.Mex., 1954-56; pres. Coop. Program in Ednl. Adminstrn., N.Mex., 1960-61; program chmn. Trans-Pecos Edn. Conf. U. Tex., El Paso, 1963-65; chmn. umbrella com. supporting grad. programs Sch. Edn. U. Mont., 1968-78; chair-discussant numerous nat. and regional meets; instr. in field, Mont. Contbr. numerous articles to profl. jours. Mem. AAUP (pres. U. Tex.-El Paso chpt. 1964-65), NEA, Philosophy of Edn. Soc. (presenter papers ann. meetings), Am. Edn. Studies Assn., Western Social Sci. Assn. (chair, panelist ann. meetings Am. studies sect.), Phi Delta Kappa, Kappa Delta Pi. Home: 604 Plymouth St Missoula MT 59801-4129 Office: U Mont Sch Edn Missoula MT 59812

FISHMAN, LILLIAN, research foundation executive; b. Calgary, Alta., Can., Apr. 28, 1915; d. Charles Simcha Waterman and Ethel (Brandeis) Guttman; m. William Harold Fishman, Aug. 6, 1939; children: Joel Sholom, Nina Esther, Daniel Lewis. BS, U. Alta., 1936; MA in Edn., Boston U., 1967. Cert. dietitian, N.Y.; cert. tchr., Mass. Rsch. asst. dept. biochemistry U. Edinburgh, Scotland, 1939-40; dietitian N.Y. Hosp., N.Y.C., 1940-41; rsch. asst. Bowman Gray Sch. Medicine, Winston-Salem, N.C., 1941-43; rsch. assoc. Sch. Medicine Tufts U., Boston, 1968-76; co-founder, scientist, asst. to pres., mgr. devel. La Jolla (Calif.) Cancer Rsch. Found., 1976-89, fgn. student coord., co-chair adv. bd., 1990—; cons. in field. Pres. Winston-Salem Hadassah, 1943-44; den mother Cub pack Brookline (Mass.) area Boy Scouts Am., 1950-53; edn. chmn. Boston Hadassah, 1960-75; dist. coord. Brookline United Fund, 1952. Recipient Deming award. Mem. Am. Jewish Com., Sigma Xi (treas. Tufts br. 1974-75). Office: La Jolla Cancer Rsch Found 10901 N Torrey Pines Rd La Jolla CA 92037-1005

FISHMAN, NORMAN, engineering consultant; b. Petaluma, Calif., July 18, 1924; s. Max and Tova (Berger) F.; m. Lillian Feinstein, Oct. 29, 1953; children: Devora Ann, David Arden. BS, U. Calif., Berkeley, 1948. Chem. engr. USDA, Albany, Calif., 1949-53; project engr. FMC Corp., San Jose, Calif., 1953-54; chem. engr. SRI Internat., Menlo Park, Calif., 1954-68, dir. polymer tech., 1968-77, cons., 1977-88; freelance cons. Menlo Park, 1988-92; pres., cons. Fishman Assocs., Inc., Menlo Park, 1992—; pres., COO, bd. dirs. Solcas Polymer Inc., San Francisco, 1992-93. Contbr. articles to profl. publs., patentee in field. Pres. Jewish Comminty Ctr., Palo Alto, 1976-79; bd. dirs. Consumer Coop. Soc., Palo Alto, 1990-93; chmn. Univ. Students Coop. Assn., Berkeley, 1947-48. Mem. Soc. Advanced Materials and Process Engring., Soc. Plastics Engring., Am. Chem. Soc., Sigma Xi. Democrat. Jewish. Home and Office: 2316 Blueridge Ave Menlo Park CA 94025-6710

FISHMAN, ROBERT ALLEN, educator, neurologist; b. N.Y.C., May 30, 1924; s. Samuel Benjamin and Miriam (Brinkin) F.; m. Margery Ann Satz, Jan. 29, 1956 (dec. May 29, 1980); children: Mary Beth, Alice Ellen, Elizabeth Ann.; m. Mary Craig Wilson, Jan. 7, 1983. A.B., Columbia U., 1944; M.D., U. Pa., 1947. Mem. faculty Columbia Coll. Physicians and Surgeons, 1954-66, asso. prof. neurology, 1962-66; asst. attending neurologist N.Y. State Psychiat. Inst., 1955-66; asst. attending neurologist Neurol. Inst. Presbyn. Hosp., N.Y.C., 1955-61, asso., 1961-66; co-dir. Neurol. Clin. Research Center, Neurol. Inst., Columbia-Presbyn. Med. Ctr., 1961-66; prof. neurology U. Calif. Med. Ctr., San Francisco, 1966—, chmn. dept. neurology, 1966-92; cons. neurologist San Francisco Gen. Hosp., San Francisco VA Hosp., Letterman Gen. Hosp.; dir. Am. Bd. Psychiatry and Neurology, 1981-88, v.p., 1986, pres., 1987. Author: Cerebrospinal Fluid in Diseases of the Nervous System, 1992; chief editor Annals of Neurology, 1993—; contbr. articles to profl. jours. Nat. Multiple Sclerosis Soc. fellow, 1956-57; John and Mary R. Markle scholar in med. sci., 1960-65. Mem. Am. Neurol. Assn. (pres. 1983-84), Am. Fedn. for Clin. Research, Assn. for Research in Nervous and Mental Diseases, Am. Acad. Neurology (v.p. 1971-73, pres. 1975-77), Am. Assn. Physicians, Am. Soc. for Neurochemistry, Soc. for Neurosci., N.Y. Neurol. Soc., Am. Assn. Univ. Profs. Neurology (pres. 1972-73), AAAS, Am. Epilepsy Soc., N.Y. Acad. Scis., AMA (sec. sect. on nervous and mental diseases 1964-67, v.p. 1967-68, pres. 1968-69), Alpha Omega Alpha (hon. faculty mem.). Home: 50 Summit Ave Mill Valley CA 94941-1819 Office: U Calif Med Center 794 Herbert C Moffitt Hosp San Francisco CA 94143

FISHMAN, WILLIAM HAROLD, cancer research foundation executive, biochemist; b. Winnipeg, Man., Can., Mar. 2, 1914; s. Abraham and Goldie (Chmelnitsky) F.; m. Lillian Waterman, Aug. 6, 1939; children—Joel, Nina, Daniel. B.S., U. Sask., Can., Saskatoon, 1935; Ph.D., U. Toronto, Ont., Can., 1939; MDhc U. Umea, Sweden, 1983; Dir. cancer rsch. New Eng. Med. Ctr. Hosp., Boston, 1958-72; rsch. prof. pathology Tufts U. Sch. Medicine, 1961-70, prof. pathology, 1970-77, dir. Tufts Cancer Rsch. Ctr., 1972-76; pres. La Jolla Cancer Rsch. Found., Calif., 1976-89, pres. emeritus, 1989—; mem. basic sci. programs merit rev. bd. com. VA, 1971-75; mem. pathobiol. chemistry sect. NIH, Bethesda, Md., 1977-81. Author in field. Rsch. Career award NIH, 1962-77; Royal Soc. Can. rsch. fellow, 1939, 17th Internat. Physiol. Congress-U.K. Fedn. fellow, 1947. Fellow AIC, AAAS; mem. Am. Assn. Cancer Rsch., Am. Soc. Biol. Chemists, Am. Soc. Cell Biology, Am. Soc. Exptl. Pathology, Histochem. Soc. (pres. 1983-84), Internat. Soc. Clin. Enzymology (hon.), Internat. Soc. Oncodevel. Biology and Medicine (hon., Abbott award 1993), Univ. Club (San Diego). Jewish. Current work: Basic rsch. on expression of placental genes by cancer cells; monoclonal antibodies; oncodevelopmental markers; immunocytochemistry. Home: 715 Muirlands Vista Way La Jolla CA 92037-6202 Office: La Jolla Cancer Rsch Found 10901 N Torrey Pines Rd La Jolla CA 92037-1005

FISK, EDWARD RAY, retired civil engineer, author, educator; b. Oshkosh, Wis., July 19, 1924; s. Ray Edward and Grace O. (Meyer) Barnes; married, Oct. 28, 1950; children: Jacqueline Mary, Edward Ray II, William John, Robert Paul. Student Marquette U., 1945-49, Fresno (Calif.) State Coll., 1954, UCLA, 1957-58; BS, MBA, Calif.-Western U.. Engr., Calif. Div. Hwys., 1952-55; engr. Bechtel Corp., Vernon, Calif., 1955-59; project mgr. Toups Engring Co., Santa Ana, Calif., 1959-61; dept. head Perliter & Soring, Los Angeles, 1961-64; Western rep. Wire Reinforcement Inst., Washington, 1964-65; cons. engr., Anaheim, Calif., 1965; assoc. engr. Met. Water Dist. So. Calif., 1966-68; chief specification engr. Koebig & Koebig, Inc., Los Angeles, 1968-71; mgr. constrn. services VTN Consol., Inc., Irvine, Calif., 1971-78; pres. E.R. Fisk Constrn., Orange, Calif., 1978-81; corp. dir. constrn. mgmt. James M. Montgomery Cons. Engrs., Inc., Pasadena, Calif., 1981-83; v.p. Lawrance, Fisk & McFarland, Inc., Santa Barbara and Orange, 1983—; pres. E.R. Fisk & Assocs., Orange, 1983—, Gleason, Peacock & Fisk, Inc., 1987-92; v.p. constrn. svcs. Wilsey & Ham, Foster City, Calif., 1993-94, ret., 1994; adj. prof. engring., constrn. Calif. State U., Long Beach, 1987-90, Orange Coast Coll., Costa Mesa, Calif., 1957-78, Calif. Poly. State U., Pomona, 1974; lectr. U. Calif., Berkeley, Inst. Transportation Studies extension, 1978—, engring. prof. programs U. Wash., 1994—, internationally for ASCE Continuing Edn.; former mem. Calif. Bd. Registered Constrn. Insps. Served with USN, 1942-43, USAF, 1951-52. Registered profl. engr., Ariz., Calif., Colo., Fla., Idaho, Ky., La., Mont., Nev., Oreg., Utah, Wash., Wyo.; registered environ. assessor, Calif.; lic. land surveyor, Oreg., Idaho; lic. gen. engring. contractor, Calif.; cert. abritator Calif. Constrn. Contract Arbitration Com. Fellow ASCE (life fellow, past chmn. exec. com. constrn. div., former chmn. nat. com. inspection 1978—), Nat. Acad. Forensic Engrs. (diplomate); mem. Orange County Engring. Council (former pres.), Calif. Soc. Profl. Engrs. (past pres. Orange County), Structural Engrs. Assn. Calif. (engrs. joint contracts documents com. 1993—), Am. Arbitration Assn. (nat. panel), U.S. Com. Large Dams, Order Founders and Patriots Am. (past gov. Calif.), Soc. Colonial Wars (dep. gov. gen. Calif. chpt.), S.R. (past dir.), Engring. Edn. Found. (trustee), Tau Beta Pi. Republican. Author: Machine Methods of Survey Computing, 1958, Construction Project Administration, 1978, 82, 88, 92, Construction Engineers Complete Handbook of Forms, 1981, 92, Resident Engineers Field Manual, 1992; co-author: Contractor's Project Guide, 1988, Contracts and Specifications for Public Works Projects, 1992. Home: PO Box 6448 Orange CA 92613-6448

FISKIN, JUDITH ANNE, artist, educator; b. Chgo., Apr. 1, 1945; d. Fred Albert and Cecile (Citron) Bartman; m. Jeffrey Allen Fiskin, Jan. 1, 1967 (div. Apr. 1975); m. Jonathan Marc Wiener, Jan. 17, 1987. BA, Pomona Coll., 1966; postgrad., U. Calif., Berkeley, 1966-67; MA, UCLA, 1969. Assoc. dean sch. art Calif. Inst. of Arts, Valencia, 1977-84, art faculty, 1977—. One-woman shows include Castelli Graphics, N.Y.C., 1976, Asher-Faure, L.A., 1991, Mus. Contemporary Art, L.A., 1992, Curt Marcus Gallery, N.Y.C., 1994, Patricia Faure Gallery, Sant Monica, Calif., 1994; exhibited in group shows at Luasanne, Switzerland, Vancouver, B.C., Internat. Ctr. for Photography, N.Y.C., San Francisco Mus. Modern Art, Corcoran Gallery Art, Washington, LaJolla (Calif.) Mus. Art and mus. in Richmond, Va., Miami, Fla., Chgo., Akron, Ohio. Cmty. funding bd. mem. Liberty Hill Found., L.A., 1994. Grantee Nat. Endowment for Arts, 1979, 90, Logan, 1986. Office: Calif Inst of Arts McBean Pkwy Valencia CA 91355

FITCH, JACK, association executive. Grad. high sch., Barry, Ill. Exec. dir. Civilian Congress, San Francisco, 1964—. Editor: (directory) Civilian Congress Annual, 1964—. Mem. Japan Soc. No. Calif., Commonwealth Club of Calif., Internat. Diplomacy Coun. of Northern Calif. Office: Civilian Congress 2361 Mission St Rm 238 San Francisco CA 94110-1813

FITCH, NOEL RILEY, writer, educator; b. New Haven, Con., Dec. 24, 1937; d. John Eckel and Dorcas (Tarr) Riley; m. Philip A. Fitch, May 29, 1958 (div. May 1986); 1 child, Gailyn R.; m. Albert Sonnenfeld, Aug. 23, 1987. BA in English, Northwestern Nazarene Coll., 1959; MA in Lit., Wash. State U., 1965, PhD in Lit., 1969. Jr. and sr. high sch. tchr. Moscow (Idaho) Pub. Schs., 1959-63; teaching asst. Wash. State U., Pullman, 1963-66, 67-68; asst. prof. Eastern Nazarene Coll., Quincy, Mass., 1966-67, 68-71; from asst. to assoc. to full prof. Point Loma Coll., San Diego, 1971-87; dept. chair lit. and fgn. langs. Point Loman Coll., San Diego, 1982-85; inst. masters of profl. writing U. So. Calif., L.A., 1990—; vis. instr. English U. So. Calif., L.A., 1987-90, Am. U., Paris, 1987-95; cons. Optical Illusions Films Jezabel Prodns., N.Y.C., 1988-92, 92-93; cons., actor Ishtar Prodns., Hollywood, 1990-92. Author: Sylvia Beach and the Lost Generation, 1983, Hemingway in Paris, 1990, Literary Cafes of Paris, 1989, Anais: The Erotic Life of Anais Nin, 1983; editor: Current, 1984-86; contbr. articles to profl. jours. Campus chair United Way, San Diego, 1974-77. Fellow Nat. Endowment for the Humanities, 1980-81; rsch. grantee NEH, 1976, 78-79, Am. Philos. Soc., 1982, Am. Coun. Learned Socs., 1984. Mem. MLA, The Authors Guild, Pen Center West. Home: 11829 Mayfield Ave Los Angeles CA 90049-5764 Office: Margret McBride Lit Agy 7744 Fay Ave Ste 201 La Jolla CA 92037

FITCH, WALTER M(ONROE), molecular biologist, educator; b. San Diego, May 21, 1929; s. Chloral Harrison Monroe and Evelyn Charlotte (Halliday) F.; m. Eleanor E. McLean, Sept. 1, 1952 (div. Mar. 28, 1988); children: Karen Allyn, Kathleen Leslie, Kenton Monroe; m. Chung-Cha Ziesel, Sept. 9, 1989. AB, U. Calif., Berkeley, 1953, PhD, 1958. USPHS postdoctoral fellow U. Calif. Berkeley, 1958-59, Stanford U., Palo Alto, Calif, 1959-61; lectr. Univ. Coll., London, 1961-62; asst. prof. U. Wis.-Madison, 1962-67, assoc. prof., 1967-72, prof., 1972-86; prof. U. So. Calif., L.A., 1986-89; prof. U. Calif.-Irvine, 1989—, prof., chmn. dept. ecology and evolutionary biology, 1990-95; prof., 1995—; vis. Fulbright lectr. London, 1961-62; NIH vis. prof. Hawaii, 1973-74; Macy Found. vis. prof. U. Calif., L.A., 1981-82; vis. prof. U. So. Calif., L.A., 1985. Editor-in-chief Molecular Biology and Evolution, 1983-93; editor Classification Literature, 1975-80; assoc. editor Jour. Molecular Evolution, 1976-80; contbr. articles to profl. jours. Mem. Cupertino Planning Commn., Calif., 1960-61, Madison Planning Commn., 1965-68; mem. Dane County Regional Planning Commn., 1968-73; chmn. Madison Reapportionment, 1979-81. Grantee NIH and NSF, 1962—. Fellow AAAS; mem. NAS, Am. Acad. Arts and Scis., Am. Soc. for Biochemistry and Molecular Biology, Am. Chem. Soc., Am. Soc. Naturalists, Biochem. Soc. (Eng.), Genetics Soc. Am., Soc. Study Evolution, Soc. Systematic Biology, Soc. for Molecular Biology and Evolution (pres. 1992-93), Linnean Soc. (London). Office: U Calif Dept Ecology & Evolutionary Biol Irvine CA 92717

FITCH, WILLIAM C., professional basketball coach; b. Cedar Rapids, Iowa, May 19, 1934. Student, Coe Coll. Basketball coach Coe Coll., Cedar Rapids, 1958-62, U. N.D., Grand Forks, 1962-67, Bowling Green State U., 1967-68, U. Minn., Mpls., 1968-70; coach Cleve. Cavaliers, 1970-79, Boston Celtics, 1979-83, Houston Rockets, 1983-88, New Jersey Nets, 1989-92, L.A. Clippers, 1994—. Named NBA Coach of Yr., 1976, 80; coach NBA championship team, 1981. Office: Los Angeles Clippers 3939 S Figueroa St Los Angeles CA 90037-1200

FITZGERALD, JERRY, security specialist; b. Detroit, Apr. 21, 1936; s. John Middleton and Jessie Lucy (Call); m. Ardra Elizabeth Finney, Dec. 1, 1962. BS, Mich. State U., 1959; MBA, U. Santa Clara, 1964; M Bus. in Econs., Claremont Grad. Sch., 1971, PhD, 1972. CISA, CDP. Indsl. engr. Parke Davis & Co., Detroit, 1959-61; acct. exec. McDonnell & Co., Detroit, 1961-62; assoc. engr. Lockheed Missiles & Space Co., Sunnyvale, Calif., 1962-66; systems analyst Singer/Friden Div., San Leandro, Calif., 1966-68; systems engr. U. Calif., San Francisco, 1968-69; assoc. prof. Calif. State Colls. & Univ., Pomona, Hayward, Calif., 1969-73; sr. mgmt. cons. SRI Internat., Menlo Pk., Calif., 1973-77; pres. Jerry FitzGerald & Assocs., Redwood City, Calif, 1977—. Author: Business Data Communications, 4th ed., 1993, Designing Controls into Computerized Systems, 2nd ed., 1990, Fundamentals of Systems Analysis, 3d ed., 1987, Internal Controls for Computerized Systems, 1981, (software/book) RANK-IT A Risk Assessment Software Tool, CONTROL-IT A Control Spreadsheet Software Tool for PCs and Compatibles; contbr. articles to profl. jours. Recipient Joseph J. Wasserman award, 1980. Mem. EDP Auditors Assn., Inst. Internal Auditors, Info. Systems Security Assn. Office: Jerry FitzGerald & Assocs 506 Barkentine Ln Redwood City CA 94065-1128

FITZGERALD, JOHN CHARLES, JR., investment banker; b. Sacramento, May 23, 1941; s. John Charles and Geraldine Edith (McNabb) F.; BS, Calif. State U. at Sacramento, 1964; MBA, Cornell U., 1966; m. Mildred Ann Kilpatrick, June 26, 1965; children—Geraldine Kathrine, Erec John. Dir. corp. planning Bekins Co., L.A., 1966-73; mgr. corp. planning Ridder Publs., Inc., L.A., 1973-75; chief fin. officer City of Inglewood (Calif.), 1975-77; treas./contr. Inglewood Redevel. Agy., 1975-77, Inglewood Housing Authority, 1975-77; v.p. mcpl. fin. White, Weld & Co., Inc., L.A., 1977-78; v.p. pub. fin. Paine Webber Jackson & Curtis, L.A., 1978-79; v.p. and mgr. for Western region, mcpl. fin. dept. Merrill Lynch Capital Markets, L.A., 1979-82, mng. dir. Western region, mcpl. fin. dept., 1982-86; mng. dir. Seidler-Fitzgerald Pub. Fin., L.A., 1986—; sr. v.p. The Seidler Cos., Inc., L.A., 1986—, also bd. dirs., mem. exec. com.; instr. fin./adminstrn. El Camino Coll., Torrance, Calif., 1977-80; bd. dirs., mem. exec. com. The Seidler Cos., Inc. Chmn. bd. dirs., exec. com., treas., chmn. fund raising com. L.A. chpt. Am. Heart Assn., 1977—; bd. dirs. Daniel Freeman Hosps. Inc., Corondelet Health Care Corp.; trustee Mt. St. Mary's Coll., L.A., 1992—; bd. dirs. Tau Kappa Epsilon Ednl. Found., Indpls., 1995—; alumni coun. mem. Johnson Grad. Sch. of Mgmt. Cornell U., real estate council. Mem. Fin. Execs. Inst., Mcpl. Fin. Officers Assn., Calif. Soc. Mcpl. Fin. Officers, League Calif. Cities, So. Calif. Corp. Planners Assn. (past pres.), L.A. Bond, Beta Gamma Sigma. Republican. Clubs: Jonathan, The Calif., Lake Arrowhead Country. Lodge: Rotary.

FITZGERALD, JOHN EDWARD, III, lawyer; b. Cambridge, Mass., Jan. 12, 1945; s. John Edward Jr. and Kathleen (Sullivan) FitzG.; m. Nancy Balik. BCE, U.S. Mil. Acad., West Point, N.Y., 1969; JD, M in Pub. Policy Analysis, U. Pa., 1975. Bar: Pa. 1975, N.Y. 1978, Calif. 1983, U.S. Supreme Ct. 1991. Commd. 2d lt. U.S. Army, 1969, advanced through grades to capt., 1971, resigned, 1972; assoc. Saul Ewing Remick & Saul, Phila., 1975-77, Shearman & Sterling, N.Y.C., 1977-78; atty. Pepsico, Inc., Purchase, N.Y., 1978-82; sr. v.p., dept. head Security Pacific Corp., Los Angeles, 1982-83; ptnr. Schlesinger, FitzGerald & Johnson, Palm Springs, Calif., 1983-87; mng. ptnr. FitzGerald & Assocs., Palm Springs, 1987—; adj. prof. law U. Pa., Temple U., U. Redlands: judge pro tem Desert Jud. Dist.; lectr. Calif. Continuing Edn. of the Bar; trustee Nat. Coun. Freedom Found., Valley Forge, Pa. Bd. dirs., vice chmn. Desert Hosp. Found.; bd. dirs. Palm Springs Boys and Girls Club, Pathfinder Ranch, Desert Youth Found., United Way. Mem. ABA, Calif. Bar Assn. (exec. com., gen. practice sect., law practice mgmt. sect.), Desert Bar Assn., Riverside County Bar Assn., Orange County Bar Assn., Assn. Trial Lawyers Am., Calif. Trial Lawyers Assn., Am. Arbitration Assn. (arbitrator), Palm Springs Polo Club, O'Donnell Golf Club (Palm Springs), Com. of 25 (Palm Springs), Monarch Bay Club, Desert Roundtable, World Affairs Coun. Home: 555 W Via Lola Palm Springs CA 92262-4372 also: 11 Grand Master Ct Monarch Beach CA 92629-4113

FITZGERALD, ROBERT LYNN, small business owner; b. Indiana, Pa., Oct. 1, 1939; s. Joseph and Jean (Smith) F.; m. Tomi Higuchi, May 30, 1991; 1 child, Robert Lynn Jr. Student, Orange Coast Coll., 1985-86; BA, U. Redlands, 1990; MA, U.S. Internat. U., 1993. Dist. mgr. Napco Sci., Portland, Oreg., 1981-88; prin., pub. Fitzgerald's Real Esate Yellow Pages, Santa Ana, Calif., 1987—; psychol. sales cons., 1990—. Hospice vol. Orange County (Calif.), Vis. Nurses Assn., 1980; founder Orange County HELP chpt., Santa Ana, 1982. Home: 2700 W Segerstrom Ave # D Santa Ana CA 92704-6547 Office: Fitzgerald's Real Estate Yellow Pages 3941 S Bristol St Ste 335 Santa Ana CA 92704-7400

FITZGERALD, TIKHON (LEE R. H. FITZGERALD), bishop; b. Detroit, Nov. 14, 1932; s. LeRoy and Dorothy Kaeding (Higgins) F. AB, Wayne State U., 1958. Ordained deacon, 1971, priest, 1978, bishop Eastern Orthodox, 1987. Enlisted U.S. Army, 1954-57; commd. 2 lt. USAF, 1960, advanced through grades to capt., 1971; air staff, 1966-71, released, 1971; protodeacon Holy Virgin Mary Russian Orthodox Cathedral, L.A., 1972-78, rector, archpriest, 1979-87; bishop of San Francisco Orthodox Ch. in Am., L.A., 1987—. Democrat. Home: 649 Robinson St Los Angeles CA 90026-3612 Office: Orthodox Ch Am Diocese of the West 650 Micheltorena St Los Angeles CA 90026-3623*

FITZGERALD, TIMOTHY KEVIN, writer; b. San Jose, Calif., Jan. 3, 1946; s. Ralph George and Bernice Christina (Huston) F. BA, San Jose State Coll., 1971, San Jose State U., 1980; MA, San Jose State U., 1985. Treas. Associated Students San Jose State Coll., 1969-70; camp bus. mgr. Boy Scouts Am., Sonora, Calif., 1973; co. budget analyst Allstate Equity Investments, San Jose, 1980; adminstrv. asst. Summer Employment of Youth program CETA, San Jose, 1981; pres. Corp. for Shared Responsibility, San Jose, 1983-84; owner/operator Raccoon Pubs., San Jose, 1991-92; freelance writer, researcher San Jose, 1992—; sec. Discovery, Inc., San Jose, 1991-93; adminstrv. trustee Inst. for Social Orgnl. Rsch., San Jose, 1992-94. Author: Essays in Capitalism, 1986, Civic Community, 1992, Inner City, 1993, (narrative) Trail to Black Mountain, 1978, poetry Impressions from Idle Rock, 1981. Mgr., candidate for State Assembly, San Jose, 1994, for San Jose City Coun., 1982; co-coord. State Green Party Platform, Calif., 1993; elected mem. Green Party County Coun., Santa Clara County, Calif., 1992-94; vol. Cmty. Companions, Inc., San Jose, 1990-91. Advanced cadet U.S. Army ROTC, 1966-67. Mem. Fellowship of Reconciliation, Sierra Club (Loma Preita chpt.), Tau Delta Phi. Office: PO Box 720594 San Jose CA 95172

FITZGERALD, VALERIE ANN, real estate company executive; b. Huron, S.D., Feb. 15, 1952; d. George Hoaglund and Donalie Ann (Young) Schumaker; m. Nelson Peltz, Mar. 11, 1977 (div. Aug. 1983); 1 child, Vanessa Lauren. BA, UCLA. V.p. Alvarez, Hyland & Young, Beverly Hills, Calif., 1989-95, The Prudential Calif. Realty, Beverly Hills, 1991—. Lobbyist Citizens Rsch. Impeach Com., N.Y.C., 1973-75. Mem. NAFE. Office: The Prudential Calif Realty 166 N Canon Dr Beverly Hills CA 90210-5304

FITZGERALD, VINCENT JAMES, controller; b. N.Y.C., Nov. 21, 1950; s. Vincent Edward and Joan Mary (Berhman) F. BA, St. John Fisher Coll., Rochester, N.Y., 1972; MBA, Northwestern U., Evanston, Ill., 1974; advanced profl. cert., NYU, 1984. CPA, Ill., N.Y. Staff acct. Deloitte Haskins & Sells, Chgo., 1974-77; sr. internal auditor Am. Hosp. Supply Corp., Evanston, 1977-79; bus. mgr. McGraw-Hill, Inc., N.Y.C., 1979-82; asst. treas. Chem. Bank, N.Y.C., 1982-84; controller Hay Group, Inc., N.Y.C., 1984-88; dir. fin. reporting Reeves Entertainment Group, L.A., 1988—. F.C. Austin scholar, 1972. Mem. AICPA, Calif. State CPAs, Acctg. Rsch. Assn. Republican. Roman Catholic. Home: 428 Delaware Ave Staten Island NY 10305-2327 Office: Reeves Entertainment Group 10877 Wilshire Blvd Los Angeles CA 90024-4341

FITZPATRICK, LOIS ANN, library administrator; b. Yonkers, N.Y., Mar. 27, 1952; d. Thomas Joseph and Dorothy Ann (Nealy) Sullivan; m. William George Fitzpatrick, Jr., Dec. 1, 1973; children: Jennifer Ann, Amy Ann. BS in Sociology, Mercy Coll., 1974; MLS, Pratt Inst., 1975. Clk. Yonkers (N.Y.) Pub. Library, 1970-73, librarian trainee, 1973-75, librarian I, 1975-76; reference librarian Carroll Coll. Library, Helena, Mont., 1976-79, acting dir., 1979, asst. prof., 1979-89, dir., 1980—, assoc. prof., 1989—; chmn. arrangements Mont. Gov.'s Pre White House Conf. on Libraries, Helena, 1977-78; mem. steering com. Reference Point coop. program for librs., 1991; mem. adv. com. Helena Coll. of Tech. Libr., 1994—. Pres. elect Helena Area Health Sci. Libraries Cons., 1979-84, pres., 1984-88; bd. dirs. Mont. FAXNET; co-chmn. interest group OCLC; chmn. local arrangements Mont. Gov.'s Pre White House Conf.; mem. adv. bd. Helena Coll. of Tech. Mem. Mont. Library Assn. task force for White House conf. 1991). Democrat. Roman Catholic. Club: Soroptimist Internat. of Helena (2d v.p. 1984-85, pres. 1986-87). Home: 1308 Shirley Rd Helena MT 59601-6635 Office: Carroll Coll Jack and Sallie Corette Libr Helena MT 59625-0099

FITZSIMMONS, (LOWELL) COTTON, professional basketball executive, broadcaster, former coach; b. Hannibal, Mo., Oct. 7, 1931; s. Clancy and Zelda Curry (Gibbs) F.; m. JoAnn D'Andrea, Sept. 2, 1978 (div.); 1 child, Gary. B.S., Midwestern Univ., Wichita Falls, Tex., M.A. Head coach, athletic dir. Moberly Jr. Coll, Moberly, Mo., 1958-67; head coach Kans. State U., Manhattan, 1967-70; head coach NBA Phoenix Suns, 1970-72, 1988-92, dir. player personnel, 1987-88; head coach NBA Atlanta Hawks, 1972-76; dir. player personnel NBA Golden State Warriors, Oakland, Calif., 1976-77; head coach NBA Buffalo Braves, 1977-78, NBA Kansas City Kings, Mo., 1978-84, NBA San Antonio Spurs, 1984-87; sr. exec. v.p. Phoenix Suns, 1992—. Recipient Coach of the Yr. award Nat. Jr. Coll. Athletic Assn., 1966, 67, Coach of the Yr. award Big 8 Conf., 1970, Coach of the Yr. award NBA, 1979, 89, Coach of the Yr. award Sporting News, St. Louis, 1979, 89; inducted into Mo. Sports Hall of Fame, Jefferson City, 1981, Nat. Jr. Coll. Basketball Hall of Fame, Hutchinson, 1985. Fellow Nat. Assn. Basketball Coaches. Office: Phoenix Suns 201 E Jefferson St Phoenix AZ 85004-2412*

FITZSIMMONS, JEFFREY LYNN, astronautical engineer, military officer; b. Alexandria, Va., Jan. 14, 1958; s. John Wayne and Joan (Straight)

F. BS in Astronautical Engr., USAF Acad., 1980; MS in Aero. and Astronautical Engr., MIT, 1984; MBA in Mgmt., Wright State U., 1991. Commd. 2d lt. USAF, 1980, advanced through grades to maj., 1992; chief integrated scheduling 6555th Aerospace Test Group, Cape Canaveral AFB, Fla., 1980-82; project officer, developmental engr. Plans & Advanced Programs, Ballistic Missile Office, Norton AFB, Calif., 1984-88; space sys. engr. Fgn. Tech. Divsn., Wright-Patterson AFB, Ohio, 1988-92; chief future upper stages Space and Missile Sys. Ctr., L.A., 1992—. Contbr. articles to profl. jours. Decorated Air Force Commendation medals USAF, 1982, 92, Air Force Meritorious Svc. medal USAF, 1988; recipient Silver Medal award Colo. Engring. Coun., 1980. Mem. AIAA (sr. mem., session chmn. space programs and tech. conf. 1993—), Am. Astronautical Soc., Nat. Space Soc., British Interplanetary Soc. Home: 1313 Mount Rainier Rd Rancho Palos CA 90275-1913 Office: SMC/SDES 160 Skynet St Los Angeles CA 90245

FITZSIMMONS, JOHN MICHAEL, physician, educator; b. Phila., Sept. 6, 1949; s. Johns Jospeh and Martha Catherine (McLouglin) F.; m. Sally Elizabeth Mauchly, June 13, 1970; children: Kathleen, Sara, Michael. BA in Math., LaSalle Coll., Phila., 1971; MD, Hahnemann Med. Coll., Phila., 1975. Diplomate Am. Bd. Ob/Gyn. Intern Hershey (Pa.) Med. Ctr., 1975-76; resident Abington (Pa.) Meml. Hosp., 1976-78; attending physician Polyclinic Med. ctr., Harrisburg, Pa., 1978-79, 81-82; instr. ob/gyn. Jefferson Med. Coll., Phila., 1979-82, asst. prof., 1982-84; asst. prof. U. Wis., Madison, 1984-86; asst. prof. U. Wash., Seattle, 1986-89, asst. dean academic affairs, assoc. prof., 1989-92, assoc. prof. oby/gyn., 1992—; assoc. dir. perinatal svcs. Tacoma (Wash.) Gen. Hosp., 1992—. Reviewer jours.; contbr. articles and abstracts to profl. jours. Mem. grant rev. com. Office of Substance Abuse Prevention, Washington, 1989-92; S.W. region rep. Wash. State Perinatal Adv. Com.; mem. Pierce County Perinatal Adv. Bd.; precinct officer Rep. Com., Tacoma, 1993, del. to county conv., 1994, del. to state conv., 1994. Mem. Am. Coll. Physician Execs., Am. Coll. Ob/Gyn., Am. Soc. Human Genetics, Soc. Perinatal Obstetricians, Teratology Soc. Republican. Roman Catholic. Home: 5001 Orca Dr NE Tacoma WA 98422-1942 Office: 314 S K St Ste 402 Tacoma WA 98405-4273

FIUMERODO, ANTHONY, airline pilot; b. Palermo, Italy, Mar. 13, 1948; came to U.S., 1960; s. Francesco Remo and Giovanna (Costa) F.; divorced; children: Flavio, Veraldo. BS in Bus. Adminstrn. with honors, U. Tenn., Knoxville, 1972; MBA with highest honors, Golden Gate U., 1984. Commd. 2d lt. U.S. Air Force, 1969, advanced through grades to capt., 1976; pilot U.S. and Turkey, 1974-89; ret. U.S. Air Force, 1989; pilot Am. Airlines, L.A., 1989—. Contbr. articles to profl. jours. Recipient Scannell award Nat. Birds Show Inc., 1992. Mem. Thousand Oaks C. of C., Alpha Kappa Phi, Beta Gamma Sigma, Phi Kappa Phi. Republican. Christian. Office: Am Airlines PO Box 92246 Los Angeles CA 90009-2246

FIX, TOBIE LYNN, special education educator; b. L.A., Aug. 25, 1961; d. Howard Jacob and Pearl (Bram) Berger; m. Thomas Fix, Aug. 25, 1985. AA, Nat. U., L.A., 1992, student, 1992—. Substitute tchr. asst. of trainable mentally handicapped Los Angeles County, Calif., 1980-85, tchr. asst. trainable mentally handicapped, 1985—; coaching asst. Spl. Olympic State Games, Los Angeles County. Recipient Vol. awards in spl. edn. Mem. Mus. of Tolerance, Huntington Libr./Gardens, L.A. Zool. Found. Democrat. Jewish. Home: 1628 Carlson Ln Redondo Beach CA 90278-4711

FIXMAN, MARSHALL, chemist, educator; b. St. Louis, Sept. 21, 1930; s. Benjamin and Dorothy (Finkel) F.; m. Marian Ruth Beatman, July 5, 1959 (dec. Sept. 1969); children—Laura Beth, Susan Ilene, Andrew Richard; m. Branka Ladanyi, Dec. 7, 1974. A.B., Washington U., St. Louis, 1950; Ph.D., MIT, 1954. Jewett postdoctoral fellow chemistry Yale U., 1953-54; instr. chemistry Harvard U., 1956-59; sr. fellow Mellon Inst., Pitts., 1959-61; prof. chemistry, dir. Inst. Theoretical Sci., U. Oreg., 1961-64, prof. chemistry, research asso. inst., 1964-65; prof. chemistry Yale U., New Haven, 1965-79; prof. chemistry and physics Colo. State U., Ft. Collins, 1979—. Mem. editorial bd. Jour. Chem. Physics, 1962-64, Jour. Phys. Chemistry, 1970-74, Macromolecules, 1970-74, Accounts Chem. Rsch. 1982-85, Jour. Polymer Sci. B, 1991-93; assoc. editor Jour. Chem. Physics, 1994—. Served with AUS, 1954-56. Fellow Alfred P. Sloan Found., 1961-63; recipient Governor's award Oreg. Mus. Sci. and Industry, 1964. Mem. NAS, Am. Acad. Arts and Scis., Am. Chem. Soc. (award pure chemistry 1964, award polymer chemistry 1991), Am. Phys. Soc. (high polymer physics award 1980), Fedn. Am. Scientists. Office: Colo State U Dept Chemistry Fort Collins CO 80523

FIX-ROMLOW, JEANNE KAY, hair care products company executive; b. Madison, Wis., June 29, 1947; d. Glen H. and Violet M. (Bohnsack) Fix; m. Paul James Romlow, Nov. 7, 1985. Student, Madison Area Tech. Sch., 1966. Mgr. Fashion Fabrics, Madison, 1973-74; promotion dir. Livesey Enterprises, Madison, 1976-77; sales assoc. First Realty Group, Madison, 1977-79; territory mgr. Aerial Beauty and Barber Supply, Madison, 1979-83; regional dir. John Paul Mitchell Systems, Santa Clarita, Calif., 1983-85, v.p., 1986-87, sr. v.p., 1987-91, exec. v.p., 1991—. Home: 11344W Bay Dr Lodi WI 53555 Office: John Paul Mitchell Systems 26455 Golden Valley Rd Santa Clarita CA 91350-2621

FLACH, VICTOR HUGO, designer, educator; b. Portland, Oreg., May 31, 1929; s. Victor H. and Eva (Huget) F. Student of, Jack Wilkinson, R. Buckminster Fuller, W.R. Hovey; BS, U. Oreg., 1952, MFA, 1957; postgrad., U. Pitts., 1959-65. Archtl., elec. engring. and cartographic draftsman with various cos. and U.S. govt. agy., 1948-62; teaching fellow, curator Henry Clay Frick Fine Arts Dept. and Gallery, U. Pitts., 1959-63; docent Frank Lloyd Wright's Fallingwater, Western Pa. Conservancy, 1963-64; prof. art, design, painting, theory and history U. Wyo., Laramie, 1965-93, prof. emeritus, 1993—; participant R. Buckminster Fuller Geodesic Prototype Projects, 1953, 59; interviewer Heritage series TV program PBS-TV, 1965; cons. Nat. Symposium on Role of Studio Arts in Higher Edn., U. Oreg., 1967. Participant: various TV programs including Arts in Practice series, 1971-77; designer multi-walled murals, U. Oreg., Eugene, 1952, Rainbow Club, 1954, Clear Lake Sch., Eugene, 1956, Sci. Ctr., U. Wyo., Laramie, 1967, sect. at Springcreek Sch., Laramie, 1995; one-man and group shows of paintings, photographs, exptl. films and drawings, 1949—; author and editor: IJHTBIW20 Poems, 1949, 12 New Painters, 1953, IN/SERT Active Anthology for the Creative, 1955-62, Gloss of the Four Universal Forms, 1959, The Anatomy of the Canvas, 1961, The Eye's Mind, 1964, The Stage, 1978, Contextualist Manifesto, 1982, Displacings & Wayfarings, 1986, JW's Orientation Mural, 1990; contbr. poems, articles and photographs to lit. jours., 1949—. With U.S. Army, 1953-55. Office: 1618 Custer Sta Laramie WY 82070-4243

FLAGG, KEOKI SCOTT, photographer; b. Honolulu, Apr. 7, 1965; s. Harry Martin and Lynn (Sher) F. BA, Conn. Coll., 1987. Mgr., owner Coll. Pro Painters, Madison, Conn., 1987, 88; freelance photographer Travel/Image Gathering, Asia, So. Hemisphere, 1988, 89, Asia, Africa, 1989-91; ski photographer, videographer Sno Motion, Olympic Valley, Calif., 1989, 92, Team Tahoe, Olympic Valley, 1993; action-sport freelance photographer Keoki Flagg Photographics, Olympic Valley, 1994—. Prodr.: (art show) Another Perspective, 1993. Named Artist of Yr., Lake Tahoe, 1993. Home: PO Box 6850 Incline Village NV 89450-6850

FLAGG, NORMAN LEE, retired advertising executive; b. Detroit, Jan. 21, 1932; s. Frank and Harriet (Brown) F.; m. Carolanne Flagg; children: James, Suzanne. BFA, U. Miami, Miami, Fla., 1958. Advt. supr. Smithkline Beckman, Phila., 1970-75, creative dir., 1975-80; owner Illusions Restaurants, Bryn Maur, Pa., 1979-87, Illusions Restaurant, Tucson, Ariz., 1984-88. Author: Shooting Blanks, 1994. With USMC, 1954-56. Recipient Diana awards Whlse Druggest Assn. 1977, Aesculapius award Modern Medicine 1978. Mem. Acad. Magical Arts.

FLAGG, ROBERT FINCH, research aerospace engineer; b. Somerville, Mass., Mar. 6, 1933; s. Donald Fairbanks and Helen Constance (Finch) F.; m. Lois-Ann Davis Laughton, June 14, 1958 (div. 1975); children: Scott, Susan, Marc. BS in Aero. Engring., MIT, 1959, MS in Aero. and Astronautical Engring., 1960; PhD in Engring. Physics, U. Toronto, Ont., Can., 1967. Teaching asst. MIT, Cambridge, 1959; rsch. assoc. U. Toronto, 1964-67; program mgr. Physics Internat. Co., San Leandro, Calif., 1967-68; dir. rsch. Holex Inc., Hollister, Calif., 1968-71; v.p. tech. ops. X-Demex Corp., Dublin, Calif., 1972-79; program mgr. Artec Assocs., Hayward, Calif., 1979-80; mgr. ordnance engring. Tracor Aerospace, San Ramon, Calif., 1980-84; tech. dir. Tracor Aerospace, Camden, Ark., 1986-90; dir. IR countermeasures Bermite div. Whittaker Corp., Saugus, Calif., 1984-85; R & D scientist Lockheed Advanced Aeros., Valencia, Calif., 1985-86; sr. engring. specialist Aerojet Ordnance, Downey, Calif., 1991—. Contbr. numerous articles to sci. and tech. jours. Staff sgt. USAF, 1950-54. Staff scholar MIT, 1954-59, N. Stewart Robinson scholar U. Toronto, 1964-67; U. Toronto Inst. Aerospace Studies scholar, rsch. fellow, Presdl. fellow U. Calif. Lawrence Berkeley Lab., 1971-72. Mem. AIAA, Am. Def. Preparedness Assn., Soc. Explosives Engrs., Internat. Pyrotechnic Soc., Sigma Gamma Tau. Republican. Home: 5793 Greenridge Rd Castro Valley CA 94552-1813 Office: Aerojet Ordnance 9236 Hall Rd Downey CA 90241-5308

FLAGLER, WILLIAM LAWRENCE, financial broker; b. Oakland, Calif., June 13, 1922; s. Albert William and Violet Dorthy (Marris) F.; B.A., San Francisco State U., 1951; degree in Library Sci., San Jose State U., 1963; m. Ruth Greiner Gilbert, Aug. 23, 1970; children by previous marriage: Vickie, David, Michael; stepchildren: Denise Gilbert La Hay, Ethan Gilbert. Registered fin. broker. Pres., LaRu Enterprises, San Jose, Calif., 1975—. Active Boy Scouts Am. Served with U.S. Army, World War II, ETO. Republican. Club: Masons. Office: PO Box 10460 San Jose CA 95157-1460

FLAHAVIN, MARIAN JOAN, artist; b. Colton, Wash., Nov. 19, 1937; d. Herbert Joseph and Margaret Thersa (McGinn) Druffel; m. G. Thomas Flahavin, Aug. 6, 1960; 1 child, John Thomas. BA in Art, Holy Names Coll., 1959; studied with, John Howard and Daniel Green. With pub. rels. Holy Names Coll., Spokane, Wash., 1959-70; artist-in-residence Spokane, 1974—; tchr. and speaker in field. Prin. work represented in galleries and shows, nation wide; prin. work includes collectible plate series, prints for benefit of children, garden sculptures of children. Mem. Pastel Soc. Am., Northwest Pastel Soc., Women Artists of Am. West, Pastel Soc. West Coast. Roman Catholic. Home and Office: RR 7 Spokane WA 99206-9801

FLAMM, MELVIN DANIEL, JR., cardiologist; b. L.A., Jan. 29, 1934; s. Melvin Daniel and Mary (Peterek) F.; m. Carla Baker, June 24, 1955; children: Scott Daniel, Bradley John, Jason Andrew, Amanda Paige. BA, UCLA, 1956; MD, Stanford U., 1960. Diplomate Am. Bd. Internal Medicine, Am. Bd. Cardiovascular Disease. Rotating intern Walter Reed Gen. Hosp., Washington, 1960-61; med. resident Stanford U., 1964-66, fellow in cardiology, 1966-68; cardiologist in pvt. practice No. Calif. Cardiology Assocs., Sacramento; clin. prof. medicine U. Calif., Davis; med. dir. Cardiac Catheterization Labs. Sutter Meml. Hosp., Sacramento, 1976-92; chmn. instl. rev. com. Sutter Comty. Hosps., 1987-93; examiner Subspecialty Bd. of Cardiovasc. Diseases of Am. Bd. Internal Medicine, 1971-75; vis. prof. cardiology Nat. Def. Med. Sch. and Vets. Gen. Hosp., Taiwan U. Sch. Medicine, 1978, Queen Mary Hosp. of Hong Kong, U. Sch. Medicine and Hong Kong Cardiologic Soc., 1978. Contbr. numerous articles to profl. jours. Trustee Sutter Hosps. Found., 1987-89. Col. M.C., USAF, 1959-74, active res., 1974-84. Fellow ACP, Am. Coll. Cardiology, Coun. on Clin. Cardiology of Am. Heart Assn. (chmn. and mem. rsch. com. and rsch. allocation com. Golden Empire chpt.); mem. AMA, Am. Fedn. Clin. Rsch., Sacramento-El Dorado Med. Assn., Calif. Med. Assn. Office: No Calif Cardiology Assocs 5301 F St Ste 117 Sacramento CA 95819-3220

FLAMMANG, SUSANN, author, publisher; b. Kenosha, Wis., June 2, 1950; d. Leslie James and Beatrice (Woodward) Flammang Sampe. Pres. The Family of God, Las Vegas, 1984—, World Harvest, 1985—, pub., editor The Family of God Newsletter, Poets for Africa, 1986—; pres. World Harvest, 1986—; producer, broadcaster Heart-to-Heart, Sta. KUNV-TV, Las Vegas; v.p. Art Affair. Author of 30 books, numerous works of poetry. Recipient numerous poetry awards including Calif. Fedn. of Poets award, 1983, Humanitarian award Clark County, 1986, Woman of Achievement award, 1987, Gov's Art award, 1985, 86. Mem. Internat. Women's Writing Guild, Internat. PEN Assn., Acad. Am. Poets. Office: The Family of God/World Harvest PO Box 34716 Las Vegas NV 89133

FLANAGAN, JOHN MICHAEL, editor, publisher; b. Bangor, Maine, Mar. 8, 1946; s. Joseph F. and Dorothy Elizabeth (Albert) F.; m. Mary Katherine Fastenau, June 22, 1990. Student, U. Notre Dame, 1963-65; BJ, U. Mo., 1970. With The News-Jour. papers, Wilmington, Del., 1970-84, mng. editor, 1982-84; editor Marin Ind. Jour., San Rafael, Calif., 1984-87; exec. editor Honolulu Star-Bulletin, 1987-93; editor, pub. Honolulu Star-Bull., 1993—. With U.S. Army, 1965-68. Office: Honolulu Star Bull PO Box 3080 Honolulu HI 96802-3080

FLANAGAN, LATHAM, JR., surgeon; b. Pitts., Dec. 2, 1936; s. Latham and Elizabeth Lansing (Bunting) Kimbrough; m. Elizabeth Ruth Losaw, June 26, 1961 (dec. May 1971); 1 child, Jennifer Ruth; m. Mary Jane Flanagan, Mar. 28, 1975; children: Sahale Ann, David Nooroa. MD, Duke U., 1961, student, 1957, MD, 1961. Diplomate Am. Bd. Surgery. Intern U. Calif., San Francisco, 1961-62, resident in surgery, 1962-66, chief resident in surgery, 1965-66; pvt. practice surgery Sacred Heart Hosp., Eugene, Oreg., 1968-84, 85—; clin. sr. instr. in surgery Oreg. Health Scis. U., Portland, 1968-84; assoc. prof. surgery U. Otago, Dunedin (New Zealand) Pub. Hosp., 1984-85; nat. surgeon Cook Islands, 1985; founder Oreg. Ctr. for Bariatric Surgery, Eugene, 1993—. Contbr. articles to profl. jours. Founder White Bird Clinic, Eugene, 1969-71; mem. adv. com. Planned Parenthood of Lane County, 1979-84, Lt. comdr. USN, 1966-68, Vietnam. Fellow ACS (pres. Oreg. chpt. 1991-92); mem. AMA, Oreg. Med. Assn., Lane County med. Soc. (com. chair 1970s), Am. Soc. Bariatric Surgery (chair ins. com. 1991-94, councillor 1994—), North Pacific Surg. Soc., Eugene Surg. Soc. (pres. 1981). Republican. Home: 4495 Pinecrest Dr Eugene OR 97405-5305 Office: 655 E 11th Ave Ste 8 Eugene OR 97401-3621

FLANARY, KATHY VENITA MOORE, librarian; b. Amherst, Tex., Jan. 15, 1946; d. Charles Edward and Jean (Willman) Moore; children: Suzanne Flanary, Charles Flanary. BA, U. Ill., 1972, MLS, 1974. Cert. profl. libr., N.Mex.; cert. tchr., N.Mex. Dir. children's libr. Hayner Pub. Libr., Alton, Ill., 1974-76; dir. Ruidoso (N.Mex.) Pub. Libr., 1978-80; libr. media specialist Horgan Libr., N.Mex. Mil. Inst., Roswell, 1985-93; libr. N.Mex. Sch. Visually Handicapped, Alamogordo, 1993—; workshop presenter Lewis & Clark Regional Libr. Systems, Ill., 1975; outreach programer Hayner Pub. Libr., 1974-76; del. Pre-White Ho. Conf., State of N.Mex., 1991. Contbr. articles to newspapers and profl. jours. Bd. dirs. Alton Symphony, 1975; mem. Altrusa, Ruidoso, 1979-84, Friend of Roswell Pub. Libr.; sec. Ruidoso Summer Festival, 1979; bd. dirs. Supts. Adv. Bd., Roswell, N.Mex., 1987-89; pres. Friends of Libr., Ruidoso, 1980-83, Parent Advocacy for Gifted Edn., 1990-92; v.p. Sunset PTA; bd. dirs. N.Mex. Libr. Found., 1992—. Recipient Svc. award Altrusa, 1979, Sunset PTA, 1989. Mem. N.Mex. Libr. Assn. (libr. devel. com., edn!. tech. roundtable vice chair 1991, chair elect 1992, co-chair state conv. local arrangements 1990-91, 2d v.p. 1993-94, 1st v.p. 1994-95, pres. 1995-96), N.Mex. Acad. and Rsch. Librs. (vice chair 1992, pres. 1993), Kiwanis (bd. dirs. 1990-92).

FLANDERS, GEORGE JAMES, mechanical engineer, engineering development manager; b. Bunker Hill, Ind., June 3, 1960; s. Melvin S. and Edith J. (Mason) F. BSME, Bradley U., 1982, MBA, 1984. Lab. engr. Materials Testing & Rsch. Lab., Peoria, Ill., 1982; rsch. design engr. Caterpillar Tractor Co., Peoria, 1982-85; staff engr. Bristol Myers Co., Englewood, Colo., 1985-86, sr. engr., bus. unit mgr. arthoscopy and reconstructive surgery products, 1986-87; group engr., Titan project bus. proposal coord. Titan Space Launch Systems, Martin Marietta Astronautics Group, Denver, 1987—; co-founder, CEO WSG Mgmt. and Holding Group, Denver, 1988—; bd. dirs., sec., chmn., investement com. chmn. Red Rock Fed. Credit Union, 1989—; ptnr. Advanced Coronary Intervention, 1994—; cons. in field. Area coord. Neighborhood Watch Program, 1988-89; crew leader 10,000 Trees Environ. Project; mem. fin. com. Littleton United Meth. Ch., 1987—. Mem. NSPE, ASME, Soc. Automotive Engrs., Sigma Phi Delta (grand pres. 1988-90, v.p. 1985-87, trustee chmn. 1988-90), Tau Beta Pi, Pi Tau Sigma, Omicron Delta Kappa. Home: 6168 S Lee St Littleton CO 80127-2561 Office: Martin Marietta Astronautics Group PO Box 179 Denver CO 80201-0179

FLANIGAN, JAMES J(OSEPH), journalist; b. N.Y.C., June 6, 1936; s. James and Jane (Whyte) F.; m. Anne Fitzmaurice, Jan. 9, 1965 (dec. Oct. 1992); children: Michael, Siobhan Jane. BA, Manhattan Coll., 1961. Fin. writer N.Y. Herald Tribune, N.Y.C. and Paris, 1957-66; bur. chief, asst. mng. editor Forbes Mag., Washington, London, Houston, L.A., N.Y.C., 1966-86; bus. columnist, sr. writer L.A. Times, 1986—. Office: LA Times Times Mirror Sq Los Angeles CA 90053

FLANNELLY, KEVIN J., psychologist, research analyst; b. Jersey City, Nov. 26, 1949; s. John J. and Mary C. (Walsh) F.; m. Laura T. Adams, Jan. 10, 1981. BA in Psychology, Jersey City State Coll., 1972; MS in Psychology, Rutgers U., 1975; PhD in Psychology, U. Hawaii, 1983. Rsch. asst. dept. psychology U. Ill., Champaign, 1972-73; rsch. intern Alcohol Behavior Rsch. Lab. Rutgers U., New Brunswick, N.J., 1973-75; rsch. scientist Edward R. Johnstone Tng. and Rsch. Ctr., Bordentown, N.J., 1975-78; teaching asst. dept. psychology U. Hawaii, Honolulu, 1980-81, rsch. asst. Pacific Biomed. Rsch. Ctr., 1981-83, asst. prof. Bekesy Lab. Neurobiology, 1983-85; rsch. statistician, statewide transp. planning office Hawaii Dept. Transportation, Honolulu, 1986-89; researcher Office of Lt. Gov., Honolulu, 1989-93; legis. dir., policy analyst energy and environ. protection com. State House of Reps., 1994; planning and policy analyst Office of Gov., Honolulu, 1994—; statis cons. U. Hawaii Sch. Nursing, Honolulu, 1986, Hawaii Dept. Health, Honolulu, 1986; staff mem. gov's. subcabinet on early childhood edn. and childcare, 1989, Hawaii task force on ednl. governance, 1991-92; mem. Gov's. Office State Planning, environ. scanning project, 1992-94; v.p., rsch. dir. Ctr. Psychosocial Rsch., Honolulu, 1987—; instr. dept. social scis. Honolulu Community Coll., 1981; ptnr. Flannelly Cons., 1991—; rsch. dir. Mktg. Rsch. Inst., 1992—; mem. State Ridesharing Task Force, 1987. Editor: Biological Perspective on Aggression, 1984, Introduction to Psychology, 1987; reviewer 8 sci. and profl. jours., 1978—; grant reviewer NSF, 1984-92; contbr. numerous articles to profl. jours. Polit. survey cons., Honolulu, 1988—; transp. cons., Honolulu, 1989—; mktg. cons., Honolulu, 1990—. Grantee NIH, 1984, Fed. Hwy. Adminstrn., 1987; N.J. State scholar N.J. Dept. Higher Edn., 1968-72. Fellow Internat. Soc. Rsch. on Aggression; mem. AAAS, Am. Psychol. Soc., Am. Statis. Assn., Internat. Soc. Comparative Psychology, N.Y. Acad. Scis., Pacific and Asian Affairs Coun., Psychonomic Soc., Sigma Xi. Office: Office of Gov Hawaii State Capitol Honolulu HI 96813

FLANNELLY, LAURA T., mental health nurse, nursing educator, researcher; b. Bklyn., Nov. 7, 1952; d. George A. Adams and Eleanor (Barragry) Mulhearn; m. Kevin J. Flannelly, Jan. 10, 1981. BS in Nursing, Hunter Coll., 1974; MSN, U. Hawaii, 1984, postgrad., 1988—. RN, N.Y., Hawaii. Psychiat. nurse Bellevue Hosp., N.Y.C., 1975, asst. head nurse, 1975-77; psychiat. nurse White Plains (N.Y.) Med. Ctr., 1978-79; community mental health nurse South Beach Psychiat. Ctr., N.Y.C., 1979-81; psychiat. nurse The Queen's Med. Ctr., Honolulu, 1981-83; crisis worker Crisis Response Systems Project, Honolulu, 1983-86; instr. nursing U. Hawaii, Honolulu, 1985-92, asst. prof., 1992—; adj. instr. nursing Hawaii Loa Coll., Honolulu, 1988, Am. Samoa Community Coll., Honolulu, 1987, 89, 90; mem. adv. bd., planning com. Psychiat. Day Hosp. of The Queen's Med. Ctr., Honolulu, 1981-82; program coord. Premenstrual Tension Syndrome Conf., Honolulu, 1984; dir. Ctr. Psychosocial Rsch., Honolulu, 1987—; program moderator 1st U.S-Japan Health Behavioral Conf., Honolulu, 1988; faculty Ctr. for Asia-Pacific Exch., Internat. Conf. on Transcultural Nursing, Honolulu, 1990; mem. bd. dirs. U. Hawaii Profl. Assembly, 1994—. Contbr. articles to profl. jours. N.Y. State Bd. Regents scholar, 1970-74; NIH nursing trainee, 1983-84; grantee U. Hawaii, 1986, 91, Hawaii Dept. Health, 1990. Fellow Internat. Soc. Rsch. on Aggression; mem. AAAS, Am. Ednl. Rsch. Assn., Am. Psychol. Soc., Am. Statis. Assn., Nat. League for Nursing, N.Y. Acad. Scis., Pacific and Asian Affairs Coun., Sigma Theta Tau. Office: U Hawaii Sch Nursing Webster Hall Honolulu HI 96822

FLATTERY, THOMAS LONG, lawyer, legal administrator; b. Detroit, Nov. 14, 1922; s. Thomas J. and Rosemary (Long) F.; m. Gloria M. Hughes, June 10, 1947 (dec.); children: Constance Marie, Carol Dianne Lee, Michael Patrick, Thomas Hughes, Dennis Jerome, Betsy Ann Bagnall; m. Barbara J. Balfour, Oct. 4, 1986. B.S., U.S. Mil. Acad., 1947; J.D., UCLA, 1955; LL.M., U. So. Calif., 1965. Bar: Calif. 1955, U.S. Patent and Trademark Office 1957, U.S. Customs Ct. 1968, U.S. Supreme Ct. 1974, Conn. 1983, N.Y. 1984. With Motor Products Corp., Detroit, 1950, Equitable Life Assurance Soc. Am., Detroit, 1951, Bohn Aluminum & Brass Co.; Bohn Aluminum & Brass Co., Hamtramck, Mich., 1952; mem. legal staff, asst. contract adminstr. Radioplane Co. (div. Northrop Corp.), Van Nuys, Calif., 1955-57; successively corp. counsel, gen. counsel, asst. sec. McCulloch Corp., Los Angeles, 1957-64; sec., corp. counsel Technicolor, Inc., Hollywood, Calif., 1964-70; successively corp. counsel, asst. sec., v.p. sec. and gen. counsel Amcord, Inc., Newport Beach, Calif., 1970-72; v.p., sec., gen. counsel Schick Inc., Los Angeles, 1972-75; counsel, asst. sec. C.F. Braun & Co., Alhambra, Calif., 1975-76; sr. v.p., sec., gen. counsel Automation Industries, Inc. (now PCC Tech. Industries Inc. a unit of Penn Cen. Corp.), Greenwich, Conn., 1976-86; v.p., gen. counsel G&H Tech., Inc. (a unit of Penn Cen. Corp.), Santa Monica, Calif., 1986-93; temp. judge Mcpl. Ct. Calif. L.A. Jud. Dist., 1987—; settlement officer L.A. Superior and Mcpl. Cts., 1991—; panelist Am. Arbitration Assn., 1991—; jud. arbitrator and mediator, jud. adminstrn. program L.A. Superior and Mcpl. Cts., 1993—. Contbr. articles to various legal jours. Served to 1st lt. AUS, 1942-50. Mem. ABA, State Bar Calif. (co-chmn. corp. law dept. com. 1978-79, lectr. continuing legal edn. program), L.A. County Bar Assn. (chmn. corp. law dept. com. 1966-67), Century City Bar Assn. (chmn. corp. law dept. com. 1979-80), Conn. Bar Assn., N.Y. State Bar Assn., Am. Soc. Corp. Secs. (L.A. regional group pres. 1973-74), L.A. Intellectual Property Law Assn., Am. Ednl. League (trustee 1988—), West Point Alumni Assn., Army Athletic Assn., Friendly Sons St. Patrick, Jonathan Club, Braemar Country Club, Phi Alpha Delta. Roman Catholic. Home and Office: 439 Via De La Paz Pacific Palisades CA 90272

FLAXER, CARL, physician; b. Lynn, Mass., Jan. 9, 1918; s. Moses M. and Rose Rachel (Shriberg) F.; m. Evelyn Esther Sachs, Dec. 3, 1944; children: Michael, Susan, Lisa, Lori. BS, Mass. Coll. Pharmacy, 1938; MD, U. Colo., 1950. Pharmacist Johnson Drug, Waltham, Mass., 1938-40, Lovell Gen. Hosp., Ayer, Mass., 1940-42; intern Fitsimons AMC, Denver, 1950-51; pvt. practice family practice Keenesburg, Colo., 1951-70, Denver, 1980-88; dir. family practice residency Mercy Med. Ctr., Denver, 1970-80; edn. chmn. Colo. Acad. Family Physicians, Denver, 1985-90, pres., 1981-82; mem. Gov.'s Adv. Commn. on Family Medicine, Denver, 1972-80. Contbr. chpts. to books: Family Practice, 1978, Critical Care Issues, 1982. Capt. Med. Corps. U.S. Army, 1951-52. Recipient Recognition award for innovative programs Colo. Hosp. Assn., 1976. Fellow Am. Acad. Family Physicians (founding mem.); mem. Colo. State Med. Soc. Home and Office: 890 Hudson St Denver CO 80220-4437

FLECK, JADE CARLSON, literature educator, registered nurse; b. Duluth, Minn., Dec. 4, 1948; d. Carl Adolph Carlson and Joyce Marie (Richeson) Beldin; m. Paul Douglas Fleck, June 25, 1983. AB in English Lit., U. Calif., Berkeley, 1974, PhD in English Lit., 1990; BA in Biblical Studies, Patten Coll., 1978. RN, Minn. Tchr. Patten Acad., Oakland, Calif., 1977-78; tchg. asst. dept. English U. Calif., Berkeley, 1980-81; adj. prof. New Coll., Berkeley, 1992—; com. on spirituality New Coll., Berkeley, 1993—, post-doctoral tutor, 1994; freelance copyeditor, 1994. Author: (chpt.) Reform and Counterreform, 1994. Pres. On Belay, 1991-92. U. Calif. Regents fellow, 1979-80. Mem. MLA, Am. Acad. Religion, Conf. on Christianity and Lit., Internat. Thomas Merton Soc., Soc. Study of Christian Spirituality, Phi Beta Kappa. Presbyterian.

FLECK, RICHARD FRANCIS, English language educator, writer; b. Phila., Aug. 24, 1937; s. J. Keene and Anne M. (DeLeon) F.; m. Maura B. McMahon, June 29, 1963; children: Richard Sean, Michelle Marie, Ann Maureen. BA, Rutgers U., 1959; MA, Colo. State U., 1962; PhD, U. N.Mex., 1970. Park ranger naturalist Rocky Mountain Nat. Pk., Colo., 1959; instr. English North Adams (Mass.) State Coll., 1963-65; prof. of English U. Wyo., Laramie, 1965-90; prof. intercultural studies, dir. humanities div. Teikyo Loretto Heights U., Denver, 1990-93, dir. humanities div., 1991-93; exch. prof. Osaka (Japan) U., 1981-82; vis. prof. SUNY, Cortland, 1988-89; dean arts and humanities C.C. Denver, 1993—. Author: Thoreau and Muir Among the Indians, 1985, Earthen Wayfarer, 1988, Critical Perspectives on Native American Fiction, 1993, (with others) John Muir: His Life and Works, 1993, (with others) World Without Violence: Essays in Honor of the 125th Anniversay of Gandhi's Birth, 1993; asst. editor Sage U. Wyo., 1965-67; editor Thoreau Jour. Quar., 1975-77; contbg. editor Paintbrush, 1986—. Dem. precinct committeman, Laramie, 1968. With USN, 1961-63. Grantee U. Wyo., 1967, 71, Wyo. State Hist. Soc., 1973, Wyo. Humanities Coun., 1979, 80. Mem. Thoreau Soc., Appalachian Mountain Club, Sierra Club. Roman Catholic. Office: CC Denver Office of Dean Arts & Humanities 1111 W Colfax Ave Denver CO 80204-2026

FLEENER, TERRY NOEL, marketing professional; b. Ottumwa, Iowa, May 26, 1939; s. Lowell F. and Freda B. (Sparks) F.; m. Jane A. Bacon, Dec. 9, 1969; children: Clinton Todd, Clayton Scott. BSME, U. Iowa, 1963. Engr. Bendix Corp., Davenport, Iowa, 1963-67, Ball Aerospace, Boulder, Colo., 1967-74; bus. mgr. Ball Aerospace, Boulder, 1974-78; v.p. gen. mgr. Entropy Ltd., Boulder, 1978-80; pres. Energy Bank, Inc., Golden, Colo., 1980-82; program mgr. Ball Aerospace, Boulder, 1982-84, dir. mktg., 1984—; pres. U.S. Rugby Assn., Colorado Springs, 1987-89, Pam-Am. Rugby Assn., Miami, 1991-93. Mem. ASME, AIAA, Am. Astron. Soc., Cryogenic Soc. Am. Office: Ball Aerospace PO Box 1062 Boulder CO 80306-1062

FLEGAL, A(RTHUR) RUSSELL, JR., toxicologist, geochemist, educator; b. Oakland, Calif., Aug. 30, 1946; s. Arthur Russell Sr. and Barbara (Warren) F.; m. Brenda Dolan, Dec. 18, 1970; children: Heather Dolan, John Arthur. BS, U. Calif., Santa Barbara, 1968; MS, Moss Landing (Calif.) Marine Labs., 1976; PhD, Oreg. State U., 1979. Rsch. assoc. Moss Landing Marine Labs., 1981-85; vis. rsch. assoc. Calif. Inst. Tech., Pasadena, 1981-93; assoc. rsch. geochemist U. Calif., Santa Cruz, rsch. geochemist, 1988-92, prof. environ. toxicology, 1992—, assoc. dean natural sci. divsn., 1994—; vis. scientist Swiss Fed. Inst. Tech., Zurich, Switzerland, 1988; assoc. dean natural sci. divsn., 1994—; vis. scientist Lawrence Livermore (Calif.) Nat. Labs., 1988—; mem. com. Nat. Rsch. Coun., Washington, 1989-93, Intergovt. Oceanographic Commn., Paris, 1989—; cons. EPA, Washington, 1989—. Contbr. chpts. to sci. texts, sects. to ency.; contbr. more than 100 articles to profl. jours. Post doctoral fellow Calif. Inst. Tech., 1980, Rsch. fellow, 1980-81. Mem. Am. Chem. Soc., Am. Geophys. Union, Soc. Environ. Toxicology and Chemistry. Office: U Calif Inst Marine Sci Santa Cruz CA 95064

FLEISCHMANN, ERNEST MARTIN, music administrator; b. Frankfurt, Germany, Dec. 7, 1924; came to U.S., 1969; s. Gustav and Antonia (Koch) F.; children: Stephanie, Martin, Jessica. B of Commerce, U. Cape Town, South Africa, 1950, MusB, 1954; postgrad., South African Coll. Music, 1954-56; MusD (hon.), Cleve. Inst. Music, 1987. Gen mgr. London Symphony Orch., 1959-67; dir. Europe CBS Masterworks, 1967-69; exec. dir. L.A. Philharm. Assn. and Hollywood Bowl, 1969-88, exec. v.p., mng. dir., 1988—; mem. French Govt. Commn. Reform of Paris Opera, 1967-68; steering com. U.S. nat. commn. UNESCO Conf. Future of Arts, 1975. Debut as condr. Johannesburg (Republic of South Africa) Symphony Orch., 1942; asst. condr. South African Nat. Opera, 1948-51, Cape Town U. Opera, 1950-54; condr. South African Coll. Music Choir, 1950-52, Labia Grand Opera Co., Cape Town, 1953-55; music organizer Van Riebeeck Festival Cape Town, 1952; dir. music and drama Johannesburg Festival, 1956; contbr. to music publs. Recipient Award of Merit, L.A. Jr. C. of C., John Steinway award, Friends of Music award, Disting. Arts Leadership award U. So. Calif., 1989, L.A. Honors award L.A. Arts Coun., 1989, Live Music award Am. Fedn. Musicians Local 47, 1991, Disting. Authors/Artists award U. Judaism, 1994. Mem. Assn. Calif. Symphony Orchs., Major Orch. Mgrs. Conf., Am. Symphony Orch. League, L.A. Philharm. Assn. (bd. dirs. 1984—), European Mozart Found. (adv. bd.), L.A. Arts Leaders (exec. com.). Office: Los Angeles Philharm Orch 135 N Grand Ave Los Angeles CA 90012-3013

FLEISHMAN, ALAN MICHAEL, marketing consultant; b. Berwick, Pa., June 28, 1939; s. Benjamin Bennet and Ruth (Sadock) F.; m. Ann Arrasmith, Aug. 3, 1963; children: Elizabeth, Gregory, Keith. BA, Dickinson Coll., 1961; postgrad., Xavier U., 1966-67, Calif. State U., Fullerton, 1968-69. Sales and mktg. planning Procter & Gamble, Cin., 1963-67; sr. product mgr. Baxter Internat., Costa Mesa, Calif., 1967-70; dir. mkgt. Allergan, Inc., Irvine, Calif., 1970-76; exec. v.p. Hudson Vitamins, West Caldwell, N.J., 1976-77; v.p. mktg. and sales Cooper Vision, Inc., Mountain View, Calif., 1977-80; pres. Alan M. Fleishman, Mktg. Cons., San Carlos, Calif., 1980—; instr. U. Calif., Berkeley, 1990—. With U.S. Army, 1961-63. Mem. Am. Mktg. Assn., Med. Mktg. Assn. Democrat. Jewish. Home and Office: 3 Bluebell Ln San Carlos CA 94070-1526

FLEMING, JUNE HELENA, city manager; b. Little Rock, June 24, 1931; d. Herman Leroy and Ethel Lucille (Thompson) Dwellingham; m. Silas W. Cullins, June 5, 1956 (div.); m. Roscoe Lee Fleming Jr., Mar. 11, 1966; children: Ethel Lucille, Roscoe Lee III. BA, Talladega Coll., 1953; MLS, Drexel U., 1954. Br. libr. Bklyn. Pub. Libr., 1954-55; high sch. libr. Little Rock Pub. Schs., 1955-56; assoc. prof. Philander Smith Coll., Little Rock, 1960-66; dir. librs. City of Palo Alto, Calif., 1968-79, asst. city mgr., 1980-92, city mgr., 1992—. Mem. adv. bd. YWCA, Palo Alto, 1984—; pres. search com. Foothill Coll., Los Altos Hills, Calif., 1994; mem. allocation com. Santa Clara United Way, San Jose, Calif., 1991-93. Mem. Internat. City Mgrs. Assn., Links, Inc., Rotary (bd. dirs.), Delta Sigma Theta (corr. sec. 1993). Methodist. Home: 27975 Roble Blanco Ct Los Altos Hls CA 94022-2413 Office: City of Palo Alto 250 Hamilton Ave Palo Alto CA 94301-2531

FLEMING, ROBERT EDWARD, English language educator; b. Shullsburg, Wis., Dec. 18, 1936; m. Esther May Bogusch, Feb. 7, 1959; 1 child, Kathleen Maria. BA, No. Ill. U., 1959, MA, 1964; PhD, U. Ill., 1967. Asst. prof. U. N.Mex., Dept. English, Albuquerque, 1967-71, assoc. prof., 1971-76, prof., 1976—, assoc. dean Coll. Arts and Scis., 1988-95; invited lectr. Gorky Inst., Moscow, Russia, 1993. Author: Willard Motley, 1978, Sinclair Lewis: Reference Guide, 1980, James Weldon Johnson, 1987, Face in the Mirror: Hemingway's Writers, 1994. Recipient Summer Rsch. stipend NEH, 1972. Mem. MLA, Western Lit. Assn., Rocky Mountain MLA, Sinclair Lewis Soc. (bd. mem., founder), Ernest Hemingway Found. (bd. mem., treas.). Office: Univ N Mex Dept English 217 Humanities Bldg Albuquerque NM 87131

FLEMMING, NAOMI VERNETA, elementary school educator; b. Las Vegas, Nev., Oct. 13, 1953; d. James Major and Mable Audrey (Mack) F. BS in Edn., U. Nev., 1976. Inventory clk. Woolco Dept. Stor, Las Vegas, 1969; student aide U.S. AEC, Las Vegas, 1971-75; telephone sales person Sears, Roebuck & Co., Las Vegas, 1973-74; clk., typist U.S. Energy, Rsch. and Devel. Adminstrn., Las Vegas, 1975-77; div. sec. U.S. Dept. Energy, Las Vegas, 1977-79; investigator U.S. Office Personnel Mgmt., Las Vegas, 1979-85; employment security specialist State of Nev., Las Vegas, 1988; counselor NutriSystem Weight Loss Ctr., Las Vegas, 1988-89; tchr. Mabel Hoggard Sixth Grade Ctr. (name now to Mabel Hoggard Math & Sci. Magnet Sch.), Las Vegas, 1988—; Title I reading tchr. Mabel Hoggard Math. and Sci. Magnet Sch., 1994—; mem. black history program com. Mabel Hoggard Sch., Las Vegas, 1989-90, student coun. advisor, 1990-91, tchr. liaison Parent Tchr. Student Assn., 1991-92, mem. Martin Luther King Jr. parade com. 1991-92, Just Say No To Drugs Computer Club advisor, 1992-93; Hoggard Magnet sch. lang. arts rep., drill team sponsor, Clark County Sch. Dist. mentor, 1993-94, Hoggard Magnet Sch. Title I reading tchr., 1994—. Mem. Martin Luther King Jr. Parade Com., 1991-92; advisor Just Say No To Drugs Club, 1992-93; chairperson hospitality com. Am. Bus. Women's Assn., 1976-77; mem. women's adv. com. U.S. Energy, R&D Adminstrn., Las Vegas, 1976-78; facilitator, vol. Fully Alive Self-Help Ctr., 1992, 93-94. Mem. Las Vegas Alumnae chpt. Delta Sigma Theta (publicist 1976-78). Democrat. Home: 1220 W Washington Ave Las Vegas NV 89106-3543 Office: Mabel Hoggard Math & Sci Magnet Sch 950 N Tonopah Dr Las Vegas NV 89106-1902

FLEMMING, STANLEY LALIT KUMAR, family practice physician, mayor; b. Rosebud, S.D., Mar. 30, 1953; s. Homer W. and Evelyn C. (Misra) F.; m. Marth Susan Light, July 2, 1977; children: Emily Drisana, Drew Anil, Claire Elizabeth Misra. AAS, Ft. Steilacoom Coll., 1973; BS in Zoology, U. Wash., 1976; MA in Social Psychology, Pacific Luth. U., 1979; DO, Coll. Osteopathic Med. Pacific, 1985. Diplomate Am. Coll. Family Practice; cert. ATLS. Intern Pacific Hosp. Long Beach (Calif.), 1985-86; resident in family practice Pacific Hosp. Long Beach, 1986-88; fellow in adolescent medicine Children's Hosp. L.A., 1988-90; clin. preceptor Family Practice Residency Program Calif. Med. Ctr., U. So. Calif., L.A., 1989—; clin. instr. Sch. Medicine U. So. Calif., L.A., 1989-90; clin. instr. Coll. Osteopathic Medicine Pacific, Pomona, Calif., 1989-90; clin. asst. prof. Family Medicine Coll. Osteopathic Medicine Pacific, Pomona, 1987—; exam. commr., expert examiner Calif. Osteo. Med. Bd., 1987-89; med. dir. Community Health Care Delivery System Pierce County, Tacoma, Wash., 1990—; clin. instr. U. Wash. Sch. Medicine, 1990—; bd. dirs. Calif. State Bd. Osteo. Physicians Examiners, 1989—, cons., 1989. Lt. col. with med. corps U.S. Army, 1976—. Named Outstanding Young Man Am., 1983, 85, Intern of Yr. Coll. Osteo. Medicine of Pacific, 1986, Resident of Yr., 1988, Alumnus of Yr., 1993, Physician of Yr., 1993; recipient Pumerantz-Weiss award, 1985. Mem. Fedn. State Bds. Licensing, Am. Osteopathic Assn., Am. Acad. Family Practice, Soc. Adolescent Medicine, Assn. Military Surgeons U.S., Assn. U.S. Army (chpt. pres.), Soc. Am. Military Engrs. (chpt. v.p.), Calif. Med. Assn., Wash. Osteopathic Med. Assn., Calif. Family Practice Soc., Long Beach Med. Assn. (com. mem.), N.Y. Acad. Sci., Calif. Med. Review Inc., Sigma Sigma Phi, Am. Legion. Episcopalian. Home: 7619 Chambers Creek Rd W Tacoma WA 98467-2015 Office: Community Health Care Delivery System Of Pierce Count Olympia WA 98504

FLETCHER, BETTY B., federal judge; b. Tacoma, Mar. 29, 1923. B.A., Stanford U., 1943; LL.B., U. Wash., 1956. Bar: Wash. 1956. Mem. firm Preston, Thorgrimson, Ellis, Holman & Fletcher, Seattle, 1956-1979; judge U.S. Ct. Appeals (9th cir.), Seattle., 1979—. Mem. ABA (Margaret Brent award 1992), Wash. State Bar Assn., Am. Law Inst., Fed. Judges Assn. (past pres.), Order of Coif, Phi Beta Kappa. Office: US Ct Appeals 9th Cir 1010 5th Ave Seattle WA 98104-1130*

FLETCHER, DONALD WARREN, microbiologist, educator; b. Phoenix, Ariz., June 8, 1929; s. Donald Warren and Ruth Marie Fletcher; children: Lisa, Timothy. BS, Oreg. State U., 1951, MS, 1953; PhD, Wash. State U., 1956. Cert. community coll. tchr., Calif. Instr. Wash. State U., Pullman, 1956-59; asst. prof. San Francisco State U., 1959-62, assoc. prof., 1962-66, prof., 1966-88, prof. emeritus, 1988—; dean coll. liberal arts U. Bridgeport, Conn., 1969-70; assoc. state univ. dean Calif. State U., Long Beach, 1975-88; exec. dir. Ctr. for Advanced Med. Tech., San Francisco, 1966-69, Commn. on Adult Edn. Calif. State U., 1987-88. Author: Microbiology, 1980; contbr. articles to profl. jours. Vice foreman grand jury, 1990-91. Fulbright fellow, 1966, 67; grantee several orgns. Fellow Calif. Acad. Sci., AAAS; mem. Am. Soc. Microbiology, Soc. for Gen. Microbiology, Sigma Xi. Home: 17817 Oriole Ct Penn Valley CA 95946-9678

FLETCHER, DOUGLAS GERALD, research scientist; b. Burlington, Vt., Nov. 15, 1957; s. John Grover Jr. and Marylin Preston (Hinsdale) F.; m. Melissa Lynn Gough, June 4, 1988. BS in Engring., U. Vt., 1979; MSME, U. Va., 1984, PhD in Mech. and Aerospace Engring., 1989. Engr. Vt. Wood Energy Corp., Stowe, 1979-80, Vt. Ski Safety Equipment Corp., Underhill, 1980-81; grad. rsch. asst. dept. mech. and aero. engring. U. Va., 1982-88; rsch. assoc. Aerospace Rsch. Lab. U. Va., Charlottesville, 1988-89; rsch. scientist NASA Ames Rsch. Ctr., Moffett Field, Calif., 1989—; lectr. dept. engring. Stanford (Calif.) U., 1995—; reviewer Optics Letters AIAA Jour., 1990—. Contbr. articles to profl. publs. Mem. AIAA, Optical Soc. Am. Mem. Green Party. Office: NASA Ames Rsch Ctr MS 230-2 Moffett Field CA 94035-1000

FLETCHER, HOMER LEE, librarian; b. Salem, Ind., May 11, 1928; s. Floyd M. and Hazel (Barnett) F.; m. Jacquelyn Ann Blanton, Feb. 7, 1950; children—Deborah Lynn, Randall Brian, David Lee. B.A., Ind. U., 1953; M.S. in L.S, U. Ill., 1954. Librarian Milw. Pub. Library, 1954-56; head librarian Ashland (Ohio) Pub. Library, 1956-59; city librarian Arcadia (Cal.) Pub. Library, 1959-65, Vallejo (Calif.) Pub. Library, 1965-70; city librarian San Jose, Calif., 1970-90, ret., 1990. Contbr. articles to profl. jours. Pres. S. Solano chpt. Calif. Assn. Neurol. Handicapped Children, 1968-69. Served with USAF, 1946-49. Mem. ALA (intellectual freedom com. 1967-72), Calif. Library Assn. (pres. pub. libraries sect. 1967), Dem. Century Club, Phi Beta Kappa. Democrat. Mem. Christian Ch. Disciples of Christ (elder, chmn. congregation 1978-79). Home: 7921 Belknap Dr Cupertino CA 95014-4973

FLETCHER, J. SUE, health educator; b. Hollister, Calif., Aug. 9, 1946; d. James R. and Lois Frances (Fletcher) Prewitt; 1 child, Jeffrey W. Cook. BSN, Calif. State U., Fresno, 1968, MS in Nursing, 1971; EdD, U. San Francisco, 1980. Instr., chmn. div. Modesto (Calif.) Jr. Coll., 1973-83; staff nurse Scenic Gen. Hosp., Modesto, 1983-90; prof. Calif. State U., Stanislaus, Turlock, 1983—. Co-Author: Essentials in Mental Health Nursing, 3d edit. Clerk Mercer City Sch. Dist Bd. Edn.; v.p. Merced County Sch. Bds. Assn. Mem. Calif. Nurses Assn. (pres. region 8 1992-94).

FLETCHER, JAMES ALLEN, video company executive; b. Toledo, Sept. 18, 1947; s. Allen Rae and Ruth Helen (Scharf) F.; m. Kathy Jane Barrett, Jan. 25, 1975. AS, West Coast U., 1977, BSEE, 1979. Electronic technician Hughes Aircraft Co., El Segundo, Calif., 1970-72; engring. technician Altec Corp., Anaheim, Calif., 1972-75, Magna Corp., Santa Fe Springs, Calif., 1975-76; engring. technician Odetics Inc., Anaheim, 1976-79, electronic engr., 1979-86; pres., founder F & B Technologies, Orange, Calif., 1986—. Served as sgt. U.S. Army, 1967-69. Mem. Soc. Motion Picture and TV Engrs., Soc. Cable TV Engrs., Mensa, Bicentennial Club. Libertarian. Office: F & B Technologies 630 N Tustin St Ste 1516 Orange CA 92667-7100

FLETCHER, LELAND VERNON, artist; b. Cumberland, Md., Sept. 18, 1946; s. Kenneth L. and Marjorie L. (Benecke) F.; m. Janis Traub, July 19, 1978; children: Nathan Fletcher, Joshua Traub. BS, U. Minn., 1972. One man shows include U. Minn. Exptl. Gallery, 1972, La Mamelle Art Ctr., San Francisco, 1976, San Jose State U. Union Gallery, 1978, Place des Nations, Maubeuge, France, 1987, Univ. Art Gallery, Calif. State U., Hayward, 1989, McHenry County Coll. Art Gallery, Crystal Lake, Ill., 1991, Lake County Mus., Calif., 1993; group exhbns. include Mus. Contemporary Art, Sao Paulo, Brazil, 1977, Urbanart '77, Vancouver, Can., 1977, Los Angeles Inst. Contemporary Art, 1978, Inst. Modern Art, Brisbane, 1978, Hansen Gallery, N.Y.C., 1978, Fendrick Gallery, Washington, 1979, 8th Internat. Print Bienale, Cracow, Poland, 1980, Cooper-Hewitt Mus., N.Y.C., 1980, Sch. Art Inst. Chgo., 1981, Metronome Gallery, Barcelona, 1981, 16th Bienal de Sao Paulo, 1981, Neue galerie der Stadt Linz, 1982, Bienal de Pontevedra, Spain, 1983, Lyng by Kunstbibliotek, Denmark, 1984, Otis Art Inst./Parsons Sch. Design, Los Angeles, 1984, 10th Internat. Print Bienale, Cracow, Poland, 1984, Mus. Arte da Univ. Fed. de Mato Grosso, Brazil, 1984, 11th Biennal Internat., Mus. Art Contemporani d'Eivissa, Spain, 1984, Intergrafik '84 Triennale, Berlin, Fiatel Muveszek Klubja Budapest, 1985, Intersection Gallery, San Francisco, 1985, Mus. Petit Format, Couvin, Belgium, 1985, 9th British Internat. Print Biennale, Bradford, Eng., 1986, Victoria and Albert Mus., London, 1986, Sculpt 87/3, Maubeuge, 1987, Fundacio la Caixa, Valencia, Spain, 1987, Acad. Belles Arts Sabadell, Barcelona, 1987, Taliesin Ctr. for Arts, Swansea, Eng., 1987, Worcester (Eng.) City Art Gallery, 1987, Symposium Sculpture en Plein Air, Maubeuge, France, 1987, Richards Gallery, Northeastern U., Boston, 1987, Montserrat Coll. Art, Beverly, Mass., 1987, 11 Internat. Print Biennale, Krakow, 1986, Skulptur Biennale '88 Royal Gardens, Copenhagen, Internat. Biennale Palais des Roi de Majorque, Perpignan, France, 1988, Fine Art Mus., Budapest, Hungary, 1988, Works gallery, San Jose Calif., 1988, Palthehuis Mus., Oldenzaal, The Netherlands, 1989, Budapest Galeria, Hungary, 1989, Stedelijk Hoger Institut, Cultural Ctr., Genk, Belgium, 1989, Inst. Contemporary Art, Clocktower Gallery, N.Y.C., 1989, Corporacion GOG, Pontevedra, Spain, 1989, Ea. Washington U., Spokane Ctr. Gallery, 1989, Munson-Williams-Proctor Inst., Sch. Art Gallery, Utica, N.Y., 1989, 44th Salon des Realities Nouvelles, Grand Palais, Paris, 1990, Buda Castle Palace, Budapest, 1990, Pensacola (Fla.) Mus. Art, 1990, Anchorage (Alaska) Mus. Art, 1990, Fundacao Democrito Rocha, Fortaleza, Brazil, 1991, Miejski Osrodek Kultury, Chelm, Poland, 1991, Bharat Bhavan, Bhopal, India, 1991, Chabot Coll., Hayward, Calif., 1992, Lake County Arts Coun., Lakeport, Calif., 1992, Artisans Gallery, Mill Valley, Calif., 1992, Greenville Mus. Art, N.C., Centro Civico Social, Alcorcon, Madrid, 1994, numerous others; represented in permanent collection at Mus. Contemporary Art, Sao Paulo, Mpls. Inst. Arts, Art Mus. of Calif. State U., Long Beach, deSaisset Mus., U. Santa Clara (Calif.), Art Inst. Chgo., Victoria and Albert Mus., London, Museen der Stadt Koln, Ludwig Mus., Cologne, Mus. Plantin-Moretus, Antwerp, Mus. de Arte Moderno, Barcelona, Bradford Mus., Eng., Kunsthalle, Hamburg, Galleria D'Arte Moderna, Trieste, Ecole des Beaux-Arts, Mus. Maubeuge, Musee de la Sculpture en plein Air, Maubeuge, Musee de Maubeuge, FMK Galeria, Budapest, Bur. for Artistic Exhibitions, Cracow, Poland, Kunsthalle Bremen, West Germany, Museu de Arte da Universidad Federal de Mato Grosso, Brazil, others. Address: 3288 Konocti Ln Kelseyville CA 95451-9131

FLETCHER, NORMAN L.S., lawyer, educator; b. Newellton, La., Feb. 17, 1937; s. Arnold Vester and Jimmielee (Almond) F.; m. Ester Wiker, Nov. 23, 1960; children: Katharine, Kimberlee. AB, Calif. State U., 1958; JD, U. Calif., 1967. Fresno County deputy D.A. Dist. Attorney's Office, Fresno, Calif., 1968-70; pvt. practice Fresno, Calif., 1970-79, Fletcher & Fogderude, Fresno, Calif., 1979-94; tchr. Barstow (Calif.) H.S., Coll., 1961-64, San Joaquin Coll. of Law, Fresno, 1975-80, Calif. State U., Fresno, 1987-88. Pres. Fig Garden P.T.A., 1973-74. Mem. Fig Garden Rotary Club (bd. dirs., 1982-84, pres. 1993-94). Republican. Episcopalian. Home: 2746 W Cromwell Ave Fresno CA 93711-0351 Office: Fletcher & Fogderude Inc 5412 N Palm Ave Ste 101 Fresno CA 93704-1943

FLETCHER, ROSE MARIE, mortgage banker, consultant; b. Oakland, Calif., Dec. 8, 1940; d. Martin George Maher and Gertrude Elizabeth (Noe) Maher McCarthy; m. Jamie Franklin Fletcher, Aug. 1, 1960; children: Roberta JoAnne, Rebecca Louise, Jamie Suzanne. Student San Jose State U., 1958-60, West Valley Coll., 1972-76. Lic. real estate broker, Calif. Formerly br. mgr. Sutro Mortgage Co., San Jose, Calif., 3 yrs.; sr. v.p. Unified Mortgage Co., Cupertino, Calif., 1981-85; owner, pres., cons. Processing Place, San Jose, 1985—; dir. ops. Mortgage Loans Am., Campbell, Calif., 1986-88; First Corp. Mortgage Co., 1988-90; cons., lectr., trainer in lending field. Mem. Calif. Assn. Residential Lenders (1st v.p. 1985, pres. 1986, 95), South Bay Assn. Mortgage Brokers (bd. dirs. 1995—), Assn. Profl. Mortgage Women (regional gov. 1980-81, Woman of Yr. 1979). Democrat. Roman Catholic. Avocations: water skiing; swimming; dancing. Home: 3704 Heppner Ln San Jose CA 95136-1505 Office: Pacific Fidelity Mortgage 260 Sheridan Ave Ste 212 Palo Alto CA 94306-2009

FLETTNER, MARIANNE, opera administrator; b. Frankfurt, Germany, Aug. 9, 1933; d. Bernhard J. and Kaethe E. (Halbritter) F. Diploma, Hessel Bus. Coll., 1953. Sec. various cos., 1953-61, Pontiac Motor Div., Burlingame, Calif., 1961-63; sec. Met. Opera, N.Y., 1963-74, asst. co. mgr., 1974-79; artistic adminstr. San Diego Opera, 1979—. Home: 4015 Crown Point Dr San Diego CA 92109-6211 Office: San Diego Opera PO Box 988 San Diego CA 92112-0988

FLICK, WILLIAM FREDRICK, surgeon; b. Lancaster, Pa., Aug. 18, 1940; s. William Joseph and Anna (Volkl) F.; m. Jacqueline Denise Phaneuf, May 21, 1966; children: William J., Karen E., Christopher R., Derrick W., Brian A. BS, Georgetown U., 1962, MD, 1966; MBA, U. Colo., 1990. Cert. Am. Bd. Surgeons, 1976. Self employed surgeon Cheyenne, Wyo., 1973-84; pres., surgeon Cheyenne Surgical Assocs., 1984-94; med. dir. Blue Cross Blue Shield of Wyo., Cheyenne, 1994—. Trustee Laramie County Sch. Dist. #1, Cheyenne, 1988-92. Maj., chief of surgery USAF, 1971-73. Fellow ACS, Southwestern Surg. Congress; mem. Am. Coll. Physician Execs., Nat. Assn. Managed Care. Republican. Roman Catholic. Office: Blue Cross Blue Shield Wyo 400 House Ave Cheyenne WY 82007-1468

FLINN, ROBERTA JEANNE, management, computer applications consultant; b. Twin Falls, Idaho, Dec. 19, 1947; d. Richard H. and Ruth (Johnson) F. Student Colo. State U., 1966-67. Ptnr., Aqua-Star Pools & Spas, Boise, Idaho, 1978—, mng. ptnr., 1981-83; ops. mgr. Polly Pools, Inc., Canby, Oreg., 1983-84, br. mgr. Polly Pools, Inc., A-One Distributing, 1984-85; comptr., Beaverton Printing, Inc., 1986-89; mng. ptnr. Invisible Ink, Canby, Oreg., 1989—. Mem. NAFE, Nat. Appaloosa Horse Club, Oreg. Dressage Soc. (pres. North Willamette Valley chpt.) Republican. Mem. Christian Ch. Home: 24687 S Central Point Rd Canby OR 97013-9743

FLINT, LOU JEAN, state education official; b. Ogden, Utah, July 11, 1934; d. Elmer Blood and Ella D. (Adams) F.; children: Dirk Kershaw Brown, Kristie Susan Brown Felix, Flint Kershaw Brown. B.S., Weber State Coll., 1968; M.Ed., U. Utah, 1974, Ed.S, 1981. Cert. early childhood and elem. edn., Utah Bd. Edn., 1968, edn. adminstrn., 1981. Master tchr. Muir Elem., Davis Sch. Dist., Farmington, Utah, 1968-77; edn. specialist Dist. I, Dept. Def., Eng., Scotland, Norway, Denmark, Holland, Belgium, 1977-79; ednl. cons. Office Higher Edn. State of Utah, Utah System Approach to Individualized Learning, Tex., S.C., Fla., Utah, 1979-81; acad. affairs officer Commn. Higher Edn. Office State of Utah, Salt Lake City, 1982—; mem. Equity Vocat. Edn. Bd., Women's Politics Caucus; adv. bd. Women and Bus. Conf.; mem. single parent employment demonstration project State of Utah, foster care citizen review pilot project State of Utah; pres. elect Utah Mental Health Assn. Named Exemplary Tchr., Utah State Bd. Edn., 1970-77, Outstanding Educator, London Central High Sch., 1979; recipient Appreciation award, Gov. of Utah, 1983-85, 93, Woman of Achievement award Utah Bus. and Profl. Women, 1985, Pathfinder award C. of C., 1988, Outstanding Educator award YWCA, 1989, Silver Apple award Utah State U., 1992. Mem. AAUW (Edn. Found. award given in her honor, 1986, named Woman Who Makes History, 1994), Nat. Assn. Women's Work/Women's Worth (Disting. Woman award 1987), Women's Polit. Caucus (Susa Young Gates award 1987), Nat. Assn. Edn. Young Children, Utah Assn. Edn. Young Children (past pres.), Women Concerned About Nuclear War, Utah Jaycee Aux. (past pres. Centerville), Crones Coun., Math Sci. Network. Mormon. Author: The Comprehensive Community College, 1980; others. Office: State of Utah Office Commr Higher Edn 355 W North Temple # 3 Triad Salt Lake City UT 84180-1114

FLINT, WILLIS WOLFSCHMIDT (WILLI WOLFSCHMIDT), artist; b. Kenton, Ohio, Dec. 27, 1936; s. Wilbur Henry and Ilo Edna (Obenour) F. Student, Art Career Sch., N.Y.C., 1957-60, Ins. Allende, San Miguel Allende, Mexico, 1961. Artist trainee Kossack Advt., Tucson, 1961; gen. boardman Mithoff Advt., El Paso, 1962-63; tech. illustrator Volt Tech. Corp., N.Y.C., 1967; gen. illustrator Salesvertising Advt., Denver, 1968; gen. boardman/cons. Burr-Brown Rsch. Corp., Tucson, 1969-71; musician, actor Paul Barons Harmonica Rascals, Bklyn., 1965-85; musician The Wild Ones, Tucson, 1982-83; muralist, San Diego, Tucson, N.Y.C., 1976-80; artist, Tucson, 1985—; originator Fantasy-Expressionism, 1984; pvt. tchr. art, Tucson, 1981-85; cons. muralist Yaqui Indian-Pascua Ctr., Tucson, 1989; freelance muralist and graphic artist Wolfschmidt & Washburn, 1994—. Author: (poetry) Best-Loved Contemporary Poems, 1979, Famous Poems of Today, 1995; contbr. poetry to local newspapers; paintings exhibited in group shows at United Way Fund Drive Exhibit, Tucson, United Servicemen's Orgn. Exhibit, Mobile, Ala., Student Union Exhibit U. Ariz., Tucson, La Galeria Instituto, San Miguel de Allende, Margarita De Mena Gallery, N.Y.C.; represented in permanent collections Mr. and Mrs. Charles Hernandez, Queens, N.Y., Mr. and Mrs. Peter Greco, Catskill, N.Y., So. Ariz. Hist. Soc., Tombstone, Ariz. With USN, 1954-57, 1979-81. Recipient scholarship Latham Found., 1958, award of merit Latham Found., 1958, letter commendation U. Ariz. Family Practice, Tucson, 1978, letter commendation Dept. Navy, San Diego, 1979. Mem. The Maverick Artists, Internat. Platform Assn. Home: 707 W Calle Progreso Tucson AZ 85705

FLOCK, ROBERT ASHBY, retired entomologist; b. Kellogg, Idaho, July 16, 1914; s. Abraham Lincoln and Florence Louise (Ashby) F.; m. Elsie Marie Ronken, Apr. 8, 1950; children: Karen Marie, Anne Louise Checkai. BS, U. Ariz., 1938, MS, 1941; PhD, U. Calif., Berkeley, 1951. Inspector Ariz. Commn. Agriculture and Horticulture, Phoenix, 1938-41, asst. entomologist, 1941-46; lab. tech. U. Calif., Riverside, 1947-52, asst. entomologist, 1952-63; entomologist Imperial County Dept. Agriculture, El Centro, Calif., 1963-85, part-time entomologist, 1985—. Contbr. articles to profl. jours. Mem. Entomol. Soc. Am., Am. Phytopathol. Soc., Pan-Pacific Entomol. Soc., AAAS, Ctr. for Process Studies, Kiwanis (pres. Imperial Valley chpt. 1984-86, Man of Yr. 1986), Sigma Xi. Republican. Methodist. Home: 667 Wensley Ave PO Box 995 El Centro CA 92244 Office: Imperial County Dept Agricu 150 S 9th St El Centro CA 92243-2801

FLOM, ROBERT MICHAEL, interior designer; b. Grand Forks, N.D., Oct. 27, 1952; s. John Nicholai and Irene Magdaline (Miller) F.; m. Holly Suzanne Schue, July 20, 1975 (div. June 1986); m. Margaret Elizabeth Moon, Oct. 15, 1988; children: Amy Michelle Moon, Jamie Bryant Moon. Student, Western Tech., 1970-71, U. N.D., 1980-83, LaSalle U., 1994-95. Asst. food and beverage mgr. Holiday Inn/Topeka Inns, Denver, 1970-71; interior designer, fl. mgr. Crossroads Furniture, Grand Forks, 1972-85; store mgr. Greenbaums, Tacoma, 1986-88, interior designer, 1986—; tng. advisor Greenbaums, Bellevue, Wash., 1988—. Mem. Am. Soc. Interior Designers (allied mem.), Autism Soc. Tacoma-Pierce County (treas. 1991—). Home: 6816 47th St W Tacoma WA 98466-4912 Office: Greenbaums 929 118th Ave SE Bellevue WA 98005-3855

FLOOD, JAMES TYRRELL, broadcasting executive, public relations consultant; b. Los Angeles, Oct. 5, 1934; s. James Joseph and Teresa (Rielly) F.; m. Bonnie Carolyn Lutz, Mar. 25, 1966; children: Hilary C., Sean L. BA in Liberal Arts, U. Calif., Santa Barbara, 1956; MA in Communications, Calif. State U., Chico, 1981. Publicist Rogers & Cowan, 1959-60, Jim Mahoney & Assocs., 1960-61, ABC-TV, San Francisco and Hollywood, Calif., 1961-64; cons. pub. relations, Beverly Hills, Calif., 1964-72; pub. relations, advt. dir. Jerry Lewis Films, 1964-72; dir. pub. rels. MTM Prodns., 1970-72; pub. relations cons. Medic Alert Found. Internat., 1976-83; owner, mgr. Sta. KRIJ-FM, Paradise, 1983-88; instr. Calif. State U. Sch. Communications, Chico, 1982-89; gen. mgr. KIXE-TV (PBS), Redding-Chico, Calif., 1991-92; media cons., 1993—. represented numerous artists including Pearl Bailey, Gary Owens, Ruth Buzzi, Allen Ludden, Betty White, Celeste Holm, Jose Feliciano, Tom Kennedy, Shirley Jones, David Cassidy, others. Pub. rels. dir. Mary Tyler Moore Prodns., 1971. Calif. media cons. Carter/Mondale campaign, 1976; mem. Calif. Dem. Fin. Com., 1982-83. Served with USNR, 1956-58. Mem. Calif. Broadcasters Assn. (bd. dirs. 1986-88).

FLOOD, SHEILA THERESA, physical therapist; b. Spokane, Wash., Jan. 23, 1958; d. Seymour Allen and Vera Rose (Peck) F.; m. Scott Lewis Kerber, Apr. 20, 1991. BS, U. Puget Sound, 1982. Phys. therapy aide Pk. Rose Care Ctr., Tacoma, 1982-83; phys. therapist Desert Hosp., Palm Springs, Calif., 1983-85, sr. phys. therapist, 1986-94; ind. contractor home health Cathedral City, Calif., 1994—, mktg. com. for rehab. svcs. Desert Hosp., Palm Springs, 1991-93, pre-operative teaching, 1991—. Named Employee of Month, Desert Hosp., 1987. Mem. AAUW (treas. 1984-89, v.p. membership 1989-91). Methodist. Home: 68-555 Los Gatos Rd Cathedral City CA 92234-8101

FLOR, LOY LORENZ, chemist, corrosion engineer, consultant; b. Luther, Okla., Apr. 25, 1919; s. Alfred Charles and Nellie M. (Wilkinson) F.; BA in Chemistry, San Diego State Coll., 1941; m. Virginia Louise Pace, Oct. 1, 1946; children: Charles R., Scott R., Gerald C., Donna Jeanne, Cynthia Gail. With Helix Water Dist., La Mesa, Calif., 1947-84, chief chemist, 1963—, supr. water quality, 1963—, supr. corrosion control dept., 1956—. 1st. lt. USAAF, 1941-45. Registered profl. engr., Calif. Mem. Am. Chem. Soc. (chmn. San Diego sect. 1965—), Am. Water Works Assn. (chmn. water quality div. Calif. sect. 1965—), Nat. Assn. Corrosion Engrs. (chmn. western region 1970), Masons. Republican. Presbyterian.

FLORA, MARY ELLEN, bishop; b. Martinsville, Va., Sept. 19, 1944; d. Paul Haden and Vivian Aston (Riggle) F.; m. Charles Richard Eckel, June 1966 (div. 1976); m. F. Slusher, Mar. 3, 1977. BA in Sociology, Queens Coll., 1966; postgrad., Oreg. State U., 1969-70. Ordained to ministry, Ch. of Divine Man, 1976. Youth program coord. Mission Dist. YMCA, San Francisco, 1966-68; pre-kindergarten tchr. Oakland (Calif.) Sch. Sys., 1968-69; jr. and sr. H.S. tchr. Singapore-Am., 1971-72; real estate speculator Oakland, Calif., 1973-76; min., bishop, tchr. Ch. of Divine Man, Everett, Wash., 1976—; co-founder Ch. of Divine Man, Seattle, Everett, Tacoma, Spokane, Bellingham, Wash., Portland, Oreg., Vancouver, B.C., Can.; vice chmn. bd. dirs., Ch. of Divine Man, 1977—. Author: Meditation: Key to Spiritual Awakening, 1991, Healing: Key to Spiritual Balance, 1992, Claivoyance: Key to Spiritual Perspective, 1992, Chakras: Key to Spiritual Opening, 1993, Cosmic Energy: The Creative Power, 1995. Del. YMCA World Youth Conf. Va. YMCA, Hilversom, Holland, 1960; scholarship Queens Coll., 1964-65, DANA scholar, 1966. Office: Ch of Divine Man 2402 Summit Ave Everett WA 98201-3256

FLORENCE, ALFRED WILLIAM, computer engineer; b. Las Vegas, N.Mex.; s. Alfonso Frank and Cora Margret (Paiz) F.; m. Harumi Uchida; children: Bryan, Daniel. BS in Math., Physics, U. N.Mex.; postgrad., UCLA, U. So. Calif. Geophysicist Shell Oil Co., L.A., 1967-68; software engr. Quotron Systems, Culver City, Calif., 1972-74, TRW, Manhattan Beach, Calif., 1974-78; supr., engr. Hughes Aircraft, El Segundo, Calif., 1968-72, 78-79; mgr., engr. Martin Marietta, Denver, 1979-92; software engring. mgr. BDM, Boulder, Colo., 1993; cons., pres. Florence Internat. Corp., Denver, 1993—. Home: 26 Dutch Creek Dr Littleton CO 80123-6502

FLORENCE, KENNETH JAMES, lawyer; b. Hanford, Calif., July 31, 1943; s. Ivy Owen and Louella (Dobson) F.; m. Verena Magdalena Demuth, Dec. 10, 1967. BA, Whittier Coll., 1965; JD, Hastings Coll. Law, U. Calif.-San Francisco, 1974. Bar: Calif. 1974, U.S. Dist. Ct. (cen. dist.) Calif. 1974, U.S. Dist. Ct. (ea. and so. dists.) Calif., 1976, U.S. Dist. Ct. (no. dist.) Calif. 1980, U.S. Ct. Appeals (9th cir.) 1975, U.S. Supreme Ct. 1984. Dist. mgr. Pacific T&T, Calif., 1969-71; assoc. Parker, Milliken, et al, Los Angeles, 1974-78; ptnr. Dern, Mason, et al, 1978-84, Swerdlow, Florence & Sanchez, A Law Corp., Beverly Hills, 1984—; pres. Westside Legal Services, Inc., Santa Monica, Calif., 1982-83. Served to lt. USNR, 1966-69, Vietnam. Col. J.G. Boswell scholar, 1961. Mem. ABA (co-chmn. state labor law com. 1988-91). Democrat. Home: 1063 Stradella Rd Los Angeles CA 90077-2607 Office: Swerdlow Florence & Sanchez 9401 Wilshire Blvd Ste 828 Beverly Hills CA 90212-2921

FLORENCE, VERENA MAGDALENA, small business owner; b. Interlaken, Switzerland, Nov. 4, 1946; came to U.S., 1967; d. Paul Robert and Marie (Raess) Demuth; m. Kenneth James Florence, Dec. 10, 1967. BA, U. Calif., Berkeley, 1974; MS, UCLA, 1979, PhD, 1982. Research scientist Procter & Gamble, Cin., 1983; adminstr. Swerdlow & Florence, Beverly Hills, Calif., 1984-89; pres., chief exec. officer, chmn. of bd. Böl Designs, Inc., L.A., 1989—. Contbr. articles to profl. jours. Mem. L.A. Computer Soc. (SIG leader). Democrat. Home and Office: 1063 Stradella Rd Los Angeles CA 90077-2607

FLORES, DAN LOUIE, history educator; b. Vivian, La., Oct. 19, 1948; s. Willie Clyde Jr. and Margaret Kathryn (Hale) F. BA, Northwestern State U., Natchitoches, La., 1971; MA, Northwestern State U., 1972; PhD, Tex. A&M U., 1978. Instr., history Northwestern State U., 1971-72; teaching asst. Tex. A&M U., College Station, 1974-78; vis. asst. prof. Tex. Tech. U., Lubbock, 1978-80, asst. prof., 1980-84, assoc. prof., 1984-90, prof., history, 1990-92; vis. prof. U. Wyo., Laramie, 1986; A.B. Hammond chair in western history U. Mont., Missoula, 1992—. Author: Jefferson and Southwestern Exploration, 1984 (Best Book on the West, Westerners' Internat., Best Book on Tex., Tex. State Hist. Assn.), Journal of an Indian Trader, 1985, Canyon Visions, 1989, Caprock Canyon Lands, 1990, The Mississippi Kite, 1993. Recipient NEH summer rsch. grant, 1983, Eugene Barker prize (for an article) U.Tex.-Arlington, 1978. Fellow Tex. State Hist. Assn. (Tullis prize for best article 1985); mem. Am. Assn. for Environ. History, Western History Assn. (Ray A. Billington prize for best article 1985), Ethnohistory Assn. Office: Dept History U Montana Missoula MT 59812

FLORES, GEORGE RAYMOND, county health officer; b. L.A., Oct. 10, 1949; s. Michael John and Carmen (Acebo) F.; m. Sonja Ludwell, Feb. 24, 1968; children: Matthew Dominic, Simone Nicole. AA, L.A. City Coll., 1976; BA, Calif. State U., L.A., 1973; MD, Utah Coll. Medicine, Salt Lake City, 1977; MPH, Harvard U., 1977. Resident in family practice U. Utah McKay Dee Hosp., Ogden, 1977-80; with USPHS, Nipomo, New Cuyama, Calif., 1980; dep. health officer County of Santa Barbara, Calif., 1981-87; program dir. Project HOPE, Guatemala, 1987-89; pub. health officer County of Sonoma, Calif., 1989—; state and local program Kennedy Sch. of Govt., Harvard U., 1992; co-chair Latino Coalition for a Healthy Calif., 1992; asst. prof. U. Calif. Sch. Medicine, San Francisco. Scholar Nat. Pub. Health Leadership Inst., 1994—. Mem. Calif. Conf. Local Health Officers (pres.-elect 1994-95). Home: 3249 Cobblestone Dr Santa Rosa CA 95404-1744 Office: Sonoma County Health Dept 3313 Chanate Rd Santa Rosa CA 95404-1707

FLORES, JOHN A., internist; b. Indio, Calif., Jan. 17, 1957; m. Gladys Dolores Flores; children: Angelina, Jacob, Matthew, Marisa, Lauren. BS in Biochemistry, U. Calif., Riverside, 1980, MS in Biochemistry, 1981; MD, U. Minn., 1986. Intern internal medicine San Fernando Valley Program UCLA, 1986-87, resident internal medicine San Fernando Valley Program, 1988-90; resident anesthesiology U. Kans. Med. Ctr., 1987-88; dir. Pain Mgmt. Clinic Beaver Med. Clinic, Redlands, Calif., 1990—, physician internal medicine, 1990—; mem. active staff Redlands Community Hosp., 1990—; instr. advanced coronary life support cert. San Fernando Valley program UCLA, 1988-89; mentor sci. ednl. enhancement svcs. health profl. mentor program Calif. Poly. State U., 1991—; preceptor med. student edn. Osteo. Sch. Medicine Coll. of Pacific, 1993-94; lectr. Med. Sch. U. Minn., 1982-84, San Fernando Valley program UCLA, 1988-89, Beaver Med. Clinic, 1992, Calif. Poly. State U., Pomona, 1992, Redlands Com. Hosp., 1994. Recipient Appreciation award Chicano/Latino Pre-Med. Student Assn. Calif. Poly State U., 1993, Appreciation award Beverly Manor Convalescent, 1993, Recognition award Coll. Osteopathic Medicine Pacific, 1993—. Mem. AMA, ACP (assoc.), Am. soc. Anesthesiologists, Am. Soc. Pain Mgmt., Am. Soc. Regional Anesthesia, Calif. Med. Assn. (alt. del. for San Bernardino County Med. Soc. 1993-94, tech. adv. com. on pain mgmt. 1994—), San Bernardino County Med. Soc. (young physicians com. 1992—, chmn. 1993—, exec. com. 1993—), Redlands C. of C. Home: 2 W Fern Ave Redlands CA 92373-5916

FLORES, ROMEO M., geologist, researcher; b. San Fernando, La Union, The Philippines, Apr. 28, 1939; came to U.S., 1960; s. Serapio C. and Gelacia M. Flores; divorced; 1 child, Alejandro N. BS in Geology, U. The Philippines, 1959; Ms in Geology, U. Tulsa, 1962; PhD in Geology, La. State U., 1966. Geologist White Eagle Oil Co., Manila, 1959-60; rsch. petrologist Amoco Rsch. Ctr., Tulsa, 1963; petroleum geologist Amoco Prodn. Co., New Orleans, 1964; asst. prof. to full prof. Sul Ross State U., Alpine, Tex., 1966-75, chmn. dept. geology, 1967-75, rsch. geologist U.S. Geol. Survey, Denver, 1975—; adj. prof. Colo. State U., Fort Collins, 1982—, N.C. State U., Raleigh, 1980—. Contbr. numerous articles to profl. jours. Fellow Geol. Soc. Am.; mem. Soc. Econ. Paleontologists and Mineralogists (Best Paper awards 1984, 90, 91), Am. Assn. Petroleum Geologists. Office: US Geol Survey MS 972 PO Box 25046 Denver CO 80225-0046

FLORES, THOMAS R., professional football team executive; b. Fresno, Calif., Mar. 21, 1937; s. Tom C. and Nellie (Padilla) F.; m. Barbara Ann Fridell, Mar. 25, 1961; children: Mark and Scott (twins), Kim. BA, Coll. Pacific, 1959; hon. doctorate, Pepperdine U. Quarterback Oakland Raiders, 1960-66; quarterback Buffalo Bills, 1967-68, Kansas City (Mo.) Chiefs, 1969-70; asst. coach Oakland (now Los Angeles) Raiders, 1972-78, head coach, from 1979; gen. mgr. Seattle Seahawks, 1989-91; past pres. Seahawks, head coach, now also gen. mgr., 1992—; player rep. AFL, 1966-68. Nat. hon. chmn. Lung Assn. Named Man of Yr. No. Calif. Lung Assn., 1979; Latino of Yr. City of Los Angeles, 1981. Democrat. Roman Catholic. Office: Seattle Seahawks 11220 NE 53rd St Kirkland WA 98033-7505*

FLORES, WILLIAM VINCENT, Latin American studies educator; b. San Diego, Jan. 10, 1948; s. William J. and Velia (Aldrete) F.; m. Carole Mary Dische, July 3, 1973 (div. Jan 1986); children: Antonio Ramon, Diana Maria. BA, UCLA, 1970; MA in Polit. Sci., Stanford U., 1971, PhD in Social Theory/Pub. Policy, 1987. Teaching & rsch. fellow Stanford (Calif.) U., 1971-72; lectr. in polit. sci. Calif. State U., Hayward, 1972-75; program coord. Project Intercept, San Jose, Calif., 1976-78; assoc. dir. Gardner Cmty. Health Ctr., San Jose, 1979-84; lectr. U. Santa Clara, Calif., 1985-87; asst. dir. Inter-Univ. Program for Latino Rsch., Stanford, 1987-88; chair dept. Chicano/Latin Am. studies Calif. State U., Fresno, 1988-92, assoc. dean Sch. of Social Scis., 1992-94. Mem. exec. com. Chicano/Latino Faculty Assn. Calif. State Univ. Sys., 1994—; chair Com. for Hispanic Ednl. Equity, Fresno, 1990-92; mem. nat. adv. bd. U.S. Students Assn., Washington, 1991-93; v.p. Latino Agenda Coalition Calif., L.A., 1984-86. Chicano Fellows Program fellow Stanford U., 1971-72; Ford Found. fellow Stanford U., 1970-74; Compton-Danforth fellow Stanford U., 1984-85.; Rockefeller Humanities fellow, 1993-94; Am. Coun. on Edn. fellow, 1993-94. Mem. Am. Anthropol. Assn., Am. Studies Assn., Nat. Assn. Chicano Studies (co-chair polit. action com. 1986), Internat. Platform Assn. Democrat. Office: Office of the Dean Sch Social Scis Fresno CA 93740-0091

FLOREY, JERRY JAY, aerospace company executive, consultant; b. Geddes, S.D., Apr. 3, 1932; s. Henry Clifford and Lizzie M. Florey; m. Mary E. Richey, Sept. 17, 1955; children: Glen David, Janet Renee. BSChemE, Oreg. State U., 1955. Cert. in electronics. From research engr. to engring. supr. Rockwell Internat., Canoga Park, Calif., 1955-66; sr. project engr. Rockwell Internat., Downey, Calif., 1966-67; successively engring. mgr., engring. dir., chief engr. Rockwell Internat., Seal Beach, Calif., 1967-85, dir. advanced systems, rsch. and tech., 1985-89; sr. staff mgr. strategic planning and market analysis McDonnell Douglas Space Co., Huntington Beach, Calif., 1989-95; propulsion systems cons., 1995—; participant on several industry workshop panels which advised USAF regarding its mil. space systems tech. planning activities. Scoutmaster Boy Scouts Am., Costa Mesa, Calif., 1970; mem. Republican Presdl. Task Force; del. at large Rep. Platform planning com. Recipient NASA Cert. Appreciation Marshall Space Flight Ctr., Huntsville, Ala., 1972, Astronaut Person Achievement award NASA, 1969, Skylab Achievement award NASA, 1973, AIAA and USAF Recognition of Svc. certs. AFSTC, 1985. Fellow AIAA (assoc., bd. dirs., nat. space and missile systems tech. activities com.); mem. Nat. Mgmt. Assn., Nat. Mktg. Soc. Am., U.S. Space Found. Home: 2085 Goldeneye Pl Costa Mesa CA 92626-4770

FLOSS, HEINZ G., chemistry educator, scientist; b. Berlin, Aug. 28, 1934; s. Friedrich and Annemarie F.; m. Inge Sauberlich, July 17, 1956; children: Christine, Peter, Helmut, Hanna. B.S. in Chemistry, Technische Universitat, Berlin, 1956, M.S. in Organic Chemistry, 1959; Dr. rer. nat. in Organic Chemistry, Technische Hochschule, Munich, W. Ger., 1961, Dr. habil. in Biochemistry, 1966; D.Sc. (hon.), Purdue U., 1986. Hilfsassistent Technische Universitat, Berlin, 1958-59; hilfsassistent Technische Hochschule, Munich, 1959-61; wissenschaftlicher asst. and dozent Technische Hochschule, 1961-66; on leave of absence at dept. biochemistry and biophysics U. Calif.-Davis, 1964-65; assoc. prof. Purdue U., 1966-69, prof., 1969-77, Lilly Disting. prof., 1977-82, head dept. medicinal chemistry, 1968-69, 74-79; prof. chemistry Ohio State U., Columbus, 1982-87, chmn. dept. chemistry, 1982-86; prof. chemistry U. Wash., Seattle, 1987—, adj. prof. biochemistry medicinal chemistry and microbiology, 1988—; vis. scientist ETH Zurich, 1970; vis. prof. Tech. U. Munich, 1980, 86, 95; mem. bio-organic and natural products study sect. NIH, 1989-93. Mem. editorial bd. Lloydia-Jour. Natural Products, 1971—, BBP-Biochemie und Physiologie der Pflanzen, 1971-84, Applied and Environ. Microbiology, 1974-84, Planta Medica, 1978-83, Jour. Medicinal Chemistry, 1979-83, Applied Microbiology and Biotech., 1984-88, Jour. Basic Microbiology, 1989—. Recipient Lederle faculty award, 1967, Mead Johnson Undergrad. Rsch. award, 1968, rsch. career and devel. award USPHS, 1969-74, Volwiler award, 1979, Humboldt sr. scientist, 1980, Newby-McCoy award 1981, award in microbial chemistry Kitasato Inst. and Kitasato U., 1988. Fellow Acad. Pharm. Scis. (Research Achievement award in natural products 1976), AAAS; mem. Am. Chem. Soc., Am. Soc. Biol. Chemists, Am. Soc. Microbiology, Am. Soc. Pharmacognosy (Rsch. award 1988), Phytochem. Soc. N.Am., Sigma Xi (Faculty Research award 1976). Home: 5609 145th Ave SE Bellevue WA 98006-4381 Office: Univ Wash Dept Chemistry Box 351700 Seattle WA 98195-1700

FLOWER, RENÉE BEVILLE, artist; b. Chgo., Oct. 22, 1950; d. Milton Oliver and Doris Lea (Beville) F.; m. Victor Allan Spiegel, June 22, 1975 (div. June 1981); m. James Anderson MacKenzie, July 31, 1982. BA in Studio Art, U. Calif., Santa Cruz, 1979. lectr. in field. Ilustrator: (books) The Complete Sylvie & Bruno, 1991, City Noise, 1994; one-woman shows include Eloise Pickard Smith Gallery, 1993; exhibited in group shows at Ste 311, Pacific Grove, 1985, Zaner Gallery, Rochester, N.Y., 1986, San Francisco Mus. Modern Art Rental Gallery, 1987, The Art Mus. Santa Cruz County, 1988, Christopher Grimes Gallery, Carmel, 1989, Susan Cummins Gallery, Mill Valley, Calif., 1990, One Market Plaza, San Francisco, 1991, Gallery 500, Elkins Park, Pa., 1992, and others.

FLOWERS, ROBERT SWAIM, medical educator, surgeon; b. Greenville, Ala., Sept. 13, 1934; children: Swain, Rob, Christian, Jonathan. BS in Chemistry and Biology, U. Ala., 1955, MD, 1960. Diplomate Am. Bd. Plastic Surgery. Intern U.S. Army Tripler Med. Ctr., 1960-61; battle group surgeon U.S. Army, 1961-63; resident gen. surgery Cleve. (Ohio) Clinic, 1963-66, resident plastic surgery, 1966-68; chmn. plastic surgery sect. Straub Clinic, Honolulu, 1968-72; chmn. dept. plastic surgery Queen's Med. Ctr., Honolulu, 1972-74; asst. clinical prof. plastic surgery U. Hawaii, 1971—; dir., prin. surgeon Plastic Surgery Ctr. of the Pacific Inc., Honolulu, 1975-93, chief, dir. Hawaii Fellowship Program for Aesthetic Surgery; co-founder Gender Identity Clinic of Hawaii U., Hawaii; on staff Queen's Med. Ctr., Honolulu, Kapiolani Children's Med. Ctr., Honolulu; vis. prof. and lectr. U. Miami, 1975, U. Calif., 1976, Stanford U., 1977, 78, 94, Emory U., 1976, U. Zagreb, Yugoslavia, 1977, U. Munich, Germany, 1979, Columbia Presbyn. U., 1983, Duke U., 1985, 86, Cleve. Clinic, 1985, UCLA, 1987, U. Louisville, 1988, 90, U. Ala., 1990, Saarland U., Germany, 1993, U. Colo., 1994, U. Toronto, 1995 and numerous others. Author (with others): Clinics in Plastic Surgery, 1977, 87, 91, Aesthetic Contouring of the Craniofacial Skeleton, 1991, Male Aesthetic Surgery, 1981, Aesthetic Breast Surgery, 1983, Cosmetic Surgery in the Oriental, 1988, Principals of Dermatologic Surgery, 1989, Aesthetic Rhinoplasty, 1993, Aesthetic Plastic Surgery, 1993 and numerous others; Contbd. numerous articles to profl. jours. Pres. congregation and ch. coun. Calvary By The Sea Luth. Ch., Honolulu, 1971-72, 77-78, 78-79, choir dir. 1969-70, 76-77, soloist 1969—, liturgist and lay minister, 1969—; bd. dirs. Honolulu Symphony, 1986-88, Friends of Ballet, 1986. Fellow Am. Coll. Surgeons; mem. AMA, Ala. Med. Soc., Am. Assn. Plastic Surgeons, Am. Soc. Plastic Surgeons, Asian Soc. of Aesthetics Plastic Surgery for Orientals (hon. founding mem.), Australasian Soc. of Aesthetics Plastic Surgery (hon. mem.), Calif. Soc. Plastic Surgeons, Can. Soc. Aesthetic Plastic Surgeons, Hawaii Med. Assn., Hawaii Plastic Surgical Socs. (co-founder), Honolulu County Med. Soc. (bd. govs. 1990-94), Internat. Soc. Aesthetic Plastic Surgeons, Internat. Soc. Clinical Plastic Surgeons, Northwest Soc. Plastic Surgeons (hon. mem.), Pan-Pacific Surgical Assn., Southeastern Soc. Plastic Surgeons (hon. mem.); Outrigger Canoe Club, Waikiki Yacht Club, The Honolulu Club. Home: 219 Paiko Dr Honolulu HI 96821 Office: Plastic Surgery Ctr of the Pacific 677 Ala Moana Blvd Ste 1011 Honolulu HI 96813-5418

FLOYD, BARBARA IRENE, newspaper editor-in-chief; b. Breckenridge, Minn., Sept. 17, 1939; d. Harry Jesse and Eugenia Elizabeth (Kirschner) Wheeler; m. Robert D. Floyd, Dec. 26, 1962; children: Brenda Swanson, Barbra-Jean Skaleberg, Bobbi-Jo, Brook. AS, N.D. State Sch. Sci., 1959; BS, Moorhead State Coll., 1961. Tchr. Columbia Heights (Minn.) H.S., 1961-63, Prescott (Ariz.) Jr. H.S., 1963-65; owner The Country Goose, Phoenix, 1983-89; editor, owner The Country Register, Phoenix, 1988-94; owner The Country Register Cafe & Tea Rm., Kennewick, Wa., 1994—; owner, tchr. B&B Ceramic Studio, Prescott, 1963-65; owner Gooseberries Tea Room, Phoenix, 1989-91. Author, editor: The Country Register Collections Cookbook, 1993. Troop leader Girl Scouts U.S., Phoenix, 1970-73; ways and means chmn. Lookout Mountain Sch. PTA, Phoenix, 1976-77. Office: The Country Register PO Box 84342 Phoenix AZ 85071-4342

FLOYD, BRETT ALDEN, mortgage banker, consultant; b. Las Vegas, Nev., Nov. 12, 1963. Branch mgr. Transamerica Fin., West Covina, Calif., 1984-89, Assocs. Fin., San Gabriel, Calif., 1989; area sales mgr. Long Beach Bank, F.S.B., Woodland Hills, Calif., 1989-94; divsn. mgr. Royal Thrift & Loan Co., L.A., 1994—; cons. Sunwest Cons., L.A., 1990—. Assoc. Ctl. Com., L.A., 1992. Republican. Home: 2747 Beldon Dr Hollywood Hills CA 90068 Office: Royal Thrift & Loan Co 11107 W Olympic Blvd Los Angeles CA 90064-1805

FLOYD, MARGUERITE MARIE (MAITA FLOYD), publisher; b. St. Jean de Luz, France, Aug. 10, 1924; came to U.S., 1946; d. Jean Louis Branquet and Felicie Ibarrart; m. Willard C. Floyd, May 1968 (dec. Sept. 1985). Cert., Mlle. Suertegaray, Hendaye, 1937; postgrad., Ste Bernadette, Pau, 1940, Ariz. State U., Tempe, 1967, Maricopa Tech., 1975-76, So. Mountain Community Coll., 1989. Customer svc. Trans World Airlines, N.Y., 1952-62; agt. Phoenix, 1962-82; pub., pres. Eskualdum Pubs., Phoenix, 1982—; lectr. caregiving, bereavement and domestic violence. Author and illustrator: Caretakers, The Forgotten People, 1988, 89, 90, Platitudes, You are Not Me!, 1991; author: Don't Shoot! My Life is Valuable, 1993; various appearances on TV, radio; lectr. Vol. Hospice Bereavement, Phoenix, 1987, victim adv. vol. Maricopa County Dist. Atty.; mem. Gov. of Ariz. Commn. Violence Against Women Task Force. Mem. Am. Bus. Women's Assn., Profl. Women in Sales, Ariz. Book Pubs. Assn., Ahwatukee Entertainers. Democrat. Roman Catholic. Home: 4749 E Ahwatukee Dr Phoenix AZ 85044-2033 Office: Eskualdun Pubs PO Box 50266 Phoenix AZ 85076-0266

FLUKE, LYLA SCHRAM (MRS. JOHN M. FLUKE), publisher; b. Maddock, N.D.; d. Olaf John and Anne Marie (Rodberg) Schram; m. John M. Fluke, June 5, 1937; children: Virginia Fluke Gabelein, John M. Jr., David Lynd. BS in Zoology and Physiology, U. Wash., Seattle, 1934, diploma teaching, 1935. High sch. tchr., 1935-37; tutor Seattle schs., 1974-75; pub. Portage Quar. mag., Hist. Soc. Seattle and King County, 1980-84. Author articles on history. Founder N.W. chpt. Myasthenia Gravis Found., 1953, pres., 60-66; obtained N.W. artifacts for destroyer Tender Puget Sound, 1966; mem. Seattle Mayor's Com. for Seattle Beautiful, 1968-69; sponsor Seattle World's Fair, 1962; charter mem. Seattle Youth Symphony Aux., 1974; bd. dirs. Cascade Symphony, Salvation Army, 1985-87; benefactor U. Wash., 1982-88, nat. chmn. ann. giving campaign, 1983-84; benefactor Sterling Circle Stanford U., MIT, 1984, Wash. State Hist. Soc., Pacific Arts Ctr.; mem. condr.'s club Seattle Symphony, 1978—. Fellow Seattle Pacific U., 1972—; mem. Wash. Trust for Hist. Preservation, Nat. Trust for Hist. Preservation, N.W. Ornamental Hort. Soc. (benefactor, life, hon.), Nat. Assn. Parliamentarians (charter mem., pres. N.W. unit 1961), Wash. Parliamentarians Assn. (charter), IEEE Aux. (chpt. charter mem., pres. 1970-73), Seattle C. of C. (women's div.), Seattle Symphony Women's Assn. (life, sec. 1982-84, pres. 1985-87), Hist. Soc. Seattle and King County (exec. com. 1975-78, pres. women's mus. league 1975-78, pres. Moritz Thomsen Guild of Hist. Soc., 1978-80, 84-87), Highlands Orthopedic Guild (life), Wash. State Hist. Soc., Antiquarian Soc. (v.p. 1986-88, pres. 1988-90, hon. mem. John Fluke Mfg. Co. 20 Year club, 1987—), Rainier Club, Seattle Golf Club, Seattle Tennis Club, U. Wash. Pres.'s Club. Republican. Lutheran. Address: 1206 NW Culbertson Dr Seattle WA 98177-3942 also: Vendovi Island PO Box 703 Anacortes WA 98221-0703

FLUOR, MARJORIE LETHA WADE, author; b. Christiansburg, Va., May 6, 1926; d. Hubert Dodd and Ida (Sowers) Wade; m. John Simon Fluor, Aug. 17, 1956 (dec. Sept. 1974); m. Thurman Moore, July 27, 1979. Author: (geneal. book) Birth and Death Records Floyd County, Virginia, 1980; co-author: (with Michael Evlanoff) Alfred Nobel The Loneliest Millionaire, 1969. Chmn. vols. ARC, 1960-62; mem. adv. bd. Children's Hosp., Orange County, 1965-68; bd. dirs. Orange County Symphony Assn., 1964-69, Orange County Community Chest, 1962-66, Salvation Army, 1963-68, YWCA, 1963-68, Girl Scouts U.S., 1977—, World Affairs Council Orange County, 1975—, mem. exec. bd. Holmes Research Ctr., Los Angeles, 1975—; spl. rep. Calif. Bicentennial Celebration Commn., 1967-69; trustee United Ch. Religious Sci., 1980-85. Recipient Headliner award Orange County Press County, 1966, Heart to God, Hand to Man award Salvation Army, 1968, Disneyland Community Service Program award, 1967, Practitioner Emeritus Recognition award Golden Circle Ch. of Religious Sci., 1988. Mem. DAR (past regent, state asst. chaplain), Freedoms Found. (life), Assistance League, Federated Rep. Women, Philanthropic Ednl. Orgn., Les Dames de Champagne (chmn. 1970-74), Ctr. Club, Balboa Bay Club, Santa Ana Country Club, Pro Am. Club, Order Ea. Star. Home: 1920 N Heliotrope Dr Santa Ana CA 92706-2538

FLYNN, ELIZABETH ANNE, advertising and public relations company executive; b. Washington, Aug. 21, 1951; d. John William and Elizabeth Goodwin (Mahoney) F. AA, Montgomery Coll., Rockville, Md., 1972; BS in Journalism, U. Md., 1976; postgrad. San Diego State U., 1976. Writer, researcher, Sea World, Inc., San Diego, 1977-79; sr. writer Lane & Huff Advt., San Diego, 1979-80; account exec. Kaufman, Lansky, Baker Advt., San Diego, 1980-82; mng. dir. Excelsior Enterprises, Beverly Hills, Calif., 1983-84; sr. account exec. Berkhemer & Kline, Inc., L.A., 1985; pres. Flynn Advt. & Pub. Rels., L.A., 1985—; cons. Coca-Cola Bottling Co. L.A., 1982-84; U.S. corr. Aeronovum mag., 1990—; v.p. mktg. Graffiti Prevention Systems, L.A., 1990-91; dir. new bus. devel. BBDO Hispanica, L.A., 1992-93; pub. rels. dir. Regional Organ Procurement Agy. So. Calif., L.A., 1994—. Bd. dirs. Friends of Reconstructive Surgery, Beverly Hills, 1983-89, Nat.

Kidney Found., 1994, So. Calif. Coalition on Donation, 1994—, also mem. steering com. Recipient Distinction cert. Art Direction Mag., 1982. Mem. NAFE, Greater L.A. Press Club. Republican. Roman Catholic. Avocations: screenwriting, short stories, painting. Address: Flynn Advt & Pub Rels 1440 Reeves St Apt 104 Los Angeles CA 90035-2950

FLYNN, RALPH MELVIN, JR., sales executive, marketing consultant; b. Winchester, Mass., May 2, 1944; s. Ralph Melvin and Mary Agnus (Giuliani) F.; m. Rose Marie Petrock (div. 1988); children: John Patrick, Marc Jeffery; m. Carolyn F. Lee; 1 child, Sean Michael. Engr. Bell Tel. Labs., Holmdel, N.J., 1966-68; tech. coord. Expts. in Art and Tech., N.Y.C., 1968-69; exec. v.p. Bestline Products, San Jose, Calif., 1969-73; pres. Internat. Inst. for Personal Achievement, Palo Alto, Calif., 1975-76, Diamite Corp., Milpitas, Calif., 1977-84; dir. mktg. IMMI, Campbell, Calif., 1973-77; v.p. internat. Neo-Life Co., Fremont, Calif., 1984—; pres. Ultra Promotions, Los Gatos, Calif., 1988-89, Score Publishing, Saratoga, Calif., 1987—; tech. cons. Robert Rauschenberg, N.Y.C., 1968; cons. Standard Oil Co., San Francisco, 1975, I.B.C., Geneva, 1984-88, 1st Interstate Bank, L.A., 1985; lectr. in field. Author: The Only Variable, 1985, Navigating towards Success, 1986; contbr. articles to profl. publs. Named adm. State of Nebr., 1987; Joseph Kaplan Trust scholar, 1961. Mem. Direct Selling Assn., Coffee Soc. (founder 1988), Rolls Royce Owners Club. Republican. Office: Coffee Soc 21265 Stevens Creek Blvd Cupertino CA 95014-5715

FLYNN, THOMAS CHARLES, banker; b. Pittsfield, Mass., July 27, 1950; s. Charles Edward and Angelina Mary (Cicurello) F.; m. Susanne Carin Ifcher; children: Matthew, Jillian. BS in Mgmt., U. Bridgeport, 1972; MBA in Fin., St. John's U., N.Y.C., 1975. Nat. bank examiner internat. div. Comptroller of Currency, Washington, 1973-75; asst. v.p., div. contr. Citibank N.A., N.Y.C., 1975-79; mgr. mgmt. adv. svcs. Price Waterhouse & Co., N.Y.C., 1979-81; v.p., dir. corp. mgmt. acctg. and reporting Bank of Am., San Francisco, 1981-85; nat. dir. cons. svcs. to fin. instns. Touche Ross, San Francisco, 1985-87; exec. v.p., dir. ops. U.S. Leasing, San Francisco, 1987-92; dir. opers. Amplicon Fin., Santa Ana, Calif., 1993-94; mng. assoc. fin. svcs. Coopers & Lybrand, L.L.P., L.A., 1994—. Career profl. advisor St. John's U.; v.p., dir. devel. Marin Theater Co. Recipient cert. of exceptional performance Comptroller of Currency, 1975. Mem. Am. Mgmt. Assn. Home: 15 Hastings Laguna Beach CA 92677-2938

FOCH, NINA, actress, creative consultant, educator; b. Leyden, The Netherlands, Apr. 20, 1924; came to U.S. 1927; d. Dirk and Consuelo (Flowerton) F.; m. James Lipton, June 6, 1954; m. Dennis de Brito, Nov. 27, 1959; 1 child, Dirk de Brito; m. Michael Dewell, Oct. 31, 1967 (div.). Grad., Lincoln Sch., 1939; studies with Stella Adler. Adj. prof. drama U. So. Calif., 1966-68, 78-80, adj. prof. film, 1987—; creative cons. to dirs., writers, prodrs. of all media; artist-in-residence U. N.C., 1966, Ohio State U., 1967, Calif. Inst. Tech., 1969-70; mem. sr. faculty Am. Film Inst., 1974-77; founder, tchr. Nina Foch Studio, Hollywood, Calif., 1973—; founder, actress Los Angeles Theatre Group, 1960-65; bd. dirs. Nat. Repertory Theatre, 1967-75. Motion picture appearances include Nine Girls, 1944, Return of the Vampire, 1944, Shadows in the Night, 1944, Cry of the Werewolf, 1944, Escape in the Fog, 1945, A Song to Remember, 1945, My Name Is Julia Ross, 1945, I Love a Mystery, 1945, Johnny O'Clock, 1947, The Guilt of Janet Ames, 1947, The Dark Past, 1948, The Undercover Man, 1949, Johnny Allegro, 1949, An American in Paris, 1951, Scaramouche, 1952, Young Man with Ideas, 1952, Sombrero, 1953, Fast Company, 1953, Executive Suite, 1954 (Oscar award nominee), Four Guns to the Border, 1954, You're Never Too Young, 1955, Illegal, 1955, The Ten Commandments, 1956, Three Brave Men, 1957, Cash McCall, 1959, Spartacus, 1960, Such Good Friends, 1971, Salty, 1973, Mahogany, 1976, Jennifer, 1978, Rich and Famous, 1981, Skin Deep, 1988, Sliver, 1993, Morning Glory, 1993; appeared in Broadway plays including John Loves Mary, 1947, Twelfth Night, 1949, A Phoenix Too Frequent, 1950, King Lear, 1950, Second String, 1960; appeared with Am. Shakespeare Festival in Taming of the Shrew, Measure for Measure, 1956, San Francisco Ballet and Opera in The Seven Deadly Sins, 1966; also many regional theater appearances including Seattle Repertory Theatre (All Over, 1972 and The Seagull, 1973); actress on TV, 1947—, including Playhouse 90, Studio One, Pulitzer Playhouse, Playwrights 56, Producers Showcase, Lou Grant (Emmy nominee 1980), Mike Hammer; series star: Shadow Chasers, 1985, War and Remembrance, 1988, LA Law, 1990, Hunter, 1990, Dear John, 1990, 91, Tales of the City, 1993; many other series, network spls. and TV films; TV panelist and guest on The Dinah Shore Show, Merv Griffin Show, The Today Show, Dick Cavett, The Tonight Show; TV moderator: Let's Take Sides, 1957-59; assoc. dir. (film) The Diary of Anne Frank, 1959; dir. (nat. tour and on-Broadway) Tonight at 8:30, 1966-67; assoc. producer re-opening of Ford's Theatre, Washington, 1968. Hon. chmn. Los Angeles chpt. Am. Cancer Soc., 1970. Recipient Film Daily award, 1949, 53. Mem. AAUP, Acad. Motion Picture Arts and Scis. (co-chair exec. com. fgn. film award, membership com.), Hollywood Acad. TV Arts and Scis. (bd. govs. 1976-77). Office: PO Box 1884 Beverly Hills CA 90213-1884

FOCHT, MICHAEL HARRISON, health care industry executive; b. Reading, Pa., Sept. 16, 1942; s. Benjamin Harrison and Mary (Hannahoe) F.; m. Sandra Lee Scholwin, May 14, 1964; 1 child, Michael Harrison. Archtl. estimator Caloric Corp., Topton, Pa., 1964-65, cost acct., 1965-66, indsl. engr., 1966-68, mgr. wage rates and standards, 1968-70; indsl. engr. Am. Medicorp. Inc., Fort Lauderdale, Fla., 1970-71; exec. dir. midwest region Am. Medicorp. Inc., Chgo., 1977-78; asst. adminstr. Cypress Community Hosp., Pompano Beach, Fla., 1971-73, adminstr., 1975-77; adminstr. Doctor's Hosp. Hollywood, Fla., 1973-75; v.p. Medfield Corp., St. Petersburg, Fla., 1978-79; v.p. ops. hosp. group Nat. Med. Enterprises, Inc., Los Angeles, 1979-81; regional sr. v.p. hosp. group Nat. Med. Enterprises, Inc., Tampa, Fla., 1981-83; pres., chief exec. officer internat. group Nat. Med. Enterprises, Inc., Los Angeles, 1983-86, pres. chief exec. officer hosp. group, 1986-91; sr. exec. v.p., dir. ops. Nat. Med. Enterprises, Inc., 1991—. Mem. Fedn. Am. Hosps. (bd. govs. 1983—), Fla. League Hosps. (bd. dirs. 1982-83). Republican. Roman Catholic. Home: PO Box 703 Santa Ynez CA 93460-0703 Office: Nat Med Enterprises Inc 2700 Colorado Ave Santa Monica CA 90404-3521

FOELL, RONALD R., builder; b. 1929. With Standard Pacific LP, 1964—; now pres., bd. dirs. Standard Pacific LP, Costa Mesa, Calif. Office: Standard Pacific Corp 1565 Macarthur Blvd Costa Mesa CA 92626-1407

FOFLYGEN, RONALD WAYNE, manufacturing executive; b. Washington, Pa., Oct. 14, 1944; s. James Wayne and Elma Grace (Dunfee) F.; m. Yvonne Emma Sinnett, Nov. 20, 1965; children: Jeffrey Wayne, Kara Leigh. BSEE, Pa. State U., 1973. Design engr. Midland-Ross Corp., Pitts., 1973-75; chief elec. engr. Crucible Steel, Inc., Midland, Pa., 1975-83; sales mgr. Advanced Tech. Sales, Inc., Pitts., 1983-84; sr. staff BDM Corp., Albuquerque, 1984-87; engring. mgr. Plasmatronics, Inc., Albuquerque, 1987-88; v.p. ops. Indsl. Lasers, Inc., Albuquerque, 1988-90; sr. engr. Martin Marietta Corp., Albuquerque, 1990-93; v.p. prodn. Cell-Robotics Inc., Albuquerque, 1993—; pres. Advanced Tech. Cons., Albuquerque, 1987—. Inventor bar hanger box fastener for elec. constrn. products, patentee in field. Elder Ambridge United Presbyn. Ch., Pa., 1984; deacon Covenant Presbyn. Ch., Albuquerque, 1988, mem. Univ. N.Mex. Hosp. Bio-Med. Engr. Devel. Consortium, Albuquerque, 1992—. With USAF, 1966-70, Viet Nam. Mem. Phi Kappa Phi, Tau Beta Pi, Sigma Tau, Eta Kappa Nu, Phi Eta Sigma, Pa. State Alumni Assn. Republican. Home: 11720 Molly Brown Ave NE Albuquerque NM 87111-5915 Office: Cell-Robotics Inc 2715 Broadbent Pky NE Albuquerque NM 87107-1634

FOGEL, NORMAN IRWIN, religious organization administrator; b. L.A., Dec. 23, 1939; s. Edward G. and Frieda (Moder) F.; m. June 25, 1987; children: Melissa, Stephanie, Jeremy. BS, UCLA, 1962. Fellow in Temple Adminstrn., 1966. Asst. dir. Temple Emanuel, Beverly Hills, Calif., 1961-65, Temple Solael, Canoga Park, Calif., 1965-66, Temple Beth Israel, San Diego, 1966-71, Brandeis-Bardin Inst., Simi Valley, 1971-78, Temple Israel, Boston, 1978-83, Stephen S. Wise Temple, Bel Air, Calif., 1983—. Chmn. planning commn. City of Simi Valley, 1975-78; mem. human rels. commn. Ventura County, 1975-78. Cpl. USAR, 1957-65. Mem. Nat. Assn. Temple Adminstrs. (pres. 1991-93, mem. exec. bd.), Union Am. Hebrew Congregations (exec. bd. 1991-93, bd. trustees, mem. Commn. on Synagogue Mgmt., exec. bd. Pacific S.W. Coun., mem. Pacific S.W. Region Bd.). Office: 15500 Stephen S Wise Dr Los Angeles CA 90077-1520

FOGO, FRED RICHARD, communications educator; b. Gary, Ind., Dec. 13, 1943; s. Dominic Guy and Elizabeth Elaine (Komenich) F.; m. Ronda Claire Robbins, Aug. 14, 1966. BA, Wabash Coll., 1967; MA, U. Nevada, 1970; PhD, U. Utah, 1990. Instr. Tahoe (Calif.) Coll., 1969-70, U. Nevada, Reno, 1970-73, Western Nevada Cmty Coll., Reno, 1974-75, U. Ariz., Tucson, 1979-80, Northern Nev. Cmty. Coll., Elko, 1975-79, 80-82, Salt Lake Cmty. Coll., 1983; mktg. rep. Wadsworth Publ. Co., Belmont, Calif., 1983-85; editorial asst. Critical Studies in Mass Communication, Salt Lake City, 1986-89; assoc. prof. comm. Westminster Coll. of Salt Lake City, 1990—. Author: I Read the News Today: The Social Drama of John Lennon's Death, 1994; contbr. articles to profl. jours. Rsch. grant Westminster Coll., 1993. Mem. Speech Communication Assn., Assn. Educators in Journalism and Mass Communications, Internat. Assn. Bus. Communicators. Democrat. Home: 860 1st Ave Salt Lake City UT 84103-3828 Office: Westminster Coll 1840 S 1300 E Salt Lake City UT 84105

FOK, AGNES KWAN, cell biologist, educator; b. Hong Kong, British Crown Colony, Dec. 11, 1940; came to U.S., 1962; d. Sun and Yau (Ng) Kwan; m. Fok, June 8, 1965; children: Licie Chiu-Jane, Edna Chiu-Joan. BA in Chemistry, Coll. Great Falls, 1965; MS in Plant Nutrition and Biochemistry, Utah State U., 1966; PhD in Biochemistry, U. Tex., Austin, 1971. Asst. rsch. prof. pathology dept. U. Hawaii, Honolulu, 1973-74, Ford Found. postdoctoral fellow, anatomy dept., 1975, asst. rsch. prof. Pacific Biomed. Rsch. Ctr., 1975-82, assoc. rsch. prof., 1982-88, assoc. rsch. prof. biology program, 1985, rsch. prof., 1988—, grad. faculty, dept. microbiology, 1977—; dir. biology program Pacific Biomed. Rsch. Ctr., 1994—. Contbr. articles to profl. jours. Mem. Am. Soc. for Cell Biology, Soc. for Protozoologists, Sigma Xi (treas. Hawaii chpt. 1979—). Office: U Hawaii Dept Microbiology Honolulu HI 96822

FOK, SAMUEL SHIU-MING, engineer, consultant; b. Macau, China, Feb. 15, 1926; came to U.S., 1947.; s. Yan-Nung and Bick-Lan (Cheong) F.; m. Ruth L. Sung, Aug. 16, 1952; children: William David Z.C., John Peter Z.Y., James Andrew Z.M. BChE, Ohio State U., 1949; MS in Chem. Engring., Case Inst. Tech., 1951, PhD in Chem. Engring., 1955. Rsch. engr. Indsl. Rayon Corp., Cleve., 1954-56; sr. staff engr. Shockley Transistor Corp., Mountain View, Calif., 1956-60; mem. tech. staff Fairchild R & D Lab, Palo Alto, Calif., 1960-70; microlithographic cons. Palo Alto, 1970-71; mask tech. mgr. Siliconix, Inc., Santa Clara, Calif., 1971-74; dep. dir. FCT Bros. Co., Ltd., Bangkok, Thailand, 1975-77; prin. engr. Perkin-Elmer Corp., Hayward, Calif., 1977-90; cons. Palo Alto, 1990—; tech. dir. Siliconix Hong Kong, 1973; application specialist Perkin-Elmer EBT Divsn., Hayward, 1977-90; primary tutor JLS Sch., Palo Alto, 1992-94. Contbr. articles to profl. jours. Chartered mem. Stanford Area Chinese Club, 1966; prin. Chinese Lang. Sch., Palo Alto, 1962-66; mem. Pacific Art League of Palo Alto, 1990. Mem. Am. Soc. Testing Materials (F-1 com.), Semiconductor Mfg. Engrs. Inst. (micropatterning com.), Am. Vacuum Soc., Soc. Photographic Instrument Engrs., Chinese Inst. Engrs. Republican. Presbyterian.

FOLDEN, NORMAN CLARK (SKIP FOLDEN), information systems executive, consultant; b. San Francisco, July 28, 1933. BS in Math./English/Engring., U.S. Mil. Acad., 1956. With IBM Corp., various locations, 1966-83; program mgr. I/S tech. IBM, Sommers, N.Y., 1983-86; owner Folden Mgmt., Westchester, N.Y., 1986-91, Las Vegas, 1991—. Home and Office: 4329 Silvercrest Ct North Las Vegas NV 89030-0116

FOLEY, DANIEL EDMUND, real estate development executive; b. St. Paul, Mar. 1, 1926; s. Edward and Gerry (Fitzgarld) F.; student U. Minn., 1941-43; m. Paula Evans, Apr. 1, 1946. Chmn. bd. Realty Ptnrs. Ltd., Los Angeles; pres. Alpha Property Mgmt. Served with AUS, 1943-46.

FOLEY, EDWARD JOSEPH, hospital administrator; b. Mpls., June 12, 1933; married. BA, U. Minn., 1957; MA, U. Calif., 1962. Mgr. gen. svcs. L.A. County-U. So. Calif. Med. Ctr., 1962-63; dir. personnel L.A. County-Harbor Gen. Hosp., 1963-67; asst. adminstr. John Wesley County Hosp., L.A., 1967-72; personnel officer L.A. County Dept. Health Svc., West Covina, Calif., 1973-75; assoc. adminstr. Rancho Los Amigos Hosp., Downey, Calif., 1975-76, adminstr., 1976-80; adminstr. L.A. County-Harbor-U. So. Calif. Med. Ctr., Torrance, Calif., 1980—. Office: UCLA Med Ctr Office of Adminstr 1000 W Carson St Torrance CA 90502-2004

FOLEY, MARY KATHLEEN, theatre arts educator; b. Chgo., Aug. 31, 1947; d. Charles Joseph and Jane Eleanor (Considine) F.; m. Roy Mendelssohn, July 2, 1979; children: Nathan Samuel, Dierdre Jane. BA, Rosemont (Pa.) Coll., 1969; Ma, U. Mass., 1975; PhD, U. Hawaii, 1979; Fulbright cert., U. Bochum, West Germany, 1970. Vis. prof. U. Hawaii, Honolulu, 1984; asst. prof. theatre arts bd. U. Calif., Santa Cruz, 1979-87, assoc. prof., 1987-92, prof., 1992—; provost Porter Coll., U. Calif., 1989—; dalang (puppeteer) U. Calif. Indonesian Arts Troupe, Santa Cruz, 1979—. Editor: Essays on Southeast Asian Performing Arts, 1992; S.E. Asia editor Asian Theatre Jour., 1984—; contbr. articles to profl. jours. Adv. com. Festival of Indonesia, N.Y., Jakarata, 1989-92; convener Coun. of Provosts, U. Calif., Santa Cruz, 1993—; artist SPECTA, Santa Cruz, 1980—, Honolulu Artists-in-Schs. program, 1975-78; bd. dirs. Vols. in Asia, Stanford, Calif., 1988-90. Fulbright grantee Fulbright Commn., 1969-70, East-West Ctr. grantee, 1975-79, Asian Cultural Coun. grantee Asian Cultural Coun., 1988, Nat. Endowment for Humanities, 1981, 93.

FOLEY, PETER WILHELM CHRISTIAN, humanities educator, researcher, translator; b. Rinteln, Germany, Nov. 11, 1961; came to U.S., 1990; s. Hervey Michael and Waltraud Gisela (Rothe) F.; m. Pia Francesca Cuneo, Aug. 4, 1990. BA, U. Keele, Staffordshire, Eng., 1985; MA, Northwestern U., 1986; DrPhil, U. Vienna, Austria, 1990. Asst. tchr. Ulrich-von-Hutten H.S., Schluechtern, Germany, 1983-84; tchg. asst. German dept. Northwestern U., Evanston, Ill., 1985-86; lectr. U. Econs., Vienna, 1986-90; vis. lectr. dept. German, U. Ariz., Tucson, 1992, lectr. humanities program, 1992—. Author: Heinrich Von Kleist and Adam Mueller, 1990; editor-in-chief Concourse newspaper, 1981-82; contbr. articles to profl. jours. Recipient tchg. award Fund for Advancement U. Econs., 1988, 89, 90; co-recipient tchg. award U. Ariz. Provost, 1994; grantee German Acad. Exch. Svc., 1983, Austrian Fgn. Study Svc., 1987-90. Mem. MLA, N.Am. Kant Soc., Fichte Soc., Am. Assn. Tchrs. German, Nat. Liberal Club (Eng.). Mem. Liberal Democrat Party (Eng.). Roman Catholic. Office: U Ariz Humanities Program Harvill Bldg Rm 343 Tucson AZ 85721

FOLEY, THOMAS MICHAEL, financial executive; b. Phila., Apr. 21, 1943; s. Thomas Bernard and Alice Mary (Machulsky) F.; m. Jean D. McCrystal, Oct. 1, 1966 (dec. 1973); children: Thomas R., Timothy J., Brian P.; m. Carolyn Jo Forbes, mar. 23, 1974; children: Kathryn A. and Jo A. (twins). BS, LaSalle U., 1965; MBA, Temple U., 1984. CPA, Pa. With Price Waterhouse, Phila., 1965-76; audit mgr. Price Waterhouse, 1970-76; v.p. corp. auditing Mack Trucks, Inc., Allentown, Pa., 1976-80; v.p. info. mgmt. Mack Trucks, Inc., 1980-85; v.p. fin., adminstrn. Albert Nipon, Inc., Phila., 1985-87; sr. v.p., chief fin. officer Phila. Stock Exch., Phila., 1987-90; v.p., chief fin. officer Print Northwest, Inc., Tacoma, 1990—; project leader, Grace Commn., Washington, 1984. Mem. AICPA, Pa. Inst. CPAs, Wash. Inst. CPAs, Fin. Execs. Inst., Printing Industry Fin. Execs. (exec. com.). Republican. Home: 12713 133rd Ave SE Rainier WA 98576-9500 Office: Print Northwest Inc PO Box 1418 Tacoma WA 98401-1418

FOLEY, THOMAS STEPHEN, lawyer, former speaker House of Representatives; b. Spokane, Wash., Mar. 6, 1929; s. Ralph E. and Helen Marie (Higgins) F.; m. Heather Strachan, Dec. 1968. B.A., U. Wash., 1951, LL.B., 1957. Bar: Wash. Partner Higgins & Foley, 1957-58; dep. pros. atty. Spokane County, Spokane, 1958-60; asst. atty. gen. State of Wash., Olympia, 1960-61; spl. counsel interior and insular affairs com. U.S. Senate, Washington, 1961-64; mem. 89th-103rd Congresses from 5th Wash. dist., Washington, D.C., 1965-94; House majority whip, 1981-86, House majority leader, 1987-89; speaker U.S. Ho. of Reps., 1989-94; ptnr. Akin, Gump, Strauss, Hauer & Feld, Spokane, 1995—; instr. law Gonzaga U., 1958-60; mem. bd. advisors Ctr. Strategic and Internat. Studies; mem. adv. council Am. Ditchley Found. Bd. overseers Whitman Coll.; bd. advisors Yale U. council; bd. dirs. Council on Fgn. Relations. Mem. Phi Delta Phi. Democrat. Office: 601 W 1st Ave Ste 2W Spokane WA 99204-0317

FOLGER, WILLIAM MONTRAVILLE, actor, journalist; b. Lockport, N.Y., May 13, 1916; s. Wayne Harrison and MayBelle Alzina (Upson) F.; widowed; children: Valerie Ely, W. Earl Folger. BS in gen. bus., U. Ill., 1938; MA in pol. sci., Syracuse U., 1975. News writer, reporter, editor National Broadcasting Co., Washington, 1944-46; news writer, newscaster Washington Post, Washington, 1946-48; news commentator Radio Station WISH, Indpls., 1950-51; pub. rels. dir. Coe Coll., Cedar Rapids, Iowa, 1952-53; trans. writer, columnist Courier-Express, Buffalo, N.Y., 1955, religion writer, columnist, 1959-73; journalism lectr. Syracuse (N.Y.) U., 1973-75; journalism prof. U. Northern Colo., Greeley, 1975-81; freelance actor Denver, 1981—. Precinet chmn. Dem. Party, Greeley, 1975-77, state conv. del., 1988; spokesman Am. Civil Liberties Union, Greeley, 1978-80; editor Colo. Environ. Coalition, 1990—. Recipient Fine Reporting award Newspaper Guild, Buffalo, 1960, Interpretive Reporting award, 1961-62, Best Theatre Ensemble award Westword, Denver, 1988, Am. Scene award Am. Fedn. TV and Radio Artists, Denver, 1988. Mem. Soc. Profl. Journalists (Colo. chpt. pres. 1977-78), Colo. Audubon Soc. (sec. 1985-88), Colo. Environ. Coalition (sec. 1983-85, editor 1990—), Religion Writers' Assn. of U.S. and Can. (pres. 1970-74). Presbyterian. Home and Office: 100 Park Ave West # 301 Denver CO 80205-3229

FOLKERTH, THEODORE LEON, cardiovascular surgeon, educator; b. Darke County, Ohio, Nov. 24, 1937; s. L.D. and Abigail Lenore (Carpenter) F.; m. Lenora Wallace, Dec. 22, 1962 (div. 1981); children: Theodore Wesley, Elizabeth Anne, Geoffrey Wallace; m. Jean. BA in Chemistry, Earlham Coll., 1959; MS in Biochemistry, Ind. U., Indpls., 1962, MD, 1965. Commd. officer USN, 1964, advanced through grades to comdr.; staff thoracic and cardiovasc. surgeon Naval Regional Med. Ctr., San Diego, 1973-77; ret., 1978; staff cardiovasc. surgeon Good Samaritan Hosp., San Jose, Calif., 1978-81; head cardiovasc. surgery Santa Rosa (Calif.) Meml. Hosp., 1981-87; pvt. practice, Oceanside, Calif., 1987—; chmn. div. cardiovasc. surgey Tri-City Med. Ctr., Oceanside, 1987—; asst. clin. prof. U. Calif., San Diego, 1975-77, assoc. clin. prof., 1987—; program dir. seminar Current Controversies in Cardiac Surgery, 1993. Fellow ACS, Soc. Thoracic Surgeons; mem. Western Thoracic Surg. Assn. Office: 3398 Vista Way Ste C204 Oceanside CA 92056-3752

FOLKMAN, STEVEN LEE, engineering educator; b. Logan, Utah, Mar. 24, 1952; s. Basil Willmet and Rachel (Zollinger) F.; m. Marianne Boudrero, June 7, 1975; children: Melanie, Jennifer, Ashley, Wendy, Jason, Dominique. BS in Nutrition & Food Sci., Utah State U., 1975, PhD in Mechanical Engring., 1990. Sr. engr. Thiokol Corp., Brigham City, Utah, 1978-80; rsch. engr. Utah State U., Logan, 1980-90, asst. prof., 1990-95, assoc. prof., 1995—; cons. Space Dynamic Lab., Logan, 1990—; energy conservation specialist State of Utah, Salt Lake City, 1980-90. Co-author: Food Engineering Fundamentals, 1983. Scoutmaster Boy Scouts Am., Logan, 1989-92. Mem. AIAA, ASME. Mem. LDS Ch. Office: Utah State U Mechanical Engring Dept Logan UT 84322-4130

FOLLETT, CAROLYN BROWN, poet, artist; b. N.Y.C., Jan. 31, 1936; d. Lorne William and Helen Rudd (Swayze) Brown; m. Alan Lee Follett; children: Jeffrey Tredwell, Paul Seward, Lorne Hillary. BA in English, Smith Coll., 1958. Copy editor, proofreader dept. publs. Stanford U., Internat. Bus. Rels., San Francisco, McCann Erickson, San Francisco, Cunningham and Walsh; designer, creator, owner, bus. mgr. The Peaceable Kingdom; art bd. dirs. Sight and Insight, Mill Valley, Calif.; bd. dirs. Marin Poetry Ctr., Marin County, Calif., de Young Mus. Art Sch., San Francisco, Art Apprentice Program, San Francisco; leader workshops Internat. Women Writers Guild; numerous poetry readings. Author: The Latitudes of Their Going, 1993, Gathering the Mountains, 1995; contbr. poetry to numerous jours.; two-person shows include O'Hanlon Gallery, Mill Valley, Calif., 1994; exhibited in group shows at Artisans Gallery, Mill Valley, 1989, Signature Gallery, San Diego, 1990, 1994, O'Hanlon Gallery, Mill Valley, 1990, 91, 92, 93, 94, Perception Gallery, Ft. Mason, San Francisco, 1991. Founding trustee San Francisco U. H.S., 1973-82; trustee, bd. chmn. Urban H.S., San Francisco, 1982-88; art vol. San Francisco Edn. Aux. Recipient numerous poetry awards; Marin Arts Coun. grant for poetry, 1995. Office: ICB Bldg # 104 480 Gate Five Rd Sausalito CA 94965

FOLLETTE, DAVID MICHAEL, cardiothoracic surgeon; b. San Francisco, July 11, 1947; s. James Henniger and Betty Ann (Kuchar) F.; m. Sandra Louise Spaulding, June 1, 1986; children: Christelle, Michael. BA, UCLA, 1969, MD, 1973. Diplomate Am. Bd. Surgery, Am. Bd. Thoracic Surgery. Intern; resident in surgery UCLA, resident in cardiothoracic surgery; dir. cardiac surgery St. John's Hosp., Santa Monica, Calif., 1982-89; assoc. prof. U. Calif., Davis, 1989—; residency dir. dept. surgery U. Calif., Davis, 1990—, co-dir. lung transplant program, 1994—. Contbr. articles to profl. jours. Sunday sch. instr. Trinity Cathedral Ch., Sacramento, 1990—. Mem. Am. Assn. Thoracic Surgeons, Soc. Thoracic Surgeons, Internat. Soc. Heart and Lung Transplant, Western Thoracic Surgery Assn., U. Calif.-Davis Surg. Assn. (sec./treas. 1993—), Sacramento Surg. Soc. (treas. 1995). Republican. Episcopalian. Office: Univ Calif Dept Surgery 4301 X St Rm 2310 Sacramento CA 95817-2214

FOLLICK, EDWIN DUANE, law educator, chiropractic physician; b. Glendale, Calif., Feb. 4, 1935; s. Edwin Fulfford and Esther Agnes (Catherwood) F.; m. Marilyn K. Sherk, Mar. 24, 1986. BA, Calif. State U., L.A., 1956, MA, 1961; MA, Pepperdine U., 1957, MPA, 1977; PhD, DTheol., St. Andrews Theol. Coll., Sem. of the Free Protestant Episc. Ch., London, 1958; MS in Libr. Sci., U. So. Calif., 1963, MEd in Instructional Materials, 1964, AdvMEd in Edn. Adminstrn., 1969; student, Calif. Coll. Law, 1965; LLB, Blackstone Law Sch., 1966, JD, 1967; DC, Cleve. Chiropractic Coll., L.A., 1972; PhD, Academia Theatina, Pescara, 1978; MA in Organizational Mgmt., Antioch U., L.A., 1990. Tchr., libr. adminstr. L.A. City Schs., 1957-68; law librarian Glendale U. Coll. Law, 1968-69; coll. librarian Cleve. Chiropractic Coll., L.A., 1969-74, dir. edn. and admissions, 1974-84, prof. jurisprudence, 1975—, dean student affairs, 1976-92, chaplain, 1985—, dean of edn., 1989—; assoc. prof. Newport U., 1982; extern prof. St. Andrews Theol. Coll., London, 1961; dir. West Valley Chiropractic Health Ctr., 1972—. Contbr. articles to profl. jours. Chaplain's asst. U.S. Army, 1958-60. Decorated cavaliere Internat. Order Legion of Honor of Immaculata (Italy); Knight of Malta, Sovereign Order of St. John of Jerusalem; knight Order of Signum Fidei; comdr. chevalier Byzantine Imperial Order of Constantine the Gt.; comdr. ritter Order St. Gereon, numerous others. Mem. ALA, NEA, Am. Assn. Sch. Librarians, L.A. Sch. Library Assn., Calif. Media and Library Educators Assn., Assn. Coll and Rsch. Librarians, Am. Assn. Law Librarians, Am. Chiropractic Assn., Internat. Chiropractors Assn., Nat. Geog. Soc., Internat. Platform Assn., Phi Delta Kappa, Sigma Chi Psi, Delta Tau Alpha. Democrat. Episcopalian. Home: 6435 Jumilla Ave Woodland Hills CA 91367-2833 Office: 590 N Vermont Ave Los Angeles CA 90004-2115 also: 7022 Owensmouth Ave Canoga Park CA 91303-2005

FOLTYN, JACQUE LYNN, sociologist, educator; b. Chgo., Jan. 31, 1955; d. John Stanley and Margaret Cecelia (Amaranthus) F. BA in Sociology, U. Calif. San Diego, 1978, MA in Sociology, 1981, PhD in Sociology, 1989. Instr. Muir Coll. Writing Program U. Calif. San Diego, La Jolla, Calif.; asst. vis. prof. U. of the Pacific, Stockton, Calif., 1989-90, U. Redlands, Calif., 1990-91; acting chair dept. cultural, social, literary studies Nat. U., San Diego, 1992; asst. prof. U. Redlands, Calif., 1992—; vis. scholar Manchester Coll., Oxford U., Eng., 1993; speaker in field. Editor: (book) Headache, 1980, Total Organization, 1983; author: (book) The Beauty Problem, 1996; (with others) Contemporary Issues in the Sociology of Death and Dying, 1995; contbr. articles to Allure mag. and Chgo. Tribune. Recipient Dissertation fellowship U. Calif. San Diego, 1984, scholarships U. Calif. San Diego. Mem. Inst. for Study of Global Conflict and Cooperation, Writing Women. Democrat. Office: U Redlands Liberal Studies 1200 E Colton Ave Redlands CA 92374-3755

FOLTZ, DONALD JOSEPH, franchise development consultant; b. Chgo., Jan. 23, 1933; s. Joseph M. and Sheldon B. (Morris) F.; m. Carol Elizabeth Seymour, Aug. 29, 1953; children: Kim Foltz Stanton, Joseph Jay. BBA, Western Mich. U., 1955, MBA, 1956. Regional mktg. mgr. Frigidaire Div. Gen. Motors Corp., Denver, 1958-60; co-founder, pres. Mr. Steak, Inc. (Jamco), Denver, 1960-70, The Mktg. Group, Inc., Denver, 1971-78, The Franchise Ctr./DJFA & Assocs., Inc., Denver, 1971—; chmn., dir. Profusion

Systems, Inc., Aurora, Colo., 1982-90; pres., dir. Franchise Network U.S.A., Inc., Aurora, 1986-88; bd. dirs. Colo. Industry Tng. Coun., Golden. Author: The College of Franchise Knowledge, 1992. Exec. dir. Runaways, Inc., Denver, 1970-82. 1st lt. U.S. Army, 1956-58. Office: Donald J Foltz & Assocs Inc 5555 Dtc Pky Ste 3210 Englewood CO 80111-3005

FONG, CARL S., systems and operations analyst; b. Sacramento, June 11, 1959; s. John Ye and Amy Fong m. Denise Lowe, Dec. 12, 1992. AS, Consumnes River Coll., 1979; BS, Calif. Polytech. Inst., 1985; postgrad., U. LaVerne, Calif., 1990-93. Tutor Calif. Polytech. Inst., Pomona, 1983, lab. cons., 1984-85; peripheral operator Security Pacific Automation Corp., Brea, Calif., 1984-85; programmer, analyst I Orange County Dept. of Edn., Costa Mesa, Calif., 1985-86, programmer, analyst II, 1986-87, systems programmer, 1987-89, systems and ops. analyst, 1989—. Mem. Assn. of MBA Execs., Mgmt. Info. System Student Assn., Data Processing Mgmt. Assn. Office: Orange County Dept of Edn 200 Kalmus Dr # 1016C Costa Mesa CA 92626-5922

FONG, DAVID, psychiatrist; b. Stockton, Calif., Mar. 20, 1921; s. Ying King and Sutie (Wong) F.; m. Nancy Nai-Sien Wong, May 8, 1955; children: Heather M., Celia L. AB, U. Calif., Berkeley, 1942; MD, U. Calif., San Francisco, 1944; grad., San Francisco Psychoanalytic, Inst. and Soc., 1964. Diplomate Am. Bd. Psychiatry and Neurology. Rotating intern San Francisco Gen. Hosp., 1944-45; resident in psychiatry Langley Porter Psychiat. Hosp. and Clinic, San Francisco, 1947-50; pvt. practice, Berkeley, 1950—; psychiatrist Student Health Svc. U. Calif., Berkeley, 1950-71; med. dir. Chinatown-North Beach clin. svcs. San Francisco Dept. Pub. Health, 1972—; cons. residency tng. program Herrick Hosp., Berkeley, 1966-71, Internat. Inst. Alameda, Oakland, Calif., 1973-75, Asian Cmty. Mental Health Svcs., Oakland, 1974-75; cons. Asian mental health component Highland Hosp., Oakland, 1976-79; lectr. Calif. STate U., Hayward, 1970-71. Mem. Mental Health Adv. Bd. Berkeley, Calif., 1972-76. Capt. U.S. Army Med. Corp., 1945-47. Fellow Am. Psychiat. Assn. (life); mem. Calif. Med. Assn., No. Calif. Psychiat. Soc., Alameda Contra-Costa Med. Assn. Office: 2232 Carleton St Berkeley CA 94704-3225

FONG, ELAINE CHUN, principal; b. Honolulu, Feb. 9, 1936; d. James Tai Yee and Esther Chun; m. James Chuck Fong, Dec. 26, 1964; children: Margery Ann, Elizabeth Ann. BA, U. Hawaii, 1958; MA, U. San Francisco, 1975. Tchr. Dept. Edn. State of Hawaii, Honolulu, 1958-61; tchr. San Francisco Unified Sch. Dist., 1961-81; dir. San Francisco Tchr. Ctr., 1981-85; prin. San Francisco Unified Sch. Dist., 1985—; cons., trainer Calif. Schs. Leadership Acad., Sacramento, 1986—; trainer Tchr. Expectations and Student Achievement, San Francisco, 1987—. Bd. dirs. Learning Through Edn. in the Arts Project, San Francisco, 1985-92. Mem. AAUW, Calif. ASCD (exec. bd.. dirs. 1993—), Nat. Coaliton for Equality in Learning, Alpha Delta Kappa (pres. 1982-84, 92-94, Calif. state historian 1994-96), Sigma Omicron Pi (v.p. 1990-92, pres. 1992-94), Phi Delta Kappa. Roman Catholic. Home: 2200 15th Ave San Francisco CA 94116-1823

FONG, HIRAM L., former senator; b. Honolulu, Oct. 15, 1906; s. Lum Fong and Chai Ha Lum; m. Ellyn Lo; children, Hiram, Rodney, Marie-Ellen Fong Gushi, Marvin-Allan (twins). AB with honors, U. Hawaii, 1930, LLD, 1953; JD, Harvard U., 1935; LLD, Tufts U., 1960, Lafayette Coll., 1960, Lynchburg Coll., 1970, Lincoln U., 1971, U. Guam, 1974, St. John's U., 1975, Calif. Western Sch. Law, 1976, Tung Wu (Soochow) U., Taiwan, 1978, China Acad., Taiwan, 1978; LHD, L.I. U., 1968. With supply dept. Pearl Harbor Navy Yard, 1924-27; chief clk. Suburban Water System, 1930-32; dep. atty. City and County of Honolulu, 1935-38; founder, ptnr. law firm Fong, Miho, Choy & Robinson, until 1959; founder, chmn. bd. emeritus Finance Factors, Grand Pacific Life Ins. Co.; founder, chmn bd. Finance Investment Co., Market City, Ltd., Fin. Enterprises Ltd.; pres. Ocean View Cemetery, Ltd.; owner, operator Sen. Fong's Plantation and Gardens, Honolulu; dir. numerous firms, Honolulu; hon. cons. China Airlines. Mem. Hawaii Legislature, 1938-54, speaker, 1948-54; mem. U.S. Senate, 1959-77, Post Office and Civil Service Com., Judiciary Com., Appropriations Com., Spl. Com. on Aging; U.S. del. 150th Anniversary Argentine Independence, Buenos Aires, 1960, 55th Interparliamentary Union (World) Conf., 1966, Ditchley Found. Conf., 1967, U.S.-Can. Inter-Parliamentary Union Conf., 1961, 65, 67, 68, Mex.-U.S. Inter-Parliamentary Conf., 1968, World Interparliamentary Union, Tokyo, 1974; mem. Commn. on Revision Fed. Ct. Appellate System, 1975—; Active in civic and service orgns.; v.p. Territorial Constl. Conv., 1950; del. Rep. Nat. Conv., 1952, 56, 60, 64, 68, 72; founder, chmn. bd. Fin. Factors Found.; founder, pres. Hiram & Ellyn Fong Found.; founder, pres., chmn. bd. Market City Found.; hon. co-chmn. McKinley High Sch. Found., 1989; bd. visitors U.S. Mil. Acad., 1971—, U.S. Naval Acad., 1974—. Served from 1st lt. to maj. USAAF, 1942-44; ret. col. USAF Res. Recipient award NCCJ, 1960, Meritorious Svc. citation Nat. Assn. Ret. Civil Employees, 1963, Horatio Alger award, 1970, citation for Outstanding Svc. Japanese Am. Citizens League, 1970, award Am. Acad. Achievement, 1971, Outstanding Svc. award Orgn. Chinese Ams., 1973, award Nat. Soc. Daus. Founders and Patriots Am., 1974, cert. Pacific Asian World, 1974, Citizen Among Citizens award Boys & Girls Clubs of Hawaii, 1991, Disting. Alumni award U. Hawaii Alumni Assn., 1991, Kulia I Ka Nu'u award Pub. Schs. Hawaii Found., 1992, Dedication and Support award McKinley Found., 1995; named to Jr. Achievement Hawaii Bus. Hall of Fame, 1995; decorated Order of Brilliant Star with Grand Cordon Republic of China, Order of Diplomatic Svc. Merit, Gwanghwan Medal Republic of Korea. Mem. Am. Legion, VFW, Lambda Alpha Internat. (Aloha chpt.), Phi Beta Kappa. Congregationalist. Home: 1102 Alewa Dr Honolulu HI 96817-1507

FONG, JULITA ANGELA, pathologist; b. Hong Kong, Oct. 11, 1933; d. Eugene F.W. and Thora W. (Wong) Chin; m. Henry S. Fong, June 8, 1959 (dec.); children: Marydaisy, Joseph E. BA, San Francisco Coll. for Women, 1954; MD, Stanford U., 1958. Diplomate Am. Bd. Pathology. Assoc. pathologist Sacramento (Calif.) Med. Ctr., 1964-74; med. dir. Physicians Clin. Lab, Sacramento, 1974-78; lab dir. Fong Diagnostic Lab, Sacramento, 1978—; assoc. clin. prof. pathology U. Calif. Davis Sch. Medicine, 1975—. Mem. AMA, Calif. Med. Assn., Sacramento-El Dorado County Med. Soc., Coll. Am. Pathologists, Am. Soc. Clin. Pathologists, Am. Med. Womens Assn., Soroptimist Internat. of Sacramento. Republican. Office: Fong Paternity Lab 7237 E Southgate Dr Sacramento CA 95823-2620

FONG, MARC ALAN, lawyer; b. Oakland, Calif., Dec. 1, 1949; s. Richard Alvin and Marie (Wong) F.; m. Rosie Fong (div. 1984); children: Marc Alan, Michael Gregory, John William (dec.); m. Suzanne Tucker, May 11, 1985. BA, Calif. State U., Hayward, 1971; JD, Lincoln U., 1977. Bar: Calif. 1978, U.S. Dist. Ct. (no. dist.) Calif. 1978, U.S. Tax Ct. 1985. Ptnr. Fong & Fong, Oakland, 1978-86, Chatzky, Fong & Fong and Fong & Fong, Oakland and San Jose, Calif., 1986—; co-founder, gen. counsel Aeron Biotech. Inc., San Leandro, Calif., 1986—. Gen. counsel, bd. dirs. Asian Bus. League, San Francisco, 1984-86; vice-chmn. western region Community Assn. Inst., Alexandria, Va., 1987-89, bd. dirs., past pres. San Francisco chpt.; co-founder Bay Area Com., San Francisco, 1986; mem. Calif. Legis. Action Com., San Francisco, 1986; bd. dirs. Peralta Cancer Rsch. Inst., Oakland, 1986, no. chpt. Leukemia Soc. Am., 1990—. Mem. Assn. Trial Lawyers Am., State Bar Assn. Calif., Calif. Trial Lawyers Assn., Alameda County Bar Assn., Lakeview Club, Harbor Bay Club. Democrat. Home: 9 Applegate Way Alameda CA 94502-7714 Office: Fong & Fong One Kaiser Pla Ste 785 Oakland CA 94612

FONG, PETER C. K., lawyer, judge; b. Honolulu, Oct. 28, 1955; s. Arthur S.K. and Victoria K.Y. (Chun) F. BBA with honors, U. Hawaii, 1977; JD, Boston Coll., 1980. Bar: Hawaii 1980, U.S. Dist. Ct. Hawaii 1980, U.S. Ct. Appeals (9th cir.) 1980, U.S. Supreme Ct. 1983. Law clk. to presiding justice Supreme Ct. Hawaii, Honolulu, 1980-81; dep. pros. atty. Pros. Atty.'s Office, Honolulu, 1981-84; with Davis, Reid & Richards, Honolulu, 1984-89; chief legal counsel, chief clk. Senate jud. com. Hawaii State Legislature, 1989—; judge per diem Dist./Family Ct., Hawaii, 1989—; ptnr. Hong, Kwock & Fong, Honolulu, 1990-91, Fong & Fong, Honolulu, 1989—; gen. legal counsel Hawaii Jr. C. of C., 1983-84; pres., bd. dirs. Legal Aid Soc. Hawaii, 1984-90; pres., 1986-87; arbitrator Hawaiian Cir. Ct., 1986—, Am. Arbitration Assn., 1989—; mediator Arbitration Forums, Inc., 1989—; mem. asset devel. and pers. coms. Chun Kim Chow, Ltd., 1989—. Editorial staff Boston Coll. Internat. and Comp. Law Rev., 1978-80. Mem. City and County Honolulu Neighborhood Bd., 1981-83; campaign treas. for Hawaii state senator, 1981-89; mem. aux. admissions com. Boston Coll. Law Sch., 1982—, major gifts com. and sustaining membership fundraising drive com. YMCA, 1988; del. Gov.'s Congress on Hawaii's internat. role, 1988; del. Hawaii Jud. Forsight Congress, 1991; mem. hearings com. Hawaii State Atty.'s Disciplinary Bd., 1991—. Recipient Pres.'s award Hawaii Jr. C. of C., 1984; named one of ten Outstanding Persons of Hawaii, 1990, 92. Mem. ABA, Hawaii State Bar Assn. (co-chmn. and vice-chmn., jud. salary com., mem. legis. com., coord. legis. resource bank, mem. task force on discplinary counsel), Hawaii Developer's Coun., Am. Judicature Soc., Hawaii Supreme Ct. Hist. Soc., Hawaii Trial Judges Assn., Nat. Coun. of Juvenile and Family Ct. Judges, Rsch. Bd. of Advisors, Assn. Trial Lawyers Am., Nat. Assn. Dist. Attys., U.S. Supreme Ct. Hist. Soc., Mortar Bd., Tu Chiang Shen (past pres.). Home: 5255 Makalena St Honolulu HI 96821-1808 Office: Fong & Fong Grosvenor Ctr-PRI Tower 733 Bishop St Ste 1550 Honolulu HI 96813-4006

FONKALSRUD, ERIC WALTER, pediatric surgeon, educator; b. Balt., Aug. 31, 1932; s. George and Ella (Fricke) F.; m. Margaret Ann Zimmermann, June 6, 1959; children: Eric Walter Jr., Margaret Lynn, David Loren, Robert Warren. B.A., U. Wash., 1953; M.D., Johns Hopkins U., 1957. Diplomate Am. Bd. Surgery, Am. Bd. Thoracic Surgery, Am. Bd. Pediatric Surgery. Intern Johns Hopkins Hosp., Balt., 1957-58, asst. resident, 1958-59; asst. resident U. Calif. Med. Ctr., Los Angeles, 1959-62, chief resident surgery, 1962-63, asst. prof. surgery, chief pediatric surgery, 1965-68, assoc. prof., 1968-71, prof., 1971—, vice chmn. dept. surgery, 1981-89; resident pediatric surgery Columbus (Ohio) Childrens Hosp. and Ohio State U., 1963-65; practice medicine specializing in pediatric surgery Los Angeles, 1965—; Mem. surg. study sect. NIH; James IV surg. traveller to, Gt. Britain, 1971. Author 3 books; mem. editl. bd. Jour. Surg. Rsch., Archives Surgery, Am. Jour. Surgery, Annals Surgery, Surgery, Current Problems in Surgery, Jour. of Pediatric Surgery, Japanese Jour. Surgery, Turkish Jour. Pediatric Surgery, Med. Video Jour. Surgery; contbr. over 600 articles to med. jours., chpts. to books. Mem. Eagle Scout. Recipient Mead Johnson award for grad. tng. surgery ACS, 1963, Golden Apple award for teaching UCLA Sch. Medicine, 1968; John and Mary R. Markle scholar in acad. medicine, 1963-68; hon. fellow Deutsche Gesellshaft für Chirurgie, Polish Assn. Pediat. Surgery. Fellow ACS (surg. forum com., bd. govs. 1978-84, pres. So. Calif. chpt. 1995-96), Am. Acad. Pediatrics (exec. bd., chmn. surg. sect. 1986-87); mem. AMA, Am. Thoracic Surg. Assn., Am. Acad. Sci., Soc. Univ. Surgeons (pres. 1972, sec. 1973-76), Calif. Med. Assn., Internat. Surg. Group (treas. 1993—), Lilliputian Surg. Soc. (chmn. 1989), L.A. County Med. Assn., Am. Surg. Assn., Pan Pacific Surg. Assn., Pacific Coast Surg. Assn. (recorder 1979-85, pres. 1989), Am. Pediatric Surg. Assn. (bd. govs. 1975-78, pres. 1989), Pacific Assn. Pediatric Surgeons (pres. 1983-84), S.W. Pediatric Soc., L.A. Pediatric Soc., Soc. for Clin. Surgery, Transplantation Soc., Pediatric Surgery Biology Club, Bay Surg. Soc., L.A. Surg. Soc. (sec. 1988-90, pres. 1991), Pithotomy Club (pres. 1956-57), Sigma Xi, Alpha Omega Alpha. Methodist. Home: 428 24th St Santa Monica CA 90402-3102 Office: U Calif Med Ctr Dept Surgery Los Angeles CA 90024

FONS, AUGUST MARION, III, protective services official, educator; b. El Paso, Tex., Jan. 29, 1951; s. August M. Jr. and Nila Anne (Scott) F.; m. Lynn Corbett; children: Trina Anne, Chelsea Marie. AA, N.Mex. Jr. Coll., 1979; BBA, Coll. of S.W., Hobbs, N.Mex., 1987. Police officer, emergency med. technician Alamogordo (N.Mex.) Dept. Police Sta., 1973-76; police officer Hobbs Police Dept., 1976-79, narcotics detective, 1979-81, from police officer to capt., 1982—; fluids engr. IMCO, Houston, 1981-82; instr. N.Mex. Jr. Coll., Hobbs, 1989—; comdr. SWAT team Hobbs Police Dept., 1987-90, instr. in officer survival N.Mex. Law Enforcement Acad., Santa Fe, 1990—. Bd. dirs. Crimestoppers, Hobbs, 1990. With USAF, 1969-73. Mem. Nat. Drug Enforcement Officers Assn., 5th Jud. Law Enforcement Assn. (pres. 1990—), Tex. Narcotics Officers Assn., N.Mex. Narcotics Officers Assn., Nat. Tactical Officers Assn., Hobbs Order of Firefighters, Fraternal Order of Police (treas. 1986-87, bd. dirs. 1994). Roman Catholic. Home: 1123 E Michigan Dr Hobbs NM 88240-3241 Office: Hobbs Police Dept 300 N Turner St Hobbs NM 88240-8302

FONZA, MILFORD R., fire protection official; b. Des Moines, Oct. 23, 1943; s. Hallie and Blossom Fonza; m. Victoria (div. 1981); children: Milford II, Joey, Lolita, Ceasura. Cert. in advance mgmt., Calif. State U., L.A., 1993. Fire fighter Des Moines Fire Dept., 1967-73; fire fighter Pasadena (Calif.) Fire Dept., 1975-79, fire engr., 1979-81, fire capt., 1981-88, fire battalion chief, 1988-91, fire marshall, 1991-93; fire chief City of Compton, Calif., 1993—; sr. advisor Fire Explore Post, Pasadena, 1984-87; Rose Bowl comdr. 1984 Olympics, Pasadena, 1984, NFL Super Bowl, 1993; fire acad. coord. Foothill Fire Acad., Pasadena, 1988-91. Author: Multi-Hazard Response Guide, 1992. With U.S. Army, 1962-65, Vietnam. Recipient Silver Merit award City of Pasadena, 1984. Mem. Nat. Forum Black Pub. Adminstrs., Internat. Fire Chiefs, Black Profl. Fire Fighters, Assn. Retarded Citizens (mem. planning com.). Office: Compton Fire Dept 201 S Acacia Compton CA 90220

FOOTE, PAUL SHELDON, business educator, consultant; b. Lansing, Mich., May 22, 1946; s. Harlon Sheldon and Frances Norene (Rotter) F. BBA, U. Mich., 1967; MBA (Loomis-Sayles fellow), Harvard U., 1971; advanced profl. cert. NYU, 1975; PhD, Mich. State U., 1983; m. Badri Seddigheh Hosseinian, Oct. 25, 1968; children: David, Sheila. Br. mgr., divl. mgr. Citibank, N.Y.C., Bombay, India and Beirut, Lebanon, 1972-74; mgr. planning and devel. Singer Co., Africa/Middle East, 1974-75; instr. U. Mich., Flint, 1978-79; lectr. acctg. Mich. State U., East Lansing, 1977; asst. prof. U. Windsor (Ont., Can.), 1979-81; assoc. prof. Saginaw Valley State Coll., University Center, Mich., 1981-82; asst. prof. Oakland U., Rochester, Mich., 1982-83; asst. prof. NYU, 1983-87; assoc. prof. Pepperdine U., Malibu, Calif., 1987-89; prof. dept. of acctg. Sch. Bus. and Econs. Calif. State U., Fullerton, 1989—; prof. Sultan Qaboos U., Muscat, Oman, 1994—; founder, pres. The Computer Coop., Inc., 1981-82. Lt. AUS, 1968-69. Haskins and Sells Doctoral Consortium fellow, 1977. Mem. Am. Acctg. Assn. Office: Sultan Qaboos U Coll Commerce & Econs, PO Box 20 Al-Khod, 123 Muscat Oman

FOOTMAN, GORDON ELLIOTT, educational administrator; b. L.A., Oct. 10, 1927; s. Arthur Leland and Meta Fay (Neal) F.; m. Virginia Rose Footman, Aug. 7, 1954; children: Virginia, Patricia, John. BA, Occidental Coll., 1951, MA, 1954; EdD, U. So. Calif., 1972. Tchr., Arcadia, Calif., 1952, Glendale, Calif., 1956; psychologist Burbank (Calif.) Schs., 1956-64, supr., 1964-70, dir. pupil personnel services, 1970-72; dir. div. ednl. support svcs. L.A. County Office Edn., Downey, Calif., 1972-91; cons. ednl. adminstrn., counseling and pscyhol. svcs., 1991—; pres. Calif. Assn. Adult Devel. and Aging, 1994—; lectr. ednl. psychology U. So. Calif., 1972-75, asst. prof. ednl. psychology, 1976—. Pres. Council for Exceptional Children, 1969-70; pres. Burbank Coordinating Council, 1969-70; mem. Burbank Family Service Bd., 1971-72. Served with AUS, 1945-47. Mem. Am. Edn. Research Assn., Am. Assn. for Counseling and Devel. (senator 1983-86, gov. coun., 1989—, exec. com. 1990—, parliamentarian 1991—, western region bd. assembly publs. editor 1985-87, chair 1988-89), Calif. Personnel and Guidance Assn. (pres. 1981-82), Calif. Assn. Sch. Psychologists and Psychometrists, Nat., Calif. (monograph editor 1977—), Assns. Pupil Personnel Adminstrs., Calif. Assn. Counselor Educators and Suprs. (trustee), Calif. Assn. Sch. Adminstrs., Calif. Soc. Ednl. Program Auditors and Evaluators (sec. 1975-76, v.p. 1976-77, pres.), Calif. Assn. Measurement and Evaluation in Guidance (sec. 1976, pres. 1979-80), Calif. Inst. Tech. Assocs., Coun. Exceptional Children (pres. Foothill chpt. 1969-70), Phi Beta Kappa, Phi Alpha Theta, Psi Chi. Republican. Presbyn. Home and Office: 1259 Sherwood Rd San Marino CA 91108-1816

FOPIANO, LOIS MAE, institute administrator, psychotherapist,; b. Hollywood, Calif., Feb. 19, 1938; d. Harry James Fopiano and Lois (Ross) Fopiano-Rose; m. George Raymond Cuthbertson, Aug. 3, 1959 (div. Dec. 1975); children: Susan Mae, William Archer. B in Home Econ., Whittier Coll., 1959; M in Spl. Edn., Mount St. Mary's Coll., 1987; M in Psychology, Profl. Sch. Psychiat. Studies, 1989; D in Clin. Hypnotherapy, Am. Inst. Hypnotherapy, 1994. Grief counselor Grant Beckstand Cancer Ctr., Long Beach, 1987-88, H.U.G.S., Honolulu, 1990-91; pvt. practice Kailua, Hawaii, 1991-92, Hilo, Hawaii, 1992-94; family crisis counselor The Inst. for Family Enrichment, Honolulu, 1991-92; family counselor MIST, Hilo, 1992-93; program adminstr. The Inst. for Family Enrichment, Hilo, 1993-94; intern Calif. Assn. Marriage and Family Therapist, Long Beach, 1987-90, Orange County, 1988-90; rsch. and presentations on superlearning to enhance learning with spl. needs children and used with hypnosis to accelerate the process of achieving desired results. Author, editor: (children's newsletter) Daily Plan-It, 1981. Pres. Winward Bus. Assn., Kailua, 1991-92. Mem. Am. Counseling Assn., Healthy Mothers Healthy Babies, Hawaii Counseling Network, Western Hawaii Health and Human Svcs. Office: 1465 Kiluea Hilo HI 96720

FORAKER, DAVID ALAN, lawyer; b. Mpls., Feb. 22, 1956; s. Crawford Jackson and Norma Jane (Settlemoir) F.; m. Nancy Jean Howard, May 9, 1987. MS, St. Cloud State U., 1978; JD, U. Oreg., 1981. Bar: Oreg. 1981; cert. bus. bankruptcy law, Am. Bankruptcy Bd. Certification. Assoc. McMenamin, Joseph, Babener, Greene & Perris, Portland, Oreg., 1981-83, Greene & Perris, Portland, 1983-84; ptnr. Greene & Markley, P.C., Portland, 1984—; mem. Oreg. Debtor Creditor Bankruptcy Rules Subcom., 1987—, chair, 1992, Oreg. Debtor Creditor Fast Track Chpt. II Subcom., 1991—; speaker Oreg. Trial Lawyers Assn., 1987, N.W. Bankruptcy Inst., 1992. Editor Oreg. Debtor-Creditor News, 1987—, editor-in-chief, 1988. Mem. ABA, Oreg. Bar Assn., Multnomah County Bar Assn., Am. Bankruptcy Inst. Democrat. Episcopalian. Office: Greene & Markley PC 1515 SW 5th Ave Ste 600 Portland OR 97201-5449

FORBES, DAVID CRAIG, musician; b. Seattle, Feb. 12, 1938; s. Douglas James and Ruby A. (Niles) F.; m. Sylvia Sterling, Aug. 29, 1965 (div. Apr. 1973); 1 child, Angela Rose. Grad., USN Sch. Music, 1957; student, Western Wash. U., 1960-64. Prin. horn La Jolla (Calif.) Civic Orch., 1958-60, Seattle Worlds Fair Band, 1962, Seattle Opera Co., 1964—, Pacific Northwest Ballet, Seattle, 1964—; asst. prin. horn Seattle Symphony Orch., 1964—; prin. horn Pacific Northwest Wagner Fest., Seattle, 1975—; instr. horn Western Wash. State U., 1969-81, Cornish Inst., Seattle, 1964-78. Served with USN, 1956-60. Mem. NARAS, Internat. Horn Soc. Home: 217 NW Market St Seattle WA 98107-3430

FORBES, KENNETH ALBERT FAUCHER, urological surgeon; b. Waterford, N.Y., Apr. 28, 1922; s. Joseph Frederick and Adelle Frances (Robitaille) F.; m. Eileen Ruth Gibbons, Aug. 4, 1956; children: Michael, Diane, Kenneth E., Thomas, Maureen, Daniel. BS cum laude, U. Notre Dame, 1943; MD, St. Louis U., 1947. Diplomate Am. Bd. Urology. Intern St. Louis U. Hosp., 1947-48; resident in urol. surgery Barnes Hosp., VA Hosp., Washington U., St. Louis. U. schs. medicine, St. Louis, 1948-52; asst. chief urology Letterman Army Hosp., San Francisco, 1952-54; fellow West Roxbury (Harvard) VA Hosp., Boston, 1955; asst. chief urology VA Hosp., East Orange, N.J., 1955-58; practice medicine specializing in urology Green Bay, Wis., 1958-78, Long Beach, Calif., 1978-85; mem. cons. staff Fairview State Hosp. U. Calif. Med. Ctr., Irvine, VA Hosp., Long Beach; asst. clin. prof. surgery U. Calif., Irvine, 1978-85; cons. Vols. in Tech. Assistance, 1986—. Contbr. articles to profl. jours. Served with USNR, 1944-46; capt. U.S. Army, 1952-54. Named Outstanding Faculty Mem. by students, 1981. Fellow ACS, Royal Soc. Medicine, Internat. Coll. Surgeons; mem. AMA, AAAS, Calif. Med. Assn., Am. Urol. Assn. (exec. com. North Ctrl. sect. 1972-75, Western sect. 1980—), N.Y. Acad. Scis., Surg. Alumni Assn. U. Calif.-Irvine, Justin J. Cordonnier Soc. Washington U., Confedn. Americana Urologia, Urologists Corr. Club, Notre Dame Club (Man of Yr. award 1965), Union League Club of Chgo., Phi Beta Pi. Republican. Roman Catholic. Home and Office: 11579 Sutters Mill Cir Gold River CA 95670-7214

FORBES, LEONARD, engineering educator; b. Grande Prairie, Alta., Can., Feb. 21, 1940; came to U.S., 1966; s. Frank and Katie (Tschetter) F.; B.Sc. with distinction in Engring. Physics, U. Alta., 1962; M.S. in E.E., U. Ill., 1963, Ph.D., 1970. Staff engr. IBM, Fishkill, N.Y. and Manassas, Va., 1970-72; IBM vis. prof. Howard U., Washington, 1972; asst. prof. U. Ark., Fayetteville, 1972-75; assoc. prof. U. Calif.-Davis, 1976-82; prof. Oreg. State U., Corvallis, 1983—; with Hewlett-Packard Labs., Palo Alto, Calif., 1978; cons. to Telex Computer Products, D.H. Baldwin, Hewlett-Packard, Fairchild, United Epitaxial Tech., Naval Ocean Systems Ctr.; organizer Portland Internat. Conf. and Exposition on Silicon Materials and Tech., 1985-87. Served with Royal Can. Air Force, 1963-66. Mem. IEEE. Contbr. articles to profl. jours. Home: 965 NW Highland Ter Corvallis OR 97330-9706 Office: Oreg State U Dept Elec Engring Corvallis OR 97331

FORBIS, RICHARD GEORGE, archaeologist; b. Missoula, Mont., July 30, 1924; s. Clarence Jenks and Josephine Marie (Hunt) F.; m. Marjorie Helen Wilkinson, Nov. 12, 1960; children: Michael, David, Amanda. B.A., U. Mont., 1949, M.A., 1950; Ph.D., Columbia U., 1955. Sr. archeologist Pacific N.W. Pipeline Corp., Western U.S., 1955-56; archeologist Glenbow Found., Calgary, Alta., Can., 1957-63; mem. faculty U. Calgary, 1963—, prof. archaeology, 1968-88, prof. emeritus, 1988—, interim chmn. dept., Killam Meml. fellow, 1977; chmn. Alta. Public Adv. Com. Hist. and Archeol. Resources, 1971-74; mem. Alta. Historic Sites Bd., 1974-78; vis. scientist Can. Nat. Museum Man, 1970. Author: Cluny: An Ancient Fortified Village in Alberta, 1977; co-author: An Introduction to the Archaeology of Alberta, Canada, 1965. Served with AUS, 1943-46. Mem. AAAS, Soc. Am. Archaeology, Can. Archaeol. Assn. (Smith-Wintemberg award 1984), Am. Anthrop. Assn., Plains Anthrop. Conf., Champlain Soc., Sigma Chi. Office: U Calgary Dept Archeology, 2500 University Dr NW, Calgary, AB Canada T2N 1N4

FORCE, ROLAND WYNFIELD, anthropologist, museum executive; b. Omaha, Dec. 30, 1924; s. Richard Erwin and Edna Fern (Collins) F.; m. Maryanne Tefft, Sept. 16, 1949. B.A., Stanford U., 1950, M.A. in Edn., 1951, M.A. in Anthropology, 1952, Ph.D. in Anthropology, 1958; D.Sci. (hon.), Hawaii Loa Coll., 1973. Acting instr. Stanford U., 1954; assoc. in ethnology Bernice P. Bishop Mus., Honolulu, 1954-56, dir., 1962-76, dir. emeritus, 1976—, holder C.R. Bishop Disting. chair in Pacific studies, 1976-77; dir. Mus. Am. Indian, Heye Found., N.Y.C., 1977-86, pres., dir., 1986-90, pres., dir. emeritus, 1990—; curator oceanic archeology, ethnology Field Mus. of Natural History, Chgo., 1956-61. Served with C.E. and Infantry AUS, 1943-46. Fellow Am. Anthrop. Assn., AAAS, Pacific Sci. Assn. (hon. life, mem. council 1966-77); mem. Sigma Xi. Home: 161 Kalaiopua Pl Honolulu HI 96822-5005

FORCE, RONALD WAYNE, librarian; b. Sioux City, Iowa, Sept. 7, 1941; s. Robert N. and Madeline (Heine) F.; m. Jo Ellen Hitch, May 31, 1964; children: Emily, Alicia. BS, Iowa State U., 1963; MA, U. Minn., 1968; MS, Ohio State U., 1975. Asst. to head dept. librs. Ohio State U., Columbus, 1968-70, head engring. librs., 1970-72, head edn./psychology libr., 1972-79; asst. dir. pub. svcs. Wash. State U. Librs., Pullman, 1979-82; asst. sci. libr. U. Idaho Libr., Moscow, 1982-84, pub. svcs. libr., 1984-85, humanities libr., 1985-88, assoc. dean libr. svcs., 1988-91, dean libr. svcs., 1991—; mem. adv. coun. Libr. Svcs. and Constrn. Act. Author: Guide to Literature on Biomedical Engineering, 1972; contbr. articles to profl. jours. Mem. Sacajawea Coun. Campfire Bd., 1980-85, mem. Pullman Dist. Campfire Com., fin. com., 1980-82, chair, 1983-84, treas., 1985, Sacajawea County Self-Study Com., 1986; mem. adv. bd. N.W. Net Info. Resources, 1994—; mem. Idaho Network Adv. Com., 1993—; mem. LSCA Adv. Coun., 1989-95. Mem. ALA, Idaho Libr. Assn. Home: 545 N Blaine St Moscow ID 83843-3626 Office: U Idaho Libr Moscow ID 83844-2371

FORD, BETTY BLOOMER (ELIZABETH FORD), health facility executive, wife of former President of United States; b. Chgo., Apr. 8, 1918; d. William Stephenson and Hortence (Neahr) Bloomer; m. Gerald R. Ford (38th Pres. U.S.), Oct. 15, 1948; children: Michael Gerald, John Gardner, Steven Meigs, Susan Elizabeth. Student, Sch. Dance Bennington Coll., 1936, 37; LL.D. (hon.), U. Mich., 1976. Dancer Martha Graham Concert Group, N.Y.C., 1939-41; model John Powers Agy., N.Y.C., 1939-41; fashion dir. Herpolscheimer's Dept. Store, Grand Rapids, Mich., 1943-48; dance instr. Grand Rapids, 1932-48; chmn. bd. dirs. The Betty Ford Ctr., Rancho Mirage, Calif. Author: autobiography The Times of My Life, 1979, Betty: A Glad Awakening, 1987. Bd. dirs. Nat. Arthritis Found. (hon.); trustee Martha Graham Dance Ctr., Eisenhower Med. Ctr., Rancho Mirage; hon. chmn. Palm Springs Desert Mus.; nat. trustee Nat. Symphony Orch.; trustee Nursing Home Adv. and Rsch. Coun. Inc.; mem. Golden Circle Patrons Ctr. Theatre Performing Arts; bd. dirs. The Lambs, Libertyville, Ill.; Sunday sch.

tchr., 1961-64. Mem. Women in Senate and House. Episcopalian. Home: PO Box 927 Rancho Mirage CA 92270-0927*

FORD, FREEMAN ARMS, manufacturing company executive; b. L.A., Feb. 24, 1941; s. Robert Freeman and Janet (Vosberg) F.; m. Diana Vhay, May 28, 1966; children: David, Kimberly, Tod, Erin. AB in Econs., Dartmouth, 1963; MS in Bus., Stanford U., 1980. Aviator USN, Alameda, Calif., 1968; prodn. mgr. Kasper Instruments, Santa Clara, Calif., 1969-71; founder, pres. FAFCO, Inc., Redwood City, Calif., 1971—; past pres. Solar Energy Industries Assn., Washington; dir. H.B. Fuller Co., St. Paul, 1976—. Patentee in field. Office: FAFCO Inc 2690 Middlefield Rd Redwood City CA 94063-3402

FORD, GERALD RUDOLPH, JR., former President of United States; b. Omaha, July 14, 1913; s. Gerald R. and Dorothy (Gardner) F.; m. Elizabeth Bloomer, Oct. 15, 1948; children: Michael, John, Steven, Susan. A.B., U. Mich., 1935; LL.B., Yale U., 1941; LL.D., Mich. State U., Albion Coll., Aquinas Coll., Spring Arbor Coll. Bar: Mich. 1941. Practiced law at Grand Rapids, 1941-49; mem. law firm Buchen and Ford; mem. 81st-93d Congresses from 5th Mich. Dist., 1949-74, elected minority leader, 1965; v.p. U.S., 1973-74, pres., 1974-77; del. Interparliamentary Union, Warsaw, Poland, 1959, Belgium, 1961, Bilderberg Group Conf., 1962; dir. The Travelers, Inc., Alexander & Alexander; adv. dir. Tex. Commerce Bancshares, Inc., Am. Express Co.; mem. internat. adv. coun. Inst. Internat. Studies. Served as lt. comdr. USNR, 1942-46. Recipient Grand Rapids Jr. C. of C. Distinguished Service award, 1948; Distinguished Service Award as one of ten outstanding young men in U.S. by U.S. Jr. C. of C., 1950; Silver Anniversary All-Am. Sports Illustrated, 1959; Distinguished Congressional Service award Am. Polit. Sci. Assn., 1961. Mem. Am., Mich. State, Grand Rapids bar assns., Delta Kappa Epsilon, Phi Delta Phi. Republican. Episcopalian. Clubs: University (Kent County), Peninsular (Kent County). Lodge: Masons. Home: care Judy Risk PO Box 927 Rancho Mirage CA 92270-0927

FORD, JAMES CARLTON, human resources executive; b. Portland, Mar. 10, 1937; s. John Bernard and Margaret (Reynolds) F.; m. Carolyn Tadina, Aug. 22, 1959; children: Scott, Michele, Mark, Brigitte, Deidre, John. BA in History, U. Portland, 1960; MS in Edn., Troy State U., 1969; MPA, U. Puget Sound, 1976. Cert. sen. profl. in human resources. Commd. 2d lt. USAF, 1960, advanced through grades to lt. col., 1976, adminstr., tng. officer, 1960-70, personnel mgmt. officer, 1971-76; dep. inspector gen. U.S. Air Force Acad., Colorado Springs, Colo., 1977-80; ret. U.S. Air Force Acad., 1980; employment mgr. Western Fed. Savs. (name changed to Bank Western), Denver, 1980-82, v.p. human resources, 1982-88, sr. v.p. mgmt. svcs., 1988-92; dir. career mgmt. AIM Exec., Inc., Cons. Svcs., 1992-95; owner Orgn./Individual Strategies, Inc., Cons., 1995—; bd. dirs. Rocky Mountain chpt. AM. Inst. of Banking, Denver; adj. prof. U. Colo., Colorado Springs, 1978-79, USAF Acad., Colorado Springs, 1978-80; adv. bd. U. Colo. Contemporary Mgmt. Program, Regis Coll. Career Svcs. Mediator Neighborhood Justice Ctr., Colorado Springs, 1980; vol. allocations com. Pikes Peak United Way, Colorado Springs, 1978-79; vol. campaign exec. Mile Hi United Way, Denver, 1986-89; vol. mgmt. cons. Tech. Assistance Svc., Denver, 1991. Mem. Assn. for Mgmt. of Orgn. Design, Soc. for Human Resource Mgmt., Adminstrv. Mgmt. Soc. Republican. Roman Catholic. Office: Orgn/Individual Strategies, Inc 975 Tari Dr Colorado Springs CO 80921

FORD, JOHN T., JR., art, film and video educator; b. Rotan, Tex., Feb. 17, 1953; s. John T. and Lala Fern (Shipley) F.; m. Betty Jean Crawford; children: Casey, Craig, Kirk. BA, U. Redlands, 1975. Cert. tchr., Calif. Tchr. art, film, video Yucaipa (Calif.) Joint Unified Sch. Dist., 1976-88; tchr. art and crafts Vacaville (Calif.) Unified Sch. Dist., 1990-92, tchr. video prodn., 1992—; cons. Dist. Fine Arts Insvc., Yucaipa, 1987; co-sponsor Art Club, Will C. Wood High Sch., Vacaville, sponsor Video Club. Creator, coord. (conceptual art) Whole School Environments, Caves, Tubes and Streamers, Forest Edge, 1980-84; creator (comml. art prints) Toy Horse Series, 1982-83. Mem. Yeoman Svc. Orgn., U. Redlands, 1972, Vacaville Sch. Dist. Tech. Com., Dist. Fine Arts Task Force, Yucaipa, 1984-87, Dist. Task Force for Vocat. Edn., 1992; interim dir. Hosanna House, Redlands, Calif., 1975; liaison Sch. Community Svc./San Bernardino County (Calif.) Fire Dept., 1980-81. Recipient Golden Bell award Calif. Sch. Bd. Research Found., 1987, Ednl. Service award Mason's, 1987-88; named one of Outstanding Young Men of Am., 1987, Tchr. of Yr. Calif. Continuation Edn. Assn., 1987-88; grantee Calif. Tchrs. Instructional Improvement Program, 1985; scholar U. Redlands, 1975. Mem. Am. Film Inst. Office: Will C Wood High Sch 998 Marshall Rd Vacaville CA 95687-5735

FORD, MICHAEL Q., not-for-profit association administrator; b. Washington, Dec. 12, 1949; s. Milton Q. and Jeanne Louise (Goltman) F.; m. Christine Ann Davies, Apr. 24, 1971 (div. June 1980); m. Elizabeth Julia Ginsberg, June 1, 1984; 1 child, Jennifer. BS in Journalism, Ohio U., 1971. Writer, reporter TV Digest, Washington, 1971-72; staff writer Coun. Better Bus. Burs., Washington, 1972-74; staff assoc. Ctr. for Study of Responsive Law, Washington, 1974; exec. dir. Coalition for Health Funding, Washington, 1975-77; dir. Office of Pub. Policy Nat. Coun. on Alcoholism, Washington, 1977-80; pres. Nat. Assn. Addiction Treatment Providers, Irvine, Calif., 1980-93; exec. dir. Nat. Nutritional Foods Assn., Newport Beach, Calif., 1994—; trustee Commn. on Accreditation of Rehab. Facilities, Tucson, 1985-91. Chmn. legis. com. Nat. Coalition for Adequate Alcoholism Programs, Washington, 1978-80, chmn., 1981. Fellow Am. Coll. of Addiction Treatment Adminstrs. Jewish. Home: 3013 Nestall Rd Laguna Beach CA 92651-2026 Office: Nat Nutritional Foods Assn 3931 MacArthur Blvd # 101 Newport Beach CA 92660

FORD, RICHARD CHRISTIAN, mortgage banker; b. San Diego, Dec. 18, 1961; s. R. and Elsa (Schuster) F. BA in Comm., San Diego State U., 1989; AS in Mktg. Mgmt., Mesa Coll., San Diego, 1989, AA in Psychology, 1989, AS in Real Estate, 1991. Comml. real estate mgr. John Burnham & Co., San Diego, 1990; govt. rev. auditor Am. Resdl., San Diego, 1991; govt. loan ins. specialist Guild Mortgage Co. Inc., San Diego, 1992-93; quality control auditor Guild Cos., Inc., San Diego, 1993-94; loan officer Am. Fidelity Mortgage, San Diego, 1994—. Editor/pubr. newsletter: Meeting People in San Diego, 1990-92; author: College Survival Guide, 1991. Mem., chair Pacific Beach Planning Com., San Diego, 1988-90; announcer LaJolla Christmas Parade, 1991-94. Mem. Speech Comm. Assn. (v.p. 1989), Nat. Platform Assn., Toastmasters of La Jolla (pres. 1992, Competent Toastmaster 1991, Able Toastmaster 1993, area gov. 1993-94). Republican. Roman Catholic. Office: Real Property Fin Svcs 8280 La Mesa Blvd La Mesa CA 91941

FORD, VICTORIA, public relations executive; b. Carroll, Iowa, Nov. 1, 1946; d. Victor Sargent and Gertrude Francis (Headlee) F.; m. John K. Frans, July 4, 1965 (div. Aug. 1975); m. David W. Keller, May 2, 1981 (div. Nov. 1985); m. Jerry W. Lambert, Mar. 30, 1991. AA, Iowa Lakes Community Coll., 1973; BA summa cum laude, Buena Vista Coll., 1974; MA in Journalism, U. Nev., Reno, 1988. Juvenile parole officer Iowa Dept. Social Services, Sioux City, 1974-78; staff reporter Feather Pub. Co., Quincy, Calif., 1978-80; tng. counselor CETA, Quincy, 1980; library pub. info. officer U. Nev., Reno, 1982-84; pub. relations exec. Brodeur/Martin Pub. Relations, Reno, 1984-87; pub. relations dir. Internat. Winter Spl. Olympics, Lake Tahoe (Calif.) and Reno, 1987-89; owner Ford Factor Pub. Rels. cons. firm, Reno, 1989—. Contbr. articles to Range Mag., other profl. jours. Mem. adv. bd. Reno Philharm., 1985-87, Reno-Sparks Conv. and Visitors Authority, 1985-93; bd. dirs. Truckee Meadows Habitat for Humanity, 1992-93, half-time exec. dir., 1994; mem. Gov.'s Com. on Fire Prevention, 1991-92; mem. U. Nev. Reno Oral History Program, 1994; bd. dirs. Nev. Women's Archives, 1994—; mem. com. Nev. Writers Hall of Fam, 1993, 94; bd. dirs. Friends of the U. Nev. at Reno Libr., 1995. Mem. NOW, Pub. Rels. Soc. Am. (charter v.p. Sierra Nev. chpt. 1986-87, pres. 1987-88), Sigma Delta Chi. Democrat. Home: PO Box 6715 Reno NV 89513-6715 Office: The Ford Factor PO Box 6715 Reno NV 89513-6715

FORDEMWALT, JAMES NEWTON, microelectronics educator, consultant, engineer; b. Parsons, Kans., Oct. 18, 1932; s. Fred and Zenia (Chambers) F.; m. Suzan Lynn Hopkins, Aug. 26, 1958 (div. June 1961); m. Elizabeth Anna Hoare, Dec. 29, 1963; children: John William, James Frederick. BS, U. Ariz., 1955, MS, 1956; PhD, U. Iowa, 1960. Sr. engr. GE Co., Evandale, Ohio, 1959-60, U.S. Semcor, Inc., Phoenix, 1960-61; sect. mgr. Motorola Semiconductor Products Div., Phoenix, 1961-66; dept. mgr. Philco-Ford Microelectronics Div., Santa Clara, Calif., 1966-68; assoc. dir. R & D Am. Microsystems Inc., Santa Clara, 1968-71; assoc. rsch. prof. U. Utah, Salt Lake City, 1972-76; dir. microelectronics lab. U. Ariz., Tucson, 1976-87; assoc. prof., lab. mgr. Ariz. State U., Tempe, 1987—, assoc. chair microelectronics, 1992—, asst. chair dept. electronic and computer tech., 1993—; cons. Integrated Cirs. Engring., Scottsdale, Ariz., 1976—, Western Design Ctr., Mesa, Ariz., 1980—; mem. semiconductor com. United Techs. Corp., Hartford, Conn., 1978-87. Author: Silicon Wafer Processing Technology, 1979; editor: Integrated Circuits, 1965; contbr.: MOS Integrated Circuits, 1972. Mem. IEEE, Internat. Soc. for Hybrid Microelectronics (chpt. pres. 1982-83), Electrochem. Soc. Home: 613 W Summit Pl Chandler AZ 85224-1556

FORDER, REG ARTHUR, publishing executive; b. Edmonton, Alberta, Canada, Jan. 4, 1943; s. William A. and Janet A. (Williams) F.; m. Eleonore J. Bergan, July 30, 1984; children: Jerry, Donna, Sharon, Mark, Dale. Grad. high sch., Canada. Mgr. Nat. Real Estate Svc., Vancouver, Canada, 1965-77; prin. Century Vending, Phoenix, 1981—; pub. Christian Communicator Mag., Phoenix, 1994—; dir. confs. Am. Christian Writers, 1981—. Author: Soulwinning: An Action Handbook for Christians, 1985. Office: Am Christian Writers PO Box 5168 Phoenix AZ 85010

FORDYCE, SAMUEL WESLEY, electrical engineer, communications company executive; b. Jackson, Miss., Feb. 28, 1927; s. Samuel Wesley and Polly Adams (White) F.; S.B., Harvard U., 1949; M.S., Washington U., St. Louis, 1953; m. Sally Gillespie, Apr. 9, 1970; children—Katherine Peake, Debbie Fordyce, Wesley, Polly. Project engr. Emerson Electric Co., St. Louis, 1949-58; mem. tech. staff Ramo Wooldridge, Los Angeles, 1958-60, Gen. Electric Tempo, Santa Barbara, Calif., 1960-62; chief engr. communications div. NASA, Washington, 1962-84; chief oper. officer Advanced Bus. Communications, Inc., McLean Va., 1986-88, cons. Cape York Space Agy., Brisbane, Australia, 1988—; pres. Riparian Research Corp., 1984—. Served with USN, 1944-46. Registered profl. engr., Mo. Assoc. fellow AIAA; sr. mem. IEEE. Clubs: St. Louis Country; Met. of Washington; Chevy Chase. Achievements include design and development of radio communications systems used on Apollo (manned lunar landing) Program. Home: 195 Sheffield Dr Santa Barbara CA 93108-2242

FORE, ANN, counselor, educator; b. Artesia, N.Mex., July 16, 1948; d. Stanley William and Jackie (Hightower) Blocker; divorced; 1 child Richard Todd. BS, Eastern N.Mex. U., Portales, 1971, MA, 1976. Instr. sociology Eastern N.Mex. U., Clovis, 1974; counselor, instr. So. Plains Jr. Coll., Plainview, Tex., 1975-76; drug and alcohol counselor U.S. Dept. Army, Ft. Hood, Tex., 1976-77; group leader Forest Svc., USDA, Estacada, Oreg., 1980-81; owner Koda Kountry Prodns., Salem, Oreg., 1990—, Women's Issues Counseling Svcs., Salem, 1985—; tchr. country western ptnr. dancing and line dancing various ednl. settings, Salem, Oreg., Portland C.C., Salem Keizer Schs. Author: Silent Cry, 1993; choreographer 1 line dances. U. N.Mex. Rsch. Dept. grantee, 1972. Mem. APGA, Willamette Writers Assn., Nat. Tchrs. Assn. for Country/Western Dance Instrs. Republican. Christian. Home and Office: PO Box 13851 Salem OR 97309-1851

FORESTER, BERNARD I., recreational equipment company executive; b. 1928. B.S. in Bus. Adminstrn., U. Ariz., 1950. Audit mgr. Price Waterhouse & Co., 1950-64; chief fin. officer, dir. Republic Corp., 1964-66; exec. v.p., gen. mgr. Anthony Industries, Inc., City of Commerce, Calif., 1966-67, pres., 1967-90, chief exec. officer, 1973—, chmn. bd., 1975—, also dir. With AUS, 1946-48. Office: Anthony Industries Inc 4900 S Eastern Ave Ste 200 Los Angeles CA 90040-2962

FORESTER, JOHN, cycling transportation engineer; b. London, Oct. 7, 1929; came to the U.S., 1940; s. Cecil Scott and Kathleen (Belcher) F. AB, U. Calif., Berkeley, 1951; MS, Calif. State U., Long Beach, 1964. Registered industrial engr., Calif. Cycling transporation engr. Sunnyvale, Calif., 1972—. Author: Statistical Selections of Business Strategies, 1968, Effective Cycling, 1976, 6th edit., 1993, Bicycle Transportation, 1977, 4th edit., 1994. Rsch. bd. bicycling com. transporation Nat. Acad. Scis., 1977-83. pres. Calif. Assn. Bicycling Orgns., 1973-76, League Am. Bicyclists, 1979-80, dir., 1976-83. Home and Office: 726 Madrone Ave Sunnyvale CA 94086-3041

FORGACS, OTTO LIONEL, forest products company executive; b. Berlin, Jan. 4, 1931; emigrated to Can., 1955; s. Joseph and Luise (Schick) Forgacs; m. Patricia Purdom Saunders, Sept. 24, 1960; children: Anthony, Stephen, Jonathan. B.Sc. in Tech., U. Manchester, Eng., 1955; Ph.D., McGill U., 1959. Pulp and paper research Inst. Can., Montreal, 1958-63; research mgr. Domtar, Ltd., Montreal, 1963-73; research dir. MacMillan & Bloedel, Ltd., Vancouver, B.C., Can., 1973-77, v.p. reserach and devel., 1977-79, sr. v.p. research and devel., 1979—; dir. Forest Engring. Inst. of Can., 1985—; dir. Zellstoff, Papierfabrik Frantschach, Austria; mem. Sci. Council B.C., 1977-83. Contbr. numerous articles tech. jours. Fellow TAPPI (chmn. research and devel. div.), Chem. Inst. Can.; mem. Can. Pulp and Paper Assn. (councillor, exec. council 1977-80). Club: Vancouver Lawn Tennis. Home: 1843 Acadia Rd, Vancouver, BC Canada V6T 1R2 Office: Noranda Inc, 4225 Kincaid St, Burnaby, BC Canada V5G 4P5

FORGAN, DAVID WALLER, retired air force officer; b. Chgo., Sept. 28, 1933; s. Harold Nye and Ruth Ada (Waller) F.; m. Shirley Dobbins, Oct. 18, 1958; children—Bruce Dobbins, Todd Macmillan. B.S. in Mktg., U. Colo., 1955; M.S. in Mgmt., George Washington U., 1966. Commd. 2d lt. U.S. Air Force, 1956, advanced through grades to maj. gen., 1985, various positions worldwide, 1956-77; dir. programs hdgrs. tactical air command U.S. Air Force, Langley AFB, Va., 1977-79; dir. force devel. U.S. Air Force, Washington, 1979-80; dep. comdr. spl. ops. command U.S. Air Force, Fort Bragg, N.C., 1980-82; asst. chief staff ops. Allied Forces Central Europe, Brunssum, The Netherlands, 1982-85; dep. chief staff ops. U.S. Air Force Europe, Ramstein Air Base, Fed. Republic Germany, 1985-87; comdr. Sheppard Tech. Tng. Ctr. Sheppard AFB, Tex., 1987-89; ret., 1989. Decorated Silver Star, D.F.C. (3), Legion of Merit, Air medal, Def. Disting. Svc. medal, Def. Superior Svc. medal; Aero Cross of Merit (Spain). Mem. Delta Tau Delta. Republican. Home: 4935 Newstead Pl Colorado Springs CO 80906-5978

FORGANG, DAVID M., museum curator; b. N.Y.C., Mar. 26, 1947; s. Joseph Hyman and Clarice (Ishbia) F.; m. Joyce Enid Blumenthal, June 15, 1968 (div. May 1979); children: Adam, Bradley. B in Anthropology, U. Ariz., 1968, M in Anthropology, 1971. Mus. curator So. Ariz. Group Nat. Pk. Svc., Phoenix, 1971-77; regional curator we. region Nat. Pk. Svc., San Francisco, 1977-82; chief curator Yosemite (Calif.) Mus. Nat. Pk. Svc., 1982—; pres. Yosemite Renaissance Art Competition, 1983-94; dir. Yosemite Artist in Residence Program, 1985—. Mariposa County advisor El Portal (Calif.) Town Planning Adv. Bd., 1984-94. Recipient Unit Award citation USDI, 1974. Democrat. Jewish. Office: Nat Pk Svc PO Box 577 Yosemite National Park CA 95389-0577

FORKERT, CLIFFORD ARTHUR, civil engineer; b. Verona, N.D., Oct. 16, 1916; s. Arthur Louis and Bessie (Delamater) F.; grad. N.D. State Coll., 1940; postgrad. M.I.T.; m. Betty Jo Erickson, July 1, 1940; children: Terry Lynn Forkert Williamson, Michael, Debra Edwards. Hwy. engr., N.D., Tex., 1937-40; hydraulic engr. Internat. Boundary Commn. Tex. on Rio Grande and Tributaries, 1940-43; constrn., topographic and cons. engr., Calif. 1946—; now civil engr., prin. Clifford A. Forkert, Civil Engr.; pres. Calif. Poly. Pomona Assos. Capt. USMCR, 1943-46. Registered civil engr. Calif., Oreg., Ariz., profl. engr., Nev., Ariz.; lic. land surveyor, Nev., Ariz. Mem. Am. Congress and Mapping (life), ASCE (life), Land Surveyors Assn. Calif. (dir.), Alumni Assn. N.D. State Coll. Died Mar. 29, 1995. Home: 20821 Skimmer Ln Huntington Beach CA 92646-6548 Office: 22311 Brookhurst St Huntington Beach CA 92646-8450

FORMAN, JOEL JON, numismatic appraiser; b. Bklyn., July 4, 1938; s. Eugene and Esther (Kushel) F.; m. Linda Joy Karel, July 5, 1964; children: Debra Ann, David Alon. BA in Math., San Diego State U., 1966; M in Computer Sci., West Coast U., 1975; M in Valuation Sci., Lindenwood Coll., 1993. Software engr. various def. contractors, San Diego, L.A., 1962-77, Hughes Aircraft Co., El Segundo, Calif., 1978-93; cert. numismatic appraiser Culver City, Calif., 1988—; importer/exporter Culver City, 1991—; numismatic advisor, cons. Simon Wiesenthal Ctr., L.A., 1979—. Contbr. articles to profl. jours. With USMC, 1958-61. Mem. Am. Soc. of Appraisers (internat. bd. examiners 1992—), Toastmasters Internat. (officer, many awards), B'nai B'rith Lodge (pres. 1971-72). Jewish. Home and Office: Ste 9G 11260 Overland Ave Apt 9G Culver City CA 90230-5532

FORMBY, BENT CLARK, immunologist; b. Copenhagen, Apr. 3, 1940; naturalized, 1991; s. John K. and Gudrun A. (Dinesen) F.; m. Irene Menck-Thygesen, June 28, 1963 (div. May 1980); children: Rasmus, Mikkel; m. Florence G. Schmid, June 28, 1980. BA in Philosophy summa cum laude, U. Copenhagen, 1959, PhD in Biochemistry, 1968, DSc, 1976. Asst. prof. U. Copenhagen, 1969-73, assoc. prof., 1973-79, prof., 1979-83; vis. prof. U. Calif., San Francisco, 1979-84; sr. scientist, dir. lab. of immunology Sansum Med. Rsch. Found., Santa Barbara, Calif., 1984—; cons. Cell Tech., Inc., Boulder, Colo., 1989—, Immunex Corp., Seattle, 1989—; med. adv. bd. Biocellular Rsch. Orgn., Ltd., London, Childrens Hosp. of Orange County, Lautenburg Ctr. for Gen. and Tumor Immunology, Hebrew U., Hadassah Med. Sch., Jerusalem, 1993—, Loran Med. Sys., Inc. Editor: Fetal Islet Transplantation, 1988, 2d edit. 1995; contbr. articles to profl. jours.; patentee on non-invasive blood glucose measurement. Grantee Juvenile Diabetes Found., 1987, 88, E.L. Wiegand Found., 1993, Santa Barbara Cottage Hosp. Rsch., 1993-94, Breast Cancer Rsch. U. Calif., 1995—. Mem. N.Y. Acad. Scis., Am. Diabetes Assn. (grantee 1985, 86, 89), Am. Fedn. Clin. Rsch., European Assn. for the Study of Diabetes. Office: Sansum Med Rsch Found 2219 Bath St Santa Barbara CA 93105-4321

FORREST, KENTON HARVEY, science educator, historian; b. Fort Lauderdale, Fla., Oct. 3, 1944; s. Harvey William and Marjorie A. (Boxrud) F. BA, Colo. State Coll., 1968; MA, U. No. Colo., 1981. Science tchr. Dunstan Middle Sch., Jefferson County Pub. Schs., Lakewood, Colo., 1968—; pres. Tramway Press, Inc., 1983—. Author: Denver's Railroads, 1981; (with William C. Jones) Denver-A Pictorial History, 1973; (with others) The Moffat Tunnel, 1978; Rio Grande Ski Train, 1984, History of the Public Schools of Denver, 1989, Route 3 Englewood, 1990, The Railroads of Coors Field, 1995. Trustee Colo. Railroad Hist. Found., Golden, 1975—, pres. 1994—; mem., 1st pres. Lakewood Hist. Soc. (Colo.), 1976; office Jeffco Credit Union. Mem. NEA (life) Colo. Assn. Sci. Tchrs., Nat. Railway Hist. Soc. (Intermountain chpt. pres. 1980-83, chmn. hist. plaque commn.), Mobile Post Office Soc. Home: PO Box 15607 Lakewood CO 80215-0007 Office: Dunstan Middle Sch 1855 S Wright St Lakewood CO 80228-3963

FORREST, SUZANNE SIMS, research historian; b. Pitts., Nov. 15, 1926; d. Clarence E. and Corinne Tousley (Landgraf) Sims; m. Stephen F. de Borhegyl, July 5, 1949 (dec. 1969); children: Ilona Maria, Stephen Ernest, Carl Robert, Christopher Francis; m. James T. Forrest, Sept. 16, 1978. BA, Ohio State U., 1948; postgrad., U. Okla., 1967; MS, U. Wis., Milw., 1973; PhD, U. Wy., 1987. Asst. to dir. Carnegie Institution Wash., Guatemala City, 1949-50, Inst. Nutrition for Cen. Am., Panama, Guatemala City, 1950-51; tchr. Milw. U. Sch., 1966-1973; coordinator, cont. edn. Alverno Coll., Milw.; dir. Albuquerque (N.M.) Museum, 1974-79; exec. dir. Wy. Council for the Humanities, Wy., 1979-81; curator Bradford Brinton Meml. Mus., Big Horn, Wy., 1988-90; bd. dirs. N.Mex. Endowment for the Humanities, 1993-95, Placitas Artists Series, 1989—. Author: Ships, Shoals and Amphoras, 1961, Museums, 1962, Secret of the Sacred Lake, 1967, The Preservation of the Village: New Mexico's Hispanics and the New Deal, 1989, Century of Faith: One Hundred Years in the Life of the Las Placitas Presbyterian Church, 1995. Bd. dirs. N.Mex. Endowment for Humanities, 1993-94. Home: 45 Cabezon Rd Placitas NM 87043-9201

FORRESTER, JAMES STUART, cardiologist, medical educator; b. Phila., July 13, 1937; s. James S. and Mildred W. (Smith) F.; m. Deborah MacAdam, 1963 (div. 1974); children: Jeffrey Lance, Brent Worth; m. Barbara Ann Bick, May 27, 1975; 1 child, Justin Bick. BA, Swarthmore Coll., 1959; MD, U. Pa., 1963. Diplomate Am. Bd. Internal Medicine; bd. cert. cardiovascular disease. Intern U. Pa. Hosp.; resident Harbor Gen. Hosp.; fellow Peter Bent Brigham Hosp.; prof. medicine UCLA, 1986—, dir. cardiovascular inst., 1993—; dir. divsn. cardiology Cedars-Sinai Med. Ctr., L.A., 1989—; George Burns and Gracie Allen prof. cardiology Cedars-Sinai Med. Ctr., L.A., 1989—. Recipient Goldman award for laser rsch. SPIE, 1990. Mem. Am. Coll. Cardiology (bd. trustees 1993—), Am. Heart Assn. (bd. dirs. 1993—, Disting. Sci. Achievement award 1990). Office: Cedars Sinai Med Ctr 8700 Beverly Blvd Los Angeles CA 90048-1804

FORSBERG, CHARLES ALTON, computer, infosystems engineer; b. Willamette, Ill., May 6, 1944; s. Delbert Alton and Margery (McCleary) F. Student, Rensselaer Poly. Inst.; BSEE, U. Wis., 1966, MSEE, 1968; postgrad., various univs. and colls. From design engr. to project leader Tektronix, Portland, Oreg., 1968-74; mgr. R&D Sidereal, Portland, 1974-80; chief engr. Computer Devel. Inc., Portland, 1980-84; pres. Omen Tech. Inc., Portland, 1984—. Developer YMODEM and ZMODEM Protocols for worldwode data transfer. Recognized for outstanding contbn. to field IBM-PC Users Group, Madison, Wis., 1988, Alamo PC Orgn., San Antonio, 1988. Home and Office: 17505V NW Sauvie Island Rd Portland OR 97231-1310

FORSDALE, (CHALMERS) LOUIS, education and communication educator; b. Greeley, Colo., Mar. 8, 1922; s. John Aaron and Wilhelmina (Thorkildsen) F.; m. Elinor Wulfekuhler, Aug. 22, 1947 (dec. 1963); children: Lynn, John; m. Joan Ida Rosengren, May 28, 1964 (div. 1966). B.A., Colo. State Coll., 1942; M.A., Columbia U. Tchrs. Coll., 1947; Ed.D., Columbia U., 1951. Instr. English Tchrs. Coll., Columbia U., N.Y.C., 1947-51; asst. prof. Tchrs. Coll., Columbia U., 1951-55, assoc. prof., 1955-58, prof. communication and edn., 1958-87, prof. emeritus, 1987; vis. assoc. prof. edn. U. So. Calif., Los Angeles, 1957; cons. in communication various businesses, industries and schs., 1965—; vis. scholar Iran Communication and Devel. Inst., Tehran, 1977. Author: Nonverbal Communication, 1974, Perspectives on Communication, 1981; Editor: (with others) Communication in General Education, 1961, 8MM Sound Film and Education, 1962. Served to 1st lt. USAAF, 1943-45. Recipient Tchrs. Coll. Disting. Alumni award Merit, 1989. Democrat. Home: 330 Otero St Santa Fe NM 87501-1906

FORSSANDER, PAUL RICHARD, inventor, artist, entrepreneur; b. Chgo., Oct. 10, 1944; m. M. Andrea Peake, Dec. 30, 1967. BA in Econs., Marian Coll., Indpls., 1967. Sales and ops. adminstr. ITT Pub., Indpls., 1967-80; v.p., gen. mgr. Kutt Inc., Boulder, Colo., 1982-86; pres., chief exec. officer Skynasaur Inc., Boulder, 1986-89; pres., chief exec. officer, founder Zephyr Co. Inc., Boulder, 1989-91, Quillum Co., 1990—, Notetote Co., Boulder, 1990-91, PRF Designs, 1991—. Inventor flying and wind powered high-tech recreational products and parts, energy generation/conservation products, writing instrument designs, gift and office products; designer glass & metal sculptures, illuminaries & table art; developed forming and finishing process. Bd. dirs. PBS Sta. KGNU, Boulder, 1983-86, EMT Assn. Colo., Boulder, 1985-88; designer of fundraising strategies for non-profit orgns. Mem. Gift Assn. Am., Nat. Sporting Goods Assn., Toy Industry Am., Nat. Soc. Fundraising Execs., Nature Conservancy, Greenpeace, Sierra Club. Home: PO Box 1010 Boulder CO 80306-1010

FORSTER, BRUCE ALEXANDER, dean; b. Toronto, Ont., Can., Sept. 23, 1948; m. Margaret Jane Mackay, Dec. 28, 1968, (div. Dec. 1979); 1 child, Kelli Elissa; m. Valerie Dale Pendock, Dec. 8, 1979; children: Jeremy Bruce, Jessica Dale. BA in Math., Econs., U. Guelph, Ont., 1970; PhD in Econs., Australian Nat. U., Canberra, 1974. Asst. prof. U. Guelph, 1973-77, assoc. prof., 1977-83, prof. econs., 1983-88; vis. assoc. prof. U. B.C., Vancouver, 1979; vis. fellow U. Wyoming, 1979-80, vis. prof., 1983-84, 87; prof. econs., 1987—, dean Coll. Bus., 1991—; vis. prof. Profl. Tng. Ctr., Ministry of Econ. Affairs, Taiwan, 1990-95; acad. assoc. The Atlantic Coun. of the U.S., cons. in field. Author: The Acid Rain Debate: Science and Special Interest in Policy Formation, 1993; co-author: Economics in Canadian Society, 1986; assoc. editor Jour. Applied Bus. Rsch., 1987, editorial adv. bd., 1987—; editorial coun. Jour. Environ. Econs. and Mgmt., 1989, assoc. editor, 1989-91; contbr. articles to profl. jours. Jayes-Qantas Vis. scholar U. Newcastle, Australia, 1983. Mem. Am. Econ. Assn., Assn. Environ. and Resource Economists, Faculty Club U. Guelph (treas. 1981-82, v.p. 1982-83, 85-86, pres. 1986-87). Avocations: weight lifting, swimming, skiing, scuba diving.

Home: 3001 Sage Dr Laramie WY 82070-5751 Office: U Wyo Coll Bus Laramie WY 82071

FORSTROM, JUNE ROCHELLE, professional society administrator; b. Douglas County, Minn., June 24, 1932; d. George Dewey and Borghild Otillia (Sahl) Nelson; m. Keith William Forstrom, June 23, 1951; children: Mark William, Dawn Rochelle. Grad. high sch., St. Paul. Adminstr. rsch. grants, coord. comm. Geol. Soc. Am., Boulder, Colo., 1973—. Republican. Lutheran. Home: 7705 Baseline Rd Boulder CO 80303-4707 Office: Geol Soc Am 3300 Penrose Pl Boulder CO 80301-1806

FORSYTH, BEN RALPH, academic administrator, medical educator; b. N.Y.C., Mar. 8, 1934; s. Martin and Eva (Lazansky) F.; m. Elizabeth Held, Aug. 19, 1962; children: Jennifer, Beverly, Jonathan. Attended, Cornell U., 1950-53; MD, NYU, 1957. Diplomate Am. Bd. Internal Medicine. Intern, then resident Yale Hosp., New Haven, 1957-60; postdoctoral fellow Harvard U. Med. Shc., Boston, 1960-61; rsch. assoc. NIH, Bethesda, Md., 1963-66; assoc. prof. med. microbiology, prof. med. coll. U. Vt., Burlington, 1966-90, assoc. dean div. health scis., 1971-85, assoc. v.p. acad. affairs, 1977-78, v.p. adminstrn., 1978-85, sr. v.p., 1985-90; sr. exec. asst. to pres. Ariz. State U., Tempe, 1990—, prof. health adminstrn. and policy, 1991—, interim v.p. adminstrv. svcs., 1991-93; interim provost Ariz. State U. West, Phoenix, 1992-93, 1992-93, provost, v.p., 1993—; sr. cons. Univ. Health Ctr., Burlington, 1986-90. Contbr. articles to profl. jours. V.p., chmn. United Way Planning Com., Burlington, 1974-75, Ops. Com., 1975-76, bd. dirs., officer, 1977-89; mem. New England Bd. Higher Edn. Com., Burlington, 1985-89; chmn. U. Vt. China Project Adv. Bd., Burlington, 1989-90. Lt. comdr. USN, 1962-63. Sinsheimer Found. faculty fellow, 1966-71. Fellow ACP, Infectious Diseases Soc. Am.; mem. Phi Beta Kappa, Alpha Omega Alpha. Office: Arizona State Univ West PO Box 37100 4701 W Thunderbird Rd Phoenix AZ 85069-7100

FORSYTH, RAYMOND ARTHUR, civil engineer; b. Reno, Mar. 13, 1928; s. Harold Raymond and Fay Exona (Highfill) F.; BS, Calif. State U., San Jose, 1952; M.C.E., Auburn U., 1958; m. Mary Ellen Wagner, July 9, 1950; children: Lynne, Gail, Alison, Ellen. Jr. engr., asst. engr. Calif. Div. Hwys., San Francisco, 1952-54; assoc. engr., sr. supervising, prin. engr. Calif. Dept. Transp., Sacramento, 1961-83, chief geotech. br., 1972-79, chief soil mechanics and pavement br., 1979-83, chief Transp. Lab., 1983-89; cons., lectr. in field. Served with USAF, 1954-56. Fellow ASCE (pres. Sacramento sect., chmn. Calif. council 1980-81); mem. Transp. Research Bd. (chmn. embankments and earth slopes com. 1976-82, chmn. soil mechanics sect. 1982-88, chmn. group 2 council 1988-91), ASTM. Contbr. articles to profl. publs. Home: 5017 Pasadena Ave Sacramento CA 95841-4149

FORTH, KEVIN BERNARD, beverage distributing industry consultant; b. Adams, Mass., Dec. 4, 1949; s. Michael Charles and Catherine Cecilia (McAndrews) F.; children: Melissa, Brian. AB, Holy Cross Coll., 1971; MBA with distinction, NYU, 1973. Div. rep. Anheuser-Busch, Inc., Boston, 1973-74, dist. sales mgr., L.A., 1974-76, asst. to v.p. mktg. staff, St. Louis, 1976-77; v.p. Straub Distbg. Co., Ltd., Orange, Calif., 1977-81, pres., 1981-93, chmn., CEO, 1986-93, also bd. dirs. Commr. Orange County Sheriff's Adv. Coun., 1988—; mem. adv. bd Rancho Santiago C.C. Coll. Dist. 1978-80; bd. dirs. Children's Hosp. of Orange County Padrinos Found., 1983-85, St. Joseph's Hosp. Found., Orange County Sports Hall of Fame, 1980-89; exec. com., bd. dirs. Nat. Coun. on Alcoholism, 1980-83; mem. pres. coun. Holy Cross Coll., 1987—; bd. dirs., pres. Calif. State Fullerton Titan Athletic Found., 1983-85, 89-90 (vol. of yr., 1991); bd. dirs. Freedom Bowl, 1984-93, v.p., 1984-85, pres., 1986, chmn., 1986-87, Anaheim Vis. and Conv. Bur., 1989-93; bd. dirs. Orangewood Children's Found., 1988-93; mem. Calif. Rep. State Cen. Com., Orange County Probation Dept. Cmty. Involvement Bd., 1992-93. Benjamin Levy fellow NYU, 1971-73; recipient Founders award Freedom Bowl, 1993. Mem. Nat. Beer Wholesalers Assn. (bd. dirs., asst. sec. 1989-90, chmn.'s award for legis. exellence 1990, sec. 1990-91, vice chmn. 1991-92, chmn. 1992-93), Calif. Beer and Wine Wholesalers Assn. (bd. dirs., exec. com., pres. 1985), Industry Environ. Coun., Holy Cross Alumni Assn., NYU Alumni Assn., Nat. Assn. Stock Car Auto Racing, Calif. State Fullerton Small Bus. Inst., Sports Car Club Am. (Ariz. state champion 1982), Beta Gamma Sigma. Roman Catholic. Club: Holy Cross (Southern Calif.). Home: 27750 Tamara Dr Yorba Linda CA 92687-5840

FORTI, CORINNE ANN, corporate communications executive; b. N.Y.C., July 26, 1941; d. Wilbur Walter and Sylvia Joan (Charap) Bastian; B.A., CUNY, 1963; m. Joseph Donald Forti, Aug. 18, 1962 (dec.); 1 child, Raina. Adminstrv. asst. Ednl. Broadcasting Corp., 1963-65; adminstrv. asst. W.R. Grace & Co., N.Y.C., 1965-67, pub. relations rep., 1967-70, mgr. info. services, 1970-79, dir. info. services, 1980-86, dir. info. and advt., 1986-87; pres. Bastian-Forti Communications, 1988-89, Forti Communications Inc., 1989—; lectr. photography and graphics Am. Mgmt. Assn. Bd. dirs. YM/YWCA Day Care, Inc. Named to Acad. Women Achievers, YWCA, 1979; recipient citation award in communications Nat. Council of Women, 1979. Mem. Am. Women in Radio and TV, Chem. Mfrs. Assn., Am. Mgmt. Assn., Women Execs. in Pub. Relations. Republican. Roman Catholic. Home and Office: 1246 Calle Yucca Thousand Oaks CA 91360-2239

FORTI, LENORE STEIMLE, business consultant; b. Houghton, Mich., Sept. 9, 1924; d. Russell Nicholas and Agnes (McCloskey) Steimle; m. Frank Forti, May 29, 1950 (dec.). BBA summa cum laude, Northwood U., 1973, Dr.Laws, 1969. Asst. corp. sec., purchasing agt. Fed. Life & Casualty Co., Detroit, 1942-53; supr. sectl. J.L. Hudson Co., Detroit, 1953-57, adminstrv. asst. to exec. v.p., 1957-86; instr. Wayne State U. and U. Mich. Adult Edn., Detroit, 1958-71; creator, dir. Seminars for Profl. People, 1971—. Co-author: The Professional Secretary; contbr. articles to profl. jours. Asst. br. dir. planning City of Detroit for Civil Def.; chmn. bd. trustees PSI Rsch. and Ednl. Found.; trustee PSI Retirement Home Complex, Albuquerque; elected dir. Property Owners and Residents Assn., Sun City West Mcpl. Govt., 1994; past pres. Women's Bd. Northwood U., Midland, Mich.; pres. parish coun. Our Lady of Lourdes Ch., Sun City West, Ariz., 1988, pres. ladies guild, 1990, pres. singles club, 1995; 1st v.p. Vol. Bur. of Sun Cities, 1989. Elected One of Detroit's Top Ten Working Women, 1969; elected to Exec. and Profl. Hall of Fame. Mem. Profl. Sec. Internat. (internat. pres. 1967-69), Future Secs. Assn. (nat. coord.), Lioness Club (pres. 1991-92), Sun City West Singles Club (pres. 1988, pres. Singles Club Ch. 1995). Republican. Roman Catholic. Home and Office: 12613 W Seneca Dr Sun City West AZ 85375-4635

FORTIER, DANA SUZANNE, psychotherapist; b. Fresno, Calif., Jan. 15, 1952; d. Dan and Louise (Metkovich) Ninkovich; m. Timothy Fortier, Jan. 29, 1994. BA in Journalism summa cum laude, Calif. State U., Fresno, 1974; BSN, Calif. State U., 1979, MSW with distinction, 1986. Registered nurse, Calif; lic. social worker, Calif. Staff nurse Valley Med. Ctr., Fresno, 1980-81; pub. health nurse Fresno County Health Dept., 1981-83; therapist II Sierra Community Hosp., Fresno, 1986-87; women's svcs. coord. Turning Point Youth Svcs., Visalia, Calif., 1987-89; psychotherapist and cons. in pvt. practice Visalia, 1989—; clins. cons. in field. Contbr. articles to profl. jours. Mem. Task Force on Pregnant Mothers, 1990—. Mem. Calif. Women's Commn. on Drugs and Alcohol, Calif. Advocacy for Pregnent Women, Soc. for Clin. Social Wk., Nat. Assn. Social Workers, Visalia Bus. and Profl. Women's Clubs. Republican. Office: 304 S Johnson St Visalia CA 93291-6136

FORTNA, VALERIÉ ANNETTE, dance and performing company owner, instructor; b. Denver, May 25, 1974; d. Russell Lloyd and Barbara F. Cert. dance educator. Dance instr., dancer Rock-Out to the Future, Denver, 1990-94; owner, dir. Dance Explosion, Littleton, Colo., 1993—, Protégé Performing Co., Littleton, 1993—; dance instr. Spring Break Jam, Ft. Lauderdle, Fla., 1994, Western Dance Expo, Laramie, Wyo., 1994; comml. actress Coor Brewing Co., Golden, Colo., 1993. Author: Guide to Student Engligh, 1993; choreographer Creative Expressions, Denver, 1993. Vol. fitness Charity 1993, Cherry Creek, Colo., 1993, Dance Explosion, Littleton, 1994. Recipient Miss Royale award Denver, 1992, Top Choreography award Kar Prodns., Denver, 1994, Top Studio award, 1995. Mem. DECA (cons., sec. 1992-93, vehicles and petroleum knowledge award 1992), Creative Expressions. Democrat. Home: 11042 Wolff Way Westminster CO 80030-2046 Office: Dance Explosion 3625 W Bowles Ave Units 7 & 8 Littleton CO 80123

FORTNER, HUESTON GILMORE, lawyer, writer, composer; b. Tacoma, Nov. 1, 1959; s. Hueston Turner Jr. and Deborah Hewes (Berry) F. BS, Tulane U., 1981; JD, U. Miss., 1985. Bar: Miss. 1986, La. 1987, U.S. Dist. Ct. (no. and so. dists.) Miss. 1986, U.S. Dist. Ct. (ea., mid. and we. dists.) La., 1987, U.S. Ct. Appeals (5th cir.) 1986, Calif. 1989, U.S. Dist. Ct. (cen. dist.) Calif. 1989. Clk. Farrer and Co., London, Miss., 1985; assoc. Cliff Finch & Assocs., Batesville, Miss., 1986; pvt. practice New Orleans, 1987-88; atty. Parker, Milliken, Clark, O'Hara & Samuelian, L.A., 1989-90; pvt. prctice L.A., 1990—; vis. lectr. Anhui U., Hefei, People's Rep. of China, Bejing Inst. of Petrochem. Tech., 1994; of counsel, Law Office of Glenn M. Rosen, Tustin, Calif., 1993—; participanted in Leicester vs. Leicester Rugby Union, 1985; assisted Queen's Counsel in Yussuf Islam (Cat Stevens) vs. Bank of Westminster P.L.C. royalties litigation 1985, Newton vs. NBC, 1988; temporary judge L.A. County mcpl. Ct., 1991—; ind. film producer. Performing musician; composer numerous mus. works; contbg. photographer Flix mag., 1993—; contbr. editor Rental, 1987-89. Grant NSF, 1976. Mem. ABA (forum com. on entertainment and sports industries), Miss. Bar Assn., La. Bar Assn., State Bar Calif., Assn. Telecommunications Attys., Broadcast Music Itnernat., Nat. Acad. Songwriters, Los Angeles County Bar Assn., Phi Alpha Delta. Presbyterian. Office: 17822 17th St Ste 404 Tustin CA 92680-2154

FORTSON, JUDITH LEE, library administrator; b. Summerville, S.C., Jan. 6, 1943; d. Julien Fulton and Mary Josephine (Thronton) F.; m. Hardy Eugene Jones, Aug. 15, 1965 (div. 1979); 1 child, Hardy Ryan; m. Frederick Irwin Dretske, May 14, 1988. BA, Baylor U., 1965; MA, U. Wisc., 1968. Instr. English Concordia Coll., Austin, Tex., 1972-76; conservation specialist Nebr. State Hist. Soc., 1977-83; head libr. western langs. collection, preservation svcs. Hoover Instn., Stanford, Calif., 1983-91; cons. Nat. Assn. Govt. Archives and Records Adminstrs. Preservation Planning Project, 1989-90, Libr. of Congress, 1989, Libr. of U. Oreg., 1988, Soc. Am. ARchivists Conservation Survey Program, 1982-83, Sioux Falls Coll., 1982; instr. Western Archives Inst., L.A., 1989-, 90, Stanford U., 1985, U. Tex., Austin, 1983; guest instr. history dept. U. Nebr., 1982-83; supr. intern program experiental edn. U. Nebr., 1982; grant reviewer Dept. Edn., 1993, NEH, 1986, 90, 92, Nat. Hist. Publs. and Records Commn., Inst. Mus. Svcs. Author: Disaster Planning and Recovery: A How-To-Do-It Manual dor Librarians and Archivists, 1992; author numerous articles to profl. jours. and reviews in field; presenter in field, 1980—. Mem. ALA, Soc. Am. Archivists (chair nominating com. 1992, mem. task force on standards 1989-90, standards bd. 1990-93, vice-chair conservation sect. 1988-90, mem. adv. com. for revision of SAA basic glossary 1988-89, mem. interim bd. on cert. 1989, program com. 1984, instr., adv. bd. mem. preservation mgmt. tng. program 1992-94, instr. numerous programs 1981-86), Spl. Librs. Assn. Office: Hoover Inst Stanford U Serra and Galvez Stanford CA 94305-6010

FORTUNE, JAMES MICHAEL, marketing executive; b. Providence, Sept. 6, 1947; s. Thomas Henry and Olive Elizabeth (Duby) F.; m. G. Suzanne Hein, July 14, 1973. Student, Pikes Peak Community Coll., Colorado Springs, Colo., 1981-83; BSBA in Computer Info. Systems, Regis Coll., 1991. Owner Fortune Fin. Svcs., Colorado Springs, Colo., 1975-79; ptnr. Robert James and Assocs., Colorado Springs, 1979-81; pres. Fortune & Co., Colorado Springs, 1981-88; sr. v.p. mktg. and editorial Phoenix Communications Group, Ltd., Colorado Springs, 1988—, also bd. dirs.; also bd. dirs.; bd. dirs. Colorado Springs Computer Systems, Am. Discount Svcs., Inc., Investor's Bookshelf, Inc., Colorado Network Engring., Inc., Custom Computers of Colo., Corp.; talk show host Sta. KRCC, fin. commentator Wall Street Report, Sta. KKHT, 1983-84. Editor Fortune newsletter, 1981-85, The Can. Market News, 1981-83; editor, pub. Penny Fortune newsletter, 1981—, The Low Priced Investment newsletter, 1986-87, Women's Investment Newsletter, 1987—, Can. Market Confidential, 1988—, Spl. Option Situations, 1988—; pub. Internal Revenue Strategies, 1990, Tax and Investment Planning Strategies for Medical Professionals, 1991; contbr. articles to profl. jours. Cons. Jr. Achievement bus. project, Colorado Springs, 1985. Sgt. U.S. Army, 1968-70, Vietnam. Mem. Direct Mktg. Assn., Elks. Office: 1837 S Nevada Ave Ste 223 Colorado Springs CO 80906-2516

FORTUNE, LOWELL, lawyer; b. Colorado Springs, Colo., Dec. 12, 1941; s. Benjamin Acres and Wilma E. (Henry) F.; m. Beverly Jane Sanborn, June 30, 1963; children: Sabrina Fortune Allen, Christina. BA, U. Denver, 1963, JD, 1966. Bar: U.S. Dist. Ct. Colo. 1966, U.S. Ct. Appeals (10th cir.) 1966, U.S. Supreme Ct. 1976. Assoc. White & Steele, Denver, 1966-71, ptnr., 1971-75; pres. Lowell Fortune, P.C., Denver, 1975-79, Fortune & Lawritson, P.C., Denver, 1979-95; pvt. practice Fortune Law Firm, P.C., Denver, 1995—. Mem. ABA, Am. Bd. Trial Advocates, Denver bar Assn., Colo. Bar Assn., Lawyers Coop. Pub. (editl. adv. bd. 1989—). Republican. Home: 5237 Bear Mountain Dr Evergreen CO 80439-5605 Office: Fortune Law Firm PC 730 17th St #940 Denver CO 80202-3502

FOSGATE HEGGLI, JULIE DENISE, producer; b. El Paso, Tex., Feb. 17, 1954; d. Orville Edward and Patricia (Ward) Fosgate; m. Bjarne Heggli, June 20, 1980; children: Elise Mai, Kristin April. BA in Broadcasting, U. So. Calif., 1976, MA in Journalism, 1978. On-board editor Royal Viking Line, San Francisco, 1978-80; editor Stentor, Trondheim, Norway, 1981; staff Grunion Gazette, Long Beach, Calif., 1981; news editor Nine Network Australia, Los Angeles, 1981-82; editor South Coast Metro News, Costa Mesa, Calif., 1981-82; v.p. The Newport Group, Newport Beach, Calif., 1982-85; exec. editor Orange County This Month, Newport Beach, 1985; exec. dir. mktg. Gen. Group Cos., Harbor City, Calif., 1985-87; sr. v.p. mktg. Automax Corp., L.A., 1987-88, Gen. Group Internat., Harbor City, Calif., 1988-90; assoc. producer Zoo Life Tv Spls., L.A., 1991; assoc. producer NBC News, Burbank, Calif., 1992-94; v.p. mktg. Western Nat., Scottsdale, Ariz., 1994—. Mem. Phi Beta Kappa. Home: # 2024 11333 N 92nd St Apt 2024 Scottsdale AZ 85260-6154 Office: Western Nat 7272 E Indian School Rd Scottsdale AZ 85251-3921

FOSSLAND, JOEANN JONES, marketing professional, consultant; b. Balt., Mar. 21, 1948; d. Milton Francis and Clementine (Bowen) Jones; m. Richard E. Yellott III, 1966 (div. 1970); children: Richard E. IV, Dawn Joeann; m. Robert Gerard Fossland Jr., Nov. 25, 1982. Student, Johns Hopkins U., 1966-67; cert. in real estate, Hogan's Sch. Real Estate, 1982. Owner Kobble Shop, Indiatlantic, Fla., 1968-70, Downstairs, Atlanta, 1971; seamstress Aspen (Colo.) Leather, 1972-75; owner Backporch Feather & Leather, Aspen and Tucson, 1975-81; area mgr. Welcome Wagon, Tucson, 1982; realtor assoc. Tucson Realty & Trust, 1983-85; mgr. Home Illustrated mag., Tucson, 1985-87; asst. pub., gen. mgr. Phoenix, Scottsdale, Albuquerque, Tricities Tucson Homes Illustrated, 1990-93; pres. ADvantage Solutions Group, Cortaro, Ariz., 1993—; power leader Darryl Davis Seminars Power Program, 1995. Designer leather goods (Tucson Mus. Art award 1978, Crested Butte Art Fair Best of Show award 1980). Voter registrar Recorder's Office City of Tucson, 1985-91; bd. dirs. Hearth Found., Tucson, 1987—, pres., 1994; bd. dirs. Ariz. Integrated Residential & Ednl. Svcs., Inc., 1989-95, pres. 1994-95); mem. Hunger Project, Holiday Project. Mem. NAFF, Women's Coun. Realtors (Tucson chpt. pres. 1995, Tucson affiliate of yr. 1991, leadership tng. grad. designation 1989), Tucson Assn. Realtors (affiliate of yr. 1988). Democrat. Presbyterian. Office: ADvantage Solutions Group PO Box 133 Cortaro AZ 85652-0133

FOSTER, DAVID RAMSEY, soap company executive; b. London, May 24, 1920; (parents Am. citizens); s. Robert Bagley and Josephine (Ramsey) F.; m. Anne Firth, Aug. 2, 1957 (dec. June 1994); children:Sarah, Victoria. Student in econs., Gonville and Caius Coll., Cambridge (Eng.) U., 1938. With Colgate-Palmolive Co. and affiliates, 1946-79, v.p., gen. mgr. Europe, Colgate-Palmolive Internat., 1961-65, v.p., gen. mgr. household products div. parent co., N.Y.C., 1965-68, exec. v.p., 1968-70, pres., 1970-75, chief exec. officer, 1971-79, chmn., 1975-79. Author: Wings Over the Sea, 1990. Trustee, Woman's Sport Found. Served to lt. comdr. Royal Naval Vol. Res., 1940-46. Decorated Disting. Service Order, D.S.C. with bar, Mentioned in Despatches (2); recipient Victor award City of Hope, 1974, Herbert Hoover Meml. award, 1976, Adam award, 1977, Harriman award Boys Club N.Y., 1977, Charter award St. Francis Coll., 1978, Walter Hagen award, 1978, Patty Berg award, 1986, Commr.'s award LPGA, 1995. Mem. Soc. Mayflower Descs. Clubs: Hawks (Cambridge U.); Royal Ancient Golf (St. Andrews, Scotland); Royal St. Georges Golf, Royal Cinque Ports Golf (life), Sunningdale Golf, Swinley Forest Golf (U.K.); Sankaty Head Golf; Racquet and Tennis (N.Y.C.); Baltusrol Golf, Mission Hills Country, Bally Bunion Golf. Home: 540 Desert West Dr Rancho Mirage CA 92270-1310

FOSTER, DUDLEY EDWARDS, JR., musician, educator; b. Orange, N.J., Oct. 5, 1935; s. Dudley Edwards and Margaret (DePoy) F. Student Occidental Coll., 1953-56; AB, UCLA, 1957, MA, 1958; postgrad. U. So. Calif., 1961-73. Lectr. music Immaculate Heart Coll., L.A., 1960-63; dir. music Holy Faith Episcopal Ch., Inglewood, Calif., 1964-67; lectr. music Calif. State U., L.A., 1968-71; assoc. prof. music L.A. Mission Coll., 1975-83, prof., 1983—, also chmn. dept. music, 1977—; mem. dist. acad. senate L.A. Community Colls., 1991-92; mem. acad. senate L.A. Mission Coll., 1993—; dir. music 1st Luth. Ch., L.A., 1968-72. Organist, pianist, harpsichordist; numerous recitals; composer O Sacrum Convivium for Trumpet and Organ, 1973, Passacaglia for Brass Instruments, 1969, Introduction, Arioso & Fugue for Cello and Piano, 1974. Fellow Trinity Coll. Music, London, 1960. Recipient Associated Students Faculty award, 1988. Mem. Am. Guild Organists, Am. Musicol. Soc., Nat. Assn. of Scholars, Acad. Senate, Town Hall Calif., L.A. Coll. Tchrs. Assn. (pres. Mission Coll. chpt. 1976-77, v.p., exec. com. 1982-84), Mediaeval Acad. Am. Republican. Anglican. Office: LA Mission Coll Dept Music 13356 Eldridge Ave Sylmar CA 91342-3200

FOSTER, GEORGE MCCLELLAND, JR., anthropologist; b. Sioux Falls, S.D., Oct. 9, 1913; s. George McClelland and Mary (Slutz) F.; m. Mary Fraser LeCron, Jan. 6, 1938; children: Jeremy, Melissa Bowerman. BS, Northwestern U., 1935; PhD, U. Calif. at Berkeley, 1941; DHL (hon.), So. Meth. U., 1990. Instr. Syracuse U., 1941-42; lectr. UCLA, 1942-43; vis. prof. U. Calif.-Berkeley, 1953-55, prof. anthropology, 1955-79, prof. emeritus, 1979—, chmn. dept., 1958-61; acting dir. Mus. Anthropology, 1955-57; lectr. pub. health, 1955-64; anthropologist Inst. Social Anthropology, Smithsonian Instn., 1943-52, dir., 1946-1952; field rsch. Calif. Indians, 1937, Spain, 1949-50, Mexico, 1940—; adviser AID, India-Pakistan, 1955, Afghanistan, 1957, Zambia, 1961, 62, Nepal, 1965, Indonesia, 1973-74, WHO, Sri Lanka, 1975, Malaysia, 1978, India, 1979, 80, 81, Manila, 1983; adviser UNICEF, Geneva, 1976. Author: Traditional Cultures and the Impact of Technological Change, 1962, Tzintzuntzan: Mexican Peasants on a Changing World, 1967, Applied Anthropology, 1969, (with B. Anderson) Medical Anthropology, 1978, Hippocrates' Latin American Legacy, 1993, others, also monographs and articles. Guggenheim fellow, 1949; fellow Center for Advanced Study in Behavioral Scis., 1969-70. Fellow Am. Anthrop. Assn. (pres. 1970, Disting. Service award 1980); mem. Southwestern Anthrop. Assn. (Disting. Research award 1981), Nat. Acad. Scis., Am. Acad. Arts and Scis., Soc. Applied Anthropology (Malinowski award 1982). Club: Cosmos (Washington). Home: 790 San Luis Rd Berkeley CA 94707-2030

FOSTER, KEN D., securities trader; b. Glendale, Calif., Oct. 9, 1951; s. Donald Jay Foster and Edith Anne (La Point) Fuhlendorfm; divorced; children: Brooke Nicole, Erica Lauren. San Diego State U. Owner furniture store, 1976-79; mem. real estate sales staff San Diego, 1979-82; account exec. Smith Barney, Harris, Upham and Drexel Burnham Lambert, San Diego, 1982-86; asst. mgr., v.p. Corp. Benefit Securities, San Diego, 1982-86; sales mgr. Investment Network of Am., San Diego, 1987-89; regional v.p. Holden Fin. Bank Mktg., San Diego, 1990-92; regional dir. Integon Cmty. Bank Mktg., San Diego, 1992-93; owner Investment Sales Mgmt., Sacramento and San Diego, 1982—; arbitrator NASD Bd. Arbitrators. Home: 3790 Riviera Dr Apt 2C San Diego CA 92109-6650

FOSTER, LAWRENCE, concert and opera conductor; b. Los Angeles, 1941. Student, Bayreuth Festival Masterclasses; studied with, Fritz Zweig. Debut as condr., Young Musicians' Found., Debut Orch., 1960; condr., mus. dir., 1960-64, condr., San Francisco Ballet, 1961-65, asst. condr., Los Angeles Philharmonic Orch., 1965-68, chief guest condr., Royal Philharmonic Orch., Eng., 1969-75, guest condr., Houston Symphony, 1970-71, condr. in chief, 1971-72, music dir., 1972-78, Orch. Philharmonique of Monte Carlo, 1979, gen. music dir., Duisburg & Dusseldorf Opera (Ger.), 1982-86, former music dir. Lausanne Chamber Orch., from 1985, now music dir. Aspen (Colo.) Music Festival and Sch.; music dir. Orquestra Ciutat de Barcelona, 1995—; guest condr. orchs. in, U.S. and Europe. (Recipient Koussevitsky Meml. Conducting prize 1966, Eleanor R. Crane Meml. prize Berkshire Festival, Tanglewood, Mass. 1966); condr. Jerusalem Symphony Orch., 1990. Address: Aspen Music Festival PO Box AA Aspen CO 81612 Office: care Harrison/Parrott, 12 Penzance, London England W11 also: ICM 8942 Wilshire Blvd Los Angeles CA 90011

FOSTER, LAWRENCE HUNT, JR., physician, plastic surgeon; b. Bakersfield, Calif., Dec. 22, 1934; s. Lawrence Hunt and Edna (Knittle) F.; m. Patricia Ann Hunt, June 4, 1956 (div. Feb. 1976); children: Mark, Martin, Linda Lauren, Bill. AA, Bakersfiels Coll., 1954; BA, U. Calif., Berkeley, 1956; MD, U Calif., San Francisco, 1959. Diplomate Am. Bd. Plastic and Reconstructive Surgery, Am. Bd. Bariatric Physicians. Intern Valley Forge (Pa.) Army Hosp., 1959-60; gen. surgery resident William Beaumont Army Hosp., El Paso, Tex., 1960-63; Mobile Army Surg. Hosp., Korea, 1963-64, Brooke Burn Unit, San Antonio, 1964-66; plastic surgery resident U. Calif. Hosp., San Francisco, 1966-68; pvt. practice San Francisco, 1968—; owner Tahoe Clinic, South Lake Tahoe, Calif., 1976—; active staff St. Francis Meml. Hosp., San Francisco, 1968-75, Mary's Help Hosp., Daly City, Calif., 1968-77, courtesy staff, 1968-75, Barton Meml. Hosp., South Lake Tahoe, Calif., 1975-84, 94-96; courtesy staff French Hosp., San Francisco, 1968-75, Mt. Zion Hosp., 1968-75, Carson Tahoe Hosp., Carson City Nev., 1981-85. Am. Bd. Cosmetic Surgery fellow, 1989—. Fellow ACS, Internat. Coll. Surgeons; mem. AMA, Am. Soc. Plastic Surgeons, Am. Soc. Plastic and Reconstructive Surgeons, Am. Soc. Bariatric Physicians, Internat. Soc. Clin. Plastic Surgeons, Internat. Soc. Aesthetic Plastic Surgeons. Republican.

FOSTER, MARY CHRISTINE, motion picture and television executive; b. L.A., Mar. 19, 1943; d. Ernest Albert and Mary Ada (Quilici) F.; m. Paul Hunter, July 24, 1982. BA, Immaculate Heart Coll., Los Angeles, 1967; M of Journalism in TV News Documentary, UCLA, 1968. Dir. research and devel. Metromedia Producers Corp., Los Angeles, 1968-71; dir. devel. and prodn. services Wolper Prodns., Los Angeles, 1971-76; mgr. film programs NBC-TV, Burbank, Calif., 1976-77; v.p. movies and mini series Columbia Pictures TV, Burbank, 1977-81, v.p. series programs, 1981; v.p. program devel. Group W. Prodns., L.A., 1981-87; ptnr. The Agency, Los Angeles, 1988-90; agt. Shapiro-Lichtman Agy., Los Angeles, 1990—; lectr. in field, 1970—. Creator: (TV series) Sullivan, 1985, Auntie Mom, 1986. Bd. dirs. Immaculate Heart High Sch., L.A., 1980—; mem. exec. com. Humanitas Awards, Human Family Inst., 1985—, L.A. Roman Cath. Archdiosesan Comm. Commn., L.A., 1986-90, Catholics in Media Exec. Com., 1992—. Mem. Women in Film (bd. dirs. 1974-78), Nat. Acad. TV Arts and Scis. Democrat. Office: 2367 W Silver Lake Dr Los Angeles CA 90039

FOSTER, MARY FRAZER (MARY FRAZER LECRON), anthropologist; b. Des Moines, Feb. 1, 1914; d. James and Helen (Cowles) LeCron; B.A., Northwestern U., 1936; Ph.D., U. Calif., Berkeley, 1965; m. George McClelland Foster, Jan. 6, 1938; children—Jeremy, Melissa Foster Bowerman. Research assoc. dept. anthropology U. Calif., Berkeley, 1955-57, 75—; lectr. in anthropology Calif. State U., Hayward, 1966-75; mem. faculty Fromm Inst. Lifelong Learning, U. San Francisco, 1980. Fellow AAAS, Am. Anthropol. Assn.; mem. Linguistic Soc. Am., Internat. Linguistic Assn., Southwestern Anthrop. Assn., Soc. Woman Geographers. Democrat. Author: (with George M. Foster) Sierra Popoluca Speech, 1948; The Tarascan Language, 1969; editor: (with Stanley H. Brandes) Symbol As Sense: New Approaches to the Analysis of Meaning, 1980, (with Robert A. Rubinstein) Peace and War: Cross-Cultural Perspectives, 1986, (with Robert A. Rubinstein) The Social Dynamics of Peace, 1988 (with Lucy J. Botscharow) The Life of Symbols, 1990. Home: 790 San Luis Rd Berkeley CA 94707-2030

FOSTER, MICHAEL WILLIAM, librarian; b. Astoria, Oreg., June 29, 1940; s. William Michael and Margaret Vivian (Carlson) F. BA in History, Willamette U., 1962; MA, U. Oreg., 1965; postgrad., So. Oreg. Coll., 1976. Tchr. Astoria High Sch., 1963-66, librarian, 1970—; tchr. Am. Internat. Sch. of Kabul (Afghanistan), 1966-70; bd. dirs. Astoria H.S. Scholarships, Inc., AG-BAG Internat. Ltd., Astoria Pacific Industries, Inc. Commr. Oreg. Arts Commn., Salem, 1983-91, Oreg. Coun. Humanities, 1994—, vice-chair, 1995—; commr. Oreg. Advs. for the Arts, 1994—; bd. dirs. Am. Cancer Soc., Clatsop County, Oreg., 1980-87, Luth. Family Svcs., 1994—, Oreg.

Arts Advocates Found., 1994—, Columbia Meml. Hosp. Found., 1992—, Edward Hall Scholarship Bd., Clatsop C.C., U. Oreg. Art Mus. Coun., 1991—, pres., 1993—; bd. dirs., treas. Astoria Cmty. Concert Assn., 1964-88, pres., 1989—; bd. dirs., treas. Ed and Eda Ross Scholarship Trust; mem. Oreg. Econ. Devel. Dept. Task Force, 1995—; adv. bd. Oreg. Symphony, 1992—. Mem. NEA, Oreg. Edn. Assn., Oreg. Edn. Media Assn., Clatsop County Hist. Soc. (bd. dirs., pres. 1983-87), Ft. Clatsop Hist. Assn. (treas. 1974-91, pres. 1991—, bd. dirs.), Astoria C. of C. (bd. dirs. 1982-88, George award 1985, pres. 1987), Lewis and Clark Trails Heritage Found., League of Historic Am. Theaters, Rotary (pres. Astoria Club 1986), Astoria Golf and Country Club, Beta Theta Pi. Republican. Roman Catholic. Home: 1636 Irving Ave Astoria OR 97103-3621 Office: Astoria High Sch Libr 1001 W Marine Dr Astoria OR 97103-5829

FOSTER, RUTH MARY, dental association administrator; b. Little Rock, Jan. 11, 1927; d. William Crosby and Frances Louise (Doering) Shaw; m. Luther A. Foster, Sept. 8, 1946 (dec. Dec. 1980); children: William Lee, Robert Lynn. Grad. high sch., Long Beach, Calif. Sr. hostess Mon's Food Host of Coast, Long Beach, 1945-46; dental asst., office mgr. Dr. Wilfred H. Allen, Opportunity, Wash., 1946-47; dental asst., bus. asst. Dr. H. Erdahl, Long Beach, 1948-50; office mgr. Dr. B.B. Blough, Spokane, Wash., 1950-52; bus. mgr. Henry G. Kolsrud, D.D.S., P.S., Spokane, 1958—, Garland Dental Bldg., Spokane, 1958—. Sustaining mem. Spokane Symphony Orch. Mem. Nat. Assn. Dental Assts., DAV Aux., DAV Comdr.'s Club, Wash. State Fedn. of Bus. and Profl. Women (dist. 6 dir.), Spokane's Lilac City Bus. and Profl. Women (pres.), Nat. Alliance Mentally Ill, Wash. Alliance Mentally Ill, Spokane Alliance Mentally Ill, Spokane Lilac City Bus. and Profl. Women (past pres.), Internat. Platform Assn., Spokane Club, Credit Women's Breakfast Club, Dir.'s Club, Inland N.W. Zool. Soc. Democrat. Mem. First Christian Ch. Office: Henry G Kolsrud DDS PS 3718 N Monroe St Spokane WA 99205-2850

FOTLAND, DAVID ALLEN, computer architect; b. Cleve., Sept. 25, 1957; s. Richard Allen and Frances Louise (Bierwagen) F.; m. Wendy Ann Rubin, May 15, 1982; children: Jonathan Edward, Alexander Michael. BSEE, MS in Computer Engring., Case Western Res. U., 1979. Mem. tech. staff Hewlett Packard, Cupertino, Calif., 1979-85; project mgr. Hewlett Packard, Cupertino, 1985-94. Author of computer go software; patentee in field. Smith scholar Case Western Res. U., Cleve., 1975. Mem. Am. Go Assn. (computer tournament organizer). Home: 4863 Capistrano Ave San Jose CA 95129-1031

FOTSCH, DAN ROBERT, elementary education educator; b. St. Louis, May 17, 1947; s. Robert Jarrel and Margaret Louise (Zimmermann) F.; m. Jacquelyn Sue Rotter, June 12, 1971; children: Kyla Michelle, Jeffrey Scott, Michael David. BS in Edn. cum laude, U. Mo., 1970; MS in Edn., Colo. State U., 1973. Cert. K-12 phys. edn. and health tchr. Mo., Colo. Tchr. phys. edn., coach North Callaway Schs., Auxvasse, Mo., 1970-71; grad. teaching asst., asst. track coach Colo. State U., Ft. Collins, 1971-73; tchr. elem. phys. edn., coach Poudre R-1 Sch. Dist., Ft. Collins, 1973—; tchr. on spl. assignment Elem. Phys. Edn. Resource, 1990- adminstrv. asst. Moore Sch., 1990-95; co-dir. Colo. State U. Handicapped Clinic, Ft. Collins, 1973-93; dir. Moore Elem. Lab. Sch., Ft. Collins, 1979—; dir. Colo. State U. Super Day Camp, 1979—; presenter for conf. in field. Contbr. articles to profl. jours. State dir. Jump Rope for Heart Project, Denver, 1981. Recipient Scott Key Acad. award, Sigma Phi Epsilon, 1969, Honor Alumni award, Coll. of Profl. Studies of Colo. State U., 1983; grantee Colo. Heart Assn., 1985; recipient Coaching Excellence award Ft. Collins Soccer Club, 1991-92. Mem. NEA, AAHPERD (exec. bd. mem. coun. on phys. edn. for children 1983-86, reviewer Jour. Phys. Edn., Recreation and Dance 198495, fitness chairperson, conv. planner 1986), ASCD, Poudre Edn. Assn., Colo. Edn. Assn., Colo. Assn. of Health, Phys. Edn., Recreation and Dance (pres. 1979-82, Tchr. award 1977, Honor award 1985), Internat. Platform Assn., Ctrl. Dist. Alliance for Health, Phys. Edn., Recreation and Dance (elem. divsn. chairperson for phys. edn. 1989—), Phi Delta Kappa (found. rep. 1985), Phi Epsilon Kappa (v.p. 1969, pres. 1970). Republican. Home: 5312 Elderberry Ct Fort Collins CO 80525-5529 Office: Moore Elem Sch 1905 Orchard Pl Fort Collins CO 80521-3210

FOTT, DAVID SAMUEL, political science educator; b. Clarksville, Tenn., Mar. 31, 1961; s. Solie Isaac and Mary Ready (Gilreath) F. BA, Vanderbilt U., 1983; AM, Harvard U., 1986, PhD, 1993. Asst. prof. polit. sci. U. Nev., Las Vegas, 1992—. Grad. fellow NSF, 1983-86; scholar Harry S. Truman Found., 1981. Mem. Am. Polit. Sci. Assn.

FOUAD, HUSSEIN YEHYA, electrical engineer; b. Cairo, July 21, 1939; came to U.S., 1963; s. Yehya and Bahga (Abdel Sayed) F.; married, 1971; children: Dalya, Basma, Rafik Daniel. BSc, Cairo U., 1960; MS, Purdue U., 1965, PhD, 1967. Registered profl. engr., Md., Ohio. Sr. engr. Babcock & Wilcox, Lynchburg, Va., 1966-67, Atomic Energy Commn., Cairo, 1967-74, Westinghouse in France, Paris, 1974-80, NUS, Gaithersburg, Md., 1980-83; pres. 3C, Inc., Richland, Wash., 1980—; sr. engr. AEP, Columbus, Ohio, 1983-89; prin. engr. Westinghouse, WHC, Richland, 1990—; adj. prof. Purdue U., West Lafayette, Ind., 1965-66, U. Md., College Park, 1980-83, Ohio State U., Columbus, 1983-89, Wash. State U., Richland, 1990—. Author: Automatic Control, 1965; contbr. articles to profl. jours.; patentee in field. Mem. IEEE, Am. Nuclear Soc., Instrument Soc. Am., Sigma Xi. Home and Office: 2469 Whitworth Ave Richland WA 99352-7753

FOURNIER, DONALD FREDERICK, dentist; b. Phoenix, Oct. 16, 1934; s. Dudley Thomas and Margaret Mary (Conway) F.; m. Sheila Ann Templeton, Aug. 5, 1957 (div. 1972); children: Julia Marguerite, Donald Frederick, John Robert, Anne Marie Selin, James Alexander; m. Nancy Colleen Hamm, July 10, 1976; children: Catharine Jacinthe, Jacques Edouard. Student, Stanford U., 1952, U. So. Calif., L.A., 1952-54; BSc, U. Nebr., 1958, DDS, 1958. Pvt. practice restorative dentistry Phoenix, 1958—; pres. Hope Mining and Milling Co., Phoenix, 1970—; chief dental staff St. Joseph's Hosp., Phoenix, 1968; vis. prof. periodontology Coll. Dentistry U. Nebr., 1985; faculty Phoenix Coll. Dental Hygiene Sch., 1968-71; investigator Ariz. State Bd. Dental Examiners, 1978-89; mem. Mercy Dental Clinic Staff, 1968-70; dir. Canadian Am. Inst. Cariology, 1986—. Contbr. articles to profl. jours. Pres. bd. trustees Osborn Sch. Dist., Phoenix, 1976; dir. Lukesmen, Phoenix, 1978-81; patrolman Nat. Ski Patrol, Phoenix, 1974-79; pres. Longview PTA, 1969; mem. adv. bd. Phoenix Crime Commn., 1969-71, Phoenix Coll. Dean's Adv. Bd., 1968-75; mem. The Phoenix House Am. Indian Rehab., 1985-86. Lt. col. (retired) Ariz. Army Res. N.G., 1958—. USPHS fellow, 1956-57, 57-58. Fellow Am. Coll. Dentists, Internat. Coll. Dentists; mem. ADA, Ariz. State Dental Assn., Pacific Coast Soc. Prosthodontists, Am. Acad. Restorative Dentistry (pres. 1991-92), Am. Acad. Gold Foil Operators, Craniomandibular Inst. (dir.), Internat. Assn. Dental Rsch., Acad. Operative Dentistry (charter), U.S. Croquet Assn., Ariz. Croquet Club, Downtown Croquet Club (pres. 1993—), Phoenix Country Club, Phi Delta Theta, Xi Psi Phi. Republican. Roman Catholic. Home: 86 E Country Club Dr Phoenix AZ 85014-5435 Office: 207 E Monterey Way Phoenix AZ 85012-2619

FOURNIER, WALTER FRANK, real estate executive; b. Northampton, Mass., Feb. 26, 1912; s. Frank Napoleon and Marie Ann F.; m. Ella Mae Karrey, May 16, 1938; children: Margaret Irene, Walter Karrey. BS in Mktg., Boston U., 1939; postgrad., Anchorage Community Coll., 1963-64, Alaska Pacific U., 1964-65. Coin sales supt. Coca Cola Co., Springfield, Mass., 1939-43; electrician foreman Collins Electric Co., Springfield, 1946-48; sales coord. for pre-fabricated homes Sears Roebuck & Co., Western Mass., 1948-49; wholesale sales rep. Carl Wiseman Steel and Aluminum Co., Great Falls, Mont., 1949-51; supt. City Electric Co., Anchorage, 1951-52; owner, adminstr. Acme Electric Co., Anchorage, 1953-64; appraiser Gebhart & Peterson, Anchorage, 1964-68; broker, owner Walter F. Fournier & Assocs., Anchorage, 1968—; pres. Alaska Mortgage Cons., Anchorage, 1968-69; owner Alaska Venture Capital, 1985—. Pres. Fairview Community Council, Anchorage, 1980-81. Served with U.S. Army, 1928-31, with USN, 1944-45, PTO. Recipient Spl. Recognition award HUD, 1967. Mem. Review Mortgage Underwriters, Inst. Bus. Appraisers, Internat. Soc. Financiers, Soc. Exchange Counselors (rep. 1970), Alaska Creative Real Estate Assn. (pres. 1978, Gold Pan award 1988), Alaska Million Plus Soc. (pres. 1983). Roman Catholic. Lodge: KC. Office: Walter F Fournier & Assocs 613 E 22nd Ave Anchorage AK 99503-2205

FOWLER, BETTY JANMAE, dance company director, editor; b. Chgo., May 23, 1925; d. Harry and Mary (Jacques) Markin; student Art Inst., Chgo., 1937-39, Stratton Bus. Coll., Chgo., 1942-43, Columbia U., 1945-47; B.A., Eastern Wash. U., 1984; 1 dau., Sherry Mareth Connors. Mem. public relations dept. Girl Scouts U.S.A., N.Y.C., 1961-63; adminstrv. asst. to editor-in-chief Scholastic Mags., N.Y.C., 1963-68; adminstrv. dir. Leonard Fowler Dancers, Fowler Sch. Classical Ballet, Inc., N.Y.C., 1959-78, tchr. ballet, 1959-61; pvt. practice Ecol. Lifestyle Advisor, 1980—; editor Bulletin, Kiwanis weekly publ., Spokane, Wash., 1978-82, adminstrv. sec. Kiwanis Club; instr. Spokane Falls Community Coll., 1978. Founder Safe Water Coalition Wash. State, 1988. Cert. metabolic technician Internat. Health Inst. Avocations: travel, reading. Address: 5615 W Lyons Ct Spokane WA 99208-3777

FOWLER, CHARLES EDWARD, JR., tennis management company executive; b. Salisbury, Md., Oct. 19, 1954; s. Charles Edward and Fern Nona (Trudeau) F. BA, La. State U., 1976; JD, Tulane U., 1979. Bar: D.C. 1980. Pacific regional dir. Peter Burwash Internat., The Woodlands, Tex., 1980-82, 89—; dir. U.S. ops. Uni-Bross Ltd., Zurich, Switzerland, 1982-89; dir. Dakota ResortWear, Kihei, Hawaii, 1993—; cons. Paniolo Coffee & Yogurt Co., Lahaina, Hawaii, 1993—. Spl. Olympics dir., Baton Rouge, 1973-75; pres. Kids Deserve A Chance, Kona, Hawaii, 1990-93. Recipient Disting. Citizen award Kids Deserve a Chance, 1972, Merit award Tulane U. Sch. Law, 1978. Mem. ABA, D.C. Bar Assn., U.S. Tennis Assn., Nat. Geog. Soc. Democrat. Roman Catholic. Home: 5400 Makena Alanui Kihei HI 96753-8435 Office: Peter Burwash Internat PO Box 959-234 Kihei HI 96753

FOWLER, DAVID, air and aerospace transportation executive; b. 1945. With U.S. Army, 1967-87; with Evergreen Air Ctr., Inc., Mcminnville, Oreg., 1987—, pres., 1990—. Office: Evergreen Air Ctr Inc 3850 Three Mile Ln Mcminnville OR 97128*

FOWLER, DONALD RAYMOND, retired lawyer, educator; b. Raton, N.Mex., June 2, 1926; s. Homer F. and Grace B. (Honeyfield) F.; m. Anna M. Averyt, Feb. 6, 1960; children: Mark D., Kelly A. BA, U. N.Mex., 1950; JD, 1951; MA, Claremont Grad. Sch., 1979, PhD, 1983. Bar: N.Mex. 1951, Calif. 1964, U.S. Supreme Ct. 1980. Atty. AEC, Los Alamos and Albuquerque, 1951-61, chief counsel Nev. Ops., 1962-63; pvt. practice, Albuquerque, 1961-62; asst., then dep. staff counsel Calif. Inst. Tech., Pasadena, 1963-72, staff counsel, 1972-75, gen. counsel, 1975-90; lectr. exec. mgmt. program Claremont Grad. Sch., Calif., 1981-84. Contbr. articles to profl. publs. Served with USAAF, 1944-46. Recipient NASA Pub. Svc. award, 1981. Mem. Calif. State Bar Assn., Fed. Bar Assn., Nat. Assn. Coll. and Univ. Attys. (exec. bd. 1979-82, 84-90, chmn. publs. com. 1982-84, pres. 1987-88, chmn. nominations com. 1988-89, chmn. honors and awards com. 1989-90, Life Mem. award 1991, Disting. Svc. award 1992), Calif. Assn. for Rsch. in Astronomy (sec. 1985-90).

FOWLER, JACK W., printing company executive; b. 1931; B.S., East Tenn. State U., 1957. Plant estimator, salesman Kingsport Press, 1952-65; western sales mgr.-books Plimpton Press, 1965-67; v.p. mktg. J.W. Clement, 1967-69; v.p., gen. sales mgr. Arcata Graphics, 1969-71; with W.A. Krueger Co., Scottsdale, Ariz., 1971—v.p. mktg. books and related products, 1971-72, v.p., gen. sales mgr., 1972-73, group v.p. books and related products, then group v.p. mag. and comml. products, 1973-76, sr. v.p. ops., then pres. and chief operating officer, 1976-78, pres., chief exec. officer, 1978—, also dir. Office: W A Krueger Co 1 Pierce Pl Ste 800 Itasca IL 60143-1253

FOWLER, JOHN ROBERT, airline executive; b. Flushing, N.Y., Dec. 12, 1947; s. James Edward and Helen Katherine (D'Elosua) F.; m. Diana L. Diekroger, May 16, 1981; children from previous marriage: Thomas J., John R., Jeanne M., James E., William. A. Student, Adelphi U., 1965-67, Pepperdine U., 1994—. Cert. comml. and instrument rated pilot; FAA Airframe and powerplant cert.; FCC advanced radio lic. Cleaner Pan Am. World Airways, Jamaica, N.Y., 1967-68, mech., 1968-71, supr., 1971-82, tech. coord. avionics, 1982-83, mgr. avionics svcs., 1983-86, dir. aircraft appearance, 1986-88, mng. dir. maintenance planning, 1988-89, v.p. maintenance and engring., 1989-91; v.p. maintenance and engring. Alaska Airlines, Seattle, 1991—. Republican. Lutheran. Office: Alaska Airlines PO Box 68900 Seattle WA 98168-0900

FOWLER, PETER NILES, lawyer; b. Hamilton, Ohio, Apr. 3, 1951; s. Richard Allen and Blanche (Niles) F. BA, John Carroll U., 1973; MA, U. Ala., Tuscaloosa, 1977, Ball State U., 1979; JD, Golden Gate U., 1984. Bar: Calif. 1984, Nev. 1986, U.S. Dist. Ct. (no. dist.) Calif. 1984, U.S. Ct. Appeals (9th cir.) 1984. Law clk. to assoc. justice Nev. Supreme Ct., Carson City, 1984-85; assoc. Lilienthal and Jacobson, San Francisco, 1985-87; ptnr. Lilienthal & Fowler, San Francisco, 1988—; adj. instr., faculty mem. Golden Gate U. Sch. Law, 1988—, Hastings Coll. of Law, 1988-91, U. San Francisco, 1991—; bd. dirs. Frameline. Contbg. author to books and articles to profl. jours. Co-chair, bd. dirs. Nat. Gay and Lesbian Task Force, Washington, 1983-89; chair, bd. dirs. Nat. Edn. Found. for Individual Rights, San Francisco, 1985—. Recipient Outstanding Leadership award Am. Cancer Soc., 1980. Mem. Nat. Lesbian and Gay Law Assn., Calif. Bar Assn., Nev. Bar Assn., San Francisco Bar Assn., Bay Area Lawyers Individual Freedom Assn., Calif. Lawyers for Arts. Democrat. Roman Catholic. Office: Lilienthal & Fowler Mills Tower 220 Montgomery St Fl 15 San Francisco CA 94104-3402

FOWLES, CHARLOTTE MARIE, English language educator; b. Little Rock, May 24, 1956; d. Lee Roy Fowles and Vera Martha (Mullins) Jones. BA, U. Wyo., 1980; postgrad., U. Nat. Automoma de Mexico, San Antonio, 1984-85. Tchr. English Carbon County Sch. Dist. 2, Hanna, Wyo., 1981-83, South San Antonio Ind. Sch. Dist., 1983-87; asst. English tchr. Japan Exch. of Teaching Ministry of Edn., Miyazaki City, Japan, 1987-89; tchr. ESL San Antonio Coll., 1989-90, Pass Lang. Square, Osaka, Japan, 1991-92; instr. English and history Seian Girls' Pvt. High Sch., Kyoto, Japan, 1992—; cons. Minaminaka Bd. Edn., Nichinan City, Japan, 1987-88. Richardson Trust scholar, 1974. Mem. Am. Fedn. Tchrs., Nat. English Tchrs., Tex. Tchrs. of English, Japanese Assn. Lang. Tchrs., Alumni of the Japan Exch. and Teaching Program, Phi Sigma Iota. Democrat. Episcopalian. Home: 3620 N College Dr Cheyenne WY 82001-1974 Office: Seian Girls Pvt HS Sumitomoseimei, Midousuji Kitamanzen-Cho Sokokuji, Kitaku Kamigyo-Ku Kyoto 602, Japan

FOWLES, JANICE, graphic designer; b. Oakland, Calif., Oct. 2, 1946; d. Grant Robert and Martha Janice (Garrett) F. BA, U. Utah, 1972, MFA, 1984. Jr. designer Whisler-Patri Assocs., San Francisco, 1972-76, Conversano & Assocs., Oakland, 1976; graphic designer Primo Angeli Graphics, San Francisco, 1976-80; designer Landor Assocs., San Francisco, 1980-81; designer, art dir. Janice Fowles Design, Salt Lake City, 1981-88; sr. graphic designer Internat. Game Tech., Reno, 1988—; assoc. instr. art dept. U. Utah, Salt Lake City, 1984-88; adj. faculty Coll. St. Francis Arts Program, Joliet, Ill., 1989—, U. Nev., Reno, 1988—. Recipient Merit award Utah AIA Soc., 1984, Award of Merit Western Art Dirs. West Coast Show, 1981, Merit award San Francisco Soc. Communication Arts, 1980, Cert. of Distinction Art Direction Mag., 1980. Home: 13820 Rancheros Dr Reno NV 89511-7375

FOX, FRANCES JUANICE, retired librarian, educator, retired; b. Vicksburg, Miss., Aug. 17, 1916; d. Willie Amercy Thaxton and Fannye Lou (Spell) Hepfer; m. Leonard John Fox, Feb. 25, 1937; children: Frances Juanice, L. John Jr., Kenneth L., Robert T., William E., Elizabeth Jean. AA, Phoenix Coll., 1959; BS in Edn., Ariz. State U., 1963, MS in Edn., Libr., 1972. Cert. kindergarten, primary, and elem. tchr., cert. libr., cert. religious edn. Diocese of Phoenix. Substitute tchr. Escambia County Sch. Dist., Pensacola, Fla., 1936-38; kindergarten tchr. Lollipop Ln. Sch., Phoenix, 1960-61, 1st United Meth. Day Sch., Phoenix, 1961-62; tchr. grade 3 Wilson Elem. Sch., Phoenix, 1962-63; summer libr. R.E. Simpson Elem. Sch., Phoenix, 1964, 65; preschool tchr. Jewish Community Ctr., Phoenix, 1967-68; libr. Audio Visual Ctr. Sts. Simon and Judge Elem. Sch., Phoenix, 1969-82; cataloger First Untied Meth. Ch. Libr., Phoenix, 1963, Baker Ctr. Ariz. State Univ. Meth. and Hillel Students Libr., Tempe, 1969; tchr. ch. sch., 1942-69, ret., 1969. Author numerous poems; co-compiler: (libr. manual) Diocese of Phoenix, 1980-81. Organizer, leader Girl Scouts Am., Birmingham, Ala., 1951, 52, Phoenix, 1976-83; leader cubs Boy Scouts Am., Birmingham, 1950-52, Phoenix, 1952-55; swim instr. ARC, Fla. Ariz., 1933, 34, 53, 54; dance instr. Circle Game and Beginning Dance, Wesley Cmty. Ctr., Phoenix, 1966, 67; tchr. ch. sch., 27 yrs., ret. 1969. Recipient Gold Poet award World Book of Poetry, 1990, Honorable Mention, Poetic Voices of Am., 1990, Internat. Achievement award Cambridge, Edn., 1994; academic scholar Phoenix Coll., Ariz. State Coll., 1959. Mem. ALA, Ariz. State Libr. Assn. (com. on continuing edn. 1979-81), Gold Star Wives of Am, Inc. (pres. 1993-94), DAV Aux. (life), Ariz. PTA (life mem., organizer, v.p.), Phi Theta Kappa, Iota Sigma Alpha Honor Soc. Methodist. Home: 2225 W Montebello Ave Phoenix AZ 85015-2327

FOX, JACK, financial service executive; b. Bklyn., Mar. 8, 1940; s. Benjamin and Rebecca (Shure) F.; m. Carole Olafson, July 8, 1987; children: Neal, Stuart. BBA, CCNY, 1961; MBA, CUNY, 1969. Sales specialist Am. Can Corp., N.Y.C., 1962-63; talent agt. Gen. Artists Corp., N.Y.C., 1963-66; bus. specialist N.Y. Times, 1966-70; pres. Ednl. Learning Systems, Inc., Washington, 1971-78; budget dir. Nat. Alliance of Bus., Washington, 1979-80; pres. Computerized Fin. Services, Rockville, Md., 1980-87; regional v.p. Govt. Funding Corp., L.A., 1987-90; owner, mgr. Jack Fox Assocs., San Diego, Calif., 1990—; founder Acctg. Resources Group, San Diego, 1993—; adj. prof. Am. U., Washington, 1983-85; tchr. fin. Montgomery Coll., Rockville, 1978-86. Author: How to Obtain Your Own SBA Loan, 1983, Starting and Building Your Own Accounting Business, 1984, 2d rev. edit. 1991, Accounting and Record Keeping Made Easy for the Self Employed, 1994. Mem. Internat. Platform Assn. Democrat. Jewish. Home and Office: 6115 Gullstrand St San Diego CA 92122-3823

FOX, JACK REX, military professional; b. Roswell, N.Mex., Feb. 10, 1948; s. Dorman Rex and Thelma (Furlong) F.; m. C. Marvine Sartin, Jan. 21, 1967; children: Troy Rex, Misty Layne. BA, N.Mex. State U., 1969; MEd, Ga. State U., 1975. Mgr. Herring Produce Co., Roswell, N.Mex., 1977-83; adminstrv. office 1st battalion N.Mex. Army Nat. Guard, Roswell, 1983-85; mobilization planner state hdqrs. N.Mex. Army Nat. Guard, Sante Fe, 1985, tng. adminstr. state hdqrs., 1985-89, plans, ops. and tng. officer, 1989-91, chief staff, 1992—; instr. Pikes Peak C.C., 1986-94. Youth baseball coach. With U.S. Army, 1969-77. Named Outstanding Young Men of Am., 1975, Dependent Youth Activity Coach of the Yr., Berlin, Germany, 1977; decorated Meritorious Svc. medal with two oak leaf clusters, Army Commendation medal with four oak leaf clusters, Army Achievement medal, Armed Forces Res. Achievement medal with two oak leaf clusters, Nat. Def. Svc. medal, Army Occupational medal, Armed Forces Expeditionary medal, Armed Forces Res. medal, Army Svc. ribbon, Overseas Svc. ribbon, Res. Overseas Svc. ribbon, others. Mem. NRA (life mem.), Nat. Guard Assn. U.S. Army, Res. Officer Assn., Mil. Order of the World Wars, Sertoma, N.Mex. Mil. Inst. Alumni Assn. (bd. dirs.), Ga. State U. Alumni Assn., N.Mex. State U. Alumni Assn., U.S. Army War Coll. Alumni Assn. Mem. Church of Christ. Office: NMex Air Nat Guard PO Box 4277 Santa Fe NM 87502-4277

FOX, JOEL DAVID, political association executive; b. Boston, Apr. 22, 1949; s. Harry L. and Freda (Berry) F.; m. Cydney M. Finkel, May 19, 1974; children: Zachary Daniel, Eric Maxwell. BA, U. Mass., 1971; MA, U. Denver, 1974. Pub. rels. staff L.A. Bicentennial Com., 1976; aide and exec. dir. Howard Jarvis Taxpayers Assn., L.A., 1979-86, pres., 1986—; internat. speaker taxes and initiative process. Contbr. articles to profl. jours. and newspapers; author Calif. ballot initiatives. Gubernatorial appointee Calif. Citizen's Commn. on Ballot Initiatives, 1993; trustee LEARN-L.A. Sch. Reform, 1991—; mem. Calif. Commn. on Transp. Investment, 1995. Office: Howard Jarvis Taxpayers Asn 621 S Westmoreland Ave Ste 202 Los Angeles CA 90005-3981

FOX, JOSEPH LELAND, utilities executive; b. Hutchinson, Kans., Aug. 1, 1938; s. George L. and Margaret V. (Crist) F.; m. Barbara Beiser, June 10, 1961 (div. 1964); 1 child, Gary; m. Norma J. Leiker, Dec. 27, 1967; 1 child, Holly. BS in Bus. and Econs., Ft. Hays State Coll., 1967. Ptnr. Fox and Co. CPAs, Denver, 1967-74; chief exec. officer, trustee Energy Resources Tech. Land, Inc. and Tell Ertl Family Trust, Boulder, Colo., 1974—; bd. dirs. Lake Eldora Corp., ERTL, Inc., New Paraho Corp. Comm. officer CAP, 1991-93. Mem. C. of C. Office: New Paraho Corp 5387 Manhattan Cir Ste 104 Boulder CO 80303-4219

FOX, KENNETH L., retired newspaper editor, writer; b. Kansas City, Mo., Mar. 18, 1917; s. Henry Hudson and Margaret Patience (Kiely) F.; m. Mary Harbord Manville, June 20, 1975. A.B., Washington U., St. Louis, 1938; student, U. Kansas City, 1939-40. With Kansas City Star, 1938-78, asso. editor, 1966-78; news analyst Sta. WDAF, Kansas City, 1948-53; war corr., Vietnam and Laos, 1964, corr., No. Ireland, 1973. Served to col. AUS, 1940-46. Decorated Bronze Star, Commendation medals with Oak Leaf Cluster; recipient 1st place editl. div. nat. aviation writing contest, 1957, 58, 59, 60, 67; named Aviation Man of Yr. for Kansas City, 1959. Mem. Am. Legion, 40 and 8, Res. Officers Assn., Ret. Officers Assn., Mil. Order World Wars, Phi Beta Kappa, Beta Theta Pi, Pi Sigma Alpha, Sigma Delta Chi. Clubs: Kansas City Press; Ariz. Home: 9796 E Ironwood Dr Scottsdale AZ 85258-4728

FOX, LORRAINE ESTHER, psychologist, human services consultant; b. S.I., N.Y., Aug. 27, 1941; d. Charles Frederick and Dorothy Elizabeth (Clohessy) F. BA, Northeastern Ill. U., 1973, MA, 1976; PhD in Clin. Psychology, Profl. Sch. Psychol. Studies, San Diego, 1989. Cert. in child care; cert. counselor and contract instr. U. Calif., Davis. Exec. dir. The Harbour, Des Plaines, Ill., 1975-81; asst. prof. Coll. St. Francis, Joliet, Ill., 1981-84; dir. clin. services Casa de Amparo, San Luis Rey, Calif., 1984-86; cons. Profl. Growth Facilitators, San Clemente, Calif., 1986—; vis. lectr. U. Ill. Chgo., 1983-84; cons. Arthur D. Little, Washington, 1979-82; contract cons. U. Calif.-Davis; internat. cons. Author tng. tapes on child care info.; various media appearances; pub. speaker; contbr. articles to profl. jours. Bd. dirs. United Ch. Child Care Ctr., Irvine; mem. adv. bd. Bienvenidos Family Svcs., L.A.; community adv. Learning Independence for Emancipation, San Diego. Mem. Calif. Assn. Child Care Workers (com. mem. 1984—, pres. Ill. chpt. 1982-84), ACLU, NOW, Psi Chi, Sierra Club. Home: 2838 Riachuelo San Clemente CA 92673-4045 Office: Profl Growth Facilitators PO Box 5981 San Clemente CA 92674-5981

FOX, LORRAINE SUSAN, marketing professional; b. L.A., Feb. 8, 1956; d. Robert Lazar and Valerie Joan (Barker) Fox; m. Clark Byron Siegel, July 19, 1981 (div. Nov. 1989). AB with distinction, Stanford U., 1979; MBA, U. Chgo., 1983. Sr. fin. analyst MacIntosh div., Apple Computer, Cupertino, Calif., 1983-84, Sun Microsystems Inc., Mountain View, Calif., 1984-85; mgr. fin. planning and analysis Sun Microsystems Inc., Mountain View, 1985-86, project mgr., 1986-88, mgr. project mgmt., 1988-90, sr. product mktg. mgr., 1990-93, mgr. mktg. strategy, 1993-95; dir. multimedia product mktg. new media divsn. Oracle Corp., Redwood Shores, Calif., 1995—. Vol. fundraiser Stanford (Calif.) U., 1983-88; vol. Sun Microsystems Community Vols., Mountain View, 1989—; alumni rep. undergrad. commn. on edn. Stanford U. Mem. Commonwealth Club, Stanford Profl. Women's Club, Churchill Club. Home: 707 Bryant St Palo Alto CA 94301-2554 Office: Oracle Corp Box 659509 500 Oracle Pky Redwood City CA 94065

FOX, MAXINE RANDALL, banker; b. Yates Ctr., Kans., Feb. 18, 1924; d. Carey Holaday and Nettie Myrrl (Herder) Randall; m. Joseph Marlin Fox, Aug. 25, 1946 (dec. 1992); children: Kathryn Lynette Fox Wilz, Jonathan Randall Fox. A in Fine Arts, Colo. Woman's Coll., 1942; B Music Edn., U. Denver, 1946. Pub. sch. music. tchr. Barr Lake (Colo.), 1942-43, Independence Sch., Fort Lupton, Colo., 1943-44, Fowler Pub. Schs., Fowler, Colo., 1944-48, 1952-54; employee The Fox Ins. Agy., Fowler, Colo., 1948-55, co-owner, 1955-86; with The Fowler (Colo.) State Bank, 1949—, vice chmn. bd. dirs., 1987—. Former mem. Fowler Libr. Bd.; mem. PEO. Mem. AAUW, DAR, First Families Ohio, Descendants Colonial Clergy (life), Fowler Hist. Soc. (past treas.), Fowler C. of C., Friends of Libr., Fowler Women's Club, Order Ea. Star, Fowler Golf Club, Pueblo Golf and Country Club. Republican. Methodist. Home: 3308 County Road Kk.75 Fowler CO 81039-9713 Office: Fowler State Bank 201 Main St Fowler CO 81039-1132

FOX, RICHARD LORAIN, political science educator; b. Toledo, Ohio, Sept. 1, 1946; s. Jack Robert and Pauline Marie (Staschke) F.; m. Sylvia

Anna Romero, Dec. 19, 1970; 1 child, Miles C.A. Student, U. Iowa, 1965-66; BA, U. N.Mex., 1975, MA, 1979. Legis. analyst City of Albuquerque City Coun., 1975-77; exec. asst. to pres. Monterey (Calif.) Inst. Internat. Studies, 1977-78; mgmt. analyst State of N.Mex. Fin. Dept., Santa Fe, 1980-88; lectr. U. N.Mex., Albuquerque, 1981—; instr. Albuquerque Tech.-Vocat. Inst., 1987—; free-lance cons. to govts. and mgmt., Albuquerque, 1988—. Contbr. articles to Century Mag., 1980-83, N.Mex. Mag., 1987. Named Young Dem. of Yr., Bernalillo County Young Dems., Albuquerque, 1972; hon. fellow John F. Kennedy Libr. Found. Mem. Acad. Polit. Sci. Democrat.

FOX, ROBERT AUGUST, food company executive; b. Norristown, Pa., Apr. 24, 1937; s. August Emil and Elizabeth Martha (Deimling) F.; m. Linda Lee Carnesale, Sept. 19, 1964; children: Lee Elizabeth, Christina Carolyn. B.A. with high honors, Colgate U., 1959; M.B.A. cum laude, Harvard U., 1964. Unit sales mgr. Procter & Gamble Co., 1959-62; gen. sales mgr. T.J. Lipton Co., 1964-69; v.p. mktg. Can. Dry Corp., 1969-72; pres., chief exec. officer, dir. Can. Dry Internat., 1972-75; exec. v.p., dir. Hunt-Wesson Foods, Inc., 1975-78; pres., chief exec. officer, dir. R.J. Reynolds Tobacco Internat. S.A., 1978-80; chmn., chief exec. officer, dir. Del Monte Corp., San Francisco, 1980-85; vice chmn. Nabisco Brands, Inc., East Hanover, N.J., 1986-87; pres., chief oper. officer Continental Can Co., Norwalk, Conn., 1988-90; chmn., chief exec. officer Clarke Hooper Am., Irvine, Calif., 1990-92, also bd. dirs.; pres. Revlon Internat., N.Y.C., 1992; pres., CEO Foster Farms, Livingston, Calif., 1993—; bd. dirs. New Perspective Fund, Growth Fund Am., Income Fund Am., Am. Balanced Fund, Clarke Hooper, plc, Crompton & Knowles Corp.; trustee Euro-Pacific Growth Fund. Trustee Colgate U. Mem. San Francisco C. of C. (bd. dir., pres. 1984), Pacific Union Club, The Olympic Club. Office: Foster Farms 1000 Davis St Livingston CA 95334-1526

FOX, STUART IRA, physiologist; b. Bklyn., June 21, 1945; s. Sam and Bess F.; m. Ellen Diane Berley; 1 child, Laura Elizabeth. BA, UCLA, 1967; MA, Calif. State U., L.A., 1967; postgrad., U. Calif., Santa Barbara, 1969; PhD, U. So. Calif., 1978. Rsch. assoc. Children's Hosp., L.A., 1972; prof. physiology L.A. City Coll., 1972-85, Calif. State U., Northridge, 1979-84, Pierce Coll., 1986—; cons. William C. Brown Co. Pubs., 1976—. Author: Computer-Assisted Instruction in Human Physiology, 1979, Laboratory Guide to Human Physiology, 2d edit., 1980, 3d edit., 1984, 4th edit., 1987, 5th edit., 1990, 6th edit., 1993, Textbook of Human Phyiology, 1984, 3d edit., 1990, 4th edit., 1993, 4th edit., 1995, Concepts of Human Anatomy and Physiology, 1986, 2d edit., 1989, 3d edit., 1992, 4th edit., 1995, Laboratory Guide to Human Anatomy and Physiology, 1986, 2d edit., 1989, 3d edit., 1992. Mem. AAAS, So. Calif. Acad. Sci., Am. Physiol. Soc., Sigma Xi. Home: 5556 Forest Cove Ln Agoura Hills CA 91301-4047 Office: Pierce Coll 6201 Winnetka Ave Woodland Hills CA 91371-0001

FOX, WARREN LEONARD JOHN, electrical engineer; b. Seattle, Mar. 30, 1966; s. John William Leonard and Karen Marie (Weiss) F.; m. Meredeth J. McMahon. BSEE cum laude, U. Wash., 1988, MSEE, 1990, PhD, 1994. Elec. engr. Applied Physics Lab., U. Wash., Seattle, 1988—, fellow, 1989-94. Mem. IEEE. Office: Applied Physics Lab U Wash 1013 NE 40th St Seattle WA 98105-6606

FOXHOVEN, MICHAEL JOHN, retail and wholesale company executive, retail merchant; b. Sterling, Colo., Mar. 2, 1949; s. Mark John and Mary Kathryn (Hagerty) F.; m. Catherine Marie Carricaburu, Feb. 16, 1980; children—Patrick Michael, Rachel Marie. Student U. Colo., 1967-70, U. San Francisco, 1971-72, postgrad. Columbia Pacific U., 1987—. Comml. sales mgr. Goodyear Tire & Rubber Co., Denver, 1978-80, area sales mgr., 1980-81, store mgr., 1981-83, wholesale mgr., 1983-84, appeared in TV commls., 1972; v.p. Foxhovens, Inc., Sterling, 1984-89; cons. Foxhoven Bros., Inc., Sterling, 1984-89; gen. mgr. General Tire, Ventura, Calif., 1989-91; area sales mgr. Bridgestone/Firestone, L.A., 1991; pres. C & M Fin. Svcs., Camarillo, Calif., 1991—; area sales mgr. Bridgestone/Firestone L.A., 1991-92, dist. mgr., 1992—; participant dealer mgmt. seminar, Akron, Ohio, 1973, 85. Mem. mgmt. adv. com. Northeastern Jr. Coll., Sterling, 1976-78; sec. Highland Park Sanitation Dist., Sterling, 1984-89. Mem. Logan County C. of C. Republican. Roman Catholic. Club: Sterling Country. Lodges: Elks, Kiwanis. Office: C & M Fin Svcs 266 Camino Castanada Camarillo CA 93010-1832

FOXLEY, CECELIA HARRISON, commissioner. BA in English, Utah State U., 1964; MA in English, U. Utah, 1965, PhD in Ednl. Psychology, 1968. English tchr. Olympus H.S., Salt Lake City, 1965-66; asst. prof. edn., assoc. dir. student activities U. Minn., Mpls., 1968-71; from asst. prof. to assoc. prof., asst. dean Coll. Edn. U. Iowa, Iowa City, 1971-81; prof. psychology Utah State U., Logan, 1981-85, from asst. v.p. student svcs. to assoc. v.p. for student svcs. and acad. affairs, 1981-85; assoc. commr. for acad. affairs Utah State Bd. Regents, Salt Lake City, 1985-93, commr., 1993—; Utah rep. Am. Coun. on Edn. Office Women in Higher Edn., 1982-92; mem. nat. adv. coun. on nurse tng. U.S. Dept. Health and Human Svcs., 1987-91; mem. nat. adv. bd. S.W. Regional Ctr. for Drug Free Schs., 1988-93; mem. edn. bd. Utah Alliance for Edn. and Humanities, 1989-93; mem. prevention subcom. Utah Substance Abuse Coordinating Coun., 1991-93; mem. exec. bd. U.S. West Comm., 1995—; mem. adv. bd. Salt Lake Buzz, 1995—; active Consortium for Women in Higher Edn. Bd., 1981-85, Utah State Libr. Bd., 1990-93, Compact for Faculty Diversity, 1994—; presenter in field; cons. in field. Author: Recruiting Women and Minority Faculty, 1972, Locating, Recruiting, and Employing Women, 1976, Non-Sexist Counseling: Helping Women and Men Redefine Their Roles, 1979; co-author: The Human Relations Experience, 1982; editor: Applying Management Techniques, 1980; co-editor: Multicultural Nonsexist Education, 1979; author chpts. to books; contbr. articles to profl. jours. Grantee Utah State Dept. Social Svcs., 1984-85, 85-86; recipient Pres. Leadership award Assn. Utah Women Edn. Adminstrs., 1990, Disting. Alumni award Utah State U., 1991. Mem. APA, Am. Assn. Counseling and Devel., Am. Coll. Pers. Assn., Nat. Forum Sys. Chief Acad. Officers, State Higher Edn. Exec. Officers (mem. exec. com. 1994—), Western Interstate Cooperative Higher Edn. (mem. exec. com. 1994—). Office: Utah State Bd Regents 3 Triad Ctr Ste 550 355 W North Temple Salt Lake City UT 84180-1205*

FOXLEY, MATTHEW C., art gallery administrator; b. Omaha, May 14, 1965; s. William C. Foxley and Paula C. Washburn. Adminstr. Mus. Western Art, Denver, 1985-87; pres. Frontier Spirit Gallery Inc., Denver, 1987—, 1st Nat. Communications, Denver, 1987—. Office: Frontier Spirit Gallery 1727 Tremont Pl Denver CO 80202-4006

FOXLEY, WILLIAM COLEMAN, cattleman; b. St. Paul, Jan. 7, 1935; s. William Joseph and Eileen (Conroy) F. BA, U. Notre Dame, 1957. Pres., chmn. bd. Foxley Cattle Co., Omaha, 1960—. Chmn. bd. Mus. Western Art, Denver. Served with USMCR, 1957-60. Republican. Roman Catholic. Office: Foxley Cattle Co 7480 La Jolla Blvd La Jolla CA 92037*

FRACCHIA, CHARLES ANTHONY, investment advisor, educator; b. San Francisco, Aug. 10, 1937; s. Charles Bartholomew and Josephine (Giacosa) F; m. Ann Escobosa, Feb. 10, 1962 (div. 1971); children: Laura E., Carla A., Charles A. Jr., Francesca S.; m. Elizabeth Ann Feaster, Aug. 15, 1987. AB in History, U. San Francisco, 1960, postgrad., 1959-61; MLS, U. Calif., Berkeley, 1976; MA in History, San Francisco State U., 1979; MA in Theology, Grad. Theol. Union, Berkeley, 1981. Stockbroker Paine Webber, San Francisco, 1961-65, J. Barth, San Francisco, 1965-70; v.p. mktg. Brennan Fin. Group, San Francisco, 1970-71; gen. mgr., analyst Walker's Manual div. Hambrecht & Quist, San Francisco, 1971-73; fin. advisor Planned Investments Inc (now IFG Network Securities, Inc.), 1981—; pres. Fracchia Capital Mgmt. Co.; instr. City Coll. San Francisco, 1980—. Author: Converted Into Houses, 1976, So This is Where You Work, 1980, Second Spring, 1980, Living Together Alone, 1979, How to Be Single Creatively, 1979, Fire & Gold: The San Francisco Story. Trustee Calif. Hist. Soc., San Francisco, 1966-76, 90—; mem. San Francisco Hist. Landmarks Adv. Bd., 1968-72; pres. San Francisco Hist. Soc., 1988—. Mem. Concordia-Argonaut Club. Democrat. Roman Catholic. Home: 2881 Jackson St San Francisco CA 94115-1145 Office: IFG Network Securities Inc PO Box 420569 San Francisco CA 94142-0569

FRAGOLA, ALBERT THOMAS, army officer; b. Pelham, N.Y., Dec. 31, 1942; s. Albert and Elizabeth Margaret (Smith) F.; m. Ardy Anderson; children: Kirsten Fragola Poteet, Deidre. BA in Social Sci., Tex. Christian U., 1974, MLA, 1976; diploma, U.S. Army Command & Gen. Staff Coll., 1983, U.S. Naval War Coll., 1994. Cert. comml. pilot FAA. Commd. warrant officer U.S. Army, 1966, advanced through grades to lt. col., 1992, aviator, 1966-71; sales support mgr. Tracor-Westronics, Ft. Worth, 1971-74; assoc. prof. mgmt. Tarrant County Jr. Coll., Hurst, Tex., 1975-85; aviation office 77th U.S. ARCOM U.S. Army, Ft. Totten, N.Y., 1985-88; exec. officer 244th aviation group U.S. Army, Glenview NAS, Ill., 1988-91; sec. to gen. staff 125th US ARCOM U.S. Army, Ft. Lawton, Wash., 1991—. Recipient DFC, Bronze Star, Meritorious Svc. medal with 2 oak leaf clusters, Air medal with 17 oak leaf clusters. Home: Us Arcom # 124th Fort Lawton WA 98199

FRAHMANN, DENNIS GEORGE, computer company executive; b. Medford, Wis., June 25, 1953; s. George Henry and Aini (Siikarla) F. BA, Ripon Coll., 1974; MS, Columbia U., 1975; postgrad., U. Minn., 1978-79. Freelance writer Mpls., 1975-77; instnl. designer Control Data Corp., Mpls., 1977-80; mgr. customer edn. Xerox Corp., L.A., 1980-84; product mgr. Xerox Corp., Palo Alto, Calif., 1984-86; nat. mktg. mgr. Xerox Corp., L.A., 1986-87, mgr., cons. rels., 1989-94, dir., trade shows, 1994—; mgr. Xerox Systems Inst., L.A., 1987-89; bd. advisors Microcomputer Graphics Conf., N.Y.C., 1986-88. Contbg. editor Mpls.-St. Paul Mag., 1977-80; contbr. articles to profl. publs., chpt. to book. Mem. Mcpl. Election Com. L.A., 1985—; mem. SilverLake Improvement Assn., L.A., 1989—; pres. Hyperion Neighborhood Assn., L.A., 1989—. Wingspread fellow Johnson Found., 1971-74. Mem. Phi Beta Kappa. Office: Xerox Corp 101 Continental Blvd El Segundo CA 90245-4530

FRAITAG, LEONARD ALAN, mechanical and manufacturing engineer; b. N.Y.C., Dec. 23, 1961; s. David and Lucille Reneé (Jay) F.; children: Shoshana Elizabeth, Aaron Joseph. BSME, San Diego State U., 1987; AA, Grossmont Coll., 1983. Design engr. Restaurant Concepts, San Diego, 1987; mech. engr. Vantage Assocs., Inc., San Diego, 1988-89; design engr. Mainstream Engrng. Co., Inc., San Diego, 1989; project engr. Pilkington Barnes Hind, San Diego, 1989—. Inventor safe product moving device for contact lens. Mem. United Faculty Grossmont Coll. Office: Pilkington Barnes Hind 8006 Engineer Rd San Diego CA 92111-1906

FRAKER, MARK ARNOTT, environmental scientist; b. Columbus, Ind., Dec. 13, 1944; s. Ralph Waldo and Carol (Arnott) F.; m. Pamela Norton, May 27, 1967 (div. Feb. 1985); 1 child, Russell; m. Donice Horton, Aug. 23, 1986. BA with honors, Ind. U., 1967, MA, 1969. Biologist, project mgr. F.F. Slaney and Co., Vancouver, Can., 1972-78; biologist, project dir. LGL Ltd., Sidney, B.C., Can., 1978-82; sr. environ. scientist BP Exploration (Alaska) Inc., Anchorage, 1982-91; wildlife, restoration program mgr. divsn. oil spill impact assessment & restoration Alaska Dept. Fish and Game, Anchorage, 1991-93; pvt. practice consulting biologist Sidney, B.C., Can., 1993—; broadcaster CBC, Vancouver, 1970-72; mem. sci. com. Internat. Whaling Com., Cambridge, Eng., 1982-91; adj. prof. U. Alaska, Anchorage, 1985-89; mem. panel NAS, 1987-92; mem. rescue team Barrow Gray Whale Rescue, 1988; mem. adv. com. on polar programs NSF, 1988-90; mem. Pacific Sci. Rev. Group for Marine Mammal Stock Assessments, 1994—; mem. Ballard Locks Pinniped-Fishery Interaction Task Force, 1994—. Author: Balaena mysticetus, 1984; also articles; mem. editorial bd. Biol. Papers of the U. of Alaska. Amb. to Peru, Anchorage Olympic Organizing Com., 1986-89. Woodrow Wilson fellow, Princeton, N.J., 1967. Mem. AAAS, Am. Soc. Mammalogists, Arctic Inst. N.Am., Ottawa Field Naturalists' Club, Can. Soc. Zoologists, Soc. for Marine Mammalogy, The Wildlife Soc., Sigma Xi.

FRAME, JOHN MCELPHATRICK, theology educator, pastor; b. Pitts., Apr. 8, 1939; s. Clark Crawford and Violet Luella (McElphatrick) F.; children by previous marriage: Deborah Rubio, Doreen Kester, David O'Donnell; m. Mary Grace Cummings, June 2, 1984; children: Justin Michael, John Alden. BA, Princeton U., 1961; BD, Westminster Theol. Sem., 1964; MPhil, Yale U., 1968. Ordained to ministry, Orthodox Presbyn. Ch., 1968. Instr. to assoc. prof. apologetics and systematic theology Westminster Theol. Sem., Phila., 1968-80; assoc. prof. apologetics and systematic theology Westminster Theol. Sem., Escondido, Calif., 1987—, prof. apologetics and systematic theology, 1988—; assoc. pastor New Life Presbyn. Ch., Escondido, 1988—, pianist, worship leader, 1980—. Author: Doctrine of Knowledge of God, 1987, Medical Ethics, 1988, Evangelical Reunion, 1991, Apologetics re the Glory of God, 1994, Cornelius Van Til: An Analysis of His Thought, 1995; contbr. numerous articles to profl. jours. Mem. Evang. Theol. Soc., Soc. Christian Philosophers, Am. Guild Organists, Am. Choir Dirs. Assn. Republican. Home: 3572 Prince St Escondido CA 92025-7616 Office: Westminster Theol Sem 1725 Bear Valley Pky Escondido CA 92027-4128

FRAME, JOHN TIMOTHY, bishop; b. Toronto, Ont., Can., Dec. 8, 1930; s. Duncan McClymont and Sarah Aitken (Halliday) F.; m. Barbara Alida Butters, Sept. 8, 1956; children—Alida Grace, Bronwyn Ruth, Monica Mary. B.A., Trinity Coll., Toronto, 1953, L.Th., 1957, S.T.B., 1961, D.D. (hon.), 1968. Ordained deacon, priest Anglican Ch. Can., 1957; minister Missions to Lakes Dist., Burns Lake, B.C., 1957-67; canon Diocese of Caledonia, 1965-67; bishop of Yukon, 1967-80; sr. bishop Province of B.C., 1971-80; acting metropolitan, 1973-75; dean of Columbia and rector Christ Ch. Cathedral, Victoria, B.C., 1980—. Home: 201 1175 Newport Ave, Victoria, BC Canada V8S 5E6 Office: 912 Vancouver St, Victoria, BC Canada V8V 3V7

FRAME, TED RONALD, lawyer; b. Milw., June 27, 1929; s. Morris and Jean (Lee) F.; student UCLA, 1946-49; AB, Stanford U., 1950, LLB, 1952; m. Lois Elaine Pilgrim, Aug. 15, 1954; children: Kent, Lori, Nancy, Owen. Bar: Calif. 1953. Gen. agri-bus. practice, Coalinga, Calif., 1953—; sr. ptnr. Frame & Matsumoto, 1965—. Trustee, Baker Mus.; dir. West Hills Coll. Found. Mem. ABA, Calif. Bar Assn., Fresno County Bar Assn., Coalinga C. of C. (past pres.), Masons, Shriners, Elks. Home: 1222 Nevada St Coalinga CA 93210-1239 Office: 201 Washington St Coalinga CA 93210

FRANCES, HARRIETTE (SHERANA), painter, printmaker, consultant; b. San Francisco; d. Anton and Mary (Panos) Vatsakis; divorced; children: Mitchell, Stephanie. Student, Calif. Sch. Fine Arts, San Francisco, 1942-45, San Francisco Art Inst., 1964-66, Tamarind Lithography Inst., Albuquerque, N.Mex., 1989, 91, 92; also studied with James Weeks, Wm. H. Brown. Dir., founder Artist's Proof Graphics Workshop, Larkspur, Calif., 1974—; part-time instr. Coll. of Marin, Kentfield, Calif., 1976-93; part-time workshop tchr. Artist's Proof Graphics Workshop, Larkspur, 1974-85. Solo and group shows include Calif. Palace of Legion of Honor Mus., San Francisco, 1968, Blanden Art Gallery, Ft. Dodge, Iowa, 1969, Hastings Coll. Gallery Art, Hastings, Nebr., 1970, San Francisco Mus. Modern Art, 1976, San Marco Gallery, San Rafael, Calif., 1981, Stanford U., 1991, Marin Theatre Co., Mill Valley, Calif., 1993; numerous nat. and internat. exhbns.; work represented in pub. and corp. collections; also travelling shows. Art auction organizer Larkspur Community Assn., 1993-94. Recipient over 60 awards including James D. Phelan award in painting, 1965. Mem. Calif. Soc. Printmakers, Marin Arts Coun. Home: 105 Rice Ln Larkspur CA 94939-2054 Office: Artists Proof Graphics Workshop 469-A Magnolia Larkspur CA 94939

FRANCESCHI, ERNEST JOSEPH, JR., lawyer; b. L.A., Feb. 1, 1957; s. Ernest Joseph and Doris Cecilia (Beluche) F. BS, U. So. Calif., 1978; JD, Southwestern U., L.A., 1980. Bar: Calif. 1984, U.S. Dist. Ct. (cen. dist.) Calif. 1984, U.S. Dist. Ct. (ea. dist.) Calif. 1986, U.S. Dist. Ct. (no. and so. dists.) Calif. 1987, U.S. Ct. Appeals (9th cir.) 1984, U.S. Supreme Ct. 1989, Pvt. practice law L.A., 1984—. Mem. Assn. Trial Lawyers Am., Calif. Trial Lawyers Assn., L.A. Trial Lawyers Assn., Trial Lawyers for Pub. Justice, Fed. Bar Assn. Office: 445 S Figueroa St Ste 2600 Los Angeles CA 90071-1630

FRANCH, NORA, re-engineering specialist; b. Kansas City, Kans., Aug. 16, 1955; d. Ernest Sr. and Frances (McQuaid) Voiles; m. Gary L. Franch. BS in Bus. Adminstrn., Nat. Coll., Denver, 1983; MSS in Applied Communications, U. Denver, 1992. Office mgr. U.S. Army, Anchorage, 1976-79; lease adminstrn. K-N Energy Co., Lakewood, Colo., 1980-83; paralegal Welborn, Dufford, Brown Law Firm, Denver, 1982-84; sec. Colo. N.G., Englewood, 1984-85, staffing specialist, 1985-86, EEO mgr., 1986-88, human resources mgr., 1988-93; reengineering specialist Defense Finance & Acctg. Svcs., 1993—; instr. Nat. Coll., 1992. Home: 2096 Sandhurst Dr Castle Rock CO 80104-2392

FRANCHINI, GENE EDWARD, state supreme court justice; b. Albuquerque, May 19, 1935; s. Mario and Lena (Vaio) F.; m. Glynn Hatchell, Mar. 22, 1969; children: Pamela, Lori (dec.), Gina, Joseph James, Nancy. BBA, Loyola U., 1955; degree in adminstrn., U. N.Mex., 1957; JD, Georgetown U., 1960; LLM, U. Va., 1995. Bar: N.Mex. 1960, U.S. Dist. Ct. N.Mex. 1961, U.S. Ct. Appeals (10th cir.) 1970, U.S. Supreme Ct. 1973. Ptnr. Matteucci, Gutierrez & Franchini, Albuquerque, 1960-70, Matteucci, Franchini & Calkins, Albuquerque, 1970-75; judge State of N.Mex. 2d Jud. Dist., Albuquerque, 1975-81; atty.-at-large Franchini, Wagner, Oliver, Franchini & Curtis, Albuquerque, 1982-90; justice N.Mex. Supreme Ct., Santa Fe, 1990—. Chmn. Albuquerque Pers. Bd., 1972, Albuquerque Labor Rels. Bd., 1972, Albuquerque Interim Bd. Ethics, 1972. Capt. USAF, 1960-66. Mem. Am. Bd. Trial Advocates, N.Mex. Trial Lawyers (pres. 1967-68), N.Mex. Bar Assn. (bd. dirs. 1976-78), Albuquerque Bar Assn. (bd. dirs. 1976-78). Democrat. Roman Catholic. Home: PO Box 75327 Albuquerque NM 87194-0327 Office: NMex Supreme Ct PO Box 848 Santa Fe NM 87504-0848*

FRANCIS, CAROLYN RAE, music educator, musician, author, publisher; b. Seattle, July 25, 1940; d. James Douglas and Bessie Caroline (Smith) F; m. Barclay Underwood Stuart, July 5, 1971. BA in Edn., U. Wash., 1962. Cert. tchr., Wash. Tchr. Highline Pub. Schs., Seattle, 1962-64; musician Olympic Hotel, Seattle, 1962-72; 1st violin Cascade Symphony Orch., 1965-78; tchr. Bellevue (Wash.) Pub. Schs., 1965-92; founder/pres. Innovative Learning Designs, Mercer Island, Wash., 1984—; profl. violinist for TV, recs., mus. shows, 1962-85; violist Eastside Chamber Orch., 1984-86; pvt. tchr. string instruments, 1959—; spkr. in-svc. workshops, convs., music educators numerous cities, 1984—, adjudicator music festivals; instr. MIDI applications for educators, 1992—. Author-pub. Music Reading and Theory Skills (curriculum series), Levels 1, 2, 1986, Level 3, 1984; contbr. articles to profl. jours., 1984—. Mem. Snohomish Indian Tribe. Bellevue Schs. Found. grantee, 1985-86, 86-87, 89-90. Mem. NEA, Am. String Tchrs. Assn. (regional mem. chmn. 1992-94), Music Educators Nat. Conf., Music Industry Coun. Office: Innovative Learning Designs 7811 SE 27th St Ste 104 Mercer Island WA 98040-2961

FRANCIS, TIMOTHY DUANE, chiropractor; b. Chgo., Mar. 1, 1956; s. Joseph Duane and Barbara Jane (Sigwalt) F. Student, U. Nev., 1974-80, We. Nev. C.C., 1978; BS, L.A. Coll. Chiropractic, 1982, Dr. of Chiropractic magna cum laude, 1984; postgrad., Clark County Community Coll., 1984-85; MS in Bio/Nutrition, U. Bridgeport, 1990. Diplomate Internat. Coll. Applied Kinesiology, Am. Acad. Pain Mgmt., Am. Naturopathic Med. Bd.; cert. kinesiologist, applied kinesiology tchr.; lic. chiropractor, Calif., Nev. Instr. dept. recreation and phys. edn. U. Nev., Reno, 1976-80; from tchng. asst. to lead instr. dept. principles & practice L.A. Coll. Chiropractic, 1983-85; pvt. practice Las Vegas, 1985—; asst. instr. Internat. Coll. Applied Kinesiology, 1990, chmn. exam review com., 1993, chmn. syllabus review com., 1994; adj. faculty The Union Inst. Coll. of Undergrad. Studies, 1993; joint study participant Nat. Olympic Tng. Ctr., Beijing, China, 1990. Charles F. Cutts scholar, 1980. Fellow Internat. Acad. Clin. Acupuncture, British Inst. Homeopathy (homeopathy diploma 1993); mem. Am. Chiropractic Assn. (couns. on sports injuries, nutrition, roentgenology, technic, and mental health), Nev. State Chiropractic Assn., Nat. Strength and Conditioning Assn., Gonsted Clin. Studies Soc., Found. for Chiropractic Edn. and Rsch., Nat. Inst. Chiropractic Rsch., Nat. Acad. Rsch. Biochemists, Phi Beta Kappa, Phi Kappa Phi (v.p. 1979-80, Scholar of the Yr. award, 1980), Delta Signa. Republican. Roman Catholic. Home: 3750 S Jones Blvd Las Vegas NV 89103-2283

FRANCISCO, WAYNE M(ARKLAND), automotive executive; b. Cin., June 14, 1943; s. George Lewis and Helen M. (Markland) F. Student, Ohio State U., 1962-63; BS in Mktg. and Acctg., U. Cin., 1967; m. Susan Francisco; children: Diana Lynn, W. Michael. Unit sales mgr. Procter & Gamble, Cin., 1967-69; mktg. mgr. Nat. Mktg. Inc., Cin., 1969-70; pres. Retail Petroleum Marketers, Inc., Cin., 1970-72, chmn. bd., chief exec. officer, Phoenix, 1972-85; chmn. bd., chief exec. officer DMC Industries, Inc., 1985—; pres., chief exec. officer Cassia Petroleum Corp., Vancouver, B.C., Can., 1980-84; bd. dirs. P.F.K. Enterprises, F.I.C. Inc., Internat. Investment and Fin. Enterprises, Inc., Alpha Realty, Inc. Class agt. 62G Culver Mil. Acad., 1987-91. Mem. Culver Legion (bd. trustees 1990—), Eugene C. Eppley Club, Phoenix Bd. Appeals, 1978-80; v.p. Cuernavaca Homeowners Assn., 1982, pres., 1983-86. Recipient Image Maker award Shell Oil Co., 1979; Top Performer award Phoenix dist. Shell Oil Co., 1979, 80. Mem. Petroleum Retailers Ariz. (pres. 1977-79), Nat. Congress Petroleum Retailers (adv. bd.), Automotive Svc. Excellence (cert.), Culver Legion (life), Studebaker Drivers Club (zone coord. Pacific S.W. 1983, nat. v.p. 1986, 87, 88, nat. pres. 1989-90, Grand Canyon chpt. pres. 1986), Avanti Owners Assn. (nat. bd. dirs. 1975-91, internat. pres. 1986-89). Republican. Lodge: Optimists (bd. dirs. Paradise Valley club 1984, sec.-treas. 1984). Office: 21824 N 19th Ave Phoenix AZ 85027-2101

FRANCKE, UTA, medical geneticist, genetics researcher, educator; b. Wiesbaden, Germany, Sept. 9, 1942; came to U.S., 1969; d. Kurt and Gertrud Müller; m. Bertold Richard Francke, May 27, 1967 (div. 1982); m. Heinz Furthmayr, July 27, 1986. MD, U. Munich, Fed. Republic Germany, 1967; MS, Yale U., 1985. Diplomate Am. Bd. Pediatrics, Am. Bd. Med. Genetics (bd. dirs. 1981-84). Asst. prof. U. Calif., San Diego, 1973-78; assoc. prof. Yale U., New Haven, 1978-85, prof., 1985-88; prof. Stanford (Calif.) U., 1989—; investigator Howard Hughes Med. Inst., Stanford, 1989—, mem. sci. rev. bd., Bethesda, Md., 1986-88; mem. mammalian genetics study sect. NIH, Bethesda, 1990—; bd. dirs. Am. Soc. Human Genetics, Rockville, Md., 1981-84. Profl. advisor March of Dimes Birth Defects Found., White Plains, N.Y., 1990, Marfan Assn., Port Washington, N.Y., 1991. Mem. Inst. Medicine of NAS (fgn. assoc.), Human Genome Orgn., Soc. for Pediatric Rsch., Soc. for Inherited Metabolic Disorders. Office: Stanford U Med Sch Howard Hughes Med Inst Beckman Ctr Stanford CA 94305*

FRANDEN, BLANCHE M., nursing educator; b. N.Y.C., June 9, 1923; d. Samuel and Rebekah (Stern) Randall; m. Robert Jacob Franden, Aug. 20, 1950; children: Richard Jules, Peter Herb, Daniel Ethan. Grad. Mass. Meml. Hosp. Sch. Nursing (now Boston U. Hosp.), 1945; B. in Vocat. Edn., Calif. State U., L.A., 1980. RN, Calif. dir. student health Mass. Meml. Hosp., Boston, 1947-49; staff nurse various hosps., N.Y., Calif., 1949-91; instr., coord. hosp. related occupations East San Gabriel Valley Regional Occupational Program, 1973-90, instr., coord., EMT 1, 1986—; program dir., instr., EMT 1 La Puente Valley Regional Occupl. Program, 1985-93; CPR instr.-trainer; mem. CPR com., local governing bd. Am. Heart Assn; mem. L.A. County Com. to Revise Curriculum for EMT1 recertification, 1992—. Author student manual. Rec. sec. Pathways to Hope chpt. City of Hope. Mem. AAUW, VFW Women's Aux., Calif. Assn. Regional Occupl. Ctrs./Programs, Am. Vocat. Assn., Calif. Assn. Health Career Educators, So. Calif. Assn. EMT Instrs. and Coords. Democrat. Jewish. Office: E San Gabriel Valley Regional Occupl Program 1024 Workman St West Covina CA 91790

FRANEY, PHILIP DAVID, county treasurer, tax collector; b. Bakersfield, Calif., Feb. 5, 1948; s. James T. and Dorothy (Ross) F.; m. Dina Cepeda, Jan. 24, 1976; children: Shelly, Dina. AA, Bakersfield Coll., 1968; BSBA, Calif. State U., Bakersfield, 1973. Supervising acct.ech. Bakersfield (Calif.) City Sch. Dist., 1973-76; systems acct., auditor, controller County of Kern, Bakersfield, 1976-81; asst. treas. County of Kern, 1981-87, treas., tax collector, 1987—; bd. dirs., Kern County Employees' Retirement Assn., Bakersfield, 1987—, Kern Flex Adv. Com., 1987—; adminstr., Kern County Deferred Compensation Plan, 1987—; panelist Asset Allocation Symposium, Carmel, 1989, Calif. Assn. County Treas.-Tax Collectors, Rohnert, 1990. Chmn. Kern County Employees' United Way, Bakersfield, 1988, Kern County Employees' Savings Bonds, 1989; mem. Kern County Speakers Bureau, 1988—, CSUB Alumni Speakers Assn., 1989—. With U.S. Army, 1968-73. Mem. Am. Soc. Pub. Adminstrs., Nat. Assn. Treas.-Fin. Officers, Calif. Assn. Pub. Retirement Systems, State Assn. County Retirement Systems, Kern County Mgmt. Coun. (treas. 1981—), Kern County Speakers Bureau, Bakersfield Coll. Found., Calif. State U. Alumni, Bakersfield East Rotary (bd. dirs. 1988-89, Paul Harris fellow 1985, 85). Republican. Office: Kern County Treas 1115 Truxtun Ave Bakersfield CA 93301-4617

FRANK, ALAN, retired psychiatry educator; b. N.Y.C., May 16, 1922; s. Lawrence Kelso and Alice Vermandoir (Bryant) F.; m. Louise Thompson, 1956 (dec. 1964); children: Alexandra, Margaret, Lucia; m. Anita Magnus, May, 1969; 1 child, Loren. BA, Columbia U., 1944, MD, 1949. Diplomate Am. Bd. Med. Examiners; cert. Am. Bd. Psychiatry and Neurology. Head psychiat. div. Student Health Service U. Colo., Boulder, 1956-67; psychiatrist Health Service Pa. State U., State College, 1967-68; asst. prof. psychiatry U. N.Mex., Albuquerque, 1968-92, prof. emeritus, 1992—; cons. in field, 1969—. Fellow Am. Psychiat. Assn. (life), Am. Orthopsychiat. Assn., AAAS, ACP; mem. N.Y. Acad. Scis. Office: 8602 Aztec Rd NE Albuquerque NM 87111-4506

FRANK, ANN-MARIE, sales administration executive; b. Omaha, July 27, 1957; d. Joseph Anthony and Louise Virginia (DiMauro) Malingagio; m. Jon Lindsay Frank, July 13, 1985; 1 child, Jon L. BA in Fine and Communication Arts, Loyola Marymount U., L.A., 1980, MBA, 1988. Sr. mktg. clk. Telautograph Corp., L.A., 1981-84; advt. asst. Automotive Dealers Mktg., L.A., 1984-85; region adminstrv. mgr. Data Gen. Corp., Manhattan Beach, Calif., 1986-90; adminstrv. customer svc. mgr. Candle Corp., L.A., 1991-92, mgr. fin. svcs. western area, 1992-93; mgr. sales adminstr. nat. ops. Candle Corp., Santa Monica, 1993—. Dir., editor: (creative drama) Patchwork, 1982 (Rochester, N.Y. trophy). Republican. Roman Catholic. Home: 3311 Raintree Ave Torrance CA 90505-6618 Office: Candle Corp 2425 Olympic Blvd Santa Monica CA 90404-4030

FRANK, DONALD HERBERT, minister; b. Rochester, N.Y., May 12, 1931; s. Oscar Edward and Mary Charlotte (Morgan) F.; m. Anne Sadlon, Aug. 27, 1955; children: Donna Lynn Frank Bertsch, John Edward, James David. BA, Bloomfield (N.J.) Coll., 1954; MDiv, McCormick Theol. Sem., 1957, MA, 1966; DD, Coll. of Idaho, 1980. Ordained to ministry Presbyn. Ch., 1957. Asst. pastor Hamburg (N.Y.) Presbyn. Ch., 1957-60; min. Christian edn. 1st Presbyn. Ch., Pompano Beach, Fla., 1960-63, First Presbyn. Ch., Santa Ana, Calif., 1966-69, Northminister Presbyn. Ch., Evanston, Ill., 1963-66; assoc. pastor Bellflower (Calif.) Presbyn. Ch., 1969-74; pastor Boone Meml. Presbyn. Ch., Caldwell, Idaho, 1974-87; organizing pastor Covenant Presbyn. Ch., Reno, Nev., 1987—; commr. Synod of Pacific, Petaluma, Calif., 1977-81, 89-94, moderator, 1994. Bd. dirs. Metro Ministry Interfaith Agy., Reno, 1988, Washoe at Risk Task Force on Pub. Edn., Reno, 1988. With USNR, 1948-53. Mem. Rotary (Paul Harris fellow 1994). Democrat. Office: Covenant Presbyn Ch 6695 Mae Anne Ave Reno NV 89523-1884

FRANK, JOE EUGENE, city planner; b. Urbana, Ill., Dec. 29, 1949. BA in design, Southern Ill. U., 1973; M in urban planning, U. Ill., 1976. City planner City of Naperville, Naperville, Ill., 1976-78, City of Ft. Collins, Ft. Collins, Colo., 1978—; exec. bd. Local Devel. Co., Inc., Ft. Collins, 1990—, Colo. Coun. of Energy Officials, Arvada, Colo., 1978-82, Historic Ft. Collins Devel. Corp., 1994—. Developed Land Devel. Guidance System, 1981, Solar Energy Policy, 1984. Recipient Ford Found. finalist, 1987, 1988. Mem. Am. Planning Assn. (Outstanding Planning award, 1982), Am. Inst. Cert. Planners, Nat. Trust For Historic Preservation. Office: City of Ft Collins 281 N College Ave Fort Collins CO 80524-2404 Home: 2945 Brumbaugh Dr Fort Collins CO 80526-6231

FRANK, KURT HOWARD, non-commissioned marine officer; b. Pueblo, Colo., Mar. 9, 1958; s. Harley Dexter and Nancy Lee (Polhill) F. BBA in Fin., Nat. U., San Diego, 1988; MA in Econs., U. Okla., Norman, 1991. lic. tax preparer. Commd. USMC, advanced through grades to gunnery sgt., 1990; sgt. support chief Operation Restore Hope, Somalia, 1992-93; team chief 2d SSCT 1st Marine Divsn., 1994—; instr. fin./econs. Hawaii Pacific U., Honolulu, 1991-92; fin. planner The Adv. Group, Diamond Bar, Calif., 1994—. Mem. Orange County Hash House Harriers (master-at-arms 1986—), Road Runners Club Am., Non-Commd. Officers Am. Home: 7747 Camnito Monarch # 109 Carlsbad CA 92009 Office: 2d SSCT 1st Marine Divsn Camp Pendleton CA 92055

FRANK, LAURIE, screenwriter; b. N.Y.C., Feb. 16, 1954; d. Howard A. and Edith Frank. BA, Yale U., 1974; cert., Am. Film Inst., Los Angeles, 1985. Assoc. producer News Close-up ABC-TV, N.Y.C., 1977-81; co-producer The Body Human CBS-TV, N.Y.C., 1981-83; dir. TV show Saturday Night Live, N.Y.C., 1983-84; dir. Cinemax Comedy Spl., Los Angeles, 1986; screenwriter Los Angeles, 1987—. Screenwriter: (with Floyd Byars) Making Mr. Right, Los Angeles, 1987, (with Alan Moyle) Love Crimes, 1992. Clubs: Elizabethan (New Haven), Fence (New Haven).

FRANK, MARGOT GILBERT, middle school educator, investor, philanthropist; b. N.Y.C., Apr. 14, 1949; d. John Jacob and Margaret (Ranger) G.; m. M Allan Frank, July 6, 1991; children: Valerie, Sandi Frank, Lisa Tharpe. BA, U. Denver, 1971. Tchr. Colo. Youth Svcs., Denver, 1971-74; tchr. ESL Aurora (Colo.) Pub. Schs., 1974-75; team leader, tchr. Jefferson County Pub. Schs., Lakewood, Colo., 1975—; trustee Gilbert and Snyder Found., Denver and N.Y.C., 1991—. Chmn. spl. event Jr. League Denver, 1991-92, chmn. fundraising evaluation, 1992-93, chmn. fin. devel., 1993-94; adv. bd. Nat. Jewish Hosp., Denver, 1992-94; v.p. spl. events Juvenile Diabetes Found., Denver, 1993—; exec. bd. mem. Family Cmty. Edn. and Support, Denver, 1994-96; chmn. Kids Helping Kids, Childrens Hosp., Denver, 1994; co-chair Elway Celebrity Auction, Elway Found., Englewood, Colo., 1993, 94; founding pres. Juvenile Diabetes Found. Alliance for Cure, Denver, 1994. Recipient Vol. award Jefferson County Schs., 1993, Vol. Recognition award Elway Found., Englewood, Colo., 1993, award for fighting child abuse Elway Found., Englewood, 1994. Mem. Nat. Assn. Fundraising Execs., Jefferson County Edn. Assn. (bd. dirs. 1986-91), Jefferson County Schs. and Bus. Alliance (steering com. 1994), Juvenile Diabetes Found. (exec. bd. dirs. 1993—), Family & Cmty. Edn. Support (bd. dirs. 1994—), Phi Delta Kappa. Home: 6882 E Center Ave Denver CO 80224 Office: O'Connell Mid Sch 1275 S Teller St Lakewood CO 80232

FRANK, MICHAEL VICTOR, risk assessment engineer; b. N.Y.C., Sept. 22, 1947; s. David and Bernice (Abrams) F.; m. Jane Griminger, Dec. 21, 1969; children: Jeffrey, Heidi, Heather. BS, UCLA, 1969; MS, Carnegie-Mellon U., 1972; PhD, UCLA, 1978. Registered profl. engr., Calif.; cert. profl. cons. to mgmt. Engr. Westinghouse Electric Corp., Pitts., 1970-72, Southern Calif. Edison, Los Angeles, 1972-74; lectr. U. Calif., Santa Barbara, 1976-77; task leader General Atomics, San Diego, 1977-81; sr. exec. engr. NUS Corp., San Diego, 1981-85; with Mgmt. Analysis Co., San Diego, 1985-86; sr. cons. PLG, Newport Beach, Calif., 1986-89; pres. Safety Factor Assocs., Inc., Encinitas, Calif., 1989—; v.p. Risk Mgmt. and Assurance Svcs., Inc., Encinitas, 1993—; tech. dir. risk and reliability studies of NASA facilities, space vehicles and nuclear facilities, space vehicles and nuclear facilities worldwide; risk assessment cons., mem. U.S. Interagy. Nuclear Safety Rev. Panel, NASA hdqrs., NASA Ames Rsch. Ctr.; cons. U.S. Nuc. Regulatory Commn.; lectr. on risk assessment at various NASA ctrs.; qualified forensic cons. in product defects and hazards; mem. tech. program com. prohabilistic safety assessment and mgmt. confs. Contbr. articles to Reliability Engring. and System Safety, Nuclear Engring. and Design, others. Mem. AIAA (sr. mem.), ASME, Soc. for Risk Analysis, Cons. Round Table, Forensic Cons. Assn. (past pres.), Nat. Bur. Profl. Mgmt. Cons. Office: 4401 Manchester Ave Ste 106 Encinitas CA 92024-4938

FRANK, PETER SOLOMON, art critic, curator; b. N.Y.C., July 3, 1950; s. Reuven and Bernice (Kaplow) F. B.A., Columbia U., 1972, M.A., 1974. Critic SoHo Weekly News, N.Y.C., 1973-76, Village Voice, N.Y.C., 1977-79, L.A. Weekly, 1988—; critic Long Beach Press-Telegram, 1993—; L.A. corr. Contemporanea, 1989-91; curatorial assoc. Ind. Curators Inc., N.Y.C. and Washington, 1974—; co-curator Documenta VI, Kassel, W. Ger., 1976-77; assoc. editor Nat. Arts Guide, Chgo., 1979-81, Art Express, N.Y.C., 1980-81; curator Exxon Nat. Exhbn. of Am. Artists, Guggenheim Mus., N.Y.C., 1980-81; art critic Diversion mag., 1983-90; mem. faculty New Sch. for Social Rsch., 1974, Pratt Inst., 1975-76, Columbia U. Sch. Arts, 1978, Claremont Grad. Sch., 1989, 92-94, 95-96, U. Calif., Irvine, 1988-90, Calif. State U., Fullerton, 1990-91, U. Calif., Santa Barbara, 1994; Am. curatorial advisor Documenta 8, 1986-87. Author: The Travelogues, 1982, Something Else Press: An Annotated Bibliography, 1983; co-author: New, Used and Improved: Art in the '80s, 1987; contbr. articles to art periodicals; assoc. editor Tracks mag., 1974-76; editor Re Dact, 1983-85, Visions, 1990—; contbg. editor Art Economist, 1981-84. Nat. Endowment for Arts art critics travel fellow, 1978; critics project fellow, 1981; Royal Norwegian Ministry of Fgn. Affairs Fluxus rsch. fellow, 1987. Mem. Internat. Assn. Art Critics, Coll. Art Assn., Internationale Künstlers Gremium. Home: PO Box 24a36 Los Angeles CA 90024-1036 Office: Visions Art Quar PO Box 24589 Los Angeles CA 90024-0589

FRANK, STEPHEN RICHARD, lawyer; b. Portland, Oreg., Dec. 13, 1942; s. Richard Sigmund Frank and Paula Anne (Latz) Lewis; divorced; children: Richard Sigmund II, Theresa Anne; m. Patricia Lynn Graves, Aug. 20, 1988; stepchildren: Brian Kinney, Mathew Kinney. AB in Econs., U. Calif., Berkeley, 1964; JD, Willamette U., 1967. Bar: Oreg., U.S. Ct. Appeals (9th cir.), U.S. Supreme Ct. Assoc. Tooze, Shenker, Duden, Creamer, Frank and Hutchison, Portland, 1967-72, ptnr., 1972—; mem. audit com. Seligman & Latz NYSE, 1981-85, bd. dirs. 1976-85. Editor Willamette Law Jour., 1967. Trustee, sec. Oreg. High Desert Mus., 1977-86; sec., bd. dirs. Palatine Hill Water Dist., 1973-77; bd. dirs. Emanuel Hosp. Found., 1980-83, Portland Ctr. for Visual Arts, 1977-82. Mem. ABA, Assn. Trial Lawyers Am., Oreg. Trial Lawyers Assn., Oreg. State Bar Assn. (dir., sec. minority scholarship program 1981—, sec.-chmn. com. worker's compensation 1974-77), Oreg. Assn. Ins. Def. Counsel, Oreg. Assn. Workers Compensation Def. Counsel. Clubs: Multnomah Athletic; City (Portland). Home: 3103 SW Cascade Dr Portland OR 97201-1813 Office: Tooze Shenker Duden Creamer Frank & Hutchison 333 SW Taylor St Portland OR 97204-2413

FRANK, THOMAS, construction design and management executive; b. Salt Lake City, Nov. 23, 1937; s. Simon and Suzanne (Seller) F. BFA, U. Utah, 1963. Lic. contractor, Utah. Owner Thomas Frank Designers & Specifiers, Salt Lake City, 1962—; owner, pres. OmmiComputer West, Salt Lake City; pres. Nova Devel. Corp.; cons. in field; instr. design, textiles and drafting LDS Jr. Coll., Salt Lake City, 1963-86; lectr. on interior design for jr. and high schs. Bus. & Industry Coop. Edn. Program; profl. adviser interior design curriculum devel. program U. Utah; mem. inter-profl. adv. coun. Utah State Bldg. Bd.; lectr., presenter seminars in field. Contbr. articles to profl. publs. Exec. v.p. Salt Lake Art Ctr., 1977-80; spl. advisor Children's Ctr.; co-chmn. spl. events Utah divsn. Am. Cancer Soc., 1978. Recipient awards U. Utah, 1962, Utah Designers Craftsman Guild, 1962, State Fair Fine Arts, 1962. Fellow Am. Soc. Interior Designers; mem. N.Am. Autocadd Users Group, Nat. Kitchen and Bath Assn. (pres. mountain states chpt. west 1991-92), Am. Soc. Interior Designers (nat. long-range planning com. 1985-87, nat. comms. area coord. 1985, nat. membership devel. com. 1986-87, nat. regional dir. 1991-92, nat. edn. com. 1981, nat. chmn. energy conservation 1980-82, nat. chpt. pres.' orientation task force 1980, nat. bd. dirs. 1977-82, chmn. regional indsl. rels. 1977-78, numerous other offices, numerous awards), AID (sec. Utah 1969-71, bd. govs. 1970-74, Utah pres. 1973-75). Home: 2360 Oakhill Dr Salt Lake City UT 84121-1520 Office: Thomas Frank Designers 3369 Highland Dr Salt Lake City UT 84106-3356

FRANKE, ADRIAN AMADEUS HARALD, natural products chemist, researcher; b. Kirchzarten, Germany, Apr. 26, 1956; s. Walter Wilhelm and Lotte (Steinberg) F. Cert. chemistry, pharmaceutical, U. Freiburg, 1980, PhD in Chemistry, 1985, post doctoral studies, 1985-87. Cons. Health Dept., Bangkok, Thailand, 1987; post doctoral fellow Dept. Sci. and Indsl. Rsch., Wellington, New Zealand, 1987-89, Univ. Hawaii chemistry dept., Honolulu, 1989, U. Hawaii zoology dept., Honolulu, 1990; post doctoral fellow U. Hawaii Cancer Rsch. Ctr., Honolulu, 1991-92, asst. specialist, 1992-94, asst. rschr., 1994—. Contbr. numerous articles to profl. jours. Recipient Rsch. fellowship German Rsch. Soc., New Zealand, 1987-89; grantee U. Hawaii, 1991, 92, Am. Cancer Soc., 1992-94, U.S. C. of C., 1994-95. Mem. Am. Chem. Soc., Am. Assn. for Cancer Rsch., European Soc. of Herbal Medicine, German Pharm. Soc. Office: Cancer Rsch Ctr 1236 Lauhala St Honolulu HI 96813-2424

FRANKEL, JAMES BURTON, lawyer; b. Chgo., Feb. 25, 1924; s. Louis and Thelma (Cohn) F.; m. Louise Untermyer, Jan. 22, 1956; children—Nina, Sara, Simon. Student U. Chgo., 1940-42; B.S., U.S. Naval Acad., 1945; LL.B., Yale U., 1952; MPA, Harvard U., 1990. Bar: Calif. 1953. Mem. Steinhart, Goldberg, Feigenbaum & Ladar, San Francisco, 1954-72; of counsel Cooper, White & Cooper, San Francisco, 1972—; sr. fellow, lectr. in law Yale U., 1971-72; lectr. Stanford U. Law Sch., 1973-75; vis. prof. U. Calif. Law Sch., 1975-76, lectr. 1992—, U. San Francisco Law Sch., 1994—. Pres. Council Civic Unity of San Francisco Bay Area, 1964-66, U. San Francisco Sch. Law, 1994—; chmn. San Francisco Citizens Charter Revision Com., 1968-70; mem. San Francisco Pub. Schs. Commn., 1975-76; trustee Natural Resources Def. Council, 1972-77, 79-92, staff atty., 1977-79, hon. trustee, 1992—; chmn. San Francisco Citizens Energy Policy Adv. Com., 1981-82. Mem. ABA, Calif. Bar Assn., San Francisco Bar Assn. Democrat. Office: Cooper White & Cooper 201 California St San Francisco CA 94111-5002

FRANKFURTH, MARK STEPHEN, computer engineer; b. West Palm Beach, Fla., Sept. 23, 1963; s. Stephen DeGraw and Rosemarie (Cerny) F. BSEE, Va. Polytechnic Inst., 1988. Electronic technician Litton/Poly-Scientific Divsn., Blacksburg, Va., 1985-88, software quality engr., 1988-90; dir. quality engring. Fire Sentry Corp., Brea, Calif., 1990-91; reliability engr. AST Rsch., Inc., Irvine, Calif., 1991-92, electromagnetic compatibility engr., 1992—; founder, pres. PegaSci. Computing consultancy, Irvine, 1986-94; cons. technology Orange County Employment Action Network, Costa Mesa, Calif., 1993—; cons. computer Kids Cancer Connection, Irvine, 1992—. Founder, operator: (online info./entertainment svc.) Irvine Information Svc., 1987-94; author: (newsletter) MicroLink Computer News, 1992-94. Bd. dirs. Office on Youth, Montgomery County, Va., 1989-90. Mem. IEEE, Am. Soc. Quality Control, Microlink Personal Computer User Group (v.p. 1993, pres. 1994). Home: 22 Creek Rd Apt 25 Irvine CA 92714-4760 Office: AST Rsch Inc 16215 Alton Pky Irvine CA 92718-3616

FRANKISH, BRIAN EDWARD, film producer, director; b. Columbus, Ohio, July 28, 1943; s. John (Jack) Fletcher Frankish and Barbara Aileen (Tondro) Gray; m. Tannis Rae Benedict, Oct. 13, 1985; children: Merlin L. Reed III, Michelle Lynn Reed. AA, Chaffey Coll., 1964; BA, San Francisco State U., 1967. Freelance producer L.A.; prin. Frankish-Benedict Entertainment, L.A. Producer (film) Vice Squad, 1981, (TV series) Max Headroom, 1987; assoc. producer: (films) Elephant Parts, 1981, Strange Brew, 1982, The Boy Who Could Fly, 1985, In the Mood, 1986; exec. producer, unit prodn. mgr. (film) Field of Dreams, 1989, Flight of the Intruder, 1990, American Me, 1991; producer, dir. (theatrical play) Timing is Everything, 1991; 1st asst. dir.: (TV shows) Big Shamus, 1979, Skag, 1979, Why Me?, 1983, Making Out, 1984, Berrengers, 1984, (films) Strange Brew, 1982, Uncle Joe Shannon, 1978, Savage Harvest, 1980, Dead and Buried, 1980, Spring Break, 1982, Brainstorm, 1982-83, The Last Starfighter, 1983, The New Kids, 1983, Aloha Summer, 1984, The Best of Times, 1985, Odd Jobs, 1985, The Fugitive, 1993, Demolition Man, 1993, Roswell, 1994; unit prodn. mgr. Second Serve, 1986, The Net, 1995; distbr.'s rep. and completion bond rep. Made in Heaven, 1986, Under Siege II: Dark Territory, 1994; other prodn. credits include: Play it Again, Sam, 1971, Everything You Always Wanted to Know About Sex..., 1972, Time to Run, 1972, Haunts, 1975, Mahogany (Montage), 1975, King Kong, 1976, The Betsy, 1977. Mem. Dirs. Guild Am., Calif. Yacht Club.

FRANKLIN, ABBY, psychotherapist; b. N.Y.C., Sept. 20, 1928; d. Theodore Edward and Eileen (Gerber) Franklin; m. Seymour E. Leventer, Dec. 22, 1963 (div. Aug. 12, 1981); children: Allan, Michael. BA, U. Mich., 1949; MSW, UCLA, 1952. Dep. probation officer L.A. Probation Dept., 1952-56; asst. dir. clin. svcs. Dubnoff Ctr., North Hollywood, Calif., 1958-68; chief social svcs. L.A. Child Achievement Ctr., Encino, Calif., 1968-74; dir. Valley Psychotherapy and Learning Group, Sherman Oaks, Calif., 1974—. Pro bono supr. San Fernando Counseling Ctr., Northbridge, Calif., 1989—; pro bono counselor Social Work Treatment Ctr., L.A., 1980—; bd. dirs., sec. Calif. Coalition for Mental Health. Mem. Calif. Soc. for Clin. Social Work (Mem. of Yr. 1991, chmn. govtl. affairs 1993—), NASW. Democrat. Jewish. Office: Valley Psychotherapy & Learning Group 13715 Ventura Blvd Sherman Oaks CA 91423

FRANKLIN, JOHN ORLAND, lawyer; b. Chgo., May 20, 1939; s. Orland Alfred and Lida Marie (Harlow) F.; m. Mary Claudia Shortman, June 10, 1961; children: Stacy Duncan, Brooke Harlow. BS in Bus., U. Ariz., 1961, JD, 1964. Bar: Ariz. 1964, U.S. Dist. Ct. Ariz. 1964, U.S. Ct. Appeals (9th cir.) 1971, U.S. Tax Ct. 1973. Asst. atty. City of Tucson, 1964-66, spl. counsel, 1966-67; pvt. practice Tucson, 1966—. Chmn. bd. Pima County Sanitary Dist., Tucson, 1966-69. Fellow Ariz. Bar Found. (founder); mem. ABA, State Bar Ariz. (chmn. fee arbitration panel 1977-87, trustee clients security trust fund 1991—, chmn. 1995-96, Recognition Svc. award 1987), Inter-Am. Bar Assn., Inter-Pacific Bar Assn., Internat. Bar Assn., Found. Tucson Parks and Recreation (charter). Republican. Episcopalian. Home: PO Box 31300 Tucson AZ 85751-1300 Office: 6375 E Tanque Verde Rd Ste 140 Tucson AZ 85715-3837

FRANKLIN, JON DANIEL, journalist, writer, educator; b. Enid, Okla., Jan. 12, 1942; s. Benjamin Max and Wilma Irene (Winburn) F.; m. Nancy Sue Creevan, Dec. 12, 1959 (div. 1976, dec. 1987); children: Teresa June, Catherine Cay; m. Lynn Irene Scheidhauer, May 20, 1988. B.S. with high honors, U. Md., 1970; LHD (hon.), U. Md., Balt. County, 1981, Coll. Notre Dame, Balt., 1982. With USN, 1959-67; reporter/editor Prince Georges (Md.) Post, 1967-70; sci. writer Balt. Evening Sun, 1970-85; assoc. prof. U. Md. Coll. Journalism, 1985-88, prof., 1988-89; prof., chmn. dept. journalism Oreg. State U., Corvallis, 1989-91; prof. journalism and creative writing U. Oreg., Eugene, 1991—. Author: Shocktrauma, 1980, Not Quite a Miracle, 1983, Guinea Pig Doctors, 1984, Writing for Story, 1986, The Molecules of the Mind, 1987. Recipient James T. Grady medal Am. Chem. Soc., 1975, Pulitzer prize for feature writing, 1979, Pulitzer prize for explanatory journalism, 1985, Carringer award Nat. Mental Health Assn., 1984, Penney-Mo. Spl. award for health reporting, 1985; named to Newspaper Hall of Fame, Md.-Del.-D.C. Press Assn. Mem. Nat. Assn. Sci. Writers, Soc Profl. Journalists, The Writers Guild, Investigative Reporters and Editors. Office: U Oreg Sch Journalism Eugene OR 97403-1299

FRANKLIN, MARSHALL, cardiologist; b. Balt., Nov. 5, 1929; s. Morton and Anna (Rothstein) F.; m. Diana Jean Page; children: M. Gregg, M. Mark, M. Brett. BS, Franklin and Marshall, 1952; MD, U. Md., 1956. Intern Duke Hosp., Durham, N.C., 1956-57; resident Charity Hosp. Tulane Svc., New Orleans, 1957-60; staff cardiac cath. lab. Cleve. Clinic, 1960-64; dir. cardiac lab. Norwalk (Conn.) Hosp., 1964-77; dir. cardiac rehab. Scripps Clinic, La Jolla, Calif., 1984-89; dir. coronary angioplasty Scripps Clinic, La Jolla, 1989-92; dir. clin. cardiology Scripps Clinic, Rancho Bernardo, 1992—. Co-author: The Heart Doctors Heart Book, 1974. Fellow Am. Coll. Physicians, Am. Coll. Cardiology, Am. Heart Assn., Am. Coll. Angiology, Am. Coll. Chest Physicians. Office: Scipps Clinic & Rsch Found 10666 N Torrey Pines Rd La Jolla CA 92037-1027

FRANKLIN, ROBERT BLAIR, cardiologist; b. Buffalo, Dec. 18, 1919; s. Wilson Gale and Frances Eunice (Sullivan) F.; m. Anne W., Jan. 16, 1969; children: Virginia, Richard, Victor, George, Robert, Kathleen. BA, Canisius Coll., Buffalo, 1940; MD, U. St. Louis, 1943. Diplomate Am. Bd. Internal Medicine, Am. Bd. Cardiovascular Diseases. Commd. U.S. Army, advanced through grades to col.; chief med. svc. 130th Sta. Hosp. U.S. Army, Heidelberg, Germany, 1955-58, comdg. officer 5th Surg. Hosp., 1958-59; chief gen. med. svc. Fitzsimons Gen. Hosp. U.S. Army, Denver, 1959-60, chief cardiology svc., 1962-65; comdg. officer 121st Evacuation Hosp. U.S. Army, Seoul, Korea, 1965-66; chief cardiology svc. Letterman Gen. Hosp. U.S. Army, San Francisco, 1966-68; chief cardiology dept. Kaiser Permanente Med. Group, Santa Clara, Calif., 1968-79; dep. comdg. officer 130th Sta. Hosp. U.S. Army, Heidelberg/Seoul/Vicenza, Italy, 1979-89; asst. clin. prof. Med. Coll. Ga., Augusta, 1953-54, U. Colo., Denver, 1963-65, Seoul Nat. U., 1965-66; guest lectr. Phy Yonsei U., Seoul, 1965-66; asst. clin. prof. U. Calif. Med. Sch., San Francisco, 1966-68, 74-79, 89—. Contbr. 35 articles to profl. jours. Decorated Legion of Merit with 3 oak leaf clusters. Roman Catholic. Home: 20 Palomino Cir Novato CA 94947

FRANKLIN, ROBERT CHARLES, probation officer; b. Falls City, Nebr., Feb. 27, 1941; s. Robert Benjamin and Grace Evelyn (Riden) F.; m. Jeanette Ilene Kritnet, Aug. 28, 1964; children: Heather T., Cynthia D. BA in Sociology, U. Nebr., 1967; MS in Psychology/Counseling, Calif. State U., Hayward, 1972. Juvenile group supr. San Mateo County Probation Dept., San Mateo, Calif., 1968-75; dep. probation officer San Mateo County Probation Dept., Redwood City, Calif., 1975-91, supervising probation officer, 1991—; pres. State Coaliton of Probation Orgns., Sacramento, 1990-91. Columnist Pres.'s Corner, Calif. Probation News, 1990-91; contbr articles to profl. jours. Served with USAF, 1959-63, Japan. Mem. Calif. Probation, Parole and Correctional Assn. (state del. chair 1990-91, bd. dirs. 1990—, state conf. chair 1994—, Chpt. Mem. of Yr. 1990, 94, Pres.'s award 1989), Toastmasters (v.p. publicity 1991—). Office: San Mateo County Adult Probation 401 Marshall St Redwood City CA 94063

FRANKS, DAVID ALLAN, communications administrator; b. Vancouver, Wash., June 1, 1958; s. Homer C. and Pearl E. (Jensen) F.; m. Tamera L. Cooper, Nov. 6, 1982; children: Caitlin, Kristin. BS, Oreg. Coll. Edn., 1980. Cert. forms cons. Forms cons. Willamette Bus. Forms, Salem, Oreg., 1982-84, Capital Bus. Forms, Salem, Oreg., 1984-88; forms and publs. mgr. Adult and Family Svcs. Div., Salem, Oreg., 1988-89; purchasing analyst Dept. Gen. Svcs. Printing Div., Salem, Oreg., 1989-90; comm. coord. Dept. of Revenue, Salem, Oreg., 1990—. Dir. Argonauts Music and Motion, Salem, 1985-88, pres. bd. dirs., 1987-88. Mem. Bus. Forms Mgr.'s Assn. (Portland pres. 1989-90), Rotary (Keizer dir. 1986-88). Home: 1180 Ridgepoint St NE Keizer OR 97303-1776 Office: Oreg Dept Revenue 955 Center St NE Salem OR 97310-2501

FRANKS, THOMAS ALLEN, editorial cartoonist; b. Mpls., Aug. 10, 1948; s. John Joseph and Edna Harriet (Johnson) F.; m. Janet Shekleton, Aug. 12, 1972 (dec. Jan. 1989); 1 child, Molly Claire; m. Lauriette C. Nielson, June 25, 1994. BA in Philosophy, St. Mary's Coll., 1970; MA in Early Childhood/Visual Handicapped, Columbia U., 1973. Vol. Peace Corps, Morocco, 1970-72; edn. cons. State of Va., Richmond, 1974-75; tchr. spl. edn. Coquille (Oreg.) Sch. Dist., 1976-79; composer, guitarist, singer Electric Bill & The Killer Watts, Portland, Oreg., 1983-84; editorial cartoonist self-syndicated, Portland, 1985—. Peace activist, Forest Grove, Oreg., 1980-94; draft councilor N.W. Draft Counciling Ctr., Portland, 1980-83; social activist Coalition for Human Dignity, Washington County, 1993. Home: 3236 NW Vaughn St Portland OR 97210-1243

FRANSON, C(ARL) IRVIN, aerospace material and process engineer, educator; b. Hibbing, Minn., Oct. 17, 1934; s. Gunnar Theodore and Ina Selena (Kamb) F.; m. Adele Esther Haselton, June 29, 1968 (div. 1969). BSChemE, Purdue U., 1956; MBA, Santa Clara U., 1963. Cert. secondary tchr., Calif. Process engr. Wyandotte (Mich.) Chem. Corp., 1956-59; materials and process engr. Lockheed Missiles and Space Co., Sunnyvale, Calif., 1959-62, staff engr., 1963-68; devel. engr. Raychem Corp., Menlo Park, Calif., 1962-63; project engr. McCormick Selph, A Teledyne Co., Hollister, Calif., 1968-69; sr. devel. engr. Johnson Controls-Globe Union, Milw., 1969-70; sr. chem. engr. Gen. Telephone-Lenkurt, San Carlos, Calif., 1970-71; sr. materials engr. Ford Aerospace (Loral), Palo Alto, Calif., 1971-91; prin., entrepreneur Sigmaform Corp., Menlo Park, 1963-66; educator Golden Gate U., San Francisco, 1973, Chabot Coll., Hayward, Calif., 1970. Contbg. author: International Encyclopedia of Composites, 1990. Treas. Valley League-San Francisco Symphony, 1987-95; docent San Francisco Symphony, 1993-95. Mem. Soc. for Advancement of Material and Process Engring. (exhibits chmn. 1986 nat. symposium, historian 1974, co-founder No. Calif. chpt. 1960), Internat. Exec. Svc. Corps. (registered), No. Calif. Golf Assn. Home: 8162 Park Villa Cir Cupertino CA 95014-4009

FRANSON, PAUL OSCAR, III, public relations executive; b. Tampa, Fla., Jan. 22, 1941; s. Paul O. and Kathleen (Collins) F.; m. Theodora L. Nelson, Dec. 29, 1959 (div. 1986); children: Chris Soden, Wendy; m. Susan Cain, Nov. 17, 1990; stepchildren: Becky, Jeremy, David, Alison. BS, Davidson Coll., 1961. Editor 73 Mag., Peterborough, N.H., 1964-67; pub. rels. dir. Motorola, Phoenix, 1968-69, Teradyne, Boston, 1970; field editor Electronics mag., Dallas, L.A., 1970-75, EDN mag., San Jose, Calif., 1975-77; editor Electronic Bus. mag., Boston, 1977-80; pres. Franson & Assocs., Inc., San Jose, 1980-90, Franson, Hagerty, 1990-92; chmn., CEO Franson, Hagerty and Assoc. Inc., 1992—. Author: The Marketing Edge, 1990; contbr. articles to profl. jours. Office: Franson Hagerty & Assocs 181 Metro Dr Ste 300 San Jose CA 95110-1344

FRANTA, GREGORY ESSER, architect, energy consultant; b. Graceville, Minn., May 17, 1950; s. Joseph Benedict and Loretta Ann (Esser) F.; m. Susan M. Holstad, June 1980; children—Lori J., Lindsay S. B.Arch., U. Colo., 1973; M.Arch. in Solar Tech., Ariz. State U., 1976. Registered architect, Colo. Prin. architect Sun Designs Architect, Aspen, Colo., 1975-78; sr. architect Solar Energy Research Inst., Golden, Colo., 1978-82; pres. Ensar, Inc., Lakewood, Colo., 1982—; founder, exec. dir. Roaring Fork Energy Ctr., Aspen, 1973-78; vice chmn. Am. Solar Energy Soc., Boulder, Colo., 1983, acting exec. dir., 1983. Author: Solar Design Workbook, 1981. Designer most energy efficient residence in U.S., 1981-84, innovative design tool, 1982 (Kansas Energy award 1984), innovative solar system and control advancing state of art in solar tech., 1983 (Idaho energy Innovation award 1984). Contbr. articles to profl. jours. Recipient award for energy innovation U.S. Dept. Energy, 1984; Energy Conservation Pacesetter award, Colo., 1984. Mem. Colo. Soc. Architects (bd. dirs. 1977-78, 83), AIA (pres. Colo. West chpt. 1977-78, v.p. Denver chpt. 1983), Nat. Energy Com., (chmn. various coms.). Home: 12819 W Ellsworth Pl Lakewood CO 80228-1611

FRANTZ, JOHN CORYDON, librarian; b. Seneca Falls, N.Y., Aug. 25, 1926; s. John Clark and Cora May (Gilbert) F.; m. Vivien May Rowan, Dec. 31, 1947; children—Sheila Heather, Keith Hunter, Jay Corydon. A.B., Syracuse (N.Y.) U., 1950, B.S., 1951, M.S., 1952. Cons. Wis. State Library, 1954-58; dir. Green Bay (Wis.) Pub. Library, 1958-61; dir. pub. library grants U.S. Office Edn., 1961-67; dir. Bklyn. Pub. Library, 1967-70, Nat. Book Com., 1970-75; exec. chmn. Pahlavi Nat. Library, Tehran, Iran, 1975-77; librarian San Francisco Pub. Library, 1977-87; bd. dirs. Reading is Fundamental, Bookmobile Services Trust, Am. Reading Council, Metro Research Libraries Council. Served with U.S. Army, 1945-47. Mem. ALA, N.Y. State, Calif. library assns. Home and Office: 1390 Market St San Francisco CA 94102-5402

FRANTZ, PAUL LEWIS, lawyer; b. Bozeman, Mont., Sept. 11, 1955; s. Walter Kirke and Charlotte Catherine (Caldwell) F. BS in Bus./ Fin., Mont. State U., 1978; JD, U. Mont., 1983; M in Internat. Mgmt., Am. Grad. Sch. Internat. Mgmt., 1985; LLM in Transnational Bus. Practice, McGeorge Sch. Law, 1992. Bar: Mont. 1983, U.S. Dist. Ct. Mont. 1983, U.S. Ct. Internat. Trade 1984, U.S. Ct. Appeals (9th cir.) 1986, N.Y. 1994. Law clk. to U.S. magistrate Billings, 1983-84; law clk. to judge U.S. Dist. Ct., Helena, 1985; with Morrow, Sedivy & Bennett, P.C., Bozeman, 1986-91, Church, Harris, Johnson & Williams, P.C., Great Falls, 1992; pvt. practice Bozeman, 1993—. Pres. Mont. Coun. for Internat. Visitors, 1990. Mem. State Bar Mont., Kiwanis. Home: 112 Sunset Blvd Bozeman MT 59715-6652

FRANZEN, DON ERIK, lawyer; b. Whittier, Calif., Dec. 8, 1949; s. Erik and Helen Franzen; m. Dale Seligman, Nov. 14, 1952; children: Alexandra, Olivia. BA in Philosophy, U. So. Calif., 1972, JD, 1975. Bar: Calif. 1975, U.S. Dist. Ct. (ctrl. dist.) Calif. 1976, U.S. Ct. Appeals (9th cir.) 1976, U.S. Dist. Ct. (so. and ea. dists.) Calif. 1978, U.S. Ct. Appeals (D.C. and 5th cirs.) 1978, U.S. Supreme Ct. 1979. Assoc. Law Offices of Harrison W. Hertzberg, 1975-81, Franzen & Assocs., 1981-85; assoc. Rubin Eagan & Feder, 1985-91, atty., 1991-93; ptnr. Funsten & Franzen, Beverly Hills, Calif., 1993—. Contbr. articles to profl. jours. Vol. counsel Advocate for the Arts, L.A., 1976-78, Artists for Econ. Action, 1977; bd. dirs. Music Ctr. Opera Assn., L.A., 1985—; legal advisor Reason Found., L.A., 1987—. Mem. ABA. Office: Funsten & Franzen 9595 Wilshire Blvd Ste 305 Beverly Hills CA 90212-2503

FRAPPIA, LINDA ANN, management executive; b. St. Paul, May 14, 1946; d. Orville Keith Ferguson and Marilyn Ardis (Morris) Bidwell; 1 child, Jennifer. Grad. high sch., Seattle. Cert. claims adminstr. Claims rep. Fireman's Fund Ins., L.A., 1965-68; adminstrv. asst. to v.p. Employee Benefits Ins., Santa Ana, Calif., 1969-72; claims specialist Indsl. Indemnity Ins., Orange, Calif., 1972-83; claims supr. CNA Ins., Brea, Calif., 1983-85; claims mgr. EBI Ins. Svcs., Tustin, Calif., 1985; v.p. United Med. Specialists, Santa Ana, Calif., 1985-91; chief exec. officer United Ind. Specialists, Santa Ana, 1990—; chief executive officer United Chiropractic Specialists, Santa Ana, 1987—; instr. Ins. Edn. Assn., Brea, 1988—; speaker Western Ins. Info. Svc., Orange, 1976-83. Mem. Calif. Mfrs. Assn., Pub. Agencies Risk Mgmt. Assn., Calif. Self-Insured Assn., Toastmasters Internat. (v.p. Orange chpt. 1978). Republican.

FRARY, RICHARD SPENCER, international consulting company executive; b. Greybull, Wyo., Jan. 29, 1924; s. Frederick Spencer and Margaret Lee Ellen (Chalfant) F.; m. Eros Hunsaker, July 19, 1946; children: Richard Jr., Lorraine, John, James. BSEE, U. Colo., 1949; postgrad., N.Mex. A&M U., 1954-55, So. Meth. U., 1956-57, U. Pa., 1958. Mgr. engring. RCA, Cherry Hill, N.J., 1952-62; v.p. Ultronic Systems Corp., Pennsauken, N.J., 1962-67; v.p. govt. systems Sperry Univac, various locations, 1967-80; v.p. research and engring. A.B. Dick Co., Niles, Ill., 1980-83; with Arthur D. Little Inc., Washington, 1983-90; pvt. practice cons. RSF Assocs., 1990—. With USMC, 1943-45, 50-51. Mem. IEEE, Assn. Computing Machinery, Am. Soc. for Info. Sci. Republican. Mormon. Home and Office: RSF Assocs 2898 Juniper Way Salt Lake City UT 84117-7159

FRASCA, ROBERT JOHN, architect; b. Niagara Falls, N.Y., May 10, 1933; s. John and Jean Marie (Delgross) F.; m. Marilyn Margaret Buys, Sept. 23, 1937; children: Jason Robert, Andrea Melina. BArch, U. Mich., 1957; M in City Planning, MIT, 1959. Registered architect, Oreg., Wash., Calif., N.Y., Ariz., Utah. Ptnr. in charge of design Zimmer Gunsul Frasca Partnership, Portland, Oreg., 1966—, chief exec. officer, 1979—; design commn. U. Wash.; vis. prof. architecture U. Mich., U. Calif., Berkeley; design juror numerous nat., state and chpt. AIA awards programs. Prin. works include Justice Ctr., 1983, KOIN Ctr., 1985, Vollum Inst. for Advanced Biomed. Rsch., 1986, Oreg. Conv. Ctr., 1990, Oreg. Mus. of Sci. and Industry, 1992, Fred Hutchinson Cancer Rsch. Ctr., 1993; contbr. articles to profl. jours. and mags. Charter adv. bd. mem. Portland State U., 1987—; trustee Nat. Bldg. Mus., Washington; bd. dirs. Assn. for Portland Progress. Fellow AIA; mem. Arlington Club (Portland), Multnomah Athletic Club, Century Club (N.Y.). Clubs: Arlington (Portland), Multnomah Athletic. Office: Zimmer Gunsul Frasca 320 SW Oak St Ste 500 Portland OR 97204-2735

FRASCH, BRIAN BERNARD, lawyer; b. San Francisco, Apr. 13, 1956; s. Norman Albert Frasch and Elizabeth Louise (Michelfelder) Milsten. BA magna cum laude, U. Calif., Santa Barbara, 1978; JD, U. Calif., Berkeley, 1982. Bar: Calif. 1982, U.S. Dist. Ct. (no. dist.) Calif. 1982, U.S. Dist. Ct. (so. dist.) Calif. 1983. Law clk. to chief judge U.S. Dist. Ct. (so. dist.) Calif., 1983-84; assoc. Graham & James, San Francisco, 1984-86, Lillick & McHose, San Diego, 1986-90; ptnr. Stephenson Prairie & Frasch, San Diego, 1990—. Assoc. editor: California Law Rev., 1981-82. Mem. ABA (litigation sect.), Calif. Bar Assn. (litigation sect.), San Diego County Bar Assn., San Diego Bldg. Owners and Mgrs. Assn. (bd. dirs. 1990—, gen. counsel), Westside Athletic Club. Office: 101 W Broadway Ste 1300 San Diego CA 92101-8214

FRASER, BRUCE DOUGLAS, JR., architect, artist; b. Corvallis, Oreg., Dec. 1, 1948; s. Bruce Douglas and Betty Adele (Lively) F.; m. Laura Jane Wells, June 18, 1972. BArch, Calif. Poly. State U., 1972. Registered architect, Calif. Artist, illustrator Hopkins Assocs., San Luis Obispo, Calif., 1972-73; planner U.S. Peace Corps, Mashhad, Iran, 1973-75; mem. archtl. staff Meyer-Merriam Assocs., San Luis Obispo, 1975-77; prin. MDW Assocs., San Luis Obispo, 1977-85, Merriam-Fraser Architecture and Planning, San Luis Obispo, 1985-87, Archtl. Office Bruce Fraser, San Luis Obispo, 1987—. Chair Bldg. Appeals Bd., Pismo Beach, Calif., 1990, Planning Commn., Pismo Beach, 1991-92, vice chair, 1990. Recipient various design awards Obispo Beautiful Assn., 1977—, Downtown Assn., 1990—. Mem. AIA (v.p. Calif. Ctrl. Coast chpt. 1985, pres. 1986). Office: Archtl Off of Bruce Fraser AIA 971 Osos Ste San Luis Obispo CA 93401

FRASER, CATHERINE ANNE, Canadian chief justice; b. Campbellton, N.B., Can., Aug. 4, 1947; d. Antoine Albert and Anne (Slevinski) Elias; m. Richard C. Fraser, Aug. 17, 1968; children: Andrea Claire, Jonathan James. BA, U. Alta., Can., 1969, LLB, 1970; ML, U. London, 1972. Assoc., ptnr. Lucas, Bishop & Fraser, Edmonton, Alta., 1972-89; justice Ct. Queen's Bench Alta., Edmonton, 1989-91; justice Ct. Appeal Alta., Edmonton, 1991-92, chief justice Alta. and NW Ter., 1992—; dir. Can. Inst. Adminstrn. Justice, 1991—. Recipient Tribute to Women award YWCA, 1987. Mem. Can. Bar Assn., Edmonton Bar Assn., Law Soc. Alta. Office: Ct Appeal Alta, Law Courts Bldg, Edmonton, AB Canada T5J OR2

FRASER, KATHLEEN JOY, poet, creative writing educator; b. Tulsa, Mar. 22, 1935; d. James Ian and Marjorie Joy (Axtell) F.; m. Jack Marshall, July 10, 1960 (div. 1970); 1 child, David Ian; m. Arthur Kalmer Bierman, June 30, 1984. BA in English Lit., Occidental Coll., 1958; doctorate, San Francisco State U., 1976. Vis. prof. writing, lectr. in poetry The Writer's Workshop, U. Iowa, Iowa City, 1969-71; writer in residence Reed Coll., Portland, Oreg., 1971-72; dir. Poetry Center San Francisco State U., 1972-75, prof. creative writing, 1972-92; founder-dir. Am. Poetry Archive, San Francisco, 1973-75; founder-editor How(ever), Jour. for poets/scholars interested in modernism and women's innovative writing, 1983-91. Author: (children's book) Stilts, Somersaults and Headstands, 1967; (poetry) What I Want (New and Selected Poems), 1974, New Shoes, 1978, Something (even human voices in the foreground), A Lake, 1984, Notes Preceding Trust, 1988, When New Time Folds Up, 1993, Collected Poems, 1966-92, 1995. Recipient Frank O'Hara Poetry prize, 1964, Dylan Thomas Poetry prize New Sch. for Social Rsch., 1964; Nat. Endowment for Arts fellow, 1978, Guggenheim fellow, 1981.

FRASER, LAURA JANE, journalist; b. Denver, Feb. 9, 1961; d. Charles Hugh and Virginia (Hart) F.; m. Jay Rorty, Sept. 9, 1995. BA, Wesleyan U., 1982. Freelance writer San Francisco, 1982-94, columnist San Francisco Bay Guardian, 1988-91; contbg. editor San Francisco Weekly, 1991-93, Health mag., San Francisco, 1992—. Contbr. articles to profl. jours. Named Outstanding Young Journalist, No. Calif. Soc. Profl. Journalists, 1989.

FRASER, RENEE, advertising executive; b. Columbus, Ohio, June 15, 1954; d. William Burval and Ruth White; m. Scott C. Fraser, Dec. 10, 1977; children: Nicole, Caneel Skye. BA, U. So. Calif., 1973, MA, 1978, PhD, 1981. Prof., lectr. U. So. Calif., L.A., 1975-76; prin. Plog Rsch., Reseda, Calif., 1977-80; v.p., dir. rsch. Young and Rubican, L.A., 1980-84; sr. v.p. Kenyon & Eckhardt, L.A., 1984-89; exec. v.p., gen. mgr. Bozell & Jacobs, L.A., 1989-91; pres., CEO Fraser & Assocs. Advtg., L.A., 1991-95; pres. Fraser Young, Santa Monica, Calif., 1995—; bd. dirs. Western States Ad Agy. Assn., Minority Advtg. Tng. Program, Calif. Ad Alliance. Author: Marketing and Creating Healthcare Systems in 3rd World Countries, 1978, Leveraging Media Dollars: The Advertiser, 1995; contbr. articles to profl. jours. V.p. bd. dirs. Vols. of Am.; bd. dirs. L.A. Youth Programs. Office: Fraser/Young 100 Wilshite Ste 440 Santa Monica CA 90401

FRASER-SMITH, ELIZABETH BIRDSEY, biologist; b. Pasadena, Calif., Apr. 19, 1938; d. William Canvin and Elizabeth Armstrong (Creswell) Birdsey; m. Antony Charles Fraser-Smith, Apr. 6, 1968; children: Julie Gaye, William Antony. BA, Stanford U., 1960, MA, 1962. From assoc. scientist to sr. scientist Lockheed Missiles and Space Co., Palo Alto, Calif., 1960-69; biologist Enviros, Los Altos, Calif., 1973-77; from biologist II to staff researcher II Syntex Rsch. Corp., Palo Alto, 1977-94; staff rechr. II Syntex Discovery Rsch. divsn. RocheHoldings, 1995—. Author articles on manned space exploration, antimicrobial rsch. and atherosclerosis; patentee in field. Mem. AAAS, Am. Soc. Microbiology, Internat. Soc. Antiviral Rsch., Nat. Wildlife Fedn., Zero Poulation Growth, Sempervirens Fund, Am. Farmland Trust, Sierra Club, Am. Heart Assn., Internat. Atherosclerosis Soc. Home: 801 Hilgard Ave # 2114 Los Angeles CA 90024-3107

FRASIER, GARY W., hydraulic engineer; b. Nebr., July 27, 1937. BS in Agrl. Engring., Colo. State U., 1959; MS in Civil Engring., Ariz. State U., 1966. Agrl. engr. USDA Agrl. Rsch. Svc., Tempe, 1959-67, rsch. hydraulic engr., 1967-78; rsch. hydraulic engr. USDA Agrl. Rsch. Svc., Tucson, 1978-86, rsch. leader, 1986-90; rsch. hydraulic engr. USDA Agrl. Rsch. Svc., Ft. Collins, Colo., 1990—. Editor Jour. Range Mgmt., 1990—, Rangelands, 1984—; contbr. numerous scientific papers to profl. jours. Fellow Soc. Range Mgmt., Soil and Water Conservation Soc. Office: USDA Agrl Rsch Svc 1701 Centre Ave Fort Collins CO 80526-2081

FRASSINELLI, GUIDO JOSEPH, retired aerospace engineer; b. Summit Hill, Pa., Dec. 4, 1927; s. Joseph and Maria (Grosso) F.; m. Antoinette Pauline Clemente, Sept. 26, 1953; children: Lisa, Erica, Laura, Joanne, Mark. BS, MS, MIT, 1949; MBA, Harvard U., 1956. Treas. AviDyne Rsch., Inc., Burlington, Mass., 1958-64; asst. gen. mgr. Kaman AviDyne div. Kaman Scis., Burlington, 1964-66; asst. dir. strategic planning N. Am. ACFT OPNS, Rockwell Internat., L.A., 1966-69; mgr. program planning Rockwell Space Systems Div., Downey, Calif., 1970-76; project leader R&D Rockwell Space Systems Div., Downey, 1976-79, chief analyst bus. planning, 1980-85, project mgr. advanced programs, 1986-94. Mem. Town Hall of Calif., L.A., 1970—; treas. Ecology Devel. and Implementation Commitment Team Found., Huntington Beach, Calif., 1971-75; founding com. mem. St. John Fisher Parish Coun., Rancho Palos Verdes, Calif., 1978-85. Recipient Tech. Utilization award, NASA, 1971, Astronaut Personal Achievement award, 1985. Fellow AIAA (assoc., tech. com. on econs. 1983-87, exec. com. L.A. sect. 1987-91); mem. Sigma Xi, Tau Beta Pi. Roman Catholic. Home: 29521 Quailwood Dr Rancho Palos Verdes CA 90275

FRAUENFELDER, HANS, physicist, educator; b. Neuhausen, Switzerland, July 28, 1922; came to U.S., 1952, naturalized, 1958; s. Otto and Emma (Ziegler) F.; m. Verena Anna Hassler, May 16, 1950; children: Ulrich Hans, Kätterli Anne, Anne Verena. Diploma, Swiss Fed. Inst. Tech., 1947, Ph.D. in Physics, 1950. Asst. Swiss Fed. Inst. Tech., 1946-52; asst. prof. physics U. Ill. at Urbana, 1952-56, assoc. prof., 1956-58, prof., 1958-92, prof. emeritus, 1992—; mem. staff Los Alamos (N.Mex.) Nat. Labs., 1992—; Guggenheim fellow, 1958-59, 73; vis. scientist CERN, Geneva, Switzerland, 1958-59, 63, 73. Author: The Mossbauer Effect, 1962, (with E.M. Henley) Subatomic Physics, 1974, 2d edit., 1991, Nuclear and Particle Physics, 1975; contbr. articles to profl. jours. Recipient Humboldt award, 1987-88. Fellow AAAS, Am. Phys. Soc. (Biol. Physics prize 1992), N.Y. Acad. Sci.; mem. NAS, Am. Inst. Physics (chmn. governing bd. 1986-93), Am. Acad. Arts and Sci., Am. Philos. Soc., Acad. Leopoldina.

FRAUNFELDER, FREDERICK THEODORE, ophthalmologist, educator; b. Pasadena, Calif., Aug. 16, 1934; s. Reinhart and Freida Fraunfelder; m. Yvonne Marie Halliday, June 21, 1959; children—Yvette Marie, Helene, Nina, Frederick, Nicholas. BS, U. Oreg., 1956, MD, 1960, postgrad. (NIH postdoctoral fellow), 1962. Diplomate Am. Bd. Ophthalmology (bd. dirs. 1982-90). Intern U. Chgo., 1961; resident U. Oreg. Med. Sch., 1964-66; NIH postdoctoral fellow Wilmer Eye Inst., Johns Hopkins U., 1967; prof., chmn. dept. ophthalmology U. Ark. Health Scis. Ctr., 1968-78, 1978—; dir. Casey Eye Inst., 1989—, Nat. Registry Drug-Induced Ocular Side Effects, 1976—; vis. prof. ophthalmology Moorfields Eye Hosp., London, 1974. Author: Drug-Induced Ocular Side Effects and Drug Interactions, 1976, 4th edit., 1995, Current Ocular Therapy, 1980, 4th edit., 1994, Recent Advances in Ophthalmology, 8th edit., 1985; assoc. editor: Jour. Toxicology: Cutaneous and Ocular, 1984—; mem. editl. bd. Am. Jour. Ophthalmology, 1982-92, Ophthalmic Forum, 1983-90, Ophthalmology, 1984-89; contbr. numerous articles lens and eye toxicity rsch. to profl. jours. Served with U.S. Army, 1962-64. FDA grantee, 1976-86; Nat. Eye Inst. grantee, 1970-87. Mem. AMA, ACS, Am. Acad. Ophthalmology, Assn. Univ. Profs. in Ophthalmology (pres. 1976), Am. Ophthalmol. Soc., Am. Coll. Cryosurgery (pres. 1977), Assn. Research in Ophthalmology. Lutheran. Clubs: Lions, Elks. Home: 13 Cellini Ct Lake Oswego OR 97035-1307 Office: Casey Eye Inst 3375 SW Terwilliger Blvd Portland OR 97201-4146

FRAUTSCHI, STEVEN CLARK, physicist, educator; b. Madison, Wis., Dec. 6, 1933; s. Lowell Emil and Grace (Clark) F.; m. Mie Okamura, Feb. 16, 1967; children—Laura, Jennifer. B.A., Harvard U., 1954; Ph.D., Stanford U., 1958. Research fellow Kyoto U., Japan, 1958-59, U. Calif.-Berkeley, 1959-61; mem. faculty Cornell U., 1961-62, Calif. Inst. Tech., Pasadena, 1962—; prof. theoretical physics Calif. Inst. Tech., 1966—; vis. prof. U. Paris, Orsay, 1977-78. Author: Regge Poles and S-Matrix Theory, 1963, The Mechanical Universe, 1986. Guggenheim fellow, 1971-72. Mem. Am. Phys. Soc. Home: 1561 Crest Dr Altadena CA 91001-1838 Office: 1201 E California Blvd Pasadena CA 91125-0001

FRAYSSINET, DANIEL FERNAND, software company executive; b. Rodez, Aveyron, France, June 25, 1956; came to U.S., 1979; s. Leon Privat and Fernande Marie (Foulquier) F.; m. Chantal Luce Hebrard, June 30, 1979 (div. 1988); m. Corinne Yollande Guillaud, Mar. 4, 1989; children: Jennifer, Malorie. BA in Math., Lycee Chaptal, Mende, France, 1974; diploma in Math., Institut Nat. des Scis. Appliquees, Villeurbanne, France, 1976, MSME, 1979. Registered mech. engr. Rsch. asst. Onser, Bron, France, 1977-78; devel. engr. Centech, Glenview, Ill., 1979-82; pres., dir. JMS Inc., Camarillo, Calif., 1985—; CEO, pres., dir. D.P. Tech. Corp., Camarillo, 1982—; dir. Acaso Bus. Ctr., Oxnard, Calif. Author: Adverse Effect of Inertia and Rigidity of Truck Colliding with Lighter Vehicle, 1979; co-author: (software) Arcade, 1979, Esprit, 1984. Mem. Soc. Mfg. Engrs., Acad. Magical Arts, Inc. Office: D P Tech Corp 1150 Avenida Acaso Camarillo CA 93012-8719

FRAZIER, GARY LAWSON, real estate investment executive; b. Houston, June 27, 1956; s. Fred Lawson and Gracie Lorraine (Moore) F.; m. Robin Alice Hansen, May 18, 1986; children: Kelsey Irene, Hannah Grace. BArch, Tulane U., 1979; MBA, U. So. Calif., L.A., 1982. Real estate devel. exec. Prudential Ins. Co., L.A., 1979-84, C. J. Segerstrom & Sons, Costa Mesa, Calif., 1984-86; real estate investment exec. Prudential Ins. Co., L.A., 1987-89, 92—, Newark, 1989-92. Mem. Internat. Coun. Shopping Ctrs.

FRAZIER, LOWELL DENNIS, journalist, public relations educator, retired naval officer; b. Cleveland, Tenn., Feb. 1, 1937; s. Charlie Thurbert and Ora Inez (Officer) F.; m. Betty Jo Guffey, Dec. 20, 1956; children: Lowell Jr., Michael, Karen, Kevin. BS in Journalism, U. Tenn., 1960; MS in Teaching, Am. U., 1973, MS in Pub. Relations, 1974; EdS, Ball State U., 1981; EdD, Tenn. State U., 1987. Reporter The Knoxville (Tenn.) Jour., 1957-61; commd. ensign USN, 1961, advanced through ranks to lt. comdr., 1968, pub. affairs officer, 1961-81; chmn. journalism dept. Def. Info. Sch., 1980-81; ret. USN, 1981; prof. pub. rels. U. Hawaii, Honolulu, 1984-92, chmn. dept., 1992—; prof. pub. rels. Mid. Tenn. State U., Murfreesboro, Tenn., 1981-84. Contbr. articles to profl. jours. Vice chmn. pub. info. com. Tenn. divsn. Am. Cancer Soc., Nashville, 1983-84, Hawaii-Pacific divns., Honolulu, 1988—. Mem. Pub. Relations Soc. Am., Internat. Assn. Bus. Communicators (chpt. v.p. 1985-87), Assn. for Edn. in Journalism and Mass Communication. Home: 95-128 Kipapa Dr Apt 408 Mililani HI 96789-1174 Office: U Hawaii Journalism Dept 2550 Campus Rd Honolulu HI 96822-2217

FRAZIER, RONALD LEE, minister; b. Quincy, Ill., Jan. 6, 1937; s. Kenneth E. and Pauline (Woodruff) F.; children: Susan Goderstad, Stephen, David. BA in Religion, Culver-Stockton Coll., 1959; postgrad., Drake U., 1959-60; M in Divinity, Christian Theol. Sch., 1962. Min. Christian edn. Ctrl. Christian Ch., Decatur, Ill., 1963-68; sr. min. Davis Meml. Christian Ch., Taylorville, Ill., 1967-77, Springfield (Ill.) 1st Christian Ch., 1977-82; internat. interim min. Creighton Christian Ch., Phoenix, 1982-84; sr. min. Mesa (Ariz.) 1st Christian Ch., 1984-86, Stockton (Calif.) 1st Christian Ch., 1986—; part-time instr. Milliken U., Decatur, 1968-75; pres. Stockton Metro Ministry, 1988-90, chair emergency food and housing com., 1991—; bd. dirs. Barton W. Stone Christian Home, Jacksonville, Ill., 1978-82, Bethesda Christian Homes, San Jose, Calif., 1986-90, Bethany Christian Homes, Los Gatos, Calif., 1986-90. Mem. adv. bd. Planned Parenthood San Joaquin County, Stockton, 1992—, Women's Ctr., Stockton, 1992—; mem. human rights com. Stockton Devel. Ctr., 1988—; mem. human svcs. task force United Way & Pvt. Industry Coun., Stockton, 1992—; bd. dirs. F.E.M.A. and Affordable Housing Coalition, San Joaquin County, Calif., 1988—; pres. United Way, 1971, campaign chair, 1982; mem. Sangmon County Sr. Citizens Bd., Springfield, 1979-80; mem. steering com. Community Svcs. to Homeless, 1986. Home: 1193 Brick Tile Cir Stockton CA 95206 Office: 1234 William Moss Blvd Stockton CA 95206-5229

FRECH, HARRY EDWARD, III, economics educator, consultant; b. St. Louis, Nov. 11, 1946; s. Harry Edward Jr. and Margaret Byrne (O'Reilly) F.; m. Carol Ann Vouga, June 8, 1968 (div. Aug. 1980); children: Jon Clayton, Justin Tyler; m. Elizabeth Chen, Apr. 9, 1983; 1 child, Michael Anthony. BS in Indsl. Engring., U. Mo., 1968; MA in Econs., UCLA, 1970, PhD in Econs., 1974. Economist HEW, Rockville, Md., 1970-72; asst. prof. econs. U. Calif., Santa Barbara, 1973-77, assoc. prof. econs., 1977-81, prof., 1981—, chmn. dept., 1993-94; vis. asst. prof. econs. Harvard U., Cambridge, Mass., 1976-77; vis. prof. U. Chgo., 1982; econs. cons. FTC, Washington, 1977—, HHS, Washington, 1973-78; expert witness U.S. Dept. Justice, Washington, 1984; adj. scholar Am. Enterprise Inst. Pub. Policy Rsch. Co-author: Public Insurance in Private Medical Markets, 1978; assoc. editor Econ. Inquiry, 1975-78; editor: Health Care in America: The Political Economy of Hospitals and Health Insurance, 1988, Regulating Doctor's Fees, 1991; co-editor Health Economics Worldwide, 1992; N.Am. editor Internat. Jour. Econs. of Bus., 1992—; mem. editl. bd. Am. Econ. Rev., 1980-82, Econ. Inquiry, 1991—; series editor Health Econs. and Pub. Policy; contbr. articles to profl. jours. Bd. dirs. Christ Luth. Ch., Goleta, Calif., 1978; co-organizer 2d World Congress on Health Econs., Zurich, Switzerland, 1990. Research grantee HEW, 1976, Found. for Research in Econs. and Edn., 1974. Mem. Am. Econ. Assn., So. Econ. Assn., Western Econ. Assn.. Republican. Home: 438 Pitzer Ct Santa Barbara CA 93117-4013 Office: U Calif Econs Dept Santa Barbara CA 93106

FREDERIC, BRAD, engineering company executive; b. 1939. BA in Math., Calif. Poly Inst., 1959; postgrad., U. Calif., 1962-67. Program mgr. Gen. Rsch. Corp., 1963-73; pres. Tecolate Rsch. Inc., Santa Barbara, Calif., 1973—. Office: Tecolote Rsch Inc 5290 Overpass Rd Ste D Santa Barbara CA 93111*

FREDERICK, JOSEPH FRANCIS, JR., hotel executive; b. Luzerne, Pa., July 13, 1933; s. Joseph Francis and Emma (Sabatini) F.; children: Joelle Ann, Joseph Francis, III; m. Elia Chavez, Nov. 22, 1989. B.S., Pa. State U., 1956. Exec. trainee Waldorf-Astoria Hotel, N.Y.C., 1956-57; asst. front office mgr. Waldorf-Astoria Hotel, 1962-63; service mgr. Statler Hilton, N.Y.C., 1963-65; dir. sales Hartford Hilton, Conn., 1965-68; gen. mgr. Hartford Hilton, 1969; resident mgr. Dallas Statler Hilton, 1968-69; gen. mgr. Netherland Hilton, Terrace Hilton hotels, Cin., 1969-74, Washington Statler-Hilton Hotel, 1974-76, New Orleans Hilton, from 1976; sr. v.p. Hilton Hotels Corp.; now pres. Kansas City Queen; bd. dirs. Conv. and Visitors Bur., New Orleans, La. World Expo; mem. exec. bd., v.p. convs. Greater New Orleans Tourist Conv. Commn.; mem. exec. com., bd. dirs. Chgo. Conv. and Tourism Bureau; active New Orleans Pvt. Industry Council. Mem. citizens com. Internat. Assn. Chiefs of Police; mem. alumni bd. Coll. Human Devel., Pa. State U.; mem. Mayor's Task Force, City of New Orleans; bd. dirs. Oddessy House. Served with USAF, 1957-62. Mem. New Orleans Hotel and Motel Assn. (pres.), Pa. State U. Alumni Assn., Chgo. C. of C. (mem. ctrl. area com.), Sigma Pi Eta, Sigma Pi. Office: Kansas City Queen 218 Delaware St Kansas City MO 64105-1259 Office: Hilton Hotels Corp 9336 Civic Center Dr Beverly Hills CA 90210-3604

FREDERICK, NORMAN L., JR., electrical engineer; b. Hopkinsville, Ky., Feb. 7, 1965; s. Norman L. and Nancy A. (Bass) F. ASES, Hudson Valley C.C., 1985; BSEE, Union Coll., Schenectady, 1987; MSEE, Syracuse U., 1990. Comm. engr. GE, Schenectady, 1986; systems engr. Rome Air Force devel. ctr. MITRE, Griffiss AFB, Rome, N.Y., 1987-89; researcher, teaching asst. Syracuse (N.Y.) U., 1989-90; R&D elec. engr. HP EESOF divsn. Hewlett Packard, Westlake Village, Calif., 1991—. Mem. IEEE, Tau Beta Pi, Eta Kappa Nu, Sigma Xi. Office: Hewlett Packard 5601 Lindero Canyon Rd Westlake Village CA 91362

FREDERICKS, PATRICIA ANN, real estate executive; b. Durand, Mich., June 5, 1941; d. Willis Edward and Dorothy (Plowman) Sexton; m. Ward Arthur Fredericks, June 12, 1960; children: Corrine Ellen, Lorraine Lee, Ward Arthur II. BA, Mich. State U., 1962. Cert. Grad. Real Estate Inst., residential broker, residential salesperson; cert. real estate broker. Assoc. Stand Brough, Des Moines, 1976-80; broker Denton, Tuscon, 1980-83; broker-trainer Coldwell Banker, Westlake Village, Calif., 1984-90; broker, br. mgr. Brown, Newbury Park, Calif., 1990-94; dir. tng. Brown Real Estate, Westlake Village, Calif., 1994—; gen. mgr., dir. mktg. Coldwell Banker

Town & Country Real Estate, Newbury Park, Calif., 1994—; dir. mktg. Coldwell Banker Town and Country, 1995—; bd. sec. Mixtec Corp., Thousand Oaks, 1984-92. Contbr. articles to profl. jours. Pres. Inner Wheel, Thousand Oaks, 1991; bd. dirs. Community Leaders Club, Thousand Oaks, 1991, Conejo Future Found., Thousand Oaks, 1989-92, Wellness Community Ventura Valley, 1994—. Named Realtor of Yr., Conejo Valley Bd. Realtors, 1991. Mem. Calif. Assn. Realtors (dir. 1988-95 regional chair 1995), Conejo Valley Assn. Realtors (sec., v.p., pres.-elect 1989-92, pres. 1993), Pres.'s Club Mich. State U., Com. 100, Inner Wheel of Thousand Oaks (pres. 1991), Cmty. Concerts Assn., Alliance for the Arts, Conejo Valley Symphony Guild, Wellness Cmty., Indian Wells Country Club, North Ranch Country Club. Home: 48143 Vista Cielo La Quinta CA 92253-2256 Office: Town and Country Coldwell Banker 2277 Michael Dr Newbury Park CA 91320-3340

FREDERICKS, WARD ARTHUR, venture capitalist, food industry consultant; b. Tarrytown, N.Y., Dec. 24, 1939; s. Arthur George and Evelyn (Smith) F.; BS cum laude, Mich. State U., 1962, MBA, 1963; m. Patricia A. Sexton, June 12, 1960; children: Corrine E., Lorrine L., Ward A. Assoc. dir. Technics Group, Grand Rapids, Mich., 1964-68; gen. mgr. logistics systems Massey-Ferguson Inc., Toronto, 1968-69, v.p. mgmt. svcs., comptr., 1969-73, sr. v.p. fin., dir. fin. Americas, 1975—; comptr. Massey-Ferguson Ltd., Toronto, Ont., Can., 1973-75; cons. W.B. Saunders & Co., Washington, 1962—; sr. v.p. mktg. Massey/Ferguson, Inc., 1975-78, also sr. v.p., gen. mgr. Tractor div., 1978-80; gen. mgr. Rockwell Graphic Sys., 1980-82; pres. Goss Co.; v.p. ops., Rockwell Internat., Pitts., 1980-84; v.p. Fed. MOG., 1983-84; chmn. MIXTEC Corp., 1984—, also dir., chmn.; principal Venture Assocs., 1993—. dir. Polyfet RF, Inc., Venture Assocs., Badger Northland Inc., MST, Inc., Calif., Tech-Mark Group Inc., Spectra Tech., Inc., Mixtec Group-Venture Capital, Inc., Unicorn Corp., Mixtec-Las Vegas, Mixtec Food Group Calif., Mixtec Signal Tech., Harry Ferguson Inc., M.F. Credit Corp., M.F. Credit Co. Can. Ltd. Bd. dirs., mem. exec. com. Des Moines Symphony, 1975-79; exec. com. Conejo Symphony, pres. 1988-90, pres. Westlake Village Cultural Found., 1991; mem. exec. com. Alliance for Arts.; pres. Conejo Valley Indsl. Assn., 1990, 93; mem. Constn. Bicentennial Com., 1987-88, LaQuinta Arts Found.; v.p. Com. Leaders Club, 1988, pres., 1989-90, pres. Westlake Cultural Found, 1991; vice chair Alliance for the Arts; regent Calif. Lutheran U., 1990— (exec. com. 1993—, chmn. acad. affairs 1993—), exec. com. 1992—, chmn. acad. affairs, 1992—. Fellow Am. Transp. Assn., 1962-63, Ramlose, 1962-63. Mem. IEEE, SAR, Am. Mktg. Assn., Nat. Council Phys. Distbn. Mgmt. (exec. com. 1974), Produce Mktg. Assn., Soc. Automotive Engrs., U.S. Strategic Inst., Tech. Execs. Forum (Tech. Corridor 100 award, 1989), Internat. Food Mfg. Assn., Produce Mktg. Assn., Toronto Bd. Trade, Westlake Village C. of C. (chmn. 1990), Cochella Valley Community Concerts Assn. (bd. dirs. 1992-95), Old Crows, Assn. for Advanced Tech. Edn., Air Force Assn., Aerospace Soc., Experimental Aircraft Assn., Mil. Order World Wars, Conf. Air Force (col.), Westlake Village C. of C. (chmn. bd. 1990-91), Republican Ctrl. Com., State of Calif., 1993—, Aviation Country Club, Community Leaders Club, Pres.'s Club Mich. State U., North Ranch Country Club, Indian Wells Country Club, Rotary, Flying Rotarians, Beta Gamma Sigma. Author: (with Edward W. Smykay) Physical Distribution Management, 1974, Management Vision, 1988; contbr. articles to profl. jours. Lutheran. Home and Office: 1640 Aspenwall Rd Westlake Village CA 91361-1704 also: 48143 Vista Cielo La Quinta CA 92253-2256 also: 41865 Boardwalk Palm Desert CA 92211-9026

FREDERICKSON, ARMAN FREDERICK, minerals company executive; b. Glenbore, Man., Can., May 5, 1918; came to U.S., 1923, naturalized, 1940; s. Albert F. and Ethel M. (Wilton) F.; m. Mary Maxine Stubblefield, Sept. 23, 1943; children—Mary Christene, Clover Diane, Penny Kathlene, Kimberly Mei, Sigrid, Janice. B.S. in Mining Engring, U. Wash., 1940; M.S. in Metall. Engring, Mont. Sch. Mines, 1942; Sc.D. in Geology, Mass. Inst. Tech., 1947. Registered profl. engr., Tex., Colo., Nev., Mo.; cert. petroleum geologist. Mining engr., chief geologist Cornucopia Gold Mines, Oreg., 1939-40; instr. mineral dressing Mont. Sch. Mines, 1941-42; research asst. Mass. Inst. Tech., 1942-43; prof. geology and geol. engring. Washington U., St. Louis, 1947-56; organizer, supr. geol. research Standard (Amoco) Oil and Gas Co., Tulsa, 1955-60; prof. geology, chmn. dept. earth and planetary sci., dir. oceanography U. Pitts., 1960-65; sr. v.p., dir. research, mgr. petroleum prospecting and mineral programs in U.S., Middle East, Africa, Latin Am., 1965-71; pres., chief engr. Sorbotec, Inc., Houston, 1971-74; pres. Global Survey, 1972—; v.p. Samoco (Panama) Challenger Desert Oil Corp., 1977-81; cons. in mining and petroleum exploration, 1971—; v.p. SAMOCO, Del., 1977-81; v.p. ops. CHADOIL, 1978-81, Crown Gems, Inc., Thailand; pres. Global-Thai Exploration Corp., Thailand; organizer, past chmn. clay minerals com. Nat. Acad. Sci.-NRC; organizer, econ. analyst land and real estate projects, Calif.; negotiator oil, gemstone and mining programs, U.S., Africa, Thailand, Middle and Far East, Latin Am., exploration specialist. Author papers in field; patentee fertilizer, oil and water pollution processes and products. Served with USNR, 1943-45. Fulbright prof. Norway, 1955. Fellow Geol. Soc. Am., Mineral Soc. Am.; mem. Am. Inst. Mining, Metall. and Petroleum Engrs., Am. Assn. Petroleum Geologists, Soc. Econ. Geologists, Geochem. Soc. Am., Underwater Soc. Am. Republican. Lutheran. numerous clubs. Home Office: Field Office 1525 Eastman Ln Petaluma CA 94952-1683 also: 301/76 Klongton-ni-ves, Soi Panich-a-non Sukhumvit 71, Bankok 10110 Prakanong Thailand

FREDERICKSON, JOHN MARCUS, insurance executive; b. Fargo, N.D., Feb. 8, 1941; s. Theodore Philip and Valerie Agnes (Stahl) F.; m. Teri Lee Engles, Apr. 12, 1986; children: Susan Kay, Marcus Alan. BSBA, U. N.D., 1966. Contract adminstr. Boeing Co., Seattle, 1966-70; western region mgr. Am. Hosp. Supply Corp., Evanston, Ill., 1970-78; account exec. Drexel Burnham, Oakland, Calif., 1978-80; regional mgr. unit trusts Merrill Lynch, San Francisco, 1981-85; div. mktg. mgr. Merrill Lynch Ins. Group, Princeton, N.J., 1985—. Office: Merrill Lynch Ins Group 531 Rolling Hills Ln Danville CA 94526-6227

FREDERKING, TRAUGOTT HEINRICH KARL, chemical engineering educator; b. Rhoden, Fed. Republic of Germany, June 21, 1926. MME, Inst. Tech., Hannover, Fed. Republic of Germany, 1954; PhD in Cryogenics, Swiss Fed. Inst., Zurich, 1960. Low temperature work ETH Zurich Helium Lab., 1957-60; prof. chem. engring. UCLA, 1961—; chair Cryogenic Engring. Conf., 1988-89; co-organizer and organizer 1st and 2d Joint Seminar (U.S.-Japan) on Magnet-Stability-Related Head Transfer, Fukuoka, 1988, L.A., 1991, 3d Seminar, Fukuoka, 1994. Recipient R.B. Scott Meml. award, 1971, Disting. Svc. award Cryogenic Engring. Conf., 1991. Fellow Am. Inst. Chem. Engrs.; mem. Am. Phys. Soc., Internat. Inst. Refrigeration, Crogenic Soc. Am., Verein Dt. Ing. Home: 11 314 Homedale St Los Angeles CA 90049

FREDMAN, FAIYA RUBENSTEIN, artist; b. Columbus, Ohio, Sept. 8, 1925; d. David and Henrietta Baum (Hassel) Rubenstein; m. Milton Fredman, Feb. 14, 1947; children: Stephen Albert, Teri Lynn. BA in Visual Arts, UCLA, 1948. One-woman shows include La Jolla (Calif.) Mus. Contemporary Art, 1968, 74, 81, U. Calif.-Riverside, Irvine, 1984, Ruth Bachofner Gallery, L.A., 1985, 88, Santa Monica, 1990, Zach/Shuster Gallery, Boca Raton, Fla., 1989, Southwestern Coll., Chula Vista, Calif., 1995; group shows include La Jolla Mus. Contemporary Arts, 1973, 78, 79, 81, 86, U. Sao Paulo (Brazil) Mus. Contemporary Art, 1980, Mus. Photog. Arts, San Deigo, 1987; represented in permanent collections Mus. Photog. Arts, Oakland (Calif.) Mus., La Jolla Mus. Contemporary Arts, Ariz. State U., Tempe. Recipient 1st prize juried show San Diego Pub. TV, 1978. Home and Studio: PO Box 2735 La Jolla CA 92038-2735

FREDMAN, HOWARD S, lawyer; b. St. Louis, Feb. 1, 1944; s. Manuel and Sydine Fredman; children: Jocelyn Bly, Amber Alexandra, Cameron Penn. BA, Princeton U., 1966; JD, Columbia U., 1969. Bar: Calif. 1970, U.S. Dist. Ct. (no. dist.) Calif. 1970, U.S. Ct. Appeals (9th cir.) 1970, U.S. Dist. Ct. (so. dist.) Calif. 1974, U.S. Dist. Ct. (cen. dist.) Calif. 1975, Temp. Emergency Ct. Appeals. Law clk. to hon. Milton Pollack U.S. Dist. Ct. (so. dist.) N.Y., N.Y.C., 1969-70; assoc. McCutchen, Doyle, Brown & Enersen, San Francisco, 1970-75; counsel, sr. atty., atty. Atlantic Richfield Co. Legal Div., L.A., 1975-87; assoc. Frandzel & Share, L.A., 1987-90, ptnr., 1991—. Mem. L.A. County Bar Assn. (chmn. antitrust sect. 1986-87, exec. com. antitrust sect. 1982-89, 91—), Princeton Club So. Calif. (chmn. alumni schs. com. 1990-95, chmn. bd. trustees 1994—). Democrat. Jewish. Office: Frandzel & Share 6500 Wilshire Blvd Fl 17 Los Angeles CA 90048-4920

FREDMANN, MARTIN, ballet artistic director, educator, choreographer; b. Balt., Feb. 3, 1943; s. Martin Joseph and Hilda Adele (Miller) F.; m. Kaleriya Fedicheva, Jan. 2, 1973 (div.); m. Patricia Renzetti, June 12, 1980. Student, Nat. Ballet Sch., Washington, 1962-64, Vaganova Sch., Leningrad, 1972. Prin. dancer The Md. Ballet, Balt., 1961-64; dancer The Pa. Ballet, Phila., 1964-65, Ballet of the Met. Opera Co., N.Y.C., 1965-66; prin. dancer Dortmund (Fed. Republic Germany) Ballet, 1973-75, Scapino Ballet, Amsterdam, Holland, 1975-76; tchr. German Opera Ballet, West Berlin, Fed. Republic Germany, 1979, Netherlands Dance Theater, 1979, Royal Swedish Ballet, 1980, San Francisco Ballet, 1981; tchr., coach Australian Ballet, 1982; tchr. Tokyo City Ballet, Hong Kong Ballet, 1985, 86, 87, London Festival Ballet, 1981-83; dir. ballet Teatro Comunale, Florence, Italy, 1984-85; artistic dir. Tampa (Fla.) Ballet, 1984-90; artistic dir. in alliance with The Tampa Ballet Colo. Ballet, Denver, 1987-90; artistic dir. Colo. Ballet, 1987—; tchr. German Opera Ballet, 1982, Ballet Rambert, London, Bat Dor summer course, Israel, 1983, Cullberg Ballet, Sweden, 1983, Hong Kong Acad. For Performing Arts, 1985, 86, 87, 89, 91, Tokyo City Ballet, 1985, 86, 87, 89, 90, Ballet West, 1990, Nat. Ballet Korea, 1991, Dance Divsn. Tsoying High Sch., Kaohsiung, Taiwan, R.O.C., 1992; guest lectr., tchr. Cen. Ballet China, Beijing Dancing Acad., P.L.A. Arts Coll., Beijing, 1990; tchr. Legat Sch., 1978, examiner, 1980; tchr. Eglevsky Sch., N.Y.C., 1980; asst. dir., ballet master Niavaron Cultural ctr., Tehran, Iran, 1978; tchr. Ballet Arts Sch. Carnegie Hall, N.Y.C., 1979-81, choreographer Estonia Nat. Theatre, USSR, 1991; dir. Marin Ballet, Calif., 1981. Choreographer Romeo and Juliet, 1983, Sachertorte, 1984, A Little Love, 1984, Ricordanza, 1986, Cinderella, 1986, Coppelia, 1987, The Nutcracker, 1987, Beauty and the Beast, 1988, Masquerade Suite, 1989, Silent Woods, 1989, The Last Songs, 1991, Centenial Suite, 1994. Mem. Am. Guild Mus. Artists, Fla. State Dance Assn., Nat. Assn. Regional Ballet. Home: 836 E 17th Ave Apt 3A Denver CO 80218-1449 Office: Colo Ballet 1278 Lincoln St Denver CO 80203-2114

FREDRICKS, ANTHONY THEO, retired lawyer; b. Georgetown, Idaho, Aug. 10, 1910; s. Charles Henry and Louella Marie (Sorensen) F.; m. Edna Nellie Pershall, Apr. 14, 1934 (dec. July 1945); children: Shirley Fay, Edna Thea, Darylann; m. Epha Jane Sutcliffe, Aug. 12, 1969 (dec. June 1995). Tchr.'s Cert., U. Idaho So. Br., Pocatello, 1931; JD, George Washington U., 1938. Bar: D.C. 1938, Mont. 1938, U. S. Dist. Ct. D.C. 1938, U.S. Ct. Appeals 1938, Idaho 1945, U.S. Dist. Ct. Idaho 1945, U.S. Supreme Ct. 1947. Spl. agt. Div. Investigations, Washington, 1938-41; referee in bankruptcy U.S. Dist. Ct. for Mont., 1941-42; assoc. counsel Reconstruction Fin. Corp., Washington, 1942-44; organizer, dir. Fed. Rent Control for Idaho, Boise, 1944-47; Idaho state counsel FNMA, Boise, 1947-51; sr. mem. law firm Boise, 1947-72; mem. Am. Bd. Arbitration, 1968. Patentee of oversnow vehicle, U.S., 1961, Norway, 1961, Fed. Republic of Germany, 1961, remote control scaffold, U.S., 1971, brakeable swivel casters, U.S., 1976. Recipient Cert. of Achievement, United Inventors and Scientists of Am., 1976. Mem. ABA, Interamerican Bar Assn. Home: S 2710 Scott Spokane WA 99203

FREDRICKS, SHIRLEY JEAN, foundation director, consultant; b. Dallas; m. Robert Emmett Fredricks; children: Laura, Robert, David, Jonathan, Lisa. BS, Marquette U. Rschr., writer USIA, Washington; nonprofit cons.; exec. dir., pres. Lawrence Welk Found., Santa Monica, Calif., 1980—; bd. dirs. L.A. Urban Funders; mem. Coun. on Founds.; adv. com. Family Philanthropy, vice chair Family Philanthropy Com.; chmn. Nat. Family Found. Conf., 1991; charter mem. L.A. Women's Movement, Santa Monica. Named Corp. Woman of Yr., Battered Women's Movement, Santa Monica, 1990; recipient Humanitarian award Nat. Conf. Christians and Jews, Santa Monica, 1993, and numerous other nonprofit awards. Mem. Soc. Calif. Assn. for Philanthropy (comms. com.). Office: Lawrence Welk Found 1299 Ocean Ave # 800 Santa Monica CA 90401

FREED, AARON DAVID, architect; b. Galva, Ill., Apr. 29, 1922; s. Charles Henry and Ruth Igeborg F.; m. Mildred Alpha Magee, Mar. 30, 1946; children—Christine Diane, Joan Anita. Grad., Am. Acad. Art, Chgo., 1942; B.S., U. Ill., 1948. With Graham Anderson Probst White (Architects), 1950-52, Durham, Anderson Freed, Seattle, 1952-79, HDR, Seattle, 1979-86; instr. U. Ill., 1947-48, U. Wash., 1961-62. Served with C.E. AUS, 1943-46. Fellow AIA.; mem. Interfaith Forum on Religion, Art and Architecture. Presbyterian. Office: 350 N 190th St Ste 316C Seattle WA 98133-3856

FREED, CURT RICHARD, pharmacology educator; b. Seattle, Jan. 14, 1943; m. Nancy F. Freed. BA, Harvard U., 1965, MD, 1969. Lic. physician, Colo. Intern then resident Harbor Gen. Hosp., Torrance, Calif., 1969-71; resident Mass. Gen. Hosp., Boston, 1971-72; postdoctoral fellow U. Calif. Med. Ctr., San Francisco, 1972-75; asst. prof. medicine and pharmacology U. Colo. Sch. Medicine, Denver, 1975-81, acting head divsn. clin. pharmacology, 1976-77, assoc. prof. medicine and pharmacology, 1981-87, prof. medicine and pharmacology, 1987-93, prof., head clin. pharm. divsn., 1993—, dir. neural tranplantation program for Parkinson's disease, 1988—. Contbg. author 3 revs. and books; contbr. 166 abstracts and 79 articles to profl. jours. Mem. rsch. com. Colo. Heart Assn., 1980-86, dir. rsch. com., 1981-84. Recipient Pharm. Mfrs. aSsn. Found. Faculty Devel. award, 1976-79; faculty scholar Harvard U., 1961; NIH grantee, 1978—. Mem. Assn. of Am. Physicians, Am. Soc. Clin. Investigation, Am. Soc. Clin. Pharm. and Therapeutics, Am. Soc. Pharmacology and Exptl. Therapeutics, Am. Soc. Neural Transplantation, Internat. Peptide Soc., Western Assn. Physicians, Internat. Soc. Devel. Neurosci., Am. Fedn. Clin. Rsch., Soc. for Neurosci., Sigma Xi. Office: U Colo Sch Medicine 4200 E 9th Ave C 237 Denver CO 80262

FREED, JOHN HOWARD, immunologist, educator; b. New Brighton, Pa., Mar. 10, 1943; s. Howard F. and Harriet M. (MacKinney) F.; m. Debora D. Freed, Dec. 19, 1971; children: Peter W., Emily F. SB, MIT, 1965; PhD, Stanford U., 1971. Postdoctoral fellow Stanford (Calif.) U., 1970-72, Albert Einstein Coll. Medicine, Bronx, N.Y., 1973-76; asst. prof. Johns Hopkins Sch. of Medicine, Balt., 1976-83; assoc. mem. Nat. Jewish Ctr. for Immunology and Respiratory Medicine, Denver, Colo., 1983-93; sr. mem. Nat. Jewish Ctr. for Immunology and Respiratory Medicine, Denver, 1993—; assoc. prof. U. Colo. Health Sci. Ctr., Denver, 1984-94, prof., 1994—. Assoc. editor Jour. Immunology, 1991-95; contbr. articles to profl. jours. Recipient postdoctoral fellowship Damon Runyon-Walter Winchell Found. N.Y.C., 1970-72, Arthritis Found., Atlanta, 1973-75; many rsch. awards NIH, Bethesda, 1976—. Mem. AAAS, Am. Assn. Immunologists. Office: Nat Jewish Ctr Immunology & Respiratory Medicine 1400 Jackson St Denver CO 80206

FREEDMAN, BART JOSEPH, lawyer; b. New Haven, Sept. 27, 1955; s. Lawrence Zelic and Dorothy (Robinson) F.; m. Esme Detweiler, Sept. 28, 1985; children: Luke Edward, Samuel Meade. BA, Carleton Coll., 1977; JD, U. Pa., 1982. Bar: Wash. 1984, U.S. Dist. Ct. (we. dist.) Wash. 1984, U.S. Ct. Appeals (9th cir.) 1985, U.S. Dist. Ct. (ea. dist.) Wash. 1988. Law clk. to chief justice Samuel Roberts Supreme Ct. Pa., Erie, 1982-83; asst. city solicitor City of Phila., 1984; assoc. Perkins Coie, Seattle, 1984-90; ptnr. Preston Gates & Ellis, Seattle, 1990—. Editor: Natural Resource Damages, 1993. Bd. dirs. Seattle Metrocenter YMCA, 1988—, chmn. 1993—; chair Sierra Club Inner City Outings Program, Seattle, 1986-90; chair bd. advisors Earth Svc. Corps/YMCA, Seattle, 1990—. Mem. ABA (com. on corp. counsel 1985—), Wash. State Bar Assn., Seattle-King County Bar Assn. (participant neighborhood legal clinics 1985-94). Office: Preston Gates & Ellis 701 5th Ave Ste 5000 Seattle WA 98104-7016

FREEDMAN, DAVID NOEL, religion educator; b. N.Y.C., May 12, 1922; s. David and Beatrice (Goodman) F.; m. Cornelia Anne Pryor, May 16, 1944; children: Meredith Anne, Nadezhda, David Micaiah, Jonathan Pryor. Student, CCNY, 1935-38; A.B., UCLA, 1939; B.Th., Princeton Theol. Sem., 1944; Ph.D., Johns Hopkins U., 1948; Litt.D., U. Pacific, 1973; Sc.D., Davis and Elkins Coll., 1974. Ordained to ministry Presbyn. Ch., 1944; supply pastor in Acme and Deming, Wash., 1944-45; teaching fellow, then asst. instr. Johns Hopkins U., 1946-48; asst. prof., then prof. Hebrew and O.T. lit. Western Theol. Sem., Pitts., 1948-60; prof. Hebrew and O.T. lit. Pitts. Theol. Sem., 1960-61, James A. Kelso prof., 1961-64; prof. O.T. San Francisco Theol. Sem., 1964-70, Gray prof. Hebrew exegesis, 1970-71, dean of faculty, 1966-70, acting dean of sem., 1970-71; prof. O.T. Grad. Theol. Union, Berkeley, Calif., 1964-71; prof. dept. Nr. Ea. studies U. Mich., Ann Arbor, 1971-92, Thurnau prof. Bibl. studies, 1984-92, dir. program on studies in religion, 1971-91; prof., endowed chair in Hebrew Bibl. studies U. Calif., San Diego, 1987—; coord. religious studies program U. Calif., 1989—; Danforth vis. prof. Internat. Christian U., Tokyo, 1967; vis. prof. Hebrew U., Jerusalem, 1977, Macquarie U., N.S.W., Australia, 1980, U. Queensland (Australia), 1982, 84, U. Calif., San Diego, 1985-87; Green vis. prof. Tex. Christian U., Ft. Worth, 1981; dir. Albright Inst. Archeol. Rsch., 1969-70, dir., 1976-77; centennial lectr. Johns Hopkins U., 1976; Dahood lectr. Loyola U., 1983; Soc. Bibl. Lit. meml. lectr., 1983, Smithsonian lectr., 1984; prin. bibl. cons. Reader's Digest, 1984, 88, 89, 90, 94; disting. faculty lectr. Univ. Mich., 1988; Stone lectr. Princeton Theol. Sem., 1989; Mowinckel lectr., Oslo U., 1991; lectr. Uppsala U., Sweden, 1991; vis. lectr. Brigham Young Ctr. Near Eastern Studies, Jerusalem, 1993. Co-author: (with J.D. Smart) God Has Spoken, 1949, (with F.M. Cross, Jr.) Early Hebrew Orthography, 1952, (with John M. Allegro) The People of the Dead Sea Scrolls, 1958, (with R.M. Grant) The Secret Sayings of Jesus, 1960, (with F.M. Cross, Jr.) Ancient Yahwistic Poetry, 1964, rev. edit., 1975, (with M. Dothan) Ashdod I, 1967, The Published Works of W.F. Albright, 1975, (with L.G. Running) William F. Albright: Twentieth Century Genius, 1975, 2d edit., 1991, (with B. Mazar, G. Cornfeld) The Mountain of the Lord, 1975, (with W. Phillips) An Explorer's Life of Jesus, 1975, (with G. Cornfeld) Archaeology of the Bible: Book by Book, 1976, Pottery, Poetry and Prophecy, 1980, (with K.A. Mathews) The Paleo-Hebrew Leviticus Scroll, 1985, The Unity of the Hebrew Bible, 1991, (with D. Forbes and F. Andersen) Studies in Hebrew and Aramaic Orthography, 1992,(with Sara Mandell) The Relationship between Herodotus' History and Primary History, 1993; co-author, editor: (with F. Andersen) Anchor Bible Series Hosea, 1980, Anchor Bible Series Amos, 1989; editor: (with G.E. Wright) The Biblical Archaeologist, Reader I, 1961, (with E.F. Campbell, Jr.) The Biblical Archaeologist, Reader 2, 1964, Reader 3, 1970, Reader 4, 1983, (with W.F. Albright) The Anchor Bible, 1964—, including, Genesis, 1964, James, Peter and Jude, 1964, Jeremiah, 1965, Job, 1965, 2d edit., 1973, Proverbs and Ecclesiastes, 1965, I Chronicles, II Chronicles, Ezra-Nehemiah, 1965, Psalms I, 1966, John I, 1966, Acts of the Apostles, 1967, II Isaiah, 1968, Psalms II, 1968, John II, 1970, Psalms III, 1970, Esther, 1971, Matthew, 1971, Lamentations, 1972, 2d edit., 1992, To the Hebrews, 1972, Ephesians 1-3, 4-6, 1974, I and II Esdras, 1974, Judges, 1975, Revelation, 1975, Ruth, 1975, I Maccabees, 1976, I Corinthians, 1976, Additions, 1977, Song of Songs, 1977, Daniel, 1978, Wisdom of Solomon, 1979, I Samuel, 1980, Hosea, 1980, Luke I, 1981, Joshua, 1982, Epistles of John, 1983, II Maccabees, 1983, II Samuel, 1984, II Corinthians, 1984, Luke II, 1985, Judith, 1985, Mark, 1986, Haggai-Zechariah 1-8, 1987, Ecclesiasticus, 1987, 2 Kings, 1988, s, 1989, Titus, 1990, Jonah, 1990, Leviticus I, 1991, Deuteronomy I, 1991, Numbers 1-20, 1993, Romans, 1993, Jude and 2 Peter, 1993, Zechariah 9-14, 1993, Colossians, 1995, 1 to 2 Timothy, 1995, Zephaniah, 1994; editor Anchor Bible Ref. Libr., Jesus Within Judaism, 1988, Archeology of the Land of the Bible, 1990, The Tree of Life, 1990, A Marginal Jew, 1991, The Pentateuch, 1991, The Rise of Jewish Nationalism, 1992, History and Prophecy, 1993, Jesus and the Dead Sea Scrolls, 1993, The Birth of the Messiah, 1993, The Death of the Messiah, 2 vols., 1994, Introduction to Rabbinical Literature, 1994, A Marginal Jew, vol. 2, 1994, The Scepter and the Star, 1995, (with J. Greenfield) New Directions in Biblical Archaeology, 1969, (with J.A. Baird) The Computer Bible, 1971, A Critical Concordance to the Synoptic Gospels, 1971, An Analytic Linguistic Concordance to the Book of Isaiah, 1971, I, II, III John: Forward and Reverse Concordance and Index, 1971, A Critical Concordance to Hosea, Amos, Micah, 1972, A Critical Concordance of Haggai, Zechariah, Malachi, 1973, A Critical Concordance to the Gospel of John, 1974, A Synoptic Concordance of Aramaic Inscriptions, 1975, A Linguistic Concordance of Ruth and Jonah, 1976, A Linguistic Concordance of Jeremiah, 1978, Syntactical and Critical Concordance of Jeremiah, 1978, Synoptic Abstract, 1978, I and II Corinthians, 1979, Zechariah, 1979, Galatians, 1980, Ephesians, 1981, Philippians, 1982, Colossians, 1983, Pastoral Epistles, 1984, 1 & 2 Thessalanians, 1985, Density Plots in Ezekiel, 1986, Exodus, 1987, Hebrews, 1988, Ruth, 1989, James, 1991, 1 & 2 Peter, 1991, 1, 2 & 3 John and Jude, 1991, Psalms, Job and Proverbs, 1992, Apocalypse, 1993, Who's Who in the Bible, 1994, Aramaic Inscriptions, 1975, (with T. Kachel) Religion and the Academic Scene, 1975, Am. Schs. Oriental Research publs; co-editor: Scrolls from Qumran Cave I, 1972, Jesus: The Four Gospels, 1973; Reader's Digest editor: Atlas of the Bible, 1981, Family Guide to the Bible, 1984, Mysteries of the Bible, 1988, Who's Who in the Bible, 1994; assoc. editor Jour. Bibl. Lit., 1952-54; editor, 1955-59; cons. editor Interpreter's Dictionary of the Bible, 1957-60, Theologisches Wörterbuch des Alten Testaments, 1970-92; editor in chief The Anchor Bible Dictionary, 6 vols., 1992; co-editor (with W.H. Propp and Baruch Halpern) The Hebrew Bible and Its Interpreters, 1990; contbr. numerous articles to profl. jours. Recipient prize in N.T. exegesis Princeton Theol. Sem., 1943, Carey-Thomas award for Anchor Bible, 1965, Layman's Nat. Bible Com. award, 1978, 3 awards for Anchor Bible Biblical Archaeol. Soc., 1993; William H. Green fellow O.T., 1944, William S. Rayner fellow Johns Hopkins, 1946, 47; Guggenheim fellow, 1959; Am. Assn. Theol. Schs. fellow, 1963; Am. Council Learned Socs. grant-in-aid, 1967, 76. Fellow U. Mich. Soc. Fellows (sr., chmn. 1980-82); mem. Soc. Bibl. Lit. (pres. 1975-76), Am. Oriental Soc., Am. Schs. Oriental Research (v.p. 1970-82, editor bull. of the Am. Schs. Oriental Rsch. 1974-78, editor Bibl. Archeologist 1976-82, dir. publs. 1974-82), Archaeol. Inst. Am., Am. Acad. Religion, Bibl. Colloquium (sec.-treas. 1960-90). Home: 950 Gilman Dr La Jolla CA 92093-0104 Office: U Calif San Diego Dept History 0104 La Jolla CA 92093

FREEDMAN, EDWARD, health services administrator, management consultant; b. Boston, Mar. 24, 1939; s. David Louis and Ada (Blume) F.; children: David, Joshua, Andrew; m. Patricia Jean Oh, July 27, 1991; children: Angela, George. BA, U. Vt., 1962; M of Urban Planning, U. Wash., 1967. Real estate broker Boston Wharf Co., 1963-64; cons. Arthur D. Little, Inc., San Francisco and Seattle, 1964-67; sr. planner Ala. State Housing Authority, Anchorage, 1967-68; asst. dir. regional med. program U. Wash. Med. Sch., Seattle, 1968-69; cons., staff Puget Sound Health Systems Agy., Seattle, 1969-72; mgr. Arthur Young and Co., Portland, Oreg., 1972-74; pres. Freedman Consulting Group, Seattle, 1964—; exec. dir. Hearing, Speech and Deafness Ctr., Seattle, 1987—. Mem. class Leadership Tomorrow, Seattle, 1992; bd. dirs., treas. Exec. Dirs. Coalition, Seattle, 1992—, Seattle Aquarium Soc., 1986-91, Internat. Dist. Community Health Ctr., Seattle, 1983-87; mem. employment com. Jewish Family Svc., Seattle. With USAR, 1962-63. Mem. Rotary, Kiwanis (Seattle bd. dirs. 1988-92). Home: 5608 89th Ave SE Mercer Island WA 98040-5031 Office: Hearing Speech Deafness Ctr 1620 18th Ave Seattle WA 98122-2739

FREEDMAN, GREGG, real estate appraisal company executive; b. Burbank, Calif., Feb. 1, 1957; s. Morton Ira and Charlotte (Chernick) F.; m. Laura Jean Anderson, May 20, 1989; 1 child, Hillary Anne. Student, Pasadena (Calif.) City Coll., U. So. Calif., Citrus Jr. Coll., Azusa, Calif., Calif. State U., L.A. Cert. gen. real estate appraiser Calif.; cert. rev. appraiser, sr. cert. prof. appraiser, cert. comml. property appraiser. Appraiser, mgr. Freedman and Freedman Cons., Monrovia, Calif., 1984-88; pres. Gregg Freedman and Assocs., Inc., Pasadena, Calif., 1988—; tchr. real estate appraisal classes Monrovia H.S. Adult Edn. Former commr. City of Duarte Econ. Devel. Coun. Mem. U. So. Calif. Alumni Assn. Home: 195 S Canon Ave Sierra Madre CA 91024-2601 Office: G Freedman & Assocs 468N Rosemead Bl Ste 103 Pasadena CA 91107

FREEDMAN, JONATHAN BORWICK, journalist, author, lecturer; b. Rochester, N.Y., Apr. 11, 1950; s. Marshall Arthur and Betty (Borwick) F.; m. Maggie Locke, May 4, 1979; children: Madigan, Nicholas. AB in Lit. cum laude, Columbia Coll., N.Y.C., 1972. Reporter AP of Brazil, Sao Paulo and Rio de Janeiro, 1974-75; editorial writer The Tribune, San Diego, 1981-90; syndicated columnist Copley News Service, San Diego, 1987-89; freelance opinion writer L.A. Times, 1990—; free-lance editorial writer N.Y. Times, 1990-91; dist. vis. lectr. and adj. faculty San Diego State U., 1990—; mem. U.S.-Japan Journalists Exch. Program, Internat. Press Inst., 1985. Author, illustrator: The Man Who'd Bounce the World, 1979; author: The Editorials and Essays of Jonathan Freedman, 1988; contbg. author: Best Newspaper Writing, From Contemporary Culture, 1991, (nonfiction) From Cradle to Grave: The Human Face of Poverty in America, 1993; freelance columnist, 1979-81; contbr. articles to N.Y. Times, Chgo. Tribune, San Francisco Examiner, Oakland Tribune, others. Moderator PBS, San Diego, 1988; bd. dirs. Schs. of the Future Commn., San Diego, 1987. Cornell

Woolrich Writing fellow Columbia U., 1972, Eugene C. Pulliam Editorial Writing fellow, Sigma Delta Chi Found., 1986, Media fellow Hoover Instn. Sanford Calif., 1991; recipient Copley Ring of Truth award, 1983, Sigma Delta Chi award, 1983, San Diego Press Club award, 1984, Spl. Citation, Columbia Grad. Sch. Journalism, 1985, Disting. Writing award Am. Soc. Newspaper Editors, 1986, Pulitzer Prize in Disting. Editorial Writing, 1987. Mem. Soc. Profl. Journalists (Disting. Svc. award 1985, Casey medal for meritorious journalism 1994), Nat. Conf. Editl. Writers, Authors Guild, Phi Beta Kappa. Jewish. Office: 4506 Adair St San Diego CA 92107-3804

FREEDMAN, MICHAEL HARTLEY, mathematician, educator; b. Los Angeles, Apr. 21, 1951; s. Benedict and Nancy (Mars) F.; 1 child by previous marriage, Benedict C.; m. Leslie Blair Howland, Sept. 18, 1983; children: Hartley, Whitney, Jake. Ph.D., Princeton U., 1973. Lectr. U. Calif., 1973-75; mem. Inst. Advanced Study, Princeton, N.J., 1975-76; prof. U. Calif., San Diego, 1976—; Charles Lee Powell chair math. U. Calif., 1985—. Author: Classification of Four Dimensional Spaces, 1982; assoc. editor Jour. Differential Geometry, Math. Rsch. Letters and Topology, 1982—, Annals of Math., 1984-91, Jour. Am. Math. Soc., 1987—. MacArthur Found. fellow, 1984-89; named Calif. Scientist of Yr., Calif. Mus. Assn., 1984; recipient Veblen prize Am. Math. Soc., 1986, Fields medal Internat. Congress of Mathematicians, 1986, Nat. Medal of Sci., 1987, Humboldt award, 1988; Guggenheim fellow, 1989, 94. Mem. Nat. Acad. Scis., Am. Assn. Arts and Scis., N.Y. Acad. Sics., Guggenheim Fellowship award, 1994. Office: U Calif San Diego Dept Math 9500 Gilman Dr La Jolla CA 92093-5003

FREELAND, DARRYL CREIGHTON, psychologist, educator; b. Omaha, Feb. 22, 1939; s. Elverson Lafayette and Lauretta Joyce (Coffelt) F.; m. Tina Anne Richmond, July 21, 1979; children—Adam Daniel, Noah Nathan, Sarah Eileen. B.S., U. Nebr., 1961; S.T.B., Fuller Theol. Sem., 1965; M.A., Calif. State U.-Fullerton, 1966; Ph.D., U. So. Calif., 1972. Lic. psychologist, Calif. Tchr. elem. schs., Calif., 1961-66; instr. Glendale Community Coll., Calif., 1966-67, Citrus Community Coll., Glendora, Calif., 1967-79; pvt. practice psychology, Laguna Niguel, Calif., 1969—; field faculty and vis. prof. Calif. State U.-Los Angeles, 1970, San Marino Community Presbyterian Ch., 1972, Calif. Sch. Profl. Psychology, Los Angeles, 1972-73, U. Calif.-Riverside, 1973, Humanistic Psychology Inst., San Francisco, 1976-79, Prof. U. Humanistic Studies, San Diego, 1983—; assoc. prof. psychology and family U.S. Internat. U., 1986—; asst. dir. clin. tng. Marriage and Family Therapy Tng., 1986-89; mem. pvt. post-secondary com. for qualitative rev. and assessment of licensure Calif. Dept. Edn., 1989-95. Finisher, Newport Beach-Irvine Marathon, 1981, San Francisco Marathon, 1982, Long Beach Marathon, 1988. Office: 30131 Town Center Dr Ste 298 Laguna Niguel CA 92677-2040

FREELAND, ROBERT FREDERICK, librarian; b. Flint, Mich., Dec. 20, 1919; s. Ralph V. and Susan Barbara (Goetz) F.; m. June Voshel, June 18, 1948; children: Susan Beth Visser, Kent Richard. BS, Eastern Mich. U., 1942; postgrad., Washington & Lee U., 1945; MS, U. So. Calif., 1948, postgrad., 1949; postgrad., U. Mich., 1950-52, Calif. State U., 1956-58, UCLA, 1960; LittD (hon.), Linda Vista Bible Coll., 1973. Music supr. Consol. Schs. Warren, Mich., 1946-47; music dir. Carson City (Mich.) Pub. Schs., 1948-49; librarian, audio-visual coord. Ford Found., Edison Inst., Greenfield Village, Dearborn, Mich., 1950-52, Helix High Sch. Library, 1952-77; librarian, prof. library sci. Linda Vista Bible Coll., 1976—; reference libr. San Diego Pub. Libr. System, 1967—; cons. edn., libr. and multimedia. Editor book and audio-visual aids review, Sch. Musician, Dir. and Teacher, 1950-75. Former deacon and elder Christian Reform Ch., libr., 1969-72, Classis archivist, 1991—; pub. affairs officer Calif. wing CAP. With USAAF, 1942-46. Named Scholar Freedoms Found., Valley Forge, Pa., 1976-80. Mem. NEA (life), ALA, Calif. Tchrs. Assn., Music Libr. Assn. So. Calif. (adviser exec. bd.), Calif. Libr. Assn. (pres. Palomar chpt. 1972-73), Sch. Libr. Assn. Calif. (treas. 1956-73), Calif. Media and Libr. Educators (charter mem.), Am. Legion (Americanism chmn. 22d dist. San Diego County, chmn. oratorical contest com. La Mesa post), Ret. Officers Assn., San Diego Aero Space Mus., San Diego Mus. Art. Home: 4800 Williamsburg Ln Apt 223 La Mesa CA 91941-4651 Office: Coll Libr 2075 E Madison Ave El Cajon CA 92019-1108

FREEMAN, DICK, professional baseball team executive; m. Judi Freeman; 1 child, Heather. BBA, U. Iowa, 1966. CPA. Acct. Peat, Marwick, Mitchell & Co., San Diego and L.A.; chief fin. officer San Diego Padres, 1981—, exec. v.p., 1986-89, pres., 1989—; mem. exec. com. Nat. League. Bd. Dirs. San Diego chpt., Imperial County chpt. March of Dimes, nat. trustee; bd. dirs. YMCA. Lt. (j.g.) USN. Mem. Rotary. Office: San Diego Padres PO Box 2000 San Diego CA 92112-2000*

FREEMAN, HERBERT JAMES, educational administrator; b. Raleigh, N.C., May 14, 1941; s. Hurley Lee and Annie Lee (Upchurch) F.; m. Ollie Faye Mack, Aug. 23, 1965 (div.). BA, Shaw U., 1963; MA, U. Nev., 1978. Cert. elem. tchr., spl. edn. tchr., elem. prin. Elem. tchr., 1963-65, 70-72; spl. edn. tchr. emotionally disturbed, 1965-70; program specialist Clark County Sch. Dist., Las Vegas, Nev., 1972-79, adminstrv. asst., 1979-80, coord. basic adult edn. program, 1984—; prin. Rex Bell Elem. Sch., Las Vegas, 1980-89, Parson Elem. Sch., 1989—; mem. Nev. State Bd. for Child Care, NAACP; choir dir. Zion United Meth. Ch., 1977—, So. Nev. Mass Meth. Chs.; registrar voter registration. Named Boss of Yr. Clark County Assn. Office Personnel, 1982, Outstanding Adminstr. of Yr. Nev. State PTA, 1992-93. Mem. Assn. Supervision & Curriculum Devel., Nat. Alliance Black Sch. Educators, Clark County Elem. Prins. Assn., Clark County Assn. Sch. Adminstrs., NAACP, Phi Delta Kappa, Kappa Alpha Psi. Democrat. Home: PO Box 4536 Las Vegas NV 89127-0536 Office: 4100 Thom Blvd Las Vegas NV 89130-2722

FREEMAN, JOHN FRANCIS, foundation executive; b. London, Feb. 18, 1940; came to U.S., 1940; BA in History, Antioch Coll., 1963; MA in European History, U. Mich., 1964, PhD in Early Modern Europe, 1969. Asst. prof. Calif. Poly., Pomona, 1966-69, Calif. State U., Northridge, 1969-71; dean West Wyoming Community Coll., Rock Springs, Wyo., 1971-74; asst. dean arts and sci. U. Wyo., Laramie, 1974-86; exec. dir. Wyo. Vol. Assistance Corp., Laramie, 1986-89; pres. Wyo. Community Found., Laramie, 1989—. Co-author: Citizens & Clergy of Grasse, 1988; contbr. articles to profl. jours. Mem. Wyo. Arts Coun., 1973-85, chmn., 1983-85. Woodrow Wilson fellow, 1963-64, Univ. fellow U. Mich., 1964-65. Mem. Agrl. Hist. Soc., French Hist. Studies, Rotary. Office: Wyo Community Found PO Box 4008 Laramie WY 82071-4008

FREEMAN, NEIL, accounting and computer consulting firm executive; b. Reading, Pa., Dec. 27, 1948; s. Leroy Harold and Audrey Todd (Dornhecker) F.; m. Janice Lum, Nov. 20, 1981. BS, Albright Coll., 1979; MS, Kennedy-Western U., 1987, PhD, 1988. Cert. systems profl., data processing specialist, info. system security profl. Acct. Jack W. Long & Co., Mt. Penn, Pa., 1977-78; comptroller G.P.C., Inc., Bowmansville, Pa., 1978-79; owner Neil Freeman Cons., Bowmansville, 1980-81; program mgr., systems cons. Application Systems, Honolulu, 1981-82; instr. Chaminade U., Honolulu, 1983—; owner Neil Freeman Cons., Kaneohe, Hawaii, 1982—. Author: (computer software) NFC Property Management, 1984, NFC Mailing List, 1984; (book) Learning Dibol, 1984. Served with USN, 1966-68, Vietnam. Mem. Nat. Assn. Accts., Am. Inst. Cert. Computer Profls., Assn. Systems Mgmt. Office: 45-449 Hoene Pl Kaneohe HI 96744-2950

FREEMAN, PATRICIA ELIZABETH, library and education specialist; b. El Dorado, Ark., Nov. 30, 1924; d. Herbert A. and M. Elizabeth (Pryor) Harper; m. Jack Freeman, June 15, 1949; 3 children. BA, Centenary Coll., 1943; postgrad., Fine Arts Ctr., 1942-46, Art Students League, 1944-45; BSLS, La. State U., 1946; postgrad., Calif. State U., 1959-61, U. N.Mex., 1964-74, EdS, Peabody Coll., Vanderbilt U., 1975. Libr. U. Calif., Berkeley, 1946-47; libr. Albuquerque Pub. Schs., 1964-67, ind. sch. libr. media ctr. cons., 1967—. Painter lithographer; one-person show La. State Exhibit Bldg., 1948; author: Pathfinder: An Operational Guide for the School Librarian, 1975, Southeast Heights Neighborhoods of Albuquerque, 1993; compiler, editor: Elizabeth Pryor Harper's Twenty-One Southern Families, 1985; editor: SEHNA Gazette, 1988-93. Mem. task force Goals for Dallas-Environ., 1977-82; pres. Friends of Sch. Librs., Dallas, 1979-83; v.p., editor Southeast Heights Neighborhood Assn., 1988-93. With USAF, 1948-49. Honoree AAUW Ednl. Found., 1979; vol. award for outstanding service Dallas Ind. Sch. Dist., 1978; AAUW Pub. Service grantee 1980. Mem. ALA, AAUW (dir. Dallas 1976-82, Albuquerque 1983-85), LWV (sec. Dallas 1982-83, editor Albuquerque 1984-88), Nat. Trust Historic Preservation, Friends of Albuquerque Pub. Libr., N.Mex. Symphony Guild, Alpha Xi Delta. Home: 3016 Santa Clara Ave SE Albuquerque NM 87106-2350

FREEMAN, RICHARD DEAN, new business start-up service company executive; b. Rushville, Ind., Nov. 27, 1928; s. Verne Crawford and Mary Phyllis (Dean) F.; m. Mary Jane Barkman, Aug. 21, 1950; children: Debra Dean, Phyllis Lynn, Richard Paul, Tom Crawford. BS in Aero. Engring., Purdue U., 1950, BS in Naval Sci. and Tactics, 1950, MS in Indsl. Mgmt., 1954. Supr. indsl. engring. Gen. Motors Corp., Warren, Ohio, 1954-58; prodn. mgr. Ramo Wooldridge div. TRW Corp., Denver, 1958-62; mgr. missile programs Hughes Aircraft Co., Los Angeles, 1962-68; v.p. E-Systems Inc., Dallas, 1968-72, Rockwell Internat. Co., Los Angeles, 1972-74; pres. Internat. Pacific Co., Newport Beach, Calif., 1974—; sr. lectr. West Coast U., L.A., 1974-78; sec. proteus Corp., Newport Beach, 1978-80; chmn. Tech. Assocs. Corp., Newport Beach, 1984-85; chief exec. officer Equicenters, Inc., Irvine, 1988—. Author: Economation Approaches, 1958, Equator, 1984 (also film); prod. documentary film Zeros of the Pacific, 1979. Cubmaster, scoutmaster, dist. chmn. Boy Scouts Am., various locations, 1966-76; mem. librs. devel. adv. com. Purdue U., 1992; mem. restoration adv. bd. Marine Corps Air Sta., Tustin, 1994; pres. bd. trustees, elder Presbyn. Ch. Capt. USMC, 1946-58, Korea. Named Man of Yr., Sigma Alpha Tau, West Lafayette, Ind., 1971; recipient Disting. Engring. Alumnus award Purdue U., 1973. Mem. Am. Inst. Indsl. Engrs., Purdue U. Alumni Assn., Nat. Eagle Scout Assn., Exch. Club of Newport Harbor, Kappa Sigma. Republican. Lodge: Masons (consistory 32 degree v.p.). Home: 3910 Topside Ln Corona Del Mar CA 92625-1628 Office: Internat Pacific Co 4199 Campus Dr # 650 Irvine CA 92715-2698

FREEMAN, VAL LEROY, geologist; b. Long Beach, Calif., June 25, 1926; s. Cecil LeRoy and Marjorie (Austin) F.; BS, U. Calif., Berkeley, 1949, MS, 1952; m. June Ione Ashlock, Sept. 26, 1959 (div. June 1962); 1 child, Jill Annette Freeman Michener; m. Elizabeth Joann Sabia, Sept. 4, 1964 (div. Oct. 1972); 1 child, Rebecca Sue Freeman Shepard; 1 stepchild, Frank J. Sabia; m. Betty M. Avey, Oct. 9, 1993. Geologist, U.S. Geol. Survey, 1949-85, Fairbanks, Alaska, 1955-57, Denver, 1957-70, 74-85, Flagstaff, Ariz., 1970-74, dep. chief coal resources br., until 1985. With USNR, 1943-45. Fellow Geol. Soc. Am. Contbr. articles to profl. jours. Home: 26 S Indiana Pl Golden CO 80401-5082

FREEMAN, WILLIAM ROSEMAN, ophthalmologist; b. N.Y.C., Aug. 21, 1953; m. Karen Fleischer; children: Elana Sarah, Samuel Robert. BA, Columbia U., 1975; student, MD, 1979. Diplomate Am. Bd. Ophthalmology; lic. physician and surgeon, Calif., N.Y. Intern Cedars Sinai Med. Ctr./U. Calif., L.A., 1979-80; resident in ophthalmology Lenox Hill Hosp., N.Y.C., 1980-83; prof. ophthalmology U. Calif. Sch. Medicine, San Diego, 1994—; chief retina svc. dept. ophthalmology U. Calif., San Diego, dir. ophthalmic photography, resident supr. dept. ophthalmology, 1985-86, adminstrv. dir. retina svcs., 1988—, dir. vitreoretinal fellowship program, 1987—, attending physician vitreo-retinal surgeon dept. ophthalmology, 1986—; staff physician ophthalmology sect. Alhambra (Calif.) Cmty. Hosp., 1984-86, Huntington Meml. Hosp., Pasadena, Calif., 1984-86; staff physician dept. ophthalmology U. So. Calif. Med. Ctr., L.A., 1985-86; staff physician Doheny Eye Hosp., L.A., 1985—; mem. fellowship rev. panel Fight for Sight Rsch. Divsn. Nat. Soc. Prevent Blindness, 1993—; lectr. and presenter in field. Sci. reviewer Am. Journ. Ophthalmology, Archives of Ophthalmology, Critical Reviews in Immunology, Experimental Eye Rsch., Investigative Ophthalmology and Visual Sci., Jour. AMA, Ophthalmology, Retina, Survey of Ophthalmology; contbr. articles to profl. jours. Francis I. Proctor Found. fellow U. Calif., 1983-84, Estelle Doheny Eye Found. fellow U. So. Calif., 1984-86. Fellow Am. Acad. Ophthalmology (Honor award 1991); mem. AMA, Am. Uveitis Soc., Aspen Retinal Detachment Soc., Assn. for Rsch. in Vision and Ophthalmology, Assn. Proctor Fellows, Fight for Sight Rsch. Div. the Nat. Soc. to Prevent Blindness, Macula Soc., Ophthalmic Microbiology and Immunology Group, Pacific Coast Oto-Ophthalmol. Soc., Retina Soc., Western Assn. for Vitreo-Retinal Edn. (founding mem.), Alpha Omega Alpha. Office: Univ Calif Shiley Eye Ctr 0946 9415 Campus Point Dr La Jolla CA 92093-0946

FREIBOTT, GEORGE AUGUST, physician, chemist, priest; b. Bridgeport, Conn., Oct. 6, 1954; s. George August and Barbara Mary (Schreiber) F.; m. Jennifer Noble, July 12, 1980 (div.); children: Jessica, Heather, George; m. Arlene Ann Steiner, Aug. 1, 1982. BD, Am. Bible Coll., Pineland, Fla., 1977; BS, Nat. Coll. NHA, International Falls, Minn., 1978; ThM, Clarksville (Tenn.) Sch. Theology, 1979; MD, Western U., Phoenix, 1982; ND, Am. Coll., 1979; MsT, Fla. Sch. Massage, 1977. Diplomate Nat. Bd. Naturopathic Examiners; ordained priest Ea. Orthodox Ch., 1983. Chief mfg. cons. in oxidative chemistry Am. Soc. Med. Missionaries, Priest River, Idaho, 1976-88; mfg. cons. Oxidation Products Internat. div. ASMM, Priest River, 1974—; chemist/oxidative chemistry Internat. Assn. Oxygen Therapy, Priest River, 1985—; oxidative chemist, scientist, priest A.S. Med. Missionaries, Priest River, 1982—; massage therapist Fla. Dept. Profl. Registration, Tallahassee, 1977-91; cons. Benedict Lust Sch. Naturopathy; lectr. in field. Author: Nicola Tesla and the Implementation of His Discoveries in Modern Science, 1984, Warburg, Blass and Koch: Men With a Message, 1990, Free Radicals and Their Relationship to Complex Oxidative Compounds, 1991, Complex Oxidative Molecules: Their Implication in the Rejuvenation of the Human Cell, 1994, History of Naturopathy or Pseudomedicalism: Naturopathy's Demise?, 1990, 95; contbr. articles to profl. jours. Recipient Tesla medal of Scientific Merit, Benedict Lust Sch. Natural Scis., 1992. Mem. Tesla Meml. Soc., Tesla Coil Builder's Assn., Internat. Bio-Oxidative Med. Found. (Disting. Spkr. award 1994), British Guild Drugless Pracititoners, Internat. Assn. for Colon Therapy, Am. Massage Therapy Assn., Am. Naturopathic Med. Assn., Am. Soc. Med. Missionaries, Am. Coll. Clinic Adminstrs., Nat. Assn. Naturopathic Physicians, Am. Psychotherapy Assn., Am. Soc. Metals, Am. Naturopathic Assn. (trustee, pres.), Internat. Traders. Home and Office: PO Box 1360 Priest River ID 83856-1360

FREIHEIT, CLAYTON FREDRIC, zoo director; b. Buffalo, Jan. 29, 1938; s. Clayton John and Ruth (Miller) F. Student, U. Buffalo, 1960. Caretaker Living Mus., Buffalo Mus. Sci., 1955-60; curator Buffalo Zool. Gardens, 1960-70; dir. Denver Zool. Gardens, 1970—. Contbr. articles to profl. jours. Named Outstanding Citizen Buffalo Evening News, 1967. Mem. Internat. Union Dirs. Zool. Gardens, Am. Assn. Zool. Parks and Aquariums (pres. 1967-68 Outstanding Service award). Home: 3855 S Monaco Pky Denver CO 80237-1271 Office: Denver Zool Gardens City Park Denver CO 80205

FREILICH, WILLIAM STUART, emergency physician; b. Chgo., Apr. 27, 1948; m. Daniela DiMarca; 1 child, Massimiliano. MD, U. Rome, 1980. Diplomate Am. Bd. Emergency Medicine, Am. Bd. Internal Medicine. Internship Cook County Hosp., Chgo., 1980-81, residency, 1981-83; attending physician San Jose (Calif.) Med. Ctr.; preceptor, instr. Stanford (Calif.) U., 1993-94. Fellow Am. Coll. Emergency Physicians; mem. ACP, Milan Med. Soc., Italy, San Francisco Med. Soc.

FREILICHER, MELVYN STANLEY, writer, educator; b. N.Y.C., Nov. 8, 1946; s. Jack and Frances (Altman) F. BA in Psychology, Brandeis U., 1968; postgrad., U. Calif., San Diego, 1972. Mem. faculty writing program lit. dept. U. Calif.-San Diego, La Jolla, 1979—; vis. faculty lit. dept. San Diego State U., 1979—. Editor mag. Crawl Out Your Window, 1985-89; book reviewer San Diego Union, 1990-92, Jour. L.A. Inst. Contemporary Arts, San Diego Mag., N.Y. Times, L.A. Times, San Diego Reader, others; contbg. guest editor Fiction Internat., 1992; contbr. fiction and essays to numerous profl. publs. Pres. United Artists Coalition, San Diego, 1977-81; pres. bd. dirs. Found. for New Lit., San Diego, 1983-89; mem. adv. bd. Inst. for Cultural Democracy, Ukiah, Calif., 1987—; coord. arts festival, San Diego Lesbian and Gay Ctr., 1979, tchr. workshop, 1994. Recipient award Nat. Endowment for Arts, Calif. Arts Coun. Lit., San Diego City Commn. on Arts and Culture. Home: 3945 Normal St Apt 5 San Diego CA 92103-3420 Office: U Calif San Diego Lit Dept 9500 Gilman Dr La Jolla CA 92093-5003

FREIMAN, PAUL E., pharmaceutical company executive; b. 1932. BS, Fordham U., 1955. Formely exec. v.p. pharm. and agribusiness Syntex USA Inc., pres., co-chief exec. officer, now pres., chief exec. officer, bd. dirs.; also pres. Syntex Corp., Palo Alto, Calif. Office: Syntex Corp 3401 Hillview Ave Palo Alto CA 94304-1320

FREIMUTH, WILLIAM RICHARD, architect; b. Crawford, Nebr., Nov. 26, 1949; s. Frank Francis and Freda (Miller) F.; m. Ann Agnes Hume, Aug. 11, 1984. BS in Arch. Studies, U. Nebr., 1979. Registered architect, N.Mex. Draftsman Clark Enersen Ptnrs. A&E, Lincoln, Nebr., 1974-79; architect intern Lescher & Mahoney A&E, Farmington, N.Mex., 1979-82; architect, ptnr. Johnson Freimuth Arch., P.C., Farmington, 1982-89; architect, CEO William Freimuth Arch. P.C., Farmington, 1989—. Prin works include Piñon Hills Mcpl. Golf Course, Anasazi Amphitheatre, Farmington Aquatic Ctr., Farmington and Bloomfield Post Office. Pres. River Reach Found., Farmington, 1988. Mem. AIA (Farmington chpt. pres. 1986, 93, N.Mex. chpt. pres. 1989, pres.-elect 1994). Republican. Roman Catholic. Home and Office: 316 N Behrend Ave Farmington NM 87401-5843

FREISE, EARL JEROME, university administrator, materials engineering educator; b. Chgo., Dec. 30, 1935; s. Otto H. and Mary A. (Hoffman) F.; m. Lenore A. Serpico, Dec. 27, 1958; children—Christopher E., Timothy P., Nora A., Lawrence M. B.S. in Metall. Engring., Ill. Inst. Tech., 1958; M.S. in Materials Sci., Northwestern U., 1959; Ph.D. in Metallurgy, U. Cambridge, Eng., 1962. From asst. prof. to assoc. prof. Northwestern U., Evanston, Ill., 1962-77; dir. research office, prof. mech. engring. U. N.D., Grand Forks, 1977-82; asst. vice chancellor research, prof. mech. engring. U. Nebr., Lincoln, 1982-87; dir. rsch. office Inst. Material. Sci., Calif. Inst. Tech., 1987—. Contbr. articles to profl. jours. Fulbright fellow, 1959-61; recipient award for Excellence in Engring. Edn., Western Electric Co., 1971. Mem. Am. Soc. Metals (v.p., pres. Chgo. chpt. 1971-72), AIME, Am. Soc. Engring. Edn. (sec.-treas. Ill.-Ind. sect. 1963-64, 73-74), Assn. Univ. Tech. Mgrs., Nat. Council Univ. Research Adminstrs. (pres. 1984-85). Office: Calif Inst Tech MC 213-6 1201 E California Blvd Pasadena CA 91125-0001

FREISER, HELEN, editor; b. Bklyn., Apr. 13, 1928; d. Jacob and Lillian (Reiss) Hammer; m. Leonard H. Freiser, Dec. 13, 1950; children: Leslie, Erik. BA, Bklyn. Coll., 1950; MLS, Columbia U., 1955. Sr. editor adult books BookList, ALA, Chgo., 1973-79; assoc. editor Hewitt Assocs., Lincolnshire, Ill., 1980-82; buyer trade books Sunshine Books, Phila., 1982-84; assoc. editor The H.W. Wilson Co., Cambridge, Mass., 1984-85; mng. editor Jour. of Shaw Hist. Libr., Klamath Falls, Oreg., 1986—. Editor: Guardhouse, Gallows and Graves, 1988. Home: 1215 SE 16th Ave Portland OR 97214-3707

FREISER, LEONARD HAROLD, engineering library director; b. N.Y.C., Feb. 9, 1928; s. Abraham and Henrietta (Graubard) F.; m. Helen Hammer, Dec. 13, 1950; children: Leslie, Erik. MusB, Manhattan Sch. Music, 1948; MA, Columbia U., 1948, MLS, 1955. Instr. music U. Sask., Can., 1948, Hunter Coll., N.Y.C., 1949, Evansville (Ind.) Coll., 1950; asst. prof. San Jose (Calif.) State Coll., 1951; trainee, br. librarian Bklyn. Pub. Library,, 1954-57; chief librarian Glens Falls (N.Y.) City Library, 1957-60, Toronto (Ont., Can.) Bd. Edn., 1960-69, Franklin Inst., Phila., 1981-83; dep. chief librarian Chgo. Pub. Library, 1970-72; dir. Wilmette (Ill.) Pub. Library, 1972-73; dir. libraries Nat. Coll. Edn., Evanston, Ill., 1972-78; pub. Am. Families Pub., 1978-81; dir. libraries, media, acad. support services Oreg. Inst. Tech., Klamath Falls, 1985-93; vis. assoc. prof. library sci. SUNY, Albany, 1959-60; pres. Chgo. Conservatory Coll., 1979-81; trustee Klamath County Public Library, 1985—; bd. govs. Shaw Hist. Library, 1985-93; chmn. Future Commn. Metro Portland, 1993—; cons. in field. Contbr. articles to mags., newspapers. Conductor Klamath Symphony, 1985-93. Mem. ALA (councillor 1963-68, chmn. spl. resolutions 1978), Am. Libr. Trustee Assn. (v.p. region X 1988-93), Pacific N.W. Library Assn. (exec. bd. 1988-93). Home: 1215 SE 16th Ave Portland OR 97214-3707 Office: Metro 600 NE Grand Ave Portland OR 97232-2736

FREITAG, PETER ROY, transportation specialist; b. L.A., Dec. 19, 1943; s. Victor Hugo and Helen Veronica (Burnes) F. Student, U. Fla., 1961-63, George Washington U., 1964-65. Chief supr. Eastern Airlines, L.A., 1965-77; tariff analyst, instr. United Airlines, San Francisco, 1977-84; mng. ptnr. Bentdahl, Freitag & Assoc., San Francisco, 1984-86; v.p. ops. PAD Travel, Inc., Mountain View, Calif., 1985-86; travel mgr. Loral Aerospace Corp, San Jose, Calif., 1986—. Co-editor: (textbook) International Air Tariff and Ticketing, 1983. Vol. San Francisco Bay chpt. Oceanic Soc., 1984-95. Mem. Silicon Valley Bus. Travel Assn., Bay Area Bus. Travel Assn. Episcopalian.

FREITAS, ANTOINETTE JUNI, insurance company executive; b. Kansas City, Mo., Feb. 14, 1944; d. Anthony P. and Mariam L. Freitas; BA, Calif. State U.-Long Beach, 1966; MA, U. So. Calif., 1974; m. Stephen R. Krajcar, July 4, 1980. Chartered life underwriter, chartered fin. cons. Counselor, U. So. Calif., 1967-70, assoc. dir. fin. aid, 1970-75; sales agt. Equitable Life Assurance Co., 1975-79, dist. mgr., San Francisco, 1979-84; pres. Group Mktg. Services, Inc., field dir. Northwestern Mut. Life, San Francisco, 1984-86; pres. Peninsula Fin. Group, Inc., 1986—; mktg. mgr. Home Life, H.L. Fin. Group, San Jose, Calif., 1986—; registered rep. W.S. Griffith Co., securities, 1987-91; pres. Peninsula Fin. Group, Inc., 1991. Recipient various sales and mgmt. awards; mem. Million Dollar Round Table. Mem. Nat. Assn. Life Underwriters, AAUW, U. So. Calif. Alumni Assn., Women Life Underwriters Conf. Republican. Episcopalian. Author: A Study in Changing Youth Values, 1974. Office: Peninsula Fin Group Inc 2995 Woodside Rd Ste 400 Woodside CA 94062-2401

FREITAS, ROBERT ARCHIBALD, JR., periodical editor and publisher; b. Camden, Maine, Dec. 6, 1952; s. Robert Archibald and Barbara Lee (Smith) G.; m. Nancy Ann Farrell, Aug. 10, 1974. BS in Physics, Harvey Mudd Coll., 1974, BS in Psychology, 1974; JD, U. Santa Clara, 1979. Dir. Space Initiative Lobbying for Space, Santa Clara, Calif., 1977-82; space automation study editor, Ames Rsch. Ctr. NASA/Am. Soc. Engring. Edn., Moffett Field, Calif., 1980-81; computer sci. study editor, Goddard Space Flight Ctr. NASA/Am. Soc. Engring. Edn., Balt., 1981-82; autonomy and human element in space study editor Ames Rsch. Ctr. NASA/Am. Soc. Engring. Edn., Moffett Field, 1983-84; editor, pub. Value Forecaster, Pilot Hill, Calif., 1988—. Author: Lobbying for Space, 1978; contbr. articles to profl. publs. Recipient Best Fact Article award Analog Sci. Fact/Sci. Fiction, 1981. Mem. AAAS, Internat. Inst. Forecasters, World Future Soc., Nat. Space Soc. (life). Republican. Office: Value Forecaster PO Box 50 Pilot Hill CA 95664-0050

FREMOUW, EDWARD JOSEPH, physicist; b. Northfield, Minn., Feb. 23, 1934; s. Fred J. and Marion Elizabeth (Drozda) F.; m. Rita Lorraine Johnson, June 26, 1960; children: Thane Edrik, Sean Fredrik. BSEE, Stanford U., 1957; MS in Physics, U. Alaska, 1963, PhD in Geophysics, 1966. Asst. prof. geophysics U. Alaska, Fairbanks, 1966-67; physicist Stanford Research Inst., Menlo Park, Calif., 1967-70, sr. physicist, 1970-75; program mgr. SRI Internat., Menlo Park, 1975-77; v.p. Phys. Dynamics, Inc., Bellevue, Wash., 1977-86; pres. Northwest Research Assocs., Inc., Bellevue, Wash., 1986—, also bd. dirs.; cons. Geophys. Inst., College, 1967-68; assoc. La Jolla (Calif.) Inst., 1981-89. Contbr. articles to profl. jours. Trustee East Shore Unitarian Ch., 1984-86; co-chair adv. com. on econ. diversification Wash. State, 1991—; bd. dirs., pres. Banchero Friends Svcs., Inc., 1994-95. Geographic feature Fremouw Peak named in his honor, 1968. Mem. IEEE, Am. Geophys. Union (Excellence in Refereeing award 1984, 89), Union Radio Sci. Internat., Stanford Club of Western Wash. (trustee 1984-86). Democrat. Unitarian Universalist. Home: 8232 F Mercer Way Mercer Island WA 98040-5621 Office: Northwest Rsch Assocs Inc PO Box 3027 Bellevue WA 98009-3027

FRENCH, CLARENCE LEVI, JR., retired shipbuilding company executive; b. New Haven, Oct. 13, 1925; s. Clarence L. Sr. and Eleanor (Curry) F.; m. Jean Sprague, June 29, 1946; children: Craig Thomas, Brian Keith, Alan Scott. BS in Naval Sci., Tufts U., 1945, BSME, 1947; ScD (hon.), Webb Inst., 1992. Registered profl. engr., Calif. Foundry engr. Bethlehem Steel Corp., 1947-56; staff engr., asst. supt. Kaiser Steel Corp., 1956-64; supervisory engr. Bechtel Corp., 1964-67; with Nat. Steel & Shipbldg. Co., San Diego, 1967-86; exec. v.p., gen. mgr. Nat. Steel & Shipbldg. Co., to 1977, pres., chief operating officer, 1977-84, chmn., chief exec. officer, 1984-

86, outside dir., 1989—; mem. maritime transp. rsch. bd. NRC. Bd. dirs. United Way, San Diego, YMCA, San Diego; past chmn., bd. dirs. Pres. Roundtable; chmn. emeritus bd. trustees Webb Inst. Lt. USN, 1943-53. Fellow Soc. Naval Architects and Marine Engrs. (hon., past pres.), Shipbuilders Council Am. (past chmn. exec. com.), ASTM, Am. Bur. Shipping; mem. Am. Soc. Naval Engrs., U.S. Naval Inst., Navy League U.S., Propeller Club U.S.

FRENCH, GLENDON EVERETT, JR., health care executive; b. Chgo., Mar. 11, 1934; s. Glendon Everett and Mabel (Eastman) French; m. Carolyn Miller, Nov. 28, 1959; children: Deborah Dalton, Glendon Everett, Catherine C. B.A. in Bus. Adminstrn., Dartmouth Coll., 1956, M.B.A., 1959. With Am. Hosp. Supply Corp., 1959-82; regional mgr. Am. Hosp. Supply Corp., New Eng., 1964-68; mktg. planning mgr. Am. Hosp. Supply Corp., 1968-69, mktg. services mgr., 1969-70; nat. sales mgr., v.p. mktg. Am. Critical Care div. Am. Hosp. Supply Corp., McGaw Park, Ill., 1970-73; pres. Am. Critical Care, 1973-82; pres. Health and Edn. Services Sector ARA Services, Inc., Phila., 1982-88; chmn., CEO Applied Immune Sci., Menlo Park, Calif., 1989-91; dir., chmn., CEO IMAGYN Med., Inc., Laguna Niguel, Calif., 1992-94, chmn. bd., 1995—; bd. dirs. Pacific Physician Svcs., Inc., Redlands, Calif., Independence One Bank, Mission Viejo, Calif., Radio Therapeutics, Inc., Mountain View, Calif., VISX, Santa Clara, Calif. Bd. dirs. Inroads, Chgo., 1976-80; mem. Dist. 106 Bd. Edn., 1977-81. Served with USNR, 1956-58. Mem. No. Ill. Indsl. Assn. (bd. dirs. 1979-82), El Niguel Country Club, Peninsula Golf and Country Club. Presbyterian.

FRENCH, KIRBY ALLAN, transportation engineer, computer programmer; b. San Angelo, Tex., Oct. 12, 1948; s. Leland Wayne French and Helen Lois (Stennet) French-Vance; m. Verda Jane Amyl Schaffer, Oct. 11, 1970; children: Tammy Lyrae, Adrian Allyn. Diploma in Computer Programming, Mkt. Tng. Inst., 1968. Transp. engr. Calif. Dept. Transp., San Bernardino, 1969—. Author: Speed Math, 1991, Trigonometric Formulas, 1991, Speed Reading, 1994. Mem. Profl. Engrs. in Calif. Govt. Home: 1257 Poplar St San Bernardino CA 92410 Office: Calif Dept Transp 247 W Third St San Bernardino CA 92401

FRENCH, PAMELA RENEE, computer and management consultant; b. Mpls., July 25, 1949; d. Ronald Charles and Ruby Jean (Bagstad) Blum; m. Kenneth Robert French, June 5, 1975. BS, U. Wis., 1971; MBA, U. N.Mex., 1989. Programmer Internat. Survey Rsch., Chgo., 1975-79; sr. sys. analyst Blue Cross/Blue Shield, Chgo., 1979-81; devel. ctr. leader bus. computing State of N.Mex., Santa Fe, 1981-85; from group leader to dep. divsn. dir. bus. computing Los Alamos Nat. Lab., 1985-93, staff cons., sr. mgmt., 1993—; commr. computing and info. sys. coun. State of N.Mex., Santa Fe., 1994—. Recipient scholarship No. States Power, 1967, Alpha Gamma Delta, 1970. Home: PO Box 853 Tesuque NM 87574-0853 Office: Los Alamos Nat Lab PO Box 1663 MS A122 Los Alamos NM 87545

FRENCH, STEPHEN WARREN, university administrator, educator, artist; b. Seattle, Sept. 6, 1934; s. George Warren and Madge Evelyn (Marshall) F. m. Hanna Clara Misch, June 10, 1956 (div. May 1971); children: Alexandra, Kenneth, Katharine; m. Toni Virginia Thunen, Aug. 14, 1974 (div. June 1979); 1 child, Elly Kinsell Thunen-French; m. Wanda Waldera, Oct. 19, 1990. BA, U. Wash., 1956, MFA, 1960. Instr. art dept. San Jose (Calif.) State U., 1960-61; from instr. to asst. prof. art dept. U. Wis., Madison, 1961-66; from asst. prof. to prof. San Jose State U., 1966—, assoc. dean Coll. Humanities and Arts, 1990—; vis. artist U. Wash., Seattle, 1972, 73, Mont. State U. Bozeman, 1970; mem. collections com. San Jose Mus. of Art, 1990—, mem. arts commn. City of San Jose, 1990-93, chair, 1993-94; vice chmn. conv. ctr. art selection com. City of San Jose, 1986-93; chmn. Art in Pub. Places Adv. Panel City of San Jose, 1991-93. One man show San Jose Mus., 1980; exhibited in group shows at Smithsonian Inst., Washington, 1965, Palace of the Legion of Honor, San Francisco, 1967, British Biennial of Graphic Art, 1969, 71, San Francisco Mus. of Modern Art, 1970. Mem. adv. com. San Jose Inst. of Contemporary Art. Sarah Denny fellow U. Wash., 1958. Mem. Coll. Art Assn., Nat. Assn. Schs. of Art & Design, Nat. Conf. of Art Adminstrs., Phi Beta Kappa, Phi Kappa Phi. Unitarian. Home: 1560 Four Oaks Cir San Jose CA 95131-2653 Office: San Jose State U 1 Washington Sq San Jose CA 95192-0088

FRENZEL, CHARLES ALFON, physics consultant; b. Port Arthur, Tex., Sept. 24, 1940; s. Alfon and Mary Estelle (Nichols) F.; m. Lydia Ann Melcher, June 2, 1973. BA in Physics, Vanderbilt U., 1969. Sr. rsch. engr. dept. elec. engring. U. Ky., Lexington, 1967-74; pres. Merlin Assocs. Inc., New Orleans, 1974-76, Coastal Sci. Assocs. Inc., Hammond, La., 1976-87; cons. on surface chemistry, Sutter Creek, Calif., 1987—; advisor to U.S. Rep. Dave Treen of La., 1982-83; tech. advisor CCI Svcs. Inc., 1987—; presenter profl. meetings. Exhbited in group shows at Roseville Arts Ctr., Calif, 1994; contbr. articles to profl. jours. Former mem. Pres. Eisenhower's Sci. Curriculum in Secondary Schs. Com. With USAF, 1966-67. Recipient best sci. paper of yr. award Jour. Can. Spectroscopy, 1970. Mem. N.Y. Acad. Scis., Sigma Xi.

FREUND, FREDRIC S., real estate broker, property manager; b. Denver, Sept. 23, 1930. AB, Brown U., 1952. Sr. v.p. Hanford, Freund & Co., San Francisco, 1973—; past adv. dir. Western Investment Real Estate Trust; bd. dirs. Berkeley Antibody Co.; instr. real estate mgmt. U. Calif. Ext.; guest lectr. Stanford U. Sch. Bus. Adminstrn. Commr. Calif. Senate Adv. Commn. on Cost Control in State Govt. Mem. Am. Soc. Real Estate Counselors (CRE, pres. no. Calif. 1987-88), San Francisco Bd. Realtors (pres. 1974-75, Realtor of Yr. 1975), Bldg. Owners & Mgrs. Assn. San Francisco, Realtors Nat. Mktg. Inst. (CCIM), Inst. Real Estate Mgmt. (CPM). Office: Hanford Freund & Co 47 Kearny St San Francisco CA 94108-5507

FREY, ALBERT, architect; b. Zurich, Switzerland, Oct. 18, 1903; came to U.S., 1930, naturalized, 1941; s. Albert and Ida (Meyer) F. Diploma architecture, Kantonales Technikum, Winterthur-Zurich, 1924. Architect with Le Corbusier, Paris, 1929; with architects' offices N.Y.C., Washington and; USDA, 1930-34, Palm Springs, Calif., 1934-37; with Philip L. Goodwin (architect on design Mus. Modern Art), 1937-39; pvt. practice architecture Palm Springs, Calif. Considered modernist master; works include Aluminaire House, L.I., N.Y., 1931 (now protected landmark, in exhnb. on internat. style Mus. Modern Art, N.Y., 1932), exhibitions include Columbia U., N.Y.C., 1993, UCSB, Palm Springs, Calif., 1993, Basel (Switzerland) Architecture Mus., 1995, Mus. Lausanne, Switzerland, 1995, Zurich, Switzerland, 1995, Gya Inst. ETH, Hönggerberg, 1995, also over 200 projects and works, mainly in Palm Springs; author: In Search of a Living Architecture, 1939; subject book: Albert Frey, Architect by Joseph Rosa, 1990, German edit., 1995. Fellow AIA. Office: Albert Frey Architect FAIA-E 686 Palisades Dr Palm Springs CA 92262-5644

FREY, HARVEY STUART, radiologist, law student; b. N.Y.C., Aug. 9, 1934; s. Louis Elliot and Lillian (Enker) F. BS in Physics, Calif. Inst. Tech., 1955; MD, UCLA, 1960, PhD in Med. Physics, 1968. Diplomate Am. Bd. Radiology (therapy). Asst. prof. radiol. therapy U. So. Calif., L.A., 1968-71; radiol. therapist St. John's Hosp., Santa Monica, Calif., 1971-73, Century City Hosp., Santa Monica, 1973-75, Western Tumor Med. Group, Santa Monica, 1975-85; NIH fellow UCLA, 1964-68; assoc. rsch. biologist UCLA, Santa Monica, 1985-88, clin assoc. prof. radiol. therapy, 1973—. Contbr. numerous articles to profl. jours. Capt. USA Spl. Forces, 1961-63. Mem. AAAS, UCLA Med. Alumni Assn. (sec. 1989), Radiation Rsch. Soc., European Soc. for Therapeutic Radiology & Oncology, Am. Endocurietherapy Soc. (co-founder, 1st pres.). Home: 552 12th St Santa Monica CA 90402-2908

FREYD, WILLIAM PATTINSON, fund raising executive, consultant; b. Chgo., Apr. 1, 1933; s. Paul Robert Freyd and Pauline Margaret (Pattinson) Gardiner; m. Diane Marie Carlson, May 19, 1984. BS in Fgn. Svc., Georgetown U., 1960. Field rep. Georgetown U., Washington, 1965-67; campaign dir. Tamblyn and Brown, N.Y.C., 1967-70; dir. devel. St. George's Ch., N.Y.C., 1971; assoc. Browning Assocs., Newark, 1972-73; regional v.p. C.W. Shaver Co., N.Y.C., 1973-74; founder, chmn. IDC, Boulder City, Nev., 1974—. Bd. dirs. Nev. Symphony Orch., 1994, N.J. Symphony Orch., 1991-94; apptd. Nev. Charitable Solicitation Task Force, 1994. Mem. Nat. Soc. Fund Raising Execs. (nat. treas. 1980-81, pres. N.Y. chpt. 1974-76, cert. 1982), Am. Assn. Fund Raising Counsel (sec. 1984-86), World Fund Raising Coun. (bd. dirs. 1995), N.Y. Yacht Club, Union League Club N.Y., Masons, Nassau Club, Circumnavigators Club. Office: IDC 2920 Green Valley Pky Ste 111 Henderson NV 89014-0407

FRIBERG, GEORGE JOSEPH, electronics company executive; m. Mary Seymour; children: Fane George, Felicia Lynn Friberg Clark. BSME, U. N.Mex., 1962, MBA, 1982, postgrad. Sales engr. Honeywell, L.A., 1962-64; laiason engr. ACF Industries, Albuquerque, 1964-66; quality assurance mgr. data systems div. Gulton Industries Inc., Albuquerque, 1966-72; mgr. mfg. Femco div. Gulton Industries Inc., Irwin (Pa.), High Point (N.C.), 1972-77; v.p. mfg. data systems div. Gulton Industries Inc., Albuquerque, 1977-86; pres., chief exec. officer Tetra Corp., Albuquerque, 1986-92, also bd. dirs.; pres., CEO Laguna Industries Inc., 1992—. Mem. N.Mex. R&D Gross Receipts Task Force, 1988-89; mem. Econ. Forum of Albuquerque; bd. dirs. Technet, 1983—, pres., 1983-84, 88-89; bd. dirs. RioTech, 1984—, treas., 1984-87; bd. dirs. Lovelace Sci. Resources subs. Lovelace Insts., 1988—, Bus. Industry Polit. Action Com., 1988-90, U. N.Mex. R.D. Anderson Bus. Sch. Found., 1988-92; bd. dirs. N.Mex. Bus. Innovation Ctr., 1986-92. Mem. Albuquerque C. of C. (bd. dirs. 1985—, polit. action com. 1983-84, chair Buy N.Mex. chpt. 1986-87, vice chmn. econ. affairs planning coun. 1987—, chmn. bd. 1990-91), N.Mex. Alumni Lettermen's Club (noonday bd. 1991, Hosanna Inc. bd. 1994—, editl. bd. N.Mex. bus. jour.). Home: 13234 Sunset Canyon Dr NE Albuquerque NM 87111-4220

FRICK, MR. See GROEBLI, WERNER FRITZ

FRICK, OSCAR LIONEL, physician, educator; b. N.Y.C., Mar. 12, 1923; s. Oscar and Elizabeth (Ringger) F.; m. Mary Hubbard, Sept. 2, 1954. A.B., Cornell U., 1944, M.D., 1946; M.Med. Sci., U. Pa., 1960; Ph.D., Stanford U., 1964. Diplomate: Am. Bd. Allergy and Immunology (chmn. 1967-72). Intern Babies Hosp., Columbia Coll. Physicians and Surgeons, N.Y.C., 1946-47; resident Children's Hosp., Buffalo, 1950-51; pvt. practice medicine specializing in pediatrics Huntington, N.Y., 1951-58; fellow in allergy and immunology Royal Victoria Hosp., Montreal, Que., Can., 1958-59; fellow in allergy U. Calif.-San Francisco, 1959-60, asst. prof. pediatrics, 1964-67, assoc. prof., 1967-72, prof., 1972—, dir. allergy tng. program, 1964—; fellow immunology Inst. d'Immunobiologie, Hosp. Broussais, Paris, France, 1960-62. Contbr. articles papers to profl. publs. Served with M.C., USNR, 1947-49. Mem. Am. Assn. Immunologists, Am. Acad. Pediatrics (chmn. allergy sect. 1971-72, Bret Ratner award 1982), Am. Acad. Allergy (exec. com. 1972—, pres. 1977-78), Internat. Assn. Allergology and Clin. Immunology (exec. com. 1970-73, sec. gen. 1985—), Am. Pediatric Soc. Club: Masons. Home: 370 Parnassus Ave San Francisco CA 94117-3609

FRICKE, MARTIN PAUL, science company executive; b. Franklin, Pa., May 18, 1937; s. Frank Albert and Pauline Jane (Wentz) F.; m. Barbara Ann Blanton, Jan. 3, 1959. BS, Drexel U., Phila., 1961; MS, U. Minn., 1964, PhD, 1967. Prog. mgr., group leader Gen. Atomics, San Diego, 1968-73; program mgr., divsn. mgr. Sci. Applications Internat. Corp., La Jolla, Calif., 1973-77, v.p., 1977-80, corp. v.p., 1980-84; sr. v.p. Systems Group, The Titan Corp., San Diego, Calif., 1984-87, exec. v.p. Techs Group, 1987-89, sr. v.p. corp. ops., 1989-93; mem. cross sect. evaluation working group, Upton, L.I., N.Y., 1970-73, U.S. Nuclear Data Com., Washington, 1970-73. Author publs. in field. Recipient postdoctoral fellowship U. Mich., Ann Arbor, 1967-68, scholarship Pa. Indsl. Chem. Co., 1956-60; grad. fellow Oak Ridge (Tenn.) Assoc. Univs., 1964-67. Fellow Am. Phys. Soc. (panel on pub. affairs 1982-84); mem. Phi Kappa Phi. Roman Catholic. Home: 2211 Caminito Preciosa Sur La Jolla CA 92037

FRIDLEY, SAUNDRA LYNN, internal audit executive; b. Columbus, Ohio, June 14, 1948; d. Jerry Dean and Esther Eliza (Bluhm) F. BS, Franklin U., 1976; MBA, Golden Gate U., 1980. Accounts receivable supr. Internat. Harvester, Columbus, Ohio, San Leandro, Calif., 1972-80; sr. internal auditor Western Union, San Francisco, 1980; internal auditor II, County of Santa Clara, San Jose, Calif., 1980-82; sr. internal auditor Tymshare, Inc., Cupertino, Calif., 1982-84, div. contr., 1984; internal audit mgr. VWR Scientific, Brisbane, Calif., 1984-88, audit dir., 1988-89; internal audit mgr. Pacific IBM Employees Fed. Credit Union, San Jose, 1989-90, Western Staff Svcs., Inc., Walnut Creek, Calif., 1990—; internal audit mgr., 1990-92; dir. quality assurance, 1992—; owner Dress Fore the 9's, Brentwood, Calif., 1994—; pres., founder Bay Area chpt. Cert. Fraud Examiners, 1990. Mem. NAFE, Friends of the Vineyards. Mem. Internal Auditors Speakers Bur., Cert. Fraud Examiners (founder, pres. Bay area chpt.), Inst. Internal Auditors (pres., founder Tri-Valley chpt.), Internal Auditor's Internat. Seminar Com., Internal Auditor's Internat. Conf. Com. Avocations: woodworking, gardening, golfing. Home: 19 Windmill Ct Brentwood CA 94513-2502 Office: Western Staff Svcs 301 Lennon Ln Walnut Creek CA 94598-2418 also: Dress Fore The 9's 613 1st St Ste 9 Brentwood CA 94513-1322

FRIED, ELAINE JUNE, business executive; b. L.A., Oct. 19, 1943; grad. Pasadena (Calif.) High Sch., 1963; various coll. courses; m. Howard I. Fried, Aug. 7, 1966; children: Donnover Michael, Randall Jay. Agt., office mgr. Howard I. Fried Agy., Alhambra, Calif., 1975—; v.p. Sea Hill, Inc., Pasadena, Calif., 1973-95. Publicity chmn., unit telephone chmn. San Gabriel Valley unit; past chmn. recipient certificate appreciation, 1987, Am. Diabetes Assn.; past publicity chmn. San Gabriel Valley region Women's Am. Orgn. for Rehab. Tng. (ORT); chmn. spl. events publicity, Temple Beth Torah Sisterhood, Alhambra, membership chmn., 1991-92, v.p. membership, 1991-93; former mem. bd. dirs., pub. relations com., pers. com. Vis. Nurses Assn., Pasadena and San Gabriel Valley, Recipient Vol. award So. Calif. affiliate Am. Diabetes Assn., 1974-77; chmn. outside Sisterhood publicity Congregation Shaarei Torah, 1993—, public rels. chair, 1993—. Co-recipient Ner Tamid award Temple Beth Torah. Contbr. articles to profl. jours. Clubs: ORT, Hadassah, Congregation Shaarei Torah Sisterhood. Speaker on psycho-social aspects of diabetes, insurance and the diabetic, ins. medicine. Home: 404 N Hidalgo Ave Alhambra CA 91801-2640

FRIED, LOUIS LESTER, information technology and management consultant; b. N.Y.C., Jan. 18, 1930; s. Albert and Tessie (Klein) F.; m. Haya Greenberg, Aug. 15, 1960; children: Ron Chaim, Eliana Ahuva, Gil Ben. BA in Pub. Adminstrn., Calif. State U., Los Angeles, 1962; MS in Mgmt. Theory, Calif. State U., Northridge, 1965. Mgr. br. plant data processing Litton systems, Inc., Woodland Hills, Calif., 1960-65; dir. mgmt. info. systems Bourns, Inc., Riverside, Calif., 1965-68, Weber Aircraft Co., Burbank, Calif., 1968-69; v.p. mgmt. services T.I. Corp. of Calif., Los Angeles, 1969-75; dir. advanced computer systems dept. Stanford Research Inst., Menlo Park, Calif., 1976-85, dir. ctr. for info. tech., 1985-86, dir. worldwide info. tech. practice, 1987-90; v.p. info. tech. cons. Stanford Rsch. Inst., Menlo Park, Calif., 1990—; cons. editor Auerbach Pubs., 1978—, Reston Pubs., 1979—; lectr. U. Calif., Riverside, 1965-69, lectr. mgmt. and EDP. Contbr. numerous articles to profl. jours., 2 textbooks. Mem. Assn. Systems Mgmt. Home: 788 Loma Verde Ave Palo Alto CA 94303-4147 Office: Stanford Rsch Inst Menlo Park CA 94025

FRIEDBERG, ALAN CHARLES, lawyer; b. Ft. Leavenworth, Kans., Dec. 22, 1945; s. Arnold Millard and Gisela Claire (Newkirk) F.; m. Jean Anderson, June 23, 1973; children—John, Michael. B.A. with honors, U. Va., 1967; J.D., Yale U., 1970. Bar: Va. 1970, Colo. 1973; U.S. Supreme Ct., 1994. Law clk. U.S. Ct. Appeals (10th cir.), Denver, 1974-75; dir. Pendleton & Sabian, P.C., Denver, 1975-95, Pendleton, Friedberg, Wilson, Hennessey & Meyer, P.C., 1995—. mem. faculty Nat. Inst. for Trial Adv., 1984, 85, 86; lectr. Continuing Legal Edn. of Colo., 1986—. Mem. ch. coun. Mt. Calvary Luth. Ch., Boulder, Colo., 1980-82, 89-91; adj. prof. law U. Denver, 1989—. Served as capt. JAG, U.S. Army, 1970-74. Decorated Bronze Star, Army Commendation medal, Vietnamese Cross of Gallantry, Vietnam Service medal. Mem. Denver Bar Assn. (vol. atty. pro bono program, Outstanding Young Lawyer of Yr. award 1981, past mem. interprofl., jud. selection and benefits com. jud. survey task force, pub. interest law com., exec. counsel young lawyers sect., chmn. 1979-80; chmn. legal service com. 1982-84), Colo. Bar Assn. (mem. bd. govs. 1992-94), ABA (mem. availability of legal services com.), Colo. Trial Lawyers Assn. (editor Trial Talk Mag. 1989—), Assn. Trial Lawyers Am., Nat. Inst. Trial Advocacy (mem. faculty, nat. sessions 1984-85, regional sessions 1984-86, deposition program 1988), Denver Law Club. Democrat. Club: Meadows (pres. 1986-87). Home: 275 Pawnee Dr Boulder CO 80303-3730 Office: Pendleton Friedberg Wilson Hennessey & Meyer PC 303 17th Ave Ste 1000 Denver CO 80203-1263

FRIEDENBERG, WALTER DREW, journalist; b. Meriden, Conn., Dec. 22, 1928; s. Gustav Edward and Adela (Drews) F.; m. Ramona Avila, May 29, 1965; children: Christopher Drew, Eric Avila, Karina Della. BA, Wake Forest U., 1949; AM, Harvard U., 1956; postgrad., U. Chgo., 1959. Reporter Rocky Mount (N.C.) Evening Telegram, 1949-50, Winston-Salem (N.C.) Jour., 1950, richmond (Va.) Times-Dispatch, 1954, Buffalo Evening News, summer 1956; fellow Inst. Current World Affairs, N.Y., 1956-60; stringer Chgo. Daily News, Fgn. News Svc., 1960; reporter Pitts. Press, 1960-61; fgn. corr. in Europe, Africa and Asia Scripps-Howard Newspaper Alliance, Washington, 1961-66, editl. writer, 1966-69; editor Cin. Post, 1969-77; European corr. Scripps-Howard Newspapers, London, 1977-79; fgn. affairs corr. Scripps Howard News Svc., Washington, 1979-81; exec. editor Santa Fe New Mexican, 1991-92; tchr. sch. journalism Ohio U. 2d lt. U.S. Army, 1951-53. Mem. Quail Run Club, Phi Beta Kappa, Omicron Delta Kappa. Address: 630 W San Francisco St # B Santa Fe NM 87501-1490 Office: Ohio U Scripps Sch Journalism Athens OH 45701-2979

FRIEDERICH, MARY ANNA, gynecology and obstetrics consultant; b. Rochester, N.Y., Nov. 15, 1931; d. Lewis Weniger and Mary Jasper (McGinnis) F.; m. John S. Savage (div. 1987); stepchildren: Steven T. Savage, Scott Allen Savage, Sandra Sue Savage DellaVilla. BA, Cornell U., 1953; MD, U. Rochester, 1957. Diplomate Am. Bd. Ob-Gyn. Intern in ob-gyn. and surgery U. Rochester, N.Y., 1957-58, asst. resident ob-gyn, 1958-59, assoc. resident and fellow ob-gyn and psychiatry, 1959-60, resident and instr. ob-gyn to chief resident, 1960-62, sr. instr. ob-gyn and psychiatry, 1963-66, asst. prof. in ob-gyn and psychiatry, 1966-68, assoc. prof. ob-gyn and psychiatry, 1968-76, clin. assoc. prof. in ob-gyn and psychiatry, 1976-86; med. dir. Planned Parenthood of Cen. and No. Ariz., 1986-89; sr. assoc. cons. in gyn. Mayo Clinc, Scottsdale, Ariz., 1990-91; med. dir. Ariz. Physicians I.P.A., 1989-93; assoc. Maricopa County Medicine Assocs., 1991-94; Maricpar Faculty Assn., 1994—; sr. assoc. ob-gyn and psychiatry Strong Meml. Hosp. of U. Rochester, 1976-84, attending ob-gyn, 1985-87; staff in gynecology Good Samaritan Hosp., Phoenix; attending ob-gyn Maricpar Med. Ctr., 1994—; speaker and presenter in field. Editor: Psychosomatic Medicine, Women's Health, Human Sexuality, Jour. of Psychosomatic Ob-Gyn, Social Sci. Medicine, Jour. of Reproductive Medicine, Ob-Gyn, Jour AMA; contbr. numerous articles to profl. jours. Bd. pensions United Meth. Ch. Western N.Y. Conf., 1975-84; bd. dirs. Rochester United Meth. Homes, Goodman Gardens, 1970-82, pres. 1979-82; chairperson personnel com. Alternatives for Battered Women, 1979-81; adminstrv. bd. Asbury First United Meth. Ch., 1984-86; bd. dirs. United Cancer Coun., 1985-86; chairperson program com. Women's Coalition of Health Ann. Health Confs., 1985-86. Mem. AMA, Am. Coll. Ob-Gyn, Am. Med. Women's Assn., Soc. for Sex Therapy and Rsch. (bd. dirs. 1983-85), Am. Soc. Colposcopy and Cervical Pathology, Am. Soc. for Psychosomatic Ob-Gyn (past pres., sec., treas., historian), Soc. for Menstrual Cycle Rsch. (sec., treas. 1981—), Assn. of Reproductive Health Profls., Phoenix Ob-Gyn Soc., Maricopa County Med. Soc., Ariz. State Med. Soc. Republican. Methodist. Home: 10559 N 104th Pl Scottsdale AZ 85258-4941

FRIEDHEIM, ROBERT LYLE, political scientist, educator; b. N.Y.C., Aug. 1, 1934; s. Joseph and Blanche (Vogel) F.; m. Robin Rudolph; children: Jessica Faulkner, Amy. AB, Columbia Coll., 1955; MA, Columbia U., 1957; PhD, U. Wash., 1962. Teaching asst., predoctoral assoc. U. Wash., 1958-61; from asst. prof. to assoc. prof. polit. sci. Purdue U., 1961-66; dir. law of sea project, profl. staff mem. Ctr. for Naval Analysis, Arlington, Va., 1966-76; prof. internat. rels., assoc. dir. inst. for marine studies U. So. Calif., 1976-89, dir. sea grant program, 1980-89, dir. sch. internat. rels., 1992—; advisor U.S. Arctic Rsch. Commn., 1986—; mem. adv. panel Office Tech. Assessment U.S. Congress, 1988-89; mem. internat. ocean sci. policy com. bd. ocean sci. and policy Nat. Rsch. Coun.; lectr., invited visitor Nat. Bur. Oceanography, Beijing, 1984; mem. adv. group Ocean Policy Roundtable, Woods Hole, 1993; del. Commn. of Califs., 1978-80. Editor: Jour. Ocean and Coastal Mgmt., Ocean Devel. and Internat. Law Jour.; contbr. articles to profl. jours. and chpts. to books; author: Negotiating the New Ocean Regime, 1993, The Seattle General Strike, 1964, (with others) Japan and the New Ocean Regime, 1984, Forecasting Outcomes of Multilateral Negotiations: Methodology, Vol. 1, 1977, The Navy and the Common Sea, 1972, others. Grantee NSF, 1978-80, 1977-78, 1974-75, ONR, 1978-80; CNA fellow, 1971-72. Mem. Am. Soc. Internat. Law, Internat. Studies Assn. (chair internat. orgn. sect. 1970-73, mem. adv. bd. environ. studies sect. 1989—). Office: U So Calif Sch Internat Rel Von Kleinsmid Ctr Rm 330 Los Angeles CA 90089

FRIEDHOFF, RICHARD MARK, computer scientist, entrepreneur; b. N.Y.C., Dec. 2, 1953; s. Arnold Jerome and Frances (Galanter) F.; m. Livia R. Antola, May 5, 1988. BA, Columbia U., 1976; MA, Yale U., 1978. Sci. cons. PBS's The Brain, N.Y.C., 1978-80; industry adviser Polaroid Corp., Cambridge, Mass., 1981-82; v.p. Internat. Sci. Exch., N.Y.C., 1982-85; pres. Visicom Corp., L.A., 1986-93; CEO, dir. rsch. InGen Corp., 1994—; cons. U. Calif., 1990-91, Silicon Graphics Inc., Rowland Inst. Sci.; spkr. Smithsonian Instn., also various corps. and sci. socs., 1989—. Author: Visualization: The 2nd Computer Revolution, 1989, 2d edit., 1991; contbr. articles to profl. jours. Dir. S & A Friedhoff Found. Fellow AAAS; mem. IEEE, Soc. for Photo Optical Instrumentation, Assn. for Computing Machinery, Authors Guild of Am., N.Y. Acad. Scis., Phi Beta Kappa. Office: InGen Corp 235 Montgomery St San Francisco CA 94104

FRIEDL, RICK, former academic administrator, lawyer; b. Berwyn, Ill., Aug. 31, 1947; s. Raymond J. and Ione L. (Anderson) F.; m. Diane Marie Guillies, Sept. 2, 1977; children: Richard, Angela, Ryan. BA, Calif. State U., Northridge, 1969; MA, UCLA, 1976; postgrad. UCLA, 1984; JD Western State U., 1987. Bar: Calif. 1988, U.S. Dist. Ct. (ctrl. dist.) Calif., 1992. Dept. mgr. Calif. Dept. Indsl. Rels., 1973-78; mem. faculty dept. polit. sci. U. So. Calif., 1978-80; pres. Pacific Coll. Law, 1981-86; staff counsel state fund, Calif., 1988-89; prin. Law Offices of Rick Friedl, 1989—. Author: The Political Economy of Cuban Dependency, 1982; tech. editor Glendale Law Rev., 1984; contbr. articles to profl. jours. Calif. State Grad. fellow, 1970-72. Mem. ABA, Calif. State Bar Assn., Los Angeles County Bar Assn., Am. Polit. Sci. Assn., Latin Am. Studies Assn., Acad. Polit. Sci., Pacific Coast Council Latin Am. Studies, Calif. Trial Lawyers Assn. Home: PO Box 2095 California City CA 93504-0095

FRIEDLAND, JACK ARTHUR, plastic surgeon; b. East Chicago, Ind., Feb. 10, 1940; s. Peter and Bettye (Manfield) F.; m. Harriet Anita Simensky, July 1, 1962; children: Margo Lynn, Jonathan Elliott, Julie I. Student, U. Wis., 1958-61; BS, Northwestern U., 1962, MD, 1965. Diplomate Am. Bd. of Surgery, Am. Bd. of Plastic Surgery, Nat. Bd. Med. Examiners. Intern in surgery NYU/Bellevue Med. Ctr., N.Y.C., 1965-66, from surg. resident to chief resident, 1966-70; resident in plastic surgery Inst. Reconstructive Plastic Surgery NYU Med. Ctr., N.Y.C., 1972-74; pvt. practice Phoenix, 1974—; chief of staff children's rehab. svc. State of Ariz., 1984-86; asst. chief of staff Phoenix Plastic Surgery Residency Program, 1974-84; attending physician Phoenix Plastic Surgery Fellowship/Mayo Clinic Residency Programs, 1985—; chief of surgery St. Luke's Hosp. Med. Ctr., Phoenix, 1981-83; chief of plastic surgery Children's Hosp., Phoenix, 1984-86; extra-mural asst. prof. plastic surgery Mayo Med. Sch., 1991—. Bd. dirs. men's arts coun. Phoenix Art Mus., 1975—, Am. Heart Assn., Phoenix, 1985-89, MADD, Phoenix, 1985-86. Maj. USAF, 1970-72. Fellow ACS; mem. AMA, Am. Soc. for Aesthetic Plastic Surgery, Inc. (pres. 1990-91), Am. Soc. Plastic and Reconstructive Surgeons, Am. Assn. Plastic Surgeons, Am. Cleft-Palate-Craniofacial Assn., Ariz. Med. Assn., Maricopa County Med. Assn., Ariz. Soc. Plastic and Reconstructive Surgeons, U. Club of Phoenix (bd. dirs. 1974-84, past pres.), Alpha Omega Alpha. Office: 101 E Coronado Rd Phoenix AZ 85004-1512

FRIEDLANDER, CHARLES DOUGLAS, investment company executive, space consultant; b. N.Y.C., Oct. 5, 1928; s. Murray L. and Jeane (Sottosanti) F.; m. Diane Mary Hutchins, May 12, 1951; children: Karen Diane, Lauren Patrice, Joan Elyse. BS, U.S. Mil. Acad., 1950; exec. mgmt. program, NASA, 1965; grad., Command and Staff Coll. USAF, 1965, Air War Coll. USAF, 1966. Command. 2d lt. U.S. Army, 1950, advanced through grades to 1st lt.; officer inf. U.S. Army, Korea, 1950-51; resigned U.S. Army, 1954; mem. staff UN Forces, Trieste, Italy, 1953-54; chief astronaut support office NASA, Cape Canaveral, Fla., 1963-67; space cons. CBS News, N.Y.C., 1967-69; exec. asst. The White House, Washington, 1969-71; pres. Western

Ranchlands Inc., Scottsdale, Ariz., 1971-74, Fairland Co. Inc., Scottsdale, 1974—; v.p. bd. dirs. Internat. Aerospace Hall of Fame, San Diego; space program cons., various cos., Boca Raton, Fla., 1967-69; mem. staff First Postwar Fgn. Ministers Conf., Berlin, 1954; radio/TV cons. space program. Author: Buying & Selling Land for Profit, 1961, Last Man at Hungnam Beach, 1952. V.p. West Point Soc., Cape Canaveral, Fla., 1964. Served to lt. col. USAFR, maj. USAR. Decorated Bronze Star V, Combat Inf. badge; co-recipient Emmy award CBS TV Apollo Moon Landing, 1960. Mem. Nat. Space Club, Explorer's Club, West Point Soc., Chosin Few Survivors Korea, NASA Alumni League.

FRIEDLANDER, SHELDON KAY, chemical engineering educator; b. N.Y.C., Nov. 17, 1927; s. Irving and Rose (Katzewitz) F.; m. Marjorie Ellen Robbins, Apr. 16, 1934; children: Eva Kay, Amelie Elise, Antonia Zoe, Josiah. BS, Columbia U., 1949; SM, MIT, 1951; PhD, U. Ill., 1954. Asst. prof. chem. engrng. Columbia U., N.Y.C., 1954-57; asst. prof. chem. engrng. Johns Hopkins, Balt., 1957-59, assoc. prof. chem. engrng., 1959-62, prof. chem. engrng., 1962-64; prof. chem. engrng., environ. health engrng. Calif. Inst. Tech., Pasadena, 1964-78; prof. chem. engrng. UCLA, 1978—, Parsons prof., 1982—, chmn. dept. chem. engrng., 1984-88; now dir. Engrng. Rsch. Ctr. for Hazardous Substance Control, Los Angeles; chmn. steering com. Ctr. for Clean Tech. UCLA, 1989-92; chmn. EPA Clean Air Sci. Adv. Com., 1978-82. Author: Smoke, Dust, and Haze, 1977. Served with U.S. Army, 1946-47. Recipient Sr. Humboldt prize Fed. Republic of Germany, 1985, Internat. prize Am. Assn. for Aerosol Rsch./Gesellschaft für Aerosolforschung/Japan Assn. for Aerosol Sci. and Tech., Fuchs Meml. award, 1990; Fulbright scholar, 1960-61; Guggenheim fellow, 1969-70. Mem. NAE, Am. Inst. Chem. Engrs. (Colburn award 1959, Alpha Chi Sigma award 1974, Walker award 1979, Lawrence K. Cecil award in environ. chem. engrng. 1995), Am. Assn. for Aerosol Research (pres. 1984-86). Office: UCLA Dept Chem Engring 5531 Boelter Hall Los Angeles CA 90024

FRIEDMAN, ALAN IRA, make-up artist; b. Inglewood, Calif., July 23, 1952; s. Albert and Adelaide Sylvia (Cassell) F.; m. Janice Gail Rudof (div. 1976); m. Eileen Margaret Fuentes, Dec. 30, 1984. AA, Valley State U., 1972; BA, Calif. State U., Northridge, 1974. Cert. profl. make-up instr., Calif. Make-up instr. Joe Blaslo Make-Up Ctr.; make-up artist Paramount Pictures, Warner Bros., Disney Studios, others, Hollywood, Calif.; seminar/craft pres. IATSE Local 706, North Hollywood, Calif. Home: PO Box 2228 Toluca Lake CA 91610-0228

FRIEDMAN, ARTHUR MEEKER, magazine editor, professional motorcycle racer; b. Chgo., Mar. 19, 1948; s. Arthur and Marchia Lois Friedman; m. Marjorie Eiko Naoye, Nov. 18, 1984; children: Brough Shepard (dec.), James Kazuo, Christen Miya. B.A. in History, Beloit Coll., 1971. Editor Cycle News West, Long Beach, Calif., 1972-74; sr. editor Cycle Guide, Compton, Calif., 1974-78; assoc. editor Motorcyclist Mag., L.A., 1978-80, editor, 1980-93, sr. editor, 1993—. Contbr. articles to mags., 1972—. Named mem. Endurance Racing Team of Yr., Western-Eastern Roadracing Assn., 1981. Office: Motorcyclist Mag 6420 Wilshire Blvd Los Angeles CA 90048-5515

FRIEDMAN, BRUCE DAVID, real estate and finance executive; b. San Francisco, May 20, 1957; s. John and Barbara F.; m Carolyn; children: Martha, Michael. B in History, U. Calif., Berkeley, 1975-80. Owner Penguin Records, San Francisco; owner, pres., dir. Gold's Gym 2nd St., San Francisco, 1988—; pres., CEO BPH Mortgage, San Francisco, 1993—; sr. v.p. Robert Wolfe & Assocs., San Francisco, 1995—. Program chmn. Econ. Round Table of San Francisco, 1993-94, pres. 1994-95. Office: Robert Wolfe & Assocs 221 Main St # 1550 San Francisco CA 94105

FRIEDMAN, DIANA PATRICIA, editor; b. Santiago, Chile, May 8, 1958; came to the U.S., 1981; naturalized, 1989; d. Leon and Louisa (Drapkin) Zeldis; m. Stanley Jampole, Oct. 16, 1981 (div. July, 1985); m. Joseph Friedman, Aug. 28, 1993. BA, Tel Aviv U., Israel, 1983; MA, Ariz. State U., 1984, MBA, 1989. Investment unit mgr. Mfs. Assn. of Israel, Tel Aviv, 1985-86; asst. editor Pacific Sociological Assn., Tempe, Ariz., 1989-91; support coord. Ctr. for Profl. Devel., Scottsdale, Ariz., 1991-95; bus. cons., Scottsdale, 1985—. Mem. Beta Gamma Sigma, Alpha Kappa Delta. Jewish. Home: 5508 E Karen Dr Scottsdale AZ 85254-8208

FRIEDMAN, DONALD M., English language educator; b. N.Y.C., Apr. 8, 1929; s. Morley Sidney and Lillian (Berlin) F.; m. Stephanie Judith Diamond, June 14, 1959; children: Elliot Michael, Gabriel Diamond. BA, Columbia U., 1949, Trinity Coll., Cambridge, Eng., 1951; MA, Trinity Coll., Cambridge, Eng., 1958; PhD, Harvard U., 1960. Supr. Trinity Coll., Cambridge, 1951-53; instr. Harvard U., Cambridge, Mass., 1960-61; from asst. prof. to prof. English U. Calif., Berkeley, 1961—; cons. Calif. Humanities Project, 1982-87, State Dept. of Edn., 1986-87. Served with U.S. Army, 1954-56, Japan. Author: Marvell's Pastoral Art, 1970. John Simon Guggenheim Found. fellow, 1974-75; U. Calif. Humanities Rsch. fellow, 1969-70, 91. Mem. MLA, Renaissance Soc. Am., Milton Soc. Am. (exec. bd. 1992-94), John Donne Soc., Phi Beta Kappa (exec. bd. 1991—, Excellence in Teaching award 1994). Home: 2933 Magnolia St Berkeley CA 94705-2329

FRIEDMAN, EMANUEL, physician, educator; b. Jersey City, N.J., Nov. 27, 1922. BS in Acctg. cum laude, L.I. U., 1942; BA in Zoology with honors, U. Calif., Berkeley, 1948; MD, U. Calif., San Francisco, 1952. Diplomate Am. Bd. Internal Medicine, Am. Bd. Gastroenterology. Rotating intern Jewish Hosp. of Bklyn., 1952-53; resident in internal medicine VA Hosp., Bronx, N.Y., 1953-55; resident in gastroenterology VA Hosp., West Haven, Conn., 1955-57; mem. hosp. staff Mills-Peninsula Hosp., Burlingame, Calif., Seton Med. Ctr., Daly City, Calif., U. Calif. Hosps., San Francisco; clin. instr. medicine Stanford (Calif.) U., 1959-69; cons. gastroenterology U. Hawaii Postgrad. Med. Edn. Program, Ctrl. Okinawa Hosp., Gushikawa City, 1973, 76, 94; vis. prof. medicine & gastroenterology Hadassan Med. Sch., Jerusalem, Israel, 1980; clin. prof. medicine U. Calif., San Francisco, 1980—; pres. MidPeninsula Physicians Med. Group, Inc., 1985; chief of staff Peninsula Hosp. and Med. Ctr., 1969-71, chmn. divsn. gastroenterology, 1971—. Pres. bd. dirs. Jewish Home for the Aged, San Francisco, 1989—; past chmn. Jewish Community Rels. Coun., San Mateo County, Jewish Community Fedn. Campaign, San Mateo County; bd. dirs. Jewish Community Fedn. San Francisco, San Mateo & Marin; v.p., bd. dirs. AIPAC No. Calif.; bd. dirs. Holocaust Ctr. No. Calif.; guest lectr. Middle Eastern affairs San Francisco City Coll.; acting med. dir. Am. Joint Distbn. Com. Med. Clinic, Addis Ababa, Ethiopia, 1990. Fellow ACP; mem. AMA, Am. Gastroent. Assn., Am. Soc. for Gastroent. Endoscopy, Am. Soc. for Internal Medicine, No. Calif. Soc. for Clin. Gastroenterology (pres. 1977), Calif. Soc. for Internal Medicine, Calif. Med. Assn., San Mateo County Med. Soc. (bd. dirs., legis. liaison com., fee rev. com., budget & fin. com.).

FRIEDMAN, GARY DAVID, epidemiologist, research facility administrator; b. Cleve., Mar. 8, 1934; s. Howard N. and Cema C. F.; m. Ruth Helen Schleien, June 22, 1958; children: Emily, Justin, Richard. Student, Antioch Coll., 1951-53; BS in Biol. Sci., U. Chgo., 1956, MD with honors, 1959; MS in Biostatics, Harvard Sch. Pub. Health, 1965. Diplomate Am. Bd. Internal Medicine. Intern, resident Harvard Med. Svcs., Boston City Hosp., 1959-61; 2d yr. resident Univ. Hosps. Cleve., 1961-62; med. officer heart disease epidemiology study Nat. Heart Inst., Framingham, Mass., 1962-66; chief epidemiology unit, field and tng. sta., heart disease ctrl. program USPHS, San Francisco, 1966-68; sr. epidemiologist divsn. rsch. Kaiser Permanente Med. Care Program, Oakland, Calif., 1968-76, asst. dir. epidemiology and biostatics, 1976-91, dir., 1991—; rsch. fellow, then rsch. assoc. preventive medicine Harvard Med. Sch., 1962-66; lectr. dept. biomedical and environ. health scis., sch. pub. health U. Calif. Berkeley, 1968—; lectr. epidemiology and biostatics U. Calif. Sch. Medicine, San Francisco, 1980—, asst. clin. prof. 1967-75, assoc. clin. prof., 1975-92 depts. medicine and family and community medicine; mem. U.S.-USSR working group sudden cardiac death Nat. Heart, Lung and Blood Inst., 1975-82, com. on epidemiology and veterans follow-up studies Nat. Rsch. Coun., 1980-85, subcommittee on twins, 1980—, epidemiology and disease ctrl. study sect. NIH, 1982-86, U.S. Preventive Svcs. Task Force, 1984-88, scientific rev. panel on toxic air contaminants State of Calif., 1988—, adv. com. Merck Found./Soc. Epidemiol. Rsch., Clin. Epidemiology Fellowships, 1990-94; sr. advisor expert panel on preventive svcs. USPHS, 1991—. author: Primer of Epidemiology, 1974, 2d edit., 1980, 3d edit., 1987, 4th edit., 1994; assoc. editor, then mem. editl. bd. Am. Jour. Epidemiology, 1988—; mem. editl. bd. HMO Practice, 1991—; contbr. over 200 articles to profl. jours., chpts. to books. Oboist San Francisco Recreation Symphony, 1990—; bd. dirs. Chamber Musicians No. Calif., Oakland, 1991—. Sr. surgeon USPHS, 1962-68. Recipient Roche award for Outstanding Performance as Med. Student; Merit grantee Nat. Cancer Inst., 1987, Outstanding Investigator grantee, 1989; named to Disting. Alumni Hall of Fame Cleve. Heights High Sch., 1991. Fellow Am. Heart Assn. (chmn. com. on criteria and methods 1969-71, chmn. program com. 1973-76, coun. epidemiol.), Am. Coll. Physicians; mem. APHA, Am. Epidemiol. Soc. (mem. com. 1982-86), Am. Soc. Preventive Oncology, Internat. Epidemiol. Assn., Internat. Soc. Twin Studies, Soc. Epidemiologic Rsch., Phi Beta Kappa, Alpha Omega Alpha, Delta Omega. Office: Kaiser Permanente Med Care Program Divsn Rsch 3505 Broadway Oakland CA 94611-5714

FRIEDMAN, GLORIA A., tennis coach; D. Nicholas Alexander and Ethel Agnes (Kalionzes) Pananides; m. Gary Thomas Friedman; children: Lori Nicole, Gary Thomas. AA, Bakersfield (Calif.) Jr. Coll., 1971; BA, U. Calif., Santa Barbara, 1973; Secondary Teaching Credential, Calif. State U., 1975, MA, 1977. Head coach women's tennis, assoc. athletic dir. Calif. State U., Bakersfield; tennis rep. So. Calif. Women's Intercollegiate Athletic Conf., 1974, 75, 76, Pacific Coast Theltic Conf., 1979, 80, 81, Calif. Collegiate Athletic Assn., 1985; tournament official Jr. Coll. and Div. II divs. Ojai Tennis Championships, 1980—; tournament dir. Roadrunner Tennis Classic, 1979-85; organizer NCAA Nat. Div. II Women's Tennis Championships, 1985—; camp dir. instr. Roadrunner Summer Tennis Camps, 1986—. Faculty rep. dean's adv. com. Calif. State U., 1983, 83, mem. substance abuse com., 1986—, chairperson Student's Athletic Assistance Program, 1987—. Named NCAA Nat. Coach of Yr. for Div. II Women's Tennis, 1987, Calif. Collegiate Athletic Assn. Coach of Yr., 1983. Mem. Bakersfield Tennis Patrons (ex-officio bd. dirs. 1978—), Kern County Tennis Council (bd. dirs. 1985—). Greek Orthodox. Office: Calif State U 912 Vista Verde Way Bakersfield CA 93309-2363

FRIEDMAN, JULES DANIEL, geologist; b. Poughkeepsie, N.Y., Oct. 24, 1928; s. Jack and Sophie (Seltzer) F.; m. Linda Diane Wheelock Sluss, May 2, 1988; children from previous marriage: Susanne K., Jack A., Lisa K.; 1 stepchild, Lori Midson. AB, Cornell U., 1950; MS, Yale U., 1952, PhD, 1958. Geologist, br. mil. geology U.S. Geol. Survey, Washington, 1953-64, geologist, br. theoretical and applied geophysics, 1964-72; geologist, br. geophysics U.S. Geol. Survey, Denver, 1973—, chief remote sensing sect., 1982-85; rep. to U.S. Army Corps Engrs. U.S. Geol. Survey, 1959; advisor to Mex. Govt., 1969, NASA, 1969, 70, Brazilian govt., 1970, Nat. Rsch. Coun. Iceland, 1966-71, USN, 1971-72; cons. tech. assistance program UN, 1971; U.S. Geol. Survey rep. Skylab visual observations team Johnson Space Ctr., NASA, 1975. Contbr. numerous articles to profl. jours. Recipient Group Achievement award NASA, 1974, Quality of Scientific Work award, 1979. Fellow Geol. Soc. Am.; mem. Am. Geophys. Union (sec., exec. com., front range br. 1982-83). Home: PO Box 471 Wheat Ridge CO 80034-0471 Office: US Geol Survey MS 964 Denver Fed Ctr Denver CO 80225

FRIEDMAN, KENNETH TODD, investment banker. BSBA, Lewis and Clark Coll., 1979; MBA, Harvard U., 1983. Fin. analyst Dresser Industries, L.A., 1979-80; fin. cons. Am. Appraisal, L.A., 1980-81; mng. dir. Houlihan, Lokey, Howard & Zukin, L.A., 1983-90; pres. Houlihan, Lokey, Howard & Zukin Capital, L.A., 1986-90, Friedman Enterprises, L.A., 1990—.

FRIEDMAN, LAWRENCE M., law educator; b. Chgo., Apr. 2, 1930; s. I. M. and Ethel (Shapiro) F.; m. Leah Feigenbaum, Mar. 27, 1955; children: Jane, Amy. AB, U. Chgo., 1948, JD, 1951, LLM, 1953; LLD (hon.), U. Puget Sound, 1977, CUNY, 1989, U. of Lund, Sweden, 1993; JD, John Marshall Law Sch., 1995. Mem. faculty St. Louis U., 1957-61, U. Wis., 1961-68; prof. law Stanford U., 1968—, Marion Rice Kirkwood prof., 1976—; David Stouffer Meml. lectr. Rutgers U. Law Sch., 1969; Sibley lectr. U. Ga. Law Sch., 1976; Wayne Morse lectr. U. Oreg., 1985; Childress meml. lectr. St. Louis U., 1987; Jefferson Meml. lectr. U. Calif., 1994. Author: Contract Law in America, 1965, Government and Slum Housing, 1968, A History of American Law, 1973, 2d edit., 1985, The Legal System: A Social Science Perspective, 1975, Law and Society: An Introduction, 1977, (with Robert V. Percival) The Roots of Justice, 1981, American Law, 1984, Total Justice, 1985, Your Time Will Come, 1985, The Republic of Choice, 1990, Crime and Punishment in American History, 1993; co-editor: (with Stewart Macaulay) Law and the Behavioral Sciences, 1969, 2d edit., 1977, (with Harry N. Scheiber) American Law and the Constitutional Order, 1978; contbr. articles to profl. jours. Served with U.S. Army, 1953-54. Recipient Triennial award Order of Coif, 1976, Willard Hurst prize, 1982, Harry Kalven prize, 1992, Silver Gavel award ABA, 1994; Ctr. for Advanced Study in Behavioral Sci. fellow, 1974-75, fellow Inst. Advanced Study, Berlin, 1985. Mem. Law and Soc. Assn. (pres. 1979-81), Am. Acad. Arts and Scis., Am. Soc. for Legal History (v.p. 1987-89, pres. 1990-91). Home: 724 Frenchmans Rd Palo Alto CA 94305-1005 Office: Stanford U Law Sch Nathan Abbott Way Stanford CA 94305-9991

FRIEDMAN, LEE STEVEN, public policy educator; b. N.Y.C., Aug. 10, 1946; s. Oliver and Beverly Norma (Wachtel) F.; m. Janet Angela Flammang, Dec. 11, 1982; children: Alexander Flammang, Jacob Flammang. AB cum laude, Dartmouth Coll., 1968; MPhil in Econs., Yale U., 1970, PhD in Econs., 1973. Prof. pub. policy U. Calif., Berkeley, 1974—; acting dean Grad. Sch. Pub. Policy, U. Calif., 1993, assoc. dean, 1993—; instr. Exec. Inst. Pub. Mgmt., 1989-90; tng. instr. Calif. Pub. Utilities Commn., 1988—; mem. external adv. com. Calif. EPA, 1993-94; mem. Calif. energy task force U. Calif., 1986-91; mem. rev. panel pay equity project Nat. Acad. Scis., 1986; cons. Nat. Econ. Devel. and Law Ctr.; mem. adv. panel NSF, 1981. Author: Microeconomic Policy Analysis, 1984; editor: Jour. Policy Analysis & Mgmt., 1989—. Recipient David N. Kershaw award Princeton U./Assn. Pub. Policy Analysis & Mgmt., 1985. Office: U Calif Grad Sch Pub Policy 2607 Hearst Ave Berkeley CA 94709-1005

FRIEDMAN, MILTON, economist, educator emeritus, author; b. Brooklyn, N.Y., July 31, 1912; s. Jeno Saul and Sarah Ethel (Landau) F.; m. Rose Director, June 25, 1938; children: Janet, David. AB, Rutgers U., 1932, LLD (hon.), 1968; AM, U. Chgo., 1933; PhD, Columbia U., 1946; LLD (hon.), St. Paul's (Rikkyo) U., 1963, Loyola U., 1971, U. N.H., 1975, Harvard U., 1979, Brigham Young U., 1980, Dartmouth Coll., 1980, Gonzaga U., 1981; DSc (hon.), Rochester U., 1971; LHD (hon.), Rockford Coll., 1969, Roosevelt U., 1975, Hebrew Union Coll., Los Angeles, 1981, Jacksonville U., 1993; LittD (hon.), Bethany Coll., 1971; PhD (hon.), Hebrew U., Jerusalem, 1977; DCS (hon.), Francisco Marroquín U., Guatemala, 1978. Assoc. economist Nat. Resources Com., Washington, 1935-37; mem. research staff Nat. Bur. Econ. Research, N.Y.C., 1937-45, 1948-81; vis. prof. econs. U. Wis., Madison, 1940-41; prin. economist, tax research div. U.S. Treasury Dept., Washington, 1941-43; assoc. dir. research, statis. research group, War Research div. Columbia U., N.Y.C., 1943-45; assoc. prof. econs. and statistics U. Minn., Mpls., 1945-46; assoc. prof. econs. U. Chgo., 1946-48, prof. econs., 1948-62, Paul Snowden Russell disting. service prof. econs., 1962-82, prof. emeritus, 1983—; Fulbright lectr. Cambridge U., 1953-54; vis. Wesley Clair Mitchell research prof. econs. Columbia U., N.Y.C., 1964-65; fellow Ctr. for Advanced Study in Behavioral Sci., 1957-58; sr. research fellow Hoover Inst., Stanford U., 1977—; mem. Pres.'s Commn. All-Vol. Army, 1969-70, Pres.'s Commn. on White House Fellows, 1971-74, Pres.'s Econ. Policy Adv. Bd., 1981-88; vis. scholar Fed. Res. Bank, San Francisco, 1977. Author: (with Carl Shoup and Ruth P. Mack) Taxing to Prevent Inflation, 1943, (with Simon S. Kuznets) Income from Independent Professional Practice, 1946, (with Harold A. Freeman, Frederic Mosteller, W. Allen Wallis) Sampling Inspection, 1948, Essays in Positive Economics, 1953, A Theory of the Consumption Function, 1957, A Program for Monetary Stability, 1960, Price Theory: A Provisional Text, 1962, (with Rose D. Friedman) Capitalism and Freedom, 1962, (with R.D. Friedman) Free To Choose, 1980, (with Rose D. Friedman) Tyranny of the Status Quo, 1984, (with Anna J. Schwartz) A Monetary History of the United States, 1867-1960, 1963, (with Schwartz) Monetary Statistics of the United States, 1970, (with Schwartz) Monetary Trends in the U.S. and the United Kingdom, 1982, Inflation: Causes and Consequences, 1963, (with Robert Roosa) The Balance of Payments: Free vs. Fixed Exchange Rates, 1967, Dollars and Deficits, 1968, The Optimum Quantity of Money and Other Essays, 1969, (with Walter W. Heller) Monetary vs. Fiscal Policy, 1969, A Theoretical Framework for Monetary Analysis, 1972, (with Wilbur J. Cohen) Social Security, 1972, An Economist's Protest, 1972, There's No Such Thing As A Free Lunch, 1975, Price Theory, 1976, (with Robert J. Gordon et al.) Milton Friedman's Monetary Framework, 1974, Tax Limitation, Inflation and the Role of Government, 1978, Bright Promises, Dismal Performance, 1983, Money Mischief, 1992, (with Thomas S. Szasz) Friedman & Szasz on Drugs: Essays on the Free Market and Prohibition, 1992; editor: Studies in the Quantity Theory of Money, 1956; bd. editors Am. Econ. Rev, 1951-53, Econometrica, 1957-69; adv. bd. Jour. Money, Credit and Banking, 1968-94; columnist Newsweek mag, 1966-84, contbg. editor, 1971-84; contbr. articles to profl. jours. Decorated Grand Cordon of the 1st Class Order of the Sacred Treasure (Japan), 1986; recipient Nobel prize in econs., 1976, Pvt. Enterprise Exemplar medal Freedoms Found., 1978, Presdl. medal of Freedom, 1988, Nat. Medal of Sci., 1988, Prize in Moral-Cultural Affairs, Instn. World Capitalism, 1993; named Chicagoan of Yr., Chgo. Press Club, 1972, Educator of Yr., Cgho. Jewish United Fund, 1973. Fellow Inst. Math. Stats., Am. Statis. Assn., Econometric Soc.; mem. Nat. Acad. Scis., Am. Econ. Assn. (mem. exec. com. 1955-57, pres. 1967; John Bates Clark medal 1951), Am. Enterprise Inst. (adv. bd. 1956-79), Western Econ. Assn. (pres. 1984-85), Royal Economic Soc., Am. Philos. Soc., Mont Pelerin Soc. (bd. dirs. 1958-61, pres. 1970-72). Club: Quadrangle. Office: Stanford U Hoover Instn Stanford CA 94305-6010

FRIEDMAN, MITCH ALAN, conservation biologist; b. Chgo., July 20, 1963; s. Ira Jerome Friedman and Francine (Hirsch) Scully. Student, Mont. State U., 1981-83; BA in Zoology, U. Wash., 1986. Ranch hand Ferguson Ranch, Cheyenne, Wyo., 1980; wildlife biologist Mont. Dept. Fish, Wildlife and Parks, Savage, Mont., 1981; fork lift operator Lustro Co., Evanston, Ill., 1982-83; framing carpenter Windward Builders, Lake Forest, Ill., 1984-85; fgn. fisheries observer Nat. Marine Fisheries, Seattle, 1985-86; organizer Wash. Earth First, Bellingham and Seattle, 1985-88, Ancient Forest Rescue Expedition, Bellingham, 1989-90; exec. dir., founder Northwest Ecosystem Alliance, Bellingham, 1989—; bd. dirs. The Wildlands Project, Portland, Hells Canyon Preservation Coun., Joseph, Oreg., North Cascades Conservation Coun., Seattle; advisors North Cascades Audubon Soc., Bellingham, 1987—, Atmosphere Alliance, Olympia, Wash., 1992—. Editor: Forever Wild: Conserving the Greater North Cascades Ecosystem, 1988, Cascadia Wild: Protecting an International Ecosystem, 1993 (Regional Bestseller 1993); contbg. editor Wild Earth, 1991; exec. producer video Nature Has No Borders, 1993. Co-chair No on 92-93, Whatcom County, Wash., 1993, Second Dist. Environ. Working Group, Bellingham, 1994. Pole Vault state medalist State of Ill., Champagne, 1981. Mem. Soc. for Conservation Biology, Natural Areas Soc., Nat. Audubon Soc., City Club Bellingham. Office: Greater Ecosystem Alliance Northwest Ecosys Alliance PO Box 2813 Bellingham WA 98227-2813

FRIEDMAN, MITCHELL SCOTT, public relations consultant; b. Flushing, N.Y., Sept. 3, 1960; s. Howard and Iris (Snyder) F.; m. Arete Susan Nicholas, Sept. 8, 1990. BA in History summa cum laude, Brandeis U., 1982; MA in Modern European History, Stanford U., 1984. Dir. adminstrv. svcs., summer sch. dir. Jr. Statesmen Found., Redwood City, Calif., 1984-88; jr. assoc., assoc. Neale-May & Ptnrs., Palo Alto, Calif., 1988-91; pub. rels. mgr. Sci. Certification Systems, Oakland, Calif., 1991-92; pres. Mitchell Friedman Comms., San Francisco, 1992—. Mem. Pub. Rels. Soc. Am., Toastmasters Internat. (numerous awards).

FRIEDMAN, PAMELA RUTH LESSING, art consultant, financial consultant; b. N.Y.C., Jan. 15, 1950; d. Fred William and Helen D. (Kahn) Lessing; m. Neil David Friedman, May 28, 1972; children: Elizabeth Lessing, Paul Lessing. BA, U. Rochester, 1972; MSLS, U. N.C., Chapel Hill, 1974. Dep. libr. Am. Soc. Internat. Law, Washington, 1974-76; with edn. dept. Nat. Air and Space Mus., Smithsonian Inst., Washington, 1976-84; ind. cons. fin. and art Boulder, Colo., 1984—; pub. C.S.B. Co., Boulder, 1989—; lectr. in fields, 1989—; cons. Denver Art Mus., 1989-91, Asian Art Coordinating Coun., Denver, 1990—. Author: (reference book) Chinese Snuff Bottles, 1990; editor: (reference book) Flight Service Directory, 1975. Rep. S.E.V.A.B., Smithsonian Instn., 1979-81, mem. exec. bd. docent coun. Nat. Air and Space Mus., 1977-81; mem. trustee coun. U. Rochester, N.Y., 19926, mem. vis. com. coll. of arts and scis. U. Rochester, 1994—; bd. dirs., mem. exec. com. bd., treas. Colo. Music Festival, Boulder, 1983-89; mem. exec. bd. Women's Incentive Fund Colo. U., Boulder, 1988—; rep. Leadership Boulder, 1986-87; v.p. bd. dirs. Lessing Found., N.Y., 1988—; mem. exec. bd. Interfaith Coun., Boulder, 1987-90; life mem. RAF Mus., 1977—. Recipient Internat. Gold Test Pin award Swiss Skiing Fedn., St. Moritz, 1975. Mem. Internat. Chinese Snuff Bottle Soc., Army and Navy Club (Washington), Beach Point Club (Mamaroneck, N.Y.), Game Creek Club (Vail, Colo.). Home and Office: 503 Kalmia Ave Boulder CO 80304-1733

FRIEDMAN, PAUL, food products executive; b. 1951. Ptnr. Cheese & Stuff, Hartford, Conn., 1972-80, P & J's Constrn., 1978-81, Prim Products, 1981-83; pres. Herb Farm, Inc., Encinitas, Calif., 1983—. Office: Herb Farm Inc 1613 Lake Dr Encinitas CA 92024-5226*

FRIEDMAN, ROBERT ERIC, lawyer; b. Berkeley, Calif., June 28, 1949; s. Howard Abraham and Phyllis Ruth (Koshland) F.; m. Kristina Kiehl, Mar. 12, 1977; children: Alison Kiehl Friedman, Anne Kiehl Friedman. AB, Harvard U., 1971; JD, Yale U., 1977. Bar: D.C. 1977. Chief spl. projects Ga. Dept. Natural Resources, Atlanta, 1971-72; fellow Health Policy Program U. Calif., San Francisco, 1972-73; policy analyst Nat. Ctr. for Productivity and Quality of Work Life, Washington, 1977-79; pres., founder Corp. for Enterprise Devel., Washington, 1979-88; chair, dir. Corp. for Enterprise Devel., San Francisco, 1988—; chair, founder Assn. for Enterprise Opportunity, San Francisco, 1990-92; bd. dirs. Levi Strauss Found., San Francisco, Rosenburg Found., San Francisco, EcoTrust, Portland, Oreg. Author: Development Report Card for the States, 1987, Safety Net as Ladder, 1988; editor: Expanding the Opportunity to Produce, 1981. Democrat. Jewish. Office: Corp for Enterprise Devel 353 Folsom St San Francisco CA 94105-2321

FRIEDMAN, SHELLY ARNOLD, cosmetic surgeon; b. Providence, Jan. 1, 1949; s. Saul and Estelle (Moverman) F.; m. Andrea Leslie Falchook, Aug. 30, 1975; children: Bethany Erin, Kimberly Rebecca, Brent David, Jennifer Ashley. BA, Providence Coll., 1971; DO, Mich. State U., 1982. Diplomate Nat. Bd. Med. Examiners, Am. Bd. Dermatology. Intern Pontiac (Mich.) Hosp., 1982-83, resident in dermatology, 1983-86; assoc. clin. prof. dept. internal med. Mich. State U., 1984-89, adj. clin. prof., 1989—; med. dir. Inst. Cosmetic Dermatology, Scottsdale, Ariz., 1986—. Contbr. aritcles to profl. jours. Mem. B'nai B'rith Men's Council, 1973, Jewish Welfare Fund, 1973. Am. Physicians fellow for medicine, 1982. Mem. AMA, Am. Osteopathic Assn., Am. Assn. Cosmetic Surgeons, Am. Acad. Cosmetic Surgery, Internat. Soc. Dermatologic Surgery, Internat. Acad. Cosmetic Surgery, Am. Acad. Dermatology, Am. Soc. Dermatol. Surgery, Frat. Order Police, Sigma Sigma Phi. Jewish. Office: Scottsdale Inst Cosmetic Dermatology 5206 N Scottsdale Rd Scottsdale AZ 85253-7006

FRIEDMANN, LYNNE TIMPANI, public relations consultant, writer; b. Lynn, Mass., Oct. 17, 1952; d. Henry and Rita Marie (Despres) Timpani; m. Marc David Friedmann, July 30, 1988. BA, Calif. State U., 1983. Account exec. Regis McKenna Pub. Rels., Costa Mesa, Calif., 1983-85; pub. info. rep. U. Calif., Irvine, 1985-88; cons. Friedmann Comms., San Diego, 1988—. Mem. Assn. for Women in Sci. (exec. bd. sec. 1994—, pub. rels. chair 1989-93), Nat. Assn. Sci. Writers, Pub. Rels. Soc. Am. Office: Friedmann Comms PO Box 1725 Solana Beach CA 92075-7725

FRIEDMANN, PERETZ PETER, aerospace engineer, educator; b. Timisoara, Romania, Nov. 18, 1938; came to U.S., 1969; s. Mauritius and Elisabeth Friedmann; m. Esther Sarfati, Dec. 8, 1964. DSc, MIT, 1972. Engrng. officer Israel Def. Force, 1961-65; sr. engr. Israel Aircraft Industries, Ben Gurion Airport, Israel, 1965-69; research asst. dept. aeronautics and astronautics MIT, Cambridge, 1969-72; asst. prof. mech., aerospace and nuclear engrng. dept. UCLA, 1972-77, assoc. prof., 1977-80, prof., 1980—; chmn. Dept. Mech Aerospace Nuclear Engrng., Los Angeles, 1988-91. Editor in chief Vertica-Internat. Jour. Rotocraft and Powered Lift Aircraft, 1980-90; contbr. numerous articles to profl. jours. Grantee NASA, Air Force Office Sci. Rsch., U.S. Army Rsch. Office, NSF. Fellow AIAA; mem. ASME (structures and materials award 1983), Am. Helicopter Soc., Sigma

Xi. Jewish. Office: UCLA MANE Dept Eng IV 48-121 Box 951597 Los Angeles CA 90095-1597

FRIEND, DAVID ROBERT, chemist; b. Vallejo, Calif., Aug. 10, 1956; s. Carl Gilbert and Roberta (Schwarzrock) F.; m. Carol Esther Warren, Dec. 17, 1983; 1 child, Ian, Michael. BS in Food Biochemistry, U. Calif., Davis, 1979; PhD in Agrl. Chemistry, U. Calif., Berkeley, 1983. Polymer chemist SRI Internat., Menlo Park, Calif., 1984-87, sr. polymer chemist controlled release and biomed. polymers dept., 1987-90, assoc. dir. controlled release and biomed. polymers dept., 1990-92, dir. controlled release and biomed. polymers dept., 1992-93; exec. dir. rsch. and product devel. Cibus Pharm., Redwood City, Calif., 1993-94, v.p. rsch. and product devel., 1994—; leader Biopharms. Rsch. Group, 1990; lectr. U. Calif. Sch. Pharmacy, San Francisco. Assoc. editor Jour. Controlled Release; contbr. articles to scholarly jours.; patentee in field. Mem. Am. Chem. Soc., N.Y. Acad. Scis., Controlled Release Soc., Am. Assn. Pharm. Sci., Sigma Xi. Democrat. Jewish. Home: 454 9th Ave Menlo Park CA 94025-1802 Office: SRI Internat Cibus Pharm 200 D Twin Dolpin Dr Redwood City CA 94065

FRIES, ARTHUR LAWRENCE, insurance broker; b. Bklyn., Aug. 21, 1937; s. Jack Edwin and Sophia (Kabat) F.; m. Cindy Ann Blum, Mar. 27, 1960; children: Stacey Jill, Todd Steven. AB, Nichols Coll., 1956; BS, Syracuse U., 1958. Registered health underwriter. Various positions ins. sales and adminstrn. various firms, N.Y.C., 1962-72; life and health ins. agt. Washington Nat. Ins. Co., Los Angeles, 1973-85; pvt. practice, N.Y.C., Los Angeles and Northridge, Calif., 1962-72, Northridge, 1982—; blood chmn. Washington Nat. Ins. Co., 1976-79; spkr., lectr., cons. on individual disability income ins. claims; cons., expert witness and negotiator for non-coan disability ins. claims. Contbr. articles to profl. jours. Chmn. memberships Vista Del Mar Men's Assn. for Orphaned Children, 1975; active Guardians Jewish Home for the Aged. Recipient Nat. Sales Achievement award L.A. Gen. Agts. and Mgrs. Assn., 1965-93, Health Ins. Quality award, 1965-92, 93, Agt. of Yr. award, 1976, 78, Nat. Quality award, 1980-91, Disting. Svc. award D.I.T.C. Rsch. Seminar, 1994. Mem. Am. Bd. Forensic Examiners, Inst. for Forensic Experts, Nat. Forensic Ctr., Nat. Assn. Life Underwriters (blood chmn. 1976-79, spkr. ann. conv. 1988, 90, 93 million dollar roundtable), Nat. Assn. Health Underwriters (life leading prodrs. roundtable), Calif. Assn. Life Underwriters, Calif. Assn. Health Underwriters (charter), L.A. Assn. Health Underwriters (conf. spkr., spkrs. chmn. 1983-84, program chmn. 1984, bd. dirs., membership chmn. 1987-88), Am. Coun. Ind. Life Underwriters, Am. Diabetic Assn. Republican. Home and Office: 11512 Porter Valley Dr Northridge CA 91326-1710

FRIES, DAVID SAMUEL, chemist, educator; b. Manassas, Va., June 22, 1945; s. Basil L. and Ruby (Sperau) F.; m. Marjie Ann Strayer, May 1, 1964; children: Susan, Jane, Corey. BA in Chemistry, Bridgewater Coll., 1968; PhD in Medicinal Chemistry, Va. Commonwealth U., 1971. Prof. medicinal chemistry U. of Pacific, Stockton, Calif., 1973—, dean grad. sch., 1993—; vis. rsch. prof. U. Groningen, The Netherlands, 1984-85, German Cancer Rsch. Ctr., Heidelberg, 1989-90; cons. on opioid drug addiction, 1975—. Contbr. articles to profl. jours. and chpts. to books. Rsch. grantee Nat. Inst. on Drug Abuse, NSF. Mem. Am. Chem. Soc., Fedn. Internat. Pharmaceutique, Am. Assn. Colls. Pharmacy, Sigma Xi, Phi Kappa Phi, Rho Chi, Phi Delta Chi. Office: U of Pacific Sch of Pharmacy Stockton CA 95211

FRIES, LITA LINDA, school system administrator; b. Merced, Calif., Feb. 16, 1942; d. Alfred Earl and Juanita Lora (Brown) Griffey; m. George Richard Fries, Feb. 3, 1962; 1 child, Damon Brant. BA, U. Calif., Berkeley, 1966; MS, Calif. State U., 1976. Cert. elem. tchr., secondary tchr., ednl. adminstrator, reading specialist. Tchr. Peace Corps, Mwanza, Tanzania, 1963-65; tchr. Oakland (Calif.) Unified Sch. Dist., 1966-74, tchr. spl. assignment, 1974-84, principal, Burckhalter, 1984-85, program mgr., 1985-90, administr., 1990-92, coord. state and fed. programs, 1992—. Mem. East Bay Reading Assn. (editor 1982-83), Pi Lamda Theta (membership chairperson 1986-88), Delta Kappa Gamma, Phi Delta Kappa. Democrat. Office: Oakland Unified Sch Dist 1025 2nd Ave Oakland CA 94606-2212

FRIESE, ROBERT CHARLES, lawyer; b. Chgo., Apr. 29, 1943; s. Earl Matthew and Laura Barbara (Mayer) F.; m. Chandra Ullom; children: Matthew Robert, Mark Earl, Laura Moore. AB in Internat. Rels., Stanford U., 1964; JD, Northwestern U., 1970. Bar: Calif. 1972. Dir. Tutor Applied Linguistics Ctr., Geneva, 1964-66; atty. Bronson, Bronson & McKinnon, San Francisco, 1970-71, SEC, San Francisco, 1971-75; ptnr. Shartsis, Friese & Ginsburg, San Francisco, 1975—; pres., bd. dirs. Custom Diversification Fund Mgmt., Inc., 1993—; dir.-co-founder Internat. Plant Rsch. Inst., Inc., San Carlos, Calif., 1978-86. Chmn. bd. suprs. Task Force on Noise Control, 1972-78; chmn. San Franciscans for Cleaner City, 1977; exec. dir. Nob Hill Neighbors, 1972-81; bd. dirs. Nob Hill Assn., 1976-78, Inst. Range and Am. Mustang, 1988—, Calif. Heritage Coun., 1977-78, Palace Fine Arts, 1992-94, San Francisco Beautiful, 1986—, pres., 1988—; chmn. Citizens Adv. Com. for Embarcadero Project, 1991—; mem. major gifts com. Stanford U.; bd. dirs. Presidio Heights Neighborhood Assn., 1993—. Mem. ABA, Assn. Bus. Trial Lawyers (bd. dirs.), Calif. Bar Assn., Bar Assn. San Francisco (bd. dirs. 1982-85, chmn. bus. litigation com. 1978-79, chmn. state ct. civil litigation com. 1983-90, new courthouse com. 1993—), Lawyers Club of San Francisco, Mensa, Calif. Hist. Soc., Commonwealth Club, Swiss-Am. Friendship League (chmn. 1971-79). Office: Shartsis Friese & Ginsburg 1 Maritime Plz Fl 18 San Francisco CA 94111-3404

FRIESECKE, RAYMOND FRANCIS, management consultant; b. N.Y.C., Mar. 12, 1937; s. Bernhard P. K. and Josephine (De Tomi) F.; BS in Chemistry, Boston Coll., 1959; MS in Civil Engring., MIT, 1961. Product specialist Dewey & Almy Chem. div. W. R. Grace & Co., Inc., Cambridge, Mass., 1963-66; market planning specialist USM Corp., Boston, 1966-71; mgmt. cons., Boston, 1971-74; dir. planning and devel. Schweitzer div. Kimberly-Clark Corp., Lee, Mass., 1974-78; v.p. corp. planning Butler Automatic, Inc., Canton, Mass., 1978-80; pres. Butler-Europe Inc., Greenwich, Conn. and Munich, Germany, 1980; v.p. mktg. and planning Butler Greenwich Inc., 1980-81; pres. Strategic Mgmt. Assocs., San Rafael, Calif., 1981—; chmn. Beyond Health Corp., 1994—; corp. clk., v.p. Bldg. Research & Devel., Inc., Cambridge, 1966-68. Author: Management by Relative Product Quality, The New Way to Manage; contbr. articles to profl. jours. State chmn. Citizens for Fair Taxation, 1972-73; state co-chmn. Mass. Young Reps., 1967-69; chmn. Ward 7 Rep. Com., Cambridge, 1968-70; vice chmn. Cambridge Rep. City Com., 1966-68; vice-chmn. Kentfield Rehab. Hosp. Found., 1986-88, chmn., 1988-91; Rep. candidate Mass. Ho. of Reps., 1964, 66; pres. Marin Rep. Coun., 1986-91; chmn. Calif. Acad., 1986-88; sec. Navy League Marin Coun., 1984-91, v.p. 94—. 1st lt. U.S. Army, 1961-63. Mem. NRA, Am. Chem. Soc., Am. Mktg. Assn., Marin Philos. Soc. (v.p. 1991-92), The Planning Forum, The World Affairs Coun. Home and Office: 141 Convent Ct San Rafael CA 94901-1335

FRIGON, JUDITH ANN, electronics executive, office systems consultant; b. Wisconsin Rapids, Wis., Feb. 11, 1945; d. Harold Leslie and Muriel Alice (Berard) Neufeld; m. Gene Roland Frigon, June 17, 1967; children: Shane P., Shannon M., Sean M. Sec., office mgr. George Chapman D.D.S., Fairfax, Va., 1971-75; owner, operator Sunset Motel, Havre, Mont., 1976-78; sec. Wash. State U. Social Research Ctr., Pullman, 1978-80; adminstrv. sec. Wash. State U. Systems and Computing, Pullman, 1980-85, office automation cons., word processing trainer, IBM profl. office system adminstr., 1983-89, microcomputer cons. and trainer, 1989—; systems analyst, programmer Wash. State U. Computing Ctr., Pullman, 1985—; owner Computer Assistance, Tng. and Svcs., Pullman, 1992—. Pres. Pullman svc. unit Girl Scouts U.S., 1983-89, v.p. inland empire coun., Spokane, Wash., 1985-89, pres., 1989-95; active Pullman Civic Trust, 1986—; mem-at-large Pullman United Way, 1988-93, admissions and allocations com., 1990-93, comm. com., 1990-93; host family for State of Wash. Jr. Miss Program, 1988—, local area judge Young Woman of Yr., 1985—. Recipient Girl Scouts Thanks badge, 1991, Wash. State U. Mom of Yr. award, 1995. Mem. Profl. Secs. Internat., Jaycees (Jayceen of Yr. 1978), Pullman Kiwanis Club. Roman Catholic. Home: 1235 NW Davis Way Pullman WA 99163-2815 Office: Wash State U Computing Ctr 2120 Computer Sci Bldg Pullman WA 99164

FRIPP, RAYMOND RALPH, pediatric cardiologist; b. Pinetown, Natal, Republic of South Africa, Sept. 22, 1946; came to U.S., 1977; s. Alfred Downing and Jessie (Purves) F.; m. Lynette Doveton, Aug. 29, 1970; children: Nicolette, Matthew, Jessica. MB, B Surgery, U. Witwatersrand, Johannesburg, Republic of South Africa, 1971. Diplomate Am. Bd. Pediatrics. Intern Grey's Hosp., Pietermaritzberg, Natal, Republic of South Africa, 1972-73, Hosp. St. Raphael, New Haven, 1973-74; resident Red Cross Children's Hosp., Cape Town, Republic of South Africa, 1975-77; resident Milton S. Hershey Med. Ctr., Hershey, Pa., 1977-78, asst. prof., 1980-85; fellow pediatric cardiology Yale U. Hosp., New Haven, 1978-80; asst. prof. U. N.Mex., Albuquerque, 1985; practice medicine specializing in pediatric cardiology Albuquerque, 1986—. Author: Techniques, Diagnostics and Advances in Nuclear Medicine, 1983, Managemnt of the Cardiac Patient Requiring Non-Cardiac Surgery, 1983. Am. Heart Assn. grantee, 1983-86. Fellow Coll. Physicians South Africa (pediatrics), Am. Bd. Pediatrics (bd. pediatric cardiology). Office: Pediatric Cardiology Assocs Ste 207 715 Dr Martin Luther King Jr Ave NE Albuquerque NM 87102-3667

FRISBEE, DON CALVIN, retired utilities executive; b. San Francisco, Dec. 13, 1923; s. Ira Nobles and Helen (Sheets) F.; m. Emilie Ford, Feb. 5, 1947; children: Ann, Robert, Peter, Dean. BA, Pomona Coll., 1947; MBA, Harvard U., 1949. Sr. investment analyst, asst. cashier investment analysis dept. 1st Interstate Bank Oreg., N.A., Portland, 1949-52; with PacifiCorp, Portland, 1953—, treas., 1958-60, then v.p., exec. v.p., pres., 1966-73, chief exec. officer, 1973-89, chmn., 1973-94; chmn. emeritus PacifiCorp., Portland, 1994—; bd. dirs. First Interstate Bancorp, Weyerhaeuser Co., Standard Ins. Co., Portland., Precision Castparts Corp., Portland, First Interstate Bank Northwest Region, Portland. Chmn. bd. trustees Reed Coll.; trustee Safari Game Search Found., High Desert Mus.; mem. cabinet Columbia Pacific coun. Boy Scouts Am.; founder Oreg. chpt. Am. Leadership Forum; mem. exec. com. Oreg. Partnership for Internat. Edn.; mem. Internat. Adv. Com. 1st lt. AUS, 1943-46. Mem. Arlington Club, Univ. Club Multnomah, Athletic Club, City Club (bd. govs., pres.). Office: PacifiCorp 1500 SW 1st Ave Portland OR 97201-5815

FRISCHKNECHT, LEE CONRAD, retired broadcasting executive; b. Brigham City, Utah, Jan. 4, 1928; s. Carl Oliver and Geniel (Lund) F.; m. Sara Jean McCulloch, Sept. 3, 1948; children: Diane Frischknecht Etherington, Jill Frischknecht Taylor, Ellen Frischknecht DePola, Amy Frischknecht Blodgett. BS in Speech, Utah State U., 1951; MA in Radio-TV, Mich. State U., 1957. Announcer sta. KID Radio, Idaho Falls, Idaho, 1951-52; producer-director sta. WKAR-TV, East Lansing, Mich., 1953-57, prodn. mgr., 1958-59, program mgr., 1960-61, gen. mgr., 1962-63; dir. sta. rels. Nat. Ednl. TV, N.Y.C., 1964-67; dir. univ. rels. Utah State U., 1969-70; dir. network affairs Nat. Pub. Radio, Washington, 1971, v.p., 1972, pres., 1973-77; communications cons., 1978—; mgr. ed. telecommunications sta. KAET-TV, Phoenix, Ariz., 1980-86; asst. gen. mgr. sta. KAET-TV, Phoenix, 1987-93; assoc. prof. radio-TV, Mich. State U., 1962-63; assoc. prof. speech Utah State U., 1968-69; lectr. Ariz. State U., 1981-82. Bd. dirs. Nat. Pub. Radio, 1973-78, Ariz. Sch. Svcs. Through Ednl. Tech., 1984-93, PSSC Legacy Fund, 1993—; bd. dirs. Pub. Svc. Satellite Consortium, 1982-90, chmn., 1987-90. Recipient Outstanding Alumnus in Communications award Mich. State U., 1973, Meritorious Svc. award in Communications, Brigham Young U., 1974, Disting. Svc. award Pacific Mountain Network, 1987. Mem. LDS Ch. Home: 8100 East Camelback Rd #180 Scottsdale AZ 85251-2754

FRISHBERG, NANCY JO, computer researcher; b. Mpls., Nov. 9, 1948; d. Morton Charles and Alyse Sue (Goldsman) F.; 1 child, Janet Seiden. AB with honors, U. Calif., Berkeley, 1970; MA, U. Calif., San Diego, 1973, PhD, 1976. Rsch. asst. Lab. for Lang. Studies, Salk Inst., LaJolla, Calif., 1970-73; rsch. assoc. Interpreting Svcs. Nat. Tech. Inst. for Deaf-Rochester (N.Y.) Inst. Tech., 1973-75; asst. prof. linguistics Hampshire Coll., Amherst, Mass., 1975-78; dir. sign lang. rsch. NYU Deafness Rsch. and Tng. Ctr., N.Y.C., 1978-80; pvt. practice cons. sign lang. and interpretation N.Y.C., 1980-85; liberal arts specialist IBM-Academic Info. Systems, Milford, Conn., 1985-87; staff asst., dir. sci. ctrs. IBM, Milford, 1987-89; inst. fellow User Interface Inst., IBM Watson Rsch., Yorktown Heights, N.Y., 1989-92; lic. support engr. Apple Computer, 1991-94; mem. adv. bd. ENFI Project Gallaudet U., Washington, 1988-90, Project Common Ground, 1991-94. Author: Interpreting: An Introduction, 1986, rev. edit., 1990; mem. editorial bd. Jour. of Interpretation, 1991—. Mem. Assn. Software Design (bd. dirs.), Registry Interpreters for the Deaf (pres. N.Y.C. metro 1980-82), Assn. for Computers and Humanities (exec. coun. 1989-91), Sign Instrs. Guidance Network (nat. evaluation team 1977-84), Linguistic Soc. Am., Internat. Interactive Comm. Soc. (Mark of Excellence award 1990).

FRISHMAN, EILEEN STEINBERG, accountant; b. N.Y.C., Oct. 5, 1946; m. Robert Jules Frishman, June 10, 1967; 2 children. BS in Edn., CCNY, 1967; MA in Edn., U. Conn., 1971; MS in Acctg., Pace U., 1986. CPA. Tchr. Vernon (Conn.) Pub. Schs., 1967-70; ednl. psychologist Granby (Conn.) Pub. Schs., 1971-72; owner, mgr. retail store, East Hartford, Conn., 1972-75; instr. acctg. and fin. Lockyear Coll., Evansville, Ind., 1986-87; field auditor Ind. Dept. Revenue, Evansville, 1987-88; staff acct. Yale & Seffinger, P.C., Denver, 1988-89; asst. tax mgr. Gt.-West Life Assurance Co., Englewood, Colo., 1989—; adj. instr. fin. U. Evansville, 1987. Author: Enjoy Home Winemaking, 1972, rev. 1976. Mem. AICPA, Colo. Soc. CPA's. Home: 5361 S Geneva Way Englewood CO 80111-6222

FRISK, JACK EUGENE, recreational vehicle manufacturing company executive; b. Nampa, Idaho, Jan. 22, 1942; s. Steinert Paul and Evelyn Mildred (Letner) F.; m. Sharon Rose Caviness, Aug. 3, 1959; 1 dau., Toni. With Ideal of Idaho, Inc., Caldwell, purchasing mgr., 1969-75, gen. mgr., sec.-treas., 1975-82; sales mgr. Traveleze Industries div. Thor Industries, Sun Valley, Calif., 1982-88; owner, pres. Crossroads Industry div. Cross Enterprises Inc., Mesa, Ariz., 1988-92; dir. mktg. western divsn. Chariot Eagle, Inc., Ocala, Fla., 1992-95; gen. mgr. Chariot Eagle West, Inc., Phoenix, 1995—. Episcopalian. Home: 1430 N Parsell Cir Mesa AZ 85203-3713 Office: 5635R W Van Buren Ave Phoenix AZ 85043

FRITCHER, EARL EDWIN, civil engineer, consultant; b. St. Ansgar, Iowa, Nov. 24, 1923; s. Lee and Mamie Marie (Ogden) F.; m. Dorsille Ellen Simpson, Aug. 24, 1946; 1 child, Teresa. BS, Iowa State U., 1950. Registered civil engr., Calif. Project devel. engr. dept. transp. State of Calif., Los Angeles, 1950-74, traffic engr. dept. transp., 1974-87; pvt. practice cons. engr. Sunland, Calif., 1987—; consulting prin. traffic engr. Parsons DeLeuw Inc., 1990—; cons. traffic engr. DeLeuw Cather Internat., Dubai, United Arab Emerates, 1994. Co-author: Overhead Signs and Contract Sign Plans, 1989; patentee in field. Served to 2d lt. USAF, 1942-46, 50-51. Mem. Iowa State Alumni Assn. Republican. Methodist. Clubs: Verdugo Hills Numismatic (Sunland), Glendale Numismatic.

FRITZ, ETHEL MAE HENDRICKSON, writer; b. Gibbon, Nebr., Feb. 4, 1925; d. Walter Earl and Alice Hazel (Mickish) Hendrickson; BS, Iowa State U., 1949; m. C. Wayne Fritz, Feb. 25, 1950; children: Linda Sue, Krista Jane. Dist. home economist Internat. Harvester Co., Des Moines, 1949-50; writer Wallace's Farmer mag., Des Moines, 1960-64; free-lance writer, 1960—. Chmn. Ariz. Council Flower Show Judges, 1983-85; media rels. Presdl. Inaugural Com., 1988. Accredited master flower show judge. Mem. Women in Communications (pres. Phoenix profl. chpt.; nat. task force com. 1980—), Am. Soc. Profl. and Exec. Women, Am. Home Econs. Assn., SW Writers' Conf., Ariz. Authors Assn., Phi Upsilon Omicron, Kappa Delta. Republican. Methodist. Club: PEO. Author: The Story of an Amana Winemaker, 1984, Prairie Kitchen Sampler, 1988, The Family of Hy-Vee, 1989.

FRITZ, RENE EUGENE, JR., manufacturing executive; b. Prineville, Oreg., Feb. 24, 1943; s. Rene and Ruth Pauline (Munson) F.; B.S. in Bus. Adminstrn., Oreg. State U., 1965; m. Sharyn Ann Fife, June 27, 1964; children—Rene Scott, Lanz Eugene, Shay Steven, Case McGarrett. Sales mgr. Renal Corp., Albany, Oreg., 1965-66, Albany Machine and Supply, 1965-66; pres. Albany Internat. Industries, Inc., 1966-85, Wood Yield Tech. Corp., 1972-85, Albany Internat. D.I.S.C., 1972-85, Automation Controls Internat., Inc., Albany, 1975-85; co-founder, chmn. Albany Titanium Inc., 1981-89; prin. Torwest Capital, 1989; founder, pres. WY Tech. Corp., 1984-89, R. Fritz & Assocs., 1987-89; pres. Chief Execs. Forum, 1989—, Fritz Group Inc., 1989—; fin. planner, investment banker M&A, Vancouver, Wash., 1991—. Pres., Oreg. World Trade Coun., 1982—; trustee U.S. Naval Acad. Found., Annapolis, Md., 1988—. Mem. Oreg. State Alumni, Forest Products Rsch. Soc., Young Pres. Orgn. Presbyterian. Clubs: Rotary, Elks. Patentee computer controlled machinery.

FRIZZELL, WILLIAM KENNETH, architect; b. Knox City, Tex., Dec. 10, 1928; s. Thomas Paul and Kelphia (Williams) F.; children: Jane, John Callender. B.A. magna cum laude in Architecture, Princeton U., 1950; M.A., U. Okla., 1954. Prin. Frizzell Architects, Santa Barbara. Works this country, abroad.; Works include Camelback Inn, Scottsdale, Ariz, Loews Paradise Valley Resort, Paradise Valley, Ariz., Sheraton Hammamet Hotel, Tunisia, Yves St Laurent Boutique, N.Y.C., N.Y.C., Becton-Dickenson-Endevco electronics facility, San Juan Capistrano, Calif., Omar Kahyam Hotel, Cairo, Dysan Corp. Bldgs, Santa Clara, Calif., Monarch Hotel, San Francisco, Paradise Valley Hotel, Scottsdale, Ariz., Loews Ventana Canyon Hotel, Tucson, Park Hyatt Hotel, Santa Monica, Calif., Red Lion Hotel, Glendale, Calif., Shutters Hotel, Santa Monica, Calif. Served to lt. (j.g.) USNR. Mem. AIA. Office: 619 Pilgrim Terrace Dr Santa Barbara CA 93101-3928

FROEB, DONALD FORREST, lawyer, former state judge; b. N.Y.C., Sept. 21, 1930; s. Augustus Charles and Marion (Furgueson) F.; m. Alice Keir, May 22, 1954; children: Deborah, Leslie, Peter, James. BA, Williams Coll., 1952; JD, Cornell U., 1959. Assoc., ptnr. Ryley, Carlock & Ralston, Phoenix, 1959-68; judge Superior Ct. Ariz., Phoenix, 1968-74, Div. 1 Ariz. Ct. Appeals, Phoenix, 1974-88; with Lowry, Froeb & Clements (formerly Lowry & Froeb, P.C.), Phoenix, 1988-90; of counsel Mitten, Goodwin & Raup, Phoenix, 1990—; mem. Ariz. Commn. on Jud. Conduct, 1983-87; mem. adv. com. appellate rules Jud. Conf. U.S., 1987-94. Bd. dirs. Phoenix Chamber Music Soc., 1960-85, pres. 1980-85. Capt. USAFR, 1953-69. Mem. ABA, Ariz. Bar Assn., Maricopa County Bar Assn., Rotary. Republican. Episcopalian. Home: 516 E Kaler Dr Phoenix AZ 85020-4050 Office: Mitten Goodwin & Raup 3636 N Central Ave Ste 1200 Phoenix AZ 85012-1942

FROEHLICH, ROBERT ELMER, association director, management consultant; b. Milw., Dec. 1, 1942; s. Elmer Alfred and Lucille (Miesler) F.; m. Virginia Owens, Aug. 29, 1965; children: Karen Lynn, Andrew Robert, William Scott. DVM, Iowa State U., 1966; MBA, Keller Sch. Mgmt., 1987. Owner Grafton (Wis.) Vet. Hosp., 1974-89; dir. mgmt. svc. Am. Animal Hosp. Assn., Denver, 1989—. Author: Successful Financial Management for the Veterinary Practice, 1987. Crusade chmn. Am. Cancer Soc., Ozaukee County, Wis., 1987-88. Capt. U.S. Army, 1966-68. Mem. Am. Vet. Med. Assn., Am. Animal Hosp. Assn. (hosp. dir., speaker 1988—, cons. 1989—), Colo. Vet. Med. Assn., Wis. Vet. Med. Assn., Milw. Vet. Med. Assn. (pres. 1975-76). Lutheran. Home: 8875 W Cornell Pl Lakewood CO 80227-4501

FROELICH, BEVERLY LORRAINE, foundation director; b. Vancouver, B.C., Can., Oct. 23, 1948; came to U.S., 1968; d. Kenneth Martin and Ethel (Seale) Pulham; m. Eugene Leonard Froelich, Dec. 26, 1971; children: Craig, Grant. Cert. in fundraising, U. So. Calif., 1986; profl. designation in pub. rels., UCLA, 1987. Cert. fund raising exec. Contract analyst Universal Studios, Calif., 1986-71; exec. dir. Olive View, UCLA Med. Ctr. Found., Sylmar, Calif., 1987—; pres. Beverly Froelich Pub. Rels., Sherman Oaks, Calif., 1988-90; prin. Tracy Susman & Co., Sherman Oaks, 1986-88. Co-author: (program) Overcoming Chronic Arthritis Pain, 1989; contbg. writer hosp. earthquake preparedness guidelines Hosp. Coun. So. Calif., 1991. Founder San Fernando Valley br. Arthritis Found., Encino, 1983, pres., 1983-87, mktg. com.; exec. com. Jeopardy "Balancing the Odds" Found.; bd. dirs. health care com. VICA, Futures IV com., United Way; devel. com. Crespi H.S. Recipient Nat. Vol. Svc. award Arthritis Found., 1986, Jane Wyman Humanitarian award Arthritis Found., 1991, Disting. Svc. award Arthritis Found., 1990. Mem. Nat. Soc. Fund Raisers (exec. com. San Fernando Valley chpt.), Valley Industry and Commerce Assn., UCLA Alumni Assn., Publicity Club of L.A. Home: 14152 Valley Vista Blvd Sherman Oaks CA 91423 Office: Olive View Med Ctr Found 14445 Olive View Dr Cott M Sylmar CA 91423

FROHMADER, FREDERICK OLIVER, lawyer; b. Tacoma, Wash., Mar. 12, 1930; s. Frederick William and Elizabeth May (Farrell) F.; m. Brenda Frohmader (dec.); children: Fred Albert Aubert, Frederick William, Lisa Kim. BCS, Seattle U., 1953; LLB, Gonzaga U., 1960, JD, 1967. Bar: Wash. Lawyer in pvt. practice, Tacoma, 1960—; with Pierce County Prosecutor, Tacoma, 1961-62; represented various Wash. Indians and Indian tribes in their fishing and hunting rights under various treaties signed with U.S., 1962-83. Served to 1st lt. U.S. Army, 1953-56. Mem. Wash. State Bar Assn., Wash. State Trial Lawyers Assn., Elks. Christian. Home: 629 S Winnifred St Tacoma WA 98465-2538 Office: 1130 S 11th St Tacoma WA 98405-4017

FROHNEN, RICHARD GENE, journalism educator; b. Omaha, Mar. 26, 1930; s. William P. and Florence E. (Rogers) F.; student U. Nebr., Omaha, Mo. Valley Coll., 1948-52; BA, Calif. State U., 1954; MS, UCLA 1961; EdD, Brigham Young U., 1976; grad. Army War Coll., 1982 m. Harlene Grace LeTourneau, July 4, 1958; children: Karl Edward, Eric Eugene. Bus. mgr. athletics and sports publicity dir. U. Nebr., Omaha, 1951-52; pub. rels. dir. First Congl. Ch. Los Angeles, 1953-54, 58-59; writer Los Angeles Mirror News, 1959; gen. assignment reporter, religion editor Los Angeles Times, 1959-61; prof. journalism, dean men Eastern Mont. Coll., Billings, 1961-65; N.W. editor, editorial writer Spokesman-Review, Spokane, 1965-67, also editor Sunday mag.; prof. journalism U. Nev., Reno, 1967-79; exec. dir. devel. Coll. of Desert/Copper Mountain, 1982-85, Ariz. Health Scis. Ctr., Tucson, 1986-90; pub. rels. devel. officer Sch. Med. Scis. U. Nev., 1969-75; adj. prof. mgmt., dir. grad. pros. in Mgmt. U. Redlands (Calif.), 1979-85, 91—; adj. prof. comm. Calif. State Univ., Dominguez Hills, 1991—; cons. Instl. Advancement, Long Beach, Calif., 1990—. Mem. exec. bd. Nev. area coun. Boy Scouts Am., 1968-76, coun. commr., 1973-74, v.p., 1975-76; mem. exec. bd. Yellowstone Valley coun. Boy Scouts Am., 1961-65, coun. pres. 1963-64; v.p. Catalina coun. Boy Scouts Am., 1987-90; mem. exec. bd. Long Beach Area Coun., 1990-93; founder, mng. dir. Gt. Western Expdns., 1958-90; adminstrv. asst. to Gov. of Nev., 1985. Served to 1st lt. USMC, 1954-58; now col. Res., ret. Recipient Silver Beaver award Boy Scouts Am., 1974, Pres.' Vol. Action award Coll. Desert/Copper Mountain, 1984, Outstanding Faculty award U. Redlands, 1984; named to Benson High Sch. Hall of Fame, Omaha, 1988. Mem. Assn. Edn. Journalism, Am. Legion, Res. Officers Assn. U.S., Marine Corps Assn., Marine Corps Res. Officers Assn., Am. Humanics Found., Internat. Platform Assn., Nat. Soc. Fund Raising Execs., Planning Execs. Inst., Internat. Communication Assn., Religion Newswriters Assn., Navy League, Semper Fidelis Soc., Am. Mgmt. Assn., Assn. Am. Med. Colls. Group on Pub. Affairs, Counc. for Advancement and Support Edn., Res. Officers Assn. U.S., Assn. for Healthcare Philanthropy, Kiwanis, Lions, Rotary, Kappa Tau Alpha, Alpha Phi Omega, Soc. Profl. Journalists, Sigma Delta Chi (sec.-treas. chpt.). Episcopalian. Office: 210 Grand Ave No 105 Long Beach CA 90803

FROILAN, VICENTE SINGZON, educator; b. Catbalogan, Philippines, Dec. 18, 1946; came to U.S., 1989; s. Mariano and Maria (Singzon) F. BS in Comml. Sci., San Beda Coll., 1968; BS in Edn., Jose Rizal Coll., 1988. Head prodn. svcs. unit Ctr. Ednl. Television, Quezon City, Philippines, 1968-71; exec. dir. Leyte Filiniana Cutural Found., Tacloban City, Philippines, 1971-89; tchr. Karilagan Finishing Sch., Quezon City, 1975-79; prof. San Beda Coll., Manila, Philippines, 1974-89; dir. adminstrn. Gran Hotel, Tacloban City, Philippines, 1976-85; sr. adminstr. State Bar Calif., L.A., 1989—. Author: Media Education, 1985, Business Management in Christian Perspective, 1987; columnist: The Bedan, 1966-68 (Gold medal 1968); editor-in-chief The Spires jour., 1965-68 (Gold medal 1968). Dir. Boy Scouts of the Philippines, Manila, 1985. With Philippine Mil., 1963-65. Roman Catholic. Office: State Bar of Calif 1149 S Hill St Los Angeles CA 90015

FROLICK, PATRICIA MARY, retired elementary education educator; b. Portland, Oreg., May 17, 1923; d. Fred Anthony and Clara Cecelia (Riverman) F. BS in Edn., Marylhurst Coll., 1960; MS in Edn., Portland State U., 1970; student, U. Oreg., 1975; MA in Theology, St. Mary's Coll., Moraga, Calif., 1977. Joined Roman Cath. Order Sisters of Holy Names of Jesus and Mary, 1943. Left order in 1974. Elem. sch. tchr. Catholic Sch. System, Oreg., 1943-69; tchr., libr. Hood River Pub. Schs., 1970-74, Bend-La Pine (Oreg.) Pub. Schs., 1981-93; ret., 1993; part-time tchr's. asst., Portland, 1993—. Mem. NEA, Oreg. Edn. Assn., Met. Mus. Art (assoc.), Nat. Mus.

Women in Arts (charter). Democrat. Roman Catholic. Home: 3465 SE 153rd Ave Portland OR 97236-2265

FROMM, HANNA, educational administrator; b. Nuremberg, W.Ger., Dec. 20, 1913; d. David and Meta (Stiebel) Gruenbaum; m. Alfred Fromm, July 4, 1936; children—David, Caroline Fromm Lurie. Grad. in choreography and music Folkwang Sch. Dancing and Music, Univ. Essen, Germany, 1934; D.Pub. Service (hon.), U. San Francisco, 1979. Served with ARC, World War II; exec. dir. and co-founder Fromm Inst. Lifelong Learning, U. San Francisco, 1975—. Co-founder Music in the Vineyards, Saratoga, Calif.; bd. dirs. Amnesty Internat., Nat. Council of Fine Arts Museums; former bd. dirs. Young Audiences, Community Music Ctr., Legal Aid to Elderly, San Francisco Chamber Music Soc.; coordinating com. geriatric curriculum and program U. Calif.-San Francisco; dir. Nat. Council on Aging. Recipient Living Legacy award Women's Internat. Ctr., 1990. Mem. Psychoanalytic Inst. of San Francisco Jewish. Club: Met. (San Francisco). Home: 850 El Camino Del Mar San Francisco CA 94121-1018 Office: 538 University Center 2130 Fulton St San Francisco CA 94117-1080

FROMSON, MURRAY, communications educator, journalist; b. N.Y.C., Sept. 1, 1929; s. Alfred and Frances (Segal) F.; m. Dodi H. Grumbach, May 27, 1961; children: Aliza Bental, Derek Ross. AA in Journalism, L.A. City Coll., 1949; cert. Japan studies, Sophia U., Tokyo, 1954. Reporter The Mirror, L.A., 1950; corr. The AP, San Francisco, Seoul, Tokyo, Singapore, Bangkok, 1953-60, NBC News, L.A., Bangkok, Saigon, Moscow, Hong Kong, Chgo., 1960-61, CBS News, L.A., 1962-76; moderator, producer Calif. Pub. Broadcasting, Sacramento, 1980-83; prof. U. Southern Calif., L.A., 1982—; dir. Ctr. for Internat. Journalism U. So. Calif., L.A., 1985—, interim dir. Sch. of Journalism, 1994—; spl. cons. to pres. U. Calif. Systemwide Adminstrn., Berkeley, 1979; dep. campaign mgr. for media Gov. Jerry Brown, Sacramento, 1978; bd. dirs. Calif. First Amendment Coalition, Sacramento; founding mem. Reporters Com. for Freedom of the Press, Washington, D.C. Staff sgt. U.S. Army, 1951-52, Korea, Japan. Recipient Outstanding Interpretive Reporting from Vietnam, Overseas Press Club, 1975, Outstanding Spot News Reporting from Vietnam, 1975. Mem. Asia Soc., Japan Am. Soc., Nat. Com. U.S.-China Rels., L.A. Com. on Fgn. Rels., Com. to Protect Journalists (N.Y.). Jewish. Office: Univ So Calif University Park GFS 326A Los Angeles CA 90089-1695

FRONT, THEODORE, music company executive; b. Darmstadt, Germany, Nov. 26, 1909; s. Hersz and Ryfka (Jankowiak) F. Student, Univ. Munich, 1928-29. Asst. stage dir. Hessisches Landestheater, Darmstadt, 1929-31, Staedtische Oper, Berlin, 1931-33; various positions N.Y.C., 1938-50; asst. to the owner Gateway to Music, L.A., 1950-58; founder Theodore Front Musical Literature, Inc., L.A., 1961—. Democrat. Jewish. Home: 360 S Burnside Ave Apt 1B Los Angeles CA 90036-5401 Office: Theodore Front Musical Lit 16122 Cohasset St Van Nuys CA 91406-2909

FRONTIERE, GEORGIA, professional football team executive; m. Carroll Rosenblum, July 7, 1966 (dec.); children: Dale Carroll, Lucia; m. Dominic Frontiere. Pres., owner L.A. Rams, NFL, 1979—. Bd. dirs. L.A. Boys and Girls Club, L.A. Orphanage Guild, L.A. Blind Youth Found. Named Headliner of Yr., L.A. Press Club, 1981. Office: LA Rams 2327 W Lincoln Ave Anaheim CA 92801-5102*

FROST, EVERETT LLOYD, academic administrator; b. Salt Lake City, Oct. 17, 1942; s. Henry Hoag Jr. and Ruth Salome (Smith) F.; m. Janet Owens, Mar. 26, 1967; children: Noreen Karyn, Joyce Lida. BA in Anthropology, U. Oreg., 1965; PhD in Anthropology, U. Utah, 1970. Field researcher in cultural anthropology Taveuni, Fiji, 1968-69; asst. prof. in anthropology Ea. N.Mex. U., Portales, 1970-74, assoc. prof., 1974-76, asst. dean Coll. Liberal Arts and Scis., 1976-78, dean acad. affairs and grad. studies, 1978-80, v.p. for planning and analysis, dean rsch., 1980-91, dean grad. studies, 1983-88; pres., 1991—; cons., evaluator N. Ctrl. Assn. Accreditation Agy. for Higher Edn., 1989—, mem. rev. bd., 1993—; bd. dirs. Quality N.Mex., 1st Savs. Bank of Clovis and Portales, N.Mex., Plains Regional Med. Ctrs., Clovis and Portales; bd. mem. emeritus N.Mex. First; commr. Western Interstate Commn. for Higher Edn., 1993—; pres. Lone Star Athletic Conf. Pres.'s Commn., 1992—; chmn. rsch. com. N.Mex. First, 1989-91. Chmn. N.Mex. Humanities Coun., 1980-88; mem. N.Mex. Gov.'s Commn. on Higher Edn., 1983-86; mem. exec. bd. N.Mex. First, 1987—; bd. dirs. Roosevent Gen. Hosp., Portales, 1989—; pres. bd. dirs. San Juan County Mus. Assn., Farmington, 1979-82; vice chair Portales Pub. Schs. Facilities Com., 1990—. NDEA fellow, 1969-70; grantee NEW, 1979-80, NSF, 1968-69, Fiji Forbes, Ltd., 1975-76, others. Fellow Am. Anthropol. Assn., Am. Assn. Higher Edn., Soc. Coll. and Univ. Planning, Assn. Social Anthropologists Oceania, Anthropol. Soc. Washington, Sch. Am. Rsch., Western Assn. Grad. Deans, Current Anthropology (assoc.) Polynesian Soc., Phi Kappa Phi.

FROST, MARK, director, producer, writer; b. N.Y.C.. Studied acting, directing and playwriting, Carnegie Tech., Pitts. Television writer Universal Pictures; lit. assoc. Guthrie Theater, Mpls.; playwright-in-residence Midwestern Playwright's Lab. Writer episodes (TV series) Sunshine, The Six Million Dollar Man; author: (plays) The Nuclear Family, Heart Trouble; writer, story editor, exec. story editor (TV series Hill Street Blues (Writers Guild award, Emmy nomination); writer, prodr., dir. (documentry) The Road Back, PBS; writer, assoc. prodr. (feature film) The Believers, 1987; creator (with David Lynch, TV series) Twin Peaks (Peabody award, 2 Emmy nominations); creator, exec. prodr. (TV series) Am. Chronicles; writer, dir. (feature film) Storyville, 1992; author (novels): The List of Seven (Edgar award nominee 1995, Nat. Bestseller 1995), The Six Messiahs, 1995. Office: Mark Frost Prodns PO Box 1723 North Hollywood CA 91614-0723

FROST, STERLING NEWELL, arbitrator, mediator, management consultant; b. Oklahoma City, Dec. 21, 1935; s. Sterling Johnson and Eula Dove (Whitford) F.; m. Patricia Joyce Rose, Aug. 18, 1957; children: Patricia Diane Wiscarson, Richard Sterling, Lindy Layne Harrington. BS Indsl. Engring., U. Okla., Norman, 1957; MS Indsl. Engring., Okla. State U., 1966. Registered profl. engr., Okla. Calif. Asst. mgr. acctg. Western Electric, Balt., 1972-73, mgr. indsl. engring., Chgo., 1973-75, mgr. devel. engring., 1975-76, mgr. acct. mgmt., San Francisco, 1976-78, dir. staff, Morristown, N.J., 1978-79; gen. mgr. distbn. & repair AT&T Techs., Sunnyvale, Calif., 1979-85, area v.p. material mgt. svcs. AT&T Info. Systems, Oakland, Calif., 1985-87, ops. v.p. material mgmt. svcs., San Francisco, 1988-89; dir. configuration ops. Businessland, Inc., San Jose, Calif., 1989-90, dir. svcs. support, 1990-91; exec. v.p. Isotek, Tiburon, Calif., 1991; v.p., gen. mgr. Tree Fresh, San Francisco, 1991-92; CFO Prima Pacific, Inc., Tiburon, 1992-93; mgmt. cons., arbitrator/mediator, Sterling Solutions, Tiburon, 1994—; bd. dirs. Contract Office Group, San Jose, 1983—, chmn., 1984—. Bd. dirs. Santa Clara County YMCA, San Jose, Calif., 1981-84. Recipient Man of Day citation Sta. WAIT Radio, Chgo. Mem. Nat. Soc. Prof. Engrs. (chmn. edn. com. 1969-70), Am. Inst. Indsl. Engrs. (pres. bd. dirs. 1966-68), Okla. Soc. Profl. Engrs. (v.p. 1968-69). Republican. Baptist.

FRUCHTER, JONATHAN SEWELL, research scientist, geochemist; b. San Antonio, June 5, 1945; s. Benjamin and Dorothy Ann (Sewell) F.; m. Cecelia Ann Smith, Mar. 31, 1973; children: Diane, Daniel. BS in Chemistry, U. Tex., 1966; PhD in Geochemistry, U. Calif., San Diego, 1971. Research assoc. U. Oreg., Eugene, 1971-74; research scientist Battelle Northwest, Richland, Wash., 1974-79, mgr. research and devel., 1979-87, staff scientist, 1987-91, 94—, tech. group leader, 1991-94. Contbr. numerous articles to profl. jours. Mem. AAAS, Am. Chem. Soc., Phi Beta Kappa, Phi Kappa Phi. Office: Battelle NW PO Box 999 Richland WA 99352-0999

FRUCHTMAN, MILTON ALLEN, film and television producer, director; b. N.Y.C.; s. Benjamin M. and Fanny (Ryan) F.; m. Eva Sternberg; children: Eleanor, Jordan. BS, Columbia U., MS. Dir. NBC, N.Y.C., 1956—; pres. Odyssey Prodns., Inc., N.Y.C., 1958-60; exec. producer Capital Cities Communications, N.Y.C., 1960-74; pres. Visual Media Ltd., Banff, Alta., Can., 1974—; tchr. grad. seminar Yale U., Adelphi U., Banff Sch. Fine Arts; sr. cons. Can. Broadcasting Corp., 1974—; cons. in field. Producer, dir.: (1st color series) High Adventure, CBS, 1957, (1st worldwide electronic news program) Verdict for Tomorrow, 1961 (Peabody award 1962), The Secret of Michaelangelo: Every Man's Dream, ABC, 1968 (Peabody award 1969), Dance Theater of Harlem, PBS, 1973, Those Who Sing Together, CBC, 1987, Search for the Western Sea, CBC, 1989. Recipient awards for TV work including; Peabody award U. Ga., 1962, 69; Emmy award Nat. Acad. TV Arts and Scis., 1962; Gold Hugo award Chgo. Film and TV Festival, 1973; N.Y. Film Festival award, 1974, 77; Martin Luther King Festival award, 1974; award Ohio State U., 1974; Am. Film Festival award, 1974. Mem. Dirs. Guild Am., Columbia U. Alumni Assn. Address: PO Box 1979, Banff, AB Canada T0L 0C0

FRUDDEN, RONALD, agricultural products executive; b. 1941. With King City (Calif.) Packing Co., Inc., 1970—; dir. Frudden Produce, Inc., King City, Calif., 1971—; with Growers Vegetable Express, Salinas, Calif., 1986—; now ptnr. Office: Growers Vegetable Express 1219 Abbott St Salinas CA 93901-4504*

FRUMKIN, GENE, writer, educator; b. N.Y.C., Jan. 29, 1928; s. Samuel and Sarah (Blackman) F.; B.A. in English, UCLA, 1951; m. Lydia Samuels, July 3, 1955 (dec.); children—Celena, Paul. Exec. editor Calif. Apparel News, Los Angeles, 1952-66; asst. prof. English, U. N.Mex., Albuquerque, 1967-71, assoc. prof., 1971-88, prof. 1988-94, prof. emeritus, 1994—. Mem. Associated Writing Programs, Hawaii Literary Arts Council, Pen West. Author: The Hawk and the Lizard, 1963; The Orange Tree, 1965; The Rainbow-Walker, 1968; Dostoevsky and Other Nature Poems, 1972; Locust Cry: Poems 1958-65, 1973; The Mystic Writing-Pad, 1977; Loops, 1979; Clouds and Red Earth, 1982, A Sweetness in the Air, 1987, Comma in the Ear, 1990, Saturn Is Mostly Weather: Selected and Uncollected Poems, 1992; mem. editorial bd. Blue Mesa Rev.; co-editor San Marcos Rev., 1976-83; The Indian Rio Grande: Recent Poems from 3 Cultures (anthology), 1977; editor: Coastlines Lit. Mag., 1958-62, N.Mex. Quar., 1969. Home: 3721 Mesa Verde Ave NE Albuquerque NM 87110-7723

FRUSH, JAMES CARROLL, JR., real estate development company executive; b. San Francisco, Oct. 18, 1930; s. James Carroll and Edna Mae (Perry) F.; m. Patricia Anne Blake, Oct. 29, 1960 (div. 1977); children: Michael, Gloria; m. Carolyn Fetter Bell, Aug. 23, 1978; 1 child, Stephen. BA, Stanford, 1953; postgrad., U. Calif., San Francisco, 1957-58; MA, Saybrook Inst., 1981, PhD, 1985. Ptnr. James C. Frush Co., San Francisco, 1960-70; v.p., bd. dir. Retirement Residence, Inc., San Francisco, 1964-70, pres., 1970—; pres. Nat. Retirement Residence, San Francisco, 1971-89, Casa Dorinda Corp., 1971-89; chairperson Retirement Residence Inc. Ala., Daphne, 1995—; pres. Marin Shakespeare Festival, 1971-73, James C. Frush Found., 1972-78; adj. prof. gerontology, psychology and theology Spring Hill Coll., Mobile, Ala., 1988—; adj. prof. counseling edn. U. South Ala., Mobile; bd. dirs. Gwynned Inc., Blue Bell, Pa. Author (with Benson Eschenbach): The Retirement Residence: An Analysis of the Architecture and Management of Life Care Housing, 1968, Self-Esteem in Older Persons Following a Heart Attack: An Exploration of Contributing Factors, 1985; contbr. articles to profl. jours.; producer ednl. films. Bd. dirs. San Francisco Sr. Ctr., 1973-78, Found. to Assist Calif. Tchrs. Devel. Inc., 1987-89; mem. adv. bd. Christus Theol. Inst., Spanish Ft., Ala., 1992-95; mem. ethics com. adv. bd. Westminster Village, Spanish Ft., 1994—. Mem. Gerontol. Soc., Southeastern Psychol. Assn., Assn. for Anthropology and Gerontology, Stanford Alumni Assn., RSVP (adv. bd. Mobile chpt. 1988-94), C.G. Jung Soc. of Gulf Coast (pres.), Ala. Humanities Found. Speakers Bur. (presenter 1993-94, 94-95). Office: care T Pimsleur 2155 Union St San Francisco CA 94123-4003

FRUTKOFF, GARY, production designer; b. Mineola, N.Y., May 6, 1951; s. Harold and Melanie (Feist) F. Cartoonist Rip Off Press, San Francisco, 1970-73; freelance design and illustrator Marin, Calif., 1973-83; freelance glass sculptor Farallon Studios and others, Marin, 1983-88; freelance prodn. designer L.A., 1989—. Asst. art dir. (feature films) K-9, 1988, Pacific Heights, 1989, Darkman, 1989; prodn. designer (feature films) By the Sword, 1991, Best of the Best II, 1992, King of the Hill, 1992, Fallen Angels, 1993, D2 The Mighty Ducks, 1993, Devil in a Blue Dress, 1994.

FRY, JUDY ARLINE, hypnotherapist; b. Great Falls, Mont., July 25, 1938; d. Ernest Leroy and Leota M. (Lyon) Workman; m. Kenneth J. Fry, Nov. 11, 1956 (div. 1974); children: Kenneth J., Kathy K. Student, Calif. State U., Northridge, 1978. Cert. clin. hypnotherapist. Co-owner, dir. Artistic Designs in Iron, Huntington Beach, Calif., 1969-73; ops. mgr., sales coord., purchasing agt. Komfort Industries Inc., Santa Ana, Calif., 1974-75; corp. adminstr. OEM accounts Greer Hydraulics, Inc., City of Commerce, Calif., 1975-81; office svc. supr. Pacific Pumps/Dresser Industries, Inc., Huntington Park, Calif., 1981-83, aftermarket order entry mgr., 1983-84; ops. dir., dir. pub. rels. Calif. Assn. Real Estate Investors, Laguna Niguel, 1986-87; founder, co-owner Advance Resource Ctr., Garden Grove, Calif., 1987-94, North Las Vegas, 1994—. Author two books. Mem. Nat. Mgmt. Assn., United Hypnotherapists Calif., Internat. Assn. Clin. Hypnotherapists (past pres. Orange County chpt.). Home: 4404 Fenton Ln North Las Vegas NV 89030-0141 Office: Advance Resource Ctr 4404 Fenton Ln North Las Vegas NV 89030-0141

FRY, STEPHEN MICHAEL, music librarian; b. Boise, Idaho, Jan. 5, 1941; s. Homer N. and Alice F.; m. Frances Talbott-White, Jan. 26, 1963; children: John, Kenneth. BA in Music, U. Calif., Riverside, 1964; MA in Music, Claremont (Calif.) Grad. Sch., 1965; MSLS, U. So. Calif., L.A., 1969. Music libr. U. Calif., Riverside, 1966-70; prof. of music Ind. U. of Pa., Indian, Pa., 1970-72; music libr. Northwestern U., Evanston, Ill., 1973-75, UCLA, 1975—; presenter confs. in field; cons. Anton Brees Carillon Libr., Mountain Lake Sanctuary, Lake Wales, Fla., 1972-82; reader Project for the Oral History of Music in Am., N.Y., 1976; cons. in field; dir. Westside Jazz Ensemble, 1989—. Author: California's Musical Wealth, 1985, The Story of the All Women's Orchestras in California, 1985; music editor: American National Biography, 1994—; contbr. articles to profl. jours. Mem. Soc. for Preservation of Film Music (trustee 1986—, sec. 1990—), Music Libr. Assn. (bd. dirs. 1979-81, 95—), Soc. for Preservation of Musical Heritage of So. Calif. (bd. advs. 1988—). Republican. Office: UCLA Music Libr 1102 Schoenberg Hall Univ Calif Los Angeles CA 90095-1490

FRYE, HELEN JACKSON, federal judge; b. Klamath Falls, Oreg., Dec. 10, 1930; d. Earl and Elizabeth (Kirkpatrick) Jackson; m. William Frye, Sept. 7, 1952; children: Eric, Karen, Heidi; 1 adopted child, Hedy; m. Perry Holloman, July 10, 1980 (dec. Sept. 1991). BA in English with honors, U. Oreg., 1953, MA, 1960, JD, 1966. Bar: Oreg. 1966. Public sch. tchr. Oreg., 1956-63; with Riddlesberger, Pederson, Brownhill & Young, 1966-67, Husband & Johnson, Eugene, 1968-71; trial judge State of Oreg., 1971-80; U.S. dist judge Dist. Oreg. Portland, 1980—. Office: US Dist Ct 706 US Courthouse 620 SW Main St Portland OR 97205-3037

FRYE, JUDITH ELEEN MINOR, editor; b. Seattle; d. George Edward and Eleen G. (Hartelius) Minor; student UCLA, 1947-48, U. So. Calif., 1948-53; m. Vernon Lester Frye, Apr. 1, 1954. Acct., office mgr. Colony Wholesale Liquor, Culver City, Calif., 1947-48; credit mgr. Western Distbg. Co., Culver City, 1948-53; ptnr. in restaurants, Palm Springs, L.A., 1948, ptnr. in date ranch, La Quinta, Calif., 1949-53; ptnr., owner Imperial Printing, Huntington Beach, Calif., 1955—; editor, pub. New Era Laundry and Cleaning Lines, Huntington Beach, 1962—; registered lobbyist, Calif., 1975-84. Mem. Textile Care Allied Trade Assn., Laundry & Dry Cleaning Suppliers Assn., Calif. Coin-op Assn. (exec. dir. 1975-84, Cooperation award 1971, Dedicated Svc.award 1976), Nat. Automatic Laundry & Cleaning Coun. (Leadership award 1972), Women Laundry & Drycleaning (past pres., Outstanding Svc. award 1977), Printing Industries Assn., Master Printers Am., Nat. Assn. Printers & Lithographers. Office: 22031 Bushard St Huntington Beach CA 92646-8409

FRYE, KAROLYN FAYE, dietitian, educator; b. Chesterfield, Ill., Sept. 27, 1936; d. Myron V. and Ruth A. (Ewin) Gahr; m. Jacob C. Frye, Feb. 16, 1963; children: Michael J., David C. AA, Mesa C.C., 1978; BS, Ariz. State U., 1981, MEd, 1983, postgrad., 1982. Sch. food svc. dir. dist. 18 Gila River Indian Cmty., Sacaton, Ariz., 1983-85; adminstrv. dietitian SunHealth Corp., Sun City, Ariz., 1985-88; dietary cons., owner Nutrition Unltd., Chandler, Ariz., 1988—; dir. support svcs. Friendship Retirement Corp. DBA Glencroft Care Ctr., Glendale, Ariz., 1993—; mgmt. chair Ctrl. Ariz. Dietetic Assn., Phoenix, 1985, 86, 87, nominating com., 1992-93; adj. faculty Ctrl. Ariz. Coll., 1984—. Author: (dietetic edn. program) Management Functions, 1994, Management Practicum, 1994. Mem. Am. Dietetic Assn. (registered), Ariz. Dietetic Assn. (mgmt. co-chair 1987-88, sec. 1988, 89, 90, legis. com. 1988-89, 90, 91, nominating com. 1990-91, edn. chair 1992-93, mgmt. chair 1994—, arrangements chair annual meeting 1993—), Am. Soc. Parenteral and Enteral Nutrition, Cetral Phoenix Scleraderma Found. (med. bd.). Home: 1120 W Ivanhoe St Chandler AZ 85224-3566 Office: Glencroft Care Ctr 8641 N 67th Ave Glendale AZ 85302-4308

FRYE, WILLIAM EMERSON, physicist, engineer; b. Detroit, June 20, 1917; s. Nels and Lillie (Hagman) F.; m. Elizabeth K. Sayler, June 13, 1942 (dec. 1990); children: Ann, James. AA, Danville (Ill.) Jr. Coll., 1935; AB, U. Ill., 1937, MS, 1938; PhD, U. Chgo., 1941. Group leader, then asst. sect. head Naval Rsch. Lab., Washington, 1942-46; group leader N.Am. Aviation, Inc., L.A., 1946-48; staff mem. Rand Corp., Santa Monica, Calif., 1948-56; dept. mgr. Lockheed Missiles and Space Co., Palo Alto, Calif., 1956-59, consulting scientist, 1959-68, staff scientist, 1968—; rsch. adv. com. NASA, Washington, 1960-64; lectr. in engring. UCLA, 1948-56; lectr. in elec. engring. Stanford (Calif.) U., 1960, 62, 64, 68. Editor: Impact of Space Exploration on Society, 1965. Calendar editor Coun. for Arts, Palo Alto, 1964-68. Recipient Meritorious Civilian Svc. award Naval Rsch. Lab., 1947. Assoc. fellow AIAA; mem. Am. Astronautical Soc. (bd. dirs. 1960-64), Am. Phys. Soc., Sigma Xi, Phi Beta Kappa. Democrat. Unitarian. Home: 536 Lincoln Ave Palo Alto CA 94301-3232

FRYER, GLADYS CONSTANCE, nursing home medical director, educator; b. London, Mar. 28, 1923; came to U.S., 1967; d. William John and Florence Annie (Dockett) Mercer; m. Donald Wilfred Fryer, Jan. 20, 1944; children: Peter Vivian, Gerard John, Gillian Celia. MB, BS, U. Melbourne, Victoria, Australia, 1956. Resident Box Hill Hosp., 1956-57; postdoctoral fellow Inst. of Cardiology, U. London, 1958; med. registrar Queen Victoria Hosp., Melbourne, Australia, 1958; cardiologist Assunta Found., Petaling Jaya, Malaysia, 1961-64; fellow in advanced medicine London Hosp., U. London, 1964; clin. research physician U.S. Army Clin. Research Unit, Malaysia, 1964-66; physician to pesticide program U. Hawaii, 1967-68; internist Hawaii Permanente Kaiser Found., Honolulu, 1968-73; practice medicine specializing in internal medicine Honolulu, 1973-88; med. dir. Hale Nani Health Ctr., Honolulu, 1975-89, Beverly Manor Convalescent Ctr., Honolulu, 1975-89; vis. pediatric cardiac depts. Yale U., Stanford U., U. Calif., 1958; asst. clin. prof. medicine John Burns Sch. Medicine U. Hawaii, 1968-89; vis. geriatrics dept. U. Capetown, 1990; med. cons. Salvation Army Alcohol Treatment Facility, Honolulu, 1975-81; physician to skilled nursing patients VA, Honolulu, 1984-88; preceptor to geriatric nurse practitioner program U. Colo., Honolulu, 1984-85; lectr. on geriatrics, Alzheimer's disease, gen. medicine, profl. women's problems, and neurosci., 1961—; mem. ad hoc due process bd. Med. Care Evaluation Com., 1982-88, Hospice Adv. Com., 1982-88; mem. pharmacy com. St. Francis Hosp. Clin. Staff, 1983-89, chmn. 1983-84. Contbr. articles to profl. jours. Mem. adv. com. Honolulu Home Care St. Francis Hosp., 1974-87; mem. adv. bd. Honolulu Gerontology Program, 1983-89, Straub Home Health Program, Honolulu, 1984-87; mem. sci. adv. bd. Alzheimers Disease and Related Disorders Assn., Honolulu, 1984-89; mem. long term care task force Health and Community Svcs. Coun. Hawaii, 1978-84. Special Ops. Exec., War Office, London, 1943-44. Recipient Edgar Rouse Prize in Indsl. Medicine, U. Melbourne, 1955, Outstanding Supporter award Hawaii Assn. Activity Coordinators, 1987. Fellow ACP; mem. AAAS, Hawaii Med. Assn. (councillor 1984-89), Honolulu County Med. Soc. (chmn., mem. utilization rev. com. 1973-89), World Med. Assn., Am. Geriatrics Soc., N.Y. Acad. Sci. Episcopalian.

FRYER, ROBERT SHERWOOD, theatrical producer; b. Washington, Nov. 18, 1920; s. Harold and Ruth (Reade) F. B.A., Western Res. U., 1943. Producer: (Broadway plays) (with others) A Tree Grows in Brooklyn, 1951, (with others) By the Beautiful Sea, 1954, Wonderful Town, 1953, The Desk Set, Shangri-La, Auntie Mame, Redhead, There Was a Little Girl, Advise and Consent, A Passage To India, Hot Spot, Roar Like a Dove, Sweet Charity, Chicago, 1975, The Norman Conquests, 1976, California Suite, 1976, On the Twentieth Century, 1977, Sweeney Todd, 1978, Merrily We Roll Along, The West Side Waltz, 1981, Noises Off, 1983, Benefactors, 1985, Wild Honey, 1987, Hapgood, 1989, (films) The Boston Strangler, 1968, Abdication, 1973, Mame, 1973, Great Expectations, 1974, Voyage of the Damned, 1976, The Boys from Brazil, 1978, Prime of Miss Jean Brodie 1969, Travels with My Aunt, 1973, The Shining 1979, Chicago, artistic dir., 1972-90; cons., 1990—; Ahmanson Theatre, Ctr. Theatre Group, L.A.; author: Professional Theatrical Management New York City, 1947. Bd. dirs. Kennedy Ctr.; trustee, exec. com. John F. Kennedy Ctr., Washington. Served as capt. AUS, 1941-46; maj. Res. Decorated Legion of Merit.; Rockefeller Found. fellow. Mem. Episcopal Actors Guild (v.p.), League of N.Y. Theatres (bd. govs.). Office: Producer Cir Co 1350 Ave of the Americas Penthouse New York NY 10019

FRYKMAN, GEORGE AXEL, history educator, researcher; b. South San Francisco, Calif., Apr. 30, 1917; s. Axel George and Esther Sophia (Hultberg) F.; m. Elizabeth Marie Fulton, June 14, 1942; children: Alice, Jean, Mary. BA in History, San Jose State U., 1940; MA in History, Stanford U., 1947, PhD in History, 1955. Cert. gen. secondary edn., Calif. Tchr. English and social studies Kerman (Calif.) H.S., 1941-42; instr. western civilization Stanford (Calif.) U., 1949-50; instr. history Wash. State U., Pullman, 1950-51, asst. libr., instr. history, 1951-53, from instr. history to prof. history, 1953-87, asst. to dean Grad. Sch., 1961-64, prof. of history emeritus, 1987—. Co-editor: (symposium) Changing Pacific Northwest, 1988; author: (univ. history) Creating the People's University, 1990; adv. editor: Wash. State Ency. Americana, 1959-64; book rev. editor: The Historian, 1964-66; mem. editl. adv. bd. Pacific N.W. Quar., 1980-94. Capt. USAF, 1942-46. Democrat. Lutheran. Home: SE1015 Spring St Pullman WA 99163

FRYMER, MURRY, columnist, theater critic, critic-at-large; b. Toronto, Ont., Can., Apr. 24, 1934; came to U.S., 1945; s. Dave and Sylvia (Spinrod) F.; m. Barbara Lois Grown, Sept. 4, 1966; children: Paul, Benjamin, Carrie. BA, U. Mich., 1956; student Columbia U., 1958; MA, NYU, 1964. Editor Town Crier, Westport, Conn., 1962-63, Tribune, Levittown, N.Y., 1963-64; viewpoints editor, critic Newsday, L.I., N.Y., 1964-72; asst. mng. editor Rochester Democrat & Chronicle, N.Y., 1972-75; Sunday and feature editor Cleve. Plain Dealer, 1975-77; editor Sunday Mag., Boston Herald Am., 1977-79; film and TV critic San Jose Mercury News, Calif., 1979-83, theater critic, 1983—, columnist, 1983—; instr. San Jose State U., Cleve. State U., judge Emmy awards NATAS, 1968. Author, dir. musical revue Four by Night, N.Y.C., 1963; author (play) Danse Marriage, 1955 (Hopwood prize 1955). Served with U.S. Army, 1956-58. Recipient Best Columnist/Critic award Calif. Publishers Assn., 1993; named Best Columnist, Peninsula Calif. Press Club, 1993. Home: 1060 Moongate Pl San Jose CA 95120-2031 Office: San Jose Mercury News 750 Ridder Park Dr San Jose CA 95131-2432

FU, LEE-LUENG, oceanographer; b. Taipei, Republic of China, Oct. 10, 1950; s. Yi-Chin and Er-Lan (Chen) F.; m. Cecilia C. Liu, Mar. 26, 1977; 1 child, Christine. BS, Nat. Taiwan U., Taipei, 1972; PhD, MIT, 1980. Postdoctoral assoc. MIT, Cambridge, Mass., 1980; mem. tech. staff Jet Propulsion Lab., Pasadena, Calif., 1981-85, tech. group supr., 1986-93, project scientist, 1988—, lead scientist/ocean scis., 1994, sr. rsch. scientist, 1994; chmn. TOPEX/POSEIDON sci. working team NASA, Washington, 1988—, mem. EOS sci. steering com., 1985-87, mem. NSCAT sci. working team, 1986—. Contbr. articles to profl. publs. Recipient Laurels award Aviation Week and Space Tech., 1993, CNES medal French Space Agy., 1994, Exceptional Achievement medal NASA, 1994. Mem. AAAS, Am. Geophys. Union, Am. Meteorol. Soc., Oceanography Soc. Office: Jet Propulsion Lab MS 300-323 4800 Oak Grove Dr Pasadena CA 91109-8001

FUCHIGAMI, LESLIE HIRAO, horticulturist, researcher; b. Lanai, Hawaii, June 11, 1942; s. Susumi and Shigeko (Sakamura) F.; m. Elaine Rei Kisaba, June 1, 1963; children: Sheila Shigeko, Michelle Michiko, Tammy Tamiko, Summer Sachiko, Shane Satomi. MS, U. Minn., St. Paul, 1964, PhD, 1970. From asst. to assoc. prof. Oreg. State U., Corvallis, 1970-80, prof., 1980—; chairperson dept. horticulture U. Hawaii, Honolulu, 1981-82, acting asst. dir. Coll. Tropical Agr. and Human Resources, 1990. Assoc. editor Environ. Horticulture Jour., 1984—; contbr. over 50 articles to profl. jours. Grantee USDA, 1986-88, 87-91, 89-92, Binat. Agrl. R & D Fund, 1988-91. Fellow Am. Soc. for Hort. Sci. (v.p. rsch. 1991-93, assoc. editor

1983-86, Ornamentels Publ. award 1987, Cross-Commodity Publ. award 1990). Office: Oreg State U Dept Horticulture Corvallis OR 97331-2911

FUCHS, BETH ANN, research technician; b. Moberly, Mo., July 22, 1963; d. Larry Dale and Marilyn Sue (Summers) Williams; m. Fred Albano Fuchs Jr., Sept. 30, 1989. AA, Cottey Coll., 1983; BS in Engring., U. N.Mex., 1987. Bookkeeper, chemistry technician U. N.Mex., Albuquerque, 1984-88; rsch. engr. Sandia Nat. Labs., Albuquerque, 1988—. Contbr. articles to profl. jours. Mem. Am. Vacuum Soc. Republican. Home: 336 Espejo St NE Albuquerque NM 87123-1111 Office: Sandia Nat Labs Mail Stop 0603 Divsn 1321-1 PO Box 5800 Albuquerque NM 87185-0603

FUCHS, ROLAND JOHN, geography educator, university administrator; b. Yonkers, N.Y., Jan. 15, 1933; s. Alois L. and Elizabeth (Weigand) F.; m. Gaynell Ruth McAuliffe, June 15, 1957; children: Peter K., Christopher K., Andrew K. BA, Columbia U., 1954, postgrad., 1956-57; postgrad., Moscow State U., 1960-61; MA, Clark U., 1957, PhD, 1959, DSc (hon.), 1995. Asst. prof. to prof. emeritus U. Hawaii, Honolulu, 1958—; chmn. dept. geography U. Hawaii, 1964-86, asst. dean to assoc. dean coll. arts and scis., 1965-67, dir. Asian Studies Lang. and Area Ctr., 1965-67, adj. rsch. assoc. East West Ctr., 1980—, spl. asst. to pres., 1986; vice rector UN U., Tokyo, 1987-94; dir. Internat. Start Secretariat, 1994—; vis. prof. Clark U., 1963-64, Nat. Taiwan U., 1974; mem. bd. internat. orgns. and programs Nat. Acad. Scis., 1976-81, chmn., 1980-81, mem. bd. sci. and tech. in devel., 1980-85; mem. U.S. Nat. Commn. for Pacific Basin Econ. Coop., 1985-87; sr. advisor United Nations U., 1986. Author, editor: Geographical Perspectives on the Soviet Union, 1974, Theoretical Problems of Geography, 1977, Population Distribution Policies in Development Planning, 1981, Urbanization and Urban Policies in the Pacific-Asia Region, 1987, Megacities: The Challenge of the Urben Future, 1994; asst. editor Econ. Geography, 1963-64; mem. editl. adv. com. Soviet Geography: Rev. and Translation, 1966-85, Geoforum, 1988—, African Urban Quar., 1987, Global Environ. Change, 1990—, Asian Geographer, 1991—. Ford Found. fellow, 1956-57; Fulbright Rsch. scholar, 1966-67. Mem. Am. Geog. Union, Internat. Geog. Union (v.p. 1980-84, 1st v.p. 1984-88, pres. 1988-92, past pres. 1992—), Assn. Am. Geographers (Hon. award 1982), Am. Assn. Advancement Slavic Studies (bd. dirs. 1976-81), Pacific Sci. Assn. (coun. 1978—, exec. com. 1986—, sec. gen.-treas. 1991—), Academia Europaea (fgn.). Home: 1200 N Nash St Arlington VA 22209

FUCHS, THOMAS, writer; b. L.A., Dec. 2, 1942; s. Daniel and Susan (Chessen) F. BA, U. Calif., Santa Barbara, 1965. Freelance writer, 1966—; dir. rsch. Wolper Prodns., L.A., 1966-69; staff writer You Asked for It, L.A., 1982; staff writer Ripley's Believe It or Not ABC-TV, L.A., 1983-85; mem. Theater West, Los Angeles. Writer: (TV series pilot) Escape, (TV spls.) What Would You Pay for Yesterday, Henry Fonda: An American Legacy, Crimes of Passion, Mysteries of the Bible, (one-act plays) Two Old Friends, Yea, Beethoven!, (films) Dinosaur, 1987, Two Old Friends, 1987, A Night of Miracles, 1990, (corp. films) Ralson Purina, Occidental Petroleum, Universal Studios Tour, Mobil Oil, Bank of Am., Simon Wiesenthal Ctr., (series episodes) Mysteries of the Bible, 1994; author: The Hitler Fact Book, 1990; contbr. articles to L.A. Times, New West, WGA Jour., New Obs., Hollywood Reporter, Travel & Leisure. Mem. acquisitions com. Hollywood Expn., Los Angeles. Mem. Writers Guild Am. Home: 1427 N Hayworth Ave Apt D West Hollywood CA 90046-3818

FUCHS, VICTOR ROBERT, economics educator; b. N.Y.C., Jan. 31, 1924; s. Alfred and Frances Sarah (Scheiber) F.; m. Beverly Beck, Aug. 29, 1948; children: Nancy, Fredric, Paula, Kenneth. BS, NYU, 1947; MA, Columbia U., 1951, PhD, 1955. Internat. fur broker, 1946-50; lectr. Columbia U., N.Y.C., 1953-54, instr., 1954-55, asst. prof. econs., 1955-59; assoc. prof. econs. NYU, 1959-60; program assoc. Ford Found. Program in Econ. Devel. and Adminstrn., 1960-62; prof. econs. Grad. Ctr., CUNY, 1968-74; prof. community medicine Mt. Sinai Sch. Medicine, 1968-74; prof. econs. Stanford U. and Stanford Med. Sch., 1974—, Henry J. Kaiser Jr. prof., 1988—; v.p. research Nat. Bur. Econ. Research, 1968-78, mem. sr. research staff, 1962—. Author: The Economics of the Fur Industry, 1957; (with Aaron Warner) Concepts and Cases in Economic Analysis, 1958, Changes in the Location of Manufacturing in the United States Since 1929, 1962, The Service Economy, 1968, Production and Productivity in the Service Industries, 1969, Policy Issues and Research Opportunities in Industrial Organization, 1972, Essays in the Economics of Health and Medical Care, 1972, Who Shall Live? Health, Economics and Social Choice, 1975; (with Joseph Newhouse) The Economics of Physician and Patient Behavior, 1978, Economic Aspects of Health, 1982, How We Live, 1983, The Health Economy, 1986, Women's Quest for Economic Equality, 1988, The Future of Health Policy, 1993; contbr. articles to profl. jours. Served with USAAF, 1943-46. Fellow Am. Acad. Arts and Scis., Am. Econ. Assn. (disting.; pres. 1995); mem. Inst. Medicine of NAS, Am. Philos. Soc., Sigma Xi, Beta Gamma Sigma. Home: 796 Cedro Way Stanford CA 94305-1032 Office: Dept Econ Stanford U Stanford CA 94305-6072

FUERSTENAU, DOUGLAS WINSTON, mineral engineering educator; b. Hazel, S.D., Dec. 6, 1928; s. Erwin Arnold and Hazel Pauline (Karterud) F.; m. Margaret Ann Pellett, Aug. 29, 1953; children: Lucy, Sarah, Stephen. BS, S.D. Sch. Mines and Tech., 1949; MS, Mont. Sch. Mines, 1950; ScD, MIT, 1953; Mineral Engr., Mont. Coll. Mineral Sci. and Tech., 1968; hon. doctorate degree, U. Liege, Belgium, 1989. Asst. prof. mineral engring. MIT, 1953-56; sect. leader, metals research lab. Union Carbide Metals Co., Niagara Falls, N.Y., 1956-58; mgr. mineral engring. lab Kaiser Aluminum & Chem. Corp., Permanente, Calif., 1958-59; assoc. prof. metallurgy U. Calif., Berkeley, 1959-62, prof. metallurgy, 1962-86, P. Malozemoff prof. of mineral engring., 1987-93; prof. grad. sch. U. Calif.-Berkeley, 1994—, Miller research prof., 1969-70, chmn. dept. materials sci. and mineral engring., 1970-78; bd. dirs. Homestake Mining Co.; mem. Nat. Mineral Bd., 1975-78; Am. rep. Internat. Mineral Processing Congress Com., 1978—. Editor: Froth Flotation-50th Anniversary Vol., 1962; co-editor-in-chief: Internat. Jour. of Mineral Processing, 1972—; contbr. articles to profl. jours. Recipient Alexander von Humboldt Sr. Am. Scientist award Fed. Republic of Germany, 1984, Frank F. Aplan award The Engring. Found., 1990; Japan Soc. Promotion of Sci. rsch. fellow, 1993. Mem. NAE, AIChE, Am. Inst. Mining and Metall. Engrs. (chmn. mineral processing divsn. 1967, Robert Lansing Hardy gold medal 1957, Rossiter W. Raymond award 1961, Robert H. Richards award 1975, Antoine M. Gaudin award 1978, Mineral Industry Edn. award 1983, Henry Krumb disting. lectr. 1989, hon. 1989), Soc. Mining Engrs. (bd. dirs. 1968-71, Disting. mem.), Am. Chem. Soc., Russian Fedn. Acad. Natural Scis. (fgn. mem.), Sigma Xi, Theta Tau. Congregationalist. Home: 1440 Le Roy Ave Berkeley CA 94708-1912

FUHLRODT, NORMAN THEODORE, former insurance executive; b. Wisner, Nebr., Apr. 24, 1910; s. Albert F. and Lena (Schafersman) F.; student Midland Coll., 1926-28; A.B., U. Nebr., 1930; M.A., U. Mich., 1936; m. Clarice W. Livermore, Aug. 23, 1933; 1 son, Douglas B. Tchr., athletic coach high schs., Sargent, Nebr., 1930-32, West Point, Nebr., 1932-35; with Central Life Assurance Co., Des Moines, 1936-74, pres., chief exec. officer, 1964-72, chmn. bd., chief exec. officer, 1972-74, also dir. Named Monroe St. Jour. Alumnus of Month, U. Mich. Grad Sch. Bus. Adminstrn. Gen. chmn. Greater Des Moines United campaign United Community Service, 1969-70. Former bd. dirs. Des Moines Center Sci. and Industry. Fellow Soc. Actuaries. Home: 230 W Laurel St Apt 606 San Diego CA 92101-1466

FUHRMAN, KENDALL NELSON, software engineer; b. Evansville, Ind., Aug. 1, 1962; s. Ronald Charles and Mildred Elaine (Gulley) F.; m. Susan Ann Bagstad. BS in Computer Sci. and Math., U. Denver, 1984; postgrad., Colo. State U., 1988. Assoc. engr. Am. TV & Communications, Englewood, Colo., 1982-84; mem. tech. staff Hughes Aircraft Corp., Englewood, 1984-85; software engr. Ampex Corp., Golden, Colo., 1985-87, sr. software engr., 1987-88, project leader, 1988-92; project leader Ohmeda, Louisville, Colo., 1992-94; pres. founder Evolving Video Techs., 1994—; cons. in field, Arvada, Colo., 1990—. Contbr. articles to profl. jours.; patentee antialising algorithm, graphics rendering. Mem. Assn. for Computing Machinery, IEEE, Spl. Interest Group Graphics, Spl. Interest Group Computer Human Interaction, Phi Beta Kappa. Home: 8417 Pierson Ct Arvada CO 80005-5238 Office: Evolving Video Tech Corp 7850 Vance Dr Ste 210 Arvada CO 80003-2128

FUJITA, JAMES HIROSHI, history educator; b. Honolulu, July 24, 1958; s. George Hideo and Teruko (Miyano) F. BA, U. Hawaii, 1980, MA, 1983. Grad. asst. U. Hawaii at Manoa, Honolulu, 1980-85, lectr. history, 1986—; lectr. history Kapiolani C.C., Honolulu, 1987—; lectr. Elderhostel Program, Honolulu, 1992. Mem. NEA, Hawaii State Tchrs. Assn., World History Assn., U. Hawaii Profl. Assembly, Phi Alpha Theta. Office: Kapiolani C C 4303 Diamond Head Rd Honolulu HI 96816-4421

FUJITANI, MARTIN TOMIO, software quality engineer; b. Sanger, Calif., May 3, 1968; s. Matsuo and Hasuko Fujitani. BS in Indsl. and Systems Engring., U. So. Calif., 1990. Sec. Kelly Svcs., Inc., Sacramento, 1987; receptionist Coudert Bros., L.A., 1988; rsch. asst. U. So. Calif., L.A., 1988-89; math. aide Navy Pers. Rsch. and Devel. Ctr., San Diego, 1989; quality assurance test technician Retix, Santa Monica, Calif., 1989-90; software engr. Quality Med. Adjudication, Inc., Rancho Cordova, Calif., 1990-92; test engr. Worldtalk Corp., Los Gatos, Calif., 1993-94; quality engr. Lotus Devel. Corp., Mountain View, Calif., 1994—. Assemblyman Am. Legion Calif. Boys State, 1985. Recipient Service Above Self award East Sacramento Rotary, 1986. Mem. Am. Soc. Quality Control, Sacramento Sr. Young Buddhist Assn. (treas. 1990-91), Gen. Alumni Assn. U. So. Calif. (life). Home: 205 Milbrae Ln Apt 2 Los Gatos CA 95030-5459 Office: Lotus Devel Corp 800 El Camino Real W Mountain View CA 94040

FUKUDA, NAOMI NOBUKO, medical/surgical nurse; b. Guam, Mar. 10, 1963; d. Reginald Y. and Michiko (Hanzawa) F. AS in Nursing, U. Hawaii, Honolulu, 1983, BSN, 1985, MSN, 1988. Cert. med.-surg. nurse. Staff nurse Kaiser Med. Ctr., Honolulu, 1985-88; clin. staff nurse Kaiser Permanente Hosp., Honolulu, 1988—. Mem. Hawaii Nurse's Assn., Sigma Theta Tau. Home: 94-270 Makapipipi St Mililani HI 96789-2774

FUKUHARA, HENRY, artist, educator; b. L.A., Apr. 25, 1913; s. Ichisuke and Ume (Sakamoto) F.; m. Fujiko Yasutake, Aug. 18, 1938; children: Joyce, Grace, Rackham, Helen. Student with Edgar A. Whitney, Jackson Heights, N.Y., 1972, Rex Brandt, Corona del Mar, Calif., 1974, Robert E. Wood, 1975, Carl Molno, Woodside, N.Y., 1976. Exhibited in group shows at Friends World Coll., Lloyds Neck, N.Y., 1980, Elaine Benson Gallery, Bridgehampton, N.Y., 1979, 83, Nat. Invitational Watercolor, Zaner Gallery, Rochester, N.Y., 1981, Fire House Gallery, 1982, Parrish Art Mus., 1982, Japan-R.I. Exchange Exhibit, Provincetown, R.I., 1986, Kawakami Gallery, Tokyo, 1986, Setagaya Mus. Art, Tokyo, 1988-91, 5th Ann. Rosoh Kai Watercolor Exhbn. Meguro Mus. Art, Tokyo, 1991, 6th Ann. Rosoh Kai Watercolor Exhbn. Meguro Mus. Art, 1992, 93-95, Stary Sheets Galleries Exhbn., Irvine, Calif., 1992-94, Living Legends, Mira Mesa Colls., 1994; represented in permanent collections at Heckscher Mus., Huntington, N.Y., Abilene Mus. Fine art, Nassau Community Coll., SUNY-Stony Brook, Los Angeles County Mus. Art, Blaine County Mus., Chinook, Mont., Ralston Mus., Sydney, Mont., San Bernardino County Mus., Redlands, Calif., 1984, Riverside Mus. Art, Calif., 1985, Gonzaga U., Spokane, Wash., 1986, Nagano Mus. Art, Japan, 1986, Contemporary Mus. of Art, Hiroshima, 1988, Santa Monica (Calif.) Coll., 1988; instr. Watercolor Venice (Calif.) Adult Sch., 1992-93, tchr. watercolor. Recipient Purchase award Nassau Community Coll., 1976; Best in Show, Hidden Pond, Town of Islip, 1978, Strathmore Paper Co., 1979, Creative Connections Gallery award Foothills Art Ctr., Golden, Colo., 1984, Judges Choice, Mont. Minature Art Soc. 7th Ann International Show, Working with Abandoned Control, 1993, others. Mem. Nat. Watercolor Soc., Ala. Watercolor Soc., Pitts. Watercolor Soc., Nat. Drawing Assn. Subject of profl. publs. Address: 1214 Marine St Santa Monica CA 90405-5815

FUKUMOTO, BERT KEN, lawyer; b. Yokohama, Japan, July 30, 1955; came to U.S., 1973; s. Herbert Tadao and Kikuko (Takagi) F.; m. Karen Dee Randolph, Aug. 10, 1985; children: Ken, Derek. BA, U. Oreg., 1978, JD, 1981. Bar: Oreg. 1981. Instr. law, dir. acad. support U. Oreg., Eugene, 1982-84, dir. career placement, 1983-84; ptnr. Lane Powell Spears Lubersky, Portland, 1984—; bd. dirs. exec. com. Pacific N.W. Internat. Trade Assn., Portland, 1986-88. Active City Club, Portland, Japan-Am. Soc., Portland, World Affairs Coun., Portland, N.W. Regional China Coun., Portland. Mem. ABA, Oreg. State Bar Assn. (exec. com. civil rights sect. 1988-90), Multnomah County Bar Assn., Internat. Bar Assn., Asia Pacific Lawyers Assn. Office: Lane Powell Spears Lubersky 520 SW Yamhill St Ste 800 Portland OR 97204-1331

FUKUMOTO, LESLIE SATSUKI, lawyer; b. Los Angeles, Mar. 10, 1955; parents: Robert Fukumoto and Florence Teruko Kodama Kuroda. BA, U. Hawaii, 1977; JD, William S. Richard Sch. Law, 1980. Bar: Hawaii 1980, U.S. Dist. Ct. Hawaii 1980, U.S. Ct. Appeals (9th cir.) 1981. Dep. pub. defender State of Hawaii, Honolulu, 1980-81; assoc. Pyun, Kim & Okimoto, Honolulu, 1981-83; ptnr. Pyun, Okimoto & Fukumoto, Honolulu, 1983-84; sole practice Honolulu, 1984-85; ptnr. Fukumoto & Wong, Honolulu, 1985-93, Tanaka & Fukumoto, Honolulu, 1993-94; prin. Fukumoto Law Corp., Honolulu, 1994—; bd. dirs. Alexander Bros., Ltd., Honolulu. Assoc. editor U. Hawaii Law Rev., 1979-80. Mem. Assn. Trial Lawyers Am. Club: Honolulu. Office: 1001 Bishop St Ste 976 Honolulu HI 96813-3429

FUKUSHIMA, BARBARA NAOMI, financial consultant; b. Honolulu, Apr. 5, 1948; d. Harry Kazuo and Misayo (Kawasaki) Murakoshi; m. Dennis Hiroshi Fukushima, Mar. 23, 1974; 1 child, Dennis Hiroshi Jr. BA with high honors, U. Hawaii, 1970; postgrad. Oreg. State U., 1971, 73, U. Oreg., 1972. Intern, Coopers & Lybrand, Honolulu, 1974; auditor Haskins & Sells, Kahului, Hawaii, 1974-77; pres. Book Doors, Inc., Pukalani, 1977—; pres. Barbara N. Fukushima CPA, Inc., Wailuku. 1979—; sec. treas. Target Pest Control, Inc., Wailuku, 1979—; internal auditor, acct. Maui Land & Pineapple Co., Inc., Kahului, 1977-80; auditor Hyatt Regency Maui, Kaanapali, 1980-81; ptnr. D & B Internat., Pukalani, 1980-91; instr. Maui Community Coll., Kahului, 1982-85; fin. cons. Merrill Lynch, Pierce, Fenner & Smith, Inc., 1986—. Recipient Phi Beta Kappa Book award, 1969. Mem. AICPA, Hawaii Soc. C.P.A.s, Bus. and Profl. Women's Club. Tenrikyo. Home: 1088 Bishop St Apt 1612 Honolulu HI 96813-3120 Office: 1001 Bishop St Penthouse Honolulu HI 96813

FUKUYAMA, KIMIE, medical educator; b. Tokyo, Dec. 11, 1927; came to U.S., 1956; MD, Tokyo Women's Med. Coll., 1949, PhD, 1963; MS, U. Mich., 1958. Resident dermatology Tokyo Med. Coll., 1950-55; asst. prof. Tokyo Women's Med. Coll., 1961-64; lectr. U. Calif., San Francisco, 1965-67, asst. prof. in residence, 1967-72, assoc. prof. in residence, 1972-78, prof. in residence, 1978—, vice chmn., 1980—, dir. postgrad. tng., 1976—. Mem. Am. Acad. Dermatology (life), Japanese Assn. for Dermatology (hon.), Soc. for Investigative Dermatology (patron). Office: U Calif 533 Parnassus Ave San Francisco CA 94122-2722

FULCO, ARMAND JOHN, biochemist; b. Los Angeles, Apr. 3, 1932; s. Herman J. and Clelia Marie (DeFeo) F.; m. Virginia Loy Hungerford, June 18, 1955 (div. July 1985); children: William James, Lisa Marie, Linda Susan, Suzanne Yvonne; m. Doris V.N. Goodman, Nov. 29, 1987. B.S. in Chemistry, UCLA, 1957, Ph.D. in Physiol. Chemistry, 1960. NIH postdoctoral fellow Lipid Labs. UCLA, 1960-61; NIH research fellow dept. chemistry Harvard U., Cambridge, Mass., 1961-63; biochemist, prin. investigator Lab. Nuclear Medicine and Radiation Biology, UCLA, 1963-80; asst. prof. dept. biol. chemistry UCLA (Med. Sch.), 1965-70, assoc. prof., 1970-76, prof., 1976—, prin. investigator lab. biomed. and environ. scis., 1981-93; prin. investigator lab. structural biology/molecular med. UCLA-Dept. of Energy, 1993—; cons. biochemist VA, Los Angeles, 1968-79; mem. UCLA Molecular Biology Inst., 1991—; co-dir. Lipid-Hormone Core Lab., UCLA, 1989—. Author: (with J.F. Mead) The Unsaturated and Polyunsaturated Fatty Acids in Health and Disease, 1976; contbr. over 90 articles to sci. jours. Served with U.S. Army, 1952-54. Mem. Am. Chem. Soc., Am. Soc. Biochem. and Molecular Biology, Am. Oil Chemists Soc., AAAS, Am. Soc. Microbiology, Harvard Chemists Assn., Sigma Xi. Office: Lab Structural Biology Molecular Medicine UCLA 900 Veteran Ave Los Angeles CA 90024

FULD, FRED, III, computer consultant, financial consultant; b. San Pedro, Calif., July 31, 1952; s. Fred Jr. and Gloria Mary F.; m. Sharon Elizabeth Fuld; 1 child, Fred IV. BA in Bus., Rockford Coll., 1974, BA in Econs., 1974; postgrad., Heriot-Watt U., Berkeley/Edenburgh. Cert. tchr. credential, Calif.; Registered Investment Advisor, SEC, 1981. Investment mgr. San Diego Securities, 1974-78; market maker Pacific Stock Exch., San Francisco, 1978-79; v.p. CGR Conss., San Francisco, 1979-83; pvt. practice fin., computer cons. Concord, Calif., 1983—. Author: (software) Personal Financial Planning, 1984, (software) Asset Allocation, 1986, (software) Business Valuation, 1986; author: Stock Market Secrets, 1985, 101 Most Asked Questions about the MAC, 1992. Mem. Mensa Soc. (life), The Magic Castle (life). Office: 3043 Clayton Rd Concord CA 94519-2730

FULD, STEVEN ALAN, financial advisor, insurance tax planning specialist; b. Balt., Aug. 20, 1963; s. George Joseph Fuld and Nancy (Morstein) Boltz; m. Julie Michelle Glaser, Jan. 21, 1989; 1 child, Zachary Aaron. Student, Calif. State U., Northridge, 1981-85; postgrad., Am. Coll., 1991—. CLU, ChFC. Agt. Lincoln Nat. Life, Tarzana, Calif., 1984-85; ptnr. The Skyline Group, Encino, Calif., 1985—; mem. extended faculty Am. Coll., 1990-92; lectr. Georgetown U., Nat. Assn. Health Underwriters, Nat. Assn. Life Underwriters, Calif. Soc. CPAs, Internat. Soc. Appraisers, March of Dimes, City Nat. Bank, L.A. Bus. Jour., Forth Fin. Network, others. Contbg. author: Business Insurance Law and Practice, 1989; contbr. articles to profl. jours. Trustee Temple Beth Haverim; mem. planned giving com. Arthritis Found. Named Man of Yr., Pacific S.W. Region, Fedn. Jewish Men's Clubs, 1993. Mem. Am. Soc. CLU and ChFC (lectr., bd. dirs. San Fernando Valley chpt. 1989-92, Disting. Svc. award 1990, 92), Beverly Hills Estate Counselors Forum (bd. dirs. 1992-95), Conejo Valley Estate Counselors Forum (founder), Nat. Assn. Life Underwriters, Assn. for Advanced Life Underwriting, Temple Beth Haverim Men's Club (pres.), Temple Beth Haverim (trustee, v.p. ways and means 1993-95). Office: The Skyline Group Second Fl 15928 Ventura Blvd Encino CA 91436-2754

FULKERSON, WILLIAM MEASEY, JR., college president; b. Moberly, Mo., Oct. 18, 1940; s. William Measey and Edna Frances (Pendleton) F.; m. Grace Carolyn Wisdom, May 26, 1962; children: Carl Franklin, Carolyn Sue. BA, William Jewell Coll., 1962; MA, Temple U., 1964; PhD, Mich. State U., 1969. Asst. to assoc. prof. Calif. State U., Fresno, 1981—; asst. to pres. Calif. State U.-Fresno, 1971-73; assoc. exec. dir. Am. Assn. State Colls., Washington, 1973-77; acad. v.p. Phillips U., Enid, Okla., 1977-81; pres. Adams State Coll., Alamosa, Colo., 1981-94, State Colls. in Colo., 1994—; interim pres. Met. State Coll., Denver, 1987-88. Author: Planning for Financial Exigency, 1973; contbr. articles to profl. jours. Commr. North Ctrl. Assn., Chgo., 1980—; bd. dirs. Acad. Collective Bargaining Info. Svc., Washington, 1976, Office for Advancement Pub. Negro Colls., Atlanta, 1973-77, Colo. Endowment for Humanities, 1988—. Named Disting. Alumni William Jewell Coll., 1982, Outstanding Alumnus Mich. State U. Coll. Comm., Arts & Scis., 1987. Mem. Am. Assn. State Colls. and Univs. (parliamentarian, bd. dirs. 1992-94), Am. Coun. on Edn. (bd. dirs.), Assn. Pub. Coll.s and Univs. Pres.s (pres. 1994-95), Nat. Assn. Sys. Heads, Alamosa C. of C. (dir., pres. 1984 Citizen Yr. award), Nat. Assn. of Syss. (pres. 1994—), Rotary. Office: State Colls in Colo 1580 Lincoln St Ste 750 Denver CO 80203-1509

FULLER, EDWIN DANIEL, hotel executive; b. Richmond, Va., Mar. 15, 1945; s. Ben Swint and Evelyn (Beal) F.; m. Denise Kay Perigo, July 17, 1969. Student, Wake Forest U., 1965; BSBA, Boston U., 1968; postgrad., Harvard Sch. Bus., 1987. Security officer Pinkerton Inc., Boston, 1965-68; with sales dept. Turn Bridges Marriott Hotel, Arlington, Va., 1972-73; nat. sales mgr. Marriott Hotels & Resorts, N.Y.C., 1973-76; dir. nat. and internat. sales Marriott Hotels & Resorts, Washington, 1976-78; v.p. mktg. Marriott Hotels & Resorts, 1978-82; gen. mgr. Marriott Hotels & Resorts, Hempstead, N.Y., 1982-83, Marriott Copley Place, Boston, 1983-85; v.p. ops. Midwest region Marriott Corp., Rosemont, Ill., 1985-89; v.p. ops. Western and Pacific regions Marriott Corp., Santa Ana, Calif., 1989-90; sr. v.p., mng. dir. Marriott Hotels & Resorts-Internat., Washington, 1990-93; exec. v.p., mng. dir. internat. lodging Marriott Internat. Lodging, Washington, 1994—; chmn. bd. dirs. SNR Reservation System, Zurich, Switzerland, 1979-81; bd. dirs. Boston U. Hotel Sch., 1984—, Mgmt. Engrs. Inc., Reston, Va.; treas. MEI Pacific Honolulu, 1985—; bd. dirs. Queensway Hotel, Hong Kong, 1989-93; chmn. Fuller Properties, Laguna Hills, Calif., 1990—. Pres. Boston U. Gen. Alumni Assn., 1993—, v.p., 1990-93; v.p. Boston U. Sch. Mgmt. Alumni Bd., 1985—; mem. adv. bd. Boston U. Hospitality Mgmt. Sch., 1985—; trustee Boston U., mem. exec. com. bd. trustees, 1994—. Capt. U.S. Army, 1968-72, Vietnam. Decorated Bronze Star. Mem. Boston U. Alumni Coun. (v.p.), Harvard Sch. Bus. Advanced Mgmt. Program (fund agt.), Sigma Alpha Epsilon, Delta Sigma Pi. Republican. Home: 25362 Derby Hl Laguna Hills CA 92653-7835 Office: Marriott Hotels & Resorts 1 Marriott Dr Washington DC 20058-0001

FULLER, JAMES WILLIAM, financial director; b. Rochester, Ind., Apr. 3, 1940; s. Raymond S. and Mildred (Osteimeier) F.; children: Kristen Anne, Glen William. AA, San Bernardino (Calif.) Valley Coll., 1960; BS, San Jose (Calif.) State U., 1962; MBA, Calif. State U., 1967. V.p. Dean Witter, San Francisco, 1967-71, Shields & Co., San Francisco, 1971-74; dir. fin. programs SRI Internat., Menlo Park, Calif., 1974-77; sr. v.p. N.Y. Stock Exch., N.Y.C., 1977-81, Charles Schwab & Co., San Fransico, 1981-85; pres. Bull & Bear Corp., N.Y.C., 1985-87; dir. Bridge Info. Systems, San Fransico, 1987—; bd. dirs. Action Trac Inc., L.A., Current Techs. Inc., Vancouver, B.C., Environ. Scis. Inc., San Diego; chmn. bd. dirs. Pacific Rsch. Inst., 1992—. Dir. Securities Industry Protection Corp., Washington, 1981-87, Global Econ. Action Inst., N.Y.C., 1989—; trustee U. Calif., Santa Cruz. Lt. USN, 1963-66. Mem. The Family Club (San Francisco), Olympic Club (San Francisco), Jonathon Club (L.A.), Univ. Club (N.Y.C.), The Lincoln Club (San Francisco), Polit. Com. for Econ. Growth, Internat. Platform Assn., Newcomer Soc., World Affairs Coun., Coun. on Formulations (San Francisco com.), Commonwealth Club. Republican. Presbyterian. Home: 2584 Filbert St San Francisco CA 94123-3318 Office: Bridge Info Systems 555 California St San Francisco CA 94104-1502

FULLER, KENNETH ROLLER, architect; b. Denver, Mar. 7, 1913; s. Robert Kenneth and Nelle Grace (Roller) F.; m. Gertrude Alene Heid, June 16, 1938; children: Robert K. II, Richard H. Student in archtl. engring., U. Colo., 1932-35; student in engring., U. Denver, 1935-36; student in architecture, U. Ill., 1936-37. Registered architect, Colo. Archtl. draftsman Robert K. Fuller, Denver, 1937-40, chief draftsman, 1941-42; architect, engr. U.S. Engrs., Denver and Nebr., 1942-46, architect, 1947-48; ptnr., architect Fuller Fuller & Fuller, Denver, 1949-64; prin. Fuller & Fuller, Denver, 1965-70; pres., owner Fuller Fuller & Assocs., Denver, 1971-81, semi-retired, 1982—; archtl. cons., 1973-76; instr. in architecture U. Colo., Denver, 1947-48. Author: 100 Years of Architecture Roeschlaub-Fuller, 1873-1973, 1973; co-author: Robert S. Roeschlaub—Architect of the Emerging West, 1873-1923, 1987. Recipient Honor award U. Colo. Coll. of Design and Planning, 1983, Award of Merit, Am. Assn. State and Local History, 1989. Mem. AIA (chmn. membership com. Colo. chpt. 1951-60, bd. dirs. Colo. chpt. 1960-63, author history Colo. chpt. 1985-86, Combined Service award with Colo. Soc. Architects and Denver, North, South and West chpts. 1980, honored with nat. fellowship 1984, Colo. Architect of Yr. 1989), Colo. Soc. Architects-AIA (fellow emeritus 1985, permanent corp. trustee and sec./treas. ednl. fund 1966—, Disting. Service award 1970, Outstanding Service Cert. 1974), Colo. Hist. Soc. (hon. curator 1981), Nat. Trust for Hist. Preservation, Grand County Hist. Soc., Nat. Rifle Assn., Sigma Chi. Republican. Presbyterian. Lodge: Lions (bd. dirs. Denver 1964-66, 76-77, 35 Yr. Old Monarch award 1987). Home: 1932 Hudson St Denver CO 80220-1459 Office: Fuller Fuller & Assocs 1615 California St Ste 508 Denver CO 80202-3714

FULLER, ROBERT KENNETH, architect, urban designer; b. Denver, Oct. 6, 1942; s. Kenneth Roller and Gertrude Ailene (Heid) F.; m. Virginia Louise Elkin, Aug. 23, 1969; children: Kimberly Kirsten, Kelsey Christa. BArch, U. Colo., 1967; MArch and Urban Design, Washington U., St. Louis, 1974. Archtl. designer Fuller & Fuller, Denver; architect, planner Urban Research and Design Ctr., St. Louis, 1970-72; prin. Fuller & Fuller Assocs., Denver, 1972—. Past pres. Denver East Ctrl. Civic Assn.; pres. Country Club Improvement Assn.; bd. dirs. Cherry Creek Steering Com., Horizon Adventures, Inc. Mem. AIAA (past pres. Denver chpt.), Colo. Arlberg Club, Phi Gamma Delta, Delta Phi Delta. Home: 2244 E 4th Ave Denver CO 80206-4107 Office: 3320 E 2nd Ave Denver CO 80206-5302

FULLER, WILLIAM ROGER, mathematics and physics educator; b. North Kingston, R.I., Nov. 4, 1949; s. Roger William and Stefania Theresa (Minta) F. BS, Trinity Coll., Hartford, Conn., 1971; MS, Ind. U., 1972,

MA, 1976, PhD, 1979. Tchr. St. Joseph's High Sch., South Bend, Ind., 1976-77, Holy Cross Jr. Coll., Notre Dame, Ind., 1978-80; assoc. prof. U. Portland, Oreg., 1980—; cons. St. Mary's Acad., Portland, 1983. Contbr. articles to profl. jours. 1st lt. USAF, 1973. Mem. Am. Math. Soc., Soc. for Indsl. and Applied Math., Am. Inst. Physics (referee 1983—), Am. Assn. Physics Tchrs., Internat. Assn. Mathematical Physics, Sigma Pi Sigma. Republican. Roman Catholic. Office: U Portland 5000 N Willamette Blvd Portland OR 97203-5743

FULLERTON, GAIL JACKSON, university president emeritus; b. Lincoln, Nebr., Apr. 29, 1927; d. Earl Warren and Gladys Bernice (Marshall) Jackson; m. Stanley James Fullerton, Mar. 27, 1967; children by previous marriage—Gregory Snell Putney, Cynde Putney Mitchell. B.A., U. Nebr., 1949, M.A., 1950; Ph.D., U. Oreg., 1954. Lectr. sociology Drake U., Des Moines, 1955-57; asst. prof. sociology Fla. State U., Tallahassee, 1957-60; asst. prof. sociology San Jose (Calif.) State U., 1963-67, asso. prof., 1968-71, prof., 1972-91, dean grad. studies and research, 1972-76, exec. v.p. univ., 1976-78, pres., 1978-91; ret., 1991; bd. dirs. Assoc. Western Univs., Inc., 1980-91; mem. sr. accrediting commn. Western Assn. Schs. and Colls., 1982-88, chmn., 1985-86; mem. Pres.'s Commn. Nat. Collegiate Athletic Assn., 1986-91; bd. dirs. Am. Coll. Assn., 1991. Author: Survival in Marriage, 2d edit, 1977, (with Snell Putney) Normal Neurosis: The Adjusted American, 2d edit, 1966. Carnegie fellow, 1950-51, 52-53; Doherty Found. fellow, 1951-52. Mem. Phi Beta Kappa, Phi Kappa Phi, Chi Omega. Home: 1643 Tompkins Hill Rd Fortuna CA 95540-9728

FULLMER, DANIEL WARREN, psychologist, educator; b. Spoon River, Ill., Dec. 12, 1922; s. Daniel Floyd and Sarah Louisa (Essex) F.; m. Janet Satomi Saito, June 1980; children: Daniel William, Mark Warren. B.S., Western Ill. U., 1947, M.S., 1952; Ph.D., U. Denver, 1955. Post-doctoral intern psychiat. div. U. Oreg. Med. Sch., 1958-61; mem. faculty U. Oreg., 1955-66; prof. psychology Oreg. System of Higher Edn., 1958-66; faculty Coll. Edn. U. Hawaii, Honolulu, 1966—, now prof., 1974—; pvt. practice psychol. counseling; cons. psychologist Grambling State U., 1960-81; founder Free-Family Counseling Ctrs., Portland, Oreg., 1959-66, Honolulu, 1966-74; co-founder Child and Family Counseling Ctr., Waianae, Oahu, Hawaii, Kilohana United Meth. Ch., Oahu, 1992; pres. Human Resources Devel. Ctr., Inc., 1974—; chmn. Hawaii State Bd. to License Psychologists, 1973-78. Author: Counseling: Group Theory & System, 2d. edit., 1978, The Family Therapy Dictionary Text, 1991, MANABU, Diagnosis and Treatment of a Japanese Boy with a Visual Anomaly, 1991; co-author: Principles of Guidance, 2d. edit., 1977; author (counselor/cons. training manuals) Counseling: Content and Process, 1964, Family Consultation Therapy, 1968, The School Counselor-Consultant, 1972; editor: Bulletin, Oreg. Coop Testing Service, 1955-57, Hawaii P&G Jour., 1970-76; assoc. editor: Educational Perspectives, U. Hawaii Coll. Edn. Served with USNR, 1944-46. Recipient Francis E. Clark award Hawaii Pers. Guidance Assn., 1972, Thomas Jefferson award for Outstanding Pub. Svc., 1993; named Hall of Fame Grambling State U., 1987. Mem. Am. Psychol. Assn., Am. Counseling Assn. (Nancy C. Wimmer award 1963). Methodist. Office: 1750 Kalakaua Ave Apt 809 Honolulu HI 96826-3725

FULLMER, DONALD KITCHEN, insurance executive; b. Rockyford, Colo., Apr. 11, 1915; s. George Clinton and Florence E. (Kitchen) F.; m. June 5, 1934 (dec. 1987); children: Robert E., Maxine Fullmer Vogt, Phyllis R. Fullmer Danielson. CLU, Am. Coll. Life Underwriting, 1962. Lic. ins. agt., Wash. Life underwriter N.Y. Life, Aberdeen, Wash., 1954-74; ind. gen. agt. Aberdeen, Wash., 1974-81; life underwriter MONY, Bellingham, Wash., 1983-88; ret. County chmn. Rep. Party, Grays Harbor, Wash., 1964-69, mem. state exec. com., 1971-72. With U.S. Army, 1945. Mem. N.W. Wash. Assn. Life Underwriters, Wash. State Assn. Life Underwriters (pres. 1968-69), Twin Harbor Life Underwriters, Masons. LDS. Home: 5464 Bell West Dr Bellingham WA 98226-9033

FULLMER, STEVEN MARK, banker; b. San Francisco, Mar. 15, 1956; s. Thomas Patrick and Patricia Ann (Carroll-Boyd) F.; m. Rhonda Lynnette Bush, Nov. 8, 1992; 1 child, Wesley Stevenson. BA in Chemistry, Willamette U., 1978, BA in Biology, 1978; MBA, Ariz. State U., 1993. Sr. engr., project leader Honeywell Large Computer Products, Phoenix, 1981-86; bank officer, cons., infosecurity cons. First Interstate Bank, Phoenix, 1987—; cons. J.A. Boyd & Assocs., San Francisco, 1985—, ImaginInc. Consulting, Phoenix, 1985—. Contbr. articles to profl. jours. Mem. exec. bd. Grand Canyon coun. Boy Scouts Am., scoutmaster, 1983-88, commr., 1988-92, dist. chmn., 1995; founder, lt. comdr. Maricopa County Sheriff's Adj. Posse, 1982-93; pres. Heard Mus. Coun.; rehabber Liberty Wildlife. Recipient Order of Merit Boy Scouts Am., 1988, Nat. Disting. Commr. award Boy Scouts Am., 1990, Nat. Founder's award Boy Scouts Am., 1991, Silver Beaver award Boy Scouts Am., 1994. Mem. Am. Inst. for Cert. Computer Profls. (cert. data processor 1985), Mensa, KC (membership dir. 1988), Phi Lambda Upsilon, Phi Eta Sigma, Kappa Sigma, Alpha Chi Sigma, Sigma Iota Epsilon, Beta Gamma Sigma. Republican. Roman Catholic. Office: First Interstate Bank 1150 E University Tempe AZ 85281

FULLMER, TERRY LLOYD, tax consultant, business consultant; b. Driggs, Idaho, June 23, 1939; s. W. Leigh and Addie B. (Harris) F.; m. Beverly Ann Lowe, July 9, 1970; children: Jody, Wendy, Dana, Christopher, Kelly. AA, Ricks Coll., Rexburg, Idaho, 1959; BA, Brigham Young U., 1963. Enrolled agt.; accredited tax advisor; cert. tax profl. Vol. Peace Corps, Dominican Republic, 1963-65; tchr. Modesto (Calif.) High Sch., 1967, Ganesha High Sch., Pomona, Calif., 1968-69; ins. broker Continental Casualty Ins., L.A., 1969-71; tax cons., owner Fullmer & Assocs., Orange, Calif., 1972—. Trustee Gail Pattison Youth Leadership Trust, Orange, 1986—; chair steering com. Orange Sch Dist., 1988. Mem. Nat. Enrolled Agts. Assn., Calif. Soc. Enrolled Agts., Orange County Soc. Enrolled Agts., Nat. Soc. Tax Profls., Orange C. of C. (pres., bd. dirs.). Mem. LDS Ch. Home: 5251 Pasatiempo Dr Yorba Linda CA 92686-4308 Office: Fullmer & Assocs 2133 W Chapman Ave Ste M Orange CA 92668-2329

FULTON, NORMAN ROBERT, home entertainment company executive; b. Los Angeles, Dec. 16, 1935; s. Robert John and Fritzi Marie (Wacker) F.; AA, Santa Monica Coll., 1958; BS, U. So. Calif., 1960; m. Nancy Butler, July 6, 1966; children: Robert B., Patricia M. Asst. v.p. Raphael Glass Co., Los Angeles, 1960-65; credit adminstr. Zellerbach Paper Co., Los Angeles, 1966-68; gen. credit mgr. Carrier Transicold Co., Montebello, Calif., 1968-70, Virco Mfg. Co., Los Angeles, 1970-72, Superscope, Inc., Chatsworth, Calif., 1972-79; asst. v.p. credit and adminstrn. Inkel Corp., Carson, Calif., 1980-82; corp. credit mgr. Gen. Consumer Electronics, Santa Monica, Calif., 1982-83; br. credit mgr. Sharp Electronics Corp., Carson, Calif., 1983—. Served with AUS, 1955-57. Fellow Nat. Inst. Credit (cert. credit exec.); mem. Credit Mgrs. So. Calif., Nat. Notary Assn. Home: 9 Vista Loma Box 2280 Rancho Mirage CA 92270

FULTON, RICHARD DELBERT, dean; b. Missoula, Mont., Feb. 5, 1945; s. C. Dulane and E. Benita (Lyon) F.; m. Suzanne Lee Mathews, Nov. 5, 1976; children: David Amil, Effie Lee. BA in English, Ea. Mont. Coll., 1967; MA in English, U. S.D., 1969; PhD in English, Wash. State U., 1975. Instr. U. Md., College Park, 1970-71; asst. dean Wash. State U., Pullman, 1975-82, 83-84; dean in residence Coun. Grad. Schs., Washington, 1982-83; assoc. dean Iona Coll., New Rochelle, N.Y., 1984-86; provost Rocky Mountain Coll., Billings, Mont., 1986-89; dean of faculty Clark Coll., Vancouver, Wash., 1989—; cons. Coun. Grad. Schs., 1983; chair personnel com. Wash. Instrnl. Commn., 1990. Co-editor: Henry Fielding: An Annotated Bibliography, 1980, Union List of Victorian Serials, 1985; editor: Victorian Periodicals Rev., 1993; contbr. numerous articles and revs. on Victorian periodicals and European lit. Bd. dirs. United Way, Pullman, 1976-78. Mem. Rsch. Soc. for Victorian Periodicals (pres. 1989— bd. dirs. 1984—), North Am. Conf. British Studies, Am. Assn. Higher Edn., Nat. Coun. Instrnl. Adminstrs. Democrat. Episcopalian. Office: Clark Coll 1800 E Mcloughlin Blvd Vancouver WA 98663-3509

FULTZ, PHILIP NATHANIEL, management analyst; b. N.Y.C., Jan. 29, 1943; s. Otis and Sara Love (Gibbs) F.; m. Bessie Learleane McCoy, Mar. 11, 1972. AA in Bus., Coll. of the Desert, 1980; BA in Mgmt., U. Redlands, 1980, MA in Mgmt., 1982. Enlisted USMC, 1967, advanced through grades to capt., 1972, served in various locations, 1964-78, resigned commn., 1978; CETA coord. County of San Bernardino, Yucca Valley, Calif., 1978-85; contract analyst Advanced Technology, Inc., Twentynine Palms, Calif., 1985-88; spl. transit analyst Omintrans, San Bernardino, Calif., 1988-89; tech. analyst Atlantic Rsch. Corp. (formerly Calculon Corp.), Twentynine Palms, Calif., 1988—; mgmt. analyst Marine Corps Base, Twentynine Palms, Calif., 1991—. Founding dir., Unity Home Battered Women's Shelter, Joshua Tree, Calif., 1982, Morongo Basin Adult Literacy; bd. dirs. Twentynine Palms Water Dist., 1991—. Mem. Rotary (sec. Joshua Tree chpt. 1983-85). Republican. Home: 73477 Desert Trail Dr Twentynine Palms CA 92277-2218 Office: Morale Welfare & Recreation Marine Corp Base Twentynine Palms CA 92277-2302

FUNG, K. C., economics educator; b. Hong Kong, Mar. 2, 1955; s. Wing-Kwong and Yin-Chu (Hung) Fung; m. Nancy Fung-Justin; 1 child, Kristina Fung. BA, Swarthmore Coll., 1979; MA, U. Wis., 1983, PhD, 1984. Asst. prof. Mount Holyoak Coll., South Hadley, Mass., 1984-89; asst. prof. U. Calif., Santa Cruz, 1989-93, assoc. prof., 1993—; vis. asst. prof. Stanford U., Palo Alto, Calif., 1988-89; sr. staff economist coun. Econ. Advisors, Washington, 1992-93; cons. World Bank, Washington, 1993—. Contbr. articles to profl. jours. Rsch. grantee Pacific Rim U. Calif., 1991, 92, Inst. Global Conflict and Cooperation, 1991. Mem. Am. Econs. Assn. Office: U Calif Dept Econs Santa Cruz CA 95064

FUNK, MILTON ALBERT, real estate broker; b. Cantonement, Okla., Oct. 12, 1918; s. John Anton and Cornelia Elizabeth (Schwake) F.; m. Earline Myrtle Burkholder, Feb. 15, 1937; children: DeAnne Funk Kiralla, Gary Milton. Cert. in real estate, UCLA, 1960. Owner Realty Sales & Exchange Co., South Gate, Calif., 1961—; sec.-treas. Apt. Investments, Inc., South Gate, 1961—; dir. Apple Valley View Water Assn., cons. to Los Angeles Apartment Assn. Directory, 1987. Served with arty. AUS, 1944-46, PTO. Mem. Calif. Assn. Realtors (regional v.p. 1969, dir.), S.E. Bd. Realtors (pres. 1966, dir. 1980), Los Angeles County Apt. Assn. (dir., sec.), Laguna Shores Owners Assn. (pres.), VFW, Downey and South Gate C. of C's. Home: 11714 Bellflower Blvd Downey CA 90241-5426 Office: 3947 Tweedy Blvd South Gate CA 90280-6119

FUNK, SUSAN E., management consultant; b. Manhattan, Kans., Oct. 28, 1957; d. John William and Dorothy Elizabeth (Hamilton) F.; m. Gordon Louis Fuglie, June 11, 1994. BA, Yale U., 1979; MBA, Stanford U., 1985. Legis. asst. Congressman Tom Coleman, Washington, 1979-83; assoc. dir. AMI St. Joseph Hosp., Omaha, 1985-89; asst. adminstr. Charter Hosp. Glendale, Ariz., 1989; assoc. Laventhol & Horwath, L.A., 1990; pres. Applied Healthcare Rsch., Inc., Santa Clarita, Calif., 1990-92, The Kailos Group, Inc., L.A., 1993—. Bd. mem. Am. Heart Assn., Greater L.A. affiliate, 1991-95, chair orgnl. planning and devel., 1994-95, chair met. divsn., 1991-93; bd. mem. BeeveFound. for Eye and World Health, Verdugo City, Calif., 1991-94. Recipient Exceptional Svc. award Am. Heart Assn. Greater L.A., 1991. Mem. Am. Coll. Healthcare Execs., Women in Health Adminstrn., Healthcare Fin. Mgmt. Assn., L.A. County Bar Assn. (healthcare law sect.). Office: The Kailos Group Inc 2255 Ronda Vista Dr Los Angeles CA 90027-4641

FUNKE, JULIE ANN, real estate broker; b. Indpls., May 3, 1950; d. Paul R. and Rosetta A. (Freeman) Wheeler; m. William R. Funke, Jan. 25, 1969 (div. 1976); 1 son, Brian Dean; m. Benjamin H. Wolfenberger, Apr. 25, 1981 (dec. 1987). Student Ind. U. Customer service rep. Herff Jones, Indpls., 1975-76; rep. trainee Maury Boyd & Assocs., 1976-77, customer service rep., 1977-82, v.p., 1983-90; broker Pinnacle Peak Realty, Scottsdale, 1993—. Mem. Nat. Assn. Realtors, Scottsdale Assn. Realtors, Women in Comm., Am. Soc. Assn. Execs., Coll. Fraternity Editors Assn., Profl. Fraternity Assn. (dir. 1982-86), Gamma Phi Beta (internat. officer 1985-87). Republican. Office: 8787 E Pinnacle Peak Rd Ste 100 Scottsdale AZ 85255

FUNSTON, GARY STEPHEN, publishing and advertising executive; b. Phila., July 7, 1951; s. Ralph Gaylord and Adele Rose (DeCintio) F.; m. Nancy Eileen Clark (div. 1974); 1 child, Stephen Blake. Student, DeAnza Coll., 1969-73, San Jose State U., 1973-75. Store mgr. Smith & Foley Shoes Inc., Sunnyvale, Calif., 1970-75; sales rep. The Hoover Co., San Jose, Calif., 1975-78, GTE Directories Corp., Santa Clara, Calif., 1978-81; ptnr., sec., treas. Mailco Advt. Inc., Milpitas, Calif., 1981-83; owner, cons. ADCOM, San Jose, 1983-85; dir. sales mgr. Lomar Trans Western Publs., Ft. Lauderdale, Fla., 1985-87; mgr. sales, mktg. Ameritel, San Diego, 1987-89; regional sales dir. United Advt. Publs., Union City, Calif., 1989—; sales cons. Republic Telcom, San Jose, 1983-84; mgmt. cons. Norcal Directory Co., San Jose, 1984-85; advt. cons. Yellow Page Programs, San Jose, 1983-85. Contbr. articles to profl. jours. Mem. CAP, Mountain View, Calif., 1983-84; com. mem. Housing Ind. Found., San Jose, 1991-95, dinner sponsor, 1991-94, fundraiser, 1991-95. Mem. Calif. Apt. Assn. (suppliers coun. 1990—, chmn. suppliers com. 1993, 95, industry stds. com. 1994, mem. exec. com. 1995—, bd. dirs. 1995—), Solano-Napa Rental Housing Assn., Tri-County Apt. Assn. (com. mem. 1989—), Rental Housing Owners Assn. So. Alameda County (bd. dirs. 1994, Mem. of Yr. award 1992), Highland Swingers Golf Club (treas. 1990—). Republican. Roman Catholic. Home: 1228 Bell St Sacramento CA 95825-3515 Office: For Rent Mag 32950 Alvarado Niles Rd # 510 Union City CA 94587-3106

FUNTE-RADFORD, DEIDREA LEA, interior designer, consultant; b. Mason City, Iowa, Oct. 3, 1955; d. William August and Beverly Mae Funte; m. Robert Keith Radford, Oct. 3, 1987; children: Lindsay Rai, Chelsea Kae. BFA in Interior Design, Grandview Jr. Coll., Des Moines, 1977; postgrad., Ariz. State U., 1978. Resident designer, contract mgr. SSC, Phoenix, 1980-88; interior designer Trans Designs, Atlanta, 1988-90; interior designer, cons. De's Igns, Scottsdale, Ariz., 1988—; archtl. specifications cons., Archs. and Engrs. Svc., Mission Viejo, Calif., 1992—. Mem. Am. Soc. Interior Design (allied, cert.).

FUREN, SHIRLEY ANN, marketing professional; b. Pomona, Calif., Sept. 12, 1936; d. Orville Emmett and Mary Evelyn (Carmack) Strickland; m. Ralph R. Rickel, Sept. 3, 1954 (div.); children: Lynda Diane, Lorrie Anne, Stanley Rupert; m. Walter E. Furen, Sept. 25, 1976. B Univ. Studies with distinction, U. N.Mex., 1975; Massage Therapist, Healing Arts Inst., Roseville, Calif., 1994. Cert. massage therapist, Calif. Adminstrv. asst. Psychiat. Inst. Am., Washington, 1977; exec. sec. Am. Assn. Schs. Podiatric Medicine, Washington, 1978-79; sales assoc. realtor Merrill Lynch Realty, Washington and Md., 1980-88; owner Spheres, Roseville, 1991—. Vol. Andrea Lambert, M.F.C.C., Gold River, Calif., 1992-95; vol. hostess Ted Gaines for City Coun., Roseville, 1993; vol. fundraiser Matrix Gallery, Sacramento, Crocker Art Mus., Sacramento; staffer Matrix Gallery Aux., 1994—; wedding coord. Culinary Guild, Trinity Cathedral, 1989—. Mem. ASCE (chmn. 1992, 93), Sacramento Capital Club, Mercedes Benz Assn. Episcopalian. Home and Office: Spheres 3370 Emerson Dr Roseville CA 95661-7901

FUREY, SHERMAN FRANCIS, JR., lawyer; b. Pocatello, Idaho, June 1, 1919; s. Sherman Francis and Julia Bartlett (Falls) F.; m. Jo Ann Horton, Feb. 18, 1951; children—Jan Furey Thompson, Stephen Horton (dec.), Sherman Francis III, Terrill Kay Furey Rust. B.A., U. Idaho, 1946, J.D., 1947. Bar: Idaho 1947, U.S. Dist. Ct. Idaho 1947, U.S. Ct. Appeals (9th cir.) 1955. Asst. atty. gen. State of Idaho, 1947-48; asst. U.S. atty. Dist. of Idaho, Boise, 1948-49, U.S. atty., 1953-57, 69-70; ptnr. Doane & Furey, Boise, 1949-51; sole practice, Salmon, Idaho, 1951-53, 57-69, 70-81; of counsel, Furey & Furey, Salmon, 1981—. Mayor, City of Salmon 1959-61; chmn. Citizen's Com. on Legis. Compensation 1976-83. Served to capt. USAAF 1941-45. Decorated Disting. Flying Cross, Air medal with 3 oak leaf clusters. Mem. Idaho Bar Assn. Republican. Episcopalian. Office: Furey & Furey 116 N Center St Salmon ID 83467-4255

FURIMSKY, STEPHEN, JR., freelance writer; b. Coalton, Ill., Aug. 4, 1924; s. Stephen Sr. and Anna (Petricko) F.; m. Dorothy Conrad, June 8, 1946 (dec. Nov. 1989); children: Stephen III, Karen Ann Segal, Daniel Michael, Melany; m. Janet Fay Green, Dec. 16, 1991; step-children: Bruce Emerson, Peni Emerson, Kara Welliver, Beth Emerson. AB, U. Chgo., 1951; MS in Internat. Affairs, George Washington U., 1967; grad., Air War Coll., 1967. Instr. in polit. sci. Craven Community Coll., New Bern, N.C., 1975-80; owner San Diego Sod, San Marcos, Calif., 1981-84; spl. advocate juvenile ct. Voices for Children, San Diego, 1985-91; sports editor, health and fitness editor Enterprise Newspaper, Fallbrook, Calif., 1989-91. Candidate state senate, N.C., 1978. Col. USMC, 1942-73. Decorated Legion of Merit, D.F.C., Bronze Star, Air medal, Cross of Gallantry (Vietman). Mem. VFW (life), Am. Legion. Republican. Eastern Orthodox. Home: 58 Desert Rain Ln Henderson NV 89014-2915

FURLOTTI, ALEXANDER AMATO, real estate development company executive; b. Milan, Italy, Apr. 21, 1948; came to U.S., 1957; s. Amato Vittorio and Polonia Concepcion (Lopez) F.; m. Nancy Elizabeth Swift, June 27, 1976; children: Michael Alexander, Patrick Swift, Allison Nicole. BA in Econs., U. Calif. Berkeley, 1970; JD, UCLA, 1973. Bar: Calif. 1973, U.S. Dist. Ct. (9th cir.) 1973. Assoc. Alexander, Inman, Kravetz & Tanzer, Beverly Hills, Calif., 1973-77, ptnr., 1978-80; ptnr. Kravetz & Furlotti, Century City, Calif., 1981-83; pres. Quorum Properties, L.A., 1984—; dir., CEO Transmar N.V., Netherland Antilles, 1984—. Trustee Harvard-Westlake Sch., L.A., 1989—, Yosemite Nat. Inst., San Francisco, 1990-92. Recipient Grand award Pacific Coast Bldrs. Conf., 1993, Golden Nugget award, 1993, Grand award Nat. Assn. Homebuilders, 1993. Mem. Am. Bar Assn., Urban Land Inst., The Beach Club. Republican. Episcopalian. Office: Quorum Properties 12121 Wilshire Blvd Ste 950 Los Angeles CA 90025-1172

FURLOW, MARY BEVERLEY, English language educator; b. Shreveport, La., Oct. 14, 1933; d. Prentiss Edward and Mary Thelma (Hasty) F.; divorced, 1973; children: Mary Findley, William Prentiss, Samuel Christopher; m. William Peter Cleary, Aug. 1, 1989. BA, U. Tenn., 1955, MEd, 1972; MA, Governors State U., 1975; cert. advanced study, U. Chgo., 1987. Mem. faculty Chattanooga State C.C., 1969-73, Moraine Valley C.C., Palos Hills, Ill., 1974-78; mem. English faculty Pima C.C., Tucson, 1978—; cons. in field. Contbr. author: Thinking on the Edge, 1993. Named one of Outstanding Educators of Am., 1973. Fellow Internat. Soc. Philos. Enquiry; mem. DAR, Internat. Soc. Appraisers, Internat. Soc. Philos. Enquiry, Ariz. Antiquarian Guild, Cincinatus Soc., Jr. League, Mensa, Holmes Socs., Clan Chattan Soc., Daus. of Confederacy, Alpha Phi Omega (Tchr. of Yr. 1973), Pi Beta Phi. Democrat. Episcopalian. Home: 1555 N Arcadia Ave Tucson AZ 85712-4010 Office: Pima CC 8202 E Poinciana Dr Tucson AZ 85730-4645

FURMAN, DAVID STEPHEN, art educator, artist; b. Seattle, Aug. 15, 1945; s. Stanley Albert and Lenore (Silverman) F.; m. Luann Lovejoy, Dec. 17, 1983. BA, U. Oreg., 1969; MFA, U. Wash., 1972. Prof. Otis/Parsons, L.A., 1975, Calif. State U., L.A., 1976, Colo. Mt. Coll., Vail, 1976-78, Claremont (Calif.) Grad. Sch., 1973—; prof., studio arts Pitzer Coll., Claremont, 1973—. One-man shows include: Tortue Gallery, Santa Monica, Calif., 1985, 87, 89, 91, Elaine Horwitch Gallery, Santa Fe, 1989, Margulies Taplin Gallery, Miami, Fla., 1990, O.K. Harris Works of Art, N.Y.C., 1990, Judy Youvens Gallery, Houston, 1993. NEA fellow, 1975, 86-87, Fulbright fellow, 1979, sr. artist fellow, 1990. Mem. Nat. Coun. Edn. of Ceramic Arts, Am. Crafts Coun. Home: 4739 N Glen Ivy Rd La Verne CA 91750-2311 Office: Pitzer Coll 1050 N Mills Ave Claremont CA 91711-3908

FURMAN, JAMES MERLE, foundation executive; b. Kansas City, Mo., Apr. 3, 1932; s James Merle and Audrey Eldena (Phillips) F.; m. Carol Ann McGhee, June 10, 1977; children: Mark Carter, Douglas Walter. BA, Ohio State U., 1954; LLD (hon.), Ill. Coll., 1976; L.H.D. (hon.), Nat. Coll. Edn., 1978, Govs. State U., 1981, Roosevelt U., 1984, Coll. of Sante Fe, 1992; EdD (hon.), So. Ill. U., 1981. Research assoc. Ohio Legis. Service Commn., Columbus, 1955-61; dir. Community Research, Inc., Dayton, 1962-64; exec. officer Ohio Bd. Regents, Columbus, 1964-70; dir., exec. coordinator Wash. State Council on Higher Edn., Olympia, 1970-74; exec. dir. Ill. Bd. Higher Edn., Springfield, 1975-80; v.p. MacArthur Found., Chgo., 1980-81, exec. v.p., 1981-90; dir. MacArthur Found., 1985—; mem. exec. com. State Higher Edn. Planning Commns., U.S. Office Edn.; bd. advisors Fund for the Improvement of Postsecondary Edn.; mem. student fin. assistance study group HEW; chmn. midwest region White House Fellow panel, 1984-86; mem. corp. adv. bd. U. Md.; mem. panel on politics and state univ. Carnegie Found.; mem. mgmt. adv. com. Northwestern U.; mem. bd. Donor's Forum. Trustee Loyola U., Bradley U.; chmn. Govs. Com. on Tax Reform, Nat. Task Force on Higher Edn. and Pub. Interest, Ill. Com. on Higher Edn. Scope, Structure and Productivity; bd. dirs. Sante Fe Cmty. Trust, Calif. Higher Edn. Policy Study Ctr., Inst. Am. Indian Affairs Found., N.Am. Inst.; trustee Coll. Sante Fe. Mem. Edn. Commn. of States, Western Interstate Commn. on Higher Edn., State Higher Edn. Exec. Officers (pres. 1979-80), Nat. Center for Higher Edn. Mgmt. Systems (chmn.).

FURMAN, WILL, film producer, director, cinematographer, writer; b. Washington, D.C., Aug. 29, 1940; s. William Jr. F.; m. Norma Doane, Oct. 1, 1972; children: Laurie, Linda, Rick. BA, San Francisco State U., 1962, MA, 1965. Prodr. Guild, Bascom & Bonfigli, Inc., San Francisco, 1964-66; prodr., dir. Walter Landor & Assoc., San Francisco, 1966-67; prodr., dir., owner Furman Films, San Francisco, 1967-82; prodr., dir., pres. Furman Films, Inc., San Francisco, 1982—. Recipient Cine Golden Eagle award Coun. for Internat. Nontheatrical Events, 1965, 78, 80, 83, 85, 88, 91. Mem. Independent Documentary Assn., Independent Feature Project. Republican. Clubs: Bohemian. Office: Furman Films Inc PO Box 1769 Venice CA 90291

FURNARY, ANTHONY PAUL, surgeon, educator; b. Johnstown, Pa., Apr. 29, 1958; m. Julia Rosalyn Breslin, June 17, 1989; children: Alicia Rose, James Emerich. AB cum laude with distinction in Biochemistry, Dartmouth Coll., 1980; MD, Thomas Jefferson U., 1984. Diplomate Am. Bd. Thoracic Surgery, Am. Bd. Surgery Cert., Nat. Bd. Med. Examiners; lic. physician, Pa., Oreg., Alaska; lic. advanced trauma life support instr. Intern dept. surgery Thomas Jefferson U. Hosp., Phila., 1984-85, sr. resident dept. surgery, 1985-88, chief resident dept. surgery, 1988-89; resident in cardiothoracic surgery Allegheny Gen. Hosp., Pitts., 1989-90, chief resident in cardiothoracic surgery, 1991-92; rsch. fellow divsn. cardiothoracic surgery Allegheny-Singer Rsch. Inst., Pitts., 1990-91; staff surgeon Children's Cardiac Ctr. Oreg. Emanuel Hosp., Portland, 1992—; staff surgeon St. Vincent Heart Inst. St. Vincent Hosp. & Med. Ctr., Portland, 1992—; asst. prof. dept. surgery VA Hosp., Portland, 1992—; mem. pharmacy and therapeutics com. Allegheny Gen. Hosp., 1991, joint clin. care com., 1990-92; dir. cardiovascular rsch. VA Hosp., 1992—, dir. cardiac surgery database devel. St. Vincent Heart Inst., 1992—, dir. clin. rsch., 1992—. Contbr. articles to med. jours. Vol. Birthright of Pa., 1988-92; mem. alumni exec. com. Jefferson Med. Coll., 1982-84; class agent for alumni giving The Mercersburg Acad., 1976—; treas. Housestaff Assn. Thomas Jefferson U., 1986-87. Recipient Resident Rsch. award Pa. Assn. Thoracic Surgery, 1991. Fellow ACS (assoc.); mem. AMA (del. resident physicians sect. 1991-92, Burroughs Wellcome Leadership award 1991), Soc. Thoracic Surgeons (candidate group), Am. Coll. Cardiology (affiliate), Am. Soc. Artificial Organs (traveling fellow 1991), Oreg. Thoracic Soc., Phila. Med. Rugby Club (pres. 1981-84), Dartmouth Coll. Alumni Assn. (treas., chmn. scholarship fund Dartmouth Club Western Pa. 1990-92),Phi Delta Alpha (social chmn. 1979-80). Office: Starr Wood Cardiac Group 9155 SW Barnes Rd Ste 240 Portland OR 97225-6629

FURNAS, DAVID WILLIAM, plastic surgeon; b. Caldwell, Idaho, Apr. 1, 1931; s. John Doan and Esther Bradbury (Hare) F.; m. Mary Lou Heatherly, Feb. 11, 1956; children: Heather Jean, Brent David, Craig Jonathan. AB, U. Calif.-Berkeley, 1952, MS, 1957, MD, 1955. Diplomate Am. Bd. Surgery, Am. Bd. Plastic Surgery (dir. 1979-85, sr. examiner 1986—). Intern U. Calif. Hosp., San Francisco, 1955-56, asst. resident in surgery, 1956-57; asst. resident in psychiatry, NIMH fellow Langley Porter Neuropsychiat. Inst. U. Calif., San Francisco, 1959-60; resident in gen. surgery Gorgas Hosp., C.Z., 1960-61; asst. resident in plastic surgery N.Y. Hosp., Cornell Med. Center, N.Y.C., 1961-62; chief resident in plastic surgery Cornell U. Svc., VA Hosp., Bronx, N.Y., 1962-63; registrar Royal Infirmary and Affiliated Hosps., Glasgow, Scotland, 1963-64; assoc. in hand surgery U. Iowa, 1965-68, asst. prof. surgery, 1966-68, assoc. prof., 1968-69; assoc. prof. surgery, chief div. plastic surgery U. Calif., Irvine, 1969-74, prof., chief div. plastic surgery, 1974-80, clin. prof., chief div. plastic surgery, 1980—; surgeon East Africa Flying Drs. Svc., African Med. and Rsch. Found., Nairobi, Kenya, 1972-73; plastic surgeon S.S. Hope, Nicaragua, 1966, Sri Lanka, 1968; mem. Balakbayan med. mission Mindanao and Sulu, The Philippines, 1980, 81, 82; overseas vis. prof. plastic surgery Ednl. Found., 1994. Contbr. chpts. to textbooks, articles to med. jours.; author, editor 6 textbooks; assoc. editor Jour. Hand Surgery, Annals of Plastic Surgery, Jour. Craniofacial Surgery. Expedition leader Explorer's Club Flag 171 Skull Surgeons of the Kisii

Tribe, Kenya, Flag 44 Skull Surgeons of the Marakwet Tribes, Kenya, 1987. Capt. Med. Corps, USAF, 1957-59; col. Med. Corps., USAR, 1989-92. Recipient Golden Apple award for teaching excellence U. Calif.-Irvine Sch. Medicine, 1980, Kaiser-Permanente award U. Calif.-Irvine Sch. Medicine, 1981, Humanitarian Service award Black Med. Students, U. Calif. Irvine, 1987, Sr. Research award (Basic Sci.) Plastic Surgery Ednl. Found., 1987; named Orange County Press Club Headliner of Yr., 1982. Fellow ACS, Royal Coll. Surgeons Can., Royal Soc. Medicine, Explorers Club, Royal Geog. Soc.; mem. AMA, Calif. Med. Assn., Orange County Med. Assn., Am. Soc. Plastic and Reconstructive Surgeons (bd. dirs. 1970-73), Am. Soc. Reconstructive Microsurgery, Soc. Head and Neck Surgery, Am. Cleft Palate Assn., Am. Soc. Surgery of Hand, Soc. Univ. Surgeons, Am. Assn. Plastic Surgeons (trustee 1983-86, treas. 1988-91, v.p. 1993-94, pres.-elect 1994, pres. 1995), Am. Soc. Aesthetic Plastic Surgery, Am. Soc. Maxillofacial Surgeons, Assn. Acad. Chmn. Plastic Surgery (bd. dirs. 1986-89), Assn. Surgeons East Africa, Pacific Coast Surg. Assn., Internat. Soc. Aesthetic Plastic Surgery, Internat. Soc. Reconstructive Microsurgery, Internat. Soc. Craniomaxillofacial Surgery, Pan African Assn. Neurol. Sci., African Med. and Rsch. Found. (bd. dirs. U.S.A. 1987—), Muthaiga Club, Ctr. Club, Club 33, Univ. Club., Phi Beta Kappa, Alpha Omega Alpha. Office: U Calif Div Plastic Surgery Irvine Med Ctr 101 The City Dr S Orange CA 92668-3201

FURNIVAL, GEORGE MITCHELL, petroleum and mining consultant; b. Winnipeg, Man., Can., July 25, 1908; s. William George and Grace Una (Rothwell) F.; m. Marion Marguerite Fraser, Mar. 8, 1937; children: William George, Sharon (Mrs. John M. Roscoe), Patricia M., Bruce A. BSc, U. Man., Can., 1929; MA, Queens U., Can., 1933; PhD, MIT, 1935. Field geologist in Man., Ont., N.W.T., and Que., 1928-36; asst. mine supt. Cline Lake Gold Mines, Ltd., 1936-39; geologist Geol. Survey Can., No. and Southwestern Sask., 1939-42; from 1942-70 employed by the Standard Oil Co. Calif. (Chevron) subs. including following positions: dist. geologist Standard Oil Co. of Calif. (Chevron Standard, Ltd.), Calgary, Alta., 1942-44, asst. to chief geologist, 1944-45, field supt. So. Alta., 1945-46, mgr. land and legal dept., 1948-50, v.p. land and legal, dir., 1950-52, v.p. legal, crude oil sales, govt. rels., dir., 1952-55; pres., dir. Dominion Oil, Ltd., Trinidad and Tobago, 1952-60; v.p. exploration, dir. Calif. Exploration Co., Chevron Overseas Petroleum, Inc., San Francisco, 1955-63; staff asst. land to v.p. exploration and land Standard Oil Co. of Calif., 1961-63; chmn. bd., mng. dir. West Australian Petroleum Pty., Ltd. (Chevron operated), Perth, 1963-70; dir. mines Dept. Mines and Natural Resources, Man., 1946-48; v.p., dir. Newport Ventures, Ltd., Calgary, 1971-72; v.p. ops., dir., mem. exec. com. Brascan Resources, Ltd., Calgary, 1973-75, sr. v.p., dir., 1975-77, sr. cons., 1977-78; pres., CEO, dir. Western Mines Ltd. Brascan, 1978-80, exec. v.p., divsn. gen. mgr. Westmin Resources Ltd. Brascan, also dir., mem. exec. com., 1981-82; pres., acting gen. mgr. Coalition Mining, Ltd.; pres., COO, dir. Lathwell Resources Ltd., 1983-84; cons. petroleum and mining, 1985—; founder Man. Geol. Survey, 1946; dir. Cretaceous Pipe Line Co., Ltd., Austen & Butta Pty., Ltd., Western Coal Holdings, Inc., Quest Explorations Ltd., San Antonio Resources Inc.; del. Interprovincial Mines Ministers Conf., several years; sec. Winnipeg Conf., 1947. Elected to Order of Can., 1982. Scholarship in mining geology named in his honor, U. B.C., Can. Fellow Royal Soc. Can., Geol. Soc. Am., Geol. Soc. Can., Soc. Econ. Geologists, Am. Assn. Petroleum Geologists (hon. life); mem. Engring. Inst. Can., Canadian Inst. Mining and Metallurgy (hon. life mem., past br. chmn., dist. councillor, v.p., chmn. petroleum div., Distinguished Service award 1974, Selwyn G. Blaylock gold medal 1979), Australian Petroleum Exploration Assn. (hon. life mem., chmn. com. West Australian petroleum legislation, councillor, state chmn. for Western Australia), Australian Am. Assn. in Western Australia (councillor), Assn. Profl. Engrs., Geologists and Geophysicists of Alta. (hon. life mem., Centennial award 1985), Coal Assn. of Can. (bd.dirs.). Clubs: Calgary Golf and Country, Calgary Petroleum, Ranchmen's. Author numerous govt. and co. papers, reports, reference texts, also sci. articles to profl. jours. Home: 1315 Baldwin Cres SW, Calgary, AB Canada T2V 2B7

FURSE, ELIZABETH, congresswoman, small business owner; b. Nairobi, Kenya, 1936; came to U.S., 1958, naturalized, 1972; m. John Platt; 2 children (from previous marriage). BA, Evergreen State Coll., 1974; postgrad., U. Wash., Northwestern U., Lewis & Clark Coll. Dir. Western Wash. Indian program Am. Friends Svc. Com, 1975-77; coord. Restoration program for Native Am. Tribes Oreg. Legal Svc., 1980-86; co-owner Helvetia Vineyards, Hillsboro, Oreg.; mem. 103rd-104th Congresses from 1st Oreg. dist., 1993—. Co-founder Oreg. Peace Inst., 1985. Office: 316 Cannon HOB Washington DC 20515

FURST, ARTHUR, toxicologist, educator; b. Mpls., Dec. 25, 1914; s. Samuel and Doris (Kolochinsky) F.; m. Florence Wolovitch, May 24, 1940; children: Carolyn, Adrianne, David Michael, Timothy Daniel. A.A., Los Angeles City Coll., 1935; A.B., UCLA, 1937, A.M., 1940; Ph.D., Stanford U., 1948; Sc.D., U. San Francisco, 1983. Mem. faculty, dept. chemistry San Francisco City Coll., 1940-47; asst. prof. chemistry U. San Francisco, 1947-49, assoc. prof. chemistry, 1949-52; assoc. prof. medicinal chemistry Stanford Sch. Medicine, 1952-57, prof., 1957-61; with U. Calif. War Tng., 1943-45, San Francisco State Coll., 1945; rsch. assoc. Mt. Zion Hosp., 1952-82; clin. prof. pathology Columbia Coll. Physicians and Surgeons, 1969-70; dir. Inst. Chem. Biology; prof. chemistry U. San Francisco, 1961-80, prof. emeritus, 1980—, dean grad. div., 1976-79; vis. fellow Battelle Seattle Research Center, 1974; Michael vis. prof. Weizmann Inst. Sci., Israel, 1982; cons. toxicology, 1980—; cons. on cancer WHO; mem. com., bd. mineral resources NRC. Contbr. over 250 articles to profl. and ednl. jours. Bd. trustees Pacific Grad. Sch. Psychology. Recipient Klaus Schwartz Commemorative medal Internat. Toxological Congress, Tokyo, 1986, Profl. Achievement award UCLA Alumni Assn., 1992. Fellow Acad. Toxicological Scis. (diplomate), AAAS, Am. Coll. Nutrition, Am. Coll. Toxicology (nat. sec., pres. 1985), N.Y. Acad. Scis., Am. Inst. Chemists; mem. Am. Soc. Pharmacology and Exptl. Therapeutics, Am. Soc. Pharmacology and Exptl. Therapeutics, Am. Chem. Soc., Am. Assn. Cancer Research, Soc. Toxicology, Sigma Xi, Phi Lambda Upsilon. Home: 3736 La Calle Ct Palo Alto CA 94306-2620 Office: U San Francisco Inst Chem Biology San Francisco CA 94117-1080

FURST, DANIEL ERIC, medical educator. AB cum laude, Johns Hopkins U., 1964, MD, 1968. Diplomate Nat. Bd. Medicine, Am. Bd. Internal Medicine. Med. intern Johns Hopkins U., Balt., 1968-69, med. resident, 1969-70; fellow rheumatology UCLA Med. Ctr., 1973-75, asst. prof., 1977-82; fellow clin. pharmacology U. Calif. Med. Ctr., San Francisco, 1975-77; assoc. prof. medicine/rheumatolgoy U. Iowa Coll. Medicine, Iowa City, 1982-87; clin. prof. medicine/rheumatology Robert Wood Johnson Med. Sch., U. Medicine/Dentistry of N.J., New Brunswick, N.J., 1987-92; dir. anti-inflammatory/pulmonary clin. rsch. Ciba-Geigy Pharms., Summit, N.J., 1987-92; dir. clin. rsch. programs Va. Mason Med. Ctr., Seattle, 1992-94; clin. prof. medicine U. Washington, Seattle, 1992—; clin. dir. Va. Mason Rsch. Ctr., 1993—, dir. arthritis clin. rsch., 1994—; vis. prof. McMaster U., Hamilton, Ont., Can., 1989, U. Ind., Inpls., 1990, St. Vincent's Hosp., S.I., N.Y., NYU, 1991, Med. Coll. N.Y., Albany, 1993, Hoffman-LaRoche, Switzerland, 1994, Yakima, Wash., 1994; spkr. numerous cons.; cons. Pfizer, Inc., 1993—, Sanofi, 1993—, Hoffman-LaRoche, 1994—; active numerous profl. coms. Žditor: (with others) Nonsteroidal Anti-Inflammatory Drugs, 1987, Drugs for Rheumatic Disease, 1987, Immunomodulators in the Rheumatic Diseases, 1990, Second Line Agents (DMARDS) in the Rheumatic Diseases, 1992, Nonsteroidal Anti-Inflammatory Drugs, 2nd Edition, 1994; editorial reviewer numerous jours.; contbr. chpts. to books and articles to profl. jours. Capt. M.C., USAF, 1970-73. Fellow Am. Coll. Physicians; mem. Am. Rheumatism Assn., Am. Soc. Clin. Pharmacology and Therapeutics, N.Y. Acad. Scis., Washington State Med. Assn., King County Med. Soc. Office: Va Mason Rsch Ctr 1000 Seneca St Seattle WA 98101-2744

FURUKAWA, DEAN KELII, psychotherapist; b. Seattle, Mar. 22, 1952. BA in Psychology, Social Psychology and Rsch. cum laude, Calif. State U., Northridge, 1974; M of Social Welfare, UCLA, 1978, D of Social Welfare, 1984. Lic. clin. social worker, Calif., Mont. Asst. vol. program coord. L.A. County Probation Dept., 1975-76; family counselor Family Svc. L.A., 1976-77; counselor III Harbor Regional Ctr. for Developmentally Disabled Citizens, 1977-80; rsch. interviewer Alcoholism Rsch. Ctr. UCLA Sch. Psychiatry, 1981-82; sr. social worker, clin. coord., acting dir. Gateways Hosp. and Mental Health Ctr., 1983-88; children's social worker III Adoptions Bur. L.A. County Dept. Children's Svcs., 1988-89; primary therapist, social worker Rivendell Psychiat. Ctr., Billings, 1989-91, clin. cons., 1991; psychotherapist, cons. Billings, 1990—; prof. rank lectr. Ea. Mont. Coll., 1990; clin. cons. Yellowstone Treatment Ctrs., 1991-93. Editor: Asian-American Students Assn. Newsletter, 1973-74; contbr. articles to profl. jours. Mem. exec. bd. Asian Pacific Family Outreach, 1978-80; mem. exec. com. Asian-Am. Social Workers, 1978-80; mem. adv. bd. Positive Alternative for Student Success, 1979-80; active Billings Therapist Support Group, 1990-92. DHEW Child Welfare Adminstrn. scholar UCLA, 1977-78; pub. health svc. fellow UCLA, 1981-83. Mem. NASW. Office: PO Box 21373 Billings MT 59104

FUTA, BARYN S., telecommunications industry executive; b. 1955. BA, U. San Francisco, 1976; JD, U. Calif., 1979. Assoc. Fleischmann & Walsh, 1980-83; atty. Nat. Assn. Pub. TV, 1983-88; COO Cable TV Labs., Louisville, 1988—. Office: Cable TV Labs 400 Centennial Pky Louisville CO 80027-1266*

FYFE, JO SUZANNE, artist; b. Omak, Wash., May 8, 1941; d. Richard Henry and Evelyn B. (Garigen) Storch; m. William E. Fyfe, Sept. 30, 1961; children: Amy, James. BA in Fine Arts, Wash. State U., 1964, MFA, 1968. Instr. dept. fine arts Spokane Falls C.C., 1965—, dept. chair, 1978-84, 89—; adj. faculty Wash. State U. Extension, 1964-72. Exhibited in one-person shows at Chase Gallery, Spokane, Spokane Civic Theatre, Mus. Native Am. Culture, Spokane, Nica Gallery, Pullman, Wash., Earlham Coll., Richmond, Va., others; group shows include Whitworth Coll., Spokane, Seattle Ctr., Oreg. State U., Corvallis; pub. art comms. include City of Spokane Fire Sta. Outdoor Sculpture, 1992, Washington State Arts Commn. Triptych-mixed media, Cashmere; works in corp. and pvt. collections in U.S., East Asia, Africa, No. Europe. Mem. ops. bd. Mus. Native Am. Cultures, 1989-91; mem. art adv. com. Cheney Cowles State Mus., 1969-71; pres. bd. dirs. Riverfront Arts Festival Celebration 81, 1979-81. Office: Spokane Falls CC 3410 W Fort George Wright Dr Spokane WA 99204-5204

FYKE, KENNETH JOHN, hospital administrator; b. Sept. 11, 1940; m. L. Dawn Fyke. BS in Pharmacy, U. Sask., 1962; cert. work and method study, B.C. Work Study Sch., 1965; cert. hosp. admnistrn., Can. Hosp. Assn., 1967; Master in Health Svcs. Adminstrn., U. Alta., 1971. Various adminstrv. posts Sask., 1962-69; with study project provincial lab. svcs. Province of N.B., 1970; adminstr. South Sask. Hosp. Centre, Regina, 1972-73; exec. dir. Sask. Hosp. Svcs. Plan, 1973-75; assoc. dep. minister health Province of Sask., 1975-79, dep. minister health, 1979-84; pres., CEO, Greater Victoria Hosp. Soc., B.C., 1984—; bd. dirs. Health Labour Rels. Assn. B.C.; coord. comprehensive health svcs. study Regina hosps., 1972; mem. Govt. apptd. Task Force examine funding Coll. Medicine, U. Sask., 1978; mem. exec. programs com. Treas. Bd. Govt. Sask., 1979-84; mem. Can. del. WHO Assembly, Geneva, 1981, 82, Pan-Am. Health Conf., Washington, 1982; mem. community adv. coun. U. Victoria, 1984; adj. prof. Sch. Health Info. Sci. U. Victoria, 1985—; clin. asst. prof. faculty medicine, U. B.C., 1986—; asst. prof. dept. health adminstrn. U Toronto, 1989—; mem. exec. com. Assn. Can. Teaching Hosps., 1988-92; mem. policy com. Victoria Health Project, 1988-92; commr. Royal Commn. Health Care and Costs, Province B.C., 1990-91. Contbr. articles to profl. jours.; speaker, presenter in field. Office: Greater Victoria Hosp Soc, 35 Helmcken Rd, Victoria, BC Canada V8Z 6R5

FYLER, PATRICIA ANN, nurse, small business owner; b. Pittsfield, Mass., Aug. 20, 1928; d. Clarence Augustus and Elaine Agnes (Carruthers) McConkey; m. Robert Parmelee Fyler, Oct. 4, 1949; children: Deborah, Rebecca, Pamela, Nancy, Cynthia. BS, U. Redlands, 1985. Staff to head nurse Berkshire Med. Ctr., Pittsfield, 1949-54; staff nurse, operating room St. Francis Hosp., Lynwood, Calif., 1954-57; staff nurse, operating room St. Jude Hosp., Fullerton, Calif., 1958-62, relief charge nurse, 1962-67, charge nurse, 1967-78, asst. supr. emergency dept., 1978-80; mgr. emergency dept. St. Jude Hosp., Yorba Linda, Calif., 1980-89; owner, pres. Fyler Assocs./ Multi-Specialty Legal Nurse Cons., Brea, Calif., 1990—; staff RN St. Jude Med. Ctr., Fullerton, 1989—. Active local sch. bd., PTA, youth orgns., continuing learning experience. Mem. Am. Assn. Legal Nurse Cons. (pres. Orange County), Emergency Nurses Assn. (numerous offices, CEN). Office: Fyler Assocs 2138 Westmoreland Dr Brea CA 92621-6059

GAÁL, VIOLETTA, retired social worker, massage therapist; b. Bucharest, Romania, May 1, 1931; came to the U.S., 1957; d. Gábor and Rozália (Turzai) G.; m. Alex Balogh, Sept. 14, 1953 (div. May 1965); 1 chilb, Gábor. BA, Sacramento State U., 1962. Cert. social worker, Calif.; cert. massage therapy, Calif. Adminstr. State Planning Bur., Budapest, Hungary, 1950-54; stock clk. Ladies Dress Shop, Sacramento, Calif., 1957-61; social worker Welfare Dept., Sacramento, 1963-65, Oakland, Calif., 1965-80; pvt. practice massage therapist San Francisco, 1986—; mil. contractor, watch-clock repair, 1978-81. Author: Spiral; translator: Idegen a Királyok Völgyében, 1993, Jézus Misztikus élete, 1993. Republican. Home: 4099 Howe St Apt 101 Oakland CA 94611-5204

GABBARD, DANA CHESTER, library assistant; b. San Diego, Apr. 28, 1962; s. Dana Ray and Patricia Ann (Corbin) G. BA, U. So. Calif., L.A., 1987. Libr. asst. Southwestern U., L.A., 1987—; v.p. So. Calif. Transit Advocates, 1995—; panel organizer San Diego (Calif.) Comic Conv., 1992—. Pub., editor: Duckburg Times, 1980—; contbr. articles to jours. Active Coalition Econ. Survival, L.A., 1988, ACLU, L.A., 1989-93, Housing L.A., Calif., 1990-92, So. Calif. Transit Advocates, 1994—. Mem. Internat. Animation Soc., Spumco Secret Membership Lodge. Home: #362 3010 Wilshire Blvd # 362 Los Angeles CA 90010-1146

GABLER, ROBERT CLAIR, retired research chemist; b. Phila., June 6, 1933; s. Robert Clair Sr. and Mary Elizabeth Cecilia (Allen) G.; m. Joan Wyatt, Feb. 1969 (div. July 1975); m. Beatriz Salazar, July 22, 1983. BA, Johns Hopkin's U., 1955; MS, Fla. State U., 1957. Chemist E. I. DuPont de Nemours & Co., Inc., Kinston, N.C., 1959-61; rsch. chemist U.S. Bur. of Mines, College Park and Avondale, Md., 1961-78, 78-87; supervising rsch. chemist U.S. Bur. of Mines, Albany, Oreg., 1987-94. Contbr. articles to profl. jours.; patentee in field. Vol. emergency med. technician Kent Island Vol. Fire Dept., Stevensville, Md., 1984-87, Jefferson (Oreg.) Rural Fire Protection Dist., 1987—. With U.S. Army, 1957-59. Mem. Metall. Soc., Am. Inst. Metall. Mining and Petroleum Engrs., Sigma Xi. Democrat. Roman Catholic. Home: 12752 Centerwood Rd SE Jefferson OR 97352-9219

GABOW, PATRICIA ANNE, internist; b. Starke, Fla., Jan. 8, 1944; m. Harold N. Gabow, June 21, 1971; children: Tenaya Louise, Aaron Patrick. BA in Biology, Seton Hill Coll., 1965; MD, U. Pa. Sch. Medicine, 1969. Diplomate Am. Bd. Internal Medicine, Am. Bd. Nephrology, Nat. Bd. Med. Examiners; lic. Md., Colo. Internship in medicine Hosp. of U. of Pa., 1969-70; residency in internal medicine Harbor Gen. Hosp., 1970-71; renal fellowship San Francisco Gen. Hosp. and Hosp. of U. Pa., 1971-72, 72-73; instr. medicine divsn. renal diseases, asst. prof. U. Colo. Health Scis. Ctr., 1973-74, 74-79, assoc. prof. medicine divsn. renal diseases, prof., 1979-87, 87—; chief renal disease, clin. dir. dept. medicine Denver Gen. Hosp., 1973-81, 76-81, dir. med. svcs., 1981-91; CEO, med. dir. Denver Health and Hosps., 1992—; faculty assoc. U. N.C., Chapel Hill, 1992-93; reviewer Kidney Internat., New Eng. Jour. of Medicine; intensive care com. Denver Gen. Hosp., 1976-81, med. records com., 1979-80, ind. rev. com., 1978-81, continuing med. edn. com., 1981-83, animal care com., 1979-83; student adv. com. U. Colo. Health Scis. Ctr., 1982-87, faculty senate, 1985, 86, internship adv. com., 1977-92; exec. com. Denver Gen. Hosp., 1981—, chmn. health resources com., 1988-90, chmn. pathology search com., 1989, chmn. faculty practice plan steering com., 1990-92. Mem. editorial bd. EMERGINDEX, 1983—, Am. Jour. of Kidney Disease, 1984—, Western Jour. of Medicine, 1987—, Annals of Internal Medicine, 1988-91, Jour. of the Am. Soc. of Nephrology, 1990—; contbr. numerous articles, revs. and editorials to profl. publs., chpts. to books. Mem. Mayor's Safe City Task Force, 1993; mem. sci. adv. bd. Polycystic Kidney Rsch. Found., 1984—, chmn., 1991; mem. sci. adv. bd. Nat. Kidney Found., 1991—; mem. Nat. Pub. Health and Hosps. Inst. Bd., 1993. Recipient Sullivan award for Highest Acad. Average in Graduating Class, Seton Hill Coll., 1965, Pa. State Senatorial scholarship, 1961-65, Kaiser Permanente award for Excellence in Teaching, 1976, Ann. award to Outstanding Woman Physician, 1982, Kaiser Permanente Nominee for Excellence in Teaching award, 1983, Seton Hill Coll. Disting. Alumna Leadership award, 1990; named one of The Best Doctors in Am., 1994-95; grantee Bonfils Found., 1985-86, NIH, 1985-90, 91-96. Mem. Denver Med. Soc., Colo. Med. Soc., Am. Soc. Nephrology, Internat. Soc. Nephrology, Am. Coll. Physicians, Am. Fedn. Clin. Rsch., Am. Physiol. Soc., Polycystic Kidney Disease Rsch. Found. (sci. advisor 1984—), Western Assn. Physicians, Nat. Kidney Found. (sci. adv. bd. 1987—), Women's Forum of Colo., Inc., Assn. Am. Physicians. Roman Catholic. Office: Denver Gen Hosp 777 Bannock St Denver CO 80204-4507

GABRIEL, DIERDRE CHANDRA, dietitian; b. San Jose, Calif., Nov. 2, 1956; d. Donald Reese and Margaret Jean (Hall) A. BS, Calif. State U., Sacramento, 1986; MS, Bridgeport U., 1992. Radiologic technologist Mercy San Juan Hosp., Sacramento, 1979-85; clin. dietitian L.A. County-U. So. Calif. Med. Ctr., 1989-92; renal dietitian Satellite Dialysis, San Jose, Calif., 1992—. Mem. Am. Dietetic Assn., Am. Assn. Diabetes Educators. Office: Satellite Dialysis Ctrs Inc 2121 Alexian Dr San Jose CA 95116-1906

GABRIEL, MICHAEL, hypnotherapist, educator; b. Bklyn., Sept. 27, 1927; s. Benjamin and Martha (Buslow) W.; m. Marie Woltjer, May 27, 1989. BA in English, Bklyn. Coll., 1950; MA in Psychology, Sierra U., 1987; MA in English, Columbia U., 1993. Cert. hypnotherapist. Eligibility worker County of Santa Clara, San Jose, Calif., 1970-72; workshop dir. Wellhouse Seminars, San Jose, 1973—; pvt. practice San Jose, 1973—; instr. De Anza Coll., Saratoga, Calif., 1979—. Author: Remembering Your Life Before Birth, 1992; contbr. articles to profl. jours. Mem. Assn. for Past Life Rsch. and Therapies (presenter workshops 1989—).

GABRIEL, RENNIE, financial planner; b. L.A., July 27, 1948; s. Harry and Milly (Broder) Goldenhar; m. Judi Robbins, Nov. 24, 1968 (div. Feb. 1989); children: Ryan, Davida; m. Lesli Gilmore, May 5, 1990. BA, Calif. State U., Northridge, 1971; CLU, Am. Coll., 1979, Cert. Fin. Planner, 1988. Ins. agt. Prudential and Provident Mutual, Encino, Calif., 1972-78; pension cons. Shadur LaVine & Assocs., Encino, 1978-81; owner Artist Corner Gallery Inc., Encino, 1977-82; pension and fin. planner Gabriel Tolleson & Stroum, Tarzana, Calif., 1983-87; pension cons., fin. planner Shadur LaVine/Integrated Fin., Encino, 1987-90; dir. pensions U.S. Life of Calif., Pasadena, Calif., 1983; fin. planner Pension Alternatives, Encino, 1990-92, The Fin. Coach, Encino, 1993—. Contbr. articles to fin. publs. Mem. Internat. Assn. Fin. Planning (pres. San Fernando Valley chpt. 1992), Nat. Assn. Life Underwriters (Achievement award 1974, Nat. Quality award 1975, Million Dollar Round Table 1990), Internat. Assn. Fin. Planning, CLUs, Inst. Cert. Fin. Planners, Employee Assistance Profls. Assn. (treas. San Fernando Valley chpt. 1992), Apt. Assn. San Fernando Valley-Ventura County (bd. mem. 1992).

GABRIELIAN, ARMEN, computer scientist, researcher, entrepreneur; b. Tehran, Iran, Aug. 17, 1940; came to U.S. 1959; s. Levon Simon and Eliza Gabrielian; m. Tong Moon, 1974; children: Sonya Emi, Tanya Simone. BS, MIT, Cambridge, Mass., 1963; MS, MIT, 1965, PhD, 1969. Rsch. assoc. U. Waterloo, Ont., Can., 1969-71; postdoctoral fellow U. So. Calif., L.A., 1971-72; ind. cons. L.A., Newport Beach, 1972-77; sr. sys. analyst Fluor Corp., Irvine, Calif., 1977-78; sr. scientist Hughes Aircraft Co., Fullerton, Calif., 1979-87; tech. dir. Thomson-CSF, Inc., Palo Alto (Calif.) Rsch. Ops., Palo Alto, Calif., 1987-91; pres. UniView Systems, Mountain View, Calif., 1991—. Contbr. articles to profl. jours. Mem. IEEE, Assn. for Computing Machinery, Internat. Soc. for Measurement and Control, Sigma Xi, Tau Beta Pi, Eta Kappa Nu.

GABRIELSEN, PAUL THOMAS, financial planner consultant, educational administrator, clergyman; b. Bonners Ferry, Idaho, Aug. 1, 1929; s. Gabriel and Edna Cecelia (Roen) G.; m. Karen Elaine Johnk, July 18, 1954; children: Virginia Kay Gabrielsen Evans, Stephen Paul. BA, Concordia Coll., 1952; MTh, Luther Theol. Sem., 1956; MA, U. Chgo., 1958, U. Minn., 1963; PhD, U.S. Internat. U., 1976. Ordained to ministry, Luth. Ch., 1956; registered prin. NASD. Owner Coll. Contractors, Moorhead, Minn., 1950-58; pastor North Cape Evangelical Luth. Ch., Franksville, Wis., 1958-60; chaplain Augsburg Coll., Mpls., 1960-61; faculty mem., counselor Golden Valley Luth. Coll., Mpls., 1961-70; real estate broker, fin. cons., ptnr. Capital Growth Planning, San Diego, 1970-76; dir. planned giving Luth. Bible Coll., Issaquah, Wash., 1976—; pvt. practice, charitable fin. cons. Kirkland, Wash., 1988—; registered rep. Fin. Network Investment Corp., Bellevue, Wash., 1988-94. Author: Why Doesn't God?, 1965; contbr. articles to profl. publs. Mem. Wash. Planned Giving Coun., Kiwanis. Home: 12414 89th Pl NE Kirkland WA 98034-2606 Office: Luth Bible Coll 4221 228th Ave SE Issaquah WA 98027-9264

GABRIELSON, SHIRLEY GAIL, nurse; b. San Francisco, Mar. 17, 1934; d. Arthur Obert and Lois Ruth (Lanterman) Ellison; m. I. Grant Gabrielson, Sept. 11, 1955; children: James Grant, Kari Gay. BS in Nursing, Mont. State U., 1955. RN, Mont. Staff and operating room nurse Bozeman (Mont.) Deaconess Hosp., 1954-55, 55-56; staff nurse Warm Springs State Hosp., 1955; office nurse, operating room asst. Dr. Craft, Bozeman, 1956-57; office nurse Dr. Bush, Beach, N.D., 1957-58; pub. health nurse Wibaux County, 1958-59; staff and charge nurse Teton Meml. Hosp., Choteau, Mont., 1964-65; staff pediatric and float nurse St. Patrick Hosp., Missoula, Mont., 1965-70; nurse, insvc. dir. Trinity Hosp., Wolf Point, Mont., 1970-79; ednl. coord. Community Hosp. and Nursing Home, Poplar, Mont., 1979—; coord. staff devel. Faith Luth. Home, Wolf Point, 1980-81; CPR instr. ARC, Am. Heart Assn., Great Falls, Mont., 1979—; condr. workshops and seminars; program coord., test proctor for cert. nursing assts., 1989—; preceptor for student nurses in rural health nursing clin. U. N.D., 1993—. Author: Independent Study for Nurse Assistants, 1977. Former asst. camp leader Girl Scouts U.S.A.; former mother advisor, bd. dirs. Rainbow Girls; pres. Demolay Mothers Club, 1977; bd. dirs. Mont. div. Am. Cancer Soc., 1984-90, mem. awards com., 1986-89; founder Tri-County Parkinson's Support Group, N.E. Mont. Recipient Lifesaver award Am. Cancer Soc., 1987, Svc. award ARC, 1989, Health and Human Svcs. award Mont. State Dept., 1990, U.S. Dept. Health award, 1990, Outstanding award, U.S. HHS, Mont. Health Promotion award Dept. Health and Environ. Scis. Mem. ANA, Mont. Nurses Assn. (mem. commn. on continuing edn. 1977-91, chmn. 1984-86), Order Eastern Star (Worthy grand matron 1995—), Alpha Tau Delta (alumni pres. 1956). Presbyterian. Home: 428 Hill St Wolf Point MT 59201-1244 Office: Community Hosp-Nursing Home PO Box 38 Poplar MT 59255-0038

GAC, FRANK DAVID, materials engineer; b. Granite City, Ill., Mar. 26, 1951; s. Frank John and Betty Marie (Kasprovich) G.; m. Christina Lynn McMullen, Aug. 12, 1973; children: Jessie Lynn, Benjamin Thomas. BS in Ceramic Engring., U. Ill., 1973; MS in Ceramic Engring., U. Mo., Rolla, 1975; postgrad., U. N.Mex., 1982-83; PhD in Materials Sci. and Engring., U. Wash., 1989. Registered profl. engr., N.Mex. Mem. staff Los Alamos (N.Mex) Nat. Lab., 1975-78, sect. leader, 1980-83, staff mem., 1983-84, advanced study candidate, 1984-85; research engr. U. Wash., Seattle, 1979-80; project leader Los Alamos (N.Mex) Nat. Lab., 1986-88, group leader, 1988—; mem. steering com. Advanced Composites Working Group, Cocoa Beach, Fla., 1981—; adj. faculty mem. N.Mex. Inst. Mining and Tech., 1991—, N.Mex. Ctr. for Micro-Engineered Ceramics, 1992—. Contbr. articles to profl. jours. Father helper Aspen Elem. Sch., Los Alamos, 1983-84; Sunday sch. supt. Trinity Bible Ch., Los Alamos, 1986, elder, 1987—; deacon, youth leader Sangre de Cristo Covenant Ch., Los Alamos, 1975-79; scoutmaster Boy Scouts Am., Granite City, 1967-69; com. mem. Young Life, Los Alamos, 1988—. Fellow A.P. Green Refractories Co., 1973-74; named Knight of St. Pat 100 Club, U. Ill., Champaign, 1973, one of Outstanding Young Men Am., 1986. Fellow Am. Ceramic Soc. (div. chmn. 1985-86, Cert. 1986, Karl Schwartzwalder Profl. Achievement Ceramic Engring. award 1988, chmn. programs and meetings com. 1987-88, trustee engring. ceramic div. 1991-94); mem. Nat. Inst. Ceramic Engrs. (coord. 1979-80, James I. Mueller Meml. Lecture award 1990), Gideons Internat. (pres. 1976), Young Life (leader 1975-79). Democrat. Home: 1559 41st St Los Alamos NM 87544-1920 Office: Los Alamos Nat Lab Mst 4 Ms # G756 Los Alamos NM 87545

GACIOCH, JOSEPH JAMES, public relations executive; b. St. Louis, July 19, 1945; s. Joseph James and Maude (Crancer) G.; m. Louise Nelson, Aug. 29, 1970; children: Joseph III, Paul D. BA in Edn., Ariz. State U., 1970. Part-time news reporter Phoenix (Ariz.) Gazette, 1966-70, news reporter, 1970-72; media rels. rep. Salt River Project, Phoenix, 1972-79, supr. pub.

info., 1979-89, mgr. media rels., 1989-91; with Motorola, Scottsdale, Ariz., 1992, mgr. media rels., 1993—. Active Valley Forward Assn., Phoenix, 1993—. Mem. Phoenix Press Club (pres. 1975), Internat. Assn. Bus. Communicators (v.p. 1985), Pub. Rels. Soc. Am. Office: Motorola Ariz Issues Mgmt 8220 E Roosevelt St Scottsdale AZ 85257-3804

GADBERRY, MICHAEL DALE, electrical engineer; b. Sullivan, Ind., Feb. 13, 1963; s. Danny D. Gadberry and Pamela P. (Smedley) Haynes; m. Jennifer L. Doane, June 5, 1982 (div. Aug. 1988); children: Ryan M., Tyler R.; m. Kathleen I. Bretoi, Oct. 7, 1989; children: Sierra A., Savannah N. BSEE, Purdue U., 1985. Rotational engr. CPSTG-Motorola, Phoenix, 1985-86; design engr. Power Products Smartmos, Phoenix, 1986; product engr. Power Products Divsn.- Thyristors, Phoenix, 1987-88; design engr. PPD-TMOS, Phoenix, 1988-92, PPD-Automotive, Phoenix, 1992-94; sr. engr. Login/Analog Tech. Group, Fact Logic Group, Chandler, Ariz., 1994—. Patentee in field. Mem. IEEE. Home: 2562 E Evergreen St Mesa AZ 85213-6012 Office: 2501 S Price Rd Chandler AZ 85248

GADBOIS, RICHARD A., JR., federal judge; b. Omaha, June 18, 1932; s. Richard Alphonse Gadbois and Margaret Ann (Donahue) Bartlett; children from previous marriage: Richard, Gregory, Guy, Geoffrey, Thomas; m. Vicki Cresap, May 14, 1993. A.B., St. John's Coll., Camarillo, Calif., 1955; J.D., Loyola U., Los Angeles, 1958; postgrad. in law, U. So. Calif., 1958-60. Bar: Calif. 1959, U.S. Dist. Ct. (cen. dist.) Calif. 1959, U.S. Supreme Ct. 1966. Dep. atty. gen. Calif., 1958-59; ptnr. Musick, Peeler & Garrett, L.A., 1959-68; v.p. Denny's Inc., La Mirada, Calif., 1968-71; judge Mcpl. Ct., L.A., 1971-72, Superior Ct., L.A., 1972-82, U.S. Dist. Ct. (cen. dist.) Calif., L.A., 1982—. Decorated knight Order of Holy Sepulchre (Pope John Paul II). Mem. ABA, Los Angeles County Bar Assn. (trustee 1966-67), State Bar Calif. (profl. ethics com. 1965-70). Republican. Roman Catholic. Home and Office: US Dist Ct 176 Courthouse 312 N Spring St Los Angeles CA 90012-4701

GADDES, RICHARD, performing arts administrator; b. Wallsend, Northumberland, Eng., May 23, 1942; s. Thomas and Emilie Jane (Rickard) G. L.T.C.L. in piano, L.T.C.L. for sch. music; G.T.C.L., Trinity Coll. Music, London, 1964; D. Mus. Arts (hon.), St. Louis Conservatory, 1983; D.F.A. (hon.), U. Mo.-St. Louis, 1984; D.Arts (hon.), Webster U., 1986. Founder, mgr. Wigmore Hall Lunchtime Concerts, 1965; dir. Christopher Hunt and Richard Gaddes Artists Mgmt., London, 1965-66; bookings mgr. Artists Internat. Mgmt., London, 1967-69; artistic adminstr. Santa Fe Opera, 1969-78, assoc. gen. dir., 1995—; gen. dir. Opera Theatre of St. Louis, 1975-85, bd. dirs., 1985—; bd. dirs. Grand Ctr., Inc., 1988—, pres., 1988-95; bd. dirs. William Matheus Sullivan Found. Mem. bd. advisors Royal Oak Found. Recipient Lamplighter award, 1982, Mo. Arts award, 1983, St. Louis award, 1983, Human Relations award Jewish-Am. Com., St. Louis, 1985, Nat. Inst. for Music Theatre award, 1986, Cultural Achievement award Young Audiences, 1987. Office: Santa Fe Opera PO Box 2408 Santa Fe NM 87504-2408

GAFFNEY, EDWARD STOWELL, scientist, technology executive; b. Bklyn., Jan. 28, 1943; s. William S. and Elizabeth Gaffney; m. Margaret Grace Walker, 1967 (div. Sept. 1975); 1 child, Sean P.; m. Susan Carroll Wasgatt, Oct. 19, 1975; children: Paul S., Joel A. BS, Yale U., 1964; AM, Dartmouth Coll., 1966; PhD, Calif. Inst. Tech., 1973. Rsch. scientist Systems, Sci. and Software, La Jolla, Calif., 1972-77, Pacifica Tech., San Diego, 1977-79; staff mem. Los Alamos (N.Mex.) Nat. Lab., 1979-86; sr. rsch. scientist Ktech Corp., Albuquerque, 1986-92; pres., chief scientist GRE Inc., Albuquerque, 1992—. Sec. Poway (Calif.) Planning and Devel. Program, 1977-79; vice chmn., chmn. Rep. Ctrl. Com., Los Alamos County, 1983-86; dir. N.Mex. Conf. of Chs., Albuquerque, 1994—, S.W. Conf., United Ch. of Christ, Phoenix, 1994—. Mem. Am. Geophys. Union. Office: GRE Inc PO Box 30863 Albuquerque NM 87190-0863

GAFFNEY, PAUL JAMES, systems architect; b. New Bedford, Mass., Nov. 10, 1966; s. James Edmund and Teresa Mary (Oliveira) G.; m. Kathrin Jean Schaumann, Sept. 1, 1990; 1 child, Leah Paige. AB, Harvard Coll., 1988. Systems anslyst John Hancock Mut. Life, Boston, 1984-86, JFK Sch. Govt., Cambridge, Mass., 1986-88; assoc. cons. CSC Ptnrs., Boston, 1988-89; dir. client/server products Uniquest, Inc., Richmond, Calif., 1989-93; sr. systems architect Charles Schwab & Co., San Francisco, 1993—. Mem. Harvard Club of Boston. U.s. Croquet Assn. Libertarian. Home: 3271 Parkwood Dr Rochester Hls MI 48306-3653 Office: Charles Schwab & Co 101 Montgomery St San Francisco CA 94104-4122

GAGARIN, DENNIS PAUL, advertising agency executive; b. Long Beach, Calif., July 9, 1952. BS in Graphic Design, San Jose State U., 1976. Art dir. Brower, Mitchell, Gum Advt., Los Gatos, Calif., 1976-79, Offield & Brower Advt., Los Gatos, 1979-82; sr. art dir. Tycer, Fultz, Bellack Advt., Palo Alto, Calif., 1982-85; head art dir. TFB/BBDO Advt., Palo Alto, 1985-87; creative dir. Lena Chow Advt., Palo Alto, 1987-90; prin., ptnr. Gagarin/McGeoch Advt. and Design, Redwood City, Calif., 1989—; prof. San Jose (Calif.) State U., 1987-90, now guest lectr.; guest art dir. Western Art Dirs. Club, Palo Alto. Recipient awards for graphic design, art direction. Office: Gagarin/McGeoch Advt-Design 493 Seaport Ct Ste 102 Redwood City CA 94063-2730

GAGE, FREDERICK ALBERT, business development executive,; b. Lynn, Mass., Oct. 19, 1924; s. Frederick A. and Agnes M. (Fitzgerald) G.; m. Barbara Jacqueline Faust, June 17, 1949; children: Frederick A. III (dec.), Alison Bailey, Andrea Kennedy, Robert W. Student, U.S. Mil. Acad., West Point, 1942-43, U. So. Calif., 1948-49; JD, Pacific Coast U., 1953. Pub. rels. officer L.A. Police Dept., 1948-51, Apt. Assn. L.A. County, 1954-55, L.A. County Employees Assn., 1956-59; exec. dir. Progress Assn. of L.A. County, 1960-79; pres. Gage Comms. Inc., Burbank, Calif., 1979—. Mem. Citizens Com. to Safeguard Am., Washington, 1970; mem. adv. bd. Calif. Senate Com. on Small Bus., 1983-90; del. mem. Commn. for Econ. Devel., Calif., 1982. Combat corr. USMC, 1943-46, PTO. Mem. Am. Econ. Devel. Coun., Progress Assn. Calif. (pres. 1993-94), West Point Soc. L.A., USMC Combat Corrs. Assn. (pres. L.A. chpt. 1969—), Am. Legion (post comdr. 1968), Mendel Rivers Breakfast Club (Washington), Sigma Delta Kappa. Home: 216 Carol Dr Ventura CA 93003-1709 Office: Gage Comm Inc 903 S Lake St Ste 101 Burbank CA 91502-2435

GAHAN, KATHLEEN MASON, small business owner, retired educational counselor, artist; b. Long Beach, Calif., May 23, 1940; d. Robert Elwyn and Jean Mason (Campbell) Fisher; m. Keith Victor Gahan, Apr. 21, 1961; children: Carrie Jean, Christie Sue. BA, Calif. State U., Long Beach, 1962, MA, 1967; student, Studio Arts Ctrs. Internat., Florence, Italy, 1992. Cert. gen. secondary educator, adminstr., Calif. Tchr. Long Beach Unified Sch. Dist., 1963-70; tchr. Porterville (Calif.) Union High Sch. Dist., 1970-76, counselor, 1976-95, ret., 1995; coord. gifted and talented edn. Porterville High Sch., 1976-83, coach acad. decathlon team, 1977-82, 85; adminstr. Counseling for Collegeable Hispanic Jrs., Porterville, 1988-90, Counseling for Ptnrship. Acad. in Bus., 1990-95; tchr. faculty and staff computer workshop Porterville High Sch., 1992-94; proprietor El Mirador Ranch, Strathmore, Calif., 1978—; salesman real estate, Porterville, 1981-82; income tax return preparer, Lindsay, Calif., 1983-84; organizer SAT preparation workshop, 1981-83. Editor: (cookbook) Mexican Cooking in America, 1974; editor (craft patterns) Glory Bee, 1979-84; group exhibits photography Porterville Coll., 1989, oil paintings, Coll. of Sequoias, 1992; one woman show Porterville Coll., 1995. Leader 4-H, Lindsay, 1971-79; mem. exec. com. Math. Sci. Conf. for Girls, Tulare County, 1982-85; adminstr. Advanced Placement Program, Porterville, 1979-95; mem. bible study Ch. of Nazarene; charter mem. Tulare County Herb Soc., 1983-85. Recipient 1st pl. Mus. Art, Long Beach, 1961, Orange Blossom Festival Art Show, Lindsay, 1988, 2d pl. Coll. of Sequoias Art Show, Visalia, 1988, Hon. mention Orange Blossom Festival Art Show, Lindsay, 1992, commendation Gov. Bd. and Dist. Adminstrn., Portersville, Calif., 1975, 82, 95; named Coach of Champion Acad. Decathlon Team, Tulare County, 1982, 85. Mem. AAUW, Am. Assn. Individual Investors, Calif. Tchrs. Assn., Women in the Senate and House, Porterville Educators Assn. Republican. Home: 1032 Mountain View Dr Lindsay CA 93247-1626

GAIBER, LAWRENCE JAY, financial company executive; b. Chgo., Mar. 20, 1960; s. Sy Bertrym and Mildred (Dickler) G. BS in Econ., U. Pa., 1982. Mgmt. intern Eisai Co. Ltd, Tokyo, 1980; dept. mgr. Anglo Am. Corp., Johannesburg, Republic of South Africa, 1982-84; pres. Sandton Fin. Group, L.A., 1984—; pres. Swellendam Fin. Group, Studio City, Calif., 1984—, also bd. dirs.; bd. dirs. Lawrand Ltd, Satellite Telecommunication, Inst. Cellular Nutritional Immunology, Introlagater, Gaiber, Introlagater, L.A. Greetings; chmn. Mechanics Express Inc. Contbr. articles to profl. jours and mags. Mem. South Africa Found., Johannesburg, 1984—, Town Hall Calif., 1986; bd. dirs. Brentwood Arts Coun.; vice chmn. western region 1986 Pres.' dinner Rep. Nat. Com., Washington. Recipient Most Active Vol. award S. African Inst. Internat. Affairs, 1983; honoree for contbns. to aspiring entrepreneurial women Mayor Tom Bradley's Office and Nat. Network of Hispanic Women, L.A., 1986. Mem. L.A. Venture Assn., L.A. C. of C., L.A. Jr. C. of C., Van Nuys C. of C., L.A. County Rep. Lincoln Club, L.A. County Young Reps., Brentwood Rep. Club (Pres. 1984—). Clubs: Wharton Bus. Sch., Calif. Yacht.

GAIBER, MAXINE DIANE, museum education director; b. Bklyn., May 6, 1949; d. Sidney and Junia Estelle (Gruberg) Oliansky; m. Stuart Gaiber, May 11, 1971; children: Scott Cory, Samantha Lauren. BA, Bklyn. Coll., 1970; MA, U. Minn., 1972. Tours & curriculum svcs. dir. Mpls. Inst. Arts, 1972-77, assoc. chair edn., 1977-79; cons. mus. edn. Field Mus./Art Inst., Chgo., 1979-82; program coord. Field Mus. of Natural History, Chgo., 1982-83; publs. dir. Art Ctr. Coll. Design, Pasadena, Calif., 1983-85; rsch. dir. Art Ctr. Coll. Design, Pasadena, 1985-86, campaign dir., 1986-88; pub. rels. officer Newport Harbor Art Mus., Newport Beach, Calif., 1988—, dir. edn. & publs., 1994—; instr. L.A. County Mus. Art, 1985—, Art Ctr. Coll. Design, Pasadena, 1986-89, Coll. DuPage, Glen Ellyn, Ill., 1981-83. Editor: Why Design?, 1987; editor/author: Mus. edn. materials, 1972—. Art vol. Mariners Sch., Newport Beach, 1989-93. Fellow Bush Found. 1976. Mem. Pub. Rels. Soc. Am., Am. Assn. Mus. (Edn. Com. rep. 1979-83). Office: Newport Harbor Art Mus 850 San Clemente Dr Newport Beach CA 92660-6301

GAILEY, CHARLES FRANKLIN, JR., maritime consultant; b. Eads, Colo., Apr. 2, 1926; s. Charles Franklin and Mary Francis (Cranston) G.; m. Dorothy J. Swarens, Jan. 29, 1950; children: John E., Dan M., Pamela E., Cheryl F. With USCG, 1943-74; commanding officer afloat USCG, Juneau, Alaska, 1966-68; dir. aux. USCG, Long Beach, Calif., 1968-72; chief mil. plans section USCG, Washington, 1972-74; with Gailey & Gailey Partnership, Oak Harbor, Wash., 1975—; dir. Real Estate Partnership, Oak Harbor, 1975—; cons. Maritime Environ. Cons., Ridgefield, Wash., 1976—. Active allocation panel United Way, Oak Harbor, Wash., 1985-94; bd. dirs. Island County United Way, 1988-91, chmn. budget and allocations com., 1989-90; vol. IRS, VITA program, Oak Harbor, 1985-95. Mem. Retired Officers Assn., Am. Legion, U.S. Golf Assn. Republican. Office: PO Box 664 Oak Harbor WA 98277-0664

GAILLARD, MARY KATHARINE, physics educator; b. New Brunswick, N.J., Apr. 1, 1939; d. Philip Lee and Marion Catharine (Wiedemayer) Ralph; children: Alain, Dominique, Bruno. BA, Hollins (Va.) Coll., 1960; MA, Columbia U., 1961; Dr du Troiseme Cycle, U. Paris, Orsay, France, 1964, Dr-es-Sciences d'Etat, 1968. With Centre National de Recherche Scientifique, Orsay and Annecy-le-Vieux, France, 1964-84; maitre de recherches Centre National de Recherche Scientifique, Orsay, 1973-80; maitre de recherches Centre National de Recherche Scientifique, Annecy-le-Vieux, 1979-80, dir. research, 1980-84; prof. physics, sr. faculty staff Lawrence Berkeley lab. U. Calif., Berkeley, 1981—; Morris Loeb lectr. Harvard U., Cambridge, Mass., 1980; Chancellor's Disting. lectr., U. Calif., Berkeley, 1981; Warner-Lambert lectr. U. Mich., Ann Arbor, 1984; vis. scientist Fermi Nat. Accelerator Lab., Batavia, Ill., 1973-74, Inst. for Advanced Studies, Santa Barbara, Calif., 1984, U. Calif., Santa Barbara, 1985; group leader L.A.P.P., Theory Group, France, 1979-81, Theory Physics div. LBL, Berkeley, 1985-87; sci. dir. Les Houches (France) Summer Sch., 1981; cons., mem. adv. panels U.S. Dept. Energy, Washington, and various nat. labs. C0-editor: Weak Interactions, 1977, Gauge Theories in High Energy Physics, 1983; author or co-author 140 articles, papers to profl. jours., books, conf. proceedings. Recipient Thibaux prize U. Lyons (France) Acad. Art & Sci., 1977, E.O. Lawrence award, 1988, J.J. Sakurai prize for theoretical particle physics, APS, 1993; Guggenheim fellow, 1989-90. Fellow Am. Acad. Arts and Scis., Am. Physics Soc. (mem. various coms., chairperson com. on women, J.J. Saburai prize 1993); mem. AAAS, NAS. Office: U Calif Dept Physics Berkeley CA 94720

GAINES, HOWARD CLARKE, lawyer; b. Washington, Sept. 6, 1909; s. Howard Wright and Ruth Adeline-Clarke Thomas Gaines; m. Audrey Allen, July 18, 1936; children: Clarke Allen, Margaret Anne. J.D., Cath. U. Am., 1936. Bar: D.C. bar 1936, U.S. Supreme Ct. bar 1946, U.S. Ct. Claims bar 1947, Calif. bar 1948. Individual practice law Washington, 1938-43, 46-47, Santa Barbara, Calif., 1948-51; asso. firm Price, Postel & Parma, Santa Barbara, 1951-54; partner Price, Postel & Parma, 1954-88; of counsel, 1989—; chmn. Santa Barbara Bench and Bar Com., 1972-74. Chmn. Santa Barbara Police and Fire Commn., 1948-52; mem. adv. bd. Santa Barbara Com. on Alcoholism, 1956-67; bd. dirs. Santa Barbara Humane Soc., 1958-69, 85-92; bd. trustees Santa Barbara Botanic Garden, 1960—, v.p., 1967-69; bd. trustees Cancer Found. Santa Barbara, 1960-77; dir. Santa Barbara Mental Health Assn., 1957-59, v.p., 1959; pres. Santa Barbara Found., 1976-79, trustee, 1979—. Fellow Am. Bar Found.; mem. ABA, Bar Assn. D.C., State Bar Calif. (gov. 1969-72, v.p. 1971-72, tres. 1971-72), Santa Barbara County Bar Assn. (pres. 1957-58), Am. Judicature Soc., Santa Barbara Club, Channel City Club. Republican. Episcopalian. Home: 1306 Las Alturas Rd Santa Barbara CA 93103-1600 Office: 200 E Carrillo St Santa Barbara CA 93101-2118

GALAMBOS, SUZANNE JULIA, editor, writer, institute administrator; b. St. Paul, May 24, 1927; d. Maxwell Alexander Bolocan-Segell and Ruth Gertrude (Labofsky) Segell; m. Andrew Joseph Galambos, Dec. 16, 1949. BA, U. Minn., 1949. Assoc. dir. The Free Enterprise Inst., L.A., 1961-92, dir., 1992—; v.p. The Universal Scientific Publs. Co., L.A., 1962-92, pres., CEO, 1992—; bd. dirs. The Universal Corp., L.A. Author: The Natives are Friendly-Well Almost, 1968, More Lasting Than Bronze, 1991; editor (essays) Thrust for Freedom, 1991. Office: The Free Enterprise Inst PO Box 4307 Orange CA 92613-4307

GALANE, MORTON ROBERT, lawyer; b. N.Y.C., Mar. 15, 1926; s. Harry J. and Sylvia (Schenkelbach) G.; children: Suzanne Galane Duvall, Jonathan A. B.E.E., CCNY, 1946; LL.B., George Washington U., 1950. Bar: D.C. 1950, Nev. 1955, Calif. 1975. Patent examiner U.S. Patent Office, Washington, 1948-50; spl. partner firm Roberts & McInnis, Washington, 1950-54; practice as Morton R. Galane, P.C., Las Vegas, Nev., 1955—; spl. counsel to Gov. Nev., 1967-70. Contbr. articles to profl. jours. Chmn. Gov.'s Com. on Future of Nev., 1979-80. Fellow Am. Coll. Trial Lawyers; mem. Am. Law Inst., IEEE, Am. Bar Assn. (council litigation sect. 1977-83), State Bar Nev., State Bar Calif., D.C. Bar. Home: 2019 Bannie Ave Las Vegas NV 89102-2208 Office: 302 Carson Ave Ste 1100 Las Vegas NV 89101-5909

GALARRAGA, ANDRES JOSE, professional baseball player; b. Caracas, Venezuela, June 18, 1961; m. Eneyda G., Feb. 18, 1984; 1 child, Andria. First baseman Montreal Expos, 1979-91, St. Louis Cardinals, 1991-92, Colorado Rockies, 1992—. Named to Nat. League All-Star Team, 1988, 93; recipient Gold Glove award, 1989-90, Silver Slugger award, 1988; Nat. League Batting Champion, 1993; named Comeback Player of Yr., 1993, MVP So. League. 1984. Office: Colorado Rockies 2850 W 20th Ave Denver CO 80211-5103*

GALBRAITH, JAMES RONALD, hotel executive; b. Crystal Falls, Mich., Mar. 18, 1936; s. Edwin and Lillian (Robichaud) G.; m. Mary Elizabeth Redington, June 23, 1962; children—Richard Lee, Timothy Scott, John Redington. BA, Calif. State U., Los Angeles, 1960. Reporter, news editor Ind. Star-News, Pasadena, Calif., 1955-60; adminstrv. asst. U.S. Congress, Washington, 1960-62; U.S. Supreme Ct. broadcaster NBC-Three Star Extra, Washington, 1962-64; mng. editor Washington World Mag., Washington, 1962-64; asst. dir. pub. relations Nat. Republican Congl. Com, Washington, 1964-69; dir. pub. relations Republican Gov.'s Assn., Washington, 1969-71, exec. dir., 1971-75; v.p. Ticor, Los Angeles, 1976-81; sr. v.p. Hilton Hotels Corp., Beverly Hills, Calif., 1981—; dep. Calif. Roundtable, San Francisco, 1976—; cons. Nat. Acad. Pub. Adminstrn., U.S. Presdl. Mgmt. Panel, Washington, 1979-80. Co-founder, mem. The Cogswell Soc., Washington, 1973—; mem. Los Angeles Pub. Affairs Officers Assn., 1977—, chmn., 1984; trustee Calif. Hist. Soc., San Francisco, 1979-86; trustee Edmund G. "Pat" Brown Inst. Govt. Affairs, L.A., 1984-87; mem. Brown Adv. Bd., 1987—; mem., fin. chmn. Statue of Liberty-Ellis Island Centennial Commn., 1985-87; bd. dirs. Conrad N. Hilton Found., 1989—, Eisenhower World Affairs Inst., 1991—. Recipient Ellis Island Medal of Honor, 1993. Mem. Nat. Press Club. Republican. Roman Catholic. Office: Hilton Hotels Corp 9336 Civic Center Dr Beverly Hills CA 90210-3604

GALBRAITH, JOHN ROBERT, insurance company executive; b. Portland, Oreg., Oct. 18, 1938; s. Maurice Kerr and Margaret Ione (Veach) G.; m. Maureen McKovich, Oct. 2, 1971 (div. Mar. 1978); children: Margaret Maureen, Marc Ryan; m. Betty Jean Irelan, Dec. 11, 1987. BA, Willamette U., 1960; MBA, U. Washington, 1962. CPA, Oreg. Staff acct. Ernst & Young, Portland, 1962-65; treas. First Pacific Corp., Portland, 1965-71; v.p., treas. Geo McKovich Cos., Palm Beach, Fla. and L.A., 1971-80; v.p., chief fin. officer SAIF Corp., Salem, Oreg., 1980-82; exec. v.p., CFO Liberty N.W. Ins. Corp., Portland, 1983—; bd. dir. Librerty N.W. Ins. Corp., Portland; bd. dir. Helmsman Mgmt. Svcs. N.W., Inc., Portland, 1987—. Bd. dirs. Liberty Health Plan, Inc., Portland, 1992—. With Army N.G., 1957-66. Mem. AICPAs, Fin. Exec. Inst., Fla. Ins. CPAs, Calif. Soc. CPAs, Oreg. Soc. CPAs, Multnomah Athletic Club. Republican. Home: 3025 NE Dunckley St Portland OR 97212-1729 Office: Liberty NW Ins Corp 825 NE Multnomah St Ste 2000 Portland OR 97232-2135

GALBRAITH, NANETTE ELAINE GERKS, forensic and management sciences company executive; b. Chgo., June 15, 1928; d. Harold William and Maybelle Ellen (Little) Gerks; m. Oliver Galbraith III, Dec. 18, 1948; children: Craig Scott, Diane Frances Galbraith Ketcham. BS with high honors with distinction, San Diego State U., 1978. Diplomate Am. Bd. Forensic Document Examiners. Examiner of questioned documents San Diego County Sheriff's Dept. Crime Lab., San Diego, 1975-80; sole prop. Nanette G. Galbraith, Examiner of Questioned Documents, San Diego, 1980-82; pres., examiner of questioned documents Galbraith Forensic & Mgmt. Scis., Ltd., San Diego, 1982—; one of keynote speakers Internat. Assn Forensic Scis., Adelaide, South Australia, 1990. Contbr. articles to profl. jours. Fellow Am. Acad. Forensic Scis. (questioned documents section, del. to Peoples Rep. of China 1986, USSR, 1988); mem. Am. Soc. Questioned Document Examiners, Southwestern Assn. Forensic Document Examiners (charter), U. Club Atop Symphony Towers, Phi Kappa Phi. Republican. Episcopalian. Office: Galbraith Forensic & Mgmt Scis Ltd 4370 La Jolla Village Dr San Diego CA 92122-1249

GALBREATH, JAMES HOWARD, portfolio manager; b. Pomona, Calif., June 15, 1946; s. Howard Leslie Galbreath and Barbara (Coles) Bradford; m. Kathryn Dougherty, Sept. 1, 1975; children: Shannon Brook, Brittany Nicole. BSBA in Fin., U. Denver, 1969. CFA. Account exec. Dean Witter, Denver, 1969-70; pres. Am. Money Mgmt., Denver, 1971-72; v.p. Chandelle Corp., Denver, 1972-74; ptnr. Stephenson and Co., Denver, 1974-82; pres. Galbreath Fin., Englewood, Colo., 1982-87; mng. dir. NWQ Investment Mgmt. Co., Englewood, 1987—; bd. dirs. Homax Corp., Bellingham, Wash.; pres. The Rockies Fund, Inc., 1983-87. Mem. Leadership Denver Assn. (bd. dirs.), Denver Soc. Security Analysis, Metro Denver Execs. Club, Rockies Club (chmn. 1983-90), Colo. Venture Capital Assn. (pres.), Econ. Club Colo. Republican.

GALBUT, MARTIN RICHARD, lawyer; b. Miami Beach, Fla., June 27, 1946; s. Paul A. and Ethel (Kolnick) G.; m. Cynthia Ann Slaughter, June 4, 1972; children: Keith Richard, Lindsay Anne. BS in Speech, Northwestern U., 1968, JD cum laude, 1971. Bar: Ariz. 1972, U.S. Dist. Ct. Ariz. 1972, U.S. Ct. Appeals (9th cir.) 1972. Assoc. Brown, Vlassis & Bain P.A., Phoenix, 1971-75; founder, ptnr. McLoone, Theobald & Galbut P.C., Phoenix, 1975-86; of counsel Furth, Fahrner, Bluemle & Mason, 1986-89; ptnr. Galbut & Assocs., P.C., Phoenix, 1989—; presenter guest "Law Talk" Cable TV; judge pro tem Maricopa County Superior Ct., 1995—. Contbr. articles to profl. jours. Chmn. Ariz. State Air Pollution Control Hearing Bd., 1984-89; mem. Govs. Task Force on Urban Air Quality, 1986, City Phoenix Environ. Quality Commn., 1987-88; bd. dirs. Men's Art Council Phoenix Art Mus.; bd. dirs. founder Ariz. Asthma Found. Clarion de Witt Hardy scholar, Kosmerl scholar. Mem. ABA, Ariz. State Bar Assn. (lectr., securities law and litigation com. and sect.), Maricopa County Bar Assn., Am. Arbitration Assn. (arbitrator, arbitrator trainer, lectr.), Nat. Assn. Securities Dealers (arbitrator, trainer and lectr.). Democrat. Jewish. Office: Galbut & Assocs PC 2425 E Camelback Rd Phoenix AZ 85016-4200

GALE, DANIEL BAILEY, architect; b. St. Louis, Nov. 6, 1933; s. Leone Caryll and Gladys (Wotowa) G.; student Brown U., 1951-53, Ecole Des Beaux Arts, Paris, 1954-55; BArch., Washington U., 1957; m. Nancy Susan Miller, June 15, 1957; children: Caroline Hamilton, Rebecca Fletcher, Daniel Bailey With Gale & Cannon, Architects and Planners, Hellmuth, Obata & Kassabaum, Inc., Architects, St. Louis, and exec. v.p. corp. devel., dir. HOK, Inc., St. Louis, 1961-79; ptnr. Heneghan and Gale, architects and planners, Aspen, Colo., 1967-69; pres., chief exec. officer Gale Kober Assocs., San Francisco, 1979-83; pvt. practice architecture, Belvedere, Calif., 1984—; pres. Program Mgmt. Inc., Belvedere, 1984—. Recipient Henry Adams prize Washington U., 1957. Mem. AIA, Singapore Inst. Architects. Home and Office: 280 Belvedere Ave Belvedere CA 94920-2425

GALE, MARADEL KRUMMEL, public policy and management educator, consultant; b. Bremerton, Wash., June 13, 1939; d. Bernhard Utz and Florence Claire (Choiniere) Krummel; m. Richard Philip Gale, June 10, 1961 (div. 1976). BA, Wash. State U., Pullman, 1961; MA, Mich. State U., East Lansing, 1967; JD, U. Oreg., 1974. Asst. prof. dept. urban and regional planning U. Oreg., Eugene, 1974-83, lectr. Sch. of Law, 1975-77, asst. prof. community svc. and pub. affairs, 1976-77, spl. asst. Office of the Pres., 1979-80, asst. dean Sch. Architecture, 1980-81, assoc. prof. dept. planning, pub. policy and mgmt., 1983—, dir. Micronesia and South Pacific program, 1988—; vis. asst. prof. Sch. Forestry, Oreg. State U., 1979-80; legis. lobbyist City of Eugene, 1975; mem. faculty U.S. Forest Svc. Land Mgmt. Planning Team, 1979-80; cons. Peace Corps./U.S. AID, Senegal, Kenya, Rwanda, 1986. Mem. adv. com. Bur. of Land Mgmt., Eugene, 1980—, The Micronesia Inst., 1992—; project dir. Peace Corps-Yap (Micronesia), 1988. Named Woman of Yr., Lane County Coun. Orgns., 1986; U.S. Info. Agy. grantee Coll. of Micronesia, 1989, U. of the Pacific, 1993, U.S. Dept. Edn. grantee, 1989, U.S. Dept. Interior grantee, 1990—. Mem. Assn. for Women in Devel., Am. Planning Assn. (sec., treas. planning and law divs. 1979-81). Office: U Oreg Dept Planning & Pub Policy Eugene OR 97403

GALES, SAMUEL JOEL, retired civilian military employee, counselor; b. Dublin, Miss., June 14, 1930; s. James McNary McNeil and Alice Francis (Smith) Broadus-Gales; m. Martha Ann Jackson (div. Jan. 1978); children: Samuel II (dec.), Martha Diane Gales Bryant, Katherine Roselein, Karlmann Von, Carolyn B., Elizabeth Angelica McCain. BA, Chapman Univ., 1981, MS, 1987. Ordained Eucharist minister, Episcopal Ch., 1985; cert. tchr., Calif. Enlisted U.S. Army, 1948, advanced through grades to master 1st sgt., 1969, ret., 1976; tchr. Monterey (Calif.) Unified Sch. Dist., 1981-82; civilian U.S. Army Directorate of Logistics, Ft. Ord, Calif., 1982-93; collateral EEOC counselor Dept. Def., U.S. Army, 1987-93; peer counselor, 1982-84. Active Family Svc. Agy., Monterey, 1979-85; rep. Episc. Soc. for Ministry on Aging, Carmel, Calif., 1980-86, Task Force on Aging, Carmel, 1983-87, vestry man, 1982-85, 91-94; ombudsman Monterey County Long-Term Care Program, Calif. Dept. for the Aging, 1993—; vol. guide Monterey Bay Aquarium Found., 1994—. Decorated Air medal. Mem. Am. Legion (post comdr. 1973-74), Forty and Eight (chef-de-gare 1979, 80), Monterey Chess Club, Comdr.'s Club Calif. (pres. Outpost 28 1981-82). Republican. Home: PO Box 919 1617 Lowell St Seaside CA 93955-3811

GALL, DONALD ALAN, data processing executive; b. Reddick, Ill., Sept. 13, 1934; s. Clarence Oliver and Evelyn Louise (McCumber) G.; m. Elizabeth Olmstead, June 25, 1960 (div. 1972); children: Christopher, Keith, Elizabeth; m. Kathleen Marie Insognia, Oct. 13, 1973; 1 child, Kelly Marie. BSME, U. Ill., 1956; SM, MIT, 1958, ME, 1960, ScD, 1964. Research engr. Gen. Motors, Detroit, 1956-57; staff engr. Dynatech Corp., Cambridge, Mass., 1959-60; mgr. ctr. systems Dynatech Corp., Cambridge, 1962-63; asst., assoc.

prof. Carnegie-Mellon U., Pitts., 1964-69; assoc. prof. surgery and anesthesiology U. Pitts. Sch. Medicine, 1969-73; vis. fellow IBM Research Lab., Rueschlikon, Switzerland, 1970-71; pres. Omega Computer Systems, Inc., Scottsdale, Ariz., 1973—. Contbr. articles to profl. jours.; inventor fuel injection system. Bd. dirs. Scottsdale Boys and Girls Club, 1982-93; mem. Scottsdale Head Honchos, 1978-87; mem. Verde Vaqueros, 1987—. Recipient Taylor medal Internat. Conf. on Prodn. Rsch. Mem. AAAS, ASME, Sigma Xi, Pi Tau Sigma, Tau Beta Pi, Phi Kappa Phi. Home: 9833 E Cortez St Scottsdale AZ 85260-6012 Office: Omega Computer Sys Inc 7272 E Indian School Rd Ste 406 Scottsdale AZ 85251-3921

GALL, DONALD ARTHUR, minister; b. Edgely, N.D., Apr. 30, 1936; s. Arthur Fred and Luella Sara (Weidenbach) G.; m. Shirley Ann Stevenson, Aug. 19, 1956 (div. Aug. 1972); children: Deborah Sue, Craig Donald, Matthew Allan; m. Patricia E. deJong, Dec. 29, 1984. BA, Yankton Coll., 1958; MDiv., MA in Religious Edn., Hartford Sem., 1962; D in Ministry, Eden Theol. Sem., 1983. Ordained to ministry United Ch. of Christ. Pastor 1st Congl. Ch., Whiting, Iowa, 1962-65; assoc. conf. minister Nebr. Conf. United Ch. Christ, Lincoln, 1965-70; dir. leadership devel. Presbyns. Associated for Common Tasks, Eugene, Oreg., 1970-72; assoc. min. 1st Congrl. Ch. United Ch. Christ, Eugene, 1972-75; assoc. conf. minister Fla. Conf. United Ch. Christ, Miami, 1975-79; program exec. Bd. Homeland Ministry, N.Y.C., 1979-86; conf. min. Iowa Conf. United Ch. Christ, Des Moines, 1986-94; sr. min. Eden United Ch. Christ, Hayward, Calif., 1995—; bd. dirs. Iowa Interch. Forum, Des Moines; pres. Iowa conf. United Chs. Christ Inc., Des Moines, 1986-94; chair Agy. for Peace and Justice, Des Moines, 1988-91; trustee United Theol. Sem., New Brighton, Minn., 1991; mem. Coun. Conf. Mins., 1986-94, Gen. Synod Com. on Structure, 1989-95; mem. exec. coun. United Ch. Christ, 1989-91. Author: THe Eleventh Hour, 1979; also articles. Bd. dirs. Mayflower Homes Inc., Grinnell, Iowa, 1986-94; pre. Emergency Family Shelter House, Eugene, Oreg., 1972-74, Fla. IMPACT, Tallahassee, 1977-79; vol. Oreg. Dem. Campaign, 1974. Named a Community Leader of Am., Community Leaders of Am., Inc., 1968. Home: 1338 Grizzly Peak Blvd Berkeley CA 94708-2130

GALL, SALLY MOORE, librettist, poet, scholar; b. N.Y.C., July 28, 1941; d. John Alexander and Betty (Clark) Moore; m. John Knox Marshall, 1961 (div. 1965); m. W. Einar Gall, Dec. 8, 1967. BA in English cum laude, Harvard U., 1963; postgrad., Columbia U., 1963-65; MA in English, NYU, 1971, PhD, 1976. vis. prof. English Drew U. Grad. Program, Madison, N.J., 1978; adj. asst. prof. English NYU, 1978-81. Opera libretti: Kill Bear Comes Home, The Singing Violin, The Little Thieves of Bethlehem; musical theatre texts: Pinocchio, Lysistrata; author: (books) Ramon Guthrie's Maximum Security Ward: An American Classic, 1984, (with M.L. Rosenthal) The Modern Poetic Sequence: The Genius of Modern Poetry, 1983 (Explicator Lit. Found. award 1984), 2d edit. 1986; editor: Maximum Security Ward and Other Poems, 1984 (Explicator Lit. Found. award 1984); versification editor: Poetry in English: An Anthology, 1987; translator Chopin's songs; contbr. articles to profl. jours., poetry to literary jours. Penfield fellow, 1973-74; recipient Key Pin and Scroll award, NYU, 1976. Mem. Nat. Opera Assn., MLA, Opera for Youth, Poets and Writers, Lyrica, Dramatists Guild, Morning Music Club of Nyack (pres. 1989-91). Democrat. Home and Office: 5820 Folsom Dr La Jolla CA 92037-7323 also: 29 Bayard Ln Suffern NY 10901

GALLAGHER, DENNIS JOSEPH, state senator, educator; b. Denver, July 1, 1939; s. William Joseph and Ellen Philomena (Flaherty) G.; BA, Regis Coll., 1961; MA, Cath. U. Am., 1968; postgrad. (Eagleton fellow) Rutgers U., 1972, 86; children: Meaghan Kathleen, Daniel Patrick. With locals of Internat. Assn. Theatrical and Stage Employees, Denver and Washington, 1956-63; tchr. St. John's Coll. High Sch., Washington, 1964-66, Heights Study Center, Washington, 1965-67, Regis U., 1967; mem. Colo. Ho. of Reps from 4th Dist., 1970-74; mem. Colo. Senate, 1974—, chmn. Dem. Caucus, 1982-84, Dem. Whip, 1985-87. Mem. Platte Area Reclamation Com., 1973-75; mem. Denver Anti-Crime Council, 1976-77; trustee Denver Art Mus.; bd. dirs. Cath. Community Services; mem. Colo. Commn. on Aging; mem. Colo. State Adv. Council on Career Edn.; mem. Victim Assistance Law Enforcement Bd., Denver, 1984—; Named Gates Found. fellow Harvard U. Mem. Colo. Fedn. Tchrs. (pres. local 1333, 1972-74), Colo. Calligrapher's Guild, Colo. History Group, James Joyce Reading Soc., Denver Pub. Library Commn. (mem. bd. dirs.). Democrat. Roman Catholic. Home: 4514 W Moncrieff Pl Denver CO 80212-1602 Office: Regis U Dept Comm 3333 Regis Blvd Denver CO 80221-1099

GALLAGHER, MARIAN GOULD, librarian, educator; b. Everett, Wash., Aug. 29, 1914; d. John H. and Grace (Smith) Gould; m. D. Wayne Gallagher, Oct. 1, 1942 (dec. 1953). Student, Whitman Coll., 1931-32; A.B., U. Wash., 1935, LL.B., 1937, M.L.S., 1939. Law librarian, instr. law U. Utah, Salt Lake City, 1939-44; law librarian U. Wash., Seattle, 1944-81; asst. prof. law U. Wash., 1944-48, asso. prof., 1948-53, prof., 1953-81, prof. emeritus, 1981—, adj. prof., 1944-84; vis. prof. law and disting. law librarian, Hastings Law Sch., San Francisco, 1982; cons. various law schs. and govt. law libraries. Mem. Gov.'s Commn. on Status of Women, 1964-71, Pres.'s Nat. Adv. Com. on Libraries, 1966-68; mem. adv. com. White House Conf. on Library and Info. Services, 1976-80; mem. council sect. on legal edn. and admissions to bar Am. Bar Assn., 1979-83. Named Disting. Alumna U. Wash. Sch. of Librarianship, 1970, Disting. Alumna U. Wash. Sch. Law, 1980, Disting. Alumna Whitman Coll., 1981. Fellow Am. Bar Found.; mem. Am. Bar Assn., Am. Assn. Law Libraries (pres. 1954-55, Disting. Service award 1966, 84), Wash. State Bar Assn., Seattle-King County Bar Assn., PEO, Mortar Bd., Order of Coif, Delta Delta Delta, Phi Alpha Delta. Presbyterian. Office: 1201 3rd Ave # 40 Seattle WA 98101-3000

GALLAGHER, PATRICK FRANCIS, anthropologist; b. Wilkinsburg, Pa., Apr. 18, 1930; s. Hugh Vincent and Mary Caroline (Denne) G.; m. Mary Ann Bridge, 1954 (div. 1965); children: Patrick Francis III, John Vincent, Lisa Bridge; m. Mary Ann Hammerel, Sept. 16, 1971 (div. 1979); children: Molly Alison, Kingman Cruxent. BA summa cum laude, U. Pitts., 1957; PhD in Anthropology, Yale U., 1964; student, Washington Sch. Psychiatry, 1968. From asst. prof. to prof. George Washington U., Washington, 1961-69; prof., dean Coll. of the Potomac, Washington, 1971-72; assoc. prof. Cerro Coso C.C., Ridgecrest, Calif., 1973-75; prof. anthropology Universidad Nacional Francisco de Miranda, Venezuela, 1979-81; lectr. Chapman Coll. Ctrs., Palmdale, Calif., 1973—; lectr. Smithsonian Instn., Washington, 1973, Davis & Elkins Coll., Elkins, W.Va., 1990-91. Author: La Pitia: An Archaeological Sequence in Northwestern Venezuela, 1976; asst. editor: Abstracts of New World Archaeology, 1961-62; illustrator: Sons of the Shaking Earth, 1959, The Entry of Man into the West Indies, 1960, Man Takes Control, 1961, Conservatism among the Iroquois at the Six Nations Reserve, 1961, Mexico, 1962; contbr. articles to profl. jours. NSF grantee, 1965, 67-68. Fellow AAAS, Royal Anthropol. Inst. of Gt. Britain and Ireland, Am. Anthrop. Assn.; mem. Asociacion Venezolana Para el Avance de la Ciencia, Archeol. Assn. Venezuela (corr.), Anthropol. Soc. Washington (coun. 1967-69), Soc. Am. Archaeology (treas.-elect 1968), Phi Beta Kappa, Sigma Xi. Home: 37459 5th St E Palmdale CA 93550-6009

GALLAGHER, ROSANNA BOSTICK, elementary educator, administrator; b. Kingman, Ariz., May 16, 1949; d. Charles Topp and Mary (Lisalda) Bostick; m. Richard Kent Gallagher, June 18, 1971; children: Richard Jonathon, Ryan Charles. BA in Elem. and Spl. Edn., U. Ariz., 1971, MA in Bilingual Adminstrn., 1986. Cert. tchr., spl. edn. tchr., adminstr., Ariz. Tchr. learning disabled students Tucson (Ariz.) Unified Sch. Dist., 1973-75, curriculum specialist Davis Sch., 1975-77, multi-cultural resource tchr., 1979-81, curriculum generalist, 1981-87, prin. Drachman Primary Magnet Sch., 1987-93, prin. Robins Elem., 1994—; mentor Prescott Coll., Tucson, 1988—; instr. U. Phoenix, Tucson, 1988—; nat. cons., presenter Curriculum Assocs. Pub., 1990—; GAPS adv. bd. Pima County Health Dept., Tucson, 1991—; pres. Teaching Rainbow Publs., Tucson,1 980-83. Author: Rainbow of Activities, 1982, Chalkboard Activities, 1985, Counting Creatures, 1990, Abracadabra ABCs, 1990, Tantos Niñoto/So Many Children, 1993, Rub-a-Dubb-Dub/Uno Dos Tres, 1993. Adv. bd. Tucson area Girl Scouts U.S., 1988; choir mem. St. Mark's Meth. Ch., Tucson, 1988-92, coord. Time-With-Children program, 1991-93; com. mem. Pima County Interfaith Coun. Edn., Tucson, 1992. Recipient Outstanding Adminstr. award Tucson Assn. Bilingual Edn., 1990, Copper Letter award City of Tucson, 1994; named Tucson Woman on the Move YWCA, 1989. Mem. Tucson Adminstrs. Assn. (bd. dirs. 1988-89), Tucson Assn. Bilingual Adminstrs. Home: 867 W Placita Mesa Fria Tucson AZ 85704-4746 Office: Robins Elem Sch 3939 N Magnetite Ln Tucson AZ 85745-9167

GALLAGHER, SARAH WOODSIDE, writer, producer; b. McKinney, Tex., Aug. 1, 1944; d. John Frank and Sarah Clare (Phillips) G. Student, Smith Coll., Northampton, Mass., 1962-63. Prodn. coord. Capital Cities, N.Y.C., 1969-70; proprietor Deep River Products, N.Y.C., 1971-77; dir. creative devel. Home Box Office, N.Y.C., 1978-82; pres. Sur la Plage Prodns., Venice, Calif. and, N.Y., 1983-89, 1993—; staff writer, story editor L.A. Law, L.A., 1990-92. Writer (with Judith Feldman): L.A. Law teleplays, 1990-92; prodr.: Man With A Gun, 1995; cons. Rule of Law, 1995. Advisor N.Y. State Senate Adv. Com., 1989—; mem. civic and charitable orgns. Emmy nominee Acad. TV Arts and Scis., L.A., 1990-91. Mem. Writers Guild of Am.

GALLAGHER, SUSAN VANZANTEN, English literature educator; b. Bellingham, Wash., Dec. 12, 1955; d. Paul and Shirley Faye (VandeKieft) VanZanten; m. John James Gallagher, June 7, 1975; 1 child, Joseph VanZanten. BA, Westmont Coll., 1978; MA, Emory U., 1981, PhD, 1982. Asst. prof. Covenant Coll., Lookout Mountain, Tenn., 1982-86; vis. asst. prof. Baylor U., Waco, Tex., 1986; asst. prof. Calvin Coll., Grand Rapids, Mich., 1986-87, assoc. prof., 1987-91, prof., 1991-93; prof. Seattle Pacific U., 1993—; dept. evaluator Samford U., Westmont Coll., N.W. Coll., 1989-93; mem. adv. bd. Christian Coll. Coalition South African Study Tour, 1994. Author: A Story of South Africa, 1991 (Choice award 1992); co-author: Literature Through the Eyes of Faith, 1989; editor: Postcolonial Literature and the Biblical Call to Justice, 1994. Mem. MLA, Conf. on Christianity and Lit. (bd. dirs. 1986-89, chair publs. 1987-89, 94—). Presbyterian. Office: Seattle Pacific Univ 3305 3rd Ave W Seattle WA 98119-1940

GALLAR, JOHN JOSEPH, mechanical engineer, educator; b. Poland, July 3, 1936; came to U.S., 1981; s. Joseph and Sophie (Gallar) Filipecki; m. Christina B. Wilczynski, June 30, 1962; 1 child, Darek A. BSME, State U. Poland, 1957, MSME, 1958; PhD in Tech. Scis., M & M Acad., 1966; professorship, Ahmadu Bello U., Zaria, Nigeria, 1980. Dir., prof. engring. Acad. State U., Poland, 1957-72; dir., prof. engring. Ahmadu Bello U., 1973-81, dir. postgrad. studies, 1976-81; with module design Timex Co., Cupertino, Calif., 1981-82; mgr. mfg. Computer Research Co., Santa Clara, Calif., 1982-84; mgr. hardware devel. Nat. Semiconductor Co., Santa Clara, 1984-85; chief robotics engr. Varian Corp., Palo Alto, Calif., 1986-93; pres., owner Frontier Engring., San Jose, Calif., 1994—; dep. vice-chancellor State U., Poland, 1970-71; cons. Enplan Corp., Kaduna, Nigeria, 1980-81, Criticare Tech., Sparks, Nev., 1985-86, also bd. dirs.; mgr. mfg. engring. Retro-Tek Co., Santa Clara, 1986. Contbr. poetry to Nat. Libr. of Poetry; contbr. articles to profl. jours.; patentee in field. Trustee, charter life mem. Presdl. Task Force, Washington, 1984; mem. Nat. Conservative Polit. Action Com., Washington, 1981. Recipient U.S. Ceremonial Flag Presdl. Task Force; Medal Merit from Pres. Ronald Reagan, Washington, 1985. Mem. NRA, Internat. Soc. Poets (life). Roman Catholic. Home: 5459 Entrada Cedros San Jose CA 95123-1418 Office: Frontier Engring 5459 Entrada Cedros San Jose CA 95123-1418

GALLAY, ALAN, history educator; b. N.Y.C., Nov. 26, 1957; s. Harold Herman and Leona (Gittenstein) G.; m. Carol Elizabeth Coleman, Aug. 1985; 1 child, Cyrana Coleman. BA in History, U. Fla., 1978; MA in History, Georgetown U., 1981, PhD in History, 1986. Vis. asst. prof. U. Notre Dame, South Bend, Ind., 1986-87, U. Miss., Oxford, 1987-88; prof. history Western Wash. U., Bellingham, 1988—; vis. prof. Harvard U., Cambridge, Mass., 1990-91; vis. lectr. U. Aukland, New Zealand, 1992. Author: The Formation of a Planter Elite, 1989; editor: Voices of the Old South, 1994, (2 vol.) The Colonial Wars of America: An Encyclopedia, 1994. Andrew W. Mellon Faculty fellow in the humanities Harvard U., Cambridge, 1990-91, J. William Fulbright fellow U.S. Info. Agy., Washington, 1992. Mem. Am. Hist. Assn., Orgn. Am. Historians, So. Hist. Assn., Ga. Hist. Soc., Inst. Early Am. History and Culture. Office: Dept History Western Wash Univ Bellingham WA 98225

GALLEGLY, ELTON WILLIAM, congressman; b. Huntington Park, Calif., Mar. 7, 1944; married; four children. Attended, Calif. State U., L.A. Businessman, real estate broker Simi Valley, Calif., from 1968; mem. Simi Valley City Coun., 1979; mayor City of Simi Valley, 1980-86; mem. 99th-104th Congresses from the 21st (now 23rd) Calif. dist., 1986—; mem. internat. rels. com., mem. judiciary com., chmn. resources subcom. on Native Am. and insular affairs; co-chair Task Force on Illegal Immigration; mem. exec. com. U.S. Ho. Reps. Rep. Study Com.; mem. Congl. Human Rights Caucus, Congl. Fire Svcs. Caucus; formerly vice-chmn., chmn. Ventura County Assn. govts., Calif. Bd. dirs. Moorpark Coll. Found.

GALLEGOS, LARRY DUAYNE, lawyer; b. Cheverly, Md., Mar. 23, 1951; s. Belarmino R. and Helen (Schlotthauer) G.; m. Claudia M. King, Oct. 1, 1994; 1 child, Will Adam. BS summa cum laude, U. Puget Sound, 1978; JD, Harvard U., 1981. Bar: Colo. 1981, U.S. Dist. Ct. Colo. 1981, U.S. Tax Ct. 1989. Assoc. Pendleton & Sabian, Denver, 1981-83; assoc. O'Connor & Hannan, Denver, 1983-86, ptnr., 1986-89; ptnr. Rossi & Judd, P.C., Denver, 1989-92, Berliner Zisser Walter & Gallegos, P.C., Denver, 1992—. Served with U.S. Army, 1972-74. Mem. ABA (real property, probate and trust law sect.), Colo. Bar Assn., Colo. Trial Lawyers Assn., Denver Bar Assn., U.S. Tennis Assn. Office: Berliner Zisser Walter & Gallegos PC 1700 Lincoln St Ste 4700 Denver CO 80203-4547

GALLEN, CHRISTOPHER CHARLES, neuroscientist, neurologist, psychiatrist; b. Phila., Dec. 28, 1950; m. Lucy M. Rayner, June 25, 1974; children: Thomas, Alice, Trevor, Clifford. BA in Philosophy, U. Fla., 1973; MD, Emory U., 1980, PhD in Biochemistry, 1981. Diplomate, cert. psychiatry Am. Bd. Psychiatry and Neurology. Intern Emory U. Sch. Medicine, Atlanta, 1980-81; psychiatry resident Stanford U. Sch. Medicine, Palo Alto, Calif., 1981-84; neuropharmacology rsch. fellow Stanford U. Sch. Medicine, Palo Alto, 1983-84; neurology resident U. Calif., San Diego, 1984-87, neurology chief resident, 1986-87, adj. asst. prof. neurology, 1988—; sr. rsch. assoc. neuropharmacology The Scripps Rsch. Inst., La Jolla, Calif., 1987-94; dir. biomagnetism lab. The Scripps Rsch. Inst., La Jolla, 1988—, adj. asst. mem. neuropharmacology, 1994—; staff neurologist Scripps Clinic and Rsch. Found., La Jolla, 1990—; cons. psychiatrist Santa Clara Valley Med. Ctr., San Jose, 1982-84, San Diego (Calif.) County Mental Health, 1986-93, cons. neurologist, 1993-94; cons. neuroscientist Biomagnetic Techs. Inc., San Diego, 1991—; sr. dir. med. and sci. svcs. Internat. Clin. Rsch., San Diego, 1994—. Contbr. articles to profl. jours. Mem. sci. scholarship and internship program Scripps Clinic & Rsch. Found., La Jolla, 1990—, human subjects com., 1991—. Fellow Soc. for Neurosci.; mem. Am. Acad. Neurology (assoc.), Western EEG Soc., N.Y. Acad. Scis. Office: Internat Clin Rsch Corp 5160 Carroll Canyon Rd San Diego CA 92121-1775

GALLETTA, JOSEPH LEO, physician; b. Bessemer, Pa., Dec. 21, 1935; s. John and Grace (Galletta) G.; m. Teresita Suarez Soler, Feb. 19, 1961; children: John II, Angela, Eric, Christopher, Robert Francis, Michael Angelo. Student, U. Pitts., 1953-56; MD, U. Santo Tomas, Manila, 1962. Intern, St. Elizabeth Hosp., Youngstown, Ohio, 1963-64; family practice medicine, 29 Palms, Calif., 1967-77, Hemet, Calif., 1977—; chief of staff 29 Palms Cmty. Hosp., 1970-71, 73-76; vice chief of staff Hi-Desert Med. Center, Joshua Tree, Calif., 1976-77; chmn. dept. family practice Hemet Valley Hosp., 1981-83, med. dir. chem. dependency dept., 1985-88; med. dir. Loma Linda (Calif.) U. Behavioral Medicine Ctr. Recovery Svc., 1994—; pres. Flexisplint, Inc.; founding mem. Hemet Hospice; former cons. Morongo Basin Mental Health Assn.; mem. adv. com. on substance abuse Riverside County, 1995—. Hon. mem. 29 Palms Sheriff's Search and Rescue, 1971-77. Bd. dirs. 29 Palms Cmty. Hosp. Dist., Morongo Unified Sch. Dist. Served with M.C. USN, 1964-67. Diplomate Am. Bd. Family Practice. Fellow Am. Geriatric Soc. (founder West Coast chpt.), Am. Acad. Family Practice; mem. Calif. Med. Assn., Riverside County Med. Assn., Am. Holistic Med. Assn. (charter), Am. Soc. Addiction Medicine, Calif. Soc. Addiction Medicine (mem. exec. coun. 1995—), Am. Acad. Family Practice, Calif. Acad. Family Practice. Roman Catholic. Established St. Anthonys Charity Clinic, Philippines, 1965; inventor Flexisplint armboards. Home: 27691 Pochea Trl Hemet CA 92544-8180 Office: Westside Medical Pla 37020 Florida Ave Hemet CA 92545-3520

GALLI, DARRELL JOSEPH, management consultant; b. Ft. Bragg, Calif., Nov. 10, 1948; s. Joseph Germain and Esther Edith (Happajoki) G.; B.A. in Transp./Internat. Bus., San Francisco State U., 1975; BS in Computer Info. Systems, 1985; MBA Golden Gate U., 1980; m. Rondus Miller, Apr. 23, 1977 (div. 1981); 1 dau., Troyan Hulda. With Pacific Gas & Electric Co., Santa Cruz, Calif., 1972-73; with Calif. Western R.R., Ft. Bragg, 1975-77, Sheldon Oil Co., Suisun, Calif, 1978-80; mgr. House of Rondus, Suisun, 1974-79; mgmt. cons., Suisun City, 1979—; instr. Solano Coll., 1979-81, Golden Gate U., 1981; mem. faculty U. Md. European div., Heidelberg, W.Ger., 1982-88; owner, mgr. Old Stewart House Bed and Breakfast, Fort Bragg, Calif., 1990—; lectr. Coll. Redwoods, Ft. Bragg, 1989—; coord. Small Bus. Mgmt. Seminar, 1980. Asst. coordinator Sr. Citizens Survey for Solano Coll. and Sr. Citizens Center, 1980; mem. Ft. Bragg City Coun., 1994—. Served with U.S. Army, 1969-71. Lic. Calif. real estate agt. Mem. Am. Assn. M.B.A. Execs., World Trade Assn., Bay Area Elec. R.R. Assn. Republican. Episcopalian. Club: Odd Fellows. Home: 321 Morrow St Fort Bragg CA 95437-3861 Office: 321 Morrow St Fort Bragg CA 95437-3861

GALLIAN, RUSSELL JOSEPH, lawyer; b. San Mateo, Calif., Apr. 24, 1948; s. Phillip Hugh and Betty Jane (Boulton) G.; m. Marian Barbara Howard, Sept. 21, 1969; children: Lisa, Cherie, Joseph, Russell, Yvette, Jason, Ryan. BS, U. San Francisco, 1969, JD with highest honors, 1974. Bar: Calif. 1974, Utah 1975, U.S. Ct. Appeals (10th cir.) 1975, U.S. Supreme Ct. 1990; CPA, Calif. Staff acct. Arthur Andersen & Co., CPAs, San Francisco, 1969-71; treas., contr. N.Am. Reassurance Life Svc. Co., Palo Alto, Calif., 1972-74; assoc. VanCott Bagley Cornwell & McCarthy, Salt Lake City, 1975-77; sr. ptnr. Gallian & Westfall, St. George, Utah, 1977—; chmn. bd. dirs. Dixie Title Co., St. George. Chmn, Tooele (Utah) City Planning Commn., 1978; atty. City of Tooele, 1978-80, Town of Ivins, Utah, 1982—, Town of Springdale, Utah, 1987-90, Town of Rockville, Utah, 1987—; commr. Washington County, 1993—; chmn. Washington County Econ. Devel. Coun., 1993—; bd. dirs. Dixie Ctr., 1993—; active Habitat Conservation Plan Steering Com. Mem. ABA, Utah State Bar Assn. (co-chmn. 1987-88), Tooele County Bar Assn. (pres. 1978-79), So. Utah Bar Assn. (pres. 1986-87). Republican. Mormon. Office: Gallian & Westfall J9 South 100 East Saint George UT 84770

GALLIK, JANICE SUSAN, finance executive; b. Akron, Ohio; d. Emil John and Antoinette Mary (Verdi) G.; children: Thomas Butowicz II, Elizabeth Henshaw. BS cum laude, U. Akron, 1965; postgrad., St. Francis Coll., 1978; MS, Ind. U., 1981; EdD, Seattle U., 1988. Mng. ptnr., treas., dir. pub. rels. Buckeye Group, Inc., Orion Inc., 1977-81; contr. D.S. Willett, Inc., 1982-85; mgr. acctg. G. Raden & Sons, Inc., 1986-89; cons. J. Gallik & Assocs., 1985—; controller Merit Steamship Agy., Inc., 1988-91; dir. adminstrv. svcs. Seattle Children's Home, 1991—; adj. faculty Seattle Pacific U. Contbr. articles to profl. jours. Trustee, bd. dirs. Columbus 500 Com., 1989—; bd. dirs. Lit. Ctr., 1988-89; bus./community rels. Bellevue Art Mus., 1983-85; bd. dirs., com. mem., dir. pub. rels. Ft. Wayne Philharmonic, 1978-81; treas., pres. Aboite River Women's Club, 1980-81; bd. dirs. Izaak Walton's League, 1980; area rep. Girl Scouts Am.; bd. dirs., pres. Zelienople Jr. Women, 1974-76; med. team search com. Zelienople, Pa., 1976. Scholl scholarship St. Francis, 1978; rsch. grant NYU Ctr. for Entrepreneurship, 1986. Mem. Seattle C. of C., Acad. Mgmt., Seattle U. Alumni Assn. (bd. govs.), Phi Delta Kappa, Alpha Delta Pi. Office: Seattle Children's Home 2142 10th Ave W Seattle WA 98119-2845

GALLISON, H(AROLD) BAILEY, SR., youth agency administrator, public relations and marketing consultant; b. Orange, N.J., Apr. 6, 1924; s. Harold Hobron and Stella Camilla (Holm) G.; m. Janet Caralee Frazier, Jun. 23, 1951 (div. Jun. 1983); children: Claudia Jean, Harold Bailey II; m. Sharilyn Leone Lemkuil Gallison, Jan. 27, 1984. Grad., U. Mo., 1948. Sales mgr. Carll Mercury Dealership, La Jolla, Calif., 1951-53; exec. dir. La Jolla Town Council, 1953-63; advt. mgr. Security Pacific Bank, San Diego, 1963-70; dir. pub. rels. Mercy Hosp., San Diego, 1970-83; sr. account exec. Citadel Comm., San Diego, 1983-85; exec. dir. Community Campership Coun., San Diego, 1985—; chmn. adv. bd. La Jolla Capital Fin. Corp., San Diego, 1991—. pres. La Jolla Civic Theatre Assn., 1973-76. With USN, 1943-46, MTO. Named Profl. of Yr., San Diego Pub. Rels. Club, 1973, Outstanding Alumni, U. Mo., 1987, Citizen of Yr., San Diego Boy Scout Coun., 1994. mem. SAR, U.S. Navy League, Ky. Col. So. Calif. (bd. dirs. 1991—), U. Mo. Alumni Assn. (past bd. dirs.), Hon. Dep. Sheriff Assn., Kiwanis Club (named Kiwanian of Yr. La Jolla chpt. 1991), Am. Legion. Republican. Presbyterian. Office: Community Campership Coun Ste 208 7510 Clairmont Mesa Blvd San Diego CA 92111-1539

GALLO, JOSEPH E., vintner; b. 1941. Various positions Gallo Sales Co., South San Francisco, 1962—, now pres. Office: Gallo Sales Co Inc 440 Forbes Blvd South San Francisco CA 94080-2015*

GALLOWAY, CLINTON EDMUND, accountant, communications executive; b. Birmingham, Ala., Nov. 30, 1951; s. Thomas Eugene and Mable (Collins) G. BS in Accountancy, No. Ariz. U., 1974. CPA, Calif. Auditor Coopers & Lybrand, San Francisco, 1975-78; stockbroker Smith, Barney, Harris & Upham, Beverly Hills, Calif., 1978-80; pres. 1st St. Securities Corp., L.A., 1981-83; prin. Clinton E. Galloway, CPA, L.A., 1983—; pres. Preferred Communications, Inc., L.A., 1983—; chief oper. officer Can. Internat. Health Svcs., St. Louis, 1988-89. Dir. L.A. Black Media Coalition, 1987-91. Mem. Calif. Soc. CPA's. Office: 10905 Venice Blvd Los Angeles CA 90034-7009

GALLUP, JANET LOUISE, business official; b. Rochester, N.Y., Aug. 11, 1951; d. John Joseph and Mildred Monica (O'Keefe) VerHulst; 1 son, Jason Hicks. BA, Hofstra U., 1973; MA (grad. asst.), Calif. State U., Long Beach., 1979. Asst. trader E.F. Hutton, N.Y.C., 1973-75, Los Angeles, 1975, instr. Calif. State U., Long Beach, 1978-79; fin. analyst Rockwell Internat., Seal Beach, Calif., 1979-85, coordinator mgmt. and exec. devel. and succession planning, 1985-91; mgr. orgn. and employee devel. activities, Hughes Aircraft, 1991—. Vol. Cedar House Ctr.-Child Abuse, Long Beach, 1976. Democrat. Roman Catholic. Office: Hughes Aircraft 1901 W Malvern Ave Fullerton CA 92633-2177

GALLUP, MARC RICHMOND, biology educator, paleontologist; b. Glendale, Calif., Sept. 25, 1949; s. Donald Ray and Gloria Muriel (Grimes) G.; m. Susan Holly Smith, Dec. 30, 1971 (div. 1994). BA in Zoology, UCLA, 1971, PhD in Biology, 1982; MA in Zoology, U. Tex., 1974. Instr. biology Santa Monica (Calif.) Coll., 1980-84; instr. Calif. State U., Northridge, 1981-83, Los Angeles Mission Coll., San Fernando, Calif., 1981-84, South Pasadena (Calif.) High Sch., 1984-86; instr. dept. biology, target sci. UCLA, 1992—; cons. Jet Propulsion Lab., Pasadena, 1985—. Cons. Los Angeles Libraries, 1974-76, Los Angeles County Mus. Natural History, 1975-84. Grantee Sigma Xi, 1977, Karl Schmidt Field Mus. Natural History, 1977, UCLA Patent, 1975, 77. Mem. NEA, AAAS, Am. Soc. Zoologists, Nat. Sci. Tchrs. Assn., Planetary Soc. Democrat. Home: 8816 S 10th Ave Inglewood CA 90305-2327 Office: LA HS Los Angeles CA 90019

GALLUS, CHARLES JOSEPH, journalist; b. Havre, Mont., Jan. 24, 1947; s. Raymond Charles and Anna Jo (Mack) G. BA in Polit. Sci. cum laude, Carroll Coll., 1969; MA in Polit. Sci., U. Mont., 1972. Bookkeeper's asst. Ellen Solem, CPA, Chinook, Mont., 1972; circulation asst. Havre Daily News, 1972-73, wire editor, reporter, photographer, 1973—. Mem. 2 study comms. Havre local govt., 1974-77, 84-86; mem. Hill County Dem. Ctrl. Com., Havre, 1974—. Mem. AP, Glacier Natural History Assn., Sagebrush Athletic Club, Soc. Profl. Journalists, KC, Sigma Delta Chi. Roman Catholic. Home: 112 3rd St # 746 Havre MT 59501-3532 Office: Havre Daily News 119 2nd St # 431 Havre MT 59501-3507

GALNICK, MITCHELL NEIL, real estate developer, lawyer; b. Chgo., Oct. 5, 1953; s, Asher Harold and Helen (Karel) G.; m. Marta Jean Bromschwig, May 17, 1980. BS in Bus. magna cum laude, U. Colo., 1975, JD, 1978. Bar: Colo., 1978; lic. real estate broker, Colo. Staff acct. Arthur Andersen & Co., Denver, 1978-79; prin. Dupler, Hult & Galnick. P.C., Boulder, Colo., 1979-88; pres. Venture Group Cos., Boulder, 1980—; mgr. Lake Valley Golf Club, Boulder, 1987—. Mem. U. Colo. Law Rev., 1976; contbr. articles to legal jours. Mem. Colo. Bar Assn., Boulder Bar Assn. (co. chmn. real estate com. 1987-88), Urban Land Inst., Nat. Golf Found., Boulder C. of C. (resource ctr. task force 1988), Boulder Country Club, U. Colo. Dirs. Club, Beta

Alpha Psi, Beta Gamma Sigma. Office: Venture Group 4400 Lake Valley Dr Longmont CO 80503-8301

GALTON, ELIZABETH, psychiatrist, psychoanalyst; b. Evesham, Eng., June 16, 1941; came to U.S., 1962; d. Herbert and Herta (Adler) G.; m. John E. Dunkelberger, June 25, 1977; 1 child, Diana. BA, U. Kans., 1963, MD, 1967. Cert. psychiatrist. Asst. clin. prof. psychiatry U. Calif., L.A., 1974—; pvt. practice psychiatry/psychoanalysis Santa Monica, Calif., 1974—. Viola player Santa Monica Symphony Orch. Fellow Am. Psychiat. Assn.; mem. So. Calif. Psychiat. Soc. (pres. 1994-95). Office: 2901 Wilshire Blvd Ste 449 Santa Monica CA 90403-4907

GALVAN, ELIAS GABRIEL, bishop; b. San Juan Acozac, Puebla, Mexico, Apr. 9, 1938; came to U.S., 1956; s. Elias and Olga (Peralta) G.; m. Zoraida Freytes, July 12, 1986, 1 child, Elias Gabriel. BA, Calif. State U.; D in Religion, Sch. Theology Claremont. Ordained deacon United Meth. Ch., 1964, ordained elder, 1970. Asst. pastor Asbury United Meth. Ch., L.A., 1964-66; pastor City Ter. United Meth. Ch., L.A., 1966-69, All Nations United Meth. Ch., L.A., 1969-71; exec. dir. ethnic planning dept. United Meth. Ch., L.A., 1971-74, dist. supt. Santa Barbara Dist., 1974-80, coun. dir. Pacific and Southwest Conf., 1980-84, bishop United Meth. Ch., Phoenix area, 1984—. 1st Hispanic bishop elected by United Meth. Ch. Avocation: tennis. Office: United Meth Ctr 1550 E Meadowbrook Ave # 200 Phoenix AZ 85014-4040

GALVAO, LOUIS ALBERTO, import and export corporation executive, consultant; b. Ponta Delgada, Sao Miguel, Portugal, July 5, 1949; came to U.S., 1969; s. Jeremias B. and Margarida M. G.; m. Antonieta A. Galvao, Oct. 26, 1966 (div. 1984); children: Marlene, Vanessa. Degree in Bus. Mgmt., Indsl. & Commerce Sch., Azores, Portugal, 1968; Dr. Universal Life (hon.), Universal Life Ch., 1991. Asst. mgr. sales J.B. Galvao Imports, Azores, 1964-68; asst. supr. Union Carbide Corp., Peabody, Mass., 1969-70, Container Corp. Am., Wakefield, Mass., 1970-73; sales dir. McCulloch Oil Corp., Lake Havash City, Ariz., 1972-74; pres. Sunset Investments Corp., Phoenix, 1974—; v.p. United Universal Enterprises Corp., Phoenix, 1985—; pres. Universal Imports, Inc., Phoenix, 1977—; dir. Global Savings & Loan Ltd., London, 1990—. mem. Nat. Rep. Congl. Com., Washington, 1982— (cert. recognition 1981, 84, 85, Campaign Kickoff award 1984, cert. merit 1992), Rep. Presdl. Task Force, Washington, 1984— (Am. flag dedicated in his honor at Rotunda of U.S. Capital bldg. 1986, life mem., mem. presdl. electiom registry 1992), Rep. Nat. Com. (cert. recognition 1990, 92), European Movement, U.K., 1990—, Social Dem. Party, Portugal, 1990—, Washington Legal Found.; charter mem. U.S. Def. Com.; del. The Presl. Trust, Washington, 1992. Recipient award U.S. Def. Com., 1984; inducted to Rep. Nat. Hall Honor Rep. Nat. Candidate Trust, 1992. Mem. Am. Mgmt. Assn., Nat. Assn. Export Cos., Profl. Fin. Assts., Heritage Bus. Club, Senatorial Club, Universal Life Ch. Roman Catholic.

GALVEZ, WILLIAM, artist; b. Cali, Colombia, 1945; came to U.S., 1963; Student, Inst. de Bellas Artes/Conservatorio, A.M.V., Cali, 1961-63; studied with Richard Peterson, Calif., 1975-79; studied with Roberto Lupetti, Carmel, Calif., 1980-83. Owner Galvez Pub., Placentia, Calif., 1991—. One-man shows include Galeria Elegante, Palm Desert, Calif., 1980, 83, Klein Art Gallery, Beverly Hills, Calif., 1981, Rainbow Promenade Galleries, Waikiki, Hawaii, 1982, Galeria Maria Luisa, Pasadena, Calif., 1984, San Gabriel (Calif.) Civic Auditorium, 1986, Galeria Figuras, Cali, 1989, 91, Dist. Libr., Placentia, Calif., 1990, Physician's Medicine Group, Long Beach, Calif., 1991, Calif. Colombian C. of C., L.A., 1992; exhibited in group shows at Pomeroy Art Gallery, Cypress, Calif., 1976, 77, 78, Fisher Galleries, Palm Springs, Calif., 1979, Ctr. Art Galleries, Honolulu, 1980, Internat. Art Exch., Anaheim Hills, Calif., 1981, New Masters Gallery, Carmel, 1982, 83, 84, 85, 86, 92, Fine Art Inst., San Bernardino Calif., 1986, Poulsen Galleries, Inc., Pasadena, 1988, 89, Simic Galleries, Inc., Carmel, Beverly Hills, La Jolla, 1988, 1990, 1991, Internat. Art. Galery, N.Y.C., 1990, Galeria Figuras, Cali, 1991, 92, 93, L.A. Art Expo, 1991, Art Fair, Placentia, 1991, Bob Hope Gala, Corona, Calif., Art Buyers Caraban, Long Beach, Calif., 1992, Laura Larkin Gallery, Del Mar, Claif., 1992, Phyllis Diller Nat. Parkinson found., L.A., 1992, Toronto (Can.) Art Exhbn., 1992, Internat. Colombian Fair, Chgo., 1992, Wayne Newton Gala, Anaheim, Calif., 1992, New England Fine Arts Inst., Boston, 1993, Poulsen Galleries, Inc., Pasadena, Calif., 1992, Internat. Art Gallery, L.A., Paris, 1993. Studio: 1312 Sao Paulo Ave Placentia CA 92670-3927 Address: PO Box 355 Placentia CA 92670-0355

GALVIN, ELIAS, bishop. Bishop Desert S.W. Diocese, Phoenix, Ariz. Home: PO Box 467 San Francisco CA 94101 Office: Desert SW Diocese 2933 E Indian School Rd # 402 Phoenix AZ 85016-6804*

GAMACHE, ADRIEN EDMOND, economist, valuation consultant; b. Manchester, N.H., Sept. 21, 1941; s. Wilfred Dolar Gamache and Madeleine Rose Gamache Burrill; m. Beatrice Irene Maurer, Mar. 19, 1966; children: Christina, Monique, Jennifer. Student, U. N.H., 1959-61; BS, Purdue U., 1963; PhD, U. Wash., 1969. Sr. analyst Arthur Andersen & Co., Seattle, 1969; analyst MacMillan Bloedel Ltd., Vancouver, B.C., Can., 1970-72; economist, analyst Black & Co., Inc., Portland, Oreg., 1973; economist H. C. Mason & Assocs., Inc., Portland, 1974-76; pres. Gamache & Assocs., Inc., Portland and Seattle, 1977-85, Pvt. Valuations, Inc., Bellevue, Wash., 1990—; assoc. prof. Coll. Forest Resources U. Wash., Seattle, 1981-86; dir. devel. svcs., appraiser Shorett & Reily, Seattle, 1986; v.p., dir. fin. svcs., dir. real estate valuation Consilium, Inc., Bellevue, 1987-90; instr. Appraisal Inst., U. Wash., Wash. Inst., ITT Rayonier, La.-Pacific Corp.; mem. faculty N.W. Securities Inst., Wash. State Bar Assn., Oreg. State Bar Assn.; bd. dirs. Robotic Container Holding Co., Bellevue, Locus, Inc., Seattle. Editor: Selling the Federal Forests, 1983. NSF fellow, 1963. Mem. Am. Soc. Appraisers (affiliate), Appraisal Inst. (affiliate). Republican. Unitarian. Home: 13325 NE 118th Ct Redmond WA 98052-2412 Office: Pvt Valuations Inc 1000 2nd Ave Ste 3450 Seattle WA 98104

GAMAL, IRWIN BERT, management consultant; b. Bklyn., Aug. 1, 1943; s. Murray and Rose (Yelinski) G.; m. Karen Ann Sawko, Aug. 24, 1974. AA, Cerritos Coll., Norwalk, Calif., 1965; BA, Calif. State U., Long beach, 1967, MA, 1972. Cert. Calif. cmty. coll. instr. Dir. tng. Vornado, Inc., Whittier, Calif., 1975-77; dir. mgmt. devel. Galardi Group, Newport Beach, Calif., 1977-81; dir. HRD divsn. Arrindell Assocs., Newport Beach, 1981; internal HRD cons. Fluor Corp., Irvine, Calif., 1981-84; dir. tng. Coldwell Banker Residential, Newport Beach, 1984-88; pres. Insight Sys. Group, Laguna Beach, Calif., 1988—; project advisor, class chmn. Pepperdine U., Malibu, Calif., 1990-92; feedback cons. Ctr. for Creative Leadership, La Jolla, Calif., 1993—; seminar leader, keynote spkr. Nat. Seminars Group, Shawnee Mission, Kans., 1993—. Contbr. articles to profl. jours. Mem. Indsl. League of Orange County. Recipient Cert. of Appreciation ACCET, 1993, Participation award Calif. Assn. Pre-paid Dental Plans, 1991, Outstanding Svc. award Coastline C.C., Fountain Valley, Calif., 1983. Mem. ASTD (dir. profl. devel. 1993—, Service award 1993), World Affairs Coun., Orange County Orgnl. Devel. Network (bd. editors 1993), Calif. State U.-Long Beach Alumni Assn. Republican. Jewish. Office: Insight Systems Group 20875 Klamath Ct Laguna Beach CA 92656

GAMBARO, ERNEST UMBERTO, lawyer, consultant; b. Niagara Falls, N.Y., July 6, 1938; s. Ralph and Teresa (Nigro) G.; m. Winifred Sonya Gambaro, June 3, 1961. B.A. in Aero. Engring. with honors, Purdue U., 1960, M.S. with honors, 1961; Fulbright scholar, Rome U., 1961-62; J.D. with honors, Loyola U., Los Angeles, 1975. Bar: Calif. 1975, U.S. Tax Ct. 1976, U.S. Supreme Ct. 1979, U.S. Ct. Appeals (9th cir.). With Aerospace Corp., El Segundo, Calif., 1962-80, counsel, 1975-80; asst. gen. counsel, asst. sec. Computer Scis. Corp., El Segundo, 1980-88; v.p., gen. counsel, sec. INFONET Svcs. Corp., El Segundo, 1988—; cons. bus. fin. and mgmt., 1988—. Recipient U.S. Air Force Commendation for contbns. to U.S. manned space program, 1969; Purdue U. Pres.'s scholar, 1959-60. Mem. ABA (internat., taxation sects.), Los Angeles Bar Assn. (exec. com. 1976—, former chmn. sect. law and tech. 1976-78, chmn. bar reorgn. com. 1981-82), Am. Arbitration Assn. Los Angeles Ctr. Internat. Comml. Arbitration (founder, bd. dirs.), Internat. Law Inst. (faculty), St. Thomas More Law Soc., Phi Alpha Delta, Omicron Delta Kappa (past pres.), Tau Beta Pi, Sigma Gamma Tau (past pres.), Phi Eta Sigma. Republican. Newspaper columnist Europe Alfresco; contbr. articles to profl. publs. Home: 6542 Ocean Crest Dr Palos Verdes Peninsula CA 90275-5400 Office: 2100 E Grand Ave El Segundo CA 90245-5024

GAMBINO, JEROME JAMES, nuclear medicine educator; b. N.Y.C., Sept. 13, 1925; m. Jacquelyn Ann Mazzola, Mar. 27, 1948; children: Charles, John, Mary Ellen, Jacquelyn. BA, U. Conn., 1950, MS, 1952; PhD, U. Calif., 1957. Asst. prof. natural scis. SUNY, New Paltz, 1957-59; research radiobiologist UCLA, 1959-61; mem. research staff Northrop Corp., Hawthorne, Calif., 1961-69; dir. edn. nuclear medicine dept. VA Med. Ctr., Los Angeles, 1969—; lectr. anatomy U. So. Calif., L.A., 1963-89, radiol. scis. UCLA, 1978—. Mem. Radiation Research Soc., Soc. Nuclear Medicine (pres. So. Calif. chpt. 1981-82). Office: West LA VA Med Ctr Nuclear Medicine 115 11301 Wilshire Blvd Los Angeles CA 90073

GAMBLE, BARBARA JEAN, dietitian and consultant; b. Garden City, Kans., June 6, 1950; d. Joe P. and Anna M. (Burgardt) Dreiling; m. Don L. Gamble, Dec. 14, 1973; 1 child, Angelene J. BS in Dietetics and Instnl. Mgmt., Kans. State U., 1972. Dietitian and dir. dietary svcs. Prowers Med. Ctr., Lamar, Colo., 1974—; cons. dietitian S.E. Colo. Hosp. and Long Term Care, Springfield, 1977—, Sand Haven Nursing Home, Lamar, 1972—, Holly Nursing Care Ctr., 1975—. Mem. Am. Dietetic Assn. (registered), Colo. Dietetic Assn., Colo. Cons. Dietitians, Cons. Dietitians with Health Care Facilities. Republican. Home: 402 Willow Valley Dr Lamar CO 81052-3917 Office: Prowers Med Ctr 401 Kendall Dr Lamar CO 81052-3993

GAMBLE, CAROL IRENE DAVIS, secondary education educator; b. Fargo, N.D., Apr. 21, 1952; d. Raymond Warren and Irene Margaret (Schroeder) Davis; m. Lawrence Herman Nelson, June 29, 1974 (div. 1983); m. Frederick Kroeger Gamble, June 9, 1984; children: Elaine Louise, John Davis. BS, N.D. State U., 1974; MS, U. Ariz., 1990. Salesperson/mgr. Gold Bond Stamp Redemption Ctr., St. Paul, 1968-80; child care food program coord. Food and Nutrition Office, Ariz. Dept. Edn., Phoenix, 1974-77; cons. dietition Child Nutrition Sect., Minn. Dept. Edn., St. Paul, 1977-78; sch. lunch specialist Food and Nutrition Office, Ariz. Dept. Edn., Phoenix, 1978-80, nutrition edn. and tng. program coord., 1980-82; food svc. specialist Federated Food, Inc., Sunnyvale, Calif., 1982-83; job specialist Jobs for Ariz. Grads., No. Ariz. U., Flagstaff, 1983-84; tchr. Emily Gray Jr. H.S., Tucson, Ariz., 1984—; instr., workshop leader in field. Contbg. author: (textbook) Child Development, Roles, Responsibilities, Resources, 1990. Recipient Citation of Merit, Ariz. Gov. Mem. NEA, Am. Assn. Family and Consumer Scis., Am. Sch. Food Svc. Assn. (cert., Pub. Rels. award 1980), Ariz. Sch. Food Svc. Assn. (past chpt. pres.), Phi Upsilon Omicron, Tau Beta Sigma. Democrat. Presbyterian.

GAMBLE, LADEANA, family mediation center official; b. Hubbard, Tex., Dec. 14, 1958; d. Raymond Austin and Iva Gail (Cornish) G. BSW, U. Nev., 1981, MSW, 1991. Probation officer Clark County Dept. Family and Youth Svcs., Las Vegas, Nev., 1981-86; family specialist family divsn. Family Mediation & Assessment Ctr. 8th Jud. Dist., Las Vegas, 1986-91, mgr. family divsn., 1991—; bd. dirs. Family and Child Treatment So. Nev., Las Vegas. Mem. Las Vegas Domestic Violence Task Force, 1992—. Mem.. ASPA, Assn. Family and Conciliation Cts. (bd. dirs.), Am. Bus. Women's Assn. (Bus. Assoc. of Yr. award 1991), Delta Sigma Theta. Office: Family Mediation and Assessment Ctr 3464 E Bonanza Rd Las Vegas NV 89101

GAMBLE, LEE ST. CLAIR, architectural and interior designer; b. St. Louis; d. James Carr and Dorothy Lee (Wharton) Gamble ; children: Lindsey Elise, Ashley Elizabeth. BS, Skidmore Coll., 1974; degree in Interior Design, N.Y. Sch. Interior Design, 1976. Asst. buyer Abraham & Strauss, Bklyn., 1974-75; mgr. Trevi Co., Pitts., 1975; buyer Saks Fifth Ave., N.Y.C., 1975-77; pres. West Wind Designs, Cody, Wyo., 1977—; owner Southfork Expdns. Ltd., Cody, 1987—; interior deisgn bus. owner Mountain Style Interiors, Steamboat Springs, 1992—; designer Deux Amis, Steamboat Springs, 1994—; cons. design Wyo. Waterfowl Park, Cody, 1984-86, bd. dirs. Bd. dirs. Desarro Woldlife Rseources, 1991—, Steamboat Springs Youth Soccer Assn., 1994—; active Steamboat Springs Hosp. Aux., 1993—. Mem. Zoo Mont. (bd. dirs. 1985—). Republican. Methodist. Office: Solitary Ventures Inc PO Box 775287 Steamboat Springs CO 80477-5287

GAMBOA, GEORGE CHARLES, oral surgeon, educator; b. King City, Calif., Dec. 17, 1923; s. George Angel and Martha Ann (Baker) G.; m. Winona Mae Collins, July 16, 1946; children: Cheryl Jan Gamboa Granger, Jon Charles, Judith Merlene Gamboa Hiscox. Pre-dental cert., Pacific Union Coll., 1943; DDS, U. Pacific, 1946; MS, U. Minn., 1953; AB, U. So. Calif., 1958, EdD, 1976. Diplomate Am. Bd. Oral and Maxillofacial Surgery. Fellow oral surgery Mayo Found., 1950-53; assoc. prof. grad. program oral and maxillofacial surgery U. So. Calif., Los Angeles, 1954—; assoc. prof. Loma Linda (Calif.) U., 1958-94, chmn. dept. oral surgery, 1960-63; pvt. practice oral and maxillofacial surgery, San Gabriel, Calif., 1955-93. Mem., past chmn. first aid com. West San Gabriel chpt. ARC. Fellow Am. Coll. Dentists (founding fellow), Am. Coll. Oral and Maxillofacial Surgeons (founding fellow), Am. Inst. Oral Biology, Internat. Coll. Dentists, So. Calif. Acad. Oral Pathology; mem. Am. Assn. Oral and Maxillofacial Surgeons, Internat. Assn. Oral Surgeons, So. Calif. Soc. Oral and Maxillofacial Surgeons, Western Soc. Oral and Maxillofacial Surgeons, Am. Acad. Oral and Maxillofacial Radiology, Marsh Robinson Acad. Oral Surgeons, Profl. Staff Assn. Los Angeles County-U. So. Calif. Med. Ctr. (exec. com. 1976—), Am. Cancer Soc. (Calif. div., profl. edn. subcom. 1977-90, pres. San Gabriel-Pomona Valley unit 1989-90), Calif. Dental Soc. Anesthesiology (pres. 1989-94), Calif. Dental Found. (pres. 1991-93), Calif. Dental Assn. (jud. coun. 1990—), San Gabriel Valley Dental Soc. (past pres.), Xi Psi Phi, Omicron Kappa Upsilon, Delta Epsilon. Seventh-day Adventist. Home: 1102 Loganrita Ave Arcadia CA 91006-4535

GAMBRELL, THOMAS ROSS, investor; b. Lockhart, Tex., Mar. 17, 1934; s. Sidney Spivey and Nora Katherine (Rheinlander) G.; m. Louise Evans, Feb. 23, 1960. MD, U. Tex., 1957. Company physician Hughes Aircraft, Fullerton, Calif., 1958-65, Chrysler Corp., Anaheim, Calif., 1962-65, L.A. Angels Baseball Team, Fullerton, 1962-64; pvt. practice medicine Fullerton, 1958-91; owner Ranching (Citrus) & Comml. Devel., Ariz., Tex., N.Y. Contbr. articles to profl. jours. Organizer of care for needy elderly, North Orange County, 1962-65. Fellow Am. Acad. Family Physicians; mem. AMA, Calif. Med. Assn., Tex. Med. Assn., Orange County Med. Assn., Mayflower Soc., Sons of Confederacy, Descendants of Royalty Living in Am. Office: PO Box 6067 Beverly Hills CA 90212-1067

GAMER, NANCY CREWS SCHAEFER, alumni relations director, fundraiser; b. Tacoma, Feb. 2, 1937; d. Norman W. and Kathryn (Gibbons) Schaefer; m. J. D. Gamer, June 14, 1960 (div. 1979); children: Jeffrey D., Michael C. BA, Mills Coll., 1959, MA, 1960. Instr. in English Lake Forest (Ill.) Coll., 1960-61, Monterey (Calif.) Peninsula Jr. Coll., 1964-65, Jacksonville (Fla.) U., 1967-69, No. Va. Community Coll., Annandale, 1969-72; tutor Claremont (Calif.) McKenna Coll., fall 1976; alumni sec. Harvey Mudd Coll., Claremont, 1977-78, adminstrv. asst., 1978-79, dir. alumni rels., 1979-91; writing tutor Claremont (Calif.) McKenna Coll., 1991—. Mem. parents bd. Claremont McKenna Coll., 1982-86; bd. dirs. ARC, Claremont, 1984, 85. Mem. Coun. for Advancement and Support of Edn. Office: Claremont McKenna Coll English Resource Ctr Claremont CA 91711

GAMLIN, JOHN PASCHALL, lawyer; b. Paris, Tenn., Nov. 27, 1964; s. Charles Thomas and Annie Laurie (Paschall) G. BA, Vanderbilt U., 1987; JD, Ohio State U., 1990. Bar: Tenn. 1990, Colo. 1991, U.S. Dist. Ct. Colo., U.S. Ct. Appeals (fed. cir.), U.S. Ct. Appeals (10th cir.). With John P. DiFalco and Assocs., P.C., Ft. Collins, Colo., 1990—. Home: 824 Grouse Cir Fort Collins CO 80524-2170 Office: John P DiFalco and Assoc PC 1136 E Stuart St Ste 4102 Fort Collins CO 80525-1173

GAMM, GORDON JULIUS, lawyer; b. Shreveport, La., July 14, 1939; s. Sylvian Willer Gamm and Leona (Gordon) Windes. BA, Drake U., 1963; JD, Tulane U., 1970. Bar: La. 1970, Mo. 1971. Ptnr. Hill & Gamm, Kansas City, Mo., 1977-79; pvt. practice Kansas City, 1979-83, 87—; sole practice Levine P.C. & Gamm, Kansas City, 1983-86. Founder Bragg's Symposium, 1980—. Mem. Mo. Bar Assn., Kansas City Bar Assn., Assn. Trial Lawyers Am. (diploma), Nat. Inst. Trial Advocacy (cert.). Office: 4450 Arapahoe Ste 106 Boulder CO 80303-3970

GAMMELL, GLORIA RUFFNER, sales executive; b. St. Louis, June 19, 1948; d. Robert Nelson and Antonia Ruffner; m. Doyle M. Gammell, Dec. 11, 1973. AA in Art, Harbor Coll., Harbor City, Calif., 1969; BA in Sociology, Calif. State U., Long Beach, 1971. Cert. fin. planner. Bus. analyst Dun & Bradstreet, Los Angeles, 1971-81; sales rep. Dun & Bradstreet, Orange, Calif., 1971-93; rep. sales Van Nuys, Calif., 1981-90; pres., sec. bd. dirs. Gammell Industries, Paramount, Calif., 1993—. Mem. Anne Banning Assistance League, Hollywood, Calif., 1981-82; counselor YWCA, San Pedro, Calif., 1983-84; fundraiser YMCA, San Pedro, 1984-85; mem. womens adv. com. Calif. State Assembly, 1984-89. Recipient Best in the West Presdl. Citation, 1981-86, 89, 90. Home: 991 W Channel St San Pedro CA 90731-1415

GAMMILL, DARRYL CURTIS, business executive; b. Milw., Jan. 20, 1950; s. Lawrence H. and Eunice B. (Birkett) G. BS, U. Colo., 1973; m. Maureen Mulcahy, Sept. 16, 1972; children: Rebecca, Bridgett, Maureen, Bryann. Lic. gen. and fin. prin.; registered options prin., sr. compliance officer, registered rep., SEC, registered investment advisor, broker dealer, real estate broker, SEC. Stockbroker, Douglas, Stanat, Inc., Denver, 1974; dir. rsch. Pittman Co., Denver, 1975; option specialist B.J. Leonard & Co., Denver, 1976; v.p. rsch., corp. fin. Neidiger, Tucker Bruner, Denver, 1977; chmn., pres., chief exec. officer G.S. Omni Corp., 1979-82; chmn., chief exec. officer Gammill and Co., 1981—; mng. ptnr. GSI Cons., 1988—; mng. ptnr. G.S. Oil, G.S. Leasing; dir. Valudyne, Inc., 1973-79; pres. Chalton Investment Svcs.; chmn., pres. Fusion Mgmt. Corp., 1981-83; chmn. Applied Fusion Rsch. & Tech. Corp., 1982, Pres. Rsch. Mgmt., 1984; gen. partner Fusion Ltd. Trustee Gammill Found.; pres. Platinium Club Inc., 1985-88; founder AudioOptics. Founder Nicholas R. Massaro Ednl. Scholarship, 1985; co-founder Opera Colo. Mem. Fin. Analysts Fedn., Nat. Assn. Security Dealers, Denver Soc. Security Analysts, IEEE, Am. Nuclear Soc., Nat. Energy Assn. (nat. chmn.), Am. Mgmt. Assn., Investment Rsch. Mgmt. Assn., U.S. Ski Assn., Optimists, Elks. Contbr. articles to profl. jours. Home: 28 Red Fox Ln Littleton CO 80127-5713

GANDELMAN, JOEL LESLIE, ventriloquist; b. New Haven, Nov. 30, 1949; s. Richard Robert and Helen (Ravinsky) G. BA, Colgate U., 1972; MS in Journalism, Northwestern U., 1973. Free-lance journalist, 1973-78; staff writer Wichita (Kans.) Eagle Beacon, 1980-82, San Diego Union, 1982-90; comic ventriloquist Raven Vent Prodns., San Diego, 1990—. Author: Tips From a Pro, 1994; contbr. articles to profl. jours. Named Hon. Ky. Col., Order Ky. Cols., 1989; named in Great Ventriloquists trading cards. Mem. Internat. Assn. Fairs and Expositions, Internat. Festivals Assn., Profl. Comedians Assn., N.Am. Assn. Ventriloquists, Western Fairs Assn., Moose Lodge. Home: 4434 Florida St Apt 2 San Diego CA 92116-4038 Office: Raven Vent Prodns PO Box 16496 San Diego CA 92176-6496

GANDHI, OM PARKASH, electrical engineer; b. Multan, Pakistan, Sept. 23, 1934; came to U.S., 1967, naturalized, 1975; s. Gopal Das and Devi Bai (Patney) G.; m. Santosh Nayar, Oct. 28, 1963; children: Rajesh Timmy, Monica, Lena. BS with honors, Delhi U., India, 1952; MSE, U. Mich., 1957, Sc.D., 1961. Rsch. specialist Philco Corp., Blue Bell, Pa., 1960-62; asst. dir. Cen. Electronics Engring. Rsch. Inst., Pilani, Rajasthan, India, 1962-65, dep. dir., 1965-67; prof. elec. engring., rsch. prof. bioengring. U. Utah, Salt Lake City, 1967—; chmn. elec. engring., 1992—; cons. U.S. Army Med. R & D Command, Washington, 1973-77; cons. to microwave and telecom. industry and govtl. health and safety orgns.; mem. Commns. B and K, Internation Union Radio Sci.; mem. study sect. on diagnostic radiology NIH, 1978-81. Author: Microwave Engineering and Applications, 1981; editor: Engineering in Medicine and Biology mag., 1987, Electromagnetic Biointeraction, 1989, Biological Effects and Medical Applications of Electromagnetic Energy, 1990; contbr. over 200 articles to profl. jours. Recipient Disting. Rsch. award U. Utah, 1979-80; grantee NSF, NIH, EPA, USAF, U.S. Army, USN, N.Y. State Dept. Health, others. Fellow IEEE (editor spl. issue Procs. IEEE 1980, co-chmn. com. on RF safety stds. 1988—, Tech. Achievement award Utah sect. 1975); mem. Electromagnetics Acad., Bioelectromagnetics Soc. (bd. dirs. 1979-82, 87-90, v.p., pres. 1991-94, d'Arsonval award 1995). Office: Univ Utah Dept Elec Engring 3280 Merrill Engring Salt Lake City UT 84112

GANDSEY, LOUIS JOHN, petroleum and environmental consultant; b. Greybull, Wyo., May 19, 1921; s. John Wellington and Leonora (McLaughlin) G.; m. Mary Louise Alviso, Nov. 10, 1945; children: Mary M., Catherine K., John P., Michael J., Laurie A. AA, Compton Jr. Coll., 1941; BS, U. Calif. Berkeley, 1943; M in Engring., UCLA, 1958. Registered profl. engr., Calif. With Richfield Oil Corp., L.A., 1943-65, process engr., processing foreman, sr. foreman, mfg. coord., 1943-61, project leader process computer control, 1961-63, light oil oper. supt., 1963-64, asst. refinery supt., 1964-65; mgr. planning Richfield div. Atlantic Richfield Co., L.A., 1966-68, mgr. evaluation products div., L.A., 1968-69, mgr. supply and transp., Chgo., 1969-71, mgr. planning and mgmt. sci., N.Y.C., 1971, mgr. supply and transp., L.A., 1971-72, mgr. coordination and supply, 1972-75, mgr. domestic crude, 1975-77; v.p. refining Lunday-Thagard Oil Co., South Gate, Calif., 1977-82; petroleum cons. World Oil Corp., L.A., 1982-85; gen. cons., 1986—; instr. chem. and petroleum tech. L.A. Harbor Coll., 1960-65; cons. on oil crops, Austria, 1991; U.S. del. in environ. affairs to Joint Inter-Govtl. Com. for Environ. Protection, USSR, 1991, asphalt tech. to Joint Inter-Govtl. Com. for Highway Design CWS, 1992; U.S. del. Econ. and Environ. Affairs, Portugal, Spain, 1994, Hist. & Econ. Affairs, Mexico, 1995. Contbr. articles to profl. jours. Served with C.E., AUS, 1944-45. Mem. AICE, Am. Chem. Soc., Calif. Soc. Profl. Engrs., Environ. Assessment Assn.. Home: 2340 Neal Spring Rd Templeton CA 93465-8413

GANDY, H. CONWAY, lawyer, state official; b. Washington, Nov. 3, 1934; s. Hoke and Anne B. (Conway) G.; m. Carol Anderson, Aug. 29, 1965; children: Jennifer, Constance, Margaret. BA, Colo. State U., 1962; JD, U. Denver, 1968. Bar: Colo. 1969, U.S. dist. ct. Colo. 1969. Pvt. practice, Ft. Collins, Colo., 1969-81; adminstrv. law judge div. Adminstrv. Hearings, State of Colo., Denver, 1981—. Dem. candidate for Colo. Senate, 1974, dist. atty., 1976. With USN, 1954-58. Mem. Colo. Bar Assn., Larimer County Bar Assn., Nat. Assn. Adminstrv. Law Judges (pres. Colo. chpt. 1985-86), Sertoma (Centurion award 1973, Tribune award 1975, Senator award 1977, 79, sec. Honor Club 1977-78, pres. Ft. Collins club 1978-79, pres. Front Range club 1988-89). Methodist. Home: 724 Winchester Dr Fort Collins CO 80526-2636 Office: PO Box 8287 Fort Collins CO 80526

GANESH, SHIVAJI L., computer engineer; b. Tirunelveli, Tamil Nadu, India, July 31, 1955; came to U.S., 1977; s. L.N. and Lalitha Kailasam; m. Akhila Shivaji Ganesh, Aug. 27, 1989. BTech in Elec. Engring., Indian Inst. Tech., Madras, 1977; MSEE, SUNY, Stony Brook, 1978; PhD in Computer Sci., U. Calif., Berkeley, 1984. Mem. tech. staff AT&T Bell Labs, Naperville, Ill., 1984-91; sr. consulting analyst AT&T-NCR, Naperville, 1992-93; engr. scientist Hewlett Packard, Cupertino, Calif., 1993—. Mem. IEEE. Office: Hewlett Packard 19111 Prune Ridge Ave Cupertino CA 95014

GANGWERE, HEATHER HENDRY, secondary education educator; b. Orange, Calif., Apr. 11, 1964; d. James Hendry and Phila Margaret (Hurter) Acuff; m. Walter Lewis Gangwere, Nov. 22, 1986. BA, U. Redlands, 1986; postgrad., San Jose State U., 1987-90. Cert. tchr., lang. devel. specialist, Calif. Resident asst. U. Redlands, Calif., 1985-86; substitute tchr. San Jose (Calif.) Sch. Dists., 1986-89; tchr. Spanish and ESL Leland High Sch. San Jose Unified Sch. Dist., 1989—, fgn. lang. dept. chair, 1991-94; interpreter Youth Unlimited Gospel Outreach, San Dimas, Calif., 1983—. Youth leader Crossroads Bible Ch., San Jose, 1990; participant Pacific Neighbors, San Jose, 1990—. Mem. Mortar Board, Sigma Delta Pi, Pi Lambda Theta, Omicron Delta Kappa. Home: 16055 Ridgecrest Ave Los Gatos CA 95030-4135

GANN, JO RITA, social services administrator, association executive; b. Talihina, Okla., June 2, 1940; d. Herbert and Juanita Rita (Fields) G. BS, Okla. Bapt. U., 1962; M Theatre Arts, Portland State U., 1970. Tchr. Oklahoma City Pub. Schs., 1962-64; teen dir., dir. health edn. YWCA, Oklahoma City, 1964-67; camp dir., teen dir. YWCA, Portland, Oreg., 1967-72; asst. dir., program coordinator YWCA, Flint, Mich., 1972-75; exec. dir. YWCA, Salem, Oreg., 1975—; chair N.W. regional staff YWCA, 1983, mem. constn. commn. YWCA, 1981-84, nat. com. to study purpose, 1988-91, del. to World Coun., Norway, 1991; CEO bus. panel Oregonian's Pub. Co. Co-author: A New Look at Supervision, 1980. Del. UN Conf. for Non-Govtl. Orgns.; internat. study del. on world econ. interdependence to Ghana, Africa; speaker Global Concerns, Salem and Portland, 1981—; mem. pres.'s council Salem Summerfest, 1985, 86. Mem. Nat. Assn. YWCA Exec. Dirs., Nat. Orgn. Female Execs., United Way Agy. Execs. (chair 1987, 88). Democrat. Office: YWCA 768 State St Salem OR 97301-3849

GANNATAL, JOSEPH PAUL, electronics engineer; b. Ventura, Calif., Sept. 9, 1955; s. Paul and Janet Mae (Carpenter) G.; m. Sandy Jean Lincoln, Jan. 14, 1984; children: Leonard Troy Garcia, Jennifer Lynn Garcia, Sarah Jean Gannatal, Samantha Leigh Gannatal. BSME, Calif. Polytech. Inst., San Luis Opisbo, 1979; M in Space Systems Tech., Naval Postgrad. Sch., 1987. Indsl. engr. Nat. Semiconductor, Santa Clara, Calif., 1979-81; spl. projects engr. Pacific Missile Test Ctr., Point Mugu, Calif., 1981—, mgr. devel. program, 1986-89, sr. exec. mgr. devel. program, 1990-94. Mem. bldg. com. Camarillo Bapt. Ch., 1984-86. Recipient Spl. Achievement award USN, 1982, 84, 94, Letter of Commendation, USN, 1983, Outstanding Svc. award, 1985, 86, 89, 90, 91, 92. Mem. AIAA, ASME, Nat. Space Soc. (pres. Ventura County chpt. 1990-92). Republican.

GANNON, ROBERT P., utility company executive. BA, U. Notre Dame, 1966; JD, U. Mont., 1969. Formerly v.p., gen. counsel Montana Power Co., Butte, Mont., until 1989, pres., 1989—, also dir., 1989—. Office: Mont Power Co 40 W Broadway St Butte MT 59701-9222

GANONG, WILLIAM F(RANCIS), physiologist, physician; b. Northampton, Mass., July 6, 1924; s. William Francis and Anna (Hobbet) G.; m. Ruth Jackson, Feb. 22, 1948; children: William Francis III, Susan B., Anna H., James E. A.B. cum laude, Harvard U., 1945, M.D. magna cum laude, 1949; DSc (hon.), Med. Coll. Ohio, 1995. Intern, jr. asst. resident in medicine Peter Bent Brigham Hosp., Boston, 1949-51; asst. in medicine and surgery Peter Bent Brigham Hosp., 1952-55; research fellow medicine and surgery Harvard U., 1952-55; asst. prof. physiology U. Calif., San Francisco, 1955-60; assoc. prof. U. Calif., 1960-64, prof., 1964-82, Jack D. and Deloris Lange prof., 1982-91, Lange prof. emeritus, 1991—, faculty research lectr., 1968, vice chmn. dept., 1963-68, chmn., 1970-87; cons. Calif. Dept. Mental Hygiene. Author: Review of Medical Physiology, 17th edit., 1995, Physiology: A Study Guide, 3d edit., 1989; editor: (with L. Martini) Neuroendocrinology, vol. I, 1966, vol. II, 1967, Frontiers in Neuroendocrinology, 1969, 71, 73, 76, 78, 80, 82, 84, 86, 88; editor-in-chief Neuroendocrinology, 1979-84; co-editor Frontiers in Neuroendocrinology, 1990—. Served with U.S. Army, 1943-46; served to capt. M.C. 1951-52. Recipient Boylston Med. Soc. prize Harvard U., 1949, A.A. Berthold medal, 1985; named Disting. Svc. mem. Assn. Med. Coll., 1988. Felow AAAS; mem. Am. Physiol. Soc. (pres. 1977-78), Assn. Chairmen Depts. Physiology (pres. 1976-77), Am. Soc. for Gravitational and Space Biology (bd. dirs. 1984-87), Soc. Exptl. Biology and Medicine (councillor 1989-93), Endocrine Soc., Chilean Endocrine Soc. (corr.), Internat. Brain Rsch. Orgn., Soc. for Neurosci., Internat. Soc. Neuroendocrinology (v.p. 1976-80). Home: 710 Hillside Ave Albany CA 94706-1022 Office: U Calif Dept Physiology San Francisco CA 94143-0444

GANSAUER, DIANE H., wildlife association executive; b. Monterey, Calif., Oct. 2, 1955; d. Osman Huston and Beryl Theresa (Nugent) Hull; m. Robert Henry Gansauer, Aug. 28, 1982; 1 child, Greta Kristen. BA, Coll. of William and Mary, 1977; MBA, U. Pitts., 1982. Devel. coord. Nat. Rehab. Hosp., Washington, 1984-87; assoc. dir. devel. Arlington (Va.) Hosp. Found., 1987-89; dir. direct response fundraising Nat. Wildlife Fedn., Washington, 1989-92; dir. devel. Western divsn. Nat. Wildlife Fedn., Boulder, 1992-93; exec. dir. Colo. Wildlife Fedn., Denver, 1994—; cons. fundraising Mailing Concepts, Poway, Calif., 1993—. Editor newsletter Colo. Wildlife, 1994—. Chmn. bd. dirs. Dance Exch., Washington, 1985-88, bd. dirs., 1984-90. Mem. Nat. Soc. Fundraising Execs. Office: Colo Wildlife Fedn 445 Union Blvd # 302 Lakewood CO 80228

GANTT, BARRY, secondary school educator; b. Germany, Dec. 18, 1945; s. Chil Meyer and Sarah Gottesman; divorced. BA, Long Island U., 1967; MA, San Francisco State Coll., 1970. Cert. secondary and jr. coll. tchr., Calif. Dir. conf. svcs. Calif. Coll. Arts and Crafts, Oakland, 1984-85; events producer, founding bd. mem. Cartoon Art Mus., San Francisco, 1985-88, adminstr., 1988-89; edn. dir. Artists in Print, San Francisco, 1986-88; English instr. West Valley Coll., Saratoga, Calif., 1990; art cons. Owl Gallery, San Francisco, 1991; English instr. Oakland (Calif.) Pub. Schs., 1992—; judge art contests, San Francisco Bay Guardian, 1980, 81, 82, 84, 85; producer Loonies Humor Salon, 1978—. Editor GRAPHITI (Artists in Print), 1981-83, CENTERLINE (Ctr. for Design), 1981-82; contbr. articles to nat. and local mags. Mem. adv. bd. Ctrl. YMCA, San Francisco, 1978-80; dep. registrar Ctrl Dem. Coun., San Francisco, 1972-80; v.p. Soc. of Separationists, San Francisco, 1980-85. Recipient fellowship PTA, San Francisco State Coll., 1970. Mem. Am. Fedn. Tchrs., Golden State Tip Toppers. Office: PO Box 20443 Oakland CA 94620-0443

GANTZ, DAVID ALFRED, lawyer, university official; b. Columbus, Ohio, July 30, 1942; s. Harry Samuel and Edwina (Bookwalter) G.; m. Susan Beare, Aug. 26, 1967 (div. Feb. 1989); children: Stephen David, Julie Lorraine; m. Catherine Fagan, Mar. 28, 1992. AB, Harvard U., 1964; JD, Stanford U., 1967, M in Jud. Sci., 1970. Bar: Ohio 1967, D.C. 1971, U.S. Ct. Internat. Trade 1983, U.S. Ct. Appeals (9th cir.) 1970, U.S. Ct. Appeals (fed. cir.) 1987, U.S. Supreme Ct. 1972. Asst. prof. law U. Costa Rica, San Jose, 1967-69; law clk. U.S. Ct. Appeals, San Francisco, 1969-70; asst. legal advisor U.S. Dept. State, Washington, 1970-77; ptnr. Cole & Corrette, Washington, 1977-83, Oppenheimer Wolff & Donnelly, Washington, 1983-90; ptnr. Reid & Priest, Washington, 1990-93, of counsel, 1993—; dir. grad. studies U. Ariz. Coll. Law, Tucson, 1993—; assoc. dir. Nat. Law Ctr. for Inter-Am. Free Trade, 1993—; panelist U.S.-Can. Free Trade Agreement, 1989-92, Am. Arbitration Assn., 1988, NAFTA, 1994—; judge OAS Adminstrv. Tribunal, 1987-95; adj. prof. Georgetown U. Law Ctr., 1982-93. Contbr. numerous articles on internat. law to profl. jours. Pres. Potomac River Sports Found., 1992-94. Mem. ABA, D.C. Bar Assn., Am. Soc. Internat. Law, Potomac Boat Club (Washington, bd. dirs. 1986-93). Home: 7112 N Corte Del Anuncio Tucson AZ 85718-7333 Office: Ariz Coll Law 1201 E Speedway Blvd Tucson AZ 85719

GANTZ, NANCY ROLLINS, nursing administrator, consultant; b. Buffalo Center, Iowa, Mar. 7, 1949; d. Troy Gaylord and Mary (Emerson) Rollins. Diploma in Nursing, Good Samaritan Hosp. and Med. Ctr., Portland, Oreg., 1973; BSBA, City Univ., 1986; MBA, Kennedy-Western U., 1987, PhD, 1991. Nurse ICU, Good Samaritan Hosp., 1973-75; charge nurse Crestview Convalescent Hosp., Portland, 1975; dir. nursing svcs. Roderick Enterprises, Inc., Portland, 1976-78, Holgate Ctr., Portland, 1978-80; nursing cons. in field of adminstrn., 1980-84; coord. CCU; mgr. ICU/CCU Tuality Community Hosp., Hillsboro, Oreg., 1984-86; head nurse intensive care unit, cardiac surgery unit, coronary care unit, Good Samaritan Hosp. & Med. Ctr., Portland, 1986-88, mgr. critical care units, 1988-92, asst. v.p. patient care svcs., 1992-93, dir. heart ctr. Deaconess Med. Ctr., Spokane, Wash., 1992-93; exec. asst. King Faisal Specialist Hosp. and Rsch. Ctr., Riyadh, Saudia Arabia, 1994—; mem. speakers bur. Nurses of Am.; mem. task force Oreg. State Health Div. Rules and Regulations Revision for Long Term Health Facilities and Hosps., 1978-79; numerous internat. and nat. speaking presentations. Contbr. chpts. to books and articles to profl. jours. Mem. Am. Nurses Assn. (cert.), Nat. League Nursing, Am. Assn. Critical Care Nurses (pres. elect greater Portland chpt. 1985-86, pres. 1986-87, bd. dirs. 1985—), Am. Heart Assn., Oreg. Heart Assn., Geriatric Nurses Assn. Oreg. (founder, charter pres.), Clackamus Assn. Retarded Citizens, AACN (chpt. cons. region 18 1987-89, mgmt. SIC region 18, 1990-92), AONE Coun. Nurse Mgrs. (bd. dirs. Region 9 1991-92, Sigma Theta Tau. Seventhday Adventist. Home: 15821 NE 19th St Vancouver WA 98684-4517

GANTZER, JOHN CARROLL, insurance company executive; b. Mpls., Sept. 21, 1947; s. Clarence Louis Gantzer and Ruey Elaine (James) Kimball; m. Barbara Jean Spevacek, Apr. 16, 1967 (div. 1981); m. Patricia Ann Magee, Nov. 26, 1983. BA, Gustavus Adolphus Coll., 1969. Trainee St. Paul Fire & Marine, 1969-71; underwriting mgr. Home Ins. Co., Phoenix, Milw. and Denver, 1971-83; asst. v.p. Mission Ins. Co., L.A., 1983-86; asst. v.p., chief underwriting officer Western Employers Ins., Santa Ana, Calif., 1986-87; cons. Mission Am. Ins., L.A., 1987-88; v.p., corp. sec. Condor Ins. Co., El Segundo, Calif., 1988—. Mem. Soc. of CPCU (south coast chpt. dir.), Alpha Kappa Psi. Republican. Home: 37301 Tampa Ct Palmdale CA 93552-4338 Office: Condor Ins Co 2361 Rosecrans Ave El Segundo CA 90245-4916

GANZ, LEO, psychologist and educator; b. Antwerp, Belgium, Apr. 2, 1931; came to U.S., 1939; s. Osias and Rose (Roisen) G.; m. Varda Peller (div.); m. Dyane Sherwood; children: Eric D., Karen J. B. Social Sci., CCNY, 1953; PhD, U. Chgo., 1959. Postdoctoral fellow Brown U., Providence, 1959-62; asst. prof. U. Calif., Riverside, 1962-65; rsch. fellow Primate Neurobiology Inst., Seattle, 1966-67; asst. prof. dept. psychology NYU, N.Y.C., 1967-68; assoc. prof. Stanford U., Palo Alto, Calif., 1968-71; prof. psychology Stanford U., 1968—. Contbr. articles to profl. jours. Recipient Citation award Current Contents, 1979. Mem. APA, Psychonomic Soc., Soc. for Neurosci., Assn. Rsch., Vision and Neurosci., Phi Beta Kappa. Home: 3082 Buena Vista Way Berkeley CA 94708-2020 Office: Stanford Univ Dept Psychology Stanford CA 94305

GARBARINO, JOSEPH WILLIAM, labor arbitrator, economics and business educator; b. Medina, N.Y., Dec. 7, 1919; s. Joseph Francis and Savina M. (Volpone) G.; m. Mary Jane Godward, Sept. 18, 1948; children: Ann, Joan, Susan, Ellen. B.A., Duquesne U., 1942; M.A., Harvard U., 1947, Ph.D., 1949. Faculty U. Calif., Berkeley, 1949—; prof. U. Calif., 1960-88, dir. Inst. Bus. and Econ. Research, 1962-88, prof. emeritus, 1988—; vis. lectr. Cornell U., 1959-60, UCLA, 1949, SUNY, Buffalo, 1972; Fulbright lectr. U. Glasgow, Scotland, 1969; vis. scholar U. Warwick; mem. staff Brookings Instn., 1959-60; vis. lectr. U. Minn., 1978; labor arbitrator. Author: Health Plans and Collective Bargaining, 1960, Wage Policy and Long Term Contracts, 1962, Faculty Bargaining: Change and Conflict, 1975, Faculty Bargaining in Unions in Transition. Served with U.S. Army, 1942-45, 51-53. Decorated Bronze Star. Democrat. Roman Catholic. Home: 7708 Ricardo Ct El Cerrito CA 94530-3344

GARBER, C(HARLES) STEDMAN, JR., oil and mining industry executive; b. Cin., Aug. 10, 1943; s. Charles Stedman Garber and Louise (Simrall) Hall; m. Robin Kimbrough, Jan. 4, 1989; children: Simrall, Christina, Ashley, Charles Stedman III. BS, U.S. Naval Acad., 1965; MBA, UCLA, 1972. Commd. ensign USN, 1965, advanced through grades to lt., 1968; ret., 1970; assoc. Blyth Eastman Dillon, L.A., 1972-76, v.p., 1976-77; mgr. corp. devel. Getty Oil Co., L.A., 1977-83, treas., 1983-84; sr. v.p. Santa Fe Internat., L.A., 1984-89, exec. v.p., chief oper. officer, bd. dirs., 1991—; pres. Santa Fe Minerals, Dallas, 1989—. Bd. dirs. Children's Home Soc., L.A., 1979-89. Mem. Calif. Club, Petroleum Club (Dallas). Office: Santa Fe Internat Corp 1000 S Fremont Ave # 4000 Alhambra CA 91803-4737

GARCHIK, LEAH LIEBERMAN, journalist; b. Bklyn., May 2, 1945; d. Arthur Louis and Mildred (Steinberg) Lieberman; m. Jerome Marcus Garchik, Aug. 11, 1968; children—Samuel, Jacob. B.A., Bklyn. Coll., 1966. Editorial asst. San Francisco Chronicle, 1972-79, writer, editor, 1979-83, editor This World,, 1983-84, columnist, 1984—; also author numerous book and movie reviews, features and profiles; Author: San Francisco; the City's Sights and Secrets, 1995; panelist (radio quiz show) Mind Over Matter; contbr. articles to mags. Vice pres. Golden Gate Kindergarten Assn., San Francisco, 1978; pres. Performing Arts Workshop, San Francisco, 1977-79. Recipient 1st prize Nat. Soc. Newspaper Columnists, 1992. Mem. Deutsche Music Verein, Media Alliance, Newspaper Guild, ACLU (bd. dirs. San Francisco chpt. 1977-79). Democrat. Jewish. Home: 156 Baker St San Francisco CA 94117-2111 Office: San Francisco Chronicle 901 Mission St San Francisco CA 94103-2905

GARCIA, CASTELAR MEDARDO, lawyer; b. Conejos, Colo., June 3, 1942; s. Castelar M. Sr. and Anna (Vigil) G.; m. Mary Elizabeth Miller, Apr. 1, 1967; 1 child, Victoria Elisabeth. BA, Adams State Coll., 1965; JD, U. Colo., 1976. Bar: Colo. 1977, U.S. Dist. Ct. Colo. 1977, U.S. Ct. Appeals (10th cir.) 1983, U.S. Ct. Appeals (4th cir.) 1988, U.S. Supreme Ct. 1984. Human resources counselor State of Oreg., Klamath Falls, 1966-68; regional dir. Colo. Civil Rights Com., Alamosa, 1970-73; dep. dist. atty. Denver, 1977-80, chief dep. dist. atty., 1980-84; pvt. practice Manassa, Colo., 1984—; owner Cumbres Ranch; town atty., Romeo, Colo., 1984—; commr. Colo. Dept. Hwys., 1991, Colo. Dept. Transp., 1991—. Mem. Colo. delegation to Cam Real Trade Corridor Consortium between U.S., Can. and Mex. With U.S. Army, 1968-70, Vietnam. Decorated Purple Heart. Mem. Colo. Bar Assn., Hispanic Bar Assn., San Luis Valley Bar Assn. Republican. Roman Catholic. Home: PO Box 443 Manassa CO 81141-0443 Office: 714 S St Manassa CO 81141

GARCIA, CURT JONATHAN, company executive; b. Whittier, Calif., Mar. 27, 1960; s. Raymond Arthur and Yvonne Emily (Bailey) G.; m. Cynthia Louise Guerra, Sept. 5, 1981; children: David, Denise, Natalie. BA in Bus. Econs., U. Calif., Santa Barbara, 1983; MS in Procurement and Acquisition Mgmt., Northrop U., L.A., 1991. Cert. profl. contracts mgr. Adminstr. New Life Christian Sch., Santa Barbara, 1983-85; contract acct. Mission Rsch. Corp., Santa Barbara, 1985-88; contr. Pneu Devices, Inc., Santa Barbara, 1988-90; treas., dir. contracts Illgen Simulation Tech., Inc., Santa Barbara, 1990-92; CFO, contracts mgr. Environ. Mgmt. Cons., Inc., Lompoc, Calif., 1992—. Mem. Nat. Contract Mgmt. Assn.

GARCIA, DAVID, agricultural products executive; b. 1953. Graduate, U. Wyo., 1975. With We. Nuclear Mining, Lander, Wyo., 1976-78, Diamond Fruit Growers, Inc., Hood River, Oreg., 1978—; now treas. Office: Diamond Fruit Growers Inc 3495 Chevron Dr Hood River OR 97031-9436*

GARCIA, EDWARD J., federal judge; b. 1928. AA, Sacramento City Coll., 1951; LLB, U. Pacific, 1958. Dep. dist. atty. Sacramento County, 1959-64, supervising dep. dist. atty., 1964-69, chief dep. dist. atty., 1969-72; judge Sacramento Mcpl. Ct., 1972-84, U.S. Dist. Ct. (ea. dist.) Calif., Sacramento, 1984—. Served with U.S. Army Air Corps, 1946-49. *

GARCIA, GORDON STANLEY, physician; b. Washington, July 26, 1959; s. Raymond Garcia and Lois Jane Cobb; m. Renee Jovita Fuentes, June 25, 1983; children: Margaux, Claire. BA, U. Calif., Berkeley, 1981; MD, U. Calif., San Diego, 1987. Diplomate Am. Bd. Pediats., Am. Bd. Internal Medicine, Am. Bd. Allergy and Immunology. Rsch. asst. Cetus Corp., Emeryville, Calif., 1981-83; staff physician Permanente Med. Group, Sacramento, 1993—; asst. clin. prof. pediats. U. Calif. Med. Sch., Davis, 1994—. Fellow Am. Acad. Pediats.; mem. Am. Coll. Allergy, Asthma, and Immunology, Am. Thoracic Soc., Am. Acad. Allergy and Immunology, Calif. Med. Assn., Sacramento-El Dorado County Med. Soc. Office: Permanente Med Group 6600 Bruceville Rd Sacramento CA 95823

GARCIA, IGNACIO RAZON, lawyer; b. Manila, Philippines, Sept. 20, 1953; came to U.S., 1969; s. Agustin Abraham and Rosario (Razon) G.; m. Lani Rae Suiso, Dec. 5, 1981; 1 child, Cristina. BA, U. Hawaii, 1976; JD, U. Notre Dame, 1979. Bar: Hawaii 1979, U.S. Dist. Ct. Hawaii 1979, Guam 1987, U.S. Dist. Ct. Guam 1987, U.S. Ct. Appeals (9th cir.), U.S. Supreme Ct., 1991. Sole practice Honolulu, 1979-89; atty. Garcia & Garcia (now Garcia, Garcia & Rosenberg), Honolulu, 1989—; del. Hawaii Jud. Conf., 1988-91; mem. Hawaii Supreme Ct. com. on rules of evidence, permanent com. on Hawaii rules of penal procedure, Com. to Rev. Hawaii Penal Code; mem. Hawaii Bd. Bar Examiners; mem. faculty Nat. Inst. Trial Advocacy, Hawaii Inst., 1989—. Mem. Hawaii-Filipino Jaycees. Recipient HanaHou award Sta. KITV, 1988. Mem. ABA, Hawaii Assn. Criminal Def. Lawyers (bd. dirs. 1986—, pres. 1985-86, 91-92), Nat. Assn. Criminal Def. Lawyers Assn., Assn. Trial Lawyers Am., Hawaii Bar Assn. (bd. dirs. 1990—), Hawaii-Filipino Lawyers Assn. Democrat. Roman Catholic. Office: 735 Bishop St Ste 308 Honolulu HI 96813-4819

GARCIA, JUAN RAMON, historian, educator; b. Sebastian, Tex., July 27, 1947; s. Juan and Maria de la Luz (Perez-Hernandez) G.; m. Rosalind Sigworth, Oct. 18, 1992; children: Mariel Shannon, Michelle Nocole, Alison Marissa. BA, DePaul U., 1971, MA, 1979; MA, U. Notre Dame, 1974, PhD, 1977. From asst. to assoc. prof. U. Mich., Flint, 1975-81; assoc. prof. U. Ariz., Tucson, 1981—, assoc. dean instrn. Coll. Social and Behavioral Scis., 1994—; dir. Mex. Am. studies U. Mich., Flint, 1975-81, chmn. affirmative action com. 1979-81, chmn. student affairs and concerns com. 1978-81; dir. U. Ariz. Teaching Ctr., 1990-94; cons. Nat. Inst. Edn. Women and Minorities divsn., Washington, 1978-81, NEA Program Devel. divsn., Washington, 1979-82; review cons. McGraw-Hill Publ.; hist. cons., host TV Sta. KUAT, 1989; hist. cons. Los Mineros, 1991; adv. bd. Tucson Pub. Libr. Writers the Purple Sage; liaison Am. with Disabilities Act., 1993—; presenter in field. Author: Operation Wetback, 1980; editor: Perspectives in Mexican American Studies, 1988-89, 92-93; contbr. articles to profl. jours. Chmn. State Bilingual Commn., Mich., 1976-80; Rockefeller Found. rev. panel S.W. Hispanic Rsch. Inst., 1989; libr., archives and pub. records com. mem. State of Ariz., 1988—. Ford Found. fellow, 1972-75; Rsch. grantee U. Ariz., 1986, NSF grantee, 1972; named Disting. prof. U. Mich., 1981. Mem. Nat. Assn. for Chicano Studies (Rocky Mountain rep., exec. coord. com., conf. site com. mem., chmn. editorial com. 1983-88), Western Social Sci. Assn. (coord. Chicano studies sect. 1983). Office: Univ Ariz Dept History 215 Social Science Tucson AZ 85721

GARCIA, MICHAEL JOHN, policical science educator; b. Denver, Mar. 26, 1948; m. Margaret Bauder, 1975. BA, Met. State Coll., 1971; MPA, U. Colo., 1974. Tchr. Denver Pub. Schs., 1972; asst. to city mgr. Arvada (Colo.) City Govt., 1974-75; housing rep. U.S. Dept. HUD, Denver, 1975-78; emergency mgmt. officer Fed. Emergency Mgmt. Agy., Denver, 1979-83; v.p. ops. Aristek Communities, Inc., Denver, 1983-86; devel. cons. pvt. practice, Denver, 1987-91; asst. prof. polit. sci. Met. State Coll., Denver, 1991—. Bd. dirs. Regional Transp. Dist., Denver, 1983-92, chnn. bd. dirs., 1989; treas. Denver Pub. Libr. Commn., 1985-92. Named Outstanding Hispanic Role Model Hispanic Ednl. Inst., Denver, 1989. Republican. Roman Catholic.

GARCIA, PAMELA MARCOTT, supermarket and real estate investments executive; b. Portland, Oreg., Nov. 22, 1957; d. Ronald K. and Patricia M. (Fessler) Marcott; m. Albert D. Garcia, June 17, 1989. BS in Bus., Oreg. State U., 1981; M in Mgmt., Northwestern U., 1988. Mem. sales mgmt. program Procter & Gamble, Portland, 1981-83; stockbroker Dean Witter Reynolds, Portland, 1983-85; mem. mktg. staff Microsoft, Redmond, Wash., 1985-87, Hewlett Packard, Vancouver, Wash., 1988-90; from v.p. to pres. Marcott Holdings Inc., Portland, 1990—; bd. dirs. Food Employers, Inc., Portland, Oreg., 1994. Bd. dirs. United Way of Oreg., Portland, 1983; vice chmn. United Grocers Fed. Credit Union, Milwaukee, Oreg., 1993-94; chmn. Child Svcs. Divsn. Recruitment Com., West Linn, Oreg., 1994. Home: 6331 Palomino Way West Linn OR 97068-2245

GARCIA-BORRAS, THOMAS, oil company executive; b. Barcelona, Spain, Feb. 2, 1926; came to U.S., 1955, naturalized, 1961; s. Thomas and Teresa (Borras-Jarque) Garcia-Julian; MS, Nat. U. Mex., 1950; postgrad. Rice U., 1955-56; m. Alia Castellanos Lima, Apr. 30, 1952; children: Erik, Angelica, Laureen, Cliff. Chief chemist Petroleos Mexicanos, Veracruz, Mex., 1950-55; rsch. engr. Monsanto, Texas City, Tex., 1956-60; pilot plant mgr. Cabot and Foster Grant Co., 1960-69; engring. mgr. Signal Chem. Co., Houston, 1969-71; mgmt. and engring. cons., Covina, Calif., 1971-73; project mgr. Occidental Petroleum Co., Irvine, Calif., 1973-79; fleet and indsl. mgr. internat. ops. Wynn Oil Co., Fullerton, Calif., 1979-87; dir. export Sta-Lube, Inc., Rancho Dominguez, Calif., 1987-91; prin. U.S. Products Corp., Las Vegas, Nev.; internat. bus. cons. Covina, Calif. Mem. Internat. Mktg. Assn., Am. Inst. Chem. Engrs., Am. Chem. Soc. Author: Manual for Improving Boiler and Furnace Performance, 1983; contbr. articles to profl. jours. Home: 1430 E Adams Park Dr Covina CA 91724-2925 Office: 516 S 4th St Las Vegas NV 89101-6513

GARCIA-BUNUEL, LUIS, neurologist; b. Madrid, Spain, Feb. 24, 1931; s. Pedro Garcia and Concepcion Bunuel; came to U.S., 1956, naturalized, 1965; B.A., Universidad de Zaragoza, 1949, B.S., 1949, M.D., 1955; m. Virginia M. Hile, June 30, 1960. Intern, Universidad De Zaragoza Hosp. Clinico, 1955-56 resident in neurology Georgetown U., Washington, 1956-59; NIH fellow in neurochemistry dept. pharmacology, Washington U., St. Louis, 1959-61; practice medicine specializing in neurology St. Louis, 1959-61; instr. neurology Jefferson Med. Coll., Phila., 1961-64, asst. prof. neurology, 1964-67; asst. prof. neurology U. N.Mex., Albuquerque, 1967-72; chief neurology service VA Hosp. Portland, Oreg., 1972; asso. prof. neurology, U. Oreg. Health Center, 1972-84; chief staff Phoenix VA Med. Ctr., 1984—. Diplomate Am. Bd. Neurology and Psychiatry. Fellow Am. Acad. Neurology; mem. AAAS, Am. Soc. Neurochemistry, Oreg. Neuropsychiat. Soc., Portland Myasthenia Gravis Assn. (med. adv. bd.), Sigma Xi, Phi Kappa Phi. Contbr. articles to profl jours.

GARDIN, JOHN GEORGE, II, psychologist; b. Renton, Wash., Jan. 5, 1949; s. John George and Charlotte (Larabee) G.; m. Dana Rothrock, Oct. 22, 1986; children: Greg, Gina, Bret; 1 stepchild, Angie West. BS in Chemistry, Seattle U., 1971; BS in Psychology, U. Wash., 1972; MS in Psychology, Portland State U., 1975; PhD in Psychology, U. Tenn., 1986. Lic. psychologist. Clinician Luth. Family Svcs., Portland, Oreg., 1978-80; mental health specialist Probation Dept. Oreg. State, Roseburg, 1980-81; exec. dir. ADAPT, Roseburg, 1981-85; psychologist, ptnr. South Coast Psychol., Irvine, Calif., 1986-91; assoc. prof. psychiatry U. Calif. Irvine, Dana Point, Calif., 1988-90; med. dir. Chem. Dependency Charter Hosp., Corona, Calif., 1990-91; ptnr. LifeOne, Irvine, 1991-92; pvt. practice psychology Newport Beach, Calif., 1991—; psychologist, founder, clin. dir. Genesis Psychol. Assocs., Newport Beach, 1992—; bd. dirs. Kangaroo Kids Ctr. Medically Fragile Children, 1992—. Pres. Alcohol/Drug Program Dirs. of Oreg., 1984; bd. dirs. Oreg. State Coun. on Alcoholism, 1983; mem. Counselors Credentials Task Force, Oreg., 1984. Mem. APA, Calif. State Psychol. Assn., Am. Athletic Union, Japan Karate-Do Fedn. Office: Genesis Psychol Asoscs 2900 Bristol St Ste D-107 Costa Mesa CA 92626-5981

GARDINER, LESTER RAYMOND, JR., lawyer; b. Salt Lake City, Aug. 20, 1931; s. Lester Raymond and Sarah Lucille (Kener) G.; m. Janet Ruth Thatcher, Apr. 11, 1955; children: Allison Gardiner Bigelow, John Alfred, Annette Gardiner Weed, Leslie Gardiner Crandall, Robert Thatcher, Lisa Gardiner West, James Raymond, Elizabeth, David William, Sarah Janet. BS with honors, U. Utah, 1954; JD, U. Mich., 1959. Bar: Utah 1959, U.S. Dist. Ct. Utah 1959, U.S. Ct. Apls. (10th cir.) 1960. Law clk., U.S. Dist. Ct., 1959; assoc. then ptnr. Van Cott, Bagley, Cornwall & McCarthy, Salt Lake City, 1960-67; ptnr. Gardiner & Johnson, Salt Lake City, 1967-72; ptnr. Christensen, Gardiner, Jensen & Evans, 1972-78; ptnr. Fox, Edwards, Gardiner & Brown, Salt Lake City, 1978-87, ptnr. Chapman & Cutler, 1987-89, ptnr. Gardiner & Hintze, 1990-92; CEO and pres. Snowbird Ski and Summer Resort, Snowbird Corp., 1993—; reporter, mem. Utah Sup. Ct. Com. on Adoption of Uniform Rules of Evidence, 1970-73, mem. com. on revision of criminal code, 1975-78; master of the bench Am. Inn of Ct. I, 1980-90; mem. com. bar examiners Utah State Bar, 1973; instr. bus. law U. Utah, 1965-66; adj. prof. law Brigham Young U., 1984-85. Mem. Republican State Central Com. Utah, 1967-72, mem. exec. com. Utah Rep. Party, 1975-78, chmn. state convs., 1980, 81; mem. Salt Lake City Bd. Edn., 1971-72; mem. bd. dirs. Salt Lake City Pub. Library, 1974-75; trustee Utah Sports Found., 1987-91, 93—, Salt Lake City Visitors and Conv. Bur., 1988-91, mem. exec. com., 1993—. Served to 1st lt. USAF, 1954-56. Mem. ABA, Utah State Bar Assn., Sons of Utah Pioneers, Utah Ski Assn. (mem. pub. com. 1994—), Rotary. Mormon. Office: Snowbird Corp Sandy UT 84092

GARDINER, NANCY ELIZABETH, environmental and water resources consultant; b. Boston, June 22, 1964; d. Henry Louis and Elizabeth Mary (Getek) Gorczyca; m. Michael Aaron Gardiner, Aug. 19, 1989. AB in Geology magna cum laude, Smith Coll., 1986; MS in Geology, U. Wis., 1988. Project hydrogeologist Warzyn Engring., Madison, Wis., 1988-89; sr. project scientist Woodward-Clyde Cons., Oakland, San Diego, Calif., 1989—. Contbr. articles to profl. jours. Mem. Am. Water Resources Assn., Am. Water Works Assn., Sigma Xi, Phi Beta Kappa. Democrat. Home: 3765 Fenwick Dr Spring Valley CA 91977 Office: Woodward-Clyde Cons PO Box 12681 Oakland CA 94604-2681

GARDNER, AUTREY THADDEUS, JR., industrial technology educator; b. Scottsboro, Ala., Aug. 5, 1939; s. Autrey Thaddeus and Faye Louise (Kennamer) G.; m. Joyce Elva Keel; children: Tracey Anne, Autrey Thaddeus III. BSBA, U. Ala., 1962; postgrad., U. N.D., 1967-70; MA in Communications, U. No. Colo., 1983; postgrad., U. Wy., 1987—. Cert. indsl. technologist. Commd. 2d lt. USAF, Amarillo AFB, Tex., 1962; advanced through grades to major USAF, various locations, 1972; chief of plans 351st Strategic Missile Wing, Whiteman AFB, Mo., 1973-74, supr. maintenance,

1974-76; maintenance staff officer 3901st Strategic Missile Squadron, Vandenberg AFB, Calif., 1976-80; dir. tng. 90th Strategic Missile Wing, F.E. Warren AFB, Wyo., 1980-83; ret. USAF, 1983; asst. prof. So. Ill. U., F.E. Warren AFB, Wyo., 1983—, faculty rep., 1983—. Contbr. articles to profl. jours. Mem. Nat. Assn. Indsl. Technologists, Inst. Indsl. Engrs., Am. Soc. Safety Engrs., Air Force Assn., Ret. Officers Assn. (pres. 1993), Warren AFB Officers Club (bd. dirs. 1982-83), Phi Kappa Phi, Kappa Delta Pi. Republican. Mem. Ch. of Christ. Home: 3300 Carey Ave Cheyenne WY 82001-1269 Office: So Ill U 90 MSSQ/MSE Fe Warren AFB WY 82005

GARDNER, BOOTH, governor; b. Tacoma, Aug. 21, 1936; m. Jean Gardner; children—Doug, Gail. B.A. in Bus., U. Wash., 1958; M.B.A., Harvard U., 1963. Asst. to dean Sch. Bus. Adminstrn., Harvard U., Cambridge, Mass., 1966; dir. Sch. Bus. and Econs., U. Puget Sound, Tacoma, 1967-72; pres. Laird Norton County, 1972-80; mem. Wash. Senate, 1970-73; county exec. Pierce County, Tacoma, 1981-84; gov. State of Wash., 1985-89, 89—. Co-founder Central Area Youth Assn. Seattle; trustee U. Puget Sound. recipient Harold W. McGraw, Jr. prize in edn., McGraw-Hill, 1993. Office: Office of Gov Legislature Bldg As-13 Olympia WA 98504

GARDNER, DAVID CHAMBERS, education educator, psychologist, business executive, author; b. Charlotte, N.C., Mar. 22, 1934; s. James Raymond and Jessica Mary (Chambers) Bumgardner m. Grace Joely Beatty, 1984; children: Joshua Avery, Jessica Sarah. BA, Northeastern U., 1960; MEd, Boston U., 1970, EdD, 1974; PhD, Columbia Pacific U., 1984. Diplomate Am. Bd. Med. Psychotherapists. Mgr. market devel. N.J. Zinc Co., N.Y.C., 1961-66, COMINCO, Ltd., Montreal, Que., Can., 1966-68; dir. Alumni Ann. Giving Program, Northeastern U., Boston, 1968-69; dir. career and spl. edn. Stoneham (Mass.) Pub. Schs., Boston, 1970-72; assoc. prof. div. instructional devel. and adminstrn. Boston U., 1974—; sr. ptnr. Gardner Beatty Group, 1990—; coord. program career vocat. tng. for handicapped, 1974-82, chmn. dept. career and bus. edn., 1974-79, also dir. fed. grants, 1975-77, 77-79; co-founder Am. Tng. and Rsch. Assocs., Inc., chmn. bd., 1979-83, pres., chief exec. officer, 1984—; dir. La Costa Inst. Lifestyle Mgmt., 1986-87. Author: Careers and Disabilities: A Career Approach, 1978; co-author: Dissertation Proposal Guidebook: How to Prepare a Research Proposal and Get It Accepted, 1980, Career and Vocational Education for the Mildly Learning Handicapped and Disadvantaged, 1984, Stop Stress and Aging Now, 1985, Never Be Tired Again, 1990; co-author The Visual Learning Guide series, 1992, 93, 94, 95, Internet for Windows: America Online Edition, 1995, others; editor Career Edn. Quar., 1975-81; contbr. articles to profl. jours. With AUS, 1954-56. U.S. Office Edn. fellow Boston U., 1970, U.S. Office Edn.-Univ. Boston rsch. fellow, 1974. Fellow Am. Assn. Mental Deficiency (Ann. Profl. Tchr. and Rsch. award Region X 1979); mem. Nat. Assn. Career Edn. (bd. dirs., past pres.), Coun. for Exceptional Children, Ea. Ednl. Rsch. Assn. (founding dir.), Am. Vocat. Assn., Phi Delta Kappa, Delta Pi Epsilon. Home: 7618 Nueva Castilla Way Carlsbad CA 92009-8137 Office: The Gardner Beatty Group 7618 Nueva Castilla Way Carlsbad CA 92009-8137

GARDNER, DAVID PIERPONT, foundation executive; b. Berkeley, Calif., Mar. 24, 1933; s. Reed S. and Margaret (Pierpont) G.; m. Elizabeth Fuhriman, June 27, 1958 (dec.); children: Karen, Shari, Lisa, Marci. BS, Brigham Young U., 1955, DH (hon.), 1981; MA, U. Calif., Berkeley, 1959, PhD, 1966; LHD (hon.), U. Utah, 1983, Internat. Christian U., 1990; LLD (hon.), U. of the Pacific, 1983, U. Nev., Las Vegas, 1984, Westminster Coll., 1987, U. Notre Dame, 1989, Brown U., 1989, Pepperdine U., 1992; HHD (hon.), Utah State U., 1987; D honoris causa, de l' Universite de Bordeaux, 1988. Dir. Calif. Alumni Found., U. Calif. at Berkeley, 1962-64; asst. to the chancellor, asst. prof. higher edn. U. Calif. at Santa Barbara, 1964-67, asst. chancellor, asst. prof. higher edn., 1967-69, vice chancellor, exec. asst., assoc. prof. higher edn., 1969-70; v.p., prof. higher edn. U. Calif., Santa Barbara, 1971-73; pres., prof. higher edn. U. Utah, Salt Lake City, 1973-83; pres., prof. edn. U. Calif., Berkeley, 1983-92; pres. William and Flora Hewlett Found., Menlo Park, Calif., 1993—; vis. fellow Clare Hall, Cambridge U., 1979, life mem., 1979—; bd. dirs. John Alden Fin. Corp., 1st Security Corp., Fluor Corp.; mem. coun. Hong Kong U. Sci. and Tech. Author: The California Oath Controversy, 1967; mem. editorial bd. Higher Edn. Quarterly; contbr. articles to profl. jours. Bd. dirs. George S. And Dolores Dore Eccles Found., Getty Trust, Hewlett Found., Nature Conservancy, Tanner Lectures on Human Values; past chmn. Southwestern dist. Rhodes Scholarship Selection Com.; mem. pres.'s com. Arts and the Humanities, 1994—. Decorated Legion of Honor (France), knight comdr. Order of Merit (Germany); recipient Benjamin P. Cheney medal East Wash. U., 1984, James Bryant Conant award Edn. Commn. of States, 1985, Hall of Fame award Calif. Sch. Bds. Rsch. Found., 1988; named 40th anniversary disting. fellow Fulbright Found., 1987, Alumnus of Yr., U. Calif., Berkeley. Fellow Am. Acad. Arts and Scis.; mem. Nat. Acad. Pub. Adminstrn., Am. Philos. Soc., Nat. Acad. Edn., Calif. C. of C., Phi Beta Kappa (hon.), Phi Kappa Phi (hon.). Office: William and Flora Hewlett Found 525 Middlefield Rd Ste 200 Menlo Park CA 94025-3447

GARDNER, FRANCESCA MARROQUIN, lawyer, consultant; b. New Haven, Aug. 17, 1940; d. John William and Aida (Marroquin) G.; m. John Robert Reese, Sept. 5, 1964 (div. 1986); children: Jennifer Marie, Justine Francesca. BS in Math., Stanford U., 1962, LLB, 1965. Bar: Calif. 1966, U.S. Dist. Ct. Calif. 1966, U.S. Ct. Appeals (9th cir.) 1966. Legal assoc. Crist Peters Donegan & Brenner, Palo Alto, Calif., 1965-66, Covington & Burling, Washington, 1967, Heller Ehrman White & McAuliffe, San Francisco, 1969-72; mng. ptnr. Gardner Reese Co., San Francisco, 1980-90; program officer James Irvine Found., San Francisco, 1986-92; cons., lawyer The Gardner Group, San Francisco, 1993—; mem. Coun. for the Humanities and Scis., Stanford (Calif.) U., 1982-90; part time rschr. Hambrecht & Quist, San Francisco, 1984-85; bd. dirs. Life Plan Ctr., San Francisco. Co-editor: (book of quotations) Know or Listen to Those Who Know, 1974. Mem. Calif. Bar Assn., Town and Country Club, Stanford Assocs., Stanford Alumni Assn. Home: 3970 Clay St San Francisco CA 94118-1624 Office: The Gardner Group 177 Post St Ste 910 San Francisco CA 94108-4712

GARDNER, HOMER JAY, electrical engineer; b. El Paso, Tex., Apr. 4, 1942; s. George R. and Faye E. (Folkers) G.; m. Roxy Diane Tolley, Jan. 29, 1966; children: Roger, Shannon, Stefanie. BSEE, Brigham Young U., 1968; MS, Colo. State U., 1973. Devel. engr. IBM Corp., Boulder, Colo., 1968-90; sr. engr. Exabyte Corp., Boulder, 1990—. Patentee in field. Mem. Colo. State Electronics Adv. Com., Denver, 1980-83, chmn., 1982. Mem. IEEE. Republican. Mormon. Home: 8138 Captains Ln Longmont CO 80501-7727 Office: Exabyte 1745 38th St Boulder CO 80301-2603

GARDNER, JAMES HARKINS, venture capitalist; b. Evanston, Ill., July 15, 1943; s. James Floyd and Charlotte (Hoban) G.; m. Shirley Jane Bisset, June 22, 1968 (div. 1980); 1 child, Warren Lee; m. Shannon Lee Greer, Nov. 19, 1982; 1 child, Charlotte Greer. BS, Purdue U., 1965; MBA, Harvard U., 1968. V.p. Geomet, Inc., Rockville, Md., 1970-78; pres. Risk Mgmt. Resources, Inc., San Francisco, 1979-91; COO KinderCare Learning Ctrs., Inc., Montgomery, Ala., 1991-93; pres., COO, dir., Discovery Zone, Inc, 1994—; mng. gen. ptnr., Media Venture Ptnrs., 1995—; del. White House Conf. on Small Bus., 1986; treas. No. Calif. With USPHS, 1968-70. Mem. Nat. Fedn. Ind. Bus. (Calif. guardian coun., dir. Calif. polit. action com., fed. liaison 1988-91), Ind. Adminstrs. Assn. (bd. dirs. 1989-91, v.p. 1991), Commonwealth Club Calif. (San Francisco), Masons, Sigma Nu. Office: Media Venture Ptnrs 150 Post St Ste 740 San Francisco CA 94108

GARDNER, KATHLEEN HARMON, development administrator; b. Dallas, June 18, 1947; d. Hal Ray and Mary Lois (McKean) Harmon; m. Sherman Donald Gardner, June 27, 1969 (div. May 1988); children: Mark D., Todd H., Scott D., Lisa K. BS, U. Utah, 1969. Cert. tchr. Utah, Ky., Calif. Elem. tchr. Glendover Sch., Lexington, Ky., 1969-71, John Thomas Dye Sch., Bel Air, Calif., 1971-74; mktg. asst. Utah Symphony, Salt Lake City, 1989-90; gen. mgr. Elliot and Assocs., Salt Lake City, 1990-91; assoc. dir. devel. Ballet West, Salt Lake City, 1991-92, dir. devel., 1992—. Contbr. articles to Cottonwood Collections, Discover Utah. Del. Utah Rep. Party, Salt Lake City, 1984; active Utah PTA, Salt Lake City, 1980—. Mem. Utah Soc. Fundraisers. Mormon. Home: 4782 Naniloa Dr Salt Lake City UT 84117-5547 Office: Ballet West 50 West 200 South Salt Lake City UT 84101

GARDNER, LEONARD BURTON, II, former industrial automation engineer; b. Lansing, Mich., Feb. 16, 1927; s. Leonard Burton and Lillian Marvin (Frost) G.; m. Barbara Jean Zivi, June 23, 1950; children: Karen Sue, Jeffrey Frank. B.Sc. in Physics, UCLA, 1951; M.Sc., Golden State U., 1953, Sc.D. in Engring., 1954; M.Sc. in Computer Sci, Augustana Coll., Rock Island, Ill., 1977. Registered profl. engr.; cert. mfg. engr. Instrumentation engr. govt. and pvt. industry, 1951-89; prof. and dir. Ctr. for Automated Integrated Mfg., 1982—; with computerized systems Naval Electronic Systems Engring. Ctr., San Diego, 1980-82; founder, dir. Automated Integrated Mfg., San Diego; cons. govt. agys. and industry, lectr., adj. prof. vaious univs. and colls., sci. advisor state and nat. legislators, 1980—, speaker in field. Author: Computer Aided Robotics Center; editor: Automated Manufacturing. Contbg. author: Instrumentation Handbook, 1981; contbr. numerous articles to tech. jours. Recipient award U.S. Army. Fellow IEEE; sr. mem. Soc. Mfg. Engrs. (Pres.'s award 1984); mem. ASTM, Nat. Soc. Profl. Engrs., Calif. Soc. Profl. Engrs., Sigma Xi. Home: 416 Sugar Maple Ln Cincinnati OH 45246

GARDNER, NORD ARLING, management consultant; b. Afton, Wyo., Aug. 10, 1923; s. Arling A. and Ruth (Lee) G.; BA, U. Wyo., 1945; MS, Calif. State U., Hayward, 1972, MPA, 1975; postgrad. U. Chgo., U. Mich., U. Calif.-Berkeley; m. Thora Marie Stephen, Mar. 24, 1945; children: Randall Nord, Scott Stephen, Craig Robert, Laurie Lee. With U.S. Army, 1941 Commd. 2d lt., 1945, advanced through grades to lt. col., 1964; ret., 1966; personnel analyst Univ. Hosp., U. Calif.-San Diego, 1966-68; coordinator manpower devel. U. Calif.-Berkeley, 1968-75; univ. tng. officer San Francisco State U., 1975-80, personnel mgr., 1976-80; exec. dir. CRDC Maintenance Tng. Corp., non-profit community effort, San Francisco, 1980-85; pres., dir. Sandor Assocs. Mgmt. Cons., Pleasant Hill, Calif., 1974-86, 91—; gen. mgr. Vericlean Janitorial Service, Inc.; in-charge bus. devel. East Bay Local Devel. Corp., Oakland, Calif., 1980-85; incorporator and pres. Indochinese Community Enterprises, USA, Ltd., Pleasant Hill, Calif., 1985-87; freelance writer, grantsmanship cons., 1987—; ptnr. Oi Kit Bldg. Maint. Svc., 1988-91; dir. univ. rels. Internat. Pacific U., San Ramon, Calif., 1990—, exec. dir., bd. dirs. Internat. Pacific Inst., 1994— ; cons. Phimmasone Internat. Import-Export, Richmond, Calif., Lao Lanx-Xang Assn., Oakland Refugee Assn., 1988-90; instr. Japanese, psychology, supervisory courses, 1977-78; bd. dirs. New Ideas New Imports, Inc. Author: To Gather Stones, 1978. Adv. council San Francisco Community Coll. Dist. Decorated Army Commendation medal. Mem. Ret. Officers Assn., Am. Soc. Tng. and Devel., No. Calif. Human Resources Council. Am. Assn. Univ. Adminstrs., Internat. Personnel Mgrs. Assn., Coll. and Univ. Personnel Assn., Commonwealth Club of Calif., U. Calif.-Berkeley Faculty Club, San Francisco State U. Faculty Club, Army Counter Intelligence Corp Vets., Inc. Republican. Home: 2995 Bonnie Ln Pleasant Hill CA 94523-4547 Office: Internat Pacific Inst 1 Annabel Ln Ste 214 San Ramon CA 94583-1342

GARDNER, PAUL ALLEN, biology educator; b. Philipsburg, Pa., Nov. 28, 1950; s. Roscoe Bert and Vera Rose (Biddle) G.; m. Ann Hales, Apr. 23, 1975; children: Charity, Katie. BS in Biology, Pa. State U., 1974; MS in Zoology, BYU, 1977; PhD in Zoology, No. Ariz. U., 1987. Rsch. asst. U. Utah, Salt Lake City, 1977-79; surg. technician Flagstaff (Ariz.) Med. Ctr., 1979-89; assoc. prof. biology Snow Coll., Ephraim, Utah, 1989—; mem. steering com., chmn. rsch. and monitoring com. Utah Ptnrs. in Flight, Salt Lake City, 1993—. Contbr. articles and photographs to ednl. publs. incl. Ranger Rick and Am. Biology Tchr. Varsity coach, scoutmaster Boy Scouts Am., Flagstaff and Ephraim, 1985-91. With U.S. Army, 1968-71. Mem. Human Anatomy and Physiology Soc., Nat. Assn. Biology Tchrs., Am. Ornithologists Union, Cooper Ornithol. Soc., Western Bird Banding Assn. Home: 120 E 100 S # 60 2 Ephraim UT 84627-1449 Office: Snow Coll Dept Biology 150 College Ave Ephraim UT 84627

GARDNER, PETER ALSTON, electronic warfare systems engineer; b. Columbus, Ohio, June 26, 1954; s. Lowell and Mary (Pratt) G.; m. Robin Ilene Beveridge, May 24, 1981; children: Daniel, Kendra, Kimberly, Dara. BS in Math., Norwich U., 1976; postgrad., Johns Hopkins U., 1980-82; student, Nat. Cryptologic Sch., 1980-82. Signal analyst intern Nat. Security Agy., Ft. Meade, Md., 1980-82; software engr. Nat. Security Agy. Computer Scis. Corp., Falls Church, Va., 1982; systems engr. survivable systems group GTE Corp-Comm. Sys. Divsn., Needham, Mass., 1982-85; systems engr. systems divsn. Dynamics Rsch. Corp., Wilmington, Mass., 1985-86; staff systems engr. EWSO dept. Magnavox ESC, Ft. Wayne, Ind., 1986-89; electronic warfare systems engr. avionics dept. Naval Air Warfare Ctr.-WPNSDIV, China Lake, Calif., 1989-91; electronic warfare systems engr. info. and electronic warfare directorate Naval Air Warfare Ctr.-WPNDIV, China Lake, Calif., 1991—. With U.S. Army, 1976-79, with Res. 1979—. Decorated Achievement medal, Commendation medal. Mem. N.G. Assn. U.S., N.G. Assn. Calif., Res. Officers Assn., Armed Forces Comm. and Electronics Assn., Assn. Old Crows. Republican. Home: 1232 W Tamarisk Ave Ridgecrest CA 93555-5914 Office: Naval Air Warfare Ctr WPNSDIV Code C2381 1 Adminstration CL China Lake CA 93555

GARDNER, RAY DEAN, JR., lawyer; b. Huntington Park, Calif., July 9, 1954; s. Ray Dean Gardner Sr. and Wanda Lou (Banks) Goldman; m. Elizabeth Louise Davis, Dec. 28, 1976; 1 child, John Davis. BA, Humboldt State U., 1977; JD, U. Calif., San Francisco, 1981. Bar: Alaska 1981, U.S. Dist. Ct. Alaska 1981, U.S. Ct. Appeals (9th cir.) 1981, U.S. Supreme Ct. 1985, Colo. 1989, Wis. 1991. Assoc. Hartig, Rhodes, Norman, Mahoney & Edwards, Anchorage, 1981-85, ptnr., 1985-89; sr. counsel The Pittsburg & Midway Coal Mining Co. (A Chevron Co.), Denver, 1989—. Bd. dirs. Resource Devel. Council for Alaska Inc., 1985-89, Alaska Mineral and Energy Resource Edn. Fund, 1987-89. Alfred C. Piltz scholar Humboldt State U., 1975; Calif. State fellow, 1978-81. Mem. Am. Mining Congress (coal leasing com.), Colo. Bar Assn. (mineral, bus. and environ. sects.), Denver Bar Assn., Alaska Bar Assn. (exec. com. natural resources sect. 1984-87, chmn. bus. law sect. 1985-86, corp. code revision subcom. 1985-87), Wis. Bar Assn., Alaska Assn. Petroleum Landmen, Alaska Miners Assn. (state oversight com. 1985-86), Anchorage C. of C. (chmn. state legis. com. 1986-88, bd. dirs. 1988-89). Presbyterian. Home: 2715 Comanche Dr Salt Lake City UT 84108-2810 Office: Pitts & Midway Coal Mining Co 6400 S Fiddlers Green Cir Englewood CO 80111-4950

GARDNER, ROBERT ALEXANDER, career counselor, career management consultant; b. Berkeley, Calif., Sept. 16, 1944; s. Robert Sr. and Eleanor Ambrose (Starrett); m. Sandie Gardner, Mar. 22, 1987; 1 stepdau., Heather. BA, U. Calif., Berkeley, 1967; MA, Calif. State U., Chico, 1974; MS, San Francisco State U., 1992. Registered profl. career counselor; nat. cert. career counselor. Div. personnel officer Wells Fargo Bank, San Francisco; dir. personnel Transamerica Airlines, Oakland, Calif.; instr. U. Calif., Berkeley; career counselor, career mgmt. cons. Gardner Assocs., Oakland; bd. dirs. Vocats. Svcs.; adj. faculty mem. John F. Kennedy U., Walnut Creek, Calif. Author: Achieving Effective Supervision, 1984, rev. edit. 1989, Managing Personnel Administration Effectively, 1986, Career Counseling: Matching Yourself to a Career, 1987. Mem. Am. Counseling Assn., Nat. Career Devel. Assn., Calif. Career Devel. Assn., Calif. Assn. for Counseling and Devel., Internat. Assn. Career Mgmt. Profls., Internat. Assn. of Personal and Profl. Coaches, Rotary (Paul Harris fellow). Home: 42 Aronia Ln Novato CA 94945-1805 Office: Gardner Assocs 3873 Piedmont Ave Ste 12 Oakland CA 94611-5370

GARDNER, SANDRA LEE, nurse, outreach consultant; b. Louisville, Dec. 1, 1946; d. Jane Marie (Schwab) Gardner. Nursing diploma, Sts. Mary and Elizabeth Hosp., Louisville, 1967; BSN magna cum laude, Spalding Coll., 1973; MS, U. Colo., 1975, Pediatric Nurse Practitioner, 1978. RN. Premature coordinator Meth. Evang. Hosp., Louisville, 1967-71; charge nurse Children's Hosp., Louisville, 1971-73; staff/charge nurse Children's Hosp., Denver, 1973-74, perinatal outreach coord., 1974-76; asst. prof. U. Colo. Sch. Nursing, 1976-79; co-founder, vice chmn. bd. dirs. Denver Birth Ctr., 1977-79; dir., cons. Profl. Outreach Consultation, Aurora, Colo., 1980—; founding mem. Colo. Perinatal Car Council, Denver, 1975—; founding dir. Neonatal Nursing Edn. Found., Aurora, 1982—. Co-editor: Handbook of Neonatal Intensive Care, 1985, 89; contbr. articles to profl. jours. Foster parent educator Dept. Social Svcs., 1976-78; in pub. edn. KVOD Radio/Channel 2, Denver, 1978; nursing supr. 9 Health Fair, Denver, 1980. Recipient Gerald L. Hencemann award March of Dimes, Denver, 1978. Mem. ANA (Book of Yr. 1986, 89), Nat. Neonatal Nurses Assn. Democrat. Home: 12095 E Kentucky Ave Aurora CO 80012-3233

GARDNER, WILLIAM ALLEN, electrical engineering educator; b. Palo Alto, Calif., Nov. 4, 1942; s. Allen Frances McLean and Francis Anne Demma; m. Nancy Susan Lenhart Hall, June 19, 1966. MS, Stanford U., 1967; PhD, U. Mass., Amherst, 1972. Engr. Bell Telephone Labs., North Andover, Mass., 1967-69; asst. prof. U. Calif., Davis, 1972-77, assoc. prof., 1977-82, prof. elect. engring., 1982—; pres. Statis. Signal Processing Inc., 1982—; chmn., organizer workshop on Cyclostationary Signals, NSF, Air Force Office of Sci. Rsch., Army Rsch. Office, Office Naval Rsch. Author: Introduction to Random Processes with Applications to Signals and Systems, 1985, 2d edit., 1989, Statistical Spectral Analysis: A Nonprobabilistic Theory, 1987, Cyclostationarity in Communications and Signal Processing, 1994; contbr. over 100 articles to profl. jours.; patentee in field. Recipient disting. engring. alumnus award U. Mass., 1987; grantee Air Force Office Sci. Rsch., 1979-82, 92-93, NSF, 1983-84, 89-94, Electromagnetic Sys. Labs., 1984-92, Army Rsch. Office, 1989-94, Office of Naval Rsch., 1991-94. Fellow IEEE (S.O. Rice Prize Paper award in Comm. Theory, 1988); mem. AAAS, European Assn. Signal Processing (Best Paper award 1986), Sigma Xi, Eta Kappa Nu, Tau Beta Pi. Office: U Calif Dept Elec and Engring Davis CA 95616

GAREY, DONALD LEE, pipeline and oil company executive; b. Ft. Worth, Sept. 9, 1931; s. Leo James and Jessie (McNatt) G.; BS in Geol. Engring., Tex. A&M U., 1953; m. Elizabeth Patricia Martin, Aug. 1, 1953; children: Deborah Anne, Elizabeth Laird. Reservoir geologist Gulf Oil Corp., 1953-54, sr. geologist, 1956-65; v.p., mng. dir. Indsl. Devel. Corp. Lea County, Hobbs, N.Mex., 1965-72, dir., 1972-86, pres., 1978-86; v.p., dir. Minerals, Inc., Hobbs, 1966-72, pres., dir., 1972-86, chief exec. officer, 1978-82; mng. dir. Hobbs Indsl. Found. Corp., 1965-72, dir., 1965-76; v.p. Llano, Inc., 1972-74, exec. v.p., chief operating officer, 1974-75, pres., 1975-86, chief exec. officer, 1978-82, also dir.; pres., chief exec. officer, Pollution Control, Inc., 1969-81; pres. NMESCO Fuels, Inc., 1982-86; chmn., pres., chief exec. officer Estacado Inc., 1986—, Natgas Inc., 1987—; pres. Llano Co2, Inc., 1984-86; cons. geologist, geol. engr., Hobbs, 1965-72. Chmn., Hobbs Manpower Devel. Tng. Adv. Com., 1965-72; mem. Hobbs Adv. Com. for Mental Health, 1965-67; chmn. N.Mex. Mapping Adv. Com., 1968-69; mem. Hobbs adv. bd. Salvation Army, 1967-78, chmn., 1970-72; mem. exec. bd. Conquistador coun. Boy Scouts Am., Hobbs, 1965-75; vice chmn. N.Mex. Gov.'s Com. for Econ. Devel., 1968-70; bd. regents Coll. Southwest, 1982-85. Capt. USAF, 1954-56. Registered profl. engr., Tex. Mem. Am. Inst. Profl. Geologists, Am. Assn. Petroleum Geologists, AIME, N.Mex. Geol. Soc., Roswell Geol. Soc., Rotary. Home: 315 E Alto Dr Hobbs NM 88240-3905 Office: Broadmoor Tower PO Box 5587 Hobbs NM 88241-5587

GARFEIN, ARTHUR DOUGLAS, psychiatrist, psychoanalyst; b. Bklyn., Oct. 29, 1942; s. Abraham and Flora G. (Geshwind) G.; m. Anita B. Burnett, Nov. 18, 1967; children: Jennifer, Joshua. AB, Bucknell U., 1964; MD, U. Louisville, 1968. Diplomate Am. Bd. Psychiatry and Neurology. Intern Jackson Meml. Hosp.-U. Miami (Fla.) Sch. Medicine, 1968-69; resident in psychiatry U. Colo., Denver, 1969-72; pvt. practice Littleton, Colo., 1974—; med. dir. behavioral health svcs. Porter Meml. Hosp., Denver, 1989—; asst. clin. prof. psychiatry U. Colo. Health Scis. Ctr., Denver, 1990—; chmn. Colo. Psychiat. Care; mem. faculty Denver Inst. Psychoanalysis, coord. advanced psychotherapy seminar, 1988—; cons. in field. Pres. Goddard Neighborhood Assn., Littleton, Colo., 1988-90, Assn. Mental Affiliation with Israel, Colo. chpt., Highlands Park, Ill., 1986-88. lt comdr. USN, 1972-74. Fellow Am. Psychiat. Assn.; mem. Colo. Psychita. Assn. (chmn. rev. com. 1984-86), Denver Psychoanalytic Soc. (ethics com. 1988—). Home: 3986 W Bowles Ave Littleton CO 80123-6582

GARG, MEENA, physician, neonatologist; b. New Delhi, July 18, 1954; came to U.S., 1979; d. Prem Chand and Sarla Gupta; m. Satyakam Garg, Oct. 10, 1978; children: Shruti, Medha. Grad. in intermediate sci., U. Delhi, 1971, BS, B in Surgery, 1975. Intern U. Zambia Sch. Medicine, Lusaka, 1976-77, sr. resident, registrar in pediatrics, 1977-79; resident in pediatrics Martin Luther King Jr. Gen. Hosp., L.A., 1980-83; pediatrician Kaiser Permanente, L.A., 1983-84; fellow in neonatology and pediatric pulmonology Children's Hosp., L.A., 1985-87; asst. prof. clin. pediatrics U. So. Calif. Sch. Medicine, Children's Hosp., L.A., 1988—; coord. Fellowship Program in Neonatal-Perinatal Medicine, U. So. Calif. Sch. Medicine, L.A., 1991—; conf./symposium presenter. Contbr. numerous articles to profl. jours. Office: Children's Hosp 4650 W Sunset Blvd Los Angeles CA 90027-6016

GARGIULO, FRANCA, marketing and communications consultant; b. N.Y.C., Sept. 11, 1962; d. Theodore Luigi and Gloria (Moschella) G. BS in Fgn. Svc., Georgetown, 1984; postgrad., Coll. of Europe, 1985-86. With internat. mktg. dept. Seagate Tech., Scotts Valley, Calif., 1987-88, LSI Logic, Milpitas, Calif., 1988-89; dir. U.S. Bur. Census, Monterey, Calif., 1989-90; cons. on comm. and mktg., Monterey, 1990—; advisor Washington Workshops Found., 1982-85; regional mgr. Nat. Assn. Mfrs., 1993—. Exec. v.p. Calif. Republican League; active Calif. Rep. Com. Mem. League United L.Am. Citizens, Am. Bus. Women's Assn., Monterey History and Art Assn. Roman Catholic. Home and Office: PO Box 2426 Monterey CA 93942-2426

GARLAND, CEDRIC FRANK, epidemiologist, educator; b. La Jolla, Calif., Nov. 10, 1946; s. Cedric and Eva (Caldwell) Garagliano. B.A., U. So. Calif., 1967; M.P.H., UCLA, 1970, DPH, 1974. Asst. prof. Johns Hopkins U., Balt., 1974-81; assoc. prof. U. Calif. Sch. Medicine, La Jolla, 1981—. Contbr. chpts. to books, articles to profl. jours. Chmn. info. resources Physicians for Social Responsibility, San Diego, 1982—. Recipient Aristotle award for acad. excellence UCLA, 1974; Golden Apple award for Teaching Excellence Johns Hopkins U., 1980; Environ. Health Coalition Disting. Service award, 1984; NIH Research Career award, 1982. Fellow Am. Coll. Epidemiology; mem. Am. Coll. Epidemiol., Soc. Epidemiol. Research, Sierra Club (chmn. Save Our Shore 1982—, disting. achievement award 1984). Roman Catholic. Office: Dept Family & Preventive Medicine U Calif Dept 0631C 9500 Gilman Dr La Jolla CA 92093-5003

GARLAND, G(ARFIELD) GARRETT, sales executive, golf professional; b. Lakewood, Ohio, Dec. 17, 1945; s. Garfield George and Lois Marie (Calavan) G. BA, U. Colo., 1974. Broker Marcus & Millichap, Newport Beach, Calif., 1982-84; v.p. Pacific Coast Fed., Encino, Calif., 1984-85; dir. of acquisitions Prudential Investment Fund, L.A., 1985-86; v.p. A.S.A.I., L.A. and Tokyo, 1986-89; dir. sales Lojack Corp., L.A., 1989—; pres. Collegiate Scholarship Svcs. of Am., 1991-92; cons. Centinela Hosp. Fitness Inst. Mem. Pres.'s Coun. on Competitiveness, 1992, Childhelp USA. Capt. U.S. Army, 1967-71. Mem. VFW, PGA of Am., L.I.F.E. Found., Am. Legion, World Affairs Coun., Internat. Platform Assn., U.S. Ski Team, Natural Historic Preservation Trust. Home: 3846 Via Dolce Marina Del Rey CA 90292 Office: Lojack Corp 9911 W Pico Blvd Los Angeles CA 90035-2703

GARLOUGH, WILLIAM GLENN, marketing executive; b. Syracuse, N.Y., Mar. 27, 1924; s. Henry James and Gladys (Killam) G.; m. Charlotte M. Tanzer, June 15, 1947; children: Jennifer, William, Robert. BEE, Clarkson U., 1949. With Knowlton Bros., Watertown, N.Y., 1949-67, mgr. mfg. svcs., 1966-67; v.p. planning, equipment systems div. Vare Corp., Englewood Cliffs, N.J., 1967-69; mgr. mktg. Valley Mould div. Microdot Inc., Hubbard, Ohio, 1969-70; dir. corp. devel. Microdot Inc., Greenwich, Conn., 1970-73, v.p. corp. devel., 1973-76, v.p. adminstrn., 1976-77, v.p. corp. devel., 1977-78; v.p. corp. devel. Am. Bldg. Maintenance Industries, San Francisco, 1979-83; pres. The Change Agts., Inc., Walnut Creek, Calif., 1983—; bd. dirs. My Chef Inc.; mem. citizens adv. com. to Watertown Bd. Edn., 1957. Bd. dirs. Watertown Community Chest, 1958-61; ruling elder Presbyn. Ch. With USMCR, 1942-46. Mem. Am. Mgmt. Assn., Inst. Mgmt. Cons. (cert.), Bldg. Svc. Contractors Assn., Internat. Sanitary Supply Assn., Mensa, Am. Mktg. Assn., TAPPI, Assn. Corp. Growth (pres. San Francisco chpt. 1984-85, v.p. chpts. west 1985-88), Lincoln League (pres. 1958), Am. Contract Bridge League (life master), Clarkson Alumni Assn. (Watertown sect. pres. 1955), No. N.Y. Contract Club (pres. 1959), No. N.Y. Bridge Club, Tau Beta Pi. Home: 2557 Via Verde Walnut Creek CA 94598-3451 Office: The Change Agts Inc 2557 Via Verde Walnut Creek CA 94598-3451

GARN, SUSAN LYNN, secondary computer graphics educator; b. Astoria, Oreg., July 12, 1948; d. Everett Leslie and Jeanne Esther (Linquist) G. BA in Art, U. Nev., Reno, 1970; MEd in Ednl. Adminstrn. and Higher Edn., U. Nev., Las Vegas, 1990. Tchr. art Desert Sands Unified Sch. Dist., Indio, Calif., 1973-74; art. resource tchr. Trinity County Schs., Weaverville, Calif., 1974-75; multi-subject tchr., primarily in visual arts Clark County Sch. Dist., Las Vegas, 1975-80, 87—; missionary Ch. Jesus Christ of Latter-Day Saints, 1980-82; tchr. English, reading Jordan Sch. Dist., Sandy, Utah, 1982-84; lead community sch coord. Lincoln County Sch. Dist., Newport, Oreg., 1984-87; sole propr. Sue Garn and Kids Art, Las Vegas, 1988—; presenter at profl. confs.; long term substitute tchr. Chemawa Indian Sch., Salem, Oreg., 1984. Work displayed at Educators as Artists exhibit, 1990, 92, 93. Named Tchr. of Yr. Nev. State PTA, 1990; Excellence in Edn., CCSD, 1991. Mem. Nat. Art Edn. Assn. (mid. level liaison 1993-94, past pres. cadre, Nev. Art Educator of Yr. award 1993), Art Educators So. Nev. (pres. 1990-92), Art Educators Nev. (pres. 1992-94). Home: 3709 El Jardin Ave Las Vegas NV 89102-3821 Office: Advanced Techs Acad 2501 Vegas Dr Las Vegas NV 89106

GARNAND, GARY L., produce broker; b. Twin Falls, Idaho, Oct. 28, 1946; s. Vay R. and Maxine S. (Campbell) G.; m. Lori A. Allgaier, June 28, 1975; children: Stacy, Kristen. BS in Mktg./Mgmt., U. Idaho, 1970. Sales mgr. Chef Reddy Foods, Othello, Wash., 1970-71; pres. Garnand Mktg., Inc., Twin Falls, Idaho, 1971—, The N.W. Connection, Inc., Twin Falls, 1984—; cons. PMA Product Acad., Washington, 1991—; chmn. UFFVA Onion Divsn., Washington, 1986-87. Advisor Job's Daus. #56, Twin Falls, 1993—. Mem. Masons, Elks, Vandal Booster Bd. (v.p. 1989—), U. Idaho Magic Valley Alumni Assn. (v.p. 1989), Sigma Alpha Epsilon (Merit key 1985, Outstanding Alumni 1989). Republican. Episcopalian. Home: 1068 Wildwood Dr Twin Falls ID 83301-8117 Office: Garnand Mktg Inc 320 2nd Ave N Twin Falls ID 83301-5958

GARNER, GIROLAMA THOMASINA, educational administrator, educator; b. Muskegon, Mich., Sept, 15, 1923; d. John and Martha Ann (Thomas) Funaro; student Muskegon Jr. Coll., 1941; B.A., Western Mich. U., 1944, M.A. in Counseling and Guidance, 1958; Ed.D., U. Ariz., 1973; m. Charles Donald Garner, Sept. 16, 1944 (dec.); 1 dau., Linda Jeannette Garner Blake. Elem. tchr., Muskegon and Tucson, 1947-77; counselor Erickson Elem. Sch., Tucson, 1978-79; prin. Hudlow Elem. Sch., Tucson, 1979-87, adj. prof. U. Ariz., 1973—, Tuscon Pima Community Coll., 1981—, Prescott Coll., 1986—; mem. Ariz. Com. Tchr. Evaluation and Cert., 1976-78; del. NEA convs. Active ARC, Crippled Children's Soc., UNESCO, U.S.-China People's Friendship Assn., DAV Aux., Rincon Renegades; bd. dirs. Hudlow Community Sch., 1973-76. Recipient Apple award for teaching excellence Pima Community Coll., 1982. Mem. Nat. Assn. Sci. Tchrs., Tucson Edn. Assn., Ariz. Edn. Assn., NEA, Assn. Supervision and Curriculum Devel., AAUW, Tucson Adminstrs., Pima County Retired Tchrs., Delta Kappa Gamma, Kappa Rho Sigma, Kappa Delta Pi. Democrat. Christian Scientist. Home: 6922 E Baker St Tucson AZ 85710-2230 Office: 502 N Caribe Ave Tucson AZ 85710-2242

GARNER, JERRYLE GAIL, food service executive, management consultant; b. Santa Ana, Calif., Dec. 27, 1940; d. Alton W. Fish and Isabel B. deRossett Fish Katana; m. Douglas R. Hurlbert, Nov. 19, 1960 (div. Jan. 1983); 1 child, Angela Renee Hurlbert Peterson; m. Hale E. Garner, Feb. 14, 1984 (div. July 1986). AA in Liberal Arts, Long Beach City Coll., 1965; BA in Sociology, Calif. State U., Long Beach, 1969; cert. in early edn., U. Idaho, Moscow, 1971. Tchr. Manzanita Elem. Sch., Merlin, Oreg., 1971-74; adminstrv. asst. McDonald's of Logan, Utah, 1975-80; office mgr. Logan Sr. High Sch., 1980-82; pres., CEO Jeranbi, Inc., Logan, 1994—; owner/operator McDonald's of Logan, Brigham City, Trementon, Hyrum, Utah, 1983—; pres. IMCA, Salt Lake City, 1986-88; sec.-treas., mem. steeing com. Nat. Operators Adv. Bd., Oak Brook, Ill., 1988-92; mem. steering com. Regional Operators Adv. Bd., Denver, 1988-92. Exec. bd. gov.'s club Rep. State Com., Salt Lake City, 1988-90; trustee CAA/Ellen Eccles Theatre, Logan, 1991-93, Utah Festival Opera Co., Logan, 1991-94; chmn. adv. bd. Rep. Nat. Com., Washington, 1993-94. Recipient Beautificaiton award Salt Lake City Tribune, 1990, 91. Mem. AAUW, Logan C. of C. (bd. dirs. 1987-89), Women Operators- Network-McDonald's, Old Main Soc., Big Blue Club (exec. bd.), Pres.'s Touchdown Club. Republican. Congregatinoalist. Home: 237 N 1170 E Logan UT 84321-4836 Office: Jeranbi Inc 60 E Center St Ste 109 Logan UT 84321-4664

GARNER, LYNN EVAN, mathematics educator; b. Ontario, Oreg., July 19, 1941; s. Evan Bowen and Sarah Melba (Despain) G.; m. Marjorie Kaye Waite, Sept. 9, 1960; children: Kaylene, Bradley, Kristen, Alisse, Brian. BS, Brigham Young U., 1962; MA, U. Utah, 1964; PhD, U. Oreg., 1968. Instr. to prof. Brigham Young U., Provo, Utah, 1962—; instr. Waterford Sch., Provo, 1978-89, Meridian Sch., Provo, 1989—; cons. Hewlett Packard Edn. Adv. Com., Corvallis, Oreg., 1992—. Author: Outline of Projective Geometry, 1981, Calculus and Analytic Geometry, 1988, Calculus with H/P Calculators, 1990, Calculus with the HP48, 1992, 94. Mem. Am. Math. Soc., Math. Assn. of Am., Pi Mu Epsilon, Sigma Xi. Mem. Ch. LDS. Office: Brigham Young U 283 Tmcb Provo UT 84602-1044

GARNETT, DANIEL JOSEPH, general surgeon; b. Waukegan, Ill., Aug. 21, 1942; s. Robert and Eleanor Elizabeth (Ryan) G.; m. Stephanie Ann McCarty, Nov. 24, 1971; children: David Bryan, Michael Clarke. AB, Dartmouth Coll., 1964, B in Med. Sci., 1965; MD, Columbia U., N.Y.C., 1967. Diplomate Am. Bd. Surgery. Straight surg. intern Harborview Hosp., Seattle, 1969-70; resident in gen. surgery Swedish Hosp. Med. Ctr., Seattle, 1970-73, chief resident, 1973-74; practice surgery Seattle, 1974—. Lt. USNR, 1968-70. Fellow ACS, Seattle Surg. Soc.; mem. AMA, Wash. State Med. Assn., King County Med. Soc., Trout Unltd. Office: 1801 NW Market St Ste 401 Seattle WA 98107-3909

GARON, CLAUDE FRANCIS, laboratory administrator, researcher; b. Baton Rouge, Nov. 5, 1942; s. Ivy Joseph and Janith (Latil) G.; m. Sally Sheffield; children: Michele, Anne, Julie. BS, La. State U., 1964, MS, 1966; PhD, Georgetown U., 1970. Predoctoral fellowship La. State U., Baton Rouge, 1964-66; predoctoral traineeship Georgetown U., Washington, 1966-69; postdoctoral fellowship Nat. Inst. Allergy and Inf. Diseases, Bethesda, Md., 1971-73, staff fellowship, 1971-73, sr. staff fellowship, 1973-74, rsch. microbiologist, 1974-81; head electron microscopy Rocky Mountain Labs., Hamilton, Mont., 1981-85, chief pathobiology, 1985-89, chief lab. vectors and pathogens, 1989-94; chief microscopy br. Rocky Mountain Labs., Hamilton, 1994—; bd. govs. Ctr. Excellence in Biotech., Missoula, Mont., 1988—; faculty affiliate U. Mont., 1989—. Mem. editorial bd. Jour. Clin. Microbiology, 1993. Recipient award of merit NIH, 1979, Dirs. award, 1988. Mem. Am. Soc. for Microbiology, Am. Soc. Biochemistry and Molecular Biology, Microscopy Soc. Am., Am. Soc. Rickettsiology, Pacific N.W. Electron Microscopy Soc., Lions (pres. Hamilton 1989-90). Office: Rocky Mountain Labs Microscopy Br 903 S 4th St Hamilton MT 59840-2932

GARR, CARL ROBERT, manufacturing company executive; b. Olean, N.Y., Apr. 4, 1927; s. Frederick H.J. and Mary Magdalene (Zimmerman) G.; m. Arlene Crawford, Dec. 20, 1947; children: Christine Garr Weber, Anne Garr Shields, Elizabeth Garr Reese. B.S. in Physics, Kent State U., 1950; M.S. in Physics, Case Inst. Tech., 1953, Ph.D. in Metall. Enging. 1957. Supr. engring. Bettis plant Westinghouse Co., 1956-58; supt. tech. services, nuclear fuel ops. Olin Mathieson Chem. Corp., 1958-62; dir. engring. and research Albuquerque div. ACF Industries Inc., N.Y.C., 1962-68, v.p. research and devel., 1968-70; v.p. ACF Industries, Inc., N.Y.C., 1976-82; pres., chief exec. officer Polymer Corp. subs. ACF Industries, Inc., Reading, Pa., 1970-76, 1984-86, chmn., 1987—; pres., chief exec. officer Empire Steel Castings, Inc., Reading, 1982-84; v.p. Chesebrough-Pond's Inc., 1984-86; chief exec. officer, chmn. bd. Bank of Pa., Reading, 1988-92; vice-chmn. Dauphin Deposit Corp., 1988-92; bd. dirs. Carpenter Tech. Corp., Bank of Pa. Served with USN, 1944-46. Mem. Am. Soc. Metals, Sigma Xi. Club: Berkshire Country (Reading), The Boulders Club (Carefree, Ariz.). Home: 2017 Meadow Gln Wyomissing PA 19610-2719

GARRETSON, OWEN LOREN, engineer; b. Salem, Iowa, Feb. 24, 1912; s. Sumner Dilts and Florence (White) G.; m. Erma Mary Smith, Jan. 23, 1932; children: John Albert, Owen Don, Susan Marie, Leon Todd. Student, Iowa Wesleyan Coll., 1930-32; BS, Iowa State U., 1937. Registered profl. engr., Okla., N.Mex., Iowa, Mo. Engr. Bailey Meter Co., Cleve., 1937, St. Louis, 1937-38; engr., dist. mgr. Phillips Petroleum Co., Bartlesville, Okla., 1938-39, Amarillo, Tex., 1939-40, Detroit, 1940-41; mgr. product supply and transp. div. Phillips Petroleum Co., Bartlesville, 1942-44, mgr. engring. devel. div., 1944-46, mgr. spl. porducts engring. devel. div., 1946-47; pres. Gen. Tank & Steel Corp., Roswell, N.Mex., United Farm Chem. Co.; pres., dir. Garretson Equipment Co., Mt. Pleasant, Iowa; v.p., dir. Valley Industries, Inc., Mt. Pleasant; pres., dir. Garretson Carburetion of Tex., Inc., Lubbock; v.p., dir. Sacra Gas Co. Roswell, 1957-58; exec. v.p., dir. Arrow Gas. Co. & Affiliated Corps., Roswell, N.Mex., Tex., Utah, 1958-60; asst. to pres. Nat. Propane Corp., Hyde Park, N.Y.; pres., chmn. bd. Plateau, Inc. Oil Refining, Farmington, N.Mex., 1960-82, also bd. dirs.; chmn. bd. S.W. Motels, Inc., Farmington; organizing dir. Farmington Nat. Bank, 1964; cons. Suburban Propane Gas Corp. Whippany, N.J. Contbr. articles to profl. jours.; 42 patents issued in several fields. Mem., past pres. Farmington Indsl. Devel. Svc., N.Mex. Lidquefied Petroleum Gas Commn., 1955-76, chmn., 1956-58; mem. Iowa Gov.'s Trade Commn. to No. Europe, 1970, Iowa Trade Mission to Europe, 1979; mem. com. natural gas/liquefied natural gas Internat. Petroleum Expn. and Congress, 1970-71; mem. Nat. Coun. Crime and Delinquency. Recipient Merit award Iowa Wesleyan Coll. Alunmi Assn., 1968, Profl. Achievement Engring. citation Iowa State U., 1986. Mem. ASME, NSPE, Nat. Liquefied Petroleum Gas Assn. (bd. dirs., Disting. Svc. award 1979), Am. Petroleum Inst., Nat. Petroleum Refiner's Assn. (bd. dirs., pres.), Ind. Refiners Assn. Am., Agrl. Ammonia Inst. Memphis (bd. dirs.), N.Mex. Liquefied Petroleum Gas. Assn. (pres., bd. dirs.), Ind. Petroleum Assn. Am., N.Mex. Acad. Sci., Am. Soc. Agrl. Engrs., Am. Soc. Automotive Engrs., N.Mex. Amigos., Am. Inst. Chem. Engrs., Newcomen Soc. N.Am., Soc. Indsl. Archeology, Ancient Gassers (sec., pres.), 25 Yr. Club Petroleum Industry, Masons, Rotary, Phi Delta Theta, Tau Beta Pi. Home: 500 E La Plata St Farmington NM 87401-6940 Office: PO Box 108 Farmington NM 87499-0108

GARRETSON, ROBERT MARK, financial executive; b. Greeley, Colo., Nov. 3, 1951; s. Loren Neville and Marilyn Elizabeth (Ruwaldt) G.; m. Susan Anita Carlson, Apr. 28, 1973; children: Jennifer, Christopher, Courtney, Timothy. BSBA, Colo. State U., 1974, MS in Taxation, 1982. CPA, Colo. Staff acct. Lloyd Spawn & Assocs., Ft. Collins, Colo., 1974-76; controller Pearse Electronics, Inc., Wheatridge, Colo., 1976-78, Environ. Rsch. & Tech., Ft. Collins, 1978-80; v.p. Ctr. St., Inc., Loveland, Colo., 1980-82; chief fin. officer Simons, Li & Assocs., Ft. Collins, 1982-92; owner Robert M Garreston, CPA, 1992—; CFO Welsh Engring. Sci. and Tech., Inc., Reno, 1995—. Chmn. fin. com. Christ United Meth. Ch., Ft. Collins, 1983-86, auditor, 1988; asst. scout master Ft. Collins area Boy Scouts Am., 1985-89. Mem. AICPA, Colo. Soc. CPAs. Republican. Office: 5212 Wisteria Ct Fort Collins CO 80525-5530

GARRETSON, STEVEN MICHAEL, elementary education educator; b. L.A., Nov. 2, 1950; s. Fredrick Harmon and Mildred (Mason) G.; m. Candice Kay Clouse, Sept. 23, 1972; children: Joshua Steven, Amanda Jeanine. BA, U. Calif., Irvine, 1972, tchr. credential, 1974; postgrad., U. Calif., Santa Barbara, 1973; MA, U. San Francisco, 1980. Cert. tchr., adminstr., Calif. Tchr. Irvine Unified Sch. Dist., 1974—; energy conservation cons. Irvine Unified Sch. Dist., 1981-85, grant writer, 1983—, archtl. design cons., 1975—, mentor tchr., 1984-86; presenter state social studies conf., 1980. Mem. Irvine Tchrs. Assn. (grievance chmn. 1980-82, treas., 1977-78, v.p., 1978-79, contract negotiator, 1976-84, 89-93, benefits mgmt. bd. 1990—, pres. 1993—), Phi Delta Kappa. Roman Catholic. Office: Northwood Elem Sch 28 Carson Irvine CA 92720-3313

GARRETT, DENNIS ANDREW, police official; b. Phoenix, Feb. 9, 1940; s. Lynn Patrick and Louise A. (Yates) G.; m. Joan Marie Braun, June 12, 1980. AA, Glendale Community Coll., 1975; BS magna cum laude, No. Ariz. U., 1980; MPA, Ariz. State U., 1985. Officer Phoenix Police Dept., 1963-69, sgt., 1969-72, lt., 1972-75, capt., 1975-80, maj., 1980, asst. police chief, 1980-91, police chief, 1991—. Chmn. St. Jerome's Sch. Bd., Phoenix, 1978-79, NAACP, Boys & Girls Club Met. Phoenix; mem. Valley Leadership, Phoenix, 1985—; bd. dirs. Friendly House, YMCA; officer Ariz. Police Officer Stds. and Tng. Bd. Mem. ASPA (pres. Ariz. chpt. 1988-89), Internat. Assn. Chiefs Police, Ariz. Assn. Chiefs Police, Ariz. Hispanic C. of C., Nat. Orgn. Black Law Enforcement Execs., Fraternal Order Police, Rotary, Phi Kappa Phi. Republican. Roman Catholic. Office: Phoenix Police Dept 620 W Washington St Phoenix AZ 85003-2108

GARRETT, JOHN CECIL, newspaper editor; b. Atlanta, Jan. 26, 1936; s. Cecil H. and Eunice (Hildebrand) G.; m. Judith Love Sligh, Aug. 22, 1959. BS in Journalism, Fla. State U., 1958. Sports writer Atlanta Jour., 1958-59; sports editor Albany (Ga.) Herald, 1959-61, Sarasota (Fla.) Jour. & Herald Tribune, 1961-68; asst. sports editor The Press-Enterprise, Riverside, Calif., 1968-78, sports editor, 1978—. Mem. Associated Press Sports Editors (chair western region 1984-85). Republican. Presbyterian. Office: The Press-Enterprise PO Box 792 Riverside CA 92502-0792

GARRIDO, AUGIE, university athletic coach. Head coach Calif. State Fullerton Titans, 1973-87, 1991—, U. Ill., 1987-91. Named 4th Winningnest active divsn. IA coach, 1103 victories. Office: Calif State Fullerton PO Box 34080 Fullerton CA 92634-9480*

GARRIGUS, CHARLES BYFORD, retired literature educator; b. Benton, Ill., June 13, 1914; s. Charles Byford and Ailene Marie (Fowler) G.; m. Ferne Marie Fetters, Dec. 28, 1936 (dec.); children: Marmarie (dec.), Charles, Richmond, Karis, Rose Ann. AB, U. Ill., 1936, MA, 1937. Prof. humanities King's River Coll., Reedley, Calif., 1949-73; Calif. poet laureate for life, 1966—. Author: California Poems, 1955, (poems) Echoes of Being, 1975, (novels) Brief Candel, 1987, Chas and The Summer of '26, 1994; editor: Modern Hamlet, 1950. Mem. Calif. Assembly, 1958-66. Democrat. Methodist. Home: PO Box 554 Cayucos CA 93430

GARRIS, SIDNEY REGINALD, artist management company executive; b. N.Y.C., Dec. 31, 1922; children: Brian, Michael, Ellen, Robin Garris Kaplan. Student, U. So. Calif., Pepperdine U. Jazz disk jockey Symphony Sid, N.Y.C., 1937; violist Artie Shaw Band, 1941; with various radio stas., N.Y.C., Ohio, Mich., Calif.; ptnr. Greif-Garris Mgmt., Palm Springs, Calif.; owner, mgr. New Christy Minstrels, 1962—; guest condr. L.A. Philharm., Royal Philharm. London, Atlanta Pops, Tokyo Symphony, Seattle Symphony, numerous other major orchs. throughout world; co-founder L.A. Neophonic Orch. Former mem. bd. dirs. Young Musicians Found., L.A.; participant New Am. Orch.; former mem. L.A. Philharm. Inst.; mem. Maxine Waters Com. for Ho. of Reps.; candidate for mayor City of Palm Springs, 1992; vice-chmn. PSTV Channel 17, Time Warner Cable, Palm Springs. Wiht USN, World War II. Home and Office: Mesquite Canyon Estates 2112 Casitas Way Palm Springs CA 92264-8214

GARRISON, BETTY BERNHARDT, mathematics educator; b. Danbury, Ohio, July 1, 1932; d. Philip Arthur and Reva Esther (Meter) Bernhardt; m. Robert Edward Kvarda, Sept. 28, 1957 (div. 1964); m. John Dresser Garrison, Jan. 17, 1968; 1 child, John Christopher. BA, BS, Bowling Green State U., 1954; MA, Ohio State U., 1956; PhD, Oreg. State U., 1962. Teaching asst. Ohio State U., Columbus, 1954-56; instr. Ohio U., Athens, 1956-57, San Diego State Coll., 1957-59; teaching asst. Oreg. State U., Corvallis, 1959-62; asst. prof. San Diego State U., 1962-66, assoc. prof., 1966-69, prof., 1969—. Reviewer of articles and books, 1966—; contbr. articles to profl. jours. NSF fellow, 1960-61, 61-62. Mem. Am. Math. Soc., Math. Assn. Am. Home: 5607 Yerba Anita Dr San Diego CA 92115-1027 Office: San Diego State U Math Dept San Diego CA 92182

GARRISON, F. SHERIDAN, transportation executive. CEO Am. Freightways, Harrison, Ark., 1956-79; chmn. bd., pres., CEO Am. Freightways, Inc., Harrison, Ark., 1982—, Am. Freightways Corp., Harrison, 1982—, Garrison Corp., Harrison, 1982—. Office: Am Freightways 2200 Forward Dr Harrison AR 72601-2004*

GARRISON, GENE KIRBY, artist, writer, photographer; b. Clayton, Del., Aug. 11, 1925; d. Leighton Bradley and Adelaide (Stevens) Kirby; m. Elbert Wingate Garrison; children: Robert Kirby, David Andrew. AA, Phoenix Coll., 1964. Author: Widow... or Widow-to-Be?, 1991; co-author: From Thunder to Breakfast, 1978; exhibits include Desert Artists, Inc., Cave Creek, Ariz., 1983—, es Posible Gallery, Scottsdale, Ariz., 1992—, Imagine Gallery, Scottsdale, 1988—. Literary arts com. Foothills Cmty. Found., Carefree, Ariz., 1994—; historian Desert Foothills Cmty. Theater, Carefree, 1975-95. Mem. Desert Foothills Woman's Club, Desert Artists, Inc. (founder), Sonoran Arts League.

GARRISON, LLOYD ROBERT, marketing and sales professional; b. Buffalo, Aug. 10, 1942; s. Lloyd Roscoe and Lois Elizabeth (Schwalb) G.; m. Marion E. Loucks, Mar. 17, 1979. BA in Polit. Sci., Calif. State U., L.A., 1975; MA in Polit. Sci., Calif. State U., 1977; postgrad., Clairmont Grad. Sch., 1977-79. Sr. sales engr. Ferro Corp., Cleve., 1980-85, W.R. Grace & Co., Lexington, Mass., 1985-93; internat. bus. mgr. Hampshire Chem. Corp., Lexington, Mass., 1993—. Patentee fire retardant urethane, 1963. Mem. Soc. Plastics Engrs., The Applied Pulp Paper Inst. Democrat. Home and Office: 2443 Prospect Dr Upland CA 91784

GARRISON, U. EDWIN, military, space and defense products manufacturing company executive; b. 1928. BSME, Miss. State U., 1951. With Thiokol Corp., Ogden, Utah, 1952—, from v.p. to pres. aerospace group, 1983-89, past pres., CEO, 1989—; chmn. bd. dirs. Thiokol Corp., Ogden, 1991—. With USN, 1946-48. Office: Thiokol Corp 2475 Washington Blvd Ogden UT 84401-2300*

GARRISON-FINDERUP, IVADELLE DALTON, writer; b. San Pedro, Calif., Oct. 4, 1915; d. William Douglas and Olive May (Covington) Dalton; m. Fred Marion Garrison, Aug. 8, 1932 (dec. Nov. 1984); children: Douglas Lee, Vernon Russell, Nancy Jane; m. Elmer Pedersen Finderup, Apr. 8, 1994. BA, Calif. State U., Fresno, 1964; postgrad., U. Oreg., 1965, U. San Francisco, 1968. Cert. secondary tchr., Calif. Tchr. Tranquillity (Calif.) High Sch., 1964-78, West Hills Coll., Coalinga, Calif., 1970-74; lectr. in field. Author: Roots and Branches of Our Garrison Family Tree, 1988, Roots and Branches of Our Dalton Family Tree, 1989, The History of James' Fresno Ranch, 1990, 3d edit., 1993, There is a Peacock on the Roof, 1993. Mem. DAR (sec.), Archaeology Inst. Am., Frazier Clan N.Am., Fresno City and County Hist. Soc. (life), Fresno Archaeology Soc. (sec.), Children of the Am. Revolution (sr. pres.), Westerners Internat., Fresno Gem and Mineral Soc., Thora # 11 Dannebrog, Friends of the Libr. Republican. Lutheran. Office: Garrison Libr 3427 Circle Ct E Fresno CA 93703-2403

GARROP, BARBARA ANN, elementary education educator; b. Chgo., Sept. 2, 1941; d. Marshall and Esther (Barbakoff) Stickles; widowed; children: Alana Beth, Stacy Lynn. AA with honors, Wright Jr. Coll., Chgo., 1961; BA with honors, Roosevelt U., 1963; MS with honors, Calif. State U., Hayward, 1982. Cert. elem. tchr., reading specialist, Calif. Tchr. Von Humboldt Sch., Chgo., 1963-64, Haugan Sch., Chgo., 1964-67; primary grades reading specialist Mt. Diablo Sch. Dist., Concord, Calif., 1979-80, Mills Elem. Sch., Benicia, Calif., 1980-87, Mary Farmar Sch., Benicia, 1987—; mentor tchr. Benicia Unified Sch. Dist., Benicia, 1989, 92; inst. tchr. leader Calif. Lit. Project, 1991-93; instr. Chapman U. Acad. Ctr., Fairfield, Calif., spring, 1992; mem. reading delegation to China citizen amb. program People to People Internat., 1993. Author phonic manual, 1982; featured in article Woman's Day mag., 1982; contbr. reading program to Excellence In Educational Programs Throughout Solano County, 1994-95; contbg. author Celebrating The National Reading Initiative, 1988. Bd. dirs. Sisterhood of Congregation B'nai Shalom, Walnut Creek, Calif., 1987-88. Grantee Reading Is Fundamental, 1979-80. Mem. NEA, Internat. Reading Assn., Calif. Reading Assn. (Achievement award 1984), Constra Costa Reading Assn., Calif. Tchrs. Assn., AAUW, Pi Lambda Theta. Jewish. Lodge: B'nai Brith Women (v.p. Columbus, Ohio 1971-72, pres. Walnut Creek 1973-74). Office: Mary Farmar Sch 901 Military W Benicia CA 94510-2558

GARRUTO, JOHN ANTHONY, cosmetics executive; b. Johnson City, N.Y., June 18, 1952; s. Paul Anthony and Katherine Helen (DiMartino) G.; m. Denise Kitty Conlon, Feb. 19, 1971 (div. May 1978); 1 child, James Joseph; m. Anita Louise, May 12, 1979 (div. Sept. 1984); 1 child, Christopher Russell; m. Debra Lynn Brady (div. Dec. 1986); m. Michelle Bartok, Apr. 2, 1988. BS in Chemistry, SUNY, Binghamton, 1974; AAS in Bus. Adminstrn., Broome Coll., 1976. Rsch. chemist Lander Co. Inc., Binghamton, 1974-77; rsch. dir. Lander Co. Inc., St. Louis, 1977-79, Olde Worlde Products, High Point, N.C., 1979-81; v.p. rsch. and devel. LaCosta Products Internat., Carlsbad, Calif., 1981-89; chief ops. officer Randall Products Internat., Carlsbad, 1989-91; pres. Dermasearch Internat., 1991-92; chief tech. officer Innovative Bioscis. Corp., Oceanside, Calif., 1992—; cons. Trans-Atlantic Mktg., Binghamton, 1975-78; instr. cosmetic sci UCLA, 1991, UCLA Ext. Mem. AAS, Am. Chem. Soc., Soc. Cosmetic Chemists (newsletter editor 1980-81, publicity chmn. 1984—, edn. chmn. 1987, sec. beauty industry west), Fedn. Am. Scientists, N.Y. Acad. Scis. Office: Innovative Bioscis Corp # 115-116 4168 Avenida De La Plata Oceanside CA 92056-6033

GARRUTO, MICHELLE BARTOK, cosmetic company executive; b. Youngstown, Ohio, Feb. 18, 1961; d. Albert James and Judith Ann (Phillips) Bartok; m. John Anthony Garruto, Apr. 2, 1988; 1 child, Catherine Michelle. BS in Physiol. Psychology, U. Calif., Santa Barbara, 1983. Emergency med. technician, 1984—. Asst. to phys. therapist Santa Barbara Phys. Therapy, 1983-84, Escondido (Calif.) Phys. Therapy, 1984-85; regional sales rep. Ft. Dodge Labs., San Francisco, 1985-87; owner North Coast Therapeutics, Oceanside, Calif., 1987-92; CEO Innovative Bioscis. Corp., 1992—. Mem. Nat. Women's Fitness Assn., Women's Enterprise Network, Soc. Cosmetic Chemists, Beauty Industry West (pub. rels. dir. 1991-92, Internat. Spa and Fitness Assn. sponsor Ironman competition 1989). Home: PO Box 232839 Encinitas CA 92023-2839 Office: Innovative Bioscis Corp 4168 Avenida De La Plata Oceanside CA 92056-6033

GARRY, STACEY LYNNE, pathologist; b. Bakersfield, Calif., Sept. 20, 1952; d. Stancil Lee Buchanan and Nona Ethel (Pyle) Finn; m. Edward David Garry, Dec. 18, 1982. Student, Bakersfield Coll., 1970-73; BS in Zoology, Idaho State U., 1982; MD, U. Calif., San Francisco, 1986. Diplomate Am. Bd. Med. Examiners, Am. Bd. Pathology-Anatomic and Clin. Pathology, Am. Bd. Pathology-Hematology. Lab. asst. Kern Med. Ctr., Bakersfield, 1968-72; med. lab. technician Bannock Regional Med. Ctr., Pocatello, Idaho, 1976-77, Pocatello Regional Med. Ctr., 1976-82; resident U. Utah, Salt Lake City, 1986-91; pathologist lab. med. cons. Sunrise Hosp., Las Vegas, Nev., 1991—; dir. LMC Labs., Las Vegas, Nev., 1992—; cons. U. Utah Cardiovascular Inst., Salt Lake City, 1988-91, Associated & Regional Univ. Pathologists, Salt Lake City, 1989-91, Dermatopathology Inc., Murry, Utah, 1987-91, HGM Laser Inc., Salt Lake City, 1987-89, Symbion Inc., Vancouver, B.C., 1987-91; lectr. Utah State Health Dept., Utah, Oreg., Idaho, Ill. and Wis. State Med. Tech. Soc., Bannock Regional Med. Ctr. Fellow Coll. Am. Pathologists (resident forum chmn. 1990-91, vice chmn. 1989-90, resident & young physicians sect. 1991-94, planning com. 1990-93, com. pathology enhancement 1992—); mem. AMA (del. 1983-85, 86-90, 92—), Utah State Med. Assn. (del. 1986-90), U. Utah Housestaff Assn. (pres. 1988-90), Soc. for Hematopathology, CAP-HOD (del.), Phi Kappa Phi. Home: 1500 Commanche Dr Las Vegas NV 89109-3113 Office: LMC Labs Sunrise Hosp Maryland Pky Las Vegas NV 89109-1627

GARRY, WILLIAM JAMES, magazine editor; b. San Francisco, May 8, 1944; s. William James Garry and Nancy Jean (Gaillard) Chadwick; m. Jean Ann Romano, 1989; 4 stepchildren. B.A., Dartmouth Coll., 1966; M.F.A., Columbia U., 1969. Mng. editor True mag., N.Y.C., 1971-72; exec. editor Epicure mag., N.Y.C., 1972-74; mng. editor spl. publs. House Beautiful mag., N.Y.C., 1975-77; editor Free Enterprise mag., N.Y.C., 1977-79; mng. editor Bon Appetit mag., L.A., 1980-85, editor-in-chief, 1985—. Mem. Am. Soc. Mag. Editors, Soc. Profl. Journalists. Office: Bon Appetit 6300 Wilshire Blvd Los Angeles CA 90048-5202

GARSIDE, LARRY JOE, research geologist; b. Omaha, May 2, 1943; s. Edwin Joseph and Ruby Anne (Weaver) G.; m. Terri Marie (Nelson), Sept. 11, 1993. BS in Geology, Iowa State U., 1965; MS in Geology, U. Nev., 1968. Lab. asst. Iowa State U., Ames, 1965; rsch. asst. U. Nev., Reno, 1965-68; econ. geologist Nev. Bur. Mines & Geology, Reno, 1968-84, chief geologist, dep. dir., 1985-87, acting dir., 1987-88, rsch. geologist, 1988—; exec. sec. Nev. Oil & GAs Conservation Commn., Reno, 1974-75. Contbr. numerous articles to profl. jours. Fellow Geol. Soc. of Am.; mem. Am. Assn. Petroleum Geologists, Soc. Econ. Geologists, Assn. Exploration Geochemists, Geol. Soc. Nev. (pres. 1973-74, sec., treas. 1969-70), Nev. Petroleum Soc. (sec., treas. 1986), Geothermal Resource Coun. (charter). Home: 2670 Margaret Dr Reno NV 89506-8651 Office: Nev Bur of Mines & Geology U Nev #178 Reno NV 89557-0088

GARSKE, JAY TORING, geologist, oil and minerals consultant; b. Fargo, N.D., Jan. 5, 1936; s. Vincent Walter and Margaret Anna (Toring) G.; m. Margo Joan Galloway, Aug. 31, 1957 (div. Mar. 1989); children: Mara Jayne, Brett Andrew; m. Carol Jean Apker, Apr. 24, 1993. BS in Geology, U. N.D., 1957. Geologist Superior Oil Co., Rocky Mountain Region, 1959-62; pvt. practice cons. geologist Denver, 1962—; pres., bd. dirs. Kudu Oil Corp., Denver, 1982—, Garske Energy Corp., Denver, 1984—, Frontier Gold Resources, Inc., Denver, 1987-92, Omega Oil Corp., Denver, 1992—. 1st lt. U.S. Army, 1958-59. Mem. Am. Assn. Petroleum Geologists, Am. Soc. Photogrammetry and Remote Sensing, Rocky Mountain Assn. Geologists, Colo. Mining Assn., Sigma Gamma Epsilon. Home: 1583 S Spruce St Denver CO 80231-2615 Office: Jay T Garske Consulting Geologist 1660 S Albion St Ste 710 Denver CO 80222-4023

GARSON, ARNOLD HUGH, newspaper editor; b. Lincoln, Nebr., May 29, 1941; s. Sam B. and Celia (Stine) G.; m. Marilyn Grace Baird, Aug. 15, 1964; children: Scott Arnold, Christopher Baird, Gillian Grace, Megan Jane. BA, U. Nebr., 1964; MS, UCLA, 1965. Reporter Omaha World-Herald, 1965-69; reporter Des Moines Tribune, 1969-72, city editor, 1972-75; reporter Des Moines Register, 1975-83, mng. editor, 1983-88; editor San Bernardino (Calif.) County Sun, 1988—. Recipient Pub. Svc. Reporting award Am. Polit. Sci. Assn., 1969, Prof. Journalism award U. Nebr. at Omaha, 1969, John Hancock award for excellence in bus. and fin. journalism, 1979, Mng. Editors Sweepstakes award Iowa AP, 1976. Mem. Am. Soc. Newspaper Editors, Calif. Soc. Newspaper Editors, Assoc. Press Mng. Editors, Soc. Profl. Journalists. Jewish. Home: 201 Campbell Ave Redlands CA 92373-6831 Office: San Bernardino County Sun 399 N D St San Bernardino CA 92401-1518

GARSTANG, ROY HENRY, astrophysicist, educator; b. Southport, Eng., Sept. 18, 1925; came to U.S., 1964; s. Percy Brocklehurst and Eunice (Gledhill) G.; m. Ann Clemence Hawk, Aug. 11, 1959; children—Jennifer Katherine, Susan Veronica. B.A., U. Cambridge, 1946, M.A., 1950, Ph.D., 1954, Sc.D., 1983. Research assoc. U. Chgo., 1951-52; lectr. astronomy U. Coll., London, 1952-60; reader astronomy U. London, 1960-64, asst. dir. Obs., 1959-64; prof. astrophysics U. Colo., Boulder, 1964-94, chair faculty assembly, 1988-89, prof. emeritus, 1994—; chmn. Joint Inst. for Lab. Astrophysics, 1966-67; cons. Nat. Bur. Standards, 1964-73; v.p. commn. 14 Internat. Astron. Union, 1970-73, pres., 1973-76; Erskine vis. fellow U. Canterbury, N.Z., 1971; vis. prof. U. Calif., Santa Cruz, 1971. Editor: Observatory, 1953-60; Contbr. numerous articles to tech. jours. Recipient Excellence in Svc. award U. Colo., 1990. Fellow Am. Phys. Soc., AAAS, Optical Soc. Am., Brit. Inst. Physics, Royal Astron. Soc.; mem. Am. Astron. Soc., Royal Soc. Scis. Liege (Belgium). Home: 830 8th St Boulder CO 80302-7409 Office: U Colo JILA Boulder CO 80309-0440

GARTNER, HAROLD HENRY, III, lawyer; b. L.A., June 23, 1948; s. Harold Henry Jr. and Frances Mildred (Evans) G.; m. Denise Helene Young, June 7, 1975; children: Patrick Christopher, Matthew Alexander. Student, Pasadena City Coll., 1966-67, George Williams Coll., 1967-68, Calif. State U., Los Angeles, 1969; JD cum laude, Loyola U., Los Angeles, 1972. Bar: Calif. 1972, U.S. Dist. Ct. (cen. dist.) Calif. 1973, U.S. Ct. Appeals (9th cir.) 1973. Assoc. Hitt, Murray & Caffray, Long Beach, Calif., 1972; dep. city atty. City of L.A., 1972-73; assoc. Patterson, Ritner & Lockwood, L.A., 1973-79; mng. ptnr. all offices Patterson, Ritner, Lockwood, Zanghi & Gartner, L.A., Ventura, Bakersfield, and San Bernardino, Calif., 1991—; instr. law Ventura Coll., 1981. Recipient Am. Jurisprudence award Trusts and Equity, 1971. Mem. ABA, Calif. Bar Assn., Ventura County Bar Assn., Nat. Assn. Def. Counsel, Assn. So. Calif. Def. Counsel, Ventura County Trial Lawyers Assn., Direct Relief Internat. (bd. trustees). Republican. Club: Pacific Corinthian Yacht. Home: 6900 Via Alba Camarillo CA 93012-8279 Office: Patterson Ritner Lockwood Zanghi & Gartner 3580 Wilshire Blvd Ste 900 Los Angeles CA 90010-2501

GARTNER, WILLIAM JOSEPH, company executive, business owner; b. Sterling, Ill., Mar. 2, 1942; s. Leonard P. and Dorothy L. Gartner; m. Susan Louise Nicol, Aug. 22, 1964 (div. 1991); children: Kathryn, Kimberly, Andrea; m. Jennifer Farrell, Dec. 31, 1992. BS, Lewis U., 1963; postgrad., Northwestern U., 1972-74. Rsch. chemist Burgess Battery Co., Freeport, Ill., 1963-64, U.S. Gypsum Co., Des Plaines, Ill., 1963-68; project mgr. DeSoto Chem., Des Plaines, 1966-69; pres. Aqualab, Inc., Bartlett, Ill., 1970-86, Halex, Inc., Bartlett, 1981—, Reflex, Inc., Scottsdale, Ariz., 1986-93; owner, pres. Bolin Labs., Inc., Scottsdale, 1993—; cons. Aqualab, Inc., Bartlett, 1986—, Nat. Environ. Test, London, 1986—, Associated Mills, Inc., Chgo., 1984—, Westrend, Inc., Phoenix, 1987—. Author: Toxin, 1988; patentee in field. Leader Girl Scouts USA, Elgin, Ill, 1976-82. Mem. Am. Coun. of Ind. Labs.

GARVEY, DORIS BURMESTER, environmental administrator; b. N.Y.C., Oct. 3, 1936; d. William Henry and Florence Elizabeth (Sauerteig) Burmester; m. Gerald Thomas John Garvey, June 6, 1959; children: Deirdre Anne, Gerald Thomas John Jr., Victoria Elizabeth. BA with honors, Wilson Coll., 1958; MA with honors, Yale U., 1959. Rsch. assoc. Princeton U., N.J., 1967-76; environ. scientist Argonne (Ill.) Nat. Lab., 1976-84; staff mem. Los Alamos (N.Mex.) Nat. Lab., 1984-86, regulatory compliance officer, 1986-89, sect. leader environ. protection group, 1989-92, dep. group leader, environ. protection group, 1992-94, leader sitewide Environ. Impact Statement project, 1994—. Contbr. articles to profl. jours. Bd. dirs. N.Mex. Repertory Theater, Santa Fe, 1987-88; mem. Environ. Improvement Bd., Glen Ellyn, Ill., 1980-82. Mem. AAUW, N.Mex. Hazardous Waste Soc., Women in Sci., Gov.'s Task Force Emergency Response, Nat. Assn. Environ. Profls., Phi Beta Kappa. Democratic. Roman Catholic. Home: 368 Calle Loma Norte Santa Fe NM 87501-1278 Office: Los Alamos Nat Lab PO Box 1663 MS M889 Los Alamos NM 87545

GARVEY, EVELYN JEWEL, mental health nurse; b. Carrizozo, N.Mex., Aug. 23, 1931; d. Everett E. and Jewel A. (Bullard) Bragg; m. Robert J. Garvey, July 10, 1949; children: Nancy, Annie, Catherine, Robert, Michael, Betty. AD, Ea. N.Mex. Coll., 1972. RN, N.Mex.; cert. EMT., N.Mex. Staff nurse N.Mex. Rehab. Ctr., Roswell, 1972; staff nurse Villa Solano State Sch., Roswell, 1972-79, DON, 1979-81; staff nurse Ft. Stanton (N.Mex.) Hosp., 1981-95, Sunset Villa Nursing Home, Roswell, N.Mex., 1995—.

GARVEY, JUSTINE SPRING, immunochemistry educator, biology educator; b. Wellsville, Ohio, Mar. 14, 1922; d. John Sherman and Lydia Kathryn (Johnsten) Spring; m. James Emmett Garvey, June 15, 1946; children: Johanna Xandra Kathryn, Michaela Garvey-Hayes. BS, Ohio State U., 1944, MS, 1948, PhD, 1950. Analytical chemist Sun Oil Refinery Lab., Toledo, 1944-46; Office of Naval Rsch. predoctoral fellow in microbiology U. Rochester, N.Y., 1946-47; AEC predoctoral fellow microbiology Ohio State U., Columbus, 1948-50; rsch. fellow chemistry Caltech, Pasadena, Calif., 1951-57, sr. rsch. fellow chemistry, 1957-73, rsch. assoc. chemistry, 1973-74; assoc. prof. biology Syracuse (N.Y.) U., 1974-78, prof. immunochemistry, 1978-89, emeritus, 1990—; vis. assoc. biology Caltech, 1990—; bd. sci. counselors Nat. Inst. Dental Rsch., NIH, Bethesda, Md., 1979-82; ad hoc study sects. NIH, Bethesda, 1979-88. Co-author: (textbook) Methods in Immunology, 1963, 2d edit., 1970, 3d edit., 1977; editorial bd. Immunochemistry Jour., 1964-71, Immunological Methods Jour., 1971-77; contbr. 125 articles to profl. jours. Grantee NIAID, 1951-72, NSF, 1977-79, Nat. Inst. on Aging, 1978-87, Nat. Inst. Environ. Health Scis., 1980-88. Mem. AAAS, Am. Assn. Immunologists, N.Y. Acad. Scis., Sigma Xi.

GARY, JAMES FREDERICK, business and energy advising company executive; b. Chgo., Dec. 28, 1920; s. Rex Inglis and Mary Naomi (Roller) G.; m. Helen Elizabeth Gellert, Sept. 3, 1947; children: David Frederick, John William, James Scott, Mary Anne. BS, Haverford (Pa.) Coll., 1942. With Wash. Energy Co. and predecessors, Seattle, 1947-67; v.p. Wash. Energy Co., 1956-67; pres., chief exec. officer Pacific Resources Inc., Honolulu, 1967-79, chmn., chief exec. officer, 1979-84, chmn., 1985, chmn. emeritus, 1986—, internat. bus. and energy advisor, 1987—; bd. dirs. Dole Food Co., Inc., Hawkins Oil and Gas Inc., Tulsa, Kennedy Assocs., Inc., Seattle, Am. European Spl. Opportunities Fund, Washington, Unisyn Biowaste Tech.; chmn. bd. dirs. Inter Island Petroleum, Inc.; bd. dirs. Episcopal Homes Hawaii, The Salk Inst. Coun., La Jolla. Mem. Pacific Coast Gas Assn., 1965-75, pres., 1974-75; pres. Chief Seattle coun. Boy Scouts Am., 1966-67, Aloha coun., 1973-74, mem. nat. coun., 1964—, v.p. Western region, 1978-85, pres., 1985-91, also bd. dirs.; chmn. Aloha United Way, 1978, pres., 1979-80, chmn., 1980; mem. bd. regents U. Hawaii, 1981-89; trustee Hawaii Loa Coll., 1968-85, Linfield Coll., McMinnville, Oreg., 1983-89; mem. bd. mgrs. Haverford Coll., 1983-92; bd. dirs. Rsch. Corp. of U. Hawaii, 1971-77, chmn., 1974-77, Hawaii Ednl. Coun.; bd. dirs., officer, trustee Oahu Devel. Conf., Hawaii Employers Coun., Friends of East-West Ctr., Honolulu Symphony Soc., East-West Ctr. Internat. Found.; chmn. Hawaii Cmty. Found., 1987-92, mem. bd. govs., 1987-94; mem. bd. regents Chaminade U., 1991-93. Capt. AUS, 1942-46. Recipient Pres.' trophy Pacific Gas Assn., 1960, Disting. Eagle award Boy Scouts Am., 1972, Silver Beaver award, 1966, Silver Antelope award, 1976, Silver Buffalo award, 1988. Mem. Am. Gas Assn. (bd. dirs. 1970-74), Nat. LP-Gas Assn. (bd. dirs. 1967-70), Am. Petroleum Inst., Inst. Gas Tech. (trustee 1975-86), Hawaii Econ. Coun., Nat. Petroleum Coun., Hawaii Dist. Export Coun., Japan-Hawaii Econ. Coun., U.S Nat. Com. for Pacific Econ. Cooperation, Pacific Basin Econ. Coun. (chmn. U.S. com. 1985-86), Japan-Am. Soc. Honolulu, Ctr. for Strategic and Internat. Studies-Pacific Forum, Honolulu Commn. on Fgn. Rels., Hawaii C. of C. (chmn. 1979). Episcopalian. Clubs: Pacific Union (San Francisco); Oahu Country, Waialae Country, Outrigger Canoe, Pacific, Plaza (Honolulu); Seattle Tennis, Wash. Athletic Rainier (Seattle). Office: 130 Merchant St Ste 1080 Honolulu HI 96813-4426

GARY, RICHARD N., lawyer; b. L.A., May 27, 1943. AB, U. Calif., Berkeley, 1965, JD, 1968. Bar: Calif. 1969. Mem. Thelen, Marrin, Johnson & Bridges, San Francisco, chmn. mgmt. com., 1992—. Office: Thelen Marrin Johnson & Bridges Two Embarcadero Ctr San Francisco CA 94111

GARZA, DEBORAH JANE, educational administrator; b. L.A., July 25, 1952; d. Nicholas and Mary Jane (Hover) Maloof. AA in Gen. Edn., Rio Hondo Coll., 1973; BA in Sociology, Calif. State U., Fullerton, 1978; MS in Sch. Mgmt., U. La Verne, 1988. Calif. life teaching credential; bilingual cert. competence; cert. sch. adminstr.; profl. adminstr. svcs. credential. Bilingual classroom tchr. Norwalk (Calif.)-La Mirada Unified Sch. Dist., 1981-87, 89—, categorical aid program specialist, 1987-88; instrnl. specialist Whittier (Calif.) City Sch. Dist., 1987-88; master tchr. Norwalk (Calif.)-La Mirada Unified Sch. Dist., 1985-90, dist. mentor tchr., 1989-90, presenter/instr., 1991—; panel mem. ednl. tv. broadcast Schooling and Language Minority Students, 1990. Treas. Edmondson Sch. PTA, Norwalk, 1989—. Recipient Merit Scholarship award U. of La Verne (Calif.) Faculty, 1991, Hon. Svc. award Edmondson Sch. PTA, Norwalk, 1992; named Tchr. of Yr., Edmondson Sch., 1990. Mem. Calif. Assn. for Bilingual Edn., Assn. Calif. Sch. Adminstrs., Norwalk-La Mirada Adminstrs. Assn.

GARZA, OSCAR, newspaper editor. Daily calendar editor-arts L.A. Times, Calif. Office: Los Angeles Times Times Mirror Sq Los Angeles CA 90053

GASKELL, CAROLYN SUZANNE, librarian; b. Glen Cove, N.Y., Aug. 14, 1954; d. Duane Uson and Betty Jane (Slabach) G. BA, Pacific Union Coll., 1976; MA, U. Denver, 1977. Circulation libr. Walla Walla Coll., College Place, Wash., 1978-89, dir. librs., 1989—. Mem. ALA, Assn. Seventh-day Adventist Librs. (pres.-elect 1991-92, pres. 1992-93). Office: Walla Walla Coll Peterson Meml Libr 204 S College Ave College Place WA 99324-1139

GASKILL, HERBERT LEO, accountant, engineer; b. Seattle, July 1, 1923; s. Leo Dell and Vesta Rathbone (Dahlen) G.; m. Margaret Helen Jenkins, Mar. 1, 1944 (div.); children—Margaret V., Herbert Leo; m. Opal Jordan, June 13, 1992; 1 child, Ann. B.S. and M.S. in Chem. Engring., U. Wash., 1949, M.B.A., 1976. C.P.A., Wash. Asst. prof. dental materials, exec. officer dept. dental materials Sch. Dentistry, U. Wash., 1950-56; ops. analyst The Boeing Co., Seattle, 1958-71, mktg. cons. govt. programs, 1972-74; pvt. practice acctg., Seattle, 1976-80; hazardous waste mgr. Boeing Co., Seattle, 1980-86, project mgr. Western Processing Remediation, 1986-95, ret. 1995. Active Seattle Art Mus., Pacific Northwest Aviation Hist. Found. Served to lt. (j.g.) USNR, 1941-46. TAPPI fellow, 1956; U. Wash. Engring. Expt. Sta. fellow, 1957. Mem. Wash. Soc. C.P.A.s. Contbr. articles to profl. jours. Home: 1236 NE 92nd St Seattle WA 98115-3135

GASPAR, ANNA LOUISE, retired elementary school teacher, consultant; b. Chgo., May 12, 1935; d. Miklos and Klotild (Weiss) G. BS in Edn., Northwestern U., 1957. Cert. elem. tchr., Calif. Tchr. 6th grade Pacific Palisades Elem. Sch., L.A., 1957-58; tchr. 1st grade Eastman Street Elem. Sch., L.A., 1959, Glassell Park, L.A., 1959-62, Stoner Ave. Elem. Sch., L.A., 1962-67; 2nd-4th grade tchr. Brentwood Elem. Sch., L.A., 1967-78; tchr. 4th and 5th grades Brockton Avenue Elem. Sch., L.A., 1978-90; est. The Swakopmund Tchrs. Resource Ctr., Namibia, 1991-93; English tchr. The Atlantic Sr. Primary Sch., Swakopmund, Namibia, 1992; career info. cons. Peace Corps., 1991—; substitute tchr. various schs., Las Vegas, 1994—. Vol. Peace Corps, 1991-93, Nat. Peace Corps Assn., 1991-93; mem. Hadassah, Bet Knesset Bamidbar, Las Vegas Art Mus. Mem. Internat. Platform Assn., So. Nev. Ret. Tchrs. Assn., Calif. Ret. Tchrs. Assn., Northwestern U. Alumni Assn. Democrat. Jewish. Home: 2700 Hope Forest Dr Las Vegas NV 89134-7322

GASPAR, MAX RAYMOND, surgeon; b. Sioux City, Iowa, May 10, 1915; s. Edgar Mathias and Mabel Agnes (Teefey) G.; m. Virginia Hunter, June 2, 1938 (div. Nov. 1968); children: Karen, Thomas, James, Susan, Mary Ann; m. Lia Sylvia Rista, Jan., 25, 1969. BA, Morningside Coll., 1936; BS, U. S.D., 1938; MD, U. So. Calif., 1941. Diplomate Am. Bd. Surgery, Am. Bd. Surgery with Spl. Competence in Vascular Surgery. Instr. in surgery U. So. Calif., L.A., 1947-48, Coll. Med. Evangelists, L.A., 1948-50, UCLA, 1950-53; asst. clin. prof. surgery Coll. Med. Evangelists, 1953-55, asst. prof. surgery, 1955-59; assoc. clin. prof. surgery Loma Linda U., 1959-63, clin. prof. surgery, 1963-66; clin. prof. surgery U. So. Calif., 1966-90, emeritus prof. surgery, 1990—; chief surgery L.A. County/UCLA Harbor Gen. Hosp., 1958; attending surgeon L.A. County/U. So. Calif. Gen. Hosp., 1955-91, consulting surgeon, 1991—; dir. vascular surgery Loma Linda U., 1956-66. Author: (textbook) Peripheral Arterial Disease, 1981; contbr. numerous articles to profl. jours. and chpts. to books. Dir. Cath. Welfare Bd., Long Beach, Calif., 1960-62, Am. Heart Assn., Long Beach, 1964-65, Am. Cancer Soc., Long Beach, 1967-70; trustee St. Mary's Found., Long Beach, 1985-94. Lt. USN, 1943-46. Recipient Alumnus of Yr. award U. So. Calif., 1979, Disting. Svc. medal L.A. County/U. So. Calif. Med. Ctr., 1983. Fellow Am. Coll. Surgeons; mem. Am. Surg. Assn., Soc. for Clin. Vascular Surgery (pres. 1979-81), Soc. Internat. de Chirurgie, Soc. for Vascular Surgery. Republican. Roman Catholic. Office: 7020 Western Ave Buena Park CA 90621

GASPAR, ROGELIO G., laboratory technologist; b. Manila, Philippines, Mar. 12, 1965; s. Rodolfo (dec.) and Leonila (Guevarra) G.; m. Maria Regis, Apr. 6, 1988; children: Ryan Angelo, Anna Giselle. BS in Med. Tech., U. St. Tomas, Manila, 1985. Lab. asst. Inst. Forensic Sci., Oakland, Calif., 1987; lab. tech. Vet. Ref. Lab., San Leandro, Calif., 1987-89, San Francisco AIDS Found., 1988, Fleischmann's Yeast Inc., Oakland, Calif., 1988, Damon Clin. Lab., San Francisco, 1989—; med. technologist Damon Clin. Lab., Pleasanton, Calif., 1988—, U. Calif. San Francisco-Mt. Zion, 1994—. Mem. Philippine Assn. of Med. Technologist.

GASPARRINI, CLAUDIA, publishing company executive, scientist, writer; b. Genova, Italy, Apr. 25, 1941; came to U.S., 1984; d. Corrado and Tina (Pizzuti) G. D in Earth Scis., U. Rome, 1965; cert. in English, U. Cambridge, Eng., 1965, Pitman Inst., London, 1965. Sr. tech. U. Toronto, Can., 1966-67; rsch. asst. U. Toronto, 1967-70, rsch. assoc., 1970-72; phys. scientist II Geol. Survey Can., Ottawa, 1973; rsch. scientist Nat. Inst. for Metallurgy (now Mintek), Johannesburg, South Africa, 1974-75; ind. cons. Toronto, 1976; pres., owner Minmet Sci. Limited, Toronto, 1977—, Jacksonville, Fla., 1982-86, Tucson, 1986—; pres., owner The Space Eagle Pub. Co., Inc., Toronto, Tucson, 1986—, 88—. Author: Gold and Other Precious Metals-The Lure and the Trap, 1989, How to Get the Most Out of the Legal System Without Spending a Fortune, 1990, Gold and Other Precious Metals-From Ore to Market, 1993, Murder of the Mind-The Practice of Subtle Discrimination, 1993, When You Make the Two One, 1994, (as Gloria J. Duv) How to Run a Successful Mail Order Business by Defrauding the Public, 1995; contbr. articles to profl. jours. and books. Scientist Sci. by Mail Program, Boston Mus. Sci., 1991-92; mem. rsch. bd. advisors Am. Biog. Inst., Raleigh, N.C., 1990—; hon. mem. Internat. Biog. Ctr. Adv. Coun., Cambridge, Eng., 1992—. Recipient Cert. Appreciation Outstanding Svc. Internat. Precious Metals Inst., 1994; named hon. mem. organizing com. Internat. Conf. on Precious Metals, Kosice, Slovakia, Oct. 25-27, 1995. Mem. Can. Inst. Mining and Metallurgy, Internat. Precious Metals Inst., Soc. for Geology Applied to Mineral Deposits, Assn. Women in Sci., Ariz. Geol. Soc. Home: 6651 N Campbell Ave Apt 102 Tucson AZ 85718-1360 Office: Minmet Sci Limited PO Box 41687 Tucson AZ 85717-1687 also: 2 Lansing Sq Ste 703, Willowdale, ON Canada M2J 4P8 also: Via Ugo de Carolis 62, Rome 00136, Italy

GASSER, CHARLES SCOTT, biologist, educator; b. Ft. Benning, Ga., July 26, 1955; s. James Charles and Martha Carson (Clark) G.; m. Judy Callis, Aug. 6, 1989; 1 child, Reta Catherine. BS, U. Calif., Davis, 1973; PhD, Stanford U., 1985. Sr. rsch. biologist Monsanto Co., St. Louis, 1985-89; assoc. prof. biology U. Calif., Davis, 1989—. Recipient Presdl. Young Investigator award NSF, 1990. Office: U Calif Davis Sect Molecular Cell Biology Davis CA 95616

GASSMAN, VICTOR ALAN, cosmetics executive; b. St. Louis, Nov. 7, 1935; s. Samuel and Hilda (Scalla) G.; m. Betty Cohn, Dec. 24, 1961 (div. 1981); children: Susan L., James C.; m. Lynne Hobbs, Jan. 28, 1984; children: Michael S., Christopher S. BS, BA in Retailing, Washington U., 1957. Divisional sales mgr. Famous Barr, St. Louis, 1957-64; mdse. mgr. May Co., L.A., 1965-77; divisional mdse. mgr. J.W. Robinson, L.A., 1977-83; pres. DEPUTE-div. Dep. Corp., L.A., 1983-85, Liz Claiborne Cosmetics, N.Y.C., 1985-88, Victor Gassman & Assocs., N.Y.C., 1988-90; sr. v.p., gen. mgr. Visage Beaute' Cosmetics, Beverly Hills, Calif., 1990-91, sales, mktg. svcs. cons., 1991—. Actor in You Can't Take It With You, Hilton Head Cmty. Playhouse, 1990, The Boys Next Door, 1990, Broadway Bound, 1990; actor in Misbegotten Birthday, Murder Mystery Cruise, 1990, The Madwoman of Chaillot, Readers Theater, 1990, Americas Most Wanted, Fox-TV, 1990, Good Old Days on the Radio, Fine Arts Club, Pasadena, Calif., 1994. Dir. YMCA, Boy Scouts, United Fund, Redlands Art Assn., San Bernardino, 1965-71; v.p. Regional Econ. Devel. Coun., San Bernardino, 1970; pres. Arrowhead Allied Arts Coun., San Bernardino, 1969. Capt. U.S. Army, 1957-65. Recipient Buyer of the Yr. award May Co., 1973, Retailer of Yr. award Fragrance Found., 1982, Career Achievement award So. Calif. Cosmetic Assn., 1984, Best New Packaging / TV award Fragrance Found., 1987. Mem. Foragers Cosmetics Assn., Inland Ctr. Mchts. Assn. (pres. 1971), So. Calif. Cosmetics Assn. (bd. dirs. 1990-93), Beauty Industry West (bd. dirs. 1990—), Rotary Club. Democrat. Jewish.

GAST, NANCY LOU, chemical company executive; b. Appleton, Wis., Aug. 13, 1941; d. Harvey William Gast and June Louella (Mohr) Webster. Med. technologist Palo Alto/Stanford (Calif.) Hosp., 1963-65; med. technologist St. Vincent Hosp., Portland, Oreg., 1965-70, chemistry supr., 1970-81; tech. rep. DuPont-Diagnostic Systems, Claremont, Calif., 1981-83; sales rep. Du-Pont-Diagnostic Systems, Wilmington, Del., 1983-85; account rep. DuPont-Diagnostic Systems, Claremont, Calif., 1985-87, acct. mgr., 1987-95, exec. coun. med. products sales, 1995—. Vol. med. technologist Health Help Ctr., Portland, 1984-88; bd. dirs. Assocs. ofSisters of Holy Names of Jesus and Mary, 1984-93, co-dir, 1994—. Mem. Am. Soc. Med. Technologists, Assn. Oreg. Med. Technologists (treas. 1976-78, chmn. sci. assembly for industry 1992—), Am. Soc. Clin. Pathologists (cert. med. technologist assoc.). Republican. Roman Catholic. Office: DuPont Med Products Hoffman Estates IL 60000

GASTON, HARRISON L., guidance counselor, consultant, therapist; b. L.A., Jan. 2, 1949; s. Frank and Heddie (Schiele) G.; m. Debbra E. Davis, Jan. 18, 1992; children: Tiffany R., Trinity L., Tamika. AAS, Ft. Steilacom Coll., Tacoma, Wash., 1976; BA, Columbia Christian Coll., 1978; MEd, Lewis and Clark Coll., 1980. Cert. counselor, Wash.; registered counselor, Wash. Pers. mgmt. specialist U.S. Army, Ft. Lewis, Wash., 1973-76; mental health counselor Donald E. Long Group Home, Portland, Oreg., 1976-78; social svc. practitioner Cascade Health Care, Portland, Oreg., 1978-82; dir. counseling Ctrl. Ch. of Christ, Tacoma, Wash., 1982-85; guidance counselor Ednl. Svcs. Br., Ft. Lewis, 1984-85, Tacoma Sch. Dist., 1985—; cons., therapist Casey Family Program, Tacoma, 1991—; mem. profl. edn. adv. bd. Pacific Luth. U., Tacoma, 1992—. Mem. Urban League, Tacoma, 1985—, NAACP, Tacoma, 1985—. Recipient Outstanding Contbn. award Internat. Youth Assn., 1981. Fellow NEA, Wash. Edn. Assn., Tacoma Ministerial Assn., Am. Counseling Assn., Wash. Assn. for Multicultural Counseling and Devel.

GASTON, MARGARET ANNE, business educator; b. Regina, Sask., Can., Aug. 28, 1930; Came to U.S., 1948.; d. William Julius and Mary Josephine (Collins) Grogan; 1 child, Robert Brian. BA in Bus. Edn., Cen. Wash. U., 1959; MEd, Western Wash. U., 1972; postgrad., Boston U., 1984. Cert. tchr. K-12, cert. vocat. tchr., Wash. Bus. educator Manson (Wash.) Sch. Dist., 1956-59; instr. K-12 Eastmont Sch. Dist., East Wenatchee, Wash., 1959-63; instr. Shoreline Community Coll., Seattle, 1969-70; instr., chmn. dept. bus. Skagit Valley Coll. Whipbey Campus, Oak Harbor, Wash., 1970-90; part-time instr. bus. edn. Wenatchee Valley Coll., 1959-65. Contbr. articles to profl. jours. Fellow Western Wash. U., Bellingham, 1968-69. Mem. AAUW, NEA, Wash. Edn. Assn., Bus. and Profl. Women, Delta Pi Epsilon. Home: 118 S 12th St Mount Vernon WA 98273-4036

GASTON, RANDALL WALLACE, chief of police; b. Lake Charles, La., Mar. 18, 1944; s. Wallace Howard and Mary Jean (Hubbs) G.; m. Linda Lou Lockwood; children: Debora Gaston Ricks, Aaron, Bryan, Allison. BS, Long Beach State Coll., 1971; MPA with honors, U. So. Calif., 1974; grad., FBI Nat. Acad., 1982. Police officer Anaheim (Calif.) Police Dept., 1965-69, police sgt., 1969-73, police lt., 1973-83, police capt., 1983-94, police chief, 1994—; instr. Orange County (Calif.) C.C.s, 1971-94. Mem. Internat. Police Chiefs Assn., Calif. Police Chiefs Assn., Orange County Police Chiefs Assn., FBI Nat. Acad. Assocs., Kiwanis Club of Greater Anaheim (bd. dirs. 1990-95), Phi Kappa Phi. Office: Anaheim Police Dept 425 S Harbor Blvd Anaheim CA 92805

GATCHELL, HOWELL LAMBORN, JR., radio and television news executive; b. Balt., Jan. 2, 1948; s. Howell Lamborn and Priscilla Elizabeth (Jones) G. BA, Earlham Coll., 1969. News reporter Sta. WAVI/WDAO (FM), Dayton, 1970; program and news dir. Sta. WKAL AM/FM, Rome, N.Y., 1974-76; news dir. Sta. KUZZ/KKXX (FM), Bakersfield, Calif., 1976-80, Sta. KYNO AM/FM, Fresno, Calif., 1980-82; news anchor Sta. KCBS (AM), San Francisco, 1982-84, Sta. KSFO/KYA-FM, San Francisco, 1985-86, Sta. WCKY (AM), Cin., 1986-88; news dir. Sta. KUZZ-TV-FM/KCWR (AM), Bakersfield, 1988—. Staff sgt. USAF, 1970-74. Named Radio Reporter of Yr., 1993, 94, Best Spot News, Best Live Coverage, Best Series, AP, 1993, Best News Coverage, 1991, Best Live Coverage, 1989, Best Feature, Best Hard News, Best Spot News, Kern Press Club, 1993, Best Newscast, 1988, 89, 90, 91, 92, 94, San Francisco Press Club, 1984.

GATES, BRUCE CLARK, chemical engineer, educator; b. Richmond, Calif., July 5, 1940; s. George Laurence and Frances Genevieve (Wilson) G.; m. Jutta M. Reichert, July 17, 1967; children: Robert Clark, Andrea Margarete. BS, U. Calif., Berkeley, 1961; PhD in Chem. Engring., U. Wash., 1966. Rsch. engr. Chevron Rsch. Co., Richmond, Calif., 1967-69; from asst. prof. to assoc. prof. U. Del., Newark, 1969-77, prof. chem. engring., 1977-85, H. Rodney Sharp prof., 1985-92, assoc. dir. Ctr. Catalytic Sci. & Tech., 1977-81, dir. Catalytic Ctr. Sci. & Tech., 1981-88; prof. chem. engring. U. Calif., Davis, 1992—. Author: Catalytic Chemistry, 1992; co-author: Chemistry of Catalytic Processes, 1979; co-editor: Metal Clusters in Catalysis, 1986, Surface Organometallic Chemistry, 1988. Fulbright Rsch. grantee Inst. Phys. Chemistry U. Munich, 1966-67, 75-76, 83-84, 90-91. Mem. AIChE (Alpha Chi Sigma award 1989, William H. Walker award 1995), Am. Chem. Soc. (Del. sect. award 1985, Petroleum Chemistry award 1993). Office: Univ Calif Dept Chem Engring & Material Sci Davis CA 95616

GATES, CHARLES CASSIUS, rubber company executive; b. Morrison, Colo., May 27, 1921; s. Charles Cassius and Hazel LaDora (Rhoads) G.; m. June Scowcroft Swaner, Nov. 26, 1943; children: Diane, John

Swaner. Student, MIT, 1939-41; BS, Stanford U., 1943; DEng (hon.), Mich. Tech. U., 1975, Colo. Sch. of Mines, 1985. With Copolymer Corp., Baton Rouge, 1943-46; with Gates Rubber Co., Denver, 1946—, v.p., 1951-58, exec. v.p., 1958-61, chmn. bd., 1961—, now also chief exec. officer; chmn. bd. The Gates Corp., Denver, 1982—, chief exec. officer, from 1982, also bd. dirs.; pres. The Gates Corp., 1994—; bd. dirs. BHP Petroleum Melbourne, Australia, Tejas Gas Corp.; pres. bd. trustees Gates Found. Trustee Denver Mus. Natural History, Calif. Inst. Tech., Pasadena. Recipient Community Leadership and Service award Nat. Jewish Hosp., 1974; Mgmt. Man of Year award Nat. Mgmt. Assn., 1965; named March of Dimes Citizen of the West, 1987. Mem. Conf. Bd. (dir.), Conquistadores del Cielo, Denver Country Club, Outrigger Canoe Club, Waialae Country Club, Boone and Crockett Club, Club Ltd., Old Baldy Club, Country Club of Colo., Roundup Riders of Rockies, Shikar-Safari Internat., Augusta Nat. Golf Club, Castle Pines Golf Club. Office: Gates Corp 900 S Broadway Denver CO 80209-4010

GATES, DOROTHY LOUISE, educator; b. National City, Calif., Feb. 21, 1926; d. Harold Roger and Bertha Marjorie (Lippold) Gates. BA, U. Calif., Santa Barbara, 1949; MA, U. Hawaii, 1963, PhD, 1975; postdoctoral student U. Uppsala (Sweden), 1976, Bedford Coll., London, 1978, Cuban Ministry of Justice, 1979, Cambridge U., Eng., 1986. Dept. probation officer, Riverside County, Calif., 1950-54, 55-61; dir. La Morada, probation facility, Santa Barbara County, 1963-65; prof. sociology San Bernardino Valley Coll. (Calif.), 1965-87, prof. emeritus, 1987—; part-time tchr. criminology U. Redlands, Calif.; chmn. Riverside County Juvenile Justice and Delinquency Prevention Commn., 1971-88. Pres. Women's Equity Action League, Hawaii, 1972; mem. adv. group Riverside County Justice System, 1982. bd. dirs. San Bernardino County Mental Health Assn., Symphony Guild, Cooper Burkhart House, Riverside, Alzheimer Assn., Riverside & San Bernardino counties; mem. adv. council Ret. Sr. Vol. Program, San Bernardino; acad. pres. San Bernardino Valley Coll., 1986; pres., trustee Riverside Community Coll., 1989—. Recipient Cert. of Recognition, Riverside YWCA; named Citizen of Achievement, San Bernardino LWV, 1985; NEH fellow U. Va., 1977; named Outstanding Prof. San Bernardino Valley Coll., 1987. Mem. AAUW, LWV, Western Gerontology Assn., Am. Soc. Criminology, State of Hawaii Sociol. Soc., Calif. Probation, Parole and Correctional Assn. (award 1969), Calif. Women's Assn. Edn. and Rsch., Urban League, Kiwanis (past pres.). Address: 4665 Braemar Pl # 212 Riverside CA 92501-3017

GATES, GLODEAN KENT KERKMANN, marketing consultant; b. St. Louis, May 6, 1934; d. H. Warren and Glodean (Warthen) Kerkmann; m. Armand H. Hemon, May 25, 1957 (div.); children: Angela Hemon Sirota, Charles; m. Philip W. Gates, May 22, 1976 (div.). Student U. Mich., 1955-56; BA, UCLA, 1958. Tchr. pub. schs. Lancaster, Calif., 1965-69; sales rep. Sta. KBVM-AM, Lancaster, 1967-69; account exec. Sta. KOTE-FM, Lancaster, 1970-71, sales mgr., 1971-73; gen. sales mgr. Sta. KOTE-FM, Sta. KKZZ-AM, Lancaster, 1973, v.p., gen. mgr. Lancaster-Palmdale Broadcasting Co., Lancaster, 1974-77; regional affairs dir. Sta. KFWB News 98, Westinghouse Broadcasting & Cable, Inc., L.A., 1978-85; coord. met. program and svcs. UCLA Extension, 1985-93; guest lectr. broadcasting UCLA Extension. Mem. communications, exec. heart health coms. L.A. affiliate Am. Heart Assn.; bd. dirs. Hollywood Human Svcs. Recipient Martin R. Gainsbrugh citation Econ. News Broadcasters Assn., 1981; citation Disting. Service, Am. Heart Assn., 1981; Community Service award United Way, 1980; Achievement award Credit Counselors L.A., 1982; Champion Media award for Econ. Understanding, Amos Tuck Sch. Bus., Dartmouth Coll., 1982. Mem. Pub. Rels. Soc. Am., Pub. Info. Radio and TV Edn. Soc., So. Calif. Broadcasters Assn. Pub. Affairs Dirs., Women's Coun. Greater L.A. C. of C. (dir. 1979-80), Women in Pub. Affairs, Coro Found. Assocs., UCLA Alumni Assn. (life, mem. steering com., mem. govt. relations com., Gold Shield Alumnae Hon. 1988), Nat. Assn. Broadcasters (chmn. small market radio com.), Pi Beta Phi.

GATES, JOHN ALLEN, engineer, consultant; b. Port Huron, Mich., July 27, 1953; s. John Elmer and Margaret Inez (Morriss) G.; m. Janet Rockwell Barrington, Mar. 17, 1979 (div. Jul. 1984); children: Joseph Austin O'Brien, Christopher Lawrence Gates; m. Kathleen Louise Malloy, Apr. 13, 1985; children; John Allen Jr., Timothy Andrew, Kimberly Elizabeth. BSEE, Mich. Tech. U., 1975, MSEE, 1977. Engr. Raytheon EDL, Sudbury, Mass., 1977-79, Collins Avionics, Melbourne, Fla., 1979-80; mgr. applied tech. Parker Bros., Beverly, Mass., 1980-83; chief engr. dBX, Newton, Mass., 1984; v.p. product devel. Multipoint Comm., Sunnyvale, Calif., 1984-87; sect. mgr. GTE Gov. Sys. Corp., Mountain View, Calif., 1987-93; dir. engring. Precision Echo, Santa Clara, Calif., 1993—; cons. MMI, Santa Clara, 1986. Inventor in field. Office: Precision Echo 3105 Patrick Henry Dr Santa Clara CA 95054-1815

GATES, LISA, small business owner, chef, caterer; b. Washington, July 11, 1955; d. Chester Robert and Peggy Jean (Dalton) Gates; m. Sergio Vivoli, Nov. 3, 1978 (div. Nov. 1984); m. Mitchell Cohen, Sept. 21, 1987 (div. Febr. 1995). AA, Fleming Coll., Florence, Italy, 1974. Dir. The Am. Sch. in Switzerland, Lugano, 1974-80; counter person Bar Gelateria Vivoli, Florence, 1978-80; costumer, choreographer, scene designer English Theatre of Florence, 1978; tchr. Dance Sch. Theatre, Florence, 1978-81; sec., treas. Vivoli Da Firenze, Inc., L.A., 1981-82; event coord. Calif. Catering Co., Beverly Hills, Calif., 1983; chef, sales rep. St. Germain To Go, West Hollywood, Calif., 1984; chef, cons. Posh Affair Catering Co., L.A., 1984-87; owner, chef, party planner Lisa Gates-Vivoli Catering, L.A., 1985—; catering mgr. Maple Drive Restaurant, Beverly Hills, 1990-91; pvt. chef, 1991—. Mem. Mus. Contemporary Art, L.A., L.A. County Mus. Art, L.A. Theatre Ctr., NOW, L.A., Music Ctr. Unified Fund. Recipient Outstanding Achievement in Art award Bank of Am., Miraleste, Calif., 1972. Mem. NAFE, Am. Inst. Wine and Food, Da Camera Soc. (patron), Roundtable for Women in Foodsvc. Democrat. Home and Office: 1227 N Orange Grove Ave West Hollywood CA 90046-5311

GATES, MELODI MOSLEY, software engineer; b. Dallas, Aug. 29, 1964; d. Dan Roland and Jaynet Marie (Simpson) Mosley; m. Cary L. Gates, Dec. 24, 1985. BS in Math. and Computer Sci., Calif. State U., Long Beach, 1986; MS in Computer Sci. and Engring., U. Colo., Denver, 1995. From maintenance programmer to devel. programmer/analyst CaseWare, Inc., Costa Mesa, Calif., 1986-88; staff programmer/analyst US West Knowledge Engring., Inc., Denver, 1988-89; sr. mem. tech. staff, software engr. US West Techs., Denver, 1989—. Home: 750 S Sherman St Denver CO 80209-4037 Office: US West Techs 1475 Lawrence St Denver CO 80202-2219

GATES, MILO SEDGWICK, construction company executive; b. Omaha, Apr. 25, 1923; s. Milo Talmage and Virginia (Offutt) G.; m. Anne Phleger, Oct. 14, 1950 (dec. Apr. 1987); children: Elena, Susan, Virginia, Mariquita Anne, Milo T.; m. Robin Templeton Quist, June 18, 1988; stepchildren: Robert L. Quist, Catherine Quist, Sarah Mazzocco. Student, Calif. Inst. Tech., 1943-44; BS; B.S., Stanford U., 1944, MBA, 1948. With Swinerton & Walberg Co., San Francisco, 1955—, pres., 1976—, chmn., 1988—. Bd. dirs., trustee Children's Hosp. San Francisco; trustee Grace Cathedral, San Francisco; bd. dirs. Calif. Acad. Scis. Lt. (j.g.), USNR, 1944-46. Mem. Pacific-Union Club, Bohemian Club. Republican. Home: 7 Vineyard Hill Rd Woodside CA 94062-2531 Office: Swinerton & Walberg Co 580 California St San Francisco CA 94104-1000

GATES, ROBERT C., health system administrator; b. San Diego, Jan. 26, 1941; married. B, U. Redlands, 1962; M, Syracuse U., 1963. Administr. trainee L.A. County Adminstrn. Office, 1963-64, administrv. analyst, 1964-65, asst. administrv. analyst, 1965-66, administrv. analyst, 1966-68; assoc. administr. Orange (Calif.) County Med. Ctr., 1968-76; exec. assoc. dir. U. Calif. Irvine Med. Ctr., Orange, 1976-78; chief dep. dir. L.A. County Dept. Health Svcs., 1978-84, dir., 1984—. Office: L A County-Dept Health Svcs 313 N Figueroa St Rm 912 Los Angeles CA 90012-2659

GATES, SHELDON WILBUR, publishing executive; b. Benton Harbor, Mich., May 17, 1927; s. Charles Wilbur and Gertrude Caroline (McLane) G.; m. Betty Elaine Sauer, June 17, 1951; 1 child, Lori Kim. BS, U. Mich., 1951; MS, Ariz. State U., 1963. Radio engr. U. Mich., Ann Arbor, 1949-50; intelligence officer U.S. Govt., Washington, 1951-53; electronic engr. Motorola, Inc., Scottsdale, Ariz., 1955-60; pres., founder Jensen Tools & Alloys, Phoenix, 1964-73; cons. Phoenix, 1974-80; pub. McLane Publs., Scottsdale, 1985—. Patentee in field; contbr. articles to profl. jours.; author: (software) PC-Ratios, 1993, (book) 101 Business Ratios, 1993. With U.S. Mcht. Marines, 1945-46, PTO. Mem. Phoenix Direct Mktg. Club, Beta Gamma Sigma. Office: McLane Publs PO Box 9-c Scottsdale AZ 85252

GATES, THEODORE ALLAN, JR., software engineer; b. Washington, May 24, 1933; s. Theodore Allan and Margaret (Camp) G.;m. Anne Bissell, Sept. 8, 1955; children: Virginia Anne, Nancy Bissell, Theodore Allan III (dec.), Margaret Kenyon. Student, U. Md., 1951-53, 56-57, 68-69. Mem. staff Arthur D. Little Sys., Burlington, Mass., 1976-77, Corp. Tech. Planning, Portsmouth, N.H., 1977-78; project mgr. Honeywell Info. Sys., Phoenix, 1978-81; tech. mgr. Honeywell Info. Sys., Seattle, 1981-83; mgr. data and software engring. ISC Sys. Corp., Spokane, Wash., 1983-90; project mgr. Boeing Computer Svcs., Richland, Wash., 1990—. With U.S. Army, 1953-56, Korea. Recipient Superior Performance award Census Bur., 1958. Mem. IEEE, Assn. Computing Machinery, Boston Computer Soc., Air Force Assn., Navy League, U.S. Naval Inst., Gorilla Found., Smithsonian Assocs., Nature Conservancy, Commodores Club (Boston), Masons, Shriners. Lutheran. Home: 4800 Pheasant Ln Richland WA 99352-9563 Office: Boeing Computer Svcs BCS-R LL4-91 PO Box 1970 Richland WA 99352-0539

GATES, WILLIAM CHESTER BRUCE, geological engineering executive; b. Snohomish, Wash., Jan. 19, 1947; s. Horace Chester Gates and Bessie Lucille (Worden) Boullion; m. Stephanie Ann Gardner, Feb. 15, 1975; 1 child, Sean William. BS in Geology, Campbell U., 1975; MS in Geol. Engring., S.D. Sch. of Mines, 1985; PhD in Geology, U. Nev., 1994. Registered profl. engr., Nev., Wash.; profl. geologist, N.C., Idaho, Calif.; registered engring. geologist, Oreg.; cert. environ. mgr., Nev. Enlisted U.S. Army, 1966, direct commn. to 2d lt., 1979, advanced through grades to capt., 1983, with Spl. Forces regiment (Green Berets), 1966-79; with Spl. Forces U.S. Army, Vietnam, 1969-70; chief soils engring. lab., Environ. Hygiene Agy. U.S. Army, Aberdeen Proving Ground, Md., 1979-83, chief engring. svcs. Waste Disposal Engring. Div., 1985-89; ret. U.S. Army, 1989; ops. mgr. Environ. and Water Resources Kleinfelder Inc., Reno, 1989-94, v.p., dir. Water Resources Engring. Program, 1994—. Author: Geology of the Cities of the World, 1993; contbr. artcles to profl. jours. Mem. Assn. Engring. Geologists (chmn. Reno chpt. 1991-92, hazardous waste commn. 1983-94), Geol. Soc. Am., Internat. Assn. Engring. Geologists, Nat. Ground Water Assn., Spl. Forces Assn., Phi Kappa Phi. Office: Kleinfelder Inc 3189 Mill St Reno NV 89502-2201

GATES, WILLIAM HENRY, III, software company executive; b. Seattle, Wash, Oct. 28, 1955; s. William H. and Mary M. (Maxwell) G.; m. Melinda French, January 1, 1994. Grad. high sch., Seattle, 1973; student, Harvard U., 1975. With MITS, from 1975; founder, chmn. bd. Microsoft Corp., Redmond, Wash., 1976—, now also chief exec. officer, also dir. Recipient Howard Vollum award, Reed Coll., Portland, Oreg., 1984, Nat. medal Tech. U.S. Dept. Commerce Tech. Adminstrn., 1992; named CEO of Yr., Chief Executive mag., 1994. Office: Microsoft Corp 1 Microsoft Way Redmond WA 98052-8300*

GATTI, DANIEL JON, lawyer; b. Racine, Wis., Apr. 22, 1946; s. Daniel John and Rosemary J. (Moore) G.; m. Donna Jeane Wolfe, Mar. 30, 1984; children: Danny, DiAndra, Stephanie, David. BS, Western Oreg. State U., 1968; JD, Willamette U., 1973. Bar: Oreg. 1973, U.S. Dist. Ct. Oreg. 1973, U.S. Ct. Appeals (9th cir.) 1974, U.S. Ct. Appeals (2d cir.) 1985, U.S. Supreme Ct. 1979; cert. trial specialist. Tchr. Lake Oswego (Oreg.) High Sch., 1970; specialist in edn. law Oreg. Dept. Edn., Salem, 1973-75; pres., atty., ptnr. Gatti & Gatti, P.C., Salem, 1975—. Co-author: The Teacher and The Law, 1972, Encyclopedic Dictionary of School Law, 1975, New Encyclopedic Dictionary of School Law, 1983, The Educator's Encyclopedia of School Law, 1990. V.p., bd. trustees Western States Chiropractic Coll., Portland, Oreg., 1976—. Mem. Oreg. Bar Assn., Assn. Trial Lawyers Am., Am. Bd. Trial Advocacy (cert. as trial specialist 1987), Am. Adjudicature Soc., Illahe Club. Office: Gatti Gatti Maier & Assocs 1761 Liberty St SE Salem OR 97302-5158

GAU, WAYNE WATSON, church abbot, educational consultant; b. Honolulu, Dec. 3, 1948; s. Gordon Stanley and Bessie Wo Hop Gau. AS in Police Sci., Honolulu C.C., 1970; BA in History, U. Hawaii, Manoa, 1970; MA, St. Patrick's Sem., Menlo Park, Calif., 1973, MDiv in Theology, 1974; STD, San Francisco Theological Seminary, San Anselmo, Calif., 1992. Ordained to Celtic Evang. ministry, 1979, ordained abbot, 1981. Religion tchr. Damien Meml. H.S., Honolulu, 1974-75; religion lectr. Chaminade U., Honolulu, 1975-78, Leeward C.C., Pearl City, Hawaii, 1977-79, Kapiolani C.C., Honolulu, 1979, Windward C.C., Kaneohe, Hawaii, 1982; rector St. Columba's Ch., Honolulu, 1979-88; presbyter-abbot Cmty. of St. Columba, Honolulu, 1981—; adminstr. gen. Celtic Evang. Ch., Honolulu, 1981—; human resources mgmt. instr. Pepperdine U., Pearl Harbor, Hawaii, 1978; night min. Hawaii Coun. of Chs., Honolulu, 1977-78, 79; sr. night min. Oahu Assn. Evangs., Honolulu, 1981-83; vicar-legate, dir. Cath. Apostolic Ch., Santa Ana, Calif., 1987—; owner-cons. Optimum Edn. and Promotion, Honolulu, 1987-94; coord. The Iona Inst. for Social Ethics Tng. and Personal Devel., 1994—. Book reviewer Jour. of the Evang. Theol. Soc., 1987, 88. Mem. Neighborhood Bd. for Diamond Head, Kapahulu, St. Louis Heights, Honolulu, 1987-90; dir. St. Louis Heights Cmty. Assn., Honolulu, 1988-90. Named Knight Assn. of St. George the Martyr, 1986, Comdr. Holy Orthodox Order of St. Gregory the Illuminator, 1986, Order of the Holy Cross of Jerusalem, 1987, Ordre Souverain des Chevaliers du Saint-Sepulcre Byzantin, 1987, Knight Most Vnerable and Holy Orthodox Order of St. Basil the Great, 1989. Mem. Honolulu Acad. of Arts, Henry Bradshaw Soc. (Eng.). Republican. Office: Celtic Evang Ch PO Box 90880 Honolulu HI 96835-0880

GAUFF, SUSAN TYRRELL, marketing executive; b. Hackensack, N.J., Oct. 19, 1946; d. Donald Eugene and Henrietta Dorothy (Benson) Tyrrell; m. James Anthony Gauff, Apr. 13, 1973; children: James Timothy, Janet Gauff Anthos, David Phillip. Student, Centenary Coll., 1967. Coord. market rsch. Warner-Lambert, Morris Plains, N.J., 1967-69; coord. pub. rels. Western Union Corp., N.Y.C., 1969-73; pvt. cons. practice in communications Princeton, N.J., 1973-75; asst. mgr. advt. Electronic Assocs., Inc., West Long Branch, N.J., 1975-79; dir. communications Mohawk Data Scis., Parsippany, N.J., 1979-83, Franklin Computer Corp., Pennsauken, N.J., 1983-84; dir. advt. and sales promotion Racal-Milgo, Miami, Fla., 1984-86; dir. corp. communications Siemens Info. Systems, Boca Raton, Fla., 1986-90; dir. mktg. communications Siemens Pvt. Communications Systems and Rolm Systems, Santa Clara, Calif., 1990-91; sr. dir. market and corp. communications Siemens Rolm Comm. Inc., Santa Clara, Calif., 1991—. Named one of Outstanding Young Women of Am., 1971; recipient Tribute to Women in Industry award, 1993. Mem. Bus. Mktg. Assn. (cert., chpt. pres. 1988-89, internat. v.p. media rels. com. 1989-90, internat. sec. 1990-92, internat. treas. 1994—), Am. Mktg. Assn., Pub. Rels. Soc. Am. Avocation: golf. Office: Siemens Rolm 4900 Old Ironsides Dr Santa Clara CA 95054-1830

GAUFIN, SAMUEL OLIVER, lawyer; b. Boise, Idaho, July 14, 1954; s. David Marshall and Monica Jane (Oliver) G. m. Lynn Alison Gaufin, Mar. 22, 1986; 1 child, Samuel O. II. BS, Weber State U., 1975; JD, U. Utah, 1978. Bar: Utah, 1978, U.S. Ct. Appeals (10th cir.), 1979. From assoc. to ptnr. Van Cott Bagley, Cornwall & McCarthy, Salt Lake City, Utah, 1978-87; ptnr. Berman & O'Rorke, Salt Lake City, 1987-93, Berman, Gaufin & Tomsic, Salt Lake City, 1993—. Assoc. comment editor U. Utah Law Rev., 1972. Mem. Order of the Coif. Democrat. Congregationalist. Office: Berman Gaufin Tomsic 50 S Main St Ste 1250 Salt Lake City UT 84144-0103

GAULKE, MARY FLORENCE, library administrator; b. Johnson City, Tenn., Sept. 24, 1923; d. Gustus Thomas and Mary Belle (Bennett) Erickson; m. James Wymond Crowley, Dec. 1, 1939; 1 son, Grady Gaulke (name legally changed); m. 2d, Bud Gaulke, Sept. 1, 1945 (dec. Jan. 1978); m. 3d, Richard Lewis McNaughton, Mar. 21, 1983. B.S. in Home Econs., Oreg. State U., 1963; M.S. in L.S., U. Oreg., 1968, Ph.D. in Spl. Edn., 1970. Cert. standard pers. supr., standard handicapped learner, Oreg. Head dept. home econs. Riddle Sch. Dist. (Oreg.), 1963-66; library cons. Douglas County Intermediate Edn. Dist., Roseburg, Oreg., 1966-67; head resident, head counselor Prometheus Project, So. Oreg. Coll., Ashland, summers 1966-68; supr. librarians Medford Sch. Dist. (Oreg.), 1970-73; instr. in psychology So. Oreg. Coll., Ashland, 1970-73; library supr. Roseburg Sch. Dist., 1974-91; resident psychologist Black Oaks Boys Sch., Medford, 1970-75; mem. Oreg. Gov.'s Council on Libraries, 1979. Author: Vo-Ed Course for Junior High, 1965; Library Handbook, 1967; Instructions for Preparation of Cards For All Materials Cataloged for Libraries, 1971; Handbook for Training Library Aides, 1972. Coord. Laubach Lit. Workshops for High Sch. Tutors, Medford, 1972. Fellow Internat. Biog. Assn. (life); mem. ALA, So. Oreg. Library Fedn. (sec. 1971-73), Oreg. Library Assn., Pacific N.W. Library Assn., Am. Biog. Inst. (lifetime dep. gov. 1987—), Internat. biog. Ctr. (hon., adv. coun. 1990), Delta Kappa Gamma (pres. 1980-82), Phi Delta Kappa (historian, research rep.). Republican. Methodist. Clubs: Lodge: Order Eastern Star (worthy matron 1956-57). Home: 119 Orchard Lane Ashland OR 97520 Office: 2122 N Ramona Ave Casa Grande AZ 85222-1325

GAUNT, JANET LOIS, arbitrator, mediator; b. Lawrence, Mass., Aug. 23, 1947; d. Donald Walter and Lois (Neuhart) Bacon; m. Frank Peyton Gaunt, Dec. 21, 1969; children: Cory C., Andrew D. BA, Oberlin Coll., 1969; JD, Wash. U., St. Louis, 1974. Bar: Wash. 1974, U.S. Dist. Ct. (we. dist.) Wash. 1974, U.S. Ct. Appeals (9th cir.) 1978. Assoc. Davis, Wright, Todd, Riese & Jones, Seattle, 1974-80; arbitrator/mediator Seattle, 1981—; dir. Seattle King County Labor Law Sect., 1976-77; mem. Pacific Coast Labor Law Planning Com., 1977-83; com. vice chmn. Wash. State Task Force on Gender and Justice on the Cts., 1987-89; chmn. Wash. Pub. Employment Rels. Commn., Olympia, 1989—. Author, editor: Alternative Dispute Resolution, 1989; author: Public Sector Labor Mediation and Arbitration, Arbitration and Mediation in Washington, 2d edit., 1995. Pres. State Bd. of Wash. Women Lawyers, 1986. Mem. Nat. Acad. Arbitrators (dir. rsch. and edn. found. 1991—), Am. Arbitration Assn., Wash. State Bar Assn., Mediation Rsch. Edn. Project (cert. mediator), Wash. Women Lawyers. Office: 19670 Marine View Dr SW Seattle WA 98166-4164

GAUSTAD, RICHARD DALE, financier; b. Anchorage, Alaska, Oct. 22, 1952; s. Sidney O. and Beulah (Pierce) G.; m. Lynell Dory, May 7, 1982; children: Kelsey, Eric. MusB, Utah State U., 1974; Diploma, LDS Inst. of Religion, Logan, Utah, 1975; postgrad. in law, Newport U. Sch. of Law, 1992—. Pres. Advt. Specialists, Logan, Utah, 1975-77, Cache Card, Logan, Utah, 1976-77, Northridge Enterprises, Inc., Logan, Utah, 1977-81, Nova's Gen. Store, Salt Lake City, 1981-82; chmn. Handicapped Distbrs., Inc., Mesa, Ariz., 1990-91; pres. Phase III Mktg. Corp., Mesa, Ariz., 1982-91, Infocom Capital Corp., Gilbert, Ariz., 1992—, Western Systems, Inc., Carson City, Nev., 1989—; dir. Western Systems, Inc., Gilbert, 1989-92; pres. Factor's Clearing House, Gilbert, 1992, Infocom Capital Corp., Gilbert, 1992, Handicapped Warehouse, Inc. Author: Financial Report Series, Vol. 1, 1990, Vol. II, 1992. Mem. Gilbert C. of C. LDS. Office: Infocom Capital Corp 761 N Monterey St Ste B 102 Gilbert AZ 85233-3820 also: Factors Clearing House 425 E Guadalupe Rd Ste 103 Gilbert AZ 85234-4636

GAUTIER-DOWNES, CATHERINE HELENE, geography educator, consultant; b. Saint Denis, France, July 14, 1947; came to the U.S., 1975; d. Claude Sacha and Helene (Tournant) G.; children: Julie and Kristen. BS in Physics and Chemistry, U. Paris, 1968, MS in Physics, 1970, MS in Geophysics, 1972, PhD in Physics, Meteorology, 1976, D (state) in Physics, Meteorology, 1984. Prof. physics U. Quebec, Rimouski, 1976-78; rsch. sci., pres. Metsat, Inc., Rimouski, 1978-80; assoc. scientist U. Wis., Madison, 1980-82; assoc. rsch. Scripps Inst. Oceano U. Calif., San Diego, 1982-90; prof. U. Calif., Santa Barbara, 1990—; cons. Mission Rsch. Corp., Santa Barbara, 1990—, Gautier-Downes & Assocs., 1993—; mem. bd. trustees Univ. Space Rsch. Assn., Washington, 1993—. Recipient Rsch. grants NASA, NOAA, NSF, numerous others, 1980—. Mem. Am. Meteorol. Soc. (sci. coun. 1991—), Am. Geophysical Union, Univ. Space Rsch. Assn. (mem. bd. dirs. 1993—, sci. coun. 1989-93). Office: ICESS Ellison Hall 6th Flr Univ Calif Santa Barbara CA 93111

GAWANDE, KISHORE, economics educator, consultant; b. Baroda, Gujrat, India, Jan. 22, 1959; came to U.S., 1983; s. Shreeram P. and Chandraprabha (Nimbalkar) G.; m. Anuradha Shirke, July 14, 1986; 1 child, Dipika I. BA in Econs. with honors, St. Stephen's Coll., Delhi, India, 1979; MBA, Indian Inst. Mgmt., Bangalore, 1981; MA in Math., UCLA, 1987, PhD in Econs., 1991. Asst. prof. U. N.Mex., Albuquerque, 1991—; cons. Sandia Nat. Labs, Albuquerque, 1993—. Sloan Found. fellow, 1990-91. Mem. Am. Econ. Assn., Am. Statis. Assn. Office: U NMex Dept Econs Univ Of New Mexico NM 87131

GAWRONSKI, WODEK K., aerospace engineer; b. Jutrosin, Poland, July 16, 1944; came to the U.S., 1986.; s. Jan and Jadwiga (Kieliba) G.; m. Maria B. Koziel, Mar. 5, 1976; children: Jacob, Kaja. MS, Tech. U. Gdansk, Poland, 1967, PhD in Engring., 1970, DSc in Engring., 1975. Prof. Tech. U. Gdansk, Poland, 1968-79, Polish Acad. Scis., Gdansk, 1979-83, U. Hanover, Germany, 1983-86; NRC sr. fellow NASA Langley Rsch. Ctr., Hampton, Va., 1987-89; mem. tech. staff Jet Propulsion Lab., Calif. Inst. Tech., Pasadena, Calif., 1989—; Co-author: The Finite Element Method, 1975, The Finite Element Method in Dynamics, 1984, Model Reduction for Flexible Structures, 1989, Control and Dynamics of the Deep Space Network Antennas, 1994; contbr. articles to profl. jours. Co-author: The Finite Element Method, 1975, The Finite Element Method in Dynamics, 1984, Model Reduction for Flexible Structures, 1989, Control and Dynamics of the Deep Space Network Antennes, 1994; contbr. articles to profl. jours. Grantee Internat. Rsch. and Exch. Bd., Mich. Tech. U., 1974-75, NRC, NASA Langley Rsch. Ctr., Va., 1987, 89. Mem. AIAA (sr. mem.). Democrat. Lutheran. Home: 17908 Stillmore St Santa Clarita CA 91351-3515 Office: Calif Inst Tech Jet Propulsion Lab 4800 Oak Grove Dr Pasadena CA 91109-8001

GAY, CARL LLOYD, lawyer; b. Seattle, Nov. 11, 1950; s. James and Elizabeth Anne (Rogers) G.; m. Robin Ann Winston, Aug. 23, 1975; children: Patrick, Joel, Alexander, Samuel, Nora. Student, U. of Puget Sound, 1969-70; BS in Forestry cum laude, Wash. State U., 1974; JD, Willamette U., 1979. Bar: Wash. 1979, U.S. Dist. Ct. (we. dist.) Wash. 1979. With Taylor & Taylor, 1979-82, Taylor, Taylor & Gay, 1982-85; prin. Greenaway & Gay, Port Angeles, Wash., 1985-91, Greenway, Gay & Tassie, Port Angeles, 1991—; judge pro tem Clallam County, Port Angeles, 1981-85; commr. superior Ct., 1985-91; judge Juvenile Ct., 1985-87; instr. Guardian Ad Litem Program, Port Angeles, 1985—, Peoples Law Sch., 1989—. Bd. dirs. Cmty. Concert Assn., Port Angeles, 1982-85, 94—, pres., 1984-85, 88-89; bd. dirs. Am. Heart Assn., 1987—, Clallam County YMCA, 1988—, exec. com., 1995—; mem. adv. bd. Salvation Army, Port Angeles, 1982—; subdivsn. chmn., bd. dirs. United Way Clallam County, 1987—; bd. dirs., pres. Friends of Libr., Port Angeles, 1983-91; trustee Fisher Cove, 1988—; advisor youth in govt. program YMCA, 1986—; advisor United Meth. Youth Coun., 1987—, trustee, 1989—; chmn. long-range planning com. Port Angeles Sch. Dist. Mem. ABA (real property, probate and trust and gen. practice sects.), ATLA, Wash. Bar Assn. (real property, probate and trust sects.), Clallam County Bar Assn. (pres. 1995), Nat. Coun. Juvenile and Family Ct. Judges, Superior Ct. Judges Assn. (com.), Wash. State Trial Lawyers Assn., Kiwanis (local bd. dirs. 1982-84, pres. 1986-87, Kiwanian of Yr. 1983-84), Elks. Methodist. Home: 3220 Mcdougal St Port Angeles WA 98362-6738 Office: Greenaway Gay & Tassie 829 E 8th St Ste A Port Angeles WA 98362-6418

GAY, CHARLES W., JR., academic administrator; b. Tulsa, June 30, 1937; s. Charles W. Sr. and Juanita T. (Reeder) G.; m. Sarah E. Frost Smith, Sept. 8, 1953 (div. June 1967); children: Timothy L., Patrick N.; m. Louise M. Kiser, Dec. 22, 1967; stepchildren: Beth L., Richard E. Macatee. BS in Forest Mgmt., Okla. State U., 1962, MS in Range and Livestock Mgmt., 1964. Range rsch. asst. Santa Rita Explt. Range/U.S. Forest Svc., Tucson, Ariz., 1962; range mgmt. extension specialist to assoc. prof. N.Mex. State U., 1964-68, chief of party livestock devel. project in Paraguay, 1969-72; gen. mgr. agr. divsn. Collier Cobb and Assocs./Hudson Farms and Farm Svcs., Pike Road, Ala., 1973-79; v.p. Gay Sales and Svcs., Inc., Tulsa, 1979-83; assoc. chief of party, adj. prof. on range mgmt. project Utah State U., Rabat, Morocco, 1983-86; rsch. asst. prof. of range sci. Utah State U., Logan, 1986-87, acting dept. head range sci., 1987-88, asst. to dean for adminstrv. affairs, ext. program leader, 1989—; invited lectr. Bank of Am. Symposium, 1978, Global Natural Resources Monitoring and Assessments Conf., Venice, Italy, 1989, Icelandic Soil Conservation Svc., Iceland, 1989; invited vis. scientist N.W. Plateau Inst. of Biology, Haibei Alpine Rsch. Sta., China, 1992; co-chmn. U.S. Range Mgmt. Task Force/USDA and Mex.'s Dept. Agr. and

Water Resources. Editorial bd., assoc. editor: Arid Soil Rsch. and Rehab. jour.; contbr. articles to profl. jours. Pres. of bd. Nora Eccles Harrison Mus. of Art, 1994—; bd. dirs. USU Comty. Credit Union, 1991—; trustee, past dir. Devel. for the Logan Chamber Music Soc., 1988-89; chmn. joint com. for Mendon Ward, Boy Scouts Am., 1989-90; Dem. party chmn., Mendon, Utah dist., 1990—; mem. Kiwanis Youth Devel. Com., Logan. Recipient Phillips Petroleum Grad. Rsch. scholarship, Ala. Coop. Extension Leadership award 1978, others. Mem. Soc. Range Mgmt. (sec., chmn. internat. affairs com., others), Soc. Am. Foresters (chair range ecology work group), Am. Mgmt. Assn., Soc. Internat. Devel. (mentor), Utah Soc. Environ. Edn., Intermountain Assn. Environ. Edn. Office: Coll Natural Resources Utah State U Logan UT 84322

GAY, E(MIL) LAURENCE, lawyer; b. Bridgeport, Conn., Aug. 10, 1923; s. Emil D. and Helen L. (Mihalich) G.; m. Harriet A. Ripley, Aug. 2, 1952; children: Noel L., Peter C., Marguerite S., Georgette A. BS, Yale U., 1947; JD magna cum laude, Harvard U., 1949. Bar: N.Y. 1950, Conn. 1960, Calif. 1981, Hawaii 1988. Assoc. Root, Ballantine, Harlan, Bushby & Palmer, N.Y.C., 1949-51; mem. legal staff U.S. High Commr. for Germany, Bad Godesberg, 1951-52; law sec., presiding justice appellate div. 1st dept. N.Y. Supreme Ct., N.Y.C., 1953-54; assoc. Debevoise, Plimpton & McLean, N.Y.C., 1954-58; v.p., sec.-treas., gen. counsel Hewitt-Robins, Inc., Stamford, Conn., 1958-65; pres. Litton Gt. Lakes Corp., N.Y.C., 1965-67; sr. v.p. finance AMFAC, Inc., Honolulu, 1967-73; vice chmn. AMFAC, Inc., 1974-78; fin. cons. Burlingame, Calif., 1979-82; of counsel Pettit & Martin, San Francisco, 1982-88, Goodsill, Anderson, Quinn & Stifel, Honolulu, 1988—. Editor Harvard Law Rev., 1948-49. Pres. Honolulu Symphony Soc., 1974-78; trustee Loyola Marymount U., 1977-80, San Francisco Chamber Soloists, 1981-86, Honolulu Chamber Music Series, 1988—; officer, dir. numerous arts and ednl. orgns. 2d lt. AUS, 1943-46. Mem. ABA, State Bar of Hawaii, Pacific Club (Honolulu), Phi Beta Kappa. Republican. Roman Catholic. Home: 1159 Maunawili Rd Kailua HI 96734-4641 Office: Goodsill Anderson Quinn & Stifel PO Box 3196 Honolulu HI 96801-3196

GAY, RICHARD LESLIE, chemical engineer; b. Redlands, Calif., Nov. 17, 1950; s. Philip Leslie and Mary Frances (Finnigan) G. BS in Engring., UCLA, 1973, MS in Engring., 1973, PhD in Engring., 1976. Registered profl. engr. Calif. Rsch. asst. U. Calif., Riverside, 1969-70, UCLA, 1971-76; mem. tech. staff Rockwell Internat., Canoga Park, Calif., 1976-86; mgr. chem. engring. Rockwell Internat., Canoga Park, 1986—; mem. sub-com. for fuel performance Argonne Nat. Lab., Idaho Falls, Idaho, 1987-94. Patentee in field; contbr. articles to profl. jours. Mem. Am. Inst. Chem. Engrs., Am. Chem. Soc., Sigma Xi. Republican. Roman Catholic. Home: 10012 Hanna Ave Chatsworth CA 91311-3612 Office: Rockwell Internat 6633 Canoga Ave Canoga Park CA 91303-2703

GAYDOS, GREGORY GEORGE, political scientist, educator; b. Marblehead, Ohio, July 17, 1941; s. George Joseph Gaydos and Dorothy Margaret (Vargosick) Saunders; m. Yoko Okuda, Feb. 14, 1977. BS in Edn., Bowling Green State U., 1963, MA in History, 1965; PhD in Polit. Sci., U. Hawaii, 1977. Rsch. asst. Agy. for Internat. Devel., Honolulu, 1968-69; assoc. prof. polit. sci. Hawaii Pacific U., Honolulu, 1970—; invited participant Hawaii Com. for Humanities, Honolulu, 1979. Contbr. articles to profl. jours. Active Mayor's Com. on Pub. TV, Honolulu, 1987—. 1st lt. U.S. Army, 1965-67. Recipient award for Best French Poem of Yr., Vers Jour., 1981, Most Disting. Screenplay, Hawaii Internat. Film Festival, 1983. Mem. Lanikai Lit. League, Hawaii Sociol. Assn. (invited panelist and presenter 1979), Am. Polit. Sci. Assn., Western Polit. Sci. Assn. (invited panelist and presenter 1994). Republican. Roman Catholic. Office: Hawaii Pacific U 1166 Fort Street Mall Honolulu HI 96813-2708

GAYLORD, THOMAS ALAN, academic administrator; b. St. Paul; s. James Edward Jr. and Donna Mary (Kaess) G.; children: Thomas, Tiffany, Christopher. BS in Physics, U. Alaska, 1976; MS in Physics, U. Fla., 1977, PhD Higher Edn. Adminstrn., 1980; cert., Harvard Mgmt. Devel. Program, 1990. Rsch. asst. inst. higher edn. U. Fla., Gainesville, 1977-79, intern instnl. rsch., 1979; coord. info. sys. Ariz. State U., Tempe, 1980; asst. dir. acad. and fiscal planning/rsch. coord. info sys. Alaska Commn. on Postsecondary Edn., Juneau, 1981-82; budget/rsch. analyst U. Alaska Sys. of Higher Edn., Fairbanks, 1982-84, asst. to exec. v.p., dir. fiscal analysis and planning, 1984-86, dir. statewide office instnl. rsch., 1986-90; assoc. vice chancellor planning and CIS U. Alaska, Fairbanks, 1990—; adj. asst. prof. Human and Rural Devel. U. Alaska, Fairbanks, 1984-86, dept. math. and computer scis., 1991—; guest lectr. U. Fla., Gainesville, 1987; adj. assoc. prof. Edn. U. Alaska, Fairbanks, 1992—. Contbr. articles to profl. jours. Co-coord. March of Dimes WalkAmerica, 1989-90. Mem. Alaska Assn. for Computers in Edn., Am. Assn. for Higher Edn., Assn. for Instnl. Rsch., Coll. and Univ. Sys. Exchange, Nat. Assn. Coll. and Univ. Bus. Officers, Pacific Assn. of Collegiate Registrars and Admissions Officers, Pacific N.W. Assn. for Instnl. Rsch. and Planning, Project Mgmt. Inst., Soc. for Coll. and Univ. Planning, Student Info. Sys. Users. Home: 141 Patterson St Apt 110 Anchorage AK 99504-1377 Office: Dept Planning Computing & Info Sys 201 Eielson Bldg U Alaska Fairbanks AK 99775-0001

GAYNOR, JOSEPH, technical and management consultant; b. N.Y.C., Nov. 15, 1925; s. Morris and Rebecca (Schnapper) G.; m. Elaine Bauer, Aug. 19, 1951; children: Barbara Lynne, Martin Scott, Paul David, Andrew Douglas. B in Chem. Engring., Poly. Inst., 1950; MS, Case Western Res. U., 1952, PhD, 1955. Rsch. asst. Case Inst., Cleve., 1952-55; with Gen. Engring. Labs. GE, Schenectady, N.Y., 1955-66, mgr. R & D sect., 1962-66; group v.p. rsch. Bell & Howell Co., 1966-72; mgr. comml. devel. group, mem. pres.' office Horizons Rsch., Inc., Cleve., 1972-73; pres. Innovative Tech. Assocs., Ventura, Calif., 1973—; mem. nat. materials adv. bd. com. NAS; chmn. conf. com. 2d internat. conf. on bus. graphics, 1979, program chmn. 1st internat. congress on advances in non-impact printing techs., 1981, mem. adv. com. 2d internat. congress on advances in non-impact printing techs., 1984, chmn. publs. com. 3rd internat. congress on advances in non-impact printing techs., 1986, chmn. internat. conf. on hard copy media, materials and processes, 1990. Editor: Electronic Imaging, 1991, Procs. Advances in Non-Impact Printing Technologies, Vol. I, 1983, Vol. II, 1988, 3 spl. issues Jour. Imaging Tech., Proc. Hard Copy Materials Media and Processes Internat. Conf., 1990; patentee in field. Served with U.S. Army, 1944-46. Fellow AAAS, AIChE, Imaging Sci. and Tech. Soc. (sr., gen. chmn. 2nd internat. conf. on electrophotography 1973, chmn. bus. graphics tech. sect. 1976—, chmn. edn. com. L.A. chpt. 1978—), Am. Soc. Photobiology, Sigma Xi, Tau Beta Pi, Phi Lambda Upsilon, Alpha Chi Sigma. Home: 108 La Brea St Oxnard CA 93035-3928 Office: Innovative Tech Assocs 3639 Harbor Blvd Ste 203E Ventura CA 93001-4255

GAZDAG, GYULA, film director, educator; b. Budapest, Hungary, July 19, 1947; came to U.S., 1993; s. Ervin and Zsuzsanna (Koloizs); m. Eva Forgacs; children: Peter, Julia. MFA in Film and TV Directing, Hungarian Acad. Theater, Film, Budapest, 1969. Mem. faculty Hungarian Acad. Theater, Film and TV, Budapest, 1985—, head dept. film and TV, 1990; artist in residence Film in the Cities, St. Paul, 1988; artist in residence comm. arts dept. Coll. of Santa Fe, N.Mex., 1989-90; filmmaker in residence Am. Film Inst., L.A., 1990-91; vice chair prodn. UCLA Sch. Theater, Film and TV, 1993—; vis. prof. dept. film and TV UCLA, 1990-91; bd. dirs. European Film Coll., Ebeltoft, Denmark, 1992—; mem. exec. com. Groupement Europeen des Ecoles de Cinema et de TV, 1992—; mem. com. for feature film prodn. Hungarian Motion Picture Found., 1989-91. Writer, dir.: (feature films), The Whistling Cobblestone, 1971, Singing on the Treadmill, 1974, Swap, 1977, Lost Illusions, 1982, Stand Off, 1988, (documentary feature films) The Long Distance Runner, 1968, The Selection, 1970, The Resolution, 1972, The Long Distance Runner II, 1977, The Banquet, 1979 (Best Documentary in Hungarian Film Week 1982, Best Documentary in 1982 award Hungarian Film Critics), Package Tour, 1984, Hungarian Chronicles I-II, 1991, A Hungarian Fairy Tale, 1987 (Grand Prix Salerno Internat. Film Festival 1989, Grand Prix Festival of Phantastic Cinema, Spain 1987, Hungarian Film Critics Best Feature Film of Yr. 1987, One of Yrs. 10 Best Films, Village Voice 1988); writer, co-dir. (feature film) Lost Illusions, 1982 (Best Screenplay prize Hungarian Film Week 1983, prize Figuera da Foz Internat. Film Festival 1983); co-writer, dir., co-editor (feature films) The Whistling Cobblestone, 1971 (Best Feature Film of Yr. award Hungarian Film Critics 1972), Singing on the Treadmill, 1974; writer, dir., editor: (documentary short films) The Long Distance Runner, 1968 (Spl. prize Hungarian Short Film Festival 1969), The Selection, 1970 (Best Documentary award Köszeg Film Festival 1970); writer, co-dir., editor: (documentary feature film) The Resolution, 1972 (Best Documentary Hungarian Film Week 1984); stage work includes 35 May, Simon of the Desert, Candide, A Sunday in August, Cabaret, The Heavy Barbara, The Hothouse, The Merry Widow, Pantagleize, Tom Jones, The Tempest, The Diary of a Hungarian Poet, The Abduction from the Seraglio, The Bald Soprano; TV work includes The Good Old Times of Peace I-VIII, 1973, Women in Traditional Paloc Families, The Invasion, Our Home the Univers I-VI. Office: UCLA 405 Hilgard Ave Los Angeles CA 90024-1301

GAZELL, JAMES ALBERT, public administration educator; b. Chgo., Mar. 17, 1942; s. Albert James and Ann Marion (Bloch) G. BA in Polit. Sci. with honors, Roosevelt U., 1963, MA in Polit. Sci., 1966; PhD in Govt., So. Ill. U., 1968. Instr. Roosevelt U., Chgo., 1965, 67, So. Ill. U., Carbondale, 1966-68; asst. prof. San Diego State U., 1968-72, assoc. prof., 1972-75, prof., 1975—; cons. County San Diego, 1973, Ernst and Ernst, Detroit, 1973. Contbr. articles to profl. jours. Mem. ACLU, Am. Soc. Pub. Adminstrn., Calif. Pub. Rsch. Orgn., Nat. Assn. Ct. Mgmt., Western Govt. Rsch. Assn., Inst. Judicial Ct. Mgmt. Home: 4319 Hilldale Rd San Diego CA 92116-2135 Office: San Diego State U 5402 College Ave San Diego CA 92182-4505

GAZLEY, JEF, psychotherapist; b. Phoenix, Aug. 13, 1951; s. Al and Barbara (Holmes) G.; m. Ilene Walrath, Aug. 7, 1977 (div. Jan. 1980). BA, U. Wash., 1975; MS in Counseling, U. Ore., 1980. Cert. counselor, Ariz. Intake worker Sacred Heart Hosp., Eugene, Ore., 1977-80; social worker Centro de Armistad, Guadalupe, Ariz., 1981-82; head chemical dependence, family svcs. social worker North Behavioral Health Ctr., Phoenix, 1982-86; psychotherapist Affiliated Psychotherapists, Tempe, Ariz., 1986—; mentor, tchr. Prescott (Ariz.) Coll., 1986—. Mem. AACD, NBCC, AAMFT, NACCMHC, AMHCA, Am. Soc. Clin. Hypnosis, Internat. Soc. Clin. Hypnosis, Am. Acad. Pain Mgmt. Office: Affiliated Psychotherapists 2080 E Southern Ave # E101 Tempe AZ 85282-7521

GEBBIA PINETTI, KAREN MARIE, lawyer, educator; b. Chgo., July 21, 1958; d. Stephen L. and Doris A. (Melendez) G. BA magna cum laude, Villanova U., 1980; JD cum laude, Georgetown U., 1983. Bar: Ill. 1983, Hawaii, 1995, U.S. Dist. Ct. (no. dist.) Ill. 1983, U.S. Ct. Appeals (7th cir.) 1985. With Nachman, Munitz & Sweig, Chgo., 1983-87, Winston & Strawn, Chgo., 1987-93; asst. prof. law U. Hawaii, Honolulu, 1993—; bd. dirs. Hawaii Ctrs. for Ind. Living. Contbr. numerous articles to profl. jours. Vol. N.W. Youth Outreach, Chgo., 1990-93, Lakeview Homeless Shelter, 1990-93, La Rabida Children's Hosp., 1991-93; mem. Chgo. Coun. on Fgn. Rels., People to People Internat.; mem. project adv. bd. World Without War Coun.-Midwest; mem. bd. dirs. Hawaii Ctrs. for Ind. Living, 1995—, Hawaii Catholic Diosocean Women's Concerns Com., 1995—. Mem. ABA (bus. law sect., bus. bankruptcy com., comml. fin. svcs. com.), Ill. Bar Assn., Hawaii State Bar Assn., Seventh Cir. Bar Assn., Chgo. Bar Assn. Office: U Hawaii W S Richardson Sch Law 2515 Dole St Honolulu HI 96822-2328

GEBBIE, KRISTINE MOORE, health science educator, health official; b. Sioux City, Iowa, June 26, 1943; d. Thomas Carson and Gladys Irene (Stewart) Moore; m. Lester N. Wright; children: Anna, Sharon, Eric. BSN, St. Olaf Coll., 1965; MSN, UCLA, 1968; DPH U. Mich., 1995. Project dir. USPHS tng. grant, St. Louis, 1972-77; coord. nursing St. Louis U., 1974-76, asst. dir. nursing, 1976-78, clin. prof., 1977-78; adminstr. Oreg. Health Div., Portland, 1978-89; sec. Wash. State Dept. Health, Olympia, 1989-93; coord. Nat. AIDS Policy, Washington, 1993-94; asst. prof. Sch. Nursing Columbia U., 1994—; assoc. prof. Oreg. Health Scis. U. Portland, 1980—; chair, U.S. dept. energy secretarial panel on Evaluation of Epidemiologic Rsch. Activities, 1989-90; mem. Presdl. Commn. on Human Imunodeficiency Virus Epidemic, 1987-88. Author: (with Deloughery and Neuman) Consultation and Community Orgn., 1971, (with Deloughery) Political Dynamics: Impact on Nurses, 1975; (with Scheer) Creative Teaching in Clinical Nursing, 1976. Bd. dirs. Luth. Family Svcs. Oreg. and S.W. Wash., 1979-84; bd. dirs. Oreg. Psychoanalytic Found., 1983-87. Recipient Disting. Alumna award St. Olaf Coll., 1979; Disting. scholar Am. Nurses Found., 1989. Fellow Am. Acad. Nursing; mem. Assn. State & Territorial Health Ofcls., 1988 (pres. 1984-85, exec. com. 1980-87, McCormick award 1988), Am. Pub. Health Assn. (exec. bd.), Inst. Medicine, N.Am. Nursing Diagnosis Assn. (treas. 1983-87), Am. Soc. Pub. Adminstrn. (adminstrn. award II 1983). Office: Columbia U Sch Nursing 630 W 168th St New York NY 10032-3702*

GEBHARD, BOB, professional baseball team executive. Gen. mgr. Colorado Rockies. Office: Colo Rockies 2001 Blake St Denver CO 80205-2000

GEBHART, JOHN E., III, health products company executive; b. 1954. BS in Acctg., Widener Coll., 1976; MBA, Pepperdine U., 1988. CPA. Svc. audit mgr. Arthur Young& Co., San Jose, Calif., 1976-83; dir. fin. and adminstrn. Catalytica, Inc., Mountain View, Calif., 1984-88; with Access Health Mktg., Inc., Rancho Cordova, Calif., 1989—; now sr. v.p. corp. devel. Office: Access Health Marketing Inc 11020 White Rock Rd Rancho Cordova CA 95670-6010*

GEDDES, BARBARA SHERYL, communications executive, consultant; b. Poughkeepsie, N.Y., May 27, 1944; d. Samuel Pierson and Dorothy Charlotte (Graham) Brush; m. James Morrow Geddes, Feb. 24, 1968 (div. Dec. 1980); 1 child, Elisabeth. BA, Skidmore Coll., 1968. Project leader Four-Phase Systems, Cupertino, Calif., 1976-77, Fairchild Co., San Jose, Calif., 1979-80; mgr. tech. publs. Mohawk Data Scis., Los Gatos, Calif., 1977-79, Sytek Inc., Mountain View, Calif., 1981-83; project mgr. Advanced Micro Computers, Santa Clara, Calif., 1980-81; v.p. communications systems Strategic Inc., Cupertino, 1983-86; pres., mng. ptnr. Computer and Telecommunications Profl. Services, Mountain View, Calif., 1986—; v.p. corp. mktg., sec. First Pacific Networks, Sunnyvale, Calif., 1988-94; pres., Auration, Inc., Palo Alto, 1994—; cons. H-P, Varian, Aydin Energy, Chemelex, also others, 1972—; v.p. Conf. Recorders, Santa Clara, 1975-77; advisor Tele-PC, Morgan Hill, Calif., 1983—. Editor: Mathematics/Science Library, 7 vols., 1971. Contbr. numerous articles to mags. Mem. Santa Clara County Adoptions Adv. Bd., 1971-73, Las Cumbres Archtl. Control Commn., Los Gatos, 1983; advisor Los Altos Hills Planning Commn., Calif., 1978-79. N.Y. State Regents merit scholar, 1962. Mem. Assn. for Computing Machinery (editor 1970-72), Nat. Soc. for Performance and Instrn., Bus. and Profl. Advt. Assn., Women in Communications (pres. San Jose 1983—). Democrat. Home: 910 Mockingbird Ln Palo Alto CA 94306-3719

GEDDES, CHARLES LYNN, retired history educator; b. Corvallis, Oreg., Jan. 3, 1928; s. James Edward and Dorothy Marie (Green) G. BS, U. Oreg., 1951; AM, U. Mich., 1954; PhD, U. London, 1959. Asst. prof. Am. U. Cairo, 1956-61, U. Colo., Boulder, 1961-65; Fulbright prof. Tribubhan U., Kathmandu, Nepal, 1965-66; prof. history U. Denver, 1967-92. Author: Guide to Reference Books for Islamic Studies, 1985, A Documentary History of the Arab-Israel Conflict, 1991. Pfc. U.S. Army, 1945-46. Fellow Mid. East Inst.; mem. Am. Oriental Soc., Mid. East Studies Assn., Am. Inst. Yemeni Studies, Am. Inst. Islamic Studies (resident dir. 1965). Home: 3410 W Amherst Ave Denver CO 80236-2504 Office: U Denver Dept History Denver CO 80208

GEE, DONNA BETH, elementary education educator; b. Lubbock, Tex., Oct. 12, 1959; d. Clarence Leslie Jr. and Ada Elizabeth (Rogers) Darter; m. Billy Frank Edmond Gee, Aug. 4, 1984; children: Cassandra Beth, Joshua Trent. BS in Edn., Lubbock Christian U., 1980; MEd, Tex. Tech U., 1982, EdD, 1990. Tchr. Lubbock Ind. Sch. Dist., 1980-90; asst. prof. elem. edn. Ea. N.Mex. U., Portales, 1990—; mem. sci. evalutation team Lovington Sch. Dist., Portales, 1993-94. Mem. Internat. Reading Assn., N.Mex. Coun. Tchrs. of Math., N.Mex. Sci. Tchrs. Assn., Kappa Delta Phi, Phi Delta Kappa. Mem. Ch. of Christ. Office: Ea NMex U Sta 25 Portales NM 88130

GEE, KEN, aerospace research executive; b. Hong Kong, Aug. 31, 1965; came to the U.S., 1966; s. Bing Yoke and Yim Fong (Lee) G.; m. Alisa Wong Gee, Oct. 6, 1990. BS in Aerospace, Calif. Polytechnic, 1987, MS in Aerospace, 1990; Engr., Stanford U., 1994. Aerospace rsch. sci. MCAT Inst., San Jose, Calif., 1990—. Contbr. articles to scientific jours. including: Jour. of Aircraft, AIAA Jour. Mem. AIAA.

GEER, JOHN GRAY, political science educator; b. Johnstown, Pa., Jan. 13, 1958; s. James Henderson and Jean Alice (Gray) G.; m. Maria Melissa Farenga, June 22, 1985; children: Megan Renee, James Daniel. BA, Franklin & Marshall Coll., Lancaster, Pa., 1980; MA, Princeton U., 1982, PhD, 1986. Instr. Princeton U., 1984-86; asst. prof. Ariz. State U., Tempe, 1986-91, assoc. prof., 1991—. Author: Nominating Presidents, 1989; contbr. articles to profl. jours.; mem. editl. bd. Polit. Rsch. Quarterly, Boulder, Colo., 1993—. Mem. Phi Beta Kappa. Home: 12849 S 71st St Tempe AZ 85284-3103 Office: Dept Polit Sci Ariz State U Tempe AZ 85287

GEFFNER, DAVID LEWIS, endocrinologist; b. New York, Mar. 21, 1942; s. Samuel Benjamin and Joanne (Domb) G.; m. Patricia June Fisher, JUne 7, 1970; 1 child, Laura Simpson. BA cum laude, NYU, 1962; MD, Georgetown U., 1967. Diplomate Am. Bd. Internal Medicine, Am. Bd. Endocrinology and Metabolism, Am. Bd. Quality Assurance and Utilization Physicians, Nat. Bd. Med. Examiners. Intern in medicine VA Hosp., Bklyn., 1967-68; resident Cornell Cooperating Hosps. Staff Tng. Program, N.Y.C., 1968-71; rsch. fellow in endocrinology N.Y. Hosp., N.Y.C., 1971-72; fellow in endocrinology UCLA Wadsworth VA Hosp., L.A., 1972-73, acting asst. chief endocrinology, 1973-74; dept. head endocrinology and metabolism Cigna Med. Group Calif., L.A., 1974—; rsch. asst. Sloan-Kettering Inst. Meml. Hosp. for Cancer and Allied Diseases, 1963, chief biology group, Epidemiology sect., 1965, clin. attending, admitting and diagnostic svc., 1971-72; clin. fellow in medicine Cornell U. Med. Coll., 1969-72; asst. prof. UCLA Sch. of Medicine, 1973-74, asst. clin. prof., 1974-81, assoc. clin. prof., 1981-90, clin. prof., 1990—; Cigna (Ross Loos) INA plans, numerous coms., 1972-94 including chmn. Instn. Rev. Bd., 1990, Health Care Assessment Com., 1981-84; vice chair med. quality rev. com. Med. Bd. Calif., 1986-93. Contbr. articles to profl. jours., chpts. to books, abstracts and exhibits to profl. confs.; invited speaker nat. meetings. Bd. dirs. L.A. chpt. Am. Diabetes Assn., chmn. profl. edn. com., 1992—, exec. com. bd. dirs., rsch. and edn. com. Calif. affiliate. Fellow ACP, Am. Coll. Med. Quality (adv. ethics and policy com. Calif. chpt. 1991); mem. Am. Coll. Nuclear Medicine, Am. Assn. Clin. Endocrinology, The Endocrine Soc., L.A. County Med. Soc. (com. on patient and physician advocacy 1991—, med. staff affairs 1991-93, membership retention 1992-93), Soc. Nuclear Medicine, Calif. Med. Assn. (med. staff survey com. 1991), Thyroid Found. Am., Human Growth Found., L.A. Clin. Endocrine Rsch. Group (bd. dirs. 1983-86), Crosstown Endocrine Club, Assn. Mil. Surgeons U.S., Phi Delta Epsilon. Home: 310 16th St Santa Monica CA 90402-2218 Office: Cigna Healthplans Calif 1711 W Temple St Los Angeles CA 90026-5446

GEHB, MICHAEL, public relations executive. CFO Copithorne & Bellows, San Francisco. Office: Copithorne & Bellows 131 Steuart St # 220 San Francisco CA 94105

GEHRES, ELEANOR AGNEW MOUNT, librarian; b. Riverside, N.J., Feb. 18, 1932; d. Wilton Elbert and Mary Anna (Agnew) Mount; m. E. James Gehres, July 23, 1960. BA in English, U. Va., 1952; MA in Librarianship, U. Denver, 1968, MA in History, 1972, Cert. of Mgmt.-Bus., 1982. Elem. tchr. Norfolk County Schs., Churchland, Va., 1952-59; jr. high tchr. Sch. Dist. #11, Colorado Springs, Colo., 1959-61; librarian Sch. Dist. 1, Denver, 1961-71; asst. prof. U. Denver, 1971-73; grants coord. Colo. State Libr., Denver, 1973-74; mgr. western history/genealogy dept. Western History Dept., Denver Pub. Libr., 1974—; instr. Metro. State Coll., Denver, 1975—; bd. dirs. Colo. Hist. Records Adv. Bd., Denver, 1976—, Telecom. Bd., 1992—; hist. cons. videos: Denver: Emergence of a Great City, 1984, Colorado's Black Settlements, 1978. Author printed guide: Denver Urban Environmental Studies, 1971; co-editor: The Colorado Book, 1993; host cable TV show: Conversations, 1985—. Mem. ALA, Western History Assn., Soc. of Rocky Mountain Archivists, Colo. Libr. Assn., Colo. Corral of Westerners (sheriff 1984), Colo. History Group (pres.), Bus. and Profl. Women's Club (v.p. 1987-88), Colo. Women's Hall of Fame (bd. dirs. 1989—), Colo. Preservation Alliance (pres. 1990-93), Colo. Mt. Club, Denver Fortnightly Club, Denver Posse of Westerners, Sierra Club, Colonial Willamsburg. Home: 935 Pennsylvania St Denver CO 80203-3145 Office: Denver Pub Libr 10 W 14th Ave Pkwy Denver CO 80204

GEHRES, JAMES, lawyer; b. Akron, Ohio, July 19, 1932; s. Edwin Jacob and Cleora Mary (Yoakam) G.; m. Eleanor Agnew Mount, July 23, 1960. B.S. in Acctg., U. Utah, 1954; M.B.A., U. Calif.-Berkeley, 1959; J.D., U. Denver, 1970, LL.M. in Taxation, 1977. Bar: Colo. 1970, U.S. Dist. Ct. Colo. 1970, U.S. Tax Ct. 1970, U.S. Supreme Ct. 1973, U.S. Ct. Appeals (10th cir.) 1978, U.S. Ct. Claims 1992. Atty. IRS, Denver, 1965-80, atty. chief counsel's office, 1980—. Served with USAF, 1955-58, capt. Res. ret. Mem. ABA, Colo. Bar Assn., Am. Inst. C.P.A.s, Colo. Soc. C.P.A.s, Am. Assn. Atty.-C.P.A.s, Am. Judicature Soc., Am. Acctg. Assn., Order St. Ives, The Explorers Club, Am. Alpine Club, Beta Gamma Sigma, Beta Alpha Psi. Democrat. Contbr. articles to profl. jours. Office: 935 Pennsylvania St Denver CO 80203-3145

GEHRING, GEORGE JOSEPH, JR., dentist; b. Kenosha, Wis., May 24, 1931; s. George J. and Lucille (Martin) G.; m. Ann D. Carrigan, Aug. 2, 1982; children: Michael, Scott. DDS, Marquette U., 1955. Pvt. practice dentistry, Long Beach, Calif., 1958—. Author: The Happy Flosser. Chmn. bd. Long Beach affiliate Calif. Heart Assn.; mem. Long Beach Grand Prix com. of 300; ind. candidate for pres. of the U.S., 1988, 92. Served with USNR, 1955-58. Fellow Internat. Coll. of Denists, Am. Coll. Dentists; mem. Harbor Dental Soc. (dir.), Pierre Fauchard Acad., Delta Sigma Delta. Club: Rotary. Home: 1230 E Ocean Blvd Unit 603 Long Beach CA 90802-6908 Office: 532 E 29th St Long Beach CA 90806-1617

GEHRKE, ROBERT JAMES, physicist; b. Chgo., Nov. 20, 1940; s.Wilhelm August and Gertrude Mary (Kraemer) G.; m. Mary Louise Irwin, Oct. 12, 1963; children: Marie Therese, Julie Christine, Karen Maureen. BS, DePaul U., Chgo., 1962; MS, U. Nev., Reno, 1966. Physicist Phillips Petroleum Co., Idaho Falls, Idaho, 1965-66; sr. physicist Idaho Nuclear Corp., Idaho Falls, 1966-71; assoc. scientist Aerojet Nuclear Corp., Idaho Falls, 1971-76; sci. specialist EG&G Idaho Inc., Idaho Falls, 1976-85, unit mgr., 1985-91, sci. specialist, 1991-94; sci. specialist Lockheed Martin Idaho Techs. Co., Idaho Falls, 1994—; instr. U. Idaho Ext., Idaho Falls, 1977—; project leader Am. Nat. Stds. Inst.; IAEA expert assignment to Korea Rsch. Inst. of Standards and Science Republic of Korea, 1992. Editorial rev. bd. Radioactivity and Radiochemistry Jour., 1990—; reviewer Analytical Chemistry, 1990, Jour. of Applied Radiation and Isotopes, 1988—; contbr. articles to profl. jours. Pres. Bonneville Assn. for Retarded Citizens, Idaho Falls, 1969-70, Idaho Assn. for Retarded Citizens, Boise, 1970-71. Named Disting. Alumnus, U. Nev.-Reno, 1977; recipient UR & D 100 award "Pins Chem. Assay System", 1992. Mem. Am. Nuclear Soc. (sec. environ. scis. divsn. 1990-93, treas. 1993—, newsletter editor 1990-93, treas. isotope and radiation divsn. 1993-94, chair 1994, vice chair/chair elect 1994-95, nuclear data chmn. 1989-92, chmn. ANS-41 Stds. Subcom. on Environ. Remediation of Radioactively Contaminated Sites 1992—), Am. Chem. Soc., Health Physics Soc., Am. Nat. Stds. Inst. Roman Catholic. Office: Lockheed Martin Idaho Techs PO Box 1625 Idaho Falls ID 83415-0001

GEIDUSCHEK, JEREMY MARK, pediatric anesthesiologist; b. Ann Arbor, Mich., Jan. 8, 1958; s. E. Peter and Joyce Barbara (Brous) G.; m. Susan Elaine Thompson, Mar. 26, 1988; children: A. Max, Emma Kate. BS in Biology, Stanford U., 1979; MD, Vanderbilt U., 1983. Diplomate Nat. Bd. Med. Examiners, Am. Bd. Pediatrics, Am. Bd. Anesthesiology. Resident in pediatrics U. Wash., Seattle, 1983-86, resident in anesthesiology, 1986-88, acting asst. prof., dept. of anesthesiology, 1989-92, asst. prof., 1992—; fellow, pediatric anesthesiology Children's Hosp. & Med. Ctr., Seattle, 1988-89, attending physician dept. anesthesia and critical care, 1989—. Contbr. articles to profl. jours.; author: chpt. in books: Risk and Outcome in Anesthesia, Pediatric Anesthesia, 1992, 2d edit. 1994. Mem. Am. Soc. Anesthesiologists, Wash. State Soc. Anesthesiologists, Soc. for Pediatric Anesthesiology, Am. Acad. Pediatrics, Wash. State Med. Soc. Office: Childrens Hosp & Med Ctr 4800 Sand Point Way NE Seattle WA 98105-3901

GEIGER, RICHARD GEORGE, librarian; b. Los Angeles, Sept. 13, 1946; s. George L. and Thelma E. (Klots) G.; m. Susan L. Woods, Dec. 20, 1974; 1

child, Brendan. BA in Biology, U. Calif., Santa Barbara, 1970; BA in Art, U. Calif., 1970; M in Library and Info. Sci., UCLA, 1975. Circulation supr. art library UCLA, 1971-73, photographer/cataloger slide library, 1973-74; librarian Nat. Maritime Mus., San Francisco, 1975-76; librarian San Francisco Chronicle, 1976-80, library dir., 1984—; library mgr. San Jose Mercury News, San Jose, Calif., 1980-84. Mem. Spl. Librs. Assn. (treas. news div. 1985-87, chmn. 1988-89, pres. San Francisco Bay Region chpt. 1990-91, bd. dirs. 1993—), ALA, Blue Water Cruising Club, Spinnaker Yacht Club, Assocs. of the Nat. Maritime Mus. Libr. (pres. 1989-92). Office: San Francisco Chronicle 901 Mission St San Francisco CA 94103-2905

GEIHS, FREDERICK SIEGFRIED, lawyer; b. Omaha, Nebr., Oct. 16, 1935; s. Friederich Siegfried Sr. and Dorothy Pauline (Getzschman) G.; m. Janelle J. Jeffrey, Oct. 22, 1966; children: Jeffrey J., Danielle Desiree. BS in Bus. Adminstrn., U. Nebr., Omaha, 1957; JD, Creighton U., 1962. Bar: Nebr. 1962, U.S. Dist. Ct. Nebr. 1962, U.S. Supreme Ct. 1965, Mich. 1975, Minn. 1978, U.S. Ct. Appeals (9th cir.) 1980, Nev. 1981, U.S. Dist. Ct. Nev. 1981. Atty. City Omaha (Nebr.) Law Dept., 1962-65; pvt. practice law Omaha, 1965-71, Edina, Minn., 1978-80; asst. gen., atty. Upland Industries, Omaha, 1971-75; corp. counsel Detroit and No. Savs. and Loan, Houghton, Mich., 1975-77, Knutson Cos., Inc., Mpls., 1977-78; mng. atty. Legal Assistance N.D., Bismark, 1980; dir. litigation Clark County Legal Svcs., Las Vegas, 1980-82; atty. Bell & Young, Las Vegas, 1982-83, Harding & Dawson, Las Vegas; of counsel Hilbrecht & Assocs., Las Vegas; prin. Law Offices of Frederick Siegfried Geihs, 1991—. Sec. Young Reps., Omaha, 1965-66; treas. Forgotten Ams., Omaha, 1968-70. Mem. ABA, Minn. State Bar Assn., Nebr. State Bar Assn., Nev. Trial Lawyers Assn., Assn. Trial Lawyers Am., Western State Trial Lawyers Assn., Theta Chi, Phi Alpha Delta. Lutheran. Office: 3376 S Eastern Ave Ste 148 Las Vegas NV 89109-3367

GEIKEN, ALAN RICHARD, contractor; b. Toledo, Aug. 24, 1923; s. Martin Herman and Herta Regina G.; B.S. in Engring., Iowa State U., 1950. Engr., sec. Hot Spot Detector, Inc., Des Moines, 1950-53, sales engr., asst. gen. mgr., 1953-60; pres., owner Alan Geiken Inc., Sacramento, 1960—; cons. on grain storage. Served with USAAF, 1943-45. Mem. Am. Soc. Agrl. Engrs., Council for Agrl. Sci. and Tech., Calif. Warehousemens Assn., Calif. Grain and Feed Assn., Grain Elevator and Processing Soc. Clubs: Sacramento Engrs., Sacramento 50/50 (bd. dirs.). Lutheran. Developed electronic system to maintain healthful condition of stored grain and bulk foods. Address: PO Box 214505 Sacramento CA 95821-0505

GEIS, JOHN RICHARD, plastic surgeon; b. Denver, Mar. 18, 1929; s. Eugene Edward and Patricia Lillian (McGowan) G.; m. Joyclyn Jamie Geis; 1 child, Paula Marie Long. BA, UCLA, 1951; MS, U. Denver, 1952; MD, Northwestern U., Chgo., 1956. Diplomate Am. Bd. Plastic Surgery. Asst. prof. surgery U. Calif., San Francisco, 1984—; med. cons. Med. Bd. of Calif., Fresno, 1994-95. Capt. USAF, 1958-60. Fellow ACS; mem. Am. Soc. Plastic and Reconstructive Surgery.

GEISEL, HENRY JULES, lawyer; b. Cin., Oct. 3, 1947; s. Albert and Else Geisel; m. Ellyn Anne Levy, Sept. 1, 1975; children: Noah L., Gideon L. BS in Econs., U. Pa., 1969; JD, U. Cin., 1972. Bar: Colo. 1972, U.S. Dist. Ct. Colo. 1972. Dep. dist. atty. 20th Jud. Dist., Boulder, Colo., 1973-74, 10th Jud. Dist., Pueblo, Colo., 1974-76; assoc. John R. Naylor, Pueblo, 1976-82, Naylor & Geisel P.C., Pueblo, 1982—. Pres. Temple Emanuel, Pueblo, 1981-82, 85-88; bd. dirs. Pueblo Youth Svcs. Bur., 1978-93, sec., 1989-93; bd. dirs. Pueblo Intensive Phonics Literacy Ctr., Inc., Parkview Hosp. Found., Pueblo, 1986-93, chmn., 1988. Mem. ABA, Colo. Bar Assn., Pueblo County Bar Assn., Colo. Trial Lawyers Assn. Clubs: Pueblo Country. Office: Naylor & Geisel PC PO Box 1421 1123 N Elizabeth St Pueblo CO 81002

GEISERT, OTTO, food products executive; b. 1928. Various positions Balcom & Moe Inc., Pasco, Wash., 1958—, now pres. Office: Balcom & Moe Inc 115 W Margaret St Pasco WA 99301-3700*

GEISSERT, KATY, mayor; b. Wash., 1926; m. Bill Geissert; children: Bill Jr., Jack, Holly, Doug, Ann. BA in Journalism, Stanford U., 1948. Mem. Torrance (Calif.) City Council, 1974-86; mayor City of Torrance, 1986—; mem. Gov.'s Infrastructure Rev. Task Force, Calif. Past chmn. Torrance Park & Recreation Commn.; past mem. fin. adv. com. Torrance Sch.; past chmn. adv. bd. Calif. State U., Dominguez Hills, Torrance Salvation Army; mem. bond steering com. Torrance Library, 1967; chmn. local park bond issue steering com., 1971, Los Angeles County Sanitation Dist. Bd.; community cons. South Bay Harbor Vol. Bur.; mem. adv. bd. Torrance YWCA; bd. dirs. Switzer Ctr., region III United Way, Torrance LWV; mem. city selection com. Los Angeles County. Recipient PTA Hon. Service award, Woman of Distinction award Soroptimists, Community Service award Riviera Homeowners Assn., spl. citation Nat. Recreation & Park Assn.; named Disting. Citizen of Yr. Torrance Area C. of C., 1973, Woman of Yr. YWCA, Woman of Achievement award Redondo Marina Bus. & Profl. Women's Club. Mem. U.S. Conf. Mayors, League Calif. Cities (del., cities transp. com.), Calif. Elected Women's Assn. (bd. dirs.). Office: City of Torrance Office of Mayor 3031 Torrance Blvd Torrance CA 90503-5015

GEIST, HOWARD J., orthopedic surgeon; b. Madison, Wis., Aug. 13, 1929; s. Frederick D. and Alice M. (Stewart) G.; m. Sally R. Haase, Dec. 21, 1956; children: Dennis, Alan, Richard, Gary. BA, Dartmouth Coll., 1952; MD, Harvard U., 1955. Intern, asst. resident in surgery Barnes Hosp., St. Louis, 1955-57; resident in orthopedic surgery U. Hosps. Cleve., 1960-63; pvt. practice, Portland, Oreg., 1964—. Capt. M.C., USAF, 1957-60. Fellow Am. Acad. Orthopedic Surgeons. Home and Office: 1425 SW Upland Dr Portland OR 97221-2648

GEIST, KARIN RUTH TAMMEUS MCPHAIL, secondary education educator, realtor, musician; b. Urbana, Ill., Nov. 23, 1938; d. Wilber Harold and Bertha Amanda Sofia (Helander) Tammeus; m. David Pendleton McPhail, Sept. 7, 1958 (div. 1972); children: Julia Elizabeth, Mark Andrew; m. John Charles Geist, June 4, 1989. BS, Juilliard Sch. Music, 1962; postgrad., Stanford U., 1983-84, L'Academia, Florence and Pistoia, Italy, 1984-85, Calif. State U., 1986-87, U. Calif., Berkeley, 1991, 92. Cert. tchr., Calif.; lic. real estate agt., Calif. Tchr. Woodstock Sch., Musoorie, India, 1957, Canadian, Tex., 1962-66; tchr. Head Royce Sch., Oakland, Calif., 1975-79, 87—, Sleepy Hollow Sch., Orinda, Calif., 1985—; realtor Freeholders, Berkeley, Calif., 1971-85, Northbrae, Berkeley, Calif., 1985-92, Templeton Co., Berkeley, 1992—; organist Kellogg Meml., Musoorie, 1956-57, Mills Coll. Chapel, Oakland, 1972—; cashier Trinity U., San Antonio, 1957-58; cen. records sec. Riverside Ch., N.Y.C., 1958-60; sec. Dr. Rollo May, N.Y.C., 1959-62, United Presbyn. Nat. Missions, N.Y.C., 1960, United Presbyn. Ecumenical Mission, N.Y.C., 1961, Nat. Coun. Chs., N.Y.C., 1962; choral dir. First Presbyn. Ch., Canadian, Tex., 1962-66; assoc. in music Montclair Presbyn. Ch., Oakland, 1972-88; site coord., artist, collaborator Calif. Arts Coun. Artist; cons. music edn. videos and CD Roms Clearvue EAV, Chgo., 1993—. Artist: produced and performed major choral and orchestral works, 1972-88; prodr. Paradiso, Kronos Quartet, 1985, Magdalena, 1991, 92, Children's Quest, 1993—. Grantee Orinda Union Sch. Dist., 1988. Mem. Berkeley Bd. Realtors, East Bay Regional Multiple Listing Svc., Calif. Tchrs. Assn., Commonwealth Club (San Francisco). Democrat. Home: 7360 Claremont Ave Berkeley CA 94705-1429 Office: Templeton Co 3070 Claremont Ave Berkeley CA 94705-2630

GELBER, DON JEFFREY, lawyer; b. L.A., Mar. 10, 1940; s. Oscar and Betty Sheila (Chernitsky) G.; m. Jessica Jeasun Song, May 15, 1967; children: Victoria, Jonathan, Rebecca, Robert. Student UCLA, 1957-58, Reed Coll., 1958-59; AB, Stanford U., 1961, JD, 1963. Bar: Calif. 1964, Hawaii 1964, U.S. Dist. Ct. (cen. and no. dists. Calif.) 1964, U.S. Dist. Ct. Hawaii 1964, U.S. Ct. Appeals (9th cir.) 1964, U.S. Supreme Ct. 1991. Assoc. Greenstein, Yamane & Cowan, Honolulu, 1964-67; reporter Penal Law Revision Project, Hawaii Jud. Council, Honolulu, 1967-69; assoc. H. William Burgess, Honolulu, 1969-72; ptnr. Burgess & Gelber, Honolulu, 1972-73; prin. Law Offices of Don Jeffrey Gelber, Honolulu, 1974-77; pres. Gelber & Wagner, Honolulu, 1978-83, Gelber & Gelber, Honolulu, 1984-89, Gelber, Gelber, Ingersoll & Klevansky, Honolulu, 1990—; legal counsel Hawaii State Senate Judiciary Com., 1965; adminstrv. asst. to majority floor leader Hawaii State Senate, 1966, legal csl. Edn. Com., 1967, 68; majority counsel Hawaii Ho. of Reps., 1974; spl. counsel Hawaii State Senate, 1983. Contbr. articles to legal publs. Mem. State Bar Calif., ABA (sect. bus. law), Am. Bankruptcy Inst., Hawaii State Bar Assn. (sect. bankruptcy law, bd. dirs. 1991-93, pres. 1993). Clubs: Pacific, Plaza (Honolulu). Office: Gelber Gelber Ingersoll & Klevansky 745 Fort Street Mall Ste 1400 Honolulu HI 96813-3812

GELFAND, ERWIN WILLIAM, immunologist; b. Montreal, Quebec, Can., Mar. 10, 1941; s. Samuel and Sylvia (Nadler) G.; m. Adele Zilbert, June 22, 1967; children: Lauren, Allison. BS, McGill U., Montreal, Quebec, Can., 1962, MD, 1966. Diplomate Am. Bd. Pediatrics. Rotating intern Montreal Gen. Hosp., 1966-67; jr. asst. resident Montreal Children's Hosp., 1967-68; sr. resident Children's Hosp. Med. Ctr., Boston, 1968-69; head divsn. immunology, rheumatology Hosp. for Sick Children, Toronto, Quebec, Can., 1979-87; chmn. Nat. Jewish Ctr. for Immunology and Respiratory Medicine, Denver, 1987—. Contbr. over 400 articles to profl. jours.; mem. editorial bd. various sci. jours. Recipient Johnson award in Pediatrics, 1981; named McLaughlin Found. prof. Can. Royal Coll., 1986-87, scholar Raymond & Beverly Sackler Found., 1988-92. Fellow Royal Coll. Physicians and Surgeons. Office: Nat Jewish Ctr Immunology and Respiratory Medicine 1400 Jackson St Denver CO 80206

GELHAUS, ROBERT JOSEPH, lawyer, publisher; b. Missoula, Mont., Oct. 17, 1941; s. Francis Joseph and Bonnie Una (Mundhenk) G. A.B. magna cum laude, Harvard Coll., 1963; LL.B., Stanford U., 1968. Bar: Calif. 1970, U.S. Dist. Ct., U.S. Ct. Appeals 1970. Assoc. firm Howard, Prim, Rice, Nemerovski, Canady & Pollak, San Francisco, 1970-74; sole practice, San Francisco, 1974—; editor in chief Harcourt Brace Jovanovich Legal & Profl. Publs., Inc., 1974-78; gen. ptnr. Flolex Publs., 1973—; pres. Horizon Publs. San Francisco, Inc., 1976—; instr. econs. U. Wash., 1964-65; instr. law Stanford Law Sch., 1968-69; cons. FCC, 1968-69; asst. Calif. Law Revision Commn., 1967-68. Mem. Calif. Bar Assn., Omicron Delta Epsilon, Order Coif. Club: Harvard of San Francisco. Author: (with James C. Oldham) Summary of Labor Law, 11th edit., 1972. Home: 1756 Broadway St San Francisco CA 94109-2423

GELISH, ANTHONY, air force officer; b. Peoria, Ill., May 11, 1950; s. John Anthony Gelish and LaVada (Hersemann) Fron; m. Carol Louise Zielinski, Oct. 25, 1975 (div. June 1983); m. Linda Cheryl Wright, Apr. 24, 1985. BBA, Loyola U., Chgo., 1972; MS in Systems Mgmt., U. So. Calif., L.A., 1982. Cert. profl. logistician; diplomate Am. Coll. Healthcare Execs. Comd. 2d lt. USAF, 1972, advanced through grades to lt. col., 1992; editor JET Gazette Mil. Newspaper 82d Flying Tng. Wing, Williams Air Force Base, Ariz., 1972-76; adminstr. med. materiel and svcs. mgmt. USAF Hosp., Castle Air Force Base, Calif., 1976-80; dir. med. logistics mgmt. USAF Hosp., Pease Air Force Base, N.H., 1980-82; master instr. health svcs. adminstrn. USAF Sch. Health Care Scis., Sheppard Air Force Base, Tex., 1982-85; capital med. equipment program mgr. Office of the USAF Surgeon Gen., Brooks Air Force Base, Tex., 1986-90; chief med. contracting policy and ops. br. Office of the USAF Surgeon Gen., Brooks AFB, Tex., 1990-91; chief med. logistics mgmt. Hdqs. Pacific Air Forces, Hickam AFB, Hawaii, 1991-94, chief tech. mgmt. and integration, 1994-95; project officer Pacific Med. Network, 1995—; cons. med. digital imaging, USAF Surgeon Gen.'s Office, Bolling Air Force Base, Washington, 1985—, lectr. med. facilities mgmt., Brooks Air Force Base, Tex., 1983-95, lectr. med. capital equipment acquisition, Brooks Air Force Base, 1985-95, lectr. med. digital imaging, Bolling Air Force Base, Washington, 1985—. Mem. Consumer's Union, Mt. Vernon, N.Y., 1976—, Handgun Control Inc., Washington, 1985—. Decorated Meritorious Svc. medal, Air Force Commendation medal, Air Force Achievement medal, Air Force Good Conduct medal. Mem. Am. Coll. Healthcare Execs., Soc. Logistics Engrs., Air Force Assn. (life), Air Force Sgts. Assn. (life), Assn. Mil. Surgeons of U.S., Am. Hosp. Assn., Am. Soc. Hosp. Engring., Assn. for the Advancement of Med. Instrumentation, Soc. Photo-optical Instrumentation Engrs., Nat. Assn. Watch and Clock Collectors. Home: 91-1480 Kai'ele'ele St Ewa Beach HI 96706-4613 Office: MCHK-G 1 Jarrett White Rd Tripler Army Medical Center HI 96859

GELLMAN, GLORIA GAE SEEBURGER SCHICK, marketing professional; b. La Grange, Ill., Oct. 5, 1947; d. Robert Fred and Gloria Virginia (McQuiston) Seeburger; m. Peter Slate Schick, Sept. 25, 1978 (dec. 1980); 2 children; m. Irwin Frederick, Gellman, Sept. 9, 1989; 3 children. BA magna cum laude, Purdue U., 1969; student, Lee Strasberg Actors Studio; postgrad., UCLA, U. Calif.-Irvine. Mem. mktg. staff Seemac, Inc. (formerly R.F. Seeburger Co.); v.p. V.I.P. Properties, Inc., Newport Beach, Calif. Profl. actress, singer; television and radio talk show hostess, Indpls., late 1960s; performer radio and television commls., 1960s—. Mem. Orange County Philharm. Soc., bd. dirs. womens com.; mem. Orange County Master Chorale, Orange County Performing Arts Ctr., v.p., treas. Crescendo chpt. OCPAC Ctr. Stars, 1st v.p. membership; bd. dirs. Newport Harbor (Calif.) Art Mus., v.p. membership, mem. acquisition coun.; bd. dirs., mem. founders soc. Opera Pacific, mem. exec. com. bd. dirs.; patron Big Bros./Big Sisters Starlight Found.; mem. Visionaries Newport Harbor Mus., Designing Women of Art Inst. Soc. Calif.; pres. Opera Pacific Guild Alliance; immediate past pres. Spyglass Hill Philharm. Com.; v.p. Pacific Symphony Orch. League; mem. U. Calif. Irvine Found. Bd., mem. devel. com., pub. affairs and advocacy com.; chmn. numerous small and large fundraisers. Recipient Lauds and Laurels award U. Calif., Irvine, 1994, Gellman Courtyard Sculpture honoring contbn. to Sch. of Humanities, U. Calif., Irvine. Mem. AAUW, AFTRA, SAG, Internat. Platform Assn., Actors Equity, U. Calif.-Irvine Chancellor's Club, U. Calif.-Irvine Humanities Assocs. (founder, pres., bd. dirs.), Mensa, Orange County Mental Health Assn., Balboa Bay Club, U. Club, Club 39, Islanders, Covergirls, Alpha Lambda Delta, Delta Rho Kappa. Republican. Home: PO Box 1993 Newport Beach CA 92659-0993

GELL-MANN, MURRAY, theoretical physicist, educator; b. N.Y.C., Sept. 15, 1929; s. Arthur and Pauline (Reichstein) Gell-M.; m. J. Margaret Dow, Apr. 19, 1955 (dec. 1981); children: Elizabeth, Nicholas; m. Marcia Southwick, June 20, 1992; 1 stepson, Nicholas Levis. BS, Yale U., 1948; PhD, Mass. Inst. Tech., 1951; ScD (hon.), Yale U., 1959, U. Chgo., 1967, U. Ill., 1968, Wesleyan U., 1968, U. Turin, Italy, 1969, U. Utah, 1970, Columbia U., 1977, Cambridge U., 1980; D (hon.), Oxford (Eng.) U., 1992. Mem. Inst. for Advanced Study, 1951, 55, 67-68; instr. U. Chgo., 1952-53, asst. prof., 1953-54, assoc. prof., 1954; assoc. prof. Calif. Inst. Tech., Pasadena, 1955-56; prof. Calif. Inst. Tech., 1956-93, now R.A. Millikan prof. physics; vis. prof. MIT, spring 1963, CERN, Geneva, 1971-72, 79-80; dir. physics Santa Fe Inst., 1993—; Mem. Pres.'s Sci. Adv. Com., 1969-72; mem. sci. and grants com. Leakey Found., 1977—; chmn. bd. trustees Aspen Ctr. for Physics, 1973-79; founding trustee Santa Fe Inst., 1982, chmn. bd. trustees, 1982-85, co-chmn. sci. bd. 1985—. Author: (with Y. Ne'eman) Eightfold Way. Citizen regent Smithsonian Instn., 1974—; bd. dirs. J.D. and C.T. MacArthur Found., 1979—. NSF post doctoral fellow, vis. prof. Coll. de France and U. Paris, 1959-60; recipient Dannie Heineman prize Am. Phys. Soc., 1959; E.O. Lawrence Meml. award AEC, 1966; Overseas fellow Churchill Coll., Cambridge, Eng., 1966; Franklin medal, 1967; Carty medal Nat. Acad. Scis., 1968; Research Corp. award, 1969; named to UN Environ. Program Roll of Honor for Environ. Achievement, 1988; Nobel prize in physics, 1969. Fellow Am. Phys. Soc.; mem. NAS, Royal Soc. (fgn.), Am. Acad. Arts and Scis. (v.p., chmn. Western ctr. 1970-76), Council on Fgn. Relations, French Phys. Soc. (hon.). Clubs: Cosmos (Washington); Century Assn., Explorers (N.Y.C.); Athenaeum (Pasadena). Office: Santa Fe Inst 1660 Old Pecos Trail Santa Fe NM 87505*

GELMAN, MARCELLA TAYLOR, dietitian; b. Adel, Ga., Mar. 6, 1957; d. Emmitt Archie and Ozella (Kirkland) Taylor; m. Richard Morris Gelman, Feb. 28, 1988. BS, U. Ga., 1982; MS, Okla. State U., 1984. Storeroom mgr. food and nutrition dept. U. Ga., Athens, 1981-82; grad. tchg. asst. Okla. State U., Stillwater, 1983-84; adminstrv. dietitian Okla. Tchg. Hosps., Oklahoma City, 1984-86; vendor rels. specialist Okla. Women, Infants & Children Program, Oklahoma City, 1986-88; quality assurance consumer coord. Vons Cos., Inc., L.A., 1989-90, supr. consumer affairs, 1990—. With U.S. Army, 1975-78; maj. USAR, 1978—. Recipient Women of Achievement award San Gabriel Valley YWCA, 1991, Merit award County of L.A., 1991, Philip A. Connelly award for excellence in Army food svc. 63d Army Res. Command, 129th Evac. Hosp., 1992. Mem. Am. Dietetic Assn. (registered dietitian), Calif. Dietetic Assn. (resource panel on consumer issues 1991-95, dist. coun. 1992-94, San Gabriel Valley Dist. Dietetic Assn. (health fair coord. 1991-92, pres.-elect 1992-93, pres. 1993-94, past pres. 1994—, chmn. nominating com. 1994—), Dietitian in Bus. and Comm., Nutrition Edn. for the Public, Food Mktg. Inst. (consumer affairs coun.). Office: Vons Cos Inc PO Box 3338 Los Angeles CA 90051-1338

GELPI, MICHAEL ANTHONY, entrepreneur; b. Columbus, Ohio, Dec. 28, 1940; s. Andre and Eleanor (Amorose) G. AB, Georgetown U., 1962. Store mgr. Swan Cleaners, Columbus, 1964-65, dist. supr., 1965-68, v.p., 1968-76, exec. v.p., treas., 1976-81, also dir.; v.p. Rainbow Properties, Columbus, 1971-83, pres., 1983-85, chmn. bd., dir. The Neoprobe Corp., Columbus, 1985-89; pres., dir., CEO M.D. Personal Products, Hayward, Calif., 1992-95; bd. dirs. Health Options. Trustee Am. Cancer Soc., 1978-92, crusade chmn., 1979-84, 1st v.p., 1981-84, pres., 1984-85, chmn., 1985-87, trustee Ohio div., 1984-86, state spl. gifts chmn., 1984-86. Mem. City of Columbus AIDS Adv. Coalition, 1987-92, chmn., 1988-92; trustee Players Theatre of Columbus, 1981-88, v.p., 1985-86, pres. 1986-87; trustee German Village Hist. Soc., 1980-81; trustee Cen. Ohio Reading Svc., 1982-88, pres., 1983-85, trustee Town-Franklin Hist. Neighborhood Assn., 1979-85, v.p., 1983-85; chmn. advance gifts Bishops Ann. Appeal, 1981-86; bd. dirs. Human Rights Campaign Fund, 1985-88; trustee Geriatric Svc. Orgn., 1988-92, devel. chair, 1988-92; candidate for Ohio 12th dist. U.S. Congress, 1988, 90. 1st lt. U.S. Army, 1962-64. Roman Catholic. Recipient Vol. of Yr. award Am. Cancer Soc., 1981, Community Svc. award Columbus Dispatch, 1984, Mayor's award for Vol. Svc. to City of Columbus, 1982, 84.

GELWICKS, JUDITH CATHAY, rehabilitation and career counselor; b. Nanking, Republic of China, Nov. 26, 1948; came to U.S., 1949; d. Harold Galt and Helen (Sasse) G.; m. Michael Irwin Oshan, July 15, 1970 (div.); m. Daniel Lloyd Teie, June 10, 1992; children: Jeremiah Oshan, Marnie Oshan. BA, San Francisco State U., 1971, MS, 1976. Cert. rehab. specialist. Supr. Calif. Career Devel. Project, San Jose State U., 1981-82; rehab. counselor Calif. Workers Compensation, 1982—; co-owner Oshan & Oshan & Assocs., 1982-86; owner, adminstr. Judith Gelwicks & Co., 1986—. Profl. rehab. counselor South County Alternatives, 1976-81; founder Battered Women's Shelter, South Santa Clara County. Mem. ACA, Nat. Rehab. Assn., Calif. Assn. of Rehab. Profls., Nat. Assn. of Rehab. Profls. Office: Judith Gelwicks & Co 8339 Church St Gilroy CA 95020-4406

GENDZEL, IVAN BENNETT, psychiatrist, educator; b. N.Y.C., May 14, 1931; s. Irving Meyer and Celia (Handler) G.; m. Rella Eisendorf, June 1953 (dec. Nov. 1954); m. Lolgene Grace Nickel, May 4, 1957; children: Glen Joseph, Amy Grace. BA in Chemistry with distinction, Cornell U., 1952, MD, 1956. Intern in medicine Cornell Med. Ctr.-N.Y. Hosp., N.Y.C., 1956-57, resident in medicine, 1957-58; resident in medicine U. Calif. Med. Ctr., San Francisco, 1958-59; resident in psychiatry Stanford (Calif.) U. Med. Ctr., 1959-60, 62-64, clin. faculty dept. psychiatry and behavioral scis., 1964—, clin. assoc. prof., 1975—; pvt. practice psychiatry Palo Alto, Calif., 1964—; dep. chief psychiatry Stanford Med. Ctr., 1968-70, hosp. med. bd., 1968-70, chmn. credentials com. dept. psychiatry and behavioral scis., 1978-84, concurrent rev. com., 1978-82; staff mem. Stanford U. Hosp., 1964—; profl. adv. bd. Miramonte Mental Health Svcs., 1964-73, chmn., 1970-72. Contbr. articles to profl. jours. Profl. adv. bd. Parents Without Ptnrs., 1964-70; scoutmaster Stanford Area Coun. Boy Scouts Am., 1973-76, staff advanced adult leader tng., 1976-79, course dir., 1979, v.p./Manpower, 1980-82, v.p. ops., 1983-85, coun. pres., nat. coun. rep., 1986-87 (award of merit and Silver Beaver award 1988). With USN, 1960-62. Fellow Am. Group Psychotherapy Assn., Am. Psychiat. Assn.; mem. Mid-Peninsula Psychiat. Soc. (sec. 1969-70, pres. 1978-79), No. Calif. Psychiat. Soc., No. Calif. Group Psychotherapy Soc. (coun. 1978-86, pres. 1980-82), Network Continuing Health Educators (program com. 1985, program com. chmn. 1987). Home: 1019 Harker Ave Palo Alto CA 94301-3419 Office: 900 Welch Rd Palo Alto CA 94304-1805

GENG, HWAI-YU, manufacturing engineer, plant manager; b. Chung-King, People's Republic of China, June 15, 1946; came to U.S., 1971; s. Ruhan Wu and Rubing Geng; m. Li-mei Geng, Mar. 6, 1971; children: Amy, Julie. BS in Indsl. Engring., Chung Yuan U., Chung-li, Taiwan, 1969; MSME, Tenn. Tech. U., 1973; MBA, Ashland U., 1982. Registered engr., Calif. Asst. to plant mgr. Fruehauf Corp., Delphos, Ohio, 1973-84; mgr. indsl. engring. dept. Westinghouse Electric, Sunnyvale, Calif., 1986-93; mgr. new plant constrn. Applied Materials, Santa Clara, Calif., 1993—. Author tech. papers in field; patentee in field. Mem. Inst. Indsl. Engrs. (sr., membership v.p. 1980—), Soc. Mfg. Engrs. (sr.), Inst. Environ. Scis. (sr.). Home: 4182 Coulombe Dr Palo Alto CA 94306-3801

GENGE, KENNETH LYLE, bishop; s. Nelson Simms and Grace Winifred Genge; m. Ruth Louise Bate, 1959; three children. LTh, Emmanuel Coll., Saskatoon, Sask., 1957; BA, U. Sask., Can., 1958; BD, 1959. Parish priest The Anglican Ch. Can., 1959-85, conf. retreat ctr. dir., 1985-88; bishop Diocese of Edmonton, Alta., Can., 1988—. Office: Diocese of Edmonton, 10033 84th Ave, Edmonton, AB Canada T6E 2G6

GENGLER, SUE WONG, health educator; b. Hong Kong, Apr. 6, 1959; came to U.S., 1966; d. Tin Ho and Yuet Kum (Chan) E. BS, UCLA, 1981; MPH, Loma Linda (Calif.) U., 1990; DrPH, Loma Linda U., 1995. Cert. health edn. specialist. Asst. to the dir. Project Asia Campus Crusade for Christ, San Bernardino, Calif., 1982-83, Campus Crusade for Christ-Internat. Pers., San Bernardino, 1983-90; health educator San Bernardino County Pub. Health, 1990-92; community lab. instr., rsch. asst. dept. health promotion and edn. Loma Linda (Calif.) U. Sch. Pub. Health, 1992—. Mem. Minority Health Coalition, San Bernardino, 1990—, Com. for the Culturally Diverse, San Bernardino, 1990—; vol. Am. Cancer Soc.; chair Gt. Am. Smokeout, Inland Empire, 1991; bd. dirs. Family Svcs. Agy., San Bernardino. Named Outstanding Young Woman of Yr., 1983, Hulda Crooke Scholar, Loma Linda U., 1989; recipient Am. Cancer Soc. Rose award, 1991 (Calif.), Gaspar award, 1991 (nat.), Selma Andrews scholarship Loma Linda U., 1994. Mem. APHA, Nat. Coun. for Internat. Health, Soc. Pub. Health Edn., Loma Linda U. Alumni Assn.

GENGOR, VIRGINIA ANDERSON, financial planning executive, educator; b. Lyons, N.Y., May 2, 1927; d. Axel Jennings and Marie Margaret (Mack) Anderson; m. Peter Gengor, Mar. 2, 1952 (dec.); children: Peter Randall, Daniel Neal, Susan Leigh. AB, Wheaton Coll., 1949; MA, U. No. Colo., Greeley, 1975, 77. Chief hosp. intake service County of San Diego, 1966-77, chief Kearny Mesa Dist. Office, 1977-79, chief Dependent Children of Ct., 1979-81, chief child protection services, 1981-82; registered rep. Am. Pacific Securities, San Diego, 1982-85; registered tax preparer State of Calif., 1982—, registered rep. (prin.) Sentra Securities, 1985—; assoc. Pollock & Assocs., San Diego, 1985-86; pres. Gengor Fin. Advisors, 1986—; cons. instr. Nat. Ctr. for Fin. Edn., San Diego, 1986-88; instr. San Diego Community Coll., 1985-88. Mem. allocations panel United Way, San Diego, 1976-79, children's circle Child Abuse Prevention Found., 1989—; chmn. com. Child Abuse Coordinating Council, San Diego, 1979-83; pres. Friends of Casa de la Esperanza, San Diego, 1980-85, bd. dirs., 1980—; 1st v.p. The Big Sister League, San Diego, 1985-86, pres., 1987-89. Mem. NAFE, Inst. Cert. Fin. Planners, Internat. Assn. Fin. Planning, Inland Soc. Tax Cons., AAUW (bd. dirs.), Nat. Assn. Securities Dealers (registered prin.), Nat. Ctr. Fin. Edn., Am. Bus. Women's Assn., Navy League, Freedoms Found. Valley Forge, Internat. Platform Assn. Presbyterian. Avocations: community service, travel, reading. Home: 6462 Spear St San Diego CA 92120-2929 Office: Gengor Fin Advisors 4950 Waring Rd Ste 7 San Diego CA 92120-2700

GENINI, RONALD WALTER, history educator, historian; b. Oakland, Calif., Dec. 5, 1946; s. William Angelo and Irma Lea (Gays) G.; m. Roberta Mae Tucker, Dec. 20, 1969; children: Thomas, Justin, Nicholas. BA, U. San Francisco, 1968, MA, 1969. Cert. secondary edn. tchr., Calif.; adminstrv. svcs. credential. Tchr. Ctrl. Unified Sch. Dist., Fresno, Calif., 1970—; judge State History Day, Sacramento, 1986-94; mem. U.S. history exam. devel. team Golden State, San Diego, 1989-93; securer placement of state-registered landmarks. Author: Romualdo Pacheco, 1985, Darn Right It's Butch, 1994; contbr. articles to profl. jours. Bd. dirs. Fresno Area 6 Neighborhood Coun., 1973-74, Fresno City and County Hist. Soc., 1975-78, St. Anthony's sch. bd., Fresno, 1980-84. Named one of Outstanding Young Educators Am., Fresno Jaycees, 1978. Mem. Calif. Hist. Soc. Libertarian. Home: 1486 W Menlo Ave Fresno CA 93711-1305 Office: Ctrl HS 2045 N Dickenson Ave Fresno CA 93722-9643

GENN, NANCY, artist; b. San Francisco; d. Morley P. and Ruth W. Thompson; m. Vernon Chathburton Genn; children: Cynthia, Sarah, Peter. Student, San Francisco Art Inst., U. Calif., Berkeley. lectr. on art and papermaking Am. Ctrs. in Osaka, Japan, Nagoya, Japan, Kyoto, Japan, 1979-80; guest lectr. various univs. and art mus. in U.S., 1975—; vis. artist Am. Acad. in Rome, 1989, 94. One woman shows of sculpture, paintings include, De Young Mus., San Francisco, 1955, 63, Gumps Gallery, San Francisco, 1955, 57, 59, San Francisco Mus. Art, 1961, U. Calif., Santa Cruz, 1966-68, Richmond (Calif.) Art Center, 1970, Oakland (Calif.) Mus., 1971, Linda/Farris Gallery, Seattle, 1974, 76, 78, 81, Los Angeles Inst. Contemporary Art, 1976, Susan Caldwell Gallery, N.Y.C., 1976, 77, 79, 81, Nina Freudenheim Gallery, Buffalo, 1977, 81, Annely Juda Fine Art, London, 1978, Inoue Gallery, Tokyo, 1980, Toni Birckhead Gallery, Cin., 1982, Kala Inst. Gallery, Berkeley, Calif., 1983, Ivory/Kimpton Gallery, San Francisco, 1984, 86, Eve Mannes Gallery, Atlanta, 1985, Richard Iri Gallery, L.A., 1990, Harcourts Modern and Contemporary Art, San Francisco, 1991, 93, Am. Assn. Advancement of Sci., Washington, 1994, Anne Reed Gallery, Ketchum, Id., 1995; group exhbns. include San Francisco Mus. Art, 1971, Aldrich Mus., Ridgefield, Conn., 1972-73, Santa Barbara (Calif.) Mus., 1974, 75, Oakland (Calif.) Mus. Art, 1975, Susan Caldwell, Inc., N.Y.C., 1974, 75, Mus. Modern Art, N.Y.C., 1976, traveling exhbn. Arts Coun. Gt. Britain, 1983-84, Inst. Contemporary Arts, Boston, 1977; represented in permanent collections Mus. Modern Art, N.Y.C., Albright-Knox Art Gallery, Buffalo, Libr. of Congress, Washington, Nat. Mus. for Am. Art, Washington, L.A. County Mus. Art, Art Mus. U. Calif., Berkeley, McCrory Corp., N.Y.C., Mus. Art, Auckland, N.Z., Aldrich Mus., Ridgefield, Conn., (collection) Bklyn. Mus., (collection) U. Tex., El Paso, Internat. Ctr. Aesthetic Rsch., Torino, Italy, Cin. Art Mus., San Francisco Mus. Modern Art, Oakland Art Mus., L.A. County Mus., City of San Francisco Hall of Justice, Harris Bank, Chgo., Chase Manhattan Bank, N.Y.C., Modern Art Gallery of Ascoli Piceno, Italy, Mills Coll. Art Mus., Oakland, Calif., Mills Coll. of Art, Oakland, Calif., various mfg. cos., also numerous pvt. collections; commd. works include, Bronze lectern and 5 bronze sculptures for chancel table, 1st Unitarian Ch., Berkeley, Calif., 1961, 64, bronze fountain, Cowell Coll., U. Calif., Santa Cruz, bronze menorah, Temple Beth Am, Los Altos Hills, Calif., 1981, 17, murals and 2 bronze fountain sculptures, Sterling Vineyards, Calistoga, Calif., 1972, 73, fountain sculpture, Expo 1974, Spokane, Wash; vis. artist Am. Acad., Rome, 1989. U.S./Japan Creative Arts fellow, 1978-79; recipient Ellen Branston award, 1952; Phelan award De Young Mus., 1963; honor award HUD, 1968. Home: 1515 La Loma Ave Berkeley CA 94708-2033

GENNARO, ANTONIO L., biology educator; b. Raton, N.Mex., Mar. 18, 1934; s. Paul and Mary Lou (Gasperetti) G.; m. Virginia Marie Sullivan, May 15, 1955 (div. 1979); children—Theresa Ann, Carrie Marie, Janelle Elizabeth; m. Marjorie Lou Cox, Sept. 27, 1980. B.S., N.Mex. State U., 1957; M.S., U. N.Mex., 1961, Ph.D., 1965. Tchr. biology Las Cruces High Sch., N.Mex., 1957-58; asst. prof. biology St. John's U., Collegeville, Minn., 1964-65; prof. biology Eastern N.Mex. U., Portales, 1965—. Contbr. articles to sci. jours. Served to capt. U.S. Army, 1958-59; mem. Res., 1959-66. Recipient Presdl. Faculty award Eastern N.Mex. U., 1970, Pres.'s Faculty award for excellence in rsch., 1988; Outstanding Sci. award N.Mex. Acad. Sci., 1975. Mem. Southwestern Naturalists (treas. 1974-78), Am. Soc. Mammalogists, Herpetologists League, Sigma Xi, Phi Kappa Phi (pres. 1970-74). Roman Catholic.

GENRICH, MARK L., newspaper editor; b. Buffalo, Aug. 28, 1943; m. Allison Forbes, 1967; children: Audrey, Liza, Colby. BA, Bucknell U., 1966. Editorial writer Palladium-Item, Richmond, Ind., 1970; writing exec. Bruce Eberle & Assocs., Inc., Vienna, Va., 1975-77; dep. editor editorial pages Phoenix Gazette, 1977—; participant U.S. Army War Coll., Carlisle, Pa., U.S. Naval War Coll., Newport, R.I.; participant arms control, disarmament programs including Space & Arms talks, Geneva; chmn. New Tech. Com., Journalism in Edn. Com.; mem. various coms. Created, hosted cable TV program focus on polit. figures; regional editor The Masthead. Grantee European Cmty. Visitor Programme, 1993; recipient highest honors editl. writing, newspaper design Ariz., Western Region; highest honor Maricopa County Bar Assn.; Stanford U. media fellow, 1985. Mem. Nat. Conf. Editorial Writers (bd. dirs., included vol. Editorial Excellence), First Amendment Cong. (bd. dirs.), Soc. Profl. Journalists/Sigma Delta Chi, ABA (com. prisons, sentencing). Home: 130 W Pine Valley Dr Phoenix AZ 85023-5283 Office: The Phoenix Gazette 120 E Van Buren St Phoenix AZ 85004-2227

GENSLER, M. ARTHUR, JR., architect; b. N.Y.C., July 12, 1935; s. M. Arthur and Gertrude (Wilson) G.; m. Drucilla Cortell, Sept. 7, 1957; children—David, Robert, Kenneth, Douglas. B.A. in Architecture, Cornell U., 1957. Lic. architect, 38 states. Jr. designer Shreve, Lamb & Harmon, N.Y.C., 1958-59; project mgr. Norman & Dawbarn, Kingston, Jamaica, 1959-60, Albert Sigal & Assocs., N.Y.C. and San Francisco, 1961-63, Wurster, Bernardi & Emmons, San Francisco, 1963-65; pres., founder Gensler & Assocs., Architects, San Francisco, 1966—; mem. adv. council, mem. bldgs. and properties com. Coll. Architecture, Cornell U., Ithaca, N.Y., 1981-83. Co-author: A Rational Approach to Office Planning. Bd. dirs. World Coll. West, Petaluma, Calif., 1984-87; bd. overseers U. Calif., San Francisco; trustee World Affairs Coun., 1990—. Wity C.E., U.S. Army, 1958. Recipient Charles Goodwin Sands award Cornell U. Coll. Architecture, 1958; named charter mem. Interior Design mag. Hall of Fame, Cornell Enterpeneurs of Yr., 1995. Fellow AIA, Internat. Interior Design Assn.; mem. Inst. Bus. Designers (Star award 1992), San Francisco Planning and Urban Rsch. Assn., Bldg. Mgrs. and Owners Assn., Bay Area Coun., Urban Land Inst., San Francisco C. of C. (bd. dirs. 1984-86, 94—), Bohemian Club, Univ. Club, Bankers Club, Presidio Club. Republican. Congregationalist.

GENTILE, ANTHONY LEO, association executive, consultant; b. N.Y.C., Apr. 23, 1930; s. Leo and Grace (Leone) G.; m. Bettie Lynn, July 3, 1957; children: David Lynn, Michael Leo. BS in Geology, CCNY, 1950; MS Geol. Sci., N.Mex. Tech. U., 1957; PhD in Mineralogy, Ohio State U., 1960. Mem. tech. staff Hughes Rsch. Labs., Malibu, Calif., 1961-68, sect. head, 1968-86, program mgr., 1986-87, sr. scientist, 1987-89, cons., 1990-91; cons., exec. adminstr. Am. Assn. Crystal Growth, Thousand Oaks, Calif., 1990—. Contbr. chpt. to ency., articles to profl. jours.; patentee in field. 1st lt. USAF, 1951-54. Mem. Am. Assn. Crystal Growth (exec. com. 1977-90, pres. western sect. 1977-81, treas. 1981-84, pres., 1984-87, exec. adminstr. 1990—). Office: Am Assn Crystal Growth PO Box 3233 Thousand Oaks CA 91359-0233

GENTRY, GRANT CLAYBOURNE, food retail company executive; b. Chgo., June 5, 1924; s. Grant Claybourne and Helen C. (Cooley) G.; m. Doris L. Helsten, Sept. 8, 1943; children—Grant, Scott. J.D., DePaul U., 1949. Bar: Ill. 1949. Assoc., McKnight, McLaughton & Dunn, 1949-53; tax atty. Internat. Harvester Co., 1953-57; exec. v.p. Jewel Cos., Chgo., 1957-75, also dir.; pres., chief adminstrn. officer Great Atlantic & Pacific Tea Co., Montvale, N.J., 1975-78, also dir.; ptnr. Adamy, Foley & Gentry, Chgo., 1978-79; chmn., chief exec. officer Pantry Pride, Inc., Ft. Lauderdale, Fla., 1979-86; dir. Borman's Inc. Bd. dirs. Loyola U., Chgo. Served with AUS, 1943-46. Mem. Internat. Assn. Chain Stores (chmn.), Nat. Assn. Food Chains (past chmn.), ABA. Clubs: Blindbrook Country, Park Ridge Country, Big Canyon. Office: Bromar Inc 15 Cormorant Cir Fl 2 Newport Beach CA 92660-2975

GENTRY, JAMES WILLIAM, retired state official; b. Danville, Ill., Aug. 14, 1926; s. Carl Lloyd and Leone (Isham) G.; A.B., Fresno State Coll., 1948; M.J., U. Calif., Berkeley, 1956; m. Dorothie Shirley Hechtlinger, Mar. 18, 1967; 1 stepdau., Susan Mushkin. Field rep. Congressman B.W. Gearhart, Fresno, Calif., 1948, Assemblyman Wm. W. Hansen, Fresno, 1950, sec., 1953-56; exec. asst. Calif. Pharm. Assn., Los Angeles, 1956-69, editor, pub. Calif. Pharmacy Jour., 1956-69; pub. relations dir. PAID Prescriptions, 1963-64; dir. pub. info. comprehensive Health Planning Council, Los Angeles County, 1969; asst. adminstr., dir. pub. info. So. Calif. Comprehensive Health Planning Council, 1969-71, acting adminstr., 1971-72; exec. sec. Calif. State Health Planning Council, 1972-73, Calif. Adv. Health Council, 1973-85, fed. cons., 1986-88; Calif. Health Care Commn., 1973-75; acting public info. officer Calif. Office Statewide Health Planning and Devel., 1978-79; interim dir. Calif. Office Statewide Health Planning and Devel., 1983; mem. L.A. Civil Svc. Police Interview Bd., 1967-72; asst. sgt.-at-arms Calif. State Assembly, 1950; exec. sec. Calif. Assembly Interim Com. on Livestock and Dairies, 1954-56; mem. adv. bd. Am. Security Council; mem. Calif. Health Planning Law Revision Commn.; former mem. Calif. Bldg. Safety Bd. Mem. Fresno County Republican Central Com., 1950; charter mem. Rep. Presdl. Task Force. Served to col. AUS, 1949-50, 50-53; Korea. Decorated Legion of Merit, Bronze Star medal, Commendation Ribbon with metal pendant ; recipient pub. awards Western Soc. Bus. Publns. Assn., 1964-67. Mem. Am. Assn. Comprehensive Health Planning, Pub. Relations Soc. Am., Ret. Officers Assn. (life), Allied Drug Travelers So. Calif., L.A. Press Club, Mil. Police Assn., Res. Officers Assn. (life), Assn. U.S. Army, U.S. Senatorial Club, The Victory Svcs. Club of London, Pi Gamma Mu, Phi Alpha Delta. Sigma Delta Chi. Editor: Better Health, 1963-67; Orientation Conf. Comprehensive Health Planning, 1969; Commentary, 1969-71. Editorial adv. Pharm. Svcs. for Nursing Homes: A Procedural Manual, 1966. Editor: Program and Funding, 1972; Substance Abuse, 1972. Home: 902 Commons Dr Sacramento CA 95825-6647

GENTRY, JEANNE LOUISE, lecturer, writer; b. Portland, Oreg., Sept. 12, 1946; d. Louis Darell and Mary Louise (Lane) G.; m. Gini Mario Martini, June 13, 1965 (div. 1968); children: Deborah Corinna Martina, Darell James Martini; m. David Guy Gorrell, Feb. 19, 1982 (div. 1994). Student, Northwestern Coll. Bus., Portland, 1968, Mt. Hood Community Coll., Gresham, Oreg., 1986. Receptionist, sec. to pres. Met. Printing Co., Portland, 1969-73; adminstrv. asst. Lifespring, Inc., Portland, 1974-77; cons. Jeanne Mort Co., Boring, Oreg., 1978-80; office mgr. Beef Palace Provisioners, Gresham, 1980-82; bus. cons. Boring, 1983-90; owner Good As New Doll Hosp., Boring, 1990-92; adminstrv. projects mgr. Profl. Svc. Industries, Portland, 1992—. Co-compiler: Lebanon Pioneer Cemetery, 1991, rev. edit. 1995. Mem. Geneal. Coun. Orgn. (sec. 1991-94), Nat. Geneal. Soc., Fellowship of Brethren Genealogists, Geneal. Forum of Oreg. (Newsletter staff), Ind. Geneal. Soc. (charter), East Tenn. Hist. Soc., Oreg. Hist. Cemeteries Assn. (pres. 1992—), Pellissippi Geneal. and Hist. Soc., Lebanon Geneal. Soc. Home: 16385 SE 232nd Dr Boring OR 97009-9124

GENTRY, ROGER LEE, research wildlife biologist; b. Bakersfield, Calif., Mar. 19, 1938; s. Roger Howard and Harriette Viola (Childs) G.; children: Melissa Gentry O'Brien, Erin Childs, Alison Neville. BA, Calif. State U., San Francisco, 1962, MA, 1966; PhD, U. Calif., Santa Cruz, 1970. Post-doctoral fellow Mawson Inst. for Antarctic Rsch., U. Adelaide, Australia, 1970-71; rsch. faculty U. Calif., Santa Cruz, 1971-74; rsch. wildlife biologist Nat. Marine Mammal Lab., NOAA, Seattle, 1974—; participant FAO Consultation on Marine Mammals, Bergen, Norway, 1976; mem. U.S. del. to the Standing Sci. Com. for the Interim Conv. on North Pacific Fur Seals, Moscow, 1980, 84, Ottawa, Can., 1982, Washington, 1983; rschr. and presenter in field. Co-author: Fur Seals: Maternal Strategies on Land and at Sea, 1986, The Status, Biology, and Ecology of Fur Seals, 1987; contbr. articles to profl. jours. Petty officer second class USCG, 1958-60. Grantee NASA, 1973-74, Nat. Geog. Soc., 1985-86, 86-87, 90-91. Mem. AAAS, Am. Soc. Mammalogists, Animal Behavior Soc., Soc. for Marine Mammalogy, The Oceanography Soc. Office: NOAA Nat Marine Mammal Lab C15700 7600 Sand Point Way NE # C15700 Seattle WA 98115-6349

GENUNG, SHARON ROSE, pediatrician; b. Williamsport, Pa., Oct. 6, 1951; d. Joseph Patrick and Jeanette (Mossendew) Lynch; m. Norman Bernard Genung, June 9, 1973; children: Jeffrey, Sarah. BS in Microbiology cum laude, Mich. State U., 1973; MS in Clin. Microbiology, U. Ark., 1979, MD, 1984. Lic. physician, Wash., Ark. Clin. resident in pediatrics Wright State U./Children's Med. Ctr., Dayton, Ohio, 1987; dir. pediatrics USAF Hosp. Fairchild, Spokane, Wash., 1987-88, dir. med. svcs., 1988-91; pvt. practice in pediats. Kapstaffer, Maixner & Genung, Spokane, 1991—; instr. in pediatric advanced life support, neonatal resuscitation. Contbr. articles to profl. jours. Maj. USAF M.C., 1980-91. Fellow Am. Acad. Pediatrics; mem. So. Med. Assn., Wash. State Soc. Pediatrics, Spokane Med. Soc., Spokane Pediatric Soc., Spokane Women's Assn. Physicians, Alpha Omega Alpha. Office: Kapstaffer Maixner & Genung 105 W 8th Ave Ste 318 Spokane WA 99204-2318

GEOFFEY, RUTH, director activities, artist; b. Brno, Czechoslovakia, July 2, 1915; came to U.S., 1951; d. Theodor and Else (Moser) Huber; m. Joseph Reiner (dec.). BA in Fine Arts, UCLA, 1968. Fashion designer Berlin, 1935-38; freelance illustrator Shanghai, 1939-40; head art dept. Manila-Am. Sch., 1945-62; freelance artist L.A. and San Francisco, 1968-80; dir. activities and programs Aldersly, 1984—. Mem. Marin Watercolor Sco., AAUW. Jewish. Home: 50 Pikes Peak Dr San Rafael CA 94903-1122

GEOFFRION, MOIRA MARTI, artist, educator; b. Olney, Md., July 11, 1944; d. Fritz and Gertrude (Austin) Marti; m. Charles Geoffrion, 1965; children: Sabrina, Damien. BFA, Boston U., 1965; MFA, So. Ill. U., 1974. From asst. prof. to full prof. art Notre Dame (Ind.) U., 1974-86; prof. and head dept. art U. Ariz., Tucson, 1986-91, sculpture area dir., 1991-96; vis. artist 12 univs. and colls. including U. Colo., Boulder, U. Mont., Missoula, San Jose State U., U. Cin., U. Ind., Bloomington, U. No. Ill., DeKalb. One-woman shows include Rancho Linda Vista Gallery, Oracle, Ariz., Gallery Route One, Calif., Tucson Mus. Art, Zaks Gallery, Chgo., Plieades Gallery, N.Y., 14 Sculptors Gallery, N.Y.; exhibited in group shows at Process Space Festival Traveling Exhbn., Plovdiv, Sophia, Baltchik, Bulgaria, All Around Ariz., NAU Galleries, Am. Artists Invitational, Gallery 10-10, St. Petersburg, Russia 1990, Chgo. Navy Pier Show, others. Exxon Disting. Scholar grant, ICIP/Fulbright grant for rsch., others. Office: Univ Ariz Dept Art Tucson AZ 85721

GEORGE, ALEXANDER ANDREW, lawyer; b. Missoula, Mont., Apr. 26, 1938; s. Andrew Miltiadin and Eleni (Efstathiou) G.; m. Penelope Mitchell, Sept. 29, 1968; children: Andrew A., Stephen A. BBA honors, U. Mont., 1960, JD, 1962; postgrad. John Marshall U., 1964-66. Bar: Mont. 1962, U.S. Ct. Mil. Apls. 1964, U.S. Tax Ct. 1970. Sole practice, Missoula, 1966—; mem. adv. com. U. Mont. Tax Inst., 1973-76; adj. lectr. U. Montana Law Sch. Corp. Taxation. Pres., Missoula Civic Symphony, 1973; nat. dir. Assn. Urban and Community Symphony Orch., 1974, Mont. Eye Endowment Found.; pres. Greek Orthodox Ch., 1978, 91. Served to capt JAG U.S. Army, 1962-66. Recipient Jaycee Disting. Svc. award, 1973. Mem. State Bar Mont. (pres. 1981), Western Mont. Bar Assn. (pres. 1971), Mont. Law Found. (treas. 1986-92), Mont. Soc. C.P.A., Phi Delta Phi, Alpha Kappa Psi, Sigma Nu (alumni trustee 1966-71), Rotary (pres. 1972, state chmn. found. 1977, membership com. chmn. 1978), Ahepa (pres. 1967, state gov. 1968). Home: 4 Greenbrier Ct Missoula MT 59802-3342 Office: 269 W Front St Missoula MT 59802-4301

GEORGE, ALEXANDER LAWRENCE, political scientist, educator; b. Chicago, Ill., May 31, 1920; s. John and Mary (Sargis) G.; m. Juliette Lombard, Apr. 20, 1948; children: Lee Lawrence, Mary Lombard. AM, U. Chgo., 1941, PhD, 1958; DHL (hon.), U. San Diego, 1987; PhD (hon.), U. Lund, Sweden, 1994. Rsch. analyst OSS, 1944-45; dep. chief rsch. br. Info. Control divsn. Office Mil. Govt. for Germany, 1945-48; specialist study of decision-making and internat. rels. RAND Corp., Santa Monica, Calif., 1948-68; head dept. social sci. RAND Corp., Santa Monica, 1961-63; prof. polit. sci. and internat. rels. Stanford (Calif.) U., 1968—; lectr. U. Chgo., 1950, Am. U., 1952-56. Author: (with Juliette L. George) Woodrow Wilson and Colonel House: A Personality Study, 1956, Propaganda Analysis, 1959, The Chinese Communist Army in Action, 1967, (with others) The Limits of Coercive Diplomacy, 1971, (with Richard Smoke) Deterrence in American Foreign Policy: Theory and Practice, 1974 (Bancroft prize for Deterrence in Am. Fgn. Policy 1975), Towards A More Soundly Based Foreign Policy: Making Better Use of Information, 1976, Presidential Decisionmaking in Foreign Policy, 1980, Managing U.S.-Soviet Rivalry, 1983, (with Gordon Craig) Force and Statecraft, 1983, 3rd edit., 1995; editor: (with others) U.S. Soviet Security Cooperation: Achievements, Failures, Lessons, 1988, Avoiding War: Problems of Crisis Management, 1991, Forceful Persuasion, 1992, Bridging the Gap: Theory and Practice of Foreign Policy, 1993, (with William E. Simons) The Limits of Coercive Diplomacy, 2d. edit., 1994. Fellow Ctr. Advanced Study Behavioral Scis., 1956-57, 76-77, NIMH, 1972-73, MacArthur Prize, 1983-88, Disting. fellow U.S. Inst. Peace, 1990-91, 91-92; Founds. Fund for Rsch. in Psychiatry grantee, 1960, NSF rsch. grantee, 1971-73, 75-77. Mem. Am. Acad. Arts and Scis., Coun. on Fgn. Rels., Am. Polit. Sci. Assn., Internat. Studies Assn. (pres. 1973-74), Phi Beta Kappa. Home: 944 Lathrop Pl Stanford CA 94305-1060

GEORGE, CAROL CATHERINE, psychology educator; b. Santa Monica, Calif., Dec. 12, 1952; d. Martin S. and Ruth M. (Letcher) Yez; m. David A. George, Aug. 3, 1974; children: Laurel, Geoffrey. BA, U. So. Calif., 1974; MA, U. Calif., Berkeley, 1978, PhD, 1984. Instr. U. Calif., Berkeley, 1979; rsch. assoc. Child Devel. Project, San Ramon, Calif., 1983-84; assoc. prof. psychology Mills Coll., Oakland, Calif., 1987—. Contbr. articles to profl. jours. Fellow NICHD, 1974-79, Ctr. for Advanced Study of Behavorial Scis., 1990. Mem. AAUP (chpt. pres. 1993—), Soc. for Rsch. in Child Devel., Internat. Assn. Infant Mental Health. Office: Mills Coll Dept Psychology Oakland CA 94613

GEORGE, DONALD WARNER, newspaper editor, writer, lecturer; b. Middlebury, Conn., June 24, 1953; s. Lloyd Foster and Vivian (Minor) G.; m. Kuniko Ninomiya, Apr. 24, 1982; children: Jennifer Ayako, Jeremy Naoki. BA, Princeton U., 1975; MA, Hollins (Va.) Coll., 1977. Tchg. fellow Athens (Greece) Coll., 1975-76, Internat. Christian U., Tokyo, 1977-79; TV talk show host Japan Broadcasting Corp., Tokyo, 1977-79; freelance writer, 1980-81; travel writer San Francisco Examiner, 1981-82, sr. editor Calif. Living mag., 1982-85, sr. editor Image mag., 1985-87, travel editor, 1987—. Recipient gold award Pacific Asia Travel Assn., 1987-94). Mem. Soc. Am. Travel Writers (Lowell Thomas award 1987-94). Office: San Francisco Examiner 110 5th St San Francisco CA 94103-2918

GEORGE, FRANCIS, bishop; b. Chgo., Jan. 16, 1937. Ordained priest Roman Cath. Ch., 1963. Provincial ctrl. region Oblates of Mary Immaculate, 1973-74, vicar gen., 1974-86; bishop Diocese of Yakima, Wash., 1990—. Office: Diocese of Yakima 5301 Tieton Dr Ste A Yakima WA 98908-3479*

GEORGE, KATHRYN PAXTON, bioethics educator, researcher, consultant; b. Northville, Mich., June 12, 1943; d. Robert and Geraldine Elizabeth (Ridley) Paxton; m. Albert Louis George, Sept. 16, 1967 (div. Aug. 1984); children: Kimberly Ann, Elizabeth Francene; m. Ronald James Klimko, July 27, 1985. BA summa cum laude, Wash. State U., Pullman, 1980, MA, 1982, PhD in Genetics/Philosophy, 1985. Rsch. asst. genetics Wash. State U., Pullman, 1983, asst. prof. philosophy and vet. microbiology, 1986-89; asst. prof. philosophy U. Idaho, Moscow, 1983-87, 89-92, assoc. prof., 1992—, chair dept. philosophy, 1994—, chair, 1994—; project ethicist Bioethics Tng. Program, Idaho Health Sys. Agy., 1986-87; mem. NSF oversight group Coll. Engring. and Architecture, Wash. State U., 1990-93; lectr. in field. Contbr. articles to Signs, Biology & Philosophy, Between the Species, Agr. and Human Values, Jour. Agrl. Ethics, Jour. Sustainable Agr., Anthrozoös; bd. editors: Jour. Sustainable Agr., 1990—. Recipient GTE Found. Lectureship award, 1988, 92; NEH summer seminar, 1990; NSF fellow, 1990. Mem. Am. Inst. Biol. Scis., Am. Philos. Assn., Soc. for Agr., Food and Human Values (exec. coun. 1991-92), Athena (pres. 1991-92), Phi Beta Kappa. Democrat. Home: 401 Morrill Hall Moscow ID 83843-2461 Office: U Idaho 401 Morrill Hall Moscow ID 83844-3016

GEORGE, LESLIE EARL, protective services official; b. Eldrado, Okla., July 12, 1930; s. Earl Haskel and Cuba Mae (Huddleston) G.; m. Eleanor Mae Hart, Nov. 20, 1955; children: Leslie Earl Jr., Rickie Dwayne, Jeffery Scott, Gregory Allen. AA, East L.A. Coll., 1966; BA in Mgmt., Redlands U., 1983. Reinforcing iron worker Blue Diamond Corp., L.A., 1949-53; reinforcing ironworker foreman Triangle Steel Co., Vernon, Calif., 1953-54; fire fighter City of El Monte (Calif.) Fire Dept., 1955-56, fire engr., 1956-57, fire capt., 1957-61, adminstrv. capt., 1961-66, fire battalion chief, 1966-91, fire chief, 1991—. Bd. dirs., pres. Boys' Club El Monte, 1993. With U.S. Army, 1951-53. Mem. Calif. Conf. Arson Investigators (life, pub., editor), Rotary (pres., sec., program chmn.). Home: 2627 E Maureen St West Covina CA 91792-2215 Office: 3615 Santa Anita Ave El Monte CA 91731-2428*

GEORGE, LLOYD D., federal judge; b. Montpelier, Idaho, Feb. 22, 1930; s. William Ross and Myrtle (Nield) G.; m. LaPrele Badouin, Aug. 6, 1956; children: Douglas Ralph, Michele, Cherie Suzanne, Stephen Lloyd. BS, Brigham Young U., 1955; JD, U. Calif., Berkeley, 1961. Ptnr. Albright, George, Johnson & Steffen, 1969-71, George, Steffen & Simmons, 1971-74; judge U.S. Bankruptcy Ct. (Nev. dist.), 1974-84, U.S. Dist. Ct. Nev., 1984—, now chief judge; justice of peace Clark County, Nev., 1962-69. Served with USAF, 1955-58. Office: US Dist Ct 300 Las Vegas Blvd S Fl 3 Las Vegas NV 89101-5812*

GEORGE, MARY GAE, music educator; b. Seattle, Wash., May 4, 1930; d. Howard Ruskin and Gwynnyefred A. E. (Craig) Gaetz; m. David Thorp, June 14, 1952 (div. Mar. 1955); 1 child, Jennifer Gae Fellows; m. Jon P. George, Aug. 31, 1965 (dec. Jan. 1982). MusB, Yale U., 1952. Cert. music tchr., Md., Fla., Utah. Instr. Montgomery Coll., Rockville, Md., 1960-65, Contemporary Sch. Music, Rockville, 1971-81; pres. Artistry at the Piano, Inc., Orange City, Fla., 1982—; founder, dir. Artistry Alliance, Orange City, 1983—; pres., exec. editor Artistry Press Internat., Orange City, 1990—; pres., prodr. Artistry Prodns., Orange City, 1991—; co-dir. GreyWolf, Orange City, 1993—; com. mem. pedagogy cert. programs Nat. Conf. on Piano Pedagogy, 1984—; founder, dir. Artistry Ensemble Festival Stetson U., DeLand, Fla., 1985-88; guest lectr. European Piano Tchrs. Assn. Internat. Conv., Eng., 1987-89, MTNA Symposium on Computer Assisted Music Instn., Wichita, Kans. and Salt Lake City, 1988-89; founder, dir. Nat. Conf. on Pedagogy and Performance, 1989; chmn. Ind. Music Tchrs. Forum for State of Fla., 1989-92; cons. The New Sch. for Music Study, Princeton U. Author: The Art of Movement, 1992; co-author: Artistry at the Piano, 1982, Formingreforming, 1991. Mem. Music Tchrs. Nat. Assn., Fla. State Music Tchrs. Assn. (bd. dirs. 1986-92), Md. State Music Tchrs. Assn., Utah Music Teachers Assn., Kindermusik Tchrs. Assn. Home: 10830 S 1000 E Sandy UT 84094-5928

GEORGE, MARY SHANNON, state senator; b. Seattle, May 27, 1916; d. William Day and Agnes (Lovejoy) Shannon; B.A. cum laude, U. Wash., 1937; postgrad. U. Mich., 1937, Columbia U., 1938; m. Flave Joseph George; children—Flave Joseph, Karen Liebermann, Christy, Shannon Lowrey. Prodn. asst., asst. news editor Pathe News, N.Y.C., 1938-42; mem. fgn. editions staff Readers Digest, Pleasantville, N.Y., 1942-46; columnist Caracas (Venezuela) Daily Jour., 1953-60; councilwoman City and County of Honolulu, 1969-74; senator State of Hawaii, 1974-94, asst. minority leader, 1978-80, minority policy leader, 1983-84, minority floor leader, 1987, minority leader, 1987-94, chmn. housing com., 1993, transp. com., 1981-82; mem. Nat. Air Quality Adv. Bd., 1974-75, Intergovtl. Policy Ady. Com. Trade, 1988-93, White House Conf. Drug Free Am., 1988. Vice chmn. 1st Hawaii Ethics Commn., 1968; co-founder Citizens Com. on Constl. Conv., 1968; vice-chmn. platform com. Republican Nat. Conv., 1976, co-chmn., 1980; bd. dirs. State Legis. Leaders Found., 1993-94, Hawaii Planned Parenthood, 1970-72, 79-86, Hawaii Med. Services Assn., 1972-86; mem. adv. bd. Hawaii chpt. Mothers Against Drunk Driving, 1984—. Recipient Jewish Men's Club Brotherhood award, 1974, Disting. Svc. award Hawaii Women Lawyers, 1991, Mahalo award Friends of Libr. Hawaii, 1991; Outstanding Legislator of Yr. award Nat. Rep. Legislators Assn., 1985; named Woman of Yr., Honolulu Press Club, 1969, Hawaii Fedn. Bus. and Profl. Women, 1970; Citizen of Yr., Hawaii Fed. Exec. Bd., 1973, 76. Mem. LWV (pres. Honolulu 1966-68), Mensa, Phi Beta Kappa. Author: A Is for Abrazo, 1961. Home: 782G N Kalaheo Ave Kailua HI 96734-1910

GEORGE, MICHAEL P., investment banker, lawyer; b. Rapid City, S.D., July 13, 1950; s. Abner Hunter and Mary Catherine (Shannon) G.; m. Virginia Ann Zuccaro, June 10, 1972; children: Michaela Frances, Aimee Bannister, Hunter Grafton. BA, U. Notre Dame, 1972; JD, Georgetown U., 1975. Bar: D.C. 1975. Assoc. O'Connor & Hannon, Washington, 1975-78; v.p. Lehman Bros., N.Y.C., 1978-84; mng. dir. 1st Boston Corp., San Francisco, 1984-92, J.P. Morgan & Co., San Francisco, 1992—; mem. Calif. Debt Adv. Com., Sacramento, 1984—. Mem. exec. com. of bd. dirs. Californians for Better Transp., Sacramento, 1988-93; pres. Ross (Calif.) Sch. Found., 1991-92. Mem. Phi Beta Kappa. Roman Catholic. Home: PO Box 1722 Ross CA 94957-1722 Office: JP Morgan & Co 101 California St Fl 38 San Francisco CA 94111-5802

GEORGE, NICHOLAS, criminal defense lawyer, entrepreneur; b. Seattle, July 11, 1952; s. Harry and Mary (Couroune) G.; children: Harry Nicholas, James Michael. BA in Polit. Sci. cum laude, Whitman Coll., 1974; MBA in

Mktg. and Corp. Planning, U. Chgo., 1979; JD, U. Puget Sound, 1989. Bar: Wash. 1991, U.S. Dist. Ct. (we. dist.) Wash. 1991, U.S. Ct. Appeals (9th cir.) 1991, U.S. Tax Ct. 1992, U.S. Dist. Ct. (ea. dist.) Wash. 1994, U.S. Supreme Ct. 1994. Fin. cons. Pacific Western Investment Co., Lynnwood, Wash., 1975-77; planning dir. Clinton Capital Ventures, Seattle, 1979-81; corp. planning mgr. Tacoma Boatbldg., 1981-83; pres. MegaProf Investors, Bellevue, Wash., 1983-89; practice trial-settlement law business Seattle, 1989—; free-lance coll. counselor, Seattle, 1980—. Author: Legitimacy in Government: Ideal, Goal, or Myth? 1974. Bd. auditor St. Demetrios Greek Orthodox Ch., Seattle, 1982-83; bd. dirs. Hellenic Golfers Assn., Seattle, 1981-83. Mem. ABA, Assn. Trial Lawyers Am., Wash. State Bar Assn., Wash. Assn. Criminal Def. Lawyers, Wash. State Trial Lawyers Assn., Fed. Bar Assn., Nat. Assn. Criminal Def. Lawyers, Tacoma-Pierce County Bar Assn., Seattle-King County Bar Assn., Wash. Defender Assn., Wash. State Hist. Soc., Am. Inst. Archeol., Rotary, Wash. Athletic Club, Phi Alpha Delta. Republican. Greek Orthodox. Home: 8422 NE 27th Pl Bellevue WA 98004-1656 Office: 801 2d Ave Ste 1418 Seattle WA 98104-1509

GEORGE, PETER T., orthodontist; b. Akron, Ohio; s. Tony and Paraskeva (Ogrenova) G.; BS Kent State U., 1952; DDS, Ohio State U., 1956; cert. in orthodontics Columbia U., 1962; children: Barton Herrin, Tryan Franklin. Pvt. practice orthodontics, Honolulu, 1962—; cleft palate cons. Hawaii Bur. Crippled Children, 1963—; asst. prof. Med. Sch., U. Hawaii, Honolulu, 1970—; lectr. in field. Mem. Hawaii Gov.'s Phys. Fitness Com., 1962-68; mem. Honolulu Mayor's Health Coun., 1967-72; mem. med. com. Internat. Weightlifting Fedn., 1980-84; chmn. bd. govs. Hall of Fame of Hawaii, 1984; bd. dirs. Honolulu Opera Theatre, 1986-91, chmn. bd. Hawaii Internat. Sports Found., 1988-91. Served to capt. Dental Corps, U.S. Army, 1956-60. Olympic Gold medallist in weightlifting, Helsinki, 1952, Silver medallist, London, 1948, Melbourne, 1956; six times world champion; recipient Disting. Service award Hawaiian AAU, 1968; Gold medal Internat. Weightlifting Fedn., 1976; named to Helms Hall of Fame, 1966. Diplomate Am. Bd. Orthodontics. Fellow Am. Coll. Dentistry, Internat. Coll. Dentistry; mem. Hawaii Amateur Athletic Union (pres. 1964-65), U.S. Olympians (pres. Hawaii chpt. 1963-67, 80—), Am. Assn. Orthodontists, Honolulu Dental Soc. (pres. 1967-68), Hawaii Dental Assn. (pres. 1978), Hawaii Soc. Orthodontists (pres. 1972). Editor Hawaii State Dental Jour., 1965-67. Inventor appliance to prevent sleep apnea. U.S. weightlifting coach USSR, 1979, asst. coach Olympic weightlifting team, 1980. Home and Office: 1441 Kapiolani Blvd Ste 520 Honolulu HI 96814-4403

GEORGE, RONALD M., judge; b. L.A., Mar. 11, 1940. AB, Princeton U., 1961; JD, Stanford U., 1964. Bar: Calif. 1965. Dep. atty. gen. Calif. Dept. Justice, 1965-72; judge L.A. Mcpl. Ct., L.A. County, 1972-77; judge Superior Ct. Calif., L.A. County, 1977-83, supervising judge criminal divsn., 1983-84; assoc. justice 2d dist., divsn. 4 Calif. Ct. Appeal, L.A., 1987-91; assoc. justice Calif. Supreme Ct., San Francisco, 1991—. Mem. Calif. Judges Assn. (pres. 1982-83). Office: Calif Supreme Court 303 2nd St South Tower San Francisco CA 94107

GEORGE, RUSSELL LLOYD, lawyer, legislator; b. Rifle, Colo., May 28, 1946; s. Walter Mallory and Eleanora (Michel) G.; m. Neal Ellen Moore, Nov. 24, 1972; children: Russell, Charles, Thomas, Andrew. BS in Econs., Colo. State U., 1968; JD, Harvard Law Sch., 1971. Bar: Colo. Shareholder Stuver & George, P.C., Rifle, 1976—. state rep. dist. 57 Colo. Gen. Assembly, 1993—. Fellow Colo. Bar Found.; mem. Colo. Bar Assn., Rotary Internat., Masonic Lodge. Republican. Methodist. Home: 1300 E 7th St Rifle CO 81650-2123 Office: Stuver & George PC PO Box 907 120 W 3d St Rifle CO 81650

GEORGE, SEBASTIAN, hematologist, oncologist; b. Palai, Kerala, India, Jan. 24, 1943; came to the U.S., 1974; s. Varkey and Anna George; m. Juliet Augustine George, Jan. 26, 1954; children: David, Michael. MB, BChir, Christian Med. Coll., Punjab, India, 1968, MD, 1973. Cert. internal medicine, hematology and oncology. Internal medicine residency Christian Med. Coll., Punjab, 1968-73; intern, chief resident internal medicine St. Francis Med. Ctr., Trenton, N.J., 1974-76; hematology-oncology fellow U. Wis., Madison, 1976-79; dir. oncology inpatient svc. Mt. Sinai Med. Ctr., Milw., 1979-81; staff mem. Eisenhower Med. Hosp., Rancho Mirage, Calif., 1981—; also chief sect. of oncology/hematology, 1985-94; asst. clin. prof. dept. medicine U. Wis., Madison, 1979-81, Mount Sinai Green Med. Ctr., Milw., 1979-81; med. dir. Mount Sinai Green Tree Hospice, Glendale, Wis., 1980-81; asst. clin. prof. U. So. Calif., L.A., 1985-90; chmn. Pain Clinic ad hoc com. Eisenhower Meml. Hosp., Rancho Mirage, 1988-89; spkr., rschr. and investigator in field; dir. Bone Marrow Transplant Program, Cancer and Blood Inst. of Desert. Contbr. articles to profl. jours. Coord. Melanoma Found. Fund Raising, La Quinta, Calif., 1992; bd. mem. Cancer Prevention and Early Detection, Am. Cancer Soc., 1993-94. Mem. ACP, Am. Soc. Clin. Oncology, Am. Soc. Internal Medicine, Wis. Oncology Group, Wis. Hematology Study Group, Riverside County Med. Soc., Am. Cancer Soc. (bd. mem. Desert Palms unit, prevention and early detection com. Calif. divsn.), Assn. No. Calif. Oncologists (bd. mem.). Office: Cancer and Blood Inst 39000 Bob Hope Dr Rancho Mirage CA 92270-3221

GEORGE, THOMAS FREDERICK, chemistry educator; b. Phila., Mar. 18, 1947; s. Emmanuel John and Veronica Mather (Hansel) G.; m. Barbara Carol Harbach, Apr. 25, 1970. B.A. in Chemistry and Math., Gettysburg (Pa.) Coll., 1967; M.S. in Chemistry, Yale U., 1968, Ph.D., 1970. Rsch. assoc. MIT, 1970; postdoctoral fellow U. Calif., Berkeley, 1971; mem. faculty U. Rochester, N.Y., 1972-85; prof. chemistry U. Rochester, 1977-85; dean Faculty Natural Sci. and Math., prof. chemistry and physics SUNY-Buffalo, 1985-91; provost, acad. v.p., prof. chemistry and physics Wash. State U., Pullman, 1991—, 1991—; Disting. vis. lectr. dept. chemistry U. Tex., Austin, 1978; lectr. NATO Advanced Study Inst., Cambridge, Eng., 1979; Disting. speaker dept. chemistry U. Utah, 1980; Disting. lectr. Air Force Weapons Lab., Kirtland AFB, N.Mex., 1980; mem. com. recommendations U.S. Army Basic Sci. Research, 1978-81; lectr. NATO Summer Sch. on Interfaces under Photon Irradiation, Maratea, Italy, 1986—; organizer NSF workshop on theoretical aspects of laser radiation and its interaction with atomic and molecular systems Rochester, N.Y., 1977; vice chmn. 6th Internat. Conf. Molecular Energy Transfer, Rodez, France, 1979; chmn. Gordon Rsch. Conf. Molecular Energy Transfer, Wolfeboro, N.H., 1981; Mem. program com. Internat. Conf. on Lasers, San Francisco, 1981-83, ACS Symposium on Recent Advances in Surface Sci., Rochester sect., 1982, Internat. Laser Sci. Conf., Dallas, 1985, external rev. com. for chemistry Gettysburg Coll., 1984, awards com. ACS Procter and Gamble student prizes in chemistry, 1982-83, Free-electron Laser peer rev. panel Am. Inst. Biol. Sci. Med., alt., bd. trustees Calspan-UB Rsch. Ctr., 1989—; organiser APS Symposium on Laser-Induced Molecular Excitation/Photofragmentation, N.Y., 1987; co-organizer ACS Symposium on Phys. Chemistry High-Temp. Supercondrs., L.A., 1988; co-organizer MRS Symposium on High-Temperature Superconductors, Alfred, N.Y., 1988; chmn. SPIE Symposium on Photochemistry in Thin Films, L.A., 1989; mem. internat. program adv. com. Internat. Sch. Lasers and Applications, Sayanogorsk, East Siberia, USSR, 1989; lectr. on chemistry at cutting edge Smithsonian Instn./Am. Chem. Soc., Washington, 1990; mem. internat. adv. com. Xth Vavilov Conf. Nonlinear Optics, Novosibirsk, USSR, 1990; Am. coord. NSF Info. Exchange Seminar for U.S.-Japan Program of Cooperation in Photoconversion and Photosynthesis, Honolulu, 1990; mem. exec. bd. N.Y. State Inst. on Superconductivity, 1990-91; mem. ONT/ASEE rev. panel for Engring. Edn. postdoctoral fellowship program, 1990; mem. rev panel rsch. experiences for undergrads of sci. and tech. rsch. ctrs., NSF, 1989, mem. rev. panel grad. res. traineeships NSF, 1992; cons., lectr. in field. Co-author: (textbook) Notes in Classical and Quantum Physics, 1990; also 490 papers in field; mem. editl. bd. Molecular Physics, 1984-90, Jour. Cluster Sci., 1989—; mem. adv. bd. Jour. Phys. Chemistry, 1980-84; mem. adv. editl. bd. Chem. Physics Letters, 1979-81, Chem. Materials, 1989; mem. editl. bd. Jour. Quantum Nonlinear Phenomena (Soviet jour.), 1991—; editor-at-large Marcel Dekker, 1989—; editor: Photochemistry in Thin Films, 1989; co-editor: Chemistry of High-Temperature Superconductors, Vol. I, 1987, Vol. II, 1988, ACS Symposium Series; feature editor Jour. of Optical Soc. of Am., Spectrochimica Acta, Optical Engring. Tchr., scholar Camille and Henry Dreyfus Found., 1975-85; bd. mgrs. Buffalo Mus. Sci., 1986; mem. exec. bd. N.Y. State Inst. on Superconductivity, 1990-91; mem. canvassing com. ACS; mem. external rev. com. for chemistry Gettysburg Coll., 1984; mem. NEASC site visit team Boston U., ten-yr. accreditation, 1989; bd. dirs. Wash. State Inst. for Pub. Policy, 1991—; trustee Wash. State U. Found., 1991—; bd. dirs. Wash. Tech. Ctr., 1992—; mem. exec. com. Northwest Acad. Forum, 1992—, chmn. 1994—; mem. review panel Grad. Rsch. Traineeships, NSF, 1992. Sloan fellow, 1976-80, postdoctoral fellow, 1990, Guggenheim fell recipient Disting. Alumni award Gettysburg Coll., 1987, Harrison House award ACS, 1980, Peter Debye award ACS, 1986-88, Pure Chemistry award ACS, 1989—. Fellow Am. Phys. Soc., N.Y. Acad. Scis. (steering com. Inst. Superconductivity 1987—, steering com. Ctr. for Advanced Tech. in Health-Care Instruments and Devices 1988-90), Soc. Photo-Optical Instrumentation Engrs.; mem. AAAS, Am. Chem. Soc. (exec. com. phys. div. 1979-82, 85-89, 94—, vice chmn. 1985-86, chmn.-elect 1986-87, chmn. 1987-88), European Phys. Soc., Royal Soc. Chemistry (Marlow medal and prize 1979), Coun. Colls. Arts Sci., Phi Beta Kappa, Sigma Xi (exec. com. U. Rochester 1984-85). Democrat. Lutheran. Office: Wash State U Office Provost 422 French Adminstrn Bldg Pullman WA 99164

GEORGIADES, GABRIEL GEORGE, aerospace engineering educator; b. Amarousion, Greece, Nov. 23, 1956; came to U.S., 1975; s. George Gabriel Georgiades and Evanthia Spyrou (Ioannou) Georgiadou. BA in Physics cum laude, Jacksonville U., 1979; B. Aerospace Engring., Ga. Inst. Tech., 1979; MS in Aerospace Engring., Pa. State U., 1982. Engr. in tng., Ga. Structural engr. Piper Aircraft Corp., Lock Haven, Pa., 1979-80; prof. aircraft structures Embry-Riddle Aero. U., Prescott, Ariz., 1982-85; prof. aerospace engring. Calif. State Poly. U., Pomona, Calif., 1985—; cons. Naval Weapons Ctr., China Lake, Calif., 1985—, Lockheed Aircraft Svc. Co., Ontario, Calif., 1991—, Field Svc. & Maintenance Co., North Palm Springs, Calif., 1991—, Wyle Labs., El Segundo, Calif., 1992—. Author: Aerospace Structures Lab Manual, 1988. Advisor Minority Engring. Program, Pomona, 1987—, Math. Engring., Sci. Achievement Program, Claremont, Calif., 1988—, Soc. Hispanics in Sci. and Engring., Pomona, 1989—. Recipient Cert. of Achievement, NATO, Belgium, 1974, C.W. Brownfield Meml. award U.S. Jaycees, Lock Haven, 1980. Mem. AIAA (Disting. Svc. award 1985), Aerospace Edn. Assn., Aerial Phenomena Rsch. Orgn., Soc. Automotive Engrs., Sigma Gamma Tau. Orthodox. Office: Calif State Poly U Aerospace Engring 3801 W Temple Ave Pomona CA 91768-2557

GEORGINO, SUSAN MARTHA, city redevelopment services administrator; b. Phila., Apr. 1, 1950; d. Joseph Francis and Eleanor (Kelly) Boyle; m. Richard Romano (div.); 1 child, Sean; m. Victor Georgino, Oct. 2, 1988; 1 child, Michael. BA, Calif. State U., L.A., 1975, MPA, 1983. Adminstrv. officer Maravilla Found., Montebello, Calif., 1978-81; adminstrv. analyst City of Burbank (Calif.), 1982-84, project mgr., 1984-87, asst. dir. community devel., redevel. adminstr., 1987-89; dir. redevel. svcs., deputy exec. dir. City of Brea (Calif.), 1989—; bd. dirs. Calif. Redevel. Assn. Bd. officer Soroptimist Internat., Brea, 1991; active La Providencia Guild, Burbank, 1990, Parks and Recreation Commn., Burbank, 1991; vice chair City of Burbank's Performing Arts Grant Awards Program. Mem. Nat. Assn. Redevel. and Housing Ofcls. (bd. dirs. 1986-87), Calif. Assn. Econ. Devel. Ofcls., Orange County Consortium (bd. dirs.), Lambda Alpha Internat. (bd. dirs. Orange County chpt.). Roman Catholic. Office: City of Brea One Civic Ctr Circle Brea CA 92621

GEORGITIS, WILLIAM JOHNSON, endocrinologist, medical educator; b. Bangor, Maine, Aug. 7, 1947; p. William James and Mary Helen (Wyman) G.; m. Betsy Comeau; children: Jonathan, Elizabeth, Kate, Emily. AB in Chemistry magna cum laude, Bowdoin Coll., 1969; MD, Boston U., 1973. Diplomate Am. Bd. Internal Medicine; diplomate Am. Bd. Endocrinology and Metabolism. Intern Maine Med. Ctr., Portland, 1973-74, resident internal medicine, 1974-76; staff Mid-Maine Med. Ctr., 1976-79; endocrinology fellow Fitzsimons Army Med. Ctr., Aurora, Colo., 1979-81; asst. chief endocrine svc. Brooke Army Med. Ctr., San Antonio, 1981-84; staff endocrinologist Fitzsimons Army Med. Ctr., Aurora, Colo., 1984-87; asst. chief endocrine svc. Fitzsimons Army Med. Ctr., Aurora, 1987-91, 91—; asst. chief medicine svc. 21st Evacuation Hosp., Ft. Hood, Tex., 1991; asst. clin. prof. U. Colo. Health Scis. Ctr., Denver, 1984-91, assoc. clin. prof., 1991—; physician instr. Maine Med. Ctr., Portland, 1976; courtesy staff Mid-Maine Med. Ctr., 1979-84; attending staff Ctrl. Maine Family Practice Residency Program, 1976-79; preceptor Boston U. Sch. Medicine, Cmty. Medicine Diagnosis, 1978, U. Vt. Med. Ctr., Cmty. Preceptorship Program, 1979; cons. Ctrl. Maine Med. Edn. Consortium Program, 1977-79; clin. instr., clin. asst. prof. U. Tex. Health Sci. Ctr., San Antonio, 1982-84; cons. San Antonio (Tex.) State Chest Hosp., 1982-84, DOD Region III USA MEDDAC's endocrinology, 1984—; presenter in field. Contbr. chpts. to books and articles to profl. jours. Col. USAR, 1979-84, U.S. Army, 1994—. Decorated Army Commendation medal, 1987, with oak leaf cluster, 1991, Army Achievement medal, 1988, S.W. Asia Svc. ribbon, 1991, Liberation of Kuwait medal, 1991; named Golden Ball honoree Am. Diabetes Assn.-Colo. Affiliate, 1994; recipient Peter Forsham award for academic contbns. to mil. endocrinology, 1995. Fellow ACP; mem. Am. Thyroid Assn., Endocrine Soc., Am. Diabetes Assn., Colo. Soc. for Endocrinology and Metabolism, Soc. Uniformed Endocrinologists (sci. program dir. 1992-93). Home: 7938 S Pontiac Way Englewood CO 80112-3115

GEORGOPOULOS, DEAN ELIAS, film producer, real estate developer; b. Manchester, N.H., Nov. 2, 1963; s. Louis James and Aphrodite (Zoulamis) G. U. N.H. V.p. ops. Famous Ski Togs Factory Outlets, N.H., Vt., Mass., Maine, 1978-82, Jim's Oxford Shop, Manchester, N.H., 1982, 86; gen. mgr. U. N.H. Hockey, Durham, 1982-86, 89; bus. affairs The Bus Boys, L.A., 1986-88; v.p. ops. Am. Computer Products, Salem, N.H., 1990; mgr. The Barn Sporting Goods, Newton, Mass., 1990; sales assoc. Smtih Barney Harris Upham Brokerage, White Plains, N.Y., 1991; film prodr. Rocky Point Prodns., L.A., 1990-93; redeveloper The Shannon Co., Woodland Hills, Calif., 1991-94; film prodr. Kosmos Entertainment Group, Malibu, Calif., 1993—; MIS cons. The Mus. of Flying, Santa Monica, Calif., 1990, The Cockpit, N.Y.C., 1991, LMH Prodns., Studio City, Calif., 1993—; prodn. cons. Infinity Vision Entertainment, Delmar, Calif., 1993—. Campaign coord. Georgopoulos for Congress, Manchester, N.H., 1986, Georgopoulos for Gov. Coun., Manchester, N.H., 1984; campaign worker Sununu for Gov., Manchester, N.H., 1982, Nixon re-election, Manchester, N.H., 1972. Mem. U.S. Hockey, 1968—. Republican. Greek Orthodox. Home: 143 Little Bay Rd Newington NH 03801 Office: Kosmos Entertainment Group 20006 D Pacific Coast Hwy Malibu CA 90265

GER, SHAW-SHYONG, accountant; b. Kaohsiung, Taiwan, Nov. 19, 1959; s. Jing-Ru and Jui-Mei (Lee) G. BA in econs., Nat. Taiwan U., Taipei, 1981; MBA, Ariz. State U., 1986, M in acctg., 1989. Rsch. asst. Ariz. State U., Tempe, 1988-89; contr. CLH Internat., Inc., Tempe, 1989—. Recipient All Am. Scholar award U.S. Achievement Acad., 1989. Mem. Assn. MBA Exec., Nat. Geog. Soc., Inst. Cert. Mgmt. Accts., Beta Gamma Sigma. Address: PO Box 601 Tempe AZ 85280-0601

GERBA, CHARLES PETER, microbiologist, educator; b. Blue Island, Ill., Sept. 10, 1945; s. Peter and Virginia (Roulo) G.; m. Peggy Louise Scheitlin, June 6, 1970; children: Peter, Phillip. BS in Microbiology, Ariz. State U., 1969; PhD in Microbiology, U. Miami, 1973. Postdoctoral fellow Baylor Coll. Medicine, Houston, 1973-74, asst. prof. microbiology, 1974-81; assoc. prof. U. Ariz., Tucson, 1981-85, prof., 1985—; cons. EPA, Tucson, 1980—, World Health Orgn., Pan Am. Health Orgn., 1989—; advisor CRC Press, Boca Raton, Fla., 1981—. Editor: Methods in Environmental Virology, 1982, Groundwater Pollution Microbiology, 1984, Phage Ecology, 1987; contbr. numerous articles to profl. and sci. jours. Mem. Pima County Bd. Health, 1986-92; mem. sci. adv. bd. EPA, 1987—. Named Outstanding Research Scientist U. Ariz., 1984, 92, Outstanding Rsch. Team, 1994. Fellow AAAS (environ. sci. and engring.), Am. Soc. Microbiology (divsn. chmn. 1982-83, 87-88, pres. Ariz. chpt. 1984-85, councilor 1985-88); mem. Internat. Assn. Water Pollution Rsch. (sr. del. 1985-91), Am. Water Works Assn., Am. Acad. Microbiology, Am. Acad. Microbiol. Home: 1980 W Paseo Monserrat Tucson AZ 85704-1329 Office: U Ariz Dept Microbiology and Immunology Dept Water and Soils Tucson AZ 85721

GERBER, BARRY ELDON, data processing executive, consultant, writer; b. L.A., May 12, 1942; s. Harry and Elsie (Lubin) G.; m. Jane Bernette Margo, June 7, 1962; children: Margot, Karl, Georg. BA, UCLA, 1964, MA, 1966, CPil, 1972. Prof. Calif. State U., Fullerton, 1968-77; dep. dir. Community Cancer Control, L.A., 1977-82; v.p. info. systems Zenith Ins., Encino, Calif., 1983-85; rsch. assoc. Neuropsychiatric Inst. UCLA, 1982-83, dir. Social Sci. Computing, 1985-94; dir. ctr. high performance computing U. Guadalajara, 1993-94; internat. cons. in field. Contbg. editor PC Week Ziff Davis, 1988-90; editor Network Computing, CMP Publs., 1990—; contbr. articles to profl. jours.

GERBER, JOHN G., medical educator; b. Budapest, Hungary, May 30, 1946. BA, Queens Coll., 1968; MD, Med. Coll. Va., 1972. Intern in psychiatry Denver Gen. Hosp., 1972-73; intern in medicine St. Louis U. Hosps., 1973-74; resident in medicine Med. Coll. Va., Richmond, 1974-76; postdoctoral fellow divsn. clin. pharmacology Vanderbilt U. Sch. Medicine, Nashville, 1976-77; postdoctoral fellow divsn. clin. pharmacology U. Colo. Sch. Medicine, Denver, 1977-78, asst. prof. medicine and pharmacology, 1978-82, assoc. prof. medicine and pharmacology, 1982-89, prof. medicine and pharmacology, 1989—, acting head divsn. clin. pharmacology, 1992-93; vis. scientist Wadsworth VA Med. Ctr., Ctr. for Ulcer Rsch. and Edn., L.A., 1986-87; speaker in field. Reviewer various jours. in field; contbr. articles, revs. to profl. jours., chpts. to books. NIH fellow, 1976-77, 77-78; grantee Am. Heart Assn., 1980-85; recipient Clin. Pharmacology award Burroughs Wellcome, 1985-90. Mem. Am. Fedn. Clin. Rsch., Am. Soc. Pharmacology and Exptl. Therapeutics, Colo. Soc. Internal Medicine, Western Soc. Clin. Investigation, Western Soc. Clin. Rsch., Am. Heart Assn., Colo. Heart Assn., Am. Soc. Internal Medicine, Am. Soc. Clin. Pharmacology and Therapeutics, Western Assn. Physicians. Office: U Colo Health Scis Ctr Divsn Clin Pharmacology 4200 E 9th Ave Denver CO 80220-3706

GERBRACHT, ROBERT THOMAS (BOB GERBRACHT), painter, educator; b. Erie, Pa., June 23, 1924; s. Earl John and Lula Mary (Chapman) G.; m. Delia Marie Paz, Nov. 27, 1952; children: Mark, Elizabeth, Catherine. BFA, Yale U., 1951; MFA, U. So. Calif., 1952. Cert. tchr., Calif. Art tchr. William S. Hart Jr. and Sr. High Sch., Newhall, Calif., 1954-56; stained glass artist Cummings Studios, San Francisco, 1956-58; art tchr. McKinley Jr. High Sch., Redwood City, Calif., 1958-60, Castro Jr. High Sch., San Jose, Calif., 1960-79; portrait artist, tchr. San Jose, San Francisco, 1979—; instr. art Coll. of Notre Dame, Belmont, Calif., 1955-60, San Jose City Coll., 1967-71, Notre Dame Novitiate, Saratoga, 1976-79, U. Calif., Santa Cruz, 1980-81; art cons. Moreland Sch. Dist., Campbell, Calif., 1979-80; instr. nationwide workshops, Calif., Colo., Fla., Mass., N.Mex., N.Y., S.C., Vt., Wash., Wis., Mex., 1980—. Represented in permanent collection Triton Mus. Art, Santa Clara, Calif.; portraits include Marie Gallo, Mrs. Bruce Jenner, Austin Warburton, Rev. Cecil Williams; subject of articles in Today's Art and Graphics, Art and Antique Collector, Am. Artist, U.S. ART. Cpl. U.S. Army, 1943-46. Recipient Am. Artist Achievement award Tchr. of Pastels, 1993. Mem. San Jose Art League (Best of Show award 1983, 84), Pastel Soc. Am., Pastel Soc. West Coast (advisor, Best of Show award 1988), Calif. Pastel Soc. (advisor), Soc. Western Artists (trustee, Best of Show award 1982, 85, 90, Best Portrait award 1984), Oil Painters Am. Home: 1301 Blue Oak Ct Pinole CA 94564-2145

GERHARD, NANCY LUCILE DEGE, counselor, educator; b. St. Paul, July 23, 1939; d. Carl H. and Mildred L. (Toenjes) Dege; m. Rick A. Gerhard, June 25, 1960; children: Geoffrey Austin, Mark Alan. BS in Elem. Edn. magna cum laude, Gustavus Adolphus Coll., 1960; MA in Sch. and Guidance Counseling, Chapman U., 1978. Cert. English tchr., guidance counselor, elem. tchr., adminstr., Calif. Tchr. English Orange (Calif.) Unified Sch. Dist., 1987-93, mentor tchr., 1990-93, coach Middle Sch. Demonstration Program, 1990-93, h.s. counselor, 1993—; mem. Calif. Lang. Arts Instructional Materials Evaluation Panel, 1988; cons. UCI Writing Project, Calif. Lit. Project. Mem. ASCD, NEA, Coun. for Basic Edn., Calif. Tchrs. Assn., Orange Unified Edn. Assn. Office: Orange High Sch 525 N Shaffer St Orange CA 92667-6824

GERHART, DOROTHY EVELYN, insurance executive, real estate professional; b. Monett, Mo., Apr. 20, 1932; d. Manford Thomas and Norma Grace (Barrett) Ethridge; m. Robert H. Gerhart, Apr. 11, 1952 (div. Dec. 1969); children: Sandra Gerhart Kreamer, Richard A., Diane Gerhart Lacey. Grad. high sch., Tucson; student, U. Ariz., 1950-53. Lic. real estate broker. Owner, pres. Gerhart Ins., Inc., Tucson, 1967-70, 89—; agt. Mahoney-O'Donnell Agy., Tucson, 1970-73, Gerhart & Mendelsoh Ins., Tucson, 1973-78; agt., mgr. personal lines dept. Tucson Realty and Trust, 1978-83; ins. agt. San Xavier Ins. Agy., Tucson, 1985-89; pres. Gerhart Ins., Inc., Tucson, 1989-93, Koty-Leavitt Ins., Inc. (formerly Gerhart Ins., Inc.), Tuscon, 1993—, Gerhart Realty, Inc., Tucson, 1993—. Vol. Palo Verde Psychiat. Hosp. Mem. Nat. Fedn. Ind. Bus., Ind. Ins. Agts. Tucson (bd. dirs. 1973, 74, v.p. 1975, pres. 1976, First Woman Pres.), Fed. Home Life Ins. Co. (Pres.'s Club award 1986), Nat. Fedn. Small Bus., Altrusa Club of Tucson (bd. dirs. 1984, membership chmn. 1985, fund raising chmn. 1986). Republican. Address: PO Box 13421 Tucson AZ 85732-3421 Office: Gerhart Realty Inc 3208 E Fort Lowell Rd Ste 108 Tucson AZ 85716-1625

GERICKE, PHILIP OTTO, Spanish language educator; b. Ukiah, Calif., Dec. 24, 1936; s. Otto Luke and Catherine Rose (Levi) G.; m. Patricia Ann Halpern, July 12, 1985; children: Elissa M., Teresa A., Otto L., Thomas N. BA, U. Calif., Riverside, 1958; MA, U. Calif., Berkeley, 1960, PhD, 1965. Assoc. Spanish U. Calif., Riverside, 1962-63, lectr. Spanish, 1963-64, asst. prof. Spanish, 1966-71, assoc. prof. Spanish, 1971-78, prof. Spanish, 1978-94, prof. Spanish emeritus, 1994—; asst. prof. fgn. langs. San Fernando Valley State Coll., Northridge, Calif., 1964-66. Editor, translator: Historical Notes on Lower California (Manuel C. Rojo), 1972; editor: Alfonso de Toledo Invencionario, 1992; contbr. articles to profl. jours. Mem. MLA, Am. Assn. Tchrs. Spanish and Portuguese, Philological Assn. of Pacific Coast, Assn. Internat. de Hispanistas, Phi Beta Kappa. Democrat. Office: U Calif Dept Spanish And Portu Riverside CA 92521

GERINGER, JAMES E., governor; b. Wheatland, Wyo., Apr. 24, 1944; m. Sherri Geringer; children: Jen, Val, Rob, Meri, Beckie. BS in Mechanical Engring., Kans. State U., 1967. Commd. officer USAF; with contract administration Mo. Basin Power Project's Laramie River Sta., 1977-79; elected mem. Wyo. Legislature, 1982; farm owner, 1987—; participant in various space devel. programs, Calif., devel. variety Air Force and NASA space boosters including launches of reconnaissance satellites, the NASA Viking Mars lander, an upper stage booster for the space shuttle and the Global Positioning Satellite System; chief of computer programming at a ground receiving station for early warning satellites. Mem. Nat. Fedn. Ind. Bus., Am. Legion, Farm Bur., Farmer's Union, Rotary, Lions, Ducks Unlimited, Pheasants Forever, C. of C. Lutheran. Office: Office of the Gov State Capitol Cheyenne WY 82002

GERKING, SHELBY D., economics educator; b. Bloomington, Ind., Dec. 1, 1946; s. Shelby D. and Louisa B. (Pfretzschner) G.; m. Janet Lynn Shumway, Sept. 1, 1967. BA in Econs., Ind. U., 1968, PhD in Econs., 1976; MBA in Fin., U. Wash., 1970. Asst. prof. econs. Ariz. State U., Tempe, 1974-78, Ind. U., Bloomington, 1977-78; assoc. prof. U. Wyo., Laramie, 1978-82, prof., 1982—, asst. to pres., 1988-92; exec. dir. Wyo. State Sci. Tech. and Energy Authority, Laramie, 1989-93. Author: Stochastic Imput-Output Models, 1976; also numerous articles. Mem. Wyo. Econ. Devel. and Stblzn. Bd., Cheyenne, 1988-93; bd. dirs. Laramie Econ. Devel. Corp., 1988—. Mem. AAAS, Am. Econ. Assn., Regional Sci. Assn. (councillor 1985-88, co-editor Rev. 1979-86). Home: 2526 Mountain Shadow Ln Laramie WY 82070-5353 Office: U Wyo Dept Econs PO Box 3985 Laramie WY 82071-3985

GERLACH, WILLIAM EDWARD, agriculturist; b. Eau Claire, Wis., Sept. 28, 1950; s. Edward B. and Marie A. G.; m. Cheryl Ann Hamilton, Aug. 1988; 1 child, Ian Hunter. BA in Econ., U. Wis., 1972; MS Agrl. and Managerial Econ., U. Calif., Davis, 1981. English tchr. Peace Corps., Danané, West Africa, 1972-74; pers. recruiter Peace Corps./Vista, N.Y.C., San Francisco, 1975-79; rsch. asst. U. Calif., Davis, 1980-81; commodity analyst, economist Calif. Farm Bur. Fedn., Sacramento, 1981-88; patent mgmt., mkt. rsch., strategic planning U. Calif. Tech. Transfer Office, Alameda, 1988—. Vol. tchr. Ctr. for New Americans, Concord, 1991—. With Peace Corps., 1972-74. Home: 775 Miller Ave Martinez CA 94553-1348

GERMAN, DONALD FREDERICK, physician; b. San Francisco, Oct. 2, 1935; m. Marilyn Sue King; children: Susan, Charles, Donald. BS, U. San Francisco, 1956; MD, U. Calif., San Francisco, 1960. Diplomate Am. Bd. Pediats., Am. Bd. Allergy and Immunology. Intern Kaiser Found. Hosp., San Francisco, 1960-61, resident in pediats., 1963-65, resident, fellow in allergy, 1966-68; staff pediatrician Kaiser Med. Ctr., Santa Clara, Calif., 1965-66, staff allergist, 1968-69; chief dept. allergy Kaiser Permanente Med. Ctr., San Francisco, 1969—; assoc. clin. prof. pediatrics U. Calif. Med. Sch., San Francisco, 1991—. Capt. USAF, 1961-63. Fellow Am. Acad. Pediats., Am. Coll. Allergy and Immunology, Am. Acad. Allergy and Immunology. Office: Kaiser Permanente Med Ctr Allergy Dept 1635 Divisadero St Ste 101 San Francisco CA 94115

GERMAN, WILLIAM, newspaper editor; b. N.Y.C., Jan. 4, 1919; s. Sam and Celia (Norack) G.; m. Gertrude Pasenkoff, Oct. 12, 1940; children: David, Ellen, Stephen. B.A., Bklyn. Coll., 1939; M.S., Columbia U., 1940; Nieman fellow, Harvard U., 1950. Reporter, asst. fgn., news, mng., exec. editor, editor San Francisco Chronicle, 1940—; editor Chronicle Fgn. Service, 1960-77; mng. editor KQED, Newspaper of the Air, 1968; lectr. U. Calif., Berkeley, 1946-47, 68-70. Editor: San Francisco Chronicle Reader, 1962. Served with AUS, 1943-45. Mem. AP Mng. Editors Assn., Am. Soc. Newspaper Editors, Commonwealth Club of Calif. (pres. 1995). Home: 150 Lovell Ave Mill Valley CA 94941-1883 Office: San Francisco Chronicle 901 Mission St San Francisco CA 94103-2905

GERNER, ANDRE ANTHONY, air force officer; b. Redwood City, Calif., July 8, 1957; s. Sebastian and Anna (Schmidt) G.; m. Terri Kay Donaldson, Sept. 8, 1984; children: Andre S., Joseph A. Student, U. Santa Clara, 1975-77; BS in Aero. Engring., USAF Acad., 1981; MS in Aero. and Astro. Engring., U. Wash., 1982; postgrad., USAF Test Pilot Sch. Class 91A, 1991. Commd. 2d lt. USAF, 1981, advanced through grades to lt. col., 1994; prin. rschr. NASA Ames Rsch. Ctr., Moffett Field, Calif., 1983; pilot 384th AREFS & 384th BMW, McConnell AFB, Kans., 1984-87, 32d AREFS, Barksdale AFB, La., 1987-90; exptl. test pilot USAF, Edwards AFB, Calif., 1991-94; rsch. fellow RAND, Santa Monica, Calif., 1994-95; instr. aero. engring. USAF Acad., USAFA, Colo., 1995—. Contbr. articles to profl. publs. Mem. AIAA (sr. mem., 1st place award aerospace scis. meeting 1982). Republican.

GEROU, PHILLIP HOWARD, architect; b. Natick, Mass., July 20, 1951; s. James Francis and Enid (Meymaris) G.; m. Cheri Rodgers, Nov. 24, 1979; children: Gregory Bedford, Sara Christine. BArch, U. Nebr., 1974, MArch, 1975. Architect Denver, 1970-77; project mgr. Henningson, Durham, Richardson, Denver, 1978-82; dir. architecture Daniel Mann Johnson Mendenhall, Denver, 1982-85; v.p., dir. comml. design Downing Leach Architects, Boulder, 1985-86; prin., designer Gerou & Assocs. Ltd., Evergreen, Colo., 1986—; design cons. Kilimanjaro Children's Hosp., Tanzania, 1988-91, World Alpine Ski Championships, Vail, Colo., 1988. Pres. Colo. Soc. of Architects Ednl. Fund., Denver, 1986; del. State Rep. Assembly, Denver, 1986; trustee Rockland Community Ch., Denver, 1986-89. Recipient Citation award Nat. Assn. of Remodeling Industry, 1991, Design Excellence Wood, Inc., 1990, Citation award, 1990. Fellow AIA (pres. Colo. chpt. 1986, bd. dirs. 1981-87, nat. dir. 1991-94, v.p. 1995, conf. chair Western Mtn. region 1990, spl. recognition award 1990), Nat. Coun. Archl. Adminstrn. Bds. (examiner 1985). Republican. Mem. United Ch. of Christ. Office: 2942 Evergreen Pky Ste 404 Evergreen CO 80439-7909

GEROW, LYNN BURDETTE, JR., psychiatrist; b. Reno, Nev., Jan. 19, 1942; s. Lynn Burdette and Nell Juanita (Lozano) G.; m. Ann Marie Prida, Dec. 20, 1965; 1 child, James Byron. BS, U. Nev., Reno, 1963; MD, McGill U., Montreal, Quebec, Can., 1967. Diplomate Am. Bd. Psychiatry and Neurology, Nat. Bd. Med. Examiners; lic. Calif., Nev. Intern Walter Reed Gen. Hosp., Washington, 1967-68; resident in psychiatry Letterman Gen. Hosp., San Francisco, 1968-71; fellow in Cmty. Psychiatry, Ctr. for Tng. in Cmty. Psychiatr y, Mental Health Adminstrn., Langley Porter Inst., San Francisco, 1969-71; fellow in child psychiatry Letterman Gen. Hosp. and Langley Porter Neuropsychiat. Inst., San Francisco, 1971-73; asst. chief and dir. tng. Child Psychiatry Svc. Letternam Gen. Hosp., San Francisco, 1973-75; clin. instr. of psychiatry U. Calif. Sch. Medicine, San Francisco, 1974-75; mem. com. for protection of human subjects U. Nev., Reno, 1978-80; pvt. practice psychiatry Reno, Nev., 1975—; from asst. clin. prof. to assoc. clin. prof. dept. psychiatry and behavioral scis. U. Nev. Sch. Medicine, Reno, 1979-86; attending psychiatrist Washoe Med. Ctr., 1975-93, asst. chmn. dept. psychiatry, 1976-77, chmn., mem. exec. com., 1978-80, 82-84; attending psychiatrist St. Mary's Hosp., VA Hosp., Reno, 1975, Truckee Meadows Hosp., Reno, 1981-82, Sparks Family Hosp., Reno, 1983-94; psychiat. cons. Nev. Blue Shield, 1976-84; trustee Washoe Med. Ctr., 1980-86, chmn. budget and fin. com., 1982-86. Lt. col. U.S. Army Med. Corps, 1967-75. Lt. col. U.S. Army Med. Corps, 1967-75. Fellow Am. Acad. Disability Evaluating Physicians; mem. AMA, Am. Psychiat. Assn., Nev. State Med. Assn., Washoe County Med. Soc., Nev. Psychiat. Assn., Am. Acad. Psychiatry and the Law, Am. Acad. Forensic Scis., Nat. Assn. Disability Evaluating Physicians, Am. Occupational Med. Assn. Office: 50 Kirman Ave Ste 301 Reno NV 89502-1178

GERRODETTE, CHARLES EVERETT, real estate company executive, consultant; b. Alderwood Manor, Wash., June 18, 1934; s. Honoré Everett and Marjorie Violet (Stapley) G.; m. Laurine Carol Manley, Mar. 16, 1956 (div. 1977); children: Stephen Everett, Suzanne Gerrodette Prince; m. Diane Marie Drumm, Dec. 6, 1984. BA in Bus. Adminstrn., U. Wash., 1956, postgrad., 1959; postgrad., NYU, 1956-57. Credit analyst and corr. comml. credit dept. Chase Manhattan Bank, N.Y.C., 1956-57; reviewing appraiser Prudential Ins. Co. Am., Seattle, 1959-67; v.p., sr. loan officer real estate group Seattle 1st Nat. Bank, 1967-90; pres., CEO, Portal Pacific Co., Inc., Seattle, 1990—; real estate advisor, fin. cons. Charles E. Gerrodette, MAI, Seattle, 1990—; instr. appraising Shoreline C.C., Seattle, 1974-76. Contbg. author: Prentice Hall Ency. of Real Estate Appraising, 3d edit., 1978. Mem. blue ribbon com. for planning Shoreline Sch. Dist., Seattle, 1974-75. With U.S. Army, 1957-59. Mem. Am. Arbitration Assn. (panel of arbitrators), Appraisal Inst. (MAI designation 1972, officer, bd. dirs. Wash.-B.C. chpt. 1980-89, pres. 1984, nat. fin. and adminstrn. com. 1982-87, nat. governing counselor 1987-89, nat. fin. com. 1990—), Mortgage Bankers Assn. (income property com.), Columbia Tower Club, Lambda Alpha, N.W. Grad. Assn. Theta Delta Chi (trustee 1960-70, past pres.). Episcopalian. Office: 2125 1st Ave Apt 1204 Seattle WA 98121-2118

GERRY, DEBRA PRUE, psychotherapist; b. Oct. 9, 1951; d. C.O. and Sarah E. Rawl; m. Norman Bernard Gerry, Apr. 10, 1981; 1 child, Gisele Psyche Victoria. BS, Ga. So. U., 1972; MEd, Armstrong State U., 1974; PhD, U. Ga., 1989. Cert. Ariz. Bd. Behavioral Health Examiners. Spl. edn. tchr. Chatham County Bd. Edn., Savannah, Ga., 1972-74; edn. and learning disabilities resource educator Duval County Bd. Edn., Jacksonville, Fla., 1974-77; ednl. resource counselor spl. programs adminstr. Broward County Bd. Edn., Ft. Lauderdale, Fla., 1977-81; pvt. practice Scottsdale, Ariz., 1990—. Contbr. author coll. textbooks; contbr. articles to profl. jours. Vol., fundraiser, psychol. cons., group leader Valley AIDS Orgns., Phoenix, 1990-94; fundraiser Hosp. Health Edn. Programs, Scottsdale, 1992-93; mem. com. for women's issues Plz. Club, Phoenix, 1992-93; pres. Laissez Les Bon Temps Rouler, Wrigley Club, Phoenix, 1993-95. Recipient Rudy award Shanti Orgn., 1991. Mem. APA, NOW, Am. Counseling Assn., Nat. Assn. Women Bus. Owners, Assn. for Multicultural Coun., Assn. for Specialists in Group Work, Mensa, Phi Delta Kappa, Kappa Delta Epsilon, Sigma Omega Phi, Kappa Delta Pi. Office: 6210 E Thomas Rd Ste 209 Scottsdale AZ 85251-7003

GERSTEL, MARTIN STEPHEN, pharmaceutical company executive; b. Norwalk, Conn., June 26, 1941; s. Sydney Charles and Ethel Lorraine (Kurtz) G.; m. Shoshana Wechsler, Apr. 5, 1982. B.S., Yale U., 1964; M.B.A., Stanford U., 1968. Vice-pres. fin. Alza Corp., Palo Alto, Calif., 1968-79, sr. v.p., 1979-80, exec. v.p., 1980-82, pres., 1982-87, co-chmn., chief exec. officer, 1987-93, dir. 1993—. Office: Alza Corp PO Box 10950 950 Page Mill Rd Palo Alto CA 94304-1012

GERSTELL, A. FREDERICK, aggregates/asphalt/concrete manufacturing exec; b. 1938. AB, Princeton U., 1960. Vice pres. mktg., dir. Alpha Portland Cement Co., 1960-75; v.p. Calif. Portland Cement Co., L.A., 1975-81, pres., chief operating officer, 1981-84; pres., chief operating officer CalMat Co., L.A., 1984-88, pres., chief exec. officer, chief operating officer, 1988-90; chmn.bd., pres., chief exec. officer/chief operating officer CalMat Co., 1990—. Trustee emeritus The Lawrenceville (N.J.) Sch. With USAR 1960-66. Mem. Merchants and Mfrs. Assn. (dir.), Nat. Stone Assn. (bd. dirs., exec. com.). Office: CalMat Co 3200 N San Fernando Rd Los Angeles CA 90065-1415

GERSTMAN, BUDDY BURT, health science educator; b. Bklyn., May 30, 1954; s. Joseph and Bernadine Joyce (Barnett) G.; m. Maureen Linda Gerstman, May 23, 1985; children: Emily, Deborah, Efrem, Jordan. BA, SUNY, Binghamton, 1976; DVMS, Cornell U., 1980; MPH, U. Calif., Berkeley, 1984; PhD, U. Calif., Davis, 1989. Pvt. practice as veterinarian No. Calif., 1980-85; epidemiologist FDA, Rockville, Md., 1985-90; assoc. prof. San Jose (Calif.) State U., 1990—. Contbr. articles to sci. jours. Mem. APHA, Internat. Soc. Pharmacoepidemiology, Soc. for Epidemiologic Rsch.

GERTENRICH, ROGER L., dentist, mayor; b. Oak Park, Ill., June 12, 1934; s. Roger L. and Muriel V. (Heurlin) G.; m. Caryl Joan Harrington, Dec. 20, 1935; children: Jill, Julie, Amy, Peter. AB, Ripon Coll.; DDS, Northwestern U. Councilman Salem City, Oreg., 1979-84, coun. pres., 1982; chmn. Salem Budget Com., 1981; mem. Salem Urban Renewal, Pringle Creek Adv. Com., 1972-79; mem. Downtown Devel. Bd., 1979; mem. post coun. tenure Salem Budget Com., 1988-90; past pres. Save the Elsinore Com.; facilitator methadone task force Oreg. Dept. Human Resources, Drug & Alcohol, 1992-93; mem. children's svcs. divsn. Citizen's Review Bd., 1993; past pres. Baker Sch. LSAC Com.; past pres. Marion County Health Coun.; adv. on pub. emergency dental care MPY Dental Soc.; cmty. rep. Statesman Jour. Newspaper Editl. Bd., 1990. Lt. med. svc. corps. U.S. Army. Mem. Oreg. Fishing Club. Office: PO Box 2082 Salem OR 97308

GERTH, DONALD ROGERS, university president; b. Chgo., Dec. 4, 1928; s. George C. and Madeleine (Canavan) G.; m. Beverly J. Hollman, Oct. 15, 1955; children: Annette, Deborah. BA, U. Chgo., 1947, AM, 1951, PhD, 1963. Field rep. S.E. Asia World Univ., 1950; asst. to pres. Shimer Coll., 1951; Admissions counselor U. Chgo., 1956-58; assoc. dean students, admissions and records, mem. dept. polit. sci. San Francisco St. U., San Francisco, 1958-63; assoc. dean instnl. relations and student affairs Calif. State Univ., 1963-64; chmn. commn. on extended edn. Calif. State Univs. and Colls., 1977-82; dean of students Calif. State U., Chico, 1964-68, prof. polit. sci., 1964-76, assoc. v.p. for acad. affairs, dir. internat. programs, 1969-70, v.p. acad. affairs, 1970-76; co-dir. Danforth Found. Research Project, 1968-69; coordinator Inst. Local Govt. and Public Service, 1968-70; pres., prof. polit. sci. and public adminstrn. Calif. State U., Dominguez Hills, 1976-84; pres., prof. govt. and adminstrn. Calif. State U., Sacramento, 1984—; past chair Accrediting Commn. for Sr. Colls. and Univs. of Western Coll. Assn.; chmn. admissions coun. Calif. State U.; bd. dirs. Ombudsman Found., L.A., 1968-71; com. continuing edn. Calif. Coordinating Coun. for Higher Edn., 1963-64; lectr. U. Philippines, 1953-54, Claremont Grad. Sch. and Univ. Ctr., 1965-69. Co-author: The Learning Society, 1969; author, editor: An Invisible Giant, 1971; contbg. editor Education for the Public Service, 1970, Papers on the Ombudsman in Higher Education, 1979. Mem. pers. commn. Chico Unified Sch. Dist., 1969-76, chmn., 1971-74; adv. com. on justice pgorams Butte Coll., 1970-76; mem. Varsity Scouting Coun., 1980-84; chmn. United Way campaign Calif. State Univs., L.A. County, 1981-82; bd. dirs. Sacramento Area United Way, campaign chmn., 1991-92, exec. com., 1991—, vice chmn., 1992-94, chmn.-elect, 1994-95, chmn., 1995—; mem. bd. dirs. South Bay Hosp. Found., 1979-82; mem. The Cultural Commn., L.A., 1981-84; mem. com. govtl. rels. Am. Coun. Edn. Capt. USAF, 1952-56. Mem. Internat. Assn. Univ. Pres. (chmn. N.Am. coun., pres.-elect), Am. Polit. Sci. Assn., Am. Soc. Pub. Adminstrn., Soc. Coll. and Univ. Planning, Western Govtl. Rsch. Assn., World Affairs Coun. No. Calif., Assn. Pub. Adminstrn. Edn. (chmn. 1973-74), Western Polit. Sci. Assn., Am. Assn. State Colls. and Univs. (bd. dirs.), Calif. State C. of C. (edn. com.), Assn. Governing Bds. of Univs. and Colls., Sacramento Club (bd. dirs.), Comstock Club. Democrat. Episcopalian. Home: 11463 Forty Niner Cir Gold River CA 95670-7852 Office: Calif State U 6000 J St 206 Sacramento CA 95819-6022

GERTZ, DAVID LEE, homebuilding company executive; b. Denver, July 30, 1950; s. Ben Harry and Clara (Cohen) G.; m. Bonnie Lee Schulein, June 2, 1973; children: Joshua, Eva. BS, U. Colo., 1972; MBA, U. Colo., Denver, 1993. Real estate broker Crown Realty, Denver, 1972-73; pres. Sunshine Plumbing Co., Lakewood, Colo., 1974-76, Sunshine Diversified, Inc., Lakewood, 1976—, Sunshine Master Builders, Ltd., Lakewood, 1990—; sec.-treas. Wight Lateral Ditch Co., Lakewood, 1987-91. Builder of custom homes and toxin free homes for allergy sensitive people. Cub master pack 135 Cub Scouts Am., Lakewood, 1989-91; asst. scout master troop 135 Boy Scouts Am., Lakewood, 1991-94; bd. dirs. Hebrew Ednl. Alliance, Denver, 1991-94; mem. Anti-Defamation League, Denver, 1989—. Scholar, Evans Scholars, U. Colo., 1968-72. Mem. Home Builders Assn. of Colo. (energy com. 1986—, Lakewood coord. com. 1986—, Jeffco coord. com. 1986—), Jeffco Bd. Realtors. Office: Sunshine Master Builders 8125 W Belleview Ave Littleton CO 80123-1203

GERWICK-BRODEUR, MADELINE CAROL, marketing and sales professional; b. Kearney, Neb., Aug. 29, 1951; d. Vern Frank and Marian Leila (Bliss) Gerwick; m. David Louis Brodeur; 1 child, Maria Louise. Student, U. Wis., 1970-72, U. Louisville, 1974-75; BA in Econs. magna cum laude, U. N.H., 1979; postgrad., Internat. Trade Inst., Seattle. Cert. cycles cons. Indsl. sales rep. United Radio Supply Inc., Seattle, 1980-81; mfrs. rep. Ray Over Sales Inc., Seattle, 1981-82; sales engr. Tektronix, Inc., Kent, Wash., 1982-83; mktg. mgr. Zepher Industries, Inc., Burien, Wash., 1983-85, Microscan Systems Inc., Tukwila, Wash., 1986.; market devel. URS Electronics, Inc., Portland, 1986-88; sr. product specialist Fluke Corp., 1989—; bd. dirs., sec. Starfish Enterprises Inc., Tacoma, 1984-87; com. chmn. Northcon, Seattle and Portland, 1984-86, 88, 90; speaker to Wash. Women's Employment and Edn., Tacoma, 1983—. Recipient Jack E. Chase award for Outstanding Svc. and Contbr. Northcon Founder's Orgn., 1988. Mem. Electronic Mfrs. Assn. (sec. 1982, sec.-treas. 1988, v.p. 1989), Inst. Noetic Scis., Phi Kappa Phi. Office: Fluke Corp MS270D PO Box 9090 Everett WA 98206-9090

GESHELL, RICHARD STEVEN, lawyer; b. Colorado Springs, Colo., Aug. 6, 1943; s. Peter Steven and Ann Elizabeth (Irwin) G.; m. Carol Ann Reed, Sept. 6, 1965; 1 child, Carmen Marie. BA in Chemistry, Ariz. State U., 1965; JD, U. Nebr., 1968. Bar: Nebr. 1968, U.S. Dist. Ct. Nebr. 1968, Hawaii 1983, U.S. Dist. Ct. Hawaii 1983, U.S. Ct. Appeals (9th cir.) 1984, U.S. Supreme Ct. 1986. Mem. Robak and Geshell, Columbus, Nebr., 1968-83; ptnr. R. Steven Geshell, Honolulu, 1983—. Served to capt. USAR, 1974-83. Mem. Assn. Trial Lawyers Am., Nebr. Bar Assn., Hawaii Bar Assn., Hawaii Trial Lawyers Assn., Blue Key (pres. 1964-65), Mid-Pacific C. C., Elks (chief forum 1984, past exalted ruler, trustee), Phi Sigma Kappa (past house mor, past v.p.). Republican. Home: 1155 Kaluanui Rd Honolulu HI 96825-1357 Office: 6600 Kalanianaole Hwy Ste 116 Honolulu HI 96825-1280

GESLEY, MARK ALAN, physicist, engineer; b. San Diego, Sept. 26, 1955; s. Edward Mark and Karen Kathleen (Oswald) G.; m. Gail Susan Moak, Mar. 1, 1983; children: Joseph Mead, Jared James, Edward Brennan. BA in Physics, Reed Coll., 1977; PhD in Applied Physics, Oreg. Grad. Inst. Sci. & Tech., 1985. Postdoctoral fellow IBM/T.J. Watson Rsch. Ctr., Yorktown Heights, N.Y., 1985-87; adv. engr. GTD div. IBM, East Fishkill, N.Y., 1987-88; Etec Systems, Inc., Hayward, Calif., 1988-94, sr. staff engr., 1994—; v.p. engring., 1995—. Contbr. over 20 articles to profl. jours. Exch. student Am. Field Svc., Brazil, 1972. Mem. Am. Phys. Soc., IEEE lithography, Phi Beta Kappa, Sigma Xi. Office: Etec Systems Inc 26460 Corporate Ave Hayward CA 94545-3914

GESNER, BRUCE DAVID, consulting company executive; b. Fall River, Mass., May 7, 1938; s. Norval Garfield Jr. and Margaret Lena (Glynn) G.; m. Claudette Jeannine Labreche, June 6, 1959 (div. Apr. 1991); children: Jeannine Catherine, Bruce David Jr., Jacqueline Marie, Michael Steven; m. Barbara Phyllis Whittiker, May 11, 1991. BS in Chemistry, Southeastern U. Mass., 1960; PhD in Physical Organic Chemistry, U. Idaho, 1963. Mem. tech. staff Bell Labs., Murray Hill, N.J., 1963-69; supr. PWB group Bell Labs., Whippany, N.J., 1969-71; supr. materials chemistry Bell Labs., Norcross, Ga., 1971-77; sr. field rep. Bell Labs., Omaha, 1978-82, San Francisco, 1982-84; divsn. mgr., liaison Bellcore, San Francisco, 1985; exec. dir. technology Pacific Bell, San Ramon, Calif., 1986-90; owner, operator Qualitel Cons. Group, Danville, Calif., 1990—. PAtentee in field. Sec., treas. Puddingstone Heights Country Club, Parsippany, N.J., 1970-71; treas. Smoke Rise (Ga.) Cmty Club, 1976-77. Mass. State scholar, 1959, 60; Nat Defense fellow, 1960-63. Mem. AAAS, Am. Chem. Soc., Calif. Acad. Sci. (pres. cir. 1991-94), Phi Kappa Phi, Sigma Xi. Home: 1300 Fountain Springs Cir Danville CA 94526-5625 Office: Qualitel Cons Group 900 Bush St Apt 903 San Francisco CA 94109-6394

GESTRING, CLARK KENT, oil field well evaluation service executive; b. Denver, Apr. 20, 1949; s. Harlan Dale and Martha Betty Gestring; m. Patrice Kennedy, June 22, 1974; 1 child, Michael. BS in Geol. Engring., Colo. Sch. Mines, 1971; MBA, U. Denver, 1981, M Internat. Mgmt., 1994. Registered profl. engr., Colo. Sr. geologist NL Baroid Petroleum Surveys, Houston, 1974-79; dir. field plants Enron Corp., Denver, 1980-91; pvt. cons. Denver, 1991; COO WWS Log Svcs., Lakewood, Colo., 1991—. Capt. USAR, 1972-84. Mem. Soc. Petroleum Engrs., Soc. Profl. Well Log Analysts, Denver Well Log Soc. (v.p. 1993-94). Office: WWS Log Svcs Inc 12600 W Colfax Ave Ste A270 Lakewood CO 80215-3733

GETIS, ARTHUR, geography educator; b. Phila., July 6, 1934; s. Samuel J. and Sophie Getis; m. Judith M. Marckwardt, July 23, 1961; children: Hilary Hope Tarazi, Victoria Lynn, Anne Patterson Tibbetts. BS, Pa. State U., 1956, MS, 1958; PhD, U. Wash., 1961. Asst. instr. geography U. Wash., 1960-61; asst. prof. Mich. State U., 1961-63; faculty Rutgers U., New Brunswick, N.J., 1963-77; prof. geography Rutgers U., 1969-77, dir. grad. programs in geography, 1970-73, chmn. New Brunswick geography dept., 1971-73; prof. geography U. Ill., Urbana-Champaign, 1977-90; prof. geography San Diego State U., 1990—, doctoral program coord., 1990-92; Stephen/Mary Birch Found. Endowed Chair of Geog. Studies, 1992—, Albert W. Johnson Univ. Rsch. Lectureship, 1995; head dept. U. Ill., 1977-83, dir. Sch. Social Scis., 1983-84; vis. lectr. Bristol U., Eng., 1966-67, UCLA, summers 1968, 74, U. B.C., 1969; vis. prof. Princeton U., 1971-74; vis. disting. prof. San Diego State U., 1989; mem. Regional Sci. Research Group, Harvard U., 1970; panelist NSF, 1981-83. Author: (with B. Boots) Models of Spatial Processes, 1978, Point Pattern Analysis, 1988, (with J. Getis and J.D. Fellmann) Geography, 1981, Human Geography, 3d edit., 1992, Introduction to Geography, 4th edit., 1994, (edited with J. Getis) The United States and Canada, 1995; editor: Geographical Systems, 1992—; contbg. editor, assoc. editor: Jour. Geography, 1972-74; mem.. editorial bd. Nat. Geog. Rsch., 1984-90, Rsch. and Exploration, 1991-95, Geog. Analysis, 1991; contbr. to profl. lit. Mem. Urbana Zoning Bd. Appeals, 1980-84; co-pres. Univ. High Sch. Parent-Faculty Orgn., 1982-83. Rutgers U. faculty fellow, 1970; East-West Center sr. fellow, 1974; NSF grantee, 1983-85, 1992-94. Mem. Assn. Am. Geographers (grantee 1964-65, vis. scientist 1970-72, chair math. models and quantitative methods splty. group 1991-92), Western Regional Sci. Assn. (bd. dirs. 1992—), Regional Sci. Assn. (pres. N.E. sect. 1973-74), Inst. Brit. Geographers, Internat. Geog. Union (sec. commn. math. models 1988—), Sigma Xi. Home: 5135 Jumilla St San Diego CA 92124-1503 Office: San Diego State U Dept Geography San Diego CA 92182

GETMAN, SHERYL MARIE, artist; b. Kalispell, Mont., Dec. 31, 1947; d. Dannie E. Loutherback and Shirley Jean (Barry) Michaelson; m. Daniel William Getman, Jan. 21, 1952; children: Guy Young, Crescent. Student, Ea. Mont. State Coll., 1968, 69, Calif State Coll., Fullerton, 1970, Mont. State U., 1974, 75, 76, Flathead Coll., Kalispell Mt., 1977, 78, Art Student's League, N.Y.C., 1988. Artist Jorgensen Pottery & Art Studio, Coram, Mont., 1978-83; owner, mgr. Spruce Park Truck Stop, Coram, 1980-83; pres., artist Sky Jordan Graphics, Kalispell, 1983-86; pres. Sky Jordan Restaurant Inc., Kalispell Mt., 1983-86; pres., artist Artistic Urges, Inc., Princeton, N.J., 1986-92; propr. Whitney Mansion Gallery and Inn, Kalispell, 1992—; v.p. Sky Deco Inc., 1989—; feature writer Penington (N.J.) Post, 1989, also freelance writer; pres. Sky East Inc., 1990—; instr. Reevaluation Counseling, Creativity Seminars, 1989—; owner Getman Studio, Santa Monica, Calif. Author: Big House of Montana, 1993; illustrator: Memoirs of Montana Fisherman, Jelinski, 1993. Vol. Siddha Meditation Ctr. Mem. Nat. League Am. Pen Women, North Star Watercolor Soc. (bd. dirs. 1987-88). Unitarian. Office: Sheryl Getman Studios 2633 Lincoln Blvd Santa Monica CA 90405-4656

GETREU, IAN E(DWIN), electronics engineer; b. Melbourne, Australia, Sept. 14, 1943; s. Leo and Matylda Getreu; m. Beverly S. Salmenson, June 5, 1983. BE with honors, U. Melbourne, 1965, M Engring. Sci., 1967; postgrad., UCLA, 1966-67; PhD, U. Calif., Berkeley, 1972. Sr. engr. Tektronix Inc., Beaverton, Oreg., 1972-79, mgr. integrated cir. computer aided design devel., 1979-83, mgr. advanced products mktg., 1983-85, scientist advanced products, 1985-86; v.p., modeling Analogy Inc., Beaverton, 1986-92, v.p. engring., 1992-94, v.p. tech. devel., 1992—, 1994—; also bd. dirs. Analogy, Inc., Beaverton, bd. dirs., 1986-90; lectr. U. New South Wales, Sydney, Australia, 1974-75; chmn. Computer Aided Network Design Com., 1980-82. Author: Modeling the Bipolar Transistor, 1976. Bd. dirs. Jewish Fedn. of Portland, 1986-93, v.p., 1989-93; chair Oreg. Am. Israel Pub. Affairs Com., 1994—. Mem. IEEE (sr.) (cirs. and systems soc. v.p. confs. 1990-91), Internat. Conf. Computer Aided Design (chmn. 1986). Home: PO Box 1356 Beaverton OR 97075-1356

GETREU, SANFORD, city planner; b. Cleve., Mar. 9, 1930; s. Isadore and Tillie (Kuchinsky) G.; B.A. in Architecture, Ohio State U., 1953; M.A. in Regional Planning, Cornell U., 1955; m. Gara Eileen Smith, Dec. 8, 1952 (div. Feb. 1983); children—David Bruce, Gary Benjamin, Allen Dana; m. Kelly Heim, Aug. 8, 1988. Resident planner Mackesey & Reps., consultants, Rome, N.Y., 1955-56; planning dir., Rome, 1956-57; dir. gen. planning, Syracuse, N.Y., 1957-59, dep. commr. planning, 1959-62, commr. planning, 1962-65; planning dir. San Jose, Calif., 1965-74; urban planning cons., 1974—; pres. Sanford Getreu, AICP, Inc., vis. lectr., critic Cornell U., 1960-65, Syracuse U., 1962-65, Stanford, 1965, San Jose State Coll., 1965, Santa Clara U., Calif. State Poly. Coll., DeAnza Coll., San Jose City Coll., U. Calif. at Berkeley; pres. planning dept. League of Calif. Cities, 1973-74; advisor State of Calif. Office of Planning and Research. Past bd. dirs. Theater Guild, San Jose, Triton Mus., San Jose. Mem. Am. Soc. Cons. Planners, Am. Planning Assn., Am. Inst. Cert. Planners, Bay Area Planning Dirs. Assn. (v.p. 1965-74, mem. exec. com. 1973-74), Assn. Bay Area Govts. (regional planning com. 1967-74). Club: Rotary. Home: 105 Coronado Ave Los Altos CA 94022-2222 Office: 4966 El Camino Real Ste 101 Los Altos CA 94022-1406

GETTY, GORDON PETER, composer, philanthropist; b. Los Angeles, Dec. 20, 1933; s. J. Paul and Ann Rork (Light) G.; m. Ann Getty; 4 children. Studied, voice with Easton Kent, piano with Robert Vetlesen, theory with Sol Joseph, 1961-62; BS, San Francisco Conservatory Music, hon. music degree, 1981; hon. music degree, Pepperdine U., 1985; hon. doctorate, Mannes Coll. Music, N.Y.C., 1986. Former cons. Getty Oil Co., dir.; former chmn. LSB Leakey Found., Pasadena, Calif., now trustee. Works include opera in two acts Plump Jack, commnd. by Globe Shakespeare Ctr., London, performed by San Francisco Symphony, 1985, also Scene One broadcast live from Davies Symphony Hall, San Francisco, Mar. 1985; Emily Dickinson Song Cycle The White Election, 30 performances U.S. and abroad, 1981-85, also broadcast live from Nat. Gallery Art, Washington, 1985; Victorian Scenes, performed San Francisco Girls Chorus U. Calif., Berkeley, WInifred Baker Choral, 1985; Nine Piano Pieces performed by Stewart Gordon, 1985; A Cappella Choruses and Piano Works broadcast live Georgetown U., Washington, Apr., 1985; author monograph on White Election, poems My Uncle's House, 1984, other poetry. Adv. dir. Met. Opera, 1977—; trustee Mannes Coll. Music, 1982—; dir. San Francisco Symphony, 1979—. Recipient Golden Plate award Am. Acad. Achievement, 1985, Achievement Arts award Northwood Inst., 1985. Office: Rourke Music Embarcado Ctr/Ste 1050 San Francisco CA 94111*

GEUTHER, CARL FREDERICK, financial services company executive; b. Phila., Sept. 17, 1945; s. Frederick and Dorothy (Ache) G.; m. Carole Peters, Apr. 2, 1970; children: Jeffrey, Lisa, Sharon. BA, Ursinus Coll., 1967; MBA, Lehigh U., 1968. CPA, N.Y. Sr. acct. Deloite Haskins & Sells, N.Y.C., 1968-72; zone controller Assocs. Fin. Services, South Bend, Ind., 1972-74; exec. v.p., chief fin. officer Aristar, Inc., Miami, Fla., 1974-86, Great Western Financial Corp., Los Angeles, 1986—. Am Inst. CPA's, N.Y. Soc. CPA's. Presbyterian. Home: 25275 Eldorado Meadow Rd Hidden Hills CA 91302-1243 Office: Aristar Life Ins Inc 20950 Warner Center Ln Woodland Hills CA 91367-6510

GEYER, DAVID WARREN, aerospace scientist, software engineer; b. Pueblo, Colo., Apr. 3, 1936; s. Warren Francis and Donna Maxine (Smith) G.; m. Winifred Jane Geyer, June 1974; children: Michael Harold, Michael David, Thomas, Martha. BSEE, U. Colo.; MSEE, NYU. Mem. tech. staff Bell Telephone Labs., Whippany, N.J., 1957-61; sr. engr., dir. Convair Divsn. Gen. Dynamics, San Diego, 1961-81; v.p. Teledyne Sys. Co., Northridge, Calif., 1981-87; gen. mgr. strategic planning Analex Corp., Albuquerque, 1987—. Author: (with others) Ivertial Guidance by Parson, 1968. Bd. dirs. Highlands Ranch (Colo.) Homeowners Assn., 1990-91. Mem. IEEE (sr.), AIAA, Assn. of Computing Machinery, Profl. Aerospace Contractors Assn. Office: Analex Corp 1650 University Blvd NE Ste 105 Albuquerque NM 87102-1730

GHANDEHARIZADEH, SHAHRAM, computer scientist and educator; b. Tehran, Iran, Dec. 10, 1965; came to U.S., 1982; s. Arastoo and Mehrangiz Ghandeharizadeh. BS, U. Wis., 1985, MS, 1987, PhD, 1990. Rsch. asst. U. Wis., Madison, 1985-90; asst. prof. computer sci. U. So. Calif., L.A., 1990—; cons. Hewlett-Packard, AT&T. Contbr. articles to profl. jours.; patentee in field. Recipient NSF Young Investigator award, 1992; grantee NSF/RIA, 1991-93, NSF, 1993—, U. So. Calif., 1991-92, 93-94, TRW, 1993—, AT&T, 1993—, Hewlett Packard, 1993—. Mem. IEEE, ACM. Office: U So Calif Dept Computer Sci Los Angeles CA 90089

GHAREEB, DONALD L., judge; b. East Grand Rapids, Mich., Oct. 28, 1930; s. Phillip Nimey and Hannah (Dabakey) G. AB in Letters and Law, U. Mich., 1952, JD, 1954. Bar: Mich. 1956, Ariz. 1969. Pvt. practice law Grand Rapids, Mich., 1956-68; adminstrv. law judge Ind. Commn. of Ariz., Phoenix, 1970-90, vice chief adminstrv. law judge, 1990—. Speaker and educator Ariz. Workers Compensation Bar, 1987—, chmn., 1993-94. U.S. Jaycees (nat. v.p. senate 1988-89, state pres. Ariz. senate 1987-88). Republican. Eastern Orthodox.

GHAZANFAR, SHAIKH MOHAMMED, economics educator, researcher; b. Jullundar, Brit. India, Apr. 1, 1937; came to U.S., 1958; s. Shaikh Mehboob and Musammat Farhat (Elahi) Bakhsh; m. Rukshsana Sharif, Aug. 16, 1965; children: Farah, Asif, Kashif. BA with honors, Wash. State U., 1962, MA in Econs., 1964, PhD in Econs., 1968. Instr. econs. Wash. State U., Pullman, 1962-64, rsch. economist, 1964, teaching asst., 1965-67, instr., 1967-68; asst. prof. U. Idaho, Moscow, 1968-72, assoc. prof., 1972-77, prof., 1977—, head dept., 1979-81, 92-94; head, 1994—; coord. internat. studies program U. Idaho, Moscow, 1990-93; vis. prof. U. Punjab, Lahore, Pakistan, fall 1974-75, U. Md., College Park, spring 1974-75, King Abdulaziz U., Jeddah, Saudi Arabia, 1983-866; mem. budget forecast Idaho Legis., 1974-93. Bd. dirs. Daily News community bd., 1992-94. Mem. Martin Luther King Day Com., Moscow, 1986-90, Latah County Task Force on Human Rights, Moscow, 1988-92; chmn. Malcom Kerr scholarship com. for high sch. students Nat. Coun. on U.S.-Arab Rels., Washington, 1988-94. Mem. AAUP, Nat. Tax. Assn., Mid Western Econ. Assn., Western Social Scis. Assn., Amnesty Internat., History of Econs. Soc. Office: U Idaho Dept Econs Moscow ID 83843

GHEEN, BETTY M., food products executive; b. 1924. V.p. Merrill Farms, Salinas, Calif. Office: Merrill Farms 1067 Merrill St Salinas CA 93901-4420*

GHENT, PEER, management consultant; b. Washington, Sept. 13, 1939; s. Pierre Mowell Ghent and Helen V. (Mork) Dyer; m. Sonya Renate Schmid, Oct. 12, 1962 (div. 1975); children: Carol R. Ghent-Singley, Erika Lynn, Peer Jr., Valerie. BCE, Cornell U., 1961; MBA, Harvard U., 1966. Registered civil engr. and land surveyor, La. Sr. ops. research analyst Office Sec. Def., Washington, 1966-69; pres. Plaskolite Inc., Columbus, Ohio, 1969-71; cons. U.S. Price Commn., Washington, 1971-72; dir. corp. devel. Buckeye Internat., Columbus, 1972-74; pres. Peterson Baby Products, North Hollywood, Calif., 1974-78; v.p., chief fin. officer Oakleaf Corp., Chatsworth, Calif., 1980-81; v.p. CMB Investment Counselors, Los Angeles, 1983-85, Stars to Go Inc., Los Angeles, 1986-88; prin. Peer Ghent & Assocs., Van Nuys, Calif., 1989-93; sr. cons. Mgmt. Action Programs, Inc., Sherman Oaks, Calif., 1993—; lectr. Grad. Sch. Mgmt. UCLA, 1979-88. Author: (with others) Computer Graphics: A Revolution in Design, 1966. Served to capt. U.S. Army, 1961-63. Democrat. Episcopalian. Home: 13422 Oxnard St Van Nuys CA 91401-4041 Office: Mgmt Action Programs Inc 4725 Hazeltine Ave Sherman Oaks CA 91423-2326

GHISELIN, BREWSTER, author, English language educator emeritus; b. Webster Groves, Mo., June 13, 1903; s. Horace and Eleanor (Weeks) G.; m. Olive F. Franks, June 7, 1929; children: Jon Brewster, Michael Tenant. A.B., UCLA, 1927; M.A., U. Calif.-Berkeley, 1928, student, 1931-33; student, Oxford U., Eng., 1928-29. Asst. in English U. Calif., Berkeley, 1931-33; instr. English U. Utah, 1929-31, 34-38, lectr., 1938-39, asst. prof., 1939-46, assoc. prof., 1946-50, prof., 1950-71, prof. emeritus, 1971, Distinguished Research prof., 1967-68; dir. Writers' Conf., 1947-66; poetry editor Rocky Mt. Rev., 1937-46; assoc. editor Western Rev., 1946-49; lectr. creativity, cons. Inst. Personality Assessment and Research, U. Calif., Berkeley, 1957-58; editorial adv. bd. Concerning Poetry, 1968—. Author: Against the Circle, 1946, The Creative Process, 1952, new paperback edit., 1985, 95, The Nets, 1955, Writing, 1959, Country of the Minotaur, 1970, (with others) The Form Discovered: Essays on the Achievement of Andrew Lytle, 1973, Light, 1978, Windrose: Poems, 1929-1979, 1980, (with others) Contemporary Authors, 1989; (poems) Flame, 1991. Bd. advisors Silver Mountain Found. Ford Found. fellow, 1952-53; recipient award Nat. Inst. Arts and Letters, 1970; Blumenthal-Leviton-Blonder prize Poetry mag., 1973; Levinson prize, 1978; William Carlos Williams award Poetry Soc. Am., 1981; Gov.'s award for arts Utah Arts Council, 1982; LHD hc, U of Utah, 1994. Mem. MLA, Utah Acad. Scis., Arts and Letters (Charles Redd award), Phi Beta Kappa, Phi Kappa Phi. also (summer): 1747 Princeton Ave Salt Lake City UT 84108-1810 also: U Utah 1747 Princeton Ave Salt Lake City UT 84108

GHOSH, ABHIJIT, electrical engineer; b. Calcutta, India, Aug. 22, 1964; came to U.S., 1986; s. Susanta Kumar and Madhuri G.; m. Eliane Setton, Dec. 1, 1993. B in Tech., Indian Inst. Tech., Kharagpur, India, 1986; MS, U. Calif., 1989; PhD, 1991. Rsch. asst. U. Calif., Berkeley, 1987-91, teaching asst., 1986-87; sr. engr. Mitsubishi Electric Rsch. Labs., Sunnyvale, Calif., 1991—; program com. Internat. Test Synthesis Workshop, IEEE, Santa Barbara, Calif., 1993—, Asian Design Automation Conf., IEEE, Japan, 1995. Author: Sequential Logic Testing and Verification, 1991, Logic Synthesis, 1994; patentee ATM Switch Architecture, 1994; contbr. articles to profl. jours. Recipient Best paper award IEEE, ACM, Orlando, Fla., 1990. Mem. IEEE, Assn. for Computing Machinery. Office: Mitsubishi Electric Rsch Labs Inc 1050 E Arques Ave Sunnyvale CA 94086

GIACOLETTO, JOSEPH RICHARD, electronics company executive; b. Clinton, Ind., Apr. 3, 1935; s. Joseph Henry and Helen Frances (Leinberger) G.; m. Ruby Marlene Humphreville, Sept. 13, 1974; children: Glenna Egan, Julie Nolan. BS, Ind. State U., 1956; MBA, U. So. Calif., 1968; hon. degree, UCLA, 1975. Mgr. procurement missile systems div. Hughes Aircraft Co., L.A., 1961-68, asst. mgr. contracts aero. systems div., 1969, asst. bus. mgr. F-15, 1970-71, asst. program mgr. ATLAS, 1972, asst. mgr. contracts, 1972-75, dir. contracts radar systems group, 1975-83, dir. contracts, group v.p., 1983-86, v.p., group v.p., 1986-87, sr. v.p., group v.p., 1987—. Chmn. El Segundo (Calif.) Ednl. Found.; bd. dirs. Thomas Jefferson Rsch. Ctr., Pasedena. With USAF, 1956-63. Office: Hughes Aircraft Co Radar Systems Group PO Box Bos # 92426 Los Angeles CA 90009

GIACOLINI, EARL L., agricultural products company executive. Vice-chmn. Sun Diamond Growers of Calif., Pleasanton. Office: Sun-Diamond Growers Calif 5568 Gibraltar Dr Pleasanton CA 94588-8544

GIACOMO, GARY CHRISTOPHER, magazine editor, journalist; b. Sacramento, Calif., Dec. 23, 1957; s. James John and Audrey Mary (Huttle) G.; m. Sherry Baker, June 15, 1979; 1 child, Matthew. AA in Cmty. Journalism, Am. River Coll., Sacramento, 1979; BA in Journalism, Calif. State U., Sacramento, 1983; postgrad., San Jose State U., 1993—. News editor Amador Ledger, Jackson, Calif., 1979-81; computer typesetting trainer Sys. Integrators, Inc., Sacramento, 1981-84, product mgr. newspapers, 1984-87; mag. editor Calif. State Firefighters Assn., Sacramento, 1987—; mem. reader panel Folio mag., Stamford, Conn., 1992-93. Mem. Western Publ. Assn. (Maggie award for Design 1990, Maggie award for Most Improved Mag. 1989), Soc. Profl. Journalists (Enterprise Reporting award 1994). Roman Catholic. Office: Calif State Firefighters 3246 Ramos Cir Sacramento CA 95827-2513

GIANELLI, WILLIAM REYNOLDS, foundation administrator, civil engineering consultant, former federal agency commissioner; b. Stockton, Calif., Feb. 19, 1919; s. John Antone and Frances Isabelle (Reynolds) G.; m. Shirley Jean Scott, Feb. 14, 1947; children: Cynthia Catherine, Patricia Duncan. BS, U. Calif., Berkeley, 1941. Staff engr. Calif. Dept. Water Resources, Sacramento, 1945-60, dir., 1967-73; ptnr. Gianelli & Murray, cons. engrs., Sacramento, 1960-66; cons. engr. Pebble Beach, Calif., 1973-81; asst. sec. of army Dept. Def., Washington, 1981-84; chmn. Panama Canal Commn., Washington, 1981-89; cons. engr. Pebble Beach, Calif., 1989—; mem. nat. com. on water quality, Washington, 1973-76; chmn. Monterey (Calif.) Peninsula Water Mgmt. Dist., 1978-80. Chmn. Water Edn. Found., Sacramento, 1985-89; chmn. Calif. State Pers. Bd., 1973-81. Maj. C.E., U.S. Army, 1941-45. Recipient Skill, Integrity, and Responsibility award Assn. Gen. Contractors N.Y., 1973, Hoover award (from 4 nat. engrs. socs.), 1988; named Constrn. Man of Yr. Engring. News Record, 1972, Pub. Works Man of Yr. Am. Pub. Works Assn., N.Y., 1973. Fellow ASCE (Pres.'s award 1987); mem. Am. Waterworks Assn. (hon.), Monterey Peninsula Country Club (pres. 1987). Republican. Episcopalian. Address: 973 Pioneer Rd Pebble Beach CA 93953-2718

GIANNETTI, RONALD ARMAND, psychologist; b. Chgo., May 21, 1946; s. Armando Eugene and Olga (Santarelli) G.; m. Carolyn Jean Openshaw, Nov. 23, 1975; 1 child, Anthony Michael. BA, U. Calif., Berkeley, 1967, PhD, 1973. Chief psychiat. assessment unit VA Med. Ctr., Salt Lake City, 1976-78; asst. prof. dept. psychiatry Ea. Va. Med. Sch., Norfolk, 1978-79; dir. Psychology Internship Tng. Program, Norfolk, 1978-81; assoc. prof. dept. psychiatry Ea. Va. Med. Sch., Norfolk, 1979-85; chair Va. Consortium for Profl. Psychology, Norfolk, 1979-88; prof. dept. psychiatry Ea. Va. Med. Sch., Norfolk, 1985-88; chair psychology programs Fielding Inst., Santa Barbara, Calif., 1988-92, dean of psychology, 1992—; cons. VA Med. Ctr., Hampton, Va., 1982-88, Ea. State Hosp., Williamsburg, Va., 1979-81. Author 41 articles, book chpts., and computer software packages in psychol. assessment and in edn. Mem. adv. bd. Gestalt and Family Inst. of Va., Gloucester, 1979-84, Info. Ctr. of Hampton Roads, Norfolk, 1979-80. Grantee Charles G. Brown Found., 1984, VA, 1977, Found. for Applied Comms. Tech., 1974. Fellow APA, Am. Psychol. Soc. (charter), Soc. for Personality Assessment; mem. Soc. for Computers in Psychology. Home: 2224 Chapala St Santa Barbara CA 93105-3907 Office: Fielding Inst 2112 Santa Barbara St Santa Barbara CA 93105-3544

GIANNOTTA, STEVEN LOUIS, neurosurgery educator; b. Detroit, Apr. 4, 1947; s. Louis D. and Betty Jane (Root) G.; m. Sharon Danielak, June 13, 1970; children: Brent, Nicole, Robyn. Student, U. Detroit, 1965-68; MD, U. Mich., 1972. Diplomate Am. Bd. Neurol. Surgeons. Surg. intern U. Mich., Ann Arbor, 1972-73, neurosurg. resident, 1973-78; asst. prof. neurosurgery UCLA, 1978-80; asst. prof. neurosurgery U. So. Calif., Sch. Medicine, L.A., 1980-83, assoc. prof. neurosurgery, 1983-89, prof. neurosurgery, 1989—; sec. Congress Neurol. Surgeons, Washington, 1986-89, v.p., 1993; pres. L.A. (Calif.) Soc. Clin. Neuroscis., 1992-93. Fellow ACS, Am. Heart Assn. (stroke coun., rsch. grantee 1980, 84), So. Calif. Neurol. Soc. (pres. 1993-94). Democrat. Roman Catholic. Office: Dept Neurosurgery Box 239 1200 N State St Los Angeles CA 90033

GIANNOTTI, STEPHEN PAUL, graphic designer; b. L.A., Oct. 25, 1952; s. John D. and Ruth C. (Crosby) G. Student, Pacific U., 1970-73. Assoc. art dir. Colortone Creative Graphics, Washington, 1973-74; lead designer Nat. Wildlife Fedn., Vienna, Va., 1974-76; sr. art dir. ROCOR Internat., Palo Alto, Calif., 1976-78; owner Giannotti Design, Portland, Oreg., 1978—; sr. art dir. Warr, Foote & Rose, Inc., Los Altos, Calif., 1982-86; lectr. in field. Recipient Gertrude B. Murphy award San Jose Art Dir.'s Club, 1983, Graphics Gallery awards Strathmore Paper Co., 1983, 91, Regional Design Annual award Print Mag., 1985, 89, Internat. Design Folder awards Crane's Paper Co., 1985, 86, 92, Internat. Gallery Superb Printing awards 1985, 86, 92, Self-Promotion Annual award How Mag., 1988, awards West Coast Art Dir.'s Club, 1989, 90, 91. Mem. Silicon Valley Am. Mktg. Assn. (art dir.). Home: 2027 NE Hancock St Portland OR 97212

GIANTURCO, PAOLA, management consulting company executive; b. Urbana, Ill., July 22, 1939; d. Cesare and Verna Bertha (Daily) Gianturco; m. David Sanderson Hill, Mar. 12, 1988; 1 child from previous marriage, Scott Sangster. BA, Stanford U., 1961; postgrad. U. So. Calif., 1971. Pub. relations dir. Joseph Magnin, San Francisco, 1961-67; pub. relations dir., account exec. Hall & Levine Advt. Agy., Los Angeles, 1968-73, v.p., account supr., 1973-76, sr. v.p., 1977-82; v.p. Dancer Fitzgerald Sample, 1982-87, exec. v.p., mgmt. supr. Saatchi and Saatchi, 1988-91; pres. The Gianturco Co., 1991—. Past bd. dirs. The Country Schs. Mem. Women in Communications, Stanford Profl. Women (past mem. bd. dirs.), Stanford Inst. Rsch. Women and Gender, Corp. Assocs. Bd., Inca Floats Adventure Travel (bd. dirs.). Home and Office: 30 Cecily Ln Mill Valley CA 94941-3300

GIAQUINTA, GERALD J., public relations executive; b. Lawrence, Mass.. BA, U. Mass.; PhD, U. So. Calif.; JD, Loyola U. Pub. relations officer Toyota Motor Sales USA, 1980-89; gen. mgr. public relations Mercedes-Benz, 1989-91; v.p. western region Mercedes-Benz of N.Am., 1991-92; pres., CEO Bob Thomas & Assocs., Venice, Calif., 1992-93; cons. Chiat/Day Advt., Venice, 1993—. Office: Bob Thomas & Associates 340 Main St Venice CA 90291-2524

GIBB, DOUGLAS GLENN, police chief; b. Makaweli, Hawaii, June 5, 1940; s. Douglas Stormont and Gwendolyn Elizabeth (Bedell) G.; m. Melanie Ululani Hardy, Nov. 16, 1963; children—Diane Nalani, Glenn Kale. BS in Bus. Adminstrn., U. Denver, 1966; cert., Nat. Execs. Inst., FBI, 1984. Patrolman Honolulu Police Dept., 1967-71, sgt., 1971-76, lt., 1976-80, capt., 1980-83, chief police, 1983—; cons. on sting projects Office Justice Assistance, Dept. Justice, 1983—; mem. Hawaii Gov.'s Planning Commn. on Crime, 1983—, Juvenile Justice Interagy. Bd., 1983—. Bd. dirs. ARC, Honolulu, 1983—; mem. exec. bd. Boy Scouts Am., Honolulu, 1983—; mem. sr. adv. council CAP, Honolulu, 1983—. Recipient cert. of merit Law Enforcement Assistance Adminstrn., Washington, 1979; named Police Officer of Yr., 200 Club, Honolulu, 1982. Mem. Hawaii Law Enforcement Officer Assn. (pres. 1983-85), Internat. Assn. Chiefs of Police (membership com. 1985), Major City Chiefs, Honolulu C. of C. (crime com. 1983—). Episcopalian. Home: PO Box 510 Kaaawa HI 96730-0510 Office: Honolulu Police Dept 801 S Beretania St Honolulu HI 96813-2501

GIBBONS, JERRY LEE, advertising executive; b. Coalinga, Calif., Feb. 10, 1936; s. James A. and Hazel Bernice (Drummond) G.; m. Alba Valdez, Feb. 22, 1963; children: Jeffery Scott, Cristin Lyn, Trisha Leigh. BA, San Jose State U., 1958. Trainee Young & Rubicam, San Francisco, 1957; account exec. McCann-Erickson, San Francisco, 1960-63; asst. to pres. Western Outdoor Markets, San Francisco, 1964; v.p., sales mgr. Naegele Outdoor Advt., Oakland, Calif., 1965-67; account exec. Blair Radio Co., San Francisco, 1968, Campbell-Ewald, San Francisco, 1969; v.p., account supr. Dailey & Assocs., San Francisco, 1970-71; co-founder, pres. Pritikin & Gibbons Communications, San Francisco, 1971-73; pres. Ayer, Pritikin & Gibbons, San Francisco, 1973-81; pres., chief exec. officer Doyle Dane Bernbach, San Francisco, 1981-87; sr. v.p. group mgmt. Foote, Cone and Belding, San Francisco, 1987-89; pres. Gibbons & Dickens, San Francisco, 1989-92; sr. v.p. Am. Assn. of Advt. agencies, San Francisco, 1992—; guest lectr. San Jose State U. and San Francisco State U., 1970-73. Mem. adv. bd. Nat. Assn. Visually Handicapped, 1968-72; bd. dirs., mem. exec. com. Oakland Symphony Orch. Assn., 1980-83; elder Montclair Presbyn. Ch., Oakland, 1974-84; bd. dirs. U.S. Orgn. for Disabled Athletes, 1987-90; mem. adv. com. Fred Finch Youth Ctr., 1987; bd. chair The Marine Mammal Ctr., 1993—. Served with U.S. Army, 1958-60. Recipient Profl. Achievement award San Jose State U., 1984. Mem. Am. Assn. Advt. Agys. (bd. govs. No. Calif. chpt., chmn. Western region), Sales and Mktg. Assn. San Francisco (chmn. publicity com. 1975-76, past pres.), San Francisco Soc. Communicating Arts (pres., dir. 1975-78), San Francisco C. of C., San Francisco Advt. Club (past pres., dir.), Alpha Delta Sigma (past pres., dir.). Office: Am Assn Advertising Agencies 130 Battery St San Francisco CA 94111-4905

GIBBS, JAMES LOWELL, JR., anthropologist, researcher; b. Syracuse, N.Y., June 13, 1931; s. James Lowell and Huldah Hortense (Dabney) G.; m. Jewelle Althea Taylor, Aug. 25, 1956; children: Geoffrey Taylor, Lowell Dabney. BA, Cornell U., 1952; postgrad., Cambridge (Eng.) U., 1954; PhD, Harvard U., 1961. Instr. anthropology U. Minn., Mpls., 1959-60, asst. prof., 1960-63, assoc. prof., 1963-66; assoc. prof. Stanford (Calif.) U., 1966-70, prof., 1970—, chmn. dept., 1987-90, Martin Luther King Jr. Centennial prof., 1988, acting dir. program in African and Afro-Am. studies, 1968-69, dean undergrad. studies, 1970-76, co-dir. Stanford-Berkeley Joint Ctr. for African Studies, 1985-87; mem. Overseas Devel. Coun., Washington, 1989—; mem. panel on democratization NRC, Washington, 1991-93. Co-author: Law in Radically Different Cultures, 1983 (cert. of merit Am. Soc. Internat. Law 1984); editor, contbr.: Peoples of Africa, 1965; co-producer, co-dir. film The Cows of Dolo Ken Paye, 1970 (Golden Eagle award Coun. on Internat. Non-Theatrical Events 1972). Mem. Minn. Commn. Against Discrimination, St. Paul, 1963-65; trustee Mills Coll., Oakland, Calif., 1970-75, Cornell U., Ithaca, N.Y., 1973-86, Carnegie Corp. N.Y., N.Y.C., 1984-91. Recipient E. Harris Harbison prize for gifted teaching Danforth Found., 1970; fellow Ctr. for Advanced Study in Behavioral Scis., 1969-70, Woodrow Wilson Internat. Ctr. for Scholars, 1976-77, sr. fellow W.E.B. DuBois Inst. for Afro-Am. Rsch., Harvard U., 1984-85. Fellow AAAS, Am. Anthrop. Assn. (exec. bd. 1969-70), Am. Studies Assn. (bd. dirs. 1966-69); mem. Sigma Xi. Democrat. Presbyterian. Home: 857 Sonoma Ter Stanford CA 94305-1024 Office: Stanford U Dept Anthropology Stanford CA 94305

GIBBS, JEWELLE TAYLOR, clinical psychologist; b. Stratford, Conn., Nov. 4, 1933; d. Julian Augustus and Margaret Pauline (Morris) Taylor; A.B. cum laude, Radcliffe Coll., 1955; postgrad. Harvard-Radcliffe Program in Bus. Adminstrn., 1959; M.S.W., U. Calif., Berkeley, 1970, Ph.D., 1980; m. James Lowell Gibbs, Jr., Aug. 25, 1956; children—Geoffrey Taylor, Lowell Dabney. Jr. mgmt. asst. U.S. Dept. Labor, Washington, 1955-56; market research coord. Pillsbury Co., Mpls., 1959-61; clin. social worker Stanford (Calif.) U. Student Health Service, 1970-74, 78-79, research assoc. dept. psychiatry, 1971-73; asst. prof. Sch. Social Welfare U. Calif., Berkeley, 1979-83, acting assoc. prof., 1983-86, assoc. prof., 1986-92, Zellerbach Prof. of social policy, 1992—, chair of faculty Sch. Social Welfare, 1993-94; pvt. practice as clin. psychologist, 1983-91; fellow Bunting Inst., Radcliffe Coll., spring, 1985. Bd. regents U. Santa Clara (Calif.), 1980-84; mem. Minn. State Commn. on Status of Women, 1963-65; co-chairperson Minn. Women's Com. for Civil Rights, 1963-65; mem. adv. coun. Nat. Ctr. for Children in Poverty, 1987—; bd. dirs. Ctr. for Populations Options, 1989-93; disting. scholar Joint Ctr. Pol. & Econ. Studies, Washington D.C., 1991-92; vis. scholar U. London, 1993, U. Toronto, 1994. NIMH fellow, 1979; Soroptimist Internat. grantee, 1978-79. Fellow Am. Orthopsychiat. Assn. (bd. dirs. 1985-86); mem. Am. Psychol. Assn., Nat. Assn. Social Workers, Western Psychol. Assn., Am. Assn. Suicidology (McCormick award 1987). Democrat. Author: Children of Color: Psychological Interventions with Minority Youth, 1989; editor, contbr. Young, Black and Male in America, 1988; mem. editorial bd. Am. Jour. Orthopsychiatry, 1980-84; bd. publs. Nat. Assn. Social Workers, 1980-82; contbr. chpts. to books and articles to profl. jours. Office: U Calif Sch Social Welfare Haviland Hall Berkeley CA 94720

GIBBS, WILLIAM HAROLD, university administrator; b. Evanston, Ill., Apr. 10, 1950; s. Harold William and Margaret Rose (Heidbreder) G. BS, Ariz. State U., 1973; MBA, U. Ill., 1975. CPA. Mgr. Price Waterhouse, Phoenix, 1975-82; chief fin. officer Apollo Group Inc., Phoenix, 1983-87; pres. U. Phoenix, 1987—. Office: U Phoenix 4615 E Elwood St Phoenix AZ 85040-1958

GIBBS, WOLCOTT, JR., writer, editor; b. N.Y.C., Apr. 5, 1935; s. Wolcott and Elinor Mead (Sherwin) G.; m. Elizabeth Lucille Villa, 1958 (div. 1979); children: William, Eric. BA, Princeton U., 1957. Publicity mgr. Doubleday & Co., N.Y.C., 1958-64; freelance writer Norwalk, Conn., 1964-67, 76-78; editor J.B. Lippincott Co., N.Y.C., 1967-70; book editor Motor Boating & Sailing Mag., N.Y.C., 1970-76, exec. editor, 1978-79; editor Yachting Mag., N.Y.C., 1979-84; exec. editor The New Yorker, N.Y.C., 1984-89; sr. editor Islands Mag., Santa Barbara, Calif., 1989—; cons. Book-of-the-Month Club, N.Y.C., 1973-84. Author: (non-fiction) Practical Sailing, 1971, Power Boating, 1973, Sailing: A First Book, 1974, Backpacking, 1975, Navigation, 1975, Advanced Sailing, 1975, The Coastal Cruiser, 1981, Cruising in a Nutshell, 1983, (fiction) Dead Run, 1988, Running Fix, 1990, Shadow Queen, 1992, Landfall, 1992, Capitol Offense, 1995. Mem. USCG Aux. Office: Islands Publ Co 3886 State St Santa Barbara CA 93105-3112

GIBLETT, PHYLIS LEE WALZ, middle school educator; b. Denver, July 17, 1945; d. Henry and Leah (Pabst) Walz; B.S.B.A. (Estelle Hunter scholar 1963, Denver Classroom Tchr.'s scholar 1963, Outstanding Bus. Edn. Student scholar 1967), U. Denver, 1967, MBA, 1969; m. Thomas Giblett, May 31, 1975; children: Leann Ruth, Douglas Henry, John Peter. Tchr. bus. Aurora (Colo.) South Middle Sch., Aurora Pub. Schs., 1967-80, 82-86, 88—, on leave, 1980-82, 86-88, chmn. bus. dept., 1972-79; evening tchr. S.E. Met. Bd. Coop Services, 1967-68, post secondary/adult classes Aurora Pub. Schs., 1972-75, C.C. Denver, North Campus, 1973, Aurora Pub. Schs. Adult Edn., 1983-84; mem. Aurora Pub. Sch. System, mem. tech. com. 1991-95, dist. tech. trainer, 1992—, steering com. shared decision making, 1990-94, zero tolerance com., 1992-94, facilitator Mentor com., 1991-92, exploratory tchr. facilitator, 1992-93; mem. dist. tech. com. South Middle Sch., Aurora Dist. Tech. Com., 1975-79; adviser chpt. Future Bus. Leaders Am., 1976-78; mem. Colo. Curriculum Specialist Com., 1976-77. Treas. Aurora Coun. PTA, 1987-89, Century Elem. Sch. PTA, 1988-89, reflections chmn., 1987-89, 90-93; mem. PTA. Named Miss Future Bus. Tchr., Phi Beta Lambda of Colo., 1965. Mem. Nat., Mountain-Plains (participant leadership conf. 1977), Colo. Bus. Edn. Assns. (pres. 1976-77), Colo. Educators for/About Bus., Am., Colo. vocat. assns., NEA, Colo., Aurora edn. assns., Delta Pi Epsilon (pres.-elect Eta chpt. 1978, pres. 1980-81). Republican. Lutheran.

GIBNEY, FRANK BRAY, publisher, editor, writer, foundation executive; b. Scranton, Pa., Sept. 21, 1924; s. Joseph James and Edna May (Wetter) G.; m. Harriet Harvey, Dec. 10, 1948 (div. 1957); children: Alex, Margot; m. Harriet C. Suydam, Dec. 14, 1957 (div. 1971); children: Frank, James, Thomas; m. Hiroko Doi, Oct. 5, 1972; children: Elise, Josephine. BA, Yale U., 1945; DLitt (hon.), Kyung Hee U., Seoul, Korea, 1974. Corr., assoc. editor Time mag., N.Y.C., Tokyo and London, 1947-54; sr. editor Newsweek, N.Y.C., 1954-57; staff writer, editorial writer Life mag., N.Y.C., 1957-61; pub., pres. SHOW mag., N.Y.C., 1961-64; pres. Ency. Brit. (Japan), Tokyo, 1965-69; pres. TBS-Brit., Tokyo, 1969-75, vice chmn., 1976—; v.p. Ency. Brit., Inc., Chgo., 1975-79; vice chmn., bd. editors Ency. Brit., Chgo., 1978—; pres. Pacific Basin Inst., Santa Barbara, Calif., 1979—; adj. prof. Far Ea. studies U. Calif., Santa Barbara, 1986—; vis. prof. Pomona Coll., 1995—; bd. dirs. U.S. Com. for Pacific Econ. Cooperation, 1988—, v.p., 1993-95; cons. com. on space and aeros. U.S. Ho. of Reps., Washington, 1957-59; vice chmn. Japan-U.S. Friendship Commn., 1984-90, U.S.-Japan Com. Edn. and Cultural Interchange, 1984-90. Author: Five Gentlemen of Japan, 1953, The Frozen Revolution, 1959, (with Peter Deriabin) The Secret World, 1960, The Operators, 1961, The Khruschev Pattern, 1961, The Reluctant Space Farers, 1965, Japan: The Fragile Super-Power, 1975, Miracle by Design, 1983, The Pacific Century, 1992, Korea's Quiet Revolution, 1993; co-author: The Battle for Okinawa, 1995; editor: The Penkovskiy Papers, 1965. Served to lt. USNR, 1942-46. Decorated Order of the Rising Sun 3d Class Japan, Order of Sacred Treasure 2d Class Japan. Mem. Council on Fgn. Relations, Tokyo Fgn. Corr. Club, Am. C.of C. (Tokyo), Japan-Am. Soc., Japan Soc. Roman Catholic. Clubs: Century Assn., Yale (N.Y.C.); Tokyo; Tavern, The Arts (Chgo.). Home: 1901 E Las Tunas Rd Santa Barbara CA 93103-1745

GIBSON, ARTHUR CHARLES, biologist, educator; b. Bronx, N.Y., Oct. 16, 1947; s. Richard Goodwin and Rosalie (Reinhardt) G.; m. Linda Lee Corey, Aug. 15, 1970; children: Heather Elizabeth, Erin Kathryn. B.A in Botany, Miami U., 1969; PhD. in Botany, Claremont (Calif.) Grad. Sch., 1973. Asst. prof. U. Ariz., Tucson, 1973-79, assoc. prof., 1979-80; assoc. prof. UCLA, 1980-82, prof., 1982—, also dir. Mildred E. Mathias Bot. Garden. Author: (with J.H. Brown) Biogeography, 1983; (with P.S. Nobel) The Cactus Primer, 1986; (with P.W. Rundel) Ecological Communities and Processes in a Mojave Dessert Ecosystem, 1995; contbr. articles to profl. jours. Office: UCLA Mildred E Mathias Bot Garden Botany Bldg Rm 124 Los Angeles CA 90095-1606

GIBSON, BROOKS, family services professional; b. Yankton, S.D., Oct. 26, 1960; s. F.E. and Garnett E. (Wells) G.; m. Jackie S. Herbel, Sept. 8, 1984; children: Garrett Brooks, Taylor Kathleen. Student, U. Nebr., 1979-83, Ariz. Coll. of The Bible, 1988-90; BS in psychology, Grand Canyon U., 1993. Regional mgr. Continental Gen. Ins. Co., Phoenix, 1979—; pastor Northwest Cmty. Ch., Phoenix, 1986-89; case worker Camelback Hosps., Phoenix, 1988-89; therapist Ariz. Bapt. Children's Svcs., Phoenix, 1989-92; pres., founder Northwest Family Svcs., Phoenix, 1990—; instr. License Exam Trainers, Phoenix, 1986-87; adj. prof. Ariz. Coll. of the Bible, Phoenix, 1990-91; speaker in field. Dir. radio fund raiser. Mem. ACA, Am. Assn. Christian Counselors, Am. Assn. Behavioral Therapists. Republican. Office: Northwest Family Svcs 706 E Bell Rd Ste 200 Phoenix AZ 85022-6642

GIBSON, DAVID BLAIR, anthropologist; b. Glendale, Calif., Dec. 21, 1954; s. David Wishart and Mary Leah (Wood) G.; m. Susan Lee Saul, Feb. 24, 1989; 1 child, David Saul. BA, UCLA, 1978, PhD, 1990; MA, Univ. Coll., Dublin, Ireland, 1982. Instr. Calif. State U., L.A., 1989—; prin. investigator Cahercommaun Project, 1984—. Editor Celtic Chiefdom, Celtic State, 1995, Tribe and Polity in Late Prehistoric Europe, 1988. Grantee U. Rsch. Expeditions Program, 1992, 94, Earthwatch, 1986, UCLA Dept. Anthropology, 1986. Mem. Am. Anthropol. Assn., Soc. for Am. Archaeology, Soc. for the Anthropology of Europe. Republican. Home: 13313 Strathern St North Hollywood CA 91605-1726 Office: Dept Anthropology CSULA 5151 St University Dr Los Angeles CA 90032

GIBSON, DAVID FREDERIC, engineering dean and educator; b. West Newton, Mass., Jan. 10, 1942; s. Lionel C. and Dorothy (McAfee) G.; m. Rebecca Harper, Aug. 24, 1964; children: Karen, Kathleen. BS in Indsl. Engring., Purdue U., 1963, MS in Indsl. Engring., 1964, PhD in Indsl. Engring., 1969. Registered profl. engr., Mont. Indsl. engr. USN, Forest Park, Ill., 1963; rsch. asst. Purdue U., West Lafayette, Ind., 1963-64, instr., 1966, asst. prof. Mont. State U., Bozeman, 1969-72; dean Arkansas Tech., Russellville, 1971-72; from assoc. prof. to prof. Mont. State U., Bozeman, 1972—, asst. dean of engring., 1977-83, dean of engring., 1983—. Contbr. articles to profl. jours. Accreditation visitor Accrediting Bd. for Engring. and Tech., N.Y.C., 1987—, mem. engring. accreditation com., 1991—; mem. Mont. Bd. Profl. Engrs. and Land Surveyors, Helena, 1983—, chmn. Grantee in field. Mem. Am. Soc. for Engring. Edn., Inst. Indsl. Engring., Nat. Soc. Profl. Engrs. (v.p., chmn. profl. engrs. in edn.), Nat. Coun. Engr. Examiners. Lutheran. Home: 2409 Springcreek Dr Bozeman MT 59715-6036 Office: Mont State U Bozeman MT 59717

GIBSON, ELISABETH JANE, principal; b. Salina, Kans., Apr. 28, 1937; d. Cloyce Wesley and Margaret Mae (Yost) Kasson; m. William Douglas Miles, Jr., Aug. 20, 1959 (div.); m. Harry Benton Gibson Jr., July 1, 1970. AB, Colo. State Coll., 1954-57; MA, San Francisco State Coll., 1967-68; EdD, U. No. Colo., 1978; postgrad. U. Denver, 1982. Cert. tchr., prin., Colo. Tchr. elem. schs., Santa Paula, Calif., 1957-58, Salina, Kans., 1958-63, Goose Bay, Labrador, 1963-64, Jefferson County, Colo., 1965-66, Topeka, 1966-67; diagnostic tchr. Cen. Kans. Diagnostic Remedial Edn. Ctr., Salina, 1968-70; instr. Loretto Heights Coll., Denver, 1970-72; co-owner Ednl. Cons. Enterprises, Inc., Greeley, Colo., 1974-77; resource coord. Region VIII Resource Access Project Head Start Mile High Consortium, Denver, 1976-77; exec. dir. Colo. Fedn. Coun. Exceptional Children, Denver, 1976-77; asst. prof. Met. State Coll., Denver, 1979; dir. spl. edn. N.E. Colo. Bd. Coop. Edn. Svcs., Haxtun, Colo., 1979-82; prin. elem. jr. high sch., Elizabeth, Colo., 1982-84; prin., spl. projects coord. Summit County Schs., Frisco, Colo., 1985—; prin. Frisco Elem. Sch., 1985-91; cons. Montana Dept. Edn., 1978-79, Love Pub. Co., 1976-78, Colo. Dept. Inst., 1974-75; cons. Colo. Dept. Edn., 1984-85, mem. proposal reading com., 1987—; pres. Found. Exceptional Children, 1980-81; pres. bd. dirs. N.E. Colo. Svcs. Handicapped, 1981-82; bd. dirs. Dept. Ednl. Specialists, Colo. Assn. Sch. Execs., 1982-84; mem. Colo. Title IV Adv. Coun., 1980-82; mem. Mellon Found. grant steering com. Colo. Dept. Edn., 1984-85; mem. Colo. Dept. Edn. Data Acquisition Reporting and Utilization Com., 1983, Denver City County Commn. for Disabled, 1978-81; chmn. regional edn. com. 1970 White House Conf. Children and Youth; bd. dirs. Advocates for Victims of Assault, 1986-91; mem. adv. bd. Alpine Counseling Ctr., 1986—; mem. placement alternatives commn. Dept. Social Svcs., 1986—; mem. adv. com. Colo. North Cen. Assn., 1988-91; sec. Child Care Resource and Referral Agy., 1992—; mem. Child Care Task Force Summit County, 1989—; mem. tchr. cert. task force Colo. State Bd. Edn., 1990-91; chair Summit County Interagy. Coord. Coun., 1989—. Recipient Vol. award Colo. Child Care Assn., 1992, Ann. Svc. award Colo. Fedn. Coun. Exceptional Children, 1981; San Francisco State Coll. fellow, 1967-68. Mem. Colo. Assn. Retarded Citizens, Assn. Supervision Curriculum Devel., Nat. Assn. Elem. Sch. Prins., North Cen. Assn. (state adv. com. 1988-91), Order Eastern Star, Kappa Delta Pi, Pi Lambda Theta, Phi Delta Kappa. Republican. Methodist. Author: (with H. Padzensky) Goal Guide: A minicourse in writing goals and behavioral objectives for special education, 1975; (with H. Padzensky and S. Sporn) Assaying Student Behavior: A minicourse in student assessment techniques, 1974; contbr. articles to profl. jours. Home: 600 W County Line Rd Hghlnds Ranch CO 80126-6508 Office: Summit County Schs Ctrl Office PO Box 7 Frisco CO 80443-0007

GIBSON, JOHN ALLAN, marketing professional; b. Albany, N.Y., May 10, 1954; s. Thomas Sinclair and May Florence (Bushnell) G.; m. Malaine C. White, Dec. 20, 1980 (div. Sept. 10, 1993); children: Rachelle M., Malcolm T., Alison E. AAS, North County Coll., 1974. Assoc. mem. Audio Engring. Soc., N.Y.C., 1979-94; tech. sales, mktg. Engring. & Recording, Phoenix, 1979—. Office: Engring & Recording 2641 E Mcdowell Rd Phoenix AZ 85008-3641

GIBSON, MELVIN ROY, pharmacognosy educator; b. St. Paul, Nebr., June 11, 1920; s. John and Jennie Irene (Harvey) G. B.S., U. Nebr., 1942, M.S., 1947, D.Sc. (hon.), 1985; Ph.D., U. Ill., 1949. Asst. prof. pharmacognosy Wash. State U., Pullman, 1949-52; assoc. prof. Wash. State U., 1952-55, prof., 1955-85, prof. emeritus, 1985—. Editor: Am. Jour. Pharm. Edn, 1956-61; editorial bd., co-author: Remington's Pharm. Sci, 1970, 75, 80, 85; editor, co-author: Studies of a Pharm. Curriculum, 1967; author over 100 articles. Served as arty. officer AUS, 1942-46. Decorated Bronze star, Purple Heart; sr. vis. fellow Orgn. for Econ. Cooperation and Devel., Royal Pharm. Inst., Stockholm, Sweden and U. Leiden (Holland), 1962; recipient Rufus A. Lyman award, 1972, Wash. State U. Faculty Library award, 1984; named Wash. State U. Faculty Mem. of Yr., 1985. Founder, charter mem. Am. Diplomates in Pharmacy.; fellow AAAS; assoc. fellow Am. Coll. Apothecaries; mem. N.Y. Acad. Sci., Am. Pharm. Assn., Am. Soc. Pharmacognosy (pres. 1964-65), Am. Assn. Coll. Pharmacy (exec. com. 1961-63, bd. dirs. 1977-79, chmn. coun. of faculties 1975-76, pres. 1979-80, Disting. Educator award 1984), U.S. Pharmacopeia (revision com. 1970-75), Am. Found. Pharm. Edn. (hon. life, bd. dirs. 1980-85, exec. com. 1981-85, vice chmn. 1982-85), AAUP, Acad. Pharm. Sci., Am. Public Health Assn., Fedn. Internat. Pharm., Am. Inst. History of Pharmacy, Am. Acad. Polit. and Social Sci., Sigma Xi, Kappa Psi (Nat. Svc. citation 1961), Rho Chi, Phi Kappa Phi, Omicron Delta Kappa. Democrat. Presbyterian. Club: Spokane. Home: 707 W 6th Ave Apt 41 Spokane WA 99204-2813

GIBSON, RICHARD INGRAM, geophysicist; b. Jonesboro, Ark., Aug. 19, 1948; s. Richard D. and Clena Vee (Ingram) G. Student, Flint (Mich.) Jr. Coll., 1966-68; BS in Geology, Ind. U., Bloomington, 1971; postgrad., U. Calif., Davis, 1972-73. Assoc. instr. geology dept. Ind. U., Bloomington, 1970-72; mineralogist Beck Analytical Svcs., Bloomington and Davis, Calif., 1971-75; geophysicist Aero Svc. Corp., Houston, 1975-76, Gulf Oil Exploration and Prodn. Co., Houston, 1976-84; dir., gravity and magnetics Everest Geotech, Denver and Houston, 1984-89; pres. Everest Geotech, Denver, 1989-91; owner Gibson Consulting, Golden, Colo., 1989—; adj. prof. geophysical field exercise, U. Ark., Dillon, Mont., 1986-88; instr. Geologic Field Sta., Ind. U., Cardwell, Mont., 1989—. Author: History of the Earth, 1994; editor, pub. (newsletter) Life After Gulf, 1984-91; contbr. articles to profl. jours. Recipient 1st prize Ednl. Exhibit, Houston Gem and Mineral Soc., 1977, 1st prize Clin. Investigation, Am. Urol. Assn., 1973, Hon. Mention award in Photography, Houston-Galveston Employees Clubs, 1980; named Outstanding Young Man in Am., 1982. Mem. Tobacco Root Geol. Soc. (co-founder, pres. 1974-77, sec., bd. dirs. 1977-81, Svc. award 1979), Am. Assn. Petroleum Geologists, Geol. Soc. Am., Soc. Exploration Geophysicists, Wyo. Geol. Assn., Mont. Geol. Soc., Rocky Mountain Assn. Geologists, Ind. U. Geology Club (pres. Bloomington chpt. 1969-70). Office: Gibson Consulting PO Box 523 Golden CO 80402-0523

GIBSON, TREVA KAY, university official; b. Harrisburg, Ill., Aug. 12, 1938; d. William Clayton and Margaret Pauletta (Heathman) Humphrey; m. Charles Hurbert Gibson, Sept. 6, 1959; children: Charles H. Jr., Eric Clayton. BS, So. Ill. U., 1960; MEd, U. Mo., St. Louis, 1972; DSc (hon.), Kazakh (USSR) State U., 1990; EdD, Ariz. State U., 1991. Tchr. Perry Cen. Jr. High Sch., Southport, Ind., 1961-64, Granite City (Ill.) High Sch., 1964-65; counselor Kelley High Sch., Benton, Mo., 1967-68, Valley Park (Mo.) High Sch., 1968-69, Hazelwood East High Sch., St. Louis, 1969-76, Bradshaw Mountain High Sch., Prescott Valley, Ariz., 1976-80; dir. placement Grand Canyon U., Phoenix, 1980-82, dean of students, 1982-89, spl. asst. to pres. for internat. rels., 1988—. Mem. World Coun. for Curriculum and Instrn., World Affairs Coun., Cooperative Svcs. Internat. Edn. Consortium, Gov.'s Ariz.-Mexico Commn. Baptist. Home: 2406 W Anderson Ave Phoenix AZ 85023-2210 Office: Grand Canyon U 3300 W Camelback Rd Phoenix AZ 85017-3030

GIBSON, VIRGINIA LEE, lawyer; b. Independence, Mo., Mar. 5, 1946. BA, U. Calif., Berkeley, 1972; JD, U. Calif., San Francisco, 1977. Bar: Calif. 1981. Assoc. Pillsbury, Madison & Sutro, San Francisco, 1980-83; ptnr. Chickering & Gregory, San Francisco, 1983-85, Baker & McKenzie, San Francisco, 1985—. Mem. ABA (employee benefits subcom. tax sect.), Internat. Found. Employee Benefit Plans, Am. Compensation Assn. (internat. compensation and benefits com.), Calif. Bar Assn. (exec. com. tax sect. 1985-88), San Francisco Bar Assn. (internat. and comparative law taxation sects.), Western Pension and Benefits Conf. (pres. San Francisco chpt. 1989-91, steering com. 1988—). Office: Baker & McKenzie 2 Embarcadero Ctr Ste 2400 San Francisco CA 94111-3909

GICLAS, HENRY LEE, astronomer; b. Flagstaff, Ariz., Dec. 9, 1910; s. Eli and Hedwig Herminna (Leissling) G.; m. Bernice Francis Kent, May 23, 1936; 1 child, Henry Lee. BS, U. Ariz., 1937; postgrad., U. Calif., Berkeley, 1939-40; PhD with honors, No. Ariz. U., 1980. Research asst. Lowell Obs., Flagstaff, 1931-44, astronomer, 1944-79, exec. sec., 1952-75; adj. prof. Ohio State U., Columbus, 1968-79, No. Ariz. U., 1972-79. Mem. Flagstaff Freeholder's Com., 1959; exec. v.p. Raymond Ednl. Found., 1971-77, pres., 1977-91. Fellow AAAS; mem. Am. Astron. Soc., Ariz. Acad. Sci., Astron. Soc. Pacific (dir. 1959-61), No. Ariz. Pioneers Hist. Soc. (pres. 1972-80), Internat. Astron. Union. Clubs: Coconino Country (pres 1962), Continental Country (adv. bd. 1972-75). Lodge: Elks. Home: 120 E Elm Ave Flagstaff AZ 86001-3213 Office: Lowell Obs Flagstaff AZ 86001

GIDDINGS, DEBRA LYNN, marketing executive, computer consultant; b. Steubenville, Ohio, July 27, 1956; m. Dwight Gene Taylor, Jan. 11, 1975 (div. 1987) 1 child, Karisa Lauren; m. Richard Coates Giddings, May 6, 1989. AA in Data Processing with highest honor, Jefferson Tech. Coll., 1981; student, U. Phoenix, 1994—. Computer cons. Toronto, Ohio, 1981-84; programmer analyst John Hancock Ins., Anaheim, Calif., 1984-85; system analyst Chiro-Med, Placentia, Calif., 1985-87; computer instr. CSI, Cerritos, Calif., 1987-88; sr. tech. trainer Symbol MSI, Costa Mesa, Calif., 1988-90; mgr. tech. pubs. Symbol Techs., Costa Mesa, 1990-91; software product mgr. Symbol Techs., Costa Mesa, 1991; market rsch. mgr. Pacific Access Computers, 1992-93; mktg. mgr. Caere Corp., Los Gatos, Calif., 1994-95; client svcs. mgr. Phoenix Pub. Sys., Inc., Monterey, Calif., 1995—; cons. World Vision, Monrovia, Calif., 1988, AT&T, Morristown, N.J., 1988, Great Western Bank, Chatsworth, Calif., 1988. Author: U Basic Programming, 1988. Mem. SPCA. Republican. Home: 24205 San Pedro Ln Carmel CA 93923-9305 Office: 8 Harris Ct Bldg A Monterey CA 93940

GIDEON-HAWKE, PAMELA LAWRENCE, fine arts small business owner; b. N.Y.C., Aug. 23, 1945; d. Lawrence Ian Verry and Lily S. (Stein) Gordon; m. Jarrett Redstone, June 27, 1964; 1 child, Justin Craig Hawke. Grad. high sch., Manhattan. Owner Gideon Gallery Ltd., L.A. and Las Vegas, 1975—; prin. Pamela L. Gideon-Hawke Pub. Rels., L.A., 1984—. Pres. San Fernando Valley West Point Parents Club, 1990—. Named Friend of Design Industry Designers West Mag., 1987. Mem. Am. Soc. Interior Designers (publicist), Internat. Soc. Interior Designers (trade liaison 1986-88), Network Exec. Women in Hosp. (pres. Las Vegas chpt., pres. Las Vegas program, L.A. chair), Internat. Furnishings and Design Assn. (pres.). Office: Gideon Gallery Ltd 8121 Lake Hills Dr Las Vegas NV 89128 also: 8748 Melrose Ave Los Angeles CA 90069-5015

GIEDT, WALVIN ROLAND, epidemiologist, educator; b. Eureka, S.D., Aug. 17, 1905; s. Theodore John Peter and Augusta Elizabeth (Pritzkau) G.; m. Lois Della Hosking, Nov. 4, 1932; children: Carol Augusta, Barbara Ellen. BS in Medicine, U. S.D., 1933; MD, U. Chgo., 1937; MPH, Johns Hopkin's U., 1941. Lab. instr. Sch. of Medicine U. S.D., Vermillion, 1933-36, asst. prof. microbiology Sch. of Medicine, 1938-40; chief epidemiologist div. S.D. Dept. Health, Pierre, 1941-43; chief epidemiologist div. Wash. State Dept. Health, Seattle, 1943-71, ret., 1971. Contbr. articles to profl. jours. With USPHS, 1941-66. Mem. Wash. State Pub. Health Assn. (past pres). Democrat. Home: 1730 Taylor Ave N Seattle WA 98109-2927

GIEL, KATHLEEN MARY, marketing executive; b. Chgo., May 11, 1953; d. Joseph John and Dorothy Carolyn Giel. BA in Botany, U. Calif., Berkeley, 1984; MBA, Stanford U., 1989. Dir., instr. Outward Bound Inc., U.S. and Internat., 1975-83; resource analyst Pacific Gas & Electric Co., San Francisco, 1985-87; mktg. analyst Apple Computer, Cupertino, Calif., 1988; quality mgr. Boise Cascade, Denver, 1989-91; dir. customer statisfaction measurement Boise (Idaho) Cascade, 1991—; adj. faculty mktg. Boise State U., 1992—. Expedition leader 1986 Mt. Kongur Expedition, China, 1986; bd. dirs. Idaho Bot. Garden, Boise, 1992—. Mem. Am. Mktg. Assn., Am. Soc. Quality Control. Home: 1115 N 23rd St Boise ID 83702-3229 Office: Boise Cascade Corp 1 Jefferson Sq Boise ID 83728-0001

GIEM, ROSS NYE, JR., surgeon; b. Corvallis, Oreg., May 23, 1923; s. Ross Nye and Goldie Marie (Falk) G.; student U. Redlands, Walla Walla Coll.; BA, MD, Loma Linda U.; children: John, David, Paul, James, Ross Nye, Matthew, Julie. Intern, Sacramento Gen. Hosp., 1952-53; resident in ob-gyn, Kern County Gen. Hosp., Bakersfield, Calif., 1956-57, in gen. surgery, 1957-61; practice medicine specializing in gen. surgery, Sullivan, Mo., 1961-70; staff emergency dept. Hollywood Presbyn. Med. Center, 1971-73, Meml. Hosp., Belleville, Ill., 1973-87, St. Elizabeth Hosp., Belleville, Ill., 1973-90; St. Luke Hosp., Pasadena, Calif., 1973-89, Doctors Hosp., Montclair, Calif. 1990—; instr. nurses, physicians, paramedics, emergency med. technicians, 1973-91. Served with AUS, 1943-46. Diplomate Am. Bd. Surgery. Fellow ACS, Am. Coll. Emergency Physicians; mem. AMA, Ill. Med. Assn., Pan Am. Med. Assn., Pan Pacific Surg. Assn., Royal Coll. Physicians (Eng.)

GIER, KARAN HANCOCK, counseling psychologist; b. Sedalia, Mo., Dec. 7, 1947; d. Ioda Clyde and Lorna (Campbell) Hancock; m. Thomas Robert Gier, Sept. 28, 1968. BA in Edn., U. Mo., Kansas City, 1971; MA Teaching in Math/Sci. Edn., Webster U., 1974; MA in Counseling Psychology, Western Colo. U., 1981; MEd Guidance and Counseling, U. Alaska, 1981; PhD in Edn., Pacific Western U., 1989. Nat. cert. counselor. Instr. grades 5-8 Kansas City-St. Joseph Archdiocese, 1969-73; ednl. cons. Pan-Ednl. Inst., Kansas City, 1973-75; instr., counselor Bethel (Alaska) Regional High Sch., 1975-80; ednl. program coord. Western Regional Resource Ctr., Anchorage, 1980-81; counselor U. Alaska, Anchorage, 1982-83; coll. prep. instr. Alaska Native Found., Anchorage, 1982; counselor USAF, Anchorage, 1985-86; prof. U. Alaska, Anchorage, 1982—; dir. Omni Counseling Svcs., Anchorage, 1984—; prof. Chapman Coll., Anchorage, 1988—; workshop facilitator over 100 workshops on the topics of counseling techs., value clarification, non-traditional teaching approaches, peer-tutor tng. Co-author: Coping with College, 1984, Helping Others Learn, 1985; editor, co-author: A Student's Guide, 1983; contbg. author developmental Yup'ik lang. program, 1981; contbr. photographs to Wolves and Related Canids, 1990, 91; contbr. articles to profl. jours. Mem. Am. Bus. Women's Assn., Blue Springs, Mo., 1972-75, Ctr. for Environ. Edn., World Wildlife Fund, Beta Sigma Phi, Bethel, Alaska, 1976-81. Recipient 3d place color photo award Yukon-Kuskokwim State Fair, Bethel, 1978, Notable Achievement award USAF, 1986, Meritorious Svc. award Anchorage Community Coll., 1984-88. Mem. Coll. Reading and Learning Assn. (editor, peer tutor sig leader 1988—, Cert. of Appreciation 1986-93, bd. dirs. Alaska state, coord. internat. tutor program, Spl. Recognition award 1994-95), AACD, Alaska Assn. Counseling and Devel. (pres. 1989-90), Alaska Career Devel. Assn. (pres.-elect 1989-90), Nat. Rehab. Assn., Nat. Rehab. Counselors, Greenpeace, Human Soc. of U.S. Wolf Haven Am., Wolf Song of Alaska. Home and Office: Omni Counseling Svcs 8102 Harvest Cir Anchorage AK 99502-4682

GIERLASINSKI, KATHY LYNN, accountant; b. Chewelah, Wash., May 21, 1951; d. John Edward and Margaret Irene (Seefeldt) Rail; m. Norman Joseph Gierlasinski, May 23, 1987. BBA, Gonzaga U., 1984. CPA, Wash. Legal sec. Redbook Pub. Co., N.Y.C., 1974-75, Howard Michaelson, Esquire, Spokane, Wash., 1975-76; sec. Burns Internat. Security Svcs., Spokane, 1977-79; sec. to contr. Gonzaga U., Spokane, 1979-81, acctg. asst., 1981-82; staff acct. Martin, Holland & Petersen, CPA's, Yakima, Wash., 1984-87; acct., supr. Strader Hallet & Co., P.S., Bellevue, Wash., 1988-91; acct. Miller & Co., P.S., Woodinville, Wash., 1991-93; pres. Gierlasinski & Assocs., P.S., Bothell, Wash., 1993—; treas. White Pass Ski Patrol, Nat. Ski Patrol Systems, Wash., 1987-90; editor, chmn. audit com. Mt. Spokane Ski Patrol, 1983-84. Mem. AICPA, Am. Soc. Women Accts. (charter, editor 1987), Wash. Soc. CPA (sec. Sammamish Valley chpt. 1990-92, pres. 1992-93, 93-94, chair adv. coun. 1995—, tax com., govt. affairs com.), Bus. and Profl. Women of Woodinville (treas. 1994-95), Northshore C. of C. Republican. Lutheran. Home: 21730 2nd Ave SE Bothell WA 98021-8202

GIESECKE, MARK ERNST, psychiatrist; b. Bloomington, Ill., Apr. 14, 1948; s. Gustav Ernst and Louise Helene (Bittner) G.; m. Susan Lane Bennett, June 20, 1969 (div. Dec. 1976); m. Linda L. Hartz, Apr. 23, 1977; children: Craig, Lauren. AB, Harvard Coll., 1969; MD, U. Pa., 1973. Diplomate Am. Bd. Psychiatry and Neurology; lic. psychiatrist, Ariz. Intern Hosp. U. Pa., 1973-74, resident in psychiatry, 1974-77, med. staff, 1977-90, from asst. dir. to dir. psychiatry svc., 1977-90, from assoc. instr. to clin. assoc. prof. psychiatry, 1976—; med. dir. The Guidance Ctr., Inc., Flagstaff, Ariz., 1990-93, med. dir. outpatient seriously mentally ill svcs., 1993—; staff dept. medicine Flagstaff Med. Ctr., 1990—; staff Aspen Hill Hosp., Flagstaff, Ariz., 1990—; quality assurance com. The Guidance Ctr., Inc., Flagstaff, 1990-93, total quality mgmt. com., medical svcs. com., 1993—; campus emergency procedures com. U. Pa., 1979-81, psychiat. leave policy com., 1982-84, alchol concerns com., 1983-90, coun. com. on sexual harassment, 1986-90, fraternity/sorority adv. bd., 1986-88; com. on lang. retirement U. Pa. Coll. Arts and Scis., 1984-87. Contbr. articles to profl. jours. Recipient Horatio C. Wood prize in pharmacology, 1973, Preceptorship award Am. Soc. Anesthesiologists, 1971. Mem. Am. Psychiat. Assn., Ariz. Psychiat. Soc., No. Ariz. Psychiat. Soc. (charter mem.), Alpha Omega Alpha (pres. U. Pa. chpt., 1972-73). Home: 420 W Havasupai Rd Flagstaff AZ 86001-1510 Office: The Guidance Ctr Inc 2187 N Vickey St Flagstaff AZ 86004

GIFFIN, GLENN ORLANDO, II, music critic, writer, newspaper editor; b. Denver, Feb. 27, 1943; s. Glenn Orlando and E. Louise (Mosler) G. B.Mus., U. Colo., 1965; M.A. in Librarianship, U. Denver, 1967. Scriptwriter, broadcaster radio Sta. KRNW-FM, Boulder, 1965-67; asst. music critic San Francisco Chronicle, 1968; asst. music librarian Norlin libraries U. Colo., 1968-70; music critic, staff writer Denver Post, 1970-73, music editor, 1973-88, book page editor, music critic, 1988—; host Soundings, Sta. KOA Radio 1985-86; curator Carson-Brierly Dance Library U. Denver, 1986—. Rockefeller Found. fellow, 1966-68; Corbett Found. fellow, 1969; Nat. Endowment for Arts grantee Dance Criticism Inst., Conn. Coll., summer 1971; named Outstanding Alumnus U. Colo., 1985. Mem. Music Library Assn., Am. Musicol. Soc., Dance Critics Assn., Music Critics Assn., Sigma Delta Chi. Office: PO Box 1709 Denver CO 80201-1709

GIFFIN, MARGARET ETHEL (PEGGY GIFFIN), management consultant; b. Cleve., Aug. 27, 1949; d. Arch Kenneth and Jeanne (Eggleton) G.; m. Robert Alan Wyman, Aug. 20, 1988; 1 child, Samantha Jean. BA in Psychology, U. Pacific, Stockton, Calif., 1971; MA in Psychology, Calif. State U., Long Beach, 1973; PhD in Quantitative Psychology, U. So. Calif., 1984. Psychometrist Auto Club So. Calif., L.A., 1973-74; cons. Psychol. Svcs., Inc., Glendale, Calif., 1975-76, mgr., 1977-78, dir., 1979-94; rschr. Social Sci. Rsch. Inst., U. So. Calif., L.A., 1981; dir. Giffin Consulting Svcs., L.A., 1994—; instr. Calif. State U., Long Beach, 1989-90; mem. tech. adv. com. on testing Calif. Fair Employment and Housing Commn., 1974-80, mem. steering com., 1978-80. Mem. Am. Ednl. Rsch. Assn., Soc. Indsl. Organizational Psychology, Am. Psychol. Assn., Personnel Testing Coun. So. Calif. (pres. 1980, exec. dir. 1982, 88, bd. dirs. 1980-92). Home and Office: 260 S Highland Ave Los Angeles CA 90036-3027

GIFFIN, WALTER CHARLES, retired industrial engineer, educator, consultant; b. Walhonding, Ohio, Apr. 22, 1936; s. Charles Maurice and Florence Ruth (Davis) G.; m. Beverly Ann Neff, Sept. 1, 1956; children—Steven, Rebecca. B. Indsl. Engring., Ohio State U., 1960, M.S., 1960, Ph.D., 1964. Registered profl. engr., Ohio. Research engr. Gen. Motors Research Labs., Warren, Mich., 1960-61; research assoc. systems research group Ohio State U., Columbus, 1961-62, instr. indsl. and systems engring., 1962-64, asst. prof., 1964-68, assoc. prof., 1968-71, prof., 1971-87, prof. emeritus, 1987—; prof. engring. U. So. Colo., Pueblo, 1987-92; ret., 1992—; cons. in field. Author: Introduction to Operations Engineering, 1971; Transform Techniques for Probability Modeling, 1975; Queueing: Basic Theory and Applications, 1978. NASA Research grantee, 1978-83. Club: Exptl. Aircraft Assn. (Oshkosh, Wis. and Pueblo, Colo.). Home: 419 Fairway Dr Pueblo West CO 81007-1852

GIFFORD, ARTHUR ROY, publishing executive, aircraft executive; b. Buffalo, Jan. 27, 1937; s. William Howard and Dorothy Ellen (Logan) G.; m. Anna Marie Boone, July 9, 1960 (div. Feb. 1974); 1 child, Douglas Alan; m. Carolyn Elaine Crowe, Dec. 20, 1974; children: Christine Michelle, Stephen Michael. BA, Butler U., 1964; postgrad., Pacific Luth. U., Tacoma, 1970; MA, U. Wash., 1975. Cert. provisional and standard secondary tchr., Wash. Passenger svc. agt. United Airlines, Seattle, 1966-67; indsl. engr. The Boeing Co., Seattle, 1967-70; prog. mgr. engring. div. Boeing Community Connection, The Boeing Co., Seattle, 1987-91; mgr. assessment reports, corp. safety, health and environ. affairs The Boeing Co., 1991-94; tchr. Fed. Way (Wash.) Sch. Dist., 1971-87; pres. Creative Approaches, Kent, Wash., 1994—. Bd. dirs. Lyric Theatre and Conservatory, Midway, Wash., 1980-82; treas. Wash. Edn. Theatre Assn., 1973-77, 85-89; treas. ArtsTime '89, Kent, Wash. State Centennial All-Arts Conf., 1987-89, long-range planning com., Kent (Wash.) View Christian Sch., 1987—; pres. PTA, Kent View Christian High Sch., 1992—; mem. precinct com. Dem. Orgn. King County, Wash., 1973-75, 93—. Democrat. Methodist. Home: 13904 SE 241st St Kent WA 98042-3315 Office: Creative Approaches PO Box 1114 Renton WA 98057

GIFFORD, ERNEST MILTON, biologist, educator; b. Riverside, Calif., Jan. 17, 1920; s. Ernest Milton and Mildred Wade (Campbell) G.; m. Jean Duncan, July 15, 1942; 1 child, Jeanette. A.B., U. Calif., Berkeley, 1942, Ph.D., 1950; grad., U.S. Army Command and Gen. Staff Sch., 1965. Asst. prof. botany, asst. botanist expt. sta. U. Calif.-Davis, 1950-56, assoc. prof. botany, assoc. botanist, 1957-61, prof. botany, botanist, 1962-87, prof. emeritus, 1988—, chmn. dept. botany and agrl. botany, 1963-67, 74-78. Author: (with A. S. Foster) Morphology and Evolution of Vascular Plants, 3d edit., 1989, (with T. L. Rost) Mechanisms and control of Cell Division, 1977; editor in chief Am. Jour. Botany, 1975-79; advisor to editor Ency. Brit.; contbr. articles on anatomy, ultrastructure and morphogenesis of higher plants to profl. jours. Served to maj. U.S. Army, 1942-46; ETO; to col. USAR, 1946-73. Decorated Bronze Star medal; named disting. contbr. Ency. Brit., 1964; NRC fellow Harvard U., 1956; Fulbright research scholar, France, 1966; John Simon Guggenheim Found. fellow, France, 1966; NATO sr. postdoctoral fellow, France, 1974; recipient Acad. Senate Disting. Teaching award U. Calif.-Davis, 1986. Fellow Linnean Soc. (London); mem. Bot. Soc. Am. (v.p. 1981, pres. 1982, merit award 1981), Internat. Soc. Plant Morphologists (v.p. 1980-84), Am. Inst. Biol. Scis., Calif. Bot. Soc., Sigma Xi. Office: U Calif Dept Botany Robbins Hall Davis CA 95616

GIFFORD, LESLIE JANE, artist, writer, educator; b. Chgo., May 20, 1947; d. Wendell W. and Nyma Jane Gifford. BS in Theatre and Dance, Skidmore Coll., 1969; student, Art Students League, N.Y.C., 1989-93, Alliance Francaise, Paris, 1977. Dancer Dance Circle, Boston, 1969-70; publicity dir. Chelsea Playhouse, Boston, 1969-70, Chelsea Theatre Ctr., Bklyn., 1971-74; artist in residence, choreographer, dir. Am. Ctr., Paris, 1978-81;

asst. to exec. prodr. The American Experience, Boston, 1986-91; tchr. N.Y. Open Ctr., N.Y.C., 1991-95; painter, writer N.Y.C. and San Francisco, 1993-95; tchr. Mindful Body, San Francisco, 1995. Dir., choreographer: (theater/dance) Black to Black, Edinburgh Festival, 1978 (Fringe First award); dir., prodr.: (ind. film) September Dogs, 1991; author, illustrator: (screenplay/book) Earth Song, 1993. Mem. San Francisco Art Inst.

GIFFORD, LISA BONNIE, interior designer; b. American Fork, Utah, Mar. 12, 1968; d. Ronald F. and Bonnie L. (Ball) Myers; m. L. Graham Gifford, Feb. 11, 1989; 1 child, Austin Lee. Cert. of completition, Mexican-N.Am. Inst. Cultural Rels., Mexico City, 1988; grad., Inst. of Religion, Logan, Utah, 1992; BA magna cum laude, Utah State U., 1993. Sec., receptionist Zion Home Furnishings, Provo, Utah, 1989; dept. mgr. Stokes Bros., Logan, 1989-92; interior designer Design Discovery, Salt Lake City, 1993, Office Essentials, Provo, 1993—; interior designer, prin. Details Drafting & Design, L.L.C., American Fork, 1993—. Acad. scholarships Utah State U., 1987-93. Mem. Am. Soc. Interior Designers (affiliate), Phi Kappa Phi, Phi Upsilon Omicron. Republican. Mem. LDS Ch. Office: Office Essentials 120 N University Ave Provo UT 84601-2820

GIGLIOTTI, RICHARD JOSEPH, nuclear security executive; b. North Adams, Mass., June 15, 1945; s. Victor and Ida (Antenucci) G.; m. Diane Carol Gigliotti; children: Gina Bianca, Victoria Marie, Richard Joseph Jr. BA, Norwich U., 1968; postgrad., Mass. State Coll., 1968-70. Police officer North Adams Police Dept., 1966-70, Wethersfield (Conn.) Police Dept., 1973-77; security supr. UNC Naval Products, Montville, Conn., 1977-78, corp. security dir., 1984-92; mgr. security UNC Recovery Systems, Charlestown, R.I., 1978-80; dir. loss prevention Colt Firearms, Hartford, Conn., 1980-84; mgr. security RUST Geotech Inc., Grand Junction, Colo., 1992—; adj. faculty Ea. Conn. State U., Willimantic, Mohegan C.C., Norwich, 1984-92; guest lectr. various colls., univs., and corps., 1978—. Author: Security Design for Maximum Protection, 1984, Emergency Planning for Maximum Protection, 1991; contbr. articles to profl. jours. Active Gov.'s and Gen. Assembly's Task Force on Pvt. Security in Conn., 1983. 1st lt. U.S. Army, 1970-73. Recipient Chief Samuel Luciano award Mcpl. Police Tng. Coun., 1974. Mem. Internat. Assn. Chiefs Police, Am. Soc. for Indsl. Security, Ret. Officers Assn., Blue Knights Law Enforcement Motorcycle Club. Roman Catholic. Office: Rust Geotech Inc PO Box 14000 Grand Junction CO 81502

GILBERT, DAVID HEGGIE, retired educational publisher, consultant; b. Healdsburg, Calif., Mar. 11, 1932; s. Lindley Dodge and Beatrice (Heggie) G.; m. Margaret Collins, Nov. 8, 1953; children: Stephen, Laura, Jennifer, Michael. Student, U. Calif. at Berkeley, 1949-51; B.A., U. of Pacific, 1956; M.A., U. Colo., 1957. Instr. English Oreg. State U., Corvallis, 1957-60; asst. prof. English Oreg. State U., 1960-64; Oreg. coll. traveler Holt, Rinehart & Winston Inc., N.Y.C., 1964-65; N.Y. acquiring editor in speech, drama and English Holt, Rinehart & Winston Inc., 1965-66; mgr. Holt, Rinehart & Winston Inc. (S.E. div.), Atlanta, 1966-67; asso. dir. U. Tex. Press, Austin, 1967-74; dir. U. Nebr. Press., Lincoln, 1975-86, Cornell U. Press., Ithaca, N.Y., 1986-89; interim dir. So. Ill. U. Press, 1992-93; cons. in field; Instr. English on TV Oreg. Coll. of Air, 1961-62; moderator Face to Face Ednl. TV, Austin, 1970-72. Mem. Democratic Exec. Com., Benton County (Oreg.), 1959-61. Served with AUS, 1953-55. Mem. Assn. Am. Univ. Presses (dir. 1974-76, 83-84, v.p. 1977-78, pres.-elect 1981-82, pres. 1982-83). Home: 196 SE 130th Dr South Beach OR 97366-9741

GILBERT, EDWARD MICHAEL, cardiology educator; b. Portsmouth, Va., Sept. 2, 1952; s. Edward Richard and Elenor (Kroeger) G.; m. Ina Judith Amber, Oct. 18, 1981 (div. June 1991); 1 child, Stephanie Amber; m. Karen Ann Allen, Dec. 7, 1991; 1 child, Robert Michael. BA in Chemistry, U. Conn., 1974; MD, Wayne State U., 1978. Diplomate Am. Bd. Internal Medicine, Am. Bd. Cardiovasc. Disease. Resident in medicine Wayne State U., Detroit, 1978-81, fellow in critical care, 1983-84; emergency room physician St. Johns Hosp., Detroit, 1981-83; fellow in cardiology U. Utah, Salt Lake City, 1984-88, asst. prof. medicine, 1988-93, assoc. prof., 1993—, dir. heart failure treatment program, 1992—; clin. assoc. physician NIH, 1988-90; med. dir. CCU, U. Utah Health Sci. Ctr., 1993-94. Contbr. over 50 articles to med. and sci. jours. Fellow Bayer Fund, 1988. Fellow Am. Coll. Cardiology (Merck fellow 1985); mem. Am. Heart Assn. (fellow clin. coun., grantee 1989-91), Am. Fedn. Clin. Rsch., Am. Alpine Club. Office: U Utah Health Sci Ctr 50 N Medical Dr Salt Lake City UT 84132-0001

GILBERT, HEATHER CAMPBELL, manufacturing company executive; b. Mt. Vernon, N.Y., Nov. 20, 1944; d. Ronald Ogston and Mary Lodivia (Campbell) G.; BS in Math. (Nat. Merit scholar), Stanford U., 1967; MS in Computer Sci. (NSF fellow), U. Wis., 1969. With Burroughs Corp., 1969-82, sr. mgmt. systems analyst, Detroit, 1975-77, mgr. mgmt. systems activity, Pasadena, Calif., 1977-82; mgr. software product mgmt. Logical Data Mgmt. Inc., Covina, Calif., 1982-83, dir. mktg., 1983, v.p. bus. devel., 1983-84; v.p. profl. services, 1984-85; mgr. software devel. Unisys Corp., Mission Viejo, Calif., 1985—. Mem. Assn. Computing Machinery, Am. Prodn. and Inventory Control Soc., Stanford U. Alumni Assn. (life), Stanford Profl. Women Los Angeles County (pres. 1982-83), Nat. Assn. Female Execs., Town Hall. Republican. Home: 21113 Calle De Paseo Lake Forest CA 92630-7037 Office: Unisys Corp 25725 Jeronimo Rd Mission Viejo CA 92691-2711

GILBERT, JO, psychologist; b. L.A., July 25, 1949; d. Joseph Raymond and Rochelle Rose (Burdman) G.; divorced; 1 child, Branden Christopher Smale. BA in Psychology cum laude, UCLA, 1972; postgrad., U. Houston, 1971-72, William Marsh Rice U., 1972-77; PhD in Clin. Psychology, Calif. Sch. Profl. Psychology, 1980. Lic. psychologist, Calif.; qualified med. evaluator. Psychol. intern, researcher, then counselor Olive St. Bridge, Fresno, Calif., 1978-80; registered psychologist FCEOC Project Pride, Fresno, 1980-82; psychologist Fox, Pick and Assocs., Napa, Calif., 1982-85; pvt. practice Napa, 1985—; ptnr. Napa-Solano Psychotherapy Svcs., 1993—; adj. faculty in forensic psychology Calif. Sch. Profl. Psychology, Berkeley, 1987; faculty U. San Francisco, 1987-88; presenter at profl. confs.; mem. Sacramento County panel ct.-appointed psychologists, Yolo County panel ct.-appointed psychologists, Solano County panel ct.-appointed psychologists. Contbr. articles to profl. publs. Mem. APA, Calif. Psychol. Assn. (assoc. sec. 1994-95), Napa Valley Psychol. Assn. (past pres.), Soc. Personality Assessment. Democrat. Jewish.

GILBERT, PAUL THOMAS, chemical development engineer; b. Chgo., July 29, 1914; s. Paul T. and Ilse (Forster) G.; m. Phyllis A. Simons, Oct. 17, 1942 (div. July 1955); children: Susan R. Sorensen, John (dec.), Brian (dec.), Wendy E. Levy; m. Hazel L. Dalton, July 9, 1955; children: Michael L. Pinizzotto, Michele L. Urquhart. BS in Chemistry, Northwestern U., 1936; postgrad., U. Wis., 1936-38; MA in Math., U. Minn., 1940; postgrad., Calif. Inst. Tech., 1941, U. Calif., Santa Barbara, 1971-74. Tchg. asst. math. U. Minn., Mpls., 1939-41; instr. math. Utah State Agrl. Coll., Logan, 1941, 43-44, U. Minn., Mpls., 1943; rsch. chemist Metalloy Corp., Mpls., 1944-46; rsch. scientist Beckman Instruments, South Pasadena, Calif., 1946-52, N.Am. Aviation, Downey, Calif., 1952-55, Beckman Instruments, Fullerton, Palo Alto, Calif., 1955-71; devel. engr. Chemistry Dept. U. Calif., Santa Barbara, 1971-93; tchr. math. NW Mil. and Naval Prep. Sch., Mpls., 1939-41, 45; tech. translator, 1946—; cons. Atomics Internat., Canoga Park, Calif., 1956-59, lectr. Fullerton Youth Mus., 1963-65, bd. dirs. Co-author (translator) Chemical Analysis by Flame Photometry, 1963; translator: Fundamentals of Analytical Flame Spectroscopy, 1979; patentee in field; contbr. articles to profl. jours. Racecourse measurer Santa Barbara Athletic Assn., 1978—. Cadet USAF, 1941-43. Mem. AAAS, Am. Chem. Soc., Am. Math. Soc., Phi Beta Kappa, Sigma Xi, Phi Eta Sigma. Home: 715 Via Miguel Santa Barbara CA 93111-2743 Office: Univ Calif Dept Chemistry Santa Barbara CA 93106

GILBERT, RETA ALICE, communications educator; b. Lacombe, Alta., Can., Dec. 10, 1936; came to the U.S., 1955; d. Percy and Elvina (Kerr) G. BS, Brigham Young U., 1959, MS, 1960; PhD, La. State U., 1967. Instr. Brigham Young U., Provo, Utah, 1959-60, La. State U., Baton Rouge, 1960-62; asst. prof. Calif. State U., Long Beach, 1962-68, U. Sask., Saskatoon, 1968-69; prof. Ea. Wash. U., Spokane, 1969—; dir. For Fgn. Students Grad. Program, Spokane, 1977-87, Office Applied Comm. Rsch., Spokane, 1989-95; chair comm. Ea. Wash. U., Spokane, 1988-90, 93-94; liaison Shanghai Inst. Fgn. Trade, Spokane, 1989-92. Contbr. articles to profl. jours. Spkr. Inland Empire World Trade Coun., Spokane, 1977-82; cons. Kobe Steel Co., Japan, 1978, City Trade Delegation, Spokane, 1982. Recipient Merit cert. Campus Compact, State of Wash., 1993. Fellow Phi Kappa Phi; mem. Soc. for Internat. Edn. (tng. and rsch. annual presenter), Speech Comm. Assn. (presenter), The Asia Soc., Asian Studies Assn., Coll. Art Assn. Office: Ea Wash Univ W 705 1st Ave Spokane WA 99204

GILBERT, RICHARD JOSEPH, economics educator; b. N.Y.C., Jan. 14, 1945; s. Michael N. and Esther (Dillon) G.; m. Sandra S. Waknitz, Sept. 7, 1974; children: Alison, David. BEE with honors, Cornell U., 1966, MEE, 1967; MA in Econs., Stanford U., 1976, PhD, 1976. Rsch. assoc. Stanford U., Calif., 1975-76; from assist. prof. to assoc. prof. econs. U. Calif., Berkeley, 1976-83; assoc. prof engring-econ. systems Stanford U., 1982-83; prof. econs. U. Calif., Berkeley, 1983—; dir. energy rsch. inst., 1983-93; prof. bus. adminstrn. U. Calif., Berkeley, 1990—; dep. asst. atty. gen. antitrust divsn. U.S. Dept. Justice, 1993-95; dir. U. Energy Rsch. Inst. U. Calif., Berkeley, 1983-93; dir. univ. energy rsch. inst. U. Calif., Berkeley, 1983—; prin., treas. Law & econs. Cons. Group, Berkeley, 1989—. Contbr. numerous articles to profl. jours.; editor scholarly jours. Adv. U.S. Dept. Energy, Washington, 1983—, World Bank, Washington, 1980—, NSF, Washington, 1985—, Calif. Inst. Energy Efficiency, Berkeley, 1990—. Fulbright scholar Washington, 1989; vis. scholar Cambridge U., 1979, Oxford U., 1979. Mem. Tau Beta Pi, Eta Kappa Nu, Sigma Xi. Office: U Calif Dept Economics Berkeley CA 94720

GILBERT, RICHARD KEITH, education educator, researcher; b. St. Louis, Apr. 23, 1958; s. William Ray and Janice Sylvia (Rephlo) G. BA, U. Calif., Santa Barbara, 1981, MA, 1990, postgrad., 1993. Secondary tchg. credential, Calif. Rschr. Marine Sci. Inst., Santa Barbara, 1979-82; rschr., coord. Catalina Island (Calif.) Marine Inst., 1983-85; sci. educator L.A. (Calif.) Unified Sch. Dist., 1985-87; sci. and calculus educator Am. Internat. Sch., Johannesburg, South Africa, 1987-89; rschr. psychotherapy U. Calif., Santa Barbara, 1990-92; cons. advanced tech. divsn. spl. projects Gen. Rsch. Corp., Santa Barbara, 1992-94; tchr., rschr. U. So. Calif., L.A., 1993—; cons. Akela Corp., 1994. Active re-election campaign Hon. Robert Lagomarsino, Santa Barbara, 1992—. Named Outstanding Tchr. Advanced Biol. Sci., NSF, Calif. State U., Northridge, 1986-87; Grad. fellow Calif. State U., U. So. Calif., 1993. Mem. AAAS, N.Y. Acad. Sci., Comparative Internat. Edn. Soc., Am. Ednl. Rsch. Assn., U.S. Naval Inst. Presbyterian. Home: 6285 Avenida Ganso Goleta CA 93117-2063 Office: U So Calif Dept Edn WPH 904 Los Angeles CA 90089-0031

GILBERT, ROBERT WOLFE, lawyer; b. N.Y.C., Nov. 12, 1920; s. L. Wolfe and Katherine L. (Oestreicher) Wolfe; m. Beatrice R. Frutman, Dec. 25, 1946; children: Frank Richard, Jack Alfred. BA, UCLA 1941; JD, U. Calif., Berkeley, 1943. Bar: Calif. 1944, U.S. Ct. Appeals. (9th cir.) 1944, U.S. Ct. Appeals. (D.C. cir.) 1976, U.S. Supreme Ct. 1959. Pres. Gilbert & Sackman, P.C. and predecessors, L.A., 1944—; judge pro tem Los Angeles Mcpl. and Superior Ct., Commr. City of L.A. Housing Authority 1953-63; bd. dirs. Calif. Housing Coun. 1955-63; U.S. faculty mem. Moscow Conf. on Law and Econ. Cooperation, 1990. Mem. Internat. Bar Assn., Interam. Bar Assn. (co-chmn. labor law and social security com.), ABA (co-chmn. internat. labor law com.), Fed. Bar Assn., L.A. Bar Assn. (past chmn. labor law sect.), Am. Judicature Soc., Order of Coif, Pi Sigma Alpha. Club: Nat. Lawyers. Contbr. articles to profl. jours. Home: 7981 Hollywood Blvd Los Angeles CA 90046-2611 Office: 6100 Wilshire Blvd Ste 700 Los Angeles CA 90048-5114

GILBERT, SANDRA M., English language educator. BA in English with high honors, Cornell U., 1957; MA, NYU, 1961; PhD, Columbia U., 1968; DLitt, Wesleyan U., 1988. Lectr. English CUNY, N.Y.C., 1963-64, 65-66, Calif. State U., Sacramento, 1967-68; asst. prof. English Calif. State U., Hayward, 1968-71; vis. lectr. English St. Mary's Coll., Moraga, Calif., 1972; assoc. prof. English Ind. U., Bloomington, 1973-75; assoc. prof. English U. Calif., Davis, 1975-80, prof. English, 1980-85, 89—; prof. English Princeton (N.J.) U., 1985-89, Charles Barnwell Strout Class of 1923 prof., 1989; chair women's studies subcom. SWADAC U. Calif., Davis, 1976-80; vis. prof. Ind. U., Bloomington, fall 1980, The Johns Hopkins U., Balt., fall 1986; panelist NEH, fall 1982, Rockefeller Found., fall 1982, women's studies Woodrow Wilson Found., fall 1985; dir. Mt. Holyoke Project Gender Context, 1983, summer 1984; mem. exec. com. Humanities Inst., 1983-87; Margaret Bundy Scott vis. prof. Williams Coll., fall 1984; Bonzall vis. prof. Stanford (Calif.) U., winter 1985; Gildersleeve professorship Barnard Coll., fall 1982; Joseph Warren Beach lectr. U. Minn., May, 1984; faculty Sch. Criticism and Theory, Northwestern U., summer 1984; mem. women's studies program com. Princeton U., 1986—, mem. creative writing program com., 1986—, acting dir. creative writing program, spring 1989; Paley lectr. The Hebrew U., Jerusalem, 1990; Danz lectr. U. Wash., Seattle, 1992; bd. advisors Literary Classics in the U.S., 1979-82; lectr. in field. Author: Acts of Attention: The Poems of D. H. Lawrence, 1972, 2d rev. edit., 1990 (alternate selection Readers Subscription 1973), In the Fourth World: Poems, 1979, The Summer Kitchen: Poems, 1983, Emily's Bread: Poems, 1984, Kate Chopin's The Awakening and Selected Stories, 1984, Blood Pressure: Poems, 1988, Wrongful Death: A Medical Tragedy, 1995, Ghost Volcano: Poems, 1995; co-author: (with Susan Gubar) The Madwoman in the Attic: The Woman Writer and the Nineteenth Century Literary Imagination, 1979 (runner-up Pulitzer Prize in non-fiction 1980), A Guide to the Norton Anthology of Literature by Women, 1985, No Man's Land: The Place of the Woman Writer in the Twentieth Century, Vol. 1, The War of the Words, 1987, Vol. 2, Sexchanges, 1989, Vol. 3, Letters Fom the Front, 1994; co-editor: (with Susan Gubar) Shakespeare's Sisters: Feminist Essays on Women Poets, 1979, Women of Letters Series, 1984—, The Norton Anthology of Literature by Women: The Tradition in English, 1985, Feminism and Modernism, 1987, (with Jackson Lears and Stanley Aronowitz) U. Minn. Press Am. Writers Series, 1984-89, Masterpiece Theatre: An Academic Melodrama, 1995, (with Wendy Barker) The House is Made of Poetry: Essays on the Art of Ruth Stone, 1995; editor: So. Ill. U. Press Series in Feminist Criticism, 1984—; poetry editor Calif. Quarterly, 1975-80; mem. editorial bd. Tulsa Studies in Women's Lit., 1980—, Poesis, 1983—, Genre, 1988—; co-editor (with Susan Gubar) Women's Studies, spring 1980, fall 1984; mem. poetry bd. Wesleyan U. Press, 1985-88; contbr. essays, poems and ficiton to profl. jours. and popular mags. Grantee Calif. State Hayward Found., 1969-70, Ind. U., 1974, U. Calif., summer 1976, 78, 79, 81; recipient Columbia U. Pres.'s fellowship, 1964-65, AAUW fellowship, 1966-67, NEH fellowship, 1980-81, Rockefeller Found. Humanities fellowship, 1982, Guggenheim fellowship, 1983, U. Calif.-Davis Humanities Inst. fellowship, 1987-88, U. Calif. Pres.'s fellowship, 1991-92, Eunice Tietjens Meml. prize, 1980, Charity Randall award Internat. Poetry Found., 1990, Woman of the Yr. award Ms. mag., 1986. Mem. MLA (nominating com. 1985-87, William Riley Parker Prize com. 1985-87, exec. com. Lit. Criticism divsn. 1985-87, exec. coun. 1981-84, exec. com. Women's Studies divsn. 1980-84, 2nd v.p., 1st v.p., pres-elect, 1994—), D.H. Lawrence Soc. (mem. exec. com. 1983-85). Office: Univ of Calif Dept of English Davis CA 95616

GILBERT, STEPHEN L., electrical engineer, chemist; b. Newark, July 26, 1943; s. Edwin O. and Theda (McPerry) G.; m. Lois Virgina Doak, Feb. 11, 1964 (div.); 1 child, Samuel Alexander Paul; m. Nancy Lee Conte, May 23, 1981 (div.); children: Nathan Thomas, Noah Charles, Samuel Zachary. BS in Chemistry, St. Joseph's Coll., Phila., 1974; postgrad., U. Pa., 1975. Rsch. assoc. UNIVAC, Blue Bell, Pa., 1965-68, RCA Corp. David Sarnoff Rsch. Ctr., Princeton, N.J., 1968-75; sr. assoc. engr. IBM, Burlington, Vt., 1978; chief engr. Fairbanks Mus. and Planetarium, St. Johnsbury, Vt., 1979; rsch. fellow and mgr. microelectronics U. Minn., Mpls., 1981-89; mgr. microelectronics U. Ariz., Tucson, 1989—; pres. Cons. Svcs., St. Johnsbury, 1975—; cons. UN Indsl. Devel. Orgn., 1984—, TelTech., Mpls., 1984—, Intel, Signetics; expert witness VTC Inc., Honeywell, Linear Tech., Briggs & Morgan, Wilson Sonsini, Goodrich & Rosati; bd. dirs. Minn. Microelectronics Lab Group; mem. fin. mgmt. State Capital Credit Union. Contbr. articles to profl. jours; patentee in field. David Sarnoff scholar RCA Corp., 1974. Mem. IEEE (sr.), AAAS, Inst. for Environ. Svcs. (sr.), Semiconductor Safety Assn., Minn. Electron Microscopy Assn., Am. Chem. Soc., Materials Rsch. Soc., Atmospheric Pressure Ionization Mass Spectrometry User Group (coord.), Electrochem. Soc. Office: U Ariz Elec & Computer Engring 1230 E Speedway Blvd Tucson AZ 85719

GILBERT, TERENCE NEIL, education educator, musician; b. Oceanside, Calif., July 19, 1944; s. Richard B. and Evaline M. (Errett) G.; 1 child, Krista L. Gilbert (div. Aug. 1971). BA in English Lit., UCLA, 1971. Teaching credential, Calif. Social svcs. supr. Nev. Social Svcs., Nevada City, Calif., 1974-82; tchr. L.A. Unified Sch. Dist., 1985—; presenter, trainer Calif. Lit. Project. Violinist Topanga (Calif.) Symphony, 1985-94. Sgt. USAF, 1985-89. Mem. United Tchrs. L.A. Office: Birmingham High School 17000 Haynes St Van Nuys CA 91406-5420

GILBERT-ROLFE, JEREMY DENTON, artist, art critic, educator; b. Tunbridge Wells, Kent, Eng., Aug. 4, 1945; came to U.S., 1968; s. Hendrik William Gilbert-Rolfe and Beatrice Alice Freeman Manger; m. Jenifer Jean Lyle, 1964 (div.); 1 child, Cyrus Jasper; m. Genevieve Anne Vagianos, 1979; 1 child, Cedric Foster. Student, Tunbridge Wells Art Sch., 1961-65, London U. Inst. Edn., 1966-67; MFA, Fla. State U., Tallahassee, 1970. Instr. Fla. State U., Tallahassee, 1968-71; lectr. Princeton (N.J.) U., 1972-78, Parsons Sch. Art, N.Y.C., 1978-80, Calif. Inst. Arts, Valencia, 1980-86; grad. advisor, prof. Art Ctr. Coll., Pasadena, Calif., 1986—; vis. prof. Queens (N.Y.) Coll., 1978-79; vis. lectr. Yale U. Sch. Architecture, New Haven, 1989-92. Author: Immanence and Contradiction, 1986, Beyond Piety, 1995; contbg. editor New Observations, N.Y.C., 1989—, Arts Mag., N.Y.C., 1990-93, Bomb, N.Y.C., 1988—; founding editor October, N.Y.C., 1975-78; author numerous articles; exhibited numerous paintings in N.Y. and elsewhere, 1972—. Criticism fellow NEA, 1974, painting fellow, 1979, 89. Mem. MLA, Internat. Assn. for Philosophy and Lit., Internat. Assn. for Word and Image Studies, Viking Eggeling Assn. Democrat. Office: 2900 Airport Ave # C Santa Monica CA 90405-6109

GILBERTSON, OSWALD IRVING, marketing executive; b. Bklyn., Mar. 23, 1927; s. Olaf and Ingeborg (Aase) Gabrielsen; m. Magnhild Hompland, Sept. 11, 1954; children: Jan Ivar, Eric Olaf. Electrotechnician, Sorlandets Tekniske Skole, Norway, 1947; BSEE, Stockholms Tekniska Institut, Stockholm, Sweden, 1956. Planning engr. test equipment design and devel. Western Electric Co., Inc., Kearny, N.J., 1957-61, planning engr. new prodn., 1963-67, engring. supr. test equipment, 1963-67, engring. supr. submarine repeaters and equalizers, 1967-69; engring. mgr. communication cables ITT Corp., Oslo, Norway, 1969-71, mktg. mgr. for ITT's Norwegian co., Standard Telefon og Kabelfabrik A/S (STK), 1971-87, STK Factory rep., 1987-89, Alcatel Kabel Norge AS Factory rep., 1989-92, Alcatel Can. Wire Inc. Factory rep., 1992-95; div. mgr. Eswa Heating Systems, Inc., 1980-87, pres., 1987-89. Hon. Norwegian consul, 1981—; apptd. Knight First Class Norwegian Order Merit, 1989. Served with AUS, 1948-52. Registered profl. engr., Vt. Mem. IEEE, Norwegian Soc. Profl. Engrs., Soc. Norwegian Am. Engrs., Sons of Norway. Patentee in field. Home and Office: 6240 Brynwood Ct San Diego CA 92120-3805

GILBERTZ, LARRY E., state legislator, entrepreneur; b. Gillette, Wyo., Feb. 3, 1929; s. Jacob A. and Lena E. (Schlautmann) G.; m. Verna Ann Howell, June 18, 1955; children: Katerine, L.D., Susan, Jay. Mgr. Gilbertz Ranch, Gillette, 1953-62, owner, 1963—; sr. ptnr. Gilbertz Co., Gillette, 1971—; pres. Gilbertz Enterprises, Gillette, 1988—; mem. Wyo. Senate, Cheyenne, 1993—; chmn. U. Wyo. Exptl. Farm, Campbell County, 1970-74. Treas. Sch. Bd. Dist. # 9, Campbell County, 1969-71; active Sch. Dist. Reorgn., Campbell County, 1970, Wyo. Ct. Reform, 1971. With U.S. Army, 1951-53, PTO. Recipient Performance Testing award U. Wyo., 1969-74, Chem. Weed Control award, 1969-74. Mem. Am. Farm Bur., Am. Legis. Exch. Coun., Am. Legion, Wyo. Stockgrowers. Republican. Catholic.

GILES, DAVID EDWARD, management consultant; b. Seattle, Jan. 1, 1950; s. Edward Carlyle Giles and Doris Margaret McKnight; m. Rhinee Wei-Fang Yeung; children: Katherine Elizabeth Yun Chee, Daniel Kai Yun. BA in Philosophy, Pacific Luth. U., 1972; MTS in Philosophy, Harvard U., 1975. CEO Marvin Co., Inc. and subs., Seattle and Portland, Oreg., 1976-89; ind. mgmt. cons., 1991—; with Russian-Am. U./Gorbachev Found., Moscow, 1991—; speaker, presenter workshops on leadership of newly legalized polit. parties, Moscow. Candidate for U.S. Ho. of Reps., 1986, 90; del. Dem. Nat. Conv., 1992. Mem. Wash. State China Rels. Coun., Bus. Execs. for Nat. Security, Physicians for Social Responsibiljity (bd. dirs., speaker), Seattle C. of C., others. Home and Office: 11305 207th Ave SE Issaquah WA 98027-8552

GILES, GERALD LYNN, psychology,learning enhancement,computer educator; b. Manti, Utah, Jan. 2, 1943; s. Bert Thorne and Sarah Jenett (Carlen) G.; m. Sharon Ruth Bleak, June 12, 1967; children: Kim, David, Kristie, Becky, Michael, Andrew, Brent, Amber. BA, U. Utah, 1968, MA, 1971. Tchr. Granite Sch. Dist., Salt Lake City, 1968-72; prof. Salt Lake Community Coll., Salt Lake City, 1972—; cons. QUE Enterprises, Salt Lake City, 1976—; mem. faculty U. Phoenix, Salt Lake City, 1986—; internat. presenter in field. Author: The Vicious Circle of Life, 1988, The Computer Productivity Planner, 1988. Chmn. Rep. voting dist., Salt Lake City, 1984-86; bishop LDS Ch., 1986-91; soccer coach; adviser Explorer Scouts. Named Outstanding Tchr. of Yr., 1986; recipient Teaching Excellence award, 1986, Excellence award Nisod, 1986. Mem. ASCD, Utah Assn. Devel. Edn., Assn. Adult and Continuing Edn. Home: 7366 Redwood Rd Apt 79 West Jordan UT 84084-3470 Office: Salt Lake C C PO Box 30808 Salt Lake City UT 84130-0808

GILES, JEAN HALL, retired corporate executive; b. Dallas, Mar. 30, 1908; d. C. D. and Ida (McIntyre) Overton; m. Alonzo Russell Hall, II, Jan. 23, 1923 (dec.); children: Marjorie Hodges, Alonzo Russell III; m. Harry E. Giles, Apr. 24, 1928 (div. 1937); 1 child, Janice Ruth; 1 adopted child, Marjean Giles. Grad. Hamilton State U., PhD (hon.), 1973. comdg. officer S.W. Los Angeles Women's Ambulance and Def. Corps., 1941-43; maj., nat. exec. officer Women's Ambulance and Def. Corps, 1944-45; capt., dir. field ops. Communications Corps of the U.S. Nat. Staff, 1951-52; dir. Recipe of the Month Club. Active Children's Hosp. Benefit, 1946; coord. War Chest Motor Corps, 1943-44; dir. Los Angeles Area War Chest Vol. Corps and Motor Corps, 1945-46; realtor Los Angeles Real Estate Exchange, 1948—, now ret.; also partner Tech. Contractors, Los Angeles. Bd. dirs. Tchr. Remembrance Day Found. Inc. Mem. Los Angeles C. of C. (women's div.), A.I.M., Los Angeles Art Assn., Hist. Soc. So. Calif., Opera Guild So. Calif., Assistance League So. Calif., Needlework Guild Am. (sect. pres. Los Angeles), First Century Families Calif., Internat. Platform Assn. Clubs: Athletic; Town Hall, The Garden (Los Angeles); Pacific Coast. Home: 616 Magnolia Ave Long Beach CA 90802-1243

GILES, WALTER EDMUND, alcohol and drug treatment executive; b. Omaha, Aug. 9, 1934; s. Walter Edmund and Julia Margaret (Shively) G.; m. Ellen M. Garton, June 13, 1953; m. Dona LaVonne Foster, Sept. 29, 1970 (dec. 1990); children: Sue, Stephen, Theresa, Marcy, Kim, Tim, Nadine, Charles; m. Yvonne Marie Fink, Nov. 29, 1991; children: Jessica Nicole Farr, Walter Edmund III. BA, U. Nebr., Lincoln, 1972, MA, 1977. Counselor VA Hosp., Lincoln, Nebr., 1969-70; coord. alcohol programs Mcpl. Ct., Lincoln; dir. Orange County Employee Assistance, Santa Ana, Calif., 1977-79; adminstr. Advanced Health Ctr., Newport Beach, Calif., 1979-81; pres. Great West Health Svcs. Inc., Orange, Calif., 1982-86, Pine Ridge Treatment Ctr. Inc., Running Springs, Calif., 1986—. Author (book) The Workbook, 1985, Intervention, 1986; host (radio show) Addictions, 1984. Mem. Nat. Assn. Alcoholism Counselors, Calif. Assn. Alcoholism Counselors.

GILGER, PAUL DOUGLASS, architect; b. Mansfield, Ohio, Oct. 13, 1954; s. Richard Douglass and Marilyn Joan (Hawkins) G. BArch, U. Cin., 1978. Registered architect, Ohio. Architect Soulen & Assocs., Mansfield, Ohio, 1976-81, PGS Architecture/Planning, Los Gatos, Calif., 1981-82, Bottomline Systems, Inc., San Francisco, 1983-85; pvt. practice San Francisco Bay Area, 1985-90; set designer Nomad Prodns. Scenic Studios, San Francisco, 1985-87; architect James Gillam, Architect, San Francisco, 1987-90, Hedgpeth Architects, Santa Rosa, Calif., 1990—, Home Planners, Inc., Tucson, 1994—; booking mgr. 1177 Club, San Francisco, 1985-86, City Cabaret, San Francisco, 1986-87; bd. dirs San Francisco Coun. Entertainment, 1987-90; project architect Lucasfilm Movie Studio Indsl. Light and Magic, San Rafael, Calif., 1991. Author: "Tune the Grand Up", the Jerry Herman Musical Revue. Recipient Ohio Community Theatre Assn. award, 1980, Theatrewest Acting award, 1983, Bay Area Critics Cir. award, 1984, 85, Cabaret Gold awards San Francisco Coun. Entertainment, 1985,86, Hollywood Dramalogue award, 1985, San Francisco Focus award, 1985. Home: 631 Spencer Ave Apt 6 Santa Rosa CA 95404-3301 Office: Hedgpeth Architects 2321 Bethards Dr Santa Rosa CA 95405-8536

GILL, BECKY LORETTE, addictionist, psychiatrist; b. Phoenix, Mar. 16, 1947; d. David Franklin and Lorette (Cooper) Brinegar; m. Jim Shack Gill, Jr., Aug. 5, 1978. BA in Biology, Stanford U., 1968; MD, U. Ariz., 1973. Diplomate Am. Bd. Psychiatry and Neurology; cert. addiction counselor; substance abuse residential facility dir., addictions specialist, clin. supr. Clerk typist Ariz. Med. Ctr. Med. Libr., Tucson, Ariz., 1970; asst. ref. libr. Ariz. Med. Ctr. Med. Libr., Tucson, 1971; surg. extern Tucson Med. Ctr., summer 1970; med. extern Fed. Reformatory for Women, Alderson, W.Va., 1972-73; commd. lt. USN, 1974, advanced through grades to capt., 1992; intern in medicine USPHS Hosp., Balt., 1973-74; resident in psychiatry Nat. Naval Med. Ctr., Bethesda, Md., 1974-77; head alcohol rehab. svc./substance abuse dept., staff psychiatrist Naval Hosp., Camp Lejeune, N.C., 1977-85; head alcohol rehab. svc./substance abuse dept., head psych. Naval Hosp., Millington, Tenn., 1985-88; head alcohol rehab. dept. Naval Hosp., Long Beach, Calif., 1988-94; head Navy Addictions Rehab. and Edn. Dept., Camp Pendleton, Calif., 1994—; mem. tumor bd. Naval Hosp., Camp Lejeune, 1977-85, cons. Tri-Command Consolidated Drug and Alcohol Counseling Ctr. Agy., 1977-85, phys. fitness program com., 1980-85, med. liaison on substance abuse, 1982-85, drug/alcohol program advisor, 1983-85, Tri-Command Consolidated Drug and Alcohol Adv. Coun., 1983-85, controlled substance abuse review subcom. of pharmacy and therapeutics com., 1984-85; watch officer Acute Care Clinic, Naval Hosp., Millington, 1985-86, cons. Counseling and Assistance Ctr., 1985-88, mem. bioethics com., chmn. med. records, utilization review com., 1985-88, exec. com. med. staff, chmn., 1986-87, psychiatric cons. to NAS Brig, 1986-88, mem. quality assurance com., 1986, mem. credentials com., 1986-87, pharmacy and therapeutics com., 1986, pos. mgmt. com., 1986-87, dir. med. svcs., 1986-88, dir. surgical svcs., 1986, commd. duty watch officer, 1986-87, watch officer acute care clinic, 1987-88, mem. Navy Drug and Alcohol adv. coun., 1987-88, preceptor to social worker, 1987-88, pos. mgmt. com., 1988, mem. commd. retention coun., 1988; also, numerous coms. at Naval Hosp., Long Beach, Calif., Naval Hosp., Camp Pendleton, Calif. Capt. USN. Recipient Commendation medal USN, 1988, meritorious svc. medal, 1994. Mem. Am. Acad. of Psychiatrists in Alcoholism and Addictions (founding mem.), Am. Soc. of Addiction Medicine, Assn. Mil. Surgeons of U.S., Addiction Profls. of N.C. (chmn. pub. info. com. 1979-80, ea. regional v.p. 1981-82, chmn. fall meeting planning com. 1983, sec. 1984-85), Nat. Assn. of Alcoholism and Drug Abuse Counselors, Calif. Assn. Alcohol and Drug Abuse Counselors, Am. Legion, U.S. Lawn Tennis Assn. (hon. life), Stanford Cap and Gown, Stanford Alumni Assn., U. Ariz. Alumni Assn., Stanford Cardinal Club. Democrat. Home: 32155 Corte Florecita Temecula CA 92592-6319

GILL, DAVID, food products executive; b. 1949. Student, Cal Poly San Luis Obispo, 1970-75. With Almaden Vineyards, Napa Valley, Calif., 1975-78; ptnr. Rio Farms, Oxnard, Calif., 1978—. Office: Rio Farms 4300 Wood Rd Oxnard CA 93033-8215*

GILL, GAIL STOORZA, public relations executive; b. Yoakum, Tex., Aug. 28, 1943. Student, North Tex. State U., U. Tex., Arlington. Acct. exec. Phillips Ramsey, Inc., 1965-71; dir. advt., pub. rels. Rancho Bernardo, Inc., 1969-71; dir., corp. comm. AVCO Comm. Developers, Inc., 1971-74; pres. The Stoorza Co., 1974-83; chmn. Stoorza Ziegaus & Metzger, Inc., San Diego, 1983—. Office: Stoorza Ziegaus & Metzger 225 Broadway Ste 1600 San Diego CA 92101-5018

GILL, GEORGE WILHELM, anthropologist; b. Sterling, Kans., June 28, 1941; s. George Laurance and Florence Louise (Jones) G.; BA in Zoology with honors (NSF grantee), U. Kans., 1963, M.Phil. Anthropology (NDEA fellow, NSF dissertation research grantee), 1970, PhD in Anthropology, 1971; m. Pamela Jo Mills, July 26, 1975 (div. 1988); children: George Scott, John Ashton, Jennifer Florence, Bryce Thomas. Mem. faculty U. Wyo., Laramie, 1971—, prof. anthropology, 1985—, chair dept. anthropology, 1993—; forensic anthropologist law enforcement agys., 1972—; sci. leader Easter Island Anthrop. Expdn., 1981; chmn. Rapa Nui Rendezvous: Internat. Conf. Easter Island Rsch., U. Wyo., 1993. Served to capt. U.S. Army, 1963-67. Recipient J.P. Ellbogen meritorious classroom teaching award, 1983; research grantee U. Wyo., 1972, 78, 82, Nat. Geog. Soc., 1980, Center for Field Research, 1980, Kon-Tiki Mus., Oslo, 1987, 89, 94, World Monuments Fund, 1989. Diplomate Am. Bd. Forensic Anthropology (bd. dirs. 1985-90). Fellow Am. Acad. Forensic Scis. (sec. phys. anthropology sect. 1985-87, chmn. 1987-88); mem. Am. Assn. Phys. Anthropologists, Plains Anthrop. Soc., Wyo. Archael. Soc. Republican. Presbyterian. Author articles, monographs; editor: (with S. Rhine) Skeletal Attribution of Race, 1990. Home: 649 Howe Rd Laramie WY 82070-6885 Office: U Wyo Dept Anthropology Laramie WY 82071

GILL, JAMES H., public relations and marketing executive. BS, Western Mich. U., 1975; MS, boston U., 1980. Tech. publs. writer Am. Motors Corp., Southfield, Mich., 1975-78; publicist Boston U., 1978-79; pub. rels. supr. Pontiac Motor, pub. rels. and advt. mgr. GM, LaGrange, Ill., 1979-85; v.p. Hill and Knowlton, Inc., Detroit, 1986-90; corp. mgr. corp. comms., mgr. media rels. & mktg. pub. rels. Nissan N.Am., Carson, Calif., 1990—. Mem. Pub. Rels. Soc. Am., Boston U. Alumni Assn.

GILL, LINDA LEE, English literature educator; b. Buffalo, Sept. 13, 1962; d. Lawrence Keith and Dawn Maria (Petrik) G. BA in English, Andrews U., Berrien Springs, Mich., 1984; MA in English Lit., Loma Linda U., Lasierra, Calif., 1986; PhD in English Lit., U. Calif., Riverside, 1992. Teaching asst. U. Calif., Riverside, 1986-92, lectr., 1992-93; lectr. Riverside C.C., 1990-93; asst. prof. English lit. Pacific Union Coll., Angwin, Calif., 1994—. Contbr. articles to profl. jours. Mem. MLA, U. Calif.-Riverside Alumni Assn., Sigma Tau Delta (advisor 1994—). Office: Pacific Union College Angwin CA 94508

GILL, REBECCA LALOSH, aerospace engineer; b. Brownsboro, Tex., Sept. 17, 1944; d. Milton and Dona Mildred (Magee) La Losh; m. Peter Mohammed Sharma, Sept. 1, 1965 (div.); m. James Fredrick Gill, Mar. 9, 1985; children: Erin, Melissa, Ben. BS in Physics, U. Mich., 1965; MBA, Calif. State U., Northridge, 1980. Tchr., Derby, Kans., 1966; weight analyst Beech Aircraft, Wichita, Kans., 1966; weight engr. Ewing Tech. Design, assigned Boeing-Vertol, Phila., 1966-67, Bell Aerosystems, Buffalo, 1967; design specialist Lockheed-Calif. Co., Burbank, 1968-79; sr. staff engr. Hughes Aircraft Missile Systems, Canoga Park, Calif., 1979-82, project mgr. AMRAAM spl. test and tng. equipment, 1982-85, project mgr. GBU-15 guidance sect., Navy IR Maverick Missile, Tucson, 1985-89, project mgr. Navy IR Maverick Missile, SLAM Seeker Prodn., 1989-92, TOSH and TOW program mgr., 1992—; sec. Nat. Cinema Corp. Com. chmn. Orgn. for Rehab. through Tng., 1971-75; speaker ednl. and civic groups. Pres. Briarcliffe East Homeowners Assn.; coord. support group Am. Diabetes Assn., chmn. com. fundraising; active NOW. Recipient Lockheed award of achievement, 1977. Mem. NAFE, Soc. Allied Weight Engrs. (dir., sr. v.p., chmn. pub. rels. com.), Aerospace Elec. Soc. (dir.), Tucson Zool. Soc. (bd. dirs.), Hughes Mgmt. Club (bd. dirs., chmn. spl. events, chmn. programs, parliamentarian, 1st v.p., pres.), Women in Def. (sec., Ariz. chpt.), Las Alturas Homeowners Assn. (v.p., pres.), Tucson Racquet Club. Republican. Office: Hughes Missile Systems Co Bldg 801 MS G25A Tucson AZ 85734

GILL, STEVEN, food products executive; b. 1949. Student, Cal Poly San Luis Obispo, Calif., 1970-75. With Bud Antle Inc., Salinas, Calif., 1975-78; ptnr. Rio Farms, L.A., 1978—. Office: Rio Farms 4300 Wood Rd Los Angeles CA 90033*

GILLAM, MAX LEE, lawyer; b. Cleve., Apr. 28, 1926; s. Max Lee and Louise (Sellers) G.; children: Marcheta, Wade, Lynn, Anne, Mary, Kate. B.S., U.S. Naval Acad., 1949; LL.B., Harvard U., 1956. Bar: Calif. 1957. With Latham, & Watkins, Los Angeles, 1956-93, sr. partner; sr. litigation counsel to asst. atty. gen. Antitrust Divsn., U.S. Dept. Justice, 1994-95. With USN, 1944-45, USAF, 1949-53. Mem. ABA, ATLA, Calif. Bar Assn., L.A. Bar Assn., Assn. Bus. Trial Lawyers.

GILLEN, KATHERINE ELIZABETH, librarian; b. Washington, May 16, 1951; d. Hugh Chisholm and Norma Marie (Provost) G. BS, U. Md., 1973, MLS, 1976; MA, U. Phoenix, 1989; grad., Citizens Police Acad., Mesa, Ariz., 1993. Librarian Maricopa County Community Coll., Phoenix, 1982-84; librarian reference and serials Mesa (Ariz.) Pub. Library, 1981-92; libr. mgr. Denver Pub. Libr., 1992; libr. USAF, Luke AFB, Ariz., 1993—. Book reviewer Libr. Jour., 1991—; contbr. short stories to mags.; pub.: Felicia's First Christmas, 1994. Class mem. Mesa Leadership Tng. and Devel., 1991-92. Mem. AAAS (reviewer 1982—), Ariz. State Libr. Assn. (exec. bd. 1991-92, serials roundtable chmn. 1991-92), Serials Specialists of Maricopa County, Mensa. Home: 600 N Litchfield Rd Goodyear AZ 85338-1267

GILLER, EDWARD BONFOY, retired government official, retired air force officer; b. Jacksonville, Ill., July 8, 1918; s. Edward Bonfoy and Ruth (Davis) G.; m. Mildred Florana Schmidt, July 2, 1943; children—Susan Ann, Carol Elaine, Bruce Carleton, Penny Marie, Paul Benjamin. B.S. in Chem. Engring, U. Ill., 1940, M.S., 1948, Ph.D., 1950. Chem. engr. Sinclair Oil Refining Co., 1940-41; commd. 2d lt. USAAF, 1942; advanced through grades to maj. gen. USAF, 1968; pilot, 1941-46; chief radiation br. (Armed Forces Spl. Weapons Project), Washington, 1950-54; dir. research directorate Air Force Spl. Weapons Center, Albuquerque, 1954-59; spl. asst. to comdr. (Office Aerospace Rsch.), Washington, 1959-64; dir. sci. and tech. Hdqrs. USAF, 1964-67; asst. gen. mgr. for mil. application U.S. AEC, 1967-72; ret. from USAF, 1972; asst. gen. mgr. for nat. security AEC, 1972-75; dep. asst. adminstr. for nat. security U.S. ERDA, 1975-77; rep. of Joint Chiefs of Staff to Comprehensive Test Ban Negotiations, Geneva, Switzerland, 1977-84; sr. scientist Pacific-Sierra Rsch. Corp., Arlington, Va, 1984-92; v.p. Trans Mar Inc., Spokane, Wash., 1992—; cons. in the field. Decorated Silver Star, D.S.M., Legion of Merit with oak leaf cluster, D.F.C., Air medal with 17 oak leaf clusters, Purple Heart; Croix de Guerre France). Fellow Am. Inst. Chemists; mem. AAAS, Am. Inst. Chem. Engrs., Sigma Xi, Alpha Tau Omega. Episcopalian. Home: 216 Wapiti Dr Bayfield CO 81122-9243 Office: Trans Mar Inc 1936 E 23rd Ave Spokane WA 99203-3802

GILLETT, GEORGE NIELD, JR., communications executive; b. Racine, Wis., Oct. 22, 1938; s. George Nield and Alyce (Herbert) G.; m. Rose Foster, Aug. 5, 1967; children: George Nield III, Alexander, Andrew, Foster. Student, Amherst Coll.; B.A., Dominican Coll., Racine, 1961. With McKinsey and Co., Inc. (mgmt. cons.), 1964-67; bus. mgr. Miami Dolphins, 1966-67; pres. Harlem Globetrotters, Inc., 1967-70, Globetrotter Communications, Inc., Chgo., 1970-76; vice-chmn. Globe Broadcasting Co., 1976-78; chmn. Wausau Fin. Corp., Wis., 1969—, Lease Mgmt. Corp., Chgo., 1973—; pres. Juneau Supply Co., Inc., 1977—, Wausau Energy Corp., 1977—; chmn. Gillett Holdings, Inc., 1978—, Gillett Communications Co., 1978—, Packerland Packing Co., Inc., 1978-94; owner, chmn. Vail Assocs., Inc., Colo., 1985—; chmn. Citizens Bank & Trust, Wausau, Wis., 1986; chmn. The Norris Farm, Inc., 1988—; dir. Endata, Inc., Third Nat. Bank, Nashville. Mem. Young Presidents Orgn.; mem. exec. com. Middle Tenn. council Boy Scouts Am.; bd. dirs. United Way; trustee U.S. Ski Edns. Found.; mem. Vail Valley Found. Mem. Am. Meat Assn., Alexis de Tocqueville Soc., Nat. Ski Areas Assn. Roman Catholic. Clubs: Racquet (Chgo.); Belle Meade Country, Onwentsia, Oneida; Colo. Ski (bd. dirs.), Cascade (Vail, Colo.); Beaver Creek, Buck Point, Honors Course, Richland, Country of the Rockies.

GILLETTE, ETHEL MORROW, columnist; b. Oelwein, Iowa, Nov. 27, 1921; d. Charles Henry and Myrne Sarah (Law) Morrow; student Coe Coll., 1939-41; BA, Upper Iowa U., 1959; MA, Western State Coll., 1969; m. Roman A. Gillette, May 6, 1944 (dec. 1992); children: Melody Ann, Richard Allan, William Robert (dec. 1993). Stenographer, Penick & Ford, Cedar Rapids, Iowa, 1941-43, FBI, Washington, 1943-44; tchr. Fayette (Iowa) High Sch., 1959-60, Jordan Jr. High Sch., Mpls., 1960-64, Montrose (Colo.) High Sch., 1964-68; family living, religion editor The News-Record, Gillette, Wyo., 1977-79, columnist Distaff Side, 1979-84. Mem. Western Writers Am., WestWind Writers/NMA (pres. 1994), Nat. Writers Club. Contbr. articles to various mags. Home: 1804 Locust Rd Montrose CO 81401-5825

GILLETTE, FRANKIE JACOBS, retired savings and loan executive, social worker, government administrator; b. Norfolk, Va., Apr. 1, 1925; d. Frank Walter and Natalie (Taylor) Jacobs; m. Maxwell Claude Gillette, June 19, 1976. BS, Hampton U., 1946; MSW, Howard U., 1948. Lic. clin. social worker; cert. jr. coll. tchr., life. Youth dir. YWCA, Passaic, N.J., 1948-50; dir. program Ada S. McKinley Community Ctr., Chgo., 1950-53; program dir. Sophie Wright Settlement, Detroit, 1953-64; dir. Concerted Services Project, Pittsburg, Calif., 1964-66, Job Corps Staff Devel., U. Calif., Berkeley, 1966-69; spl. program coordinator U.S. Community Services Adminstrn., San Francisco, 1969-83; pres. G & G Enterprises, San Francisco, 1985—; chmn. bd. dirs. Time Savs. and Loan Assn., San Francisco, 1986-87. Commr. San Francisco Human Rights Commn., 1988-93; bd. dirs. Urban Econ. Devel. Corp., 1980-93, San Francisco Conv. and Visitors Bur.; trustee Fine Arts Mus. of San Francisco, 1993—; chmn. San Francisco-Abidjan Sister City Com., 1990—. Mem. Nat. Assn. Negro Bus. and Profl. Women's Clubs (pres. 1983-87). Office: 85 Cleary Ct Apt 4 San Francisco CA 94109-6518

GILLETTE, RICHARD GARETH, physiology educator, researcher; b. Seattle, Feb. 17, 1945; s. Elton George and Hazel I. (Hand) G.; m. Sally A. Reams, Feb. 17, 1978 (div. Nov. 1988); 1 child, Jesse Robert. BS, U. Oreg., 1968; MS, Oreg. Health Sci. U., 1976, PhD, 1993. Rsch. asst. dept. otolaryngology Oreg. Health Sci. U., Portland, 1969-72, grad. rsch. asst., 1973-80; instr. physiology Western State Chiropractic Coll., Portland, 1981-85, asst. prof. physiology, 1985-93, assoc. prof. physiology, 1993—; lectr. neurosci. sch. optometry Pacific U., Forest Grove, Oreg., 1985-86; grad. rsch. asst. R.S. Dow Neurol. Sci. Inst., Portland, 1988-93, vis. scientist, 1993. Contbr. articles to profl. jours. NIH Predoctoral Tng. fellow Oreg. Health Sci. U., 1973-76; Tarter fellow Med. Rsch. Found. Oreg., 1989; NIH grantee, 1990-93, 94—. Mem. AAAS, Soc. for Neurosci., Am. Pain Soc., Internat. Assn. for Study of Pain, N.Y. Acad. Scis. Office: WSCC 2900 NE 132 Ave Portland OR 97230

GILLETTE-BAUMANN, MURIEL DELPHINE, nurse; b. Pasadena, Calif., Nov. 10, 1945; d. Edwin and Jean Helen (Fremont) Gillette; m. Larry Houston Potter, Dec. 31, 1971 (dec. 1979); children: Melissa Darlene Genevieve Potter Stephens, Bryan Scott; m. Robert George Baumann Jr., Aug. 18, 1980; 1 child, Robert George III. Student, Western Coll. for Women, Oxford, Ohio, 1963-65; BSN, UCLA, 1968; M of Nursing, Oreg. Health Scis. U., 1991. Sch. nurse, health tchr. Hawthorne (Calif.) Intermediate Sch., 1969-70; nurse St. John's Hosp., Santa Monica, Calif., 1969-71; camp nurse L.A. Girl Scout Coun., 1969-71; nurse UCLA Med. Ctr., 1967-70; ICU/CCU/pediatrics nurse Mercy Med. Ctr., Roseburg, Oreg., 1971-79; nurse Umpqua Valley Community Hosp., Myrtle Creek, Oreg., 1981-91; health edn. dir. City of Myrtle Creek, 1986-91; nurse practitioner Umpgua Nat. Forest, Roseburg and Glide, Oreg., 1991-93; camp nurse, health coord. Oreg. Trail Boy Scout Coun., Roseburg, 1991—; Western Rivers Girl Scout Coun., Roseburg, 1984-90. Musician quartet, orch., soloist; artist in oils; poet. Bd. dirs. River 'N Dell Day Care Ctr., Myrtle Creek, 1983-85; trustee Augusta Bixler Farms, Inc., Stockton, Calif., 1976—; mem. Douglas County Cancer Screening Com. Capt. USAF, 1970-89. Umpqua Valley Hosp. Aux. scholar, 1989; L.A. Watercolor Soc. traveling art collection award, 1963. Mem. UCLA Alumni Assn., Umpqua Valley Hosp. Aux., Oreg. Health Sci. U. Alumni Assn., OES, Delta Zeta. Republican. Presbyterian. Home: PO Box 668 Myrtle Creek OR 97457-0104

GILLIAM, GRANT DAVID, political consultant; b. Alton, Ill., Jan. 7, 1957; s. Richard Clark and Joan Margaret (Long) G. BA in History, Tulane U., 1979. Sales and mgmt. exec. Kent-Miller, Inc., St. Louis, 1979-81; commd. 2d lt. USAF, 1981, advanced through grades to capt., 1985; pilot 320th bomb wing USAF, Sacramento, Calif., 1982-86; instr. pilot, flight examiner 552d airborne warning control wing USAF, Okla. City, 1986-90; polit. cons. Calif. State Assembly, Sacramento, 1990—; chief exec. officer Gillham Profl. Group, 1991—. Vol. Nat. Coun. Alcoholism, Sacramento, 1984—; mem. alumni admissions com. Tulane U., Santa Clara and Sacramento, Calif., 1988—. Decorated Commendation medal, Air medal and Combat Readiness medal. Republican.

GILLIAM, EARL BEN, federal judge; b. Clovis, N.Mex., Aug. 17, 1931; s. James Earl and Lula Mae G.; m. Rebecca L. Prater; children: Earl Kenneth, Derrick James. B.A., Calif. State U., San Diego, 1953; J.D., Hastings Coll. Law, 1957. Bar: Calif. 1957. Dep. dist. atty. San Diego, 1957-62; judge San Diego Mcpl. Ct., 1963-74, Superior Ct. Calif., San Diego County, 1975-80, U.S. Dist. Ct. (so. dist.) Calif., San Diego, 1980—; head Trial Practice Dept. Western State U. Law Sch., San Diego, 1969—. Office: US Dist Ct 940 Front St San Diego CA 92101-8994

GILLIAM, JACKSON EARLE, bishop; b. Heppner, Oreg., June 20, 1920; s. Edwin Earle and Mary (Perry) G.; m. Margaret Kathleen Hindley, Aug. 11, 1943; children—Anne Meredith, Margaret Carol, John Howard; m. MarKatheryn Allender Brooks, Oct. 17, 1988. A.B., Whitman Coll., 1942; B.D., Va. Theol. Sem., 1948, S.T.M., 1949, D.D., 1969. Ordained to ministry Episcopal Ch., 1948; rector in Hermiston, Ore., 1949-53; canon St. Mark's Cathedral, Mpls., 1953-55; rector Ch. Incarnation, Great Falls, Mont., 1955-68; bishop Episcopal Diocese Mont., 1968-86; vicar St. Jude's Episcopal Ch., Hawaiian Oceanview Estates, 1987—; chmn. com. on pastoral devel., chmn. council on ministry, mem. program, budget and fin. com. Episc. Ch., 1978, pres. Province VI. Served to 1st lt. AUS, World War II. Decorated companion Order of Cross of Nails, companion Coventry Cathedral, Eng., 1974. Home: PO Box 6502 Ocean View HI 96737-6502

GILLIGAN-IVANJACK, CLAUDIA MARLENE, motion picture set artist; b. Indpls., Mar. 21, 1947; d. James Emmitt Gilligan and Pearl Helen (Bodfield) Webster; m. Melvin Chilcoat, Feb. 18, 1966 (div. Sept. 1972); children: Tami Mel-lene, Andy Martin; m. Thomas Robert Ivanjack, Aug. 18, 1988. Forman set artist Internat. Alliance Theatrical Stage Employees and Moving Picture Machine Operators Local 729, Hollywood, Calif., 1976—. Author: (poetry) Penelope Noise, 1981, Imagination, 1986, (movie script) Monopoly, 1989, (short stories) The Fish Pond, 1990 (Pen Women award 1990). Rent mediation bd. City Hawthorne, Calif., 1978-79. Mem. MENSA, Am. Nat. Hygiene Soc., N.Am. Fishing Club., Japan Karate Assn. (brown belt 1983). Republican. Home and Office: T&C Set Art 1540 Rosita Dr Simi Valley CA 93065-3030

GILLIN, JOHN CHRISTIAN, psychiatrist; b. Columbus, Ohio, Apr. 28, 1938; s. John Philip and Helen (Norgord) G.; m. Frances Davis, May 29, 1966. BA, Harvard Coll., 1961; MD, Case Western U., 1966. Intern Cleve. Met. Hosp., 1966-67; resident Stanford U., Palo Alto, Calif., 1987-89; clin. assoc. Nat. Inst. Mental Health, Bethesda, Md., 1969-71, researcher, 1971-82; prof. psychiatry U. Calif., San Diego, 1982—; staff psychiatrist San Diego VA Med. Ctr., 1982—; adj. prof. psychiatry San Diego State U., 1990—. Author: (with W.B. Mendelson and R.J. Wyatt) Human Sleep and Its Disorders, 1977. Capt. USNR. Office: U Calif San Diego CA 92093-0603

GILLIN, MALVIN JAMES, JR., lawyer; b. Norfolk, Va., Apr. 28, 1946; s. Malvin James Gillin and Jacqueline A. (Howell) Kyslowsky; m. Arleen Elizabeth Gillin: children: Christine Lynn, Malvin James III, Craig Dean. BA, U. Hawaii, 1969; JD, U. Denver, 1974. Bar: Hawaii 1975, U.S. Dist. Ct. Hawaii 1975, U.S. Ct. Appeals (9th cir.) 1983, U.S. Supreme Ct. 1983, Colo. 1984. Dep. atty. gen. State of Hawaii, Honolulu, 1975-76; pvt. practice law Honolulu, 1976—. Mem. Hawaii Bar Assn., Assn. Trial Lawyers Am. Roman Catholic. Office: 841 Bishop St Ste 450 Honolulu HI 96813-3904

GILLIS, CHRISTINE DIEST-LORGION, financial planner, stockbroker; b. San Francisco, Apr. 26, 1928; d. Evert Jan and Christine Helen (Radcliffe) Diest-Lorgion; children: Barbara Gillis Pieper, Suzanne Gillis Seymour (twins). BS, U. Calif., Berkeley, 1948; MS, U. So. Calif., 1968. Cert. fin. planner. Account exec. Winslow, Cohu & Stetson, N.Y.C., 1962-63, Paine Webber, N.Y.C., 1964-65; sr. investment exec. Shearson Hammill, Beverly Hills, Calif., 1966-72; fin. planner, asst. v.p. EF Hutton, L.A., 1972-87; 2nd v.p. Shearson Lehman Hutton, Glendale, Calif., 1988; v.p. investments Dean Witter Reynolds, Glendale, 1988-90; fin. planner, asst. v.p. W. J. Gallagher & Co., Inc., Pasadena, Calif., 1991—. Mem. AAUW (life, trustee ednl. found.), Inst. Cert. Fin. Planners, Town Hall of Calif. (life, corp. sec. 1974-75, dir., gov. 1976-80), Women Stockbrokers Assn. (founding pres. N.Y.C. 1963), Women of Wall Street West (pres. 1979-84), Navy League (life; dir.), Bus. and Profl. Women, U. Calif.-Berkeley Alumni Assn. (life), U. So. Calif. Alumni Assn. (life), Town and Gown (life), Rotary Internat. (charter, Paul Harris fellow), DESCANSO, Sunrise Club, La Canada Flintridge Club, Phi Chi Theta (life), Pasadena Bond Club. Episcopalian. Home: La Canada 959 Regent Park Dr La Canada Flintridge CA 91011 Office: W J Gallagher & Co Inc 747 E Green St Pasadena CA 91101-2119

GILLIS, JOHN SIMON, psychologist, educator; b. Washington, Mar. 21, 1937; s. Simon John and Rita Veronica (Moran) G.; m. Mary Ann Wesolowski, Aug. 29, 1959; children: Holly Ann, Mark, Scott. B.A., Stanford U., 1959; M.S. (fellow), Cornell U., 1961; Ph.D. (NIMH fellow), U. Colo., 1965. Lectr. dept. psychology Australian Nat. U., Canberra, 1968-70; sr. psychologist Mendocino (Calif.) State Hosp., 1971-72; asso. prof. dept. psychology Tex. Tech U., Lubbock, 1972-76; prof. psychology Oreg. State U., Corvallis, 1976—, chmn. dept. psychology, 1976-84; cons. VA, Ciba-Geigy Pharms., USIA, UN High Commn. for Refugees; commentator Oreg. Ednl. and Pub. Broadcasting System, 1978-79; Fulbright lectr., India, 1982-83, Greece, 1992; vis. prof. U. Karachi, 1984, 86, U. Punjab, Pakistan, 1985, Am. U., Cairo, 1984-86. Contbr. articles to profl. jours. Served with USAF, 1968-72. Ciba-Geigy Pharms. grantee, 1971-82. Mem. Am. Psychol. Assn., Western Psychol. Assn., Oreg. Psychol. Assn. Roman Catholic. Home: 7520 NW Mountain View Dr Corvallis OR 97330-9106 Office: Oreg State U Dept Psychology Corvallis OR 97331

GILLIS, NELSON SCOTT, financial executive; b. Pitts., May 6, 1953; s. Nelson Williams and Elinor (Miller) G.; m. Vickie Sue Hall, Nov. 22, 1980; children: Michael David, Matthew Daniel, Nathan Alexander. BS in Acctg., Fla. State U., 1975; postgrad. AEA Exec. Inst., Stanford, 1984. CPA, Ga.; cert. fin. planner. Audit sr., Price Waterhouse & Co., Atlanta, 1975-78; sr. acct. Siemens Energy and Automation, Inc., 1978-80; div. contr., Portland, Oreg., 1980-83; v.p. fin. Integrated Circuits Inc., Redmond, Wash., 1983-85; dir. Controls Evaluation and Audit Kaufman & Broad, Inc., Atlanta, 1985-89; v.p., contr. Sun Life Ins. Co. Am., Anchor Nat. Life Ins. Co., First Sun Am. Life Ins. Co., L.A., 1989-94, sr. v.p., controller, 1994—. Master fellow Life Mgmt. Inst.; mem. AICPA (life ins. and disability plans com., 1991-94, task force on disclosure of risks and uncertainties in the ins. industry, 1992-95), Inst. CFPs, Ins. Internal Audit Group, Life Office Mgmt. Assn. (fin. controls and reports com. 1987-90), Ga. Soc. CPAs (ins. plans com. 1988-89), Calif. Soc. CPAs (L.A. members in industry, acctg. principles/auditing standards and ins. industry coms., Ins. Acctg. and Systems Assn., Internat. Assn. for Fin. Planning, Am. Assn. Individual Investors, Fla. State Alumni Assn., Nat. Assn. Security Dealers (registered prin.), Beta Gamma Sigma, Lambda Chi Alpha. Republican. Office: Sun Life Ins Co Am/Century City 1 Sun Am Ctr MS 36-07 Los Angeles CA 90067-6022

GILLIS, PAUL LEONARD, accountant; b. Montevideo, Minn., Nov. 20, 1953; s. Joseph Hans and Verna Ruth (Sjolie) G.; m. Deborah Ann Roller, Sept. 9, 1978. BA, Western State Coll., 1975; MS, Colo. State U., 1976. CPA, Colo. Tax cons. Price Waterhouse, Denver, 1976-78; tax mgr. Price Waterhouse, Singapore, 1978-82; internat. tax mgr. Price Waterhouse, San Francisco, 1982-84; sr. mgr. Price Waterhouse, Denver, 1984-88, mng. tax ptnr., 1988—, chmn. mining industry practice, 1993—; mem. adv. coun. Colo. State U.; bd. dirs. World Trade Ctr., pres. Forest Hills Metro Dist.; lectr. World Trade Inst., San Francisco, 1982-84. Author: Accounting for Income Tax, 1988. Treas. Forest Hills Metro Dist., 1992—. Recipient 50 for Colo. award, Colo. Assn. Commerce and Industry. Fellow Colo. Soc. CPAs; mem. AICPAs, Am. Club (Singapore) (treas. 1981-82), Pinehurst Country Club, Denver Athletic Club, Harley Owners Group (Denver chpt.), Chatfield Yacht Club. Home: 22616 Forest Hills Dr Golden CO 80401-8022 Office: Price Waterhouse 950 17th St Denver CO 80202-2828

GILLISPIE, STEVEN BRIAN, systems analyst, researcher; b. Seattle, Oct. 19, 1955; s. Edwin B. and Claudia Mae (Cooper) G. BS in Physics with distinction, U. Wash., 1979, BS in Math., 1979, BS in Psychology, 1983, BA in Gen. Studies, 1983. Software specialist Fla. Computer Graphics, Seattle, 1983-84; data analyst coronary artery surgery study U. Wash., Seattle, 1985-

87, sci. programmer dept. radiology, 1987-88, systems analyst dept. radiology, 1988—. Dir. devel. med. imaging software Viewbox, 1992; contbr. articles to profl. jours. Mem. Woodland Park Zool. Soc., Seattle, 1985—; contbg. mem. Nordic Heritage Mus., Seattle, 1991—; patron The High Desert Mus., Bend, Oreg., 1991—; sponsor N.W. Women's Law Ctr., Seattle, 1992—. Mem. Soc. Nuclear Medicine, Soc. for Indsl. and Applied Math., U. Wash. Alumni Assn. (life). Office: U Wash Dept Radiology Box 356004 Seattle WA 98195-6004

GILLMAN, GRETA JOANNE, physician; b. Montreal, Quebec, Can., Aug. 18, 1945; d. Hyman and Fanny (Izenberg) G.; m. Vic Bhoopat, Oct. 17, 1970; children: Lisa, Mitchell. MD, U. Calif., Irvine, 1969. Physician specialist L.A. County Hosp., 1973—; asst. clin. prof. UCLA, 1976—. Home: 13492 Grinnell Cir Westminster CA 92683-1734 Office: LA County Hosp 10005 Flower St Bellflower CA 90706-5412

GILLMAR, JACK NOTLEY SCUDDER, real estate company executive; b. Honolulu, Oct. 18, 1943; s. Stanley Eric and Ruth Dorothy (Scudder) G.; m. Janet Thebaud, June 12, 1967; children: Emily, Bennett. BA, U. Pa., 1965; MA, Harvard U., 1967, Pacifica Grad. Inst., 1994. Vol. Peace Corps/Micronesia, East Caroline Islands, 1967-70; trustee Scudder Gillmar Estate, Honolulu, 1973—; trustee, sec. Parker Sch. Trust, Kamuela, Hawaii, 1991—. Author: Impact of an In-country Peace Corps Training Program, 1970, Specimens of Hwaiian Kapa, 1979, Beauty as Experience and Transcendence, 1994. Trustee, pres. Friendship Graden Found., Honolulu, 1971—; owner Nanue (Hawaii) Forest Preserve, 1986—. Fulbright grantee, 1990. Mem. Pacific Club. Office: Scudder Gillmar Estate PO Box 2902 Honolulu HI 96802-2902

GILLMAR, STANLEY FRANK, lawyer; b. Honolulu, Aug. 17, 1935; s. Stanley Eric and Ruth (Scudder) G.; m. Constance Joan Sedgwick; children: Sara Tamsin, Amy Katherine. AB cum laude with high honors, Brown U., 1957; LLB, Harvard U., 1963. Bar: Calif. 1963. Ptnr. Graham & James, San Francisco, 1970-92; of counsel Mackenzie & Albritton, 1993—. Co-author: How To Be An Importer and Pay For Your World Travels, 1979; co-pub.: Travelers Guide to Importing, 1980. Sec. Calif. Council Internat. Trade, 1973-92, hon. counsel, 1980-92, exec. com., 1985-92; mem. Mayor San Francisco Adv. Council Econ. Devel., 1976-82; mem. Title IX Loan Bd., 1982—, sec. 1986-92; dir. The San Francisco Ministry to Nursing Homes, 1992-94, treas., 1992-94; dir. Inverness Assn., 1995—. Served with USNR, 1957-60. Mem. ABA, Calif. State Bar, Bar Assn. San Francisco, Bankers Club (San Francisco); Villa Taverna Club, Inverness Yacht Club. Office: One Post St Ste 500 San Francisco CA 94104

GILLON, JEAN WARREN, surgeon; b. Pasadena, Calif., Aug. 11, 1951; d. John Warren and Jean (Ware) G. BA, U. Calif., Berkeley, 1972; MD, Brown U., 1984. Intern Stanford U. Med. Ctr., 1984-85, resident, 1985-87; resident R.I. Hosp., 1987-91; clin. instr. U. Calif.-San Francisco Gen. Hosp., 1992-93; asst. prof. U. Calif., San Francisco, 1993-94, fellow in vascular surgery, 1994-95.

GILLUM, GARY PAUL, librarian; b. Indpls., June 12, 1944; s. Paul Brane and Ruth Janeve (Hansing) G.; m. Lynn Ann Ruhland, July 12, 1969 (dec. July 1977); children: Grant, Adina; m. Elizabeth Bayliss, Oct. 11, 1977 (dec. Apr. 1986); children: Bonnie, David, Annalyn, Timothy; m. Signe Marie Slangerup, Dec. 19, 1987; children: Mary Jane, Amy, Emily, Kathryn, Lucy, Karl, Judith, Jed, Elizabeth, Jacob, Joseph. AA, St. John's Coll., Winfield, Kans., 1966; BA, Concordia Sr. Coll., Ft. Wayne, Ind., 1968; MLS, Brigham Young U., 1971. Music libr. Indpls.-Marion County Libr., 1968-69; gen. reference libr. Brigham Young U., Provo, 1971-75, humanities libr., 1975-80, ancient studies bibliographer, 1980-85, religion libr., 1985—, chmn. history-religion reference dept. Harold B. Lee Libr., 1990—. Editor: Of All Things! A Nibley Quote Book, 1981. Bd. dirs., treas. Utah Valley Symphony Orch., Provo, 1994—. Mem. Mormon History Assn., Phi Kappa Phi. Republican. Mem. LDS Ch. Office: Brigham Young U 4222 Harold B Lee Libr Provo UT 84602

GILMAN, CHRISTOPHER JOHN, radiologist; b. Watertown, N.Y., May 21, 1949; s. Ralph C. and Mary J. (LeVasseur) G.; m. Lynn Margules, Mar. 16, 1973; 1 child, Joshua M. AB, U. Rochester, 1971; MD, U. Ill., Chgo., 1975. Diplomate Am. Bd. Family Practice, Am. Bd. Radiology. Asst. prof. radiology U. N.Mex., Albuquerque, 1981-82, Baylor Coll. Medicine, Houston, 1982-85, Loma Linda (Calif.) U., 1986—. Mem. Am. Roentgen Ray Soc., Am. Radium Soc., Am. Bd. Family Practice (cert. qualifications in geriatric medicine), Am. Acad. Family Physicians, Am. Soc. Clin. Hypnosis. Republican. Roman Catholic. Home: 1221 San Ildefonso Los Alamos NM 87544-2854

GILMAN, JOHN JOSEPH, research scientist; b. St. Paul, Dec. 22, 1925; s. Alexander Falk and Florence Grace (Colby) G.; m. Pauline Marie Harms, June 17, 1950 (div. Dec. 1968); children: Pamela Ann, Gregory George, Cheryl Elizabeth; m. Gretchen Marie Sutter, June 12, 1976; 1 son, Brian Alexander. BS, Ill. Inst. Tech., 1946, MS, 1948; PhD, Columbia, 1952. Research metallurgist Gen. Electric Co., Schenectady, 1952-60; prof. engring. Brown U., Providence, 1960-63; prof. physics and metallurgy U. Ill., Urbana, 1963-68; dir. Materials Research Center Allied Chem. Corp., Morristown, N.J., 1968-78; dir. Corp. Devel. Center, 1978-80; mgr. corp. research Standard Oil Co. (Ind.), Naperville, Ill., 1980-85; assoc. dir. Lawrence Berkeley Lab., Calif., 1985-87, sr. scientist, 1987-93; adj. prof. UCLA, 1993—. Author: Micromechanics of Flow in Solids, 1969, Inventivity-The Art and Science of Research Management, 1992; editor: The Art and Science of Growing Crystals, 1963, Fracture of Solids, (with D.C. Drucker), 1963, Atomic and Electronic Structures of Metals, 1967, Metallic Glasses, 1973, Energetic Materials, 1993; editorial bd.: Jour. Applied Physics, 1969-72; contbg. editor Materials Tech., 1994—; contbr. papers, articles to tech. jours. Served as ensign USNR, 1943-46. Recipient Mathewson gold medal Am. Inst. Metal Engrs., 1959, Disting. Service award Alumni Assn. Ill. Inst. Tech., 1962, Application to Practice award, 1985. Fellow Am. Phys. Soc., Am. Soc. for Metals (Campbell lectr. 1966); mem. Nat. Acad. Engring., Phi Kappa Phi, Tau Beta Pi. Home: 2852 Forrester Dr Los Angeles CA 90064-4662 Office: UCLA 6532 Boelter Hall Los Angeles CA 90095

GILMAN, NELSON JAY, library director; b. Los Angeles, Mar. 30, 1938; s. Louis L. and Alice (Cohen) G.; m. Virginia L. Ford, May 27, 1961 (div. Sept. 1970); children: Justine C., Seth F.; m. Lelde B. Patvalds, Nov. 23, 1970. BS, U. So. Calif., 1959, MS, 1960; MLS, U. Calif., Berkeley, 1964. Tchr. math. dept. Pasadena (Calif.) High Sch., 1960-61, Tamalpais High Sch., Mill Valley, Calif., 1962-63; intern library adminstrn. UCLA, 1964-65, asst. to librarian, 1965-66, asst. to biomedical librarian, 1966-67, asst. biomedical librarian, 1967-69; assoc. dir. Pacific Southwest Regional Med. Library Service, UCLA, 1969-71; dir. Los Angeles County/U. So. Calif. Med. Ctr. Libraries, 1974-79; asst. prof. dept. med. edn. U. So. Calif. Sch. Med., 1971—, dir. Norris Med. Library, 1971—, dir. Health Scis. Libr. System, 1984—, assoc. dir. devel. and demonstration ctr., 1981—; assoc. dean librs., dir. planning for teaching libr. U. So. Calif., 1989-90; interim dir. Ctrl. Libr. System, 1990-91; cons. HEW, San Francisco, 1973-76, NIH, Washington, 1970-71. Assoc. editor U. So. Calif. Sch. Medicine Info. Systems Research Program, 1984-87; contbr. articles to profl. jours. Served with USAR, 1961-67. Mem. Am. Library Assn., Am. Soc. Info. Sci., Assn. Acad. Health Scis. Library Dirs. (bd. dirs. 1980-83), Med. Library Assn. (bd. dirs. 1977-79), Spl. Library Assn. Democrat. Jewish. Home: 615 22nd St Santa Monica CA 90402-3121 Office: U So Calif Norris Med Library 2003 Zonal Ave Los Angeles CA 90033-1034

GILMORE, A. DOUGLAS, retail sales executive; b. Kittery, Maine, July 21, 1947; s. Allen Johnston and Margaret Nell (McIntosh) G.; m. Joy Carolyn Gustafson, Aug. 23, 1969; children: Chelsea Jay, Allison Anne. BA, Willamette U., 1969; M Internat. Mgmt., Am. Grad. Internat. Mgmt., 1971. Acct. exec. Levi Strauss & Co., various locations, 1971-75; dist. sales mgr. Levi Strauss & Co., L.A., 1975-76; regional sales mgr. Levi Strauss & Co., San Francisco, 1977-80; dir. sales and mtkg. Levi Strauss & Co., Edmonton, Alta., Can., 1980-82; asst. gen. mgr., mktg. dir. Levi Strauss & Co., Sydney, Australia, 1982-86; v.p. mktg. Winmore Products, Bellevue, Wash., 1986-87; v.p. ops. Trans Am. Glass, Seattle, 1987-93; pres. Mail Movers, Inc., Seattle, 1993—; dir. internat. sales Eddie Bauer, Redmond, Wash., 1993—. Mem. Sydney/San Francisco Sister City Com., Sydney, 1982-85; mem. Boys and Girls Club of Mercer Island. Mem. Internat. Mktg. Soc., Am. Mktg. Assn., Sales and Mktg. Execs., Am. Nat. Club (Sydney). Home: 525 Overlake Dr E Bellevue WA 98004-5326 Office: Eddie Bauer 15010 NE 36th St Redmond WA 98052-5317

GILMORE, TIMOTHY JONATHAN, physician recruiter; b. Orange, Calif., June 24, 1949; s. James and Margaret (Swanson) G.; m. Blanche Jean Panter, Sept. 3, 1984; children: Erin, Sean and Brian (twins). BA, St. Mary's Coll., Moraga, Calif., 1971. Adminstrv. asst. Gov. Ronald Reagan, Sacramento, Calif., 1971-73; salesman Penn Mutual, Anaheim, Calif., 1973-76; asst. devel. dir. St. Mary's Coll., Moraga, 1976-81; devel. dir. St. Alphonsus Hosp., Boise, Idaho, 1981-83; adminstr. Blaine County Hosp., Hailey, Idaho, 1983-86; exec. dir. Poudre Hosp. Found., Ft. Collins, Colo., 1986-87; nat. recruiting dir. Power Securities Corp., Denver, 1987-89; cons. Horn, Fagan & Lund Exec. Search Cons., Ft. Collins, 1989; v.p. Jackson & Coker Locum Tenens, Inc., Denver, 1990-93; exec. v.p. Nationwide Tech. Placement, Ft. Collins, Colo., 1993—. Mem. Kiwanis (pres. Moraga club 1980-81, sec. Boise club 1982-83). Republican. Mem. LDS Ch. Home: 2914 Bassick St Fort Collins CO 80526-3738 Office: 300 S College Ave Fort Collins CO 80524-2802

GILMOUR, ERNEST HENRY, geology educator; b. Adin, Calif., Aug. 17, 1936; s. Harold J. and Velma Nettie (Helgerson) G.; m. Marie Jeanne Melton, June 27, 1957 (div. Sept. 1980); children: Ernest Henry Jr., William Bryce, Nadine Marie; m. Peggy June Keller, Dec. 22, 1982; 1 child, Laura Lee. BS, U. So. Calif., 1960; MS, U. Mont., 1964, PhD, 1967. Registered profl. geologist, Idaho. Engring. geologist dept. water resources State of Calif., L.A., 1956-61; instr. U. Mont., Missoula, 1964; field geologist U.S. Geol. Survey, Gt. Falls, Mont., 1964-65; mineral fuels geologist Mont. Bur. Mines and Geology, Butte, 1965-67; asst. prof. Mont. Coll. Mineral Sci. and Tech., Butte, 1965-67; prof. geology Ea. Wash. U., Cheney, 1967—, chmn. dept., 1976-87, cons. to archaeol. svcs. group, 1983-91, vice provost for grad. studies and rsch., 1987-89, sr. v.p., provost, 1989-91; teaching asst. U. So. Calif., 1960-61; cons. micropaleontologist Goudkoff and Hughes, L.A., 1967; cons. Vanguard Exploration Co., Spokane, Wash., 1969-71; dir. strategic minerals analysis project U.S. Bur. Mines, 1975-81, dir. mineral industry locations project, 1975-80; dir. domestic mining fellowship program HEW, 1975-80; cons., sr. geologist, Salisbury and Dietz, Inc., Spokane, 1978-84; v.p. IGAL, Inc., Cheney, 1984-85; reviewer grant proposals div. earth scis. NSF; also others. Mem. editorial adv. bd. N.W. Geology, 1975-85; N.W. regional editor Paleontol. Rsch. Inst. Newsletter, 1980-85; contbr. numerous articles to profl. jours. Named Engr. of Yr., Spokane sect. AIME, 1974; recipient Trustee's medal Ea. Wash. U., 1978; acad. scholar U. So. Calif., 1954; summer fellow NSF, 1961, fellow NDEA, 1961-64; grantee Mont. Bur. Mines and Geology, 1968, NSF, 1974, U.S. Bur. Mines, 1974-80, NSF, 1975, Ea. Wash. State Coll., 1975, HEW, 1975-80, Smithsonian Instn., 1986-87, U. S. Dept. Edn., 1987-93, Ea. Wash. U., 1986-87; numerous others. Fellow Geol. Soc. Am.; mem. AAAS, Paleontol. Soc. (pres. Pacific sect. 1979-80, 88-89, sec. Rocky Mountain 1985-91), Paleontol. Rsch. Instn. (life), Am. Assn. Petroleum Geologists, Internat. Bryozoology Assn., Nat. Assn. Geology Tchrs., N.W. Sci. Assn. (pres. 1975-76), Internat. Paleontol. Union, N.W. Mining Assn. (hon. life, trustee 1971-74, 81-84), Western Soc. Naturalists, Sigma Xi (life, past pres.), Sigma Gamma Epsilon, Phi Sigma, Phi Kappa Phi. Office: Ea Wash U Dept Geology Cheney WA 99004

GILSON, ARNOLD LESLIE, engineering executive; b. Perrysburg, Ohio, Apr. 10, 1931; s. Leslie Clair and Velma Lillian (Hennen) G.; B.S. in Mech. Engring., U. Toledo, 1962; m. Phyllis Mary Seiling, Sept. 15, 1951 (dec. May 1982); children—David, Jeffrey, Luann, Suzanne. Engr., Miller, Tillman & Zamis engrs., Toledo, 1962-67, regional mgr., Phoenix br., 1967-69; owner, mgr. A B S Tech. Services, Phoenix, 1969—. Served with U.S. Army, 1952; Korea. Decorated Bronze Star. Mem. Nat. Mil. Intelligence Assn. Republican. Roman Catholic. Commd. extraordinary minister, 1975. Patentee in several fields. Home: 8226 E Meadowbrook Ave Scottsdale AZ 85251-1739 Office: A B S Tech Svcs PO Box 2440 Scottsdale AZ 85252-2440

GILSON, VICKI CHERYL, county official; b. Oakland, Calif., Aug. 3, 1946; d. Robert Arthur and Ruth Estelle (Tiller) Wall; m. Larry Edward Gilson, June 21, 1969; children: Danika, Kirsten, Jeremiah, Zachary. AA, Hartnell Jr. Coll., Salinas, Calif., 1966; BS, Calif. State U., Fresno, 1968, postgrad., 1992—. Acct., auditor County of Tulare, Visalia, Calif., 1970-72; internal auditor County of Fresno, 1972-76; fin. dir. City of Dinuba, Calif., 1976-78; acct. County of Tulare, Visalia, 1983-88; fiscal mgr. County of Kings, Hanford, Calif., 1988—. Candidate Coll. for Sequoias Bd. of Trustees, Visalia, 1994. Mem. Calif. Welfare Dirs. Assn., Kings County Networking. Republican. LDS. Office: Kings County Human Svcs 1200 South Dr Hanford CA 93274

GIMBOLO, ALEKSEI FRANK CHARLES, artist, philosopher, author; b. Portland, Oreg., Mar. 29, 1956; s. Frank Charles and Evelyn (Van Pelt) G.; m. Lilli M. Colipapa, Dec. 16, 1985; children: Niko Alexander, Romaneé Alexander. Student, U. Hawaii, 1976-78, Coll. Charleston, 1979-80. Winemaker Chateau LaCaia, Hazel Green, Ala., 1980-87; artist, philosopher Portland, 1987—. Author: Illuminati Wisdom of the Enlightened Ones, 1993-95; painting pub.: Encyclopedia of Living Artist, 7th edit., 1992, 8th edit., 1993. Vice-chmn. Pre-Law Soc., Charleston, S.C., 1979; exec. com. chmn. Young Reps. of Am., Charleston, 1979; fencing coach Portland (Oreg.) State U., 1993. Office: PO Box 6754 Portland OR 97228-6754

GINDER, JOSEPH RONALD, computer company executive, software architect; b. Anderson, Ind., Apr. 9, 1958; s. Ronald E. and Rachael A. (Pike) G.; m. Susan Rose Bassett, June 13, 1976; children: Laura Susan, Benjamin Joseph, Samuel Joseph. AB in Computer Sci., Ind. U., 1980; postgrad., Carnegie-Mellon U., 1980-82. Sr. software engr. Perq Sys., Pitts., 1982-85; sr. software engr., founder Expert Technologies, Inc., Pitts., 1985-86; sr. computer scientist, mgr. Inference Corp., L.A., 1986-88, dir. tech. support, 1989-91; v.p. devel. Inference Corp., El Segundo, Calif., 1991-95; prin. computer scientist Brightware, Inc., El Segundo, 1995—. Presiding clk. Long Beach (Calif.) Friends Ch., 1988—; Friends Ctr. bd. Azusa Pacific U., 1993—. Kodak scholar, Rochester, N.Y., 1977-80; rsch. assistantship grantee Carnegie-Mellon U., Pitts., 1980-82. Mem. Assn. Computing Machinery, Am. Sci. Affiliation, Am. Assn. Artificial Intelligence. Mem. Soc. of Friends. Home: 2279 Albury Ave Long Beach CA 90815-2105 Office: Brightware Inc 550 N Continental Blvd El Segundo CA 90245

GINN, SAM L., telephone company executive; b. Saint Clair, Ala., Apr. 3, 1937; s. James Harold and Myra Ruby (Smith) G.; m. Meriann Lanford Vance, Feb. 2, 1963; children: Matthew, Michael, Samantha. B.S., Auburn U., 1959; postgrad., Stanford U. Grad. Sch. Bus., 1968. Various positions AT&T, 1960-78; with Pacific Tel. & Tel. Co., 1978—; exec. v.p. network Pacific Tel. & Tel. Co., San Francisco, 1979-81, exec. v.p. services, 1981-82, exec. v.p. network services, 1982, exec. v.p., strategic planning and adminstrn., 1983, vice chmn. bd., strategic planning and adminstrn., 1983-84; vice chmn. bd., group v.p. PacTel Cos. Pacific Telesis Group, San Francisco, 1984-86; pres. Air Touch Commn., San Francisco, 1984-87; vice chmn. bd., pres., chief exec. officer PacTel Corp. Pacific Telesis Group, San Francisco, 1986; pres., chief operating officer Pacific Telesis Group, San Francisco, 1987-88, former chmn., pres., chief exec. officer; chmn. Air Touch Commn., San Francisco, 1993—; now chmn. bd., CEO Air Touch Commn., Walnut Creek, Calif.; mem. adv. bd. Sloan program Stanford U. Grad. Sch. Bus., 1978-85, mem. internat. adv. council Inst. Internat. Studies; bd. dir. 1st Interstate Bank, Chevron Corp., Safeway, Inc. Trustee Mills Coll., 1982—. Served to capt. U.S. Army, 1959-60. Sloan fellow, 1968. Republican. Clubs: Blackhawk Country (Danville, Calif.); World Trade, Pacific-Union; Rams Hill Country (Borrego Springs, Calif.), Bankers. Office: Air Touch Commn. 2999 Oak Rd Walnut Creek CA 94596*

GINSBURG, JERRY HUGH, physician, health facility administrator; b. L.A., Mar. 22, 1943; s. Jack and Pauline (Wald) G.; m. Barbara Rever; children: Dustin, Ian. BA in English Lit., U. Calif., Berkeley, 1966; MD, U. So. Calif., 1970. Dir. Salinas-Monterey (Calif.) Heart Inst., 1985—. Pres. Am. Heart Assn., Salinas, 1988, 92. Fellow Am. Coll. Physicians, Am. Coll. Cardiology, Am. Coll. Rheumatology, Am. Coll. Chest Physicians, Coun. Am. Heart Assn.; mem. Soc. Critical Care Medicine. Office: Salinas-Monterey Heart Inst 230 San Jose St Ste 30 Salinas CA 93901-3932

GIOIA, TED, musician, writer; b. Oct. 21, 1957; m. Tara Munjee, Aug. 17, 1991. AB, Stanford (Calif.) U., 1979, MBA, 1983; BA/MA, Oxford (Eng.) U., 1981. Founder Stanford U. Jazz Studies Program, 1987—. Author: The Imperfect Act, 1988 (Deems Taylor award 1989), West Coast Jazz, 1992; pianist (recording) The End of the Open Road, 1988. Home and Office: 405 El Camino Real # 110 Menlo Park CA 94025-5240

GIORDANO, ANDREW ANTHONY, retired naval officer; b. Passaic, N.J., May 17, 1932; s. Samuel and Sarah (Pollara) G.; m. Felice Rochman, Mar. 3, 1957; children: Andrew Anthony, II, Dean James, Catherine Lisa. B.B.A. cum laude, CCNY, 1953; M.B.A. with distinction, Harvard U., 1962; student, Naval War Coll., 1965; L.H.D. (hon.), Nat. U., San Diego, 1982. Commd. ensign U.S. Navy, 1953, advanced through grades to rear adm., 1978; supply officer U.S.S. Kitty Hawk, Vietnam, 1968-70; ops. officer Aviation Supply Office, Phila., 1970-72; dir. material div. Office of Chief of Naval Ops., Washington, 1977-81; comdr. Naval Supply Systems Command, Chief Supply Corps, 1981-84; sr. v.p. control and ops. Donaldson's of Mpls. unit Allied Stores, 1984-87; exec. v.p., CFO Lamonts Corp., 1987-93; assoc. prof. acctg. George Washington U., 1966-67, Nat. U., 1970-72; prin. The Giordano Group, Ltd., Arlington, Va., 1993—; bd. dirs. Cherry, Webb & Tourraine, Graham-Field, Jos. A. Bank Inc., Nomos, Inc.; hon. pres. Naval Supply Corps Assn. Treas. Navy Marine Coast Guard Residence Found., 1993—. Decorated Legion of Merit, D.S.M. Mem. Army-Navy Country Club (chmn. bd. govs. 1993—). Roman Catholic.

GIORDANO, ANGELA MARIA, military officer; b. Harvey, Ill., Mar. 14, 1965; d. Ronald Raymond Saunders (stepfather) and Claudia Giovanna (Camilli) Pound. BS, U.S. Mil. Acad., 1987. Commd. 2d lt. U.S. Army, 1987, advanced through grades to capt., 1991; terrain analysis platoon leader 63d engr. airborne co. U.S. Army, Ft. Bragg, N.C., 1988-89, co. exec. officer 175th engr. airborne co., 1989, bn. S-1 adjutant 30th engr. airborne bn., 1989-90, co. exec. officer 1st psychol. ops. airborne bn., 1990, team chief Latin Am. 1st psychol. ops. airborne bn., 1991-92; asst. S-3 constrn. officer 555th Combat Engr. Group, Ft. Lewis, Wash., 1992-93, ops. officer, 1993-94; co. comdr. HHC, 14th Combat Engr. Bn. (Corps), Ft. Lewis, Wash., 1994—. Author, editor (Spanish handbook): Psychological Operations, 1991. Decorated Joint Army Achievement medal, Commendation medal, 2 Army Achievement medals. Mem. Am. Mensa, Soc. Am. Mil. Engrs., Assn. Grads. U.S. Mil. Acad., NAFE, Nat. Geographic Soc. Republican. Roman Catholic. Home: 6054 61st Ave SE Lacey WA 98513-4104

GIORDANO, GERARD RAYMOND, special education educator, author; b. West New York, N.J., July 25, 1946; m. Karen Fritz, July 5, 1975; children: Gabriel, Katherine Ann, Peter. BA, U. Hawaii, 1968; MA, Jersey City (N.J.) State Coll., 1973; PhD, Ohio State U., Columbus, 1975. Prof. W.Va. Coll. Grad. Studies, Charleston, 1975-76, N.Mex. State U., Las Cruces, 1976—; columnist Acad. Therapy, 1984-88. Author: (textbooks) Teaching Writing to Students with Learning Disabilities, 1984, Diagnostic and Remedial Mathematics in Special Education, 1993, Literacy Programs for Adults with Developmental Disabilities, 1995; mem. editl. bd. Jour. Learning Disabilities, 1984—, Career Devel. in Exceptional Individuals, 1989—. With U.S. Army, 1968-70, Vietnam. Mem. Las Cruces Rotary. Home: 607 Lenox Ave Las Cruces NM 88005-1309 Office: NMex State U Dept Spl Edn PO Box 30001 Las Cruces NM 88003-8001

GIOVENCO, JOHN V., hotel corporation executive; b. 1936. BS in Commerce, Loyola U., 1958. With Pannell Kerr Forster & Co., 1957-71; v.p. fin. Hilton Hotels Corp., 1972-74, sr. v.p., treas., 1974-80, exec. v.p., 1980—; pres. Hilton Nev. Corp., 1987-93, also bd. dirs.; with ITT Sheraton, 1993. Office: Hilton Hotels Corp Las Vegas Hilton Rd 175 Phillip Rd Woodside CA 94062-2625

GIOVINCO, JOSEPH, nonprofit administrator, writer; b. San Francisco, Oct. 12, 1942; s. Joseph Bivona Giovinco and Jean Andrews; m. Sally Garey, Aug. 31, 1970 (div. Mar. 1982); 1 child, Gina Lorraine. BA, U. Oreg., 1964; MA in History, San Francisco State U., 1968; PhD in History, U. Calif., Berkeley, 1973. Asst. prof. history SUNY, Albany, 1974-76; instr. multicultural studies Sonoma State U., Cotati, Calif., 1976-79; exec. dir. Hist. Mus. Found., Sonoma County, Santa Rosa, Calif., 1977-80; exec. dir. no. Calif. affiliate Am. Diabetes Assn., San Francisco, 1980-81; exec. dir. San Francisco Sch. Vols., 1981-85, Calif. Hist. Soc., San Francisco, 1985-87; dir. Ctr. Advancement & Renewal of Educators, San Francisco, 1988—. Contbr. articles to profl. pubs. Fellow, NEH and Harvard U., 1973; recipient scholarship U. Minn. Ctr. for Immigration History, Mpls., 1975; Rockefeller Found. grantee, 1977; recipient Covello prize Italian Am. Hist. Assn., 1976; named Alumnus of Yr., San Francisco State U., 1987. Roman Catholic. Office: Ctr Advancement & Renewal Educators 25550 25th Ave San Francisco CA 94116

GIPSON, GORDON, publishing company executive; b. Caldwell, Idaho, Oct. 26, 1914; s. James Herrick and Esther (Sterling) G.; m. Tryntje Heeling, Dec. 27, 1961; children—Craig, Amy. Student, Coll. Idaho. With The Caxton Printers, Ltd., Caldwell, 1935—; treas. The Caxton Printers, Ltd., 1945—, v.p., 1964—, pub., 1965—, pres., 1991—. Served with USAAF, 1942-45. Club: Elk. Home: 2211 S 10th Ave Caldwell ID 83605-5221 Office: 312 Main St Caldwell ID 83605-3235

GIPSTEIN, MILTON FIVENSON, psychiatrist, lawyer; b. Schenectady, N.Y., Aug. 31, 1951; s. Milton and Evelyn (Mannes) G.; m. Carol Grace Zippin, July 21, 1974; children: Steven Mark, Richard Seth. BA, Columbia U., 1972; MD, SUNY, Syracuse, 1976; JD, U. N.C., 1981. Bar: Mass., 1982; diplomate Am. Bd. Psychiatry and Neurology. Resident psychiat. U. N.C., Chapel Hill, 1976-79; practice medicine specializing in psychiat. Dept. Corrections N.C., Raleigh, 1979-81; med. dir. Brockton (Mass.) Dist. Ct. Clinic, 1981-86, Bridgewater (Mass.) St. Hosp., 1986-87, Charter Hosp. of Aurora, Colo., 1988-91; med. dir. of forensic svcs. Columbine Psychiatric Hosp., Littleton, Colo., 1991—; cons. med.-legal N.C. Legal Aid Soc., Raleigh, 1978-79, forensic Mass. Treatment Ctr. Sexually Dangerous, Bridgewater, 1981-88, psychiat. La. Gov.'s Task Force Mental Health, Baton Rouge, 1982; med.-legal cons. Medical Evaluators, Inc., Denver, 1991—; legal counsel indigent clients mental health Com. Pub. Counsel Services, Boston, 1982-86; lectr. mental health legal advisors com. Law and Mental Health for Mass. Supreme Ct, Boston, 1986. Cons. Pub. Health Adv. Com. Town of Sharon, Mass., 1983-84, Mental Health Legal Advisors Com. Mass. Supreme Ct., Boston, 1985-86; v.p. community affairs Heights Elem. Sch. PTA, Sharon, 1983-84; adv. com. gifted and talented Cherry Creek H.S., 1992—, Campus Middle Sch., 1993—. Mem. ABA, Mass. Bar Assn., Am. Profl. Practice Assn. Office: Columbine Psychiatric Hosp 4660 S Yosemite St # 9062 Englewood CO 80111-1227

GIRARD, DONALD ALAN, public relations executive; b. Columbus, Ohio, Jan. 26, 1951; s. Bernard Victor and Johanna Mary (Weber) G.; m. Cynthia Anne Hasekian, July 16, 1983; children: Jennifer, Catherine. BSBA, Ohio State U., 1973, MBA in Fin., 1979. Loan control officer Huntington Bancshares, Columbus, 1973-79; sr. airline analyst Lockheed Aircraft Co., Burbank, Calif., 1979-81; mgr. fin. So. Calif. Edison Co., Rosemead, Calif., 1981-85; dir. investor and pub. rels. Pacific Energy, Commerce, Calif., 1985—. Republican. Office: Pacific Energy 6055 E Washington Blvd Commerce CA 90040-2418

GIRARD, NETTABELL, lawyer; b. Pocatello, Idaho, Feb. 24, 1938; d. George and Arranetta (Bell) Girard. Student, Idaho State U., 1957-58; BS, U. Wyo., 1959, JD, 1961. Bar: Wyo. 1961, D.C. 1969, U.S. Supreme Ct. 1969. Practiced in Riverton, 1963-69; atty.-adviser on gen. counsel's staff HUD; assigned Office Interstate Land Sales Registration, Washington, 1969-70; sect. chief interstate land sales Office Gen. Counsel, 1970-73; ptnr. Larson & Larson, Riverton, 1973-85; pvt. practice Riverton, 1985—; guest lectr. at high schs.; condr. seminar on law for layman Riverton br. A.A.U.W., 1965; condr. course on women and law; lectr. equal rights, job discrimination, land use planning. Editor Wyoming Clubwoman, 1966-68; bd. editors Wyo. Law Jour., 1959-61; writer Obiter Dictum column Women Lawyers Jour., Dear Legal Advisor column Solutions for Seniors, 1988-94; featured in Riverton Ranger, 1994; also articles in legal jours. Chmn. fund dr. Wind River chpt. ARC, 1965; chmn. Citizens Com. for Better Hosp. Improvement, 1965; chmn. subcom. on polit. legal rights and responsibilities Gov.'s Commn. on Status Women, 1965-69, mem. adv. com., 1973—; rep.

Nat. Conf. Govs. Commn., Washington, 1966; local chmn. Law Day, 1966, 67, country chmn. law day, 1994, 95; mem. state bd. Wyo. Girl Scouts USA, sec., 1974-89, mem. nat. bd., 1978-81; state vol. adviser Nat. Found., March of Dimes, 1967-69; legal counsel Wyo. Women's Conf., 1977; gov. apptd. State Wyo. Indsl. Siting Coun., 1995-2001. Recipient Spl. Achievement award HUD, 1972, Disting. Leadership award Girl Scouts U.S.A., 1973, Franklin D. Roosevelt award Wyo. chpt. March of Dimes, 1985, Thanks Badge award Girl Scout Coun., 1987, Women Helping Women award in recognition of effective advancement status of women Riverton Club of Soroptimist Internat., 1990, Spl. award plaque in appreciation and recognition of 27 yrs. of svc. to State of Wyo., Wyo. Commn. for Women, 1964-92, Appreciation award Wyo. Sr. Citizens and Solutions for Srs., 1994. Mem. AAUW (br. pres.), Wyo. Bar Assn., Fremont County Bar Assn., D.C. Bar Assn., Women's Bar Assn. D.C., Internat. Fedn. Women Lawyers, Am. Judicature Soc., Assn. Trial Lawyers Am., Nat. Assn. Women Lawyers (del. Wyo., nat. sec. 1969-70, v.p. 1970-71, pres. 1972-73), Wyo. Fedn. Women's Clubs (state editor, pres. elect 1968-69, treas. 1974-76), Prog. Women's Club (pres.-elect 1994—), Riverton Chautauqua Club (pres. 1965-67), Riverton Civic League (pres. 1987-89), Kappa Delta, Delta Kappa Gamma (state chpt., hon.). Home: 224 Sunset Dr PO Box 687 Riverton WY 82501 Office: 513 E Main St Riverton WY 82501-4440

GIRARDEAU, MARVIN DENHAM, physics educator; b. Lakewood, Ohio, Oct. 3, 1930; s. Marvin Denham and Maude Irene (Miller) G.; m. Susan Jessica Brown, June 30, 1956; children—Ellen, Catherine, Laura. B.S., Case Inst. Tech., 1952; M.S., U. Ill., 1954; Ph.D., Syracuse U., 1958. NSF postdoctoral fellow Inst. Advanced Study, Princeton, 1958-59; research assoc. Brandeis U., 1959-60; staff mem. Boeing Sci. Research Labs., 1960-61; research assoc. Enrico Fermi Inst. Nuclear Studies, U. Chgo., 1961-63; assoc. prof. physics, research asso. Inst. Theoretical Sci., U. Oreg., Eugene, 1963-67; prof. physics, research assoc. Inst. Theoretical Sci., U. Oreg., 1967—, dir., 1967-69, chmn. dept. physics, 1974-76. Contbr. articles to profl. jours. Recipient Humboldt Sr. U.S. Scientist award, 1984-85. NSF research grantee, 1965-79; ONR research grantee, 1981-87. Fellow Am. Phys. Soc.; mem. AAUP. Home: 2398 Douglas Dr Eugene OR 97405-1711 Office: U Oreg Dept Physics Eugene OR 97403

GIRARDELLI, RONALD K., food products executive; b. 1949. BA, Oreg. State U., 1971. With Blue Cross, Portland, Oreg., 1971-73; pres. Diamond Fruit Growers, Inc., 1973—. Office: Diamond Fruit Growers Inc 3495 Chevron Dr Hood River OR 97031-9436*

GIRARDIN, DAVID WALTER, chaplain, military officer; b. Detroit, July 9, 1951; s. David Louis and Anna Marie (Didyk) G.; m. Barbara Kimberly White, June 27, 1976; children: David John, Emily Grace. BA in Theology, Andrews U., Berrien Springs, Mich., 1982, MDiv, 1985; postgrad., U. San Diego, 1994-95. RN, Calif. RN Harper Grace Hosp., Detroit, 1973-74, Detroit Indsl. Clinic, 1974-76; physician's asst. thoracic surgery Harper Grace Hosp., Detroit Med. Ctr., 1976-80; commd. ensign USN, 1983, advanced through grades to lt. comdr., 1994, chaplain, 1983-87; chaplain naval mobile constrn. bn. THREE USN, Port Hueneume, Calif., 1986-89; chaplain Marine Corps Recruit Depot USN, San Diego, 1989-91, chaplain USS COWPENS (CG-63), 1991-94; chaplain marriage family therapy program U. San Diego, 1994-95; chaplain U.S. Naval Sta., P.R., 1995—; trainer, cons. Leadership, Edn. and Devel. Cons., Reynoldsburg, Ohio, 1985—; pastor Minn. Conf. Seventh-Day Adventists, Three River Falls, 1984-86. Contbr. articles to newspapers and jours. Decorated Navy-Marine Corp Commendation medal, Meritorious Svc. medal, Navy Achievement medal, Southwest Asian War medal. Mem. Naval Res. Assn. (life), NRA (life), Adventist Chaplaincy Ministry, Adventist Mil. and Vets. Orgn. Office: Office of Chaplains PSC 1008 Box 3031 FPO AA 34051

GIRMAN, TANYA LYNN, dietitian; b. Bitburg, Germany, Apr. 26, 1968; came to the U.S., 1968; d. John Richard and Patricia Lynn (Cekanski) G. BS, U. Calif., Davis, 1990; MPH, U. Calif., L.A., 1993. Registered dietitian Commn. on Dietetic Registration. Clin. dietitian and rschr. West L.A. (Calif.) VA Med. Ctr., 1992—; mem. dietetic internship selection com. West L.A. VA Med. Ctr.,, 1993, dietetic internship adv. com., 1993—, bioethics com., 1993—, patient edn. com., 1993-94, chair nutrition edn. com., 1993-94, medicine ICU continuous quality improvement com., 1994—. Mem. APHA, Am. Soc. for Parenteral and Enteral Nutrition, Am. Dietetic Assn., Calif. Dietetic Assn., L.A. Dist. Dietetic Assn., Calif. Dietitians in Gen. Clin. Practice (founder, exec. bd. chair 1992—). Home: 1338 18th St Apt 5 Santa Monica CA 90404-1919 Office: West LA VA Med Ctr 11301 Wilshire Blvd # W120 Los Angeles CA 90073-1003

GIROD, FRANK PAUL, surgeon; b. Orenco, Oreg., Aug. 13, 1908; s. Leon and Anna (Gerig)úG.; m. Nadine Mae Cooper, Aug. 26, 1939; children: Judith Anne, Janet Carol, Franklin Paul, John Cooper. AB, Willamette U., Salem, Oreg., 1929; MD, U. Colo., 1938. Diplomate Am. Bd. Family Practice. Tchr. physics and chemistry, athletic coach Cortez High Sch., Colo., 1929-34; intern U. Colo., Denver, 1938-39; resident surgeon U.S. Marine Hosp., Balt., 1939-41; pvt. practice specializing in family practice and surgery Lebanon, Oreg., 1946—; bd. dirs. Lebanon Hosp., 1960—, pres. med. staff. Trustee, sec. Blue Shield Ops., Oreg., 1950-60; grand marshal Lebanon Strawberry Festival, 1988; mem. bd. Coun. of Govts. Sr. Svcs., 1991, 92. Maj. Army Med. Corp, 1942-45. Decorated Bronze Star; recipient Disting. Svc. First Citizen award Lebanon, Oreg., 1989. Mem. AMA, Oreg. Med. Assn. (trustee), Am. Acad. Family Practice, Kiwanis (pres. 1947-48). Republican. Methodist. Home: 625 E Rose St Lebanon OR 97355-4544 Office: 325 Park St Lebanon OR 97355-3300

GIROLAMI, LISA S., film producer; b. Modesto, Calif., Sept. 13, 1960; d. Guido and Kristine (White) G. BA, Calif. State U., Long Beach, 1983. Assoc. prodn. exec. Walt Disney Pictures/Touchtone, Burbank, Calif., 1985-87; prodn. exec. Buena Vista Pictures, Burbank, Calif., 1987-89; producer Theme Park Prodns. div. Walt Disney, Burbank, Calif., 1989—; show designer Walt Disney Imagineering, Glendale, Calif., 1990-92; line prodr. Disney's Virtual Reality Attraction, 1992-94; mgr. prodn. Disney Interactive Software, Burbank, 1995—. Prodn. exec. films including Honey I Shrunk The Kids, Heartbreak Hotel, DOA, Disorganized Crime, Ernest Saves Christmas, Where the Heart Is, 1989; producer theme park films including the Lottery, Monster Sound Show; prodn. coord. films including Critters, 1985; set mgr. films Reanimator, 1985, Terminator, 1984; asst. dir. films including Summers End, Calling Home; sr. asst. to v.p. prodn. films including Ruthless People, Outrageous Fortune, Color of Money, Adventures in Babysitting, Who Framed Roger Rabbit?, Good Morning Vietnam, Tough Guys, Down and Out in Beverly Hills; prodn. mgr. numerous commls. Roman Catholic. Office: Walt Disney Studios 500 S Buena Vista Burbank CA 91221

GIRON, RICK, adminstrative services manager; b. Santa Fe, N.Mex., Feb. 4, 1961; s. Bill and Frances (Chavez) G.; m. Rebecca D. Vigil, Nov. 17, 1986; 1 child, Andy. BBA, Univ. N.Mex., 1984, MPA, 1989. Adminstrn. intern City of Albuquerque Water Resources, 1983-84; systems analyst City of Albuquerque Pub. Works Dept., 1984-89, 89-90; 1st lt. N.Mex. Army Nat. Guard, 1987—, systems analyst, 1990-91, adminstrn. svcs. mgr., 1991—. Del. State Dem. Conv., Albuquerque, 1994; vol. political campaigns, 1980—. Named Outstanding Young Man of Am., 1987. Mem. ASPA (bd. dirs., treas. 1989-90, 94-95, pres.-elect 1995—), NG Officers Assn., Assn. U.S. Army, Air Def. Assn., Enlisted Assn., Albuquerque Hispano C. of C. (co-chmn. tourism and conv. com.), N.Mex. Suprs. and Profl. Assn. (bd. dirs., treas. 1991-93, pres. 1993—), KC. Democrat. Roman Catholic. Home: 4628 11th St NW Albuquerque NM 87107-3704 Office: City of Albuquerque PO Box 1293 Albuquerque NM 87103-1293

GIRTON, LANCE, economics educator; b. Brazil, Ind., July 20, 1942; s. John E. and Barbara (Wollard) G.; m. Kathy Marlock, Apr. 30, 1988; children: Derek, Lance Alan. BA in Econs., So. Ill. U., 1964; MA in Econs., U. Chgo., 1967, PhD in Econs., 1976. Instr. econs. Elmhurst (Ill.) Coll., 1968-69; asst. prof. econs. Mich. Technol. U., Houghton, 1969-71; economist internat. fin. div. Bd. Govs. FRS, Washington, 1971-78; prof. Pa. State U., College Park, 1983-84; vis. prof. U. Utah, Salt Lake City, 1977-78, prof., 1978—; assoc. professorial lectr. George Washington U., Washington, 1975-76; v.p., head rsch. Citicorp Homeowners Inc., St. Louis, 1985-86; cons. Investment Cos. Inst., Washington, 1981-83, World Bank, Washington, 1982—, Congl. Budget Office, Washington, 1980; Murphy Endowment Fund vis. scholar U. Wis., La Crosse, 1979; presenter papers, participant profl. meetings, 1973—; seminar presenter Brown U., U. Chgo., U. Pa., Pa. State U., UCLA, U. Colo., also others; referee profl. jours. Contbr. articles to profl. jours. Univ. scholar So. Ill. U., 1961-64; fellow NIMH, 1966-68. Mem. Am. Econ. Assn. Office: U Utah Dept Econs Salt Lake City UT 84112

GIRVIGIAN, RAYMOND, architect; b. Detroit, Nov. 27, 1926; s. Manoug and Margaret G.; m. Beverly Rae Bennett, Sept. 23, 1967; 1 son, Michael Raymond. AA, UCLA, 1947; BA with honors, U. Calif., Berkeley, 1950; M.A. in Architecture, U. Calif.-Berkeley, 1951. With Hutchason Architects, L.A., 1952-57; owner, prin. Raymond Girvigian, L.A., 1957-68, South Pasadena, Calif., 1968—; co-founder, advisor L.A. Cultural Heritage Bd., 1961—; vice chmn. Hist. Am. Bldgs. Survey, Nat. Park Svc., Washington, 1966-70; co-founder, mem. Calif. Hist. Resources Commn., 1970-78; co-founder, chmn. governing bd. Calif. Hist. Bldgs. Code, 1976-91, chmn. adminstrv. law, 1992—, chmn. emeritus, 1993—; chmn. Calif. State Capitol Commn., 1985—. Co-editor, producer: film Architecture of Southern California for Los Angeles City Schs, 1965; historical monographs of HABS Landmarks, Los Angeles, 1958-80; historical monographs of Califs. State Capitol, 1974, Pan Pacific Auditorium, 1980, L.A. Meml. Coliseum, 1984, Powell Meml. Libr., UCLA, 1989; designed: city halls for Pico Rivera, 1963, LaPuente, 1966, Rosemead, 1968, Lawndale, 1970 (all Calif.); hist. architect for restoration of Calif. State Capitol, 1975-82, Workman/Temple Hist. Complex, City of Industry, Calif., 1974-81, Robinson Gardens Landmarks, Beverly Hills, Calif., 1983-92, Pasadena (Calif.) Ctrl. Libr., 1982-92, Mt. Pleasant House Mus., Heritage Sq., L.A., 1972—. Mem. St. James Episcopal Ch., South Pasadena, Calif. Served with AUS, 1945-46. Recipient Archtl. Design medal U. Calif., Berkeley, 1947, Outstanding Achievement in Architecture award City of Pico Rivera, Calif., 1968, Neasham award Calif. Hist. Soc., 1982, Preservationist of Yr. award Calif. Preservation Found., 1987, L.A. Mayor's award for archtl. preservation, 1987, Gold Crown award for advancement of arts Pasadena Arts Coun., 1990, Golden Palm award Hollywood Heritage, 1990. Fellow AIA (Calif. state preservation chmn. 1970-75, state preservation coord. 1970-89, co-recipient nat. honor award for restoration Calif. State Capitol 1983, co-recipient honor award for restoration Pasadena Cen. Libr., Pasadena chpt. 1988); mem. Soc. Archtl. Historians, Nat. Trust for Historic Preservation, Calif. Preservation Found., Calif. Hist. Soc. Independent Democrat. Office: PO Box 220 South Pasadena CA 91031-0220

GISH, ROBERT FRANKLIN, English language educator, writer; b. Albuquerque, Apr. 1, 1940; s. Jesse Franklin and Lillian J. (Fields) G.; m. Judith Kay Stephenson, June 20, 1961; children: Robin Elaine Butzier, Timothy Stephen, Annabeth. BA, U. N.Mex., Albuquerque, 1962, MA, 1967, PhD, 1972. Tchr. Albuquerque Pub. Schs., 1962-67; prof. U. No. Iowa, Cedar Falls, 1968-91; dir. ethnic studies, prof. English Calif. Poly. State U., San Luis Obispo, 1991—, prof., 1992—. Author: Hamlin Garland: Far West, 1976, Paul Horgan, 1983, Frontier's End: Life of Harvey Fergusson, 1988, William Carlos Williams: The Short Fiction, 1989, Songs of My Hunter Heart: A Western Kinship, 1992, Frist Horses: Stories of the New West, 1993, North American Native American Myths, 1993, When Coyote Howls: A Lavaland Fable, 1994, Nueva Granada: Paul Horgan and the Southwest, 1995. Office: Calif Poly State U Ethnic Studies San Luis Obispo CA 93407

GISLASON, IRVING LEE, psychiatry educator; b. Nanaimo, B.C., Can., July 21, 1943; came to U.S., 1977; s. Sverrir and Helga Johina (Gislason) G.; m. Leslie Laura Hope; children: Sarah Jonina, Catherine Adair. MD, U. B.C., Vancouver, 1969. Diplomate Am. Bd. Psychiatry and Neurology; lic. psychiatrist B.C., Calif. Rotating intern Meml. Hosp. Long Beach, Calif., 1969-70; resident in psychiatry dept. psychiatry and human behavior U. Calif.-Irvine, Orange, 1972-74, fellow in child psychiatry dept. psychiatry & human behavior, 1974-76; chief resident dept. psychiatry U. B.C., 1976; staff psychiatrist U. Calif.-Irvine Med. Ctr., Orange, 1977—, dir. Child Study Ctr., 1977-89, acting chief divsn. child and adolescent psychiatry, 1980-81, assoc. dir. Child Inpatient Unit, 1984, acting chief Adolescent Inpatient Unit, 1987, dir. Child Psychiat. and Inpatient Unit, 1989-92, dir. adult psychiat. inpatient unit, 1992—, med. student ednl. coord., 1993—, dir. med. student edn. (psychiatry), 1993—; examiner Am. Bd. Psychiatry and Neurology; clin. instr. psychiatry U. B.C., 1977, U. Calif.-Irvine, 1975; chief child psychiatry consultation liaison program U. Calif.-Irvine Med. Ctr., 1977-89; cons. Greater Vancouver Mental Health Svcs., 1977; staff psychiatrist U. B.C. Sci. Ctr. Hosp., 1977; clin. prof. psychiatry U. Calif.-Irvine, 1987—, cons. staff dept. medicine psychiat. sect. Children's Hosp. of Orange County, 1981—; presenter and lectr. in field. Contbr. articles to profl. jours. Mem. adv. bd. Com. on Children's TV, NBC Studios, 1977-81. Licentiate Med. Coun. Can.; fellow Royal Coll. Physicians Can. (diplomate fellowship exam. in medicine 1976, specialist cert. 1976), Am. Acad. Child Psychiatry; mem. Can. Med. Assn. Home: 688 N Lemon Hill Tr Orange CA 92669 Office: U Calif-Irvine Med Ctr 101 The City Dr S Orange CA 92668-3201

GISSING, BRUCE, retired aerospace company executive; b. Bklyn., Nov. 28, 1931; s. Herbert John and Charlotte (Levine) G.; m. Edythe Harriet Aldort, June 24, 1954; children: Paul, Wendy, Peter, Alyson. BBA, CCNY, 1953; MBA, U. Denver, 1963. Dir. materiel 767 program BCAG-The Boeing Co., Seattle, 1977-79, dir. ops. 747 and 767 divs., 1979-83, v.p., gen. mgr. Boeing engring., 1983-84, v.p., gen. mgr. materiel div., 1984-86, v.p., gen. mgr. Renton div., 1986-87, v.p. ops., 1987-88, sr. v.p. ops., 1988-90, exec. v.p. ops., 1990-94; chmn., pres. Boeing Can., The Boeing Co., Seattle, 1988-94; ret., 1994; mem. Def. Sci. Bd., Washington, 1991-93. 1st lt. U.S. Army, 1953-55. Mem. Soc. Mfg. Engrs., Mfrs. Alliance for Productivity and Innovation, Inc. (trustee). Home: 4953 145th Ave SE Bellevue WA 98006-3546 Home: 4740 E Sunrise Dr Tucson AZ 85718

GITTLEMAN, ARTHUR PAUL, computer science and engineering educator; b. Bklyn., Oct. 7, 1941; s. Morris and Clara (Konefsky) G.; m. Charlotte Marie Singleton, June 1, 1986; 1 child, Amanda Eve. BA, UCLA, 1962, MA, 1965, PhD, 1969. Asst. prof. Calif. State U., Long Beach, 1966-70, assoc. prof., 1970-75, prof., 1975—, chair, math. and computer sci. dept., 1978-83, prof. computer sci. and engring., 1975—. Author: History of Mathematics, 1975. Mem. IEEE Computer Soc., Assn. for Computing Machinery, Math. Assn. of Am., Phi Beta Kappa. Office: Calif State U 1250 N Bellflower Blvd Long Beach CA 90840-0006

GITTLEMAN, MORRIS, consultant, metallurgist; b. Zhidkovitz, Minsk, Russia, Nov. 2, 1912; came to U.S., 1920, naturalized; s. Louis and Ida (Gorodietsky) G.; B.S. cum laude, Bklyn. Coll., 1934; postgrad. Manhattan Coll., 1941, Pratt Inst., 1943, Bklyn. Poly. Inst., 1946-47; m. Clara Konefsky, Apr. 7, 1937; children—Arthur Paul, Michael Jay. Metall. engr. N.Y. Naval Shipyard, 1942-47; chief metallurgist, chemist Pacific Cast Iron Pipe & Fitting Co., South Gate, Calif., 1948-54, tech. mgr., 1954-57, tech. and prodn. mgr., 1957-58; cons. Valley Brass, Inc., El Monte Calif., 1958-61, Vulcan Foundry, Ltd., Haifa, Israel, 1958-65, Anaheim Foundry Co. (Calif.), 1958-63, Hollywood Alloy Casting Co. (Calif.), 1960-70, Spartan Casting Co., El Monte, 1961-62; Overton Foundry, South Gate, Calif., 1962-70, cons., gen. mgr., 1970-71; cons. Familian Pipe & Supply Co., Van Nuys, Calif., 1962-72, Comml. Enameling Co., Los Angeles, 1963-68, Universal Cast Iron Mfg. Co., South Gate, 1965-71; pres. MG Coupling Co., 1972-79; instr. physics Los Angeles Harbor Coll., 1958-59; instr. chemistry Western States Coll. Engring., Inglewood, Calif., 1961-68. Registered profl. engr., Calif. Mem. Am. Foundrymen's Soc., Am. Foundrymen's Soc. So. Calif. (dir. 1955-57), AAAS, Am. Soc. Metals, N.Y. Acad. Scis., Internat. Solar Energy Soc. (Am. sect.). Contbr. to tech. jours.; inventor MG timesaver coupling, patents worldwide. Home: 17635 San Diego Cir Fountain Valley CA 92708

GIUDICI, FRANCIS, food products executive; b. 1956. Pres. L.A. Hearne Co., 1975—. Office: L A Hearne Co 512 Metz Rd King City CA 93930-2503*

GIULIANO, ARMANDO ELARIO, surgical oncologist, educator, author; b. N.Y.C., Oct. 2, 1947; s. Antonio Vincent and Victoria (Squizzaro) G.; m. Cheryl Jane Fallon, June 21, 1970; children: Christopher and Amanda (twins). BA, Fordham U., 1969; MD, U. Chgo., 1973. Diplomate Am. Bd. Surgery. Resident U. Calif., San Francisco, 1973-76, 78-80; fellow in tumor immunology UCLA, 1976-78, asst. prof. surgery, 1980-84, assoc. prof. surgery, 1984-90, dir. Breast Svc., 1980-91, asst. dean Med. Sch., 1988-91, clin. prof. surgery, 1991—, prof. surgery, 1990-91; assoc. dir., chief surg. oncology John Wayne Cancer Inst., Santa Monica, Calif., 1991—; dir. Keefer Breast Ctr. St. John's Hosp., Santa Monica, 1993—; vice chmn. com. on cancer liaison Commn. on Cancer, Chgo., 1993—, mem. com. on edn., 1990—. Mem. editorial bd. Breast Surgery Index and Revs., 1993—; contbr. more than 100 articles to profl. jours. Bd. dirs. Coastal Cities unit Am. Cancer Soc., 1993—; mem. nat. profl. adv. bd. The Wellness Cmty., L.A., 1993—. Mem. ACS (com. on surg. edn. 1989—), Soc. Surg. Oncology (chmn. edn. com. 1993), Soc. Univ. Surgeons, Am. Soc. Clin. Oncology, Pacific Coast Surg. Assn., Western Surg. Assn., Alpha Omega Alpha. Office: John Wayne Cancer Inst 1328 22nd St Santa Monica CA 90404-2032

GIUMARRA, GEORGE, JR., vintner; b. 1942. Prin. ARRA Sales Corp., Edison, Calif., 1975—, Giumarra Farms Inc., Edison, Calif., 1963—; v.p. Giumarra Vineyards Corp., Edison, Calif., 1963—; prin. Giumarra Bros. Fruit Co., Inc., L.A., 1963—. Office: Giumarra Vineyards Corp 11220 Edison Hwy Edison CA 93220*

GIUS, JULIUS, retired newspaper editor; b. Fairbanks, Alaska, Dec. 31, 1911; s. Julius and Mary (Sarja) G.; m. Elizabeth Gail Alexander, Aug. 24, 1940; children—Gary Alexander, Barbara Gail. Student, U. Puget Sound, 1930-33. Reporter Tacoma (Wash.) Times, 1929-35; founding editor Bremerton (Wash.) Sun, 1935-60; editor Ventura (Calif.) Star-Free Press, 1960-87; also editorial dir. John P. Scripps Newspapers, 1961-85. Mem. Am. Soc. Newspaper Editors, Sigma Delta Chi. Clubs: Elk, K.C, Rotarian. Home: 4675 Clubhouse Dr Somis CA 93066-9709

GIVANT, PHILIP JOACHIM, mathematics educator, real estate investment executive; b. Mannheim, Fed. Republic of Germany, Dec. 5, 1935; s. Paul and Irmy (Dinse) G.; m. Kathleen Joan Porter, Sept. 3, 1960; children: Philip Paul, Julie Kathleen, Laura Grace. BA in Math., San Francisco State U., 1957, MA in Math., 1960. Prof. math. San Francisco State U., 1958-60, Am. River Coll., Sacramento, 1960—; pres. Grove Enterprises, Sacramento, 1961—; pres. Am. River Coll. Acad. Senate, Sacramento, 1966-69; v.p. Acad. Senate for Calif. Community Colls., 1974-77; mem. State Chancellor's Acad. Calendar Com., Sacramento, 1977-79. Founder, producer Annual Sacramento Blues Music Festival, 1976—; producer Sta. KVMR weekly Blues music program, 1978—, music festivals Folsom Prison, 1979-81, Vacaville Prison, 1985. Pres. Sacramento Blues Festival, Inc., 1985—; mem. Lake Tahoe Keys Homeowners Assn., 1983—, Sea Ranch Homeowners Assn., 1977—. Recipient Spl. Service Commendation, Acad. Senate Calif. Community Colls., 1977, Spl. Human Rights award Human Rights-Fair Housing Commn., Sacramento, 1985, W.C. Handy award for Blues Promoter of Yr. Nat. Blues Found., Memphis, 1987, 1st Critical Achievement award Sacramento Area Mus. Awards Commn., 1992. Mem. Faculty Assn. Calif. Community Colls., Am. Soc. Psychical Research, Nat. Blues Found. (adv. com., W.C. Handy Blues Promoter of Yr. 1987). Home and Office: 3809 Garfield Ave Carmichael CA 95608-6631

GIVENS, STEVEN WENDELL, economic development planner; b. Mayfield, Ky., Sept. 18, 1954; s. Jaynes Wendell and Joanne G.; m. Robyn E. Cockrell, July, 1981 (dec. Oct. 1987); children: Grant Tyler, Paige; m. D'Lyn C. Ford, Apr. 27, 1991. BS, Murray State U., 1976. Edn. editor The Hobbs (N.Mex.) Daily News Sun, 1976-80; sports editor, area writer The Duncan (Okla.) Banner, 1980-85; territorial sales rep. Wm. E. Davis & Sons, Oklahoma City, 1985-87; mgr. Connie's Mexico Cafe, Wichita, Kans., 1987-88; sports editor Clovis (N.Mex.) Jour., 1988-90; edn./county govt. editor Carlsbad (N.Mex.) Current Argus, 1990-91; news editor Las Cruces (N.Mex.) Sun News, 1991-93, Rio Grande Gazette, Anthony, Tex., 1993; econ. devel. planner, comm. dir., grants technician Doña Ana County Econ. Devel. Grants, Las Cruces, 1994—; bd. dirs. The Messenger Advocate Pub., Mesilla Park, N.Mex.; v.p. AP Mng. Editors, N.Mex., 1992, 93. Contbr. articles to jours. and newspapers. Precinct organizer Clinton-Gore Rapid Response Team, Las Cruces, 1992; mem. Dem. Nat. Com., 1976—; dist. bd. Yucca coun., Boy Scouts Am., 1993—; adv. com. El Paso C.C., 1993—. Named Restaurant Mgr. of the Yr. Wichita River Festival, Old Town Assn., 1988; recipient Resolution of Appreciation, Eddy County, N.Mex., 1991. Mem. Optimist Internat. (club pres. 1980-82, lt. gov. 1982-83, gov. 1985-86, Outstanding Disting. Lt. Gov. award 1982-83, New Club Bldg. award 1982-83). Presbyterian. Office: Dona Ana County Econ Devel Grants 400 S Main St Las Cruces NM 88001-1205

GLAD, DAIN STURGIS, retired aerospace engineer, consultant; b. Santa Monica, Calif., Sept. 17, 1932; s. Alma Emanuel and Maude La Verne (Morby) G.; BS in Engring., UCLA, 1954; MS in Elec. Engring., U. So. Calif., 1963. Registered profl. engr., Calif. m. Betty Alexandra Shainoff, Sept. 12, 1954 (dec. 1974); 1 child, Dana Elizabeth; m. Carolyn Elizabeth Giffen, June 8, 1979. Electronic engr. Clary Corp., San Gabriel, Calif., 1957-58; with Aerojet Electro Systems Co., Azusa, Calif., 1958-72; with missile systems div. Rockwell Internat., Anaheim, Calif., 1973-75; with Aerojet Electrosystems, Azusa, 1975-84; with support systems div. Hughes Aircraft Co., 1984-90; with Electro-Optical Ctr. Rockwell Internat. Corp., 1990-94; cons., 1994—. Contbr. articles to profl. jours. Ensign, U.S. Navy, 1954-56; lt. j.g. Res., 1956-57. Mem. IEEE. Home: 1701 Marengo Ave South Pasadena CA 91030-4818

GLAD, SUZANNE LOCKLEY, retired museum director; b. Rochester, N.Y., Oct. 2, 1929; d. Alfred Allen and Lucille A. (Watson) Lockley; m. Edward Newman Glad, Nov. 7, 1953; children: Amy, Lisanne Glad Lantz, William E. BA, Sweet Briar Coll., 1951; MA, Columbia U., 1952. Exec. dir. New York State Young Reps., N.Y.C., 1951-57; mem. pub. rels. staff Dolphin Group, L.A., 1974-83; scheduling sec. Gov.'s Office, Sacramento, 1983-87; dep. dir. Calif. Mus. Sci. and Industry, L.A., 1987-94; ret. Mem. Calif. Rep. League, Flintridge, 1969—; mem. Assistance League of Flintridge, 1970—, Flintridge Guild Children's Hosp., 1969-89. Mem. Am. Assn. Mus., Sweet Briar Alumnae of So. Calif. (pres. 1972), Phi Beta Kappa, Tau Phi. Episcopalian.

GLADNER, MARC STEFAN, lawyer; b. Seattle, July 18, 1952; s. Jules A. and Mildred W. (Weller) G.; m. Susanne Tso (div. Feb. 1981); m. Michele Marie Hardin, Sept. 12, 1981; 1 child, Sara Megan. Student, U. Colo., 1970-73; JD, Southwestern U., 1976. Bar: Ariz. 1976, Navajo Tribal Ct. 1978. Law clk. jud. br. Navajo Nation, Window Rock, Ariz., 1976-77, gen. counsel jud. br., 1977-79; pvt. practice law Phoenix, 1979-83; ptnr. Seplow, Rivkind & Gladner, Phoenix, 1983-86, Crosby & Gladner, P.C., Phoenix, 1986—; adj. instr. Coll. Ganado, Ariz., 1978-79. Democrat. Jewish. Office: Crosby & Gladner PC 111 W Monroe St Ste 706 Phoenix AZ 85003-1720

GLADNEY, DRU CURTIS, Asian studies educator; b. L.A., Nov. 3, 1956; s. B.C. G. BA in Philosophy and Religious Studies, Westmont Coll., 1978; MA in Theology, Fuller Theol. Sem., 1981; MA in Anthropology, U. Wash., 1983, PhD in Anthropology, 1987. Fellow John D. and Catherine T. MacArthur Found. Program on Peace and Internat. Coop., 1989-90; assoc. editor Cen. Asian Survey for China and Inner Asia, 1992-93; asst. prof. anthropology dept. U. So. Calif., 1990-93; rsch. fellow Program for Cultural Studies, East-West Ctr., Honolulu, 1993—; assoc. prof. Asian studies U. Hawaii, Honolulu, 1993—; vis. prof. Bogazici U., 1992-93; mem. symposium planning com. The Dalai Lama in Hawaii, Honolulu, 1994; lectr. Smithsonian Inst., 1987. Contbr. articles to profl. book and jours. Mem. Am. Anthropol. Assn., Am. Ethnological Soc., Assn. Asian Studies, Assn. Cen. Asian Studies, Assn. Pol./Legal Anthropol., Middle Ea. Studies Assn. Office: Program Cultural Studies East-West Ctr 1777 East-West Rd Honolulu HI 96848

GLADWELL, MARILYN MEILAN, microbiologist; b. Conchas Dam, N.Mex., Nov. 30, 1938; d. Edmund H. and Henrietta M. (Hum) Chun; m. Jack Gladwell, Feb. 7, 1972; children: Linda Sue Poetsch, David S. Bailey. BS in Microbiology, U. Wash., 1960. Microbiologist Cowlitz Gen. Hosp., Longview, Wash., 1960-67; microbiologist, lab. supr., tech. supr. A O N.W., Inc. Med. Lab., The Dalles, Oreg., 1968-94, ptnr., 1971-94, pres., 1991-94; pres. The Majack Corp., The Dalles, 1994—. Computer asst. The Dalles Pub. Libr., 1994-95. Mem. Am. Soc. Med. Technologists, Am. Rose Soc. Republican. Home and Office: The Majack Corp PO Box 1207 The Dalles OR 97058-9207

GLADYSZ, JOHN ANDREW, chemistry educator; b. Kalamazoo, Aug. 13, 1952; s. Edward Matthew and Margean Alice (Worst) G. BS in Chemistry, U. Mich., 1971; PhD in Chemistry, Stanford (Calif.) U., 1974. Asst. prof. U. Calif., L.A., 1974-82; assoc. prof. U. Utah, Salt Lake City, 1982-85, prof., 1985—. Assoc. editor Chem. Revs., 1984—; mem. editorial bd. Organometallics, 1990-92, Bull. de la Société Chemique de France, 1992—. Alfred P. Sloan Found. fellow, 1980-84; Camile and Henry Dreyfus scholar and grantee, 1980-85; Arthur C. Cope scholar, 1988; recipient U. Utah Disting. Rsch. award, 1992, Humboldt award, 1994. Mem. AAAS, Am. Chem. Soc. (award in organometallic chemistry 1994), The Chem. Soc., Sigma Xi, Alpha Chi Sigma. Home: 1149 Charlton Ave Salt Lake City UT 84106-2603 Office: U Utah Dept Of Chemistry Salt Lake City UT 84112

GLAHE, FED RUFUS, economics educator; b. Chgo., June 30, 1934; s. Frederick William and Frances Evelyn (Welch) G.; m. Nancy Suzzanna Behrent, June 24, 1961; 1 child, Charles Dixon. BS in Aero. Engring., Purdue U., 1957, MS in Econs., 1963, PhD in Econs., 1964. Engr. Allison divsn. GM, Indpls., 1957-58, 58-60; ops. analyst Def. Sys. divsn. GM, Detroit, 1960-61; rsch. economist Battelle Meml. Inst., Columbus, Ohio, 1964-65; prof. U. Colo., Boulder, 1965—. Author: Macroeconomics, 1973, 77, 85, Microeconomics, 1981, 88, Concordance to Smith's Wealth of Nations, 1993. Mem. Mt. Pelerin Soc. Roman Catholic. Office: U Colo Campus Box 256 Boulder CO 80309

GLANVILLE, JOHN HART, construction executive; b. Houston, Dec. 31, 1954; s. James William and Nancy Ellen (Hart) G. BA in Architecture, Lehigh U., 1977; MS in Engring., U. Tex., 1985. From field engr. to project mgr. Turner Constrn., Houston, 1978-83; purchasing agt. Turner Constrn., Norwalk, Conn., 1986-87, bus. devel., 1987-88; mgr. spl. projects Turner Constrn., Hartford, Conn., 1988-90; project supt. Linbeck Constrn., L.A., 1990-91; constrn. mgr. Caltech, Pasadena, Calif., 1991—; rsch. asst. U. Tex., Austin, 1983-85. Author: Constructability Idea Evaluation, 1985. Mem. ASCE, Assocs. of Caltech, Sierra Club, Appalachian Trail Club, Nature Conservancy, Habitat for Humanity, Brook Club, Wee Burn Country Club. Democrat. Home: 627 S Marengo Ave Pasadena CA 91106-3627 Office: Caltech Mail Code 2 - 83 Pasadena CA 91125

GLASCO, DONALD GLEE, psychiatrist; b. Wichita, Kans., Oct. 18, 1929; s. James Edward and Nelle Josephine (Lyster) G.; m. JoAnn Lewis, June 12, 1955; children: Cheryl Ann, Suzanne, Mark. AB, U. Kans., 1947-52, MD, 1956; student, U. Zurich, Switzerland, 1953-54; cert. in pscyiatry, U. Colo., 1960. Diplomate Am. Bd. Psychiatry. Intern U. Kans. Health Svc. Ctr., Kansas City, 1956-57; resident U. Colo. Health Sci. Ctr., Denver, 1957-60; pvt. practice Littleton, Colo., 1962—; assoc. clin. prof. psychiatry U. Colo., Denver, 1963—; staff psychiatrist Denver VA Med. Ctr., 1963-76, 87—. Lt. comdr. USN, 1960-62. Fellow Am. Psychiatric Assn., Colo. Psychiatric Soc. (pres.), Ctrl. Neuro Psychiatric Assn.; mem. Colo. Med. Soc., Appahoe County Med. Soc. Office: 191 E Orchard Rd # 203 Littleton CO 80121-8055

GLASER, DONALD ARTHUR, physicist; b. Cleveland, Ohio, Sept. 21, 1926; s. William Joseph Glaser. B.S., Case Inst. Tech., 1946, Sc.D., 1959; Ph.D., Cal. Inst. Tech., 1949. Prof. physics U. Mich., 1949-59; prof. physics U. Calif., Berkeley, 1959—; prof. physics, molecular and cell biology, divsn. neurobiology U. Calif., 1964—. Recipient Henry Russel award U. Mich., 1955, Charles V. Boys prize Phys. Soc., London, 1958, Nobel prize in physics, 1960, Gold Medal award Case Inst. Tech., 1967, Golden Plate award Am. Acad. of Achievement, 1989; NSF fellow, 1961, Guggenheim fellow, 1961-62, fellow Smith-Kettlewell Inst. for Vision Rsch, 1983-84. Fellow AAAS, Fedn. Am. Scientists, The Exploratorium (bd. dirs.), Royal Soc. Sci., Royal Swedish Acad. Sci., Assn. Rsch. Vision and Ophthalmology, Neuroscis. Inst., Am. Physics Soc. (prize 1959); mem. Nat. Acad. Scis., Am. Assn. Artificial Intelligence, N.Y. Acad. Sci., Internat. Acad. Sci., Sigma Xi, Tau Kappa Alpha, Theta Tau. Office: U Calif Dept Molecular & Cell Biology Neurobiology Divsn Stanley Hall Berkeley CA 94720*

GLASER, STEVEN JAY, lawyer; b. Tacoma, Dec. 5, 1957; s. Ernest Stanley and Janice Fern (Stone) G.; 1 child, Jacob Andrew. Student, Oxford (Eng.) U., 1979; BSBA, Georgetown U., 1980; JD, John Marshall Law Sch., 1983. ABar: Ill. 1983, Ariz. 1984, U.S. Dist. Ct. Ariz. 1984, U.S. Ct. Appeals (9th and D.C. cirs.) 1984. Law clk. to judge Maricopa County Superior Ct., Phoenix, 1983-84; asst. atty. gen. State of Ariz., Phoenix, 1984-85; staff atty. Ariz. Corp. Commn., Phoenix, 1985-90; sr. atty. regulatory affairs Tucson Electric Power Co., 1990-92, mgr. legal dept., 1992-94, mgr. contracts and wholesale mktg., 1994, v.p. wholesale/retail pricing and system planning, 1994—. Mem. ABA, Ariz. Bar Assn., Ill. Bar Assn., Pima County Bar Assn., So. Ariz. Water Resources Assn. (bd. dirs. 1991-93), Georgetown U. Alumni Assn., Phi Delta Phi. Republican. Jewish. Office: Tucson Electric Power Co PO Box 711 220 W 6th St Tucson AZ 85702

GLASGOW, JANIS MARILYN, foreign language educator; b. Wooster, Ohio, Aug. 24, 1934; d. Paul Ellsworth and Edna Helen (Smith) G. BA, Case Western Reserve U., 1956; MA, U. Wis., 1958; PhD, UCLA, 1966. Grad. teaching asst. U. Wis., Madison, 1957-58, UCLA, 1958-62; asst. prof. French San Diego State U., 1962-68, assoc. prof., 1968-80, prof. French, 1980-94; maître de confs. U. Paris, 1973-74; exch. prof. French U. Nice (France), 1982; exch. prof. comparative lit. U. Nantes (France), 1985. Author: Une Esthetique de Comparaison: Balzac et George Sand, 1978; editor: George Sand: Collected Essays, 1985, Gabriel, 1988, Questions d'Art et de Littérature, 1991. Fulbright scholar, 1956-57, Robert V. Merrill Grad. scholar, 1961-62. Mem. MLA (regional del. Pacific coast 1974-75, 89-91), Am. Assn. Tchrs. French (pres. 1979-81), Am. Soc. French Acad. Palms, Mensa, Phi Beta Kappa (pres. Epsilon Assn. of Calif. 1972-73, pres. Nu chpt. of Calif. 1976-77, 88-90). Home: 713 N Grant St Wooster OH 44691-2824

GLASGOW, WILLIAM JACOB, lawyer; b. Portland, Oreg., Sept. 29, 1946; s. Joseph Glasgow and Lena (Friedman) Schiff; m. Renée Vonfeld, Aug. 30, 1969; children: Joshua, Andrew. BS magna cum laude, U. Pa., 1968; JD magna cum laude, Harvard U., 1972. Bar: Oreg. 1972, U.S. Dist. Ct. Oreg. 1972, U.S. Ct. Appeals (9th cir.) 1978. Assoc. Rives, Bonyhadi & Drummond, Portland, 1972-76, ptnr., 1976-79; ptnr. Stoel, Rives, Boley, Fraser & Wyse, Portland, 1979-83; mng. ptnr. Perkins Coie, Portland, 1983-88; sr. v.p., gen. counsel PacifiCorp Fin. Svcs. Inc., Portland, 1988-89, chmn., CEO, 1989—; sr. v.p. PacifiCorp, Portland, 1992-93, sr. v.p., CFO, 1993—; pres. PacifiCorp Holdings Inc., Portland, 1992—; pres., dir. NERCO, Inc., Portland, 1992-93. Pres. bd. trustees Oreg. Mus. Sci. and Industry, Portland, 1981; pres. N.W. Fin. Symposium, Portland, 1985; trustee Oreg. Art Inst., 1990-92, 94—, Oreg. Grad. Inst. Sci. and Tech., 1991—, Discovery Inst., 1992—; pres. Portland Met. Sports Authority, 1992—. Mem. Oreg. Bar Assn., Portland C. of C. (bd. dirs. 1983), Harvard Law Sch. Alumni Assn. (pres. Oreg. chpt. 1981). Democrat. Home: 3111 SW Talbot Rd Portland OR 97201-1673

GLASS, MICHAEL JOHN, microbiologist and researcher; b. Royal Oak, Mich., Sept. 22, 1962; s. Michael Arthur William and Caroline Blanchard (Ogden) G.; m. Johannah Estelle Stock, Feb. 1, 1992; 1 child, Michael Arthur William. BS, Mich. State U., 1985; PhD, U. Utah, 1992. Teaching asst. U. Utah, Salt Lake City, 1985-92; sr. microbiologist TRA Inc., Salt Lake City, 1992-94; sr. scientist/ptnr. WCG, Salt Lake City, 1994—; staff scientist Ctr. for Environ. Tech. U. Utah, Salt Lake City, 1995—, adj. prof. civil engring., 1994—; adj. prof. Salt Lake C.C., 1993—; bd. dirs. O.R. Svcs., Centerville, Utah. Recipient Student award Am. Soc. Virology, 1987; Nat. Inst. Cancer grantee, 1988-90, U.S. Army grantee, 1995. Mem. AAAS, Am. Soc. Microbiology, Am. Chem. Soc. Democrat.

GLASS, RICHARD STEVEN, chemistry educator; b. N.Y.C., Mar. 5, 1943; s. Emanuel David and Sylvia Cynthia (Lucks) G.; m. Susan Stern, Aug. 30, 1970; children: Ethan Charles, Lawrence Craig. BA, NYU, 1963; PhD, Harvard U., 1967. Rsch. assoc. Stanford (Calif.) U., 1966-67; sr. scientist Hoffmann La Roche, Inc., Nutley, N.J., 1967-70; asst. prof. U. Ariz., Tucson, 1970-76, assoc. prof., 1976-82, prof., 1982—; scientific adv. bd. Naxcor, Inc., Menlo Park, Calif., 1987—; cons. several cos. Editor: (book) Conformational Analysis of . . . , 1988; editorial bd. Sulfur Letters, Sulfur Reports, 1993—; patentee in field; contbr. articles to profl. jours. Grantee NSF, NIH, ACS, 1970—; sr. fellow NIH, 1988; guest scientist Hahn-Meitner Inst., Berlin, 1991. Fellow AAAS (pres. S.W. and Rocky Mountain Div. 1988); mem. Am. Chem. Soc. Office: Dept Chemistry Univ Ariz Tucson AZ 85721

GLASSER, CHARLES EDWARD, university president; b. Chgo., Apr. 3, 1940; s. Julius J. and Hilda (Goldman) G.; m. Hannah Alex, Mar. 8, 1987; children: Gemma Maria, Julian David. BA in History, Denison U., 1961; MA in Polit. Sci., U. Ill., 1967; JD, John F. Kennedy U., 1970. Bar: Calif. 1970, U.S. Ct. Appeals (9th cir.) 1970. Pvt. practice Hineser, Spellberg & Glasser, Pleasant Hill, Calif., 1971-77; dean Sch. Law John F. Kennedy U., Orinda, Calif., 1977-83, pres., 1990—; v.p., gen. counsel Western Hosp. Corp., Emeryville, Calif., 1983-90. Author: The Quest for Peace, 1986. Mem. Calif. Bar Assn. Office: John F Kennedy U 12 Altarinda Rd Orinda CA 94563-2603

GLASSHEIM, JEFFREY WAYNE, allergist, immunologist, pediatrician; b. Far Rockaway, N.Y., Sept. 16, 1958; s. Ronald Alan and Glenda (Deitch) G.; m. Paulette Renée, Apr. 16, 1989; 1 child, Elyssa Gwen. BA, Temple U., 1980; DO, U. New. Eng., 1984. Diplomate Am. Bd. Allergy and Clin. Immunology, Am. Bd. Pediatrics. Commd. 2d lt. U.S. Army, 1980, advanced through grades to maj., 1989; intern Winthrop-Univ. Hosp., Mineola, N.Y., 1984-85; resident Madigan Army Med. Ctr., Tacoma, Wash., 1985-87; fellowship Fitzsimons Army Med. Ctr., Aurora, Colo., 1990-91, chief fellow allergy-clin. immunology, 1990-91; chief allergy-clin. immunology and immunizations svcs. Silas B. Hays Army Community Hosp., Fort Ord, Calif., 1991-93; resigned U.S. Army, 1993; pvt. practice Ziering Allergy and Respiratory Ctr., Calif., 1993-94; dir. allergy-immunology dept. Pediatric Med. Group of Fresno, Calif., 1994-95; dir. allergy-immunology Northwest Med. Group, Fresno, 1995—. Contbr. articles to profl. jours. With USAR, 1994. Fellow Am. Acad. Pediatrics, Am. Acad. Allergy and Immunology, Am. Coll. Allergy and Immunology; mem. AMA, Am. Osteo. Assn., Am. Physicians Fellowship for Medicine in Israel, Calif. Soc. of Allergy and Clin. Immunology, Ctrl. Calif. Allergy Soc., Fresno-Madera Med. Soc., Calif. Med. Assn., Osteo. Physicians and Surgeons of Calif. Republican. Jewish. Office: Northwest Med Group Inc Allergy-Immunology Dept Ste 103 Fresno CA 93722

GLASSMAN, ARTHUR JOSEPH, software engineer; b. N.Y.C., Apr. 4, 1948; s. Max Samuel and Ruth Rae (Gold) G. SB in Physics, MIT, 1968; MS, Yale U., 1969; PhD, Columbia U., 1977. Sr. programmer Cubic, San Diego, 1978-79; engr. Linkabit, San Diego, 1979-80; sr. scientist Jaycor, San Diego, 1980-91; sr. software engr. SuperSet, San Diego, 1992-93, Document Scis. Corp., San Diego, 1994—. Mem. IEEE, Am. Phys. Soc., Am. Geophys. Union, Am. Stats. Assn., Math. Assn. Am.

GLATZER, ROBERT ANTHONY, marketing and sales executive; b. N.Y.C., May 19, 1932; s. Harold and Glenna (Beaber) G.; m. Paula Rosenfeld, Dec. 20, 1964; m. Mary Ann Murphy, Dec. 31, 1977; children: Gabriela, Jessica, Nicholas. BA, Haverford Coll., 1954. Br. store dept. mgr. Bloomingdale's, N.Y.C., 1954-56; media buyer Ben Sackheim Advt., N.Y.C., 1956-59; producer TV commls. Ogilvy, Benson & Mather Advt., N.Y.C., 1959-62; dir. broadcast prodn. Carl Ally Advt., N.Y.C., 1962-63; owner Chronicle Prodns., N.Y.C., 1963-73; dir. Folklife Festival, Smithsonian Inst., Washington, 1973, Expo 74 Corp., Spokane, Wash., 1973-74; pres. Robert Glatzer Assocs., Spokane, 1974—; ptnr. Delany/Glatzer Advt., Spokane, 1979-84; dir. sales/mktg. Pinnacle Prodns., Spokane; adj. faculty Ea. Wash. U., 1987—. Bd. dirs. Riverfront Arts Festival, 1977-78; bd. dirs. Comprehensive Health Planning Council, 1975-78, Spokane Quality of Life Council, 1976-82, Allied Arts of Spokane, 1976-80, Art Alliance Wash. State, 1977-81, Spokane chpt. ACLU, 1979-83, Wash. State Folklife Council, 1983—; commr. Spokane Arts, 1987—; mem. Spokane Community Devel. Bd., 1988—; mem. Shorelines Update Commn., 1988—; mem. Wash. State Small Bus. Improvement Coun., 1994—. Recipient CINE Golden Eagle award (2). Mem. Dirs. Guild Am. Democrat. Jewish. Author: The New Advertising, 1970; co-scenarist Scorpio and other TV prodns. Office: 8607 N Division St Spokane WA 99208

GLAZER, JACK HENRY, lawyer; b. Paterson, N.J., Jan. 14, 1928; s. Samuel and Martha (Merkin) G.; m. Zelda d'Angleterre, Jan. 14, 1979. BA, Duke U., 1950; JD, Georgetown U., 1956; postgrad. U. Frankfurt (W.Ger.), 1956-57; S.J.D. U. Calif.-Berkeley, 1977. Bar: D.C. 1957, Calif. 1968. Atty., GAO and NASA, 1958-60; mem. maritime div. UN Internat. Labour Office, Geneva, Switzerland, 1960; spl. legal adv. UN Internat. Telecommunication Union, Geneva, 1960-62; atty. NASA Washington, 1963-66; chief counsel NASA-Ames Research Center, Moffett Field, Calif., 1966-88; gov. Calif. Maritime Acad., 1975-78; asst. prof. Hastings Coll. Law, 1985-87; prof., assoc. dean bus. sch. San Francisco State U., 1988-92. Comdr. Calif. Naval Militia, ret. Capt. JAGC, USNR, ret. Mem. Calif. Bar Assn., D.C. Bar Assn., White's Inn (reader). Contbr. articles on internat. law to profl. jours. Home: 1110 Taylor St San Francisco CA 94108-1916 Office: White's Inn 37 White St San Francisco CA 94109-2609

GLAZER, REA HELENE See KIRK, REA HELENE

GLEASON, ALFRED M., telecommunications executive; b. 1930; married. Student, U. Oreg. With Pacific Power & Light Co. Inc., Portland, Oreg., from 1949, asst. to v.p., 1952-65, mgr. pub. accounts, 1965-68, v.p., 1968-76; pres. Pacific Telecom, Inc. (formerly Telephone Utilities, Inc.), Vancouver, Wash., 1973-82, chmn., from 1982, CEO, 1973-86, also bd. dirs.; pres. PacifiCorp, Portland, 1985-92, CEO, 1989-92, now vice chmn.; bd. dirs. Comdial Corp., Blount Inc., Tektronix, Legacy Health, Fred Meyer, Inc. Office: Pacificorp 700 NE Multnomah St Portland OR 97232-2131*

GLEASON, DOUGLAS RENWICK, marketing professional; b. Worcestor, Mass., Oct. 27, 1956; s. Sherman M. and Dolores E. (Murad) G. BA, Stanford U., 1978; MBA, UCLA, 1982. Asst. product mgr. Pepsi USA, Purchase, N.Y., 1982-83, assoc. product mgr., 1983-85; product mgr. Carnation Co., Los Angeles, 1985-87; dir. promotion Walt Disney Home Video, Burbank, Calif., 1987-90; dir. film licensing The Walt Disney Co., Burbank, 1990-91; dir. promotion Twentieth Century Fox, Beverly Hills, Calif., 1991—; v.p. publicity and promotion Twentieth Century Fox Internat., 1993—. Mem. Beta Gamma Sigma. Office: Twentieth Century Fox PO Box 900 Beverly Hills CA 90213-0900

GLEDHILL, BARTON LEVAN, veterinarian; b. Phila., Sept. 29, 1936; s. Albert and Kathryn Barton (LeVan) G.; m. Marianne Palmer, Dec. 19, 1959; children: Christopher, Rebecca. BS, Pa. State U., 1958; VMD, U. Pa., 1961; PhD, Royal Vet. Coll., Stockholm, 1966. Lic. veterinarian, Pa. Asst. prof. U. Pa., Phila., 1966-69; assoc. prof. U. Pa., 1969-72; group leader Lawrence Livermore (Calif.) Nat. Lab., 1973-75, sect. leader, 1975-80, dep. div. leader, 1980-82, div. leader, 1982-91, dep. assoc. dir., 1991-94; dep. dir. Ctr. for Healthcare Technologies, Livermore, 1994—; cons. and lectr. in field; Ortho lectr. McMaster U., Ont., 1984; Tap Pharms. lectr. Am. Fertil Soc., Washington, 1990; disting. vis. prof. U. Buenos Aires, 1991, 95; Associated Western U./U.S. Dept. Energy Disting. lectr., 1992. Contbr. articles to profl. jours.; patentee in field. Active Boy Scouts Am., 1978—. Recipient Disting. Alumni award Pa. State U., 1993. Mem. Am. Coll. Theriogeneologists (pres. 1977), Soc. for Analytical Cytology (pres. 1991-93), Am. Soc. Study Breeding Soundness (pres. 1982). Home: 21 Saratoga Ct Alamo CA 94507-2228 Office: Lawrence Livermore Nat Lab PO Box 5507 Livermore CA 94551-5507

GLEESON, JEREMY MICHAEL, physician; b. Napier, Hawkes Bay, N.Z., Nov. 20, 1953; came to U.S., 1984; s. Gerald Lynch and Helen Isobel (Benzeval) G.; m. Susan Jeryl Gladwell, Aug. 31, 1952; children: Catherine, Emily, Nicholas, Timothy. BSc, U. Auckland, N.Z., 1975, MB, ChB, 1978. Diplomate Am. Bd. Internal Medicine, Am. Bd. Endocrinology and Metabolism. Resident in medicine U. Auckland, 1979-84; chief resident in medicine U. Utah, Salt Lake City, 1984-85, fellow in endocrinology, 1985-88; assoc. investigator VA, Salt Lake City, 1988-89; endocrinologist Lovelace Med. Ctr., Albuquerque, 1989—, chmn. endocrinology, 1992—. Fellow Royal Australasian Coll. of Physicians; mem. Am. Coll. Physicians, Am. Diabetes Assn., Assn. Clin. Endocrinologists, Endocrine Soc. Office: 5400 Gibson Blvd SE Albuquerque NM 87108-4729

GLEISSNER, VICKIE SOMERS, marketing professional; b. Birmingham, Ala., Jan. 20, 1951; d. Homer Lee and Christine (Somers) Hudson; m. Frederick Bruce Gleissner, Sept. 2, 1983; 1 child, Dewar Lee. Student, U. Ala., Birmingham, 1974; BFA with honors, U. Ala., 1980. Lic. dental hygiene Ala., 1974. Artist, designer Vickie Somers Design, 1982—; mfrs. rep. Archtl. Products, Honolulu, 1992—; hospitality co-chair Constrn. Specifications Inst., Honolulu, 1992—. Scholastic scholar. Mem. Ala. Watercolor Soc., Jr. League Honolulu, Shoal Creek Club, Kappa Kappa Gamma. Republican. Episcopalian. Home: 642 Paopua Loop Kailua HI 96734-3534 Office: Archtl Products Hawaii 1164 Bishop St Ste 124 Honolulu HI 96813-2800

GLENDINNING, IAIN, airport terminal executive. Postgrad., Mass. Inst. Tech., 1974. With Pan Am., N.Y., 1974-84; pres. Aviation Mgmt., Newport Beach, Calif., 1984-87; exec. v.p. Aerotest, Inc., Santa Ana, Calif., 1986—. Office: Aerotest Inc 2062 N Bush St # 230 Santa Ana CA 92706-2884*

GLENN, CONSTANCE WHITE, art museum director, educator, consultant; b. Topeka, Oct. 4, 1933; d. Henry A. and Madeline (Stewart) White; m. Jack W. Glenn, June 19, 1955; children: Laurie Glenn Buckle, Caroline Glenn Galey, John Christopher. BFA, U. Kans., 1955; postgrad., U. Mo., 1964-69; MA, Calif. State U., 1974. Dir. Univ. Art Mus. & Mus. Studies program, from lectr. to prof. Calif. State U., Long Beach, 1973—; art cons. Archtl. Digest, L.A., 1980-89. Author: Jim Dine Drawings, 1984, Roy Lichtenstein: Landscape Sketches, 1986, Wayne Thiebaud: Private Drawings, 1988, Robert Motherwell: The Dedalus Sketches, 1988, James Rosenquist: Time Dust: The Complete Graphics 1962-92, 1993; contbg. editor: Antiques and Fine Arts, 1991-92. Vice chair Adv. Com. for Pub. Art, Long Beach, 1990-95; chair So. Calif. adv. bd. Archives Am. Art, L.A., 1980-90; mem. adv. bd. ART/LA, 1986-95, chair, 1992; mem. adv. bd. Decorative Arts Study Ctr., San Juan Capistrano, Calif., 1990—. Recipient Outstanding Contbn. to Profession award Calif. Mus. Photography, 1986. Mem. Am. Assn. Mus., Assn. Art Mus. Dirs., Coll. Art Assn., Art Table, Long Beach Pub. Corp. for the Arts (arts adminstr. of yr. 1989), Kappa Alpha Theta. Office: Univ Art Mus 1250 Bellflower Blvd Long Beach CA 90840-0004

GLENN, EDWARD PERRY, research scientist, botanist; b. Tucson, Ariz., Sept. 22, 1947; s. Edward P. and Jean (Pollack) G.; m. Sarah Glenn, Aug. 22, 1974; children: Charlotte, Edison. BA in Biology, U. Hawaii, 1969, MS in Botany, 1973, PhD in Botany, 1978. Rockefeller postdoctoral fellow Environ. Rsch. Lab. U. Ariz., Tucson, 1979-81, rsch. assoc., 1981-88, sr. rsch. scientist, 1989—; adj. prof. wildlife and fisheries, U. Ariz., Tucson, 1990—; keynote speaker numerous symposiums and confs. in field. Contbr. numerous articles to profl. jours. Office: Environmental Rsch Lab 2601 E Airport Dr Tucson AZ 85706-6905

GLENN, GUY CHARLES, pathologist; b. Parma, Ohio, May 13, 1930; s. Joseph Frank and Helen (Rupple) G.; m. Lucia Ann Howarth, June 13, 1953; children: Kathryn Holly, Carolyn Helen, Cynthia Marie. BS, Denison U., 1953; MD, U. Cin., 1957. Intern, Walter Reed Army Med. Center, Washington, 1957-58; resident in pathology Fitzsimons Army Med. Center, Denver, 1959-63; commd. 2d lt. U.S. Army, 1956, advanced through grades to col., 1977; demonstrator pathology Royal Army Med. Coll., London, 1970-72; chief dept. pathology Fitzsimons Army Med. Center, Denver, 1972-77; pres. med. staff St. Vincent Hosp., Billings, Mont.; past mem. governing bd. Mont. Health Systems Agy. Diplomate Am. Bd. Pathology, Am. Bd. Nuclear Medicine. Fellow Coll. Am. Pathologists (chmn. chemistry resources com., chmn. commn. sci. resources, mem. budget program and review com., council on quality assurance, chmn. practice guidelines com., bd. govs.), Am. Soc. Clin. Pathology, Med. Cons. to Armed Forces (chair legal and legis. com.), Midland Empire Health Assn. (past pres.), Rotary (bd. dirs. local chpt.). Contbr. to profl. jours. Home: 3225 Jack Burke Ln Billings MT 59106-1113

GLENN, JAMES D., JR., lawyer; b. Oakley, Idaho, July 1, 1934; s. Vernal D. and Vilate H. Glenn; student U. Utah, 1952-57, JD, 1960. Bar: Utah 1960, Calif. 1961, Idaho 1978. m. Alice Rexine, Dec. 14, 1956; children: Sheilagh Ann Glenn Thornock, Michelle Glenn Larson, James D. III, Deirdre, David R., Alison. Assoc. counsel Fed. Trade Commn., San Francisco, 1960-61; ptnr. Ferguson & Vohland, 1961-63, Ferguson & Glenn, 1963-65; pvt. practice, Oakland, Hayward and Fremont, Calif., 1965-77, Twin Falls, Idaho, 1987—; ptnr. Webb, Burton, Carlson, Pedersen & Paine, Twin Falls, Idaho, 1977-83; sr. ptnr. Glenn & Henrie, Twin Falls, 1983-87; counsel Norton Enterprises, Inc., Haney Seed Co. Bd. dirs. So. Alameda County (Calif.) Legal Svcs. Corp., 1969-73. Mem. Phi Kappa Phi. Republican. Mormon. Office: 127 2nd St W Twin Falls ID 83301-6019

GLEW, ANDREW FORSYTH, computer architect, inventor; b. Monteal, Que., Can., Sept. 10, 1961; came to U.S., 1985; s. Cyril Aubrey and Ruth Jean (Robinson) G. B.Eng., McGill U., 1985; MS, U. Ill., 1991. Programmer Systemes Videotex Formic, St. Laurent, Que., 1985, Gould, Urbana, Ill., 1985-88; programmer, performance analyst Motorola, Urbana, 1988-89; computer architect Intel, Hillsboro, Oreg., 1991—. Inventor numerous patents in field. Office: Intel Mailstop JF1-19 5200 NE Elam Young Pky Hillsboro OR 97124-6463

GLICK, MILTON DON, chemist, university administrator; b. Memphis, July 30, 1937; s. Lewis S. and Sylvia (Kleinman) G.; m. Peggy M., June 22, 1965; children: David, Sander. AB cum laude, Augustana Coll., 1959; PhD, U. Wis., 1965. Fellow, dept. chemistry Cornell U., Ithaca, N.Y., 1964-66; asst. prof. chemistry Wayne State U., Detroit, 1966-70, assoc. prof., 1970-74, prof., 1974-83, chmn. dept., 1978-83; dean arts and sci. U. Mo.-Columbia, 1983-88; provost Iowa State U., Ames, 1988-91, interim pres., 1990-91; sr. v.p., provost Ariz. State U., Tempe, 1991—. Contbr. articles in structural inorganic chemistry to profl. jours. Trustee EDUCOM. Office: Ariz State U Office of Provost 203 Adm Bldg Tempe AZ 85287

GLICK, REUVEN, economist; b. N.Y.C., July 19, 1951; m. Marci Gottlieb, Jan. 6, 1991. BA, U. Chgo., 1973; MA, Princeton U., 1975, PhD, 1979. Economist Fed. Res. Bank N.Y., N.Y.C., 1977-79; asst. prof. econs. and internat. bus. NYU Grad. Sch. Bus., N.Y.C., 1979-85; economist Fed. Res. Bank San Francisco, 1985-87, sr. economist, 1987-90, rsch. officer, 1990-92, asst. v.p., 1992-95; dir. Ctr. for Pacific Basin Monetary and Econ. Studies, 1992—, v.p., 1995—; vis. assoc. prof. econs. U. Calif., Berkeley, 1989; cons. World Bank, Washington, 1982-85. Contbr. articles to profl. jours. Mem. Am. Econ. Assn., Phi Beta Kappa.

GLICK, SAMUEL DAVID, entertainment/communications executive, shop owner; b. Chgo., Dec. 4, 1951; s. Eugene and Florence G.; m. N. Cheri Pavlov, Sept. 3, 1978; children: Bradley, Jory. BS in Radio and TV Comm., So. Ill. U., 1975. Producer pub. affairs programs WMAQ-TV, Chgo., 1974-76, mgr. on-air promotion, 1976-79; dir. creatives svcs. KGW-TV, Portland, Oreg., 1979-82, WNBC-TV, N.Y.C., 1982-84, KTLA-TV, L.A., 1984-85; ptnr. Davis*Glick Prodns., L.A., 1985—; mem. NBC Affiliates Promotion Adv. Com., N.Y.C., 1981-84. Inventor NBC affiliates automated sta. signature sys., 1984. Recipient Silver and Bronze awards N.Y. Internat. Film Festival. Mem. Acad. TV Arts and Scis. (N.Y. local Emmy award), Promotion and Mktg. Execs in the Electronic Media (Gold Medallion award), Hollywood Radio and TV Soc. (Internat. Broadcasting award). Office: Davis*Glick Prodns 2nd Floor 3280 Cahuenga Blvd W Fl 2 Los Angeles CA 90068-1378

GLICK, STANLEY BARTON, optometrist, photographer; b. N.Y.C., May 27, 1947; s. Samuel Saul and Ida Sonia (Merewitz) G. BA in Chemistry, George Washington U., 1970, MS in Analytical Chemistry, 1973; Masters, Armed Forces Inst. Pathology, 1972; OD, New Eng. Coll. Optometry, 1982. Cert. Dr. Optometry. Survey statistician com. Z AAUP, Washington, 1967-69; forensic pathologist Ga. Bur. Investigation, Atlanta, 1973-78; asst. Office of Gov., Atlanta; pvt. practice L.A., 1982—; ofcl. photographer Miss World Pagent, Boston, L.A., 1980—. Photographer (cover) Boston Herald Am., 1980. Pres. Claremont (Calif.) Jaycees, 1984, Merchant Assn., Fontana, Calif., 1983-84; active Fontana Jaycees, 1983-84, North Hills Jaycees, Granada Hills, Calif., 1987-91, Nat. Hist. Trust Preservation, Washington, 1989-91, World Affairs Coun., 1989-91, Northridge Hillel; election ofcl., insp. L.A. County, 1988-94; bd. dirs. Am. Jewish Com., 1987-91, Am.

Jewish Congress, 1987-91, optical divsn. United Jewish Fund, Beverly Hills, Calif.; asst. Office of Gov., Atlanta. Recipient Key to City, City of Miami Beach, 1961; scholar Fla. Sci. Study Found., 1961. Mem. Am. Optometric Assn., Am. Optometric Found., Calif. Optometric Assn. (del. congress 1989-91), San Fernando Valley Optometric Soc., Kiwanis, Calif. Yacht Club, Long Beach Single Sailors. Jewish.

GLIEGE, JOHN GERHARDT, lawyer; b. Chgo., Aug. 3, 1948; s. Gerhardt John Gliege and Jane Heidke; children: Gerhardt, Stephanie, Kristine. BA, Ariz. State U., 1969, MPA, 1970, JD, 1974. Bar: Ariz. 1974. Pvt. practice Scottsdale, Ariz., 1974-81, Flagstaff, Ariz., 1981-94, Sedona, Ariz., 1994—; prof. paralegal studies No. Ariz. U., Flagstaff, 1981-83, prof. urban planning and community devel. No., 1984—. Mem. Nat. Assn. of Bond Law. Home: PO Box 1388 Flagstaff AZ 86002-1388 Office: 2515 W Hwy Sedona AZ 86336

GLOCK, CHARLES YOUNG, sociologist; b. N.Y.C., Oct. 17, 1919; s. Charles and Philippine (Young) G.; m. Margaret Schleef, Sept. 12, 1950; children: Susan Young, James William. B.S., N.Y. U., 1940; M.B.A., Boston U., 1941; Ph.D., Columbia U., 1952. Research asst. Bur. Applied Social Research, Columbia U., 1946-51, dir., 1951-58, lectr., then prof. sociology, 1956-58; prof. sociology U. Calif. at Berkeley, 1958-79, prof. emeritus, 1979—, chmn., 1967-68, 69-71; dir. Survey Research Center, 1958-67; adj. prof. Grad. Theol. Union, 1971-79; Luther Weigle vis. lectr. Yale U., 1968. Co-author: Wayward Shepherds, The Anatomy of Racial Attitudes, Anti-Semitism in America, American Piety; sr. author: Adolescent Prejudice, To Comfort and To Challenge, Religion and Society in Tension, Christian Beliefs and Anti-Semitism, The Apathetic Majority; contbg. editor Rev. Religious Rsch. Sociological Analysis; editor: The New Religious Consciousness, Survey Research in the Social Sciences, Beyond the Classics, Religion in Sociological Perspective, Prejudice U.S.A., Unison-Newsletter of One Voice; contbr. numerous articles on social scis. Active parish edn. Luth. Ch. Am., 1970-72; mem. mgmt. com. Office Rsch. and Planning, 1973-80; bd. dirs. Pacific Luth. Theol. Sem., 1962-74, 80-86, Inst. Rsch. in Social Behavior, 1962-90, Interplayers, 1990-92; pres. Cornerhouse Fund, 1982-92; mem. adv. com. Office Rsch. and Evaluation Evang. Luth. Ch. Am., 1988—; mem. history com. Soc. Study of Religion, 1993-94, pres. One Voice, 1994—. Capt. USAAF, 1942-46. Decorated Bronze Star, Legion of Merit; recipient Roots of Freedom award Pacific bd. Anti-Defamation League, 1977; Berkeley citation U. Calif., Berkeley, 1979; Rockefeller fellow, 1941-42; fellow Center Advanced Study Behavioral Scis., 1957-58; fellow Soc. for Religion in Higher Edn., 1968-69. Fellow Soc. Sci. Study Religion (Western rep., pres. 1968-69); mem. Am. Assn. Pub. Opinion Research (v.p., pres. 1962-64, pres. Pacific chpt. 1959-60), Am. Sociol. Assn. (v.p. 1978-79), Religious Research Assn., Sociol. Research Assn. Home: 319 S 4th Ave Sandpoint ID 83864-1219

GLOOR, CHRISTOPHER BARTA, corporate professional; b. San Diego, May 6, 1949; s. Fred Gloor and Clarice Barta; m. Agathe Maria Gobertina Winter , Nov. 28, 1987. Student, U. Calif., San Diego, 1969-71. Ptnr. Middlearth, San Diego, 1969-72; pres. Middlearth Internat. Inc., San Diego, 1972—, Middlearth Internat. Inc. dba Corp. Svcs. Internat., San Diego, 1985—, Australia House, San Diego, 1988—; bd. dirs. Antak Proprietary Ltd., Queensland, Australia, 1983—; bd. dirs. Australia House, San Diego, Waldorf Sch. of San Diego, Jazz Unltd. Dance Co., San Diego, pres. 1994—. Mem. Inventors Assn. Australia, Australian-Am. C. of C. Republican. Office: Corp Svcs Internat 4009 S Hempstead Cir San Diego CA 92116-2013

GLOSS, LAWRENCE ROBERT, fundraising executive; b. Colorado Springs, Colo., Oct. 31, 1948; s. Kenneth Edwin and Clara U. (Heaker) G.; m. Betty Berg, June 4, 1977; children: Alexander Edwin, Carolyn Claire. BA, U. Denver, 1970. Dir. natl. congress on volunteerism and citizenship NCVA, Washington, 1975-76; dir. devel. Vis. Nurses Assn., Washington, 1976-77; devel. cons. Am. Lung Assn., Washington and N.Y.C., 1977-78; exec. dir. Colo. Conservation Fund, Denver, Colo., 1978-79, Rose Med. Ctr., enver, 1985-86; dir. devel. Rose Found., Denver, 1979-86; sr. campaign dir. J. Panas, Young and Ptnrs., San Francisco, 1986-88; pres. Gloss and Assocs., Denver, 1988—; adv. coun. Non-profit Mgmt.-Metro State Coll., Denver, 1994; cons. Native Am. Rights Fund, Boulder, Colo., Arts at the Sta., Denver, 1994. Guest spkr. Tech. Assistance Ctr., Denver, 1992-94; bd. dirs. Alzeimer's and Related Disorders Assn., Denver, 1985-86; bd. dirs. Woman's Sch. Network, Denver, 1984-85, Colo. PTA, Englewood, 1991-92. Mem. NSFRE (Colo. chpt. 1992-94, bd. dirs.), Nat. Assn. of Mus. Exhibitors, Colo. Planning Giving Roundtable, Nat. Com. on Planned Giving, Am. Prospect Rsch. Assn., Assn. of Healthcare Philanthropy (regional XII 1993-94). Lutheran. Home: 11126 E Stagecoach Dr Parker CO 80134-8424 Office: Gloss and Company 2755 S Locust St Ste 113 Denver CO 80222-7131

GLOSUP, LORENE See DEAN, DEAREST

GLOTH, ALEC ROBERT, retail grocery executive; b. Spokane, Wash., Mar. 26, 1927; s. Erich Carl and Ella L. (Felsch) G.; m. Catharine E. Seabloom, May 26, 1954; children: A. Stephen, Rebecca J. Parlet. Grad., Stanford exec. program Boise State U., 1975. With Albertson's, 1951—; v.p. mktg. Albertson's, Boise, Idaho, 1972-74, v.p. store planning, 1974-76, dist. mgr., 1976-77; v.p., div. mgr. Albertson's, Spokane, Wash., 1977-79; sr. v.p., regional mgr. Albertson's, Boise, 1979-81, sr. v.p. store planning, 1981—. Active Boy Scouts Am., Eagle Scout; bd. dirs. Discovery Ctr. Idaho. With U.S. Army, 1954-56. Mem. Am. Mgmt. Assn., Food Mktg. Inst. Republican. Methodist. Clubs: Exchange, Hillcrest Country, Spokane. Lodge: Elks. Home: 1193 Kingfisher Way Boise ID 83709-1237 Office: Albertson's Inc 250 E Parkcenter Blvd Boise ID 83706-3940

GLOVER, FRED WILLIAM, artificial intelligence and optimization research director, educator; b. Kansas City, Mo., Mar. 8, 1937; s. William Cane and Mary Ruth (Baxter) G.; m. Diane Tatham, June 4, 1988; 1 child, Lauren Glover; children from previous marriage: Dana Reynolds, Paul Glover. BBA, U. Mo., 1960; PhD, Carnegie-Mellon U., 1965. Asst. prof. U. Calif., Berkeley, 1965-66; assoc. prof. U. Tex., Austin, 1966-69; prof. U. Minn., Mpls., 1969-70; John King Prof. U. Colo., Boulder, 1970-87, US West Chair in System Sci., 1987—; rsch. dir. Artificial Intelligence Ctr., Boulder, 1984-90; invited disting. lectr. Swiss Fed. Inst. Tech., Lausanne, 1990—, IMAG Labs., U. Genoble, France, 1991; vis. Regents Chair in Engring, U. Tex., Austin, 1989; cons. U.S. Congress, 1984, Nat. Bur. Standards, 1986, also over 70 U.S. corps. and govt. agys., 1965—; lectr. NATO, France, Italy, Germany, Denmark, 1970, 78, 80, 82, 89, Inst. Decision Scis., 1984; bd. dirs. Mgmt. Systems, Boulder, Decision Analysis Inst., Boulder, 1974-82; chmn. bd. Analysis, Research & Computation, Austin, 1971-83; head, rsch. assoc. Global Optimization Space Constrn. Ctr., Boulder, 1988—; rsch. prin. U. Colo.-U.S. West Joint Rsch. Initiative, 1990—; prin. investigator Air Force Office Sci. Rsch, Office Naval Rsch., 1990—; invited rsch. scholar U. B.C., 1994. Author: Netform Decision Models, 1983 (DIS award 1984), Tabu Search I, 1989, Tabu Search II, 1990, Tabu Search (special vol.) 1993, Ghost Image Processes for Neural Networks, 1993, Linkages with Artificial Intelligence, 1990, Network Models in Optimization and Their Application in Practice, 1992, also others; contbr. over 200 articles on math. optimization and artificial intelligence to profl. jours. Participant Host Vis. Exchange, Nat. Acad. Scis., 1981; mem. grants com. Queen Elizabeth II fellowships, Australia and U.S., 1984; mem. U.S. nat. adv. bd. Univ. Rsch. Initiative on Combinatorial Optimization. Recipient Internat. Achievement award Inst. Mgmt. Scis., 1982, Energy Rsch. award Energy Rsch. Inst., 1983, Univ. Disting. Rsch. Lectr. award U. Colo., 1988, Rsch. Excellence prize Ops. Rsch. Soc., 1989, Nat. Best Theoretical/Empirical Rsch. Paper award Decision Scis. Inst., 1993, Computer Sci. Rsch. Excellence award Ops. Rsch. Soc. Am., 1994, Nat. Rsch. Excellence award Comp. Sci. Ops. Rsch. Soc., 1994; named first U.S. West Disting. fellow, 1987. Fellow AAAS, Am. Inst. Decision Scis (lectr. 1984, Outstanding Achievement award 1984), Am. Assn. Collegiate Schs. Bus., ICC Inst.; mem. Alpha Iota Delta. Office: U Colo Coll Bus PO Box 419 Boulder CO 80309-0419

GLOVSKY, MYRON MICHAEL, medical educator; b. Boston, Aug. 15, 1936; m. Carole Irene Parks; five children. BS magna cum laude, Tufts U., 1957, MD, 1962. Bd. cert. Nat. Bd. Med. Examiners, Am. Bd. Allergy & Immunology, Am. Bd. Diagnostic Lab. Immunology. Intern Balt. (Md.) City Hosp., 1962-63; resident New Eng. Med. Ctr., Boston, 1965-66; spl. NIH fellow allergy and immunology Walter Reed Army Inst. Rsch., Washington, 1966-68; fellow hematology and immunology U. Calif., San Francisco, 1968-69; staff physician dept. internal medicine So. Calif. Permanente Med. Group, L.A., 1969-72, dir. allergy & immunology lab., 1970-84, chief dept. allergy and clin. immunology, co-dir. residency program in allergy & clin. immunology, 1974-84, dir. pheresis unit, 1978-80; dir. L.A. County Gen. Hosp./U. So. Calif. Asthma Clinic; prof. medicine, head allergy and immunology labs. pulmonary divsn., head allergy and clin. immunology divsn. pulmonary medicine. U. So. Calif., Sch. Medicine, 1984-89, prof. pathology, 1986-89; clin. prof. medicine, clin. prof. pathology U. So. Calif., 1989—; dir. asthma and allergy referral ctr. Huntington Meml. Hosp., Pasadena, 1989—; head fellowship and career devel. program Nat. Heart Inst., NIH, Bethesda, Md., 1963-65, fellowship bd. mem., 1964-65; vis. assoc. in chemistry Calif. Inst. Tech., Pasadena, 1977—; acad. assoc. complement and allergy Nichols Inst., San Juan Capistrano, Calif., 1980—, med. dir. immunology, 1980-89; clin. prof. medicine U. Calif., L.A., 1983-84; vis. prof. clin. scholars program Eli Lilly & Co., Indpls., 1988; mem. steering com. Aspen Allergy Conf., 1988—; cons. in field. With USPHS, 1963-65. Fellow Am. Acad. Allergy; mem. AAAS, Am. Assn. Immunologists, Am. Thoracic Soc., Am. Fedn. for Clin. Rsch., Am. Coll. Allergy, Reticuloendothelial Soc., L.A. Soc. Allergy and Clin. Immunology (pres. 1979-80), Collegium Internat. Allergolicum. Home: 1961 Oak St South Pasadena CA 91030-4957 Office: Huntington Meml Hosp Asthma & Allergy Ctr 39 Congress St Pasadena CA 91105-3024

GLOWIENKA, EMERINE FRANCES, philosophy educator; b. Milw., Mar. 9, 1920; d. Clement Joseph and Sophia Maria (Dettlaff) G. PhD in Sociology, St. Louis U., 1956; PhD in Philosophy, Marquette U., 1973. Prof. philosophy and sociology San Francisco Coll. for Women, 1962-70; prof. philosophy U. San Diego, 1972-74; prof. sociology and philosophy U. N.Mex., Gallup, 1974-88, prof. emeritus, 1988—, prof. philosophy and homiletics Diocesan Sem., Gallup, N.Mex., 1974—. Contbr. articles to profl. jours. Speaker in field. Mem. Am. Cath. Philos. Assn., Am. Philos. Assn. Democrat. Roman Catholic. Home: 110 E Green Ave Gallup NM 87301-6236 Office: U NMex Gallup Br Coll 200 College Rd Gallup NM 87301-5603

GLUCKMAN, DALE CAROLYN, art museum curator; b. Detroit, Mar. 25, 1944; d. Sam and Gertrude (Wechsler) Schwartz; m. Jonathan Samuel Gluckman, Dec. 4, 1966. BA cum laude, UCLA, 1967, MA, 1986. Owner Double Happiness, L.A., 1971-76; cons. Fowler Mus. Cultural History, UCLA, 1977-78; lectr. UCLA, 1977, 87-88; advisor Am. Friends Svc. Com. Women-in-Africa Program, Bamako, Mali, 1979-81; rschr., cataloguer L.A. County Mus. Art, 1982-84, asst. curator, 1984-88, assoc. curator, 1988—; mem. adv. bd. dept. home econs., fashion design and merchandising program Calif. State U., Northridge, 1986-88; juror Calif. Fiber Artists, San Diego, 1993-94. Co-author: When Art Became Fashion: Kosode In Edo-Period Japan, 1991 (Millia Davenport award 1993), Inquest of Themes and Skills - Asian Textiles, 1989; co-curator: (exhbn.) When Art Became Fashion: Kosode in Edo-Period Japan, 1992 (Am. Assn. Museums curator's com. award 1993). Founding bd. mem. L.A.-Jakarta Sister City, L.A., 1990—. Implementation grantee Nat. Endowment Arts, Washington, 1989, profl. exch. grantee Asian Cultural Coun., N.Y., 1992, Curatorial Rsch. grantee Andrew W. Mellon Found., 1992. Mem. Costume Soc. Am. (regional bd. 1989-92), Textile Soc. Am. (founding bd. mem., membership sec. 1993—), Centre Internat D'Etude des Textiles Anciens, Assn. Asian Studies, Coll. Art Assn., Am. Assn. Museums (internat. com. on museums 1985—). Office: LA County Mus Art 5905 Wilshire Blvd Los Angeles CA 90036-4523

GLUECK, MARY A., psychiatric and mental health nurse, administrator; b. Bridgetown, Barbados; came to U.S., 1952; d. Hubert and Christina Cumming; m. Stephen G. Glueck (dec.). Grad. sch. nursing, St. Joseph's Mercy Hosp., Georgetown, Guyana. RN, Calif. Clin. svcs. mgr. med.-surg., geropsychiat. rehab. Crystal Springs Rehab. div. San Mateo County Gen. Hosp., San Mateo, Calif. Mem. Mid. Mgrs. Assn., Am. Psychiat. Nurses Assn. Home: 4505 Sandra Ct Union City CA 94587-4853

GLYNN, JAMES A., sociology educator, author; b. Bklyn., Sept. 10, 1941; s. James A. and Muriel M. (Lewis) G.; m. Marie J. Gates, Dec. 17, 1966 (div. Apr. 27, 1995); 1 child, David S. AA, Foothill Coll., 1961; BA in Sociology, San Jose (Calif.) State U., 1964, MA in Sociology, 1966. Instr. in sociology Bakersfield (Calif.) Coll., 1966—, prof. sociology, 1972—; adj. prof. Fresno (Calif.) State U., 1971-72, Chapman Coll., Orange, Calif., 1972, Calif. State U., Bakersfield, 1989—; del. acad. senate Calif. C.C., Sacramento, 1980-89; councilmember Faculty Assn. Calif. C.Cs., 1981—. Author: Studying Sociology, 1979, Writing Across the Curriculum Using Sociological Concepts, 1983, Hands On: User's Manual for Data Processing, 1986, (with Elbert W. Stewart) Introduction to Sociology, 1972, 4th edit., 1985, (with Crystal Dea Moore) Guide to Social Psychology, 1992, Understanding Racial and Ethnic Groups, 1992, Guide to Human Services, 1994, Focus on Sociology, 1994. Recipient Innovator Yr. award League Innovations C.C., 1989, Innovator Yr. award Kern C.C. Dist., 1992. Mem. Am. Sociol. Assn., Calif. Sociol. Assn. (founder, treas. 1990-92, editor newsletter 1991-92, pres., 1992-93, exec. dir. 1993—), Pacific Sociol. Assn., Population Reference Bur., World Watch Inst. Democrat. Home: 4512 Panorama Dr Bakersfield CA 93306-1354 Office: Bakersfield Coll 1801 Panorama Dr Bakersfield CA 93305-1219

GNEHM, MAX WILLI, diversified corporate excutive; b. Switzerland, July 15, 1943; s. Max Hans and Frieda G.; m. Regula B. Hunziker, Dec. 24, 1964; children: Alexandra Barbara, William Anthony. MBA, Swiss Sch. Bus., 1963; postgrad. Swiss Inst. Mktg. and Fgn. Trade Research. Asst. mgr. Maxwell Sci. Internat. Book Co., 1964-66; mgr. book and periodical div. Internat. Univ. Booksellers, N.Y.C., 1966-69; dir. Internat. div. Richard Abel Co., 1969-74; v.p. mktg. Blackwell of N.Am., Inc., Beaverton, Oreg., 1974-76, pres., 1976-79, also bd. dirs.; pres., bd. dirs. Transpacific Holding Group Ltd., Malcolm Smith, Inc, Concorde Pacific Exploration, Inc., Interpacific Printing, Inc., Hong Kong Fin. Group Ltd., Pacific Mining, Inc., 1987—; pres., chmn. bd. Swiss-Am. Investment Group, Inc., 1979—; bd. dirs. Macedon Resources Ltd., Lore Corp; mng. dir. JT Racing, 1989-90; pres, chief exec. officer Extreme Sports, Inc. 1991-92; bd. dirs. Captive Air Internat.; dir. sales, mktg. KIK Tire, Inc., 1992—; pres., chief exec. officer Softouch Mktg. Group, 1992—; chmn. bd. dirs. Danube Container a.s., Slovakia. Author: New Reference Tools for Librarians, 1965. Home: 3638 Carlsbad Blvd Carlsbad CA 92008

GO, VAY LIANG WONG, physician, medical educator, editor; b. Ozamis, The Philippines, Aug. 29, 1938; came to U.S., 1963; s. Bee and Shi G.; m. Frisca Yan-Go, Oct. 15, 1963; children: Frances, Lisa, William. AA, U. Santo Tomas, Manila, The Philippines, 1958, MD, 1963. Resident in internal medicine Mayo Clin., Rochester, Minn., 1965-66, resident in gastroenterology, 1967-69; rsch. assoc. Banting & Best Inst. U. Toronto, Can., 1969-71; asst. prof. medicine Mayo Med. Sch., Rochester, 1972-75, assoc. prof. medicine, 1975-78, prof. medicine, 1978-88; dir. divsn. digestive diseases and nutrition NIH, Bethesda, Md., 1985-88; prof., exec. chmn. dept. medicine. Sch. Medicine UCLA/NIH, 1988-92, dir. nutrition edn., assoc. dir. clin. nutrition rsch. unit, 1993—; mem. adv. com. gastrointestinal drugs FDA, 1980-83, 1990-94; chmn. nat. pancreatic cancer program Nat. Cancer Inst. Organ Systems Coord. Ctr., 1984-85; chair steering com. Internat. Symposium of Gastroenterology Hormones, 1988-90; mem. adv. com. Internat. Conf. on Brain-Gut Peptides, Beijing, 1988; chmn. Young Clinician program 10th World Congress of Gastroenterology, 1991-94; co-chair organizing com. Interanat. Symposium of Cholecystokinin, Cape Cod, Mass, 1993; mem. internat. adv. com. Internat. Conf. on Gastrointestinal Hormones and Gastrointestinal Motility, Beijing, 1993, mem. Nat. Adv. Comm. 10th Symposium of Gastrointestinal Hormones, 1994. Editor-in-chief (peer reviewed jour.) Pancreas, 1985—; co-editor (textbook) The Excorine Pancreas: Biology, Pathobiology, and Diseases, 1985, Pancreas, 2d rev. edit. 1993; assoc. editor Digestive Diseases and Sciences, 1977-82; mem. editl. bd. Regulatory Peptides, 1980-92, Digestive Diseases and Sciences, 1982-90, Gastroenterology International, 1988-90, Jour. Gastroenterology, 1989—, contbr. 290 articles and 465 abstracts to profl. jours., 100 chpts. to books. Recipient Donald C. Balfour Rsch. award Mayo Found., 1969, Sr. Exec. Svc. award HHS, 1987, Alimurong Lectr. award U. Santo Tomas Alumni Assn., 1988, Apolinaro Mabini award Assn. Philippine Physicians in Am., 1989, Disting. Lectureship, Japan Pancreas Soc., 1991 Allen Meml. Lectureship, SUNY Health Scis. Ctr, 1991, Commemorative Lectureship, 5th Internat. Symposium of Vasoactive Intestinal Polypeptides, 1991. Fellow ACP (mem. gov.'s adv. com. so. Calif. chpt. 1990-92); mem. AAAS, Am. Coll. Physician Execs., Am. Pancreatic Assn. (pres. 1978-79, 88-89, sec., treas. 1980-85), Am. Assn. Cancer Rsch., Am. Assn. Clin. Rsch., Am. Assn. Clin. Investigation, Am. Gastroenterological Assn. (cancer coun. 1975-78, rsch. com. 1977-80, 83-86), Am. Motility Soc., Am. Soc. Clin. Nutrition, Endocrine Soc., Assn. Profs. Medicine, Internat. Assn. Pancreatology, We. Soc. Physicians, Mayo Alumni Assn., Sigma Xi (pres. UCLA chpt. 1990). Roman Catholic. Office: UCLA Brain Rsch Inst 900 Veteran Ave Los Angeles CA 90095-1761

GOATES, DELBERT TOLTON, child psychiatrist; b. Logan, Utah, Apr. 14, 1932; s. Wallace Albert and Roma (Tolton) G.; m. Claudia Tidwell, Sept. 15, 1960 (div. Apr. 1994); children: Jeanette, Byron, Rebecca Lynn, Alan, Paul, Jonathan Phillip, Kendra, Michelle, George Milton; m. Julie Anderson Headley, Dec. 29, 1994. BS, U. Utah, 1953, MD, 1962; postgrad., U. Nebr., 1965, 67. Intern Rochester (N.Y.) Gen. Hosp., 1962-63; resident Nebr. Psychiat. Inst., Omaha, 1963-67; pvt. practice medicine specializing in child psychiatry Omaha, 1963-67, Albuquerque, 1967-71, Salt Lake City, 1971—; dir. psychiatry Riverdell Psychiat. Ctr., 1986-92, staff psychiatrist, 1992—; asst. prof. child psychiatry U. N.Mex., 1967-71, dir. children's svcs., 1967-71, asst. prof. pediatrics, 1969-71; clin. dir. Children's Psychiat. Ctr., Primary Children's Med. Ctr., Salt Lake City, 1971-77; med. dir. Life Line, 1990-93, Brightway Adolescent Psychiat. Hosp., 1992—; pres. Magic Mini Maker, Inc., Salt Lake City, 1972-78; chmn. bd. Intermountain Polytex, Inc. Bishop Ch. Jesus Christ Latter-day Sts., 1968-71; bd. dirs. Utah Cancer Soc., Great Salt Lake Mental Health. Served with MC, AUS, 1953-55. Mem. AMA, Orthopsychiat. Assn. Am., Utah Psychiat. Assn., Intermountain Acad. Child Psychiatry (pres. 1974-76), Pi Kappa Alpha, Phi Kappa Phi. Home: 4187 Abinadi Rd Salt Lake City UT 84124-4001 Office: 404 E 45th S # B-22 Murray UT 84107-2764

GOBALET, JEANNE GALLATIN, demographer; b. San Francisco, June 18, 1944; d. Kenneth Clyde and Eloise Carmelita (Gallatin) G.; m. Garth Lawrence Norton, Jan. 21, 1983; 1 child, Robert Gobalet Norton. AB in Sociology/History with distinction, Stanford U., 1966, MA in Edn., 1967, MA in Sociology, 1976, PhD in Sociology, 1982. Instr. social sci. San Jose (Calif.)/Evergreen C.C. Dist., 1967—; prin. Lapkoff & Gobalet Demographic Rsch. Inc., Saratoga, Calif., 1992—; geographic info. systems cons., 1990—, demography cons., 1989—. Contbr. articles to profl. jours. Mem. accreditation team Accrediting Commn. for Cmty. and Jr. Colls., 1993—. Mem. Population Assn. Am., Am. Sociol. Assn., Soc. for Applied Sociology, Toastmasters Internat., Phi Beta Kappa.

GOBAR, ALFRED JULIAN, economic consultant, educator; b. Lucerne Valley, Calif., July 12, 1932; s. Julian Smith and Hilda (Millbank) G.; B.A. in Econs., Whittier Coll., 1953, M.A. in History, 1955; postgrad. Claremont Grad. Sch., 1953-54; Ph.D. in Econs., U. So. Calif., 1963; m. Sally Ann Randall, June 17, 1957; children—Wendy Lee, Curtis Julian, Joseph Julian. Asst. pres. Microdot Inc., Pasadena, 1953-57; regional sales mgr. Sutorbilt Corp., L.A., 1957-59; market research assoc. Beckman Instrument Inc., Fullerton, 1959-64; sr. marketing cons. Western Mgmt. Consultants Inc., Phoenix, L.A., 1964-66; ptnr., prin., chmn. bd. Darley/Gobar Assocs., Inc., 1966-73; pres., chmn. bd. Alfred Gobar Assocs., Inc., Placentia, Calif., 1973—; asst. prof. finance U. So. Calif., L.A., 1963-64; assoc. prof. bus. Calif. State U., L.A., 1963-68, 70-79, assoc. prof. Calif. State U.-Fullerton, 1968-69; mktg., fin. adviser 1957—; bd. dirs. Quaker City Bancorp, Inc., So. Calif. Housing Devel.; pub. speaker seminars and convs. Contbr. articles to profl. publs. Trustee Whittier Coll., 1992—. Home: 1100 W Valencia Mesa Dr Fullerton CA 92633-2219 Office: 721 W Kimberly Ave Placentia CA 92670-6343

GOBETTI, MARIA CECILIA, acting coach, director, producer; b. Balt.; d. John Peter and Maria (Bambi) G.; m. Thomas A. Ormeny. BA, UCLA, 1962, MA, 1972. Moderator, creator WCBM Radio Talk Show, Balt., 1956—; actress N.Y. and L.A., 1962—; free-lance dir. L.A. theaters, 1972—; assoc. prof. acting UCLA, 1971-72; dir. devel. The Brillsteen Co., L.A., 1984-85; head coach, dir. The New Mickey Mouse Club, Orlando, 1990-91; pres., dir./head coach The Gobetti/Ormeny Acting Studio, Burbank, Calif., 1972—; artistic dir. The Victory and Little Victory Theaters, Burbank, 1979—. Director numerous plays, 1972—; producer more than 40 profl. plays, 1979—. Mem. Dirs. Guild Am., Actors Equity Assn., SAG, AFTRA, Women in Film, Women in Theatre, ACLU, Amnesty Internat., Save the Children. Democrat. Office: The Victory Theatre 3326 W Victory Blvd Burbank CA 91505-1542

GOBLE, ELISE JOAN H., pediatric ophthalmologist; b. Winnipeg, Man., Can., Jan. 23, 1932; d. Michael Samuel and Sarah (Corbin) Hollenberg; m. John Lewis Goble, Oct. 4, 1956; children: John Robert, Michael William. Assoc. in Music, U. Man., 1949, MD, 1956. Resident Columbia Presbyn. Eye Inst., N.Y.C., 1956-59; pvt. practice pediatric ophthalmology San Mateo, Calif., 1959—. Mem. San Mateo Sch. Health Com.; mem. Coordinating Coun. Developmental Disabilities, San Mateo; founder San Mateo chpt. Nat. Assn. Autistic Citizens. Fellow ACS, Am. Bd. Ophthalmology, Am. Bd. Pediatrics; mem. Am. Assn. Pediatric Ophthalmology & Strabismus (charter mem.), San Mateo County Med. Soc., Calif. Med. Assn. Home: 2007 New Brunswick Dr San Mateo CA 94402-4012 Office: 100 S Ellsworth Ave Ste 507 San Mateo CA 94401-3929

GOBLE, PAUL JOHN, software engineer, technical communicator; b. Rapid City, S.D., May 1, 1964; s. Benjamin Leon and Marian Grace (Zeigler) G.; m. Rogene Mae Foster, May 9, 1992. BS in Physics magna cum laude, U. Denver, 1986; MS in Computer Sci., Colo. State U., 1989. Tech. writer Mgmt. Assistance Corp. Am., Ft. Collins, Colo., 1987; systems programmer Colo. State U., Ft. Collins, 1987-89; learning products developer Hewlett-Packard Co., Colorado Springs, Colo., 1989—. Author software manuals. Dir. libr. Rocky Mountain Chamber Orch., Lakewood, Colo., 1980-86; rsch. vol. Blemar Mus., Lakewood, 1982; state del. Dems., Denver, 1984, 88; violinist Pikes Peak Civic Orch., Colordo Springs, 1990-91; bd. dirs. Holland Park Comty. Assn. Mem. IEEE, Soc. Tech. Comm., Assn. Computing Machinery, Toastmasters (sec.-tras 1991-92, pres. 1993-94, v.p. 1994-95), Phi Beta Kappa. Republican. Presbyterian. Office: Hewlett Packard Co 1900 Garden of Gods Rd Colorado Springs CO 80901

GOBLE, THOMAS LEE, clergyman; b. Anderson, Ind., July 5, 1935; s. Carl Wilbur and Agnes Irene (McVey) G.; m. Esther Charlene Callaway, June 12, 1956; children: Jeffreay Mark, Jeanette Marcelle Goble Pittman. BA, Pasadena Coll., 1956; BD, Nazarene Theol. Sem., 1959; DMin, Calif. Grad. Sch. Theology, 1972. Ordained to ministry Ch. of Nazarene, 1960, deacon, 1960. Pastor various congregations Ch. of Nazarene, 1959-87; supt. Anaheim dist. Ch. of Nazarene, Orange, Calif., 1987—; prof., Point Loma Nazarene Coll., Nazarene Bible Coll.; chmn. bd. dirs., Asian Nazarene Bible Coll., Long Beach, Calif., 1987—. Trustee, Idyllwild (Calif.) Christian Camp, 1987—, Point Loma Nazarene Coll., San Diego, 1987—. Mem. Point Loma Coll. Alumni Assn., Rotary. Office: Anaheim Dist Ch Nazarene 524 E Chapman Ave Orange CA 92666-1603

GODAGER, JANE ANN, social worker; b. Blue River, Wis., Nov. 29, 1943; d. Roy and Elmyra Marie (Hood) G. BA, U. Wis., 1965; MSW, Fla. State U., 1969. Lic. clin. social worker. Social worker III State of Wis. Dept Corrections, Wales, 1965-71; supervising psychiat. social worker I State of Calif., San Bernardino, 1972-75, La Mesa, 1975-77; psychiat. social worker State of Calif., San Bernardino, 1978-85; supr. mental health services Riverside (Calif.) County Dept. Mental Health, 1985-86; mental health counselor Superior Ct. San Bernardino County, 1986—; mem. adv. bd. Grad. Sch. Social Work Calif. State U., San Bernardino, Mental Health Assn. Mem. Nat. Assn. Social Workers, Acad. Cert. Social Workers (diplomate), Kappa Kappa Gamma Alumnae Assn. Office: Office Mental Health Counselor 700 E Gilbert St Bldg 1 San Bernardino CA 92404-5413

GODDARD, MARSHALL LEWIS, JR., fire battalion chief; b. Louisville, June 29, 1942; s. Marshall Lewis and Mildred J. (Schaefer) G.; m. Mary Margaret Smedley, Aug. 7, 1964; children: Richard Brian, Michael Lewis. Cert. of confidence Fire Sci., Mt. San Antii Coll., 1970; AA, Santa

Ana (Calif.) City Coll., 1992. Cert. chief officer, Calif. tng. chief, Calif., hazardous materials technician, Calif. Firefighter Placentia (Calif.) Fire Dept., 1965-66, engr., 1966-67, capt., 1967-70, tng. officer, 1970-72, fire marshal, 1972-74; tng. officer Santa Barbara County (Calif.) Fire Dept., 1974-75; tng. chief Santa Barbara (Calif.) Fire Dept., 1975-80, suppression chief, 1980—; pres. Orange County Tng. Officers, Orange, Calif., 1972, Tri-Counties Tng. Officers, Santa Barbara, Calif., 1975, So. Calif. Tng. Officers, 1977-78; bd. dirs. So. Calif. Foresters and Fire Wardens, 1984-86; tchr. fire sci. Santa Barbara City Coll., 1974-78, Allan Hancock Coll., Santa Maria, 1978—. Sec., treas. Jaycees City of Placentia, 1970-74; bd. dirs., v.p. Optimists Club, Santa Ynez, 1991-94. With U.S. Army 1960-63. Mem. Santa Barbara County Fire Chief Officers Assn. (pres.), Calif. Fire Chiefs Assn., Tri-Counties Fire Chiefs Assn. Republican. Methodist. Home: 182 1st St Solvang CA 93463-2809 Office: Santa Barbara County Fire Dept 4410 Cathedral Oaks Rd Santa Barbara CA 93110

GODFREY, DOUGLAS, tribologist, consultant; b. Mograth, Alberta, Can., July 12, 1918; came to U.S., 1937; s. Melvin and Eva (Jones) G.; m. Yolanda Babinsky, Jan. 1, 1947; children: Yolanda Plaza, Marsha Dees. BSChemE, U. Utah, 1942. Rsch. scientist NACA (now NASA), Cleve., 1944-55; sr. rsch. engr. Chevron Rsch. Co., Richmond, Calif., 1955-83; cons. Wear Analysis, San Rafael, Calif., 1983—; adj. prof. San Francisco State U., 1983-94. Contbr. articles to profl. jours. (3 awards). Pvt. USAF, 1942-43. Fellow Soc. Tribologists and Lubrication Engrs. (life, bd. dirs. 1956-58); mem. ASME. Home and Office: 144 Center St San Rafael CA 94901-1718

GODFREY, RICHARD GEORGE, real estate appraiser; b. Sharon, Pa., Dec. 18, 1927; s. Fay Morris and Elisabeth Marguerite (Stefanak) G.; m. Golda Fay Goss, Oct. 28, 1951; children: Deborah Jayne, Gayle Rogers, Bryan Edward. BA, Ripon Coll., 1949. V.p. 1st Thrift & Loan Assn., Albuquerque, 1959-61; pres. Richard G. Godfrey & Assocs., Inc., Albuquerque, 1961-93, owner, 1993—. Mem. Appraisal Inst. (v.p. 1981-82), Am. Right of Way Assn., Counselors of Real Estate. Baptist. Home: 1700 Columbia Dr SE Albuquerque NM 87106-3311 Office: 523 Louisiana Blvd SE Albuquerque NM 87108-3842

GODO, EINAR, computer engineer; b. Aalesund, Möre, Norway, May 31, 1926; came to U.S. 1953; s. Lars and Oline (Blindheim) G.; m. Betty Jane Graba, 1955; children: Kjell Einar, Greta Anne, Erik Lars. BS in Aero. Engring., U. Wash., 1956, BSEE, 1958, MS, 1964. Electronic designer Boeing Aerospace, Seattle, 1959-82; prime investigator Computer Devel., Bellevue, Wash., 1982—.

GODSEY, C. WAYNE, broadcasting executive; b. Lynchburg, Va., Aug. 5, 1946; s. Carl Dodge and Frances Anna (Keesee) G.; m. Anne Marie Ruzicka, Oct., 1979; children: Rebecca Susan, Patricia Anne, Thomas Lawrence. BA in English, Lynchburg Coll., 1968. Reporter Sta. WSOC-TV, Charlotte, N.C., 1969-71, news dir., 1971-74; reporter, producer Newsweek Broadcasting, N.Y.C., 1974-77; news dir. Stas. WTMJ-TV and Radio, Milw., 1977-82; v.p., gen. mgr. Sta. WTMJ-TV, Milw., 1982-84, Sta. WISN-TV, Milw., 1984-87, Sta. KOAT-TV, Albuquerque, 1987-93; exec. v.p. Pulitzer Broadcasting Co., St. Louis, 1993—; past state chmn. 1990 Red Ribbon Campaign; past chmn. Albuquerque Bus. Edn. Co., 1988-90; Eucharistic Min. Christ Prince of Peace. Bd. dirs. Easter Seal Soc., Milw., 1984-87, Better Bus. Bur., Milw., 1984-87, Big Bros. and Big Sisters, Milw., 1985-87, Centurions of St. Joseph Hosp., Milw., 1985-87, Children's Hosp. Wis., 1987-88, Great S.W. Coun. Boy Scouts Am., 1991-93; mem. N.Mex. Gov.'s Bus. Adv. Coun., 1988-90; mem. Albuquerque Bus. Edn. Compact, 1990; mem. N.Mex. Amigos; mem. N.Mex. Open Records Task Force, 1990; hon. comdr. 551st Flight Tng. Squadron KAFB, 1991-92. Mem. Nat. Assn. Broadcasters (task force on drug and alcohol abuse 1984-86), Wis. Broadcasters Assn. (chmn. legis. liaison com.), Albuquerque Econ. Forum, N.Mex. Broadcasters Assn. (bd. dirs. 1988-91), Albuquerque C. of C. (bd. dirs., Superior Svc. award 1991), Arbitron Adv. Coun., Soc. Profl. Journalists, U. N.Mex. Lobo Club (bd. dirs.), Whitmoor Country Club. Republican. Roman Catholic. Home: 938 Arlington Oaks Ter Twn And Cntry MO 63017-5902 Office: Pulitzer Broadcasting Co 101 S Hanley Rd Ste 1250 Saint Louis MO 63105-3406

GODWIN, MARY JO, editor, librarian consultant; b. Tarboro, N.C., Jan. 31, 1949; d. Herman Esthol and Mamie Winifred (Felton) Pittman; m. Charles Benjamin Godwin, May 2, 1970. BA, N.C. Wesleyan Coll., 1971; MLS, East Carolina U., 1973. Cert. libr., N.C. From libr. asst. to asst. dir. Edgecombe County Meml. Library, Tarboro, 1970-76, dir., 1977-85; asst. editor Wilson Library Bull., Bronx, N.Y., 1985-89, editor, 1989-92; dir. govt. sales The Oryx Press, Phoenix, 1993—95; dir. mktg. svc. The Oryx Press, Phoeniz, 1995—; mem. White House Conf. on Librs. and Info. Svcs. Task Force; bd. dirs. Libr. Pub. Rels. Coun., 1992-95. Bd. dirs. Friends of Calvert County Pub. Libr., 1994. Recipient Robert Downs award for intellectual freedom U. Ill. Grad. Sch. of Libr. Sci., 1992. Mem. ALA (3M/Jr. Mem. Roundtable Profl. Devel. award 1981), N.C. Libr. Assn. (sec. 1981-83), Info. Futures Inst., Ind. Librs. Exchange Roundtable (v.p., pres. elect 1994, pres. 1995—). Democrat. Episcopalian. Office: 7510 N Viadel Paraiso Scottsdale AZ 85258

GOEDDE, ALAN GEORGE, financial company executive; b. Irvington, N.J., Feb. 27, 1948; s. Albert and Herta (Konrad) G.; m. Julie S. Withers, June 30, 1981. BS in Engring., Duke U., 1970, PhD in Econs., 1978. Economist U.S. Treasury, Washington, 1976-79, Export-Import Bank, Washington, 1979-81; mgr. Arthur Andersen & Co., Chgo., 1981-84; v.p. bus. planning 1st Nat. Bank Chgo., 1984-86; dir. strategic planning The NutraSweet Co., Chgo., 1986-87; pres., CEO Mentor Internat., Northbrook, Ill., 1987-88; cons. Coopers & Lybrand, Chgo., 1988-90, Freeman & Mills, L.A., 1990-94, Putnam, Hayes and Bartlett, L.A., 1994—. Office: Putnam Hayes Bartlett Inc 520 S Grand Ave Los Angeles CA 90071-2600

GOEI, BERNARD THWAN-POO (BERT GOEI), architectural and engineering firm executive; b. Semarang, Indonesia, Jan. 27, 1938; came to U.S., 1969; naturalized, 1976; s. Ignatius Ing-Khien Goei and Nicolette Giok-Nio Tjioe; m. Sioe-Tien Liem, May 26, 1966; children: Kimberley Hendrika, Gregory Fitzgerald. BA in Fine Arts, Bandung Inst. Tech. State U. Indonesia, 1961, MA in Archtl. Space Planning, 1964; postgrad., U. Heidelberg, Germany, 1967-68. Co-owner, chief designer Pondok Mungil Interiors Inc., Bandung, 1962-64; dept. mgr., fin. advisor Gumarna Architects, Engrs. and Planners, Inc., Bandung, Jakarta, Indonesia, 1964-67; shop supr., model maker Davan Scale Models, Toronto, Ont., Can., 1968-69; chief archtl. designer George T. Nowak Architects and Assocs., Westchester, Calif., 1969-72; sr. archtl. designer Krisel & Shapiro Architects and Assocs., L.A., 1972-74; sr. supervising archtl. designer The Ralph M. Parsons A/E Co., Pasadena, Calif., 1974—; v.p. United Gruno U.S.A. Corp. Import/Export, Monterey Park, Calif., 1980-89. Mem. Rep. Presdl. Task Force, Washington, 1982—, Nat. Rep. Senatorial Com., Washington, 1983—, Nat. Rep. Congrl. Com., Washington, 1981—, Rep. Nat. Com., Washington, 1982—; active Am. Indonesian Cath. Soc. Recipient Excellent Design Achievement commendation Magneto-Hydro-Dynamics Program, 1976, Strategic Def. Initiative "Star Wars" Program, 1988, USAF Space Shuttle Program, West Coast Space-Port, 1984; scholar U. Heidelberg, 1967-68. Mem. NRA, Am. Air Gunner Assn., Tech. Comm. Soc., Indonesian Am. Soc., Dutch Am. Soc., Second Amendment Found., The Right to Keep and Bear Arms Com. Republican. Roman Catholic. Home: 154 Ladera St Monterey Park CA 91754-2125 Office: Ralph M Parsons A/E Co 100 W Walnut St Pasadena CA 91124-0001

GOERINGER, KABRENA EILEEN, chemist; b. Fairfield, Calif., Jan. 24, 1970; d. Thomas C. and Lynn E. (Fisher) Rodda; m. Scott D. Goeringer, Jan. 29, 1993. BS in Chemistry, USAF Acad., 1992; MS in Project and Sys. Mgmt., Golden Gate U., 1995. Commd. 1st lt. USAF, 1992; chief nuclear sys. tech. tech. ops. divsn. USAF, McClellan AFB, Calif., 1992-93, chief chem. analysis br., 1993—. Choir mem., mus. accompanist St. Andrew's Ch., North Highlands, Calif., 1992-94; vol. SAFE Halloween Coords., Rancho Cordova, Calif., 1994. Recipient Leadership award Nat. U., Sacramento, 1993, 94. Mem. Am. Chem. Soc. (accredited chemistry degree), McClellan AFB Officer's Club, McClellan AFB Co. Grade Officers Coun. (profl. devel. chmn. 1994-95). Republican. Episcopalian.

GOETZEL, CLAUS GUENTER, metallurgical engineer; b. Berlin, July 14, 1913; came to U.S., 1936; s. Walter and Else (Baum) G.; m. Lilo Kallmann, Nov. 19, 1938; children: Rodney G., Vivian L. Dipl.-Ing., Technische Hochschule, Berlin, 1935; PhD, Columbia U., 1939. Registered profl. engr., Calif. Research chemist, lab. head Hardy Metall. Co., 1936-39; tech. dir., works mgr. Am. Electro Metal Corp., 1939-47; v.p., dir. research Sintercast Corp. Am., 1947-57; adj. prof. NYU, N.Y.C., 1945-57, sr. research scientist, 1957-60; cons. scientist Lockheed Missiles & Space Co., Sunnyvale, Calif., 1960-78; cons. metall. engring. Portola Valley, Calif., 1978—; lectr., vis. scholar Stanford (Calif.) U., 1961-88; vis. prof. Tech. Univ. Karlsruhe, Germany, 1978-80. Author: Treatise on Powder Metallurgy, 5 vols., 1949-63; co-author: (with Lilo Goetzel) Dictionary of Materials and Process Engineering, 1995; contbr. articles to profl. jours. Recipient Alexander von Humboldt Sr. U.S. Scientist award, Fed. Republic Germany, 1978. Fellow AIAA (assoc.), Am. Soc. Metals Internat.; mem. AIME (life), Am. Powder Metallurgy Inst. (sr.), Materials Sci. Club N.Y. (life, past pres.), Inst. Materials (life, London).

GOETZKE, GLORIA LOUISE, social worker, income tax specialist; b. Monticello, Minn.; d. Wesley and Marvel (Kreidler) G. BA, U. Minn., 1964; MSW, U. Denver, 1966; MBA, U. St. Thomas, 1977. Cert. enrollment to practice before IRS. Social worker VA Med. Ctr., L.A., 1980—; master tax preparer and instr. H&R Block, Santa Monica, Calif.; clin. instr. UCLA Grad. Sch. Social Policy; adj. prof. Calif. State U. Long Beach Grad. Sch. Social Work. Mem. Nat. Assn. Social Workers (cert.). Lutheran.

GOETZL, THOMAS MAXWELL, law educator, arbitrator; b. Chgo., May 31, 1943. AB, U. Calif., Berkeley, 1965, JD, 1969. Bar: Calif. 1970. Prof. law Golden Gate U., Sch. Law, San Francisco, 1972—. Bd. dirs. Calif. Lawyers for Arts, 1979—. Office: Golden Gate U Sch Law 536 Mission St San Francisco CA 94105-2921

GOFF, JAMES ALBERT, medical center administrator, civil engineer; b. Hyannis, Mass., Sept. 16, 1941; s. James Satterlee and Evelyn Cornelia (Williams) G.; m. Gail Dorothy Smith, Aug. 24, 1963; children—James Satterlee II, Melissa Anne. B.S.C.E., U. Ill., 1963; M.H.A., U. Minn., 1972. Registered profl. engr., Ill. Asst. hosp. dir. VA Med. Ctr., Spokane, Wash., 1972-73; asst. dir. field ops. VA Central Office, Washington, 1973-74, asst. dir. field ops., San Francisco, 1974-75; dep. exec. asst. VA Med. Dist. 27, San Francisco, 1975-76; asst. dir. VA Med. Ctr., Cleve., 1976-79; dir. VA Med. Ctr., Boise, Idaho, 1979—. Bd. dirs. Statewide Health Coordinating Council, Boise, 1980-87, Idaho Health Systems Agy., Boise, 1980-87, Boise chpt. ARC, 1981-87, Univ./Community Health Scis. Assn., Boise, 1981—, v.p., 1984—; bd. dirs. United Way of Ada County, Idaho, 1984-85; adj. regent Am. Coll. Healthcare Execs., 1984-85, regent for Idaho chpt., 1985—. Served to capt. U.S. Army, 1964-67. Fellow Am. Coll. Hosp. Adminstrs. (regent for Idaho 1985—); mem. Idaho Hosp. Assn. (bd. dirs. 1987—), Fed. Health Care Execs. Alumni Assn., Fed. Exec. Council (pres. Boise chpt. 1983), Sr. Execs. Assn. (sr. exec. VA chpt. 1981—). Episcopalian. Lodge: Rotary. Office: VA Med Ctr 3801 Miranda Ave Palo Alto CA 94304-1207

GOFF, ROBERT ALLEN, environmental regulator, geologist; b. Riverton, Wyo., Mar. 29, 1963; s. Robert Loyd and Vera Louise (Dodrill) G. AS, N.W. C.C., Powell, Wyo., 1983; BS, U. Wyo., 1985; MS, U. Ala., 1990. Cert. hazardous waste insp. Asst. libr. Geophysical Inst., Fairbanks, Alaska, winter 1987-90; jr. geologist Placer Dome U.S. Inc., Nome, Alaska, 1988; hazardous waste insp. Alaska Dept. Environ. Conservation/S.E. Region, Juneau, 1990-93, hazardous waste and pollution prevention coord., 1993—. Mem. Soc. for Sedimentary Geology, Am. Assn. Petroleum Geologists (jr.), European Union of Geoscis., Smithsonian Instn. (assoc.), Am. Mus. Natural History (assoc.). Home: PO Box 22663 Juneau AK 99802-2663

GOFF, WILLIAM JAMES, librarian; b. Kansas City, Kans., May 31, 1934; s. William Ambrose and Velma Gertrude (Conley) G.; m. Janet Rosa Guthrie, Aug. 26, 1961; children: William Alexander, John Douglas. B.S., U. Mo., Kansas City, 1960; M.S., U. Wash., 1963, M.L.S., 1966. Head librarian Scripps Instn. Oceanography, La Jolla, Calif., 1966—; cons. G.K. Hall Co., Boston, 1969-76, U. Del., 1979, CICESE, Ensenada, Baja California, Mex., 1974—, Unidad, Ciencias Marinas, 1972—, Liebhardt and Weston Assocs. and Architects, La Jolla. Mem. Cardiff Town Council, Calif., 1982—. Served with USN, 1953-57. NATO fellow, Bristol, Eng., 1975; Sigma Xi award, 1983. Mem. Spl. Libraries Assn., Geosci. Info. Soc., Am. Soc. Info. Sci., ALA, Internat. Assn. Marine Sci. Libraries and Info. Ctrs., Beta Phi Mu, House of Scotland Pipe Band. Home: 2284 Manchester Ave Cardiff By The Sea CA 92007-1944 Office: U Calif Scripps Inst Oceanographic Libr 9500 Gilman Dr # 0175C La Jolla CA 92093-5003

GOFFE, ESTHER, elementary school educator; b. Devils Lake, N.D., Jan. 3, 1944; d. Harold Melvin and Myrtle Gilene (Johnson) Hanson; m. Stanley M. Goffe, July 14, 1965; 1 child, Bryan. BA, Jamestown (N.D.) Coll., 1966; postgrad., Pacific Luth. U., Tacoma, 1972. Elem. tchr. Plains (Mont.) Sch. Dist., 1966-68; elem. tchr. Sch. Dist. 216, Enumclaw, Wash., 1968—, bldg. coord. after sch. enrichment, 1989-90, trainer coop pluralism, 1990-93; dist. coord. Young Authors' Celebration, 1991-93; mem. Joint Assn./Dist. Forum, 1987-92; mem. Joint Assn./Dist. Formative Evaluation Com., 1991-93, legis. bargaining team, 1991, sec., 1991-93; mem. elem. instrnl. coun., 1994—, grade level chair, 1994—. Mem. AAUW, NEA, ASCD, Wash. ASCD, Wash. Edn. Assn. (del. rep. assembly 1990—, del. endorsement conv. 1992), Enumclaw Edn. Assn. (v.p. 1987-91, pub. rels. 1987-93, negotiator 1986-90, 94—, pres. 1990-92), Puget Sound Uniserv Coun. (pres. 1993-95), Enumclaw C. of C. (edn. com. 1990—, chair 1992-94, Peer Coach 1992-94).

GOFORTH, NATHAN DAN, police officer; b. Phoenix, Sept. 12, 1951; s. Nathan and Mabel Lettie (Deal) G.; m. Lori Ann Petersen (div. 1984). AA in Bus. Adminstrn., Glendale Community Coll., Ariz., 1974, AA in Adminstrn. Justice, 1976; BS in Pub. Programs, Ariz. State U., 1985. Second asst. mgr. Smittys Big Town, Phoenix, 1967-73, sales rep., 1975-76; sr. inventory auditor Motorola Semiconductor, Phoenix, 1973-74; police officer City Glendale, Ariz., 1976—; Interpreter for deaf Glendale Police Dept., 1976—, peer counselor, 1989—, field tng. officer, 1980—; vol. tchr. Glendale Community Coll. Police Res. Acad., 1989-94. Res. hwy. patrolman Ariz. Dept. Pub. Safety, Phoenix, 1975-76; advisor Glendale Explorer Post 469, 1978—, instl. head, 1992. Recipient Dedication to DAV award, 1990-91, Cert. of Appreciation award Independence High Sch., 1990, Outstanding Vol. Svc. award MADD, 1991. Mem. NRA, Ariz. State U. Alumni Assn., Internat. Police Assn., Frat. order of Police (treas. 1990-94, v.p. 1994-95, trustee 1995—), Ariz. Cts. Assn., Critical Incident Stress Debriefing (S.W. region), Sons of Am. Legion. Office: Glendale Police Dept 6835 N 57th Dr Glendale AZ 85301-3218

GOGARTY, WILLIAM BARNEY, oil company executive, consultant; b. Provo, Utah, Apr. 23, 1930; s. William B. and Zola (Walker) G.; m. Lois Gay Pritchett, Dec. 14, 1951; children: Laura Gay, Colleen, William Shaun, Kathlyn, Michael Barney. BS, U. Utah, 1953, PhD, 1959. Registered profl. engr., Colo. With Marathon Oil Co., Denver and Findlay, Ohio, 1959-86, sr. staff engr., Findlay, 1973-75, assoc. rsch. dir. prodn., Denver, 1975-86, ret. 1986; pvt. practice enhanced oil recovery cons., Littleton, Colo., 1986—; adj. assoc. prof. chem. engring. and metallurgy dept. U. Denver, 1967-73; cons. Ciba-Geigy Corp; mem. Nat. Petroleum Coun. chem. task group Com. on Enhanced Oil Recovery, 1982-84; cons., tchr. Dept. Tech. Cooperation, UN, India, 1986, Rogaland Rsch. Inst., Norsk Hydro and Statoil, Norway, 1987, Petromer Trend Corp., Indonesia, 1988, Petrobras, Brazil, 1989; Muskat lectr. U. Utah, 1985. Contbr. articles to profl. jours.; patentee in field. Mem. Rep. precinct com., Littleton, Colo., 1984. Served to 1st lt. AUS, 1953-55. Mem. NAE, Am. Inst. Chem. Engrs., Soc. Petroleum Engrs. (fluid mechanics and oil recovery process tech. com. 1963-65, monograph com. 1971-73, chmn. monograph com. 1973, textbook com. 1974-76, chmn. textbook com. 1976, program vice chmn. 1977-78, Lester C. Uren award com. 1980-82, chmn. award com. 1982, program com. for Soc. Petroleum Engrs./U.S. Dept. Energy Enhanced Oil Recovery Symposium 1982, Disting. lectr. 1982-83, Lester C. Uren award 1987, region II dir.-elect 1988-89, bd. dirs. 1989-90, Henry Mattson Tech. Svc. award Denver petroleum sect. 1989, Enhanced Oil Recovery Pioneer award Mid-Continent region, 1990), Sigma Xi, Tau Beta Phi, Phi Kappa Phi, Alpha Chi Sigma. Mem. LDS Ch.

GOGERTY, DAVID CALVIN, economist; b. Phoenix, Ariz., Oct. 24, 1934; s. david Leason and Lora Waunita (Hughes) G.; m. Jean Ann Waggoner, Sept. 20, 1987 (div. Dec. 1991). AB, Stanford U., 1956, AM, 1962. Economist The Rand Corp., Santa Monica, Calif., 1963-74; self employed economist L.A., 1974-75, Newport Beach, Calif., 1976-89, Irvine, Calif., 1990—; cons. Inst. for Defense Analyses, Alexandria, Va., 1988-91. Lt. (j.g.) USN, 1957-60, Japan, the Mediterranean, Antarctica. Mem. Am. Econ. Assn., Inst. Navigation, Ops. Rsch. Soc. Episcopalian.

GOGOLIN, MARILYN TOMPKINS, educational administrator, language pathologist; b. Pomona, Calif., Feb. 25, 1946; d. Roy Merle and Dorothy (Davidson) Tompkins; m. Robert Elton Gogolin, Mar. 29, 1969. BA, U. LaVerne, Calif., 1967; MA, U. Redlands, Calif., 1968; postgrad., U. Washington, 1968-69; MS, Calif. State U., Fullerton, 1976. Cert. clin. speech pathologist; cert. teaching and sch. adminstrn. Speech and lang. pathologist Rehab. Hosp., Pomona, 1969-71; diagnostic tchr. L.A. County Office of Edn., Downey, Calif., 1971-72, program specialist, 1972-74, cons. lang., 1975-76, cons. orgns. and mgmt., 1976-79, dir. adminstrv. affairs, asst. to supt., 1979-95; dep. supt., 1995—; cons. lang. sch. dists., Calif., 1975-79; cons. orgn. and mgmt. and profl. assns., Calif., 1976—; exec. dir. L.A. County Sch. Trustees Assn., 1979—. Founding patron Desert chpt. Kidney Found., Palm Desert, Calif., 1985. Doctoral fellow U. Washington, 1968; named One of Outstanding Young Women Am., 1977. Mem. Am. Mgmt. Assn., Am. Speech/Hearing Assn., Calif. Speech/Hearing Assn., Am. Edn. Research Assn. Baptist. Office: LA County Office Edn 9300 Imperial Hwy Downey CA 90242-2813

GOIN, JOHN MOREHEAD, plastic surgeon; b. Los Angeles, Mar. 29, 1929; s. Lowell Sidney and Margaret Catherine (Morehead) G.; m. Marcia Stewart Kraft, Mar. 5, 1960; children: Suzanne Jennifer, Jessica Michele. B.A. in Zoology, UCLA, 1951; M.D., St. Louis U., 1955. Diplomate: Am. Bd. Plastic Surgery (dir. 1980-86). Intern U. Calif. Med. Center, San Francisco, 1955-56; asst. resident in surgery U. Calif. Med. Center, 1956-59; asst. resident to chief resident in plastic surgery U. Calif. Med. Center, Los Angeles, 1959-62; fellow in plastic surgery Queen Victoria Hosp., East Grinstead, Sussex, Eng., 1961; pvt. practice specializing in plastic and reconstructive surgery Los Angeles, 1962—; clin. prof. surgery U. So. Calif.; chief plastic surgery Los Angeles County/U. So. Calif. Med. Center, 1971-80; head div. plastic surgery Children's Hosp. of Los Angeles, 1976-79. Author: (with Marcia Kraft Goin) Changing the Body: Psychological Effects of Plastic Surgery, 1980; Contbr. (with Marcia Kraft Goin) articles to profl. jours. Fellow ACS (gov. 1983—); mem. AMA, Calif. Soc. Plastic Surgeons (past pres.), Am. Soc. Plastic and Reconstructive Surgeons (sec. 1979-82, v.p. 1982-83, pres.-elect 1983-84, pres. 1984-85), Am. Soc. Aesthetic Plastic Surgery, Am. Assn. Plastic Surgeons, Pacific Coast Surg. Assn. Republican. Episcopalian. Home: 2500 Park Oak Dr Los Angeles CA 90068-2542 Office: 2500 Park Oak Dr Los Angeles CA 90068-2542

GOIN, OLIVE BOWN, biologist; b. Pitts., Dec. 2, 1912; d. Charles Elmer and Anne Louise (Hay) Bown; m. Coleman Goin, June 7, 1940 (dec.); children: Lynda, Coleman Jr. AB, Wellesley Coll., 1934; MS, U. Pitts., 1936. Asst. lab. mammalogy Carnegie Mus., Pitts., 1934-40; lab. instr. to asst. prof. U. Fla., Gainesville, 1942-46; rsch. assoc. Mus. of No. Ariz., Flagstaff, 1971-80; ret. Author: World Outside My Door, 1955, Introduction to Herpetology, 1962, Comparative Vertebrate Anatomy, Man and the Natural World, 1970, Introduction to Herpetology, 2d edit., 1971, Journey Onto Land, 1974, Man and the Natural World, 2d edit., 1975 (all with C.J. Goin); (with C.J. Goin and George Zug) Introduction to Herpetology, 3rd edit., 1978; contbr. numerous articles to profl. jours.

GOIN, PETER JACKSON, art educator; b. Madison, Wis., Nov. 26, 1951; m. Chelsea Miller; children: Kari, Dana. BA, Hamline U., 1973; MA, U. Iowa, 1975, MFA, 1976. Prof. art. U. Nev., Reno, 1984—. Author: Tracing the Line: A Photographic Survey of the Mexican-American Border, 1987, Nuclear Landscapes, 1991, Arid Waters: Photographs from the Water in the West Project, 1992, Stopping Time: A Rephotographic Survey of Lake Tahoe, 1992; sole exhbns. include Nora Eccles Harrison Mus. Art, Logan, Utah, 1992, Duke U. Mus. Art, Durham, N.C., 1992, Phoenix Mus. Art, 1992, Indpls. Mus. Art, 1992, Savannah (Ga.) Coll. Art and Design, 1992, Nev. Humanities Com. Travelling Exhibit, 1992 and others. Recipient grant NEA, 1981, 90. Office: Univ Nev Dept Art Reno NV 89557

GOINS, RONALD L., art director; b. Austin, Tex., Sept. 10, 1962. Graphic artist San Antonio (Tex.) Light, 1982-85; art dir. San Antonio Light Sunday Mag., San Antonio, 1982-85; graphic artist Houston Chronicle, Houston, 1985-86; graphic artist L.A. Daily News, L.A., 1986, art dir., 1986-90; publ., editor Westside Chronicle, L.A., 1990-91; art dir., creative dir. The Advocate Mag., L.A., 1992—; creative dir. Liberation Publs., L.A., 1992—. Mem. Am. Inst. Graphic Arts. Office: Liberation Publs 6922 Hollywood Blvd Fl 10 Los Angeles CA 90028-6117

GOLD, ANNE MARIE, library director; b. N.Y.C., Feb. 24, 1949; d. James Raymond and Marion Rita (Magner) Scully; m. Steven Louis Gold, Aug. 9, 1974; 1 child, Lauren Z. BA in English, St. Lawrence U., 1971; MS in Libr. Svc., Columbia U., 1972. Libr. N.Y. Pub. Libr., N.Y.C., 1972-74, Oakland (Calif.) Pub. Libr., 1975-80; head reference Solano County Libr., Fairfield, Calif., 1980-82, libr. Vallejo region, 1982-84, coord. libr. brs. and ext. svcs., 1984-86, dir. libr. svcs., 1986-90; county libr. Contra Costa County Libr., Pleasant Hill, Calif., 1990—. Mem. ALA, Pub. Libr. Assn. (Allie Beth Martin award com. 1986-88, chair 1991 nominating com. 1989-91, pub. librs. adv. bd. 1989—, bd. dirs. 1992-93, chair orgn. and planning com. met. librs. sect. 1988-89, v.p. 1991-92, pres. 1992-93, br. librs. com. small and medium sized librs. sect. 1985-87, 1988 nominating com. 1986-88), Calif. Libr. Assn. (coun. mem. 1985-87, 90-92, exec. bd. 1991-92, co-chair legis. com. 1992-93, Mem. of Year award, 1994), Calif. Inst. Librs. (nominating com. 1989, v.p. 1990-91), Calif. Soc. Librs. (com. profl. standards 1986-87), Libr. Adminstrn. and Mgmt. Assn. (program com. 1989-91), restructuring Calif. pub. libs. task force (1994-95).,. Office: Contra Costa County Libr 1750 Oak Park Blvd Pleasant Hill CA 94523-4412

GOLD, BRUCE GORDON, medical educator; b. Glen Ridge, N.J., Nov. 22, 1954; s. Martin and Zelda (Kaplan) G.; m. Jeanette Conception Bartel, Sept. 6, 1980; children: Melissa Jeanine, Sandra Anita. BA, Boston U., 1976; PhD, U. Medicine and Dentistry N.J., 1981. Rsch. fellow Sch. Medicine Johns Hopkins U., Balt., 1981-84, asst. prof. Sch. Hygiene & Public Health, 1984-85; asst. prof. Rutgers U., Piscataway, N.J., 1985-89; assoc. prof., scientist Oreg. Health Scis. U., Portland, 1989—; cons. Wheeling (W.Va.) Clinic, 1986. Author: (with others) Neuroregeneration, 1993; editor Toxicology, 1987; contbr. more than 30 articles to profl. jours. Grantee NIH, 1988-91, 91-96, Paralyzed Vets. Am., 1993-95. Mem. AAAS, Am. Assn. Neuropathologists, Internat. Soc. Neuropathology, Soc. Neurosci., Soc. Exptl. Neuropathology, Peripheral Nerve Soc. Home: 6320 Haverhill Ct West Linn OR 97068-4900 Office: Oreg Health Scis U 3181 SW Sam Jackson Park Rd Portland OR 97201-3011

GOLD, JEROME, publisher, novelist; b. Chgo., Sept. 8, 1943; s. Sidney Singman and Edith (Hoffman) G.; m. Clotilde Rita Litchfield, Aug. 20, 1965 (div. Apr. 1978); children: Jack Michael, David Charles, Leah Molina Antonia. AA, Fullerton Coll., 1968; BA, U. Mont., Missoula, 1970, MA, 1976; PhD, U. Wash., 1988. Publ. Black Heron Press, Seattle, 1984—; counselor Dept. Juvenile Rehab., Olympia, Wash., 1991—. Author: The Negligence of Death, 1984, The Inquisitor, 1991, Publishing Lives, The Prisoner's Son, 1995; co-author: Of Great Spaces, 1987; editor: Hurricanes, 1994. Sgt. U.S. Army, 1963-66, Vietnam. Mem. Internat. Assn. of Ind. Publs., Amnesty Internat. Jewish. Office: Black Heron Press PO Box 95676 Seattle WA 98145-2676

GOLD, LOIS SWIRSKY, research scientist; b. Newark, Nov. 21, 1941; d. Sidney C. and Anna S. (Adler) Swirsky; m. Stuart Milton Gold, Mar. 31, 1968; children: Alissa Sharon, Jenny Anne. Student, U. Geneva, 1961-62; AB, Goucher Coll., Towson, Md., 1963; PhD, Stanford U., 1967. Postdoctoral fellow Sys. Devel. Corp., Santa Monica, Calif., 1967-68; lectr. Sch. Pub. Policy U. Calif., Berkeley, 1968-73, assoc. specialist dept. biochemistry, 1970-73; sr. fellow Carnegie Commn. on Future of Higher Edn., Berkeley, 1970-73; dir. Carcinogenic Potency Project Lawrence Berkeley Lab. and U. Calif., Berkeley, 1978—; mem. ad hoc panel of expert reviewers Nat. Toxicology Program, 1988-91; mem. adv. bd. Harvard Ctr. Risk Analysis, 1993—, Harvard Group on Risk Mgmt. Reform, 1994-95. Contbr. articles to profl. jours. Mem. AAAS, Soc. Toxicology, Phi Beta Kappa. Home: 1345 Queens Rd Berkeley CA 94708-2113 Office: U Calif Carcinogenic Potency Database 401 Barker Hall Berkeley CA 94720

GOLD, MARVIN HAROLD, chemist, consultant; b. Buffalo, June 23, 1915; s. Max and Jennie (Frankel) G.; m. Sophye Mendelson, Aug. 31, 1940; children: Judith May Bloom, Norman Charles. BA, UCLA, 1937; PhD, U. Ill., 1940. Rsch. assoc. Northwestern U., Evanston, Ill., 1940-42; rsch. group leader The Visking Corp., Chgo., 1942-48; sr. scientist Aerojet Gen. Corp., Sacramento and Azusa, Calif., 1948-72; tech. cons./chemist Sacramento, 1972—. Contbr. articles to profl. jours.; inventor/patentee (more than 85) in chems., plastics, coatings, insulations, lubricants. Pres. People to People of Sacramento, 1962-65. Recipient Civilian Meritorious Svc. Citation USN, 1962; Anna Fuller Fund Cancer Rsch. fellow Nat. Cancer Inst., 1940-42. Mem. Am. Chem. Soc. (sec. councilor 1967-68), Sigma Xi (chpt. pres. 1966), Phi Lambda Upsilon. Jewish. Home and Office: 2601 Latham Dr Sacramento CA 95864-7141

GOLD, MICHAEL NATHAN, investment banker, management consultant; b. Chgo., May 3, 1952; s. Julius and Sarah (Blitzblau) G.; m. Cynthia Bilicki, June 19, 1976; children: Aaron Michael, Nathan Matthew. BA, Kalamazoo Coll., 1976; cert. in exec. mgmt., UCLA, 1989. Rsch. fellow Sinai Hosp., Detroit, 1976; rsch. assoc. Molecular Biological Inst., UCLA, L.A., 1976-77; lab mgr., adminstr. Biomed. Engring. Ctr. U. So. Calif., L.A., 1977-80; asst. dir. Crump Inst. for Med. Engring. UCLA, 1980-84, assoc. dir., exec. officer Crump Inst. for Med. Engring., 1984-89; chmn., pres. Therapeutic Environments Inc., Van Nuys, Calif., 1989-91; pres. Michael Gold & Assocs., Van Nuys, 1989—; mng. dir., investment banker Crimson Capital Corp. Ministry of Privatization, Czech Republic, 1991—. Mem. IEEE, Assn. for Advancement of Med. Instrumentation, Clin. Ligand Assay Soc., Am. Assn. for Med. Systems and Informatics, Sea Edn. Assn., Biomed. Engring. Soc., Internat. Soc. for Optical Engring. Office: Michael Gold & Assocs 236 W Mountain St Ste 101 Pasadena CA 91103-2968

GOLD, RICK L., federal government executive; b. Rexburg, Idaho, June 25, 1946; s. Raymond Russell and Thelma (Lee) G.; m. Anamarie Sanone, May 14, 1988; children: Nanette Phillips, Russell. BSCE, Utah State U., 1968, MSCE, 1970. Registered profl. engr., Colo., Mont., Utah. Hydraulic engr. U.S. Bur. Reclamation, Provo, Utah, 1969-73; project hydrologist U.S. Bur. Reclamation, Durango, Colo., 1973-75; regional hydrologist U.S. Bur. Reclamation, Billings, Mont., 1975-81; spl. asst. to regional dir. U.S. Bur. Reclamation, Washington, 1981-82; asst. planning officer U.S. Bur. Reclamation, Billings, 1982-83; projects mgr. U.S. Bur. Reclamation, Durango, Colo., 1983-88; regional planning officer U.S. Bur. Reclamation, Salt Lake City, 1988-90, asst. regional dir., 1990-94, deputy regional dir., 1994—; mem. water quality com. Internat. Joint Commn. Study on Garrison Divsn. Unit, Billings, 1975-77; fed. negotiator Cost Sharing and Indian Water Rights Settlement, Durango, 1986-88; chmn. Cooperating Agy. on Glen Canyon Dam EIS, Salt Lake City, 1990-94. Contbr. articles to profl. jours.; author papers. Mem. Rotary Internat., Durango, 1985-87; bd. dirs. United Way of La Plata County, Durango, 1983-88; chmn. Combined Fed. Campaign, La Plata County, 1985. Mem. ASCE, bd. dirs. U.S. Com. on Irrigation and Drainage. Office: US Bur Reclamation 125 S State St Salt Lake City UT 84138-1102

GOLD, SHIRLEY JEANNE, state legislator, labor relations specialist; b. N.Y.C., Oct. 2, 1925; d. Louis and Gussie (Lefkowitz) Diamondstein; BA in Music, Hunter Coll., 1945; MA in Behavioral Sci. (Crown-Zellerbach Corp. scholar), Reed Coll., 1962; m. David E. Gold, June 22, 1947; children: Andrew, Dana. Tchr., Portland (Oreg.) Public Schs., 1954-68; pres. Portland Fedn. Tchrs., Am. Fedn. Tchrs./AFL-CIO, 1965-72, pres. Oreg. Fedn. Tchrs., 1972-77; cons. labor relations, 1977-80; mem. Oreg. Ho. of Reps., Salem, 1980-88, majority leader, 1985-88, chmn. legis. rules, ops. and reform, human resources com., 1983-84, revenue com., 1987-88, policy and priorities com., com. of edn., commn. of states, from 1987, campaign fin. reform com., from 1987; now state senator Oreg. Senate; senate chair Edn. Com., 1989-93, Revenue and Sch. Fin. Com., 1993-95; senate mem. Rules Elections Com., Oreg. Comm. for Child Care; mem. Oreg. Tchr. Tenure Rev. Bd., 1965-72; mem. Nat. Multi-State Consortium, 1974; mem. Speak Out Oreg. com. to White House and Congress, 1978; mem. Oreg. Task Force on Tax Reform; mem. Solid Waste Regional Policy Commn., 1989-91; AFL-CIO scholar George Meany Inst., 3 times, 1976-77; commr., nat. vice chmn. Edn. Commn. of States, 1988-90; mem. Oreg. Commn. on Women. Chairperson precinct com., conv. del. Oreg. Democratic Party, 1960-80, dist. leader, chairperson edn. com., 1978-80; charter mem., mem. exec. bd., v.p. Oreg. Council for Cts., 1977-80. Named to Hunter Coll. Hall of Fame, 1985, Citizen of Yr., 1985. Mem. Hunter Coll. Alumni Assn., Reed Coll. Alumni Assn., Pacific N.W. Labor History Assn., Portland Fedn. Tchrs., Oreg. Fedn. Tchrs., Oreg. Fedn. Dem. Women, Oreg. Coalition for Nat. Health Security, Oreg. Women's Polit. Caucus, Com. on Drug Abuse, Northwest Oreg. Health System, ACLU, Coalition Labor Union Women. Jewish. Contbr. articles on labor relations to Willamette Week newspaper, 1977-80; editor Oreg. Tchr. newspaper, 1970-72. Office: S316 State St Salem OR 97301-3445

GOLD, STANLEY P., chemical company executive, manufacturing company executive; b. 1942. AB, U. Calif., 1964; JD, U. So. Calif., 1967. Ptnr. Gang Tyre and Brown, 1967—, Shamrock Holdings Inc., 1985—; pres., chief exec. officer Shamrock Holdings; chmn., CEO, dir. L.A. Gear Inc., L.A., 1992—. Office: Shamrock Holdings Inc 4444 W Lakeside Dr Burbank CA 91505-4054 also: LA Gear Inc 2850 Ocean Park Blvd Santa Monica CA 90405-2936*

GOLDAPER, GABRIELE GAY, clothing executive, consultant; b. Amsterdam, The Netherlands, May 4, 1937; came to U.S., 1949; d. Richard and Gertrud (Sinzheimer) Mainzer; married, 1957; children: Carolyn, Julie, Nancy. BA in Econs., Barnard Coll., 1959; BS in Edn., U. Cin., 1960; postgrad., Xavier U., 1962. V.p. planning, systems and material control High Tide Swimwear div. Warnaco, Los Angeles, 1974-79; v.p., customer support cons. Silton AMS, Los Angeles, 1979-80; exec. v.p., ptnr. Prisma Corp., Los Angeles, 1980-84; exec. v.p. Mindstar Prods., Los Angeles, 1984-85; gen. mgr. Cherry Lane, Los Angeles, 1985-86; dir. inventory mgmt. Barco Uniforms, Los Angeles, 1986; mgmt. cons. to clothing industry Santa Monica, Calif., 1986—; dir. corp. operation svcs. Authentic Fitness, L.A., 1993; exec. v.p. corp. LCA Intimates, 1994—; instr. Calif. State U., 1978-79, UCLA Grad. Bus. Mgmt. Sch., 1979-86, Fashion Inst. Design and Merchandising. 1985—; chmn. data processing com. Calif. Fashion Creators, 1980; mediator Los Angeles County Bar Assn.; cons. Exec. Service Corps; lectr. various colls. Author: A Results Oriented Approach to Manufacturing Planning, 1978, Small Company View of the Computer, 1979; also articles. Elected mem. Commn. on Status Women, 1985-89. Mem. Apparel Mfrs. Assn. (mgmt. systems com. 1978-80), Calif. Apparel Industries Assn. (exec. com., bd. dirs. 1980), Am. Arbitration Assn.

GOLDBECK, ROBERT ARTHUR, JR., physical chemist; b. Evanston, Ill., July 25, 1950; s. Robert Arthur Sr. and Ruth Marilyn (Nordwall) G.; m. Jennifer Jane Tollkuhn, Aug. 19, 1989; stepchildren: Jessica Kathleen Tollkuhn, Brenna Maurin Tollkuhn. BS, U. Calif., Berkeley, 1974; PhD, U. Calif., Santa Cruz, 1982. Postdoctoral fellow Stanford (Calif.) U., 1983-84, rsch. assoc., 1984-87; rsch. chemist U. Calif., Santa Cruz, 1987—; lectr. in chemistry U. Calif., 1980, 84, 86. Contbr. articles to Biophys. Jour.; contbr. articles to profl. jours. Mem. AAAS, Am. Chem. Soc., Biophys. Soc. Office: U Calif Dept Chemistry Biochem Santa Cruz CA 95064

GOLDBERG, DAVID BRYAN, biomedical researcher; b. San Bernardino, Calif., Mar. 29, 1954; s. Gus and Rose (Goldrich) G.; m. Dianne Rae, Dec. 19, 1976; children: Jason, Mark, Eric, Ashley. BA, UCLA, 1976, PhD, 1987. Rsch. asst. Calif. State U., L.A., 1976-79; rsch. assoc. UCLA, 1979-82; sci. project mgr. Alpha Therapeutic Corp., L.A., 1989—; adj. prof. Chaffey Coll., Alta Loma, Calif., 1990—. Contbr. articles to N.Y. Acad. Scis., Jour. Clin. Apheresis, Proceedings of ASCO, FASEB Jour., Fedn. Preceedings, Nat. Hemophelia Found. Mem. PTA, Alta Loma, 1991. Basic Rsch. grantee, Cancer Rsch. Ctr., 1987, 88, Cancer Seed grantee 1989; Teaching fellow, UCLA, 1982-87, Rsch. fellow II, City of Hope, Duarte, Calif., 1987-89. Mem. Fedn. Am. Socs. Experimental Biology. Office: Alpha Therapeutic Corp 1213 John Reed Ct La Puente CA 91745-2405

GOLDBERG, EDWARD MORRIS, political science educator; b. N.Y.C., May 18, 1931; s. Harry Abraham and Pauline Goldberg; children: David Powell, Natalie Pauline. BA, Bklyn. Coll., 1953; MA, U. N.Mex., 1956; PhD, U. Pa., 1965. Instr. U. Pa., Phila., 1956-59; asst. dean Calif. State U., L.A., 1968-70, dept. chmn. polit. sci., 1972-77, assoc. dean, 1981-86, asst. prof. polit. sci., 1961-66, assoc. prof. polit. sci., 1966-70, prof. polit. sci., 1970—; vis. prof. U. So. Calif., L.A., 1974; vis. asst. prof. San Diego State U., 1960-61, U. N.Mex., Albuquerque, 1959-60; cons. HUD, Washington, 1971-72, Calif. State Assembly, Sacramento, 1965; rsch. polit. scientist U. Calif., Davis, 1966, 67; rsch. cons. Taxpayers Assn. of N.Mex., Santa Fe, 1957, 60. Author more than 20 pubs. in field; assoc. editor Western Polit. Quarterly jour., 1981-84; contbr. articles to profl. jours. With U.S. Army, 1953-55. Recipient Outstanding Prof. award Calif. State U., L.A., 1985, summer fellowships NEH, 1980, 84, 89. Mem. Western Polit. Sci. Assn. (v.p. 1977-78, pres. 1978-79), So. Calif. Polit. Sci. Assn. (v.p. 1972-73, pres. 1973-74), Am. Polit. Sci. Assn., Internat. Polit. Sci. Assn. Democrat. Office: Calif State Univ Dept Polit Sci Los Angeles CA 90032-8226

GOLDBERG, FRED SELLMANN, advertising executive; b. Chgo., Jan. 22, 1941; s. Sydney Norman and Birdie (Cohen) G.; m. Jerrilyn Toby Tager, Apr. 12, 1964; children—Robin Lynn, Susanne Joy. B.S., U. Vt., 1962; M.B.A., NYU, 1964. Mktg. research mgr. P. Ballantine & Sons, Newark, 1964-67; sr. v.p., mgmt. supr. Young & Rubicam, N.Y.C., 1967-78; sr. v.p., gen. mgr. Young & Rubicam, Los Angeles, 1978-82; exec. v.p., gen. mgr. Chiat-Day, Inc., San Francisco, 1982-85; exec. v.p., chief operation officer Chiat-Day, Advt., L.A., 1985-87; pres., chief exec. officer San Francisco office Chiat-Day, Inc., San Francisco; vice chmn. Chiat/Day Advt., Inc., L.A., 1987-90; founder, chmn., CEO Goldberg Moser O'Neill Advt., San Francisco, 1990—. Republican. Jewish. Office: Goldberg Moser O'Neill 77 Maiden Ln San Francisco CA 94108-5414

GOLDBERG, FREDRIC I., investment management company executive; b. N.Y.C., July 3, 1941; s. Larry and Frances (Bender) G.; m. Nicole Henri, Jan. 19, 1992. BA, SUNY, Buffalo, 1963; MA, Ohio State U., 1965; PhD, Brandeis U., 1968. Instr. philosophy MIT, Cambridge, 1966-68; prof. San Jose (Calif.) State U., 1968-70, Mont. State U., Bozeman, 1971-73, U. Calif., Santa Cruz, 1976-78; salesman Britannica Corp., N.Y.C., 1980-82; salesman, asst. mgr. Equitable Life Ins. Co., N.Y.C., 1982-84; pres., CEO, Goldberg Capital Mgmt. Inc., Santa Fe, 1984—; writer, prodr. The World of Investments, Sta. KHFM, Albuquerque. Home and Office: RR 2 Box 650 Santa Fe NM 87505-8697

GOLDBERG, HARVEY, financial executive; b. Bklyn., Jan. 30, 1940; s. Joseph and Regina (Goldkrantz) G.; m. Joyce Baron, Nov. 22, 1962; children—Keith, Jodi. BS in Acctg., Bklyn. Coll., 1962; postgrad. CCNY, 1963. CPA, N.Y. Sr. acct. Schwartz, Zelin & Weiss CPA's, N.Y.C., 1962-66; mgr. fin. analysis Columbia Records div. CBS, Inc., N.Y.C., 1966-70; asst. controller Revlon, Inc., N.Y.C., 1970-71; treas. Central Textile, Inc., Jersey City, 1971-74; controller Marcade Group, Inc., Jersey City, 1974-81, v.p., controller, 1981-86; v.p., CFO Paul Marshall Products, Inc., subs. Marcade Group, Long Beach, Calif., 1982-86, v.p., CFO , 1988-93; v.p., CFO, Players Internat., Inc., Calabasas, Calif., 1988-93, sr. v.p., CFO, 1988-93; exec. vp., CFO Adesso, Inc., Culver City, Calif., 1994—. County committeeman Monmouth County Dem. Com., N.J., 1979-80; chmn. adv. bd. High Point Ctr., Marlboro, N.J., 1978-82; mem. Marlboro Twp. Bd. Edn., 1980-82, v.p., 1981-82; bd. dirs. Family Consultation Ctr., Freehold, N.J. , 1982-83. Mem. AICPA, N.Y. State Soc. CPA's, Met. Retail Fin. Execs. Assn. Home: 19798 Greenbriar Dr Tarzana CA 91356-5442 Office: Adesso Inc 5110 W Goldleaf Cir Ste 90 Los Angeles CA 90056-1273

GOLDBERG, HERB, psychologist, educator; b. Berlin, Germany, July 14, 1937; came to U.S., 1941; s. Jacob and Ella (Nagler) G.; 1 child, Amy Elisabeth. BA cum laude, CUNY, 1958; PhD, Adelphi U., 1963. Lic. psychologist, Calif. Pvt. practice, L.A., 1965—; prof. Calif. State U., L.A., 1965—. Author: Creative Aggression, 1972, The Hazards of Being Male, 1976, Money Madness, 1978, The New Male, 1979, The Inner Male, 1986, The New Male/Female Relationship, 1982, What Men Really Want, 1991. Mem. APA, Phi Beta Kappa. Office: 1100 Glendon Ave Bldg 939 Los Angeles CA 90024-3513

GOLDBERG, JACOB, computer scientist, researcher; b. San Francisco, June 4, 1926; s. Lawrence and Bertha (Stark) G.; m. Shula Calic, June 12, 1926; children: Michael, Ari, Dena, Loren. BSEE, U. Calif., Berkeley, 1950; MSEE, Stanford U., 1954. Jr. rsch. engr. SRI Internat., Menlo Park, Calif., 1951-53; rsch. engr. SRI Internat., Menlo Park, 1953-57, sr. rsch. engr., 1957-64, lab. dir., 1964-84, sr. staff scientist, 1984-87, sr. sci. cons., 1987-95. Contbr. 30 papers on computing; 17 patents in field. With USN, 1944-46, PTO. Fellow IEEE (life); mem. Assn. for Computing Machinery. Democrat. Jewish. Home: 3373 Cowper St Palo Alto CA 94306-3020

GOLDBERG, LEE WINICKI, furniture company executive; b. Laredo, Tex., Nov. 20, 1932; d. Frank and Goldie (Ostrowiak) Winicki; student San Diego State U., 1951-52; m. Frank M. Goldberg, Aug. 17, 1952; children: Susan Arlene, Edward Lewis, Anne Carri. With United Furniture Co., Inc., San Diego, 1953-83, corp. sec., dir., 1963-83, dir. environ. interiors, 1970-83; founder Drexel-Heritage Store Edwards Interiors, subs. United Furniture, 1975; founding ptnr., v.p. FLJB Corp., 1976-86, founding ptnr., sec. treas., Sea Fin., Inc., 1980, founding ptnr., First Nat. Bank San Diego, 1982. Den mother Boy Scouts Am., San Diego, 1965; vol. Am. Cancer Soc., San Diego, 1964-69; chmn. jr. matrons United Jewish Fedn., San Diego, 1958; del. So. Pacific Coast region Hadassah Conv., 1960, pres. Galilee group San Diego chpt., 1960-61; supporter Marc Chagall Nat. Mus., Nice, France, U. Calif. at San Diego Cancer Ctr. Found., Smithsonian Instn., L.A. County Mus., San Diego Mus. Contemporary Art, San Diego Mus. Art; pres. San Diego Opera, 1992-94. Recipient Hadassah Service award San Diego chpt., 1958-59; named Woman of Dedication by Salvation Army Women's Aux., 1992, Patron of Arts by Rancho Sante Fe Country Friends, 1993. Democrat. Jewish.

GOLDBERG, LESLIE ROBERTA, management development, employee relations and training executive; b. N.Y.C.; d. William and Margaret (Waterman) G. BA, Hunter Coll., 1969; MS, Lehman Coll., 1974. Cert. in human rels., human resources, tng. Instructional design specialist Yonkers (N.Y.) Bd. Edn., 1969-87; sales and tng. specialist Commerce Clearing House Inc., N.Y.C., 1987-89; human resources devel. cons. Sussman-Automatic Corp., N.Y.C., 1987—; tng. and devel. mgr. Kirk Paper Co., L.A., 1989-91; mgmt. edn. program mgr. Employers Group (formerly Mchts. & Mfrs. Assn.), L.A., 1992-95; human resources mgr. AIDS Project, L.A., 1995—; cons. job search skills for profls. Employment and Devel. Dept., State of Calif., 1992; counselor, cons. Worknet, L.A., 1992—; featured in Fortune Mag., TV-KHSC. Mem. ASTD, Profls. in Human Resources Assn. (program chairperson 1994).

GOLDBERG, MICHAEL ARTHUR, land policy and planning educator; b. Bklyn., Aug. 30, 1941; s. Harold and Ruth (Abelson) G.; m. Rhoda Lynne Zacker, Dec. 22, 1963 (div. 1987); children: Betsy Anne, Jennifer Hei; m. Deborah Nelson, Sept. 7, 1991. B.A. cum laude, Bklyn. Coll., 1962; M.A., U. Calif., Berkeley, 1965, Ph.D., 1968. Acting instr. Sch. Bus. Adminstrn., U. Calif., Berkeley, 1967-68; asst. prof. Faculty of Commerce and Bus. Adminstrn., U. B.C., Vancouver, 1968-71, assoc. prof., 1971-76, prof., 1976—, assoc. dean, 1980-84, dean, 1991—, Herbert R. Fullerton prof. urban land policy, 1981—; mem. Vancouver Econ. Adv. Commn., 1980-82, Can. dept. Finance Deposit Ins. adv. group, 1992-94, Can. dept. Internat. Trade, Strategic Adv. Group on Internat. Trade in Financial Svcs., 1991—; vice chmn. B.C. Real Estate Found., 1985-87, chmn. 1987-91; mem. IFC Vancouver, 1985—, vice chmn., 1985-88, chmn., 1988-89, exec. dir. 1989-91; commr. B.C. Housing Mgmt. Commn., 1989-92; bd. dirs. Imperial Parking Ltd., VLC Properties Ltd., 1991-93, Brink Hudson Lefever. 1993—. Redekop Properties, 1994—; vice chmn. Canadian Fedn. Deans of Mgmt. and Adminstrv. Scis., 1991-92, chair, 1992-94, Securities Industry Policy Adv. Com., 1995—. Author: (with G. Gau) Zoning: Its Costs and Relevance for 1980's, 1980, The Housing Problem: A Real Crisis?, 1983, (with P. Chinloy) Urban Land Economics, 1984, The Chinese Connection, 1985, (with J. Mercer) The Myth of the North American City, 1985, On Balance, 1989; editor: Recent Perspectives in Urban Land Economics, 1976, (with P. Horwood) North American Housing Markets into the Twenty-first century, 1983, (with E. Feldman) The Rites and Wrongs of Land Use Policy, 1988. Trustee Temple Sholom, 1980-84. Can. Coun. fellow, 1974-75, Social Scis. and Humanities Rsch. Coun. fellow, 1979-80, 84-85, Inst. Land Policy fellow, 1979-80, Urban Land Inst. fellow, 1984—, Homer Hoyt Inst. fellow, 1988—, recipient Can. 125th anniversary medal for service to Can., 1993. Mem. Am. Planning Assn., Western Regional Sci. Assn., Regional Sci. Assn., Canadian Regional Sci. Assn., Canadian Econs. Assn., Am. Real Estate and Urban Econs. Assn. (dir. 1978—, pres. 1984), Vancouver Bd. Trade, Lambda Alpha. Home: 934 Gale Dr, Vancouver, BC Canada V4M 2P5 Office: U BC, Dean Commerce & Bus Adminstrn, Vancouver, BC Canada V6T 1Z2

GOLDBERG, MORRIS, internist; b. N.Y.C., Jan. 23, 1928; s. Saul and Lena (Schanberg) G.; BS in Chemistry cum laude, Poly. Inst. Bklyn., 1951; MD, SUNY, Bklyn., 1956; m. Elaine Shaw, June 24, 1956; children: Alan Neil, Seth David, Nancy Beth. Intern, Jewish Hosp. Bklyn., 1956-57, resident, 1957-58, 61-62, renal fellow, 1958-59; practice medicine, specializing in internal medicine, N.Y.C., 1962-71, Phoenix, 1971—; instr. to asst. clin. prof. internal medicine State U. N.Y. Coll. Medicine, Bklyn., 1962-71; clin. investigator, metabolic research unit Jewish Hosp. Bklyn., 1962-71; cons. in field; mem. staff Phoenix Bapt., Maryvale Samaritan, Good Samaritan, St. Joseph's Hosp., Vets. Affairs Med. Ctr., Phoenix. Served to capt. M.C., U.S. Army, 1959-61. Diplomate Am. Bd. Internal Medicine. Fellow ACP; mem. AMA, Am. Soc. Internal Medicine, Am. Coll. Nuclear Physicians (charter mem.), Am. Soc. Nephrology, Am. Soc. Hypertension (charter mem.), Ariz. Med. Assn., 38th Parallel Med. Soc. S. Korea, Ariz., Maricopa County Med. Assn., Sigma Xi, Phi Lambda Upsilon, Alpha Omega Alpha. Jewish. Contb articles to med. jours. Home: 24 E Wagon Wheel Dr Phoenix AZ 85020-4063

GOLDBERG KENT, SUSAN, library director; b. N.Y.C., Mar. 18, 1944; d. Elias and Minnie (Barnett) Solomon; m. Eric Goldberg, Mar. 27, 1966 (div. Mar. 1991); children: Evan, Jessica, Joanna; m. Rolly Kent, Dec. 20, 1991. BA, SUNY, Binghamton, 1965; MS, Columbia U., 1966. Libr. N.Y. Pub. Libr., 1965-67, br. mgr., 1967-68; reference libr. Bklyn. Pub. Libr. 1971-72; reference libr. Finkelstein Meml. Libr., Spring Valley, N.Y., 1974-76; coord. adult svcs. Tucson Pub. Libr. Ariz., 1977-80, dep. dir., 1980-87; mng. dir. Ariz. Theatre Co., Tucson, 1987-89; cons., Tucson, 1989-90; dir. Mpls. Pub. Libr., 1990-95; dir. L.A. Pub. Libr., Calif., 1995—. mem. adj. faculty Pima Community Coll., Tucson, 1978, U. Ariz., Tucson, 1978-79; commr. Ariz. Commission on the Arts, 1983-87; bd. dirs. Tejo Foster Found. Tucson, 1994—; chmn. strategic directions com. Urban Librs. Coun. Evanston, Ill., 1993—, bd. dirs. Editor: Courtly Love in the Shopping Mall, 1991; contbg. author: Critical Issues Conference 8, 1979; Public Librarianship, 1982; Reorganization in the Public Library, 1984, Against All Odds, 1994. v.p. Cultural Alliance of Tucson, 1981-82; chmn. arts and culture com. Tucson Tomorrow, 1982-87. Mem. ALA (mem. coun. 1990—), NOW (pres. Rockland County br. 1974-76), Minn. Libr. Assn., Pub. Libr. Assn. (pres. 1987-88, chmn. 1994 Nat. Convention, exec. bd. Urban Linrs. Coun., 1994—). Office: LA Pub Libr 630 W 5th St Los Angeles CA 90071-2002

GOLDBLATT, HAL MICHAEL, photographer, accountant; b. Long Beach, Calif., Feb. 6, 1952; s. Arnold Phillip and Molly (Stearns) G.; m. Shawn Naomi Doherty, Aug. 27, 1974; children: Eliyahu Yonah, Tova Devorah, Raizel, Shoshana, Reuven Lev, Eliezer Noach, Esther Bayla, Rochel Leah, Zalman Ber, Perle Sara. BA in Math., Calif. State U., Long Beach, 1975. Owner Star Publs., Las Vegas, 1975—; treas. Goldblatt, Inc., Las Vegas, 1980—; pres. SDG Computer Svc., Las Vegas, 1985—; chief fin. officer Martin & Mills Ltd., Las Vegas, 1992-93; controller Amland Devel., Las Vegas, 1993—. Photographer: (photo essays) Mikveh Yisroel, 1978, Chassidic Fabrengen, 1979, A Day at Disneyland, 1985; producer, engr.; (audio cassettes) From the Heart of My Dreams, 1980, Middle Class Dreams, 1981, Uforatzta Trio, 1982. Founder, pres. Jews for Judaism, Long Beach, 1975-82, v.p., 1983—; fundraising chmn. Friends of Lubavitch, Long Beach, 1977; bd. dirs. Congregation Lubavitch, Long Beach, 1987, 91-92. Recipient Gold Press Card award Forty Niner Newspaper, 1973, 74, Floyd Durham Meml. award for Outstanding Community Svc., 1973. Office: Amland Devel 1253 S Arville Las Vegas NV 89102

GOLDEN, BONNIE JANE, counselor; b. Chgo., Apr. 5, 1956; d. Ted and Dorothy (Kranz) Schultz; m. Norman Scott Golden, Aug. 20, 1978; 1 child, Samuel Golden. AA, S.W. Coll., Chgo., 1975; BS, U. Ill., 1977; MEd, U. Ariz., 1978. Counselor, coord. U. Ariz., Tucson, 1978-83; counselor Pima Coll., Tucson, 1987—, EEO coord., 1984-87. Co-author: Building Self-Esteem: Strategies for Success in School, 1994. Mem. Assn. Psychol. Type, Nat. Counseling Assn., Nat. Career Devel. Assn. Office: Pima CC 1255 N Stone Ave Tucson AZ 85709-3002

GOLDEN, CONSTANCE JEAN, aerospace engineer; b. Highland Park, Ill., June 8, 1939; d. Herman William and Chrystle O'Linda Leuer; BS in Math, Physics, Beloit Coll. summa cum laude, 1961; AM in Math., Harvard, 1962; PhD in Math., Stanford U., 1966, MS in Ops. research Engring., 1970; m. Charles Joseph Golden, June 13, 1962; 1 dau., Kerri Lynn. Scientist/engr. research and devel. div. Lockheed Missiles & Space Co., Sunnyvale, Calif., 1962-68, sr. scientist/engr. Palo Alto research labs., 1968-74, mgr. planning requirements and mgmt. control, missile systems div., Sunnyvale, 1975-78; program mgr. space ops. studies Ford Aerospace, Palo Alto, 1978-79, corp. strategy mgr., Detroit, 1980-81, mgr. mission ops. and tech. devel., Sunnyvale, Calif., 1982-84, mgr. adv. programs, chair corp. intelligent systems consortium, 1984-91; program mgr. network stds. and interoperability, Space and Range Systems, Loral Aerospace, Sunnyvale, Calif., 1992—; mem. comml. satellite survivability task force. Nat. Security Telecommunications Adv. Com., 1982-84; mem. Nat. Def. Exec. Res.-Fed. Emergency Mgmt. Agy.; mem. adv. council for sci. and math. Mills Coll., 1976-80; bd. trustees Beloit Coll., 1993—. NSF fellow, 1961-62; recipient Tribute to Women in Industry award, 1985-86; named Disting. Woman of Yr. Lockheed, 1976. Mem. AIAA (space systems tech. panel 1982-83, AI tech. com. 1989-92, chair space ops. stds. com., 1992—, assoc. fellow, 1992), Armed Forces Communications and Electronic Assn. (sect. dir. 1979-80), Am. Astronautical Soc. (chmn. San Francisco Bay Area sect. 1984), Soc. Women Engrs. (fellow 1982, past pres. San Francisco Bay Area sect., past nat. scholarship chmn.), Jr. Achievement, Phi Beta Kappa (award 1960-61). Club: Toastmasters (past pres., ATM). Contbg. author: Second Careers for Women, 1975. Office: Loral Space and Range Systems 1260 Crossman Ave Sunnyvale CA 94089-1116

GOLDEN, GINA LOUISE, psychotherapist; b. Denver, June 2, 1964; d. James Alfred and Evelyn Lucille (Sellers) G.; m. Kevin DeShazer, June 3, 1995. AA, Colo. Mountain Coll., Steamboat Springs, 1987; BA magna cum laude, U. Colo., 1993, MA, 1994. Sec.-receptionist Western World Resorts, Steamboats Springs, 1983; sales assoc. Sportstalker, Steamboats Springs, 1983-84; sales and design asst. Dianna's Furniture Gallery, Steamboats Springs, 1986-87; dance tchr. Colo. Mountain Coll., Steamboats Springs, 1989-90; sales and asst. mgr., buyer 8th St. West, Steamboats Springs, 1989-92; psychotherapy intern Steamboat Mental Health, 1994; with High Country Counseling, Craig, Colo., 1994—; choreographic cons. Steamboat Springs H.S., 1989-90; dancer, performer Ballet N.W., Steamboat Springs, 1988-94; dancer, performer, choreographer Steamboat Dance Theatre, 1983-91; mentor, classroom aide Univ. Hills Elem. Sch., Boulder, 1992-93. Mem. APA (assoc.), Am. Counseling Assn., Psi Chi, Chi Sigma Iota.

GOLDEN, JULIUS, advertising and public relations executive, lobbyist, investor; b. N.Y.C., Feb. 25, 1929; s. Nathan and Leah (Michlin) G.; m. Constance Lee Carpenter, Dec. 31, 1954 (div. Mar. 1965); children: Andrew Mitchell, Juliet Deborah; m. Diana Zana George, Apr. 30, 1973; 1 child, Jeremy Philip. B.A., U. N.Mex., 1952. Asst. dir. info. U. N.Mex., Albuquerque, 1952-53; writer AP, Albuquerque, part-time 1952-53, staff writer, 1953-55, fgn. corr., S.Am., 1956-59; pres. Group West Advt./Pub. Relations Albuquerque, 1959—; dir. Diagnostek, Inc., Albuquerque, Galaxy Broadcasting Co., Albuquerque, Health Care Svcs., Inc., Albuquerque, HPI, Inc., Albuquerque, Hebenstreit Comm., Inc., Albuquerque, Electrical Products Co., Albuquerque. Author: A Time to Die, 1975. Active Bernalillo County Lung Assn., 1961-64; mem. Met. Crime Commn., Albuquerque, 1967-71; chmn., 1970-71; mem. Albuquerque Police Commn. Task Force, 1988-89. Served with AUS, 1945-48, PTO, Korea. Recipient Nat. Feature Writing award Sigma Delta Chi, 1952, E.H. Shaffer award N.Mex. Press Assn., 1953.

Mem. Pub. Relations Soc. (pres. N.Mex. chpt. 1972), Profl. Journalism Soc. (pres. 1969-70), Pub. Relations Soc. N.Mex. pres. 1972), Am. Advt. Fedn., Sigma Delta Chi. Democrat. Jewish. Clubs: Overseas Press of Am., Albuquerque Press, Petroleum, 4 Hills Country. Home: 1408 Stagecoach Ln SE Albuquerque NM 87123-4429 Office: Group West 7005 Prospect Pl NE Albuquerque NM 87110-4311

GOLDEN, MICHAEL, state supreme court justice; b. 1942. BA in History, U. Wyo., 1964, JD, 1967; LLM, U. Va., 1992. Bar: Wyo. 1967, U.S. Dist. Ct. 1967, U.S. Ct. Appeals (10th cir.) 1967, U.S. Supreme Ct. 1970. Mem. firm Brimmer, MacPherson & Golden, Rawlins, Wyo., 1971-83, Williams, Porter, Day & Neville, Casper, Wyo., 1983-88; justice Wyo. Supreme Ct., Cheyenne, 1988—; mem. Wyo. State Bd. Law Examiners, 1977-82, 86-88. Capt. U.S. Army 1967-71. Office: Wyo Supreme Ct PO Box 1737 Cheyenne WY 82003-1737*

GOLDEN, MORTON JAY, museum director; b. Bklyn., Apr. 11, 1929; s. Sam Carl and Anna (Denmark) G.; m. Evelyn Lois Gould, Oct. 6, 1956; children: Caron, Linda, Jay. BS, U. So. Calif., 1952. Dep. dir. Los Angeles County Mus. Art, 1972-82; dir. Palm Springs (Calif.) Desert Mus., 1982—; cons. M.A.P., 1984—. Treas., mem. exec. com. Greater Palm Springs Conv. and Visitors Bur., 1985—. Honor of Republic, nation of Egypt, 1978. Mem. Am. Assn. Mus. (cons. 1985-86, mem. accreditation rev. com. 1986), Calif. Assn. Mus. (chmn. bd. 1979-83, bd. dirs. 1985—), Mus. Mgmt. Inst. (sr. assoc.)., Assn. Sci. Mus. Dirs. Democrat. Jewish. Office: Palm Springs Desert Mus Inc 101 Museum Dr PO Box 2288 Palm Springs CA 92263

GOLDEN, NANCY MCALEER, fundraising consultant; b. Bridgeport, Conn., Mar. 21, 1941; d. Arthur Gordon and Nancy (Stevens) McAleer; m. Frederic Golden, Sept. 27, 1980. BA in English Lit., Russell Sage Coll., 1962; postgrad., NYU, 1978-79. Exec. asst. Pubaid S.A., London, 1965-68; mktg. info. mgr. Time-Life Books Time Inc., N.Y.C., 1968-75, gen. mgr. Selling Areas-Mktg., Inc., 1975-82, mgr. adminstrn. and tng. info. systems svcs., 1982-87; dir. membership Commonwealth Club of Calif., San Francisco, 1988-89; freelance fund-raising cons. San Francisco, 1989—. Chair holiday luncheon planning com. San Francisco Edn. Fund, 1989; vol., bd. dirs. Svcs. for the Elderly, Yorkville, 1975-87; bd. dirs., pres. condo. assn., San Francisco, 1987—; bd. dirs., pres. coop. N.Y., 1985-87. Mem. Nat. Soc. Fund Raising Execs., Cosmopolitan Club. Office: 2207 Alameda Padre Serra Santa Barbara CA 93103-1707

GOLDEN, RENÉE WAYNE, lawyer; b. N.Y.C., Oct. 20, 1930; d. Benjamn A. Weiner and Ada (Block) Zweig; 1 child, Philip Andrew. JD, San Fernando Valley Coll. Law, L.A., 1977. Bar: Calif. 1977. Pvt. practice Hollywood, Calif., 1977—. Mem. ABA, State Bar Calif., Calif. Lawyers for Arts, L.A. County Bar Assn., L.A. Copyright Soc., Beverly Hills Bar Assn. Home and Office: 8983 Norma Pl West Hollywood CA 90069

GOLDEN, THOMAS LESLIE, computer specialist, graphic design artist; b. New Orleans, Nov. 30, 1934; s. Thomas L. and Merriam A. (Riles) G.; m. Betty J. Davidson, Apr. 3, 1959; children: Chandra Kim, C. Stuart. AS, Moorpark Coll., 1976; BS, Calif. State U., Northridge, 1979. Layout designer Mor-Aire Corp., Houston, 1960-69; cobol programmer G.T.&E. Data Svcs., Marina Del Rey, Calif., 1970-77; computer analyst G.T.&E. Data Svcs., Marina Del Rey, 1979-88; control analyst Moorpark (Calif.) Coll., 1977-79; instr. data processing Ventura (Calif.) Coll., 1979; owner, mgr. Golden Graphics, Rockwall, Tex., 1985-88; MIS supr. Harris DTS, Novato, Calif., 1988-94; mem., advisor Calif. Edn. Data Processing Assn., 1978-80. Troop leader Boy Scouts Am., Houston, 1959-60. With U.S. Army, 1958-60. Recipient Houston Mus. of Art scholarship, 1952-54. Mem. Internat. Soc. Artists, British Toy Soldier Soc.

GOLDFARB, I. JAY, accountant; b. N.Y.C., Mar. 8, 1933; s. Joseph and Fay Esther (Hirschhorn) G.; m. Arlene Storch, May 8, 1955; children: Meryl, David. BA, CUNY, 1955. CPA, N.Y., Calif. Staff acct. T.D. Davidson & Co., N.Y.C., 1957-59; ptnr. Rashba & Pokart, N.Y.C., 1959-65; chief fin. officer Fabrics by Joyce Inc., N.Y.C., 1965-66; ptnr. Clarence Rainess & Co., N.Y.C., 1966-71, L.A., 1971-75; sr. ptnr. Joseph J. Herbert & Co., L.A., 1975-78; mng. ptnr. Goldfarb, Whitman & Cohen, L.A., 1978—. Mem. bd. govs. City of Hope, 1993—. Capt. USAF, 1955-57. Recipient Spirit of Life award City of Hope, 1990. Mem. AICPA, N.Y. State Soc. CPAs, Calif. Soc. CPAs, Prof. and Fin. Assoc. City of Hope (pres. 1974-76, dinner chmn. 1977-79), Boys and Girls Club San Fernando Valley (v.p. 1989, treas. 1990-93), Keystone Lodge, Masons. Office: Goldfarb Whitman & Cohen 12233 W Olympic Blvd Los Angeles CA 90064-1034

GOLDFARB, TIMOTHY MOORE, hospital administrator; b. Jerome, Ariz., Dec. 15, 1949; married. B, Ariz. State U., 1975, MHA, 1978. Adminstrv. resident Univ. Med. Ctr., Tucson, 1977-78, mgr. patient accts., 1978-79; asst. adminstr. Tucson Gen. Hosp., 1979; asst. adminstr. Univ. Med. Ctr., Tucson, 1979-83, assoc. adminstr., 1983-84; assoc. hosp. dir. Oreg. Health Scis. Univ. Hosp., Portland, 1984-89, hosp. dir., 1989—. Office: Univ Hosp 3181 SW Sam Jackson Park Rd Portland OR 97201-3011

GOLDIE, ERIC TODD, marketing professional; b. L.A., Apr. 21, 1962; s. Sheldon Myron and Sheila Marlene (Brodey) G. BA in Polit. Sci./Internat. Rels., Calif. State U., Northridge, 1993. Electronic warfare supr., petty officer first class USNR, USS Cowpens, 1982—; cable TV salesman United Cable TV Co., L.A., 1985-88; E.S.L. tchr. L.A. ORT Tech. Inst., L.A., 1988-91; life. ins. spl. agt. Northwestern Mut. Life, L.A., 1991-93; ednl. sales mgr. P.F. Collier/Macmillan Pub. Co., L.A., 1993-94; nat. mktg. mgr. Vivid/Atlantis Interactive, Van Nuys, Calif., 1994—. Pres. Calif. State U. Northridge Hillel, 1985-86; officer North San Fernando Valley Calif. Rep. Assembly, Van Nuys, 1989-91; precinct leader Graffiti Busters, Van Nuys, 1989-91; co-chair environ. com. Van Nuys C. of C., 1990-92. 2d lt. Calif. Army Nat. Guard 240th Signal Battalion, 1995—. Mem. L.A. Jewish Fedn. (Young Leadership com. co-chair 1992-93, interethnic religious subcom. chair 1986-93), U.S. Naval Inst., Am. Polit. Sci. Assn. Republican. Jewish. Home: 5735 Woodman Ave Apt 205 Van Nuys CA 91401-4470

GOLDIE, RAY ROBERT, lawyer; b. Dayton, Ohio, Apr. 1, 1920; s. Albert S. and Lillian (Hayman) G.; student U. So. Calif., 1943-44, JD, 1957; student San Bernardino Valley Coll., 1950-51; JD U. So. Calif., 1957; m. Dorothy Roberta Zafman, Dec. 2, 1941; children—Marilyn, Deanne, Dayle, Ron R. Elec. appliance dealer, 1944-54; teaching asst. U. So. Calif. Law Sch., 1956-57; admitted to Calif. bar, 1957; dep. atty. gen. State of Calif., 1957-58; sole practice, San Bernardino, 1958-87. Pres., Trinity Acceptance Corp., 1948-53. Mem. World Peace Through Law Center, 1962—; regional dir. Legion Lex, U. So. Calif. Sch. Law, 1959-75; chmn. San Bernardino United Jewish Appeal, 1963; v.p. United Jewish Welfare Fund San Bernardino, 1964-66, Santa Anita Hosp., Lake Arrowhead, 1966-69. Bd. dirs. San Bernardino Med. Arts Corp. Served with AUS, 1942-43. Fellow Internat. Acad. Law and Sci.; mem. ABA, San Bernardino County Bar Assn., Riverside County Bar Assn., State Bar Calif., Am. Judicature Soc., Am. Soc. Hosp. Attys., Calif. Trial Lawyers Assn. (v.p. chpt. 1965-67, pres. 1967-68), Am. Arbitration Assn. (nat. panel arbitrators), Coachella Valley Desert Bar Assn., Order of Coif, Nu Beta Epsilon (pres. 1956-57). Club: Lake Arrowhead Country (pres. 1972-73, 80-81), Lake Arrowhead Yacht, Club at Morningside (CFO 1992-93, sec. 1993-94). Home and Office: 1 Hampton Ct Rancho Mirage CA 92270-2585

GOLDIE, RON ROBERT, lawyer; b. San Bernardino, Calif., Apr. 6, 1951; s. Ray R. and Dorothy R. (Zafman) G.; m. Betty J. Cooper, June 13, 1983; children: Meghan Ann, Rand R., R. Cooper. Diploma, U. Paris, 1970; BA, U. So. Calif., 1972, MBA, JD, 1975. Bar: Calif. 1975, U.S. Dist. Ct. (cen., no. and so. dists.) Calif., U.S. Tax Ct., U.S. Ct. Appeals (2d, 9th and 11th cirs.). Atty. Goldie Law Corp., Los Angeles and San Bernardino, 1975-82; sole practice Los Angeles, 1982-86; prin. Law Offices of Ron R. Goldie, Los Angeles, 1986-88; sr. ptnr., chmn. bus. dept. Rosen, Wachtell & Gilbert, L.A., 1988-90; sr. ptnr. Jeffer, Mangels, Butler & Marmaro, L.A., 1990—. Republican. Jewish. Home: 14139 Beresford Rd Beverly Hills CA 90210-1067 Office: Jeffer Mangels Butler & Marmaro 2121 Avenue Of The Stars Los Angeles CA 90067-5010

GOLDING, GEORGE EARL, journalist; b. Oakdale, Calif., Aug. 26, 1925; s. Herbert Victor and Elva M. (Leydecker) G.; m. Joyce Mary Buttner, July 15, 1948; children: Earlene Golding Bigot, Brad Leslie, Dennis Lee, Frank Edwin, Charlton Kenneth, Daniel Duane. AA, Modesto Jr. Coll., 1950; BA San Francisco State Coll., 1959. Advt. salesman Riverbank News, 1949; galley bank boy, cub reporter San Bernardino Sun, 1951; editor Gustine Standard, 1952; photographer-reporter Humboldt Times, 1952-56; reporter, asst. city editor San Mateo (Calif.) Times, 1956-90; staff writer, corr. UPI; contbg. writer, photographer Nat. Motorist mag.; aviation writer, columnist Flight Log; co-author: (with Joyce Golding) Empire of Cousins, 1995. Pub. relations adviser Powder Puff Derby start. 1972. Served with U.S. Maritime Service, 1943, USAAF, 1944-46, AUS, 1950. Recipient John Swett award Calif. Tchrs. Assn., 1964; nominee McQuaid award Cath. Newsmen, 1965, 68; A.P. and Ency. Brit. photography awards, 1954-55, A.P. newswriting award, 1964. Mem. Am. Newspaper Guild, San Francisco-Oakland News Guild, Aviation/Space Writers Assn. (various awards 1983-84), Peninsula Press Club (founding dir., pres. 1976, co-chmn. awards and installation 1986-87), San Mateo County Arts Council (charter). Home: 1625 Ark St San Mateo CA 94403-1001

GOLDING, SUSAN, mayor; b. Muskogee, Okla., Aug. 18, 1945; d. Brage and Hinda Fay (Wolf) G.; children: Samuel, Vanessa. Cert. Pratique de Langue Francaise, U. Paris, 1965; BA in Govt. and Internat. Rels., Carleton Coll., 1966; MA in Romance Philology, Columbia U., 1974. Asssoc. editor Columbia U. Jour. of Internat. Affairs, N.Y.C., 1968-69; teaching fellow Emory U., Atlanta, 1973-74; instr. San Diego Community Coll. Dist., 1978; assoc. pub., gen. mgr. The News Press Group, San Diego, 1978-80; city council mem. City of San Diego, 1981-83; dep. sec. bus., transp., housing State of Calif., Sacramento, 1983-84; county supr. dist. 3 County of San Diego, 1984—; mayor City of San Diego, 1992—; founder Internat. Trade Commn., San Diego, 1985; chmn. San Diego Drug Strike Force, 1987-88, Alcohol and Drug Abuse Prevention Task Force, 1988, San Diego Earthquake Preparedness Com., 1986—, San Diego Unified Disaster Council, 1989—, San Diego Regional Justice Facility Financing Agy., 1989—, Calif. Environ. Quality Act Task Force, San Diego County Bd. Suprs., 1989—; dir. Svc. Auth. for Freeway Emergencies, San Diego, 1987; mem. Gov.'s Pub. Infrastructure Task Force, Mortgage Capital Task Force, Calif. Housing Fin. Agy., Calif. Coastal Commn.; mem. San Diego County Commn. on the Status of Women; bd. dirs. San Diego County Water Authority; trustee So. Calif. Water Com., Inc.; founder Mid City Comml. Revitalization Task Force; chair Pub. Svcs. and Safety Com. San Diego City Coun., Select Com. on Affordable Rental Housing; co-chair City County Reinvestment Task Force; vice-chair Transp. and Land Use Com. of City Coun. Bd. dirs. Child Abuse Prevention Found., San Diego Conv. and Vis. Bur., Crime Victims Fund, United Cerebral Palsy, San Diego Air Quality Bd., San Diego March of Dimes, Rep. Assocs.; adv. bd. Girl Scouts U.S.; trustee So. Calif. Water Comm.; mem. Rep. State Cen. Com.; co-chair com. Presidency George Bush Media Fund, Calif.; chair San Diego County Regional Criminal Justice Coun., race rels. com. Citizens Adv. Com. on Racial Intergration, San Diego Unified Sch. Dist.; hon. chair Am. Cancer Soc's. Residential Crusade, 1988. Named one of Ten Outstanding Rep. County Ofcls. in U.S.A., Rep. Nat. Com., 1987, San Diego Woman of Achievement Soroptimists Internat., 1988, One of San Diego's Ten Outstanding Young Citizens, 1981; recipient Calif. Women in Govt. Achievement award, 1988, Alice Paul award Nat. Women's Polit. Caucus, 1987, Willie Velasquez Polit. award Mex. Am. Bus. and Profl. Assn., 1988. Mem. Nat. Assn. of Counties (chair Op. Fair Share, mem. taxation and fin. com.), Nat. Women's Forum, Kiwanis, Sigma Delta Chi. Jewish. Office: Office of the Mayor City Administration Bldg 11th Fl 202 C St San Diego CA 92101-4806

GOLDKAMP, KENNETH JAMES, civil engineer; b. San Diego, Calif., May 17, 1938; s. Sanglier Claire and Theresa Marie (Pavlinick) G.; m. Kathleen Marie Kendall, Nov. 14, 1964; children: Mary Theresa, John Christian. BS in Engring., San Diego State Coll., 1964; MS in Civil Engring., Calif. State U., San Diego, 1973. Registered profl. civil engr., Calif. Asst. civil engr. County San Diego, 1964-68; sr. civil engr. City of Chula Vista, Calif., 1968—. With USNR, 1957-59, Guam. Mem. Am. Soc. Civil Engrs. (treas. local sect.), Am. Pub. Works Assn. (dir. San Diego and Imperial sects.). Republican. Roman Catholic. Home: 8695 Chantilly Ave San Diego CA 92123-3434 Office: City of Chula Vista Pub Works Dept 276 4th Ave Chula Vista CA 91910-2631

GOLDMAN, ALVIN IRA, philosopher and educator; b. Bklyn., Oct. 1, 1938; s. Nathan and Frances (Krugman) G.; m. Holly Martin Smith, June 15, 1969; children: Raphael, Sidra. BA, Columbia U., 1960; MA, Princeton U., 1962, PhD, 1965. From asst. prof. to prof. U. Mich., Ann Arbor, 1963-80; prof. U. Ill., Chgo., 1980-83; prof. U. Ariz., Tucson, 1983-94, Regents' prof. philosophy, 1994—. Author: A Theory of Human Action, 1970, Epistemology and Cognition, 1986, Liaisons: Philosophy Meets..., 1992, Philosophical Applications of Cognitive Science, 1993. Guggenheim fellow, 1975-76, Ctr. for Advanced Study in Behavioral Scis. fellow, 1975-76, Nat. Humanities Ctr. fellow, 1981-82. Mem. Am. Philos. Assn. (Pacific divsn. pres. 1991-92), Soc. for Philosophy and Psychology (pres. 1987-88). Office: Univ of Ariz Dept Philosophy Tucson AZ 85721

GOLDMAN, MITCHEL PAUL, dermatologist; b. Miami Beach, Fla., Apr. 5, 1955; s. Arnold Leonard and Betty (Freedman) G.; children: Risa D., Melissa D. BA in Biology summa cum laude, Boston U., 1977; MD, Stanford U., 1982. Diplomate Am. Bd. Dermatology. Intern U. Calif., San Diego, 1982-83; resident UCLA, 1983-86; with Dermatology Assocs., La Jolla, Calif., 1986—; mem. staff U. Calif. San Diego Med. Ctr., Scripps Meml. Hosps., Encinitas and La Jolla, Children's Hosp., 1987—; asst. clin. prof. dermatology U. Calif., San Diego. Author 6 med. textbooks; contbr. more than 100 articles to profl. jours. Bd. dirs. San Diego chpt., Am. Cancer Soc. Fellow Am. Soc. for Dermatologic Surgery (bd. dirs. 1995—), Am. Acad. Dermatology, Am. Soc. for Laser Medicine and Surgery; mem. N.Am. Soc. Phlebology (past pres.), Am. Venous Forum (bd. dirs. 1993-95), Internat. Soc. for Edn. and Rsch. of Vascular Diseases, Internat. Soc. of Cosmetic Laser Surgeons, San Diego County Dermatol. Soc. (past pres.), Sonoran Dermatology Soc. (past pres.), Phi Beta Kappa. Office: Dermatology Assocs 9850 Genesse Ste 480 La Jolla CA 92037

GOLDMAN, SERGEY YURI, programmer, physicist; b. Saratov, Russia, Oct. 19, 1957; came to U.S., 1990; s. Yuiri Sergey and Vera Moisey (Minkin) G.; m. Lilia Sheynfeld, Aug. 25, 1991; children: Miriam, Joseph. PhD in Physics and Math., Saratov State U., 1985; MS in Environ. Sci., Oreg. Grad. Inst. Sci. & Tech., 1992. Engr., physicist Rsch. Inst. Agropribor, Saratov, Russia, 1979-90; rsch. scientist Oreg. Grad. Inst. Sci. and Tech., Portland, 1990-94; programmer, analyst Computer Sci. Corp., Portland, 1994—. Contbr. articles to profl. jours.; co-inventor 6 inventions including method of determining permeability of porous material; spectroscopic method for determining the diffusion coefficient and solubility of helium and neon in glass. Fellow AAAS. Home: 8190 SW 82nd Pl Portland OR 97223-6995

GOLDRING, STANLEY DONALD, medical instrument designer; b. St. Louis, Apr. 13, 1942; s. Ben and Ruth Goldring. BSEE, Wash. U., 1964; MSEE, U. Calif., Berkeley, 1965. Registered profl. engr., Calif. Sr. mem. of tech. staff ESL Inc., Sunnyvale, Calif., 1965-76; R & D engr., sect. mgr. Abbott Labs., Mountain View, Calif., 1977—. Inventor signal filter method, saturation levels in blood, and electro-optic coupler. Grantee NSF, 1964. Mem. Silicon Valley Biomed. Industry Coun., Eta Kappa Nu, Tau Beta Pi. Jewish. Office: Abbott Labs 1212 Terra Bella Ave Mountain View CA 94043-1824

GOLDSMITH, DONALD WILLIAM, lawyer, astronomer, writer; b. Washington, Feb. 24, 1943; s. Raymond William and Selma Evelyn (Fine) G.; m. Rose Marien, Apr. 10, 1975 (div. 1978); 1 child, Rachel Evelyn. BA, Harvard U., 1963; PhD, U. Calif., Berkeley, 1969, JD, 1983. Asst. prof. earth and space sci. SUNY, Stony Brook, 1972-74; vis. prof. Niels Bohr Inst., Copenhagen, 1977; vis. instr. physics Stanford (Calif.) U., 1983; vis. lectr. astronomy U. Calif., Berkeley, 1980-88, vis. assoc. prof., 1990-93; assoc. Pillsbury, Madison and Sutro, San Francisco, 1985-87; cons. Cosmos TV program, Los Angeles, 1978-80; pres. Interstellar Media Pubs., Berkeley, 1978—. Author: Nemesis, 1985, The Evolving Universe, 1985, Supernova!, 1989, Space Telescope, 1989, The Astronomers, 1991; (with others) The Search for Life in the Universe, 1980, 2d edit. 1992, Cosmic Horizons, 1982, Mysteries of the Milky Way, 1991; co-writer (TV programs) Is Anybody Out There, 1986, The Astronomers, 1991. Recipient 1st prize popular essays in astronomy Griffith Obs./Hughes Aircraft Corp., L.A., 1983, Best Popular Writing by a Scientist award Am. Inst. Physics, 1986, Klumpke-Roberts award for lifetime achievement Astronomy Soc. Pacific, 1990, Annenberg Found. award for edn. Am. Astron. Soc., 1995. Home: 2153 Russell St Berkeley CA 94705-1006

GOLDSMITH, JONATHAN CHARLES, pediatrician; b. Dayton, Ohio, Oct. 19, 1945; m. Delores Y. Goldsmith. AB, Dartmouth Coll., 1967; MD, NYU, 1971. Intern then resident Vanderbilt U. Hosps., 1971-74; fellow in hematology U. N.C., 1976-79; dir. Hemophilia Treatment Ctr., Children's Hosp., L.A., 1991—; prof. pediatrics and medicine U. So. Calif., L.A., 1991—. Maj. USAF, 1974-76. Office: Childrens Hosp LA 4650 W Sunset Blvd # 54 Los Angeles CA 90027-6016

GOLDSTEIN, BARRY BRUCE, biologist, researcher; b. N.Y.C., Aug. 2, 1947; s. George and Pauline (Kolodner) G.; m. Jacqueline Barbara Aboulafia, Dec. 21, 1968; children: Joshua, Jessica. BA, Queens Coll., 1968; MA, CCNY, N.Y.C., 1974; PhD, CUNY, N.Y.C., 1980; JD, U. N.Mex., 1994. Microbiologist CPC Internat., Yonkers, N.Y., 1968-71; rsch. scientist U. Tex., Austin, 1977-80; v.p. SystemCulture Inc., Honolulu, 1980-83; bioenergy/aquaculture program mgr. N.Mex. Solar Energy Inst., Las Cruces, 1983-89; pres. Ancient Seas Aquaculture Inc., Roswell, N.Mex., 1989-92, Desert Seas Aquaculture Inc., Roswell, 1990-92, Hawaii Shellfish Co., Las Cruces, 1991—; project leader Sandia Nat. Labs., Carlsbad, N.Mex., 1994—. Editl. bd. Natural Resources Jour.; contbr. articles to profl. jours. Recipient Nat. Energy Innovation award Dept. Energy, Washington, 1985; Grad. fellow CUNY, 1971, Jesse Smith Noyes fellow, 1975, Regents scholar SUNY, 1964. Mem. World Aquaculture Soc., Am. Soc. Microbiology, AAAS. Office: Hawaii Shellfish Co PO Box 4209 Albuquerque NM 87196-4209

GOLDSTEIN, BERNARD, transportation company executive; b. Rock Island, Ill., Feb. 5, 1929; s. Morris and Fannie (Borenstein) G.; m. Irene Alter, Dec. 18, 1949; children: Jeffrey, Robert, Kathy, Richard. BA, U. Ill., 1949, LLB, 1951. Bar: Iowa 1951. With Alter Co., Bettendorf, Iowa, 1951—; bd. dirs. Valley Corp.; chmn. bd. Casino Am. Inc. Pres. Quad City Jewish Fedn., 1975. Jewish.

GOLDSTEIN, DEBBE, art history educator; b. Akron, Ohio, Sept. 1, 1953; d. Max and Evelyn Eva (Goldner) G. BA, Ohio State U., 1975, postgrad., 1994—. Adminstr. The Kitchen Ctr. for Video Music and Dance, N.Y.C., 1977-78; proprietor Deborah Goldstein Arts, N.Y.C., 1978-81; program asst. L.A. County Mus.; asst. dir. spl. events Mus. Contemporary Art, L.A., 1986-88; asst. dir. admissions Art Ctr. Coll. of Design, Pasadena, Calif., 1988—; adv. bd. graphics Orange (Calif.) Coast Coll., Saddleback Coll., Mission Viejo, Calif.; guest lectr. L.A. County Mus., 1992; presenter, spkr. Bowling Green State U., 1995. Co-curator Terra Moto: The Fallen and the Saved (Robert Morris), 1994, (ltd. edit.) Where's Wallenberg? (James Rosenquist), 1995. Educator MOCA, L.A., 1993, 94; mem. Dem. County Com., County of N.Y., 1984. Mem. (affiliate) Indsl. Design Soc. Am. Democrat. Jewish. Democrat. Jewish. Office: Art Ctr Coll of Design 1700 Lida Pasadena CA 91103

GOLDSTEIN, ELLIOTT STUART, science educator; b. Bklyn., July 7, 1942; s. William and Lottie (Roth) G.; m. Suzanne Kussner, July 7, 1963; children: Andrew Richard, Hyla Lynn. BS, U. Hartford (Conn.), 1967; MS, U. Minn., 1970, PhD, 1972. Postdoctoral fellow Mass. Inst. Tech., Cambridge, 1972-74; asst. prof. zoology Ariz. State U., Tempe, 1974-78, assoc. prof., 1978—; vis. assoc. prof. Calif. Inst. Tech., Pasadena, 1981; vis. scholar Ind. U., Bloomington, 1989; cons. Maricopa County (Ariz.) Dist. Atty., 1989-91. Contbr. articles to profl. jours. Exec. bd. mem. Temple Beth Sholom of Mesa (Ariz.), 1982—, pres., 1984-85. Mem. AAAS, Soc. for Devel. Biology, Genetics Soc. Am., Sigma Xi. Jewish. Home: 2342 E Alameda Dr Tempe AZ 85282-3058 Office: Ariz State U Zoology Dept Tempe AZ 85287

GOLDSTEIN, HOWARD EDWARD, chemical engineer; b. White Plains, N.Y., June 28, 1937; s. Nathan and Matilda (Sussman) G.; m. Sheila Carrol Singer, June 18, 1961; children: David, Allen, Debra. BS in Chem. Engring., U. Ariz., 1961, MS in Chem. Engring., 1963. Engr. Lockheed Missiles & Space, Sunnyvale, Calif., 1963-67; thermodynamics engr. Applied Space Products, Palo Alto, Calif., 1967-70; from rsch. scientist to chief thermal protection materials Space Tech. Divsbn. Ames Rsch. Ctr., Moffett Field, Calif., 1970-90, chief/sr. scientist, 1990—. Contbr. articles to profl. jours.; spkr., presenter in field; holder patents in field. Recipient medal for exceptional scientific achievement NASA, 1976, numerous certificates of recognition and group awards. Fellow AIAA (thermophysics com. 1978-81, materials com. 1986-89); mem. AAAS, Am.Ceramic Soc., Am. Chem. Soc., Soc. for Advancement of Materials and Processing Engring. Office: Ames Rsch Ctr Bldg 229-3 Moffett Field CA 94035

GOLDSTEIN, MARCIA, historian, educator, law office administrator; b. Denver, Jan. 17, 1951; d. Dickerson H. and Phyllis (Selby) Tremmel; m. Jeffrey A. Goldstein, Feb. 28, 1976; 1 child, Deanna. BA in History magna cum laude, Metro. State Coll., 1982; MA in Am. History, U. Colo., 1995. Mktg. support mgr. NBI, Inc., Boulder, 1983-87; law office adminstr. Goldstein & Dodge, Denver, 1991—; instr. Arapahoe C.C., Littleton, Colo., 1994-95. Mem. Orgn. Am. Historians, Nat. Pub. History Coun., Western History Assn., Colo. Hist. Soc., Colo. Com. for Women's History (bd. dirs., pres., 1993—), Colo. History Group, Historic Denver, Inc., Denver Woman's Press Club, Denver Westerners, Phi Alpha Theta. Democrat.

GOLDSTEIN, MARK ALAN, information science and research company executive, consultant; b. Suffern, N.Y., Feb. 5, 1951; s. Harry and Betty (Cohen) G.; m. Elizabeth Ann Warren, Jan. 1, 1985. BA, SUNY, Binghamton, 1972. Pres. Advanced Tools for the Arts, Tempe, 1975-94; rsch. and devel. engr. MicroAge, Tempe, 1976-79; mgr. hybrid test engring. Medtronic/Micro-Rel, Tempe, 1980-92; pres. Internat. Rsch. Ctr., Tempe, 1992—; mem. exec. bd. Gov.'s Strategic Partnership Econ. Devel./Ariz. Tech. and Info. Coun., Phoenix, 1993-94. Mem. IEEE, Am. Soc. Info. Sci., Assn. Ind. Info. Profls., Electronic Frontier Found., Soc. competitive Intelligence Profls., World Future Soc. (bd. dirs. Phoenix chpt.), Ariz. Software Assn., Ariz. Libr. Assn., Ariz. Online Users Group (pres.). Office: Internat Rsch Ctr PO Box 825 Tempe AZ 85280-0825

GOLDSTEIN, SIR NORMAN, dermatologist; b. Bklyn. July 14, 1934; s. Joseph H. and Bertha (Docteroff) G.; B.A., Columbia Coll., 1955; M.D., SUNY, 1959; m. Ramsay, Feb. 14, 1980; children: Richard, Heidi. Intern, Maimonides Hosp., N.Y.C., 1959-60; resident Skin and Cancer Hosp., 1960-61, Bellevue Hosp., 1961-62, NYU. Postgrad. Center, 1962-63 (all N.Y.C.); ptnr. Honolulu Med. Group, 1967-72; practice medicine specializing in dermatology, Honolulu, 1972—; clin. prof. dermatology U. Hawaii Sch. Medicine, 1973—; bd. dirs. Pacific Laser. Bd. dirs. Skin Cancer Found., 1979—; trustee Dermatol. Found., 1979-82, Hist. Hawaii Found., 1981-87; pres. Hawaii Theater Ctr., 1985-89, Hawaii Med. Libr., 1987-89; mem. Oahu Heritage Council, 1986—. Served with U.S. Army, 1960-67. Recipient Henry Silver award Dermatol. Soc. Greater N.Y., 1963; Husik award NYU, 1963; Spl. award Acad. Dermatologia Hawaiiana, 1971, Outstanding Scientific Exhibit award Calif. Med. Assn., 1979, Special award for Exhibit Am. Urologic Assn., 1980, Svc. to Hawaii's Youth award Adult Friends for Youth, 1991, Nat. Cosmetic Tattoo Assn. award, 1993, Cmty. Svc. award Am. Acad. Dermatology, 1993; named Physician of Yr., Hawaii Med. Assn., 1993. Fellow ACP, Am. Acad. Dermatology (Silver award 1972), Am. Soc. Lasers Medicine & Surgery, Royal Soc. Medicine; mem. Internat. Soc. Tropical Dermatologists (Hist. and Culture award), Soc. Investigative Dermatologists, AAAS, Am. Soc. Photobiology, Internat. Soc. Cryosurgery, Am. Soc. Micropigmentation Surgery, Small Bus. Council Am. (bus. adv. council), Pacific and Asian Affairs Council, Navy League, Assn. Hawaii Artists, Nat. Stereoscopic Soc., Biol. Photog. Assn., Friends of Photography, Health Sci. Communication Assn., Internat. Pigment Cell Soc., Am. Med. Writers Assn., Physicians Exchange of Hawaii (bd. dirs.), Am. Coll. Cryosurgery, Internat. Soc. Dermatol. Surgery, Am. Soc. Preventive Oncology, Soc. for Computer Medicine, Am. Assn. for Med. Systems and Info., computer Security Inst., Japan Am. Soc. Hawaii (bd. dirs.), Pacific Telecom

Council, Hawaii State Med. Assn. (mem. public affairs com.), Hawaii Dermatol. Soc. (sec.-pres.), Hawaii Public Health Assn., Pacific Dermatol. Assn., Pacific Health Research Inst., Honolulu County Med. Soc. (gov.), Nat. Wildlife Fedn., C. of C., Preservation Action, Am. Coll. Sports Medicine, Rotary, Ancient Gaelic Nobilitary Soc. (named Knight of the Niadh Nask, 1995), Outrigger Canoe Club, Plaza Club (pres. bd. dirs. 1990-92), Chancellor's Club, Oahu Country Club. Contbr. articles to profl. jours. Office: Tan Sing Bldg 1128 Smith St Honolulu HI 96817-5139

GOLDSTEIN, NORTON MAURICE (GOLDY NORTON), public relations consultant; b. Cleve., Apr. 11, 1930; s. Jacob N. and Phyllis Ruth (Weinstein) G.; m. Judith Marcia Morris, Oct. 29, 1955; 1 child, Ann Dee. Reporter L.A. Daily News, 1952-54; writer, producer Cleve Hermann Radio-TV Sports, L.A., 1952-59; exec. v.p. Kennett Pub. Rels. Assocs., L.A., 1959-71; writer, producer Vin Scully Sports Program, L.A., 1959-64; owner, oper. Goldy Norton Pub. Rels., L.A., 1971—. Author: Official Frisbee Handbook, 1972. Founding dir. U.S. Acad. Decathlon, L.A., 1982. With U.S. Army, 1949-52, Korea. Named to Frisbee Hall of Fame, Internat. Frisbee Assn., Hancock, Mich., 1979. Mem. So. Calif. Sports Boradcasters Assn. (mem. exec. bd. 1958). Office: Goldy Norton Pub Rels 6200 Wilshire Blvd Ste 906 Los Angeles CA 90048-5810

GOLDSTEIN, SIMON, credit management executive; b. N.Y.C., Sept. 1, 1935; s. Irving Charles and Tillie (Alpern) G.; m. Roberta Dubowitz, Jan. 4, 1958 (dec. 1968); children: Shari Lynn, David. BA, U. of Redlands, 1986. Ptnr. Parkway Floor Co., Long Branch, N.J., 1958-60; counselor Synanon Found., Santa Monica, Calif., 1961-65; salesman Harry P. Hirsch Carpet Co., Beverly Hills, Calif., 1961-64; owner Distinctive Floor Coverings, Beverly Hills, 1965-67; regional mgr. Nat. Credit Svcs., L.A., 1968-78, v.p., cons., 1990—; asst. contr., nat. credit mgr. Assoc. Internat., L.A., 1979-89; internat. collections project leader Hellmann Internat. Forwarders, Long Beach, Calif., 1989-90. With U.S. Army, 1953-58, Korea. Recipient Cert. of Recognition, Calif. State Assembly, 50th Dist., 1991, Calif. Legislature Assembly Resolution, Calif. Legislature Assembly, 1992. Democrat. Jewish. Home: 13520 Kornblum Ave Hawthorne CA 90250-7644

GOLDSTEIN, STEVEN EDWARD, psychologist; b. Bronx, N.Y., Nov. 25, 1948; s. Maurice and Matilda (Weiss) G.; BS in Psychology, CCNY, 1970, MS in Sch. Psychology, 1971; EdD in Sch. Psychology, U. No. Colo., 1977. Tchr., N.Y.C. Public Schs., 1970-71, 72-73, tchr., counselor, 1974; extern in sch. psychology N. Shore Child Guidance, 1972; sch. psychologist Denver Pub. Schs., 1975; asst. prof. psychology Northeastern Okla. State U., Tahlequah, 1976-78; coord. inpatient, emergency svcs. Winnemucca (Nev.) Mental Health Center, 1978-80; dir. Desert Devel. Ctr., Las Vegas, Nev., 1980-82; sr. psychologist Las Vegas Mental Health Ctr., 1982-92; pvt. practice psychology, Las Vegas, 1983—; sr. psychologist Desert Regional Ctr., 1992—; participant NSF seminar on biofeedback, 1977. Sec. grad. coun. CUNY, 1971; pres. grad. coun. in edn. CCNY, 1971. Lic. psychologist, Nev.; cert. sch. psychologist, N.Y., Calif. Mem. APA (Nev. coord. office of profl. practice 1987-88), Biofeedback Soc. Nev. (membership dir. 1982-90), Nev. Soc. Tng. and Devel. (dir. 1982-83), So. Nev. Soc. Cert. Psychologists (pres. 1984-86). Presenter papers to profl. confs. Office: 1300 S Jones Blvd Las Vegas NV 89102-1206 also: 3180 W Sahara Ave Ste C-25 Las Vegas NV 89102-6005

GOLDSTEIN, STUART WOLF, lawyer; b. Buffalo, N.Y., Sept. 9, 1931; s. Joseph and Esther (Wolf) G.; m. Myra Saft Stuart, June 1960 (dec. Aug. 1981); children: Jeffrey, Jonathan, Meryl; m. Nancy Baynes Lux, 1993. Student, U. Buffalo, 1949-52, JD, 1955; postgrad., U. Va., 1956. Bar: N.Y. 1956, Fla. 1974, Ariz. 1977, U.S. Supreme Ct. 1960, U.S Dist. Ct. (we. dist.) N.Y. 1956, U.S. Ct. Mil. Appeals 1957, U.S. Ct. Appeals (2d cir.) N.Y., 1978, U.S. Dist. Ct. Ariz. 1981. Sole practice Buffalo, 1960-79, 82-85, Phoenix, 1980-82, 85—. Pres., founder Cystic Fibrosis Found., Buffalo, 1960; fund-raiser United Fund, United Jewish Appeal; pres. Boys League; active Erie County Spl. Task Force on Energy, Buffalo, 1978. 1st lt. JAG, U.S. Army, 1956-60. Fellow Ariz. Bar Found.; mem. Ariz. State Bar Assn., N.Y. Trial Lawyers Assn., Erie County Trial Lawyers, Ariz. Trial Lawyers Assn. (Ariz. real property sect.), N.Y. State Bar Assn., Fla. Bar Assn., Am. Arbitration Assn., Maricopa County Bar Assn., Buffalo Skating Club, Curling Skating Club (legal counsel). Office: 2702 N 3rd St Phoenix AZ 85004-1130

GOLDSTEIN, WILLIAM M., composer, producer; b. Newark, Feb. 25, 1942; s. Harry and Sylvia (Hochheiser) G. MusB, Manhattan Sch. Music, 1965, postgrad., 1965-66. Freelance composer, arranger, producer music for TV, film, theater, 1966—; composer-in-residence U.S. Army Band, Ft. Myer, Va., 1966-69. Composer, condr., arranger, producer: (feature films) Hello Again, The Bad Guys, Bingo Long Traveling All Stars, 1976, Eye For an Eye, Force Five, Norman Is That You?, Hello Again, 1987, Shocker, 1989, The Quarrel, 1991, others, (TV films) Connecticut Yankee in King Arthur's Court, 1990, Blood River, 1991, (TV spls.) Omnibus, (Emmy award nomination 1980), Happy Endings (Emmy award nomination 1983), Fame (Emmy award nomination 1983), Hero in the Family, Marilyn: The Untold Story, Mobil Showcase Theatre, others, (documentaries) Television's Greatest Commercials, Parts I-V, The Stars Salute the U.S. Olympic Team, The Mysteries of the Mind, Living Sands of Namib, others, (theater prodns.) Marat Sade, Spread Eagle Four, The Peddler, Total Sweet Success, A Bullet for Billy the Kid 1964, others, (commls.) McDonalds, Buick, Noxema, Duncan Hines, Mitsubishi, others, (records) Switched on Classics, There's No Stopping Us (Sister Sledge), My Touch of Madness (Jermaine Jackson), Old Fashioned Man (Smokey Robinson), Guys and Dolls (Grammy award nomination 1977), Oceanscape, others. Bd. dirs. Calif. State Summer Sch. for the Arts. Recipient Golden Horse award Republic of China, 1981. Mem. Acad. Motion Picture Arts and Scis. (vis. artist 1980).

GOLDSTON, BARBARA M. HARRAL, editor; b. Lubbock, Tex., Jan. 26, 1937; d. Leonard Paul and Olivette (Stuart) Harral; m. John Rowell Toman (div. 1963); 1 child, Stuart Rowell; m. Olan Glen Goldston, 1989. BE, Tex. Christian U., 1959; MLS, U. Hawaii, 1968; postgrad., Golden Gate U., 1980-82. Tchr. pub. elem. schs., various cities, Tex. and Hawaii, 1959-66; contracts abstractor, indexer Champlin Oil Co., Ft. Worth, 1963-64; adminstrv. asst. engring. Litton Industries, Lubbock, Tex., 1964-65; mgr. rsch. library Hawaii Employers' Coun., Honolulu, 1968-72; rsch. cons. Thailand Hotel Study, Touche-Ross Assocs., Honolulu, 1974; dir. med. library U. S.D.-Sacred Heart Hosp., Yankton, 1977-79; editor, adminstrv. coord. book div. ABC-Clio, Inc., Santa Barbara, Calif., 1981-88; free-lance rsch./editorial cons. Albuquerque, 1988-89; instr. Santa Fe Community Coll., 1989—; owner Sandbar Prodns., Albuquerque, 1993—; ptnr. Broome-Harral, Inc., Albuquerque, 1989—. Author, editor with others Hist. Periodical Dir., 5 vols., World Defense Forces compendium. Contbr. Boy's Ranch, Amarillo, Tex., 1987—; mem. Lobero Theater Group, Santa Barbara, 1975-76; mem., treas. Yankton Med. Aux., 1977-79. Mem. ALA, Spl. Libraries Assn., Med. Libraries Assn., Am. Soc. Info. Sci., Albuquerque C. of C., Albuquerque Conv. and Visitors Bur., Better Bus. Bur. Albuquerque, Tex. Christian U. Alumni Assn., Delta Delta Delta. Republican. Episcopalian. Home: 9300 Seabrook Dr NE Albuquerque NM 87111-5863 Office: PO Box 3824 Albuquerque NM 87190-3824

GOLDSTONE, JACK ANDREW, sociologist; b. San Francisco, Sept. 30, 1953; s. Jack Robert and Ursula (Weinberg) G.; m. Gina Belinda Saleman, Feb. 9, 1992; 1 child, Alexander. AB, Harvard U., 1976, AM, 1979, PhD, 1981. Asst. prof. Northwestern U., Evanston, Ill., 1981-84; assoc. prof. Northwestern U., 1984-88; prof. U. Calif., Davis, 1989—; dir. ctr. for comparative rsch., U. Calif., Davis, 1989-91. Author: Revolution and Rebellion, 1991 (disting. pub. award Am. Sociol. Assn. 1993); editor: Revolutions of the Late 20th Century, 1991. ACLS fellow, 1983-84, Ctr. for Advanced Studies fellow Stanford U., 1993-94. Mem. Am. Sociol. Assn., Sociol. Rsch. Assn. Office: U Calif Sociology Dept Davis CA 95616

GOLDSTONE, STEPHEN A., superintendent; b. Hollywood, Calif., Dec. 12, 1938; s. Harry and Eunice (Goldman) G.; m. Linda Goldstone, Dec. 17, 1968; children: David, Danny, Robert, Stefanie. BA, Calif. State U., Northridge, 1961, MA, 1967; EdD, U. So. Calif., L.A., 1978. Tchr. Santa Monica and L.A. Unified Sch. Dist., L.A., 1964-67; counselor George K. Potter Jr. High Sch., Granada Hills, Calif., 1967-69, registrar, 1969-70; asst. prin. Wm. S. Hart Unified H.S. Dist., Saugus, Calif., 1970-73; prin. Carl H. Lorbeer Jr. High Sch., Pomona, Calif., 1973-77; area supt. Pomona (Calif.) Unified Sch. Dist., 1977-80; supt. Albany (Calif.) Unified Sch. Dist., 1980-85, Arcadia (Calif.) Unified Sch. Dist., 1985-89, China (Calif.) Unified Sch. Dist., 1989—, Valley City Unified Sch. Dist., Vallejo, Calif., 1995—; mem. San Bernardino (Calif.) County Supt.'s Adv. Bd., U. So. Calif. Supt.'s Adv. Bd., L.A., Chaffey Coll. Cmty. Adv. Bd., Rancho Cucamonga. Pres. Chino Valley C. of C., 1994; bd. dirs. United Way/YMCA, Chino; pres. Chino Valley Rotary, 1995. Named Supt. of Yr., Assn. Calif. Sch. Adminstrs., 1994. Office: Vallejo City Unified Schs 211 Valle Vista Ave Vallejo CA 94590

GOLDSTRAND, DENNIS JOSEPH, financial planning executive; b. Oakland, Calif., July 12, 1952; s. Joseph Nelson and Frances Marie (Royce) G.; m. Judy A. Goldstrand. BSBA, Calif. State U., 1975; CLU, Am. Coll., 1986, CFC, 1988. Asst. mgr. Household Fin. Corp., San Leandro, Calif., 1975-76; registered rep. Equitable Fin. Svcs., San Francisco, 1976-79; dist. mgr. Equitable Fin. Services, San Francisco, 1979-85; ptnr. Goldstrand & Small Ins. and Fin. Services, Stockton, Calif., 1986-89; owner Goldstrand Fin. & Ins. Svcs., Stockton, 1989—. Speaker Stockton Assn. Life Underwriters, 1986; contbr. articles to Life Ins. Selling mag., 1986, 88. Mem. Stockton Estate Planning Coun., bd. dirs. 1995-96; past pres. United Way San Joaquin County Endowment Found., Inc., 1994, bd. dirs. Mem. Nat. Assn. Life Underwriters (pres. Stockton chpt. 1990-91, Life Underwriter of Yr. 1994), Am. Soc. CLU (pres. Stockton chpt. 1989-90, bd. dirs.), Calif. Assn. Life Underwriters (trustee 1995—), Million Dollar Round Table Found., Greater Stockton C. of C., Rotary, Golden Key Soc. Home: 9215 Stony Creek Ln Stockton CA 95219-4910 Office: Goldstrand Fin & Ins Svcs 5250 Claremont Ave # 230 Stockton CA 95207-5700

GOLDWYN, RALPH NORMAN, financial company executive; b. Chgo., Jan. 24, 1925; s. Herman and Rissie F. Goldwyn; B.S., UCLA, 1948; m. Joan J. Snyder, Dec. 25, 1954; children: Bob, Greg, Lisa. Partner, Arc Loan Co., L.A., 1948-52; v.p. Arc Discount Co., L.A., 1952-73; pres. Arc Investment Co., Los Angeles, 1952-73; partner First Factors, L.A., 1960-78; pres. First Comml. Fin., L.A., 1978—; dir. Roy J. Maier, Inc.; trustee UCLA Found. Served to lt. (j.g.) USN, 1943-46. Mem. World Affairs Coun., UCLA Chancellor Assns. (sustaining), Anti-Defamation League, Town Hall of Calif. Club (life), Brentwood Country Club of L.A., UCLA Bruin Club (sustaining). Jewish. Office: First Comml Fin 4221 Wilshire Blvd Ste 260 Los Angeles CA 90010-3512

GOLDZBAND, MELVIN GEORGE, psychiatrist; b. St. Louis, Nov. 6, 1929; s. Max Morris and Genevieve (Goldenson) G.; m. Marilyn Joan Miller, June 30, 1953; children: Daniel A., Lawrence J., Marjorie J. BS, U. Ill., 1950; MD, U. Chgo. Med. Sch., 1955. Diplomate Am. Bd. Psychiatry & Neurology. Intern Cook County Hosp., Chgo., 1955-56; resident VA Westside Hosp. Dept. of Psychiatry, Chgo., 1956-59; psychiatrist USNR, San Diego, 1959-61; pvt. practice psychiatry San Diego, 1961—; clin. prof., dir. forensic psychiatric tng. U. Calif., San Diego, 1967—. Author: Consulting in Child Custody, 1981, Quality Time, 1985, Custody Cases & Expert Witnesses, 2d edit., 1988. V.p. San Diego Symphony Orch., 1963-68. Named disting. alumnus U. Chgo. Med. Sch., 1992. Fellow Am. Psychiat. Assn., Am. Coll. Psychiatrists, Am. Acad. Forensic Scis.; mem. Am. Acad. Psychiatry & the Law (treas.). Office: 3342 4th Ave San Diego CA 92103-5704

GOLITZ, LOREN EUGENE, dermatologist, pathologist, clinical administrator, educator; b. Pleasant Hill, Mo., Apr. 7, 1941; s. Ross Winston and Helen Francis (Schupp) G.; MD, U. Mo., Columbia, 1966; m. Deborah Burd Frazier, June 18, 1966; children: Carrie Campbell, Matthew Ross. Intern, USPHS Hosp., San Francisco, 1966-67, med. resident, 1967-69; resident in dermatology USPHS Hosp., Staten Island, N.Y., 1969-71; dep. chief dermatology, 1972-73; vis. fellow dermatology Columbia-Presbyn. Med. Ctr., N.Y.C., 1971-72; asst. in dermatology Coll. Physicians Surgeons, Columbia, N.Y.C., 1972-73; vice-chmn. Residency Rev. Com. for Dermatology, 1983-85. Earl D. Osborne fellow dermal. pathology Armed Forces Inst. Pathology, Washington, 1973-74; assoc. prof. dermatology, pathology Med. Sch. U. Colo., Denver, 1974-88; prof., 88—; chief dermatology Denver Gen. Hosp., 1974—; med. dir. Ambulatory Care Ctr., Denver Gen. Hosp., 1991—. Diplomate Am. Bd. Dermatology, Nat. Bd. Med. Examiners. Fellow Royal Soc. Medicine; mem. Am. Soc. Dermatopathology (sec., treas. 1985-89, pres.-elect 1989, pres. 1990), Am. Acad. Dermatology (chmn. coun. on clin. and lab. svcs., coun. sci. assembly 1987-91, bd. dirs. 1987-91, chmn. 1991), Soc. Pediatric Dermatology (pres. 1981), Soc. Investigative Dermatology, Pacific Dermatol. Assn. (exec. com. 1979-89, sec.-treas. 1984-87, pres. 1988), Noah Worcester Dermatol. Soc. (publs. com. 1980, membership com. 1989-90), Colo. Dermatol. Soc. (pres. 1978), Am. Bd. Dermatology Inc. (chmn. part II test com. 1989—, exec. com. 1993—, v.p. 1994, pres. elect 1995), Colo. Med. Soc., Denver Med. Soc., AMA (residency rev. com. for dermatology 1982-89, dermatopathology test com. 1979-85), Denver Soc. Dermatopathology, Am. Dermatol. Assn. Editorial bd. Jour. Cutaneous Pathology, Jour. Am. Acad. Dermatology, Advances in Dermatology (editorial bd. Current Opinion in Dermatology), Women's Dermatologic Soc., So. Med. Assn., Internat. Soc. Pediatric Dermatology, Am. Contact Dermatitis Soc., Am. Soc. Dermatologic Surgery, Physicians Who Care, Am. Bd. Med. Specialties (del.), N.Y. Acad. Scis., AAAS, Brit. Assn. Dermatologists (hon.), Brazilian Soc. Dermatology (hon.), U. Mo. Med. Alumni Orgn. (bd.govs. 1993—); contbr. articles to med. jours. Home: 11466 E Arkansas Ave Aurora CO 80012-4106 Office: Denver Gen Hosp Dept Dermatology 777 Bannock St # 0146 Denver CO 80204-4507

GOLLEDGE, REGINALD GEORGE, geography educator; b. Dungog, Australia, Dec. 6, 1937; came to U.S., 1963; s. Lance Golledge; m. Margaret Ruth Mason, 1961 (div. 1974); children: Stephanie, Linda; m. Allison Louise Cahill; children: Bryan, Brittany. BA with honors, U. New Eng., Australia, MA, 1961; PhD, U. Iowa, 1966. Asst. prof. U. B.C., Vancouver, 1965-66; asst. prof. Ohio State U., Columbus, 1966-67, assoc. prof., 1967-71, prof. geography, 1971-77; prof. geography U. Calif., Santa Barbara, 1977—, chmn. dept., 1980-84; dir. Rsch. Unit for Spatial Cognition and Choice, Santa Barbara, 1990—. Co-author: Analytical Behavioral Geography, 1987; co-editor: Behavioral Problems in Geography, 1982, Behavioral Modelling in Geography and Planning, 1988, A Ground for Common Search, 1988, Behavior and Environment, 1993. Fellow Guggenheim Found., 1987. Fellow AAAS; mem. Assn. Am. Geographers (Honors award 1981), Psychometric Soc., Regional Sci. Assn., Inst. Australian Geographers (hon. life), Gamma Theta Upsilon. Home: 267 Forest Dr Goleta CA 93117-1108 Office: U Calif Dept Geography Santa Barbara CA 93106

GOLLEHER, GEORGE, food company executive; b. Bethesda, Md., Mar. 16, 1948; s. George M. and Ruby Louise (Beecher) G.; div.; 1 child, Carly Lynn. BA, Calif. State U., Fullerton, 1970. Supr. acctg. J.C. Penney, Buena Park, Calif., 1970-72; systems auditor Mayfair Markets, Los Angeles, 1973, v.p., CFO, 1982-83; controller Fazio's, Los Angeles, 1974-78; group controller Fisher Foods, Ohio, 1978-79; v.p. fin. Stater Bros. Markets, Colton, Calif., 1979-82; sr. v.p., CFO Boys Markets Inc., Los Angeles, 1983—. Office: Food 4 Less of Southern Cal 777 S Harbor Blvd La Habra CA 90631-6839

GOLLOB, HARRY FRANK, psychology educator; b. Newark, June 7, 1939; s. Joseph S. and Doris C. (Stevens) G.; m. Maureen M. Morris, Sept. 4, 1959; children: Steven P., David J., Kenneth J. BA cum laude, U. Denver, 1960; MS, Yale U., 1962, PhD, 1965. Asst. to assoc. prof. of psychology U. Mich., Ann Arbor, 1965-69; asst. to assoc. rsch. psychologist Mental Health Rsch. Inst., Ann Arbor, 1965-69; assoc. prof. psychology U. Denver, 1969-73, prof. psychology, 1973—, chmn. dept. psychology, 1978-79, 91-93; cons. in field. Mem. editorial bd. Jour. Exptl. Social Psychology, 1974-79, Multivariate Behavioral Rsch., 1971—, Social Psychology Quar., 1992—; contbr. articles to profl. jours. NIMH grantee, 1969-72, 76-79, 84-88, NSF grantee, 1976-79. Fellow APA, Am. Psychol. Soc.; mem. Am. Statis. Assn., Psychometric Soc., AAAS, Multivariate Exptl. Psychologists (sec., treas. 1984-86), Ednl. Statisticians. Home: 8590 E Nichols Ave Englewood CO 80112-2735 Office: U Denver Dept Psychology 2155 S Race St Denver CO 80210-4633

GOLOMB, BEATRICE ALEXANDRA, physician, medical researcher; b. L.A., May 16, 1959; d. Solomon A. Golomb; m. Terrence Joseph Sejnowski, Mar. 25, 1990. BS in Physics, U. So. Calif., L.A., 1979; PhD in Biology, U. Calif. at San Diego, La Jolla, Calif., 1988, MD, 1989. Resident VA Hosp. West L.A., 1990-93, chief resident, 1993-94; Robert Wood Johnson clin. scholar U. Calif., L.A., 1994—. Recipient Solomon Scholars award UCLA, 1992, 93. Mem. Phi Kappa Phi. Home: 672 San Mario Dr Solana Beach CA 92075 Office: UCLA Dept Medicine 10833 Le Conte Ave Los Angeles CA 90024

GOLSTON, JOAN CAROL, psychotherapist; b. Vancouver, B.C., Can., Aug. 10, 1947; came to U.S., 1958; d. Stefan and Lydia Barbara (Fruchs) G. Student, Reed Coll.; BA, U. Wash., 1977, MSW, 1979. Cert. social worker. Clin. supr. Crisis Clinic, Seattle, 1975-77; psychiatric social worker Valley Gen. Hosp., Renton, Wash., 1979-82; psychotherapist pvt. practice, Seattle, 1981—; sch. counselor Northwest Sch., Seattle, Seattle Acad.; clin. cons. outpatient dept. Valley Cities Cmty. Mental Health, Renton, 1991, Seattle Counseling Svcs., 1991—, emergency svcs., 1975-89; cons., trainer and presenter in field. Contbr. articles to profl. jours. Bd. dirs. Open Door Clinic, Seattle, 1975-76, Northwest Family Tng. Inst., Seattle, v.p., 1990, pres., 1991, mem. exec. com., 1988-91; mem. adv. bd. Ctr. Prevention of Sexual and Domestic Violence, 1993—, AIDS Risk Reduction Project Sch. Social Work U. Wash., 1988-93. Nat. Merit scholar, 1964. Mem. NASW (diplomate), Wash. State chpt. NASW (mem. com. on ethics 1992—), Internat. Soc. Study of Dissociation, Internat. Soc. Trauma Stress Studies, Acad. Cert. Social Workers. Office: 726 Broadway Ste 303 Seattle WA 98122-4337

GOLTZ, MARK NEIL, environmental engineer; b. Bklyn., July 1, 1951; s. Seymour and Harriet (Champagne) G.; m. Mi Suk So, Feb. 14, 1977; children: Hugh, Eric. BSEE, Cornell U., 1972; MS in Sanitary Engring., U. Calif., Berkeley, 1973; PhD in Environ. Engr., Stanford U., 1986. Commd. 2d lt. USAF, 1972, advanced through grades to lt. col., 1989, ret., 1993; assoc. prof. environ. engring. Air Force Inst. Tech., Wright-Patterson AFB, Ohio, 1986-93; acting assoc. prof. dept. civil engring. Stanford (Calif.) U., 1993—, asst. dir. Western Region Hazardous Substance Rsch. Ctr.; Mem. Environ. Mgmt. Bd., Wright-Patterson AFB, 1988-90. Contbr. articles to profl. jours. Treas. Dayton (Ohio) Jr. Strings Orch., 1992-93. Recipient Air Force Mil. Engr. of Yr., NSPE, 1992, Air Force Sci. Achievement award USAF, 1987, Air Force Meritorious Svc. medal USAF, 1978, 82, 93. Mem. Soc. Am. Mil. Engrs. (bd. dirs. Kittyhawk Post 1990-93), Assn. Environ. Engring. Profs., Am. Geophys. Union, Water Environment Fedn. Home: 1413 S Mary Ave Sunnyvale CA 94087-4041 Office: Stanford U Dept Civil Engring Stanford CA 94305-4020

GOLUB, GENE HOWARD, computer science educator, researcher; b. Chgo., Feb. 29, 1932; s. Nathan and Bernice (Gelman) G. BS in Math., U. Ill., 1953, MA in Math.-Stats., 1954, PhD in Math., 1959; Tech. Dr. (hon.), Linköping U., 1984; Dr. honoris causa, U. Grenoble, 1986, U. Waterloo, 1987, U. of Dundee, 1987, Katholieke Univ. Leuven, Belgium, 1992; hon. degree, U. Ill., 1991, U. Waterloo, 1987. Assoc. prof. Stanford U., 1966-70, prof., 1962—, Fletcher Jones prof. computer sci., 1991, chmn. dept. computer sci., 1980-84, dir. sci. computing/computational math.; founder NA-net; mem. adv. com. on computer sci. NSF, 1982-84. Author: (with Gerard Meurant) Resolution Numerique des Grandes Systems Lineaires, 1983, (with Charles Van Loan) Advanced Matrix Computations, 1984, rev. edit., 1989, (with James M. Ortega) Scientific Computing and Differential Equations: An Introduction to Numerical Methods, 1992, Scientific Computing: An Introduction with Parallel Computing, 1993; contbr. articles to profl. jours.; assoc. editor various jours., 1967-79; editor: Numerische Mathematik, 1978; founding editor SIAM Jour. on Matrix Analysis and Applications. Recipient Alumni Honor award U. Ill., Urbana, 1984; hon. fellow St. Catherine's Coll., Oxford U., Eng., 1983; Guggenheim fellow, 1987. Fellow AAAS (hon.); mem. NAS, NAE, Am. Acad. Arts & Scis., Soc. for Indsl. and Applied Math. (mem. coun. 1975-77, trustee 1982—, pres. 1985-87, vis. lectr. 1976-77, founder, editor Jour. Sci. and Statis. Computing 1980—), U.S. Nat. Com. for Math., Royal Swedish Acad. Engring. Scis. Home: 576 Constanzo St Palo Alto CA 94305-8418 Office: Stanford U Dept U Bldg 460 Dept Computer Sci Stanford CA 94305

GOLUBIC, THEODORE ROY, sculptor, designer, inventor; b. Lorain, Ohio, Dec. 9, 1928; s. Ivan and Illonka (Safar) G.; m. Rose Andrina Ieraci-Golubic, Nov. 27, 1958; children: Vincivan, Theodore E., Victor, Georjia. Student Ohio State U., Columbus, 1947-48; BFA in Painting, Miami U., Oxford, Ohio, 1951; student Syracuse U., 1955; MFA in Sculpture, U. Notre Dame, 1957. Asst. to Ivan Mestrovic, 1954-60; guest tchr. U. Notre Dame, 1959; urban planner redevel. dept., South Bend, Ind., 1960-65; sculpture cons., Rock of Ages Corp., 1965-67; instr. Cen. Mo. State U., 1969; instr. San Diego Sculptors' Guild, 1970-71; artist-in-residence Roswell (N.Mex.) Mus. and Art Ctr., 1971-72; sculptor, designer, inventor, 1958—; works include: 4 dimensional sun environ. design, South Bend, Ind., Limestone relief sculpture Cathedral of the Nativity, Dubuque, Iowa, The Crypt Series, ROA Corp., Barre, Vt., bronze St. John Bapt., Lorain, Ohio, 4 pt. surface pick-up, 3 dimensional interconnected integrated cir., multilevel S.I.P. package, isolated heatsink bonding pads, semiconductor chip module (Eureka award Motorola, Inc.), Phoenix, mahogany bas relief U. San Diego. With U.S. Army, 1951-53. Mem. Coll. Art Assn. Am., Internat. Sculpture Ctr. Contbr. articles to profl. jours.

GOLUM, ROBERT BRUCE, journalist; b. Long Beach, Calif., May 6, 1956; s. Abraham and Irma (Berman) G.; m. Pamela Joan Ruben, Sept. 4, 1983. BA in Journalism, San Diego State U., 1978. Reporter Chula Vista (Calif.) Star News, 1978-79, Women's Wear Daily, N.Y.C., 1979-84, Investor's Daily, Los Angeles, 1984—. Mem. ACLU, Los Angeles, 1985-86. Democrat. Jewish.

GOMAN, JON GIFFORD, university chaplain, educator; b. Corvallis, Oreg., Nov. 7, 1946; s. Edward Gordon and LaVerne Pruden Goman; m. Elizabeth Nisbet Marty; children: Nicholas, Jessica, Timothy. BA with honors, U. Puget Sound, 1968; D of Religion, Claremont Sch. Theology, 1976. Assoc. rector St. Michael & All Angels, Issaquah, Wash., 1976-78; tchr. Episcopal Theol. Sch., Claremont, Calif., 1979-81; priest-in-charge Holy Nativity Episcopal Ch., L.A., 1979-81; Episcopal chaplain Oreg. State U., Corvallis, 1981—; tchr. Linn-Benton C.C., Albany, Oreg., 1984—, Ctr. for the Diaconate, Scio, Oreg., 1984—; chmn. Dept. Ministry in Higher Edn. Diocese of Oreg., 1992—. Author: A Few Words on the Book of Common Prayer, 1993; author, editor: A Bibliography of Secondary Sources for the Gospel Readings of the Eucharistic Lectionary, 1993. Danforth fellow, 1968. Office: St Anselm of Canterbury 2615 NW Arnold Way Corvallis OR 97330-5308

GOMBOCZ, ERICH ALFRED, biochemist; b. Vienna, Austria, Aug. 29, 1951; came to U.S., 1990; s. Erich and Maria (Mayer) G.; m. Gisela M. Dorner, June 12, 1973 (div. Apr. 1992); 1 child, Manfred Alexander (dec.). Cert., T.U., Vienna, 1970-75. With Fed. Inst. for Food Analysis and Rsch., Vienna, 1975-90, head of sect. dept. biochem. analysis, 1980-90, contbr. Cen. Lab. Info. Mgmt. System, 1987-90; chmn. scientific adv. bd. LabIntelligence, Inc., Menlo Park, Calif., 1989—, v.p., dir. rsch., 1989—; speaker and lectr. in field. Editor: Computers in Electrophoresis; contbr. articles to profl. jours.; patentee in field. Postdoctoral Rsch. award NIH, Bethesda, Md., 1985-86, 88. Mem. Internat. Assn. for Cereal Chemistry, Internat. Electrophoresis Soc., Am. Electrophoresis Soc. Roman Catholic. Office: Lab Intelligence Inc 177 Jefferson Dr Menlo Park CA 94025-1114

GOMES, DANIEL, historian educator; b. Ocean Falls, B.C., Can., Sept. 17, 1960; s. Inocencio Amado and Anna (Kanelopoulos) G. BA, U. B.C., 1988; MA, U. Md., 1991; postgrad., U. Calif. Tchg. asst. U. Md., Balt., 1990-91, U. Calif., Santa Barbara, 1991-95; cons. Micro-Computer Facilities, Balt., 1990-91; intern Nat. Archives, 1990. Co-author: Sifting Through the Ashes: Lessons Learned From the Painted Cave Fire, 1993; contbg. author The Ency. of African Am. Civil Rights, 1992; editl. asst. The Public Historian, Santa Barbara, 1991-95. Mem. NAACP, Am. Hist. Assn., Orgn. Am. Historians, Ctr. for Study of Presidency, Phi Alpha Theta, Omicron Delta Kappa. Home: 439 E 51st Ave, Vancouver, BC Canada V5X 1C8

GOMEZ, DAVID FREDERICK, lawyer; b. Los Angeles, Nov. 19, 1940; s. Fred and Jennie (Fujier) G.; m. Kathleen Holt, Oct. 18, 1977. BA in Philosophy, St. Paul's Coll., Washington, 1965, MA in Theology, 1968; JD, U. So. Calif., 1974. Bar: Calif. 1975, U.S. Dist. Ct. (cen. dist.) Calif. 1975,

U.S. Dist. Ct. (ea. dist.) Calif. 1977, Ariz. 1981, US. Dist. Ct. Ariz. 1981, U.S. Ct. Claims 1981, U.S. Ct. Appeals (9th cir.) 1981, U.S. Supreme Ct. 1981; ordained priest Roman Cath. Ch., 1969. Staff atty. Nat. Labor Relations Bd., Los Angeles, 1974-75; ptnr. Gomez, Paz, Rodriguez & Sanora, Los Angeles, 1975-77, Garrett, Bourdette & Williams, San Francisco, 1977-80, Van O'Steen & Ptnrs., Phoenix, 1981-85; pres. David F. Gomez, PC, Phoenix, 1985—; mem. faculty Practicing Law Inst., 1989. Author: Somos Chicanos: Strangers in Our Own Land, 1973; co-author Advanced Strategies in Employment Law, 1988. Mem. ABA, Maricopa County Bar Assn., Los Abogados Hispanic Bar Assn., Nat. Employment Lawyer's Assn., Calif. State Bar Assn., Ariz. State Bar Assn. (com. on rules of profl. conduct 1991—, civil jury instructions com. 1992-94, peer rev. com. 1992—). Democrat.

GOMEZ, EDWARD CASIMIRO, physician, educator; b. Key West, Fla., Nov. 30, 1938; s. Edward C. and Francisca (Pijuan) G.; m. Barbara Jeanne Wilson, 1960 (div. 1979); 1 child, Marielle Elise; m. Ellen Elizabeth Mack, 1980. AB in Biol. Scis., Johns Hopkins U., 1960; MD, U. Miami, 1965, PhD, 1971. Diplomate Am. Bd. Dermatology; bds. cert. spl. competence in dermopathology. Pediatric intern U. Miami, Fla., 1966-67, resident in dermatology, 1969-72; research coordinator Dept. Dermatology Mt. Sinai Med. Ctr., Miami Beach, Fla., 1972-75, dermatopathology fellow, 1976-77; assoc. prof. dermatology NYU, 1977-80; prof. dermatology Sch. Medicine U. Calif., Davis, 1980-91, prof. emeritus, 1991—, assoc. dean for affiliate programs, 1983-86, assoc. dean for clin. affairs, 1987-90; regional chief of staff VA Western Region, San Francisco, 1991-93; assoc. chief staff No. Calif. Sys. Clinics, Pleasant Hill, 1993—; asst. chief to chief dematology sect. VA Med. Ctr., N.Y.C., 1977-80; assoc. chief to chief of staff, VA Med. Ctr., Martinez, Calif., 1983-86; mem. VA Dermatology Field Adv. Group, Washington, 1978-80, task force on Chloracne, 1979-84; cons. U.S. Army Med. Research and Devel. Command, Frederick, Md., 1979-80, Johnson and Johnson Corp., New Brunswick, N.J., 1979-80; expert witness FDA, Washington, 1978; Gov.'s appointee Med. Quality Rev. Com., Alameda and Contra Costa counties, Calif., 1984-87. Editor 1 book; contbr. articles to profl. jours. Served to lt. comdr., USNR, 1967-69. Fellow Soc. Investigative Dermatology, Am. Acad. Dermatology; mem. Am. Fedn. Clin. Research, Am. Soc. Dermatopathology, Am. Coll. Physician Execs., Alpha Omega Alpha, Phi Kappa Psi. Republican. Office: No Calif Sys Clinics 2300 Contra Costa Blvd Pleasant Hill CA 94523

GOMEZ, LOUIS SALAZAR, college president; b. Santa Ana, Calif., Dec. 7, 1939; s. Louis Reza and Mary (Salazar) G.; m. Patricia Ann Aboytes, June 30, 1962; children: Louis Aboytes, Diana Maria, Ramon Reza. Student, Calif. State Poly. U., 1959-65; BA, Calif. State U., San Bernardino, 1971; MA, Calif. State U., 1975; EdD, U. So. Calif., L.A., 1987. Cert. tchr., counselor, adminstr., Calif. Tchr., counselor San Bernardino City Schs., 1971-76; human rels. coord. San Bernardino Valley Coll., 1976-78, counselor, 1978-82, coord. of counseling, 1982-87; asst. dean student svcs. Crafton Hills Coll., Yucaipa, Calif., 1987-89, dean student svcs., 1989-90, acting pres., 1990-92, pres., 1992—; lectr. Calif. State U., San Bernardino, 1976-81, mem. adv. bd., 1987—. Bd. dirs. Redlands YMCA. Mem. San Bernardino Valley Coll. Faculty Assn. (treas. 1980-82), Faculty Assn. Calif. Community Colls., San Bernardino Community Coll. Dist. Mgmt. Assn., Kiwanis (pres. San Bernardino chpt. 1982). Democrat. Roman Catholic. Home: 10682 Berrywood Cir Yucaipa CA 92399-5924 Office: Crafton Hills Coll 11711 Sand Canyon Rd Yucaipa CA 92399-1742

GOMEZ, MARTIN, library director. Dir. Oakland (Calif.) City Pub. Libr. Office: Oakland City Public Library 125 14th St Oakland CA 94612-4310

GÓMEZ, RAFAEL, Hispanic studies educator; b. Bogotá, Colombia, Aug. 27, 1953; came to U.S., 1967; s. José Antonio and Julia (Rodriguez) G.; m. Frauke Loewensen, Apr. 20, 1990. PhD, Ind. U., 1993. From assoc. instr. to lectr. Ind. U., Bloomington, 1984-89; asst. prof. Monterey (Calif.) Inst. Internat. Studies, 1990-93, head Hispanic studies dept., 1993—. Fulbright grantee, Germany, 1987; Nat. Hispanic scholar Nat. Hispanic Assn., 1987-88; Agapito Rey fellow. Mem. MLA, Ctr. for Cuban Studies. Home: 128 Seeno St Monterey CA 93940-2320 Office: Monterey Inst Internat Stud 425 Van Buren St Monterey CA 93940-2623

GÓMEZ, RICARDO JUAN, philosophy educator; b. Buenos Aires, Jan. 23, 1935; came to U.S., 1976; s. Inocencio A. and Maria T. (Pianzola) G.; m. Maria J. Proaño. MA, Ind. U., 1978, PhD, 1982. Prof. U. LaPlata, Argentina, 1967-76; prof. methodology U. Buenos Aires, 1970-76, prof. logic, 1970-74; prof. philosophy of sci. U. Quito, 1978-82; prof. philosophy and sci. Nat. U., Mex., 1978, 82 summer; asspc. prof. philosophy Calif. State U., L.A., 1983-87, prof., 1987—; dir. Inst. of Logic of Philosophy of Sci., La Plata, 1970-76; dean Sch. of Arts and Letters, La Plata, 1973-74. Author: Scientific Theories, 1977, Neoliseralism and Pseudoscience, 1995; contbr. articles to profl. jours. Mem. Philosophy of Sci. Assn., Am. Philos. Assn., N.Am. Kant Soc., Soc. for Philosophy Tech., Honors Soc. for Internat. Scholars, Sogedad Filbosofia Iberoamericana. Office: Philosophy Dept Calif State U 5151 State University Dr Los Angeles CA 90032

GONDA, HARRY HENRIK, psychiatrist; b. Mako, Hungary, Apr. 17, 1915; came to U.S., 1949, naturalized, 1954; s. Joseph and Regina (Frankel) G.; m. Clara Turai-Lichtig, May 6, 1939; children: John Richard, Robert Dale. Baccalaureate summa cum laude, Matura Realgymnasium, Debrecen, Hungary, 1933; MD cum laude, U Debrecen, 1939. Diplomate Am. Bd. Psychiatry and Neurology; lic. physician, N.Y., Calif.; cert. mental health adminstr.; lic. sch. psychiatrist, N.Y.C. Rotating intern Univ. Hosps., Debrecen, 1940-41; resident in internal medicine Chevra Kadisha Hosp., Nagyvarad, Hungary, 1941-42; resident Neuropsychiat. Inst., U. Debrecen, 1945; fellow in child psychiatry Bklyn. Juvenile Guidance Ctr., 1959, Jewish Bd. Guardians, 1960-61; dep. dir. Suffolk Psychiat. Hosp., to 1970; med. dir. South Shore Child Guidance Ctr., Freeport, N.Y., 1970-79; staff psychiatrist South Nassau Communities Hosp., Oceanside, N.Y., 1975-80; psychiat. cons. Student Health Svc. Calif. State U., Long Beach, 1979-91; psychiat. cons. Long Beach Mental Health Ctr.-Children's Day Treatment Ctr., 1980—; pvt. practice adult psychiatry, 1957-80, child and adolescent psychiatry, 1961-80; asst. clin. prof. psychiatry Albert Einstein Coll. Medicine, 1966-74; asst. prof. clin. psychiatry SUNY, Stony Brook, 1976-80. Fellow Am. Psychiat. Soc.; mem. Med. Soc. State of N.Y., Soc. for Adolescent Psychiatry, N.Y. State Hosps. Med. Alumni Assn. (sec. 1976-80). Home: 11 Mayapple Way Irvine CA 92715-2714 Office: Los Angeles Cou Dept Mental Health Long Beach CA

GONG, CAROLYN LEI CHU, real estate agent; b. Visalia, Calif., July 10, 1949; d. Robert C. and Lynn P. (Low) G. BA in Health Sci., Calif. State U., Long Beach, 1973; MA in Sociology, Calif. State U., L.A., 1980. Cert. jr. coll. tchr., Calif. Social worker County of L.A., El Monte, Calif., 1974-76, children treatment counselor, 1976-81; children svcs. worker County of L.A., Norwalk, 1981-89; real estate agt. Coldwell Banker, Diamond Bar, Calif., 1989-90, First Team Real Estate, Dana Point, Calif., 1991-92, Grubb & Ellis Real Estate, Dana Point, Calif., 1994—, 1994—. Mem. NAFE, Nat. Assn. Realtors (Mult-million Prodn. award 1989—), Calif. Assn. Realtors, Asian Bus. League, Tennis Connection. Republican. Home: 33144 Ocean Rdg Dana Point CA 92629-6010 Office: Grubb & Ellis Real Estate 34105 Coast Hwy Dana Point CA 92629

GONG, HENRY, JR., physician, researcher; b. Tulare, Calif., May 23, 1947; s. Henry and Choy (Low) G.; m. Janice Wong; children: Gregory, Jaimee. BA, U. of the Pacific, 1969; MD, U. Calif., Davis, 1973. Diplomate Am. Bd. Internal Medicine, 1977, Pulmonary Disease subspecialty bd., 1980. Resident in medicine Boston U., 1973-75; fellow in pulmonary medicine UCLA Med. Ctr., 1975-77; asst. prof., then assoc. prof. Sch. Medicine UCLA, 1977-89, prof. medicine, 1989-93; assoc. chief pulmonary div. UCLA Med. Ctr., 1985-92; chief Environ. Health Svc. Rancho Los Amigos Med. Ctr., 1993—; prof. medicine U. So. Calif., 1993—; dir. Environ. Exposure Lab., UCLA, 1988-93; mem. pub. health and socio=econs. task force South Coast Air Quality Mgmt. Dist., El Monte, Calif., 1989-90. Contbr. articles to rsch. publs., chpts. to books; editorial bd. Jour. Clin. Pharmacology, 1983—, Heart and Lung Jour., 1984-92, Am. Jour. Critical Care, 1992—. Elder on session Pacific Palisades Presbyn. Ch., 1984-86, 89-91. Fellow Am. Coll. Chest Physicians (pres. Calif. chpt. 1991-92), Am. Coll. Clin. Pharmacology; mem. Am. Thoracic Soc., Am. Fedn. Clin. Rsch., Western Soc. Clin. Investigation, Air and Waste Mgmt. Assn., Phi Eta Sigma, Phi Kappa Phi. Office: Environ Health Svc Rancho Los Amigos Med Ctr 7601 Imperial Hwy Downey CA 90242-3456

GONG, MAMIE POGGIO, secondary education educator; b. San Francisco, June 26, 1951; d. Louis and Mary Lee (Lum) G.; m. Andy Anthony Poggio. BA, U. Calif., Berkeley, 1973, postgrad., 1981-83, MEd, 1982. Tchr. Oakland (Calif.) Unified Sch. Dist., 1974-84, Palo Alto (Calif.) Unified Sch. Dist., 1984—; cons., writer Nat. Clearinghouse for Bilingual Edn., Washington, 1984; cons. ARC Assocs., Oakland, 1983; rsch. asst. dept. edn. Stanford U., 1987-89. Co-author: Promising Practices: A Teacher Resource, 1984. Recipient Kearney Found. award, 1969, others. Mem. Tchrs. English to Speakers Other Langs. (presenter 1990 conf.), Calif. Assn. Tchrs. English to Speakers Other Langs. Democrat. Office: Palo Alto Unified Sch Dist 25 Churchill Ave Palo Alto CA 94306-1005

GONZALES, ANTHONY RALPH, industrial engineer; b. Quincy, Wash., Oct. 5, 1959; s. Jess and Alvina (Gonzales) G.; m. Carla L. Williams, Nov. 3, 1990; children: Jacob, Jarod. AAA, Wenatchee Valley Coll., 1979, AA, 1987; BS, Cen. Wash. U., 1990. Prodn. supr., then quality assurance supr. Lamb Weston, Quincy, Wash., 1979-86, process quality supr., 1986-89, shift supt., 1989-90, indsl. engr., 1990—. Councilman City of Quincy, 1993—, planning commn., 1992-93. Mem. Inst. Cert. mgmt. Accts., Kiwanis. Republican. Home: 901 2nd Ave SE Quincy WA 98848-1534 Office: Lamb West West PO Box 368 Industrial Tract Quincy WA 98848-0368

GONZALES, RICHARD JOSEPH, lawyer; b. Tucson, Mar. 5, 1950; s. Diego D. and Helen O. (Olivas) G.; m. Julie D. Gonzales; children: Adrianne, Laura, Beau, Barry, Jordan. BA, U. Ariz., 1972, JD, 1975. Bar: Ariz. 1976, U.S. Dist. Ct. Ariz. 1976, U.S. Ct. Appeals 1976, U.S. Supreme Ct. 1993. Asst. pub. defender Pima County Pub. Defenders Office, Tucson, 1976-77; dep. atty. criminal div. Pima County Atty.'s Office, Tucson, 1977-80; ptnr. Gonzales & Villarreal, P.C., Tucson, 1980—; assoc. instr. bus. law Pima Community Coll.,Tucson, 1977, criminal law, 1978-80; judge pro tem Pima County Superior Ct., 1983—; magistrate City of South Tucson, 1982-85; spl. magistrate City of Tucson, 1982-85; comn. appellate ct. appointments, 1991-95. Mem. Tucson Tomorrow, 1984-87, Citizen's adv. coun. Sunnyside Sch. Dist., 1986-88; chmn. com. Udall for Congress 2d Congl. Dist., United Way Hispanic Leadership Devel. Program, 1984-85, vice-chmn., 1983-84, chmn., 1984-85; bd. dirs. Girls Club of Tucson, Inc., 1980-81, Teatro Carmen, Inc., 1981-85, Sunnyside Devilaides, Inc., 1982-83, Alcoholism Coun. Tucson, 1982-83, Crime Resisters, 1984-85, La Frontera Ctr., Inc., 1985—, Crime Prevention League, 1985; gen. counsel U. Ariz. Hispanic Alumni; bd. dirs. U. aAriz. Law Coll. Assn., 1984-95, Am.-Israel Friendship League, 1990—, Tucson Internat. Mariachi Conf., 1990—. Named one of Outstanding Young Men of Am. U.S. Jaycee's, 1980; recipient Vol. of Yr. award United Way Greater Tucson, 1985, Cmty. Svc. award Ariz. Minority Bar Assn., 1992, Citizen Svc. award U. Ariz. Hispanic Alumni, 1995. Fellow Ariz. Bar Found.; mem. ABA, Ariz. Bar Assn., Pima County Bar Assn., Assn. Trial Lawyers Am., Ariz. Trial Lawyers Assn. (bd. dirs.), Nat. Orgn. on Legal Problems of Edn., Supreme Ct. Hist. Soc., Univ. Ariz. Alumni Assn. (bd. dirs. 1988-91), Tucson 30, Phi Delta Phi. Democrat. Roman Catholic. Lodge: Optimists (Optimist of Yr. 1981). Office: Gonzales & Villarreal PC 3501 N Campbell Ave Tucson AZ 85719-2032

GONZALES, RICHARD L., fire department chief. AA in Fire Sci. Tech., Red Rocks C.C., 1988; BS summa cum laude in Bus. Adminstrn., Regis U., 1991; MA, Harvard U., 1991; student, U. Colo. Firefighter Denver Fire Dept., 1972-75, mem. fire prevention bureau, dist. 5 roving officer, 1976-79, mem. training divsn., 1980-81, dist. roving officer firefighter, 1981-82, capt. firefighter pumper 2 and 27, 1982-85, asst. chief, 1985-87, chief fire dept., 1987—; Mem. Nat. Fire Protective Assn. Urban Fire Forum, Internat. Assn. Fire Chiefs, Metro Fire Chiefs Assn., Denver Metro Fire Chiefs Assn., Colo. State Fire Chiefs Assn., Urban Fire Forum, IAFF Local 858 Negotiating Team; bd. trustees Nat. Fire Protection Assn., 1992-95. Mem. adv. bd. U. Colo. Denver Sch. of Pub. Affairs, Red Rocks C.C., Denver Ptnrs., KAZY Denver Marathon; bd. trustees Nat. Multiple Sclerosis Soc.; bd. dirs. Rocky Mountain Poison Drug Found., Chic Chicana, Golden Gloves Charity. Recipient Outstanding Achievement award Hispanics of Colo., 1987; named Young Firefighter of the Yr., 1981. Office: Denver Fire Dept 745 W Colfax Ave Denver CO 80204-2612*

GONZALES, RICHARD ROBERT, academic administrator; b. Palo Alto, Calif., Jan. 12, 1945; s. Pedro and Virginia (Ramos) G.; m. Jennifer Ayres; children: Lisa Dianne, Jeffrey Ayres. AA, Foothill Coll., 1966; BA, San Jose (Calif.) State U., 1969; MA, Calif. Poly. State U., San Luis Obispo, 1971; grad. Def. Info. Sch., Def. Equal Opportunity Mgmt. Inst. Counselor student activities Calif. Poly. State U., San Luis Obispo, 1969-71, instr. ethnic studies, 1970-71; counselor Ohlone Coll., Fremont, Calif., 1971-72, coord. coll. readiness, 1971; counselor De Anza Coll., Cupertino, Calif., 1972-78, mem. community speakers bur., 1975-78; counselor Foothill Coll., Los Altos Hills, Calif., 1978—, mem. community speakers bur., 1978—; instr. Def. Equal Opportunity Mgmt. Inst., 1984—. Mem. master plan com. Los Altos (Calif.) Sch. Dist., 1975-76; vol. worker, Chicano communities, Calif.; active mem. Woodside (Calif.) Recreation Commn. With Calif. Army N.G., now maj. Adj. Gen. Corps, USAR. Recipient Counselor of Yr. award Ohlone Coll., 1971-72; Masters and Johnson Inst. fellow. lic. marriage family child counselor, Calif. Mem. ACA, Am. Coll. Counseling Assn., Calif. Assn. Marriage and Family Therapists, Calif. Community Coll. Counselor Assn. (former pres.), Calif. Assn. Counseling and Devel. (former pres. Hispanic Caucus), Calif. Assn. for Humanistic Edn. and Devel., Calif. Assn. for Multi-Cultural Counseling, Res. Officers Assn., La Raza Faculty Assn. Calif. Community Colls., Nat. Career Devel. Assn., Phi Delta Kappa, Chi Sigma Iota. Democrat. Office: Foothill Coll Los Altos CA 94022

GONZALES, RON, county supervisor; b. San Francisco; m. Alvina Gonzales; 3 children: Miranda, Rachel, Alejandra. BA in Community Studies, U. Calif., Santa Cruz. Formerly with Sunnyvale (Calif.) Sch. Dist., City of Santa Clara, Calif.; then human resource mgr. Hewlett-Packard Co.; market program mgmt. cons. state and local govts.; mem. city council City of Sunnyvale, 1879-87, mayor, 1982, 87; mem. bd. suprs. Santa Clara County, 1989—; bd. chair, 1993; bd. of transit suprs. Santa Clara County, 1989; bd. dirs. Joint Venture: Silicon Valley, The Role Model Program, Bay Area Biosci. Ctr., Nat. Hispanic U. Office: Office of the Bd of County Supr 70 W Hedding St San Jose CA 95110-1705

GONZALES, STEPHANIE, state official; b. Santa Fe, Aug. 12, 1950; 1 child, Adan Gonzales. Degree, Loretto Acad. for Girls. Office mgr. Jerry Wood & Assocs., 1973-86; dep. sec. of state Santa Fe, 1987-90, sec. of state, 1991; bd. dirs. N.Mex. Pub. Employees Retirement, N.Mex. State Convassing Bd., N.Mex. Commn. Pub. Records. Mem. exec. bd. N.Mex. AIDS Svc.; mem. Commn. White House Fellowships. Mem. Nat. Assn. Secs. State, United League United Latin Am. Citizens (women's coun.). Office: Office of the Sec of State State Capital Rm 420 Santa Fe NM 87501

GONZÁLEZ, ARTHUR ELISEO, architectural designer; b. L.A., Oct. 18, 1949; s. Robert and Soledad (Guitron) G.; m. Robin Reid Worley, June 10, 1978. BFA, BA, U. So. Calif., 1970; MA, U. Tex., 1981. Commd. 2d lt. USAF, 1970, advanced through grades to capt., 1980; arch. USAF Civil Engring., worldwide, 1970-83; arch. interior design Palm Springs, Calif., 1984—; cons. Patch Assocs., Anchorage, 1985-86, Design West, Palm Springs, 1985-87, Marriott Hotels, national, 1989-92. Designer olympic fountain, 1986 (honorable mention 1987). Vol. Anchorage Conv. and Visitors Bur., 1984-87 (Vol. of Yr. 1987), Anchorage Concert Assn., 1985-87, Anchorage Olympic Com., 1986. Republican. Roman Catholic. Office: González/French Archs PO Box 730 APO AA 34042

GONZALEZ, ELIZABETH FARR, accountant, management consultant; b. San Diego, July 24, 1946; d. Michael Ibs and Elizabeth (Sibley) G. AB in History, Stanford U., 1968; MA in History, U. Calif., Riverside, 1970; postgrad., George Mason U., 1984-87, U. Richmond, 1986, Rice U., 1989. Dir. rsch. and ref. Am. Symphony Orch. League, Washington, 1984-87; dir. fin. Syracuse (N.Y.) Symphony, 1986-87; dir. mktg. and pub. rels. Albany (N.Y.) Symphony, 1986-88, Fla. Philharm., Ft. Lauderdale, 1988; contr. Cellular One-Richmond, Va., 1985-87; Recell produce planner Celltech, Inc., Houston, 1987-90; acct. Camp Fire of the Ctrl. Coast, Arroyo Grande, Calif., 1994-95; contr. Raiice Publishing, Atascadero, Calif., 1995—; cons. Omaha Symphony, 1988, Fla. Philharm. Orch., 1988, Camp Fire of Kern County, Bakersfield, Calif., 1994, various cellular telephone cos., 1990-92. Author: (manual) Financial Planning and Reporting for Symphony Orchestras, 1986. Tutor San Luis Obispo (Calif.) Literacy Coun., 1992-93; mem. City of Morro Bay (Calif.) Cable Bd., 1992-93. Mem. Inst. Mgmt. Accts. (v.p. profl. edn. Ctrl. Coast chpt. 1994—), Ctrl. Coast Women's Soccer Assn. (publicity dir. 1994—), Stanford Club of Ctrl. Coast. Republican. Episcopalian. Home: 1297 15th St Los Osos CA 93402-1415

GONZALEZ, ENRICO RAUL, art educator, artist; b. N.Y.C., July 1, 1967; s. Edward John Gonzalez and Barbara Elaine Giné. Student, U. Idaho, 1985-87; BAFA, U. N.Mex., 1990. Instr. art Art Masters Acad., Albuquerque, 1989-92; prin. designer, dir. Boca Grande Studios Inc., Albuquerque, 1994—; owner Erg Fine Art Ltd.; design cons. Del Campillo Design Ltd. Furniture Design, Albuquerque, 1989-90, Creative Colaboration, Ltd., Albuquerque, 1990-91, Danzig Distbrs. Inc., Spokane, Wash., 1990-92. Mem. Sigma Phi Epsilon (N.Mex. alpha chpt. bd. dirs. 1988-89). Republican. Roman Catholic. Home: 3501 Indian School Rd NE Albuquerque NM 87106-1142

GONZALEZ, IMELDA, medical nurse; b. Orange, Calif., Mar. 11, 1963; d. Margarito Vazquez and Rosa (Acevedo) G. AS in Liberal Arts, Rancho C.C., Santa Ana, Calif., 1984; AS in Nursing, Pacific Union Coll., 1987, BSN, 1989. RN. Staff nurse White Meml. Med. Ctr., L.A., 1988-89, Univ. Calif., Irvine, 1989—. Author: Spanish English Medical Dictionary, 1992, Spanish for NeoNatal Intensive Care Part I, 1992, (cassette) Basic Spanish Course, 1992. Comdr., dir. Med. Cadets of Seventh Day Adventist, 1994-95. Mem. Pathfinders (master guide, counselor, tchr.). Home: 18862 E Vine Ave Orange CA 92669-3542

GONZALEZ, IRMA ELSA, federal judge; b. 1948. BA, Stanford U., 1970; JD, U. Ariz., 1973. Law clk. to Hon. William C. Frey U.S. Dist. Ct. (Ariz. dist.), 1973-75; asst. U.S. atty. U.S. Attys. Office Ariz., 1975-79, U.S. Attys. Office (ctrl. dist.) Calif., 1979-81; trial atty. antitrust divsn. U.S. Dept. Justice, 1979; ptnr. Seltzer Caplan Wilkins & McMahon, San Diego, 1981-84; judge U.S. Magistrate Ct. (so. dist.) Calif., 1984-91; ct. judge San Diego County Superior Ct., 1991-92; dist. judge U.S. Dist. Ct. (so. dist.) Calif., San Diego, 1992—; adj. prof. U. San Diego, 1992. Trustee San Diego Mus. Man; pres. Girl Scout Women's Adv. Cabinet. Mem. ABA, Calif. Bar Assn., San Diego County Bar Assn., Ariz. Bar Assn., Pima County Bar Assn., Nat. Assn. Women Judges, Nat. Coun. U.S. Magistrates, Lawyers' Club San Diego, Calif. Judges Assn., Thomas More Soc., La Raza Lawyers, Am. Inns of Ct. Office: Edward J. Schwartz US Courthouse 940 Front St Rm 11 San Diego CA 92101-8994*

GONZALEZ, JESUS MANUEL, social work associate; b. Cardenas, Cuba, Feb. 12, 1957. Student, Boston Coll., 1980; BA, Met. State Coll., 1995. Cert. flight attendant. Customer svc. mgr. Air Fla., Miami, 1982-86; airline steward Arrow Air, Miami, 1986-88; cmty. outreach coord. AIDS Edn. Program, Colo. AIDS Project, Denver, 1987-89; epidemiologist II STD/AIDS Edn. and Tng. Program Colo. Dept. Health, Denver, 1989-93; social work assoc. pediatric infectious diseases Children's Hosp., Denver, 1993—. Contbr. articles to profl. jours. Mem. edn. adv. com. Am. Found. AIDS Rsch., Colo. HIV/AIDS Consumer Info. Task Force, material rev. panel ARC, material rev. com. Ctr. for Health Policy Devel., Inc., material rev. panel Colo. Dept. Edn.; bd. dirs. The Masske Project, Denver Health and Hosps., Gay and Lesbian Cmty. Ctr. Colo., 1989-93, Legal Ctr. for People with Disabilities, 1991-92. Home: 1347 Lafayette St Denver CO 80218-2305 Office: Children's Hosp Campus B055 Ped Infectious Diseases 1056 E 19th Ave Denver CO 80218-1088

GONZÁLEZ, MARÍA R., Spanish language educator; b. Torreon, Mex., Dec. 6, 1949; came to U.S., 1966; d. Victor F. and Margarita (González) G. TS, Imperial Valley Coll., 1975; BA, U. Calif., Santa Barbara, 1978, MA, 1980; PhD, U. Calif., Irvine, 1991. Instr. Spanish St. Michael Prep. H.S., El Toro, Calif.; part-time instr. Spanish Imperial (Calif.) Valley Coll.; grad. student asst. U. Calif., Irvine; asst. prof. Spanish Humboldt State U., Arcata, Calif., Calif. State U., Chico; counselor Calipatria (Calif.) H.S., 1981-83. Mem. Chicano Latino Coun., Chico, 1993, H.A.C.E., Chico, 1993. Recipient grant Calif. State U., 1994. Home: 37 Cameo Dr Apt 1 Chico CA 95926-0865 Office: Calif State Univ Dept Fgn Lang and Lits Chico CA 95929-0825

GONZALEZ, MARTIN MICHAEL, television industry executive; b. L.A., June 18, 1955; m. Susan Louise Byrne, Apr. 12, 1981; children: Andrew, Cristina. BA in Mass Communications, Calif. State U., 1978; MA in Journalism, Ohio State U., 1993. Videotape editor Sta. KCRA-TV, Sacramento, 1979-81, producer, host monthly mag. program, 1980-87, gen. assignment reporter, 1980-87; East Bay bur. chief Sta. KGO-TV, San Francisco, 1987—, substitute sports and news anchor, 1987—; instr. Ohio State U., 1992-93, Cosumnes River Coll., Sacramento, 1986-87, Diablo Valley Coll., Pleasant Hill, Calif., 1995. Kiplinger fellow Ohio State U., 1992-93. Office: 2300 Contra Costa Blvd. #105 Pleasant Hill CA 94553

GONZÁLEZ, NATALIE LOUISE, dietitian; b. Taos, N.Mex., Oct. 12, 1949; d. Gustavo Adolfo González and Nora Ruth (Martinez) Graeme; m. William H. Green, Feb. 7, 1970. BS in foods & dietetics, U. N.Mex., 1971; postgrad, U. Hawaii, 1971; MS in cmty. health edn., U. N.Mex., 1975. Cert. dietitian, Wash. Student dietitan U. N.Mex., Albuquerque, 1969-70; dietary cons. Albuquerque, 1971-73, ptnr. in housecleaning bus., 1973-74; ptnr. in catering bus. Mumms, Albuquerque, 1973-74; nutrition cons. U. N.Mex. Sch. of Medicine, Albuquerque, 1974-75, Wash. State Dept. of Health, Olympia, Wash., 1976-92; health svcs. adminstrn. Wash. State Dept. of Health, Olympia, 1992—; diversity com. Dept. of Health, Olympia, 1993—. Contbr. articles to profl. jours., contbr. chpt. to book. Pres. governing bd. Western Wash. Area Health Edn. Ctr., Seattle, 1993-95; hunger com. Dept. Cmty. Devel. Wash., Olympia, 1991-94. Mem. Am. Dietetic Assn. (practice group, bd. dirs. 1978-94), Wash. State Dietetic Assn. (pres. 1986-87), Wash. State Food & Nutrition Coun. (pres. 1978, 84), Assn. State and Territorial Pub. Health Nutrition Dirs. (Outstanding Accomplishment award 1992, legis. liaison 1988-94). Democrat. Roman Catholic. Home: PO Box 1629 Milton WA 98354-1629 Office: Dept Health P O Box 47852 Olympia WA 98504-7852

GONZALEZ-DEL-VALLE, LUIS TOMAS, Spanish language educator; b. Nov. 19, 1946. BA in Spanish cum laude, Wilmington Coll.-U. N.C., Wilmington, 1968; MA in Spanish and Spanish-Am. Lits., U. Mass., 1972; Phd in Spanish and Spanish-Am. Lits. five coll. coop. program, Amherst Coll., Hampshire Coll., Mt. Holyoke Coll., Smith Coll., U. Mass., 1972. Asst. prof. modern langs. Kans. State U., 1972-75, assoc. prof. modern langs., 1975-77; assoc. prof. modern langs. and lits. U. Nebr., Lincoln, 1977-79, prof. modern langs. and lits., 1979-86; prof. Spanish and Portuguese U. Colo., Boulder, 1986—, chmn. dept. Spanish and Portuguese, 1986—; reading cons. South-Western Pub. Co., Inc., 1974, Eliseo Torres & Sons, 1974; dir. Ibero-Latin Am. Studies Ctr., 1987—; lectr. in field. Author: La nueva ficciōn hispanoamericana a traves de M.A. Asturias y G. Garcia Marquez, 1972, La ficciōn breve de Valle-Inclán, 1990, El Canon: Reflexiones Sobre la Recepciōn Literaria-Teatral, 1993; co-author: Luis Romero, 1979; gen. editor: Anales de la literatura española contemporánea, 1975—, Siglo xx/20th Century, 1985—; editor: Jour. Spanish Studies: 20th Century, 1972-80, Studies in 20th Century Lit., 1975-79, Annual Bibliography of Post-Civil War Spanish Fiction, 1977-82; contbr. articles, essays, book revs. to profl. jours. Recipient Postdoctoral Rsch. award Coun. for Internat. Exch. Scholars, 1984, 500th Rsch. Award Spanish Fgn. Ministry, 1992; grantee Coun. on Rsch. and Creative Work, U. Colo., 1986-87, Com. for Ednl. & Cultural Affairs, U. Nebr.-Lincoln, Chancellor's Rsch. Initiation Fund, U. Nebr.-Lincoln, 1980-81, Rsch. Coun., U. Nebr.-Lincoln, 1978, 79; Sr. Faculty Summer Rsch. fellow Rsch. Coun., U. Nebr.-Lincoln, 1978, Woodrow Wilson Dissertation fellow, 1971-72, Univ. fellow U. Mass., 1968-69, 70-72, Grad. fellow, 1969-70. Mem. Conf. Editors of Learned Jours. (bd. dirs. 1987—), MLA, Spain's Pen Club (founding 1984), Assn. Colegial de Escritores (spl. rep. to U.S., v.p.), Assn. de Escritores y Artistas Espanoles (U.S. rep.), Fgn. Lang. Adminstrs. of Colo., North Am. Acad. of Spanish Lang. (corrs. mem.), Assn. Europea de Profesores de Espanol, Am. Assn.

Tchrs. Spanish and Portuguese, Soc. Spanish and Spanish-Am. Studies (bd. dirs. 1975—), 20th Century Spanish Assn. (exec. sec. 1982—), Circulo de Cultura Panamericano (exec. coun. 1972), Cervantes Soc. Am., Nebr. Fgn. Lang. Assn., Phi Kappa Phi, others. Home: 1875 Del Rosa Ct Boulder CO 80304-1800 Office: U Colo Dept Spanish Portugues Boulder CO 80309

GONZÁLEZ-TRUJILLO, CÉSAR AUGUSTO, Chicano studies educator, writer; b. L.A., Jan. 17, 1931; s. José Andalón and Camerina (Trujillo) González; m. Bette L. Beattie, Aug. 30, 1969. BA, Gonzaga U., 1953, MA, Licentiate in Philosophy, 1954; MST, Licentiate in Sacred Theology, U. Santa Clara, 1961; postgrad., UCLA, 1962-65. Tchr. Instituto Regional Mex., Chihuahua, Mex., 1954-57; community devel. specialist Centro Laboral Méx., México D.F., Mex., 1965-68; supr. ABC Headstart East L.A., L.A., 1968-69; employment counselor Op. SER, San Diego, 1969-70; prof., founding chair dept. Chicano studies San Diego Mesa Coll., 1970—; founding chairperson Raza Consortium, San Diego, 1971-72; cons. Chicano Fedn. San Diego, Inc., 1987-89. Author poetry, short fiction and criticism; editor, asst. editor lit. jours., 1976—; contbr. numerous articles to profl. jours. Mem. Ednl. Issues Coordinating Com., L.A., 1968-69; founding bd. dirs. Mex.-Am. Adv. Com. to Bd. of Edn., L.A., 1969. Fulbright-Hays fellow, Peru, 1982, NEH fellow, 1984; recipient Cmty. Svc. award Chicano Fedn. San Diego Inc., 1982, Teaching Excellence award Nat. Inst. Staff and Orgnl. Devel., 1983, Outstanding Tchr. San Diego Mesa Coll., 1985, 95, Editor's Choice award Poet Mag., 1993, Cesar Chavez Social Justice award, 1994, Latina Latino Indigenous People Coalition award, 1995; named Outstanding Tchr. and Scholar, Concilio of Chicano Studies for San Diego, Imperial Valley and Baja, Calif., 1990; Spl. Congl. recognition, 1995. Mem. Am. Fedn. Tchrs., Nat. Assn. Chicano Studies, La Raza Faculty Assn., Chicano Fedn. San Diego County, Centro Cultural De La Raza (past bd. dirs.), Poets and Writers, Asociación Internacional de Hispanistas. Democrat. Roman Catholic. Office: San Diego Mesa Coll 7250 Mesa College Dr San Diego CA 92111-4902

GOOCH, ROBERT FRANCIS, lawyer; b. San Bernardino, Calif., May 1, 1918; s. Elmer Nicholas and Genevieve Agnes (Rodczweicz) G.; m. Virginia M. Gerardi, July 26, 1947; children—Patrick, Mary Gooch-Wallis, Teresa Gooch Ross, Melissa Gooch-Stevens. B.A., UCLA, 1939; LL.B., Stanford U., 1942. Bar: Calif. 1946. Sole practice, Hawthorne, Calif., 1946-54, Los Angeles, 1968-84; sr. ptnr. Gooch & Barrett, Hawthorne, 1954-64, Gooch & Jones, Hawthorne, 1965-68, Gooch & Feingold, Los Angeles, 1984—; mem. adv. com. Los Angeles Dist. Atty. Office, 1964; mem. arbitration panel Am. Arbitration Assn., Los Angeles, Bd. dirs. St. Anne's Found., Los Angeles, 1951—, pres., 1971-72. With USAF, 1942-45. Mem. Am. Judicature Soc., ABA, Los Angeles County Bar Assn., Calif. State Bar Assn. Republican. Roman Catholic. Office: Gooch and Feingold 11340 W Olympic Blvd Bldg 178 Los Angeles CA 90064-1611

GOOD, DEBORAH ANNE, art therapist, counselor, consultant; b. Lancaster, Pa., June 15, 1950; d. Amos Huber and Pauline Ann (Gehman) G. BA in Art Edn., Edinboro (Pa.) U., 1972; MA in Art Edn./Art Therapy, U. N.Mex., 1983, doctoral candidate, 1991—. Registered art therapist; lic. profl. clin. counselor, lic. art therapist, N.Mex. Art tchr. Sarah Reed Children's Home, Erie, Pa., 1972; art tchr., case mgr. Harborcreek Sch. for Boys, Erie, 1973-76; art therapist, pediatric oncology and hemophilia U. N.Mex. Hosp., Albuquerque, 1983-84; art therapist, educator N.Mex. Sch. for the Deaf, Santa Fe, 1984-85; dir. expressive thearpy Charter Hosp., Albuquerque, 1986-90; head art therapy program Southwestern Coll., Santa Fe, 1989-94, 95—; pvt. practice art therapist, counselor for visually impaired Albuquerque Pub. Schs., 1991—; art therapist, counselor Family Therapy of Albuquerque, 1990—. Contbr. articles to profl. jours. Bd. dirs. Very Spl. Arts Santa Fe, 1985. Mem. Am. Art Therapy Assn. (dir. 1990-92, 95—, Disting. Svc. award 1993), N.Mex. Art Therapy Assn. (bd. dirs. 1985-88, pres. 1985, 88, Disting. Svc. award 1991). Democrat. Home: 2449 Pueblo Bonito Ct NW Albuquerque NM 87104-1916 Office: Family Therapy Albuquerque 8600 Academy Rd NE Albuquerque NM 87111-1107

GOOD, REBECCA MAE WERTMAN, learning and behavior disorder counselor, hospice nurse; b. Barberton, Ohio, May 13, 1943; d. Frederick Daniel Wertman and Freda Beam Wertman Lombardi; m. William Robert Good Jr., Aug. 15, 1964; children: William Robert III, John Joseph, Matthew Stephan. Diploma, Akron Gen. Med. Ctr., Ohio, 1964; BS in Psychology, Ramapo Coll., Mahwah, N.J., 1986; MA in Counseling, NYU, 1990. RN, N.Y.; nat. cert. counselor. Staff nurse Green Cross Gen. Hosp., Cuyahoga Falls, Ohio, 1965-68; staff nurse, relief supr., psychiat. nurse F.D.R. VA Hosp., Montrose, N.Y., 1971-72; geriatric staff and charge nurse Westledge Extended Care Facility, Peekskill, N.Y., 1972-77; infirmary and ICF nurse St. Dominics Home, Orangeburg, N.Y., 1981-83; allergy and immunology nurse Dr. Andre Codispoti, Suffern, N.Y., 1979-89; rsch. asst. counselor NYU, N.Y.C., 1989-90; Rockland advocate Student Advocacy Inc., White Plains, N.Y., 1989-90; exec. dir. Rockland County Assn. for Learning Disabled, Orangeburg, 1990-91; life skills counselor Bd. Coop. Edn., West Nyack, N.Y., 1991-93; learning and behavior disorders counselor, Suffern, 1991-93, Salt Lake City, 1994—; hospice nurse United Hospice Rockland, 1991-93; assessment and referral counselor/case mgr. CPC Olympus View Hosp., Salt Lake City, 1994—. Co-chmn. Rockland County Coordinating Coun. for Devel. Disabled Offenders, New City, N.Y., 1990-93; bd. visitors Rockland Children's Psychiat. Ctr., Orangeburg, 1991-93, sec., 1992; mem. U.S. Congressman Benjamin Gilman's Handicapped Adv. Com., Rockland County, 1985-94; pres. Ramapo Ctrl. Sch. Dist. Spl. Edn. PTA, 1982-86. Ramapo Coll. of N.J. Pres.'s scholar, 1986. Mem. ACA, Utah Counselors Assn., Children and Adults with Attention Deficit Disorders (coord. Rockland chpt. 1992-93), Hospice Nurses Assn., Nurse Healers Profl. Assn., Utah Networker Nurse Healers Profl. Assn. Episcopalian. Home and Office: 7730 S Quicksilver Dr Salt Lake City UT 84121-5500

GOOD, WILLIAM ZEV, physician; b. Wilno, Poland, Apr. 27, 1924; s. Dov Ber and Chana (Kopelowicz) Gdud; m. Pearl Esterowicz, June 7, 1953; children: Leonard James, Michael Daniel, Anne Margaret. MD, U. Turin, Italy, 1951; postgrad. in comprehensive medicine, NYU Postgrad. Med. Sch., 1953-54. Bd. cert. Acad. Family Practice. Rotating intern St. Elizabeth Hosp., Elizabeth, N.J., 1952-53; ob-gyn. resident Cumberland Hosp., Bklyn., 1954-55; pvt. practice family medicine La Puente, Calif., 1956—. Mem. Am. Jewish Com., 1980. Mem. AMA, Calif. Med. Assn., Calif. Acad. Family Practice, Am. Acad. Family Practice, Zionist Orgn. of Am. Jewish. Office: 1840 N Hacienda Blvd La Puente CA 91744-1143

GOODALL, JACKSON WALLACE, JR., restaurant company executive; b. San Diego, Oct. 29, 1938; s. Jackson Wallace and Evelyn Violet (Koski) G.; m. Mary Esther Buckley, June 22, 1958; children: Kathleen, Jeffery, Suzanne, Minette. BS, San Diego State U., 1960. With Foodmaker, Inc., San Diego, 1963—, pres., 1970—, chief exec. officer, 1979—, chmn. bd., 1985—; founder, bd. dir. Grossmont Bank, La Mesa, Calif.; bd. dirs. Thrifty Drug Stores Inc., Van Camp Seafood Inc.; owner, dir., bd. dirs. San Diego Padres Baseball Club. Bd. dirs. Greater San Diego Sports Assn.; mem. Pres.'s Coun. San Diego State U.; chmn. Child Abuse Prevention Found.; dir. San Diego Hall Champions. Recipient Golden Chain award, 1982, Silver Plate award Internat. Foodsvc. Mfg. Assn., 1985; named Disting. Alumni of Yr. San Diego State U., 1974, 89, Golden Chain Operator of Yr. Multi Unit Food Svc. Operators, 1988, State of Israel Man of Yr., 1987, Citizen of Yr. City Club of San Diego, 1992, Marketer of Yr. Acad. Mktg. Sci., 1992; inducted into San Diego Bus. Hall of Fame, 1992. Mem. Am. Restaurant Assn., Fairbanks Ranch Country Club (founder), Univ. Club of San Diego, San Diego Intercollegiate Athletic Coun., Kadoo Club of N. Am. Republican. Office: Foodmaker Inc 9330 Balboa Ave San Diego CA 92123-1516

GOOD-BROWN, SUE ANN, nurse, small business owner; b. Webster City, Iowa, Nov. 29, 1960; d. George G. and Faye Joann (Simms) Good; m. Scot Warren Brown, Sept. 24, 1988; 1 child, McKenna; 1 step child, Lindsey. AD in Pol. Sci., Miles Community Coll., Miles City, Mont., 1981, ADN, 1983; cert., Sheffield Sch. of ID, 1990. RN, Mont. Owner, artist Redwater Pearl, Circle, Mont., 1985—; RN McCone County Pub. Health, Circle, 1990—; nurse McCone County Hosp., Circle, 1983-90, McCone County MAF and Nursing Home, Circle, 1992. Dir. McCone County Ann. Health Fair; active McCone County MSU Ext. Adv. Bd., 1992—, Mont. State Ext. Adv. Bd., 1992-96; svc. unit mgr. GSUSA. Mem. NRA, NOW, NAFE, NFIB, McCone County Sheepgrowers, Make it Yourself with Wool (dist. dir.), Mont. Woolgrower Women. Methodist. Home: PO Box 138 Circle MT 59215-0138

GOODBY, JEFFREY, advertising agency executive. Grad., Harvard Univ., 1973. Political reporter Boston; began advt. career with J. Walter Thompson; with Hal Riney & Ptnrs. San Francisco; prin., creative dir. Goodby, Berlin & Silverstein, San Francisco, 1983—. Office: Goodby Berlin & Silverstein 921 Front St San Francisco CA 94111-1426*

GOODCHILD, LESTER FRANCIS, higher education educator; b. Lackawanna, N.Y., Apr. 30, 1948; s. Thomas J. and Mary June (Devoy) Walczak; m. Wynn Evelyn Johnson, Sept. 20, 1980. BA, U. St. Thomas, 1970; MDiv with high honors, St. Meinrad Sch. Theology, 1975; MA, Indiana U., Bloomington, 1979; PhD, U. Chgo., 1986. Dir. project respond St. Meinrad (Ind.) Seminary, 1971-72; assoc. instr. dept religious studies Ind. U., 1973; supr. pastoral edn. St. Meinrad Sch. Theology, 1973-74, teaching asst. dept. ch. hist., 1974; dir. aged ministry program St. Joseph's Hosp., Huntingberg, Ind., 1973-74; deacon St. Andrew's Ch., Joliet, Ill., 1974, St. Paul the Apostle Ch., Joliet, 1975; cons. residential property ops., regional property mgr., property mgr. Lehndorff Mgmt. U.S.A. Ltd., Chgo., 1976-78; property mgr. The Habitat Co., Chgo., 1979-81; rsch. asst. ctr. for continuing edn. U. Chgo., 1979-81; instr., mentor Sch. for New Learning DePaul U., Chgo., 1981-88, dir. suburban campuses, 1987; asst. prof. higher edn. coll. edn. dept. profl. studies Iowa State U., Ames, 1988-89; adjunct rsch. assoc. ctr. for study of higher edn. Pa. State U., University Park, 1989-90; assoc. prof. edn., coord. higher edn. program coll. edn. U. Denver, 1990—; vis. lectr. sch. edn. Loyola U., Chgo., 1989-90; presenter in field. Co-editor Association for the Study of Higher Education Reader on the History of Higher Education, 1989, Administration as a Profession: Formal Programs in the Study of Higher Education, 1991; asst. editor (refereed jour.) Religion & Edn., 1989—; assoc. editor (annual vol.) Higher Education: Handbook of Theory and Research, 1992—; mem. editorial bd. Jour. Gen. Edn., 1990-94, Review of Higher Edn., 1992—, History of Higher Edn. Ann., 1994—; contbr. articles and book reviews to profl. jours., chpts. to books. Election judge City of Chgo., 1976. Travel grantee U. Notre Dame, 1982, NEH, 1989; mini grantee Iowa State U., 1989; faculty rsch. grantee U. Denver, 1992, faculty internat. rsch. grantee; scholar Meinrad Sch. Theology, 1971-75, Ind. U., 1973. Mem. AAUP, Am. Assn. for Higher Edn., Am. Cath. Hist. Assn., Am. Ednl. Rsch. Assn. (proposal reviewer 1985, 88-92), Am. Hist. Assn., Am. Coll. Pers. Assn., Assn. Study Higher Edn. (registration com. 1984, program com. 1987, futures com. 1987-89, welcoming com. 1988—, chair disseration of yr. award com. 1990, task force on edn. in 21st century, 1990-92, chair cirriculum, learning and instruction com. 1990—, annual conf. evaluation com. 1992, proposal reviewer 1988—), Nat. Orgn. Legal Problems Edn., Hist. Edn. Soc., Midwest Philosophy Edn. Soc., Nat. Coun. on Religion and Pub. Edn. (article reviewer 1990—). Democrat. Roman Catholic. Home: 5667 S Geneva St Englewood CO 80111-3726 Office: U Denver Coll Edn 2450 S Vine St Denver CO 80208

GOODEY, ILA MARIE, psychologist; b. Logan, Utah, Feb. 1, 1948; d. Vernal P. and Leona Marie (Williams) Goodey. BA with honors in English and Sociology, U. Utah, 1976; Grad. Cert. Criminology, U. Utah, 1976, MS in Counseling Psychology, 1984, PhD in Psychology, 1985. Speech writer for dean of students U. Utah, Salt Lake City, 1980-89, psychologist Univ. Counseling Ctr., 1984—; cons. Dept. Social Services, State of Utah, Salt Lake City, 1983—; pvt. practice psychology Consult West, Salt Lake City, 1985-86; pub. relations coordinator Univ. Counseling Ctr., 1985—; cons. Aids Project, U. Utah, 1985—; pvt. practice psychology, Inscapes Inst., Salt Lake City, 1987-88; writer civic news Salt Lake City Corp., 1980—; mem. Senator Orrin Hatch's Adv. Com. on Disability Oriented Legis., 1989—. Author book: Love for All Seasons, 1971, Poemspun, 1994, Tapestry, 1995; play: Validation, 1979; musical drama: One Step, 1984. Contbr. articles to profl. jours. Chmn. policy bd. Dept. State Social Service, Salt Lake City, 1986—; campaign writer Utah Dem. Party, 1985; appointed to Utah State Legis. Task Force on svcs. for people with disabilities, 1990; chmn. bd. Utah Assistive Tech. Program, 1990—. Recipient Creative Achievement award Utah Poetry Soc., 1974, English SAC, U. Utah, 1978, Leadership award YWCA, 1989, Nat. Golden Rule award J.C. Penny, Washington, 1989, 90, Volunteerism award State of Utah, 1990; Ila Marie Goodey award named in honor. Mem. AAUW, Am. Psychol. Assn., Utah Psychol. Assn., Internat. Platform Assn., Mortar Board, Am. Soc. Clin. Hypnosis, Utah Soc. Clin. Hypnosis, Soc. Psychol. Study Social Issues, League of Women Voters, Phi Beta Kappa, Phi Kappa Phi, Alpha Lambda Delta. Mormon. Clubs: Mormon Theol. Symposium, Utah Poetry Assn. Avocations: theatrical activities, creative writing, travel, political activities. Office: U Utah Counseling Ctr 2450 SSB Salt Lake City UT 84112

GOODING, GRETCHEN ANN WAGNER, physician, educator; b. Columbus, Ohio, July 2, 1935; d. Edward Frederick and Margaret (List) Wagner; m. Charles A. Gooding, June 19, 1961; children: Gunnar Blaise, Justin Mathias, Britta Meghan. BA magna cum laude, St. Mary of the Springs Coll., Columbus, 1957; MD cum laude, Ohio State U., 1961. Diplomate Am. Bd. Diagnostic Radiology. Intern Univ. Hosps., Columbus, 1961-62; rsch. fellow Boston City Hosp., 1962-63, Boston U., 1963-65; with dept. radiology U. Calif., San Francisco, 1975—, assoc. prof. in radiology, 1981-85, prof., vice chmn., 1986—; asst. chief radiology VA Med. Ctr., San Francisco, 1978-87, chief radiology, 1987—, chief ultrasonography, 1975—; chair com. acad. pers. U. Calif., San Francisco, 1993-94; speaker in field. Co-editor Radiologic Clinics of N.Am., 1993—; mem. editorial bd. San Francisco Medicine, 1986-95, Applied Radiology, 1987-89, Current Opinion in Radiology, 1992-93, The Radiologist, 1993—, Emergency Radiology, 1993—; contbr. articles to profl. jours. Fellow Am. Coll. Radiology (mem. commn. on ultrasound 1984-95), Am. Inst. Ultrasound in Medicine (bd. govs. 1981-84, chair convention program 1986-88, Presdl. Recognition award 1984); mem. AMA, San Francisco Med. Soc. (chmn. membership com. 1992-94, bd. dirs. 1995), RSNA (course com. 1984-88, tech. exhibit com. 1992-95), Bay Area Ultrasound Soc. (pres. 1979-80), Soc. Radiologists Ultrasound (chair membership com. 1991-93), ARRS, AUR, CRS, Calif. Med. Assn., Am. Assn. Women Radiologists (pres. 1984-85, trustee 1991-94), VA Chiefs of Radiology Assn. (pres.-elect, pres. 1994-95), San Francisco Radiological Soc. (pres. 1990-91), Hungarian Radiological Soc. (hon.). Office: VA Med Ctr Radiology Svc 4150 Clement St San Francisco CA 94121-1545

GOODMAN, BEATRICE MAY, real estate professional; b. Rehoboth, Mass., Nov. 12, 1933; s. Manuel Silva and Mercy Elizabeth (Mayers) Bettencourt; m. Sam R. Goodman, Sept. 15, 1957; children: Mark, Stephen, Christopher. BS, Marymount Coll., 1980. Pres. Bettencourt Draperies, Rehoboth, Mass., 1955-56; asst. mgr. Leo H. Spivack Furniture, L.I., N.Y., 1956-57; asst. designer Lillian Decorators, L.I., N.Y., 1957-58; asst. buyer Macy's N.Y., N.Y.C., 1958-59; pres. Beatrice & Beverly, Mt. View, Calif., 1980-82; realtor Coldwell Banker, Menlo Park, Calif., 1984—; pres. The Added Touch, Atherton, Calif., 1984-91; realtor Cornish & Carey Realtors, Menlo Park, Calif., 1991—. Den mother Boy Scouts Am., N.Y.C., 1970-76; active Peninsula Vols., Palo Alto, 1974—, Internat. Friendship Force. Mem. Nat. Bd. Realtors, Orgn. for Rehab. Tng. Home: 60 Shearer Dr Atherton CA 94027-3957 Office: Cornish & Carey 1000 El Camino Real Menlo Park CA 94025-4327

GOODMAN, CHARLES SCHAFFNER, JR., food product executive, consultant; b. Phila., Nov. 15, 1949; s. Charles Schaffner Sr. and Dorothy Ruth (Irwin) G. BA, U. Pa., 1971. Warehouse and distb. mgr. Odyssey Records, Santa Cruz, Calif., 1974-75; mgr. Paradiso's, Santa Cruz, Calif., 1978-79; sales mgr. Mask Prodns., Chatsworth, Calif., 1980; regional sales mgr. Harmony Foods, Inc., Santa Cruz, 1981-83, nat. sales mgr., 1983-85, nat. sales mgr. foodsvc., 1985-88, v.p. foodsvc., 1988-90; owner, pres. Creative Mktg. Group, Soquel, Calif., 1990—; bd. dirs. Noema Software. Mem. No. Calif. Food Svc. Mktg. Assn., The Foodsters. Home: 4713 Soquel Creek Rd Soquel CA 95073-9657 Address: PO Box 5271 Santa Cruz CA 95063-5271 Office: Creative Mktg Group PO Box 1736 Soquel CA 95073-1736

GOODMAN, CHRISTOPHER BETTENCOURT, cytogeneticist; b. N.Y.C., June 8, 1967; s. Sam Richard and Beatrice May (Bettencourt) G. BS in Biol. Scis., Calif. Poly. State U., San Luis Obispo, 1990; MS in Human Cytogenetics, Hofstra U., 1994; postgrad., Foothill Coll., 1995. Tutor for learning disabled students Calif. Poly. State U., 1988-90; student tchr., asst. Hofstra U., Hempstead, N.Y., 1992-94; human cytogeneticist MediGene Inc., Yonkers, N.Y., 1993-94; technician Outland, Menlo Park, Calif., 1984—; cons. ShredMax, Atherton, Calif., 1994—; mem. U.S. Dept. HHS, 1992—. EMT, Emergency Med. Svcs., San Luis Obispo, 1990. Mem. AAAS, Am. Soc. Human Genetics, Genetics Soc. Am., N.Y. Acad. Scis., Churchill Club, Beta Theta Pi. Republican. Jewish. Home and Office: 60 Shearer Dr Atherton CA 94027-3957

GOODMAN, GWENDOLYN ANN, nursing educator; b. Davenport, Iowa, Aug. 7, 1955; d. Merle Erwin and Loraine Etta (Mahannah) Langfeldt; m. Mark Nathan Goodman, Oct. 24, 1982; children: Zachary Aaron, Alexander Daniel. BS in Nursing, Ariz. State U., 1977. RN, Ariz. Staff nurse surg. fl. and intensive care unit St. Luke's Hosp. and Med. Ctr., Phoenix, 1977-81; staff nurse intensive care unit Yavapai Regional Med. Ctr., Prescott, Ariz., 1981-82; instr. nursing Yavapai Coll., Prescott, 1982-88, cons., 1986; part-time staff nurse Ariz. Poison Control Ctr., Phoenix, 1980-81; mem. profl. adv. com. Home Health Agy. Yavapai Regional Med. Ctr., 1988-93. Mem. Sigma Theta Tau. Democrat. Home: PO Box 450 Prescott AZ 86302-0450

GOODMAN, JOSEPH WILFRED, electrical engineering educator; b. Boston, Feb. 8, 1936; s. Joseph and Doris (Ryan) G.; m. Hon Mai Lam, Dec. 5, 1962; 1 dau., Michele Ann. B.A., Harvard U., 1958; M.S. in E.E., Stanford U., 1960, Ph.D., 1963. Postdoctoral fellow Norwegian Def. Rsch. Establishment, Oslo, 1962-63; rsch. assoc. Stanford U., 1963-67, asst. prof., 1967-69, assoc. prof., 1969-72, prof. elec. engring., 1972—; vis. prof. Univ. Paris XI, Orsay, France, 1973-74; dir. Info. Systems lab., dept. elec. engring., Stanford U., 1981-83, chmn., 1988—; William E. Ayer prof. elec. engring. Stanford U., 1988—; cons. to govt. and industry, 1965—; v.p. Internat. Comm. for Optics, 1985-87, pres., 1988-90, past pres., 1991-93. Author: Introduction to Fourier Optics, 1968, Statistical Optics, 1985, (with R. Gray) Fourier Transforms: An Introduction for Engineers; editor: International Trends in Optics, 1991; contbr. articles to profl. jours. Recipient F.E. Terman award Am. Soc. Engring. Edn., 1971, Frederic Ives Medal, 1990, Optical Soc. Am. Fellow Optical Soc. Am. (dir. 1977-83, editor jour. 1978-83, Max Born award 1983, Frederick Ives award 1990, Esther Hoffman Beller medal 1995, v.p. 1990, pres.-elect 1991, pres. 1992, past pres. 1993), IEEE (edn. medal 1987), Soc. Photo-optical Instrumentation Engrs. (bd. govs. 1979-82, 88-90, Dennis Gabor award 1987); mem. NAE, Electromagnetics Acad. Home: 570 University Ter Los Altos CA 94022-3523 Office: Stanford U Dept Elec Engring McCullogh 152 Stanford CA 94305

GOODMAN, LINDSEY ALAN, furniture manufacturing executive, architect; b. L.A., Nov. 17, 1957; s. Ira and Wilma Carolyn (Sanders) G.; m. Joan Frances Radditz, July 7, 1990; 1 child, Alexandra Isabelle. BA, UCLA, 1980; MArch, Calif. State Poly. U., Pomona, 1983. Registered architect. Project designer Bertram Berenson, Architect, Claremont, Calif., 1983; job capt. Architecture & Planning, San Rafael, Calif., 1985-86, Barry Archtl. Design Group, Santa Barbara, Calif., 1986-87; project architect Architects West, Santa Barbara, 1987-89; prin. L.A. Goodman, Architect, Santa Barbara, 1989-91; v.p. IWI/Internat., Chino, Calif., 1992—; ptnr. IWI/Capital Devel., Chino, 1991—. Author: (poem) The Camargue, 1987. Mem. adv. coun. Santa Barbara Mus. Natural History, 1988-89, 95—, trustee, 1989-95; patron Santa Barbara Civic Light Opera. Recipient Richard J. Neutra Meml. award, 1983. Mem. AIA, Internat. Platform Assn., Royal Archtl. Inst. Can. (internat.). Office: IWI/Internat 15044 La Palma Dr Chino CA 91710-9669

GOODMAN, MARY A., photographer; b. Hartford, Conn., July 24, 1934; d. Allan S. and Carlyn Rhoda (Leicher) G. BS in Edn., NYU, 1958; MA in Spl. Edn., Columbia U., N.Y.C., 1961; MSW, Simmons Coll. Social Wk., Boston, 1965. Free lance photographer various locations, 1975—. Photography of notable persons include His Royal Highness Prince of Wales, Her Majesty, Queen Elizabeth, The Queen Mother, Sir Michael Tippett, O.M., Sir Yehudi Menuhin, Dame Morgot Fonteyn, Dame Alicia Markova, many others. Mem. Friends of Photography, Ansel Adams Ctr., San Francisco. Mem. Nat. Soc. Arts and Letters (Tucson br.), N.Y. Acad. Sci., Royal Photographic Soc. G.B. (sec./membership sect. Journalism group 1976-79, pictorial portfolio group 1991—), Royal Photographic Soc. Pacific br., Photographic Soc. Am., Internat. Ctr. Photography, The Photographer's Gallery, Ctr. for Creative Photography, Soc. Southwestern Authors, Resources for Women. Home: 6266 N Campbell Ave Tucson AZ 85718-3150

GOODMAN, MAX A., lawyer, educator; b. Chgo., May 24, 1924; s. Sam and Nettie (Abramomitz) G.; m. Marlyene Monkarsh, June 2, 1946; children: Jan M., Lauren A., Melanie Murez. A.A., Herzl Jr. Coll., 1943; student, Northwestern U., 1946-47; J.D., Loyola U., 1948. Bar: Calif. 1948; cert. family law specialist. Sole practice Los Angeles, 1948-53; ptnr. Goodman, Hirschberg & King, Los Angeles, 1953-81; prof. law Southwestern U. Sch. Law, Los Angeles, 1966—; lectr. Calif. Continuing Edn. of the Bar, 1971—; editorial cons. Bancroft Whitney, San Francisco, 1986—. Contbr. articles to profl. jours. Served to cpl. U.S. Army, 1943-45. Mem. ABA (chmn. law sch. curriculum family law sect. 1987-88), State Bar Calif. (del. conf. dels. 1972, 80-87, 91, exec. com. family law sect. 1981-85), Los Angeles County Bar Assn. (chmn. family law sect. 1971-72, editor family law handbook). Office: Southwestern U Sch of Law 675 S Westmoreland Ave Los Angeles CA 90005-3905

GOODMAN, MURRAY, chemistry educator; b. N.Y.C., July 6, 1928; s. Louis and Frieda (Bercun) G.; m. Zelda Silverman; Aug. 26, 1951; children: Andrew, Joshua, David. BS magna cum laude with honors in Chemistry, Bklyn. Coll., 1949; PhD, U. Calif., Berkeley, 1953; DSc honoris causa, CUNY, Staten Island, 1995; PhDhonoris causa, CUNY, 1995, D in sci., 1995; D (hon.), U. Ioannina, Greece, 1995. Asst. prof. Polytechnic Inst., Bklyn., 1956-60, assoc. prof., 1960-64, prof. chemistry, 1964-71, dir. polymer rsch. inst., 1967-71; prof. chemistry U. Calif.-San Diego, La Jolla, 1971—, chmn. dept. Chemistry, 1976-81; vis. prof. U. Alta., Can., 1981, Lady Davis Vis. Prof., Hebrew U., Jerusalem, 1982; William H. Rauscher lectr. Rensselaer Poly. Inst., 1982. Editor Biopolymers Jour., 1963—; contbr. numerous articles to profl. jours. Recipient Alumnus medal Bklyn. Coll., 1964, Scoffone medal U. Padova, 1980, Humboldt award 1986, Max-Bermann medal 1991, Givaudan-Roure award Assn. Chemo-reception Scis., 1992; NRC fellow Cambridge (Eng.) U., 1955-56. Fellow AAAS; mem. Am. Chem. Soc., Am. Peptide Soc. (Pierce award 1989), Am. Soc. Biol. Chemists, The Chem. Soc. Eng., Biophys. Soc., Coun. for Chem. Rsch. (sci. adv. bd.), U.S. Nat. Commn., Acad. Creative Endeavors, Sigma Xi, Phi Beta Kappa. Home: 9760 Blackgold Rd La Jolla CA 92037-1115 Office: U Calif San Diego Dept Chemistry # 0343 La Jolla CA 92093

GOODMAN, ROBERT MERWIN, agriculturalist, plant biologist, university educator; b. Ithaca, N.Y., Dec. 30, 1945; s. Robert Browning and Janet Edith (Pond) G.; 1 child, Nathan Mansfield. Student, Johns Hopkins U., 1963-65; B.Sc., Cornell U., 1967, Ph.D., 1973. Vis. rsch. fellow John Innes Inst., Norwich, Eng., 1973-74; asst. prof. U. Ill., Urbana, 1974-78; assoc. prof. U. Ill., 1978-81, prof., 1981-83; exec. v.p. R&D Calgene, Inc., Davis, Calif., 1982-90; sr. scholar-in-residence NRC, 1990-91; vis. prof. U. Wis., Madison, 1990-91, prof., 1991—; mem. Bd. on Agr., NRC, 1986-91, chair com. on exam. plant sci. rsch. programs U.S., 1990-92, Commn. on Life Sci.; bd. dirs. Calgene, Inc., 1984-88, Genetic Resources Comms. Systems, Inc., Cornell Rsch. Found., Inc., Lakeside Biotech., Inc.; mem. NSF Task Force: Biol., Behavioral and Social Scis. Looking to 21st Century, 1990-91; cons. W.K. Kellogg Found., 1990-94; chmn. oversight com. collabrative crop rsch. program McKnight Found. Editor: Expanding the Use of Soybeans, 1976; assoc. editor Virology, 1976-94; mem. editl. bd. Plant Molecular Biology-Molecular Breeding, 1994—. Pres. Channing-Murray Found., Urbana, Ill., 1976-78; bd. dirs. Sacramento Sci. Ctr., 1989-90. NSF-NATO postdoctoral fellow, 1973. Mem. AAAS, Am. Phytopathol. Soc., Am. Chem. Soc., Am. Soc. Virology, Internat. Soc. Plant Molecular Biology. Office: U Wisconsin 1630 Linden Dr Madison WI 53706-1520

GOODMAN, SAM, food products executive. With Durkee Sharht, L.A.; pres. Mayfair Packing. Office: Mayfair Packing Co Inc 2070 S 7th St San Jose CA 95112-6010*

GOODMAN, SAM RICHARD, electronics company executive; b. N.Y.C., May 23, 1930; s. Morris and Virginia (Gross) G.; m. Beatrice Bettencourt, Sept. 15, 1957; children—Mark Stuart, Stephen Manuel, Christopher Bettencourt. BBA, CCNY, 1951; MBA, NYU, 1957, PhD, 1968. Chief acct. John C. Valentine Co., N.Y.C., 1957-60; mgr. budgets and analysis Gen. Foods. Corp., White Plains, N.Y., 1960-63; budget dir. Crowell Collier Pub. Co., N.Y.C., 1963-64; v.p., chief fin. officer Nestle Co., Inc., White Plains, 1964; chief fin. officer Aileen, Inc., N.Y.C., 1973-74, Ampex Corp., 1974-76; exec. v.p. fin. and adminstrn. Baker & Taylor Co. div. W.R. Grace Co., N.Y.C., 1976-79, Magnuson Computer Systems, Inc., San Jose, Calif., 1979-81; v.p., chief fin. officer Datamac Computer Systems, Sunnyvale, Calif., 1981; pres. Nutritional Foods Inc., San Francisco, 1983-84; chmn., chief exec. officer CMX Corp., Santa Clara, Calif., 1984-88; dir., sr. v.p. Masstor Systems Corp., Santa Clara, 1988—; pvt. cons. Atherton, Calif., 1990—; sr. mgmt. cons. Durkee/Sharlit, 1991—; pres. Mayfair Packing Co., 1991—; mng. dir. Quincy Pacific Ptnrs., L.P., 1992—; pres., CEO Mayfair Packing Co., San Jose, Calif., 1991-94; pvt. cons. SRG Assocs., 1994—; lectr. NYU Inst. Mgmt., 1965-67; asst. prof. mktg. Iona Coll. Grad. Sch. Adminstrn., 1967-69; prof. Golden Gate U., 1974—; prof. fin. and mktg. Pace U. Grad. Sch. Bus. Adminstrn., 1969-79. Author 7 books, including Controller's Handbook; contbr. articles to jours. Lt. (j.g.) USNR, 1951-55. Mem. Fin. Execs. Inst., Nat. Assn. Accts., Am. Statis. Assn., Am. Econs. Assn., Planning Execs. Inst., Am. Arbitration Assn., Turnaround Mgmt. Assn. Home and Office: 60 Shearer Dr Atherton CA 94027-3957

GOODMAN, WILLIAM LEE, commercial pilot; b. Butte, Mont., May 15, 1946; s. William Lonzo and Phyllis Hilma (White) G.; m. Susan Margaret Thompson, Nov. 29, 1969; children: Kathryn, Margaret, William. BS in Computer Sci., Oreg. State U., 1968; MBA, City U., Seattle, 1982; postgrad., Seattle U.; postgrad. in def. econs., U.S. Naval War Coll., 1986. Cert. airline transport pilot, flight engr., control tower operator, flight instr., FAA. Systems analyst Mohawk Data Scis. Corp., Portland, Oreg., 1974-76; air traffic controller FAA, Pendleton, Oreg., 1976-78; pilot Trans Internat. Airlines, Oakland, Calif., 1978; aerospace engr. Boeing Comml. Airplane Co., Seattle, 1978-86; pilot USAIR, Washington, 1986—. Editor Boeing Tng. Ctr. newsletter Intercom, 1980-82; contbg. editor Boeing Customer Service mag. Advisor, 1982-86. V.p. Homeowners Assn., Auburn, 1982-85. Served to comdr. USNR, 1968-89, Vietnam. Mem. Airline Pilots Assn. (chmn. local air safety 1994—). Republican. Home: 2912 202nd Avenue Ct E Sumner WA 98390-9022

GOODRICH, GLORIA JEAN, federal agency administrator; b. Lima, Ohio, Feb. 21, 1934; d. Orville John and Lila Mae (Rigel) Mortimer; m. Merlin Virgil Goodrich, June 6, 1953; children: Sandra Kay, Gregory Lynn, Geoffrey Virgil. Student, Owosso Coll., 1952-55, 67-68, Muskegon (Mich.) Community Coll., 1971-73. Cert. legal asst., 1988. Estimator E.H. Sheldon & co., Muskegon, 1975-77; dep. clk. U.S. Fed. Ct., Tucson, 1977-81, supr., 1982-94; ret., 1994. Tchr. ch. sch., Ohio, Mich., Ariz., 1950—; leader Boy Scouts Am. and Girl Scouts U.S., Mich., 1966-71; mem. Tucson Clean and Beautiful. Mem. Ariz. Assn. for Ct. Mgmt., Tucson Assn. Legal Assts., Nat. Assn. for Female Execs. Avocations: walking, reading, sewing, teaching, needlework.

GOODSON, JOHN EARL, civil engineering executive; b. Merced, Calif., Oct. 19, 1945; s. Vincent Bernard and Dorothy Mae (Taber) G.; m. Mary Haley Cook, Sept. 5, 1970; children: Montgomery Vincent, Garett Champlin. AA, San Jose City Coll., 1969, BS in Civil Engring., 1971; MS in Civil Engring., Purdue U., 1972. Registered profl. civil engr., Oreg., Calif. Transp. planning specialist Tudor Engring. Co., San Francisco, 1972-73; assoc. transp. planner Sacramento Regional Area Planning Commn., 1973-74; transp. engr. Parsons Brinckerhoff-Quade & Douglas, San Francisco, 1974-75; transp. planning engr. Lane County Pub. Works Dept., Eugene, Oreg., 1975-82, county engr., 1982, pub. works dir., 1982—; student aide-civil engr. Contra Costa County Pub. Works Dept., Martinez, Calif., summers 1968-70; rsch. asst. joint hwy. rsch. project Purdue U., West Lafayette, Ind., 1971-72; mem. trans. tech. adv. com. AOC; supporting mem. Transp. Rsch. Bd. Mem. Am. Pub. Works Assn., Oreg. Assn. County Engrs. and Surveyors (sec.- treas. 1988, pres.- elect 1989, pres. 1990, Award of Merit 1987, County Engr. of Yr. 1988), Inst. Transp. Engrs. (assoc., mem. com. 5B-8). Home: 792 E 39th Pl Eugene OR 97405-4538 Office: Lane County Pub Works Dept 3040 N Delta Rd Eugene OR 97408-1636

GOODWILL, MARGARET JANE, artist; b. L.A., Sept. 27, 1950; d. David and Erna Pauline (Kremser) G.; m. James Vincent Erickson, Sept. 6, 1980. Student, U. Calif., Santa Barbara, 1968-70; BFA cum laude, Calif. Coll. Arts and Crafts, 1972. Graphic artist Proarts, Oakland, Calif., 1970-71; creative art dir. Am. Analysis Corp., San Francisco, 1974-76; dir. Lone Wolf Gallery, San Francisco, 1982-84; prin., artist Calif. and Hawaii, 1984—. One-woman shows include Lone Wolf Gallery, 1985, Wrubel Gallery, Berkeley, Calif., 1988, 3660 On The Rise, Honolulu, 1995, 3660 On The Rise, Honolulu; two-person shows include St. Mary's Coll., Moraga, Calif., 1973, Hewlett-Packard Corp. Hdqrs., 1990, 94, 95, Stanford U., Calif., 1991, 95, C.C.P. Gallery, Honolulu, 1992, PacTel Hdqrs., 1992, SunSoft Hdqrs., Calif., 1992, Tandem Hdqrs., Calif., 1992, Raleigh Studios, Hollywood, Calif., 1993, TRW Hdqrs., Oakland, Calif., 1993, Crouching Lion Gallery, Oahu, Hawaii, 1994, Return to Paradise, Honolulu, 1994; exhibited in group shows San Francisco Art Festival, 1971, 72, A Gallery, Palm Desert, Calif., 1986, Banaker Gallery, Walnut Creek, Calif., 1988, 90, Trans Am. Pyramid, San Francisco, 1990, Recycle Art Hawaii 95, Honolulu, Pacific Bell hdqrs., Concord, Calif., 1992, murals for Prevention Cruelty to Animals Hdqrs., San Francisco, 1980, Wave Nightclub, Waikiki, Hawaii, 1991, illustrations for So. Poverty Law Ctr., Memphis, 1991, Cosmo, CD cover designs; Hawaii Pub. TV, The Breaks; fabric design Sonali Corp.; design and illustration Dolphin Shirt Co., ITP Hawaii. Recipient 1st prize Ossining (N.Y.) Women's Club, 1968, Poughkeepsie (N.Y.) Art Ctr., 1968, merit award Delta Art Show, Antioch, Calif., 1971; N.Y. State Regent's scholar, 1968, Walnut Creek Civic Arts scholar, 1970. Mem. Calif. Coll. Arts and Crafts Alumni Assn., Mus. Contemporary Art of Hawaii, Bishop Mus., Nat. Geog. Soc., Smithsonian Assocs.

GOODWIN, ALFRED THEODORE, federal judge; b. Bellingham, Wash., June 29, 1923; s. Alonzo Theodore and Miriam Hazel (Williams) G.; m. Marjorie Elizabeth Major, Dec. 23, 1943 (div. 1948); 1 son, Michael Theodore; m. Mary Ellin Handelin, Dec. 23, 1949; children: Karl Alfred, Margaret Ellen, Sara Jane, James Paul. B.A., U. Oreg., 1947; J.D., 1951. Bar: Oreg. 1951. Newspaper reporter Eugene (Oreg.) Register-Guard, 1947-50; practiced in Eugene until, 1955; circuit judge Oreg. 2d. Jud. Dist., 1955-60; assoc. justice Oreg. Supreme Ct., 1960-69; judge U.S. Dist. Ct. Oreg., 1969-71; judge U.S. Ct. Appeals for (9th cir.), Pasadena, Calif., 1971-88, chief judge, 1988-91, sr. judge, 1991—. Editor Oreg. Law Rev., 1950-51. Bd. dirs. Central Lane YMCA, Eugene, 1956-60, Salem (Oreg.) Art Assn., 1960-69; adv. bd. Eugene Salvation Army, 1956-60, chmn., 1959. Served to capt., inf. AUS, 1942-46, ETO. Mem. Am. Judicature Soc., Am. Law Inst., ABA (ho. of dels. 1986-87), Order of Coif, Phi Delta Phi, Sigma Delta Chi, Alpha Tau Omega. Republican. Presbyn. Club: Multnomah Athletic (Portland, (Oreg.). Office: US Ct Appeals 9th Cir PO Box 91510 125 S Grand Ave Pasadena CA 91105-1652

GOODWIN, JOANNE LORRAINE, historian, educator; b. Seattle, Aug. 23, 1949; d. Roy Goodwin and Vera (Bedgisoff) Locks. BFA, U. Wash., 1973; MA, Sarah Lawrence Coll., 1983; PhD, U. Mich., 1991. Asst. prof. history U. Nev., Las Vegas, 1991—; chair Nev. Women's Archives Adv. Bd., U. Nev., 1994-95. Contbr. articles to profl. jours. Recipient Rsch. award Nev. Humanities Com., 1993, Faculty Recognition award U. Nev. Las Vegas Alumni Assn., 1993, Am. Coun. of Learned Soc. fellowship, 1995-96, Nat. Endowment for the Humanities Summer Rsch. award, 1995-96. Mem. AAUW, Orgn. Am. Historians (mem. membership com. 1993—), Am. Hist. Assn., Social Sci. History Assn. Office: Univ Nev 4505 S Maryland Pky Las Vegas NV 89154-9900

GOODWIN, JOHN ROBERT, lawyer, educator; b. Morgantown, W.Va., Nov. 3, 1929; s. John Emory and Ruby Iona G.; m. Betty Lou Wilson, June 2, 1952; children: John R., Elizabeth Ann Paugh, Mark Edward, Luke Jackson, Matthew Emory. B.S., W.Va. U., 1952, LLB, J.D., 1964. Bar: W.Va., U.S. Supreme Ct. Formerly city atty., county commr., spl. pros. atty., then mayor City of Morgantown; prof. bus. law W.Va. U.; prof. hotel and casino law U. Nev., Las Vegas; Author: Legal Primer for Artists, Craftspersons, 1987, Hotel Law, Principles and Cases, 1987. Served with U.S. Army, Korea. Recipient Bancroft-Whitney award in Constl. Law'; named Outstanding West Virginian, State of West Virginia. Democrat. Author: Twenty Feet From Glory; Business Law, 3d edit.; High Points of Legal History; Travel and Lodging Law; Desert Adventure; Gaming Control Law; editor Hotel and Casino Letter; past editor Bus. Law Rev., Bus. Law Letter. Home: Casa Linda 48 5250 E Lake Mead Blvd Las Vegas NV 89115-6751

GOODWIN, KEMPER, retired architect; b. Tempe, Ariz., Apr. 28, 1906; m. Mary McGhee (dec.); children: Mary Helen Goodwin Flanagan, Kathleen Goodwin Bales, Michael Kemper. Student, U. So. Calif., 1924-28. Various positions El Paso, Tex., Dallas, Texarkana, Shreveport, Kansas City and Chgo., 1931-35; architect Lescher & Mahoney, Phoenix, 1935-42, Del E. Webb Constrn., Phoenix, 1942-45; prin. Michael and Kemper Goodwin, 1945—; ret., 1988. Prin. works include various bldgs. Ariz. State U., Tempe, Casa Grande, Ariz., Coolidge, Ariz., Safford, Ariz., Globe, Ariz., Holbrook, Ariz., Kingman, Ariz., other schs. and indsl. bldgs. in Phoenix. Fomer mem. Tempe City Coun.; chmn. Tempe United Fund campaign; mem. local coun. Boy Scouts Am. Recipient Citizen award Am. Legion, 1962. Fellow AIA (past pres. Cen. Ariz. chpt.); mem. Ariz. Soc. Architects (past sec. and pres.), State Bd. Tech. Registration, Nat. Coun. Archtl. Registration Bds., Tempe Hist. Soc., Tempe C. of C., Exec. Club, Ariz. Country Club, Rotary. Address: 4814 S Birch St Tempe AZ 85282-7209

GOODWIN, MARCY, architectural coordinator, consultant; b. San Diego, Mar. 11, 1948; d. Don and Beverly (Stern) G. BFA, Chouinard Art Sch., 1965-69; MFA in Painting, Claremont Grad. Sch., 1969-71. Exhibition coordinator Office of Charles & Ray Eames, Venice, Calif., 1977-79, curator Inventions exhibit, 1977-79; exhibition cons. IBM, Armonk, N.Y., 1980-81; mus. cons. R. Meier & Assocs. Architect, N.Y.C., 1982; bldg. project dir. Mus. Contemporary Art, Los Angeles, 1980-86, Tech. Ctr. Silicon Valley, San Jose, Calif., 1986-87, San Francisco Mus. Modern Art, 1987-89, Napa (Calif.) Valley Arts Found., 1988, Chgo. Mus. Contemporary Art, 1989-90, Wellesley (Mass.) Coll. Art Mus., 1989; bldg. program cons. Mus. Contemporary Art, Chgo., 1988, Craft and Folk Art Mus., L.A., Andy Warhol Mus., Pitts., 1990-92, Latino Mus., L.A., 1991-92, Santa Barbara Mus. Art, 1991-92, Scripps Coll., 1991, Bronx Acad. Arts, 1991, Hoover Dam Visitors Ctr., 1991, Tech. Ctr. Silicon Valley, 1991-92, L.A. County Mus. of Art, Calif., 1993, Walker Art Ctr., Mpls., 1994, Milw. Art M,us., Wis., 1994, Nelson Atkins Mus. of Art, Kansas City, Mo., 1994-95, Jewish Mus. of San Francisco, 1995; curator Automobile and Culture exhibit Mus. Contemporary Art, L.A., 1982-83; design cons. San Diego Arts Ctr., 1984-86, curator On the Drawing Bd. exhibit, 1984-85, J. Jerde exhibit, 1985-86; panelist, speaker Nat. Conf. on Arts and the Handicapped, Washington, 1975, West Weew conf. Pacific Design Ctr., Los Angeles, 1984; panel moderator conf. on architecture and art AIA, Los Angeles, 1985; panel moderator annual meeting Am. Assn. Mus., Los Angeles, 1986; spl. speaker, seminar dir. Am. Assn. Art Mus. Dirs., Ann. Conf., 1988. Author: LA/ACCESS, 1980-81; contbr. articles to Los Angeles Mag. Calif. Arts Commn. grantee, 1974, 75.

GOODWIN, MARTIN BRUNE, radiologist; b. Vancouver, B.C., Can., Aug. 8, 1921; came to U.S., 1948; m. Cathy Dennison, Mar. 7, 1980; 1 child, Suzanne; stepchildren: Chuck Glikas, Dianna; 1 child from previous marriage, Nancijane Goodwin Hilling. BSA in Agriculture, U. B.C., 1943, postgrad., 1943-44; MD, CM, McGill U. Med. Sch., Montreal, Can., 1948. Diplomate Am. Bd. Med. Examiners, lic. Med. Coun. Can.; cert. diagnostic and therapeutic radiology Am. Bd. Radiology; cert. Am. Bd. Nuclear Medicine. Intern Scott & White Hosp., Temple, Tex., 1948-49; fellow radiology Scott & White Clinic, 1949-52, mem. staff, 1952-53; instr. U. Tex., Galveston, 1952-53; radiologist Plains Regional Med. Ctr., Clovis, N.Mex.; radiologist Plains Regional Med. Ctr., Portales, N.Mex., pres. med. staff; chief radiology De Baca Gen. Hosp., Ft. Sumner, N.Mex.; cons. Cannon AFB Hosp., Clovis; pvt. practice radiology Clovis, Portales, Ft. Sumner and Tucumcari, 1955—; adj. prof. health scis. Ea. N.Mex. U., 1976-77; adj. clin. prof. health scis. We. Mich. U., 1976-78. Apptd. N.Mex. Radiation Tech. Adv. Coun., N.Mex. Bd. Pub. Health; former chmn. N.Mex. Health and Social Svcs. Bd.; mem. Regional Health Planning Coun.; treas. Roosevelt County Rep. Ctrl. Com. Capt. U.S. Army M.C., 1953-55; Col. USAF M.C., 1975-79. Fellow AAAS, Am. Coll. Radiology, Am. Soc. Thoracic Radiologists (founder); mem. N.Mex. Med. Soc. (various coms., chmn. joint practice com., councillor bd. dirs.), N.Mex. Radiol. Soc. (past pres.), N.Mex. Thoracic Soc. (past councillor, 3 coms.), N.Mex. Med. Review Assn. (bd. dirs.), N.Mex. Med. Soc. Found. for Med. Care (bd. dirs. 1975—, former v.p., former treas.), County Med. Soc. (past pres., past v.p., past sec.), Clovis C. of C. (chmn. civic affairs com.), Clovis Elks Lodge (past exalted ruler), Clovis Noonday Lions Club (past sec.). Republican. Presbyterian. Home: 505 E 18th St Portales NM 88130-9201

GOODWIN, SAMUEL MCCLURE, officer; b. N.Y.C., Dec. 3, 1916; s. Samuel Rivington and Pearl Estelle (McClure) G.; m. DuVal Rutledge Roberts, July 14, 1949 (div. Aug. 1955); children: Samuel McClure Jr., Charles DuVal; m. Christjane Thom, May 25, 1957; 1 child, Peter Bouton. BS in Mil. Sci., U.S. Military Acad., 1940; MA in Internat. & Pub. Affairs, The George Washington U., 1971. Platoon leader, staff officer, squadron comdr. 6th Armored Clavary, USA, France, Germany, USA, France, Germany, 1940-45; div. staff officer 24th Inf. Div., Korea, 1953-55; theater army staff officer Hawaii and, Vietnam, 1965-66; sr. advisor 1st Rep. Korea Army, 1966-67; commanding gen. U.S. Army Berlin Brigade, Berlin, Germany, 1967-69; dep. cmdr., chief staff U.S. Army III Corps., Ft. Hood, Tex., 1969-70. Pres. Santa Fe Coun. on Internat. Rels., Santa Fe, N.Mex., 1972-78; bd. dirs. Vol. Involvement Svc., Sante Fe., 1978-84; bd. dirs., treas. Visitor Hospitality Cen., Santa Fe., 1984-90. Decorated Disting. Svc. medal U.S. Army, 1970, Legion of Merit (3), 1945. 67, 69, Silver Star medal, 1945, Bronze Star medal, 1945, Disting. Alumnus N. Mex., Inst., 1993. Mem. Kiwanis Internat. (hon.), Assn. U. S. Army, U.S. Armor Assn., U.S. Cavalry Assn., Nat. Assn. Uniformed Svcs., Ret. Officers Assn., Mil. Order WW. Democrat. Home and Office: Crossed Sabers Ranch Cerrillos NM 87010

GOODWIN, SANDRA JOAN, management trainer, consultant; b. St. Louis, Sept. 30, 1937; d. Robert Earl and Irma Josephine (Modray) Balencia; m. Earl Victor Goodwin II, July 22, 1980; children: Kathleen Anne, Kristine Annette. Student, Wash. U.; MS in exec. mgmt., U. Calif., Riverside, 1986. Adminstrv. aide Washington U., St. Louis, 1955-65; mgmt. cons. Hughes Heiss & Assocs., San Mateo, Calif., 1975-79; budget analyst San Bernardino (Calif.) County, 1979-80, mgmt. cons., 1980-82, data processing projects mgr., 1982-83, chief edn. and info. services, 1983-87, exec. post dep. county admnstr. officer, 1987-88; owner Mgmt. Assocs. Tng. and Cons. Services, San Bernardino, 1982—. State chairperson Calif. Regional Criminal Justice Planning Bd., San Mateo, 1974-78, regional vice chairperson; exec. asst. San Mateo Bd. Suprs., 1978. Coro Found. scholar, 1976. Mem. Am. Soc. Pub. Adminstrn., Nat. Acad. Polit. Scientists, Am. Soc. Tng. Devel., LWV (chairperson fin., tng. bur. 1973-78), Bus. and Profl. Women, League of Women Voters. Democrat. Lutheran. Home: 648 Palo Alto Dr Redlands CA 92373-7321 Office: Mgmt Assocs PO Box 8505 San Bernardino CA 92412-8505

GOOKIN, THOMAS ALLEN JAUDON, civil engineer; b. Tulsa, Aug. 5, 1951; s. William Scudder and Mildred (Hartman) G.; m. Leigh Anne Johnson, June 13, 1975 (div. Dec. 1977); m. Sandra Jean Andrews, July 23, 1983. BS with distinction, Ariz. State U., 1975. Registered profl. engr., Calif., Ariz., Nev., land surveyor Ariz., hydrologist. Civil engr., treas. W.S. Gookin & Assocs., Scottsdale, Ariz., 1968—. Chmn. adv. com. Ariz. State Bd. Tech. Registration Engring., 1984—. Recipient Spl. Recognition award Ariz. State Bd. Tech. Registration Engring., 1990. Mem. NSPE, Ariz. Soc. Profl. Engrs. (sec. Papago chpt. 1979-81, v.p. 1981-84, pres. 1984-85, named Young Engr. of Yr. 1979, Outstanding Engring. Project award 1988), Order Engr., Ariz. Congress on Surveying and Mapping, Am. Soc. Civil Engrs., Ariz. Water Works Assn., Tau Beta Pi, Delta Chi (Tempe chpt. treas. 1970-71, sec. 1970, v.p. 1971), Phi Kappa Delta (pres. 1971-73). Republican. Episcopalian. Home: 10760 E Becker Ln Scottsdale AZ 85259-3868 Office: W S Gookin & Assocs 4203 N Brown Ave Scottsdale AZ 85251-3946

GORAB, LAWRENCE NED, urologist; b. Jersey City, Nov. 18, 1938; s. Nadeem and Lillian (McLoof) G.; m. Jane Reilly, May 8, 1965; children: Lawrence N. Jr., Elizabeth J., Edward R., William W. BA, Rutgers U., 1960; MD, Georgetown U., 1964. Diplomate Am. Bd. Urology. Intern Hackensack (N.J.) Hosp., 1964-65; resident in gen. surgery Georgetown U. Hosp., Washington, 1965-66; resident in urology Thomas Jefferson U. Hosp., Phila., 1968-71; urologist Colorado Springs (Colo.) Med. Ctr., 1971—; staff physician Penrose Hosp., Colorado Springs, 1971—, St. Francis Hosp., Colorado Springs, 1971—, Meml. Hosp., Colorado Springs, 1971—. Capt. U.S. Army, 1966-68. Fellow ACS; mem. AMA, Am. Urol. Assn., Am. Fertility Soc., Am. Assn. Clin. Urologists, Colo. Med. Soc., El Paso County Med. Soc., Rocky Mountain Urol. Soc., South Ctrl. Sect. Am. Urol. Assn. Office: Colorado Springs Med Ctr 209 S Nevada Ave Colorado Springs CO 80903-1994

GORANS, GERALD ELMER, accountant; b. Benson, Minn., Sept. 17, 1922; s. George W. and Gladys (Schneider) G.; m. Mildred Louise Stallard, July 19, 1944; 1 child, Gretchen. BA, U. Wash., Seattle, 1947. CPA, Wash. With Touche, Ross & Co., CPAs and predecessor, Seattle, 1947-88; ptnr. Touche, Ross & Co. (name changed to Deliotte & Touche 1989), 1957-88, in charge Seattle office, 1962-82, mem. policy group, adminstrv. com., 1964-69, dir., 1974-83, sr. ptnr., 1979-88, chmn. mgmt. group, 1982-88, ret., 1988; bd. trustee Washington Inst., 1994—. V.p. budget and fin. Seattle Worlds Fair, 1962; chmn. budget and fin. com. Century 21 Ctr., Inc., 1963-64; mem. citizens adv. com. Seattle Lic. and Consumer Protection Com., 1965; head profl. div. United Way King County, Seattle, 1963-64, head advanced gifts div., 1965, exec. v.p., 1966, pres., 1967; trustee United Way Endowment Fund, 1984-90; adv. bd. Seattle Salvation Army, 1965-80, treas., 1974-80; fin. com. Bellevue Christian Sch., 1970-77; citizens adv. bd. pub. affairs Sta. KIRO-TV, 1970-71; treas., bd. dirs., exec. com. Scandinavia Today in Seattle, 1981-83; treas., bd. dirs. Seattle Citizens Coun. Against Crime, 1972-80, pres., 1976, 77; bd. dirs. U. Wash Alumni Fund, 1967-71, chmn., 1971; trustee U. Wash. Pres.'s Club, 1980-83; bd. dirs., chmn. devel. com. N.W. Hosp. Found., 1977-83; bd. dirs., treas. N.W. Hosp., 1981-86; chmn. fin. com., vice chmn. bd. Health Resources N.W., 1986-89, bd. dirs., 1986—, chmn. bd., 1989-90; chmn. fin. com. Com. for Balanced Regional Transp., 1981-91; co-chmn. United Cerebal Palsy Seattle Telethon, 1986; chmn. fin. com. fund raising Mus. Flight, 1983-87; mem. assoc. bd. Pacific Scis. Ctr., Seattle, 1986-95; active Japanese/Am. Conf. Mayors and C. of C. Pres. vice chmn. U.S. del., 1989-91; chmn. fin. com. Napa Valley Club Homeowners Assn.; bd. dirs., chmn. fin. com. Napa Valley Club Homeowners Assn., 1992—; bd. dirs., 1st pres. 600 Pk. Ter. Condominium Assn., 1993—. Lt. (j.g.) USNR, 1943-45. Recipient Honor award Sr. Svcs. of Seattle and King County, 1990. Mem. AICPA (chmn. nat. def. com. 1969-75, mem. spl. investigation com. 1984-87), Nat. Office Mgmt. Assn. (past pres.), Wash. Soc. CPAs (Outstanding Pub. Svc. award 1988), Seattle C. of C. (chmn. taxation com. 1970-71, bd. dirs. 1971-74, 76-79, 80-81, 85—, exec. com. 1980-83, v.p. 1981-84, 1st vice chmn. 1983-84, chmn. 1984-85, vice chmn. facilities fund dr. 1982-84), Nat. Def. Exec. Res., Nat. Club Assn. (bd. dirs. 1984-93, sec. and mem. exec. com. 1991-93), Assn. Wash. Bus. (bd. dirs. 1983-86). Home: 612 Bellevue Way SE Bellevue WA 98004-6633 also: 122 Valley Club Cir Napa CA 94558-2064 Office: Deloitte & Touche 700 5th Ave Ste 4500 Seattle WA 98104-5000

GORDER, CHERYL MARIE, book publisher; b. Brookings, S.D., Nov. 7, 1952; d. Shirley William and Arlene Opal (Barenklau) Seas; m. Dale Martin Gorder, Dec. 30, 1972 (June 1, 1992); 1 child, Sarah Lynne. BA, S.D. State U., 1974. Mgr. regional auctions Blue Bird Pub., Tempe, Ariz., 1974-85, pub., 1985—; cons. NIMTEC, Inc., Chandler, Ariz., 1991-92. Author: (book) Home Schools: An Alternative, 1985, Homeless: Without Addresses in America, 1988, Home Business Resource Guide, 1989, Green Earth Resource Guide, 1991, Multicultural Education Resource Guide, 1995; editor: Who's Who in Antiques, 1986, Real Dakota, 1988, Home Education Resource Guide, 1989, Spacedog's Best Friend, 1989, Dr. Christman's Learn to Read Book, 1990, They Reached for the Stars, 1990, The Sixth Sense: Practical Tips for Everyday Safety, 1990, Under Two Heavens, 1991, Survival Guide to Step-Parenting, 1992. Recipient Benjamin Franklin award Pub.'s Mktg. Assn., 1989. Mem. Pub. Mktg. Assn., Am. Bus. Women's Assn., Ariz. Book Pub. Assn. Office: Blue Bird Pub 1739 E Broadway Rd Ste 306 Tempe AZ 85282-1628

GORDLY, AVEL LOUISE, state legislator, community activist; b. Portland, Oreg., Feb. 13, 1947; d. Fay Lee and Beatrice Bernice (Coleman) G.; 1 child, Tyrone Wayne Waters. BS in Adminstrn. of Justice, Portland State U., 1974. Phone co. clk. Pacific West Bell, Portland, 1966-70, mgmt. trainee, 1970-74; work release counselor Oreg. Corrections Divsn., Portland, 1974-78, parole and probation officer, 1974-78; dir. youth svcs. Urban League of Portland, 1979-83; dir. So. Africa program Am. Friends Svc. Com., Portland, 1983-89, assoc. exec. sec., dir. Pacific N.W. region, 1987-90; freelance writer Portland Observer, Portland, 1988-90; program dir. Portland House of Umoja, 1991; mem. Oreg. Ho. of Reps., Portland, 1991—, mem. joint ways and means com., adv. mem. appropriations com., rules and reorgn. com., low income housing com., energy policy rev. com., others; mem. joint ways and means com. on edn., mem. adv. bd. appropriations, mem. gov. drug and violent crime policy bd., mem. Oreg. liquor control commn. task force, mem. sexual harrassment task force, mem. Hanford waste bd., mem. gov. commn. for women; mem. Gov's. Commn. for Women, Gov.'s Drug and Violent Crime Policy Bd.; originator, producer, host Black Women's Forum, 1983-88; co-producer, rotating host N.E. Spectrum, 1983-88. Mem. corrections adv. com. Multnomah Cmty.; mem. adv. com. Oregonians Against Gun Violence; mem. Black Leadership Conf.; treas., bd. dirs. Black United Fund; co-founder, facilitator Unity Breakfast Com.; co-founder Sisterhood Luncheon; past project adv. bd. dirs. Nat. Orgn. Victims Assistance; past citizen chmn. Portland Police Bur.; past mem. coordinating com. Portland Future Focus Policy Com.; past coord. Cmty. Rescue Plan; past vice chmn. internat. affairs Black United Front; past sec. Urban League Portland, past vice chmn. and exec. com.; past adv. com. Black Ednl. Ctr.; past vice chmn. Desegregation Monitoring; also past adv. com., past chmn. curriculum com., other past orgn. coms. Recipient Outstanding Community Svc. award NAACP, 1986, Outstanding Women in Govt. award YWCA, 1991, Girl Scout-Community Svc. award, 1991, N.W. Conf. of Black Studies-Outstanding Progressive Leadership in the African-Am. Community award, 1986, Community Svc. award Delta Sigma Theta, 1981, Joint Action in Community Svc.-Vol. and Community Svc. award, 1981, Quality of Life Photography award Pacific Power & Light Co., 1986; Am. Leadership Forum Sr. fellow, 1988. Mem. NAACP.

GORDON, ALAN LESLIE, internist; b. Chgo., June 12, 1931; s. Lee Stanley and Doree (Leslie) G.; m. Babs Schneider, Aug. 8, 1954; children: Leslie, Todd, Jill, Peter. BS, U. Ill., 1952; MB, U. Ill., Chgo., 1953, MS in Biochemistry, 1955, MD, 1955. Diplomate Am. Bd. Internal Medicine (bd. govs. 1987-93). Intern Cook County Hosp., Chgo., 1955-56; fellow in internal medicine Mayo Clinic, Rochester, Minn., 1958-61; asst. to staff Mayo Clinic, Rochester, 1967-68; founding dir. residency program in internal medicine Good Samaritan Hosp., Phoenix, 1967-68; founding chmn. Ariz. Coun. for Grad. Med. Edn., Phoenix, 1989-93; pvt. practice specializing in internal medicine Phoenix, 1962—; clin. prof. of medicine U. of Ariz. Contbr. numerous articles to profl. jours. Bd. dirs. Valley Big Brothers, Phoenix, 1965-66; pres. Ariz Heart Assn., Phoenix, 1971-72; chmn. Physicians' sect. United Way, Phoenix, 1977; v.p. bd. trustees St. Joseph Hosp., 1990—; adv. bd. fellowship, selection com. scholarship, comn. on med. manpower Flinn Found., Phoenix, 1983-92. Lt. cmmdr. USN, 1956-58. Recipient Meritorious Rsch. award Borden Found., 1955, A. Ashley Rousuck award Mayo Clinic, 1962, Outstanding Tchr. award St. Joseph's Hosp., 1969, 84, Dirs. award, 1992, Alumni award U. Ariz., 1994. Master ACP (bd. govs., exec. com. 1980-84, Laureate award 1986); mem. Ariz. Soc. Internal Medicine (pres. 1974-76), Maricopa County Med. Assn. (pres. 1975-81), Mayo Clinic Alumni Assn. (bd. dirs. 1975-81, residency rev. com. for internal medicine 1984-90), Alpha Omega Alpha. Home: 5823 N 37th Pl Paradise Vly AZ 85253-5001 Office: 2200 N 3rd St Phoenix AZ 85004-1401

GORDON, BEATRICE SCHNEIDER, English literature educator; b. Chgo., July 10, 1934; d. Edward S. and Ada (Walder) Schneider; m. Alan L. Gordon, Aug. 8, 1954; children: Leslie, Todd, Jill, Peter. Student, Vassar Coll., 1952-53, Northwestern U., 1953-54; BA, Ariz. State U., 1987, MA, 1989. Cert. in med. tech. Med. technologist Louis A. Weiss Hosp., Chgo., 1955-56, Med. Specialists, Ltd., Phoenix, 1971-77; art sales cons. Gallery 10, Scottsdale, Ariz., 1977-81; teaching asst. dept. English Ariz. State U., Tempe, 1988-89; instr. Am. lit. No. Ariz. U., Phoenix, 1990; instr. Honors Coll. Ariz. State U., Tempe, 1992—, faculty assoc. dept. English, 1990—; mem. screening com., scholarships Flinn Found., Phoenix, 1991—. Author articles and book revs.; presenter in field. Chpt. chmn. Am. Heart Assn., Phoenix, 1973; pres. guild and com. chair Heard Mus., Phoenix, 1960s-87; pres.

women's bd. Ariz. Kidney Found., Phoenix, 1980s. Recipient Silver medallion svc. award Am. Heart Assn., 1973, Bronze medallion 1972, Disting. Pub. Svc. award Med. Soc. Maricopa County, 1983, Meritorious award United Way Campaign, Phoenix, 1983. Mem. MLA, Nat. conf. Tchrs. English, Am. Soc. Clin. Pathologists, Golden Key, Sigma Tau Delta. Republican. Jewish. Home: Paradise Valley AZ Office: Ariz State U Dept English DEN 0302 Tempe AZ 85287

GORDON, BRADLEY B., pharmaceutical research executive; b. 1954. MBA, U. So. Calif., 1981. Gen. ptnr. EMC Venture Ptnrs., San Diego, 1981-86; pres. Access Ptnrs., San Diego, 1986-87; ptnr. Viagene, Inc., San Diego, 1987—. Office: Viagene Inc 11055 Roselle St San Diego CA 92121-1204*

GORDON, CLAUDE EUGENE, musician; b. Helena, Mont., Apr. 5, 1916; s. James Austin and Nellie G. (Elge) G.; m. Genevieve Alice Pentecost, Apr. 19, 1936 (dec. 1988); children: Gary Anthony, Steven Robert; m. Patricia J. Kasarda, Sept. 22, 1990. D of Music and Letters (hon.), La Sierra U., 1992. Trumpeter NBC, CBS, Motion Pictures, L.A., 1937-69; 1st trumpet big bands, stage shows, hotels, L.A., 1937-44, CBS, Hollywood, 1944-56; orch. leader L.A. and nationwide, 1950-69; condr. TV mus., stage shows for stars, L.A., Reno and Las Vegas, Nev., 1960-69; lectr., instr. clinics Mich. U., No. Ill. U., Fla. State U., North Tex. State U., others, 1970-87; instr. Glaude Gordon Internat. Brass Workshop, La Sierra U., Riverside, Calif.; recorded for all major labels. Author: Brass Playing Is No Harder Than Deep Breathing, The Physical Approach to Elementary Brass Playing, Systematic Approach to Daily Practice, Daily Trumpet Routines, Tongue Level Exercises, 30 Velocity Studies; annotator: Arban Complete Method, 1982; instrument designer: CG Benge trumpet, 1960, Claude Gordon Selmer trumpet, 1977, (mouthpiece) CG Personal for trumpet, coronet and fluglehorn, 1974.

GORDON, EMMAJEAN ELIZABETH, farmer, investor, consultant; b. Fresno, Calif., Dec. 10, 1920; d. John Peter and Emilie (Kromberg) Wagenleitner; div. 1976; children: Marilyn Gordon Johnson, Glenda Rouzaud Farrer. Bus. cert., 4 C's Bus. Sch., 1941; provision teaching credential, Fresno State U., 1942; BA, Chico State U., 1955, MA, 1963. Lic. tchr., supervision, adminstr. edn., life credentials. Tchr. Fresno (Calif.) County Schs., 1945-47, Shasta County Schs., Redding, Calif., 1947-49, Enterprise Elem. Sch., Redding, 1949-58; tchr. team sports and crafts Redding Recreation Dept., 1945-47, 49-58; tchr. Redding Elem. Sch., Bonneyview, 1958-59; tchr., counseler Enterprise High Sch., Redding, 1959-63, counselor, 1963-83; beauty cons. Mary Kay Cosmetics, Fresno, 1988—; farmer Fresno, 1978—; investor E.J. Gordon Enterprises, Fresno, 1976—; mem. salary com. Shasta-Union High Dist., Redding, 1973-75. Ch. choir leader Redding Ch., 1948-52; bd. mem., chmn. Redding Jr. Acad., 1973-76; chmn. county sr. adv. Shasta Coll., Redding, 1983-84, mem. med. adv. bd., 1979-82; mem. adv. bd. Shasta County Woman's Refuge, Redding, 1980-83. Named Gold Star Foster Parent, Shasta County Foster Parent Assn., 1968, 86; recipient Golden Nike award Bus. and Profl. Women, Reading, 1983. Mem. NEA (life), AAUW (life), NAFE, Women in Agr. and Raisen Wives, Shasta Retired Tchrs. Assn. (life), Fresno Bus. and Profl. Women (scholarship chmn. 1989—, sec. 1990), Calif. Fedn. Fig Garden Women's Club, Profl. Women's Bowling Club, Palm Lakes Women's Golf Assn., Edison Social Club Women's Aux., Woodard Esec. Estates Condo Assn. (beautification chmn. 1989-91). Republican.

GORDON, GLORIA KATHLEEN, business association executive, magazine editor; b. Kerrville, Tex., Feb. 13, 1938; d. Candler Ross and Gertrude (Beitel) Gordon; m. Dale H. Fietz, Feb. 23, 1957 (div. 1983); children: Martha Fietz O'Brien, Diane Fietz, Kathleen Fietz. BA in English, U. Tex., 1958. Prod., quality control assoc. Cahners Pub. Co., Denver, 1961-68; editorial asst. Ski Racing mag., Denver, 1968-69; prod. mgr. Meat Industry mag., Mill Valley, Calif., 1965-71; prod. dir. Guidance Industries, Mill Valley, Calif., 1971-72; cons. pub. rels. Gloria Graphics, Corte Madera, Calif., 1978-80; mng. editor Pacific Food Svc. News, Sausalito, Calif., 1980-83; v.p. communications Internat. Assn. Bus. Communicators, San Francisco, 1983—; bd. dirs. Marin Music Conservatory, Tiburon, Calif. Editor Communication World mag.; contbr. articles to profl. jours. Recipient Gold Key award Pub. Rels. News, 1991. Mem. Am. Soc. Assn. Execs., Pub. Rels. Soc. Am. Office: Internat Assn Bus Communicators 1 Hallidie Plz Ste 600 San Francisco CA 94102-2818

GORDON, HELEN HEIGHTSMAN, English language educator, writer; b. Salt Lake City, Sept. 7, 1932; d. Fred C. and Florence Isabel Heightsman; m. Norman C. Winn, Aug. 10, 1950 (div. Sept. 1972); children: Bruce Vernon Winn, Brent Terry Winn, Holly Winn Willner; m. Clifton Beverly Gordon, Feb. 17, 1974. Student, U. Utah, 1959-62; BA in English and Edn., Calif. State U., Sacramento, 1964, MA in English, 1967; EdD, Nova U., 1979. Cert. tchr., Calif.; lic. counselor, Calif. Stenographer, payroll clk. Associated Food Stores, Inc., Salt Lake City, 1951-59; part-time instr. in remedial English U. Utah, Salt Lake City, 1960-61; tchr. high sch. Rio Americano High Sch., Sacramento, 1965-66; assoc. prof., counselor Porterville (Calif.) Coll., 1967-74; prof., counselor Bakersfield (Calif.) Coll., 1974—; chair lang. arts divsn. Porterville Coll., 1971-74; coord. women's studies Bakersfield Coll., 1977-78, adminstrv. intern, 1982-83; dir. region V, English Coun. of Calif. Two Yr. Colls., 1990-92; articulation coord. Bakersfield Coll., 1992-93. Author: (textbook) From Copying to Creating, 2d edit., 1983, Developing College Writing, 1989, Wordforms, Book I & II, 2d edit., 1990, Interplay: Sentence Skills in Context, 1991, Voice of the Vanquished: The Story of the Slave Marina and Hernan Cortes, 1995. Founder, 1st pres. Writers of Kern, Bakersfield, 1993; guest mem. editl. bd. Bakersfield Californian Newspaper, 1988; past pres. Unitarian Fellowship of Kern County, Bakersfield, 1976-78. Calif. Fund for Instruction grantee, 1978; U. Utah scholar, 1959-62. Mem. NEA, Am. Assn. Women in Cmty. and Jr. Colls. (founder Bakersfield chpt., pres., program chair 1988-91), Nat. Coun. Tchrs. of English, Faculty Assn. Calif. Cmty. Coll., Textbook Authors Assn. (charter), LWV (pres. Bakersfield chpt. 1981-83, 89-90), Calif. Writers Club. Democrat. Home: 6400 Westlake Dr Bakersfield CA 93308-6519 Office: Bakersfield Coll 1801 Panorama Dr Bakersfield CA 93305-1219

GORDON, HELEN WILCOX, church librarian; b. Grand Forks, N.D., Feb. 14, 1919; m. Earl W. Gordon, 1948; children: Paul, Carol. BA, Scripps Coll., Claremont, Calif., 1940; Diploma in Nursing, Johns Hopkins Sch. Nursing, 1943. RN, Calif. Pub. health nurse Health Dept., Newton County, Mo., 1952-54; sch. nurse Pasadena (Calif.) Sch. Dist., 1966-68; libr. First United Meth. Ch., Pasadena, 1991—. 1st lt. Nurse Corps, U.S. Army, 1945-47. Mem. The Ch. and Synagogue Librs. Assn. (pres. Los Angeles County chpt. 1994). Methodist. Office: First United Methodist Ch 500 E Colorado Blvd Pasadena CA 91101-2027

GORDON, HUGH SANGSTER, JR., fire services administrator; b. Winnipeg, Manitoba, Can., July 6, 1949; s. Hugh Sangster Sr. and Margaret Forbes (Johnston) G. BS, U. N.D., 1973, MS, 1975. Cert. arena and pool mgr., fireman. Gen. mgr. recreation commn. City of Flin Flon, Can., 1978-81; supr. field house City of Saskatoon, Can., 1982-84, arena mgr., 1984-85; mgr. facility ops. dept. park and recreation City of Regina, Can., 1985-87, acting. dir. parks and recreation dept., 1986-87, dir. fire svcs., 1987—. Recipient Cert. of Devoted Civil Svc., City of Saskatoon, 1985. Mem. Can. Assn. Fire Chiefs, Saskatchewan Assn. Fire Chiefs (v.p. 1987—). Mem. United Ch. Can. Office: Regina Fire Dept, Box 1790, Regina, SK Canada S4P 3C8*

GORDON, JUDITH, communications consultant, writer; b. Long Beach, Calif.; d. Irwin Ernest and Susan (Perlman) G.; m. Lawrence Banka, May 1, 1977. BA, Oakland U., 1966; MS in Libr. Sci., Wayne State U., 1973. Researcher Detroit Inst. of Arts, 1968-69; libr. Detroit Pub. Libr., 1971-74; caseworker Wayne County Dept. Social Svcs., Detroit, 1974-77; advt. copywriter Hudson's Dept. Store, Detroit, 1979; mgr. The Poster Gallery, Detroit, 1980-81; mktg., corp. communications specialist Bank of Am., San Francisco, 1983-84; mgr., consumer pubs. Bank of Am., 1984-86; prin. Active Voice, San Francisco, 1986—. Contbr. edit. The Artist's Mag., 1988-93; contbr. to book Flowers: Gary Bukovnik, Watercolors and Monotypes, Abrams, 1990. Vol. From the Heart, San Francisco, 1992, Bay Area Book Festival, San Francisco, 1990, 91, Aid & Comfort, San Francisco, 1987, Save Orch. Hall, Detroit, 1977-81, NOW sponsored abortion clinic project. Recipient Nat. award Merit, Soc. Consumer Affairs Profls. in Bus., 1986, Bay Area Best award, Internat. Assn. Bus. Communicators, 1986, Internat. Galaxy award, 1992. Mem. Internat. Assn. Bus. Communicators, Nat. Writers Union, Freelance Editorial Assn., AAUW, Graphic Arts Coun., Women's Nat. Book Assn., Media Alliance, Friends of City Arts and Lectrs., ZYZZYVA (bd. dirs.). Office: 899 Green St San Francisco CA 94133-3756

GORDON, KENNETH JAY, aerospace engineer; b. Boston, Jan. 31, 1968; s. Michael Jeffrey Gordon and Judith Ann (Davis) Lapp. BS in Engring., U. Mich., 1989; MS in Aerospace Engring., U. So. Calif., L.A., 1991. Sr. mem. tech. staff The Aerospace Corp., El Segundo, Calif., 1989—; guest lectr. Calif. Tech., USAF Acad., U. So. Calif., U. Mich., others, 1991-94. Spkr., student advisor Youth Motivation Task Force, L.A., 1990-93; student mentor Rebuild L.A., Inc., 1993. Mem. AIAA (vice chair membership 1992-93, mem. astrodynamics stds. com. 1991-92, disting. svc. award 1993), Mich. Soc. Profl. Engrs. (v.p. student chpt. 1987-89, Engring. Student of Yr. 1989), Vulcans Sr. Honor Soc., Tau Beta Pi, Sigma Gamma Tau. Office: The Aerospace Corp PO Box 92957 M4/948 Los Angeles CA 90009-2957

GORDON, LEONARD, sociology educator; b. Detroit, Dec. 6, 1935; s. Abraham and Sarah (Rosen) G.; m. Rena Joyce Feigelman, Dec. 25, 1955; children: Susan Melinda, Matthew Seth, Melissa Gail. B.A., Wayne State U., 1957; M.A., U. Mich., 1958; Ph.D., Wayne State U., 1966. Instr. Wayne State U., Detroit, 1960-62; research dir. Jewish Community Council, Detroit, 1962-64; dir. Mich. area Am. Jewish Com., N.Y.C., 1964-67; asst. prof. Ariz. State U., Tempe, 1967-70, assoc. prof., 1970-77, prof., 1977—, chmn. dept. sociology, 1981-90, assoc. dean for acad. programs Coll. Liberal Arts and Scis., 1990—; cons. OEO, Maricopa County, Ariz., 1968. Author: A City in Racial Crisis, 1978, (with A. Mayer) Urban Life and the Struggle To Be Human, 1979, (with R. Hardert, M. Laner and M. Reader) Confronting Social Problems, 1984, (with J. Hall and R. Melnick) Harmonizing Arizona's Ethnic and Cultural Diversity, 1992. Sec. Conf. on Religion and Race, Detroit, 1962-67; mem. exec. bd. dirs. Am. Jewish Com., Phoenix chpt., 1969-70. Grantee NSF, 1962, Rockefeller found., 1970, 84. Fellow Am. Sociol. Assn.; mem. Pacific Sociol. Assn. (v.p. 1978-79, pres. 1980-81), AAUP, Soc. Study Social Problems (chair C. Wright Mills award com. 1988, treas. 1989—), Ariz. State U. Alumni Assn. (faculty dir. 1981-82). Democrat. Jewish. Home: 13660 E Columbine Dr Scottsdale AZ 85259 Office: Ariz State U Coll Liberal Arts and Scis Office for Acad Programs Tempe AZ 85287

GORDON, MARC STEWART, pharmacist, scientist; b. Cleve., June 13, 1958; s. Eugene and Eileen (Israel) G.; m. Diane Southwell, Aug. 11, 1985; children: Evan, Emma. BS in Pharmacy, U. Mich., 1982. Registered pharmacist, Calif. Staff rschr. II, mgr. Syntex Rsch., Palo Alto, Calif., 1982-94; sr. scientist Inhale Therapeutic Systems, Palo Alto, Calif., 1995—. Contbr. numerous articles to profl. jours. Mem. Am. Assn. Pharm. Scientists, Am. Pharm. Assn., Santa Clara County Pharmcists Assn., No. Calif. Pharm. Discussion Group, Rho Chi. Home: 1474 Samedra St Sunnyvale CA 94087-4054 Office: Inhale Therapeutic Systems 1001 E Meadow Circle Palo Alto CA 94303

GORDON, MARVIN JAY, physician; b. Balt., Jan. 11, 1946; s. Joseph Nathan and Sarah Henrietta (Seidel) G.; m. Linda Susan Merican, Dec. 23, 1968 (div. Oct. 1984); m. Myra Eleanor Sklar, Jan. 27, 1985; children: David, Joseph, Allison, Lisa. BS, U. Md., College Park, 1965; MD, U. Md., Balt., 1969. Diplomate Am. Bd. Internal Medicine, Am. Bd. Gastroenterology, Am. Bd. Quality Assurance and Utilization. Resident in internal medicine U. Md., Balt., 1969-72, Gastroenterology fellowship, 1972-74; pvt. practice Laguna Beach, Calif., 1976—. Contbr. articles to profl. jours. Pres. Temple Beth El, Laguna Niguel, Calif., 1984-85. Major USAF, 1974-76. Fellow Am. Coll. Gastroenterology; mem. Am. Gastroenterol. Assn. Home and Office: 31852 S Coast Hwy Ste 300 Laguna Beach CA 92677-3288

GORDON, MILTON ANDREW, academic administrator; b. Chgo., May 25, 1935; s. Herrmann Andrew Gordon and Ossie Bell; m. Margaret Faulwell, July 18, 1987; children: Patrick Francis, Vincent Michael; 1 stepchild, Michael Faulwell. BS, Xavier U. La., New Orleans, 1957; MA, U. Detroit, 1960; PhD, Ill. Inst. Tech., 1968; postgrad., Harvard U., 1984. Teaching asst. U. Detroit, 1958-59; mathematician Lab. Applied Scis. U. Chgo., 1959-62; part-time tchr. Chgo. Pub. Sch. System, 1962-66; assoc. prof. math. Loyola U., Chgo., 1966-67; dir. Afro-Am. Studies Program Loyla U., Chgo., 1971-77; dean Coll. Arts and Scis., prof. math. Chgo. State U., 1978-86; v.p. acad. affairs, prof. math. Sonoma State U., Rohnert Park, Calif., 1986-90; pres., prof. math. Calif. State U., Fullerton, 1990—; bd. dirs. Associated We. Univs., Inc.; hon. admissions counselor United States Naval Acad., 1979; mem. exec. coun. Calif. State U., 1990; rep. for Calif. univs.Am. Assn. State Colls. and Univs., 1992; commn. on leadership devel. Am. Coun. on Edn., 1992; nat. task force on gender equality Nat. Collegiate Athletic Assn., 1992-94, pres.'s commn., 1994—; commr. joint commn. on accoutability reporting project Am. Assn. of State Colls. and Univs./Nat. Assn. of State Univs. and Land Grant Colls., 1994—. Contbr. articles to profl. jours. Chmn. Archdiocese of Chgo. Sch. Bd., 1978-79; bd. govs. Orange County Community Found., Costa Mesa, Calif., 1990—, NCCJ, 1991—; bd. dirs. United Way of Orange County, Irvine, Calif., 1991, Pacific Symphony Orch., Santa Ana, 1993—; bd. adv. St. Jude Med. Ctr., Fullerton, Calif., 1992, Partnership 2010, Orange County, 1994. Recipient cert. of appreciation Community Ch. Santa Rosa, Calif., 1988, Tree of Life award Jewish Nat. Fund, 1994; named Adminstr. of Yr., Chgo. State U., 1979. Mem. Am.conf. Acad. Deans (chmn. bd. dirs. 1983-85), Am. Assn. Univ. Adminstrs. (bd. dirs. 1983-86), Calif. Coalition of Math., Sigma Xi, Phi Beta Delta. Roman Catholic. Office: Calif State Univ Office of President PO Box 34080 Fullerton CA 92634-9480

GORDON, PETER LOWELL, immigration administrator; b. Powell, Wyo., Feb. 16, 1953; s. John Eric Gordon and Carol Mae (Peterson) Olson; m. Shigeko Masunaga, Apr. 16, 1983 (div. Feb. 24, 1992); m. Mitsuko Natsume, Sept. 18, 1993. BA in Polit. Sci., Criminal Justice, Calif. State U., L.A., 1975. Asst. cook Country Kitchen, LaCrosse, Wis., 1970-71; asst. mgr. Ky. Fried Chicken, Tujunga, Calif., 1975-76, Parasol Restaurant, Alhambra, Calif., 1976-77; border patrol agt. Immigration and Naturalization Svc., Dept. Justice, San Diego, 1977-80; immigration insp. Immigration and Naturalization Svc., Dept. Justice, Anchorage, 1980-83; immigration examiner Immigration and Naturalization Svc., Dept. Justice, L.A., 1983-87; legalization mgr. Immigration and Naturalization Svc., Dept. Justice, Laguna Niguel, Calif., 1987-90, immigration mgr., 1990—. Co-developer (nat. data base) Legalization Adjustment Processing System, 1987 (Commr.'s award 1987); co-designer Western Svc. Ctr., 1989; co-author Western Svc. Ctr. Guidelines, 1989. Spkr. Am. Immigration Lawyers Assn., So. and Northern Calif. chpts.; contbr. Dedicatioin and Everlasting Love to Animals. Mem. Nat. Space Soc., Immigration Officer Assns., Fedn. for Am. Immigration Reform. Republican. Lutheran.

GORDON, ROBERT EUGENE, lawyer; b. L.A., Sept. 20, 1932; s. Harry Maurice and Minnie (Shafer); 1 child, Victor Marten. BA, UCLA, 1954; LLB, U. Calif., Berkeley, 1959, JD, 1960; cert., U. Hamburg, Fed. Republic Germany, 1960. Bar: Calif. 1960. Assoc. Lillick, Geary, McHose, Roethke & Myers, Los Angeles, 1960-64, Schoichet & Rifkind, Beverly Hills, Calif., 1964-67; ptnr. Baerwitz & Gordon, Beverly Hills, 1967-69, Ball, Hunt, Hart, Brown & Baerwitz, Beverly Hills, 1970-71; of counsel Jacobs, Sills & Coblentz, San Francisco, 1972-78; ptnr. Gordon & Hodge, San Francisco, 1978-81; sole practice San Francisco, 1981-84, Sausalito, Calif., 1985-89; pvt. practice Corte Madera, Calif., 1989—; adj. prof. entertainment law Hastings Coll. of Law, San Francisco, 1990-91, U. Calif., Berkeley, 1992. Served to 1st lt. U.S. Army, 1954-56. Mem. ABA (forum com. on entertainment and sports law, exec. com. music sect.), San Francisco Bar Assn., Los Angeles Copyright Soc. (bd. trustees 1970-71), Copyright Soc. of the USA. Home: 35 Elaine Ave Mill Valley CA 94941-1014 Office: 5725 Paradise Dr Ste 840 Corte Madera CA 94925-1222

GORDON, ROBERT WILLIAM, editor; b. N.Y.C., Apr. 29, 1946; s. David William and Elizabeth (Marshal) G. BA in Journalism, CCNY, 1968; MA in English, NYU, 1970. Editor Showcase mag., N.Y.C., 1970-72; freelance reader Players Press Inc., N.Y.C., 1965-72, assoc. editor, 1972-74, editor, 1974-76, sr. editor, 1976-78, v.p. editls., assoc. publ., 1978—; editl./script cons. Empire Entertainment, Hollywood, Calif., 1979-84; editl. cons. New World Studios, Hollywood, 1985-87; bd. dirs. Players U.S.A., Studio City, Calif. Author (play) Once Around the Park, 1985 (Best New Play 1987), (books) Writing for Stage, 1990, Classic Theatre, 1990, Working in the Field, 1990. Bd. dirs. Western Ednl. Theatre, Studio City, 1979—. Office: Players Press Inc PO Box 1132 Studio City CA 91614-0132

GORDON, ROGER L., savings and loan association executive. Formerly sr. exec. v.p., COO San Francisco Fed. Savs. & Loan Assn., pres., CEO, 1990—. Office: San Francisco Fed Savs & Loan 88 Kearny St San Francisco CA 94108-5530

GORDON, RUBY DANIELS, retired nursing educator, counselor; b. Camden, Ark., Dec. 28, 1927; d. Fred Jewell and Etta Matilda (Watson) Daniels; m. DeVore Basil Gordon, Sept. 1, 1946 (div. 1950); children: Sally Ann Gordon, Lynne Gordon. Diploma, St. Monica's Hosp., Phoenix, 1949; BS, Ariz. State U., 1959, MA, 1962, PhD, 1975. Instr. basic scis. St. Joseph Hosp. Sch. Nursing, Phoenix, 1962-67; chairperson dept. nursing Glendale (Ariz.) C.C., 1967-80; prof. Phoenix Coll., 1980-92; counselor Glendale C.C., 1993—. Mem. ANA, NEA, ACA, Ariz. Nurses Assn., Nat. League for Nursing, Ariz. League for Nursing, Am. Soc. Aging, Am. Assn. for the History of Nursing, Nat. Coun. on the Aging, Assn. for Adult Devel. and Aging, Nat. Career Devel. Assn.

GORDON, STEVEN ERIC, animator, designer; b. Hollywood, Calif., Mar. 23, 1960; s. Wilfred Isadore and Tamara (Bernstein) G.; m. Judith Katherine Ball, June 27, 1981; children: Scott Conrad, Eric Alexander. Grad. high sch., Granada Hills, Calif. Asst. animator Bakshi Prodns., Hollywood, 1977-79, animator, 1979-80; animation dir. Bakshi Prodns., Sun Valley, Calif., 1981-82; layout artist Filmation Studios, Hollywood, 1980-81; animator Disney Pictures, Burbank, Calif., 1982-87; dir. animation Rich Animation, Burbank, Calif., 1987—; owner The Animator's Gallery, 1994—; story bd. artist Disney TV, Burbank, 1984-91, DIC Enterprises, Burbank, 1986-88; comml. animator Playhouse Pictures, Hollywood, 1986-88, Baer Animation Co., Inc., Hollywood, 1989-90, Cool Prodn., Burbank, 1990-92, Film Roman, North Hollywood, 1991. Democrat. Home: 32449 Scandia Dr Running Springs CA 92382 Address: PO Box 2829 Running Springs CA 92382-2829

GORDON, WALTER, architect; b. Buffalo, Sept. 8, 1907; s. Walter William and Florence (Green) G.; m. Margaret Murray, July 4, 1936. B.S., Princeton U., 1930, M.F.A. in Architecture, 1932; spl. student, Yale U., 1936-37, U. Paris, France, 1934. Curator San Francisco Mus. Art, 1937-39; asst. dir. Portland (Oreg.) Art Mus., 1939-41; practicing architect Portland, 1946-58; dean Sch. Architecture, U. Oreg., 1958-62; faculty mem. Reed Coll., 1962-65; sr. partner Gordon & Hinchliff, architects, 1962-72; prin. Walter Gordon, architect, 1972—; design cons. Portland Devel. Commn., 1962-76, Eugene Renewal Agy., 1972-80, Salem (Oreg.) Renewal Agy., 1973-82; mem. Gov.'s Adv. Com. for Preservation Yaquina Head, 1977-80, Oreg. Bd. Architect Examiners, 1956-58, Portland Art Commn., 1955-57, Oreg. Capitol Planning Commn., 1959-68. Prin. works include Southwest Hills Libr., Portland, Alpha Phi sorority house, Corvallis, Oreg. libr., dormitories, faculty residence Marylhurst Coll., Portland, Pub. Libr., Toledo, Oreg., visitor's lodge, infirmary Trappist Abbey, Lafayette, Oreg., parish hall, chapel Sacred Heart Ch., Newport, Oreg., numerous residences, Pacific N.W. Trustee Portland Art Mus., 1947-51. Fellow A.I.A. (mem. nat. edn. com. 1960-62); mem. Phi Beta Kappa. Clubs: City of Portland (v.p. 1971-72), University. Home and Office: 105 NW Wade Way Newport OR 97365-1426

GORDON, WILL, information system specialist; b. 1943. BA, BS, U. Miami, 1965. Field supr. Traveler's Ins., 1969-75; mgr. Cubic Corp., San Diego, 1975-81; pres. Intertech Corp.; program mgr. Ford Aerospace & Comm., Phila., 1986-88; pres. Applied Data Tech, Inc., San Diego, 1988—. With U.S. Army, 1966-69. Office: Applied Data Tech Inc 10151 Barnes Canyon Rd San Diego CA 92121*

GORE, THOMAS GAVIN, insurance and securities broker; b. Pittsburg, Kans., Feb. 8, 1939; s. Harold Gavin and Mary Adele (Brinn) G.; m. Lorraine Elizabeth Riley, Sept. 3, 1960; children: Robert, Gregory. BA, Kans. U., 1962. CLU; ChFC. Agt. Transamerica Life Ins. Co., L.A., 1962-67; br. mgr. Transamerica Life Ins. Co., Newport Beach, Calif., 1968-75; pres. Thomas Gore & Assocs., Inc., Newport Beach, Calif., 1976—. Mem. Million Dollar Round Table, Nat. Assn. Life Underwriters, Assn. Advanced Life Underwriters, Santa Ana Country Club (bd. dirs. 1989—). Republican. Office: Thomas Gore & Assocs Inc 535 Anton Blvd Costa Mesa CA 92626-1947

GOREN, BRUCE NEAL, television engineer, computer graphics company executive; b. N.Y.C., Jan. 6, 1956; s. Seymour and Elaine (Popkin) G. BA, CUNY, Queens, 1978; MA, Bowling Green State U., 1979. Lic. gen. class FCC radiotelephone operator. Paste-up artist Ad Design, Inc., College Point, N.Y., 1977-78; grad. teaching asst. Bowling Green (Ohio) State U., 1979; prodn. asst. Sta. KGAN-TV (formerly Sta. WMT-TV), Cedar Rapids, Iowa, 1980; broadcast engr. Sta. WQAD-TV, Moline, Ill., 1980-81; master control engr. Cable News Network, Atlanta, 1981-82; engr. Sta. WSB-TV, Atlanta, 1982-84; on-air supr. The Post Group, Hollywood, Calif., 1984; TV engr. Sta. KLCS-TV, Los Angeles, 1984-95, CSI Videosystems, L.A., 1995—; owner, artist Cheap Computer Graphics, Hollywood, 1986—; contbg. editor, columnist TV Tech. Mag., Austin, Tex., 1991—. Contbr. numerous articles to profl. jours. and mag. Regents scholar N.Y., 1973, Kodak Visual scholar U. Iowa, 1979. Mem. Spl. Interest Group on Computer Graphics, Assn. for Computing Machinery, Soc. Motion Picture and TV Engrs., Mensa. Home: 28938 Morningside Dr Castaic CA 91384-2414

GORENBERG, ALAN EUGENE, physician; b. Japan, Apr. 30, 1959; s. Daniel and Louise Gorenberg; m. Beverly J. Juan, June 24, 1984. BS in Biology, U. Calif., Irvine, 1981; MD, Loma Linda U., 1986. Diplomate Am. Bd. Internal Medicine, Am. Bd. Allergy and Immunology. Pvt. practice San Bernardino, Calif., 1991—, Victorville, Calif., 1991—. Office: 2130 N Arrowhead Ave Ste 101 San Bernardino CA 92405-4023

GORHAM-SMITH, R(OSELLA) DORITA, direct mail and marketing company executive; b. Washington, Mar. 2, 1948; d. Herman Homer and Julia Rosella (Corker) Gorham; children: Shannon W. Smith, S. Joline Smith. AA, St. Louis Inst., Clayton, Mo., 1966; student, No. Va. Community Coll., Saddleback Valley Community; advanced cert., Alexandria (Va.) Sch. Music, 1968. Tchr. Alexandria Sch. Music, 1963-64, asst. dir., 1966-76; mgr. Deese Cosmetics, Beltsville, Md., 1976-78; R&D rep. Nat. Assn. Broadcasters, Washington, 1978-80; pres., owner U.S. Mail & Mktg. Corp., Paramount, Calif., 1990—. Coord. Inner City Music Appreciation, Alexandria, 1968-70; vol. Alexandria/Laguna Hills Pub. Schs., Va., Calif., 1975-89; activist Learning Disabled Programs, Va., 1980-86; mem. scholarship bd. Oakwood Sch., Annandale, Va., 1982-84; mem. Bd. Edn., Laguna Hills, Calif., 1987. Winner Guild Piano Competition, Washington, 1966; recipient Am. Lyricist award, 1978; St. Louis Inst. Music scholar, 1965; Top 100 L.A. Women-Owned Businesses, 1994. Mem. Direct Mail Club Calif., Nat. Assn. Women Bus. Owners, L.A. and Paramount C. of C., Pi Mu. Office: US Mail & Mktg Corp 7027 Motz St Paramount CA 90723-4842

GORMAN, BARBARA ROSE, secretarial service administrator; b. Terre Haute, Ind., Apr. 12, 1945; d. Arthur Clarence and Lena (Laney) Bitts; m. Claude R. Gorman Jr., Apr. 10, 1970. Grad. high sch., Terre Haute. Sec. Levin bros. Wholesale, Terre Haute, 1963-64, Ind. State U., Terre Haute, 1965-70, Firestone Tire and Rubber Co., Salinas, Calif., 1971-73; sales rep. Avon Corp., Aurora, Colo., 1976-79; sec. for regional dir. Jafra Cosmetics, Aurora, 1980-83; prin. B.G. Typing Svc., Lakewood, Colo., 1987-92. Mem. NAFE. Home: 4591 S Buckley Way Aurora CO 80015-1957

GORMAN, BRIAN DEAN, investment professional; b. Rockford, Ill., Feb. 13, 1954; s. Benjamin Lee and Joyce (Bartlett) G.; m. Weezie Dunn, Jan. 4, 1974; children: Kellie, Bill, Charlie, Hunter. Student, Shimer Coll., Mt. Carroll, Ill., 1972; BA in History with honors, Mont. State U., 1987. Staff mgr. Guaranteed Life Ins. Co., Gainesville, Fla., 1974-76; v.p. Furniture City, Consumers Warehouse, Inc., Gainesville, 1976-81; owner So. Furniture Distbrs., Inc. (dba Affordable Furniture and Beds; Affordable Sofas, Alpha Mortgage), Gainesville and Bozeman, Mont., 1981-91; mortgages purchase and sales profl. Alpha Mortgage Investments, Bozeman, 1983—. Home: 8004 Pinon Pl Bozeman MT 59715-8929 Office: Alpha Mortgage Investments 8004 Pinon Pl Bozeman MT 59715-8929

GORMAN, BRUCE CHARLES, health care executive; b. Washington, Jan. 14, 1949; s. Edward David and Dora (Hallen) G.; m. Judy Ann Jackl, Jan. 1, 1982; children: Marcus, Kate. BA with honors, U. Md., 1972; M in City and Regional Planning, Rutgers U., 1974. Dir. mktg. Select Health, Emeryville, Calif., 1984-87; adminstr. Aetna Life Ins. Co., Walnut Creek, Calif., 1987-89; v.p. Am. Biodyne, South San Francisco, 1989-93, Medco Behavioral Care Systems, South San Francisco, 1993—; mgmt. cons., Berkeley, Calif., 1976-82. Contbr. articles to profl. jours. Cons. Community Organizing Project, San Francisco, 1979-82, Galleria de la Raza, San Francisco, 1982-83. Named one of Outstanding Young Men Am., 1982. Mem. No. Calif. Employee Benefits Coun., Behavioral Health Care Inst., Omicron Delta Epsilon. Democrat. Jewish. Office: Medco Behavioral Care Corp 400 Oyster Point Blvd South San Francisco CA 94080-1904

GORMAN, MICHAEL JOSEPH, library director, educator; b. Witney, Oxfordshire, Eng., Mar. 6, 1941; came to U.S. 1977; s. Philip Denis and Alicia F. (Barrett) G.; m. Anne Gillett, Mar. 6, 1962 (div. 1992); children—Emma, Alice. Student, Ealing Sch. Librarianship, 1964-66. Dir. gen. services dept. Univ. Library U. Ill., Urbana, 1977-88, acting univ. librarian, 1986-87; prof. library adminstrn. U. Ill., Urbana, 1977-88; vis. prof. U. Chgo. Library Sch., 1984, 86-88, U. Calif., Berkeley, 1989-91; dean libr. svcs. Calif. State U., Fresno, 1988—; vis. lectr. U. Ill. Grad. Sch. Library Sci., Urbana, 1974-75; bibliog. cons. Brit. Library Planning Secretariat, 1972-74; head cataloguing Brit. Nat. Bibliography 1969-72. Author: A Study of the Rules for Entry and Headings in the Anglo-American Cataloguing Rules, 1967, 68, Format for Machine Readable Cataloguing of Motion Pictures, 1973, Concise AACR2, 1980, 2d edit., 1990, Technical Services Today and Tomorrow, 1990, (with Walt Crawford) Future Libraries, 1995, others; editor: Anglo-American Cataloguing Rules, 2d edit., 1978, rev., 1988, Catalogue and Index, 1973, Non Solus, 1981, Crossroads, 1986, Convergence, 1990; contbr. articles to profl. jours., chpts. to books. Fellow Brit. Libr. Assn.; mem. ALA (Margaret Mann citation 1979, mem. coun. 1991-95, Melvil Dewey medal 1992), Libr. Info. and Tech. Assn. (mem.-at-large exec. bd. 1982-85). Office: Calif State U Henry Madden Libr 5200 N Barton Ave Fresno CA 93740-8014

GORMAN, MICHAEL STEPHEN, construction executive; b. Tulsa, Aug. 3, 1951; s. Lawrence Matthew and Mary Alice (Veith) G.; m. Sheryl Lane McGee, Feb. 19, 1972; children: Kelley Lane, Michael Ryan. Student, Colo. State U., 1970, 71. With McGee Constrn. Co., Denver, 1972-74, with sales and estimating dept., 1974-78, gen. mgr., 1978-80, pres., owner, 1980-91; pres. Wisor Group, Boulder, 1990—; cons. in remodeling and custom home building; presenter seminars in field. Mem. Nat. Assn. Remodeling Industry Metro Denver (chmn. membership svcs. com. 1987-91, bd. dirs., pres. 1982-91, regional v.p. 1987-89, nat. sec. 1990-91, Man of Yr. 1982, Regional Contractor of Yr. 1988).

GORMAN, RUSSELL WILLIAM, marketing executive, consultant; b. Glen Ridge, N.J., Aug. 17, 1927; s. William Francis and Emily (Weldon) G.; m. Mieko Deguchi, June 19, 1956. BS, U.S. Merchant Marine Acad., 1949. Lic. mcht. marine, chief mate. Lic. officer Moore McCormack Lines Inc., N.Y., 1949-53; dir. tng. Chevron Shipping Co., San Francisco, 1957-77; mgr. orgn., adminstrn. Utah Internat. Corp., San Francisco, 1977-84; pres. Lumier Inc., San Francisco, 1984-85; v.p. John F. Perry Assocs., Concord, Calif., 1986; pres. Market Devel. Assocs., Danville, Calif., 1986-94; sr. v.p. Aegis Fin. Svcs., 1993—; pres., dir. Perfect Wash US, 1993—; bd. dirs. Norlock Tech. Inc., San Mateo, Calif., Internat. Tech. Assocs. Santa Clara, Calif. Chmn. Calif. Vets. Coalition for Bush, 1988; mem. Sec. of Def. Adv. Bd. on Naval History, 1990—; vice chmn. Sec. of Interior Adv. Commn. on San Francisco Maritime Hist. Park, 1992—; chmn. U.S.S. Missouri and Allied Forces Meml.; adv. speaker Peter Wilson for Senate Campaign, 1988. Lt. USN, 1954-57, rear adm. USNR, 1980-87. Decorated Legion of Merit with gold star. Mem. Navy League of the U.S. (v.p. Pacific Ctrl. region 1989—), Res. Officers Assn. of the U.S. (v.p. Navy sect. 1990-92), Naval Res. Assn. (nat. v.p. surface/subsurface 1990—), Oakland C. of C. (vice chmn. mil. affairs com. 1990—). Republican. Methodist. Home: 46 Willowview Ct Danville CA 94526-1945

GORMÈZANO, KEITH STEPHEN, editor, arbitrator; b. Madison, Wis., Nov. 22, 1955; s. Isadore and Miriam (Fox) G.; m. Emma Lee Rogers, Aug. 17, 1986 (div. Nov. 1990). BGS, U. Iowa, 1977, postgrad. in pub. affairs, 1979-80; postgrad. in law, U. Puget Sound, 1984-86. Pub. Le Beacon Presse, Seattle, 1980-89; real estate agt. Jim Stacy Realty, Seattle, 1988-89; arbitrator Better Bus. Bur. Greater Seattle, 1987—; arbitrator Puget Sound Multi-Listing Assn., 1988-89, Nat. Assn. Securities Dealers, 1989—, Ford Consumer Appeals Bd., 1991-92, Harborview Med. Ctrs., 1990-91, 92-93, Up. Improvement Found., 1980-81; joint labor mgmt. com. Puget Fin. Svcs. U. Wash. Med. Ctr., 1990-91, 92-93; pub. info. officer; vol. VISTA, 1982-83; dir. ACJS, Inc., 1981-82. Editor M'godolim, 1980-81, Funding Bull. U. Wash. Health Scis. Grantseekers, 1991; pub., editor Beacon Rev., 1980-89. Vice chmn. Resource Conservation Commn., Iowa City, 1979-80; bd. dirs. Seattle Mental Health Inst., 1981-83, Youth Advocates, Seattle, 1984, Atlantic St. Ctr., 1984; mem. City of Seattle Animal Control Commn., 1984-86, vice chmn., 1985-86, chmn., 1986; mem. Selective Svc. System, 1982—, vice chmn. civilian rev. bd. 742, 1985—; mem. Wash. State Local Draft Bd. # 18, mem. controlled choice appeals bd. Seattle Sch. Dist., 1989; patient collection rep. U. Wash., 1990-91, Harborview Med. Ctrs., 1990-91, 92-93; mem. Ford Consumer Appeals Bd., 1991-93, Ford Motor Co. Dispute Settlement Bd., 1991-93, Joint Labor-Mgmt. Com., Patient Fin. Svcs., U. Wash. Med. Ctr., 1990-91, 92-93, Temple B'nai Torah; mem. coordinating com. edn. after dark program Jewish Fedn. Greater Seattle, 1991-92, exec. bd. thirty-something plus Jewish Community Ctr., 1991-92; active Congregation Eitz Or; co-facilitator Polyfidelity Group, 1995. Named Citizen of the Day Sta. KIXI Radio, 1982. Mem. League United Latin Am. Citizens Amigos (chair 1984-86), U. Iowa Alumni Assn. Democrat. Jewish. Office: 501 N 36th St Ste 330 Seattle WA 98103-8613

GORMLEY, FRANICS XAVIER, JR., social worker; b. Boston, Apr. 27, 1953; s. Francis Xavier and Catherine Caroline (Ireland) G. Student, Massasoit Community Coll., 1973; BA in Psychology, U. Mass., Boston, 1981; MSW, U. Wash., 1984. Cert. social worker. Coordinator Gerontology Career Program Elder Fest, Chico, Calif., 1981; mgr. Arnold's Restaurant, Cardiff, Wales, 1981-82; med. social worker Harborview Med. Ctr., Seattle, 1983-84; psychotherapist Seattle Counseling Svc., 1982-88; clin. social worker Pain Ctr. Swedish Hosp., Seattle, 1984-88, Valley Med. Ctr., Renton, Wash., 1987-88; clin. social worker AIDS program, virology clinic Univ. Hosp., Seattle, 1988-94; sr. social worker, oncology and HIV/AIDS clin. specialist The Queen's Med. Ctr., Honolulu, 1994—; speaker U. Wash Sch. Social Work Graduation Class, 1984, Social Sensitivity in Health Care U. Wash., 1985—; coord. Coping with AIDS Swedish Hosp. Tumor Inst., 1985; participant Coun. of Internat. Fellowship Italia, Placement Servizi Socio-Sanitari AIDS-Roma, 1991; guest speaker Sta. KIRO-TV, Seattle, 1985, Sta. KPLZ, Seattle, 1985; presentor psychosocial aspects HIV/AIDS Northwest AIDS Edn. & Tng. Ctr. Program, U. Wash. Med. Ctr., 1992, clin. mgmt. of patient with HIV/AIDS El Rio Health Ctr., Pima Colo. Pub. Health Dept., 1992; cons. Assn. Workers Resources, Seattle, 1985—; practicum instr. U. Wash. Seattle Sch. Social Work, 1989—; preceptor, intern Residency Tng. Project Sch. of Medicine/Health Scis., Univ. Wash; HIV/AIDS planning coun. Seattle/King County Pub. Health Dept., 1993; com. for the 25th health scis. open house U. Wash. Editor abstract form Comprehensive Multi-Disciplinary Documentation, Western U.S.A. Pain Soc., 1986; contbr. articles to profl. jours. Mem. Seattle Aids Network, 1985—. Mem. NASW (mem. bd. Wash. state chpt. 1988-90), Acad. Cert. Social Workers, Occupational Social Work Orgn. of NASW, Coun. Internat. Fellowship, U. Wash. Alumni Assn., U. Mass. Alumni Assn., Green Key Soc. Democrat. Office: The Queen's Med Ctr Social Work Dept 1301 Punchbowl St Honolulu HI 96813-2413

GORNEY, RODERIC, psychiatry educator; b. Grand Rapids, Mich., Aug. 13, 1924; s. Abraham Jacob Gorney and Edelaine (Roden) Harburg; m. Carol Ann Sobel, Apr. 13, 1986. BS, Stanford U., 1948, MD, 1949; PhD in Psychoanalysis, So. Calif. Psychoanalytic Inst., 1977. Diplomate Am. Bd. Psychiatry and Neurology. Pvt. practice psychiatry San Francisco, 1952-62; asst. prof. UCLA, 1962-71, assoc. prof., 1971-73, prof. psychiatry, 1980—, dir. psychosocial adaptation and the future program, 1971—; faculty So. Calif. Psychoanalytic Inst. Author: The Human Agenda, 1972. Served with USAF, 1943-46. Fellow AAAS, Acad. Psychoanalysis, Am. Psychiatric Assn. (essay prize 1971), Group for Advancement of Psychiatry. Office: UCLA Neuropsychiatric Inst 760 Westwood Plz Los Angeles CA 90024-8300

GORT, PAMELA J., sales executive; b. Pitts., Nov. 16, 1955; d. William J. and Evelyn A. Gort. BA, Georgetown U., 1977; MBA, So. Meth. U., 1992. Info. analyst Haskell Toxicology Lab., Newark, Del., 1977-82; profl. sales rep. DuPont Pharms., Dallas, 1982-85; profl. hosp. rep. DuPont Pharms., Houston, 1985-88, clin. liaison, 1988-91; dist. mgr. DuPont Pharms., Dallas, 1991-93; assoc. bus. dir. DuPont Pharms., Irvine, Calif., 1994—. Office: DuPont Pharms 15615 Alton Pky Ste 230 Irvine CA 92718-3307

GORTON, SLADE, senator; b. Chicago, Ill., Jan. 8, 1928; s. Thomas Slade and Ruth (Israel) G.; m. Sally Jean Clark, June 28, 1958; children: Tod, Sarah Jane, Rebecca Lynn. AB, Dartmouth Coll., 1950; LLB with honors, Columbia U., 1953. Bar: Wash. 1953. Assoc. law firm Seattle, 1953-65; ptnr. law firm, 1965-69; atty. gen. State of Wash., Olympia, 1969-81; U.S. Senator from Wash., 1981-87, 89—; ptnr. Davis, Wright & Jones, Seattle, 1987-89; mem. Wash. Ho. of Reps., 1959-69, majority leader, 1967-69, Nat. Republican Senatorial com., Indian Affairs/Labor & Human Resources com., budget com.; chmn. commerce, sci., & transp. subcom. on consumer affairs, fgn. commerce & tourism, appropriations subcom. Interior & Related Agys. Trustee Pacific Sci. Center, Seattle, found. mem., 1977-78; mem. Pres.'s Consumer Adv. Council, 1975-77; mem. Wash. State Law and Justice Commn., 1969-80, chmn., 1969-76; mem. State Criminal Justice Tng. Commn., 1969-80, chmn., 1969-76. Served with AUS, 1946-47; to 1st lt. USAF, 1953-56; col. USAFR (ret.). Mem. ABA, Wash. Bar Assn., Nat. Assn. Attys. Gen. (pres. 1976-77, Wyman award 1980), Phi Delta Phi, Phi Beta Kappa. Clubs: Seattle Tennis, Wash. Athletic (Seattle). Office: US Senate 730 Hart Senate Bldg Washington DC 20510

GOSANKO, GARY NICOLAS, lawyer; b. Seattle, Mar. 28, 1954; s. Clarence N. and Louella Mae Gosanko; m. Ann Valarie Rice, May 23, 1992. BA in Econs. cum laude, Wash. State U., 1977; JD magna cum laude, U. Puget Sound, 1983. Bar: Wash. Law clk. Honorable Herbert Swanson, Wash. State Ct. Appeals, Seattle, 1983-85; pvt. practice Seattle, 1985—. Mem. Assn. Trial Lawyers Am., Wash. State Trial Lawyers. Office: 701 5th Ave Ste 6850 Seattle WA 98104-7016 Office: 805 164th St SE Ste 101 Mill Creek WA 98012-6316

GOSE, CELESTE MARLENE, writer; b. Laramie, Wyo., Jan. 2, 1959; d. Richard Vern Gose and Agnes Jean (Allen) McGreggor. BS, U. Wyo., 1984; student, U. UNA, Belo Horizonte, Brazil, 1982. Freelance writer Scottsdale, Ariz., 1990—; writer Today's Ariz. Woman. N.Mex. prodn. coord. (feature movies) Twins, 1988, Young Guns, 1988, (cable) The Tracker, 1987, asst. prodn. coord. (feature movies) Outrageous Fortune, The Sunday Disney Movie; asst. unit publicist The Milagro Beanfield War, 1986; casting asst. (television) Lonesome Dove, 1988, Sparks, 1989, The Fantastiks, 1995; author: Your Daggar or Mine?, 1991, (song lyrics) Awake Inside a Dream, 1990, Caught in Eternity, 1990, Drum Sticks on the Moon, 1990, Sometimes, Somewhere, 1994, Stardust and Loneflower, 1994, Coyotes Don't Bark, 1995, The Reluctant Actress, Have No Regrets. Mem. Ariz. 602-Film Prodr's. Warehouse, Women in Comm., Internat. Arabian Horse Assn., Brazilian Inst. Ariz., Ariz. Club. Republican. Home and Office: 31206 N 65th St Cave Creek AZ 85331-6126

GOSE, KAREN KAMARA, state arts administrator; b. Seattle, July 4, 1955; d. Alvin Frederick Jr. and Donna Muriel (Malde) Kamara; m. Michael Gordon Gose, Mar. 20, 1978; children: John Michael, Elisabeth Jane. BA, The Evergreen State Coll., 1982. Adminstrv. asst. to v.p. and provost The Evergreen State Coll., Olympia, Wash., 1983-86; arts program mgr. II Wash. State Arts Commn., Olympia, 1986-88, 1988-90, asst. dir., 1990-93, acting exec. dir., 1993-94, exec. dir., 1994—; bd. dirs. Western States Arts Fedn., Santa Fe. Editor: Peoples of Washington, 1989. Office: Wash State Arts Commn 234 E 8th Ave Olympia WA 98504-2675

GOSE, RICHARD VERNIE, lawyer; b. Hot Springs, S.D., Aug. 3, 1927. MS in Engring., Northwestern U., 1955; LLB, George Washington U., 1967; JD, George Washington U., 1968. Bar: N.Mex. 1967, U.S. Supreme Ct. 1976, Wyo. 1979; registered prof. engr., N.Mex., Wyo.; children: Beverly Marie, Donald Paul, Celeste Marlene. Exec. asst. to U.S. Senator Hickey, Washington, 1960-62; mgr. E.G. & G., Inc., Washington, 1964-66; asst. atty. gen. State of N.Mex., Santa Fe, 1967-70; pvt. practice law, Santa Fe, 1967—, Santa Fe/Prescott, 1979—; assoc. prof. engring. U. Wyo., 1957-60; owner, mgr. Gose & Assocs., Santa Fe, 1967-78; pvt. practice law, Casper, Wyo., 1978-83; pres. Argosy Internat., Inc., 1994—; co-chmn. Henry Jackson for Pres., M.Mex., 1976, Wyo. Johnson for Pres., 1960. With U.S. Army, 1950-52. Mem. N.Mex. Bar Assn., Wyo. Bar Assn., Yavapai County Bar Assn., Masons, Phi Delta Theta, Pi Tau Sigma, Sigma Tau. Methodist. Home and Office: PO Box 3998 Prescott AZ 86302-3998

GOSS, GEORGIA BULMAN, translator; b. N.Y.C., Dec. 1, 1939; d. James Cornelius and Marian Bright (McLaughlin) Bulman; m. Douglas Keith Goss, Dec. 21, 1957; children: Kristin Anne, David. BA, U. Mich., 1961. Libr., High Altitude Obs., Boulder, Colo., 1963-64, U.S. Bur. Standards, Boulder, 1964-65; cons. editor Spanish lang. pilots' tng. manual, 1981-82; freelance translator, Englewood, Colo., 1982—. Mem. U. Mich. Alumni Assn., Phi Sigma Iota. Republican. Episcopalian. Home and Office: D-1 # 105 7755 E Quincy Ave # 105 Denver CO 80237-2312

GOSS, JEROME ELDON, cardiologist; b. Dodge City, Kans., Nov. 30, 1935; s. Horton Maurice and Mary Alice (Mountain) G.; m. Lorraine Ann Sanchez, Apr. 20, 1986. BA, U. Kans., 1957; MD, Northwestern U., 1961. Diplomate Am. Bd. Internal Medicine, Am. Bd. Cardiology (fellow, bd. govs. 1981-84). Intern Met. Gen. Hosp., Cleve., 1961-62; resident Northwestern U. Med. Ctr., Chgo., 1962-64; fellow in cardiology U. Colo., Denver, 1964-66; asst. prof. medicine U. N.Mex., Albuquerque, 1968-70; practice medicine specializing in cardiology N.Mex. Heart Clinic, 1970—; mem. bd. alumni counsellors Northwestern U. Med. Sch., 1977-89, mem. nat. alumni bd., 1991—; chief dept. medicine Presbyn. Hosp., Albuquerque, 1978-80, mem. exec. com., 1980-82, bd. dirs. cardiac diagnostic svcs., 1970—. Contbr. articles to profl. jours. Bd. dirs. Presbyn. Heart Inst., Ballet West N.Mex., N.Mex. Symphony Orch.; pres. Albuquerque Mus. Found. Lt. comdr. USN, 1966-68. Nat. Heart Inst. research fellow, 1965-66; named one of Outstanding Young Men Am., Jaycees, 1970; recipient Alumni Service award Northwestern U. Med. Sch., 1986. Fellow ACP, ACC, Coun. Clin. Cardiology of Am. Heart Assn., Soc. Cardiac Angiography; mem. Albuquerque-Bernalillo County Med. Soc. (sec. 1972, treas. 1975, v.p. 1980), Alpha Omega Alpha. Republican. Methodist. Office: NMex Heart Clinic 1001 Coal Ave SE Albuquerque NM 87106-5205

GOSSAGE, JAMES DEARL, quality control administrator; b. Bellingham, Wash., Oct. 16, 1937; s. Dearl Lars and Ilene Loretta (Babcock) G. Test technician final acceptance Martin Marietta Corp., Littleton, Colo., 1959-62; photo asst., photo printer Hagelstein Bros. Studio, N.Y.C., 1963-64; photo printer Gilbert Photo Svc., N.Y.C., 1964-73; with evaluation/AV equipment dept. Ednl. Products Info. Exch. Inst., N.Y.C., 1973-74; troubleshooter audio A Total Electronics Svc., Bellingham, Wash., 1978; quality dept. adminstrv. aide Pioneer Magnetics, Santa Monica, Calif., 1980—; systems operator bull. bd. system the original Off Off Broadway BBS, Santa Monica, 1990—. Photo contbr. to books; photo documentor of Off Off Broadway. Active Com. to Restore Constitution. With U.S. Army, 1956-59. Mem. Nat. Health Fedn., Ancentry Rsch. Club. Home: 1223 Broadway # 322 Santa Monica CA 90404-2707

GOSSARD, EARL EVERETT, physicist; b. Eureka, Calif., Jan. 8, 1923; s. Ralph Dawson and Winifred (Hill) G.; m. Sophia Poignand, Nov. 21, 1948; children: Linda Margaret, Kenneth Earl, Diane Winifred. BA, UCLA, 1948; MS, U. Calif., San Diego, 1951; PhD in Phys. Oceanography, Scripps Instn. Oceanography, 1956. Meteorologist Navy Electronics Lab., San Diego, 1949-55, head radio meteorol. sect., 1955-61; head radio physics div. Navy Electronics Lab. (name now Naval Ocean Systems Ctr.), San Diego, 1961-71; chief geoacoustics program Wave Propagation Lab., NOAA, Boulder, Colo., 1971-73, chief meteorol. radar program, 1973-82; sr. rsch. assoc. Coop. Inst. for Rsch. in Environ. Scis. U. Colo., Boulder, 1982—. Co-author: (with Hooke) Waves in the Atmosphere (Disting. Authorship award Dept. Commerce 1975), 1973; (with Strauch) Radar Observation of Clear Air and Clouds (Disting. Authorship award Dept. Commerce 1985); editor: Radar Observation of the Clear Air, 1980; contbr. over 74 articles to profl. jours. 1st lt. USAAF, 1943-46, CBI. Recipient Silver medal Dept. Commerce, 1976, Citation Am. Geophys. Union, 1986. Fellow Am. Meteorol. Soc.; mem. Nat. Acad., Internat. Union Radio Sci. (past chmn. U.S. Commn. F.). Republican. Presbyterian. Home: 1088 Kelly Rd W Sugarloaf Star Rt Boulder CO 80302 Office: U Colo Campus Box 449 Boulder CO 80309

GOSSELIN, KENNETH STUART, minister; b. Altus, Okla., Aug. 9, 1932; s. George Clairo and Florence May (Stebbins) G.; m. P. Rodene Tayar, Sept. 8, 1962; children: Mark Alan, Kimberly Sue, Anna Jouree, Sabrina Kay. BA, Oklahoma City U., 1954; STM, Perkins Sch. Theology, 1958; MA, Claremont (Calif.) Grad. Sch., 1967. Cert. tchr., Calif. Community coll. campus minister Wesley Found., Tex. Christian U., Ft. Worth, 1958-64; minister to youth 1st Meth. Ch., Riverside, Calif., 1964-66; assoc. minister Community Meth. Ch., Sepulveda, Calif., 1967-69; minister St. Matthew's Meth. Ch., Newbury Park, Calif., 1969-71; assoc. minister Christ Ch. United Meth., Tucson, 1971-73; minister Nestor United Meth. Ch., San Diego, 1973-83, Pacific Beach (Calif.) United Meth. Ch., 1983-85; sr. minister Christ United Meth. Ch., San Diego, 1985-90; minister Lemon Grove (Calif.) United Meth. Ch., 1990-94, 1st United Meth. Ch., San Francisco, 1994—; radio announcer, editor Religion in the News, Sta. KFMB, San Diego County Ecumenical Conf., 1979-91; mem. ordained ministry com. United Meth. Dist., San Diego, 1982-91; mem. communications com. Calif.-Pacific Conf. U. Meth. Ch., Pasadena and L.A., 1988—. Entertainer, clown Muscular Dystrophy Assn. Telethon, San Diego, 1973-92, Spl. Olympics, Am. Cancer Soc., Children's Hosp., San Diego Symphony, etc. Danforth Found. grantee, 1956-57. Mem. Am. Acad. Religion, Clowns Am., World Clown Assn., San Diego State U. Clown Club. Democrat. Home: 900 N Workman St San Fernando CA 91340-1750 Office: 1st United Meth Ch 1525 Glenoaks Blvd San Fernando CA 91340-1739

GOSSETT, JEFFREY ALAN, professional football player; b. Charleston, Ill., Jan. 25, 1957. BS in Phys. Edn., Eastern Ill. U., 1982. With Kansas City Chiefs, 1981-82, Cleve. Browns, 1983-84, 85-87; punter Portland USFL, 1985; with Houston Oilers, 1987; punter L.A. Raiders, 1988—. Named punter The Sporting News NFL All-Pro team, 1991. Office: L.A. Raiders 332 Center St El Segundo CA 90245-4047*

GOSSETT, RICHARD GERALD, management consultant; b. Chgo., Aug. 29, 1963; s. William Terrance Gossett and Phyllis Catherine Swarberg. Student, U. Tulsa, 1981; BS in Mech. Engring., Northwestern U., Evanston, Ill., 1985, M in Mfg. Engring., 1986; MBA, Harvard U., 1992. Mem. tech. staff AT&T Bell Labs. Inc., Columbus, Ohio, 1986-89; sr. engr. GE Co., Worthington, Ohio, 1989-90; cons. N.Y. Cons. Ptnrs., N.Y.C., 1992-93, Andersen Cons., L.A., 1993—. Whirlpool fellow Ctr. for Mfg. Engring., Evanston, 1985. Republican. Roman Catholic. Home: 1920 6th St Apt 355 Santa Monica CA 90405-1273 Office: Andersen Consulting 633 W 5th St Los Angeles CA 90071-2005

GOTCHER, JAMES RONALD, lawyer; b. Dallas, Jan. 18, 1947; s. James Bentley and Elga Audra (Dyess) G.; m. Satoko Hata, June 20, 1970; 1 son, James Kensuke. B.A. magna cum laude in History, Calif. State U.-Long Beach, 1972; postgrad. U. Hawaii, 1972-73; J.D., Loyola U., Los Angeles, 1976. Bar: Calif. 1976 (cert. legal specialist immigration & nationality law), U.S. Supreme Ct. 1980. Assoc. Gruber & Kelman, 1976-77; ptnr. Gotcher & Shapiro, 1977-81; ptnr. Aberson, Lynes & Gotcher, 1982-89; counsel Coudert Brothers, 1989-93; prin. Law Offices of James R. Gotcher, 1993—. Mem. Town Hall of Los Angeles. Served with USAF, 1965-68. Decorated Bronze Star. Mem. Los Angeles County Bar Assn. (chmn. immigration law sect. 1983-84), Am. Immigration Lawyers Assn., ABA. Republican. Clubs: University (Los Angeles). Author: Comprehensive guide to U.S. Nonimmigrant Visas, 1983; contbr. articles to legal jours. Address: 15303 Ventura Blvd Fl 9 Sherman Oaks CA 91403-3110

GOTHOLD, STUART E., school system administrator, educator; b. L.A., Sept. 20, 1935; s. Hubert Eugene and Adelaide Louise (Erickson) G.; m. Jane Ruth Soderberg, July 15, 1955; children: Jon Ernest, Susan Louise, Eric Arthur, Ruth Ann. BA, Whittier Coll., 1956, MA in Edn., 1961, LLD (hon.), 1988; EdD, U. So. Calif., 1974. Tchr. grades 1-9 El Rancho Sch. Dist., Pico Rivera, Calif., 1956-61, prin. jr. h.s., 1961-66; curriculum cons. L.A. County Office Edn., 1966-70; asst. supt. South Whittier (Calif.) Sch. Dist., 1970-72, supt., 1972-77; asst. supt. L.A. County Office Edn., Downey, 1977-78, chief dep. supt., 1978-79, supt., 1979-94; asst. dean, clin. prof. Sch. Edn. U. So. Calif., L.A., 1994—; asst. dean Sch. Edn. U. So. Calif., 1994—; mem. adv. bd. Nat. Ctr. Fgn. Lang., 1984—, Nat. Comp Systems, Des Moines, 1990—; charter mem. Edn. Insights, Detroit, 1990—. Author: (book) Inquiry, 1970, Decisions-A Health Edn. Curriculum, 1971. Recipient Alumni Merit award USC, 1993, Alumni Achievement award, 1986; named Dist. Educator Calif. State U., 1993. Republican. Roman Catholic. Home: 10121 Pounds Ave Whittier CA 90603-1649 Office: U So Calif WPH 802 Los Angeles CA 90090-0031

GOTO, SHINYA, cardiologist, researcher; b. Tokyo, Apr. 4, 1961; came to U.S., 1992; s. Kouichi and Yoshiko G.; m. Mami Goto, June 29, 1988; children: Shinichi Goto, Ippei Goto. MD, Keio U., DMS, 1992. Instr. Keio U. Hosp., Tokyo, 1986-90, clin. asst. prof., 1990-92; rsch. assoc. The Scripps Rsch. Inst., La Jolla, Calif., 1992—; med. cons. Chiyoda Mut. Life Ins., Tokyo, 1989-92, Tokyo Assn. of Banks, 1989-92; rsch. cons. Ajinomoto Co. Ltd., Kanagawa, Japan, 1994. Author: Clinical Manual of Arrhythmia, 1992; contbr. scientific papers to profl. jours. Grantee Japanese Ministry Edn., 1992, 93, Chiyoda Mut. Found., 1992, Uehara Meml. Fund, 1994. Mem. Am. Heart Assn., Japanese Coll. Cardiology, Japanese Soc. Circulation, Japanese Soc. Thrombosis and Hemostatis. Office: The Scripps Rsch Inst. 10666 N Torrey Pines Rd La Jolla CA 92037-1027

GOTTENBORG, DAVID ANDREW, natural gas executive; b. Portland, Oreg., Apr. 14, 1955; s. Russell Baldwin and Dorothy Marie (Arneson) G.; m. Jean Ellen O'Day, July 29, 1978; children: Erin, Drew. BA, Colo. Coll., 1977; JD, U. Denver, 1981. Bar: U.S. Supreme Ct. 1988. Assoc. Davis, Graham & Stubbs, Denver, 1981-88; mng. ptnr. Fountainhead Resources, Ltd., Denver, 1988—; pres., chmn. Colo. Natural Gas Assistance Corp., Denver, 1988—; chmn. bd. dirs. Colo. Natural Gas Assistance Found., Denver, 1988—, Colo. Equity Fund, Inc., Denver, 1990—. Co-author: American Law Mining, 2d edit., 1985 (6 vols.); editorial cons. (book) Law of Federal Oil & Gas Leases, 2d edit., 1985 (2 vols.); contbr. author Mineral Law Newsletter, 1987-88; contbr. articles to profl. jours. Bd. dirs., chmn. Children's Legal Clinic, Denver, 1984—; pres., chmn. Denver Young Reps., 1987; bd. dirs. Colo. Sci. Ctr., Denver, 1983-85; mem. Colo. State Commn. on Jud. Performance, 1993—. Named one of 50 for Colo. by Colo. Assn. Commerce & Industry, 1987-88. Mem. Denver Bar Assn., Colo. Bar Assn. Lutheran.

GOTTFRIED, EUGENE LESLIE, physician, educator; b. Passaic, N.J., Feb. 26, 1929; s. David Robert and Rose (Chill) G.; m. Phyllis Doris Swain, Aug. 16, 1957. AB, Columbia U., 1950, MD, 1954. Cert. Nat. Bd. Med. Examiners, Am. Bd. Internal Medicine. Intern Presbyn. Hosp., N.Y.C., 1954-55, asst. resident in medicine, 1957-58; resident Bronx (N.Y.) Mcpl. Hosp. Ctr., 1958-59, fellow in medicine, 1959-60; asst. instr. medicine Albert Einstein Coll. Medicine Yeshiva U., N.Y.C., 1959-60, instr., 1960-61, assoc., 1961-65, asst. prof., 1965-69; assoc. prof. medicine Cornell U. Med. Coll., N.Y.C., 1969-81, assoc. prof. pathology, 1975-81; clin. prof. dept. lab. medicine U. Calif., San Francisco, 1991-93, prof., 1993—, vice chmn. dept. lab. medicine, 1981—; hosp. appointments include asst. vis. physician Bronx Mcpl. Hosp. Ctr., 1960-66, assoc. attending physician, 1966-69; assoc. attending physician N.Y. Hosp., N.Y.C., 1969-81, assoc. attending pathologist, 1975-81, dir. lab. clin. hematology, 1969-81; chief lab. medicine San Francisco Gen. Hosp. Med. Ctr., 1981—, dir. clin. labs., 1981—; chair area com. hematology Nat. Com. for Clin. Lab. Stds., 1995—. Assoc. editor Jour. Lipid Research, 1971-72, 75-77; mem. editorial bd. Jour. Lipid

Research, 1972-77. Chmn. area com. on hematology, Nat. Com. for Clin. Lab. Stds., 1995—. Lt. comdr. USNR, 1955-57. Recipient Career Scientist award Health Research Council City of N.Y., 1964-72. Fellow Am. Soc. Hematology, Internat. Soc. Hematology, ACP, Acad. Clin. Lab. Physicians and Scientists; mem. AAAS, Phi Beta Kappa, Alpha Omega Alpha. Office: San Francisco Gen Hosp Clin Labs 1001 Potrero Ave San Francisco CA 94110-3518

GOTTI, MARGARET LYNN, library administrator; b. Detroit, July 31, 1944; d. Frank Mathias and Betty Louise (Lee) Sieger; m. Cyriac Thannikary, Nov. 13, 1965 (div. Feb. 1973); 1 child, Luke Anthony; m. Marcos T. Perez, Mar. 1973 (dec. Oct. 1973); m. Lui Gotti, Dec. 23, 1984. AB, U. Detroit, 1968; MLS, Pratt Inst., 1969; postgrad., NYU, 1976-77. Cert. librarian, N.Y. Sr. librarian Queens Pub. Library, Jamaica, N.Y., 1969-77; library dir. El Centro Pub. Library, El Centro, Calif., 1977—; county libr./cons. Imperial County Free Libr., 1993—; vice chmn., chmn. Serra Coop. Libr. Sys., San Diego, 1980-82. Pres. Hist. Site Found., El Centro, 1988, 82, 93, sec., 1989, trustee, 1989—, v.p., 1991—; fin. sec. St. Elizabeth Luth. Ch., El Centro, 1988; active numerous civic coms., fundraising events; mem. comm. and arts task force Imperial County Arts Coun.; coord. arts and culture com. City of El Centro Strategic Plan. Title IIB fellow Pratt Inst., 1968-69. Mem. ALA, AAUW (v.p. El Centro 1988), Calif. Libr. Assn., Toastmasters (v.p. El Centro 1987-88), Soroptomists (treas. El Centro 1978, corr. sec. 1990-91, 1st v.p. 1991—, pres. 1992-93, 2d v.p. 1995-96), Women of Moose (sr. regent El Centro 1988-89). Democrat. Lutheran. Home: 1531 W Heil Ave El Centro CA 92243-3135 Office: El Centro Pub Libr 539 W State St El Centro CA 92243-2928

GOTTLIEB, ALAN MERRIL, advertising, fundraising and broadcasting executive, writer; b. L.A., May 2, 1947; s. Seymour and Sherry (Schutz) G.; m. Julie Hoy Versnel, July 27, 1979; children: Amy Jean, Sarah Merril, Alexis Hope, Andrew Michael. Grad. Georgetown U., 1970; BS, Nuclear Engring., U. Tenn., 1971. Press sec. Congressman John Duncan, Knoxvill, Tenn., 1971, regional rep., Young Ams. for Freedom, Seattle, 1972, nat. dir. Young Ams. for Freedom, Washington, 1971-72; nat. treas. Am. Conservative Union, Washington, 1971—, bd. dirs., 1974—; pres. Merril Assocs., 1974—; chmn. Citizens Com. for Right to Keep and Bear Arms, Bellevue, Wash., 1972—, exec. dir., 1973; pres. Ctr. Def. of Free Enterprise, Bellevue 1976—, Second Amendment Found., Bellevue, 1974—; pub. Gun Week, 1985—, The Gottlieb-Tartaro Report, 1995—; bd. dirs. Nat. Park User Assn., 1988—, Am. Polit. Action Com., 1988—, Coun. Nat. Policy, bd. govs., 1985—, Svc. Bureau Assn., pres., dir., 1974—, Chancellor Broadcasting, Inc, Las Vegas, Nev., 1990-93; pres. Sta. KBNP Radio, Portland, 1990—, Evergreen Radio Network, Bellevue, 1990-93, Westnet Broadcasting Inc., Bellevue, 1990, Sta. KSBN Radio, Spokane, 1995—; chmn. Talk Am. Radio Network, 1994—. With U.S. Army, 1968-74. Recipient Good Citizenship award Citizens Home Protective Assn., Honolulu, 1978, Cicero award Nat. Assn. Federally Licensed Firearms Dealers, Fla., 1982, Second Amendment award Scope, 1983, 91, Outstanding Am. Handgunner award, Am. Handgunners Award Found., Milwaukee, Wisc., 1984, Roy Rogers award, Nat. Antique Arms Collectors Assn., Reno, Nev., 1987, Golden Eagle award, Am. Fedn. Police, Washington, 1990. Mem. NRA. Republican. Author: The Gun Owners Political Action Manual, 1976, The Rights of Gun Owners, 1981, Rev. edit., 1991, The Gun Grabbers, 1988, Gun Rights Fact Book, 1989, Guns For Women, 1988, The Wise Use Agenda, 1989, Trashing the Economy, 1993, Things You Can Do To Defend Your Gun Rights, 1993, Alan Gottlieb's Celebrity Address Book, 1994.

GOTTLIEB, DANIEL SETH, lawyer; b. Los Angeles, Sept. 19, 1954; s. Seymour and Blanche Joyce (Kaufman) G.; m. Marilynn Jeanne Payne, July 21, 1985; children: Gwendolyn Z., Rebecca Lucinda. BA summa cum laude, Columbia U., 1976; JD, Harvard U., 1980. Bar: Wash. 1980, U.S. Dist. Ct. (we. dist.) Wash. 1980. Assoc. Riddell, Williams, Bullitt & Walkinshaw, Seattle, 1980-86, ptnr., 1986—; coord. S.E. Legal Clinic, Seattle, 1984-86. Mem. Seattle Fremont Adv. Com. Recipient Achievement award Seattle-King County Econ. Devel. Coun., 1990. Mem. ABA, Nat. Assn. Bond Lawyers, Wash. State Bar Assn., Seattle-King County Bar Assn. (treas. 1993-95, second v.p. 1995-96, bd. dirs. young lawyers divsn. 1987-90, treas. 1987-88, vice-chmn. 1988-89, chmn. 1989-90, chmn. legal info. and referral clinics com. 1986-87), Wash. State Assn. Mcpl. Attys., Wash. Coun. Sch. Attys., Wash. State Soc. Hosp. Attys., Bainbridge Island-North Kitsap Jewish Chavurah (v.p. & sec. 1993-95). Jewish. Home: 16684 Agate Pass Rd NE Bainbridge Is WA 98110-3064 Office: Riddell Williams Bullitt & Walkinshaw 1001 4th Ave Ste 4400 Seattle WA 98154-1101

GOTTLIEB, LEONARD, association administrator; b. Santa Monica, Calif., Apr. 12, 1923; s. Charles and Sarah Gottlieb; m. M. Elizabeth Gottlieb, 1943; children: Thomas Byron, Robert John, Mary Lou. AA, L.A. Trade Tech. Coll., 1943; student, UCLA, 1958, Calif. State U., L.A., 1960. Chief field dep. L.A. City Coun., 1957-67; campaign mgr. Spencer-Roberts & Assocs., L.A., 1967-69; exec. dir. So. Calif. Kidney Found., L.A., 1969-75; dir. devel. Nat. Kidney Found., N.Y.C., 1975-79; regional dir. Nat. Kidney Found., L.A., 1983-91, dir. planned giving, 1991—; legis. analyst II City of L.A., 1980-83. Author: Fund Raising: The How To's, 1976. Mem. life Calif. PTA, 1954; mem. Friends of Sport. Recipient L.A. City Coun. commendation resolution, 1969. Fellow Nat. Kidney Found. Profl. Staff Assn., Planned Giving Coun. So. Calif., Nat. Com. on Planned Giving, Nat. Health Agys. Planned Giving Roundtable, Optimist Internat. Venice H.S. Alumni Assn. Office: Nat Kidney Found 3140 Grand View Blvd Los Angeles CA 90066-1027

GOTTLIEB, SHERRY GERSHON, author, editor; b. L.A., Apr. 6, 1948; d. Harry L. and Evelyn Jellen) Gershon; m. David Neil Gottlieb, Aug. 12, 1971 (div. 1973). BA in Dramatic Arts, U. Calif., Berkeley, 1969. Exec. sec. Budget Films, L.A., 1970-72; script reader United Artists, L.A., 1971-74; owner A Change of Hobbit bookstore, L.A. and Santa Monica, Calif., 1972-91; class coord. UCLA Extension, 1982. Author: Hell No, We Won't Go! Evading the Draft During the Vietnam War, 1991, Love Bite, 1994. Named Spl. Guest of Honor, Westercon, 1979. Mem. PEN USA. Democrat.

GOTTSCHALK, ADELE M., surgeon; b. N.Y.C., Dec. 28, 1941; d. Otto George and Ada Mae Gottschalk. BS, CUNY, 1963; MD, SUNY, Buffalo, 1967. Intern and resident surgery U. Chgo. (Ill.) Hosp. and Clinics, 1968-70; resident surgery Michael Reese Hosp., Chgo., 1970-71, U. San Diego (Calif.) Hosp., 1971-73; gen. surgeon Kaiser Hosp. Harbor City, Calif., 1973—. Office: Kaiser Hosp Harbor City 1050 Pacific Coast Hwy Harbor City CA 90710-3509

GOTTSTEIN, BARNARD JACOB, retail and wholesale food company executive, real estate executive; b. Des Moines, Dec. 30, 1925; s. Jacob B. and Anna (Jacobs) G.; children: Sandra, James, Ruth Anne, David, Robert; m. Rachel Landau, July, 1986. BA in Econs. and Bus., U. Wash., 1949; LLD (hon.), U. Alaska, Fairbanks, 1991. Pres. J.B. Gottstein & Co., Anchorage, 1953-90; chmn. bd. Carr-Gottstein Inc., Anchorage, 1974-90; ret., 1990—; dir. United Bank Alaska, Anchorage, 1975-86. Commr. Alaska State Human Rights Commn., 1963-68; del. Dem. Nat. Conv., 1964, 68, 76, 88, 92; committeeman Dem. Nat. Com., 1976-80; v.p. State Bd. Edn., Alaska, 1983-87, pres., 1987-91. Served with USAF, 1944-45. Jewish. Office: Carr-Gottstein Properties 550 W 7th Ave # 1540 Anchorage AK 99501

GOUGH, AIDAN RICHARD, legal educator, consultant; b. L.A., May 22, 1934; s. James Albert and Marian (Ford) G. AB, Stanford U., 1952, AM, 1957; JD, Santa Clara U., 1962; LLM, Harvard U., 1966. Bar: Calif. 1963, U.S. Dist. Ct. (no. dist.) Calif. 1963, U.S. Supreme Ct. 1966. Dep. probation officer Santa Clara County Juvenile Ct., San Jose, Calif., 1956-60; prof. law Santa Clara U., 1962—; alt. referee, judge pro tem Juvenile div. Santa Clara County Superior Ct., 1963-88; reporter juvenile justice standards Nat. Joint Commn., N.Y.C., 1971; vis. prof. law Stanford U., 1971; vis. prof. London Sch. Econs., 1973; active Dist. VII med. quality com. Calif. State Bd. Med. Quality Assurance, San Mateo, Calif., 1976-84; cons. emergency legal medicine Stanford (Calif.) Med. Ctr., 1978—, San Francisco Gen. Hosp. Med. Ctr., 1982—; legal advisor Calif. State Council Emergency Nurses Assn., Long Beach, Calif., 1980—; bd. dirs. Lifeguard HMO, Milpitas, Calif., 1982-92. Co-author, editor: Beyond Control: Status Offenders in the Juvenile Court, 1977. Co-chmn. bioethics com. Santa Clara County Med. Soc., San Jose, 1968; mem. profl. stds. com. Santa Clara County Med. Soc., 1968, multiple casualty com., 1980—; emergency svcs. advisor and spl. counsel, County of Santa Cruz, 1989—. Law Teaching fellow Harvard U., 1965-66, Ford Found. fellow, 1965; recipient Outstanding Service to Medicine, Santa Clara County Med. Soc., 1978, Nat. Emergency Nursing Disting. Svc. award Nat. Bd. Emergency Nursing, 1987. Mem. ABA, Calif. Bar Assn., Santa Clara County Bar Assn., Am. Coll. of Legal Medicine, Internat. Soc. on Family Law (exec. council), Nat. Health Lawyers Assn. Republican. Roman Catholic. Home: 2320 Park Ave Santa Clara CA 95050-6030 Office: Santa Clara U School Of Law Santa Clara CA 95053

GOUGH, HARRISON GOULD, psychologist, educator; b. Buffalo, Minn., Feb. 25, 1921; s. Harry B. and Aelfreda (Gould) G.; m. Kathryn H. Whittier, Jan. 23, 1943; 1 child, Jane Kathryn Gough Rhodes. AB summa cum laude, U. Minn., 1942, AM (Social Sci. Research Council fellow 1946-47), 1947, PhD, 1949. Asst. prof. psychology U. Minn., 1948-49; asst. prof. U. Calif.-Berkeley, 1949-54, assoc. prof., 1954-60, prof., 1960-86, prof. emeritus, 1986—, assoc. dir. Inst. Personality Assessment and Research, 1964-67, dir., 1973-83, chmn. dept. psychology, 1967-72; cons. VA, 1951—; dir. cons. Psychologists Press, Inc., 1956—; mem. research adv. com. Calif. Dept. Corrections, 1958-64, Calif. Dept. Mental Hygiene, 1964-69, Gov.'s Calif. Adv. Com. Mental Health, 1968-74, citizens adv. council Calif. Dept. Mental Hygiene, 1968-71; clin. projects research review com. NIMH, 1968-72. Served to 1st lt. AUS, 1942-46, 1986. Recipient U. Calif. the Berkeley citation, 1986, Bruno Klopfer Disting. Contbn. award Soc. Personality Assessment, 1987; Fulbright research scholar, Italy, 1958-59, 65-66; Guggenheim fellow, 1965-66. Mem. Am., Western psychol. assns., Soc. Personality Assessment, Internat. Assn. Cross-Cultural Psychology, Académie National de Psychologie, Soc. Mayflower Desc., Phi Beta Kappa. Clubs: Commonwealth (San Francisco), Capitol Hill (Washington). Author: Adjective Check List, California Psychological Inventory, other psychol. tests; chmn. bd. editors U. Calif. Publs. in Psychology, 1956-58; cons. editor Assessment, 1993—, Jour. Cons. and Clin. Psychology, 1956-74, 77-84, Jour. Abnormal Psychology, 1964-74, Jour. Personality and Social Psychology, 1981-84, Med. Tchr., 1978-84, Cahiers d'Anthropologie, 1978-84, Population and Environment: Behavioral and Social Issues, 1977-80; Current Psychol. Research and Revs., 1985-93, Pakistan Jour. Psychol. Research, 1985—, Jour. Personality Assessment, 1986—, Psychological Assesment, 1991-92, Psychopathology and Behavioral Assessment, 1992—; assoc. editor Jour. Cross-Cultural Psychology, 1969-81. Home: PO Box 909 Pebble Beach CA 93953-0909 Office: U Calif Inst Personality and Social Rsch Berkeley CA 94720

GOUGH, WILLIAM CABOT, engineer; b. Jersey City, Aug. 22, 1930; s. William Lincoln and Lillian May (Mansmann) G.; m. Marion Louise McConnell, Apr. 27, 1957; children: Barbara Louise, William Scott. BS in Engring., Priceton U., 1952, MA in Engring., 1953; postgrad., Harvard U., 1966-67. Registered prof. engr., Calif. Adminstr. engr. Civilian Power Program AEC, Washington, 1953-55, indsl. info. officer, 1958-60, tech. asst. for systems, plans and programs, div. controlled thermonuclear rsch., 1960-74; project engr. nuclear aircraft program USN, Washington, 1955-58; program mgr. fusion power Electric Power Rsch. Inst., Palo Alto, Calif., 1974-77; sr. DOE/EPRI energy program coord., tech. dir. Office Program Assessment and Integration U.S. Dept. of Energy, San Francisco and Palo Alto, 1977-81; dir. DOE Site Office Stanford Linear Accelerator Ctr. Stanford (Calif.) U., 1981-88; ret., 1988; pres. Found. for Mind-Being Rsch., Los Altos, Calif., 1980—; bd. dirs. Sage Seminars, Inc., San Francisco, 1984-88, MERU Found., San Anselmo, Calif., 1988-93; mem. bd. advisors Bonny Found., Salina, Kans., 1990—; mem. physics of humanity coun. Inst. Heart Math., Boulder Creek, Calif., 1993—. Contbr. articles and chpts. to tech. jours. and texts. With USN, 1955-58. Mem. AAAS, Am. Nuclear Soc., N.Y. Acad. Sci., Fedn. Am. Scientists, Soc. for Sci. Exploration, Internat. Soc. Study of Subtle Energies and Energy Medicine (jour. adv. bd. 1990—), World Future Soc., Common Cause, UN Assn. Home and Office: 442 Knoll Dr Los Altos CA 94024-4731

GOUL, RICHARD MASSON, lawyer; b. Long Beach, Calif., Feb. 27, 1958; s. Richard Dean and Gloria (Masson) G.; m. Karen Leslie Thorp, Apr. 10, 1992. BA in Polit. Sci., U. So. Calif., L.A., 1983; postgrad., Oxford U., Eng., 1985; JD, Loyola U., L.A., 1988. Bar: Calif. Writer various publs., 1978-86; city atty. L.A. City Atty.'s Office, 1986-89; dep. dist. atty. Los Angeles County Dist. Atty.'s Office, L.A., 1989—. Author legislation: Pub. Resources Code 5164, Calif., 1993. Mem. sch. bd. Cerritos (Calif.) Community Bd., 1979-85, pres. 1984. Roman Catholic. Office: Los Angeles County Dist Atty's Office 210 W Temple Los Angeles CA 90012-3210

GOULD, CLIO LAVERNE, electric utility and irrigation district exec.; b. Madison, S.D., Feb. 20, 1919; s. Howard Bennett and Moneta Kay (Herrick) G.; student Walla Walla Coll., 1948, U. Wash. Extension, 1954, U. Calif. at San Diego Extension, 1962, Capital Radio Enging. Inst. Corr., 1958-62; diploma elec. engring. Internat. Corr. Schs., 1958; m. Mildred May Newell, Apr. 13, 1942; children: George Marcus, Deanna May (Mrs. Terry L. Paxton). With astronautics div. Gen. Dynamics Corp., San Diego, 1956-66, sr. design engr. research and devel. Atlas and Centaur space vehicles, 1956-62; supt. power and pumping depts. Wellton Mohawk Irrigation & Drainage Dist., Wellton, Ariz., 1966-76, gen. mgr., 1976—. treas. Liga Internat., Inc., San Diego, 1964-65; mem. Colorado River Task Force, 1987-90; mem. exec. bd. ARiz. Agrl. Bus. Coun., 1980-86, v.p.; sec./treas. Irrigation and Electrical Dist. Assoc., 1987—; commr. Ariz. State Water Commn., 1989. Served with AUS, 1941-45; PTO. Recipient Performance award Gen. Dynamics Corp., 1963. Registered profl. engr., Ariz. Mem. IEEE (sr.), AIAA, Nat., Ariz. (pres. chpt. 1977-78) socs. profl. engrs., Photog. Soc. Am., Nat. Water Resources Assn., Ariz. State Reclamation Assn., Colorado River Water Users Assn. (bd. dirs. 1982-92, exec. com. 1984-92), Ariz. Agri-Bus. Council (exec. bd. 1980-87, v.p. 1981). Republican. Seventh-day Adventist (elder 1956-92, chmn. bldg. com. 1970-73). Home: RR 1 Box 4 Wellton AZ 85356-9801 Office: RR 1 Box 19 Wellton AZ 85356-9801

GOULD, D. JOY, social services administrator; b. Annapolis, Md., Oct. 30, 1951; d. Sidney and Portia (Greenblatt) G. B in Psychology, Webster Coll., 1973; MPA, Calif. State U., Dominguez Hills, 1981. Cert. alcholism counselor. Adminstrv. mgr. Wayback Inn-Social Model Detox Ctr., 1978-81; dir. alcohol abuse program Hollywood Cmty. Svcs., 1981-85; dir. recovery svcs., acting exec. dir. People in Progress, Inc., 1985-86; program mgr. Pacifica Cmty. Hosp., 1986-88; dir. outpatient svcs. L.A. Ctrs. for Alcohol and Drug Abuse, 1988-89; dir. drug/alcohol studies program Pacific Oaks Coll., Pasadena, Calif., 1991-92; exec. dir. Helpline Youth Counseling, Inc., Norwalk, Calif., 1989—; founder and dir. Calif. Inst. for Counseling Studies, Pasadena, 1993—; prof. alcohol drug studies program Pacific Oaks Coll., 1989—; cons. youth residental program CLARE Found., Inc., 1986-87; treas. bd. dirs., chair fin. com. So. Calif. Women's Substance Abuse Task Force, Inc., 1987—; cons. chem. dependency rehab. program Redgate Meml. Hosp., 1988. Cons., contbr. chpts. to book: Coping With Sibling Rivalry, 1989. Office: Helpline Youth Counseling 12330 Firestone Blvd Norwalk CA 90650-4324

GOULD, JULIAN SAUL, lawyer; b. L.A., Apr. 15, 1924; s. David H. and Jeanette (Palm) G.; m. Norma Patricia Gould; 1 child, Paul Julian. Student, U. So. Calif., 1946-48; JD, Southwestern U., L.A., 1950. Bar: Calif. 1950. Lawyer in pvt. practice L.A., 1950—. Named Alumnus of Yr., Southwestern U., 1972. Mem. Hollywood Bar Assn. (pres. 1978), Am. Legion (comdr. 24th Dist. 1960), Southwestern U. Alumni Assn. (pres. 1972), Masons (32 deg., Shriners.

GOULD, MARTHA BERNICE, retired librarian; b. Claremont, N.H., Oct. 8, 1931; d. Sigmund and Gertrude Heller; m. Arthur Gould, July 29, 1960; children: Leslie, Stephen. BA in Edn., U. Mich., 1953; MS in Library Sci., Simmons Coll., 1956; cert., U. Denver Library Sch. Community Analysis Research Inst., 1978. Childrens librarian N.Y. Pub. Libr., 1956-58; adminstr. library services act demonstration regional library project Pawhuska, Okla., 1958-59; cons. N.Mex. State Libr., 1959-60; childrens librarian then sr. childrens librarian Los Angeles Pub. Libr., 1960-72; acctg. dir. pub. srvices, reference librarian Nev. State Libr., 1972-74; pub. services librarian Washoe County (Nev.) Libr., 1974-79, asst. county librarian, 1979-84, county librarian, 1984-94; ret., 1994. Contbr. articles to jours. Treas. United Jewish Appeal, 1981; bd. dirs. Temple Sinai, Planned Parenthood of Nev.; trustee RSVP, North Nevadans for ERA; No. Nev. chmn. Gov.'s Conf. on Libr., 1990; mem. bd. Campaign for Choice, No. Nev. Food Bank, Nev. Women's Fund (Hall of Fame award 1989); mem. No. Nev. NCCJ, Washoe County Quality Life Task Force, 1992—; chair Sierra (Nev.) Cmty. Access TV; presdl. appointee Nat. Commn. on Libr. and Info. Sci., 1993-97; mem. adv. bd. Partnership Librs. Washoe County. Recipient Nev. State Libr. Letter of Commendation, 1973, Washoe County Bd. Commrs. Resolution of Appreciation, 1978, ACLU of Nev. Civil Libertarian of Yr. 1988, Freedom's Sake award AAUW, 1989, Leadership in Literacy award Sierra chpt. Internat. Reading Assn., 1992, Woman of Distinction award 1992, Nev. Libr. Assn. Libr. of Yr., 1993. Mem. ALA (bd. dirs., intellectual freedom roundtable 1977-79, intellectual freedom com. 1979-83, coun. 1983-86), ACLU (bd. dirs. Civil Libertarian of Yr. Nev. chpt. 1988, chair gov.'s conf. for women 1989), Nev. Libr. Assn. (chmn. pub. info. com. 1972-73, intellectual freedom com. 1975-78, govt. rels. com. 1978-79, v.p., pres.-elect 1980, pres. 1981, Spl. Citation 1978, 87, LIbr. of Yr. 1993).

GOULD, WILLIAM AWSWORTH, ecologist and musician; b. Mpls., Feb. 12, 1956; s. John Douglas and Mary Elvira (Ravlin) G. BS in Biology, U. Minn., 1989, MS in Plant Biology, 1992; postgrad., U. Colo., 1992—. Pres. Useless Records, Mpls., 1987-94; dir. Arctic Field Rsch. Program, Boulder, 1987-93; pres. Inst. for Advanced Field Edn., Boulder, 1994—; exploration leader Arctic Field Rsch. program, 1977—. Producer, composer: Early Useless, 1988, Human, 1989, Last Year, 1990, Invisible Audience, 1992. Office: U Colo CB 450 Boulder CO 80309

GOULDTHORPE, KENNETH ALFRED PERCIVAL, publisher, state official; b. London, Jan. 7, 1928; came to U.S., 1951, naturalized, 1956; s. Alfred Edward and Frances Elizabeth Finch (Callow) G.; m. Judith Marion Cutts, Aug. 9, 1975; children: Amanda Frances, Timothy Graham Cutts. Student U. Westminster (formerly Regent St. Poly.), 1948-49, Bloomsbury Tech. Inst., 1949-50; diploma City and Guilds of London, 1949; student, Washington U., 1951-52. Staff photographer St. Louis Post-Dispatch, 1951-55, picture editor, 1955-57; nat. and fgn. corr. Life mag., Time, Inc., N.Y.C., 1957-65, regional editor Australia-New Zealand, 1966-68, editorial dir. Latin Am., 1969-70; editor Signature mag., N.Y.C., 1970-73; mng. editor Penthouse mag., N.Y.C., 1973-76, pub. cons., 1976-79; editor, exec. pub. Adventure Travel mag., Seattle, 1979-80; sr. ptnr. Pacific Pub. Assocs., Seattle, 1981-83; editor, pub. Washington mag., 1984-89; vice chmn. Evergreen Pub. Co., 1984-89; dir. tourism, State of Wash., 1989-91; pub./cons., writer, 1991—; dir. Grand Fir Pub. Corp., 1994—; tchr. design, editorial techniques Parsons Sch. Design, N.Y.C.; lectr., contbr. elementary schs. lit. progs. Served with Royal Navy, 1946-48. Decorated Naval Medal and bar; recipient awards of excellence Nat. Press Photographers Assn., AP and UP, 1951-57, Pres.' medal Ea. Wash. U., 1986; certs. excellence, Am. Inst. Graphic Arts, 1971, 72, 73, Communication Arts, 1980, 81, 84; spl. award, N.Y. Soc. Publs. Designers, 1980. Mem. Regional Pubs. Assn. (v.p., pres., Best Typography award 1985, Best Spl. Issue 1989), Western Publs. Assn. (Best Consumer Mag. award, Best Travel Mag. awards, 1980, Best Regional and State Mag. award 1985, 86, 88, Best New Publ. award 1985, Best Column award 1985, Best Signed Essay 1986, 87, Best Four-Color Layout 1985, Best Four Color Feature Design), City and Regional Mag. Assn. (William Allen White Bronze awards), Time/Life Alumni Soc., Sigma Delta Chi. Episcopalian. Nominated for Pulitzer Prize for coverage of Andrea Doria disaster, 1956; contbr. articles, photographs to nat. mags., books by Life mag. Home: 3049 NW Esplanade Seattle WA 98117-2624

GOULET, WILLIAM DAWSON, marketing professional; b. Hartford, Conn., Sept. 24, 1941; s. Henry J.K. and Elizabeth Bryne (Dawson) G. BA in English, Marietta Coll., 1963. Field service rep. Conn. Gen. Life Ins. Co., Hartford, 1963-65; sales promotion assoc. Phoenix Mut. Life Ins. Co., Hartford, 1965-69; dir. sales promotion Pacific Nat. Life Ins. Co., San Francisco, 1969-70; v.p. sales and mktg. E.F. Hutton Life Ins. Co., San Francisco, 1970-79; sr. v.p., fin. planning Prudential-Bache, San Francisco, 1979; v.p. GUMP's, San Francisco, 1980-91, mem. exec. com., 1981-91, mktg. cons., 1991-; pres. Campton Advt. Agy., 1980-91; dean ins. faculty Life Ins. Industry Sch., Williamsburg, Va., 1974; mktg. cons. U. of the Pacific, Stockton, Calif., 1972-80. Bd. dirs. Mus. Soc. San Francisco, 1984-90, Friends of Recreation and Parks, 1980—, v.p. bd. dirs. 1986; mem. adv. bd. The McLean Home, Simsbury, Conn., 1985; mem. hon. bd. govs. The World Corp. Games, San Francisco, 1988; trustee Performing Arts Libr. and Mus., 1990, v.p. bd. 1991, pres. bd. 1992—, Asian Art Mus. Found., 1992-94. Sgt. USAR, 1963-69. Recipient Lawrence award Life Advertisers Assn., Vancouver, B.C., Can., 1979, Disting. Alumni Lectr. award Marietta Coll., 1985. Mem. San Francisco Grand Prix Assn. (adv. bd. 1986), Western Retail Mktg. Assn. (bd. dirs. 1989). Democrat. Roman Catholic. Home and Office: PO Box 155 Ross CA 94957-0155

GOVAN, GLADYS VERNITA MOSLEY, retired critical care and medical surgical nurse; b. Tyler, Tex., July 24, 1918; d. Stacy Thomas and Lucy Victoria (Whitmill) Mosley; m. Osby David Govan, July 20, 1938; children Orbrenett K. (Govan) Carter, Diana Lynn (Govan) Mosley. Student, East Los Angeles Coll., Montebello, Calif., 1951; lic. vocat. nurse, Calif. Hosp. Med. Ctr., L.A., 1953; cert., Western States IV Assn., L.A., 1978. Lic. vocat. nurse, Calif.; cert. in EKG. Intravenous therapist Calif. Hosp. Med. Ctr., cardiac monitor, nurse; ret. Past pres. PTA, also hon. mem., 1963—; charter mem. Nat. Rep. Presdl. Task Force; active L.A. World Affairs Coun., 1992, 93.

GOWDY, MIRIAM BETTS, nutritionist; b. Nelsonville, Ohio, Jan. 9, 1928; d. Charles Donald and Lillian Mary (Linscott) B.; m. Robert Averill Gowdy, Oct. 12, 1950 (div. 1977); children: Carol Jo, Robert Jr., Bruce. BA in Home Econs., Ohio Wesleyan U., 1949; student, Duke U., 1949-50, Calif. State U., L.A., 1975-76. Registered dietitian. Dietitian L.A., 1977-91; cons. Nat.-in-Home Health, Van Nuys, Calif., 1984-87; clin. dietitian Lake Mead Hosp., 1991-94; pvt. practice cons. nutritionist Las Vegas, Nev., 1994—. Mem. Am. Diabetes Assn. (cons. San Fernando Valley Unit 1976-80, bd. dirs. N.W. chpt. 1977-82), So. Nev. Dietetic Assn. (mem. chmn. 1991-92, pres. 1993-94), Cons. Nutritionists (chmn.-elect So. Calif. chpt. 1979-81), Calif. Dietetic Assn. (chmn. diabetes care practice 1979-81), Am. Heart Assn. (mem. gov. bd. N.W. chpt. 1988-89), Sierra Club, Nat. Audubon Soc. Republican. Methodist. Home and Office: 9713 White Cloud Dr Las Vegas NV 89134-7840 Office: 9713 White Cloud Dr Las Vegas NV 89134-7840

GOZANI, TSAHI, nuclear physicist; b. Tel Aviv, Nov. 25, 1934; came to U.S., 1965; s. Arieh and Rivcca (Meiri) G.; m. Adit Soffer, Oct. 14, 1958; children: Mor, Shai Nachum, Or Pinchas, Tal. BSc, Technion-IIT, Haifa, Israel, 1956, MSc, 1958; DSc, Swiss Fed. Inst. Tech. (ETH), Zurich, Switzerland, 1962. Registered profl. nuclear engr., Calif.; accredited nuclear material mgr. Rsch. physicist Israel Atomic Energy Commn., Beer-Sheva, 1962-65; rsch. assoc. nuclear engring. dept. Rensselaer Poly. Inst., Troy, N.Y., 1965-66; sr. staff scientist General-Atomic & IRT, San Diego, 1966-70, 71-75; prof. applied physics Tel Aviv U., 1971; chief scientist, div. mgr. Sci. Applications Internat. Corp., Palo Alto and Sunnyvale, Calif., 1975-84; v.p., chief scientist Sci. Applications Internat. Corp., Sunnyvale, 1984-87; corp. v.p. Sci. Applications Internat. Corp., Santa Clara, Calif., 1987-93, sr. v.p., 1993—; Lady Davis vis. prof. Technion-Israel Inst. Tech., 1983-84; bd. dirs. Radiation Sci. Inst., San Jose State U. Author: Active Non-Destructive Assay of Nuclear Materials, 1981; co-author: Handbook of Nuclear Safeguards Measurement Methods, 1983; contbr. over 150 articles to profl. jours. Recipient 1989 Laurel award Aviation Week Jour., R&D 100 awd, 1988, Most Innovative New Products, nominee for the Safe Skies award Conway Data Inc., 1991, 92, 93. Fellow Am. Nuclear Soc.; mem. Am. Phys. Soc., Inst. Nuclear Materials. Office: Sci Applications Internat Corp 2950 Patrick Henry Dr Santa Clara CA 95054-1813

GRABARZ, DONALD FRANCIS, pharmacist; b. Jersey City, Sept. 18, 1941; s. Joseph and Frances (Zotynia) G.; m. Joan Isoldi, Aug. 13, 1966; children: Christine, Robert, Danielle. BPharm, St. Johns U., N.Y.C., 1964. Lic. pharmacist, N.Y., Vt. Dir. qualtiy control and assurance Johnson and Johnson Co., New Brunswick, N.J., 1965-72; dir. quality assurance and regulatory affairs Bard Parker div. Becton Dickinson, Franklin Lakes, N.J., 1972-76; asst. corp. dir. regulatory affairs Becton Dickinson, 1976-80; corp. dir. regulatory affairs C.R. Bard Inc., Murray Hill, N.J., 1980-85; v.p. regulatory affairs, qualtiy assurance Symbion Inc., Salt Lake City, 1985-86; cons., pres. DFG & Assocs., Inc., Salt Lake City, 1986—; mng. dir. Internat. Regulatory Consultants, L.C., Salt Lake City, Boston, also U.K., 1987—;

lectr. Inst. for Applied Tech., Inst. Internat. Rsch., Ernest & Young, Salt Lake C. C.; adj. prof. Salt Lake City C.C., 1993—. Co-author, technical advisor, editor Inspection and Recall Film; co-author: Science, Technology, and Regulation in a Competetive Environment, 1990; contbr. articles to profl. jours. Bd. dirs. v.p., asst. treas. Am. Lung Assn., N.J., 1972-75; chmn. Drug Edn., DuPage County, Ill., 1968. Mem. Health Industry Mfg. Assn. (chmn. Legal and Regulatory commn. 1983), Regulatory Affairs Profl. Soc. (lectr.), Am. Soc. Quality Control, Am. Mfr. Med. Instrumentation Assn., Am. Pharm. Assn., Food and Drug Law Inst., Cottonwood Country Club (bd. dirs., treas. 1995—). Office: DFG & Assocs PO Box 17801 Salt Lake City UT 84117-0801

GRABER, SUSAN P., judge; b. Oklahoma City, July 5, 1949; d. Julius A. and Bertha (Fenyves) G.; m. William June, May 3, 1981; 1 child, Rachel June-Graber. BA, Wellesley Coll., 1969; JD, Yale U., 1972. Bar: N.Mex. 1972, Ohio 1977, Oreg. 1978. Asst. atty. gen. Bur. of Revenue, Santa Fe, 1972-74; assoc. Jones Gallegos Snead & Wertheim, Santa Fe, 1974-75, Taft Stettinius & Hollister, Cin., 1975-78; assoc., then ptnr. Stoel Rives Boley Jones & Grey, Portland, Oreg., 1978-88; judge, then presiding judge Oreg. Ct. Appeals, Salem, 1988-90; assoc. justice Oreg. Supreme Ct., Salem, 1990—. Mem. Gov.'s Adv. Coun. on Legal Svcs., 1979-88; bd. dirs. U.S. Dist. Ct. of Oreg. Hist. Soc., 1985—, Oreg. Law Found., 1990-91; mem. bd. visitors Sch. Law, U. Oreg., 1986-93. Mem. Oreg. State Bar (jud. adminstrn. com. 1985-87, pro bono com. 1988-90), Ninth Cir. Jud. Conf. (chair exec. com. 1987-88), Oreg. Jud. Conf. (edn. com. 1988-91, program chair 1990), Oreg. Appellate Judges Assn. (sec.-treas. 1990-91, vice chair 1991-92, chair 1992-93), Am. Inns of Ct. (master), Phi Beta Kappa. Office: Oreg Supreme Ct 1163 State St Salem OR 97310-1331

GRABOWSKI, DIANE MARIETTA, registered dietitian, nutrition educator; b. Detroit, May 5, 1959; d. W. George and Maryanne (Studnicki) G.; m. Gary A.W. Nepa, Sept. 9, 1994. AA, U. Ctrl. Fla., 1978; BS, Clemson (S.C.) U., 1981, MS, 1983. Nutrition educator, cons. Pritikin Longevity Ctr., Santa Monica, Calif., 1983-87, 90—; adminstr./asst. food svc. dept. The Westin Hotel, Denver, 1987-90. Author: The L.A. Diet, 1986. Mem. Humane Soc. Am. J.H. Mitchell scholar, 1981. Mem. Am. Dietetic Assn. Republican. Roman Catholic. Office: Pritikin Longevity Ctr 1910 Ocean Front Walk Santa Monica CA 90405-1014

GRACE, JOHN WILLIAM, electrical company executive; b. Swissville, Pa., May 29, 1921; s. Joseph and Ruth Margaret (Bailey) G.; student Am. TV Inst. Tech., 1950; BEE, Drexel U., 1960; m. Ruth Delores Schroeder, Nov. 25, 1950; children: Martha, Joan, Nancy, John William. Technician missiles and surface radar div. RCA, Moorestown, N.J., 1950-56, design engr., 1956-60, project engr., 1960-66; mgr. engring. and sci. exec. EG & G, Inc., Las Vegas, Nev., 1966-73, mgr. bus. devel. operational test and evaluation, Albuquerque, 1973-77; engring. mgr. Instrumentation div., Idaho Falls, Idaho, 1977-79, mgr. systems project office, 1979, mgr. instrumentation program office, 1979-82, mgr. engring. spl. products div., 1982-84, mgr. tech. resources, 1984-91, retired 1991. Active Boy Scouts Am., 1969-71. Served with USNR, 1941-45. Mem. IEEE, Instrument Soc. Am. (dir. sci. instrumentation and research div.), Assn. Old Crows, Am. Legion (post adj. vice comdr. 1950). Episcopalian (pres. couples retreat 1969-70). Patentee contradirectional waveguide coupler. Home: 8311 Loma Del Norte Dr NE Albuquerque NM 87109-4901 Office: EG&G Spl Projects Divsn 821 Grier Dr PO Box 93747 Las Vegas NV 89193-3474

GRACE, KAY SPRINKEL, management consultant; d. Robert Lee and Marian (Boyles) S.; children: Michael, Andrew, Greg. BA in Comms.-Journalism, Stanford U., MA in Edn. Dir. grad. ann. giving, dir. spl. gifts Santa Clara U.; fund devel. dir. The Children's Health Coun., Palo Alto, Calif.; orgnl. cons. San Francisco, 1987—; cons. clients include Philharmonia Baroque Orchestra, Grace Cathedral, Calif. Hist. Soc., The Children's Health Coun., San Francisco Food Bank, Djerassi Resident Artists Program, and numerous others; core faculty mem. The Fund Raising Sch., Ind. U.; panelist/speaker numerous orgns. including Nat. Soc. Fund Raising Execs., Assn. Hosp. Philanthropy, Devel. Execs. Roundtable, others; presenter confs. in field. Author publs. in field. Fund-raising vol. Stanford U., nat. chair Ann. Fund. Recipient Gold Spike award, Stanford U., 1979, Outstanding Achievement award, Stanford Assocs., 1989, numerous others.

GRACE, WILLIAM PERSHING, petroleum geologist, real estate developer; b. Mineral Point, Mo., Sept. 19, 1920; s. William Francis and Bertha Luciel (Nephew) G.; m. Jeannette Marie Grace, March 28, 1942 (dec.); children: Joyce Medaris, Pamela Grace, Sonia Scott, Patricia Lawser. Student, Corpus Christi U., 1946-47; B in Geology, Tex. Tech. U., 1947-50; student (GRI), U. Colo. Extension, 1968-69. Capt. USAF, 1940-46; regional geologist Anderson-Prichard Oil Corp., San Antonio, Tex., 1950-62; real estate broker Grace Reality, Aurora, Colo., 1963-66; pres. Kimberley Homes, Construction, Aurora, 1966-72; pres., broker Grace-Scott-Cooper Corp., Aurora, 1972—. pres. Friends of the Aurora Pub. Library, 1967, trustee mem. 1978; chmn. Adams County Rep. Party, 1970-72; mem. vocat. edn. coun. Sch. Dist. 285, 1989—. Named Colorado of Yr. Colo. State Libr. Assn., 1988. Mem. Am. Assn. Petroleum Geologists (del. House of Dels. 1961-62), Nat. Assn. Realtors, Rocky Mountain Assn. Petroleum Geologists, Colo. Assn. Realtors, Colo. State Friends and Trustee Assn., Denver Petroleum Club, Aurora Bd. Realtors (treas. 1979, Realtor of Yr. 1980), Aurora C. of C. (dir. 1966-68, Man of Yr. 1980), Aurora Kiwanis (internat. del. in Nice, France, 1993, lt. gov. Rocky Mountain divsn. 1992, sec. 1965, pres. 1972), Sixty Five Roses Found., Sigma Gamma Epsilon. Lutheran. Home: 2797 S Xanadu Way Aurora CO 80014

GRAD, LAURIE BURROWS, food editor; b. L.A., June 17, 1944; d. Abe and Ruth (Levinson) Burrows; m. Peter N. Grad, Feb. 11, 1968; 1 child, Nicholas Newfield. BA, U. Pa., 1966. Fashion model N.Y.C., 1965-67, food writer, 1973--; food editor L.A. Mag., 1977--; TV chef Hour Mag., L.A., 1980-87. Author: Dining in Los Angeles, 1979, Make it Easy in the Kitchen, 1982, Make it Easy Entertaining, 1984 (Tastemaker award 1985), Make it Easy, Make it Light, 1987. Mem. Mem. Am. Inst. Wine and Food, Internat. Assn. Cooking Profls., Alzheimer's Disease and Related Disorders Assn. (hon. bd. dirs.). Home: 1250 Beverly Green Dr Los Angeles CA 90035-1017

GRADDY, ELIZABETH ANN, economics educator; b. Harrisburg, Ark., Sept. 25, 1950; d. Henry T. and Catherine E. (Burrow) G.; m. Glen A. Reed; children: Acacia, Alexandra. BA with highest honors, Memphis State U., 1974; PhD, Carnegie-Mellon U., Pitts., 1984. Asst. prof. U. So. Calif., L.A., 1984-90, assoc. prof., 1990—; vice dean Sch. Pub. Adminstrn. U. So. Calif., 1994—. Contbr. articles to profl. jours. HEW doctoral fellow, 1980-84. Mem. Am. Econ. Assn., Assn. Pub. Policy Analysis and Mgmt., Econometric Soc., Inst. Mgmt. Sci., Western Econ. Assn., Sigma Xi. Office: U So Calif Von Kleinsmid Ctr Los Angeles CA 90089

GRADY, DOLORES ANNE, academic administrator, educator, consultant; b. Wiesbaden, Germany, Apr. 24, 1958. BA, U. No. Colo., Greeley, 1980, MA, 1983; PhD, LaSalle U., L.A., 1994. Cert. tchr., 1987. Instr. Denver Tech. Coll., 1987, Adelphi Bus. Coll., 1984-87; assoc. prof. Colo. Tech. Coll., 1994; project mgr. Advanced Skills Edn. Program/Basic Skills Edn. Program Pikes Peak C.C., Ft. Carson, Colo., 1991-93; tng. mgr. Matrix Mktg., Colo., 1993—; adj. prof. Chapman U., Colorado Springs, Colo., 1991—; tng. mgr. Matrixx Mktg., 1993—. Bd. dirs. Pikes Peak Mental Health Action League, Jr. League Colorado Springs. Mem. Am. Soc. Tng. and Devel. Home: 2111 Lockhaven Dr Colorado Springs CO 80909-2037

GRADY, JEFFREY O., system engineering consultant; b. Old Town, Maine, Apr. 12, 1934; s. Robert Fulton and Ava (Johnson) G.; m. Jane Ellis, Apr. 23, 1960; children: Kimberly C., Jeffrey Rex, Patrick O. BA in math., San Diego State U., 1981; MS in system mgmt., U. Southern Calif., 1986. Customer training instr. Librascope, Glendale, Calif., 1964-65; engr. Teledyne Ryan Aeronautical, San Diego, 1965-82; engr. convair div. Gen Dynamics, San Diego, 1982-84, system devel. mgr. space systems div., 1984-92, projects systems engring., 1992-93; prin. Jeffrey O. Grady System Engring., San Diego, 1993—. Author: System Requirements Analysis, 1993, System Integration, 1994, System Engineering Planning and Enterprise Identity, 1995; editor Jour. of Nat. Coun. on Sys. Engring., 1994—. Mem. Nat. Coun. on Systems Engring. (sec. 1992, founding mem.), Soc. Concurrent Engring., AIAA.

GRAEBEL, WILLIAM PAUL, engineering educator; b. Manitowoc, Wis., July 15, 1932; s. Adolph Fred and Erna Violet (Huhn) G.; m. June Erna Ness, June 12, 1954; children: Jeffrey Paul, Susan Kay. B.S., U. Wis.-Madison, 1954, M.S., 1955; Ph.D., U. Mich., 1959. Registered profl. engr., Nev. Mem. tech. staff Bell Telephone Labs., Whippany, N.J., 1955-56; instr. engring. U. Mich., 1956-59, asst. prof., 1959-62, asso. prof., 1962-67, prof., 1967-91, prof. emeritus, 1991—; design specialist Douglas Aircraft Co., Santa Monica, Calif., 1962; summer visitor Nat. Ctr. Atmospheric Rsch., Boulder, Colo., 1963; rsch. collaborator Centre d'Etudes Nucleaires de Grenoble, France, 1979; rsch. scientist Netherlands Ophthalmic Rsch. Inst., Amsterdam, 1979; sr. design analyst Westinghouse Marine Div., 1981; vis. prof. Stanford (Calif.) U., 1987; mem. summer faculty Sandia Nat. Labs., Albuquerque, 1989; adj. prof. U. Nev. Las Vegas, 1991—; pres. Nev. Engring. R&D Systems, 1993—; cons. in field. Contbr. numerous articles to profl. jours. Fellow AIAA (assoc.); mem. ASME, Sigma Xi. Unitarian. Home: 6452 Viewpoint Dr Las Vegas NV 89115-7052

GRAF, BOB LEE, secondary education educator; b. Hayes, Kans., Jan. 12, 1949; s. Gilbert Joseph and Elizabeth (Windholtz) G.; m. Suzie Elise Allen, Aug. 16, 1980; children: David Lee, Timothy Allen. BA, U. No. Colo., Greeley, 1971; MA, Adams State Coll., Alamosa, Colo., 1981. Cert. tchr., Colo. Tchr., coach St. Philomena Sch., Denver, 1972-74, Ctrl. Cath. H.S., Denver, 1974-76, Summit County H.S., Frisco, Colo., 1976-80; cross country/track coach Adams State Coll., Alamosa, 1980-81; dir. Blue Mountain Rural Youth Camps, Florissant, Colo., 1981—; activities dir., tchr., coach Wasson H.S., Colorado Springs, Colo., 1982—; speaker and presenter in field. Contbr. articles to Colo. Coach. Caucus chmn. Dem. Party, Lake George, Colo., 1986-88; bd. dirs. Summit County Hist. Soc., Frisco, 1978-80; fire warden Teller County Fire Dept., Florissant, 1986-88; mem. Teller County Search and Rescue, Woodland Park, Colo., 1983-86; res. dept. sheriff Park County, 1990—. Mem. NEA, U.S. Track and Field Ofcls. (master; internat. track ofcl. 1981, Olympic ofcl.), Colo. Edn. Assn., U.S. Track Coaches Assn., Am. Camping Assn., Colorado Springs Edn. Assn., Colo. H.S. Coaches Assn. (bd. dirs. 1991—), Colo. H.S. Track Coaches Assn. (exec. sec. 1991—), Colo. Track and Field Ofcls. Assn. (pres. 1988-90), Phi Delta Kappa. Home: PO Box 146 11227 Park County Rd 98 Florissant CO 80816 Office: Wasson HS 2115 Afton Way Colorado Springs CO 80909-1921

GRAF, ERVIN DONALD, municipal administrator; b. Crow Rock, Mont., Mar. 9, 1930; s. Emanuel and Lydia (Bitz) G.; m. Carolyn Sue Robinson, Mar. 15, 1956 (div. 1958); m. Eleanor Mahlein, Apr. 13, 1959 (dec. Oct. 1990); children: Debra, Belinda, Corrina, Melanie (dec.), Ervin Jr. Enlisted U.S. Army, 1948; served two tours of duty in Vietnam; ret. U.S. Army, 1972; with office and maintenance staff Greenfields Irrigation Dist., Fairfield, Mont., 1972-77, sec. to Bd. Commrs., 1977-95; ret., 1995. Decorated Bronze star with oak leaf cluster. Mem. Am. Legion (all offices Post #80 and Dist. 8 incl. dist. comdr.). Democrat. Lutheran. Home: 211 6th St N Fairfield MT 59436-0565 Office: Greenfields Irrigation Dist Central Ave W Fairfield MT 59436

GRAF, GARY LYNN, career officer; b. Tucson, Ariz., May 4, 1952; s. Milton Frank and Margret Francis (Prausa) G.; m. Jane Elizabeth Bentley, July 25, 1987. BS, U.S. Naval Acad., 1974. Commd. ensign USN, Annapolis, Md., 1970; advanced through grades to comdr. USN, 1989; div. officer USS Flasher USN, Mare Island, San Diego, Calif., 1975-79; leading engring. officer, Nuclear Prototype Tng. Unit USN, Idaho Falls, Idaho, 1979-81; ops. officer USS Pollack USN, San Diego, 1982-85, ASW officer Carrier Group Seven, 1985-87; exec. officer USS Mariano G. Vallejo USN, Charleston, S.C., 1987-89; chief staff officer Submarine Squadron Seven USN, Pearl Harbor, Hawaii, 1990-91; commdg. officer USS Pintado USN, 1992—. Decorated 3 Navy Commendation medals, Navy Achievement medal. Home: 92-127 Leipapa Way Kapolei HI 96707-1343 Office: USS Pintado SSN672 FPO AP 96675-2352

GRAF, HANS, conductor; b. Austria, Feb. 15, 1949. Studied with Franco Ferrera and Arvid Jonsons. Music dir. Orch. Symphonica De Eurskadi, San Sebastian, Spain. Conductor: Royal Liverpool Philharmonic, Santa Ceclia Orch., Leningrad Philharmonic, Cologne and Rai Milano. Office: Calgary Philharmonic Orchestra, 205 8th Ave SE, Calgary, AB Canada T2G 0K9

GRAF, JOSEPH CHARLES, retired foundation executive; b. Jersey City, Sept. 10, 1928; s. John Bernard and Josephine C. (Stanley) G.; stepmother Margaret C. (Toomey) G.; m. Joleen Schovee; children: Claire Graf Ludwig, Joseph Charles, Michelle Graf Allison, Mary Ellen, Thomas S., Richard J., stepchildren: Thomas R. Schovee, Stephen W. Schovee, Kathryn L. Schovee. BS, Seton Hall U., 1949; MBA, U. Pa., 1954. Trainee, Prudential Ins. Co., Newark, 1954-55, systems analyst, 1955-56, asst. research analyst, 1956-58, research analyst, 1958-61, investment analyst, 1961-63, sr. investment analyst, 1963-64, Houston, 1964-67; v.p. So. Nat. Bank, Houston, 1967-69; fin. adv. Quintana Petroleum Corp., Houston, 1969-79, investment mgr., 1979-84; dir. Alamo Group Inc., Legacy Trust Co., Triten Corp., 1969-88; mem. investment com. trust dept. Cullen Bank & Trust, 1974-92; cons. research com. Houston C. of C., 1966-71; exec. sec. Cullen Found., 1974-93; ret., 1993. Bd. govs., v.p. Center for Retarded, Inc., Houston, 1978-86, trustee, 1982-87; bd. dirs. Alley Theatre, 1981-83; dir. Wharton Club (Houston), 1983-93. Served with AUS, 1951-53. Mem. Houston Fin. Analysts (pres. 1973-74, dir. 1974-77), Country Club Castle Pines (Colo.). Home: 3119 Ramshorn Dr Castle Rock CO 80104-9073

GRAFE, WARREN BLAIR, cable television executive; b. N.Y.C., June 22, 1954; s. Warren Edward and Maree Lee (Ahn) G.; m. Pamela Arden Rearick, Mar. 8, 1980 (div. Nov. 1982). Student Kendall Coll., 1974-75, U. Wis.-Platteville, 1975-76; BA, Ind. U., 1979. Sales rep., Sta. WGTC-FM, Bloomington, Ind., 1979-84, account exec., coop. coord., 1980-84; nat. sales rep. Stas. WTTS-WGTC, Bloomington, 1984; sales rep. Sta. KLFF-KMZK, Phoenix, 1985; account exec. Rita Sanders Advt. and Pub. Rels. Agy., Tempe, Ariz., 1985, Am. Cable TV, Phoenix, 1985-86, Dimension Media Svcs., Phoenix, 1986-89, Greater Phoenix Interconnect, 1989-95, CABLERep/Phoenix, 1995—. Recipient Nat. Sales 1st award, Cable TV Advt. Bur., 1986, 2d award, 1987, 3d award, 1991, 4th award, 1994; named one of Cable's Best Top Ten Cable Advt. Sales Reps. in Country, Cable Avails, 1995. Mem. Tempe C. of C. (ambassador 1986), Chandler (Ariz.) C. of C., Mesa (Ariz.) C. of C. Office: CABLERep/Phoenix 2020 N Central Ave #400 Phoenix AZ 85004

GRAFF, NORMAN IRWIN, psychiatrist; b. Chgo., Aug. 26, 1921; s. Morris David and Mollie (Ginsberg) G.; m. Phyllis Lenore Firestone, Aug. 14, 1946; children: Marc David, Wendy Lynne, Steven Martin, Douglas B. B of Edn., Chgo. Tchrs. Coll., 1942; BS, U. Chgo., 1949, MD, 1949. Intern USPHS, San Francisco, 1949-50; resident VA Hosp., Topeka, 1950-53; sr. asst. surgeon MEd. Ctr. Fed. Prisoners, Springfield, Mo., 1953-55; psychiatrist pvt. practice, San Mateo, Calif., 1955—; staff psychiatrist VA Hosp., Menlo Park, Calif., 1990-94; clin. assoc. prof. emeritus Stanford (Calif.) U., 1960—. Mem. San Mateo Mental Health Bd. With U.S. Army, 1942-46, USPHS, 1950-55. Fellow Am. Psychiat. Assn. (life); mem. No. Calif. Psychiat. Assn. (pres. 1965). Home: 250 Sierra Dr Hillsborough CA 94010-6935

GRAFFIS, JULIE ANNE, interior designer, entrepreneur; b. Houston, Jan. 4, 1960; d. Robert B. and Dorothy Gean (Weempe) Hyde; m. William B. Graffis, May 29, 1988; 1 child, Aaron James Hehr. Student, U. St. Thomas, Houston, 1977, Portland C.C., The Dalles, Oreg., 1984-85; AA, North Seattle C.C., 1987. Cert. window fashions profl. assoc., specialist, master Window Fashions Cert. Program. Co-owner Mosier (Oreg.) Shell Svc., 1981-85; quality control mgr. Town & Country Jeep-Eagle, Seattle, 1986-87; cons. Giovi Ford-Mercury, Pullman, Wash., 1988-89; prin., CEO, Interiors by JAG, Vancouver, Wash., 1990—; mem. Allied Bd. of Trade; cons. Habitat for Humanity, Vancouver, 1992—; lectr., presenter interior design workshops. Bus. ptnr. Hough Elem. Found. and Sch.; patron Pilchuck Glass Sch. Mem. NAFE, BBB, Wondow Fashions Edn. and Design Resource Network, Greater Vancouver C. of C. (liaison bus. and edn. partnership 1992—, amb. 1993-95), Inst. Managerial and Profl. Women. Office: Interiors by JAG 1605 F St Vancouver WA 98663-3445

GRAFFT, WILLIAM DAVIS, retired school system administrator; b. Ventura, Calif., Dec. 9, 1929; s. Clark Francis and Aileen (Willard) G.; m. Marilyn Eloise Church, June 16, 1951; children: Katherine, Paul. AB, U. Calif., Berkeley, 1951, MA, 1959, EdD, 1966. Cert. tchr. and adminstr., Calif. Tchr. pub schs., Oakland, Calif., 1951-52, 55-60, prin., 1960-64; prin. Maxwell Park Sch., Oakland, 1964-65, Ralph J. Bunche Sch., Oakland, 1965-68, Glorietta Sch., Orinda, Calif., 1968-70; asst. supt. Orinda Union Sch. Dist., 1970-78; supr. Mountain View (Calif.) Sch. Dist., 1978-92; chmn. Santa Clara Supts., Santa Clara County, Calif., 1989-91; bd. dirs. Whitney Edn. Found., Los Altos, Calif., 1983-87; speaker, presenter in field. Contbr. articles to profl. jours. Pres., bd. dirs. Life's Garden Sr. Housing, Sunnyvale, Calif., 1985-89; bd. dirs. United Way, Mountain View, 1986-89, YMCA, Mountain View, 1983-87; mem. support com. NASA/Ames Mountain View Space Ctr., 1988-92; sponsor Scaife Scholarship Found.; ednl. activities dir. Friends of Ctr. Performing Arts. Lt. comdr. USNR, 1952-55, Pacific. Recipient Outstanding Adminstr. award Women Leaders in Edn., 1992, Red Triangle award YMCA, 1992, commendation Santa Clara County Suprs., 1992, commendation Calif. Legislature, 1992; Spl. honoree Boy Scouts Am., 1992. Mem. NEA, Individualized Instrn. Assn. (pres. 1978), Assn. Calif. Sch. Adminstrs. (Supt. of Yr. 1992). Democrat. Presbyterian. Home: 313 Lester Ct Santa Clara CA 95051-6543

GRAFTON, FREDERICK WELLINGTON, artist; b. Middletown, Conn., May 3, 1952; s. Frederick Meeker and Catherine (Simmons) G. BFA with honors, Calif. Coll. Arts and Crafts, Oakland, 1976. watercolor instr. Assoc. Students U. Calif., Berkeley. Represented in permanent collections at Met. Mus. Art, Chase Manhattan Bank, N.Y., Art Inst. Chgo., Arco Ctr. Visual Art, L.A., Bank Am., San Francisco, Meridian Bldg., San Francisco; one-man shows include Grapestake Gallery, San Francisco, 1980, 83, Galleria Del Cavallino, Venice, Italy, 1981, San Jose (Calif.) Mus. Art, 1982; group shows include Bay Area Works on Paper, Seoul and San Francisco Exch., USIS Gallery, South Korea, 1983, Dealers Choice, San Francisco and L.A. Recipient Watercolor award Calif. State Expo, 1978. Mem. Emeryville Artists Coop. Home and Office: 1420 45th St # 30 Emeryville CA 94608-2906

GRAGER, STEVEN PAUL, financial planner; b. Everett, Wash., July 18, 1964; s. Clara A. Grager; m. Courtney A. Van Detta, June 27, 1987; 1 child, Emma D. BA in Mktg.magna cum laude, Seattle Pacific U., 1986; MBA in Fin., U. Chgo., 1991. CLU; ChFC; CFP; registered investment advisor. Fin. cons. H.D. Vest Fin. Svcs., Irving, Tex., 1987-91; mktg. dir. Mut. of N.Y., San Francsico, 1991-92; fin. planner Mut. of N.Y., Bellevue, Wash., 1992-94; regional v.p. Pacific Mut., Seattle, 1994—; investment advisor Steven P. Grager & Assocs., Seattle, 1992—. Co-chair Giving Something Back, Chgo., 1989-91; v.p. Toastmasters, Chgo., 1990-91. Arthur Andersen scholar Seattle Pacific U., 1984; Student Activities grantee U. Chgo., 1990. Mem. NALU, Am. Soc. CLU. Republican. Presbyterian. Home: 5720 17th Ave NE Seattle WA 98105-2510 Office: Pacific Mutual 700 Newport Center Dr Newport Beach CA 92660-6307

GRAHAM, CLYDE BENJAMIN, JR., physician; b. Hannibal, Mo., Jan. 15, 1931; s. Clyde Benjamin and Eileen (Legan) G.; m. Pearl Louise Relling, Sept. 7, 1956; 1 dau., Leslie Eileen. Student, Wash. State U., 1948-49; BA with highest honors, U. Ill., 1954; MD, U. Wash., 1958. Diplomate: Am. Bd. Radiology. Intern Children's Hosp. and Med. Ctr., Seattle, 1958-59; resident in radiology U. Wash. Affiliated Hosps., 1959-62; faculty radiology and pediatrics U. Wash. Sch. Medicine, Seattle, 1963—; prof. U. Wash. Sch. Medicine, 1974—; dir. pediatric radiology U. Wash. Hosp., 1964—; dir. radiology Children's Hosp. and Med. Ctr.; cons. pediatric radiology Madigan Gen. Hosp., others; vis. radiologist Pediatric Clinic, Karolinska Inst., Stockholm, 1964. Contbr. articles to profl. publs. Named to Hall of Fame Nat. Wheelchair Basketball Assn., 1979; James Picker Found. fellow, 1962-64; scholar, 1964-66. Fellow Am. Coll. Radiology, Am. Acad. Pediatrics; mem. Soc. Pediatric Radiology (past dir.), Am. Roentgen Ray Soc., Radiological Soc. N.Am., Pacific Coast Pediatric Radiologists Assn. (past pres.), Alpha Omega Alpha. Home: 5116 Kenilworth Pl NE Seattle WA 98105-2841 Office: Children's Hosp & Med Ctr PO Box 5371 Seattle WA 98105-0371

GRAHAM, DANIEL EDWARD, economic development executive; b. Kansas City, Mo., Jan. 2, 1947; s. William C. and Helen (Fidler) G.; m. Julia Gregory, Sept. 1987 (div. Feb. 1991); children: Matthew William and Douglas Edward (twins). BS in History, U. Ctrl. Ark., 1971. Cert. econ. developer; cert. econ. devel. fin. profl. Adminstrv. asst. Killeen (Tex.) Bd. Devel., 1975-80; econ. devel. cons. Tex. Econ. Devel. Commn., Austin, 1980-85; exec. dir. Marshall (Tex.)-Harrison County Industries, 1985-87, Hempstead County Econ. Devel. Corp., Hope, Ark., 1987; pres. San Marcos (Tex.) Econ. Devel. Corp., 1988-89; exec. dir. San Juan County Econ. Devel. Corp., Farmington, N.Mex., 1989-92; econ. devel. dir. City of Louisville, Colo., 1992; exec. dir. Otero County Econ. Devel. Corp., Alamogordo, N.Mex., 1993—; assoc. Glenn-James & Assocs., Grand Junction, Colo., 1991-93. Instr. ARC, Austin, Tex., 1980-85. Mem. Am. Econ. Devel.Coun., N.Mex. Indsl. Devel. Execs. Assn., Am. C. of C. Researchers Assn., Rotary (dir. 1991). Republican. Office: Otero County Econ Devel Coun Ste 4 1401 S White Sands Blvd Alamogordo NM 88310-7264

GRAHAM, DENIS DAVID, retired curriculum coordinator, marriage and family therapist, education counsultant; b. Santa Rosa, Calif., Oct. 21, 1941; s. Elbert Eldon and Mildred Bethana (Dyson) G.; m. Margaret Katherine Coughlan, Aug. 31, 1968; children: Kathleen Ann, Todd Cameron (dec.). BS in Edn., U. Nev., 1964, MEd, 1973, MA, 1982. Cert. for ednl. personnel; lic. marriage and family therapist, Nev.; nat. cert. counselor Nat. Bd. for Cert. Counselors. Tchr. vocat. bus. edn. Earl Wooster High Sch., Reno, 1964-66, chmn. dept. bus. edn., 1966-67; state supr. bus. and office edn. Nev. Dept. Edn., Carson City, 1967-70, adminstr. vocat. edn. field svcs., 1970-74, asst. dir., 1974-78, vocat. edn. cons., 1978-85; edn. curriculum specialist Washoe County Sch. Dist., Reno, 1985-89, curriculum coord., 1989-94; ret., 1994; pres. Midpoint Inc., 1994—. marriage and family counselor Severance & Assocs., Carson City, 1983-85, Mountain Psychiat. Assocs., 1985-87; mem. tng. and youth employment council S.W. Regional Lab. for Ednl. Research and Devel., Los Alamitos, Calif., 1982, mem. career edn. council, 1980-81. Editor Council of Chief State Sch. Officers' Report: Staffing the Nation's Schools: A National Emergency, 1984. Contbr. articles to profl. jours. bd. dirs. U. Nev.-Reno Campus Christian Assn., 1988-90; adv. com. Truckee Meadows Community Coll., Reno, 1988-94; mem. Gov.'s Crime Prevention Com., Carson City, 1979-83, Atty. Gen.'s Anti-Shoplifting Com., Carson City, 1974-78, Gov.'s Devel. Disabilities Planning Council, Carson City, 1977-79; bd. dirs. Jr. Achievement No. Nev., 1989-92, sec., mem. exec. com., 1990-91; bd. dir. Friends of the Coll. of Edn. U. Nev., Reno, 1995—. Recipient award for svc. Bus. Edn. Assn. of No. Nev., 1973, Svc. award YMCA, 1962, 63, Helping Hand award Procter R. Hug High Sch., 1993-94, Bill Trabert Meml. award Nev. Dept. Edn. and Nev. Vocat. Assn., 1994. Mem. Am. Vocat. Assn., Nat. Assn. Vocat. Edn. Spl. Needs Pers. (Outstanding Svc. award region V 1982), Assn. Suprs. & Curriculum Devel., Am. Assn. Marriage and Family Therapy, Am. Counseling Assn., Nev. Vocat. Assn. (Outstanding Svc. award 1991, Bill Trabert Meml. award Excellence in Occupational Edn. 1994), Internat. Assn. Marriage and Family Counselors, U. Nev. Reno Alumni Assn. (exec. com. 1971-75), Phi Delta Kappa, Phi Kappa Phi. Democrat. Methodist.

GRAHAM, JAMES HERBERT, dermatologist; b. Calexico, Calif., Apr. 25, 1921; s. August K. and Esther (Choudoin) G.; m. Anna Kathryn Luiken, June 30, 1950 (dec. May 1987); children: James Herbert, John A., Angela Joann; m. Gloria Boyd Flippin, July 29, 1989. Student, Brawley Jr. Coll., 1941-42; AB, Emory U., 1945; MD, Med. Coll. Ala., 1949. Diplomate: Am. Bd. Dermatology (dir. 1977-87, v.p. 1985-86, pres. 1986-87, Disting. Service medal 1987); diplomate in dermatopathology Am. Bd. Dermatology and Am. Bd. Pathology. Intern Jefferson-Hillman Hosp., Birmingham, Ala., 1949-50; resident in dermatology VA Center and UCLA Med. Center, 1953-56; clin. asst. instr. in medicine UCLA, 1954-56; Osborne fellow and NRC fellow in dermal pathology Armed Forces Inst. Pathology, Washington, 1956-58; vis. scientist Armed Forces Inst. Pathology, 1958-69, chmn. dept. dermatopathology, 1980-88; registrar Registry of Dermatopathology, Armed

Forces Inst. Pathology, 1980-88, also program dir. dermatopathology, 1979-88; program dir. dermatopathology Walter Reed Army Med. Center, Washington, 1979-88; asst. prof. dermatology and pathology Temple U., 1958-61, assoc. prof., 1961-65, prof. dermatology, 1965-69, assoc. prof. pathology, 1965-67, prof. pathology, 1967-69; prof. medicine, chief div. dermatology, prof. pathology, dir. sect. dermal pathology and histochemistry U. Calif., Irvine, 1969-78; chief dermatology U. Calif. Med. Ctr., Irvine, 1977-78; prof. emeritus Coll. Medicine, U. Calif., 1978—; head sect. dermatology Orange County (Calif.) Med. Center, 1969-73; cons. dermatology VA Hosp., Long Beach, Calif., 1969-73; chief dermatology sect. VA Hosp., 1973-78, acting chief med. service, 1976; cons. dermatology, dermal pathology Regional Naval Med. Center, San Diego, 1969-82, Long Beach, 1969-78, Camp Pendleton, Calif., 1972-78; cons. dermatology, dermal pathology Meml. Hosp. Med. Center, Long Beach, 1972-86, Fairview State Hosp., Costa Mesa, Calif., 1969-78; cons. for career devel. for rev. clin. investigator applications VA Central Office, Washington, 1973-78; Disting. Eminent physician VA physician and dentist-in-residence program, 1980-88; mem. organizational com. Am. Registry Pathology, Armed Forces Inst. Pathology, Washington, 1976-77; mem. exec. com. Am. Registry Pathology, Armed Forces Inst. Pathology, 1977-78; prof. dermatology, clin. prof. pathology Uniformed Services U. of Health Scis., Bethesda, Md., 1979-88, prof. emeritus, 1989—; program dir. dermatopathology Naval Hosp. and Scripps Clin. and Rsch. Found., San Diego, 1991-94; head divsn. dermatopathology, dept. pathology Scripps Clinic and Rsch. Found., LaJolla, Calif., 1994, ret., 1994. Sr. author: Dermal Pathology, 1972; contbr. articles to profl. publs. Served with M.C. USNR, 1949-53. Named Disting. Alumnus, Med. Coll. Ala., 1994. Mem. AMA and Accreditation Coun. for Grad. Med. Edn. (residency rev. subcom. for dermatopathology 1974-87, mem. residency rev. com. dermatology 1977-87, chmn. 1984-87, cert. of merit 1960), Soc. Investigative Dermatology, U.S. and Can. Acad. Pathology, Am. Soc. Investigative Pathology, Am. Dermatol. Assn. (essay award 1958, v.p. 1986-87), Am. Soc. Dermatopathology (pres. 1975-76, Founder's award 1990, rep. to bd. of mem. Am. Registry Pathology, 1988-92), Dermatopathology Club (pres. 1980-81), Assn. Mil. Dermatologists, Am. Acad. Dermatology (dir. 1974-77, 82, v.p. 1980-81, rep. to bd. mems. Am. Registry Pathology 1977-78), N.Am. Clin. Dermatologic Soc. (hon.), 1973, Pa. Acad. Dermatology, Pacific Dermatol. Assn. (dir. 1972-75, hon. mem. 1981), Dermatology Found., Leader's Soc., Washington Dermatol. Soc. (spl hon.), Phila. Dermatol. Soc. (pres. 1967-68, hon. mem. 1994), San Diego Dermatol. Soc., Cutaneous Therapy Soc., Alpha Omega Alpha. Club: Cosmos (Washington).

GRAHAM, JAN, state attorney general; b. Salt Lake City. BS in Psychology, Clark U., Worcester, Mass., 1973; MS in Psychology, U. Utah, 1977, JD, 1980. Bar: Utah. Ptnr. Jones, Waldo, Holbrook & McDonough, Salt Lake City, 1979-89; soliciter gen. Utah Atty. Gen.'s Office, Salt Lake City, 1989-93; atty. gen. State of Utah, 1993—; adj. prof. law U. Utah Law Sch.; bar commr. Utah State Bar, 1991; master of bench Utah Inns Ct. VII; mem. Utah Commn. on Justice in 21st Century; bd. dirs. Jones, Waldo, Holbrook & McDonough; bd. trustees Coll. Law U. Utah (pres.). Fin. devel. chair YWCA; chair Ctrl. Bus. Improvement Dist.; mem. Salt Lake City Olympic Bid Com. 1988 Games. Named Woman Lawyer Yr. Utah, 1987. Mem. Am. Arbitration Assn. (nat. panel arbitrators), Women Lawyers Utah (co-founder, mem. exec. com.). Office: 236 State Capitol Building Salt Lake City UT 84114-1202*

GRAHAM, LINDA MARIE, museum director, photographer; b. Worcester, Mass., Dec. 16, 1947; d. Henry William Russell and Rose Marie (Magnan) Ohlson; m. Douglas John Merton Graham, Feb. 14, 1984; 1 child, Isis Marina. Freelance photographer, 1969—; co-dir. The Turner Mus., Denver, 1981—, trustee, 1983—. Exhibited in group shows, New East End Gallery, Provincetown, Mass., 1989, Foothills Art Ctr., Golden, Colo., 1990, Photo Mirage Gallery, Denver, 1990, Alternative Arts Alliance, Denver, 1990. Chair music performabce Jr. Symphony Guild, Denver, 1992-93. Mem. Unity Ch. Home and Office: The Turner Mus 773 Downing St Denver CO 80218-3428

GRAHAM, LOIS CHARLOTTE, retired educator; b. Denver, Mar. 20, 1917; d. James Washington Brewster and Martha Wilhemina (Raukohl) Plunkett; m. Milton Clinton Graham, June 30, 1940 (dec.); children: Charlotte, Milton, Charlene, James. Student, Okla. City U., 1935-36; AB, Ouachita Bapt. U., 1939; postgrad., U. Nev., Reno, 1953, 63, 68, Ark. State U., 1954, 59. Cert. tchr., Colo., Nev., Ark. Tchr. Fairmount Sch., Golden, Colo., 1939-40, Melbourne (Ark.) Sch., 1940-41, Blytheville (Ark.) Jr. H.S., 1944-45, Hawthorne (Nev.) Elem. Sch., 1952-81; substitute tchr. Mineral County Sch. Dist., Hawthorne, 1988-94; sr. resource cons. dept. geriatrics U. Nev.-Reno Med. Sch., 1988-90, del. to Rural Health Conf., Hawthorne, 1990; officer Mineral County Tchrs. Assn., 1955-65; ad hoc com. Nev. State Tchrs., 1965. Mem. Mineral County Emergency Planning Com., 1991—; asst. to pres. High Sch. PTA, Hawthorne, 1958, Elem. PTA, Hawthorne, 1961; pianist, choir dir., tchr. various chs., 1927—; active Older Am. Friends of Libr. Recipient Disting. Svc. award. Mem. AAUW (membership v.p. 1988-91, pres. 1991-92, 94-95, 96—), AARP (pres. 1995—), Ret. Pub. Employees of Nev. (membership v.p.), Older Ams., Delta Kappa Gamma (v.p. 1991-92). Republican. Baptist. Home: PO Box 1543 Hawthorne NV 89415-1543

GRAHAM, MARGARET KATHERINE, secondary school educator; b. Grass Valley, Calif., Dec. 21, 1941; d. Carroll Joseph and Mary Barbara (Clark) Coughlan; m. Denis David Graham, Aug. 31, 1968; 1 child, Kathleen Ann. BA, U. Nev., 1963. Cert. secondary tchr., Nev. Case aide Catholic Social Svcs., San Francisco, 1963-64; tchr. Sparks (Nev.) H.S., 1965-67; history tchr. Carson City (Nev.) H.S., 1968-71; tchr. 7th/8th grades St. Teresa's Catholic Sch., Carson City, 1983-87; sex edn. tchr. Washoe County Sch. Dist., Reno, Nev., 1988—; sex edn. adv. bd. Carson City Sch. Dist., 1984-85. Mem. NEA, Washoe County Tchr.'s Assn., PEO, Serra Club (treas. 1992). Democrat. Roman Catholic. Office: Washoe County Sch Dist 425 E 9th St Reno NV 89512-2800

GRAHAM, PAMELA SMITH, distributing company executive, artist; b. Winona, Miss., Jan. 18, 1944; d. Douglas LaRue and Dorothy Jean (Hefty) Smith; m. Robert William Graham, Mar. 6, 1965 (div.); children: Jennifer, Eric; m. Thomas Paul Harley, Dec. 4, 1976; stepchildren: Tom, Janice. Student U. Colo., 1962-65, U. Cin., 1974-76. Cert. notary pub., Colo. Profl. artist, craft tchr., art exhibitor Colo., N.J., Ohio, 1968-73; property mgmt. and investor Cin., 1972-77; acct., word processor Borden Chem. Co. div. Borden, Inc., Cin., 1974-78; owner, pres. Hargram Enterprises, Cin., 1977-81; owner, pres. Graham & Harley Enterprises. Morrison, Colo., 1981—; tchr.; cons. County committeewoman Bergen County, N.J., 1972, clk. of session, 1975-79, conv. chmn., 1981; campaign chmn. United Appeal, 1977; lifeline telephone counselor Suicide Hotline, 1985—; victim advisor Abusive Men Exploring New Directions, 1986—. Recipient numerous awards for art exhibits including, bus. achievements, 1962—. Mem. NAFE, United Sales Leaders Assn., Nat. Museum of Women in Arts, Colo. Artists Assn., Evergreen Artists Assn. (bd. dirs., pres. 1990, 91), Colo. Calligraphers Guild, Gilpin County Arts Assn., Foothills Art Ctr., Alpha Gamma Chi, Kappa Kappa Gamma. Republican. Clubs: Mt. Vernon Country Club, Queen City Racquet. Office: Graham & Harley Enterprises 4303 S Taft St Morrison CO 80465-1425

GRAHAM, PRISCILLA MANN, librarian; b. Highland Park, Ill., Jan. 3, 1915; d. William David and Isabel (Browning) Mann; m. Myron J. Graham, Oct. 14, 1939; children: Wendy Stevens, Peter Mann, Robert Allen. Student, Northwestern U., 1936; BS, Calif. Poly. State U., 1970; MLS, San Jose State U., 1972. Ref. libr. Calif. Poly State U. Libr., San Luis Obispo, 1970-80; substitute libr. Cuesta C.C., San Luis Obispo, 1988-91; staff Historic Preservation Survey, City of San Luis Obispo, 1980-85. Trustee City Libr., San Luis Obispo, 1968-69, mem. cultural heritage com., 1981-91. Am. Beautiful grantee, 1972. Mem. AAUW, LWV, Libr. Assn. Calif. Poly., Alpha Phi, Beta Phi Mu. Home: 61 Los Palos Dr San Luis Obispo CA 93401-7725

GRAHAM, ROBERT ARLINGTON, newspaper entertainment editor; b. Pitts., May 14, 1938; s. Kenneth Erret and Bette Dee (Locke) G. Arts editor San Francisco Chronicle. Office: San Francisco Chronicle 901 Mission St San Francisco CA 94103-2905

GRAHAM, ROBERT KLARK, lens manufacturer; b. Harbor Springs, Mich., June 9, 1906; s. Frank A. and Ellen Fern (Klark) G.; A.B., Mich. State U., 1933; B.Sc. in Optics, Ohio State U., 1937; O.D. (hon.), 1987; hon. Dr. Ocular Sci., So. Calif. Coll. Optometry, 1988; children (by previous marriage)-David, Gregory, Robin, Robert K., Janis, Wesley; m. Marta Ve Everton; children: Marcia, Christie. With Bausch & Lomb, 1937-40; Western mgr. Univis Lens Co., 1940-44, sales mgr., 1945-46; v.p., dir. research Plastic Optics Co., 1946-47; pres., chmn. bd. Armorlite, Inc., 1947-78; lectr. optics Loma Linda U.; assoc. prof. So. Calif. Coll. Optometry, 1948-60. Co-founder (with Hermann J. Muller) Repository for Germinal Choice; trustee Found. Advancement of Man; bd. dirs. Inst. for Research on Morality; bd. dirs. Intra-Sci. Research Found., v.p., 1980; founder Graham Sci. Ctr., Escondido. Recipient Herschel Gold medal Germany, 1972, Feinbloom award Am. Acad. Optometry, 1987, Glenn Fry medal Physiol. Optics, 1992; named Disting. Alumnus, Ohio State U., 1987.. Fellow AAAS; mem. Am. Inst. Physics Profs., Optical Soc. Am., Am. Acad. Optometry, Rotary Club, Mensa, Sigma Xi. Republican. Author: The Evolution of Corneal Contact Lenses; The Future of Man; also articles in sci. publs. Inventor variable focus lens, hybrid corneal lens; directed devel. hard resin lenses. Home: 3024 Sycamore Ln Escondido CA 92025-7433 Office: Graham Internat Plz Ste 300 2141 Palomar Airport Rd Carlsbad CA 92009-1423

GRAHAM, STEVEN PIDDINGTON, entertainment production company executive; b. San Juan, P.R., May 26, 1962; s. Charles Paul and Gayle Ann (Piddington) G. BA in Motion Picture and Video, Brooks Inst. Photography, Santa Barbara, Calif., 1988. Freelance photographer, 1980—; prodn. asst. Handmade Films, L.A., 1989; operator, technician Lynn Greenberg Teleprompting, Newhall, Calif., 1989-91; pres. PC Prompting Sys., Sherman Oaks, Calif., 1992—. Author teleprompting software Scrollmaster, 1992; creator, inventor portable jib arm teleprompting equipment, 1992. Vol. L.A. Works, 1993. Mem. NABET (Local 53). Republican. Lutheran. Home: 4261 Dixie Canyon Ave Apt 4 Sherman Oaks CA 91423-3970

GRAHAM, SUSAN BRANDT, gynecologist, anthropologist; b. Oklahoma City, Oct. 26, 1946; d. Clinton H. and Lois (Casbeer) Brandt; m. G. Gordon Graham, Nov. 28, 1969 (div. Aug. 1994); 1 child, Brandt Gordon. BA, U. Okla., 1967; MA, U. Ariz., 1970, PhD, 1975; MD, U. Kans., Kansas City, 1985. Diplomate Am. Bd. Ob-Gyn.; lic. physician, N.Mex. Lab asst. in anthropology Stovall Mus., U. Okla., Norman, 1965-67; naturalist U.S. Nat. Park Svc., Grand Canyon, Ariz., summers 1968-70; asst. prof. anthropology U. Mo., Kansas City, 1976-81; resident in ob-gyn. U. N.Mex. Hosp., Albuquerque, 1985-89; gynecologist, obstetrician Women's Med. Specialists P.C., Albuquerque, 1989-93; gynecologist, owner Susan Brandt Graham, MD, PhD, PC, Albuquerque, 1994—; mem. gynecology peer rev. com. St. Joseph Healthcare System, Albuquerque, 1993—; mem. U.S. Med. Licensing Examination Test Writing Com., 1995—. Author articles. Woodrow Wilson Nat. fellow, 1967-68, U. Ariz. grad. scholar, 1969-70, U. Kans. med. scholar, 1985-89. Fellow Am. Coll. Ob-Gyn. (mem. com. on Indian affairs 1991-94), Am. Anthrop. Assn.; mem. Soc. for Med. Anthropology, N.Mex. Med. Soc. (mem. med.-legal panel 1990—), Greater Albuquerque Med. Assn., Mensa. Office: 101 Hospital Loop NE Ste 111 Albuquerque NM 87109-2100

GRAHAM, SUSAN LOIS, computer science educator, consultant; b. Cleve, Sept. 16, 1942; m., 1971. A.B. in Math., Harvard U., 1964; M.S., Stanford U., 1966, Ph.D. in Computer Sci., 1971. Assoc. research scientist, adj. asst. prof. computer sci. Courant Inst. Math. Sci., NYU, 1969-71; asst. prof. computer sci. U. Calif., Berkeley, 1971-76, assoc. prof., 1976-81, prof., 1981—; vis. scientist, Stanford U., 1981; adv. com. NSF div. computer and computation rsch., 1987-92, program for sci. and tech. ctrs., 1987-91; mem. MIT vis. com. for elec. engring. and computer sci., 1989—; mem. Nat. Rsch. Coun. div. on physical sci., math., and applications, 1992—. Co-editor Communications, 1975-79; editor Transactions on Programming Languages and Systems, 1978-92. NSF grantee. Fellow AAAS; mem. IEEE, Assn. Computing Machinery, Nat. Acad. Engring. Office: U Calif-Berkeley Computer Sci Div EECS Berkeley CA 94720

GRAHAM, TONI, writer; b. San Francisco, June 24, 1945; d. Joseph Foster and Maxine E. (Johnson) Avila; m. J. Richard Graham, Nov. 23, 1972 (div. 1987); 1 child, Salvatore Z. BA, New Coll. Calif., 1989; MA in English, San Francisco State U., 1992. Lectr. dept. creative writing San Francisco State U., 1992; thesis advisor lectr. MA in Writing program U. San Francisco, 1993—. Contbr. short fiction to mags., including Playgirl, Short Story Rev., Am. Fiction 88, Five Fingers Rev., Miss. Rev., Ascent, Clockwatch Rev., Miss. Mud, San Francisco Rev. Harrold scholar, 1986; recipient Calif. Short Story Competition award, 1987, Herbert Wilner Meml. Short Story award, 1994; story Shadow Boxing cited in Pushcart Prize XIV-Best of the Small Presses, 1989. Mem. MLA, Assoc. Writing Programs, Hemingway Soc., Golden Key Honor Soc. Home: 345 Prospect Ave San Francisco CA 94110-5509

GRAHAM-ROGERS, CHARLES THEODORE (TED ROGERS), metapsychologist, lecturer; b. N.Y.C., Oct. 8, 1907; s. Charles T. and May (Church) G-R.; B.S., Wagner Coll., 1933; M.S., San Diego State U., 1962; certificate in counseling U. So. Calif., 1965; D.Sc., Miss. State Christian Coll., 1969; C.H., Dominion Coll., 1975; Ph.D., Newport U., 1977; Ph.D. in Metapsychology, U. Humanistics Studies, 1978; M.S.D., Inst. Metapsychology, 1980; m. Consuelo Yvonne d'Aguilar, March 11, 1933 (dec. July 1975); 1 dau., Patricia Suzanne. Dir. delinquency prevention N.Y.C. schs., 1934-39; assistant dir. personnel tng. Pub. Works Adminstrn., N.Y.C., 1940-41; mem. N.Y. State Div. Parole, 1941-46; chief probation officer San Diego County, San Diego, 1947-67; cons., researcher parapsychology, psychic phenomena, survival, metaphys. healing, 1967—; dir. Ctr. for Edn. and Research, 1965-78; chmn. metapsychology U. Humanistic Studies, 1977-78, mem. psychology faculty, 1977-83 , dean Inst. Metapsychology, 1981—; dir. Voyage of Discovery Internat. Inst. Metapsychology, 1982-89, Project Exploration, 1988-93; guest lectr. San Diego State Coll., 1948; lectr. Calif. Western U., 1958-61; lectr., hon. fellow Lynwood Fellowship, Eng., 1984-93; cons. Nat. Probation and Parole Assn., Ariz. Correctional Study, 1958; cons. Deliquency Control Inst., Ariz. State U., 1959-64; cons. Youth Studies Ctr. U. So. Calif., 1963-65, youth problems Bishopric of Fiji, 1966; mem. County Parole Bd., 1961-67; mem. com. Probation Study, Dependent Child Study, State of Calif., 1963-67; mem. profl. advisory com. social work curriculum San Diego State Coll., 1959-61; probation adv. com. Calif. Youth Authority, 1958-67; v.p., chmn. research com. Parapsychology Found., lectr., 1962-67. Served to capt. USAAF, 1942-46; PTO. Recipient Legion of Honor, Order of DeMolay. Fellow World Assn. Soc. Psychiatry, Royal Soc. Health, Inst. Parapsychol. Research, Coll. Psychic Studies, Am. Orthopsychiatric Assn.; mem. Am. Soc. Psychical Research, Am. assns. social psychiatry, British Soc. for Psychical Rsch., Acad. Parapsychology and Medicine, Assn. for Humanistic Psychology, Soc. for Sci. Study of Religion, Acad. Religion and Psychical Research, Nat. Assn. Social Workers (charter), Acad. Religion and Mental Health, Internat. Assn. Metapsychology (pres. 1980—), So. Calif. Soc. Psychical Research, Cosmosophy Soc. (pres. 1965-80), Am. Assn. Study Mental Imagery, Assn. Transpersonal Psychology, Spiritual Frontiers Fellowship, Calif. Probation, Parole and Correctional Assn. (pres. 1961-62), Acad. Certified Social Workers, Church's Fellowship for Psychic Studies, Theosophical Soc., Pi Sigma Alpha. Contbr. articles to various publs. Address: Colina de La Costa 7301-F Alicante Rd Carlsbad CA 92009-6217

GRAJEWSKI, JULIAN, law librarian, educator; b. Porto Potenza Picena, Macerata, Italy, Feb. 10, 1946; came to U.S., 1960; s. Anthony and Santa (Grandinetti) G.; m. Agnes Murray Mutch, Sept. 28, 1970 (div. Dec. 1976); children: Keir Ewan, Naomi Isabel; m. Elisabet Appel, Dec. 31, 1986, 1 child, Janusz Antares. BA, SUNY, Plattsburgh, 1974; MA in English, Concordia U., Montreal, 1977; MLS, U. Ariz., 1991. Instr. Pima County C.C., Tucson, 1983-92; law libr. Dept. of Corrections, Winslow, Ariz., 1992—. Author: Liberation, 1970; contbr. short story to Free Fire Zone: Short Stories by Vietnam Veterans, 1973; contbr. articles to Pig Iron Press, East Campus Caldera, Magill's Critical Survey of Short Fiction. Organizer Dem. Party, various locations, 1975—. With U.S. Army, 1966-68, Vietnam. Mem. MLA. Democrat. Roman Catholic.

GRALAPP, MARCELEE GAYL, librarian; b. Winfield, Kans., Nov. 2, 1931; d. Benjamin Harry and Lelia Iris G. BA, Kansas State Teacher's Coll., 1952; MA, U. Denver, 1963. Children's libr. Hutchinson Pub. Libr., Kans., 1952-57, Lawrence Pub. Libr., Kans., 1957-59; assoc. libr. Boulder Pub. Libr., Colo., 1959-66, libr. dir., 1966—; vis. faculty U. Denver, 1965-66, 67, Kans. State Teacher's Coll., Emporia, 1965. Chmn. state plan for libr. devel. Libraries-Colo., 1974; city staff liaison Boulder Arts Commn., 1979—; bd. dirs. Boulder Ctr. for Visual Arts, 1975-79; treas. Irving Libr. Network, Inc. Recipient Governor's award Colo. Council on Arts and Humanities, 1981. Mem. ALA, Mountain Plains Libr. Assn., Colo. Libr. Assn. (legis. com. 1970-78, Lifetime Achievement award 1992), Boulder Hist. Soc., Boulder Philharm. Soc., Chautauqua Assn., Denver Art Mus., Delta Kappa Gamma. Democrat. Home: 3080 15th St Boulder CO 80304-2614 Office: Boulder Pub Libr PO Drawer H 1000 Canyon Blvd Boulder CO 80306

GRAMES, GEORGE MILLER, human services administrator, physician; b. Phila., Apr. 28, 1934; s. Constantine and Margaret Louise (Whitcomb) G.; m. Betty Ann Rhodes, June 16, 1957; children: Cheryl Lynn, Rae Ann, Barry Scott. BA, Columbia Union Coll., 1956; MD, Loma Linda U., 1960. Diplomate Am. Bd. Internal Medicine, Am. Bd. Nephrology, Am. Bd. Nuclear Medicine. Intern Walter Reed Gen. Hosp., 1960-61, resident internal medicine, 1961-64; asst. prof. radiology Loma Linda (Calif.) U. Med. Ctr., 1971-76, from assoc. prof. to prof. medicine, 1976-91; adminstr. Redlands (Calif.) Hemodialysis Ctr., 1993—; dir. residency tng. program for internal medicine Loma Linda U. Med. Ctr., 1986-90; cons. in field. Contbr. articles to profl. jours. Pres. Epsilon chpt. Alpha Omega Alpha, 1975. Maj. U.S. Army, 1960-67. Fellow ACP; mem. Am. Soc. Nephrology, Am. Soc. Nuclear Medicine, Inland Soc. Nephrology, Internat. Soc. Internal Medicine, Alpha Omega Alpha. Office: Inland Nephrology 1210 Indiana Ct Redlands CA 92374-2896

GRAMMATER, RUDOLF DIMITRI, retired construction executive; b. Detroit, Nov. 29, 1910; s. D.M. and Amelia (Busse) G.; m. Fredricka W. Cook, Aug. 18, 1943, 1 child, Douglas. Student, Pace Coll., 1928-32; LLB, Lincoln U., 1937. Bar: Calif. 1938; CPA Calif. With Bechtel Corp., San Francisco, 1941-73, treas., v.p., 1955-62, v.p., 1962-71, dir., 1960-73, cons., 1973, v.p., dir. subsidiaries, 1955-71. Mem. ABA, AICPA, Calif. Soc. CPAs, Calif. Bar Assn., Menlo Country Club. Home: 50 Mounds Rd Apt 302 San Mateo CA 94402-1257

GRAMS, THEODORE CARL WILLIAM, librarian, educator; b. Portland, Oreg., Sept. 29, 1918; s. Theodore Albert and Emma Elise (Boehne) G. B.A., U. Wash., 1947; postgrad. Harvard Law Sch., 1947-48; M.S. in L.S., U. So. Calif., 1951. Land title asst. U.S. Bonneville Power Adminstrn., Portland, 1939-45, accountant, 1948-50, librarian, 1951-52; head cataloger, lectr. Portland State U. Library, 1952-59, dir. processing services, 1960-83, prof., 1969-87, prof. emeritus, 1988—. Pres. Portland Area Spl. Librns., 1954-55; panelist on impact new tech. on info. scis. Am. Soc. Info. Sci., 1974, panelist on Libr. Congress svcs., 1976. Author: Allocation of Joint Costs of Multiple-Purpose Projects, 1952, Textbook Classification, 1968; editor: Procs. 4th Am. Soc. Info. Scis. Midyear Meeting, 1975, Special Collections in the Libraries of the Pacific Northwest, 1979, Disaster Preparedness and Recovery, 1983, Technical Services: The Decade Ahead (in Beyond 1984: The Future of Technical Services), 1983. Panelist on community action N.W. Luth. Welfare Assn. Conf., 1969; mem. adv. council Area Agy. on Aging, 1974-75; commr. City-County Commn. Aging, Portland-Multnomah County, 1975-80. Bd. dirs. Hub-Community Action Program, Portland, 1967-70, Project ABLE, 1972-74. HEW Inst. fellow, 1968-69. Mem. Am. Library Assn., AAUP, Multnomah Athletic Club, Beta Phi Mu. Lutheran. Home: 6653 E Carondelet Dr Tucson AZ 85710-2150

GRAN, ROBERT, engineering company executive; b. 1942. PhD, Calif. Inst. Tech., 1970. Sec. head TRW Sys., Redondo Beach, Calif., 1970-73; sr. rsch. engr., divsn. mgr. Flow Rsch. Inc., L.A., 1973-76; chief sci. Dynamics Tech., Inc., Torrance, Calif., 1976—. Office: Dynamics Tech Inc 21311 Hawthorne Blvd Torrance CA 90503-5602*

GRANDY, JAY FRANKLIN, fruit processing executive; b. Murray, Ky., July 21, 1939; s. Rodney Leon and Marion Elizabeth (Birchall) G.; m. Jane Ann Howard, June 26, 1965; children—Joanna, Sharon. B.S. in Physics, Auburn U., 1961; M.B.A., Siena Coll., 1969. With Gen. Electric, 1961-77; mktg. mgr. FMC, Cedar Rapids, Iowa, 1977-81, gen. mgr., Fresno, Calif., 1981-82; pres. Snokist Growers, Yakima, Wash., 1984—. Served to 1st lt. U.S. Army, 1962-64. Home: 4203 Fellows Dr Yakima WA 98908-2266 Office: Snokist Growers PO Box 1587 Yakima WA 98907-1587

GRANGER, ARTHUR EARLE, geologist; b. Salt Lake City, Mar. 15, 1911; s. Louis Edwin and Sarah (Dibble) G.; m. Leona Pearce, June 23, 1937; children: Penelope, Arthur, Pamela, Sallee, Christine. BA, U. Utah, 1934; MS, U. Wash., 1937; PhD, Am. Internat. U., Pasadena, Calif., 1960. Registered geologist, Calif. Engr. U.S. Forest Svc., Salt Lake City, 1934-36; teaching asst. U. Wash., Seattle, 1936-38; geologist U.S. Geol. Survey, Washington, 1938-54; chief geol. engr. U.S. Steel Corp., San Francisco, 1954—55; chief geologist U.S. AEC, Grand Junction, Colo., 1955-63; owner Arthur E. Granger Co., Reno, Nev., 1964—. Fellow Soc. Econ. Geologists; mem. Am. Assn. Petroleum Geologists. Home and Office: 3300 Clearacre Ln Reno NV 89512-1408

GRANLUND, THOMAS ARTHUR, engineering executive, consultant; b. Spokane, Wash., Mar. 1, 1951; s. William Arthur and Louise (Urie) G.; m. Jean MacRae Melvin, May 25, 1974 (div. Feb. 1991). BS, Wash. State U., 1973, BA, 1973; MBA, Gonzaga U., 1982. Engring. adminstr. Lockheed Aeronautical Systems Co., Burbank, Calif., 1978-91; mgmt. cons., 1991—. Co-author: (screenplay) Identities, 1988, Flash, 1989. 1st lt. USAF, 1973-78. Mem. Wash. State U. Alumni Assn. Home: 20924 Ben Ct Santa Clarita CA 91350-1418

GRANT, CHARLES WAYNE, computer scientist; b. Castro Valley, Calif., Oct. 13, 1956; s. Charles Alvin and Delores Mae (Bramlett) G. AS in Electronics Engring. Tech., BS in Electronics Engring. Tech., DeVry Inst. Tech., Ariz., 1978; MS in Computer Sci., U. Calif., Davis, 1981, PhD in Computer Sci., 1992. V.p. engring. Custom Engring. Inc., Phoenix, 1976-78; computer scientist Lawrence Livermore (Calif.) Nat. Lab., 1978-92, mem. postdoctoral rsch. staff, 1993—; cons. Waltrip and Assocs., Sacramento, 1992-93. Author: Introduction to the UCSD P-System, 1981, IEEE Tutorial on Computer Graphics: Image Synthesis, 1987. Mem. IEEE, Assn. for Computing Machinery, Tri Valley Stargazers (bd. dirs. 1994-95). Home: PO Box 2551 Livermore CA 94551-2551

GRANT, EMON HOWARD, JR., advertising agency executive; b. Palestine, Tex., Jan. 8, 1942; s. Emon Howard and Evelyn Mauline (Hudson) G.; m. Mary Cathleen Kelly, Jan. 21, 1966 (div. June 1977); m. Lynn Wilson, Apr. 7, 1978 (div. Aug. 1985); m. Linda Darlene Hogue, Mar. 23, 1991. AA, South Plains Coll., Levelland, Tex., 1962; BA, Tex. Tech. Coll., 1965. Announcer KLBK Radio, Lubbock, Tex., 1964-66; announcer KHOB Radio, Hobbs, N.Mex., 1966, program dir., 1969-71; asst. mgr. KBIM Radio, Roswell, N.Mex., 1971-74, account exec., 1978-89; cons. KRSY Radio, Roswell, 1974-78, morning talk show host, 1989—; CEO, chmn. bd. Grant and Co. Advt., Roswell, 1992—. Author: Calendar, 1987, Politics in Roswell, 1989, Someday I'll Find Tomorrow, 1986; (screenplay) Ticket, 1993. Commr. Planning and Zoning Commn., Roswell, 1982-84; city councillor City of Roswell, 1984-88; commn. City Planing and Zoning, Roswell, 1988-91 (mem. extraterritorial zoning authority 1984-88, chmn. 1987-88), Planning and Zoning, Chaves County, N.Mex., 1991—. With U.S. Army, 1966-68. Recipient Cert. of Recognition City Coun., Roswell, 1988, County Commn., Chaves County, 1988. Mem. Elks, Masons, Eagles. Democrat. Mem. Worldwide Ch. Home and Office: Grant and Co Advt Inc 1601 E Gallina Rd Roswell NM 88201-8951

GRANT, JAMES RUSK, business owner; b. Malvern, Ark., July 22, 1939; s. James Rusk and Maxie (Thompson) G.; m. Diane Grant, June 2, 1978; children from a previous marriage: Michele Rene, Michael Reed. AA in Psychology, Orange Coast U., 1975; BS in Human Svcs., Calif. State U., Fullerton, 1977. V.p. Internat. Recruiting, Van Nuys, Calif., 1978-88; mgr. Snelling & Snelling, Inc., Sunnyvale, Calif., 1988-89; pres. Nugent & Grant, Inc., Santa Clara, Calif., 1989—, Searchnet, Hillsboro, Oreg. Mem. Emergency Ham Radio Santa Clara, Van Nuys Masonic Blue Lodge, San

Jose Scottish Rite Masons, Shriners. Republican. Office: Searchnet 3931 NE Brogden St Hillsboro OR 97124

GRANT, JOHN BARNARD, writer; b. Hartford, Conn., Mar. 23, 1940; s. Ellsworth S. and Marion (Hepburn) G.; m. Ann Halterman, May 28, 1965; children: Jason, Schuyler. BA, U. Calif., Berkeley, 1965. Phys. edn. and outdoor skills tchr. Green Valley Sch., Orange City, Fla., 1966-68; math. and English tchr. Deerborne Sch., Coral Gables, Fla., 1969-70; charter sailboat capt. Bradenton Beach, Fla., 1968-69; dir. devel. Calif. Outward Bound, Palo Alto, 1970-71; writer, editor, and pub. Los Gatos and Sebastopol, Calif., 1971—. Author: The Geocentric Experience, 1972, (with Katharine Houghton) Two Beastly Tales, 1975, Skateboarding, 1976, (with Jim Gault) The World of Women's Gymnastics, 1976, Ins and Outs of Soccer, 1983, (with Laeh Maggie Garfield) Companions in Spirit, 1985, The Unamericans in Paris, 1988, (play) Joan, 1989; contbr. numerous stories and poems to mags. With USMC, 1960-64. Mem. Musicians Union (local 292).

GRANT, JOHN CARRINGTON, advertising executive; b. St. Louis, Feb. 2, 1937; s. George Nelson Whitfield and Mary Frances (Tissier) G.; m. Judith Ann Thompson, Oct. 20, 1962; children: Christopher, Susan. Student Westminister Coll., 1960; BS, Washington U., St. Louis, 1969. Account mgr. Darcy, McManus & Masius, St. Louis, N.Y.C. and San Francisco, 1960-68; with Gardner Advt., St. Louis, 1963-66, McCann-Erickson, Seattle, 1974-75; stockbroker Dean Witter, San Francisco, 1968-74; with Tracy-Locke/BBDO, 1975-80; pres. Grant Pollack Advt., Denver, 1980-85; v.p. Brock & Assocs., Denver, 1985-86; dir. Univ. rels. U. Denver, 1987-89; pres. Grant & Assocs., 1989—; pres. CEO The Advertising Consortium, 1989—; mem. faculty Met. State Coll., Denver, 1981-82. Mem. Denver Advt. Fedn. Clubs: Denver Athletic, Oxford.

GRANT, LEWIS O., agricultural products executive, meteorology educator; b. Washington, Pa., Mar. 29, 1923; s. Lewis F. and Rita J. (Jacqmain) G.; m. Patricia Jean Lovelock, July 23, 1949; children: Ann, Nancy, Brenda, Andrew, Laura. BS, U. Tulsa, Okla., 1947; MS, Calif. Inst. Tech., Pasadena, 1948. Meteorological cons. Water Resources Devel. Corp., Pasadena, Calif., 1948-54, Denver, 1948-54; rschr. and rsch. dir. Am. Inst. Aerological Rsch., Denver, 1954-59; asst. prof., assoc. prof. to prof. atmospheric sci. dept. Colo. State U., Ft. Collins, 1959-93, emeritus prof., 1993—; pres. Piedmont Farms, Inc., Wellington, Colo., 1975—; cons. Colo. Legis., Denver, 1971-73. Contb. to profl. jours. Scout master, com. chmn. Boy Scouts of Am.; pres. Partner Communities, Ft. Collins, Colo., 1988; elder Presbyn. Ch., 1980; 1st lt. U.S. Field Artillery, 1943-46. Recipient Vincent J. Schaefer award Weather Modification Assn., 1991. Fellow Am. Meterological Assn.; mem. Colo. Weather Modification Advisory's Assn. (pres. 1970), Nat. Sci. Found. (atomospheric sci. sect. adv. com. 1970), Nat. Acad. Sci. (sect. chmn. 1975-76), Organic Farming Rsch. Found. (bd. mem. 1995). Republican. Presbyterian. Office: Piedmont Farms Inc 1020 W County Rd 72 Wellington CO 80549 also: Colo State U Dept Atmospheric Sci Fort Collins CO 80523

GRANT, MICHAEL ERNEST, educational administrator, institutional management educator; b. L.A., June 6, 1952; s. Ernest Grant and Shirley Ruth (George) G. BA in Spanish, Calif. State U., Long Beach, 1974, MA in Edn. Adminstrn., 1978; EdD, Pepperdine U., 1984. Cert. elem., secondary, and community coll. tchr., bilingual and cross-cultural edn., adminstr. Tchr. kindergarten through adult edn. Long Beach Unified Sch. Dist., 1975-83, tchr. 5th grade, 1975, tchr. 6th grade, 1975-76, bilingual multicultural specialist, 1976-78, tchr. 6th, 7th and 8th grades, 1978-79, mgmt. program specialist, 1979-80, adminstr., program specialist, 1980-81, vice prin., 1981-83; asst. prof. tchr. edn. Calif. State U., San Bernardino, 1986-88; prin. dir. IMPACT/TEACH, assoc. prof. ednl. psychology and adminstrn. Calif. State U., Long Beach, 1988-91; pres., founder Mykulphone Teleteach, Long Beach, 1991—; asst. part-time instr. tchr. edn. Grad. Sch. Edn., Calif. State U., Long Beach, 1983-86. Contbr. articles to profl. jours. Pepperdine U. scholar, 1983-84; Calif. State U. grantee, 1988-89, 89-90, 89-91. Mem. NEA, Assn. Calif. Sch. Adminstrs., Nat. Assn. Tchr. Educators, Nat. Coun. States In-Svc. Edn., Nat. Black Congress Faculty, Calif. Faculty Assn., Calif. State Intersegmental Coordination Coun., Calif. Black Faculty and Staff Assn., Calif. Assn. Tchr. Educators, Calif. Edn. Rsch. Assn., Intersegmental Coordinating Coun. Democrat. Baptist. Home and Office: 270 N Cañon Dr Ste 1220 Beverly Hills CA 90210-9999 Office: Calif State U Grad Sch Edn 1250 N Bellflower Blvd Long Beach CA 90840-0006

GRANT, RICHARD EARL, nursing administrator; b. Spokane, Wash., Aug. 27, 1935; s. Conrad Morrison and Sylva Celeste (Sims) G.; m. Susan Kimberly Hawkins, Mar. 17, 1979; children: Paaqua A., Camber Do'otsie O. BSc cum laude, U. Wash., 1961; MEd, Whitworth Coll., 1974; PhD, Wash. State U., 1980. Cert. ins. rehab. specialist; cert. case mgr. Supr. nursing Providence Hosp., Seattle, 1970-72; asst. prof. nursing Wash. State U., Spokane, 1972-78; dir. nursing Winslow (Ariz.) Meml. Hosp., 1978-79; adminstr. psychiat. nursing Ariz. State Hosp., Phoenix, 1979-80; asst. prof. Ariz. State U., Tempe, 1980-83; assoc. prof. Linfield Coll., Portland, Oreg., 1983-86, Intercollegiate Ctr. for Nursing Edn., Spokane, 1986-88; sr. med. care coord. Fortis Corp., Spokane, 1988-92; med. svcs. cons. CorVel Corp., Spokane, 1992-95; owner Richard Grant & Assocs., Spokane, 1995—; cons. Ariz. State Hosp., 1980-82, Pres.'s Commn., Washinton, 1981-83, U. No. Colo., Greely, 1985-86; area med. svcs. cons., 1992—. Author: The God-Man-God Book, 1976, Publications of the Membership (Conaa), 1983, 3d rev. edit., 1985, 4th rev. edit., 1988, Predetermined Careplan Handbook-Nursing, 1988; contbr. articles to profl. jours. Judge Student Space Shuttle Project, Portland, 1983, N.W. Sci. Expo, Portland, 1983. With U.S. Army, 1953-56. Grantee NIMH, U. Wash., 1961; named one of top Hopi Scholars, Hopi Tribe, Second Mesa, Ariz., 1981. Mem. AAAS, Nat. League for Nursing, Wash. League for Nursing (v.p. 1988-90), Coun. on Nursing and Anthropology (editor 1982-90), N.Y. Acad. Scis., Case Mgmt. Soc. Am., Sigma Theta Tau.

GRANT, SANDRA KAY, adult education educator; b. Honolulu, Hawaii, Sept. 1, 1948; d. Wallace Everett and Setsuko (Shiozawa) G.; m. Ageel Moin Chishty, Jan. 1, 1983 (div. May 1989). BS, Weber State U., 1974. Cert. tchr. level 4 math., Utah. Tchr. N. Davis Jr. High Sch., Clearfield, Utah, 1973, Bonniville High Sch., Riverdale, Utah, 1973, Roy (Utah) High Sch., 1974; lectr. Weber State U., Ogden, Utah, 1974-87; instr. Ogden-Weber Applied Tech. Ctr., Ogden, 1987—; initiated first statewide Light on Literacy conf., 1992. Author, compiler: ATC Cook Book, 1989; author: Applied Mathematics, 1990. Grantee Utah State Office of Edn., 1990, 92, 93. Mem. ASCD, Am. Assn. Adult Edn., Am. Vocat. Assn., Nat. Coun. Tchrs. Math., Utah Vocat. Assn., Utah Coun. Tchrs. Math., Utah State Ednl. Resource Libr. (adv. 1992—), Utah State Adult Edn. Suprs., Utah Assn. Adult, Community and Continuing Edn. (bd. dirs. 1992-95, pres.-elect), Utah Literacy and Adult Edn. Coalition (bd. dirs. 1991——), N. Utah Literacy Coalition (co-chmn. 1992—), Mountain Plains Adult Edn. Assn. Home: 2963 Jefferson Ave Ogden UT 84403-0136 Office: Ogden-Weber Applied Tech Ct 559 Avc Ln Ogden UT 84404-6704

GRANT, STEPHEN R., construction executive, lawyer; b. 1939. LLB, U. Calif., Berkeley, 1966. With McCurcheon, Doyle, Brown & Emerson, San Francisco, 1966-89, Nat. Projects, Inc., 1989—. Office: National Projects Inc 720 Park Blvd Boise ID 83712-7714*

GRANT, SURLENE GEORGETTE, public information officer; b. Redwood City, Calif., Apr. 25, 1959; d. George Gene and Surlene (Jackson) G. BS in Journalism, Northwestern U., 1981. Multicultural edn. dir. YWCA, Palo Alto, Calif., 1981-83; pub. relations dir. Bay Area Urban League, Oakland, Calif., 1983-85; legis. aide Calif. State Senate, Sacramento, 1985-86; asst. press sec. speakers office Calif. Assembly, 1987; pub. info officer City of Oakland, Calif., 1987-94; project mgr. Pub. Affairs Mgmt., San Francisco, 1994—. Author: Chronological History of Jerusalem Baptist Church, 1986. Mem. YWCA, Palo Alto, 1986—; campaign worker Bradley for Gov., Sacramento, 1986; mem. Dem. State Cen. Com., 1987. Named Employee of Yr., Bay Area Urban League, Oakland, 1985. Mem. Pub. Relations Soc. Am. (bd. dirs. East Bay chpt.), Black Women Organized for Polit. Action, Bay Area Black Journalist Assn., Women's Econ. Agenda Project (past bd. dirs.). Democrat. Baptist. Office: Pub Affairs Mgmt 101 The Embarcadero Ste 210 San Francisco CA 94612

GRASS, GEORGE MITCHELL, IV, pharmaceutical executive; b. Bryn Mawr, Pa., Dec. 31, 1957; s. George Mitchell III and Irma Lucy (Schaffer) G. PharmD, U. Nebr., Omaha, 1980; PhD, U. Wis., 1985. Lic. pharmacist. Staff rschr. Syntex Rsch., Palo Alto, Calif., 1985-91; pres. Precision Instrument Design, Tahoe City, Calif., 1987—; cons. Costar Corp., Cambridge, Mass., 1990—, various pharm. cos., 1991—; co-founder Raptor Graphics, Snohomish, Wash. Contbr. numerous articles to profl. jours. Recipient Ebert prize Jour. Pharm. Sci., 1989. Mem. AAAS, Am. Assn. Pharm. Scientists, Sigma Xi.

GRASSI, JAMES EDWARD, recreational facility executive director; b. Oakland, Calif., Nov. 19, 1943; s. Dante Carlos and Mae Johanna (Condon) G.; m. Mary Louise Etter, Apr. 10, 1965; children: Daniel James, Thomas William. BS in Recreation Adminstrn., Calif. State U., Hayward, 1966; MPA, Calif. State U., 1971. Ordained to ministry Evangelical Ch.,1992. Recreation supr. Oakland (Calif.) Pks. & Recreation, 1964-66; adminstrv. asst. East Bay Regional Pk. Dist., Oakland, 1966-76; dep. town mgr. Town of Moraga, Calif., 1976-86; exec. dir. Let's Go Fishing & FOCAS Ministries, 1986—; dir. Calif. Recreational Fisheries Counsel, Sacramento, 1968-74; trustee Christian Heritage Coll. Bd., El Cajon, Calif., 1989—; nat. speaker on Bldg. Strong Families. Author: (booklet) Ultimate Fishing Challenge, 1990, (pamphlet) Anchoring Your Lives in Christ, 1990; The Ultimate Fishing Challenge-Discipleship, 1994; co-host TV show Fishing Tales, 1988-91; contbr. articles to profl. jours.; freelance writer on outdoor sports. Bd. dirs. Rotary Internat., 1976-86, YMCA, Hayward, 1977-70. Recipient Legis. Resolution Appreciation and Accomodation, Disting. Employee award Moraga Town Counsel, 1986, Presdl. plaque Calif. Pks. & Recreation Soc., 1980. Mem. U.S. Trout Farmers Aquaculture Assn., Nat. Assn. Evangs. Republican. Evangelical. Home: 22 Del Rio Ct Moraga CA 94556-2031 Office: Lets Go Fishing PO Box 434 Moraga CA 94556-0434

GRASSO, MARY ANN, theatre association administrator; b. Rome, N.Y., Nov. 3, 1952; d. Vincent and Rose Mary (Pupa) Grasso. BA in Art History, U. Calif., Riverside, 1973; MLS, U. Oreg., 1974. Dir. Warner Rsch. Collection, Burbank, Calif., 1975-84; mgr. CBS TV/Docudrama, Hollywood, Calif., 1984-88; exec. dir. Nat. Assn. Theatre Owners, North Hollywood, Calif., 1988—; instr. theatre arts UCLA, 1980-85, Am. Film Inst., L.A., 1985-88. Screen credits: The Scarlet O'Hara Wars, This Year's Blonde, The Silent Lovers, A Bunnies Tale, Embassy. Mem. Nat. Assn. Theatre Owners (exec. dir.), Bus. and Profl. Women's Assn. (Woman of Achievement award 1983), Acad. Motion Pictures Arts and Scis., Friends of The Motion Picture Pioneers, Phi Beta Kappa. Democrat. Office: Nat Assn Theatre Owners 4605 Lankershim Blvd # 340 North Hollywood CA 91602-1818

GRASSO, MONICA MARIE, home health nurse; b. Albany, N.Y., July 30, 1964; d. Ralph Joseph and Joanna Anna (Haponski) G. BSN, U. No. Colo., Greeley, 1987. RN, Colo. Staff nurse oncology St. Joseph Hosp., Denver, 1987-90; staff nurse ob-gyn. Univ. Hosp., Denver, 1990-92; home health nurse Presbyn. St. Luke Hosp., Denver, 1992, Denver Vis. Nurses Assn., 1992—. Merit scholar U. No. Colo., 1987. Mem. ANA.

GRAUBART, JEFFREY LOWELL, entertainment lawyer; b. Chgo., Aug. 18, 1940; s. John H. and Florence R. G.; m. Mary Linda Carey, June 24, 1973; children: Joshua Gordon, Noah Carey. BS in Fin., U. Ill., 1962; JD, Northwestern U., Chgo., 1965. Bar: Ill. 1965, Calif. 1968, N.Y. 1980. Assoc. Curtis Friedman & Marks, Chgo., 1965-67, Capitol Records, Inc., Los Angeles, 1968-70; prin. Hadfield, Jorgensen, Graubart & Becker, San Francisco, 1970-81; counsel Frankfurt, Garbus, Klein & Selz, P.C., N.Y., 1981-85; prin. Strote, Graubart & Ashley, P.C., Beverly Hills, Calif. and N.Y., 1986-87; counsel Cohen & Luckenbacher, L.A., 1988-90, Engel & Engel, L.A., 1991-92; sec. Paramount Growers, Inc., Delano, Calif., 1968-70; v.p., dir. London Internat. Artists, Ltd., Los Angeles, 1969-70, Jazz Images, Inc., N.Y.C., 1983-86; adj. prof. NYU, 1982-85; lectr. Columbia U. Sch. Law, N.Y.C., 1982-85, UCLA, 1988—, U. So. Calif., 1988—. Contbr. articles to profl. jours. and mags. Counsel San Francisco Jazz Found., 1980-81. Recipient Deems Taylor award ASCAP, 1981. Mem. NARAS (San Francisco chtp. legal counsel 1973-93, gov. 1973-85, gov. and legal counsel N.Y. chpt. 1982-85, gov. L.A. chpt. 1988-92), Calif. Copyright Conf. (dir. 1995—), Internat. Fedn. Festival Orgns. (dir. 1994—), Inter-Pacific Bar Assn., Beverly Hills Bar Assn. (chair internat. law sect. 1995—), Internat. Radio and TV Soc., Country Music Assn., Assn. of the Bar of the City of N.Y., Soc. Preservation of Film Music (trustee 1989—), v.p. 1991-94). Lodges: B'nai Brith (N.Y. and Los Angeles); Golden Gate (San Francisco) (v.p. 1974-75), Entertainment Industry Unit L.A. (founder, trustee 1988—). Office: 2029 Century Park E Ste 2700 Los Angeles CA 90067-3013

GRAVES, DAVID WILLIAM, winery executive; b. Oakland, Calif., Oct. 26, 1952; s. James Washington and Barbara Jean (Wagner) G.; m. Elizabeth Peterson McKinne, July 14, 1990. BS, U. Calif., Santa Cruz, 1975. Cellar worker Chappellet Vineyards, Rutherford, Calif., 1978, Joseph Phelps Vineyards, St. Helena, Calif., 1979, Domaine Chandon, Yountville, Calif., 1980, Mt. Eden Vineyards, Cupertino, Calif., 1981; co-founder Saintsbury, Napa, Calif., 1981—; pres., treas. Carneros Quality Alliance, Napa, 1988—; pres. Pinot Noir: Am., Napa, 1989-90. Mem. Am. Soc. Enology and Viticulture (profl. mem.), U. Calif. Santa Cruz Alumni Assn. (alumni councillor 1987—). Democrat. Office: Saintsbury 1500 Los Carneros Ave Napa CA 94559-9742

GRAVES, EARL WILLIAM, JR., journalist; b. Kodiak, Alaska, June 30, 1950; s. Earl William Graves, Sr. and Lola (Olson) Raab; m. Karin Ann Steichen, July 30, 1972; children: Emma, Mark, Max. BA in English with honors, U. Puget Sound, 1972; MA in English, Western Wash. State U., 1976. Tchr. English Naselle (Wash.) High Sch., 1972-74, Clatskanie (Oreg.) High Sch., 1975-77; police reporter Coeur d'Alene (Idaho) Press, 1978-79, city editor, 1980-82, mng. editor, 1983-84; sr. reporter Bulletin, Bend, Oreg., 1984-86; edn. reporter News and Observer, Raleigh, N.C., 1986-87; state edn. reporter News and Observer/Raleigh Times, 1987—. Author: Poisoned Apple, 1995. Recipient Outstanding Svc. award N.C. chpt. Phi Delta Kappa, 1988, Third Prize So. Journalism Feature Reporting award Inst. for So. Studies, 1989, N.C. Sch. Bell award N.C. Assn. Educators, 1989, Benjamin Fine award Nat. Assn. Secondary Sch. Prins., 1989, First Pl. Gen. News Reporting award N.C. Press Assn., 1990, First Pl. Edn. Reporting award Pacific Northwest Excellence in Journalism, Soc. Profl. Journalists, 1991, 92, Media award Assn. Retarded Children Oreg., 1992, Second Pl. Spot News Reporting award Best of West, 1992, Second Pl. Best Writing award Oreg. Newspaper Pubs. Assn., 1993, Excellence in Edn. award Oreg. Assn. Supervision and Cirriculum Devel., 1993. Mem. Edn. Writers Assn. (sec., bd. dirs. 1990—, Spl. Citation Nat. Awards for Edn. Reporting 1987, 91, Second Pl. Newspaper Series award 1989, Second Pl. Nat. Awards Edn. Reporting 1989). Democrat. Office: Oregonian 1320 SW Broadway Portland OR 97201-3469

GRAVES, PATRICK LEE, lawyer; b. Pasadena, Calif., Sept. 16, 1945; s. James Edward and Virginia (Dudley) G.; children: Carrie Kathleen, Michael Partick. AS, Citrus Jr. Coll., Glendora, Calif., 1969; BS, Calif. State Polytechnic U., 1973; BS in Law, Western State U., 1973, JD, 1975. Bar: Calif. 1975, U.S. Dist. Ct. (cen. dist.) Calif. 1976, U.S. Ct. Appeals (9th cir.) 1978, U.S. Supreme Ct. 1980. Assoc. Lynberg & Watkins, Los Angeles, 1975-80, ptnr., 1981-93; ptnr. Graves & King, Upland, Calif., 1993—; settlement officer Los Angeles Superior Ct., 1988—, arbitrator, 1981—; arbitrator San Bernardino Superior Ct., 1990—. judge pro tem L.A. Superior Ct., 1992—. Sustaining mem. Rep. Nat. Com., Washington, 1979—; mem. Nat. Rep. Congl. Com., 1980—. Mem. ABA, Los Angeles County Bar Assn., San Bernardino County Bar Assn., Assn. So. Calif. Defense Counsel (chmn. 1988), Defense Research Inst., Upland (Calif.) C. of C. Home: 1724 Brentwood Ave Upland CA 91784 Office: Graves & King 1317 W Foothill Blvd Ste 200 Upland CA 91786-3674

GRAVES, THOMAS DAYLE, psychology educator; b. Concordia, Kans., July 21, 1936; s. Byron W. and Hazel Agnes (McGowan) G.; m. Patricia Louise McGintie, Apr. 22, 1961; children: Kelly, Kerry, Karleen. BA, Adams State Coll., 1965, MA, 1966; EdD, U. No. Colo., 1974. Lic. profl. counselor, Colo. Pers. adminstr. Martin-Marietta Corp., Denver, 1958-64; instr. Mesa State Coll., Grand Junction, Colo., 1966-74, prof. psychology, 1975—; cons. Dixson's Inc., Grand Junction, 1976-77, Occidental Oil Shale, Grand Junction, 1976-77, Job Corps, Colbran, Colo., 1978-79, Union Oil Co.,Grand Junction, 1982-85, U.S. Sack Corp., Grand Junction, 1995. Author: Practicum Manual for Undergraduate Students, 1988, Internship Manual for Undergraduate Students, 1989. With U.S. Army, 1956-58. Mem. APA, ACA, Colo. Counseling Assn., Am. Mental Health Counseling Assn. Democrat. Roman Catholic. Home: 2719 8th Ct Grand Junction CO 81506-8203 Office: Mesa State Coll Box 2647 Grand Junction CO 81502

GRAVITZ, SIDNEY ISAAC, aerospace engineer; b. Balt., June 28, 1932; s. Philip Benjamin and Sophie (Korim) G.; m. Phyllis Bilgrad, June 14, 1964; children: Deborah Anne, Elizabeth Ellen. BS, MIT, 1953, MS, 1954, AeroE, 1957. Rsch. engr. aero. engring. dept. MIT, Cambridge, 1952-57; dynamics group engr. N.Am. Aviation, Columbus, Ohio, 1957-60; engr. mgr. Boeing Co., Seattle, 1960-90; cons. Mercer Island, Wash., 1990—; mem. space shuttle design criteria working group NASA, 1970; mem. panel Radio Tech. Commn. Aero., 1980-81; mem. panel Naval Rsch. Adv. Com., 1990; lectr. in field. Contbr. articles to Vibration, Flutter, Surface Transp. Loaned exec. United Good Neighbor Fund, King County, Wash., 1968; regional chair alumni fund dr. MIT, 1970, mem. ednl. coun., 1974-77. 1st lt. USAF, 1954-56. Scholar MIT, 1949, fellow, 1956. Fellow AIAA (assoc.); mem. ASME, Sigma Xi, Sigma Gamma Tau. Home: 8428 SE 62nd St Mercer Island WA 98040-4923

GRAY, ALFRED ORREN, journalism educator, research and communications consultant; b. Sun Prairie, Wis., Sept. 8, 1914; s. Charles Orren and Amelia Katherine (Schadel) G.; m. Nicolin Jane Plank, Sept. 5, 1947; children—Robin, Richard. B.A., U. Wis.-Madison, 1939, M.A., 1941. Reporter-correspondent-intern U. Wis.-Madison and Medford newspapers, 1937-39; free-lance writer, 1938-41, 51-57; intelligence investigator U.S. Ordnance Dept., Ravenna, Ohio, 1941-42; hist. editor, chief writer U.S. Office Chief Ordnance Service, ETO, Paris and Frankfurt, Germany, 1944-46; asst. prof. journalism Whitworth Coll., Spokane, Wash., 1946-48, assoc. prof., 1948-56, head dept. journalism, adviser student publs., 1946-80, prof., 1956-80, prof. emeritus, 1980—, chmn. div. bus. and communications arts, 1958-66, chmn. div. applied arts, 1978-79; cons. research and communications Spokane, 1980—; dir. Whitworth News Bur., 1952-58; prin. researcher, writer 12 hist. and ednl. projects. Author: The History of U.S. Ordnance Service in the European Theater of Operations, 1942-46, Not by Might, 1965, Eight Generations from Gondelsheim: A Genealogical Study, 1980; co-author: Many Lamps, One Light: A Centennial History, 1984; editor: The Synod Story, 1953-55; mem. editorial adv. bd. Whitworth Today mag., 1989-90; contbr. articles to newspapers, mags., jours.; advisor All-Am. coll. newspaper; editorial reader Am. Presbyns.: The Jour. of Presbyn. History, 1992—. Scoutmaster Troop 9, Four Lakes Coun., Boy Scouts Am., Madison, Wis., 1937-41; chmn. Pinewood Addition Archtl. Com., Spokane, 1956—; dir. Inland Empire Publs. Clinic, Spokane, 1959-74; mem. ho. of dels. Greater Spokane Council of Chs., 1968-71; judge Goodwill Worker of Yr. awards Goodwill Industries Spokane County, 1972; vice-moderator Synod Wash.-Alaska, Presbyn. Ch. (U.S.A.), 1966-67; bd. dirs. Presbyn. Hist. Soc., 1984-90, 91-94, exec. com., 1986-90, chmn. hist. sites com., 1986-90; mem. Am. Bd. Mission Heritage Commn. for Sesquicentennial of Whitman Mission, 1986; elder Spokane 1st Presbyn. Ch., 1962—, clk. of session, 1984-86, mem. Inland Empire Presbytery Com. for Bicentennial of Gen. Assembly, 1988-89, Inland Empire Presbytery, mem. com. on justice and peacemaking, 1988-95; Dem. precinct official, Spokane, 1988-92. Served with AUS, 1942-46. Decorated Bronze Star and Army Commendation medals; recipient Printers Ink trophy Advt. Assn. West, 1953, citation Nat. Coun. Coll. Publ. Advisers, 1967, Outstanding Teaching of Journalism award Whitworth Coll. Alumni Assn., 1972; named Disting. Newspaper Adviser in U.S., Nat. Coun. Coll. Publ. Advisers, 1979. Mem. Assn. for Edn. in Journalism, Ea. Wash. Hist. Soc., Coll. Media Advisors (hon.), Ea. Washington Geneal. Soc., N.Am. Mycol. Assn., U. Wis. Alumni Assn. Half Century Club, Spokane First Presbyn., Phi Beta Kappa (pres. profl. chpt. 1949-50, 67-68, 70-71). Democrat. Home: 304 W Hoerner Ave Spokane WA 99218-2124

GRAY, AUGUSTINE HEARD, JR., computer consultant; b. Long Beach, Calif., Aug. 18, 1936; s. Augustine Heard Gray and Elizabeth (Dubois) Jordan Gray; m. Averill Forneret, Dec. 27, 1959. SB, MIT, 1959, SM, 1959; PhD, Calif. Inst. Tech., 1964; MBA, Pepperdine U., 1981. Asst. prof. dept. elec. and computer engring. U. Calif., Santa Barbara, 1964-68, assoc. prof., 1968-75, prof., 1975-80; v.p. Signal Tech. Inc., Santa Barbara, 1980-88; v.p. SmartStar Corp., Goleta, Calif., 1988-90, sr. scientist, 1990-92; owner A.H. Gray Cons., 1993—. Co-author: Linear Prediction of Speech, 1976; contbr. articles to profl. jours. Fellow IEEE. Democrat. Home: 88039 Leeward Dr Florence OR 97439-9003

GRAY, DEBORAH MARY, medical corporation executive; b. Sydney, N.S.W., Australia, Feb. 4, 1952; came to U.S., 1973; d. Anthony Eric and Mary Patricia (O'Mullane) Gray; m. Theodore Ralph Culbertson, July 31, 1971 (div. 1979); m. Scott Cameron Struthers, Jan. 31, 1981 (div. 1988). Student St. Petersburg Jr. Coll., 1978-85, Eckerd Coll., 1988-90. Fin. counselor Wuesthoff Meml. Hosp., Rockledge, Fla., 1973-75; adminstrv. dir. Dresden & Ticktin, MDs, P.A., St. Petersburg, Fla., 1976-80; exec. dir., v.p. Am. Med. Mgmt., Inc., Clearwater, Fla., 1980-90; pres., dir. All Women's Health Ctr., Inc., St. Petersburg, 1980-90, All Women's Health Ctr. North Tampa, Inc., Fla., 1980-90, All Women's Health Ctr. Tampa, Inc., 1980-90, Women's Ob-Gyn. Ctr. Countryside, Inc., 1984-90, All Women's Health Ctr. Sarasota, Fla., 1980-90, All Women's Health Ctr. Ocala, Fla., 1980-90, All Women's Health Ctr. Gainesville, Fla., 1981-90, Lakeland Women's Health Ctr., Fla., 1980-90, Ft. Myers Womens Health Ctr., Fla., 1980-90, All Women's Health Ctr. Jacksonville, Fla., 1980-90, Nat. Women's Health Svcs., Inc., Clearwater, Fla., 1983-90, D.M.S. of Ft. Myers, Inc., 1985-90, Alternative Human Svc., 1979; treas., v.p., dir. Birthing Mgmt. Inc., 1985-90; healthcare cons., 1990-92; N.Am. mgr. Cowra Wines, Australia, 1991-95; owner, sole proprietor The Australian Wine Connection, Breckenridge, Colo., 1992—; dir. Perinatal Ct. Ga. Bapt. Med. Ctr., 1990-92. Mem. bd. agy. that facilitates hard to place children adoptions One Ch. One Child, 1990-94.

GRAY, DONALD ALLAN, computer software international sales executive; b. Palo Alto, Calif., Jan. 27, 1964; s. Thomas Leighton and Audrey May (MacGregor) G. BS, U. So. Calif., 1987. Corp. trainer Computer Solutions, Internat., L.A., 1987-89; regional sales mgr. V.I. Corp., Newport Beach, Calif., 1989-91; internat. sales dir. Talarian Corp., Mountain View, Calif., 1991-93, 1993—; bus. plan devel. mgr. Occidental Petroleum, L.A., 1988-89, Armand Hammer Mus. Art and Cultural Ctr. Home: PO Box 391673 Mountain View CA 94039-1673 Office: Talarian Corp 444 Castro St Mountain View CA 94041-2017

GRAY, DONOVAN MICHAEL, cultural development specialist; b. July 14, 1948; s. Stanley Hermann and Maxine Abbott (Cushing) G. BA in Community Arts Devel., The Evergreen State Coll., 1976, MPA in Cultural Policy, 1982. Grants coord. The Evergreen State Coll., Olympia, Wash., 1980-82; local liaison Oreg. Arts Commn., Salem, 1982-85; fundraiser Meany Hall for Performing Arts, Seattle, 1986-88; dir. Western Arts Mgmt. Inst., Ashland, Oreg., 1987-90; pub. info., grant panel system mgr. Nev. State Coun. on Arts, Reno, 1990-91; ptnr. Withers and Gray Project Mgmt. and Consultancy, Medford, 1991-93; exec. dir. Network of Local Arts Agys. of Wash. State, Olympia, 1993—; part-time devel. assoc. The Evergreen State Coll., Olympia, 1993—; mem. cultural study tour to No. Ireland, Brit. Coun., 1991. Photographs exhibited in shows at Exclusive Accents Gallery, Jacksonville, Oreg., 1990, Rental/Sales Gallery, Rogue Gallery, Medford, 1990-93, 4th St. Gallery and Garden Cafe, Ashland, Oreg., 1992; author: Cultural Equation: The Sum of the Arts, 1989, The Arts Add Up, 1990, Southern Oregon Media Directory, 1990; contbr. articles to profl. publs.; editor, pub. agy. newsletters, 1972-92. Bd. dirs. western divsn. Assn. Am. Dance Cos., 1973-74; mem. Seattle Ctr. Visual Arts adv. com. Seattle Arts Commn., 1973; mem. dance adv. coun. City of Seattle Parks Dept., 1973-74; mem. adv. bd. Western Humanities Ctr., UCLA, 1974-75; mem. expansion arts panel Nat. Endowment for Arts, 1977-78, mem. arts adminstrn. tng. task force locals program, 1989; treas. bd. dirs. Neighborhood Arts Programs Nat. Orgn. Com., 1978-79; mem. adv. bd. Rural Arts Svcs., Mendocino, Calif., 1988-90; chmn. adv. com. Washington State Bldg. for the Arts, 1994—. Named One of Outstanding Community Arts Developers in U.S., Arts Reporting Svc., 1984. Home: 1916 Washington St SE # A Olympia WA 98501-2956

GRAY, GARY MICHAEL, physician, researcher, educator; b. Seattle, June 4, 1933; s. Max Leslie Gray and Irene Helen Thibeau; m. Mary A. Lassila, Aug. 1957; children: David, Peter, Jeffrey, Michael, Jason. BS in Chemistry and Math., Seattle U., 1955; MD, U. Wash., 1959. Diplomate Am. Bd. Internal Medicine. Intern, then jr. asst. resident Bellevue Hosp., N.Y.C., 1959-61; sr. asst. resident Univ. Hosp. Cleve., 1961-62; fellow in gastroenterology Univ. Hosp., Boston, 1962-64; asst. prof. medicine Stanford (Calif.) U. Sch. Medicine, 1966-70, assoc. prof., 1970-77, prof., 1977—, chief gastroenterology div., 1971-88, dir. digestive disease ctr., 1987—; mem. rev. com. NIH-Nat. Inst. Digestive, Diabetes and Kidney Disease, 1972-78; mem. Am. Inst. Nutrition. Author: Scientific American Medicine, 1979—; mem. editorial bd. Gastroenterology; contbr. articles to profl. jours. Captain M.C., U.S. Army, 1964-66. Recipient Career Devel. award USPHS, 1970-75; USPHS grantee, 1967—. Mem. Assn. Am. Physicians, Am. Gastroent. Assn. (bd. govs. 1980-84), Am. Soc. for Clin. Investigation, Am. Soc. Biol. Chemistry & Molecular Biology, Am. Chem. Soc., Am. Clin. and Climatol. Soc. Democrat. Office: Stanford U Med Ctr 300 Pasteur Dr Palo Alto CA 94304-2203

GRAY, GAVIN CAMPBELL, II, computer information engineer, computer consultant; b. Levittown, N.Y., Sept. 16, 1948; s. Gavin Campbell Gray and Pauline Louise (Bauerschmidt) Gowen; m. Catherine Ann West, Aug. 23, 1969; children: Jeffrey William, Tamara Pauline. Student, U. Wis., Milw., 1966-71. Programmer, analyst Equitable Variable Life Ins., Farmingdale, N.Y., 1975-77; analyst, programmer Atty.'s Title Svcs., Orlando, Fla., 1977-78; systems analyst Cert. Grocers, Ocala, Fla., 1978-80; supr. R & D, Clay Electric Coop., Keystone Heights, Fla., 1980-86; mgr. info. svcs. Coldwell Banker Relocation Svcs., Mission Viejo, Calif., 1986—; mem. Guide Internat. Bus. Rules Standards Project, 1994-95, Asymetrix Corp. Adv. Coun. Author: IBM GIS Usage for IMS/DLI, 1979; developer software Map-Paint for CICS, methodology Path Evaluation Method (PEM), TRANS-FLOW Programming, Tier Diagramming Method. Mem. IEEE, ANSI (mem. accredited standards com. 1994—), Assn. Computing Machinery, Data Adminstrn. Mgmt. Assn. Internat., Math Assn. Am., Am. Psychol. Assn., Internat. Platform Assn., IEEE Computer Soc., IEEE Engring. Mgmt. Soc., N.Y. Acad. Scis., Am. Mus. Natural History, Zool. Soc. San Diego, Nat. Eagle Scout Assn., Am. Mensa Ltd., Intertel. Office: Coldwell Banker Relocation Svcs 27271 Las Ramblas Mission Viejo CA 92691-6386

GRAY, JAN CHARLES, lawyer; b. Des Moines, June 15, 1947; s. Charles Donald and Mary C. Gray; 1 child, Charles Jan. BA in Econs., U. Calif., Berkeley, 1969; MBA, Pepperdine U., 1986; JD, Harvard U., 1972. Bar: Calif. 1972, D.C. 1974, Wyo. 1992. Law clk. Kindel & Anderson, L.A., 1971-72; assoc. Halstead, Baker & Sterling, L.A., 1972-75; sr. v.p., gen. counsel and sec. Ralphs Grocery Co., L.A., 1975—; owner Am. Presidents Resorts, Custer, S.D., Glenrock, Wyo., 1983—, Big Bear (Calif.) Cabins-Lakeside, 1988—, Sta. KGOS/KERM, Torrington, Wyo., 1993—, Sta. KRAL/KIQZ, Rawlins, Wyo., 1993—, Sta. KZMX, Hot Springs, S.D., 1993—, Sta. KFCR, Custer, S.D., 1992—, Sta. KQLT-FM, Casper, Wyo., 1994—; judge pro tem L.A. Mcpl. Ct., 1977-85; instr. bus. UCLA, 1976-85, Pepperdine MBA Program, 1983-85; arbitrator Am. Arbitration Assn., 1977—; media spokesman So. Calif. Grocers Assn., 1979-90, Calif. Grocers Assn., 1979—, Calif. Retailers Assn., 1979—; real estate broker, L.A., 1973—. Contbg. author: Life or Death, Who Controls?, 1976; contbr. articles to profl. jours. Trustee South Bay U. Coll. Law, 1978-79; mem. bd. visitors Southwestern U. Sch. Law, 1983—; mem. L.A. County Pvt. Industry Coun., 1982—, exec. com. 1984-88, chmn. econ. devel. task force, 1986-89, chmn. mktg. com. 1991-93; mem. L.A. County Martin Luther King, Jr. Gen. Hosp. Authority, 1984—; mem. L.A. County Aviation Commn, 1986-92, chmn., 1990-91; L.A. Police Crime Prevention Adv. Coun., 1986—; Angelus Plaza Adv. Bd., 1983-85; bd. dirs. RecyCAL of So. Calif., 1983-89; trustee Santa Monica Hosp. Found., 1986-91, adv. bd., 1991—; mem. L.A. County Dem. Cen. Com., 1980-90, L.A. City Employees' Retirement System Comsn., 1993—; del. Dem. Nat. Conv., 1980. Recipient So. Calif. Grocers Assn. award for outstanding contbns. to food industry, 1982; Calif./Nev. Soft Drink Assn. appreciation award for No on 11 Campaign, 1983. Mem. ABA, Calif. Bar Assn., L.A. County Bar Assn. (exec. com. corp. law depts. sect. 1974-76, 79—, chmn. 1989-90, exec. com. barristers sect. 1974-75, 79-81, trustee 1991-93, jud. evaluation com. 1993—, nominating com. 1994), San Fernando Valley Bar Assn. (chmn. real property sect. 1975-77, L.A. Pub. Affairs Officers Assn., L.A. World Affairs Coun., Calif. Retailers Assn. (supermarket com.), Food Mktg. Inst. (govt. rels. com., benefits coun. 1993—, chmn. lawyers and economists 1994—), So. Calif. Bus. Assn. (bd. dirs. 1981—, mem. exec. com. 1982—, sec. 1986—, chair 1991—), Town Hall L.A., U. Calif. Alumni Assn., Ephebian Soc. L.A., Harvard Club of So. Calif., Phi Beta Kappa. Home: 2793 Creston Dr Los Angeles CA 90068-2209 Office: PO Box 54143 Los Angeles CA 90054-0143

GRAY, KARLA MARIE, state supreme court justice. BA, Western Mich. U., MA in African History; JD, U. Calif., San Francisco, 1976. Bar: Mont. 1976, Calif. 1977. Law clk. to Hon. W. D. Murray U.S. Dist. Ct., 1976-77; staff atty. Atlantic Richfield Co., 1977-81; pvt. practice law Butte, Mont., 1981-84; staff atty., legis. lobbyist Mont. Power Co., Butte, 1984-91; judge Supreme Ct. Mont., Helena, 1991—. Mem. Mont. Supreme Ct. Gender Fairness Task Force. Fellow Am. Bar Found., Am. Judicature Soc., Supreme Ct. Hist. Soc.; mem. State Bar Mont., Silver Bow County Bar Assn. (past pres.), Nat. Assn. Women Judges. Office: Supreme Ct Mont Justice Bldg Rm 323 215 N Sanders St Helena MT 59601-4522

GRAY, PATRICIA JOYCE, court administrator; b. Carlsbad, N.Mex., Feb. 5, 1951; d. Owen Corbett and Bobby Jo (Jones) G.; m. Patrick A. Edwards, Oct. 29, 1981 (div. June 1990). Student, U. Nev., Las Vegas, 1974-77. Receptionist, clk. Nationwide Fin., Las Vegas, 1969-70; dep. clk. U.S. Bankruptcy Ct. for Dist. Nev., Las Vegas, 1970-74, chief dep. clk., 1974-75, chief clk., 1975-79, clk. of ct., 1979—; mem. bankruptcy work measurement sub-com. of com. on adminstrn. bankruptcy system Jud. Conf. U.S., 1989-91; mem. tng. and edn. com. U.S. Bankruptcy Cts. Adminstrv. Office U.S. Cts., 1990-91; mem. Bankruptcy Work Measurement subcom. of Clerk's adv. com. Adminstrv. Office U.S. Cts., 1992-93, local rules subcom. Dist. Nev., 1991—. Mem. Space and Facilities Ad Hoc Task Force on Personnel of Adminstrv. Office of U.S. Cts., 1994—, 9th Cir. Task Force on Race, Religious, and Ethnic Fairness, 1994—; mem. bd. dirs. of Clark County, Nev. chpt. ARC, 1994—. Mem. Nat. Conf. Bankruptcy Clks., Fed. Ct. Clks. Assn. Rebublican. Office: US Bankruptcy Ct Foley Fed Bldg 300 Las Vegas Blvd S Las Vegas NV 89101-5812

GRAY, PAUL WESLEY, university dean; b. Cicero, Ill., Jan. 30, 1947; s. Harry B. and Audrey (Tong) G.; m. Rachel E. Boehr, June 3, 1967; children: John M., Janel E., Robert B. BA, Faith Baptist Bible Coll., Ankeny, Tex., 1970; ThM, Dallas Theol. Sem., 1975; MS in Libr. Sci., East Tex. State U., 1977, EdD, 1980; MA, Tex. Woman's U., 1989. Dorm dir. Buckner Baptist Benevolences, Dallas, 1971-75; dir. community living residence IV Dallas County Mental Health/Mental Retardation, Dallas, 1975-78; cataloger W. Walworth Harrison Pub. Libr., Greenville, Tex., 1978-81; v.p. Golden Triangle Christian Acad., Garland, Tex., 1979-83; dir. libr. LeTourneau U., Longview, Tex., 1983-88; dean computer svc. and univ. libr. Azusa (Calif.) Pacific U., 1989—. Mem. ALA, Calif. Libr. Assn., So. Calif. Area Theol. Libr. Assn., Foothill Libr. Consortium. Republican. Baptist. Office: Azusa Pacific U 901 E Alosta Ave Azusa CA 91702-2701

GRAY, PHILIP HOWARD, psychologist, educator; b. Cape Rosier, Maine, July 4, 1926; s. Asa and Bernice (Lawrence) G.; m. Iris McKinney, Dec. 31, 1954; children: Cindelyn Gray Eberts, Howard. M.A., U. Chgo., 1958; Ph.D., U. Wash., 1960. Asst. prof. dept. psychology Mont. State U., Bozeman, 1960-65; assoc. prof. Mont. State U., 1965-75, prof., 1975-92; ret., 1992; vis. prof. U. Man., Winnipeg, Can., 1968-70; chmn. Mont. Bd. Psychologist Examiners, 1972-74; speaker sci. and geneal. meetings on ancestry of U.S. presidents. Organizer Folk art exhbns. Mont. and Maine, 1972-79; author: The Comparative Analysis of Behavior, 1966, (with F.L. Ruch and N. Warren) Working with Psychology, 1963, A Directory of Eskimo Artists in Sculpture and Prints, 1974, The Science That Lost Its Mind, 1985, Penobscot Pioneers, vol. 1, 1992, vol. 2, 1992, vol. 3, 1993, vol. 4, 1994, vol. 5, 1995; contbr. numerous articles on behavior to psychol. jours.; contbr. peotry to lit. jours. With U.S. Army, 1944-46. Recipient Am. and Can. research grants. Fellow AAAS, APA, Am. Psychol. Soc., Internat. Soc. Rsch. on Aggression; mem. NRA (life), SAR (v.p. Sourdough chpt. 1990, pres. 1991-95, trustee 1989), Nat. Geneal. Soc., New Eng. Hist. Geneal. Soc., Gallatin County Geneal. Soc. (charter, pres. 1991-93), Deer Isle-Stonington Hist. Soc., Internat. Soc. Human Ethology, Descs. Illegitmate Sons and Daus of Kings of Britain, Piscataqua Pioneers, Order Desc. Colonial Physicians and Chirugiens, Flagon and Trencher, Order of the Crown of Charlemagne. Republican. Home: 1207 S Black Ave Bozeman MT 59715-5633

GRAY, RICHARD ARDEN, transportation executive; b. Ft. Bragg, Calif., Oct. 29, 1935; s. Arden Howard and Marion Florence (Coolidge) G.; m. Roberta Jeanne Montna, Feb. 5, 1955; children: Mark Alan, Laura Ann, Deborah Marie, Lisa Lynn. AA, Yuba Coll., 1955; BA, Calif. State U., 1957. Cert. coll. instr., Calif. Deputy sheriff Yuba County Sheriffs Dept., Marysville, Calif., 1957; traffic officer Calif. Hwy. Patrol, Ventura, 1958-60, Yuba City, 1961-68; sgt. field ops. officer Calif. Hwy. Patrol, Gardena, 1969-71; lt. exec. officer Calif. Hwy. Patrol, Van Nuys, 1972-76; lt. area comdr. Calif. Hwy. Patrol, Chico, 1977-88; wholesale, retail distbr. Dick Gray Enterprises, Chico, 1989-94; instr. Yuba Coll., Marysville, 1965-67, Calif. fish and game hunter safety program, Chico, 1982-86; profl. driver, transporter motor homes, 1989—. Chmn. citizen rev. com. United Way of Butte County, Chico, 1984 (outstanding achievement 1984-86), fundraising campaign chmn. 1986, pres. bd. dirs. 1985; pres., bd. dirs. No. Calif. Counties Exch. Club Child Abuse Prevention Ctr., Chico, 1987-91. With USNR, 1953-61. Recipient Individual Excellence Outstanding Cmty. Svc. award United Way Butte and Glenn Counties, 1994-95. Mem. Calif. Hwy. Patrolmen Assn., RV Club, Elks (honors 1988, pres. 1988-89), Breakfast Exch. Club (pres., bd. dirs. 1980-81), Exch. Club Greater Chico (sponsor 1983). Republican.

GRAY, RICHARD MOSS, retired college president; b. Washington, Jan. 25, 1924; s. Wilbur Leslie and Betty Marie (Grey) G.; m. Catherine Claire Hammond, Oct. 17, 1943; children: Janice Lynn Gray Armstrong, Nancy Hammond Gray Schultz. BA, Bucknell U., 1942; MDiv summa cum laude, San Francisco Theol. Sem., 1961; PhD, U. Calif., Berkeley, 1972; doctorate degree (hon.), World Coll. West, 1988. Writer, creative dir. N.W. Ayer & Son, Phila., 1942-58; univ. pastor Portland State U., Oreg., 1961-68; founder, pres. World Coll. West, Petaluma, Calif., 1973-88, pres. emeritus, 1988—; bd. dirs. World Centre, San Francisco, Lifeplan Ctr. Author poetry Advent, 1989. Bd. dirs. Citizens Found. Marin, San Rafael, Calif., 1988—, Marin Ednl. Found., 1989-92; ruling elder Presbyn. Ch. U.S.A. Named Disting. Alumnus of Yr. San Theol. Sem., 1988, Marin Citizen of Yr. Citizens Found., 1988; recipient Svc. to Humanity award Bucknell U., 1992. Mem. Phi Beta Kappa.

GRAY, ROBERT DONALD, mayor; b. Quincy, Ill., May 6, 1924; s. James Arthur and Katherine Elnora (Moore) G.; m. Marie Dolores Albert, July 15, 1951; children: Michael S., Sheilah C. Student, Washington & Jefferson Coll., 1945-47; BSEE, Okla. State U., 1949; postgrad., Northwestern U. Electrolysis engr. Sinclair Refining Co., 1949-50; North Atlantic field mgr. navigation/communication systems USAF, 1950-51; cons. Lockheed Aircraft Ga. Co., 1951-52; sr. devel. engr. Harris Corp., 1952-54; dir. Gen. Telephone Electronics, Mountain View, Calif., 1954-66; dir. reliability and quality control Gen. Dynamics/Electronics, Rochester, N.Y., 1961-62; v.p. rsch./devel. Lockheed Missiles/Space Co., Sunnyvale, Calif., 1966-79; pres. Gray Assocs., Internat. Air Traffic Control System, Los Altos, Calif., 1980-87; mayor City of Los Altos, Calif., 1993—. With USN, 1941-45; ETO. Mem. IEEE (sr.), Los Altos Golf and Country Clu, Phi Kappa Psi. Republican. Home: 270 Valencia Dr Los Altos CA 94022-2258

GRAY, RONALD FREDERICK, college administrator, engineer; b. Salina, Kans., Feb. 12, 1944; s. Roland Arlington and Dorothy Lavera (Beals) G.; m. Sharon Ann Reich, June 8, 1968; 1 child Darren Scott Gray. BSME, S.D. Sch. Mines and Tech., Rapid City, 1966. Profl. Engr.- Mech. Sr. engr. The Boeing Co., Seattle, 1966-71; product test engr. Ford Motor Co., Dearborn, Mich., 1972-73; sr. engr. The Boeing Co., Seattle, 1973-74; dir. phys. plant S.D. Sch. of Mines and Tech., Rapid City, S.D., 1974-88, Mesa State Coll., Grand Junction, Colo., 1988—. Me. Assn. of Phys. Plant Adminstrs. Office: Mesa State Coll 1175 Texas Ave Grand Junction CO 81501-7605

GRAY, THOMAS STEPHEN, newspaper editor; b. Burbank, Calif., Aug. 22, 1950; s. Thomas Edgar and Lily Irene (Ax) G.; m. Barbara Ellen Bronson, Aug. 27, 1977; children: Jonathan Thomas, Katherine Marie. BA, Stanford U., 1972; MA in English, UCLA, 1976. Teaching assoc. UCLA, 1976-77; reporter L.A. Daily News, 1977-79, editorial writer, 1979-84, editorial page editor, 1984—. Recipient 1st Place award Editorial Writing Greater L.A. Press Club, 1988, Inland Daily Press Association, 1993. Office: Daily News Editorial Pages PO Box 4200 Woodland Hills CA 91365-4200

GRAY, WALTER P., III, museum director, consultant; b. San Francisco, Aug. 8, 1952; s. Walter Patton II and Elsie Josephine (Stroop) G.; m. Mary Amanda Helmich, May 23, 1980. BA in History, Calif. State U., Sacramento, 1976. Rschr. Calif. State R.R. Mus., Sacramento, 1977-80, curator, 1980-81, 85-90, archivist, 1981-85, dir., 1990—; cons. in field, 1976—. Contbr. articles to profl. jours. Democrat. Buddhist. Office: California State Railroad Museum 111 I St Sacramento CA 95814-2204

GRAY, WILLIAM HIRAM, university dean; b. San Jose, Calif., Feb. 5, 1947; s. William H. Jr. and Barbara (Wilcox) G.; m. Kelsey Gray, July 12, 1980; children: Ashley Troy, Karlin Nola. AA, San Jose City Coll., 1968; BA, U. Calif., Davis, 1970; MA, Wash. State U., 1972; PhD, Portland State U., 1984. Rsch. asst., assoc. Wash. State U., Pullman, 1970-72; ext. agt. Wash. State U., Bellingham, 1972-76; ext. chair Wash. State U., Vancouver, 1976-81; program adminstr., dir. Wash. State U., Pullman, 1981-87; dean Wash. State U., Spokane, 1987—. Contbr. articles to profl. jours. Trustee Econ. Devel. Coun., Spokane, 1988-93; dir. Spokane Unltd., 1988—, Deaconnes Med. Ctr., Spokane, 1992—; trustee Spokane Symphony, 1992—; trustee, founder N.W. Mus. Health & Sci., 1988. With U.S. Army, 1967-73. Ford Found. fellow, Washington, 1975, Kellogg fellow Resources for the Future, Washington, 1986, Paul Harris fellow Rotary Internat., 1992. Mem. Cmty. Devel. Soc. Am. (chpt. pres. 1978-80). Home: 3444 S Lincoln Dr Spokane WA 99203-1626 Office: Wash State U 601 W 1st Ave Spokane WA 99204-0317

GRAYBEAL, LYNNE ELIZABETH, lawyer; b. Seattle, May 21, 1956; d. John Olin and Janie Marie (Everly) G.; m. Scott Harron, Oct. 7, 1989. Student, Pomona Coll., 1974-76; BA, Colby Coll., 1979; JD, U. Puget Sound, 1983. Bar: Wash. 1983, U.S. Dist. Ct. (we. dist.) Wash. 1983. Rsch. asst. Charles River Assocs., Boston, 1979-80; assoc. Bogle & Gates, Seattle, summer 1982, 83-85; assoc. Monroe, Stokes, Eitelbach & Lawrence, P.S., Seattle, 1986-89, prin., 1990-92; ptnr. Riddell, Williams, Bullitt & Walkinshaw, 1992—. Sec. Bathhouse Theatre, 1984-86, v.p., 1987; bd. dirs. Wash. Vol. Lawyers for ARts, 1985-89; v.p., bd. dirs. Seattle Found. for Motion Picture ARts, 1988-89. Mem. ABA (chmn. unfair competition trade identity subcom. 1987-88), Wash. State Bar Assn. (chmn. intellectual and indsl. property sect. 1988-89), Wash. State Patent Law Assn., Wash. Women Lawyers (treas. 1989-91, pres. 1992), Greater Seattle C. of C. (curriculum com. 1989-91, Leadership Tomorrow class 1988-89). Home: 2215-2d Ave N 3037 38th Ave W Seattle WA 98199-2512 Office: Foster Pepper & Shefelman 1111 Third Ave Ste 3400 Seattle WA 98101*

GRAYBILL, DAVID WESLEY, chamber of commerce executive; b. Council Bluffs, Iowa, Apr. 8, 1949, s. John Donald and Dorothy Lorraine (King) G.; m. Kortney Loraine Steinbeck, Aug. 17, 1974; 1 child, Darcy Lorraine. BA in Journalism, U. Iowa, 1971. Cert. econ. developer, Chamber exec. Adminstrv. asst. Iowa City C. of C., 1972-74; exec. v.p. Brighton (Colo.) C. of C., 1974-77; pres. Fremont (Nebr.) C. of C., 1977-83; pres., chief exec. officer Tacoma-Pierce County C. of C., 1983—; pres. Nebr. C. of C. Execs., 1981-82; treas. NE Nebr. Econ. Devel. Dist., 1980-83. Charter mem. Gov.'s Small Bus. Improvement Com., Wash., 1984-86; presiding elder Tacoma (Wash.) Reorganized LDS Ch. Mem. Am. Econ. Devel. Coun. (bd. dirs. 1985-87), Am. C. of C. (bd. dirs. 1990-94), Wash. C. of C. Execs. (pres. 1988-89, bd. dirs. 1988-90), Rotary (bd. dirs. Tacoma 1985-87). Office: Tacoma-Pierce County C of C PO Box 1933 Tacoma WA 98401-1933

GRAYMAN, GLEN, emergency medicine physician; b. L.A., May 24, 1949; s. Martin Grayman and Elaine Joy (Fagnan) Burakoff; m. Betty Jane Kerling, Aug., 1972 (div. 1978); m. Karla Ellen Rodine, Mar. 19, 1982; children: Dane Martin, Britta Jensen. BA with highest honors, U. Calif., Riverside, 1970; MD, UCLA, 1974. Diplomate Nat. Bd. Med. Examiners, Am. Bd. Emergency Medicine, Am. Bd. Internal Medicine, Am. Bd. Quality Assurance & Utilization Review Physicians; BLS, ACLS, ATLS, PALS. Intern L.A. County-Harbor Gen. Hosp., Torrance, Calif., 1974-75, resident, 1975-77; emergency physician Desert Hosp., Palm Springs, Calif., 1977—; med. dir. emergency/trauma ctr. Desert Hosp., 1989—, chmn. dept. emergency medicine, 1990-91; pres. Desert Emergency Physicians Med. Group, Palm Springs, 1989—; med. dir. dept. emergency med. svcs. Crafton Hills Coll., Yucaipa, Calif., 1983-90; med. dir. Heart to Heart Emergency Med. Instrn. Co., 1987-90, Western Nurse Specialists, Inc., 1986-91; physician specialist, cons. 1984 Olympic Games, L.A., 1984; asst. clin. prof. UCLA, 1985—, clin. instr., 1982-85. Contbr. articles to profl. jours. Bd. dirs. Riverside county chpt. Am. Heart Assn., 1981-84. Fellow Am. Coll. Emergency Physicians; mem. Am. Coll. Physician Execs., AMA, Calif. Med. Assn., Riverside County Med. Assn. (bd. councilors 1988-90, mediation and med. care com. 1987-88, disaster and emergency med. care com. 1993—), Palm Springs Acad. Medicine (pres. 1991-92, sec. 1989-90), Phi Beta Kappa, Alpha Omega Alpha. Jewish. Office: Desert Hosp 1150 N Indian Canyon Dr Palm Springs CA 92262-4872

GRAYSON, ELLISON CAPERS, JR., human resources executive; b. St. Paul, Sept. 7, 1928; s. Ellison Capers and Inez (Santos) G.; m. Jean Mason, Dec. 26, 1953; children: Darby, William. BA, U. Minn., 1950; LHD (hon.), Nat. U., San Diego, 1984. CLU. Gen. agt. Home Life Ins. Co. N.Y., San Francisco, 1955-81; prin. dep., asst. sec. USN, Washington, 1981-84; dir. mktg. and devel. Pvt. Sector Coun., 1985; cons. Washington, 1985-86; sr. v.p. Boyden Internat., San Francisco, 1987-90; ptnr. Spencer Stuart, San Francisco, 1990—; bd. dirs. StellarNet, Inc., San Francisco; advisory bd. Clark/Bardes, Inc., Dallas. Commr. City and County of San Francisco, 1978-81; pres. bd. dirs. St. Mary's Hosp. and Med. Ctr., San Francisco, 1972-75; co-chmn. nat. finance com. Bush for Pres; bd. regents St. Ignatius Coll. Preparatory, San Francisco. Capt. USN, 1952-55. Named Eagle Scout Boy Scouts Am., 1944; recipient Nat. Brotherhood award Nat. Assn. Christians and Jews, San Diego, 1984. Mem. Sovereign Mil. (knight 1978), Order of St. John of Jerusalem, Knights of Malta, Bohemian Club, Met. Club (Washington), Villa Taverna Club (San Francisco), St. Francis Yacht Club, Army Navy Club, Alfalfa Club (Washington). Republican. Roman Catholic. Home: 95 Sea Cliff Ave San Francisco CA 94121-1122 Office: Spencer Stuart # 3700 525 Market St # 3700 San Francisco CA 94105-2708

GRAYSON, SANDRA MARIE, educator; b. San Bernardino, Calif., Dec. 7, 1965; d. William Melvin and Ethelyn Ann (Gueno) Slush; m. Jimmie Robert Grayson, Jr., Nov. 29, 1985. BA in English, Hawaii Pacific U., 1988; MA in English, Calif. State U., Long Beach, 1991; PhD, U. Calif., Riverside, 1994. English tchr. Paramount (Calif.) Unified Sch. Dist., 1989-91; prof. Calif. State U., Long Beach, 1993-95, Bentley Coll., Waltham, Mass., 1995—; cons. Dymally Internat. Group, Inc., Ingelwood, Calif., 1993—; state chairperson Nat. Assn. of African Am. Studies Nat. Conf., 1994—; presenter in field. Editor (newsletter) Network 2000 Newsletter, 1994—; contbr. articles to profl. jours. Rsch. grantee U. Calif., Riverside, 1994; recipient Chun and Julia Afong Liberal Arts award Hawaii Pacific U., 1988, Cert. of Merit Hawaii Pacific Univ. Honors Program, 1988. Mem. NAACP, MLA, ASCD, Nat. Coun. Tchrs. English, Nat. Assn. of African Am. Studies.

GRAZIANO, JOSEPH A., computer company executive; b. 1945. CPA, Merrimack Coll. With Ernst & Whinney, Boston, Rolm Corp., 1976-81; CFO Apple Computer, Inc., Cupertino, Calif., 1981-85, 89—, also exec. v.p., also dir.; CFO, v.p. finance Sun Microsystems, Inc., 1987-89. Office: Apple Computer Inc 20525 Mariani Ave Cupertino CA 95014-6201*

GRAZIOLI, ALBERT JOHN, JR., real estate management executive; b. Honolulu, Jan. 24, 1954; s. Albert John and Kathryn (DeVane) G.; m. Caroline Ann Wilson, Aug. 29, 1981. BA, Rice U., 1976. Lic. real estate broker. Sales cons. Coldwell Banker Comml. Real Estate, L.A., 1980-85, sr. sales mgr., 1985-87; v.p. devel. The Koll Co., L.A., 1987-90; project dir. Gemtel Corp., Pasadena, Calif., 1990-91; pres. Grazioli Devel. Co., Pasadena, 1991-92; v.p. The McGregor Co., L.A., 1992; asset mgr. Citicorp, L.A., 1992-93; v.p. Institutional Realty Advisors, L.A., 1993—. Mem. Jonathan Club (chmn. jr. com., cmty. rels. com., entertainment com., membership com., audit and fin. com., mem. rels. com.). Republican. Office: Instnl Realty Advisors 6300 Wilshire Blvd Ste 1400 Los Angeles CA 90048-5202

GREALISH, JEANNE BLAIR, voice educator; b. Gastonia, N.C., Aug. 25, 1935; d. Lewis Hall and Helen Hansel (Sams) G. BA, Meredith Coll., 1957; MusM, New England Conservatory, 1959, artist's diploma, 1961; postgrad., Vienna Acad. Music, 1961-65. Lectr. U. N.Mex., Albuquerque, 1965-72; coord. grants and tours N.Mex. Symphony, Albuquerque, 1972-77; devel. dir. Sandia Preparatory Sch., Albuquerque, 1978-87; pvt. practice Jeanne Grealish Studio of Voice, Albuquerque, 1987—; performed throughout U.S. and Europe, 1961—; cons. Opera S.W., Albuquerque, 1991, Santa Fe (N.Mex.) Preparatory Sch., 1990, Santa Fe Symphony Orch., 1992, Hospice of the Rio Grande, 1994—; conducted master classes in various schs. and colls., 1980—. Contbr. articles to profl. jours. Artists chmn. June Music Festival, Albuquerque, 1988-94; mem. adv. com. Alliance for Arts Edn., Santa Fe; panelist N.Mex. Arts Divsn., Santa Fe, 1993; bd. dirs. alumni bd. New Eng. Conservatory, Boston; bd. dirs. Nat. Conf. Christians and Jews, Albuquerque. Mem. Opera Unltd. (bd. dirs., ednl. dir.), Music and Arts at St. Michaels (chmn.), Nat. Assn. Tchrs. Singing, N. Mex. Music Tchrs. Assn., Nat. Music Tchrs. Assn., Sigma Alpha Iota Alumnae (pres. 1991-94). Republican. Episcopalian. Home and Office: 1226 Morningside Dr NE Albuquerque NM 87110-6171

GREASER, CONSTANCE UDEAN, automotive industry executive; b. San Diego, Jan. 18, 1938; d. Lloyd Edward and Udean Greaser. BA, San Diego State Coll., 1959; postgrad. U. Copenhagen Grad. Sch. Fgn. Students, 1963, Georgetown U. Sch. Fgn. Service, 1967; MA, U. So. Calif., 1968; Exec. MBA, UCLA, 1981. Advt., publicity mgr. Crofton Co., San Diego, 1959-62; supr. Mercury Publs., Fullerton, Calif., 1962-64; supr. engring. support services div. Arcata Data Mgmt., Hawthorne, Calif., 1964-67; mgr. computerized typesetting dept. Continental Graphics, Los Angeles, 1967-70; v.p., editorial dir. Sage Publs., Inc., Beverly Hills, Calif., 1970-74; head publs. RAND Corp., Santa Monica, Calif., 1974-90; mgr. communications Am. Honda Motors Co., Torrance, Calif., 1990—. Mem. nat. com. Million Minutes of Peace Appeal, 1986, Nat. Info. Standards Orgn., 1987-93, nat. com. Global Cooperation for Better World, 1988. Recipient Berber award Graphic Arts Tech. Found., 1989. Mem. Women in Bus. (pres. 1977-78), Graphic Comm. Assn. (bd. dirs. 1994—), Soc. for Scholarly Pubs. (nat. bd. dirs.), Women in Communication, Soc. Tech. Communication, Brahma Kumaris World Spiritual Orgn. Co-author: Quick Writer-Build Your Own Word Processing Users Guide, 1983; Quick Writer-Word Processing Center Operations Manual, 1984; editor: Urban Research News, 1970-74; mng. editor Comparative Polit. Studies, 1971-74; contbr. articles to various jours. Office: Am Honda Motor Co 1919 Torrance Blvd Torrance CA 90501-2722

GREAT, DON CHARLES, composer, music company executive; b. Medford, Oreg., Mar. 11, 1951; s. Donald Charles Sr. and Anna Marie (Huff) G.; m. Andrea Louise Gerber, Oct. 31, 1970. Student, UCLA, 1975-76, 83-86, Dick Grove Sch. Music, 1983-87. Freelance songwriter Metro-Goldwyn-Mayer Records, 20th Century Records, Bell Records, Los Angeles, 1968—; pres. Don Great Music, Inc., Los Angeles, 1972—. Composer music for TV shows including Who's the Boss? (ABC), 227 (NBC), The Jeffersons (CBS), Gimme a Break (NBC), A Different World (NBC), Fact of Life (NBC), Unsolved Mysteries (NBC), Amen (NBC), Freddies Nightmares (Lorimar-Warner Bros. TV), Saved By the Bell (NBC Disney), One Day at a Time (CBS), Married With Children (Fox/Columbia Pictures), Small Wonder (Fox TV), 1978—, Different Strokes (NBC), BJ and the Bear (NBC), Silverspoons (NBC), Sheriff Lobo (NBC), Incredible Hulk (CBS), Sanford (NBC), Real People (NBC), Crimetime After primetime (CBS), Candid Camera, Tales From the Crypt, In Living Color (Fox-TV), Laugh-In, Baby Races. Mem. Broadcast Music, Inc. (Best Music Score of Yr. award 1986, named TV Composer of Yr. 1986).

GREAVER, HARRY, artist; b. L.A., Oct. 30, 1929; s. Harry Jones and Lucy Catherine (Coons) G.; m. Hanne Synnestvedt Nielsen, Nov. 30, 1955; children—Peter, Paul, Lotte. BFA, U. Kans., 1951, MFA, 1952. Assoc. prof. art U. Maine, Orono, 1955-66; exec. dir. Kalamazoo Inst. Arts, 1966-78; dir. Greaver Gallery, Cannon Beach, Oreg., 1978—; mem. visual com. Mich. Coun. Arts, 1976-78. One-man exhbns. include Baker U., Baldwin, Kans., 1955, U. Maine, Orono, 1958, 59, Pacific U., 1985; group exhbns. include U. Utah Mus. Fine Arts, 1972-73, Purdue U., 1977, Drawings/U.S.A, St. Paul, 1963, San Diego Mus., 1971, Rathbun Gallery, Portland, Oreg., 1988; 10-yr. print retrospective Cannon Beach Arts Assn., 1989. Mem. adv. bd. Haystack Ctr. for the Arts, Cannon Beach, 1988-91. Recipient Purchase award Nat. Endowment Arts, 1971; grantee U. Maine, 1962-64. Mem. Cannon Beach Arts Assn., 1986-88. Address: PO Box 120 Cannon Beach OR 97110-0120

GREBER, ROBERT MARTIN, financial investments executive; b. Phila., Mar. 15, 1938; s. Joseph and Golda (Rubin) G.; m. Judith Ann Pearlstein, Dec. 23, 1962; children: Matthew, Jonathan. B.S. in Fin., Temple U., 1962; grad., Sch. Mgmt. and Strategic Studies, 1982-84. Account exec. Merrill Lynch, Phila., 1962-68; portfolio mgr. v.p. Afuture Funds Inc., Lima, Pa., 1968-70; instl. account exec. Merrill Lynch, Phila., 1970-75; officer, mgr.-v.p. Merrill Lynch, Los Angeles, 1975-79; chief fin. officer Lucasfilm Ltd., Los Angeles, 1979-80; pres., CEO Lucasfilm Ltd., San Rafael, Calif., 1980-84, Diagnostic Networks, Inc., San Francisco, 1984-87; ptnr. Leon A. Farley Assocs., San Francisco, 1988-90; pres., COO The Pacific Stock Exch., 1990—; bd. dirs. Sonic Solutions. Bd. dirs. KQED Pub. Broadcasting Sys., San Francisco, 1983, chmn. bd., 1988; bd. dirs. Film Inst. No. Calif., Marin Symphony Orch., 1981-83, Sonic Solutions, 1993—; trustee Western Behavior Scis. Inst., La JOlla, 1982-89; vice chmn. Assn. Am. Pub. TV, 1992-94; trustee Beryl Buck Inst. for Edn., 1990-93. With Army NG, 1959-60. Mem. Assn. Am. Pub. Television (vice chmn. 1991-93). Office: Pacific Stock Exchange Inc 115 Sansome St San Francisco CA 94104-3601

GRECO, GINA LYN, French language and literature educator; b. New Orleans, Apr. 23, 1964; d. Claude A. and Beryl E. (Bagert) G.; m. Gaetano DeLeonibus, Dec. 19, 1992. BA, Emory U., 1985; MA, Princeton U., 1989, PhD, 1992. Asst. prof. Portland State U., Portland, Oreg., 1992—. Contbr. articles to profl. jours. Mellon Found. fellow, 1986-92. Mem. MLA (mem. com. emerging techs. pedagogy and rsch. 1994—), Medieval Acad. Am., Medieval Acad. The Pacific, Phi Beta Kappa. Office: Portland State U Dept Fgn Langs & Lit PO Box 751 Portland OR 97207-0751

GREEAR, MICHAEL ALLYN, employment counselor and consultant; b. Chehalis, Wash., Dec. 9, 1962; s. William Allyn and Ina Jeanette (Aust) G. BA in Philosophy and Lit., N.W. Nazarene Coll., Nampa, Idaho, 1987. Job coach, crew leader Reliable Enterprises, Centralia, Wash.; employment counselor/cons. ARC Inc. of Ada County, Boise, Idahl; employment cons. Boise Area businesses, 1991-94. Songwriter, musician (rec.) Boneflower, 1994. Supporter Snake River Alliance, Boise, KBSU Pub. Radio, Boise. Office: ARC Inc of Ada County 4402 Albion St Boise ID 83705-1324

GREELEY, RONALD, geology educator; b. Columbus, Ohio, Aug. 25, 1939; s. Edward T. and Elizabeth J. (Graf) G.; m. Cynthia Ray Moody, Aug. 28, 1960; 1 child, Randal Robert. BS in Geology, Miss. State U., 1962, MS in Geology, 1963; PhD in Geology, U. Mo., Rolla, 1966. Geologist Standard Oil Co., Lafayette, La., 1966-67; rsch. scientist NASA-Ames Rsch. Ctr., Moffett Field, Calif., 1967-69; postdoctoral rsch. assoc. NASA-Ames Rsch. Ctr., Moffett Field, 1969-71; rsch. assoc. physics dept. U. Santa Clara, Moffett Field, 1971-77; prof. geology and Ctr. for Meteorite Studies, Ariz. State U., Tempe, 1977—; chmn. dept. Ariz. State U., 1986-90; rsch. fellow Physics and Astronomy Dept. U. London Observatory, Eng., 1975-80; vis. assoc. prof. Divsn. of Geol. and Planetary Sci., Calif. Inst. Tech., Pasadena, 1976-77; adj. prof. Dept. of Geol. Scis., SUNY Buffalo, 1976-80; Overseas Fellow Churchill Coll. and Dept. of Earth Scis., Cambridge, Eng.; cons. French space science review, 1978, UNESCO Physics of Desertification, Trieste, 1979, Khartoum, 1984, Impact Cratering proposal, Royal Soc., London, 1980, Wind Tunnel Project, Kuwait Inst. Sci. Rsch., 1986-88; Regent's prof. Ariz. State U., 1994; organizer, convenor for numerous NASA courses, coms., workshops, confs. Author: (with M.H. Carr) Volcanic Features of Hawaii-A Basis for Comparison with Mars, 1980, (with B.C. Murray and M.C. Malin) Earthlike Planets, 1981, (with Iversen) Wind as a Geological Process: Earth, Mars, Venus and Titan, 1985, Planetary Landscapes, 1987, 2d edit., 1994; (with R. Batson) Planetary Mapping, 1990; eitl. bd. Icarus, 1984—; assoc. editor, contbr. numerous articles to profl. jours. Capt. U.S. Army, 1967-69. Recipient Pub. Svc. medal NASA, 1977, Disting. Rsch. award Ariz. State U., 1981-82, Oustanding Mentor of Grad. Students award, 1988, Group Achievement award NASA, 1991, 92, 93. Fellow Geol. Soc. Am. (chmn. planetary geology divsn.); mem. Am. Geophys. Union, Am. Assn. Advancement of Sci., Meteoritical Soc. Office: Ariz State U Dept Geology Tempe AZ 85287

GREEN, ADELINE MANDEL, psychiatric social worker; b. St. Paul; d. Meyer and Eva Ulanove; B.S., U. Minn., M.S.W.; m. Nathan G. Mandel (div.); children—Meta Susan (Mrs. Richard Katzoff), Myra (Mrs. Jeffrey Halpern); m. Maurice L. Green. Past investigator, Ramsey County Mothers Aid and Aid to Dependent Children, Ramsey County Welfare Bd., St. Paul; then psychiat. social worker Wilder Child Guidance Clinic, St. Paul; then psychiat. social worker, supr. outpatient psychiatry clinic U. Minn. Hosps., Mpls., subsequently supr., clin. instr. psychiatry-social service, outpatient psychiatry clinic; currently in pvt. practice family and marriage counseling South Bay Clinic. Past pres. St. Paul sect. Council Jewish Women; past chmn. Diagnostic Clinic for Rheumatic Fever-Wilder Clinic, St. Paul; assoc. Family and Child Psychiat. Med. Clinic. Lic. clin. social worker. Mem. Nat. Assn. Social Workers, Acad. Certified, Social Workers, Minn. Welfare Conf., Am. Assn. Marriage and Family Counselors, Brandeis U. Women. Democrat. Home: 1091 Sea Terrace Ln Costa Mesa CA 92627-4035 Office: South Bay Psychiatric Clinic Ste 225 14651 S Bascom Los Gatos CA 95030

GREEN, ALLAN WRIGHT, winery owner; b. L.A., May 24, 1949; s. Aaron Gus and Jean Carol (Haber) G. BA in Art, UCLA, 1971, MA in Design, 1974. Winery owner/operator Greenwood Ridge Vineyards, Philo, Calif., 1980—. Mem. Anderson Valley Winegrowers Assn. (pres. 1991-93). Democrat.

GREEN, BONNIE JEAN, early childhood administrator; b. Crookston, Minn., Oct. 23, 1950; d. Francis Romain and Dorothy Marion (Boatman) Bagne; m. Steven Douglas Wedger, July 21, 1973 (div. Feb. 1985); m. Charles Edward Green Jr., June 15, 1985; stepchildren: Andrew Green, Russell Green. BS in Edn. magna cum laude, U. N.D., 1972; cert. human rels., Minn. State U., 1973; postgrad., U. Minn., 1975-83. Cert. elem./early childhood edn. adminstr. Math/reading tutor bilingual students U. N.D., Grand Forks, 1969-71; 1st grade tchr. Park Rapids (Minn.) Ind. Sch. Dist., 1972-73; asst. dir./curriculum writer, tchr. Child Devel. and Learning Ctr., Burnsville, Minn., 1973-75, dir., 1975-87; caring ministry outreach Luth. Ch. of Incarnation, Davis, Calif., 1990—; facilitator-parent edn. program Dakato County Vo-Tech, 1973-78; advisor, cons. Dakota County Childcare Coun., 1977-83; advisor, tchr. cert. program Augsburg Coll., Mpls., 1977-78; supr. student tchrs. Coll. of St. Catherine, Augsburg, St. Paul, 1977-87; cons. Minn. Edn. for Young Children, 1978, State of Minn., 1979-81, Am. Luth. Ch., Mpls., 1981-83; cons., kindergarten curriculum Burnsville Sch. Dist., 1983; liaison coord. Head Start Program, Burnsville, 1985-87. Vol. Prince of Peace Luth. Ch., Burnsville, 1975-87 facilitator parents of divorce, 1984-87; vol. Yolo Wayfare Ctr., Woodland, Calif., 1992; bd. dirs. Riverwoods Homeowners Assn. Arch. Control, 1978-85; mem., vol. Holy Cross Luth., Wheaton, Ill., 1987-89, Luth. Ch. of Incarnation, Davis, 1989—, curriculum planner, 1989; publicity chair, bd. dirs. U. Calif. Farm Circle, Davis, 1989—; fundraiser Wheaton (Ill.) Newcomers, 1987-89. Mem. Nat. Assn. for Edn. Young Children, PEO (guard, treas.), Pi Lambda Theta. Home and Office: 39648 Lupine Ct Davis CA 95616-9756

GREEN, BRIAN GERALD, marketing executive; b. Missoula, Mont., Sept. 5, 1954; s. Gerald Jay and Ruth Anne (Althaus) G.; m. Robin Lee McIntyre, May 10, 1980; 1 child, Sean Brian. ASEE, Clark Coll., 1976; BS in Electronics Engrng. Tech., Oreg. Inst. Tech., Klamath Falls, 1978; MBA, U. Hartford, 1988. Cert. electronic technician. Field engr. Triad Systems Corp., Hartford, Conn., 1978-79; midwest regional mgr. Triad Systems Corp., Chgo., 1979-81; Northwest regional mgr. Triad Systems Corp., Portland, Oreg., 1981-83; northeast area mgr. Triad Systems Corp., Bristol, Conn., 1983-88, Canadian svc. mgr., 1987-88; western area mgr. Triad Systems Corp., Tracy, Calif., 1988-89; world wide svc. mgr. Sysgen, Inc., Milpitas, Calif., 1989-91; svc. mktg. mgr. Sony Corp. Am., San Jose, 1991-93; self employed cons., 1993; bus. mgr. REPAC, Inc., Forest Park, Ga., 1993-94; market segment mgr. AirTouch Cellular Data Group, Walnut Creek, Calif., 1994—. Mem. Assn. for Svcs. Mgmt. Internat., Masons (Southington, Conn. and Vancouver, Wash. chpts.), Scottish Rite (Hartford), Sphinx Shrine (Hartford). Republican. Methodist. Home: 12140 Carnegie Dr Tracy CA 95376-9149

GREEN, CHARLES WALTER, newspaper editor; b. Longmont, Colo., Jan. 11, 1947; s. Walter C. and Esther M. (Hansen) G. B.A., U. Colo., 1969. Reporter Denver Post, Inc., 1968-72, city editor, 1972-74, exec. city editor, 1974-80, asst. mng. editor, 1980-83, editorial page editor, 1983—; instr. U. Colo., 1977-79. Named Colo. Journalist of Yr. Sigma Delta Chi, 1978, Outstanding Alumnus U. Colo., 1982. Mem. Colo. Press Assn. (dir.), Am. Soc. Newspaper Editors, Nat. Conf. Editorial Writers (bd. dirs.), Denver Press Club (pres. 1978-79). Clubs: Tournament Players, Lakewood Country. Office: Denver Post 1560 Broadway Denver CO 80202-5133

GREEN, CYRIL KENNETH, retail company executive; b. Portland, Oreg., June 11, 1931; s. Lionel and Nora Evelyn (Walker) G.; m. Beverly Ann Hutchinson, July 24, 1950; children: Kenneth James, Teri Ann, Tamara Jo Green Easton, Kelly Denise Green Van Horn. Student pub. schs., Portland. Salesperson Fred Meyer Inc., Portland, Oreg., 1947-53, mgr. food dept., 1953-57, supr. food div., 1957-60, buyer food div., 1960-64, head buyer food div., 1964-67; gen. mgr. Roundup Co. subs. Fred Meyer Inc., Spokane, Wash., 1967-70; dir. ops. Fred Meyer Inc., Portland, Oreg., 1970-72, pres., 1972—, chief operating officer, from 1972; vice chmn., bd. dirs. Oreg. Trail chpt. ARC, Portland, 1984-89; bd. dirs. Marylhurst Coll., Portland, 1987—. Office: Fred Meyer Inc 3800 SE 22nd Ave Portland OR 97202-2918*

GREEN, DANIEL FRED, forester; b. Seattle, Feb. 28, 1947; s. Fred Davis and Rowena Anne (Pratt) G.; m. Janice Marie Bachman, Sept. 9, 1967 (div. 1979); children: Kelly Colleen, Wendy Alicia; m. Susan Dell Plaisance, Dec. 28, 1984. BS in Forest Mgmt., Oreg. State U., 1969; MS in Forest Sci., U. Idaho, 1976. Forester Oreg. State Forestry Dept., Forest Grove, 1971-73; Millicoma area forester Oreg. State Forestry Dept., Coos Bay, 1973-76; assoc. prof., extension agt. Oreg. State U., Oregon City, 1976-84; owner Green Tree Farm, Oregon City, 1976—; v.p. Woodland Mgmt. Inc., Lake Oswego, Oreg., 1984—; vis. prof. Tech. Inst. of Costa Rica, Cartago, 1984. Vol., host Experiment in Internat. Living, Oregon City, 1986-93; host World Learning, 1994—; pres. Environ. Learning Ctr., Oregon City, 1978, Environ. Edn. Assn. of Oregn., 1979; chmn. natural resources com. Ptnrs. of the Americas, Oreg. and Costa Rica, 1990-93. Mem. Soc. Am. Foresters (chmn. Portland chpt. 1980, state chmn.-elect 1995), Clackamas County Farm Forestry Assn. (pres. 1986-88), Oreg. State U. Forestry Alumni Bd. (chmn. 1994-95). Republican. Office: Woodland Mgmt Inc 5285 Meadows Rd Ste 282 Lake Oswego OR 97035-3228

GREEN, DAVID LEROY, accountant; b. Pocatello, Idaho, Apr. 27, 1946; s. Urban Lyndon and Rebecca (Jorgensen) G. BS, Brigham Young U., 1970, M in Acctg., 1972. CPA Idaho. Staff acct. M. Green & Co., Tulare, Calif., 1972-75; office mgr. M. Green & Co., Coalinga, Calif., 1974-75; staff acct. Haskins & Sells CPAs, Twin Falls, Idaho, 1975-76; sr. acct. Deloitte Haskins & Sells, Twin Falls, Idaho, 1976-78; mgr. Beckstead Cooper Co., Twin Falls, Idaho, 1978-81; mgr. Beckstead Cooper Jiroves, Las Vegas, Nev., 1981-82, pntr., 1982-83; owner, ptnr. Green & Gwinn, Pocatello, 1983—. Mem. AICPA, Idaho Soc. CPAs (chmn. taxation com. 1994-95), Rotary. Office: Green & Gwinn CPA 405 W Whitman PO Box 247 Pocatello ID 83204

GREEN, DAVID OLIVER, JR., sculptor, designer; b. Enid, Okla., June 29, 1908; s. David Oliver Green and Ina (Christmas) McBride; m. Jaxine Rhodes Green, Aug. 20, 1929 (dec. Dec. 1983); m. Lilian Stone DeLey, Mar. 15, 1986 (dec. May 1986). Student, Am. Acad. Art, Chgo., 1926, Nat. Acad. Art, 1927. Letterer Nat. Playhouses, Chgo., 1925-30; with lettering/layout Chgo. Herald-Examiner, Chgo., 1931-32; freelance designer London Guarantee Bldg., Chgo., 1932-33; layout artist Charles Daniel Frey Advt., Chgo., 1933-36; package designer Sears Roebuck, Chgo., 1936-37; art dir. advt. Mills Industries, Chgo., 1947-40; prodn. illustrator McDonald Douglas Aircraft, Long Beach, Calif., 1940-42; draftsman Calif. Inst. Tech., Pasadena, Calif., 1943-45; prof. sculpture Otis Art Inst., L.A., 1946-69; Prin. works include Altadena Libr. Bldg., Calif., Lytton Savs. and Loan, Hollywood, Calif.; author: La Partida/The Contest, 1957. Recipient Golden Crown award Pasadena Arts Coun., 1984. Mem. Pasadena Soc. Artists, Soc. for Calligraphy, Pasadena Photochrome Soc. Home and Studio: 176 Jaxine Dr Altadena CA 91001-3818

GREEN, FERDERICK BARDON, photographer; b. L.A., Feb. 2, 1948; s. Fred Watson and Frederika Elvira (Bardon) G.; m. Lon M. Green, 1992; children: Nicholas Bardon, Bryan Frederick. BA, San Fernando Valley State Coll, 1971; MS, Calif. State U., 1974. Salesman, pub. photographer Asanuma Corp., L.A., 1974-75; wilderness camera mgr. Wilderness Studio, Lake Tahoe, Nev., 1976-86; owner Wilderness Studio, 1986—; guest spkr. Profl. Photographers Am. Nat. Convention, 1993. Rep. U.S. Postal Commn., Douglas County, 1990. Recipient Profl. Student Participation award, Calif. State U., 1972. Mem. Profl. Photographers Am. (Nat. Merit Print award 1989, Kodak Gallery award 1992, winner Fuji Masterpiece Award 1992-94), Sierra Nev. Assn. Profl. Photographers (v.p. 1987, pres. 1994), Tahoe Douglas C. of C. (exec. bd. treas.), Clan Buchanan Soc., Sigma Xi. Republican. Episcopalian. Home: PO Box 1610 Zephyr Cove NV 89448-1610 Office: Wilderness Studio PO Box 12218 Zephyr Cove NV 89448-4218

GREEN, FLORA HUNGERFORD, lactation consultant, nurse; b. Mason City, Iowa, June 23, 1941; d. Mac Willard and Ethel Elizabeth (Hill) Hungerford; m. Ronald Eugene Green, Aug. 3, 1974; children: Elizabeth Jane, Marjorie Ann. Diploma, Meth-Kahler Sch. of Nursing, 1963; BS in Biology, Westmar Coll., 1964; BS in Nursing, Case Western Res. U., 1968; MA in Edn. Media, U. Minn., 1971. RN, Idaho, Calif., Iowa; cert. lactation cons., lamaze instr. Ednl. programmer U. Wis., Milw., 1970-72; asst. prof. nursing Idaho State U., Pocatello, 1972-76; dir. ins-svc. and patient edn. Bingham Meml. Hosp., Blackfoot, Idaho, 1976-77; staff nurse St. Agnes' Hosp., Fresno, Calif., 1979-81, Eden Hosp., Castro Valley, Calif., 1981-83; pvt. practice lactation cons. Fremont, Calif., 1985—; staff nurse high risk obstet. dept. Stanford U. Hosp., 1989-90, Kaiser Hosp.; obstet. nurse Kaiser Permanente Med. Ctr., Hayward, 1991—; cons. media div. J.B. Lippincott Co., Phila., 1973-80; bd. dirs. Bay Area Lactation Assn., Daly City, Calif. Chmn. Blacow Sch. emergency and safety com., Fremont, 1987-88, 92-93; bd. dirs. Fresno Montessori Sch., 1980-81, Bannock County ARC, Pocatello, 1976-77; emergency svcs. disaster cons. Idaho State U., Bannock County Red Cross, Bannock County, Pocatello, Idaho, 1972-77. Mem. AAUW, NAACOG, So. Alameda ASPO (co-chairperson 1987-88), Internat. Lactation Cons. Assn., Internat. Childbirth Edn. Assn., Sons of Norway, Sigma Theta Tau. Lutheran.

GREEN, FRANCIS WILLIAM, investment consultant; b. Locust Grove, Okla., Mar. 17, 1920; s. Noel Francis and Mary (Lincoln) G.; B.S., Phoenix U., 1955; M.S. in Elec. Engring., Minerva U., Milan, Italy, 1959; M.S. in Engring., West Coast U., Los Angeles, 1965; m. Alma J. Ellison, Aug. 26, 1950 (dec. Sept. 1970); children: Sharmon, Rhonda; m. Susan G. Mathis, July 14, 1973 (div. July 1979). With USN Guided Missile Program, 1945-49; design and electronic project engr. Falcon missile program Hughes Aircraft Co., Culver City, Calif., 1949-55; sr. electronic engr. Atlas missile program Convair Astronautics, San Diego, 1955-59; sr. engr. Polaris missile program Nortronics div. Northrop, Anaheim, Calif., 1959-60; chief, supr. electronic engr. data systems br. Tech. Support div. Rocket Propulsion Lab., USAF, Edwards AFB, Calif., 1960-67, dep. chief tech. support div., 1967-69; tech. adviser Air Force Missile Devel. Ctr., Holloman AFB, N.Mex., 1969-70, 6585 Test Group, Air Force Spl. Weapons Ctr., Holloman AFB, from 1970; pvt. investment cons., 1978—. Bd. examiners U.S. CSC; mem. Pres.'s Missile Site Labor Relations Com.; cons. advanced computer and data processing tech. and systems engring.; mem. USAF Civilian Policy Bd. and Range Comdrs. Coun; brig. gen., comdr. 2d brigrade State Milit. Forces; comdr. State Mil. Forces, 1989—; mem. State Guard Assn. U.S. Served as pilot USAAF, 1941-45. Fellow Am. Inst. Aeros. and Astronautics; mem. IEEE, Nat. Assn. Flight Instrs. Contbr. articles to profl. jours. Home and Office: 2345 Apache Ln Alamogordo NM 88310-4851

GREEN, HARRY WESTERN, II, geology/geophysics educator; b. Orange, N.J., Mar. 13, 1940; s. Harry Buetel and Mabel (Hendrickson) G.; children from previous marriage: Mark, Stephen, Carolyn, Jennifer; m. Maria Manuela Marques Martins, May 15, 1975; children: Alice, Miguel, Maria. AB in Geology, UCLA, 1963, MS in Geology and Geophysics, 1967, PhD in Geology and Geophysics with distinction, 1968. Postdoctoral research assoc. materials sci. Case Western Res. U., Cleve., 1968-70; asst. prof. geology U. Calif., Davis, 1970-74, assoc. prof., 1974-80, prof., 1980-92; chmn., 1984-88; prof. geology and geophysics U. Calif., Riverside, 1993—; dir. Inst. Geophysics and Planetary Physics, 1993-95, electron microscope facility, 1995—, vice chancellor for rsch., 1995—; exch. scientist Université de Nantes, France, 1973, prof. associeé, 1978-79, dir. analytical electron microscopy facility, 1994—; vis. prof. Monash U., Melbourne, Australia, 1984; specialist advisor World Bank Program, China U. of Geoscis., Wuhan, People's Republic of China, 1988; adj. sr. rsch. scientist Lamont-Doherty Earth Obs., Columbia U., 1989—, Vetlesen vis. prof., 1991-92; expert advisor geophysics rev. panel NSF, 1991-94. Contbr. articles to books and profl. jours. Grantee NSF, 1969—, Dept. Energy, 1988-94. Fellow Mineral Soc. Am., Am. Geophys. Union (N.L. Bowen award 1994, Francis Birch lectr. 1995); mem. AAAS, Materials Rsch. Soc., Sigma Xi. Office: Inst Geophysics and Planetary Physics U Calif Riverside CA 92521 also: Office Rsch Affairs U Calif Riverside CA 92521

GREEN, HILARIE CATTELL, financial consultant; b. Meadeville, Pa., Oct. 25, 1959; d. Ronald E. Hicks and Jowaine L. (Cattell) Humphrey; m. John Andersen Green; 1 child, Brice Cattell. BS in Biochemistry, SUNY, Plattsburgh, 1981; MBA in Fin., U. Pitts., 1985. ChFA. Rsch. scientist Enzo Biochem., Inc., N.Y.C., 1981-82; researcher Sch. of Medicine U. Pitts., 1983; assoc. scientist Carnegie Mellon U., Pitts., 1983-84; v.p. Wilshire Assocs., Santa Monica, Calif., 1986—. Co-chair LaSalle-Adams Neighborhood Assn., L.A., 1991—. Mem. L.A. Soc. Fin. Analysts, Assn. Investment Mgmt. and Rsch. Office: Wilshire Assocs 1299 Ocean Ave Santa Monica CA 90401-1004

GREEN, JACK, geology educator; b. Poughkeepsie, N.Y., June 19, 1925; s. Louis and Marie (Harris) G.; m. Renee Jean Utley, Sept. 21, 1952; children: Kathy, Jeffrey, Nathan, Teresa, Terrence, Ronald. BS, Va. Poly. Inst. and State U., Blacksburg, 1950; PhD, Columbia U., 1954. Registered geologist, Calif.; cert. environ. inspector. Geologist Std. of Calif., La Habra, 1953-59; rsch. geologist Rockwell Internat., Downey, Calif., 1959-65, McDonnell Douglas Corp., Huntington Beach, Calif., 1965-70; prof. geology Calif. State U., Long Beach, 1970—; cons. in field; mem. adv. com. Idaho Nat. Engring. Lab., 1990—; lectr. in field. Sr. editor: Atlas of Volcanic Landforms, 1971. With U.S. Army, 1943-46. NASA grantee, 1972, fellow, 1981; invitee geothermal rsch. grp. Peoples Rep. of China, Tibet, 1984. Mem. Am. Astron. Soc. Home: 941 Via Nogales Palos Verdes Peninsula CA 90274-1661 Office: Calif State U Long Beach Dept Geolog Scis Long Beach CA 90840

GREEN, JAMES CRAIG, data systems company executive; b. Gladstone, Mich., Apr. 19, 1933; s. Albert Keene and Margaret Josephine (Craig) G.; student Coll. of Gt. Falls, 1951-53, UCLA, 1962; m. Catherine Maxwell, Nov. 1, 1957; children: Cindi, Shelley, Nancy, James W., Robert. Clk., carrier U.S. Post Office, Gt. Falls, Mont., 1951-57; clk. office and sales Mont. Liquor Control Bd., Gt. Falls, 1957-59; payroll clk. Herald Examiner, Hearst Publs., L.A., 1959-67, data processing mgr., 1967-75, data processing ops. mgr. corp. hdqrs. Hearst Publs., N.Y.C., 1975-78; gen. mgr., v.p. Computer/Data Inc., Billings, Mont., 1978-83; mgr. customer service Big Sky Data Systems, Billings, Mont., 1983-84; pres. FACTS, Inc., 1985—; tax cons., L.A., 1962-75. Cub Scout leader, com. chmn., L.A. coun. Boy Scouts Am., 1973-75; pres. Bus. Office Employees Assn. L.A., 1963-66. Area commr. Black Otter coun. Boy Scouts Am., 1982-84, com. chmn., 1982-84; bd. govs. Spokane unit Shrine Hosp. Crippled Children, 1993—, hosp. chmn. Al Bedoo Shrine, 1992—. With USNR, 1951-59. Recipient degree of Chevalier, De Molay Cross of Honor, Legion of Honor degree.; cert. data processing mgr. Mem. Data Processing Mgrs. Assn., Rainbow Girls Grand Cross of Colors Shrine, L.A. Masonic Press Club. Clubs: Masons, Blue Lodge, York Rite, Scottish Rite, Shrine Grotto (charter mem. Gt. Falls), DeMolay (chpt. advisor 1983-92, state advisor 1982-92). Writer, negotiator contract Bus. Office Employees Assn., L.A., 1965.

GREEN, JERSEY MICHAEL-LEE, lawyer; b. Washington, Feb. 29, 1952; m. Jonelle Sue Burke, May 12, 1988. BA in criminology, U. Md., 1976; JD, Syracuse U., 1983. Bar: Colo. 1983, U.S. Dist. Ct. Colo. 1983, U.S. Ct. Appeals (10th cir.) 1983, U.S. Tax Ct. 1983, U.S. Ct. Appeals (9th cir.) 1987, U.S. Supreme Ct. 1988, U.S. Ct. Appeals (2d cir.) 1990, U.S. Dist. Ct. Ariz. 1994. Atty. Wagner & Waller, P.C., Denver, 1983-86, Waller, Mark & Allen, P.C., Denver, 1986-89, Orten & Hindman P.C., Denver, 1989-90, Elrod, Katz, Preeo, Look, Moison & Silverman, P.C., Denver, 1990—. Mem. exec. com. staff Lawyers for Romer, Denver, 1986; precinct committeeman, 1989-92. Recipient Syracuse (N.Y.) Def. Group scholarship, 1982. Mem. Assn. Trial Lawyers Am., Colo. Trial Lawyers Assn., Arapahoe County Bar Assn., Syracuse U. Alumni Assn. (pres. Colo. 1987-89). Democrat. Office: Elrod Katz Preeo Look Moison & Silverman PC 1120 Lincoln St Ste 1100 Denver CO 80203-2139

GREEN, JOEY, writer; b. Miami, Fla., May 26, 1958; s. Robert Morris and Barbara Sandra Green; m. Deborah Ann White, Sept. 7, 1987; 1 child, Ashley Jordan. BFA, Cornell U., 1980. Contbg. editor Nat. Lampoon, N.Y.C., 1981-83, Spy mag., N.Y.C., 1985-87; copywriter J. Walter Thompson USA, N.Y.C., 1983-85; Hong Kong, 1988; sr. copywriter Walt Disney World, Orlando, Fla., 1990-91, Lord Dentsu & Ptnrs., L.A., 1991-92, Tracy-Locke Advt., L.A., 1993. Author: Cornell Widow Hundredth Anniversary Anthology, 1981, Hellbent on Insanity, 1983, The Unofficial Gilligan's Island Handbook, 1987, The Get Smart Handbook, 1993, The Partridge Family Album, 1994. Recipient Clio award, 1983. Mem. ACLU, Greenpeace. Democrat.

GREEN, JONATHAN WILLIAM, museum administrator and educator, artist, author; b. Troy, N.Y., Sept. 26, 1939; s. Alan Singer and Frances (Katz) G.; m. Louise Lockshin, Sept. 16, 1962 (div. 1985); children: Raphael, Benjamin; m. Wendy Hughes Brown, Aug. 12, 1988. Student, MIT, 1958-60, Hebrew U., 1960-61; BA, Brandeis U., 1963, postgrad., 1964-67; MA, Harvard U., 1967. Photographer Jonathan Green, Photography, Boston, 1966-76, Ezra Stoller Assocs., Mamaroneck, N.Y., 1967-68; prof. MIT, Cambridge, Mass., 1968-76; dir. Creative Photography Lab MIT, Cambridge, 1974-76; editor Aperture Books and Periodical, N.Y.C., 1972-76; prof. Ohio State U., Columbus, 1976-90; dir. Wexner Ctr. Visual Arts/Univ. Gallery Fine Art Wexner Ctr. Arts/Univ. Gallery Fine Art, Columbus, 1981-88; founding dir. Ohio State U., Columbus, 1981-90; dir. Calif. Mus. Photography, U. Calif., Riverside, 1990—; prof. U. of Calif., Riverside, 1990—; cons. Nat. Endowment for Arts, Washington, 1975-76, 85, 88, 94, Harry N. Abrams, Pubs., N.Y.C., 1982-84, Oxford U. Press, N.Y.C., 1977-82, Polaroid Corp., Cambridge, 1976; co-founder Visible Lang. Workshop, MIT Media Lab., 1973. Author: American Photography, 1984 (Nikon Book of Yr. award 1984, Benjamin Citation 1986), The Snapshot, 1974 (N.Y. Type Dirs. Club award 1974), Camera Work: A Critical Anthology, 1973 (Best Art Book award 1973); editor, essayist James Friedman: Color Photographs 1979-1982, 1982, Housing a Program: Architecture as Logic, Architecture as Symbol, The Garden of Earthly Delights: Photographs by Edward Weston and Robert Mapplethorpe, 1995, Pedro Meyer: Truths & Fictions, 1995; editor Rudolf Baranik Elegies: Sleep Napalm Night Sky, 1987; represented in permanent collections Mus. Fine Arts, Boston, Mus. Fine Art, Houston, Cleve. Mus. Art, Va. Mus. Fine Art, Richmond, Princeton U. Art Mus., Bell System Collection, Moderna Museet, Stockholm, Ctr. for Creative Photography, Tucson, De Saisset Art Gallery and Mus., Internat. Ctr. Photography, N.Y.C., MIT, Mpls. Inst. Arts; photographs pub.: American Images: New Work by Twenty Contemporary Photographers, 1979, Aperture, 1972, 73, 74, 25 Years of Record Houses, 1981, Architectural Record, Architecture and Urbanism, Progressive Architecture, A Field Guide to Modern American Architecture. Danforth fellow, 1963-67, NEA

Photographer fellow, 1978, AT & T fellow, 1979. Office: California Museum Of Photography Downtown Hist Pedestrian Mall 3824 Main St Riverside CA 92501-3624

GREEN, JOSEPH MARTIN, psychiatrist, educator; b. Mt. Horeb, Wis., July 19, 1925; s. Joseph Marinus and Agnes Helene (Dahle) G.; m. Ruth Mary Fenner, June 17, 1952 (div. Dec. 1975); children: Richard C., Karen S., Jeffrey M. Student, U. Wis., 1946-48; MD, Northwestern U., 1952. Diplomate Am. Bd. Psychiatry and Neurology, Am. Bd. Child Psychiatry. Intern Wesley Meml. Hosp., Chgo., 1952-53; resident and fellow in child psychiatry Menninger Found., Topeka, 1953-57; clin. dir. Kans. Treatment Ctr. for Children, Topeka, 1956-59; practice medicine specializing in child psychiatry Tucson, 1961-73; med. dir. for children LaFrontera Ctr., Tucson, 1973-76; dir. of child and adolescent psychiatry U. Wis., Madison, 1976-88, prof. emeritus of psychiatry, 1989—; mem. gov.'s adv. com. on mental health, Phoenix, Ariz., 1965-66; cons. Arizona Acad., Phoenix, 1968; chief examiner Am. Bd. Psychiatry and Neurology, Evanston, Ill., 1974-82, Child Psychiatry; del. Am. Bd. Med. Specialties, Chgo., 1974-75; councillor psychiatry Joint Commn. Accreditation of Hosps., Chgo., 1977-79; cons. NIMH, Washington, 1977-81; faculty to gov.'s Spouses Seminar, Madison, Wis., 1986. Author: (with others) Basic Handbook of Child Psychiatry, 1979; contbg. author Group for Advancement of Psychiatry pubs., 1972, 73, 82, Internat. Encyclopedia Neurol Psychiatry, Psychoanalysis and Psychology, 1977; reviewer Am. Jour. Psychiatry and Jour. Child Psychiatry, 1971, 75-80, 82; sect. editor Treatment of Psychiat. Disorders, 1989. Founding bd. dirs. Big Bros. Tucson, 1964-67. Served as pvt. U.S. Army, 1943-46, ETO. Fellow Am. Psychiat. Assn. (pres. Ariz. chpt. 1966-67, pres. So. Wis. chpt. 1981-82), Am. Orthopsychiat. Assn. (v.p. 1973-74), Am. Acad. Child Psychiatry (councillor 1983-86); mem. AMA (residency rev. com. for psychiatry 1978-82), Soc. Prof. Child Psychiatry (pres. 1986-88), Group Advancement Psychiatry (com. chmn. 1972-76). Democrat.

GREEN, KATHERINE ELIZABETH, federal agency administrator; b. Seattle, Mar. 30, 1940; d. James Ellis and Sarah Katherine (Morgenroth) Flaherty; m. William Charles Green, Feb. 14, 1971; 1 child, Brian Patrick. AB in Psychology, Whitman Coll., 1962. Claims and field rep. Social Security Adminstrn., San Francisco, 1962-68; ops. supr. Social Security Adminstrn., Walnut Creek, Calif., 1968-69; health ins. specialist Social Security Adminstrn., Balt., 1969-71; ops. supr. Social Security Adminstrn., San Francisco, 1971-72, tng. specialist, 1972-74, quality appraisal/mgmt. info. mgr., 1974-76, fin. mgmt. officer, 1977-91, tng. officer, 1991—. Rschr., compiler book: The Descendants of Patrick and Barbara (Scanlon) Flaherty, 1992. Mem. Sch. Site Coun., Brisbane, Calif., 1984-91, 93-95, chair, 1992-93. Mem. New Eng. Hist. Geneal. Soc., Minn. State Hist. Soc., Ind. State Hist. Soc., Mothers' Club St. Ignatius H.S. Democrat. Roman Catholic. Office: Social Security Adminstrn 75 Hawthorne St San Francisco CA 94105-3919

GREEN, MARC EDWARD, editor; b. Cleve., Mar. 11, 1943; s. Emery S. and Aileen (Goldman) G.; m. Ellen Wilson, June 29, 1969; children: Alec, Matthew. BA, Amherst Coll., 1965; MA, Harvard U., 1966. Instr. in English George Washington U., Washington, 1971-74; screenwriter Warner Bros., Sydney Pollack Prodn., Martin Ransahoff Prodn., L.A., CBS/Paramount, Tri-Star Pictures, others, L.A., 1970-92; adminstr./editor Nat. Health Law Program, L.A., 1982-87; editor The Grantsmanship Ctr., L.A., 1991—. Co-author: Hollywood Dynasties, 1984, Outrageous Conduct, 1988, Hollywood on the Couch, 1993. Mem. Writers Guild of Am. Office: The Grantsmanship Ctr 1125 W 6th St Los Angeles CA 90017

GREEN, MARILYN VIRGINIA, writer; b. Grand Rapids, Mich., Nov. 6, 1948; d. John Robert and Virginia (Tuthill) G.; m. Drew A. McCalley, Apr. 14, 1979. BA, Mich. State U., 1970. Author: Intergenerational Programming in Libraries, 1979, The Button Lover's Book, 1991. Mem. Peninsula Stitchery Guild, San Francisco, 1977—.

GREEN, MARJORIE, automotive distribution, import and manufacturing company executive; b. N.Y.C., Sept. 27, 1943; d. Benjamin Maxon and Harriet (Weslock) Gruzen; m. Thomas Henry Green, May 31, 1964. Student Antioch Coll., 1961-63, CCNY, 1964-65. Adminstrv. asst. ednl. research U. Calif.-Berkeley, 1965-76; v.p., co-owner Automotion, Santa Clara, Calif., 1973—. Adv. bd. Import Car mag. Mem. Am. Fedn. State, County and Mcpl. Employees (pres. U. Calif. chpt. 1967), Porsche Club Am (v.p. Golden Gate region 1974, treas. region 1975). Home: 10666 W Loyola Dr Los Altos CA 94024-6513 Office: Automotion 193 Commercial St Sunnyvale CA 94086-5202

GREEN, MARJORIE BILLER, educational administrator; b. Boston, Nov. 5, 1939; d. David Wolfe and Martha S. (Rosenthal) Biller; m. Jason I. Green, Mar. 17, 1963; children: Nancy Elke, David Charles, Matthew Adam. AB cum laude, Boston U., 1961, MA, 1964; postgrad., U. Calif., Berkeley, 1961-62, UCLA, 1973-78. Ednl. cons. Rand Corp., Los Angeles, 1977-78; coordinator Wilshire Community Edn. Complex, Los Angeles, 1979-80; cons. Los Angeles Unified Sch. Dist., 1980-83; exec. dir. Calif. Coalition Pub. Edn., Los Angeles, 1985-87; dir. western states edn. Anti-Defamation League of B'nai B'rith, Los Angeles, 1987—. Mem. Mayor Bradley's Edn. Adv. Com., Los Angeles, 1979—; del. Dem. Nat. Conv., San Francisco, 1984; chairperson 24th Congl. Dist. Women-to-Women campaign, Los Angeles, 1984; mem. Los Angeles Commn. Sex Equity, 1984—; bd. dirs. Community Relations Conf. So. Calif., 1984, bd. dirs., 1985—; bd. dirs. Para los Niños, Los Angeles, 1984—; bd. dirs. community relations com. Jewish Fedn. Council So. Calif., 1986, chmn. edn. commn., 1986—. Recipient Outstanding Service award Los Angeles Unified Sch. Dist., 1981-82, Outstanding Contbn. award Los Angeles Commn. Sex Equity, 1983, citation Calif. Assembly, 1986, Euclan award U. Calif., 1986. Mem. LWV, Phi Beta Kappa, Phi Delta Kappa. Home: 218 Lorraine Blvd Los Angeles CA 90004-3812 Office: Anti-Defamation League Dir Western States Edn 15248 Dickens St Sherman Oaks CA 91403-3339

GREEN, MELANIE JANE, speech-language pathologist; b. Fremont, Calif., Nov. 23, 1968; d. Robert Lucian and Frances Eileen (Jones) G. BA in Communicative Disorders, Calif. State U., Fullerton, 1992; MS in Speech Lang. Pathology, U. Redlands, 1994. Child care coord. Calvary Chapel of Fullerton (Calif.), 1986-87; speech pathologist aide Providence Speech and Hearing Ctr., Orange, Calif., 1988-90; activities asst. Western Neuro Care Ctr., Tustin, Calif., 1989-90; speech-lang. pathology paraprofl. Long Beach, Calif., 1990—; speech-lang. pathologist Newport Lang., Speech, and Audiology Ctr., Newport Beach, 1994—. Mem. Autism Soc. Am., Nat. Student Speech and Hearing Assn. Home: PO Box 5679 Newport Beach CA 92662-5679

GREEN, MICHAEL, foundation administrator; b. Niagara Falls, N.Y., Jan. 6, 1943; s. Joseph and Vivian Hughes (Egbert) G. AB in Sociology, U. Pa., 1967; MA in Polit. Sci., Temple U., 1974; MA in Environ. Planning, Calif. State U., 1980; cert. computer ops., DeAnza Coll., 1986; cert. non-profit fundraising, U. Wash., 1992, cert. documentary video prodn., 1995. Land use analyst Praeger, Kavanagh & Waterbury, N.Y.C., Camden, N.J., 1967-68; legis. analyst Guam Territorial Legis., 1970; fin. analyst Assn. Am. Colls., Washington, 1971-72; environ. planner Calif. Dept. Transp., Sacramento, 1974-77; econ. analyst Inst. Internat. Law and Econ. Devel., Washington, 1977-78; econ. analyst dept. commerce Dept. Commerce U.S. V.I., St. Thomas, 1980-81; CEO Found. for Early Devel., San Francisco, Kingston and Bellingham, Wash., 1987—. Contbr. articles to profl. jours. and rsch. studies. Mem. Pacific N.W. Grantmakers Forum, Kiwanis (chmn. major emphasis Bellingham Meridian chpt. 1992-93). Republican. Office: Found for Early Devel 1430 Birchwood Ave Apt 209 Bellingham WA 98225-1382

GREEN, MICHAEL FOSTER, neuropsychologist, educator; b. Sewickley, Pa., July 5, 1956; s. May J. and Victoria Lia (Grunberg) G. BA, Oberlin Coll., 1979; PhD, Cornell U., 1984. Assoc prof. UCLA, 1992—; health sci. specialist West L.A. VA Hosp., 1992—. Editl. bd. Cognitive Neuropsychiatry; contbr. numerous articles to profl. jours. Grantee NIMH, 1988-94, Janssen Rsch. Found., 1993—. Mem. Am. Psychol. Soc., Soc. Rsch. Psychopathology (exec. bd. 1985—), Internat. Neuropsychol. Soc. Office: UCLA Rsch Ctr Box 6022 Camarillo CA 93011

GREEN, MICHAEL I., physicist; b. Suffern, N.Y., Mar. 21, 1930; s. Herman and Sylvia Katherine (Silverman) G.; m. Susan Lea Simon, Feb. 6, 1959; children: Deborah, William Harold. BS, U. Ala., 1953; PhD, Wayne State U., Detroit, 1972. Engr. Westinghouse, Bloomfield, N.J., 1955-57; sr. scientist Lockheed Rsch. Labs., Palo Alto, Calif., 1958-63, Bendix Rsch. Labs., Detroit, 1963-64; cons. Detroit, 1964-74; instr. Wayne State U., 1972-74; accelerator physicist Lawrence Berkeley Lab, Berkeley, Calif., 1974—; dir. Internat. Magnetic Measurement Workshop, 1981—; instr. CERN Acc. Sch., 1992; vis. scientist Superconducting Super Collider Lab., 1992—, European Synchrotron Radiation Facility, Grenbole, France, 1988; cons. in field, 1986—, reviewer jour. articles, 1986—. Contbr. articles to profl. jours. Leader Boy Scouts Explorer Scouts, N.Y., Ala., Calif., 1953—; mem. Dem. Cen. Com., Santa Clara County, Calif., 1961-63. With U.S. Army, 1953-55. Mem. Am. Physical Soc., IEEE, AAAS, Soaring Soc. Am., Pacific Soaring Coun. (v.p. 1984-85), Ames Soaring Club (v.p. 1982-83), Sigma Xi. Jewish. Home: 117 Rheem Blvd Orinda CA 94563-3620 Office: Lawrence Berkeley Lab 1 Cyclotron Rd Berkeley CA 94720

GREEN, PAUL CECIL, management consultant; b. Oconto, Nebr., Sept. 8, 1919; s. Paul Simpson Green and Ruth Adelaide (Kennedy) Elder; m. Carole Jean Pass, Dec. 21, 1964. BSBA, U. Nebr., 1941; MBA, Harvard U., 1948. CLU. Dir. sales Continental Assurance Co., Chgo., 1948-62, v.p. mktg., 1962-73; v.p. mktg. USLIFE Corp., N.Y.C., 1973-75; sr. v.p. Helmich, Miller and Pasek, Inc., Chgo., 1975-81; pres. Paul C. Green and Assocs., Ltd., Green Valley, Ariz., 1981—; chmn. bd. CLU Jour., Bryn Mar, Pa. Contbr. articles to profl. jours. Precinct capt. Young Repubs., Chgo.; bd. dirs. Green Valley Recreation, Inc.; exec. bd. Green Valley Coordinating Council; pres. Foothills IV Homeowners Assn., Green Valley. Lt. col. USAF, 1942-46. Recipient Achievement award City of Hope, 1977, 78. Mem. Am. Soc. Chartered Life Underwriters, Internat. Assn. Fin. Planners, Life Ins. Mktg. and Research Assn. (chmn. various coms.), Harvard Bus. Sch. Club (Phoenix chpt.), Country Club of Green Valley. Presbyterian. Home: 551 S Paseo Del Cobre Green Valley AZ 85614-2321 Office: PO Box 1448 Green Valley AZ 85622-1448

GREEN, RICHARD KEVIN, special effect company executive; b. Detroit, Mar. 2, 1957; s. Jack and Dorothy (Clayman) G. BA, Mich. State U., 1979. Field prodr. ABC News, Washington, 1979-81; pres. R. Green Prodns., Seattle, 1982-88, Wildfire Inc., L.A., 1989—. Developer black light spl. effects for film, TV, concerts including The Doors, Bill and Ted's Bogus Journey, The Lawnmower Man, Star Trek 6, Singles, Disney parks, Michael Jackson tour, billboards and others. Big brother Big Bros., L.A., 1990. Office: Wildfire Inc 11250 Playa Ct Culver City CA 90230-6127

GREEN, RICHARD R., communications executive; b. 1937. BA, Colo. Coll., 1959; MA, SUNY, Albany, 1964; PhD, U. Wash., 1968. Prodn. engr. Sta. KIRO-TV, Seattle, 1965-72; with Hughes Aircraft, L.A., 1972-77, ABC Videotape Post Prodn., Hollywood, Calif., 1977-79; dir. CBS Advanced TV Labs., Stamford, Conn., 1980-83; sr. v.p. broadcast ops. & engring. PBS, Washington, 1984-88; pres., CEO Cable TV Labs., Louisville, Colo., 1988—. Office: Cable TV Labs 400 Centennial Pky Louisville CO 80027-1266*

GREEN, ROBERT SCOTT, biotechnology company executive; b. N.Y.C., Aug. 7, 1953; s. Morris and Sophie (Weinstock) G.; m. Jill Susan Bolhack, June 24, 1979; children: Melissa, Meredith. BA, CUNY, 1974; JD, Fordham U., N.Y.C., 1977. Bar: N.Y. 1978, D.C. 1979. Assoc. Paul, Weiss, Rifkind, Wharton & Garrison, N.Y.C., 1979-87; v.p. Kaplan Capital Mgmt. Inc., N.Y.C., 1987-89; pres. Vega Biotechs., Inc., Tucson, 1989-92; pres., bd. dirs. Applitech Inc., Tucson, 1992—; mng. dir. Fusion Assocs., Ltd., Tucson, 1990-91; bd. dirs. Hearing Innovations, Inc., Tuscon. Contbr. articles to profl. jours. Mem. N.Y. State Bar Assn. Office: Applitech Inc 6741 N Saint Andrews Dr Tucson AZ 85718-2618

GREEN, RONNIE DAVID, education educator; b. Roanoke, Va., June 17, 1961; s. Charles M. and Frances Evelyn (Cahoon) G.; m. Jane O. Pauley, Aug. 2, 1986; children: Justin Lucas, Benjamin Nathaniel, Kelli Noelle. BS, Va. Polytech. Inst., Blacksburg, Va., 1983; MS, Colo. State U., 1985; PhD, U. Nebr., 1988. Grad. asst. Colo. State U., Ft. Collins, 1983-85, U. Nebr., Lincoln, 1985-88; asst. prof. Tex. Tech. U., Lubbock, 1988-94; assoc. prof. Colo. State U., 1994—. Contbr. articles to profl. jours. Pres. Lubbock Presbyn. Community Ch., 1991-93; ordained elder, vocal soloist Westminster Presbyn. Ch., Lubbock, 1988-94. Rsch. grantee, 1988-93. Mem. Am. Soc. Animal Sci., Nat. Block and Bridle Club (nat. sec./treas. 1992-96), Nat. Cattlemen's Assn., Tex. and Southwestern Cattle Raisers Assn., Tex. Cattel Feeders Assn. Office: Colo State Univ Dept Animal Scis Fort Collins CO 80523

GREEN, RUSSELL PETER, management consultant; b. N.Y.C., Dec. 13, 1942; s. Arthur William and Sarah (Mintz) G.; m. Carolee Madsen, June 21, 1964 (div. June 1981); m. Ibolya Farkas, Dec. 14, 1992; children: Peter Gregory, Caroline Veronica, Donna Frances. AB, Cornell U., 1964, MBA, 1965. Fin. analyst Doubleday & Co., Garden City, N.Y., 1967-72; acctg. mgr. Burroughs Corp., Goleta, Calif., 1972-76; controller MCR Tech., Goleta, 1976-79; dir. fin. Browne Engring., Carpinteria, Calif., 1980-83, Pentabs, Santa Barbara, Calif., 1983-85; v.p. fin. Eyeglasses Unltd., Inc., Santa Barbara, 1985-86; dir. fin. Investors Retirement & Mgmt. Corp., Carpinteria, 1986-90; contr. McGhan Med. Corp., Santa Barbara, Calif., 1990-92; pres. R.P. Green & Assoc., Santa Barbara, 1979—; contr. Game Keeper, Inc., Goleta, 1992-93, CFO, 1994—; CFO CTR, Inc., Santa Barbara, 1993—; bd. dirs. MCR Techs., Game Keeper, Inc. Home and Office: 224 W De La Guerra St # C Santa Barbara CA 93101-3756

GREEN, STEVEN J., retail executive; b. 1945; married;. Chmn. World Properties Research and Sterling Capital, 1969-74; pres. Inprojet Corp., 1975-79; chmn. KDT Industries, Inc., 1979-84; chmn., pres. HRT Industries, Inc. subs. McCrory Crop., Los Angeles, 1984—, formerly chief exec. officer, also bd. dirs.; now chmn. Samsonite Corp., New York, 1988—. Office: Samsonite 11200 E 45th Ave Denver CO 80239-3018

GREEN, STEVEN MORRIS, research scientist; b. L.A., June 3, 1962; s. Sidney and Cecily (Golden) G. BS in Aero. Engring., U. Calif., Davis, 1984; MS in Aero. & Astronautics, Stanford U., 1988. Aerospace engr. NASA, Moffett Field, Calif., 1985—. Mem. AIAA. Office: NASA Ames Rsch Ctr M/S 210-9 Moffett Field CA 94035-1000

GREEN, WENDY C.H., behavioral ecologist, researcher; b. Cin., Feb. 22, 1948; d. Francis and Virgie Marie (Bernhardt) Hortenstine; m. Steven Green, Sept. 23, 1969 (div. Jan. 1978); m. Aron Rothstein, Feb. 15, 1980. BA, CUNY, 1979, PhD, 1987. Grad. teaching asst. dept. biology CUNY, 1979-86; lectr. in ecology U. Autonomo, Santo Domingo, Dominican Rep., 1987; adj. assoc. prof. dept. environ. resource science U. Nev., Reno, 1988-89, post-doctoral fellow dept. biology, 1990-91, adj. rsch. assoc., 1992—; cons. biologist Wind Cave Nat. Park, S.D., 1982-84, Etosha Nat. Park, Nambia, 1992—. Contbr. articles to sci. jours. including Behavioral Ecology, Animal Behavior, Jour. Zool. (London), and Ethology. Recipient Rsch. grant Chgo. Zool. Soc., 1991, 93, World Wildlife Fund, 1993; Rsch. award Nat. Geographic Soc., Nambia, 1992—. Fellow AAUW; mem. Grad. Women in Science, Animal Behavior Soc. Office: Dept Biology U Nevada Reno NV 89557

GREEN, WILLIAM PORTER, lawyer; b. Jacksonville, Ill., Mar. 19, 1920; s. Hugh Parker and Clara Belle (Hopper) G.; m. Rose Marie Hall, Oct. 1, 1944; children: Hugh Michael, Robert Alan, Richard William. BA, Ill. Coll., 1941, JD, Northwestern U., Evanston, Ill., 1947. Bar: Ill. 1947, Calif. 1948, U.S. Dist. Ct. (so. dist.) Tex. 1986, U.S. Ct. Customs and Patent Appeals, U.S. Patent and Trademark Office 1948, U.S. Ct. Appeals (fed. cir.) 1982, U.S. Ct. Appeals (5th and 9th cir.), U.S. Supreme Ct. 1948, U.S. Dist. Ct. (cen. dist.) Calif. 1949, (so. dist.) Tex.1986. Pvt. practice L.A., 1947—; mem. Wills, Green & Mueth, L.A., 1974-83; of counsel Nilsson, Robbins, Dalgarn, Berliner, Carson & Wurst, L.A., 1984-91; of counsel Nilsson, Wurst & Green L.A., 1992—; del. Calif. State Bar Conv., 1982—, chmn., 1986. Bd. editors Ill. Law Rev., 1946; patentee in field. Mem. L.A. world Affairs Coun., 1975—; deacon local Presbyn. Ch., 1961-63. Mem. ABA, Calif. State Bar, Am. Intellectual Property Law Assn., L.A. Patent Law Assn. (past. sec.-treas., mem. bd. govs.), Lawyers Club L.A. (past treas., past sec., mem. bd. govs., pres. 1985-86), Los Angeles County Bar Assn. (trustee 1986-87), Am. Legion (past post comdr.), Northwestern U. Alumni Club So. Calif., Big Ten Club So. Calif., Town Hall Calif. Club, PGA West Golf Club (La Quinta, Calif.), Phi Beta Kappa, Phi Delta Phi, Phi Alpha. Republican. Home: 3570 Lombardy Rd Pasadena CA 91107-5627 Office: Nilsson Wurst & Green 707 Wilshire Blvd Ste 3200 Los Angeles CA 90017-3514

GREENAWALD, GLENN DALE, social studies trainer, curriculum developer, researcher; b. Pitts., May 26, 1947; s. Glenn Victor and June (Scheller) G. BA, U. Pitts., 1969; MA, U. Minn., 1973; DA, Carnegie-Mellon U., 1978. Cert. social studies tchr., Pa. Tchr. Anoka (Minn.)-Hennepin Sch. Dist., 1969-70, Hempfield Sch. Dist., Greensburg, Pa., 1970-75; teaching asst., rsch. asst. Carnegie-Mellon U., Pitts., 1975-78; staff assoc. Social Sci. Edn. Consortium, Boulder, Colo., 1978-82; dir. social studies W.Va. Dept. Edn., Charleston, 1982-85; dir. Learning Improvement Svcs., Nederland, Colo., 1985—; staff assoc. Social Sci. Edn. Consortium, Boulder, 1987-91; dir. Ctr. for Teaching Social Sci. U. No. Colo., Greeley, 1991-93; exec. dir. Colo. Close Up, 1985—. Author: (with Betty Dillon Peterson) Staff Development in the Social Studies, 1979, Washington Close Up Current Issues Teachers Guide, 1990, The Railroad Era, 1991. Mem. Amnesty Internat., Sierra Club, Legal Def. Fund, Colo. Mountain Club. Recipient numerous grants. Mem. ASCD, Nat. Coun. for Social Studies (chmn. archives com. 1990—, co-chmn. citizenship com. 1981), Coun. of State Social Studies Specialists; Coll. and Univ. Faculty Assembly, Social Studies Specialist Assn., Wash. Coun. for Social Studies, Minn. Coun. for Social Studies, Colo. Coun. for Social Studies (regional dir. 1992, pres. 1994—), Phi Delta Kappa. Home and Office: Box 681 Nederland CO 80466

GREENBERG, ARNOLD ELIHU, water quality specialist; b. Bklyn., Apr. 13, 1926; s. Samuel and Minnie (Gurevitz) G.; m. Shirley E. Singer, Aug. 2, 1952; children: Noah J., Seth M. BS, CCNY, 1947; MS, U. Wis., 1948; SM, MIT, 1950; postgrad., U. Calif., Berkeley, 1970-75. Rsch. engr., biologist U. Calif., Berkeley, 1950-54; asst. chief labs. Calif. Dept. Health Svcs., Berkeley, 1954-82; lab. mgr. East Bay Mcpl. Utility Dist., Oakland, Calif., 1982-91; cons., 1991—; instr. in engring. extension U. Calif., 1963—; instr. Contra Costa Coll., San Pablo, Calif., 1968-82; cons. Lawrence Berkeley Lab., 1973-84; vis. fellow Israel Inst. Tech., Haifa, 1981. Editor: Standard Methods for the Examination of Water and Wastewater, 1971, 75, 81, 85, 89, 92, 95, Laboratory Procedures for the Examination of Seawater & Shellfish, 1985. Col. USPHS, 1955—. Recipient APHA award for excellence, 1993. Mem. APHA, Am. Acad. Microbiology, Am. Water Works Assn. (hon.).

GREENBERG, BARRY MICHAEL, talent executive; b. Bklyn., Nov. 9, 1951; s. Aaron Herbert and Alice Rhoda (Strauss) G.; m. Susan Kay Greenberg, Feb. 19, 1990; 1 child, Samuel Jacob; 1 child by previous marriage: Seth Grahame-Smith. BA, Antioch U. Dir. B'nai B'rith, Phila., 1976-80; acting dir. Jewish Nat. Fund, L.A., 1980-81; chmn. Celebrity Connection, Beverly Hills, Calif., 1981—; co-founder Beverly Hills Air Force Co. Mem. Air Force adv. bd. USAF; mem. Wilshire Community police adv. bd. L.A. Police Dept.; mem. 50th Anniversary of WWII com. U.S. Dept. Def.; mem. pub. safety steering com. L.A. 4th Councilmatic Dist.; mem. exec. bd. CDC Bus. Responds to AIDS program; co-founder Windsor Watch; bd. dirs. Windsor Sq. Assn.; charter past pres. entertainment industry unit B'nai B'rith. With USAF, 1969-75. Mem. Def. Orientation Conf. Assn., Air Force Pub. Affairs Alumni Assn. Jewish. Office: Celebrity Connection 8306 Wilshire Blvd # 2659 Beverly Hills CA 90211-2382

GREENBERG, BYRON STANLEY, newspaper and business executive, consultant; b. Bklyn., June 17, 1919; s. Albert and Bertha (Getleson) G.; m. Helena Marks, Feb. 10, 1946; children: David, Eric, Randy. Student, Bklyn. Coll., 1936-41. Circulation mgr. N.Y. Post, 1956-62, circulation dir., 1962-63, bus. mgr., 1963-72, gen. mgr., dir., 1973-79; sec., dir. N.Y. Post Corp., 1966-75, treas., dir., 1975-76, v.p., 1976-81; v.p., dir. Leisure Systems, Inc., 1978-80; pres., chief exec. officer, dir. Games Mgmt. Services, Inc., 1979-80. Bd. dirs. 92d St YMHA, 1970-71, Friars Nat. Found., 1981-82. Served with AUS, 1942-45. Mem. Friars Club. Home and Office: 2560 S Grade Rd Alpine CA 91901-3612

GREENBERG, DAVID PAUL, pediatrician, researcher; b. L.A., Aug. 22, 1956; s. Richard Charles and Henrietta (Friedman) G.; m. Melanie Wolf-Greenberg, June 28, 1981; children: Henry Brian, Rebecca Suzanne. BS in Biology, U. Calif., Irvine, 1978; MD, Baylor Coll. Medicine, 1982. Diplomate Am. Bd. Pediatrics, 1987, Am. Bd. Pediatric Infectious Diseases, 1994. Intern, resident pediatrics U. Calif., Irvine, 1982-85; fellow in pediatric infectious diseases Harbor-UCLA Med. Ctr., Torrance, 1985-88, asst. prof. pediatrics, 1988—, assoc. dir. Ctr. for Vaccine Rsch., 1990—. Contbr. articles to profl. jours. Mem. Men's Club Temple Beth Shalom, Long Beach, Calif., 1994—. Grantee NIH, 1991, 94, various pharmaceutical cos., 1988-95. Fellow Am. Acad. Pediatrics; mem. Am. Soc. Microbiology, Am. Acad. Pediat. (chpt. 2 infectious disease com. 1988—), Infectious Disease Soc. Am., We. Soc. Pediat. Rsch., Pediat. Infectious Disease Soc. Office: Harbor-UCLA Med Ctr Dept Pediatrics 1124 W Carson St Bldg E-6 Torrance CA 90502

GREENBERG, JOANNE, author, anthropologist; b. Bklyn., Sept. 24, 1932; m. Albert Greenberg, 1955; children: David, Alan. Assoc. prof. anthropology Colo. Sch. of Mines; speaker in field. Author: The King's Persons, 1963, I Never Promised You a Rose Garden, 1964, The Monday Voices, 1965, Summering: A Book of Short Stories, 1966, In This Sign, 1970, Rites of Passage, 1972, Founder's Praise, 1976, High Crimes and Misdemeanors, 1979, A Season of Delight, 1981, The Far Side of Victory, 1983, Simple Gifts, 1986, Age of Consent, 1987, Of Such Small Differences, 1988, With The Snow Queen, 1991, No Reck'ning Made, 1993. Recipient H. and E. Daroff Meml. award, 1963, Fromm Reichmann award, 1967, Kenner award, 1971, Christopher award, 1971, Rocky Mountain Women's Inst. award, 1983, Cmty. Grange award, Denver Pub. Libr. Bookplate award, 1990, Colo. Author of Yr. award, 1991. Home: 29221 Rainbow Hills Rd Golden CO 80401-9708

GREENBERG, MARVIN, retired music educator; b. N.Y.C., June 24, 1936; s. Samuel and Rae (Sherry) G.; B.S. cum laude, N.Y. U., 1957; M.A., Columbia U., 1958, Ed.D., 1962. Tchr. elem. schs., N.Y.C., 1957-63; prof. music edn. U. Hawaii, Honolulu, 1963-93, prof. emeritus, 1993, ret., 1993, rsch. cons. Ctr. for Early Childhood Rsch., 1969-71; edn. adminstr. Model Cities project for disadvantaged children Family Svcs. Ctr., Honolulu, 1971-72. Cons. western region Volt Tech. Svcs., Head Start program, 1969-71; Head Start worker, 1972-75; Child Devel. Assoc. Consortium rep., 1975—. Recipient several fed. and state grants for ednl. rsch. and curriculum projects. Mem. Hawaii Music Educators Assn., Music Educators Nat. Conf., Soc. for Rsch. in Music Edn., Coun. for Rsch. in Music Edn. Author: Teaching Music in the Elementary School: Guide for ETV Programs, 1966; Preschool Music Curriculum, 1970; Music Handbook for the Elementary School, 1972; Staff Training in Child Care in Hawaii, 1975; Your Child Needs Music, 1979, Teachers Guides Honolulu Symphony Children's Concerts, 1980—; also over 100 articles. Home: 2575 Kuhio Ave # 19-2 Honolulu HI 96815-3971

GREENBERG, MAXWELL ELFRED, lawyer; b. Los Angeles, Mar. 11, 1922; s. Abe Lewis and Annette Friedman G.; children: Jan Greenberg LeVine, Richard E., David J., Jonathan A.; m. Asha Saund. A.B. cum laude, UCLA, 1941; LL.B. magna cum laude, Harvard U., 1949. Bar: Calif. 1950, Ill. 1959. Practiced law Los Angeles, 1950—; research atty. Justice Roger Traynor, Calif. Supreme Ct., San Francisco, 1949-50; sr. mem. Greenberg, Bernhard, Weiss, Rosin, Inc., Los Angeles, 1954-84, Jeffer, Mangels, Butler and Marmaro, Los Angeles, 1985—; pres. Greater Ariz. Savs. & Loan Assn., Phoenix, 1961-66, chmn. bd., 1966-72, chmn. exec. com., 1972-73; adj. prof. law UCLA, 1972-74. Author, editor, pub.: various legal outlines Calif. Bar Rev. Course, 1953-73. Nat. chmn. Anti-Defamation League, 1978-82, hon. chmn., 1983—; pres. Anti-Defamation League Found., 1984-89; chmn. community rels. com., v.p. Jewish Fedn.-Coun. Greater L.A., 1975-77; chmn. bd. Rural Devel. Corp., 1969-70; v.p. L.A. Police Commn., 1980-84; chmn. state adv. com. to U.S. Commn. on Civil Rights, 1985-87. 1st lt. AUS, 1942-46. Mem. State Bar Calif., Ill., Am. bar assns., Phi Beta Kappa, Pi Gamma Mu, Pi Lambda Phi. Democrat. Home: 315 15th St Santa Monica CA 90402-2211 Office: Jeffer Mangels Butler & Marmaro 2121 Avenue Of The Stars Fl 10 Los Angeles CA 90067-5010

GREENBERG, MORTON PAUL, lawyer, insurance broker, advanced underwriting consultant; b. Fall River, Mass., June 2, 1946; s. Harry and Sylvia Shirley (Davis) G.; m. Louise Beryl Schindler, Jan. 24, 1970; 1 child, Alexis Lynn. BSBA, NYU, 1968; JD, Bklyn. Law Sch., 1971. Bar: N.Y. 1972; CLU Am. Coll., 1975. Atty., Hanner, Fitzmaurice & Onorato, N.Y.C., 1971-72; dir., counsel, cons. on advanced underwriting The Mfrs. Life Ins. Co., Toronto, Ont.,Can., 1972—; mem. sales ideas com. Million Dollar Roundtable, Chgo., 1982-83; 4th ann. George M. Graves meml. lectr., 1991; speaker on law, tax, and advanced underwriting to various profl. groups, U.S., Can. Author: (tech. jour.) ManuBriefs. Mem. ABA, N.Y. State Bar Assn., Assn. for Advanced Life Underwriting (mem. bus. ins. and estate planning steering com., 1989-93), Internat. Platform Assn., Nat. Assn. Life Underwriters , Denver Assn. Life Underwriters, Am. Soc. CLU, NYU Alumni Assn., Stern Sch. Bus. Alumni Assn. Office: 7617 N Sunrise Trl Parker CO 80134-6915

GREENBERG, MYRON SILVER, lawyer; b. L.A., Oct. 17, 1945; s. Earl W. and Geri (Silver) G.; m. Shlomit Gross; children: David, Amy, Sophie, Benjamin. BSBA, UCLA, 1967, JD, 1970. Bar: Calif. 1971, U.S. Dist. Ct. (cen. dist.) Calif. 1971, U.S. Tax Ct. 1977; CPA, Calif. Staff acct. Touche Ross & Co., L.A., 1970-71; assoc. Kaplan, Livingston, Goodwin, Berkowitz, & Selvin, Beverly Hills, 1971-74; ptnr. Dinkelspiel, Steefel & Levitt, San Francisco, 1975-80; ptnr. Steefel, Levitt & Weiss, San Francisco, 1981-82; pres. Myron S. Greenberg, a Profl. Corp., Larkspur, Calif., 1982—; professorial lectr. tax. Golden Gate U.; instr. U. Calif., Berkeley, 1989—. Author: California Attorney's Guide to Professional Corporations, 1977, 79; bd. editors UCLA Law Rev., 1969-70. Mem. San Anselmo Planning Commn., 1976-77; bd. dirs. Bay Area Lawyers for Arts, 1979-80, Marin County chpt. Am. Heart Assn. (bd. dirs., pres. 1984-90); mem. adv. bd. cert. program in personal fin. planning U. Calif., Berkeley, 1991—. Mem. ABA, AICPA, Marin County (Calif.) Bar Assn. (bd. dirs. 1994—), Real Estate Tax Inst. of Calif. Continuing Edn. Bar (planning com.), Larkspur C. of C. (bd. dirs. 1985-87). Democrat. Jewish. Office: 700 Larkspur Landing Cir Larkspur CA 94939-1715

GREENBERG, ROGER L., plastic and reconstructive surgeon; b. Cedar Rapids, Iowa, Feb. 15, 1936; m. Mary F. BS, U. Mich., 1958; MD, Wayne State U., 1962. Diplomate Am. Bd. Plastic Surgeon. Gen. surgery resident Calif. Pacific Med. Ctr., San Francisco, 1962-67, chmn. dept. plastic surgery, 1979-89; plastic surgery fellow Cronin-Brauer Clinic, Houston, 1967-69; pvt. practice San Francisco, 1969—. Contbr. articles to profl. jours. Mem. AMA, Am. Soc. Plastic Surgeons, Calif. Med. Soc., Calif. Soc. Plastic Surgeons (pres. 1993, med. dir. alliance 1992—), San Francisco Med. Soc. Office: 525 Spruce St San Francisco CA 94118-2616

GREENBERGER, MARTIN, computer and information scientist, educator; b. Elizabeth, N.J., Nov. 30, 1931; s. David and Sidelle (Jonas) G.; A.B., Harvard, 1955, A.M., 1956, Ph.D., 1958; m. Liz Greenberger; children: Kari, David, Beth Jonit, Jonah Ben, Jilly Sal. Teaching fellow, resident adviser, staff mem. Computation Lab., Harvard, Cambridge, 1954-58; mgr. applied sci. IBM, Cambridge, 1956-58; asst. prof. mgmt. Mass. Inst. Tech., Cambridge, 1958-61, assoc. prof., 1961-67; prof., chmn. computer sci., dir. info. processing Johns Hopkins U., Balt., 1967-72, prof. math. scis., sr. research asso. Center for Met. Planning and Research, 1972-75, prof. math. scis., 1978-82; IBM chair in tech. and policy UCLA Anderson Grad. Sch. Mgmt., 1982—; dir. UCLA Ctr. Digital Media, 1995—; pres. Council for Tech. and the Individual, 1985—; mgr. systems program Electric Power Research Inst., Palo Alto, Calif., 1976-77; Isaac Taylor vis. prof. Technion-Israel Inst. Tech., Haifa, 1978-79; vis. prof. Internat. Energy Program, Grad. Sch. Bus., Stanford U., 1980; vis. prof. policy and analysis MIT Media Lab., 1988-89. Mem. computer sci. and engring. bd. NAS, 1970-72; chmn. COSATI rev. group NSF, 1971-72; mem. evaluation com. Internat. Inst. for Applied Systems Analysis, Laxenburg, Austria, 1980; mem. adv. panels, Office Tech. Assessment, GAO, U.S. Congress; cons. IBM, A.T.&T., CBS, Rand Corp., Morgan Guaranty, Arthur D. Little, TRW, Bolt, Beranek & Newman, Brookings Inst., Resources for Future, Electric Power Rsch. Inst., Atlantic Richfield, Rockwell Internat., Security Pacific Corp, John F. Kennedy Sch. of Govt. Harvard U. Mem. overseers' vis. com. Harvard U., 1975-81; founder and mem. working groups Energy Modeling Forum, Stanford U., 1978-81; mem. adv. com. Nat. Center Analysis of Energy Systems Brookhaven Nat. Lab., 1976-80, chmn., 1977; mem. rev. com. Energy and Environment div. Lawrence Berkeley Lab., 1983, applied sci. div., 1986-88; chmn. forum on electronic pub., Washington program Annenberg, 1983-84; co-founder ICC Forum, 1985; chmn. Roundtable in Multimedia, 1990—; trustee Educom, Princeton, N.J., 1969-73, chmn. council, 1969-70. With USAF, 1952-54, USAFR, 1954-60. NSF fellow, 1955-56; Guggenheim fellow U. Calif., Berkeley, 1965-66. Fellow AAAS (v.p., chmn. sect. T 1973-75); mem. Phi Beta Kappa, Sigma Xi. Author: (with Orcutt, Korbel and Rivlin) Microanalysis of Socioeconomic Systems: A Simulation Study, 1961; (with Jones, Morris and Ness) On-Line Computation and Simulation: The OPS-3 System, 1965; (with Crenson and Crissey) Models in the Policy Process: Public Decision Making in the Computer Era, 1976; (with Brewer, Hogan and Russell) Caught Unawares: The Energy Decade in Retrospect, 1983. Editor: Management and The Computer of the Future, 1962, republished as Computers and the World of the Future, 1964; Computers, Communications, and the Public Interest, 1971; (with Aronofsky, McKenney and Massy) Networks for Research and Education, 1973; Electronic Publishing Plus: Media for a Technological Future, 1985, Technologies for the 21st Century, Vol. 1, On Multimedia, Vol. 3, 1990, Multimedia in Review, Vol. 5, 1992, Content and Communication, 1994. Office: UCLA Anderson Grad Sch Mgmt Los Angeles CA 90024

GREENBLATT, STEPHEN J., English language educator; b. Cambridge, Mass., Nov. 7, 1943; s. Harry J. and Mollie (Brown) G.; m. Ellen Jane Schmidt, April 27, 1969; children: Joshua, Aaron. BA, Yale U., 1964, M. in Philosophy, 1968, PhD, 1969; BA, Cambridge U., England, 1966. Prof. English U. Calif., Berkeley, 1969—; vis. prof. Peking U., Beijing, 1982, Oxford (Eng.) U., 1988, U. Bologna, Italy, 1988, U. Chgo., 1989, U. Trieste, 1991, U. Florence, 1992, Ecole des Hautes Etudes, Paris, 1989, Harvard U., Cambridge, Mass., 1990-94, Istituto Italiano per gli Studi Filosofici, Naples, 1994, U. Ala., 1994. Author: Three Modern Satirists: Waugh, Orwell, and Huxley, 1965 (Lloyd Mifflin prize 1964), Sir Walter Raleigh, 1970, Renaissance Self-Fashioning, 1980, Shakespearean Negotiations, 1988, Learning to Curse, 1990, Marvelous Possessions, 1991; editor: Allegory and Representation, 1981, Power of Forms, 1982, Representing the English Renaissance, 1988, Redrawing the Boundaries of Literary Study in English, 1992, New World Encounters, 1992. Recipient Porter prize, 1969, Brit. Coun. prize, 1982, James Russell Lowell prize MLA, 1989; Fulbright scholar, 1964-66, Woodrow Wilson scholar, 1966; Guggenheim fellow, 1975, 83. Fellow Am. Acad. Arts and Scis. Office: U Calif Dept of English Berkeley CA 94720

GREENE, ADDISON KENT, lawyer, accountant; b. Cardston, Alta., Can., Dec. 23, 1941; s. Addison Allen and Amy (Shipley) G.; m. Janice Hanks, Aug. 30, 1967; children: Lisa, Tiffany, Tyler, Darin. BS in Acctg., Brigham Young U., 1968; JD, U. Utah, 1973. Bar: Utah 1973, Nev. 1974, U.S. Tax Ct. 1979. Staff acct. Seidman and Seidman, Las Vegas, Nev., 1968-69, Peat Marwick Mitchell, Los Angeles, 1969-70; atty. Clark Greene & Assocs., Ltd., Las Vegas, 1973—; instr. Nev. Bar Rev., Las Vegas, 1975-78; bd. dirs. Cumorah Credit Union. Mem. Citizen's for Responsible Gov't, Las Vegas, 1979—; asst. dist. com. mem. Boy Scouts Am., Las Vegas, 1985—. Mem. ABA, Utah Bar Assn., Nev. Bar Assn., Nev. Soc. CPA's (assoc.), Am. Assn., Pension Actuaries (assoc.). Republican. Mormon. Office: Clark Greene & Assocs Ltd 3770 Howard Hughes Pky Ste 195 Las Vegas NV 89109-0940

GREENE, ALBERT LAWRENCE, hospital administrator; b. N.Y.C., Dec. 10, 1949; s. Leonard and Anne (Birnbaum) G.; m. Jo Linda Anderson, Sept. 3, 1972; children: Stacy, Jeremy. BA, Ithaca Coll., 1971; MHA, U. Mich., 1973. Adminstrv. asst. Harper Hosp., Detroit, 1973-74, asst. adminstr., 1974-77, assoc. adminstr., 1977-80; adminstr. Grace Hosp., Detroit, 1980-84, Harper Hosp., Detroit, 1984-87; pres., chief exec. officer Sinai Samaritan Med. Ctr., Milw., 1988-90, Alta Bates Med. Ctr., Berkeley, Calif., 1990—; bd. dirs. Acuson Corp., Calif. Assn. Hosps. and Health Sys., Hosp. Coun. No. and Ctrl. Calif. Trustee Huron Valley Hosp., Milford, Mich., 1984-87. Mem. Am. Coll. Healthcare Execs., Young Pres. Orgn., Rotary, Blackhawk Country Club, Lakeview Club. Home: 3819 Cottonwood Dr Danville CA 94506-6007 Office: Alta Bates Med Ctr 2450 Ashby Ave Berkeley CA 94705-2067

GREENE, ALVIN, service company executive, management consultant; b. Pitts., Aug. 26, 1932; s. Samuel David and Yetta (Kroff) G.; BA, Stanford U., 1954, MBA, 1959; m. M. Louise Sokol, Nov. 11, 1977; children: Sharon, Ami, Ann, Daniel. Asst. to pres. Narmco Industries, Inc., San Diego, 1959-62; adminstrv. mgr., mgr. mktg. Whittaker Corp., L.A., 1962-67; sr. v.p. Cordura Corp., L.A., 1967-75; chmn. bd. Sharon-Sage, Inc., L.A., 1975-79; exec. v.p., chief operating officer Republic Distbrs., Inc., Carson, Calif., 1979-81, also dir.; chief operating officer Memel, Jacobs & Ellsworth, 1981-87, 87—; pres. SCI Cons., Inc.; dir. Sharon-Sage, Inc., True Data Corp.; vis. prof. Am. Grad. Sch. Bus., Phoenix, 1977-81. Chmn. bd. commrs. Housing Authority City of L.A., 1983-88 . Served to 1st lt., U.S. Army, 1955-57. Mem. Direct Mail Assn., Safety Helmet Mfrs. Assn., Bradley Group. Office: 11990 San Vicente Blvd Ste 300 Los Angeles CA 90049-6608

GREENE, FRANK SULLIVAN, JR., investment management executive; b. Washington, Oct. 19, 1938; s. Frank S. Sr. and Irma O. Greene; m. Phyllis Davison, Jan. 1958 (dec. 1984); children: Angela, Frank, Ronald; m. Carolyn W. Greene, Sept. 1990. BS, Washington U., St. Louis, 1961; MS, Purdue U., 1962; PhD, U. Santa Clara (Calif.), 1970. Part-time lectr. Washington U., Howard U., Am. U., 1959-65; pres., dir. Tech. Devel. Corp., Arlington, Tex., 1985-92; pres. Zero One Systems, Inc. (formerly Tech. Devel. of Calif.) Santa Clara, Calif., 1971-87, Zero One Systems Group subs. Sterling Software Inc., 1987-89; asst. chmn., lectr. Stanford U., 1972-74; bd. dirs. Networked Picture Systems Inc., 1986, pres., 1989-91, chmn., 1991-94; gen. ptnr. New Vista Capital, Palo Alto, Calif., 1994—. Author two indsl. textbooks; also articles; patentee in field. Bd. dirs. NCCJ, Santa Clara, 1980—, NAACP, San Jose chpt., 1986-89; bd. regents Santa Clara U., 1983-90, trustee, 1990—; mem. adv. bd. Urban League, Santa Clara County, 1986-89, East Side Union High Sch., 1985-88. Capt. USAF, 1961-65. Mem. IEEE, IEEE Computer Soc. (governing bd. 1973-75), Assn. Black Mfrs. (bd. dir., 1974-80), Am. Electric Assn. (indsl. adv. bd., 1975-76), Fairchild Rsch. and Devel. (tech. staff, 1965-71), Bay Area Purchasing Coun. (bd. dir. 1978-84), Security Affairs Support Assn. (bd. dir. 1980-83), Sigma Xi, Eta Kappa Nu, Sigma Pi Phi.

GREENE, HOWARD E., JR., pharmaceutical executive; b. 1943. Harvard U., 1967. With McKinsey & Co., Chgo., 1967-74, Baxter Travenol, San Diego, 1974-78; CEO Hybritech, Inc., San Diego, 1979-86; gen. ptnr. Biovest Ptnrs., San Diego, 1986-91; with Cytel Corp., 1991—, now chmn. bd. Office: Cytel Corp 3525 Hopkins Ct San Diego CA 92121*

GREENE, JAMES FIEDLER, real estate executive; b. Rochester, Minn., Feb. 15, 1958; s. Laurence Francis and Rosalyn Estelle (Ravits) G. BA, Colo. Coll., 1980; MBA, U. Denver, 1987. Lic. real estate broker, Colo. V.p. CB Comml. Group, Denver, 1982—. Mem. Alumni awards com. Colo. Coll., Denver, 1986—; bd. dirs. I Have A Dream Found. Club: Colo. Coll. Gold, Denver Athletic Colo. Office: CB Comml Group 1050 17 St Ste 800 Denver CO 80265-0801

GREENE, JOHN THOMAS, JR., federal judge; b. Salt Lake City, Nov. 28, 1929; s. John Thomas and Mary Agnes (Hindley) G.; m. Kay Buchanan, Mar. 31, 1955; children: Thomas B., John B., Mary Kay. B.A., U. Utah, 1952, J.D., 1955. Bar: Utah 1955. Law clk. Supreme Ct. Utah, Salt Lake City, 1954-55; asst. U.S. atty. Dist. Utah, Salt Lake City, 1957-59; partner firm Marr, Wilkins & Cannon, Salt Lake City, 1959-69, Cannon, Greene & Nebeker, Salt Lake City, 1969-74, Greene, Callister & Nebeker, Salt Lake City, 1974-85; judge U.S. Dist. Ct. Utah, 1985—; spl. asst. atty. gen. State of Utah, 1965-69; spl. grand jury counsel Salt Lake County, 1970; pres. Utah Bar Found., 1971-74, trustee, 1971-88. Author: sect. on mining rights American Law of Mining, 1965; contbr. articles to profl. jours. Pres. Community Svcs. Coun., Salt Lake City area, 1971-73; chmn. Utah Bldg. Authority, 1980-85; mem. Utah State Bd. Regents, 1983-86. Mem. Utah Bar Assn. (pres. 1970-71, chmn. jud. com. 1971-76, chmn. com. post. law sch. tng. 1985-89), ABA (Utah del. to ho. of dels. 1975-81, 82-93, mem. bd. govs. 1988-91, mem. spl. com. delivery legal svc. 1975-81, coun. gen. practice sect. 1974-82, chmn. spl. com. on environ. law 1971-75, mem. adv. com. Nat. Legal Svc. Corp. 1975-81, com. youth edn. law 1991-94, chmn. standing com. on jud. selection, tenure and compensation 1985-88), Am. Law Inst. (mem. adv. com. on restatement of law governing lawyers), Judicial Conf. U.S. (com. ct. adminstrn. and case mgmt. 1990—), Order of Coif, other. Mem. LDS Ch. Office: US Courthouse 350 S Main St Salt Lake City UT 84101-2106

GREENE, LAURENCE WHITRIDGE, JR., surgical educator; b. Denver, Jan. 18, 1924; s. Laurence Whitridge Sr. and Freda (Schmitt) G.; m. Frances Steger, Sept. 16, 1950 (dec. Dec. 1977); children: Charlotte Greene Kerr, Mary Whitridge Greene, Laurence Whitridge III; m. Nancy Kay Bennett, Dec. 7, 1984. BA, Colo. Coll., 1945; MD, U. Colo., 1947; postgrad., U. Chgo., 1948-50. Diplomate Am. Bd. of Surgery. Intern St. Lukes Hosp., Denver, 1947-48; sr. intern in ob./gyn. U. Chgo. Lying-In Hosp., 1948-49; surg. resident U. Cin. Gen. Hosp., 1952-55, sr. surg. resident, 1955-57, chief surgery resident, 1957-58; clin. surgery asst. Sch. of Medicine U. Colo., Denver, 1958-61, clin. instr. Sch. of Medicine, 1961-67, asst. clin. prof. Sch. of Medicine, 1967-75, assoc. clin. prof. Sch. of Medicine, 1975-87, clin. prof. Sch. of Medicine, 1987—; adj. prof. zoology and physiology U. Wyo., Laramie, 1970-80; mem. staff Ivinson Meml. Hosp., Laramie, 1958—; chmn. Wyo chpt. Com. on Trauma, 1973-89; tchr., mem. adv. staff U. Colo. Med. Sch., Denver, 1958-83; mem. advisor, surgeon U. Wyo. Athletics, Laramie, 1975-80, Wyo. Hwy. Patrol, 1950—. Contbr. numerous articles to profl. jours. Lt. M.C. (s.g.) USN, 1950-52, Korea. Fellow ACS; mem. Am. Assn. for Surgery of Trauma, Southwestern Surgery Congress, Western Surg. Assn., Mont Reed Soc., Masons, Shriners, Sigma Xi. Republican. Episcopalian.

GREENE, MICHAEL C., art association administrator. Pres., CEO NARAS, Santa Monica, Calif. Office: NARAS 3402 Pico Blvd Santa Monica CA 90405-2118

GREENE, RICHARD BOYD, JR., marketing and sales executive; b. Boston, July 31, 1962; s. Richard B. and Joy C. (Cudd) G.; m. Lynn Susan Lippoldt, Aug. 24, 1991. BBA, U. Wis., Milw., 1985; MBA, U. Phoenix, San Jose, Calif., 1994. Sales rep. Campbell Soup Co., Des Plaines, Ill., 1985, sales specialist, 1985-87; mgr. trade svcs. Selling Areas Mktg., Inc., Chgo., 1987-88; regional dir. Selling Areas Mktg., Inc., San Ramon, Calif., 1988-91; dir. Info. Resources, Inc., San Francisco, 1991-94; v.p. Nielsen Mktg. Rsch., Fremont, Calif., 1994—. Mem. Am. Mktg. Assn. Republican. Methodist.

GREENE, RICHARD MARTIN, artist; b. Utica, N.Y., Oct. 30, 1953; s. Stuart Merwin and Lois Claire (Friedlander) G. BS, MIT, 1974. Exhibit developer The Exploratorium, San Francisco, 1974-76, 80-82; artist San Francisco, 1976-80; programmer Jandel Corp., Sausalito, Calif., 1983-84; artist, inventor San Francisco, 1984—; computer cons., San Francisco, 1984—; artist-in-residence The Exploratorium, San Francisco, 1986-87. Contbr. articles to profl. jours.; inventor, patentee graphic input apparatus; exhibited in group show at IBM Think Pocket, Tokyo, 1984-89. Vol. tutor San Francisco Unified Sch. Dist., 1985-88. Mem. Green Party. Home and Office: 845 Misty Hills Ln Sebastopol CA 95472-5028

GREENE, ROLAND ARTHUR, literature educator; b. Henderson, Nev., Oct. 8, 1957; s. Roland Earl and Dorita (Pallais) G. AB, Brown U., 1979; MA, Princeton U., 1982, PhD, 1985. Asst. prof. dept. English Harvard U., Cambridge, Mass., 1984-89; assoc. prof. Harvard U., Cambridge, 1989-92; prof. dept. English, program in comparative lit. U. Oreg., Eugene, 1993—. Author: Post-Petrarchism, 1991. Recipient sr. fellowship Am.. Coun. of Learned Socs., 1992-93, Mellon fellowship Stanford Humanities Ctr., 1992-93. Mem. MLA, Renaissance Soc. Am., Shakespeare Assn. Am., Am. Comparative Lit. Assn. (sec.-treas.). Office: Univ Oreg Program in Comparative Lit 5242 Univ Oreg Eugene OR 97403-5242

GREENE, SHARON LOUISE, computer executive director; b. Washington, Sept. 8, 1960; d. Gary Edward and Lorna Sybil (Herzog) G; m. Jeffrey D. Lally. Student U. Colo., 1980-82. Office mgr. Irving Kerner Literary Agy., Boulder, 1979-81; mgr. Alpha Micro Users Soc., Boulder, 1979-88 , editor, 1983—, meeting planner, 1984—, sec.-treas., 1983-86; exec. dir. Alpha Micro Users Soc., 1988—; cons. Club Mac, Boulder, 1984-85. Mem. NAFE. Am. Soc. Assn. Execs., Meeting Planners Internat. Democrat. Jewish. Avocations: fishing; camping; hiking; reading; sports. Office: Alpha Micro Users Soc 619 Florida Ave Longmont CO 80501-6419

GREENE, WENDY SEGAL, special education educator; b. New Rochelle, N.Y., Jan. 9, 1929; d. Louis Peter and Anne Henrietta (Kahan) Segal; m. Charles Edward Smith (div. 1952); m. Richard M. Greene Jr. (div. Mar. 1967); children: Christopher S., Kerry William, Karen Beth Greene Olson; m. Richard M. Greene Sr., Aug. 29, 1985 (dec. 1986). Student, Olivet Coll., 1946-48, Santa Monica Coll., 1967-70; BA in Child Devel., Calif. State U., Los Angeles, 1973, MA in Elem. Edn., 1975. Cert. tchr., Calif. Counselor Camp Watitoh, Becket, Mass., 1946-49; asst. tchr. Outdoor Play Group, New Rochelle, 1946-58; edn. sec. pediatrics Syracuse (N.Y.) Meml. Hosp., 1952-53; with St. John's Hosp., Santa Monica, Calif., 1962-63; head tchr. Head Start, L.A., 1966-77; tchr. spl. edn. L.A. Unified Sch. Dist., 1977—, Salvin Spl. Edn. Ctr., L.A., 1977-85, Perez Spl. Edn. Ctr., L.A., 1986-; instr. mktg. rsch. for motivational rsch. Anderson-McConnell Agy., 1966; mentor tchr. L.A. Unified Sch. Dist., 1992—. Contbr. to house organ of St. John's Hosp.; co-editor of newspaper for Salvin Sch., L.A. and The Eagle, Perez Sch., L.A., 1988—. Bd. dirs. Richland Ave. Youth House, L.A., 1960-63, Emotional Health Assn., L.A., 1961-66, Richland Ave. Sch. PTA, 1959-63; vol. Hospice of St. Joseph Hosp., Orange, Calif., 1985—; mem. cmty. adv. com. spl. edn. Tustin Unified Sch. Dist., 1994. Mem. AAUW, So. Calif. Assn. Young Children, Olivet Coll. Alumni Assn., United Tchrs. L.A., Westside Singers (L.A.), Kappa Delta Pi. Jewish. Home: 14291 Prospect Ave Tustin CA 92680-2316

GREENE LLOYD, NANCY ELLEN, infosystems specialist, physicist; b. Worcester, Mass., Nov. 4, 1947; d. William Arthur II and Dorothy Goddard (Fuller) Green; children: Ellen Dorothy, Gwyneth Tegan; m. Stephen C. Lloyd, July 25, 1992. BS in Physics, Ohio State U., 1969, MS in Physics, 1971. Instr. physics U. Colo., Colorado Springs, 1971-73; physics programmer U. N.Mex., Albuquerque, 1973-76; data analyst Los Alamos (N.Mex.) Nat. Lab., 1975-77, programmer, 1977-78, mem. tech. staff controlled thermonuclear reaction divsn., 1978-81, mem. tech. staff Accelerator Tech. div., 1981-84, mem. tech. staff adminstrv. data processing divsn., 1984-85, mem. tech. staff dynamic experimentation divsn., 1985-94, staff mem. supr., 1989-90, acting sect. leader, 1990-91, acting dep. divsn. leader, 1992, chief ops. explosives tech. and applications divsn., 1992-94, mem. tech. staff environ., safety, and health divsn. Instl. Affairs Office, 1994—; speaker in field. Vol. Los Alamos Schs., 1980-88, Fountain Valley Sch., Colo., 1990-91. Nat. Merit scholar, Mich. State U., 1965, Nat. Defense Edn. Act Title IV fellow, Ohio State U., 1969. Mem. N.Mex. Digital Equipment Computer Users Soc. (exec. com. 1984-87, 88-90, registration chair computer conf. 1984-87, vice-chair 1988-89, publicity 1989-90), VAX Computer Local Users Group (chmn. 1981-82, sec. 1989-92), NAFE, IEEE, Toastmasters Internat. Office: Los Alamos Nat Lab PO Box 1663 K491 Los Alamos NM 87545-0600

GREENER, YIGAL, biomedical researcher; b. Petach-Tikva, Israel, May 10, 1937; came to U.S., 1965; s. Yehuda and Maniya (Vallinchik) G.; 1 child, Iris; m. Stella Limor, Aug. 21, 1966; children: Anat, Gilat. BA, NYU, 1968, MS, 1970, PhD, 1977. Rsch. technician Einstein Coll. Medicine, N.Y.C., 1968-79, assoc. in medicine, 1977-79; mgr., assoc. dir. Baxter/Travenol, Round Lake, Ill., 1979-87; assoc. dir., safety assessment Sterling Drug, Rensselaer, N.Y., 1987-92; dir., pre-clin. Molecular Biosystems, San Diego, 1992—. With Israel Def. Forces, 1956-59. Jewish. Office: MBI 10030 Barnes Canyon Rd San Diego CA 92121-2722

GREENFIELD, ROSEANNE, English and history educator; b. L.A., Nov. 21, 1960; d. Irwin and Fay Sally (Rosen) Greenfield; m. Francis Weng Fai Thong, June 24, 1990. BA in Am. Studies, Calif. State U., Fullerton, 1983, MA in Am. Studies, 1990; MA in TESOL, U.S. Internat. U., San Diego, 1992. Cert. in secondary and adult edn. Instr. English and second lang. Feng Chia U., Tai Chung, Taiwan, 1984-85; instr. adult edn. Fed. Correctional Inst., Terminal Island, Calif., 1985-86; English specialist Nat. Taiwan Normal U., Taipei, 1987-88; instr. English as second lang. Calif. State U., Long Beach, 1988, Rancho Santiago C.C., Santa Ana, Calif., 1991; instr. English as second lang., history Garden Grove (Calif.) Sch. Dist., 1988-92; chair Spanish and English dept. Colegio Maya Internat. Sch., Guatemala City, Guatemala, 1992-93; English specialist Chinese Internat. Sch., Hong Kong, 1993—; guest lectr., trainer Calif ESL Tng. Conf., Hanoi and Ho Chi Minh Cities, Vietnam, summer, 1991; cross-cultural edn. exchange mem. Calif. State U., Tai Chung, Taiwan, 1984-85; staff intern Orange County Register, Santa Ana, Calif.; staff writer Daily Titan, Fullerton, Calif.; editor, staff writer, Daily 49er, Long Beach. Contbg. author: New Ways of Teaching Speaking, 1994; contbr. articles to profl. jours. Mem. draft bd. U.S. Selective Svc. Sys., Orange County, Calif., 1982-94; bd. dirs. Huntington Beach Environ. Bd., 1980-82. Mem. Tchrs. of English to Spkrs. Other Langs., Ptnrs. Internat. Student Alumni Assn. (bd. dirs. 1990—), Am. Studies Student Assn. (bd. dirs. 1980-92), Phi Beta Delta. Home: 17300 Santa Clara St Fountain Valley CA 92708

GREENFIELD, SARAH C., school counselor; b. Rochester, N.Y., July 7, 1937; d. George Stoner and Margaret (Sidebotham) Curtice; m. James D. Greenfield, June 3, 1961. BA, U. Rochester, 1959; Ma in Edn., Ariz. State U., 1968, M of Counseling, 1970, PhD, 1975. Biochem. lab. technician Strong Meml. Hosp., Rochester, N.Y., 1959-61, Pabst Biochem. Lab., Milw., 1962-63; counselor, tutor Alum Rock Sch. Dist., San Jose, Calif., 1977; sch. counselor Chinle (Ariz.) Unified Sch. Dist., 1977—. Vol. crisis worker ADABI, Chinle, 1989—; vol. Heard Mus., Phoenix, 1965-71; mem. exec. bd. Interfaith Counseling N.W., Phoenix, 1972-73, Heard Mus. Gift Shop, 1970. Rockefeller Found. fellow, 1972. Mem. Am. Counseling Assn., Ariz. Counseling Assn. Presbyterian. Home: 6608 N 20th St Phoenix AZ 85016 Office: Chinle Jr HS PO Box 587 Chinle AZ 86503

GREENHALL, CHARLES AUGUST, mathematician; b. N.Y.C., May 5, 1939; s. A. Frank and Miriam (Housman) G. BA, Pomona Coll., 1961; PhD, Calif. Inst. Tech., 1966. Rsch. assoc. Jet Propulsion Lab., Pasadena, Calif., 1966-68; asst. prof. U. So. Calif., L.A., 1968-73; with Jet Propulsion Lab., Pasadena, 1973—, mem. tech. staff, 1981—. Contbr. articles to profl. jours; patentee of frequency stability measurement. Mem. IEEE, Am. Math. Soc., Math. Assn. Am., Soc. Indsl. and Applied Maths. Republican. Home: 1836 Hanscom Dr South Pasadena CA 91030-4008 Office: Jet Propulsion Lab # 298-100 4800 Oak Grove Dr Pasadena CA 91109-8001

GREENHOUSE, LYNN, physician; b. Garden City, Kans., Feb. 11, 1956; d. Arnold Hillel and Louise Lynn Greenhouse; m. Douglas James Bruha, June 10, 1989. BA magna cum laude, Miami U. Ohio, Oxford, 1977; MA, Johns Hopkins U., 1979; MD, U. Nev., 1992. Policy analyst office spl. projects U.S. Dept. Energy, Washington, 1979-81; rep. gas mktg., compliance analyst Petro-Lewis Corp., Denver, 1981-84; asst. v.p. investor rels. Derand Resources Corp., Arlington, Va., 1984-86; med. enrolled health care program U. Nev., Reno, 1987-92; med. resident U. Internal Medicine, Reno, 1992—; presenter in field. Contbr. articles and abstracts to profl. jours. Mem. ACP, AMA, Phi Beta Kappa, Phi Kappa Phi.

GREENHUT, SAUL EPHRIAM, biomedical researcher, engineer; b. Detroit, May 27, 1961; s. Frederick Sanford and Lillian (Rosen) G.; m. Nancy Jean Cronk, Sept. 8, 1985; children: Adam, Jonathan. BSE summa cum laude, U. Mich., 1983, MS in Bioengring., 1984, PhD in Bioengring., 1991. Rsch. engr. Newark Beth-Israel Med. Ctr., 1984-85; computer coord. William Beaumont Hosp., Royal Oak, Mich., 1985-88; rsch. asst. U. Mich., Ann Arbor, 1986-91; rsch. scientist Telectronics Pacing Sys., Englewood, Colo., 1991—. Contbr. articles to profl. jours.; inventor in field. Vol., staff aide Families First, Aurora, Colo., 1992-93. Fellow U. Mich., 1983-84. Mem. IEEE, Internat. Soc. Computerized Electrocardiology (conf. session chmn. 1993, Young Investigator hon. mention 1990). Democrat. Jewish. Office: Telectronics Pacing Sys 7400 S Tucson Way Englewood CO 80112-3938

GREENLAW, ROGER LEE, interior designer; b. New London, Conn., Oct. 12, 1936; s. Kenneth Nelson and Lyndell Lee (Stinson) G.; children—Carol Jennifer, Roger Lee. BFA, Syracuse U., 1958. Interior designer Cannell & Chaffin, 1958-59, William C. Wagner, Architect, L.A., 1959-60, Gen.

Fireproofing Co., Los Angeles, 1960-62, K-S Wilshire, Inc., L.A., 1963-64; dir. interior design Calif. Desk Co., L.A., 1964-67; sr. interior designer Bechtel Corp., L.A., 1967-70; sr. interior designer, project mgr. Daniel, Mann, Johnson, & Mendehall, L.A., 1970-72, Morganelli-Heumann & Assos., L.A., 1972-73; owner, prin. Greenlaw Design Assos., Glendale, Calif., 1973—; lectr. UCLA; mem. adv. curriculum com. Mt. San Antonio Coll., Walnut, Calif., Fashion Inst. Design, L.A.; bd. dirs. Calif. Legis. Conf. Interior Design. Past scoutmaster Verdugo council Boy Scouts Am.; pres. bd. dirs. Unity Ch., La Crescenta, Calif., 1989-91. Mem. Am. Soc. Interior Designers (treas. Pasadena chpt. 1983-84, 1st v.p. 1985, pres. 1986-87, chmn. So. Calif. regional conf. 1985, nat. dir. 1987—, nat. com. legis., nat. com. jury for catalog award, speaker ho. dels., nat. bd. dirs., medallist award, regional v.p., nat. chair ethics com., nat. exec. com., v.p., treas. 1992 Calif. legislative conf. interior design, chmn. standards task force, pres. 1994-95), Glendale C. of C. (bd. dirs.), Adm. Farragut Acad. Alumni Assn., Delta Upsilon. Republican. Lodge: Kiwanis (bd. dirs.). Home: 2100F Valderas Dr Glendale CA 91208-1328 Office: 3901 Ocean View Blvd Montrose CA 91020-1514

GREENLICK, VICKI RUTH, film producer; b. Detroit, Nov. 15, 1961; d. Merwyn Ronald and Harriet Pauline (Cohen)Greenlick; m. Bernard Joseph Bottomly, Aug. 27, 1988; 1 child, Elizabeth Ann Bottomly. Student, Oberlin (Ohio) Coll., 1979-83. Office mgr. Friends of Les AuCoin, Portland, Oreg., 1985-87; prodn. asst. Signature Prodns., Portland, Oreg., 1987, prodn. coord., 1987-88, producer, 1988-89; exec. producer Signature Films, Portland, Oreg., 1989—. Producer tv comml. (Advt. Age Best 1989, Clio finalist, Emmy finalist). Co-chmn. Cascade Awards Festival, Portland, 1991, 92; mem. Hysterectomy Info. Com., Portland, 1990. Mem. Assn. Ind. Comml. Producers, Oreg. Media Prodn. Assn., Portland Advt. Fedn. Democrat.

GREENSPAN, ADAM, radiologist, educator; b. Przemysl, Poland, May 28, 1935; s. Bernard and Eugenia (Wert) G.; m. Barbara Lynn Warshofsky, Mar. 31, 1985; children: Ludwig, Samantha, Michael. MD, Med. Acad. Worclaw, Poland, 1958, DMS, 1965. Med. diplomate; cert. in radiology. Asst. prof. radiology Mt. Sinai Sch. Medicine, N.Y.C., 1977-79, assoc. prof. radiology, 1979-85; assoc. prof. radiology N.Y.U. Sch. Medicine, N.Y.C., 1986-87; assoc. prof. radiology and othopaedic surgery Sch. Medicine U. Calif., Davis, 1987-88; prof. radiology and orthopaedic surgery N.Y.U. Sch. Medicine, 1988—. Author: Orthopaedic Radiology, 1988, 2d edit., 1993, Radiology of the Arthritides, 1990, Imaging of the Spine, 1993. Recipient Physician's Recognition awards AMA, 1974, 77, 81, 92, 94. Fellow N.Y. Acad. Medicine; mem. Internat. Skeletal Soc., Am. Coll. Radiology, Radiol. Soc. N.Am., Assn. Univ. Radiologists, Am. Roentgen Ray Soc. Office: Univ Calif Davis Radiology 2516 Stockton Blvd Sacramento CA 95817

GREENSPAN, EVAN MARTIN, music industry executive; b. Phila., Sept. 11, 1957; s. Robert Philip and Sylvia (Fisher) G.; m. Liz F. Rifkin, Dec. 19, 1987. BA, U. Pa., 1979; MFA, U. Calif., L.A., 1980. Freelance entertainment writer Twelve Signs, Inc., L.A., 1979; staff tech. writer Trainex Corp., Westminster, Calif., 1981; condr., music dir. Charles Brown Enterprises, L.A., 1981-82; mgr. music adminstrn. Alan Landsburg Products, L.A., 1982-85; dir. music clearance Bob Banner Assocs., L.A., 1985-87; pres., CEO Evan M. Greenspan, Inc., Studio City, Calif., 1987—; bd. mem. Calif. Copyright Conf., L.A., 1986—, v.p., 1993-94, pres., 1994—; guest lectr. So. Meth. U. L.A. Workshop, 1986—, UCLA Continuing Edn. Program, 1992—. Film music supr.: Amelia Earhart: The Final Flight, 1994; tv music composer, 1983-87. Bd. mem. exec. com. La. chpt. Shaare Zedek Hosp. in Jerusalem, Israel, 1990—; supporting contbr. The Starlight Found., L.A., Chabad House, L.A. Mem. ASCAP (writer mem., pub. mem.), Assn. Ind. Mus. Pubs., Nat. Acad. Songwriters.

GREENSTEIN, MERLE EDWARD, import and export company executive; b. Portland, Oreg., June 22, 1937; s. Sol and Tillie Germaine (Schnitzer) G.; m. Patricia Ellen Graves, April 5, 1971; children: Randall Dale, Todd Aaron. BA, Reed Coll., 1959. Pres. Acme Trading and Supply Co., Portland, 1963-82; chmn. MMI Group, Portland, 1982-91, Internat. Devel. Assocs., Portland, 1991—; com. mem. ISRI, Washington, 1987-89; mem. dist. export coun. U.S. Dept. Commerce, 1980—. Chmn. fin. Portland Opera, 1966; bd. dirs. Met. YMCA, 1964-67; del. to China, State of Oreg. Ofcl. Trade Mission, 1979; chmn. Western Internat. Trade Group, 1981-82; mem. State of Oreg. Korea Commn., 1985-90; fin. chmn. Anne Frank exhibit, Portland; joint chmn. bldg. camapign Oreg. Mus. Sci. and Industry; bd. dirs. Waverly Children's Home; bd. cons. Unilearn Corp. Recipient President's E for Export, U.S. Dept. Commerce, 1969; named Citizen of the Week, City of Portland, 1953. Mem. Rolls Royce Owners Club (London), City Club, Tualatin Country Club, Masons, Shriners. Office: Internat Devel Assocs 6731 NE 47th Ave Portland OR 97218-1205

GREENWADE, LANCE ERIC, scientific visualization specialist, mathematician; b. Napa, Calif., July 4, 1957; s. Gerald Gordon and Karen Rae (Smit) G.; m. Margaret Marie Rosa, July 18, 1981; children: Zachary Ray, Benjamin Gordon. BA, Humboldt State U., 1982; MS, Mont. State U., 1984. Lectr. Mont. State U., Bozeman, 1981-85; staff scientist Los Alamos (N.Mex.) Nat. Lab., 1985-86; sr. scientist Idaho Nat. Engring. Lab., Idaho Falls, 1986-87, scientific specialist, 1987—; Graphics chair Cray User Group, 1992—; INEL rep. Sandia-Los Alamos Tech. Exch. Com., 1987—. Mentor Los Alamos Sci. Program, 1985-86, Science NOW, Idaho Falls, 1990-91. Mem. IEEE, IEEE Computer Soc., Assn. Computing Machinery, SIGGRAPH, AEC Sportsman Club (v.p. 1992-93, pres. 1993-94). Home: 601 E 97th S Idaho Falls ID 83404-7762 Office: Idaho Nat Engring Lab 1155 Foote Dr Idaho Falls ID 83402-1835

GREENWAY, FRANK LYONS, III, medical educator; b. Petaluma, Calif., Jan. 15, 1945; s. Frank Lyons Jr. and May Beth (Behrens) G.; m. Jan Ellen Matthews Gardner, June 24, 1967; 1 child, Scott; m. Teresa Maria Valencia, Jan. 2, 1972; children: Greg, Lenore. BA in Biology, Stanford U., 1966; MD, UCLA, 1970. Diplomate Nat. Bd. Med. Examiners, Am. Bd. Internal Medicine, Am. Bd. Endocrinology and Metabolism. Intern Harbor Gen. Hosp., Torrance, Calif., 1970-71, resident in internal medicine, 1971-73, fellow in endocrinology and metabolism, 1973-75; from instr. to asst. clin. prof. medicine UCLA Sch. Medicine, 1975-85, assoc. clin. prof. medicine, 1985-93, clin. prof. medicine, 1993—; prof. medicine Pennington Biomed. Rsch. Ctr., La. State U., Baton Rouge, 1995—; panel mem. NIH Consensus Devel. Conf. on Gastrointestinal Surgery for Severe Obesity, Bethesda, Md., 1991; dir. med. edn. for 3rd and 4th yr. clin. clks. from Autonomous U. Guadalajara Med. Sch. Marina Mercy Hosp., 1976-84, mem. credentials com., 1975-76, mem. med. records com., 1975-76, chmn. ICU/CCU com., 1976-79, mem. ER disaster com., 1976-81, chief of medicine, 1977-79, vice chief medicine, 1979-80, chmn. med. ICU com., 1980-81, mem. dietary com., 1980, mem. med. exec. com., 1977-79, mem. infection/transfusion com., 1977-79, mem. medicine com., 1975-81; mem. ER disaster com. Centinela Hosp., L.A., 1975-76; mem. utilization com. Daniel Freeman Hosp., Inglewood, Calif., 1975-76, chief of medicine, 1983-84, vice chief of staff, 1984-88, mem. pharmacy and therapeutics com., 1986-87, 88—, chmn. outpatient utilization com., 1987-88, mem. credentials com., 1988-89; chmn. med. edn. com. Wash. Hosp., Culver City, Calif., 1983-86, mem. med. exec. com., 1982-88; chief of medicine Wash. Med. Ctr., 1986-88, mem. medicine com., 1984—; preceptor for 3rd yr. med. student Coll. Osteo. Medicine the Pacific, 1986; manuscript reviewer Am. Jour. Clin. Nutrition, Obesity Rsch., Endocrine Practice, Internat. Jour. Obesity; cons. and lectr. in field. Mem. editorial bd. Obesity Update, 1985-88; contbr. articles to profl. jours. Maj. U.S. Army N.G., 1970-77. Doffelmeyer scholar Stanford U., 1962-66; recipient Merit award L.A. Surg. Soc., 1975, Disting. Teaching award Harbor-UCLA Med. Ctr., 1986, Alumni award UCLA Sch. Medicine, 1970; recipient numerous rsch. grants, 1974-93. Fellow ACP; mem. Am. Diabetes Assn., Am. Fedn. Clin. Rsch., Am. Inst. Nutrition, Am. Soc. Clin. Nutrition, The Endocrine Soc., N.Am. Soc. for Study of Obesity (pub. affairs com. mem. 1989-93). Office: Pennington Biomed Rsch Ctr 6400 Perkins Rd Baton Rouge LA 70808-4124

GREENWAY, MARLENE LAURA, archaeologist; b. San Diego, Nov. 3, 1940; d. Edward Judd Hill and Erna Lydia (Ehmke) Wells; m. James Carl Greenway, June 22, 1957 (div. 1974); children: James Shean, Terry Lee, Marla Kay. AA in Philosophy with highest honors, Coll. of Redwoods, 1979; postgrad., U. Calif., Irvine, 1981; BA in Anthropology, Humboldt State U., 1984; MA in Cultural Resource Mgmt., Sonoma State U., Rohnert Park, Calif., 1988. Lic. fixed wing single engine aircraft pilot. Staff archaeologist Arcata (Calif.) Resource Area, 1988-91; dist. lead archaeologist Clear Lake Resource Area, Bur. Land Mgmt., Ukiah, Calif., 1991—; mem. Mendocino County Archeol. Commn., 1988-94. Mem. Soc. Am. Archaeology, Soc. Calif. Archaeology, Historic Mining Assn., Lake County Hist. Soc., Pi Gamma Mu. Republican. Home: 1725 Camellia Dr Mckinleyville CA 95521-4093 Office: Bur Land Mgmt 2550 N State St Ukiah CA 95482-3023

GREENWELL, ROGER ALLEN, scientist; b. Santa Maria, Calif., Dec. 4, 1941; s. George C. and Bessie Florence (Sutton) G.; m. Jeannine Pendleton, July 25, 1969; 1 child, George Eli. AA, Hancock Jr. Coll., 1961; BS, Calif. Poly. Coll., 1968; MS, U.S. Internat. U., 1974, DBA, 1981. Mathematician Naval Weapons Ctr., China Lake, Calif., 1968, ops. research analyst, Corona, Calif., 1969-70; ops. research analyst Comdr. Naval Forces, Vietnam, 1968-69; mathematician Naval Electronics Lab. Ctr., San Diego, 1970-77; scientist Naval Ocean Systems Ctr., San Diego, 1977-84; v.p., dir. advanced tech. disvn. Sci. and Engring. Assoc., Inc., 1984—; cons. fiber optics and econ. analysis; mem. NATO Research Study Group, 1983—. Served with U.S. Army, 1964-67. Decorated Bronze Star. Mem. AIAA, IEEE, ACS, Internat. Soc. Optical Engrs., Ops. Research Soc. Am., Inst. Mgmt. Sci., Soc. Allied Weight Engrs., Optical Soc. Am. Home: 3778 Eagle St San Diego CA 92103-3958 Office: 2878 Camino Del Rio S Ste 315 San Diego CA 92108-3844

GREENWELL, RONALD EVERETT, communications executive; b. Louisville, Oct. 28, 1938; s. Woodrow M. and Christine (Comer) Gossett G.; m. Diane J. Greenwell, Mar. 18, 1967; children: Wendy, Robin. With Motorola Inc., Schaumburg, Ill., 1962-94, sr. v.p., gen. mgr. communications internat. group, 1986-94; pres. Motorola Communications Internat. Inc., Schaumburg, Ill., 1986-94, ret., 1994; bd. dirs. United Comms. Industry PCC, Bangkok, Thailand. Mem. N.C. Ctr. for World Langs. and Culture (bd. dirs.). Home: 30 Canyon Ridge Dr Sandia Park NM 87047

GREENWOOD, RICHARD M., finance company executive, bank executive; b. Fargo, N.D., 1947. Grad., U. Idaho, 1972, Am. Grad. Sch. Internat. Mgmt., 1974. Formerly exec. v.p., CFO Calfed Inc., L.A.; now pres., CEO, dir. Citadel Holding Corp., Glendale, Calif., 1992—. Office: Citadel Holding Corp 600 N Brand Blvd Glendale CA 91203-1241

GREER, DARRELL STEPHEN, production operator, finance executive; b. St. Louis, July 4, 1949; s. Roger James and Florence Marie (Kelly) G.; m. Rosemary Fowler, 1973 (div. 1975); m. Louise Marie Kemp, June 25, 1993. BA in Philosophy, Calif. State U., L.A., 1981. Cert. notary pub., Calif. Advanced through grades to staff sgt. USAF; with ticket dept. L.A. Dodgers, 1982-92; motivational cons. Darrell Greer & Assocs., L.A., 1984-86; ops. asst. Smith-Barney, Albuquerque, 1988-95; prodn. operator Motorola Ceramics Products, Albuquerque, 1995—. Mem. Rio Rancho Mayor's Graffiti Task Force. Mem. AFTRA, Screen Actors Guild, Non-Commd. Officers Assn., Mensa (film critic monthly rev. column Lament mag. L.A. chpt. 1987-92), Masons (chaplain). Home: 516 Star Villa Cir SE Rio Rancho NM 87124-2927 Office: Motorola Ceramics Products 4800 Alameda Blvd Albuquerque NM 87110

GREER, HOWARD EARL, former naval officer; b. Tyler, Tex., May 1, 1921; s. Earl Abner and Ollie (Lightfoot) G.; m. Dale Price, Nov. 1, 1986; children—Margaret, Darby, David, Briand, Holly, Howard. Student, Tyler Jr. Coll., 1939-40; B.S., U.S. Naval Acad., 1943; M.B.A., George Washington U., 1965. Commd. ensign U.S. Navy, 1943, advanced through grades to vice adm., 1975; comdr. Aircraft Carrier Hancock, 1967-69, Carrier Force, Vietnam, (4 tours), Naval Air Forces, U.S. Atlantic Fleet, Norfolk, Va., 1975-78; dir. CEDAM Internat.; with Hughes Aircraft. Decorated D.S.M. (2), Legion of Merit (4), Knights of Malta Order St. John of Jerusalem. Mem. Assn. Naval Aviation (trustee), Golden Eagles (early pioneer naval aviators, Tailhook Assn., Naval Res. Assn. Republican. Methodist. Clubs: Outrigger Canoe; Oahu Country. Home: 1121 Waieli St Honolulu HI 96821-1244

GREER, JERRY DEAN, forester; b. Marshfield, Mo., Sept. 12, 1941; s. Ivan Lee and Mary Ellen (Young) G.; m. Karen Sue Evans, Oct. 7, 1961 (div. Jan. 1979); children: Richard Dean, Mary Kathryn Anne; m. Suzanne Karol French, Jan. 23, 1979 (div. Jan. 1989); 1 child, Cassandra Jeri-Lynn. BS in Forestry, U. Mo., 1964. Work project leader Forest Svc./USDA, Mountainair, N.Mex., 1966-68; recreation/lands staff Forest Svc./USDA, Pecos, N.Mex., 1968-70; recreation/lands/fire staff Forest Svc./USDA, Happy Jack, Ariz., 1970-72; recreation/lands staff Forest Svc./USDA, Flagstaff, Ariz., 1972-75; dist. ranger Forest Svc./USDA, Sedona, Ariz., 1975-78, Albuquerque, 1978-84; project mgr. remote sensing Forest Svc./USDA, Houston/Salt Lake City, 1984-88; resources staff officer Forest Svc./USDA, Bedford, Ind., 1988-91; br. chief planning and ecosys. mgmt. Forest Svc./USDA, McCall, Idaho, 1991—; reviewer sci. books for children Boston U. Sch. Edn., 1991—. Editor: Remote Sensing in the Forest Service, 1988, 90, 92, 94; contbg. editor Uptime Mag., 1987-88; author: (booklet) Techniques of Supervision of Volunteers, 1987; contbr. numerous articles to profl. jours. Bd. dirs. Keep Sedona Beautiful, 1977-78; trustee, bd. dirs. N.Mex. Crime Prevention Assn., Albuquerque, 1984; sec., bd. dirs. Greater Albuquerque Vols. Assn., 1982, 83; mem. com. Flagstaff Area Transp. Study, 1974-75; mem. N.Mex. Disting. Pub. Svc. Awards Coun., Santa Fe, 1984. Curators Freshman scholar, U. Mo., 1959, Richard M. Higgins Endowment Fund scholar, 1961. Mem. AAAS, Soc. Am. Foresters (chpt. chmn., chpt. sec.-treas.), Forest History Soc., Am. Soc. Photogrammetry and Remote Sensing, Soc. of Photo-Optical Instrumentation Engrs., Planetary Soc. Home: PO Box 1971 Mc Call ID 83638 Office: USDA Forest Svc Payette Nat For PO Box 1026 Mc Call ID 83638

GREER, MARTIN BRAD, computer executive; b. Salt Lake City, Sept. 26, 1957; s. Douglas Kerr and Lucille (Meyer) G.; m. Shari Rothenstein Leigh, Dec. 31, 1979; children: Shannon Leigh, Krista Heather. BS, MIT, 1981. Sys. engr. Rockwell Internat., Downey, Calif., 1979-80; bus. cons. Tymshare, Denver, 1981-83; sr. cons. Telic Corp., Denver, 1983-85; v.p. tech. svcs., cons. Miaco Corp., Denver, 1985—; spkr. and presenter in field. Author: In Search of the Golden Fleece, 1990; contbr. articles to profl. jours. Founding mem. MIT Enterprise Forum Colo., Denver, 1986-87; advisor MIT Ednl. Coun., Denver, 1988—, Belleview Acad. Adv. Com., Denver, 1991—; cons. Stay-in-Sch. Program, Denver, 1993.

GREEVER, JANET GROFF, history educator; b. Philadelphia, Sept. 12, 1921; m. William St. Clair Greever, Aug. 24, 1951; 1 child. BA, Bryn Mawr Coll., 1942, MA, 1945; MA, Harvard U., 1951, PhD, 1954. Resident head grad. houses Radcliffe Coll., Cambridge, Mass., 1947-48; resident head undergrad. hall Bryn Mawr (Pa.) Coll., 1949-51, instr. history, 1949-50; asst. prof. history Wash. State U., Pullman, 1962-63, U. Idaho, Moscow, 1965-66; ind. rschr., lectr. history Moscow, Idaho, 1954—; interim lectr. history Whitman Coll., Walla Walla, Wash., 1978; regional admissions cons., interviewer Bryn Mawr Coll., 1955-81. Author: Jose Ballivian y El Oriente Boliviano, 1987. bd. dirs. U. Idaho Libr. Assocs., Moscow, 1979-81, pres. 1980-81. Pa. State scholar, 1938-42, History fellow Bryn Mawr (Pa.) Coll., 1944-45, Margaret M. Justin fellow AAUW, Washington, 1948-49; grantee Lucius N. Littauer Found., N.Y.C., 1948-49. Mem. Am. Hist. Assn. (life), Conf. on Latin. Am. History (life), Latin Am. Studies Assn., Soc. for Am. Archaeology (life), Archaeol. Inst. Am. (life), Phi Alpha Theta. Home: 315 S Hayes St Moscow ID 83843-3419

GREEVER, MARGARET QUARLES, mathematics educator; b. Wilkensburg, Pa., Feb. 7, 1931; d. Lawrence Reginald and Ella Mae (LeSueur) Quarles; m. John Greever, Aug. 29, 1953; children: Catherine Patricia, Richard George, Cynthia Diane. Cert. costume design, Richmond Profl. Inst., 1952; student, U. Va., 1953-56; BA in Math., Calif. State U., Los Angeles, 1963; MA in Math., Claremont Grad. Sch., 1968. Cert. tchr. specializing in Jr. Coll. math., Calif. Tchr. math. Chaffey Unified High Sch. Dist., Alta Loma, Calif., 1963-64, Los Angeles Unified Sch. Dist., 1964-65, Chino (Calif.) Unified Sch. Dist., 1965-81; from asst. prof. to prof. Chaffey Coll., Alta Loma, 1981—, phys. sci. divsn. chmn., 1985-92; dean, phys., life, health sci., 1992—. Mem. LWV, Nat. Coun. Tchrs. Math., Am. Math. Assn. Two-Yr. Colls., Calif. Math. Coun., Assn. Calif. C.C. Adminstrs., Assn. Instr. Adminstrs., Women in Higher Edn., Pi Lambda Theta. Office: Chaffey Coll 5885 Haven Ave Rancho Cucamonga CA 91737-3002

GREGERSEN, MAX A., structural, earthquake and civil engineer; b. Blackfoot, Idaho, Apr. 6, 1951; s. Garth Clifford and Ella Lavere (Adamson) G.; m. Berneitta Ann Pieper, July 24, 1982; children: Dusty Rae, Molly Malinda. BS in Civil Engring., U. Utah, 1976. Registered profl. engr. Ala., Alaska, Ark., Calif., Del., Fla., Ga., Idaho, Ind., Ill., Kans., La., Maine, Mich., Minn., Miss., Mo., Mont., Nev., N.J., N.Y., N.C., N.D., Ohio, Okla., Pa., S.C., Tenn., Tex., Utah, Vt., Wash., Wis., Wyo., Alta. Can., P.R.; cert. structural engr. Civil/structural engr. Kellogg-Rust Engring., Salt Lake City, 1976-83; mgr. civil/structural engring. dept. Ford, Bacon & Davis, Inc., Salt Lake City, 1983—; corr. mem. 1994, Fed. Emergency Mgmt. Agy. Nat. Earthquake Hazards Reduction Program; seismic provisions tech. subcoms. for steel and concrete structures Bldg. Seismic Safety Coun., Washington, 1977, seismic provisions update com. for steel strucres, 1992—; mem. applied tech. coun. Fed. Emergency Mgmt. Agy.-sponsored ATC-33 Project devel. guidelines for seismic rehab. existing bldgs. concrete team, 1993—; mem. curriculum adv. bd., lectr. dept. civil engring. U. Utah, 1993—. Mem. ASCE, Am. Concrete Inst. (com. 369 Seismic repair and rehab. 1992—), Nat. Inst. Bldg. Scis., Earthquake Engring. Rsch. Inst., Constrn. Specifications Inst., Structural Engrs. Assn. Utah, Steel Structures Painting Coun., North Am. Geosynthetics Soc., Internat. Geotextile Soc., Internat. Conf. Bldg. Ofcls., Bldg. Ofcls. and Code Adminstrs. Internat., So. Bldg. Code Congress Internat., Assn. Profl. Engrs., Geologists, and Geophysicists Alta. Office: Ford Bacon and Davis Inc 375 Chipeta Way PO Box 58009 Salt Lake City UT 84158-0009

GREGG, KENNETH STEPHEN, computer scientist; b. Lakewood, Ohio, July 13, 1960; s. John Frederick and Evelyn Mae (Lutrey) G.; m. Theresa Mae Liska, Sept. 5, 1981. BS, Mich. State U., 1983; MS, U. Tex. at Dallas, Richardson, 1988. Software design engr. Tex. Instruments Inc., Lubbock, 1983; programmer/systems analyst Tex. Instruments Inc., Sherman, 1983-84; software design engr. Tex. Instruments Inc., Dallas, 1984-85; software engr., sr. software engr. InteCom Inc., Allen, Tex., 1985-88, lead sr. software engr., 1989; software design engr. Microsoft Corp., Redmond, Wash., 1989-90, OEM liaison, testing architect, 1990-91, Windows NT base test mgr., 1991-92, Windows NT test and performance mgr., 1992-94; sr. dir. software engring. Artisoft, Inc., Tucson, 1994—. Recipient Sch. award Am. Legion, Lakewood, Ohio, 1978. Mem. Assn. for Computing Machinery. Mormon. Home: 8301 N Westcliff Dr Tucson AZ 85743-1044 Office: Artisoft 691 E River Rd Tucson AZ 85704-5824

GREGG, LUCIUS PERRY, JR., aerospace executive; b. Henderson, N.C., Jan. 16, 1933; s. Lucius Perry and Rachel (Jackson) G.; m. Doris Marie Jefferson, May 30, 1959 (dec. Nov. 1980); 1 child, Lucius Perry III; m. Beverly E.E. Ward, Jan. 3, 1994. BSEE, U.S. Naval Acad., 1955; MS in Aero and Astronautics, MIT, 1961; AMP Program, Harvard U., 1975; D of Sci. (hon.), Grinnell Coll., 1973. Pilot, aircraft commdr. mil. air command USAF, 1956-59; project scientist Air Force Office Scientific Rsch., Washington, 1961-65; dir., rsch. coord., assoc. dean sci. Northwestern U., Evanston, Ill., 1965-69; program officer Alfred P. Sloan Found., N.Y.C., 1969-72; pres. First Chgo. U. Finance Corp., Chgo., 1972-79; v.p. First Nat. Bank Chgo., 1972-79; v.p. corp. planning Bristol-Myers Co., N.Y.C., 1979-83; dir. nat. pub. rels., v.p. gov. rels. Citibank/Citicorp, N.Y.C., 1983-87; v.p. pub. affairs N.Y. Daily News, N.Y.C., 1987-89; v.p. corp. communications Hughes Aircraft Co., L.A., 1989—; vis. com. on aero and astronautics MIT, Cambridge, 1971-79; vis. com. on physics Harvard U., Cambridge, 1973-79; mem. commn. on human resources Nat. Acad. Sci., Washington, 1973-78; vice chmn., bd. dirs. Corp. for Pub. Broadcasting, Washington, 1975-81; bd. trustees W Net Pub. TV, N.Y.C., 1981-89; bd. dirs. Chgo. Coun. on Fgn. Rels., Chgo., 1975-79; mem. academic bd. U.S. Naval Acad., Annapolis, Md., 1971-81; mem. NASA U. Rels., Washington, 1968-72; chmn. bd. Tulane U., New Orleans, 1972-82; trustee Roosevelt U., Chgo., 1976-79; mem. Ill. Commn. on Urban Gov., Chgo., 1976-79, Chgo. Mayor's Coun. Econ. Advisors, Chgo., 1976-79; intelligence rev. com. Chgo. Police Depart., 1977-79. Maj. USAF, 1965-85. Named Engr. of Yr. Washington Acad. Sci., 1964, One of 10 Outstanding Young Men Chgo. Jr. Assn. Commerce and Industry, 1966. Office: Hughes Aircraft Co PO Box 80028 Los Angeles CA 90080-0028

GREGGS, ELIZABETH MAY BUSHNELL (MRS. RAYMOND JOHN GREGGS), retired librarian; b. Delta, Colo., Nov. 7, 1925; d. Joseph Perkins and Ruby May (Stanford) Bushnell; m. Raymond John Greggs, Aug. 16, 1952; children: David M., Geoffrey B., Timothy C., Daniel R. BA, U. Denver, 1948. Children's librarian Grand Junction (Colo.) Pub. Library, 1944-46, Chelan County Library, 1948, Wenatchee (Wash.) Pub. Library, 1948-52, Seattle Pub. Library, 1952-53; children's librarian Renton (Wash.) Pub. Library, 1957-61, dir., 1962, br. supr. and children's services supr., 1963-67; area children's supr. King County Library, Seattle, 1968-78, asst. coordinator children's services, 1978-86; head librarian Valley View Library of King County Library System, Seattle, 1986-90; cons., organizer Tutor Ctr. Library, Seattle South Community Coll., 1969-72; mem. Puget Sound (Wash.) Council for Reviewing Children's Media, 1974—, chmn., 1974-76; cons. to children's TV programs. Editor: Cayas Newsletter, 1971-74; cons. to Children's Catalog, Children's Index to Poetry. Chmn. dist. advancement com. Kloshee dist. Boy Scouts Am., 1975-78; mem. Bond Issue Citizens Group to build new Renton Libr., 1958, 59; mem. exec. bd. Family Edn. and Counseling Ctr. on Deafness, 1991-94. Recipient Hon. Service to Youth award Cedar River dist. Boy Scouts Am., 1971, Award of Merit Kloshee dist., 1977, winner King County Block Grant, 1990. Mem. ALA (Newbery-Caldecott medal com. 1978-79, com. chmn. 1983-84; membership com. 1978-80, Boy Scouts com. children's svcs. div. 1973-78, chmn. 1976-78, exec. bd. dirs. Assn. for Libr. Svc. to Children 1979-81, mem. coun. 1985-92, chmn. nominating com. 1986-87, councillor 1989-92, exec. bd. 1989-92, exec. com. 1989-92, coun. orientation com. 1987-89), Wash. Libr. Assn. (exec. bd. children's and young adult svcs. div. 1970-78, chmn. membership com. 1983-90, publs. com. 1988-92, emeritus 1991, mem. elections com.), King County Right to Read Coun. (co-chmn. 1973-77), Pierce-King County Reading Coun., Wash. State Literacy Coun. (exec. bd. 1971-77), Wash. Libr. Media Assn. (jr. high levels com. 1980-84), Pacific N.W. Libr. Assn. (young readers' choice com. 1981-83, chmn. div. 1983-85, exec. bd. 1983-85). Methodist. Home: Unit 49 201 Union Ave SE Renton WA 98059-5176

GREGO-HEINTZ, DONNA MARIE, pediatric physical therapist; b. Phila., July 3, 1956; d. Joseph Francis and Rosemarie (Damico) Grego; m. Stephen Eugene Heintz, Aug. 28, 1982; children: Emily, Lauren, Audrey. BS, U. Del., 1978. Cert. phys. therapist. Staff phys. therapist Nat. Jewish Hosp., Denver, 1978-79, Swedish Med. Ctr., Denver, 1979-80; phys. therapy dept. chief First Creek Sch., Aurora, Colo., 1980-84; pediatric therapy coord. Rose Med. Ctr., Denver, 1984-88; clin. instr. U. Colo., Denver, 1988-94; owner, pediatric phys. therapist Theracare, P.C., Englewood, Colo., 1989—. Vol. Alternatives Pregnancy Ctr., Denver, 1986—. Mem. Am. Phys. Therapy Assn. (regional dir. 1986-88), Neurodevel. Treatment Assn., Pediatric Therapist Interest Group (v.p. 1981-83). Republican. Home: 3734 S Ventura Way Aurora CO 80013-3438 Office: Theracare PC 6851 S Holly Cir Ste 240 Englewood CO 80112-1041

GREGOR, DOROTHY DEBORAH, librarian; b. Dobbs Ferry, N.Y., Aug. 15, 1939; d. Richard Garrett Heckman and Marion Allen (Richmond) Stewart; m. A. James Gregor, June 22, 1963 (div. 1974). BA, Occidental Coll., 1961; MA, U. Hawaii, 1963; MLS, U. Tex., 1968; cert. in Library Mgmt., U. Calif., Berkeley, 1976. Reference libr. U. Calif., San Francisco, 1968-69; dept. libr. Pub. Health Libr. U. Calif., Berkeley, 1969-71, tech. services libr., 1973-76; reference libr. Hamilton Libr., Honolulu, 1971-72; head serials dept. U. Calif., Berkeley, 1976-80, assoc. univ. libr. tech. svcs. dept., 1980-84, univ. libr., 1992-94; ret., 1994; chief Shared Cataloging div. Libr. of Congress, Washington, 1984-85; univ. libr. U. Calif.-San Diego, La Jolla, 1985-92, OCLC asst. to pres. for acad. and rsch. libr. rels., 1995—; instr. sch. libr. and info. studies U. Calif., Berkeley, 1975, 76, 83; cons. Nat. Libr. of Medicine, Bethesda, Md., 1985, Ohio Bd. Regents, Columbus, 1987; trustee Online Computer Libr. Ctr., asst. to pres. for acad. and rsch. libr. rels., 1995—. Mem. ALA, Libr. Info. Tech. Assn., Program Com. Ctr. for Rsch. Libs. (bd. chair 1992-93, Hugh Atkinson award 1994).

GREGORY, CALVIN, insurance service executive; b. Bronx, N.Y., Jan. 11, 1942; s. Jacob and Ruth (Cherchian) G.; m. Rachel Anna Carver, Feb. 14, 1970 (div. Apr. 1977); children—Debby Lynn, Trixy Sue; m. 2d, Carla Deane Deaver, June 30, 1979. A.A., Los Angeles City Coll., 1962; B.A., Calif. State U.-Los Angeles, 1964; M.Div., Fuller Theol. Sem., 1968; M.R.E., Southwestern Sem., Ft. Worth, 1969; Ph.D. in Religion, Universal Life Ch., Modesto, Calif., 1982; D.Div. (hon.), Otay Mesa Coll., 1982. Notary pub., real estate lic., casualty lic., Calif.; ordained to ministry Am. Baptist Conv., 1970. Youth minister First Bapt. Ch., Delano, Calif., 1964-65, 69-70; youth dir. St. Luke's United Meth. Ch., Highland Park, Calif., 1969-70; tchr. polit. sci. Maranatha High Sch., Rosemead, Calif., 1969-70; aux. chaplain U.S. Air Force 750th Radar Squadron, Edwards AFB, Calif., 1970-72; pastor First Bapt. Ch., Boron, Calif., 1971-72; ins. agt. Prudential Ins. Co., Ventura, Calif., 1972-73, sales mgr., 1973-74; casualty ins. agt. Allstate Ins. Co., Thousand Oaks, Calif., 1974-75; pres. Ins. Agy. Placement Service, Thousand Oaks, 1975—; head youth minister Emanuel Presbyn. Ch., Los Angeles, 1973-74; owner, investor real estate, U.S., Wales, Eng., Can., Australia. Counselor YMCA, Hollywood, Calif., 1964, Soul Clinic-Universal Life Ch., Inc., Modesto, Calif., 1982. Mem. Apt. Assn. Los Angeles, Life Underwriter Tng. Council. Republican. Clubs: Forensic (Los Angeles); X32 (Ventura). Lodge: Kiwanis (club speaker 1971). Office: Ins Agy Placement Svc PO Box 4407 Thousand Oaks CA 91359-1407

GREGORY, ELEANOR ANNE, artist, educator; b. Seattle, Jan. 20, 1939; d. John Noel and Eleanor Blanche G.; BA, Reed Coll., 1963; MFA, U. Wash., 1966; MEd, Columbia U., 1978, EdD., 1978. Art tchr. Seattle Pub. Schs., 1970-75; instr. N.Y.C. C.C., 1977, Manhattan C.C., N.Y.C., 1978; asst. prof. N.Mex. State U., Las Cruces, 1978-79; asst. prof. art Purdue U., West Lafayette, Ind., 1979-82, West Tex. State U., Canyon, 1982-84; mgr. Watson's Crick Gallery, West Lafayette, 1982-83; lectr. Calif. State U., Long Beach, 1985-87, L.A. Unified Sch. Dist., 1988—. One woman shows: Columbia U. Tchrs. Coll., 1976, Watson's Crick Gallery, West Lafayette, 1980, 81, Gallery I, Purdue U., 1980, W. Tex. State U., 1983, Amarillo Art Ctr., 1984, Sch. Visual Concepts, Seattle, 1985; group shows include: El Paso (Tex.) Art Mus., 1979, Ind. State Mus., Indpls., 1980, Lafayette (Ind.) Art Mus., 1982, T. Billman Gallery, Long Beach, 1987; represented in permanent collection: Portland (Oreg.) Art Mus. Mem. Nat. Art Edn. Assn. (pres. women's caucus chpt. 1988-90, v.p.-elect Pacific region 1994—), N.Y. Soc. Scribes, L.A. Soc. Calligraphy, Internat. Soc. Edn. Through Art, Art Educators of L.A. (pres. 1993-95). Episcopalian.

GREGORY, JAMES, actor; b. N.Y.C., Dec. 23, 1911; s. James Gillen and Axemia Theresa (Ekdahl) G.; m. Ann Catherine Miltner, May 25, 1944. Grad. high sch. Actor, 1936—. Actor: (summer stock prodns.) Deer Lake, Pa., 1936-37, 39, Millbrook, N.Y., 1938, Braddock Heights, Md., 1940, Buck's County Playhouse, New Hope, Pa., 1941, Ivy Tower Playhouse, Spring Lake, N.J., 1951, (Broadway shows) Key Largo, 1939, Journey to Jerusalem, 1940, In Time to Come, 1941, Dream Girl, 1945, All My Sons, 1947, Death of a Salesman, 1948-49, Dead Pigeon, 1954, Fragile Fox, 1955, Desperate Hours, 1956-57, (films) The Young Strangers, 1955, Al Capone Story, 1955, Gun Glory, 1956, Nightfall, 1956, The Big Caper, 1956, A Distant Trumpet, 1961, Underwater Warrior, 1962, PT-109, 1965, The Sons of Katie Elder, 1967, The Manchurian Candidate, 1967, Captain Newman, M.D, 1967, Million Dollar Duck, 1968, Clam Bake, 1967, Secret War of Harry Frigg, 1968, Beneath the Planet of the Apes, 1970, The Hawaiians, 1970, Shoot Out, 1971, The Late Liz, 1971, $1,000,000. Duck, 1971, The Strongest Man in the World, 1974, The Main Event, 1979, Wait Til Your Mother Gets Home, 1982, X-15, Death of a Salesman, also 5 Matt Helm pictures, (TV shows) Big Valley, Bonanza, Gunsmoke, Rawhide, Playhouse 90, Climax, Alfred Hitchcock Presents, Twilight Zone, Quincy, as Inspector Luger in Barney Miller, Mr. Belvedere, 1986. Served with USNR, USMCR, 1942-45, PTO. Mem. Soc. Preservation and Encouragement Barber Shop Quartet Singing Am. Club: Hollywood Hackers, Golf. Home: 55 Cathedral Rock Dr Unit 33 Sedona AZ 86351-8624*

GREGORY, JOEL PATRICK, geologist, consultant; b. Danville, Va., Aug. 19, 1956; s. Andrew Harrison and Christine (Burton) G.; m. Bernardine Gayle Zimmerman, Mar. 27, 1982 (div. May 1986). BS in Geology, Coll. William and Mary, 1978; MS in Geology, U. N.C., 1982. Tchg. tchg. asst. Dept. Geology, U. N.C., Chapel Hill, 1978-79, lab. asst., 1979-80, rsch. asst., 1980-81; rsch. asst. U.S. Geol. Survey, Denver, 1981; prodn. geologist Gulf Oil Exploration and Prodn. Co., Okla. City, 1981-84; exploration geologist Enserch Exploration, Inc., Dallas, 1984-91; consulting geologist Pinedale, Wyo., 1991—. Compiler map; contbr. articles to profl. jours. NSF Rsch. grantee, 1977. Mem. Am. Assn. Petroleum Geologists (cert.), Geol. Soc. Am., Sigma Gamma Epsilon. Home and Office: PO Box 1329 Pinedale WY 82941-1329

GREGORY, NELSON BRUCE, motel owner, retired naval officer; b. Syracuse, N.Y., Aug. 4, 1933; s. Nelson Bruce and Josephine (Sully) G.; m. Bonnie K. Bannowsky, May 2, 1961 (div. 1970); children: Elizabeth Jo, Jennifer Kay; m. Patricia Ann Greenhalgh, Oct. 15, 1977 (div. 1994); children: Peter Ward, Annette Frances, Michael John, Geoffrey Charles. BS, N.Y. Maritime Coll., 1955; postgrad., USN Pilot Tng., Pensacola, Fla., 1955-57; grad., NATO Weapons Sch., Oberammergau, Fed. Republic of Germany, 1966; diploma, Joint Warfare Sch., Salisbury, Eng., 1967, USN Counter Insurgency, Little Creek, Va., 1968, USAF Space Ops., Montgomery, Ala., 1969. Commd. ens. USN, 1955, advanced through grades to lt. comdr., 1964; operational pilot airborne Early Warning Squadron 2 USN, Patuxent River, Md., 1957-60; flight instr. Airborne Early Warning Tng. Unit USN, Patuxent River, 1960-63; command pilot Air Devel. Squadron 6 USN, McMurdo Sound, Antarctica, 1963-64; airspace control officer NATO, Naples, Italy, 1964-68; chief pilot Naval Support Activity, Danang, Vietnam, 1968-69; space intelligence analyst NORAD, Colorado Springs, Colo., 1969-71; operational pilot Electronic Warfare Squadron 33 USN, Norfolk, Va., 1971-74; ops. officer Nat. Parachute Test Range USN, El Centro, Calif., 1974-75; ret. USN, 1975; owner, gen. mgr. Bonneville Motel, Idaho Falls, Idaho, 1975—; bd. dirs. Am. Trowel Inns, 1976-78. Patron Idaho Falls Symphony/Opera Theater, 1980—; mem. Better Bus. Bur., 1989; POW return sponsor, 1973. Decorated Air medals (3) USN; recipient Vietnamese Gallantry Cross Republic of Vietnam, 1969; Gregory Ridge in Antarctica named for him, 1964. Mem. Ret. Officers Assn. (life), Idaho Falls C. of C., Elks. Republican. Presbyterian. Home: 2000 S Yellowstone Hwy Idaho Falls ID 83402-4325

GREGORY, THOMAS LANG, restaurant chain executive; b. Detroit, 1935. Grad., Mich. State U., 1957. Pres. Sizzler Restaurants Internat., L.A.; v.p. Collins Foods Internat. Inc. Office: Sizzler Restaurants 12655 W Jefferson Blvd Los Angeles CA 90066-7008

GREGORY, WILLIAM EDGAR, psychologist; b. Steelville, Mo., Nov. 13, 1910; s. Edward Clark and Rilla Frances (Edgar) G.; m. Ella Virginia Sausser, Mar. 10, 1937 (dec. 1953); 1 child, William Edgar Jr.; m. Muriel Holden Van Gilder, June 10, 1956. BA, Colo. Coll., 1933; postgrad., U. Chgo., 1933-36; BD, Chgo. Theol. Sem., 1936; PhD, U. Calif., Berkeley, 1955. Ordained to ministry United Ch. of Christ, 1937. Asst. min. Jefferson Park Congl. Ch., Chgo., 1934-36; editorial assoc. Advance, Boston, 1936-37; pastor West Congl. Ch., Concord, N.H., 1937-39; acting supt. Ft. Berthold Indian Mission, Elbowoods, N.D., 1939-40; chaplain U.S. Army, 1940-45; dir. ministry svcs. pers. and vets. San Francisco Coun. of Chs., 1945-47; dir. rsch. N. Calif. Coun. of Chs., San Francisco, 1947-48; prof. psychology Coll. of Pacific, Stockton, Calif., 1938—; prof. emeritus U. Pacific, Stockton, 1981—; instr. U. Md. abroad, Verona, Italy, 1965. Mem. APA, Am. Sociol. Assn., Am. Anthropol. Assn., Soc. for Sci. Study Religion, DAV. Democrat. Home: 976 W Mendocino Ave Stockton CA 95204-3024

GREIG, WILLIAM TABER, JR., publishing company executive; b. Mpls., Apr. 16, 1924; s. William Taber and Margaret Naomi (Buckbee) G.; m. Doris Jane Walters, June 23, 1951; children: Kathryn Ann Greig Rowland, William Taber, III, Gary Stanley, Doris Jane. B.Arch., U. Minn., 1945. Jr. exec. Bur. Engraving, Mpls., 1946-48; partner, mgr. Praise Book Publns., Mound, Minn., 1948-50; v.p., exec. v.p., gen. mgr. Gospel Light Publs., 1950-76; pres., owner Gospel Light Publs., Ventura, Calif., 1976—, chmn., 1983—; bd. dirs. Lighthouse Ptnrs. Bookstores, Gospel Lit. Internat.; founder, chmn. bd. St. Petersburg (Russia) Pub. Ruling elder Presbyn. Ch. (U.S.A.); bd. dirs., chmn. Joy of Living Bible Studies, 1978—; trustee Latin Am. Mission, Concerts of Prayer Internat., 1988—; chmn. John Perkins Found., 1990—. Served to lt. (j.g.) USNR, 1943-46. Mem. Evang. Christian Pubs. Assn. (co-founder 1974, bd. dirs., pres. 1981-83). Republican. Clubs: Verdugo, Tower. Home: 347 Lupine Way Ventura CA 93001-2201 Office: Gospel Light Publs 2300 Knoll Dr Ventura CA 93003-7308

GREINER, ROBERT PHILIP, lawyer, real estate broker; b. Herkimer, N.Y., July 3, 1930; s. Max Henry and Margaret Mary (O'Hara) G. BA, U. Rochester, 1951; MBA, Syracuse U., 1957; LLB, UCLA, 1964. Bar: Calif. 1965; CPA, Calif.; lic. real estate broker, Calif. Pvt. practice acct., CPA, 1962-64; lawyer L.A. (Calif.) Pub. Defenders Office, 1965-87; pvt. practice lawyer and real estate broker Calif., 1987—. Pres. Guide Dog Boosters, Los Alamitos, Calif., 1984. Staff sgt. USAF, 1951-55. Home and Office: 730 Natalie Dr Windsor CA 95492-8870

GREINER MAKENNA, CARRIE ANN, religious science practitioner; b. Denver, Sept. 25, 1959; d. Rodney Earl and Ruth Ellen (Brunskill) G.; m. Craig Evan Rouse, Oct. 8, 1993. BFA, Colo. State U., 1982. Cert. massage therapist. Graphic designer office of comm. Colo. State U., Ft. Collins, 1982-83, prodn. artist Collegian newspaper, 1982-83; art dir. Cimarron Prodns., Denver, 1984-85; owner design bus. The Solution Rm., Denver, 1985-86; massage in pvt. practice Denver, 1986-92; religious sci. practitioner Mile Hi Ch., Denver, 1991—; mgr. corp. comm. First Trust Corp., Denver, 1986—. Democrat.

GREMBOWSKI, EUGENE, insurance company executive; b. Bay City, Mich., July 21, 1938; s. Barney Thomas and Mary (Senkowski) G.; m. Teresa Ann Frasik, June 27, 1959; children: Bruce Allen, Debora Ann. AA, Allan Hancock U., 1963; BA, Mich. State U., 1967; MBA, George Washington U., 1972. Cert. profl. contracts mgr.; cert: CLU. Enlisted USAF, 1955, commd. 2d lt., 1968, advanced through grades to capt., 1971; pers. officer USAF, Goldsboro, N.C., 1968-70; chief of procurement USAF, Cheyenne, Wyo., 1971-73; contract analyst USAF, Omaha, 1973-76; chief of contracting USAF, Atwater, Calif., 1976-79; ret. USAF, 1979; office supr. Farmers Ins. Group of Cos., Merced, Calif., 1980-85, office mgr., 1985-86; corp. fleet mgr. L.A., 1986—. Author: Governmental Purchasing: Its Progression Toward Professional Status, 1972. Cubmaster Boy Scouts Am., Goldsboro, 1968; com. chmn. Am. Heart Assn., Merced-Mariposa, Calif., 1985, sec.-treas., 1986. Decorated Commendation medals, 1965, 70, 79; recipient Meritorious Svc. medals Office of the Pres., 1973, 76. Mem. Nat. Contract Mgmt. Assn., Nat. Assn. Fleet Adminstrs., Automotive Fleet and Leasing Assn., Am. Legion, Air Force Assn. (life), Ret. Officers Assn. (life). Office: Farmers Group Inc 4750 Wilshire Blvd Los Angeles CA 90010-4603

GREN, CONRAD ROGER, auditor; b. Medford, Oreg., Aug. 11, 1955; s. Donald Oswald and Jean Viola (Hoefs) G.; m. Barbara June Kyle, Sept. 5, 1982; children: Eric Conrad Kyle, Kari June Elizabeth, Laura Jean Alyssa. BSBA, Walla Walla Coll., 1978. Acct. bus. office Walla Walla Coll., College Place, Wash., 1974-75, food preparer, cashier for food svc., 1975-77, reader Theology dept., 1975-76; inventory return Northrup, King & Co., Portland, Oreg., 1976-77; audit clk. Corps of Engrs., NPD Audit, Walla Walla, Wash., 1977-78; auditor Corps of Engrs., NPD Audit, Portland, Oreg., 1979-82, 83—; acct. Forest Svc., Deschutes Nat. Forest, Bend, Oreg., 1978-79, Portland Dist., Corps of Engrs., 1982-83; pres. Green Heritage Imaging, Inc., Clackamas, Oreg. Elder Sunnyside Seventh-day Adventist Ch., Portland, 1988-91, mem. ch. and family life coun., 1991-92; constituent del. triennial meeting Oreg. Conf. Seventh-day Adventists, 1992, spl. edn. session, 1993, 95, mem. fin. com., 1993—. Democrat. Home: 21601 SE Edward Dr Clackamas OR 97015-8755 Office: US Army Corps Engrs N Pacific Div 220 NW 8th St Ste 409 Portland OR 97208-2870

GRENFELL, GEORGE ALBERT, JR., assistant district attorney; b. Modesto, Calif., Mar. 19, 1941; s. George Albert Sr. and Margaret (Armbrust) G.; m. Mary Louise Vieira, May 22, 1971; children: Richelle Louise, Trisha Lynn. BSBA in Econs., Saint Mary's Coll., 1963; JD, Humphrey's Law Sch., 1968. Bar: Calif., 1970. Dep. dist. atty. Tulare County Dist. Atty. Office, Visalia, Calif., 1970-74; asst. dist. atty., adminstr. Fresno (Calif.) Dist. Atty. Office, 1974—; cons. L.A. County Adminstrv. Office, 1980-81; mem. CSNet Workgroup Dept. HHS-Office Child Support Enforcement, Washington, 1988, Calif. rep. time and activity standard com., 1989; mem. Statewide Automated Child Support System Policy Mgmt. Adv. Com. State Dept. Social Svcs., Sacramento, 1989—. Bd. dirs., v.p. Tulare County Legal Aid Soc., Visalia, 1973-77, Fresno County pvt. ind. coun. Parenting Oportunities Program, 1991-93; bd. dirs., sec., treas. The Lakes Homeowners Assn., Visalia, 1988-89; mem. child support vision for excellence task force State Dept. Social Svcs., 1992. Recipient Disting. Faculty award, Nat. Dist. Attys. Assn., 1976; named Outstanding Individual Mgr. State Dept. Social Svcs., 1989, Outstanding Individual Achievement (Mgr.) Nat. Child Support Enforcement Assn., 1990. Mem. Calif. Family Support Coun. (bd. dirs., pres. 1975-76, chmn. automation com. 1989-91, Truly B. Knox 1977), Calif. State Bar Assn., Calif. Dist. Attys. Assn. (AB 407 Task Force 1995), Fresno County Bar Assn., Nat. Child Support Enforcement Assn., E Clampus Vitas (chpt. 855), San Joaquin Fine Woodworkers Assn. (pres. 1986-88, newsletter editor, 1989-91). Republican. Roman Catholic. Home: 5536 W Prospect Ave Visalia CA 93291-9278 Office: Dist Atty Family Support 2220 Tulare St Fresno CA 93721-2104

GRENFELL, GLORIA ROSS, freelance journalist; b. Redwood City, Calif., Nov. 14, 1926; d. Edward William and Blanch (Ross) G.; m. June 19, 1948 (div. Nov. 15, 1983); children: Jane, Barbara, Robert, Mary. BS, U. Oreg., 1948, postgrad., 1983-85. Coll. bd., retail sales Meier & Frank Co., Portland, Oreg., 1945; book sales retailer J.K. Gill & Co., Portland, Oreg., 1948-50; advisor Mt. Hood Meadows Women's Ski Program, Oreg., 1968-78; corp. v.p. OK Delivery System, Inc., Oreg., 1977-82; ski instr. Willamette Pass, Oreg., 1983-85, Mt. Shasta, 1986; Campfire girls leader Portland, 1958-72; freelance journalist Marina, Calif., 1986—. Mem. Assn. Jr. League Internat., 1957-87; mem. Monterey County Mental Health Adv. Commn., 1994—, So. Poverty Law Ctr., 1994—, No. Mariposa County History Ctr., Calif. Recipient Golden Poles award Mt. Hood Meadows, 1975. Mem. Soc. Profl. Journalists, Profl. Ski Instrs. Am., U.S. Ski Coaches Assn., Calif. State Sheriffs' Assn. (assoc.), Monterey History and Art Assn., Yosemite Assn., Monterey Sports Ctr., Friends of Sea Otter, Mariposa County C. of C., Monterey Bay Area Nat. Alumnae Panhellenic, Order Ea. Star, Mortar Bd., Kappa Alpha Theta. Democrat. Episcopalian. Home and Office: 3128 Crescent Ave Lot 9 Marina CA 93933-3131

GRENIER, JUDSON A., JR., history educator; b. Indpls., Mar. 6, 1930; s. Judson A. Sr. and Beatrice Olivia (Bjeldanes) G.; m. Nancy Hicks, Aug. 9, 1954; children: Karen, Eric, Jonathan, Caddie. BA, U. Minn., 1951; MA, U. Calif., Berkeley, 1952; PhD in History, UCLA, 1965. Teaching asst. U. Calif., Berkeley, 1951-52; analyst IPS U.S. Dept. of State, Washington, 1952; reporter L.A. Mirror-News, 1958, 59; instr. El Camino Coll., Torrance, 1956-65; prof. Calif. State U., Dominguez Hills, 1966—; vis. lectr. UCLA, 1965-66; mem. acad. senate Calif. State U., 1974-83, sec., 1976-78, vice chmn., 1979-80, dir. oral history project, 1986-89, 94—; cons. El Pueblo St. Historic Park, L.A., 1980-83, City of Gardena, Calif., 1980-87, City of Torrance, Calif., 1980-82, City of Redondo Beach, Calif., 1985-87, L.A. County Dept. of Edn., 1979-81. Author: California Legacy: Watson-Dominguez Family, 1987; edit. cons. Calif. History; contbr. articles to profl. jours. Recipient Community Disting. Svc. award Calif. State U., 1987; NEH fellow, 1984, Huntington-Haynes fellow, 1985, Newberry Fellow, 1991. Mem. Am. Hist. Assn., Hist. Soc. of So. Calif. (v.p. 1981-83), L.A. 200 (hist. and edn. coms. 1978-81), L.A. Bicentennial Com. (hist. team 1973-76). Home: 587 33rd St Manhattan Beach CA 90266-3405 Office: Calif State U 1000 E Victoria St Carson CA 90747-0001

GRENNAN, CYNTHIA, school superintendent; b. Sterling, Ill., Jan. 4, 1938; d. Francis John and Elza (Pippert) G. B.S., Ill. State U., 1959; M.A., Ariz. State U., 1964. Tchr. Palatine Sch. Dist., Ill., 1959-61, Chandler Sch. Dist., Ariz., 1961-64, Anaheim Union High Sch. Dist., Calif., 1964-67, counselor, 1972-76, psychologist, 1972-76, asst. prin. to asst. supt., 1976-79, supt., 1979—; state supt. com. Assn. Calif. Sch. Adminstrs., Burlingame, Calif., 1984—. Episcopalian. Office: Anaheim Union High Sch Dist PO Box 3520 Anaheim CA 92803-3520*

GRESHAM, ROBERT LAMBERT, JR., insurance company executive; b. Portland, Oreg., Oct. 11, 1943; s. Robert L. and Barbara (Jones) G.; m. Judy L. Norris, Dec. 7, 1974. BS, U. So. Calif., 1965. CPCU. Adjuster Ins. Co. of NoAm., L.A., 1966-68; mgr. R.L. Gresham & Co., Inc., Las Vegas, Nev., 1968-72, pres., 1980—; mem. editorial rev. bd. Adjusters Reference Guide, Omaha, 1980—; dir. Nat. Panel Select Adjusters Cos., Harahan, La., 1985—. Pres. Fraternal Order of Eagles, Las Vegas, 1978, Fraternal Order of Police, Las Vegas, 1973; bd. dirs. Las Vegas Jaycees, 1972. With USNR, 1961-70. Mem. Nev. State Claims Assn. (pres. 1976-77, Nev. Claimsman of Yr. 1973), Calif. Assn. Ind. Ins. Adjusters (pres. 1986-87), Affiliated Ins. Adjusters (pres. 1977-78), So. Nev. Claims Assn. (pres. 1973-74), Nat. Assn. Ind. Ins. Adjusters (pres. 1992), CPCU (pres. So. Nev. chpt. 1983-84). Office: R L Gresham & Co Inc 1200 S 4th St Las Vegas NV 89104-1046

GRETZINGER, WILDA VIRGINIA, educator; b. Charleston, W.Va., Apr. 16, 1927; d. John Lewis and Josephine McChesney (Criser) Hall; m. Charles Elwin Davis (dec.); m. Robert Evans Gretzinger (dec.); children: Paul, George, Mark. BS in Edn., U. South Ala., 1978. Cert. tchr., Oreg. Gen. sys. v.p. Aerospace Software Co., Tarzana, Calif., 1968-70; mem. editing staff Santa Susana Mag., Westlake Village, Calif., 1972-73; tchr. U. South Ala. Am. U. Cairo (Egypt), 1982; dir. Mobile (Ala.) Internat. Festival, 1982-87; lectr. on Egypt and Rome civic orgns. and schs. Ala., Fla., La., Miss., 1982-87; lectr. on Am. Indian Annette von Droste Coll., Friedrichshafen, Germany, 1991; lectr. on Egypt Aloha H.S., Portland, Oreg., 1992; substitute tchr. State of Oreg., Portland, 1992—; tutor Oreg. Literacy Inc., Portland, 1994; field trip coord. Mobile Sch. Sys. and Sister Cities, 1982-87; excavator, illustrator U. South Ala., Dauphin Island, 1976, Moorpark (Calif.) Coll., 1972; actress Horizon Players, Simi Valley, Calif., 1970-72. Author: (play) Dear Uncle Sam (Hon. mention award 1974). Vice chmn. recycling com. Sylvan Heights Homeowners Assn., Portland, 1994; weekend coord. guide for Oakleigh Antebellum Home, Mobile Hist. Preservation Soc., 1973-76; dir. Mobile Internat. Youth Assn., 1982-87. Recipient award Nat. Aerospace Edn. Assn., 1974-75, Northridge Cultural Arts and Hist. Assn., 1972. Mem. DAR (rec. sec., def. chmn. Tristan de Luna chpt. 1987, Honors award 1970-72), Kappa Kappa Iota. Episcopalian. Home: 14645 SW Quail Ln # 0-105 Beaverton OR 97007-8534

GREYSON, JEROME, chemist, consultant, educator; b. N.Y.C., Nov. 7, 1927; m. Jacqueline Vis, July 27, 1957; children: Clifford, Ann, Paul. BA, Hunter Coll., 1950; PhD in Chemistry, Pa. State U., 1956. Mem. tech. staff Bell Telephone Labs., Murray Hill, N.J., 1956-57, IBM Rsch. Labs., Yorktown Heights, N.Y., 1957-62; phys. chemistry group leader Stauffer Chem. Co., Richmond, Calif., 1962-64; supr. environ. chemistry N.Am. Rockwell, Canoga Park, Calif., 1964-70; dir. blood chem. devel. Miles Labs., Inc., Elkhart, Ind., 1970-82; tech. dir. Precision Sci. Co., Chgo., 1982-86; owner, mgr. J & JG Assocs., Conifer, Colo., 1986—; adj. faculty Metro State Coll., Denver; presented in field to profl. meetings, symposia and confs., 1966-81, including 10th Internat. Congress on Clin. Chemistry, Mexico City, 1978, 3d European Congress Clin. Chemistry, Brighton, Eng., 1979, 1st South East Asian and Pacific Congress Clin. Biochemistry, Singapore, 1979, Analytica 80, Munich, 1980, Mexican Assn. Clin. Biochemistry, Mexico City, 1981, XXXI Italian Congress Clin. Pathology, Sicily, 1981. Author: Carbon, Sulfur, and Nitrogen Pollutants and Their Determination in Air and Water, 1990; contbr. articles to Diabetes Care, Am. Lab., Biotechniques, Trial, Jour. Auto. Chemistry, Clin. Chemistry, Jour. Immunological Methods, Analytical Chemistry, Jour. Chem. and Engring. Data, Yale. Sci. Mag., Jour. Phys. Chemistry, Desalination, Jour. Polymer Sci., Jour. Electrochem. Soc., also others. With USNR, 1945-46, PTO. Mem. Am. Chem. Soc. Office: J & JG Assocs 10742 S Timothys Rd Conifer CO 80433-8220

GRIER, CHARLES CROCKER, forestry educator; b. Pasadena, Calif., Sept. 1, 1938; s. Charles Horace and Priscilla Mary (Crocker) G.; m. Jeannie Kathleen Conway, Aug. 20, 1960; 1 child, Charles Christopher. BS in Forestry, U. Wash., 1968, PhD, 1972. Rsch. assoc. in forestry Oreg. State U., Corvallis, 1972-76; rsch. asst. prof. forestry U. Wash., Seattle, 1976-80, assoc. prof., then prof. forestry, 1980-85; prof. forestry No. Ariz. U., Flagstaff, 1985-91; prof., head dept. forest resources Coll. Natural Resources, Utah State U., Logan, 1991-93; prof., dept. head forest scis. Colo. State U., Ft. Collins, 1993—. Contbr. articles to sci. jours. Grantee NSF, 1976, 77, 80, 84, U.S. Dept. Man and Biosphere Consortium, Costa Rica, 1980. Mem. Ecol. Soc. Am., Soil Sci. Soc. Am., Sigma Xi, Xi Sigma Pi. Office: Colo State U Dept Forest Scis Colorado State University CO 80523

GRIER, JAMES EDWARD, hotel company executive, lawyer; b. Ottumwa, Iowa, Sept. 7, 1935; s. Edward J. and Corinne (Bailey) G.; m. Virginia Clinker, July 4, 1959; children: Michael, Susan, James, John, Thomas. BSc, U. Iowa, 1956, JD, 1959. Bar: Iowa 1959, Mo. 1959. Mng. ptnr. Hillix, Brewer, Hoffhaus & Grier, Kansas City, Mo., 1964-77, Grier & Swartzman, Kansas City, 1977-89; pres. Doubletree Hotels Corp., Phoenix, 1989-94; chmn. Sonoran Hotel Capital, Inc., Phoenix, 1994—; bd. dirs. Iowa Law Sch. Found., Iowa City, St. Joseph Hosp. and Med. Ctr., Phoenix, Homeward Bound, Phoenix. Home: 3500 E Lincoln Dr Phoenix AZ 85018-1010 Office: Sonaran Hotel Capital 2425 E Camelback Rd Ste 450 Phoenix AZ 85016-4236

GRIER, WILLIAM E., petroleum company executive; b. 1933; married. BA, Claremont Men's Coll., 1954; MBA, Stanford U., 1961. Sales rep. Western Ops., Inc., 1961-76; v.p. mktg. Chevron Oil Europe, Inc., 1976-77; v.p. indsl. relations Chevron Oil U.S.A., Inc., 1977-78; with parent co. Chevron Corp., 1958—, wholesale specialist, 1966-67, asst. to pres., 1967-69, div. mgr. mktg., San Diego and Seattle, 1969-71, div. mgr., Seattle, 1971-78, v.p. corp. indsl. relations, 1978-81, v.p. foreign div., asst. to pres., 1981-84, v.p., Can., 1984—. Served with U.S. Army, 1955-57. Office: Chevron Corp 555 Market St San Francisco CA 94105-2801

GRIESCHE, ROBERT PRICE, hospital purchasing executive; b. Berkeley, Calif., July 21, 1953; s. Robert Bowen and Lillian (Price) G.; m. Susan Dawn Albers, June 8, 1985 (div. Apr. 1989); 1 child, Sara Christine. AA, Coll. of the Canyons, Valencia, Calif., 1984. Warehouse supr. John Muir Hosp., Walnut Creek, Calif., 1973-82; purchasing mgr. Henry Mayo Newhall Hosp., Valencia, 1982-85; materials mgr. Foothill Presbyn. Hosp., Glendora, Calif., 1985-87; materials mgmt. dir. Huntington Meml. Hosp., Pasadena, Calif., 1987—; chmn. Huntington Employee Campaign, 1990-92. V.p. Coll. of the Canyons Found., Valencia, 1985-90. Named to Outstanding Young Men of Am., 1988. Mem. Calif. Cen. Svc. Assn. (charter). Republican. Presbyterian. Home: 3651 Cosmos Ct Palmdale CA 93550-5748 Office: Huntington Hosp 100 W California Blvd Pasadena CA 91105-3010

GRIESON, RONALD EDWARD, economist, educator; b. N.Y.C., Mar. 8, 1943; s. Hans and Stella Grieson; m. Barbara Anne Auel, Aug. 29, 1970. BA with honors, CUNY, 1964; MA, U. Rochester, 1966, PhD, 1969. Asst. prof. econs. MIT, Cambridge, Mass., 1969-72; assoc. prof. econs. CUNY, N.Y.C., 1972-74, Columbia U., N.Y.C., 1974-79; vis. prof. econs. Princeton U., N.J., 1979-80; prof. econs. U. Calif., Santa Cruz, 1980—; cons. DRI/McGraw-Hill, Cambridge, 1976—. Editor 4 books; editor Jour. Urban Econs., 1974—, Nat. Tax Jour., 1992-94; contbr. chpts. to books, articles to profl. jours. NSF fellow, 1964; Herbert Lehman fellow, 1966-69; recipient various grants. Mem. Am. Econs. Assn., Econometric Soc., Nat. Tax Assn. Home: 27 Ridgecrest Dr Scotts Valley CA 95066 Office: U Calif Dept Econs/SSI Santa Cruz CA 95064

GRIFFEY, KEN, JR. (GEORGE KENNETH GRIFFEY, JR.), professional baseball player; b. Donora, Pa., Nov. 21, 1969. Grad. high sch., Cin. Outfielder Seattle Mariners, 1987—. Recipient Gold Glove award, 1990-94; named to All-Star team, 1990-93, Sporting News Am. League Silver Slugger team, 1991, 93-94, Sporting News All-Star team, 1991, 93-94. Office: Seattle Mariners PO Box 4100 411 1st Ave S Seattle WA 98104-2860*

GRIFFEY, STEPHEN MICHAEL, veterinarian; b. Ringgold, Ga., June 27, 1963; s. Roy Lee and Earlene Peters G.; m. Rebecca Mae Echols, Nov. 9, 1991; 1 child, Alexandra Mary-Margaret. B of Vet. Sci., Tex. A & M U., 1987, DVM, 1989. Lic. Tex. Bd. Vet. Med. Examiners. Vet. asst. Tex. A & M Large Animal Hosp., College Station, 1982, Town North Vet. Hosp., Dallas, 1983-86, Tex. A & M Lab. Animal Resources Ctr., College Station, 1986-87; vet. libr. Tex. A & M Vet. Libr., College Station, 1987-88; pathology resident U. Calif. Vet. Hosp., Davis, 1989-91; staff pathologist

VMTH and comparative pathology lab. U. Calif., Davis, 1991-92; grad. student comparative pathology U. Calif., 1992-94, pathologist Sch. Vet. Medicine dept. of pathology, 1994—; chmn. West Coast Vet. Pathology Conf., Davis, 1992; pathology cons. U. Calif.-Davis Med. Ctr., Dept. Radiology, Sacramento, 1993-94, Innerdyne Inc., Palo Alto, Calif., 1993-94. Contbr. articles to Jour. Vet. Surgery, Vet. Pathology Jour. and others. Pathology scholar C. L. Davis Found., 1992. Mem. Am. Vet. Med. Assn., Am. Assn. Vet. Lab. Diagnosticians, C. L. Davis Found. for Advancement of Vet. and Comparative Pathology. Office: U Calif Dept of Pathology Sch of Vet Medicine Davis CA 95616

GRIFFIN, DEWITT JAMES, architect, real estate developer; b. Los Angeles, Aug. 26, 1914; s. DeWitt Clinton and Ada Gay (Miller) G.; m. Jeanmarie Donald, Aug. 19, 1940 (dec. Sept. 1985); children: Barbara Jean Griffin Holst, John Donald, Cornelia Caulfield Claudius, James DeWitt (dec.); m. Vivienne Dod Kievenaar, May 6, 1989. Student, UCLA, 1936-38; B.A., U. Calif., 1942. Designer Kaiser Engrs., Richmond, Calif., 1941; architect CF Braun & Co., Alhambra, Calif., 1946-48; pvt. practice architecture Pasadena, Calif., 1948-50; prin. Goudie & Griffin Architects, San Jose, Calif., 1959-64, Griffin & Murray, 1964-66, DeWitt J. Griffin & Assocs., 1966-69; pres. Griffin/Joyce Assocs., Architects, 1969-80; chmn. Griffin Balzhiser Affiliates (Architects), 1974-80; founder, pres. Griffin Cos. Internat., 1980—; founder, dir. San Jose Savs. and Loan Assn., 1965-75, Capitol Services Co., 1964-77, Esandel Corp., 1965-77. Pub. Sea Power mag, 1975-77; archtl. works include U.S. Post Office, San Jose, 1966, VA Hosp, Portland, 1976, Bn. Barracks Complex, Ft. Ord, Calif., 1978. bd. dirs. San Jose Symphony Assn., 1973-84, v.p. 1977-79, pres. 1979-81; active San Jose Symphony Found., 1981-86, v.p. 1988-90; bd. dirs. Coast Guard Acad. Found., 1974-87, Coast Guard Found., 1987-90; founder, bd. dirs. U.S. Navy Meml. Found., 1978-80, trustee, 1980—; trustee Montalvo Ctr. for Arts, 1982-88. Served to comdr. USNR, 1942-46, 50-57. Recipient Navy Meritorious Pub. Svc. medal, 1971, Disting. Service medal Navy League of U.S., 1973; Coast Guard Meritorious Pub. Svc. medal, 1975; Navy Disting. Pub. Svc. medal, 1977; Coast Guard Disting. Pub. Svcs. medal, 1977. Fellow Soc. Am. Mil. Engrs.; mem. AIA (emeritus), U.S. Naval Inst., Navy League U.S. (pres. Santa Clara Valley coun. 1963-66, Calif. state pres. 1966-69, nat. dir. 1967—, exec. com. 1968—, pres. 12th region 1969-71, nat. v.p. 1973-75, nat. pres. 1975-77, chmn. 1977-79), U.S. Naval Sailing Assn., Naval Order of U.S., Confrevre de la Chaine des Rotisseurs, Wash. Athletic Club (Seattle), St. Francis Yacht Club, Commonwealth of San Francisco Club, Phi Gamma Delta. Republican. Congregationalist. Home and Office: 8005 NE Hunt Club Ln Hansville WA 98340-9756

GRIFFIN, GLORIA JEAN, elementary school educator; b. Emmett, Idaho, Sept. 10, 1946; d. Archie and Marguerite (Johnson) G. AA, Boise (Idaho) Jr. Coll., 1966; BA, Boise Coll., 1968; MA in Elem. Curriculum, Boise State U., 1975. Cert. advanced elem. tchr., Idaho. Tchr. music, tutor, Boise; sec. Edward A. Johnson, atty., Boise; tchr. Head Start, Boise; elem. tchr. Meridian (Idaho) Sch. Dist., 1968—; developer multi-modality individualized spelling program; co-developer program for adapting curriculum to student's individual differences. Author: The Culture and Customs of the Argentine People As Applied to a Sixth Grade Social Studies Unit. Sec. PTA. Named Tchr. of Yr., Meridian Sch. Dist., 1981. Mem. NEA, Internat. Reading Assn., Idaho Edn. Assn., Meridian Edn. Assn. (bldg. rep.), Idaho Reading Coun., Orton Dyslexia Soc., Horizons Reading Coun., Alpha Delta Kappa (rec. sec.). Office: Silver Sage Elem Sch 7700 Snohomish St Boise ID 83709-5975

GRIFFIN, JAMES EDWARD, real estate consultant; b. Fall River, Mass., Jan. 27, 1941; s. James Edward and Marion Beatrice (Johnsen) G. AA, Napa (Calif.) Coll., 1965; BS, Calif. State U., Sacramento, 1967. CPA, Calif., Nev. Auditor Authur Young & Co., San Francisco, 1967-69, Providence, 1969-71; v.p. fin. R.I. Land Co., Providence, 1971-79; treas. Moss Land Co., Sacramento, 1979-82; chief fin. officer Equi-Real Devel. Co., Sacramento, 1982-84, Am. Nev. Co., Henderson, Nev., 1984-90; exec. v.p., chief oper. officer Am. Nev. Co., 1990-93; prin. cons. Griffin & Co., Las Vegas, 1993—; sec.-treas. acctg. adv. coun. UNLV, 1991, chmn. 1993. Recipient Bus. Adminstrn. award Bank Am., 1965. Fellow Nev. Soc. CPAs; mem. AICPA, Inst. Mgmt. Accts. (treas. Las Vegas chpt. 1991, bd. dirs. 1990), Calif. Soc. CPAs, Urban Land Inst. (assoc.), Constrn. Fin. Mgmt. Assn., Am. Fin. Assn. Home: 7550 Pearwood Ct Las Vegas NV 89123-0546 Office: Griffin & Co 7550 Pearwood Ct Las Vegas NV 89123-0546

GRIFFIN, (ALVA) JEAN, entertainer; b. Detroit, June 1, 1931; d. Henry Bethel White and Ruth Madelyn (Gowen) Durham; m. Francis Jay Griffin, July 8, 1958 (dec.); stepchildren: Patra, Rodney; 1 adopted child, Donald; children: Rhonda Jean, Sherree Lee. Student, Anderson Coll., 1952-53; DD (hon.), Ministry of Salvation, Chula Vista, Calif., 1990, Ministry of Salvation, 1990. Ordained minister, 1990. Supr. Woolworth's, Detroit, 1945-46; operator, supr. Atlantic Bell Telephone Co., Detroit, 1947-51, Anderson, Ind., 1952-56; sec. to div. mgr. Food Basket-Lucky Stores, San Diego, 1957-58; owner, mgr. Jay's Country Boy Markets, Riverside, Calif., 1962-87; entertainer, producer, dir., singer Mae West & Co., 1980—; owner The Final Touch, Colorado Springs; tchr. art Grant Sch., Riverside, 1964-65; tchr., adviser Mental Retarded Sch., Riverside, 1976-77; instr. Touch for Health Found., Pasadena, Calif., 1975-79; cons., hypnotist, nutritionist, Riversaide, 1976-79; mem., tchr. Psi field parapsychology. Mem. Rep. Presdl. Task Force, 1983. Recipient svc. award Rep. Presdl. Task Force, 1986. Mem. Parapsychology Assn. Riverside (pres. 1981-82). Mem. Ch. of Religious Science New Thought. Home: 201 W Chapel Rd Sedona AZ 86336-7031

GRIFFIN, JIM ALLAN, librarian; b. Claremore, Okla., Dec. 11, 1947; s. Jimmie Lee and Dorothy Lee (Rathfon) G. BA, Calif. State U., Turlock, 1970; MLS, San Jose State U., 1978. Substitute tchr. Stanislaus County, Modesto, Calif., 1970-71, clerical/libr. asst., 1972-79, libr. I, 1979-81, libr. II, 1982-92, lib. III, br. libr. mgr., 1992—. Mem. Save Our Libr., Stanislaus County, 1992. Mem. Am. Libr. Assn., Bay Area Young Adult Librs., Am. Saluki Assn. (past rsch. chmn.), Saluki Club Greater San Francisco (bd. dirs.). Home: 10607 Workman Rd Oakdale CA 95361-8530 Office: Stanislaus County Free Libr Turlock Br 550 N Minaret Ave Turlock CA 95380-4137

GRIFFIN, JOSEPH EDWARD, multimedia and telecommunications executive; b. Chgo., June 9, 1947; s. George G. and Helen M. G.; m. Donna Jean Kalteux, Sept. 30, 1978; children: David C., Amanda Jo, Jessica. BS, U. Ill., 1970; MBA, DePaul U., 1980. Brand mgr. Hart Schaffner & Marx, Chgo., 1970-73; product planner Victor Bus., Products, Chgo., 1973-77; dir. mktg. Pioneer Electronics, Moonachie, N.J., 1977-82; nat. sales mgr. Philips Consumer Electronics, N.Y.C., 1982-83; dir. New Bus. Devel. AT&T, Basking Ridge, N.J., 1983-89; dir. bus. devel. VISA Internat., San Francisco, 1990-92; sr. dir. ptnrs. and licensing Gen. Magic, Sunnyvale, Calif., 1992—. Mem. Stanford/MIT Venture Lab, 1992—; bd. dirs. Global Svc. Leadership Coun. With USAR, 1968-74. Mem. Am. Mktg. Assn. (conf. chmn. 1987—), Info. Industry Assn., Electronic Funds Transfer Assn., Alpha Kappa Psi. Office: Gen Magic 420 Mary Ave Sunnyvale CA 94086

GRIFFIN, KIRSTEN BERTELSEN, nursing educator; b. Oakland, Calif., Mar. 23, 1940; d. Elmer V. and Helen E. (Hansen) Bertelsen; children: Colleen Hime Risvold, Sean W., Patrick C.; m. John R. Griffin. Diploma, Samuel Merritt Coll. Nursing, 1961; BA, U. Redlands, 1982; A in Bus., Advantage-Health Edn., 1992. Pvt. practice cons./stress trainer San Jacinto, Calif.; cons. Calif. State Dept. Edn., Sacramento, 1979—; program dir. nursing asst. program Riverside (Calif.) County Office Edn., 1984—, parttime instr. Mt. San Jacinto (Calif.) Coll., 1989; part-time staff nurse acute psychiat. unit Hemet (Calif.) Med. Ctr.-Behavioral Health; advisor, judge Health Occupation Students Am., 1990—; rater Nurse Asst. Tng. Assessment Program, 1992—. Youth advisor, judge Vocat. Indsl. Clubs Am., 1977-88; instr. ARC, Am. Heart Assn. Recipient Women Helping Women award Soroptimists, 1989. Mem. Calif. Assn. Health Career Educators (pres.-elect 1984-85, pres. 1985-86), Beta Sigma Phi (Order of Rose award, Laureate 1995). Home: 3109 La Travesia Dr Fullerton CA 92635

GRIFFIN, LINDA SUE, appraiser; b. Oakdale, Calif., Aug. 23, 1947; d. Raymond Emil and Betty Arlene (Holloway) Anderson; m. Jim A. Griffin, Sept. 2, 1972. AA, Modesto (Calif.) Jr. Coll., 1968; BA, Calif. State U. Stanislaus, Turlock, 1976. Eligibility worker Stanislaus County Dept. Social Svcs., Modesto, Calif., 1969-80; appraiser Stanislaus County Assessor, Modesto, 1980—. Mem. Am. Saluki Assn. (sec. 1991-94), Saluki Club Greater San Francisco (sec. 1994—), LWV. Home: 10607 Workman Rd Oakdale CA 95361-8530 Office: Stanislaus County Assessor PO Box 1068 1100 H St Modesto CA 95353-1068

GRIFFIN, MERV EDWARD, former entertainer, television producer, entrepreneur; b. San Mateo, Calif., July 6, 1925; s. Mervyn Edward and Rita (Robinson) G.; m. Julann Elizabeth Wright, May 18, 1958 (div. June 1976); 1 son, Anthony Patrick. Student, San Mateo Coll., 1942-44; L.H.D., Emerson Coll., 1981. Chmn. bd. MGP (Merv Griffin Prodns.), Beverly Hills, Calif.; owner 17 radio stas. in Hartford, Albany, Providence Liberty Broadcasting; owner Teleview Racing Patrol Inc., Miami, Fla., Video Racing Patrol Inc., Seattle, Beverly Hilton Hotel, Beverly Hills, Calif.; chmn. Resorts Internat., Atlantic City and The Bahamas, Griffin Group, Inc., Beverly Hills. Performer, Merv Griffin Show radio sta. KFRC, San Francisco, 1945-48, vocalist, Freddy Martin's Orch., 1948-52; contract player, star: So This is Love, Warner Bros., 1953-55; TV master ceremonies, 1958—, Merv Griffin Show, NBC-TV, 1962-63, Westinghouse Broadcasting Co., 1965-69, CBS-TV, 1969-72, syndication, 1972-86; currently producing: Wheel of Fortune, Jeopardy. Trustee Dr. Armand Hammer United World Coll. of Am. S.W. Club: Bohemian (San Francisco). Office: Merv Griffin Enterprises 9860 Wilshire Blvd Beverly Hills CA 90210-3115 also: The Griffin Group 780 Third Ave New York NY 10017-2024 also: Sta WPOP-AM PO Box 31-1410 Newington Br Hartford CT 06131*

GRIFFIN, STEPHEN, food products executive; b. 1955. With Griffin Produce Co., Inc., 1976—, now pres.; sec., treas. Misioneros Inc., Salinas, Calif., 1979—; ptnr. Banner Farms, Salinas, Calif., 1981—, Sonora Packing, Salinas, Calif., 1990-91. Office: Griffin Produce Co Inc 1129 Harkins Rd Salinas CA 93901-4407*

GRIFFIN, SYLVIA GAIL, reading specialist; b. Portland, Oreg., Dec. 13, 1935; d. Archie and Marguerite (Johnson) G. AA, Boise Jr. Coll., 1955; BS, Brigham Young U., 1957, MEd, 1967. Cert. advanced teaching, Idaho. Classroom tchr. Boise (Idaho) Pub. Schs., 1957-59, 61-66, 67-69, reading specialist, 1969-90, 91—, early childhood specialist, 1990-91; tchr. evening Spanish classes for adults, 1987-88; lectr. in field; mem. cons. pool U.S. Office Juvenile Justice and Delinquency Prevention, 1991—. Author: Procedures Used by First Grade Teachers for Teaching Experience Readiness for Reading Comprehension, The Short Story of Vowels, A Note Worthy Way to Teach Reading. Advisor in developing a program for dyslexics Scottish Rite Masons of Idaho, Boise. Mem. NEA, AAUW, Internat. Reading Assn., Orton Dyslexia Soc., Horizon Internat. Reading Assn., Idaho Edn. Assn. (pub. rels. dir. 1970-72), Boise Edn. Assn. (pub. rels. dir. 1969-72, bd. dirs. ednl. polit. involvement com. 1983-89), Alpha Delta Kappa. Office: 5007 Franklin Rd Boise ID 83705-1106

GRIFFIN, W. C., bishop. Bishop Ch. of God in Christ, Albuquerque. Office: Ch of God in Christ 3322 Montclaire Dr NE Albuquerque NM 87110-1702

GRIFFIN, WILLIAM STANLEY, scientist, researcher; b. St. Joseph, Mo., Apr. 13, 1935; s. William Mellican and Mary Florence (Whitlock) G.; m. Loretta Mae Chanon, July 24, 1965; children: Loretta Lynn, Edward W., Eric J., Evan H., Gene S. Student, U. Mo., 1953-54; BS, MS, MIT, 1958, M in Engring, ScD, 1963. Aerospace engr. NASA, Cleve., 1963-68; aerospace engr., asst. for engring. devel., corp. labs. Northrop Corp., Hawthorne, Calif., 1968-77; chief scientist Hughes Aircraft Co., El Segundo, Calif., 1977—; cons. cardiovascular rsch. St. Vincents Hosp. Cleve., 1964-67. Patentee in field. 1st lt. USAF, 1963-65. Mem. ASME, AIAA, Am. Def. Preparedness Assn. Republican. Methodist. Office: Hughes Aircraft E0-E1/D125 1200 E El Segundo Blvd El Segundo CA 90245

GRIFFIS, STANLEY DOUGLAS, county manager; b. Odum, Ga., Oct. 25, 1942; s. John Randall and Hattie Lou (Dubberly) G.; m. Pamela Stewart, Aug. 8, 1945; children: David, Jeffrey, Michelle. BBA, U. Okla., 1963; MBA, Mich. State U., 1969; PhD, St. Louis U., 1981. Commd. 2d lt. USAF, 1968, advanced through grades to maj., 1981; assoc. prof. USAF Acad., 1976-81; ret. USAF, 1982; pres. Griffco, Colorado Springs, 1982-87; dir. fin. and adminstrv. svcs. El Paso County, Colorado Springs, 1987-89; dir. fin. Douglas County, Castle Rock, Colo., 1989; county mgr. Pinal County, Florence, Ariz., 1989—; grad. prof. Regis Coll., Colorado Springs, 1983-87; adj. prof. Ctrl. Ariz. Coll., Florence, 1989—. Decorated with Vietnamese Cross of Gallantry, Bronze star. Democrat. Office: Pinal County PO Box 827 Florence AZ 85232-0827

GRIFFITH, JOHN GORDON, real estate company officer; b. Council Bluffs, Iowa, Dec. 16, 1931; s. Frank L. and Geneva (Seitz) F.; children: Stephen John, Jessica Geneva. BS, Iowa State U., 1953. Chief exec. officer Centurion & Real Estate Investment Co., Newport Beach, Calif., 1973—; bd. dirs. Bio-Trends Internat., Sacramento. 2d lt. USAF, 1953-54. Mem. BIA. Office: Centurion & Real Estate Investment Co 2043 Westcliff Dr Ste 201 Newport Beach CA 92660-5510

GRIFFITH, ROBERT DOUGLAS, broadcasting company executive; b. Detroit, June 6, 1947; s. Robert Douglas and Betty (Kohaida) G.; m. Marsha M. Sassin, May 8, 1969 (div. 1973); 1 child, Jeffery Robert; m. Lynn Marie Johnston, July 27, 1985. Student, Wayne State U.; student, Macomb Coll. Account exec. McGauren Guild Radio, Detroit, 1972-77; account exec. ABC Radio, Los Angeles, 1977-78; mgr. western region RFO Radio Sales, Los Angeles, 1978-79; gen. sales mgr. Sta. KMET, Los Angeles, 1979-82; gen. mgr. Sta. KFI KOST, Los Angeles, 1982-84, Sta. KYSR-FM, Los Angeles, 1984—. Sponsor Calif. Spl. Olympics, 1985. Recipient award City of Los Angeles, 1985, Calif. Spl. Olympics, 1985. Mem. So. Calif. Broadcasters Assn. Office: Sta KYSR-FM 3500 W Olive Ave Ste 250 Burbank CA 91505-4628*

GRIFFITH, WILLIAM SAMUEL, adult education educator; b. Johnstown, Pa., Nov. 25, 1931; s. Samuel Nelson and Myrtle Irene (Hess) G.; m. Beverly Ann Breland, Aug. 21, 1964; children: Thomas Nelson, Kathryn Ann, Rebecca Leigh. BS in Dairy Sci., Pa. State U., 1953; MS in Dairy Sci., La. State U., 1955; PhD in Adult Edn., U. Chgo., 1963. Asst. farm dir. Sta. KDKA, Pitts., 1952; rsch. assoc. La. State U., Baton Rouge, 1954; asst. prof. Va. Poly. Inst., Blacksburg, 1955-62; asst. prof. U. Chgo., 1963-67, assoc. prof., 1968-77; vis. lectr. U. Wis., Madison, 1979; prof. U. B.C., Vancouver, Can., 1977—; vis. lectr. N.C. State U., Raleigh, 1971, 88, Pa. State U., University Park, 1989; chmn. Commn. of Profs. of Adult Edn., 1969-71. Sr. editor (book series): Handbook of Adult Education in the U.S., 1980-81; mem. editl. com. Jour. Extension, 1970-76; cons. editor Adult Edn. Quar., 1968—, Adult Basic Edn., 1990—. Bd. dirs. Planned Parenthood Fedn., Ottawa, Ont., Can., 1989-94; pres. Point Roberts (Wash.) Registered Voters' Assn., 1993—; charter mem. Rep. Presdl. Task Force, 1989—. Rsch. grantee Adult Edn. Assn. U.S.A., 1980, Fulbright sr. rsch. grantee, Australia, 1972-73; travelling fellow Brit. Coun., Eng., 1982. Mem. Am. Assn. Adult and Continuing Edn. (pres. 1990-91), N.W. Adult Edn. Assn. (pres. 1986-87, Meritorious Svc. award 1988), Ill. Adult Edn. Assn. (pres. 1969-70, rsch. to practice award 1980), N.Y. Acad. Scis., Lion's Paw Alumni Assn., Sigma Xi (U. B.C. chpt. sec.-treas. 1992—), Phi Delta Kappa. Lutheran. Home: PO Box 1189 1677 Seymour Pl Point Roberts WA 98281 Office: Univ BC, 5760 Toronto Rd, Vancouver, BC Canada V6T 1L2

GRIFFITH JOYNER, FLORENCE DELOREZ, track and field athlete; b. L.A., Dec. 21, 1959; d. Robert and Florence Griffith; m. Al Joyner; 1 child: Mary Ruth Joyner. Student, Calif. State U., Northridge, UCLA; PhD (hon.), Am. U., Washington, 1994. Co-owner NUCO Nails, Camarillo, Calif., 1994—; Designed line of sportswear, and uniforms for NBA Ind. Pacers. Actress (prin. role film) The Chaser, (recurring role TV drama) Santa Barbara, guest 227 TV situation comedies; host, commentator various sports events; guest numerous talk shows. Co-chairperson Pres. Coun. on Phys. Fitness & Sports, 1993—, founder The Florence Griffith Joyner Youth Found. Winner Silver medal Summer Olympics, L.A., 1984, 3 Gold medals, 1 Silver medal Summer Olympics, Seoul, Republic of Korea, 1988; U.S. Olympic Com. Sports Woman of the Year 1988, TAC Jesse Owens outstanding track and field athlete, 1988, Internat. Jesse Owens award Most Outstanding amateur athlete, 1988, Tass News Agy. Sports Personality of Yr., 1988, Internat. Fedn. Bodybuilders Most Outstanding Physique 1980s, 1988, UPI and AP Sportswoman of the year, 1988; named Athlete of Yr. Track and Field, 1988, recipient of the Harvard Found. award for outstanding contribution to the field of athletics, 1989, Essence Mag's. Sports award Extraordinary Accomplishments in Athletics, 1989, Golden Camera award from German Advt. Industry, 1989, James E. Sullivan Meml. award as most outstanding athlete in Am., 1989. Office: Florence Griffith Joyner Youth Foundation 30021 Tomas Ste 300 Rancho Santa Margarita CA 92688 also: NUCO Nails Inc PO Box 67 Camarillo CA 93011

GRIFFITHS, ARTHUR R., professional hockey team executive. Chmn., gov. Vancouver (Can.) Canucks. Office: Vancouver Canucks, 100 N Renfrew St, Vancouver, BC Canada V5K 3N7*

GRIFFITHS, MARIAN E. (MIMI GRIFFITHS), government administrator; b. Chgo., June 9, 1948; d. Robert Henry and Dora Irene (MacAllister) G. BA, Eastern Ill. U., Charleston, 1971, MS in LS, 1973. Audiovisual libr. Vincennes (Ind.)/Knox County Pub. Libr., 1973-74; dir. Olney (Ill.) Carnegie Pub. Libr., 1974-81; coord. adminstrv. code unit Ill. Sec. of State, Springfield, 1981-83, adminstr. adminstrv. code div., 1983-89; rules mgr. Ariz. Sec. of State, Phoenix, 1990-91, dir. pub. svcs. dept., 1991—; cons. Okla. Sec. of State/Div. Librs. Editor: Arizona Blue Book, 1993-1994, 1994; author, editor: (booklets) Illinois Administrative Code Style Manual, 1985-89, Arizona Notary Public Handbook, 1993; author articles. Mem. Nat. Assn. Secs. of State (exec. sec. adminstrv. codes and registers sect. 1984-87, exec. sec. emeritus 1987—, Plaque of Appreciation 1985, Resolution of Recognition 1987), Nat. Assn. Desktop Pubs. Republican. Methodist. Home: 6348 N 7th Ave Apt 7 Phoenix AZ 85013-1353 Office: Ariz Sec of State Office 1700 W Washington St Fl 7 Phoenix AZ 85007-2814

GRIGGS, GAIL, marketing executive; b. 1937. Grad., U. Chgo., U. Chgo. Instr. Chgo. Art Inst., Roosevelt U., Chgo., Evergreen State U., Olympia, Wash.; with Griggs-Anderson, Inc., 1979—, now pres. Office: Griggs-Anderson Inc 308 SW 1st Ave Fl 4 Portland OR 97204-3400*

GRIGSBY, JILL SPENCER, sociology educator; b. West Palm Beach, Fla., Mar. 8, 1954; d. Andrew Harris and Gilmah (Spencer) G.; m. John Mackenzie Light, Oct. 29, 1977; 1 child, Janet Mackenzie Light. ScB, Brown U., 1976, AM, 1977; MA, Princeton U., 1981, PhD, 1983. Rsch. assoc. U. Mich., Ann Arbor, 1987-80; asst. prof. Pomona Coll., Claremont, Calif., 1983-89, assoc. prof., 1989—; rsch. assoc. U. So. Calif., L.A., 1990-91. Coauthor: Society & Population, 1992; editor: (newsletter) Pomona Valley Zero Population Growth, 1994. Mem. Am. Sociol. Assn., Gerontol. Soc. Am., Population Assn. Am. Office: Pomona Coll 425 N College Claremont CA 91711

GRILLO, LEO, actor, photographer, animal rescuer; b. Lawrence, Mass., Feb. 6, 1949; s. Leo F. Sr. and Carmela M. (DeLucia) G.; m. Stacy Grillo; 1 child, Erica. BS in speech, Emerson Coll., Boston, 1970. Actor Glendale, Calif., 1965—; pres., founder Dedication and Everlasting Love to Animals Inc., Glendale, 1979—, Living Earth Prodns., 1990—, Horse Rescue Am., 1991—; founder, pres. DELTA Rescue Netherlands, DELTA Rescue Italy. Author: (with others) Landscam, 1988, Is This the Place?; producer, host Safe House, (TV show) Delta Rescue Story; contbr. articles to mags. Mem. Screen Actors' Guild, AFTRA, Actors Equity Assn. Home: PO Box 11523 Glendale CA 91226-7523 Office: DELTA PO Box 9 Glendale CA 91209-0009

GRILLO, TERRY WILSON, public relations executive; b. San Mateo, Calif., May 1, 1947; s. Wilson August and Clara Athalie (Dougherty) G.; m. Maryann Ilona Torok, Oct. 23, 1976; children: Sarah Rose, Caitlin Scarlett, Dominic Nathan. AA, Coll. San Mateo, 1969; BA, U. Nevada, 1975. Newsman Associated Press, Reno, Nev., 1975-77; news editor Sierra Sun, Truckee, Calif., 1977-79; pub. affairs reporter Menlo-Atherton Recorder, 1979-81; reporter, editor Ledger-Dispatch, Jackson, Calif., 1981-85; owner Plug Street Communications, 1986-88; pub. rels. rep Georgia-Pacific Corp., Martell, Calif., 1988; editorial cons., PR cons. Sierra Citizen Alliance for Resources & Environ., Plymouth, Calif., 1991—. Dir. Volcano Com. Svcs. Dist., Volcano, Calif., 1986-89. Recipient Crystal award Internat. Assn. Bus. Communicates, 1992. Mem. Pub. Rels. Soc. Am., Italian Benevolent Soc., Amador C. of C. (dir. 1992—). Democrat. Roman Catholic. Office: Georgia-Pacific Corp Highway 49 Martell CA 95654

GRILLY, EDWARD ROGERS, physicist; b. Cleve., Dec. 30, 1917; s. Charles B. and Julia (Varady) G.; m. Mary Witholter, Dec. 14, 1942 (dec. 1971); children: David, Janice; m. Juliamarie Andreen Langham, Feb. 1, 1973. BA, Ohio State U., 1940, PhD, 1944. Rsch. scientist Carbide & Carbon Chemicals Corp., Oak Ridge, Tenn., 1944-45; asst. prof. Chemistry U. N.H., Durham, 1946-47; mem. staff U. Calif. Nat. Lab., Los Alamos, N.Mex., 1947-80, cons., 1980—. Contbr. articles to books and profl. jours. Mem. N.Mex. House of Reps., Santa Fe, 1967-70, Los Alamos County Coun., Los Alamos, 1976-78. Mem. Am. Physical Soc., Kiwanis Club, Los Alamos Golf Club (pres. 1974-75). Republican. Home: 705 43rd St Los Alamos NM 87544-1807

GRIM, J(OHN) NORMAN, biology educator, electron microscopy consultant; b. Santa Barbara, Calif., Sept. 8, 1933; s. John Charles and Meada Fern (VanNorman) G.; m. Carole Ann Werly, June 20, 1954; children: Stephen Jay, Kristine Louise Grim Weisskopf. BA, U. Calif., Santa Barbara, 1956; MA, UCLA, 1960; PhD, U. Calif., Davis, 1967. Rsch. technician Sch. Medicine UCLA, 1959-60; rsch. technician Zoology Dept. U. Calif., Davis, 1960-67; biology professor No. Ariz. U., Flagstaff, 1967-94; prof. emeritus, 1994—; pvt. cons., Flagstaff, 1975—; dir. No. Ariz. U. Electron Microscope Facility, Flagstaff, 1968-90. Reviewer books, rsch. articles; contbr. 38 articles to profl. jours. Commr. Boy Scouts Am., Flagstaff, 1989-91, 93—. Col. USAR, ret. Grantee NSF, 1980, 89-90, U.S. Dept. of Army, 1971-74. Mem. Am. Microscopical Soc., Soc. Protozoologists, Ariz. Soc. Electron Microscopy (pres. 1970-71, 78-79), Soaring Soc. Am., Am. Aviation Hist. Soc., Sigma Xi. Home: 3610 N Paradise Rd Flagstaff AZ 86004-1611 Office: No Ariz U Biology Dept Box 5640 Flagstaff AZ 86011

GRIMES, JOSEPH EDWARD, computer science educator; b. Bloomington, Ill., Sept. 28, 1941; s. Edward A. and Mary C. (Kleemann) G.; m. Mary Rae Tures, Aug. 8, 1964; children: Joe, Therese, Christine, Michael, Matthew, Mark. BA, St. Ambrose U., Davenport, Iowa, 1963; MS, Ill. State U., 1968; PhD, Iowa State U., 1973. Tchr., coach Cen. Cath. High Sch., Bloomington, 1963-66; civil engr. McLean County Hwy. Dept., Bloomington, 1966-68; instr. Iowa State U., Ames, 1968-73; prof. computer sci. Calif. Poly. State U., San Luis Obispo, 1973—, mgr. computer svcs., 1986-87; cons. NASA, Moffett Field, Calif., 1974—, Xerox Corp., Santa Clara, Calif., 1989—; mem. Naval Ship Weapons Engring. Sta., Port Hueneme, Calif., 1987-90; expert witness NCR Corp., 1984-89, Ford Motor Corp., 1989, State of Calif., 1992. Contbr. articles to profl. jours. Dir. referees San Luis Obispo Youth Soccer, 1982—; chmn. fin. coun., mem. pastoral coun. Old Mission, San Luis Obispo, 1985-89. Mem. Am. Statis. Assn., Assn. for Computing Machinery, Computing Soc. of IEEE, Mu Sigma Rho. Roman Catholic. Home: 650 Evans Rd San Luis Obispo CA 93401-8121 Office: Calif Poly State U Dept Computer Sci San Luis Obispo CA 93407

GRIMES, RUTH ELAINE, city planner; b. Palo Alto, Calif., Mar. 4, 1949; d. Herbert George and Irene (Williams) Baker; m. Charles A. Grimes, July 19, 1969 (div. 1981); 1 child, Michael; m. Roger L. Sharpe, Mar. 20, 1984; 1 child, Teresa. AB summa cum laude, U. Calif., Berkeley, 1970, M in City Planning, 1972. Rsch. and evaluation coord. Ctr. Ind. Living, Berkeley, 1972-74; planner City of Berkeley, 1974-76, sr. planner, 1983—, analyst, 1976-83; bd. dirs. Vets. Asssistance Ctr., Berkeley, pres., 1978-93; bd. dirs. Berkeley Design Advisors, treas., 1987-94. Author: Berkeley Downtown Plan, 1988; contbr. numerous articles to profl. jours. and other publs. Bd. dirs. Berkeley-Sakai Sister City Assn., 1994—, pres., 1995—, Ctr. Ind. Living. Honored by Calif. State Assembly Resolution, 1988; Edwin Frank Kraft scholar, 1966. Mem. ASPA, Am. Inst. Cert. Planners, Am. Planning Assn., Mensa, Lade Merrit Joggers and Striders (sec. 1986-89, pres. 1991-93), Lions Internat. (bd. dirs. Berkeley club 1992-94), U. Calif. Coll. Environ. Design Alumni Assn. (bd. dirs., treas. 1994—). Home: 1330 Bonita Ave Berkeley CA 94709-1925 Office: City of Berkeley 2121 Mckinley Ave Berkeley CA 94703-1519

GRIMLEY, CYNTHIA PATRIZI, rehabilitation consultant, special education educator; b. Sharon, Pa., Mar. 29, 1958; d. James Donald and Delores Virginia (Maykowski) Patrizi; m. Kevin Neil Grimley, Apr. 11, 1987; children: Ronald James, Jennifer Rose. BS, Youngstown (Ohio) State U., 1981; MS, Calif. State U., 1986. Lic. multiple subject tchr., spl. edn. and elem. tchr., severely handicapped edn. tchr., Ohio, Pa.; specialist credential, Calif.; cert. rehab. counselor, case mgr. Residential program worker, supr., classroom tchr. Mercer County Assn. for the Retarded, Hermitage, Pa., 1980-82; tchr. spl. edn. Hermitage Sch. Dist., 1982-83; cons. property mgmt. Lorden Mgmt. Co., Covina, Calif., 1983-84; tchr. spl. edn. Fullerton (Calif.) Elem. Sch. Dist., 1984-87; vocat. rehab. cons. Profl. Rehab. Cons., Santa Ana, Calif., 1986-89, Pvt. Sector Rehab., Fullerton, 1989—i. Contbr. curriculum, articles in field. Coach Spl. Olympics, Fullerton, 1982-87; sec. So. Calif. Rehab. Exch., 1989, mem.-at-large, 1990, treas., 1991. Polish Art Club scholar, 1977. Fellow Am. Bd. Vocat. Experts, Am. Acad. Pain Mgmt.; mem. NEA, Nat. Assn. Rehab. Profls. in the Pvt. Sector, Calif. Assn. Rehab. Profls., Assn. Retarded Citizens. Democrat. Roman Catholic. Office: Pvt Sector Rehab 2555 E Chapman Ave Ste 300 Fullerton CA 92631-3618

GRIMM, BOB, food products executive; b. 1954. With Grimmway Enterprises, Inc., Bakersfield, Calif., 1975—, now v.p. Office: Grimmway Enterprises Inc 18071 Zerker Rd Bakersfield CA 93312*

GRIMM, LARRY LEON, psychologist; b. Goshen, Ind., Aug. 16, 1950; s. Warren Arden and Elizabeth Ann (Rassi) G.; m. Ann Mae Nelson, July 16, 1977; 1 child, Kirsten Ann. BS in Elem. Edn., No. Ariz. U., 1975, MA in Early Childhood Edn., 1977, EdD in Ednl. Psychology, 1983. Lic. psychologist; cert. sch. psychologist, elem. tchr. Ariz., Nat. Tchr. elem. sch. Page (Ariz.) Unified Dist., 1975-76; grad. asst. Coll. Edn., No. Ariz. U., Flagstaff, 1976; tchr. elem. sch. Litchfield Sch. Dist., Litchfield Park, Ariz., 1976-80; grad. assoc. dept. ednl. psychology No. Ariz. U., Flagstaff, 1980-81; sch. psychologist intern Peoria (Ariz.) Unified Dist., 1981-82; adj. faculty Grand Canyon Coll., Phoenix, 1982; sch. psychologist Child Study Services, Prescott (Ariz.) Unified Sch. Dist., 1982-87; adj. assoc. prof. No. Ariz. U., Flagstaff, 1984—, vis. faculty, 1987-88; postdoctoral fellow in pediatric psychology Child Devel. Ctr. Georgetown U. Med. Ctr., Washington, 1988-89; pvt. practice, 1989—; cons. in field; presenter at convs. Contbr. articles to profl. jours. Chmn. project devel. com. Infant & Toddler Network, 1989-92; mem. family resource ctr. adv. bd. Yavapai Regional Med. Ctr., 1990—. Mem. Am. Psychol. Assn. (publs. com. div. 16), Ariz. Assn. Sch. Psychologists (bd. dirs. No. Ariz., regional dir. 1983-84, pres. 1986-87, newsletter editor, 1986-87, Pres.'s award 1985, 88, 89), Nat. Assn. Sch. Psychologists (Ariz. del. fiscal adv. com. 1987-88, Capitol Network 1988-89), Soc. Pediatric Psychologists, Christian Assn. Psychol. Studies. Republican. Office: 143 N McCormick St Ste 204 Prescott AZ 86301

GRIMM, REINHOLD, humanities educator; b. Nuremberg, Germany, May 21, 1931; s. Eugen and Anna (Käser) G.; m. Anneliese E. Schmidt, Sept. 25, 1954; 1 dau., Ruth Sabine. Student, U. Erlangen, Germany, 1951-56, Ph.D., 1956; student, U. Colo., 1952-53; Dr. honoris causa, Georgetown U., 1988. Faculty German lit. U. Erlangen, 1957-61, U. Frankfurt, Germany, 1961-67; vis. prof. Columbia, also N.Y.U., spring 1967, U. Va., fall 1978; Alexander Hohlfeld prof. German U. Wis., 1967-80, Vilas prof. comparative lit. and German, 1980-90; presdl. prof. German and comparative lit. U. Calif., Riverside, 1990-92; mem. Inst. for Research in Humanities, U. Wis., spring 1981. Author: numerous books including Nach dem Naturalismus: Essays zur modernen Dramatik, 1978, Von der Armut und vom Regen: Rilkes Antwort auf die soziale Frage, 1981, Love, Lust and Rebellion: New Approaches to Georg Büchner, 1985, Echo and Disguise: Studies in German and Comparative Literature, 1989, Versuche zur europäischen Literatur, 1994; editor: numerous books, jours. including Monatshefte, 1979-90, German Quar., 1991-94, Deutsche Romantheorien, 2d edit., 1974, Deutsche Dramentheorien, 3d edit., 1981; co-editor: numerous books, yearbooks including Basis, 1970-80, Brecht Yearbook, 1971-81; contbr. articles to profl. jours. Recipient Förderungspreis der Stadt Nürnberg, 1964; Guggenheim fellow, 1969-70; Hilldale award, 1988. Mem. MLA, Am. Assn. Tchrs. German (hon., pres. 1974-75), PEN. Home: 6315 Glen Aire Ave Riverside CA 92506-5304

GRIMM, ROD, food products executive; b. 1946. Pres. Grimmway Enterprises, Inc., Bakersfield, Calif., 1965—. Office: Grimmway Enterprises Inc 18071 Zerker Rd Bakersfield CA 93312*

GRIMMER, BEVERLEY SUE, church administrator, maritime agency agent; b. Olathe, Kans., June 9, 1950; d. Edward Mathines Rice and Jessie LaVaun (Cade) Waymire; m. Danny Joe San Romani, June 4, 1977 (div. May 1991); 1 child, Justin (dec.); m. Gary G. Grimmer, June 21, 1992. Student, Kans. State Tchrs. Coll., 1968-71, U. Kans., 1975-77. Employee trainer, dept. mgr. T.G.&Y. Stores, Emporia, Kans., 1968-70; office mgr. Office of Staff Judge Adv. 3d Armored Div., Frankfurt, Fed. Republic of Germany, 1971-75, Don W. Lill, Atty. at Law, Emporia, 1976-77; instr., sub. tchr. Kodiak (Ala.) C.C. and Kodiak Pub. Sch. System, 1979-81; legal sec. Kaito & Ishida, Honolulu, 1983-84; adminstr. Alcantara & Frame, Honolulu, 1984-86; ind. contractor Hughes Hubbard & Reed, N.Y., Honolulu, 1986-88; paralegal Carlsmith, Ball, Wichman, Murray, Case, Mukai & Ichiki, Honolulu, 1988-91; spl. agt. Vanuatu (Hawaii) Maritime Agy., 1989—; ch. adminstr. Ctrl. Union Ch., Honolulu, 1991-94; owner Gentle Memories, Kailua, Hawaii, 1995—; Gubernatorial coun. appointee Juvenile Justice State Adv. Coun., 1993-94; mem. women's health week com. State of Hawaii, Commn. on Status of Women, 1994. 1st v.p. Christmas in April Oahu, 1995, bd. dirs., 1995—; auction pub. chair Acad. Arts Guild, 1993; mem. Contemporary Arts Mus.; cmty. rels. and arrangements chairs for Tuxes 'n Tails Black and White Ball, Hawaiian Human Soc., 1993, 94; mem. Hawaii Lupus Found.; bd. dirs. Armed Forces YMCA, 1995—. Recipient Order of Golden Swivel Shot award Comdt. USCG, 1981, 89, 1st Runner-up Maritime Week Maritime Employee award Propeller Club U.S., 1986, Letter of Appreciation, Dept. Navy, 1983, Cert. of Commendation, U.S. Army, 1975. Mem. Am. Heart Assn. (chair Celebrity Celebration 1994), Coast Guard Officers' Spouses Club (nominating chair 1989, pres. 1982, 87, 88), Awa Lau Wahine (Coast Guard rep. 1988, 87, corr. sec. 1983, Boutiki chair 1982), Rotary (vice chair Friends of Foster Kids Picnic 1994, chair 1995), Jr. League (cmty. v.p. 1993, rec. sec. 1990), Navy League, Propeller Club Port of Honolulu (bd. govs. alt. 1990), Hawaii Legal Aux. (v.p. 1994, pub./publs. chair 1994). Republican. Episcopalian. Home: 159 Kakahiaka St Kailua HI 96734-3474 Office: Gentle Memories 159 Kakahiaka St Kailua HI 96734-3474

GRIMSBO, RAYMOND ALLEN, forensic scientist; b. Portland, Oreg., Apr. 25, 1948; s. LeRoy Allen and Irene Bernice (Surgen) G.; m. Barbara Suzanne Favreau, Apr. 26, 1969 (div. 1979); children: John Allen, Kimberly Suzanne; m. Charlotte Alice Miller, July 25, 1981 (div. 1994); children: Sarah Marie, Benjamin Allen. BS, Portland State U., 1972; D of Philosophy, Union for Experimenting Colls. & Univs., Cin., 1987. Diplomate Am. Bd. Criminalistics; cert. profl. competency in criminalistics DEA Rschr. Registration. Med. technician United Med. Labs., Inc., Portland, 1969-74; criminalist Oreg. State Police Crime Lab., Portland, 1975-85; pvt. practice forensic science Portland, 1985-87; pres. Intermountain Forensic Labs., Inc., Portland, 1987—; adj. instr. Oreg. Health Scis. U., Portland, 1987—; adj. prof. Portland State U., 1986-88, adj. asst. prof., 1988—; clin. dir. Intermountain Forensic Labs., Inc., 1988-92, Western Health Lab., Portland; adj. faculty mem. Union Inst.; mem. substance abuse methods panel Oreg. Health Div. Contbr. articles to profl. jours. Fellow Royal Microscopical Soc., Am. Acad. Forensic Scientist; mem. ASTM, STM, Soc. Forensic Haemogenetics, N.W. Assn. Forensic Scientists, Internat. Assn. Bloodstain Pattern Analysts, Internat. Electrophoresis Soc., Internat. Assn. Identification, Internat. Assn. Forensic Toxicologists, Pacific N.W. Forensic Study Club, New Horizons Investment Club. Home: 16936 NE Davis St Portland OR 97230-6239 Office: Intermountain Forensic Labs Inc 11715 NE Glisan St Portland OR 97220-2141

GRIN, LEONID, conductor; b. Dniepropetrovsk, Ukraine, June 19, 1947; came to U.S., 1981; s. Gavriil and Ita (Sklar) Grinshpun; m. Marina Gusak, Apr. 25, 1970; children: Radmila, Daniel. BMus, Dniepropetrovsk Music Coll., 1966; MusM, Onesin's Music Inst., 1971; MusM in Conducting, Moscow State Conservatory, 1975, DMus, 1977. Assoc. condr. Moscow Philharm. Symphony Orch., 1977-79; prof. conducting U. Houston, 1983-86; prin. guest condr. Tampere (Finland) Philharm Orch., 1988-90, music dir., condr., 1990-94; music dir., condr. San Jose (Calif.) Symphony Orch., 1992—; guest condr. various orchs. in Denmark, Sweden, Norway, Finland, Eng., Scotland, Israel, Germany, The Netherlands, Italy, Belgium, Spain, Portugal, New Zealand, USA, Can., many others. Recs. include music by Tchaikovsky, Procofrev, Shostakovitch, all 6 symphonies by Errki Mellartin. Office: San Jose Symphony Orchestra 495 Almaden Blvd San Jose CA 95113-1604

GRINDAL, MARY ANN, sales professional; b. Michigan City, Ind., Sept. 9, 1942; d. James Paxton and Helen Evelyn (Koivisto) Gleason; m. Bruce Theodore Grindal, June 12, 1965 (div. Sept. 1974); 1 child, Matthew Bruce. BSBA, Ind. U., 1965. Sec. African studies program Ind. U., Bloomington, 1965-66; rsch. aid Ghana, West Africa, 1966-68; exec. sec. div. biol. scis. Ind. U., Bloomington, 1968-69; office asst. Dean of Students office Middlebury (Vt.) Coll., 1969-70; exec. sec. Remo, Inc., North Hollywood, Calif., 1974-76; sec., asst. to product mgrs. in cosmetic and skin care Redken Labs., Canoga Park, Calif., 1976-79; various sec. and exec. sec. positions L.A., 1979-81, 85-89; exec. sec. Sargent Industries, Burbank, Calif., 1981-85; sales asst. Chyron Graphics, Burbank, Calif., 1989—. Author of poems and essays. Mem. DAR (chpt. registrar 1988-91, chpt. regent 1991-94, chpt. chmn. pub. rels. and pub. 1994—, state chmn. Am. Heritage 1994—), Nat. Soc. Colonial Dames (rec. sec. 1989-90), Daughters of Union Vets. of Civil War, 1861-1865, Inc., Finland Soc. Episcopalian.

GRINELL, SHEILA, museum director; b. N.Y.C., July 15, 1945; d. Richard N. and Martha (Mimiless) G.; m. Thomas E. Johnson, July 15, 1980; 1 child, Michael; stepchildren: Kathleen, Thomas. BA, Radcliffe Coll., 1966; MA, U. Calif., Berkeley, 1968. Co-dir. exhibits and programs The Exploratorium, San Francisco, 1969-74; promotion dir. Kodansha Internat., Tokyo, 1974-77; traveling exhbn. coord. Assn. Sci. Tech. Ctrs., Washington, 1978-80, exec. dir., 1980-82, project dir. traveling exhbn. Chips and Changes, 1982-84; assoc. dir. N.Y. Hall of Sci., 1984-87; exec. dir. Ariz. Sci. Ctr., Phoenix, 1993—; cons. Optical Soc. Am., 1987, Nat. Sci. Ctr. Found., 1988, Interactive Video Sci. Consortium, 1988, Assn. Sci. Tech. Ctrs., 1988-89, Found. for Creative Am., 1989-90, Am. Assn. for World Health, 1990, Children's TV Workshop, 1991, Sciencenter, 1991, SciencePort, 1991, The Invention Factory, 1992, N.Y. Bot. Garden, 1992-93. Author: Light, Sight, Sound, Hearing: Exploratorium '74, 1974; editor A Stage for Science, 1979, A New Place for Learning Science: Starting and Running A Science Center, 1992. Fulbright teaching asst., 1966; hon. Woodrow Wilson fellow, 1967. Fellow AAAS; mem. Am. Assn. Mus., Phi Beta Kappa. Office: Ariz Sci Ctr 147 E Adams St Phoenix AZ 85004-2331

GRINGS, ELAINE ETHEL, research animal scientist, nutritionist; b. L.A., Feb. 19, 1956; d. William Washburn and Hilda Caroline (Balster) G. BS, U. Calif., Davis, 1977; MS in Range Sci., Colo. State U., Ft. Collins, 1979; PhD in Animal Sci., Wash. State U., Pullman, 1986. Rsch. asst. Colo. State U., 1977-79; range conservationist Bur. Land Mgmt., U.S. Dept. Interior, Meeker, Colo., 1979-82; rsch. asst. Wash. State U., 1982-85, rsch. assoc., 1986-87; rsch. assoc. U. Idaho, Moscow, 1988-91; rsch. animal scientist Agrl. Rsch. Svc., USDA, Miles City, Mont., 1991—. Contbr. articles to Jour. Animal Sci., Jour. Dairy Sci., Jour. Range Mgmt., others. Mem. AAUW (treas. Miles City br. 1994), Am. Soc. Animal Sci., Soc. for Range Mgmt., Am. Dairy Sci. Assn., Coun. for Agrl. Sci. and Tech., Assn. of Women in Sci. Home: PO Box 1572 Miles City MT 59301-1572 Office: USDA-ARS Ft Keogh Livestock/Range Rsch Lab Rte 1 Box 2021 Miles City MT 59301

GRISET, ROBERT PAUL, publisher; b. Santa Monica, Calif., May 30, 1951. BS in Animal Sci., Calif. Poly. State U., 1974; MS in Animal Sci., N.Mex. State U., 1977, MBF in Bus. Fin., 1977; PhD in Equine Reproductive Physiology, Colo. State U., 1982. Pres., CEO Robert Griset Industries, Inc., Mission Hills, Calif., 1976—; sr. portfolio mgr., equities analyst RGI-Fin. Svcs., Mission Hills and Malibu, Calif., 1979—; pres., pub. Agritech Pub. Group, Inc., Mission Hills, 1985—. Mem. Am. Soc. for Prevention of Cruelty to Animals, Tree People. Office: Agritech Pub Group Inc PO Box 950553 Mission Hills CA 91395-0553

GRISEZ, JAMES LOUIS, physician, plastic surgeon; b. Modesto, Calif., Feb. 25, 1935; s. John Francis and Josephine Marie (Tournamu) G.; m. Valerie Ann Marron, Mar. 20, 1960 (div. Oct. 1992); m. Diane Madeline Skidmore, Mar. 7, 1989; children: James, Stephen, Suzanne, Kathleen. MD, St. Louis Sch. Medicine, 1960. Diplomate Am. Bd. Plastic and Reconstructive Surgery. Intern D.C. Gen. Hosp., Washington, 1960-61; resident med. ctr. Georgetown U., Washington, 1961-64; resident plastic and reconstructive surgery ctr. St. Francis Meml. Hosp., San Francisco, 1964-66; military surgeon Brook Army Med Ctr., San Antonio, 1966, Second Gen. Hosp., Landstuhl, Germany, 1966-69; pvt. practice Napa, Calif., 1969-82, Salinas, Calif., 1982-90, Kailua-Kona, Hawaii, 1993—, Gilroy, Calif., 1995—; active staff mem. St. Louise Hosp., Kona Hosp., South Valley Med. Ctr., Hazel Hawkins; chief staff St. Helena Hosp., 1977-78, exec. com. 1973-80; radio talk show host All About Plastic Surgery, sta. KRNY, 1986-88. Contbr. articles to med. jours. Mem. Am. Cancer Soc. (pres. 1988-90), Am. Soc. Plastic and Reconstructive Surgeons, Calif. Soc. Plastic and Reconstructive Surgeons, Hawaii Plastic Surgery Soc. Home: 8675 Muir Dr Gilroy CA 95020 Office: 8375 Church St Gilroy CA 95020

GRISMORE, ROGER, physics educator, researcher; b. Ann Arbor, Mich., July 12, 1924; s. Grover Cleveland and May Aileen (White) G.; m. Marilynn Ann McNinch, Sept. 15, 1950; 1 child, Carol Ann. BS, U. Mich., 1947, MS, 1948, PhD, 1957; BS in Computer Sci., Coleman Coll., 1979. From asst. to assoc. physicist Argonne (Ill.) Nat. Lab., 1956-62; assoc. prof. physics Lehigh U., Bethlehem, Pa., 1962-67; specialist in physics Scripps Inst. Oceanography, La Jolla, Calif., 1967-71, 75-78; prof. physics Ind. State U., Terre Haute, 1971-74; from mem. staff to sr. scientist JAYCOR, San Diego, 1979-84; lectr. Calif. Poly. State U., San Luis Obispo, 1984-92, lunar sample investigator, 1994—, 1994—. Contbr. numerous articles to profl. jours. Served as ensign USNR, 1945-46, PTO. Mem. AAAS, Am. Phys. Soc., Am. Geophys. Union, Sigma Xi. Home: 535 Cameo Way Arroyo Grande CA 93420-5574 Office: Calif Poly State U Dept Physics San Luis Obispo CA 93407

GRISSOM, LEE ALAN, state official; b. Pensacola, Fla., Sept. 7, 1942; s. Levi Aaron and Virginia Sue (Olinger) G.; m. Sharon Kay Hasty, May 14, 1966; children: David, Jonathan, Matthew, Andrew. BA in Pub. Adminstrn., San Diego State U., 1965, M in City Planning, 1971. Sr. research assoc. Western Behavioral Scis. Inst., La Jolla, Calif., 1965-73; mgr. planning div. Greater San Diego C. of C., 1973-74, gen. mgr., 1974-75, pres., chief operating officer, 1975-92; exec. dir. Coun. on Calif. Competitiveness, Gov's. Coun. Econ. advisors; mem. NFL Super Bowl Task Force; mem. bd. and exec. com. San Diego Holiday Bowl. Host (TV program) The City Game, 1972-75. Trustee Calif. State U., 1984-91, fin. com.; chmn. collective bargaining com., chair legis. com.; bd. dirs. Armed Forces YMCA, Econ. Devel. Corp.; chmn. San Diego Housing Commn., 1983-86, Pres.'s adv. bd., San Diego State U., 1983—; mem. Calif. Econ. Devel. Task Force, 1983—; adv. com. Fed. Home Loan Mortgage Corp.; mem. exec. com. Am.'s Cup Task Force. Named Outstanding Young Citizen San Diego Jaycees, 1976; named Outstanding Young Citizen Calif. Jaycees, 1977, one of 10 Outstanding Young Men in Am. U.S. Jaycees, 1978, Outstanding Alumnus San Diego State U., 1987. Republican. Lodge: Rotary. Office: Gov Pete Wilson Sacramento CA 95814

GRISWOLD, MARTHA KERFOOT, social worker; b. Oklahoma City, Mar. 22, 1930; d. John Samuel III and Frances (Mann) Kerfoot; m. George Littlefield Griswold, Jan. 28, 1967. AB, Occidental Coll., 1951; MRE, U. So. Calif., 1956, postgrad., 1962. Cert. social worker. Teen dir. Toberman Settlement, San Pedro, Calif., 1954-56; social worker County of L.A., 1956-62, 1969-72; dir. program to integrate disabled children Internat. Inst., L.A., 1979-80; cons. community orgn. L.A., 1980-84; dir. LIV Disability Resources Ctr., Altadena, Calif., 1984—; instr. Calif. State U., L.A., 1966-68, 1983-84; chair Childrens' Adv. Com. L.A. County Dept. Mental Health, 1985-86; coordinator So. Calif. Conf. on Living Long Term with Disability, 1985-87. Co-host, prodr. radio program on disability Challenge, Sta. KPFK-FM, 1987—, host. prodr. cable TV program on disability issues LIVstyles, 1992—. Mem. Pasadena (Calif.) City Disability Issues Com., 1984-86, Pasadena Strategic Planning Task Force, 1985-86, City of Pasadena commn. disability access; mem. coun. on aging and long-term care Region 2 United Way, L.A., chairperson, 1989-90; mem. Pasadena Awareness: A Cmty. Effort for Disabled (PACED v.p.), 1983—. Recipient 1986 award So. Calif. Rehab. Assn. Mem. AAUW, NASW, Californians for Disability Rights, Acad. Cert. Social Workers, Health and Social Svc. Workers with Disabilities. Congregationalist. Office: LIV Ctr 943 E Altadena Dr Altadena CA 91001-2033

GRITTER, GORDON WILLIAM, psychiatrist; b. Falmouth, Mich., Apr. 26, 1927; s. John and Jeanette Remerie (Schoolland) G.; m. Willa Kenoyer, Apr. 8, 1961 (div. 1977); children: John W., Judith A., Jeanette D., James L.; m. Dianne N. Long, June 20, 1981; children: Stacy K., Curtis D. AB, Calvin Coll., 1951; MD, Boston U., 1955. Diplomate Am. Bd. Psychiatry and Neurology, Nat. Bd. Med. Examiners, Royal Australian and New Zealand Coll. Psychiatrists. Intern Butterworth Hosp., Grand Rapids, Mich., 1955-56; resident and sr. resident Langley Porter Neuropsychiat. Inst., San Francisco, 1956-61; staff psychiatrist San Francisco (Calif.) Gen. Hosp., 1961-62; pvt. practice San Francisco, 1962-73; chief psychiatrist Shiawassee County Mental Health, Owosso, Mich., 1973-76; cons. psychiatrist Wellington (New Zealand) Hosp. Bd., 1976-79; assoc. prof. Mich. State U., East Lansing, 1979-82; staff psychiatrist Atascadero (Calif.) State Hosp., 1982-84, clin. and med. dir., 1984—; clin. asst. and assoc. prof. U. Calif., San Francisco, 1965-73-84—. Lay reader, sr. warden, standing com., dep. Episcopal Ch., Calif. and Mich., 1962—. 1st lt. U.S. Army, 1945-47. Recipient Gov.'s Managerial Performance award State of Calif., 1986, 89. Fellow Am. Psychiat. Assn. (life); mem. AMA, Am. Acad. Psychiatry and Law, Physicians for Social Responsibility, Internat. Physicians for Prevention Nuclear War (Nobel Peace prize 1985), World Psychiat. Assn. Home: 313 San Miguel Ave San Luis Obispo CA 93405-2135 Office: Atascadero State Hosp PO Box 7001 Atascadero CA 93423-7001

GROAH, LINDA KAY, nursing administrator and educator; b. Cedar Rapids, Iowa, Oct. 5, 1942; d. Joseph David and Irma Josephine (Zitek) Rozek; diploma St. Luke's Sch. Nursing, Cedar Rapids, 1963; student San Francisco City Coll., 1976-77; BA, St. Mary's Coll., Moraga, Calif., 1978; BS in Nursing, Calif. State U.; MS in Nursing, U. Calif.; m. Patrick Andrew Groah, Mar. 20, 1975; 1 child, Kimberly; stepchildren: Nadine, Maureen, Patrick, Marcus. Staff nurse to head nurse U. Iowa, 1963-67; clin. supr., dir. oper. and recovery room Michael Reese Hosp., Chgo., 1967-73; dir. oper. rooms Med. Ctr. Cen. Ga., Macon, 1973-74; dir. oper. and recovery rooms U. Calif. Hosps. and Clinics, San Francisco, 1974-90, asst. dir. hosps. and clinics, 1982-86; divsn. dir. Kaiser Found. Hosp., San Francisco, 1990—; asst. clin. prof. U. Calif. Sch. Nursing, San Francisco, 1975—; cons. to oper. room suprs., to div. ednl. resources and programs Assn. Am. Med. Colls., 1976—; condr. seminars. Mem. Nat. League for Nurses, Am. Nurses Assn. (vice chmn. operating room conf. group 1974-76), Assn. Oper. Room Nurses (com. on nominations 1979-84, treas. 1985-87, 93-95, bd. dirs. 1991-93, pres.-elect 1995—, pres. found., 1992-95, Excellence award in Preoperative Nursing 1989), Ctr. for Study Dem. Instns. Author: Perioperative Nursing Practice, 1983, 3d edit., 1995; contbr. articles on operating room techniques to profl. jours. and textbooks; author, producer audio-visual presentations; author computer software. Home: 5 Mateo Dr Belvedere Tiburon CA 94920-1071 Office: 3020 Bridgeway Ste 299 Sausalito CA 94965-2839

GROAT, JENNY HUNTER (LAVIDA JUNE GROAT), painter, artist, choreographer, writer; b. Modesto, Calif., Aug. 30, 1929; d. Leo Hunt and Lola Tuttle (Atwood) Miller; m. Maurice Frederick Groat, Jan. 15, 1955. AA in Music, San Joaquin Delta, 1950. Modern dance tchr. Dominican Schs., San Rafael, Calif., 1952-54; dance dir., tchr. Reed Coll., Portland, Oreg., 1954-56 summers; co-founder, artistic dir., tchr. various dance coops., San Francisco Bay Area, 1951-61; founder, dir., tchr., soloist, choreographer Dance West: The Jenny Hunter Sch. and Dance Co., San Francisco, 1962-68; invited art tchr. Internat. workshops, 1983—; tchr. art calligraphy Coll. of Marin, Kentfield, Calif., 1980-90; tchr.-mentor art classes Lagunitas, Calif., 1987—; tchr., tng. for creative dance Dancers and Artists, Bay area, 1955—; mast classes, dance Bay area groups, colls. and univs., 1958-68; organizer panel discussions on art Jenny Hunter Sch., Dance West, San Francisco, 1963. One-woman shows include Claudia Chapline Gallery, Stinson Beach, Calif., 1994, 93, Gallery One, Petaluma, 1994, Zen Ctr., San Francisco, 1993, 90, Bechtel Ctr. Stanford U., 1993, Marin County Civic Ctr. Libr., San Rafael, San Geronimo Valley Cultural Ctr., 1990, Detroit Pub. Libr., 1988, Markings Gallery, Berkeley, Calif., 1985, Fairfax (Calif.) Pub. Libr., 1981-82, Lyford Ho., Tiburon, Calif., 1982, Palace Legion of Honor Theatre, 1967, 68, 65; numerous group exhbns. including Klingspor Mus., Germany, 1983, Grand Palais, Paris, 1990; permanent collections include Nat. Mus. Women in Arts, Washington, U. Tex., Austin, Harrison Collection-San Francisco Pub. Libr.; represented in many pvt. collections. Grantor scholarships for child and adult dancers Jenny Hunter Dance West Sch., 1962-68; founder, mentor, tchr. Grass Root Scribes, Marin County, Calif., 1987-89; curator, art exhbns. Coll. of Marin and Kentfield, and Fairfax (Calif.) Libr., 1980-82. Grantee for art work in modern dance City of San Francisco, 1968; recipient Golden Quill award Calligraphic Soc. of Ariz., 1986. Mem. Colo. Calligrapher's Guild (hon.), Friends of Calligraphy, Marin Soc. of Artists (life), Soc. for Calligraphy (L.A.), Marin Arts Coun. Democrat. Buddhist.

GROBER, MATTHEW SCOTT, biologist, educator; b. N.Y.C., Nov. 19, 1959; s. Ronald Leonard and Roberta Lois (Stone) G.; m. Debra LeBlanc, Aug. 17, 1985; children: Aaron Jacob LeBlanc, Mia LeBlanc, Cory LeBlanc. BS, Calif. State U., Long Beach, 1981; PhD, UCLA, 1988. Pres., co-founder Maritech Inc., Long Beach, 1982-84; teaching fellow dept. biology UCLA, 1982-88; NIH postdoctoral fellow sect. neurobiology and behavior Cornell U., Ithaca, N.Y., 1988-92; asst. prof. zoology dept. biol. sci. U. Idaho, Moscow, 1992—; cons. Law Offices of Marc Grober, Nenana, Alaska, 1990-92. Contbr. articles and abstracts to profl. jours. Fellow Smithsonian Tropical Rsch. Inst., 1984; recipient Nat. Rsch. Svc. award NIH, 1988-92; grantee NSF, NIH, 1992—. Mem. Internat. Soc. for Neuroethology, Animal Behavior Soc., Am. Soc. Zoologists, Soc. for Neurosci., AAAS, Western Soc. Naturalists, Sigma Xi. Democrat. Jewish. Home: 1628 Hillcrest Dr Moscow ID 83843-9210 Office: U Idaho Dept Biol Scis Moscow ID 83843

GROBER, MICHAEL, computer industry professional; b. St. Petersburg, Russia, Aug. 13, 1955; came to U.S., 1987; s. Miney and Tonya (Nikanorova) G. BA in English, St. Petersburg Coll., 1980; MSME, St. Petersburg Inst. Tech., 1977; M of Engring., Cornell U., 1989. Cert. translator. Design engr. Torgmash Design Co., St. Petersburg, 1977-81; engr., rschr. City Gas Co., St. Petersburg, 1981-87; libr. rschr. Cornell U. Libr., Ithaca, N.Y., 1988-89; engring. counselor JVS, San Francisco, 1989-93; program coord. Sun Mircosystems, Mountain View, Calif., 1993—; cons. Bank of Am., San Francisco, 1991-92; bd. dirs. EI Internat., Pacifica, Calif. Contbr. articles to profl. jours. Pres. local chpt. Young Profls. Orgn., St. Petersburg, 1978, 80. Mem. Am. Translators Assn., Assn. for Computing Machinery.

GROCE, EWIN PETTY, lawyer; b. Ft. Worth, Dec. 19, 1953; s. Charles Tillman and Mary Elizabeth (Hill) G.; m. Elisita Bernis Groce, Oct. 29, 1982; children: Tamara Roxanne, Jonathan Paul, Meghan Elizabeth. BA cum laude, U. Tex., 1979; postgrad., Golden Gate Seminary, 1982; JD, Whitter Law Sch., 1989; postgrad., Fuller Seminary. Bar: Kans. Supreme Ct. 1990, Mo. Supreme Ct. 1991, U.S. Dist. Ct. (ea. dist.) Kans. 1990, U.S. Dist. Ct. (we. dist.) Mo. 1991. Paralegal Groce & Groce Law Offices, Ft. Worth, 1979-81, Abraham Liao Law Offices, Monterey Park, Calif., 1987-88; paralegal litigation dept. Charles M. Finkel Law Offices, Beverly Hills, Calif., 1988-90; lawyer Ewin Groce Law Offices, Overland Park, Kans., 1990—; lectr. continuing legal edn. Consiliators Training Workshop, Kansas City, Mo., 1991—. Author numerous poems. Worked with immigrant Chinese for Evang. Formosan Ch., L.A., 1983-90; vol. mediatorChristian Conciliation Svc., L.A., 1989-90, Kansas City, 1990—, bd. dirs., 1990—; First Amendment law advisor Metro Vineyard Fellowship, Kansas City, 1990-92; cons. immigration law Grace Training Ctr., Kansas City, 1991-92. Mem. ABA, Assn. Trial Lawyers Am., Christian Legal Soc., Christian Conciliation Svc, Kansas City (mediators panel). Republican. Office: Law Offices Abraham C Liao 300 S Garfield Ave Monterey Park CA 91754-3336

GRODY, MARK STEPHEN, public relations executive; b. Milw., Jan. 1, 1938; s. Ray and Betty (Rothstein) G.; m. Karen Goldstein, Mar. 6, 1965 (div. 1972); 1 child, Laura; m. Susan Tellem, Mar. 25, 1979 (div. 1989); 1 child, Daniel. BS, U. Wis., 1960. Pub. rels. exec. GM, Detroit, 1961-74; v.p. pub. affairs Nat. Alliance of Businessmen, Washington, 1973-74; v.p. Carl Terzian & Assocs., L.A., 1974-75; chmn. Mark Grody Assocs. and Grody Tellem Comm., Inc. (now The Rowland Co.), L.A., 1975-90; pres. Mark Grody Assocs., L.A., 1975-90; exec. v.p., gen. mgr. Ogilvy Adams & Rinehart, L.A., 1993—. Capt. U.S. Army, 1960. Mem. Pub. Rels. Soc. Am., Industry Edn. Coun. of Calif. (bd. dirs.), Nat. Alliance of Bus./West (bd. dirs.), Mountain Gate Country Club, L.A. Sports Club, Beverly Hills Country Club. Office: Ogilvy Adams & Rinehart 11766 Wilshire Blvd Ste 900 Los Angeles CA 90025-6538

GRODY, WAYNE WILLIAM, physician; b. Syracuse, N.Y., Feb. 25, 1952; s. Robert Jerome and Florence Beatrice (Kashdan) G.; m. Gaylen Ducker, July 8, 1990. BA, Johns Hopkins U., 1974; MD, Baylor Coll. Medicine, 1977, PhD, 1981. Diplomate Am. Bd. Pathology, Am. Bd. Med. Genetics; lic. physician, Calif. Intern/resident UCLA Sch. Medicine, 1982-85, postdoctoral fellow, 1985-86, asst. prof., 1987-93, assoc. prof., 1993—; panelist Calif. Children's Svcs., 1987—, USFDA, Washington, 1989—; mem. DNA tech. com. Pacific Southwest Regional Genetics Network, Berkeley, Calif., 1987—; med., tech. cons. and writer Warner Bros., NBC, Tri-Star, CBS, others, 1987—; mem. molecular genetics com. Coll. Am. Pathology, Am. Coll. Med. Genetics, Nat. Com. on Clin. Lab. Stds., others. Contbg. editor: MD Mag., 1981-91; assoc. editor Diagnostic Molecular Pathology, 1993—; contbr. articles to profl. jours. Recipient best paper award L.A. Soc. Pathology, 1984, Joseph Kleiner Meml. award Am. Soc. Med. Technologists, 1990; Basil O'Connor scholar March of Dimes Birth Defects Found., 1989. Mem. AAAS, AMA, Am. Soc. Clin. Pathology (DNA workshop dir. 1988—), Am. Soc. Human Genetics, Coll. Am. Pathologists (scholar award 1987), Soc. Inherited Metabolic Disorders, Western Soc. Pediatric Rsch., Am. Coll. Med. Genetics (mem. DNA com.). Democrat. Jewish. Office: UCLA Sch Medicine Divsn Med Genetics & Molecular Pathology Los Angeles CA 90024-1732

GROEBLI, WERNER FRITZ (MR. FRICK), professional ice skater, realtor; b. Basel, Switzerland, Apr. 21, 1915; s. Fritz and Gertrud (Landerer) G.; m. Yvonne Baumgartner, Dec. 30, 1954. Student architecture, Swiss Fed. Inst. Tech., 1934-35. Lic. realtor, Calif. Chmn. pub. relations com. Profl. Skaters Guild Am., 1972—. Performed in ice shows, Patria, Brighton, Eng., 1937; command performance in, Marina, London, 1937, Symphony on Ice, Royal Opera House, 1937; mem. Ice Follies, 1939-81, partner (with Hans Mauch) in comedy team Frick & Frack, 1939-53; solo act as Mr. Frick (assisted by comedy team), 1955-81; numerous TV appearances including Snoopy on Ice, 1973, Snoopy's Musical on Ice, 1978, Sportsworld, NBC-TV, 1978, Donnie and Marie Osmond Show, 1978, Mike Douglas Show, 1978, Dinah Shore Show, 1978; films include Silver Skates, 1942, Lady Let's Dance, 1943, Jinxed, 1981; interviewed by Barbara Walters NBC Today, 1974; appeared in Christmas Classics on Ice at Blue Jay Ice Castle, 1991. Served with Swiss Army, 1934-37. Named Swiss jr. skating champion, 1934; named to Madison Sq. Garden Hall of Fame for 10,000 performances in Ice Follies, 1967, U.S. Figure Skating Assn. World Hall of Fame, 1984; recipient Hall of Fame Ann. award Ice Skating Inst. Am. Mem. SAG, Profl. Skaters Guild Am., Swiss Club of San Francisco (hon.). Office: care US Figure Skating Assn 20 1st St Colorado Springs CO 80906-3624

GROENEVELD, DAVID PAUL, plant ecologist; b. Harvey, Ill., Mar. 20, 1952; s. Robert D. and Ruth M. (Terranova) G. BA, U. Colo., 1975, MA, 1977; PhD, Colo. State U., 1985. Rsch. asst. Inst. Arctic and Alpine Rsch., Boulder, Colo., 1972-76; cons., pres. GEOS, Inc., Telluride, Colo., 1977-81; plant ecologist Inyo County Water Dept., Bishop, Calif., 1981—; cons. Resource Mgmt. Cons., Bishop, 1983—; mem. tech. group Inyo City/City of L.A., 1983—; tech. advisor Great Basin Air Pollution Control Dist., Bishop, 1985—; mem. mined land reclamation expert's panel, Denver, 1980. Contbr. articles to profl. jours. Mem. Ecol. Soc. Am., Range Soc. Am. (life). Home: 618 Keough St Bishop CA 93514-2534 Office: Inyo County Water Dept 163 May St Bishop CA 93514-2709

GROENINGER, EDWARD JOHN, air force officer; b. Rockford, Ill., Aug. 19, 1947; s. Edward Vincent and Elizabeth Jane (Mariga) G.; m. Marsha Powell Curran, Dec. 20, 1969; children: Elizabeth Joy, Matthew Lee, Luke William. BS in Edn., Ill. State U., 1969; MS in Edn., No. Ill. U., 1972; MBA, Golden Gate U., 1985; Grad., USAF Squadron Officer Sch., 1979, USAF Fighter Weapons Sch., 1980, RAF Staff Coll., 1987, USAF Air War Coll., 1991. Math tchr. Roosevelt Jr. High Sch., Bellwood, Ill., 1969-70, Fremd High Sch., Palatine, Ill., 1970-72; commd. 2d lt. USAF, 1973, advanced through grades to col., 1995; F-4 pilot Spangdahlem AB, Germany, 1975-77, F-4 instr. pilot, 1977-78; F-4 instr. pilot George AFB, Calif., 1978-80, F-4 weapons and tactics instr. pilot, 1980; Mirage III weapons and tactics instr. pilot RAAF Base Williamtown, Australia, 1980-83; F-4 figher weapons instr. pilot George AFB, Calif., 1983-84; wing weapons officer George AFB, 1984-85, fighter weapons flight comdr., 1985-86, squadron ops. officer, 1985-86; tactical weapons unit staff officer RAF Bentley Priory, Eng., 1988-90; chief current plans br. Hdqrs. NORAD, Peterson AFB, Colo., 1991-92, chief current and counterdrug planning divsn., 1992, chief forces planning divsn., 1993-94, dep. dir. comdr.-in-chief support group, 1994—. Active Boy Scouts Am. Mem. Air Force Assn. Roman Catholic. Home: 3220 Windjammer Dr Colorado Springs CO 80920-4424 Office: Hdqs NORAD/CX 250 S Peterson Blvd Ste 116 Peterson AFB CO 80914-3285

GROFF, DAVID CLARK, JR., lawyer; b. Detroit, June 16, 1946; s. David Clark and Marguerite (Lowrie) G.; children: Eric W., Paul D. BA in Polit. Sci., U. Mich., 1968, JD, 1972. Bar: Wash. 1972, U.S. Dist. Ct. (we. dist.) Wash. 1972, U.S. Ct. Appeals (9th cir.) 1972. Assoc. Davis, Wright & Jones, Seattle, 1972-78; ptnr. Davis Wright Tremaine (previously Davis, Wright & Jones), Seattle, 1978-92, Groff & Murphy, Seattle, 1992—. Author: Washington Constrn. Law, 1980-91; mem. editorial bd. Mich. Law Rev., 1971-72; contbr. articles to legal jours. Bd. govs. Wash. Spl. Olympics, 1990—; bd. trustees Seattle Repertory Theatre, 1992—. Mem. ABA (steering com. on Constrn. Forum 1987-90), Wash. State Bar Assn. (bd. dirs., sect. pub. contracts and pvt. constrn. law 1987-90), Order of Coif. Home: 1700 36th Ave Seattle WA 98122-3419 Office: Groff & Murphy 1191 2nd Ave Ste 1900 Seattle WA 98101-2933

GROFF, DAVID HUSTON, academic administrator, director, educator; b. Sacramento, Feb. 15, 1945; s. Philip David and Harriett (Huston) G.; m. Elizabeth Ussher, Sept. 16, 1969; children: Rebecca, Julia. BA, U. Calif., Davis, 1967; MA, Stanford (Calif.) U., 1972, PhD, 1980. Asst. prof. history and humanities Reed Coll., Portland, Oreg., 1976-87, dean of students, 1983-87; asst. dir. div. continuing edn. Linfield Coll., McMinnville, Oreg., 1987-93; dir. Linfield Coll., Portland, 1988—. Author: (chpt. in book) African Bourgeoisie, 1987, Law and Colonialism in Africa, 1987; contbr. articles to profl. jours. Woodrow Wilson Found. fellow, 1967, Ford Found. fellow, 1973, NEH fellow, 1986. Mem. Assn. Concerned Africa Scholars (nat. exec. sec. 1987-90), Am. Hist. Assn., African Studies Assn. Office: Linfield Coll Portland Campus 2255 NW Northrup St Portland OR 97210-2952

GROGAN, STANLEY JOSEPH, educational educator, consultant; b. N.Y.C., Jan. 14, 1925; s. Stanley Joseph and Marie (Di Giorgio) G.; AA, Am. U., 1949, BS, 1950, MA, 1955; degree, Industrial Coll. of Armed Forces Air War Coll., 1972; MS, Calif. State Coll., Hayward, 1973; EdD, Nat. Christian U., 1974; m. Mary Margaret Skroch, Sept. 20, 1954; 1 child, Mary Maureen. Pers. asst., recruitment asst. CIA, Washington, 1954-56; disting. grad. acad. instr., allied officer course, Maxwell AFB, Ala., 1962; asst. prof. air sci. U. Calif., Berkeley, 1963-64, Chabot Coll., 1964-70, Oakland Unified Sch. Dist., 1962-83, Hayward Unified Sch. Dist., 1965-68; instr. ednl. methods, edn. rsch. methods of instrn. Nat. Christian U., 1975—, Nat. U. Grad. Studies, Belize, 1975—; pres. SJG Enterprises, Inc., cons., 1963—. Asst. dir. Nat. Ednl. Film Festival, 1971. Pub. rels. cons., 1963—. Bd. dirs. We T.I.P., Inc., 1974. With AUS, 1945; lt. col. USAFR, 1948-76; col. Calif. State Mil. Res. Decorated Air medal with oak leaf cluster; recipient citation Korea, 1963; RCVP Korean Vets. Assn. medal, 1994; named to Hon. Order Ky. Cols. Commonwealth of Ky., 1970, Outstanding Secondary Educators of Am. 1972. Mem. NRA (life), VFW (life), DAV (life), Am. Def. Preparedness Assn. (life), Night Fighter Assn. (nat. publicity chmn. 1967), Air Force Assn., Res. Officers Assn., Phi Delta Kappa, Am. Soc. Indsl. Security (cert. protection profl.), Nat. Def. Exec. Res., Marines Meml., Contbr. articles to profl. jours. and newspapers. Home: 2585 Moraga Dr Pinole CA 94564-1236

GROH, RUPERT JAMES, JR., judge; b. Richland Center, Wis., Dec. 5, 1933; s. Rupert James Sr. and Sadie Lenora (Mathews) G.; m. Evelyn Theresa Rausch, June 14, 1958; children: Rupert J. III, Thomas M., Jonathan C., Peter Christian. AB, Ripon Coll., 1955; JD, Marquette U., 1960. Bar; Wis. 1960, Ill. 1065, Calif. 1976, U.S. Dist. Ct. (ea., we. dists.) Wis. 1960, U.S. Dist. Ct. (no. dist.) Ill. 1964, U.S. Dist. Ct. (no. dist.) Ind. 1965, U.S. Ct. Claims 1965, U.S. Tax Ct. 1965, U.S. Ct. Appeals (7th cir.) 1970, U.S. Supreme Ct. 1965. Trial atty. civil rights and tax divs. U.S. Dept. Justice, Washington, 1960-65; v.p. gen. counsel Benefit Trust Life Ins. Co., Chgo., 1965-69; ptnr. Wildman, Harrold, Allen & Dixon, Chgo., 1969-75; prof. law, asst. dean U. Pacific, Sacramento, 1975-84; magistrate judge U.S. Dist. Ct. (we. dist.) Wis., Madison, 1984-91, U.S. Dist. Ct. (ctrl. dist.) Calif., L.A., 1991—. 1st lt. USAR, 1955-63, Mil. Intelligence. Mem. ABA (legal edn. sect.), Ill. State Bar Assn., State Bar Wis., State Bar Calif., Gideons, Navy League, Law Club Chgo. Lutheran. Office: US Dist Ct Ctrl Dist Calif 312 N Spring St Los Angeles CA 90012-4701

GRONLI, JOHN VICTOR, college administrator, minister; b. Eshowe, South Africa, Sept. 11, 1932; s. John Einar and Marjorie Gellet (Hawker) G.; came to U.S., 1934, naturalized, 1937; BA, U. Minn., 1953; MDiv, Luther Theol. Sem., 1958, DMin, 1978; MA, Pacific Luth. U., 1975; m. Jeanne Louise Ellertson, Sept. 15, 1952; children: Cheryl Marie Mundt, Deborah Raechel Hokanson, John Timothy, Peter Jonas, Daniel Reuben. Ordained to ministry, 1958; pastor Brocket-Lawton Luth. Parish, Brocket, N.D., 1958-61; Harlowton (Mont.) Luth. Parish, 1961-66; sr. pastor St. Luke's Luth. Ch., Shelby, Mont., 1966-75; missionary Paulinum Sem., Otjimbingwe, Namibia, 1975-76; dean, chmn. dept. philosophy and humanities Golden Valley Luth. Coll., Mpls., 1976-85; dir. Summer Inst. Pastoral Ministry, Mpls., 1980-85, sr. pastor Pella Luth. Ch., Sidney, Mont., 1985-95; pres., CEO GEHM Inc., Martinsdale, Mont., 1991—, cons. for orgnl. comms., 1995—. Bd. dirs. Mont. Assn. Chs., 1973-75, Richland Homes, Sidney, Mont., 1990-94, Ea. Mont. Mental Health Assn., 1993-94; sec. bd. for communications and mission support Am. Luth. Ch., 1973-75; mem. dist. coun. Rocky Mountain Dist., 1963-75, sec., 1963-70; mem. S.African affairs task force SEM Dist., 1978-79; dean S.W. Mont. Conf. Evang. Luth. Ch. in Am.; faculty No. Rockies Inst. Theology, 1986—; trustee Luth. Bible Inst., Seattle, 1986-92. Mem. personnel and guidance assns., Am., Minn. coll. personnel assns. Editor: Rocky Mountain Dist. Yearbook, 1963-70; Rocky Mountain Views, 1973-75; contbr. to Lutheran Standard, 1973-77; contbr. articles to religious jours.

GRONNING, LLOYD JOSEPH, engineering company executive, civil engineer; b. Tacoma, July 12, 1951; s. Neil Roland and Marie Sarafica (Buettner) G.; m. Robyn Mary McAtavey, May 29, 1971; children: John, Jenny, Margaret. BSCE, U. Notre Dame, 1973; MSCE, Colo. State U., 1976; MBA, U. Denver, 1983. Registered profl. engr. Colo., Wyo., N.Mex. Design engr., resident insp. Nelson, Haley, Patterson and Quirk, Greeley, Colo., 1972-76; project engr. M&I Cons. Engrs., Ft. Collins, Colo., 1976-77; mgr. water resources City of Thornton, Colo., 1977-80, utilities dir., 1980-84; pres. Gronning Engring. Co., Denver, 1984—. Mem. ASCE, Cons. Engrs. Council Colo., Am. Waterworks Assn., Colo. Water Congress, Internat. Water Supply Assn. Democrat. Roman Catholic. Home: 9916 Wagner Ln Westminster CO 80030-2527 Office: Gronning Engring Co 12050 Pecos St Ste 100 Denver CO 80234-2080

GROOMS, LARRY WILLIS, newspaper editor; b. Searcy, Ark., Dec. 1, 1945; s. Willis Martin and Ida Mae (Self) G.; m. Diane Valeska Marland, Oct. 13, 1984; children: Richard, Robert. BS in Orgnl. Behavior, U. San Francisco, 1986. Reporter Port Arthur (Tex.) News, 1967; sports editor Antelope Valley Press, Palmdale, Calif., 1967-68; reporter Daily Ledger-Gazette, Lancaster, Calif., 1968-71; reporter, city editor Salinas Californian, 1971-81; exec. v.p. Salinas C. of C., 1981-83; co-owner PR Plus Advt. & PR, Salinas, 1983-86; city editor Antelope Valley Press, 1986-90, editor-in-chief, 1990—; bd. dirs. Lancaster (Calif.) Econ. Devel. Corp. Bd. dirs. Antelope Valley Cultural Found., 1991—. Mem. Calif. Soc. Newspaper Editors, Suburban Newspapers of Am. Office: Antelope Valley Press 37404 Sierra Hwy Palmdale CA 93550-9343

GROSE, ANDREW PETER, association executive; b. Washington, July 16, 1940; s. Peter Andrew and Mildred (Holsten) G.; m. Jacqueline Stamm, Aug. 17, 1963; children: Peter Andrew II, Tracey Christine. BS with high honors, U. Md., 1962, MA, 1964. Mem. legis. staff Fla. Ho. of Reps., Tallahassee, 1972-74; research dir. Nev. Legislature, Carson City, 1974-83; chief of staff Office of Gov. Nev., Carson City, 1983-84, dir. econ. devel., 1984-90; dir. western region Coun. of State Govt., San Francisco, 1990—; mem. exec. com. Nat. Conf. State Legislatures, Denver, 1982-83. Author: Florida Model City Charter, 1974; mem. editorial bd. Nev. Rev. of Bus. and Econs., Reno, 1976—. Chmn. coun. on ministries 1st United Meth. Ch., San Francisco, 1994-95; active Habitat for Humanity. Served to capt. USAF, 1964-70, to brig. gen., Res. Recipient Spl. citation Nev. Library Assn., Carson City, 1981. Mem. Air Force Assn., Res. Officers Assn., Nat. Assn. State Devel. Agys. (1st v.p.), Western Govt. Rsch. Assn. (pres. 1993-95), Kiwanis (pres. 1981-82, bd. dirs. 1994). Democrat. Home: 405 Hazelwood Ave San Francisco CA 94127-2129 Office: Coun State Governments 121 2nd St Fl 4 San Francisco CA 94105-3608

GROSE, ELINOR RUTH, retired elementary education educator; b. Honolulu, Apr. 23, 1928; d. Dwight Hatsuichi and Edith (Yamamoto) Uyeno; m. George Benedict Grose, Oct. 19, 1951; children: Heidi Diane Hill, Mary Porter, John Tracy, Nina Evangeline. AA, Briarcliff Jr. Coll., 1948; postgrad., Long Beach State U., 1954-55; BS in Edn., Wheelock Coll., Boston, 1956; MA in Edn., Whittier Coll., 1976. Cert. tchr., Mass., N.Y., Calif. Reading tchr. Cumberland Head Sch., Plattsburgh, N.Y., 1968-70; master tchr. Broadoaks Sch., Whittier (Calif.) Coll., 1971; reading tchr. Phelan/Washington Schs., Whittier, 1971-73; elem. tchr. Christian Sorensen Sch., Whittier, 1978-94, ret., 1994; cons. Nat. Writing Projet, 1987—, South Basin Writing Project, Long Beach, 1987—; team tchr. Young Writers' Camp, Long Beach State U., 1988. First v.p. Women's League of Physicians Hosp., Plattsburgh, 1970; asst. to Christian, Jewish and Muslim pres., v.p.s of Acad. Judaic, Christian and Islamic Studies 6th Assembly World Coun. Chs., Vancouver, 1983. Named Companion of the Order of Abraham, Acad. for Judaic, Christian and Islamic Studies, 1987. Mem. NEA, Calif. Tchrs. Assn., Whittier Elem. Tchrs. Assn., English Coun. of Long Beach. Presbyterian. Home: 6085 E Brighton Ln Anaheim CA 92807

GROSS, ALLEN, engineer; b. Bklyn., Dec. 28, 1937; s. David and Ann (Green) G.; div.; 1 child: Lisa Rachel. BS in Chem. Engring., CCNY, 1960; MSME, Rensselaer Poly. Inst., 1963. Engr. Pratt & Whitney, East Hartford, Conn., 1960-63; project engr. Rocketdyne, Canoga Park, Calif., 1963-65; tchr. West Coast U., L.A., 1963-68; instr. U. So. Calif., Europe and Asia, 1968-70; project engr. Aerospace Corp., El Segundo, Calif., 1965-68, 70—. Developed, pub. numerous reports, space sensor cost model. Office: Aerospace Corp PO Box 92957 El Segundo CA 90245

GROSS, BEATRICE MARIE, public relations manager; b. Wheatridge, Colo., Jan. 10, 1963; d. Billie G. and Monique M. (Hommes) G. BS, Met. State Coll. Denver, 1988, student Pub. Rels. Strategies, 1994; student Real Estate Mkt. Analysis, U. Colo. Denver, 1990. Office adminstr., legal sec. De Muth & Kemp, Denver, 1984-88; from receptionist, sec. to pub. rels. mgr. Beta West, Inc., Denver, 1988—. Mem. Pub. Rels. Soc. Am. Home: 4747 W 30th Ave Denver CO 80212-1634 Office: Beta West Inc 1050 17th St Ste 1000 Denver CO 80265-0101

GROSS, BRUCE L., insurance executive; b. Butte, Mont., Aug. 13, 1944; s. Raymond Leon and Eudessa May (Evans) G.; m. Dorna Parkinson, July 15, 1967 (dec. 1980); m. Carolyn O. Hart, Sept. 5, 1980; children: Shellie, Jason, Robert, Michael, Alex, Jill. BS in Bus. Mgmt., Ariz. State U., 1967, MS in Criminal Justice, 1978. Gen. mgr. Rays Markets, Inc., Kingman, Ariz., 1972-75; dir. vending ops. Ariz. State U., Tempe, 1975-78; dir. R&D Collegiate Products, Inc., Tulsa, 1978-79; owner, CEO Lafayette Electronics, Prescott, Ariz., 1979-80; pres., CEO Groco, Inc., Provo, Utah, 1980-84, Intermountain Planning, Inc., Provo, 1984-89, Ind. Systems, Inc., Salt Lake City, 1989—; bd. dirs., mem. ethics com. Nat. Indian Gaming Assn., Mpls.; mem. Pollard Bd. Govs., Houston, 1986-88. Capt. U.S. Army, 1968-72, Viet Nam. Mem. Internat. Legion Intelligence, Mensa. Republican. Mem. LDS Ch. Home: 1645 E 480 S Pleasant Grove UT 84062-3303

GROSS, GEORGE CLAYBURN, English language educator; b. Wilmington, Calif., May 14, 1922; s. Henry and Rebecca Ada (Bachman) G.; m. Marlo Vane Mumma, Apr. 30, 1941; children: George Timothy, John Henry. BA in English, San Diego State Coll., 1948, MA in English, 1950; PhD in English, U. So. Calif., L.A., 1963. Cert. gen. secondary tchr., Calif. Tchr. English Grossmont H.S., El Cajon, Calif., 1948-49; instr. English San Diego State Coll., 1949-51; head English dept. Grossmont H.S., El Cajon, 1951-61; grad. teaching asst. U. So. Calif., L.A., 1959-60; from asst. to assoc. to full prof. San Diego State U., 1961-85, assoc. dean faculty pers., 1970-72, dean of faculty affairs, 1972-81, prof. English, 1981-85, prof. English emeritus, 1985—; cons. Sweetwater Sch. Dist., Chula Vista, Calif., 1967-68, Calif. State Com. on Pub. Edn., Berkeley, 1967; lectr. in field. Contbr. articles to scholarly jours. 2d lt. U.S. Army, 1943-45, ETO. Scholar U. So. Calif., 1960. Mem. AAUP (officer 1969-70, chpt. v.p.), MLA, Keats-Shelley Assn., Phi Beta Kappa (chpt. sec. 1977-80, spl. award 1985), Phi Kappa Phi (chpt. pres. 1969-70, svc. award 1985). Home: 4025 Citradora Dr Spring Valley CA 91977-1127 Office: San Diego State U Dept English San Diego CA 92182

GROSS, HAL RAYMOND, bishop; b. Walla Walla, Wash., Jan. 15, 1914; s. John J. and Millie (Hale) G.; m. Evelyn Blythe Kerr, July 22, 1933; 1 dau., Patricia Ann Gross Simmons. Student, Oreg. State U., 1931-36; J.D., Willamette U., 1939; student, Ch. Div. Sch. of Pacific, 1946, D.D., 1965. Bar: Oreg. bar 1939. Pvt. practice in Corvallis, 1939-42; atty. Oreg. Unemployment Compensation Commn., 1942-44; ordained to ministry Episcopal Ch., 1946; pastor U. Oreg., 1946-47; rector St. Paul's Ch., Oregon City, 1947-61; archdeacon Episcopal Diocese Oreg., 1961-65; suffragan bishop Oreg., 1965-79; ret., 1979; mem. exec. council Episcopal Ch., 1975-79; vice chmn. Ho. of Bishops, 1976-79. Trustee Ch. Div. Sch. of Pacific, 1950-55, 72-73. Mem. Oreg. Bar Assn., Phi Delta Theta. Democrat. Club: Rotary (hon.). Home: 8255 SW Fairway Dr Wilsonville OR 97070-9419

GROSS, JOSEPH FRANCIS, retired bio-engineering educator; b. Plauen, Fed. Republic of Germany, Aug. 22, 1932; s. Joseph and Helen (Doelling) G. BSChemE, Pratt Inst., 1953; PhDChemE, Purdue U., 1956. Research engr., staff mem. Rand Corp., Santa Monica, Calif., 1958-72; prof. chem. engring. U. Ariz., Tucson, 1972-92, emeritus prof. chem. engring. and physiology, 1992—, head chem. engring. dept., 1975-81, dir. Ariz. rsch. labs. microcirculation divsn., 1981—. Editor: Mathematics of Microcirculation Phenomena, 1980; co-editor: Finite Elements in Biomechanics, 1982; contbr. articles to profl. jours. Recipient Humboldt U.S. Sr. Scientist award Alexander von Humboldt Found., 1979. Fellow AIAA (assoc.), AICE, Am. Inst. Med. and Biol. Engrs. (founding mem.), ASME; mem. Am. Physiol. Soc., Microcirculatory Soc. (pres. 1976-77), Internat. INst. Microcirculation (sec., treas. 1983—), Internat. Soc. Biorheology (treas. 1982-86). Home: PO Box 41445 Tucson AZ 85717-1445 Office: U Ariz Dept Physiology Tucson AZ 85724

GROSS, MICHAEL DAVID, lawyer; b. Brookings, S.D., Dec. 16, 1946; s. Guilford Carroll and Hope Allison (Blewitt) G.; m. Susan Kaye Doner, Aug. 16, 1969; 1 son, Christopher Michael. BA, No. State Coll., Aberdeen, S.D., 1969; JD, U. S.D., 1972. Bar: Colo. 1976, U.S. Dist. Ct. Colo. 1976. Text writer Shepard's, Inc., Colorado Springs, Colo., 1973-76; ptnr. Barber & Gross, Colorado Springs, 1976-80, Gross & Andersson, Colorado Springs, 1980-84, Andersson, Gerig, Gross & Lederer, P.C., 1985-86, pvt. practice, Colorado Springs, 1986—. Bd. dirs., officer Colorado Springs Civic Theatre, 1979-81. Served to capt. USAR, 1969-76. Mem. ATLA, Colo. Trial Lawyers Assn., Order Barristers. Republican. Episcopalian. Club: Torch (pres. 1982-83) (Colorado Springs). Home: 515 Pluto Dr Colorado Springs CO 80906-1025 Office: 1771 S 8th St Colorado Springs CO 80906

GROSS, RICHARD PHILIP, retired business executive; b. San Francisco, Aug. 13, 1903; s. Louis and Ida (Solomon) G.; m. Marion Brownstone, Dec. 7, 1924 (dec. 1981) 1 child, Richard P. Jr. (dec.); m. Lila North, Jan. 8, 1982 (dec. 1982); m. Ruth Heller, Mar. 21, 1987. Student, Stanford U., 1924. Sec. Nat. Smelting Co., San Francisco, 1923-26; salesman Louis Forester, San Francisco, 1926-28; gen. ptnr. Richard P. Gross and Co., San Francisco, 1928-41, Kanter and Gross, San Francisco, 1941-46; gen. ptnr. Stone and Youngberg, San Francisco, 1946-75, ltd. ptnr., 1975—; bd. dirs. David Rabb Real Estate Investment Trust; gov. San Francisco Curb Exch., 1932-38, pres. 1935-38; gov. San Francisco Stock Exch., 1949-50, Pacific Coast Stock Exch., San Francisco, 1957, 58, 68. Mem. Concordia-Argonaut Club (bd. dirs. 1935), City Club. Republican. Jewish. Home: 999 Green St San Francisco CA 94133-3662

GROSS, SHARON RUTH, forensic psychologist, researcher; b. L.A., Mar. 21, 1940; d. Louis and Sylvia Marion (Freedman) Lackman; m. Zoltan Gross, Mar. 1969 (div.); 1 child, Andrew Ryan; m. Ira Chroman, June 1994. BA, UCLA, 1983; MA, U. So. Calif., L.A., 1985, PhD, 1991. Tech. Rytron, Van Nuys, Calif., 1958-60; computress on tetrahedral satellite Space Tech. Labs., Redondo Beach, Calif., 1960-62; owner Wayfarer Yacht Corp., Costa Mesa, Calif., 1962-64; electronics draftsperson, designer stroke-writer characters Tasker Industries, Van Nuys, 1964-65; pvt. practice cons. Sherman Oaks, Calif., 1965-75, 77-80; printed circuit bd. designer Systron-Donner, Van Nuys, Calif., 1975-76; design checker, tech. writer Vector Gen., Woodland Hills, CAlif., 1976-77; undergrad. adv. U. So. Calif., L.A., 1987-89, rsch. asst. prof., rsch. assoc. social psychology, 1991—; Owner Attitude Rsch. Legal and Orgnl. Cons. Contbr. chpts. to books. Mem. ACLU, L.A., 1991. Recipient Haynes Found. Dissertation fellowship U. So. Calif., 1990. Mem. APA (student dissertation rsch. award 1991), AAAS, Computer Graphics Pioneers, Am. Psychol. Soc., Western Psychol. Assn. Democrat. Jewish. Office: U So Calif Dept Psychology Los Angeles CA 90089-1061

GROSS, WILLIAM H., financial analyst, insurance company executive; b. Middletown, Ohio, Apr. 13, 1944; children: Jeff, Jennifer. BA in Psychology, Duke U., 1966; MBA in Fin., UCLA, 1971. Chartered Fin. Analyst. Investment analyst Pacific Mut. Life Ins. Co., Newport Beach, Calif., 1971-73, sr. analyst, 1973-76, asst. v.p., Fixed Income Securities, 1976-78, 2d v.p., Fixed Income Securities, 1978-80, v.p. Fixed Income Securities, 1980-82; mng. dir. Pacific Investment Mgmt. Co. subs. Pacific Mut. Life Ins. Co., Newport Beach, Calif., 1982—; regular panelist Wall Street Week with Louis Rukeyser TV program. Mem. L.A. Soc. Fin. Analysts. Office: Pacific Investment Mgmt Co 840 Newport Ctr Dr PO Box 9000 Newport Beach CA 92660

GROSSETETE, GINGER LEE, gerontology administrator, consultant; b. Riverside, Calif., Feb. 9, 1936; d. Lee Roy Taylor and Bonita (Beryl) Williams; m. Alec Paul Grossetete, June 8, 1954; children: Elizabeth Gay Blech, Teri Lee Zeni. BA in Recreation cum laude, U. N.Mex., 1974, M in Pub. Adminstrn., 1978. Sr. ctr. supr., Office of Sr. Affairs, City of Albuquerque, 1974-77, asst. dir. Office of Sr. Affairs, 1977—; conf. coord. Nat. Consumers Assn., Albuquerque, 1978-79; region 6 del. Nat. Coun. on Aging, Washington, 1977-84; conf. chmn. Western Gerontol. Soc., Albuquerque, 1983; del. White House Conf. on Aging from N.Mex., 1995. Contbr. articles to mags. Campaign dir. March of Dimes N.Mex., 1966-67; pres. Albuquerque Symphony Women's Assn., 1972; mem. exec. com. Jr. League Albuquerque, 1976; mem. Gov.'s Coun. on Phys. Fitness, 1987-91, chmn. 1990-91. Recipient N.Mex. Disting. Pub. Service award N.Mex. Gov.'s Office, 1983, Disting. Woman on the Move award YWCA, 1986. Fellow Nat. Recreation and Pk. Assn. (bd. dirs. S.W. regional coun. rep., bd. dir. leisure and aging sect., pres. N.Mex. chpt. 1983-84, Outstanding Profl. award 1982); mem. Am. Soc. Pub. Adminstrn. (pres. N.Mex. coun. 1987-88), S.W. Soc. on Aging (pres. 1984-85, bd. dirs., Outstanding Profl. award 1991), U. N.Mex. Alumni Assn. (bd. dirs. 1978-80, Disting. Alumni award 1985), Las Amapolas Garden Club (pres. 1964), Pi Alpha Alpha, Chi Omega (pres. alumni 1959-60), Pi Lambda Theta. Home: 517 La Veta Dr NE Albuquerque NM 87108-1403 Office: Office of Sr Affairs 714 7th St SW Albuquerque NM 87102-3814

GROSSKOPF, BARRY, psychiatrist, consultant; b. Breslau, Germany, Nov. 1, 1945; came to U.S., 1949; s. Israel and Evelyn (Mendolwicz) G.; m.

Myrna Ethel Slotsky, Aug. 14, 1966 (div. July 1983); children: David Dylan, Lauren Rebecca; m. Wendy Lustbader, Mar. 1, 1987. BS with high honors, U. Fla., 1966; MD, U. Miami, 1970. Diplomate Am. Bd. Psychiatry and Neurology. Intern Va. Mason Hosp., Seattle, 1970-71; resident in psychiatry U. Wash., Seattle, 1974-77; pvt. practice, 1977-91; cons. psychiatrist Cedar Hills, Maple Valley, Wash., 1990—; Helped establish migrant worker clinic, Perrine, Fla., 1968, outreach program Dade County Jail, Miami, 1968; with Appalachia Project AMSA, Lebanon, Va., 1969; gen. practice Group Health Coop. Puget Sound, Burien, Wash., 1971; founder Comprehensive Cmty. Family Practice Clinic, Glenville, W.Va., 1972; county pub. health officer Gilmer County, W.Va., 1972-74; physician cons. outreach for older adults King County Dept. Pub. Health, Seattle, 1977-78; spkr., lectr. in field. With USPHS, 1972-74. Recipient Pioneer award Nat. Health Svc. Corps, 1992. Mem. Am. Psychiat. Assn., Wash. State Psychiat. Assn., Wash. Assn. Community Psychiatrists, King County Med. Soc. Jewish. Office: Cedar Hills 15900 227th Ave SE Maple Valley WA 98038-6207

GROSSMAN, GEORGE STEFAN, library director, law educator; b. Poltar, Czechoslovakia, May 31, 1938; m. Suzi Herczeg, 1960; 1 child, Zoltan. B.A., U. Chgo., 1960; LL.B., Stanford U., 1966; M.A. in Library Sci., Brigham Young U., 1971. Bar: Calif. 1966, Minn. 1974. Tech. processes law librarian U. Pa., 1966-68; assoc. prof. law, law librarian U. Utah, 1968-70, prof., law librarian, 1970-73; prof., dir. law library U. Minn., 1973-79, Northwestern U., Chgo., 1979-93; with U. Calif., Davis, 1993—; cons. to univs. Author: Legal Research: Historical Foundations of the Electronic Age, 1994; contbr. articles to legal jours. Mem. Indian rights com. ACLU, 1973-92, pres. Utah affiliate, 1972-73, bd. dirs. Ill. affiliate, 1982-87. Mem. Am. Assn. Law Libraries, Internat. Assn. Law Libraries. Office: U Calif Sch Law Libr King Hall Davis CA 95616

GROSSMAN, RICHARD, obstetrician/gynecologist; b. Phila., July 13, 1943; s. Louis I. and Emma May (MacIntyre) G.; m. Gail Sise, June 18, 1966; children: David, Bryan. BA, Swarthmore Coll., 1965; MD, U. Pa., 1969; MPH, Loma Linda U., 1993. Diplomate Am. Bd. Ob.-Gyn. Med. intern Hartford (Conn.) Hosp., 1969-70; gen. practitioner Presbyn. Med. Svcs., Questa, N.Mex., 1970-73; resident in ob-gyn. U. N.Mex., Albuquerque, 1973-76; obstetrician-gynecologist, shareholder Durango (Colo.) OB-GYN Assocs. PC, 1976—; contract gynecologist Planned Parenthood of the Rocky Mountains, Durango, 1976—; obstetrician-gynecologist Hosp. General Castañer, P.R., 1983-84; clin. asst. prof. U. N.Mex., Albuquerque, 1976—, U. Colo., Denver, 1990—; preceptor U. N.Mex. Dept. Family Practice, Albuquerque, 1976—. Patentee for Improved Condom, Needle Safety Guard; contbg. author gynecologist's column Woman's World, 1984-88; contbr. articles to profl. jours. Recipient Cert. of Appreciation Colo. Assist Alliance, Denver, 1993, Plaques of Appreciation Hosp. General Castañer, P.R., 1984, Planned Parenthood of Rocky Mountains, Denver, 1991, LaPlata County Prevention Ptnrs., Durango, 1994. Fellow Am. Coll. Ob-Gyn.; mem. APHA (chair membership com., sect. population, family planning & reproductive health), Assn. Reproductive Health Profls., Nat. Coun. for Internat. Health, Soc. for Advancement of Contraception. Quaker. Office: Durango OB-GYN Assocs PC 375 E Park Ave # 3C Durango CO 81301

GROSSMAN, ROBERT JAMES, architect; b. Spokane, Wash., Feb. 3, 1936; s. George Christian and Corinne (Shelton) G.; m. Shirley Rozelle, Aug. 7, 1956; children: Kevin James, Heidi Rozelle. B Archtl. Engring. with highest honors, Wash. State U., 1959. Lic. architect, Wash. Architect Heylman-Trogdon, Spokane, 1962-64, Trogdon-Smith, Architects, Spokane, 1964-72; prin. architect Trogdon-Smith-Grossman, TSG Architects, Spokane, 1973-83; mng. prin. N.W. Archtl. Co. (A Joint Venture), Spokane, 1979-83; pres., prin. N.W. Archtl. Co., P.S., Seattle, 1983-85, mng. prin., 1986—; coord. architect for site planning and devel. Expo'74 World's Fair, Spokane, 1971-74; mem. adv. coun. Sch. Architecture Wash. State U., Pullman, 1986-93, mem. adv. bd. Coll. Engring. and Architecture, 1991—. Prin. works include 15 elem. schs., Spokane, sch. projects, pvt. and pub. projects. Bd. dirs., pres. Salvation Army-Booth Care Ctr., Spokane, 1972-85; bd. dirs. Med. Svc. Corp., Spokane, 1984-86; mem. state adv. bd. Lien Law Reform, 1990; founding pres. Downtown Exch. Club of Seattle Found., 1990—; mem. adv. bd. for master planning Children's Hosp., Seattle, 1991-94; vice chair Wash. State Archs. and Engrs. Legis. Coun., 1994—. 1st. lt. C.E., U.S. Army, 1960-62. Recipient Disting. Svc. award Govt. State of Wash. and State Commn. for Expo '74, 1974. Mem. AIA (pres. Spokane chpt. 1976), Wash. State Coun. Architects (bd. dirs. 1975-78), Wash. State U. Alumni Assn. (Alumni Achievement award 1990), Exch. Club (bd. dirs. 1988-91). Office: NW Archtl Co 303 Battery St Seattle WA 98121-1419

GROSSMAN, SEYMOUR, gastroenterologist; b. Newark, July 5, 1933; s. Abraham and Sally Gertrude (Pilchman) G.; m. Bonnie Jane Simon Grossman, June 26, 1955; children: Michael Joseph, Deborah Joan. Student, MIT, 1950-53; MD, NYU Coll. Medicine, 1957. Diplomate Am. Bd. Internal Medicine, 1964; cert. Gastroenterology, 1969. Rotating intern Cleve. Metro. Gen. Hosp., 1957-58; internal medicine resident, 1958-61; rsch. fellow, clin. trainee N.Y. Hosp.-Cornell Med. Ctr., 1961-63; clin. instr. Cornell U. Med. Ctr., 1963-65, U. Calif. Sch. Medicine, San Francisco, 1965-67; clin. asst. prof. U. Tex. Sch. Medicine, San Antonio, 1967-69; asst. clin. prof. U. Calif. San Francisco, 1967-75, assoc. clin. prof., 1975-84, clin. prof., 1984—; pres. staff assn. Kaiser Found. Hosp., 1974, mem. libr. com., 1974—, chmn., 1974-82, mem. well-being com., 1983—. Contbr. articles to profl. jours. Mem. Am. Gastroent. Assn., Am. Soc. for Gastrointestinal Endoscopy, No. Calif. Soc. for Clin. Gastroenterology (pres. 1984), Phi Lambda Upsilon. Home: 2661 Cedar St Berkeley CA 94708-1933 Office: Kaiser Permanente 280 W Macarthur Blvd Oakland CA 94611-5642

GROSSMAN, YAFFA LINDA, plant physiological ecologist; b. Upland, Calif., Sept. 22, 1955; d. Sherwin Alvin and Adele Eleanor (Nye) G. BA in Math., Amherst Coll., 1978; MS in Botany, U. Mass., 1981; PhD in Botany, U. Calif., Davis, 1993. Co-coord. Amherst (Mass.) Water Conservation Project, 1980-81; rsch. assoc. Pub. Affairs Office, Ecol. Soc. Am., Washington, 1987-89; grad. fellow, teaching asst. U. Calif., Davis, 1982-87, rsch. asst., 1989-92, post grad. researcher, 1993—; steering com. network for grad. and faculty women U. Calif., Davis, 1984-87; sci. rsch. task force Water Supply Citizen's Adv. Com., Commonwealth of Mass., 1980-82; participant Biotech. Network, Washington, 1987-89. Contbr. articles to Ecology, Tree Physiology, Annals of Botany, Hort Sci. Mem. Amherst Town Meeting, 1981-82. Mem. AAAS, Am. Soc. Plant Physiologists, Ecol. Soc. Am., Bot. Soc. Am., Am. Soc. Hort. Sci. Office: U Calif Dept Pomology Davis CA 95616

GROUSSMAN, RAYMOND G., diversified utility and energy company executive, lawyer; b. Price, Utah, Dec. 15, 1935; s. Raymond K. and Gene E. (Goetzman) G.; m. Marilyn Kaye Jensen, Mar. 16, 1964; children: Katherine Anne Hajeb, Laura Kaye Hunter, Daniel Ray, Adam J. B.S., U. Utah, 1961, J.D., 1966. Bar: Utah 1965, U.S. Supreme Ct. 1978. Police officer Salt Lake City Police Dept., 1962-66; mem. firm Amoss & Groussman, Salt Lake City, 1966-69; staff atty. Utah Legal Services, 1969-70; chief dep. Salt Lake County atty., 1970-71; assoc. Pugsley, Hayes, Watkiss, Campbell & Cowley, Salt Lake City, 1971-74; gen. counsel Mountain Fuel Supply Co., Salt Lake City, 1974-84; v.p. Mountain Fuel Supply Co., 1977-84; v.p., gen. counsel Questar Corp., 1984—; bd. dirs. Wexpro Co., Celsius Energy Co. Bd. dirs. Children's Svc. Soc. Utah, 1976-77; trustee Ft. Douglas Mil. Mus., 1976-84; bd. advisers Energy Law Ctr., U. Utah Coll. Law, 1978—; mem. criminal law revision com. Utah Legis. Coun.; bd. dirs. Utah Legal Svcs., 1970-78; United Way of Salt Lake City, 1982-89; mem. bd. litigation Mountain States Legal Found., 1990—. With U.S. Army, 1957-60, lt. comdr. USCGR, 1967-85, ret. Mem. ABA, Fed. Energy Bar Assn., Am. Gas Assn., Pacific Coast Gas Assn. (chmn. legal adv. coun. 1979-80, 93-94), Salt Lake County Bar Assn., Salt Lake Legal Defenders Assn. (dir. 1978—), Am. Corp. Counsel Assn. (bd. dirs. Intermountain chpt. 1990-94), Salt Lake City C. of C., Sigma Alpha Epsilon, Delta Theta Phi. Office: Questar Corp 180 E 100 S Salt Lake City UT 84139-1000

GROUT, MARILYN ANN, geologist, researcher; b. Albion, N.Y., July 10, 1943; d. Harold Miller and Arline Caroline (Klafehn) Higley; m. Richard Vernon Grout, Nov. 26, 1965. BS in Edn., SUNY, Brockport, 1964; MS in Geology, U. Colo., 1981, PhD in Geology, 1990. Tchr. Centereach (N.Y.) Schs., 1964-65, Dept. Def., Yokota AFB, Japan, 1966-69, Paxton (Mass.) Schs., 1969-70; tchg. asst. dept. geology U. Colo., Boulder, 1978-79; geol. field asst., geologist U.S. Geol. Survey, Denver, 1981-88, rsch. geologist, 1988—. Contbr. numerous articles on natural fracture systems to profl. jours. Fellow Geol. Soc. Am.; mem. Am. Assn. Petroleum Geologists (Best Paper award 1992), Internat. Assn. Structural/Tectonic Geologists, Rocky Mountain Assn. Geologists, Fluorescent Mineral Soc., Franklin/Ogdensburg Mineral Soc. Office: US Geol Survey Fed Ctr MS 913 Box 25046 Denver CO 80225

GROVE, ANDREW S., electronics company executive; b. Budapest, Hungary, 1936; married; 2 children. B.S., CCNY, 1960, DSc (hon.), 1985; Ph.D., U. Calif.-Berkeley, 1963; DEng (hon.), Worcester Poly. Inst., 1989. With Fairchild Camera and Instrument Co., 1963-67; pres., COO, Intel Corp., Santa Clara, Calif., 1967-87, pres., CEO, 1987—, also bd. dirs. Recipient medal Am. Inst. Chemists, 1960, Merit cert. Franklin Inst., 1975, Townsend Harris medal CCNY, 1980, Enterprise award Profl. Advt. Assn., 1987, George Washington award Am. Hungarian Found., 1990, Citizen of Yr. award World Forum Silicon Valley, 1993, Exec. of Yr. award U. Ariz., 1993, Achievement medal AEA, 1993, Heinz Family Found. award for tech. and economy, 1995. Fellow IEEE (Achievement award 1969, J.J. Ebers award 1974, Engring. Leadership Recognition award 1987), Acad. Arts and Scis.; mem. Nat. Acad. Engring. Office: Intel Corp PO Box 58119 2200 Mission College Blvd Santa Clara CA 95052-8119*

GROVE, DOUGLAS DAVID, insurance company executive; b. Oakland, Calif., Aug. 6, 1957; s. David Malley and Kathleen Lillian (Hogan) G.; m. Gail DeBenedictis, Sept. 12, 1992. BS in Bus. Adminstrn., U. Pacific, Stockton, Calif., 1980. CPCU. Property underwriter trainee, underwriter Kemper Group, San Francisco, 1980-85; comml. account underwriter Northbrook Property & Casualty Co., San Francisco, 1985-86; comml. underwriter Chubb Ins. Cos., San Francisco, 1986-87; sr. underwriter nat. accounts Fireman's Fund Ins. Cos., San Rafael, Calif., 1987-88, exec. underwriter nat. accounts, 1988-93; exec. underwriter nat. brokerage unit Fireman's Fund, Novato, Calif., 1993—. Mem. Cert. Property and Casualty Underwriters, Assocs. in Risk Mgmt. Office: Fireman's Fund Ins Co Nat Broker Ctr 777 San Marin Dr Novato CA 94998-0001

GROVER, JAMES ROBB, chemist, editor; b. Klamath Falls, Oreg., Sept. 16, 1928; s. James Richard and Marjorie Alida (van Groos) G.; m. Barbara Jean Ton, Apr. 14, 1957; children: Jonathan Robb, Patricia Jean. BS summa cum laude, valedictorian, U. Wash., Seattle, 1952; PhD, U. Calif., Berkeley, 1958. Rsch. assoc. Brookhaven Nat. Lab., Upton, N.Y., 1957-59, assoc. chemist, 1959-63, chemist, 1963-67, chemist with tenure, 1967-77, sr. chemist, 1978-93, rsch. collaborator, 1993—; cons. Lawrence Livermore (Calif.) Nat. Lab., 1962; assoc. editor Ann. Rev. of Nuclear Sci., Ann. Revs., Inc., Palo Alto, Calif., 1967-77; vis. prof. Inst. for Molecular Sci., Okazaki, Japan, 1986-87; vis. scientist Max-Planck Inst. für Strömungsforschung, Göttingen, Fed. Republic Germany, 1975-76. Contbr. numerous articles to profl. jours. With USN, 1946-48. Mem. Am. Chem. Soc. (chmn. nuclear chemistry and tech. 1989), Am. Phys. Soc., Triple Nine Soc., Sigma Xi, Phi Beta Kappa, Phi Lambda Upsilon, Zeta Mu Tau, Pi Mu Epsilon. Libertarian. Presbyterian. Home and Office: 1536 Pinecrest Ter Ashland OR 97520-3427

GROVER, STUART RALPH, management consultant; b. Newark; s. Sidney and Edith Norma (Glazer) G. BA, U. Wis., 1965, MA, 1966, PhD, 1971. Asst. prof. history Vanderbilt U., Nashville, 1971-75, Witteberg U., Springfield, Ohio, 1975-77, Ohio State U., Columbus, 1977-78; assoc. dir. continuing edn. Ohio State U., Columbia, 1979-81; pub., editor Northside Herald, Columbus, Ohio, 1981-82; dir. pub. rels. Mus. History & Industry, Seattle, 1982-84; pres. Stuart Grover & Assocs., Seattle, 1984-90, The Collins Group, Inc., Seattle and Portland, Oreg., 1990—; nat. panelist NEH Challenge Grant Program, 1989, 90; presenter in field. Contbr. articles to profl. jours. Bd. dirs. Allied Arts, 1987-88, Artist Trust, 1987-88, Seattle/King County Conv. and Visitors Bur., 1984-89, Friends of Chamber Music, Portland, Oreg., 1992—; mem. oversight com. African-Am. Heritage Ctr. Project City of Seattle Dept. Community Devel., 1987; mem. tech. adv. group for hist. bldg. code State Bldg. Code Coun., 1990; founder Oreg. Artist Trust, 1993-94, Group Health Found., 1994—; active Seattle Leadership Tomorrow, 1987. Recipient Young Scholar award NEH, 1975-75. Home: 2204 NE Klickitat St Portland OR 97212-2461 Office: The Collins Group Inc 101 Stewart St Ste 840 Seattle WA 98101-1048

GROVES, MARTHA, newspaper writer. Computer writer L.A. Times. Office: LA Times Times Mirror Sq Los Angeles CA 90012-3816

GROVES, SHERIDON HALE, orthopedic surgeon; b. Denver, Mar. 5, 1947; s. Harry Edward Groves and Dolores Ruth (Hale) Finley; m. Deborah Rita Threadgill, Mar. 29, 1970 (div. Apr. 1980); children: Jason, Tiffany; m. Nanely Marie Lamont, July 1, 1980 (div. Dec. 1987); 1 child, Dolores; m. Elaine Robbins, Feb. 7, 1991. BS, U.S. Mil. Acad., 1969; MD, U. Va., Charlottesville, 1976. Commd. 2nd lt. US Army, 1969, advanced through grades to maj.; surg. intern US Army, El Paso, Tex., 1976-77, orthopedic surgery resident, 1977-80; staff orthopedic surgeon US Army, Killeen, Tex., 1980-83; resigned US Army, 1983; staff emergency physician various emergency depts. State of Tex., 1983-84, 87; emergency dept. dir. Victoria (Tex.) Regional Med. Ctr., 1984-86; med. dir. First Walk-In Clinic Victoria, 1986-87; tchr. U. Tex. Med. Br., Galveston, 1986-90; emergency dept. dir. Gulf Coast Med. Ctr., 1988-89; with Amerimed Corp., 1990-92, Primedex Corp., 1992-93; clinic med. dir, staff orthopedic surgeon Pain Relief Network, 1993—; lectr. Speakers Bur., Victoria, 1984-86, Cato Inst., Ludwig Von Mises Inst. Contbr. articles to profl. jours. Mem. Victoria Interagy. Council Sexual Abuse, 1984-86; treas. bd. dirs. Youth Home Victoria, 1986-90. Recipient Physician's Recognition award AMA, 1980, 83, 86, 89, 92. Fellow Am. Acad. Neurologic and Orthopedic Surgeons; mem. Soc. Mil. Orthopedic Surgeons, Am. Coll. Emergency Physicians, Tex. Med. Found., Assn. Grads. of U.S. Mil. Acad. (life), Am. Assn. Disability Evaluation Physicians, Coalition of Med. Providers, Am. Coll. Sports Medicine, Am. Running and Fitness Assn. (cert. recognition 1987), Internat. Coll. Surgeons (vice regent), Internat. Martial Arts Assn., Hurricane Sports Club of Houston, Smithsonian Assocs., So. Calif. Striders Track Club.

GROVES, WILLIAM RALPH, actor; b. Barnesville, Ohio, Jan. 7, 1922; s. William Roy and Mary Lee (Bailey) G.; m. Ruby Elizabeth Groves, Oct. 12, 1942 (dec. 1963); children: Andrea Duffy, Nancy Spiker; m. Alice Joy Crawford, May 17, 1973. Student, Ohio State U., 1946-49; student, Franklin U., 1949-50. Radio, TV announcer various stas., Ohio, Ill., Tex., 1951-56; film, TV actor various studios, Hollywood, Calif., 1956—; owner, operator, dir., writer Groves' Lincoln Cabin Theater, Morongo Valley, Calif., 1986—. Screenwriter: Thunder on the Rio, 1958, Teenage Scarface, 1962; playwright: (stage plays) The Life and Times of Abraham Lincoln. Mem. Desert Theatre League, Palm Springs, Calif., 1988— (pres. 1989-90). Sgt. USAAF, 1940-45. Named Best Actor in Drama, Desert Theatre League, 1989, Outstanding Playwright, 1990, Best Dir., 1992, Best Stage Drama, 1993. Mem. Dramatists Guild, Screen Actors Guild (hon.), Am. Legion. Home: 8768 Desert Willow Trl Morongo Valley CA 92256-9516

GRUBAUGH, STEVEN JACK, education educator; b. Robinson, Ill., Oct. 8, 1946; s. Andrew Jackson and Evelyn Jane (Reeder) G.; m. Barbara Irene Steele; children: Anna Kathryn, Jessica Jo. BA in English, Calif. State U., Sonoma, 1970; MA in Reading, U. No. Colo., 1975, EdD, 1981. Cert. English and Reading tchr., Colo. Tchr. reading & English Reed Jr. High Sch., Loveland, Colo., 1975-79; workshop co-dir. U. No. Colo., Greeley, 1978-79, teaching asst., 1979-81; asst. prof. U. New Orleans, 1981-87, assoc. prof., 1987-91; prof. U. Nev., Las Vegas, 1991—; bd. dirs. Spl. Plan to Upgrade Reading, New Orleans, 1983-84, La. Reading Assn., 1983-84; cons. in field. Contbr. articles to profl. jours. Grantee in field including La. Edn. Quality Support Fund. Mem. La. Coll. Tchrs. of Reading (sec., treas. 1988-90, pres. 1991), Coll. Reading Internat. Reading Assn. (parlimentarian 1984-86), Colo. Internat. Reading Assn., Thompson Council of the Internat. Reading Assn. Democrat. Episcopalian. Home: 1805 Walker Ln Henderson NV 89014-4015 Office: U Nev Dept Instrnl & Curr Studies 4505 S Maryland Pky Las Vegas NV 89154-3005

GRUBB, DAVID H., construction company president; b. 1936; married. BSCE, Princeton U.; MSCE, Stanford U. With Swinerton and Walberg Co., San Francisco, 1964—, sr. v.p., then exec. v.p. SF San Structural div., exec. v.p. ops., now pres., also bd. dirs.; pres. Lindgren Holdings Inc., 1993—; chmn. bd. Conelly Construction Inc., 1993—. Office: Swinerton & Walberg Co 580 California St San Francisco CA 94104-1000*

GRUBB, L(EWIS) CRAIG, investment company executive, consultant; b. Canton, Ohio, June 1, 1954; s. Lewis G. and Janet M. (Hornback) G.; m. Carol Elizabeth Norvell, Dec. 19, 1981; children: Carie Lynne, Chelsea Michelle. Student, W.Va. Wesleyan Coll., 1972-74. Regional rep. IDS/Am. Express Corp., Tucson, 1982-84; v.p. Mut. Benefit Fin. Group, Tucson, 1984-86, Am. Fin. Cos. (formerly Estate Fin. Services Ltd.), Tucson, 1986-88; also bd. dirs. Estate Fin. Svcs. Ltd., Tucson; fin. cons. Merrill Lynch, Tucson, 1989-94; investment advisor Rauscher, Pierce, Refsnes, Tucson, 1994—. Trustee Carondelet Found., Tucson, 1995, chmn. investment and fin. com., 1995—; bd. dirs. Desert Survivors Inc., Tucson, 1984-86, Carondelet Health Care Sys., 1995—, mem. fin. com., 1995—; chmn. investment com. Carondelet Found., 1995—, trustee, chmn. investment com., chmn. fin. com., 1995—. Mem. Masons. Republican. Home: 10621 E Sundance Cir Tucson AZ 85749-9540 Office: Rauscher Pierce Refsnes 3561 E Sunrise Dr Ste 125 Tucson AZ 85718-3204

GRUBER, ANDRAS, physician, researcher; b. Budapest, Hungary, Jan. 10, 1954; came to U.S., 1986; s. Gyula Foky Gruber and Edit Kardos; m. Anna Szemere, Nov. 1, 1975; 1 child, Nora. BS, Radnòti Sch. of Eötvös L. U., Budapest, 1972; MD, Semmelweis Med. U., Budapest, 1979. Cert. in internal medicine. Resident Postgrad. Med. Sch., Budapest, 1979-84, mem. med. staff, 1984-85; mem. med. staff Szönyi Tibor Hosp., Vác, Hungary, 1985-86; postdoctoral fellow Scripps Clinic and Rsch. Found., La Jolla, Calif., 1986-89, rsch. assoc., 1989-91; sr. rsch. assoc. The Scripps Rsch. Inst., La Jolla, 1991—, asst. mem., 1992—, adj. asst. mem., 1994—; assoc. med. dir. DepoTech Corp., La Jolla, 1994—; lectr. in field, 1986—. Contbr. 31 articles to profl. jours., also book chpts., abstracts; patentee in field. Rsch. fellow Immuno Ag. Austria/Scripps Clinic, 1986, Am. Heart Assn./Calif. Affiliate, 1989; rsch. grantee U. Calif. Tobacco-Related Disease Rsch. Program, 1991. Mem. Soc. of Fellows of Scripps Clinic & Rsch. Found., Internat. Soc. Thrombosis & Hemostasis, Am. Heart Assn. Coun. on Thrombosis, N.Y. Acad. Scis. Office: DepoTech Corp 11025 N Torrey Pines Rd La Jolla CA 92037-1030

GRUCHALLA, MICHAEL EMERIC, electronics engineer; b. Houston, Feb. 2, 1946; s. Emeric Edwin and Myrtle (Priebe) G.; m. Elizabeth Tyson, June 14, 1969; children: Kenny, Katie. BSEE, U. Houston, 1968; MSEE, U. N.Mex., 1980. Registered profl. engr., Tex. Project engr. Tex. Instruments Corp., Houston, 1967-68; group leader EG&G Washington Analytical Services Ctr., Albuquerque, 1974-88; engring. specialist EG&G Energy Measurements Inc., Albuquerque, 1988—; cons. engring., Albuquerque; lectr. in field, 1978—. Contbr. articles to tech. jours.; patentee in field. Judge local sci. fairs, Albuquerque, 1983—. Served to capt. USAF, 1968-74. Recipient R&D 100 award, 1991, Gen. Mgr.'s Vision award Dept. Energy, 1994. Mem. IEEE, Instrumentation Soc. Am., Planetary Soc., N.Mex. Tex. Instruments Computer Group (pres. 1984-85), Sigma Xi, Tau Beta Pi, Eta Kappa Nu. Office: EG&G Energy Measurements Inc Kirtland Ops PO Box 4339 Albuquerque NM 87196-4339

GRUEN, CLAUDE, economist, consultant; b. Bonn, Aug. 17, 1931; came to U.S., 1938; s. Walter and Elsbet (Bronne) G.; m. Nina Jaffe Gruen, Sept. 11, 1960; children: Les, Dale, Adam, Joshua, Aaron. BBA, U. Cin., 1954, MA, 1962, PhD, 1964. Instr. Xavier U., Cin., 1963-64; lectr. U. Calif., Berkeley, 1964-70; economist Arthur D. Little Inc., San Francisco, 1964-70; pres., prin. economist Gruen Gruen & Assocs., San Francisco, 1970—; dir. Rreef Am. Reit, Inc., 1994—. Co-author: Low and Moderate Income Housing, 1972; contbg. editor Instl. Real Estate Letter, 1991—; contbr. articles to profl. jours. Capt. USAF, 1954-57. Mem. Urban Land Inst. (mixed use coun.), Western Regional Sci. Assn., Am. Assn. Econs., Lambda Alpha Real Estate. Jewish. Office: Gruen Gruen & Assocs 564 Howard St San Francisco CA 94105-3002

GRUENBERG, MAX F., JR., lawyer; b. San Francisco, Sept. 25, 1943; s. Max Foorman Gruenberg and Dorothy (Lilienthal) Schnier; children: Bruce Leonard, Daniel Suchanan. BA, Stanford, 1965; JD, UCLA, 1970. Bar: Alaska 1970, Calif. 1971, D.C. 1972, U.S. Supreme Ct. 1980. Pvt. practice Anchorage, 1974—; ptnr. Gruenberg & Clover, Anchorage, 1984—; mem. Alaska Ho. of Reps., 1985-92, majority leader, 1987-88, 91-92. Lt. (j.g.) USNR, 1965-67. Fellow Am. Acad. Matrimonial Lawyers. Office: Gruenberg & Clover 2909 Arctic Blvd # 203 Anchorage AK 99503-3810

GRUENWALD, GEORGE HENRY, new products development management consultant; b. Chgo., Apr. 23, 1922; s. Arthur Frank and Helen (Duke) G.; m. Corrine Rae Linn, Aug. 16, 1947; children: Helen Marie Gruenwald Orlando, Paul Arthur. BS in Journalism, Northwestern U., 1947; student, Evanston Acad. Fine Arts, 1937-38, Chgo. Acad. Fine Arts, 1938-39, Grinnell Coll., 1940-41. Asst. to pres. UARCO, Inc., Chgo., 1947-49; creative dir., mgr. mdse. Willy-Overland Motors Inc., Toledo, 1949-51; new products, brand and advt. mgr. Toni Co./Gillette, Chgo., 1951-53; v.p., creative dir., account supr. E.H. Weiss Agy., Chgo., 1953-55; exec. v.p., mgmt. supr. North Advt., Chgo., 1955-71; pres., treas., dir. Pilot Products, Chgo., 1963-71; pres., dir. Advance Brands, Inc., Chgo., 1963-71; owner Venture Group, 1971—; exec. v.p., dir. Campbell Mithun Inc., Mpls. and Chgo., 1971-72; pres., dir. Campbell Mithun Inc., 1972-79, chmn., dir., 1979-81, CEO, dir., 1981-83, chief creative officer, dir., 1983-84; vice-chmn., dir. Ted Bates Worldwide, N.Y.C., 1979-80; mgmt. cons. new products, 1984—. Author: New Product Development-What Really Works, 1985, 2d edit. 1992, New Product Development-Responding to Market Demand, 1992, (workbook) New Product Development Checklist: From Mission to Market, 1991, (videos) New Products Seven Steps to Success, 1988, New Product Development, 1989; editor-in-chief Oldsmobile Rocket Ctr. mag., 1955-65, Hudson Family mags., 1953-56, expert columnist Mktg. News, 1988—; contbr. articles to profl. jours.; editor, pub. rels. specialist. Trustee Chgo. Pub. TV Assn., 1969-73, Mpls. Soc. Fine Arts, 1975-83, Linus Pauling Inst. Sci. and Medicine, Palo Alto, 1984-92, advisor, 1992-95, trustee, 1995—; chmn., v.p. chmn. class reps. Northwestern U. Alumni Fund Coun., Chgo., 1965-68; trustee, chmn., chmn. exec. com. Twin Cities Pub. TV Corp., 1971-84; trustee Minn. Pub. Radio Inc., 1973-77, vice chmn., 1974-75; bd. dirs., exec. com. Pub. Broadcasting Svc., Alexandria, Va., 1978-86, 88-94, mem. comm. adv. com., 1993—; vice chmn. Task Force on Funding, 1991-92, lay rep., 1971—; lay rep. Am.'s Pub. TV Stas., Washington, 1971—, del.; bd. dirs. St. Paul Chamber Orch., 1982-84, San Diego Chamber Orch., 1986-88; mem. adv. bd. San Diego State U. Pub. Broadcasting Cmty., 1986—, pub. rels. specialist, editor. With USAF, 1943-45, MTO. Recipient Hermes award Chgo. Federated Advt. Clubs, 1963; Ednl. TV awards, 1969, 71, 86. Mem. Am. Assn. Advt. Agys. (mgmt. com. 1976-84), Nat. Soc. Profl. Journalists, Am. Inst. Wine and Food (bd. dirs. 1985-92), So. Calif. Advt. Media Soc. Office: PO Box 1696 Rancho Santa Fe CA 92067-1696

GRUENWALD, JAMES HOWARD, association executive, consultant; b. Cin., Aug. 30, 1949; s. Howard Francis and Geraldine Emma (Mueller) G. BS, Xavier U., 1971. Cert. profl. in recreation and leisure svc., Ill. Rep. pub. rels. Cath. Youth Orgn., Cin., 1969-72; advtransp. sales rep. Spade Trucking Co., Cin., 1972-73; field rep. Ohio Dept. Transport, Columbus, 1973-76; editorial, sales rep. Cin. Suburban Newspaper, 1976-77; asst. devel. dir. Cin. Art Acad., 1977-79; nat. exec. dir. Say Soccer USA, Cin., 1979-93; co-founder, exec. dir. U.S. Indoor Soccer Orgn., 1985-90; bd. dirs. Buckeye Men's Baseball, Cin., 1982-90, chmn. 1982-86, 89-90; dir. Amateur Athletic Union, Indpls., 1983-85; assoc. dir. of devel., Am. Youth Soccer Organization, L.A., 1993—. cert. trainer Am. Coaches Effectiveness Program, Champaign, Ill., 1983-92. Contbr. articles to profl. jours including Jour. Nat. Recreation and Parks, 1983, Jour. Ohio Parks and Attractions, 1985, Jour. Mich. Leisure, 1986, Strategies, AAPHER, 1989. Editor: jour. Touchline, 1980-92, Parents Guide to Soccer, 1985-92. Candidate for city coun. City of St. Bernard, Ohio, 1977; mem. adv. bd. Church Parish, Cin., 1974-76. Recipient Exec. Dir. Svc. award Say Soccer USA, 1979; State of Mich. Community Svc. award, 1986. Mem. Nat. Council Youth Sports Dirs., Nat. Recreation and Parks Assn., Mich. Recreation and Parks Assn. (Community Service award 1986), Soc. for Non Profits. Avocations: hiking, reading, writing, teaching, conducting workshops. Home: 2706 Embassy Row Indianapolis IN 46224-2962 Office: 5403 W 138th St Hawthorne CA 90250-6431

GRUFF, ERIC STEPHEN, inorganic chemist; b. N.Y.C., Oct. 24, 1963; s. Jules and Muriel Ruth (Sobol) G. BS in Chemistry, Rensselaer Poly. Inst., Troy, N.Y., 1985; PhD in Chemistry, SUNY, Stony Brook, 1990. Postdoctoral rsch. fellow Salk Inst., La Jolla, Calif., 1990-92; scientist Molecular Biosystems, Inc., San Diego, 1992—. Contbr. articles to profl. jours. Mem. Am. Chem. Soc., Sigma Xi (travel awardee 1990). Home: 9004 Pimpernel Dr San Diego CA 92129-3601 Office: MBI 10030 Barnes Canyon Rd San Diego CA 92121-2722

GRULLÓN, KENNETH EMANUEL, obstetrician-gynecologist; b. N.Y.C., Nov. 17, 1964; s. Emanuel A. Grullón and Mary M. Febo-Grullón; m. Jennifer L. Centeno, June 2,. 1991. BA magna cum laude, Harvard Coll., 1986; MD, U. Calif., San Francisco, 1991. Diplomate Nat. Bd. Med. Examiners. Instr. Med. Scholars Program, San Francisco, 1987-90; med. intern U. Calif., San Francisco, 1991-92, resident, 1992—; med. paralegal Bennett and Poland, San Francisco, 1990-91. Author: (poster) Society Gynecologic Investigation, 1991. Co-founder Mission Hill Afternoon Program, Boston, 1983-86; mem. Chicanos/Latinos Health Edn., San Francisco, 1988-90. Harvard Coll. scholar, 1982-86, Rotary Found. scholar, Lima, Peru, 1987. Jr. fellow Am. Coll. Ob-gyn.; mem. AMA, Calif. Med. Assn., Calif. Hispanic AMA. Democrat. Roman Catholic. Office: U Calif 400 Parnassus Ave San Francisco CA 94122-2721

GRUMBLING, HUDSON VIRGIL, JR., internist; b. Indiana, Pa., Aug. 21, 1936; s. Hudson Virgil and Mildred Alice (Seanor) G.; m. Frances Wood Welchans, June 18, 1960; children: Matthew Virgil, Mark David, Daniel Frank, Ruth Maree. BA, U. Mich., 1958; MD, U. Pa., 1962. Bd. cert. internal medicine; med. lic., Ariz., Pa. Intern Akron (Ohio) Gen. Hosp., 1962-63; commd. ensign USNR, 1959; commd. lt. USN, 1963, advanced through grades to capt., 1979; resident internal medicine Phila. Naval Hosp., 1966-69; staff physician Annapolis (Md.) Naval Hosp., 1969-71; resigned USN, 1971; capt. USNR, 1979—; active staff physician Altoona (Pa.) Hosp., 1971-73, W.O. Boswell Meml. Hosp., Sun City, Ariz., 1973—; courtesy staff physician Del E. Webb Meml. Hosp., Sun City West, Ariz., 1987—; chief med. staff W.O. Boswell Meml. Hosp., Sun City, 1990-92; med. dir. Royal Sun West Nursing Ctr., Avondale, Ariz., 1992—; bd. dirs. Suan Health Corp., Sun City. Mem. ACP, AMA, Maricopa County Med. Assn., Ariz. Med. Assn., Naval Res. Assn. Republican. Home: 280 E Campina Dr Litchfield Park AZ 85340-4221 Office: 13640 N Plaza Del Rio Blvd Peoria AZ 85381-4848

GRUNLOH, HOWARD JAMES, research and development company executive; b. San Diego, Aug. 26, 1957; s. Louis F. and Bernice T. (Vaisnoras) G.; m. Sheila C. Ross, Nov. 21, 1987 (Mar. 1993); 1 child, Brian J. BS, U. Calif., San Diego, 1982. Engring. aide Gen. Atomics, San Diego, 1979-82, engr., 1983-87, sr. engr., 1987-90, assoc. staff engr., 1990-91, project mgr., 1991-94, bus. action team, 1994—. Mgmt. com. Greater San Diego Sci. and Engring. Fair, 1983—, chmn. judging, 1983—. Recipient Harvard Book award Harvard Soc., 1974. Mem. Am. Soc. Metals, Am. Nuclear Soc. Office: Gen Atomics 3550 General Atomics Ct San Diego CA 92121-1122

GRUNWALD, JOSEPH, economist; b. Vienna, Austria, June 25, 1920; came to U.S., 1938, naturalized, 1943; s. Arthur and Marie (Laub) G.; m. Sheila Katz, June 2, 1949; children: Peter, Kenneth, Timothy. BS, John Hopkins U., 1943; PhD, Columbia U., 1950. Pers. mgr. Comfy Mfg. Co., Balt., 1940-43; lectr. Rutgers U., New Brunswick, N.J., 1946-47, Columbia U., 1947; asst. prof. Adelphi U., Garden City, N.Y., 1947-50; econ. adviser to gov. P.R., acting dir., econ. div. P.R. Planning Bd., 1950-52; prof. CCNY, 1952-54; prof. econs. U. Chile, 1954-61; dir. Inst. Econs., 1954-61; prof. econs. Yale U., New Haven, 1961-63; lectr. Johns Hopkins U. Sch. Advanced Internat. Studies, Washington, 1963-73; mem. adv. panel Office Tech. Assessment, U.S. Congress, 1986-91; dep. asst. sec. for econ. policy bur. Inter-Am. Affairs, Dept. State, Washington, 1976-77; adj. prof. econs. George Washington U., 1972-84; sr. fellow The Brookings Instn., Washington, 1963-84; founding pres. Inst. Americas, La Jolla, 1984-88; adj. prof. econs. Grad. Sch. Internat. Refs. and Pacific Studies, U. Calif.-San Diego, La Jolla, 1985—; cons. Ford Found., 1960-85; com. indsl. and transp. rsch. U.S.-Brazil, Nat. Acad. Scis., 1966-68, 70. Author: National Budgeting in Norway, 1950; (with others) Economic Development of Puerto Rico, 1951; The Economic Development of Chile, 1956; (with others) Latin American Trade Patterns, 1965; (with P. Musgrove) Natural Resources in Latin American Development, 1970; (with others) Latin American Economic Integration, 1972; (with K. Flamm) The Global Factory, 1985; editor: Latin America and the World Economy, 1978; mem. editorial bd. Latin Am. Rsch. Rev., 1977-80. Mem. adv. bd. Hispanic Found., Library of Congress, 1964-79; mem. com. experts Alliance for Progress, 1963-68; Com. Internat. Exch. of Persons, 1971-73; com. eminent persons UNIDO, Vienna, Austria, 1977-78. Decorated Order Bernando O'Higgins, Chile, 1969. Mem. Social Sci. Rsch. Coun.-Am. Coun. Learned Soc. (chmn. joint coms.), Am. Econ. Assn., Internat. Devel. Soc., Internat. Assn. Rsch. in Income and Wealth, Latin Am. Studies Assn. (v.p. 1975, pres. 1976). Home: 15071 Tierra Alta Del Mar CA 92014-3928 Office: U Calif IR/PS La Jolla CA 92093-0519

GRUSHKIN, DONALD ADAM, psychologist; b. Encino, Calif., Mar. 20, 1965; s. Arnold Gerald and Beverly Kay (Steinberg) G. BA, Gallaudet U., 1985, MA, 1987; postgrad., U. Arizona, 1992—. Cert. sch. psychologist. Sch. psychologist Va. Sch. for the Deaf, Hampton, 1988-89, Beverly (Mass.) Sch. for the Deaf, 1989-90, Lexington Sch. for the Deaf, N.Y.C., 1990-92; residential aide Ariz. Sch. for the Deaf, Tucson, 1992—; instr. Am. Sign Lang. U. Ariz., Tucson, 1994. Jewish.

GRUTTER, JUDITH APPLEY, career counselor; b. Montclair, N.J., Nov. 24, 1942; d. Lawrence Asa and Ruth (Wilson) Appley; m. Karl Grutter, Aug. 26, 1966 (div. Jan. 1971); m. William Karl Schatz, Nov. 26, 1976. BA in English, Syracuse U., 1969; MS in Counseling, Calif. State U., 1976. Cert. career counselor; registered profl. career counselor Calif. Career counselor Calif. State U., L.A., 1971-76, L.A. County Schs., 1976-81; coord. grad. programs in career counseling Calif. State U., Northridge, 1981-90; ptnr. Webb, Grutter, Helander & Assocs., Pasadena, Calif., 1990-94; prin. G/S Cons., So. Lake Tahoe, Calif., 1978—; trainer, conf. presenter in field, 1976—. Mem. Nat. Career Devel. Assn. (recipient merit award 1993, named career counselor of yr. 1994), Calif. Career Devel. Assn. (exec. bd. 1983—, pres. 1989-90), Assn. for Psychol. Type (tng. faculty 1993—). Democrat. Office: G/S Consultants PO Box 7855 South Lake Tahoe CA 76158

GRUTZ, JAMES ARTHUR, lawyer; b. Dubuque, Iowa, Oct. 24, 1940; s. Clarence Peter and Edna Evelyn (Nelson) G.; m. Kate Boyle, Aug. 20, 1941; children: Kristin, Rachel, Karrin, Adam, Brendan. BA, Loras Coll., 1963; JD, Northwestern U., 1966. Bar: Wash. 1967, U.S. Dist. Ct. (we. dist.) Wash. 1968, U.S. Ct. Appeals (9th cir.) 1972, U.S. Supreme Ct. 1979. Law clk. Wash. Supreme Ct., Olympia, 1967-68; assoc. Jackson, Ulvestad & Goodwin, Seattle, 1968-74; ptnr. Jackson, Ulvestad, Goodwin & Grutz, Seattle, 1974-81, Goodwin, Grutz & Scott, Seattle, 1981—. Mem. ABA, Wash. Bar Assn., Seattle-King County Bar Assn., Assn. Trial Lawyers Am., Wash. Trial Lawyers Assn. Roman Catholic. Office: Goodwin Grutz & Scott 1928 One Union Sq # 600 Univ Seattle WA 98101

GRUVER, WILLIAM RAND, II, journalist, educator; b. N.Y.C., June 18, 1936; s. Henry and Anne Catherine (Lauer) G.; m. Lila Hean Gruver, Sept. 15, 1961 (dec.); children: Catherine, Robin; m. Barbara Anne Boone, Mar. 4, 1984; 1 child, Renée. BA in Polit. Sci., Columbia U., 1960, MA in Journalism, 1961. Pub. affairs exec. Carl Byoir & Assocs., N.Y.C., 1964-69; dep. press sec. to Senator Robert Kennedy, U.S. Senate, Washington, 1967-68; polit. editor CBS News, N.Y.C. and L.A., 1969-76; polit. corr. Jack Anderson Column, Washington, 1976-82; news dir., anchor U.A. Columbia Cable, Nutler, N.J., 1983-85; commentator, corrs. Stas. KFYI, KFLR, KHEG and KHEP, Phoenix, 1992—; mng. editor Fourth Estate News Svc., Phoenix; mem. faculty Ariz. State U. Walter Cronkite Sch. Journalism and Telecom., Tempe, 1986—. Author: Since 1789, 1971, Last Act, Ed Meese, Man in the Middle, 1994; contbr. numerous articles to mags. and newspapers. Former exec. sec. Calif. Dem. Com., L.A.; former chmn. Ft. Lee (N.J.) Consumer Commn.; media cons. 3 to U.S. senators, Washington. Ensign USN, 1953-57. Mem. AFTRA (sec., bd. dirs.), Soc. Profl. Journalists, Assn. Univ. Tchrs., Am. Legion, Beta Sigma Tau. Home: 3341 W Pershing Ave Phoenix AZ 85029-1236 Office: Fourth Estate News Svc PO Box 39094 Phoenix AZ 85069-9094

GRYC, GEORGE, geologist; b. St. Paul, Minn., July 27, 1919; s. Anthony Stanley and Lillian (Teply) G.; m. Jean L. Funk, Feb. 4, 1942; children: James, Stephen, Christina, Paula, Georgina. BA, U. Minn., 1940, MS, 1942; postgrad., Johns Hopkins U., 1946-49. Geologist Alaskan Br. U.S. Geol. Survey, Washington, 1943-63; chief Alaskan br. U.S. Geol. Survey, Menlo Park, Calif., 1963-76, regional geologist, 1976; chief Office of Nat. Petroleum Resource in Alaska U.S. Geol. Survey, Anchorage, 1976-82; dirs. rep. Western region U.S. Geol. Survey, Menlo Park, 1982-95, gen. chmn. Circum-Pacific Map Project, 1982—. Recipient Meritorious Svc. award Dept. of Interior, Washington, 1974, Disting. Svc. award, 1978; named Hon. Mem., Alaska Geol. Soc., 1987. Fellow Geol. Assn. Am., Sigma Xi; mem. Am. Assn. Petroleum Geologists (editor), Paleontological Soc., Cosmos Club Washington. Office: US Geol Survey MS 144 345 Middlefield Rd Menlo Park CA 94025-3561

GRZANKA, LEONARD GERALD, writer, consultant; b. Ludlow, Mass., Dec. 11, 1947; s. Stanley Simon and Claire Genevive (Rozkuszka) G. BA, U. Mass., 1972; MA, Harvard U., 1974. Asst. prof. Gakushiun U., Tokyo, 1975-78; pub. rels. specialist Pacific Gas and Electric Co., San Francisco, 1978-80; sales promotion writer Tymshare Transaction Svcs., Fremont, Calif., 1980-81; account exec. The Strayton Co., Santa Clara, Calif., 1981-82; mng. editor Portable Computer Mag., San Francisco, 1982-84; prin. Grzanka Assocs., San Francisco, 1984-86; San Francisco bur. chief Digital News, 1986-91; battery program cons. Bevilacqua Knight Inc., Oakland, Calif., 1991—; staff asst. Electric Power Rsch. Inst./U.S. Advanced Battery Consortium, Palo Alto, Calif., 1991—; lectr. Golden Gate U., San Francisco, 1985-87. Author: Neither Heaven Nor Hell, 1978; translator, editor: (art catalog) Masterworks of Japanese Crafts, 1977; translator: (book chpt.) Manajo: The Chinese Preface to the Kokinwakashu, 1984 (Literary Transl. award 1984). Sgt. USAF, 1965-69. Fellow Danforth Found., 1974. Mem. United Anglers Calif., Harvard Club of San Francisco (bd. dirs. 1984-88, Cert. Appreciation 1986, 88), Phi Beta Kappa, Phi Kappa Phi. Home: 2909 Madison St Alameda CA 94501-5426 Office: BKI 501 14th St # 210 Oakland CA 94612-1405 also: EPRI 3412 Hillview Ave Palo Alto CA 94303

GUARDINO, SAL, food executive; b. 1922. Farmer Stockton, Calif., 1942—; v.p. Sunniland Fruit Inc., Stockton. Office: Sunniland Fruit Inc 1350 Report Ave Stockton CA 95205-3054*

GUARINO, PETER ROSERIO, corporate lawyer; b. Bklyn., June 22, 1958; s. Peter André and Rosalie Dorothy (Fontana) G. Student, Tulane U., 1976-78; BA, Rutgers U., 1980; JD, Suffolk U., Boston, 1989. Bar: N.Y. 1989, Mass. 1990. Legal asst. Monarch Resources, Inc., N.Y.C., 1981-85; sr. legal asst Colonial Mgmt. Assoc., Inc., Boston, 1985-89; atty. The Dreyfus Corp., N.Y.C., 1989-91; asst. gen. counsel G.T. Capital Mgmt., San Francisco, 1991—. Mem. com. Cystic Fibrosis Found., San Francisco, 1991-95, leadership com. ARC, 1995—. Mem. ABA. Home: 1921 Hyde St San Francisco CA 94109-2050 Office: GT Capital Mgmt Inc 50 California St San Francisco CA 94111-4624

GUARRERA, JOSEPH ANTHONY, city administrator, company director; b. Bklyn., June 12, 1934; s. Antonio and Irene (Tringo) G.; m. Susan D. Hayes, Aug. 8, 1959; children: Dyan, Joseph Jr. AA, East L.A. Jr. Coll., 1961; BS, Calif. State U., L.A., 1968, MS, 1973. Field dir. Cath. Youth Orgn., L.A., 1958-63; recreation supr. City of Torrance, Calif., 1963-64, City of Alhambra, Calif., 1964-65; dir. parks and recreation City of Monrovia, Calif., 1965-72; dir. cmty. svcs. City of Azusa, Calif., 1972—; pres. Capital Enterprises, Duarte, Calif., 1968—, Monrovia Ice Co., Duarte, 1979—. Parade chair Golden Days Assn., Azusa, 1975—; softball umpire, 1968-93. With U.S. Army, 1954-56. Mem. So. Calif. Mcpl. Athletic Fedn. (pres. 1980, Svc. award 1974, Citation award 1976, Merit award 1977, Spl. Achievement award 1992), Calif. Park and Recreation Soc. (pres. 1973, bd. dirs. 1981, Merit award 1974). Democrat. Roman Catholic. Office: City of Azusa 320 N Orange Pl Azusa CA 91702-3430

GUAY, GORDON HAY, postal service executive, marketing educator, consultant; b. Hong Kong, Aug. 1, 1948; came to U.S., 1956; s. Daniel Bock and Ping Gin (Ong) G. AA, Sacramento City Coll., 1974; BS, Calif. State U., Sacramento, 1976, MBA, 1977; PhD, U. So. Calif., 1981. Mgmt. assoc. U.S. Postal Svc., Sacramento, 1980-82, br. mgr., 1982-83, fin. mgr., 1983-84, mgr. quality control, 1984-86, mgr. tech. sales and svcs. divsn., 1986-91, dir. mktg. and comm., 1991—; assoc. prof. bus. adminstrn., mktg. and mgmt. Calif. State U., Sacramento, 1981-85; prof. mktg. Nat. U., San Diego, 1984—; pres. Gordon Guay and Assocs., Sacramento, 1979—; cons. Mgmt. Cons. Assocs., Sacramento, 1977-79. Author: Marketing: Issues and Perspectives, 1983; also articles to profl. jours. With U.S. Army, 1968-70. Recipient Patriotic Svc. award U.S. Treasury Dept., San Francisco, 1985. Fellow Acad. Mktg. Sci.; mem. NEA, AAUP, Am. Mgmt. Assn., Am. Mktg. Assn. (Outstanding Mktg. Educator award 1989), Am. Soc. Pub. Adminstrn., Soc. Advancement Mgmt. (Outstanding Mem. 1976), Assn. MBA Execs. Democrat. Office: US Postal Svc 3775 Industrial Blvd West Sacramento CA 95799-0100

GUBINS, SAMUEL, museum administrator; b. N.Y.C., Nov. 10, 1942; s. Jack and Mae (Sorin) G.; m. Eleanor Bush, June 27, 1965; children: Sara Rebecca, Tamar Rachel. BA, Reed Coll., 1964; PhD, Johns Hopkins U., 1970. Asst. prof. econs. Haverford Coll., Pa., 1968-74, v.p. fin., 1974-81; sr. v.p., treas. Acad. Natural Scis., Phila., 1981-95; treas. Am. Type Culture Collection, 1993. Co-author: Macroeconomics, 1974. Contbr. articles to profl. publs. ; chmn., Pa. Humanities Council, 1987-90. Mem. Am. Econ. Assn., Soc. Indsl. and Applied Math (treas. 1982—). Home: 1028 Paradise Way Palo Alto CA 94306 Office: Annual Reviews Inc 4139 El Camino Real Way Palo Alto CA 94303-0139

GUDMUNDSEN, RICHARD AUSTIN, physicist; b. Salt Lake City, Dec. 27, 1922; s. Austin Gudmundsen and Myrl Goodwin; m. Bernice Sayre, Jan. 1, 1925; children: Joyce, Scott Austin, Mark Richard, Annette, Lee Karl, Eileen. Student, U. Wis., Milw., 1942-43, U. Utah, 1943; B. Engring. in Mech. Engring., U. So. Calif., L.A., 1947, PhD in Physics, 1955. Office of Naval Rsch. fellow U. So. Calif., L.A., 1949-51; mgr. semiconductor labs. Hughes Aircraft Co., Culver City, Calif., 1952-59; pres. Quantum Tech. Labs., Santa Ana, Calif., 1960-63; mgr. lasers and electrooptics Rockwell Internat., Anaheim, Calif., 1963-70, dir. advanced tech., 1970-81; pres. Perceptrix, Inc., Santa Ana, 1982—. Contbr. numerous tech. articles to profl. jours. With U.S. Army, 1943-45, ETO. Decorated Bronze Star. Mem. IEEE (sr.), Am. Phys. Soc., Autonetics Sigma Xi Club (pres. 1975), Sigma Delta Omega, Tau Beta Pi. Republican. Mem. LDS Church. Home: 12052 Larchwood Ln Santa Ana CA 92705-3102

GUDORF, GREG DAVID, marketing and sales executive; b. St. Mary's, Ohio, Mar. 11, 1960; s. David L. and Marion M. (fowler) G.; m. cheryl Ann Brackman, May 12, 1979; children: Eric Michael, Troy Gregory. AS in Bus., Sinclair C.C., Dayton, Ohio, 1986; BA in Mgmt., Antioch U., 1990. V.p. sales Gudorf & Sons, Minster, Ohio, 1978-81; v.p. new bus. MCC, Inc., Dayton, Ohio, 1981-85; gen. mgr. URI, Inc., Cin., 1985-89; dir. sales and mktg. Gen. Instrument, San Diego, 1990-94; v.p. mktg. and sales Chaparral Comms., San Jose, 1994—; instr. Small Bus. Mgmt. Kettering (Ohio) Adult Sch., 1989-90. Republican. Roman Catholic. Home: 430 Dolores Ct Pleasanton CA 94566-7668 Office: Chaparral Comms 2450 N 1st St San Jose CA 95131-1002

GUENTER, SCOT MICHAEL, social sciences educator; b. Port Allegany, Pa., July 30, 1956; s. Fritz Edward and Mary (Connors) G. BA, Pa. State U., 1978; MA, U. Md., 1981, PhD, 1986. Tchg. asst., lectr. U. Md., College Park, 1978-86; lectr. Johannes Gutenberg U., Mainz, Germany, 1981-82; asst. prof. Wichita (Kans.) State U., 1986-87, Dickinson Coll., Carlisle, Pa., 1987-89; asst. to assoc. prof. San Jose (Calif.) State U., 1989—. Author: The American Flag 1777-1924, 1990; editor Raven: A Journal of Vexillology, 1994—; mem. editorial bd. Proteus: A Jour. of Ideas, 1990—; contbr. articles to profl. jours. Bd. dirs. Aris Project, San Jose, 1994—. Nat. merit scholar, 1974. Mem. Am. Studies Assn., Calif. Am. Studies Assn. (v.p. 1992-94, pres. 1994-95), Am. Culture Assn., N.Am. Vexillological Assn. (v.p. 1989-91, pres. 1991-94, Driver award 1985), Golden Gate Area Vexillological Assn., Phi Beta Kappa. Democrat. Roman Catholic. Home: 201 S Fourth St 617 San Jose CA 95112 Office: San Jose State U Dept Am Studies San Jose CA 95192-0092

GUENTHER, ROBERT STANLEY, II, investment and property executive; b. Orange, Calif., Sept. 29, 1950; s. Robert Stanley and Fanny Newman (Shaw) G. BA in Psychology, U. Calif., Santa Barbara, 1975; BA in Sociology, U. Calif., 1975. Pvt. practice Templeton, Calif., 1975—. Home and Office: 7245 El Pomar Dr Templeton CA 93465-8641

GUERARD, ALBERT JOSEPH, retired modern literature educator, author; b. Houston, Nov. 2, 1914; s. Albert Leon and Wilhelmina (Macartney) G.; m. Mary Maclin Bocock, July 11, 1941; children—Catherine Collot, Mary Maclin, Lucy Lundie. A.B., Stanford U., 1934, Ph.D., 1938; A.M., Harvard U., 1936. Instr. Amherst (Mass.) Coll., 1935-36; mem. faculty Harvard U., Cambridge, Mass., 1938-61, successively instr. English, asst. prof., assoc. prof., 1948-54, prof., 1954-61; prof. Stanford (Calif.) U., 1961-85, Albert L. Guerard prof. lit., 1965-85. Author: The Past Must Alter, 1937, Robert Bridges, 1942, The Hunted, 1944, Maquisard, 1945, Joseph Conrad, 1947, Thomas Hardy, 1949, Night Journey, 1950, Andre Gide, 1951, Conrad the Novelist, 1958, The Bystander, 1958, The Exiles, 1963, The Triumph of the Novel: Dickens, Dostoevsky, Faulkner, 1976, The Touch of Time: Myth, Memory and the Self, 1980, Christine/Annette, 1985, Gabrielle, 1992, The Hotel in the Jungle, 1995; co-editor: The Personal Voice, 1964. Served as tech. sgt. psychol. warfare br. AUS, World War II. Rockefeller fellow, 1946-47; Fulbright fellow, 1950-51; Guggenheim fellow, 1956-57; Ford fellow, 1959-60; Nat. Found. Arts fellow, 1967-68; Nat. Found. Humanities fellow, 1974-75; recipient Paris Review Fiction prize, 1963. Mem. Am. Acad. Arts and Scis., Phi Beta Kappa, Pen Cen. West. Home: 635 Gerona Rd Palo Alto CA 94305-8452

GUERBER, STEPHEN CRAIG, community foundation executive; b. Corvallis, Oreg., Oct. 2, 1947; s. Allen Lewis and Thelma Mae (Gilson) G.; m. Donna Kay Panko, Feb. 4, 1968; children: Dani Michelle, Patrick Jason, Suzanne Aleece. BA, Idaho State U., 1969. Bus. editor The Idaho Statesman, Boise, 1970-73; info. svcs. dir. Jim Hawkes Advt., Boise, 1973-74; asst. alumni dir. Idaho State U., Pocatello, 1974-76; pub. rels. mgr. U.S. West Communications, Boise, 1976-88; dir. info. U.S. West Found., Boise, 1988-91; mgr. community affairs U.S. West Communications, Boise, 1991-93; exec. dir. Idaho Cmty. Found., 1993—. Councilman City of Eagle, 1984-88, mayor, 1988—; bd. dirs. Assn. Idaho Cities, 1988-94, Silver Sage coun. Girl Scouts U.S.A., 1990-93, Am. Festival Ballet, 1984-88, Simplot Vol. Award, 1988; mem. Ada Planning Assn., 1985—, Fourth Idaho Dist. Jud. Coun., 1988—, Ada County Centennial Commn., 1989-90. Recipient Outstanding Pub. Svc. Award Social Svc. Adminstrn., 1983, Profl. Achievement award Idaho State U. Coll. Arts and Scis., 1991; named Idaho Disting. Citizen The Idaho Statesman, 1988. Democrat. Baptist. Home: 699 Ranch Dr Eagle ID 83616-5115 Office: Idaho Cmty Found 205 N 10th St Ste 650 Boise ID 83702-5725

GUERRA, ANNA O'BANNON, nurse educator, maternal/women's health nurse; b. Cleve., July 27, 1949; d. Charles Grant and Anita Pauline (Norman) O'Bannon; m. Francisco Javier Guerra, Dec. 27, 1970; children: Brandon Michael, Elisa Catherine . BSN, Tex. Woman's U., 1971; MS, U. Ariz., 1990. RN, Tex., Ariz. Head nurse Hall-Bennett Hosp., Big Spring, Tex., 1971; relief staff nurse Incirlik CDI Hosp., Adana, Turkey, 1972-74; family planning nurse Okaloosa County Pub. Health Dept., Ft. Walton Beach, Fla., 1974-75; charge nurse Plano (Tex.) Cmty. Hosp., 1977-79; staff nurse Presbyn. Hosp., Dallas, 1979-80; charge nurse St. Francis Hosp. and Birth Ctr., Colorado Springs, Colo., 1980-81; per diem nurse Tucson Med. Ctr. and Northwest Hosp., 1986-90; mem. faculty Pima C.C. Sch. of Nursing, Tucson, 1986-90; perinatal nurse, clin. educator Healthdyne Perinatal Svcs., Tucson, 1991-92; lectr. U. Ariz. Coll. of Nursing, Tucson, 1992—; mem. multiple coms. U. Ariz. Coll. Nursing; childbirth edn. instr., presenter in field. Leader Cub Scouts, 1984-86, chmn. pack com., 1986-87; leader Girl Scouts, 1987-89; host family Amphi High Sch.-Hermosillo Student Exch. Program, 1990-92. Recipient Highest Recruitment of Leaders award Boy Scouts Am., 1987, Outstanding Leadership award Girl Scouts U.S., 1988. Fellow Nightingale Soc.; mem. AWHONN, Pima County Healty Mothers/Healthy Babies Coalition, Sigma Theta Tau (sec. Beta Mu chpt. 1993-95). Home: 1200 E Placita Ardilla Tucson AZ 85718-2910 Office: U Ariz Coll Nursing Tucson AZ 85721

GUETTICH, BRUCE MICHAEL, sporting goods company executive; b. Lansing, Mich., Aug. 4, 1957; s. Randolph Otto and Ingiborg (Lintner) G.; m. Shelby Angela Kindig, June 21, 1956. Grad. h.s., Portland, Oreg. Ski and binding technician Glacier's Edge, Portland, 1972-76; ski shop mgr. Glacier's Edge West, West Slope, Oreg., 1976-79, Beyond Repair, Steamboat Springs, Colo., 1979-81; sales and promotions dir. Kenncorp Internat., Vancouver, Wash., 1981-83; founder, pres., dir. World Footbag Assn., Golden, Colo., 1983—; founder, dir. Internat. Footbag Adv. Bd., Golden, 1983—. Author, editor: (mag.) Footbag World, 1983—; author: (manual) Footbag Instructional Manual, 1986; actor, author: (instrnl. video) Footbag Basics, 1987; author, editor: (instrnl. video) Tricks of the Trade, 1990. Office: World Footbag Assn # 7 1317 Washington Ave # 7 Golden CO 80401-1915

GUETZKOW, HAROLD, international politics educator; b. Milwaukee, Wis., Aug. 16, 1915; s. Albert Charles and Teckla (Prinz) G.; m. Lauris Lynette Steere, Sept. 17, 1944; children: James, Gay, Daniel. BA, U. Chgo., 1936; PhD, U. Mich., 1948. Instr., asst prof. U. Mich., Ann Arbor, 1945-50; assoc. prof., prof. Carnegie Inst. Tech., Pitts., 1950-57; prof., Fulcher chair Northwestern U., Evanston, Ill., 1957-85, Fulcher prof. emeritus, 1985—; sr. intern U.S. Dept. State, Washington, 1969-70, UN Secretariat, N.Y.C., 1970-71; rsch. scholar in Ea. Europe, Latin Am., Asia, Africa, Fulbright, 1981, 83, 84, 87. Co-author, editor Simulated International Processes, 1981; co-author, co-inventor: (classroom game) Inter-Nation Simulation Kit, 1966. Mem. Internat. Studies Assn. (pres. 1987), Am. Polit. Sci. Assn., Internat. Soc. Polit. Psychology. Home and Office: 715 Quetta Ave Apt B Sunnyvale CA 94087-1249

GUGELCHUK, GARY MICHAEL, academic administrator; b. Williamson, W.Va., May 25, 1953; s. Tony and Sally E. (Bevins) G. BA, Ohio State U., 1975, MA, 1976, PhD, 1985. Curriculum developer Ohio U., Athens, 1985-86; asst. prof. Health Profl. Edn. Coll. Osteopathic Medicine Pacific, Pomona, Calif., 1986-92; assoc. prof. Health Profl. Edn. Coll. Osteopathic Medicine Pacific, Pomona, 1992—, dir. office of grants, 1989—, asst. to v.p. acad. affairs, 1993—; mem. adv. com. IGC project Soc. Tchrs. of Family Medicine, Kansas City, Mo., 1993—; cons. Am. Assn. Colls. of Osteopathic Medicine, Rockville, Md., 1994. Contbr. articles to profl. jours. Adv. com. Cmty. Wellness Partnership, Violence Prevention project, Pomona, 1994—; adv. com. LULAC Nat. Edn. Ctr., Pomona, 1988-92. Fellow Am. Anthropol. Assn., Soc. for Applied Anthropology; mem. Am. Ednl. Rsch. Assn., Am. Folklore Soc., Phi Beta Kappa, Phi Kappa Phi. Office: Coll Osteopathic Medicine of the Pacific 309 E 2d St Pomona CA 91766

GUGGENHEIM, SUZANNE, company executive; b. Budapest, Hungary, June 6, 1944; came to U.S., 1981; d. Elisabeth Marton; m. Alan A. Guggenheim, Mar. 20, 1974; 1 child, Valerie. BA in Polit. Sci., Inst. of Polit. Sci., Paris, 1968; M in Law, U. Paris, 1968, MA in English, 1970. COO UNI, Paris, 1968-77; chancellor U. of French Antilles and Guyana, Guadeloupe, 1977-80; pres. Apasica, 1980-81; COO DBCS, Stockton, Calif., 1982-88; realtor Wine County Realtors, Lodi, Calif., 1988-89; real estate broker Camino Realty, Oxnard, Calif., 1989-92; exec. v.p., broker CIS Real Estate, Newbury Park, Calif., 1992—. Mem. Calif. Rep. Party, 1991—; alt. Ventura County Ctrl. Com., 1991—; mem. Thousand Oaks City Social Svcs. Funding Com.; pres. Conejo Valley Rep. Women, 1993—, Conejo Valley Women's Club, 1992-94; chmn. Sch. Site Coun. Maple Elem., 1993-94; mem. Parent Assn., 1st v.p. 1993-96; mem. Conejo Valley Sch. Dist. Adv. Coun., 1992-94; 1st v.p. Thousand Oaks CRA. Mem. Rotary Club of Newbury Park (bd. dirs. 1992-94). Home: 3265 Peppermint St Newbury Park CA 91320-5039 Office: CIS Real Estate 1560 Newbury Rd 204 Thousand Oaks CA 91320

GUGGENHEIM-BOUCARD, ALAN ANDRE ALBERT PAUL EDOUARD, business executive, international consultant; b. Paris, May 12, 1950; came to U.S., 1981, naturalized, 1991; s. Jacques and Micheline (Raffalovich) Guggenheim; m. Suzanne Marton, Mar. 20, 1974; 1 child, Valerie. BS, U. Paris, 1971; MSCE, Ecole Speciale des Travaux Publics, Paris, 1974; MBA in Finance, U. Paris, 1975; grad., French Command-Gen. Staff

Res. Coll., 1981. Asst. prof. math. Nat. Sch. Arts and Architecture, Paris, 1972-75; civil engr. Societe Routiere Colas, Paris, 1976-77, French Antilles, 1977-78; chief exec. officer, exec. dir. C.R.P.G., Pointe A Pitre, Guadeloupe, 1978-81; chief exec. officer, chmn. San Joaquin Software Systems, Inc., Stockton, Calif., 1982-86, CalCar Investment Svcs., Inc., Newbury Park, Calif., 1983—; bd. mem. Sucmanu, Paris, 1976-82; bd. of organizers Pacific State Bank, Stockton, Calif., 1985-87. Exec. Editor newsletter L'Action Universitaire, 1970-76. Mem. French Res. Policy Rev. Bd., Paris, 1971-77; mem. Ventura County Rep. Cen. Com., Rep. Presdl. Task Force, Rep. Campaign Coun.; candidate Rep. 37th Assembly Dist., Calif.; mem. cen. com. Calif. Rep. Party, 1992—. Maj. French Res., 1981. Recipient Gold Medal Omnium Technique Holding, 1975. Fellow Engr. and Scientist France; mem. AAS, ADPA, Assn. U.S. Army, Yosemite Club, Rotary. Roman Catholic. Home: 3265 Peppermint St Newbury Park CA 91320-5039 Office: 1560 Newbury Rd # 204 Newbury Park CA 91320

GUGGENHIME, RICHARD JOHNSON, lawyer; b. San Francisco, Mar. 6, 1940; s Richard E. and Charlotte G.; m. Emlen Hall, June 5, 1965 (div.); children: Andrew, Lisa, Molly; m. Judith Perry Swift, Oct. 3, 1992. AB in Polit. Sci. with distinction, Stanford U., 1961; JD, Harvard U., 1964. Bar: Calif. 1965, U.S. Dist. Ct. (no. dist.) Calif. 1965, U.S. Ct. Appeals (9th cir.) 1965. Assoc. Heller, Ehrman, White & McAuliffe, 1965-71, ptnr., 1972—; spl. asst. to U.S. Senator Hugh Scott, 1964; bd. dirs. Comml. Bank of San Francisco, 1980-81, Global Savs. Bank, San Francisco, 1984-86. Mem. San Francisco Bd. Permit Appeals, 1978-86; bd. dirs. Marine World Africa USA, 1980-86; mem. San Francisco Fire Commn., 1986-88, Recreation and Parks Commn., 1988-92; chmn. bd. trustees San Francisco Univ. High Sch., 1987-90; trustee St. Ignatius Prep. Sch., San Francisco, 1987—. Mem. Am. Coll. Probate Counsel, San Francisco Opera Assn. (bd. dir.), Bohemian Club, Wine and Food Soc. Club, Olympic Club, Chevaliers du Tastevin Club (San Francisco), Thunderbird Country Club (Ranch Mirage, Calif.). Home: 2621 Larkin St San Francisco CA 94109-1512 Office: Heller Ehrman White & McAuliffe 333 Bush St San Francisco CA 94104-2806

GUGLIELMO, EUGENE JOSEPH, computer scientist; b. Bklyn., Nov. 23, 1958; s. Anthony and Carlotta Sylvia (Grossi) G.; m. Nancy Eleanor Booth, Aug. 13, 1983; children: Tiffany, Trevyn, Kyle, Quentyn. BS in Computer Sci., St. John's U., 1979; MS in Computer Sci., Calif. State U., Chico, 1987; PhD in Computer Sci., Naval Postgrad. Sch., 1992. Computer asst. St. John's U., Jamaica, N.Y., 1977-79; mem. tech. staff Bell Telephone Labs., Whippany, N.J., 1979-80; sys. designer AT&T Comm., Piscataway, N.J., 1980-85; computer scientist Naval Air Warfare Ctr., China Lake, Calif., 1985-94; cons. IBM Cons. Group, Boulder, Colo., 1994; software engr. Monterey Bay Aquarium Rsch. Inst., Pacific Grove, Calif., 1994—. Contbr. articles to profl. jours. Mem. IEEE, IEEE Computer Soc., Assn. for Computational Linguistics, Assn. Computing Machinery (Info. Retrieval, Artificial Intelligence), N.Y. Acad. Scis. Roman Catholic. Home: 35 Bayview Rd Elkhorn CA 95012

GUICE, JOHN THOMPSON, retired air force officer; b. Kosciusko, Miss., Nov. 5, 1923; s. Gustave Nathaniel and Anne Mae (McCool) G.; m. Charlotte Webb, Mar. 8, 1949; children—John Thompson, James G., Steven L., Thomas A., Joseph D. B.S. in Engring, U.S. Mil. Acad., 1947; M.S. in Internat. Relations, George Washington U., 1966; disting. grad., Air Command and Staff Coll., 1962, Air War Coll., 1966. Commd. 2d lt. U.S. Army, 1947; advanced through grades to maj. gen. USAF, 1974; tactical and interceptor pilot, 1947-55; officer Air N.G. and N.G., 1956—; dep. dir. Air N.G., 1974-77, dir., 1977-81, ret., 1981. Decorated Legion of Merit, Air Force D.S.M. Mem. Air Force Assn., N.G. Assn., Sigma Chi. Home: 4901 N Calle Luisa Tucson AZ 85718-4925

GUIDERA, ELLEN MARIE, entertainment industry executive; b. Rockville Center, N.Y., Nov. 22, 1957. BA in Econs. cum laude, Middlebury (Vt.) Coll., 1980; MBA, Harvard Bus. Sch., 1986. Legis. asst. U.S. Ho. of Reps., Washington, 1981-84; dep. rsch. dir. Elliot Richardson for Senate Campaign, Boston, 1984; dir. licensing Walt Disney Co., Burbank, Calif., 1986-89, v.p. new bus. devel., 1992—; dir. Walt Disney Co., Hong Kong, 1989-91; dir. new bus. devel. Walt Disney Co., Bombay, India, 1991-92. Co-chmn. Calif. Assn. Hong Kong; mem. HBS Cmty. Action Group. Home: 332 N Palm Dr Apt 306 Beverly Hills CA 90210-4108 Office: Walt Disney Co 500 S Buena Vista St Burbank CA 91521-0001

GUILBERT, IRENE WEST, educational consultant; b. Camp Verde, Ariz., Oct. 11, 1930; d. Irving Coleman and Amy Elaine (Stock) West; m. Lionel Ward Guilbert, Apr. 12, 1952 (div. May 1985); children: Marion Elizabeth, Lynelle Marie, Marjorie Ann. BA in Secondary Edn., U. Ariz., 1952; MEd in Elem. Edn., Ariz. State U., 1982. Cert. elem. and secondary tchr., prin., Ariz. Tchr. pub. schs. Ariz., 1954-78, 81-83; developer, demonstrator nat. diffusion network U.S. Office Edn., Mesa, Ariz., 1978-85, asst. state facilitator, 1983-85; instrnl. specialist Ariz. Dept. Edn., Phoenix, 1985-88; pres. Ednl. Directions, Inc., Glendale, Ariz., 1985-91, prin., 1988—; adj. prof. No. Ariz. U., Flagstaff, 1985-88; mem. Nat. Diffusion Network, U.S. Dept. Edn.; cons. on math., lang. arts, mgmt. and motivation, early childhood, integrated learning, classroom mgmt. Author: Big Tee Math Books, 1986, Math Pages, 1987. Community chmn. Girl Scouts U.S.A., 1958-71; pres. PTA, 1957. Mem. ASCD, NAESP, Ariz. Sch. Adminstrs., Federated Woman's Club (pres.), Mensa, Phi Delta Kappa, Pi Lambda Theta, Alpha Delta Kappa (pres., southwestern regional scholar 1980). Republican. Unitarian.

GUILFOYLE, BILL, securities executive; b. 1957. With Benham Group, San Francisco; sr. v.p. mktg. G T Global Fin. Svcs., San Francisco, 1987—. Office: G T Global Financial Svc 50 California St Fl 27 San Francisco CA 94111-4624*

GUILL, JOHN RUSSELL, architect; b. Hanford, Calif., Jan. 18, 1959; s. George Russell and Julia G.; m. Debra Kay McGuire, Oct. 6, 1984; children: Laura Kay, Alexander Russell. Student, Reedley Coll., 1977-78, Harvard U., 1981; BS cum laude, Calif. State U., Fresno, 1981. Lic. architect, Calif. Draftsman Lew & Patnaude Architects, Fresno, Calif., 1980-83; designer Temple Andersen Moore Architects, Fresno, Calif., 1983-84; project mgr. Edwin S. Darden Architects, Fresno, 1984; sr. architect Stevens Design Group, Mt. Shasta, Calif., 1984—. Planning commn. Mt. Shasta City, 1988-95, chmn., 1990-91; mem., chmn. bd. trustees Meth. Ch., Mt. Shasta, 1990-94. Mem. AIA, Phi Kappa Phi, Epsilon Pi Tau, Elks. Republican. Office: 205 N Mount Shasta Blvd Mount Shasta CA 96067-2901

GUILLEMIN, ROGER C. L., physiologist; b. Dijon, France, Jan. 11, 1924; came to U.S., 1953, naturalized, 1963; s. Raymond and Blanche (Rigollot) G.; m. Lucienne Jeanne Billard, Mar. 22, 1951; children: Chantal, Francois, Claire, Helene, Elizabeth, Cecile. B.A., U. Dijon, 1941, B.Sc., 1942; M.D., Faculty of Medicine, Lyons, France, 1949; Ph.D., U. Montreal, 1953; Ph.D. (hon.), U. Rochester, 1976, U. Chgo., 1977, Baylor Coll. Medicine, 1978, U. Ulm, Germany, 1978, U. Dijon, France, 1978, Free U. Brussels, 1979, U. Montreal, 1979, U. Man., Can, 1984, U. Turin, Italy, 1985, Kyung Hee U., Korea, 1986, U. Paris, Paris, 1986, U. Barcelona, Spain, 1988, U. Madrid, 1988, McGill U., Montreal, Can., 1988, U. Claude Bernard, Lyon, France, 1989. Intern, resident univs. hosps. Dijon, 1949-51; asso. dir., asst. prof. Inst. Exptl. Medicine and Surgery, U. Montreal, 1951-53; asso. dir. dept. exptl. endocrinology Coll. de France, Paris, 1960-63; asst. prof. physiology Baylor Coll. Medicine, 1953-57, assoc. prof., 1957-63, prof., dir. labs. neuroendocrinology, 1963-70, adj. prof., 1970—; adj. prof. medicine U. Calif. at San Diego, 1995—; resident fellow, chmn. labs. neuroendocrinology Salk Inst., La Jolla, Calif., 1970-89, adj. rsch. prof., 1989-94; Disting. Sci. prof. Whittier Inst., 1989—; adj. prof. medicine U. Calif., San Diego, 1995—. Decorated chevalier Legion d'Honneur (France), 1974, officer, 1984; recipient Gairdner Internat. award, 1974; U.S. Nat. Medal of Sci., 1977; co-recipient Nobel prize for medicine, 1977; recipient Lasker Found. award, 1975; Dickson prize in medicine, 1976; Passano award sci., 1976; Schmitt medal neurosci., 1977; Barren Gold medal, 1979; Dale medal Soc. for Endocrinology U.K., 1980, Ellen Browning Scripps Soc. medal Scripps Meml. Hosps. Found., 1988. Fellow AAAS; mem. NAS, Am. Physiol. Soc., Am. Peptide Soc. (hon.), Assn. Am.Physicians, Endocrine Soc. (pres. 1986), Soc. Exptl. Biology and Medicine, Internat. Brain Rsch. Orgn., Internat. Soc. Rsch. Biology Reprodn., Soc. Neuro-scis., Am. Acad. Arts and Scis., French Acad. Scis. (fgn. assoc.), Academie Internationale de Medecine (fgn. assoc.), Swedish Soc. Med. Scis. (hon.), Academie des Scis. (fgn. assoc.), Academie Royale de Medecine de Belgique (corr. fgn.), Internat. Soc. Neurosci. (charter), Western Soc. Clin. Rsch., Can. Soc. Endocrinal Metabolism, (hon.), Club of Rome. Office: Whittier Inst 9894 Genesee Ave La Jolla CA 92037-1221

GUINN, KENNY C., utility company executive; b. 1936; married. BA, Calif. State U., Fresno, MA; EdD, Utah State U. Supt. Clark County Sch. Dist.; v.p. adminstrn. Nev. Savs. and Loan Assn. (PriMerit Bank), 1978-80, pres., chief operating officer, 1980-85, chief exec. officer, 1985-92, now chmn. bd.; pres. Southwest Gas Corp., 1987-88, chmn., chief exec. officer, 1988-93; now chmn. bd. S.W. Gas Corp. Office: PriMerit Bank 3300 W Sahara Ave Las Vegas NV 89102-6066 also: SW Gas Corp 5241 Spring Mountain Rd Las Vegas NV 89150-0001

GUINN, LINDA ANN, environmental lawyer; b. Idaho Falls, Idaho, Feb. 5, 1956; d. Denzel K. and Wanda Alice (Woodruff) Jenson; m. Gary Douglas Guinn, Oct. 9, 1976; children: Mindy, Aaron. AAS in Radiation Safety, Ea. Idaho Tech. Coll., Idaho Falls, 1981; BS in Systematics and Ecology, U. Kans., 1988, JD, 1990. Bar: Idaho 1991; cert. environ. mgr. Health physics technician Westinghouse Idaho Nuclear, Idaho Falls, 1981-84; pres. Radon & Environ. Profls., Lawrence, Kans., 1986-88; atty. EG&G Idaho, Idaho Falls, 1990-93, sr. atty., 1993-94; sr. cons. EG&G Environ., Denver, 1994-95; gen. counsel Rocky Mountain Remediation Svcs., LLC, Golden, Colo., 1995—; instr. undergrad. and grad. U. Idaho, Idaho Falls, 1991-94; bd. dirs., mem. environ. law sect. Idaho Bar, 1993-94. Author articles. Atty. coach Idaho Students Mock Trials, Eagle Rock Jr. H.S., 1992-93; precinct committeeman Idaho Republican Party, Idaho Falls, 1973-74; active Girl Scouts of Am., Kans., 1984-89. Named Best Oralist Nat. Environ. Law Moot Ct., 1989. Mem. ABA, Idaho Health Physics Soc. (chair pub. rels. com. 1983-84), Idaho Assn. Commerce and Industry (environ. com. 1992-94), Kans. U. Environ. Law Soc. (pres. 1988-89), Mensa (pres.). Home: 9750 Peacock St Denver CO 80221-5749

GUINOUARD, DONALD EDGAR, psychologist; b. Bozeman, Mont., Mar. 31, 1929; s. Edgar Arthur and Venabell (Ford) G.; m. Irene M. Egeler, Mar. 30, 1951; children: Grant M., Philip A., Donna I. BS, Mont. State U., Bozeman, 1954; MS, Mont. State U., 1955; EdD, Wash. State U., Pullman, 1960; postdoctoral, Stanford U., 1965; grad., Indsl. Coll. of the Armed Forces, 1964, Air War Coll., 1976. Lic. psychologist, Ariz., counselor, Wash., Mont.; cert. secondary tchr. and sch. adminstr., Wash., Mont. Advanced through grades to col. USAFR, 1946-84, ret., 1984; dir. counseling Consol. Sch. Dist., Pullman, Wash., 1955-60; assoc. prof. Mont. State U., Bozeman, 1960-66; field selection officer Peace Corps, U.S., S.Am., 1962-68; prof. counseling, counseling psychologist Ariz. State U., Tempe, 1966-90; prof. emeritus, 1990; co-owner Forensic Cons. Assocs., Tempe, 1970—; pvt. practice, 1990—; admissions liaison officer USAF Acad., Colo. Springs, 1967-84; assessment officer Fundamental Edn. Ctr. for the Devel. of the Latin American Community, Patzcuaro, Mex., 1963-64; expert witness on vocat. and psychol. disability for fed. and state cts. Contbr. articles to profl. jours. Mem. Ariz. Psychol. Assn., Am. Assn. Counseling & Devel., Reserve Officers Assn. Democrat. Methodist. Home: 112 E Cairo Dr Tempe AZ 85282-3606

GUINOUARD, PHILIP ANDRE, restaurant executive; b. Pullman, Wash., Apr. 9, 1960; s. Donald Edgar and Irene (Egeler) G.; m. Miquela Teresa Padilla, Feb. 16, 1988; childern: Mia, Angela. Student, Mesa (Ariz.) Community Coll. Dir. quality Garcia's, Phoenix, 1978-84; area spr. El Pollo Asado Inc., Phoenix, 1985-89; gen. mgr. Quinto Patio, Evergreen, Colo., 1989-90, Garcia's, Littleton, Colo., 1990—, Quila's Fresh Mexican Cantina, 1993-94; field tng. mgr. Internat. House of Pancakes, 1994-95; pres., CEO Sub & Munch, 1995—. Mem. Colo. Restaurant Assn. Home: 1714 W Manor St Chandler AZ 85224-5105 Office: 230 W Baseline Rd #103B Tempe AZ 85283

GULA, WILLIAM PETER, physicist; b. Cleve., Dec. 5, 1939; s. Steve William and Anna Regina (Dudek) G.; m. Anne Amy Albrink, May 27, 1972 (div. July 1980); m. Dolores Jeanne Tory, June 11, 1983. BS, Spring Hill Coll., 1964; MS, Columbia U., 1968, PhD, 1972. Tech. staff mem. Los Alamos (N.Mex.) Nat. Lab., 1972—; sci. advisor Dept. Energy, Germantown, Md., 1990-92; advisor Nat. Rsch. Coun., Washington, 1989-93. Mem. IEEE, AAAS, Assn. for Computing Machinery, Am. Phys. Soc. Home: 116 La Vista Dr Los Alamos NM 87544-3437 Office: X-DO MS B218 Los Alamos Nat Lab Los Alamos NM 87545

GULASEKARAM, BALASUBRAMANIAM, psychiatrist, educator; b. Sri Lanka, Mar. 10, 1946. MBBS, U. Ceylon, Colombo, Sri Lanka, 1970. Diplomate Am. Bd. Psychiatry and Neurology. Resident Westchester County Med. Ctr. N.Y. Med. Coll., 1976-79; sr. psychiatrist Met. State Hosp., Norwalk, Calif., 1984—; asst. clin. prof. dept. psychiatry U. Calif., Irvine, 1991—. Mem. AMA, Am. Psychiat. Assn. Office: 16510 Bloomfield Ave Cerritos CA 90703-2115

GULDAHL, MARTIN GRANVILLE, software engineer; b. Seattle, Oct. 1, 1961; s. Alt and Harriet Florence (Houghton) G. BSEE, U. Utah, 1991. Design engr. Evans & Sutherland Computer Corp., Salt Lake City, 1992—. Mem. IEEE, Phi Kappa Phi, Tau Beta Pi. Home: 1418 S 1100 E Apt 18 Salt Lake City UT 84105-2428 Office: Evans & Sutherland Computer Corp 600 Komas Dr Salt Lake City UT 84108-1229

GULICK, PETER VANDYKE, lawyer; b. Honolulu, Feb. 15, 1930; s. Willard Clark and Harriet (Winch) G.; m. Kathryn Christen, June 23, 1952 (div. Mar. 1987); children: Willard, Sarah, Scott. AB, Princeton U., 1952; postgrad. Stanford U., 1952-53; LLB, U. Wash., 1956. Bar: Wash. 1956, U.S. Dist. Ct. (we. dist.) Wash. 1956, U.S. Ct. Appeals (9th cir.) 1957. Mem. Foster, Pepper & Riviera, Seattle, 1956-78; pvt. practice, Bellevue, Wash., 1979—. Scoutmaster, dist. Round Table commr., chief Seattle coun. Boy Scouts Am., 1971-77; pres. Lake Heights Community Club, 1960; commr. Newport Hills Sewer Dist., 1966-72. Recipient dist. merit award Boy Scouts Am., 1976. Mem. ABA, Wash. State Bar Assn., Seattle-King County Bar Assn. Office: 855 106th Ave NE Ste 200 Bellevue WA 98004-4309

GULL, PAULA MAE, nephrology nurse, medical/surgical nurse; b. L.A., Mar. 7, 1955; d. Gerald Henry and Artemis (Cubillas) Balzer; m. Randell Jay Gull, July 10, 1976. AA, Cypress (Calif.) Coll., 1976; AS with high honors, Rancho Santiago Coll., Santa Ana, Calif., 1985; BSN with high honors, Calif. State U., 1993. Cert. med. surg. nurse, nephrology nurse. Staff RN U. Calif. Irvine Med. Ctr., Orange, Calif., 1986-87, asst. nurse mgr., 1987-88, nurse mgr., 1988; med.-surg. nurse N000, 1990—; renal transplant coord. V.C.I. Med. Ctr. Mem. Am. Nephrology Nurses Assn. Mormon. Home: 24974 Enchanted Way Moreno Valley CA 92557-6410

GULMAN, PAUL JAMES, engineer; b. Staten Island, N.Y., Nov. 24, 1951; s. Marcel John and Margaret Mary (Ferrick) G. B of Engring., The Cooper Union, N.Y.C., 1973. Registered profl. engr., Colo. Mech. design engr. Bindery Systems div. Harris Corp., Easton, Pa., 1973-77; mech. project engr. Colo. Conveyor Corp., Lakewood, 1977-78; prodn. engr. Ball Corp., Westminster, Colo., 1978-85; staff engr. Martin Marietta Corp., Denver, 1985-90; engring. cons. in pvt. practice Wheat Ridge, Colo., 1990-93; prin. EVA West, Inc., Denver, 1993—; mem. NASA Space Assembly and Servicing Working Group, Houston, 1991-92. Mem. Mass Transit Com., City of Wheat Ridge, 1979-83, chair, 1980-83. Mem. AIAA, NSPE, Profl. Engrs. Colo. (dir. 1983-85, chair Mathcounts com. 1987-92, pres. Met. chpt. 1986-87, Outstanding Svc. award 1984, 89, 91, Appreciation award 1992), Aircraft Owners and Pilots Assn., Denver Electric Vehicle Coun. Republican. Roman Catholic. Home: 4315 Ammons St Wheat Ridge CO 80033-4445

GUMPPERT, KARELLA ANN, federal government official; b. N.Y.C., Oct. 16, 1942; d. Leonard Lewis and Florence M. Gumppert. AB in Polit. Sci., George Washington U., 1963, postgrad., 1963-65. Lic. in real estate sales, Md., 1984. Editor to Bd. Govs. Fed. Res. Sys., Washington, 1966-67; editorial asst. Jour. of Maritime Law and Commerce, N.Y.C., 1969-71; adminstr. NYU Law Sch., N.Y.C., 1968-73; law asst. White & Case and other firms, N.Y.C., Boston, Hartford, 1974-80; vol. asst. U.S. Presdl. Inaugural Com., Washington, 1981; confidential asst. The White House Staff, Washington, 1981; publs. asst. Congressional Budget Office, Washington, 1982-84; credit summarizer Xerox Corp., Arlington, Va., 1985-86; asst. in govtl. affairs Mut. Omaha, Washngton, 1988; land law adjudicator U.S. Dept. Interior, Anchorage, 1991—. Author, illustrator: (children's book) An Adventure, 1949; founding editor lit. mag. Springboard, 1959; mem. editorial bd. newspaper Amicus Curiae, 1964-65. Charity asst. Girl Scouts U.S.A., N.Y.C., 1952-54, Christian Assn., N.Y.C., 1959-61, Wesley Found., Washington, 1962-63; vol. asst. N.Y. Rep. County Com., 1959-62, Conn. Reps. State Com., Hartford, 1979-80. Recipient numerous scholarships, 1957-60. Mem. NAFE, Nat. Trust for Hist. Preservation, Nat. Audubon Soc., Women's Nat. Rep. Club, Subscribers of Anchorage Symphony Orch. Office: PO Box 1319 Anchorage AK 99510-1319

GUMUCIO, FERNANDO RAUL, foods and beverage company executive; b. Bolivia, Sept. 9, 1934; s. Julio F. G.; children: Linda, Julie, Cynthia, Beverly. B.S., U. San Francisco, 1957; M.B.A., St. Mary's Coll., 1977. Dir. mktg. Latin Am. Del Monte, Mexico, 1963-68; group product dir. Del Monte Corp., San Francisco, 1971-73, dir. sales and product mgmt., 1973-74, v.p. mktg., 1973-80, pres. dry grocery and beverage products group, 1980-85, group v.p., 1985-87, pres. Del Monte U.S.A. operating group, 1985-87; dir. Basic Am. Foods, San Francisco; mem., exec. bd. Nat. Food Producers Assn., Washington. Active Boy Scouts Am.; bd. regents St. Mary's Coll. Republican. Roman Catholic. Clubs: St. Francis Yacht; World Trade (San Francisco). Office: Del Monte Corp 1 Market Pla PO Box 3575 San Francisco CA 94119-0116

GUND, GEORGE, III, financier, professional sports team executive; b. Cleve., May 7, 1937; s. George and Jessica (Roesler) G.; m. Mary Theo Feld, Aug. 13, 1966; children: George, Gregory. Student, Western Res. U., Menlo (Calif.) Sch. Bus. Engaged in personal investments San Francisco, 1967—; cattle ranching Lee, Nev., 1967—; partner Calif. Seals, San Francisco, 1976-77; pres. Ohio Barons, Inc., Richfield, 1977-78; chmn. bd. Northstar Fin. Corp., Bloomington, Minn., from 1978; formerly chmn. bd. Minn. North Stars, Bloomington; chmn., co-owner San Jose Sharks, NHL, San Jose, CA, 1991—; dir. Ameritrust Cleve.; vice-chmn. Gund Investment Corp., Princeton, N.J.; chmn. North Stars Met Center Mgmt. Corp., Bloomington; v.p. hockey Sun Valley Ice Skating, Inc., Idaho. Chmn. San Francisco Internat. Film Festival, 1973—; mem. sponsors council Project for Population Action; adv. council Sierra Club Found.; mem. internat. council Mus. Modern Art, N.Y.C.; collectors com. Nat. Gallery Art; bd. dirs. Calif. Theatre Found., Bay Area Ednl. TV Assn., San Francisco Mus. Art, Cleve. Health Museum, George Gund Found., Cleve. Internat. Film Festival, Sun Valley Center Arts and Humanities, U. Nev. Reno Found., Sundance Inst. Served with USMCR, 1955-58. Clubs: Calif. Tennis (San Francisco), University (San Francisco), Olympic (San Francisco); Union (Cleve.), Cleve. Athletic (Cleve.), Kirkland Country (Cleve.), Rowfant (Cleve.); Ranier (Seattle). Office: 1821 Union St San Francisco CA 94123-4307

GUNDERSEN, JOAN REZNER, historian, educator; b. Chgo., Nov. 9, 1946; d. Charles Louis and Lois Gladys (Baskin) Rezner; m. Robert Peter Gundersen, Sept. 13, 1969; 1 child, Kristina. BA, Monmouth Coll., 1968; MA, Coll. William and Mary, 1969; PhD, U. Notre Dame, 1972. Adj. faculty Ind. U., South Bend, 1971-74; vis. asst. prof. Vanderbilt U., Nashville, 1974-75; asst. to full prof. St. Olaf Coll., Northfield, Minn., 1975-90; founding prof. Calif. State U., San Marcos, 1989—. Author: Before the World Confessed, 1987, The Anglican Ministry in Virginia, 1989; co-author: American History at a Glance, 1974, 78, 94, America: Changing Times, 1980, 83; bd. editors: Mid-America, 1988—, Virginia Magazine of History, 1992—; contbr. articles to profl. jours. Bd. dirs., pres. Northfield Hist. Soc., 1980-89; mem. exec. bd. Episcopal Women's History Project, 1988—; bd. dirs. San Marcos Boys and Girls Club, 1991—. Named Outstanding Young Alumnus, Monmouth Coll., 1978, Outstanding Faculty Advisor, Phi Alpha Theta, 1989, Outstanding Course grant Am. Soc. for 18th Century Studies, 1992. Mem. AAUW, Am. Hist. Assn. (Pacific Coast br. coun. mem.), So. Hist. Assn. (membership com. 1986, 88, 89, 93), Women Historians of the Midwest (pres. 1988-90), Alpha Xi Delta (chpt. treas. 1966-68). Episcopalian. Home: 1218 Huntington Rd San Marcos CA 92069-5436 Office: Calif State Univ San Marcos CA 92096

GUNDERSEN, PAUL MARTIN, SR., Aleut tribe leader, fisherman; b. Nelson Lagoon, Alaska, Jan. 16, 1921; s. Martin G. and Katie (Sawa) G.; m. Emma Endersen (div. Mar. 1965); children: Butch, Kathleen, Romona, Beverly, Dale; m. Justine Gundersen, Nov. 29, 1977; 1 child, Theo. GED, Dellingham, Alaska. Pres. Nelson Lagoon Tribal Coun., 1972-93, Nelson Lagoon Corp., 1974-93. Chmn. Nelson Lagoon Adv. Bd., 1980-93. With U.S. Army, 1941-45. Office: Native Village of Nelson Lagoon PO Box 13-NLG Nelson Lagoon AK 99571-9999

GUNDERSON, CLARENCE JOSEPH, JR., lawyer, judge advocate; b. Honolulu, Apr. 12, 1949; s. Clarence Joseph Gunderson and Evaline K. (Rodrigues) Awa; m. Betsey Hughes, June 14, 1975; children: Christine-Elyse, Claire-Charisse, Joanne, Jon-Erik, Jason. AA, Windward C.C., 1974; BA, U. Hawaii, 1975, JD, 1983. Bar: Hawaii 1984, U.S. Dist. Ct. Hawaii, U.S. Ct. Mil. Appeals. Police officer Honolulu Police Dept., 1971-72; bank ops. officer Bank of Hawaii, Honolulu, 1977-80; assoc. atty. Law Offices, Honolulu, 1983-85; dep. atty. gen. State Atty. Gen., Honolulu, 1985-87; N.G. judge adv. Hawaii N.G., Honolulu, 1987—. Maj. USAF, 1967-71, 75-77. Mem. ABA, Fed. Bar Assn., Hawaii State Bar Assn. Home: 6996 Niumalu Loop Honolulu HI 96825-1644 Office: Office of Adj Gen 3949 Diamond Head Rd Honolulu HI 96816-4413

GUNDERSON, CLEON HENRY, management consultant corporation executive; b. Great Falls, Mont., June 5, 1932; s. Leon H. and Mona (Emmett) G.; m. Virginia Ellen Hudson, Aug. 26, 1972; children: Craig H., Robert S., Laura E. BS, Inst. Tech., Dayton, Ohio, 1971, Mont. State U., 1957; MAPA, U. Okla., 1975. Communications engr. Mountain States Tel & Tel, Helena, Mont., 1953-54; aerospace engr. Boeing Co., Seattle, 1957-58; commd. 2nd lt. USAF, 1958, advanced to col., 1974, ret., 1976; pres. Precision Prodn. & Engring., Walla Walla, Wash., 1976-79, Western Skies Energy Systems, Spokane, Wash., 1979-88, Computer Central, Olympia, Wash., 1988-90, C.H. Gunderson & Assocs., Littlerock, Wash., 1990—; Mem. Am. Inst. Elec. Engrs., Seattle, 1957-60, Am. Inst. Indsl. Engrs., Spokane, 1982-85. Inventor heatexchange solar panels, comml. solar panels. Decorated Silver Stars, Disting. Flying Crosses, Purple Heart, Air medals. Mem. Soc. Mfg. Engrs. (sr. mem.), Soc. Mil. Engrs., Nat. Assn. Small Businesses, Toastmasters Internat., Walla Walla C. of C., Canto Blanco Gun Club (Madrid, v.p. 1973-75, Scott Air Force Base Gun Club (v.p. 1975-76), Spokane Gun Club. Republican. Home: 13001 Littlerock Rd PO Box 246 Littlerock WA 98556-0246 Office: C H Gunderson & Assocs PO Box 246 Littlerock WA 98556-0246

GUNDERSON, ELMER MILLARD, state supreme court justice, law educator; b. Mpls., Aug. 9, 1929; s. Elmer Peter and Carmaleta (Oliver) G.; m. Lupe Gomez, Dec. 29, 1967; 1 son, John Randolph. Student, U. Minn., U. Omaha, 1948-53; LL.B., Creighton U., 1956; LL.M., U. Va., 1982; LL.D., Calif. Western Sch. Law; student appellate judges seminar, N.Y. U., 1971; LL.D., U. Pacific. Bar: Nebr. 1956, Nev. 1958. Atty.-adviser FTC, 1956-57; pvt. practice Las Vegas, 1958-71; justice Nev. Supreme Ct., 1971-89, now sr. justice; instr. bus. law So. regional div. U. Nev.; lectr., author bulls. felony crimes for Clark County Sheriff's Dept.; counsel Sheriff's Protective Assn.; mem. legal staff Clark Council Civil Def. Agy.; legal counsel Nev. Jaycees. Compiler, annotator: Omaha Home Rule Charter; project coordinator: Juv. Orientation Manual, 1974. Chmn. Clark County Child Welfare Bd., Nev. central chpt. Nat. Multiple Sclerosis Soc.; hon. dir. Spring Mountain Youth Camp. Served with U.S. Army. Recipient A.J.S. Herbert Harley award. Mem. Am., Nebr., Nev. bar assns.; Mem. Inst. Jud. Adminstrn., Am. Law Inst., Am. Trial Lawyers Assn., Am. Judicature Soc., Phi Alpha Delta, Alpha Sigma Nu. Office: Nev Supreme Ct 100 N Carson St Carson City NV 89701-4717

GUNDERSON, TED LEE, security consultant; b. Colorado Springs, Colo., Nov. 7, 1928. BBA, U. Nebr. Sales rep. George A. Hormel Co., Austin, Minn., 1950-51; spl. agt. in charge U.S. Dept. Justice FBI, Los Angeles, Dallas, Memphis, Phila., 1951-79; internat. security cons. Ted L. Gunderson & Assocs., Santa Monica, Calif., 1979—; cons. Calif. Narcotic Authority.

Author: How to Locate Anyone Anywhere, 1989, Be Smart, Be Safe, 1994; appeared on numerous nat. and local TV and radio talk shows; prodr. TV documentary on Satanism. Mem. Bel Air U.S. Navy League, Internat. Assn. Chiefs of Police, Internat. Footprinters Assn., Philanthropic Found. (Los Angeles chpt.), Royal Soc. Encouragement of Arts, Mfrs. and Commerce, Sigma Alpha Epsilon.

GUNDZIK, MICHAEL JOHN, health insurance executive; b. Berkeley, Calif., July 27, 1961; s. Michael George Gundzik and Arline Martineau Rustin. BS cum laude, U. Colo., 1983; MBA, U. Chgo., 1986. Computer programmer/analyst Am. Mgmt. Systems, Lakewood, Colo., 1983-84; free-lance computer programmer/analyst Denver, 1984; summer intern Citicorp, Port-Au-Prince, Haiti, 1985; assoc. The First Boston Corp., N.Y.C., 1986-88; health ins. broker Gundzik & Assocs., Inc., Denver, 1988—. Mem. Nat. Assn. Life Agts., Centennial Assn. Life Agts., Assn. of Health Ins. Agts. Office: Gundzik & Assocs Inc 1801 Broadway Ste 250 Denver CO 80202-3828

GUNN, MICHELA FAITH, psychiatrist; b. Chgo., Feb. 27, 1940; d. Samuel Albert and Elsie (Chestler) G.; m. Martin B. Gelber, Jan. 22, 1970. BS in Chemistry, U. Miami, 1961, MD, 1965. Intern L.A. County-U. So. Calif. Med. Ctr., 1965-66, resident, 1966-68, 68-70, ward chief, 1971-87, clin. instr. psychiatry, 1971-73, clin. asst. prof., 1973-79, clin. assoc. prof., 1979—; psychiatrist pvt. practice, Beverly Hills, Calif., 1970—. Mem. Women's Archtl. League, L.A., 1971—, Gamble House, PAsadena, Calif., 1974—. L.A. County-U. So. Calif. fellow, 1970-71. Mem. So. Calif. Psychiat. Soc. (mem. ethics com. 1987—). Democrat. Jewish. Home and Office: 12268 Canna Rd Los Angeles CA 90049

GUNNELL, DALE RAY, hospital administrator; b. Logan, Utah, May 21, 1936; married. BA, U. Utah, 1963, MA, 1977. Dir. med. records U. Utah Hosp., Salt Lake City, 1969-70, dir. budget, 1970-74, asst. adminstr., 1974-81, assoc. adminstr., 1981-92, COO, 1992—, now assoc. v.p. Contbr. articles to profl. jours. Home: 269 Shari Cir Bountiful UT 84010-3017 Office: Univ of Utah Hospital & Clinics 50 N Medical Dr Salt Lake City UT 84132-0001

GUNST, ROBERT ALLEN, consumer products executive; b. Chgo., Apr. 8, 1948; s. Melville A. and Lois Ellibee G.; m. Karen Kemp, Sept. 5, 1970; children: Graham, Katherine. BA in Econs., Dartmouth Coll., 1969; MBA, U. Chgo., 1971. Asst. v.p. First Nat. Bank Chgo., 1969-75; sr. v.p., chief fin. officer Victoria Sta., Larkspur, Calif., 1975-82; v.p. fin. and adminstrn. PepsiCo Foods Internat. div. PepsiCo Inc., Dallas, 1982-84; sr. v.p. La Petite Boulangerie Inc. subs. PepsiCo Inc., Mill Valley, Calif., 1984-86; sr. v.p., chief fin. officer Shaklee Corp., San Francisco, 1987—, also bd. dirs.; mem. adv. bd. Byers Inc., Hartford; pres., chief oper. officer The Good Guys!, San Francisco. Mem. San Francisco Zool. Soc. (bd. dirs.), Bankers Club, City Club.

GUNSTREAM, ROBBY DEAN, music society executive; b. Pasadena, Calif., Sept. 23, 1951; s. Robby Nelman and Dorothy Jean (Poole) G.; m. Mareth Sinclair, June 6, 1981; children: Corbin Sinclair, Caroline E. Stuart, Colin Saunders Poole. MusB, U. So. Calif., 1974; MusM, Yale U., 1976. Staff assoc. Nat. Assn. Schs. of Music, Reston, Va., 1976-79; asst. dean Conservatory of Music Wheaton (Ill.) Coll., 1979-83; exec. dir. Coll. Music Soc., Missoula, Mont., 1983—. Recipient cert. Ctr. for Black Music Research, Chgo., 1987. Episcopalian. Office: Coll Music Soc 202 W Spruce St Missoula MT 59802-4202

GUNSUL, BROOKS R. W., architect; b. Seattle, Aug. 7, 1928; s. Frank Justus and Phyllis (Webster) G.; m. Marilyn Thompson, Aug. 26, 1950; children: Robin, Karen, David, Jana. B.S. in Archtl. Engring., Wash. State U., 1952. Registered architect, Oreg., Wash., Ill., N.Y. Architect Stewart & Richardson architect, Portland, 1952-57, Scott & Payne, Portland, 1957-59, Wolff & Zimmer, 1959-65; ptnr. Wolff, Zimmer Gunsul. Frasca, Portland, 1966-77; ptnr. Zimmer Gunsul Frasca, Portland, 1977, Seattle, 1987—, L.A., 1988—; mem. adv. com. Wash. State U. Dept. Architecture, Pullman, 1983-93, found. adv. bd., 1994-96; dir., founder Architecture Found., Portland, 1980-88. Contbr. articles to profl. jours. Chmn. adv. com. Oreg. Maritime Ctr. and Mus. Served with U.S. Army, 1946-47. Recipient Wash. State U. Achievement award, 1991. Fellow AIA (Firm of Yr. award 1991), Portland Yacht Club, Multnomah Athletic Club. Office: Zimmer Gunsul Frasca Partnership 320 SW Oak St Ste 500 Portland OR 97204-2735

GUNTER, EMILY DIANE, communications executive, marketing professional; b. Atlantic City, N.J., Apr. 5, 1948; d. Fay Gaffney and Verlee (Wright) G.; children: Saliha, Kadir, Amin, Shedia. BA in Math. Stats., Am. U., 1970, postgrad. computer sci., 1971; postgrad. mktg., San Diego C.C., 1986. Traffic engr. C&P Bell, Washington, 1970-71; market analyst Market Towers Inc., Atlantic City, N.J., 1978-79; outside plant engr. N.J. Bell, Atlantic City, 1979-81; market analyst Empcor Group, Atlantic City, 1981-83; outside plant engr. Pacific Bell, San Diego, 1983-91, account exec., 1991-93; exec. v.p. Black Am. of Achievement, Inc., San Diego, 1994-95; pres. Gunter Devel. Enterprises, 1987—; lectr. women and minorities in engring. and math. Princeton (N.J.) U., 1979-81, Atlantic C.C., Atlantic City, 1979-81; customer coord. Pacific Bell-Telsam, San Diego, 1983-85; prof. math. Grossmont Coll., 1992—, instr. super learning skills seminar, 1992—. Author: Superlearning 2000: The New Technologies of Self-Empowerment, 1993, Supermath 2000: How to Learn Math Without Fear, 1993, Achieve Goals 2000: A Personal Handbook for the Lifelong Learner, 1995. Bd. dirs. Lead, San Diego, Atlantic City Transp. Authority, 1981-82, San Diego Urban Math. Collaborative; trustee Reuben H. Fleet Sci. Found., 1989, San Diego Sci. Found., 1989—, 1990 class Lead-Leadership Edn. Awareness Devel., San Diego; mem. steering com. United Negro Coll. Fund, San Diego; mem. Atlantic City Urban Area Transp. Commn., 1982-83; mem. Am. Humanics Bd. U. San Diego, 1991—; pres. bd. dirs. World Beat Cultural Ctr., Balboa Park, Calif., 1992-93. Mem. African Am. Womens Conf. Democrat. Islamic. Home: PO Box 152121 San Diego CA 92195-2121 also: Gunter Devel Enterprises PO Box 152121 San Diego CA 92195-2121

GUNTER, WILLIAM DAYLE, JR., physicist; b. Mitchell, S.D., Jan. 10, 1932; s. William Dayle and Lamerta Berniece (Hockensmith) G.; m. Shirley Marie Teshera, Oct. 24, 1955; children—Maria Jo, Robert Paul. B.S. in Physics with distinction, Stanford U., 1957, M.S., 1959. Physicist Ames Research Ctr. NASA, Moffett Field, Calif., 1960-81, asst. br. chief electronic optical engring., 1981-85; pvt. practice cons. Photon Applications, San Jose, Calif., 1985—. Patentee in field. Contbr. articles to profl. jours. Served with U.S. Army, 1953-55. Recipient Westinghouse Sci. Talent Search award, 1950; various awards NASA; Stanford U. scholar, 1950. Mem. Am. Assn. Profl. Cons., Optical Soc. Am., IEEE (sr.), Am. Phys. Soc., Soc. Photo-Optical Instrumentation Engrs., Planetary Soc., Nat. Space Soc., NASA Alumni League. Office: Photon Applications 5290 Dellwood Way San Jose CA 95118-2904

GUNTY, CHRISTOPHER JAMES, newspaper editor; b. Hometown, Ill., Oct. 13, 1959; s. Harold Paul and Therese Agnes (Kohs) G.; m. Nancy Louise Blanton, July 10, 1982; children: William, Amy, Timothy. BA, Loyola U., Chgo., 1981. Circulation mgr. The Chgo. Catholic, 1981-83, assoc. mnging. editor, 1983, mng. editor, 1983-85; editor, mng. editor The Catholic Sun, Phoenix, 1985—. Author: He Came to Touch Us, 1987; co-author videotape script The Pope in Arizona, 1987. Contbr. articles to spl. Catholic news svcs. as well as papers where employed. Mem. Fiesta Bowl Com., Phoenix, 1987-92. Named Honoree Summer U. Internat. Cath. Union of the Press, Switzerland, 1988. Mem. Cath. Press Assn. (bd. dirs. 1988—, sec. 1990-92, v.p. 1994—), Assoc. Ch. Press, Ariz. Newspapers Assn., Ariz. Press Club, Soc. Profl. Journalists. Roman Catholic. Office: The Catholic Sun 400 E Monroe St Phoenix AZ 85004-2336

GUPTA, BARBARA MACKAY, mathematics educator; b. Berkeley, Calif., Nov. 6, 1948; d. William Robert and Joanne Coby (Williams) Mackay; m. Yogendra Mohan Gupta, June 21, 1975; children: Anjuli Monica, Sonia Michelle. BA in Elem. Edn., Washington State U., 1970, postgrad., 1987—. Cert. tchr., Wash. Tchr. Edison Elem Sch., Walla Walla, Wash., 1970-75; from tchr. and math. dept. chair to prin. middle campus Pinewood Pvt. Sch., Los Altos, Calif., 1976-81; curriculum cons. Pullman, Wash., 1981—. Eisenhower Spl. Project grant Office the Supt. Pub. Instrn., Pullman, Wash., 1993-94. Mem. ASCD, AAUW, Nat. Coun. Tchrs. Math., Am. Ednl. Rsch. Assn., Assn. for Women in Sci. Home and Office: SW 845 Mies Pullman WA 99163

GUPTA, BIMLESHWAR PRASAD, mechanical engineer, manager; b. Jaipur, Raj, India, May 17, 1946; s. Hari Prasad and Sarla D. (Agarwal) G.; m. Rajni Garg, Dec. 10, 1974; children: Anjli, Neeraj. BSME, U. Jodhpur, India, 1968; MSME, U. Minn., 1971, MBA, 1974. Registered profl. engr., Colo. Engr. Honeywell Inc., Mpls., 1971-76, sect. mgr., 1976-78; program and div. ops. mgr. Nat. Renewable Energy Lab., Golden, Colo., 1978—; lectr. in field; chairperson nat. and internat. confs. on solar thermal rsch. Guest editor spl. edit. The Energy Jour., 1987; contbr. articles to profl. jours. Mem. ASME (assoc. editor jour. 1983-85, guest editor spl. issue 1984), Internat. Solar Energy Soc., India Assn. Colo. (exec. com. 1983-84, pres. 1991), U. Minn. Alumni Assn., Toastmasters (pres. Lakewood 1985, bd. govs. F-2 area 1988-89). Home: 14373 W Bayaud Pl Golden CO 80401-5339 Office: Nat Renewable Energy Lab 1617 Cole Blvd Golden CO 80401

GUPTA, PRAVEEN, engineering executive, software engineer; b. Sambhal, India, May 24, 1959; came to U.S., 1983; s. Jai P. and Kanti (Baranwal) Vaish; m. Reeta Gupta, Dec. 4, 1985; 1 child, Ankur. BS in Physics, M.S. U., Baroda, India, 1978; MSc, U. Roorkee, India, 1980; MTech, Indian Inst. Sci., Bangalore, 1982; MS in Computer Sci., U. Tex., Arlington, 1988; MBA, Golden Gate U., 1995. Systems analyst Tata Consultancy Svcs., Delhi, 1982-84; sr. software engr. Gearhart Industries, Inc., Ft. Worth, 1984-88; sr. electronic systems engr. Electrocom Automation, Inc., Arlington, 1988-90; engring. mgr. Internat. Computers Ltd., Santa Clara, Calif., 1990-94, Raynet Corp., Menlo Park, Calif., 1994-95, Octel Comm. Corp., Milpitas, Calif., 1995—. Mem. IEEE. Home: 34712 Teal Common Fremont CA 94555-2857

GUPTA, SUNEEL KUMAR, pharmacologist; b. Yamuna Nagar, India, Sept. 6, 1957; came to U.S., 1987; s. Inder Sain and Kaushalaya (Devi) G.; m. Shahida Naseem, May 24, 1991. MPharm with 1st class honors, Indu U., Varanasi, India, 1981; student, Inst. of Cost and Works Acctg., Calcutta, 1983-84; PhD, U. Manchester, Eng., 1987. Mfg. pharmacist Hindustan Ciba-Geigy Ltd., Kandla, India, 1981-85; postdoctoral fellow U. Calif., San Francisco, 1987-89; staff scientist ALZA Corp., Palo Alto, Calif., 1989-91, rsch. scientist, 1991-92, mgr. clin. pharmacology, 1992-93, assoc. dir. clin. pharmacology, 1994—. Contbr. articles to profl. jours. Recipinet Frederick Craven Moore award U. Manchester, 1985-87. Mem. Am. Soc. Clin. Pharmacology and Therapeutics, Am. Assn. Pharm. Scientists, Am. Coll. Clin. Pharmacology. Office: ALZA Corp 2400 Hanover St Palo Alto CA 94304-1113

GURAK, STANLEY JOSEPH, mathematics and computer science educator; b. Troy, N.Y., June 14, 1949; s. Joseph Steven and Viola Catherine (Trela) G. BS in Math. and Physics, SUNY, Stony Brook, 1971; PhD in Math., UCLA, 1975; MS in Computer Sci., U. Calif., San Diego, 1987. Lectr. math. UCLA, 1975-76; asst. prof. Fla. State U., Tallahassee, 1976-77; asst. prof. U. San Diego, 1977-80, assoc. prof., 1980-83, prof. math. and computer sci., 1983—, head dept. math. and computer sci., 1988-91; vis. rsch. fellow U. New South Wales, Sydney, Australia, 1983, McQuarie U., Sydney, 1992. Contbr. articles to profl. jours. Chancellor's Intern fellow UCLA, 1971. Mem. Am. Math. Soc., Math. Assn. Am., Sigma Pi Sigma. Office: U San Diego Dept Math and Computer Sci Alcala Pk San Diego CA 92110

GURASH, JOHN THOMAS, insurance company executive; b. Oakland, Calif., Nov. 25, 1910; s. Nicholas and Katherine (Restovic) G.; student Loyola U. Sch. Law, Los Angeles, 1936, 38-39; m. Katherine Mills, Feb. 4, 1934; 1 child, John N. With Am. Surety Co. N.Y., 1930-44; with Pacific Employers Ins. Co., 1944-53; pres., organizer Meritplan Ins. Co., 1953-59; exec. v.p. Pacific Employers Ins. Co., 1959-60, pres., 1960-68, chmn., bd., 1968-76; v.p. Ins. Co. N. Am., 1966-70; exec. v.p., dir. INA Corp., 1968-69, chmn., pres., CEO, 1969-74, chmn., CEO, 1974-75, chmn. bd., 1975, chmn. exec. com., 1975-79; chmn. bd. CertainTeed Corp., 1978-92; chmn. bd. dirs. Horace Mann Educators Corp., Springfield, Ill., 1989—; dir. St. Gobain Corp., chmn.bd. dirs., 1991-92. Trustee emeritus Occidental Coll., L.A.; former trustee Orthopaedic Hosp., Los Angeles; bd. dirs. Weingart Found. Mem. Pa. Soc., Newcomen Soc. N.Am., Am. Soc. French Legion of Honor, Knights of Malta, Calif. Club, Pine Valley (N.J.) Golf Club, L.A. Country Club, Sr. Golf Assn. of So. Calif., Annandale Golf Club, Valley Hunt Club. Office: 1000 Wilshire Blvd Ste 610 Los Angeles CA 90017-2457

GURGIN, VONNIE ANN, social scientist; b. Toledo, Nov. 20, 1940. B.A., Ohio State U., 1962; M.A., U. Calif., Berkeley, 1966; D.Criminology, 1969. Research asst. Calif. Dept. Mental Hygiene, San Francisco, 1962-64; research sociologist U. Calif., Berkeley, 1964-66; dir. cons. services Survey Research Center, 1967-68, asst. prof. criminology, 1968-71; research sociologist Social Sci. Research and Devel. Corp., Berkeley, 1966-67; sr. research criminologist Stanford Research Inst. (now SRI Internat.), Menlo Park, Calif., 1971-72; research dir. Inst. Study Social Concerns, Berkeley, 1972—; asst. chief resource for cancer prevention and epidemiology sect. Calif. Tumor Registry, Calif. Dept. Health Services, Emeryville, 1981-86; dir. survey research No. Calif. Cancer Ctr., Belmont, 1982-86; dir. SEER programs No. Calif. Cancer Ctr., 1986; cons.; mgr. dept. family and community health Calif. Med. Assn., San Francisco, 1993—; pres. bd. dirs. Inst. Study Social Concerns, Berkeley; bd. dirs. Elmwood Coll., Berkeley, 1992—. Author reports, monographs, articles. Bd. dirs. Rsch. Guild, Sacramento, 1983-86. Mem. AAAS, Am. Sociol. Assn. Address: 1099 Sterling Ave Berkeley CA 94708-1728

GURNSEY, KATHLEEN WALLACE, state legislator; b. Donnelly, Idaho; d. Robert G. and Thelma (Halferty) Wallace; m. Vern L. Gurnsey, May 7, 1950; children: Kristina Johnson, Steve, Scott. BA in Bus. Adminstn., Boise State U., 1976. Mem. Idaho Ho. of Reps., Boise, 1974—. Bd. dirs. YMCA, Boise; elder, pres. Women's Assn. First Presbyn. Ch.; bd. dirs. Fundsy, St. Luke's Aux.; mem. Def. Adv. Com. Women in the Svc., Dept. Def., 1982-84. Named Disting. Citizen Idaho Statesman, Woman of Yr. Soroptimist, Woman Achievment Altrusa Club, Outstanding Alumna Boise State U., 1991. Mem. AAUW (Outstanding Community Svcs. award 1991), Bus. and Profl. Women, Jobs Daus. (Bethel guardian honored queen). Republican. Presbyterian. Home: 1111 W Highland View Dr Boise ID 83702-1319

GURWITZ-HALL, BARBARA ANN, artist; b. Ayer, Mass., July 7, 1942; d. Jack and Rose (Baritz) Gurwitz; m. James M. Marshall III, Mar. 12, 1966 (div. 1973); m. William D. Hall, May 3, 1991; legal guardian: Samantha Hollinger. Student, Boston U., 1960-61, Katherine Gibbs Sch., Boston, 1961-63. Represented by Karin Newby Gallery, Tubac, Ariz.; represented by Wilde-Meyer Gallery, Scottsdale, Ariz.; Artist-in-residence Desert House of Prayer, Tucson, 1989-91; oblate mem. Benedictine Sisters Perpetual Adoration, 1986—. One-artist shows: YWCA, Bklyn., 1977, Henry Hicks Gallery, Bklyn., 1978, Misty-Mountain Gallery, Tubac, Ariz., 1987, Karin Newby Gallery, Tubac, 1989; exhibited in group shows: Becket (Mass.) Art Ctr., 1978, Winter Gallery, Tucson, 1980, Johnson Gallery, Bisbee, Ariz., Hilltop Gallery, Nogales, Ariz., 1981, Scharf Gallery, Sante Fe, 1982, Data Mus., Ein Hod, Israel, 1985, C.G. Rein Gallery, Santa Fe, 1986, New West Views Tubac Ctr. for Arts, 1985, Mesquite Gallery, Patagonia, Ariz., 1986, Beth O'Donnell Gallery, Tucson, 1989, Karin Newby Gallery, 1989—, Wilde-Meyer Gallery, Scottsdale, Ariz., 1991—, ArtWest, Art Collector's Gallery, Tulsa, 1992, Ann. Juried Festival Show, 1989, 90, 91, 92, 93, 94,95, Mountain Oyster Club Ann. Western Art Show, Tucson, 1994, Phoenix Mus. League, 1994; represented in permanent collections: Diocese of Tucson, N.J. Sambul & Co., N.Y.C., Goldman Sachs & Co., N.Y.C., Data Mus., Israel, Desert House of Prayer, Tucson, Ethical Culture Soc., Bklyn., St. Andrews Episcopal Ch., Nogales, Tubac Elem. Sch., numerous private collections U.S., Eur. Mem. Tubac Village Coun., 1979-86; bd. dirs. Pimeria Alta Hist. Soc., Nogales, Ariz., 1982-84; creator Children;s Art Walk, Tubac Sch. System and Village Coun., 1980; set designer, choreographer ann. De Anza Ann. Pageant, Tubac Ctr. Arts, 1982—; apstoral asst. St. Ann's Parish, Tubac, 1986-89; team mem. R.C.I.A. Our Lady of the Valley Parish, Green Valley, Ariz., 1994—. Mem. Santa Cruz Valley Art Assn. (hon. mention ann. juried show 1989-95, Best of Show award 1989, award for excellence 1992), Assn. Contemplative Sisters.

GUSTAFSON, CHARLES IVAN, hospital administrator; b. Chadron, Nebr., June 29, 1931; s. Archie and Adelia (Bawnes) G.; BS, U. Wash., 1953; MHA, U. Mich., 1957; m. Donna Rae Gustafson; children: Laura Kay, Brian Charles, James Robert, Jennifer Kaye. Asst. adminstr. Good Samaritan Hosp., Portland, Oreg., 1957-58; adminstr. Rogue Valley Meml. Hosp., Medford, 1958-80, bd. dirs., 1979; chief exec. officer G.N. Wilcox Meml. Hosp. and Health Center, Kauai, Hawaii, 1980-83; adminstr. Deaconess Hosp., Spokane, Wash., 1983-84; hosp. dir. King Fahad Hosp., Al-Baha, Saudi Arabia, 1984-88; adminstrv. dir. Hamad Med. Ctr., Doha, Qatar, 1989-93; sr. v.p. corp. devel. Brim, Inc., Portland, Oreg., 1993—; bd. dirs. So. Oreg. Ednl. Co. Mem. Gov.'s Com. on Comprehensive Health Planning, 1968-72; mem. Oreg. Health Commn. Bd. dirs. Shakespearean Festival, Ashland, Oreg., Rogue Valley Health Found., 1979—. Served with AUS, 1953-55. Fellow Am. Coll. Hosp. Adminstrs.; mem. Am. Hosp. Assn. (Oreg. del. 1968-70), Oreg. Assn. Hosps. (pres. 1968-69), Nat. Assn. Hosp. Devel., Am. Assn. Hosp. Planning. Republican. Episcopalian. Home: 1870 Hoone Rd Koloa HI 96756-9791

GUSTAFSON, RANDALL LEE, city manager; b. Sidney, Nebr., Nov. 11, 1947; s. Robert John and Hilda Lydia (Sims) G.; m. Cynthia Ann Taylor, Oct. 18, 1974. Student, U. Kans., 1965-68, Rockhurst Coll., 1968-70; BS in Pub. Adminstrn., Upper Iowa U., 1992. City mgr. City of Bonner Springs, Kans., 1970-77; bus. owner Lambquarters, Dix, Nebr., 1977-83; city mgr. City of Aurora, Mo., 1983-85, City of Sterling, Colo., 1985—; bd. dirs. Logan Area Devel. Co., Sterling. Bd. dirs. Fire and Police Pension Assn. Colo., Denver, 1987—, 13th Jud. Dist. Community Corrections, Brush, Colo., 1988-90; mem. Colo. Mcpl. League Policy Com., Denver, 1987-89. Recipient Disting. Svc. award Jaycees, 1976. Mem. Internat. Assn. City Mgmt. (full mem.), Colo. Assn. City Mgmt., Am. Soc. for Pub. Adminstrn., Govs. Fin. Assn., Rotary, Elks. Republican. Lutheran. Office: Centennial Sq Sterling CO 80751

GUSTAFSON, SALLY A., counselor, cosmetologist, educator; b. Olympia, Wash., Sept. 21, 1947; d. Thomas Buchanan and Dorothy May (Long) Ness; m. Douglas Carl Gustafson, Oct. 2, 1967; children: Troy Douglas, Tristan Suzan. Cert. cosmetologist, Mr. Roberts Beauty Coll., Tacoma, Wash., 1966; cert. counselor, Maranatha Inst., Oakley, Calif., 1994. Cosmetology instr. Calif. Beauty Coll., Pleasant Hill, 1969-70; mgr. Jafra Cosmetics, Antioch, Calif., 1970-84; cosmetologist J.C. Penney, Antioch, Calif., 1991—; counselor Pittsburg (Calif.) Christian Assembly, Calif., 1994—. Office: Pittsburg Christian Ctr 1210 Stoneman Ave Pittsburg CA 94565-5458

GUSTAVSON, JOAN ELLEN CARLSON, psychologist; b. Bingham Canyon, Utah, Feb. 26, 1947; d. Leonard Alfred and Melba Ellen (Brown) Carlson; m. Carl Roger Gustavson, June 6, 1964; children: Andrew Roger, Eric Cris. BS, N.D. State U., Fargo, 1982. Interviewer coord. Galveston (Tex.) Family Health Mental Health Survey Project, 1986-87; asst. rsch. dir. Psychiat. Ethology Lab., U. Tex. Med. Br., Galveston, 1985-89; owner Body Image Distortion and Dissatisfaction Evaluation. Editor: Roses and Catails: A Collection of Readings in Human Sexuality, 1981; contbr. articles to profl. jours. Named One of the Outstanding Young Women of Am., 1982. Mem. Am. Inst. Biol. Sci., Am. Psychol. Soc., Western Psychol. Assn., N.Y. Acad. Sci., Sigma Xi, Phi Kappa Phi. Home: 243 W Calle Monte Vista Dr Tempe AZ 85284-2261

GUSTAVSON, MARK STEVEN, lawyer; b. Berkeley, Calif., Jan. 3, 1951; s. Dean Leonard and Barbara (Knight) G.; m. Janet Daly, Jan. 24, 1974; children: Eric Karl, Stephen Earl, Jennifer Ann. BA in Philosophy magna cum laude, U. Utah, 1973, JD, 1976. Bar: Utah 1976. Gen. counsel The Gustavson Group, Inc., Salt Lake City, 1976-91; pvt. practice Salt Lake City, 1976-82; sr. ptnr. Gustavson & Williams Attys., 1983-85, Gustavson, Hall & Williams, Salt Lake City, 1985-86, Gustavson, Schultz, Hall & Williams, Salt Lake City, 1986-93; corp. counsel, sec. Christensen Boyles Corp., Salt Lake City, 1993—; pres. Concours Automotive Restoration, Inc., 1981—; adj. prof. philosophy Utah C.C., 1991; mem. devel. com. Tanner Humanities Ctr., U. Utah. Columnist Scale Auto Enthusiast, Car Modeler, Model Car Jour.; contbr. articles to prol. jours. Founder Nat. Model Car Builders' Mus. Faculty scholar, U. Utah, 1972-73. Mem. Utah Bar Assn., Salt Lake County Bar Assn., Sunstone Found., Owl and Key. Libertarian. Mormon. Office: Christensen Boyles Corp 4446 W 1730 S Salt Lake City UT 84104-4703

GUTHRIE, DAVID NEAL, marketing executive; b. Paris, Tex., Feb. 12, 1941; s. Wesley Neal and Marie (Oliver) G.; m. Ramona Jeanne Busch, Feb. 6, 1959; children: David Jr., Scott, Laure. Student, San Antonio Coll., 1959-62, U. Tex., 1962-63, U. Tex., Arlington, 1965-66, U. Mo., 1970-72. From systems analyst to sales mgr. Sperry Univac, St. Louis, 1967-80; sales rep. Computer Sharing Svcs. Inc., St. Louis, 1980-83, Tandem Computers, Inc., St. Louis, 1983-84, Sykes Datatronics, Inc., St. Louis, 1984-85; sales rep. Cray Rsch., Inc., Colorado Springs, 1985-88, mktg. mgr., 1988-93; sales mgr. Thinking Machines Corp., 1993—. With USMCR, 1957-59. Fellow Mensa. Republican. Home: 42 Jessana Hts Colorado Springs CO 80906-7902 Office: Thinking Machines Corp 105 E Vermijo Ste 550 Colorado Springs CO 80903-2241

GUTHRIE, EDGAR KING, artist; b. Chenoa, Ill., May 12, 1917; s. David McMurtrie and Emily Henrietta (Streid) G.; m. Eva Ross Harvey, Dec. 8, 1945 (dec. Jan. 1978); children: Melody Bliss Johnson, Mark King Guthrie. BEd, Ill. State U., 1939; MA, Am. U., 1958; graduate, Command and General Staff Coll., Ft. Leavenworth, Kan., 1967. Artist W.L. Stensgaard Co., Chgo., 1939-40, The Diamond Store, Phoenix, 1941-42; presentation artist CIA, Washington, 1955-72; instr. Columbia Tech. Inst., Arlington, Va., 1966-72; owner, later ptnr. Guthrie Art & Sign Co., Winchester, Va., 1976—; instr. U. Hawaii, Lihue, 1980-81; cartoonist The Kauai Times, Lihue, 1981-90; owner Alo-o-oha-ha-ha Caricatures, Lihue, Honolulu, 1980—; cons., artist Shenandoah Apple Blossom Festival, Winchester, 1975-78; cartoonist Internat. Salon of Caricature, Montreal, Can., 1976-77; co-chmn. Kauai Soc. of Artists Art Show, Lihue, 1981. One man shows include 50 Yrs. of Painting-A Retrospective, Lihue, 1984; inventor Artists' Kit; Filmic Artist: (documentary film) The River Nile, 1960 (NBC Emmy Award). Bd. dirs. Civil Def., Virginia Hills, 1954; publicity com. Frederick County Taxpayers Assn., Winchester, 1973, Exch. Club, Winchester, 1977. Lt. col. U.S. Army, 1942-54. Decorated Purple Heart, Bronze Star with oak leaf cluster; recipient Spl. Merit award Boy Scouts Am. Aloha Coun., Lihue, 1982. Mem. Mus. of Cartoon Art, U.S. Naval Combat Artist, Daniel Morgan Mus. (contbr. 1976), Nat. Soc. Mural Painters (contbr. 1976), Allied Artists of Am. (contbr. 1977), Pastel Soc. Am. (contbr. 1977-78), Am. Watercolor Soc. (contbr. 1982—), Greek Expeditionary Forces (hon.). Mem. Ch. LDS.

GUTHRIE, JAMES BRYAN, architect; b. Chgo., Jan. 26, 1957; s. Thomas Allan and Marilyn L. (Murphy) G. BS, U. Ill., 1979, MArch, 1982. Architect Krommenhoek, McKeown Architects, San Diego, M.W. Steele, Inc., San Diego; assoc. Gast, Urban Design & Architecture, San Diego; prin. San Diego, 1989—; instr. New Sch. of Architecture, 1987—, Urban Info. Sys., 1994—. Contbr. articles to profl. jours.;. Bd. dirs. Norman Heights Community Devel. Corp, 1988—, Save Our Heritage Orgn., 1988-90; pres. Normal Heights Community Devel. Corp., 1990-94. Mem. San Diego Archt. Club (pres. 84-86), AIA, Nat. Trust Hist. Preservation, San Diego Sailing Club, Urban Land Inst., Am. Planning Assn.

GUTHRIE, PATRICIA SUE, newspaper reporter, free-lance writer; b. Buffalo, Sept. 27, 1958; d. Robert and Margaret Ann (Flagstad) G. Student, Buffalo State Coll., 1976-78, U. Buffalo, 1978-79; BS in Journalism, Northern Ariz. State U., 1983. Freelance reporter DesertWest News, Flagstaff, Ariz., 1983-85; reporter The Gallup (N.M.) Independent, 1985-88; freelance writer The Ariz. Republic and other news orgns., 1985-88; reporter The Albuquerque Tribune, 1988—. Recipient Don Bolles award Ariz. Press Club, 1986, George Polk award L.I. U., 1988, Best Investigative Series award N.M. AP Mng. Editors, 1988, Team Reporting award Scripps Howard Newspapers, 1988-89, Nat. Headliner award Atlantic City Press Club, 1989, Unity Awards in Media Lincoln U. of Mo., 1989, Pub. Svc. award N.M. Press Assn., 1989, Pub. Svc. award Mng. Editors AP, 1989, Amicus Honor for Pub. Svc. N.M. Trial Lawyers Amicus Found., 1989, Kiplinger Fellowship award Ohio State U. Journalism Grad. Sch., 1990—; named Disting. Alumnus No. Ariz. U., 1990. Mem. N.M. Press Women (awards for writing, 1987), Edn. Writers Assn., Women in Communications (Clarion award, 1989), Investigative Reporters and Editors, Sigma Delta Chi (v.p. Flagstaff student chpt. 1982-83). Office: Albuquerque Tribune PO Drawer T Albuquerque NM 87103*

GUTIERREZ, MARY CECILIA, vocational school counselor; b. Albuquerque, Oct. 1, 1952; m. Joey A. Gutierrez, Nov. 27, 1971. BA in Psychology magna cum laude, U. N.Mex., 1988, MA in Counseling, 1989. Lic. profl. counselor, cert. counselor. Counselor Gen. Rehab. Svc., Albuquerque; clin. therapist Family & Children's Svc., Albuquerque, Horgares, Inc., Albuquerque, New Day, Inc., Albuquerque; coord. spl. populations Albuquerque Tech./Vocat. Inst., 1993—; instr., cons. Supervisory Inst., Albuquerque, 1994—; mem. adv. bd. Men in Transition Project, Albuquerque, 1994—; mem. cultural diversity task force Albuquerque Pub. Schs., 1993—. Mem. AMHCA, ACDA, NMCA, NMMHCA, NMCDA, Am. Counseling Assn., Phi Kappa Phi, Phi Beta Kappa. Home: 12204 Emperor NE Albuquerque NM 87123 Office: Albuquerque Tech Vocat Inst 525 Buena Vista SE Albuquerque NM 87106

GUTIERREZ-MEDINA, HECTOR, Spanish interpreter; b. Mexico City, Mex., Feb. 3, 1951; came to U.S., 1963; s. Benjamin and Emily (Gutierrez) M.; m. Cheryl Ann Creech, June 29, 1985; 1 child, Sabrina. AA, East L.A. Coll., 1975; BA, UCLA, 1978. Spanish ct. interpreter L.A., 1980—. Mem. Am. Translators Assn., Calif. Ct. Interpreters Assn. Democrat. Roman Catholic. Home: 3869 Bluff St Torrance CA 90505-6359

GUTMAN, GEORGE ANDRE, molecular biologist, educator; b. Domme, France, Sept. 15, 1945; came to U.S., 1947; s. Peter M. and Frances F. (Reitman) G.; m. Janis Lynn Schonauer, Dec. 30, 1977; children: Pierre Daniel, Marie Elizabeth. AB, Columbia Coll., 1966; PhD, Stanford U., 1973. Postdoctoral fellow Stanford (Calif.) U., 1973-74, Walter and Eliza Hall Inst. Med. Rsch., Melbourne, Australia, 1974-76; asst. prof. U. Calif., Irvine, 1976-82, assoc. prof., 1982-89, prof., 1989—. Fulbright Hays fellow, 1966-67, Arthritis Found. rsch. fellow, 1974-77; USPHS grantee, 1978-90; recipient Rsch. Career Devel. award USPHS, 1978-83. Fellow Am. Assn. for Advancement of Sci.; mem. Am. Assn. Immunology. Office: U Calif Dept Microbiol Molec G Irvine CA 92717

GUTOW, BERNARD SIDNEY, packaging manufacturing company executive; b. Chgo., Nov. 11, 1939; s. Max and Betty (Warshawsky) G.; m. Carol Lerch, June 5, 1960; children: Jeffrey, Bryon. BS in Engring., U. Ill., 1961, MS in Engring., 1962; MBA, U. Santa Clara, 1965. Registered profl. engr., Ill. Sr. engr. Lockheed Missiles, Sunnyvale, Calif., 1962-65; project engr. U.S. Steel Co., Chgo., 1965-67; engr., prin. A.T. Kearney Co., Chgo., 1967-78; dir. Shaklee, San Francisco, 1978-79; v.p. H.S. Crocker, San Bruno, Calif., 1979-85; v.p., gen. mgr. First Data Resources subs. Am. Express Corp., Tustin, Calif., 1985-88; gen. ptnr., Mgmt. Resource Ptnrs., Redwood Shores, Calif., 1988—. Editor: Plant Engineering Management, 1974; pres., CEO Bayline Ptnrs., Bayline Paper Supply, Union City, Calif., 1991—; contbr. articles to profl. jours. Pres. Morton Grove Park Dist., Ill., 1973-78; mem. Morton Grove Youth Commn., 1973-78. Recipient Plaque, Morton Grove Park Dist., 1978; cert. Soc. Mfg. Engrs., Chgo., 1975, Bronze award Internat. Film and TV Festival N.Y., N.Y.C., 1984. Mem. ASME (chpt. chmn. 1972-73). Home: 3263 La Mesa Dr San Carlos CA 94070-4244

GUTSCHE, STEVEN LYLE, physicist; b. St. Paul, Nov. 10, 1946; s. Lyle David and Phyllis Jane (Stubstad) G.; divorced; children: Kristina, Angela; m. Marilyn D. Maloney, Oct. 4, 1980; children: Taylor Steven, Daniel Mark. BS, U. Colo., 1968; MS, U. Calif., Santa Barbara, 1970. Physicist USN Pacific Missile Range, Point Mugu, Calif., 1968-71; staff scientist Mission Rsch. Corp., Santa Barbara, 1971-76, group leader, 1977-79, div. leader, 1979—, v.p., 1987—; pres., 1989—; also bd. dirs. Mission Rsch. Corp., Santa Barbara. Contbr. articles to tech. publs. Presbyterian. Office: Mission Rsch Corp 735 State St # 719 Santa Barbara CA 93101-3351*

GUTSCHICK, VINCENT PETER, biologist, educator; b. Berwyn, Ill., July 24, 1945; s. Vincent William and Frances Genevieve (Stonich) G.; married; 1 child, David Duncanson. BS in Chemistry, U. Notre Dame, 1966; PhD, Calif. Inst. Tech., 1972. NSF postdoctoral fellow U. Calif., Berkeley, 1971-72; J.W. Gibbs Instr. Yale U., New Haven, Conn., 1972-75; dir.'s postdoctoral fellow Los Alamos (N.Mex.) Nat. Lab., 1975-77, cons., 1977-78, staff mem., 1978-85; assoc. prof. N.Mex. State U., Las Cruces, 1985-91, prof., 1991—; vis. fellow CSIRO, Canberra, Australia, 1991, Carnegie Inst. Plant Biology, Stanford, Calif., Australian Nat. U, Canberra, 1994; program officer NSF, Washington, 1992-93; disting. vis. fellow Latrobe U., Melbourne, Australia. Author: A Functional Biology of Crop Plants, 1987; contbr. numerous articles to profl. jours.; patentee in field. Mem. Am. Soc. Plant Physiologists, Am. Inst. Biol. Scis., Ecol. Soc. Am. Democrat. Office: NMex State U Dept Biology 3AF Las Cruces NM 88003

GUTTENTAG, WILLIAM SIDNEY, television producer; b. Bklyn., Jan. 27, 1958; s. Jack and Doris W. G.; m. Marina Brodskaya. BA, U. Pa., 1979; postgrad., Am. Film Inst., 1979-80. Writer, producer CBS News, N.Y.C., 1989; writer, producer, dir. ABC News, N.Y.C., 1990-93, Nat. Geographic TV, Washington, 1993, Home Box Office, N.Y.C., 1986—. Writer, prodr.: (documentary film) You Don't Have to Die, 1988 (Acad. award 1989); writer, prodr., dir.: Crack USA: County Under Siege, 1989 (Acad. award nomination 1990), Death on the Job, 1991 (Acad. award nomination 1992); writer, prodr., dir.: (documentary TV spl.) The Cocaine War: Lost in Bolivia, 1992, Blues Highway, 1994 (Acad. award nomination 1995). Recipient Ace award Nat. Acad. Cable TV, 1990, 93, Scott Newman award Scott Newman Found., 1990. Mem. Acad. Motion Picture Arts and Scis.

GUTTERMAN, SHEILA MAYDET, lawyer; b. Mendota, Ill., Jan. 28, 1944; d. Simon and Anne (Koopersmith) Maydet; m. Gary Gutterman, Aug. 15, 1965; children: Steven, Sara. BA cum laude, U. Mich., 1965, MA in Guidance and Counseling cum laude, 1967; JD, U. Denver, 1987. Bar: Colo. 1988; cert. basic mediation and advanced family and custody mediation. Assoc. Larry Litvak P.C., Denver, 1987-90; pvt. practice Denver, 1990—; mem. planning com. and faculty Keystone (Colo.) Child Custody Conf.; nat. lectr. on family law Barbri Bar Rev. Active Unted Way, Human Svcs., Rose Hosp., Nat. Jewish Hosp., Children's Diabetes Found., Graland Country Day Sch. Fellow Colo. Bar Found.; mem. Colo. Bar Assn. (membership chair family law sect., bd. govs. 1992—, alternate dispute resolution, professionalism com.), Exec. Coun. Family Law (chair Barrister's Benefit Ball 1993-94, pro bono fundraiser), Colo. Trial Lawyers, Colo. Women's Bar, Denver Bar Assn. (1st v.p. 1995, maint. legis. com., Vol. Lawyer of Yr. 1994), Arapahoe Bar Assn. (mediation credentials com.), Phi Alpha Delta. Office: 400 S Colorado Blvd # 900 Denver CO 80222-1237

GUTTERSEN, MICHAEL, cattle rancher; b. San Francisco, Mar. 26, 1939; s. William L. and Grace Tooee (Smith) Vogler; m. Penny Leonora Quinn, Aug. 29, 1959; children: Michael William, Arthur Roy, Shawn Patrick. Student, U. Col., 1957-58. Foreman Crow Creek Ranch, Ault, Colo., 1960-61; owner/mgr. Flying G Ranch, Briggsdale, Colo., 1961-86; pres. Two E Ranches Inc., Greeley, Colo., 1969-86, PX Ranch, Elko, Nev., 1969-71, Indian Creek Ranch, Encampment, Wyo., 1970-83, Lake Farms Co., Eaton, Colo., 1969-86; gen. ptnr. Guttersen & Co./Guttersen Ranch, Kersey, Colo., 1986—; mgr. ins. agy. Am. Nat. Ins. Co., Greeley, 1962-70; owner FGF Ins. Brokers, Inc., Greeley, 1962-70. Bd. dirs. United Way, Weld County, Colo., 1979-81, Greeley Philharmonic Orch., 1991-94, Nat. Cowboy Hall of Fame, Oklahoma City, 1994—. With U.S. Army, 1958-60. Mem. Nat. Cattlemens Assn., Colo. Cattlemens Assn., Colo. Cattle Feeders Assn., Tex. and S.W. Cattle Raisers Assn., Weld County Livestock Assn., Greeley Country Club. Republican. Roman Catholic. Home: Woods Lake Farm 13696 RD 74 Eaton CO 80615 Office: Guttersen Ranch PO Box 528 Kersey CO 80644-0528

GUTTMAN, IRVING ALLEN, opera stage director; b. Chatham, Ont., Can., Oct. 27, 1928; s. Shea and Bernetta (Schaffer) G. Opera student, Royal Conservatory Music, Toronto, Ont., 1947-52. Asst. to Herman Geiger Torel of Can. Opera Co., Toronto, 1948-52; dir., under Pauline Donalda Montreal (Que., Can.) Opera Guild, 1959-68. Founding artistic dir., Vancouver (B.C., Can.) Opera Assn., 1960-74, artistic dir., Edmonton (Alta., Can.) Opera Assn., from 1966, Man. (Can.) Opera Assn., Winnipeg, from 1972; dir. numerous TV productions of opera, including first full-length TV opera for, CBC French Network, 1953, operatic productions for numerous U.S. opera cos., also Can. and European cos.; founding artistic dir., Opera Group, Courtenay Youth Music Camp; author: The Unlikely Pioneer-David Watmough, 1987. Decorated Centennial medal, Queen Elizabeth Jubilee medal, Order of Can., 1988, Alberta Govt. award of Excellence, 1989; named to Edmonton Hall of Fame, 1989. Mem. Canadian Equity, Am. Guild Musical Artists.

GUY, BASIL, French literature educator; b. Lynn, Mass., Apr. 12, 1926; s. Basil J.T. and Emma May (Houchin) G. BA, Bowdoin Coll., 1949; MA, Yale U., 1951, PhD, 1955. Instr. U. Calif., Berkeley, 1954-62, prof., 1962-91, prof. emeritus, 1991—; coun. mem. Phi Beta Kappa, Berkeley, 1985—; bd. mem. Am. Soc. 18th Century Studies, 1985-90, Nouvelles Annales Ligne, Brussels, 1986—. Author: French Image of China, 1963; editor: Ligne Oeuvres Choisies, 1979, Varlet Domestic Correspondence, 1985, Ligne Coup d'Oeil, 1992. With U.S. Army, 1944-46, ETO. Fulbright scholar, 1953-54; Commn. for Relief of Belgium fellow Belgian-Am. Ednl. Found., 1960-61, Guggenheim fellow, 1964-65. Office: U Calif 4125 DW Berkeley CA 94720

GUY, MICHELLE, computer professional. Student, Ft. Lewis Coll., 1989-92, U. Colo., 1992—. Customer svc./sales rep. First Interstate Bank, Denver, 1991-93; tech. asst. for regional sys. engr. mgr. Sprint, N.Y.C., 1993; computer lab. advisor U. Colo., Computing, Info. and Network Svcs. Dept., Denver, 1993—; assoc. software engr. Analex, Littleton, Colo., 1994—. Named Presdl./Continuing scholar, Regents scholar, Gene Haskell scholar, Microsoft scholar. Mem. Assn. for Computing Machinery, Soc. Women Engrs. (treas. 1994—), Golden Key Honor Soc. (v.p. 1994—), Tau Beta Pi.

GUY, MILDRED DOROTHY, retired secondary school educator; b. Brunswick, Ga.; d. John and Mamie Paul (Smith) Floyd; BA in Social Sci., Savannah State Coll., 1949; MA in Am. History, Atlanta U., 1952; postgrad. U. So. Calif., U. Colo.; m. Charles H. Guy, Aug. 18, 1956 (div. 1979); 1 child, Rhonda Lynn. Tchr. social studies L.S. Ingraham High Sch., Sparta, Ga.; tchr. English and social studies North Jr. High Sch., Colorado Springs, 1958-84; ret., 1984; cooperating tchr. Tchr. Edn. Program, Col. Coll., 1968-72. Fund raiser for Citizens for Theatre Auditorium, Colorado Springs, 1979; bd. dirs. Urban League, 1971-75; del. to County and State Dem. Conv., 1972, 76, 80, 84, 92; mem. Pike's Peak Community Coll. Council, 1976-83; mem. Colo. Springs Opera Coun. of 500, 1984-88; mem. nominating com. Wagon Wheel council Girl Scouts U.S.A., 1985-87; active Fine Arts Ctr., Pikes Peak Hospice. Recipient Viking award North Jr. High Sch., 1973, Woman of Distinction award Girls Scouts Wagon Wheel Coun., 1989, 94; Outstanding Black Woman of Colorado Springs award, 1975; named Pacesetter, Atlanta U., 1980-81, Outstanding Black Educator of Yr., Black Educators of Dist. II, Colorado Springs, 1984; Outstanding Ednl. Service award Colo. Dept. and State Bd. Edn., 1983, Dedicated Service award Pikes Peak Community Coll., 1983; Outstanding Community Leadership award Alpha Phi Alpha, 1985; award Colo. Black Woman for Polit. Action, 1985, Sphinx award, 1986; named in recognition sect. Salute to Women, Colorado Springs Gazette Telegraph, 1986. Mem. LWV (Colo. chpt.), Negro Hist. Assn., Women's Found. Colo.; life mem. NAACP (Golden Heritage), NEA, AAUW, Colo. Coun. Social Studies, Assn. Study Afro-Am. Life and History, Women's Ednl. Soc. Colo. Coll. (bd. mgrs. 1992—), Alpha Delta Kappa, Alpha Kappa Alpha (pres. 1985). Baptist. Home: 3132 Constitution Ave Colorado Springs CO 80909-2177

GUY, RICHARD P., state supreme court justice; b. Coeur d'Alene, Idaho, Oct. 24, 1932; s. Richard H. and Charlotte M. Guy; m. Marilyn K. Guy, Nov. 16, 1963; children: Victoria, Heidi, Emily. JD, Gonzaga U., 1959. Bar: Wash. 1959, Hawaii 1988. Former judge Wash. Superior Ct., Spokane, from 1977; now justice Wash. Supreme Ct., Olympia. Capt. USAS. Mem. Wash. State Bar, Spokane County Bar Assn. Roman Catholic. Office: Wash Supreme Ct PO Box 40929 Temple of Justice (AV-11) Olympia WA 98504*

GUYAN, CHERYL ANN, nurse; b. Worcester, Mass., June 4, 1964; d. Ronald John and Linda Ellen (Stone) Denault; m. William James Guyan, July 19,. 1986; 1 child, Jeffrey. BS in Nursing, Salve Regina Coll., Newport, R.I., 1986. RN, Ariz., Calif., Mass.; cert. CCRN; cert. oncology nurse; cert. ACLS instr. Nurse St. Joseph's Hosp., Tucson, 1986-87; charge nurse Univ. Med. Ctr., Tucson, 1987-90; nurse clinician St. Joseph's Hosp., Savannah, 1990-92, ICU nurse mgr., 1992-94;; charge nurse Univ. Med. Ctr., Tucson, 1987-90; critical care RN Meth. Hosp., Arcadia, Calif., 1994—; mem. numerous coms. St. Joseph's Hosp., Savannah, Ga., 1990-94; critical care educator, Meth. Hosp., Arcadia, Calif., 1995—. Leader Cancer Support Group. Mem. AACN, Oncology Nursing Soc., Ga. Assn. Nursing Execs., Sigma Phi Sigma. Republican. Home: 6881 Rovato Pl Alta Loma CA 91701-8586

GUYNN, STEFANIE CAROL, social work administrator, trainer, consultant; b. N.Y.C., Apr. 25, 1938; d. David L. and Beatrice (Gould) Blum; m. William Howard Guynn, July 31, 1965; children: Jessica Rachel, Noah David. BA magna cum laude, Barnard Coll., 1959; postgrad., Harvard U. and Radcliffe Coll., 1959-61; MSW, U. Calif., Berkeley, 1970. Lic. clin. social work, Calif.; diplomate in clin. social work Am. Bd. Examiners in Clin. Social Work. Librarian U. Calif., Berkeley, 1961-66; psychiat. social worker Calif. State Dept. Mental Hygiene, Oakland, 1972-74; social casework specialist II children svcs. Contra Costa County Social Service Dept., Richmond, Calif., 1974-84; social work supr. II children svcs. Contra Costa County Social Service Dept., Martinez, Calif., 1984-88; social svc. div. mgr. Contra Costa County Social Service Dept., Martinez, El Sobrante, Hercules, Calif., 1988—; field work instr. U. Calif. Sch. Social Welfare, Berkeley, 1985-88, Sacramento State U., 1987-88; trainer for child protective svcs. workers Calif. State Dept. Social Svcs. and Calif. State U. Fresno; mem. adv. com. employment and econ. status of women Contra Costa County Bd. Suprs., 1990-91; mem. Contra Costa County Mgmt. Coun., 1994—; mem. dean's avd. com. U. Calif. Sch. Social Welfare, 1989-91; lectr. in field at various univs. and colls.; cons. in field. Woodrow Wilson fellow, 1959-60; Radcliffe Coll. grantee, 1960-61; NIMH fellow, 1966-67, Calif. State Dept. Mental Hygiene fellow, 1967-68; N.Y. State scholar, 1955-59; mem. field work adv. bd. U. Calif. Sch. Social Welfare, Berkeley, 1988-89. Mem. Nat. Assn. Social Workers (cert., continuing edn. faculty 1991—, regional dir., bd. dirs. Calif. chpt. 1989-91), Berkeley Women's Health Ctr. (bd. dirs. 1993), Phi Beta Kappa. Jewish. Home: 643 Vincente Ave Berkeley CA 94707-1523 Office: Social Service Dept Contra Costa County 151 Linus Pauling Dr Hercules CA 94547-1822

GUYTON, ROBERT ARMOUR, JR., secondary school educator, business administrator; b. Memphis, Nov. 13, 1957; m. Dia Rodriguez, Mar. 9, 1989; children: Kristen Colleen, Robert Christopher. Student, Glendale C.C., 1975-78; BS in Polit. Sci., Ariz. State U., 1980, BA in Edn., 1986; MA in Edn., Ednl. Adminstrn., Calif. State U., Bakersfield, 1994. Cert. social sci. tchr., Calif. History tchr. Mesa (Ariz.) High Sch., 1986; English and social studies tchr. Summit High Sch., 1988-90; govt., econs. and computer sci. tchr. Nueva High Sch., 1990—; summer sch. tchr. Kern Valley H.S., 1989, North H.S., 1991, Vista East H.S., 1993; presenter in field. Contbr. articles to profl. publs. Capt. U.S. Army, 1980-90. Willard fellow Capstone Econs., 1993. Mem. Calif. ASCD, Calif. Continuing Edn. Assn., Hist. Miniatures and Gaming Soc., KC. Republican. Roman Catholic. Home: 5103 Shadow Lake Dr Bakersfield CA 93313-4369

GUYTON, SAMUEL PERCY, retired lawyer; b. Jackson, Miss., Mar. 20, 1937; s. Earl Ellington and Eulalia (Reynolds) G.; m. Jean Preston, Oct. 11, 1959; children: Tamara Reynolds, William Preston, David Sage. BA, Miss. State U., 1959; LLB, U. Va., 1965. Bar: Colo. 1965, U.S. Dist. Ct. Colo. 1965, U.S. Tax Ct. 1977, U.S. Ct. Appeals (10th cir.) 1965, U.S. Ct. Appeals (5th cir.) 1981. Ptnr., Holland & Hart, Denver, 1965-92; ret., 1992; faculty Am. Law Inst. ABA, 1976-88. Sec., trustee Colo. Hist. Found., 1971-92, pres., 1983-87; trustee Music Assn. Aspen and Aspen Music Festival, 1980-88; precinct com. chmn. Dem. Party, 1968-70; mem. Gov.'s mansion preservation com., 1989-92, mem. adv. com., 1989-92; Capt. USAF, 1959-62. Fellow Am. Coll. Tax Counsel (bd. regents 1985-92, chmn., pres. 1989-91), Am. Tax Policy Inst. (trustee 1989-92, v.p. 1989-92); mem. ABA (sect. taxation 1967-92, chmn. sect.'s com. on agr. 1980-82), Colo. Bar Assn. (tax coun. 1983-86, sec. 1983, chmn. 1985-86), Colo. Bar Found., Greater Denver Tax Csls. Assn. (chmn. 1978), Law Club Denver, Little River Lectures Assn. (bd. dirs., v.p.), Am. Alpine Club (life), Colo. Mountain Club (life), Eleanore Mullen Weckbaugh Found. (trustee), Humphreys Found. (sec., treas., trustee), Colo. Trail Found. (trustee), Colo. Mountain Club Found. (dir.). Mem. Unity Ch. Co-author: Cattle Owners Tax Manual, 1984, Supplement to Federal Taxation of Agriculture, 1983, Colorado Estate Planning Desk Book, 1984, 90; contbr. articles to jours., mags.; bd. advs. Agrl. Law Jour., 1978-82; mem. editorial bd. Jour. Agrl. Tax and Law, 1983-92. Home and Office: 12345 W 19th Pl Lakewood CO 80215-2516

GUZY, MARGUERITA LINNES, secondary education educator; b. Santa Monica, Calif., Nov. 19, 1938; d. Paul William Robert and Margarete (Rodowski) Linnes; m. Stephen Paul Guzy, Aug. 25, 1962 (div. 1968); 1 child, David Paul. AA, Santa Monica Coll., 1959; student, U. Mex., 1959-60; BA, UCLA, 1966, MA, 1973; postgrad. in psychology, Pepperdine U., 1988-92; cert. bilingual competence, Calif., 1994. Cert. secondary tchr., quality review team ednl. programs, bilingual, Calif. Tchr. Inglewood (Calif.) Unified Sch. Dist., 1967—, chmn. dept., 1972-82, mentor, tchr., 1985-88; clin. instr. series Clin. Supervision Levels I, II, Ingelwood, 1986-87; clin. intern Chem. Dependency Ctr., St. John's Hosp., Santa Monica, 1988-92; lectr. chem. and codependency St. John's Hosp., Santa Monica, 1992—; tchr. Santa Monica Coll., 1975-76; cons. bilingual edn. Inglewood Unified Sch. Dist., 1975—, lead tchr. new hope program at-risk students, 1992; cons. tchr. credentialing fgn. lang. State of Calif., 1994; sch. rep. restructuring edn. for state proposal, 1991—; mem. Program Quality Rev. Team Pub. Edn., Calif., 1993; mem. Supt.'s Com. for Discrimination Resolution, 1994-95. Author: Elementary Education: "Pygmalian in the Classroom", 1975, English Mechanics Workbook, 1986. Recipient Teaching Excellence cert. State of Calif., 1986; named Tchr. of Yr., 1973, 88. Mem. NEA, Calif. Tchrs. Assn., Inglewood Tchrs. Assn. (local rep. 1971-72, tchr edn. and profl. services com. 1972-78), UCLA Alumnae Assn. (life), Prytanean Alumnae Assn. Republican. Club: Westside Alano (Los Angeles)(bd. dirs., treas. 1982-83). Lodge: Masons. Office: Monroe Jr High Sch 10711 S 10th Ave Inglewood CA 90303-2015

GWIN, BILLY JOE, transportation executive; b. Baker, Oreg., Apr. 30, 1946; s. Billy Rex and Ellen Jo (Moyer) G. Licensed customs broker. Messenger to v.p. Geo. S. Bush & Co., Inc., Seattle, 1967-92; mgr. consulting svcs. Tower Group Internat., Seattle, 1992—. Chmn. Port of Seattle/Tacoma-Lynx, 1988-91. With USAF, 1964-66. Mem. Customs Brokers and Internat. Freight Forwarders Assn. Wash. State (treas., v.p., pres. 1990-91), Australia New Zealand Am. Soc. (treas.-sec. 1987-90), Transp. Club Seattle (bd. dirs., sec.-treas. 1985-89). Office: Tower Group Internat 821 2nd Ave Ste 1400 Seattle WA 98104-1519

GWINN, MARY ANN, newspaper reporter; b. Forrest City, Ark., Dec. 29, 1951; d. Lawrence Baird and Frances Evelyn (Jones) G.; m. Richard A. King, June 3, 1973 (div. 1981); m. Stephen E. Dunnington, June 10, 1990. BA in Psychology, Hendrix Coll., 1973; MEd in Spl. Edn., Ga. State U., 1975; MA in Journalism, U. Mo., 1979. Tchrs. aide DeKalb County Schs., Decatur, Ga., 1973-74, tchr., 1975-78; reporter Columbia (Mo.) Daily Tribune, 1979-83; reporter Seattle Times, 1983—, now natural resources and maritime reporter; instr. extension div. U. Wash., Seattle, 1990. Recipient Charles Stewart Mott Found. award for edn. reporting, 1980, C.B. Blethen award for enterprise reporting Blethen Family, Seattle, 1989, Pulitzer Prize for nat. reporting, 1990. Mem. Newspaper Guild. Office: Seattle Times PO Box 70 1120 John St Seattle WA 98111*

GWINN, MARY DOLORES, philosopher; b. Oakland, Calif., Sept. 16, 1946; d. Epifanio and Carolina (Lopez) Cruz; m. James Monroe Gwinn, Oct. 23, 1965; 1 child, Larry Allen. Student, Monterey Peninsula Jr. Coll., 1965. Retail store mgr. Consumer's Distbg. divsn. May Co., Hayward, Calif., 1973-78; mktg. rep. Dale Carnegie Courses, San Jose, Calif., 1978-79; founder, pres. Strategic Integrations, Ariz.'s Innovative Bus. Devel. Ctr., Scottsdale, 1985—; speaker St. John's Coll. U. Cambridge, England, 1992; founder, pres. Internat. Inst. for Conceptual Edn., Scottsdale, 1993—, Gwinn Genius Inst., 1995—. Founder new fields of study Genistics and NeuroBus.; contbr. articles to profl. jours. Republican. Home and Office: 5836 E Angela Dr Scottsdale AZ 85254-6410

GWINNETT, JAMES RANDALL, telecommunications industry executive; b. Statesboro, Ga., July 23, 1950; s. Lonnie Warden and Evelyn Matilee (Sowell) G.; m. Catherine Ann Reeves, July 2, 1975 (div. Dec. 1983). Grad. high sch., Statesboro, Ga. Lic. private pilot. Ops. mgr. Atlanta dist. United Technologies Comm., St. Louis, 1975-77, project mgr. Metromedia Project, 1977-79, project mgr. network accts., 1979-81, nat. accts. ops. mgr., 1981-82, nat. acct. mgr., 1982-83; v.p. ops. Executone Telecom., Phoenix, 1983-84, v.p., gen. mgr., 1984-85; PBX sys. mgr. NEC Am., Inc., Dallas, 1988-92; sr. acct. mgr. NEC Am., Inc., Tampa, Fla., 1992; v.p., gen. mgr. Interwest Comm. Corp., Denver, 1992—. Staff sgt. USAF, 1968-72. Republican. Methodist. Home: 9057 E Mississippi # 14204 Denver CO 80231 Office: Interwest Comm Corp 1313 S Clarkson St Denver CO 80210-2234

GWON, ARLENE, ophthalmologist; b. N.Y.C., Sept. 21, 1943; d. William and Mamie Gwon; m. Patrick Francis Sheehy, 1970; children: Brian, Laura. BA, SUNY, 1964, MD, 1968. Diplomate Am. Bd. Ophthalmology. Ophthalmologist pvt. practice, Newport Beach, Calif., 1973—; assoc. clin. prof. U. Calif., Irvine, 1991—; med. rsch. investigator Allergan Inc., Irvine, 1993—; chmn. Hoag Meml. Hosp. IRB, Newport Beach, 1991—. Patentee in field. Office: Allergan Inc 2525 Dupont Dr Irvine CA 92713 also: 1401 Avocado Ste 903 Newport Beach CA 92660

GWOZDZIOWSKI, JOANNA MONICA, research analyst; b. L.A., Sept. 23, 1959; d. Czeslaw Jan and Helena Wanda (Skomra) G.; m. Nevin Derrick Whiteley, Sept. 27, 1986. BA, UCLA, 1982; MPhil, Oxford (Eng.) U., 1986, PhD, 1994. Personal asst. to M.P., London, 1981-82; cons. RAND Corp., Santa Monica, Calif., 1989-90; pvt. practice polit. risk cons. Manhattan Beach, Calif., 1990-92; vis. fellow Ctr. for Internat. and Strategic Affairs, UCLA, 1986-92; adj. fellow Ctr. for Internat. Studies, U. So. Calif., 1987-88. Pers. recruiter and trainer L.A. Olympic Organizing Com., 1982-84. Edn. abroad scholar UCLA, Stirling U., 1981-82; overseas rsch. student grantee Brit. Govt., 1986; recipient U.S. State Dept. Fascell Fellowship to U.S. Embassy in Warsaw, 1991—. Mem. Internat. Inst. for Strategic Studies, Am. Assn. for the Advancement of Slavonic Studies, Acad. Polit. Sci., L.A. World Affairs Coun., United Oxford and Cambridge U. Club, Oxford and Cambridge Club L.A. Home and Office: 309 Evening Star Ln Newport Beach CA 92660-5704

GWYNN, ANTHONY KEITH (TONY GWYNN), professional baseball player; b. L.A., May 9, 1960; m. Alicia; children: Anthony, Anisha Nicole. Student, San Diego State U. Player minor league teams Walla Walla and Amarillo, Hawaii, 1981-82; with San Diego Padres, 1981—. Winner Nat. League batting title, 1984, 87, 88, 89; recipient Gold Glove award, 1986-87, 89-91; mem. All-Star team, 1984-87, 89-94; named MVP N.W. League, 1981, Sporting News Nat. League Silver Slugger team, 1984, 86-87, 89, 94, Sporting News Nat. League All-Star Team, 1984, 86-87, 89, 94. Office: San Diego Padres PO Box 2000 San Diego CA 92112-2000*

GYLSETH, DORIS (LILLIAN) HANSON, librarian; b. Helena, Mont., May 26, 1934; d. Richard E. and Lillie (Paula) Hanson; m. Arlie Albeck, Dec. 26, 1955 (div. Apr. 1964); m. Hermann M. Gylseth, Apr. 29, 1983 (dec. Aug. 1985). BS in Edn., Western Mont. Coll. Edn., 1958; MLS, U. Wash., 1961. Tchr. Helena Sch. Dist., 1955-56, Dillon (Mont.) Elem. Sch., 1957-59, Eltopia (Wash.) Unified Sch. Dist., 1959-60; sch. libr. Shoreline Sch. Dist., Seattle, 1960-64, Dept. of Def., Chateauroux, France, Hanau, Fed. Republic Germany, Tachikawa, Japan, 1964-68, Long Beach (Calif.) Unified Sch. Dist., 1968-70; br. libr. Long Beach Pub. Libr., 1970-74, coord. children's svcs., 1974-85; libr. Long Beach (Calif.) Unified Sch. Dist., 1986-94; realtor Century 21, All Pacific, 1994—. Bd. dirs. Children's Svcs. divsn. Calif. Libr. Assn., 1985, Literary Guild of Orange County, 1993—; co-chmn. Long Beach Authors Festival, 1978-86; mem. planning coun. Third Pacific Rim Conf. on Children's Lit., UCLA, 1986. Mem. So. Calif. Coun. on Lit. for Children and Young Poeple (bd. dirs. 1974-88, pres. 1982-84), Helen Fuller Cultural Carrousel (bd. dirs. 1985—), Friends of Long Beach Pub. Libr. (bd. dirs. 1988—), Zonta (pres. 1978-80). Home: 5131 Kingscross Rd Westminster CA 92683-4832 Office: Century 21 A First Choice 7662 Edinger Huntington Beach CA 92647

HA, CHONG WAN, state government executive; b. Chin-ju, Kyung-Nam, South Korea, Oct. 25, 1938; came to U.S., 1963; s. Kyung-sik and Kyung-Nam (Park) H.; m. Karen Hye-Ja Han, Aug. 19, 1968; children: Jean Frances, Julie Ann. BA in Econs., UCLA, 1970; cert. in exec. mgmt., The Peter F. Drucker Mgmt. Ctr., 1984; MA in Mgmt., Claremont (Calif.) Grad. Sch., 1985. Sr. systems analyst Atlantic Richfield Co., Los Angeles, 1972-78; asst. v.p. 1st Interstate Services Co., Los Angeles, 1978-85; v.p. Ticor Title Ins. Co., Los Angeles, 1985-91; assoc. dir. MCA/Universal Studios, 1991; dir. State of Calif. Stephen P. Teale Data Ctr., Sacramento, 1991—; mem. exec. com. Calif. Forum on Info. Tech.; mem. adv. bd. Govt. Tech. Conf., 1994. Res. police officer Monterey Park (Calif.) Police Dept., 1981-82; bd. dirs. Asian Pacific Alumni Assn., UCLA, 1988, Asian Pacific Am. Legal Found., L.A., 1988, Korean Youth Ctr., Korean Am. Music Acad.; mem. alumni coun. Claremont Grad. Sch., 1993. Recipient Peter Drucker Ctr. Alumni award, 1994, Calif. State Atty. Gen. award, 1994. Mem. Soc. of Info. Mgmt., Leadership Edn. for Asian Pacifics, UCLA Chancellers Circle. Home: 5625 Adobe Rd Rocklin CA 95765-4529

HAAG, CAROL ANN GUNDERSON, marketing professional, consultant; b. Mpls.; d. Glenn Alvin and Genevieve Esther (Knudson) Gunderson; m. Lawrence S. Haag, Aug. 30, 1969; 1 child, Maren Anne. BJ, U. Mo., 1969; postgrad., Roosevelt U., Chgo., 1975—. Pub. relations writer, advt. copywriter Am. Hosp. Supply Corp., Evanston, Ill., 1969-70; asst. dir. pub. relations Rush-Presbyn. St. Luke's Med. Ctr., Chgo., 1970-71; asst. mgr. pub. and employee communications Quaker Oats Co., Chgo., 1971-72, mgr. editorial communications, 1972-74, mgr. employee communications programs, 1974-77; dir. pub. relations Shaklee Corp., San Francisco, 1978-82; pres. CH & Assocs., San Francisco, 1982-84; dir corp. communications BRAE Corp., San Francisco, 1984; dir. mktg. St. Francis Meml. Hosp., San Francisco, 1985-89, dir. mktg. and planning svcs., 1989-91; ptnr. Haag & Rohan, San Francisco, San Diego, 1991—; cons. in field. Bd. dirs. Calif. League Handicapped; mem. adv. bd. San Francisco Spl. Olympics; mem. pub. relations com. San Francisco Recreation and Parks Dept., San Francisco Vol. Bur. Recipient 1st place cert. Printing Industry Am., 1972, 74, 1st place spl. comm. award Internat. Assn. Bus. Communicators, 1974, 1st place citation Chgo. Assn. Bus. Communicators, 1974, gold award Healthcare Mktg. Reports, 1989, 90. Mem. NATAS, Indsl. Com. Coun., Pub. Rels. Soc. Am., San Francisco C. of C. (grad. leadership program 1991, bd. dirs. leadership coun.), San Francisco Press Club. Home and Office: 133 Fernwood Dr Moraga CA 94556-2315

HAAG, CARRIE H., sports association executive. BA, Purdue U., 1972; MA, Ea. Ky. U., 1977, EdS, 1978; postdoctoral work, U. N.C., 1978-79. Phys. edn. tchr. Sch. Dist. # 65, Evanston, Ill., 1973-76; grad. asst. Ea. Ky. U., Richmond, 1977-78, U. N.C., Greensboro, 1978-79; asst. to exec. dir. Assn. for Intercollegiate Athletics for Women, Washington, D.C., 1979-80; dir. nat. championships Assn. for Intercollegiate Athletics for Women, Washington, 1980-82; asst. dir. athletics Dartmouth Coll., Hanover, N.H., 1982-84; cons. Washington, D.C., 1989-90; asst. dir. athletics Cen. Conn. State U., New Britain, 1990-92; exec. dir. U.S. Field Hockey Assn., Colorado Springs, Colo., 1984-88, 92—; del., moderator New Agenda I: Nat. Women in Sports Conf., Washington, 1983; panelist U.S. Olympic Acad. X, Colorado Springs, 1986; U.S. del. Internat. Hockey Fedn. Congress, Brussels, Belgium, 1986, Internat. Olympic Acad., Olympia, Greece, 1987; del. House of Dels. U.S. Olympic Com., 1985-88; grant author and project dir. U.S. Olympic Found., 1986-88; mem. safety com. U.S. Olympic Tng. Ctr. Complex, 1988; mem. applied strategic planning team Nat. Assn. for Girls and Women in Sport, 1988, v.p. bd. dirs., 1990-92. Office: US Field Hockey Assoc 1750 E Boulder St Colorado Springs CO 80909*

HAAG, KEN LEE, public works director; b. Columbus, Mont., Dec. 20, 1939; s. Edward Peter and Ruth Virginia (Bell) H.; m. Marie Eileen Carlson, Oct. 24, 1959; children: Pamela Marie Clower, Vincent E., Richard Lee. BSCE, Mont. State U., 1962. Civil engr. U.S. Dept. of Interior, Billings and Miles City, Mont., 1962-65; sales engr. Armco Steel Corp., Billings, 1965-69; field and office engr. N.L. Garrick Constr. Co., Missoula, Mont., 1969-71; asst. city engr. City of Billings, 1971-72, city engr., 1972-77, pub. works dir., 1977—. Mem. Mont. League of Cities and Town Program Com., Helena, 1991-94, State of Mont. Solid Waste Mgmt. Plan com., Helena, 1992-93, Regional Tech. Assistance Program, Bozeman, Mont., 1990-92; bd. dirs. Billings Bright n' Beautiful Bd., 1990-94. Mem. ASCE (Ea. br. Mont. sect. pres. 1973-74, Outstanding Young Engr. award 1973, Disting. Svc. award 1994), Am. Pub. Works Assn. (pres.-elect 1994, region IX dir. 1991-94, Rocky Mountain chpt. pres. 1984-85), Billings C. of C. (managed growth com.). Office: Pub Works Dept City of Billings 510 N Broadway 4th Fl Billings MT 59101

HAAGE, ROBERT MITCHELL, retired history educator, organization leader; b. Garden City, Kans., Mar. 10, 1924; s. William Russell and Mayme Levice (Mitchell) H.; m. Lila Marie Baker, Sept. 7, 1947; children: Lori Deane, Lisa Anne, Melanie Sue. BA, Southwestern Coll., 1947; MDiv, Garrett Bibl. Inst., 1952. Cert. tchr., Kans., Calif. Min. Meth. Ch., Copeland, Kans., 1947-48, Meth. Chs., Ingleside, Spring Grove, Ill., 1948-50; asst. min. First Meth. Ch., Emporia, Kans., 1952-53; tchr. core curriculum Marshall Intermediate Sch., Wichita, Kans., 1953-56; tchr. U.S. history Bellflower (Calif.) High Sch., 1956-57; tchr. math. Chaffey Joint Union High Sch. Dist., Ontario, Calif., 1957-59; tchr. U.S. history and econs. Chaffey Joint Union High Sch. Dist., 1959-85; 1st faculty pres. Montclair High Sch., 1959-60; founding pres. Inland Empire Counties Coun. for Social Studies, San Bernardino, Calif., 1961-62; dean student activities Western CUNA Mgmt. Sch., Pomona Coll., Claremont, Calif., 1980-84; treas. Tchrs. Adv. Group/Tchrs. Farm and Ranch Co-op, 1984-93. Conservation editor Desomount Dustings Newsletter, 1990-92, gen. editor, 1993—. Founding officer Chaffey Dist. Employees Fed. Credit Union, Ontario, 1964-69; pres., bd. dirs. Chaffey Fed. Credit Union, Ontario, 1979-87, dir., 1969—; officer, bd. govs. Mt. Baldy chpt. Calif. Credit Union League, Pomona, 1977-86; bd. dirs., treas. Upper Westwood Homeowners Assn., Pomona, 1982-84, 91-92; conservation chair Desomount Environ. Orgn.; mem. Nat. Wildlife Fedn. Recipient We Honor Ours award Calif. Tchrs. Assn., 1985, Outstanding Svc. award Associated Chaffey Tchrs., 1985. Mem. Univ. Club Claremont (sec.-v.p.-pres. 1986-92, editor newsletters 1986-90, bd. dirs. 1993—, chair fin. com. 1993—, Leadership award 1992), Toastmasters Club 12 (pres. 1964-65, Best Evaluator award 1982, 83, 85), Sierra Club, Fedn. of Western Outdoor Clubs (v.p. So. Calif. chpt. 1990—, gen. v.p. 1994—), Phi Delta Kappa (pres. 1977-78, Disting. Svc. award 1978), Kappa Delta Pi (hon. soc. in edn. 1953—). Democrat. Home: 9541 Tudor Ave Montclair CA 91763-2219

HAARSAGER, SANDRA LYNN, author, communications educator; b. West Plains, Mo., Sept. 17, 1946; Victor Everett and Melba Louise (Rowlett) Smith; m. James Barry Watkinson, June 15, 1969 (div. Oct. 1975); m. Dennis Lee Haarsager, Jan. 1, 1977; children: Anna Lynn, Andrew Lee, Jennie Ella. BA in English Lit. and Psychology, Coll. of Idaho, Caldwell, 1968; MPA, Boise State U., 1982; PhD in Am. Studies, Wash. State U., 1990. Cert. tchr. secondary schs., Idaho. Reporter and spl. edits. editor Times-News, Twin Falls, Idaho, 1965-69; health & edn. reporter, reviewer and consumer affairs editor Idaho Statesman, Boise, 1972-75; asst. to supt. pub. instrn. Idaho Dept. Edn., Boise, 1975-78; asst. dir. devel. Wash. State U., Pullman, 1978-79; dir. univ. info. svcs. U. of Idaho, Moscow, 1979-83, from instr. to assoc. prof., 1988—, coord. Am. Studies Program, 1994—; reporter and editor Idahonian/Daily News, Moscow, 1983-85; gen. mgr. News-Rev. Pub. Co., Moscow, 1985-88; columnist Daily News, Moscow, 1986—; bd. dirs. N.W. Region, Coun. for Advancement and Support of Edn., 1981-82, pub. reviewer; condr. seminars in field; lectr. in field; judge Idahonian/Daily News "Our Town" series, 1989, Utah Press Assn. contest, 1984, Lewiston Morning Tribune, Top Stories of the Decade, 1990, others. Author: Bertha Knight Landes of Seattle - Big City Mayor, 1994, Organized Womanhood: Women's Clubs and Cultural Politics in the Pacific Northwest, 1875-1915; author monograph: Student Rights and Responsibilities, 1978; contbr. articles, book revs. to profl. jours.; referee Canon-Jour. of Rocky Mountains Am. Studies Assn., 1992—, Journalism Monographs, 1991—, Journalism Quar., 1991—, Am. Journalism, 1993—; editl. adv. bd. Idaho--The University Mag., 1983-84. Mem. cmty. adv. coun. Lewiston (Idaho) Tribune, 1981-82; task force leader Idaho Conf. on Women, Boise, 1977; mem. juvenile justice coun. Idaho Law Enforcement Planning Commn., Boise, 1976-78; mem. Wash. Idaho Symphony Chorus, 1981-84, 90-93; bd. dirs. Boise Hotline, 1974-75. Recipient Edn. Media award for columns and editls. on edn. Idaho Assn. Sch. Adminstrs., 1984, Excellence in Pub. Info., Coun. for Advancement and Support of Edn., 1981, Excellence in Broadcast Media, 1979, 80; grantee John Calhoun Smith Fund, 1991-92, 92-93, 93-94, U. Idaho Rsch. Found., 1990, 94, Office of Acad. Affairs of U. Idaho, 1990. Mem. Pacific N.W. Am. Studies Assn. (treas. 1990—), Soc. History of Tech., Am. Journalism Historians Assn., Assn. for Edn. in Journalism and Mass Comm. (rsch. chair, sec., qualitative studies 1993—), U. Idaho Alumni Assn. (bd. dirs. 1992—), N.W. Comm. Assn., Ida State Parent Tchr. Assn. (life, Svc. to Edn. award 1977), Idaho Press Club (Best Columnist award 1988, Best Feature Writer 1975), Moscow C. of C. (bd. dirs. 1982-83, co-chmn. cmty. rels./membership com. 1986-88), Phi Kappa Phi. Unitarian. Office: Univ of Idaho Sch of Communication Moscow ID 83843-1072

HAAS, BRADLEY DEAN, clinical pharmacist, consultant; b. Albion, Nebr., Nov. 24, 1957; s. Ernest Duane Jr. and Joy Lou (Fusselman) H. Student, Kearney State Coll., 1976-78; PharmD with distinction, U. Nebr., Omaha, 1981. Registered pharmacist, Nebr., Colo.; cert. hosp. pharmacy residency, basic life support instr. and provider, advanced cardiac life support instr. and provider. Resident hosp. pharmacy U. Nebr. Med. Ctr., Omaha, 1981-82; intensive care clin. pharmacist Mercy Med. Ctr., Denver, 1982-85; home care pharmacist Am. Abbey Homecare, Englewood, Colo., 1985; pharmacy dir. Charter Hosp. of Aurora, Colo., 1989-90; clin pharmacy coord. Porter Meml. Hosp., Denver, 1987-92; asst. dir. clin. pharmacy svcs. Luth. Med. Ctr., Wheat Ridge, Colo., 1992-94; dir. pharmacy Integrated Pharmacy Solutions, Inc./Pru Care Pharmacies, Denver, 1994—; cons. Porter Meml. Hosp. Chronic Pain Treatment Ctr., 1987-89, Charter Hosp., 1989-90; adj. asst. prof. pharmacy U. Colo., 1983—; mem. leadership adv. coun. sch. pharmacy U. Colo., 1987-89; mem. adv. bd. Instl. and Managed Healthcare, Ortho Biotech, Inc., 1992—; mem. State Colo./ Medicare D.U.R. Com., 1992—. Author, co-author in field. Vol. Colo. Hosp. Pharmacists Week, Poison Prevention Week, KUSA-TV Health Fair; lectr. Pathfinder's Youth Group- Careers Day; active Colo. Trust. Named Disting. Young Pharmacist of the Year Marion Labs., Colo., 1987, one of Outstanding Young Men of Am., 1987; recipient Acad. Scholarship U. Nebr. Med. Ctr, 1978-81, Excellence in Pharmacy Practice award U. Colo. Sch. Pharmacy, 1988; Marjorie Merwin Simmons Meml. scholar U. Nebr. Found. Fund., 1980; scholar VFW, 1978-81. Mem. Am. Soc. Hosp. Pharmacists (state chpt. grants program selection com. 1989, nominations com. 1990-91, ho. of dels. 1987, 90-92, Acad. Managed Care Pharmacy, Colo. Soc. Hosp. Pharmacists (Hosp. Pharmacy Practitioner Excellence award 1988, 89, presdl. officer 1987-89, chair numerous couns. and coms.). Home: 10115 Granite Hill Dr Parker CO 80134 Office: Integrated Pharmacy Solutions/PruCare Pharmacy 4643 S Ulster St Ste 1000 Denver CO 80237-2867

HAAS, CATHERINE MAY, performing arts executive; b. Gillingham, Kent, England, May 21, 1942; came to the U.S., 1960; d. Hugh and Evelyn May (Appleby) Fraser; m. Henry Haas, July 7, 1963; children: David M., Susan M., Kimberly A. BA in Polit. Sci., Pacific Luth. U., 1984. Resources coord. Planned Parenthood Pierce County, Tacoma, Wash., 1980-81; cmty. rels. dir. Greater Lakes Mental Health Found., Tacoma, 1985-86; mng. dir. Tacoma Actors Guild, 1986—. Chair Pierce County Ethics Commn., 1983, State Human Rights Commn., Wash., 1983-90; active Tacoma 2010 Com., 1994. Named Newsmaker of Tomorrow Tacoma News Tribune/Time Mag., 1983, Outstanding Alumnus Pacific Luth. U., 1991. Fellow Am. Leadership Forum; mem. Theatre Communications Group, Jr. League, Nat. Coun. Jewish Women (life), Tacoma C. of C. (chair mktg. task force 1992-94), Rotary. Office: Tacoma Actors Guild 901 Broadway Fl 6 Tacoma WA 98402-4415

HAAS, EDWARD LEE, business executive, consultant; b. Camden, N.J., Nov. 9, 1935; s. Edward David and Mildred (Wynne) H.; m. Maryann Lind, Dec. 27, 1958; children: John Eric, Gretchen Lind. BA, LaSalle U., 1958; postgrad., Temple U., 1960—. Mgr. systems devel. RCA Corp., Cherry Hill, N.J., 1966-71; mgr. computer tech. svcs. Gencorp, Akron, Ohio, 1971-74; sr. mgr. computer applications R & D Ernst & Young, Cleve., 1974-75; dir. nat. systems group Ernst & Young, LLP, 1976-77; nat. dir. data processing and software products Ernst & Young, 1977, nat. ptnr., 1978-82, cons. ptnr., 1983—. 1st lt. arty. U.S. Army, 1958-59. Mem. Data Processing Mgmt. Assn., Assn. Systems Mgmt., Assn. Inst. for Cert. Computer Profls., Plantation Country Club, Union League of Phila. Republican. Roman Catholic. Office: 515 S Flower St Los Angeles CA 90071-2201

HAAS, HARL HENRY, judge; b. Cape Girardeau, Mo.; s. Harl H. and Berniece Mary (Taylor) H.; m. Mary Lou Haas, Apr. 12, 1986; children: Amy Taylor, Holly Rae. LLB with honors, Willamette U., 1961. Bar: Oreg. 1961, U.S. Dist. Ct. Oreg., U.S. Supreme Ct. Ptnr. Bailey Swink and Haas, 1961-73, Haas and Benzinger, 1981-84; mem. Oreg. State Ho. Reps., 1969-71, Oreg. State Senate, 1971-73; dist. atty. Multnomah County, Oreg., 1973-81; judge Multnomah County Cir. Ct., Portland, 1984-85; spkr., presenter in field; mem. legis. com., budget com. State Jud. Dept., 1992-94, mem. jud. conduct com., 1988-89; mem. Adv. Com. on Prison Terms and Parole Stds., 1988; mem. exec. Oreg. Jud. Conf., 1993-94; mem. jud. adminstrn. com. Oreg. State Bar, 1991-93, mem. pres-media-bar com., 1989-91; lectr. Nat. Jud. Coll., Oreg. Trial Lawyers Assn., Oreg. Def. Lawyers Assn. Comment editor Willamette Law Rev., 1961; contbr. articles to profl. publs. Vice chmn. Oreg. Law Enforcement Coun., 1975-78, vice chmn., 1978-80; bd. dirs. Nat. Orgn. for Crime Victims' Assistance, 1978-80; mem. task forces, cons. Nat. Dist. Attys. Assn., 1978-80, treas., 1977, v.p., 1978-81; mem. Gov.'s Spl. Task Force on Corrections, 1979-81; mem. Gov.'s Commn. on Organized Crime, 1973-81; pres. Oreg. Dist. Attys. Assn., 1979; del. Dem. Nat. Conf., 1974; keynote spkr. Oreg. Dem. Conv., 1971; chmn. Muskie for Pres., 1971. Recipient Disting. Svc. award, Outstanding Prosecutor award Nat. Dist. Attys. Assn., 1980. Mem. ABA (vice chmn. jud. adminstrn. divsn. com. on jury stds. 1990-95, del. nat. conf. 1992-95, co-chair task force), Oreg. Cir. Ct. Judge's Assn. (pres. 1993-94). Office: 1021 SW 4th Ave Portland OR 97204-1123

HAAS, JUNE F., special education educator, consultant; b. Burien, Wash., June 5, 1934; d. Carl Edwin and Mary Rebecca (Best) Flodquist; m. Frank M. Haas, June 21, 1958; children: Michael Edward, Katherine June Haas Dunning. BA in Elem. Edn., Psychology, U. Wash., 1956; MS in Early Childhood Edn., Oreg. Coll. Edn., 1975. Tchr. Haines (Alaska) Borough Sch. Dist., 1956-76, spl. edn. tchr., 1976-86, gifted, talented coord., 1978-87, migrant edn. tchr., 1986-87; instr. U. Alaska, Haines, 1984-85; cons. Ednl. Cons. Svcs., Haines, 1987—; instr. World Conf. Gifted/Talented Children, Hamburg, Germany, 1985, Sydney, Australia, 1989, 2d Gifted Asian Conf. on Giftedness, Taipei, Taiwan, 1992, World Conf. Gifted/Talented Children, Toronto, Can., 1993 ; coach Alaska Future Problem Solving Program, 1982-87; del. Citizen Ambassador Program Russia, Siberia, Hungary, 1991; del./presentor U.S./Russia Joint Conf. Edn., Moscow, 1994. Pres. Bus. and Profl. Women's Clubs, Alaska, 1973-74; pres. Am. Legion Aux., Alaska, 1990-91, nat. exec. com., 1991-92, mem. nat. edn. com., 1991-92; bd. dir. Am. Cancer Soc., Alaska, 1976—; chmn. we divsn. Nat. Edn. Com., 1992-93. Mem. World Coun. Gifted/Talented Children, Coun. Exceptional Children, Bus. and Profl. Women's Club (v.p. 1972-73, Woman of Yr. 1972), Am. Legion Aux. (nat. jr. activities com., western divsn. chmn. 1993-94, mem. citizens flag alliance 1994-95), Lynn Canal Community Players (nat. drama festival com. 1983), Haines Women's Club (pres. 1988-90), Pioneers of Alaska (pres. 1990-91). Methodist. Home and Office: Ednl Cons Svcs PO Box 97 Haines AK 99827-0097

HAAS, PETER E., SR., retired manufacturing company executive; b. San Francisco, Dec. 20, 1918; s. Walter A. and Elise (Stern) H.; m. Josephine Baum, Feb. 1, 1945; m. Mimi Lurie, Aug., 1981; children: Peter E., Michael Stern, Margaret Elizabeth. Student, Deerfield Acad., 1935-36; A.B., U. Calif., 1940; MBA cum laude, Harvard, 1943. With Levi Strauss & Co., San Francisco, 1945—; exec. v.p. Levi Strauss & Co., 1958-70, pres., 1970-81, chief exec. officer, 1976-81, chmn. bd., 1981-89, chmn. exec. com., 1989—; dir. emeritus AT&T. Trustee San Francisco Found., 1984—; assoc. Smithsonian Nat. Bd., 1988—; bd. dirs. No. Calif. Grantmakers, 1989—; former mem. exec. com. Strive for Five; former mem. Golden Gate Nat. Recreation Area Adv. Com.; Former pres. Jewish Welfare Fedn.; former trustee Stanford U.; former dir., vice chmn. San Francisco Bay Area Council; former trustee United Way of San Francisco Bay Area; former pres. Aid to Retarded Children; former bd. govs. United Way of Am. Recipient Alexis De Tocqueville Soc. award, United Way Am., 1985; named CEO of Yr., Fin. World mag., 1981, Bus. Statesman of Yr., Harvard Bus. Sch., 1982; Baker scholar, 1940. Office: Levi Strauss & Co PO Box 7215 San Francisco CA 94120-7215

HAAS, ROBERT DOUGLAS, apparel manufacturing company executive; b. San Francisco, Apr. 3, 1942; s. Walter A. Jr. and Evelyn (Danzig) H.; m. Colleen Gershon, Jan. 27, 1974; 1 child, Elise Kimberly. BA, U. Calif., Berkeley, 1964; MBA, Harvard U., 1968. With Peace Corps, Ivory Coast, 1964-66; fellow White House, Washington, 1968-69; assoc. McKinsey & Co., 1969-72; with Levi Strauss & Co., San Francisco, 1973—, sr. v.p. corp. planning and policy, 1978-80, pres. new bus. group, 1980, pres. operating groups, 1980-81, exec. v.p., COO, 1981-84, pres., CEO, 1984-89, CEO, chmn. bd., 1989—, also bd. dirs.; pres. Levi Strauss Found., mem. global leadership team. Hon. dir. San Francisco AIDS Found.; trustee Ford Found.; bd. dirs. Bay Area Coun.; past bd. dirs. Am. Apparel Assn. White House fellow, 1968-69. Mem. Brookings Inst. (trustee), Bay Area Com., Conf. Bd., Coun. Fgn. Rels., Trilateral Commn., Calif. Bus. Roundtable, Meyer Freidman Inst. (bd. dirs.), Phi Beta Kappa. Office: Levi Strauss & Co 1155 Battery St San Francisco CA 94111-1230

HAAS, ROBERT JOHN, aerospace engineer; b. Dayton, Ohio, Apr. 14, 1930; s. Robert J. Haas and Harriett (Longstreth) Bevan; m. Florence A. Eldred, June 6, 1952 (div. June 1984); adopted children: Jeffrey (dec.), Lisa Haas Cappuccio; m. Gayle F. Byrne, Dec. 14, 1984; stepchildren: Patrick Barton, Marissa Barton; children: Amber Haas, Robert J. Haas III. Student, U.S. Mil. Acad., 1948-51; BS in Petroleum Engring., U. Tulsa, 1954. Petroleum engr. Skelly Oil Co., Tulsa, 1953-54; propulsion engr., supr. Marquardt, Van Nuys, Calif., 1957-64; mgr. rocket programs Marquardt, Van Nuys, 1964-69, dir. test and facilities, 1969-72, gen. mgr. environ. systems, 1972-75; plant gen. mgr. Williams Internat., Ogden, Utah, 1975-79; sr. v.p. engring. Williams Internat., Walled Lake, Mich., 1979-86; sr. v.p. product planning and mktg. Williams Internat., Walled Lake, 1986-90; sr. advisor, cons. Las Vegas, Nev., 1990—; cons. Marquardt, Van Nuys, 1961-75. Author: Approach to Aerospace Plane Propulsion, 1960. Lectr. and advisor Weber State Coll., U. Utah and various high schs. and clubs., 1975-79; pres. Marquardt Mgmt. Club, 1971. 1st lt. USAF, 1954-56. Mem. AIAA, Navy League (lifetime). Republican. Roman Catholic. Home: PO Box 33126 Las Vegas NV 89133-3126 Office: Haas Enterprize PO Box 33126 Las Vegas NV 89133-3126

HAAS, WALTER A., JR., retired apparel company executive, professional baseball executive; b. San Francisco, Jan. 24, 1916; s. Walter Abraham and Elise (Stern) H.; m. Evelyn Danzig, 1940; children: Robert D., Elizabeth Haas Eisenhardt, Walter J. BA, U. Calif., Berkeley, 1937; MBA, Harvard U., 1939; hon. degree, Wheaton Coll., 1983. Chief exec. officer Levi Strauss & Co., San Francisco, 1958-76, now hon. chmn. exec. com. bd. dirs.; owner, mng. gen. ptnr. Oakland (Calif.) Athletics Baseball Co.; bd. dir. Bank of Am., Bank Am. Corp., UAL, Inc., Mauna Kea Properties, Pacific Tel. Co.; trustee The Bus. Enterprise Trust; former bd. dir. Bank of Am. Bd. dirs. Nat. Park Found.; mem. adv. coun. Reading is Fundamental, Inc.; mem. SRI Internat. Adv. Coun.; mem. Nat. Commn. on Pub. Svc; former mem. Trilateral Commn.; former mem. exec. com., former regional chmn. Nat. Alliance Businessman; former mem. Presdl. Adv. Coun. for Minority Enterprise, Presdl. Task Force on Internat. Devel., 1970, Nat. Ctr. for Voluntary Action, Citizens Commn. on Pvt. Philanthropy and Pub. Needs; former mem. vis. com. Harvard Bus. Sch.; former mem. intercollegiate athletics adv. bd. U. Calif.; former dir. Hunters Point Boys' Club, San Francisco Boys' Club, Bay Area Urban League, Mt. Zion Hosp.; campaign chmn. United Bay Area Crusade, 1956, also bd. dirs.; former chmn. Radio Free Europe, No. Calif.; commr. San Francisco Parking Authority, 1953; former trustee Ford Found., Com. for Econ. Devel.; former co-chmn. bus. steering com. Nat. Cambodia Crisis Com. Named a Leader of Tomorrow Time mag., 1953, Chief Exec. Officer of Yr. Fin. World mag., 1976, Alumnus of Yr., U. Calif. at Berkeley, 1984; recipient Jefferson award Am. Inst. Pub. Service, 1977, Alumni Achievement award Harvard Grad. Sch. Bus., 1979, Chancellor's award U. Calif. at Berkeley Found., 1982, The Alexis De Tocqueville Society award United Way Am., 1985. Mem. Mfrs. and Wholesalers Assn. San Francisco, (pres. 1951), Nat. Urban League (former dir.), Phi Beta Kappa, Alpha Delta Phi. Office: Levi Strauss & Co PO Box 7215 San Francisco CA 94120-7215 also: Oakland Athletics Oakland/Alameda County Coliseum Oakland CA 94621*

HAAS, WALTER J., professional baseball team executive; S. Walter A. Jr. and Evelyn (Danzig) H.; m.; 3 children. Former pres. Goldmine Records; exec. v.p. Oakland (Calif.) A's, Am. League, 1980-88, chief oper. officer, 1988-89, former pres., former chief exec. officer, now chmn., COO. Trustee Evelyn and Walter A. Haas, Jr. Fund, Marin County Day Sch. Office: care Oakland A's Oakland Coliseum 7000 Coliseum Way Oakland CA 94621-1918*

HAASE, ROBERT WILLIAM, executive bottle water company; b. Seattle, June 1, 1950; s. William Delbert and Jeanette Lillian (Lewis) H.; m. Rae Ann Gaedeke (div. Sept., 1979); children: Adam Douglas, Jessica Lynn; m. Constance Elizabeth Jones, July 22, 1989; stepchilden: Stephanie Marie Remus, Samantha Kate Remus. Student, Brevard Coll., 1968-70, St. Andrews Coll., 1970-71. Supr. Fla. Guard Rail Co., Hollywood, Fla., 1971-73; prodn. mgr. Starline Corp., Pompano Beach, Fla., 1973-74; cabinet maker Kramer Woodworking, Washington, Va., 1974-75; ptnr. Country Cupboards, Washington, 1975-77, Nature's Foods, Washington, 1975-77; owner, designer Robert Haase Furniture Design, Washington, 1978-84; gen. mgr., bd. sec. Polar Water Co., Inc., Stockton, Calif., 1984—. Bd. dirs. Better Bus. Bur. Mid. Counties, Stockton, Calif., 1990—, vice-chmn. Mem. Calif. Bottled Water Assn. (pres.), San Joaquin Employers Coun. (bd. dirs.), Stockton United Soccer Club (past pres. bd.), Rotary Club Stockton. Presbyterian. Office: Polar Water Co Inc PO Box 511 1029 W Fremont St Stockton CA 95203-2795

HABBESTAD, KATHRYN LOUISE, writer; b. Spokane, Wash., Sept. 29, 1949; d. Bernard Malvin and Gertrude Lucille (Westberg) H. BA, U. Wash., 1971; postgrad., Seattle U., 1981-82. Mgr. bus. Seattle Sun, 1974-75; analyst, dep. dir. Research and Planning Office, Seattle, 1975-83; account exec. Southmark Fin. Services, Seattle, 1983-84; stockbroker Interstate Securities, New Bern, N.C., 1985-86; co-founder, assoc. pub. Havelock (N.C.) News, 1986-87; owner ISIS Enterprises, Spokane, 1988—; writer Spokane; sec.-treas. Seattle Sun Pub. Co., 1974-75, Veritas Services, Seattle, 1978-83; chmn. Energy Com. Nat. Congress for Community Econ. Devel., Washington, 1979-82; pub. The Gnus, 1988. Treas. Havelock Chili Festival, 1985-87. Mem. Internat. Platform Assn., Mensa. Home and Office: 3822 131st Ln SE # L-6 Bellevue WA 98006-1362

HABEDANK, GARY L., brokerage house executive; b. Glendive, Mont., Feb. 17, 1944; s. Otto T. and Arleen T (Miller) H.; m. Kathryn Ann Czyhold, June 18, 1967; children: Silke, Anne. BBA, Pacific Lutheran U., 1966; postgrad., U. Mont., 1966-67. CFP, 1980. 1st v.p. and asst. br. mgr. Smith Barney Inc., Tacoma, 1968—; Adv. coun. John Nuveen & Co., Chgo., 1986—; adv. bd. Planned Giving & Fin. Bd. of Visitors. Trustee Tacoma Art Mus., 1984-90; trustee, pres. Tacoma Philharm., Inc., 1977-83; sec. Annie Wright Sch., 1985-91; mem. Christ Episc. Ch. (vestry, fin. chmn. 1987-91). Recipient Community Svc. award Jr. League of Tacoma, 1990. Mem. Tacoma Club, Tacoma Elks, Boy Scouts Am. Republican. Episcopalian. Home: 3 N Rosemount Way Tacoma WA 98406-7117 Office: Tacoma Fin Ctr 1145 Broadway Ste 1400 Tacoma WA 98402-3523

HABERLIN, WILLIAM EARL, real estate company executive; b. Honolulu, Mar. 26, 1925; s. Earl William Haberlin and Mary Constance (Ferreira) Burroughs; m. Mildred Frances Copley, July 1, 1945; children: James William, Laura Joyce, Judith Ann, Brian Jon. AA, U. Calif., Berkeley, 1944; MBA, Harvard U., 1956. Asst. v.p. United Calif. Bank, L.A., 1963-65; sr. economist Stanford Rsch. Inst., South Pasadena, Calif., 1965-67; sr. v.p. Union Bank, L.A., 1967-81; v.p., corp. sec. Watson Land Co., L.A., 1981—. Contbr. articles to profl. jours. Mem. Pvt. Industry Coun., L.A., 1990—. Comdr. USN, 1943-63. Mem. Rotary Club of L.A., Harvard-Radcliff Club of So. Calif., Harvard Bus. Sch. Alumni Assn., Assn. for Corp. Growth, Assn. for Bus. Economists, Jonathan Club.

HABERMANN, NORMAN, restaurant group executive; b. Hillside, N.J., 1933. Grad., Rutgers U., 1955; postgrad., Golden Gate U. Sch. Bus. Adminstrn., 1968. Former pres., now chmn. Restaurant Enterprises Group Inc., Irvine, Calif.; chief oper. officer Carrows Restaurants, Santa Barbara, Calif.; bd. dirs. Elephant Bar Restaurants Inc., Taco Villa Inc., Jeremiah's Restaurants Inc., Grace Food Co., Bruner Corp. Inc., Rayne Aquatechs. Inc. Office: Restaurant Enterprises Group Inc 1 Park Plz Ste 900 Irvine CA 92714-5999 also: Gilbert/Robinson Inc 47th & Main St Box 16000 Kansas City MO 64112

HACHMEISTER, JOHN H., lawyer, educator, mediator; b. Chgo., Nov. 24, 1944; s. Howard E. and Leah (Mace) H.; m. Lydia E. McCarver, Jan. 8, 1982; children: Steven, Mellissa, Rachel. BA in Polit. Sci., Cen. State U., Edmond, Okla., 1978; postgrad., Oklahoma City U., 1980-82; JD, Southwestern U., L.A., 1984. Bar: Calif. Technician Am. Chain & Cable, Franklin Park, Ill., 1972-76; assoc. Somers, Hall, et al., Gardena, Calif., 1985-90, Spray, Gould & Bowers, L.A., 1990-92, Fiore, Nordberg, et al, Irvine, Calif., 1992-94; pvt. practice Redondo Beach, Calif., 1994—; owner Jack's Imagination Enterprises, Redondo Beach, 1988—; asst. prof. Calif. State U., Northridge; cons., facilitator Oklahoma City Coalition of Neighborhood Assns., 1972-82; speaker in field. Author: (poetry) Colorado Cowboy Poetry Gathering, 1993; co-inventor solder jig for multi-wire cables, 1992. Candidate for state sen. Dem. party, Torrance, Calif., 1990, Ho. of Reps., Oklahoma City, 1978; del. Dem. party convs. Okla. and Calif., 1974-92; mem. Mayor's Transp. Task Force, Oklahoma City, 1976-80; lt. gov. Okla. Intercollegiate Legis., 1977-78; judge Southwestern U. Moot Ct. Competition, Santa Ana, Calif., 1993. Named to Outstanding Young Men of Am. Mem. Calif. Bar Assn., Greenpeace. Home and Office: 2112 Warfield Ave Apt 4 Redondo Beach CA 90278-1447

HACKBARTH, DEAN ROBERT, manufacturing executive; b. Ridgewood, N.J., July 12, 1958; s. Robert Van Hoven and Doris Ruth (Hudson) H.; m. Robin Lee Hounshell, July 15, 1978; children: Jenny Ruth, Taylor Robert. Student, Arapahoe C.C., Littleton, Colo., 1976-77; grad., Denver Auto and Diesel Coll., 1978. Laborer, welder's helper, welder, fitter Zimkor Industries, Littleton, 1976-79; laser technician, machinist Viner Mfg., Evergreen, Colo., 1979-84; machinist, laser specialist, dept. head Midwest Machine Products, Arvada, Colo., 1984-87; laser cons., sales rep. Bond's Custom Mfg., Arvada, 1987, plant mgr., 1987-89, laser specialist, technician, 1990—; mfg. mgr. GBC Inc., Lakewood, Colo., 1990—; laser cons. users and mfrs., 1990—; condr. trade show seminars on indsl. laser applications. Republican. Baptist. Office: GBC Inc 190 S Union Blvd Lakewood CO 80228-2222

HACKBARTH, DOROTHY ALICE, association executive; b. Naperville, Ill., Apr. 21, 1921; d. Walter Dewey and Nellie Louise (Staffeldt) Eichelberger; m. Charles Alfred Hackbarth, Oct. 24, 1942; children: Christofer Lee, Cathleen, Timothy Scott. BA, U. Calif., Berkeley, 1964. Cert. secondard tchr., Calif. Clk. Elgin (Ill.) Watch Factory, 1940-42; sec. Lucien Lelong, Chgo., 1942-43; telephone operator Hinsdale (Ill.) Telephone Co., 1943-44; dress designer Naperville, Ill., 1947-55; tchr. Oakland (Calif.) Unified Sch. Dist., 1965-66, Berkeley Unified Sch. Dist., 1966-78; pres., chief exec. officer Unesco Assn./USA, Inc., Oakland, Calif., 1978—; pres. UN Assn./Alameda City, Oakland, 1968-73; chair Fgn. Lang. Dept. Martin Luther King Sch., Berkeley, 1969-73. Chair Nat. French Contest, Oakland, Calif., 1968-70. Fellowship UNESCO, 1971; recipient Excellence in Teaching award Berkeleyans for Acad. Excellence, 1977; scholarship Calif. PTA, 1977. Mem. Calif. Alumni Assn. Home and Office: 5815 Lawton Ave Oakland CA 94618-1510

HACKER, RICHARD CARLETON, author; b. Chgo., Sept. 10, 1942; s. Silvio Insana and Lillian Padorr. BA, Ariz. State U., 1965. Author: The Muzzleloading Hunter, 1981, The Christmas Pipe, 1986, The Ultimate Pipe Book, 1984-88, The Ultimate Cigar Book, 1993. Mem. Confrerie de Maitre de Pipie de St. Claude, L'Academie Internationale de La Pipe. Office: PO Box 634 Beverly Hills CA 90213-0634

HACKER, THOMAS OWEN, architect; b. Dayton, Ohio, Nov. 4, 1941; s. Homer Owen and Lydia (McLean) H.; m. Margaret (Brooks) Stewart, Mar. 21, 1965; children: Jacob, Sarah, Alice. BA, U. Pa., 1964, MArch, 1967. Registered arch., Oreg.; registered Nat. Coun. Archtl. Registration Bds. Intern architect Office of Louis I. Kahn, Phila., 1964-70; mem. faculty architecture U. Pa., Phila., 1967-69, U. Oreg., Eugene, 1970-84; design prin. Thomas Hacker and Assocs. Architects P.C., Portland, Oreg., 1983—; vis. profl. architecture, U. Oreg., 1985—, U. Idaho, Moscow, 1991-92, Ariz. State U., Tempe, 1986-87, U. Tex., Austin, 1986. Prin. works include Biomed. Info. Comm. Ctr., Oreg. Health Scis. U. (Design Excellence award AIA), Sch. Nursing, Oreg. Health Scis. U. (Design Excellence award 1992, Regional Honor award AIA 1993), Portland Art Mus., High Desert Mus., Bend, Oreg.; designer crystal vase for Steuben Inc., Watzek Libr. renovation and addition, Spokane Pub. Libr., Western Treasure Valley Cultural Ctr., Ontario, Oreg., Yellowstone Art Ctr., Billings, Mont., others. Bd. visitors Sch. Architecture, U. Oreg., 1987-89; mem. Portland Design Commn., 1989—. Mem. AIA. Office: 34 NW 1st Ave Ste 406 Portland OR 97209-4017

HACKETT, CAROL ANN HEDDEN, physician; b. Valdese, N.C., Dec. 18, 1939; d. Thomas Barnett and Zada Loray (Pope) Hedden; BA, Duke, 1961; MD, U. N.C., 1966; m. John Peter Hackett, July 27, 1968; children: John Hedden, Elizabeth Bentley, Susanne Rochet. Intern. Georgetown U. Hosp., Washington, 1966-67, resident, 1967-69; clinic physician DePaul Hosp., Norfolk, Va., 1969-71; chief spl. health services Arlington County Dept. Human Resources, Arlington, Va., 1971-72; gen. med. officer USPHS Hosp., Balt., 1974-75; pvt. practice family medicine, Seattle, 1975—; mem. staff, chmn. dept. family practice Overlake Hosp. Med. Ctr., 1985-86; clin. asst. prof. Sch. Medicine U. Wash. Bd. dirs. Mercer Island (Wash.) Preschool Assn., 1977-78; coordinator 13th and 20th Ann. Inter-profl. Women's Dinner, 1978, 86; trustee Northwest Chamber Orch., 1984-85. Mem. AAUW, Am. Acad. Family Practice, King County Acad. Family Practice (trustee 1993-94), King County Med. Soc. (chmn. com. TV violence), Wash. Med. Soc., DAR, Bellevue C. of C., NW Women Physicians (v.p. 1978), Seattle Symphony League, Eastside Women Physicians (founder, pres.), Sigma Kappa, Wash. Athletic Club, Lakes Club, Seattle Yacht Club. Episcopalian. Home: 4304 E Mercer Way Mercer Island WA 98040-3826 Office: 1414 116th Ave NE Bellevue WA 98004-3801

HACKETT, DWIGHT VERNON, business owner; b. Modesto, Calif., Mar. 21, 1945; s. Kenneth Gordon and Rosalind (Odell) H.; m. Mary McEwen, July 20, 1970; children: Matthew Dwight, Timothy Dylan. Student, San Frnacisco Art Inst., 1969-70. Mgr. Nambe Mills, Santa Fe, N.Mex., 1971-80; pres. Art Foundry, Inc., Santa Fe, 1980—, Hackett Foundry, Inc., L.A., 1988-91; exhibition curator St. John's Coll., Santa Fe, 1986, Coll. Santa Fe, 1994. Director, publisher: Art Foundry Editions, 1991—. Bd. dirs. Ctr. Contemporary Arts, Santa Fe, 1988—. Office: Art Foundry Inc PO Box 8107 Santa Fe NM 87504-8107

HACKETT, JOHN PETER, dermatologist; b. N.Y.C., Feb. 10, 1942; s. John Thomas and Helen (Donohue) H.; m. Carol A. Hedden, July 27, 1968; children: John, Elizabeth, Susanne. AB, Holy Cross Coll., 1963; MD, Georgetown U., 1967. Diplomate Am. Bd. Internal Medicine, Am. Bd. Dermatology. Intern Georgetown U. Hosp., 1967-68, resident, 1968-69; fellow Johns Hopkins Hosp., 1972-75, chief resident, 1975; practice medicine specializing in dermatology Seattle, 1975—; chmn. bd. dirs. NW Dental Ins. Co., 1989-92; clin. asst. prof. dermatology U. Wash., 1976-88, clin. assoc. prof., 1988—; active staff Swedish Hosp., Providence Hosp.; cons. Wash. State Dept. Labor and Industries, 1992—; pres. Psoriasis Treatment Ctr., Inc., 1978-80; cons. physician Children's Orthopedic Hosp. Contbr. articles to profl. jours. Bd. dirs. Mercer Island Boys and Girls Club, 1976-81, Seattle Ctr. for Blind, 1979-80, N.W. Chamber Orch., 1983-86. Served to lt. condr. USNR, 1969-71. Mem. Am. Acad. Dermatology, Seattle Dermatol. Soc. (pres. 1981-82), Soc. Investigative Dermatology, Am. Contact Dermatitis Soc., Wash. State Med. Soc., King County Med. Soc. (chmn. media rels. com. 1977-80, grievance com. 1991—), Wash. Physicians Ins. Exch. (chmn. actuarial subcom. 1983-85, chmn. subscribers adv. com. 1986-90, audit com. 1988-92, fin. com. 1990-92), Wash. Athletic Club, Seattle Yacht Club, Lakes Club, Rotary. Office: 1500 Cabrini Tower 901 Boren Ave Seattle WA 98104-3508

HACKETT, LOUISE, personnel services company executive, consultant; b. Sheridan, Mont., Nov. 11, 1933; d. Paul Duncan and Freda A. (Dudley) Johnson; m. Lewis Edward Hackett, June 24, 1962; 1 child, Dell Paul. Student U. Oreg., 1959-61; BA, Calif. State U.-Sacramento, 1971. Legal sec. Samuel R. Friedman, Yreka, Calif., 1952-58, Barber & Cottrell, Eugene, Oreg., 1958-59; paralegal Elmer Sahlstrom, Eugene, 1959-62; legis. aide Calif. Legislature, Sacramento, 1962-72; owner Legal Personnel Services, Sacramento, 1973-78, corp. pres., 1979—; pres. Legalstaff, Inc., 1987—; curriculum adv. dept. bus. Am. River Coll., Sacramento, 1974-79; founder, adminstr. Pacific Coll. Legal Careers, Sacramento, 1973-84; cons. legal edn. Barclay Schs., Sacramento, 1984; active Sacramento Employees Adv. Coun. Designer, pub. Sacramento/Yolo Attys. Directory, 1974—. Author operations manual and franchise training textbook; contbr. articles to profl. jours. Adv. bd. San Juan Sch. Dist., 1975-84. Mem. Calif. Assn. Personnel Cons., Sacramento Council Pvt. Edn. (pres. 1976-77), Pi Omega Pi. Clubs: Sierra Sail and Trail, Soroptimist Internat. Lodge: Order of Rainbow. Avocations: skiing, sailing, gardening, horseback riding. Office: Legal Personnel Svcs 1415 21st St Sacramento CA 95814-5208 also: 433 California St Ste 904 San Francisco CA 94104-2013 also: 2103 Landings Dr Mountain View CA 94043-0839 also: 111 N Market St Ste 404 San Jose CA 95113-1101

HACKETT, RALPH, agricultural products supplier; b. 1954. With Suma Fruit Internat., Phila., 1975-89; with Suma Fruit Internat. USA, 1989—, now CEO. Office: Suma Fruit International USA 1810 Academy Ave Sanger CA 93657-3739*

HACKETT, RANDALL SCOTT, engineer; b. Grand Rapids, Mich., Oct. 1, 1943; s. Hugh Jerry and Phyllis (Weekes) H.; m. Lyn Susan Swanson, Jan. 11, 1964; children: Katherine Eileen and Elizabeth Evelyn (twins), Kimberly Michele. AA, West Valley Jr. Coll., 1970; BS, Calif. State U., San Jose, 1972. Technician Allen Electronics, Mountain View, Calif., 1963-64, Fairchild Semiconductor, Mountain View, 1964-66, IBM, San Jose, Calif., 1966-68; from assoc. engr. to sr. assoc. engr. IBM, San Jose, 1968-78, staff engr., 1978-89, adv. engr., 1989-94; computer cons., CEO Pacheco Labs., Inc., Gilroy, Calif., 1994—. Inventor slave processor, measurement control unit, spelling checking typewriter. Republican. Lutheran. Home: 11048 Alessi Ct Gilroy CA 95020-9123 Office: Pacheco Labs Inc 11048 Alessi Ct Gilroy CA 95020-9123

HACKNEY, ROBERT WARD, plant pathologist, nematologist, parasitologist, molecular geneticist, commercial arbitrator; b. Louisville, Dec. 11, 1942; s. Paul Arnold and Ovine (Whallen) H.; m. Cheryl Lynn Hill, June 28, 1969; 1 child, Candice Colleen. BA, Northwestern U., 1965; MS, Murray State U., 1969; PhD, Kans. State U., 1973. Postgrad. rsch. nematologist U. Calif., Riverside, 1973-75; plant nematologist Calif. Dept. Food and Agr., Sacramento, 1975-85, sr. plant nematologist, supr. 1985-89, sr. plant nematologist, specialist, 1989—; comml. arbitrator Am. Arbitration Assn., 1980—; chmn. Calif. Nematode Diagnosis Adv. Commn., Sacramento, 1981—. Contbr. articles to profl. jours. Hon. dep. Sheriff, Sacramento, 1982-83. Served with USMC, 1966. NSF grantee, 1974. Mem. Soc. Nematologists, Internat. Council Study of Viruses and Virus Diseases of the Grape, Delta Tau Delta, Sigma Xi. Democrat. Baptist. Home: 2024 Flowers St Sacramento CA 95825-0422 Office: Calif Dept Food & Agriculture Plant Pest Diagnostic Ctr 3294 Meadowview Rd Sacramento CA 95832-1437

HACKWORTH, THEODORE JAMES, JR., city official; b. Denver, Nov. 7, 1926; s. Theodore James and Thelma B. (Hill) H.; m. Doris Evelyn Larson, Dec. 31, 1947; children—James Robert, Joan Evelyn Grady, Linda Jean Hoffman. B.A., U. Denver, 1955. Sales mgr. Continental Baking Co., Denver, 1950-64; mktg. exec. Sigman Meat Co., Denver, 1964-76; v.p. sales Pierce Packing Co., Billings, Mont., 1976-79; city councilman City of Denver, 1979—, pres., 1983-84; cons. EPA. Mem. Denver pub. schs. bd. edn., 1971-77; dir. Urban Drainage and Flood Control Dist., 1981-84; dir. Met. Wastewater Reclamation Dist., 1982—, sec., 1984-85, chmn. elect 1988-89, chmn., 1989—; mem. Denver Regional Council Govts., 1979-94, vice chmn., 1981-83, chmn., 1984-86; neighborhood commr. Boy Scouts Am., 1968-69, Western Dist. commr., 1970-71; pres. Harvey Park Improvement Assn., 1969; chmn. Denver Met. Library Task Force, 1982. Served with USAF, 1945-47. Mem. Nat. Assn. Regional Council (bd. dirs. m., chmn. surface trans. task force, pres. 1987-89). Republican. Club: Mt. Vernon Country. Contbr. articles to EPA jours. Home: 3955 W Linvale Pl Denver CO 80236-2212 Office: 3110 S Wadsworth Blvd # 304 Denver CO 80227-5507

HADA, JOHN JUJI, East Asian international affairs educator; b. San Francisco, Apr. 16, 1927; s. Jutaro James and Katsuyo (Noma) H.; m. Mitzi Mutsumi Egusa, May 27, 1951; children: Elayne Naomi, Matthew Stuart Jun, Sterling Theodore, Leslie Anne. BA in Philosophy and History, U. San Francisco, 1972, MA in History, 1973, EdD in Edn., 1981; PhD in Anthrop. Linguistics, U. Tokyo, Japan, 1986. Col. U.S. Army, 1944-71; fgn. svc. officer Embassy of U.S.A., Tokyo, 1982-86; sr. Fulbright fellow Nat. Lang. Rsch. Inst., Tokyo, 1986-88; prof. Tohoku Nat. U., Sendai, Japan, 1988-93, U. San Francisco, 1993—, Coll. of Notre Dame, Belmont, Calif., 1994—; rschr. Ctr. for the Pacific Rim, U. San Francisco, 1993—. Author: The Anatomy of the All Japan Federation of Self-Governing Students: Its Evolution and Dimensions of Japanese Student Activism in the Postwar Period. Decorated D.S.C., U.S. Army, 1966, Legion of Merit, U.S. Army, 1966. Mem. Nat. Japanese Am. Hist. Soc. (dir. 1994—). Democrat. Roman Catholic. Home: 1429 23rd Ave San Francisco CA 94122-3305 Office: U San Francisco 2130 Fulton St San Francisco CA 94117-1080

HADAS, ELIZABETH CHAMBERLAYNE, publisher; b. Washington, May 12, 1946; d. Moses and Elizabeth (Chamberlayne) H.; m. Jeremy W. Heist, Jan. 25, 1970 (div. 1976); m. Peter Eller, Mar. 21, 1984. A.B., Radcliffe Coll., 1967; postgrad. Rutgers U., 1967-68; M.A., Washington U., St. Louis, 1971. Editor U. N.Mex. Press, Albuquerque, 1971-85; dir., 1985—. Mem. Assn. Am. Univ. Presses (pres. 1992-93). Democrat. Home: 2900 10th St NW Albuquerque NM 87107-1111 Office: U NMex Press 1720 Lomas Blvd NE Albuquerque NM 87106-3807

HADAVI, FOUAD FRED, interior designer; b. Ahvaz, Khuzistan, Iran, Apr. 16, 1956; came to U.S., 1977; s. Majid and Fatemeh (Salamipour) H. BS in Archtl. Engring., Roger Williams Coll., 1981. Engr. Ea. Cabinet Co., Glendale, N.Y., 1981-82, Hochberg Bros. Schan, Inc., Bklyn., 1982-84; interior designer Walker Group/CNI, L.A. and N.Y.C., 1984-90; owner, founder Tustin (Calif.) Design Group, 1991-93; interior designer Design and Interiors, L.A., 1994—. Recipient Unsong Hero award Walker Group/CNI. Mem. Calif. Coun. for Interior Design (cert.), Am. Soc. Interior Designers, Inst. of Store Planners (assoc.). Home: 2370 Paseo Circulo Tustin CA 92680-9021 Office: Design I Interiors 4056 Del Rey Ave Marina Del Rey CA 90292

HADDAD, EDMONDE ALEX, public affairs executive; b. Los Angeles, July 25, 1931; s. Alexander Saleeba and Madeline Angela (Zail) H.; m. Harriet Ann Lenhart; children: Mark Edmonde, Brent Michael, John Alex. AA, Los Angeles City Coll., 1956; BA, U. Southern Calif., 1958; MA, Columbia U., 1961. Staff writer WCBS Radio News, New York, 1959-61; news commentator, editor KPOL AM/FM Radio, Los Angeles, 1961-67, dir., pub. affairs, 1967-73; exec. dir. Los Angeles World Affairs Council, 1973-84; pres. L.A. World Affairs Coun., 1984-88; deputy asst. sec. of State for Pub. Diplomacy Dept. State, U.S. Govt., Wash., 1987-88; mem. steering com., moderator Conf. environ., L.A., 1989-90; pres. Nat. Coun. World Affairs Orgns., 1981-83; pres. Radio and TV News Assn. So. Calif., 1965-66; sr. fellow Ctr. Internat. Rels., U. Calif., L.A., 1991—; bd. dirs. Pen Ctr. USA West. Contbg. author: How Peace Came to the World,, 1985; founder, pub. World Affairs Jour. Quar., 1981. Bd. dirs. PEN Ctr. USA West, 1994—, World Affairs Coun., Ventura County, 1995—. Recipient Am. Polit. Sci. Assn. award for Disting. Reporting of Pub. Affairs, 1967. Mem. Friends of Wilton Pk. (exec. com. So. Calif.). Democrat. Home: 582 Pacific Cove Dr Port Hueneme CA 93041-2175

HADDAD, EDWARD RAOUF, civil engineer, consultant; b. Mosul, Iraq, July 1, 1926; came to U.S., 1990; s. Raouf Sulaiman Haddad and Fadhila (Sulaiman) Shaya; m. Balquis Yousef, July 19, 1961; children: Reem, Raid. BSc, U. Baghdad, Iraq, 1949; postgrad., Colo. State U., 1966-67. Project engr., cons. Min. Pub. Works, Baghdad, 1949-63; arbitrator Engring. Soc. & Ct., Kuwait City, Kuwait, 1963-90; tech. advisor Royal Family, Kuwait, 1987-90; cons. pvt. practice Haddad Engring., Albuquerque, 1990—. Organizer Reps. Abroad, Kuwait, 1990. Recipient Hon. medal Pope Paul VI of Rome, 1973. Mem. ASCE, NSPE, KC (chancellor 1992), Am. Arbitration Assn., Sierra Internat. (trustee), Lions (bd. dirs. 1992), Inventors Club (bd. dirs. 1992). Address: 143 General Arnold St NE Apt A Albuquerque NM 87123-2535

HADDAD, FARID SAMI, educator; b. N.Y.C., May 4, 1922; s. Sam Abraham and Lamia Nicholas (Morcos) H.; m. Huda F. Fawaz, Sept. 19, 1949; children: Sami, Ranwa, Ziad. BA, Am. U., 1941, MD, 1948. Intern Am. U. Hosp., Beirut, Lebanon, 1948-49; resident Orient Hosp., Beirut, Lebanon, 1949-50, Presbyn. Hosp., Chgo., 1951-53; asst. in urology U. Ill., Chgo., 1951-53; spl. fellow Meml. Hosp., N.Y.C., 1953-54; attending urologist, attending surgeon, chief of staff Orient Hosp., Beirut, 1957-74; attending urologist, attending surgeon Marj'uyun (Lebanon) Govt. Hosp., 1972-77; chief urologist, chief surgeon Obeid Hosp., Riyadh, Saudi Arabia, 1977-81, chief of staff, 1979-81; chief urology VA Med. Ctr., Phoenix, 1981-93; clin. assoc. prof. surgery U. Ariz., Tucson, 1987—. Author: Directory of Medical Alumni, 1957-67, The Prostate - Your Gland, 1963, Directory of AUB, 1967, Hadith for Omar, 2d edit., 1969, Medical Ethics Law, 1969, Bareme des honoraires chirurgicaux, 1970, Catalogue of Medical Manuscripts, 1984, Guide to Diagnostic Imaging Vol. 4, 1984, Vol. 5, 1984; editor: History of Arab Medicine, 1975; contbr. articles to profl. jours. Mem. AMA, Atheneum of History of Medicine Buenos Aires (corr. mem.), Syrian Soc. Hisotry of Scis., Am. Assn. History of Sci., Maricopa County Med. Assn., Phoenix Urological Assn., Ariz. Med. Assn., Assn. VA Surgeons, Ariz. Urological Soc., Assn. Mil. Surgeons N.Am., History Sci. Soc., Arab Am. Med. Assn., Alpha Omega Alpha. Evangelical. Home and Office: 4332 E Piccadilly Rd Phoenix AZ 85018-5447

HADDAD, WISAM BOULOS, surgeon; b. Amman, Jordan, Mar. 4, 1954; came to U.S., 1973; s. Boulos Somail and Tammam Mufaddi (Hawatmeh) H.; m. Rozanne Charlie Carrubba, June 12, 1977; children: Angie, Laila, Laura. BS, Andrews U., 1976; MD, Loma Linda U., 1979. Diplomate Am. Bd. Surgery. Intern, resident in surgery Loma Linda (Calif.) U. Sch. Medicine, 1980-85, instr. Sch. Medicine, 1984-85, asst. prof. surgery, 1988—; assoc. in surgery Riverside (Calif.) Gen. Hosp., 1985-95, chmn. tumor bd., 1988-94; dir. trauma svcs. Riverside (Calif.) Gen. Hosp, 1994-95; spkr., lectr. to med. socs., med. convs., among others. Chmn. tobacco task force Am. Cancer Soc., Inland Empire, Calif., 1993—. Fellow ACS; mem. Soc. Loma Linda U. Surgeons (pres. 1993—). Home: 969 Talcey Ter Riverside CA 92506-7517 Office: Beaver Med Clinic 2 W Fern Ave Redlands CA 92373

HADDIX, CHARLES E., legislative and regulatory consultant; b. Astoria, Oreg., Nov. 23, 1915; s. Charles H. and Mattie Lee (Wilson) H.; grad. U.S. Maritime Officers Sch., 1943; grad. in traffic mgmt. Golden Gate U., 1951; m. Betty Lee Wylie, Aug. 22, 1948; children—Bruce W., Anne C., C. Brian. Nat. sales mgr. Radio Sta. KLX, Oakland, Calif., 1953-55; West Coast mgr. Forjoe & Co., 1955-60; v.p. Calif. Spot Sales, 1958-60, Radio Calif., KLIP, Fowler, Calif., 1961-63; med. sales rep. Ives Labs., Inc., Sanger, Calif., 1964-73; state govt. rels. cons. Marion Merrill Dow Labs., Inc., 1973-87; Calif. legis. advocate, 1968-85; Ariz., Nev., N.Mex., Oreg., Wash., Idaho, Utah and Mont. legis. advocate, 1975-85. Mem. Central Calif. Forum on Refugee Affairs, 1983—, chmn. 1987-88, state forum chmn., 1988; mem. Calif. State Adv. Council on Refugee Assistance and Svcs., 1988-90; field cons. U.S. Sen. Alan Cranston, 1987-90, Calif. State Sen. Rose Ann Vuich, 1991-92; Refugee coord. Dooley for Congres Campaign, 1990, Bustamente for Assembly Campaign, 1993-94; commr. Fresno County Econ. Opportunities Commn., 1992-93; mem. Clinton Presdl. Transition Planning Found., 1993; mem. U.S. Senate Staff Club, 1987-90; field cons. Assemblyman Cruz Bustamente; dist. rep. State Sen. Jim Costa, 1995. Author: Reminiscenses of an Old Astoria House, 1992, River Travel Memories on the Columbia, 1992, An Adventure in Dredging, 1993, The Astor Street Mystery, 1994. Served with Marina Mercante Nat., Republic of Panama, 1945, U.S. Mcht. Marine, 1939-41, USCG, 1942-45. Mem. U.S. Naval Inst., Ctrl. Tex. Geneaol. Soc., Historic Waco Found., Oreg. Hist. Soc., Manuscript Soc., Clatsop County Hist. Soc., Columbia River Maritime Mus., Am. Merchant Marine Vets. (CEO Ctrl. Calif. chpt. 1994—), Commonwealth Club of Calif. (San Francisco). Address: 3218 N Mccall Ave Sanger CA 93657-9385

HADGES, THOMAS RICHARD, media consultant; b. Brockton, Mass., Mar. 13, 1948; s. Samuel Charels and Ethel Toli (Prifti) H.; m. Beth Evelyn Rastad, Oct. 22, 1988. BA in Biology magna cum laude, Tufts U., 1969; student, Harvard Sch. Dental Med., 1969-71. Announcer Sta. WOKW, Brockton, 1965-67, Sta. WTBS-FM, MIT, Cambridge, 1966-68; announcer, program dir. Sta. WTUR, Medford, Mass., 1967-69; announcer Concert Network, Sta. WBCN-FM, Boston, 1968-78, program dir., 1977-78; program dir. Sta. WCOZ-FM, Blair Broadcasting, Boston, 1978-80, Sta. KLOS-FM, ABC, Los Angeles, 1980-85; sr. programming advisor Pollack Media Group, Pacific Palisades, Calif., 1985-89; pres. Pollack/Hadges Enterprises, Pacific Palisades, 1985-89, Pollack Media Group, 1989—. Named Program Dir. of Yr., Los Angeles Times, 1981. Mem. Phi Beta Kappa. Office: Pollack Media Group 984 Monument St Ste 105 Pacific Palisades CA 90272-3858

HADLEY, ELEANOR MARTHA, economist; b. Seattle, July 17, 1916; d. Homer More and Margaret Sarah (Floyd) H. BA, Mills Coll., 1938; MA, Radcliffe/Harvard U., 1943; PhD, Harvard U., 1949. Rsch. analyst Office Strategic Svcs., Washington, 1943-44; economist Dept. State, Washington, 1944-46, GHQ-SCAP, Tokyo, 1946-47; staff mem. Pres. Trumans Commn. Migratory Labor, Washington, 1950-51; assoc. prof. Smith Coll., Northampton, Mass., 1956-65; economist U.S. Tariff Commn., Washington, 1967-74; professorial lectr. George Washington U., Washington, 1972-84; group dir. internat. div. Gen. Acctg. Office, Washington, 1974-81; vis. scholar U. Washington, Seattle, 1984—; class dean Smith Coll., Northampton, 1958-62; participant Occupation of Japan series Brit. Broadcasting Co., London, 1989; participant Power in the Pacific KCET, L.A. and Australian Broadcasting Co., 1989. Author: Antitrust in Japan, 1970; contbg. author: Political Power of Economic Ideas, 1989; contbr. to Kodansha Ency. of Japan; author articles. Vol., bd. dirs. Seattle Pub. Libr. Found., 1987—. Recipient Sacred Treasure award Emperor of Japan, 1986; Fulbright rsch. scholar, Japan, 1962-64. Mem. Assn. for Asian Studies (regional coun. mem., dir. nat. orgn., bd. dirs., 1987-89, named Disting. Lectr. 1985), U. Wash. Mortar Bd. (hon. mem.). Home: 807 SW 207th Pl Seattle WA 98166-4163

HADLEY, JANE FRANCIS, mental health nurse; b. Fort Knox, Ky., Oct. 15, 1953; d. Richard Aloyisius and Mary Elizabeth (Davis) Walsh; m. P.C. McNamara, Dec. 20, 1975 (div. Jan. 1986); 1 child, Joel; m. William Melvin Hadley, Oct. 13, 1990. BSN, U. N.Mex., 1977; MSN, U. Tex., El Paso, 1986. RN, N.Mex.; cert. family nurse practitioner. Staff nurse U. N.Mex. Hosp., Albuquerque, 1978-81; faculty Maternal Child U. Albuquerque, 1980; staff nurse Step-down Unit Presbyn. Hosp., Albuquerque, 1981; clin. faculty pediatrics Luna Vocat.-Tech. Inst., Las Vegas, N.Mex., 1982; from diabetes educator to rsch. coord. Lovelace Med. Ctr., Albuquerque, 1982-88; pharmacology faculty Diabetes Ctr. U. Va., Charlottesville, 1989; clin. educator St. Jospeh's Med. Ctr., Albuquerque, 1989-90; clin. nurse specialist Post Traumatic Stress Disorder Vet. Affairs Med. Ctr., Albuquerque, 1990-93, nurse mgr. Acute Psychiatric, 1993-95. Grantee U.S. Govt., 1979-81, ANA, 1994-95. Mem. ANA (clin. nurse specialist in med./surg., psychiatric adult mental health nurse), Am. Assn. Diabetes Educators (chpt. coun. chair 1986-87, bd. dirs. 1987-90, fin. com. chair 1987-90), Zia Assn. Diabetes Educators (pres. 1985-86), N.Mex. Nurses Assn. (com. 1992—). Republican. Home: 12712 Piru Blvd SE Albuquerque NM 87123-3825

HADLEY, PAUL BURREST, JR. (TABBIT HADLEY), chef services manager, photographer; b. Louisville, Apr. 26, 1955; s. Paul Burrest and Rose Mary (Ruckert) H. Grad. in Computer Ops. and Programming, No. Ky. Vocat. Sch., 1975. Floor mgr. reconciling dept. Cen. Trust Co., Cin., 1974-76; freelance photographer Ky., Ohio, Colo., 1975—; chef mgr. The Floradora, Telluride, Colo., 1978—; pres. Tabbit Enterprises; freelance recipe writer, Telluride, 1978—. Author poetry (Golden Poet award 1989, Silver Poet award 1990); actor: (plays) Of Mice and Men, The Exercise, Crawling Arnold, A Thousand Clowns, The Authentic Life of Billy The Kid, others. Actor The Plunge Players, Telluride; v.p. Telluride Coun. for Arts and Humanities, 1989. Mem. Plan Internat. USA, Christian Children's Fund. Home: PO Box 923 Telluride CO 81435-0923

HADSALL, DEBRA JUNE, business service and consulting executive; b. Wichita, Kans., Aug. 28, 1951; d. Doyle I. and June I. (Lonnon) Loveridge; m. Terry B. Hadsall; 1 child, Isaac J. Student, Kans. State U., Manhattan, 1969-72; BS in Bus. Adminstrn., Regis U., Denver, 1991. Program analyst in logistics and facilities planning Air Force Acctg. and Fin. Ctr., Denver, 1986-91; program analyst in planning Def. Fin. and Acctg. Svc., Denver, 1991-94; pres. Shared Visions, Inc., Aurora, Colo., 1993—. Vol. in strategic planning Cherry Creek (Colo.) Sch. Dist. Mem. The Planning Forum, Internat. Soc. for Strategic Mgmt. and Planning, World Future Soc., Denver Exec. Women in Govt., Tech. Assocs. Colo. (bd. dirs.). Methodist. Office: 12273 E Bates Cir Aurora CO 80014-3309

HAERTEL, GENEVA DILUZIO, educational researcher; b. Hazleton, Pa., July 18, 1947; d. Daniel Anthony and Eva (Socker) DiLuzio; m. Edward Henry Haertel, July 12, 1975 (div. June 1991). BS in Edn., Kent State U., 1968, PhD in Edn., 1975. Cert. tchr. K-8, Ohio. Evaluator dept. rsch. and evaluation Chgo. Pub. Schs., 1975-77; rsch. assoc. Office Ednl. Rsch., U. Ill., Chgo., 1978-80; rsch. assoc. Ctr. Rsch. in Human Devel. & Edn., Temple U., Phila., 1985-88, sr. rsch. assoc. (part time), 1990—; rsch. assoc. (part time) RMC Rsch. Corp., Mountain View, Calif., 1990-91, Evaluation Ctr., Western Mich. U., Kalamazoo, 1991-94; cons. NSF, Washington, 1977-78, Office Ednl. Rsch. and Improvement, Dept. Edn., Washington, 1991, EREAPA Assocs., Livermore, Calif., 1993—, The Rebus Inst., Burlingame, Calif., 1994—. Author: (with Patricia Wheeler) Resource Handbook on Performance Assessment and Measurement, 1993; editor: (with H.J. Walberg) International Encyclopedia of Educational Evaluation, 1989. Mem. ASCD, Am. Ednl. Rsch. Assn., Am. Evaluation Assn., Am. Psychological Assn. Home: 501 Forest Ave Apt 310 Palo Alto CA 94301-2613

HAFEY, EDWARD EARL JOSEPH, precision tool company executive; b. Hartford, Conn., June 7, 1917; s. Joseph Michael and Josephine (Pyne) H.; B.S. in Mech. Engring., Worcester Poly. Inst., 1940; postgrad. Johns Hopkins U., 1943, 44; m. Loyette Lindsey, Oct. 21, 1971; children—Joseph M., Barbara Hafey Beard, Edward F. Instr. dept. mech. enging. Worcester Tech. Inst., 1940-41; mgr. Comfort Air Inc., San Francisco, 1946-47; owner, mgr. Hafey Air Conditioning Co., San Pablo, Calif., 1947—, pres. Hafey Precision Tool, Inc., Laguna Beach, Calif., 1982—; cons. air conditioning U.S. Navy, C.E., Japan, Korea, Okinawa. Served to comdr. USNR, 1941-46. Registered profl. engr., Calif.; named Man of Year, San Pablo, 1962. Mem. Assn. Energy Engrs., Calif. Air Conditioning Service Engring. Soc., Am. Legion, Ret. Officers Assn., Sigma Alpha Epsilon. Republican. Roman Catholic. Clubs: Exchange of Laguna Beach, Marine's Meml. Office: PO Box 417 Laguna Beach CA 92652-0417

HAFNER-EATON, CHRIS, health services researcher, educator; b. N.Y.C., Dec. 9, 1962; d. Peter Robert and Isabelle (Freda) Hafner; m. James Michael Eaton, Aug. 9, 1986; children: Kelsey James, Tristen Lee. BA, U. Calif., San Diego, 1986; MPH, UCLA, 1988, PhD in Health Svcs., 1992. Cons. dental health policy UCLA Schl. Dentistry, 1989; grad. teachng asst. UCLA Sch. Pub. Health, 1987-92; health svcs. researcher UCLA, 1987-92; cons. health policy U.S. Dept. Health & Human Svcs., Washington, 1988—; analyst health policy The RAND/UCLA Ctr. Health Policy Study, Santa Monica & L.A., 1988-94; asst. prof. health care adminstrn. Oreg. State U. Dept. Pub. Health, Corvallis, 1992—; lectr. in field. Contbr. articles to profl. jours. Rsch. grantee numerous granting bodies, 1988-94. Mem. AAUW, LLLI, NOW, Am. Pub. Health Assn. (med. care sect., women's caucus), Am. Assn. World Health, Am. Alliance Health, Phys. Edn., Recreation and Dance, Oreg. Pub. Health Assn., Oreg. Health Care Assn., Assn. Health Svcs. Rsch., Soc. Pub. Health Edn., Physicians for Social Responsibility, UCLA Pub. Health Alulmni Assn., Delta Omega.

HAGA, ENOCH JOHN, computer educator, author; b. L.A., Apr. 25, 1931; s. Enoch and Esther Bouncer (Higginson) H.; student Sacramento Jr. Coll., 1948-49; AA, Grant Tech. Coll., 1950; student U. Colo., Denver, 1950, U. Calif., Berkeley, 1954, Midwestern U., 1950-54; AB, Sacramento State Coll., 1955, MA, 1958; PhD, Calif. Inst. Integral Studies, 1972, diploma tchr. Asian Culture, 1972; m. Elna Jo Wright, Aug. 22, 1957. Tchr. bus. Calif. Med. Facility, Vacaville, 1956-60; asst. prof. bus. Stanislaus State Coll., Turlock, Calif., 1960-61; engring. writer, publs. engr. Hughes Aircraft Co., Fullerton, Calif., 1961-62, Lockheed Missiles & Space Co., Sunnyvale, Calif., 1962, Gen. Precision, Inc., Glendale, Calif., 1962-63; sr. adminstrv. analyst Holmes & Narver, Inc., L.A., 1963-64; tchr., chmn. dept. bus. and math. Pleasanton Unified Dist., Pleasanton, Calif., 1964-92, coordinator computer svcs., adminstrn. and instrn., 1984-85; vis. asst. prof. bus. Sacramento State Coll., 1967-69; instr. bus. and computer sci. Chabot Coll., Hayward, Calif., 1970-89; instr. bus. and philosophy Ohlone Coll., Fremont, Calif., 1972; prof., v.p., mem. bd. govs. Calif. Inst. Asian Studies, 1972-75; pres., prof. Pacific Inst. East-West Studies, San Francisco, 1975-76, also mem. bd. govs.; dir. Certification Councils, Livermore, Calif., 1975-80; mem., chmn. negotiating team Amador Valley Secondary Educators Assn., Pleasanton, Calif., 1976-77, pres., 1984-85. With USAF, 1949-52, with USNR, 1947-49, 53-57. Mem. Internat. Assn. for Computer Information Systems (exec. dir. 1970-74). Coordinating editor Total Systems, 1962; editor Automation Educator, 1965-67, Automated Educational Systems, 1967, Data Processing for Education, 1970-71, Computer Techniques in Biomedicine and Medicine, 1973; contbg. editor Jour. Bus. Edn., 1961-69, Data Processing mag., 1967-70; author and compiler: Understanding Automation, 1965; author: Simplified Computer Arithmetic, Simplified Computer Logic, Simplified Computer Input, Simplified Computer Flowcharting, 1971-72, Before the Apple Drops, 15 Essays on Dinosaur Education, 1994, Exploring Prime Numbers on Your PC, 1994, TAROsolution, A Complete Guide to Interpreting the Tarot, 1994, The 2000-Year History of the Haga-Helgøy and Krick-Keller Families, Ancestors and Descendants, 1994; editor Data Processor, 1960-62, Automedica, 1970-76, FBE Bull., 1967-68. Home: 983 Venus Way Livermore CA 94550-6345

HAGAN, ALFRED CHRIS, federal judge; b. Moscow, Idaho, Jan. 27, 1932; s. Alfred Elias and Irene Lydia (Wells) H.; m. Doreen M. Auve, July 10, 1953; children: Chris E., Martha Ann, Peter M. BA, U. Idaho, 1953, JD, 1958. Bar: Idaho 1958, U.S. Dist. Ct. Idaho 1958. Asst. atty. gen. State of Idaho, Boise, 1958, dist. judge, 1967-77; dep. pros. atty. Ada County, Boise, 1959; pvt. practice Boise, 1960-67, 77-84; U.S. bankruptcy judge Dist. of Idaho, Boise, 1985—. 1st lt. USAF, 1953-55. Mem. Nat. Conf. Bankruptcy Judges. Office: MSC 040 550 W Fort St Boise ID 83724-0101

HAGAN, ALFRED JOHN, marketing and economics educator; b. N.Y.C., Jan. 24, 1937; s. Joseph and Mary Madeline (Quinn) H.; children: Michael, Matthew; m. Monica J. Smith, Feb. 2, 1995. BS, U. Maine, Orono, 1962; MBA, Ind. U., 1964; PhD, U. Tex., 1970. Asst. prof. U. Tex., Austin, 1969-70, Ariz. State U., Tempe, 1970-76; assoc. prof. U. Tex., Odessa, 1976-78, Pepperdine U., Malibu, Calif., 1978-80, Am. Grad. Sch. Internat. Mgmt., Glendale, Ariz., 1980-82; prof. Calif. State U., Fullerton, 1982-83, Pepperdine U., Culver City, Calif., 1983—; cons. U.S. and fgn. govts., 1965—. Author: Economy of the Multinational Corporation, 1986; co-author: Marketing: An Environmental Approach, 1976; co-editor: Sustainable Economic Business Growth in Latin America, 1993; illustrator: Silverplated Flatware, 1979; contbr. articles to profl. jours. Served as sgt. USAF, 1954-58. Research grantee Ford and Carnegie Founds., Guatemala, Mex., 1965—. Mem. Acad. Internat. Bus., Acad. Mktg. Sci., Western Mktg. Educators,Pi Sigma Epsilon; fellow Sigma Iota Epsilon. Republican. Episcopalian. Lodge: Masons. Office: Pepperdine U 400 Corporate Pt Culver City CA 90230-7615

HAGE, STEPHEN JOHN, radiology administrator, consultant; b. Chgo., July 22, 1943; s. Steve and Irene (Lewandowski) H.; m. Constance Louise Simonis, June 10, 1967. AAS, YMCA C.C., Chgo., 1970. Registered radiol. tech. Staff tech. Highland Park (Ill.) Hosp., 1966-68; chief radiotherapy tech. VA Hines (Ill.) Hosp., 1968-70; chief radiology tech. Gottlieb Meml. Hosp., Melrose Park, Ill., 1970-71; radiology adminstr. S. Chgo. County Hosp., 1971-79; adminstrv. dir. radiology Cedars-Sinai Med. Ctr., L.A., 1979-93; CEO HumiPerfect Co., Chatsworth, Calif., 1994—; cons. Computer Sci. Corp., El Segundo, Calif., 1983—. Contbr. articles to profl. jours. Served with USMC, 1961-64. Recipient 1st pl. Essay award Ill. State Soc. Radiol. Technicians, 1966. Mem. Am. Hosp. Radiology Adminstrs. (charter), Am. Soc. Radiol. Technologists, AAAS, Phi Theta Kappa. Home and Office: HumiPerfect 22115 Halsted St Chatsworth CA 91311-4027

HAGEL, JOHN, III, management consultant; b. Berlin, N.H., Sept. 14, 1950; s. John Jr. and Evelyn Gertrude (Parent) H.; m. Laura Leeann Call, Sept. 11, 1987. BA, Wesleyan U., 1972; PhB, Oxford U., 1974; MBA, Harvard U., 1978, JD, 1978. Bar: Mass. 1978. Cons. Boston Cons. Group, 1978-80; pres. Sequoia Group, Larkspur, Calif., 1980-82; v.p. Atari, Inc., Sunnyvale, Calif., 1982-83, sr. v.p., 1983-84; sr. engagement mgr. McKinsey and Co., N.Y.C., 1984-91, prin., 1987—, McKinsey & Co., San Francisco, 1991—. Author: Alternative Energy Strategies, 1976, Assessing The Criminal, 1977; contbr. articles to profl. jours. Keasbey Found. fellow, 1972-74. Mem. ABA, Mass. Bar Assn. Episcopalian.

HAGEMAN, JAMES C., rancher; b. Douglas, Wyo., Mar. 2, 1930; s. Fred August and Ruth (Shaw) H.; m. Marion Malvin, May 19, 1956; children: Julia Newman, James P., Rachel Rubino, Hugh, Harriet Dewey, Ted Yellowwolf. Owner, operator ranch Ft. Laramie, Wyo., 1961—. Chair edn. com. Wyo. Ho. of Reps., Cheyenne, 1990—; chmn. sch. bd. exec. com. Wyo. tockgrows, Torrington. Republican. Home: HC 72 Box 340 Fort Laramie WY 82212-9601

HAGEN, EDNA MAE, retired nurse; b. Jasper, Ark., Nov. 30, 1932; d. Eugene and Dovie (Combs) Keef; m. Harry Hagen, Jan. 4, 1952; children: Catherine, Harry, Jr. ADN, Santa Barbara Coll., 1973. RN, Calif. Staff nurse Cottage Hosp., Santa Barbara, Calif., 1970-74; head nurse to pvt. physician L.A. Price, M.D., Inc., Santa Barbara, 1974-95; ret., 1995. Mem. U.S. Army Med. Corps, 1951-52. Mem. ANA, CNA.

HAGEN, GLENN W(ILLIAM), lawyer; b. Detroit, July 8, 1948; s. William A. and Lilian (Abrolat) H.; m. Cynthia Winn, July 21, 1984. BS in Chemistry, U. Ala., 1970; JD, Valparaiso U., 1973. Bar: Mich. 1973, U.S. Dist. Ct. (we. dist.) Mich. 1974, Colo. 1981, U.S. Dist. Ct. Colo. 1982. Ptnr. Peters, Seyburn & Hagen, Kalamazoo, 1973-76; dep. city atty. City of Battle Creek, Mich., 1976-79; staff and regulatory counsel CF&I Steel Corp., Pueblo, Colo., 1979-81; gen. counsel Commonwealth Investment Properties Corp., Littleton, Colo., 1981-82; assoc. Berkowitz & Brady, Denver, 1982-83, Zarlengo, Mott, Zarlengo & Winbourn, Denver, 1983-87; pvt. practice Denver, 1987—; lectr. on law office mgmt. Del. Colo. Rep. Com., 1986, 90, 92, 94; referee property tax appeals Douglas and Jefferson Counties. Mem. ABA (young lawyers exec. coun. 1978-81, chmn. small bus. enterprises 1986, regional dir. constabars 1992-94, nat. editors conf. 1995), Mich. Bar Assn. (young lawyers exec. coun. 1976-80), Colo. Bar Assn. (chmn. long-range planning com. 1983-86, gen. practice exec. coun. 1985—, chmn. small firm sect. 1991—, law office mgmt. com. 1995—, chmn. budget com. 1987-89, mem. svcs. com. 1987-89, bus. law sect. 1986—, alt. dispute resolution com. 1990—), Denver Bar Assn., Douglas-Elbert County Bar Assn., Colo. Lawyers for Arts, Am. Arbitration Assn. (lectr. law office mgmt.). Lutheran. Home: 2303 E Lansdowne Pl Hghlnds Ranch CO 80126-4936 Office: One Norwest Ctr Ste 3901 1700 Lincoln St Denver CO 80203-4501

HAGEN, KIRK DEE, mechanical engineer, educator; b. Ogden, Utah, July 12, 1953; s. Darius and Ellen Virginia (Hicks) H.; m. Jan Rowley, June 9, 1978; children: Kathryn, Jennifer, Alec, Daniel. BS in Physics, Weber State Coll., Ogden, 1977; MSME, Utah State U., 1981; PhD in Mech. Engring., U. Utah, 1989. Sr. engr. Hercules Aerospace, Magna, Utah, 1980-86; prin. engr. Unisys Corp., Salt Lake City, 1986-92; asst. prof. mech. engring. tech. Weber State U., Ogden, 1993—; adj. prof. engring. Salt Lake C.C., Salt Lake City, 1991-93. Contbr. articles to profl. jours. Blazer scoutleader Boy Scouts Am., Centerville, Utah, 1990-91. Mem. ASME, Am. Soc. Engring. Edn., Boy Scouts Am. (varsity scoutleader), N.Y. Acad. Scis., Sigma Xi. Mem. LDS Ch. Home: 582 N 220 E Centerville UT 84014-1836 Office: Weber State U Ogden UT 84408

HAGENBUCH, JOHN JACOB, investment banker; b. Park Forest, Ill., May 31, 1951; s. David Brown and Jean Iline (Reeves) H.; m. Christy Ann Nichols; children: Henry, Hunter, Hilary, Hunter Scott, Will. AB magna cum laude, Princeton U., 1974; MBA, Stanford U., 1978. Assoc., Salomon Bros., N.Y.C., 1978-80, v.p., San Francisco, 1980-85; gen. ptnr. Hellman & Friedman, 1985-93; owner, John J. Hagenbuch & Co., San Francisco, 1993—; gen. ptnr. M&H Realty Ptnrs., L.P., 1993—; bd. dirs. AOF II, Inc., Story First Comm. Inc. Bd. govs. San Francisco Symphony, Town Sch. for Boys, William H. Donner Found. Mem. Burlingame Country Club, Pacific-Union Club, Calif. Tennis Club, Villa Taverna Club, Menlo Circus Club. Office: M&H Realty Ptnrs Ste 2160 353 Sacramento St San Francisco CA 94111

HAGENBUCH, RODNEY DALE, stock brokerage house executive; b. Saxville, Wis.; s. Herbert Jenkin and Minnie Leona (Hayward) Hagenbuch; children: Kris, Beth, Patricia; m. LaVerne Julia Scoonover, Sept. 1, 1956. BS, Mich. State U., 1980; Grad., L.A. Children's Hosp. Inst., of Rsch. Cert. fin. mgr. Designer Olds div. Gen. Motors, Lansing, Mich., 1960-66; institutional account exec. Merrill Lynch, Lansing, 1966-75, institutional mgr., 1975-80; sales mgr. Merrill Lynch, Columbus, Ohio, 1980-82; sr. resident v.p. Merrill Lynch, Tacoma, 1982-93, L.A., 1993—. Bd. dirs. Tacoma Club, 1989-93, treas. 1990, pres. 1993, L.A. Acad. Finance, 1993—, Valley Hosp. Found., 1994—, L.A. United Cerebral Palsey, 1994—; adv. bd. Charles Wright, 1989-93; mem. econ. devel. bd. City of Tacoma, 1986-93, chmn. 1987-88; pres. Downtown Tacoma Assn., 1986; chmn. Corp. Coun. for the Arts, 1986, L.A. United Way, 1993—; pres. Tacoma Symphony, 1988; chmn. Human Resources Commn., Meridian Twp., 1972-74, Meridian Planning Commn., Lansing, 1964-70, Meridian Police and Fire Com., Lansing, 1964-70; pres. adv. bd. U. Wash., Tacoma, chmn. 1992; mem. State Wash. Arts Stabilization Bd., Tacoma Art Mus. Bd., sec. 1992; legis. chmn. N.W. Securities Industry Assn.; campaign chmn. Pierce County United Way Bd., 1991-92; non-resident dir. Tacoma (Calif.) Art Mus., 1994—; econ. cons. Tacoma (Calif.) Urban League, 1983-93; bd. dirs. Valley Hosp. Found., 1994—. Recipient Outstanding Citizen award Mcpl. League Pierce County, 1988; named Nat. Vol. of Yr., Urban League Western Divsn., 1987. Mem. Tacoma C. of C. (bd. dirs.), Forward Washington (bd. dirs.), L.A. Children's Hosp. Rsch. Inst. (bd. govs. 1994—). Home: 3627 Dixie Canyon Ave Sherman Oaks CA 91423-4823

HAGENS, WILLIAM JOSEPH, state official, public health educator; b. Bay City, Mich., June 3, 1942; s. Francis Bernard and Lillian May (O'Neill) H.; m. Noel Scantlebury, Apr. 15, 1967; children: Clara O'Neill, Nicholas Barlow. BA, Saginaw Valley Coll., 1969; MA, Wayne State U., 1971. Mem. adj. faculty Wayne State U., Detroit, 197l; VISTA vol. Pierce County Legal Assistance, Tacoma, 197l-73; sr. policy analyst Wash. Ho. of Reps., Olympia, 1974—; instr. Pacific Luth. U., Tacoma, 1979-81; clin. prof. Sch. Pub. Health U. Wash., Seattle, 1984—, mem. vis. com. Sch. Nursing, 1993; mem. health policy project George Washington U., Washington, 1985—; bd. dirs. Area Health Edn. Ctr., Seattle, 1988-90; mem. Nat. Acad. State Health Policy, 1990—; mem. adv. com. Wast. State Ctr. Health Stats. Contbg. author: Analyzing Poverty Policy, 1975. Participant AIDS symposium Pasteur Inst., Paris, 1987. Recipient Pres. award Wash. State Pub. Health Assn., 1986, Animal award Wash. State Pub. Health Assn., 1994; NIMH fellow, 1979, WHO internat. travel fellow, 1991. Mem. Am. Pub. Health Assn., Am. Polit. Sci. Assn., Policy Studies Orgn., English Speaking Union, World Affairs Coun., Pi Sigma Alpha. Home: 3214 N 27th St Tacoma WA 98407-6208 Office: Wash State Ho of Reps PO Box 40740 Olympia WA 98504-0740

HAGENSTEIN, WILLIAM DAVID, forester, consultant; b. Seattle, Mar. 8, 1915; s. Charles William and Janet (Finigan) H.; m. Ruth Helen Johnson, Sept. 2, 1940 (dec. 1979); m. Jean Kraemer Edson, June 16, 1980. BS in Forestry, U. Wash., 1938; MForestry, Duke, 1941. Registered profl. engr., Wash., Oreg. Field aid in entomology U.S. Dept. Agr., Hat Creek, Calif., 1938; logging supt. and engr. Eagle Logging Co., Sedro-Woolley, Wash., 1939; tech. foreman U.S. Forest Svc., North Bend, Wash., 1940; forester West Coast Lumbermen's Assn., Seattle and Portland, Oreg., 1941-43, 45-49; sr. forester FEA, South and Central Pacific Theaters of War and Costa Rica, 1943-45; mgr. Indsl. Forestry Assn., Portland, 1949-80; exec. v.p. Indsl. Forestry Assn., 1956-80, hon. dir., 1980-87; pres. W.D. Hagenstein and Assocs., Inc., Portland, 1980—; H.R. MacMillan lectr. forestry U. B.C., 1952, 77; Benson Meml. lectr. U. Mo., 1966; S.J. Hall lectr. indsl. forestry U. Calif. at Berkeley, 1973; cons. forest engr. USN, Philippines, 1952, Coop. Housing Found., Belize, 1986; mem. U.S. Forest Products Trade Mission, Japan, 1968; del. VII World Forestry Congress, Argentina, 1972, VIII Congress, Indonesia, 1978; mem. U.S. Forestry Study Team, West Germany, 1974; mem. sec. Interior's Oreg. and Calif. Multiple Use Adv. Bd., 1975-76; trustee Wash. State Forestry Conf., 1948-92, Keep Oreg. Green Assn., 1957—, v.p., 1970-71, pres., 1972-73; adv. trustee Keep Wash. Green Assn., 1957—; co-founder, dir. World Forestry Ctr., 1965-89, v.p., 1965-79; hon. Dir. for Life, 1990. Author: (with Wackerman and Michell) Harvesting Timber Crops, 1966; Assoc. editor: Jour. Forestry, 1946-53; columnist Wood Rev., 1978-82; contbr. numerous articles to profl. jours. Trustee Oreg. Mus. Sci. and Industry, 1968-73. Served with USNR, 1933-37. Recipient Hon. Alumnus award U. Wash. Foresters Alumni Assn., 1965, Forest Mgmt. award Nat. Forest Products Assn., 1968, Western Forestry award Western Forestry and Conservation Assn., 1972, 79, Gifford Pinchot medal for 50 yrs. Outstanding Svc. Soc. Am. Foresters, 1987, Charles W. Ralston award Duke Sch. Forestry, 1988. Fellow Soc. Am. Foresters (mem. coun. 1958-63, pres. 1966-69, Golden Membership award 1989); mem. Am. Forestry Assn. (life, hon. v.p. 1966-69, 74-92, William B. Greeley Forestry award 1990), Commonwealth Forestry Assn. (life), Internat. Soc. Tropical Foresters, Portland C. of C. (forestry com. 1949-79, chmn. 1960-62), Nat. Forest Products Assn. (forestry adv. com. 1949-80, chmn. 1972-74, 78-80), West Coast Lumbermen's Assn. (v.p. 1969-79), David Douglas Soc. Western N. Am., Lang Syne Soc., Hoo Hoo Club, Xi Sigma Pi (outstanding alumnus Alpha chpt. 1973). Republican. Home: 3062 SW Fairmount Blvd Portland OR 97201-1439 Office: 921 SW Washington St Ste 803 Portland OR 97205-2826

HAGER, SHIRLEY ANN, school counselor; b. Urbana, Mo., June 21, 1947; d. James Earnest and Willa Lou (Wilson) Mabary; divorced; children: Jeffrey, Bradley, Nicholas. BS with highest honors, N.W. Mo. State U., Maryville, 1969; MA, U. Colo., Denver, 1994. Cert. in counseling phychology; cert. sch. counselor, Colo.; nat. cert. counselor. Tchr. home econs. Cedar Rapids (Iowa) Cmty. Schs., 1969-70, Waka Secondary Sch., Biu, Nigeria, 1970-73; food svc. supr. Marshall Field and Co., Chgo., 1973-74; extension home economist Iowa State U., Ames, 1975-78; tchr. teen parents Douglas County Sch. Dist., Castle Rock, Colo., 1991-93; counselor Douglas County Sch. Dist., Highlands Ranch, Colo., 1994—; mem. teen parenting adv. bd. Douglas County Sch. Dist. Betty Seely Martin scholar Farm Bur., Red Oak, Iowa, 1965. Mem. ACA, AAUW (memberhsip chmn. 1978-81), Southglenn Country Club (sec. bd. dirs. 1989-92), Kappa Omicron Phi. Methodist. Home: 985 E Briarwood Cir S Littleton CO 80122-1222 Office: Cresthill Mid Sch 9195 S Cresthill Ln Highlands Ranch CO 80126

HAGER, THOMAS ARTHUR, editor, writer; b. Portland, Oreg., Apr. 18, 1953; s. Donald Preston and Betty Jeanne (Buehner) H.; m. Lauren Jeanne Kessler, July 7, 1984; children: Jackson Kessler, Zane Kessler, Elizabeth Kessler. BS in Biology, Portland State U., 1976; MS in Microbiology, Oreg. Health Scis. U., 1978; MS in Journalism, U. Oreg., 1981. Writer Eugene, Oreg., 1981—; editor Aster Pub., Eugene, 1982-83, U. Oreg., Eugene, 1985-95; asst. prof. U. Oreg., Eugene, 1987—, dir. comms., 1994—. Author: Force of Nature: The Life of Linus Pauling, 1995; co-author: Staying Young, 1987; founding editor LC Mag., 1983; editor Old Oreg. mag., 1985-95; founding editor Oreg. Quar., 1994; contbr. articles to mags. Recipient Case 1 award, 1986, 91. Mem. U. Oreg. Alumni Assn. (ex-officio mem. bd.). Office: U Oreg Office of Comm Eugene OR 97403

HAGEY, ROBIN GREENE, writer; b. Phila., Oct. 4, 1954; d. Howard Gilbert and Cynthia (Davis) G.; m. Stephen Michael Hagey, Jan. 4, 1986; children: Justin Taylor, Sara Davis. BA, Barnard Coll., 1976; MIA, Columbia Univ., 1980, MS, 1981. Assoc. editor Meeting News Mag., N.Y.C., 1980-82; money/careers editor Self Mag., N.Y.C., 1982-83; adminstr. Fund for Journalism Jewish Life, Bethesda, Md., 1988-90; reporter/editor United Press Internat., Pitts., Washington,, Jerusalem, 1983-90; freelance writer L.A. Times, 1993-94. Founding mem. Parent Ptnrs., Washington, 1992. Home: 2179 Flintridge Ct Thousand Oaks CA 91362-1741

HAGGARD, JOEL EDWARD, lawyer; b. Portland, Oreg., Oct. 10, 1939; s. Henry Edward and Kathryn Shirley (O'Leary) H.; m. Mary Katherine Daley, June 8, 1968; children: Kevin E., Maureen E., Cristin E. BSME, U. Notre Dame, 1961; M in Nuclear Engring., U. Okla., 1963; JD, U. Wash., 1971. Bar: Wash. 1971, U.S. Dist. Ct. (we. dist.) Wash. 1971, U.S. Ct. Appeals (9th cir.) 1971, U.S. Supreme Ct. 1971. Nuclear engr. Westinghouse Corp. Bettis Atomic Power Lab., Pitts., 1963-67; research engr. aerospace div. The Boeing Co., Seattle, 1968; engr., mgmt. cons. King County Dept. Pub. Works, Seattle, 1969-71; assoc. Houghton, Cluck, Coughlin & Riley, Seattle, 1971-74, ptnr., 1975-76; pvt. practice law Seattle, 1977, 85—; ptnr. Haggard, Tousley & Brain, Seattle, 1978-84; judge marriage tribunal, Archdiocese of Seattle, 1975-90; chmn. Columbia River Interstate Compact Commn., 1975—; arbitrator King County Superior Ct., 1986—. Contbr. articles to profl. jours. Past bd. trustees, mem. exec. com., past sec. Seattle Symphony. Mem. ABA, Wash. Bar Assn. (past chmn. environ. law sect., fee arbitration com., past mem. rules of profl. conduct com.), Seattle-King County Bar Assn., Rainier Club, Wash. Athletic Club, Astoria Golf and Country Club, Magnolia Cmty. Club (past pres., bd. dirs.). Office: 1200 5th Ave Seattle WA 98101-1127

HAGGERTY, CHARLES A., electronics executive. Student, U. St. Thomas. Pres., chief exec. officer, chmn. bd. dirs. IBM, 1964-92; pres., COO Western Digital Corp., Irvine, Calif., 1992—. Office: Western Digital Corp PO Box 19665 Irvine CA 92713-9665*

HAGGERTY, FRANCIS JAMES, manufacturing engineer; b. L.A., June 14, 1959; s. Eugene and Pauline H. BS in Engring. and Applied Sci., Calif. Inst. Tech., 1981; postgrad., U. Chgo., 1982-83. Devel. engr. Branson/Internatl. Plasma Corp., Hayward, Calif., 1981-82, 83-84; field svc. engr. Leybold Heraeus Technologies, San Jose, Calif., 1985-86; devel. engr. Ampex Corp., Redwood City, Calif., 1987-88; maintainence engr. Nat. Semiconductor, Santa Clara, Calif., 1988-89; mfg. engr. Intrex Divsn./Courtaulds, Sylmar, Calif., 1989; field svc. engr. Gen. Signal Thinfilm Co., Fremont, Calif. and, Burlington, Vt., 1990-91; field engr. ASM Am., Burlington, 1991-95; field svc. rep. Transpacific Tech., Sunnyvale, Calif., 1995—; Metron Tech. Corp. Office: Metron Tech Corp 770 Lucerne Dr Sunnyvale CA 94086

HAGOPIAN, JACOB MICHAEL, documentary film producer, political scientist, educator; b. Harpoot, Armenia, Oct. 20, 1913; s. Michael and Aghavmie (Shatanian) H.; m. Antoinette L. Hobden, Sept. 8, 1961; children: Michael, Jeanne, David, William. AB, U. Calif., Berkeley, 1937, MA, 1938; MA, Harvard U., 1940, PhD, 1943; LLD, La Verne (Calif.) U., 1989. Instr. econ. Oreg. State U., Corvallis, 1946; instr. polit. sci. U. Calif., L.A., 1946-48; asst. prof. Am. U. Beirut, 1948-49; adj. prof. history, econs., polit. sci. Bernares (India) Hindu U., 1949-50; pres. Atlantis Prodns., Thousand Oaks, Calif., 1952—, chmn., 1994—; chmn. Armenian Film Found., Thousand Oaks, 1979—. Producer numerous TV documentary films including The Nile River, 1949, The Armenian Case, 1977, The Forgotten Genocide, 1977 (2 emmy nominations), A Century of Silence..Problems of The American Indian, 1978, Strangers in A Promised Land, 1984; also corporate films including Thousand Oaks a Place To Grow, 1982, Museum, Gateway To Perception, 1965, numerous others. Founding pres. Conejo Valley Hist. Soc., 1964-68; founding chmn. Ventura County Cultural Heritage Bd., 1967-71; mem. master plan devel. com. City of Thousand Oaks, 1970-72, chmn. open space com., 1975-76; mem. pres. adv. coun. Calif. Lutheran Coll., 1972—; mem. Conejo Valley C. of C., 1970-75; ruling elder Emmanuel Presbyn. Ch., 1964—; mem. Rotary Internat., 1965-78, hon. mem. 1979-94; chmn. vision 20/20 com. Conejo Future Found., 1989-90, mem. bd. trustees, 1984-90; vice chmn. Ferrahian H.S. Bd. Trustees. Staff sgt. Air Force, 1943-45. Recipient Americanism award Daughters of the Am. Revolution, over 150 awards for films. Mem. Am. Polit. Sci. Assn., Writer's Guild of Am., Internat. Motion Picture and Lectrs. Assn., Internat. Travel-Adventurer's Film Guild, Armenian Profl. Soc., Harvard Club, Adventurer's Club, Explorer's Club. Office: Armenian Film Found 2219 E Thousand Oaks Blvd Thousand Oaks CA 91362

HAGSTRUM, JEAN HOWARD, language professional, educator; b. St. Paul, Mar. 26, 1913; s. Andrew and Sadie Gertrude (Fryckberg) H.; m. Ruth Pritchett, June 29, 1941; children: Katherine Jeanne, Phyllis Ann. AB summa cum laude, U. Minn., 1933; MA, Northwestern U., 1938; PhD, Yale U., 1941; DHL (hon.), North Park Coll., 1966, U. Chgo., 1985, U. Minn., 1986. Instr. English and speech North Park Coll., Chgo., 1934-38; chief allocation sect. U.S. Office Censorship, 1942-44; mem. faculty Northwestern U., Evanston, Ill., 1940-42, 46-81; prof. English Northwestern U., 1957-81, chmn. dept., 1958-64, 73-74, John C. Shaffer prof., 1970-81; vis. lectr. at univs., Copenhagen, Lund, Stockholm, Uppsala, Gothenburg, Aix-en-Provence, Delhi, Bombay, Srinagar; mem. presdl. adv. com. Yale Ctr. for Brit. Art and Brit. Studies, 1972-81; Phi Beta Kappa vis. scholar, 1983-84, English vis. scholar U. Ariz., 1992—. Author: Samuel Johnson's Literary Criticism, rev. edit, 1967, The Sister Arts, 1958, William Blake: Poet and Painter, 1964, (with others) A Community of Scholars, 1968, (with James Gray) Sermons of Samuel Johnson, 1979, Sex and Sensibility: Ideal and Erotic Love from Milton to Mozart, 1980, The Romantic Body: Love and Sexuality in Keats, Wordsworth, and Blake, 1985, Eros and Vision: Restoration to Romanticism, 1989, Esteem Enlivened by Desire: The Couple from Homer to Shakespeare (Comparative Literary Studies Scaglione prize 1993), 1992. Trustee Newberry Library, 1964—. Served with AUS, 1944-46. Recipient Disting. Service award Phi Beta Kappa Assn., Chgo.; Fulbright research fellow Italy, 1953-54; Fulbright research fellow India, 1972, 82; grantee Am. Philos. Soc., 1952, 59, 76; fellow Newberry Library, Chgo., 1953, 57; sr. fellow Clark Library, UCLA, 1970; fellow Huntington Library, 1974, 83; fellow Guggenheim Found., 1974-75; fellow NEH, 1976-77; Mellon sr. fellow Nat. Humanities Ctr., 1985-87; Rockefeller Found. fellow, Bellagio, Italy, 1987. Fellow AAAS, mem. MLA (exec. council 1968-72), Swedish Hist. Soc. Home: 35 Cochise Ln Bisbee AZ 85603-9722

HAGUE, DONALD VICTOR, museum director; b. Salt Lake City, Dec. 28, 1926; s. Roger Frank and Fawn (Robison) H.; m. Lorna Dangerfield, Aug. 27, 1947; children—Alan, Kevin, Steven, Bryan, Karen. B.S. in Zoology, U. Utah, 1951, M.A. in Art History (Nat. Endowment Arts fellow 1973), 1975; grad., Mus. Mgmt. Inst., U. Calif., Berkeley, 1979. Archtl. draftsman Scott & Beecher, Salt Lake City, 1948-50; artist, designer Mus. Anthropology, U. Utah, 1950-51; designer Salt Lake Cabinet & Fixture Co., 1952-54; chief artist Ft. Worth Mus. Sci. and Industry, 1954-58; graphic arts supr. Sperry Rand Corp., Salt Lake City, 1958-65; curator exhibits Utah Mus. Natural History, U. Utah, 1965-73, dir. mus., 1973—, univ. instr. zoology, 1966—; guest lectr. mus. studies, sci. illustrators, cons. in field, 1954—; chmn. task force public edn. Utah Antiquities Com., 1976; mem. adv. bd. Hansen Planetarium, 1970-73. Author articles in field. Mem. Salt Lake Sister Cities Com., 1975-78; chmn. community council South High Sch., 1975-79. Served with USNR, 1945-46. Mem. Am. Assn. Museums, Internat. Council Museums, Assn. Sci. Mus. Dirs., Western Museums Assn. (v.p., 1972-74), Utah Museums Assn. (pres. 1972-74, award excellence 1976), Nat. Wildlife Fedn. Club: U.Utah Faculty. Office: Utah Mus Natural History U Utah Salt Lake City UT 84112

HAHN, BETTY, artist, photographer, educator; b. Chgo., Oct. 11, 1940; d. Eugene Joseph and Esther Josephine (Krueger) H.; widowed. A.B., Ind. U., 1963, M.F.A., 1966. Asst. prof. photography Rochester (N.Y.) Inst. Tech., 1969-75; prof. art U. N.Mex., Albuquerque, 1976—. One-woman shows include Smithsonian Instn., Washington, 1969, Ctr. Photographic Studies, Louisville, 1971, Focus Gallery, San Francisco, 1974, Sandstone Gallery, Rochester, N.Y., 1978, Blue Sky Gallery, Portland, Oreg., 1978, Susan Spiritus Gallery, Newport Beach, Calif., 1977, 82, Witkin Gallery, N.Y.C., 1973, 79, Washington Project for the Arts, 1980, Ctr. Creative Photography, Tucson, 1981, Columbia Coll. Gallery, Chgo., 1982, Port Washington Pub. Library, N.Y., 1984, Mus. Fine Arts, Mus. N.Mex, Santa Fe, 1986, Lehigh U., 1988, U. Mass., Amherst, 1989, Andrew Smith Gallery, Santa Fe, 1991, U. N.Mex. Art Mus., Albuquerque, 1994. Named Honored Educator, Soc. for Photog. Edn., 1984; Nat. Endowment Arts grantee, 1977-78, 82-83; N.Y. State Council Arts grantee, 1976. Mem. Soc. Photog. Edn., Coll. Art Assn., Evidence Photographers Internat. Council. Office: Univ N Mex Art Dept Albuquerque NM 87131

HAHN, ELLIOTT JULIUS, lawyer; b. San Francisco, Dec. 9, 1949; s. Leo Wolf and Sherry Marion (Portnoy) H; m. Toby Rose Mallen; children: Kara Rebecca, Brittany Atira Mallen, Michael Mallen. BA cum laude, U. Pa., 1971, JD, 1974; LLM, Columbia U., 1980. Bar: N.J. 1974, Calif. 1976, D.C. 1978, U.S. Dist. Ct. N.J. 1974, U.S. Dist. Ct. (cen. dist.) Calif. 1976, U.S. Supreme Ct. 1980. Assoc. von Maltitz, Derenberg, Kunin & Janssen, N.Y.C., 1974-75; law clk. L.A. County Superior Ct., 1975-76; atty. Atlantic Richfield Co., L.A., 1976-79; prof. Summer in Tokyo program Santa Clara Law Sch., 1981-83; assoc. prof. law Calif. Western Sch. Law, San Diego, 1980-85; atty. Morgan, Lewis & Bockius, L.A., 1985-87; assoc. Whitman & Ransom, L.A., 1987-88, ptnr., 1989-93; ptnr. Sonnenschein Nath & Rosenthal, L.A., 1993—; vis. scholar Nihon U., Tokyo, 1982; vis. lectr. Internat. Christian U., Tokyo, 1982; adj. prof. law Southwestern U. Sch. Law, 1986—, Pepperdine U. Law Sch., 1986—; lectr. U. Calif., Davis, Law Sch. Orientation in U.S.A. Law Program, 1994—. Author: Japanese Business Law and the Legal System, 1984; contbr. chpt. on Japan to The World Legal Ency.; contbg. editor Internat. Calif. Bus. Law Reporter; internat. law editor Calif. Bus. Law Reporter. Vice-chmn. San Diego Internat. Affairs Bd., 1981-85; bd. dirs. San Diego-Yokohama Sister City Soc., 1982-85, L.A.-Nagoya Sister City Soc., 1986—; mem. master planning com. City of Rancho Palos Verdes, Calif., 1989-91; advisor, exec. com. Calif. Internat. Law Sect., 1990-91, appointee exec. com., 1991-94, vice-chmn., 1992-93, chair, 1993-94; appointee, trustee Palos Verdes Libr. Dist., 1993. Mem. ABA, State Bar of Calif., L.A. County Bar Assn. (bd. dirs. internat. sect., exec. com. Internat. Legal Sec. 1987—, appointee pacific rim com. 1990—, chmn. 1995—), Assn. Asian Studies, U. Pa. Alumni Club (pres. San Diego chpt. 1982, pres. coun. Phila., 1983), Anti-Defamation League, Japanese-Am. Soc. Legal Studies (book rev. editor Seattle 1983-85). Jewish. Office: Sonnenschein Nath & Rosenthal 601 S Figueroa St Ste 1500 Los Angeles CA 90017-5720

HAHN, ERWIN LOUIS, physicist, educator; b. Sharon, Pa., June 9, 1921; s. Israel and Mary (Weiss) H.; m. Marian Ethel Failing, Apr. 8, 1944 (dec. Sept. 1978); children: David L., Deborah A., Katherine L.; m. Natalie Woodford Hodgson, Apr. 12, 1980. B.S., Juniata Coll., 1943, D.Sc., 1966; M.S., U. Ill., 1947, Ph.D., 1949; D.Sc., Purdue U., 1975. Asst. Purdue U., 1943-44; research assoc. U. Ill., 1950; NRC fellow Stanford, 1950-51, instr., 1951-52; research physicist Watson IBM Lab., N.Y.C., 1952-55; assoc. Columbia U., 1952-55; faculty U. Calif., Berkeley, 1955—, prof. physics, 1961—, assoc. prof., then prof. Miller Inst. for Basic Rsch., 1958-59, 66-67, 85-86; Eastman vis. prof. Balliol Coll., Oxford, Eng., 1988-89; cons. Office Naval Rsch., Stanford, 1950-52, AEC, 1955—; spl. cons. USN, 1959; adv. panel mem. Nat. Bur. Stds., Radio Stds. div., 1961-64; mem. NAS/NRC com. on basic rsch.; advisor to U.S. Army Rsch. Office, 1967-69; faculty rsch. lectr. U. Calif., Berkeley, 1979. Author: (with T.P. Das) Nuclear Quadrupole Resonance Spectroscopy, 1958. Served with USNR, 1944-46. Fellow Guggenheim Found., 1961-62, 69-70, NSF, 1961-62; recipient prize Internat. Soc. Magnetic Resonance, 1971, Humboldt Found. award, 1977, 94, Alumni Achievement award Juniata Coll., 1986, citation U. Calif., Berkeley, 1991; co-winner prize in physics Wolf Found., 1984; named to Calif. Inventor Hall of Fame, 1984; vis. fellow Brasenose Coll., Oxford U., 1969-70, life hon. fellow, 1984—. Fellow AAAS, Am. Phys. Soc. (past mem. exec. com. div. solid state physics, Oliver E. Buckley prize 1971); mem. NAS (co-recipient Comstock prize in electricity, magnetism and radiation 1993), Slovenian Acad. Scis. and Arts (fgn.), French Acad. Scis. (fgn. assoc.). Home: 69 Stevenson Ave Berkeley CA 94708-1732 Office: U Calif Dept Physics 367 Birge Berkeley CA 94720

HAHN, HAROLD THOMAS, physical chemist, chemical engineer; b. N.Y.C., May 31, 1924; s. Gustave Hahn and Lillie Martha (Thomas) H.; m. Bennie Joyce Turney, Sept. 5, 1948; children: Anita Karen, Beverly Sharon, Carol Linda, Harold Thomas Jr. Student, Hofstra U., 1941-43; BSChemE, Columbia U., 1943-44; PhD in Chemistry, U. Tex., 1950-53. Chem. engr. Manhattan Dist. U.S. Army, Los Alamos, N.Mex., 1945-47; chem. engr. U. Calif., Los Alamos, 1947-50; sr. scientist Gen. Electric Co., Hanford, Wash., 1953-58; sect. chief, chem. research dept. Phillips Petroleum Co., Idaho Falls, Idaho, 1958-64; sr. staff scientist Lockheed Missiles & Space Co., Palo Alto, Calif., 1964-92; private cons., 1992—. Contbr. articles to profl. jours.; patentee in field. Pres. Edgemont Gardens PTA, Idaho Falls, 1963-64; commr. cub scout div. Stanford area council Boy Scouts Am., Palo Alto, 1973-76, also cubmaster pack 36, 1973-80, chmn. troops 36 and 37, 1975-77; mem. adminstrv. bd. Los Altos Meth. Ch. Served to col. U.S. Army, 1944-46, with res., 1946-84, col. res. ret. Humble Oil Co. fellow, 1952, Naval Bur. Ordnance fellow, 1953. Fellow Am. Inst. Chemists; mem. AIAA, Magnetics Soc. IEEE (elected sr. mem.), Calif. Acad. Scis., Internat. Platform Assn., Am. Chem. Soc., Sigma Xi, Phi Lambda Upsilon, Kappa Rho. Republican. Home and Office: 661 Teresi Ln Los Altos CA 94024-4162

HAHN, HELENE B., motion picture company executive; b. N.Y.C.. BA, Hofstra U.; JD, Loyola U., Calif., 1975. Bar: Calif. 1975. V.p. bus. affairs Paramount Pictures Corp., L.A., sr. v.p. bus. affairs, 1983-84; sr. v.p. bus. and legal Walt Disney Studios, Burbank, Calif., 1984-87, exec. v.p., 1987-94; with Dreamworks, 1994—. Recipient Frontrunner award in bus. Sara Lee Corp., 1991, Big Sisters Achievement award, 1992, Clairol Mentor award, 1993, Women in Bus. Magnificent Seven award, 1994.

HAHN, JOAN CHRISTENSEN, drama educator, travel agent; b. Kemmerer, Wyo., May 9, 1933; d. Roy and Bernice (Pringle) Wainwright; m. Milton Angus Christensen, Dec. 29, 1952 (div. Oct. 1, 1971); children: Randall M., Carla J. Christensen Teasdale; m. Charles Henry Hahn, Nov. 15, 1972. BS, Brigham Young U., 1965. Profl. ballroom dancer, 1951-59; travel dir. E.T. World Travel, Salt Lake City, 1969—; tchr. drama Payson High Sch., Utah, 1965-71, Cottonwood High Sch., Salt Lake City, 1971—; dir. Performing European Tours, Salt Lake City, 1969-76; dir. Broadway theater tours, 1976—. Bd. dirs. Salem City Salem Days, Utah, 1965-75; regional dir. dance Latter-day Saints Ch., 1954-72. Named Best Dir. High Sch. Musicals, Green Sheet Newspapers, 1977, 82, 84, 90, Utah's Speech Educator of Yr., 1990, 91, named to Nat. Hall of Fame Ednl. Theatre Assn., 1991; recipient 1st place award Utah State Drama Tournament, 1974, 77, 78, 89, 90, 91, 94, 95, Tchr. of Yr. award Cottonwood High Sch., 1989-90, Limelight award, 1982, Exemplary Performance in teaching theater arts Granite Sch. Dist., Salt Lake City, 1982; named to Nat. Hall of Fame, Ednl. Theatre Assn., 1991, Cottonwood H.S. Hall of Fame, 1995; named Outstanding Educator, Utah Ho. Reps., 1995. Mem. Internat. Thespian Soc. (sponsor 1968—, internat. dir. 1982-84, trustee 1978-84), Utah Speech Arts Assn. (pres. 1976-78, 88-90), NEA, Utah Edn. Assn., Granite Edn. Assn., Profl. Travel Agts. Assn., Utah High Sch. Activities Assn. (drama rep. 1972-76), AAUW (pres. 1972-74). Republican. Mormon. Avocations: reading; travel; dancing. Home: 685 S 1st E PO Box 36 Salem UT 84653-0036 Office: Cottonwood High Sch 5715 S 1300 E Salt Lake City UT 84121-1023

HAHN, MARK STEPHEN, computer security specialist, educator; b. L.A., June 13, 1953; s. Lester Curtis and Sandra Donelen (Bailey) H. BS in Computer Sci., Calif. Polytech. State U., 1976. Programmer Gesco Corp., Fresno, Calif., 1976-80; security analyst Northrop, El Segundo, Calif., 1980, SKK, Inc., Rosemont, Ill., 1980-82; security specialist Gesco Corp., Fresno, 1982-83, mktg. support specialist, 1983-84; computer security specialist Candle Corp., L.A., 1984-88, 91-92, instr., 1988-91; security cons. Coles Myer, Ltd., Melbourne, Australia, 1986; sr. cons. Vanguard Integrity Profls., Orange, Calif., 1992—. Contbr. articles to profl. jours. Mem. EDP Auditors Assn., Computer Sci. Inst., Alpha Epsilon Pi (chpt. pres. 1975, bd. govs. 1975, Outstanding Scribe 1974). Home: 11684 Ventura Blvd 895 Studio City CA 91604

HAHN, WOODY, sports association executive. Grad., Wash. State U. Athletic dir. Ea. Mont. Coll., until 1987; commr. Great Northwest Conf., 1988—, Continental Divide Cond., 1989—; active NCAA West Region Men's Basketball Adv. Com. Mem. Nat. Assn. Collegiate Dirs. Athletics, Volleyball Coaches' Assn., Basketball Coaches' Assn., NCAA Divsn. II Commrs. Assn. Office: Pacific West Conf PO Box 2002 Billings MT 59103-2002*

HAHN, YUBONG, electro-optics company executive; b. Seoul, Oct. 26, 1942; came to U.S., 1961; s. Chi-Gin Hahn and Bok-Hee Chung; m. Myung-Ok Hahn, June 6, 1970; children: Steven, Denise. PhD in Physics, U. Mo., Rolla, 1971. V.p. CVI Laser Corp., Albuquerque, 1972-79; with Optics Co., Seoul, Korea, 1979-83; pres. Rocky Mountain Instrument Co., Longmont, Colo., 1983—. Mem. Soc. Photog. Instrument Engrs., Soc. Photo-Optical Instrumentation Engring. Office: Rocky Mountain Instruments 1501 S Sunset St Longmont CO 80501-6750

HAIG, DAVID M., property and investment management specialist; b. New Rochelle, N.Y., May 20, 1951; s. Alexander Salusbury and Joan (Damon) H.; m. Myrna B. Murdoch, Oct. 1, 1983. Student, Marlboro Coll., 1974. Trustee Estate of S.M. Damon, Honolulu, 1982—; bd. dirs. First Hawaiian, Inc., First Hawaiian Bank, Honolulu. Bd. dirs. YMCA Met. Honolulu, 1985—, YMCA USA, Chgo., 1990—, Aloha United Way, 1990—. Mem. Oahu Country Club, Waialae Country Club, Rotary. Office: 1132 Bishop St Ste 1511 Honolulu HI 96813-2830

HAILE, BENJAMIN CARROLL, JR., retired chemical engineer, mechanical engineer; b. Shanghai, China, Apr. 6, 1918; came to U.S., 1925; s. Benjamin Carroll and Ruth Temple (Shreve) H.; m. Lola Pauline Lease, Dec. 28, 1957; children: Thomas Benjamin, Ronald Frederick. BS, U. Calif., Berkeley, 1941; cert., Harvard-MIT, 1945; postgrad., U. So. Calif., 1950-51. Registered profl. chem. and mech. engr., Calif. Chem. engr. Std. Oil of Calif. (Chevron), San Francisco, El Segundo, Calif., 1941-43, 46-48; sr. project chem. engr. C.F. Braun & Co., Alhambra, Calif., 1948-50, 54-56, 67-71, 72; contract chem. and mech. engr. Dow Chem., Stearns-Roger, Fluor et al, Tex., Colo., Ill., 1951-54, 56-57; sr. process engr. Aerojet-Gen. Corp., Sacramento and Covina, Calif., 1957-67; mech. engr. So. Calif. Edison Co., Rosemead, Calif., 1972-84; pvt. practice chem. engr. Fontana and Montclair, Calif., 1986, 88, 92; sr. mem. tech. staff Ralph M. Parsons Co., Pasadena, Calif., 1971, 88-91. 2d lt. USAAF, 1943-46. Mem. NSPE (life, Sacramento chpt. pres. 1960-62), Am. Inst. Chem. Engrs. (mem. emeritus), Toastmasters Internat. (chpt. v.p. 1979, Outstanding Toastmaster 1984), Psi Upsilon. Republican. Home: 159 N Country Club Rd Glendora CA 91741-3919

HAILE, LAWRENCE BARCLAY, lawyer; b. Atlanta, Feb. 19, 1938; m. Ann Springer McCauley, March 28, 1984 (dec. Apr. 1994); children: Gretchen Vanderhoof, Eric McKenzie, Scott McAllister. B.A. in Econs, U. Tex., 1958, LL.B., 1961. Bar: Tex. 1961, Calif. 1962. Law clk. to U.S. Judge Joseph M. Ingraham, Houston, 1961-62; pvt. practice law San Francisco, 1962-67, L.A., 1967—; instr. UCLA Civil Trial Clinics, 1974, 76; lectr. law Calif. Continuing Edn. of Bar, 1973-74, 80-89; mem. nat. panel arbitrators Am. Arbitration Assn., 1965—. Assoc. editor: Tex. Law Rev, 1960-61; contbr. articles profl. publs. Mem. State Bar Calif., Tex., U.S. Supreme Ct. Bar Assn., Internat. Assn. Property Ins. Counsel (founding mem., pres. 1980), Vintage Auto Racing Assn. (bd. dirs.), Vintage Motorsports Coun. (pres.), Phi Delta Phi, Delta Sigma Rho. Office: Haile & Simon 12304 Santa Monica Blvd Ste 300 Los Angeles CA 90025

HAILE, MARCUS ALFRED, retired chemistry educator; b. Haviland, Kans., Oct. 14, 1930; s. William Oral and Myrna May (Stotts) H.; m. Lynne Helene Hunsucker, Mar. 20, 1964; children: Marta Helene, Cavan William. BS, Pepperdine U., 1955; Master, U. No. Iowa, 1968. Cert. secondary tchr., Calif. Tchr. chemistry Hamilton High Sch., L.A., 1957-67; prof. chemistry L.A. City Coll., 1969-94, also pres. acad. senate, 1972-73. Author: Experimental General Chemistry, 1973, 76, Gen. Analytical Chemistry, 1987; contbr. articles to profl. jours. Chmn. Amateur Athletic Union So. Calif. Swimming U.S. Swim, Los Angeles, Ventura and Santa Barbara Counties, Calif., 1980-81. Served with U.S. Army, 1950-52. NSF grantee, 1967-68. Mem. Am. Chem. Soc., Am. Fedn. Tchrs., Thoroughbred Owners Calif. Democrat. Home: 22404 Kearny St Calabasas CA 91302-5861

HAINES, DAVID WAYNE, commercial printing executive; b. Everett, Wash., Jan. 28, 1956; s. Vernon Pringle and Norma Zee (Robinson) H.; m. Yvonne Alice Watts, Apr. 21, 1979; children: Kenneth David, Corry Daniel. BA in Visual Comm. Edn., Western Wash. U., 1978. System mgr. K & H Printers, Everett, 1979-81, sales rep., 1981-84, sales mgr., 1984-87, gen. mgr., 1987-91, pres., 1991-94; v.p. Pacific Printing Industries, Seattle, 1992-94, chmn., 1995; treas. Pacific Printing Industries, Seattle, 1991-92. Bd. dirs. ARC, Everett, 1985-89, Boy Scouts Am., Everett, 1991—; chmn. Cub Scouts Pack 16, Mukilteo, Wash., 1991-92; chair 24 hour challenge Am. Cancer Soc., Everett, 1991-92. Recipient Gold Eagle, Boy Scouts Am., 1992. Mem. Rotary Club. Office: K & H Printers Inc 1611 Broadway Everett WA 98201-1723

HAINES, IRENE LOIS, librarian; b. Nespelem, Wash., Aug. 1, 1951; d. William H. Haines and Eula Jean (Roberts) Rogers. AA in Theatre and Libr. Sci., Fort Wright Coll., 1976, BA with hons., 1976; MLS, U. Wash., 1987. Cert. libr., Wash. Libr. supr. Colville Tribal Libr., Nespelem, 1980-82; coord. libr. asst. Seattle (Wash.) Pub. Libr., 1983-87, pub. svc. libr., 1987-88, br. team leader, 1988—; human diversity trainer Exec. Diversity Svcs., Seattle, 1989-92. Contbr. articles to jours. Bd. dirs. AFSCME Local 2083C, Seattle, 1984-88; bd. dirs. Colville Indian Libr. Assn., 1981-82. Mem. Magnolia Community Club, Magnolia C. of C., Cen. Area C. of C. (bd. dirs. 1988-93), Colville Confederated Tribes. Democrat. Office: Magnolia Br Libr 2801 34th Ave W Seattle WA 98199-2602

HAINES, JIM ALLEN, architect; b. Escondido, Calif., Apr. 28, 1946; s. Allen Ray and Arlene Haines; m. Margaret Amanda Howell, Apr. 4, 1982; children: Amanda Christine, Evan Scott. BArch with distinction, Wash. State U., 1972. Lic. architect, Wash., Idaho; cert. bldg. insp., Wash. Structural draftsman Atwood-Hinzman Cons. Structural Engrs., Spokane, Wash., 1972-74; archtl. draftsman Tan-Brookie Kundig Architects, Spokane, 1974-76; architect E.M. Hicks Architects, Spokane, 1976-78; bldg. tech. Spokane County Bldg. Dept., 1979-84; prin. Haines Archtl. Svcs., Spokane, 1985—. With U.S. Army, 1967-69, Vietnam. Mem. Constrn. Specifications Inst. (program chmn. 1985-86, pres. 1989-90), Phi Kappa Phi. Presbyterian. Office: Haines Archtl Svcs 3516 W Rosamond Ave Spokane WA 99204-2032

HAINES, SALLY STEWART, public relations practitioner; b. Phoenix, Mar. 1, 1955; d. Biven and Nancy Sue (Spurlock) Stewart; children: Padraic Haines, Colin Haines. BS in Broadcast Journalism, Ariz. State U., 1977, BA in Edn., 1980. Staff writer, media rep. Salt River Project, Phoenix, 1979-81; copy editor Mesa (Ariz.) Tribune, 1981-82; mktg. adminstrv. asst. Phoenix chpt. ARC, 1983; pub. info. asst. City of Scottsdale, Ariz., 1983-84; bus. editor, asst. city editor Scottsdale Progress, 1984-86; comms. mgr. Mesa Conv. and Visitors Bur., 1986-90; mgmt. asst. Neighborhood Improvement and Housing Dept., City of Phoenix, 1990-92, Pub. Info. Office, City of Phoenix, 1992-93; sr. media rels. rep. Ariz. Pub. Svc., Phoenix, 1993—. Mem. com. Fiesta Bowl, Phoenix, 1987-89; mem. pub. rels. com. Juvenile Diabetes Found., Phoenix, 1990; mem. pub. rels. com. Children's Garden Ground Breaking, Phoenix, 1993. Mem. Pub. Rels. Soc. Am. (accredited, bd. dirs. 1991-93, assembly del. 1993-95). Office: Ariz Pub Svc 2 Arizona Ctr 400 N 5th St Phoenix AZ 85004-3902

HAINES, THOMAS DAVID, JR., lawyer; b. Dallas, Oct. 30, 1956; s. Thomas David Sr. and Carol V. (Mullins) H.; m. Nanette Cluck, Mar. 1, 1986. BS in Polit. Sci., Okla. State U., 1979; JD, U. Okla., 1982. Bar: Okla. 1982, N.Mex. 1983, U.S. Ct. Appeals (10th cir.) 1983, U.S. Dist. Ct. N.Mex. 1983. Assoc. Hinkle, Cox, Eaton, Coffield & Hensley, Roswell, N.Mex., 1982-87, ptnr., 1988—. Contbg. editor N.Mex. Tort and Worker's Compensation Reporter, 1987-90. Youth sponsor First United Meth. Ch., Roswell, 1986-88. Mem. State Bar Assn. N.Mex. (com. on continuing legal edn., young lawyers divsn. 1989—, mem. med.-legal rev. commn. 1988—), Chaves County Bar Assn., N.Mex. Def. Lawyer's Assn., N.Mex. Trial Lawyer's Assn., Phi Delta Phi, Phi Kappa Phi. Republican. Office: Hinkle Cox Eaton Coffield & Hensley 400 N Pennsylvania Ave Ste 700 Roswell NM 88201-4777

HAIR, KITTIE ELLEN, secondary educator; b. Denver, June 12, 1948; d. William Edward and Jacqueline Jean (Holt) H. BA, Brigham Young U., 1971; MA in Social History, U. Nev., Las Vegas, 1987. cert. tchr., Nev. Health educator Peace Corps, Totota, Liberia, 1971-72; tchr. Clark County Sch. Dist., Las Vegas, Nev., 1972-77, 1979—; chair dept. social studies Clark County Sch. Dist., Las Vegas, 1993-95; missionary Ch. Jesus Christ Latter-Day Saints, Alta., Can., 1977-79. Recipient Outstanding Faculty award U. Nev./Southland Corp., Las Vegas, 1991. Mem. NEA, Nat. Coun. for Social Scis., Clark County Tchrs. Assn., Phi Kappa Phi, Phi Alpha Theta, Delta Kappa Gamma. Democrat. Office: Advanced Technologies Acad 2501 Vegas Dr Las Vegas NV 89106

HAKEEM, MUHAMMAD ABDUL, artist, educator; b. N.Y.C., Oct. 15, 1945; s. Cheveland and Ruby (Rountrea) Marshall; m. Sheron Fatima, Nov. 27, 1987. Student of sculpture and painting, Pratt Inst., Pietrasanta, Italy, 1972; BFA, Pratt Inst., 1974; MA, Tchr. Coll., 1976; MEd, Columbia U., 1980; postgrad., U. Colo., 1994—. Artist N.Y. Daily News, 1976-78; asst. technician Bklyn. Mus., 1980-81, instr. African Art, 1981; tchr. Holy Rosary Sch., Bklyn., 1982-89; arts and crafts specialist Fresh Air Fund Camp, Fishkill, N.Y., 1983 summer, Camp Merrimac, Contoo Cook, N.H., 1986-88 summer; art tchr. Yonkers (N.Y.) Pub. Sch., 1989-90; adj. prof. Naropa Inst., Boulder, 1991-93. Exhibited in group shows at Bklyn Mus., 1973, Lynn Kottler Galleries, 1974, Hansen Galleries, 1974, Galleries Internat., 1975, Community Gallery, 1977, Waverly Gallery, Inc., 1977, Allan S. Park Gallery, 1978, Greenwich Bar and Restaurant, 1979, Macy Gallery, 1980, West Side Story, 1981, Lynn Kottler Galleries, 1981, World Trade Expo-Keane Mason Gallery, 1981, Tabor Gallery, 1982, Gallery II, St. George, Utah, 1984, Beulahland, 1986, Morin-Miller Galleries, 1987, 89, Ednl. Alliance, 1988, Steamboat Springs (Colo.) Art Coun./Eleanor Bliss Ctr. for the Arts of the Depot (hon. mention), 1992, Boulder (Colo.) Art Ctr., 1993, Louisville (Colo.) Arts Ctr., 1993, Emmanuel Gallery-U. Colo., Denver, 1994, Cross Gallery, Boulder, 1995—; contbr. articles to profl. jours. art tchr. Lower East Side Cmty. Sch., N.Y.C., 1976-77, Urban League, Bklyn., 1969 summer; counselor Office of Cath. Edn., Bklyn., 1987-88; mem. customer panel Regional Transp. Divsn.; bd. dirs. Arts and Humanities Assembly of Boulder. Winner Cheekwood Nat. Contemporary Painting Competition, Cheekwood Mus. Art, Tenn., 1993. Mem. Colo. Artists Register, Kappa Delta Pi (Kappa chpt.). Home: 2900 Aurora Ave Apt 312 Boulder CO 80303-2237

HAKIM, BESIM SELIM, architecture and urban design educator; b. Paris, July 31, 1938; came to U.S., 1978; s. Selim D. and Meliha M. (Yamulki) H.; m. Fatina S. Hijab, Oct. 31, 1963 (div. July 1983); children: Omar, Lena, Sara; m. Mariam B. Bashayan, Dec. 31, 1984; 1 child, Malak. BArch, Liverpool (Eng.) U., 1962; M Architecture and Urban Design, Harvard U., 1971. Registered architect, Ariz. Asst. prof. Tech. U. of Nova Scotia, Halifax, Can., 1967-74, assoc. prof., 1974-80, adj. rsch. prof., 1980-83; adj. assoc. prof. U. N.Mex., Albuquerque, 1981-82; assoc. prof. King Fahd U. of Petroleum and Minerals, Dhahran, Saudi Arabia, 1984-85; assoc. prof. Coll. of Architecture and Planning King Faisal U., Dammam, Saudi Arabia, 1985-93; ind. scholar and cons.; vis. prof. McGill U., Montreal, 1974, Tech. Inst. Architecture & Urbanism in Tunis, Tunisia, 1975, King Saud U., Riyadh, Saudi Arabia, 1982, 87, 89, 92, MIT, 1977, scholar, 1981; cons. to Skidmore, Owings & Merrill, Architects/Engrs., Chgo., Keith Graham & Assocs., Architects, Halifax, Nova Scotia and others; architect, engr. King Khaled Internat. Airport, Riyadh, Saudi Arabia, 1983-84. Prin. works include urban design downtown Halifax, N.S., 1971-74, Coors Corridor Plan, Albuquerque, Hist. Old Town, Albuquerque, 1981-83, 11 custom-built houses, an eight-story office bldg., hosp. renovations/additions, apt. bldgs. and a religious facility, U.S., Can., Mid-East; author: (book) Arabic-Islamic Cities: Building and Planning Principles, 1986, 2d edit., 1988, (monograph) Sidi Bou Sa'id Tunisia: A Study in Structure and Form, 1978; contbr. numerous articles, revs., and tech. reports to profl. publs. Recipient citation for rsch. Progressive Architecture, 1987, Edn. Honors award AIA, 1990. Mem. AIA, Am. Inst. Cert. Planners, Am. Planning Assn., Assn. Collegiate Schs. of Architecture, Middle East Studies Assn. N.Am., Halifax Bd. Trade (civic affairs com.). Home: 1832 Field Dr NE Albuquerque NM 87112-2834

HAKKILA, EERO ARNOLD, nuclear safeguards technology chemist; b. Canterbury, Conn., Aug. 4, 1931; s. Jack and Ida Maria (Lillquist) H.; m. Margaret W. Hakkila; children: Jon Eric, Mark Douglas, Gregg Arnold. BS in Chemistry, Cen. Conn. State U., 1953; PhD in Analytical Chemistry, Ohio State U., 1957. Staff mem. Los Alamos (N.Mex.) Nat. Lab., 1957-78, assoc. group leader safeguard systems, 1978-80, dep. group leader, 1980-82, group leader, 1982-83, project mgr. internat. safeguards, 1983-87, program coord.,

1987—. Editor: Nuclear Safeguards Analysis, 1978; contbr. numerous articles to profl. jours. Fellow Am. Inst. Chemists; mem. N.Mex. Inst. Chemists (pres. 1971-73), Am. Chem. Soc., Am. Nuclear Soc. (exec. com. fuel cycle and waste mgmt. div. 1984-86), Inst. Nuclear Materials Mgmt. Office: Los Alamos Nat Lab PO Box 1663 Los Alamos NM 87544-0600

HALBERG, CHARLES JOHN AUGUST, JR., mathematics educator; b. Pasadena, Calif., Sept. 24, 1921; s. Charles John August and Anne Louise (Hansen) H.; m. Ariel Arfon Oliver, Nov. 1, 1941 (div. July 1969); children—Ariel (Mrs. William Walters), Charles Thomas, Niels Frederick; m. Barbro Linnea Samuelsson, Aug. 18, 1970 (dec. Jan. 1978); 1 stepchild, Ulf Erik Hjelm; m. Betty Reese Zimprich, July 27, 1985. B.A. summa cum laude, Pomona Coll., 1949; M.A. (William Lincoln Honnold fellow), UCLA, 1953, Ph.D., 1955. Instr. math. Pomona Coll., Claremont, Calif., 1949-50; assoc. math. UCLA, 1954-55; instr. math. U. Calif.-Riverside, 1955-56, asst. prof. math., 1956-61, assoc. prof. math., 1961-68, prof. math., 1968—, vice chancellor student affairs, 1964-65; dir. Scandinavian Study Center at Lund (Sweden) U., 1976-78; docent U. Goteborg, Sweden, 1969-70; bd. dirs. Fulbright Commn. for Ednl. Exchange between U.S. and Sweden, 1976-79. Author: (with John F. Devlin) Elementary Functions, 1967, (with Angus E. Taylor) Calculus with Analytic Geometry, 1969. Served with USAAF, 1945-46. NSF fellow U. Copenhagen, 1961-62. Mem. Math. Assn. Am. (chmn. So. Calif. sect. 1964-65, gov. 1968), Am. Math. Soc., Swedish Math. Soc., Sigma Xi, Phi Beta Kappa. Home: PO Box 2724 Carlsbad CA 92018-2724

HALBY, ANTHONY WAYNE, insurance agent; b. Mesa, Ariz., Nov. 22, 1949; s. Tony and Linda (Mawson) H.; m. Charlene T. Pavao, Aug. 21, 1971; children: Gabriella Marie, Matthew James, Mark Anthony, Michael Alfred, Joseph Christopher. BS in Mktg., BS in Mgmt., Woodbury U., 1971. Pvt. practice ins. sales La Crescenta, Calif. and Nevada City, Calif., 1971—. Named to Leading Producers Roundtable Nat. Assn. Health Underwriters, 1982, 88, 90, 91, 92, 93. 94. Mem. L.A. Assn. Health Underwriters (founder, bd. dirs. 1981-83, pres. 1982-83), (charter) Calif. Assn. Health Underwriters (pres. 1990-91), Nat. Assn. Health Underwriters (trustee 1992-94), Sacramento Assn. Health Underwriters (pres. 1988-90). Republican. Roman Catholic. Home: 11534 Country View Way Grass Valley CA 95945-7607 Office: 313 Railroad Ave # 201 Nevada City CA 95959-2835

HALE, BRUCE DONALD, marketing professional; b. Oak Park, Ill., Dec. 21, 1933; s. Edward Garden and Mildred Lillian (Pelc) H.; m. Nancy Ann Novotny, July 2, 1955 (div. 1976); children: Jeffrey Bruce, Karen Jill Hale; m. Connie Luella Green Gunderson, Apr. 21, 1979. BA in Econs., Wesleyan U., Middletown, Conn., 1955. Trainee Caterpillar Tractor Co., Peoria, Ill., 1955-56, dealer tng. rep., 1956-59; dist. rep. Caterpillar Tractor Co., Albuquerque, 1959-62; asst. sales mgr. Rust Tractor Co., Albuquerque, 1962-65; gen. sales mgr. Rust Tractor Co., Albuqerque, 1965-71, v.p. sales, 1971-81, v.p. mktg., 1981—; bd. dirs. Mega Corp., Albuquerque. Mem. Am. Mining Congress, Soc. Mining Engrs., Associated Contractors N.Mex., Associated Equipment Distbrs., Rocky Mountain Coal Mining Inst., N.Mex. Mining Assn., Albuquerque Country Club. Home: 9508 Layton Pl NE Albuquerque NM 87111-1368 Office: Rust Tractor Co 4000 Osuna Rd NE Albuquerque NM 87109-4423

HALE, CARL DENNIS, electronics company executive; b. Oakland, Calif., July 12, 1949; s. William Francis and Irene Helegard (Knoth) H.; children: Telissa, Desiree, Michael. BS, San Jose State U., 1974; mfg. studies program, Gen. Electric Co., San Jose, 1976; MBA, St. Mary's Coll., Moraga, Calif. Prodn. planner Gen. Electric, San Jose, Calif., 1974-77; mfg. engr. Gen. Electric, Paterson, N.J., 1977-78; advisor, prodn. mgr. Gen. Electric Co., San Jose, 1978-79; materials mgr. Spectra Physics, Mountain View, Calif., 1979-81; factory parts mgr. Hewlett-Packard, Mountain View, 1981-82; materials mgr. Hewlett-Packard, Santa Clara, 1982-86; mgr. prodn. sect. Hewlett-Packard, San Jose, 1986-88, materials mgr. rsch. and devel., 1988-89; logistics mgr. Hewlett-Packard, Santa Clara, 1989—; part time instr. San Jose State U., 1985—. Author: (manuals) Material Requirements Planning, 1981, Conceptual Manufacturing, 1983, How to Professionally Qualify Suppliers, Apics Internat. Conf., 1987, Building World Class Service in Suppliers, Inst. for Internat. Rsch. Conf., 1990. Mem. Am. Prodn. and Inventory Control Soc. (cert. prodn. and inventory mgmt.), Club Sport. Republican. Roman Catholic. Home: 3102 3 Lakemont Dr San Ramon CA 94583 Office: Hewlett-Packard 370 W Trimble Rd San Jose CA 95131-1008

HALE, CHARLES RUSSELL, lawyer; b. Talpa, Tex., Oct. 17, 1916; s. Charles L. and Exa (Evans) H.; m. Clementine L. Moore, Jan. 5, 1946; children: Robert R., Norman B. A.B., Stanford U., 1939; J.D., Fordham U., 1950. Bar: N.Y. 1950, Calif. 1953. Supr., United Geophys. Co., Pasadena, Calif., 1940-46; mem. patent staff Bell Telephone Labs., N.Y.C., 1947-48, Sperry Gyroscope Co., Great Neck, N.Y., 1948-51; practiced in Pasadena, 1951-54; ptnr. Christie, Parker & Hale, Pasadena, 1954-87; retired, 1987. Mem. ABA, Am. Patent Law Assn., San Diego County Bar Assn., IEEE. Clubs: Rancho Santa Fe (Calif.) Golf. Home: PO Box 616 Rancho Santa Fe CA 92067-0616 Office: Christie Parker & Hale 350 W Colorado Blvd Pasadena CA 91105-1855

HALE, DANIEL CUDMORE, lawyer; b. Denver, Nov. 5, 1944; s. George Ellis and Dorothy Ann (Cudmore) H.; children: Brad, Tessa. BS in Mktg., U. Colo., 1967, JD, 1971. Bar: Colo. 1971, U.S. Dist. Ct. Colo. 1971, U.S. Ct. Appeals (10th cir.) 1971, U.S. Supreme Ct. 1979. Clk. to judge U.S. Dist. Ct., Denver, 1971-72; chief trial dep. Boulder Dist. Atty.'s Office Colo., 1973-76; atty. Miller, Gray & Hale, Boulder, 1976-84; ptnr. Miller, Hale & Harrison, Boulder, 1984—; cert. instr. search and seizure State of Colo., 1980—; instr. trial advocacy U. Colo., 1987—. Bd. dirs. Boulder County Bd. of Developmental Disabilities, Boulder, 1982-88, pres., 1984-85. Mem. Boulder County Bar Assn. (sec., treas. 1977-79, bd. govs. 1985-89, 92—, pres.-elect 1989, pres. 1990-91), Colo. Bar Assn., Nat. Assn. Criminal Def. Lawyers, Assn. Trial Lawyers Am., Colo. Criminal Def. Bar, Calif. Attys. for Criminal Justice. Democrat. Home: 792 Pine Brook Rd Boulder CO 80304-0456

HALE, DAVID FREDRICK, health care company executive; b. Gadsden, Ala., Jan. 8, 1949; s. Millard and Mildred Earline (McElroy) H.; BA, Jacksonville State U.; m. Linda Carol Sadorski, Mar. 14, 1975; children: Shane Michael, Tara Renee, Erin Nicole, David Garrett. Dir. product mgmt. Ortho Pharm. Corp. Divsn. Johnson & Johnson, Raritan, N.J., 1978-80; v.p. mktg. BBL Microbiology Systems divsn. Becton Dickenson & Co., Cockeysville, Md., 1980-81, v.p., gen. mgr., 1981-82; sr. v.p. mktg. and bus. devel. Hybritech, Inc., San Diego, 1982, pres. 1983-86, CEO, 1986-87; pres., CEO Gensia, Inc., San Diego, 1987—, chmn. bd. dirs. 1991; mem. bd. dirs. Genta, Inc., Dura Pharmaceuticals, Gensia, Inc., Pharm. Rsch. & Mfrs. Assn., Francis Parker Sch., Biotechnology Ind. Orgn., Calif. Healthcare Inst., Biocom San Diego; chmn. San Diego Econ. Devel. Corp., Viagene, Inc.; founder CONNECT; mem. bd. advisors UCSD Med. Ctr.; chmn. Mayor's Bus. and Econ. Devel. Coun. Mem. Young Pres.'s Orgn. Republican. Episcopalian Home: 13023 Aguamarina Pt San Diego CA 92128-1522

HALE, DEAN EDWARD, social services administrator; b. Balt., Aug. 4, 1950; s. James Russell and Marjorie Elinor (Hoerman) H.; m. Lucinda Hoyt Muniz, 1979; children: Christopher Deane, Lydia Alice JeeSoo. BASW, U. Pa., 1975; postgrad. U. Oreg., 1976, U. London, 1974, U. Mont., 1968-71, Portland State U., 1993. Dir. recreation Hoffman Homes for Children, Gettysburg, Pa., 1970; social worker Holt Adoption Program, Inc., Eugene, Oreg., 1975-78; supr. social svcs. Holt Internat. Children's Svcs., Eugene, 1978-84, Asia rep., 1984-90, program mgr., 1990-94, interim dir. internat. programs, 1994-95, dir., China, 1995—; guest lectr. U. Oreg.; cons. internat. child welfare, 1982—; co-founder Family Opportunities Unltd. Inc., 1981—. Author: Adoption, A Family Affair, 1981, When Your Child Comes Home, 1986. Pres. Woodtique Heights Homeowners Assn., 1980-91, bd. dirs.; pres. Our Saviour's Luth. Ch., 1981-85; bd. dirs. Greenpeace of Oreg., 1979-84; cons., campaign worker Defazio for Congress 1988, 1987-90; mem. Westside Neighborhood Quality Project, 1988—. Named Outstanding New Jaycee, Gettysburg Jaycees, 1971. Mem. Nat. Assn. Social Workers (bd. dirs. 1978-80, sec. 1979-80), Nat. Assn. Christian Social Workers, Acad. Cert. Baccalaureate Social Workers. Home: 931 Taylor St Eugene OR 97402-4451 Office: PO Box 2880 1195 City View St Eugene OR 97402-3325

HALE, JAMES LEROY (JOHN HALE), forensic document analyst, consultant; b. Prescott, Ariz., Oct. 30, 1941; s. James LeRoy Sr. and Grace Viola (Nichols) H.; m. Cathy Jo Johnsmiller, Feb. 21, 1951; children: Kathryn, Lora Ann, Debra Lynn; m. Susan Gail Jeffries, July 4, 1964 (div. Sept. 1974). AA in Police Sci., Glendale C.C., 1974; student, Ariz. State U., 1974-78. Diplomate Am. Bd. Forensic Document Examiners. Surveyor's aide U.S. Bur. Reclamation, Phoenix and Yuma, Ariz., 1964-65; with Ariz. Hwy. Patrol, Yuma and Wickenburg, Ariz., 1965-70; undercover narcotics enforcement agt. Ariz. Dept. Pub. Safety, 1970-72; forensic document analyst Ariz. Dept. Pub. Safety Questioned Document Lab., Phoenix, 1972-85, No. Ariz. Forensic Lab., Chino Valley, 1985—; cons. and expert witness; lectr.-instr. Am. Inst. Banking, Phoenix, 1982-90; instr. Ariz. law enforcement officer adv. coun. acads., 1978-85. Editor forensic newsletter Southwestern Examiner, 1981-83; author rsch. articles; presenter in field. Mem. Chino Valley Town Coun., 1988-93; pres., bd. dirs. Hi-Desert Artists, Chino Valley, 1988-90, 92-93. Served with U.S. Army, 1959-62, Korea. Recipient numerous appreciation awards. Mem. Southwestern Assn. of Forensic Document Examiners (founder, past pres., bd. dirs.). Republican. Baptist. Home: 1331 E Red Cinder Rd Chino Valley AZ 86323-5461 Office: No Ariz Forensic Lab PO Box 411 Chino Valley AZ 86323

HALE, NATHAN ROBERT, architect; b. Battle Creek, Mich., July 20, 1944; s. Nathan Shirley and Gertrude Anges (Barnes) H.; m. CarolAnn Purrington, May 28, 1966; children: Marilyce, Maile, Martha. B.A., Syracuse U., 1967, B.Arch., 1971. Dir., Architects Hawaii, Honolulu, 1971—. Served with AUS, 1968-70, Vietnam. Mem. Hawaii C. of C. (exec. com. 1994—), AIA (bd. dirs. 1984, pres. 1992), Econ. Devel. Corp. Honolulu (chair 1993—), Rotary Club (bd. dirs. 1986-88), Friends of Children's Advocacy Ctr. (pres. 1991, 93, bd. dirs. 1986—). Office: Architects Hawaii Ltd Pacific Tower 300 1001 Bishop St Honolulu HI 96813-3429

HALE, VIOLET ELAINE, director food service, master graphoanalyst; b. Atwood, Kans.; d. Frank and Lola Mae (Threlkel) Wederski; m. Everett David Hale, June 25, 1948; children: Diana Elaine, Chester Duane, Ray Don. Student, IGAS, 1980. Asst. food svc. dir. Manitou Springs (Colo.) Sch., 1967-84, ret., 1984. Author poems, songwriter; inventor cap shaper dryer, sliced bread stacker. Mem. Manitou Springs Hist. Soc. (v.p. 1989-92). Methodist.

HALER, LAWRENCE EUGENE, technology educator, councilman; b. Iowa City, Iowa, Jan. 24, 1951; s. Eugene Hilbert and Mary Elizabeth (Hans) H.; m. Jenifer Lea Leitz, June 1, 1974. BA, Pacific Luth. U., 1974. Reactor operator UNC Nuclear Industires, Richland, Wash., 1974-80, lead cert. instr., 1980-81, mgr. tng. adminstrn., 1981-82, sr. ops. analyst, 1982-85; sr. specialist Gen. Physics Corp., Columbia, Md., 1985-86; sr. instr. Rockwell Hanford Ops., Richland, 1986-88; tech. instr. Westinghouse Hanford Co., Richland, 1988-89, sr. specialist instr., 1989—; chmn. bd. dirs. Benton-Franklin County Bd. Health, Richland, Sci. and Tech. Park, Richland; vice chmn. Benton-Franklin Regional Coun. Govts., 1994. Chmn. Benton County Reps., Richland, 1976-78, state committeeman, 1988-90; councilman, mayor pro-tem City of Richland, 1990—; active comty. econ. devel. com. Nat. League of Cities. Mem. Richland C. of C. (chmn. legis. affairs com. 1988-93), Richland Kiwanis (pres. 1994—). Lutheran. Home: PO Box 1319 Richland WA 99352-1319 Office: Richland City Coun 505 Swift Blvd Richland WA 99352-3510

HALEY, ANNE ELIZABETH, library director; b. Oct. 4, 1946; m. James F. Shepherd. BA in History, French, U. Puget Sound, 1968; MLS, U. Wash., 1970. Libr. trainee San Diego (Calif.) Pub. Libr., 1968-69; libr. Pierce County Libr., Tacoma, 1970-73; ext. coord. Fort Vancouver (Wash.) Regional Libr., 1973-77; dir. Walla Walla Pub. Libr., Wash., 1977—; lectr. U. Wash. Grad. Sch. Libr. and Info. Sci., 1986, 89, 91, 92; speaker/panelist various libr. assns.; del. head US Observer Del., UNESCO, Paris, 1990; chair statements writing process Wash. Gov.'s Conf. on Librs., 1991; chmn. Wash. Adv. Coun. on Librs., 1979-81; chmn. S.E. Libr. Svc. Area, 1979; chmn. Interstate Libr. Planning Coun., 1975-76. Book reviewer; contbr. articles to profl. jours. Planning facilitator Moscow/Latah County Libr., 1991; chmn. Libr. Legis. Day, Olympia, 1985, 86; mem. Walla Walla Art Club, Walla Walla Women's Reading Club, PEO, Walla Walla Country Club, Walla Walla Symphony Guild; chmn. Symposium on Creativity, Walla Walla Symphony Soc. 75th Celebration, 1981; parliamentarian Jr. Club Walla Walla, 1982-83; 2d v.p. Camp Fire Coun., 1986-88, treas., 1988-80, sec., 1985-86, chmn. ct. svc. com., 1980-83; pub. svc. divsn. chair United Way Campaign, 1985-87; bd. dirs. Exchange Club, 1988-89; pres. Allied Arts Coun., 1981-82, treas., 1980-81, 82-90; founding pres. Project Read, Walla Walla, 1986-89; chmn. budget and allocations com. United Way, 1991-93, mem., 1989-93; day leader Leadership Walla Walla C. of C., 1992, 93; mem. steering com. City Mgr. Recruitment, 1992; chmn. adv. com. Helpline, 1992-94; pres. United Way Walla Walla County, 1993-94. Recipient Disting. Alumnus award U. Wash. Grad. Sch. Libr. & Info. Sci., 1994. Mem. ALA (chmn. internat. rels. com. 1990-91), Pacific N.W. Libr. Assn. (1st v.p./pres. 1993-95, rep. 1977-79, chmn. pub. libr. divsn. 1977-79, chmn. local arrangements 1972), Wash. Libr. Assn. (ALA councilor 1987-92, ALA coun. 1995—, pres. 1983-85, 1st v.p., chmn. legis. planning com., chmn. budget com. 1981-83, Pres.'s award 1992), Exch. Club (Builders of Pride recognition award 1988). Home: 644 Boyer Ave Walla Walla WA 99362-2308 Office: Walla Walla Pub Libr 238 E Alder St Walla Walla WA 99362-1943

HALEY, JOHN DAVID, petroleum consulting company executive; b. Denver, Mar. 16, 1924; s. Peter Daniel and Margaret Dorothy (O'Haire) H.; m. Annie Loretta Breeden, June 20, 1951; children: Laura, Patricia, Brian, Sharon, Norine, Kathleen. Profl. engr. Colo. Sch. Mines, 1948. Registered profl. engr., Colo., Okla. Petroleum engr. Creole Petroleum, Venezuela, 1948-50, field engr. Texaco Inc., La., 1950-52; staff engr. Carter Oil (Exxon), Tulsa, 1954-56; petroleum cons. Earlougher Engring., Tulsa, 1956-61, resident mgr., Denver, 1961-62; v.p. prodn. Anschutz Corp., Denver, 1962-86; v.p. Circle A Drilling, Denver, 1967-78; dir. Circle A Mud, Denver, 1983-86; pres. Greylock Pipeline, Denver, 1983-86, Anschutz Pipeline, Denver, 1984-86; pres. Haley Engring. Inc., 1987—; mem. pres.'s council Colo. Sch. Mines, 1985—; bd. dirs. Alumni Assn., 1992—, pres., 1995. Rep. committeeman, Littleton. Lt. comdr. USNR, 1943-46, 52-54. Mem. Soc. Petroleum Engrs. (bd. dirs. Denver chpt. 1965), Soc. Petroleum Evaluation Engrs. (bd. dirs. 1992-95), Ind. Petroleum Assn. Mountain States, Am. Petroleum Inst. (citation for service), Internat. Assn. Drilling Contractors, Rocky Mountain Oil & Gas Assn. (bd. dirs. 1988—), Soc. Profl. Well Log Analysts, Petroleum Club (Denver chpt.). Roman Catholic. Home: 561 E Caley Dr Littleton CO 80121-2212

HALEY, RHOBERTA JONES, family nurse practitioner, educator; b. San Bernardino, Calif., Nov. 23, 1955; d. Orlyn Lee and Gara K. Jones; children: Sara, Adam. BSN, Calif. State U., 1977; MN, UCLA, 1982. Cert. family nurse practitioner, Calif. Family nurse practitioner Kaiser Permanente HMO, San Diego, 1982-87; lectr. San Diego State U., 1992-94, U. San Diego Sch. Nursing, 1992-94; nurse Ctr. for Womens' Medicine, San Diego, 1994—. Mem. Calif. Nurses Assn., Calif. Coalition Nurse Practitioners, Gamma Gamma chpt. Sigma Theta Tau (past pres.). Home: 1683 Hacienda Dr El Cajon CA 92020-1361

HALEY, SALLY FULTON, artist; b. Bridgeport, Conn., June 29, 1908; d. John Poole and Elizabeth (Akers) H.; m. Michele Russo, June 29, 1935; children: Michael Haley, Gian Donato. BFA, Yale U., 1931. One-woman shows include Marylhurst Coll., 1965, Maryhill Mus. Fine Arts, Washington, 1975, Portland Art Mus., 1960, 75, Woodside Gallery, Seattle, 1971, 76, 79, Gov's. Office, Oreg. State Capitol, 1976, Wentz Gallery, Pacific N.W. Coll. Art, 1984, Fountain Gallery Art, Portland, 1962, 72, 77, 80, 81, 84, 86; exhibited in group shows Stewart Gallery, Boston, 1947, San Francisco Mus. Art, 1949, Walker Art Ctr., Mpls., 1954, Denver Art Mus., 1956, 57, 3d Pacific Coast Biennial Exhbn., 1960, Francis J. Newton's Collection, Bush House, 1964, Seattle Ctr. Art Pavilion, 1976, Womans Bldg., L.A., 1977, Laura Russo Gallery, 1993, Oreg. Group Show, Expn. '86 World's Fair, Vancouver, B.C.; represented in permanent collections Fred Myer Trust, Wash. State U., State Capitol Bldg., Salem, Portland Art Mus., The Laura Russo Gallery, Portland, Lynn McAllister Gallery, Seattle, Barby Investment Co., AT&T, Kaiser Found., numerous others; retrospective, Marylhurst Coll., 1993. Named Artist of Yr. Neighbor Newspaper Community, Portland, 1984; recipient Woman of Achievement award YWCA, 1988, Govs. award for the Arts, 1989, Poster award, 1982, Hubbard award Hubbard Mus., Ruidoso Downs, N.Mex., 1990-91.

HALFANT, GARY D., small business owner; b. Washington, Aug. 1, 1953; s. Manny and Jean Frances (Eddinger) H.; m. Gwyn Reneé Jones, Dec. 24, 1987 (div. Apr. 1992); 1 child, Garic David. Grad. high sch., Sacramento. Pres. G's Herbs, Sacramento, 1974-78, G's Herbs Internat., Ltd. (now G's Seasonings Co.), Portland, Oreg., 1978-92.

HALFORD, SHARON LEE, crime victim services administrator, victimologist, educator; b. Clifton, Colo., July 22, 1946; d. Robert Lee and Florence V. (Kubly) Eighmy; m. Allen A. Dreher, Jan. 29, 1967 (div. Jan. 1979); children: Heidi Ann, Gretchen Christine, Kirsten Beth; m. Donald Gary Halford, May 23, 1986. BS in Edn., U. Colo., 1969; postgrad., U. Denver, 1981-83; M in Criminal Justice, U. Colo., 1987. Legal asst. 1st Jud. Dist. Atty., Golden, Colo., 1979-81, legal rschr., 1981-83; victim witness coord. 18th Jud. Dist. Atty., Englewood, Colo., 1983-92; mem. faculty Aurora (Colo.) C.C. Criminal Justice Dept., 1989—, Colo. Faculty Adv. Coun., 1993—. Contbg. author, editor: Colorado Crime Victims Rights Contitutional Amendment Outreach Manual and Implementation Manual, 1992-93. Mem. Domestic Violence Task Force, Douglas County, Colo., 1985-92, Arapahoe County, Colo., 1985-94; trainer Rape Assistance and Awareness Program, Denver, 1985-91, MADD, 1990-92, Colo. Victim Witness Coord. Coalition, 1991; mem. 18th Judicial Dist. Child Advocacy Ctr. Com., 1990—, Gov.'s Victims' Compensation and Assistance Coord. Com., 1991—, Colo. Victim Asst. and Law Enforcement Bd., 1991—, Criminal Justice Educators Task Force, 1992—, Colo. Corrections Consortium, 1992—, Colo. Crime Victim Rights Constl. Ammendment Com., 1990—; sec. Colo. Faculty Adv. Coun., 1993—; com. chair Colo. PACT Project, 1993—. Fellow Nat. Orgn. for Victim Assistance, Nat. Victim Ctr.; mem. Colo. Orgn. for Victim Assistance (pres.), S.W. Criminal Justice Educators Assn., Nat. Criminal Justice Educators Assn., Nat. Criminal Justice Assn., Am. Criminal Justice Assn., Internat. Platform Speakers Assn. Democrat. Methodist. Office: CC Aurora 16000 E Centretech Pky Aurora CO 80011-9057

HALFPENNY, JAMES CARSON, scientist, educator, author; b. Shreveport, La., Jan. 23, 1947; s. Donald Frazier and Dorothy (Carson) H. BS, U. Wyo., 1969, MS, 1970; PhD, U. Colo., 1980. Various positions with govt. conservation agys., parks and univ conservation programs, 1966—; coord. long-term ecol. rsch. program U. Colo., Boulder, 1980-91; rsch. assoc. Inst. Arctic and Alpine Rsch., U. Colo., 1980-87, 92, fellow, 1987-91, affiliate, 1991—; instr. Teton Sci. Sch., Kelly, Wyo., 1980—, affiliate, 1992—, Aspen (Colo.) Ctr. for Environ. Studies, 1984—, Yellowstone (Wyo.) Inst., 1984—, Rocky Mountain Nature Assn., 1987, 90, 92; pres. A Naturalist's World, Boulder, 1985—; staff trainer Colo. Div. Wildlife, 1979, 83, 91, sci. advisor 1982-85; staff trainer Yellowstone Nat. Park, 1985-86, 88, Grand Teton Nat. Park, 1990, Rocky Mountain Nat. Park, 1992; grant proposal rev. bd. NSF, 1984—, Nat. Geog. Sci., 1984—; trustee Thorne Ecol. Inst., Boulder, 1982-84; mem. Indian Peaks Wilderness Area Adv. Panel, Boulder, 1982-86, others; speaker mammal tracking, alpine and winter ecology, Republic of China's endangered wildlife. Author: A Field Guide to Mammal Tracking, 1986, Winter: An Ecological Handbook, 1989; editor (booklets) Mountain Rsch. Sta.: its environment and rsch., 1982, Long Term Ecol. Rsch. in the U.S.: a network of rsch. sites, 1982, 83, 84; contbr. articles to profl. jours. and mags. on nat. history. Mem. sci. adv. panel EOP program U. Colo., 1982-84; mem. sci. coun. Greater Yellowstone Coalition; bd. advisors Teton Sci. Sch., Moran, 1985-89; bd. dirs. Nat. Outdoor Leadership Sch., Lander, Wyo., 1975-80, chmn., 1978-79. With USNR, 1969-71, Vietnam. Decorated Navy Achievement medal with combat "v", Vietnamese Gallantry Cross with palm (Republic Vietnam); recipient Roosevelt Meml. grant Am. Mus. Natural History, 1979, Walker Van Riper grant U.Colo., 1979, Kathy Lichty Fund grant U. Colo., 1979, Book Plate award Denver Pub. Libr. Friends Found. Fellow The Explorer Club; mem. AAAS, Ecol. Soc. Am., Am. Inst. Biol. Scis., Am. Soc. Mammalogists, Internat. Soc. Cryptozoology, Southwestern Assn. Naturalists, N.W. Sci. Assn., Colo.-Wyo. Acad. Sci., Orgn. Biol. Field Stas., Sci. Coun. Greater Yellowstone Coalition, Sigma Xi. Office: A Naturalist's World PO Box 989 300 Scott Gardiner MT 59030

HALL, ALAN HERMAN, toxicologist, educator; b. South Bend, Ind., Jan. 8, 1949; s. Herman and Thelma D. (Dennie) H.; m. Priscilla K. Hall, July 8, 1967; 1 child, Stephanie A. BA with honors, Ind. U., South Bend, 1973; MD, Ind. U., Indpls., 1977. Diplomate Am. Bd. Emergency Medicine and subspecialty board in med. toxicology, Am. Bd. Med. Toxicology; lic. physician, Tex., Colo. Intern Thomason Gen. Hosp., El Paso, 1977; resident U. Tex. Health Scis. Ctr., San Antonio, 1978-79; fellow U. Colo. Health Scis. Ctr., Denver, 1984-86, sr. cons. Rocky Mountain Poison and Drug Ctr., 1986—, asst. prof. pediatrics, 1987-92, clin. asst. prof. preventive medicine and biometrics, 1992—; mem. faculty U. Colo.; editor-in-chief Tomes and Tomes Plus Info. Sys., Micromedex, Inc., Denver. Guest editor study cases; reviewer jours.; contbr. numerous articles to profl. jours. Mem. peer rev. com. Agy. for Toxic Substances and Disease Registry, 1988-90; mem. State of Colo. Air Quality Sci. Adv. Bd., 1992—. Maj., MC, USAFR, hon. ret. Fellow Am. Coll. Emergency Physicians; mem. AMA, Am. Med. Writers Assn., Am. Coll. Emergency Physicians, Am. Acad. Clin. Toxicology, Am. Coll. Med. Toxicology, Am. Coll. Occupl. and Environ. Medicine, Am. Coll. Med. Toxicology, Colo. Med. Soc., Colo. Coll. Emergency Physicians, Rocky Mountain Acad. Occupl. and Environ. Medicine, Denver Med. Soc., Nat. Environ. Health Assn., Aerospace Medicine Assn., Soc. USAF Flight Surgeons, others. Republican. Home: 85 Santa Fe Mountain Dr Evergreen CO 80439-4921

HALL, ANTHONY ELMITT, plant physiologist; b. Tickhill, Yorkshire, Eng., May 6, 1940; came to U.S., 1964; s. Elmitt and Mary Lisca (Schofield) H.; m. Bretta Reed, June 20, 1965; children: Kerry, Gina. Student, Harper Adams Agrl. Coll., Eng., 1958-60; student in agrl. engring., Essex Inst. Agrl. Engring., Eng., 1960-61; BS in Irrigation Sci., U. Calif., Davis, 1966, PhD in Plant Physiology, 1970. Farmer Dyon House, Austerfield, Eng., 1955-58; extension officer Ministry of Agr., Tanzania, 1961-63; research asst. U. Calif., Davis, 1964-70, asst. research scientist, 1971; research fellow Carnegie Inst., Stanford, Calif., 1970; prof. U. Calif., Riverside, 1971—, cons. on African agrl. devel., 1974—, chmn. dept botany and plant scis., 1994—. Editor: Agriculture in Semi-Arid Environments, 1979, Stable Isotopes and Plant Carbon-Water Relations, 1993; adv. editor (jour.) Irrigation Sci.; tech. editor (jour.) Crop Sci.; mem. editorial adv. bd. Field Crops Research, Vigna Crop Adv. Com. USDA; contbr. articles to profl. jours. Fellow Am. Soc. Agronomy, Crop Sci. Soc. Am.; mem. Am. Soc. Plant Physiologists, Scandinavian Soc. Plant Physiology, Alpha Zeta, Gamma Sigma Delta, Phi Beta Kappa, Phi Kappa Phi. Office: U Calif Dept Botany and Plant Scis Riverside CA 92521

HALL, BLAINE HILL, librarian; b. Wellsville, Utah, Dec. 12, 1932; s. James Owen and Agnes Effie (Hill) H.; married, 1959; children: Suzanne, Cheryl, Derek. BS, Brigham Young U., 1960, MA, 1965, MLS, 1971. Instr. English, Brigham Young U., Provo, Utah, 1963-72, humanities librarian, 1972—; book reviewer Am. Reference Book Ann., 1984—. Author: Collection Assessment Manual, 1985, Saul Bellow Bibliography, 1987, Jerzy Kosinski Bibliography, 1991, Jewish American Fiction Writers Bibliography, 1991; editor: Utah Libraries, 1972-77 (periodical award ALA 1977); contbr. articles to profl. jours. Bd. dirs. Orem (Utah) Pub. Libr., 1977-84; mem. Orem Media Rev. Commn., 1984-86; chmn. Utah Adv. Commn. on Librs. With U.S. Army, 1953-54, Korea. Mem. ALA (coun. 1988-92), Utah Library Assn. (pres. 1980-81, Disting. Svc. award 1989), Mountain Plains Library Assn. (bd. dirs. 1978-83, editor newsletter 1978-83, pres. 1994—, grantee 1979, 80, Disting. Svc. award 1991), Phi Kappa Phi. Mormon. Home: 230 East 1910 South Orem UT 84058 Office: Brigham Young U Provo UT 84602

HALL, BRENDA DENISE, preschool special education educator; b. Twin Falls, Idaho, Nov. 21, 1955; d. Benjamin Harold and Beulah Faye (Gay) Blades; m. Ervin Earl Hall, Oct. 16, 1982; children: Chandi DeLyn, Shandra ErLyn. BA in Edn., N.W. Nazarene Coll., 1978, BA in Spl. Edn., 1980; MA in Spl. Edn., Boise State U., 1991; MA in Sch. and Cmty. Counseling, Albertson Coll. Idaho, 1994. Cert. tchr., Idaho. 3rd grade tchr. Meridian (Idaho) Primary, 1978-79; 2d grade tchr. Acequia (Idaho) Elem., 1979-80; spl. edn. tchr. Hagerman (Idaho) Elem., 1980-83, 1st grade tchr., 1985-88, chpt. I ESL tchr., 1988-94; spl. edn. tchr. Hagerman Sch. Dist., 1983-85;

presch. primary spl. edn. tchr. Wendell (Idaho) Elem., 1994—; cons. Adult-Child Devel. Ctr., Twin Falls, Hagerman Elem.; rep., v.p., pres. Magic Valley Young Authors, Twin Falls. Children Ministries leader Ch. of the Nazarene, Gooding, Idaho, 1980—; advocate for edn. young children. Recipient Idaho State Dept. of Edn. award for exceptional ednl. program for preschoolers, 1995. Mem. Nat. Assn. Edn. Young Children, Idaho Assn. Edn. Young Children, Snake River Assn. Edn. Young Children. Office: Wendell Elem PO Box 10 Wendell ID 83355-0010

HALL, CARL ALBIN, artist; b. Washington, Sept. 17, 1921; s. Walter Robert and Ella Loretta (Stant) H.; m. Phyllis Naomi Blake, July 12, 1944; children: Merrilee (dec.), Carol, Lisa, Eric. Student, Meinzinger Art Sch., Detroit, 1939-42. Assoc. prof., artist in residence Willamette U., Salem, Oreg., 1947-86. Dxhibited in group shows including Whitney Mus., N.Y., Art. Inst. of Chgo., Corcoran Gallery, Washington, Palace of the Legion of Honor, San Francisco, Carnegie Gallery, Met. Mus., Nat. Acad. N.Y., Seattle Art Mus., Phila. Mus., Bklyn. Mus., Butlar Art Inst., Denver Mus., Munson-Williams Proctor Inst., Boston Mus. Art, Wichita Art Mus., Detroit Inst. of Arts, Portland Art Mus., Cleve. State U. Art Gallery, 1994, others; permanent collections include Swope Art Gallery, Terre Haute, Ind., Boston Mus. of Fine Arts, Whitney Mus., Springfield (Mass.) Art Inst., Detroit Inst. Art, U. Tenn., Ea. Oreg. Coll., Coos Bay (Oreg.) Mus., Oreg. State U., Orchestral Hall, Detroit, Portland Art Mus., Williams Coll. Mus. Art, Wichita (Kans.) Art Mus., Oregon State Supreme Ct. Bldg., Salem, numerous pvt. collections. With U.S. Army, 1942-46. Arts and Letters grant Nat. Inst. of Arts and Letters, 1949; NEH fellowship Willamette U., 1985; recipient Excellence in the Arts award Salem Art Commn., City of Salem, 1976. Mem. Portland Art Mus. Home: 4626 Pettyjohn Rd S Salem OR 97302-9485

HALL, CARYL RONNIE, technology support analyst; b. N.Y.C., May 11, 1949; d. Jacob Sidney and Marian (Werner) Brod; m. Richard Wein, June 20, 1970 (div. 1981); m. Roger Wayne Hall, July 3, 1982; 1 stepchild, Christy. AAS, Fashion Inst. Tech., 1969; BA in Mgmt., U. Redlands, 1981. Supr. word processing Coldwell Banker Mgmt. Corp., L.A., 1973-75; sr. text processing operator Jet Propulsion Lab., Pasadena, Calif., 1975-77; office automation analyst Union Oil Co., L.A., 1977-79; supr. word processing GE, El Monte, Calif., 1979-81; supr. sales support Wang Labs., Culver City, Calif., 1981-87; sr. systems cons. Wang Labs., L.A., 1987-88; sr. mktg. specialist western ops. Wang Labs., Los Angeles, 1988-90; tng. and support specialist western region Heitman Fin. Ltd., Beverly Hills, Calif., 1990-92; tech. support analyst Times Mirror Corp., L.A., 1992—. Mem. NAFE. Club: Toastmasters (Los Angeles).

HALL, CHARLES FREDERICK, space scientist, government administrator; b. San Francisco, Apr. 7, 1920; s. Charles Rogers and Edna Mary (Gibson) H.; m. Constance Vivienne Andrews, Sept. 18, 1942; children—Steven R., Charles Frederick, Frank A. B.S., U. Calif., Berkeley, 1942. Aero. research scientist NACA (later NASA), Moffett Field, Calif., 1942-60; mem. staff space projects NACA (later NASA), 1960-63; mgr. Pioneer Project, NASA, 1963-80. Recipient Disting. Service medal NASA, 1974, Achievement award Am. Astronautical Soc., 1974, Spl. Achievement award Nat. Civil Service League, 1976, Astronautics Engr. award Nat. Space Club, 1979. Home: 817 Berry Ave Los Altos CA 94024-5416

HALL, CHARLES MCALLISTER, writer; b. Mt. View, Wyo., Nov. 27, 1930; s. Henry Vernon and Eleanor (McAllister) H.; m. Frankie Jane Taylor, Oct. 11, 1957; children: Kathy Jenine, Jonathan, Jared, James, Jeanette, Juli. BA, Brigham Young U., 1958, MA, 1960. Tchg. asst. French Brigham Young U., Provo, Utah, 1958-60; tchr. German Pasco (Wash.) H.S., 1960-63; instr. French Columbia Basin Coll., Pasco, 1963-72; tchg. asst. Russian U. Utah, Salt Lake City, 1968-69; profl. genealogist Global Rsch. Sys., Salt Lake City, 1978-82; freelance writer Salt Lake City, 1972—. Author: Atlantic Bridge to Germany, Vols. 1-9, 1974-95. With U.S. Army, 1953-55. Mem. Fedn. East European Famuly History Societies (pres. 1992—), Palatines to Am. (pres. 1975-77). Mem. LDS Ch.

HALL, CYNTHIA HOLCOMB, federal judge; b. Los Angeles, Feb. 19, 1929; d. Harold Romeyn and Mildred Gould (Kuck) Holcomb; m. John Harris Hall, June 6, 1970 (dec. Oct. 1980);. A.B., Stanford U., 1951, J.D., 1954; LL.M., NYU, 1960. Bar: Ariz. 1954, Calif. 1956. Law clk. to judge U.S. Ct. Appeals 9th Circuit, 1954-55; trial atty. tax div. Dept. Justice, 1960-64; atty.-adviser Office Tax Legis. Counsel, Treasury Dept., 1964-66; mem. firm Brawerman & Holcomb, Beverly Hills, Calif., 1966-72; judge U.S. Tax Ct., Washington, 1972-81, U.S. Dist. Ct. for central dist. Calif., Los Angeles, 1981-84; cir. judge U.S. Ct. Appeals (9th cir.), Pasadena, Calif., 1984—. Served to lt. (j.g.) USNR, 1951-53. Office: US Ct Appeals 9th Cir 125 S Grand Ave Pasadena CA 91105-1621

HALL, DAVID RAMSAY, architect; b. Lansing, Mich., Oct. 24, 1945; s. Harold Wendell and Sarah Katherine (Schlademan) H.; m. Catherine Anne Weeks, Dec. 23, 1967; children: Sarah Catherine, Rebecca Jane. BArch, Wash. State U., 1968. Registered architect, Wash. Designer, draftsman Earl Flansburgh & Assocs., Cambridge, Mass., 1968-70, NBBJ, Seattle, 1970, Mel Streeter & Assoc., Seattle, 1971-72; designer, ptnr. Henry Klein Partnership, Architects, Mt. Vernon, Wash., 1972—. Author, designer, contbr. articles to profl. publs. Commr. Dike Dist. # 19, Skagit County, Wash., 1984—; mem. adv. bd. Wash. State U., Pullman, 1990—; bd. dirs. Self Help Housing, Mt. Vernon, 1980-84. Recipient Progressive Architecture Design award, 1972, Honor award Cedar Shake & Shingle, 1991, Am. Wood Coun., 1993. Mem. AIA (bd. dirs. N.W. chpt. 1985-88, Honor award Seattle chpt. 1991, N.W. chpt. 1991, 94, Commendation award Seattle chpt. 1987). Home: 585 Farm To Market Rd Edison WA 98232 Office: Henry Klein Partnership 314 Pine St #205 Mount Vernon WA 98273

HALL, DAVID STANLEY, aerospace transportation executive; b. Oak Park, Ill., Jan. 12, 1935; s. Clifford Francis and Alice Elizabeth (Brandenburger) H.; m. Arlene Carole Denzler, June 7, 1957 (div. 1984); children: Sheridan, D. Michael, Tina; m. LaNette Vinson, July 21, 1984 (div. 1991); m. Roseann Hannon, July 31, 1992. BEE, Ill. Inst. Tech., 1957; MS, U. So. Calif., 1972. Cert. air transport pilot; registered profl. safety engr., Calif. Flight test engr. Lockheed Advanced Devel., Burbank, Calif., 1962-66; sr. flight test engr. Garrett AiResearch, Phoenix, Ariz., 1967-69, sr. product safety specialist, 1973-78; lectr. U. So. Calif., L.A., 1969-72; pres. Hall Rsch. Assocs., Phoenix, 1979-90; lectr. Ariz. State U., Tempe, 1973-86, Internat. Ctr. for Aviation Safety, Lisbon, 1986-89; cons. NASA/Goddard, Greenbelt, Md., 1979-84, Nat. Taiwan U., 1971. Contbr. numerous articles to profl. jours. Founding bd. chmn. Scottsdale (Ariz.) Christian Acad., 1968. Lt. USN, 1957-62. Mem. AIAA, SAE, Internat. Soc. Air Safety Investigators, Mensa. Home: 2111 Lido Cir Stockton CA 95207-6014

HALL, GORDON R., retired state supreme court chief justice; b. Vernal, Utah, Dec. 14, 1926; s. Roscoe Jefferson and Clara Maud (Freestone) H.; m. Doris Gillespie, Sept. 6, 1947; children: Rick Jefferson, Craig Edwin. B.S., U. Utah, 1949, LL.B., 1951. Bar: Utah 1952. Solo practice Tooele, Utah, 1952-69; county atty. Tooele County, 1958-69; judge 3d Jud. Dist. Utah, 1969-77; assoc. justice Supreme Ct. Utah, 1977-81, chief justice, 1981-94; of counsel Snow, Christensen & Martineau, Salt Lake City, 1994—; chmn. Utah Jud. Coun., 1983-94; pres. Conf. Chief Justices, 1988-89; chmn. Nat. Ctr. State Cts., 1988-89; pres. Utah Assn. Counties, 1965; mem. Pres.'s Adv. Com. OEO, 1965-66. Served with U.S. Maritime Svc., 1944-46. Mem. ABA, Utah Bar Assn. Office: Snow Christensen Martineau 11th Fl PO Box 45000 10 Exchange Pl Salt Lake City UT 84145

HALL, HAL, writer, economic, political, social and religious critic; b. Colby, Kans., June 7, 1911; s. Robert Ellsworth and Sarah (Myers) H.; m. Liane Hanft, May 23, 1947; children: Robert Eric, Alan Rae, Ronald Frederick. Student Lewis Inst., 1933-34; BA in Econs. U. Ill., 1939. Journeyman welder various shipyards, Oakland, Calif., 1941-43; with Mil. Govt., 16th Armored Div., 1943-46; journeyman carpenter, San Jose, Calif., 1946-49; house designer and builder, Calif., Colo., 1949-53; co-owner, co-operator Red Mountain Lodge, Ouray, Colo., 1953-80. Author: The Great Conflict, 1943, Even to the Last Man, 1960, The Wealth of Persons, 1968, Collectivism and Freedom, 1976, The Sleeping Dragon, 1981, rev. edit., 1986, The Road to Freedom, 1989. Supporter of equalitarian democracy. Address: PO Box 129 Ouray CO 81427-0129

HALL, HAROLD ROBERT, retired computer engineer; b. Bakersfield, Calif., Feb. 7, 1935; s. Edward Earl and Ethel Mae (Butner) H.; m. Tenniebee May Hall, Feb. 20, 1965. BS, U. Calif., Berkeley, 1956, MS, 1957, PhD, 1966. Chief engr. wave-filter div. Transonic, Inc., Bakersfield, 1957-60; chief design engr. Circuit Dyne Corp., Pasadena and Laguna Beach, Calif., 1960-61; sr. devel. engr. Robertshaw Controls Co., Anaheim, Calif., 1961-63; research engr. Naval Command, Control and Ocean Surveillance Ctr., rsch. and devel. divsn. Navy Research Lab., San Diego, 1966-95; bd. dirs. Circuit Dyne Corp., Pacific Coil Co. Recipient Thomas Clair McFarland award U. Calif., Berkeley, 1956, NSF fellow, 1957. Mem. IEEE, Acoustical Soc. Am., Phi Beta Kappa. Home: 5284 Dawes St San Diego CA 92109-1231 Office: Naval Command Control & Ocean Surveillance Ctr Rsch & Devel Divsn San Diego CA 92152-5352

HALL, HOWARD PICKERING, engineering and mathematics educator; b. Boston, July 8, 1915; s. George Henry and Elizabeth Isabel (McCallum) H.; m. Ellen Marguerite Ide, June 25, 1945 (dec. 1984); children: Charlotte McCallum, Stephanie Wilson, Lindsey Louise, Gretchen Elizabeth. AB, Harvard U., 1936, MS, 1937, DSc, 1951. Registered structural engr., Ill., 1953. Instr., civil engring. Brown U., Providence, 1937-38; structural analyst Mark Linenthal, Engr., Boston, 1938-39; instr., asst. prof., assoc. prof. civil engring. Northwestern U., Evanston, Ill., 1939-56; design engr, field engr. Porter, Urquart, Skidmore, Owings, Merrill, Casablanca, Fr. Morocco, 1951-53; dean, sch. engring., acad. v.p. Robert Coll., Istanbul, Turkey, 1956-68; dir. of studies, acting headmaster St. Stephen's Sch., Rome, 1968-72; prof. math. Iranzamin Internat., Tehran, Iran, 1973-80; math. tchr. Vienna Internat. Sch., 1980-83, Copenhagen Internat. Sch., 1983-86; cons. S.J. Buchanan, Bryan, Tex., Eng., 1955. Contbr. articles to profl. jours. Served to Capt. U.S. Army, 1942-46, ETO. Recipient Clemens Herschel award Boston Soc. Civil Engrs., 1954. Mem. Sigma Xi. Home: 301 SW Lincoln St Apt 1101 Portland OR 97201-5031

HALL, JEAN ANN, veterinarian, educator; b. Roseburg, Oreg., July 26, 1957; d. Robert A. and Eleanor Carol (Barter) H.; m. Stephen F. Callahan, Aug. 13, 1988; children: Ty, Clay, Travis. BS, Oreg. State U., 1981; DVM summa cum laude, Wash. State U., 1982; MS, Colo. State U., 1987, PhD, 1989. Diplomate Am. Coll. Vet. Internal Medicine; lic. vet. Oreg., Wash., Mass. Intern Angell Meml. Animal Hosp., Boston, 1982-83; clinician in medicine and surgery Brookline Animal Hosp., Boston, 1983-84; resident in small animal internal medicine Colo. State U., Ft. Collins, 1984-87; postdoctoral fellow Oreg. Health Scis. U., Portland, 1989-90; asst. prof. vet. medicine Oreg. State U., Corvallis, 1990—; lectr., cons., and presenter in field. Contbr. chpts. to books and articles and abstracts to profl. jours. Recipient Travel award Fedn. Am. Socs. Exptl. Biology, 1987; grantee Ralston-Purina Co., 1991, faculty Oreg. State U., 1993, IAMS Co., 1994, Mark Morris Inst., 1994. Mem. AVMA, Am. Motility Soc. (Travel award 1986, 88), Am. Animal Hosp. Assn., Oreg. Vet. Med. Assn., Comparative Gastroenterology Soc., Phi Kappa Phi, Alpha Psi, Phi Zeta. Home: 560 SW Lookout Dr Corvallis OR 97333-4032 Office: Oreg State U Coll Vet Medicine Magruder Hall 105 Corvallis OR 97331-4802

HALL, JILL, composition and literature educator; b. Denver, Apr. 24, 1959; d. David Michael and Alice Jean (Powell) H. BA, U. Colo., 1981, BS, 1981, MA, 1985; PhD, U. So. Calif., 1993. Discussion leader U. Colo., Boulder, 1983-84, teaching asst., 1984-85; asst. lectr., writing tutor U. So. Calif., L.A., 1986-92; lectr. composition and lit. Oxnard (Calif.) Coll., 1993—; conf. moderator Far West Popular Culture Assn., Las Vegas, Nev., 1991. Author: (with others) Dictionary of British Literary Characters, 1993; editor, manuscript reviewer jour. The Writing Instr., 1988-92; contbr. articles to profl. jours. Mem. MLA, Calif. Am. Studies Assn., Far West Popular Culture Assn., Mark Twain Cir. Democrat.

HALL, JOSEPHINE WEISSMAN, obstetrician/gynecologist; b. N.Y.C., Dec. 29, 1937; d. Jacob Eliah and Sonia Hall; m. Jearld Wayne Hall, June 20, 1971; children: Michael, Gillian, James, Jesse, Cameron. BA, Swarthmore Coll., 1959; MD, Chgo. Med. Sch., 1963. Diplomate Am. Bd. Ob-gyn. Resident Albert Einstein Coll. Medicine, N.Y.C., 1964-68; pvt. practice Washington, 1968-69; with Mound Bayou (Miss.) Cmty. Hosp., 1969-70; ob-gyn. Ross Coos Med. Group, L.A., 1970-71; instr. dept. Ob-gyn. U. So. Calif. Coll. Medicine, L.A., 1972-73; clin. prof. ob.-gyn. U. So. Calif., L.A., 1989—; pvt. practice L.A., 1973—; bd. dirs. alumni bd. govs. Chgo. Med. Sch. mem. Glendale (Calif.) Nat. Charity League. Recipient Disting. Alumnus award The Chgo. Med. Sch., 1988. Fellow Am. Bd. Ob-gyn. Office: 1910 W Glenoaks Blvd Glendale CA 91201-1616

HALL, JULIA FRANCES, psychologist; b. Reno, May 14, 1944; d. Ross Moore and Helen May (McCormick) H. BS, U. Oreg., 1968; MS, Portland State U., 1970; PhD, Calif. Sch. Profl. Psychology, 1977. Lic. psychologist, Oreg., Calif. Psychologist Beaverton, Oreg., 1980-94, Marion County Mental Health, Salem, Oreg., 1994—; with employee assistance program Manful Curtis Engring., Beaverton, 1992-94. Bd. dirs. Metro Crisis, Portland, 1981-83; vol. therapist Cascade AIDS Project, Portland, 1986—. Mem. APA, Western Psychol. Assn., Oreg. Psychol. Assn. (ethics com.), Portland Psychol. Assn. Democrat. Office: 4320 SW 110th Ave Beaverton OR 97005-3009

HALL, JULIE JANE, community health nurse, administrator; b. Berkeley, Calif., Jan. 14, 1951; d. Dale Oliver and Patricia Martha (Krone) Hall; m. Norman Charles Weinstein, Mar. 22, 1986. ADN, Boise State U., 1980, BS, 1983. Cert. community health nurse. Staff nurse St. Luke's Regional Med. Ctr., Boise, Idaho, 1980-84; hospice nurse Mountain States Tumor Insts., Boise, 1983-84; staff devel. coord. Hillcrest Care Ctr., Boise, 1986-87; asst. mgr. St. Alphonsus Home Health, Boise, 1990-95; dir. prevention and community care St. Alphonsus Regional Med. Ctr., Boise, 1995—, dir. prevention and cmty. care. Mem. APHA, Idaho Hosp. Assn. Home Care Soc. (pres. 1993-94), Leadership Boise (v.p. 1994-95), Idaho Orgn. Nurse Execs., Idaho Nurses Assn., Sigma Theta Tau.

HALL, LARRY D., energy company executive, lawyer; b. Hastings, Nebr., Nov. 8, 1942; s. Willis E. and Stella W. (Eckoff) H.; m. Jeffe D. Bryant, July 5, 1985; children: Scott, Jeff, Mike, Bryan. BA in Bus., U. Nebr., Kearney; JD, U. Nebr. Bar: Nebr., Colo. Ptnr. Wright, Simmons, Hancock & Hall, Scottsbluff, Nebr., 1967-71; atty., asst. treas. KN Energy Inc., Hastings, 1971-73, dir. regulatory affairs, 1973-76; v.p. law divsn. KN Energy Inc., Lakewood, Colo., 1976-82, sr. v.p., 1982-85, exec. v.p., 1985-88, pres., COO, 1988-94, pres., CEO, 1994—, also bd. dirs., 1988-94, pres., CEO, 1994—, 1994—; bd. dirs. Colo. Assn. Commerce and Industry, Gas Rsch. Inst., Colo. Alliance for Bus., MLA, Rocky Mountain Oil and Gas Assn. Mem. ABA, Fed. Energy Bar Assn., Nebr. Bar Assn., Colo. Bar Assn., Pres. Assn., Midwest Gas Assn. (chmn.), INGAA, MGA, CAB (bd. dirs.), Hiwan Country Club, Elks, Club 30. Presbyterian. Home: 1892 Sugarbush Dr Evergreen CO 80439 Office: KN Energy Inc PO Box 15265 Lakewood CO 80215

HALL, LAWRENCE JOHN, physics educator; b. Perivale, U.K., Sept. 9, 1955; came to U.S., 1977; s. Kenneth and Patricia Kathleen (Stock) H.; m. Paula Louise Petti, June 27, 1982; children: Geoffrey Kenneth, David Lawrence. BA, Oxford U., Eng., 1977; MA, Harvard U., 1978, PhD, 1981. Miller fellow U. Calif., Berkeley, 1981-83, from asst. prof. to prof. physics, 1986—; from asst. to assoc. prof. Harvard U., Cambridge, Mass., 1983-86; mem. physics adv. com. Fermilab, Chgo., 1991—. Contbr. over 110 articles in rsch. jours. Recipient Presdl. Young Investigator award NSF, 1987-92. Fellow Am. Phys. Soc. Office: Univ of Calif Dept Physics Berkeley CA 94720

HALL, LOIS RIGGS, former state senator, former symphony orchestra administrator; b. Beeville, Tex., May 22, 1930; d. Ira Franklin and Pearl Ophelia (McCoy) Riggs; m. Walter William Hall, Dec. 28, 1950 (dec.); children: Robert Macfarlane, Elaine Denise, Judith Lea. Student, Tex. Women's U., 1947-49, U. Tex., Austin, 1949-50. Exec. sec. N.Mex. Symphony Orch., Albuquerque, 1975-93; mem. N.Mex. Senate, 1980-85, ret. . Active Boy Scouts Am., Girl Scouts U.S.A., Officers Wives Clubs; 2d v.p. Albuquerque Symphony Women's Assn.; bd. dirs. Friends of Music, 1986-88; treas., publicity dir. N.Mex. Aviation Assn. Republican. Home: 620 Ortiz Dr NE Albuquerque NM 87108-1447

HALL, MADELYN GAEL PRIEBE, medical librarian; b. Seattle, May 4, 1951; d. Thomas Taylor and Donna Marie (Moore) Priebe; m. Dennis Earl Hall, Sept. 30, 1972; children: Christopher, Kilmeny. BA in Elem. Edn., Western Wash. U., 1973; MEd in Early Childhood Edn., Columbus (Ga.) Coll., 1984; cert. program in libr. mgmt., U. Wash., 1991. Libr. asst. Whatcom County Libr. System, Bellingham, Wash., 1973-75; substitute tchr., Raymond, Wash., 1976-77; gen. clk. libr. br. U.S. Army Recreation Svcs., Ft. Polk, La., 1977-78; libr. technician U.S. Army Recreation Svcs., Aschaffenburg, Germany, 1979-81; acad. coord., head tchr. basic skills edn. program U.S. Army, Ft. Benning, Ga., 1982-85; libr. Merrill Reeh Ophthalmology Libr., Good Samaritan Hosp. and Med. Ctr., Portland, Oreg., 1985-92, dir. librs., 1992-94; med. libr. S.W. Wash. Med. Ctr. Libr., Vancouver, 1994—; presenter in field; rep. regional adv. com. from Oreg. to Regional Med. Libr., Nat. Library Medicine, 1994-96. Author: Pediatric Ophthalmology Consumer Resource File, 1988, 3d edit., 1993. Mem. Med. Libr. Assn. (chmn. registration and hospitality Pacific N.W. chpt. 1993), Oreg. Health Scis. Libr. Assn. (sec. 1993), Assn. Visual Sci. Librs. (sec. 1990-91, chmn. 1992-93), Wash. Med. Libr. Assn., Portland Area Health Scis. Librs., Kappa Delta Pi. Democrat. Episcopalian. Office: SW Wash Med Ctr Libr Svcs 400 NE Mother Joseph Pl PO Box 1600 Vancouver WA 98668

HALL, MARIAN ELLA See ROBERTSON, MARIAN ELLA

HALL, MARK EDWARD, archaeologist; b. Louisville, Sept. 4, 1960; s. David B. and Judy A. (Wallace) H. BS in Engring., U. Ky., 1982; MS in Engring., U. Calif., Berkeley, 1985, MA in Anthropology, 1986, PhD in Anthropology, 1992. Teaching asst. dept. anthropology U. Calif., Berkeley, 1987-92, lectr. extension program, 1992—, researcher Archaeol. Rsch. Facility, 1993—; project engr. Pyromet Industries, San Carlos, Calif., 1990-93. Contbr. articles to profl. publs. Office: Archaeol Rsch Facility Kroeber Hall Berkeley CA 94720

HALL, PHILIP G., engineering executive; b. 1941. BS in Civil Engring., U. Mich., 1963, MS in Civil Sanitary Engring., 1966. With Peace Corps., 1963-64; with CH2M Hill, Inc., 1966-87, ctrl. dist. mgr., 1987-90, vice chmn. bd., 1990-93, chmn. bd., 1993—. Office: CH2M Hill Cos Ltd 4565 SW Research Way Corvallis OR 97333-1063*

HALL, RICHARD DENNIS, agribusiness and international trade writer; b. Troy, N.Y., Apr. 12, 1935; s. Dennis John and Clara Eleanor (Hanson) H.; m. Joyce Ann Huntington, June 7, 1957; children: Brian Huntington, Roger Hanson. BS, Boston U., 1957. Gen. assignment reporter Worcester (Mass.) Telegram and the Evening Gazette, 1957-60; city hall reporter, columnist Springfield (Mass.) Union, 1960-65; reporter Fresno (Calif.) Bee, 1965-77, agr. water reporter, 1977-79; Washington corr. McClatchy Newspapers, 1979-83; agribus. writer Fresno (Calif.) Bee, 1983-91, ret., 1991; mem. 9th Ann. Conf. European and Am. Journalists, Maastricht, The Netherlands, 1985. Author: Fresno County in the 20th Century, 1987, Hanford Hometown America, 1990; contbg. editor Calif. Farmer mag., 1986—. Docent local history tours, Hanford, Calif., 1987. Recipient Agribus. Invitation award, Taiwan, 1983. Home and Office: 1978 Mulberry Dr Hanford CA 93230-2046

HALL, ROBERT EMMETT, JR., investment banker, realtor; b. Sioux City, Iowa, Apr. 28, 1936; s. Robert Emmett and Alvina (Faden) H.; m. Marna Thiel, 1969. BA, U. S.D., 1958, MA, 1959; MBA, U. Santa Clara, 1976; grad. Am. Inst. Banking, Realtors Inst. Grad. asst. U. S.D., Vermillion, 1958-59; mgr. ins. dept., asst. mgr. installment loan dept. Northwestern Nat. Bank of Sioux Falls, S.D., 1959-61, asst. cashier, 1961-65; asst. mgr. Crocker Nat. Bank, San Francisco, 1965-67, loan officer, 1967-69, asst. v.p., asst. mgr. San Mateo br., 1969-72; v.p., Western regional mgr. Internat. Investments & Realty, Inc., Washington, 1972—; owner Hall Investment Co., 1976—; pres. Almaden Oaks Realtors, Inc., 1976—; instr. West Valley Coll., Saratoga, Calif., 1972-82, Grad. Sch. Bus., U. Santa Clara (Calif.), 1981—. Treas., Minnehaha Leukemia Soc., 1963, Lake County Heart Fund Assn., 1962, Minnehaha Young Republican Club, 1963. Mem. Am. Inst. Banking, San Mateo C. of C., Calif. Assn. Realtors (vice chmn.), Beta Theta Pi. Republican. Roman Catholic. Clubs: Elks, Rotary (past pres.), K.C., Almaden Country, Mercedes Benz Calif. Home: 6951 Castlerock Dr San Jose CA 95120-4705 also: PO Box 458 Tahoma CA 96142 also: 8864 Rubicon Dr Rubicon Bay CA 96142 Office: Hall Enterprises 6501 Crown Blvd Ste 106 San Jose CA 95120-2903

HALL, SHAWN RICHARD, museum director; b. Southington, Conn., Feb. 8, 1960; s. Albert William and Lorraine Louise (Lorey) H.; m. Debora Marie McEachin, Apr. 11, 1992; 1 child, Heather Ashley. BA, Harvard U., 1983; MA, Calif. State U., 1994. Social worker Rite of Passage, Schurz, Nev., 1986-89; asst. curator of history Nev. State Mus., Carson City, Nev., 1989-90; asst. dir. Northeastern Nev. Mus., Elko, Nev., 1991-94, dir., 1994—; sec. Northeastern Nev. Cultural Commn., 1994—. Author: Guide to the Ghost Towns and Mining Camps, 1981, The Western Public Lands: A Growing Crisis, 1986, Romancing the Nevada's Past, 1993. Mem. Am. Assn. Mus., Nev. Mus. Assn. (sec. 1993-95), Desert Sunrise Rotary (newsletter editor 1992-95, pres.-elect 1995). Office: Northeastern Nev Mus 1515 Idaho St Elko NV 89801

HALL, TENNIEBEE M., editor; b. Bakersfield, Calif., May 21, 1940; d. William Elmer and Lillian May (Otis) Hall; m. Harold Robert Hall, Feb. 20, 1965. BA in Edn., Fresno State Coll., 1962; AA, Bakersfield Coll., 1960. Cert. tchr., Calif. Tchr. Edison (Calif.) Sch. Dist., 1962-65; substitute tchr. Marin and Oakland Counties (Calif.), Berkeley, 1965-66; engring. asst. Pacific Coil Co., Inc., Bakersfield, 1974-81; editor United Ostomy Assn., Inc., Irvine, Calif., 1986-91. Co-author: Treating IBD, 1989, Current Therapy in Gastroenterology, 1989; author, designer: Volunteer Leadership Training Manuals, 1982-84; contbr. articles to Ostomy Quar., 1973—. Mem. Pacific Beach Town Coun., San Diego, 1977—; campaign worker Maureen O'Connor (1st woman mayor of city), San Diego, 1986; mem. Nat. Digestive Diseases Adv. Bd., NIH, Washington, 1986-91; mem. planning and devel. bd. Scripps Clinic and Rsch. Found. Inflammatory Bowel Disease Ctr., San Diego, 1993—; various vol. activities, 1966-74, 81-86. Recipient Outstanding Svc. award VA Vol. Svc., Bur. of Vets. Affairs, Washington, 1990. Mem. Nat. Assn. Parliamentarians, United Ostomy Assn. Inc. (regional program dir. 1980-84, pres. 1984-86, Sam Dubin award 1983, Industry Adv. award 1987), Crohn's and Colitis Found. Am. (nat. trustee 1986—, nat. v.p. 1987-92). Home and Office: 5284 Dawes St San Diego CA 92109-1231

HALL, WILLIAM E., engineering and construction company executive; b. Washington, Sept. 5, 1942; s. George W. and Jane F. (Brogger) H.; m. Lavinia Swift, Sept. 21, 1974; children: Deborah A., Douglas E., L. Jane, Elizabeth D. BSChemE, Va. Poly. Inst. and State U., 1963, MSChemE, 1964; postgrad., Stanford U., 1991. Process engr. Stone & Webster Engring. Co., Boston, 1967-70; project mgr. Stone & Webster Engring. Co., London, 1970-76, N.Y.C., 1976-78; regional bus. devel. mgr. Stone & Webster Engring. Co., Houston, 1978-79; prin. project mgr. RM Parsons Co., Pasadena, Calif., 1979-81, sr. v.p., 1989-92; pres. Ralph M. Parsons Co., Pasadena, Calif., 1992—; prin. project mgr. Saudi Arabia Parsons Ltd., Yanbu, 1981-84, mng. dir., 1984-89; bd. dirs. Proye Parsons, Caracas, Venezuela, Latisa; alt. dir. Constrn. Industry Inst., Austin, Tex., 1990-92, dir. 1992—. CHmn. Tournament of Life, Pasadena, 1990-92. Mem. Am. Inst. Chem. Engrs. Republican. Lutheran. Office: Ralph M Parsons Co 100 W Walnut St Pasadena CA 91124*

HALLAM, ROBERT J., performing company executive, consultant; b. Edmonton, Alta., Can., Oct. 24, 1952; s. Donald Robert and Mary (Dutton) H.; m. Sydney Ann Scott, Oct. 5, 1984; 1 child, Robert Ian. MusB, U. Alta., 1976, MBA, 1983. Adminstrv. mgr. Edmonton Opera, 1983-85, gen. mgr., 1985-89, gen. dir., 1989-91; gen. dir. Vancouver (B.C.) Opera, Can., 1991—; dir. Opera Am., Washington, 1987-93, treas., 1990—; bd. dirs., vice chmn. Vancouver Cultural Alliance, 1994—. Office: Vancouver Opera, 845 Cambie St Ste 500, Vancouver, BC Canada V6B 4Z9

HALLENBECK, HARRY C., architect. Architect State of Calif., Sacramento. Recipient Edward C. Kemper award Archtl. Inst. Am., 1994. Office: Divsn of the State Arch Gen Svcs Divsn 400 P St Fl 5 Sacramento CA 95814-5345 also: 7485 Rush River Dr # 333 Sacramento CA 95831-5259

HALLENBECK, POMONA JUANITA, artist; b. Roswell, N.Mex., Nov. 12, 1938; d. Cleve and Juanita Henriette (Williams) H.; children: Cheryl Ellis, Cynthia Ellis-Ralph, Catherine Ellis-Timmons. AA, Ea. N.Mex. U., 1965; BFA, Art Student's League, 1976; postgrad., Pan Am. Art Sch., 1976-77. Mgr. Paul Anderson Photography, San Antonio, Tex., 1951-54; tchr. Roswell (N.Mex.) Ind. Sch. Dist., 1960-64; dir., instr. Sketchbox Sch. Art, Galveston, Tex., 1965-71; monitor etching class Art Student's League, N.Y.C., 1975-77; dir., instr. Alleyworks Atlier, Austin, Tex., 1978-81; dir., proprietor, artist Sketchbox Studio, Roswell, 1982-94; instr. Elderhostel program Ghost Ranch, Abiquiu, N.Mex, 1984-94; coord. Calender project Ghost Ranch, Abiquiu, N.Mex., 1992—; owner, proprietor Pomona's Accent Line, Roswell, 1986-94, cons., 1988-94; artist, demonstrator Roswell (N.Mex.) Mus. and Art Ctr., 1981-90, Roswell (N.Mex.) Ind. Sch., 1982-90. Illustrator: (book covers) Julian of Norwich, Nachman, Pseudo Dionysius, Classics of Western Spirituality, Naming the Powers, Unmasking the Powers, Engaging the Powers, Ghost Ranch Cookbook; exhibited in Southwest Expressions Gallery, Chgo., 1990, 91, Claire's Mountain Village, Ruidoso, N.Mex., 1990-94, Roswell Fine Art Mus., 1994, Artisan Gallery, Austin, 1995, Blaire Carnehan Fine Art, San Antonio, 1995, Ramsey House Gallery, Cissimaron, N.Mex., 1995, Trading Post, 1995. Mem. Roswell Assurance Home for Children, 1990, Ghost Ranch Compadres, Santa Fe, 1990-94, People for the Ethical Treatment of Animals, 1994; arts convener silent auction, Ghost Ranch, 1995. Recipient scholarship Altrusa Club, 1973, Purchase award Am. Artist, N.Y.C., 1975; named best of show Ghost Ranch Compadre show, N.Mex., 1990, Altusa Fashion Show, N.Mex., 1990; grantee Whitney Enterprises, San Diego, 1990, artist-in-residence grantee Ghost Ranch, Santa Fe, 1992. Mem. AAUW, Internat. Platform Assn., Nat. Platform Assn., Soc. Illustrators, Taos Fine Arts Assn., N.Mex. Watercolor Soc., Western Colo. Watercolor Soc., Supts. Salon of Paris (Bronze medal 1988), Ghost Ranch Found. Ctr., Roswell Mus. and Art Ctr., U.S. Humane Soc., Roswell (N.Mex.) Humane Soc. Democrat. Presbyterian. Office: Sketchbox Studio of Art 3737 EGP Rd Roswell NM 88201

HALLER, EUGENE ERNEST, materials scientist, educator; b. Basel, Switzerland, Jan. 5, 1943; s. Eugen and Maria Anne Haller; m. Marianne Elisabeth Schlittler, May 27, 1973; children: Nicole Marianne, Isabelle Cathrine. Diploma in Physics, U. Basel, 1967, PhD in Physics, 1970. Postdoctoral asst. Lawrence Berkeley (Calif.) Lab., 1971-73, staff scientist, then sr. staff scientist, 1973-80, faculty sr. scientist, 1980—; assoc. prof. U. Calif., Berkeley, 1980-82, prof. materials sci., 1982—; co-chmn. Materials Rsch. Soc. Symposia, Boston, 1982, 89, Internat. Conf. on Shallow Levels in Semiconductors, Berkeley, 1984, 94; rev. com. instrument div. Brookhaven Nat. Lab., Upton, N.Y., 1987-93; mem. Japanese tech. panel on sensors NSF-Nat. Acad. Sci., Washington, 1988; vis. prof. Imperial Coll. Sci., Tech. and Medicine, London, 1991. Editorial adv. bd. Jour. Phys. and Chem. Solids, 1993—; contbr. to numerous profl. publs. U.S. Sr. scientist award Alexander von Humboldt Soc., Germany, 1986, Max-Planck Rsch. award, 1994; rsch. fellow Miller Inst. Basic Rsch., Berkeley, 1990. Fellow Am. Phys. Soc.; mem. AAAS, Materials Rsch. Soc., Swiss Phys. Soc., Sigma Xi. Office: U Calif Berkeley 553 Evans Hall Berkeley CA 94720

HALLETT, JANE MARTIN, writer, educator; b. Belleville, Ill., May 9, 1933; d. Cecil Lawrence and Clara Harriet (Haskins) M.; m. Christian E. Heiligenstein, Aug. 29, 1953 (div.); children: Eric Lee Heiligenstein, Lynn Heiligenstein Caffrey. BA, U. Ill., 1955; MA, Ill. State U., 1984. Mgr. Spanish Internat. Tourist Office, St. Louis, 1968-70; promotional dir. Northwoods Mall, Peoria, Ill., 1971-73; tour leader Fine Arts Soc. and Peoria Art Guild, 1982-85; arts coord. Meth. Med. Ctr., Peoria, 1984-85; mus. educator U. Okla. Mus. Art, Norman, 1985-87; freelance writer, reporter Peoria Observer, WCBU, WHOI-TV, Peoria, The Pantagraph, Bloomington, Ill., New Art Examiner, Chgo., 1974-79; guest curator Laumeier Sculpture Park, St. Louis, 1983; mus. rep. Okla. Art Edn. Assn., Oklahoma City, 1985-87; mem. Okla. Alliance for Art Edn., Oklahoma City, 1985-87; grants com. Tucson/Pima Arts Coun., Tucson, 1991-93. Co-author children's activity book series, 1988—. Co-chair Pub. Arts Com. of Peoria City Beautiful, 1975-78; mem. Pub. Art and Cmty. Design Com., Tucson, 1991—. Multi-cultural heritage grantee Tucson/Pima Arts Coun., 1992, 93. Mem. Internat. Sculpture Ctr., Am. Assn. Museums, Pub. Rels. Soc. Am., Spanish Colonial Arts Soc., Assocs. Art History U. Ariz. (cmty. bd.). Office: PO Box 64216 Tucson AZ 85728-4216

HALL-HACKLEY, CAROL ANN, public relations educator, consultant; b. Sacramento, Mar. 20, 1940; d. Charles Peter and Alice Marian (Schmidt) Cusick; m. William E. Hall, Sept. 1, 1966 (dec. Aug. 1991); children: Kevin Dennis, Kimberlee Marian Hall Floyd; m. T. Cole Hackley, Apr. 10, 1993. BA, Calif. State U., Sacramento, 1961; MA, Ohio State U., 1984, PhD, 1985; D, . Pub. rels. dir., tchr. Lincoln Unified Schs., Stockton, Calif., 1961-63; advt. promotion copy writer, columnist Honolulu (Hawaii) Star-Bulletin, Hawaii Newspaper Agy., 1964; instr. U. Nebr., Lincoln, 1964-66, Ohio State U., Columbus, 1972-80, 82-85; exec. dir. Jour. Assn. Ohio Schs., Columbus, 1974-80, 82-85; asst. prof. U. Hawaii, Honolulu, 1980-82; assoc. prof. pub. rels. comm. dept. U. Pacific, Stockton, 1985—, chair comm. dept., 1992-94; pub. rels. cons. Hall and Hall Prescriptive Pub. Rels., Stockton, 1987-91; prof.-in-residence Edelman Pub. Rels. Worldwide, Sydney, London and San Francisco, 1990—. Chmn. bd. Mountain Valley Multiple Sclerosis, Stockton, 1989-91. em. Pub. Rels. Soc. Am. (accredited, mem. internat. sect., internat. pub. rels. exec. com. 1995, v.p. Oakland/ East Bay chpt. 1994, del. nat. assembly 1995), Internat. Comm. Assn. Home: 2618 Sheridan Way Stockton CA 95207-3246 Office: Univ of the Pacific 3601 Pacific Cir Stockton CA 95211-0110

HALLICK, RICHARD BRUCE, biochemistry educator; b. Glendale, Calif., Jan. 15, 1946; s. John and Rosa Elizabeth (Coates) H.; m. Margaret Ann Thomas West, Feb. 14, 1989; 1 child, Deborah Hallick Mundorf. BA, Pomona Coll., 1967; PhD, U. Wis., 1971. Postdoctoral rsch. assoc. U. Calif., San Francisco, 1971-73; asst. prof. U. Colo., Boulder, 1973-79, assoc. prof., 1980-83, prof., 1983-84; prof. biochemistry U. Ariz., Tucson, 1984—; vis. scientist Weizmann Inst. Sci., Rehovot, Israel, 1982; cons. Agrigenetics, Boulder, 1981-87; expert witness on DNA evidence, U.S. Dist. Ct., Pima, Cochise, Maricopa Counties, 1992—, in dist. and superior cts., Phoenix, Albbuquerque, 1992—; faculty senator U. Ariz., 1994-96. Exec. editor: Nucleic Acids Rsch. jour., 1989—. Rsch. grantee NIH, 1993-97. Mem. AAAS, Am. Soc. Biol. Chemists, Internat. Soc. Plant Molecular Biologists, Am. Soc. Biochemists and Molecular Biologists, Am. Soc. Plant Physiologists. Episcopalian. Office: Univ Ariz Biosciences West 524 Tucson AZ 85721

HALLIDAY, JOHN MEECH, investment company executive; b. St. Louis, Oct. 16, 1936; s. William Norman and Vivian Viola (Meech) H.; m. Martha Layne Griggs, June 30, 1962; children: Richard M., Elizabeth Halliday Traut. BS, U.S. Naval Acad., 1958; MBA, Harvard U., 1964. Dir. budgeting and planning Automatic Tape Control, Bloomington, Ill., 1964-66; dir. planning Ralston-Purina, St. Louis, 1966-67, v.p. subsidiary, 1967-68, dir. internat. banking, 1967-68; v.p. Servicetime Corp., St. Louis, 1968-70; assoc. R.W. Halliday Assocs., Boise, Idaho, 1970-87; v.p. Sawtooth Comm. Corp., Boise, 1970-73, Comdr. Corp., 1979-81; pres., CEO, bd. dirs. ML Ltd., San Francisco, 1979—, H.W.L. Inc., San Francisco, 1985-93; pres. Halliday Labs., Inc., 1980-91; exec. v.p., bd. dirs. Franchise Fin. Corp. Am., Phoenix, 1980-85; bd. dirs., v.p. Harvard Bus. Sch. Assn. No. Calif., 1980-87; bd. dirs. FFAC, Irvine, Calif., 1989-92; pres., CEO, bd. dirs. Cycletrol Diversified Industries, Inc., 1992—; guest lectr. U. Calif. Berkeley, 1991—. Pres. Big Bros. San Francisco, 1978-81; trustee, pres. U. Calif.-Santa Cruz Found., 1988—. Lt. comdr. USNR, 1958-66. Mem. Restaurant Assn. (v.p. 1969-70), Olympic Club (San Francisco), Scott Valley Tennis Club (Mill Valley, Calif.). Republican. Episcopalian. Home: 351 Corte Madera Ave Mill Valley CA 94941-1013 Office: 625 Market St Ste 602 San Francisco CA 94105-3308

HALLIDAY, WILLIAM ROSS, retired physician, speleologist, writer; b. Atlanta, May 9, 1926; s. William Ross and Jane (Wakefield) H.; m. Eleanore Hartvedt, July 2, 1951 (dec. 1983); children: Marcia Lynn, Patricia Anne, William Ross III; m. Louise Baird Kinnard, May 7, 1988. BA, Swarthmore Coll., 1946; MD, George Washington U., 1948. Diplomate Am. Bd. Vocat. Experts. Intern Huntington Meml. Hosp., Pasadena, Calif., 1948-49; resident King County Hosp., Seattle, Denver Children's Hosp., L.D.S. Hosp., Salt Lake City, 1950-57; pvt. practice Seattle, 1957-65; with Wash. State Dept. Labor and Industries, Olympia, 1965-76; med. dir. Wash. State Div. Vocat. Rehab., 1976-82; staff physican N.W. Occupational Health Ctr., Seattle, 1983-84; med. dir. N.W. Vocat. Rehab. Group, Seattle, 1984, Comprehensive Med. Rehab. Ctr., Brentwood, Tenn., 1984-87; dep. coroner, King County, Wash., 1964-66. Author: Adventure Is Underground, 1959, Depths of the Earth, 1966, 76, American Caves and Caving, 1974, 82; co-author: (with Robert Nymeyer) Carlsbad Cavern: The Early Years, 1991; editor Jour. Spelean History, 1968-73; contbr. articles to profl. jours. Mem. Gov.'s North Cascades Study Com., 1967-76; mem. North Cascades Conservation Coun., v.p., 1962-63; pres. Internat. Speleological Found., 1981-87; asst. dir. Internat. Glaciospeleological Survey, 1972-76. Served to lt. comdr. USNR, 1949-50, 55-57. Recipient medal Geol. Soc. China; named Alumnus of Yr., George Sch., 1992. Fellow Am. Coll. Chest Physicians, Nat. Speleological Soc. (bd. govs. 1988-94, chmn. Hawaii Speleological Survey 1989—, chmn. Internat. Symposia on Vulcanospeleology, chmn. Internat. Union Speleology Commn. on Volcanic Caves 1990—), We. Speleological Survey (dir. 1957-83, dir. rsch. 1983—), Explorers Club; mem. AMA, Soc. Thoracic Surgeons, Wash. State Med. Assn., Tenn. State Med. Assn., King County Med. Soc., Am. Fedn. Clin. Rsch., Am. Spelean History Assn. (pres. 1968), Brit. Cave Rsch. Assn., Nat. Trust (Scotland), Mountaineers Club (past trustee), Seattle Tennis Club.

HALLIN, KARL-ELIV JOHANN, industrial process control company executive; b. Stockholm, Sweden, Apr. 14, 1951; s. Emil Lennart Teodor and Liv Anna (Skogvang) H. BS, U. Alberta, Edmonton, Alberta, Can., 1973; PhD in Chemistry/Spectroscopy, U. B.C., Vancouver, B.C., Can., 1977. Rsch. assoc. Nat. Rsch. Coun./Herzberg Inst. of Astrophysics, Ottawa, Ont., Can., 1978-79; engr. Sentrol Systems Ltd., Downsview, Ont., Can., 1979-82; prin. scientist Valmet Sentrol, Downsview, 1982-89; sr. scientist Devron Hercules, Inc., North Vancouver, B.C., Can., 1989-92; sr. staff scientist Measurex Corp., Cupertino, Calif., 1992—. Recipient Sci. scholarship Nat. Rsch. Coun. Can., U. B.C., 1973-77. Mem. Instrument Soc. of Am., IEEE. Office: Measurex Corp One Results Way M/S 5244 Cupertino CA 95014-5991

HALLOCK, C. WILES, JR., athletic official; b. Denver, Feb. 17, 1918; s. Claude Wiles and Mary (Bassler) H.; m. Marjorie Louise Eldred, Mar. 23, 1944; children: Lucinda Eldred Hallock Rinne, Michael Eldred. A.B., U. Denver, 1939. Sports info. dir. U. Wyo., 1949-60, track coach, 1952-56; sports info. dir. U. Calif., Berkeley, 1960-63; dir. pub. relations Nat. Collegiate Athletic Assn., 1963-68; dir. Nat. Collegiate Sports Services, 1967-68; commr. Western Athletic Conf., 1968-71; exec. dir. Pacific-8 Conf. (now Pacific-10 conf.), San Francisco and Walnut Creek, Calif., 1971-83; historian Pacific 10 Conf., 1983. Mem. Laramie (Wyo.) City Council, 1958-60. Served to lt. comdr. USNR, World War II. Decorated Air medal; mem. Nat. Football Found. and Hall of Fame Honors Ct. Mem. Nat. Collegiate Athletic Assn., Nat. Assn. Collegiate Dirs. Athletics (Corbett award 1983), Collegiate Commrs. Assn., Coll. Sports Info. Dirs. Am. (Arch Ward award 1963), Football Writers Assn. Am. (past dir.), U.S. Basketball Writers Assn., Lambda Chi Alpha. Presbyn. Home: 235 Western Hills Dr Pleasant Hill CA 94523-3167 Office: 800 S Broadway Walnut Creek CA 94596-5218

HALLORAN, JAMES VINCENT, III, technical writer; b. Greenwich, Conn., May 12, 1942; s. James Vincent and Rita Lucy (Keator) H.; m. Barbara Sharon Case, Sept. 7, 1974. BME, Cath. U. Am., 1964; MBA, U. Chgo., 1973. Mktg. rep. Rockwell Internat., El Segundo, Calif., 1973-76, bus. area mgr., 1976-80, bus. analysis mgr., 1980-84; asst. dir. market analysis H. Silver & Assocs. Inc., Torrance, Calif., 1984-87, dir. mktg., 1987-90; program mgr. Tech. Tng. Corp., Torrance, 1990-91; prin. Bus. Info. & Analysis, Redondo Beach, Calif., 1991-94; mgr. spl. projects Wyle Labs., El Segundo, Calif., 1994—. Commr. Redondo Beach Housing Adv. and Appeals Bd., 1985-89; mem. citizens adv. bd. South Bay Union High Sch. Dist., Redondo Beach, 1983. Capt. USAF, 1964-68. Libertarian. Home: 612 S Gertruda Ave Redondo Beach CA 90277-4245 Office: Wyle Labs 128 Maryland St El Segundo CA 90245

HALLOWELL, M. BROOKE, speech pathologist, educator; b. Trenton, N.J., Mar. 20, 1961; d. Ralph P. Hallowell and Janet Louise (Hoag) Smith; m. Richard G. Linn, Aug. 11, 1984; children: Nicholas, Elizabeth. AB, Brown U., 1983; MS, Lamar U., 1986; PhD, U. Iowa, 1991. Cert. speech-lang. pathologist, Ohio, Calif. Instr. Lamar U., Beaumont, Tex., 1985-86, Wright State U., Dayton, Ohio, 1990-92; speech-lang. pathologist TheraTx, Inc., Rehab. Am., Dayton, 1992-93; asst. prof. neurolinguistics U. No. Calif., Marin County, 1993—, dir. Sch. Langs. and Linguistics, 1993—; cons., speech-lang. pathologist Alta Therapies, No. Calif., 1994—; con. Latin Lang. Cons., Dayton, 1992-93. Bd. dirs. U. No. Calif., 1993—; mem. Leadership Novato, Calif., 1993—; mem. Econ. Devel. Com., Novato, 1994—. Fulbright scholar, 1983-84. Mem. MLA, TESOL, Am. Speech-Lang.-Hearing Assn., Calif. Speech-Lang.-Hearing Assn., Am. Coun. on Tchg. Fgn. Langs., Internat. Assn. Tchrs. English as Fgn. Lang., Marin County C. of C., Marin Coun. of Aging, Phi Beta Kappa, Sigma Xi, Phi Beta Delta. Office: U No Calif 101 San Antonio Rd Petaluma CA 94952-9524

HALLSTROM, CAROL ROGOFF, human relations professional. BA cum laude, Beaver Coll., 1963; JD, Boston U., 1975. Bar: Mass., 1975. Staff atty. Ctr. for Criminal Justice, Boston, 1975-80; founding dir. Community Mediation Program of San Diego, 1981-86, San Diego Immigration Law Coalition, 1986-89, San Diego Legalization Appeals Project, 1987-89; dir. San Diego Law Ctr., 1981-89; regional dir. Nat. Conf. (former Nat. Conf. of Christians and Jews), San Diego, 1990—; community devel. counselor Action for Boston Community Devel., Boston; dir. People for Human Rights, Phila.; field sec. student/non-violent coord. com., Amite County, Miss. Contbr. articles to profl. jours., publs. Adv. bd. U.S. Border Patrol Citizens, 1994; trustee San Diego Coalition for Equality, 1992—; mem. Civil Unrest Task Force, County of San Diego, 1992—; pres. selection com. Urban League of San Diego, 1993; mem. Blue Ribbon Commn. on Violent Crime, City of San Diego, 1991-92; mem. conf. com. Internat. Assn. Civilian Oversight of Law Enforcement, 1992; bd. govs. DIFFA, San Diego, 1989—; bd. dirs. San Diego Urban League, vice-chmn. 1989-91, sec. 1988-89; bd. dirs. Jewish Community Rels. Com., more.*. Recipient numerous community svc. awards including Community Svc. Recognition, San Diego County Office of Edn., 1989, Human Dignity Ordiance Task Force, 1990, Human Rels. award San Diego County Human Rels. Commn., 1989, others.

HALLSTROM, ROBERT CHRIS, government actuary; b. Sacramento, June 8, 1953; s. Clifford Clarence and Billee June (Plunkett) H.; m. Pamela Jane Pracht, Apr. 25, 1987; 1 child, Kelsey Kathlene. BA in Math. with honors, Calif. State U., Sacramento, 1974, MS in Math., 1976. Cert. math. tchr. c.c., Calif. Asst. actuary Transam. Ins. Co., L.A., 1976-80; actuary Cal-Farm Ins. Co., Sacramento, 1980-84; instr. math. Sacramento City Coll., 1985, Sierra Coll., Rocklin, Calif., 1985; sr. casualty actuary Calif. Dept. Ins., San Francisco, 1985—. Fellow Casualty Actuarial Soc.; mem. Internat. Actuarial Assn. Office: Calif Dept Ins 425 Market St San Francisco CA 94105-2406

HALOPOFF, WILLIAM EVON, industrial designer, consultant; b. Los Angeles, May 31, 1934; s. William John Halopoff and Dorothy E. (Foote) Lawrence; m. Nancy J. Ragsdale, July 12, 1960; children: Guy William and Carolee Nichole. BS, Art Ctr. Coll. Design, 1968. Internat. indsl. design cons. FMC Corp. Cen. Engring. Lab., Santa Clara, Calif., 1969-81; mgr. indsl. design Tandem Computers, Cupertino, Calif., 1981-93; design cons. Halopoff Assocs., San Jose, Calif., 1984—. Patentee in field. Served with U.S. Army, 1957-59. Mem. Indsl. Designers Soc. Am., Soc. Automotive Engrs. (chmn. subcom. 29 1979-85). Home: 17544 Holiday Dr Morgan Hill CA 95037-6303

HALPENNY, DIANA DORIS, lawyer; b. San Francisco, Jan. 18, 1951; d. William Frederick and Doris E. Halpenny; m. Gregory D. Prowell, Aug. 28, 1982. BA, Calif. State Coll., 1973; JD, Univ. Pacific, 1980. Bar: Calif. 1980. Bookkeeper/sales clerk Farmers Empire Drugs, Santa Rosa, Calif., 1971-73; activity dir. Beverly Manor Convalescent Hosp., Anaheim, Calif., 1973-74; instructional aide Los Angeles County Supt. Schs., Downey, Calif., 1974-76, sub. tchr., 1976-77; assoc. Littler, Mendelson, Fastiff & Tichy, San Jose, Calif., 1980-82, Walters & Shelburne, Sacramento, Calif., 1982-84, Kronick Moskovitz Tiedemann & Girard, Sacramento, 1984-85; legal advisor Pub. Employment Rels. Bd., 1985-87; gen. counsel San Juan Unified Sch. Dist., 1987—. Founding mem. In-house Sch. Attys No. Calif.; past pres. no. sect. Sch. Law Study Sect. County Counsels Assn., 1991-92; mem. legal adv. com. Calif. Sch. Bd. Assn. Edn. Legal Alliance; mem. exec. bd. Calif. Edn. Mandated Cost Network, 1987—. Mem. ABA, Calif. Bar Assn., Calif. Coun. Sch. Attys. (v.p. programs 1993, pres.-elect 1994, pres. 1995), Sacramento County Bar Assn., Trayner Honor Soc., Order of Coif. Republican. Lutheran. Office: San Juan Unified Sch Dist 3738 Walnut Ave Carmichael CA 95608-3054

HALPENNY, LEONARD CAMERON, water resources consultant, hydrologist; b. Winnipeg, Manitoba, Can., June 21, 1915; came to U.S., 1926, naturalized, 1939; s. Jasper and Lillian Hartley (Brown) H.; m. Cora Elizabeth Jett, Jan. 25, 1941; children: Carol Jean, Philip Cameron. BS in Petroleum Engring., U. Tex., 1938; postgrad., U. Ariz., 1958. Registered profl. engr., Ariz., N.Mex., Utah; registered geologist, Ariz., Calif. Hydrologist U.S. Geol. Survey, Austin, Tex., 1937-39, Tucson, 1939-41; field engr. Marathon Oil, Hobbs, N.Mex., 1941-43; hydrologist U.S. Geol. Survey, Tucson, 1945-51, dist. chief, 1951-55; cons. hydrologist World Mining Consultants, Angola, 1955-57; cons. water resources Water Devel. Corp., Tucson, 1957—; hydrology cons. Ctrl. El Palmar, Cagua, Venezuela, 1959-88; spl. master Cappaert v. U.S., U.S. Dist. Ct., Las Vegas, 1973-78; expert witness for many water lawsuits. Co-inventor water stage recorder (Nash Conservation award); contbr. articles to several mags. With U.S. Army, 1943-45, ETO. Mem. ASCE, Am. Assn. Petroleum Geologists, Am. Geophys. Union, Am. Water Resources Assn., Am. Water Works Assn., Ariz. Geol. Soc., Ariz. Hydrol. Soc. (founding mem. Tuscon chpt.), Ariz. Water and Pollution Control Assn., Internat. Assn. Sci. Hydrology, Internat. Soc. Sugar Cane Technologists, Nat. Water Well Assn., U.S. Com. on Irrigation Drainage and Flood Control. Home and Office: Water Devel Corp 3938 E Santa Barbara Ave Tucson AZ 85711-4744

HALPERN, LINDA CARAY, minister, author, poet; b. Oakland, Calif., Dec. 27, 1947; d. Philip Courtney and Melba Caray (Eble) Rude; m. Melford Duane Barker, Oct. 26, 1968 (div. 1981); children: Jeffrey Duane Barker, Scott Duane Barker (dec.); m. Maurice Halpern, Apr. 4, 1993 (div. 1994). Student, U. Calif., Westwood, 1965; cert. interior design, Internat. Corr. Sch., 1987; MSc, U. Metaphysics, Studio City, Calif., 1995; postgrad., 1995—. Ordained minister, metaphysical practitioner. Nurse various dr.'s offices, Azusa, Calif., 1969-82; owner beauty salon Upland, Calif., 1972-81; owner Italian restaurant Montclair, Calif., 1983-86; mgr., interior designer Standard Brands Paint Co., Calif., 1986-89; interior designer Upland, Calif., 1987-90; author, artist Flagstaff, Ariz., 1992—; pastoral counselor, 1995. Author: Crisis to Creativity, 1993; contbr. poetry to anthologies including The Coming of Dawn Anthology, Poetic Voices of American, Memories Anthology, Helicon, Inspirations in Ink. Bd. dirs., coach Upland Am. Little League, Calif., 1981-82. With U.S. Army, 1967-68. Recipient Editor's Choice award Nat. Libr. Poetry, 1993, Accomplishment of Merit award Creative Arts and Sci. Enterprises, 1993. Mem. Internat. Soc. Poets (charter lifetime mem., adv. panel 1993—), Internat. Order Job's Daus. (honored queen 1962-66), Beta Sigma Phi (pres. 1965). Republican.

HALPERN, NORA R., museum director, art curator; b. N.Y.C., Dec. 5, 1960; d. Ben and Lois Julie (Gordon) H.; m. Kerry Bryan Brougher, Aug. 9, 1987; 1 child, Emily Clara Brougher. BA, UCLA, 1983, MA, 1990. Curator Frederick Weisman Collections, L.A., 1983-90; founding dir. Frederick R. Weisman Mus. Art, Malibu, Calif., 1992-94; dir. fine arts, Los Angeles; asst. v.p. Sothebys, Beverly Hills, Calif., 1995—; adj. prof. Pepperdine U., Malibu, 1992—; art cons., lectr., writer, critic L.A., 1983—. Editor: Frederick R. Weisman Foundation of Art, Vol. II, 1985, Selections from Frederick R. Weisman Art Foundation, 1987, Dynaton, Before and Beyond, 1992. Vol. Art Walk Venice, Calif., Venice Family Clinic, 1985—; trustee L.A. Inst. Contemporary Art, 1983-87, bd. dirs. Helena Rubenstein fellow Whitney Mus. Am. Art, 1981-82. Mem. Art Table. Office: Sothebys 9665 Wilshire Blvd Beverly Hills CA 90212

HALPERT, LESLIE DEAN, engineering executive; b. N.Y.C., Oct. 25, 1953; s. Albert Lee and Charlotte (Batcher) H.; m. Mary Elise Copley, Oct. 23, 1988. Student, Calif. Poly. U., 1971-76; BS in Aerospace Engring., Northrop U., 1987. Design engr. NAA, Rockwell Internat., El Segundo, Calif., 1976-80, sr. master dimensions engr., 1981-93; sr. design engr. Lockheed Corp., Burbank, Calif., 1980-81; pres., chief exec. officer Allen Indsl. Supply, Inc., Burbank, 1993—. Mem. AIAA. Office: Allen Indsl Supply Inc 1711 W Burbank Blvd Burbank CA 91506-1312

HALPIN, TIMOTHY PATRICK, former air force officer; b. Worcester, Mass., Mar. 13, 1960; s. Daniel Joseph Halpin and Angelina (Ferranti) Wilkes; m. Rachel Esther Hanneman, Aug. 3, 1991; children: Alyssia Kristin, Patrick Stephan, Joseph Marvin. BBA in Mgmt., U. Mass., 1982; MBA, Embry-Riddle Aero. U., 1994; postgrad., Regent U., 1995—. Commd. 2d lt. USAF, 1982, advanced through grades to capt., 1986; instr. electronic warfare USAF, various locations, 1984-89, 93d Bomb Wing, Castle AFB, Calif., 1989-95; resigned, 1995. Decorated DFC, Air medal (3). Mem. VFW. Republican. Christian. Home: 5972 Jake Sears Cir # 102 Virginia Beach VA 23464-5123

HALSEY-BRANDT, GREG, mayor. BA in Geography, U. B.C., MA in Geography. Town planner, alderman, 1981-90; mayor City of Richmond, B.C., 1990—; mem. Vancouver Regional Transit Commn.; chmn., dir. Greater Vancouver Regional Dist. Mem. Planning Inst. B.C., Richmond C. of C. Office: Office of the Mayor, 6911 No 3 Rd, Richmond, BC Canada V6Y 2C1

HALTEMAN, ELLEN LOUISE, librarian; b. Cleve., Sept. 7, 1947; d. Eber Kingdon and Mary Ann (Geyer) H.; divorced; 1 child, Anna Sharane Schwartz. AB, Washington U., 1969; MA, U. Calif., Davis, 1976; MLS, U. Calif., Berkeley, 1979. Libr. Calif. State Railroad Mus., Sacramento, 1981—. Author: Northern California Art Exhibition Catalogues -- 1878-1915, 1990, California Art Research -- 1936-1937, 1987, San Francisco Art Exhibition Catalogues, 1981. Bd. dirs. Davis Sch. Arts Found., 1993—. Mem. ALA, Spl. Librs. Assn. Office: Calif State Railroad Mus 111 I St Sacramento CA 95814-2204

HALVERSON, STEVEN THOMAS, lawyer, real estate executive; b. Enid, Okla., Aug. 29, 1954; s. Robert James Halverson and Ramona Mae (Ludke) Selenski; m. Diane Mary Schueller, Aug. 21, 1976; children: John Thomas, Anne Kirsten. BA cum laude, St. John's U., 1976; JD, Am. U., 1979. Bar: Va. 1979. Asst. project dir. ABA, Washington, 1977-79; with Briggs & Morgan, St. Paul., 1980-83; v.p. M.A. Mortenson Cos., Mpls., Denver, Seattle, 1984—; bd. dirs. Associated Gen. Contractors Colo., Ctr. for New West, Greater Denver Corp, Denver Partnership, Rocky Mountain World Trade Ctr. Co-author: Federal Grant Law, 1982; contbr. articles to profl. jours. Bd. dirs. Regis U., Central City Opera. Republican. Roman Catholic. Home: 2013 Montane Dr E Golden CO 80401-8099 Office: MA Mortenson Cos 1875 Lawrence St Ste 600 Denver CO 80202-1847

HALVORSEN, JAN LA RAYNE, library services manager; b. Chgo., Aug. 30, 1941; d. La Vern Grant and Dorothy Ethelyn (Johnston) Kelley; m. Wayne Lee Halvorsen, Nov. 5, 1958 (div. Feb. 1975); children: Jon Alan, Kathryn Lynn. BA in Polit. Sci. with honors, Calif. State Poly. U., 1975; M in Pub. Adminstrn., U. Calif., Riverside, 1977; MLS, UCLA, 1990. Ops. supr. City of Huntington Beach (Calif.) Libr., 1984-90, libr. svcs. mgr. support and extension svcs., 1991—; guest lectr. mcpl. fin. Calif. State Poly. U., Pomona, 1986, 87; guest lectr. libr. mgmt. UCLA, 1989; intenr devel. office UCLA, 1988, Mayor Tom Bradley's city econ. devel. office City of L.A., 1989. Founder family literacy program U.S. Dept. Health Edn. and Welfare, Huntington Beach, 1993; dir. ARIDAY, Costa Mesa, Calif., 1994; v.p. Mgmt. Employees Orgn., Huntington Beach, 1986, pres., 1987. Community Devel. grantee Huntington Beach Dept. Housing Urban Devel., 1994. Mem. ALA, Am. Soc. Pub. Adminstrn., Calif. Libr. Assn. (chair women's devel. conf. 1991-92), Acad. Polit. Sci., Soroptimist Internat. (newsletter, del. 1991-92, 92-93, v.p. 1993-94, pres. 1994—). Home: 15682 Mayflower Ln Huntington Beach CA 92647-2807 Office: Huntington Beach Libr 7111 Talbert Ave Huntington Beach CA 92648-1232

HALVORSEN, ROBERT ALFRED, JR., radiologist, educator; b. N.Y.C., Oct. 12, 1948; s. Robert Alfred and Dorothy Deeble (Stalcup) H. BS in Chemistry, U. Miami, 1970, MD, 1974. Rotating intern St. Mary's Med. Ctr., Long Beach, Calif., 1974-75; resident in radiology U. Tex., San Antonio, 1977-80, instr., 1980; fellow ABD imaging Duke U., Durham, N.C., 1980-81, from asst. prof. to assoc. prof., 1981-87; assoc. prof. U. Minn., Mpls., 1987-90; prof., vice-chmn. radiology and medicine U. Calif., San Francisco, 1990—; chief radiology San Francisco Gen. Hosp., 1990—; chmn. re-engring. work group Dept. Pub. Health, San Francisco, 1994, steering com. County Info. Sys. Network. Contbr. numerous papers to sci. jours., 15 book chpts. Alternate del. Rep. Party, Mpls., 1989. Cadet USCG, 1966-67. Fellow Am. Coll. Radiology; mem. Soc. Computed Body Tomography and Magnetic Resonance (chmn. standards com. 1993-95), Soc. Gastrointestinal Radiology (Roscoe Miller award for best paper 1989), Assn. Univ. Radiologists (exec. com. 1990-95, chmn. Stauffer award com. 1993-95), Soc. Emergency Radiologists (chmn. program com.). Home: 37 Mountain View Rd Fairfax CA 94930-1912 Office: San Francisco Gen Hosp Dept Radiology 1001 Potrero Ave San Francisco CA 94110-3518

HALVORSON, ALFRED RUBIN, mayor, consultant, education educator; b. Milan, Minn., Jan. 22, 1921; s. Chris and Alice (Kleven) H.; m. Dorothy F. Boxrud, Apr. 23, 1944; children: Gary A., Joan D. Halvorson Felice. BS, U. Minn., 1944, PhD, 1949. County extension agt. Agr. Extension Svc. of Minn., St. Paul, 1945; soil fertility researcher Oreg. State U., Klamath Falls, 1949-54; extension agronomist Purdue U., Lafayette, Ind., 1954-57; extension soil scientist Wash. State U., Pullman, 1957-86, prof. emeritus, 1986—; cons. ACF & Shirley Fetilizer Ltd., Brisbane, Australia, 1964, Saudi Arabia Farming Ops., Riyadh, 1984, U.S. AID, Sanaa, North Yemen, 1987. City councilman, City of Pullman, 1987-91, mayor, 1991—. With M.C. U.S. Army, 1945. Mem. Kiwanis (chair com. Pullman chpt.). Republican. Lutheran. Home and Office: 325 SE Nebraska St Pullman WA 99163-2239

HALVORSON, ARDELL DAVID, research leader, soil scientist; b. Rugby, N.D., May 31, 1945; s. Albert F. and Karen (Mygland) H.; m. Linda Kay Johnston, Apr. 11, 1966; children: Renae, Rhonda. BS, N.D. State U., 1967; MS, Colo. State U., 1969, PhD, 1971. Soil scientist Agr. Rsch. Svc., USDA, Sidney, Mont., 1971-83; soil scientist Agr. Rsch. Svc., USDA, Akron, Colo., 1983-88, rsch. leader, 1988-94; lab. dir. USDA-Agr. Rsch. Svc., Mandan, N.D., 1994—. Contbr. more than 120 articles to profl. jours. Fellow Am. Soc. Agronomy (assoc. editor 1983-87), Soil Sci. Soc. Am. (chmn. div. S-8, 1989), Soil and Water Conservation Soc. (chpt. pres. 1991); mem. Crop Sci. Soc. Am., Elks. Office: USDA Agrl Rsch Svc PO Box 459 Mandan ND 58554-0459

HAM, GARY MARTIN, psychologist; b. Lincoln, Nebr., Feb. 6, 1940; s. Wendell E. and Sally Bertha (Lind) H.; m. Helene Stearnes; children: Jeffery M., Shari L., Michael A., Dante A. BS in Psychology, Wash. State U., 1963, MS in Psychology, 1965; PsyD, Newport U., 1988. Lic. psychologist, Calif.; cert. tchr., Calif, counselor. Clin. psychologist Riverside (Calif.) County Dept. Mental Health, 1967—; tchr., cons., pub. speaker, researcher Riverside County Dept. Mental Health, 1967—; instr. U. Calif. Riverside, Chapman U. Clin. psychologist Riverside County, Critical Incidents Disaster Response Team, 1985—, ARC Disaster Team. 1st lt. USAF, 1964-67. Mem. APA, ASCD, Am. Mental Health Counselors Assn., Am. Critical Incident Stress Found., Calif. Psychol. Assn., Air Force Soc. Psychologists, Psi Chi, Sigma Phi Epsilon. Office: Riverside County Dept Mental Health 9990 County Farm Rd Riverside CA 92503-3518

HAMACHEK, TOD RUSSELL, manufacturing executive; b. Jan. 3, 1946; m. Barbara Callister, 1969; children: Mark, Elizabeth. BA, Williams Coll., 1968; MBA, Harvard U., 1970. Nat. sales mgr. Harris Corp., Westerly, R.I., 1970-74; asst. to pres. Gt. Western Malting Co., Vancouver, Wash., 1974-76, v.p. sales, 1976-79; pres., chief exec. officer Gt. Western Malting Co., Vancouver, Oreg., 1979-84; pres., chief ops. officer Penwest, Ltd., Bellevue, Wash., 1984-85, pres., chief exec. officer, 1985—; sr. v.p. Univar Corp., Seattle, 1982-84; bd. dirs. N.W. Natural Gas Co., Dekalb Genetics Corp., The Seattle Times Co., Blethen Corp. Bd. dirs., pres. 100 Club Wash.; bd. dirs. Pacific Sci. Ctr., Va. Mason Hosp.; trustee Lakeside Sch., Seattle Found. (vice-chmn.), Wash. Roundtable, Lewis & Clark Coll. Mem. PNW, Young Pres.' Orgn., U. Wash. Grad. Sch. Bus. Adminstrn. (past chmn. adv. bd.). Office: Penwest Ltd PO Box 1688 Bellevue WA 98009-1688

HAMADA, DUANE TAKUMI, architect; b. Honolulu, Aug. 12, 1954; s. Robert Kensaku and Jean Hakue (Masutani) H.; m. Martha S.P. Lee, Dec. 22, 1991; children; Erin, Robyn. BFA in Environ. Design, U. Hawaii, 1977, BArch, 1979. Registered architect, Hawaii, Guam, Florida, Puerto Rico. Intern Edward Sullam, FAIA & Assocs., Honolulu, 1979-80; assoc. Design Ptnrs., Inc., Honolulu, 1980-86; prin. AM Ptnrs., Inc., Honolulu, 1986—. Chmn. 31st Ann. Cherry Blossom Festival Fashion Show, Honolulu, 1982, 32d Ann. Cherry Blossom Festival Cooking Show, 1983, mem. steering com., 1982, 83. Recipient Gold Key award for Excellence in Interior Design Am. Hotel and Motel Assn., 1990, Renaissance '90 Merit award Nat. Assn. Home Builder's Remodeler Coun., Merit award Honolulu mag., 1990, Cert. of Appreciation PACDIV USN, 1992. Mem. AIA (Sch. medal 1979), Constrn. Specifications Inst., Nat. Coun. Archtl. Registration Bds., Colegio de Arcquitectos de P.R., Japanese C. of C. Hawaii, Japan-Am. Soc., Hawaiian Astron. Soc. Office: AM Ptnrs Inc 1164 Bishop St Ste 1000 Honolulu HI 96813-2824

HAMAI, JAMES YUTAKA, business executive; b. L.A., Oct. 14, 1926; s. Seizo and May (Sata) H.; B.S., U. So. Calif., 1952, M.S., 1955; postgrad. bus. mgmt. program industry exec., UCLA, 1963-64; m. Dorothy K. Fukuda, Sept. 10, 1954; 1 child, Wendy A. Lectr. chem. engring. dept. U. So. Calif., Los Angeles, 1963-64; process engr., sr. process engr. Fluor Corp., Los Angeles, 1954-64; sr. project mgr. central research dept. Monsanto Co., St. Louis, 1964-67, mgr. research, devel. and engring. graphic systems dept., 1967-68, mgr. comml. devel. New Enterprise div., 1968-69; exec. v.p., dir. Concrete Cutting Industries, Inc., Los Angeles, 1969-72; pres., dir. Concrete Cutting Internat., Inc., Los Angeles, 1972-78, chmn. bd., 1978—; cons. Fluor Corp., Los Angeles, 1970-72; dir. Intech Systems Co., Ltd., Tokyo, Cutting Industries Co., Ltd., Tokyo, Techno Trading Co., Ltd., Tokyo; internat. bus. cons. Served with AUS, 1946-48. Mem. Am. Inst. Chem. Engrs., Am. Mgmt. Assn., Tau Beta Pi, Phi Lambda Upsilon. Club: Rotary (gov. dist. 1982-83). Home: 6600 Via La Paloma Palos Verdes Peninsula CA 90275-6449 Office: PO Box 700 Wilmington CA 90748-0700

HAMBIDGE, DOUGLAS WALTER, archbishop; b. London, Mar. 6, 1927; emigrated to Can., 1956; s. Douglas and Florence (Driscoll) H.; m. Denise Colvill Lown, June 9, 1956; children: Caryl Denise, Stephen Douglas, Graham Andrew. A.L.C.D., London U., 1953, B.D., 1958, D.D., 1969. Ordained deacon Church of England, 1953, priest, 1954, consecrated bishop, 1969; asst. curate St. Mark's Ch., Dalston, London, 1953-55; priest-in-charge St. Mark's Ch., 1955-56; incumbent All Saints Ch., Cassiar, B.C., Can., 1956-58; rector St. James Parish, Smithers, B.C., 1958-64, North Peace Parish, Ft. St. John, B.C., 1964-69; canon St. Andrew's Cathedral, 1965; lord bishop of Caledonia, 1969-80, New Westminster, B.C., 1980-81; lord archbishop of New Westminster and metropolitan of B.C., 1981-93; prin. St. Mark's Theol. Coll., Dar es Salaam, Tanzania, 1993—; asst. bishop Diocese of Dar es Salaam, Dar es Salaam, 1993—; mem. Anglican Consultative Coun., 1985-93. Mem. Vancouver Club, Arbutus Club.

HAMBRECHT, WILLIAM R., venture capitalist; b. 1935; married; 5 children. Student, Princeton U. Broker Francis I. DuPont & Co., San Francisco; mng. ptnr. Hambrecht & Quist, San Francisco, now pres., chief exec. officer, dir.; bd. dirs. People Express, Inc. Office: Hambrecht & Quist One Bush St San Francisco CA 94104

HAMBURG, DANIEL (DAN HAMBURG), congressman; b. St. Louis, 1948; m. Carrie Hamburg, 1972; 4 children. BA with honors in History, Stanford U., 1970; MA in Philosophy and Religion, Calif. Inst. Integral Studies, 1992. Founder, tchr. Mariposa Sch., 1970-80; dir. Ukiah Valley Child Devel. Ctr., 1970-80; exec. dir. North Coast Opportunities Inc., 1986-93; bd. suprs. Mendocino County, Calif., 1981-85; dir. cultural studies program People's Republic of China, 1984-90; mem. 103d Congress from 1st Calif. Dist., 1993—. Mem. Rotary. Democrat. Office: Ho of Reps 114 Cannon Bldg Washington DC 20515-0003*

HAMBURGER, ROBERT N., pediatrics educator, consultant; b. N.Y.C., Jan. 26, 1923; s. Samuel B. and Harriet (Neufeld) H.; m. Sonia Gross, Nov. 9, 1943; children: Hilary, Debre (dec.), Lisa. BA, U. N.C., 1947; MD, Yale U., 1951. Diplomate Am. Bd. Pediatrics, Am. Bd. Allergy and Immunology. Instr., asst. clin. prof. sch. medicine Yale U., New Haven, 1951-60; assoc. prof. biology U. Calif. San Diego, La Jolla, 1960-64, assoc. prof. pediatrics, 1964-67, prof., 1970-90, prof. emeritus, 1990—, asst. dean sch. medicine, 1964-70, lab. dir., 1970—, head fellows tng. program allergy and immunology divsn., 1970-90; cons. various cos., Calif., Sweden, Switzerland, 1986—; bd. dirs. Pathfinder Holding Corp. Author 1 book; contbr. articles to profl. jours.; patentee allergy peptides, allergen detector. Vol. physician, educator Children of the Californias, Calif. and Baja California, Mex., 1993—. 1st lt. Air Corps, U.S. Army, 1943-45. Grantee NIH and USPHS, 1960-64, 64-84; Fulbright fellow, 1980, Disting. fellow Am. Coll. Allergy, Asthma, Immunology, 1986. Mem. U. Calif. San Diego Emeriti Assn. (pres. 1992-94). Office: U Calif San Diego Allergy Immunology Lab La Jolla CA 92093-0950

HAMBY, DRANNAN CARSON, chemist, educator; b. Duncan, Okla., Nov. 16, 1933; s. Wellington Vernon and Dessie A. (Miller) H.; m. Beverly R. Reinhart, Apr. 3, 1951; children: Mark, Marcy. BA, Linfield Coll., McMinnville, Oreg., 1955; MA, Oreg. State U., Corvallis, 1962, PhD, 1968. Chemist Linfield Rsch. Inst., McMinnville, 1956—, dir., 1962-78; from asst. prof. to prof. chemistry Linfield Coll., 1962—; vis. rsch. engr. UCLA, 1975-76, Brigham Young U., Provo, Utah, 1991-92; instr. Nat. Outdoor Leaders Sch., Lander, Wyo., 1983—. Mem. McMinnville City Coun., 1976-80. Fulbright scholar, Germany, 1955-56. Mem. Electrochem. Soc., Mt. Hood Ski Patrol, Sierra Club, Sigma Xi. Democrat. Home: 232 Oregon Way Mcminnville OR 97128 Office: Chemistry Dept Linfield College Mcminnville OR 97128

HAMERSLOUGH, WALTER SCOTT, health and physical education educator; b. Needles, CA, Dec. 15, 1935; s. Walter Kenneth and Frances (Brown) H.; m. V. Darlene Berdan, Dec. 17, 1961; children: Kenneth Scott, Rhonda Darlene. BA, La Sierra Coll., 1958; MA, U. Redlands, 1964; EdD, U. Oreg., 1971. Tchr. Fairview Elem. Sch., San Bernardino, Calif., 1958-59, Loma Linda (Calif.) Elem. Sch., 1959-60; hist., phys. edn. tchr. Loma Linda Acad., 1960-63; prof. health and phys. edn., chair La Sierra U., Riverside, Calif., 1963—; cons. YMCA, Intercommunity Home for Exceptional Children. Coach Alvord Pony League, 1978-80 (v.p., 1980), Alvord Little League, 1975-78. Mem. Am. Coll. Sports Medicine, Am. Alliance for Health, Phys. Edn., Nat. Intramural Sports Assn., SDA Health, Phys. Edn. Recreation Assn. (exec. dir. 1983—), Western Coll. Phys. Edn. Soc. (So. Calif. Rep. 1981-87), Phi Epsilon Kappa. Republican. Adventist. Office: La Sierra U Health Phys Edn Dept Riverside CA 92515

HAMES, WILLIAM LESTER, lawyer; b. Pasco, Wash., June 21, 1947; s. Arlie Franklin and Nina Lee (Ryals) H.; m. Pamella Kay Rust, June 3, 1967; children: Robert Alan, Michael Jonathan. BS in Psychology, U. Wash., 1974; JD, Willamette U., 1981. Bar: Wash. 1981, U.S. Dist. Ct. (ea. dist.) Wash. 1982, U.S. Ct. Appeals (9th cir.) 1985, U.S. Dist. Ct. (we. dist.) Wash. 1985. Counselor Wash. Juvenile Ct., Walla Walla, Wash., 1974-76; reactor operator control rm. United Nuclear Inc., Richland, Wash., 1976-77; assoc. Sonderman, Egan & Hames, Kennewick, Wash., 1981-84, Timmons & Hames, Kennewick, 1984-86, Sonderman, Timmons & Hames, Kennewick, 1987-88; ptnr. Hames, Anderson & Whitlow, Kennewick, 1988—; bd. dirs. eastern Wash. bankruptcy sect. Fed. Bar Assn. Mem. Am. Trial Lawyers Assn., Wash. State Bar Assn. (chmn. legal assts. com.), Wash. State Trial Lawyers Assn., Benton-Franklin County Bar Assn. Democrat. Methodist. Home: 410 W 21st St Kennewick WA 99337 Office: Hames Anderson & Whitlow PO Box 5498 Kennewick WA 99336-0498

HAMI, LISA SUZANNE, laboratory supervisor, medical technologist; b. Balt., July 24, 1964; d. Paul Frederick Jr. and Marjorie Anne (Cook) Fox.; m. Aliakbar Hami, Mar. 16, 1991; children: Nima John, Maryann Melissa. BS, U. Md., 1986. Med. tech. U. Md. Med. Sys., Balt., 1985-90; supr. cryopreservation lab. U. Colo. Hosp., Denver, 1990—; lectr. CACMLE, Denver, 1994. Contbr. articles to profl. jours. Mem. Internat. Soc. Hematother and Graft Engring. (bd. dirs. 1993—). Office: U Colo U Hosp 4200 E 9th Ave Box B-190 Denver CO 80262

HAMILL, CAROL, biologist, writing educator; b. San Diego, July 15, 1953; d. William David Sr. and Katharine Louise (Garlock) H.; divorced; 1 child, Jason John Voutas. Student, San Diego State U., 1972-73, Worcester State Coll., 1975-78; BS in Natural Scis., Worcester State Coll., Riverside, 1980; postgrad., Calif. State U., San Bernardino, 1986-92, U. La Verne, 1994—. Lab. asst. Worcester State Coll., 1976-78; ind. biologist Calif., 1983-86; lab. asst. Calif. State U., San Bernardino, 1987-88; mem. adj. faculty Riverside C.C., 1990-93; lab. asst. dept. biochemistry U. Calif., Riverside, 1979-80, writing instr., 1992—; freelance writer, 1988—; speaker in field. Contbr. articles to Off Duty, Natural Food and Farming, Country Rev., Sr. Highlights, Our Town, Palm and Pine, and others, over 50 articles to nat. and local mags. Mem. publicity com. Orange Empire Rwy. Mus., Perris, Calif., 1989-92. Mem. AAAS, N.Y. Acad. Scis. (publicity com. 1989-92), Ecol. Soc. Am. Democrat. Episcopalian. Home: 11681 Dalehurst Rd Moreno Valley CA 92555-1909 Office: PO Box 7960 Moreno Valley CA 92552-7960

HAMILTON, ALLEN PHILIP, financial advisor; b. Albany, Calif., Oct. 17, 1937; s. Allen Philip Sr. and Barbara Louise (Martin) H.; m. Mary Williams, July 18, 1981 (div. Mar. 1987). BA in Bus. Mgmt., St. Mary's U., San Jose, Calif., 1961; AA, Contra Costa State Coll., 1957; Bus. Assoc. degree, NW Mo. State U., 1969; postgrad., San Jose State U., 1959-61. Cert. fin. planner. Fin. advisor Consolidated Investment Svcs., Kansas City, Mo., 1968-70; pres., chief exec. officer Balanced Mgmt. Assn., Mission, Kans., 1969-72, Advanced Svc. Assn., Overland Park, Kans., 1971-78; divisional mgr. Waddell & Reed, Inc., Kansas City, 1978-81; sr. v.p., regional dir. WZW Fin. Svcs., Kansas City, 1981-86; exec.v.p. Skaife & Co., Orinda, Calif., 1986-88; v.p., mktg. dir. Consolidated Securities Corp., Walnut Creek, Calif., 1988; sr. dir. and cert. trainer Club Am., Inc., L.A., 1990—; CFP, prin. Hamilton Fin. Adv., Am. Investment Svcs., Pleasant Hill., Calif., 1989—; silver mktg. distbr., corp. trainer, Can. mktg. distbr. and trainer Nikken, Inc. Internat., numerous fgn. countries, 1991—; sales mgr., ind. distributor, sales trainer Alpine Industries, 1992—; prin. advisor Environ. Solutions Internat.; exec. dir. Environ. Air Quality and Health Found.; sr. dir. Club Am. OTC Pink Shts., L.A., 1990-92; presdl. dir. FundAmerica, Irvine, Calif., 1988—; guest speaker in field. Author: (with others) The Financial Planner A New Profession, 1986. Asst. dist. commr. Boy Scouts Am., Kansas City, Kans., 1970-79; corp. dir. United Campaign, Overland Park, Kans., 1965-73; active TV show Kidney Found., Kansas City, Mo., 1969-70; sr. arbitrator San Francisco Bay Area Better Bus. Bur., 1986—. Lt. U.S. Army, 1963-65. Recipient Citation Nat. Campaign Re-election 1992, 1992m Senatorial Commn. Rep. Senatorial Inner Circle, 1991. Mem. Inst. Cert. Fin. Planners, Internat. Assn. for Fin. Planning (v.p., bd. dirs. 1982-87, practitioner div.), Registry of Fin. Planning Practitioners, Mt. Diablo Distbrs. Assn. Republican. Home: 2265 Gladwin Dr Walnut Creek CA 94596-6332

HAMILTON, CALVIN SARGENT, planning consultant, retired city official; b. Lakeland, Fla., Dec. 12, 1924; s. Calvin Ralph and Francelia (Sargent) H.; m. Glenda Chapelle, Aug. 24, 1975; children: John, Hallam, Charles. B.A. in Landscape Architecture, U. Ill., 1949; M.City Planning, Harvard U., 1952; research fellow, U. Coll., U. London, 1953. Planning cons. Project East River, Dept. Def., Cambridge, Mass., 1952, Harland Bartholomew & Assos., St. Louis, 1953-55; exec. dir. Met. Planning Dept., Indpls., 1955-60, Pitts. Planning Dept., 1960-64; pres. Integrated Devel. Svcs., Inc., 1989—; planning dir. Los Angeles City Planning Dept., 1964-86; planning and urban design, landscape designs cons. Los Angeles, 1986—; plan cons. Athens, Greece, 1983, Sao Paulo, Brazil, 1968, Guatemala City, 1972, Limosol, Cypress, 1983, Shanghai Harbor, People's Republic China, 1983, New Delhi and Bombay, 1988; past mem. faculty Ind. U., U. Pitts., UCLA, U. So. Calif., Harbor Coll.; faculty mem. Calif. Poly. U., Pamona, 1990—; vis. lectr. numerous U.S. and fgn. univs., 1968—; L.A. and Pcific Rim countries coord. Internat. Mega Cities Program, 1988; del. to internat. sems. USIS; mem. Miracle Mile Coalition Bd.; v.p. Beautification Com., Carthay Circle Assn. Bd. Author papers, city plans. Founder Historic Landmarks Found., Indpls., 1959; co-founder Pitts. History and Landmarks Found., 1962; founder L.A. Goals Program, 1965-72; exec. com. Bldg. Research Adv. Bd., NAS, 1971-80; environ. quality officer, L.A.,1978-86; trustee Hubbard Trust, Boston, 1973—; bd. dirs. Los Angeles Conservancy, 1980, Ctr. for Mcpl. Planning, N.Y.C.; v.p., mem. gen. bd. Nat. Council Chs., 1963-70; chmn. Civic Ctr. Authority, 1983-86; chmn. adv. bd. landscape architecture UCLA, 1984—; planning rep. Pacific Presbytery to Synod of So. Calif. and Hawaii, 1989; mem. session Wilshire Presbyn. Ch., 1984—. With USAAF, 1942-46. Recipient Bronze tablet U. Ill., 1949, 1st Honor award for Los Angeles Planning Assn. Am. Planning Assn., 1983; 1st honor award for Los Angeles energy plan Am. Planning Assn.; named one of 25 greater contbrs. to L.A. in preceding 25 yrs. by L.A. Mag.; Rotary Internat. Found. fellow, 1952; grantee West German Govt., 1971, French Govt., 1983. Fellow Am. Soc. Landscape Architects (Bradford Williams medal 1973, Nat. Merit award 1987), Am. Geog. Soc.; mem. Am. Inst. Cert. Planners, AIA (hon. assoc. So. Calif. chpt.), Nat. Inst. Bldg. Scis. (exec. com. cons. council), Am. Shore and Beach Preservation Assn., So. Calif. Assn. Govts. (past chmn. council planning), Internat. Assn. Royal Town Planning Inst. (London), Lambda Alpha (v.p. L.A. chpt. 1989—), Phi Kappa Phi. Democrat.

HAMILTON, CHARLES EDWARD, JR., communication consultant; b. Balt., Dec. 22, 1957; s. Charles Edward and Dorothy Isabel (Gettel) H. BA in Internat. Studies, Johns Hopkins U., 1978; MA in Journalism, U. Minn., 1979; PhD in Pub. Comm., U. Md., 1994. Contract specialist U.S. Dept. Energy, Washington, 1979-81; mgr. human devel. programs Corp. for Pub. Broadcasting, Washington, 1981-85; instr. U. Md., College Park, 1985-88, 90; interim gen. mgr. WWOZ-FM, New Orleans, 1988; asst. gen. mgr. WBJC-FM, Balt., 1988-89; vis. asst. prof. George Washington U., Washington, 1989-90; mgr. Jack Straw Prodns., Seattle, 1990-92; pres. Charles Hamilton Comm. Svcs., Seattle, 1985—; tng. cons. KCMU-FM, Seattle, 1992; bd. dirs., tng. cons. Earth on the Air, Seattle, 1991-92; trainer Pyramid Comm. Internat., Washington, 1988; rsch. cons. Ctr. for TV Rsch., U. Leeds, Eng., 1987. Editor: Analysis of the Skills Used in Public Broadcasting's Key Jobs, 1985; contbr. articles to profl. jours. Mem. Nat. Fedn. Community Broadcasters (judge Golden Reel awards 1991), Nat. Assn. Broadcasters (judge Crystal Radio awards 1990). Home and Office: Charles Hamilton Comm Svcs 400 Harvard Ave E # 306 Seattle WA 98102-4900

HAMILTON, CHARLES HOWARD, metallurgist; b. Pueblo, Colo., Mar. 17, 1935; s. George Edwin and Eva Eleanor (Watson) H.; m. Joy Edith Richmond, Sept. 7, 1968; children: Krista Kathleen, Brady Glenn. BS, Colo. Sch. Mines, 1959; MS, U. So. Calif., 1965; PhD, Case Western Res. U., 1968. Research engr. Space div. Rockwell Internat., Downey, Calif., 1959-65; mem. tech. staff Los Angeles div. Rockwell Internat., 1968-75; tech. staff, phys. metallurgy Sci. Ctr., Thousand Oaks, Calif., 1975-77, group mgr. metals processing, 1977-79, prin. scientist, 1979-81, dir. materials synthesis and processing dept., 1982-84; assoc. prof. Washington State U., Pullman, 1984-87, prof., 1987—; chmn. Rockwell Corp. tech. panel, materials research and engring; co-organizer 1st Internat. Symposium Superplastic Forming, 1982, Internat. Conf. on Superplasticity and Superplastic Forming, 1988. Sr. editor Jour. Materials Shaping Tech.; dep. editor Scripta Metallurgica et Materialia, 1989—; contbr. tech. articles to profl. publs.; patentee advanced metalworking and tech. Named Rockwell Engr. of Yr., 1979; recipient IR 100 award Indsl. Research mag., 1976, 80. Fellow Am. Soc. Metals; mem. AIME (shaping and forming com.), Sigma Xi. Home: 410 SE Crestview St Pullman WA 99163-2213

HAMILTON, DARDEN COLE, flight test engineer; b. Pitts., Nov. 28, 1956; s. Isaac Herman Hamilton and Grace osborne (Fish) thorp; m. Linda Susanne Moser, Aug. 7, 1976; children: Christopher Moser Hamilton, Elijah Cole Hamilton. BS in Aeronautics, St. Louis U., Cahokia, Ill., 1977; postgrad. in aeronautical tech., Ariz. State U. Lic. pilot, airframe and power mechanic; cert. instr. NRA. Engr. McDonnell Douglas Aircraft Co., St. Louis, Mo., 1977-80; group leader, engring. Cessna Aircraft Co., Wichita, Kans., 1980-83, sr. flight test engr., 1983-85; sr. flight test engr. Allied-Signal Aerospace Co., Phoenix, 1986-92; flight test engr. specialist Allied-Signal Aerospace Co., 1992—. Editor Family Proponent Newsletter, 1994—. Tierra Buena precinct commiteeman Rep. Party; vol. coord. legis. dist. 16 campaign John Shadegg for Congress; mem. adult edn. dept. Rivers Cmty. Ch.; del. Ariz. dist. 16 Ariz. Rep. Conv., 1995—. Mem. Soc. Flight Test Engrs., Ariz. State Rifle and Pistol Assn. (life). Republican. Lodge: Masons. Home: 4501 W Paradise Ln Glendale AZ 85306-2729 Office: Allied-Signal Aerospace Co Allied Signal Engines Inc 111 S 34th St Phoenix AZ 85034-2802

HAMILTON, DAVID MIKE, publishing company executive; b. Little Rock, Feb. 25, 1951; s. Ralph Franklin and Mickey Garnette (Chappell) H.; m. Carol Nancy McKenna, Oct. 25, 1975; children: Elisabeth Michelle, Caroline Ellen. BA, Pitzer Coll., 1973; MLS, UCLA, 1976. Cert. tchr. library sci., Calif. Editor Sullivan Assocs., Palo Alto, Calif., 1973-75; curator Henry E. Huntington Library, San Marino, Calif., 1976-80; mgr. prodn., mktg. William Kaufmann Pubs., Los Altos, Calif., 1980-84; pres. The Live Oak Press, Palo Alto, 1984—; cons. editor, gen. ptnr. Sensitive Expressions Pub. Co., Palo Alto, 1985—; consulting dir. AAAI Press, 1994—. Author: To the Yukon with Jack London, 1980, The Tools of My Trade, 1986; contbg. author (jour.) Small Press, 1986, Making a Digital Book, 1995; (books) Book Club of California Quarterly, 1985, Research Guide to Biography and Criticism, 1986. Sec. vestry Trinity Parish, Menlo Park, 1986, bd. dirs., 1985-87; trustee Jack London Ednl. Found., San Francisco; bd. dirs. ISYS Forum, Palo Alto, 1987—; pres. site coun., mem. supt.'s adv. com. Palo Alto Unified Sch. Dist. Mem. ALA, Coun. on Scholarly, Med. and Ednl. Publs., Am. Assn. Artificial Intelligence (bd. dirs. 1984—, dir. publs.), Bookbuilders West (book show com. 1983), Author's Guild, Soc. Tech. Communication (judge 1984), Assn. Computing Machinery (chmn. pub. com. 1984), Soc. Scholarly Pubs., Sierra Club, Book Club Calif. Democrat. Episcopalian. Home: 2620 Emerson St Palo Alto CA 94306-2310 Office: The Live Oak Press PO Box 60036 Palo Alto CA 94306-0036

HAMILTON, DONALD BENGTSSON, author; b. Uppsala, Sweden, Mar. 24, 1916; s. Bengt L.K. and Elise (Neovius) H.; m. Kathleen Stick, 1941 (dec. Oct. 28, 1989); children: Hugo, Elise, Gordon, Victoria. B.S., U. Chgo., 1938. Writer and photographer, 1946—. Creator Matt Helm series; author books including Death of a Citizen, 1960, The Wrecking Crew, 1960, The Removers, 1961, The Silencers, 1962, Murderer's Row, 1962, The Ambushers, 1963, The Ravagers, 1963, The Shadowers, 1964, The Devastators, 1965, The Betrayers, 1966, The Menacers, 1968, The Interlopers, 1969, The Intriguers, 1972, The Intimidators, 1974, The Terminators, 1975, The Terrorizers, 1977, The Retaliators, 1976, The Poisoners, 1971, Cruises with Kathleen, 1980, The Mona Intercept, 1980, The Revengers, 1982, The Annihilators, 1983, The Infiltrators, 1984, The Detonators, 1985, The Vanishers, 1986, The Demolishers, 1987, The Frighteners, 1989, The Threateners, 1992, The Damagers, 1993; contbr. articles on hunting, yachting, and photography to mags. Mem. Mystery Writers Am., Western Writers Am., Outdoor Writers Assn. Am. Office: PO Box 1141 Old Saybrook CT 06475-5141

HAMILTON, DONALD EMERY, librarian; b. Calgary, Alta., Can., Oct. 11, 1938; s. George Emery and Clarice Edna (Bird) H.; m. Sally, Aug. 18, 1961; children: Jennifer, George. BA, Mt. Allison U., 1964; MSL, Western Mich. U., Kalamazoo, 1970. Tchr. English New Liskeard (Ont., Can.) Bd. Edn., 1964-66; tchr. English and libr. Cen. Huron Bd. Edn., Clinton, Ont., 1966-68; libr. Lake of the Woods Bd. Edn., Kenora, Ont., 1968-71; edn. libr. U. Victoria, B.C., 1971—, acting head ref. libr., 1987-91, adj. asst. prof. sch. librarianship, 1988—, sponsor Pearson Programs, 1978-87; cons. in field. Columnist Sch. Librs. Can. Mem. Can. Sch. Libr. Assn. (pres. 1973-74, M.B. Scott award of merit 1988). Home: 1020 Pentrelew Pl, Victoria, BC Canada V8V 4J6 Office: U Victoria Curriculum Libr, PO Box 1800, Victoria, BC Canada V8W 2Y2

HAMILTON, GARY GLEN, sociology educator; b. Ellsworth, Kans., Nov. 17, 1943; s. Glen G. and Ethel (Livingston) H.; m. Eleanor Shufelt; 1 child, Justine. BA, U. Kans., 1965; MA, U. Wash., PhD, 1975. From asst. to full prof. sociology U. Calif., Davis, 1974-93, chmn. dept., 1986-89, dir. Internat. Program on East Asia Bus. & Devel., 1987-93; prof. sociology U. Wash., Seattle, 1993—. Author: (with Nicole Biggart) Governor Reagon, Governor Brown, 1984; editor: Business Networks and Economic Development in East and Southeast Asia, 1991; translator: (with Wang Zheng) From the Soil, The Foundations of Chinese Society, 1992; contbr. articles to profl. jours. Served to 1st lt. U.S. Army, 1966-69, Vietnam. Fulbright-Hays fellow, Tunghai U., Taiwan, 1984-85; recipient Outstanding Teaching award U. Calif.-Davis, 1982-83; NSF grantee, 1978-81, 86-89; Guggenheim fellow, 1989-90. Mem. Am. Sociol. Assn., Assn. Asian Studies. Office: U Wash Dept Sociology Seattle WA 98195

HAMILTON, HARRY LEMUEL, JR., academic administrator; b. Charleston, S.C., May 26, 1938; s. Harry Lemuel and Velma Fern (Bell) H.; m. LaVerne McDaniel, June 26, 1965 (div. 1978); children: David M., Lisa L. BA in Physics, Beloit Coll., 1960; MS in Meteorology, U. Wis., 1962, PhD in Meteorology, 1965. Asst. prof. atmospheric sci. SUNY, Albany, 1965-71, assoc. prof., 1971-90, dir. ednl. opportunity program, 1968-71, chairperson atmospheric sci., 1976-83; dean undergrad. studies, assoc. v.p. academic affairs SUNY, 1983-88; rsch. scientist GE, Schenectady, N.Y., 1973-75; sr. v.p., provost Chapman U., Orange, Calif., 1990—. Trustee Beloit (Wis.) Coll., 1972—; bd. dirs. Albany Med. Ctr., 1988-90, Mohawk Hudson Community Found., 1988-90; pres. Empire State Inst. for Performing Arts, Albany, 1986-90. Mem. Am. Meteorol. Soc., Am. Assn. for Higher Edn., Sigma Xi. Office: Chapman U 333 N Glassell St Orange CA 92666-1011

HAMILTON, JAMES DOUGLAS, economics educator; b. Denver, Colo., Nov. 29, 1954; s. Warren Bell and Alcita Victoria Hamilton; m. Marjorie Ann Flavin, Aug. 6, 1983; children: Laura Diane, Richard Gregory. BA, Colo. Coll., 1977; MA, U. Calif., Berkeley, 1981, PhD, 1983. From asst. prof. to assoc. prof. to prof. econs. U. Va., Charlottesville, 1981-92; prof. econs. U. Calif., San Diego, 1992—; vis. prof. U. Calif., San Diego, 1984-85, rsch. advisor Fed. Res. Bank, Richmond, Va., 1989-92. Assoc. editor Jour. Econ. Dynamics and Control, 1988—, Jour. Bus. and Econ. Statistics, 1991—, Econometrica, 1992—, Rev. Econs. and Statistics, 1993—, Jour. Money, Credit and Banking, 1993—. Grad. fellow NSF U. Calif., 1978-81; rsch. grantee NSF, 1988—. Mem. Am. Econ. Assn., Econometric Soc., Soc. Econ. Dynamics and Control. Office: U Calif San Diego Dept Econs San Diego CA 92093-0508

HAMILTON, JERALD, musician; b. Wichita, Kans., Mar. 19, 1927; s. Robert James and Lillie May (Rishel) H.; m. Phyllis Jean Searle, Sept. 8, 1954; children: Barbara Helen, Elizabeth Sarah, Catharine Sandra. MusB, U. Kans., Lawrence, 1948, MusM, 1950; postgrad., Royal Sch. Ch. Music, Croydon, Eng., summer 1955, Union Theol. Sem. Sch. Sacred Music, N.Y.C., summer 1960; studies with, Laurel Everette Anderson, Andre Marchal, Catharine Crozier, Gustav Leonhardt. From instr. to asst. prof. organ and theory Washburn U., Topeka, 1949-59; dir. Washburn Singers and Choir, 1955-59; asst. prof. organ, dir. univ. singers and chorus Ohio U., Athens, 1959-60; asst. prof. organ and ch. music U. Tex., Austin, 1960-63; lectr. ch. music Episcopal Theol. Sem. S.W., Austin, 1961-63; mem. faculty U. Ill., Urbana-Champaign, 1963-88, prof. music, 1967-88, prof. emeritus, 1988—; organist, choirmaster chs. in Kans. and Tex., 1942-63; organist, choirmaster Episcopal Ch. St. John the Divine, Champaign, 1963-88; organist, choirmaster St. John's Cathedral, Albuquerque, 1988-93, organist-choirmaster emeritus, 1994—; mem., chmn. commn. ch. music Episc. Diocese Kans., 1951-59; mem. bishop's commn. ch. music Episc. Diocese of Springfield, 1978-80, 82-88; concert organist, 1955—; with Phyllis Stringham Concert Mgmt. Author (with Marilou Kratzenstein) Four Centuries of Organ Music, Detroit Studies in Music Bibliography No. 51, 1984. Fulbright scholar, 1954-55. Mem. Assn. Anglican Musicians, Am. Guild Organists, Omicron Delta Kappa, Pi Kappa Lambda, Phi Mu Alpha. Episcopalian. Home: 27 Abajo Dr Edgewood NM 87015

HAMILTON, JUDITH ANN, human resources professional; b. Humboldt, Nebr., Nov. 19, 1946; d. Donald Leonard and Betty June (Warner) Stalder; m. Rodney Gene Hamilton, Mar. 23, 1973; 1 child, Russell Allen. BBA, U. Denver, 1990; cert. mgmt. devel., U. Colo., 1984. Cert. sr. profl. in human resources. V.p. adminstrn. Particle Measuring Systems Inc., Boulder, Colo., 1979-85; dir. human resources Access Graphics, Inc., Boulder, 1990-93; prin. Solutions Resource Group, Santa Fe, 1994—; speaker Colo. Bus. Educators Conf., Denver, 1991; event judge Future Bus. Leaders Am., Colo., 1991. Chairperson Bus. Adv. Com., Adams County Sch. Dist. 12, Colo. Named Bus. Person of Yr., Future Bus. Leaders Am., 1991. Mem. Soc. Human Resource Mgmt., Colo. Human Resource Assn., No. N.Mex. Human Resource Assn. (basic reading tutor Santa Fe literacy program), Human Resource Mgmt. Assoc. Albuquerque, N. Mex., Boulder Area Human Resource Assn. (dir. 1992, 93), program Com. for N. Mex. State Conf. of SHRM (chair). Office: 4350 Airport Rd Ste 5-435 Santa Fe NM 87505-6503

HAMILTON, MARTA, research scientist; b. L.A., Jan. 28, 1957; d. Walter Joseph and Shirley Ann (Patterson) Wardzinski; m. Steven Dee Hamilton, June 2, 1979. BS in Chemistry, Southeastern Mo. State U., 1979; PhD in Analytical Chemistry, Purdue U., 1983. Rsch. scientist Eli Lilly & Co., Indpls., 1983-90, mgr. quality control labs., 1990-92; pharm. industry bus. devel. mgr. Hewlett Packard Analytical Products Group, Wilmington, Del., 1992-94; rsch. strategy group Inflammation Rsch. Amgen, Inc., Thousand Oaks, Calif., 1994-95; head lab. Amgen Boulder (Colo.), Inc., 1995—; mem. external adv. bd. Ctr. Bioanalytical Chemistry, Lawrence, Kans., 1992—. Mem. Am. Chem. Soc., Am. Assn. Pharm. Scis. Home: 4297 Vinca Ct Boulder CO 80304 Office: Amgen Boulder Inc 3200 Walnut St Boulder CO 80304

HAMILTON, MARTIN ALVA, statistician, consultant; b. Lander, Wyo., June 18, 1939; s. Alva Wester and Ruth Margaret (King) H.; m. Mary Talovich, Dec. 2, 1967; children: Wade, Katrina, Gordon. BS, U. Wyo., 1961, MS, 1962; PhD, Stanford U., 1968. Statistician Nat. Cancer Inst., Bethesda, Md., 1968-70, Mont. State U., Bozeman, 1970—; prof. Mont. State U., Bozeman, 1980; dir. Mont. State U. Cons. Svcs., Bozeman, 1988-90; acting dir. Ctr. for Biofilm Engring., Bozeman, 1991-92. Contbr. chpts. to books and articles to profl. jours. Scientist USPHS, 1968-70. Recipient Fulbright scholarship Fulbright Commn., U. Aberdeen, Scotland, 1962-63, Rsch. Career Devel. award Nat. Inst. Environ. Health Sci., Research Triangle Park, N.C., 1979, Wiley Faculty award for meritorious rsch. Mont. State U., Bozeman, 1984. Mem. AAAS, Am. Statis. Assn. (editorial bd. 1981-82), The Biometric Soc. (regional com. mem. 1983-85), Inst. Math. Stats., Soc. for Epidemiologic Rsch., Com. of Pres.' of Statis. Socs. (treas. 1986-88). Office: Dept Math Scis Mont State Univ Bozeman MT 59717-0240

HAMILTON, PENNY RAFFERTY, research executive, writer, educator; b. Altoona, Pa., Feb. 18, 1948; d. William E. and Lois B. (Noel) Rafferty; m. William A. Hamilton, Dec. 21, 1971. AA, Columbia (Mo.) Coll., 1968; BA, Columbia (Md.) Coll., 1976; MA, U. Nebr., 1978, PhD, 1981; postdoctoral studies, Menninger Found., Topeka, 1984. Community educator U.S. Forces in Europe, Fulda, Fed. Republic of Germany, 1972-74; health educator Nebr. State Govt., Lincoln, 1974-84; v.p. Advanced Rsch. Inst., Winter Park, Colo., 1984—; spl. features editor, newspaper columnist Sun Newspapers/Capital Times, Lincoln, 1982-91; dir. pub. affairs Sta. KHAT-KMXA, Lincoln, 1986-92. Bd. dirs. Grand County Pet Pals, 1992—, Grand County Aviation Assn., 1992—, Friends of Granby Airport, 1992—. Set world and nat. aviation speed record, 1991. Home: PO Box 2001 Granby CO 80446-2001 Office: Advanced Rsch Inst PO Box 3499 Winter Park CO 80482-3499

HAMILTON, PHILLIP DOUGLAS, lawyer; b. Pasadena, Calif., Oct. 16, 1954; s. Ivan and Annette O. (Brown) H.; m. Gerry Messner, Sept. 17, 1976 (div. Feb. 1984); m. Janet L. Hester, Apr. 22, 1984; children: Melissa, John, Mark Charles. BA, U. Pa., 1976; JD, Pepperdine U., 1979. Bar: Calif. 1979, U.S. Dist. Ct. (cen. dist.) Calif. 1980. Assoc., Offices of James J. DiCesare, Santa Ana, Calif., 1979-84; sole practice, Newport Beach, Calif., 1984—. Bd. dirs. Juvenile Diabetes Found., Orange County, 1988, pres., 1989, 90, 91. Recipient Am. Jurisprudence award, 1980. Mem. Assn. Trial Lawyers Am., Orange County Trial Lawyers Assn., Calif. Trial Lawyers Assn., Calif. Trial Lawyers Polit. Action Com., Orange County Bar Assn. Republican. Presbyterian. Office: 5 Hutton Centre Dr Ste 950 Santa Ana CA 92707-5819

HAMILTON, RONALD RAY, minister; b. Evansville, Ind., May 6, 1932; s. Floyd Ray Hamilton and Ruby Dixon (Chism) Hahn; m. Norma Jean Robertson, Mar. 25, 1956; children: Ronnetta Jean, Andrea, Robert Rae. BA, U. Evansville, 1955; BD, Garrett Theol. Sem., 1958, MDiv, 1972; PhD, Oxford Grad. Sch., Eng., Dayton, Tenn., 1989. Ordained elder United Meth. Ch. Minister Scobey (Mont.) Meth. Ch., 1958-61, St. Andrew Meth. Ch., Littleton, Colo., 1961-67; sr. minister First Meth. Ch., Grand Junction, Colo., 1967-75, Christ United Meth. Ch., Salt Lake City, 1975-80, Littleton United Meth., 1980-86, U. Park United Meth., Denver, 1986-91. Author: The Way to Success, 1972, The Greatest Prayer, 1983, A Chosen People, 1986; editor jour., 1978. Recipient Spl. award Mental Health Assn., Mesa County, Colo., 1974, Goodwill Rehab. Inc., 1975. Mem. Lions Club, Rotary Club, Civitan (chaplain 1964-67). Republican. Home: 4509 E Frye Rd Phoenix AZ 85044-7601

HAMILTON, RUTH HELLMANN, design company owner; b. Millboro, S.D., Oct. 15; d. Walter Otto and Laura Ethel (King) Hellmann; m. Gordon Eugene Hamilton, June 11, 1950; children: Kristin Goodnight, Bret Hamilton, Lori O'Toole, Lynnelle Anderson. AB, Nebr. Wesleyan U., Lincoln, 1948; MEd and Humanities, So. Meth. U., 1952. Owner, chief exec. officer Sonoran Desert Designs, Tucson, 1976-95; lectr. Ariz. Desert Mus., Tucson, 1985-86, Tohono Chul Mus., Tucson, 1986-95, Prescott Coll., Tucson, 1987, Tucson Bot. Gardens, 1985-95, Elderhostel, 1991-92; tchr. design student classes. Exhibited displays for Old Pueblo Mus. at Foothills Mall, 1987-90; demonstrations of desert designs Ariz. State Conv. Garden Clubs N.Mex., 1987, 89; one-woman shows at Tucson Garden Club, 1988, 90; original designs published by Nat. Coun. Garden Clubs Calendars, 1984, 87, 89, 95. Mem. pub. svcs. bd. KVOA-TV, 1969-74. Mem. Los Cerros Garden Club (pres. 1984-85, 94-95). Home: 7720 N Sendero De Juana Tucson AZ 85718-7517

HAMILTON, SCOTT SCOVELL, professional figure skater, former Olympic athlete; b. Toledo, Aug. 28, 1958; adopted s. Ernest Scovell and Dorothy (McIntosh) H. Grad. high sch., Bowling Green, Ohio, 1976; student, Metro State Coll., 1979. nat. spokesman Discover Card youth programs, 1995—. Amateur competitive career includes Nat. Figure Skating Championships: jr. men's 1st pl., 1976, sr. men's 9th pl., 1977, 3d pl., 1978, 4th pl., 1979, 3d pl., 1980, 1st pl., 1981, 82, 83, 84, Mid-Western Figure Skating Championships: sr. men's 3d pl., 1977, 78, 79, Norton Skate Championships (now Skate Am.): men's divsn. 1st pl., 1979, 80, 81, 82, South Atlantic Figure Skating Championships: sr. men's divsn. 1st pl., 1980, Eastern Figure Skating Championships: sr. men's 1st pl., 1980, 81, 82, 83, 84, World Figure Skating Championships: men's divsn. 5th pl., 1980, 1st pl. 81, 82, 83, 84, Nat. Sports Festival Championships: 1st pl. men's divsn., 1981; Winter Olympics: men's divsn. 5th pl., Lake Placid, N.Y., 1980, 1st pl., Sarajevo, Yugoslavia, 1984, Nippon Hoso Kykai Figure Skating Championships, men's divsn. 1st pl., 1982, Golden Spin of Zagreb Championships, men's divsn. 1st pl., 1983; Profl. competitive career includes Nutrasweet/NBC-TV World Profl. Figure Skating Championships mens. divsn., 1st pl., 1984, 86, 2d pl., 85, 87, 88, 89, 91; World Challenge Champions/ABC-TV men's divsn., 2d pl., 1985, 1st pl., 1986; U.S. Open men's divsn. 1st pl., 1990, 2d pl., 1991, Diet Coke Profl. Skaters Championship men's divsn. 1st pl., 1992, Hershey's Kisses Pro-Am. Figure Skating Championships 2d Place Men's divsn. 1993, Sun Valley Men's Outdoor Championship 2d pl., 1994, The Gold Championship men's divsn. 1st pl., 1994, Can. Profl. Skating Championship men's divsn. 1st pl., 1994, Fox's Rock and Roll Skating Championship men's divsn. 1st pl., 1994; profl. performances include Nat. Arena Tour Ice Capades, 1984-85, 85-86, star Scott Hamilton's Am. Tour, 1986-87, 1990-91, co-star Concert On Ice, Harrah's Hotel, Lake Tahoe, Nev., 1987, spl. guest star Festival On Ice, Nat. Theatre Tour, 1987, star Discover Card Stars On Ice Nat. Arena Tour, 1987-88, 88-89, star Festival On Ice, Harrah's Hotel, 1988, guest star ABC-TV spl. Ice Capades With Kirk Cameron, 1988, A Very Special Christmas, ABC-TV, 1988, An Olympic Calgary Christmas, ABC-TV, 1988, star and mus. comedy and acting debut Broadway On Ice, Harrah's Hotel and Nat. Theatre Tour, 1989; CBS-TV Sports Figure Skating Commentator 1984-91 various skating competitions and CBS-TV coverage Winter Olympics, Albertville, France, 1992, Lillehammer, Norway, 1994; star, dir., producer Scott Hamilton's Celebration On Ice, Sea World of Calif., 1988, Scott Hamilton's Time Traveler: An Odyssey On Ice, Sea World of Calif., 1989; host, guest star TV spl. A Salute To Dorothy Hamill, 1988; star, co-producer Discover Card Stars On Ice, Nat. Arena Tour, 1989-91; guest star CBS-TV spl. Disney's Christmas on Ice, 1990; co-producer, star Discover Card Stars on Ice Nat. Arena Tour, 1991-92; co-host, star HBO TV spl. Vail Skating Festival, 1992; co-prodr., star Discover Card Stars on Ice Nat. Arena Tour, 1992-93, 93-94, 94-95, Canadian Nat. Tour, 1995; guest TV spl. A Disney Christmas on Ice, 1992, CBS-TV spl. Disney on Ice, 1992, HBO-TV spl. Vail Skating Festival, 1993, Skates of Gold I, Boston, 1993, Skates of Gold II, Cin., 1994, CBS-TV Disney Fantasy on Ice, 1993, CBS-TV spl. Nancy Kerrigan & Friends, 1994, CBS-TV spl. Disney's Greatest Hits, 1994, CBS-TV spl. Dreams on Ice, 1995; creator original concepts in arena figure skating. Cons. Friends of Scott Hamilton Found. named in his honor to fundraise and benefit youth oriented causes throughout U.S., 1988, Scott Hamilton's Friends and Legends 1st Annual Celebrity Charity Golf Tournament, Ford's Colony, Williamsburg, Va., 1991; participant fund-raising Athletes for Reagan, March of Dimes, Am. Cancer Soc., Spl. Olympics, Starlight Found., United Way Adoption Home Socs., Make A Wish Found, Big Bros., 1984 Athletes For Bush, Adult and Ped. AIDS Rsch., Edn. and Funding, 1988—, Homeless, 1989—, Great Am. Workout for Pres.'s Coun. Phys. Fitness & Sports, 1990, 92; nat. spokesman Discover Card youth programs, 1995—. Winner Olympic Gold medal, Sarajevo, 1984; U.S. Olympic Com. awards and honors include carrier Am. Flag in opening ceremonies Lake Placid, 1980, Figure Skating Athlete of Yr., 1981, 82, 83, 84, Athlete of Yr., 1981, Olympic Spirit award, 1987; recipient Olympia award Southland Corp., 1984, Achievement award March of Dimes, 1984, Colo. Athlete of Yr. award Denver Athletic Club, 1984, Most Courageous Athlete award Phila. Sportswriters Assn., 1985, Profl. Skater of Yr. award Am. Skating World mag., 1986, Jacques Favart award Internat. Skating Union, 1988, The Crown Royal Achievement award from House of Seagrams and Jimmy Heuga Ctr., 1991, Clairol's Personal Best award, 1991, Spirit of Giving award U.S. Figure Skating Assn., 1993, 9th Ann. Great Sports Legends award Nick Buonoconti Fund The Miami Project, 1994, Ritter F. Shumway award U.S. Figure Skating Assn., 1994; inducted U.S. Olympic Hall of Fame, 1990, World Figure Skating Hall of Fame, 1990; honoree nat. com. for adoption, 1992. Hon. mem. Phila. Skating Club, Humane Soc. Republican. Office: 4242 Van Nuys Blvd Sherman Oaks CA 91403-3710

HAMLIN, EDMUND MARTIN, JR., engineering manager; b. Utica, N.Y., June 9, 1949; s. Edmund Martin and Catherine Mary (Humphreys) H.; m. Nancy Ann Christensen, June 26, 1971; 1 child, Benjamin John (dec.). BSEE, Clarkson U., 1971; MBA, UCLA, 1993. Lic. airframe and powerplant mechanic, 1994. Engr. NASA Flight Rsch. Ctr., Edwards, Calif., 1971-75; sr. engr. NASA Flight Rsch. Ctr., Edwards, 1976-79; project engr. Sundstrand Energy Systems Div., Belvidere, Ill., 1975-76; sr. engr. Teleco Oilfield Svcs., Meriden, Conn., 1979-80, mgr. electronic systems, 1980-83, the sr. staff engr., 1984; sr. engr. NASA Ames-Dryden, Edwards, Calif., 1984-85; asst. chief flight sys. NASA Ames-Dryden, Edwards, 1990-94, asst. dir. rsch., 1994—, 1994—. Inventor: position measurement system, 1976, method for determining and correcting magnetic interference in boreholes, 1988, method for computing borehold azimuth while rotating, 1989. Pres. bd. trustees Tehachapi (Calif.) Unified Sch. Dist., 1989-94. Mem. AIAA, Instrument Soc. Am., Aircraft Owners and Pilots Assn., Exptl. Aircraft Assn. Home: 22220 Valley Vista Dr Tehachapi CA 93561-9549 Office: NASA Ames-Dryden Flight Rsch Facility PO Box 273 Edwards CA 93523-0273

HAMLIN, SUSAN ELIZABETH, lawyer, educator; b. Boise, Idaho, Nov. 15, 1966. BA, U. Idaho, 1989, JD, 1992. Bar: Idaho 1992. Lectr. U. Idaho, Moscow, 1990-92; legal extern U.S. Atty.'s Office, Boise, 1991; law clk. Atty. Gen., Boise, 1992, Idaho Dist. Judge and Snake River Adjudication, 1992-93; dep. atty. gen. Idaho Dept. Water Resources, Boise, 1993—. Assoc. mem. Idaho Law Rev., 1990-91. Mem. ABA, Idaho Trial Lawyers Assn., Idaho Vol. Lawyers for the Arts, Idaho Water User Assn., Phi Alpha Theta (pres. 1987-88), Alpha Gamma Delta (pres. 1987-88). Office: Idaho Dept Water Resources 1301 N Orchard St Boise ID 83706-2237

HAMM, CATHARINE MARGARET, journalist; b. Syracuse, N.Y., June 6, 1954; d. Joseph Francis and Genevieve Margaret (Fleming) H. BA, McPherson Coll., 1976. Dep. mng. editor Kansas City (Mo.) Star, 1990-92; mng. editor The Sun, San Bernardino, Calif., 1993—. Bd. dirs. Read Aloud, San Bernardino, 1993-94. Mem. Soc. of Newspaper Design, Calif. Soc. of Newspaper Editors. Office: The Sun 399 N D St San Bernardino CA 92401-1518

HAMM, GEORGE ARDEIL, retired secondary education educator, hypnotherapist, consultant; b. San Diego, Aug. 13, 1934; s. Charles Ardeil and Vada Lillian (Sharrah) H.; m. Marilyn Kay Nichols, July 1, 1972; children—Robert Barry, Charles Ardeil II, Patricia Ann. B.S. in Music, No. Ariz. U., 1958, M.A. in Music Edn., 1961; M.A. in Ednl. Adminstrn., Calif. Lutheran Coll., 1978, M.S. in Guidance and Counseling, 1981. Cert. secondary sch. tchr., adminstr. pupil personnel services, Calif., clinical hypnotherapist. Tchr. music Needles (Calif.) High Sch., 1958-61; music sociology, psychology tchr, counselor Hueneme High Sch., Oxnard, Calif., 1961-93; ret. founder Nat. Judo Inst., Colorado Springs, Colo., Coll. Sport Sci., Nat. Judo Inst.; cons. applied sport hypnotherapy; creator teaching program. Served with USMC, 1953-55; Korea. Mem. Am. Fedn. Tchrs., Am. Council Hypnotist Examiners, U.S. Judo Assn. Inc. (6th degree black belt of Ju Jitsu, sr. level coach of Judo, 1980, cert. rank examiner), Phi Delta Kappa, Kappa Delta Pi. Republican. Mormon. Contbr. numerous articles to nat. and internat. Judo jours. Pioneer ednl. hypnosis. Home: 2560 Ruby Dr Oxnard CA 93030-8607

HAMM, GERHARD CORNELIUS, business executive; b. Berlin, Nov. 17, 1936; came to the U.S., 1959; s. Wilhelm C. and Else (Schulz) H.; m. Pamela Kim Hamm, 1975 (div. 1985); children: Christian, Natascha. Abitur, Tannenberg Schule, Berlin, 1956; BSc, U. Calif., Berkeley, 1965, MBA, 1966. Asst. to wholesale mgr. Mercedes-Benz of Can., Vancouver, 1959-63; asst. to v.p. corp. devel. Pfizer, Internat., N.Y.C., 1966-67; sales mgr. Eurocars of Hawaii, Ltd., Honolulu, 1968-82, Continental Cars, Ltd., Honolulu, 1982-93; v.p., bd. dirs. Condominium Assn., Honolulu, 1977-79. Bd. dirs. Neighborhood Bd., Honolulu, 1989-90. Mem. Honolulu Acad. Art, Bishop Mus. Home: 1930 Alaweo St Honolulu HI 96821-1304

HAMM, WILLIAM GILES, banking executive; b. Washington, Dec. 29, 1942; s. John Edwin and Letty Belle (Wills) H.; m. Kathleen Kelley, Sept. 5, 1970; 1 child, Giles Alexander. AB, Dartmouth Coll., 1964; MA, U. Mich., 1966, PhD, 1969. Budget examiner Bur. of the Budget, Washington, 1969-72; chief HUD br. Office of Mgmt. & Budget, Washington, 1972-76; dep. assoc. dir. Office of Mgmt. & Budget, 1976-77; legis. analyst Calif. Legis., Sacramento, 1977-86; v.p. World Savs. & Loan, Oakland, Calif., 1986-91; sr. v.p. Fed. Home Loan Bank of San Francisco, 1991-92, exec. v.p., COO, 1992—. Bd. visitors Duke U., Durham, 1986-89, U. Calif., Davis, 1986-93. Recipient William A. Jump award, Civil Svc. Commn., 1975, Presdl. commendation, 1973, 74. Fellow Nat. Acad. Pub. Adminstrn., Coun. for Excellence in Govt.; mem. Commonwealth Club, Phi Beta Kappa, Phi Kappa Phi. Office: Fed Home Loan Bank San Francisco 600 California St San Francisco CA 94108-2704

HAMMAN, STEVEN ROGER, vocational rehabilitation specialist; b. Santa Monica, Calif., Nov. 2, 1946; s. Roy Ernest H. and Joan Barbara (Werner) Scott; m. Christine Frances Solomon, May 29, 1976; children: Zachary Charles, Tamara Edith, Bryan Joseph. AA, Northeastern Colo. U., 1967; BA, Colo. State Coll., 1970; MA, U. No. Colo., 1972; MS, Drake U., 1981. Cert. vocat. expert, rehab. counselor, ins. rehab. specialist. Social worker Poudre-Thompson Transp. Corps, Ft. Collins, Colo., 1974-78; placement specialist Missoula (Mont.) Rehab. Ctr., 1978-80; rehab. counselor Adolph Coors Co., Golden, Colo., 1981; rehab. counselor, br. mgr. Nat. Rehab. Cons., Duluth, Minn., 1981-82; Mont. case svcs. dir. Nat. Rehab. Cons., Missoula, 1982-83; case svcs. dir. Northwest U.S. Nat. Rehab. Cons., Spokane, Wash., 1983-86; rehab. cons., pres., chief exec. officer Vocability, Inc., Post Falls, Idaho, 1986—; counselor, trainer Community Corrections Program, Ft. Collins, 1976. Community organizer VISTA, Clay, W.Va., 1973-74; pres., bd. dirs. Mountain Van Spl. Transp., Missoula, 1980; bd. dirs. Heritage Place I and II, Coeur d'Alene Homes Inc.; mem. coun. Calvary Luth. Ch., Post Falls. Mem. Nat. Assn. Rehab. Practitioners in the Private Sector., Vocat. Evaluation and Work Adjustment Assn. (registered cons. Americans with Disabilities Act). Office: Vocability Inc PO Box 772 Post Falls ID 83854-0772

HAMMARGREN, LONNIE, lieutenant governor; b. Dec. 25, 1937; married. BA, U. Minn., 1958, MA in Psychol., 1960, BS, 1964, MD, 1964, MS in Neurosurgery, 1974. Diplomate Am. Bd. Neurological Surgery; med. license Nev., Minn. Flight surgeon for the astronauts NASA Manned Space Craft Ctr.; lt. gov., pres. of the senate State of Nev., 1995—; assoc. clin. prof. neurosurgery U. Nev. Sch. Medicine, Reno; clin. assoc. prof. surgery U. Calif., San Diego, 1982; chair Commn. Econ. Devel., Commn. Tourism; bd. dirs. Nev. Dept. Transp. Bd. regents U. and C.C. Sys. Nev., 1988-94; adv. bd. mem. Gov.'s com. for Employment of Handicapped; mem. State Bd. Edn., 1984-88; bd. mem. March of Dimes, Aid to Adoption of Spl. Kids. Mem. Spinal Cord Injury Program of Nev. (pres.), Cancer Soc., Aerospace Med. Assn., U Med. Ctr. Rehabilitation Unit (dir.), U. Med. Ctr. (chmn. neurosurgery dept.), Help Them Walk Again Found. (Nat. Dir.), Spina Bifida and Hydrocephalus Soc. (med. dir.), Internat. Ctr. for Rehabilitation Engring. (med. dir.), Pacific World Med. Found. (treas.), Paramed. and Emergency Care Bd. (adv.). Office: Capitol Complex Carson City NV 89710

HAMMEL, EUGENE ALFRED, anthropologist; b. N.Y.C., Mar. 18, 1930; s. William Jonathan and Violet Nancy (Brookes) H.; m. Joan Marie Swingle, Jan. 26, 1951; children—Kenneth, Bruce, Deborah, Richard. A.B. in Anthropology, U. Calif., Berkeley, 1951, Ph.D. in Anthropology, 1959. Asst. prof. U. N.Mex., Albuquerque, 1959-61; asst. prof. U.Calif., Berkeley, 1961-63, assoc. prof., 1963-66, prof., 1966—; mem., chmn. Joint Com. on E. Europe, N.Y., 1972-75, Math. Soc. Sci. Bd., 1975-78; chmn. NRC Commn. on Population, Washington, 1983-86. Author: Power in Ica, 1969; Ritual Relations and Alternative Social Structures in the Balkans, 1968; co-author: Statistical Studies of Historical Social Structure, 1978; contbr. articles to profl. jours. Mem. Sierra Club, San Francisco, 1952—. Served to lt. U.S. Army, 1951-54. Guggenheim Found. fellow, 1965; fellow Ctr. Advanced Study Behavioral Sci., Stanford, 1962. Fellow Am. Anthropol. Assn. (exec. bd. 1968-70); mem. Am. Ethnol. Soc. (pres. 1985), Population Assn. Am., Internat. Union for Scientific Study of Population, Nat. Acad. Scis. Office: U Calif Dept Anthropology 2232 Piedmont Ave Berkeley CA 94704

HAMMELL, GRANDIN GAUNT, real estate consultant; b. Rumson, N.J., Aug. 10, 1945; s. Grandin Kenneth and Catherine Elizabeth (Conklin) H.; m. Darlene Faye Settje, Nov. 21, 1972; children: Grandin Jeffrey, Heidi Grechen. B of Bus. Sci., Calif. State U., Los Angeles, 1979; grad., Realtor Inst., 1994. V.p. Security Pacific Bank, N.A., Los Angeles, 1973-87; exec. v.p. The Wellington Group, Rolling Hills Estate, Calif., 1987-89; bus. cons. Cambridge Bus. Forms, Burbank, Calif., 1991-93; real estate cons. Fowler Real Estate Better Homes & Gardens, Boulder, Colo., 1993—; speaker seminars on estate planning, so. Calif., 1983-90. Exec. producer radio program The World of Money. Mem. planned giving com. of So. Calif. chpt. Arthritis Found., 1987-93; v.p. Burbank Ednl. Found., 1984-93; chmn. fund raising com. L.A. County Natural History Mus. Mem. Glendale Estate Planning Commn., Burbank C. of C. (ednl. com. 1989-93, devel. com.). Office: Fowler Real Estate Better Homes & Gardens 2970 Wilderness Pl Ste 200 Boulder CO 80301-5412

HAMMER, JAN HAROLD, television station manager; b. Boise, Idaho, May 28, 1939; s. Frederick Allen Hammer and Violet (Gardner) Goicoechea; m. Jane M. Hammer, June 15, 1957 (div. 1972); children: Julie, Christopher, Angela, Gregory. Student, Ea. Mont. Coll., 1963-64, Boise State Coll., 1965-66. Nat. sales mgr. KIVI/KPVI TV, Boise, 1972-77; campaign mgr. Gov. John V. Evans, Idaho, Boise, 1978, spl. asst., 1977-79; congl. candidate Idaho's First Congl. Dist., Boise, 1980; nat. sales mgr. KOKI-TV, Tulsa, 1981-85; gen. sales mgr. KTTY-TV, San Diego, 1985-86; gen. mgr. KJCT-TV, Grand Junction, Colo., 1986—; head govt. rels. we. dist. ABC-TV Affiliates Assn., 1986—. Creator TV awareness campaign on environ. Colo. Cares, 1990. Advisor Mesa County Econ. Devel. Coun., Grand Junction, 1986—; dir. Mus. of Western Colo., Grand Junction, 1987-91; dir. Rural Colo. Pvt. Industry Coun., Denver. Staff sgt. U.S. Army, 1956-64. Recipient Best TV News Story award Colo. Broadcasters Assn., Denver, 1988. Mem. Nat. Assn. Broadcasters, The Jefferson Awards, Grand Junction Lion's Club (dir. community betterment com. 1986—). Democrat.

Roman Catholic. Home: 2673 Catalina Dr Grand Junction CO 81506-1756 Office: KJCT-TV 8 Foresight Cir Grand Junction CO 81505-1014

HAMMER, SHARON ARLENE, library director; b. Seattle, July 26, 1938; d. Chauncey Rockhold Marshall and Dorothy Elizabeth (Antic) Ulbrickson; m. M. Wayne Mullins, Sept. 2, 1957 (div. June 1967); 1 child, Michael Wayne (dec.); m. Donald Jay Hammer, Aug. 23, 1969; children: Marjory Backstrum, Bonnie Moore, Polly Collier, Robert, Andy. BA in History, U. Wash., 1969, MLS, 1971, mgmt. program cert., 1982. Supr. serials and circulation Boeing Aerospace Libr./Seattle U. Libr., 1961-69; establisher basic libr. for learning disabled Bellevue (Wash.) Adaptive Learning Ctr., 1971; handicapped/elderly libr. program dir. Seattle Pub. Libr., 1972-74, dir. Wash. libr. for blind and physically handicapped, 1974-78; asst. dir. undergrad. libr. svcs. U. Wash. Librs., Seattle, 1978-83, acting libr. pers. officer, 1980-81; county libr. Marin County Free Libr., San Rafael, Calif., 1983-88; dir. Ft. Vancouver Regional Libr., Vancouver, Wash., 1988—; conf. speaker, workshop presenter, libr. edn. instr. Contbr.: Against All Odds: Case Studies on Library Financial Management, 1994. Mem. Am. Libr. Assn. (Wash. chpt. councilor 1975-79, coun.-at-large 1983-87, chair coun. resolutions com.), Pub. Libr. Assn. (mem. polit. effectiveness com., pub. policy for pub. librs. sect. transition, nominating and fee-based svcs. coms.), Assn. Specialized and Coop. Libr. Agys., Assn. Coll. and Rsch. Librs., Assn. Com. on Orgn., Libr. Info. and Tech. Assn., Libr. Instrn. Roundtable, Washington Libr. Assn. (pres. 1994—, Pres. award 1993, mem. exec. bd., numerous coms.). Office: Ft Vancouver Regional Libr 1007 E Mill Plain Blvd Vancouver WA 98663-3504

HAMMER, SUSAN W., mayor; b. Monrovia, Calif., Dec. 21, 1938; d. James Nathan and Katrine (Krutzsch) Walker; m. Philip Hammer, Sept. 4, 1960; children: Philip, Hali, Matthew. BA in History, U. Calif., Berkeley, 1960. Svc. rep. Pacific Telephone Co., Berkeley, 1960-61; staff asst. Peace Corps, Washington, 1962-63; councilwoman City of San Jose, Calif., 1980-81, 83-90, spl. asst. to mayor, 1981-82, vice mayor, 1985-87, mayor, 1991—. Bd. dirs. San Jose Mus. Art, 1971-90,, pres., 1978-80; mem. governing bd. NCCJ, 1978—; mem. adv. bd. Community Found. Santa Clara County, 1978—; mem. Santa Clara County Transp. Com., 1976-77, Santa Clara County Juvenile Justice Commn., 1974-80, San Jose Fine Arts Comm., 1980, Victim-Witness Adv. Bd., 1977—, Children's Health Coun. San Jose, 1981-89, Santa Clara Valley Leadership Program, 1986—, Childrens Shelter Project, 1991—, Am. Leadership Forum, 1992—; past chmn. parents adv. com. Trace Sch. Recipient Rosalie M. Stern Community Svc. award U. Calif., 1975, Disting. Citizen of San Jose award Exch. Club, 1979, Investment in Leadership award Coro Found., 1985, Tzedek award for honor, compassion and community svc. Temple Emanu-El, 1987, Recognition award YWCA, Santa Clara County, 1989, resolution of commendation Assn. for Responsible Alcohol Control, 1990, Woman of Achievement award The Women's Fund, 1990, Dox Quixote award Nat. Hispanic U., 1991, Friends of Bay Area Mcpl. Elections Com. award, 1991. Democrat. Office: Office of Mayor 801 N 1st St Rm 600 San Jose CA 95110-1704*

HAMMERBACK, JOHN CLARK, communications educator; b. San Francisco, Oct. 6, 1938; s. William Joseph and Susan (Ridzik) H.; m. Jean Melton, Aug. 29, 1965; children: Kristen, Karen. BA, San Francisco State Coll., 1962; MA, U. Okla., 1965; PhD, Ind. U., 1970. Teaching asst. dept. speech communication U. Okla., Norman, 1963-65, Ind. U., Bloomington, 1965-68; prof. speech communication Calif. State U., Hayward, 1968—, chmn. dept. speech and drama, 1972-79, affirmative action liason officer, 1986-88, asst. v.p. rsch. faculty affairs, 1988-91, assoc. dean, 1993—; lectr. U. N.Mex., Albuquerque, 1977, Oreg. State Coll., 1989, San Jose State U., 1993; lectr. Rotary, Kiwanis, Lions; speechwriter for local polit. candidates, Fremont, Calif., 1978—; dir. Conf. in Rhetorical Criticism, 1987-93. Author: A War of Words: Chicano Rhetoric of the 1960s and 1970s, 1985, In Search of Justice: Studies in Speech Communication in the Indiana Tradition, 1987; contbr. articles, papers, and book reviews to profl. publs. Bd. dirs. Community Counseling and Edn. Ctr., Fremont; v.p. Greater Kimber Area Homeowners Assn., 1984. Faculty Research grantee Calif. State U., Hayward, 1975; Meritorious Service award, 1985. Mem. Western Speech Comm. Assn. (2d v.p. 1979-80, mem. legis. assembly 1974-77, chmn. 1980, 1st v.p. 1981-82, chief conv. planner 1982-83, pres. 1983-84, assoc. editor jour. 1979-81, 84-87, 90—, disting. svc. award com. 1985, nominating com. 1984, chmn. mem. com. 1980, mem. search com. 1989), Rhetoric Soc., Speech Communication Assn. (com. on coms. 1985—, program planner and vice chair, chmn. pub. address divsn. 1994, nominating com. and legis. assembly 1995), Execs. Club (pres. 1991). Home: 203 Fisalia Ct Fremont CA 94539-3028 Office: Calif State U Hayward CA 94539

HAMMERSLEY, FREDERICK HAROLD, artist; b. Salt Lake City, Jan. 5, 1919; s. Harold Frederick and Anna Maria (Westberg) H. Student, U. Idaho, 1936-38, Chouinard Art Sch., 1940-42, 46-47, Ecole des Beaux Arts, Paris, France, 1945, Jepson Art Sch., 1947-50. Tchr. Jepson Art Sch., L.A., 1948-51, Pomona Coll., Claremont, Calif., 1953-62, Pasadena (Calif.) Art Mus., 1956-61, Chouinard Art Sch., L.A., 1964-68, U. N.Mex., Albuquerque, 1968-71; guest artist Tamarind Inst., Albuquerque, 1973, 88, 91. On-man shows include Owings-Dewey Fine Arts, Santa Fe, 1992, Richard Levy Gallery, Albuquerque, 1993, Mulvane Art Mus., Washburn U., Topeka, 1993, Corcoran Gallery, 1994others; works shown in gruop exhibits at M. Knoedler Gallery, Smithsonian Inst., Corcoran Gallery of Art, Albright-Knox Mus. Art, Butler Inst. Am. Art, others; represented in permanent collections Corcoran Gallery Art, San Francisco Mus. Modern Art, LA County Mus. Art, others. Sgt. U.S. Signal Corps and Infantry, 1942-46. John Simon Guggenheim fellow in painting, 1973; grantee Nat. Endowment for the Arts, 1975-77; recipient numerous purchase awards. Home and Office: 608 Carlisle Blvd SE Albuquerque NM 87106-1510

HAMMETT, BENJAMIN COWLES, psychologist; b. L.A., Nov. 18, 1931; s. Buell Hammett and Harriet (Cowles) Graham; m. Ruth Finstrom, June 18, 1957; children: Susan Hood, Sarah, Carol Bress, John. BS, Stanford U., 1957; PhD, U. N.C., 1969. Lic. psychologist, Calif. Staff psychologist Children's Psychiat. Ctr., Butner, N.C., 1965-67; sr. psychologist VA Treatment Ctr. for Children, Richmond, Va., 1968-71; asst. prof. child psychiatry Va. Commonwealth U., Richmond, 1968-71; instr. psychology Western Grad. Sch. Psychology, 1980—; pvt. practice clin. psychology Palo Alto, Calif., 1972-92; rsch. psychologist, 1992—; affiliate staff mem. O'Connor Hosp., San Jose, Calif., 1980-84; v.p. bd. dirs. Mental Rsch. Inst., Palo Alto, 1982-83, pres. bd. dirs., 1983-85, treas. 1990-92, mem. staff, 1992—, bd. dirs. emeritus, 1992—. Co-author chpts. two books. Scoutmaster Boy Scouts Am., 1952-54; treas. John B. Cary Sch. PTA, Richmond, Va., 1969-70; vol. Peninsula Conservation Ctr., Palo Alto, 1983—, Calif. Acad. Scis., San Francisco, 1987—. 1st lt. Civil Air Patrol, 1969. Named Eagle Scout, 1947; grantee NIMH, 1970. Mem. Am. Psychol. Assn., Am. Psychol. Soc., Am. Group Psychotherapy Assn., Internat. Transactional Analysis Assn. (cert. clin. mem.), Assn. Applied Psychophysiology and Biofeedback, Biofeedback Soc. Calif., Calif. Psychol. Assn., Assn. for the Advancement of Gestalt Therapy, El Tigre Club Stanford U. (sec. 1954), Nat. Parks and Conservation Assn. (bd. trustees 1995—). Democrat. Unitarian. Home: 301 Lowell Ave Palo Alto CA 94301-3812

HAMMOND, ALAN DAVID, public speaker; b. Bristol, Eng., Dec. 21, 1936; s. Alan Trevor and Edith Cavell (Tucker) H.; m. Jean Louise Hobson, Sept. 15, 1967. BEd, U. B.C., Vancouver, 1967. Pub. speaking counselor The Emissaries, Loveland, Colo., 1966-90, exec. dir., 1982-92; founder, pres. The Auralia Found., Loveland, 1993—; founder, pres. Emissary Found. Internat., Loveland, 1982-90, Renaissance Bus. Assocs., Loveland, 1983-90, Renaissance Edn. Assocs., Loveland, 1985-91; adv. to bd. dirs. Whole Health Inst., 1984-89, Assn. for Responsible Comm., Corona, Calif., 1984-89. Co-author anthology-talks, 1979; author numerous booklets; contbr. articles to profl. jours. With RAF, 1955-57. Home and Office: The Auralia Found PO Box 214 Masonville CO 80541

HAMMOND, BERT DORSEY, retired social science educator, counselor, consultant; b. Nashville, Feb. 9, 1925; s. Arthur and Mattie Dorsey; m. Mildred E. Keller, Dec. 25, 1947; children: Deborah Bert Dorsey Jr., Christopher, Mark, Michael. BS in Social Sci., Ohio State U., 1950; MEd in Pub. Sch. Adminstrn.-Social Sci., Cornell U., 1955; postgrad., U. So. Calif., 1966-67, Oxford (Eng.) U., 1985-86. Tchr. history, internat. rels. and psychology Oxnard (Calif.) High Sch., 1958-67; exec. dir. Project Open Future, Claremont (Calif.) Coll.s, 1967-68, asst. dir. for admissions and cmty. rels., 1968-70; dir. Urban Affairs Ctr., Calif. State Poly. U., Pomona, 1970-75, counselor, prof., 1975-92; emeritus Calif. State Poly. U., 1992—; envoy L.A. Olympic Organizing Com. to Nat. Olympic Coms. Chad, Togo, Benin, Ivory Coast, Mali, and Gabon, 1984; participant, bd. advisors African Agrl. Devel., Tech., Ecology and Society Conv., Pomona, 1985. Prodr., interviewer Africa World, Sta. KJLH, L.A., 1981-83, Family Tree, Sta. KPFK, L.A., 1983-85; contbr. articles to profl. jours. Mem. L.A. Mayor's Task Force on Africa, 1984—, Sister City Program of City of L.A., for Lusaka, 1984—. With U.S. Army, WWII, 1944-46, Korea, 1951-53; capt. U.S. Army Res., 1965. Home: 416 Taylor Dr Claremont CA 91711-4137

HAMMOND, HOWARD DAVID, retired botanist and editor; b. Phila., Feb. 10, 1924; s. Clarence Elwood Jr. and Myrtle Iva (Sprowles) H.; m. Sarah Lichtenberg, Apr. 30, 1955; 1 child, Julia Ethel. BS, Rutgers U., 1945, MS, 1947; PhD, U. Pa., 1952. Asst. prof. U. Del., Newark, 1957-58, Howard U., Washington, 1958-68; from asst. prof. to assoc. prof. SUNY, Brockport, 1968-83; assoc. editor N.Y. Bot. Garden, Bronx, 1984-92. Co-editor: Floristic Inventory Tropical Countries, 1989. Mem. Am. Inst. Biol. Scis., Bot. Soc. Am., Torrey Bot. Club (editor 1976-82, 87-92, pres. 1992), Sigma Xi. Home: 4025 Lake Mary Rd Apt 33 Flagstaff AZ 86001-8608

HAMMOND, JUDY MCLAIN, business services executive; b. Downey, Calif., June 24, 1956; d. Ernest Richard and Bernice Elaine (Thompson) McLain; m. Dennis Francis Hammond, Aug. 15, 1981. BS in Mgmt., Pepperdine U., 1982; MBA, U. So. Calif., 1986. Br. mgr. Kelly Svcs., Encino, Calif., 1978-81; mktg. mgr. Payco Am. Corp., Encino, 1981-83, GC Svcs. Corp., Santa Ana, Calif., 1983-86; pres. Resource Mgmt. Svcs. Inc., Norwalk, Calif., 1986—; founder, pres. The Debt Marketplace, Inc., Norwalk, 1994—; founder, pres. The Debt Marketplace, Inc., 1994—; cons., expert in collection and recovery. Author: Collect More From Collection Agencies. Mem. Toastmasters. Office: 10440 Pioneer Blvd Ste 2 Santa Fe Springs CA 90670-3742

HAMMOND, M(ARY) ELIZABETH HALE, pathologist; b. Salt Lake City, Jan. 5, 1942; d. Edward Girard and Ruth (Hansen) Hale; m. John Morgan Hammond, Dec. 30, 1964; children: Jonathan Hale, Thomas Hale, Kathleen Hale. BS, U. Utah., 1963, MD, 1967. Diplomate Am. Bd. Pathology. Intern U. Utah Sch. Medicine, Salt Lake City, 1967-68; USPHS fellow Karolinska Inst., Stockholm, 1968-69; resident, fellow Mass. Gen. Hosp., Boston, 1970-74, staff pathologist, 1974-77; instr. Harvard Med. Sch., Boston, 1974-76, asst. prof. of pathology, 1976-77; pathologist LDS Hosp., Salt Lake City, 1977—, dir. electron microscopy lab., 1978-92, chmn. dept. of pathology, 1992—, med. staff pres., 1995—; assoc. prof. U. Utah Sch. Medicine, Salt Lake City, 1978-91, prof., 1991—; dir. cardiac pathology Utah CARDIAC, Salt Lake City, 1986—, adj. assoc. prof. internal medicine, 1991; mem. Radiation Therapy-Oncology Group, 1986—; chmn. pathology com., 1986-92, tumor repository com., 1993; ad hoc reviewer Nat. Cancer Inst., 1986—. Author: Pathology of Mediastinum, 1990; editor: Solid Organ Transplant Pathology, 1994; mem. editl. bd. Jour. Heart Transplant, 1990-93, Cardiovascular Pathology, 1991, Jour. Radoncology Biology Physics, 1989, assoc. editor, 1995; guest editor Ultrastructural Pathology, 1991-92; contbr. over 100 articles to profl. publs., chpts. to books. Bd. dirs. Deseret Found., Salt Lake City, 1977-94, chmn. rsch. com., 1985-94. Rsch. scholar Am. Cancer Soc., 1974-77. Fellow Am. Coll. Chest Physicians, Am. Soc. Clin. Pathology, Coll. Am. Pathology (vice chmn. cancer com.); mem. U.S. and Can. Acad. Pathology, Am. Assn. Pathology, Am. Assn. Immunology, Cardiovascular Pathology Soc. (councillor 1988-91), Soc. for Ultrastructural Pathology (councillor 1989-91, pres. 1993-95), Soc. for Heart Transplantation, Utah Soc. Pathologists (pres. 1982-85), Utah Med. Ins. Assn. (bd. govs. 1987-92), Phi Beta Kappa, Alpha Omega Alpha. Democrat. Mem. LDS Ch. Office: LDS Hosp Dept Pathology 8th Avenue St Salt Lake City UT 84143

HAMP-LYONS, LIZ, language educator, consultant; b. Northampton, Eng., May 25, 1946; came to U.S., 1986; m. Brian Wood; 1 child, Nicholas; m. Michael Lyons; 1 child, Christopher. DipEd, U. Exeter, Eng., 1975, MEd, 1977; PhD, U. Edinburgh, 1986. Asst. lectr. Tech. Coll., Northampton, 1971-72; lectr. Coll. of Further Edn., Northampton, 1972-75; dir. studies Am. Ednl. Coll., Patras, Greece, 1977-78; lectr. U. Azebaijan, Tabriz, Iran, 1978; sr. lectr. Universiti Sains Malaysia, Pinang, 1978-80; ESL curriculum coord. We. Ill. U., Macomb, 1980-82; fellow U. Edinburgh, 1982-86; asst. prof. U. Mich., Ann Arbor, 1986-90; assoc. prof. U. Colo., Denver, 1990—; cons. in writing assessment Brit. Coun., London, 1983-89, Australian Ministry of Immigration and Employment, Sydney, 1993, 94, Ednl. Testing Svc., Princeton, N.J., 1992—. Author: Research Matters, 1984, Study Writing, 1987; author, editor: Assessing Second Language Writing in Academic Contexts, 1991. Recipient Duke of Edinburgh's prize English Speaking Union, 1984; U. Colo. Denver fellow, 1994-95. Mem. Internat. Lang. Testing Assn. (founding mem.), TESOL, Coll. Composition and Comm. Assn. Office: U Colo Denver 4033 E 17th Ave Denver CO 80220-1010

HAMPSON, NEIL BRADLEY, physician; b. Seattle, May 17, 1955; s. Floyd Franklin Jr. and Mary Louise (Bradley) H.; m. Diane Kimberly Bourque, June 24, 1978; children: Lindsay Ann, Courtney Lynn. BS, U. Wash., 1977, MD, 1981. Diplomate Am. Bd. Med. Examiners, Am. Bd. Internal Medicine, Pulmonary Disease, Critical Care Medicine. Intern U. Iowa Hosps. and Clinics, Iowa City, 1981-82, resident, 1982-84; staff physician sect. pulmonary and critical care Virginia Mason Clinic, Seattle, 1988—, med. dir. hyperbaric medicine dept., 1989—; regional coord. northwestern region Divers Alert Network, 1989—; deputy med. dir. respiratory therapy dept. Virginia Mason Hosp., 1991—; assoc. prof. medicine Duke U. Med. Ctr., Duryam, N.C., 1987-88; clin. instr. medicine U. Wash., Seattle, 1990-92, clin. asst. prof. medicine, 1992—. Contbr. chpts. to books and articles to profl. jours. U. Wash. Student Rsch. Tng. program fellow, 1977, U. Wash. Sch. Medicine Alumni fellow, 1978, Rsch. Tng. fellow Am. Lung Assn., Am. Thoracic Assn., 1986-88, Pulmonary fellow Allen and Hanburys Respiratory Inst., 1990—; R.H. Williams Med. Rsch. award, 1980. Fellow Am. Coll. Physicians, Am. Coll. Chest Physicians; mem. AMA, Am. Fedn. Clin. Rsch., Am. Thoracic Soc., Internat. Soc. Oxygen Transport to Tissue, Wash. State Med. Assn., Wash. Thoracic Soc., King County Med. Soc., Undersea and Hyperbaric Med. Soc., U. Wash. Med. Alumni Assn. (bd. trustees 1992—), Phi Beta Kappa. Office: Virginia Mason Clinic 1100 9th Ave Seattle WA 98101-2756

HAMPTON, CAROLYN SEEBA, small business owner, minister; b. Palo Alto, Calif., Nov. 11, 1949; d. Robert F. and Beverly M. (Engley) Seeba; m. David Charles Hampton, Apr. 22, 1972; children: Nathan Christopher, Rebekah Ruth. BA, Lewis and Clark Coll., 1971; MDiv, San Francisco Theol. Sem., 1978; cert. in small bus. mgmt., Tillamook Bay C.C., 1994. Ordained to ministry Presbyn. Ch. (USA), 1978; cert. Christian educator. Various clerical positions librs. and shops, Calif., Oreg., 1968-71; mem. clerical staff Lewis and Clark Libr., Portland, Oreg., 1971-75; libr. aide San Francisco Theol. Sem., San Anselmo, Calif., 1975-76; intern St. John's Presbyn. Ch., Camas, Wash., summer 1976; curriculum libr. San Francisco Theol. Sem., San Anselmo, 1976-78; co-assoc. pastor Bethany Presbyn. Ch., Grants Pass, Oreg., 1978-84; co-pastor 1st Presbyn. Ch., Phoenix, Oreg., 1984-85; contract curriculum writer Presbyn. Ch. (U.S.A.), Louisville, 1986-87; temp. supply pastor Mount Laki Presbyn. Ch., Klamath Falls, Oreg., 1987; chaplain Phoenix (Oreg.) Vol. Fire Dept., 1986-88; co-pastor Yoked Parish Presbyn. Ch., Pacific City & Cloverdale, Oreg., 1988-92; chaplain Nestucca Rural Fire Protection Dist., Cloverdale, 1988—; owner Circuit Rider Books of Oreg., Pacific City, 1993—; cons. Christian edn. to various chs., workshops and tchrs., 1987-88; mem. Chrsistian nurture div. Cascades Presbytery, 1979-81, 84-92, chmn. ch. officer devel. team, 1986-88; commr. to 199th Gen. Assembly, Presbyn. Ch. (USA), 1987. Author: (instrnl. text) Teaching Media: A Guide to Making and Using Your Own Audio-Visual Materials, 1973, (Sunday sch. curriculum) The Big Little School Curriculum, 1981-84, (ch. sch. course) Bible Discovery, 1987. Active Tillamook Emergency Svcs. Chaplaincy, 1994—, United Presbyn. Women, 1977—; troop leader Girl Scouts U.S.A., 1988-93; den leader, chmn. pack com. Cub Scouts, 1986-88; program parent Block Home, 1984-88; convenor Rogue C.C. United Campus Ministry Bd., 1981-84; vol. mgr. Cascades Remote Bookshore, 1988-91. Mem. AAUW (life). Home and Office: Circuit Rider Books Oreg PO Box 788 35625 Lower Loop Rd Pacific City OR 97135-0788

HAMPTON, RICHARD OWEN, research plant pathologist/virologist, educator; b. Dalhart, Tex., Feb. 17, 1930; s. Christopher C. and Marian Martha (Wise) H.; m. Willa Mae Johnson, June 12, 1954; children: Kevin Ray, Audrey C. BS in Agr., U. Ark., 1951; MS in Plant Pathology, Iowa State U., 1954, PhD in Plant Pathology, 1957. Asst. plant pathologist Wash. State U., Prosser, 1957-61; rsch. plant pathologist USDA Agr. Rsch. Svc., Prosser, 1961-65, Corvallis, Oreg., 1965—; project and lab. dir. USDA Agr. Rsch. Svc., Oreg. State U., Corvallis, 1965—; crop adv. com. USDA Agr. Rsch. Svc. Crop Germplasm Coordination, 1980-95. Author: Serological Detection and Identification of Viral and Bacterial Pathogens, 1990; contbr. over 160 articles to profl. jours. Recipient grants for rsch., several seed cos., Idaho, Wash., Oreg., 1965—. Mem. Am. Phytopathological Soc. (chair germplasm 1993-95), Nat. Pea Improvement Assn. (pres. 1988-90, exec. com. 1986-95, Meritorious Svc. award 1991). Republican. Baptist. Office: USDA ARS Dept Botany & Plant Pathol Oreg State Univ Corvallis OR 97331-2902

HAMPTON, SHELLEY LYNN, hearing impaired educator; b. Muskegon, Mich., Nov. 27, 1951; d. Donald Henry and Ruth Marie (Heinanen) Tamblyn; m. John Pershing Hampton Jr., Aug. 10, 1985; 1 child, Sarah Elizabeth. BA, Mich. State U., 1973, MA, 1978. Cert. tchr., Wash., Mich., N.Y. Tchr. presch. thru 3d grade N.Y. State Sch. for Deaf, Rome, 1973-78; cons. Ingham Intermediate Sch. Dist., Lansing, Mich., 1978-81; hearing impaired coord. Shoreline Sch. Dist., Seattle, 1981—; N.W. rep. Bur. of Edn. Handicapped, N.Y.C., 1978; N.Y. del. Humanities in Edn., 1977; adv. bd. State Libr. for the Blind, Lansing, 1980-81; adj. prof. Mich. State U., 1979-81, Seattle Pacific U., 1984-86; participant World Cong. Edn. and Tech., Vancouver, B.C., 1986; computer resource technician Spl. Programs, 1988-92, collegial team leader, 1992—; rep. Site-Based Mgmt. Coun., Seattle, 1992—. Writer: Social/Emotional Aspects of Deafness, 1983-84. Del. N.Y. State Assn. for Edn. of Deaf, N.Y.C., 1974-78; N.Y. del. Humanities in Edn., 1977; mem. bd. Plymouth Congl. Ch., Seattle, 1983-87. Recipient Gov.'s Plaque of Commendable Svc., State of Mich., 1981; grantee State of Wash., 1979, 82, Very Spl. Arts Festival, 1979-81; recipient Outstanding Svc. award Mich. Sch. for the Blind, 1980. Mem. NEA, Wash. State Edn. Assn., Shoreline Edn. Assn., Alexander Graham Bell Assn., Regional Hearing Impaired Coop. for Edn., Internat. Orgn. Educators of the Hearing Impaired, U.S. Pub. Sch. Caucus, Conf. Ednl. Adminstrs. Serving the Deaf. Home: 14723 62nd Dr SE Everett WA 98208-9383 Office: Shoreline Hearing Program 16516 10th Ave NE Seattle WA 98155-5904

HAMRAH, KALLEN MICHAEL, securities trader; b. Plainfield, N.J., June 11, 1952; s. Kallen and Marrie (McFadden) H.; m. Dale Coddington, Aug. 30, 1971 (div. Sept. 10, 1975); m. Rosemarie Ann Lopes, Aug. 30, 1980; children: Kirk, Rachel, Michael, Jessica. BS in Fin., San Jose State U., 1986. Home bldr. Dunellen, N.J., 1970-74; microwave technician, quality engr., project planner govt. Avantek, Milpitas, Calif., 1980-86; registered rep. Waddell and Reed, Capitola, Calif., 1986—. With USN, 1974-80. Republican. Office: Waddell and Reed 1500 41st Ave Ste 3 Capitola CA 95010-2907

HAMREN, NANCY VAN BRASCH, bookkeeper; b. L.A., Feb. 2, 1947; d. Milton Carl and Winifred (Taylor) Van Brasch; m. Jerome Arthur Hamren, Feb. 14, 1981; children: Emily Allison, Meredith Ann. Student, Pasadena City Coll., 1964-65, San Francisco State Coll., 1966-67, U. Oreg., 1975-79. Bookkeeper/office mgr. Springfield Creamery, Eugene, Oreg., 1969—, also bd. dirs.; originator Nancy's Yogurt, Nancy's Cultured Dairy Products. Active mem. Oreg. Shakespearean Festival, Ashland, 1986, Oreg. Nat. Abortion Rights Action League, Sta. KLCC-PBS Radio; bd. dirs. BRING Recycling. Mem. Audubon Soc., N.Am. Truffling Soc., The Wilderness Soc., Oreg. Pub. Broadcasting, Buhl (Idaho) Arts Coun., Conservation Internat. Democrat. Unitarian. Home: 1315 Ravenswood Dr Eugene OR 97401-1912 Office: Springfield Creamery 29440 Airport Rd Eugene OR 97402-9524

HAMRICK, JOSEPH EUGENE, JR., information services specialist; b. Chapel Hill, N.C., Feb. 4, 1954; s. Joseph Eugene Sr. and Emily Southerland (Cole) H.; m. Elaine Kay Metcalf, Oct. 2, 1982; children: Aubrie Nicole, Allison Laurel, Wendy-Anne Alisa, Claire Elise. BS in Computer and Mmt. Sci, Met. State Coll., Denver, 1989. Cert. system profl. Inst. for Cert. Computer Profls. Programmer, analyst Aviation Mgmt. Systems, Denver, 1980-83; mgr., AVsoft devel. PHH Aviation Systems, Golden, Colo., 1983-86; programmer, analyst Columbine Systems, Inc., Golden, 1986-88; dir., info. svcs. Property Asset Mgmt., Denver, 1988—; cons., pres. Bridgeware, Denver, 1985—. Cons. Terry Considine U.S. Senate Campaign, Denver, 1985-86. Sgt. USAF, 1975-79. Presbyterian. Home: 2272 S Grape St Denver CO 80222-6263 Office: Property Asset Mgmt 1873 S Bellaire St Denver CO 80222-4358

HAN, ITTAH, lawyer, political economist, high technology, computer engineering and financial strategist; b. Java, Indonesia, Jan. 29, 1939; came to U.S., 1956, naturalized, 1972; s. Hongtjioe and Tsuiying (Chow) H. BS in Mech. Engring. and Elec. Engring., Walla Walla Coll., 1960; MA in Math., U. Calif., Berkeley, 1962; BA in French, U. Colo., 1965, MS in Elec. Engring., 1961; MSE in Computer Engring., U. Mich., 1970; MS in Computer Sci., U. Wis., 1971; MBA in Mgmt., U. Miami, Fla., 1973; BA in Econs., U. Nev., 1977; MBA in Tax, Golden Gate U., 1979, MBA in Real Estate, 1979, MBA in Fin., 1980, MBA in Banking, 1980, MPA in Adminstrv. Orgn. and Mgmt., 1984, ME in Computer Engring. U. Idaho, 1991, JD, Whittier Coll., 1991, PhD. in Ethics & Tech. The Union Inst., 1994. Bar: Calif. 1992; cert. fin. planner. Salesman, Watkins Products, Walla Walla, Wash., 1956-60; instr. Sch. Engring. U. Colo., Denver, 1964-66; systems engr. IBM Corp., Oakland, Calif., 1967-69, Scidata Inc., Miami, Fla., 1971-72; chief of data processing Golden Gate Bridge, Hwy. and Transp. Dist., San Francisco, 1973-74; mgr. info. systems tech. and advanced systems devel. Summa Corp., Las Vegas, Nev., 1975-78; mgr. systems devel. Fred Harvey Inc., Brisbane, Calif., 1978-80; chmn. corp. systems steering com., mgr. systems planning Amfac Hotel & Resorts, Inc., 1978-80; tax strategy planner, innovative turnaround fin. strategy planner, chief exec. Ittahhan Corp., 1980-95; exec. v.p. Developers Unltd. Group, Las Vegas, 1982-84; v.p. Fidelity Fin. Co., Las Vegas, 1984-85; exec. v.p. John H. Midby and Assocs., Las Vegas, 1982-84, 1986-95; sec., treas., dir. River Resorts Inc., Las Vegas, 1983-84; sec., treas. Goldriver Ltd., Las Vegas, 1983-84; pres. Weststar Gen. Ptnr. Co., 1984-85, Developers Group Service Co., 1984-86; chief exec. officer, pres. Very High Tech. Polit. Economy Turnaround Management Strategist, Inc., 1986-95; chief exec. officer, pres. Artificial Intelligence Computer Engring. and Expert Systems Engring., Inc. (named changed to Turnaround Strategist & Artificial Intelligence Engring., Inc.), 1986—; pres. Orion Land Devel. Co., Las Vegas, 1987-89, Very High Tech. Computer Engring., Inc., Las Vegas, 1988-95; instr. U. Nev. Sch. Elec. Engring., Reno, 1981; systems designer, cons. in field. Mem. IEEE, Internat. Bd. of Stds. and Practices for CFP, Inc., Calif. Bar Assn., Assn. Computing Machinery, Am. Assn. Artificial Intelligence, Am. Math. Assn., Inst. Cert. Fin. Planners, Am. Contract Bridge League. Republican. Home and Office: 2501 Fulano Way Las Vegas NV 89102-2034

HAN, JAMES SEBASTIAN, commercial real estate broker, consultant; b. Seoul, Korea, Sept. 17, 1967; came to U.S., 1974; s. Donald S. and Mi C. Han. BA, U. Nev., 1993. Assoc. Coldwell Banker, Las Vegas, 1989-90; sr. cons. Americana Comml., Las Vegas, 1990-94; sr. assoc. Indsl. Property Group, Las Vegas, 1994—. Office: Industrial Property Group 4435 S Eastern Ave Las Vegas NV 89119-7826

HAN, JIAWEI, computer scientist, educator; b. Shanghai, China, Aug. 10, 1949; came to U.S., 1979; arrived in Can., 1987; s. Yu-chang Han and Jia-zhi Wang; m. Yandong Cai, July 3, 1979; 1 child, Lawrence. BSc, USTC, Beijing, China, 1979; MSc, U. Wis., 1981, PhD, 1985. Asst. prof. Northwestern U., Evanston, Ill., 1986-87, Simon Fraser U., Burnaby, B.C., Can., 1987-91; assoc. prof. Simon Fraser U., Burnaby, 1991-95, prof., 1995—. Contbr. articles to profl. jours. Grantee NSF, 1986-88, NSERC, 1988—. Mem. IEEE (conf. program com. 1990-95), ACM, Assn. Logic Programming. Office: Simon Fraser Univ, Sch Computing Sci, Burnaby, BC Canada V5A 1S6

HAN, JUNGHYUN, computer scientist; b. Seoul, Korea, Apr. 6, 1963; came to U.S. 1989; s. Kyuho and Kumsun (Koo) H.; m. Kyungok Lee, Feb. 3, 1964; 1 child, Jeehee. BS, Seoul Nat. U., 1988; MS, U. Cin., 1991. Rsch. asst. U. Cin., 1990-91; rsch. assoc. U. So. Calif., L.A., 1992—. Recipient Univ. Grad. Scholarship U. Cin., 1990-91. Mem. IEEE, ASME, Assn.

Computing Machinery. Home: 8208 Summertime Ln Culver City CA 90230-4570 Office: U So Calif University Park Los Angeles CA 90089

HAN, MAO-TANG, surgeon, researcher; b. Jinan, Shandong, China, Aug. 28, 1934; came to U.S., 1989; s. Houngwen Han and Shie Sun; m. Hui-Fong Wang, Aug. 28, 1960; children: Han Qiang, Han Shan. Student, Chee-Loo U., 1951-52; MD, Tongj Medical Sch., Wuhan, China, 1952-57. Resident gen. surgery Simo (Province of Yunan) Dist. Hosp., 1957-60, Tonjee Teaching Hosp. Medical U. Tonjee, Wuhan, Province of Hubei, 1960-61; resident in pediatric surgery Tianjin Children's Hosp., Tianjin, 1963-64, chief resident in pediatric surgery, 1963-64, attending surgeon, 1965-84; postgrad. fellow Shanghai Chest Hosp., 1975-76; vis. physician dept. surgery The Mayo Clinic, Rochester, Minn., 1979-82; chief surgeon dept. surgery Tianjin Children's Hosp., Tianjin, 1984-89; assoc. editor Chinese Jour. Pediat. Surgery; organizer 1st and 2d Internat. Symposia on Pediat. Surgery of China, 1984, 88. Contbr. chpts. to books; contbr. articles to profl. jours. Mem. Assn. of Chinese Pediatric Surgery, Chinese Medical Assn., Am. Coll. Chest Physicians, Asian Assn. Pediatric Surgeons, Pacific Assn. Pediatric Surgeons. Home: 4633 41st Ave NE Seattle WA 98105-3905 Office: Childrens's Hosp & Med Ctr 4800 Sand Point Way NE Rm E-626 Seattle WA 98105-3901

HAN, ZHONG-SHENG, neurobiologist, researcher; b. Cheng Cheng, Shaanxi, China, Apr. 15, 1953; came to U.S., 1992; s. Hong-Bin and Pei-Qin (Wang) H.; m. Xiu-Ying Qiao, Oct. 1, 1982; children: Lee Han, Fee Han. BS, Shanxi Med. Coll., 1976, MS, 1982; PhD, Fourth Med. U., 1988; postgrad., Oxford U., 1990-91, Barrow Neurol. Inst., 1992—. Resident doctor for occupational diseases Weinan (Shaanxi) Inst. Sanitation and Antiepidemic, 1977-78, rsch. fellow dept. physiology Shaanxi Acad. Chinese Medicine and Pharmacology, Xian, 1983-84; lectr. dept. neurobiology Inst. Neurosci., Fourth Med. U., Xian, 1988-89; postdoctoral fellow MRC unit dept. pharmacology Oxford (Eng.) U., 1990-91; postdoctoral fellow dept. neurobiology Barrow Neurol. Inst., Phoenix, 1992-94; rsch. assoc. Dow Neurol. Scis. Inst., Portland, Oreg., 1995—; lectr. dept. physiology Fourth Mil. Med. U., Xi'an, China, 1983; lectr. dept. brain rsch. Xi'an Med. U., 1984; lectr. dept. physiology Shanxi Med. Coll., Taiyuan, China, 1987, lectr. dept. neurobiology, 1988; lectr. Shanghai (China) Inst. Physiology, 1989; lectr. summer sch. on neurosci. program U. Oxford, 1991. Author revs. and abstracts; contbr. articles to profl. jours. Mem. Pain Mgmt. Delegation to S.E. Asia, U.S. Citizen Ambassador Programs, 1993. Grantee Nat. Natural Sci. Found. China, 1985-88, 1988-89. Mem. U.S. Soc. Neurosci., Chinese Anatomy Soc., Chinese Physiology Soc. Office: Dow Neurol Inst 1120 NW 20th Ave Portland OR 97209

HANAUER, JOE FRANKLIN, real estate executive; b. Stuttgart, Fed. Republic Germany, July 8, 1937; came to U.S., 1938; s. Otto and Betty (Zurndorfer) H.; m. Jane Boyle, Oct. 20, 1972; children: Jill, Wendy, Jason, Elizabeth. BS, Roosevelt U., 1963; postgrad., U. Chgo. Pres. Thorsen Realty, Oak Brook, Ill., 1974-80; sr. v.p. Coldwell Banker, Newport Beach, Calif., 1980-83, pres., 1984, chmn. bd., CEO, 1984-88; prin. Combined Investments LP, Laguna Beach, Calif., 1989—; chmn. Grubb & Ellis Co., San Francisco, 1993; bd. dirs. MAF Bancorp, Chgo.; chmn. policy adv. bd. Joint Ctr. for Housing Studies Harvard U. Bd. dirs. Chgo. Chamber Orch., 1976-82; trustee Roosevelt U. Mem. Nat. Assn. Realtors (exec. com.). Home: 105 S La Senda Dr Laguna Beach CA 92677-3311 Office: Combined Investments LP 361 Forest Ave Ste 200 Laguna Beach CA 92651-2146

HANBY, JOHN ESTES, JR., technology management executive; b. Washington, May 3, 1941; s. John E. Sr. and Winnifred (Parker) H.; m. Elaine J. Nett, July 13, 1968; children: John, Christina. BSChemE, Ga. Inst. Tech., 1963; MS, Inst. Paper Chemistry, 1965, PhD, 1968. Rsch. engr., supr. Crown Zellerbach Corp., Camas, Wash., 1970-76; mgr. tech. R&D Crown Zellerbach Corp., Portland, Oreg., 1976-78; plant mgr. Crown Zellerbach Corp., Florence, Ky., 1978-80; mfg. mgr. Crown Zellerbach Corp., Portland, 1980-81; asst. resident mgr. Crown Zellerbach Corp., Wauna, Oreg., 1981-86; bus. mgr. communication papers James River Corp., Wauna, 1986-89; v.p. tech. James River Corp., Camas, 1989—. Scoutmaster Boy Scouts Am., 1968—91. Capt. USAR, 1963-70. Mem. Tech. Assn. Pulp & Paper Industry, Paper Industry Mgmt. Assn., Tau Beta Pi, Phi Kappa Phi. Office: James River Corp 349 NW 7th Ave Camas WA 98607-2042

HANCE, ANTHONY JAMES, retired pharmacologist, educator; b. Bournemouth, Eng., Aug. 19, 1932; came to U.S., 1958; s. Walter Edwin and Jessie Irene (Finch) H.; m. Ruth Anne Martin, July 17, 1954; children: David, Peter, John. BSc, Birmingham U., 1953, PhD, 1956. Rsch.fellow in electrophysiology Birmingham U., Eng., 1957-58; rsch. pharmacologist UCLA, 1959-62; rsch. assoc. pharmacology Stanford U., Palo Alto, Calif., 1962-65, asst. prof., 1965-68; assoc. prof. U. Calif., Davis, 1968-94, ret. prof. emeritus, 1994. Contbr. articles to profl. jours. Mem. AAAS, Am. Soc. for Pharmacology and Exptl. Therapeutics, Biomed. Engring. Soc., Assn. for Computing Machinery. Home: 1103 Radcliffe Dr Davis CA 95616-0944 Office: U Calif Med Sch Dept Med Pharmacology & Toxicology Davis CA 95616-8654

HANCHETT, WILLIAM A. BARTON, mechanical engineer, designer; b. San Francisco, June 11, 1928; s. William A. Barton Sr. and Tempest Caroline (Wilder) W.; m. Jane Elizabeth Connell, Apr. 6, 1948; children: William A. Barton III, Barbara Lee, Marc Connell. BSBA, SUNY, 1976; BSME, Cath. U. Am., 1980, MSME, 1981. Cert. sr. safety engr. Commd. 2d lt. U.S. Army, 1952, advanced through grades to col., 1971, retired, 1975; dir. Hanchett Engring., Springfield, Va., 1975-81, Ojai, Calif., 1981—; program dir. Advanced Tech., Camarillo, Calif., 1982-88; dist. mgr. Am. Mgmt. Systems Inc., Port Hueneme, Calif., 1988-93. Named hon. mayor Bretten-Badden, Fed. Republic of Germany, 1964-66; decorated Legion of Merit (twice), Joint Svcs. Commendation medal, Army Commendation medal (three times), Vietnam medal of Valor (twice); recipient Engring. Recognition award Cath. U. Amer., 1980. Mem. ASME, Soc. Am. Mil. Engrs. (bd. govs. 1986-89), Am. Soc. Safety Engrs., Systems Safety Soc., Am. Soc. Indsl. Security (vice-chmn. 1989-90, 95—), Am. Soc. Naval Engrs. Republican. Club: Mil. Officer (bd. govs.). Home: 2585 Valley Meadow Ct Oak View CA 93022-9513 Office: Hanchett Engring Assoc 2585 Valley Meadow Ct Ste B Oak View CA 93022-9513

HANCIULESCO, BARBU, architectural design professional; b. Bucharest, Romania, Aug. 6, 1936; came to U.S., 1981; s. Toma and Constantza H.; m. Alexandra Hanciulescu, Oct. 31, 1971; children: Roxanne, Arina. Student, architecture, Architectural Sch., Bucharest, 1954; MD in Mech. Engring., Faculty of Engring., Bucharest, 1969; student, film and TV, I. Marcota, Hollywood, Calif., 1988; student, plumbing and engring., UCLA, 1989. Architect Project Bucharest, 1954-69, mech. engr., 1969-80; mech. engr. McDonald Engring., Calif., 1981-86; pres. B.H. Design Group, Hollywood, 1986—; radio producer Am. Radio Network, L.A., Hollywood, 1994—; pres. B.H. Group Archtl. and Mech. Engring. Consulting Firm, L.A., 1986-93. Designer mech. systems for hotels, housing, others, 1969—; inventor toilet vent seat, 1988, solar system/drinking water producer, 1992. Republican. Greek Orthodox. Office: BH Design Group 7095 Hollywood Blvd # 839 Los Angeles CA 90028-8903

HANCOCK, DON RAY, researcher; b. Muncie, Ind., Apr. 9, 1948; s. Charles David and June Lamoine (Krey) H. B.A., DePauw U., 1970. Community worker Fla. Meth. Spanish Ministry, Miami, 1970-73; seminar designer United Meth. Seminars, Washington, 1973-75; info. coord. SW Rsch. and Info. Ctr., Albuquerque, 1975—; cons. State Planning Coun. on Radioactive Waste Mgmt., Washington, 1980-81; task force mem. Gov.'s Socioecon. Com., Santa Fe, 1983; pub. adv. bd. WIPP Socioecon. Study, Albuquerque, 1979-81. Writer mag. articles. Bd. chmn. Roadrunner Food Bank, Albuquerque, 1981-92, N.Mex. Coalition Against Hunger, 1978-85; bd. dirs. Univ. Heights Assn., Albuquerque, 1977-82, 85, 88-89, 90-95, United Meth. Bd. of Ch. and Society, Washington, 1976-80. Democrat. Office: SW Rsch and Info Ctr PO Box 4524 Albuquerque NM 87196-4524

HANCOCK, EMILY STONE, psychologist; b. Syracuse, N.Y., Nov. 18, 1945; d. Theodore McLennan and Eleanor Sackett (Stone) H.; m. Philip Yenawine, Aug. 28, 1965 (div. 1970); 1 child, Tad. BA, Syracuse U., 1971; MSW, Boston U., 1974; EdD, Harvard U., 1981. Lic. clin. social worker, Mass., Calif.; ACSW. Clin. social worker Children's Hosp., Boston, 1974-77; pvt. practice Mass., Calif., 1976—; co-founder, therapist Divorce Resource Ctr., Cambridge, 1976-78; teaching fellow Harvard U., 1978-79; counselor Alameda County Superior Ct., Oakland, 1982—; screening coord. U. Calif., San Francisco Dept. Pediatrics, 1982-85; faculty Ctr. for Psychol. Studies, Albany, Calif., 1982—; chairwoman Askwith Symposium and Colloquia, Cambridge, 1979. Author: The Girl Within, 1989; editor: Harvard Ednl. Rev., 1979-81; contbr. articles to numerous profl. jours. Fellow HEW, 1972-74, Danforth Found., 1978-80, NIMH, 1981-82; grantee Radcliffe Coll., 1978, 80, Woodrow Wilson Found., 1980. Mem. APA, Acad. Cert. Social Workers, Phi Beta Kappa, Phi Kappa Phi. Home and Office: 1230 Glen Ave Berkeley CA 94708-1841

HANCOCK, EUGENE MERRILL, dietitian; b. Blackfoot, Idaho, Feb. 14, 1939; s. Clawson Brott and Margaret Amanda (Poulsen) H.; m. Barbara Jean Anderson, May 29, 1965; children: Susan, Douglas, Jean, Rebecca, Amanda, Rachel. Diploma, Ricks Coll., Rexburg, Idaho, 1959; BS, Brigham Young U., 1966. Registered dietitian. Dietetic intern Olka, State U., Stillwater, 1966-67; prodn. mgr. U. N.Mex. Food Svc., Albuquerque, 1967-69; asst. mgr. Brigham Young U. Dining Svc., Provo, Utah, 1969—. Voting dist. chmn. Rep. Party, Orem, Utah, 1986-87. With USAR, 1962-65. Mem. Am. Dietetic Assn., N.Mex. Dietetic Assn., Utah Dietetic Assn., Nat. Assn. Coll. and Univ. Food Svc. LDS. Office: Brigham Young Univ 180 SASC PO Box 21840 Provo UT 84602-1840

HANCOCK, HERBERT JEFFREY (HERBIE HANCOCK), composer, pianist, publisher; b. Chgo., Apr. 12, 1940; s. Wayman Edward and Winnie (Griffin) H.; m. Gudrun Meixner, Aug. 31, 1968. Student, Grinnell (Iowa) Coll., 1956-60, Roosevelt U., Chgo., 1960, Manhattan Sch. Music, 1962, New Sch. Social Research, 1967. owner-pub. Hancock Music Co., 1962—, founder Hancock and Joe Prodns., 1989—; pres. Harlem Jazz Music Center, Inc. Performed with Chgo. Symphony Orch., 1952, Coleman Hawkins, Chgo., 1960, Donald Byrd, 1960-63, Miles Davis Quintet, 1963-68; recorded with Chick Corea; scored films Blow Up, 1966, The Spook Who Sat By the Door, 1973, Death Wish, 1974, A Soldier's Story, 1984, Jo Jo Dancer, Your Life is Calling, 1986, Action Jackson, 1988, Colors, 1988, Harlem Nights, 1989, Livin' Large, 1991; scored and appeared in film 'Round Midnight, 1986 (Academy award best original score 1986); albums include Takin' Off, 1963, Succotash, 1964, Speak Like a Child, 1968, Fat Albert Rotunda, 1969, Mwandishi, 1971, Crossings, 1972, Sextant, 1972, Headhunters, 1973, Thrust, 1974, The Best of Herbie Hancock, 1974, Man-Child, 1975, The Quintet, 1977, V.S.O.P., 1977, Sunlight, 1978, An Evening with Herbie Hancock and Chick Corea in Concert, 1979, Feets Don't Fail Me Now, 1979, Monster, 1980, Greatest Hits, 1980, Lite Me Up, 1982, Future Shock, 1983, (with Foday Musa Suso) Village Life, 1985, (with Dexter Gordon) The Other Side of 'Round Midnight, 1987, Perfect Machine, 1988, Jamming, 1992, Cantaloupe Island, 1994, Tribute to Miles, 1994, Dis Is Da Drum, 1995. Recipient citation of achievement Broadcast Music, Inc., 1963; Jay award Jazz mag., 1964; critics poll for talent deserving wider recognition Down Beat mag., 1967; 1st place piano category, 1968, 69, 70; composer award, 1971; All-Star Band New Artist award Record World, 1968; named top jazz artist Black Music mag., 1974; recipient Grammy award for best rhythm and blues instrumental performance, 1983, 84, for best jazz instrumental composition (co-composer), 1987, best jazz instrumental performance, 1995. Mem. Nat. Acad. Rec. Arts and Scis., Jazz Musicians Assn., Nat. Acad. TV Arts and Scis., Broadcast Music. Club: Pioneer (Grinnell Coll.). Address: Hancock Music 1250 N Doheny Dr Los Angeles CA 90069-1723

HANCOCK, NANNETTE BEATRICE FINLEY, mental health educator, consultant; b. Birmingham, Ala., Aug. 24, 1937; d. James L. and Minnie (Mason) Finley; m. Frank J. Hancock Jr., Dec. 27, 1958 (div. May 1976); children: Andria Denise, Frank J. III, Cheryl René. BSN, Dillard U., 1958; MPH in Pub. Health, U. Calif., Berkeley, 1970; PhD in Psychology, Western Colo. U., 1977; MA in Clin. Psychology, John F. Kennedy U., 1991. Lic. marriage, family and child therapist. 2d lt. staff nurse U.S. Army Nurse's Corp, Denver, 1958-59; staff nurse, head nurse St. Francis Hosp., Evanston, Ill., 1960-64, Richmond (Calif.) Hosp., 1964-65; sch. nurse Richmond Unified Sch. Dist., 1965-69; prof. Contra Costa Coll., San Pablo, Calif., 1970—; pvt. practice mental health cons. Richmond, 1977—; founder, owner Nannette's Beauty and Figure Salon, 1982-86; head mental health component Bay Area Black Consortium for Quality Health Care AIDS Minority Health Initiative, Oakland, Calif., 1994—. Mem. Social Heritage Group, 1964—, human rels. com., 1966-70, Easter Hill Meth. Ch., 1964—. Col. Army Nurse's Corp. USAR, 1978—. Mem. Calif. Assn. Marriage and Family Therapy, Calif. Nurse's Assn., Bay Area Assn. Black Psychologists, Res. Officer's Assn. Home: 4801 Reece Ct Richmond CA 94804-3444 Office: 1440 Broadway Ste 209 Oakland CA 94612-2022

HANCOCK, N(EWELL) LES(LIE), accountant; b. Pitts., Apr. 13, 1943; s. Newell Francis and Mildred Helen (Bouverouz) H.; m. Margaret Ann Kendric, Nov. 30, 1968; children: Michelle Lynn, Jennifer Ann, Marie Noelle. BSBA, U. Denver, 1966; postgrad., various schs., 1969—. CPA, Colo. Supr. Pannell, Kerr, Forster, Denver and Atlanta, 1969-78; mgr. Wolf & Co. of Colo., Inc., Denver, 1978-79, 83-84; supr. Kafoury, Armstrong & Co., Reno, 1979-82; pvt. practice acctg. Arvada, Colo. and Reno, 1982—; mgr. Ashby, Armstrong & Co., Denver, 1984-87; asst. contr. 1st Resorts Inc. and Great Am. Mgmt. Group Inc., Lakewood, Colo., 1987-89; group leader subcontract auditing sect. Nat. Renewable Energy Lab., Golden, Colo., 1989—. Served to 1st lt. U.S. Army, 1966-69. Mem. AICPA, Colo. Soc. CPAs (report rev. com. 1984-90, pvt. co. practice com. 1990-93, accountancy regulation com. 1993-94, mem. rels. com. 1994—), Nev. Soc. CPAs (bd. dirs. Reno chpt. 1982-83, auditing stds. com. 1981-82, vice chmn. acctg. principles com. 1981-83), Hospitality Accts. Assn. (sec. 1976-77). Republican. Baptist. Office: PO Box 740535 Arvada CO 80006-0535

HANCOCK, S. LEE, lawyer; b. Knoxville, Tenn., Aug. 11, 1955; s. Melton Donald and Alma Helen (McDaniel) H.; m. Kathleen Ann Koll, July 26, 1986. BS summa cum laude, Southwest Mo. State U., 1975; JD cum laude, So. Meth. U., 1979. Bar: Mo. 1979, U.S. Dist. Ct. (we. dist.) Mo., U.S. Tax Ct. 1982, U.S. Ct. Claims Calif. 1983, Calif. 1988, U.S. Supreme Ct., 1992; CPA, Mo. Assoc. Blackwell, Sanders, Matheny, Weary & Lombardi, Kansas City, Mo., 1979-83, ptnr., 1984-88; ptnr. Allen, Matkins, Leck, Gamble & Mallory, Newport Beach, Calif., 1988—. Bd. dirs. U. Calif./Orange County Venture Forum, 1988—, Orange County Cmty. Found., 1991—, sec., 1994—. Mem. ABA, Young Execs. Am. (bd. dirs. Orange County chpt. 1992—, pres. 1994-95), Calif. Bar Assn., Mo. Bar Assn., Orange County Bar Assn., Lawyers Assn. Kansas City (pres. young lawyers sect. 1986-87, bd. dirs. 1986-87), Order of coif, Mensa. Republican. Home: 4 Hampshire Ct Newport Beach CA 92660-4933 Office: Allen Matkins Leck Gamble & Mallory 1800 Von Karman Fl 4 Newport Beach CA 92715

HANCOCKS, DAVID MORGAN, museum director, architect; b. Kinver, Worcestershire, Eng., May 5, 1941; came to U.S., 1972; s. Cecil and Eva Alice (Morgan) H.; m. Anthea Page Cook, Feb. 16, 1982; children: Samuel Morgan, Thomas David, Morgan Page. BSc with honors, U. Bath, Eng., 1966, BArch with honors, 1968. Registered architect, U.K. Architect Zool. Soc. London, 1968-69, West of Eng. Zool. Soc., Bristol, 1970-72; design coord. Woodland Pk. Zool. Gardens, Seattle, 1973-74, dir., 1975-84; pvt. practice design Melbourne, Australia, 1985-89; exec. dir. Ariz.-Sonora Desert Mus., Tucson, 1989—; cons. Singapore Zool. Gardens, 1979-89, Zool. Soc. Victoria, Australia, 1986-89, Mus. of Victoria, 1994; mem. adv. bd. U. Ariz. Press, U. Ariz. Sch. Renewable Natural Resources. Author: Animals and Architecture, 1971, Master Builders of the Animal World, 1973 (writing award State of Wash. Govs. 1974), 75 Years: A History of Woodland Park Zoological Gardens, 1979. Bd. dirs. Allied Arts, Seattle, 1976-85, Chamber Music Soc., Seattle, 1984-85; adv. coun. Sch. of Renewable Natural Resources, U. Ariz.; adv. bd. U. Ariz. Pres s. Fellow Discovery Inst., Seattle; recipient Disting. Svc. award Am. Soc. Landscape Architects, 1975, Outstanding Pub. Employee of Yr. award Seattle Mcpl. League, 1983, WPZS medal Woodland Pk. Zool. Soc., 1991. Mem. Am. Assn. Mus., Am. Assn. Zool. Pks. and Aquariums, Am. Assn. Bot. Gardens and Arboreta, Internat. Coun. Mus., Royal Inst. Brit. Architects (assoc.). Home: 6760 N Placita Manzanita Tucson AZ 85718-1226 Office: Ariz-Sonora Desert Mus 2021 N Kinney Rd Tucson AZ 85743-8918

HAND, DALE L., pharmacist; b. Boise, Idaho, Oct. 21, 1947; s. Robert Ray and Evelyn Mabel (McKenzie) H.; m. Gloria J. Lassen, Dec. 19, 1970; children: Travis D., Jason D. Student, Walla Walla Coll., 1965-66; B Pharmacy, Idaho State U., 1970; MS in Health Svcs. Adminstrn., Coll. St. Francis, Joliet, Ill., 1985. Intern Clinic Pharmacy, Pocatello, Idaho, 1968-70; pharmacognosy lab. tchng. asst. Idaho State U., 1969-70; hosp. pharmacy internship St. Luke's Hosp., Boise, 1970-71, clin. staff pharmacist, 1971-77; various to dir. pharmacy svcs. Porter Meml. Hosp., Denver, 1981-92, adminstrv. dir. dept. pharm. care, 1992—; pharmacy extern preceptor U. Colo., 1981—; cons. pharmacist McNamara Hosp. and Nursing Home, Fairplay, Colo., 1981-83; cons. Edn. Design, Inc., 1993—; lectr. in field.; chmn. various hosp. coms. Contbr. articles to profl. jours. Bd. dirs. Arapahoe Sertoma, 1991—. Mem. Am. Soc. Hosp. Pharmacists, Colo. Soc. Hosp. Pharmacists, Colo. Pharmacal Assn., Rho Chi. Seventh-Day Adventist. Home: 7269 W Chestnut Dr Littleton CO 80123-5699 Office: Porter Meml Hosp 2525 S Downing St Denver CO 80210-5817

HAND, HARLAND JULIUS, garden designer, consultant, retired educator; b. Fairmont, Minn., July 17, 1922; s. Ernest Richard and Emma Lena Louise (Saggau) H. Student, U. Minn., 1940,-42, 45; BA, MA, U. Calif., Berkeley, 1952. Florist Sheridan & Bell, San Francisco, 1948-58; tchr. biology, physiology, art Oakland (Calif.) Pub. Schs., 1952-82; science dept. head McClymond's High Sch., Oakland, 1965-74; garden designer pvt. practice, San Francisco Bay area, 1970—; garden writer various publs., 1977—; lectr. various Calif. Garden Clubs, 1976-80. Contbr. articles on gardening to various mags. and newspapers, chpt. to book, The American Man's Garden. Vol. designer of plantings for City of El Cerrito, Calif., 1975-85. Sgt. U.S. Infantry, 1942-45, ETO. Recipient Commendation City of El Cerrito, 1986; named Man of Yr. Calif. Garden Clubs, Inc., 1978. Mem. Calif. Horticultural Soc. (pres. 1975-76, coun. 1972-76, lectr., Garden award 1990), Friends of U. Calif. Botanical Gardens, Berkeley (lectr., bd. dirs.), Am. Rock Garden Soc. (lectr.), Strybing Arboretum Soc. (lectr.). Home and Office: Harland Hand Garden Design and Consultation 825 Shevlin Dr El Cerrito CA 94530-3050

HANDAGAMA, PREM JOSEF, hematopathologist, researcher; b. Colombo, Sri Lanka, May 7, 1953; came to U.S., 1979; s. William Granville and Daisybelle (Abeykoon) H. B of Vet. Sci., U. Sri Lanka, 1977; PhD in Comparative Pathology, U. Calif., Davis, 1985. Lic. in vet. medicine, Calif. Asst. lectr. dept. para-clin. studies Sch. Vet. Medicine U. Sri Lanka, 1977-78; dist. vet. dept. animal prodn. and health Govt. of Sri Lanka, 1978-79; adj. instr. dept. clin. pathology Sch. Vet. Medicine U. Calif., Davis, 1984-85; postdoctoral rsch. fellow dept. pathology Sch. of Medicine U. Calif., San Francisco, 1985-86, asst. specialist dept. pathology, 1986-87, vis. asst. rsch. pathologist, 1987-89, asst. rsch. hematopathologist, 1989—. Contbr. 20 articles to profl. jours.; author 11 abstracts; invited lectr. in field. Rsch. fellow Am. Heart Assn., 1987-89; grantee NHLBI, 1992-94, Am. Heart Assn., 1992-94. Mem. AAAS, Am. Soc. Histochemists and Cytochemists, Am. Heart Assn. (coun. on thrombosis), Am. Soc. Vet. Clin. Pathology, Am. Soc. Hematology, Calif. Vet. Med. Assn., Calif. Acad. Sci., Sierra Club. Office: Univ Calif San Francisco Dept Pathology Box 0506, HSW-501 San Francisco CA 94143

HANDEL, NEAL, plastic surgeon, researcher; b. L.A., Sept. 2, 1947; s. Max and Ruth (Masovetski) H. BA, Columbia U., 1969; MD, Yale U., 1973. Diplomate Am. Bd. Plastic Surgery. Plastic and reconstructive surgeon The Breast Ctr., Van Nuys, Calif., 1982—, assoc. med. dir., 1982—; mem. adv. bd. Ctr. for Devel. Biology Calif. State U., Northridge, 1985—. Contbr. articles to profl. jours. Rsch. grantee Am. Soc. Aesthetic Plastic Surgery, 1991. Fellow ACS; mem. Am. Soc. Plastic and Reconstructive Surgery, Calif. Soc. Plastic and Reconstructive Surgeons. Office: The Breast Ctr 14624 Sherman Way Ste 506 Van Nuys CA 91405

HANDEL, WILLIAM KEATING, advertising and sales executive; b. N.Y.C., Mar. 23, 1935; s. Irving Nathaniel and Marguerite Mary (Keating) H.; m. Margaret Inez Sitton; children: William Keating II, David Roger. BA in Journalism, U. S.C., 1959, MA in English Lit. 1960. Account supr. Ketchum, MacLeod & Grove, Pitts., 1960-67; mgr. advt. and pub. rels. ITT Gen. Controls, Glendale, Calif., 1967-80; mgr. corp. comm. Fairchild Camera and Instrument Corp., 1980-84; dist. mgr. Cahners Pub. Co., 1984-90; founder, chief exec. officer Tri-Dimensional Mktg. Communications Agy., 1990-91, Penton Pub. Co., 1991—; pub. rels. counsel Calif. Pvt. Edn. Schs., 1978-87; chmn. exhibits Mini/Micro Computer Conf., 1977-78. Bd. dirs. West Valley Athletic League; bd. dir. L.A. chpt. USMC Scholarship Found.; pub. rels. cons. Ensenada, Mexico Tourist Commn., 1978; chmn., master of ceremonies USMC Birthday Ball, L.A., 1979-82. With USMC, 1950-53. Decorated Silver Star, Bronze Star, Purple Heart (4), Navy Commendation medal with combat V; recipient Pub. Svc. award L.A. Heart Assn., 1971-73. Mem. Bus. and Profl. Advt. Assn. (cert. bus. communicator, past pres.), 1st Marine Divsn. Assn., Navy League (bd. dir.), AdLinx Golf Club of So. Calif., Torrey Pines Golf Club, Griffith Pk. Golf Club, Nueva España Boat Club, Bajamar Country Club, Ensenada Country Club, Ensenada Fish and Game Club (Baja, Mex.), U. S.C. Alumni Club (pres. L.A. chpt.), Sigma Chi (chpt. adv.). Republican. Roman Catholic. Home: 2428 Badajoz Pl Carlsbad CA 92009-8006

HANDELL, ALBERT GEORGE, artist; b. Bklyn., 1937. Student, Art Students League N.Y.C., 1968, Grande Chaumiere and Louvre, Paris, 1961-65. leader painting workshops, nationwide. One-man shows include The Fitzgerald Gallery, N.Y.C., 1961-63, A.C.A. Gallery, N.Y.C., 1966, Eileen Kuhlich Gallery, N.Y.C., 1973, Guild Gallery, N.Y.C., 1979, Berkshire Mus. Art, Pittsfield, Mass., 1975, Schenectady (N.Y.) Mus., 1976, Albany (N.Y.) Inst. History and Art, 1977; exhibited in group shows at Ventana Gallery, Santa Fe, N.Mex., Shriver Gallery, Taos, N.Mex.; works listed in publs. including Pastel Painting Step by Step (Elinor Lathrop Sears), 1966, How to Paint Portraits in Pastel (Joe Singer), 1971, How to Paint Figures in Pastel (Joe Singer), 1973; subject of articles in publs. including Am. Artist mag., S.W. Profile, Art Gallery Internat., S.W. Art., Focus/Santa Fe, Art of the West, subject of books Oil Painting Workshop, 1979, Pastel Painting Workshop, 1981, Intuitive Composition, 1989, Intuitive Light, 1995. Recipient more than 70 awards from ann. exhbns. including Allied Artists Am., N.Y.C., Audubon Artists Am., N.Y.C., Nat. Acad. Design, N.Y.C., Acad. Artists Am., Springfield, Mass., Pastel Soc. Am., N.Y.C., Butler Inst. Am. Art, Youngstown, Ohio, SUNY, Albany, U. Utah, Salt Lake City, Nat. Arts Club, N.Y.C., The Schenectady Mus., Berkshire Mus. Art, Pittsfield, Albany Inst. History and Art; named to Pastel Hall of Fame, Pastel Soc. Am., 1987; grantee John F. and Anna Lee Stacy Found., Montreal, Can., Elizabeth T. Greenshields Found., Montreal. Address: PO Box 9070 Santa Fe NM 87504-9070

HANDFORD, JACK, fashion education consultant; b. Piedmont, Mo., Aug. 4, 1917; s. Jack and Ethel Collins (Bunyard) H.; m. Virginia Lee Snigg, Sept. 19, 1942 (dec. 1983). BFA, Chouinard Art Inst., L.A., 1946; MFA, Kensington U., Glendale, Calif., 1977; EdD, Kensington U., 1978. Apparel designer Chic Lingerie, L.A., 1946-50; instr. Chouinard Art Inst., L.A., 1946-61; apparel designer Calif. Girl, L.A., 1952-56; designer/owner Handford Ent., Inc., L.A., 1956-72; dir./owner Calif. Fashion Inst., L.A., 1961-72; instr. UCLA Ext., 1972-83; assoc. chmn. fashion dept. Otis/Parsons, L.A., 1981-89; guest lectr. Calif. Dept. Edn., Sacramento, 1964-69, Calif. State U., L.A., 1969-79; part-time instr. Fullerton Coll., 1975-83; conductor/planner in field; mem. various fashion adv. bds. Author: Professional Patternmaking, 1974, 2nd edit. 1984, Professional Pattern Grading, 1980; contbr. articles to profl. jours. With USNR, 1942-45. Fellow Costume Soc. Am. (nat. bd. dirs. 1977-86, reg. pres. 1977-79); mem. Calif. Fashion Designers (pres. 1950-52), Costume Coun. (bd. dirs. 1978-80). Episcopalian. Home: 2500 Honolulu Ave Apt 105 Montrose CA 91020-1876

HANDLER, MARK S., retail executive; b. 1933; married. Student, U. Ill.; B.S., Roosevelt U., 1957; M.S., N.Y.U., 1958. With R.H. Macy & Co. Inc., N.Y.C., 1958—; mdse. adminstr. Bamberger's (subs. R. H. Macy & Co. Inc.), Newark, 1962-65, v.p., mdse. adminstr., 1965-67, sr. v.p. merchandising, 1967-71, pres., 1979, chmn., chief exec. officer, 1979-80, also bd. dirs.; pres., dir. R. H. Macy & Co. Inc., N.Y.C., 1980-92; co-chmn., co-CEO Bullock's (subs. R. H. Macy & Co. Inc.), N.Y.C., 1992—. Served with U.S. Army, 1953-55. Office: Bullock's 760 Market St San Francisco CA 94120

HANDLEY, SUE ANN, professional quiltmaker, educator; b. Decatur, Ill., Feb. 22, 1955; d. Max Bail and Virginia Ellen (Paul) Handley; m. Gregory

Alan Poteat, June 28, 1975 (div. 1992); children: Brian, Zachary. Student, Antelope Valley Jr. Coll., Lancaster, Calif., 1983-85. Tchr. quilting Sr. Citizen Ctr., Lancaster, 1984-85, House of Fabrics, Palmdale, Calif., 1984-88; lectr. quilting Palmdale Sch. Dist., 1984-88; vol. St. Andrew's Priory, Valyermo, Calif., 1983—; quiltmaker MGM Studios, Hollywood, Calif., 1990; banner maker So. Calif. Renewal Communities, Anaheim, 1986; lectr. First Presbyn. Ch., Palmdale, 1991, Palmdale Elks Lodge, 1991, othrs. Completed more than 400 quilts; contbr. to Quilter's Newsletter. Recipient 1st place award Inland Empire Quilt Guild, Riverside, Calif., 1990, 3d place award Smoky Mountain Quilt Competition, 1982, Best of Show award Antelope Valley Fair, Lancaster, 1978; Calif. State champion Calif. State Fair Bd., Sacramento, 1979. Mem. Am. Quilters Soc. (included in calendar 1994). Democrat. Roman Catholic. Home: 38563 Jacklin Ave Palmdale CA 93550-4019 Office: Sue's Custom Quilting 38563 Jacklin Ave Palmdale CA 93550-4019

HANDRON, DEANNE WESTFALL, management consulting executive; b. Hollywood, Calif., Jan. 6, 1955; d. Winfield Sidney Westfall and Joy Elaine (Hobbs) Friedman; m. Michael Anthony Handron, Dec. 3, 1983; children: Matthew, Jonathan, Caitlin. BA, U. So. Calif., 1977; MBA, Cornell U., 1979. Cert. mgmt. cons. Inst. Mgmt. Cons. Cons. Arthur Young & Co., San Jose, Calif., 1979-82; mgr. Arthur Young & Co., San Jose, 1982-85; prin. Arthur Young & Co., L.A., 1986-88; ptnr. Arthur Young & Co., Seattle, 1988-90; dir. n.w. cons. group Ernst & Young, Seattle, 1990—. Office: 22518 SE 46th Pl Issaquah WA 98027-6812

HANDS, D(OUGLAS) WADE, economics educator; b. Lafayette, Ind., Apr. 22, 1951. BS in Econs., U. Houston, 1973; MA in Econs., Ind. U., 1977, PhD in Econs., 1981. Assoc. instr. dept. econs. Ind. U., Bloomington, 1976-79; asst. prof. econs. U. Puget Sound, Tacoma, 1980-86, assoc. prof., 1986-92, prof., 1992—; vis. assoc. prof. U. Notre Dame, Ind., fall 1991. Author: Introductory Mathematical Economics, 1991, Testing, Rationality and Progress: Essays on the Popperian Tradition in Economic Methodology, 1993; contbr. articles and books revs. to profl. jours. Recipient Lieber Assoc. Instr. award Ind. U., 1980; John Lantz jr. faculty fellow U. Puget Sound., 1984, Burlington No. Found. grantee, 1986, 92, Martin Nelson grantee, 1987, 89, 91, John Lantz sr. sabbatical fellow, 1994. Mem. Am. Econ. Assn., History of Econs. Soc., Internat. Network for Econ. Method, Philosophy of Sci. Assn. Home: 4826 Marine View Dr Tacoma WA 98422 Office: U Puget Sound Dept Econs Tacoma WA 98416

HANDS, ELIZABETH S. (ELIZABETH S. GELTZ), nutrition analysis software company executive; b. Richmond, Va.; d. Benjamin Franklin and Tempe (Stewart) Hunt; m. Robert B. Geltz, Nov. 9, 1974; children: Terese Hands, James Hands, David Hands. Student, MIT, 1957-58; BA, Willamette U., 1969. Planner, statistician Gov.'s Planning Dept., Salem, Oreg., 1969-70; self employed in mktg. and fin. cons. Salem, 1970-74; sr. mgmt. analyst Gov.'s Exec. Dept., State of Oreg., Salem, 1974-75, sr. budget analyst, 1975-79; mgr. budget and fin. Port of Portland, Oreg., 1979-81; founder, CEO, pres. ESHA Rsch., Salem, 1981—; co-founder, bd. dirs. Capitol Health Care/HMO Ins., 1972-88. Author: The Food Finder, several edits., 1987-94; editor, author: (software) The Food Processor, 1985-94, Genesis, 1981-94. Mem. urban renewal planning coms., Salem, 1966-70. Mem. Focus Group. Home: 606 Juntura Way SE Salem OR 97302-3964 Office: ESHA Rsch 4263 Commercial St SE Salem OR 97302-3938

HANDSCHUMACHER, ALBERT GUSTAVE, retired corporate executive; b. Phila., Oct. 20, 1918; s. Gustave H. and Emma (Streck) H.; children: Albert, David W., Megan, Karin, Melissa. B.S., Drexel Inst. Tech., 1940; diploma, U. Pitts., 1941, Alexander Hamilton Inst., 1948. Prodn. mgr. Jr. Motors Corp., Phila., 1938-40; sales engr. Westinghouse Electric Co., Pitts., 1941; with Lear, Inc., Grand Rapids, Mich., 1945-57; beginning as sales mgr. central dist., successively asst. to pres., asst. gen. mgr., v.p. and gen. mgr., sr. v.p., dir. sales, pres., dir. Lear, Inc., 1959-62; v.p., gen. mgr. Rheem Mfg. Co., 1957-59; pres., dir. Lear Siegler, Inc., 1962-65; underwriting mem. Lloyd's of London. Trustee Drexel U., Am. Heart Assn.; mem. coun. UCLA Internat. Student Ctr. Maj. USAAF, 1942-45. Recipient 60th Anniversary Alumni award for outstanding achievements and services field of indsl. mgmt. Drexel U., 1951, Outstanding Alumni award, 1971; Man of Year award City of Hope, 1970; Man of Year award Nat. Asthma Assn., 1978; named to Abington High Sch. Hall of Fame, 1989. Mem. Jonathan Club, Astro Club (Phila.). Home: 1100 Stone Canyon Rd Los Angeles CA 90077-2918

HANDWERKER, LISA, medical anthropologist, public health consultant; b. Bklyn., May 2, 1958; d. Sol and Minnie (Geller) H. Student, Emory U., 1976-78; BA, Oberlin Coll., 1980; MPH, U. Calif., Berkeley, 1985; PhD, U. Calif., San Francisco, Berkeley, 1993. Cert. labor coach, ARC standard first aid, CPR for Profl. Rescuer, sr. life saving, swim instr. Pvt. tchr. ESL Tapei, Taiwan, 1981, Jackson Mann Cmty. Sch., Boston, 1982-83, Beijing (China) Med. U., 1985; tchg. asst. U. Calif. Berkeley, U. Calif. Berkeley Ext. Program, 1987-89; post-doctorate rsch. scholar U. Calif., Berkeley, 1994—, rsch. scholar Beatrice M. Bain Rsch. Ctr., 1994—; policy and legis. analyst, cons. World Inst. on Disability, Berkeley, 1995—; adj. faculty Calif. Inst. Integral Studies, San Francisco; field rschr., exchange student Sch. Pub. Health, Policy and Planning Program, U. Guadalajara, Mexico, 1984; cons. Internat. Child Resource Inst., Berkeley, 1985-86; rschr. Western Consortium for the Health Professions, San Francisco, 1986-87; field rschr. Highland Hosp. Ob-Gyn. Clinic, Oakland, Calif., 1988, others; presenter in field. Editor: Coun. on Anthropology and Reproduction Newsletter, 1993—; contbr. articles to profl. jours. Labor coach, translator Highland Hosp. and Asian Health Svcs., Oakland, 1987-88, 91—; cmty. health worker Berkeley (Calif.) Free Clinic, 1984-85. Recipient Oberlin Coll. Grad. Student Alumni award, 1988-89, Predoctoral award Assn. for Women in Sci., 1990, NSF Doctoral Dissertation Improvement award, 1990-91, Fulbright-Hays Doctoral Dissertation award, 1990-91, Sorpotomist Internat. award, 1991-92, Wenner-Gren Anthropol. Assn. doctoral dissertation award, 1995. Office: Beatrice M Bain Rsch Inst Univ Calif Berkeley Berkeley CA 94704

HANDZLIK, JAN LAWRENCE, lawyer; b. N.Y.C., Sept. 21, 1945; s. Felix Munso and Anna Jean Handzlik; children: Grant, Craig, Anna. BA, U. So. Calif., 1967; JD, UCLA, 1970. Bar: Calif. 1971, U.S. Dist. Ct. (cen. dist.) Calif. 1971, U.S. Ct. Appeals (9th cir.) 1971, U.S. Supreme Ct. 1975, U.S. Tax Ct. 1979, U.S. Dist. Ct. (no. dist.) Calif. 1979, U.S. Dist. Ct. (ea. dist.) Calif. 1981, U.S. Dist. Ct. (so. dist.) Calif. 1982, U.S. Ct. Appeals (2d cir.) 1984, U.S. Ct. Internat. Trade 1984. Law clk. to Hon. Francis C. Whelan, U.S. Dist. Ct. (cen. dist.) Calif., L.A., 1970-71; asst. U.S. atty. fraud and spl. prosecutions unit criminal div. U.S. Dept. Justice, L.A., 1971-76; assoc. Greenberg & Glusker, L.A., 1976-78; ptnr., prin. Stilz, Boyd, Levine & Handzlik, P.C., L.A., 1978-84; prin. Jan Lawrence Handzlik, P.C., L.A., 1984-91; ptnr. Kirkland & Ellis, L.A., 1991—; del. U.S. Ct. Appeals (9th cir.) Jud. Conf., L.A., 1983-85; counsel to ind. Christopher Commn. study of the L.A. Police Dept., 1991; dep. gen. counsel to Hon. William H. Webster, spl. advisor to L.A. Police Commn. for the investigation of L.A. Police Dept.'s Response to Urban Disorders, 1992; mem. adv. com. for Office of L.A. County Dist. Atty., 1994—. Mem. editl. adv. bd. DOJ Alert, 1994-95. Bd. dirs. Friends of Child Advs., L.A., 1987-91, Inner City Law Ctr., L.A., 1993—; mem. bd. judges Nat. and Calif. Moot Ct. Competition Teams, UCLA Moot Ct. honors program. Mem. ABA (sects. criminal justice nat. com. on white collar crime, 1991—, co-chair securities fraud subcom. 1994—, mem. Calif. white collar crime com., mem. exec. com. 1993—, vice chairperson 1994—, mem. litigation, criminal litigation com. 1989—), Fed. Bar Assn., State Bar Calif. (sects. on criminal law and litigation), L.A. County Bar Assn. (mem. coms. on fed. ct. 1988—, chairperson criminal practice subcom. 1989-90, fed. appts. evaluation 1989-93, white collar crime def. 1991—, mem. exec. com. 1991—), Nat. Assn. Criminal Def. Lawyers. Office: Kirkland & Ellis 300 S Grand Ave Ste 3000 Los Angeles CA 90071-3140

HANES, JOHN GRIER, lawyer, state legislator; b. Cheyenne, Wyo., 1936; s. Harold H. and Mary Elizabeth (Grier) H.; m. Liv Paul; children: Greg, Clint. BS in Bus. Adminstrn., U. Wyo., 1958, JD, 1960. Bar: Wyo. 1960, U.S. Ct. Appeals (10th cir.) 1960, U.S. Ct. Mil. Appeals, 1960, U.S. Supreme Ct. 1964. Dep. sec. of state State of Wyo., 1963-65; prijn. Burke, Woodard & Bishop, Cheyenne, 1965-90, of counsel, 1990—; atty. Wyo. Senate, 1967-71; mcpl. judge City of Cheyenne, 1970-73; mem. Burke, Woodard & Bishop, P.C. and predecessor firms, Cheyenne, Wyo., until 1990, of counsel, 1990—; mem. Wyo. Ho. of Reps., 1993—. Vol. Cheyenne Frontier Days; mem. Heels; Rep. precinct committeeman, 1976-94. With U.S. Army JAGC. Mem. C. of C., Rotary (pres. 1982-83, dist. gov. 1990-91), Sigma Nu. Home: 848 Creighton St Cheyenne WY 82009-3231 Office: 600 Boyd Bldg 1720 Carey Ave Cheyenne WY 82001-4429

HANEY, RAYMOND LEE, gas and electric company executive; b. Piedmont, Kans., Dec. 9, 1939; s. Carl Wilburn and Imogene (Johnson) H.; m. Linda Jo Amis, Nov. 2, 1967; children: Laura Jo, Paul Lee, Kevin Seth, Kimberly Ann, Keith Andrew. B.S., Brigham Young U., 1970, M.B.A., 1972. Mgr. fin. services San Diego Gas and Electric Co., 1979-80, mgr. fin. services, asst. treas., 1980-81, treas., 1981-83, v.p. fin., treas., 1983—; chief fin. officer Califia Co., San Diego. Served with USN, 1957-60. Mem. Fin. Execs. Inst., Nat. Corp. of Corporate Treas. Republican. Mormon. Home: 1906 Marlinda Way El Cajon CA 92021-1154 Office: San Diego Gas & Electric Co PO Box 1831 San Diego CA 92112-4150

HANEY, ROBERT LOCKE, retired insurance company executive; b. Morgantown, W.Va., June 14, 1928; s. John Ward and Katherine Eugenia (Locke) H. BA, U. Calif., Berkeley, 1949. Sr. engr. Pacific Telephone Co., San Francisco, 1952-58; mgmt. analyst Lockheed Missiles & Space Co., Sunnyvale, Calif., 1958-64; sr. cons. John Diebold, N.Y.C., 1964-65; sr. indsl. economist Mgmt. & Econs. Research, Inc., Palo Alto, Calif., 1965-67; prin. economist Midwest Research Inst., Kansas City, Mo., 1967-69; dir. mktg. coordination Transam. Corp., San Francisco, 1969-73; staff exec. Transam. Ins. Corp., L.A., 1974-82; 2d v.p. Transam. Life Cos., L.A., 1982-93; ret., 1993; cons. in field. Co-author: Creating the Human Environment, 1970. Lt. (j.g.) USN, 1949-52. Mem. Scabbard & Blade. Republican. Episcopalian. Home: 2743 Tiburon Ave Carlsbad CA 92008-7908

HANF, JAMES ALPHONSO, poet, government official; b. Chehalis, Wash., Feb. 3, 1923; s. William G. and Willa DeForest (Davis) H.; m. Ruth G. Eyler, Aug. 16, 1947; 1 child, Maureen Ruth. Grad. Centralia Jr. Coll., 1943, DLitt (hon.) World U. Ariz., 1980 Naval architect technician P.F. Spaulding, naval architects, Seattle, 1955-56, Puget Sound Bridge & Dredge Co. (Wash.), 1953-55, Puget Sound Naval Shipyard, 1951-53, 56-93; cons. Anderson & Assocs., ship bldg.; cons. The Rsch. Bd. Advs., Am. Biographical Inst., Inc.; guest lectr. on poetry and geneal. rsch. methods to various lit. socs., 1969—; contbr. hundreds of poems to lit. jours., anthologies and popular mags.; poetry editor Coffee Break, 1977-82. Recipient Poet Laureate Recognition award Internat. Biog. Centre of Cambridge, Eng., grand prize World Poetry Soc. Conv., 1985, 86, , 90, Golden Poet award World of Poetry in Calif., 1985-90, Silver Poet award Calif. sponsored nat. contest, 1989, numerous other awards. Judge poetry contest, Australia and India, 1985; named Man of Yr. Abaas, 1989—; named Internat. Eminent Poet Internat. Poet Acad. of Madras, India, 1987. Mem Internat. Poetry Soc. (Poet Laureate Wash. State award 1981), World of Poetry Soc. (Golden Poet award 1985-88, Poet Laureate award 1979), Kitsap County Writers Club (pres. 1977-78), Internat. Fedn. Tech. Engrs., Nat. Hist. Locomotive Soc., Kitsap County Hist. Soc., Puget Sound Geneal. Soc., Western World Haiku Soc., Olympic Geneal. Soc. (pres. 1974-75), N.Y. Poetry Forum, World Poets Resource Ctr., Literarische Union, Académie Européenne des Scis., Des Arts Et Des Letters (corr.), Internat. Soc. Poets Md. (hon. charter), Internat. Platform Assn., Calif. Fedn. Chaparral Poets, World Sadhak Soc. (hon.), Nat. Libr. Poetry (hon. mem.). Baptist. Home: PO Box 374 Bremerton WA 98337-0075

HANFF, PETER EDWARD, librarian, bibliographer; b. Jacksonville, Fla., Jan. 23, 1944; s. George E. and Mildred Todd (Stringer) H.; m. Judith A. Baker, Jan. 22, 1974 (div. 1979). BA, U. Calif., Santa Barbara, 1966; MLS, UCLA, 1967. Librarian Library of Congress, Washington, 1967-69; librarian, fellow Lilly Library, Ind. U., Bloomington, 1969-70; librarian Bancroft Library, U. Calif., Berkeley, 1970—, acting dir., 1990-95, dep. dir., 1995—; lectr. on book collecting U. Calif. Extension, 5 campuses, 1978, 79. Author: Bibliographia Oziana, 1976, 2d edit., 1988; mem. editl. bd. Rare Books and Manuscripts Librarianship, 1986-93; contbr. articles to various publs. Mem. ALA, Assn. Coll. and Rsch. Librs. (appointments and nominating com. 1989-90), Am. Pty. Hist. Assn. (trustee 1993—), Internat. Wizard of Oz Club (bibliography editor 1976—, pres. 1978-86, 95—, recipient L. Frank Baum Meml. award 1978), Grolier Club (N.Y.C.), Colophon Club (San Francisco), Roxburghe Club (San Francisco). Home: 1083 Euclid Ave Berkeley CA 94708-1639 Office: U Calif Bancroft Library Berkeley CA 94720

HANG, SOEI-SHIN, design engineer; b. Hong Kong, Apr. 17, 1967; came to U.S., 1985; d. Loisniwati (Ongko Widjaja) Soemedi; m. Brian Shing, Sept. 19, 1992. BS in Computer Sci., BSEE, Washington U., St. Louis, 1989; MSEE, UCLA, 1991. Design engr. Cylink Co., Sunnyvale, Calif., 1991-92, sr. design engr., 1992—; participant Internat. Conf. Acoustic and Signal Processing, 1992, Custom Integrated Cir. Conf., 1993. Mem. IEEE.

HANIFEN, RICHARD CHARLES, bishop; b. Denver, June 15, 1931; s. Edward Anselm and Dorothy Elizabeth (Ranous) H. B.S., Regis Coll., 1953; S.T.B., Cath. U., 1959, M.A., 1966; J.C.L., Pontifical Lateran U., Italy, 1968. Ordained priest Roman Catholic Ch., 1959; asst. pastor Cathedral Parish, Denver, 1959-66; sec. to archbishop Archdiocese Denver, 1968-69, chancellor, 1969-76; aux. bishop of Denver, 1974-83; 1st bishop of Colorado Springs, Colo., 1984—. Office: Bishop of Colo Springs 29 W Kiowa St Colorado Springs CO 80903-1403

HANKET, ARTHUR ANTHONY, actor, marketing and sales analyst, consultant; b. Ft. Belvoir, Va., June 23, 1954; s. Arthur P. and Jimsy A. (Murphree) H.; 1 child, Peter Colot. BA in Theater Arts, U. Va., 1976; MFA in Acting, Fla. State U., 1978. Mktg. profl. Metler Assocs., N.Y.C., 1979-82; mktg./sales prof. The N.Y. Times, N.Y.C., 1982-84; mktg./rsch./mgmt. profl. Atwood Richards Inc., N.Y.C. and Irvine, Calif., 1985—; sole propr., pres. TeleMarketing Cons., L.A. Author: National Poetry Review, 1994; appearences include (TV shows) Knots Landing, Married with Children, Andre's Mother, Beauty, One Life to Live, Another World; (theatre) Playwright's Horizons, N.Y.C., Pub. Theater, N.Y.C., Lamb's Theater, N.Y.C., N.Y. Theater Workshop, Hudson Guild Theater, N.Y.C., WPA Theater, N.Y.C., CSC Repertory, N.Y.C., Guthrie Theater, Mpls., The Actor's Gang, La Jolla (Calif.) Playhouse, Long Beach (Calif.) Opera Co., Hartford (Conn.) Stage So., Alley Theater, Phila. Drama Guild, Calif. Shakespeare Festival, Ala. Shakespeare Festival.

HANKINS, HESTERLY G., III, computer systems analyst, inventor, educator; b. Sallisaw, Okla., Sept. 5, 1950; s. Hesterly G. and Ruth Faye (Jackson) H. BA in Sociology, U. Calif., Santa Barbara, 1972; MBA in Info. Systems, UCLA, 1974; postgrad., Golden Gate U., 1985-86, Ventura Coll., 1970, Antelope Valley Coll., 1977, La Verne U., 1987; student, NRI McGraw-Hill Sch. Writing, Washington, 1993—. Cert. community coll. tchr., Calif. Applications programmer Xerox Corp., Marina Del Rey, Calif., 1979-80; computer programmer Naval Ship Weapon Systems Engring. Sta. of Port Hueneme, Oxnard, Calif., 1980-84; spl. asst. to chief exec. officer Naval Air Sta. of Moffett Field, Mountain View, Calif., 1984-85; mgr. computer systems project Pacific Missile Test Ctr., Oxnard, 1985-88, MIS Def. Contract Adminstrn. Svcs. Region, L.A., 1988-94; ret. MIS DEf. Contract Adminstrn. Svcs. Region, L.A., 1994; instr. writing Nat. U., Inglewood, Calif., 1994—; instr. bus. West Coast U., Camarillo, Calif., 1985; core adj. faculty Nat. U., L.A., 1988—; lectr. bus. Golden Gate U., Los Altos, Calif., 1984; instr. computer sci. Chapman Coll., Sunnyvale, 1984, Ventura (Calif.) Coll., 1983-84; cons. L.A. Police Dept., Allison Mortgage Trust Investment Co.; minority small bus. assn. cons. UCLA. Author: Campus Computing's Accounting I.S. As A Measurement of Computer Performance, 1973, Campus Computer, 1986, Network Planning, 1986, Satellites and Teleconferencing, 1986, Quotations, 1992, Quotable Expressions and Memorable Quotations of Notables, 1993, Idea Bank, 1993, Product Rating System, 1993, Training Base Model, 1993, Sound Seal/Shield, 1994, My Biographical Profile. Mem. St. Paul United Meth. Ch., Oxnard, Calif., 1986-87; fundraiser YMCA Jr. Rodeo, Lake Casitos, Calif.; key person to combine fed. campaign United Way. Named One of Outstanding Young Men in Am. U.S. Jaycees, 1980, Internat. Leader of Achievement and Man of Achievement, Internat. Biog. Centre, Cambridge, Eng., 1988, 20th Century award for achievement Internat. Biog. Centre, Cambridge, Eng., 1994. Mem. Nat. Assn. Accts., Calif. Assn. Accts., Intergovtl. Council on Tech. Info. Processing, Assn. Computing Machinery (recipient Smart Beneficial Suggestion award 1984), IEEE Computer Soc., Fed. Mgrs. Assn., Alpha Kappa Psi (sec. 1972-73). Office: Nat Univ PO Box 34931 Los Angeles CA 90034-0931

HANKS, EUGENE RALPH, land developer, cattle rancher, retired naval officer; b. Corning, Calif., Dec. 11, 1918; s. Eugene and Lorena B. Hanks; m. Frances Elliot Herrick, Mar. 4, 1945; children: Herrick, Russell, Stephen, Nina. Student, Calif. Poly. Coll., 1939-41, U. So. Calif., 1949-50, Am. U., 1958-59; grad., Command and Staff Coll., Norfolk, Va., 1960. With Naval Aviation Flight Tng.,V-5 Program USN, 1941-42, commd. ensign, 1942, advanced through grades to capt., 1963; carrier fighter pilot, Am. Ace, six victories, 1942-45; test pilot Naval Air Test Ctr., 1946-48; mem. Navy Flight Exhbn. Team Blue Angels, 1950; commdg. officer fighter squadrons including Navy's 1st squadron of F4 Phantoms, Mach II Missile Fighters, Miramar, Calif., 1952-61; 1st ops. officer U.S.S. Constellation, 1961-62; dir. ops. Naval Missile Test Ctr., 1963-66; test dir. Joint Task Force Two, Albuquerque, 1966-69; ret., 1969; owner, developer Christmas Tree Canyon, Cebolla Springs and Mountain River subdivs., Mora, N.Mex., 1969-95. Decorated Navy Cross, DFC with star (2), Air medal (7), Legion of merit; named Citizen of Yr., Citizen's Com. for Right to Bear Arms, 1987, 93, to Dun and Bradstreet's Million Dollar Club. Mem. Ret. Officers Assn., Am. Fighter Aces Assn., Combat Pilots Assn., Assn. Naval Aviation, Am. Forestry Assn., NRA, Blue Angels Assn., Naval Aviation Museum Found., Legion of Valor. Republican. Home and Office: Christmas Tree Canyon PO Box 239 Mora NM 87732-0239

HANKS, LAWRENCE MICHAEL, ecologist, entomologist; b. Livermore, Calif., Jan. 26, 1953; s. Amos Mefford and Janet Marilyn (Frager) H. BS, U. Calif., Davis, 1978; MS, U. Nev., 1982; PhD, U. Md., 1991. Postdoctoral fellow U. Calif., Riverside, 1989-93; asst. rsch. entomologist, 1994—. Contbr. articles to profl. jours. Recipient Robert Malcolm scholarship U. Calif., Davis, 1976, Hebert Kroft scholarship, 1977, Gahan scholarship U. Med., 1984, 86; grantee Sigma Xi, 1981. Mem. Entomol. soc. Am., Ecol. Soc. Am., Entomol. Soc. Wash., Soc. for the Study of Evolution, Phi Kappa Phi. Office: U Calif Dept Entomology Riverside CA 92521

HANKS, MERTON EDWARD, professional football player; b. Dallas, Tex., Mar. 12, 1968. BA, liberal arts, U. Iowa, 1990. With San Francisco 49ers, 1991—. Office: San Francisco 49ers 4949 Centennial Blvd Santa Clara CA 95054-1229

HANKS, SUSAN BUDLONG, physical therapist; b. Evanston, Ill., May 13, 1942; d. Joseph Lyman and Geraldine (Handley) Budlong; divorced; children: Paul Joseph, Nicole Susanne. BS in Phys. Medicine, U. Wis., 1964. Staff phys. therapist Rehab. Inst. Oreg., 1964-66; staff phys. therspist Oreg. Health Scis. U., Child Devel. and Rehab. Ctr., 1967—; pvt. practice phys. therapy Portland, Oreg., 1978-89; cons. Albany (Oreg.) Pub. Schs., 1977, Salem (Oreg.) Pub. Schs., 1978-79, Idaho State Hosp. and Tng. Ctr., Nampa, 1978-79, Ea. Oreg. State Hosp. and Tng. Ctr., Pendleton, 1980, Clark Inst. for Restorative Tech., Battleground, Wash., 1980, Newberg Sch. Dist., 1980-82, McMinnville Sch. Dist., 1981-82, Woodburn Sch. Dist., 1982, Fairview State Hosp., 1981-89; presenter workshops in field. Author: Education and Therapeutic Interventions in Rett Syndrome, 1989; contbr. articles to profl. jours. Mem. Am. Phys. Therapy Assn., Oreg. Phys. Therapy Assn., Neurodevel. Treatment Assn., Phi Kappa Phi. Anglican. Office: Child Devel & Rehab Ctr 707 SW Gaines St Portland OR 97201-2998

HANLEY, JOAN CORETTE, vineyard owner; b. Missoula, Mont., Jan. 25, 1933; d. John Earl and Elsie (Pauly) Corette; m. Donald Lee Hanley, Mar. 26, 1953; children: Lee, Dean, Scott, Mark, Elise. Student, Stanford U., 1951-52, Mont. State Coll., 1953, Northwestern U., 1953; BA in Speech, U. Wash., 1955. Cert. clin. competence speech pathology and audiology. Speech pathology and audiologist, 1955-74; owner, gen. ptnr. Miramonte Vineyards, Temecula, Calif., 1973—; dir. Ctrl. City Speech and Hearing Clinic, Calif. State U., Long Beach, 1978-80; dir. pub. affairs Monaghan Co., Rancho Palos Verdes, Calif., 1990-91; corp. dir. So. Calif. Edison Co., SCE Corp., 1980—; bd. dirs. Harbor-UCLA Rsch. and Edn. Inst. Trustee Pomona Coll., Claremont, Calif., 1982—; bd. dirs. Calif. Agrl. Edn. Found., 1989—, Greater L.A. United Way, Inc., 1971-94; co-chair So. Calif., Campaign for U. Wash., 1989-92; chmn. Harbor S.E. region bd. dirs. Greater L.A. United Way; chmn. fundraising com. Holy Trinity Cath. Ch., San Pedro, Calif., 1991-95; bd. dirs., exec. com. Greater L.A. United Way; mem. Commn. on Agr. and Higher Edn. State Calif., 1994-95. Republican. Roman Catholic.

HANLEY, KEVIN LANCE, maintenance manager; b. Oil City, Pa., Nov. 25, 1961; s. Harold Edward and Helen Louise (Banta) H.; m. Patricia Yolanda DeLeon, Sept. 29, 1984; children: Jennifer Jessica, Kevin Lance Jr. Grad. high sch., Titusville, Pa.; diploma, McDonald's Regional Hdqs., L.A., 1986. Maintenance supr. Paschen Mgmt. Corp. McDonald's, Camarillo, Calif., 1980-86, asst. mgr., 1986-88, 95—, maintenance cons., 1988-89; mgr. phys. plant Westmont Coll., Santa Barbara, Calif., 1988—; apartment mgr. Bartlein & Co., Ventura, Calif., 1990—; storekeeper USNR, Port Hueneme, Calif., 1994—; gen. cons. "r" Cleaning Maintenance, Santa Paula, Calif., 1989-91. Sec.-treas. Ch. of God of Prophecy, Ventura, Calif., 1987—, co-pastor, 1988—. With USNR, 1994—. Republican. Office: Westmont Coll 955 La Paz Rd Santa Barbara CA 93108-1023

HANLIN, RUSSELL L., citrus products company executive; b. Sioux Falls, S.D., 1932; married. Student, U. Wash., Los Angeles City Coll. With Sunkist Growers, Inc., Van Nuys, Calif., 1951—, advt. mgr., 1964-72, v.p. mfg., mkt. research and devel., products group, 1972-78, former chief exec. and chief operating officer, pres., 1978—, also dir. Served with U.S. Army, 1953-55. Office: Sunkist Growers Inc 14130 Riverside Dr Sherman Oaks CA 91423-2313

HANLY, JERI RYAN, computer science educator; b. Evansville, Ind., Oct. 31, 1949; d. Charles Keith and Elizabeth (McIntyre) Ryan; m. Brian Vaughan, Aug. 25, 1968; children: Eric Josef, Kevin Frederick. BS in Edn., U. So. Ala., 1970; MA in Romance Langs., U. Mich., 1975; MS in Computer Sci., U. Wyo., 1984. Instr. of French and Russian Interlochen (Mich.) Arts Acad., 1970-73; lectr. in computer sci. U. Wyo., Laramie, 1980—; rsch. collaborator Naval Weapons Ctr., China Lake, Calif., 1984-92; software engring. seminar instr. IBM-US Edn., 1988-91. Author: Problem Solving and Program Design in C, 1993, C Program Design for Engineers, 1994. Mem. Assn. for Computing Machinery. Baptist. Office: U Wyo Computer Sci Dept PO Box 3682 Laramie WY 82071-3682

HANNA, HARRY MITCHELL, lawyer; b. Portland, Oreg., Jan. 13, 1936; s. Joseph John and Amelia Cecelia (Rask) H.; m. Patricia Ann Shelly, Feb. 4, 1967; 1 child, Harry M. Jr. BS, U. Oreg., 1958; JD, Lewis and Clark Coll., 1966. Bar: Oreg. 1966, U.S. Tax Ct. 1967, U.S. Dist. Ct. Oreg. 1970, U.S. Supreme Ct. 1971, U.S. Ct. Appeals (9th cir.) 1973, U.S. Ct. Claims 1973. Airport mgr. Port of Portland, 1964-66; mng. ptnr. Hanna & Purella, Portland, 1966-80, Niehaus, Hanna, Murphy, Green, Holloway & Connolly, Portland, 1980-88; shareholder, v.p. Hanna, Kerns & Strader, P.C., Portland, 1988—; judge pro-tempore U.S. Dist. Ct. Oreg., 1973-78; adj. prof. N.W. Sch. Law, Lewis and Clark Coll., Portland, 1976-77. Trustee Emanuel Med. Ctr. Found., 1989—; pres. Ctrl. Cath. H.S. Bd., 1992-95. Mem. ABA, Fed. Bar Assn., Oreg. State Bar Assn., Multnomah Bar Assn., Rotary (pres. East Portland club 1989-90). Office: Hanna Kerns & Strader PC 1300 SW 6th Ave Ste 300 Portland OR 97201-3461

HANNA, NABIL, biomedical engineer; b. 1944. PhD in Immunology, Hebrew U., Israel. Lectr. Hebrew U., Israel, 1973-78; rsch. sci. NCI-Frederick Cancer Rsch. Ctr., 1978-81; dir. SmithKline Beecham, 1981-90; now with IDEC Pharm. Corp., San Diego, 1991—. Office: IDEC Pharm Corp 11011 Torreyana Rd San Diego CA 92121*

HANNA, ROBERT CECIL, lawyer; b. Albuquerque, July 28, 1937; s. Samuel Gray and Orvetta (Cecil) H.; BA, U. N.Mex., 1959, JD, 1962. Bar: N.M1962, Hawaii 1974, U.S. Supreme Ct. 1970; practiced in Albuquerque, 1962-70, 72—; organizer, dep. dir. Micronesian Legal Svcs. Corp., Trust Ter. Pacific Islands, 1970-71; practiced in Hilo; Hawaii, 1974; ptnr. Cotter,

Atkinson, Kitts, Kelsey & Hanna, Ortega, Snead, Dixon & Hanna, Albuquerque, 1975-77; owner, pres., prin. Robert C. Hanna & Assocs., Albuquerque, 1978-80, 88—; pres. Sedco Internat. USA, Inc., Albuquerque, 1977-79, Suncastle Builders, Inc., Albuquerque, 1978—, Am. Legal Consortium, A Chartered Law Firm, 1984—, The Garden Spa Resort, 1995—; gen. counsel Casas de Sueños The Bed and Breakfast Company, 1991—, Zephyr Mgmt. Co., 1991—; ptnr. Contemporary Devel. Inc., 1989—, N.Mex. Real Estate Consortium Ltd., 1986—; mem. Bd. Bar Commrs., Trust Ter. Pacific Islands, 1971-72. Bd. dirs. Found. for Life Action (nonprofit), L.A., 1990—; founder, pres., bd. dirs. Casa de Sueños Found. (nonprofit), 1993—. Recipient award Rocky Mountain Mineral Law Found., 1962; Pub. Svc. award Micronesian Legal Services Corp. Bd. Dirs., 1972. Mem. Hawaii Bar Assn., N.Mex. Bar Assn., Albuquerque Bar Assn. Home and Office: 310 Rio Grande Blvd SW Albuquerque NM 87104-1477

HANNA, SARA L., English language educator; b. Greencastle, Ind., July 9, 1943; d. George William and Hazel Frieda (Ahl) H. BA, Ind. U., 1966, PhD, 1985; MPhil, Yale U., 1969. Assoc. instr. Ind. U., Bloomington, 1980-85; asst. prof. N.Mex. State U., Las Cruces, 1985-90; assoc. prof. N.Mex. Highlands U., Las Vegas, 1990—. Contbr. articles to profl. publs. Tutor, bd. dirs. Las Vegas/San Miguel Literacy, 1993—; rschr. Hist. Preservation Com., Las Vegas, 1990—; vol. San Miguel Search & Rescue, Las Vegas, 1993—, Santa Fe Nat. Forest Trails, Las Vegas, 1993—. NDEA fellow, 1966-69; NEH grantee, 1992. Mem. MLA, Shakespeare Assn. Am., New Chancer Soc., Renaissance Soc. Am., Phi Beta Kappa, Phi Kappa Phi (sec.-treas. 1994—).

HANNA, WILLIAM JOHNSON, electrical engineering educator; b. Longmont, Colo., Feb. 7, 1922; s. William Grant and Anna Christina (Johnson) H.; m. Katherine Fagan, Apr. 25, 1944; children: Daniel August, Paul William. BSEE, U. Colo., 1943, MS, 1948, D in Elec. Engring., 1951. Registered profl. engr., Colo., Kans. Mem. faculty U. Colo., 1946-91, prof. elec. engring., 1962-91, prof. emeritus, 1991—; cons. in field; mem. Colo. Bd. Engring. Examiners, 1973-85. Author articles, reports. Served to 1st lt. AUS, 1943-46. Recipient Faculty Recognition award Students Assn. U. Colo., 1956, 61, Alfred J. Ryan award, 1978, Archimedes award Calif. Soc. Profl. Engrs., 1978, Outstanding Engring. Alumnus award U. Colo., 1983, Faculty Service award, 1983; named Colo. Engr. of Yr. Profl. Engrs. Colo., 1968; named to Hon. Order of Ky. Cols. Mem. IEEE, Am. Soc. Engring. Edn., Nat. Soc. Profl. Engrs. (pres. Colo. 1967-68), Nat. Coun. Engring. Examiners (pres. 1977-78, Disting. Svc. award with spl. commendation 1990), AIEE (chmn. Denver 1961-62). Republican. Presbyterian. Club: Masons. Home and Office: 27 Silver Spruce Nederland Star Rt Boulder CO 80302-9604

HANNE, WILLIAM GERON, training development professional, educator; b. Kansas City, Kans., Dec. 30, 1938; s. William Homer and Iris Marie (Geron) H.; m. Anne Katherine Strobach Hanne, Nov. 26, 1960; children: Matthew William, Brian Robert, Mark Andrew, Eric Joseph. BS in Mil. Sci., U.S. Mil. Acad., 1960; MS in Geography, U. Ill., 1968; PhD in Adult/Higher Edn., U. Md., 1991. Commd. lt. U.S. Army, 1960, advanced through grades to col., 1982, ret., 1989; sr. edn./tng. officer Nat. Security Agy., Ft. Meade, Md., 1989-90; pres. MBME Cons., Sierra Vista, Ariz., 1990—; program mgr. Mandex, Inc., Sierra Vista, 1992—; adj. faculty Cochise Coll., Sierra Vista, 1990—. Author, editor: Landscape Atlas of USSR, 1971; contbr. chpt. to book and articles to profl. jours. com. chmn., scoutmaster Boy Scouts Am., Mass., R.I., Pa., Va., 1974-83. Decorated Legion of Merit; named Master Inst., Nat. Cryptologic Sch., Ft. Meade, 1989. Mem. Optimist. Home: 7154 E Dakota St Hereford AZ 85615-9327 Office: Mandex Inc 7154 E Dakota Rd Ste B Hereford AZ 85615-9327

HANNEN, JOHN EDWARD, bishop; b. Winnipeg, Man., Can., Nov. 19, 1937; s. Charles Scott and Mary Bowman (Lynds) H.; m. Alana Susan Long, June 24, 1977; children—Rebecca Meghann, Meredith Alana. B.A., McGill U., 1959; G.O.E., Coll. of Resurrection, Mirfield, Eng., 1961. Ordained deacon Anglican Ch., 1961, ordained priest, 1962. Asst. curate Diocese of Birmingham, Eng., 1961-64; priest-in-charge Hart Hwy. Diocese of Caledonia, Chetwynd, B.C., Can., 1965-67; assoc. priest Diocese of Caledonia, Greenville, B.C., 1967-68; priest-in-charge Diocese of Caledonia, Port Edward, B.C., 1968-71, Kincolith, B.C., 1971-80; bishop Diocese of Caledonia, Prince Rupert, B.C., 1981—; senator Vancouver Sch. Theology, B.C., 1981-85; mem. inter ch.-interfaith relations com. Gen. Synod, Anglican Ch. of Can., 1983-89. Chmn. bd. trustees Nishga Sch. Dist., Naas River, B.C., 1977-78; mem. exec. com. Nishga Tribal Council, Naas River, 1974—. Office: Synod Office, PO Box 278, Prince Rupert, BC Canada V8J 3P6

HANNUM, GERALD LUTHER (LOU HANNUM), retired tire manufacturing company official; b. Syracuse, N.Y., May 31, 1915; s. Ralph Charles and Coral (Snyder) H.; m. Carolyn Russell Osgood, Nov. 29, 1941; children: Nancy, Susan, Jean. AB, Syracuse U., 1937; MA, Kent State U., 1971. Supr. forecasting and inventory control B.F. Goodrich, Arkon, Ohio, 1961-67; econ. planning specialist, staff for v.p. planning B.F. Goodrich Co., 1967-75, econ. planner, 1946-75; ret., 1975. Councilman City of Medford, Oreg., 1977-82, 89-92, mayor, 1983-86; bd. dirs. United Way, Medford, 1986—; pres. Crater Lake coun. Boy Scouts Am., 1987-90. Lt. USNR, 1943-52, PTO. Recipient Silver Beaver award Boy Scouts Am., 1987. Mem. League Oreg. Cities (pres. 1983, Richards award 1989), Rotary. Home: 2900 Seckel St Medford OR 97504-8150

HANOWELL, ERNEST GODDIN, physician; b. Newport News, Va., Jan. 31, 1920; a. George Frederick and Ruby Augustine (Goddin) H.; m. Para Jean Hall, June 10, 1945; children: Ernest D., Deborah J. Hanowell Orick, Leland H., Dee P. Hanowell Martinmaas, Robert G. Diplomate Am. Bd. Internal Medicine. Intern USPHS Hosp., Norfolk, Va., 1948-49; resident in internal medicine USPHS Hosp., Seattle, 1952-55; fellow cardiology New Eng. Ctr. Hosp., Boston; chief medicine USPHS Hosp., Ft. Worth, 1955-57; dept. chief medicine USPHS Hosp., Boston, 1957-59; chief medicine USPHS Hosp., Memphis, 1964-65, Monterey County Gen. Hosp., 1969-70; ret. med. dir., col. USPHS; mem. IM and Cardiology staff Kaiser Permanente Med. Group, Sacramento, 1971-87; writer Auburn, Calif., 1987—; clin. asst. Tufts Med. Sch., 1960-61; cons. chest disease Phila. Gen. Hosp., 1960-61; asst. prof. U. Md. Med. Sch., 1961-64; instr. U. Tenn. Med. Sch., 1964-65; asst. clin. prof. Sch. Medicine, U. Calif., Davis, 1973-81; mem. attending staff Cardiac Clinic Stanford U. Med. Sch. 1967-69. Mem. sch. bd. Salinas, Calif., 1968-69; bd. dirs. Am. Heart Assn., Tb and Health Assn. Served with AUS, 1943-46. Fellow ACP, Am. Coll. Chest Diseases; mem. AWA, Crocker Art Mus. Assn., Comstock Club (Sacramento), Phi Chi. Home and Office: 1158 Racquet Club Dr Auburn CA 95603-3042

HANRETTA, ALLAN GENE, psychiatrist, pharmacist; b. Galveston, Tex., June 24, 1930; s. Aloysius Thomas and Genevieve M. (Feeney) H.; m. Carolyn Jean Jacobs, Sept. 4, 1954; children: Allan Thomas, Patrice M., Mark D. BS in Pharamcy, U. Tex., Austin, 1952, BA in Arts and Sci., 1957; MD, U. Tex., Galveston, 1959. Diplomate Am. Bd. Psychiatry and Neurology. Gen. rotating intern USPHS Hosp., San Francisco, 1959-60; resident in psychiatry U. Tex. Med. Br., Galveston, Tex., 1960-63; fellow in clin. electroencephalography Meth. Hosp.-Tex. Med. Ctr., Houston, 1963-64; pvt. practice, Santa Barbara, 1964-83; chief staff Dani's Psychiat. Hosp., Santa Barbara, 1971-79; mem. med. staff Cottage Hosp., St. Francis Hosp., Goleta Valley Community Hosp., Camarillo State Hosp., 1964—. Lectr. Santa Barbara Pharm. Assn., 1975. Lt. (j.g.) USN, 1952-54. Recipient contbn. to pharmacy award Santa Barbara Pharm. Assn., 1975. Mem. AMA, Am. Psychiat. Assn., So. Calif. Psychiat. Assn., Santa Barbara Psychiat. Soc. (pres. 1977-79). Home: 3728 Calle Cita Santa Barbara CA 93105-2411

HANSCH, JOACHIM HORST, music director; b. Bad Grund, Hartz, Germany, Oct. 5, 1946; came to U.S., 1976; s. Frank and Johanna (Klimke) H. Intermediate Cert., Blacktown, Australia, 1959; Leaving Cert., Parramatta, Australia, 1961. Broadcast Operators Cert. Proficiency, Marconi Sch. Wireless, "B.O.C.P.", 1964. Audio tech. A.W.A., Sydney, Australia, 1964-65, mastering engr., 1965-70; mastering engr. Festival Records, Sydney, Australia, 1970-76; mastering engr. Kendun Recorders, L.A., 1976-77, studio mgr., mastering engr., 1977-79; studio mgr., mastering engr. Artisan Sound Recorders, Hollywood, Caif., 1979-81; owner, engr. Dinkum Recording Svc., Hollywood, Caif., 1981-88; dir. music Cannon Films, Beverly Hills, Calif., 1988-89; dir. Pathe Comm. Co., Beverly Hills, Calif., 1989-90, MGM, Culver City, 1990-92; pres. edel Am. Records, Inc., North Hollywood, Calif., 1992-94; ind. cons., 1994—. Mem. NARAS, Audio Engring. Soc. Office: Joachim Horst Hansch Penthouse 1220 15250 Ventura Blvd Sherman Oaks CA 91403

HANSELL, WALTER WHITE, lawyer; b. Phila., Sept. 16, 1959; s. Norris and Margaret White (Corry) H.; m. Amy Lottman, Sept. 23, 1989; children: Abigail Jean, Marian White. BA, U. Ill., 1981; JD, U. Calif., Berkeley, 1984. Bar: Calif. 1984, U.S. Dist. Ct. (no. dist.) Calif. 1984, U.S. Dist. Ct. (ea. dist.) Calif. 1992. Investment adviser self-employed, Urbana, Ill., 1980-81, San Francisco, 1981-84; assoc. atty. Cooper, White & Cooper, San Francisco, 1984-90, ptnr., 1991—; govt. rels. com. chair, dir. Women in Cable, San Francisco Bay Area Chpt., 1988-92. Vol. atty. Vol. Legal Svcs. Project and Homeless Assistance Project Bar Assn., San Francisco, 1985-94; mem. Ferguson Twp. Democratic Party, 1994—. Recipient Wiley Manuel Pro Bono Svc. award State Bar Calif., 1990-94. Mem. Women in Cable, Bay Area Cable Club, Communications Law Forum, ABA, State Bar Calif., Bar Assn. San Francisco, Florissant Valley Jaycees (bd. dirs, 1990-95, pres. 1995), St. Louis High Alumni (bd. dirs. 1994—), St. Louis U. Bus. Sch. Alumni (bd. dirs. 1995—). Home: 1049 Harvard Rd Piedmont CA 94610-1128 Office: Cooper White & Cooper 201 California St # 1700 San Francisco CA 94111-5002

HANSEN, ANNE MOLONEY, parent educator; b. L.A., Dec. 6, 1947; d. Donald Joseph and Madeliene Marie (Sartoris) M.; m. Ronald Paul Hansen, June 21, 1969; children: Emily, Sarah, Claire, Reid, Jeremy. BA in Psychology, Immaculate Heart Coll., L.A., 1969; MA in Ednl. Psychology, Calif. State U., 1986. Tchr. Archdiocese of L.A., 1969-75; parent educator PACE-Parent and Child Edn., Camarillo, Calif., 1986—; parent edn. cons. Pleasant Valley Hosp., Camarillo, 1986-93, Westlake (Calif.) Med. Ctr., 1989—, Archdiocese of L.A., 1990—. Author (column) Tidings Newspaper, 1994—. Democrat. Roman Catholic.

HANSEN, ARTHUR AUGUST, history educator; b. Hoboken, N.J., Oct. 10, 1938; s. Haakon and Anna (Stover) H.; m. Roberta Johnson, June 30, 1962 (div. June 1977); m. Debra Gold Hansen, June 25, 1977. BA in History, U. Calif., Santa Barbara, 1960, PhD in History, 1972. Instr. dept. English U. Calif., Santa Barbara, 1961, teaching asst. dept. history, 1963-65; tchr. dept. English Tustin (Calif.) Union High Sch., 1962-63; instr. dept. history Reading (Eng.) Coll., 1965; instr. divsn. social scis. Santa Ann (Calif.) Coll., 1966; asst. prof. dept. history Calif. State U., Fullerton, 1966-72, assoc. prof., 1972-77, prof., 1977—, coord. grad. studies dept. history, 1985-88; vis. prof. dept. history Calif. Poly. State U., San Luis Obispo, 1979-80; dir. Japanese Am. Project oral history program Calif. State U., Fullerton, 1972—, vice-chair dept. history, 1988-91, dir. oral history program dept. history, 1975-79, 87-89, 91—; chair conf. program Oral History Assn. ann. meeting, Long Beach, Calif., 1986, S.W. Oral History Assn. ann. meeting, Hemet, Calif., 1990, Reno, Nev. 1991. Author: The British Intellectual and Americanization, 1972; editor: Voices Long Silent: An Oral Inquiry into the Japanese American Evacuation, 1974, Manzanar Martyr; An Interview With Harry Y. Ueno, 1986, The Harvest of Hate, 1986, Reflections on Shattered Windows: Promises and Prospects for Asian American Studies, 1988, Sekinin (Duty Bound), 1989, Japanese American World War II Evacuation History Project, 1990-94; contbr. articles profl. jours.; co-editor Jour. Orange County Studies, 1988-91; editor Oral History Rev., 1981-87. Bd. dirs. Hist. and Cultural Found. Orange County, Calif., 1985-87; coun. mem. Nat. Scholars Adv. Coun., Japanese Am. Nat. Mus., 1990—. Calif. State U. faculty summer grantee, 1985, 89, 92, faculty travel grantee, 1986, faculty rsch. grantee, 1977, 81. Mem. Oral History Assn. (coun. mem. 1991-94), S.W. Oral History Assn. (v.p. 1990-91, pres. 1991-92, exec. coun. 1989-93), Am. Hist. Assn., Japanese Am. Hist. Soc. So. Calif., Pacific Hist. Assn., Radical History Assn., Western Hist. Assn., Asian Am. Studies Assn., Orgn. Am. Historians, Phi Alpha Theta. Office: Calif State U Dept History Fullerton CA 92634

HANSEN, BERNT ALLAN, lawyer; b. Longview, Wash., Mar. 29, 1941; s. Bernt Andrew and Wilma Leah (Simon) H.; m. Carole Tuttle, June 8, 1968; children: Matthew, Nicolai, Rachel. BS, Portland State U., 1965; sr. dep. dist. atty., U. Oreg., 1971. Bar: Oreg. 1972, U.S. Dist. Ct. Oreg. 1981. Dep. dist. atty. Lane County, Oreg., 1972-73, Yamhill County, Oreg., 1973-80; pvt. practice McMinnville, Oreg., 1980—. Planning commr. City of McMinnville, 1977-84, councilman, 1985-93. With U.S. Army, 1965-68. Mem. Yamhill County Bar Assn. (pres. 1981-82), ATLA, Oreg. Trial Lawyers Assn., Oreg. Criminal Def. Lawyers Assn., 12th Jud. Dist. Bar Assn. (pres. 1975-76), Rotary (pres. 1995—). Home: 922 N Galloway St Mcminnville OR 97128-3831 Office: 638 E 5th St PO Box 597 Mcminnville OR 97128

HANSEN, CARL FREDERICK, chemistry educator; b. Owatonna, Minn., June 11, 1921; s. Clifford Franklin and Lumetta Gladys (Swanson) H.; m. Alice Adelaide Underleak, July 11, 1946 (div. 1968); children: David R., Richard F., George H. BA, Carleton Coll., 1943; MS, Stanford U., 1948; D of Engring., Nagoya U., 1982. Aeronautical rsch. scientist Ames Aerospace Lab. NACA, Mountain View, Calif., 1950-59; chief physics br. Ames Rsch. Ctr. NASA, Mountain View, Calif., 1959-61, 67-82; head earth & astro scis. GM Defense Rsch. Lab., Santa Barbara, Calif., 1961-67; pres. JAI Assoc., Inc., Mountain View, 1985-89; rsch. prof. chem. physics inst. U. Oreg., Eugene, 1989—; vis. prof. aerospace engring. Nagoya (Japan) U., 1982, Indian Inst. Sci., Bangalore, 1983, Nat. Cheng Kung U., Taiwan, 1984-85, vis. prof. mech. engring. MIT, Cambridge, 1965-66; pres. Hansen Rsch. Assocs., Eugene, 1989—. Author: Molecular Physics of Equilbrium Gases, 1976, Rate Process in Gas Phase, 1983; contbr. articles to profl. jours. Treas. Com. Sch. Improvement, Palo Alto, Calif., 1958-59; bd. dirs. Orchard Farms Assn., San Jose, Calif., 1969-81. Sgt. USAF, 1943-46. Fellow AIAA (assoc., v.p. No. Calif. chpt. 1960); mem. Aircraft Owners and Pilots Assn., Elks. Independent. Office: U Oreg Physics Dept Eugene OR 97403

HANSEN, CAROL LOUISE, English language educator; b. San Jose, Calif., July 17, 1938; d. Hans Eskelsen and Thelma Josephine (Brooks) Hansen; m. Merrill Chris Davis, July 17, 1975 (div. 1978). BA in English, San Jose State U., 1960; MA in English Lit., U. Calif., Berkeley, 1968; PhD in English Lit., Ariz. State U., 1975. Asst. prof. English City Coll. San Francisco, Calif., 1985—, Coll. San Mateo, Calif., 1987—. Author: Woman as Individual in English Renaissance Drama, 1993. Active Grace Cathedral, San Francisco. NDEA fellow, English-Speaking Union fellow for rsch. in Eng. Ariz. State U., 1972. Mem. Virginia Woolf Soc. Episcopalian. Office: City Coll San Francisco 50 Phelan Ave San Francisco CA 94112

HANSEN, CHRISTINE MERRI, music educator; b. Inglewood, Calif., Dec. 26, 1954; d. Oluf Steffen and Betty Jane (Henderson) H. PharmD, U. So. Calif., L.A., 1979; AA in Music, piano tchg. cert., Golden West Coll., 1993. Cert. pharmacist; cert. piano tchr. Clin. pharmacist, lectr. pharmacology Cottage Hosp., Santa Barbara, Calif., 1979-87; pvt. math and sci. tutor Calif., 1987—; math. and sci. tutor Golden West Coll. Tutoring Ctr., Huntington Beach, Calif., 1991-93; model La Belle Agy., 1990-91, John Robert Powers Agy., 1991-93; pvt. piano tchr. Writer, pub.: (newsletter) Our Generation. City of Huntington Beach and Mercury Savs. scholar Golden West Coll., 1975, Gift of Music scholar Golden West Coll., Huntington Beach, 1992.

HANSEN, CORAL JUNE, nurse practitioner, respiratory therapist; b. Seattle, June 5, 1950; d. Raymond Leland and Rosalie (Van Deman) H. Cert. in respiratory therapy, Seattle Cen. Coll., 1975; BS in Nursing summa cum laude, Seattle U., 1987; M in Psychosocial Nursing magna cum laude, U. Wash., 1990. Registered respiratory therapist, Wash.; RN, Wash.; advanced RN practitioner with prescriptive authority; cert. clin. specialist in adult mental health/psychiat. nursing. Respiratory therapist Cura-Care Inc., Modesto, Calif., 1975-84, Northwest Hosp., Seattle, 1984-88; critical care and rehab. nurse University Hosp., Seattle, 1986-87; psychiat. nurse jail psychiat. health Seattle Dept. Pub. Health, 1991; psychiat. nurse Minerth-Meier Psychiat. Unit, Seattle, 1991—; pvt. practice psychotherapy/counseling adult mental health Seattle, 1991—. Contbr. letters to profl. jours. Profl. Nurse Traineeship grantee NIH, 1988-89. Mem. ANA, Assn. Advanced Practice Psychiat. Nurses, DAR, Sigma Theta Tau. Home: PO Box 75193 Seattle WA 98125-0193 Office: PO Box 75193 Seattle WA 98125-0193

HANSEN, CURTIS LEROY, federal judge; b. 1933. BS, U. Iowa, 1956; JD, U. N.Mex., 1961. Bar: N.Mex. Law clk. to Hon. Irwin S. Moise N.Mex. Supreme Ct., 1961-62; ptnr. Snead & Hansen, Albuquerque, 1962-64, Richard C. Civerolo, Albuquerque, 1964-71, Civerolo, Hansen & Wolf, P.A., 1971-92; dist. judge U.S. Dist. Ct., N.Mex., 1992—. Mem. ABA, State Bar N.Mex., Albuquerque Bar Assn., Am. Coll. Trial Lawyers, Am. Bd. Trial Advocates, Albuquerque Country Club, Albuquerque Petroleum Club. Office: 500 Gold Ave Sw 11th Fl PO Box 1309 Albuquerque NM 87103•

HANSEN, DAVID LEE, sales and marketing executive; b. Chgo., Aug. 14, 1941; s. Ralph Richard and Catherine Margaret (Cox) H.; m. Donna Jean Wessel, Sept. 7, 1963 (div. Aug. 1986); children: Robert, Kristin, Donald; m. Patricia Ann Wood, Mar. 27, 1987; 1 child, Jason. BS in Chemistry, S.D. Sch. Mines/Tech., 1964. Chemist, product mgr. Nuclear Chicago, Des Plaines, Ill., 1964-76; v.p. Immuno Nuclear Corp., Stillwater, Minn., 1976-79; owner, operator North Star Resort, Marcell, Minn., 1979-82; product mgr. Packard Instrument Co., Des Plaines, 1982-84; dir. ops. Totalmed, San Rafael, Calif., 1984; pres. Stress Control Ctrs., San Rafael, 1984; product mktg. mgr. Gould Imaging, Fremont, Calif., 1984-87; product mgr. Bio-Rad Labs., Richmond, Calif., 1987-90; bus. analyst ind. contracts, Sunnyvale, Calif., 1990—; cons. Frost & Sullivan Market Intelligence Rsch., Mountain View, Calif., 1987-91, Conceptual Mktg. Internat., Fremont, 1990-92; dir. sales and mktg. Gen. Am., Inc., 1992-95; pres. Hansen Info. Svcs., Inc., 1995—. Patentee in field; contbr. articles to profl. jours. Election officer Santa Clara County, Mountain View, 1990-95; del. Rep. party, Marcell, Minn., 1989-90; bldg. commn. Marcell Twp., 1979-81. Mem. AAAS, Am. Chem. Soc., Assn. Cytogenetic Technologists. Presbyterian. Home and Office: 1659K Belleville Way Sunnyvale CA 94087-3926

HANSEN, DEBRA GOLD, library science educator, historian; b. Orange, Calif., Sept. 16, 1953; d. James M. and Emma Jean (Sommerville) Gold; m. Arthur A. Hansen, June 25, 1977. BA in History, Calif. State U., Fullerton, 1975, MA in History, 1979; MLIS, UCLA, 1983; PhD in History, U. Calif., Irvine, 1988. Editor oral history program Calif. State U., Fullerton, 1975-79; editor Chinese Am. Oral History project UCLA Asian Am. Studies Ctr., 1982-83; hisotry bibliographer, reference libr. Honnold Libr. Claremont (Calif.) Colls., 1984-89; archivist Anaheim (Calif.) History Archives Anaheim Pub. Libr., 1989-90; asst. prof. sch. libr. & info. sci. San Jose (Calif.) State U., 1989—. Author: Strained Sisterhood: Gender and Class in the Boston Female Anti-Slavery Society, 1993; contbr. articles and revs. to profl. jours.; resources editor Jour. Orange County Studies, 1988-92; assoc. editor Oral History Rev., 1980-87; editor newsletter Am. Soc. Indexers, 1980-82. U. Calif. Regent's fellow, 1983-84; Calif. State U. summer fellow, 1992; rsch. grantee U. Calif., 1986, Am. Philos. Soc., 1994; recipient Chancellor's Patent Fund award U. Calif., 1986. Mem. ALA, Orgn. Am. Historians, Radical Historians, Oral History Assn., Soc. Calif. Archivists. Democrat. Office: San Jose State U Sch Libr & Info Sci Fullerton Campus PO Box 1450 CSU-Fullerton Fullerton CA 92634

HANSEN, DONALD CURTIS, manufacturing executive; b. Marinette, Wis., Mar. 13, 1929; s. Curtis Albert and Dagmar Anne (Johnson) H.; m. Joan Mary Crant, Nov. 9, 1973. BBA, Carroll Coll., 1952. Purchasing agt. Prescott/Sterling Co., Menominee, Mich., 1954-62; mfrs. rep. Don C. Hansen Assocs., Phoenix, 1962-63; sales mgr. Karolton Envelope Co., San Francisco, 1964-72; owner, pres. San Francisco Envelope Co., 1972-79; owner Curtis Swann Cards, San Francisco, 1977-79; pres., owner Don C. Hansen, Inc. (doing bus. as The Envelope Co.), Oakland, Calif., 1979—. Mgr., organizer Twin City Civic Chorus, Menominee, 1959; bd. dirs. Menominee C. of C., 1958. Served with U.S. Army, 1952-54. Mem. Envelope Printing Specialists Assn. (bd. dirs. 1983—, pres. 1983-84), Envelope Mfrs. Assn. Am., San Francisco Lithograph and Craftsmans Club, Printing Industries of No. Calif. (bd. dirs. 1980-94), San Francisco Tennis Club (bd. govs. 1989-92), Terravita Country Club (Scottsdale, Ariz.), Masons, Shriners. Republican. Office: The Envelope Co PO Box 23853 Oakland CA 94623-0853

HANSEN, FLORENCE MARIE CONGIOLOSI (MRS. JAMES S. HANSEN), social worker; b. Middletown, N.Y., Jan. 7, 1934; d. Joseph James and Florence (Harrigan) Congiolosi; m. James S. Hansen, June 16, 1959 (dec. Nov. 1989); 1 child, Florence M. BA, Coll. New Rochelle, 1955; MSW, Fla. State U., 1960; PhD, Union Inst., 1992. Caseworker, Orange County Dept. Pub. Welfare, N.Y., 1955-57, Cath. Welfare Bur., Miami, Fla., 1957-58; supr. Cath. Family Service, Spokane, Wash., 1960, Cuban Children's Program, Spokane, 1962-66; founder, dir. social service dept. Sacred Heart Med. Ctr., 1968-85, dir. Kidney Ctr., 1967-91. Asst. in program devel. St. Margaret's Hall, Spokane, 1961-62; trustee Family Counseling Svc. Spokane County, 1981—, also bd. dirs.; mem. budget allocation panel United Way, 1964-76, mem. planning com., 1968-77, mem. admissions com., 1969-70, chmn. projects com. 1972-73; mem. kidney disease adv. com. Wash.-Alaska Regional Med. Program, 1970-73. Mem. Spokane Quality of Life Commn., 1974-75; vol. Primary Health Care Nangoma Health Ctr., 1992—; cons. CARE Internat., Zambia, 1993—. Recipient Ursula Laurus citation Coll. New Rochelle, 1990, Angela Merici medal, 1995. Mem. Nat. Assn. Social Workers (Wash. chpt. pres. 1972-74, Wash. State Social Worker of Yr. 1991, Nat. Social Worker of Yr. 1991), Acad. Cert. Social Workers (charter). Roman Catholic. Home: 5609 W Northwest Blvd Spokane WA 99205-2039 Office: Nangoma Health Ctr, Box 830022, Mumbwa Zambia

HANSEN, FREDERIC J., state environmental agency director; b. Portland, Oreg., Mar. 22, 1946; s. Vernon Edward and Ella Freda (Schacher) H. BA in Math. and History, U. Oreg., 1968; MA in History, McMaster U., 1969; postgrad., Johns Hopkins U., 1970. Asst. historian U.S. Nat. Park Service, Washington, 1970; office mgr. U.S. Senate, Washington, 1970-71; exec. asst. U.S. Ho. of Reps., Washington, 1971-75; spl. asst. to pres. Clemency Bd. for Vietnam Era Veterans, Washington, 1975; exec. officer Peace Corps., Washington, 1975-77; dep. dir. office of the pres. Fed. Cash Mgmt. Project, Washington, 1977-78; chief dep. state treas. State of Oreg., Salem, 1978-84; dir. Oreg. Dept. of Environ. Quality, Portland, 1984-94; dep. administr. EPA, Washington, 1994—; co-chair hazardous waste identification rule com., EPA; task force air implementation, EPA; mem. environ. futures com. Sci. Adv. bd. to EPA, 1993-94; mem. groundwater adv. com. Urban Inst., 1989-90, relative risk reduction com. Sci. Adv. bd. to EPA, 1989-90, Gov.'s State Agy. Growth Coun., 1990-94, State EPA com. 1989-94; active Nat. Com. on Superfund. Woodrow Wilson Nat. Found. vis. fellow, 1987—. Mem. Phi Eta Sigma, Phi Beta Kappa. Office: EPA 401 M St SW Washington DC 20460

HANSEN, J. WOODFORD, agricultural products supplier; b. 1948. Owner of affiliate Hansen Ranch, Camarillo, Calif., 1968—; with Seaboard Produce, Oxnard, Calif., 1979—, now pres. Office: Seaboard Produce 601 Mountain View Ave Oxnard CA 93030-7203•

HANSEN, JAMES LEE, sculptor; b. Tacoma, Wash., June 13, 1925; s. Hildreth Justine and Mary Elizabeth Hansen; m. Annabelle Hair, Aug. 31, 1946 (dec. Sept. 1993); children: Valinda Jean, Yauna Marie; m. Jane Lucas, May 13, 1994. Grad., Portland Art Mus. Sch. Mem. faculty Oreg. State U., Corvallis, 1957-58, U. Calif., Berkeley, 1958, Portland State U., 1964-90. One-man shows include Fountain Gallery, Portland, Oreg., 1966, 69, 77-81, U. Oreg. Art Mus., Eugene, 1970, Seligman (Seders Gallery), Seattle, 1970, Portland Art Mus., 1971, Cheney Cowles Meml. Mus., Spokane, Wash., 1972, Polly Freidlander Gallery, Seattle, 1973, 75, 76, Smithsonian Instn., Washington, 1974, Hodges/Banks Gallery (now Linda Hodges Gallery), Seattle, 1983, Abanté Gallery, Portland, 1986, 88, 92; group exhbns. include N.W. Ann. Painters and Sculptors, Seattle, 1952-73, Oreg. Ann. Painters and Sculptors, Portland Art Mus., 1952-75, Whitney Mus. Am. Art, N.Y.C., 1953, Santa Barbara (Calif.) Mus. Art, 1959-60, Denver Art Mus., 1960, San Francisco Art Mus., 1960, Smithsonian Instn., Washington, 1974, Wash. State U., Pullman, 1975; represented in permanent collections Graphic Arts Center, Portland State Capitol, Olympia, Wash., U. Oreg., Eugene, Salem (Oreg.) Civic Center, Clark Coll., Vancouver, Wash., Portland Art Mus., Transit Mall, Portland, Fresno (Calif.) Mall, Seattle Art Mus., Gresham Town Fair (Oreg.), Oreg. Health Scis. U., Portland, various banks and schs., numerous commns.; represented by Abanté Gallery, Portland, Soma Gallery, San Diego. Address: 28219 NE 63rd Ave Battle Ground WA 98604-7107

HANSEN, JAMES VEAR, congressman; b. Salt Lake City, Utah, Aug. 14, 1932; s. J. Vear and Sena C. H.; m. Ann Burgoyne H., 1958; children—Susan, Joseph James, David Burgoyne, Paul William, Jennifer. B.S., U. Utah, 1960. Mem. Utah Ho. of Reps., 1973-80, speaker of house, 1979-80; mem. 97th-104th Congresses from 1st Utah dist. 97th-103rd Congresses from 1st Utah dist., Washington, D.C., 1981—; pres. James V. Hansen Ins. Agy., Woodland Springs Devel. Co.

HANSEN, JULIA, music educator; b. Peoria, Ill., Feb. 5, 1934; d. Sherman and Mabel (Nubson) Almanrode; m. Joseph Shakes, June 1, 1957 (div.); children: David Shakes, Diane Shakes, Jonathan Shakes. BMusic with honors, Oberlin Conservatory Music, 1955; MMusic with highest honors, Mich. State U., 1956; MS in Counseling, U. LaVerne, Calif., 1986. Cert. tchr. music and counseling Calif. Community Colls. Tchr. Skyline Coll., San Bruno, Calif., 1977—, counselor, 1988-89; pvt. tchr. piano, music theory and composition, 1958—; tchr. piano, theory and ensembles San Francisco City Coll., 1972-76; guest lectr. in field. Author: Music Reading for Beginners, 1986, Handbook for Counselors and Music Students, 1988, The Art of Performing Bamboo Instruments of Bali, 1992; contbr. articles to Piano Guild Notes. Mem. Coun. for the Arts, Palo Alto, Calif. Oberlin Conservatory scholar, 1951-55; Mich. State U. fellow, 1955-56. Mem. Coll. Music Soc., Music Tchrs. Nat. Assn., Nat. Guild Piano Tchrs., Music Assn. Calif. Community Colls., Soc. for Ethnomusicology. Office: Skyline Coll Creative Arts Dept San Bruno CA 94066

HANSEN, LELAND JOE, communications executive; b. Spokane, Wash., Mar. 26, 1944; s. Herman Johnny and Emma Irene (Borth) H.; m. Jonni Krajeski, Apr. 15, 1979. Creative dir., dir., producer Mel Blanc and Assocs., Beverly Hills, Calif., 1971-73; creative dir., writer, producer, dir. nat. TV and radio commls. and entertainment programs ABC Watermark, Universal City, Calif., 1973-80; pres., chief exec. officer, writer, producer, dir. film and TV GDE Prodns. Inc., Sherman Oaks, Calif., 1980-87; sr. writer, dir. video svcs. Rockwell Internat., Canoga Park, Calif., 1987—; voice-over artist nat. TV and radio. Dir. American Top Forty, 1973-77, The Elvis Presley Story, Soundtrack of the Sixties; creator, producer, dir. Alien Worlds, 1973-80. Founding mem. Am. Forces Radio, Saigon, Socialist Republic of Vietnam, 1963-64. Served with U.S. Army, 1962-65, Vietnam. Recipient Belding award The Advt. Club Los Angeles, 1977. Mem. AFTRA.

HANSEN, LEONARD JOSEPH, author, journalist; b. San Francisco, Aug. 4, 1932; s. Einar L. and Margie A. (Wilder) H.; m. Marcia Ann Rasmussen, Mar. 18, 1966 (div.); children: Barron Richard, Trevor Wilder. AB in Radio-TV Prodn. and Mgmt., San Francisco State U., 1956, postgrad. 1956-57; cert. IBM Mgmt. Sch., 1967. Jr. writer Sta. KCBS, San Francisco, 1952-54; assoc. producer and dir. Ford Found. TV Rsch. Project, San Francisco State U., 1955-57; crew chief on live and remote broadcasts Sta. KPIX-TV, San Francisco, 1957-59, air promotion dir. and writer Sta. KPIX-TV, San Francisco, 1959-60; pub. rels. mgr. Sta. KNTV-TV, San Jose, Calif., 1961; radio and TV promotion mgr. Seattle World's Fair, 1962; pub. relations and promotion mgr. Century 21 Ctr., Inc., Seattle, 1963-64; pub. rels. dir. Dan Evans for Gov. Com., Seattle, 1964; propr., mgr. Leonard J. Hansen Pub. Rels., Seattle, 1965-67; campaign mgr. Walter J. Hickel for Gov. Com., Anchorage, 1966; exec. cons. to Gov. of Alaska, Juneau, 1967; gen. mgr. No. TV, Inc., Anchorage, 1967-69; v.p. mktg. Sea World, Inc., San Diego, 1969-71; editor, pub. Sr. World Publs., Inc., San Diego, 1973-84; chmn. Sr. Pubs. Group, 1977-89; speaker and mktg. cons. to sr. citizens, 1984-92; panelist, pub. affairs radio programs, 1971-92; lectr. journalism San Diego State U., 1975-76. Writer weekly syndicated column Mainly for Seniors, 1984—, syndicated column Travel for Mature Adults, 1984—; writer, journalist The Mature Market; contbg. editor Mature Life Features, news/feature syndicate, 1987-90; chmn. Mature Mkt. Seminars, 1987-90; author Life Begins at 50-The Handbook for Creative Retirement Planning, 1989; pres., pub. Mature Market Editorial Svcs., 1991—. Founding mem. Housing for Elderly and Low Income Persons, San Diego, 1977-78; mem. Mayor's Ad Hoc Adv. Com. on Aging, San Diego, 1976-79; vice chmn. Housing Task Force, San Diego, 1977-78; bd. dirs. Crime Control Commn., San Diego, 1980; del. White House Conf. on Aging, 1981. Served with U.S. Army, 1953-55. Nat. Press Found. fellow, 1994; recipient numerous service and citizenship awards from clubs and community orgns. Fellow Nat. Press Found.; mem. Pub. Rels.Soc. Am. (accredited), Soc. Profl. Journalists (Best Investigative Reporting award 1979), Internat. Platform Assn., San Diego Press Club (Best Newswriting award 1976-77, Headliner of Yr. award 1980), Am. Assn. Travel Editors (profl. mem.). Home and Office: 10 Town Plz Ste 313 Durango CO 81301-5104

HANSEN, LISA YOUNG, municipal agency administrator; b. Rexburg, Idaho, Apr. 28, 1957; d. Rulon Squires and Lucille Cole (Young) McCarrey; m. Darrel Chancy Hansen, Mar. 23, 1984. A, Ricks Coll., 1977; student, Harvard U., summers 1977, 78, Brigham Young U., 1980-82. Geneal. clk. Stevensons Geneal. Ctr., Provo, Utah, 1977; typesetter, news clk. Valley News, Rexburg, Idaho, 1977-78; credit clk. Credit Bur. Idaho Falls, 1982-83; adminstrv. asst. Bonneville County Civil Defense, Idaho Falls, 1983—; speaker in field; radiol. defense officer State of Idaho, Bureau of Disaster Services, 1984—; sec. Bonneville Tricentennial Commn., 1983—, Bonneville Flood Control Coordinatig com., 1983—, Bonneville Bicentennial of the Constn. com., 1983—. Editor: Bonneville Tricentennial Commn. Newsletter; contbr. articles to profl. jours. Rep. United Way, Idaho Falls, 1986; vote clerk Bonneville County Elections Dept., Idaho Falls, 1980, 81; mem. Bonneville County Centennial Com., Nat. Coordinating Coun. Emergency Mgmt. Mem. Am. Civil Def. Assn. (co-resolutions chmn. 1985-87), Idaho Civil Def. Assn., Bonneville County Employees Assn. (pres. 1989), Bonneville County Humane Soc., Humane Soc. of U.S., Am. Soc. for Prevention of Cruelty to Animals, People for the Ethical Treatment of Animals, Doris Day Animal League, Nat. Wildlife Fedn., Nat. Coordinating Coun. on Emergency Mgmt., Lambda Delta Sigma. Republican. Mormon. Home: 874 Goldie St Idaho Falls ID 83402-4727 Office: Bonneville County Civil Def 605 N Capital Ave Idaho Falls ID 83402-3582

HANSEN, LOWELL HOWARD, physician; b. Clay Center, Kans., Dec. 26, 1929; s. Howard E. and Emma E. (Nochtigal) H.; m. Jesse J. Johnson, Sept. 1, 1951; children: Susan, Rebecca, Sheree, Kathryn, Peter. BS, Wheaton (Ill.) Coll., 1951; MD, U. Colo., 1955. Diplomate Am. Bd. Radiology. Pvt. practice Denver, 1958-64; resident in radiology Denver Gen. Hosp., 1964-66; radiologist Mett. Radiologists, P.C., Denver, 1966—. With USPHS, 1955-58. Fellow Am. Coll. Radiology; mem. Radiol. Assn. N.Am., Rocky Mountain Radiol. Soc. (pres. 1978). Office: 7475 Dakin St Ste 400 Denver CO 80221-6918

HANSEN, MARGARET, food executive; b. 1952. With affiliate Hansen Ranch, Camarillo, Calif., 1973—; sec. Seaboard Produce, Oxnard, Calif., 1979—. Office: Seaboard Produce 601 Mountain View Ave Oxnard CA 93030-7203*

HANSEN, MICHAEL JOSEPH, association executive, writing educator; b. Chgo., Nov. 18, 1930; s. Max J. and Helen J. Hansen; m. Alice Pauline Hamilton, Jan. 19, 1957; 1 child, Michael Hamilton. AA in Acctg., City Colls. Chgo., 1950; student, Syracuse U., 1953; BA in English, U. Chgo., 1958, MA in English, 1960. C.C. tchg. cert. in English and Russian. Russian lang. specialist USAF, Europe, 1951-55; instr. Valparaiso (Ind.) U., 1960-61; adminstr., asst. prof. City Colls. Chgo., Ill., 1962-72; asst. dir. Pima Assn. Govts., Tucson, 1973—; adj. writing instr. Pima C.C., Tucson, 1983—. Author: (novelet) Ransom, 1977. Chmn., mem. Pima Coll. Bd. Govs., Tucson, 1978-82; mem. Ariz. Juvenile Justice Adv. Coun., Phoenix, 1981-87; vice chmn. Crime Resisters Exec. Bd., Tucson, 1983; arbitrator Better Bus. Bur., Tucson, 1987—.

HANSEN, NANCY C. URDAHL, special education educator; b. Tacoma, May 17, 1940; d. Arthur Selmer and Doris Lavina (Perry) Urdahl; m. John Raymond Hansen, Apr. 2, 1966 (div.); children: John Raymond, Julia Amy. BA, U. Puget Sound, 1969; postgrad., Gov.'s State U., 1972-73; AA, Seattle C.C., 1978; MEd, U. Wash., 1979. Cert. spl. edn. tchr., Wash. Tchr. Grace Migrant Sch., Park Forest, Ill., 1970-71, Rainbow Valley Child Care Ctr., Seattle, 1977-78; tchr. aide Highline Pub. Schs., Seattle, 1978, Experimental Edn. Unit U. Wash., Seattle, 1978; vol. coord. Camp Fire Inc., Seattle, 1979-80; researcher Mott Rehab. Svcs., Mountlake Terrace, Wash., 1980-82; tchr. South Kitsap Sch. Dist., Port Orchard, Wash., 1980-82, resource rm. tchr., 1982—; advisor, tchr. Micro-Society (Econ. medel for sch.), 1994—; interviewer King County Interagy. Project U. Wash., Seattle, 1978-80; sec. Queen Anne Juvenile Ct. Conf. Com., Seattle, 1976-78. Contbr. articles to profl. jours. Mem. citizen adv. group Piecre County Comprehensive Plan, Tacoma, 1992; co-coord. Keep Wash. Liveable, Tacoma, 1990; sec., co-founder Peninsula Neighborhood Assn., Gig Harbor, Wash., 1988-91, bd. dirs., 1992; coord. & co-founder Peninsula Stream Monitors, Gig Harbor, 1992-95. Mem. Wash. Edn. Assn., South Kitsap Edn. Assn., Learning Disabilities Assn. Wash., Alpha Phi Sorority.

HANSEN, PETER ULRICH, art educator; b. Honolulu, July 18, 1965; s. Peter Ulrich and Martaret (Röthe) H. BFA, Md. Inst. Coll.of Art, 1989. Art tchr. Punahou Sch., Honolulu, 1989—, supr. peer counseling svcs., 1990—. Fellow Am. Craft Coun., Glass Arts Soc., Hawaii Craftsman. Office: Punahou Sch 1601 Punahou St Honolulu HI 96822-3336

HANSEN, ROBERT DENNIS, educational administrator; b. San Francisco, July 17, 1945; s. Eiler Cunnard and Muriel Lenore (Morrison) H.; BA, U. San Francisco, 1967, MA in Counseling and Guidance, 1971, MA in Supervision and Adminstrn., 1973; EdD, U. La Verne, 1988; m. Karen Calder, Apr. 21, 1990; children from a previous marriage: April Michelle, Alison Nicole, Andrew Warren. Tchr., dept. chmn., counselor, dir. student affairs, attendance officer South San Francisco Unified Sch. Dist., 1968-74, coordinator, asst. prin. Jurupa Unified Sch. Dist., Riverside, Calif., 1974-78; prin., asst. supt. San Gabriel (Calif.) Sch. Dist., 1978-91; supt. Rosemead (Calif.) Sch. Dist., 1991—; adj. prof. U. La Verne, Calif., 1988—. Exec. bd. South San Francisco PTA, 1968-74; bd. dirs. West San Gabriel YMCA; mem. parade formation com. Pasadena (Calif.) Tournament of Roses. Recipient Hon. Service award Calif. State PTA. Mem. U. San Francisco Edn. Alumni Soc. (pres. 1972-73), Nat. Assn. Year-Round Edn., U. San Francisco Alumni Assn., Am. Assn. Sch. Adminstrs., Assn. Calif. Sch. Adminstrs., Assn. for Supervision and Curriculum Devel., Phi Delta Kappa. Republican. Episcopalian. Mason (32 deg.). Home: 2650 Country Club Dr Glendora CA 91741-4029 Office: Rosemead Sch Dist 3640 Rio Hondo Ave Rosemead CA 91770-2041

HANSEN, ROBERT GUNNARD, philatelist, entrepreneur; b. Chgo., Aug. 16, 1939; s. Earl F. and Mildred E. (Hargrave) H.; A.A., Lincoln Coll., 1960; B.A., Culver Stockton Coll., 1962; M.B.A., U. So. Calif., 1966; postgrad. UCLA Extension, 1962-67; m. Bertha Golds, Aug. 10, 1960; children—Karin Lee, Lisa Marie. With Litton Industries, 1962-63, Sterer Engring., 1963-69; mktg. and contracts ofcl. Santa Barbara Research Ctr., 1969-73; pres., chief exec. officer, R.G. Hansen & Assocs., Santa Barbara, 1974— ; pres., owner The Silver Penny and Santa Barbara Stamp & Coin, 1969—; owner, CEO, pres. Univ. Travel Bureau, 1990—; guest lectr. Santa Barbara City Coll. Mem. Am. Vacuum Soc., Am. Philatelic Soc. (life), Am. Numismatic Assn., Hawaii Numismatic Assn., Sci. and Engring. Coun. Santa Barbara (pres. 1989), Token and Medal Soc., Masons, York Rite. Scottish Rite, Shriners, Royal Order of Scotland, Channel City, Royal Arch Masons, Rotary Internat. (Paul Harris fellow 1990). Research and publs. on cryogenics, electro-optics, infrared radiation; patentee in field. Republican. Presbyterian. Office: 631 Chapala St Santa Barbara CA 93101-3311

HANSEN, RODNEY ALLAN, city official; b. Evanston, Wyo., Aug. 22, 1956; s. Delbert Rodney and Marilyn Jean (Cook) H.; m. A. Irene Fessler, June 30, 1977; children: Jeffery Scott, Jessica Jean. Grad. high sch., Evanston. Mcpl. svc. worker City of Evanston, 1977-90, employee adv. bd., 1980-84; gen. supt. ops. Intermodal Surface Transp. Efficiency Act Bd., 1990—; bd. dirs. Uinta County Weed Pest, Evanston. Pres. Uinta Coordinating Coun., Evanston, 1990-94. Mem. Am. Water Works Assn. (scholar 1992), Wyo. Mont. Safety Coun. Office: City of Evanston 1200 Main St Evanston WY 82930-3316

HANSEN, RONALD GREGORY, civil engineer; b. Waipahu, Hawaii, Aug. 22, 1929; s. Erling M. and Geraldine J. (Nettleton) H.; m. Theresa J. Cunningham, Feb. 5, 1955; children: Eric L., Karen A., Maureen A., Timothy E. BCE, U. Santa Clara, 1952; MSCE, U. So. Calif., 1958, postgrad., 1958-66; M in Pub. Adminstrn., U. Alaska, 1981. Lic. civil engr., Alaska, Wash., Oreg., Calif. Engr. Calif. Dept. Water Resources, Los Angeles, 1957-67; sr. engr. Water Quality Control Bd., Los Angeles, 1967-71; chief water pollution control State of Alaska, Juneau, 1971-79; sr. engr. KCM Inc. and EMPS Engring, Juneau, 1980-85; pres. Hansen Engring., Juneau, 1985—. Former scoutmaster, mem. bldg. com. S.E. Alaska, Boy Scouts Am.; mem., chmn. Juneau Parks and Recreation Adv. Com., 1983-91. Served to lt. col., C.E., USAR. Mem. ASCE, NSPE (nat. dir. 1993—), Am. Water Works Assn., Water Environ. Fedn., Am. Acad. Environ. Engrs., Am. Water Resources Assn., Internat. Water Resources Assn., Rotary (Juneau-Gastineau club pres.-elect 1995). Republican. Roman Catholic. Home and Office: Hansen Engring 4117 Birch Ln Juneau AK 99801-8909

HANSEN, SHARON M., state agency administrator, policy analyst; b. Port Angeles, Wash., Sept. 28, 1935; d. Herbert Milton and Caryl (Heslin) McGee; m. Janis T. Hansen, Sept. 2, 1956; children: Andrew John, Matthew Thomas. BA, U. Wash., 1957, cert. in Mgmt., 1988. Planner Office of Cmty. Devel., State Wash., Olympia, Wash., 1974-75; exec. dir. Pierce County Assn. for Retarded Citizens, Tacoma, 1975-80; resource mgr. Dept. Social and Health Svcs., State Wash., Tacoma, 1980-82; planner Dept. Social and Health Svcs., State Wash., Olympia, Wash., 1982-84; exec. dir. Developmental Disabilities Planning Coun., State Wash., Olympia, Wash., 1984-91; analyst Family Policy Coun., State Wash., Olympia, Wash., 1992-94; dir. Tacoma-Pierce County Commn. on Children, Youth and Families, 1994—; bd. dirs. Nat. Assn. Developmental Disabilities Coun., Washington, D.C., 1985-90, v.p. 1990-91; cons. Westside Regional Ctr., Calif., 1987, N.J. Developmental Disabilities Coun., 1991, Govt. India Ministry of Welfare, 1991. Contbd. articles to profl. jours. Fulbright Hayes lectureship, 1991. Home: 714 N Stadium Way Tacoma WA 98403-2826 Office: Tacoma-Pierce County Com on Children 3629 South D Street Tacoma WA 98408

HANSEN, THOMAS CARTER, college athletics conference commissioner; b. Seattle, Nov. 30, 1937; s. Herbert and Marjorie Jean (Jordan) H.; m. Melva Marie Fuhr, Oct. 11, 1962; children: Sarah Marie Hansen Reeves, Bryan Thomas. BA, U. Wash., 1959. Reporter The Columbian, Vancouver, Wash., 1959-60; dir. pub. rels. Pacific-10 Conf., San Francisco, 1960-67; dir. pub. rels. NCAA, Kansas City, Mo., 1967-71, asst. exec. dir., 1971-83; commr. Pacific-10 Conf., Walnut Creek, Calif., 1983—. Author: (chpt.) Administration for Athletic Programs, 1987. Mem. Kiwanis Club, Vancouver, 1959-60, San Francisco, 1960-67, Kansas City, 1967-83. Mem. Nat. Assn. Collegiate Dirs. of Athletics (exec. com. 1988-92, Adminstrv. Excellence award 1994), Collegiate Commrs. Assn. (pres. 1992, 93), Football Found. Hall of Fame (honors ct. 1994—). Republican. Lutheran. Office: Pacific 10 Conf 800 S Broadway Ste 400 Walnut Creek CA 94596-5218

HANSEN, WAYNE RICHARD, radioecologist; b. Rice Lake, Wis., Aug. 6, 1939; s. Richard Lyman and Helen Ann (Nethig) H.; m. Nancy Jane Rohde, Sept. 10, 1960; children: Richard W., William R. BS, U. Wis., Eau Claire, 1961; MS, U. Kans., 1963; PhD, Colo. State U., 1970. Diplomate Am. Bd. Health Physics (bd. dirs. 1990—). Health physicist U. Colo., Boulder, 1963-67, Bur. Radiol. Health, Rockville, Md., 1970-71, EPA, Washington, 1971-75; sr. radiobiologist NRC, Washington, 1975-77; group leader environ. surveillance Los Alamos Nat. Lab., 1977-84, dep. div. leader health, safety and environ., 1984-87, chief scientist environ. rsch., 1987-90, group leader environ. scis., 1990—; sr. scientist accident response group Dept. Energy, Albuquerque, 1986-94. Contbr. articles to profl. jours., chpt. to book. Vice chmn. N.Mex. Gov.'s Radiation Tech. Adv. Coun., Sante Fe, 1983-93. Fellow AAAS; mem. Health Physics Soc. (coun. Rio Grande chpt. 1988-90), N.Mex. Acad. Sci. Lutheran. Home: 557 Bryce Ave Los Alamos NM 87544-3607 Office: Los Alamos Nat Lab PO Box 1663 # J495 Los Alamos NM 87544-0600

HANSMA, HELEN GREENWOOD, biophysics researcher; b. Oakland, Calif., Dec. 5, 1945; d. James Hays and Jean (McMinn) Greenwood; m. Paul Kenneth Hansma, Dec. 27, 1968; children: Scott, Joy. AB, Earlham Coll., 1967; MA, U. Calif., Berkeley, 1969; PhD, U. Calif., Santa Barbara, 1974. Staff rsch. assoc. U. Calif., Berkeley, 1969-72; postdoctoral assoc. U. Calif., L.A., 1976; postdoctoral assoc. U. Calif., Santa Barbara, 1975, asst. rsch. biologist, 1977-79, 88-93, assoc. rsch. biologist, 1993—; sci. cons. Isla Vista Sch., Goleta, Calif., 1980-89. Contbr. numerous articles to profl. jours. Mem. AAAS, Grad. Women in Sci. Democrat. Roman Catholic. Office: Univ of Calif Dept Of Physics Santa Barbara CA 93106

HANSON, DENNIS MICHAEL, medical imaging executive; b. Cleve., Aug. 20, 1943; s. John Joseph and Victoria (Tucholski) H. BBA, Cleve. State U., 1971; MPH, U. Pitts., 1974. Asst. adminstr. Huron Rd. Hosp., Cleve., 1974-76; adminstr. asst. Mt. Sinai Med. Ctr., Cleve., 1976-80; dir. radiology U. Louisville, Ky., 1980-84, assoc. prof., 1982-86; sr. cons. Honeywell, Mpls., 1986-87; mgr. radiology U. N.C., Chapel Hill, 1987-90; mgr. diag. imaging Kaiser Hosp., Honolulu, 1990—. Councilman City of Meadowbrook Farm, Ky., 1982-86. With USAF, 1961-65. Named Ky. Colonel, 1984. Fellow Am. Coll. Healthcare Execs.; mem. Am. Hosp. Assn., Am. Hosp. Radiology Adminstrs. Office: Kaiser Permanente 3288 Moanalua Rd Honolulu HI 96819-1469

HANSON, EILEEN, principal; b. Camden, N.J., Mar. 3, 1948; d. Thomas Edward and Rita Theresa (Madison) Bannan; m. Kenneth Wesley Hanson, Mar. 22, 1975; 1 child, Michelle Eileen. BA, San Diego State U., 1970; teaching cert., Calif. State U., Dominguez Hills, 1974, cert. adminstr., 1976. Prin. St. Anthony Sch., El Segundo, Calif., 1976-80; dir. St. Charles Catechetical Program, San Diego, 1980-87; prin. Holy Family Sch., San Diego, 1987-92, St. Pius X Sch., Chula Vista, Calif., 1992—; grant project coord. for Cath. Schs. San Diego, 1992-94. Mem. ASCD, Nat. Cath. Educators Assn., Greater Math. Assn., San Diego Child Care and Devel. Com., San Diego Alcohol and Tobacco Edn. Assn., Western Assn. Schs. Colls. (accreditation chair). Home: 942 Grove Ave Imperial Beach CA 91932-3347 Office: 37 E Emerson St Chula Vista CA 91911-3507

HANSON, GEORGE PETER, retired research botanist, real estate investor; b. Conde, S.D., July 20, 1933; s. George Henry and Rosa Wilhelmina (Peterson) H.; m. Barbara Jean Graves, Aug. 20, 1958; children: David, Carole, Heather, Peter; m. Gloria Ann Gauntt, June 1, 1969. BS in Agronomy, S.D. State U., 1956, MS in Plant Breeding, 1958; PhD in Genetics, Ind. U., 1965. Asst. prof. biology Thiel Coll. Greenville, Pa., 1962-65; asst. prof. botany Butler U., Indpls., 1965-67; sr. biologist L.A. State and County Arboretum, Arcadia, Calif., 1968-82; real estate investor, 1971—. Mem. Apt. Assn. of Greater L.A. Methodist. Contbr. numerous articles in field to profl. jours. Home: 1345 W Haven Rd San Marino CA 91108-2018

HANSON, GERALD WARNER, retired county official; b. Alexandria, Minn., Dec. 25, 1938; s. Lewis Lincoln and Dorothy Hazel (Warner) H.; m. Sandra June Wheeler, July 9, 1960; 1 child, Cynthia R. AA, San Bernardino Valley (Calif.) Coll., 1959; BA, U. Redlands (Calif.), 1979; MA, U. Redlands, 1981; EdD, Pepperdine U., 1995. Cert. advanced metrication specialist. Dep. sealer San Bernardino (Calif.) County, 1964-80, div. chief, 1980-85, dir. weights and measures, 1985-94. Mem. Redlands Rent Rev. Bd., 1985—; bd. dirs. House Neighborly Svc., Redlands, 1972-73, Boys Club, Redlands, 1985-86; mem. Redlands Planning commn., 1991—. With USN. Fellow U.S. Metric Assn. (treas. 1986-88, 92—); mem. NRA (life), Nat. Conf. on Weights and Measures (asst. treas. 1986-94), Western Weights and Measures Assn. (pres. 1987-88), Calif. Assn. Weights and Measures Ofcls. (1st v.p. 1987), Calif. Rifle and Pistol Assn. (life), Masons, Shriners, Kiwanis (treas. Redlands club 1983—). Home: 225 E Palm Ave Redlands CA 92373-6131

HANSON, HOWARD PAUL, environmental research scientist; b. Peoria, Ill., Jan. 1, 1950; s. Edwin Eugene and Marilyn (Sedgwick) H.; m. Claire Marie Smith, Mar. 26, 1983. BS in Aero. and Astro. Engring., U. Ill., 1972; PhD in Atmospheric Sci., U. Miami, Fla., 1979. Rsch. assoc. NRC, Washington, 1979-81; rsch. assoc. Coop. Inst. for Rsch. in Environ. Scis., U. Colo., Boulder, 1981-85, fellow and assoc. dir., 1985—, sr. rsch. assoc., 1991—; vis. scientist Nat. Ctr. Atmospheric Rsch., Boulder, 1985; mission scientist NASA, NOAA, 1981-87; cons. Jason Group, LaJolla, Calif., 1991. Contbr. articles to profl. jours.; editor, guest editor: Modelling and Prediction of the Upper Layers of the Ocean, 1977, Deep-Sea Research, GATE Supplement II, 1979, Progress in Oceanography, 1981. NRC fellow, 1979-81; rsch. grantee NSF, NASA, Office Naval Rsch., NOAA, DOE, 1981—; recipient NASA Group Achievement award, 1991. Mem. Am. Meteorol. Soc., Am. Geophys. Union, The Oceanography Soc., Sigma Xi, Tau Beta Pi. Office: CIRES/U Colo Boulder CO 80309-0216

HANSON, JOHN J., lawyer; b. Aurora, Nebr., Oct. 22, 1922; s. Peter E. and Hazel Marion (Lounsbury) H.; m. Elizabeth Anne Moss, July 1, 1973; children from their previous marriages—Mark, Eric, Gregory. A.B., U. Denver, 1948; LL.B. cum laude, Harvard U., 1951. Bar: N.Y. bar 1952, Calif. bar 1955. Assoc. firm Dewey, Ballantine, Bushby, Palmer & Wood, N.Y.C., 1951-54; ptnr. firm Gibson, Dunn & Crutcher, L.A, 1954—; mem. exec. com. Gibson, Dunn & Crutcher, 1978-87, adv. ptnr, 1991—. Contbr. articles to profl. jours. Trustee Palos Verdes (Calif.) Sch. Dist., 1969-73. Served with U.S. Navy, 1942-45. Fellow Am. Coll. Trial Lawyers; mem. Am. Bar Assn., Los Angeles County Bar Assn. (chmn. antitrust sect. 1979-80), Bel Air Country Club. Home: 953 Linda Flora Dr Los Angeles CA 90049-1630 Office: Gibson Dunn & Crutcher 333 S Grand Ave Los Angeles CA 90071-1504

HANSON, KENNETH MERRILL, physicist; b. Mt. Vernon, N.Y., Apr. 17, 1940; s. Orville Glen and Marion (Chamberlain) H.; m. Earle Marie Low, June 1964 (div. July 1989); children: Jennifer Anne, Keith Merrill. BE in Physics, Cornell U., 1963; MS in Physics, Harvard U., 1967, PhD in Physics, 1970. Rsch. assoc. Lab. of Nuclear Studies, Ithaca, N.Y., 1970-75; mem. staff Los Alamos (N.Mex.) Nat. Lab., 1975—. Author: (with others) Radiology of Skull and Brain, 1979, Image Recovery, 1987; contbr. articles to profl. jours. Recipient Award Excellence, Dept. Energy, 1986. Fellow Soc. Photo Optical Instrumentation Engrs. (program com. imaging conf. 1984—); mem. IEEE (sr.), Am. Phys. Soc., Opt. Soc. Am. Office: Los Alamos Nat Lab MS-P940 Los Alamos NM 87545

HANSON, NOEL RODGER, management consultant; b. L.A., Jan. 19, 1942; s. Albert and Madelyne Gladys (Pobanz) H.; B.S. in Indsl. Mgmt., U. So. Calif., 1963, M.B.A. in Fin., 1966; m. Carol Lynn Travis, June 17, 1967; 1 son, Eric Rodger. Asst. dir. alumni fund, then dir. ann. funds U. So. Calif., 1964-66; asst. to Walt Disney for Cal-Arts, Retlaw Enterprises, Glendale, Calif., 1966-68; asst. dir. joint devel. Claremont U. Center, 1968-69; v.p. adminstrn. Robert Johnston Co., Los Angeles, 1969-70; partner Hale, Hanson & Co., Pasadena, Calif., 1970-82, Hanson, Olson & Co., 1982—; pres. Pasadena Services, Inc., 1977—; dir. Pasadena Fin. Cons., Inc., Wilihire Funding, Inc., 1988—. Trustee Oakhurst Sch., Pasadena, 1973-75; bd. advisers Girls Club Pasadena, 1977—; mem. U. So. Calif. Assos., 1979—, U. So. Calif. Commerce Assos., 1965—. Republican. Presbyterian. Club: Jonathan (Los Angeles). Address: 1051 La Loma Rd Pasadena CA 91105-2208

HANSON, NORMAN, lawyer; b. Roy, Mont., Feb. 12, 1916; s. Peder and Ida S. (Olson) H.; m. Constance Brown, Sept. 5, 1946; children: David, Margaret, Sara. BA with honors, U. Mont., 1937, JD with honors, 1940. Bar: Mont. 1940, U.S. Dist. Ct. Mont. 1940, U.S. Supreme Ct. 1960. Assoc. Brown and Davis, Billings, Mont., 1940; spl. agent FBI, Washington, 1941-42; assoc., ptnr. Brown, Davis and Hanson, Billings, 1946-51; ptnr. Coleman, Jameson and Lamey, Billings, 1952-57; ptnr. Crowley, Haughey, Hanson, Toole and Dietrich, Billings, 1958-88, of counsel, 1989—; spl asst. to Atty. Gen. of U.S., 1954-55; trustee Rocky Mountain Mineral Law Found., Denver, 1969—, pres. 1982-83; lectr. bus. law Montana State U., Billings, 1989. Editor: Mont. Law Rev., 1939-40; contbr. articles to profl. jours. Bd. dirs. Mont. Heart Assn., 1956-62, Sch. Dist. 2, numerous community orgs.; com. mem. Governor's Com. Edn. Served to maj. USAF, 1943-46. Mem. State Bar Mont., Yellowstone County Bar Assn. (pres. 1955-56). Republican. Congregational. Clubs: Rotary (Billings) (pres. 1965-66), Billings Petroleum. Lodge: Masons. Home: 2026 Pryor Ln Billings MT 59102-1656 Office: Crowley Haughey Hanson Toole & Dietrich PO Box 2529 Billings MT 59103-2529

HANSON-SMITH, ELIZABETH, English language educator, computer consultant; b. Bridgeport, Conn., Oct. 28, 1942; d. Arthur Christian and A. Elizabeth H.; m. Jack H.L. THompson, Nov. 25, 1979; children: Aaron Virgil, Paul, Cairbre A.H. Smith. AB in English, Smith Coll., 1964; postgrad., Hochschule St. Gallen, 1964-65; MA in English, Stanford U., 1967; postgrad., U. Paris, 1967-68; PhD in English and Comparative Lit., Stanford U., 1972. Dir. writing adj. program Calif. State U., Sacramento, 1976-80; tchr.-trainer Ministry of Edn., China, 1980-81, Maurice Thorez Inst. Fgn. Langs. and Am. Coun. for Collaboration in Lang. Study, Moscow, 1989-90; prof. English Calif. State U., Sacramento, 1971-95, coord. TESOL grad. program, 1984-95; chair Ryan Act com. arts. and scis. Calif. State U., Sacramento, 1974-75; bd. govs. Calif. Maritime Acad., Vallejo, 1978-80; English lang. cons. Univ. Grants Commn. and Asia Found., Sri Lanka, 1984; curriculum cons. Ministry of Edn. and USAID, Belize, 1986; coord. conv. computer room Calif. Assn. TESOL, 1991-93. Contbg. editor CAELL Jour., 1992—; contbr. articles to profl. jours. Stanford Dissertation fellow, 1967-70; Smith Coll. Alumnae scholar, 1960-64. Mem. TESOL (chair CALL IS 1994-95), Calif. Assn. TESOL, Phi Beta Delta.

HANTOS, PETER, computer engineer; b. Budapest, Hungary, Apr. 13, 1949; came to U.S., 1979; s. Andor and Terry (Graf) H. MSEE, Tech. U. Budapest, 1973, PhD, 1980. Asst. prof. Tech. U. Budapest, 1973-79, U. Calif., Santa Barbara, Calif., 1979-82. Contbr. articles to profl. jours. Mem. IEEE (sr.), Assn. Computing Machinery. Office: Xerox Corp 701 S Aviation Blvd # 102 El Segundo CA 90245-4806

HANUSEY, RICHARD DMYTRO, library director; b. Phila., Nov. 30, 1945; s. Richard and Adela Francias (Mackunas) H.; m. Kathleen Mary Morrow, Oct. 2, 1971; children: Keala, Amanda. Student, E. Stroudsburg State U., 1971; Diploma in Libr. Sci., U. Hawaii, 1973. Cert. libr. Libr. asst. dept. planning State of Hawaii, Honolulu, 1973-75; libr. Picatinny Arsenal, Dover, N.J., 1975-77; adminstrv. libr. U.S. Army Area Spt. Group, Livorno, Italy, 1977-80; libr. dir. U.S. Army, Norddeutschland, Bremerhaven, Germany, 1980-86; adminstrv. libr. Fort Drum/10th Mt. Divsn., Watertown, N.Y., 1986-88; libr. dir. U.S. Army, Pacific, Schofield Bar, Hawaii, 1988—; chmn. mng. info systems U.S. Army/Dept. Community Action, Fort Shafter, Hawaii, 1992—; mem. army libr. com. dept. info. resources, U.S. Army, Washington, 1991—, libr. career planning bd., 1991—; mem. joint army-state ednl. schs. adv. coun., Honolulu, 1992—. Mem. Parent's Sch. Assn., Honolulu, 1994. Fellow Hawaii Libr. Assn., ALA. Office: U S Army/Pacific Appe-CFA Libr ACTV Fort Shafter HI 96858-5100

HANZLIK, RAYBURN DEMARA, lawyer; b. Los Angeles, June 7, 1938; s. Rayburn Otto and Ethel Winifred (Membery) H.; m. Susan Evans, Sept. 28, 1963; children: Kristina, Rayburn N., Alexander, Geoffrey. B.S., Principia Coll., 1960; M.A., Woodrow Wilson Sch. Fgn. Affairs, U. Va., 1968; J.D., U. Va., 1974. Bar: Va. 1975, D.C. 1977. Staff asst. to Pres. U.S., Washington, 1971-73; asso. dir. White House Domestic Council, 1975-77; of counsel firm Danzansky Dickey Tydings Quint & Gordon, Washington, 1977-78, Akin Gump Hauer & Feld, Washington, 1978-79; individual practice law Los Angeles, 1979-81; adminstr. Econ. Regulatory Adminstrn., Dept. Energy, Washington, 1981-85; ptnr. Heidrick and Struggles, Inc., 1985-91, McKenna & Hanzlik, Irvine, Calif., 1991-92; chmn. Lanxide Sports Internat., Inc., San Diego, 1992-95, Stealth Propulsion Internat., Ltd., San Diego, Calif. and, Melbourne, Australia, 1994—. Contbg. author: Global Politics and Nuclear Energy, 1971, Soviet Foreign Relations and World Communism, 1965. Alt. del. Republican Nat. Conv., 1980; dir. Calif. Rep. Victory Fund, 1980. Served to lt. USN, 1963-68, Vietnam. Mem. ABA, Va. Bar Assn., D.C. Bar Assn., Am. Legion. Republican. Christian Scientist.

HAPNER, KENNETH DALE, biochemistry educator; b. Goshen, Ind., May 7, 1939; s. Kenneth Jefferson and Mildred Jean (Umbenhour) H.; m. Sara Ann Williams, May 10, 1965 (div. 1973); 1 child, Clara Ann; m. Sharon Jo Fitzwater, June 11, 1977. BA in Chemistry/Biology, Wabash Coll., 1961; Phd in Biochemistry, Ind. U., 1966. Postdoctoral U. Wash., Seattle, 1966-68, acting asst. prof., 1968-69; asst. prof. Mont. State U., Bozeman, 1969-73, assoc. prof., 1973-84, prof., 1984—. Author (chpts. in book) Immunity in Arthropods, 1986; contbr. articles to profl. jours. Mem. Air Quality Task Force, Bozeman, 1993—. NSF rsch. grantee, 1985, 93. Mem. Am. Soc. Biochemistry Molecular Biology, Am. Entomology Assn., Protein Soc. Office: Dept Biochemistry 616 L Johnson Hall Mont State U Bozeman MT 59717

HAPPEL, KENNETH MALCOLM, computer scientist; b. N.Y.C., June 8, 1949; s. Carl Frederick and Katherine King (Kehlor) H.; m. Riemke Rip, 1974 (div. 1977); m. Marie-Jose Kaasenbrood, Feb. 14, 1990 (div. 1995); 1 child, Lieneke. Student, U. Calif., Santa Barbara. Quality engr. EMI Holland Prodns., Haarlem, Netherlands, 1975-77; tech. dir. Technovation, Arnhem, Netherlands, 1978-82; Synterials Plc., London, 1982-83; CEO, founder Devtech Bv., Heerlen, 1984-89; sr. staff engr. Gen. Dynamics Electronics, San Diego, 1989-91; CEO, chmn. Omnigon, San Diego, 1991—. Inventor Hyperknowledge; research in artificial intelligence, virtual reality & advanced materials. Mem. IEEE, Assn. for Computing Machinery, Eurographics. Republican.

HAQ, ABID, physician; b. Nairobi, Kenya, Mar. 28, 1953; came to U.S. 1989; s. Mohamed Abdul and Sarwat Ara (Ghauri) H.; m. Ayesha Mansoor Ahmad; children: Amyr, Myra. MB, BCh, Ain Shams U., Cairo, 1984. Med. officer Coast Province Gen. Hosp., Mombasa, Kenya, 1984-86; sr. house officer Nat. Pub. Health Lab. Svcs., Nairobi, 1986-87; registrar U. Nairobi, Dept. Surgery, 1987-89; intern in internal medicine U. Calif. at Davis, VA Med. Ctr., Martinez, Calif, 1991-92; resident in internal medicine U. Calif. at San Francisco, Alameda County Med. Ctr., Oakland, Calif., 1992-94; staff physician urgent care dept. internal medicine Kaiser Permanente Med. Ctr., Santa Clarita, Calif., 1994—. Author: A Blow to Islam, 1978; contbr. articles to profl. jours. Exec. com. Kenya Scouts Coun., Nairobi, 1987-89. Mem. AMA, ACP, Royal Soc. Health. Muslim. Home: 17744 Hillsboro Pl Santa Clarita CA 91351-4200

HARA, ERNEST HIDEO, architect; b. Honolulu, Nov. 15, 1909; s. Kaichi and Maki (Yamane) H.; m. Claire Hanako Nishigawa, Nov. 27, 1937; children—John Masayuki, Ann Misayo, Michael Takao. B.Arch., U. So. Calif., 1935. Registered architect. Architect Ernest H. Hara, Honolulu, 1941-56; pres. Ernest H. Hara & Assocs., Inc., Honolulu, 1957—. Trustee Punahou Sch., Honolulu, 1969-85, Honolulu Acad. Arts, Honolulu, 1967-81 , Found. for Study in Hawaii and Abroad, Honolulu, 1969; mem. Japan-Hawaii Econ. Council, Honolulu, 1971—. Recipient Fourth Class Order of the Rising Sun, Japanese Govt., 1984. Fellow AIA. Clubs: Waialae Country, Pacific (Honolulu). Home and Office: Ernest H Hara & Assocs Inc 1st Fl 1018 Kemole Ln Honolulu HI 96826-2316

HARAD, GEORGE JAY, manufacturing company executive; b. Newark, Apr. 24, 1944; m. Beverly Marcia Harad, June 12, 1966; children: Alyssa Dawn, Matthew Corde. BA, Franklin and Marshall Coll., 1965; MBA with high distinction, Harvard Bus. Sch., 1971. Staff cons. Boston Cons. Group, 1970-71; asst. to sr. v.p. housing Boise (Idaho) Cascade Corp., 1971; asst. to v.p. Boise Cascade Corp., Palo Alto, Calif., 1971; fin. mgr. Boise Cascade Realty Group, Palo Alto, Calif., 1972-76; mgr. corp. devel. Boise Cascade Corp, Palo Alto, Calif., 1976-80; dir. retirement funds, risk mgmt. Boise Cascade Corp., 1980-82, v.p., contr., 1982-84, sr. v.p., chief fin. officer, 1984-89, exec. v.p., chief fin. officer, 1989-90, exec. v.p. paper, 1990-91; pres., COO Boise Cascade Corp, Palo Alto, Calif., 1991-94, pres., CEO, 1994—; chmn., CEO, 1995; chmn., bd. dirs. Boise Cascade Corp.; chmn., dir. Boise Cascade Office Products Corp., Rainy Fiver Forest Products, Inc.; bd. dirs. Allendale Ins. Co., Inst. Paper Sci. and Tech.; mem. Am. Paper Inst., Bus. Roundtable. Founder, pres. Boise Coun. for Gifted and Talented Students, 1977-79; bd. dirs. Boise Philharm. Assn., 1983-84; dir. bd. trustees Coll. Idaho, 1986-91. Grad. Prize fellow Harvard Grad. Sch. Arts and Scis., 1965-69, Frederick Roe fellow Harvard U. Sch. Bus., 1971; George F. Baker scholar, 1970-71. Mem. Nat. Assn. Mfrs. (bd. dirs.), Phi Beta Kappa, Century Club (Boston), Arid Club, Crane Creek Country Club. Home: 224 E Braemere Rd Boise ID 83702-1710 Office: Boise Cascade Corp PO Box 50 Boise ID 83728-0050

HARA-ISA, NANCY JEANNE, graphic designer; b. San Francisco, May 14, 1961; d. Toshiro and Masaye (Nakahira) Hara; m. Stanley Takeo Isa, June 15, 1985. Student, UCLA, 1979-82; BA in Art and Design, Calif. State U., L.A., 1985. Salesperson May Co., L.A., 1981; svc. rep. Hallmark Cards Co., L.A., 1981-83; prodn. artist Calif. State U., L.A., 1983, Audio-Stats Internat. Inc., L.A., 1983; prodn. asst. Auto-Graphics Inc., Pomona, Calif., 1984-85, lead supr., 1985-86; art dir., contbg. staff writer CFW Enterprises, Burbank, Calif., 1987-88; graphic designer, prodn. mgr. Bonny Jularbal Graphics, Las Vegas, Nev., 1988-90; graphic designer Weddle Caldwell Advt., Las Vegas, 1990-92; owner Nancy Hara-Isa Designs, 1992—; graphic artist Regional Transp. Commn. of Clark County, Las Vegas, 1993—; freelance designer Caesar's Palace. Writer Action Pursuit Games mag. Parade asst., mem. carnival staff Nisei Week, L.A., 1980-84; asst., mem. Summit Orgn., L.A., 1987—. Mem. NAFE, Women in Profl. Graphic Svcs. (acting 1st v.p. 1990, 2d v.p. 1991), Women in Comms. Republican. Presbyterian. Home: 367 Cavos Way Henderson NV 89014-3555

HARALICK, ROBERT MARTIN, electrical engineering educator; b. N.Y.C., Sept. 30, 1943; s. David and Yetta (Stier) H.; m. Joy Gold, Aug. 20, 1967 (div. July 1977); 1 child, Tammy-Beth; m. Linda G. Shapiro, Feb. 12, 1978 (div. Aug. 1992); 1 child, Michael Aaron; m. Ihsin T. Phillips, Dec. 1993. BA, U. Kans., 1964, BS, 1966, MS, 1967, PhD, 1969. Asst. prof. elec. engring. U. Kans., Lawrence, 1969-71, assoc. prof., 1971-75, prof., 1975-78; prof. Va. Poly. Inst. and State U., 1979-84; v.p. rsch. Machine Vision Internat., Ann Arbor, Mich., 1984-86; Boeing Clairmont Egtvedt prof. elec. engring., adj. prof. computer sci. U. Wash., Seattle, 1986—; pres. Mnemonics Inc., 1979—; co-dir. NATO Advanced Study Inst. Image Processing, 1978; co-chmn. NATO Advanced Study Inst. on Image Processing, 1980, Robust Computer Vision Workshop, 1990, 92, 94; vice chmn. 5th Internat. Conf. on Pattern Recognition, Miami, 1980; dir. NATO Advanced Study Inst. on Pictorial Data Analysis, 1982; adj. prof. Ctr. Bioengring. U. Wash., Seattle, 1988—; program chmn. 10th annual ICPR Conf. on Pattern Recognition Systems and Applications, 1990; program co-chmn. Internat. Conf. on Document Analysis and Recognition, 1991. Author: (with T. Creese) Differential Equations for Engineers, 1977; Pictorial Data Analysis, 1983, (with L. Shapiro) Computer and Robust Vision, Vol I and II, 1992; editor: (with J. C. Simon) Issues in Digital Image Processing, 1980, Digital Image Processing, 1981; assoc. editor Computer Vision, Graphics and Image Processing, 1975-93, Pattern Recognition, 1977-93, Communication of the ACM, Image Processing, 1982-92, IEEE Transactions on Systems, Man and Cybernetics, 1979-88, IEEE Transactions on Image Processing, 1992—, Jour. of Electronic Imaging, 1994—; mem. editorial bd. IEEE Transactions on Pattern Analysis and Machine Intelligence, 1981-84, IEEE Expert, 1986-90, Machine Vision and Applications, 1987—, Real Time Imaging, 1994—, mem. editl. com. IEEE Transactions on Pattern Analysis and Machine Intelligence, 1979-84, mem. adv. bd. IEEE Transactions on Pattern Analysis and Machine Intelligence, 1984-93, Image and Vision Computing, 1984-93; mem. adv. program com. Structural & Syntactic Pattern Recognition, 1990; contbr. over 400 articles to profl. jours.; digital computer art exhibitions include William Rockhill Nelson Gallery, Kansas City, Mo., 1971, Nat. History Mus., U. Kans., 1971, Dulin Gallery Art, 1971 (2 purchase awards), Nat. Invitational Print Show, U. R.I., 1972, Fla. State U., 1972, San Diego State Coll., 1972. Recipient Dow Chem. Young Outstanding Faculty award Am. Soc. Engring. Educators, 1975, Outstanding Young Elec. Engrs. Honorable Mention award Eta Kappa Nu, 1975, Best Paper award 5th Ann. Symposium on Automatic Imagery Pattern Recognition, 1975, Best Paper award Pattern Recognition Soc., 1989; NSF faculty fellow, 1977-79. Fellow IEEE, IAPR; mem. IEEE Computer Soc. (chmn. pattern analysis and machine intelligence tech. com. 1975—, acoustics, signal and speech processing, sys., man and cybernetics, pattern recognition tech. subcom. 1975-81, data structures and pattern recognition subcom. 1975-81, biomed. pattern recognition subcom. 1975-81, internat. assn. for pattern recognition gov. bd. 1986—, program com. pattern and image processing conf. 1978, 4th internat. joint conf. on pattern recognition 1978, conf. B-pattern recognition methods and sys. program com. 11th internat. conf. on pattern recognition 1992, structural and syntactic pattern recognition 1992, 2d internat. conf. on document analysis and recognition 1993, chairperson various workshops and confs., Cert. Appreciation award 1978, 84), Pattern Recognition Soc., Am. Assn. Artificial Intelligence, Assn. Computing Machinery. Home: 8651 Inverness Dr NE Seattle WA 98115-3987 Office: U of Wash Dept of Elec Engring Seattle WA 98195

HARALSON, LINDA JANE, communications executive; b. St. Louis, Mar. 24, 1959; d. James Benjamin and Betty Jane (Myers) N.; married. BA summa cum laude William Woods Coll., 1981; MA, Webster U., 1982. Radio intern Stas.-KFAL/KKCA, Fulton, Mo., 1981; paralegal Herzog, Kral, Burroughs & Specter, St. Louis, 1981-82; staffing coordinator, then mktg. coordinator Spectrum Emergency Care, St. Louis, 1982-85, mktg. mgr., 1985-87; dir. mktg. and recruitment Carondelet Rehab. Ctrs. Am., Culver City, Calif., 1987—; mktg. dir. outpatient and corp. services Calif. Med. Ctr., Los Angeles, 1987-88; mktg. dir. Valley Meml. Hosp., Livermore, Calif., 1988-89; account exec. Laurel Communications, Medford, Oreg., 1989-91; community rels. dir. Rogue Valley Med. Ctr., Medford, 1991—. Party chmn. Heart Assn., St. Louis, 1982—; bd. dirs. Am. Lung Assn. Oreg. Recipient Flair award Advt. Fedn. St. Louis, 1984, Hosps. award Hagen Mktg. Research and Hospitals mag., 1984; presdl. acad. scholar William Woods Coll., Fulton, 1977-81. Mem. IABC, NAFE, Am. Mktg. Assn., So. Oreg. Advt. Profls., Britt Music Festivals, Alpha Phi Alumnae Assn. (pres. chpt. 1985-87). Republican. Presbyterian. Avocations: running, travel, sports, French, needlepoint. Office: Roque Valley Medical Ctr 2825 Barnett Road Medford OR 97504

HARARY, KEITH, psychologist; b. N.Y.C., Feb. 9, 1953; s. Victor and Lillian (Mazur) H.; m. Darlene Moore, Oct. 22, 1985. BA in Psychology, Duke U., 1975; PhD, Union Inst., 1986. Crisis counselor Durham (N.C.) Mental Health Ctr., 1972-76; rsch. assoc. Psychical Rsch. Found., Durham, 1972-76; rsch. assoc. dept. psychiatry Maimonides Med. Ctr., Bklyn., 1976-79; dir. counseling Human Freedom Ctr., Berkeley, Calif., 1979; rsch. cons. SRI Internat., Menlo Park, Calif., 1980-82; design cons. Atari Corp., Sunnyvale, Calif., 1983-85; pres., rsch. dir. Inst. for Advanced Psychology, San Francisco, 1986—; freelance sci. journalist, 1988—; invited lectr. Duke U., 1995; lectr. in field; adj. prof. Antioch U., San Francisco, 1985, 86; guest lectr. Lyceum Sch. for Gifted Children, 1985-89; vis. rschr. USSR Acad. Scis., 1983; rsch. cons. Am. Soc. for Psychical Rsch., 1971-72, Found. for Rsch. on Nature of Man, 1972. Co-author: Who Do You Think You Are? Explore Your Many-Sided Self With the Berkeley Personality Profile, 1994, 30-Day Advanced Psychology Series, 1989-91, The Mind Race, 1984, 85; contbr. more than 100 articles to Omni, Jour. Am. Soc. Psychical Rsch., Psychology Today, Exceptional Human Experience, Magical Blend, ASPR Newsletter, Jour. Near Death Studies, others. Mem. APA, Am. Psychol. Soc., Assn. for Media Psychology. Home and Office: 2269 Chestnut St # 875 San Francisco CA 94123-2607

HARBAUGH, DANIEL PAUL, lawyer; b. Wendell, Idaho, May 18, 1948; s. Myron and Manuelita (Garcia) H. BA, Gonzaga U., 1970, JD, 1974. Bar: Washington 1974, U.S. Dist. Ct. (ea. dist.) Wash. 1977, U.S. Ct. Appeals (9th cir.) 1978. Asst. atty. gen. State of Wash., Spokane, 1974-77; ptnr. Richter, Wimberley & Ericson, Spokane, 1977-83, Harbaugh & Bloom, P.S., Spokane, 1983—; bd. dirs. Spokane Legal Svcs., 1982-86; bd. govs. LAWPAC, Seattle, 1980-92. Bd. dirs. Spokane Ballet, 1983-88; chpt. dir. Les Amis du Vin, Spokane, 1985-88; mem. Spokane County Civil Svc. Commn., 1991—, Gonzaga U. Pres'. Coun., 1991—. Mem. ABA, Wash. State Bar Assn. (spl. dist. counsel 1982-95, mem. com. rules for profl. conduct 1989-92, mem. legis. com. 1995—), Spokane County Bar Assn., Wash. State Trial Lawyers Assn. (v.p. 1988-89, co-chair worker's compensation sect. 1992, 93, spl. select com. on workers' corp. 1990—, forum 1994—, vice chmn. 1994—, mem. legis. com. 1995—), ATLA, Nat. Orgn. Social Security Claimants Reps., Internat. Wine & Food Soc. (pres. local chpt. 1989-91, cellar master), Alpha Sigma Nu, Phi Alpha Delta. Democrat. Roman Catholic. Clubs: Spokane, Spokane Country. Office: Harbaugh & Bloom PS PO Box 1461 N 9 Post Ste 210 Spokane WA 99210

HARBAUGH, JOHN WARVELLE, applied earth sciences educator; b. Madison, Wis., Aug. 6, 1926; s. Marion Dwight and Marjorie (Warvelle) H.; m. Josephine Taylor, Nov. 24, 1951 (dec. Dec. 25, 1985); children: Robert, Dwight, Richard. BS, U. Kans., 1948, MS, 1950; PhD, U. Wis., 1955. Prodn. geologist Carter Oil Co., Tulsa, 1951-53; prof. geol. sci. Stanford U., 1955—. Author: (with G. Bonham-Carter) Computer Simulation in Geology, 1981, (with D. M. Tetzlaff) Simulating Clastic Sedimentation, 1989, (with P. Martinez) Simulating Nearshore Environments, 1993, (with R. Slingerland and K. Furlong) Simulating Clastic Sedimentary Basins, 1994. Recipient Haworth Disting. Alumni award U. Kans., 1968, Krumbein medal Internat. Assn. Math. Geologists, 1986. Fellow Geol. Soc. Am.; mem. Am. Assn. Petroleum Geologists (Levorsen award 1970, Disting. Svc. award 1987). Republican. Home: 683 Salvatierra St Stanford CA 94305-8539 Office: Stanford U Dept Geological Sciences 105 Mitchell Stanford CA 94305-2115

HARBISON, JOHN ROBERT, management consultant; b. Phila., Mar. 1, 1953; s. Robert James III and Elizabeth (Thompson) H.; m. Renata Kawczynski, May 25, 1980; children: Peter, Robert. AB, Harvard U., 1975, MBA, 1980; MS, NYU, 1976. CPA, N.Y. Sr. acct. KPMG Peat Marwick, N.Y.C., 1975-78; v.p. Booz, Allen & Hamilton, L.A., 1980—; leader aerospace practice Booz, Allen & Hamilton, Bethesda, Md., 1990—, also bd. dirs. Contbr. articles to various publs. Home: 916 Via Panorama Pls Vrds Est CA 90274-1636 Office: Booz Allen & Hamilton 5220 Pacific Concourse Dr Los Angeles CA 90045-6277

HARBORD, ANNE MARIE, consulting dietetics company executive; b. Detroit, Nov. 9, 1954; d. Lionel Joseph and Mary Ellen (Beaushaw) H.; m. Scott H. Reed, May 27, 1978 (div. Apr. 1980); m. Charles Bloom, June 18, 1988; children: Erica, Mark Alexander. BS in Dietetics, Mich. State U., 1976; MS Nutrition, Food Mgmt., Calif. Poly. U., 1985. Registered dietition, Calif. Clin. dietitian Saga Foods Co., Kalamazoo, 1976-78; cardiac dietition Anaheim (Calif.) Meml. Hosp., 1978; dir. dietary svcs. Care Enterprises, Orange, Calif., 1978-88; owner, mgr. Geriatric Nutrition Mgmt., Encinitas, Calif., 1988—; speaker in field; quality assurance cons. Health Care div. ARA Living Ctrs. and Retirement Homes, Verduga Hills, Calif., 1979; spl. project coord. Calif. Dieticians in Health Care, 1995—. Pub. (continuing edn. prog.) Nutritional Problems in the Elderly; editor: Dietary Policy and Procedure Manual for Long-Term Care, 1984, Recipes Standardized for Long-Term Care, 1986. Calif. Dietetic Assn. grad. scholar, 1984. Mem. Am. Dietetic Assn., Calif. Assn. Health Facilities (chmn. cons. dietitian practice group 1981-85, treas. 1990-91), Am. Soc. Enteral and Parenteral Nutrition, San Diego Dietetic Assn. (edn. chmn. 1988-89, dist. rep. 1989-91). Roman Catholic. Home and Office: Geriatric Nutrition Mgmt 5027 Nighthawk Way Oceanside CA 92056-5447

HARBOUR, KEVIN GEORGE, sales executive; b. Modesto, Calif., Aug. 20, 1957; s. George and Juanita (Deceuser) H.; m. Donna Denese Harbour, Apr. 12, 1984; children: James, Kevin Jr., Leia. BA, UCLA, 1979; postgrad., Pepperdine U., 1992—. Sales rep. Xerox Corp., Woodland Hills, Calif., 1979-81; ednl. sales cons. Tandy Corp., Beverly Hills, Calif., 1981-82; account rep. A. B. Dick Co., Culver City, Calif., 1982-83; sales rep. Digital Equipment Corp., L.A., 1984-86, account mgr., 1986-90, sales unit mgr., 1990-93, br. sales mgr., 1984—; prin. cons. Bus. Mgmt. Sys., 1994—. Active Baldwin Hills Youth Sports; precinct fundraiser Councilman Daniel Tabor campaign, Inglewood, Calif., 1982-90; fundraiser campaigns Mayor Elihu Harris, Oakland, Calif., 1989, Jesse Jackson Presdl. Campaign, L.A., 1984-88. Recipient Honor awards Baldwin Hills Youth Sports, 1989-94. Mem. UCLA Alumni Assn., Bruin Club, Kappa Alpha Psi (pres. alumni chpt. 1989-91), Svc. awards 1984-91).

HARCOURT, MICHAEL FRANKLIN, premier of Province of British Columbia; b. Edmonton, Alta., Can., Jan. 6, 1943; s. Frank Norman and Stella Louise (Good) H.; m. Mai-Gret Wibecke Salo, June 26, 1971; 1 son, Justen Michael. B.A., U. B.C., 1965, LL.B., 1968. Bar: B.C. 1969. Founder dir. Vancouver Community Legal Assistance Soc., 1969-71; partner firm Lew, Fraser & Harcourt, 1971-79; pres. Housing & Econ. Devel. Consulting Firm, Vancouver, from 1977; alderman City of Vancouver, 1972-80; mayor, 1980-86, mem. Legis. Assembly, 1986—, leader, New Dem. Party of British Columbia, 1987—, former leader of opposition, leader of govt.; asst. dir. Justice Devel. Commn., Vancouver; dir. Housing Corp. B.C. Mem. Law Soc. B.C. New Democrat. Mem. United Ch. Can. Office: Legislative Assembly, Parliament Bldgs, Victoria, BC Canada V8V 1X4

HARCOURT, ROBERT NEFF, educational administrator, journalist; b. East Orange, N.J., Oct. 19, 1932; s. Stanton Hinde and Mary Elizabeth (Neff) H. BA, Gettysburg Coll., 1958; MA, Columbia U., 1961. Cert. guidance, secondary edn., career and vocat. guidance, N.Mex. Social case worker N.J. State Bd. Child Welfare, Newark and Morristown, 1958-61; asst. registrar Hofstra U. and asst. to evening dean of students CCNY, 1961-62; housing staff U. Denver, 1962-64; fin. aid and placement dir. Inst. Am. Indian Arts, Santa Fe, 1965—; appointed by corp. pres. to adv. bd. Genre Ltd. Art Pubs., L.A., 1986—; nat. color ad participant The Bradford Exchange, Chgo., 1986—. Donor Am. Indian Libr. collection Gettysburg (Pa.) Coll.; active Santa Fe Civic Chorus, 1977-78; art judge 3d, 4th ann. Aspen Fundraiser Nat. Mus. Am. Indian, 1993, 94. With U.S. Army, 1954-56; Ger. Named Hon. Okie, Gov. Okla., 1970; decorated Nat. Def. medal; postmasters fellow U. Denver, 1962-64; col. a.d.c. to N.Mex. Gov. David F. Cargo, 1970; Disting. Alumni award Gettsburg Coll. Alumni Assn., 1995. Mem. Am. Contract Bridge League (exec. bd. Santa Fe unit; life master), SAR, Santa Fe Coun. Internat. Rels., Am. Assn. Counseling and Devel., Inst. Am. Indian Arts Mus. (founders cir. 1992), Internat. Platform Assn., Assn. Specialists in Group Work (charter), Adult Student Personnel Assn. (charter), Southwestern Assn. Indian Affairs, Neff Family Hist. Soc., Phi Delta Kappa (past mem. exec. bd. local chpt.), Alpha Tau Omega, Alpha Phi Omega, Safari Club Internat. Home: 2980 Viaje Pavo Real Santa Fe NM 87505-5344 Office: Inst Am Indian Arts CSF Campus Santa Fe NM 87504

HARDAWAY, TIMOTHY DUANE, basketball player; b. Chgo., Sept. 12, 1966. Student, U. Tex. at El Paso. With Golden State Warriors, 1989—. Named to NBA All-Rookie team, 1990, All-Star team, 1991, 92, 93. Office: care Golden State Warriors Oakland Coliseum Arena Oakland CA 94621*

HARDEN, MARVIN, artist, educator; b. Austin, Tex.; s. Theodore R. and Ethel (Sneed) H. BA in Fine Arts, UCLA, 1959, MA in Creative Painting, 1963. Tchr. art Calif. State U., Northridge, 1968—, Santa Monica (Calif.) City Coll., 1968; mem. art faculty UCLA Extension, 1964-68; mem. visual arts fellowship, painting panel NEA, 1985. One-man shows include Ceeje Galleries, L.A., 1964, 66, 67, L.A. City Coll., 1968, Occidental Coll., L.A., 1969, Whitney Mus. Am. Art, N.Y.C., 1971, Eugenia Butler Gallery, L.A., 1971, Rath Mus., Geneva, Switzerland, 1971, Irving Blum Gallery, L.A., 1972, Los Angeles Harbor Coll., 1972, David Stuart Galleries, L.A., 1975, Coll. Creative Studies, U. Calif., Santa Barbara, 1976, James Corcoran Gallery, L.A., 1978, Newport Harbor Art Mus., 1979, L.A. Mcpl. Art Gallery, 1982, Conejo Valley Art Mus., 1983, Simard Gallery, L.A., 1985, The Armory Ctr. for the Arts, Pasadena, Calif., 1994; group shows include U.S. State Dept. Touring Exhbn., USSR, 1966, Oakland (Calif.) Mus. Art, 1966, UCLA, 1966, Mpls. Inst. Art, 1968, San Francisco Mus. Art, 1969, Phila. Civic Ctr. Mus., 1969, Mus. Art, R.I. Sch. Design, 1969, N.S. State Mus., 1969, Everson Mus. Art, Syracuse, 1969, La Jolla (Calif.) Mus., 1969, 70, High Mus. Art, Atlanta, 1969, Flint (Mich.) Inst. Arts, 1969, Ft. Worth Art Center Mus., 1969, Contemporary Arts Assn., Houston, 1970, U. N.Mex., 1974, U. So. Calif., 1975, Bklyn. Mus., 1976, Los Angeles County Mus. Art, 1977, Newport Harbor Art Mus., 1977, Frederick S. Wight Gallery, UCLA, 1978, Cirrus Editions, Ltd., L.A., 1979, Franklin Furnace, N.Y.C., 1980, Art Ctr. Coll. Design, L.A., 1981, Alternative Mus., N.Y.C., 1981, Laguna Beach Mus. (Calif.), 1982, L.A. Inst. Contemporary Art, 1982, Mus. Contemporary Art, Chgo., 1983, Mint Mus., Charlotte, N.C., 1983, DeCordova and Dana Mus. and Park, Lincoln, Mass., 1983, Equitable Gallery, N.Y.C., 1984, L.A. Municipal Art Gallery, 1984, 1985, Cirrus, L.A., 1986, 1990, Heal the Bay, Surfboard Art Invitational, 1990, Pasadena Armory Ctr. for the Arts, 1992, Claremont Coll. West Gallery, L.A., 1992, Grolier Club, N.Y.C., 1993, Calif. State U., San Luis Obispo, 1994, Cheney Cowles Mus., Spokane, Wash., 1995, Louis Stern Fine Art, L.A., 1995, Porter Troup Gallery, San Diego, 1995; represented in permanent collections include Whitney Mus. Am. Art, N.Y.C., Mus. Modern Art, N.Y.C., N.Y. Pub. Libr. Spence Collection, Getty Ctr. for Arts and Humanities, Los Angeles County Mus. Art, Atlantic Richfield Co. Corp. Art Coll., Grunwald Ctr. Graphic Arts UCLA, City of Los Angeles, Metromedia, Inc., L.A., San Diego Jewish Community Center, Berkeley (Calif.) U. Mus., Home Savs. & Loan Assn., L.A., also pvt. collections. Bd. dirs. Images & Issues, 1980-86; mem. artists adv. bd. L.A. Mcpl. Art Gallery Assn., 1983-86. Recipient UCLA Art Council award, 1963, Disting. Prof. award Calif. State U. Northridge, 1984, Exceptional Merit Service award Calif. State U. Northridge, 1984; Nat. Endowment Arts fellow, 1972; awards in Visual Arts, 1983; Guggenheim fellow, 1983. Mem. L.A. Inst. Contemporary Art (co-founder 1972). Home:

PO Box 1793 Cambria CA 93428-1793 Office: Calif State U Northridge 18111 Nordhoff St Northridge CA 91330-0001

HARDEN, PATRICK ALAN, journalist, news executive; b. Twickenham, Eng., Aug. 13, 1936; s. Ernest William and Annie Ceridwen (Jones) H.; m. Connie Marie Graham, Nov. 2, 1963; children: Marc Graham, Ceri Marie. Cert. in journalism, Ealing (Eng.) Tech. Coll., 1957. With UPI, 1960-78; regional exec. UPI, London, 1968-69; European picture mgr. UPI, London and Brussels, 1969-72; regional exec. UPI, Detroit, 1973-75; gen. mgr. UPI Can. Ltd., Montreal, 1976-78, UP Can., Toronto, 1979-82; dir., sec. UP Can., 1979-82; treas. UPI Can. Ltd.; gen. mgr. Edmonton (Alta.) Sun, 1982-84, pub., 1984-92; v.p. Toronto Sun Pub. Corp., 1989-94; v.p., bur. chief Washington, 1992-94; Washington columnist Toronto Sun Pub. Corp., 1994—. Mem. senate U. Alta, 1991-92. Recipient Merit award City of Edmonton, 1992. Mem. Can.-Am. Bus. Coun. (bd. dirs.), Nat. Press Club.

HARDEN, WILLIAM L., airport executive. Various positions Oakland (Calif.) Internat. Airport, mgr. gen. aviation, 1990-93; mgr. airport ops. San Diego Internat. Airport, 1993—; mem. adv. bd. aviation dept. Mesa Coll., San Diego. Civil svc. commr. City of Martinez, Calif.; mem. curriculum adv. bd. mgmt. and supervision dept. Diablo Valley Coll. Office: San Diego Internat Airport Lindbergh Field PO Box 488 San Diego CA 92112-0488*

HARDER, KELSIE T., artist, educator; b. Trenton, Tenn., Mar. 8, 1942; s. Kelsie Brown Harder and Geneva Lee (Tomlin) Carlson; m. Kumiko Tanaka, Oct. 2, 1991; children: Samuel Armstrong, Tsunami Tomlin and Tanaka Solomon (twins). Student, Claremont (Calif.) Men's Coll., 1960-61, Escuela de Bellas Artes, Morelia, Mex., 1961, Ventura Coll., 1961-62; BA, U. Nev., 1973-75. Artist self-employed, 1957-96; prof. Truckee Meadows C.C., Reno, 1978-96; Ventura (Calif.) Coll.; chmn. art dept. Truckee Meadows C.C., 1982-91. Contbr. articles to profl. jours., mags., textbooks; 25 one-man shows; represented in over 100 collections. Recipient numerous regional and national awards including YWCA Silver cert. for Outstanding Community Svc., No. Nev., 1972. Office: Truckee Meadows CC 7000 Dandini Blvd Reno NV 89512-3901

HARDER, WENDY WETZEL, marketing and communications executive; b. Oceanside, Calif., Feb. 14, 1951; d. Burt Louis Wetzel and Marjorie Jean Evans; m. Peter Nicholas Harder, Dec. 1, 1984; 1 child, Jonathan Russell. AA, Palomar Coll., 1971; BA in Comms., U. So. Calif., 1973; MBA, Pepperdine U., 1988. Pub. rels. dir. Orange County Cmty. Devel. Coun., Santa Ana, Calif., 1975-76; anchor, assoc. producer KOCE-TV (PBS), Huntington Beach, Calif., 1976-82; sr. adminstr. comms. Mission Viejo (Calif.) Co., 1983, mgr. corp. affairs, 1984-85, dir. corp. affairs, 1985-91, v.p. corp. affairs, 1991-93, v.p., mktg. and corp. comms., 1993—; chmn. Lake Mission Viejo Mgmt. Com., 1993—. Bd. dirs. Dunaj Internat. Dance Ensemble, Costa Mesa, Calif., 1985—; bd. dirs. Saddleback Coll. Found., Mission Viejo, 1988-94, 1st v.p., 1988, 93; 1st v.p. Aliso Viejo (Calif.) Community Found., 1988-92, pres., 1992—; pres. Alegria Guild Children's Hosp. at Mission, Mission Viejo, 1994. Recipient MAME award Sales and Mktg. Coun., Orange County, 1990, 91, 92, Woamn of Yr. award, Saddleback Valley Bus. and Profl. Women, 1992; named Palomar Coll. Alumna of Yr., Palomar Coll. Found., 1989, Emmy award Best Local News, 1980. Mem. Orange County Press Club (best feature release award 1983), Pub. Rels. Soc. Am. (Protos, Spl. Events award 1986), Radio and TV News Assn. (Best Feature 1980, Best Investigative News Report 1981), Working Women Soc. (Best Feature award 1980). Republican. Lutheran. Home: 22551 Tindaya Mission Viejo CA 92692-1330 Office: Mission Viejo Co 26137 La Paz Rd Mission Viejo CA 92691-5309

HARDESTY, DONALD LYNN, anthropology educator; b. Terra Alta, W.Va., Sept. 2, 1941; s. Ezra J. and Mary A. (Jenkins) H.; m. Susan A. Bennett, Aug. 29, 1969. AB in Anthropology, U. Ky., 1964; MA in Anthropology, U. Oreg., Eugene, 1967, PhD in Anthropology, 1972. Prof. U. Nev., Reno, 1968—; pres. Soc. for Hist. Archaeology, 1987. Author: Ecological Anthropology, 1977, Archaeology of Mining, 1988; co-editor: Environment and Society, 1974, Others Knowing Others, 1994. Home: 5000 E Lakeridge Ter Reno NV 89509-5807

HARDIE, GEORGE GRAHAM, casino executive; b. Cleve., Aug. 19, 1933; s. William M. and Helen (Graham) H.; children: George Graham Jr., Jennifer. With sales dept. Hardie Bros., Pitts., later various mgmt. positions, operator dist. sales agys.; owner, driver, trainer, racer standardbred horses, 1963—; owner, mgr. Profile, Inc., Las Vegas, 1973—; founder, mng. ptnr. Bell Gardens Bicycle Club Casino, 1984-94; mayor City of Cathedral City, Calif., 1988-90, mayor pro tem, 1990-92; owner, mgr. Profile Comm. Inc., 1990—, Hardie's Nut Kettle Inc., 1990—; owner, mgr. investment and acquisitions co. The Hardie Group, 1990—; owner Emerald Meadows Ranch, 1989—. Active cmty. and civic affairs. Recipient Congl. award, 1987; commendation L.A. County Suprs., 1987, L.A. County Office Dist. Atty., 1987; resolution Calif. Senate, 1987, cert. of recognition City of Bell Gardens, 1987. Mem. Calif. Harness Drivers Guild (past pres.), Western Standardbred Assn. (past bd. dirs.), Golden State Greyhound Assn. (organizer, pres. 1973), Bell Gardens C. of C. (pres. 1986). Office: Hardie Group Inc 3900 Paradise Rd Ste 235 Las Vegas NV 89109

HARDING, ANNA KRISTINE, education educator; b. Mercersburg, Pa., June 2, 1950; d. Obed Jalmer and Anna Ruth (Guss) Williamson; children: Anika Sarah, Benjamin Joel, Paul Steven. BS in Cmty. Health and Health Edn., U. Oreg., 1972; PhD in Health, Oreg. State U., 1990. Registered environ. sanitarian, Oreg.; cert. tchr., Oreg. Environ. sanitatian trainee and lab. technologist Lane County Health Dept., Eugene, Oreg., 1972-73; subs. tchr. Corvallis (Oreg.) Sch. Dist., 1973; environ. sanitarian Linn County Health Dept., Albany, Oreg., 1974-75; water quality specialist Timberhill Homeowners Assn., Corvallis, 1984-87; grad. teaching asst., instr. Oreg. State U., Corvallis, 1987-90, asst. prof., dir. environ. health program, 1990—; instr. Linn Benton C.C., Corvallis, 1974-75; rschr. Coimbatore, Tamil Nadu, India, 1988-89; environ. justice task group, 1993—; mercury working group Oreg. Dept. Environ. Quality, 1994; nat. environ. goals roundtable group U.S. EPA, 1994—; presenter in field. Contbg. author: Access to Health, 2nd Edit., 1990; contbr. articles to profl. jours. Composting edn. com. Benton County, 1991-93, AIDS edn. com., 1989-92; unit coord. Health and Human Performance Combined Funds, 1991; vol. Boy Scouts Am., Corvallis, 1990—; mission and outreach bd. First Congl. Ch., 1992-93. Grantee Internat. Pub. Health Conf., 1991, 94, Oreg. Dept. Eniron. Quality, 1992-93, Internat. Environ. Health Conf., 1992-93, Coll. Health and Human Performance, 1992-94, Oreg. State U. Rsch. Office, 1993-94, EPA, 1994-95. Mem. APHA, Am. Assn. for World Health, Assn. Oreg. Faculties, Nat. Coun. for Internat. Health, Nat. Environ. Health Assn., Oreg. Environ. Health Assn., Womens Internat. Pub. Health Network. Democrat. Congregationalist. Office: Oreg State Univ Waldo Hall Dept Public Health Corvallis OR 97331-6504

HARDING, CAROL ELAINE, English language educator; b. Bellingham, Wash., Oct. 22, 1953; d. Bruce C. and Lenna J. (Deutsch) H.; m. Kyle R. Jansson, June 26, 1982; children: Bryn, Tyra. BA, U. Oreg., 1974, MA, 1976; PhD, Ind. U., 1985. Instr. Wash. State U., Pullman, 1982-84; vis. prof. Linfield Coll., McMinnville, Oreg., 1985-86; instr. Chandler-Gilbert C.C., Chandler, Ariz., 1992-94; lectr. Western Oreg. State Coll., Monmouth, 1994—, writing coord., 1995—. Author: Merlin and Legendary Romance, 1988. Vol. Albany (Oreg.) Pub. Libr., 1985-87; mem. Crossroads Internat., Corvallis, Oreg., 1985-92; treas. Beyond War, Linn-Benton Counties, Oreg., 1985-89. Mem. MLA, Medieval Acad. Am., Internat. Arthurian Soc., Mid-Valley Writing Consortium. Office: Western Oregon State Coll Dept of English Monmouth OR 97361

HARDING, JIM, state agency executive, energy policy specialist; b. Oakland, Calif., Aug. 17, 1952; s. Robert Eugene and Ebba (Bisgaard) H. Student, Bowdoin Coll., 1969-72; BA, U. San Francisco; postgrad., U. Calif., Berkeley, 1989-90. Energy program dir. Friends of the Earth, Inc., San Francisco, 1972-76; advisor to commr./chmn. Calif. Energy Commn., Sacramento, 1976-79; exec. dir. Internat. Project for Safe Energy Paths, San Francisco, 1979-85; sr. assoc. MHB Tech. Assocs., Inc., San Jose, Calif., 1985-90; asst. dir. Wash. State Energy Office, Olympia, 1990-92, acting dir., 1993, asst. dir., 1994—; policy dir. Northwest Power Planning Coun., 1995—; cons. Can. Internat. Devel. Agy., Ottawa, Ont., 1980-85, Calif. Pub. Utilities Commn., San Francisco, 1985-90, Paul, Weiss, Rifkind, Wharton & Garrison, N.Y.C., 1987-90, Md. Pub. Counsel, Balt., 1988-90. Author: Nuclear Power in the U.S., Europe and U.S.S.R., 1985, Plutonium 1986, 1986, Washington State Energy Strategy, 1992; co-author: Social and Economic Criteria for High Level Waste Management, 1984. Mem. steering com. Keystone (Colo.) Ctr. for Conflict Resolution, 1977-82; mem. Calif. Regulatory Reform Commn., Sacramento, 1979-80; com. mem. NAS, Washington, 1980-84; gov.'s rep. Nat. Marine Fisheries Svc., Portland, Oreg., 1991—. Recipient Adminstr.'s award for exceptional pub. svc. Bonneville Power Adminstrn., 1991, award of merit Soc. for Tech. Communication, 1991. Mem. AAAS. Home: 1725 Arbutus St NE Olympia WA 98506-3201 Office: NWPPC 1110 Capitol Way Olympia WA 98501

HARDING, KAREN ELAINE, chemistry educator and department chair; b. Atlanta, Sept. 5, 1949; d. Howard Everett and Ruth Evangeline (Lund) H.; m. Bruce Roy McDowell, Aug. 30, 1975. BS in Chemistry, U. Puget Sound, Tacoma, 1971; MS in Environ. Chemistry, U. Mich., 1972; postgrad., Evergreen State Coll., 1972, 84, Yale U., 1986, Columbia U., 1991. Chemist Environ. Health Lab., Inc., Farmington, Mich., 1972-73, U. Mich. Med. Sch., Ann Arbor, 1973-75; instr. chemistry Schoolcraft Coll., Livonia, Mich., 1975-77; chair chemistry dept. Pierce Coll., Tacoma, 1977—; adj. prof. U. Mich., Dearborn, 1974-77; instr. S.H. Alternative Learning Ctr., Tacoma, 1980-83, Elderhostel, Tacoma, 1985-89. Mem. County Solid Waste Adv. Com., Tacoma, 1989—, Superfund Adv. Com., Tacoma, 1985-89, Sierra Club, Wash., 1989—; mem., past pres. Adv. Com. Nature Ctr., Tacoma, 1981-87. Faculty Enhancement grantee Pierce Coll., 1990; recipient Nat. Teaching Excellence award, 1991. Mem. NW Assn. for Environ. Studies (treas. 1985—), Am. Chem. Soc., Ft. Steilacoom Running Club (race dir. 1986—). Office: Pierce Coll 9401 Farwest Dr SW Tacoma WA 98498-1919

HARDING, RAY MURRAY, JR., lawyer; b. Logan, Utah, Nov. 23, 1953; s. Ray M. Sr. and Martha (Rasmussen) H.; children: Michelle, Nicole, Justin. BS, Brigham Young U., 1975; JD, J. Reuben Clark Law Sch., 1978. Bar: Utah 1978. Ptnr. Harding & Harding, American Fork and Pleasant Grove, Utah, 1978-85; owner Harding & Assoc., American Fork and Pleasant Grove, 1986—; atty. Lindon City and Pleassant Grove City, Utah, 1983—, Alpine City, 1985-94, American Fork, Utah, 1985—. Bd. trustees Utah Valley State Coll., 1986—, chmn., 1991-93. Named Businessman of Yr., Future Bus. Leaders of Am., 1983. Mem. ABA, ATLA, Utah State Bar Assn., Utah Trial Lawyers Assn., Utah County Bar Assn., Utah Elephant Club, Pleasant Grove C. of C. (pres. 1983), Kiwanis (local bd. dirs. 1982-83). Republican. Mormon. Home: 11165 N Yarrow Cir Highland UT 84003 Office: Harding & Assoc 110 S Main St Pleasant Grove UT 84062-2631 also: 306 W Main St American Fork UT 84003-2230

HARDING, RUSSELL JOHN, environmental administrator; b. Lower Hutt, New Zealand, Nov. 12, 1956; s. Stanley Raymond and Joan Murray Harding; 1 child, Hamish Alexander. BA, Waikato U., Hamilton, New Zealand, 1978; M in Pub. Policy, Victoria U., Wellington, New Zealand, 1983, PhD, 1991. Clk. Ministry of Agr., Hamilton, 1977; recruitment officer State Svcs. Commn., Hamilton, 1978-80; policy adv. officer Ministry of Transport, Wellington, 1981-84; sr. exec. officer Ministry of Agr. and Fisheries, Wellington, 1985-88; natural resource cons. Wellington, 1989-90; spl. cons. N. Pacific Fish Mgmt. Coun., Anchorage, 1991-92; adminstr. Oreg. Grad. Inst., Portland, 1993-94; mgr. standards and assessments Water Quality divsn. Oreg. Dept. Environ. Quality, Portland, 1995—. Contbr. articles to profl. jours. Chair Amnesty Internat. Group, Wellington, 1982-87; treas. Wellington Childcare Assn., 1989. Recipient Sir Desmond Todd Meml. prize in politics Victoria U. Wellington, 1991. Mem. ASPA, Pu. Adminstrn. Theory Network. Jewish. Office: Oreg Dept Environ Quality 811 W 6th Ave Portland OR 97204

HARDING, TERESA J., interior designer; b. L.A.; d. Edward Joseph Harding and Jane Elizabeth (Gunter) Kruse; divorced. BA, U. Okla. Cert. interior designer, Calif. Buyer lamps and accesories W & J Sloane, San Francisco; interior designer W & J Sloane, Beverly Hills, Calif.; interior designer, owner Harding Interior, L.A. Mem. Brentwood Homeowners Assn., L.A., 1994; treas. Nat. Charity League, 1994—. Mem. Nat. Charity League (treas. 1994—), Achievement Rewards for Coll. Scientists, Colleagues Helpers in Philanthropic Svcs. (hon.), Am. Soc. Interior Design. Home: 11421 Waterford St Los Angeles CA 90049-3438

HARDING, WAYNE EDWARD, III, accountant; b. Topeka, Sept. 29, 1954; s. Wayne Edward and Nancy M. (Gean) H.; BS with honors in Bus. Adminstrn., U. Denver, 1976, MBA, 1983; m. Janet Mary O'Shaughnessy, Sept. 5, 1979 (div. Mar. 1985); m. Karen Ruttan, Oct. 10, 1987. Partner, HKG Assocs., Denver, 1976-77; staff auditor Peat, Marwick, Mitchell & Co., Denver, 1976-78; auditor Marshall Hornstein, P.C., Wheat Ridge, Colo., 1978-79; sr. auditor Touche Ross & Co., Denver, 1979-80; controller Mortgage Plus Inc., 1980-81; sec.-treas. Sunlight Systems Energy Corp., 1980-81; ptnr. Harding, Newman, Sobule & Thrush, Ltd., Denver, 1981-82; pvt. practice specializing in microcomputer applications and litigation support, 1982-89; acct., v.p. Great Plains Software, Fargo, N.D., also dir. CPA ptnr. rels.; founder Discount Computer Rentals, Inc., 1985; dir. Harding Transp., Harding Tech. Leasing, Crown Parking Products; lectr. to various profl. groups on computer tech. Class agt., mem. alumni council Phillips Exeter Acad., Exeter, N.H., 1973-83, class agt., 1993—; bd. dirs., treas. Legal Center for Handicapped Citizens, Denver, 1979-80; vol. Denver Bridge, 1984-85. Mem. AICPA (instr., mem. tech. rsch. com. 1994—), Colo. Soc. CPAs (chmn. CPE com. 1987-89, instr., mem. bd. dirs. 1994—), Beta Alpha Psi, Pi Gamma Mu, Beta Gamma Sigma. Libertarian. Mem. editorial bd. Practical Acct. Mag.; contbr. articles in field of microcomputers to profl. jours. including Jour. Acctg. on Micro Computers. Home: 6029 S Kenton Way Englewood CO 80111-5727 Office: 6000 E Evans Ave Denver CO 80222-5406

HARDISON, DONALD LEIGH, architect; b. Fillmore, Calif., Mar. 23, 1916; s. Leigh Winter and Myrtle Glenn (Thorpe) H.; m. Betty Jane Decker, June 14, 1942; children—Stephen Decker, Janet Leigh Hardison Brown. A.B., U. Calif.-Berkeley, 1938. Lic. architect, Calif. Prin. Hardison & Assocs., Richmond, Calif., 1948-56; ptnr. Hardison & Komatsu, Richmond, 1956-64; pres. Hardison & Komatsu, San Francisco, 1965-78; chmn. bd. Hardison Komatsu Ivelich & Tucker, San Francisco, 1978-87. Prin. works include Sonoma State Coll. Residence Hall, 1972 (AIA award 1977), Chevron Cafeteria-Tech. Ctr., Richmond, 1981, McAllister Tower, San Francisco, 1982, (co-architect) U. Calif.-Berkeley Student Ctr. Complex, 1970 (AIA award 1970). Mem. Richmond Planning Commn., 1952-55; mem. Calif. Commn. on Housing and Community Devel., 1969-74; bd. dirs. Art Ctr., Richmond, 1965-70, Richmond Mus. of History, 1990—. Fellow AIA (bd. dirs. 1978-80, chancellor Coll. Fellows 1985, pres. East Bay chpt. 1954, pres. Calif. council 1965, Calif. council Disting. Service citation 1984). Republican. Presbyterian. Club: Commonwealth (San Francisco). Lodge: Rotary (pres. Richmond, Calif. 1986-87). Office: Hardison Komatsu Ivelich & Tucker 400 2nd St San Francisco CA 94107-1402

HARDISON, ROY LEWIS, marketing professional; b. Brea, Calif., Sept. 5, 1929; s. Arthur Abbott and Norma Doris (Lovering) H.; m. Frances Lucille Jacobsen, Aug. 21, 1949; children: Martin Arthur, Bradley Lewis, Steven Dean. BS in Econ. Entom., U. Calif., Berkeley, 1951. With sales Calif. Spray Chem., Modesto, 1951-59; asst. br. mgr. Chevron Chem. Co. (formerly Calif. Spray Chem.), Lindsay, Calif., 1960-61; br. mgr. Chevron Chem. Co., Yuba City, Calif., 1962-67; asst. dist. mgr. Chevron Chem. Co., Woodland, Calif., 1968-70; dist. mktg. specialist Chevron Chem. Co., Modesto, Calif., 1970-73; cen. coast dist. rep. Chevron Chem. Co., Salinas, Calif., 1973-75; mgr. East Asia Chevron Chem. Internat., Inc., Tokyo, 1976-84; prod. prom. specialist Chev. Chem. Co., Fresno, Calif., 1984-86; with regulatory affairs Moyer Products, Inc., Fresno, 1987-92; tech./market devel. profl. Best Sulfur Products Inc., Fresno, Calif., 1992—. Mem. Hazardous Materials Control Resources Inst., Lions (sec., pres. 1954—). Republican. Presbyterian. Home: 7332 N Pacific Ave Fresno CA 93711-0571 Office: Best Sulfur Products Inc 5427 E Central Ave Fresno CA 93725-9336

HARDWAY, JAMES EDWARD, vocational specialist; b. Pueblo, Colo., Nov. 26, 1944; s. William Jeremiah and Margaret Ann (Rinker) H.; m. Mary Frances Walker, Sept. 9, 1967; children: Tina Marie, Catherine Ann, William James. BA, U. So. Colo., 1969; MS, U. Wis.-Stout, Menomonie, 1971; postgrad., U. Toledo, 1972—. Cert. vocat. evaluator, work adjustment specialist. Counselor Pueblo (Colo.) Diversified Industries, 1969-70; vocat. evaluator Penta County Vocat. Schs., Perrysburg, Ohio, 1971-82; dept. mgr. Magic City Enterprises, Cheyenne, Wyo., 1982-88; case mgr. Profl. Rehab. Mgmt., Cheyenne, 1989-91, regional mgr., 1992-94; pvt. practice vocational expert Cheyenne, 1994—; speaker State of Ohio Spl. Needs Conf., Ohio, 1972-80; cons. Wyo. State Tng. Sch., Lander, 1977. Pres. bd. dirs. Laramie County Community Action, Cheyenne; bd. dirs. Handicapped Employment Agy., Cheyenne, Wyo. Alzheimer's Assn. With U.S. Army, 1962-65. Fellow Am. Bd. Vocat. Experts; mem. Kiwanis (bd. dirs.).

HARDY, BEN(SON) (B.), orchid nursery executive; b. Oakland, Calif., Nov. 22, 1920; s. Lester William and Irene Isabell (Bliss) H.; student pub. schs., Oakland, Calif., Concord, Calif.; grad. photo Intelligence Sch., Denver, 1949. Served as enlisted man U.S. Navy, 1942-48; joined USAF, 1948, advanced through grades to capt., 1957; with 67th Reconnaissance Squadron, Korea, 1951-52, Hdqrs. Squadron, Thule AFB, 1956, resigned, 1957; material requirements analyst-coord. Teledyne Ryan Aero. Co., San Diego, 1958-73, 83—; dispatcher-coord. Cubic Western Data Co., San Diego, 1977-80; owner-ptnr. orchid nursery. Pres. Exotic Plant Soc., 1976-78, 81-84, San Diego Gesneriad Soc., 1978; dir. 23d Western Orchid Congress, 1979. Author: (with John Klemme) The Orchid Badge Collector's Guide, 1993. Decorated Bronze Star; recipient Letter of Commendation NASA, also others. Mem. Am. Orchid Soc. (life), N.Z. Orchid Soc., San Diego County Orchid Soc. (life, pres. 1972-73, 75-76), Pacific Orchid Soc. Hawaii, Hoya Soc. Internat. (pres. 1981-83), Cymbidium Soc. Am., Orchid Digest Corp., Auckland Orchid Club, Orchid Badge Club Internat. (found. 1988, pres. 1991—). Home: 9443 E Heaney Cir Santee CA 92071-2919

HARDY, BLAINE CARMON, history educator; b. Vernal, Utah, Dec. 24, 1934; s. Blaine C. and LaRue Mignon (Hunting) H.; m. Kamillia Marlene Compton, July 31, 1954; children: Melody, Cristine, David, Amelia, Robin. BA, Wash. State U., 1957; MA, Brigham Young U., 1959; PhD, Wayne State U., 1963. Asst. prof. Brigham Young U., Provo, Utah, 1961-66; prof. history Calif. State U., Fullerton, 1966—. Author: Solemn Covenant, 1992 (Best Book award Mormon Hist. Assn. 1993); contbr. articles to profl. publs. Office: Calif State U Fullerton Dept History 800 N St College Blvd Fullerton CA 92634

HARDY, CHARLES EXTER, III, minister; b. Atlanta, Dec. 22, 1960; s. Charles Exter Jr. and Loretta (Westmoreland) H.; m. Claudia Gail Barton, Jan. 11, 1986; children: Lauren Nicole, Charles Exter IV. BS in Agr., U. Tenn., 1982; MDiv, Golden Gate Sem., 1987. Youth minister Stock Creek Bapt. Ch., Knoxville, Tenn., 1981-82, Cen. Bapt. Ch., Waycross, Ga., 1982-83, Rollingwood Bapt. Ch., San Pablo, Calif., 1983-84; minister to deaf El Camino Bapt. Ch., Sacramento, 1984; youth min. Narwee (N.S.W. Australia) Bapt. Ch., 1985; asst. pastor First Bapt. Ch., El Sobrente, Calif., 1986-87; pastor First Bapt. Ch., Winters, Calif., 1987-90, First So. Bapt. Ch., Davis, Calif., 1991—; participant mission trips to Indonesia, 1986, Jamaica, 1988, Ecuador, 1990, Argentina, 1992, Kenya, 1994. Author: (play) Cheap Show, 1990. Mem. Winters (Calif.) Ministerial Assn. (pres. 1989-90), Sacramento Assn. So. Bapt. Chs. (moderator 1995). Home: 2650 Belmont Dr Davis CA 95616-1539

HARDY, DAVID WHITTAKER, III, artist, educator; b. Dallas, Oct. 5, 1929; s. David Whittaker and Elnor Virginia (Randlett) H.; m. Sally Hofman; 1 child, Anne Louise. Student, Austin Coll., 1947-48, So. Meth. U., 1949-50, U. Colo., 1949, Am. Acad., 1953-56, Art Students League, 1956-59, Sch. Visual Art, 1957-58, Laney Coll., 1972-75, Calif. Coll. Arts & Crafts, 1979-85; studied with, Marion Virginia Randall Randlett, 1941-49, Ramon Froman, 1950-53, William Moseby, 1954-56, Joseph Van Der Brock, 1953-56, Antonin Sterba, 1953, Frank Mason, 1957-58, Robert Beverly Hale, 1958-59, Jack Potter, 1958. Instr. pvt. art classes., 1960—; owner, operator 13th Street Crafts Garden, Oakland, Calif., 1973-76; instr. art Mendocino (Calif.) Art Ctr., 1973-74, Calif. Coll. Arts and Crafts, Oakland, 1979-86; art buyer Hall of Justice, Hayward, Calif.; guest Wurlizer Found., Toas, N.Mex., 1965; docent tng. program Fine Arts Mus., San Francisco, 1982, 86; guest lectr. U. Calif., Bekerley, 1981, 82. one-man shows include North Park, Dallas, 1964, Pantechnicon Gallery, San Francisco, 1970, Arden Van Wijk Gallery, Saratoga, Calif., 1984, Hemisfair Art, Witte Meml. Mus., San Antonio, 1968, Soc. Western Artists, M.H. De Young Mus., San Francisco, 1970, San Francisco Ann., 1971, Audubon Artists, Nat. Acad., N.Y., 1973, Alma Gilbert Galleries, Inc., Burlingame, Calif., 1992, others; numerous pvt. collections in U.S. and abroad. Recipient 1st pl. painting Alameda County Fair, 1973, Valley Arts Assn., 1973. Mem. Berkeley Art Festival Guild (pres. 1972-77), Soc. Western ARtists, Lillian Paley Ctr. Visual Arts (bd. trustees 1974-78). Home: 4220 Balfour Ave Oakland CA 94610-1750 Office: The Atelier 5010 Telegraph Ave Oakland CA 94609-2014

HARDY, ERWIN, entrepreneur, inventor; b. Winter Garden, Fla., Nov. 21, 1964; s. James and Ethel (Brown) H.; m. Rachel I. Hardy; 1 child, Erwin II. BS in Bus. Adminstrn., Bethune-Cookman Coll., Daytona Beach, Fla., 1988; MBA, Nat. U., San Diego, 1992. Computer lab. asst. Bethune-Cookman Coll., 1984-88; mgr. trainee Family Bargain Ctr., San Diego, 1990-91; chief exec. officer Creid, Inc., San Diego, 1991—. Inventor high-tech. products. With USN, 1988-90. Home: 1329 3rd Ave # 171 Chula Vista CA 91911-4302

HARDY, LOIS LYNN, educational seminar training company executive; b. Seattle, Aug. 20, 1928; d. Stanley Milton and Helen Berniece (Conner) Croonquist; m. John Weston Hardy, July 29, 1951 (div. 1974); children: Sarah Lynn, Laura Lynn; m. Joseph Freeman Smith, Jr., Apr. 18, 1981; stepchildren: Nancy Smith Willis, Martha Smith Dahlquist. BA, Stanford U., 1950, MA, 1952; postgrad., U. Calif., Berkeley, 1957-78, U. San Francisco, 1978-81. Cert. life secondary tchr., life counselor, adminstr., Calif.; lic. career and ednl. counselor, Calif. Tchr., counselor Eastside Union High Sch. Dist., San Jose, Calif., 1951-55; dir. Lois Lynn Hardy Music Studio, Danville, Calif., 1955-69; high sch. tchr. San Ramon Unified Sch. Dist., Danville, 1969-71, counselor, 1971-83; dir. Growth Dynamics Inst., Alamo, Calif., 1976—; instr. Fresno (Calif.) Pacific Coll., 1976-79, Dominican Coll., San Rafael, Calif., 1979—; cons., trainer Personal Dynamics Inst., Mpls., 1976—, Performax Internat., Mpls., 1979—, San Jose Unified Sch. Dist., 1986-86, Novato (Calif.) Unified Sch. Dist., 1985-86, IBM, San Francisco, 1984, corp. and ednl. cons., 1951—. Author: How To Study in High School, 1952, 3d edit., 1973; (with B. Santa) How To Use the Library, 1954; How To Learn Faster and Succeed: A How to Study Workbook For Grades 1-14, 1982, rev., 1985; author various seminars; contbr. numerous articles to profl. jours. Choir dir., organist Community Presbyn. Ch., Danville, 1966-68, elder, 1974-75; speaker to numerous orgns., 1955—. Named Musician of Yr., Contra Costa County, 1978, Counselor of Yr., No. Calif. Personnel and Guidance Assn., 1980; Olive S. Lathrop scholar, 1948, AAUW scholar, 1950; recipient Colonial Dames prize in Am. History, 1950. Mem. Am. Assn. Counseling and Devel., Calif. Assn. Counseling and Devel., Calif. Tchrs. Assn., Calif. Career Guidance Assn., Nat. Speakers Assn., Am. Guild Organists, Stanford U. Alumni Assn., Calif. Assn. for the Gifted, Delta Zeta. Democrat. Presbyterian. Office: Growth Dynamics Inst PO Box 1053 Alamo CA 94507-7053

HARDY, WAYNE RUSSELL, insurance broker; b. Denver, Sept. 5, 1931; s. Russell Hinton and Victoria Katherine (Anderson) H.; m. Carolyn Lucille Carvell, Aug. 1, 1958 (July 1977); children: James Russell Hardy, Jann Miller Hardy. BSCE, U. Colo., 1954; MS in Fin. Svcs., Am. Coll., 1989. CLU; ChFC. Western dist. mgr. Fenestra, Inc., San Francisco, 1956-63; ins. and investment broker John Hancock Fin. Svcs., Denver, 1963—, Wayne R. Hardy Assocs., Denver, 1963—; speaker convs. and sales seminar, 1977, 81, 84, 85, 89; chmn. John Hancock Agt.'s Adv. Com., 1983-84; active State of Colo. Ins. Adv. Bd., 1991-93. Chmn. Colo. Coun. Camera Clubs, Denver, 1962; bd. dirs. Porter Charitable Found., Denver, 1983-85; deacon, class pres. South Broadway Christian Ch., 1961-65; mem. Denver Art Mus., Denver Botanic Gardens, Rocky Mountain Estate Planning Coun., Alliance Francaise. Capt. U.S. Army, 1954-56. Mem. Am. Soc. CLU and ChFC (pres. Rocky Mountain chpt. 1990-91), Nat. Assn. Life Underwriters (pres. Denver chpt. 1983-84, Nat. Quality award 1968), Nat. Football Found. (bd. dirs. Denver chpt. 1992—), Million Dollar Round Table (life), U. Colo. Alumni (bd. dirs. 1990-92), U. Colo. Alumni C Club (bd. dirs. 1972-74),

Univ. Club, Greenwood Athletic Club, Village Tennis Club, Rocky Mountain Optimist Club (pres. 1984-85). Republican. Home: 6178 E Hinsdale Ct Englewood CO 80112-1534 Office: 621 17th St Ste 935 Denver CO 80293-0901

HARE, PAUL DEHAVEN, public safety official; b. Salamanca, N.Y., Feb. 3, 1936; s. Edwin Lawrence and Mary Elizabeth (DeHaven) H.; m. Gene Marie Hurlbut, May 5, 1959; children: Scott, Shawn, Shelly. BS in Sociology, U. Rochester, 1973. Cert. polygraphist Nat. Acad. Lie Detection. Investigator L.A. Sheriff's Dept., 1962-70, Palm Springs (Calif.) Police Dept., 1976-83; security cons. Paul Hare & Assocs., Palm Springs, 1984-90; dir. pub. safety Cabazon Band Mission Indians, Indio, Calif., 1991—; bd. advisor Calif. Polygraph Examination Assn., 1984-88; security advisor, cons. Cabazon Band Mission Indians, 1984-90. City commr., mem. personnel bd. City of Palm Springs, 1983-86. Sgt. USAF, 1954-62. Mem. Internat. Assn. Chiefs of Police, Masons (sr. deacon 1973—), Royal Arch (high priest 1975-76), Scottish Rite, Am. Legion (comdr. 1973—), Rotary (Palm Springs pres. 1988-89, Indio bd. dirs. 1993-94). Office: Cabazon Pub Safety Dept 84-245 Indio Springs Dr Indio CA 92203-3405

HARGISS, JAMES LEONARD, ophthalmologist; b. Manhattan, Kans., June 15, 1921; s. Meade Thomas and Julia Baldwin (Wayland) H.; m. Helen Natalie Berglund, July 19, 1947; children: Phillip M., Craig T., D. Reid. BS, U. Wash., 1942; MD, St. Louis U., 1945; MSc in Medicine, U. Pa., 1952. Diplomate Nat. Bd. Med. Examiners, Am. Bd. Ophthalmology. Intern U.S. Naval Hosp., PSNS Bremerton, Washington, 1945-46; resident physician G.F. Geisinger Meml. Hosp. and Foss Clinic, Danville, Pa., 1949-51; practice medicine specializing in ophthalmic surgery Seattle, 1951-58; ophthalmic surgeon Eye Assocs. N.W., Seattle, 1958—, pres., 1962-91, CEO, 1985-91; asst. clin. prof. Sch. Medicine, U. Wash., 1995—. Contbr. chapter to book, 1987, articles to Ophthalmology, 1964-80. Dist. chmn. King County Rep. Cen. Com., 1962-70. Served as physician/surgeon with USNR, 1945-48. Recipient Citation of Merit Washington State Med. Assn., 1959, Cert. of Award Am. Acad. Ophthalmology and Otolaryngology, 1975; Wendell F. Hughes fellow, 1960. Fellow AMA (Cert. of award 1960), Am. Coll. Surgeons, Am. Acad. Ophthalmology (honor award), Am. Soc. Ophthalmic Plastic and Reconstructive Surgery (charter) (Lester T. Jones award 1979), De Bourg Soc. of St. Louis U., Lions (Lake City pres. 1960-61), Alpha Omega Alpha. Office: Eye Assocs NW 1101 Madison St #600 Seattle WA 98104-1320

HARGREAVES, GEORGE JULIAN, landscape architect; b. Atlanta, Nov. 12, 1952; s. George Julian and Carolyn Lucille (Snyder) H.; children: Joseph, Rebecca, Kate. B of Landscape Architecture, U. Ga., 1977; M of Landscape Architecture, Harvard U., 1979. Prin. Hargreaves Assocs., San Francisco, 1980—; vis. prof. Calif. Polytech. Inst., 1981, U. Ill., 1984, U. Va., 1985, Harvard U., 1986-88; lectr. in field. One man shows include Harvard U., 1987, Ohio State U., 1988, U. Minn., 1988, Iowa State U., 1988, U. Toronto, 1988, N.C. State U., 1988, Pa. State U., 1988; works published in European, Am. and Japanese jours.; contbr. articles to profl. jours. Recipient Henry Herring Meml. medal Nat. Sculpture Soc., 1988, Design award Am. Inst. Architects, 1985, Pacific Coast Builders Gold Nugget award, 1984; Hubert B. Owens fellow, 1977. Mem. Am. Soc. Landscape Architects (chmn. jury, Excellence award 1986, 87), Am. Acad. Rome (Landscape Architecture award 1988).

HARGROVE, JOHN JAMES, federal judge; b. Bay Shore, N.Y., May 4, 1942; s. John A. and Cecelia L. Hargrove; m. Jane A Nagle, Oct. 21, 1967; children: David, Kristin, Kelly, Kathryn. BAin Polit. Sci., U. Notre Dame, 1964, JD, 1967. Bar: N.Y. 1968, Calif. 1971. Atty. Gant & Asaro, San Diego, 1972-76; ptnr. Weeks, Willis, Hoffman & Hargrove, San Diego, 1976-79, Strauss, Kissane, Davis & Hargrove, San Diego, 1979-83, Britton & Hargrove, San Diego, 1983-84; prin. John J. Hargrove & Assocs., San Diego, 1984-85; judge U.S. Bankruptcy Ct., San Diego, 1985—; adj. prof. Calif. Western Sch. Law, 1986. Coach University City Bobby Sox Softball Team; lector Our Mother of Confidence Roman Cath. Ch.; trustee U. Notre Dame, 1987-89. Lt. col. USMCR, 1968-90. Mem. U. Notre Dame Alumni Assn. (bd. dirs. 1985-89, pres. 1988-89). Republican. Office: US Bankruptcy Ct So Dist Calif 325 W F St San Diego CA 92101-6017

HARKER, ROGER GEORGE, manufacturing company executive; b. Silver City, N.Mex., Jan. 28, 1945; s. Robert Asa Geraldine (Smiley) H.; m. Sheryl Martin, Oct., 1973; children: Matthew, Bradley, Amanda. BSEE, U. Calif., Berkeley, 1966. V.p. engring. Bently Nev. Corp., Minden, 1971-76, exec. v.p., gen. mgr., 1976-86, pres., 1986—, also bd. dirs.; bd. dirs. Bently Nev. Corp. Trustee St. Mary's Found. Mem. ASME, Am. Petroleum Inst., Instrument Soc. Am. Office: Bently Nev Corp PO Box 157 Minden NV 89423-0157

HARKESS, NANCY ROBYN, public relations, marketing executive; b. Altadena, Calif., May 14, 1944; d. Cecil Henry and Mary Dorothy (Spriggs) Murray; m. George Robert Harkess III, June 30, 1986; children: Deanna Lynn, Craig Robert. AA in Broadcasting, Clark County C.C., Las Vegas, 1981; BA in Journalism, U. Nev., Las Vegas, 1983, MA in English, 1994. Instr. U. Nev., Las Vegas, 1984-87; employee comms. E.G.& G., Las Vegas, 1988-94; pub. affairs officer Dept. Energy, Las Vegas, 1994—; pres. Mardor Corp., Las Vegas, 1991—. Editor Focus Mag. 1988— (Bronze Quill 1994). Co-chair WalkAm., Las Vegas, 1992-94; mem. Leadership Las Vegas, C. of C., 1993—; mem. steering com. KNPR Pub. Radio, 1991—. Mem. AAUW, Internat. Assn. Bus. Communicators (pres. 1992—, Silver Six award 1992, Bronze Quills, 1989, 90, 91, 92, 94), Pub. Rels. Soc. Am., Las Vegas C. of C. (edn. com.). Democrat. Roman Catholic. Home: 808 Sweeney Ave Las Vegas NV 89104-1656 Office: Dept Energy 2753 S Highland Dr Las Vegas NV 89109-1007

HARKINS, CRAIG, management consultant; b. Boston, May 1, 1936; s. Edwin Craig and Shirley Nadine (Pike) H.; m. Betty Letitia Hester, June 17, 1961 (div. 1985); children: Daniel, Sean, Lance; m. Donna Marie Hamlin, Sept. 1, 1990; 1 child Angelika. BA, Colby Coll., Waterville, Maine, 1958; MA, NYU, 1959; Profl. Dipl., Columbia U., N.Y.C., 1963; PhD, Rensselaer Poly. Inst., Troy, N.Y., 1978. Computer operator Pacific Mutual, L.A., 1957; reporter Evening Independent, St. Petersburg, Fla., 1960-61; pub. rels. mgr. IBM, N.Y./Calif, 1961-82; mgmt. cons. Hamlin Harkins Ltd., San Jose, 1982—. Co-editor: Guide to Writing Better Technical Papers, 1982; contbr. numerous articles to profl. jours. Sec. Hudson River Sloop Restoration, Poughkeepsie, N.Y., 1972-76; communications/mktg. com. United Way, Santa Clara, Calif., 1981—; mem. mktg. com. San Jose Cleve. Ballet, 1991—. With USMCR, 1961-66. Mem. Internat. Communication Assn., Peninsula Mktg. Assn., Soc. for Tech. Communication (bd. dirs. 1980-81), IEEE Profl. Communications Soc. (sec. 1977-80). Democrat. Roman Catholic. Home: 1301 Mariposa Ave San Jose CA 95126-2624 Office: Hamlin Harkins Ltd 1611 The Alameda San Jose CA 95126-2202

HARLAN, DAVID, reporter; b. Portland, Oreg., July 24, 1955; s. Dale Morgan and Joyce (Niedemeyer) H. BJ, U. Oreg., 1983, B in History, 1983. News editor The Clackamas County Review, Milwaukie, Oreg., 1984-85; reporter, community editor The Enterprise Courier, Oregon City, Oreg., 1985-86; corr. The Oregonian, Oregon City, Oreg., 1985-86; bus. reporter The Daily Astorian, Astoria, Oreg., 1986—. Recipient 1st and 2d pl. Bus. and Econ. Reporting awards Oreg. Newpaper Pubs. Assn., 1986, 1st pl. Consumer and Environ. Affairs Reporting award Pacific N.W. Soc. of Profl. Journalists "Excellence in Journalism Competition", 1988. Democrat. Presbyterian. Office: The Daily Astorian 949 Exchange St Astoria OR 97103-4605

HARLAN, KATHLEEN T. (KAY HARLAN), business consultant, professional speaker and seminar leader; b. Bremerton, Wash., June 9, 1934; d. Floyd K. and Rosemary (Parkhurst) Troy; m. John L. Harlan, Feb. 16, 1952 (div. 1975); children: Pamela Kay, Kenneth Lynwood, Lianna Sue; m. Stuart Friedman, Nov. 10, 1991. Chair Kitsap-North Mason United Way, 1968-70; owner, operator Safeguard N.W. Systems, Tacoma, 1969-79; devel., mgr. Poulsbo (Wash.) Profl. Bldg., 1969-75; pres. Greenapple Graphics, Inc., Tacoma, 1976-79; owner, mgr. Iskrem Hus Restaurant, Poulsbo, 1972-75; pres. Bus. Seminars, Tacoma, 1977-82; owner, mgr. Safeguard Computer Ctr., Tacoma, 1982-91; owner Total Systems Ctr., Tacoma, 1983-88; mem. Orgnl. Renewal, Inc., Tacoma, 1983-88; assoc. mem. Effectiveness Resource Group, Inc., Tacoma, 1979-80; pres. New Image Confs., Tacoma, 1979-82; speaker on mgmt. and survival in small bus.; CEO Manage Ability, Inc., profl. mgmt. firm, 1991—; bus. mgr. Another Door to Learning, 1993—. Contbg. author: Here is Genius!, 1980; author small bus. manuals. Mem. Wash. State br. Boundary Rev. for Kitsap County, 1970-76, Selective Svc. Bd. 19, 1969-76; co-chair Wash. State Small Bus. Improvement Coun., 1986; del. White House Conf. on Small Bus., 1986; chair Wash. State Conf. on Small Bus., 1987; mem. exec. bd. Am. Leadership Forum, 1988-94; dir. Bus. Leadership Week, Wash. State, 1990—; chair Pro-Tech Pierce County, 1992-94; chair Allenmore Hosp., 1993—; founding mem. Multicare Health Found., 1995—. Recipient Nellie Cashman award; named Woman Entrepreneur of Yr. for Wash. State, 1986, 87. Mem. Tacoma-Pierce County C. of C. (lifetime exec. bd. 1985—, chair spl. task force on small bus. for Pierce County 1986-89, treas. 1987-88, chair-elect 1988-90, chair 1990-91).

HARLAN, RAYMOND CARTER, communication executive; b. Shreveport, La., Nov. 13, 1943; s. Ross E. and Margaret (Burns) H.; m. Nancy K. Munson, Sept. 3, 1966 (div. 1978); children: Kathleen Marie, Patrick Raymond; m. Sarah J. Kinzel, Sept. 1, 1979 (div. 1982); m. Linda Frances Gerdes, Mar. 30, 1985; stepchildren: Kimberly Jo Gillis, Kellie Leigh Raffa, Ryan William Gerdes. BA in Speech and Drama cum laude, Southwestern U., 1966; MA in English, U. Tex., 1968; MA in Speech & Theatre Arts, Bradley U., 1976. Commd. 2d lt. USAF, 1968, advanced through grades to maj., 1980, ret., 1988; pres. ComSkills Tng., Aurora, Colo., 1988—; asst. prof. Bradley U., Peoria, Ill., 1972-76; instr., asst. prof., course dir. Air Force Acad., Colorado Springs, 1976-81; asst. prof. Air Force Inst. Tech., Dayton, Ohio, 1987-88; internat. trainer Inst. for Internat. Rsch., London, 1990-92. Author: The Confident Speaker, 1993; co-author: Telemarketing That Works, 1991, Interactive Telemarketing, 1995; contbr. articles and revs. to profl. jours. Decorated Air Force Commendation medal with three oak leaf clusters, Air Force Meritorious Svc. medal with one oak leaf cluster; recipient George Washington Honor Medal Freedom Found., 1983, Leo A. Codd award Am. Def. Preparedness Assn., 1st Prize ann. poetry contest Ariz. State Poetry Soc., 1979. Mem. ASTD, Nat. Writers Assn., Air Force Assn., Ret. Officers Assn., Assn. for Bus. Comm. Lutheran. Office: ComSkills Tng 17544 E Wesley Pl Aurora CO 80013-4174

HARLANDER, LESLIE ALBERT, naval architectural consultant; b. Crockett, Calif., Jan. 26, 1923; s. Albert Charles and Hilma Louise (Hedstrom) H.; m. June Hildegarde Rodgers, Oct. 3, 1943 (dec. Mar. 1983); children: George, Penny, Leslie; m. Rowena Noldner, May 21, 1983. BSME, U. Calif., Berkeley, 1951; MS in Naval Architecture and Marine Engring., MIT, 1955; postgrad., Sch. Nuclear Sci. and Engring., 1956. Design draftsman Moore Drydock Co., Oakland, Calif., 1951-54; engr. Matson Navigation Co., San Francisco, 1955-56, mgr. engring. devel., 1957-63, v.p. engring. and maintenance, 1964-67, v.p. engring. and marine ops., 1968-70; v.p. ops. Am. Pres. Lines, San Francisco, 1971-77; cons., prin. L.A. Harlander & Assocs., Richmond, Calif., 1977—; owner Cal-Coast Marine, Inc., Richmond, 1977—. Contbr. numerous articles to profl. jours.; patentee in field. Recipient Gibbs medal NAS, 1988. Mem. Soc. Naval Architects and Marine Engrs. (MIT scholarship 1954, Jerry Land medal 1987), St. Francis Yacht Club, Richmond Yacht Club, Sigma Xi. Republican. Office: L A Harlander & Assocs PO Box 1874 Gardnerville NV 89410-1874

HARLEY, HALVOR LARSON, banker, lawyer; b. Atlantic City, Oct. 7, 1948; s. Robison Dooling and Loyde Hazel (Gauhnauer) H. B.Sc., U. S.C., 1971, M.A., 1973; J.D., Widener U., 1981. Bar: Pa. 1982, D.C. 1989. Staff psychologist Columbia Area Mental Health Ctr., S.C., 1971-73; dir. Motivational Research Consultants, Columbia, 1973-79; psychologist Family Ct. Del., Wilmington, 1979, sole practice law, Phila., 1982; v.p. investment banking Union Bank, L.a., 1982-88; v.p., mgr. Tokai Bank, Newport Beach, Calif., 1988—. Bar: U.S. Ct. of Appeals (3rd cir.), 1987, U.S. Dist. Ct. (ea. dist.) Pa., 1987, D.C. 1988, U.S. Supreme Ct., 1988, U.S. Ct. Appeals D.C. 1989. Author: Help for Herpes, 1982; also articles. Fundraiser Orange County Performing Arts Ctr., 1983-84; vol. Hosp. Ship HOPE, Sri Lanka, 1968-69; bd. dirs., v.p. exec. com. Alzheimers Assn. Orange County; bd. dirs. Lido Sands Homeowners Assn., Newport Beach, Calif., 1984-85, Calif. Bankers Assn., United Cerebral Palsy of Orange County (chmn. Bastile Day com.). Mem. Orange County Bankers Assn., Assn. Trial Lawyers Am., Am. Judicature Soc., Indsl. League Orange County (membership com. 1983-84), Am. Bankers Assn., World Trade Ctr. Assocs. Orange County (directing com. 1983-85), Orange County Performing Arts Fraternity, Psi Chi (chpt. pres. 1971-73). Home: 5015 Lido Sands Dr Newport Beach CA 92663-2403 Office: Mellon Bank 4695 MacArthur Ct Ste 240 Newport Beach CA 92660

HARLOCK, MICHAEL J., architect. BArch, U. Mich.; MArch, U. Calif., Berkeley. Registered arch., Calif. Sr. planner Planning Dept. City of Novato; sr. project. mgr. Whistler-Patri, until 1986; joined SGPA Architecture and Planning, Lafayette, Calif., 1986—, assoc., 1987-88, sr. assoc., 1988—. Prin. works include Xerox Corp., Sunnyvale, Calif., Sand City Hotel, Monterey, Calif., Hills Bros. Mixed Use, San Francisco, Sierra Point Comml. Ctr., San Francisco, Monterey/Blossom Hill Ctr., San Jose, Calif., Mervyn's Cochrane Plz., Morgan Hill, Calif, numerous others. Mem. AIA (Honor award), Am. Inst. Cert. Planners, Am. Planning Assn. Office: SGPA Architecture and Planning 49 Stevenson St 800 Lafayette CA 94549

HARLOW, CHARLES VENDALE, JR., finance educator, consultant; b. Long Beach, Calif., May 18, 1931; s. Charles Vendale and Lucille (Morris) H.; m. Luann Jones, July 6, 1956; children: Jeffrey, Pamela, John. BA, Stanford U., 1953; MBA, U. So. Calif., 1960, DBA, 1968. Ptnr. Harlow & Harlow Investments, Long Beach, 1955-68; pres. Cambistics, Inc., Long Beach, 1968-88; asst. prof. Calif. State U., Long Beach, 1968-71, assoc. prof., 1971-75, prof. fin., 1975-94; prof. fin. Pepperdine U., 1995—; mng. dir. Cambistics Securities Corp., Long Beach, 1990—. Co-author: The Commodity Futures Trading Guide, 1969 (100 Best Books in Bus. award), The Futures Game, 1974, How to Shoot From the Hip Without Getting Shot in the Foot: Making Smart Strategic Choices Every Day, 1990. 1st lt. USMC, 1953-55. NSF grantee, 1968. Republican. Office: Cambistics PO Box 15596 Long Beach CA 90815-0596

HARLOW, STEVEN MICHAEL, banker; b. Houston, Sept. 15, 1963; s. Harvey Lee Harlow and Dorothy Jean Boulton; m. Angelia D. Wesch, Oct. 9, 1993. BBA, U. Tex., 1986. CPA, Tex. Credit analyst Bank One Tex. N.A., Houston, 1986-87, credit analyst supr., 1987, comml. loan rep., 1987-88, comml. loan officer, 1988-89, asst. v.p., 1989-91, v.p., 1991-92; v.p. Seafirst Bank, Tacoma, Wash., 1992—; youth job program advisor Seafirst Bank, 1994—. Vol. income tax asst. IRS, various locations, 1988-89; recruiting chmn. Multiple Sclerosis Club, 1989-90; pres. jr. bd. Am. Cancer Soc., 1989-90, bd. dirs., treas. Houston unit, 1989-92; bd. dirs. S.W. Alternate Media Project, 1990-91; mem. Tacoma-Pierce County C. of C. (leadership program 1995). Mem. AICPA, Tex. Soc. CPAs (bd. dirs. Houston chpt. 1992, chmn. young CPA com. Houston chpt. 1991-92), Wash. Soc. CPAs, U. Tex. Ex-Students Assn., Forum Club (Houston), Houston Sierra Club (bd. dirs., vice chmn., 1990-91, outings leaders 1989-93), Rotary Internat. (G.S.E. team to the Netherlands 1992). Home: 4102 N 38th St Tacoma WA 98407-5619 Office: Seafirst Bank 950 Pacific Ave Fl 5 Tacoma WA 98402-4410

HARMAN, JANE FRANK, congresswoman, lawyer; b. N.Y.C., June 28, 1945; d. A. N. and Lucille (Geier) Lakes; m. Sidney Harman, Aug. 30, 1980; children: Brian Lakes, Hilary Lakes, Daniel Geier, Justine Leigh. BA, Smith Coll., 1966; JD, Harvard U., 1969. Bar: D.C. 1969, U.S. Ct. Appeals (D.C. cir.) 1972, U.S. Supreme Ct. 1975. Spl. asst. Commn. of Chs. on Internat. Affairs, Geneva, Switzerland, 1969-70; assoc. Surrey & Morse, Washington, 1970-72; chief legis. asst. Senator John V. Tunney, Washington, 1972-73; chief counsel, staff dir. Subcom. on Rep. Citizen Interests, Com. on Judiciary, Washington, 1973-75; adj. prof. Georgetown Law Ctr., Washington, 1974-75; chief counsel, staff dir. Subcom. on Constl. Rights, Com. on Judiciary, Washington, 1975-77; dep. sec. to cabinet The White House, Washington, 1977-78; spl. counsel Dept. Def., Washington, 1979; ptnr. Manatt, Phelps, Rothenberg & Tunney, Washington, 1979-82, Surrey & Morse, Washington, 1982-86; of counsel Jones, Day, Reavis & Pogue, Washington, 1987-92; mem. 103rd Congress from 36th Calif. dist., 1992—; mem. vis. coms. Harvard Law Sch., 1976-82, Kennedy Sch. Govt., 1990—. Counsel Dem. Platform Com., Washington, 1984; vice-chmn. Ctr. for Nat. Policy, Washington, 1981-90; chmn. Dem. Nat. Com. Nat. Lawyers' Coun., Washington, 1986-90. Mem. Phi Beta Kappa. Democrat. Office: US House Reps 325 Cannon House Office Bldg Washington DC 20515-0536 Office: 5200 W Century Blvd Ste 960 Los Angeles CA 90045-5900 also: 3031 Torrance Blvd Torrance CA 90503-5015*

HARMEL, HILDA HERTA See PIERCE, HILDA

HARMON, CLIFF F., artist; b. L.A., June 26, 1923; s. Artemas Henry and Helen Leone (Lindsey) H.; m. Barbara Sayre; 1 child, Jonathan Henry. Student, Bisstram Sch. Fine Arts, Taos Valley Art Sch., Black Mountain Coll. Wood tool pattern maker Douglas Aircraft Co., Santa Monica, Calif., 1954-59; wood model builder Electronic Splty. Co., L.A., 1959-61; owner art gallery Taos, N.Mex., 1962—. One-man shows include N.Mex. Mus. Fine Art, Santa Fe, 1952, Stables Art Gallery, Taos, 1965-69, 71, 73, 75, 77, 79, Total Arts Gallery, Taos, 1978, Suzanne Brown Gallery, Ariz., 1985, New Directions Gallery, Taos, 1989; exhibited in group shows at Dallas Mus. Fine Arts, 1949, Mus. N.Mex. Art Gallery, Santa Fe, 1952, Arts & Humanities Coun. Invitational Travelling Exhibit, 1971, Cunningham Meml. Art Gallery, Bakersfield, Calif., 1971, Phoenix Art Mus., N.Mex. Mus. Fine Arts, Stables Gallery, 1973, Rotunda Gallery, London, 1973, Okla. Art Ctr., Oklahoma City, 1974, Colo. Women's Coll., Denver, 1975, 17th Ann. Eight State Exhbn., Okla., 1975, Munson Gallery, Santa Fe, 1978, Fall Festival of Arts, Taos, 1984-85, El Cielo Grande de Taos, 1986-89, Harwood Mus., Taos, 1987, 91, Civic Ctr., Taos, 1990-93, Taos Art Assn., 1991, 93, 94 (1st pl., Blue Ribbon 1994); represented in various permanent pub. collections. With USCG, 1942-46, PTO. Recipient 1st, 2d and 3d prizes Glendale Art Assn., 1960, 1st premium N.Mex. State Fair Art Exhbn., 1968, 3d prize 1st Biennial Five State Art Exhibit, 1971. Mem. Taos Art Assn. (artist mem., pres.). Home and Office: Torreon Gallery Box 202 234 Las Cruces Rd Taos NM 87571

HARMON, JOHN EMERY, public housing agency executive; b. Salem, Oreg., Apr. 23, 1949; s. Clarence Vernon and Doris (Emery) H.; m. Tonja-Jolene Gail Streeter, June 5, 1981; children: Shanna, Wendi, Kelsey. BA in Polit. Sci. with honors, Calif. State Poly. U., 1971. Cert. pub. housing mgr. Housing mgmt. officer HUD, San Francisco, 1972-75; housing mgmt. officer Office of Indian Programs HUD, 1976-77; acting dir./asst. to dir. Alameda County Housing Authority, Hayward, Calif., 1977; acting asst. dir. Napa (Calif.) Housing Authority, 1977-78; asst. exec. dir./acting exec. dir. Butte County Housing Authority, Gridley, 1978; exec. dir. Sutter County Housing Authority, Yuba City, 1978-83; chief of housing mgmt. Sacramento (Calif.) Housing and Redevel. Agy., 1983-86, asst. dir. housing, 1986-88; exec. dir. Bellingham (Wash.)-Whatcom County Housing Authorities, 1988—. Vice-pres. Bellingham Devel. Assn., 1993-94; mem. adv. bd. Community Devel., Bellingham, 1994—. Recipient Cert. of Excellence award for mgmt. ops. U.S. Dept. Housing and Urban Devel., 1991, 92, 93. Mem. ASPA, Assn. Wash. Housing Authorities (v.p., pres. 1988—), Nat. Assn. Housing and Redevel. Ofcls. (award of merit for resident svcs. coord. program 1993, Harborview tax credit housing devel. 1994, Pacific Rim rated bond housing devel. 1994, Creekside Meadows tax credit housing devel. 1995—). Office: Bellingham/Whatcom County Housing Authorities 208 Unity St Bellingham WA 98225

HARMON, WARREN WAYNE, geography educator; b. Colton, Calif., Feb. 13, 1936; s. Renick Elkin and Henrietta Frances (Stûwich) H.; m Margaret Ann Schonberger, Nov. 21, 1959; children: Andrea Jane, Fritz Warren. AA, San Bernardino Valley Coll., 1958; BA, San Diego State Coll., 1961, MA, 1964. Lic. secondary tchr., Calif. Chmn. social sci. Roosevelt Jr. High Sch., San Diego, 1962-66; geography instr. Mesa Coll., San Diego, 1966; geography instr. Grossmont Coll., El Cajon, Calif., 1967-84, div. coord., 1984, prof. geography, dept. chmn. of earth scis., 1984-89, dean humanities & social scis., 1989-90, dean math., phys. and behavioral scis. div., 1990-92, prof. geography, 1992—; geog. cons. UCLA, 1986-88. Author: Geography of California, 1976; co-author Geographic Perspectives on American Westward Expansion, 1986; contbr. articles to profl. jours. Co-founder So. Calif. Tourette Syndrome Assn., Mission Viejo, Calif, 1974; chief Indian Guides, La Jolla, Calif., 1978. Named Outstanding Educator of Am., Fuller and Dees, 1974, Disting. Chair of Sci. Grossmont Coll., 1988-89. Mem. San Diego County Social Sci Adv. Coun., Nat. Coun. for Geog. Edn., Calif Geography Soc. (exec. bd. mem. 1978), Calif. Geog. Alliance (charter mem.), Fulbright Alumni Assn. (Fulbright scholar 1970-71), La Jolla Play Readers Club, Gamma Theta Upsilon. Democrat. Methodist. Office: Grossmont Coll 8800 Grossmont College Dr El Cajon CA 92020-1765

HARMS, GLENN EDWARD, minister, pastor; b. Newton, Kans., Jan. 8, 1939; s. Ed and Minnie (Rutschman) H.; m. Helen L. Janzen, Feb. 20, 1959; children: David Edward, Debbie Kaye. Grad. in pastoral theology, Western Bible Coll., Denver, 1969. Ordained to ministry Bapt. Ch., 1969. Pastor Calvary Bapt. Ch., Chadron, Nebr., 1969-71; pastor, founder Foothills Bapt. Ch., Loveland, Colo., 1971—. Mem. High Plains Bapt. Fellowship (founding mem.), Internat. Fellowship of Bapts. Republican. Office: Foothills Bapt Ch 4000 W 22nd St Loveland CO 80538-8613

HARNEY, FRANCIS PAUL, mechanical engineer, consultant; b. Rochester, N.Y., July 18, 1960; s. James Joseph and Regina Dolores H. BSME, U. Rochester, 1983; M Engring. in Engring. Mgmt., U. Colo., Boulder, 1995. Registered profl. engr., Colo. Media devel. engr. Storage Tech., Inc., Louisville, Colo., 1986-90, staff engr. libr. devel., 1990-93, staff engr. libr. enhancements, 1993-94, staff engr. mechanical integrity, 1994—; cons. in field Boulder, Colo., 1991—. Mem. ASME, Nat. Eagle Scout Assn. Home: 535 W Hackberry St Louisville CO 80027 Office: Storage Tech Inc 2270 S 88th St # 0196 Louisville CO 80028-0001

HARNEY, WILLIAM JOHN, JR., electronics engineer; b. Bennington, Vt., Mar. 2, 1954; s. William John and Marjorie Grace (Bowker) H.; m. Deborah June Banes, May 20, 1978; children: William Richard, Geoffrey Scott, Elizabeth June. Student, U.S. Naval Acad., 1972-74, Drexel U., 1974-75; BSEE, U Md., 1977; postgrad., George Washington U., 1979-83. Electronics engr. David Taylor Rsch. Ctr., Annapolis, Md., 1978-83, electronics engr., supr., 1983-92; electronics engr., range mgr. Naval Surface Warfare Ctr., SEAFAC, Ketchikan, Alaska, 1992—; cons., owner Electronic & Instrumentation Systems, Ketchikan, 1984—. Served with USN, 1972-74. Mem. Fed. Exec. Assn. (v.p. 1994-95), Greater Ketchikan C. of C. Republican. Roman Catholic. Home: 5351 Shoreline Dr N Ketchikan AK 99901-9032 Office: Naval Surface Warfare Ctr/ SEAFAC PO Box 5637 Ketchikan AK 99901

HARNICHER, DAVID JOHN, insurance company executive; b. Warren, Ohio, Sept. 3, 1950; s. John Paul and Irene Louise (Metro) H.; married, 1983. BS in Bus. Adminstrn., Ohio State U., 1973, MBA, 1979. Life underwriters tng. coun. fellow. Mem. sales staff Burroughs Corp., Columbus, Ohio, 1973-74; cost coord. Rockwell Internat. Corp., Columbus, Ohio, 1974-79; mgmt. cons. Vredenberg & Assocs., McLean, Va., 1979-82; developer The Harnicher Co., Houston, 1982-89; broker rep. The Paul Revere Ins. Co., Houston, 1989-91; gen. mgr. The Paul Revere Ins. Co., Salt Lake City, 1991—. Fellow Life Underwriters Tng. Coun.; mem. Nat. Assn. Health Underwriters, Nat. Assn. Life Underwriters. Office: Paul Revere Ins Co 349 S 200 E Ste 570 Salt Lake City UT 84111-2821

HARNSBERGER, THERESE COSCARELLI, librarian; b. Muskegon, Mich.; d. Charles and Julia (Borrell) Coscarelli; B.A. cum laude, Marymount Coll., 1952; M.L.S., U. So. Calif., 1953; postgrad. Rosary Coll., River Forest, Ill., 1955-56, U. Calif., Los Angeles Extension, 1960-61; m. Frederick Owen Harnsberger, Dec. 24, 1962; 1 son, Lindsey Carleton. Free-lance writer, 1950—; librarian San Marino (Calif.) High Sch., 1953-56; cataloger, cons. San Marino Hall, South Pasadena, Calif., 1956-61; librarian Los Angeles State Coll., 1956-59; librarian dist. library Covina-Valley Unified Sch. Dist., Covina, Calif., 1959-67; librarian Los Angeles Trade Tech. Coll., 1972—; med. librarian, tumor registrar Alhambra (Calif.) Community Hosp., 1975-79; tumor registrar Huntington Meml. Hosp., 1979—; pres., dir. Research Unltd., 1980—; free lance reporter Los Angeles' Best Bargains, 1981—; med. library cons., 1979—; reviewer various cookbooks, 1991—. Author numerous poems. Chmn. spiritual values com. Covina Coordinating Council, 1964-66; chmn. Neighborhood Watch, 1976—. Winner poetry contest Pasadena Star News, 1993. Mem. ALA, Internat. Women's Writing

Guild, Calif. Assn. Sch. Librarians (chmn. legis. com.), Covina Tchrs. Assn., AAUW (historian 1972-73), U. So. Calif. Grad. Sch. Libr. Sci. (life), Am. Nutrition Soc. (chpt. Newsletter chmn.), Nat. Tumor Registrars Assn., So. Calif. Tumor Registrars Assn., Med. Libr. Assn., So. Calif. Libr. Assn., So. Calif. Assn. Law Libr., Book Publicists So. Calif., Am. Fedn. Tchrs. (exec. bd. part-timers 1994, alt. exec. bd. local # 1521 coll. guild 1994—), Coll. Guild, Calif. Libr. Assn., Assn. Poetry Bibliographers, Faculty Assn. Calif. Community Colls., Immaculate Heart Coll. Alumnae Assn., Assistance League Pasadena, Loyola Marymount Alumnae Assn. (coord. 1986), Pi Lambda Theta. Author: (poetry) The Journal, 1982, To Julia: in Memoriam; contbr. articles to profl. jours., poems to newspapers. Office: 2809 W Hellman Ave Alhambra CA 91803-2737

HARO, MARIA-PAZ, Spanish language and culture educator; b. Valencia, Spain; came to U.S., 1965; d. Jose-Maria and Maria-Luisa (Sabater) H.; m. Joaquin Valdes, Dec. 20, 1965. Lic. Fil. y Letras, U. Valencia, Spain, 1963; PhD, U. Madrid, 1967. Prof. Spanish and chair fgn. langs. Lone Mountain Coll., San Francisco, 1966-78; prof. and dir. Spanish lang. program Stanford (Calif.) U., 1978—; prin. investigator Bay Area Fgn. Lang. Project, Stanford, 1990-94; cons. UNESCO, 1986-89, Ednl. Testing Svc., Princeton, N.J., 1992—, State Dept. Edn., Sacramento, 1988—. Co-author: (textbooks) Foundation Course in Spanish, 1978, Cada Vez Mejor, 1990. NEH fellow, Tulane U., New Orleans, 1975; Mellon Found. grantee, Rio de Janeiro, Brazil, 1985; recipient Walter Gores award for Excellence in Tchg., Stanford U., 1987. Mem. MLA (grantee 1993), Am. Coun. on Teaching of Fgn. Langs., Calif. Lang. Tchr. Assn., Fgn. Lang. Assn. No. Calif., Am. Assn. Fgn. Lang. Suprs., Asociación de doctores y licenciados españoles en Estados Unidos. Office: Stanford Univ Dept Spanish and Portuguese MC2014 Stanford CA 94305

HAROLD, FRANKLIN MARCEL, research scientist; b. Frankfurt Germany, Mar. 16, 1929; came to U.S., 1947; s. Walter Morton and Hermine (Reiss) H.; m. Ruth Laura Catsiff, Feb. 7, 1954; 1 dau., Lynn Stephanie. BS, CCNY, 1952; PhD, U. Calif.-Berkeley, 1955; D in Natural Scis. (hon.), U. Osnabrück, 1984. Various positions Nat. Jewish Ctr. for Immunology and Respiratory Medicine, Denver, 1959—, U. Colo. Med. Sch., Denver, 1963—; rsch. prof. Colo. State U., Ft. Collins, 1989—; vis. fellow Australian Nat. U., Canberra, 1975. Author: The Vital Force-A Study of Bioenergetics, 1986. Served with U.S. Army, 1955-57. Fulbright fellow, Teheran, 1969-70. Mem. Am. Soc. Biol. Chemists, Am. Soc. Microbiology. Home: 908 Edwards St Fort Collins CO 80524-3824 Office: Colorado State U Dept Biochemistry Fort Collins CO 80523-0001

HAROLD, RUTH LAURA, research biologist; b. N.Y.C., July 16, 1931; d. Oscar and Mae (Remstein) Catsiff; m. Franklin M. Harold, Feb. 7, 1954; 1 child, Stephanie L. BA, U. Ariz., 1952; MA, U. Calif., Berkeley, 1954. Various tech. rsch. positions U. Calif., Berkeley, 1954-56, Calif. Inst. Tech., Pasadena, 1957-59, U. Colo., Denver, 1959-61; rsch. biologist Nat. Jewish Hosp. and Rsch. Ctr., Denver, 1961-72, rsch. assoc., 1978-89; rsch. assoc. Colo. State U., Ft. Collins, 1989—. Editor Newsletter of the Zoosporic Fungi, Ft. Collins, 1992—; artist watercolor paintings, India ink wash drawings, bot. illustrations, 1988—; scientist-author 20 scholarly rsch. articles in peer-reviewed jours., 1956—. Precinct com. chair Dem. Party, Denver, 1972-74; del. Dem. State Conv., Denver, 1972, 74; mem., com. chair LWV, Denver, 1966-68. Mem. Am. Soc. Microbiology, Am. Mycological Soc., Guild of Natural Sci. Illustrators. Office: Colo State U Dept Biochemistry Fort Collins CO 80523

HAROUN, ANSAR M., forensic psychiatrist, educator; b. Pakistan, Nov. 29, 1947; m. Nasra Haroun, 1977. Student, U. London; MB, BChir, King Edward Med. Coll., 1975; M in Med. Sci. in Cmty. Medicine, U. Nottingham, Eng., 1979. Diplomate Am. Bd. Psychiatry and Neurology, Am. Bd. Child and Adolescent Psychiatry. Fellow in cmty. medicine U. Nottingham Med. Sch., 1976-79; med. intern resident physician in psychiatry Yale U. Sch. Medicine, 1980-84; fellow in psychiat. pub. health Yale U. Sch. Pub. Health, 1984-85; fellow in pediatric psychiatry Columbia U. Coll. Physicians and Surgeons, N.Y.C., 1985-87; forensic psychiatrist Superior Ct. Calif., San Diego, 1987—; asst. clin. prof. psychiatry U. Calif. Sch. Medicine, San Diego; adj. prof. U. San Diego Sch. Law. Author: Insomnia and Depression in General Practice, 1979, Clinical Guidelines for Involuntary Outpatient Treatment, 1990. Maj. M.C., USAR, 1984—. Recipient Ciba award Royal Soc. Medicine; Royal, Religious and Ancient Found. of Christ's Hosp. scholar, Roosevelt scholar. Fellow Royal Soc. Health; mem. Am. Acad. Psychiatry and Law (child psychiatry and law com.), Am. Psychiat. Assn., Am. Soc. Law and Medicine, Am. Coll. Utilization Rev. Physicians, Am. Coll. Forensic Psychiatry. Office: Superior Ct Calif Forenis Psychiatry Clinic County Courthouse Rm 1003 San Diego CA 92101-3814

HARPER, ANTHONY, counselor, singer; b. Clarksville, Tenn., Jan. 6, 1952; s. Hal L. and Kathryn A. (Reding) H.; m. Mary K. McGrane, July 1972 (div. Nov. 1974); 1 child, Amy; m. Mary J. Breshears. BA, USNY, 1984; MEd, Coll. Idaho, 1986; postgrad., Liberty U., Calif. Coast U., 1989—, Liberty U., Calif. Coast U. Tv switcher engr. KISU TV, Pocatello, Idaho, 1977-78, KIFI TV, Idaho Falls, Idaho, 1979; singer various locations, 1978—; founder, exec. dir., counselor Shiloh Counseling Ctr., Boise, Idaho, 1987—; guest spkr. in field. Author: (test and manual) Spiritual Relationship Scale, 1990. Republican. Office: PO Box 1829 Boise ID 83701-1829

HARPER, DONALD CALVIN, dean; b. Claresholm, Alta., Can., Oct. 31, 1942; s. William James and Effie Mabel (Slonaker) H.; m. Kathleen Ann Paton, May 18, 1968; children: Christopher Bradley, Angela Dawn. BA, U. Alta., Edmonton, 1963, MA, 1970. Rsch. asst. exec. coun. Province of Alta., 1966-67, rsch. asst. dept. of youth, 1967-69; instr. sociology Grande Prairie Regional Coll., Alta., 1969-71, registrar, 1971-74, registrar, dir. student svcs., 1974-79, dir. student and community svcs., 1979-80, instr. humanities and social scis., 1980-81, chairperson acad. devel., 1981-84, dean acad. and applied studies, 1984-93; mem. task force Worth Royal Com. Ednl. Planning, 1970-71; chairperson acad. coun. Gran Prairie Regional Coll., 1969-70, 78-80; mem. Alta Coun. Admissions & Transfer, 1974-77, 79-82, 89-92; chairperson com. Sr. Acad. Officers, Alta, 1990-92. Pres. Grande Prairie Little Theatre, 1978-80, 94-95, Crohn's and Colitis Found. of Can., G.P. chpt.; bd. dirs. Prairie Gallery, 1980-81, 84-86, other community bds.; regional dir. Alta. Fedn. Home and Sch. Assns., 1990-92; mem. Can. Program adv. com. Assn. Can. C.C., 1991-93. Home: 8517 100A St, Grande Prairie, AB Canada T8V 3C4

HARPER, GLORIA JANET, artist, educator; children: Dan Conyers, Jan Shriver. Student, Famous Artists Sch., 1967-69, 69-71; BA in Comml. Art, Portland C.c., 1981; postgrad., Valley View Art Sch., 1982-89, Carrizzo Art Sch., 1983-88, Holdens Portrait Sch., 1989; studied with Daniel Greene, 1989, postgrad. in paralegal studies. Cert. art educator. Artist, art instr. Art By Gloria, Pendleton, Oreg., 1980—; owner Art By Gloria Art Sch. and Gallery, Pendleton, 1991—; lectr., workshop presenter in field, 1980—. Paintings and prints included in various mags. Mem. NAFE, Water Color Soc. Am., Nat. Mus. Women in Arts, So. Career Inst. Profl. Legal Assts. (area rep.), Profl. Legal Assts., Pendleton C. of C. Home: PO Box 1734 Pendleton OR 97801-0570 Office: Art By Gloria 133 S Main St Pendleton OR 97801-2214

HARPER, JOSEPH STAFFORD, theater educator, performer; b. Washington, June 21, 1959; s. Joseph Garfield and Helen Jean (Wingfield) H.; m. Elizabeth Saxon Leach, June 23, 1990; 1 child, Samantha Elizabeth Leach. BFA, Howard U., 1982; MS in Ednl. Adminstrn., Pepperdine U., 1995. Instr. Children's Theatre Howard U., Washington, 1981-82; dir. drama St. Andrews Episcopal Sch., Bethesda, Md., 1982-85; chmn. performing arts Episcopal High Sch., Bellaire, Tex., assoc. arts coord., 1985-92; chmn. performing arts Rev. Canon Thomas G. Clarke Campbell Hall Sch., North Hollywood, Calif., 1993—, dir. of summer programs, 1994—. Mem. Internat. Thespian Soc., Theatre Edn. Assn., Ednl. Theatre Assn., Am. Alliance Theatre and Edn., So. Calif. Theatre Educators Assn. Home: 1411 N Brighton St Burbank CA 91506-1205 Office: Campbell Hall Sch 4533 Laurel Canyon Blvd North Hollywood CA 91607-4122

HARPER, KIMBALL TAYLOR, ecologist, educator; b. Oakley, Idaho, Feb. 15, 1931; s. John Mayo and Mary Ella (Overson) H.; m. Caroline Frances Stepp, June 7, 1958; children: Ruth L., James K., Gay A., Denise C., Karla D., Steven S.. BS, Brigham Young U., 1958, MS, 1960; PhD, U. Wis., 1963. Range technician U.S. Forest Svc., Moab and Moticello, Utah, 1957-58; range scientist U.S. Forest Svc., Ogden, Utah, 1958-59; rsch. asst. U. Wis., Madison, 1959-63; asst. prof., then assoc. prof. U. Utah, Salt Lake City, 1963-73; prof. Brigham Young U., Provo, Utah, 1973—, chmn. dept. botany and range sci., 1973-76; vis. scholar U. Calif., Berkeley, 1984-85; mem. Mono Lake com. NRC, Washington, 1986-87. Editor, co-author: Intermountain Biogeography, 1978, Ecological Impacts of Weather Modification, 1981, Natural History of the Colorado Plateau and Great Basin; mem. editorial bd. Great Basin Naturalist, 1977-87; contbr. numerous articles to profl. jours. Ward bishop LDS Ch., Spanish Fork, Utah, 1978-83. Served as cpl. U.S. Army, 1953-55, Korea. Grantee NSF, U.S. Forest Svc., U.S. Bur. Land Mgmt., U.S. Army., 1965—. Fellow AAAS; mem. Am. Bot. Soc., Ecol. Soc. Am. (editor, mem. editorial bd. jour. 1965-67, 1975-79), Soc. for Range Mgmt., Am. Inst. For Biol. Scis., Soc. for Study Evolution, Brit. Ecol. Soc., Phi Kappa Phi. Republican. Home: 410 S 300 E Spanish Fork UT 84660-2422 Office: Brigham Young U Dept Botany And Range Provo UT 84602

HARPER, RICHARD HENRY, film producer, director; b. San Jose, Calif., Sept. 15, 1950; s. Walter Henry and Priscilla Alden (Browne) H.; m. Ann Marie Morgan, June 19, 1976; children: Christine Ann, Paul Richard, James Richard. Show designer Walt Disney Imagineering, Glendale, Calif., 1971-76; motion picture producer, dir. Harper Films, Inc., La Canada, Calif., 1976—. Producer, dir. (films) Impressions de France, Disney World, Fla., 1982, Magic Carpet Round the World, Disneyland, Tokyo, 1983, American Journeys, Disneyland, Calif., 1985, Collecting American, Nat. Gallery Art, Washington, 1988, Hillwood Mus., Washington, 1989, Journey Into the 4th Dimension for Sanrio World, Journey Into Nature for Sanrio World, Japan, 1990, Masters of Illusion, Nat. Gallery of Art, Washington, 1992. Recipient more than 150 awards world-wide for outstanding motion picture prodn. including Silver trophy Cannes Internat. Film Festival, 2 Gold awards Internat. Festival of the Ams., 1981, 82, 14 Golden Eagle C.I.N.E. awards, 1977-92, Emmy award Nat. Acad. TV Arts and Scis., 1993. Mem. Acad. of Motion Picture Arts and Scis.

HARPER, RICHARD HILTON, marketing executive; b. North Vancouver, B.C., Can., Apr. 19, 1947; came to U.S., 1961; s. Robert Hilton and Gladys Ellen (Barker) H.; m. Jeani Marie Bevacqua, Nov. 2, 1968; children: Jodie Marie, Blake Hilton. Grad., Sales Tng. Inst., Seattle, 1971. Letter carrier U.S. Postal Svc., Seattle, 1970-72; sales rep. Lang Distbg. Co., Seattle, 1972-74; dist. mgr. K&L Distbrs., Inc., Bellevue, Wash., 1974-81; gen. mgr. Premium Distbrs., Inc., Seattle, 1981-83; pres. J.B.H., Inc., Edmonds, Wash., 1983—. Pres. bd. trustees Cmty. Foun., Edmonds, 1992—; pres. bd. dirs. Home Care Wash., Seattle, 1990-91; bd. advocates Clothes for Kids, Lynnwood, Wash., 1992—; organizer capital campaign Little Red Sch. House, Lynnwood, 1990, Pathways for Women, Mountlake Terrace, Wash., 1991; co-founder Snohomish County Cmty. Found., Edmonds, 1992; organizer The Neutral Zone, Mountlake Terrace, 1993. Staff sgt. USAF, 1966-70, Vietnam. Mem. Pacific N.W. Grantmakers Forum (membership com. 1992—).

HARPER, ROBERT LEVELL, pharmaceutical company executive; b. Wichita, Kans., Nov. 11, 1942; s. Cleo Levell and Mary Florence (Weaver) H.; m. Margaret Lucille Madden, Jan. 20, 1961 (div. 1980); children: Douglas Warren, Susan Denise; m. Maria Elain Davis, June 20, 1981; stepchildren: Laura Elaine Emery, Melissa MacAlpin Emery. Cert. med. rep., Sterling Mgmt. Inst. Sales rep. Dorsey Labs. div. Sandoz Pharms., Tulsa, 1967-70; mgr. key accounts Sandoz Pharms., Houston, 1970-72; div. mgr. Dorsey Pharms. div. Sandoz Pharms., Kansas City, Mo., 1972-85; mgr. govt. affairs Sandoz Pharms., Sacramento, 1985—; rotating mgr. Sandoz Pharms., East Hanover, N.J., 1985. Donor Kansas City Coll. Osteo. Medicine, 1973; co-founder first aid program state CAP, Oklahoma City, 1973; leader youth program YMCA, Johnson County, Mo., 1977-79; leader youth baseball Johnson County, 1976-79; del. Nat. Baseball Congress, Houston, 1971, 72, 73; mem. med. edn. for srs. SRx Regional Program, 1985—. With USAFR, 1960-64. Recipient appreciation award Calif. State Firemen's Assn., Sacramento, 1987. Mem. Nat. Assn. Legis. Svcs., Calif. Medication Edn. Coalition, Calif. Mfrs. Assn., Pharm. Mfrs. Assn., Calif. Derby. Home: 11370 Tunnel Hill Way Gold River CA 95670-7240

HARPER, SHARYNE RAE, social services administrator; b. Crescent City, Calif., Nov. 10, 1946; d. Joseph Fairchilds Hostler and Sylvia (Stewart) White; m. Richard J. Harper; children: Michele L.S. Vagle, Lisa L.R. Irvine. AA with highest honors, Coll. of Redwoods, 1974; BS, Humboldt State U., 1976, MBA, 1992. Tax preparer, checker H&R Block, Inc., Eureka, Calif., 1971-73; tax mgr., preparer EBS Tax Svc., Eureka, 1973-74; bookkeeper United Indian Health Svcs., Inc., Trinidad, Calif., 1973-76, fiscal officer, 1976-82, fiscal officer, asst. dir., 1982-91, dep. dir., 1991—. Election judge County of Humboldt, Eureka, 1976—; server No. Calif. Indian Devel. Coun., Eureka, 1973—. Mem. Calif. Employer Coun. (treas. 1992-94), Employer Adv. Coun. (sec. 1987-93, reg. v.p. 1994—, pres. 1993—), Am. Mgmt. Assn., Soc. for Human Resource Mgrs., North Coast Human Resource Coun. Office: United Indian Health Svcs Ma-We-Mor View Ln Trinidad CA 95570

HARPER, VERA JEAN, convalescent home activity director, music therapist; b. Spokane, Wash., Apr. 20, 1925; d. James Young Wellington and Lucia Annie (Bisbee) Wilson; m. Glenn F. Harper, June 26, 1946 (div. 1982); children: David, Ruth Ann. Student, Wash. State U., 1944-46. Storekeeper Naval Supply Depot, Spokane, 1943-45; libr. attendant Wash. State U., Pullman, 1945-52; sec. Pullman (Wash.) Pub. Schs., 1952-57; piano tchr. Pullman, 1960-62, Des Moines, Wash., 1965—; activity coord. Midway Manor Convalescent, Des Moines, 1971—. Mem. com. for small area of King County annexed to Des Moines; mem. choir, deacon Presbyn. Ch. Recipient Appreciation award Friend to Friend Greater Seattle, Des Moines, 1985; named to Hall of Fame, Wash. Health Care Assn., 1993. Mem. Nat. Cert. Coun. Activity Profls. (cert. activity dir., bd. dirs. 1991—), Nat. Assn. Activity Profls. (regional state contact 1989-90, conv. co-chmn. 1987-90), Wash. State Assn. Activity Profls. (pres. 1987-89, Activity Dir. of Yr. 1991), Kiwanis (sec., treas. Kiwanian of Yr. 1991-92). Home: 23449 25th Ave S Des Moines WA 98198-8717

HARPSTER, ROBERT EUGENE, engineering geologist; b. Olney, Ill., Sept. 25, 1930; s. Christian Edward and Margaret (Tatum) H.; m. Carol Ann Dewald, Nov. 25, 1977; step-children: Larry Britt, Charla Britt. BS, Beloit Coll., 1952; MA, U. Tex., 1957. Registered geologist Calif.; cert. engring. geologist Calif., cert. quality assurance lead auditor. Petroleum geologist Geo Svc. Co., Abilene, Tex., 1952; engring. soil instr. Corp Engrs., Ft. Belvoir, Va., 1952-54; project geologist Bechtel Corp., Vernon, Calif., 1956-57; sr. project engr. geologist dept. water resources State Calif., Sacramento, 1957-73; sr. project engr. geologist Woodward-Clyde Cons., San Francisco, 1973-80, mgr. and implementator for internat. engring. projects, v.p. quality assurance/applied sci., 1980-88; quality assurance, organizer and implementor Woodward-Cyde Coms., Las Vegas, Nev., 1988-93; sr. quality assurance specialist, design rev. MACTEC, CER/SAIC, Las Vegas, Nev., 1993—; mem. tech. rev. bds. U.S. Gov. and pvt. industries, San Francisco, 1972—; instr. Antelope Community Coll., Lancaster, Calif., 1969-72; del. People to People, USSR, 1991. Author: Selected Clays used for Dam/Fills Construction, 1979, Methods of Investigating Faults, 1979. coach swimming Antelope Valley YMCA, Lancaster, 1969-72. Sgt. U.S. Army, 1952-54. Fellow Geological Soc. Am., Assn. Engring. Geologist (mem. chmn., v.p. 1961-63, vice chmn. 1959-62), Am. Soc. Civil Engrs., Am. Soc. for Quality Control, Earthquake Engr. Rsch. Inst., Interanl Clay Mineral Soc. Home: 5735 Buena Vista Ave Oakland CA 94618-2120 Office: CER Corp Ste 664 Ste 656 101 Convention Ctr Las Vegas NV 89109

HARRELL, GARY PAUL, lawyer; b. Texas City, Tex., July 8, 1952; s. James Eugene Jr. and Mary Alice (Worley) H.; m. Leigh Evans, May 27, 1978. BS, U. Tex., 1977, MA, 1979; cert. mgmt. healthcare facilities, UCLA, 1984; JD cum laude, Lewis & Clark Coll., 1991. Bar: Oreg. 1991, U.S. Dist. Ct. (federal dist.) Oreg. 1991; diplomate Am. Coll. Healthcare Execs. Staff/charge nurse Healthcare Facilties, Austin, Tex., 1972-78; gen. mgr. Nursing Support Svcs., Austin, 1978-80; dir. edn. Downey (Calif.) Cmty. Hosp., 1980-84; v.p. patient care Grande Ronde Hosp., La Grande, Oreg., 1984-88; assoc. Lane Powell Spears Lubersky, Portland, Oreg., 1990-94; ptnr. Harrell & Nester, Portland, 1994—; adj. prof., asst. prof. Calif. State U., Long Beach, 1980-84; pres. Oreg. State Bd. Nursing, Portland, 1987-90. With USNR, 1970-74. Recipient Am. Jurisprudence award, 1989. Mem. Oreg. Assn. Nurse Attys. (treas., past. pres.), Healthcare Fin. Mgmt. Assn. (Oreg. chpt., bd. dirs. 1995—). Office: Harrell & Nester 140 SW Arthur St Ste 200 Portland OR 97201-4766

HARRELL, LYNN MORRIS, cellist; b. N.Y.C., Jan. 30, 1944; s. Mack and Marjorie (Fulton) H.; m. Linda Blandford, Sept. 7, 1976. Student, Juilliard Sch. Music, Curtis Inst. Music. Piatigorsky prof. cello U. So. Calif., L.A., 1987-93; prof. internat. cello studies Royal Acad. Music, London, 1988-93, prin., 1993-95; artistic dir. L.A. Philharm. Inst., 1988-91. Prin. cellist, Cleve. Orch., 1963-71; debut Carnegie Hall, N.Y.C., 1963 ; soloist with maj. orchs. U.S. and Europe: rec. artist London/Decca Records, EMI/Angel, RCA, CBS, Deutsche Gramaphon. Recipient 1st Piatigorsky award, Grammy award, 1981, 87, 88; co-recipient 1st Avery Fisher award, 1975. Office: care IMG 22 E 71st St New York NY 10021-4911

HARRICK, JIM, university athletic coach. Head coach NCAA Divsn. 1A basketball, ranked #4 UCLA Bruins, 1992, head coach NCAA Divsn. 1A basketball champions, 1995. Office: UCLA 405 Hilgard Ave Los Angeles CA 90024-1301*

HARRIETT, JUDY ANNE, medical equipment company executive; b. Walterboro, S.C., July 22, 1960; d. Billy Lee and Loretta (Rahn) H. BS in Agrl. Bus./Econs., Clemson U., 1982. Sales rep. III Monsanto Corp., Atlanta, 1982-85; surg. stapling rep. Ethicon, Inc., Johnson & Johnson Corp., Somerville, N.J., 1985-87; dist. sales mgr. Imed Corp., San Diego, 1987—, regional tng. coord., 1992-93; mem. pres. adv. panel, 1991, 92, mem. pres. club, 1993. Author: Time and Territory Management, 1984. Com. mem. Multiple Sclerosis Fund Raising Benefit, Knoxville, Tenn., 1988, 89, Women's Ctr. Benefit, Knoxville, 1990. Mem. NAFE. Republican. Home: 21620 Mayhew Rd Mooresville NC 28115-8661 Office: Imed Corp 9775 Businesspark Ave San Diego CA 92131-1642

HARRIGAN, NICHOLAS PAUL, military officer; b. Santa Monica, Calif., Aug. 27, 1969; s. Michael John and Kathleen Karyl (Krock) H. BSME, Carnegie Mellon U., 1991. Commd. USN, advanced through grades to lt. j.g., 1991-93; instr. Carnegie Mellon U. Naval ROTC, Pitts., 1991; student NFO CTW-6, Pensacola, Fla., 1991-93; radar intercept officer VF-2 VF-124, San Diego, Calif., 1993—.

HARRIMAN, JOHN HOWLAND, lawyer; b. Buffalo, Apr. 14, 1920; s. Lewis Gildersleeve and Grace (Bastine) H.; m. Barbara Ann Brunmark, June 12, 1943; children—Walter Brunmark, Constance Bastine, John Howland. A.B. summa cum laude, Dartmouth, 1942; J.D., Stanford U., 1949. Bar: Calif. 1949. Assoc. firm Lawler, Felix & Hall, Los Angeles, 1949-55; asst. v.p., then v.p. Security Pacific Nat. Bank, Los Angeles, 1955-72; sr. v.p. Security Pacific Nat. Bank, 1972-85; of counsel Argue Freston Pearson Harbison & Myers, 1985-86; sec. Security Pacific Corp., 1971-85; dir. Master Metal Works. Mem. L.A. adv. coun. Episcopal Ch. Found., 1977-79; mem. Republican Assocs., 1951—, trustee, 1962-72; mem. Calif. Rep. Central Com., 1956-69, 81—, exec. com., 1960-62, 81-84; mem. L.A. County Rep. Central Com., 1958-70, exec. com., 1960-62, vice chmn., 1962; chmn. Calif. 15th Congl. Dist. Rep. Central Com., 1960-62, Calif. 30th Congl. Dist. Rep. Central Com., 1962; treas. United Rep. Fin. Com. L.A. County, 1969-70; chmn. L.A. County Reagan-Bush campaign, 1980, co-chmn., 1984; exec. dir. Calif. Rep. Party, 1985-86. With USAAF, 1943-46. Mem. Am. Bar Assn., Am. Soc. Corp. Secs. (pres. Los Angeles region 1970-71), State Bar Calif., Los Angeles Bar Assn., Town Hall Los Angeles, Phi Beta Kappa, Theta Delta Chi, Phi Alpha Delta. Clubs: Beach (Santa Monica, Calif.); California (Los Angeles); Lincoln, Breakfast Panel (pres. 1970-71).

HARRIMAN, THOMAS JARVIS, JR., lawyer; b. Buffalo, N.Y., Apr. 29, 1946; s. Thomas Jarvis and Eleanor Harrington (Levet) H.; m. Janice Kathleen King, July 7, 1970. Student, Swarthmore Coll., 1963-64; AB, U. Calif., Berkeley, 1971, JD, 1974. Bar: Calif. 1974, Am. Samoa, 1978. Sr. atty. Calif. Supreme Ct., San Francisco, 1975-78; asst. pub. defender Office Pub. Defender, Pago Pago, Am. Samoa, 1979-81; founder, gen. ptnr. Law Offices of Tom Harriman, Sebastopol, Calif., 1981—. Editor: (law rev.) Samoan Pacific Law Jour., 1978-79; author: (mag.) The New Pacific, 1979-81. Cons. Legislature Am. Samoa, Pago Pago, 1978-81. With S.C., U.S. Army, 1967-68, Vietnam. Mem. Western Sonoma County Hist. Soc. (pres. 1994—). Office: Law Offices Tom Harriman 5462 Mcfarlane Rd Sebastopol CA 95472

HARRINGTON, CHARLES LEE, judge, retired; b. Berkeley, Calif., Feb. 5, 1932; s. Harris Clifford and Thelma Aileen (Lee) Harrington; m. Febe Forster, Dec. 29, 1956; children: Kathleen Harrington Guerra, Aileen Harrington Parsons, Jane Harrington Erdiakoff. BSBA, U. Calif., Berkeley, 1953; JD, U. Calif., San Francisco, 1963. Bar: N.Mex., Calif. Pvt. practice Albuquerque and Roswell, N.Mex., 1964-68; dep. county counsel Alameda County Counsel's Office, Oakland, Calif., 1969-86; ct. commr./judge pro tem Alameda County Superior Ct., Oakland, 1986-94; mem. bioethics com. Alameda-Contra Costa Med. Assn., Oakland; panelist on continuing edn. of the Bar, Berkeley, calif., 1972-80; panelist The Rutter Group, Encino, Calif., 1989. Bd. dirs. pres. Moraga (Calif.) Hist. Soc., 1975-78; bd. dirs. Big C Soc., Berkeley, 1979-83; bd. dirs., v.p., sec. Friends of Cal Crew, Berkeley, Calif., 1987—; bd. dirs. Oakland (Calif.) Strokes, 1975-83. 1st lt. USAF, 1954-58; lt. col. USAF Res., retired 1984. Decorated 2 Air Force Commendation medals. Mem. Friends of Cal Crew (bd. dirs., sec. 1987—), Moraga Hist. Soc. (pres. 1975—), Alameda County Bar Assn., State Bar of N.Mex., Calif. State Bar. Republican. Home: 105 La Quinta St Moraga CA 94556-1024 Office: PO Box 185 Moraga CA 94556-0185

HARRINGTON, GLENN LEWIS, insurance company executive; b. Fitchburg, Mass., Dec. 18, 1942; s. Lewis Lowe and Eleanor Frances (Mansfield) H.; m. Marcia Anne Browning, Sept. 3, 1971. Ed., Gordon Coll., 1960-63, Suffolk U., 1963-64. Underwriter Hartford Life Ins. Co., Boston, 1964-66; mktg. mgr. Dentsply Internat., York, Pa., 1966-70; asst. v.p. mktg. Family Life Ins. Co., Seattle, 1971-88; v.p. mktg. Family Life and Merrill Lynch Life Ins. Cos., Seattle, 1988—. V.p. , trustee Seattle Opera, mem. planned giving com. Seattle Art Mus. Mem. Royal Philatelic Soc., Rainier Club. Home: PO Box 99689 Seattle WA 98199-0689 Office: Merrill Lynch Life Ins Co Seattle WA 98101

HARRINGTON, JOHN LEONARD, JR., hospital administrator; b. Pitts., Feb. 1, 1955; s. John Leonard and Marilyn (Rice) H.; m. Krisann Jacobs, May 31, 1980 (div. July 1987); m. Coleen Christine Attanucci, Dec. 31, 1988; children: Jennifer Lynne, Zachary Scott Dyer, Heather Leigh. BS magna cum laude, U. Pitts., 1977, MPH, 1980. Adminstrv. resident Phoenix Gen. Hosp., 1979-80, asst. v.p., 1980-83; asst. adminstr. Good Samaritan Med. Ctr., 1983-85, assoc. adminstr., 1985-89; assoc. adminstr. Thunderbird Samaritan Med. Ctr., Glendale, Ariz., 1989-91; ctr. adminstr. Cigna Healthplan of Ariz., 1991—. Mem. Ariz. Sr. Olympics Steering Com., Phoenix, 1983-91, chmn., 1988-89, bd. dirs. 1989-90; mem. planning com. of bd. YMCA, Phoenix, 1988-89. Mem. Health Adminstrs. Forum Ariz. (sec.-treas. 1983, pres. 1984), Am. Coll. Healthcare Execs. (regents adv. com. 1984—, Fache fellow, 1989), Ariz. Hosp. Assn. Republican. Roman Catholic. Home: 433 E Tierra Buena Ln Phoenix AZ 85022-3034 Office: Cigna Healthplan 755 E Mcdowell Rd Phoenix AZ 85006-2519

HARRINGTON, MARY EVELINA PAULSON (POLLY HARRINGTON), religious journalist, writer, educator; b. Chgo.; d. Henry Thomas and Evelina (Belden) Paulson; m. Gordon Keith Harrington, Sept. 7, 1957; children: Jonathan Henry, Charles Scranton. BA, Oberlin Coll., 1946; postgrad., Northwestern U., Evanston, Ill., Chgo., 1946-49, Weber State U., Ogden, Utah, 1970s, 80s; MA, U. Chgo.-Chgo. Theol. Sem., 1956. Publicist Nat. Coun. Chs., N.Y.C., 1950-51; mem. press staff 2d assembly World Coun. Chs., Evanston, Chgo., 1954; mgr. Midwest Office Communication, United Ch. of Christ, Chgo., 1955-59; staff writer United Ch. Herald, N.Y.C., St. Louis, 1959-61; affiliate missionary to Asia, United Ch. Bd. for World Ministries, N.Y.C., 1978-79; freelance writer and lectr., 1961—; corr. Religious News Svc., 1962—; prin. lectr. Women & Family Life in Asia series to numerous librs., Utah, 1981, 81-82; pub. rels. coord. Utah Energy

Conservation/Energy Mgmt. Program, 1984-85; tchr. writing Ogden Community Schs., 1985-89; adj. instr. writing for publs. Weber State U., 1986—; instr. Acad. Lifelong Learning, Ogden, 1992—, Eccles Community Art Ctr., Ogden, 1993—; dir. communication Shared Ministry, Salt Lake City, 1983—; chmn. communication Intermountain Conf., Rocky Mountain Conf., Utah Assn. United Ch. of Christ, 1970-78, 82—, Ind. Coun. Chs., 1960-63; chmn. communication Ch. Women United Utah, 1974-78, Ogden rep., 1980—. Editor: Sunshine and Moonscapes: An Anthology of Essays, Poems, Short Stories, 1994; contbr. numerous articles and essays to religious and other publs. Pres. T.O. Smith Sch. PTA, 1976-78, Ogden City Coun. PTA, 83-85; assoc. dir. Region II, Utah PTA, Salt Lake City, 1981-83, mem. State Edn. Commn., 1982-87; chmn. state internat. hospitality and aid Utah Fedn. Women's Clubs, 1982-86, v.p. Ogden dist., 1990-92, pres. Ogden dist., 1992—; trustee Family Counseling Svc. No. Utah, Ogden, 1983—; Utah rep. to nat. bd. Challenger Films, Inc., 1986—; state pres. Rocky Mountain Conf. Women in Mission, United Ch. of Christ, 1974-77, sec., 1981-84, vice moderator Utah Assn., 1992-94. Recipient Ecumenical Svc. citation Ind. Coun. Chs., 1962, Outstanding Local Pres. award Utah PTA, 1978, Outstanding Latchkey Child Project award, 1985, Cmty. Svc. award City of Ogden, 1980, 81, 82, Celebration of Gifts of Lay Woman Nat. award United Ch. of Christ, 1987, Excellence in the Arts in Art Edn. award Ogden City Arts Commn., 1993, Spirit of Am. Woman in Arts and Humanities award Your Cmty. Connection, Ogden, 1994; Utah Endowment for Humanities grantee, 1981, 81-82. Mem. Nat. League Am. Penwomen (chmn. Utah conv. 1973, 11 awards for articles and essays 1987-95, 1st pl. news award 1992), AAUW (state edn. rep. 1982-86). Democrat. Home and Office: 722 Boughton St Ogden UT 84403-1152

HARRINGTON, MATTHEW JEROME, public relations company executive; b. Boston, May 25, 1962; s. John Michael and Ellen Patricia (White) H.; m. Elizabeth Ann Abell, Aug. 16, 1986; children: Elizabeth Phelps, Lauren Shippen. BA, Denison U., 1984. Account exec. Daniel J. Edelman Inc., N.Y.C., 1984-85; sr. account exec. R.C. Auletta Inc., N.Y.C., 1985-87; v.p. Dewe Rogerson Inc., N.Y.C., 1987-91; v.p., dir. investor rels. Edelman Pub. Rels. Worldwide, N.Y.C., 1991-93; sr. v.p. fin. svcs. Edelman Publ Rels. Worldwide, San Francisco, 1993—. Fellow Nat. Investor Rels. Inst.; mem. Brit.-Am. C. of C., Pub. Rels. Soc. Am., Univ. Glee Club N.Y.C. Democrat. Roman Catholic. Office: Edelman Pub Rels Worldwide 350 California St San Francisco CA 94104-1402

HARRINGTON, WALTER HOWARD, JR., judge; b. San Francisco, Aug. 14, 1926; s. Walter Howard and Doris Ellen (Daniels) H.; B.S., Stanford, 1947; J.D., Hastings Coll., U. Calif., 1952; m. Barbara Bryant, June 1952 (div. 1973); children: Stacey Doreen, Sara Duval; m. 2d, Hertha Bahrs, Sept. 1974. Admitted to Calif. bar, 1953; dep. legislative counsel State of Calif., Sacramento, 1953-54, 55; mem. firm Walner & Harrington, Sacramento, 1954; dep. dist. atty. San Mateo County, Redwood City, Calif., 1955-62; pvt. practice in Redwood City, 1962-84; judge San Mateo County Mcpl. Ct., 1984-90, Superior Ct., 1990—. Chmn., San Mateo County Criminal Justice Council, 1971-76, San Mateo County Adult Correctional Facilities Com., 1969-71; pro tem referee San Mateo County Juvenile Ct., 1967-72. Served as ensign USNR, 1944-46. Mem. San Mateo County Bar Assn. (pres. 1969, editor publs. 1964-74), State Bar Calif. (editorial bd. 1968-81, vice chmn. 1969, 74-75, chmn., editor 1975-76), San Mateo County Legal Aid Soc. (pres. 1971-72), Order of Coif, Delta Theta Phi. Republican. Episcopalian. Office: Hall of Justice 401 Marshall St Redwood City CA 94063-1636

HARRINGTON-LLOYD, JEANNE LEIGH, interior designer; b. L.A.; d. Peter Valentine and Avis Lorraine (Brown) Harrington; m. James Wilkinson, Dec. 17, 1966 (div. Mar. 1976); m. David Lloyd, Nov. 27, 1985. BS in Psychology, U. Utah, 1984; cert., Salt Lake Sch. Interior Design, 1985; MS in Mgmt., Marylhurst Coll., 1990. With Mary Webb-Davis Agy., L.A., 1970; model, actress McCarty Agy., Salt Lake City, 1983-85; contract designer Innerspace Design, Salt Lake City, 1985-89; space planning and utilization mgr. U.S. Bancorp, Portland, Oreg., 1991—. Mem. Internat. Facilities Mgmt. Assn. Democrat. Home: 4580 SW Natchez Ct Tualatin OR 97062-8769

HARRIS, APRIL LEE (APRIL LEE HILL), higher education public relations professional; b. Defiance, Ohio, Sept. 18, 1953; d. James Robert and Betty Jeanne (George) Hill; m. James Edward Harris, May 27, 1978; 1 child, James Richard. BS, Bowling Green State U., 1975. Writer Ohio Dept. Econ. & Community Devel., Columbus, 1975-77; coord. alumni involvement programs Office Devel. and Alumni Affairs Bowling Green (Ohio) State U., 1977-80, dir. spl. svcs., 1980-84, assoc. dir. devel. for pub. rels., 1984-86; health communicator Baylor Coll. of Medicine, Tex. Med. Ctr., Houston, 1986-91; prin. Harris Comms., Logan, Utah, 1993—; adj. prof. comm. Utah State U., 1994—, devel. officer Coll. Humanities, Arts & Social Scis., 1995—; publ. Events newsletter for spl. events planners in edn., 1993—; speaker various groups, schs. and orgns. Author: Special Events: Planning for Success, 1988, Raising Money and Cultivating Donors through Special Events, 1991; contbr. chpt. to Library Development. Recipient nat. silver medal Coun. Advancement and Support of Edn., 1989, Ellis media award Am. Heart Assn., 1991, gold excalibur award Pub. Rels. Soc. Am., 1992. Republican. Office: Harris Communications PO Box 3311 Logan UT 84323-3311

HARRIS, BARBARA HULL (MRS. F. CHANDLER HARRIS), social agency administrator; b. L.A., Nov. 1, 1921; d. Hamilton and Marion (Eimers) Baird; m. F. Chandler Harris, Aug. 10, 1946; children: Victoria, Randolph Boyd. Pres., Victoria Originals, 1955-62. Student, UCLA, 1939-41, 45-47. Ptnr.J.B. Assocs., cons., 1971-73; statewide dir. vols. Children's Home Soc. Calif., 1971-75. L.A. County Heart Sunday chmn. L.A. County Heart Assn., 1965, bd. dirs., 1966-69; mem. exec. com. Hollywood Bowl Vols., 1966-84, chmn. vols., 1971, 75; chmn. Coll. Alumni of Assistance League, 1962; mem. exec. com. Assistance League So. Calif., 1964-71, 72-80, 83-89, pres., 1976-80; bd. dirs. Nat. Charity League, L.A., 1965-69, 75, sec., 1967, 3d v.p., 1968; ways and means chmn., dir. L.A. Am. Horse Show, 1969; dir. Coronet Debutante Ball, 1968, ball bd. chmn., 1969-70, 75, 84, mem. ball bd., 1969—; pres. Hollywood Bowl Patroness com., 1976; v.p. Irving Walker aux. Travelers Aid, 1976, 79, pres., 1988-89; pres. So. Calif. alumni council Alpha Phi, 1961, fin. adviser to chpts. U. So. Calif., 1961-72, UCLA, 1965-72; benefit chmn. Gold Shield, 1969, 1st v.p., 1970-72; chmn. Golden Thimble III Needlework Exhbn., Hosp. of Good Samaritan, 1975; bd. dirs. UCLA Affiliates, 1976-78, KCET Women's Council, 1979-83, Region V United Way, 1980-83; pres. Jr. Philharmonic Com., 1981-82; bd. dirs. L.A. Founder chpt. Achievement Rewards for Coll. Scientists, 1980-91, pres., 1984-85; pres. L.A. County chpt. Freedom Found. of Valley Forge. Recipient Outstanding Svc. award L.A. County Heart Assn., 1965, Outstanding Alumna Ivy award Alpha Phi, 1969, Outstanding Alumni award for community service UCLA, 1978, Mannequin's Eve award, 1980, Outstanding Bd. Mem. of Yr. award Assistance League of So. Calif., 1989-90. Mem. Hollywood C. of C. (dir. 1980-81). Home: 7774 Skyhill Dr Los Angeles CA 90068-1232

HARRIS, BENJAMIN KEITH, rheumatologist; b. Stambaugh, Mich., Dec. 24, 1937; s. Edward and Dorothy M. Harris; m. Janis Lee Finkleman, May 24, 1985; children: Eric, Jason, Jay, Jamie, Jill. BA with highest distinction, Northwestern U., 1959; MD cum laude, Yale U., 1963. Diplomate Am. Bd. Internal Medicine (internal medicine and rheumatology). Intern Univ. Hosps. Cleve., 1963-64, resident in internal medicine, 1966-68, fellow in rheumatology, 1968-70; pvt. practice Phoenix, 1970—; rheumatology sect. chief Good Samaritan Med. Ctr., Phoenix, 1973-80, St. Joseph's Hosp. and Med. Ctr., Phoenix, 1974—; clin. lectr. internal medicine U. Ariz. Coll. Medicine, Tucson, 1986—. Bd. dirs. Phoenix Chamber Music Soc., 1976-86, Greater Phoenix chpt., Austic Soc. Am., 1973-76, Ctrl. Ariz. chpt., Arthritis Found., 1973—. Capt. M.C., 1964-66. Recipient Nat. Vol. Svc. citation Arthritis Found., 1978. Fellow ACP, Am. Coll. Rheumatology (network physician, com. rheumatologic care); mem. Phi Beta Kappa. Republican. Jewish. Office: Arthritis Specialists Ariz 1300 N 12th St Ste 304 Phoenix AZ 85006-2813

HARRIS, BOB, investment company executive; b. 1948. MBA, U. Calif., Berkeley, 1970. With Alex Brown & Sons, San Francisco, 1970-89; gen. ptnr. Harris Unterberg, San Francisco, 1989—. Office: Harris Unterberg 275 Battery St Ste 2980 San Francisco CA 94111-3339*

HARRIS, CHRISTIE LUCY, author; b. Newark, Nov. 21, 1907; d. Edward and Matilda (Christie) Irwin; m. Thomas A. Harris, Feb. 13, 1932; children: Michael, Moira, Sheilagh, Brian, Gerald. Tchrs. cert., Provincial Normal Sch., Vancouver, B.C., Can., 1925. Tchr. B.C., 1925-32; free-lance scriptwriter Canadian Broadcasting Corp. radio, 1936-63; women's editor B.C. News Weekly, Abbotsford, 1951-57. Author: Raven's Cry, 1966, Mouse Woman books (3), 1976, 77, 79, The Trouble With Princesses, 1980, Something Weird Is Going On, 1994, others. Decorated Order of Can., 1981; recipient Can. Book of Yr. medal for Children's book, 1967, 77; Can. Council Children's Lit. prize, 1981. Mem. Writers' Union Can. (life). Address: 430 Arnold Ave, Victoria, BC Canada V8S 3M2

HARRIS, CLAUDE, fire department chief. Fire chief Seattle Fire Dept. Office: Seattle Fire Dept Office of the Chief 301 2nd Ave S Seattle WA 98104-2618

HARRIS, CYNTHIA VIOLA, educational administrator; management consultant; b. San Francisco, Aug. 18, 1948; d. Gilbert and Mary Lee (Barnes) H. BA in Speech, San Francisco State U., 1970, MA in Counseling, 1975; EdD, Nova U., 1987. U. Cert. tchr., adminstr., Calif. Tchr. Martin L. King Elem. Sch., Oakland, Calif., 1971-74; teaching v.p., Peratta Year Round Sch., Oakland, 1974-80, prin., 1980-86, coordinator staff devel., 1986-90, dir. staff devel., 1990-91, coord. recruitment 1991—, asst. coord. to supt. community, parents and bus. partnerships, 1992—; part-time mgmt. cons. year-round educ., leadership; guest lectr. Mills Coll., LaVerne U; coord. Community, Parents and Bus. Partnership. Bd. dirs. Wiley Manuel Law Found., Charles Harrison Mason Scholarships; chair minority caucus New Oakland Com. Nominated Outstanding Woman of Am., Alpha Kappa Alpha, 1981; recipient Capwell's Networker award, 1985; named Outstanding Youth Leader, Nat. Bus. and Profl. Bd., 1981. Mem. Nat. Assn. Female Execs., Nat. Assn. Prins., United Adminstrs. Oakland, Alliance Black Educators, Black Summit (internat. enrollment mgr.), Glamor Working Women's Panel, Phi Delta Kappa. Democrat. Mem. Pentecostal Ch. Club: Coalition of 100 Black Women. Author: (teaching manual) All about Us, 1980.

HARRIS, DALE RAY, lawyer; b. Crab Orchard, Ill., May 11, 1937; s. Ray B. and Aurelia M. (Davis) H.; m. Toni K. Shapkoff, June 26, 1960; children: Kristen Dee, Julie Diane. BA in Math., U. Colo., 1959; LLB, Harvard U., 1962. Bar: Colo. 1962, U.S. Dist. Ct. Colo. 1962, U.S. Ct. Appeals (10th cir.) 1962, U.S. Supreme Ct. 1981. Assoc. Davis, Graham & Stubbs, Denver, 1962-67, ptnr., 1967—, chmn. mgmt. com., 1982-85; spkr., instr. various antitrust seminars; bd. dirs. Lend-A-Lawyer, Inc., 1989-94. Mem. campaign cabinet Mile High United Way, 1986-87, chmn., atty. adv. com., 1988, sec., legal counsel, trustee, mem. exec. com. 1989-94; trustee The Spaceship Earth Fund, 1986-89; trustee, Legal Aid Found. Colo., 1989-95; mem. devel. coun. U. Colo. Arts & Scis. dept., 1985-93; area chmn. law sch. fund Harvard U., 1978-81; bd. dirs. Colo. Judicial Inst., 1994—; steering com. Youth-At-Work, 1994, School-To-Work, 1995—. With USAR, 1962-68. Fellow Am. Bar Found.; mem. ABA (antitrust and litigation sects.), Colo. Bar Found., Colo. Bar Assn. (chmn. antitrust com. 1980-84; coun. corp. banking and bus. law sect. 1978-83, bd. govs. 1991-95, exec. com. 1993-94), Denver Bar Assn. (chmn. Centennial Com. 1990-91, pres.-elect 1992-93, pres. 1993-94, bd. trustees 1992-95), Colo. Assn. Corp. Counsel (pres. 1973-74), Denver Law Club (pres. 1976-77), The Two Percent Club (exec. com., 1994—), Citizens Against Amendment 12 Com. (exec. com. 1994), Phi Beta Kappa, Univ. Club, Union League Club (Chgo.), Rotary (Denver). Home: 2032 Bellaire St Denver CO 80207-3722 Office: Davis Graham & Stubbs 370 17th St PO Box 185 Denver CO 80201

HARRIS, DARRYL WAYNE, publishing executive; b. Emmett, Idaho, July 29, 1941; s. Reed Ingval and Evelyn Faye (Wengreen) H.; m. Christine Sorenson, Sept. 10, 1965; children: Charles Reed, Michael Wayne, Jason Darryl, Stephanie, Ryan Joseph. B.A., Brigham Young U., 1966. Staff writer Deseret News, Salt Lake City, 1965, Post-Register, Idaho Falls, 1966-67; tech. editor Idaho Nuclear Corp., Idaho Falls, 1967-68; account exec. David W. Evans & Assos. Advt., Salt Lake City, 1968-71; pres. Harris Pub., Inc., Idaho Falls, 1971—; pub. Potato Grower of Idaho mag., 1972—, Snowmobile West mag., 1974—, Sugar Producer mag., 1974—, Blue Ribbon mag., 1987-90; Modstock mag., 1992—; pub. SnowAction mag., 1987—, Western Guide to Snowmobiling, 1988—, Houseboat Mag., 1990—, Pontoon and Deck Boat Mag., 1995—. Campaign mgr. George Hansen for Congress Com., 1974, 76; campaign chmn. Mel Richardson for Congress Com., 1986; 1st counselor to pres. Korean Mission, Ch. Jesus Christ of Latter-day Saints, Seoul, Korea, 1963, area public communications dir., Eastern Idaho, 1976-86; High Priest, LDS Ch., 1987-91, high coun. Idaho Falls Ammon Stake, 1987-91; founder Blue Ribbon Coalition, 1987; v.p. Teton Peaks Council Boy Scouts Am., 1987-92; publicity chmn. Upper Snake River Scout Encampment, 1988; founder , pres. Our Land Soc., 1989-92. Mem. Agr. Editors Assn., Internat. Snowmobile Industry Assn. (Best Overall Reporting journalism award 1979, 80), Western Publs. Assn., World Champion Cutter and Chariot Racing Assn. (historian 1966-80), Nat. Snowmobile Found. (founder 1988), Kappa Tau Alpha. Lodge: Idaho Falls Kiwanis (pres. 1978, Disting. Club Pres. award 1978). Office: Harris Pub Inc 520 Park Ave Idaho Falls ID 83402-3516

HARRIS, DAVID JACK, artist, painter, educator; b. San Mateo, Calif., Jan. 6, 1948; s. Jack McAllister and Audrey Ellen (Vogt) H. BA, San Francisco State U., 1971, MA, 1975. Dir. Galerie de Tours, San Francisco, 1971-72; lectr. Chabot Coll., Hayward, Calif., 1975-80; interior designer David Harris Assocs., San Mateo, 1975-85; freelance artist, painter San Mateo, 1975—; art cons. David Harris Assocs., Belmont, Calif., 1980—; v.p. Coastal Arts League Mus., Half Moon Bay, Calif., 1988—; ptnr., art dir. Fine Art Pub., Palo Alto, Calif., 1989—; bd. dirs. 1870 Gallery and Studios, Belmont, 1978—, gallery dir., 1989—, owner, partner HSW Gallery, San Francisco. Painter murals Chartered Bank of London, 1979, Caesar's Hotel, Las Vegas, 1984, Pacific Telephone, San Francisco; author mus. catalog California Concepts, 1988; rep. in permanent collections: Ask Computer, Palo Alto, Shared Fin., Harris Corp, Bain and Co., San Francisco, Verilink, Litton Industries, Foothill Bank, Los Altos, Chartered Bank of London, San Francisco, Stanford U., Palo Alto, Golden Nugget Hotel, Atlantic City, Nat. Bank of Detroit, Crisafi, Sciabica, Woodward, D.J. Crisafi and Co., Sheraton Grande, L.A., 1st Am. Title Guaranty Co., Walt Disney, Voysys Corp., Spieker Ptnrs., others. Recipient Purchase award North Cen. Washington Mus., 1988. Mem. Internat. Soc. Interior Designers, Coastal Arts League Mus. (v.p. 1988—, Zoe Tierny award 1988). Home and Office: 1870 Ralston Ave Belmont CA 94002-1859

HARRIS, DAVID JOEL, foundation executive; b. Miller, S.D., Sept. 22, 1950; s. Joel Chips and Amy Ruth (Rietz) H.; m. Susan Claire Hagius, June 30, 1979; children: John, Jennifer. BA, Earlham Coll., Richmond, Ind., 1972; MS, Purdue U., 1975; PhD, U. Hawaii, 1983. Vis. rsch. asst. Internat. Ctr. Tropical Agr., Cali, Colombia, 1975-76; rsch. assoc. U. Hawaii, Honolulu, 1976-83; sr. rsch. fellow Internat. Ctr. Tropical Agr., 1984-87; mgr. Calif.-Nev. United Meth. Found., San Francisco, 1988-92, exec. v.p., 1992—; treas. Nat. Assn. United Meth. Found., 1992-94. Contbr. articles to profl. jours. Pres. Mothers Against Drunk Driving, Sonoma County, Calif., 1989-91. Recipient Lubrizol award, 1971; Purdue grad. fellow, 1972; NSF fellow, 1973. Mem. Nat. Coun. of Planned Giving (No. Calif. chpt.), Commonwealth Club of Calif., Phi Beta Kappa. Methodist. Home: 355 Gemma Cir Santa Rosa CA 95404-2733 Office: Calif Nev United Meth Found 1579 Farmers Ln Ste 283 Santa Rosa CA 95405-7535

HARRIS, DAVID THOMAS, immunologist; b. Jonesboro, Ark., May 9, 1956; s. Marm Melton and Lucille Luretha (Buck) H.; m. Francoise Jacqueline Besencon, June 24, 1989; children: Alexandre M., Stefanie L. BS in Biology, Math. and Psychology, Wake Forest U., 1978, MS, 1980, PhD in Microbiology and Immunology, 1982. Fellow Ludwig Inst. Cancer Rsch., Lausanne, Switzerland, 1982-85; rsch. asst. prof. U. N.C., Chapel Hill, 1985-89; assoc. prof. U. Ariz., Tuscon, 1989—; cons. Teltech, Inc., Mpls., 1990—, Advanced Biosci. Resources, 1994—; bd. sci. advisors Cryo-Cell Internat., 1992—; bd. dirs. Ageria, Inc., Tucson; dir. Cord Blood Stem Cell Bank, 1993—; sci. dir. Gene Therapy, 1994—; mem. Ariz. Cancer Ctr., Steele Meml. Children's Rsch. Ctr., Ariz. Arthritis Ctr. Program. Co-author chpts. to sci. books, articles to profls. jours.; reviewer sci. jours.; co-holder 2 scientific patents. Grantee local and fed. rsch. grants, 1988—. Mem. AAAS, Am. Assn. Immunologists, Reticuloendothelial Soc., Internat. Soc. Hematotherapy and Graft Engring., Internat. Soc. Devel. and Comparative Immunology, Scandanavian Soc. Immunology, Sigma Xi. Democrat. Mem. Ch. of Christ. Office: U Ariz Dept Microbiology Bldg 90 Tucson AZ 85721

HARRIS, DEBRA SUE, development engineer; b. Colorado Springs, Sept. 16, 1961; d. Donald Scott and Patricia Darlene (Vrbas) Johnson; m. Larry James Harris, May 21, 1983. BS in Elec. Engring., U. Colo., 1983; BS in Computer Sci., 1983. Operator Hewlett Packard, Colorado Springs, Colo., 1981-83; CAD engr. United Tech. Microelectronics, Colorado Springs, Colo., 1983-89, section mgr. Phys. Design, 1989-92, team leader engring., 1992-93, engr., 1993—. Mem. Toastmasters, Eta Kappa Nu. Office: United Tech Microelectronic 1575 Garden Of The Gods Rd Colorado Springs CO 80907-3415

HARRIS, DIANE, history educator; b. Austin, Tex., May 11, 1961; d. Robert Sidney and Sandra Lou (Robbins) H.; m. Eric H. Cline. BA in Classics, Stanford U., 1983; MA in Classical Archaeology, Princeton U., 1990, PhD in Classical Archaeology, 1991. Instr. history of Ancient Greek Art and Archaeology St. John's U., Athens, Greece, 1988, 89; vis. instr. history Portland (Oreg.) State U., 1990-91; assoc. prof. history Calif. State U., Fresno, 1991-95; asst. prof. classical archeology classics dept. U. Cin., 1995—; vis. assoc. prof. U. Cin., 1994—; cons. Harper Collins Pubs., 1994, Prentice-Hall Pubs., 1992; lectr. in field. Author: The Inventory Lists of the Parthenon Treasures, 1991; contbr. articles to profl. jours. Advisor, founder Hillel of Calif. State U.-Fresno, 1991—. Fulbright scholar to Greece, 1987-88; NEH travel grantee, summers 1992, 94, Calif. State U.-Fresno rsch. grantee, 1992-93, 93-94, 94—, Portland State U. grantee, 1990-91; Hencken Prize Travel grantee, 1989, Spears Travel grantee, 1986, Spears and Berry Funds grantee, 1985; Doreen C. Spitzer fellow, 1988-89, Princeton U. fellow, 1983-87, Seeger fellow, 1986. Mem. Archaeol. Inst. Am. (bd. dirs., v.p., San Joaquin Valley chpt. 1991—), Am. Philol. Assn. (Women's Classical Caucus), Inst. for Classical Studies (London), Fulbright Alumni Assn., Fresno County Archaeol. Soc. (bd. dirs. 1991—, co-v.p. programming 1994—), Calif. Classical Assn. (so. sect.), Classical Assn. Pacific N.W., Assn. Ancient Historians, Am. Classical League, Am. Hist. Assn., Alumni Assn. of Am. Sch. Classical Studies in Athens (nat. nominating com. 1990-91). Democrat. Jewish. Home: 3433 Ruther Ave Cincinnati OH 45220 Office: U Cin Blegen Libr ML0226 Cincinnati OH 45220-0226

HARRIS, EDWARD A., producer, writer, director; b. Elizabeth, N.J., Dec. 14, 1946; s. Howard E. and Bernice W. Harris; m. Chris Garrison, May 16, 1987. Student music composition and theory, U. Okla., 1964-67, Los Angeles Community Coll., 1977, UCLA, 1978. Singer, songwriter, 1962—; pres., exec. producer Myriad Prodns., Los Angeles, 1965—; creative dir. Myriad Graphics, Los Angeles, 1976—; producer, assoc. dir. Columbia Music Hall, Hartford, Conn., 1972-75; film and TV producer, 1971—; multi-media entertainment cons., Los Angeles, 1977—; field producer Good Morning Am., also Good Night Am., ABC-TV, 1975-77; exec. producer, dir. The Act Factory, Los Angeles, 1977-83; sr. ptnr. Myriad-Fritz Prodns., Los Angeles, 1977-83; v.p. Sports Prodns., Am. Videogram, Inc., Los Angeles, 1986-87; ptnr. Myriad/Knox Prodns., Los Angeles, 1987-92, H-two-O Prodns., L.A., 1987-92; exec. producer Gateway Group, San Francisco, 1974-75; dir. Performance Evaluation Workshop, Los Angeles Songwriter's Expo, 1978-83; co-dir. SPVA Performing Arts Workshop, Los Angeles, 1980; exec. dir. Nat. Sports Found., L.A., 1993—. Composer over 30 songs; exec. producer: (TV show) The National Sports Tributes, 1991—; producer: (TV sports mag.) The Clubhouse, 1982—, (TV series) Boating World, ESPN, 1987-92. Pres. Wintonbury Mall Mchts. Assn., Bloomfield, Conn., 1971-72. Mem. Am. Fedn. Musicians, AGVA, Soc. for Preservation of Variety Arts, Alpha Epsilon Pi, Kappa Kappa Psi.

HARRIS, ELIHU MASON, mayor; b. L.A., Aug. 15, 1947; m. Kathy Neal, Aug. 14, 1982. BS in Polit. Sci. with honors, Calif. State U., 1968; M in Pub. Adminstrn., U. Calif., Berkeley, 1969; JD, U. Calif., Davis, 1972. Bar: Calif., D.C. Pvt. practice Calif., 1977-78; formerly mem. Calif. Legis. Assembly, from 1978; now mayor City of Oakland, Calif.; prof. pol. sci. and adminstrn. of justice Calif. State U., Hayward and Sacramento campuses. Former chmn. Joint Legis. Audit Com., Assembly Com. on Fair Employment Practices and the Select Com. on Judicial Eficiency and Improvement, also former mem. Ways and Means, Judiciary, and Health and Transp. coms.; mem. Niagara Movement Dem. Club. Dr. Martin Luther King Rsch. fellow U. Calif. Davis Sch. Law; finalist White House Fellowships competition, 1977-78. Mem. ABA (exec. dir. 1975-77), NAACP, Charles Houston Bar Assn., Calif. Assn. Black Lawyers, Black Am. Polit. Assn. Calif. (former chmn.), Kappa Alpha Psi. Office: Office of Mayor 1 City Hall Plz Oakland CA 94612-1929*

HARRIS, ELLEN STERN, foundation administrator, public policy educator, writer; b. Los Angeles, Nov. 2, 1929; d. Herman Jastro Stern and Geraldine (Rosenberg) Wayne; divorced; children—Tom, Jane. Pub. affairs workshop instr. Communications Workers Am., Los Angeles, 1977-78; instr., program coordinator, moderator, guest lectr. UCLA, 1972—; exec. dir. Pub. Access Producers Acad., Beverly Hills, Calif., 1983—; consumer advocate columnist Los Angeles Times, 1971-78; consumer advisor Times Mirror Satellite Cable/Apple Prodns, 1981; producer, host TV program Who's In Charge, Sta. KPFK-TV, 1979-80, Consumer Connection program Sta. KCRW-TV, 1979; co-host consumer edn. TV series NBC, 1975. Trustee Sta. WETA-TV-AM, Washington, 1975-78; coordinator Calif. Friends of Pub. Broadcasting, 1976-80; exec. sec. Council for Planning and Conservation, 1967-73, Friends of Santa Monica Mountains Parks, 1965-66; exec. dir. Fund for Environment, 1970—; asst. founder Ctr. for Study Democratic Insts., 1964; bd. dirs. Bay Inst. of San Francisco, 1982-86, Friends of Beverly Hills Pub. Library, 1982-83; mem. cable adv. com. Beverly Hills City council, 1986, Mayor's adv. com. on Beverly Hills Water, 1986; adv. bd. Calif. Tomorrow, 1967-83, Urban Environment Found., 1977-79, Town Hall of Calif., 1976—, Los Angeles Conservancy, 1978—; mem. AIA Land Use Task Force, 1972-74; bd. dirs. Met. Water Dist. So. Calif., 1978-81; chmn. Mayor's Adv. Com. on cable TV, City of Beverly Hills, 1982-83, 85; vice chmn. Calif. Coastal Zone Conservation Commn., 1972-76; mem. spl. com. access conveners City of L.A., 1990—; mem. EMF consensus group Calif. Pub. Utilities Commn., 1991-92; mem. recreation and pks. commn. City of Beverly Hills, 1991—, vice chair, 1991-92, chair, 1992-93; mem. electromagnetic fields sci. adv. cons. Calif. Dept. Health Svcs., 1994—; mem. Fed. Coastal Zone Mgmt. Adv. Com., 1973-75, Los Angeles County Environ. Quality Control Com., 1970-73, Los Angeles County Beach Adv. Com., 1970-73, Los Angeles-Ventura Regional Water Quality Control Bd., 1966-70, Dist. Atty's. Community Adv. Council for Los Angeles County, 1976-82, Calif. Atty. Gen's Environ. Task Force, 1970-79, others. Named Woman of Yr., Los Angeles Times, 1969, Voorhis Disting. Visitor, Claremont Colls. and Calif. Poly., 1991; honored by Sierra Club, 1969, Audubon Soc., 1969; Clarence Darrow Found., 1978; recipient Am. Motors Conservation award, 1970; World Communications award UN Assn., 1983. Home and Office: PO Box 228 Beverly Hills CA 90213-0228

HARRIS, ELLIOTT SHOLES, office products executive; b. Providence, Sept. 16, 1924; s. Myer and Esther (Sholes) H.; m. Shirley Harris, June 3, 1947; children: Barbara Ann Gordon, Jeffrey B. BA, U. R.I., 1940; MBA, U. Pa., 1949. Regional sales mgr. Revlon, Inc., N.Y.C., 1949-59; nat. sales mgr. Lindy Pen Co., Inc., L.A., 1954-66, v.p. sales and mktg., 1966-72, bd. dirs., 1972—; pres., CEO Harris Office Supplies, San Diego, 1972—; cons. Nat. Office Products Assn.; arbitrator Nat. Panel Consumer Arbitrators, San Diego, 1980—. Sgt. U.S. Army, 1944-46, ETO. Bd. dirs. BBB. Home: 4624 Pavlov Ave San Diego CA 92122-3834

HARRIS, EMMA EARL, nursing home executive; b. Viper, Ky., Nov. 6, 1936; d. Andrew Jackson and Zola (Hall) S.; m. Ret Haney Marten Henis Harris, June 5, 1981; children: Debra, Joseph, Wynona, Robert Walsh. Grad. St. Joseph Sch. Practical Nursing. Staff nurse St. Joseph Hosp., Bangor, Maine, 1973-75; office nurse Dr. Eugene Brown, Bangor, 1975-77; dir. nurses Fairborn Nursing Home, Ohio, 1977-78; staff nurse Hillhaven Hospice, Tucson, 1979-80; asst. head nurse, 1980. Author: Thoughts on Life, 1988. Vol. Heart Assn., Bangor, 1965-70, Cancer Assn., Bangor, 1965-70. Mem. NAFE. Democrat. Avocations: theatre, opera. Home: 530 E Flores St Tucson AZ 85705-5723

HARRIS, F. CHANDLER, retired university administrator; b. Neligh, Nebr., Nov. 5, 1914; s. James Carlton and Helen Ayres (Boyd) H.; m. Barbara Ann Hull, Aug. 10, 1946; children: Victoria, Randolph Boyd. AB, UCLA, 1936. Assoc. editor Telegraph Delivery Spirit, Los Angeles, 1937-39; writer, pub. service network radio programs University Explorer, Sci. Editor, U. Calif., 1939-61; pub. information mgr. UCLA, 1961-75, dir., 1975-82, dir. emeritus, 1982—. Mem. pub. relations com., western region United Way, 1972-75; bd. dirs. Am. Youth Symphony, Los Angeles, 1978—, v.p., 1983—; bd. dirs. Hathaway Home for Children, 1982-88. Recipient 1st prize NBC Radio Inst., 1944; Harvey Hebert medal Delta Sigma Phi, 1947, Mr. Delta Sig award, 1972; Adam award Assistance League Mannequins, 1980, Univ. Service award UCLA Alumni Assn., 1986. Mem. Western Los Angeles Regional C. of C. (dir. 1976-80), U. Calif. Retirees Assn. Los Angeles (pres. 1985-87), Sigma Delta Chi, Delta Sigma Phi (nat. pres. 1959-63). Club: UCLA Faculty (sec. bd. govs. 1968-72). Editor Interfraternity Research Adv. Council Bull., 1949-50, Carnation, 1969-80, Royce Hall, 1985. Home: 7774 Skyhill Dr Los Angeles CA 90068-1232

HARRIS, FREDERICK PHILIP, retired philosophy educator; b. Portland, Oreg., Aug. 28, 1911; s. Philip Henry and Nellie Louise (Humpage) H.; m. Hester Almira Larson, July 15, 1943; children: Judith, Jacquelyn, Jennifer, Elizabeth, Marcia, Frederick (dec.). AB, Willamette U., 1935; MA, Columbia U., 1937, PhD, 1944; cert. in Japanese, U. Mich., 1944. Tutor Horace Mann Sch. for Boys, N.Y.C., 1935-41; instr. English Rutgers U., New Brunswick, N.J., 1941-42; psychologist Bur. Psychol. Svcs., U. Mich., Ann Arbor, 1946; assoc. prof. philosophy Case Western Res. U., Cleve., 1946-55, chmn. dept., 1948-57; headmaster Am. Sch. in Japan, Tokyo, 1957-66; prof. Oreg. State U., Corvallis, 1967-80, chmn. dept. philosophy, 1967-76; Fulbright vis. prof. faculty edn. Kyoto (Japan) U., 1955-57; prof. Rockefeller Found. Am. Studies Seminar, Doshisha U. Japan, 1956; vis. prof. U. Oreg., Eugene, summer 1950, U. Hawaii, Honolulu, summer 1966, Lewis & Clark Coll., Portland, 1966-67; dir. Oreg. Study Ctr. Waseda U., Tokyo, 1977-80; vis. prof. Grad. Sch. Commerce Waseda U., 1980, Open Coll., 1982-92; pres. Tokyo Internat. Co., 1986-92; advisor Japan Intercultural Comm. Soc., Tokyo, 1980-82. Author: The Neo-Idealist Political Theory, 1944; editor: The Teaching of Philosophy, 1950; editor Perspectives, Japan Intercultural Comm. Soc., 1981-82. Trustee Internat. Sch., Nagoya, Japan, 1963-66, Sendai Am. Sch., Japan, 1963-65. Staff sgr. U.S. Army, 1942-45. Fulbright grantee, Kyoto, 1955, 56; Frederick Philip Harris Libr. named in his honor Am. Sch. in Japan, Tokyo, 1966. Mem. Am. Philos. Assn., Asiatic Soc. Japan (counselor 1986-89), Japan English Forensics Assn., Dem. Nat. Com., Common Cause, Nature Conservancy, Wilderness Soc., Nat. Wildlife Fedn. Methodist. Home: 3050 SW Ridgewood Ave Portland OR 97225-3363

HARRIS, GUY HENDRICKSON, chemical research engineer; b. San Bernardino, Calif., Oct. 2, 1914; s. Edwin James and Nellie Mae (Hendrickson) H.; m. Elsie Mary Dietsch, Mar. 15, 1940; children: Alice, Robert, Mary, Sara. AA, San Bernardino Valley Coll., 1934; BS, U. Calif., Berkeley, 1937; AM, Stanford U., 1939, PhD, 1941. Analytical chemist Shell Devel. Co., Emeryville, Calif., 1937-38; organic chemist William S. Merrell Co., Cin., 1941-45; rsch. chemist Fiber Bd., Emeryville, 1945-46; from organic chemist to assoc. scientist The Dow Chem. Co., Pittsburg, Calif., 1946-62; assoc. scientist The Dow Chem. Co., Walnut Creek, Calif., 1964-82; sr. lectr. U. Ghana, Legon Accra, 1962-64; chmn. dept. chem. John F. Kennedy U., Orinda, Calif., 1964-69; pvt. practice cons. Concord, Calif., 1982-88; chmn. dept. chemistry JFKU, 1964-69; rsch. engr. U. Calif., Berkeley, 1988—. Contbr. K & O Encyclopedia Chem. Tech., 1964, 74, 84, Reagents in Mineral Tech., 1990. Fellow AAAS, Royal Soc. Chemistry; mem. Am. Inst. Mining Engrs., Sigma Xi. Roman Catholic. Home: 1673 Georgia Dr Concord CA 94519-1921 Office: Univ California 386 Hearst Mining Bldg Berkeley CA 94720

HARRIS, HELEN JOSEPHINE, foundation administrator; b. Phila.; d. John and Grace Melley; m. Robert Irvin Harris; children: Robert, Jim, Rich. Grad. high sch., Phila. Pres., founder Retinitis Pigmentosa Internat., Woodland Hills, Calif., 1973—. Recipient Humanitarian award, Pierce Coll., Woodland Hills, 1984, Leadership award, YWCA, L.A., 1986. Mem. Women in Film, L.A. C. of C., Woodland Hills C. of C. Democrat. Roman Catholic. Office: RP Internat 23241 Ventura Blvd # 115 Woodland Hills CA 91364-1003

HARRIS, HOWARD JEFFREY, marketing and printing company executive; b. Denver, June 9, 1949; s. Gerald Victor and Leona Lee (Tepper) H.; m. Michele Whealen, Feb. 6, 1975; children: Kimberly, Valerie. BFA with honors, Kansas City Art Inst., 1973; M. of Indsl. Design with honors, Pratt Inst., 1975; postgrad. Graphic Arts Research Center, Rochester Inst. Tech., 1977; cert. mktg. exec., U. Utah, 1987. Indsl. designer Kivett & Myers, Architects, 1970-71; indsl. designer United Research Corp., Denver, 1971-72; indsl. designer, asst. to v.p., pres. JFN Assos., N.Y.C., 1972-73; dir. facility planning Abt & Assos., Cambridge, Mass., 1973-74; v.p. design, prodn., and research Eagle Direct, Denver, 1974—; pres. Eagle Direct, Denver. Mem. Indsl. Designers Soc. Am., Graphic Arts Tech. Found., Design Methods Group, The Color Group, Nat. Assn. Counsel for Children, Am. Advt. Fedn., Nat. Assn. Printers and Lithographers (bd. dirs.). Democrat. Jewish. Office: 5105 E 41st Ave Denver CO 80216-4420

HARRIS, JAMES MARTIN, architect; b. Lead, S.D., Apr. 30, 1928; s. James Reynolds and Amy B. (Martin) H.; m. Enid Lou Vondy, June 26, 1955; children—Jini Lynn Harris Selig, Kristen Marie Harris Landau. B.Arch., U. Oreg., 1954. Registered architect, Wash., Oreg. Founder James M. Harris Architect, Tacoma, Wash., 1960; with Harris, Reed, Litzenberger & Tsang; of counsel to Harris Tsang Architects, 1988—. Co-author: Norway, 1969; contbr. articles to profl. jours. Pres. Downtown Tacoma Assn., 1984; founding co-chmn. Downtown Area Revitalization Task Force, Tacoma, 1980; bd. dirs. Better Bus. Bur., 1981-84; chmn. bd. visitors U. Oreg. Sch. Architecture and Allied Arts; chmn. Tacoma-Vladivostok (Russia) Sister City Com., 1990—; mem. exec. bd. Rainier coun. Boy Scouts Am., 1992—. Lt. (j.g.) USNR, 1946-48. Mem. AIA (coll. fellows, nat. bd. dirs. 1976-78, nat. v.p. 1979, nat. long-range planning com., del. people to people exch. to China, 1981, to Australia and New Zealand, 1988, various commns. and design juries), Tacoma Lawn and Tennis Club, Rotary (bd. dirs. 1981-84, pres. 1993-94), Elks. Republican. Episcopalian. Office: 3624 N Union Ave Tacoma WA 98407-6139

HARRIS, JAMES MICHAEL, museum director; b. San Francisco, Mar. 24, 1947; s. Alfred James and Pearl Olga (Slavich) H.; m. Vivian Toni Ferrara, Mar. 20, 1987 (div. Mar. 1992); 1 child, Michael James. BA, San Diego State U., 1971. Rsch. assoc. San Diego State U., 1971-73; assoc. dir. San Diego Taxpayers Assn., 1973-75, exec. dir., 1976-79; govt. rels. dir. Rohr Industries, San Diego, 1975-76; chief of staff City of San Diego, 1979-83; CEO Harris & Lee, San Diego, 1983-90; exec. dir. San Diego Auto Mus., 1990—; cons. Souplantation Restaurants, San Diego, 1977-83, Fuego Zero, San Diego, 1989-90, Couveé Comm., San Diego, 1989-90, Deanna Kay Products, Carlsbad, Calif., 1989-90; bd. dirs. Ctrl. Balboa Park Assn., Inter-Mus. Promotional Coun. Rschr. (book) Public Finance in the San Diego S.M.S.A., 1972, Shifting Public Functions and the Distribution of Tax Burden by Economic Class, 1972. Bd. dirs. Alumni Assn. San Diego State U., 1977-79; San Diego county coord. Yes on Lottery Campaign, Woodward/McDowell, San Diego, 1984; expert witness San Diego County Grand Jury, 1977, 78; charter rev. com. mem. San Diego County, 1984. Recipient 20 Outstanding Young Citizens of San Diego award San Diego Jr. C. of C., 1977, Man of Distinction award San Diegans Inc., 1979. Office: San Diego Automotive Mus 2080 Pan American Plz San Diego CA 92101-1636

HARRIS, JEREMY, mayor; s. Ann Harris; m. Ramona Sachiko Akui Harris. BA, BS in Marine Biology, U. Hawaii, 1972; M in Population and Environmental Biology and Urban Ecosystems, U. Calif., Irvine. Lectr. oceanography, biology Kauai C.C.; instr. on reef walks on Kauai U. Hawaii Sea Grant Program; del. Hawaii Constl. Conv., 1978; chmn. Kauai County Council; exec. asst. to Mayor Frank F. Fasi City and County of Honolulu, 1985-86, mng. dir. of Honolulu, 1986-94, mayor, 1994—. Named Pub. Adminstr. of Yr. Am. Soc. Pub. Adminstrn., 1993, 94; recipient Merit award Internat. Downtown Assn., others. Office: Office of the Mayor 530 S King St Honolulu HI 96813

HARRIS, JOSEPH, retired biochemistry educator; b. Balt., Dec. 2, 1919; s. Philip and Bess (Green) H.; m. Irene Dorothy Brown, Mar. 5, 1944; children: Donald Jeffrey, Mark Lindsay. BS, U. Md., 1947; MA, Johns Hopkins U., 1949, PhD, 1952. Responsible investigator Baxter Labs., Inc., Morton Grove, Ill., 1952-54; instr. U. Colo., Denver, 1954-55; asst. prof. biochemistry Albany (N.Y.) Med. Coll., 1955-62; head neurochemistry lab. Barrow Neurol. Inst., Phoenix, 1962-75; rsch. prof. Ariz. State U., Tempe, 1965-75, prof., 1975-89; prof., assoc. chmn. dept. chemistry, 1975-86; prof. emeritus Ariz. State U., Tempe, 1990—; vis. rsch. prof. Royal N. Shore Hosp., Sydney, N.S.W., 1969; exchange scientist U.S. Nat. Acad. Scis., Hungary, 1971; vis. prof. Oxford U., Oxford, U.K., 1981. Cons. editor monograph, Pi-Interactions in Biological Systems, 1969; co-editor: Metal Ions in Neurology and Psychiatry, 1985; contbr. articles to profl. jours. Bd. dirs. Am. Heart Assn., Ariz., 1971-90; project advisor Ariz. Commn. Post Secondary Edn., Phoenix, 1985-87; adv. bd. Cen. Ariz. Consortium Internat. Edn., 1987-89. Capt. U.S. Army, 1944-46; ETO. Travel grantee Burroughs Wellcome Found., 1981. Fellow AAAS, N.Y. Acad. Scis.; mem. Am. Chem. Soc., Am. Soc. for Neurochemistry, Biochem. Soc., Biophys. Soc., Sigma Xi. Home: 2131 E Geneva Dr Tempe AZ 85282-4039 Office: Ariz State Univ Dept Chemistry and Biochemistry Tempe AZ 85287-1604

HARRIS, KEVIN MICHAEL, library manager, investigative specialist; b. Falls City, Kans., Nov. 14, 1950. AA, Skagit Valley Jr. Coll., 1971; BA in English, Western Wash. U., 1973; cert. legal asst., Bellingham Tech. Sch., 1986; cert. investigative specialist, Exec. Security Internat., 1992. Asst. mgr. Whatcom County Libr. System, Bellingham, 1982—; investigative legal asst. Vol. Lawyer Program, Bellingham, 1986-93; investigative specialist Harris and Assocs., Ferndale, Wash., 1992—; res. police officer Ferndale Police Dept., 1993—. Mem. Custer Sportsmen's Club (life, legis. chmn. 1991—, chief instr. 1993—), Double Action Tng. Acad. (staff mem. 1995). Office: Ferndale Community Libr PO Box 1209 Ferndale WA 98248-1209

HARRIS, KRISTINA LEE, management/computer consultant; b. Reno, Nev., Oct. 30, 1966; d. Donald Chesley and Nancy (Watson) Pfaff; m. Charles Macloren Harris, Nov. 14, 1989. BS, Thomas Edison State Coll., 1993; postgrad., U. Nev., 1994—. Lic. air traffic contr. Ops. officer, cons. Mylan's Enterprises Mgmt., Inc., 1993-94; pres. Apogee Self-Mktg. Cons., Reno, Nev., 1993—. Contbg. author, editor The Eclectic Collection, 1993-94. With U.S. Army, 1986-90.

HARRIS, LORI RENEE, dietitian, educator; b. Patterson, Calif., Oct. 14, 1964; d. Arland and Phyllis Mae Erlandson; m. Robert Ray Harris, Jan. 9, 1988; children: Tyler Jordan, Julia Danielle. BS, Calif. Poly. State U., 1986. Dir. dietary Riverbluff Convalescent, Riverbank, Calif., 1986-87; dietetic intern L.A. County U. Southern Calif. Medical Ctr., L.A., 1987; dir. dietary Cmty. Psychiatric Ctr. Vista Del Mar, Ventura, Calif., 1988; clin. dietitian Kino Cmty. Hosp., Tucson, 1988-91; chief clin. dietitian Santa Monica (Calif.) Med. Ctr., 1992; nutrition educator Emanuel Med. Ctr., Turlock, Calif., 1992—; cons. St. Joe's Hosp., Tucson, 1989, N.W. Hosp., Tucson, 1990-91. Contbr. articles to profl. jours. Mem. Am. Dietetic Assn., Calif. State U. Assn., Golden Empire Dist.-Stanislaus Area Subgroup (pres. 1993-94). Office: Emanuel Med Ctr 825 Delbon Ave Turlock CA 95382-2016

HARRIS, MARCUS WILLIAM, construction executive; b. Colorado Springs, Colo., Oct. 19, 1960; s. Garvan Benjamin and Wanda Lou (Hall) H.; m. Carla Ann Ploman, July 24, 1981; children: Crystal, Kelli, Mitchell. V.p. Dick-Con, San Diego, 1978—. Mem. site coun. bd. Alpine (Calif.) Sch. Dist., 1990-92. Mem. Nat. Assn. Home Builders (spike 1992—), Constrn. Purchasing Assn. (v.p. 1991-92, pres. 1993-94), Am. Youth Soccer Orgn. (bd. dirs., reg. commr. 1992-94). Republican. Lutheran. Office: Dick-Con 4500 Imperial Ave San Diego CA 92113-1922

HARRIS, MARTIN STEPHEN, aerospace engineering executive; b. Greenville, S.C., Nov. 23, 1939; s. Vitruvius Aiken and Clara Margaret (Thackston) H.; m. Helen C. Dean, Sept. 7, 1963 (div. May 1980); children: Dean, Susan, James; m. Prudence Cooper Bolstad, Jan. 20, 1990 (dec. Mar. 10, 1993). BS in Physics, Furman U., 1962; MS in Physics, Fla. State U., 1967; ret., USAF, 1982. Commd. 2d lt. USAF, 1962, advanced through grades to maj., 1973, ret., 1982; sr. project engr. Hughes Aircraft Co., El Segundo, Calif., 1982-84, section head, 1984-86, space vehicle mgr., 1986-89, asst. program mgr., 1989—. Mem. Sigma Alpha Epsilon.

HARRIS, MARY BIERMAN, psychology educator; b. St. Louis, Feb. 9, 1943; d. Norman and Margaret (Loeb) Bierman; m. Richard Jerome Harris, June 14, 1965; children: Jennifer, Christopher, Alexander. BA, Radcliffe U., 1964; MA, Stanford U., 1965, PhD, 1968. From asst. prof. to full prof. U. N.Mex., Albuquerque, 1968—; vis. assoc. prof. Ohio State U., Columbus, 1974-75; vis. prof. U. NSW, Australia, 1981-82, U. Ga., 1988-89; mem. adv. bd. Nat. Inst. Edn. N.Mex. State U. Project, Las Cruces, 1978-80; cons. NIH, Washington, 1980-81. Author: Basic Statistics for Behavioral Science Research, 1995; editor: Classroom Uses of Behavior Modification, 1972; contbr. articles to profl. jours. Bd. dirs. Rio Grande Planned Parenthood, Albuquerque, 1984-95. Rsch. grantee NIH Heart, Lung and Blood Inst., 1985-87. Mem. Am. Psychol. Soc., Am. Ednl. Rsch. Assn., Phi Beta Kappa, Sigma Xi. Democrat. Office: U N Mex Coll Edn Albuquerque NM 87131

HARRIS, MICHAEL GENE, optometrist, educator, lawyer; b. San Francisco, Sept. 20, 1942; s. Morry and Gertrude Alice (Epstein) H.; BS, U. Calif., 1964, M. Optometry, 1965, D. Optometry, 1966, MS, 1968; JD, John F. Kennedy U., 1985; children: Matthew Benjamin, Daniel Evan. Bar: Calif., U.S. Dist. Ct. (no. dist.) Calif. Assoc. practice optometry, Oakland, Calif., 1965-66, San Francisco, 1966-68; instr., coord. contact lens clinic Ohio State U., 1968-69; asst. clin. prof. optometry U. Calif., Berkeley, 1969-73, dir. contact lens extended care clinic, 1969-83, chief contact lens clinic, 1983—, assoc. clin. prof., 1973-76, asst. chief contact lens svc., 1970-76, assoc. chief contact lens svc., 1976—, lectr., 1978-80, sr. lectr., 1980—, vice chmn. faculty Sch. Optometry, 1983-85, prof. clin. optometry, 1984-86; clin. prof. optometry, 1986—, dir. residency program, 1993—, asst. dean, 1994—; John de Carle vis. prof. City U., London, 1984; vis. rsch. fellow U. New South Wales, Sydney, Australia, 1989; sr. vis. rsch. scholar U. Melbourne, Australia, 1989, 92; pvt. practice optometry, Oakland, Calif., 1973-76; mem. ophthalmic devices panel, med. device adv. com. FDA, 1990—; lectr., cons. in field; mem. regulation rev. com. Calif. State Bd. Optometry; cons. hypnosis Calif. Optometric Assn., Am. Optometric Assn.; cons. Nat. Bd. Examiners in Optometry, Soflens div. Bausch & Lomb, 1973—, Barnes-Hind Hydrocurve Soft Lenses, Inc., 1974-87, Pilkinton-Barnes Hind, 1987—, Contact Lens Rsch. Lab., 1976—, Wesley-Jessen Contact Lens Co., 1977—, Palo Alto VA, 1980—, Primarius Corp., Cooper Vision Optics Alcon, 1980—; co-founder Morton D. Sarver Rsch. Lab., 1986; Planning commr. Town of Moraga, Calif., 1986, vice-chmn., 1987-88, chmn. 1988-90; mem. Town Coun., Moraga, Calif., 1992—, , vice mayor, 1994—, Medi-Cal. Adv. Planning Commn., 1993—, chair, 1994—; founding mem. Young Adults div. Jewish Welfare Fedn., 1965—, chmn. 1967-68; commr. Sunday Football League, Contra Costa County, Calif., 1974-78. Charter Mem. Jewish Community Ctr. Contra Costa County; founding mem. Jewish Community Mus. San Francisco, 1984; Para-Rabbinic, Temple Isaiah, Lafayette, Calif., 1987, bd. dirs., 1990; life mem. Bay Area Coun. for Soviet Jews, 1976; bd. dirs. Jewish Community Rels. Coun. of Greater East Bay, 1979—, Campolindo Homeowners Assn., 1981—; pres. student coun. John F. Kennedy U. Sch. Law, 1984-85. Fellow U. Calif., 1971; Calif. Optometric Assn. Scholar 1965, George Schneider Meml. scholar, 1964. Fellow Am. Acad. Optometry (diplomate cornea and contact lens sect.; chmn. contact lens papers; mem. contact lens com. 1974—, vice chmn. contact lens sect. 1980-82, chmn. 1982-84, immediate past chmn. 84-86, chmn. jud. com. 1989—, chmn. by-laws com. 1989—), Assn. Schs. and Colls. Optometry (coun. on acad. affairs), AAAS, Prentice Soc.; mem. Assn. for Rsch. in Vision and Ophthalmology, Am. Optometric Assn. (proctor 1969—, cons. on hypnosis, mem. contact lens sect., mem. position papers com., com. on ophthalmic standards, subcom. on testing and certification), Calif. Optometric Assn., Assn. Optometric Contact Lens Educators, Am. Optometric Found., Mexican Soc. Contactology (hon.), Nat. Coun. on Contact Lens Compliance, Internat. Soc. Contact Lens Rsch., Calif. State Bd. Optometry (regulation rev. com.), Calif. Acad. Scis., U. Calif. Optometry Alumni Assn. (life), ABA, Assn. Trial Lawyers Am., Calif. Trial Lawyers Assn., Calif. Young Lawyers Assn., Contra Costa Bar Assn., Mus. Soc., JFK U. Sch. Law Alumni Assn., Benjamin Ide Wheeler Soc. U. Calif., Mensa. Democrat. Lodge: B'nai B'rith. Editor current comments sect. Am. Jour. Optometry, 1974-77; editor Eye Contact, 1984-86, assoc. editor The Video Jour. Clin. Optometry, 1988—, consulting editor Contact Lens Spectrum, 1988—; editor: Problems in Optometry, Special Contact Lens Procedures; Contact Lenses and Ocular Disease, 1990; contbr. chpts. to books; author various syllabuses; contbr. articles to profl. pubs.

HARRIS, MICHAEL HATHERLY, educational administrator; b. Indpls., Sept. 8, 1940; s. John Edward and Bessie (Hatherly) H.; widowed; children: Christopher, Erik, Megan. BA, Macalester Coll., 1966; MA, U. Denver, 1970. Account exec. Benson Optical Co., Mpls., 1966-70; tchr. Adams County Sch. Dist. 14, Commerce City, Colo., 1970-75, dir. student svcs., 1975-80; prin. Portland (Oreg.) Pub. Schs., 1980—. Mem. Met. Youth Commn., Portland. Mem. Oreg. Assn. for Alternative Edn. (pres. 1988, lobbyist, Spl. Svc. award 1993, treas. 1994), Portland Assn. Mid. Sch. Prins. (pres. 1994-95). Home: 11970 NW Dumar Ln Portland OR 97229-3959 Office: Portland Pub Schs 501 N Dixon St Portland OR 97227-1804

HARRIS, MORGAN, zoologist educator; b. St. Anthony, Idaho, May 25, 1916; s. Archibald Overton and Augusta Pearl (Lewelling) H.; m. Marjorie Ruth Mason, Aug. 10, 1940 (dec. Aug. 1955); children—Roger Mason, Ronald Morgan; m. Anne Harris, Aug. 3, 1987. A.B. with highest honors, U. Calif. at Berkeley, 1938, Ph.D., 1941; George Leib Harrison postdoctoral research fellow, U. Pa., 1941-42; Merck sr. postdoctoral fellow, U. Paris, 1953-54. Teaching asst. dept. zoology U. Calif. at Berkeley, 1938-41, instr. zoology, 1945-46, asst. prof., 1946-50, assoc. prof., 1950-56, prof., 1956-83, prof. emeritus, 1983—, vice chmn. zoology, 1952-57, chmn., 1957-63, Miller research prof., 1963-65; research asst. dept. biology Stanford, 1942-44; instr. zoology U. Wash., 1944-45; Research aviation physiology OSRD, 1942-44; mem. cell biology study sect., div. research grants NIH, 1958-60, 61-63, mem. nat. adv. gen. med. scis. council, 1963-65. Author: Cell Culture and Somatic Variation, 1964, also research papers. Guggenheim fellow Cambridge, Eng., 1960-61. Mem. Tissue Culture Assn. (pres. 1958-60), Soc. Gen. Physiologists, Internat. Soc. Cell Biology (exec. com. 1964-72, treas. 1968-72), Am. Soc. Cell Biology (mem. exec. council 1964-68), Soc. for Growth and Devel., Internat. Fedn. for Cell Biology (exec. com. 1972-76), Am. Soc. Zoologists, Phi Beta Kappa, Sigma Xi, Phi Sigma (Scholarship medal 1937-38). Clubs: American Alpine (N.Y.C.); Sierra (Calif.). Home: 605 Plateau Dr Kensington CA 94708-1135

HARRIS, NANCY HOWARD, paper conservator, writer; b. Utica, N.Y., Nov. 5, 1949; d. William Page Harris and Gertrude (Howard) Owens; div. 1980. BA with honors, U. Mich., 1972; MA in Art History, NYU, 1975, diploma in Conservation, 1977. Grad. fellow NYU, 1977-78; paper conservator Detroit Inst. Arts, 1978-80; sr. paper conservator Harry Ranson Humanities Rsch. Ctr., U. Tex., Austin, 1980-82; paper conservator Gen. Libr., U. Calif., Berkeley, 1983—; cons. Cartoon Art Mus., San Francisco, 1986—, JFK U. Ctr. for Mus. Studies, San Francisco, 1987-88, State Archives, Sacramento, 1992; sec. Bay Area Art Conservation Guild, San Francisco, 1982-85. Contbr. articles to profl. jours. Recipient grant NEA, 1979, 80, NEH, 1985, Dept. of Edn., 1988, 91, 92. Episcopalian. Office: Libr Univ Calif Rm 416 Doe Berkeley CA 94720

HARRIS, ORVILLE D., transportation executive. CEO Arco Transp. Alaska, Anchorage. Office: Arco Transp Alaska 550 W 7th Ave Anchorage AK 99501-3510

HARRIS, RICHARD ANTHONY SIDNEY, trust company executive; b. Bklyn., Dec. 22, 1940; s. Stanley Sidney and Rose (Franquelli) H.; m. Sharon Lynne Harvey, Dec. 21, 1975; 1 child, Aaron Nathaniel Graeme. Student St. John's U., Jamaica, N.Y., 1958-61. Adminstr. Harris Trust, N.Y.C., 1972—, trustee, 1972—; adminstr. Beehive Trading Co., Provo, Utah, 1980—, Aaron Reseda Med., Calif., 1976—; pres. Reseda Mgmt., 1976—, also dir. Mem. Am. Assn. Individual Investors, Internat. Platform Assn., Heritage Found. Roman Catholic. Office: PO Box 386 Albion CA 95410-0386

HARRIS, RICHARD JEROME, psychology educator; b. Vicksburg, Miss., May 17, 1940; s. Frederick Arthur and Mary Elizabeth (Gieselbreath) H.; m. Mary Margaret Bierman, June 14, 1965; children: Jennifer Mary, Christopher Richard, Alexander Norman. Student, Calif. Inst. Tech., 1958-61; BS, U. Wis., 1963; MA, Stanford U., 1966, PhD, 1968. Instr., acting co-chmn. psychology & sociology dept. Talladega (Ala.) Coll., 1965-66; psychology rsch. assoc. Palo Alto VA Hosp., Mountain View, Calif., 1967-68; lectr. Stanford (Calif.) U., 1968; asst. prof. U. N.Mex., Albuquerque, 1968-72; assoc. prof. psychology U. N.Mex., 1972-83, prof. psychology, 1983—; vis. assoc. prof. Ohio State U., Columbus, 1974-75, vis. prof. U. Ga., Athens, 1988-89; action editor Jour. Personality Social Psychology, 1979; mem. edit. bd. Jour. Experimental Social Psychology, 1977-90. Author: A Primer of Multivariate Statistics, 1975, 2d rev. edit., 1985, An Analysis of Variance Primer, 1994; contbr. articles to profl. jours. Vis. fellow, U. New South Wales, Kensington, Australia, 1981-82. Fellow Am. Psychol. Soc., Soc. Personality and Social Psychology; mem. Soc. Multivariate Experimental Psychology, Soc. Experimental Social Psychology, Psychonomic Soc., Soc. Applied Multivariate Rsch. (pres. 1977-79), Soc. Advancement Social Psychology. Democrat. Home: 1719 Rita Dr NE Albuquerque NM 87106-1129 Office: U N Mex Dept Psychology Albuquerque NM 87131

HARRIS, ROBERT FRANCIS, psychoanalyst, psychiatrist; b. Wellington, Kans., May 4, 1944; s. Francis Benjamin and Cleta Catherine (Wempe) H.; m. Stephanie Diane Brown, Sept. 9, 1978; 1 child, Makenzie Brown-Harris. BS summa cum laude, St. Louis U., 1966; MD, Stanford U., 1971; grad., San Francisco Psychoanalytic Inst., 1991. Diplomate Am. Bd. Psychiatry and Neurology. Intern St. Mary's Hosp., San Francisco, 1971-72; resident Stanford (Calif.) U., 1972-75; pvt. practice Palo Alto, 1975—; psychiatrist Stanford U. Hosp., 1975—; vol. clin. faculty Stanford U., 1975—, clin. assoc. prof., 1986—, mem. clin. faculty com., 1978-82, chmn. clin. faculty com., 1980-81, mem. task force on psychiat. edn., 1987-89, mem. curriculum com., 1988—; personal and supervising analyst Psychoanalytic Inst. No. Calif., San Francisco, 1991; mem. ext. divsn. San Francisco Psychoanalytic Inst., 1981—; asst. prof. Pacific Grad. Sch. Psychology, Menlo Park, Calif., 1980-84, 86-90; mem. clin. faculty psychiat. residency program Dept. Mental Health Svcs., County of San Mateo, Calif., 1984-89; vol. faculty Family Svcs. Assn. of the Mid-Peninsula, Palo Alto, 1978-80. Author: (with others) Violence and the Struggle for Existence, 1970; contbr. articles to profl. jours. Mem. Am. Psychoanalytic Assn., San Francisco Psychoanalytic Soc., Am. Psychiat. Assn., Am. Group Psychotherapy Assn., No. Calif. Group Psychotherapy Soc. Office: 780 Welch Rd Ste 207 Palo Alto CA 94304-1518

HARRIS, ROBERT GEORGE, illustrator; b. Kansas City, Mo., Sept. 9, 1911; s. Harry George and Lena Mary (Stevens) H.; m. Marjorie Elnora King, Dec. 26, 1935; children: Craig, Marcia. Student, Kansas City Art Inst., 1928-30, Art Students League, N.Y.C., 1931-32, Grand Cen. Art Sch., N.Y.C., 1931-32. illustrator Sat. Evening Post, Ladies Home Jour., McCall's, Cosmopolitan, RedBook, Good Housekeeping, 1939-65; portrait painter Justice Dept., Washington, Union Pacific R.R., N.Y.C., Ariz. State U., Beta Sigma Phi Hdqrs., Seabury Western Theol. Sem., many corp. and family portraits, 1965—. Mem. Soc. Illustrators (life). Home: PO Box 1124 Carefree AZ 85377-1124

HARRIS, ROGER J., mortgage company executive, entrepreneur; b. Chgo., Nov. 20, 1930; s. Stanley and Mary (Koba) Pokwinski; married, 1948 (div. Jan. 1970); 1 child, Linda; m. Betty J. Henry, Nov. 21, 1971. BS in Commerce, Roosevelt U., Chgo., 1956; postgrad., Loyola U. Law Sch., Chgo., 1959-62. Systems sales rep. Univac, Chgo., 1953-55; merchandising systems analyst Montgomery Ward, Chgo., 1956-62; cons. Haskins & Sells, Chgo., 1962-65; prin. A.T. Kearney, L.A., 1965-70; bus. cons. Roger J. Harris and Assocs., Inc., Calif. and Alaska, 1970—; chmn. bd. dirs., CEO Mortgage Co. Alaska; chmn. of bd. Mortgage Co. of Alaska; conf. leder Am. Mgmt., Assn., L.A., 1970-82. Mem. Am. Soc. of Accts., Small Bus. Adminstrn. (chmn. score/ACE program 1990-91). Office: 1844 W Northern Lights Blvd Anchorage AK 99517-3342

HARRIS, ROXANNA MARIE, emergency room nurse; b. Kansas City, Kans., July 16, 1950; d. Alvin Thomas Harris and Emilia Frances (Scigliano)

Harris-Douthat. Lic. paramedic, Med. Ctr., Independence, Mo., 1985; ADN, Fort Scott (Kans.) C.C., 1991. RN, Kans.; cert. ACLS, PALS instr., CPR, BLS. Paramedic Sac-Osage Hosp., Osceolo, Mo., 1988-91, Mercy Hosp., Fort Scott, Kans., 1991-92; emergency rm. travel nurse Am. Home Health, O.P., Kans., 1993-94, Yukon Kuskokwim Delta Regional Hosp., Bethal, Alaska, 1994—; instr. pediat. advanced life support. CPR instr. Am. Heart Assn., Fort Scott, Kansas City, 1985-92. Mem. Emergency Rm. Nurses Assn.

HARRIS, SHELDON HOWARD, history educator; b. Bklyn., Aug. 22, 1928; s. Peter Harris and Bertha Perry; m. Sheila J. Black, Oct. 30, 1955; children: Robin L., David A. AB cum laude, Bklyn. Coll., 1949; MA, Harvard U., 1950; PhD, Columbia U., 1958. Lectr. Bklyn. Coll., 1957-58; assoc. prof. New Bedford (Mass.) Inst. Tech., 1958-63; prof. Calif. State U., Northridge, 1963-91, prof. emeritus, 1991—. Author: Paul Cuffe, 1972, Factories of Death, 1994; contbr. articles to profl. jours. Rsch. grantee various orgns. Mem. Am. Hist. Assn., Sierra Club. Home: 17144 Nanette St Granada Hills CA 91344-1409

HARRIS, SIGMUND PAUL, physicist; b. Buffalo, Oct. 12, 1921; s. Nathan N. and Ida (Lebovitz) H.; m. Florence Katcoff, Sept. 19, 1948; 1 child, Roslyn. BA cum laude, SUNY, Buffalo, 1941, MA, 1943; postgrad., Yale U., 1943; PhD, Ill. Inst. Tech., 1954. Physicist Metall. Lab. U. Chgo., 1943-44; jr. scientist Los Alamos (N.Mex.) Nat. Lab., 1944-46; assoc. physicist Argonne Nat. Lab., Chgo., 1946-53; sr. physicist Tracer Lab., Inc., Boston, 1954-56; sr. research engr. Atomics Internat., Canoga Park, Calif., 1956-64; head physics sect. research div. Maremont Corp., Pasadena, Calif., 1964-66; from asst. prof. to full prof. L.A. Pierce Coll., Woodland Hills, Calif., 1966-86, prof. physics emeritus, 1986—; cons. Space Scis. Inc., Monrovia, Calif., 1968—. Author: Introduction to Air Pollution, 1973. Patentee method for measuring power level of nuclear reactor, apparatus for producing neutrons. Mem. Am. Nuclear Soc., Am. Assn. Physics Tchrs., Am. Phys. Soc., Phi Beta Kappa, Sigma Xi. Home: 5831 Saloma Ave Van Nuys CA 91411-3018 Office: 6201 Winnetka Ave Woodland Hills CA 91371-0001

HARRIS, TIM RAY, sports promoter, agent; b. Inglewood, Calif., Dec. 21, 1961; s. Leo and June (Glazier) H. BA, UCLA, 1984. Athlete maj. indoor soccer league, various teams, 1984-89; COO Forum Sports, Inglewood, 1989—; sports agt. Manhattan Beach, Calif., 1992—. Office: Forum Sports 3900 W Manchester Blvd Inglewood CA 90305-2200

HARRIS, WARREN LYNN, development engineer; b. Albuquerque, May 8, 1966; s. Jerry Dale and Viola Guadalupe (Gutierrez) H. BS, Ariz. State U., 1988. Programming mgr. I.P.C. Computer Svcs., Inc., Tempe, Ariz., 1985-89; software systems engr. Intel Corp., Chandler, Ariz., 1990; dir. software R&D Pics, Inc., Tempe, 1990-91; dir. software R&D, parics div. Ansoft Corp., Tempe, 1991-94; devel. engr. Ansoft Corp., Phoenix, 1994—. Mem. IEEE, Assn. for Computing Machinery, Golden Key Nat. Honor Soc., Mortar Bd., Upsilon Pi Epsilon. Office: Ansoft Corp Parics Div 6210 W Minnezona Ave Phoenix AZ 85033-2125

HARRISON, BHANU JOY, social worker; b. Evanston, Ill., June 15, 1954; d. Peter William and Brigitta Julia (de le Roi) Norgaard; m. Robert Lee Harrison, July 24, 1993. BA, SUNY, 1991; MSW, N.Mex. Highlands U., 1994. Lic. massage therapist, natural therapeutic specialist, N.Mex.; lic. social worker. Pvt. practice body centered psychotherapy Vitality Works, Albuquerque, 1984—, massage therapist, 1984—; instr. N.Mex. Sch. Natural Therapeutics, Albuquerque, 1985—. Mem. NASW, Am. Massage Therapy Assn., Phi Kappa Phi.

HARRISON, CAROL ANNE, librarian; b. Eastcote, Middlesex, England, July 23, 1952; came to U.S., 1983; d. Louis Arthur and Isabel Violet (Tayler) H.; m. David Leland Combs, May 7, 1986; children: Skylar Harrison Combs. BA with honors, U. Birmingham, England, 1973; diploma in librarianship, Coll. Librarianship, Wales, 1978. Editorial asst. British Film Inst., London, 1974-76; libr. asst. Westminster City Librs., London, 1976-77; asst. libr. Luton (England) Coll. Higher Edn., 1978-80; asst. tutor libr. Leeds (England) Polytechnic, 1980-82; reference libr. Southeastern Mass. U., N. Dartmouth, 1983; reference/tech. reports libr. UCLA, 1984-87; rsch. libr. Twentieth Century Fox Film Corp., Beverly Hills, Calif., 1987-90, 91-92, head rsch. libr., 1992—. Mem. Am. Libr. Assn.

HARRISON, CAROLE ALBERTA, museum curator, restaurateur, civic worker; b. Dayton, Ohio, Jan. 16, 1942; d. Chester Arthur and Mildred Irene (Focke) Shaw; student U. Dayton, 1959-60, U. Colo., 1960-61; children: Amelia Holmes, Ann Elizabeth, Abigail Shaw. With Council for Pub. TV, Channel 6, Inc., Denver, 1972-78, Hist. Denver, Inc., 1973-93; owner Harrison Enterprises, Inc., 1982—; general mgr. The Denver Petroleum Club, The Denver Club; dir. devel. Sewall Rehab. Center, Denver, 1979-80; exec. v.p. Marilyn Van Derbur Motivational Inst., Inc., 1980-82. Bd. dirs. Center for Public Issues, Denver, 1979-82, Passages, 1982-88, Hall of Life, 1981-83, Historic Denver, 1982-84, Denver Firefighters Mus., 1979—; bd. dirs. KRMA-TV Vols., 1970—, pres., 1973-74; founder Com. for Support of Arts, Denver, 1978-79; chmn. Graland Country Day Sch. Auction, 1979, 80, Channel 6 Auction, 1971, 72, Colo. Acad. Auction, 1980, The Hundred Most Interesting Women in Denver, 1988; mem. Denver Mayor's Task Force on Infrastructure Fin., 1988-90; bd. dirs. Met. Denver and Colo. Conv. and Visitors Bur. Named Outstanding Bus. Woman of the Yr. Colo. Woman's C. of C., 1991. Mem. Leadership Denver Alumni Assn. (dir. 1980-82), Colo. Restaurant Assn., Denver C. of C. (govt. relations com. 1983-87, state local affairs council 1987-88, urban affairs), Women's Forum. Home: 490 Jackson St Denver CO 80206 Office: 555 17th St Ste 3700 Denver CO 80202

HARRISON, CHARLES WAGNER, JR., applied physicist; b. Farmville, Va., Sept. 15, 1913; s. Charles Wagner and Etta Earl (Smith) H.; m. Fern F. Perry, Dec. 28, 1940; children—Martha R., Charlotte J. Student, U.S. Naval Acad. Prep. Sch., 1933-34, U.S. Coast Guard Acad., 1934-36; BS in Engring., U. Va., 1939, EE, 1940; SM, Harvard U., 1942, M of Engring., 1952, PhD in Applied Physics, 1954; postgrad., MIT, 1942, 52. Registered profl. engr., Va., Mass. Engr. Sta. WCHV, Charlottesville, Va., 1937-40; commd. ensign U.S. Navy, 1939, advanced through grades to comdr., 1948; research staff Bur. Ships, 1939-41, asst. dir. electronics design and devel. div., 1948-50; research staff U.S. Naval Research Lab., 1944-45, dir.'s staff, 1950-51; liaison officer Evans Signal Lab., 1945-46; electronics officer Phila. Naval Shipyard, 1946-48; mem. USN Operational Devel. Force Staff, 1953-55; staff Comdg. Gen. Armed Forces Spl. Weapons project, 1955-57; ret. U.S. Navy, 1957; cons. electromagnetics Sandia Nat. Labs., Albuquerque, 1957-73; instr. U. Va., 1939-40; lectr. Harvard U., 1942-43, Princeton U., 1943-44; vis. prof. Christian Heritage Coll., El Cajon, Calif., 1976. Author: (with R.W.P. King) Antennas and Waves: A Modern Approach, 1969; contbr. numerous articles to profl. jours. Fellow IEEE (Electronics Achievement award 1966, best paper award electromagnetic compatibility group 1972); mem. Internat. Union Radio Sci. (commn. B), Electromagnetics Acad., Famous Families Va., Sigma Xi. Home: 2808 Alcazar St NE Albuquerque NM 87110-3516

HARRISON, ETHEL MAE, financial executive; b. Ft. Dodge, Iowa, June 11, 1931; d. Arthur Melvin and Grace Gwendolyn (Hall) Cochran; m. Cleo Arden Goss, June 17, 1951 (div. 1962); m. Clarence Hobert Harrison, Dec. 23, 1965 (dec. Feb. 1993). Dipl., Internat. Corres. Schs., Riverside, Calif., 1986. Tax preparer Goss Tax Svc., Riverside, 1953-61; tax preparer H & R Block, Inc., Riverside, 1972-84, supr./bookkeeper, 1974-79; owner, pres. Ethel Harrison's Tax Svc., Riverside, 1984—. Mem. NAFE, Riverside Tax Cons. Assn. (sec. 1988—), Am. Soc. Profl. and Exec. Women, Am. Inst. Profl. Bookkeepers, Soc. of Calif. Tax Profls., Nat. Assn. Tax Cons., Nat. Soc. Tax Profls., Nat. Assn. Tax Preparers, Inland Soc. Tax Cons., Nat. Taxpayers Union. Home and Office: 10460 Gramercy Pl Riverside CA 92505-1359

HARRISON, GLENN RUSSELL, mathematics educator; b. Albany, Oreg., Apr. 28, 1939; s. Russell B. and Altha E. (Green) H.; m. Carol Ann Stowe, June 16, 1962; children: Nancy Ann, Sherry Lynn. BS, Oreg. State U., 1961, EdM, 1965; MS, U. Oreg., 1973. Cert. math. tchr., Oreg. Tchr. Cen. Linn Sch. Dist., Halsey, Oreg., 1961—; instr. Linn-Benton Community Coll., Albany, 1978—; mem. Nat./Oreg. Tchrs. Edn. Accreditation Team, Oreg. and Calif., 1970's-80's, Oreg. Tchr. Standards and Practices Commn., 1971-74; mem., vice chair, chair Oreg. Pers. Mgmt. Adv. Com., 1979-83; speaker Am. Assn. Colls. of Tchr. Edn., Chgo., 1975. Author: (intro.) Remembering When/A Pictoral History of Albany, Vol. I, II, III, 1990; contbr. articles to profl. jours. Mem. long range planning com. Greater Albany Pub. Schs., 1980; mem., chair Albany Elem. Bd., 1969-74; mem., chair budget com. City of Albany, 1979-87; mem., vice chair, chair Oreg. PERS Bd., 1987-91; mem. Linn County Historic Resources Commn., 1993—. Mem. long range planning com. Greater Albany Pub. Schs., 1980; mem., chair Albany Elem. Bd., 1969-74; mem., chair budget com. City of Albany, 1979-87; mem., chair Oreg. PERS Bd., 1987-91. Mem. NEA (bd. dirs. Washington 1975-78, program budget com. 1976-78), Oreg. Edn. Assn. (bd. dirs. 1972-79, exec. com. 1973-78, bidget com. 1973-79, Dick Barss tchr. Rights award 1979), Cen. Linn Edn. Assn. (pres., bargaining spokesperson, grievance chair), Oreg. Calif. Trails Assn. (v.p.), Oreg. Hist. Soc., Linn County His. Mus. (adv. com. 1990), Linn County Hist. Soc. (treas. 1988, pres. 1989), Nat. Coun. Tchrs. Math., Oreg. Coun. Tchrs. Math. Democrat. Presbyterian.

HARRISON, HAROLD HENRY, physician, scientist, educator; b. Oak Park, Ill., Mar. 18, 1951; s. Orlow Harold and Wanda Odell (Olesczynski) H.; m. Brenda E. Naccari, 1993; 1 child, Amelia. BS in Biochemistry with honors, U. Ill., 1972; MD, U. Ill., Chgo., 1979, PhD, 1979. Diplomate Nat. Bd. Med. Examiners, Am. Bd. Pathology. Resident in internal medicine U. Ill. Hosps., Chgo., 1979-80; resident lab. medicine Northwestern U. Hosp., Chgo., 1980-83; asst. prof. U. Chgo. Med. Sch., 1984-92; asst. dir. clin. chemistry U. Chgo. Hosps., 1984-86, dir. spl. chemistry, toxicology and molecular pathology, 1986-90, dir. protein and genetic chemistry, 1990-92, staff physician, 1984-92; staff physician United Blood Svcs., Chgo., 1981-84; dir. clin. pathology, med. dir. Phoenix Labs., 1992—, Genetrix, Inc., Scottsdale, Ariz., 1992—; assoc. dir. Southwest Biomedical Rsch. Inst., Scottsdale, 1992—; chair workshop program Genetics Task Force Ill., Chgo., 1988; sr. clin. lectr. pathology Med. Sch., U. Ariz., Tucson, 1993—; lectr. in field. Contbr. articles to profl. publs. Adelmann Fund scholar, 1976, T. B. Sachs scholar, 1975, V. S. Yarros scholar, 1974, Edmund J. James scholar, 1969-72. Fellow Coll. Am. Pathologists (inspector 1992), Am. Soc. Clin. Pathologists; mem. Am. Coll. Med. Genetics, Am. Coll. Physician Execs., Am. Soc. Human Genetics, Am. Assn. Clin. Chemistry, Sigma Xi, Phi Eta Sigma. Office: Genetrix/SBRI 6401 E Thomas Rd Scottsdale AZ 85251-6005

HARRISON, HELEN HERRE, writer, volunteer, advocate; b. Harrisburg, Pa., Aug. 23, 1946; d. Edward Albert Herre Jr. and Rebecca Irene (Allen) Webster; (stepfather) Donald Steele Webster; m. Alfred Craven Harrison Jr., Apr. 4, 1970; children: Edward Alfred, Amy Ruth. AB, U. Calif., Berkeley, 1968. Writer St. Martin's Press, 1976—. Author: The Premature Baby Book: A Parent's Guide for Coping and Caring in the First Years, 1983; edited: Parent to Parent Newsletter, 1978-80, Support Lines, 1984; contbg. column for Twins Mag., 1984-88; editorial adv. bd. Twins Mag., 1988—. Mem. Phi Beta Kappa. Home: 1144 Sterling Ave Berkeley CA 94708-1757

HARRISON, ISOM, librarian. BS in Chemistry, Rust Coll., 1970; MS in Organic Chemistry, U. of the Pacific, 1978. Tech. info. specialist Lawrence Livermore (Calif.) Nat. Lab., 1973-82, supr. br. librs., 1980-82, asst. mgr. rsch. info. group, 1983-86, libr. divsn. mgr., 1991—; tech. info. specialist Chem. Info. System, 1982-83; libr. svcs. mgr. Clorox Co., Pleasanton, Calif., 1986-91; presenter, tchr., coord. workshops in field. Contbr. articles to profl. publs. Home: 1648 Bonaire Cir Stockton CA 95210-5677

HARRISON, JOHN CONWAY, state supreme court justice; b. Grand Rapids, Minn., Apr. 28, 1913; s. Francis Randall and Ethlyn (Conway) H.; m. Ethel M. Strict; children—Nina Lyn, Robert Charles, Molly M., Frank R., Virginia Lee. LLD, George Washington U., 1940. Bar: Mont. 1947, U.S. Dist. Ct. 1947. County atty. Lewis and Clark County, Helena, Mont., 1934-60; justice Mont. Supreme Ct., Helena, 1961—. Pres. Mont. TB Assn., Helena, 1951-54, Am. Lung Assn., N.Y.C., 1972-73, Mont. coun. Boy Scouts Am., Great Falls, Mont., 1976-78. Col. U.S. Army. Mem. ABA, Mont. Bar Assn., Kiwanis (pres. 1953), Sigma Chi. Home: 215 S Cooke St Helena MT 59601-5143 Office: Mont Supreme Ct 215 N Sanders St Helena MT 59601-4522

HARRISON, KEN L., holding company and electric utility executive; b. Bakersfield, Calif., Oct. 14, 1942. BS, Oreg. State U., 1964, MA, 1966. Cert. fin. analyst. V.p. 1st Interstate Bank, Portland, Oreg., 1966-75; asst. to pres. Portland Gen. Electric Co., 1975-78, v.p., 1978, chief fin. officer, 1978-80, sr. v.p., 1980-87, pres., 1987-88, also bd. dirs., chmn. bd., pres., chief exec. officer; chmn. bd., chief exec. officer Portland Gen. Corp., also bd. dirs.; chmn., chief exec. officer Portland Gen. Electric Co. Office: Portland Gen Corp 121 SW Salmon St Portland OR 97204-2901

HARRISON, WALTER ASHLEY, physicist, educator; b. Flushing, N.Y., Apr. 26, 1930; s. Charles Allison and Gertrude (Ashley) H.; m. Lucille Prince Carley, July 17, 1954; children: Richard Knight, John Carley, William Ashley, Robert Walter. B. Engring. Physics, Cornell U., 1953; M.S., U. Ill., 1954, Ph.D., 1956. Physicist Gen. Elec. Research Labs., Schenectady, 1956-65; prof. applied physics Stanford (Calif.) U., 1965—, chmn. applied physics dept., 1989-93; scientific adv. bd. Max Planck Inst., Stuttgart, Germany, 1989-92. Author: Pseudopotentials in the Theory of Metals, 1966, Solid State Theory, 1970, Electronic Structure and the Properties of Solids, 1980; editor: the Fermi Surface, 1960, Proceedings of the International Conference on the Physics of Superconductors, 1985, Proceedings of the International Conference on Materials and Mechanisms of High-Temperature Superconductivity, 1989. Guggenheim fellow, 1970-71; recipient von Humboldt sr. U.S. scientist award, 1981, 89, 94; vis. fellow Clare Hall, Cambridge U., 1970-71. Fellow Am. Phys. Soc. Home: 817 San Francisco Ct Stanford CA 94305-1021 Office: Stanford U Dept Applied Physics Stanford CA 94305

HARRISON, WILLIAM CRAIG, computer company executive; b. Chickasha, Okla., June 5, 1940; s. Odie Webb and Sarah (Boone) H.; m. Susan Marie Jenne, Sept. 10, 1970; children: Richard Scot, Robin Alaine. BS in Physics, Tex. Tech. U., 1962; PhD in Physics, Fla. State U., 1970; MBA in Fin., Temple U., 1983. Rsch. fellow Harvard U., Cambridge, Mass., 1970-71, Rutgers, The State U. N.J., New Brunswick, 1972-74; sr. sci. programmer Boeing Computer Svcs., Phila., 1974-76, supr. sci. computing, 1976-78, mgr. sci. computing, 1978-90; mgr. sci. computing Boeing Computer Svcs., Seattle, 1990-92, mgr. delivery sys., 1992-95; dir. Delivery Sys., 1995—. Mem. Am. Phys. Soc., Assn. Computing Machinery. Home: 1528 E Interlaken Blvd Seattle WA 98112-2125 Office: Boeing Internat & Support Svcs Seattle WA 98112

HARRISON, WILLIAM ORVILLE, physician; b. Longview, Wash., July 9, 1938; s. Orville William and Ruth Ellen (McMilan) H.; m. Susan Marie Connelly, Dec. 29, 1965 (div. Jan. 1994); children: Scott William, John Andrew. Student, U. Vienna, Austria, 1960; AB in Biology, Stanford U., 1961; postgrad., U. Oreg., Eugene, 1961-62; MD, U. Md., 1962-66. Diplomate Am. Bd. Preventive Medicine. Commd. ensign USN, 1962, advanced through grades to capt., 1979; intern Oak Knoll Naval Hosp., Oakland, Calif., 1966-67; med. submarine officer U.S.S. Kamehameha USN, Pearl Harbor, Hawaii, 1967-69; resident in internal medicine Naval Regional Med. Ctr., Oakland, 1969-72; sr. rsch. fellow U. Wash., Seattle, 1972-74; head infectious diseases br. U.S. Naval Hosp., San Diego, 1974-81, chmn. clin. investigation dept., 1981-84, dir. HIV/AIDS br., 1985-88, commdg. officer med. clinics NTC, 1984-85, ret., 1988; AIDS specialist San Diego, 1988-94; clin. svcs. dir. Reynolds Electrical Engring. Co., Las Vegas, Mercury, Nev., 1994—; pvt. practice North Las Vegas, 1994—; cons. epidemiologist Calif. Dept. Health Svcs., Sacramento, 1985-95; cons. physician Calif. Dept. Corrections, Frontera, Calif., 1991-94. Contbr. articles to profl. jours. Recipient Sir Henry Wellcome medal Assn. Mil. Surgeons of U.S., 1980. Fellow ACP, Am. Coll. Preventive Medicine, Infectious Diseases Soc. Am.; mem. Christian Med. Soc. (trustee 1988-92), Am. Venereal Disease Assn. (sec.-treas. 1980-88), Alpha Omega Alpha. Republican.

HARROP, DONALD BRUCE, film company executive. Student, U. Utah, 1948-51. With mktg. and sales Nehi Beverage Co., Salt Lake City, 1951-53, Dixie Cup Co., Eaton, Pa., 1953-55; mktg. and sales mgmt. exec. Am. Greetings Corp., Cleve., 1955-68; v.p., regional sales dir. The World Acad., Inc., Cin., 1968-70; pres. Don Harrop & Assocs., 1975-82; gen. mgr. The Best Western Chieftain Inn, Chambers, Ariz., 1982-85; exec. dir. in mktg. and sales The Journey Assocs., Inc., Phoenix, 1985-89; exec. v.p., chief operating officer Filosa Films Internat., Inc., Beverly Hills, Calif., 1990—; ind. contractor Simmons Market Rsch. Bur., N.Y.C. With U.S. Army, 1945-47. Home: 7202 E Ed Rice Ave Mesa AZ 85208-2713

HARROUN, DOROTHY SUMMER, painter, educator; b. El Paso, Tex., Nov. 29, 1935; d. Daniel Stuart and Eleanor (Flowers) H. BFA, U. N.Mex., 1957; postgrad., U. Paris, Sorbonne, 1957-58; MFA, U. Colo., 1960. One woman shows: The Gondolier Gallery, Boulder, Colo., 1961, 62, Sta. KAFE-FM Gallery, San Francisco, 1963, 64; Lovelace-Bataan Hosp., Albuquerque, 1976, 79; Eastern N.Mex. U., 1981, Rathaus, Kelkheim, Germany, N.Mex. State U.; group shows include Whitte Mus., San Antonio, 1960, shows in Hyannis, Mass., Waterbury, Conn., Newport, R.I., 1964-65, Mus. N.Mex., Santa Fe, 1966, Ogunguit (Maine) Art Ctr., 1977, Am. Watercolor Soc. 112th Ann., N.Y.C., 1979, Coos Art Mus., Coos Bay, Oreg., 1980, Western Slope Show, Montrose, Colo., 1981, 82, Ga. Watercolor Soc. Open, 1983, Western Fedn. Watercolor Socs., 1984, 85, 86, 88, Sun Carnival Art Show, El Paso, 1984, Western Fedn. Watercolor Socs., 1984, 85, 86, 87, 88, El Paso Mus. Art, 1987, N.Mex. Watercolors show Gov's Gallery, State Capitol, 1988, State Fair Fine Arts Gallery, Albuquerque, 1988, Ch. Farm House Mus., London, 1988-89, St. John's Coll., Santa Fe, 1991, Gallery of the Rep., Santa Fe, 1993, On Water, Santa Fe, 1994, Magnifico Invitational Keynote Show, Albuquerque, 1995; represented in permanent collections U. N.Mex., U. Colo., Fine Arts Mus., Carlsbad, N.Mex., also pvt. collections in U.S., France, Italy, Germany; art dir. Wood-Reich Advt. Agy., Boulder, 1960-61; lectr. U. Colo., Boulder, 1961-62; tchr. art Langley-Porter Neuropsychiat. Inst. U. Calif., 1963; lectr. San Francisco State Coll., 1964-65; tchr. Art Ctr. Sch., Albuquerque, 1975-79; tchr. watercolor, drawing U. N.Mex., 1980-81. Pres. fine arts alumni bd. U. N.Mex., 1989—. Fulbright scholar. Mem. Artist Equity Assn. (pres. Albuquerque chpt. 1977-79), AAUW (state cultural dir.), Nat. League Am. Pen Women (pres. Albuquerque br. 1982-83), N.Mex. Watercolor Soc. (v.p. 1984, pres. 1985). Author and illustrator: Take Time to Play and Listen, 1963, Phun-y Physics, 1975; illustrator: Mini Walks on the Mesa, 1989, also painted portraits of first and third pres.' of U. N.Mex. Home: 1365 Thunder Rdg Santa Fe NM 87501-8875

HARRUS, ALAIN SIMON, marketing professional; b. Casablanca, Morocco, Aug. 25, 1955; came to U.S., 1979; s. David and Helen (Ifergan) H.; m. Carol Beth Ronis, July 26, 1981; children: Isaac Alexander, Rachel Beth Julie. BS in Math. and Physics, U. Paris, 1978, MS in Physics, 1979; PhD, Temple U., 1984. Tech. staff AT&T Bell Labs., Allentown, Pa., 1985-89; sr. tech. Novellus Systems, San Jose, Calif., 1989-90, dir. chem. vapor deposition, 1990-93, dir. strategic mktg., 1994—; dir. chem. vapor desosition LAM Rsch., Fremont, Calif., 1993-94. Patentee in field; contbr. articles to profl. jours. Mem. IEEE, Am. Phys. Soc., Electrochem. Soc. Home: 517 Patricia Ln Palo Alto CA 94303-2856 Office: Novellus Systems 81 Vista Montana San Jose CA 95134-1510

HARSHA, PHILIP THOMAS, aerospace engineer; b. N.Y.C., Feb. 22, 1942; s. Palmer and Catherine (Redinger) H.; m. Jean Ann Quinn, Oct. 23, 1965; children: Peter Charles, Evan Michael. BS in Engring. Sci., SUNY, Stony Brook, 1962, MS in Engring. Sci., 1964; PhD in Aerospace Engring., U. Tenn., 1970. Combustion rsch. engr. Gen. Electric Co., Cin., 1964-67; lead rsch. engr. Aro, Inc., Arnold Engring. Devel. Ctr., Tenn., 1969-74; rsch. specialist R&D Assoc., Marina Del Rey, Calif., 1974-76; div. mgr. Sci. Applications Internat. Corp., Chatsworth, Calif., 1976-85; chief aero. scientist Lockheed Aero. Systems Group, Burbank, Calif., 1985-88; chief project engr. Rocketdyne div. Rockwell Internat., Canoga Park, Calif., 1988-90; dep. program dir. Nat. Aero-Space Plane Program, 1990-95; program mgr. N.Am. Aircraft divsn. Rockwell Internat., Seal Beach, Calif., 1994—, 1994—. Contbr. articles to profl. jours. Recipient Disting. Alumnus award U. Tenn. Space Inst., 1984. Mem. AIAA, ASME, N.Y. Acad. Sci., Sigma Xi. Republican. Methodist. Home: 7235 Cirrus Way West Hills CA 91307-1416 Office: Rockwell Internat N Am Aircraft Divsn PO Box 3644 Seal Beach CA 90740

HARSTAD, KENNETH GUNDER, mechanical engineer, researcher; b. Hillsboro, N.D., Mar. 8, 1939; s. Henry J. and Ruth J. Harstad. BSME, U. N.D., 1961; MS, MIT, 1962; PhD, Calif. Inst. Tech., 1967. Mem. tech. staff Jet Propulsion Lab., Pasadena, Calif., 1967—. Contbr. articles to profl. jours. Office: Jet Propulsion Lab 4800 Oak Grove Dr Pasadena CA 91109-8001

HART, ANNE, author; b. N.Y.C., Nov. 18, 1941; BS in Creative Writing, English, NYU, 1964; MA in Creative Writing, English, San Diego State U., 1979; diploma Hollywood Scriptwriting Inst., 1984; diploma Alexandra Inst. Painting, San Diego, 1988. Pres. Anne Hart Prodns., Writing Cons. Author more than 40 books including In The Chips: 101 Ways to Make Money with your Personal Computer, 1985, High Paying Jobs in Six Months or Less, 1984, Understanding Robotics, 1985, Careers in Robotics, 1985, Careers in Aerospace, 1985, Homehealth Careers, 1993, Winning Resumes for Computer Personnel, 1994, (novels) Psyche Squad, The One Who Invented Writing, 1991, (CD-ROM) How To Write Video & Multimedia Scripts, The Idealist Adventures, 1994, and various short stories; co-author: Winning Tactics for Women Over 40, 1988, (screenplay and novel) Midnight Shift, 1989, Playpen Hostages, 1989, (screenplay) Black Snow Melting, 1990, Why so Many Thousands of American Children Are MIssing Overseas, 1991, Midnight Shift, Writing For the New Media, 1994; columnist Careers and the Internet; contbr. articles to various publs., film scripts, 2 novelettes and collections of short stories. Office: PO Box 4333 San Diego CA 92164-4333

HART, BONITA ELLEN, registered dietitian analyst; b. Rolla, N.D., Aug. 3, 1940; d. Delmar Lee and Ellen Vivien (Nicholas) Lovitt; m. Patrick Dennis Hart; children: Patrick Michael Hart, Lorene Ellen Hart. BS, Colo. State U., 1963; post grad., U. Calif. Berkeley, 1963-65, Seattle City U., 1978-84. Cert. dietitian. Clin. instr., dietetic intern Letterman Gen. Hosp., San Francisco, 1964-66; chief prodn. and svc. Letterman Gen. Hosp., 1964-66; food svc. dir. North Hollywood (Calif.) Cmty. Hosp., 1966-71; v.p. Hyatt Med. Enterprises, Encino, Calif., 1971-87, Am. Med. Internat., Beverly Hills, Calif., 1971-87; pres. Food and Nutrition Mgmt. Svcs., Inc., North Hollywood, 1987—. Author, editor: Clinical Diet Manual, 1971—, tng. manuals, pamphlets; lectr. in field. 1st lt. U.S. Army, 1962-66. Mem. AFTRA, Am. Dietetic Assn., Am. Soc. for Hosp. Food Svc. Adminstrs., Calif. Dietetic Assn., L.A. Dist. Dietetic Assn., Washington Dietetic Assn. Roman Catholic. Home: 6548 Charlesworth Ave North Hollywood CA 91606-1220

HART, DONALD PURPLE, bishop; b. N.Y.C., Apr. 22, 1937; s. Donald Buell Hart and Ann Wentworth (Ayres) Herrick; m. Elizabeth Ann Howard, Sept. 8, 1962; children: Sarah, Thomas. BA, Williams Coll., 1959; B of Divinity, Episc. Div. Sch., Cambridge, Mass., 1962. Curate Ch. of the Redeemer, Chestnut Hill, Mass., 1962-64; priest-in-charge Good Shepherd Mission, Huslia, Alaska, 1964-69; diocesan staff Native Ministry, Anchorage, Alaska, 1969-73; rector St. Matthew's Ch., Fairbanks, Alaska, 1973-83, St. James Ch., Keene, N.H., 1983-86; bishop Diocese of Hawaii, Honolulu, 1986-94, The Epsiopal Divinity Sch., Honolulu, 1994—. Chmn. St. Andrew's Priory Sch., Honolulu, 1986—, Seabury Hall Sch., Makawao, Hawaii, 1986—, St. John's Sch., Tumon Bay, Guam, 1986—; bd. govs. Iolani Sch., Honolulu, 1986—. Office: Episcopal Divinity Sch 99 Brattle St Cambridge MA 02138-3402

HART, EDWARD LEROY, poet, educator; b. Bloomington, Idaho, Dec. 28, 1916; s. Alfred Augustus and Sarah Cecilia (Patterson) H.; m. Eleanor May Coleman, Dec. 15, 1944 (dec. Dec. 1990); children: Edward Richard, Paul LeRoy, Barbara, Patricia; m. Leah Yates Bryson, Apr. 30, 1993. BS, U. Utah, 1939; MA, U. Mich., 1941; DPhil (Rhodes scholar), Oxford (Eng.) U., 1950. Instr. U. Utah, Salt Lake City, 1946; asst. prof. U. Wash., Seattle, 1949-52; asst. prof. Brigham Young U., Provo, Utah, 1952-55, assoc. prof., 1955-59, prof., 1959-82, prof. emeritus, 1982—; vis. prof. U. Calif., Berkeley, 1959-60, Ariz. State U., summer 1968. Author: Minor Lives, 1971, Instruction and Delight, 1976, Mormom in Motion, 1978; (poems) To Utah, 1979, Poems of Praise, 1980; More Than Nature Needs, 1982, God's Spies, 1983; contbr. articles to profl. jours. Lt. USNR, 1942-46. Am. Philos. Soc. grantee, 1964; First prize in poetry and biography Utah State Inst. Fine Arts, 1973,75; Fulbright-Hays sr. lectr. Pakistan, 1973-74; recipient Charles Redd award Utah Acad., 1976, Coll. Humanities Disting. Faculty award Brigham Young U., 1977. Fellow Am. Coun. Learned Socs., Found. Econ. Edn.;

mem. MLA, Rocky Mountain MLA, Am. Soc. 18th Century Studies, Utah Acad. Sci., Arts and Letters, Phi Beta Kappa, Phi Kappa Phi. Democrat. Mormon. Home: 1401 Cherry Ln Provo UT 84604-2848 Office: Brigham Young U Dept English Provo UT 84602

HART, ELDON CHARLES, educator; b. Plain City, Utah, Mar. 1, 1915; s. Charles Walter and Mildred (England) H.; m. Julina Smith, June 8, 1938; children: Eldon, Julina, Mildred, Lewis. BA, Brigham Young U., 1938; BS, U. Ill., 1939, MA, 1940, PhD, 1963. Coll. adminstr. Ricks Coll., Rexburg, Idaho, 1940-80; physics libr. U. Ill., Urbana, 1961-64; pres., instr. Aero Technicians, Inc., Rexburg, 1972—. Mem. Rotary Internat. Republican. Mem. LDS. Office: Aero Technicians Inc PO Box 7 Rexburg ID 83440-0007

HART, HOWARD FRANKLIN, lawyer; b. Syracuse, N.Y., Sept. 5, 1947; s. Earl E. and Leona (Altman) H.; m. Helene Hayat, May 23, 1985; 1 child, Sarah. AB, Cornell U., 1969; JD, Harvard U., 1972. Bar: N.Y. 1973, Calif. 1982. Assoc. Hughes Hubbard & Reed, N.Y.C., 1972-80; ptnr. Hughes Hubbard & Reed, N.Y.C., L.A., 1980-86, Rodi, Pollock, Pettker, Galbraith, & Phillips, L.A., 1986-89; v.p., gen. counsel Carlsberg Mgmt. Co., Santa Monica, Calif., 1989—.

HART, JEAN MACAULAY, clinical social worker; b. Bellingham, Wash.; d. Murry Donald and Pearl N. (McLeod) Macaulay; m. Richard D. Hart, Feb. 3, 1940 (dec. Mar. 1973); children: Margaret Hart Morrison, Pamela Hart Horton, Patricia L.; m. Lawrence Duling, Jan. 20, 1979 (dec. May 1992); children: Lenora Daniel, Larry, Jane. BA, Wash. State U., 1938; MSW, U. So. Calif., 1961. Lic. clin. social worker, Calif.; accredited counselor, Wash. Social worker Los Angeles County, 1957-58; children's service worker Dept. Children's Services, Los Angeles, 1958-59; program developer homemakers services project Calif. Dept. Children's Services, Los Angeles, 1962-64, developer homemaker cons. position, 1964-66; supr. protective services Dept. Children's Services, Los Angeles, 1966-67; dep. regional service adminstrn. Dept. Los Angeles County Children's Services, 1967-76; adminstr. Melgon Home for Developmental Disability, 1985-86. Mem. Portals Com., Los Angeles, 1974, Travelers Aid Bd., Long Beach, Calif. 1969. Recipient Nat. award work in community, spl. award for work with emotionally disturbed Com. for Los Angeles, 1974. Mem. AAUW, Nat. Assn. Social Workers (former delegate), Acad. Cert. Social Workers. Republican. Congregationalist. Club: Wing Point Golf and Country (Bainbridge Island, Wash.).

HART, JOSEPH H., bishop; b. Kansas City, Mo., Sept. 26, 1931. Ed., St. John Sem., Kansas City, St. Meinrad Sem., Indpls. Ordained priest Roman Catholic Ch., 1956; consecrated titular bishop of Thimida Regia and aux. bishop Cheyenne Wyo., 1976; apptd. bishop of Cheyenne, 1978. Office: Bishop's Residence 2121 Capitol Ave PO Box 426 Cheyenne WY 82003-0468

HART, MARIAN GRIFFITH, retired reading educator; b. Bates City, Mo., Feb. 5, 1929; d. George Thomas Leon and Beulah Winiferd (Hackley) Griffith; m. Ashley Bruce Hart, Dec. 23, 1951; children: Ashley Bruce Hart II, Pamela Cherie Hart Gates. BS, Cen. Mo. State Coll., 1951; MA, No. Ariz. U., 1976. Title I-Chpt. I reading dir. Page (Ariz.) Sch. Dist.; Title I dir. Johnson O'Malley Preschool, Page Sch. Dist.; dist. reading dir. Page Sch. Dist. Contbr. articles to profl. jours. and children's mags. Vol., organizer, mgr., instr. Page Community Adult Lit. Program; lifetime mem. Friends of Page Pub. Libr., sec. bd., 1990-91. Mem. Lake Powell Inst. (bd. dirs., sec. 1993—, Page Main St. Vol. of Yr. 1992), Lake Powell Inst. Behavioral Health Svcs. (bd. mem. 1995), Delta Kappa Gamma (pres. chpt. 1986-90, historian 1990-92, Omicron state coms., scholarship 1988-89, nominations 1991), Beta Sigma Phi (pres. chpt., v.p. chpt.). Home and Office: 66 S Navajo Dr PO Box 763 Page AZ 86040

HART, MICHAEL JOHN, environmental management; b. Manchester, N.H., July 7, 1946; s. Wilfred Norman and Agnes Hedvega (Filipowitz) H.; m. G. Mary Falvey, Aug. 15, 1976; children: Jocelyn Elizabeth, Catherine Mary. BA, Colo. U., 1968; MBA, Denver U., 1989. Radio announcer Sta. KRNW, Boulder, Colo., 1971-73; resource mgr. Flatiron Cos., Boulder, Colo., 1973-79; v.p. Flatiron Sand & Gravel, Boulder, Colo., 1979-89; pres. Hart & Assocs., Boulder, Colo., 1989—; chmn. of bd. Thorne Ecol. Inst., Boulder, 1991-93; pres. Colo. Rock Products Assoc., Denver, 1989; bd. dirs. Nat. Aggregates Assoc., Silver Springs, Md., 1992, Nat. Sand and Gravel Assoc., Silver Spring, 1983-86. Contbr. articles to profl. jours. Mem. LWV, BOulder, 1992, Pvt. Industry Coun., Boulder, 1989, Sch. Dist./Capital Needs Com., Boulder, 1990-92. Named Man of Yr., Colo. Sand & Gravel Assoc., 1979. Mem. Soc. for Ecol. Restoration, Assn. State Wetland Mgrs., Environ. Law Inst., Colo. Water Congress, Nat. Stone Assn., Nat. Aggregates Assn., Beta Gamma Sigma. Office: Hart and Assocs 2255 Meadow Ave Boulder CO 80304-1626

HART, MILFORD E., psychotherapist; b. Cambridge, Mass., Apr. 10, 1945; s. I. Lester and Florence D. (Robinson) H.; m. Magdalena Herrera, Jan. 14, 1977; children: Joaquin, Norma, Jeremy, Thomas, Katherine. BA, U. No. Colo., 1968, MA, 1992. Real estate broker ERA Ken Rice, Aurora, Colo., 1980-83; pvt. practice psychotherapy Greeley & Ft. Morgan, Colo., 1992—; real estate broker ERA Questor Real Estate Corp., Aurora, 1984-85, pvt. real estate broker, Denver, 1985-89; instr. psychology Morgan C.C., Ft. Morgan, 1993—; fin. counselor CCCS, Greeley, Colo., 1989—; mem. adv. bd. Family Self-Suffeciency, Greeley, 1993-94. Author poems; contbr. articles to profl. jours. Mem. Weld County Dem. Com., Greeley, 1967-68; vol. United Farm Workers, Weld County, 1966-69, Cath. Comty. Svcs., Greeley, 1989—; area dir. women's program U.S. Slowpitch Softball Assn., Weld County, 1990-93; chair grievance com. Aurora Bd. Realtors; chair polit. affairs Greeley Bd. Realtors. Recipient John A. Love Book award U. No. Colo., 1968; grantee Cmty. Correction, 1993-94, Morgan C.C., 1994. Mem. ACA, Am. Mental Health Counseling Assn., Colo. Housing Counseling Coalition (v.p.), Internat. Assn. Counselors and Therapists. Democrat. Office: 705 8th Ave Greeley CO 80631-3955

HART, MONROE MONTE, English language and literature educator; b. Buena Park, Calif., Mar. 30, 1930; s. Montie Hart and Mabel Eliza Howard; m. Mary Federinic, 1953 (div. 1990); chilren; Stephanie Ann Hart Brazell, Laura Lee Hart Zemple, Marlyssa Lynn Hart West. BA in English and Speech, UCLA, 1957; MA in English, Long Beach (Calif.) State U., 1958; MA in Radio, TV and Film, Calif. State U., Northridge, 1977. Tchr. L.A. City Unified Schs., Tujunga, Calif., 1958-90. Author: English One, 1970, From Experience, A Rhetoric Reader, 1974, English Mechanics, 1978; contbr. scripts, short stories, poems and articles to profl. jours. Pioneered pub. access State of Calif.; organized 1st Pub. Access Found., L.A. Served with U.S. Army, 1951-53, Korea. Home and Office: 5393 Godbey Dr La Canada CA 91011-1872

HART, RUSS ALLEN, telecommunications educator; b. Seguin, Tex., June 30, 1946; s. Bevelly D. and Hattie V. (Reeh) H.; m. Judith Harwood, 1984 (div. 1986); m. Patricia Barrios, Mar. 22, 1987. BA, Tex. Tech. U., 1968; MA, U. Ariz., 1976; PhD, U. Wyo., 1984. Chief cinematographer, producer-dir. dept. med-TV-film, health sci. ctr. U. Ariz., Tuscon, 1973-77; instr., coord. ednl. TV and cinematography U. Wyo., Laramie, 1977-81; assoc. prof., dir. biomed. communication Mercer U., Macon, Ga., 1981-84; prof., dir. instructional telecommunications Calif. State U., Fresno, 1984-92, prof., assoc. dir. computing, comm. and media svcs., 1992—; condr. ednl. confs.; tech. cons. for distance edn. Contbr. articles to profl. jours. Served to capt. USAF, 1968-73. Recipient Cert. Merit, Chgo. Internat. Film Festival, 1975, 1st pl. INDY Indsl. Photography award, 1976, 2d pl. INDY Indsl. Photography award, 1975, Silver plaque Chgo. Internat. Film Festival, 1978, Winner of case study competition Internat. Radio and TV Soc., 1989, Bronze Telly award, 1992, 93, Crystal Shooting Star award, 1993, 94, Cine Golden Eagle award, 1994. Mem. Assn. for Ednl. Comms. and Tech. (rsch. session chmn. 1983), Am. Assn. Adult and Continuing Educators (mem. eval. task force 1986), Broadcast Edn. Assn., Health Sci. Comms. Assn. (mem. continuing edn. subcom. 1983), Biol. Photog. Assn. (film judge 1975), Alliance for Distance Edn. in Calif. (founding mem. 1991), Ednl. Telecom. Consortium of Ctrl. Calif. (founding mem. 1993), Phi Delta Kappa. Office: Calif State U Dept Computing Comm and Media Svcs Fresno CA 93740

HART, TIMOTHY RAY, lawyer, dean; b. Portland, Jan. 5, 1942; s. Eldon V. and Wanda J. (Hillyer) H.; m. Mary F. Barlow, Aug. 31, 1964 (div. Dec. 1975); children: Mark, Matthew, Marisa, Martin; m. Annette Bryant, Aug. 8, 1981. AA, San Jose City Coll., 1968; BA, San Jose State U., 1970; MA, Wash. State U., 1973; JD, San Joaquin Coll. Law, Fresno, Calif., 1983. Bar: Calif. 1983, U.S. Dist. Ct. (ea. dist.) Calif. 1983. Police officer City of Santa Clara, Calif., 1965-71; chief of police U. Idaho, Moscow, 1971-73; crime prevention officer City of Albany, Oreg., 1973-75; instr. criminal justice Coll. of Sequoias, Visalia, Calif., 1975-81, dir. paralegal dept., 1981-83, chmn., dir. adminstrn. justice div., 1983-88; assoc. dean instruction, 1988—; sole practice, Visalia, 1983—. Bd. dirs. Sprout Ranch for Deaf Children, Tulare County Humane Soc. With USAF, 1960-63. Mem. ABA, Calif. Bar Assn., Assn. Trial Lawyers Am., Assn. Criminal Justice Educators, Am. Criminal Justice Assn., Delta Phi. Mennonite. Home: 3039 W Packwood Ct Visalia CA 93277-7923 Office: Coll of Sequoias 915 S Mooney Blvd Visalia CA 93277-2214

HARTENBACH, DAVID LAWRENCE, school system administrator; b. St. Louis, Dec. 6, 1934; s. Henry Charles and Loretta S. (Schwarz) H. BA, St. Louis U., 1958, MEd, 1960; EdD in Sacred Theology, U. No. Colo., 1981. Cert. adminstr., Colo. Adminstrv. intern St. Louis U. H.S., 1966-67, asst. prin., 1967-68; prin. Regis H.S. Archdiocese of Denver, 1968-70; prin. Benton Harbor (Mich.) H.S., 1970-72; prin. W.C. Hinkley H.S. Aurora (Colo.) Pub. Schs., 1972-77, exec. dir. H.S.'s, 1977-86, assoc. supt. instrn., 1986-89, assoc. supt. aux., 1989-93, supt. schs., 1993—; mem. state com. Colo. North Ctrl. Assn., Greeley, 1976-83. Membership chmn. Centennial Dist. Unit PTA, Aurora, 1993—; mem. human rels. com. City of Aurora, 1978-84. Named Colo. Supt. of Yr., Nat. Sch. Bds. Assn., 1995; grantee Ford Found., 1965-66, Nat. Acad. Rsch. in Vocat. Edn., 1979. Mem. ASCD, Nat. Assn. Secondary Sch. Prins. (nat. com. large secondary schs. 1980-83, adminstrv. intern J. Lloyd Trump grantee 1966-67), Am. Assn. Sch. Adminstrs., Colo. Assn. Sch. Bds., Colo. Assn. Sch. Execs., Kiwanis (past pres. Centennial chpt.). Office: Aurora Pub Schs 1085 Peoria St Aurora CO 80011-6203*

HARTER, LAFAYETTE GEORGE, JR., economics educator emeritus; b. Des Moines, May 28, 1918; s. Lafayette George and Helen Elizabeth (Ives) H.; m. Charlotte Mary Toshach, Aug. 23, 1950; children—Lafayette George III, James Toshach, Charlotte Helen. B.A. in Bus. Adminstrn, Antioch Coll., 1941; M.A. in Econs, Stanford, 1948, Ph.D., 1960. Instr. Menlo Coll., Menlo Park, Cal., 1948-50; instr. Coll. of Marin, Kentfield, Calif., 1950-60; prof. econs. dept. Oreg. State U., 1960-85, prof. emeritus, 1985—, chmn. dept., 1967-71; mem. panel arbitrators Fed. Mediation and Conciliation Service, 1965—, Oreg. Conciliation Service, 1967—; mem. Univ. Centers for Rational Alternatives. Author: John R. Commons: His Assault on Laissez-faire, 1962, Labor in America, 1957, Economic Responses to a Changing World, 1972; editorial bd. Jour. Econ. Issues, 1981-84. Assoc. campaign chmn. Benton United Good Neighbor Fund, 1970-72, campaign chmn., v.p., 1972-73, pres., 1973-74, vice chmn.; pub. mem. Adv. Commn. on Unemployment Compensation, 1972, 73, chmn., 1974-78; Bd. dirs. Oreg. Coun. Econ. Edn., 1971-89; pub. mem. local profl. responsibilities Oreg. State Bar Assn., 1980-83; pub. mem. Oreg. Coun. on Ct. Procedures, 1985-93, bd. mem. Community Econs. of Corp., Community Econ. Stabilization Corp. Lt. comdr. USNR, 1941-46. Mem. AAUP, Am. Arbitration Assn. (pub. employment disputes panel 1970-92), Am. Western Econ. Assns., Indsl. Rels. Rsch. Assn., Am. Assn. for Evolutionary Econs., Oreg. State Employees Assn. (v.p. faculty chpt. 1972, pres. 1973), Am. Assn. Ret. Persons (pres. local chpt. 1992-93), Corvallis Retirement Village (fin. com.). Democrat. Mem. United Ch. of Christ (moderator 1972, 73; mem. fin. com. Oreg. conf. 1974-82, dir. 1978-81, mem. personnel com. 1983-85). Home: 3755 NW Van Buren Ave Corvallis OR 97330-4952

HARTER, PENNY, poet, English educator; b. N.Y.C., Apr. 9, 1940; d. George and Barbara (Kingsley) H.; m. Charles H. Bihler, 1960 (div. 1980); children: Charles, Nancy Etline; m. William J. Higginson, May 31, 1980. BA in English Edn., Douglass Coll., New Brunswick, N.J. Tchr. Woodbridge Twp. Bd. Edn., Woodbridge, N.J., 1978-83; tchr. English Madison (N.J.) High Sch. and Jr. Sch., 1983-91, Santa Fe (N.Mex.) Prep. Sch., 1991—; adj. instr. English, Union County Coll., Cranford, N.J., 1987-89; editor From Here Press, Santa Fe, 1979—; cons. in writing and teaching of writing, 1972—. Author: (poems) House by the Sea, 1975, Lovepoems, 1981, In the Broken Curve, 1984, The Price of Admission, 1986, The Monkey's Face, 1987, At the Zendo, 1993, Stages and Views, 1994, Shadow Play: Night Haiku, 1994, Grandmother's Milk, 1995, others; contbr. to numerous anthologies and periodicals. Recipient Arnold Gingrich Meml. award N.J. State Coun. on Arts, 1978, Honorable Mention awrd Chester H. Jones Found. Nat. Poetry Competition, 1988, Mary Carolyn Davies Meml. award Poetry Soc. Am., 1987; N.J. State Coun. on Arts fellow in writing, 1985, 88, Geraldine R. Dodge Found. fellow in teaching of writing, 1985. Mem. PEN N.Mex., PEN Internat., Poetry Soc. Am., Haiku Soc. Am. (pres. 1986). Office: care From Here Press PO Box 2740 Santa Fe NM 87504-2740

HARTFORD, JANE DAVIS, textile artist; b. Erick, Okla., Aug. 21, 1927; d. Bunyon Hoyt and Lonie Lee (Jeter) Davis; m. Thomas James Hartford, Jr., June 15, 1951; children: Jane Anne, Thomas James III. BFA, U. Okla., 1949; postgrad., Parson's Sch. Design, 1949; MA, U. Louisville, 1960. Interior designer Marshall Field and Co., Chgo., 1950-51; art therapist Norton Meml. Infirmary, Louisville, 1958-59; artist, tchr. Utah Arts Coun., Salt Lake City, 1980; bd. dirs., founding mem., chmn. ways and means com. Intermountain Weavers Conf., Phoenix, 1980-83. Exhibited in group shows at Small Expressions '85, Mass., 1985, Small Expressions '87, Calif., 1987, Convergence '86, Toronto, Can., 1991, Conf. So. Calif. Handweavers, 1991, Nat. Cathedral, Washington, 1992. Vol. demonstrator Pioneer Trails State Park, Salt Lake City, 1976-88. Mem. Handweavers Guild Am. (bd. dirs. 1980-88, pres. 1983-85, chmn. bd. dirs. 1985-88), MM Atwater Weavers Guild Utah (life, pres. 1974-75), Las Tejedoras de Santa Fe y los Alamos (v.p. 1991-93,chair 1993-95), P.E.O. (recording corr. sec., guard 1991-92), Pi Beta Phi (historian 1946-47). Episcopalian. Home: 500 Washington Ave Santa Fe NM 87501-1123

HARTFORD, MARGARET ELIZABETH (BETTY HARTFORD), social work educator, gerontologist; b. Cleve., Dec. 12, 1917; d. William A. and Inez (Logan) H. BA, Ohio U., 1940; MS, U. Pitts., 1944; PhD, U. Chgo., 1962. Dir. youth svc. YWCA, Canton, Ohio, 1940-42; program cons. Intercultural Rels. Am. Svc. Inst., Pitts., 1943-48, exec. dir., 1948-50; prof. social work Case Western Res. U., Cleve., 1950-75; founding dir. Sch. Gerontology U. So. Calif., L.A., 1975-77, prof. gerontology, social work, 1977-83, prof. emeritus, 1983—; instr. Claremont (Calif.) Adult Sch. Dist., 1983—, mentor/tchr. adult edn., 1990—; instr. retirement Pasadena (Calif.) City Coll., 1983-84, Mt. San Antonio Coll., 1988-90; cons. pre-retirement, retirement planning to corps. and ednl. systems, various cities, 1980—; free-lance writer, cons., lectr. 1970—. Author: Groups in Social Work, 1973, (workbook) Making the Best of the Rest of Your Life, 1982, Leaders Guide to Making the Best of the Rest of Your Life, 1986; contbr. monthly column on successful aging Pomona Valley Cmty. Svcs. on Aging Newsletter, monthly column on transitions to Tempo mag.; contbr. numerous articles to profl. publs. Commr. human svcs. City of Clairmont, 1986-89, city coun. observer LWV, 1994-95; trustee Mt. San Antonio Gardens Retirement Com., 1985-92, sec., 1988-91; v.p. Mt. San Antonio Gardens Club Coun. Residents Orgn., 1991—, area chmn., 1994—, trustee Corp. Pilgrim Pl. Ret. Cmty., chmn. health and svcs. com., 1987-94; bd. dirs., trustee Vol. Assn. Rancho Santa Ana Bot. Gardens, 1991—; chmn. vol. pers. com. St. Ambrose Episcopal Ch., Claremont, 1988—. Named Outstanding Contbn. to Social Work, Alumni Assn. Schs. Social Work U. So. Calif., 1984, Outstanding Contbr. Social Group Work, Com. Advancement of Group Work, Toronto, Ont., Can., 1985, Woman of Yr., Trojan Women U. So. Calif., 1976, Woman of Yr., YWCA of Pomona Valley, 1989, Vol. of Yr., L.A. County Coun. on Aging, 1990; recipient Dart award for Innovative Teaching, U. So. Calif., 1974, 1st pl. award at juried show Am. Assn. Chinese Brush Painting, 1987, 2nd pl. short story Sedona Writers Contest, Hon. Mention non fiction, 1989, County Commnr. Citation State of Calif. Ho. of Reps., Outstanding Contbn. award Mt. San Antonio Gardens Retirement Cmty., 1994, Contbn. to Srs. award Pomona Valley Cmty. Svcs., 1994. Fellow Gerontol. Soc. Am.; mem. AAUW, Nat. Assn. Social Workers (cert., nat. chmn. 1962-64, group work sect., chmn. Cleve. chpt. 1969-72), Am. Soc. Aging (chmn. program com. 1983-85, City of Claremont com. on aging, chmmn. 1991, program chair 1985-94), Delta Kappa Gamma, Alpha Xi Delta. Episcopalian. Home: 918 Harrison Ave Claremont CA 91711-4129

HARTH, ROBERT JAMES, music festival executive; b. Louisville, June 13, 1956; s. Sidney and Teresa O. H.; m. Melanie Lynn Pope; 1 child, Jeffrey David Harth Curtis. B.A. in English, Northwestern U., 1977. Assoc. mgr. Ravinia (Ill.) Festival Assn., 1977-79; v.p., gen. mgr. Los Angeles Philharm. Assn., 1979-89, Hollywood Bowl, 1979-89; pres., chief exec. officer Aspen (Colo.) Music Festival and Sch., Music Assocs. of Aspen, Inc., 1989—. Office: Aspen Music Festival-Sch 2 Music School Rd Aspen CO 81611

HARTING, TRIP, equine trainer; b. Takoma, Md., Jan. 8, 1946; s. Frederick George Jr. and Claire Charlotte (McMullen) H. BA, Roanoke Coll., 1968; MA, Georgetown U., 1971. Dressage judge Am. Horse Shows Assn., N.Y.C., 1972; chmn. dressage com. U.S. Pony Clubs, Lexington, Ky., 1994; chmn. jr. young rider com. U.S. Dressage Fedn., Lincoln, Nebr., 1991. Sgt. U.S. Army, 1968-70. Office: PO Box 691842 West Hollywood CA 90069-8842

HARTINGER, PATRICIA BERNARDINE CURRAN, elementary school educator; b. Monterey, Calif., Sept. 16, 1935; d. John George and Myra Hall Curran; m. Walter Hartinger, Nov. 14, 1959; children: Maureen, John. AA with honor, Monterey Peninsula Coll., 1955; BA with great distinction, San Jose State U., 1958; postgrad., U. Calif., Santa Cruz, U. Santa Clara. Cert. life sch. libr., jr. high sch., child devel. Libr. San Jose (Calif.) State Coll., 1956-58, Milpitas (Calif.) Sch. Dist., 1960-62, Alma Coll., Los Gatos, Calif., 1963-65, Santa Clara (Calif.) Pub. Libr., 1966-69; tchr. Westerner Schs., Los Gatos, 1975-82, Town & Country Pre-Sch., San Jose, Calif., 1982-83, St. Frances Cabrini Sch., San Jose, 1983-85, St. Lucy Sch., Campbell, Calif., 1985-93, St. Lawrence The Martyr Sch., Santa Clara, Calif., 1993-94; substitute tchr. Diocese of San Jose, 1994—, Sacred Heart Sch., Saratoga, Calif., 1995—; curriculum writer in field. Author: Earthquake of Apr. 18, 1906 in the Santa Clara Valley, 1973 (cash award), History of Santa Clara Valley Handweavers Guild, 1988; contbr. articles on Peace Edn. to various pubs., recipes to Sunset Mag. Vol. tchr. Lyceum of Santa Clar County for Gifted Children, San Jose, 1974-80; vol. libr. Santa Clara Valley Med. Ctr., San Jose, 1962-63, Los Gatos Elem. Sch. Dist., 1968-75; tchr. of religion pre-sch. Diocese of San Jose, 1971-80; mem. Nat. Audubon Soc., 1981—; Nature Conservancy, 1990—. Recipient Kiwanis Club scholarship San Jose State U., 1956, Delta Delta Delta Sorority scholarship, 1957-58. Mem. Nat. Coun. for Social Studies, Calif. Coun. Social Studies, Calif. Assn. Edn. Young Children, Santa Clara County Reading Coun., Santa Clara Valley Handweavers (founding), San Jose State U. Key Club, Phi Alpha Theta, Phi Kappa Phi. Democrat. Home: 16155 Jacaranda Way Los Gatos CA 95032-3627

HART-KEPLER, VIRGINIA LYNN, nurse, educator; b. Chico, Calif., Dec. 17, 1953; d. Lloyd G. and Patricia B. Hart; m. William Edward Kepler, Mar. 21, 1987. AA, Pasadena City Coll., 1976; BSN, Calif. State U., L.A., 1980; FNP, UCLA, 1986, M in Nursing, 1987. Cert. family nurse practitioner. part time nurse practictioner K. Norris Cancer Hosp. Employee Health Svc., L.A. Active in community working with homeless and underprivileged. Recipient Audrienne H. Moseley Rsch. Fund award. Mem. Am. Acad. Nurse Practitioners, Calif. Coalition of Nurse Practitioners, Assn. Christian Therapists, Sigma Theta Tau.

HARTLEY, ALBERT EDWARD, insurance agent; b. Seattle, Mar. 17, 1924; s. Edward Albert and Gertrude (Lachance) H.; m. Eileen Barnawell, Mar. 8, 1945 (div. May 1973); 1 child, Kevin B.; m. Marny W. Woodsmall, May 17, 1974. BA in Econs., Berea Coll., 1947. CLU, chartered fin. con. Am. Coll. Ins. agt. Prudential Ins. Co., Trenton, Mich., 1957-84, Sun Plan Fin. Svcs., Tucson, 1984—. Bd. dirs., treas. Cooperative Svcs., Detroit, 1967-80. Democrat. Office: Sun Plan Fin Svcs 3208 E Ft Lowell Rd Ste 105 Tucson AZ 85716-1625

HARTMAN, ANDREW PAUL, JR., hospital association administrator; b. Phila., Apr. 3, 1945; s. Andrew Paul and Katherine Jane (Howell) H.; m. Diane Margaret Walton, July 12, 1969; children: Robert Jacob, Ashley Nicole. BSBA, U. Fla., 1967; MBA, U. Mont., 1971; M in Hosp. Adminstrn., Washington U., St. Louis, 1976. Asst. adminstr. Warner Brown Hosp., El Dorado, Ark., 1976-79; assoc. adminstr. Warner Brown Hosp., El Dorado, 1979-81, Lester E. Cox Med. Ctr., Springfield, Mo., 1981-83; adminstr. Breech Med. Ctr., Lebanon, Mo., 1983-88; chief exec. officer Steamboat Springs (Colo.) Hosp. Assn., 1988—. V.p. Lacede County chpt. Am. Cancer Soc., Lebanon, Mo., 1987-88, bd. dirs., 1986-88. Capt. USAF, 1967-74. Mem. Am. Coll. Healthcare Execs. (regents adv. coun. 1988—), Lebanon Rotary (sec. 1986-88), Steamboat Springs Rotary, Voluntary Hosps. of Am. Mountain States (bd. dirs. 1988—). Office: N Valley Rehab Hosp 340 W East Ave Chico CA 95926-7238

HARTMAN, HYMAN, biochemist; b. Montreal, June 5, 1936; s. Cecil Nathan and Hadassah (Weissenberg) H.; m. Berl Mendelson Hartman, Sept. 15, 1960; children: Rebecca, Deborah. BSc in Biochemistry, McGill U., Montreal, 1957; PhD in Biochemistry, Columbia U., 1963. Postdoctoral fellow dept. molecular biology MIT, Cambridge, Mass., 1964-68; rsch. assoc. dept. molecular biology U. Calif., Berkeley, 1968-74; asst. prof. dept. human genetics Sackler Med. Sch., U. Tel-Aviv, Israel, 1974-76; rsch. scientist Children's Hosp., Harvard Med. Sch., Boston, 1977-80; rsch. scientist dept. earth sis. MIT, 1980-87; rsch. assoc. dept. computer sci. U. Calif., Berkeley, 1988-90, rsch. assoc. dept. soil sci., 1991—; dir. Inst. for Advanced Studies in Biology, Berkeley, 1991—; mem. NASA Exobiology Peer Rev. Panel, 1980-85; mem. com. on planetary biology and chem. evolution Space Sci. Bd., Nat. Acad. Sci., 1984-87. Co-editor: Search for the Universal Ancestor, 1987, Clay Minerals and the Origin of Life, 1986, The Origin and Evolution of the Cell, 1992; contbr. articles to profl. jours. Office: Inst Advanced Studies Biol 880 Spruce St Berkeley CA 94707-2043

HARTMAN, ROBERT LEROY, artist, educator; b. Sharon, Pa., Dec. 17, 1926; s. George Otto and Grace Arvada (Radabaugh) H.; m. Charlotte Ann Johnson, Dec. 30, 1951; children: Mark Allen, James Robert. B.F.A., U. Ariz., 1951, M.A., 1952; postgrad., Colo. Springs Fine Arts Center, 1947, 51, Bklyn. Mus. Art Sch., 1953-54. Instr. architecture, allied arts Tex. Tech. Coll., 1955-58; asst. prof. art U. Nev., Reno, 1958-61; mem. faculty dept. art U. Calif., Berkeley, 1961—, prof., 1972-91, prof. emeritus, 1991—, chmn. dept., 1974-76; mem. Inst. for Creative Arts, U. Calif., 1967-68. One man exhbns. include, Bertha Schafer Gallery, N.Y.C., 1966, 69, 74, Santa Barbara Mus. Art, 1973, Cin. Art Acad., 1975, Hank Baum Gallery, San Francisco, 1973, 75, 78, San Jose Mus. Art, 1983, Bluxome Gallery, San Francisco, 1984, 86, U. Art Mus., Berkeley, 1986, Instituto D'Arte Dosso Dossi, Ferrara, Italy, 1989, Victor Fischer Galleries, San Francisco, 1991, Triangle Gallery, San Francisco, 1992, 93, 95; group exhbns. include Richmond Mus., 1966, Whitney Mus. Biennial, 1973, Oakland Mus., 1976, San Francisco Arts Commn. Gallery, 1985 (award), Earthscape Expo '90 Photo Mus., Osaka, Japan, 1990, In Close Quarters, American Landscape Photography Since 1968, Princeton Art Mus., 1993, Facing Eden: 100 Years of Landscape Art in The Bay Area, San Francisco, 1995; represented in permanent collections, Nat. Collections Fine Arts, Colorado Springs Fine Arts Center, Corcoran Gallery, San Francisco Art Inst., Roswell Mus., Princeton Art Mus. U. Calif. humanities research fellow, 1980. Office: U Calif Dept Art Berkeley CA 94720

HARTMAN, ROSEMARY JANE, special education educator; b. Gainesville, Fla., Aug. 24, 1944; d. John Leslie and Irene (Bowen) Goddard; m. Alan Lynn Gerber, Feb. 1, 1964 (div. 1982); children: Sean Alan, Dawn Julianne Silva, Lance Goddard; m. Perry Hartman, June 27, 1992. BA, Immaculate Heart Coll., 1967; MA, Loyola U., 1974. Cert. resource specialist. Tchr. L.A. Unified Schs., 1968-78; resource specialist Desert Sands Unified Sch. Dist., Palm Desert, 1978-83, Palm Springs Unified Schs., 1983—. Co-author: The Twelve Steps of Phobics Anonymous, 1989, One Day At A Time in Phobics Victorious, 1992; founder Phobics Victorious, 1992. Mem. Am. Assn. Christian Counselors (charter). Office: Phobics Victorious PO Box 695 Palm Springs CA 92263-0695

HARTMAN, TERRY A., filmmaker; b. Waukegan, Ill.. BFA, Art Ctr. Sch., L.A., 1971. Fellow in clin. hypnotherapy. Dir. Terry Hartman Studio,

Portland, Oreg., 1974-82; creative dir. Needham Worldwide, Auckland, New Zealand, 1983-85; dir. Hong Kong Films, 1986; writer, dir. Hartman Films, Portland, 1988—; dir. PSI Creative Internat., Portland; v.p. Second Breath, Inc., Portland, Making the Difference, Inc.; exec. producer, Vagabond Video, Portland. Producer: (TV commls.) Am. Cancer Soc., 1990 (Nat. Citation/Telly 1992), (video) New Voice Club, 1993 (Telly), (documentary) Perrier Investments, 1994 (Telly). Mem. Assn. Ind. Film/Video Makers.

HARTMAN-IRWIN, MARY FRANCES, retired language professional; b. Portland, Oreg., Oct. 18, 1925; d. Curtiss Henry Sabisch and Gladys Frances (Giles) Strand; m. Harry Elmer Hartman, Sept. 6, 1946 (div. June 1970); children: Evelyn Frances, Laura Elyce, Andrea Candace; m. Thomas Floyd Irwin, Apr. 11, 1971. BA, U. Wash., 1964-68; postgrad., Seattle Pacific, 1977-79, Antioch U., Seattle, Wash., 1987, Heritage Inst., Seattle, Wash., 1987. Lang. educator Kennewick (Wash.) Dist. # 17, 1970-88; guide Summer Study Tours of Europe, 1971-88. Sec. Bahai Faith, 1971-94, libr., Pasco, Washington, 1985-88; trustee Mid. Columbia Coun. Girl Scouts USA; mem. Literacy Coun. Fulbright summer scholar, 1968. Mem. NEA, Wash. Edn. Assn., Kennewick Edn. Assn., Nat. Fgn. Lang. Assn., Wash. Fgn. Lang. Assn., Literacy Coun. Home: 1119 W Margaret St Pasco WA 99301-4134

HARTNELL, AGNES E., dietitian, educator; b. Covington, Ohio; d. Richard Fowler and Margaret Louella (Crook) Albery; m. William F. Hartnell; divorced; children: Jan Hancock, Hanna. BS in Home Econs., Ohio State U., 1937; BS in Edn., U. Akron, 1955; MS in Edn., U. Ariz., 1962; EdD in Adminstrn. and Supervision, Ariz. State U., 1968. Cert. tchr., Ariz. Home economist Columbus (Ohio) Electric Co.; educator in univ. and H.S. Ohio, Calif., Ariz., 1953-57; home econs. dept. chair Phoenix Coll., 1977-88; cons., instr. Ctrl. Ariz. Coll., Coolidge, 1988—; TV/radio instr. PBS, Ariz. State U., Tempe, 1970-88; registered dietician, cons., Phoenix, 1988—; cons. prisons, Native Ams., colls., Ariz., 1970-77; mem. nat. adv. bd. Future Homemakers Am., 1958, 70, State of Ariz., Ariz. Dietetic Assn., Home Econs. Assn., Hero, Phoenix Coll., Ctrl. Ariz. Coll., 1970—. Author: (study guide) Nutrition Concepts and Controversies, 3d edit., 1988, (textbook) Child Nutrition Practicum, 1994, Outsmarting the Migraine Headache, 1995; contbr. articles to profl. jours. Resource nutrition spkr. 1st United Meth. Ch., Phoenix, 1990—; resident mem. The Mountain Club, Prescott, Ariz., 1982—; del. China Assns. for Sci.-Tech., Peking, 1988. Recipient Star award Chandler, Ariz., 1967-68, Hosp. Aux. Mem. Am. Dietetic Assn., Am. Home Econs. Assn. (cert.), Am. Soc. of Interior Designers, Ret. Edn. Assn., Home Econs. in Bus., Ohio State U. Alumni Assn., Ariz. State U. Alumni Assn., Delta Gamma, Omicron Nu. Republican. Home and Office: 520 W Clarendon Ave Unit E5 Phoenix AZ 85013-3428

HARTNESS, SANDRA JEAN, venture capitalist; b. Jacksonville Fla., Aug. 19, 1944; d. Harold H. and Viola M. (House) H. AB, Ga. So. Coll., 1969; postgrad., San Francisco State Coll., 1970-71. Researcher Savannah (Ga.) Planning Commn., 1969, Environ. Analysis Group, San Francisco, 1970-71; dir. Mission Inn, Riverside, Calif., 1971-75; developer Hartness Assocs., Laguna Beach, Calif., 1976—; ptnr. Western Neuro-Care Ctr., Tustin Calif., 1983-89; pres. Asset Svcs., Inc., 1981—. V.p., mem. bd. dirs. Evergreen Homes, Inc., 1986-90. Recipient numerous awards for community svc. Democrat. Office: Hartness Assocs 32612 Adriatic Dr Monarch Beach CA 92629-3510

HARTOUNI, VALERIE ANNE, political science educator; b. Newton, Mass., May 5, 1955; d. Edward and Jacqueline Anne (Priest) H. BA in Polit. Studies, Pitzer Coll. of Claremont Coll, 1977; PhD in History of Consciousness, U. Calif., Santa Cruz. Lectr. Stanford U., Calif., 1985-87; asst. prof. polit. sci. Williams Coll., Williamstown, Mass., 1988-90; asst. prof. comms. & women's studies U. Calif., San Diego, 1990—; reader U. Minn. Press, Mpls., Signs., Mpls., Women & Politics. Mem. Am. Polit. Sci. Assn. Office: U Calif Dept Comms 9500 Gilman Dr La Jolla CA 92093-5003

HARTSHORN, TERRY O., health facility administrator; b. 1944. Adminstrv. sec. Centinela Valley Hosp., Inglewood, Calif., 1965-68, adminstrv. asst., 1969; adminstr., cons. Community Health Svc., USPHS, L.A., 1969-71; adminstr. Luth. Hosp. Soc. So. Calif., L.A., 1971-73, Moore-White Med. Clinic, L.A., 1973-76; chmn. Pacificare Health Systems, Inc., Cypress, Calif., 1977—; chmn., pres., CEO Pacificare Health Systems, Inc., Burbank, Calif., 1993—; chmn. bd., pres., CEO UniHealth Am., Inc., Burbank, 1993—. Office: Unihealth Am 4100 W Alameda Ave Fl 4 Burbank CA 91505-4153

HARTWICK, THOMAS STANLEY, aerospace company executive; b. Vandalia, Ill., Mar. 19, 1934; s. William Arthur and Bernice Elizabeth (Daniels) H.; m. Alberta Elaine Lind, June 10, 1961; children: Glynis Anne, Jeffrey Andrew, Thomas Arthur. BS, U. Ill., 1956; MS, UCLA, 1958; PhD, U. So. Calif., 1969. Mgr. quantum electronics dept. Aerospace Corp., El Segundo, Calif., 1973-75, asst. dir. electonics research lab., 1975-79; mgr. electro-optical devel. lab. Hughes Aircraft Co. subs. Gen. Motors Corp., El Segundo, 1979-82, chief sci. advanced tactical programs, 1982-83; mgr. electro-optics research ctr. TRW Corp., Redondo Beach, Calif., 1983-86, mgr. microelectrics ctr., 1986-90, program mgr., 1990—; chmn., bd. dirs. Laser Tech., Inc., Hollywood, Calif.; cons. mem. U.S. Dept. Def. Adv. Group on Electronic Devices, Washington, 1977—, group C chmn., 1988-94; mem. Japan/U.S. Tech. Assessment Team, Washington, 1984; mem. Army Rsch. Labs. Adv. Bd., 1993—. Contbr. articles to profl. jours.; inventor FAR Infrared Laser, 1975. Mem. Am. Phys. Soc., Optical Soc. Am., (com. mem. 1976-79), Am. Def. Preparedness Assn. (dep. chmn. West Coast seminar 1987-88). Office: TRW Inc One Space Park 1 Space Park Blvd Rm 2830 Redondo Beach CA 90278-1001

HARTWIG, ROBERT ALLEN, JR., international trade accountant; b. Mason City, Iowa, June 9, 1958; s. Robert Allen and Shirley June (Orvis) H.; m. Glenda Gayle Grubbs, Aug. 18, 1979; children: David Christian, Amanda Gayle. BBA in Acctg. and Fin., U. Iowa, 1980; Cert. in Applied Internat. Mktg. & Mgmt., Front Range Coll., 1993. CPA, Colo. Auditor Alexander Grant & Co., Denver, 1980-84; acct. III, systems analyst City of Aurora, Colo., 1984; chief acct. City of Westminster, Colo., 1984-89; fin. dir. City of Greenwood Village, Colo., 1989-91; prin. Hartwig & Assocs., CPA, PC, 1991—; bd. dirs. Front Range Coll. Found. City councilman City of Westminster, 1989-93; chmn. Jefferson County Air Show Com., 1994—; precinct capt. Jefferson County Rep. Ctrl. Com., 1989-94, dist. capt., 1994—, campaign mgr., 1992—; precinct capt. Nat. League Cities, 1989-93. Mem. Govt. Fin. Officers Assn. (spl. rev. com. 1985-86, cert. achievement for excellence in fin. reporting 1984-87), Govtl. Acctg. Stds. Bd. (com. on acctg., auditing, and fin. reporting 1986-87), Colo. Soc. CPAs (CPAs in industry, govt. and edn. com. 1989-90), Colo. Assn. Mcpl. Tax Auditors, Metro North C. of C., Broomfield C. of C. Lutheran. Home: 6612 W 113th Ave Broomfield CO 80020-7245 Office: Hartwig and Assocs CPA PC 2 Garden Ctr Ste 303 Broomfield CO 80020

HARTZELL, IRENE JANOFSKY, psychologist; b. L.A. Vor-Diplom, U. Munich, 1961; BA, U. Calif., Berkeley, 1963, MA, 1965; PhD, U. Oreg., 1970. Lic. psychologist, Calif., Wash., Ariz. Psychologist Lake Washington Sch. Dist., Kirkland, Wash., 1971-72; staff psychologist VA Med. Ctr., Seattle, 1970-71, Long Beach, Calif., 1973-74; dir. parent edn. Children's Hosp., Orange, Calif., 1975-78; clin. psychologist Kaiser Permanente, Woodland Hills, Calif., 1979—; clin. instr. dept. pediatrics U. Calif. Irvine Coll. Medicine, 1975-78. Author: The Study Skills Advantage, 1986; contbr. articles to profl. jours. Intern Oreg. Legislature, 1974-75. U.S. Vocat. Rehab. Adminstrn. fellow U. Oreg., 1966-67, 69. Mem. APA, Western Psychol. Assn., Pi Lambda Theta.

HARVEY, CANNON Y., railway company executive, lawyer; b. Washington, Nov. 16, 1940. BA, U. Mo., 1962; MA, Harvard U., 1963, LLB cum laude, 1966. Bar: Colo. 1966. Formerly v.p., gen. counsel, mem. Holme Roberts & Owen, Denver; gen. counsel So. Pacific Transp. Co., San Francisco, 1990-94; sr. v.p. fin. and law So. Pacific Rail Corp., Denver, 1994—. Office: So Pacific Rail Corp 1860 Lincoln St 14th Fl Denver CO 80295

HARVEY, DONALD, artist, educator; b. Walthamston, Eng., June 14, 1930; s. Henry and Annie Dorothy (Sawell) H.; m. Elizabeth Clark, Aug. 9, 1952; children—Shan Mary, David Jonathan. Art tchrs. diploma, Brighton Coll. Art, 1951. Art master Ardwyn Grammar Sch., Wales, 1952-56; mem. faculty dept. art U. Victoria, B.C., Can., 1961—; now prof. painting U. Victoria. One man exhbns. include, Albert White Gallery, Toronto, 1968, retrospective, Art Gallery of Victoria, 1968; represented in permanent collections, Nat. Gallery Can., Montreal Mus., Albright-Knox Mus., Seattle Art Mus. Mem. accessions com. Art Gallery of Victoria, 1969-72. Can. Council fellow, 1966. Mem. Royal Can. Acad. of Arts (full academician), Can. Group Painters, Can. Painters and Etchers. Home: 1025 Joan Crescent, Victoria, BC Canada V8S 3L3 Office: Univ of Victoria, Victoria, BC Canada

HARVEY, ELAINE LOUISE, artist, educator; b. Riverside, Calif., Mar. 1, 1936; d. Edgar Arthur and Emma Louise (Shull) Siervogel; m. Stuart Herbert Harvey, June 16, 1957; children: Kathleen Robin, Laurel Lynn, Mark Stuart. BA with highest honors, with distinction, San Diego State U., 1957. Cert. gen. elem. tchr., Calif. Tchr. Cajon Valley Schs., El Cajon, Calif., 1957, 58; free-lance artist El Cajon, 1975—; tchr. Athenaeum Sch. Music & Art, 1990—; juror various art exhbns., Calif., 1983—; lectr., 1984—; tchr. painting seminars, 1987—. Editor: Palette to Palate, 1986; contbr. The Artists Mag., 1987, 94, The New Spirit Watercolor, 1989, Calif. Art Rev., 1989, The Artists So. Calif., 1989, Splash, 1990, Splash II, 1992, Watercolor Techniques for Releasing the Creative Spirit, 1992, Collage Techniques, 1994, The Artistic Touch, 1994. Trustee San Diego Mus. Art, 1985, 86; leader El Cajon Coun. Girl Scouts of U.S., 1968; vol. art tchr., San Diego area pub. schs., 1975-78; choral dir. Chapel of Valley United Meth., 1991—. Recipient Merit award La. Watercolor Soc., 1984, Arches Canson Rives award Midwest Watercolor Soc./Tweed Mus., Greenbay, Wis., 1984, Winsor Newton award Midwest Watercolor Soc./Neville Mus., Duluth, Minn., 1985, McKinnon award Am. Watercolor Soc. 1985, Creative Connection award Rocky Mountain Nat. Exhbn., 1986, 1st Juror's award San Diego Internat. Watercolor Exhbn., 1986, Dassler Mochs award Adirondacks Exhbn. of Am. Art, 1988, Arjomari/Arches/Rives award Watercolor West, Brea Cultural Ctr., 1990. Mem. Nat. Watercolor Soc. (bd. dirs. 1987-88, elected juror 1989), Watercolor West (bd. dirs. 1986-88, 94), West Coast Watercolor Soc. (pres. 1992—), San Diego Watercolor Soc. (pres. 1979-80, chmn. internat. exhbn. 1980-81, Silver Recognition award 1986), San Diego Mus. Art Artists Guild (pres. 1985-86, bd. dirs. 1986-87, 90—) Western Fedn. Watercolor Socs. (del. 1983-91), Rocky Mountain Nat. Watermedia Soc., Allied Artists Am., Grossmont Garden Club (Elson Creativity Trophy 1977, 79). Home and Studio: 1602 Sunburst Dr El Cajon CA 92021

HARVEY, GREGORY ALAN, microcomputer technology educator, consultant; b. Harvey, Ill., Feb. 15, 1949; s. Kenneth Herman and Mildred Faye (Pounds) H. BA, U. Ill., 1970; teaching credential, San Francisco State U., 1982. Mem. drafting and design staff Bechtel Engring., San Francisco, 1973-81; computer cons., prin. Harvey & Assocs., San Francisco, 1981—; prin. Media of the Minds, 1993—; computer cons. PCTeach, Inverness, Calif., 1984-91; profl. lectr. Golden Gate U., 1992. Author: (computer books) Communication in Writing, 1984, Mastering SuperCalc 3, 1985, Mastering Q&A, 1986, Lotus 1-2-3 Desktop Companion, 1987 WordPerfect Desktop Companion, 1987, Mastering WordStar, 1987, Lotus 1-2-3 Instance Reference, 1988, WordPerfect Instant Reference, 1988, DOS Instant Reference, 1988, Understanding HyperCard, 198, HyperTalk Instant Reference, 1988, The Complete Lotus 1-2-3 Handbook, 1989, Mastering PageMaker on the MacIntosh, 1990, Encyclopedia WordPerfect, 1990, Que's WordPerfect Windows QuickStart, 1991, Que's Lotus 1-2-3 Windows QuikStart, 1991, PCWorld's WordPerfect Windows, 1991, Greg Harvey's Excel 4 Handbook Windows, 1992, Greg Harvey's Excel 4 Handbook MacIntosh, 1992, IDG's 1-2-3 for Dummies, 1992, IDG's DOS for Dummies Command Reference, 1993, Windows for Dummies Command Reference, 1993, WordPerfect for Dummies Command Reference, 1993, WordPerfect 6 DOS Handbook, 1993, More Excel for Dummies, 1994, Excel 5 for Mac for Dummies, 1994, Windows 95 for Dummies Quick Reference, 1995. Mem. Internat. Interactive Comm. Soc., Berkeley Macintosh Users Group. Democrat. Zen Buddhist. Home: 60 Kylewood Pl Inverness CA 94937-9717 Office: Harvey & Assocs PO Box 1175 Point Reyes Station CA 94956-1175

HARVEY, J. R., utilities company executive; b. 1937; married. BS, U. Mo., 1960. Gas engr. Ill. Power Co., 1960-66; with Wash. Water Power Co., Spokane, 1966—, various engring. and mgmt. positions, 1966-80, asst. v.p., asst. to pres., 1980, v.p. ops., 1980-84, exec. v.p., 1984-85, chief operating officer, exec. v.p., 1985—. Office: Wash Water Power Co 1411 E Mission Ave Spokane WA 99202-2617

HARVEY, JAMES GERALD, educational consultant, counselor, researcher; b. California, Mo., July 15, 1934; s. William Walter and Exie Marie (Lindley) H. BA Amherst Coll., 1956; MAT (fellow), Harvard U., 1958, MEd, 1962. Asst. to dean grad. sch. edn. Harvard U., Cambridge, Mass., 1962-66, dir. admissions, fin. aid, 1966-69; dir. counseling service U. Calif., Irvine, 1970-72; ednl. cons., Los Angeles, 1972—. Author: (ednl. materials) HARVOCAB Vocabulary Program, 1985—. 1st lt. USAF, 1958-61. Amherst Mayo-Smith grantee, 1956-57; UCLA Adminstrv. fellow, 1969-70. Mem. Am. Ednl. Research Assn., Nat. Council Measurement in Edn., Am. Counseling Assn. Address: 1845 Glendon Ave Los Angeles CA 90025-4653

HARVEY, JAMES ROSS, finance company executive; b. Los Angeles, Aug. 20, 1934; s. James Ernest and Loretta Berniece (Ross) H.; m. Charlene Coakley, July 22, 1971; children: Kjersten Ann, Kristina Ross. B.S. in Engring., Princeton U., 1956; M.B.A., U. Calif., Berkeley, 1963. Engr. Chevron Corp., San Francisco, 1956-61; acct. Touche, Ross, San Francisco, 1963-64; chmn. bd. Transamerica Corp., San Francisco, 1965—; bd. dirs. Airtouch Comm. Inc., McKesson Corp., Charles Schwab Corp. With U.S. Army, 1958-59. Mem. Bohemian Club, Pacific-Union Club, Fly Fishers Club (London). Office: Transam Corp 600 Montgomery St San Francisco CA 94111-2702

HARVEY, JANE R., investment company executive; b. Tarrytown, N.Y., Oct. 13, 1945; d. Fred W. and Margaret (White) Rosenbauer. Student, U. Ariz., Iona Coll., Coll. Fin. Planning; grad., Pace U. Lic. ins. counselor; registered fin. cons. Registered rep. KMS Fin. Svcs., Inc., Tucson, acct. exec., 1994—. Contbr. articles to profl. jours. Active Resources for Women. Mem. NAFE, Internat. Assn. Fin. Planning (past bd. dirs., v.p. membership So. Ariz. chpt., pres. 1994—), Internat. Assn. Registered Fin. Planners (bd. govs., speaker conv.), Internat. Assn. Registered Financial Cons. (bd. dirs. 1995—), Am. Bus. Womens Assn., Am. Assn. Individual Investors, Tucson C. of C. Office: KMS Financial Services 5620 N Kolb Rd #171 Tucson AZ 85715

HARVEY, JOSEPH EMMETT, construction executive; b. L.A., Dec. 4, 1951; s. Emmett Allan and Mary Summerall (Anderson) H. BA in Psychology with distinction, U. Hawaii, 1974; postgrad., U.S. Internat. U., 1975-76. Ops. mgr. C.S. Goodale Co., San Diego, 1977-84; sales mgr. Dunn & Co., San Diego, 1985-89; constrn. mgr. Comml. Shelving, Inc., Honolulu, 1989-92; constrn. exec. Skylights of Hawaii, Honolulu, 1992—. Program coord. Crisis House, El Cajon, Calif., 1975-79. Mem. Bldg. Industry Assn., Constrn. Specifications Inst. (dir. 1994—, asst. chair western region tech. com. 1994—, constrn. document tech. cert. 1995, Merit award 1993), Rotary (Svc. award 1993), Phi Beta Kappa.

HARVEY, JOSEPH PAUL, JR., orthopedist, educator; b. Youngstown, Ohio, Feb. 28, 1922; s. Joseph Paul and Mary Justinian (Collins) H.; m. Martha Elizabeth Toole, Apr. 12, 1958; children: Maryalice, Martha Jane, Frances Susan, Helen Lucy, Laura Andre. Student, Dartmouth, 1939-42; M.D., Harvard, 1945. Diplomate: Nat. Bd. Med. Examiners. Intern Peter Bent Brigham Hosp., Boston, 1945-46; resident Univ. Hosp., Cleve., 1951-53, Hosp. Spl. Surgery, N.Y.C., 1953-54; instr. orthopedics Cornell Med. Coll., N.Y.C., 1954-62; mem. faculty Sch. Medicine, U. So. Calif., Los Angeles, 1962-92; prof. orthopedic surgery U. So. Calif., 1966-92, prof. emeritus, 1992—; chmn. sect. orthopedics Sch. Medicine, U. So. Calif., 1964-78; dir. dept. orthopedics U. So. Calif.-Los Angeles County Med. Center, 1964-79, mem. staff, 1979—. Editor-in-chief: Contemporary Orthopedics. Served to capt. AUS, 1946-48. Exchange orthopedic fellow Royal Acad. Hosp., Upsala, Sweden, 1957. Fellow Western Orthopedic Assn., Am. Acad. Orthopedic Surgery, A.C.S., Am. Soc. Testing Materials; mem. AMA, Calif. Med. Assn., Los Angeles County Med. Assn., Am. Rheumatism Assn., Am. Orthopedic Assn., Internat. Soc. Orthopedics and Truamatology. Club: Boston Harvard. Home: 2050 Lorain Rd San Marino CA 91108-2548 Office: 39 Congress St Pasadena CA 91105-3024

HARVEY, STEWART CLYDE, pharmacologist, retired educator; b. Denver, Feb. 16, 1921; s. John Alden and Marie Bronson (Barfoot) H.; m. Joyce Contance Payne, Dec. 27, 1947 (dec. June 1964); children: Janet Ann Harding, Stephen John; m. Eunice Marie Munk, July 2, 1965. BA, U. Colo., 1943, postgrad., 1946; PhD, U. Chgo., 1948. Instr. U. Colo., Boulder, 1943-46; instr., chmn. pharmacology Dental Coll. U. Tex., Houston, 1948-49; instr. pharmacology U. Utah, Salt Lake City, 1949-51, asst. prof. pharmacology, 1951-53, assoc. prof. pharmacology, 1953-74, prof. pharmacology, 1974-88, prof. emeritus, 1988—; vis. prof. U. Southampton, Eng., 1972-73; mem. rev. panel on pharmacology and toxicology NIH, Bethesda, Med., 1965-66; mem. Utah Heart Rsch. Com., Salt Lake City, 1955-66; cons. com. on drugs AMA, Chgo.; mem. panel on rev. antacids FDA, Bethesda, 1972-74; ad hoc cons. Med. Letter, NSF; cons., expert witness on alcohol and drugs to various cts., 1952-90. Author chpts. in books; assoc. editor Remington's Pharm. Scis., 1963-90, Circulation Rsch., 1958-63. Chmn. 1st senatorial dist. Utah Dem. Party, Salt Lake City, 1953-62; scoutmaster Boy Scouts of Am., Salt Lake City, 1957-65; charter mem. Utah Environ. Ctr., Salt Lake City, 1970-72; mem. Citizens Adv. Panel to U.S. Army Engrs., Ogden, Utah, 1970-72. Rsch. grantee NIH, Am. Heart Assn., Utah Heart Assn., Gividan-Delawana. Democrat. Home: 1652 Yale Ave Salt Lake City UT 84105-1720

HARVEY-MELLEBY, MARY ANN, public relations executive; b. Pottstown, Pa., Mar. 28, 1945; d. W. Harold and C. La Verne (Noble) Bealer; m. Thomas Richard Harvey, June 17, 1967 (div. 1991); children: John Lathrop II, Scott Richard; m. Michael Rolf Melleby, Feb. 18, 1995. Diploma in nursing, Thomas Jefferson U., 1966; BA, U. LaVerne, 1979, postgrad., 1990. RN, Calif., Pa., N.Y. Nurse Phoenixville (Pa.) Hosp., 1966-67; head nurse St. Joseph's Hosp., Syracuse, N.Y., 1967-70; bldg. mgr. Upstate Med. Ctr., SUNY, Syracuse, 1970-72; dir. community rels. Queen of the Valley Hosp., West Covina, Calif., 1979-86; asst. adminstr. Hillcrest Homes, LaVerne, Calif., 1986-90; cons. Hillcrest Homes, LaVerne, 1990—; pub. rels. dir. Coll. Osteo. Medicine of Pacific, Pomona, Calif.; lectr. colls. and univs. so. Calif., 1979-90; speaker healthcare. Contbr. articles to religious mags. Rep. committeewoman, adv. Senator Bill Campbell, Whittier, Calif., 1983-87; coord. LaVerne Centennial Com., 1986; mem. various local campaign coms., 1980—. Recipient Golden Advocate award Healthcare Pub. Rels. and Mktg. Assn., L.A., 1983, 85. Mem. AAUW, Brethern Health and Welfare Assn. (past pres.), West Covina C. of C. (pres. 1985-86, Bus. Woman of Yr. 1984). Mem. Brethern Ch. Home and Office: 427 E Walker Rd San Dimas CA 91773-2045

HARVIE, J. JASON, administrative aide, secretary; b. Seattle, Wash., Dec. 12, 1937; s. James Joseph Harvie and Betty Clair (Walton) Krussow; m. Maureen W.Y. Johnson, June 12, 1970 (div. Sept. 1980). Cert. Law Enforcement, U. Guam, Agana, 1973, Grad. Basic Police Acad., 1973, Advanced Police Technology, 1974; Diploma, San Francisco Police Acad., 1980. Police officer II Gov. of Guam/Dept. Pub. Safety, Agana, 1972-77; chief dept. safety and secutiy U. Calif. Hastings/Coll. of Law, San Francisco, 1978-82; chief patrol officer San Francisco Parking Authority, 1982-84; aide H.E. Sheik Abdullah O. Mahdi, Pebble Beach, Calif., 1984—. Decorated Navy Achievement medal USN; named Knight Chevalier, Grand Knight/Police Hall of Fame, Miami, 1989; recipient Legion of Honor award Am. Police Hall of Fame, Miami, 1990. Mem. Am. Fedn. Police, Calif. Peace Officers Assn., Marine's Meml. Club, Am. Police Hall of Fame. Republican. Episcopalian. Home: PO Box 1018 Pebble Beach CA 93953 Office: PO Box 1541 Pebble Beach CA 93953-1541

HARVIE, KEITH WILLIAM, orthopaedic surgeon; b. Cornith, N.Y., July 20, 1940; s. Donald Edwin and Gussie (Sclar) H.; m. Betty Kramer, June 10, 1964; children: Lois Rebecca, Joel Seaton. BA, Yeshiva U., 1961; DO, Kirksville Coll., 1965. Pvt. practice Orthopedic Cons. Ltd., Albuquerque, 1974—; chmn. dept. surgery St. Joseph Heights Hosp., Albuquerque, 1981-92. Pres. Jewish Fedn. Greater Albuquerque, 1992-94. Fellow Am. Osteo. Bd. Surgery, Internat. Coll. Surgeons, Am. Acad. Orthopedic Surgeons, AOAO, NASS, ITS. Office: 4325 Carlisle Blvd NE Albuquerque NM 87107-4810

HARWICK, BETTY CORINNE BURNS, sociology educator; b. L.A., Jan. 22, 1926; d. Henry Wayne Burns and Dorothy Elizabeth (Menzies) Routhier; m. Burton Thomas Harwick, June 20, 1947; children: Wayne Thomas, Burton Terence, Bonnie Christine Foster, Beverly Anne Carroll. Student, Biola, 1942-45, Summer Inst. Linguistics, 1945, U. Calif., Berkeley, 1945-52; BA, Calif. State U., Northridge, 1961, MA, 1965; postgrad., MIT, 1991. Prof. sociology Pierce Coll., Woodland Hills, Calif., 1966-95, pres. acad. senate, 1976-77, pres. faculty assn., 1990-91, chair dept. for philosophy and sociology, 1990-95; co-founder, faculty advisor interdisciplinary religious studies program Pierce Coll. Author: (with others) Introducing Sociology, 1977; author: Workbook for Introducing Sociology, 1978. faculty rep. Calif. Community Coll. Assn., 1977-80. Alt. fellow NEH, 1978. Mem. Am. Acad. Religion, Soc. Bibl. Lit., Am. Sociol. Assn. Presbyterian. Home: 19044 Superior St Northridge CA 91324-1845 Office: LA Pierce Coll 6201 Winnetka Ave Woodland Hills CA 91371-0001

HARWICK, MAURICE, lawyer; b. L.A., Feb. 6, 1933; m. Saowapa Butranon, July 4, 1970; children: Manasnati, Manasnapa. AA, L.A. City Coll., 1954; JD, Southwestern U., 1957. Bar: Calif., 1958; U.S. Supreme Ct., 1962. Dep. dist. atty. County of Los Angeles, 1958-60; pvt. practice law, Santa Monica, Calif., 1960—; judge pro tem Municipal Ct., 1966-67, 80-81, 85—; past advisor to dist. atty. Los Angeles County. Chmn. bd. rev. Los Angeles Community Colls. and City Schs.; mem. Project Safer Calif. gov.'s com., 1974-75. Mem. ABA, Calif. Bar Assn., Los Angeles County Bar Assn., Dist. Attys. Assn. L.A., Criminal Cts. Bar Assn. (pres. 1972, bd. govs.), Assn. Trial Lawyers Am., Los Angeles County Dist. Attys. Assn., Vikings. Office: 2001 Wilshire Blvd Ste 600 Santa Monica CA 90403-5684

HARWOOD, BRIAN DENNIS, securities industry executive; b. London, Feb. 3, 1932; arrived Can., 1953; s. William Henry and Catherine Mary (O'Brien) H.; m. Diane Louise McLean, Sept. 1, 1988. Ed. pvt. schs., London. Fgn. exch. cashier Thos. Cook & Sons, London, 1949-50, 52-53; to br. mgmt. Bank of Montreal, Vancouver and Montreal, Can., 1953-62, 64-70; lending officer Security First Nat. Bank, L.A., 1963-64; with Canaccord Capital Corp (formerly L.O.M. Western Securities Ltd.), Vancouver, 1970—, exec. v.p., 1975-87, pres., chief oper. officer, 1987-94; vice chmn., 1994—; also bd. dirs. Canaccord Capital Corp (formerly L.O.M. Western Securities Ltd.), Vancouver; past chmn. and dir. Can. Investor Protection Fund; bd. dirs. West Can. Depository Trust Co. Sgt. Brit. Army, 1950-52. Mem. Investment Dealers Assn. Can. (bd. dirs., nat. and exec. coms. 1989-94), Vancouver Stock Exch. (bd. govs. 1985-94, vice chmn. 1989, chmn. 1991-93), Royal Vancouver Yacht Club, Vancouver Lawn Tennis Club, Terminal City Club. Office: Canaccord Capital Corp, 609 Granville St PO Box 10337, Vancouver, BC Canada V7Y 1H2

HARWOOD, JAMES WILLIAM, surgeon; b. N.Y.C. BA, Villanova U., 1964; MD, U. Pa., 1974. Intern U. Calif., San Diego, 1974-75; resident U. Calif., San Francisco, 1975-80; oncological surgeon Santa Rosa (Calif.) Meml. Hosp., 1992—; chief of surgery Santa Rosa Cmty. Hosp., 1995—; asst. prof. Sch. Medicine U. Calif., San Francisco, 1992—. With Bd. Found. for Health Care, Sonoma County, 1994. Lt. USN, 1966-69. Fellow Am. Coll. Surgeons (fellow No. Calif. br.), Naffziger Surg. Soc., Project Hope Alumni Assn. Office: 1111 Sonoma Ave Ste 320 Santa Rosa CA 95405-4820

HARZ, G. MICHAEL, lawyer; b. N.Y.C., Apr. 18, 1951; s. Victor and Arlene (Nadohl) H. BSCE, Cornell U., 1973; JD, U. Denver, 1989. Bar: Colo. 1989. Pres. Zibeq Enterprises, N.Y.C., 1975—. Regent scholar N.Y. State Edn. Dept., 1969-73; recipient Nat. Collegiate Legal Studies award U.S. Achievement Acad., 1988,. Home: 1156 Aspen Dr Evergreen CO 80439-4804

HASAN, MAHMOOD UL, secondary school educator; b. Dibai, India, Aug. 12, 1945; came to U.S. 1981; s. Qazi Saeed and Khursheed (Zehra) Ahmad; m. Olga Marie Feixova, Dec. 4, 1976 (div. July 1993); children: Shaun, Talib; m. Ghazala Qamar Omar, Sept. 10, 1993. BSc with honors, U. Karachi, Pakistan, 1964; MSc, U. Karachi, 1965; BEd, U. New Brunswick, Fredericton, Can., 1973. Lectr. Habib Tech. Inst., Nawabshah, 1965-66, S.M. Sc. Coll., Karachi, 1966-67; tchr. Lake Manitoba Sch., Vogar, 1975-81; instructional asst. San Jose (Calif.) City Coll., 1985-88; tchr. San Francisco Unified Sch. Dist., 1988—. Author (computer software) Pascal Tutor, 1993. Mem. Calif. Tchrs. Assn., San Francisco Math. Tchrs. Assn., Pakistan Engrs. and Scientists Assn. Islam. Home: 4176 Sophia Way San Jose CA 95134-1522 Office: Phillip and Sala Burton Acad High Sch 400 Mansell St San Francisco CA 94134

HASEGAWA, NORIKO, artist; b. Nyuzen-machi, Japan, Apr. 10, 1933; came to U.S., 1971; d. Shosaku and Natsu (Nagare) Ikari; m. Jun Hasegawa, Aug. 20, 1971; children: Emi H. Lee., Naomi. BS, Toyama U., 1956; MS, Pvt. Sch. Ikebana, 1965; PhD, Tokyo U., 1971. Cert. pharmacist. Chief chemist Grelan Pharm. Lab., Tokyo, 1956-71; cons. Grelan Pharm. Lab., 1971-73. Exhbns. include Pal Springs Desert Mus. All Media, 1994, Triton Mus. Watercolor, 1994 (award 1994), Phila. Watercolor Club, 1992 (award 1993), N.W. Watercolor Soc., 1992 (award 1993-94), Rocky Mountain Nat. Watermedia, 1986, 89, 94 (award 1994), Adirondacks Nat. Exhbn. Am. Watercolors, 1983-89, 91-93 (awards 1984, 93), Nat. Watercolor Soc., 1987-93, 94 (award 1994), Nat. Assn. Women Artists, 1992-94 (awards 1993, 94), Audubon Artists, Inc., 1987-95 (awards 1987-90, 95), Midwest Watercolor Soc., 1985, 1987-90, 93-94 (awards 1985-89), France-Japan Exhbn., 1993-94, Grand Palais, Paris, Tokyo Metro. Mus. Art, Osaka City Mus. Art. Mem. Nat. Assn. Women Artists (Grehner watercolor awards 1993-94), Nat. Watercolor Soc., West Coast Watercolor Soc., Audubon Artists, Inc. (awards 1987-90), Midwest Watercolor Soc. (awards 1985, 87, 89), Watercolor West.

HASENKAMP, BRUCE HENRY, foundation executive; b. Bklyn., May 12, 1938; s. Henry Ernst Hasenkamp and Ruth Frances (Hoyer) Savage; m. Inta Sarma Macs, May 13, 1973; 1 child, Peter Andris Henry. AB cum laude, Dartmouth Coll., 1960; JD, Stanford U., 1963. Bar: Calif. 1964, N.Y. 1964, U.S. Dist. Ct. (no. dist.) Calif. 1964, U.S. Ct. Appeals (9th cir.) 1964, U.S. Dist. Ct. (so. dist.) N.Y. 1968, U.S. Supreme Ct. 1968. Assoc. Simpson Thacher and Bartlett, N.Y.C., 1963-68; asst. dean law sch. Stanford (Calif.) U., 1968-73; dir. Pres.'s Commn. on White House Fellowships, Washington, 1974-77; dir. pub. affairs Shaklee Corp., San Francisco, 1978-82; exec. v.p. The Hannaford Co., San Francisco, 1983-85; v.p. The Asia Found., San Francisco, 1985-86, Hosp. Council No. Calif., San Mateo, 1986-89; exec. dir. St. Francis Found., San Francisco, 1989—; mem. Pres.'s Commn. on White House Fellowships, 1981-91, Calif. Med. Bd., 1987—, pres., 1993-94. Trustee World Affairs Coun. No. Calif., San Francisco, 1981-88, Hillsborough City Sch. Dist., 1985-93; vice chmn. Hillsborough Recreation Commn., 1989-91; steering com. Bay Area Coun., San Francisco, 1980-82, dep. Calif. Roundtable, San Francisco, 1980-82; pres. Calif. Rep. League, 1971-73; asst. sec. Calif. Reps., 1973-74; dir. Coun. of Better Bus. Bur., 1980-84. Mem. Direct Selling Assn. (bd. dirs. 1981-82), Calif. State Bar Assn. (ho. dels. 1971), Fedn. of State Med. Bds. of U.S. (editl. bd. 1989-95, bd. dirs. 1993—, treas. 1995—), Commonwealth Club of Calif. (gov. San Francisco 1981-85), Univ. Club Capitol Hill Club (Washington), Sigma Phi Epsilon (nat. dir. 1973-87, grand pres. 1991-93). Mem. Anglican Ch. Home: 2435 Skyfarm Dr Hillsborough CA 94010-6343 Office: St Francis Found Ste 1208 900 Hyde St San Francisco CA 94109

HASHIMOTO, LLOYD KEN, communications executive; b. Cheyenne, Wyo., Sept. 21, 1944; s. Harry H. and Bettie M. (Kadota) H. Student in chemistry, 1963-65, student in elec. engring., 1969-72, student in edn., 1979; BSin Vocat. Edn., U. Wyo., 1992. Prin. Teltron Electronics, Laramie, Wyo., 1972—; audio visual technician U. Wyo., Laramie, 1972—; mem. internat. panel Electronics Mag., 1974, 76; instr. workshops and seminars High Tech to a Lay Person, 1978; instr. workshop radio direction finding, 1988—; mem. edn. steering com. U. Wyo. Grad. Mountain Folk Sch., 1993-94. Contbr. articles to profl. jours. Program chmn., unit and dist. commr. Snowy Range dist. Boy Scouts Am., Laramie, 1985—, instr. Longs Peak Coun. With U.S. Army, 1965-69. Recipient award of merit Boy Scouts Am., 1991, Silver Beaver award Boy Scouts Am., 1993, Disting. Commr. award Boy Scouts Am., 1994. Mem. IEEE, Assn. Ednl. Comms. Tech. (assoc. audio visual technician S.E. Wyo. chpt.), Soc. Internat. Devel., Assn. for Field Svc. Mgrs. Internat., Am. Legion, Masons (cryptic Masons youth leadership award for Wyo. 1994), Shriners. Home: 504 S 26th St Laramie WY 82070-4932 Office: Teltron Electronics PO Box 1049 Laramie WY 82070-1049

HASKELL, DONALD, agricultural products executive; b. 1928. Chmn. bd. M.H. Sherman Co., Newport Beach, Calif., 1960—, Tejon Ranch Co., Lebec, Calif. Office: Tejon Ranch Co 4436 Lebec Rd Lebec CA 93243*

HASKELL, DONALD MCMILLAN, lawyer; b. Toledo, July 2, 1932; s. Irwin Wales and Grace (Lee) H.; m. Carol Jean Ross, June 19, 1954; children: Deborah Lee, Catherine Jean, David Ross. BA, Coll. of Wooster, 1954; JD, U. Mich., 1957. Bar: Ill. 1957, U.S. Dist. Ct. (no. dist.) Ill. 1958, U.S. Ct. Appeals (7th cir.) 1960, U.S. Supreme Ct. 1963, U.S. Ct. Appeals (10th cir.) 1974, Oreg. 1990. Ptnr. McKenna, Storer, Rowe, White & Haskell and predecessors, Chgo., 1957-75; sr. ptnr. Haskell & Perrin, Chgo., 1975-89, of counsel, 1989—; mem. Oreg. Bd. Bar Examiners, 1991-94, chmn., 1993-94. Fellow Am. Bar Found., Ill. Bar Found.; mem. ABA (ho. of dels. 1982-92, bd. govs. 1987-90), Law Club Chgo., Legal Club Chgo., Astoria Country Club. Republican. Lutheran. Home: 600 W Lexington Ave Astoria OR 97103-5726 Office: Wecoma Ptnrs Ltd PO Box 777 100 16th St Astoria OR 97103-3634 also: Haskell & Perrin 200 W Adams St Ste 2600 Chicago IL 60606-5233

HASKINS, MARIAN MCKEEN, nursing administrator; b. N.Y.C., Jan. 27, 1954; d. Sean and Margaret (Hegarty) McKeen; m. Thomas Creed Haskins, Sept. 27, 1981. BS in Nursing, Hunter Coll., N.Y.C.; MA in Marriage, Family and Child Counseling, Calif. Family Study Ctr., Burbank. Lic. marriage, family and child counselor. Critical care registry nurse Critical Care Svcs., Inc., L.A., 1978-79; staff devel. cons.-instr. Profl. Med. Educators, Northridge, Calif., 1979; clin. nurse III respiratory intensive care unit UCLA, 1979-81; counselor marriage, family and child svcs. Encino, Calif., 1989-94; critical care edn. coord. Daniel Freeman Meml. Hosp., Inglewood, Calif., 1981-89, profl. nurse, case mgr., 1990—. Recipient Outstanding Nurse award UCLA, 1980; Named one of Top Ten Nurses in State of Calif., 1993. Mem. Calif. Assn. Marriage and Family Therapists, Am. Assn. Marriage and Family Therapists. Home: 22566 Cardiff Dr Santa Clarita CA 91350-3028 Office: Daniel Freeman Meml Hosp Nursing Adminstrn 333 N Prairie Ave Inglewood CA 90301-4501

HASLAM, GERALD WILLIAM, writer, educator; b. Bakersfield, Calif., Mar. 18, 1937; s. Fredrick Martin and Lorraine Hope (Johnson) H.; m. Janice Eileen Pettichord, July 1, 1961; children: Frederick W., Alexandra R., Garth C., Simone B., Carlos V. BA, San Francisco State U., 1963, MA, 1965; PhD, Union Grad. Sch., 1980. Instr. English San Francisco State U., San Francisco, 1966-67; asst. prof. English Sonoma State U., Rohert Park, Calif., 1967-70, assoc. prof. English, 1970-74, prof. English, 1971—; adj. prof. Union Grad. Sch., Cin., 1984—, The Nat. Faculty, Atlanta, 1984—. Editor various anthologies; author various booklets, monographs, film scripts, (fiction) Okies: Selected Stories, 1973, Masks: A Novel, 1976, The Wages of Sin: Collected Stories, 1980, Hawk Flights: Visions of the West, 1983, Snapshots: Glimpses of the Other California, 1985, The Man Who Cultivated Fire and Other Stories, 1987, That Constant Coyote: California Stories, 1990, Condor Dreams and Other Fictions, 1994, The Great Tejon Club Jubilee, 1995, (non-fiction) Coming of Age in California, 1990, The Other California, 1990, The Great Central Valley: California's Heartland, 1993. With U.S. Army, 1958-60. Creative Writing fellow Calif. Arts Coun., 1989; recipient Benjamin Franklin award, 1993, Bay Area Book Reviewers' Non-fiction award, 1994, Commonwealth Club medal for Calif., 1994, Merit award Assn. State & Local History, 1994. Mem. PEN U.S.A. West (Josephine Miles award 1990), Western Lit. Assn. (bd. dirs., past pres.), Calif. Studies Assn. (steering com., founding mem.), Calif. Hist. Assn., Calif. Tchrs. Assn., San Francisco State U. Alumni Assn. (life), Union Inst. Alumni Assn., Multi-Ethnic Lit. of U.S. (founding mem.), Robinson Jeffers Assn. (founding mem.), Sierra Club, The Nature Conservancy, Calif. Trout (founding mem.), Tulare Basin Archeology Group, Save the American River Assn. Roman Catholic. Office: Sonoma State U 1801 E Cotati Ave Rohnert Park CA 94928-3613

HASLER, GEOFF JULIAN, marketing consultant; b. Sydney, New South Wales, Australia, Dec. 9, 1947; came to U.S., 1984; s. Arthur Ralph and Patricia Elsa (Riley) H.; m. Sandra Anne Richards, May 30, 1969 (div. 1983); 1 child, Timothy J.; m. Mary Jane Leimer, Sept. 29, 1990. BA in Econs., U. Sydney, 1970. Journalist Sydney Morning Herald, 1967-70; econs. master Oakhill Coll., Castle Hill, New South Wales, Australia, 1970-72; mng. dir. Peninsula Newspapers Pty. Ltd., New South Wales, 1972-75; lectr. Murdoch U., Perth, West Australia, 1975-78; mng. dir. Australian Bus. Book. Pubs., Sydney, 1978-84; pres. Internat. Pub. Svcs. Inc., L.A., 1984-88, Winning Mktg. Strategies, Santa Barbara, Calif., 1988—. Author: How to Advertise Your Business, 1978; editor (newsletter) Winning Marketing Strategies, 1988—. Episcopalian. Office: Winning Mktg Strategies Inc 1235 Coast Village Rd Ste G Santa Barbara CA 93108-2731

HASPIEL, GEORGE SIDNEY, writer, illustrator; b. St. Louis, Jan. 1, 1929; s. Harry Hyman and Ceilia (Edelstein) H.; m. Margaret Fleming, Dec. 23, 1973; children: Erica, Adam, Lisa. AB, Washington U., St. Louis, 1951; MS, 1953; PhD, Pa. State U., 1961. Dir. Audiology Clinic Tulane U., New Orleans, 1953-54; clin. audiologist Northwestern U., Evanston, Ill., 1954-56; co-dir. Outpatient Audiology Pa. State U., State College, 1956-60; dir. Hunter Coll., N.Y.C., 1960-64; co-dir. Pa. State U., State College, 1964-69; pvt. practice St. Lukes Hearing and Speech Ctr., San Francisco, 1969-91; exec. dir. St. Lukes Corr. Dental-Facial Deformities, San Francisco, 1988-91, St. Lukes Cognition and Learning Ctr., San Francisco, 1988-91; dir. Dragon Press Pub. Co., San Francisco, 1988—; dir. Lang. Rsch. Jewish Guild for the Blind, N.Y.C., 1962-66; dir. Title III Project Cupertino (Calif.) Pub. Schs., 1973-76; adv. bd. Sr. Adv. Group, San Francisco, 1987-90. Author: (test) Discrimination By Identification of Pictures, 1961, Children's Articulation Test, 1990, (books) Lipreading for Children, 1988, Language Activities for Children, 1989. Fellow Am. Speech and Hearing Assn. Democrat. Jewish. Home: 127 Sycamore Ave Mill Valley CA 94941-2821

HASSAN, TOM ANDREW, land developer; b. San Diego, Jan. 11, 1964; s. Mervyn Leslie and Sylvia O.R. (Fry) H. BA in Communications and Broadcasting, Pepperdine U., 1985. Account exec. pub. rels. and mktg. Cooper & Assocs., Santa Monica, Calif., 1984-85; prodn. coord. Lorne Greene Prodns., Santa Monica, 1985-86; asst. mgr. ops. DeLaurentiis Entertainment Group, Beverly Hills, Calif., 1986-87; mgr. ops. TMS Pictures/ The Movie Store, L.A., 1987; dir. film acquisitions TMS Pictures/ The Movie Store, 1988-90; project mgr. HCH Land Co. Ltd., 1991—; guest speaker Pepperdine U., Malibu, Calif., 1988, UCLA; rep. Am. Film Market, L.A., 1988. Creator of Pop-A-Thought greeting cards. Mem. Am. Film Inst., Am. Mgmt. Assn. Republican. Home: 1969 Kings Ave, West Vancouver, BC Canada V7V 2B6 Office: 1030 W Georgia St, Vancouver, BC Canada V6E 2Y3

HASSEBROEK, LYLE G., engineering company executive; b. 1941. BSCE, U. Wis., 1963. With CH2M Hill Inc., Corvallis, Oreg., 1963—, ea. dist. mgr., 1983-90, pres., 1990—. Office: CH2M Hill Corp 4565 SW Research Way Corvallis OR 97333-1063*

HASSELL, H(UGH) ROBERT, manufacturing company executive; b. Portland, Oreg., Mar. 6, 1945; s. Albert Errol and Margaret Mary (Thon) H.; m. Judy Terjeson, June 13, 1970; children: Molly Anne, Tiah Marie, Wolf. BS in Econs., Portland State U., 1972. Computer ops. supr. Consol. Freightways, Portland, 1968-72; mgr. systems and programming divs. Multnomah County, Portland, 1972-75; gen. mgr. Mgmt. Info. Systems Freightliner Corp., Portland, 1975—; pres. bd. dirs. Key Computer Sys. Internat., Inc. With U.S. Army, 1966-68. Mem. Oreg. Club of Portland (pres. elect), Phi Gamma Delta. Home: 11275 SW Viewmount Ct Tigard OR 97223-3731 Office: Freightliner Corp 4747 N Channel Ave Portland OR 97217-7613

HASSON, STEVEN J., chairman board of county commissioners; b. Spokane, Wash., July 29, 1950; s. John W. and Arden L. (Whitehead) H.; m. Janet S., June 12, 1982; children: Jenny Lynn, Nicholas Ryan, Paul Andrew. BA in Urban & Regional Planning, Eastern Wash. U., 1982, BA in Earth Sci. magna cum laude, 1982. Cert. journeyman carpenter. Self-employed bldg. contractor Wash., 1973-82; urban planner Spokane (Wash.) County Planning Dept., 1983; pk. and recreation planner Spokane (Wash.) Pks. Dept., 1984; utility planner Spokane (Wash.) County Utilities Dept., 1985, mgr. aquifer protection area, 1986, mgr. sewer and water protection svcs., 1987; county commr. Spokane County, 1988-92, 1992—, hearing examiner officer, 1993—. Past chmn., mem. Spokane County Health Dist., 1989—; vice chmn. Eastern Wash. Area Agy. on Aging, 1989—; past pres., mem. Magnuson Club, Spokane, 1986—; exec. bd. Spokane Transit Authority, 1989—; exec. bd. mem. Solid Waste Authority, 1995—, Spokane County Air Pollution Control Authority, 1995—, Spokane Regional Transp. Coun. With U.S. Army, 1975-76. Recipient Cert. of Merit, Nat. Dean's List, 1981, 82, Achievement award Planning Assn. of Wash., 1984. Mem. Spokane Valley Bus. Assn., Am. Planning Assn., Wash. State Assn. Counties, Citizens League (founding mem. 1986—), Spokane Club, Spokane Valley C. of C., Spokane City C. of C. Republican. Home: 2020 S Pierce Rd Spokane WA 99206-5687 Office: Spokane County Commr Office 1116 W Broadway Ave Spokane WA 99260-2052

HASSOUNA, FRED, architect, educator; b. Cairo, Mar. 26, 1918; s. Amin Sami and Dawlat (Mansour) H.; came to U.S., 1948, naturalized, 1953; diploma in architecture with honors Higher Sch. Fine Arts, Cairo, 1940; diploma in Egyptology with 1st class honors U. Cairo, 1944; diploma in civic design U. Liverpool (Eng.), 1946; M.Arch., M.S. in Pub. Adminstrn., U. So. Calif., 1950; m. Verna Arlene Dotter, Mar. 9, 1950. Architect, curator Cairo Mus., Egypt, 1940-44; lectr. archaeology and architecture Alexandria U., Egypt, 1944-45, 47-48; dir. planning Huyton-with-Roby Urban Dist. Council, Huyton, Eng., 1946-47; lectr. city planning U. So. Calif., 1950-55; architect Kistner, Wright and Wright, architects and engrs., Los Angeles, 1952-53; project architect Welton Becket and Assocs., architects and engrs., Los Angeles, 1954-56, Albert C. Martin and Assocs., architects and engrs., 1956-58; faculty architecture East Los Angeles Coll., 1958-75, prof. architecture, head dept. architecture; prof., head dept. architecture Saddleback Coll., 1975-83; pvt. planning cons., architect, Los Angeles, 1950-75, Laguna Niguel, 1975—. Mem. indsl. tech. adv. bd. Calif. State U. at Long Beach, 1963-83; mem. adv. bd. on environ. and interior design U. Calif., Irvine, 1976-83; pres. Calif. Council Archtl. Edn., 1977; mem. liaison com. architecture, landscape architecture, urban and regional planning in Calif. higher edn., 1976-83. Registered architect, Calif.; recipient hon. cultural doctorate World U. Roundtable, Benson, Ariz., 1983. Fellow Internat. Inst. Arts and Letters (life); mem. emeritus AIA, Am. Planning Assn. Home and Office: 31242 Flying Cloud Dr Laguna Niguel CA 92677-2716

HASSRICK, PETER HEYL, museum director; b. Phila., Apr. 27, 1941; s. Royal Brown and E. Barbara (Morgan) H.; m. Elizabeth Drake, June 14, 1963; children: Philip Heyl, Charles Royal. Student, Harvard U., 1962; BA, U. Colo., 1963; MA, U. Denver, 1969. Tchr. Whiteman Sch., Steamboat Springs, Colo., 1963-67; also bd. dirs. Whiteman Sch., Steamboat Springs; curator of collections Amon Carter Mus., Ft. Worth, 1969-75; dir. Buffalo Bill Hist. Ctr., Cody, Wyo., 1976—. Author: Frederic Remington, 1973, The Way West, 1977, (with others) The Rocky Mountains, 1983, Treasures of the Old West, 1984, (with others) Frederic Remington, The Masterworks, 1988, (with others) Frontier America, 1988, Charles M. Russell, 1989. Office: Buffalo Bill Hist Ctr PO Box 1000 Cody WY 82414-1000

HASTINGS, L(OIS) JANE, architect, educator; b. Seattle, Mar. 3, 1928; d. Harry and Camille (Pugh) H.; m. Norman John Johnston, Nov. 22, 1969. B.Arch., U. Wash., Seattle, 1952, postgrad. in Urban Planning, 1958. Architect Boeing Airplane Co., Seattle, 1951-54; recreational dir. Germany, 1954-56; architect (various firms), Seattle, 1956-59, pvt. practice architecture, 1959-74; instr. archtl. drafting Seattle Community Coll., part-time 1969-80; owner/founder The Hastings Group Architects, Seattle, 1974—; lectr. design Coll. Architecture, U. Wash., 1975; incorporating mem. Architecta (P.S.), Seattle, 1980; pres. Architecta (P.S.), from 1980; mem. adv. bd. U. Wash. YWCA, 1967-69; mem. Mayor's Com. on Archtl. Barriers for Handicapped, 1974-75; chmn. regional public adv. panel on archtl. and engring. services GSA, 1976; mem. citizens adv. com. Seattle Land Use Adminstrn. Task Force, from 1979; AWIU guest of Soviet Women's Con., 1983; speaker Pacific Rim Forum, Hong Kong, 1987; guest China Internat. Conf. Ctr. for Sci. and Tech. of the China Assn. for Sci. and Tech., 1989; mem. adv. com. Coll. architecture and urban planning U. Wash., 1993; mem. accreditation team U. Oreg. Coll. Architecture, 1991, N.J. Inst. Tech. Sch. Architecture, 1992. Design juror for nat. and local competitions, including Red Cedar Shingle/AIA awards, 1977, Current Use Honor awards, AIA, 1980, Exhibit of Sch. Architecture award, 1981; Contbr. to: also spl. features newspapers, articles in profl. jours. Sunset mag. Mem. bd. Am. Women for Internat. Understanding, del. to, Egypt, Israel, USSR, 1971, Japan and Korea, 1979, USSR, 1983; mem. Landmarks Preservation Bd. City of Seattle, 1981-83; mem. Design Constrn. Rev. Bd. Seattle Sch. Dist., 1985-87; mem. mus. con. Mus. History and Industry, 1987—; leader People to People del. women architects to China, 1990. Recipient AIA/The Seattle Times Home of Month Ann. award, 1968; Exhbn. award Seattle chpt. AIA, 1970; Environ. award Seattle-King County Bd. Realtors, 1970, 77,; AIA/House and Home/The American Home Merit award, 1971, Sp. Honor award Wash. Aggregates and Concrete Assn., 1993, Prize bridge Am. Inst. Steel Contrn., 1993; Honor award Seattle chpt. AIA, 1977, 83; Women Achievement award Past Pres. Assembly, 1983, Washington Women and Trading Cards, 1983; Nat. Endowment for Arts grantee, 1977; others; named to West Seattle High Sch. Hall of Fame, 1989, Woman of Achievement Matrix Table, 1994; named Woman of Distinction, Columbia River Girl Scout Coun., 1994. Fellow AIA (pres. Seattle chpt. 1975, pres. sr. council 1980, state exec. bd. 1975, NW regional dir. 1982-87, 86, Seattle chpt. found. bd. 1985-87, Bursar Coll. Fellows 1989-90, internat. rels. com. 1988-92, vice chancellor 1991, chancellor 1992, Seattle chpt. medal 1995), Internat. Union Women Architects (v.p. 1969-79, sec. gen. 1985-89, del. UIA Congress, Montreal 1990), Am. Arbitration Assn. (arbitrator 1981—), Coun. of Design Professions, Assoc. Woman Contractors, Suppliers and Design Cons.'s, Allied Arts Seattle, Fashion Group, Tau Sigma Delta, Alpha Rho Chi (medal). Office: The Hastings Group-Architects 1516 E Olive Way Seattle WA 98122-2130

HASTINGS, MERRILL GEORGE, JR., publisher, marketing consultant; b. Dedham, Mass., May 12, 1922; s. Merrill G. and Emita E. (Zeil) H.; m. Priscilla G. Brayton, July 31, 1948; children: William, Deborah. Educ., Bowdoin Coll., 1946. Chmn. bd., pres. Skiing Pub. Co., Denver, 1950-64, Colorado Mag., Inc., Denver, 1964-77, Mountain Bus. Pubs., Denver, 1972-77, Hastings, Johnsus & White, Vail, Colo., 1977-79, Energy Pub. Co., Denver, 1980-82, Pulse Pubs., Denver, 1985-87, Living Will Ctr., Denver, 1990—, Colo. Mag. LLC, Denver, 1994—. Founder Nat. Cancer Survivors Day, 1988. Served with Brit. Army, 1944-45. Recipient Austrian IXth Winter Olympic medal, Innsbruck, 1964. Mem. Colo. Press Assn. Home: Sunnyvail Rnch Mc Coy CO 80463 Office: 1250 Poppy Creek Rd Mc Coy CO 80463

HASTRICH, JEROME JOSEPH, bishop; b. Milw., Nov. 13, 1914; s. George Philip and Clara (Dettlaff) H. Student, Marquette U., 1933-35; BA, St. Francis Sem., Milw., 1940, MA, 1941; student, Cath. U. Am., 1941. Ordained priest Roman Cath. Ch., 1941; assigned to Milw. Chancery, 1941; curate St. Ann's Ch., Milw., St. Bernard's Ch., Madison, Wis.; asst. chaplain St. Paul U. Chapel, then U. Wis.; sec. to bishop of Diocese U. Wis., Madison, Wis., 1946-52; chancellor Diocese Madison, Wis., 1952-53; apptd. vicar gen. Diocese Madison, 1953, domestic prelate, 1954, protonotary apos., 1960; aux. bishop, 1963-67, titular bishop of Gurza and aux. of Madison, 1963; pastor St. Raphael Cathedral, Madison, 1967-69; bishop Gallup, N.Mex., 1969-90, ret.; diocesan dir. Confraternity Christian Doctrine, 1946—, St. Martin Guild, 1946-69; aux. chaplain U.S. Air Force, 1947-67; pres. Latin Am. Mission Program; sec. Am. Bd. Cath. Missions; vice chmn. Bishop's Com. for Spanish Speaking; mem. subcom. on allocations U.S. Bishops Com. for Latin Am.; founder, episcopal moderator Queen of Americas Guild, 1979—; pres. Nat. Blue Army of Our Lady of Fatima, 1980—. Mem. Gov. Wis. Commn. Migratory Labor, 1964—. Club: K.C. (hon. life mem.). Home: PO Box 1777 Gallup NM 87305-1777

HASWELL, T. CLAYTON, newspaper editor; b. Evanston, Ill., July 21, 1949; s. H.A. and Frances (Ellis) H.; m. Sarah D. Mott, Nov. 13, 1981; 1 child, Sam. BA, U. So. Calif., 1971. Sports editor Anchorage Times, 1973-74; reporter The Australian, Brisbane, 1975, The Christchurch (New Zealand) Press, 1976; mng. editor Anchorage Daily News, 1977-81; editor AP, Boston and Mpls., 1981-89; exec. editor, v.p. Lesher Comm., Walnut Creek, Calif., 1990—. Mem. Am. Soc. Newspaper Editors, AP Mng. Editors, Calif. Soc. Newspaper Editors (v.p., bd. dirs.). Office: Contra Costa Times PO Box 5088 Walnut Creek CA 94596-0088

HATAI, THOMAS HENRY, international marketing professional; b. Tokyo, Dec. 27, 1937; came to U.S., 1951; s. Isamu Herbert and Kiyoko (Kume) H.; m. Geraldine Hatai, Jan. 19, 1970 (div. 1978); children: Dickson Y., Keio Gijuku Yochisha. BS, Woodbury Coll., 1965. Supr. internat. dept. Union Bank, L.A., 1964-66; with mgmt. United Airlines, L.A., 1966-69; v.p. far east Travel Systems Internat., Oakbrook, Ill., 1969-75; pres. Hatai Internat., L.A., 1975-78; pres., chief exec. officer Pace Mktg., Inc., La Habra, Calif., 1978—; founder, vice chmn. bd. dirs., CEO Yamamo Cosmetics Inc., 1991—; pres., CEO Yamamo Products Inc. (dba AVEC), 1992—; bd. dirs. Grand Five Corp., Bangkok, Thailand; pres. D.B.H. Global, Ltd., La Hambra, 1993—. Illustrators: The Marty Story, 1954, The St. Meinrad Story, 1954. Mem. United Internat. Club (bd. dirs. 1969 Japan), U.S. C. of C. Republican. Home: 8544 Buena Tierra Pl Buena Park CA 90621-1002 Office: D B H Global Ltd 1251C S Beach Blvd La Habra CA 90631-6301

HATAMI, MARVIN, architect, educator, urban designer; b. Tehran, Iran, Feb. 14, 1925; came to U.S., 1955, naturalized, 1961; s. Fazlolah and Fahime Hatami; m. Bernice Vann Hecke, 1958 (div. 1972); children: Todd Adrian, Darius Mark, Brenna Celest; m. Judith Ann Anderson, Sept. 1991. BSCE, U. Tehran, 1949; BArch, U. Colo., Boulder, 1958; MArch, Yale U., 1961. Registered arch., Colo. Designer, draftsman various archtl. firms, Denver and N.Y.C., 1957-64; ptnr. Baume, Polivnick & Hatami, Denver, 1964-67; v.p. architecture URS Corp., Denver, 1974-76; prof. interior design U. Denver Sch. Arts, 1972-74; prin. Marvin Hatami & Assocs. URS Corp., 1967—; prof. adj. Sch. Architecture and Planning U. Colo., Denver, 1987, assoc. prof. architecture and urban design, 1988—, dir. interior design program; adj. assoc. prof., vis. lectr. U. Colo., Boulder and Denver Ctr., 1970-82; presenter, speaker in field; mem. Adv. Panel for Urban Design Guidelines and Source Book, Denver, 1983-84. Prin. works include Denver Skyline Urban Renewal Project, Communitas, The Galleria, Auraria Higher Edn. Ctr., St. Francis Interfaith Ctr., Denver, Fisk Planetarium, U. Colo., Boulder, Traylor Elem. Sch., Denver, Pacific Place, Denver, Glenarm Place, Denver; also pvt. residences, preservation and renovation projects; contbr. articles to profl. jours. Mem. Friends Contemporary Arts, 1965-74, Denver Civic Ctr. Assn., 1973, chmn. Nat. Com. on Regional Devel. and Natural Resources; mem. task force Downtown Area Plan, Denver, 1984-85. Recipient citation Progressive Architecture, 1963, 70, design award, 1975; honor award for design excellence HHD, 1970, 1st award for inner elegance Denver Bd. Realtors, 1979; winner design competition Boulder Civic Ctr., 1969, design competition for low income housing Denver Housing Authority, 1976; Alumni scholar U. Colo., 1957; ednl. grantee Yale U., 1961. Fellow AIA (chmn. nat. com. on regional devel. and resources, Commn. on Environ. Denver chpt., mem. urban design com. 1981—, ednl. com. Colo. chpt. 1985-88, design award westeern region 1981); mem. Profl. Sci. Instrs. Am. (cert.), City Club Denver, Tau Beta Pi, Sigma Tau. also: Univ of Colorado At Denver 494 Columbine St Denver CO 80206-4247 Office: U Colo New Coll Architect and Planning Campus Box 236 PO Box 173364 Denver CO 80217-3364

HATCH, ELVIN JAMES, anthropology educator; b. Tulare, Calif., Sept. 20, 1937; s. Raymond K. and Elvera (Anderson) H.; m. Deanna Elizabeth Fries; children: Kristen Lee, Catherine Anderson. BA, Fresno State Coll., 1959; PhD, UCLA, 1968. Lectr. anthropology U. Calif., Santa Barbara, 1967-68, asst. prof. anthropology, 1968-74, assoc. prof. anthropology, 1974-79, prof. anthropology, 1979—, chair dept. anthropology, 1978-84; mem. editorial com. U. Calif. Press, Berkeley, 1986-91, co-chair editorial com., 1988-91. Author: Theories of Man and Culture, 1973, Biography of a Small Town, 1979, Culture and Morality, 1983, Respectable Lives, 1991. Mem.

Am. Anthropol. Assn. Office: Dept Anthropology Univ Calif Santa Barbara CA 93106

HATCH, GARY LAYNE, English educator, writer; b. South Jordan, Utah, Sept. 15, 1964; s. LaRelle J. and Jacqueline Deanna (Roberts) H.; m. AnneMarie Henrichsen, May, 31, 1986; children: Aubrey, Carson. BA in English, Brigham Young U., 1988; PhD in English, Ariz. State U., 1992. Field rep. LDS Ch., Copenhagen, Denmark, 1983-85; instr. LDS Missionary Tng. Ctr., Provo, Utah, 1986-88; teaching assoc. Ariz. State U., Tempe, 1988-92; asst. prof. Brigham Young U., Provo, 1992—; assoc. composition coord. English dept. Brigham Young U., 1993—; moderator H-Rhetor Electronic Conf., U. Ill., Chgo., 1993—. Author, editor: B.H. Robert's The Truth, The Way, The Life, 1994; contbr. articles. to profl. jours. Kennedy Ctr. rsch. grantee Brigham Young U., Provo, 1994; Regent scholar 1991, 92. Mem. Nat. Coun. Tchrs. of English, Internat. Soc. Social Argumentation, Internat. Soc. for History of Rhetoric, 18th Century Scottish Studies Soc., Brigham Young Scholar Assn. (pres.). Democrat. Office: English Dept Brigham Young U 3146 Jhkb Provo UT 84602-1031

HATCH, GEORGE CLINTON, television executive; b. Erie, Pa., Dec. 16, 1919; s. Charles Milton and Blanche (Beecher) H.; m. Wilda Gene Glasmann, Dec. 24, 1940; children: Michael Gene Zbar, Diane Glasmann Orr, Jeffrey Beecher, Randall Clinton, Deepika Hatch Ogsbury. AB, Occidental Coll., 1940; MA in Econs., Claremont Coll., 1941; HHD (hon.), So. Utah State U., 1988. Pres. Communications Investment Corp., Salt Lake City, 1945—; chmn. Double G Comm. Corp., Salt Lake City, 1956—; dir. Republic Pictures Corp., Los Angeles, 1971-94; pres. Sta. KVEL, Inc., 1978-94; pres. Standard Corp., Ogden, 1993—; past mem. Salt Lake adv. bd. First Security Bank Utah; past chmn. Rocky Mountain Pub. Broadcasting Corp.; past chmn. bd. govs. Am. Info. Radio Network; past bd. govs. NBC-TV Affiliates. Past pres. Salt Lake Com. on Fgn. Relations; past mem. Utah Symphony Bd., Salt Lake City; past chmn. Utah State Bd. Regents, 1964-85. Recipient Svc. to Journalism award U. Utah, 1966, silver medal Salt Lake Advt. Club, 1969, Disting. Svc. award Utah Tech. U., 1984. Mem. Nat. Assn. Broadcasters (past pres., radio bd. dirs., ambassador to Inter-Am. mtgs. in Latin Am. 1962), Utah Broadcasters Assn. (past pres., Mgmt. award 1964, Hall of Fame award 1981), Salt Lake City Advt. Club (silver medal 1969), Phi Beta Kappa, Phi Rho Pi (life). Democrat. Office: Sta KUTV 2185 S 3600 W Salt Lake City UT 84119-1121

HATCH, JOHN DAVIS, design consultant, art historian; b. Oakland, Calif., June 14, 1907; s. John Davis and Gethel (Gregg) H.; m. Olivia Phelps Stokes, Oct. 14, 1939; children: John Davis VI, Daniel Lindley, James Stokes, Sarah Stokes Saeger. Student, U. Calif., 1926-28; student Far Eastern Studies, Harvard U., 1931; student Near East Studies, Princeton U., summer 1938; student Am. Studies, Yale U., 1940; MA in Classical Studies, St. John's Coll., 1993. Landscape architect Santa Barbara, Calif., 1925, Seattle, 1928; exec. sec. Seattle Art Inst., 1928-29, dir., 1929-31; v.p. Western Assn. Art Museums, 1929-30; surveyed facilities and materials for Far Eastern studies in U.S. and Can., 1931-32, Am. studies in U.S. colls. and univs. for Am. Council Learned Socs., 1938-39; dir. U.S. art projects in New Eng., 1933-34; mem. McDowell Colony, 1938; asst. dir. Isabella Stewart Gardner Mus., Boston, 1932-35, Carnegie Corp., N.Y., 1935-37; founder, adviser So. Negro Colls. Coop. Exhibits Group, 1936-41; founder Am. Artist Depository, 1937, Am. Drawing Ann., 1940, Commn. on Art Studies, 1938; Dir. Albany Inst. History and Art, 1940-48; chmn. Albany-Nijmegen Holland Com., 1948; vis. prof. U. Oreg., 1948-49, U. Calif., summer 1949, U. Mass., summer 1971; dir. Norfolk Mus. Arts and Scis., 1950-59; pres. Phelps Stokes Corp., 1959-62; coordinating adviser, acting chmn. fine arts div. Spelman Coll., Ga., 1964-70; v.p. Nevada Co.; Chmn., founder Old Curtisville, 1965, pres. emeritus, 1981—; former trustee Lenox Sch., Hoosac Sch.; hon. keeper Cape Henry Light House, Assn. for Preservation Va. Antiquities, 1948—. Author: American sect. Great Drawings of All Times, 1962, Historic Survey of Painting in Canada, 1946, Historic Church Silver in the Southern Diocese of Virginia, 1952; Editor: Parnassus, 1937-39, Albany County Hist. Assn. Record, 1941-48, Early Am. Industries Chronicle, 1942-49; 100 Am. drawings, Dublin, London, Paris, 1976-77; had pioneer exhibit The Negro Artist Comes of Age, 1943, Painting in Canada, 1944, Thomas Cole, 1942, Outdoor Sculptors of Berkshires, 1978. Donated (with others) Anson Phelps Stokes Ref. Libr. to U. Liberia, 1980. Fellow Morgan Library, Met. Mus. N.Y., Nat. Gallery, Washington. Mem. Master Drawing Assn. (hon. trustee, founder 1962), Am. Drawing Soc. (adv. bd.), Am. Assn. Mus. (founder N. Eastern conf. 1941, S.E. conf. 1951); founding mem. Internat. Mus. Assn. Episcopalian. Clubs: Rotary, Grolier (N.Y.C.), Cosmos (Washington), Quail Run (Santa Fe), Harvard Musical (Boston). Home: 640 Camino Lejo Santa Fe NM 87505-7510

HATCH, ORRIN GRANT, senator; b. Homestead Park, Pa., Mar. 22, 1934; s. Jesse and Helen (Kamm) H.; m. Elaine Hansen, Aug. 28, 1957; children: Brent, Marcia, Scott, Kimberly, Alysa, Jess. B.S., Brigham Young U., 1959; J.D., U. Pitts., 1962; LLD (hon.), U. Md., 1981; MS (hon.), Def. Intelligence Coll., 1982; LLD (hon.), Pepperdine U., 1990, So. Utah State U., 1990. Bar: Pa. 1962, Utah 1962. Ptnr. firm Thomson, Rhodes & Grigsby, Pitts., 1962-69, Hatch & Plumb, Salt Lake City, 1976; mem. U.S. Senate from Utah, 1977—, past chmn. labor and human resources com., chmn. Senate judiciary com., joint com. on taxation, com. on Indian affairs. Author ERA Myths and Realities, 1983; contbr. articles to newspapers and profl. jours. Recipient Outstanding Legislator award Nat. Assn. Rehab. Facilities, Legislator of Yr. award Am. Assn. Univ. Affiliated Programs, Legis. Leadership award Health Profl. Assn., many others. Mem. Am., Nat., Utah, Pa. bar assns., Am. Judicature Soc. Republican. Mormon. *

HATCH, SCOTT ALEXANDER, wildlife research biologist; b. June 7, 1952; s. William Todd and Evelyn Doris (Peterson) H.; m. Martha Ann Laughlin, Sept. 21, 1974; children: Kyle Evelyn, Megan Elise. BS summa cum laude, U. Wash., 1975; MS, U. Alaska, 1979; PhD, U. Calif., Berkeley, 1985. Wildlife biologist Denver Wildlife Rsch. Ctr., U.S. Fish & Wildlife Svc., Anchorage, 1981-85, supervisory wildlife biologist, 1985-93; supervisory wildlife biologist Nat. Biol. Survey, Alaska Rsch. Ctr., Anchorage, 1993—. Contbr. numerous articles to profl. jours. Mem. Am. Ornithologists, British Ornithologists Union, Assn. Field Ornithologists, Soc. Northwestern Vertebrate Biology, Colonial Waterbird Soc., Cooper Ornithol. Soc., Wilson Ornithol. Soc., Peacific Seabird Group (life, chmn. 1988, founder, chmn. standing com. seabird monitoring 1992—), Phi Beta Kappa, Phi Kappa Phi, Xi Sigma Pi. Office: Nat Biol Survey 1011 E Tudor Rd Anchorage AK 99503-6103

HATCH, STEVEN GRAHAM, publishing company executive; b. Idaho Falls, Idaho, Mar. 27, 1951; s. Charles Steven and Margery Jane (Doxey) H.; BA, Brigham Young U., 1976; postgrad. mgmt. devel. program U. Utah, 1981; m. Rhonda Kay Frasier, Feb. 13, 1982; children: Steven Graham, Kristen Leone, Cameron Michael, Landon Frasier. Founder, pres. Graham Maughan Enterprises, Provo, Utah, 1975—, Internat. Mktg. Co., 1980—; dir. Goldbrickers Internat., Inc. Sec., treas. Zions Estates, Inc., Salt Lake City, Kansas City, Mo. Eagle Scout Boy Scouts Am., 1970; trustee Villages of Quail Valley, 1984-88. Recipient Duty to God award, 1970; missionary France Mission, Paris 1970-72, pub. rels. dir. 1972. Mem. Provo Jaycees, Internat. Entrepreneurs Assn., Mormon Booksellers Assn., Samuel Hall Soc. (exec. v.p. 1979), U.S. C. of C., Provo C. of C. (chmn. legis. action com. 1981-82, mem. job svc. employer com.), Rotary Club (Provo pres. 1995—). Republican. Mormon. Office: Graham Maughan Pub Co 50 E 500 S Provo UT 84606-4809

HATCHER, HERBERT JOHN, biochemist, microbiologist; b. Mpls., Dec. 18, 1926; s. Herbert Edmond and Florence Elizabeth (Larson) H.; m. Beverly J. Johnson, Mar. 28, 1953 (dec. July 1985); children: Dennis Michael, Steven Craig, Roger Dean, Mark Alan, Susan Diane, Laura Jean; m. Louise Fritsche Nelson, May 24, 1986; children: Carlos Howard Nelson, Kent Robert Nelson, Carolyn Louise Tyler. BA, U. Minn., 1953, MS, 1964, PhD, 1965. Bacteriologist VA Hosp., Wilmington, Del., 1956-57; microbiologist Smith, Kline, French, Phila., 1957-60, Clinton (Iowa) Corn Processing, 1966-67; microbiologist, biochemist Econs. Lab. Inc., St. Paul, 1967-84; biochemist EG&G Idaho Inc., Idaho Falls, 1984-90; co-owner B/CG Cons. Svcs., Idaho Falls, 1990—; affiliate prof. U. Idaho; adj. prof. Mont. State U., Bozeman; cons. EG&G Idaho, Inc., Idaho Falls, Henkel Corp. N.J., 1986. Chmn. bd. edn. Cross of Christ Luth. Ch., Coon Rapids, Minn., 1974-76; pres. chpt. Aid Assn. Luths., Idaho Falls, 1986; pres.-elect St. Johns Luth. Ch., 1988, pres., 1989. With USNR, 1945-46. Mem. Am. Chem. Soc. (fuel divsn.).

HATCHER, JOHN CHRISTOPHER, psychologist; b. Atlanta, Sept. 18, 1946; s. John William and Kay (Carney) H.; BA, U. Ga., 1968, MS, 1970, PhD, 1972. Psychologist, Clayton Mental Health Ctr., Atlanta, 1971-72; dir. intern tng. psychology svc. Beaumont Med. Center, El Paso, Tex., 1972-74; dir. family therapy program Langley Porter Inst., U. Calif., San Francisco, 1974-88, dir. ctr. for study of trauma, San Francisco, 1989—; adj. prof. dept. psychology U. Tex., 1972-74, dept. ednl. psychology and guidance, 1972-74; asst. clin. prof. psychology U. Calif., San Francisco, 1974-80, assoc. clin. prof., 1980-86, clin. prof., 1986—; cons. city and state govts. in U.S., Europe, Mexico, Asia, Far East; internat. cons. in hostage negotiation, kidnapping and terrorism chmn., Mayors Commn. on Family Violence, San Francisco, 1974-77; advisor arson task force San Francisco Fire Dept., 1977-81; advisor U.S. State Dept., 1985-90; advisor U.S. Congress Task Force on Tech. and Terrorism, 1990-91; adv. bd. Nat. Firehawk Found., 1980-86; advisor CBS-TV, 1975-80; spl. asst. to Mayor of San Francisco in charge of People's Temple Jonestown Case, 1978-80; mem. Calif. State Legis. Task Force on Missing Children, 1987-89; adv. bd. Nat. Minority Vietnam Vet. PTSD Study, 1991; prin. investigator U.S. Dept. Justice Families of Missing Children Project, Reunification of Missing Children Project, Obstacles to Recovery in Parental Abduction Project; assoc. investigator NIMH Adult and Adolescent Response to Distaster Project, U.S. Dept. Justice Models Treatment for Families of Missing Children Project. Fellow Am. Psychol. Assn. (chmn. com. hostage families, predsl. task force on violence and the family); mem. Calif. Psychol. Assn. (chmn. task force on terrorism, disting. humanitarian award, 1991, chmn. divsn. edn. and tng.), Soc. Police and Criminal Psychology, Assn. Advancement Psychology, Am. Family Therapy Assn., Internat. Council Psychologists, Phi Kappa Phi. Author: (with Himelstein) Handbook of Gestalt Therapy, 1976; (with Brooks) Innovations in Counseling Psychology, 1977, (with Gaynor) Psychology of Child Firesetting, 1987; assoc. editor Am. Jour. Family Therapy; sr. editor Family Therapy Jour., mem. editorial bd. Family Psychology Jour., Jour. Traumatic Stress; newsletter: Workplace Violence and Behavior; co-author (film) Workplace Violence: First Line of Defense. Office: U Calif Dept Psychiatry 401 Parnassus Ave Box GMO San Francisco CA 94143-6401

HATFIELD, CHARLES DONALD, newspaper executive; b. Huntington, W.Va., June 15, 1935; s. Howard Donald and LaUna (Wilson) H.; m. Sandra Gail Soto, June 11, 1955; children: John Christopher, Lisa, Joel Thomas. BA, Marshall Coll., 1977. Mem. sports staff Huntington Advertiser, 1953-60, asst. news editor, 1960-67, mng. editor, 1972-79; news editor Herald-Advertiser, Huntington, 1967-69, mng. editor, 1969-72; exec. editor Herald-Dispatch, Huntington, 1979-82, pub., editor, 1982-85; regional v.p. Gannett Co., Inc. E., Huntington, 1985-86; pub., editor and regional v.p. Tucson Citizen and Gannett West, 1986—. Author: Don Hatfield Cleans Out His Attic, 1986. Bd. dirs. United Way, Tucson, 1987—, Pima County Econ. Devel., Tucson, 1988—, Tucson Mus. Art, 1989—. Mem. AP Mng. Editors Assn. (treas 1986-88), Am. Soc. Newspaper Editors, Am. Newspapers Pubs., Ariz. Newspaper Assn., La Paloma Club, Tucson Country Club. Office: Tucson Citizen PO Box 26767 Tucson AZ 85726-6767

HATFIELD, MARK O., senator; b. Dallas, Oreg., July 12, 1922; s. Charles Dolen and Dovie (Odom) H.; m. Antoinette Kuzmanich, July 8, 1958; children: Mark, Elizabeth, Theresa, Charles. A.B., Willamette U., 1943; A.M., Stanford U., 1948. Instr. Willamette U., 1949, dean students, assoc. prof. polit. sci., 1950-56; mem. Oreg. Ho. of Reps., 1951-55, Oreg. Senate, 1955-57; sec. State of Oreg., 1957-59, gov., 1959-67; U.S. senator from Oreg., 1967—, chmn. appropriations com.; mem. energy and natural resources com., rules and adminstrn. com., joint printing com., joint libr. com.; mem. select com. Indian Affairs, Republican Policy Com.; chmn. Appropriations subcom. on transp. & related agencies. Author: Not Quite So Simple, 1967, Conflict and Conscience, 1971, Between A Rock and A Hard Place, 1976; co-author: Amnesty: The Unsettled Question of Vietnam, 1976, Freeze! How You Can Help Prevent Nuclear War, 1982, The Causes of World Hunger, 1982; co-author: What About the Russians, 1984. Served to lt. j.g. USN, 1943-45, PTO. Recipient numerous hon. degrees. Republican. Baptist. Office: US Senate 711 Hart Senate Bldg Washington DC 20510

HATFIELD, PAUL GERHART, federal judge, lawyer; b. Great Falls, Mont., Apr. 29, 1928; s. Trueman LeRoy and Grace Lenore (Gerhart) H.; m. Dorothy Ann Allen, Feb. 1, 1958 (dec. Aug. 1992); children: Kathleen Helen, Susan Ann, Paul Allen. Student, Coll. of Great Falls, 1947-50; LL.B., U. Mont., 1955. Bar: Mont. bar 1955. Assoc. firm Hoffman & Cure, Gt. Falls, Mont., 1955-56, Jardine, Stephenson, Blewett & Weaver, Gt. Falls, 1956-58, Hatfield & Hatfield, Gt. Falls, 1959-60; chief dep. county atty. Cascade County, Mont., 1959-60; dist. ct. judge 8th Jud. Dist., Mont., 1961-76; chief justice Supreme Ct. Mont., Helena, 1977-78; U.S. Senator from Mont., 1978-79; U.S. dist. judge for Dist. of Mont., Gt. Falls, 1979—; chief judge, 1990—; Vice chmn. Pres.'s Council Coll. of Great Falls. Author standards for criminal justice, Mont. cts. Served with U.S. Army, 1951-53. Korea. Mem. Am., Mont. bar assns., Am. Judicature Soc. Roman Catholic. Office: US Dist Ct PO Box 1529 Great Falls MT 59403-1529

HATHAWAY, LOLINE, zoo and botanic park curator; b. Whittier, Calif., June 27, 1937; d. Richard Franklin and F. Nadine (Applegate) H.; 1 child, Patrick Paul Kundtz. BA, Reed Coll., Portland, Oreg., 1959; PhD, Washington U., St. Louis, 1969. Instr. St. Louis U., 1966-68; curator of edn. Chgo. Zool. Soc., Brookfield, Ill., 1968-71; cons. on terrestrial biology Ryckman, Edgerly, Tomlinson & Assocs., St. Louis, 1972-75; marina mgr. Lake Piru (Calif.) Recreation Area, 1976-77; curator, dir. Navajo Nation Zool. and Botanical Park, Window Rock, Ariz., 1983—. Vice chmn., chmn. City of Santa Fe Springs (Calif.) Traffic Commn., 1979-83; mem. Navajo Estates Vol. Fire Dept., Yah-ta-hey, N.Mex., 1984-85; bd. dirs. Hathaway Ranch Mus., Santa Fe Springs, 1986-93, Gallup Cmty. Concerts Assn., 1994—; leader 4-H Club, 1989—. Mem. AAAS (vice chmn. S.W.-Rocky Mountain div. sci. edn. sect. 1983-84, chmn. 1984-85), AAUW (scholarship com. Gallup 1992—), Am. Assn. Zool. Parks and Aquariums, Am. Assn. Bot. Gardens and and Arboretums, Assn. Living. Hist. Farms and Agr. Mus., Am. Inst. Biol. Scis., Sierra Club (Ozarks chpt. founder, bd. dirs., sec. Gt. Lakes chpt. 1963-72). Democrat. Home: 27 S LaChee PO Box 4172 Yah-ta-hey NM 87375 Office: Navajo Nat Zool and Bot Pk PO Box 9000 Window Rock AZ 86515-9000

HATHAWAY, STANLEY KNAPP, lawyer; b. Osceola, Nebr., July 19, 1924; s. Franklin E. and Velma Clara (Holbrook) H.; m. Roberta Louise Harley, Nov. 26, 1948; children—Susan Garrett, Sandra D'Amico. A.B., U. Nebr., 1948, LL.B., 1950; LL.D., U. Wyo., 1975. Bar: Nebr. 1950, Wyo., 1950, U.S. Dist. Ct. Wyo., Nebr., Mont. 1950, U.S. Supreme Ct. 1964. Sole practice, Torrington, Wyo., 1950-66; gov. Wyo., 1967-75; assoc. Hathaway, Speight & Kunz, Cheyenne, Wyo., 1975—; dir. Apache Corp., Houston, Key Wyo. Bankshares, Cheyenne, Wyo.; county atty. Goshen County (Wyo.), 1955-62; gov. State of Wyo., 1967-75; sec. U.S. Dept. Interior, 1975. Served with USAAF, 1943-45. Decorated Air medals with 5 clusters. Mem. ABA, Wyo. State Bar Assn. Republican. United Episcopalian. Clubs: Lions, Masons (Cheyenne); Shriners (Rawlins, Wyo.). Office: Hathaway Speight & Kunz One Pioneer Ctr Cheyenne WY 82001

HATHAWAY, WILLIAM ELLISON, pediatrics educator; b. Ardmore, Okla., Jan. 13, 1929; s. Elmer Gray and Bertha Mae (Underwood) H.; m. Helen Sue White, Aug. 23, 1956; children: Elizabeth, Jennifer, William, Thomas, Margaret, Joseph, Katherine. BA, U. Okla., 1950, MD, 1954. Intern USN Hsop., Bremerton, 1954-55; resident in pediatrics N.Y. Hosp., N.Y.C., 1957-59; fellow in hematology U Colo. Sch. Med., Denver, 1959-60, asst. prof. pediatrics, 1964-67, assoc. prof., 1967-73, prof. pediatrics, 1973-88, prof. emeritus, 1988—; pvt. practice pediatrics Colorado Springs, Colo., 1960-61; instr. pediatrics U. Ky. Med. Ctr., Lexington, 1961-63, asst. prof. pediatrics, 1963-64; dir. hemophilia programs U. Colo. Med. Ctr., Denver, 1967-88; vis. prof. U. Ariz. Med. Ctr., Tucson, 1992—. Author: (with others) Immunologic Deficiency Diseases in Man, 1968, (with others) Hemophilia and New Hemorrhagic States, 1970, , Advances in Pediatrics, 1972, Care of the Critically Ill Cild, 1972, (with others) Immunologic Disorders in Infants and Children, 1973, Clinics in Perinatology, 1975, Current Problems in Pediatric Hematology, 1975, Current Pediatric Therapy, 1976, The Critically Ill Child, 1977, (with R.R. Montgomery) Kidney Disease: Hematologic and Vascular problems. 1977, (with J. Bonnar) Perinatal Coagulation, 1978, (with R.R. Montgomery) Pediatric Clinics of North America, 1980, Haemostasis and Thrombosis, 1981, Pediatrics, 1982, Current Pediatric Therapy, 1982, Standardization of Coagulation Assays: An Overview, 1982, Current Pediatric Therapy, 1984, Current Therapy in Neonatal-Perinatal Medicine, 1985, Practical Pediatric Therapy, 1985, Management of Musculoskeletal Problems in Hemophilia, 1986, Blood Component Therapy of Neonatla Disease, 1986, Primary Pediatric Care, 1987, Current Pediatric Diagnosis and Treatment, 1987, 1987 Yearbook of Pediatrics, 1987, Haemostasis and Thrombosis, 1987, Pediatrics, 1987, Current Therapy in Pediatrics-2, 1989, Immunologic Disorders in Infants and Children, 1989, Hematologic Disorders in Maternal-Fetal Medicine, 1990, Current Pediatric Diagnosis and Treatment, 10th edit., 1991, Perinatal Thrombosis and Haemostasis, 1991, Hematology: Basic Principles and Practice, 1991, (with others) Vitamin K and Vitamin-K Dependent Proteins: Analytical, Physiological and Clinical Aspects, 1993, Pediatric Therapy, 1993, Haemostasis and Thrombosis in Obstetrics and Gynaecology, 1992, Fetal and Neonatal Physiology, 1992; (with W.W. Hay, J.R. Groothuis, J.E. Paisley) Current Pediatric Diagnosis and Treatment, 1993; (with S.H. Goodnight Jr.) Disorders of Hemostasis and Thrombosis: A Clinical Guide, 1993; contbr. numerous articles to profl. jours. Comdr. USNR, 1955-57. Mem. Internat. Soc. Thrombosis Haemostasis, Am. Soc. Hematology, Am. Pediatric Soc., Soc. Pediatric Rsch. Home: 450 N Mountain Side Pl Tucson AZ 85745-9126 Office: U Colo Health Sci Ctr Dept Pediatrics 4200 E 9th Ave Denver CO 80220-3706

HATHAWAY-BATES, JOHN HUGH, company executive; b. Oxford, Eng., Nov. 7, 1940; came to U.S., 1979; s. Percival Hugh and Freda Elizabeth (Hathaway-Taylor) Bates; m. Holly Dee, Nov. 5, 1986; children: Sarah, Christina, Raymond, Matthew, David. Grad., Southfield Sch., Oxford, Eng., 1956. Agt. United Friendly Ins. Co., Oxford, 1961-67; dir. Hunts Group, Oxford, 1967-71; pres. John Hathaway-Bates & Assocs., Oxford, 1971-76, Ubbink Telmrose Ltd., Bicester, Eng. & Doesburg, Holland, 1976-79; corp. v.p., internat. dir. mktg. Environetics Inc., London and N.Y.C., 1979-81; pres. Asigan Internat. Inc., Beverly Hills, Calif., 1981-83, The Bus. Forum Inc., Beverly Hills, 1983—; profl. spkr. mktg. & tactical mgmt. Author: Tactics, 1988, Fast Track Marketing in a Global Economy, 1993; (course) American Management Association: Executive Guide to Facilities Design, 1982. With RAF, 1957-61. Anglican. Office: The Bus Forum Inc 9250 Wilshire Blvd Ste 220 Beverly Hills CA 90212-3344

HATHERILL, JOHN ROBERT, toxicologist, educator; b. Waterford, Mich., Aug. 20, 1953; s. John William and Anna Marie (Morin) H. MS, Ea. Mich. U., 1978; PhD, U. Mich., 1985. Med. technologist U. Mich., Ann Arbor, 1976-78, sr. clin. chemist, 1979-86, rsch. assoc., 1980-85; sr. scientist Ciba-Geigy Pharms., Summit, N.J., 1986-87; rsch. dir. Stanford (Calif.) U., 1987-89; prof. U. Calif., Santa Barbara, 1990—; adj. prof. UCLA, 1990—. Contbr. articles to profl. jours., chpts. to books. Judge, mem. adv. bd. Calif. State Sci. Fair, L.A., 1992. Fellow World Ctr. for Exploration (bd. dirs. 1985); mem. Soc. Toxicology, Am. Soc. Clin. Pathologists, N.Y. Acad. Sci., Sigma Xi, Gamma Alpha. Home: 71 Via Colinas Thousand Oaks CA 91362

HATHEWAY, ALSON EARLE, mechanical engineer; b. Long Beach, Calif., Nov. 15, 1935; s. Earle Miller and Carla (Barnhart) H.; m. Robin Lewis, Aug. 24, 1968; children: Jason Teale, Teale. BSME, U. Calif., Berkeley, 1959. Registered profl. engr., Calif. Engr. Boeing Aerospace Co., Seattle, 1959-60, Ford Aerospace Co., Newport Beach, Calif., 1960-66; mgr. Xerox Corp., Pasadena, Calif., 1966-72, Hughes Aircraft Co., Culver City, Calif., 1972-76, Gould Inc., El Monte, Calif., 1976-79; pres. Alson E. Hatheway Inc., Pasadena, 1979—; instr. U. La Verne, Calif., 1989. Editor: Procs. Structural Mechanics of Optical Systems II, 1987, Procs. Precision Instrument Design, 1989; contbr. articles to profl. jours. Fellow Soc. Photo-Optical Instrumentation Engrs. (instr. 1987—, conf. chmn. 1987, 89, 91, 94, program chmn. 1990, 91); mem. AIAA (sr., chmn. San Gabriel Valley sect. 1992-93), ASME, NSPE, Am. Soc. Precision Engrs., Calif. Soc. Profl. Engrs. (treas. 1965-66), Optical Soc. So. Calif. (pres. 1986—), Opto-Mech. Engring. and Precision Instrument Design Working Group (chmn. 1992-94), Assn. Old Crows. Home: 419 S Meridith Ave Pasadena CA 91106-3512 Office: 595 E Colorado Blvd Ste 400 Pasadena CA 91101-2039

HATTER, TERRY JULIUS, JR., federal judge; b. Chgo., Mar. 11, 1933. A.B., Wesleyan U., 1954; J.D., U. Chgo., 1960. Bar: Ill. 1960, Calif. 1965, U.S. Dist. Ct. 1960, U.S. Ct. Appeals 1960. Adjudicator Chgo., 1960-61; assoc. Harold M. Calhoun, Chgo., 1961-62; asst. pub. defender Cook County Chgo., 1961-62; asst. U.S. atty. No. Dist. Calif., San Francisco, 1962-66; chief counsel San Francisco Neighborhood Legal Assistance Found., 1966-67; regional legal svcs. dir. Exec. Office Pres. OEO, San Francisco, 1967-70; exec. dir. Western Ctr. Law and Poverty, L.A., 1970-73; exec. asst. to mayor, dir. criminal justice planning L.A., 1974-75; spl. asst. to mayor, dir. urban devel., 1975-77; judge Superior Ct. Calif., L.A., 1977-80, U.S. Dist. Ct. (cen. dist.) Calif., L.A., 1979—; lectr. Police Acad., San Francisco Police Dept., 1963-66, U. Calif., San Diego, 1970-71, Colo. Jud. Conf., 1973; assoc. clin. prof. law U. So. Calif. Law Ctr., L.A., 1970-74, mem. bd. councilors; prof. law Loyola U. Sch. Law, L.A., 1973-75; mem. faculty Nat. Coll. State Judiciary, Reno, 1974. V.p. Northbay Halfway House, 1964-65; vice chmn. Los Angeles Regional Criminal Justice Planning Bd., 1975-76; mem. Los Angeles Mayor's Cabinet Com. Econ. Devel., 1976-77, Mayor's Policy Com., 1973-77, chmn. housing econ. and community devel. com., City Los Angeles, 1975-77, chmn. housing and community devel. tech. com., 1975-77; vice chmn. Young Dems. Cook County, 1961-62; chmn. bd. Real Estate Coop; bd. dirs. Bay Area Social Planning Coun., Contra Costa, Black Law Center L.A., Nat. Fedn. Settlements & Neighborhood Ctrs., Edn. Fin. & Governance Reform Project, Mexican Am. Legal Def. & Ednl. Fund, Nat. Health Law Program, Nat. Sr. Citizens Law Ctr., Calif. Law Ctr., L.A. Regional Criminal Justice Planning Bd.; mem. exec. com. bd. dirs. Constl. Rights Found; trustee Wesleyan Univ. Meth. Ch.; mem. bd. visitors U. Chgo. Law Sch. Mem. NAACP (exec. com., bd. dirs. Richmond chpt.), Nat. Legal Aid & Defender Assn. (dir., vice chmn.), L.A. County Bar Assn. (exec. com.), Am. Judicature Soc., Charles Houston Law Club, Phi Delta Phi, Order Coif. Office: US Dist Ct 312 N Spring St Los Angeles CA 90012-4701*

HATTON, GLENN IRWIN, medical educator; b. Chgo., Dec. 12, 1934; s. Irwin Alfred and Anita (Clauson) H.; m. Patricia J. Dougherty, Oct. 6, 1954; children: James D., William G., Christopher J., Jennifer K., Tracey E. BA, North Ctrl. Coll., Naperville, Ill., 1960; MA, U. Ill., 1962, PhD, 1964. Asst. prof. Mich. State U., East Lansing, 1965-68, assoc. prof., 1968-73, prof., 1973-92, neuroscience program dir., 1978-92; prof. U. Calif., Riverside, 1992—, chair dept. neurosci., 1992—; cons. NIH, Washington, 1992—. Recipient Javits Neurosci. Investigator award Nat. Inst. Neurol. Disorders and Stroke, 1986-92, 93—. Mem. Assn. Neurosci. Depts. and Programs (pres. 1994-95), Soc. for Neurosci., Physiol. Soc. (London), Am. Physiol. Soc., Am. Assn. Anatomists, Soc. Gen. Physiologists. Office: U Calif Dept Neuroscience Riverside CA 92521

HATZENBELER, MICHAEL JOSEPH, academic director; b. Richland, Wash., June 3, 1966; s. Gary Francis and Mary Joan (Grady) H.; m. Peggy Carreau, Aug. 10, 1990. Student, U. Wash., 1984-88. Asst. field dir. Citizen Toxic Cleanup Campaign, Seattle, 1988-89; county coord. vol. leadership project Disabilities Rsch. and Info. Coalition, Seattle, 1989; asst. campaign dir. citizen outreach project Wash. Pub. Interest Rsch. Group, Seattle, 1989, campaign dir. citizen outreach project, 1989-90; grant cons. drug edn. coop. Ednl. Svc. Dist. # 114, Bremerton, Wash., 1990; program coord. Bremerton/Kitsap County DWI Task Force, Bremerton, Wash., 1990-92; dir. devel. and pub. rels. Acad. of the Pacific, Honolulu, 1992—. Vice chair Assn. Cmty. DWI Task Force Coords., 1991-92; mem. Citizens United to Reform the Electoral System, 1991; vol. Children's Initiative Campaign Com., 1989, Jim McDermott for Congress Campaign, 1988, George Fleming for Lt. Gov. Campaign, 1988, Retain Senator Gene Lux Campaign, 1988, Referendum 40-Anti-Nuclear Waste Dump Campaign, 1986, Initiative 547 - Growth Mgmt. Campaign, 1991; chmn. bd. dirs. Washington Pub. Interest Rsch. Group, 1987-88, U. Wash. chpt., 1986-87. Home: 1630 Makiki St Apt B303 Honolulu HI 96822-4434 Office: Acad of the Pacific 913 Alewa Dr Honolulu HI 96817-1503

HAUBER, JANET ELAINE, mechanical engineer; b. Milw., July 21, 1937; d. Ralph Joseph and Ethel Esther (Forsyth) H. BME, Marquette U., 1965; MS, Stanford U., 1967, PhD, 1970. Rsch. metallurgist dept. chemistry Lawrence Livermore (Calif.) Nat. Lab., 1970-73, project leader, 1973-74, sect. leader, facility mgr., 1974-76, dep. div. leader, 1976-78, dep. div. leader mech. engring. dept., 1978-86, dep. assoc. dept. head, 1986-87, sect. leader, 1987-93; engr.-at-large, 1993—. Contbr. articles to profl. jours. Ford Foudn. fellow Stanford U., 1965, ASTM fellow, 1967. Mem. AAUW (v.p. 1992-93), Soc. Women Engrs., Sigma Xi, Math./Sci. Network (bd. dirs. 1994—, treas. 1995—). Office: Lawrence Livermore Nat Lab PO Box 808 Livermore CA 94551-0808

HAUCK, DENNIS WILLIAM, author, technical writer; b. Hammond, Ind., Apr. 8, 1945; s. Floyd William and Wilma (Frey) H. AA in Math., Ind. U., 1964-67; MS in Math., U. Vienna, Austria, 1972. Editor IUFOR Svcs. Inc., Munster, Ind., 1973-76; mng. editor Countrywide Publs., N.Y.C., 1976-80; tech. writer EPCO Inc., Reno, 1980-83, Odenberg Inc., Sacramento, Calif., 1984-91; freelance writer Sacramento, 1991—; cons. in field. Editor Jour. of Ufology, 1973-76; author: William Shatner: A Biography, 1992, The Alchemical Works of Gottlieb Latz, 1992, Haunted Places Guidebook, 1993, First Matter, 1993, Captain Quirk, 1995. Active mem. Greenpeace, San Francisco. Mem. Authors Guild, Soc. for Tech. Comm., Nat. Writers Club, Calif. Writers Club, Nat. Writers Union. Office: Hauck Editorial Svcs 5550 Franklin Blvd Ste 101 Sacramento CA 95820-4700

HAUCK, JOANN RAE, secondary education educator; b. San Bernardino, Calif., Sept. 27, 1946; d. Victor Ray and Irene Theresa (Schumacher) Starkweather; m. Robert James Hauck, Nov. 18, 1992. BS in Secondary Edn., Idaho State U., 1987; MEd in Sch. Counseling, Albertson Coll. of Idaho, 1994. Cert. vocat. guidance counselor, secondary vocat. bus. edn. tchr., Idaho. Bus. tchr. Mackay (Idaho) Jr./Sr. H.S., 1987—. Mem. ACA, NEA, Idaho Counselors Assn., Nat. Bus. Edn. Assn., Idaho Edn. Assn. Home: PO Box 599 Mackay ID 83251-0599 Office: Mackay Jr/Sr High Sch PO Box 390 Mackay ID 83251-0390

HAUENSTEIN, DONALD HERBERT, JR., computer consultant; b. Canton, Ohio, Dec. 29, 1942; s. Donald Herbert and Mary Alice (Andrichs) H.; m. Maria Del Socorro Moreno, June 5, 1965 (div. Apr. 1979); children: Carlos Ian, Marissa Renee; m. Carol King, May 28, 1988. B in Indsl. Engring., Ohio State U., 1970, MS in Indsl. Engring., 1970; MBA, U. Houston, 1977; exec. mgmt. program, UCLA, L.A., 1986. Indsl. engr. Schlumberger Well Svcs., Houston, 1970-72, supr. of methods, 1972-75; mgr. engring. svcs. Dresser Atlas, Houston, 1975-80; mgr. mfg. engring. VETCO Offshore, Ventura, Calif., 1980-83; dir. mfg. engring. HR Textron, Valencia, Calif., 1983-88; dir. spl. projects HR Textron, Valencia, 1988-90; owner, retail Abacus Computer Svcs., Saugus, 1990—. Pres. St. Christopher's Sch. Bd., Houston, 1976-79, bd. dirs. Orchard Ln. Condominium Assn., Oxnard, Calif., 1986, Arbor Park Condominium Assn., 1987. With USAF, 1961-65. Mem. Tau Beta Pi, Alpha Pi Mu. Republican. Roman Catholic. Home: 28025 Tupelo Ridge Dr Santa Clarita CA 91354-1326 Office: Abacus Computer Svcs 23001 Soledad Canyon Rd Saugus CA 91350-2635

HAUGEN, MARY MARGARET, state legislator; b. Camano Island, Wash., Jan. 14, 1941; d. Melvin Harry and Alma Cora (Huntington) Olsen; m. Basil Badley; children: Mary Beth Fisher, Katherine Heitt, Richard, James. Mem. Wash. Ho. Reps., Olympia, 1982-1992, past mem. natural resources com., transp. com., mem. joint legis. com. on criminal justice system; mem. Wash. Senate, Olympia, 1993—; chmn. govt. ops. com., transp. com., natural resource com., law and justice com. Wash. State Senate. Mem. Camano Homeowners Assn.; mem. United Meth. Ch. Mem. LWV, Stanwood Camano Soroptomists. Democrat. Lodge: Order Ea. Star. Home: 1268 N Olsen Rd Camano Island WA 98292-8708 Office: Wash State Legislature JAC Wac # 414 Olympia WA 98504

HAUK, A. ANDREW, federal judge; b. Denver, Dec. 29, 1912; s. A.A. and Pearl (Woods) H.; m. Jean Nicolay, Aug. 30, 1941; 1 dau., Susan. AB magna cum laude, Regis Coll., 1935; LLB, Cath. U. Am., 1938; JSD (Sterling fellow), Yale U., 1942. Bar: Calif. 1942, Colo. 1939, D.C. 1938, U.S. Supreme Ct. 1953. Spl. asst. to atty. gen., counsel for govt. antitrust div. U.S. Dept Justice, Los Angeles, Pacific Coast, Denver, 1939-41; asst. U.S. atty., Los Angeles, 1941-42; with firm Adams, Duque & Hazeltine, Los Angeles, 1946-52; individual practice law Los Angeles, 1952-64; asst. counsel Union Oil Co., Los Angeles, 1952-64; judge Superior Ct., Los Angeles County, 1964-66; U.S. dist. judge Central Dist. Calif., 1966—, chief judge, 1980-82, now sr. judge, chief judge emeritus; instr. Southwestern U. Law Sch., 1939-41; lectr. U. So. Calif. Law Sch., 1947-56; vice chmn. Calif. Olympic Com., 1954-61; ofcl. VIII Olympic Winter Games, Squaw Valley, 1960; Gov. Calif.'s del. IX Olympic Games, Innsbruck, Austria, 1964. Bd. dirs. So. Calif. Com. for Olympic Games. Served from lt. to lt. comdr., Naval Intelligence USNR, 1942-46. Recipient scroll Los Angeles County Bd. Suprs., 1965, 66, 75; Alumnus of Yr. Regis Coll., 1967; named to Nat. Ski Hall of Fame, 1975. Mem. Los Angeles County Bar Assn. (chmn. pleading and practice com. 1963-64, chmn. Law Day com. 1965-66), State Bar Calif. (corps. com., war work com. past vice-chmn.), ABA (com. criminal law sect.), Fed. Bar Assn., Lawyers Club Los Angeles, Am. Judicature Soc., Am. Legion, Navy League, U.S. Lawn Tennis Assn., Far West Ski Assn. (Nat. Sr. Giant Slalom champion 1954), Yale Law Sch. Assn. So. Calif. (dir., past pres.), Town Hall. Clubs: Yale of So. Calif. (dir. 1964-67), Newman; Valley Hunt (Pasadena); Jonathan (Los Angeles). Office: US Dist Ct 312 N Spring St Los Angeles CA 90012-4701

HAULENBEEK, ROBERT BOGLE, JR., government official; b. Cleve., Feb. 24, 1941; s. Robert Bogle and Priscilla Valerie (Burch) H.; BS, Okla. State U., 1970; m. Rebecca Marie Talley, Mar. 1, 1965; children—Kimberly Kaye, Robert Bogle, III. Micro paleon. photographer Pan Am. Rsch. Co., Tulsa, 1966-67; flight instr. Okla. State U., 1970; air traffic control specialist FAA, Albuquerque, 1970-73, Farmington, N.Mex., 1973-78, flight svc. specialist, Dalhart, Tex., 1978-80, Albuquerque, 1980—; staff officer CAP, Albuquerque, 1970-73, Farmington, 1974-78, advanced through grades to col., 1988, dir. ops. for hdqrs., 1981-86, N.Mex. Wing dep. commdr., 1986-88, N.Mex. Wing comdr., 1988-91, N.Mex. Wing dir. sr. programs, 1993—; mem. faculty Nat. Staff Coll., Gunter Air Force Sta., Montgomery, Ala., 1981-82; dir. South West Region Staff Coll., Albuquerque, 1986. With U.S. Army, 1964-65. Recipient Meritorious Svc. award CAP, 1978, 81, 82, Lifesaving award, 1982, Exceptional Svc. award, 1981, Distng. Svc. award, 1991. Mem. Exptl. Aircraft Assn., Nat. Assn. Air Traffic Specialists (facility rep. 1978-86), Nat. Assn. Flight Instrs., Aircraft Owners and Pilots Assn. Republican. Presbyterian. Home: 5229 Carlsbad Ct NW Albuquerque NM 87120-2322

HAUN, DAVID HARDING, government official; b. Ogden, Utah, Oct. 11, 1953; s. Wallace Edmund and Nadine (Harding) H. BA, Weber State U., 1975; MPA, Am. U., 1979. Staff asst. com. on aeronautical and space scis. U.S. Senate, 1975-77, staff mem., 1977; rsch. analyst gov.'s com. on exec. reorgn. State of Utah, 1977-78; dist. office mgr. no. Utah office U.S. Bur. of the Census, 1980; rsch. analyst Gov.'s Agenda for the 80's Commn., 1981; dep. assessor Weber County Assessor's Office, 1985-88, dept. assessor, reappraisal supr., 1988-91, sys. adminstr., reappraisal supr., 1991-92; city councilman 3d mcpl. ward Ogden City Coun., 1989-92; assessor Weber County, 1992—; adj. prof. Weber State U., 1991; mem. human devel. policy com. Nat. League of Cities, 1990-91, energy, environ. and natural resources policy com., 1982-83; ; mem. Ogden City budget adv. com. on fin. affairs, 1985-86; mem. Utah League of Cities and Town Resolutions Com., 1983; mem. Utah Energy Devel. and Conservation Coun., 1983, Weber Area Coun. of Govts., 1981-83; mgr. TCS Printing Svcs., 1982-84; mem. Ogden Energy Commn., 1983. Mem. Am. Soc. of Pub. Adminstrn., Internat. Assn. of Assessing Officers, Utah Assn. of Counties (mem. legis. com. 1992—, by-laws revision com. 1992-93, bd. dirs. 1994—). Office: Weber County Assessor 2549 Washington Blvd Ste 201 Ogden UT 84401

HAUN, JOHN DANIEL, petroleum geologist, educator; b. Old Hickory, Tenn., Mar. 7, 1921; s. Charles C. and Lydia (Rhodes) H.; m. Lois Culbertson, June 30, 1942. AB, Berea Coll., 1948; MA, U. Wyo., 1949, Ph.D., 1953. Registered profl. engr., Colo. Geologist Stanolind, Amoco, Vernal, Utah, 1951-52; v.p. Petroleum Research Corp., Denver, 1952-57; mem. faculty dept. geology Colo. Sch. Mines, Golden, 1955-80; prof. Colo. Sch. Mines, 1963-80, part time, 1980-85, emeritus prof., 1983—; cons. Barlow & Haun, Inc., Evergreen, Colo., 1957-90; cons. Potential Gas Agy., 1966-78, mem. com., 1978—; mem. adv. com. Colo. Water Pollution Control Commn., 1969-70; mem. adv. council Kans. Geol. Survey, 1971-76; del. Internat. Geol. Congress, Sydney, Australia, 1976; U.S. rep. Internat. Com. on Petroleum Res. Classification UN, N.Y.C., 1976-77; mem. oil shale adv. com. Office of Tech. Assessment, Washington, 1976-79, mem. U.S. natural gas availability adv. panel, 1983; mem. Colo. Oil and Gas Conservation Commn., 1977-87, vice-chmn., 1983-85, chmn. 1985-87; mem. energy resources com. Interstate Oil and Gas Compact Commn., 1978—; mem. exec. adv. com. Nat. Petroleum Coun., 1968-70, 79-89, mem. com. on unconventional gas sources, 1978-80; com. on Arctic oil and gas resources, 1980-81; mem. U.S. Nat. Com. on Geology Dept. Interior and NAS, 1982-89, chmn., 1985-87; mem. com undiscovered oil and gas resources, 19881-91, com. status and rsch. objectives in solid-earth scis.: critical assessment, 1988-92, Nat. Rsch. Coun.; del. Internat. Geol. Congress, Paris, 1980, Moscow, 1984; mem. Colo. Oil and Gas legis. com., 1993-94. Editor: The Mountain Geologist, 1963-65, Future Energy Outlook, 1969, Methods of Estimating the Volume of Undiscovered Oil and Gas Resources, 1975; asst. editor: Geologic Atlas of the Rocky Mountain Region, 1972; co-editor: Subsurface Geology in Petroleum Exploration, 1958, Symposium on Cretaceous Rocks of Colorado and Adjacent Areas, 1959, Guide to the Geology of Colorado, 1960; contbr. articles to profl. jours. Served with USCG, 1942-46. Recipient Disting. Svc. award Am. Assn. Petroleum Geologists, 1973, Disting. Alumnus award U. Wyo., 1986, Disting. Alumnus award Berea Coll., 1989, Outstanding Prof. award Colo. Sch. Mines, 1973, Halliburton award Colo. Sch. Mines, 1985. Fellow Geol. Soc. Am., AAAS; mem. Am. Assn. Petroleum Geologists (editor 1967-71, pres. 1979-80, hon. mem. 1984, Sidney Powers Meml. award 1995), Am. Inst. Profl. Geologists (v.p. 1974, pres. 1976, exec. com. 1981-82, Ben H. Parker Meml. award 1983), Am. Geol. Inst. (governing bd. 1976, 79-82, sec.-treas. 1977-78, v.p. 1980-81, pres. 1981-82, Ian Campbell medal 1988), Rocky Mountain Assn. Geologists (sec. 1961, 1st v.p. 1964, pres. 1968, hon. mem. 1974), Soc. Econ. Paleontologists and Mineralogists, Am. Petroleum Inst. (com. exploration 1971-73, 78-88), Nat. Assn. Geology Tchrs., Wyo. Geol. Assn. (hon. life), Colo. Sci. Soc. (hon. life), Sigma Xi, Sigma Gamma Epsilon, Phi Kappa Phi. Home: 1238 County Road 23 Evergreen CO 80439

HAUSDORFER, GARY LEE, mortgage banker; b. Indpls., Mar. 26, 1946; s. Walter Edward and Virginia Lee (Bender) H.; AA, Glendale Coll., 1966; BS, Calif. State U.-L.A., 1968; m. Debora Ann French, Dec. 17, 1966; children: Lisa Ann, Janet Lee. Rsch. officer Security Pacific Bank, L.A., 1968-73; v.p., mgr. W. Ross Campbell Co., Irvine, Calif., 1973-81; sr. v.p. Weyerhaeuser Mortgage Co., Irvine, 1982-87; exec. v.p., ptnr. L.J. Melody & Co. of Calif., 1987-89; pres. Hausdorfer Co., 1989—. pres. The Diamond Group, 1994—; Councilman, City of San Juan Capistrano, 1978-94, mayor, 1980-81, 84-85, 88-90; chmn. Capistrano Valley Water Dist., 1980-81, San Juan Capistrano Redevel. Agy., 1983-84, 85-86, South Orange County Leadership Conf.; bd. dirs. Orange County Trans. Corridor Agy., Orange County Transit Dist.; chmn. Orange County Transp. Authority. Recipient cert. of commendation Orange County Bd. Suprs., 1981, congl. commendation, 1985, Theodore Roosevelt Conservation award Pres. Bush, 1990. Mem. Mortgage Bankers Assn. Am., Calif. Mortgage Bankers Assn., Orange County Mortgage Bankers Assn. (dir. 1979-80), Calif. League of Cities. Republican.

HAUSEL, WILLIAM DAN, economic geologist; b. Salt Lake City, July 24, 1949; s. Maynard Romain and Dorthy (Clark) H.; m. Patricia Kemp, Aug. 14, 1970; children: Jessica Siddhartha, Eric Jason. BS in Geology, U. Utah, 1972, MS in Geology, 1974. Astronomy lectr., Hansen Planetarium, Salt Lake City, 1968-72; rsch. asst. U. Utah, 1972-74; teaching asst. U. N.Mex., Albuquerque, 1974-75; project geologist Warnock Cons., Albuquerque, 1975; geologist U.S. Geol. Survey, Casper, Wyo., 1976-77; staff geologist Geol. Survey of Wyo., Laramie, 1977-81, dep. dir., 1981-91, sr. econ. geologist, 1991—; cons. Western Gold Exploration and Mining, Anchorage, 1988, 89, Chevron Resources, Georgetown, Mont., 1990, Fowler Resources, Phillipsburg, Mont., 1992, A and E Diamond Exploration, Calif., 1993, Echo Bay Exploration, U.S., 1994; assoc. curator mineralogy Wyo. State Mus., Cheyenne, 1983-90; state rep. and divsn. head Shorin-Ryu Karate, JUKO-KAI Internat., Wyoming, 1994-95. Author: Partial Pressures of Some Lunar Lavas, 1972, Petrogenesis of Some Representative Lavas, Southwestern Utah, 1975, Exploration for Diamondiferous Kimberlite, 1979, Gold Districts of Wyoming, 1980, Ore Deposits of Wyoming, 1982, Geology of Southeastern Wyoming, 1984, Minerals and Rocks of Wyoming, 1986, The Geology of Wyoming's Precious Metal Lode and Placer Deposits, 1989, Economic Geology of the South Pass Greenstone Belt, 1991, Economic Geology of the Cooper Hill Mining District, 1992, Mining History and Geology of Wyoming's Metal and Gemstone Districts, 1993, Geology, Mining Districts, and Ghost Towns of the Medicine Bow Mountains, 1993, Diamonds, Kimberlite and Lamproite in the United States, 1994, Pacific Coast Diamonds-An Unconventional Source Terrane, 1995, Economic Geology of the Seminoe Mountains Greenstone Belt, 1994, The Great Diamond Hoax of 1872, 1995; contbr. over 250 articles to profl. jours. and 2 books. Grantee NASA, 1981, Office of Surface Mining, 1979, U. Wyo., 1981-92, U.S. Geol. Survey Coop. Geologic Mapping Initiative, 1985-88, Union Pacific Resources, 1991, 92, 93, 94. Mem. Wyo. Geol. Assn., Wyo. Profl. Geologists, Soc. Econ. Geologists, U. Utah Geology Club (pres. 1969-71), Laramie Bushido Dojo Karate (pres. 1985-88), U. Wyo. Campus Shotokan Karate Club (instr. 1988-93), Shorin-Ryu Karate Club (U. Wyo. Campus headmaster 1993—), Juko-Kai Internat., Internat. Okinawan Martial Arts Union, Black Belts of the Faith Internat. Avocations: karate (5th degree black belt), sketching, astronomy. Home: 4238 Grays Gable Rd Laramie WY 82070-6911 Office: Geol Survey of Wyo PO Box 3008 Laramie WY 82071-3008

HAUSER, DANIEL EUGENE, state assemblyman; b. Riverside, Calif., June 18, 1942; s. Norman Eugene and Vivian (Barnes) Clover; m. Donna June Dumont, July 13, 1963; children: Dawn Marie Hauser Durbin, Douglas Eugene. B in History, Humboldt State U., 1965. Ins. investigator Gen. Adjustment Bur., Eureka, Calif., 1965-67, Fireman's Fund Ins. Co., Eureka, Calif., 1967-84; assemblyman State of Calif., Sacramento, 1982—. Scout master Boy Scouts Am., Eureka/Arcata, Calif., 1965-85, bd. dirs., 1992—; city councilman City of Arcata, 1974-82, mayor, 1978-82; chmn. Fisheries Legis. Task Force, Pacific states, 1985—, Forestry Legis. Task Force, Pacific states, 1986—. Named Legislator of Yr., Planning and Conservation League Sacremento, 1991, Disting. Legislator, Regional Coun. Rural Counties Sacramento, 1993. Democrat. Lutheran.

HAUSER, GERARD ALAN, communication educator; b. Buffalo, N.Y., May 20, 1943; s. Albert Clement Hauser and Ann John Michalakes; m. Jean Marie Brown, Aug. 14, 1965; children: Gerard, Jr., Kirsten. BA, Canisius Coll., 1965; MA, U. Wis., 1966, PhD, 1970. Asst. prof. Pa. State U., University Park, 1969-73, assoc. prof., 1973-87, prof., 1987-93; prof. U. Colo., Boulder, 1993—; dir. univ. scholars program, Pa. State U., 1987-93; chmn. comm. dept. U. Colo., Boulder, 1993—. Author: Introduction to Rhetorical Theory, 1986; co-editor: Philosophy and Rhetoric jour., 1990-93. Mem. Internat. Soc. for History of Rhetoric, Rhetoric Soc. of Am., Speech Comm. Assn., We. States Commn. Assn. Office: Univ Colo 94 Hellems Hall Boulder CO 80309-0270

HAUSMANN, WERNER KARL, pharmaceutical executive; b. Edigheim, Germany, Mar. 9, 1921; came to U.S., 1948, naturalized, 1954; s. Carl and Johanna (Sprenger) H.; m. Helen Margaret Vas, Sept. 29, 1949; 1 child, Gregory. M.S. in Chem. Engring., Swiss Fed. Inst. Tech., 1945, D.Sc., 1947. Cert. quality engr. Research fellow U. London, 1947-48; research assoc. Rockefeller Inst. Med. Research, N.Y.C., 1949-57; research group leader Lederle Labs., Pearl River, N.Y., 1957-66; assoc. dir. quality control Ayerst Labs., Rouses Point, N.Y., 1966-71; dir. quality control Stuart Pharms., Pasadena, Calif., 1971-74; dir. quality assurance, analytical research and devel. Adria Labs., Inc., Columbus, Ohio, 1974-84; cons. Columbus, Ohio, 1985-86, San Diego, 1986—; freelance fiction writer, 1989—. Patentee in antibiotics; contbr. articles to profl. jours. Pres. Ednl. TV Assn., 1970-71; radiation officer CD, 1962-66; scoutmaster, 1941-45. Served to 1st lt. Swiss Army, 1941-46. Fellow Royal Soc. Chemistry, Chem. Soc. London, Am. Inst. Chemists, N.Y. Acad. Scis., AAAS, Am. Soc. Quality Control (chmn. Columbus sect.); mem. Acad. Pharm. Scis., Am. Soc. Biol. Chemists, Am. Chem. Soc., Am. Soc. Microbiology, Parenteral Drug Assn., Am. Assn. Individual Investors, Nat. Writers Assn. Presbyterian. Office: 4332 Post Rd San Diego CA 92117-1145

HAUSSMANN, NORMAN JOSEPH, printing account executive; b. Cleve., Oct. 30, 1940; s. Karl Fredrick and Rose Hilda Josephine (Buchholz) H.; m. Virginia Lee Dow, Dec. 29, 1962; children: Deborah, Patricia, Kathleen. AA, L.A. City Coll., 1960; BS, Calif. State U., L.A., 1962. Aviation officers tng. USN, Pensacola, Fla., 1962-63; naval flight officer USN, 1963-66; printing acct. exec. Anderson Lithograph, L.A., 1966-73, Triangle Lithograph, L.A., 1973-83, Overland Printers, Hawthorne, Calif., 1983-92, So. Calif. Graphics, Culver City, 1992—; naval air reservist Naval Air Sta. Pt. Mugu, Oxnard, Calif., 1963-84; commanding officer Patrol Squadron 65, USN Pt. Mugu, Oxnard, Calif., 1981-83. Recipient Vietnam War Decorations, USN, 1966, Letters of Commendation, USN, 1983. Mem. Ret. Officers Assn., Naval Res. Assn. Republican. Roman Catholic. Office: So Calif Graphics 8432 Steller Dr Culver City CA 90232-2425

HAVDALA, ELLEN, business executive; b. Chgo., Feb. 13, 1966; d. Henri Solomon and Sandra Lee (Abrams) H. BA magna cum laude, Harvard U., 1988. Fin. analyst First Boston Corp., N.Y.C., 1988-90, Chilmark Ptnrs. and Zell-Chilmark Fund, L.P., Chgo., 1990-93; v.p. Scott Sports Group, Boulder, Colo., 1993—. Mem. Harvard Club (Chgo.). Jewish. Home: 2735 Pine St Apt 3 Boulder CO 80302-3800

HAVEKOST, DANIEL JOHN, architect; b. Fremont, Nebr., May 12, 1936; s. Alvin Deidrich and Magdalen (Osterman) H.; m. Patricia Jo Haney, June 6, 1959 (div. June 1983); children: Christopher, Karen; m. Sandra Schwendemann, Aug. 29, 1993. Lic. architect, Colo., Calif., Tex., N.D.; cert. Nat. Council Archtl. Registration Bds. Designer Papachristou & Assoc., Denver, 1959-61; architect Anshen & Allen, San Francisco, 1961-62; assoc. Hornbein & White, Denver, 1962-63; ptnr. Papachristou & Havekost, Denver, 1963-64; prin. Havekost & Assocs., Denver, 1964-71; pres. HWH Assocs., Inc., Denver, 1971-91, Havekost & Lee Architects P.C., Denver, 1991—; vis. lectr. U. Colo., Denver, 1969, 72, 82; sec., treas. Encore Devel. Corp., Denver, 1984-91. Prin. works include Encore Redevel. (AIA award 1985,86), Grant Street Mansion (Colo. Soc. Architects, AIA award 1979), Reverend's Ridge (Western Mountain Region AIA award 1973, Havekost Residence Western Mountain Region AIA award 1971). Bd. dirs. Denver Cmty. Design Ctr., 1968-72, Hist. Paramount Found., Denver, 1980-94, Hist. Denver, 1978-82; panel mem. Gen. Svcs. Adminstrn., Denver, 1978-79, mem. plan enforcement rev. and variation com., Denver, 1970-76. Served with USNR, 1954-62. Recipient Archtl. Excellence awards WOOD Inc., 1968-82, Honor award for Adaptive Re-use, Historic Denver, 1975, WOOD Design award Nat. Cattlemen's Hdqrs., 1982. Fellow AIA (pres. Denver chpt. 1978-81, chmn. Colo. chpt. govt. affairs com. 1984-91, pres. Colo. chpt. 1981-83, Colo. hist. preservation officer 1982—, recipient Fisher Traveling award of Colo. AIA Ednl. Fund 1988, excellence archtl. design award 1960). Office: Havekost & Lee Architects PC 1121 Grant St Denver CO 80203-2301

HAVELIN, JULIA, political scientist, economist; b. Phila., May 29, 1958; d. Dudley and Marie (Firman) H. BA in French, Grinnell Coll., 1981; BSN, U. Iowa, 1982; MPH, U. South Fla., 1990; MA in Internat. Rels., U. So. Calif., 1994; postgrad., U. So. Calif., L.A., 1995—. Rsch. asst. U. South Fla., Tampa, 1991-92; emergency room nurse various hosps., Clearwater, Fla., 1984-92; emergency rm. nurse Assoc. Health Profls., L.A., 1992—. Vol. RN Clearwater Free Clinic, 1984-87; vol. RN and interpreter, Iowa City Free Clinic, 1982-84; dir. Tuberculosis Control Program, Clinica Para las Americas, L.A., 1993—. Mem. Latin Am. Studies Assn., Phi Beta Kappa, Sigma Theta Tau. Office: Assoc Health Profls 6095 Bristol Pky Ste 100 Culver City CA 90230

HAVENS, CANDACE JEAN, planning consultant; b. Rochester, Minn., Sept. 13, 1952; d. Fred Z. and Barbara Jean (Stephenson) H.; m. Bruce Curtis Mercier, Feb. 22, 1975 (div. Apr. 1982); 1 child, Rachel; m. James Arthur Renning, Oct. 26, 1986; children: Kelsey, Sarah. Student, U. Calif., San Diego, Darmouth Coll., Am. U., Beirut, 1973-74; BA in Sociology, U. Calif., Riverside, 1977; MPA, Harvard U., 1994. Project coord. social svc. orgn. Grass Roots II, San Luis Obispo, Calif., 1976-77; planning enforcement technician City San Luis Obispo, 1977-81, asst. planner, 1981-83; assoc. planner City of San Luis Obispo, 1983-86, coord. parking program, 1986-88, spl. asst. to city adminstr., mgr. constr. libr. and parking structures, 1989, planning cons., 1991-94; mgmt. rsch. specialist Bank of Boston, 1994—. Past pres. Nat. Charity League, Riverside; mem. San Luis Obispo Med. Aux., 1986—, San Luis Obispo Arts coun., 1986—; pres. bd. dirs. San Luis Obispo Children's Mus., 1990-91, pres. 1990-91, CFO, 1993. Mem. AAUW, San Luis Obispo Med. Aux., Toastmasters (sec. 1986-87, v.p. 1987-88, pres. 1989-90, treas. 1991-92). Office: PO Box 1395 San Luis Obispo CA 93406-1395

HAVER, JURGEN F., marketing consultant; b. Joliet, Ill., July 16, 1932; s. Elmer William and Hermina (Peters) H.; B.A., Wartburg Coll., 1956; m. Jane Suzanne Merrill, Apr. 13, 1985; children: Jason, Kyra. Feature writer Daily Peoples Press, Owatonna, Minn., 1959-60; editor Lyon County Independent, Marshall, Minn., 1960-62; asst. advt. dir. Burpee Seed Co., Phila., 1962-66; advt. mgr. for Organic Gardening, Theater Crafts and Quinto Lingo, promotion dir. for Prevention, Rodale Press, Emmaus, Pa., 1966-67; promotion of electronics mag. staff Kiver Pubs., Chgo., 1968-69; advt. dir. Henry Regnery Co., Chgo., 1969-70; pub. relations dir. Hess's Dept. Stores, Allentown, Pa., 1970-76; cons. Haver Mktg., Albuquerque, N.Mex., 1976—; co-founder U. N.Mex. Inst. for Entrepreneurial Success; faculty mktg. Moravian Coll., U. Pa. Sch. Dentistry, Pa. State U. Mem. Internat. Bus. Writers (past pres.), Am. Mktg. Assn. (past pres.). Author: Personalized Guide to Marketing Strategy, 1982; contbr. articles to profl. jours. Address: 11515 Manitoba NE Albuquerque NM 87111

HAVERSTRAW, DEAN L., information systems executive; b. Minot, N.D., Aug. 25, 1961; s. Raymond Haverstraw and Marilyn Jane Skeem Haines; m. Pam Webber, June 16, 1984; children: Sarah Gayle, Hayley Ray. BS cum laude, Western Wash. U., 1985. Programmer Allsop Inc., Bellingham, Wash., 1985-87, programmer analyst, 1987-88, sys. analyst, 1988-89, data processing mgr., 1989-91, dir. info. sys., 1991—; cons. Knowledge Factory, Bellingham, Wash., 1989—; advisor Bellingham Schs. Tech. Coun., 1993-95. Mem. APICS, Seattle Pick User Group, West Wash. U. Alumni Assn. Home: 3835 Del Bonita Way Bellingham WA 98226 Office: Allsop Inc 4201 Meridian Bellingham WA 98226

HAVILAND, JOHN BEARD, anthropology and linguistics educator; b. San Francisco, Mar. 20, 1947; s. Morrison Chandler and Mary Elizabeth (Mooney) H.; m. Leslie Knox McCullough, Sept. 9, 1966; m. Lourdes De Leon, Sept. 8, 1986; children: Sophie Beard Haviland, Maya Lolen Deveraux Haviland, Isabel Haviland. AB in Philosophy cum laude, Harvard Coll., 1966; postgrad. Filosofiska Institutionen, Stockholms Universitet, 1967; PhD in Social Rels.-Social Anthropology, Harvard U., 1972; postgrad., Australian Nat. U., 1972. Teaching fellow in social rels. Harvard U., 1967-70, asst. prof. social anthropology, 1971-74; rsch. fellow dept. anthropology, rsch. sch. Pacific studies Inst. Advanced Studies, Australian Nat. U., 1975-80, sr. rsch. fellow, 1980-82; investigador Titular 'C', Instituto de Investigaciones Antropológicas Universidad Nacional Autónoma de México, 1983-84; fellow Ctr. Advanced Study in Behavioral Scis., Stanford, Calif., 1985-86; vis. assoc. prof. linguitics and anthropology Reed Coll., Portland, Oreg., 1986-88, prof. linguistics and anthropology, 1989—; field dir. Harvard Chiapas project, 1971; vis. asst. prof. dept. anthropology U. Chgo.; vis. lectr. cursillo on Lenguaje, Cultura y Sociedad en el Area Tzotzil, Centro de Estudios Mayas, Instituto de Investigaciones Filológicas, Universidad Nacional Autónoma de México, 1982, vis. prof., 1985; vis. fellow dept. anthropology, rsch. sch. Pacific studies, Australian Nat. U., 1982-85; vis. prof. Maestría de Lingüística, Escuela Nacional de Antropología e Historia, Mex., 1985; Freie wissenschaftliche Mitarbeiter, Max-Planck-Gesellschaft, Projektgruppe für Kognitive Anthropologie, Berlin and Forschungsgruppe für Kognitive Anthropologie am MPI für Psycholinguistik, Nijmegen, Netherlands, 1990-92; researcher in field. Author: (with Tulo Gordon) Milbi: Aboriginal Tales from Queensland's Endeavour River, 1979; author: Sk'op Sotz'leb; El Tzotzil de San Lorenzo Zinacantán, 1981; mem. editorial bd. Multilingua, Jour. Cross-cultural and Interlanguage Communication; contbr. numerous articles to profl. jours. Nat. Merit scholar Harvard Coll., 1966; Thord Grey fellow

Am. Scandinavian Found., 1967; doctoral rsch. fellow NIMH, 1972; postdoctoral fellow in sci. NATO, 1972; fellow Harry Frank Guggenheim Found., 1985-86; grantee NSF, 1985-86. Mem. Am. Anthropological Assn., Linguistic Soc. Am., Seminario Permanente de Estudios Chicanos, DEAS/INAH (Mex.). Office: Reed Coll Dept Linguistics/Anthropology 3203 SE Woodstock Blvd Portland OR 97202-8138

HAVIS, ALLAN STUART, playwright, theatre educator; b. N.Y.C., Sept. 26, 1951; s. Mickey and Esther H. BA, CCNY, 1973; MA, Hunter Coll., 1976; MFA, Yale U., 1980. Film animation tchr. Guggenheim Mus., N.Y.C., 1974-76; playwriting tchr. Dramatist Guild, N.Y.C., 1985-87, Ulster County C.C., Stoneridge, N.Y., 1985-88; prof. theatre U. Calif.-San Diego, La Jolla, 1988—. Author: (novel) Albert the Astronomer, 1979, (plays) Morocco, 1986 (HBO award), Lilith, 1991, (anthology) Plays by Allan Havis, 1989, (play) A Vow of Silence, 1995. Dramaturg Young Playwrights Festival, N.Y.C., 1984, juror, 1993; juror N.J. Arts Coun., Trenton, 1987; panelist Theatre Communications Group, N.Y.C., 1987; juror McKnight Playwriting Fellowship, 1995. Playwriting fellow Nat. Endowment for the Arts, 1986, Rockefeller Found., 1987, Guggenheim Found., 1987-88; recipient New American Plays award Kennedy Ctr./Am. Express, Washington, 1988. Mem. Circle Repertory Lab. Democrat. Jewish. Office: Dept of Theatre Univ Calif-San Diego La Jolla CA 92093

HAVLEN, ROBERT JAMES, astronomer, non-profit society administrator; b. Utica, N.Y., Sept. 16, 1943; s. Frank James and Marian Whitmore (Briggs) H.; m. Carolyn Anne Wolf, Sept. 2, 1967; children: Pamela Ruth, Naomi Lynn. BS, U. Rochester, 1965; PhD, U. Ariz., 1970. Staff astronomer European So. Obs., Santiago, Chile, 1970-77; vis. lectr. U. Va., Charlottesville, 1977-79; asst. to dir. Nat. Radio Astronomy Obs., Charlottesville, 1979-88; head obs.svcs. Nat. Radio Astronomy Obs., Socorro, N.Mex., 1988-93; exec. dir. Astron. Soc. Pacific, San Francisco, 1993—. Contbr. rsch. papers to profl. jours. Mem. Am. Astron. Soc., Internat. Astron. Union. Office: Astron Soc Pacific 390 Ashton Ave San Francisco CA 94112-1722

HAVRAN, WENDY LYNN, immunologist; b. Houston, Sept. 1, 1955; d. George Anton and Myra Laverne (Faulkner) H. BS, Duke U., 1977; PhD, U. Chgo., 1986. Sr. rsch. technician Med. Ctr. Duke U., Durham, N.C., 1977-79, rsch. analyst Med. Ctr., 1980-82; postdoctoral fellow U. Calif., Berkeley, 1987-91; asst. prof. Scripps Rsch. Inst., La Jolla, Calif., 1991—; speaker, Greece, 1989—. Contbr. articles to profl. jours. Vol. Hyde Park Food Pantry, Chgo., 1984-86; Sunday Sch. tchr., Chgo. and N.C., 1978-86. Lucille P. Markey Scholar, Miami, Fla., 1989—, Mary Gibbs Jones Scholar Jones Found., Houston, 1973-77. Mem. Am. Assn. Immunologists (Travel award 1989). Office: Scripps Rsch Inst Dept Immunology Imm 8 10666 N Torrey Pines Rd La Jolla CA 92037-1027

HAWK, DAWN DAVAH, secondary education educator; b. Dodge, Nebr., Apr. 14, 1945; d. Fred John and Marcella Martha (Kunes) Lerch; m. Floyd Russell Hawk, June 14, 1969. BAE, Wayne State Coll., 1967. Cert. tchr., Nebr., Iowa, Ariz. English tchr. Tekamah (Nebr.) Pub. Sch., 1967-69, West Lyon Community Schs., Inwood, Iowa, 1970-74, Norfolk (Nebr.) Cath. Schs., 1974-85; English tchr., libr. Beemer (Nebr.) Pub. Schs., 1969-70; English and reading tchr. San Manuel (Ariz.) Sch. Dist., 1986—; chair adaptive edn. dept. San Manuel (Ariz.) High Sch., 1992-93; tutor in field. Active Catalina Luth. Ch., Tucson, 1991-93. Recipient Cooper Found. award for excellence in teaching U. Nebr., 1983; NEG edn. grantee, 1987, 89, 91, 95. Mem. NEA, Nat. Coun. Tchrs. English, Internat. Reading Assn., Ea. Pinal Lit. Coun., Ariz. English Tchrs. Assn., Tucson Area Reading Coun. (bd. advisors), San Manuel Tchrs. Assn. Republican. Home: 3950 E Hawser St 5 Tucson AZ 85737-9534 Office: San Manuel HS PO Box 406 San Manuel AZ 85631-0406

HAWK, FLOYD RUSSELL, secondary school educator; b. Fresno, Calif., Oct. 7, 1945; s. Floyd Edward and Velma Irene (Lyon) H.; m. Dawn Davah Lerch, June 14, 1969. BA in Bus., Wayne State Coll., 1971. Cert. tchr. Ariz. Tchr. W. Lyon Pub. Schs., Inwood, Iowa, 1970-74, Norfolk (Nebr.) Cath. Schs., 1974-76, Madison (Nebr.) Pub. Schs., 1977-85, Young (Ariz.) Pub. Schs., 1985-86, San Manuel (Ariz.) High Sch., 1986-; state rep. Nat. Coaches Assn., Madison, Nebr., 1980-82; bd. dirs. Pinal County Adult Literacy, San Manuel. Mem. adv. bd. Multiple Sclerosis Soc. NEH grantee, 1995. Mem. NEA, Ariz. Edn. Assn., Nat. Coun. Social Studies, Ariz. Bus. Edn. Assn., Ariz. Hist. Soc., Optimist Club (pres. 1972, lt. gov. 1973). Republican. Lutheran. Office: San Manuel HS PO Box 406 San Manuel AZ 85631

HAWK, STEVE J., magazine editor; b. Pensacola, Fla., Aug. 14, 1955; s. Frank Hagen and Nancy Jo (Skaggs) H.; m. Pamela Mary Higgins; 1 child, Wilson Henry. BA in Eng., U. Calif., Santa Barbara, 1977. Staff writer The Citizen, Solana Beach, Calif., 1979-80, Blade-Tribune, Oceanside, Calif., 1980-81, Times-Advocate, Escondido, Calif., 1981-84, Orange County Register, Santa Ana, Calif., 1984-90; editor Surfer Magazine, San Juan Capistrano, Calif., 1990—; freelance writer Us, Harper's, Alaska Airlines Mag., L.A. Times, 1980-94. Editor: Notes from the Jungle's Edge: The Journalism of Barry Farrell, 1988. Office: Surfer Magazine PO Box 1028 Dana Point CA 92629-5028

HAWKANSON, DAVID ROBERT, theatre company executive; b. Sept. 21, 1946; s. Robert O. and Jane (Crosby) H.; m. Ann-Sara Mathews, Nov., 1980 (div. Sept. 1983). BA, Lawrence U., 1969. Bus. mgr. The Guthrie Theatre, Mpls., 1971-72, assoc. mgr., 1972-74; asst. dir. spl. projects Nat. Endowment for the Arts, Washington, 1974-75; guest adminstr. Am. Conservatory Theatre, San Francisco, 1975-76; mng. dir. Ariz. Theatre Co., Tucson, Phoenix, 1976-85, Hartford (Conn.) Stage Co., 1985-93, Crossroads Theatre Co., New Brunswick, N.J., 1994—; chmn., panelist theatre program and Challenge Grant program Nat. Endowment for Arts, 1975-93; cons. Found. for Ext. and Devel. Am. Profl. Theatre, N.Y.C., 1975-85; artistic advisor Fund New Am. Plays, Kennedy Ctr. for Performing Arts, 1990—. Mem. Tucson Mayor's Arts Task Force, 1980-82; vice chmn. Tucson Tomorrow, 1980-84; mem. exec. com. Ariz. for Cultural Devel., Phoenix, 1980-85; incorporator Inst. of Living, Hartford, 1991-93. Mem. Theatre Comm. Group (trustee, sec. treas. 1982-91), Am. Arts Alliance (trustee, treas. 1982-91), League of Resident Theatres (exec. com. 1986—). Office: 350 W 57th St Apt 16C New York NY 10019-3763

HAWKE, SIMON NICHOLAS, writer, educator; b. N.Y.C., Sept. 30, 1951; s. Valentin Michael and Helga Ellen (Hartewelt) Yermakov. Student, Am. U., 1969-70; BA in Comms., Hofstra U., 1974; postgrad., U. Ariz., 1993-94; M in English and History, Western N.Mex. U., 1994. instr. Colo. Mountain Coll. Summer Writers Conf., instr. in fiction writing, Pima C.C., Tucson, 1992—; instr. Pima Writers workshop, 1992; instr. Gila Writers Conf., Western N.Mex. U., Silver City, 1994; dir. Sonora Writers Workshop, 1995; spkr. 23rd ann. N.Mex. Sci. Fiction Conf., Albuquerque, 1991, 94, Circle Ouroboros Fantasy Conf., Meridien, Miss., 1991, Boise Fantasy Arts Conf., 1991, Once Upon a Con Fantasy Conf., Boulder, Colo., 1990, 91, 92, MileHiCon Sci. Fiction Conf., Telluride, 1979, 80, 81, U. Ariz., 1994. Author: (pub. as Nicholas Yermakov) Journey from Flesh, 1981, Last Communion, 1981, Fall into Darkness, 1982, Epiphany, 1982, Clique, 1982, Jehad, 1984; (pub. as Simon Hawke) The Ivanhoe Gambit, 1984, The Timekeeper Conspiracy, 1984, The Pimpernel Plot, 1984, The Zenda Vendetta, 1985, The Nautilus Sanction, 1985, The Khyber Connection, 1986, The Argonaut Affair, 1987, Psychodrome, 1987, The Wizard of Fourth Street, 1987, The Shapechanger Scenario, 1988, The Dracula Caper, 1988, The Wizard of Whitechapel, 1988, Steele, 1989, The Lilliput Legion, 1989, Cold Steele, 1989, The Wizard of Sunset Strip, 1989, Killer Steele, 1990, Jagged Steele, 1990, The Hellfire Rebellion, 1990, Renegade Steele, 1990, The Wizard of Rue Morgue, 1990, Target Steele, 1990, The Cleopatra Crisis, 1990, To Stalk a Spectre, 1991, Samurai Wizard, 1991, The Wizard of Santa Fe, 1991, The Sixgun Solution, 1991, The Reluctant Sorcerer, 1992, The Nine Lives of Catseye Gomez, 1992, Sons of Glory, 1992, The Romular Prize, 1993 (N.Y. Times Bestseller), The Outcast, Call to Battle, 1993, The Inadequate Adept, 1993, The Wizard of Camelot, 1993, The Wizard of Lovecraft's Care, 1993 (Locus Bestseller), The Patrian Transgression, 1994, The Seeker, 1994, The Nomad, 1994, Whims of Creation, 1995, The Broken Blade, 1995; author numerous sci. fiction. short stories to anthologies. Home: HCR-1 Box 466 Tucson AZ 85736 Office: c/o Russel Galen/S Chichak Galen Lit Agy 381 Park Ave S New York NY 10016-8806

HAWKES, ELIZABETH LAWRENCE (BONNIE HAWKES), health facility administrator; b. Bryn Mawr, Pa., May 28, 1944; d. Edward Bettle and Anna Correy (Keen) Scull; m. Geoffrey Neale Hawkes, Aug. 12, 1972. BA in Chemistry, Hood Coll., 1966; cert. in occupational therapy, U. Pa., 1968; cert. in health care mgmt., B.C. Inst. Tech., Can., 1981; MS in Health Care Mgmt., U. B.C., 1988. Therapist Mary Bridge Children's Hosp., Tacoma, 1968-72; staff occupational therapist Pearson Hosp., Vancouver, B.C., 1972-74; staff occupational therapist Lions Gate Hosp., North Vancouver, B.C., 1974-76, sr. occupational therapist, 1976-78, supr. occupational therapy, 1978-82; rschr. med. engring. dept. surgery U. B.C., Vancouver, 1983-84, lectr., 1981-86, clin. instr., 1981-93; cons. health services North Vancouver, 1983—; adminstrv. dir. clin. practice unit Vancouver Gen. Hosp., 1992-93; coord. quality improvement Vancouver Hosp. and Health Scis. Ctr., 1993—; bd. dirs. Lions Gate Med. Rsch. Found., 1988-89. Contbr. articles to profl. jours. Bd. dirs. First Aid Ski Patrol, (coordinator 1977-79) (patrol 1973-80); first aid instr. St. John Ambulance, 1977-80, CPR instr. 1978. Mem. B.C. Soc. Occupational Therapists, Can. Coun. Health Svcs. Execs. Home: # 14-3634 Garibaldi Dr, North Vancouver, BC Canada V7H 2X5 Office: Vancouver Hosp Health Sci Ctr Quality Improvement Team, 855 W 12th Ave, Vancouver, BC Canada V5Z1M9

HAWKES, GLENN ROGERS, psychology educator; b. Preston, Idaho, Apr. 29, 1919; s. William and Rae (Rogers) H.; m. Yvonne Merrill, Dec. 18, 1941; children—Kristen, William Ray, Gregory Merrill, Laura. B.S. in Psychology, Utah State U., 1946, M.S. in Psychology, 1947; Ph.D. in Psychology, Cornell U., 1950. From asst. prof. to prof. child devel. and psychology Iowa State U., Ames, 1950-66, chmn. dept. child devel., 1954-66; prof. human devel., rsch. psychologist U. Calif., Davis, 1966-89, prof. emeritus, 1990—, acad. coord. Hubert Humphrey fellowship program, 1990—, assoc. dean applied econs. and behavioral scis., 1966-83, chmn. dept. applied behavioral scis., 1982-86, chmn. teaching div., 1970-72, prof. behavioral scis. dept. family practice, Sch. Medicine; vis. scholar U. Hawaii, 1972-73, U. London, 1970, 80, 86; bd. dirs. Creative Playthings Inc., 1962-66. Author: (with Pease) Behavior and Development from 5 to 12, 1962; (with Frost) The Disadvantaged Child: Issues and Innovations, 1966, 2d edit., 1970; (with Schultz and Baird) Lifestyles and Consumer Behavior of Older Americans, 1979; (with Nicola and Fish) Young Marrieds: The Dual Career Approach, 1984. Contbr. numerous articles to profl. and sci. jours. Served with AUS, 1941-45. Recipient numerous research grants from pvt. founds. and govtl. bodies; recipient Iowa State U. faculty citation, 1965, Outstanding Service citation Iowa Soc. Crippled Children and adults, 1965, citation Dept. Child Devel., 1980, Coll. Agrl. and Environ. Scis., 1983; named hon. lt. gov. Okla., 1966. Home: 1114 Purdue Dr Davis CA 95616-1736 Office: U Calif Internat House 10 College Park Davis CA 95616

HAWKEY, PHILIP A., city manager; b. Lima, Ohio, Sept. 26, 1946; s. George D. and Beatrice A. (Coon) H.; m. Dena Spanos, Oct. 18, 1969; children: George, Aaron, Ann. BA, Baldwin-Wallace Coll., 1968; MA, Ohio State U., 1972; JD, Cleve. State U., 1975. Bar: Ohio, 1976. Adminstrv. asst. City of Cleve., 1972-76; city adminstr. City of Wooster, Ohio, 1976-79; city mgr. City of Kettering, Ohio, 1979-82; dep. city mgr. City of Cin., 1982-86; city mgr. City of Toledo, 1986-90, City of Pasadena, Calif., 1990—; bd. dirs. Calif. City Mgmt. Assn. Mem. adv. coun. State and Local Legal Ctr., Washington. Mem. Internat. City Mgmt. Assn. (v.p.). Home: 1136 Wotkyns Dr Pasadena CA 91103-2838 Office: City Hall 100 N Garfield Ave Pasadena CA 91101-1726

HAWKINS, CHARLES EUGENE, private investigator, security consultant; b. Dallas, Feb. 1, 1941; s. Eugene Rupert and Artie Velma (Ward) H.; m. Frances Annetta Rader, Aug. 26, 1961; children: Tracy Lynn, René Launette. Student, Arlington State Coll., 1964-65, Palomar Coll., 1974-77. Lic. pvt. investigator, Calif. Machine operator Sunstrand Aviation, Denver, 1962-63; machinist Bell Helicopter, Hurst, Tex., 1963-69; mgr. Womack Machine Supply, Ft. Worth, 1969-70; owner, mgr. Escondido (Calif.) Karate, 1970-77; pres. Western Survival Enterprises, San Diego, 1977-91; owner, dir. Action Assocs., San Diego, 1991—. Contbr. articles to profl. publs. Internal affairs chmn. Am. Tae Kwon Do Assn., Little Rock, 1984, tournament chmn., 1986. With USN, 1958-62. Mem. Am. Soc. Indsl. Security, Calif. Inst. Profl. Investigators (charter mem.), Tae Kwon Do Internat. (pres.), Kiwanis Internat. (bd. dirs.). Office: Action Associates 5173 Waring Rd San Diego CA 92120-2705

HAWKINS, DAVID RAMON, psychiatrist, writer, researcher; b. Milw., June 3, 1927; s. Ramon Nelson and Alice-Mary (McCutcheon) H.; children: Lynn Ashley, Barbara Catherine. BS, Marquette U., 1950; MD, Med. Coll. Wis., Milw., 1953; PhD, Columbia Pacific U., 1995. Med. dir. North Nassau Mental Health Ctr., Manhasset, N.Y., 1956-80; dir. rsch. Brunswick Hosp., L.I., N.Y., 1968-79; pres. Acad. Orthomolecular Psychiatry, N.Y.C., 1970-80; dir. Inst. Spiritual Rsch., Sedona, Ariz., 1979-88, The Rsch. Inst., Sedona, 1988—; pres. Attractor Rsch., Sedona, 1989—, Veritas Pub., Sedona, 1995—; bd. dirs. Huxley Inst. Biosocial Rsch., N.Y.C., 1970-80; chmn. Inst. Advanced Theoretical Rsch., 1993—; guest lectr. U. Notre Dame, Harvard U., U. W.Va., U. Mich., 1970-88; guest on TV news and interview shows including McNeal-Lehrer, Barbara Walters, Today, 1972-76; chief of staff Mingus Mountain RTC, 1995; cons. psychiatrist MJL Hosp., Cottonwood, Ariz., 1995; cons. USN, Dept. Health Edn. Welfare, Congress. Author: (with Linus Pauling) Orthomolecular Psychiatry, 1973, Force vs. Power, 1995; contbr. articles to profl. jours. With U.S. Navy, 1945-46, PTO. Decorated knight Sovereign Order St. John of Jerusalem; Rsch. grantee N.Y. State Dept. Mental Hygiene, annually, N.Y. State Legis., 1967-87; recipient Mosby Book award, 1953. Mem. AMA, APA, Ariz. Med. Soc., Ariz. Psychiat. Soc., Alpha Omega Alpha. Office: Rsch Inst HC 2 Box 817 Sedona AZ 86336-9711

HAWKINS, DEBRA LYNN, software development administrator; b. L.A., Dec. 29, 1949; d. Sam and Justine (Mlynar) Wysowski; m. Robert James Hawkins, Oct. 19, 1979 (div. Dec. 1988); children: Ian W., Jeffrey S. Grad., high sch., Whittier, Calif., 1968. Cert. masonry contractor, Calif. Sr. customer svc. rep. Delta Airlines, Santa Ana, Calif., 1982-88; owner R.J. Constrn., Walnut, Calif., 1988-91; v.p. Unique Devels., Pahrump, Nev., 1991—. Roman Catholic. Home: 2300 N Jason Pahrump NV 89041-9730 Office: Unique Developments PO Box 6000 Pahrump NV 89041-6000

HAWKINS, JAMES VICTOR, state official; b. Coeur d'Alene, Idaho, Sept. 28, 1936; s. William Stark and Agnes M. (Ramstedt) H.; m. Gail Ruth Guernsey, June 19, 1959; children—John William, Nancy Clare. B.S., U. Idaho, 1959; postgrad., Am. Savs. and Loan Inst., 1960-67, Pacific Coast Banking Sch., 1970—. Mgmt. trainee Gen. Telephone Co. of N.W., Coeur d'Alene, 1959-60; asst. mgr. First Fed. Savs. & Loan Assn., Coeur d'Alene, 1960-67; v.p., gen. mgr. Idaho S.W. Devel. Co., Boise, 1967-68; v.p., trust officer First Security Bank of Idaho, N.A., Boise, 1968-72; pres. Statewide Stores Inc., Boise, 1972-82; spl. projects adminstr. Lucky Stores Inc., 1982-84; pvt. practice fin. cons. Boise, 1984-87; dir. dept. commerce State of Idaho, Boise, 1987—. Bd. dirs., chmn. adv. bd. Coll. Bus. and Econs. U. Idaho; bd. dirs. Idaho Coun. Econ. Edn., Boise United Fund, Boise Art Assn.; pres., mem. U. Idaho Found.; exec. bd. Coun. State Community Affairs Agys.; bd. dirs., pres. Nat. Assn. State Devel. Agys.; mem. Indsl. Devel. Rsch. Coun.; mem. exec. com. Coun. State and Community Devel. Agys.; bd. dirs. Idaho Total Quality Inst.; chmn. Idaho R.R. Adv. Coun. Named Outstanding Young Idahoan Idaho Jr. C. of C., 1967; Eagle Scout. Mem. Am. Inst. Banking, Boise C. of C., U. Idaho Alumni Assn. (mem. exec. bd.), Elks, Coeur d'Aleue, Rotary, Crane Creek Country Club, Arid Club (Boise), Phi Gamma Delta. Episcopalian. Home: 163 E Ridgeline Dr Boise ID 83702-6517

HAWKINS, RICHARD MICHAEL, lawyer; b. Nevada City, Calif., July 23, 1949; s. Robert Augustus and Virginia June (Hawke) H.; m. Linda Lee Chapman, Sept. 27, 1975; child, Alexandra Michelle. BS in Math., U. Calif., Davis, 1971; JD, U. Calif., San Francisco, 1974; LLM in Taxation, U. Pacific, 1983. Bar: Calif. 1974, U.S. Dist. Ct. (ea. dist.) Calif. 1974, U.S. Dist. Ct. (no. dist.) Calif. 1982, U.S. Ct. Claims 1982, U.S. Tax Ct. 1982, U.S. Ct. Appeals (9th cir.) 1982, U.S. Supreme Ct. 1982. From assoc. to ptnr. Larue & Francis, Nevada City, 1974-76; ptnr. Larue, Roach & Hawkins, Nevada City, 1977-78; of counsel Berliner & Ellers, Nevada City; ptnr. Berliner, Spiller & Hawkins, Nevada City, 1981; sole practice Grass Valley, Calif., 1981—. Bd. dirs. 49ers Fire Dist., Nevada City, 1977-81, 89—, asst. fire chief, 1981-83, fire chief, 1983-89. Mem. ABA, Calif. State Bar (cert. specialist in estate planning, trust and probate law 1990), Nevada County Bar Assn. (v.p. 1976), Order of Coif, Phi Kappa Phi. Republican. Roman Catholic. Home: 14762 Banner Quaker Hill Rd Nevada City CA 95959-8813 Office: 10563 Brunswick Rd Ste 2 Grass Valley CA 95945-7801

HAWKINS, RICHARD SCOTT, physician; b. Portland, Oreg., Aug. 25, 1947; s. Richard Harlan and Mildred Elizabeth (Blair) H.; m. Sonya Lee Balleisen, Dec. 14, 1974; 1 child, Lisa Kirstan. BS in Chemistry, Lewis and Clark Coll., 1969; MD, U. Oreg., 1973. Diplomate Am. Bd. Family Practice, Nat. Bd. Med. Examiners. Intern St. Paul-Ramsey Hosp., St. Paul, 1973-74; pvt. practice Tacoma, Wash., 1978—; mem. active med. staff St. Joseph Hosp., Tacoma, 1978—, Tacoma Gen. Hosp., 1978—, Ctrl. Meml. Hosp., Toppenish. 1974-78; mem. staff Allenmore Hosp., Tacoma, 1978—, sec. med. staff, 1982, 83, trustee, 1985-86; program physician, med. dir. Tacoma-Pierce County Methadone Maintenance Program, 1978—. Gen. med. officer, clin. dir. Yakima Indian Health Ctr., Toppenish, 1974-78; bd. dirs. Yakima Valley chpt. ARC, 1976-78; mem. adminstrv. bd. Mason United Meth. Ch., Tacoma, 1988, 89; bd. dirs. Family Counseling Svc. of Tacoma Pierce County, 1989—, chair, 1992—; trustee Pierce County Med. Bur., 1992—. With USPHS, 1974-78. Fellow Am. Acad. Family Physicians; mem. AMA, Wash. State Med. Assn. (del. 1983-85, vice spkr. ho. of dels. 1985-92, spkr. ho. of dels. 1992—, trustee 1985—), Pierce County Med. Soc. (trustee, exec. com. 1983-87, v.p. 1983, 84, pres. 1986), Pierce County Acad. Family Physicians (sec. 1980, 81, pres. 1982), Wash. Acad. Family Physicians (spkr. ho. of dels. 1993—, trustee 1993—), Am. Soc. Addiction Medicine, Am. Inst. Parliamentarians, Nat. Assn. Parliamentarians, Tacoma Ind. Practice Assn. (bd. dirs. 1988—, pres. 1989-92), Kiwanis (bd. dirs. Tacoma chpt. 1987-89). Office: Allenmore Med Ctr Ste B-7005 South 19th St and Union Ave Tacoma WA 98405-1891

HAWKINS, ROBERT LEE, health facility administrator; b. Denver, Feb. 18, 1938; s. Isom and Bessie M. (Hugley) H.; m. Ann Sharon Hoy, Apr. 28, 1973; children: Robert, Jeanne, Julia, Rose. AA, Pueblo Jr. Coll., 1958; BS, So. Colo. State Coll., 1965; MSW, U. Denver, 1967. Psychiat. technician Colo. State Hosp., Pueblo, 1956-58, 1962-63, occupl. therapist asst., 1964-65, clin. adminstr. psychiat. team, 1969-75, dir. cmty. svcs., 1975-92, asst. supt. clin. svcs., 1992—, supr. vol. services, 1975—, mem. budget com., 1975—; asst. supt. clin. svcs., 1992—; counselor (part-time) Family Svc. Agy., Pueblo, 1968-69, exec. dir., 1969-70; mem. faculty U. So. Colo., 1968-75; ptnr. Human Resource Devel., Inc., 1970-75; mem. Nat. Adv. Com. on Instnl. Quality and Integrity, U.S. Dept. Edn., Washington, 1993—. Mem. Pueblo Positive Action Com., 1970; chmn. adv. bd. Pueblo Sangre de Cristo Day Care Center, 1969-72; chmn. Gov.'s So. Area Adv. Council of Employment Service, 1975-76, chmn. Pueblo's City CSC, 1976-77, Pueblo Cmty. Corrections, 1985-87, Pueblo Civil Svc. Commn., 1988—; commr. Pueblo Housing Authority, 1986—, Colo. Commn. Higher Edn., 1987—, USED Commn. for Ednl. Quality & Integrity, 1993—; mem. gov.'s adv. com. Mental Health Stds., 1981—; mem. Colo. Juvenile Parole Bd., 1977; bd. dirs. Pueblo United Fund, 1969-74, pres., 1973; bd. dirs. Pueblo Community Orgn., 1974-76, Spanish Peaks Mental Health Center, 1976—, Neighborhood Health Center, 1977-79, Pueblo Community Corrections, 1983—, Pueblo Legal Svcs., 1983—; mem. Pueblo Colo. 2010 Commn., 1994—, adv. com. YWCA, 1994—, Healthy Pueblo 2000 Task Force, 1993—. Bd. dirs. Posada Shelter for Homeless, 1990—, Boys Girls club, 1991—, ARC, 1994—, pres., 1994—. With U.S. Army 1958-62. Mem. Nat. Assn. Social Workers (nominating com. 1973-76), ACLU (dir. Pueblo chpt. 1980—), NAACP, Broadway Theatre Guild. Democrat. Methodist. Mem. Kiwanis. Home: 520 Gaylord Ave Pueblo CO 81004-1312 Office: Colo State Hosp 1600 W 24th St Pueblo CO 81003-1411

HAWLEY, NANCI ELIZABETH, public relations and communications professional; b. Detroit, Mar. 18, 1942; d. Arthur Theodore and Elizabeth Agnes (Fylling) Smisek; m. Joseph Michael Hawley, Aug. 28, 1958; children: Michael, Ronald, Patrick (dec.), Julie Anne. Pres. Tempo 21 Nursing Svcs., Inc., Covina, Calif., 1973-75; v.p. Profl. Nurses Bur., Inc., L.A., 1975-83; cons. Hawley & Assocs., Covina, 1983-87; exec. v.p. Glendora (Calif.) C. of C., 1984-85; dir. membership West Covina (Calif.) C. of C., 1985-87; exec. dir. San Dimas (Calif.) C. of C., 1987-88; mgr. pub. rels. Soc. for Advancement of Material and Process Engrs., Covina, 1988-92; small bus. rep. South Coast Air Quality Mgmt. Dist., 1992-94; bus. counselor Commerce and Trade Agy., Small Bus. Devel. Ctr., 1994; exec. v.p. Ont. (Calif.) C. of C., 1994—. V.p. Sangabriel valley chpt. Women in Mgmt. Recipient Youth Motivation award Foothill Edn. Com., Glendora, 1987. Mem. NAFE, Pub. Rels. Soc. Am., Soc. Nat. Assn. Publs., Am. Soc. Assn. execs., Nat. Assn. Membership Dirs., Profl. Communicators Assn. So. Calif., Kiwanis Internat. (sec. 1989-90, pres. West Covina 1990-91, Kiwanian of Yr. 1989), Rotary Internat. Office: Ontario C of C 121 W B St Ontario CA 91762-3502

HAWLEY, PHILIP METSCHAN, retired retail executive, consultant; b. Portland, Oreg., July 29, 1925; s. Willard P. and Dorothy (Metschan) H.; m. Mary Catherine Follen, May 31, 1947; children: Diane (Mrs. Robert Bruce Johnson), Willard, Philip Metschan Jr., John, Victor, Edward, Erin (Mrs. Kevin Przybocki), George. BS, U. Calif., Berkeley, 1946; grad. advanced mgmt. program, Harvard U., 1967. With Carter Hawley Hale Stores, Inc., L.A., 1958-93, pres., 1972-83, chief exec. officer, 1977-93, chmn., 1983-93; bd. dirs. Atlantic Richfield Co., BankAm. Corp., AT&T, Johnson & Johnson, Weyerhaeuser Co. Trustee Calif. Inst. Tech., U. Notre Dame; chmn. L.A. Energy Conservation Com., 1973-74. Decorated hon. comdr. Order Brit. Empire, knight comdr. Star Solidarity Republic Italy; recipient Award of Merit L.A. Jr. C. of C., 1974, Coro Pub. Affairs award, 1978, Medallion award Coll. William and Mary, 1983, Award of Excellence Sch. Bus. Adminstrn. U. So. Calif., 1987, Bus. Statesman of Yr. award Harvard Bus. Sch., 1989, 15th ann. Whitney M. Young Jr. award L.S. Urban League, 1988; named Calif. Industrialist of Yr. Calif. Mus. Sci. and Industry, 1975. Mem. Calif. Retailers Assn. (chmn. 1993—, dir.), Beach Club, Calif. Club, L.A. Country Club, Bohemian Club, Pacific-Union Club, Newport Harbor Yacht Club, Multnomah Club, Links Club, Phi Beta Kappa, Beta Alpha Psi, Beta Gamma Sigma. Office: 444 S Flower St Ste 2280 Los Angeles CA 90071-2923

HAWLEY, ROBERT CROSS, lawyer; b. Douglas, Wyo., Aug. 7, 1920; s. Robert Daniel and Elsie Corienne (Cross) H.; m. Mary Elizabeth Hawley McClellan, Mar. 3, 1944; children—Robert Cross, Mary Virginia, Laurie McClellan. BA with honors, U. Colo., 1943; LLB, Harvard U., 1949, JD, 1989. Bar: Wyo. 1950, Colo. 1950, U.S. Dist. Ct. Colo. 1950, U.S. Dist. Ct. Wyo. 1954, U.S. Ct. Appeals (10th cir.) 1955, Tex. 1960, U.S. Ct. Appeals (5th cir.) 1960, U.S. Supreme Ct. 1960, U.S. Dist. Ct. (so. dist.) Tex. 1961, U.S. Ct. Appeals (D.C. cir.) 1961, U.S. Ct. Appeals (8th cir.) 1979, U.S. Ct. Appeals (11th cir.) 1981, U.S. Dist. Ct. (we. dist.) Tex. 1987. Assoc. Bannister Weller & Friedrich, Denver, 1949-50; sr. atty. Continental Oil Co., Denver, 1952-58, counsel, Houston, 1959-62; ptnr., v.p. Ireland, Stapleton & Pryor, Denver, 1962-81; ptnr. Dechert Price & Rhoads, Denver, 1981-83, Hawley & VanderWerf, Denver, 1983-94; sole practice, Denver, 1994—; pres. Highland Minerals, Denver; bd. dirs. Bank of Denver; speaker oil and gas insts. Contbr. articles to Oil & Gas Pubs. Bd. dirs. Am. Cancer Soc., Denver, 1967-87, treas., 1981-82; chmn. U. Colo. Devel. Found., 1960-61; bd. dirs. Rocky Mountain Arthritis Found., 1987—, sec., 1993-94, vice chmn. Colo., 1994—; mem. adv. bd. ARC, 1988—; chmn. 1st Annual Retarded Children Campaign, 1963; dir. East Seal Chpt., 1966-68; bd. dirs. Craig Hosp., 1964-68. Lt. col. U.S. Army, Korean War. Recipient Alumni Recognition award U. Colo., Boulder, 1958, Meritorious Service award Monticello Coll., Godfrey, Ill., 1967, Humanitarian award Arthritis Found., 1992, Honored Lawyer award Law Club, 1993; Sigma Alpha Epsilon scholar, 1941-43. Mem. Denver Assn. Oil and Gas Title Lawyers (pres. 1983-84), Denver Petroleum Club (pres. 1978-79), Harvard Law Sch. Assn. Colo. (pres. 1980-81), Associated Alumni U. Colo. (pres. and bd. dirs. 1956-57), Law Club, Denver (pres. 1958-59), ABA, Colo. Bar Assn., Denver Bar Assn., Tex. Bar Assn., Wyo. Bar Assn., Fed. Energy Bar Assn. (legal and lands com.), Interstate Oil and Gas Compact Comn., Harvard Alumni Assn., Rocky Mountain Oil and Gas Assn., Rocky Mountain Petroleum Pioneers (pres. 1991-92), Wyo. Pioneer Assn., Chevaliers du Tastevin, Denver Country Club, Petroleum Club, Gyro Club, Univ. Club Denver, Garden of the Gods Club (Colo. Springs), Colo. Arlberg Club, Mile High Club, U. Colo. Alumni

Club (Living Legend award). Republican. Episcopalian. Author, co-author: Landman's Handbook, Law of Federal Oil and Gas Leases, Problems of Surface Damages, Federal Oil and Gas Leases--The Sole Party in Interest Debacle. Home: 4401 E 3rd Ave Denver CO 80220-5627 Office: Ste 575 3773 Cherry Creek North Dr Denver CO 80209-3825

HAWN, WILLIAM EUGENE, health care company executive; b. Bonne Terre, Mo., May 8, 1941; s. James William and Mary Kathryn (Denman) H.; m. Linda Sharon Swingle, Jan. 19, 1964; children: Matthew Todd, Andrew James. BA, U. Mo., 1963, MPA, 1968. Asst. adminstr. USAF Hosps., Travis AFB, Calif., 1968-72, Contra Costa County Hosp., Martinez, Calif., 1972-73; assoc. adminstr. Fairmount Hosp., San Leandro, Calif., 1973-79; v.p. Alta Bates Hosp., Berkeley, Calif., 1979-86; pres. VHA-West, L.A., 1986, Northbay Health Advantage, Fairfield, Calif., 1986—; commr. City of Hayward, Calif., Human Svcs. Commn., 1978-86. Chmn. parent adv. coun. Hayward (Calif.) Sch. Dist., 1975-79. Capt. USAF, 1968-72. Recipient Gold award Alcosta/Calif. Tchrs. Assn., 1978. Fellow Am. Coll. Healthcare Execs.; mem. Rotary. Democrat. Methodist. Office: North Bay Healthcare Advantage 1200 B Gale Wilson Blvd Fairfield CA 94533-3552

HAWRANEK, JOSEPH PAUL, computer company executive, consultant; b. N.Y.C., Dec. 21, 1937; s. Joseph and Tina Woodsinger H.; m. Joanne Arlene Vinson, Mar. 21,1959; children: David Paul, Daniel Strauss, Scott Joseph;. BS in EE, U. Va., Charlottesville, 1960; MBA, U. Va., 1962; PhD, U. Pa., Phila., 1970. Mgr. IBM, Raleigh, N.C., 1966-76; dir. Nat. Semi-Conductor, Santa Clara, Calif., 1976-80, Honeywell, Phoenix, Ariz., 1980-83, Aydin Corp.-Aydin Controls, Ft. Washington, Pa., 1983; pres. Teneron Corp., Beaverton, Oreg., 1983-86, Raven Communications Inc., Phoenix, 1987-88, 89-93; v.p. ops. Telxon Corp., Akron, Ohio, 1988-89; pres. wireless divsn. Calif. Microwave, 1993; pres. Raven Communications Inc., Phoenix, 1994—. Office: Raven Communications 8724 N 67th St Paradise Vly AZ 85253-2701

HAWTHORNE, MARION FREDERICK, chemistry educator; b. Ft. Scott, Kans., Aug. 24, 1928; s. Fred Elmer and Colleen (Webb) H.; m. Beverly Dawn Rempe, Oct. 30, 1951 (div. 1976); children: Cynthia Lee, Candace Lee; m. Diana Baker Razzaia, Aug. 14, 1977. B.A., Pomona Coll., 1949; Ph.D. (AEC fellow), U. Calif. at Los Angeles, 1953; D.Sc. (hon.), Pomona Coll., 1974; PhD (hon.), Uppsala U., 1992. Research asso. Iowa State Coll., 1953-54; research chemist Rohm & Haas Co., Huntsville, Ala., 1954-56; group leader Rohm & Haas Co., 1956-60; lab. head Rohm & Haas Co., Phila., 1961; vis. lectr. Harvard, 1960, Queen Mary Coll., U. London, 1963; vis. prof. Harvard U., 1968; prof. chemistry U. Calif. at Riverside, 1962-68, U. Calif. at Los Angeles, 1968—; vis. prof. U. Tex., Austin, 1974; mem. sci. adv. bd. USAF, 1980-86, NRC Bd. Army Sci. and Tech., 1986-90; disting. vis. prof. Ohio State U., 1990; mem. dir.'s external adv. bd. divsn. M, Los Alamos (N.Mex.) Nat. Lab., 1991-94. Recipient Chancellors Research award, 1968, Herbert Newby McCoy award, 1972, Am. Chem. Soc. award in Inorganic Chemistry, 1973, Tolman Medal award, 1986, Nebr. sect. Am. Chem. Soc. award, 1979, Disting. Service in the Advancement of Inorganic Chemistry award Am. Chem. Soc., 1988, Disting. Achievements in Boron Sci. award, 1988, Bailar medal, 1991, Polyhedron Medal and prize, 1993, Chem. Pioneer award Am. Inst. Chemists, 1994, Willard Gibbs medal Am. Chem. Soc., 1994; named sr. scientist Alexander von Humboldt Found., Inst. Inorganic Chemistry U. Munich, 1990—; Sloan Found. fellow, 1963-65, Japan Soc. Promotion Sci. fellow, 1986; named Col. Confederate Air Force, 1984. Fellow AAAS; mem. U.S. Nat. Acad. Scis., Am. Acad. Arts and Scis., Göttingen Acad. Scis. (corr. mem.), Aircraft Owners and Pilots Assn., Cosmos Club, The Internat. Soc. for Neutron Capture Therapy for Cancer (mem. exec. com. 1992—, pres.-elect 1994—), Sigma Xi, Alpha Chi Sigma, Sigma Nu. Home: 3415 Green Vista Dr Encino CA 91436-4011

HAWTHORNE, NAN LOUISE, writer, editor, trainer; b. Hawthorne, Nev., Jan. 3, 1952; d. Louis Frederick Haas and Merle Forrest (Ohlhausen) Ritter; m. James Denver Tedford, Dec. 20, 1981. BS, No. Mich. U., 1981. Freelance writer, editor, indexer, Seattle, 1974—; coord. Circles of Exch., Seattle, 1984—; mgr. vols. Community Svcs. for Blind and Partially Sighted, Seattle, 1989-93; co-owner, trainer Voices, 1993—; host, co-host talk show Evergreen Radio Reading Svc., Seattle, 1989—; mgr. vols. SEattle Commns., 1993-94; columnist Seattle Vol., 1994—. Author: Loving the Goddess Within, 1991; co-indexer: Women's Book of Healing, 1988; indexer, editor: WomanSpirit Index, 1989; editor Information Guide for Blind Persons in Washington, 1990; pub. Puget Sound Vol. Mgr. Mem. Sagewoman Adv. Coun., 1988-90, Wash. State Coun. on Volunteerism and Citizen Svcs., 1992—; trainer United Way of King County Vol. Ctr., 1993—; bd. dirs., dir. vols. Ageras of King County, 1992; mem. adv. bd. Retired Sr. Vol. Program, 1995—. Mem. Assn. Vol. Adminstrn., Am. Volksport Assn., Vol. Mgrs. Breakfast Club (steering com. 1994-95). Office: Circles of Exch 9594 1st Ave NE Ste 413 Seattle WA 98115-2028

HAY, ANDREW MACKENZIE, merchant banking and commodities company executive; b. London, Apr. 9, 1928; came to U.S., 1954, naturalized, 1959; s. Ewen Mackenzie and Bertine (Buxton) H.; MA in Econs., St. John's Coll., Cambridge U., 1950; m. Catherine Newman, July 30, 1977. Commodities trader, London and Ceylon, 1950-53; v.p. Calvert Vavasseur & Co. Inc., N.Y.C., 1954-61, pres., 1962-78, pres. Calvert-Peat Inc., N.Y.C., 1978—, Andrew M. Hay, Inc.; chmn. Barretto Peat Inc., N.Y.C., 1974-88; Pacific NW cons. Am. Assn. Exporters and Importers, 1982—; radio and TV appearances. Mem. adv. com. on tech. innovation Nat. Acad. Scis., 1978; bd. dirs. Winston Churchill Found.; treas., trustee World Affairs Coun. Oreg., 1986—; apptd. Her Majesty's hon. Brit. consul, 1987; dean Oreg. Counsular Corps, 1991. Capt. Brit. Army. Decorated comdr. Order Brit. Empire. Mem. Am. Importer Assn. (pres. 1977-79), Pacific N.W. Internat. Trade Assn. (exec. dir. 1986—), Brit. Am. C. of C. (pres. 1966-68), Philippine Am. C. of C. (pres. 1977-79), St. George's Soc. (bd. dir.), St. Andrew's Soc. (bd. dir.), Recess Club, Downtown Assn. (N.Y.C.), U. Club, Arlington Club. Episcopalian. Author: A Century of Coconuts, 1972. Home and Office: 3515 SW Council Crest Dr Portland OR 97201-1403

HAY, JOHN LEONARD, lawyer; b. Lawrence, Mass., Oct. 6, 1940; s. Charles Cable and Henrietta Dudley (Wise) H.; 1 child, Ian. AB with distinction, Stanford U., 1961; JD, U. Colo., 1964. Bar: Colo. 1964, Ariz. 1965, D.C. 1971. Assoc. Lewis and Roca, Phoenix, 1964-69, ptnr., 1969-82; ptnr. Fannin, Terry & Hay, Phoenix, 1982-87, Allen, Kimerer & LaVelle, Phoenix, 1987-94, Gust Rosenfeld, Phoenix, 1994—; bd. dirs. Ariz. Life and Disability Ins. Guaranty Fund, 1984—, chmn., 1993—. Mem. Dem. Precinct Com., 1966-78, Ariz. State Dem. Com., 1968-78; chmn. Dem. Legis. Dist., 1971-74; mem. Maricopa County Dem. Cen. Com., 1971-74; bd. dirs. ACLU, 1973-78; bd. dirs. Community Legal Svcs., 1983-89, pres., 1987-88; bd. dirs. Ariz. Club, 1994—. Mem. ABA, Maricopa County Bar Assn. (bd. dirs. 1972-85), Ariz. State Bar Assn., Assn. Life Ins. Counsel, Ariz. Licensors and Franchisors Assn. (bd. dirs. 1985—, pres. 1988-89), Ariz. Civil Liberties Union (bd. dirs. 1967-84, pres. 1973-77, Disting. Citizen award 1979). Home: 201 E Hayward Ave Phoenix AZ 85020-4037 Office: Gust Rosenfeld 201 North Cen Ave Ste 3300 Phoenix AZ 85073

HAY, JOHN WOODS, JR., retired banker; b. Rock Springs, Wyo., Apr. 23, 1905; s. John Woods and Mary Ann (Blair) H.; A.B., U. Mich., 1927; m. Frances B. Smith, Dec. 28, 1948; children—Helen Mary, John Woods III, Keith Norbert, Joseph Garrett. Pres., dir. Rock Springs Nat. Bank, 1947-95, Rock Springs Grazing Assn., 1939-95, Blair & Hay Land & Livestock Co., Rock Springs, 1949—. Former trustee, v.p. William H. and Carrie Gottsche Found. Mem. Sigma Alpha Epsilon. Republican. Episcopalian. Clubs: Masons, Shriners, Jesters, Rotary. Home: 502 B St Rock Springs WY 82901-6213 Office: 333 Broadway St Rock Springs WY 82901-6242

HAY, RICHARD LAURENCE, theater scenic designer; b. Wichita, Kans., May 28, 1929; s. Laurence Charles and Ruth Mary (Rhoades) H. BA, Stanford U., 1952, MA, 1955. Tech. dir., designer Oreg. Shakespeare Festival, Ashland, 1953-55, prin. scenic designer, 1970—; instr. drama Stanford U., Palo Alto, Calif., 1957-62, assoc. prof., 1965-69; assoc. artistic dir. for design Denver Ctr. Theater Co., 1984-91; freelance scenic designer Guthrie Theater, Mpls., Am. Conservatory Theater, San Francisco, Mo. Repertory Theater, Kansas City, Mark Taper Forum, Los Angeles, Old Globe Theater, San Diego, Berkekey (Calif.) Repertory Theater, others; theatre designer: Source and Space Theatres, Denver Ctr. Theatre Co., New Old Globe Theatre and Festival Stage, Old Globe Theatre, San Diego, Intiman Theatre, Seattle, Black Swan, Angus Bowmer Theatre, Elizabethan Stage, Oreg. Shakespeare Festival. Author: (with others) A Space for Magic: Stage Settings by Richard L. Hay, 1979; exhibitor Prague Quadriennial, 1987, U.S. Inst. Theatre Tech. Biennial Scenography Expn., 1984, 88, 90. Bd. dirs. U.S. Inst. Theatre Tech., 1994—. Recipient Critics award Hollywood (Calif.) Drama-Logue, 1982, 85, 86, 89, Gov's. award for the Arts State of Oreg., 1989; Fulbright grantee, 1955. Mem. United Scenic Artists, U.S. Inst. Theatre Tech. (bd. dirs.), League Hist. Am. Theaters. Democrat. Congregationalist. Home: 707 Liberty St Ashland OR 97520-3140 Office: Oreg Shakespeare Festival PO Box 158 Ashland OR 97520-0158

HAY, SHERMAN COLIN, artist, art educator; b. San Jose, Calif., Sept. 12, 1948; s. Leslie Drew and Barbara Jane (Farrote) H.; m. Stacy Alexandra Blum, July 18, 1981; children: Garin Sherman, Monica Courtney. Student, San Jose City Coll., 1966, 67, 71, L.A. Pierce Coll., 1970-71; BA in Art, Hayward (Calif) State U., 1976; MA in Art, Humboldt State U., Arcata, Calif., 1979. Cert. tchr. fine and applied arts C.C., Calif. Co-owner, master printer Stratum Editions, Arcata, Calif., 1979-81; instr. handmade paper Coll. of the Redwoods, Eureka, Calif., 1980; visual art instr. William James Assn., Santa Cruz, Calif., 1983-84, 90-91; artist in residence Calif. Arts Coun., Sacramento, 1984-86,, 87-90, 91-94; artist in the librs. State Libr. System, Sonora, Calif., 1987; art instr. Columbia (Calif.) Jr. Coll., 1994—; judge fine arts divsn. Solano County Fair, 1990, 91, 5th Ann. Countours, Ctrl. sierra Arts Coun., Sonora, 1990. Artist: exhibits include (handmade paper) Lodi Art Annual, 1988 (purchase award), Calif. State Fair (award of excellence 1988, 93), 35th ann. Nat. Soc. Painters, N.Y.C., (hon. mention 1988), Internat. Juried Art Competition , Scarsdale, N.Y. (cert. of excellence), Bradford Studios, Sonora, Calif., 1994. Donated Artwork for Auction, Ctrl. Sierra Arts Coun., 1989, 90,91, 92, KVIE, Channel 6, Sacramento, 1993, donated sculpture for art scholarships auction, New Leaf Garden Gallery, Berkeley, Calif., 1994. With USMC, 1967-70. Recipient award of merit for papermaking and painting, Nat. Congress of Art, Salt Lake City, 1988, Sculpture award Pub. Art Commn. Calauaras County Libr., 1995. Mem. Ctrl. Sierra Arts Coun. Home: 19076 North Dr Jamestown CA 95327-9613 Office: PO Box 5211 Sonora CA 95370

HAY, WILLIAM CHARLES, professional hockey team executive; b. Saskatoon, Sask., Can., Dec. 9, 1935; s. Charles and Florence (Miller) H.; m. Nancy Ann Woodman, Aug. 24, 1957; children: Pam, Penny, Donald. B.S. in Geology, Colo. Coll., 1958. Profl. hockey player Chgo. Black Hawks, 1958-67; mgr. Sedco Drilling Co., Calgary, Alta., 1967-70, gen. mgr., from 1970; gen. mgr. Hi-Tower Drilling Co., Calgary, Alta., from 1970; formerly pres., chief operating officer Hockey Can.; pres. Calgary Flames Hockey Club, NHL, 1991—; also alternate governor Calgary Flames. Office: Calgary Flames, PO Box 1540 Sta M, Calgary, AB Canada T2P 3B9

HAY, WILLIAM WINN, natural history and geology educator; b. Dallas, Oct. 12, 1934; s. Stephen J. and Avella (Winn) H. BS, So. Meth. U., 1955; postgrad. U. Zurich, Switzerland, 1955-56; MS, U. Ill., 1958; PhD, Stanford U., 1960. Mem. faculty dept. geology U. Ill., Urbana, 1960-73; mem. faculty Rosenstiel Sch. Marine and Atmospheric Sci., U. Miami., Fla., 1968-82, chmn. div. marine geology, 1974-76, interim dean, 1976-77, dean, 1977-80; pres. Joint Oceanographic Instn., Inc., Washington, 1979-82; dir. U. Colo. Mus., Boulder, 1982-87; prof. geol. scis., fellow Coop. Inst. for Rsch. in Environ. Sci., U. Colo., Boulder, 1983—; prof. GEOMAR, Christian-Albrechts U., Kiel, Germany, 1990—; mem. adv. panel sedimentary and geochem. processes Joint Oceanographic Instns. for Deep Earth Sampling, 1989-92, chmn., 1994—; mem. sci. adv. com. Ocean Margin Drilling Program, 1979-83; mem. exec. com. div. ocean sci. NSF, 1982-85. Editor: Studies in Paleo-Oceanography, 1974. Univ. Coll. London fellow, 1972—; recipient Francis P. Shepard medal Soc. Econ. Paleontologists and Mineralogists, 1981, Best Paper award Gulf Coast sect., 1970; Alexander von Humboldt Found. prize, 1991-92; F.C. Donders Prof. U. Utrecht, 1993. Fellow Geol. Soc. Am., Geol. Soc. (London), Coop. Inst. Rsch. in Environ. Scis.; mem. Am. Assn. Petroleum Geologists. Office: U Colorado Dept Geological Scis Campus Box 250 Boulder CO 80309 also: Geomar, Wischhofstr 1-3, D24148 Kiel Germany

HAYASE, LINDA MICHI, direct mail company executive; b. Honolulu, Oct. 22, 1963; d. Glenn Atsuo Shimada and Amy Ayako (Takeda) Wong; m. Alan Hisashi Hayase. BBA, U. Hawaii, 1985. Lic. life ins. solicitor, registered issuer of securities, Hawaii. Salesperson McInerny, Honolulu, 1982-83; clk. U. Hawaii Bd. Regents, Honolulu, 1982-84; sales rep. A.L. Williams, Honolulu, 1984, sales mgr., 1984-85, dist. mgr., 1985, div. mgr., 1986; traffic prodn. mgr., account exec. DiCarlo Advt. Agy., Honolulu, 1986-87; account exec. Pearlman, Wohl, Olshever, Marchese, L.A., 1987-88; fin. cons. Merrill Lynch, Pierce, Fenner & Smith, Inc., Santa Ana, Calif., 1988-90; acct. exec. HomeFed Ins./GNA Securities, Santa Ana, Calif. 1990-92; investment exec. Pacific First Investment Svcs., San Bernardino, Calif. 1992-93; v.p. investments Great Western Fin. Svcs., 1993; pres./owner Hawaiian Island Express. Mem. Nat. Assn. Securities Dealers (cert.), Asian Pacific Women's Network, Home Office and Bus. Opportunities, Alpha Beta Chi (chpt. sec. 1983-84, chpt. pres. 1984-85). Republican. Office: 5753-G E Santa Ana Canyon # 3500 Anaheim CA 92807

HAYDEN, ANN MARIE, family nurse practitioner; b. St. Peter, Minn., Aug. 8, 1960; d. William H. and Roseila Cora (Mueller) H. BSN, U. Minn., 1982, MA in Indsl. Rels., 1986; MSN/Family Nurse Practitioner, U. San Diego, 1994. RN, Minn., Calif. Human resources intern Republic/Northwest Airlines, Mpls., 1982-86; staff nurse, charge nurse U. Minn. Hosps.; clin. nurse specialist cardiovascular and thoracic surgery Minn. Heart and Lung Inst., 1988-89; clin. nurse specialist cardiothoracic surgery U. Calif. San Diego Med. Ctr., 1989—, heart/lung transplant coord., 1989—; lectr., presenter in field. Contbr. articles to profl. jours. Mem. coun. on cardiovascular nursing Am. Heart Assn., 1988—. Mem. AACN, Internat. Soc. Heart and Lung Transplantation (edn. chmn. nursing com.), N.Am. Transplant Coords. Assn. (grantee 1990). Home: 4344 Corte Al Fresco San Diego CA 92130-2160 Office: U Calif San Diego Med Ctr 225 Dickinson St San Diego CA 92103-1910

HAYDEN, CEDRIC L., state legislator, dentist; b. Eugene, Oreg., Aug. 4, 1934; s. Jesse and Gwendolen (Lampshire) H.; m. Marilyn Adele Jaekel, Dec. 27, 1961; children: Jonathan, Christopher, Matthew, Cedric Ross, Kaminda. BS, U. Oreg., 1957; DMD, Washington U., St. Louis, 1960; MPH, Loma Linda U., 1979. Dentist Antioch (Calif.) Dental Group, 1963-65; missionary Seventh Day Adventist Ch., Port of Spain, Trinidad, 1965-69; dentist Hayden Family Dentistry Group, Eugene, Oreg., 1970—; legislator Oreg. Ho. of Reps., Salem, 1985—, chmn. house com. on transp., house com. on gen. govt., 1991—, asst. majority leader, asst. caucus leader, 1991—. Lt. (s.g.) USN, 1960-63. Fellow Am. Dental Soc. Anesthesiology. Republican. Home: 43676 E Bilyeu Creek Dr Scio OR 97374-9378

HAYDEN, RON L., library director; b. San Pedro, Calif., Dec. 24, 1948; s. Larnie Alphonsis and Myrtie Louise (Pilcher) H.; m. Marilee Ann Brubaker, May 30, 1971 (dec. June 1978); m. Susan Ann Huffman, Jan. 1, 1982. AA, Golden West Coll., 1969; BA, Long Beach State U., 1972; MLS, Fullerton U., 1974. Reference sr. libr. Huntington Beach (Calif.) Libr., 1975-79, pub. svc. libr., 1979-86, libr. dir., 1986—; liason Libr. Patrons Assn., Huntington Beach, 1986—. Author: Collection Development Library Journal, 1979. Recipient Award of Excellence Calif. S.W. Recreation Park Conf., 1990. Mem. ALA (Libr. in Media award, Best of Show award 1990), Calif. Libr. Assn., Friends Libr., So. Calif. Tennis Assn., Rotary (bd. dirs., vocat. chmn. 1988—). Home: 609 21st St Huntington Beach CA 92648-3318 Office: Huntington Beach Libr 7111 Talbert Ave Huntington Beach CA 92648-1232*

HAYEK, CAROLYN JEAN, retired judge; b. Portland, Oreg., Aug. 17, 1948; d. Robert A. and Marion L. (DeKoning) H.; m. Steven M. Rosen, July 21, 1974; children: Jonathan David, Laura Elizabeth. BA in Psychology, Carleton Coll., 1970; JD, U. Chgo., 1973. Bar: Wash. 1973. Assoc. firm Jones, Grey & Bayley, Seattle, 1973-77; sole practice law, Federal Way, Wash., 1977-82; judge Federal Way Dist. Ct., 1982-95; ret., 1995. Task force mem. Alternatives for Wash., 1973-75; mem. Wash. State Ecol. Commn., 1975-77; bd. dirs. 1st Unitarian Ch. Seattle, 1986-89, vice chair 1987-88, pres., 1988-89; den leader Cub Scouts Mt. Rainier coun. Boy Scouts Am., 1987-88, scouting coord., 1988-89; bd. dirs. Twin Lakes Elem. Sch. PTA. Recipient Women Helping Women award Federal Way Soroptimist, 1991, Martin Luther King Day Humanitarian award King County, 1993, Recognition cert. City of Federal Way Diversity Commn., 1995. Mem. AAUW (br. pres. 1978-80, 90-92, chmn. state level conf. com. 1986-87, mem. diversity com. 1991—, state bd. mem. 1995—), ABA, Wash. Women Lawyers, Wash. State Bar Assn., King County Dist. Ct. Judges Assn. (treas., exec. com. 1990-91, 92-93, com. chmn., chair and rules com. 1990-91, 92-94), Elected Wash. Women (dir. 1983-87), Nat. Assn. Women Judges (nat. bd. dirs., dist. bd. dirs. 1984-86, chmn. rules com. 1988-89, chmn. bylaws com. 1990-91), Fed. Way Women's Network (bd. dirs. 1984-87, 88-91, 95—, pres. 1985, program co-chair 1989-91, co-editor newsletter), Greater Fed. Way C. of C. (dir. 1978-82, sec. 1980-81, v.p. 1981-82), Sunrise Rotary (com. svc. chair, bd. dirs., membership com., Federal Way chpt. 1991—, exchange officer 1994—), Washington Women United, 1995—. Republican. Address: PO Box 24494 Federal Way WA 98093-1494

HAYES, BYRON JACKSON, JR., lawyer; b. L.A., July 9, 1934; s. Byron Jackson and Caroline Violet (Scott) H.; m. DeAnne Saliba, June 30, 1962; children: Kenneth Byron, Patricia DeAnne. Student, Pomona Coll., 1952-56; BA magna cum laude, Harvard U., LLB cum laude, 1959. Bar: Calif. 1960, U.S. Supreme Ct. 1963. Assoc., McCutchen, Black, Verleger & Shea, L.A., 1960-68, ptnr., 1968-89; ptnr. Baker & Hostetler, 1990—. Trustee L.A. Ch. Extension Soc. United Meth. Ch., 1967-77, pres., 1974-77, chancellor ann. conf. Pacific and S.W., 1979-86; Dir., pres. Pacific and S.W. United Meth. Found., 1978-84. Named Layperson of yr. Pacific and S.W. Ann. Conf., United Meth. Ch., 1981; recipient Bishop's award United Meth. Ch., 1992. Mem. ABA, Am. Coll. Mortgage Attys. (regent 1984-90, 91—, pres. 1993-94), Calif. Bar Assn., Assn. Real Estate Attys., L.A. County Bar Assn. (chmn. real property sect. 1982-83), Toluca Lake Property Owners Assn. (sec. 1990-94), Pomona Coll. Alumni Assn. (pres. 1984-85), Lakeside Golf Club (Toluca Lake, Calif.). Office: Baker & Hostetler 600 Wilshire Blvd Fl 10 Los Angeles CA 90017-3212

HAYES, CECIL EDWARD, physicist; b. Memphis, May 11, 1941; s. Thomas Jackson and Laura Katherine (West) H.; m. Joyce Elaine Wittebort, June 21, 1969; children: Elaine Marie, John Alexander. BS in Engring. Physics, Cornell U., 1964; AM in Physics, Harvard U., 1966, PhD in Physics, 1973. Rsch. asst. dept. physics Harvard U., Cambridge, Mass., 1968-73; rsch. assoc. dept. physics Rutgers U., New Brunswick, N.J., 1973-76; postdoctoral rsch. assoc./teaching fellow physics U. Utah, Salt Lake City, 1976-79, rsch. asst./rsch. assoc. prof., 1979-82; sr. physicist Applied Sci. Lab., GE Med. Sys., Milw., 1982-91; adj. asst. prof. dept. med. physics U. Wis., Madison, 1988-93; assoc. prof. dept. radiology U. Wash., Seattle, 1993—; cons. GE Med. Sys., Milw., 1991—, Superconductor Technologies, Santa Barbara, Calif., 1993-94. Patentee in field (12); contbr. numerous articles and abstracts to jours., chpts. to books. NSF fellow, 1964-66; John McMullen Regional scholar, 1959-62, Owens-Ill. scholar, 1962-64. Mem. Am. Phys. Soc., Soc. for Magnetic Resonance in Medicine, Phi Eta Sigma, Tau Beta Pi (Meml. prize for best 5th yr. rsch. project in engring. physics). Office: Univ of Washington Dept Radiology RC-05 1959 NE Pacific St Seattle WA 98195-0004

HAYES, CLAUDE QUINTEN CHRISTOPHER, research scientist; b. N.Y.C., Nov. 15, 1945; s. Claude and Celestine (Stanley) H. BA in Chemistry and Geol. Sci., Columbia U., 1971, postgrad., 1972-73; postgrad., N.Y. Law Sch., 1973-75; JD, Western State Law Sch., 1978. Cert. community coll. tchr. earth scis., phys. sci., law, Calif. Tech. writer Burroughs Corp., San Diego, 1978-79; instr. phys. scis. Nat. U., San Diego, 1980-81; instr. bus. law, earth scis. Miramar Coll., 1978-82; sr. systems analyst Gen. Dynamics Convair, 1979-80, advanced mfg. technologist, sr. engr., 1980-81; pvt. practice sci. and tech. cons. Calif., 1979—; instr. phys. sci., phys. geography, bus. law San Diego Community Coll. Dist., 1976-82, 85-90; U.S. Dept. Def. contractor Def. Nuclear Agy., Strategic Def. Initiative Agy., USAF, Def. Advance Rsch. Projects Agy., 1986—, U.S. Army, 1991—; adj. prof. phys. chemistry San Diego State U., 1986-87; bus. and computer sci. def. rsch. contractor to Maxwell Labs., Naval Ocean Sys. Ctr.; tech. cons. Pizza Hut, Inc., Carts of Colo., Smiths Industries. Contbr. articles to profl. jours.; patentee in field. Mem. Am. Chem. Soc., N.Y. Acad. Sci., Am. Inst. Aero. and Astronautics. Home and office: 3737 3rd Ave Apt 308 San Diego CA 92103-4133

HAYES, DEBORAH, musicology educator, college administrator; b. Miami, Fla., Dec. 13, 1939; d. Lauffer Truby Hayes and Margaret Hayes Parsons. AB, Oberlin Coll., 1960; AM, Stanford U., 1961, PhD, 1968. Instr. U. Colo., Boulder, 1968-70, asst. prof., 1970-78, assoc. prof. musicology, 1978—, assoc. dean Coll. of Music, 1994—. Author: Peggy Glanville-Hicks: A Bio-Bibliography, 1990, Peter Sculthorpe: A Bio-Bibliography, 1993; contbr. articles to profl. publs.; feature editor Internat. Alliance for Women in Music, 1993—; contbr. articles to profl. jours. Mem. Am. Musicological Soc. (com. on status of women 1991-94), Sonneck Soc. Home: 3290 Darley Ave Boulder CO 80303-6412 Office: U Colo Campus Box 301 Boulder CO 80309

HAYES, DELBERT J., athletic company executive; b. 1935. BA, Wash. State U., 1957. CPA, Wash. Acct. Price, Waterhouse & Co., 1961-69, Linn-Pacific, 1969-70; ptnr. Hayes, Nyman & Co., 1972-75; treas. Nike, Inc., Beaverton, Oreg., 1975-80, exec. v.p., 1980—, also bd. dirs. Office: Nike Inc 3900 SW Murray Blvd Beaverton OR 97005-2319

HAYES, EDWARD CARY, management consultant; b. Chgo., Dec. 28, 1937; s. Edward Bean and Helen Frances (Walker) H.; m. Rosemary Triggs, Sept. 10, 1972, (div. July 1976). BA magna cum laude, Swarthmore Coll., 1960; MA in Polit. Sci., U. Calif., Berkeley, 1962, PhD in Polit. Sci., 1968. Postdoctoral fellow U. Chgo., 1968-69; asst. prof. polit. sci. U. Wis., Milw., 1969-72, Ohio U., Athens, 1972-76; dir. econ. devel. program U.S. Cath. Conf., Columbus, 1976-78; dir. employment tng. ACCESS, San Diego, 1979-82; founder, pres. Metro Assocs., San Diego, 1982-90; pres. Communi Corp., 1990-94; sr. analyst High Tech. Solutions, Inc., San Diego, 1994—; vis. scholar Inst. Gov. Studies U. Calif., 1991-92. Author: Power Structure and Urban Politics, 1972, Public Administration on Three Continents, 1978, A Fire That Won't Go Out, 1984, The Hidden Wealth of Cities, 1989. Grantee NSF, 1971. Mem. Am. Soc. Pub. Adminstrn., Am. Polit. Sci. Assn., Christian Mgmt. Assn., Mensa. Office: High Tech Solutions Inc 4858 Mercury St Ste 106 San Diego CA 92111

HAYES, ERNEST M., podiatrist; b. New Orleans, Jan. 21, 1946; s. Ernest M. and Emma Hayes; m. Bonnie Ruth Beigle, Oct. 16, 1970. B.A., Calif. State U., Sacramento, 1969; B.S., Calif. Coll. Podiatric Medicine, San Francisco, 1971, D.P.M., 1973. Resident in surg. podiatry Beach Community Hosp., Buena Park, Calif., 1973-74, dir. residency program, 1974-75; practice podiatry, Anaheim, Calif., 1974-80, Yreka, Calif., 1980—; sr. clin. instr. So. Calif. Podiatric Med. Center, Los Angeles, 1975-78; vice chmn. podiatry dept. Good Samaritan Hosp., Anaheim, Calif., 1978-79; mem. med. staff Mercey Med. Ctr., Mt. Shasta, Calif. Bd. dirs. Little Bogus Ranches Home Owners Assn., 1981-83, pres., 1983-84. Fellow Nat. Coll. Foot Surgeons; mem. Am. Assn. Podiatric Physicians and Surgeons, Am. Coun. Cert. Podiatric Physicians and Surgeons (cert.), Kiwanis. Baptist. Home: PO Box 958 Yreka CA 96097-0958 Office: 1009 S Main St Yreka CA 96097-3324

HAYES, GEORGE NICHOLAS, lawyer; b. Alliance, Ohio, Sept. 30, 1928; s. Nicholas John and Mary Irene (Fanady) H. B.A., U. Akron, 1950; M.A., Western Res. U., 1953, LL.B., 1955. Bar: Ohio 1955, U.S. Dist. Ct. Alaska 1957, Alaska 1959, U.S. Ct. Appeals (9th cir.) 1958, U.S. Supreme Ct. 1964, Wash. 1972. Mcpl. ct. prosecutor, asst. county prosecutor Portage County, Ravenna, Ohio, 1955-57; asst. U.S. atty. Fairbanks and Anchorage (Alaska), 1957-59; dep. atty. gen. State of Alaska, 1959-62; dist. atty. 3d Jud. Dist., Anchorage, 1960-62; atty. gen., Juneau, Alaska, 1962-64; spl. counsel to Gov., State of Alaska on earthquake recovery program at Washington, 1964; ptnr. Delaney, Wiles, Hays, Reitman & Brubaker, Inc., Anchorage, 1964-92, of counsel, 1992—. Mem. ABA, Washington State Bar Assn., Alaska Bar Assn., Ohio Bar Assn., Anchorage Bar Assn., Am. Coll. Trial Lawyers. Democrat. Office: Delaney Wiles Hayes Reitman & Brubaker 1007 W 3rd Ave Anchorage AK 99501-1917

HAYES, GLADYS LUCILLE ALLEN, state community care official, poet, writer; b. Havelock, Nebr., Nov. 29, 1913; d. Harry Arthur and Louise (Vogel) Allen; m. James Franklin Hayes, Oct. 5, 1943; children: J. Allen, Warren Andrew. Secretarial diploma, Lincoln (Nebr.) Sch. Commerce, 1932; student, Santa Clara U., 1950-60; BS in Media Studies, Sacred Heart U., Fairfield, Conn., 1989, exec. MBA, 1991. Cert. profl. religion tchr. Archdiocese of San Francisco. Exec. tech. sec. McCormick-Selph div. Teledyne Corp., Hollister, Calif., 1960-65; adminstrv. asst. to v.p. Greater Bridgeport Regional Narcotics Program, Inc., Bridgeport, Conn., 1979-81; adminstrv. asst. to scientists and engrs. CBS Lab. div. CBS Inc., Stamford, Conn., 1968-76; sec. to Nobel laureate and physicist Dennis Gabor, Dsc, FRS U. London, U.S.; corp. sec. Automated Power Systems, Inc., Bridgeport, 1976-90; owner, mgr. GA Secretarial Svc., Stratford, Conn., 1980-91; secretarial asst. Conn. Community Care, Inc., Stratford, Conn., 1986-91; sec., environ. resources U.S. Army Corps Engrs., Elmendorf AFB, Anchorage, Alaska, 1992-93; substitute tchr. Anchorage Sch. Dist., 1992-93; cmty. svc. rep. Alaska Dept. Corrections, Juneau, 1994—; radio broadcaster Fairfield U., 1985-90. Former residential fund raising chmn. ARC, Gilroy, Calif.; former motion picture chmn. St. Mary's Sch., Gilroy, also past pres. Mothers' Guild, former mem. Edn. Commn.; former fundraiser March of Dimes; mem. various choirs and choral groups, Calif., Conn., Alaska; mem. Nat. Coun. on Aging; tchr. religion Archdiocese of San Francisco, Diocese of Lincoln, 1933-67, Archdiocese of Bridgeport, 1968-72. Recipient Excellence in Aging award Conn. Community Care, Inc., 1989, prize for photograph City of Bridgeport, 1987, Pope Pius X Medal of Honor, 1959. Mem. Nat. Honor Soc. Republican. Roman Catholic.

HAYES, JEANNE, information services executive; b. Chgo., Oct. 22, 1942; d. Raymond John and Margaret (Burke) H.; m. Thomas T. Olkowski, Aug. 5, 1967; 1 child, Colin F. Hayes. BA, Marquette U., 1965; postgrad., U. Mich., 1965-67. Tchr. Southfield (Mich.) Pub. Schs., 1965-67, Clarksville (Ind.) Pub. Schs., 1967-69, Jefferson County Schs., Lakewood, Colo., 1969-70; v.p. product devel. Curriculum Info. Ctr., Denver, 1972-78; gen. mgr. Denver office Market Data Retrieval, Shelton, Conn., 1979-80; pres. Quality Education Data, Inc., Denver, 1981—. Mem. Denver Athletic Club, Jr. Symphony Guild. Democrat. Home: 9 Albion St Denver CO 80220-5610 Office: Quality Edn Data Inc 1600 Broadway Denver CO 80202-4927

HAYES, MARGARET MARY, physician; b. Aberdeen, S.D., Sept. 24, 1952; m. Eric S. Berman. BS, Portland State U., 1989; MD, Oreg. Health Scis. U., 1994. Dir. faculty profl. svcs. coun. Oreg. Health Scis. U., Portland, 1989-91, student rep., mem. new course approval and curriculum com., 1991—; resident family medicine Oreg. Health Scis. U., 1994—; papers presented at Nat. Congress of Family Practice Residents and Student, Kansas City, Mo., 1993, Child Abuse Response and Evaluation Svcs. (CARES), Emanuel Children's Hosp., 1993, Nat. Rural Health Assn. Annual Conf., San Francisco, 1994. Vol. health care worker Neighborhood Health Clinics, Inc., Mulnomah County N.E. H.S. Recipient John Snow Inc. scholarship Nat. Rural Health Assn., 1994. Mem. AMA (Nat. Leadership award 1994), Am. Acad. Family Physicians, Am. Med. Student Assn., Am. Med. Women's Assn., Multnomah County Med. Soc. (trustee 1993-94), Oreg. Med. Assn. (steering com., domestic violence task force), Oreg. Acad. Family Physicians (sci. assembly com.), Soc. Tchrs. Family Medicine (Rsch. Forum award 1993), Physician's for Social Responsibility. Office: Oreg Health Scis U-EJH 3181 SW Sam Jackson Park Rd Portland OR 97201-3011

HAYES, MARY ESHBAUGH, newspaper editor; b. Rochester, N.Y., Sept. 27, 1928; d. William Paul and Eleanor Maude (Seivert) Eshbaugh; B.A. in English and Journalism, Syracuse (N.Y.) U., 1950; m. James Leon Hayes, Apr. 18, 1953; children—Pauli, Eli, Lauri Le June, Clayton, Merri Jess Bates. With Livingston County Republican, Geneseo, N.Y., summers, 1947-50, mng. editor, 1949-50; reporter Aurora (Colo.) Advocate, 1950-52; reporter-photographer Aspen (Colo.) Times, 1952-53, columnist, 1956—, reporter, 1972-77, assoc. editor, 1977-89, editor in chief, 1989-92, contbg. editor, 1992—; contbg. editor Destinations Mag., 1994—. tchr. Colo. Mountain Coll., 1979. Mem. Nat. Fedn. Press Women (1st prizes in writing and editing 1976-80), Colo. Press Women's Assn. (writing award 1974, 75, 78-85, sweepstakes award for writing 1977, 78, 84, 85, 91, 92, 93, also 2d place award 1976, 79, 82, 83, 94, 95, Woman of Achievement 1986). Mem. Aspen Community Ch. Photographer, editor: Aspen Potpourri, 1968, rev. edit., 1990. Home: PO Box 497 Aspen CO 81612-0497 Office: Box E Aspen CO 81612

HAYES, ROBERT B., communications executive; b. Seattle, Mar. 9, 1942; m. Donna-Marie Hayes; children: Robert Jr., Kendall, Justin. BA in Pub. Rels., San Jose State U., 1965. Pub. rels. rep. Sylvania Electronic Systems, 1965-66; account exec. Ruder & Finn, Inc., 1967-68; pub. rels. mgr. paper group Boise Cascade Corp., Boise, Idaho, 1968-71, press rels. mgr. corp. comms., 1971-72, dir. corp. comms., 1972-80, 81—; v.p. pub. affairs Gould, Inc., 1980; mem. Pub. Rels. Seminar. Past trustee Boise Art Mus.; past chmn. pub. rels. com. United Way Ada County; past pres. FUNDSY, Inc., bd. dirs.; bd. dirs. Boise River Festival. Mem. Pub. Rels. Soc. Am., Am. Forest & Paper Assn. (comms. steering com.), Nat. Assn. Mfrs. (past mem. pub. rels. coun.), Greater Boise C. of C. (past chmn. pub. rels. com.). Office: Boise Cascade Corp PO Box 50 Boise ID 83728-0050

HAYES, ROGER MATTHEW, deputy sheriff; b. Youngstown, Ohio, May 27, 1943; s. Roger and Edith (Wellendorff) H.; m. Carolyn Starr; children: Troy, Matthew, Todd, Adam, Trent, Sarah. BA, Columbia Coll., 1992; postgrad., U. Colo. Dep. sheriff Arapahoe County (Colo.) Sheriff Dept., 1986—. Past pres. Arapahoe County Rep. Men's Club; pres. Fraternal Order of Police, Greenwood Village, Colo.; mem. mil. acad. selection com. U.S. Senator William Armstrong, Denver, 1982, White House Adv. Team, Reagen/Bush, Denver, 1982. Sgt. USMC, 1963-66, Vietnam. Recipient medal of Merit Air Force Assn., Washington, 1984. Mem. Am. Soc. Pub. Adminstrs., Am. Sociol. Assn. Home: 1857 S Union Blvd Lakewood CO 80228-3973

HAYES, STEVEN LEE, lawyer; b. Ft. Smith, Ark., Oct. 12, 1947; s. Fred B. and Frances S. (Stanley) H.; m. Paula M. Webster, Apr. 30, 1990; 1 child, Nicole S. BA in History, U. Ark., 1969; LLB, U. San Francisco, 1979. Bar: Calif. 1979. Ptnr. Pritzker & Hayes, L.A., 1979-83, pres., 1983-92; pvt. practice L.A., 1992—; pres. Citizens for an Alt. Tax System, L.A., 1990—. Contbr. articles to profl. jours. Mem. Phi Beta Kappa. Home and Office: Citizens for an Alt Tax System 1015 Oneonta Dr Los Angeles CA 90065-4255

HAYES, THOMAS A., credit manager; b. Rockford, Ill., Nov. 4, 1959; s. Robert E. and Barbara C. Hayes; m. Carol E. Hayes, July 20, 1991. BS in Fin., No. Ill. U., 1982; MBA, U. Ill., Chgo., 1988. Credit analyst First Nat. Bank Freeport, Ill., 1982-84; account mgr. MNC Fin., Oak Brook, Ill., 1984-89; credit mgr., v.p. CIT Group/Credit Fin. Inc., L.A., 1989—. Performer Scandia Dancers. Libertarian. Methodist. Home: 12207 Summertime Ln Culver City CA 90230-4588 Office: CIT Group 1925 Century Park E Los Angeles CA 90067-2701

HAYMAN, RICHARD WARREN JOSEPH, conductor; b. Cambridge, Mass., Mar. 27, 1920; s. Fred Albert and Gladys Marie (Learned) H.; m. Maryellen Daly, June 25, 1960; children: Suzanne Marie, Olivia Kathryn. D Hum. (hon.), Detroit Coll. Bus., 1980. Free-lance composer, arranger 20th Century Fox, Warner Bros., MGM, Universal Film Studios; music arranger, dir. Vaughn Monroe Orch. records and TV show, N.Y.C., 1945-50; chief arranger Arthur Fiedler and Boston Pops Orchestra, 1950-88; mus. dir. Mercury Record Corp., N.Y.C., 1950-65, Time-Mainstream Records, N.Y.C., 1960-70; prin. pops condr. Detroit Symphony Orchs., St. Louis, Birmingham (Ala.), Hartford (Conn.), Calgary (Can.), Grand Rapids (Mich.) Symphony Orch., London (Ont., Can.) Orch. Composer: No Strings Attached, Dansero, Skipping Along, Carriage Trade, Serenade to a Lost Love, Olivia, Suzanne, Freddie the Football; recorded and released 30 C.D.'s on Naxos Internat. Records with own symphony orch., 1990-91. Recipient Best Instrumental Record award Sta. WERE, Cleve., 1963, Best TV Comml. Jingle award Nat. Acad. Rec. Arts and Scis., (N.Y.C.), 1960; star dedicated to him on Hollywood Blvd Walk of Fame. Mem. Nat. Acad. Rec. Arts and Scis., ASCAP, Am. Fedn. Musicians. Roman Catholic. Office: Richard Hayman Prodns 784 US Highway 1 Ste 22-b North Palm Beach FL 33408 also: St Louis Symphony Orch 718 N Grand Blvd Saint Louis MO 63103

HAYMOND, J. BRENT, chemical company executive, state legislator; b. Provo, Utah, Sept. 18, 1936; s. Edwin James and Helen (Harmer) H.; m. Marilyn Woodward, June 20,1959 (div. 1971); children: Michael, Diane, David, Mary Ann; m. Janis S. Haymond, Dec. 20, 1975; 1 child, Eric James; stepchildren: Cathy, Pam, David; foster children: Debbie, Dawnette. BS, Brigham Young U., 1960; MBA, Northwestern U., 1962. Mgr. mktg. IBM, Seattle, 1962-70; mgr. data ctr. EDP, Vancouver, B.C., 1971-72; v.p. McKesson Drug Co., San Francisco, 1973-75; v.p., gen. mgr. Martin Wolfe, San Diego, 1976-78; pres. Weidmar Comm., Provo, 1979-82, Intex Corp., Springville, Utah, 1983-95; mem. Utah State Ho. Reps., 1991—. Mayor City of Springville, Utah, 1982-86; bd. dirs. Utah Mcpl. Assn. Power, Sandy, 1984-93, Springville World Folkfest, 1985-93; pres. bd. dirs. Springville Mus. Art, 1988-93; chair house Appropiations Human Svcs. & Health. Mem. C. of C., Kiwanis. Republican. Mem. LDS Ch. Home: 164 W 200 S Springville UT 84663-1812

HAYNE, HARRIET ANN, state legislator, rancher; b. Puget Island, Washington, Sept. 11, 1922; d. Albert Greger and Angeline Marie (Benjaminsen) Danielsen; m. Jack McVicar Hayne, Apr. 3, 1946; children: Mary Joan, John David, Alice Sue, Nancy Ann. Student, Healds Bus. Coll., San Francisco, 1941-42, Wash. State U., 1946-47. Rep. Mont. Legis. Assembly, 1979-80, 84—. Precinct, then state committeewoman, vice-chmn., active various campaigns Mont. Reps., Pondera County, 1964. Served as staff sgt. USMC, 1943-45. Mem. Am. Nat. Cattlewomen, Nat. Order Women Legislators, Am. Farm Bur., Am. Legion Aux., Am. Legion, Women Marines Assn., Nat. Fedn. Rep. Women. Lutheran.

HAYNER, HERMAN HENRY, lawyer; b. Fairfield, Wash., Sept. 25, 1916; s. Charles H. and Lillie (Reifenberger) H.; m. Jeannette Hafner, Oct. 24, 1942; children: Stephen, James K., Judith A. BA, Wash. State U., 1938; JD with honors, U. Oreg., 1946. Bar: Wash. 1946, Oreg. 1946, U.S. Dist. Ct. Wash. 1947, U.S. Ct. Appeals (9th cir.) 1947. Asst. U.S. atty. U.S. Dept. Justice, Portland, Oreg., 1946-47; atty. City of Walla Walla, Wash., 1949-53; ptnr. Minnick-Hayner, Walla Walla, 1949-93; mem. Wash. State exec. bd. U.S. West, Seattle, 1988—. Regent Wash. State U., Pullman, 1965-78; dir. YMCA, Walla Walla, 1956-67. Lt. col. Infantry, 1942-46. Decorated Bronze Star medal and four Battle Stars; recipient Disting. Svc. award Jr. C. of C., 1951, Wash. State U. Alumni award, 1988. Fellow ABA, Am. Coll. Trust & Estate Counsel; mem. Wash. State Bar Assn., Walla Walla County Bar Assn. (pres. 1954-55), Walla Walla C. of C. (merit award 1977, dir. 1973-88), Rotary (pres. 1956-57), Walla Walla Country Club (pres. 1956-57). Republican. Lutheran. Home: 1508 Ironwood Dr PO Box 454 Walla Walla WA 99362-9254 Office: Minnick-Hayner PO Box 1757 Walla Walla WA 99362-0348

HAYNER, JEANNETTE CLARE, state legislator; b. Jan. 22, 1919; m. Herman H. Hayner, 1942; children: Stephen A., James K., Judith A. BA, U. Oreg., 1940, JD, 1942, PhD (hon), Whitman Coll., 1992. Atty. Bonneville Power Co., Portland, Oreg., 1943-47; mem. Wash. Ho. of Reps., 1972-76, Wash. Senate from Dist. 16, 1977-92, minority leader, 1979-80, 83-86, majority leader, 1981-82, 87-92; dist. chmn. White House Conf. on Children and Youth, 1970; dir. Standard Ins. Co. Portland, 1974-90. Mem. Walla Walla Dist. 140 Sch. Bd., 1956-63, chmn. bd., 1959-61; mem. adv. bd. Walla Walla Youth and Family Svc. Assn., 1968-72; active YWCA, 1968-72; chmn. Walla Walla County Mental Health Bd., 1970-72; former mem. Wash. Coun. on Crime and Delinquency, Nuclear Energy Coun., Bonneville Power Regional Adv. Coun., State Wash. Organized Crime Intelligence Adv. Bd.; mem. Coun. State Govts. Governing Bd.; former asst. whip Republican Caucus. Mem. Wash. State Centennial Commn.; bd. dir. Washington Inst. for Policy Studies, 1992—; bd. dir. chmn. bd. TV Washington. Recipient Merit award Walla Walla C. of C., Pres's. award Pacific Luth. Univ., 1982, Pioneer award U. Oreg., 1988, Lifetime Achievement award Wash. State Ind. Colls., 1991, Washington Inst. Columbia, 1991; named Legislator of Yr. Nat. Rep. Legislators' Assn., 1986, Chairman's award, 1989, Wash. Young Rep. Citizen of Yr., 1987, Legislator of Yr. Nat. Rep. Legislators Assn., 1989. Mem. Oreg. Bar Assn., Delta Kappa Gamma (hon.), Kappa Kappa Gamma. Lutheran. Home: PO Box 454 Walla Walla WA 99362

HAYNES, CALEB VANCE, JR., geology and archaeology educator; b. Spokane, Wash., Feb. 29, 1928; m. Elizabeth Hamilton, Jan. 11, 1954 (div. 1991); 1 child, Elizabeth Anne.. Student, Johns Hopkins U., 1947-49; degree in geol. engring., Colo. Sch. Mines, 1956; PhD, U. Ariz., 1965. Mining geology cons., 1958-60; sr. project engr. Am. Inst. Research, Golden, Colo., 1956-60; sr. engr. Martin Co., Denver, 1960-62; geologist Nev. State Mus. Tule Springs Expedition, 1962-63; research asst. U. Ariz., Tucson, 1963-64, asst. prof. geology, 1965-68, prof. geoscis., anthropology, 1974—, Regents prof., 1991—; assoc. prof. So. Meth. U., Dallas, 1968-73, prof., 1973-74. Served with USAF, 1951-54. Guggenheim fellow 1980-81, Smithsonian sr. post doctoral fellow, 1987 ; grantee NSF, Nat. Geographic Soc., others. Fellow AAAS, Geol. Soc. Am. (Archeol. Geology award 1984); mem. NAS, Am. Quaternary Assn. (pres. 1976-78), Soc. Am. Archaeology (Fryxell award 1978), Sigma Xi. Office: U Ariz Dept Anthropology Tucson AZ 85721

HAYNES, EMILY LOUISE, secondary school educator; b. Schenectady, N.Y., Aug. 24, 1957; d. Richard Alexander and Janet Marie (Cisar) Fish; m. Mark Munro Haynes, Aug. 11, 1990; 1 child, Tamara Marie. BS, Cornell U., 1979; PhD in Biophysics, Syracuse (N.Y.) U., 1988. Cert. tchr. in secondary sci., Colo. Rsch. scientist Bristol Labs., Syracuse, 1979-81, Molecular Therapeutics, Inc., West Haven, Conn., 1987-88; postdoctoral fellow U. Colo., Boulder, 1988-89; sci. tchr. Jefferson High Sch., Edgewater, Colo., 1992—. Mem. AAAS, Nat. Sci. Tchrs. Assn. Office: Jefferson High Sch 2304 Pierce St Edgewater CO 80214

HAYNES, GARY ANTHONY, archaeologist; b. Long Beach, Calif., Sept. 30, 1948; s. Ellsworth Wallace and Martha Louise (Ryan) H. BA, U. Md., 1970; MA, Cath. U. Am., 1978, PhD, 1981. Vis. asst. prof. anthropology Cath. U. Am., Washington, 1981; assoc. prof. lectr. George Washington U., Washington, 1982; research assoc. anthropology dept. Smithsonian Inst., Washington, 1981-85; asst. prof. anthropology U. Nev., Reno, 1985-88, assoc. prof. anthropology, 1988—; founder, vice-chmn. bd. Zimbabwe (Africa) Nat. Parks Research Trust, 1987—. Author: Mammoths, Mastodonts, and Elephants, 1991; editor: Nev. Archaeologist, 1987—; contbr. articles to profl. jours. Active Scientist Exchange Acad. Scis. U.S. Nat. Research Council, 1987. Smithsonian Inst. fellow, 1980; grantee Nat. Geog. Soc., 1981-88, 91, Leakey Found., 1990, 91. Mem. Soc. Am. Archeology (Fryxell com. chmn. 1986-89), Am. Quaternary Assn., Soc. Vertebrate Paleontology, Zimbabwe Sci. Assn., Nev. Archaeol. Assn. (exec. com. 1987—), Arctic Inst. N.Am. Office: U Nev Dept Anthropology Reno NV 89557

HAYNES, JAMES EARL, JR., association executive; b. Bakersfield, Calif., Oct. 11, 1943; s. James E. and Ruth M. (Campbell) H.; m. Norma Beth Jordan, Feb. 10, 1978; 1 child, Andrew Jordan. B.A. in Journalism, Los Angeles State Coll., 1967. Asst. mgr. West Covina C. of C., Calif., 1966-68; mgr. Monterey Park C. of C., Calif., 1968-72; gen. mgr. ops. San Francisco C. of C., 1972-76; pres. Phoenix C. of C., 1976—; mem. bd. regents Insts. for Orgn. Mgmt. U.S. C. of C.; vice chmn. Western Internat. U. Bd. dirs. Western Internat. U. Mem. Am. C. of C. Execs. (bd. dirs., past chmn.), Ariz. C. of C. Mgrs. Assn. Office: Phoenix Chamber of Commerce 34 W Monroe St Phoenix AZ 85003-1708

HAYNES, MICHAEL SCOTT, SR., resource specialist; b. Hancock, Mich., Feb. 16, 1948; s. Russell L. and Hildegard Eleanor (Habel) H.; m. Joan Loree Donaldson, July 25, 1968; children: Michael Jr., Andrew Lloyd, Gregory Alan. BA in History, Calif. Luth. U., 1970; MS in Spl. Edn., Learning Disabled, Calif. State U., Long Beach, 1993. Cert. tchr. elem. edn., Calif., cert. resource specialist tchr., handicapped specialist, Calif. Tchr. elem. edn. Rio Lindo Sch., El Rio, Calif., 1970-71, Trinity Luth. Day Sch., Hawthorne, Calif., 1973-82; tchr. elem. edn. L.A. Unified Sch. Dist., 1982-88, learning handicapped specialist, 1988-90, resource specialist tchr., 1990—; tchr. chair Am. Luth. Edn. Assn., 1979-82; trustee L.A. Edn. Alliance Restructuring, 1992—; sec. sch. site United Tchrs. L.A., 1991-94. Scoutmaster Boy Scouts Am., 1983-90. With USCG, 1975-85. Recipient Wood badge Boy Scouts Am., 1983. Mem. Calif. Assn. Resource Specialists (univ. liaison 1991-92), So. Calif. Chihuahua Club, Inc. (sec. 1992-94), Orange Empire Dog Club, Kappa Delta Pi, Phi Delta Kappa. Office: El Sereno Mid Sch 2839 N Eastern Ave Los Angeles CA 90032-2701

HAYNES, WILLIAM ERNEST, lawyer, financial consultant, educator; b. Peoria, Ill., Aug. 22, 1936; s. Clarence Ernest and Lucille Ann Haynes; m. Willette Lancia Rothschild, Dec. 2, 1972; children: Lancia Ann, Sharon Elizabeth. BA in Fin., Loras Coll., Dubuque, Iowa, 1959; JD, Marquette U., Milw., 1964; MBA in Bus. Econs., Loyola U., Chgo., 1969. Bar: Wis. 1964, Ill. 1965, Calif. 1970; cert. specialist taxation law, Calif. Corp. counsel Gen. Fin. Co., Evanston, Ill., 1964-69; asst. contr. internat. tax Wells Fargo Bank, San Francisco, 1969-76; tax counsel Kaiser Aluminum and Chem. Corp., Oakland, Calif., 1976-79; prin. Law Offices of William E. Haynes and Assocs., San Francisco, 1979—; chief fin. officer Pacific Rim Ptnrs. Ltd., San Francisco, 1989—; pres. Gryphon Group Ltd., econ. cons., 1981-86; prin. The Bus. Mart Bus. Brokers, San Francisco, 1987—; prof. taxation, adj. faculty, McLaren Coll. of Bus., U. San Francisco; lectr. on law, taxation and fin. Mem. adv. com. on edn. State Bar of Calif.; bd. dirs. Meals on Wheels of San Francisco. With U.S. Army, 1959-61. Mem. ABA, Calif. Bar Assn., Am. Econs. Assn., San Francisco Internat. Tax Group, Internat. Assn. Fin. Planners, Calif. Hist. Soc., San Francisco Mus. Soc., World Affairs Council, Civil Air Patrol (capt.). Republican. Roman Catholic. Lodge: Rotary, Elks. Office: 50 California St Ste 1400 San Francisco CA 94111-4683

HAY-ROE, VICTOR, plastic surgeon; b. Edmonton, Alta., Can., Dec. 23, 1930; s. Edmund Archer and Ruth Mildred (Maddison) Hay-Roe; m. Elizabeth Mae Davison, May 8, 1953 (div. 1978); children: Glenn Cameron, Elizabeth Diane, Scott Richard; m. Lynn Siu, Apr. 19, 1980. BSc, U. Alta., 1953, MD, 1955. Resident in surgery Queen's Hosp., Honolulu, 1956-59; resident in plastic surgery U. Pitts. Sch. Medicine, 1963-66; chief of plastic surgery Honolulu Med. Group, Inc., 1967—; clin. assoc. prof. plastic surgery, U. Hawaii, Honolulu, 1973—; trip leader, Interplast plastic surgery team to Samoa, 1978, Jamaica, 1988, 90. Mem. Hawaii Plastic Surgery Soc. (pres. 1986-88), Northwest Soc. Plastic Surgeons, Am. Soc. Plastic and reconstructive Surgeons. Republican. Home: 2277 Halekoa Dr Honolulu HI 96821 Office: Honolulu Med Group Inc 550 S Beretania St Honolulu HI 96813-2405

HAYS, BONNIE LINN, county official; b. Silverton, Oreg., Aug. 21, 1950; d. Lacy Emmett and Ethel Marie (Hunt) Bowlsby; m. Robert Verne Hays, Mar. 21, 1972 (dec. Aug. 1976); m. Arthur J. Lewis, Aug. 22, 1981. BS, Oreg. State U., 1972; postgrad. Portland State U., 1973-74, Rocky Mt. Inst., 1982, Sch. Pub. Adminstrn. Lewis & Clark Coll., Northwestern Sch. Law, 1985-87. Cert. tchr. secondary edn., Oreg. Tchr. high sch. Astoria Sch. Dist., Oreg., 1972-75; ins. agt. Equitable Life Assurance Co., Portland, Oreg., 1975-77; br. mgr. Transamerica Title Ins. Co., Beaverton, Oreg., 1977-82; county commr. Washington County, Hillsboro, Oreg., 1981-95; advisor Washington County Community Corrections, Hillsboro, 1983-93, elected chmn., bd. commrs., 1987-95; candidate exec. officer Metro Gen. Election, 1994; dir. State Job Tng. Coordinating Council, Salem, Oreg., 1985-88, Multnomah-Washington Pvt. Industry Council, Portland, 1983-87; project dir. Washington County Driving Under the Influence of Intoxicants Act Com., Hillsboro. Mem. Commn. on Accreditation for Corrections, 1985-92; pres. Washington County Visitors Assn., 1989-90; bd. dirs. Un Lugar para Niños, Hillsboro, 1984-94; bd. mgmt., chmn. YMCA of Washington County, Beaverton, 1983-89; corp. bd. dirs. YMCA of Columbia-Williamette, 1987-89; bd. dirs. Tualatin Valley Econ. Devel. Corp., 1987—, Washington County Roundtable for Youth, 1988-93, El Centro Cultural, 1989-94, Washington County Hist. Soc., Hillsboro, 1985-89, pres., 1986-88; mem. Young Reps. of Oreg., Salem, 1984-89; mem. Oreg. Episc. Sch. Wetlands Adv. Com., 1986; head of delegation Dalsuh (Korea) Tech. Exch. Team Mcpl. Govts., 1991. Named One of Washington County's 10 Most Influential People, Valley Times Newspaper Poll, 1985, Woman of Distinction, Environ. Columbia River Girl Scout coun., 1992. Mem. Am. Corrections Assn., Assn. Oreg. Counties (com. pub. safety and human resources 1982-90, vice chmn. 1982, chmn. 1986-90, 1st v.p. 1990, pres. 1990-91), Nat. Assn. Counties (justice and pub. safety steering com. 1987-92, energy & environ. steering com. 1994), Multnomah Athletic Club. Republican. Roman Catholic. Avocation: gourmet cooking. Home: 5469 NW Deerfield Way Portland OR 97229-1757 Office: Washington County Courthouse 155 N 1st Ave Hillsboro OR 97124-3072

HAYS, DANIEL WILLIAM, writer, counselor, lecturer; b. Medford, Oreg., Sept. 1, 1944; s. James Franklin and Celia Helena (Reinhart) H. B.S. in Humanities, So. Oreg. Coll., 1966; M.S. in Humanities, 1968; M.S. in Psychol. Counseling, U. Oreg., 1982. Writer/supr. Merrie Eng., Ashland, Oreg., 1968-72; editor/writer Cygnus Communications, Eugene, Oreg., 1975-79; publicity dir. Jamil, Eugene, 1979; instr. English, U. Oreg., Eugene, 1979-80; writer Landmark Design, Eugene, 1980-82; communication trainer State of Oreg., Salem, 1982-86, editor Mgmt. Insight, 1982-86; free-lance writer for newspapers and mags., 1972—; book and theatre critic Salem Statesman Jour., 1994—; pvt. practice counseling, Ashland, Eugene and Salem, 1966—; actor Oreg. Shakespeare Festival, Ashland, 1964-68, stage mgr., 1969. Theatrical dir., 1969—; lectr. on Shakespeare and the occult, 1968—. Editor, Homefinder mag., 1975-77, Eugene Living 1977-79. Researcher, writer Citizens for Better Govt., Ashland, 1968; writer, coordinator Sister City Com., Ashland, 1970. Carpenter Found. scholar, 1962-66; Oreg. Shakespearean Festival scholar, 1968; Theatre Guild scholar U. Oreg., 1972. Democrat. Home: 1523 Salishan St SE Salem OR 97302-3339

HAYS, DIANA JOYCE WATKINS, consumer products company executive; b. Riverside, Calif., Aug. 29, 1945; d. Donald Richard and Evelyn Christine (Kolvoord) Watkins; m. Gerald N. Hays, Jan 30, 1964 (div. Jan. 1970), 1 child, Tad Damon. BA, U. Minn., 1975, MBA, 1982. Dir. environ./phys. sci. Sci. Mus. Minn., St. Paul, 1972-76; dir. mktg. rsch. No. Natural Gas Co., Omaha, 1977-78; mktg. asst., asst. product mgr. Gen. Mills, Inc., Mpls., 1978-81; product mgr. ortho pharms. Consumer Products div. Johnson & Johnson, Raritan, N.J., 1981-82, product dir. home diagnostics, 1982-86; mktg. dir. new market devel. Consumer Products div. Becton Dickinson & Co., Franklin Lakes, N.J., 1986-90; dir. home diagnostics worldwide program Becton Dickinson Advanced Diagnostics Div. Becton Dickinson & Co., Balt., 1990-93; founder, pres. Exec. Computing Solutions, Inc., Vista, Calif., 1991—; product mktg. mgr. Jostens Learning Corp., San Diego, 1994—; chmn. energy exhibit com. Assn. Sci.-Tech. Ctrs., Washington, 1974-75. Producer Ecologenie, 1975. Recipient Tribute to Women and Industry award YWCA, 1989. Mem. Am. Mktg. Assn., NAFE, Twin Mgmt. Forum, Am. Assn. of Health Svcs. Mktg., Capital PC User Group, Beta Gamma Sigma (life). Republican. Roman Catholic. Office: Jostens Learning Corp 9920 Pacific Heights Blvd San Diego CA 92121-4330

HAYS, HOWARD H. (TIM HAYS), editor, publisher; b. Chgo., June 2, 1917; s. Howard H. and Margaret (Mauger) H.; m. Helen Cunningham, May 27, 1947 (div. Dec. 1988); children: William, Thomas; m. Susie Gudermuth, Sept. 1992. BA, Stanford U., 1939; LLB, Harvard U., 1942. Bar: Calif. 1946. Spl. agt. FBI, 1942-45; reporter San Bernardino (Calif.) Sun, 1945-46; asst. editor Riverside (Calif.) Daily Press, 1946-49, editor, 1949-65, editor, co-pub., 1965-83, editor, pub., chief exec. officer, 1983-88, editor, chmn., chief exec. officer, 1989-92, chmn. bd., 1992—; Mem. Pulitzer Prize Bd., 1976-86; mem. AP Bd., 1980-89, vice chmn. 1988-89. Bd. visitors John S. Knight Fellowships for Profl. Journalism U. So. Calif., 1991-93; mem. nat. com. Washington U. Sch. of Art, 1992—. Recipient Dist. award Calif. Jr. C. of C., 1951; named Pub. of Year Calif. Press Assn., 1968. Mem. Calif. Bar Assn., Am. Soc. Newspaper Editors (dir. 1969-76, pres. 1974-75), Stanford Alumni Assn. (dir. 1970-74), Internat. Press Inst. (chmn. Am. com. 1971-72, mem. exec. bd. 1977-83), Am. Press Inst. (bd. dirs. 1973—, chmn. 1978-83), New Directions for News (bd. dirs. 1987-92), Nature Conservancy Calif. (bd. dirs. 1982-86), Kappa Tau Alpha. Home: 3724 Utah Pl Saint Louis MO 63116-4831 Office: Press-Enterprise PO Box 792 3512 14th St Riverside CA 92502-0792

HAYS, JONATHAN FINCHER, newspaper executive; b. L.A., Oct. 29, 1955; s. Daniel Mauger and Esther (Fincher) H.; divorced; 1 child, Rachel Elizabeth. BA in History, U. So. Calif., L.A., 1981; MBA in Mktg., Claremont Grad. Sch., 1985. Mem. staff Press Enterprise Co., Riverside, Calif., 1981-83; account exec. CBS, Inc., L.A., 1985-87; account exec. Press Enterprise Co., Riverside, 1987-90, asst. gen. mgr., 1990-94, gen. mgr., exec.

v.p., 1987-90. Democrat. Office: Press Enterprise Co 3512 14th St Riverside CA 92504

HAYS, RICK F., public relations executive; b. St. Joseph, Mo., Oct. 27, 1952; s. William Andy and Alma LaVonne (Temple) H.; m. Jane Reid, Aug. 16, 1975; children: Matthew Patrick, Benjamin Reid, Lara Elizabeth. BS in Journalism, U. No. Colo., 1973. Editor Town & Country News, Greeley, Colo., 1973-74; pub. relations rep. Mountain Bell, Greeley, 1974-77; pub. relations supr. Mountain Bell, Tucson, 1977-79; pub. relations mgr. Mountain Bell, Denver, 1979-83; dir. regional pub. rels. U S WEST Communications, Boise, Idaho, 1984—; mem. mktg. com. Boise Area Econ. Devel. Coun., 1987—; chair Idaho Bus. Week, 1991; chair edn. com. IACI, 1993-94; exec. com. ID Sch. Improvement Com., 1993—. Coach Capital Youth Soccer, 1986-93; mem. troop com. Boy Scouts Am., 1989-94; mem. strategic com. Idaho Edn. Project, 1990-91; mem. exec. bd. Ada County United Way, Boise, 1991—; mem. adv. bd. Boise Sch. Ptnrs. in Edn., 1991—; active Schs. 2000, 1992—; mem. ecumenical commn. Cath. Ch., 1990—. Recipient award Idaho Assn. Supervision and Curriculum Devel., 1990; named Outstanding Young Man, 1992. Mem. Pub. Rels. Soc. Am. (bd. dirs. 1988—), Jaycees (bd. dirs. Greeley, Colo. 1976-77). Roman Catholic. Office: US WEST Comm 999 Main St Fl 11 Boise ID 83702-9001

HAYS, RONALD JACKSON, naval officer; b. Urania, La., Aug. 19, 1928; s. George Henry and Fannie Elizabeth (McCartney) H.; m. Jane M. Hughes, Jan. 29, 1951; children: Dennis, Michael, Jacquelyn. Student, Northwestern U., 1945-46; B.S., U.S. Naval Acad., 1950. Commd. ensign U.S. Navy, 1950, advanced through grades to adm., 1983; destroyer officer Atlantic Fleet, 1950-51; attack pilot Pacific Fleet, 1953-56; exptl. test pilot Patuxent River, Md., 1956-59; exec. officer Attack Squadron 106, 1961-63; tng. officer Carrier Air Wing 4, 1963-65; comdr. All Weather Attack Squadron, Atlantic Fleet, 1965-67; air warfare officer 7th Fleet Staff, 1967-68; tactical aircraft plans officer Office Chief Naval Ops., 1969-71; comdg. officer Naval Sta., Roosevelt Roads, P.R., 1971-72; dir. Navy Planning and Programming, 1973-74; comdr. Carrier Group 4, Norfolk, Va., 1974-75; dir. Office of Program Appraisal, Sec. of Navy, Washington, 1975-78; dep. and chief staff, comdr. in chief U.S. Atlantic Fleet, Norfolk, Va., 1978-80; comdr. in chief U.S. Naval Force Europe, London, 1980-83; vice chief naval ops. Dept. Navy, Washington, 1983-85; comdr. in chief U.S. Pacific Command, Camp H.M. Smith, Hawaii, 1985-88; pres., chief exec. officer Pacific Internat. Ctr. for High Tech. Rsch., Honolulu, Hawaii, 1988-92; tech. cons., 1992—. Decorated D.S.M. with 3 gold stars, Silver Star with 2 gold stars, D.F.C. with silver star and gold star, Legion of Merit, Bronze Star with combat V, Air Medal with numeral 14 and gold numeral 3, Navy Commendation medal with gold star and combat V. Baptist. Home and Office: 869 Kamoi Pl Honolulu HI 96825-1318

HAYWARD, FREDRIC MARK, social reformer; b. N.Y.C., July 10, 1946; s. Irving Michael and Mildred (Feingold) H.; m. Ingeborg Beck, Aug. 18, 1971 (div. 1974); 1 child, KJ. BA, Brandeis U., Waltham, Mass., 1967; MA, Fletcher Sch. Law & Diplomacy, Medford, Mass., 1968, MALD, 1969. Exec. dir. Men's Rights, Inc., Boston, 1977—; vis. lectr. Tufts U., Medford, Mass., 1979; lectr. in field; conductor workshops in field; mem. adv. bd. Ctr. for Men's Studies, 1988-93; host, prodr. The SacraMENshow. Author 3 published anthologies; contbg. editor: The Liberator, Forest Lake, Minn., 1988-89; contbg. writer Spectator, Berkeley, Calif., 1988—; contbr. articles to profl. jours. Farrell fellowship on Men, 1989; Fletcher Sch. Law and Diplomacy fellow, 1967-69; recipient award of Excellence Nat. Coalition of Free Men, 1993. Mem. Nat. Congress for-Men (bd. dirs. 1981-90), Am. Fedn. TV and Radio Artists, Men. Internat. (bd. dirs. 1982-86), Sacramento Valley Men's Coun., Children's Rights Coun. Office: Mr Inc PO Box 163180 Sacramento CA 95816-9180

HAYWORTH, JOHN DAVID, JR., congressman, sportscaster, commentator, broadcaster; b. High Point, N.C., July 12, 1958; s. John David and Gladys Ethel (Hall) H.; m. Mary Denise Yancey, Feb. 25, 1989; children: Nicole Irene, Hannah Lynne. BA in Speech and Polit. Sci., N.C. State U., 1980. Sports anchor, reporter Sta. WPTF-TV, Raleigh, N.C., 1980-81, Sta. WLWT-TV, Cin., 1986-87; sports anchor Sta. WYFF-TV (formerly Sta. WFBC-TV), Greenville, S.C., 1981-86, Sta. KTSP-TV, Phoenix, 1987-94; congressman, Ariz. U.S. House Reps., Washington, D.C., 1995—; radio commentator; play-by-play broadcaster. Dist. committeeman Ariz. Rep. Com., Scottsdale, 1988-89; bd. dirs. Am. Humanics Found., Ariz. State U., Tempe, 1991-92; chmn. Scout-A-Rama, Theodore Roosevelt coun. Boy Scouts Am., 1991-92. Recipient honor roll award Atlantic Coast Conf., 1977, Young Am. award Unharrie coun. Boy Scouts Am., 1979, Friend of Edn. award Sch. Dist. Greenville County, 1985, Sch. Bell/Friend of Edn. award S.C. Dept. Edn., 1985. Mem. Rotary (bd. dirs. Phoenix 1989-90). Baptist. Office: US House Reps 1024 Longworth House Office Bldg Washington DC 20515-0306*

HAZEKAMP, PHYLLIS WANDA, library director; b. Chgo.; d. John Edward and Mary Ann (Demski) Wojciechowski. BA, De Paul U., 1947; MSLS, La. State U., 1959; postgrad., Santa Clara U. Cert. tchr., Calif., Ariz. Libr. Agrl. Experiment Sta., U. Calif., Riverside, 1959-61; tech. libr. Lockheed Tech. Libr., Palo Alto, Calif., 1962-63; asst. law libr. Santa Clara (Calif.) U. Law Sch., 1963-72; libr. dir. Carmelite Seminary, San Jose, Calif., 1973-78; reference libr. San Jose State U., 1978-79; libr. SAI Engrs., Santa Clara, 1980-81; libr. dir. Palmer Coll. Chiropractive, San Jose, 1981-90, Camp Verde (Ariz.) Community Libr., 1990—; mem. Cultural Commn., Santa Clara, 1968-72; pres. Santa Clara Art Assn., 1973-74. Mem. Kiwanis Internat. (bd. dirs. 1992-93). Office: Camp Verde Community Libr 130 Black Bridge Loop Rd Camp Verde AZ 86322

HAZEL, JOANIE BEVERLY, elementary educator; b. Medford, Oreg., Jan. 20, 1946; d. Ralph Ray Lenderman and Vivian Thelma (Holtane) Spencer; m. Larry Aydon Hazel, Dec. 28, 1969. BS in Edn., So. Oreg. Coll., Ashland, 1969; MS in Edn., Portland State U., 1972; postgrad., U. Va., 1985. Elem. tchr. Beaverton (Oreg.) Schs., 1972-76, Internat. Sch. Svcs., Isfahan, Iran, 1976-78; ESL instr. Lang. Svcs., Tucker, Ga., 1983-84; tchr. Fairfax (Va.) Schs., 1985-86; elem. tchr. Beaverton (Oreg.) Schs., 1990—. Mem. AAAS, U.S. Hist. Soc., Platform Soc., Smithsonian Instn., Am. Mus. Natural History, Nat. Mus. Women in Arts, U.S. Hist. Soc., The United Nations, The Colonial Williamsburg Found., Wilson Ctr., N.Y. Acad. Scis. Home: 9247 SW Martha St Portland OR 97224-5577

HAZEN, PAUL MANDEVILLE, banker; b. Lansing, Mich., 1941; married. BA, U. Ariz., 1963; MBA, U. Calif., Berkeley, 1964. Asst. mgr Security Pacific Bank, 1964-66; v.p. Union Bank, 1966-70; chmn. Wells Fargo Realty Advisors, 1970-76; with Wells Fargo Realty Advisors, San Francisco, 1979—, exec. v.p., mgr. Real Estate Industries Group, 1979-80, mem. exec. office Real Estate Industry Group, 1980, vice-chmn. Real Estate Industries Group, 1980-84, pres., chief oper. officer Real Estate Industries Group, 1984—, also dir. Real Estate Industries Group, 1984—; pres., treas. Wells Fargo Mortgage & Equity Trust, San Francisco, 1977-84; with Wells Fargo & Co., San Francisco, 1978—, from exec. v.p. to vice-chmn., pres., chief operating officer, 1978-95, chmn, CEO, 1995—, also dir.; trustee Wells Fargo Mortgage & Equity Trust; bd. dirs. Pacific Telesis Group. Office: Wells Fargo Bank NA 420 Montgomery St San Francisco CA 94104-1205*

HAZEWINKEL, VAN, manufacturing executive; b. L.A., Oct. 2, 1943; s. Ben J. and Betty J. (Bishop) H.; m. Linda Bennett, Sept. 11, 1965; children: Van, Karey. BS, Calif. State U., Long Beach, 1967. With Daily Indsl. Tools Inc., Costa Mesa, Calif., 1959—, v.p., 1966-78, pres., 1978—. Founding mem. bd. dirs. Greater Irvine (Calif.) Indsl. League, 1970-73. Mem. Soc. Mfg. Engrs. Office: 3197D Airport Loop Dr Costa Mesa CA 92626-3420

HEACOX, RUSSEL LOUIS, mechanical engineer; b. Big Timber, Mont., Feb. 7, 1922; s. Charles Lewis and Gladys Ellen (Gibson) H.; m. Jacqueline J. Jewett, Sept. 22, 1944 (dec. 1974); children: William J., Teri Bertoli; m. Ketty Hansine Jorgenson, Dec. 22, 1976. BSME, U. Wash., 1950. Registered profl. engr., Calif. Equipment design engr. P & Z Co. Inc., South San Francisco, Calif., 1966-74; owner Heacox Engring. Designs, Tiburon, Calif., 1974—. Capt. USMC, 1943-46, PTO. Mem. NSPE, Crane Certification Assn., Scottish Rite Shrine Assn., Masons. Home and Office: 131 Esperanza St Tiburon CA 94920-1914

HEAD, DWIGHT TERRY, art educator; b. Sacramento, Nov. 21, 1964; s. Robert Lee and Frances (Powell) H. AA in Computer Sci., MTI Bus. Coll., Sacramento, 1989; AA, Sacramento City Coll., 1991. Freelance graphic artist D.T. Head Graphics, Sacramento, 1982—; painter, demonstrator Sacramento State Fair, 1993-94; art educator Sacramento Sch. Dist., 1992—; art instr. Crocker Art Mus., Sacramento, 1993—; art instr. on bd. dirs. Celebration Arts, Visual Arts; art instr. Children Art Festival, Sacramento, 1993. Recipient Third Pl. in Fine Art Show, Sacramento County Fair, 1994. Mem. Assn. Hawaii Artist, Salvador Dali Mus. Home: PO Box 8936 Honolulu HI 96830-0936

HEAD, SAMUEL, community development executive; b. Tampa, Nov. 20, 1948; m. Karen Theresa Grant, Oct. 24, 1988; children: Samuel Sherman, Shaunda Denise, Jonathan Spencer. BS, Fla. A&M U., 1970; MA in Mgmt., Nat. U., San Diego, 1989; MPA, Golden Gate U., 1993. Dir. comml. revitalization Nev. Econ. Devel. Co., Las Vegas, 1984-85; sr. mgmt. analyst Clark County, Las Vegas, 1985-92; interim city mgr. City of Seaside, Calif., 1993-94, asst. city mgr., cmty. devel. dir., 1992-95; prin. The HEAD Group, Henderson, Nev., 1995—. Commr. Monterey County Film Commn., Monterey, Calif., 1992-94. Mem. Internat. City Mgr. Assn., Nat. Forum for Black Pub. Adminstrs., Am. Soc. Pub. Adminstrn., Uptown Kiwanis (Las Vegas) (pres., sec., 1986-92, Meritorious award 1988), Alpha Phi Alpha (pres., sec. 1967—, 25 yr award 1992). Republican. Baptist. Office: The HEAD Group PO Box 50252 Henderson NV 89016

HEADDING, LILLIAN SUSAN (SALLY HEADDING), writer, forensic clairvoyant; b. Milw., Jan. 1, 1944; d. David Morton and Mary Davis (Berry) Coleman; m. James K. Hill (div. 1976); children: Amy Denise; m. John Murray Headding (div. 1987). BA, U. Nev., 1975; MA, U. Pacific, 1976. With Gimbels, Milw., 1963-65; spl. assignment g2 USAPIC U.S. Women's Army Corp., 1963; retail mgr. Frandisco Corp., N.Y.C., 1965-66; dist. mgr. Anita Shops, Los Angeles, 1966-68; store mgr. Clothes Closet, Sunnyvale, Calif., 1969-70; owner Lillian Headding Interiors & Comml. Design, Pittsburg, Calif., 1976-88; mfrs. rep. and assoc. J.G. West, San Francisco, 1989-91; Karate instr. Sch. of the Tiger, Pleasant Hill, Calif., 1988-94, 1st degree black belt, 1973; clairvoyant, psychic cons. on numerous crime and missing persons cases, U.S., Can., Eng. and France, 1972—. Author: (as Sally Davis): When Gods Fall; author short stories, poetry. Bd. dirs. and co-founder Cmty. Action Against Rape, Las Vegas, 1972-75; self-def. expert Las Vegas Met. Police Dept., 1972-75, North Las Vegas (Nev.) Police Dept.; co-supr. Family & Children's Svcs., Contra Costa County, Calif., 1985-86. Mem. AAUW, People for Ethical Treatment of Animals, Walnut Creek Writers Group (pres.), Berkeley Women's Writer Group, Philippine Hawaiian Black Belters Assn. Democrat. Jewish. Office: 5333 Park Highlands Blvd #33 Concord CA 94521-3718

HEADLEE, ROLLAND DOCKERAY, association executive; b. Los Angeles, Aug. 27, 1916; s. Jesse W. and Cleora (Dockeray) H.; m. Alzora D. Burgett, May 13, 1939; 1 dau., Linda Ann (Mrs. Walter Pohl). Student, UCLA, 1939. Asst. mgr. Par Assocs., Los Angeles, 1935-43, Finance Assocs., 1946-58; financial cons., lectr., 1958-63; account exec. Walter E. Heller & Co., Los Angeles, 1963-66; exec. dir. emeritus Town Hall Calif., Los Angeles, 1966—; dir. Am. Internat. Bank, Mfrs. Assocs., R.H. Investment Corp. Mem. adv. bd., bd. dirs., Los Angeles council Boy Scouts Am. Served to 1st lt. AUS, 1943-46. Mem. Mensa, Los Angeles World Affairs Council, Newcomen Soc. Methodist. Clubs: Commonwealth of Calif, Economic of Detroit, Los Angeles Stock Exchange. Home: 8064 El Manor Ave Los Angeles CA 90045-1434

HEADY, FERREL, retired political science educator; b. Ferrelview, Mo., Feb. 14, 1916; s. Chester Ferrel and Loren (Wightman) H.; m. Charlotte Audrey McDougall, Feb. 12, 1942; children—Judith Lillian, Richard Ferrel, Margaret Loren, Thomas McDougall. A.B., Washington U., St. Louis, 1937, A.M., 1938, Ph.D., 1940; hon. degrees, Park Coll., 1973, John F. Kennedy U., 1974, U. N.Mex., 1993. Jr. adminstrv. technician, also adminstrv. asst. Office Dir. Personnel, Dept. Agr., 1941-42; vis. lectr. polit. sci. U. Kansas City, 1946; faculty U. Mich., 1946-67, prof. polit. sci., 1957-67; dir. Inst. Pub. Adminstrn., 1960-67; acad. v.p. U. N.Mex., Albuquerque, 1967-68; pres. U. N.Mex., 1968-75, prof. pub. adminstrn. and polit. sci., 1975-81, prof. emeritus, 1981—; Asst. to commr. Com. Orgn. Exec. Br. of Govt., 1947-49; dir., chief adviser Inst. Pub. Adminstrn., U. Philippines, 1953-54; mem. U.S. del. Internat. Congress Adminstrn. Scis., Spain, 1956, 80, Germany, 1959, Austria, 1962, Poland, 1964, Mexico, 1974; exec. bd. Inter-Univ. Case Program, 1956-67; sr. specialist in residence East-West Center, U. Hawaii, 1965; mem. Conf. on Pub. Service, 1965-70; chmn. bd. Assoc. Western Univs., 1970-71; commr. Western Interstate Commn. Higher Edn., 1972-77; mem. commns. on bus. professions and water resources, mem. exec. com. Nat. Assn. State Univs. and Land Grant Colls., 1968-75. Author: Administrative Procedure Legislation in the States, 1952, (with Robert H. Pealy) The Michigan Department of Administration, 1956, (with Sybil L. Stokes) Comparative Public Administration: A Selective Annotated Bibliography, 1960, Papers in Comparative Public Administration, 1962, State Constitutions: The Structure of Administration, 1961, Public Administration: A Comparative Perspective, 1966, rev. edit., 1979, 5th edit., 1995; contbr. profl. jours. Chmn. state affairs com. Ann Arbor Citizens Council, Mich., 1949-52; mem. exec. com. Mich. Meml.-Phoenix Project and Inst. Social Research, 1960-66; mem. Gov. Mich. Constl. Revision Study Commn., 1960-62; schs. and univs. adv. bd. Citizens Com. for Hoover Report, 1949-52, 54-58; cons. to Ford Found., 1962; chmn. Council on Grad. Edn. in Pub. Adminstrn., 1966; mem., vice chmn. N.Mex. Gov.'s Com. on Reorgn. of State Govt., 1967-70; mem. N.Mex. Am. Revolution Bicentennial Commn., 1970-73, N.Mex. Gov.'s Com on Tech. Excellence, 1969-75, Nat. Acad. Pub. Adminstrn.; mem., vice chmn. N.Mex. Constl. Revision Commn., 1994—. Served to lt. USNR, 1942-46. Recipient Faculty Disting. Achievement award U. Mich., 1964, N.Mex. Disting. Pub. service award, 1973, award of distinction U. N.Mex. Alumni Assn., 1975, Outstanding Grad. Tchr. award U. N.Mex., 1981-82, Fulbright sr. lectureship, Colombia, 1992, Waldo award for career contbns. to lit. and leadership of pub. adminstrn., 1994. Mem. Am. Polit. Sci. Assn., Am. Soc. Pub. Adminstrn. (pres. 1969-70), AAUP (chmn. com. T 1957-61), Am. Council Edn. (mem. commn. on fed. relations 1969-72), Phi Beta Kappa, Phi Kappa Phi. Presbyterian. Home: 2901 Cutler Ave NE Albuquerque NM 87106-1714

HEALEY, MARK CALVIN, biologist, educator; b. Salt Lake City, Mar. 7, 1947; children: Rachelle, Jeffrey, Christopher. BS, U. Utah, 1971, MS, 1973; PhD, Purdue U., 1976; DVM, Miss. State U., 1981. Lic. veterinarian, Utah; lic. accredited veterinarian in Utah by USDA. Teaching asst., teaching fellow U. Utah, 1970-73; grad. instr. Sch. of Vet. Medicine Purdue U., Lafayette, Ind., 1973-76; instr. Tex. A&M U., College Station, 1976-77; resident Coll. of Vet. Medicine Miss. State U., 1978-81; rsch. asst. prof. Dept. Animal, Dairy and Vet. Scis. Utah State U., Logan, 1981-83, asst. prof. Dept. Animal, Dairy and Vet. Scis., 1983-86, asst. prof. joint appointment with Dept. of Biology, 1984—, assoc. prof. Depts. Biology and Animal, Dairy and Vet. Scis., 1986-91, asst. head Dept. Animal, Dairy and Vet. Scis., 1990—, prof., 1991—; outside peer reviewer USDA/Competitive Rsch. Grants Program, 1985—. Patentee bacterial extract vaccines for veterinary application; contbr. numerous articles to profl. jours. Recipient Phi Sigma Soc. award U. Utah, 1970, Outstanding Young Men of Am. Ann. award, 1982, Prof. of Yr. award Utah State U., 1986. Mem. Am. Soc. Parasitologists, Am. Assn. Vet. Parasitologists, Rocky Mountain Conf. Parasitologists, Am. Vet. Med. Assn., Intermountain Vet. Med. Assn., Utah Vet. Med. Assn., Vet. Med. Assn. of No. Utah, Am. Soc. Microbiology, Intermountain Br. of Am. Soc. for Microbiology, Conf. Rsch. Workers in Animal Disease, Western Food Animal Disease Rsch. Conf. Office: Utah State U Coll of Agriculture Dept Animal Dairy Vet Scis Logan UT 84322-5600

HEALY, ALICE FENVESSY, psychology educator, researcher; b. Chgo., June 26, 1946; d. Stanley John and Doris (Goodman) Fenvessy; m. James Bruce Healy, May 9, 1970; 1 dau., Charlotte Alexandra. AB summa cum laude, Vassar Coll., 1968; PhD, Rockefeller U., 1973. Asst. prof. psychology Yale U., New Haven, 1973-78, assoc. prof. psychology, 1978-81; assoc. prof. psychology U. Colo., Boulder, 1981-84, prof. psychology, 1984—; rsch. assoc. Haskins Labs., New Haven, 1976-80; mem. com. NIMH, Washington, 1979-81; co-investigator rsch. contract USAF, U. Colo., 1985-86; prin. investigator rsch. contract U.S. Army Rsch. Inst., U. Colo., 1986—, Naval Tng. Systems Ctr., 1993-94. Co-author: Cognitive Processes, 2d edit., 1986; editor: Memory and Cognition, 1986-89, (with S.M. Kosslyn and R.M. Shiffrin) From Learning Theory to Connectionist Theory: Essays in Honor of William K. Estes, Vol. I, 1992, From Learning Processes to Cognitive Processes: Essays in Honor of William K. Estes, Vol. II, 1992, (with L.E. Bourne Jr.) Learning and Memory of Knowledge and Skills: Durability and Specificity, 1995; assoc. editor Jour. Exptl. Psychology, 1982-84; contbr. chpts. to books and over 100 articles to profl. jours. Recipient Sabbatical award James McKeen Cattell Fund, 1987-88; NSF Rsch. grantee, 1977-86, Spencer Found. Rsch. grantee, 1978-80. Fellow APA (exec. com. divsn. 3 1989-92, chair membership com. 1992-93), AAAS (nominating com. 1988-91, chair 1991, chair-elect psychology sect. 1994, chair psychology sect. 1995—); mem. Psychonomic Soc. (governing bd. 1987-92, publs. com. 1989-93), Soc. Math. Psychology, Rocky Mountain Psychology Assn. (pres.-elect 1993-94, pres. 1994-95, past pres. 1995—), Cognitive Sci. Soc., Univ. Club, Phi Beta Kappa, Sigma Xi. Home: 840 Cypress Dr Boulder CO 80303-2820 Office: U Colo Dept Psychology Campus Box 345 Boulder CO 80309-0345

HEALY, ANNE, sculptor; b. N.Y.C., Oct. 1, 1939; d. Robert Timothy and Mary Rita (Essig) H.; m. Richard Alois Synek, Feb. 28, 1960 (div. 1962); 1 child, Deirdre Leigh. BA, Queens Coll., 1961. One-woman exhbns. include U.S. Theatre Technicians Symposium, 1971, Solow Bldg., N.Y.C., 1971, A.I.R. Gallery, N.Y.C., 1972, 74, 78, 81, 83, CUNY Grad. Ctr., 1974, Hammarskjold Pla. Sculpture Garden, N.Y.C., 1974, 88 Pine St., N.Y.C., 1974-75, Zabriskie Gallery, N.Y.C., 1975, 78, Contemporary Art Ctr., Cin., 1976, Am.'s Cup Ave., Newport Art Assn., Susie Schochet Gallery, R.I., 1976, U. Mass., Amherst, 1976, A.I.R., N.Y.C., 1978, U. of South, Tex., 1979, San Francisco M.O.M.A. Rental Gallery, 1989; group exhbns. include Outdoor Installations, Basel, Switzerland, 1976, Paris, 1976; represented in permanent collections Solow Bldg., N.Y.C., Mus. Contemporary Crafts, N.Y.C., Dept. Cultural Affairs, N.Y.C., N.Y. Cultural Ctr., Mich. State U., Allen Art Mus., Oberlin, Ohio, CUNY Grad. Ctr.; commns. include Wayne State U. Health Care Inst., Detroit, 1979, Springfield Mus. Fine Art, Mass., 1979, City of Pitts., 1981, Prudential Life Ins., Newark, N.J., 1984, State of Wash., 1985, City of Oakland, Calif., 1986, Litton Industries, Los Colinas, Tex., 1986, Stanford U., 1990; instr. sculpture St. Ann's Sch., Bklyn., 1973-79; adj. asst. prof. Baruch Coll., CUNY, 1976-81; guest lectr. Mich. State U., 1973; vis. artist Mich. State U., 1973; guest lectr. U. Cin., 1974, 76, Smith Coll., Northampton, Mass., 1975, U. R.I., Kingston, 1975; vis. prof. U. Iowa, Iowa City, 1979; asst. prof. U. Calif. Berkeley, 1981-85, assoc. prof., 1985-94, prof. 1994—. Arts commr. for sculpture City of San Francisco, 1989—, pres. arts commn., 1992-95. Featured in numerous popular mags. and profl. jours.; contbr. articles to profl. jours. Office: U Calif Dept Art Kroeber Hall Berkeley CA 94720

HEALY, BARBARA ANNE, insurance company executive, financial planner; b. Chgo., May 21, 1951; d. William James Healy and Eileen Mary (Dooley) Dashiell; m. Joel Feldman, June 25, 1991. BA, No. Ill. U., 1973; MBA, DePaul U., 1976. Cert. fin. planner. Dept. head, instr. St. Benedict High Sch., Chgo., 1973-76; account rep. Xerox Corp., Chgo., 1976-78, mktg. specialist, 1978-79, high volume sr. sales exec., 1979-81; western dist. mgr. McGraw Hill, N.Y.C., 1981-82; fin. planner United Resources Ins. Service, Torrance, Calif., 1982-83, sales mgr., 1983-85, exec. v.p., 1985-86; regional v.p. United Resources Ins. Service, Foster City, Calif., 1986-89; v.p., nat. mktg. dir. Met. Life Resources (formerly United Resources Ins. Svcs.), Phoenix, 1990—; Tempe, Ariz.; instr. Trenton Coll., Riverside, Ill., City Coll. Chgo., Northeastern Ill. U., Chgo., Prairie State Coll., Chicago Heights, 1976-81. Author: Financial Planning for Educators, 1987; contbr. articles to prof. jours.; speaker in field. Mem. Internat. Assn. Fin. Planners, Inst. Cert. Fin. Planners, Registry Fin. Planning Practitioners, Nat. Council Fin. Edn. Republican. Roman Catholic. Home: 10301 N 48th Pl Paradise Vly AZ 85253-1033 Office: Met Life Resources 1501 W Fountainhead Ste 650 Tempe AZ 85282-1846

HEALY, JAMES BRUCE, cooking school administrator, writer; b. Paterson, N.J., Apr. 15, 1947; s. James Burn and Margaret Mercy (Patterson) H.; m. Alice Fenvessy, May 9, 1970; 1 child, Charlotte Alexandra. BA, Williams Coll., 1968; PhD, The Rockefeller U., 1973. Mem. faculty Inst. Advanced Study, Princeton, N.J., 1973-75; J.W. Gibbs instr. physics Yale U., New Haven, Conn., 1975-77, research affiliate, 1977-80; dir. Healy-Lucullus Sch. French Cooking, New Haven, 1978-80, Boulder, Colo., 1980—; cons. Claudine's, Denver, 1985-86; vis. instr. Salem (Mass.) State Coll., 1984, and various culinary schs. Author: Mastering the Art of French Pastry, 1984, The French Cookie Book, 1994; contbr. articles and revs. on restaurants and cooking to mags. and profl. jours. Mem. Internat. Assn. Cooking Profls. (cert.), Confederation Nationale des Patissiers, Glaciers, et Confiseurs de France. Presbyterian. Home and Office: Healy-Lucullus Sch French Cooking 840 Cypress Dr Boulder CO 80303-2820

HEALY, KIERAN JOHN PATRICK, lighting designer, consultant; b. London, June 6, 1957; came to U.S., 1980; citizen of Ireland.; s. Denis Finbarr and Dawn Josephine (O'Hannigan) H.; m. Debra Leslie Liebling, Jan. 6, 1990; 1 child, Conor Thomas. Student, Isleworth Polytechnic, Middlesex, Eng., 1975-76. Lighting designer Music, The Who, 1976-80, The Rolling Stones, U.S.A., 1980; v.p. Showlites, L.A., 1980-81; freelance in TV, lighting designer, 1982-89; dir. photography Klages Group Inc, Hollywood, Calif., 1989—. Lighting designer for TV programs, including Live Aid, Liberty Weekend Opening Ceremonies, Gracelands in Africa, Arsenio Hall Show, other spls. Mem. Nat. Acad. Cable Programming (ACE Nomination 1988), Acad. TV Arts and Scis. (Emmy Nominations 1984, 87, 89, 92), Assn. Cinemotograph Techs. and Allied Trades, Internat. Photographers Guild. Roman Catholic. Office: The Klages Group Inc 1438 N Gower St Los Angeles CA 90028-8383

HEALY, SONYA AINSLIE, health facility administrator; b. Sudbury, Ont., Can., Apr. 7, 1937; came to U.S., 1949; d. Walter B. and Wilma A. Scott; m. Richard C. Healy, Jr., Dec. 16, 1961. Diploma, Good Samaritan Hosp., West Palm Beach, Fla., 1958; student, U. Mass., 1963-64, NYU, 1964-66; BS, Boston U., 1969, MS in Med.-Surg. Nursing, 1974. Various staff nursing, charge nurse positions, suprs., med.-surg. and obstet. nursing, 1958-69; chmn. jr.-sr. teaching team Sch. of Nursing Melrose (Mass.) Wakefield Hosp., 1969-73; asst. dir. nurses Boston State Hosp., 1973-74; asst. dir., DON Mt. Zion Hosp. and Med. Ctr., 1974-75; asst. dir. patient care svcs., DON St. Elizabeth's Hosp., Boston, 1975-80, St. Joseph's Hosp., Nashua, N.H., 1980-82; adminstr. U. Calif. Med. Ctr., San Diego, 1982-91, corp. chief nursing officer, 1991, assoc. dir. hosp. and clinics, dir. patient care svcs., 1982—; mem. acad. affairs com., bd. trustees U. San Diego; clin. assoc. Ul. San Diego, 1984—; mem. adj. faculty San Diego State U.; mem. clin. faculty UCLA Sch. of Nursing; presenter in field. Author: The 12-hour Shift: Is It Viable?-Nursing Outlook, 1984, (handbook) Human Resource Management Handbook, 1987, Human Resources Management Handbook, 1987, Nursing Economics, 1989; mem. editorial adv. bd. dirs. OR Nurse Today; editorial rev. Nursing Economics; contbr. articles to profl. jours. Mem. ASNSA (nominations com. 1978, cert.), Am. Orgn. of Nurse Execs. (bd. dirs. 1990-92, by laws com. 1990-92), Mass. Soc. of Nursing Svcs. Adminstrs. (pres. pres. 1977), Calif. Soc. of Nursing Svc. Adminstrs. (task force on orgns. program com. 1984-85, bd. dirs. 1985-87, mem. com. 1987-88, long range planning com.), San Diego Dirs. of Nurses (sec. 1982-83, pres. 1988-89), Sigma Theta Tau (Zeta Mu chpt.).

HEARD, RONALD ROY, motion picture producer; b. Denver, Oct. 3, 1947; s. John Arthur and Louise Marie (Smith) H.; m. Kim Widing Aug. 12, 1967 (div. 1969). BS, Colo. State U., 1969; postgrad., U. Colo., 1969-72, U. Paris/Sorbonne, 1964-65. Prodn. design/stage mgr. The Rolling Stones, London, 1969-86; property/set dresser Universal Studios, Universal City, Calif., 1978-79, Warner Bros. Studios, Burbank, Calif., 1979-80; producer stage plays Hollywood, 1980-85; music video cons. L.A., 1984—; corres. CBS Network News, Chgo., 1971-72; writer/photographer UPI/Nat. Geographic/Denver Post, 1969-73; ptnr. Silver Screen Ptnrs. II and III, L.A., 1986—; CEO, pres. Radio Safari, 1991—; pres. Brightstar Entertainment dba Liberty Tree Studios, 1994—; owner Yankee Pride Ent., North Hollywood, Calif., 1986—. Exec. com. Dem. Party, Larimer County, Colo., 1972-79; Dem. candidate for Ho. of Rep., 1972, 76. Named honorary citizen of S.D. by Gov. Richard Kneip, 1972. Mem. Am. Film Inst., Smithsonian Instn., Statue of Liberty/Ellis Island Cen. Commn. Democrat.

HEARLE, KEVIN JAMES, poet, educator; b. Santa Ana, Calif., Mar. 17, 1958; s. H. David and L. Patricia (Flaherty) H.; m. Elizabeth Ellen Henderson, Nov. 26, 1983. AB in English with distinction, Stanford U., 1980; MFA in English, U. Iowa, 1983; MA in Lit., U. Calif., Santa Cruz, 1990, PhD in Lit., 1991. Poet, 1979—; teaching asst. U. Calif., Santa Cruz, 1987-91, lectr., 1993; lectr. San Jose (Calif.) State U., 1992-94; poet-in-the-schs. Iowa Ctr. for the Arts, Iowa City, 1982; teaching asst. U. Iowa, Iowa City, 1982-83; instr. Coe Coll., Cedar Rapids, Iowa, 1983-84; participant Nat. Endowment for Humanities Summer Seminar on Am. Indian Lit., U. Ill., Chgo., 1994. Author: Each Thing We Know Is Changed Because We Knew It and Other Poems, 1994; poetry co-editor Quarry West, 1988-92; reviewer Am. Lit., 1992—, We. Am. Lit., 1992—, Steinbeck Newsletter, 1992—; editl. bd. Steinbeck Newsletter, 1995—; asst. editor Viking Critical Library Edition of The Grapes of Wrath, 2d edit., 1995; contbr. poetry and articles to jours. Mem. MLA, Robinson Jeffers Assn., Internat. John Steinbeck Soc., We. Lit. Assn., PEN Ctr. West USA. Home: 320 N Palm Dr Apt 304 Beverly Hills CA 90210-5804

HEARN, ANTHONY CLEM, computer scientist; b. Adelaide, Australia, Apr. 13, 1937; came to the U.S., 1962; s. Clem and Elma Frances (Almond) H.; m. Jo Elaine Johnson, May 16, 1970; children: Alison Margaret, David John. Degree, U. Adelaide, 1958, degree in math. with honors, 1959; PhD in Theoretical Physics, U. Cambridge, 1962. Prof. physics U. Utah, Salt Lake City, 1971-78, prof. computer sci., 1973-81, dir. computer sci. div., 1973-74, chmn. dept. computer sci., 1974-80; head info. scis. dept. RAND Corp., Santa Monica, Calif., 1980-84, corp. rsch. staff mem., 1984-90, resident scholar, 1990—; cons. USRA Sci. Coun., 1980, Lawrence Livermore Nat. Labs., 1980, Hewlett Packard Corp., Palo Alto, Calif., 1983, NSF Adv. Com. for Advanced Scientific Computing, 1984. Shell Commonwealth scholar, 1958; Alfred P. Sloan Found. fellow, 1967-69. Fellow Cambridge Philos. Soc., mem. Am. Phys. Soc., Spl. Interest Group on Symbolic and Algebraic Manipulation (chmn. 1981-83). Office: Rand 1700 Main St Santa Monica CA 90401-3208

HEARN, CHARLES VIRGIL, minister; b. Westport, Ind., Sept. 4, 1930; s. Forrest V. and Emma Florence (Marsh) H.; Ph.D., Thomas A. Edison U., 1972; D.D., Trinity Hall Coll. and Sem., 1977; diploma Palm Beach Psychotherapy Tng. Center, 1976; m. Linda Elmendorf; children by previous marriage—Debra Lynn, Charles Gregory, Martin Curtis. Ordained to ministry Methodist Ch., 1958; pastor various Meth. chs., Ind., Tex., Wyo., Calif., 1958-70; interpersonal minister St. Alban's Ch. of the Way, San Francisco, 1974—; clergyman and counselor Green Oak Ranch Boys Camp, Calif., 1969-70; dir. rehab. Mary-Lind Found., Los Angeles, 1970-71; med. asst. Fireside Hosp., Santa Monica, Calif., 1971-72; dir. alcoholism program Patrician Hosp., Santa Monica, 1972-74; propr., exec. dir. Consultation & Referral, Santa Monica, 1974—. Vice chmn. Western Los Angeles Alcoholism Coalition, 1974-78; pres. bd. dirs. Trinity Hall Coll. and Sem. Served with U.S. Army, 1951-53; Korea. Decorated Bronze Star; diplomate Am. Bd. Examiners in Psychotherapy, Bd. Examiners in Pastoral Counseling. Fellow Am. Acad. Behavioral Sci., Internat. Council Sex Edn. and Parenthood of Am. U.; mem. Am. Ministerial Assn. (pres. 1981—), Nat. Assn. Alcoholism Counselors, Calif. Assn. Alcoholism Counselors, Cons. on Alcoholism for Communities, Nat. Council Family Relations, Am. Coll. Clinic Adminstrs., Assn. Labor-Mgmt. Adminstrs. Democrat. Contbr. numerous articles on psychotherapy to profl. publs. Office: 1244 11th St Apt D Santa Monica CA 90401-2018

HEARNE, JOHN Q., telecommunications executive; b. San Francisco, June 10, 1948; s. John P. and Genevieve (Carolan) H.; m. Elizabeth Michaels, 1977; children: Jennifer, Brendan, Megan. BA in Math. summa cum laude, UCLA, 1970; JD, Stanford U., 1973. Bar: Calif. 1974, D.C. 1977. Assoc. Fisher, Wayland, Cooper & Leader, Washington, 1977-82, ptnr., 1983-89, of counsel, 1990—; owner, chmn. Point Communications Co., 1988—; $D; chmn. Gold Coast Broadcasting Co., 1994—, 1994—. Contbr. articles to profl. jours. Woodrow Wilson Nat. fellow, 1970. Mem. Fed. Comm. Bar Assn. (chmn. common carrier practice com. 1984-87, chmn. access to records com. 1987-88), Cellular Telecomm. Industries Assn. (bd. dirs. 1990-94), Surfrider Found., U.S. Surfing Fedn., Nat. Scholastic Surfing Assn., Malibu Surfing Assn., Rotary (chmn. environ. com.), Phi Beta Kappa.

HEARST, JOHN EUGENE, chemistry educator, researcher, consultant; b. Vienna, Austria, July 2, 1935; came to U.S., 1938; s. Alphonse Bernard and Lily (Roger) H.; m. Jean Carolyn Bankson, Aug. 30, 1958; children—David Paul, Leslie Jean. B.E., Yale U., 1957; Ph.D., Calif. Inst. Tech., 1961; D.Sc. (hon.) Lehigh U., 1992. Postdoctoral researcher Dartmouth Coll., Hanover, N.H., 1961-62; prof. chemistry U. Calif., Berkeley, 1962—, Miller rsch. prof., 1970-71, sr. rsch. scientist Lawrence Berkeley Lab., 1980—, dir. div. chem. biodynamics, 1986-89; Disting. lectr. Purdue U., 1986; Merck Centennial lectr. Lehigh U., 1992, Robert A. Welch Found. lectr., 1992; cons., bd. dirs. HRI Rsch. Inc., 1980—, Steritech Inc., Concord, Calif., 1992—; cons. Oncor, Inc., 1993—. Author: Contemporary Chemistry, 1976. Editor: General Chemistry, 1974; exec. editor Nucleic Acids Rsch., 1990-93. Bd. dirs. U. No. Calif., 1993—. Recipient NSF sci. profl. devel. award, 1977-78; John Simon Guggenheim fellow, 1968-69, European Molecular Biology Orgn. sr. fellow, 1973-74. Mem. AAAS, Am. Chem. Soc., Biophys. Soc., Am. Soc. Biol. Chemists, Am. Soc. for Photobiology (coun., pres. elect 1990-91, pres. 1991-92, Rsch. award 1994). Home: 101 Southampton Ave Berkeley CA 94707-2036 Office: U Calif Dept Chemistry #1460 Berkeley CA 94720-1460

HEARST, ROSALIE, philanthropist, foundation executive; b. Oklahoma City, Mar. 7; d. Mathis O. and Audell Bertha (Clary) Wynn; m. George Randolph Hearst, Sr., July 16, 1958. Student, Oklahoma City Coll., UCLA. Hearst rep. U.S. Senate Youth Program; pres. George Randolph Hearst Meml. Found. for Diabetic Edn.; pres. Rosalie Hearst Ednl. Found.; bd. dirs. Elvirita Lewis Found; life mem. Eisenhower Med. Ctr., Pathfinders, Tiempo de Los Ninos, Desert Hosp. Aux., Desert Press Club, Coll. of the Desert Aux., Internat. Orphans; bd. dirs. Pathfinder's Ranch Boys' Club; past bd. dirs. numerous charitable orgns.; trustee emeritus The Bob Hope Cultural Ctr.; coord. Officers' Wives Vol. Svcs. Dibble Gen. Hosp., Palo Alto; coord. Am. Women's Vol. Svcs. Sawtelle Hosp. L.A.; created Rosalie and George Hearst Fellowship in Ophthalmology U. Calif Berkeley. Named Woman of Yr. City of Hope, 1971, Disting. Woman Northwood Inst. Midland, Mich., 1988; recipient award for Lifetime Achievement in Community Service Palm Springs Women's Press Club. Home: 550 Camino Del Sur Palm Springs CA 92262

HEARTH, FRED E., librarian, educator; b. Klamath Falls, Oreg., Sept. 15, 1937; s. Fred and Mary Pearl (Harris) H. BA cum laude, San Diego State U., 1959, MA, 1964; MA in LS, U. Minn., 1970. Cert. in med. librarianship. Tech. librarian 3M Co., St. Paul, 1972-73; asst. prof., asst. dir. St. Paul Campus Librs. U. Minn., 1974-76; asst. dir. readers svcs. San. Francisco State U. Libr., 1976-81, asst. dir. adminstrv. svcs., 1981-83; dir. Armacost Libr. U. Redlands, Calif., 1983-94, interim access svcs. libr., 1994—; info. systems cons. San Bernardino Valley Mcpl. Water Dist., San Bernardino, Calif., 1994—; bd. dirs. Coop. Libr. Agy. for Systems and Svcs., 1989-91. Mem. editorial bd. Coll. and Rsch. Librs. News, 1986-90; contbr. articles to profl. jours. Served with U.S. Army, 1961-63. Mem. ALA (career mem., ret.), Kappa Delta Pi, Phi Beta Mu. Democrat. Episcopalian.

HEATH, EDWARD V., rubber company executive; b. Denver, Mar. 11, 1938; s. Raymond J. and Lois Heath; m. M. Jane Jobe, Aug. 15, 1961; children: Kent, Gregory. BA, Colo. Coll., 1960; B of Fgn. Trade, Thunderbird Sch., 1962; MBA, U. Denver, 1963. Sales corr. Gates Export Co., Denver, 1962-63; spl. rep. Mid. East Gates Export Corp., Beirut, 1963-67; mgr. mktg. devel. Gates Europe, Brussels, 1967-68; export mgr. Millers Falls Co., Greenfield, Mass., 1968-71; mgr. mktg. Latin Am. Stanley Works, New Britain, Conn., 1971-76; gen. mgr. Stanley Colombia, Cali, 1976-79; pres. Huge & Sons Inc., Houston, 1979-84; dir. internat. mktg. Gates Rubber Co., Denver, 1984-85, dir. export ops., 1985-94, mng. dir. Latin Am. ops., 1994—. Mem. Soc. Mfg. Engrs., Overseas Automotive Coun. Republican. Presbyterian. Home: 4272 E Orchard Pl Littleton CO 80121-3172

HEATH, GARY BRIAN, manufacturing firm executive, engineer; b. Pueblo, Colo., Nov. 5, 1954; s. William Sidney Heath and Eleanor Aileen (Mortimer) Svedman, (stepfather) Donald Svedman; m. Francine Marie Tamburelli, Apr. 28, 1990. BSME, U. So. Colo., 1979; MBA, U. Phoenix, 1984. Engr. ADR Ultrasound Corp., Tempe, Ariz., 1979-81; sr. engr. Technicare Ultrasound, Englewood, Colo., 1981-83; engring. mgr. COBE Labs., Inc., Lakewood, Colo., 1983-89; dir. mfg. COBE BCT, Inc., Lakewood, 1989—; Patentee fluid flow transfer device, pressure diaphragm for fluid flow device. Mem. Soc. Mfg. Engrs., Soc. Plastics Engrs. Home: 2436 S Dover Ct Lakewood CO 80227-3109 Office: COBE BCT INC 1201 Oak St Lakewood CO 80215-4409

HEATH, HUNTER, III, endocrinology researcher, educator; b. Dallas, June 8, 1942; s. Hunter Jr. and Velma M. (Brandon) H.; m. Glenna A. Witt, July 25, 1965; 1 child, Ethan Ford. BA in Chemistry, Tex. Tech Coll., 1964; MD, Washington U., St. Louis, 1968. Intern, then resident in medicine U. Wis. Hosps., Madison, 1968-70; fellow in endocrinology and metabolism Walter Reed Army Med. Ctr., Washington, 1970-72; chief endocrinology sect. Letterman Army Med. Ctr., San Francisco, 1972-74; rsch. fellow in biochemistry and metabolism Grad. Sch. Medicine Mayo Clinic, Rochester, Minn., 1974-76, from asst. prof. to prof. medicine, cons./rschr. endocrinol., 1976-91, head endocrine rsch. unit, 1984-88, assoc. dir., dir. clin. rsch. ctr., 1986-88; dir. for rsch. Mayo Clinic, Scottsdale, Ariz., 1988-90; prof. medicine, chief divsn. endocrinology, metabolism and diabetes U. Utah, Salt Lake City, 1991—; mem. adv. com. NIH, Bethesda, Md., 1985-88; pres., bd. dirs. Advances in Mineral Metabolism, Inc., Rochester, 1986-89, treas. 1994—; mem. select panel of physicians FAA, Washington, 1986-87. Bd. dirs. Utah affiliate Am. Diabetes Assn., 1992-93; bd. dirs. Utah affiliate Arthritis Found., 1993—; mem. Sch. Dist. Task Force on Lang. Arts Edn., Rochester, 1984. Maj. U.S. Army, 1970-74. Fellow ACP (editl. bd. 1985-88); mem. Am. Soc. for Clin. Investigation, Am. Soc. for Bone Mineral Rsch. (councillor 1985-88), Endocrine Soc. (publs. com. 1985-88), Western Assn. Physicians, Exptl. Aircraft Assn. (chmn. aeromed. adv. coun. Oshkosh, Wis. 1987-89, vice chmn. 1993—). Office: U Utah Sch Medicine 50 N Medical Dr Rm 4c116 Salt Lake City UT 84132-0001

HEATH, SCOTT RICHARD, instructional designer, hypermedia developer; b. Ypsilanti, Mich., Apr. 19, 1951; ss. Roger and Elizabeth Heath; m. Linda Elaine Smoke, Aug. 25, 1990; 1 child, Sarah Anne. AB in Visual and Environ. Studies magna cum laude, Harvard Coll., 1973; BA in Gen. Writing, U. Colo., Denver, 1980, MA in Instrnl. Tech., 1993. Pvt. practice graphic design Denver, 1973-76; prodn. asst. Denver Mo., 1973-76; tech. writer Denver Software Co., 1981-82; tech. writer R & D Champion Software Corp., 1983-84; pvt. practice tech. writing, 1984-91; intern, cons. Tech. Info. Assocs., 1992-93; rsch. asst. instrnl. tech. divsn. Sch. Edn. U. Colo., Denver, 1991-93; mem. transfusion medicine edn. project rsch. dept. Bonfils Blood Ctr., Denver, 1993—; tech. writer AT&T, U.S. West, 1984-91. Contbr. articles to profl. publs. Black belt (shodan) Denver Aikidokai. Mem. Soc. Tech. Comm., Assn. Computing Machinery, Assn. Ednl. Comm. and Tech. (co-presenter paper conv. 1993). Quaker.

HEATH, STEPHEN RICHARD, communications executive; b. Santa Rosa, Calif., June 19, 1947; s. Richard Signor and Florence Orene (Hosford) Stage; m. Dorell Marie Van Ausdale, Dec. 22, 1972; children: Robert Duryea Deats, Sandra Jean Slider. BA in Journalism, Calif State U., Sacramento, 1970. From customer rels. adminstr. to residence svc. ctr. mgr. Pacific Tele., Sacramento, 1977-80; from comm. planner to advt. mgr. Pacific Tele., San Francisco, 1980-81; dir. mass comm. Pacific Tele./Bell, Sacramento, 1981-85; dir. corp. comm. Pacific Bell, San Francisco, 1985-88; exec. asst. to chmn./CEO Pacific Telesis Group, San Francisco, 1985-88; dep. comm. dir. Californians Against Unfair Tax Increases, Sacramento, 1988; comm. dir. Sutter Health, Sacramento, 1989-91, v.p. for comm., 1991—. bd. dirs., exec. com. mem., chmn. comm. com., founding chmn. United Way, Sacramento; active exec. leadership program U. Calif. Davis Grad. Sch. Mgmt.; past bd. dirs. Calif. Hosps. Polit. Action Com., Sacramento Child Abuse Prevention Coun., Calif. State U. Sacramento Alumni Assn., Carmichael C. of C.; past team capt. Am. Lung Assn. Celebrity Waiters Luncheon; past bd. dirs. v.p. Sacramento Theatre Co.; past co-chmn. Sacramento Camellia Festival Assn. Stephen Kyle scholar Calif. State U., 1968; recipient Richard Hardie Meml. award for outstanding cmty. svc. United Way, Sacramento, 1993, Crystal award Internat. Assn. Bus. Communicators, Calif., 1989-93. Mem. Am. Soc. for Health Care Mktg. and Pub. Rels. (nat. conf. planning com. and panel moderator 1993, profl. devel. com. 1993-94, concurrent session presenter 1992-94), Health Care Mktg. & Pub. Rels. Soc. No. Calif. (conf. panel moderator 1992), Am. Coll. Healthcare Execs. (assoc.), Sacramento Urban League (sec., past chmn., exec. com. mem.), Calif. Newspaper Publ. Assn. (local unit sec.-treas.), Sacramento Press Club, Calif. Press Assn. Office: Sutter Health 2800 L St Sacramento CA 95816-5616

HEATHCOCK, CLAYTON HOWELL, chemistry educator, researcher; b. San Antonio, Tex., July 21, 1936; s. Clayton H. and Frances E. (Lay) H.; m. Mabel Ruth Sims, Sept. 6, 1957 (div. 1972); children: Cheryl Lynn, Barbara Sue, Steven Wayne, Rebecca Ann; m. Cheri R. Hadley, Nov. 28, 1980. BSc, Abilene Christian Coll., Tex., 1958; PhD, U. Colo., 1963. Supr. chem. analysis group Champion Paper and Fiber Co., Pasadena, Tex., 1958-60; asst. prof. chemistry U. Calif.-Berkeley, 1964-70, assoc. prof., 1970-75, prof., 1975—, chmn., 1986-89; chmn. Medicinal Chemistry Study Sect., NIH, Washington, 1981-83; mem. sci. adv. coun. Abbott Labs., 1986—. Author: Introduction to Organic Chemistry, 1976; editor-in chief Organic Syntheses, 1985-86, Jour. Organic Chemistry, 1989—; contbr. numerous articles to profl. jours. Recipient Alexander von Humboldt U.S. Scientist, 1978, Allan R. Day award, 1989, Prelog medal, 1991, Centenary medal Royal Soc. Chemistry, 1995. Mem. AAAS, Am. Acad. Arts and Scis., Am. Chem. Soc. (chmn. divsn. organic chemistry 1985, Ernest Guenther award 1986, award for creative work in synthetic organic chemistry 1990, A.C. Cope scholar 1990), Nat. Acad. Scis., Royal Soc. Chemistry (Centenary medal 1995), Am. Soc. Pharmacology. Home: 5235 Alhambra Valley Rd Martinez CA 94553 Office: U Calif Dept Chemistry Berkeley CA 94720

HEATON, CULVER, architect; b. Los Angeles, Jan. 3, 1912. B.Arch., U. So. Calif., 1936. With Culver Heaton, FAIA, Thomas Zartl, AIA and Assocs., Architects, Pasadena, Calif., 1941—. Prin. works include Muir High Sch, Pasadena; 300 ch. projects, including Covenant Presbyn. Ch, Long Beach, St. Peter's By The Sea Presbyn. Ch, Portuguese Bend, Anaheim United Meth. Ch; comml. projects include Ralph C. Sutro Co. Hdqrs, Los Angeles, Allianz Ins. Co, Los Angeles and N.Y.C. Fellow AIA (pres. Pasadena 1951, dir. 1952, treas. Calif. council 1952, dir. 1958); mem. Guild Religious Architecture (western regional dir. 1969-70). Address: Culver Heaton & Assocs 774 N Lake Ave Pasadena CA 91104-4557

HEATON, JEAN, early childhood educator; b. Equality, Ill., Feb. 27, 1933; d. Lytle and Loretta (Drone) Mossman; m. Fred T. Heaton, June 10, 1954 (div. Dec. 1979); children: Fred T., Laura, Sheri; m. Michael Marticorena, Mar. 14, 1987; children: Michael, Maria. BS in Home Econs., Southern Ill. U., 1955, MS in Edn., 1958; PhD in Child Devel., Early Childhood Edn, Fla. State U., 1971. Cert. secondary educator Ill., Fla., Calif. Tchr. Corham (Ill.) High Sch., 1955-57; rsch. asst. Southern Ill. U., Carbondale, 1957-58; tchr. Jefferson High Sch., Tampa, Fla., 1958-60, Hamilton Jr. High Sch., Oakland, Calif., 1960-61; prof. San Francisco State U., 1961-94; ednl. cons. Dept. Home and Cmty. Devel., U. Monrovia, Liberia, 1982, Calif. State Dept. Edn., 1974-76; mem. adv. bd. Skyline Coll., 1973-94, coord. Study Tours; presenter at profl. confs. Contbr. articles to profl. jours. and newsletters. Recipient Meritorious Performance award SFSU, 1986 and 1989. Mem. Infant/Toddler Consortium San Francisco Bay Area (exec. com. 1988-93), San Francisco/San Mateo Child Care Consortium (exec. com. 1987-93), Calif. Coun. on Children and Youth (exec. com. Region II 1982-90), San Francisco Assn. for Edn. Young Children (pres. 1990-92), AAUW (exec. com. San Mateo br. 1981-83), Pi Lambda Theta, Omicron Nu.

HEBE, JAMES L., trucking executive. Chmn., pres., ceo Freightliner Corp., Portland, Or. Office: Freightliner Corp PO Box 3849 Portland OR 97208-3849

HEBERT, ALVIN JOSEPH, chemist; b. Los Angeles, Sept. 15, 1932; s. Antonio and Grace Erma (Loggie) H.; children: John Scott, Cheryl Marie. AA, El Camino Coll., 1957; BS, UCLA, 1959; PhD, U. Calif., Berkeley, 1963. Fellow Lawrence-Berkeley (Calif.) Lab., 1962-64, sr. staff scientist nuclear chemistry div., 1964-77; sr. staff scientist Altus Corp., Palo Alto, Calif., 1979-80; editor Microwave Sys. News EW Comm., 1981; sr. tech. writer Kaiser Electronics, San Jose, Calif., 1981-82; pres. Am. Electrosci. Industries, Valencia, Calif., 1986—; substitute tchr. Torrance Unified Sch. Dist., 1989—; cons. U. Calif. dept. Geology and Geophysics, Berkeley, 1977, Pres. of U.S., 1976-81; rschr. in gravity, astrophysics and cosmology. Author: Gravity, The Alpha Force, 1994; contbr. articles to profl. jours.; inventor in field. Mem. nominating com. Kaiser Elem. Sch. PTA, Oakland, Calif., 1971-72; sch. rep. to Master Plan Citizen's Com., 1972-73; mem. selection com. Master Plan Area Coordinator, Oakland Pub. Schs., 1973-74. Served with U.S. Army, 1953-54. Mem. Am. Phys. Soc., AAAS, Yosemite Natural History Assn., Sigma Xi. Democrat. Office: Am Electroscience Found 1639 1/2 Cabrillo Ave Apt 42 Torrance CA 90501-2820

HECHT, CHIC, ambassador, former senator; b. Cape Giradeau, Mo., Nov. 30, 1928; m. Gail Hecht; children: Lori, Leslie. B.S., Washington U., St. Louis, 1949; postgrad., Mil. Intelligence Sch., Ft. Holibird, Mo., 1951. Mem. Nev. State Senate, 1966-74, Rep. minority leader, 1968-72; mem. U.S. Senate from Nev., 1982-89, mem. Banking, Housing and Urban Affairs Com., chmn. housing and urban affairs subcom., mem. Energy and Natural Resources Com., mem. Senate Select Com. on Intelligence; amb. to The Bahamas, 1989-93. Served with U.S. Army, 1951-53. Mem. Nat. Counter Intelligence Corps. (past pres.), Nat. Mil. Intelligence Assn.

HECHT, HAROLD MICHAEL, retail executive; b. Buffalo, Oct. 17, 1939; s. Harold Michael and Elizabeth (Liveright) Hl; m. Brenda Clucas, June 16, 1962; children: Elizabeth, Thomas, John, Christopher. BSBA, Dartmouth Coll., 1961, MBA, 1962. Merchandise mgr. br. store Stuart & Co., Balt., 1965-68; v.p. br. stores Hecht Co., Washington, 1968-69; v.p., mgr. gen. merchandise Meier & Frank, Portland, Oreg., 1969-72; exec. v.p. G. Fox & Co., Hartford, Conn., 1972-75; exec. v.p. sales promotions and merchandising The Broadway Dept. Stores, Los Angeles, from 1975, chmn. bd. dirs., chief exec. officer; exec. v.p. Carter Hawley Hale Stores Inc., Los Angeles, 1990, pres., 1991—. Mem. adv. bd. Fashion Inst., Los Angeles; bd. dirs. NCCJ, San Marino Schs. Found., 1984—. Mem. Merchants and Manufactors Assn. (bd. dirs.). Clubs: Jonathan (Los Angeles); Princeton (N.Y.C.); Annandale Golf (Pasadena, Calif.). Office: Carter Hawley Hale Stores 444 S Flower St Los Angeles CA 90071-2901

HECHT, SASANNA BETTINA, architect/design educator. BSc, U. Chgo., 1972; MA, U. Calif., Berkeley, 1976; PhD of Geography, U. Calif., 1982. Vis. prof. Ctr. Advanced Amazonian Studies Fed. Univ. of Para, Brazil, 1977-78; vis. asst. prof., asst. prof. Grad. Sch. Architecture UCLA, 1982-89, assoc. prof. Grad. Sch. Architecture and Urban Planning, 1989—; vis. asst. prof. Dept. Geography U. Chgo., 1985; cons. Ford Found., Rockefeller Found., Pew Charitable Trusts, W. Alton Jones, NSF, Gaia Found., USAID, Colombia Corp. Araracuara, Brazil Ministry Agr., German Aid Agy., Dominican Republic Plan Sierra, Rainforest Action Network, Conservation Internat., World Wildlife Fund, World Bank, InterAm. Bank, UN; exhibited at Smithsonian Instn., Mus. Goeldi, Belem, Consortium of Ams. Columbian Exhibit; tech. advisor (film) Saviors of the Forest, 1990. Co-author: (with Alexander Cockburn) Fate of the Forest: Developers, Destroyers and Defenders of the Amazon, 1989; editor: Amazonia: Agriculture and Land Use Research, 1982; co-editor: (with T. Downing, H. Pearson, C. Downing) Development or Destruction: Deforestation and the Livestock Industry in Latin America, 1992, (with M. Altieri) Agroecology and Small Farm Development, 1990, (others) People and the Tropic Forest: A Research Report from the U.S. Man and Biosphere Program, 1987. Fellow Heinz Found. Latin Am., 1994-95, MacArthur Found. Internat. Peace and Security, 1989-90, Fulbright U. Minas Gerais, 1984, Tinker Found. Travel, 1982, NAS Travel, 1982; grantee Latin Am. Studies Ctr., 1992-93, 91-92, UNESCO/CEPREMAP, 1991-92, Oakridge Nat. Lab., 1991, Ford Found., 1991, Jessie Smith Noyes Found., 1989-90, Internat. Studies and Overseas Programs, 1989-90, 88-89, Man and Biosphere Program, 1988-89.

HECHT, SCOTT JAMES, mechanical engineering executive; b. Powell, Wyo., Oct. 6, 1959; s. Robert N. and Jackie Louise (Corbett) H.; m. Janice Neilson, Aug. 21, 1981; children: Kristin, Jessica, Nathan, Jason. BSME, Brigham Young U., 1984, MSME, 1985. Registered professional engineer, Wyo., Mont., Idaho. Staff engr. SSR Engrs., Billings, Mont., 1985-90; pres. Western Engring. Inc., Powell, 1990—. Mem. IEEE, ASME, Nat. Assn. Corrosion Engrs. Republican. Mem. LDS Ch. Office: Western Engring Inc 871 Road 19 Powell WY 82435-9510

HECHTER, MARC STEVEN, management consultant; b. N.Y.C., May 25, 1952; s. Leon Hechter and Rebecca Naomi Hall Hoge; div. 1985; children: Brandon Christopher, Whitney Marie; m. Mamie May Chinn, Dec. 20, 1987. BA, U. Nev., Las Vegas, 1975, MPA, 1979. Mgmt. analyst Regional Transp. Commn., Las Vegas, 1978-79; prin. planner Clark County Dept. Comprehensive Planning, Las Vegas, 1979-83; adminstr. Nev. Housing Div., Carson City, 1983-86; v.p. Donaldson, Lufkin and Jenrette Securities Corp., N.Y.C. and L.A., 1986-87; sr. mgmt. analyst Clark County Dept. Fin., Las Vegas, 1987-88; exec. asst. to gov. State of Nev., Carson City, 1988-89; contract lobbyist, polit. cons. Wadhams and Assocs., Inc., Las Vegas and Carson City, 1989, 90-91; v.p. Zions First Nat. Bank, Las Vegas, 1989-90; asst. gen. mgr. State Indsl. Ins. System, Carson City, 1991-93; prin., CEO Jayne, Hechter and Co., Inc., Las Vegas, 1993-95; sr. v.p. fin. Saxton Inc., Las Vegas, Nev., 1995—; adj. instr. polit. sci. and history We. Nev. C.C. Past bd. dirs. Nev. Opera Assn. Mem. Pi Kappa Phi, Pi Sigma Alpha. Republican. Episcopalian. Home: 3456 Distinction Ct Las Vegas NV 89129-6728

HECK, GARY L., security management company executive; b. Great Lakes, Ill., Oct. 31, 1952; s. Walter John and Alice Edna (Vogan) H.; m. Tracy Carolyn Mayer, Sept. 9, 1984; children: Tera Lee, Breyana Marie. AAS, Delta Coll., 1972; BS, Mich. State U., 1974. Cert. protection profl. Police officer Ludington (Mich.) Police Dept., 1974-75; undercover narcotics investigator Thumb Intelligence Group, Cass City, Mich., 1975-77, Jefferson County Sheriffs Dept., Madras, Oreg., 1977-78; police patrolman Lansing Police Dept., 1978-86; chief of security Trammell Crow Co., Dallas, 1986-88; security mgr. Am. Patrol and Guard, Denver, 1988-90; dir. life safety and security Trammell Crow Co., Denver, 1990-95, Vector Property Svcs., Denver, 1995—; cons. emergency response task force Bldg. Owners and Mgrs. Assn., Denver, 1992—. Contbr. North Shore Animal League, Chgo., 1992—; walker March of Dimes, Denver, 1993. Mem. Am. Soc. for Indsl. Security, Downtown Denver Security Assn. (bd. dirs.), Nat. Fire Protection Assn., Nat. Parks and Conservation Assn., Sierra Club, World Wildlife Fund, Planetary Soc. Home: PO Box 18429 Denver CO 80218-0429 Office: Vector Property Svcs 1200 17th St Ste 1130 Denver CO 80202-5811

HECKATHORN, WILLIAM GARY, military officer; b. Steubenville, Ohio, Mar. 8, 1946; s. George Edward and Mary Virginia (Varner) H.; m. Laura Ann Druga, June 7, 1970; children: Jason William, Sally Ann. Bachelor Aeronautical and Astronautical Engring., Ohio State U., 1969, MS, 1970; PhD, U. Ill., 1985. Navigator 346th bomb squadron USAF, Westover AFB, Mass., 1972-73; B-52 radar navigator 17th bombardment wing USAF, Wright Patterson AFB, Ohio, 1973-75; instr. navigator 452 flying tng. squadron USAF, Mather AFB, Calif., 1975-79; test project mgr. air def. tactical air command USAF, Tyndall AFB, Fla., 1980-82; chief of test and evaluation hypersonic glide vehicle USAF, Wright Patterson AFB, 1985-87, dir. airlift and tng. systems, 1987-90, dir. airlifte and tng. systems, program exec. officer tactical and airlift systems, 1990-91; program mgr. Global Positioning System Sattelite and Control Segments, 1991-94; dir. advanced weapons survivability Philips Lab., Kirkland AFB, N.Mex., 1994—; program mgr.'s course Def. Systems Mgmt. Coll., Ft. Belvoir, Va., 1987, Air War Coll., Maxwell AFB, Ala., 1984-85. Contbr. articles to profl. jours. Tchr. Aley United MEth. Ch., Beavercreek, Ohio, 1988-91, St. Peters Presbyn. Ch., 1993-94; coach YMCA, 1986-88, Boy Youth Soccer Assn., 1989-90, BCAA, 1991, Am. Youth Soccer Assn., 1991-94. Mem. AIAA (sr.), Air Force Assn., Masons, Tau Beta Pi. Office: PL/WS 3550 Aberdeen Ave SE Kirtland AFB NM 87117

HECKENLIVELY, JOHN ROBERT, ophthalmology educator; b. Denver, Jan. 24, 1946; s. H.M. and Dora H. AB, Oberlin Coll., 1968; MD, U. Colo., 1972. Intern U. Utah Med. Ctr., Salt Lake City, 1972-73; resident in ophthalmology U. Ky. Med. Ctr., Lexington, 1973-76; fellow in retina UCLA/Jules Stein Eye Inst., L.A., 1976-77; asst. prof. ophthalmology UCLA/Jules Stein Eye Inst., 1978, assoc. prof. ophthalmology, 1983, prof.

ophthalmology, 1988—; fellow in genetics Johns Hopkins Hops., Balt., 1977-78; dir. UCLA Visual Physiology Lab., 1979—, Hereditary Retinal Disease Ctr., Jules Stein Eye Inst., 1992—. Author: (textbook) Retinitis Pigmentosa, 1988; author/editor: Principles and Practice of Clinical Electrophysiology of Vision, 1992; editor: Pattern Electroretinogram, 1984, Retinal Diseases, 1992; editorial bd. Metabolic and Pediatric Ophthalmology, Documenta Ophthalmologica; ad hoc reviewer NIH; editor Internat. Soc. for Clin. Electrophysiology of Vision, 1982-90. Adv. bd. Blue Cross of Calif., 1987—. Recipient Jules Stein Tribute award RP Internat. Found., Woodland Hills, Calif., 1986, award NIH, Bethesda, Md., 1987-96. Fellow Am. Acad. Ophthalmology (chair retina sec. 1983-92), Royal Coll. Ophthalmologists; mem. Macula Soc., Ophthalmic Genetic Study Club, Am. Soc. Human Genetics, Oxford Ophthal. Congress, Am. Ophthal. Soc., L.A. Acad. Medicine. Office: UCLA Jules Stein Eye Inst 100 Stein Plaza Los Angeles CA 90024

HECKLER, GERARD VINCENT, lawyer; b. Utica, N.Y., Feb. 18, 1941; s. Gerard Vincent and Mary Jane (Finocan) H. BA, Union Coll., Schenectady, 1962; JD, Syracuse U., 1970; MA in Clin. Psychology, Antioch U., 1994; postgrad., The Fielding Inst., 1995—. Bar: Ill. 1971, Calif. 1980, Mass. 1986, N.Y. 1986, U.S. Supreme Ct. 1985. Assoc. Martin, Craig, Chester & Sonnenschein, Chgo., 1970-73, Goldstein, Goldberg & Fishman, Chgo., 1973-76; ptnr. Heckler & Enstrom, Chgo., 1976-80; pvt. practice law L.A., Irvine, 1980-85; sr. trial atty. Law Office of Harden Bennion, L.A., 1985-87, Rafferty & Polich, Cambridge, Mass., 1987-8; trial atty. Acret, Gropman & Turner, L.A., 1989-92; instr. trial skills and evidence Calif. State Bar, 1987—; judge pro tem L.A. Mcpl. Ct., 1991—. Lt. USCG, 1964-67, Vietnam. Mem. Calif. State Bar (Bd. Govs. commendation 1986), L.A. County Bar Assn., Acad. Family Mediators, Ill. Bar Assn., Mass. Bar Assn., N.Y. Bar Assn. Office: 4 Hutton Centre Dr Ste 300 Santa Ana CA 92707-5784

HECKMAN, JAMES KENT, metallurgical engineer; b. Berwyn, Ill., July 13, 1962; s. William Vincent and Elaine Heckman. BS in Metallurgical Engring., U. Ill., 1984. Process engr. Motorola Semiconductor, Phoenix, 1984-86, Motorola Govt. Group, Chandler, Ariz., 1986-91; staff process engr. Motorola Semiconductor, Chandler, Ariz., 1991—. Inventor and contbr. in field. Office: Motorola 1300 N Alma School Rd Chandler AZ 85224-2939

HECKMAN, RICHARD AINSWORTH, chemical engineer; b. Phoenix, July 15, 1929; s. Hiram and Anne (Sells) H.; m. Olive Ann Biddle, Dec. 17, 1950; children: Mark, Bruce. BS, U. Calif., Berkeley, 1950, cert. hazardous mgmt. U. Calif., Davis, 1985. Registered profl. engr., Calif. With radiation lab. U. Calif., Berkeley, 1950-51; chem. engr. Calif. Rsch. & Devel. Co., Livermore, 1951-53; assoc. div. leader Lawrence Livermore Nat. Lab., 1953-77, project leader, 1977-78, program leader, 1978-79, energy policy analyst, 1979-83, toxic waste group staff engr., 1984-86, waste minimization project leader, 1986-90; div. dir. hazardous waste mgmt. Nationwide Technologies, Inc., Oakland, 1990-91; mng. dir. Heckman & Assocs., 1991-92; v.p. environ. scis. Pan Am. Resources Inc., Pleasanton, Calif., 1992—, also bd. dirs.. Mem. Calif. Radioactive Materials Forum. Co-author: Nuclear Waste Management Abstracts, 1983; patentee in field. Bd. dirs. Calif. Industries for Blind, 1977-80, Here and Now Disabled Svcs. for Tri-Valley, Inc., 1980. Calif. Fellow Am. Inst. Chemists, Acad. Hazardous Materials Mgmt.; mem. AAAS, Am. Acad. Environ. Engrs. (diplomate), Am. Chemistry Soc., Am. Inst. Chem. Engrs., Am. Nuclear Soc., Soc. Profl. Engrs., Water Environ. Fedn., Air and Waste Mgmt. Assn., Internat. Union Pure and Applied Chemistry (assoc.), Nat. Hist. Soc., N.Y. Acad. Scis., Internat. Oceanographic Soc., Environ. Assessment Assn. (registered environ. assessor Calif.), World Trade Club, San Francisco, Commonwealth Club San Francisco, Richmond Yacht Club, Island Yacht Club (commodore 1971), Midget Ocean Racing Club (sta. 3 commodore 1982-83), U.S. Yacht Racing Union, Midget Ocean Racing Assn. No. Calif. (commodore 1972). Home and Office: Pan Am Resources Environ Scis Dept 5683 Greenridge Rd Castro Valley CA 94552-2625

HECKMANN, RICHARD ANDERSON, zoology educator; b. Salt Lake City, Dec. 7, 1931; married; 5 children. BS in Zoology, Utah State U., 1954, MS in Zoology, 1958; postgrad., U. Calif., Davis, 1958-60, U. Pacific, 1959, U. Hawaii, 1960-61, U. Wash., 1963, U. Calif., Berkeley, 1963, 66; PhD in Zoology, Mont. State U., 1970; postgrad., Imperial Coll., Eng., 1976, U. Utah, 1985-86. Teaching asst. Utah State U., 1957; rsch. asst. U. Calif., 1958-59, teaching asst., 1959-61; instr. Contra Costa Coll., 1962-67; teaching asst. Mont. State U., 1968-70; asst. prof. Calif. State U., Fresno, 1970-72; prof. Brigham Young U., Provo, Utah; lectr. Calif. State U., Fresno, 1970; cons. U.S. Forest Svc., 1962, Niagara Chem. Co., 1964, 65, 67, Westinghouse Electric Corp., 1974, 75, 76, Central Utah Project, 1974, Diking Utah Lake Proposal Team, 1976, BLM Deep Creek Mts. and Big Creek Impact Studies, Vaughn Hansen Assocs., 1978, NARL Nielsen, Maxwell & Wangsgaard Engrs., Noorlander Corp., 1979, 80; dir. Rsch. Team to Guatemala; vis. prof. USSR, Poland, Nat. Acad. Sci., 1989. Author: Laboratory Manual for Biology Part I and II, 1966, Healing and Bacteriocidal Properties of Selected Herbal Extracts, 1988; co- author: (Clark, Glen) Atlas of Animal Parasites, 1974; editorial bd. Calif. Fish and Game Mag., 1974, Jour. Wildlife Diseases, 1974; patentee in field; Contbr to numerous profl. jours. Recipient Faculty Rsch. awards, 1972, 73, 74, 75, Silver Beaver award Boy Scouts of Am., 1989; grantee NSF, 1971, 72, 75, Utah Divsn. Wildlife Resources, 1975, 78, 79, Westinghouse Corp., 1976, Ariz. Fuels Corp., 1977, 78, 79, Naval Artic Rsch. Lab. U. Alaska, 1979, Utah Power and Light, 1979, Schering Corp., 1984, Brigham Young U., 1987-89, Binational Agrl. Rsch. Devel. Fund, 1986, 87, 88, 89, Nev. Divsn. Wildlife Resources, 1986, 87, 88-89; Pauley Rsch. fellow, 1960, 61, NSF, 1963, 66; Carl Raymond Grey scholar, 1950; honored by Farmer to Farmer Program USAID, 1988, 89. Mem. Am. Inst. Fishery Rsch. Biologist, Soc. of Protozoologist, Soc. of Parasitologists, Am. Fisheries Soc. (fish health sect., fish culture sect., pub. com., chmn. profl. standards com., mem. endangered species com.), World Malocologist's Soc., Utah Pub. Health Assn. Office: Brigham Young U Dept Zoology Provo UT 84602

HECOX, WALTER EDWIN, economics educator; b. Denver, Sept. 23, 1942; s. Morris Brown and Elizabeth (Rogers) H.; m. Ann Elizabeth Gourlay, Dec. 26, 1970; children: Sarah, Eric. BA in Econs., Colo. Coll., 1964; MA in Econs., Syracuse U., 1967, PhD in Econs., 1969. Research economist US Aid/Pakistan, Lahore, 1968, U.S. Mil. Acad., West Point, N.Y., 1969-70; project supr. Nat. Resources Dept. State of Colo., Denver, 1979-81; adv. trade and tariffs Ministry of Fin., Nairobi, Kenya, 1982-84; from asst. prof. to assoc. prof. econs. Colo. Coll., Colorado Springs, 1970-85, prof., 1985—; sr. lect. Fulbright program, Islamabad, Pakistan, 1976-77; vis. scientist Internat. Inst. for Applied Systems Analysis, Vienna, 1981; cons. Ford Found., Islamabad, 1976-77, Kenyan Minister of Fin., Nairobi, 1982, U.S. Aid/Kenya, Nairobi, 1984, U.S. Aid/Sudan, Khartoum, 1985-86. Contbr. articles to profl. jours. Served to capt. U.S. Army, 1969-70. Fulbright scholar, 1964-65, Nat. Def. Edn. Act fellow, 1965-69, Sr. fellow Grand Canyon Trust, 1994—. Mem. Am. Econ. Assn., Western Social Sci. Assn., assn. Environ. and Resource Economists, Soc. Internat. Devel., African Studies Assn. Office: Colo Coll Econs Dept Colorado Springs CO 80903

HEDINE, KRISTIAN EINAR, lawyer; b. Whitefish, Mont., July 14, 1956; s. Duane Rodney and Edna Louise (Welz) H.; m. Kathy Ilene Schirmer, Apr. 14, 1984; 1 child, Kjirsten Dayle; 1 stepchild, Jarred P. BS in Psychology, U. Wash., 1978; JD, U. Kans., 1982. Bar: Wash. 1982, U.S. Dist. Ct. (ea. dist.) Wash. 1982, U.S. Bankuptcy Ct. (ea. dist.) Wash. 1982, U.S. Ct. Appeals (9th cir.) 1994. Intern Reese & Baffney P.S., Walla Walla, Wash., 1981-82; assoc. Reese, Baffney, Schrag & Siegel, P.S., Walla Walla, 1982-86; ptnr. Reese, Baffney, Schrag, Siegel & Hedine, P.S., Walla Walla, 1986-95, Reese, Baffney, Schrag & Hedine, P.S., Walla Walla, Wash., 1995—; dep. city atty. City of Walla Walla, 1982—; bd. dirs. bankruptcy sect. Fed. Bar Assn. Ea. Dist.; spl. dist. counsel Wash. State Bar Assn., 1989—. Bd. dirs. Exchange Club of Walla Walla, 1986-87, Walla Walla Block Watch Com., 1984—. Mem. ABA, Assn. Trial Lawyers Am., Am. Bankruptcy Inst., Wash. Trial Lawyers Assn., Bankruptcy Ct. Ea. Dist. Wash. (local rules adv. com.), Elks. Office: Reese Baffney Schrag & Hedine Baker Bldg 8 S 2d Ave 7th Fl Walla Walla WA 99362

HEDRICK, BASIL CALVIN, state agency administrator, ethnohistorian, educator, museum and cultural institutions consultant; b. Lewistown, Mo., Mar. 17, 1932; s. Truman Bloice and M. LaVeta (Stice) H.; m. Anne Kehoe, Jan. 19, 1957 (div. 1979); 1 dau., Anne Lanier Hedrick Caraker; m. Susan Elizabeth Pickel, Oct. 2, 1980. A.B., Augustana Coll., Rock Island, Ill., 1956; MA, U. Fla., 1957; PhD, Inter-Am. U., Mex., 1965; cert., U. Vienna, Strobl, Austria, 1956. Asst. prof., assoc. prof., prof. So. Ill. U., Carbondale, 1967-74, asst. dir. Univ. Mus., 1967-70, dir. Univ. Mus. and Art Galleries, 1970-77, dean internat. edn., 1972-74; asst. dir. Ill. Div. Mus., Springfield, 1977-80; prof. history U. Alaska, Fairbanks, 1980-88, dir. U. Alaska Mus., 1980-88, dir. inter. affairs, 1985-87; founder, dir. Div. Mus., Archaeology and Publs. State of Mich., Lansing, 1988-91; museum/gallery cons., 1991—; dir. mktg. Rosalie Whyel Mus. Doll Art, Bellevue, Wash., 1991—; Fulbright sr. lectr., Brazil, 1972; mem. nat. register adv. panel, Ill., 1977-80; mem. Alaska Coun. on Arts, Anchorage, 1983-85; chmn. Fairbanks Hist. Preservation Commn., 1982-88; mem. Alaska Land Use Coun.; bd. dirs. Alaska Hist. Preservation Found., 1986-88; mem. Gov.'s Revitalization Task Force, Lansing, Mich., mem. ethnic coun., Mich., 1988-89; bd. dirs. East King County Visitors Bur., 1993—; officer, bd. dirs. Wash. Mus. Assn., 1993—. Author: (with others) A Bibliography of Nepal, 1973, (with Carroll L. Riley) The Journey of the Vaca Party, 1974, Documents Ancillary to the Vaca Journey, 1976, (with C.A. Letson) Once Was A Time, a Wery Good Time: An Inquiry into the Folklore of the Bahamas, 1975, (with J.E. Stephens) In the Days of Yesterday and in the Days of Today: An Overview of Bahamian Folkmusic, 1976, It's A Natural Fact: Obeah in the Bahamas, 1977, Contemporary Practices in Obeah in the Bahamas, 1981; compilations and collections, 1959-69; editor: (with J. Charles Kelley and Riley) The Classic Southwest: Readings in Archaeology, Ethnohistory and Ethnography, 1973, (with J. Charles Kelley and Riley) The Mesoamerican Southwest: Readings in Archaelogy, Ethnohistory and Ethnology, 1974, (with Riley) Across the Chichimec Sea, 1978; (with others) New Frontiers in the Archaeology and Ethnohistory of the Greater Southwest, 1980; Trans. of Ill. Acad. Sci., 1979-81, (with Susan Pickel-Hedrick) Ethel Washington: The Life and Times of an Eskimo Dollmaker, The Role of the Steamboat in the Founding and Development of Fairbanks, Alaska, 1986, (with Susan Savage) Steamboats on the Chena, 1988; co-editor: Led Zeppelin live, 1993, 94; author and editor of various other publications; contbr. articles to profl. jours. Chmn. Goals for Carbondale, 1972; active various local state, nat. polit. campaigns. Mem. NMA (bd. dirs. 1989-91), Am. Assn. Mus. (leader accreditation teams 1977—, sr. examiner), Ill. Archaeol. Soc. (pres. 1973-74), Mus. Alaska, Assn. Sci. Mus. Dirs., Midwest Mus. Conf. (treas. 1977-80), Western Mus. Assn., Wash. Mus. Assn. (bd. dirs. 1994—), BD Arts (bd. dirs. 1995—), Phi Kappa Phi.

HEDRICK, JOSEPH WATSON, JR., retired judge; b. Fresno, Calif., Nov. 29, 1924; s. Joseph Watson and Kathryn (Watson) H.; m. Coleena Alice Wade, June 17, 1949; children—Joseph Wade, Robert S. BS, U. Calif.-Berkeley, 1950; LLB, U. Calif.-San Francisco, 1952. Bar: Calif. 1953. Assoc. Rowell Lamberson & Thomas, Fresno, 1953; mcht., Fresno, 1954; atty. Fresno County Legal Services, Inc., 1967; ptnr. Lerrigo, Thuesen & Thompson, Fresno, 1971, Lerrigo, Thuesen, Walters, Nibler & Hedrick, Fresno, from 1972; judge Modesto div. Ea. Dist. Calif., U.S. Bankruptcy Ct., 1980-94; ret., 1994. Served with AUS, 1943-46. Office: US Bankruptcy Ct PO Box 5276 Modesto CA 95352-5276

HEDRICK, WALLACE EDWARD, business executive; b. Malad, Idaho, Nov. 11, 1947; s. Clarence Franklin and Beth S. Hedrick; BS, U. Nev., Reno, 1970; MA, U. No. Colo., Greeley, 1974; m. Jerrie S. Deffenbaugh, Nov. 20, 1980; children: Ann Elizabeth, Ryan Wallace, Hallie Sue. Regional dir. No. Idaho, Idaho Planning and Cmty. Affairs Agy., Moscow, 1970-73, assoc. chief, Boise, 1973-75; project dir. Pacific N.W. Regional Commn., Boise, 1975-76; pres. Resources N.W., Inc., Boise, 1976-88; dir. Idaho State Lottery, 1988-95; pres. Tri West Lotto Bd., 1993-95; pres. Resources Northwest, Boise, 1995—. Sec.-treas. Idaho Citizens for Responsible Govt., 1978-80; trustee, chmn. Joint Sch. Dist. 2, 1985—; trustee Meridian Sch. Bd.; bd. dirs. Boise Family YMCA, 1994—; exec. com. North Am. Assn. State and Provincial Lotteries. Served with USAR, 1971. Mem. Multi State Lottery Assn. (pres. 1994-95), N.Am. Assn. of State and Provincial Lotteries (regional dir.). Democrat. Home: 9413 Knottingham Dr Boise ID 83704-2234 Office: Resources Northwest PO Box 578 Boise ID 83704

HEE, VIVIAN SANAE MITSUDA, principal; b. Honolulu, Hawaii, May 16, 1946; d. Hozumi and Kimiyo (Ueno) Mitsuda; m. Richard K.F. Hee, Aug. 24, 1968. BA in Elem. Edn., U. Hawaii, 1970, MA in Edn. Adminstrn., 1989. Cert. tchr., sch. adminstr., state edn. adminstr. Hawaii. Elem. tchr. Dept. Edn. Dist., Windward, Hawaii, 1970-77; itinerant tchr. Dept. Edn. Dist., Kaneohe, Hawaii, 1977-83; state resource tchr. Dept. Edn. State, Honolulu, Hawaii, 1983-85, state specialist gifted talented, 1985-88; vice prin. Kapunahala Elem. Sch., Kaneohe, Hawaii, 1989-89, August Ahrens Elem. Sch., Waipahu, Hawaii, 1990-91; prin. T. Jefferson Elem. Sch., Honolulu, Hawaii, 1991—; cons. U. Hawaii, Hilo, 1989—, Consortium for Teaching Asian Pacific Children, 1989; adv. com. Tchrs. Edn. Com. for Gifted, U. Hawaii, 1986-89; mem. State Supt. Task Force, 1990-91, Diamond Head Mental Health Svc. Bd., 1993—. Contbr. author: (book) Scope/ Sequence Gifted Curr., 1988; assoc. editor: (mag.) U. Hawaii Educational Perspective, 1989; contbr. to profl. journs. and mags. Cons. Center for Gifted Native Hawaiian Children, Hilo, 1989—, Hawaii Assn. for Gifted, 1988; outreach assoc. John Hopkins Univ., Hawaii, 1990—; judge Senator R. Bryd. Scholarship, Hawaii, 1985-88; mem. Red Cross, Hawaii, 1980—. With Naval Intelligence Reserve, 1965-70. Recipient Outstanding Svc. award Ser Teens of Hawaii, 1988, Meritorious Svc. award Hawaii Assn. for Gifted, 1988, Outstanding Svc. award Johns Hopkins U. Ctr. for Talented Youth, 1994; Masters Program scholar U. Hawaii, 1989; Grantee to China East West Center, U. Hawaii, 1989, to Japan East West Center, U. Hawaii, 1990. Mem. Assn. Supervision Curriculum Devel. (bd. dirs. 1988—), Hawaii Assn. Supervision Curriculum Devel. (pres. 1992-93), Nat. Assn. Elementary Sch. Principals, 1989—, Alliance for Drama, East West Center Alumni Assn., Delta Kappa Gamma. Office: Jefferson Elem Sch 324 Kapahulu Ave Honolulu HI 96815-4033

HEEGER, DAVID J., psychology educator; b. Berkeley, Calif., Oct. 3, 1961; s. Alan J. and Ruth (Chadacoff) H.; m. Anne Gelman, Oct. 21, 1990; 1 child. BA, U. Pa., 1983, MS in Edn., 1985, PhD, 1987. Rsch. assoc. Stanford (Calif.) U., 1990-91; rsch. scientist NASA-Ames Rsch. Ctr., Moffett Field, Calif., 1991; asst. prof. Stanford U., 1991—. Contbr. articles to profl. jours.; patentee in field. Rsch. fellow U. Pa., Phila., 1983-87, Vis. fellow SRI Internat., Menlo Park, Calif., 1984-85, Postdoctoral Rsch. fellow MIT Media Lab., Cambridge, Mass., 1987-90, Fairchild Found. Postdoctoral fellow, 1987, Sloan Rsch. Found. fellow, 1994; NIH Rsch. grantee, 1993; recipient David Marr prize Internat. Conf. Computer Vision, London, 1987. Office: Stanford U Dept Psychology Stanford CA 94305

HEEGER, JACK JAY, public relations consultant; b. Sioux City, Iowa, Oct. 18, 1930; s. Lester and Etta (Grossman) H.; m. Fern E. Rubenstein, Feb. 14, 1954 (dec. May 1987); children: Lloyd, Marshall, Laurie; m. Heddy L. Swierstra, Sept. 2, 1989. MBA, Calif. State U., 1985. Accredited in pub. rels. Reporter Sioux City (Iowa) Jour., 1954-55, UPI, L.A., 1955-57; asst. dir. pub. rels. Revell, Inc., Venice, Calif., 1957-59; mgr. west coast Carl Byoir & Assoc., L.A., 1959-69; owner, cons. Jack J. Heeger Pub. Rels., L.A., 1969-70, 84—; exec. staff mem. Braun & Co., L.A., 1970-74; v.p. pub. affairs Sunkist Growers, Inc., Sherman Oaks, Calif., 1974-84; lectr. Calif. State U., L.A., 1986-87, Long Beach, 1987-90; assoc. prof. emeritus Calif. State U., 1990-92. Contbr. articles to profl. jours. Sgt. USMC, 1951-53. Fellow Pub. Rels. Soc. Am. (pres. L.A. chpt. 1973, named disting. profl. 1976, Cmty. Svc. award 1991).

HEEKIN, VALERIE ANNE, telecommunications technician; b. Santa Monica, Calif., Nov. 7, 1953; d. Edward Raphael and Jane Eileen (Potter) H. AA, L.A. Valley Coll., 1980; BS magna cum laude, Calif. Baptist Coll., 1987. Telecommunications technician Pacific Bell Co., N. Hollywood, Calif., 1971—; pres. Odyssey Adventures, Inc., Sylmar, Calif., 1987—. Pres. Parkwood Sylmar Homeowners Assn., 1981-89; activist civil rights. Republican. Roman Catholic. Office: Odyssey Adventures PO Box 923094 Sylmar CA 91392-3094

HEERMANS, JOHN MICHAEL, electrical, chemical engineer; b. The Dalles, Oreg., Nov. 24, 1958; s. Donald Jerome and Motrona A. H.; m. Karen Marie Hudson, Nov. 8, 1987. BS in Chem. Engring., U. Calif., Santa Barbara, 1983; MSEE, U. So. Calif., L.A., 1989. Engr. Grumman Aerospace Corp., Nas Pt. Mugu, Calif., 1983-86; project engr. Hughes Aircraft Co., El Segundo, Calif., 1986-94; engr. specialist Loral Def. Sys., Litchfield Park, Ariz., 1994—. Republican. Seventh-Day Adventist. Office: Loral Def Sys MS 5122 PO Box 85 Litchfield Park AZ 85340

HEFFERN, RICHARD ARNOLD, author; b. Orange, Calif., July 24, 1950; s. Frank Schnepp Heffern and Mary Claire (Dominguez) Elliott; m. Matilde Lopez, Aug. 21, 1971; children: Christina Marie, Richard Arnold Jr. Student, Fullerton Coll., 1968-71, Calif. State U., Fullerton, 1971-75. Lab. technician Natural Products Devel. Corp., Orange, 1971-76; sr. editor Trinity Ctr. Press., Beaumont, Calif., 1974-77; freelance Santa Ana, Calif., 1971—. Author: The Herb Buyers Guide, 1973, The Complete Book of Ginseng, 1976, Secrets of the Mind-Altering Plants of Mexico, 1974, The Use of Herbs in Weight Reduction, 1975, Time Travel: Myth or Reality, 1977; cons.: (book) New Age Nutrition, 1974, Elementary Treatise in Herbology, 1974, Dictionary of Health and Nutrition, 1976, Advanced Treatise in Herbology, 1978.

HEFFLINGER, LEROY ARTHUR, agricultural manager; b. Omaha, Feb. 14, 1935; s. Leroy William and Myrtle Irene (Lampe) H.; m. Carole June Wickman, Dec. 23, 1956; children: Dean Alan, Andrew Karl, Roger Glenn, Dale Gorden. BS in Fin., U. Colo., 1957. Mgr. Hefflinger Ranches, Inc., Toppenish, Wash., 1963-73; pres. Hefflinger Ranches, Inc., 1973—; bd. dirs. Hop Adminstrv. Com., Portland, Oreg., 1980-86; trustee Agr. and Forestry Edn. Found., Spokane, Wash., 1988-94, vice chmn., 1993-94. Vestryman, bd. dirs. St. Michael's Ch., Yakima, Wash., 1969-74; mem. capital campaign com. Heritage Coll., Toppenish, 1990-91. Capt. USAF, 1958-63. Mem. Hop Growers Am. (bd. dirs., past pres.), Hop Growers Wash. (bd. dirs., past treas.), Beta Theta Pi. Republican. Episcopalian. Office: Hefflinger Ranches Inc PO Box 47 Toppenish WA 98948-0047

HEFFNER, JOHN EDWARD, medical educator; b. Long Beach, Calif., Dec. 29, 1948; s. Jack Nathan and Hazel Leticia (Davies) H.; m. Ann Louise Vasen, July 10, 1976; children: John Nathan, James Edward. Student, U. So. Calif., L.A., 1970; MD, UCLA, 1974. Internist Tri-City Hosp., Oceanside, Calif., 1978-80; critical care physician Penrose Hosp., Colorado Springs, Colo., 1982-85; dir. ICU Med. U. S.C., Charleston, 1985-90; dir. ICU St. Joseph's Hosp. and Med. Ctr., Phoenix, Ariz., 1990-94, chmn. acad. internal medicine, program dir. internal med., 1992—. Author: Pulmonary Pearls, 1989; editor: Critical Care Pearls, 1990, Internal Medicine Pearls, Cardiology Pearls. Fellow ACP, Am. Coll. Chest Physicians; mem. Am. Thoracic Soc. Office: St Josephs Hosp & Med Ctr 350 W Thomas Rd Phoenix AZ 85013-4409

HEFFRON, MICHAEL EDWARD, computer scientist; b. Battle Creek, Mich., Dec. 18, 1949; s. Michael Richard and Maxine Beverly (Piper) H.; m. Louella Mae Thompson, Apr. 12, 1969; children: Karen, Jennifer. BS in Computer Sci., Ariz. State U., 1986. Engring. asst. Motorola, Inc., Scottsdale, Ariz., 1977-81; calibration lab. supr. ADR Ultrasound, Tempe, Ariz., 1982-83; engring. aide Motorola, Inc., Scottsdale, 1983-86; v.p. CyberSoft, Inc., Tempe, Ariz., 1986-90; engr. Injection Rsch. Specialists, Inc., Colorado Springs, Colo., 1990-91; software devel. mgr. Injection Rsch. Specialists Co. div. Pacer Industries, Colorado Springs, 1991-92; sr. systems engr. Computer Data Systems Inc., Rockville, Md., 1992-93; software engr. Coergon, Inc., Boulder, Colo., 1993—. Patentee in field. Served with USAF, 1970-77. Mem. IEEE Computer Soc. (affiliate), Assn. Computing Machinery. Republican. Pentecostal Ch. Office: Coergon Inc 1050 Walnut St Ste 426 Boulder CO 80302-5143

HEFLEY, JOEL M., congressman; b. Ardmore, Okla., Apr. 18, 1935; s. J. Maurice and Etta A. (Anderson) H.; m. Lynn Christian, Aug. 25, 1962; children: Janna, Lori, Juli. B.A., Okla. Baptist U., 1957; M.S., Okla. State U., 1963. Exec. dir. Community Planning and Research, Colorado Springs, Colo., 1966-86; mem. Colo. Ho. of Reps., 1977-78, Colo. Senate, 1979-87, 100th-103rd Congresses from 5th Colo. dist., 1987—; mem. armed svcs. com., mem. natural resources com., mem. small bus.-SBA com. Republican. Baptist. Clubs: Rotary, Colorado Springs Country. Office: House of Representatives 2442 Rayburn Bldg Washington DC 20515-0005

HEFTI, FRANZ F., neuroscientist, educator; b. Zurich, Switzerland, Dec. 22, 1947; came to U.S., 1978; s. Fridolin and Charlotte (Hunziker) H.; m. Zena P. Bottani, Aug. 5, 1974; children: Marco M., Prisca D. MS, U. Zurich, Switzerland, 1972, PhD, 1976. Rsch. asst., dept. pharmacology U. Zurich, 1974-77; rsch. assoc. MIT, Cambridge, Mass., 1978-80, Max Planck Inst., Munich, W. Germany, 1980-81; head of rsch. lab. Sandoz Ltd., Basel, Switzerland, 1982-85; assoc. prof. neurology U. Miami, Fla., 1985-89; James E. Birren prof. gerontology U. So. Calif., L.A., 1989—; dir. dept. neurosci. Genentech Inc., South San Francisco, Calif., 1993—. Contbr. over 200 articles to sci. jours.; editor: Progress in Parkinson Research, 1988, and other books in field. Fellowship Swiss Nat. Sci. Found., 1978, Alex. von Humboldt Stiftung, Bonn, W. Germany, 1980; grantee Alzheimer's Disease Found., Chgo., 1985, Nat. Parkinson Found., Miami, 1985, 88, NIH, Washington, 1987, NSF, Washington, 1988; Nomination to Parkinson Rsch. Scholar, Nat. Parkinson Found., Miami, 1988, Robert Bing Prize Swiss Acad. Med. Scis., 1988. Mem. Soc. for Neuroscience, European Neuroscience Soc., Internat. Soc. for Neurochemistry, Internat. Brain Rsch. Orgn. Office: Genentech Inc 460 Pt Bruno Blvd South San Francisco CA 94080

HEGARTY, WILLIAM KEVIN, medical center executive; b. Sask., Can., Feb. 14, 1926; came to U.S., 1951; s. William Alexander and Lila (Taylor) H.; m. Doreen Alice Symon, Sept. 8, 1951; children—Kelley, Kerry, Michael. B. Commerce, U. Man., 1949; M.H.A., Northwestern U., 1953. Exec. dir. Calif. Hosp., Los Angeles, 1966-69; v.p. Lutheran Hosp. Soc., Los Angeles, 1969-74; vice chmn. Huntington Meml. Hosp., Pasadena, Calif., 1974-90; ret.; Bd. dirs. Blue Cross of So. Calif. Contbr. articles to profl. jours. Mem. Am. Hosp. Assn., Calif. Hosp. Assn. (pres. 1977, Outstanding Service award), Hosp. Council So. Calif. (pres. 1973), Assn. Am. Med. Colls. Congregationalist. Club: Rotary Internat. Home: 341 Fairway Dr Alisal Ranch Solvang CA 93463

HEGEDUS, JOHN S., medical products executive; b. 1929. With Am. Home Products, N.Y., 1968-77, Revlon Health Care, N.Y., 1977-86, Sterling Drug, N.Y., 1986-92, Genelabs Tech, Inc., Redwood City, Calif., 1992—. Office: Genelabs Tech Inc 505 Penobscot Dr Redwood City CA 94063-4737*

HEICKSEN, MARTIN HENRY, retired archaeology-biblical literature educator; b. Columbus, Mont., Apr. 17, 1911; s. Henry Martin and Bertha Ann (Crawford) H.; m. Amanda Eldora Bolstad, July 18, 1938; children: Byron Homer, Gerald Eugene, Darlene Joyce. AB, San Francisco State U., 1955, MA, 1957. Life C.C. anthropology credential, Calif. Min., pastor 4 Assemblies of God chs., Mont., 1936-42; exec. sec.-treas. Mont. dist. coun. Assembly of God, 1942-47; instr. Ctrl. Bible Coll., Springfield, Mo., 1947-48; prof. bibl. lit. Bethany Coll., Santa Cruz, Calif., 1948-67; assoc. prof. archaeology Wheaton (Ill.) Coll., 1967-71; vis. prof. archaeology Cabrillo Coll., Aptos, Calif., 1974-76; prof. archaeology and O.T., Omega Tng. Ctr., San Jose, Calif., 1976-79, St. James Coll., Pacifica, Calif., 1980-90; ret., 1990; field archaeologist San Francisco State U. and U. Calif., Berkeley, 1950-63; archaeologist, photographer Dothan (Jordan) Archaeol. Expdn., 1964; dir. Tekoa (Israel) Archaeol. Expdn., 1968-71; cons. archaeologist, Santa Cruz, 1971-76. Author: Settlement Patterns in Jordan, 1966, Tekoa: Excavations in 1968, 1969, Tekoa, Historical and Cultural Profile, 1970; author, photographer: Zondervan, Pictorial Ency.-Bible, 5 vols., 1975. Rsch. grantee Am. Philos. Soc., 1964. Mem. Near East Archaeol. Soc. (sec. 1969-94). Republican. Baptist. home: 412 Gay Pl Billings MT 59102-4730

HEIDBREDER, GAIL, architect, educator; b. Balt., Jan. 20, 1941; d. Gerald August and Ora Henderson (Longley) H.; children: Laura Temple Lundin, John Temple. BA, Stanford U., 1966, postgrad., 1975-78, 93—. Registered architect, Calif. With various firms, 1969-85; owner Gail Heidbreder, AIA-Architect, Porterville, Calif., 1985—; instr. architecture, constrn. and CADD, Coll. of Sequoias, Visalia, Calif., 1990—. Mem. AIA. Office: Coll of Sequoias 915 S Mooney Visalia CA 93277

HEIDIG, ELIZABETH ANNE, lawyer; b. Grand Rapids, Mich., Apr. 25, 1959; d. Eugene Michael and Betty Jane (Tobin) Skazinski; m. Edward G. Heidig II, Aug. 13, 1988. BA, Grand Valley State Coll., Allendale, Mich., 1981; JD, Thomas Cooley Law Sch., 1984. Bar: Calif. 1986, U.S. Dist. Ct. (cen. dist.) Calif. 1988. Assoc. Berris & Seton, Century City, Calif., 1985-86, Law Offices of Michael J. Rand, Encino, Calif., 1986-89; officer Sacramento Ct. Appointed Spl. Advocates, 1991-93. Fellow Nat. Trust for Hist. Preservation, 1990; appointee Calif. Commn. Tchr. Credentialing. Mem. ABA. Roman Catholic.

HEIDRICH, FRED EDMUND, III, medical educator; b. Toledo, Ohio, Oct. 9, 1949; s. Fred Edmund Jr. and Jean Alvina (Manthey) H.; m. Joyce Hiu-Mui Ling, Aug. 31, 1974; children: Melissa, Bryan. BA, U. Calif., San Diego, 1971; MD, Stanford U., 1976; MPH, U. Wash., 1981. Diplomate Am. Bd. Family Practice with cert. in geriatrics. Residency in family practice U. Wash., 1976-79; sr. fellow U. Wash. Med. Sch., Seattle, 1979-81; family physician, resident faculty mem. Group Health Coop., Seattle, 1981-94; clin. assoc. prof. U. Wash., Seattle, 1988—; vis. prof. U. Malaysia, Kuala Lumpur, 1991, Nat. Taiwan U., Taipei, 1987; grant reviewer Group Health Found., Seattle, 1987—; reviewer Jours. of Family Practice, 1981—. Computer programmer for ednl. film Myoglobin, 1971. Vol. physician Cmty. Health Clinics, Seattle, 1981—; Sunday sch. tchr. Univ. Congl. Ch., Seattle, 1983—. First alumni scholar Stanford Alumni Assn., 1975, Chancellor's scholar U. Calif., 1967. Mem. Am. Acad. Family Physicians, Soc. Tchrs. of Family Practice. Office: Group Health Coop 200 15th E Seattle WA 98112

HEIDT, RAYMOND JOSEPH, insurance company executive; b. Bismarck, N.D., Feb. 28, 1933; s. Stephen Ralph and Elizabeth Ann (Hirschkorn) H.; BA, Calif. State U., San Jose, 1963, MA, 1968; PhD, U. Utah, 1977; m. Joyce Ann Aston, Jan. 14, 1956; children: Ruth Marie, Elizabeth Ann, Stephen Christian, Joseph Aston. Claims supr. Allstate Ins. Co., San Jose, Calif., 1963-65; claims mgr. Gen. Accident Group, San Francisco, 1965-69; owner, mgr. Ray Heidt & Assocs., Logan, Utah, 1969-76; v.p. claims Utah Home Fire Ins. Co., Salt Lake City, 1976—; with Utah State U., 1970-76; dir. Inst. for Study of Pacifism and Militarism; vice-chmn. Benton County Parks and Recreation Bd., 1987-90. Active Kennewick Hist. Preservation Commn., 1989-90, 1st chmn., 1989-90, Magna Area Coun., 1992, pres. 1993-94; bd. trustees, sec. treas. Utah Ethnic and Mining Mus., 1994—. With U.S. Army, 1952-57. Decorated Bronze Star. Mem. Southeastern Wash. Adjusters' Assn. (pres. 1988-90), Utah Claims Assn. (pres. 1977-78), Lions, Am. Legion. Mormon. Republican. Home: 437 Pleasants Dr Nampa ID 83651

HEIFETS, LEONID, microbiologist, researcher; b. Russia, Jan. 5, 1926; came to U.S., 1979; s. Boris and Luba Heifets; m. Seraphima Apsit, Jan. 1955 (div. July 1978); children: Michael, Herman. MD, Med. Inst., Moscow, 1947, PhD, 1953; DSc, Acad. Med. Scis., Moscow. Asst. prof. Med. Inst., Arkhangelsk, Russia, 1950-54, assoc. prof., 1954-57; lab. dir. Mechnikov Rsch. Inst., Moscow, 1957-69; sr. researcher Inst. for Tuberculosis, Moscow, 1969-78; rsch. fellow Nat. Jewish Hosp., Denver, 1979-80; lab. dir. Nat. Jewish Ctr., Denver, 1980—; asst. prof. Colo. U., Denver, 1980-86, assoc. prof., 1986-92, prof. microbiology, 1992—; mem. com. on bacteriology Internat. Union Against Tuberculosis, Paris, 1986—. Author: Effectiveness of Vaccination, 1968; author, editor: Drug Susceptibility, 1991; mem. editorial bd. Antimicrobial Agents and Chemotherapy, Washington; contbr. articles to profl. jours. Mem. Am. Soc. Microbiology. Office: Nat Jewish Ctr Immunology Respiratory Med 1400 Jackson St Denver CO 80206-2761

HEIFNER, JACK L., writer; b. Corsicana, Tex., Mar. 31, 1946; s. Lee and Naomi (Norris) H. BFA, So. Meth. U., 1968. Author: (plays) Casserole, 1975, Vanities, 1976, Patio/Porch, 1978, Music-Hall Sidelights, 1978, Star Treatment, 1980, Running on Empty, 1982, Tornado, 1983, Smile, 1983, Tropical Depression, 1984, Natural Disasters, 1985, Leader of the Pack, 1985, Twister, 1986, Bargains, 1987, American Beauty, 1988, Home Fires, 1991, There She Is, 1991, Boys' Play, 1992, Heartbreak, 1992, Sing Baby Sing, 1993, The Lemon Cookie, 1993, Clara Period, 1995, Comfort and Joy, 1995, (films) Miss Bikini, 1993, Wide Place in the Road, 1994, also TV scripts. Office: care Brad Kalos Internat Creative Mgmt 40 W 57th St New York NY 10019

HEILMAN, JOHN EDWARD, engineering consultant; b. Chgo., Mar. 20, 1936; s. Frederick John and Kathryn Grace (Schnider) H.; BS in Food Engring., Ill. Inst. Tech., 1961; m. Virginia Lois Anderson, Jan. 28, 1956; children—Wayne John, Warren Wesley. Engr. grocery products div. Armour & Co., Chgo., 1959-61, lab. technician, 1958, foreman, 1958-59; process engr. Central Soya Co., Inc., Ft. Wayne, Ind., 1962-65, supt., Chgo., 1965-68; sr. process engr. Continental Grain Co., Chgo., 1968-75, dir. engring. process div., N.Y.C., 1975-77, asst. v.p. process div., 1977-79; v.p. world oilseeds group, 1979-91; prin. Heilman Consulting Group, 1991—. Mem. Nat. Fire Protection Assn. (sectional com. solvent extraction, sectional com. agrl. dusts), Am. Oil Chemists Soc. (mem. bd. govs., pres. found.). Republican. Methodist. Home and Office: 6135 Moorfield Ave Colorado Springs CO 80919-4802

HEILMAN, MARLIN GRANT, photographer; b. Tarentum, Pa., Sept. 29, 1919; s. Marlin Webster and Martha (Grant) H.; widowed; 1 child, Hans. BA in Econs., Swarthmore Coll., 1941. Prin. Grant Heilman Photography, Inc., Lititz, Pa., 1948—. Author and photographer: Farm Town, 1974, Wheat Country, 1977, FARM, 1988; photographer: Psalms Around us, 1970. Capt. U.S. Army, 1941-45. Decorated Bronze Star, Croix de Guerre, French Army, 1945, Hon Legionaire Firs Clas, French Fgn. Legion, 1943.

HEIMANN, JANET BARBARA, volunteer trail consultant; b. Santa Cruz, Calif., Dec. 18, 1931; d. John Louis and Charlotte Lucina (Burns) Grinnell; m. Richard Frank Gustav, July 10, 1953; children: David Robert, Gary Alan, Kathleen Janet. BS, U. Calif., Berkeley, 1954. Vol. trail rschr. Monterey County Pks. Dept.; appointee Carmel Valley Trail Adv. Com., 1993—. Pres. Folsom Freedom Trails, Placer County, Calif., 1980-83; chmn. Adopt-a-Trail, Folsom Lake Trail Patrol, Placer County, 1986-88; bd. dirs. Loomis Basin Horseman Assn., Placer County, 1986-87. Mem. AAUW. Republican. Home: 11565 Mccarthy Rd Carmel Valley CA 93924-9239

HEIMANN-HAST, SYBIL DOROTHEA, retired language arts and literature educator; b. Shanghai, May 8, 1924; came to U.S., 1941; d. Paul Heinrich and Elisabeth (Halle) Heimann; m. David G. Hast, Jan. 11, 1948 (div. 1959); children: Thomas David Hast, Dorothea Elizabeth Hast-Scott. BA in French, Smith Coll., 1946; MA in French Lang. and Lit., U. Pitts., 1963; MA in German Lang. and Lit., UCLA, 1966; diploma in Spanish, U. Barcelona, Spain, 1972. Cert. German, French and Spanish tchr., Calif. Assoc. in German lang. UCLA, 1966-70; asst. prof. German Calif. State U., L.A., 1970-71; lectr. German Mt. St. Mary's Coll., Brentwood, Calif., 1974-75; instr. French and German, diction coach Calif. Inst. of Arts, Valencia, 1977-78; coach lang. and diction UCLA Opera Theater, 1973-93, ret., 1993, lectr. dept. music, 1973-93; interviewer, researcher oral history program UCLA, 1986-93; dir., founder ISTMO, Santa Monica, Calif., 1975—; cons. interpreter/translator L.A. Music Ctr., U.S. Supreme Ct., L.A., J. Paul Getty Mus., Malibu, Calif., Warner New Media, Panorama Internat. Prodn., Sony Records, 1986—; voice-over artist; founder, artistic dir. Westside Opera Workshop, 1986—. Author of poems. UCLA grantee, 1990-91. Mem. AAUP, AFTRA, MLA, SAG, Sunset Succulent Soc. (v.p., bd. dirs., reporter, annual show chmn.), German Am. C. of C., L.A. Home and Office: 1022 17th St Apt 7 Santa Monica CA 90403-4339

HEIMBECHER, RONALD FREDERICK, information technologies director; b. Kremmling, Colo., Nov. 26, 1949; s. Fred Charles Heimbecher and Dorothy Rae (Lynch) Heimbecher Bersano; m. Lyn Dee Schlapia, June 10, 1972 (div. Nov. 1989); children: Stefan Friedrich, Lyssa Lyn. AS in Computer Sci., Parks Coll., Denver, 1981. Controller Wickes corp., throughout U.S., 1969-80; v.p. Alpha Computer Systems Inc., Longmont, Colo., 1982-87; owner Thinline Prodns., Broomfield, Colo., 1987—; mgr. info. systems City of Broomfield, Colo., 1991—; cons. Denver Theaters & Arenas, 1992-93; mem. computer sci. adv. bd. Front Range C.C., Westminster, Colo., 1991—. Author (screenplay) Love Your Eyes, 1992-93; leading actor (film) The Down Button, 1993; asst. producer vocals (recording) The Sonic Gallery, OhNo YoYo, 1993; appeared in stage performances, TV, film and recording credits. Advisor Future Bus. Leaders Am., Greeley, Colo., 1979, North Ctrl. Tech. Prep, Denver, 1993; chmn. Kern County Credit Mgrs. Assn., Bakersfield, Calif., 1980; mcpl. applications design Project Colo., Denver, 1994. Mem. Colo. Film and Video Assn., Denver Internat. Film Soc. (cons. 1987—, vol. coord. festival 1989-91), Rocky Mountain Writer's Guild. Republican. Office: City of Broomfield 1 Descombes Dr Broomfield CO 80020

HEIMBUCH, BABETTE E., bank executive; b. 1948. Student, U. Calif., 1972. Audit mgr. Peat Marwick Mitchell & Co., 1973-81; corp. contr. Zoetrope Studios, 1981-82; CFO, exec. v.p., treas. First Fed. Bank Calif. (subs. First Fed. Fin. Corp.), Santa Monica, CFO, sr. exec. v.p., treas., pres. Office: First Fed Bank Calif 401 Wilshire Blvd Santa Monica CA 90401-1416*

HEIN, KENNETH CHARLES LAWRENCE, priest, educator; b. Longmont, Colo., June 2, 1938; s. Peter Joseph and Lena Josephine (Keller) H. BA in Latin, St. Benedict's Coll., Atchison, Kans., 1964; STB, Coll. di Sant'Anselmo, Rome, Italy, 1967; ThD, U. Tübingen, Fed. Republic Germany, 1973. Benedictine monk Holy Cross Abbey, Canon City, Colo., 1960—, bus. mgr., 1985-88, treas., 1988-92; priest Roman Cath. Ch., 1969—; sem. tchr. St. Thomas Theol. Sem., Denver, 1972-74; tchr. high sch.modern langs. The Abbey Sch. Theology, Canon City, 1974-83, acad. dean, 1981-83; tchr. St. Anselm's Coll., Manchester, N.H., 1983-85; chaplain Fitzsimon's Army Med. Ctr., Aurora, Colo., 1989-92; adminstr. Holy Cross Abbey, Canon City, Colo., 1992—; bd. dirs. Theol. Inst. Holy Cross Abbey, 1974-78; mem. Med.-Moral Bd. St. Thomas More Hosp., 1980—; presenter in Anglican Roman Cath. dialog, 1975-76, med.-moral issues, 1979—. Contbr. numerous articles to profl. jours.; translator Psalms of Bible, 1989. Founder Abbey Students Aid to Poor, 1974-83; mem. Birthright, Woodbury, N.J., 1985—. Office: Holy Cross Abbey 2951 E Us Highway 50 Canon City CO 81212-2781

HEIN, MARTIN HENRY, farm manager; b. Newport News, Va., Aug. 29, 1966; s. Charles Henry and Barbara A. (Wolf) H. BA, Calif. State U., 1990. cert. farm mgr. Mgr. Hein Ranch Co., Visalia, Calif., 1986—. Mem. Am. Soc. Farm Mgrs. and Rural Appraisers (Assoc.), Pesticide Applicators Profl. Assn. Republican. Office: Hein Ranch Co 1241 E Sweet Ave Visalia CA 93292-2260

HEINDL, CLIFFORD JOSEPH, physicist; b. Chgo., Feb. 4, 1926; s. Anton Thomas and Louise (Fiala) H. B.S., Northwestern U., 1947, M.S., 1948; A.M., Columbia U., 1950, Ph.D., 1959. Sr. physicist Bendix Aviation Corp., Detroit, 1953-54; orsort student Oak Ridge Nat. Lab., 1954-55; asst. sect. chief Babcock & Wilcox Co., Lynchburg, Va., 1956-58; research group supr. Jet Propulsion Lab., Pasadena, Calif., 1959-65, mgr. research and space sci., 1965—. Served with AUS, 1944-46. Mem. AIAA, Am. Nuclear Soc., Health Physics Soc., Planetary Soc., Am. Phys. Soc. Home: 179 Mockingbird Ln South Pasadena CA 91030-2047 Office: 4800 Oak Grove Dr Pasadena CA 91109-8001

HEINECKEN, ROBERT FRIEDLI, art educator, artist; b. Denver, Oct. 29, 1931; s. Friedli Wilhelm and Mathilda Louise (Moehl) H.; m. Janet Marion Storey, Jan. 7, 1955 (div. 1980); children—Geoffrey Robert, Kathé Marie, Karol Leslie. AA, Riverside Coll., 1951; BA, UCLA, 1959, MA, 1960. Vis. faculty Harvard, 1972; Vis. faculty San Francisco Art Inst., 1970, Art Inst. Chgo., 1970; Vis. faculty Internat. Museum Photography, Rochester, N.Y., 1967, State U. N.Y. at Buffalo, 1969; prof. art UCLA, 1960-91, prof. emeritus dept. art, 1991—. One-man shows include Light Gallery, N.Y.C., Witkin Gallery, N.Y.C., Pasadena Art Mus., Focus Gallery, San Francisco, Madison (Wis.) Art Center, Friends of Photography Gallery, Carmel, Calif., Internat. Mus. Photography, Foto Forum, Universitat Kassel, Gallery Min, Tokyo, Art Inst. of Chgo.; exhibited in group shows at Mus. Modern Art, N.Y.C., Whitney Mus., N.Y.C., Nat. Gallery Can., Ottawa, Camden Arts Center, London, Eng.; represented in permanent collections Internat. Mus. Photography, Rochester, Mus. Modern Art, N.Y.C., Fogg Art Mus., Cambridge, Mass., San Francisco Mus. Art, Oakland (Calif.) Mus. Art, Library of Congress, Washington, Pasadena Mus. Art; represented by Pace/MacGill Gallery, N.Y.C., Ctr. for Creative Photography, U. Ariz. Trustee Friends of Photography, Carmel, 1974-75. Served with USMCR, 1953-57. Guggenheim fellow, 1975; Nat. Endowment for Arts grantee, 1977, 81, 86. Mem. Soc. for Photog. Edn. (chmn. bd. dirs. 1970-72). Office: 10300 Viretta Ln Los Angeles CA 90077-2724 also: UCLA Dept Art 405 Hilgard Ave Los Angeles CA 90024-1301

HEINER, DOUGLAS CRAGUN, pediatrician, educator; b. Salt Lake City, July 27, 1925; s. Spencer and Eva Lillian (Cragun) H.; m. Joy Luana Wiest, Jan. 8, 1946; children: Susan, Craig, Joseph, Marianne, James, David, Andrew, Carolee, Pauli. BS, Idaho State Coll., 1946; MD, U. Pa., 1950; PhD, McGill U., 1969. Intern Hosp. U. Pa., Phila., 1950-51; resident, fellow Children's Med. Ctr., Boston, 1953-56; asst. prof. pediatrics U. Ark. Med. Ctr., Little Rock, 1956-60; assoc. prof. pediatrics U. Utah Med. Ctr., Salt Lake City, 1960-66; fellow in immunology McGill U., Montreal, 1966-69; prof. of pediatrics Harbor-UCLA Med. Ctr., Torrance, 1969-94; prof. emeritus UCLA Sch. Medicine, 1994—. Author: Allergies to Milk, 1980; contbr. over 150 original articles to profl. jours. and chpts. to books; editorial bd.: Journal of Allergy and Clinical Immunology, 1975-79, Allergy, 1981—, Journal of Clinical Immunology, 1981—. Scoutmaster Boy Scouts Am., Salt Lake City, Rancho Palos Verdes, Calif., 1963-66, com. chmn. Rancho Palos Verdes, 1979-81; high coun. mem. Mormon Ch., Rancho Palos Verdes, 1983-86. 1st lt. U.S. Army, 1951-53. Recipient Disting. Alumni award Idaho State U., 1987. Fellow Am. Pediatric Soc., Am. Acad. Allergy and Clin. Immunology (food allergy com. 1981—), Am. Coll. Allergy and Immunology; mem. Soc. for Pediatric Rsch., Western Soc. for Pediatric Soc. (Ross award 1961), Am. Assn. Immunologists, Clin. Immunology Soc., Am. Acad. Pediatrics. Republican. Office: 745 N 500 W Provo UT 84601-1546

HEINER, LAWRENCE ELDEN, mineral company executive; b. Grand Junction, Colo., Aug. 24, 1938; s. Larry R. and Lola T. (Hall) H.; m. Virginia E. Doyle, Aug. 29, 1959; children: L. Timothy, Lawrence A. BS in Mining Engring., U. Alaska, 1961, MS in Mineral Preparation Engring., 1966. Registered profl. engr., Alaska, profl. land surveyor, Alaska. Assoc. prof. U. Alaska, Fairbanks, 1964-70; v.p. Resource Assocs. Alaska, Fairbanks, 1970-79, pres., 1979—; pres. NERCO Minerals Co., Fairbanks, 1982—; v.p. NERCO, Inc., Portland, Oreg., 1982-86; pres. NERCO Oil & Gas Inc., 1986—. Contbr. articles to profl. jours. Mem. State of Alaska Bd. Engring. and Archtl. Examiners, Fairbanks, 1979, Fairbanks Council Econ. Devel., 1984. Named Outstanding Mining Grad., U. Alaska, 1961; Outstanding Alumnus U. Alaska Sch. Mining Engring., 1984; Outstanding Businessman of Yr., U. Alaska Sch. Bus., 1984. Mem. AIME, Am. Mining Congress (bd. govs. western region 1985—, chmn. western div. 1986—). Office: NERCO Minerals Co 500 NE Multnomah St Portland OR 97232-2023

HEINISCH, ROBERT CRAIG, sales and marketing executive, consultant; b. Lakewood, Ohio, Nov. 17, 1941; m. Nancy Marhefka; children: Robert, Noreen, Matthew. Part owner C.F. Heinisch & Assocs., Akron, Ohio, 1964-67; sales promotion mgr. Foster and Kleiser div. Metromedia, Inc., Ohio, 1969-70; account exec. Foster and Kleiser div. Metromedia, Inc., 1970-71, mktg. svcs. mgr., 1971-72; mktg. svcs. mgr. Foster and Kleiser div. Metromedia, Inc., Dallas, Fort Worth, 1972-83, Calif., 1983-84; dir. mktg. svcs. to v.p. dir. mktg. svcs. Foster and Kleiser div. Metromedia, Inc., 1984-86; dir. mktg. Bowers Imaging Technologies, Berkeley, Calif., 1987-88; dir. mktg. Metromedia Technologies, L.A., 1988-90, v.p. internat. sales, 1990—; cons. Martin Outdoor Advt., The Pegasus Group, Triad Outdoor. Contbr. articles to profl. jours. Mem. dir. adv. com. Cleve. State U., 1970; mem. Super Sesqui Commn., Cleve., 1971. With U.S. Army, 1967-69. Home: 23525 Via Farol Valencia CA 91355-3025 Office: Metromedia Technologies 1320 N Wilton Pl Los Angeles CA 90028-8527

HEINLEIN, OSCAR ALLEN, former air force officer; b. Butler, Mo., Nov. 17, 1911; s. Oscar A. and Katherine (Canterbury) H.; B.S., U.S. Naval Acad., 1932; M.S., Calif. Inst. Tech., 1942; M.S. in Mech. Engring., Stanford, 1949; certificate in mining U. Alaska, 1953; grad. Air War Coll., 1953; student spl. studies U. Ariz., 1956-57, Eastern Wash. U., Clark County Community Coll., Las Vegas, Nev., 1988, U. Nice, France; D.D., Universal Sem., 1970; AA Clark County Community Cm. Catharine Anna Bangert, May 1, 1933 (div. Apr. 1937); 1 dau., Catharine Anna; m. 2d, Mary Josephine Fisher, Aug. 25, 1939 (dec. Dec. 1977); 1 son, Oscar Allen III; m. 3d, Suzanne Birke, Feb. 23, 1980; 1 son, Michael Andre Bertin. Marine engr. Atlantic Refining Co., Phila., 1934; civil engr. Annapolis Mineral Devel. Co., Calif., 1935-37; enlisted as pvt. U.S. Army, 1937, advanced through grades to col., 1944; comdr. Ladd AFB, Alaska, 1953-54, 11th Air Div., Fairbanks, Alaska, 1954, Air Force Logistics Command Support Group, Vandenberg AFB, Calif., 1960-65, prof. air sci. U. Ariz., Tucson, 1955-58; insp. Gen. Mobile Air Materiel Area, Ala., 1958-60; ret. 1965; now cons.; pres. O.A. Heinlein Merc. Co., Butler, Mo., 1934—; vis. prof. U. Nev., Reno; dep. dir. civil def. Boulder City, Nev., 1967; dir., sec. Boulder Dam Fed. Credit Union, 1973-79; mem. Boulder City Police Adv. Com., 1976; ordained minister Bapt. Ch., 1976. Active Boy Scouts Am. Mem. Clark County (Nev.) Republican Central Com., 1966, Exec. com., 1970; mem. Rep. Central Com., 1966; Rep. candidate Nev. Assembly, 1972; mem. Boulder City Charter Commn. Mem. community coll. adv. bd. U. Nev., 1970. Served with USN, 1928-32; to 2d lt. USMC, 1932-34. Decorated Legion of Merit, Air medal, Army, Navy and Air Force commendation medals. Mem. Inst. Aero. Scis., Am. Meteorol. Soc., Nat. Research Assn., Am. Radio Relay League, SAR, Am. Polar Soc., VFW, Daedalians, Mensa, So. Nev. Amateur Radio Club, Inst. Amateur Radio, Quarter Century Wireless Assn., Ret. Officers Assn., Air Force Assn., Nat. Rifle Assn. (life), Armed Forces Communications and Electronics Assn., USS Nevada Assn., CAP, Am. Legion, Am. Assn. Ret. Persons, West Coast Amateur Radio Service, Soc. Wireless Pioneers. Mason, Nev. Rifle and Pistol Assn. (bd. dirs.), Vet. Wireless Operator's Assn. Clubs: MM (San Diego); Intertel (Ft. Wayne, Indiana); Missile Amateur Radio (pres. 1961-65 Vandenberg AFB); Explorers (N.Y.C.); Arctic Circle Prospectors', High Jumpers (Fairbanks, Alaska); Boulder City Gem and Mineral; Stearman Alumnus; Marines Memorial (San Francisco). Author: Big Bend County, 1953. Inventor. Home: 107 Wyoming St Boulder City NV 89005-2818

HEINS, MARILYN, college dean, pediatrics educator, author; b. Boston, Sept. 7, 1930; d. Harold and Esther (Berow) H.; m. Milton P. Lipson, 1958; children: Rachel, Jonathan. A.B., Radcliffe Coll., 1951; M.D., Columbia U., 1955. Diplomate Am. Bd. Pediatrics. Intern N.Y. Hosp., N.Y.C., 1955-56; resident in pediatrics Babies Hosp., N.Y.C., 1956-58; asst. pediatrician Children's Hosp. Mich., Detroit, 1959-78; dir. pediatrics Detroit Receiving Hosp., 1965-71; asst., assoc. dean student affairs Wayne State U. Med. Sch., Detroit, 1971-79; assoc. dean acad. affairs U. Ariz. Med. Coll., Tucson, 1979-83, vice dean, 1983-88, prof. pediatrics, 1985-88. Author: (with Anne M. Seiden) Child Care/Parent Care, 1987; mem. editorial bd. Jour. AMA, 1981-91; contbr. articles to profl. jours. Bd. dirs. Planned Parenthood So. Ariz., 1983, pres., 1988-89, Ariz. Ctr. for Clin. Mgmt.,1991—, Nat. Bd. Med. Examiners, 1983-88; mem. adv. bd. So. Ariz. Women's Fund, 1992—, Ariz. State Hosp., 1985-88. Recipient Alumni Faculty Service award Wayne State U., 1972, Recognition award, 1977, Women on the Move Achievement award YWCA Tucson, 1983; mem. Ariz. Ctr. Clin. Mgmt. 1990—. Fellow Am. Orthopsychiat. Assn., Am. Acad. Pediatrics; mem. Assn. Am. Med. Colls. (chair group on student affairs 1976-79), Am. Hosp. Assn. (chmn. com. med. edn. 1985), Soc. Health and Human Values, Women in Sci. and Engring. U. Ariz. (bd. dirs. 1979-88), Exec. Women's Council Tucson, Ariz. Med. Assn. (com. on med. svc. 1985-87), Pima County Med. Soc., Pima County Pediatric Soc., Ambulatory Pediatric Assn., AAAS, Am. Pub. Health Assn. Home: 6530 N Longfellow Dr Tucson AZ 85718-2416

HEINY, ROBERT WAYNE, special education educator; b. Oakland, Calif., Jan. 28, 1936; s. Edwin Wayne and Martha Mary (Wilkinson) H.; m. Joan Marie Umscheid, Dec. 28, 1956; children: Lawrence Wayne, Leanne Lynn, Loren Charles, Layne Pahl, Lora Joy. BA, U. LaVerne, 1960; MA, Calif. State U., L.A., 1964; PhD, U. Ill., 1969. Passenger agt. United Airlines, San Francisco, 1957-59; tchr. Azusa (Calif.) Unified Sch. Dist., 1960-63; instr. in spl. edn. U. Ill., Champaign, 1967-68; assoc. prof. edn. U. N.C., Chapel Hill, 1968-70; assoc. prof. spl. edn. George Peabody Coll., Nashville, 1970-75; dir. edn. and tng. Wassaic (N.Y.) Devel. Ctr., 1975-76; sr. rsch. assoc. Brandeis U., Waltham, Mass., 1976-80; asst. to pres. and other titles U. LaVerne, Calif., Calif., 1981-87; spl. cons. to pres. Am. Armenian Internat. Coll., LaVerne, 1984-87; assoc. prof. spl. edn. Ill. State U., Normal, 1989-93; dir. Mont. Ctr. on Disabilities, Billings, 1993-94; prof. spl. edn. and ednl. founds. Mont. State U., Billings, 1993—; sr. ptnr. Robert Heiny Assocs., 1978-89. Editor spl. feature issues Peabody Jour. Edn., 1972; contbr. articles to profl. jours., chpts. to books. Bd. dirs. Ill. Spl. Olympics, Normal, 1992-93, MARC Ctr., Bloomington, Ill., 1992-93, Mashdots Coll., Pasadena, Calif., 1992—; legis. liaison Ill. Spl. Edn. Coalition, Springfield, 1991-92. Recipient Bronze medal Coun. for Advancement and Support of Edn., 1985. Mem. ASCD, Coun. for Exceptional Children, Am. Assn. on Mental Retardation. Mem. Ch. of the Brethren. Office: Mont Ctr on Disabilities 1500 N 30th St Billings MT 59101-0245

HEINZ, DON J., agronomist; b. Rexburg, Idaho, Oct. 29, 1931; s. William and Berniece (Steiner) H.; m. Marsha B. Hegsted, Apr. 19, 1956; children: Jacqueline, Grant, Stephanie, Karen, Ramona, Amy. BS, Utah State U., 1958, MS, 1959; PhD, Mich State U., 1961; grad., Stanford U. Exec. Program, 1982. Assoc. plant breeder Experiment Sta. Hawaiian Sugar Planters' Assn., Aiea, 1961-66, head dept. genetics and pathology, 1966-78, asst. dir., 1977-78, v.p. and dir., 1979-85, pres., dir. experiment sta., 1986-94; ret.; cons. Hawaiian Sugar Planters Assn., Philippines, Egypt, Colombia, Reunion; mem. adv. com. plants Hawaii Dept. Agriculture, 1970-94, Pres. Nat. Commn. Agriculture and Rural Devel. Policy, 1988-91. Contbr. articles to sci. jours. on sugarcane breeding, cytogenetics, cell and tissue culture techniques, and sugarcane culture. Served with USAF, 1951-54. Mem. AAAS, Internat. Soc. Sugar Cane Technologists (chmn. com. germplasm and breeding 1975-86), Sigma Xi. Mem. LDS Ch. Home: PO Box 352 Island Park ID 83429-0352

HEINZ, RONEY ALLEN, civil engineering consultant; b. Shawano, Wis., Dec. 29, 1946; s. Orville Willard and Elva Ida (Allen) H.; m. Judy Evonne Olney, Oct. 30, 1965. BSCE, Mont. State U., 1973. Surveyor U.S. Army Corps Engrs., Seattle, 1966-73; civil engr. Hoffman, Fiske, & Wyatt, Lewiston, Idaho, 1973-74, Tippetts-Abbott-McCarthy-Stratton, Seattle, 1977-79; asst. editor Civil Engring. Mag. ASCE, N.Y.C., 1974-77; constrn. mgr. Boeing Co., Seattle, 1979-83; owner, gen. mgr. Armwavers Ltd., South Bend, Wash., 1983—; pres. Great Walls Internat. Inc., Elma, Wash., 1993—; mem. dams and tunnels del. to China, People to People Internat., Spokane, 1987; mem. U.S. com. on Large Dams. Asst. editor Commemorative Book Internat. Congress on Large Dams, 1987; contbr. articles to profl. publs., including Civil Engring. Mag., Excavator Mag., Internat. Assn. for Bridge and Structural Engring., Japan Concrete Inst., others. Dir. Canaan Christians Fund, Aberdeen, 1993—; bd. dirs. Seaman's Ctr., Aberdeen, Wash., 1990—. Recipient First Quality award Asphalt Paving Assn. Wash., 1991. Mem. ASCE (sec. met. sect. 1975-76, assoc. mem. forum), ASTM (Student award 1973), U.S. Com. On Large Dams. Republican. Lutheran. Office: Armwavers Ltd PO Box 782 South Bend WA 98586-0782

HEINZE, DAVID C., business administration educator; b. Paterson, N.J., June 3, 1941; s. E. Charles and Susan (Jen) H. BS in Math., Ariz. State U., 1963, PhD in Quantitative Bus. Analysis, 1969; MS in Actuarial Sci., U. Wis., 1964. Prof. bus. Rochester (N.Y.) Inst. Tech., 1969-74, Va. Commonwealth U., Richmond, 1974-79, No. Ariz. U., Flagstaff, 1979-81, Calif. State U., Chico, 1981—; cons. Eastman Kodak, Rochester, 1971-74, Omark, Oroville, Calif., 1984. Author: Statistical Decision Analysis for Management, 1973, Management Science, 1978, 82, Fundamentals of Managerial Statistics, 1980; contbr. articles to profl. jours. Knapp fellow, NDEA fellow. Mem. Phi Kappa Phi. Office: Calif State U. Dept. Bus Chico CA 95929

HEINZE, RUTH-INGE, Asian studies educator, researcher, writer; b. Berlin, Nov. 4, 1919; came to U.S., 1955; d. Otto and Louise (Preschel) H. Gr. Latinum, Interpreter Coll., Berlin, 1967; BA, U. Calif., Berkeley, 1969, MA, 1971, PhD, 1974. Producer, writer Ednl. Broadcast, Berlin,

1963-73; lectr. U. of Chiang Mai, Thailand, 1971-72; staff rsch. asst. human devel. dept. U. Calif., San Francisco, 1974, rsch. assoc. Ctr. for S.E. Asian Studies, 1974—; lectr. Mills Coll., Oakland, Calif., 1974; adj. faculty Saybrook Inst., San Francisco, 1984—, Calif. Inst. for Integral Studies, 1984—. Author: The Role of the Sangha in Modern Thailand, 1977, Tham Khwan - How to Contain the Essence of Life, 1982, Trance and Healing in Southeast Asia Today, 1988, Shamans of the 20th Century, 1991, The Search for Visions, 1994. Prodr. Universal Dialogue Series, Berkeley, 1979—; nat. dir. Ind. Scholars of Asia, 1981—; bd. dirs. Oakland Asian Cultural Ctr., 1987—. Recipient grant Am. Inst. for Indian Studies, 1975,78, Fulbright-Hays Rsch. grant, 1978-79. Mem. Internat. Assn. for Study of Traditional Asian Medicine, Internat. Soc. for Study of Subtle Energies and Energy Medicine, Internat. Soc. for Shamanic Rsch., Parapsychology Rsch., Group Spiritual Emergency Network, Nat. Pictographic Soc., Ind. Scholars of Asia, Assn. for Asian Studies. Home and Office: 2321 Russell St Apt 3A Berkeley CA 94705-1959

HEISTER, CARLA GAYLE, library director; b. Rock Falls, Ill., May 16, 1950; d. Andrew George and Elizabeth Mary (Brooks) Fisher; m. Robert Allen Heister, Aug. 2, 1980; children: Leah Elizabeth, Ellen Clare. BS in Biology, No. Ill. U., 1979, MA in Libr. Sci., 1982; MS in Biol. Scis., U. Ill., 1989. Libr. Ill. Natural History Survey, Champaign, 1982-92; dir. Quinney Libr. Utah State U. Coll. Natural Resources, Logan, 1992—. Co-compiler: The Natural Resources of Illinois, 1987. Mem. Am. Soc. Info. Sci., Utah Soc. for Environ. Edn., Spl. Librs. Assn. (chair environ. and resource mgmt. div. 1993-94). Presbyterian. Office: SJ and Jessie E Quinney Nat Resources Rsch Libr UMC 5260 Logan UT 84322

HEITLER, BRUCE F., entrepreneur; b. Denver, June 12, 1945; s. Emmett H. and Dorothy (Shwayder) H.; m. Susan Kaye McCrensky, June 6, 1971; children: Abigail, Sara, Jesse, Jacob. BA, Yale U., 1967, JD, 1972; MCP, U. Calif., Berkeley, 1969. Bar: Colo. 1973. Assoc. Holme Roberts & Owen, Denver, 1972-74; project mgr. Cen. Devel. Group, Denver, 1974-76; pres. Heitler Devel., Inc., Denver, 1976—; vice chmn., bd. dirs. Nexus Greenhouse Corp., Northglenn, Colo., 1982-93; pres., bd. dirs. Colo. Biogenix, Inc., Denver; owner, operator Discovery Door Children's Ctr., Denver, 1990—; vice-chmn. Lowry AFB Redevel. Authority, 1994—. Trustee E. Roosevelt Inst. for Cancer Rsch., Denver, 1975-94, Social Sci. Found. U. Denver, 1989—; active Yale Devel. Bd., New Haven, 1986-90. Mem. Colo. Yale Assn. (pres. 1991-93), Assn. Yale Alumni (bd. govs. 1994—), Cactus Club (pres. 1986-88). Jewish. Office: Heitler Devel Inc Ste B203 1410 Grant St Denver CO 80203-1846

HEITMAN, GREGORY ERWIN, state official; b. Lewiston, Idaho, June 7, 1947; s. Elmer William and Carmelita Rose Ann (Kinzer) H.; m. Phyllis Ann Pryor, Sept. 25, 1982. BS in Math., U. Idaho, 1969, MBA, 1971; student, Wash. State U., 1965-67. Student communications dir. Assoc. Students U. Idaho, Moscow, 1970-72, advisor, apt. mgr. dept. housing, 1971-72; traffic fatality analyst Idaho Dept. Transp., Boise, 1973-74; ops. mgr. Region IV Health & Welfare State of Idaho, Boise, 1974-78, supr. computer svcs., div. environ. in health and welfare, 1978-85; supr. field svcs., program dir. Idaho Vital Statistics, Boise, 1985—; acting dir. Idaho Ctr. for Health Statistics, Boise, 1988-89, spl. asst. program and policy devel., 1989—; mem. med. records adv. com. Boise State U., 1987—, cons., lectr. 1987—. Active various charitable orgns.; precinct committeeman Dem. of Latah County, 1972; election day coord. Ada County, 1986; vol. Am. Cancer Soc., 1990, Easter Seals, 1992. Mem. Idaho Pub. Health Assn., Assn. Vital Records and Health Statistics, Idaho Pub. Employees Assn., Assn. Govt. Employees. Roman Catholic. Home: 5103 Shalecrest Ct Boise ID 83703-3442 Office: Idaho Vital Stats PO Box 83720 Boise ID 83720-0002

HEJHALL, ROY CHARLES, electrical engineer; b. Duluth, Minn., Aug. 11, 1932; s. Charles Joseph Hejhall and Florence Mary (Patwell) Wales; m. Virginia Lee Hoke, June 9, 1956 (div. 1968); children: Jeffrey, Jody, Julie; m. Audrey Ruth Bailey, June 28, 1970. BS in Engring., U.S. Naval Acad., 1956.; Commd. ensign USN, 1956, advanced through grades to lt., 1961; tech. staff Motorola, Phoenix, 1961—; tech. advisor Am. Radio Relay League, Newington, Conn., 1977—. Contbr. articles to profl. jours. Mem. Elks. Republican. Office: Motorola 5005 E Mcdowell Rd Phoenix AZ 85008-4229

HELD, JAY ALLEN, pastor; b. Canton, Ohio, Dec. 15, 1961; s. Earl E. and E. Jean (Robinson) H.; m. Laureen Elizabeth Allen, Mar. 19, 1988. BS in Theology, Bapt. U. Am., 1985, postgrad.; MA in Counseling, Western Sem., 1990, MDiv, 1994; MA in Missions, Grace Theol. Sem., 1990. Ordained to ministry Canton Baptist Temple, 1990. Inner-city missionary Forest Hills Bapt. Ch., Decatur, Ga., 1980-84; asst. to pastor Allgood Rd. Bapt. Ch., Marietta, Ga., 1984-85, Eastland Bapt. Ch., Orlando, Fla., 1985; tchr. high sch. Eastland Christian Sch., Orlando, 1985; inner-city missionary North Portland Bible Fellowship, Portland, 1989-91, Mt. Sinai Community Bapt. Ch., Portland, 1991-94; urban pastor North Bapt. Ch., 1994—; camp counselor Camp C.H.O.F., Dalton, Ohio, summer, 1981, 82; adolescent counselor Youth Guidance Assn., Portland, 1986-88; program dir. Youth Outreach, Vancouver, Wash., 1988-89; tchr. North Portland Bible Clubs, 1989; instr. North Portland Bible Coll., 1991—. Mem. Oreg. Gang Task Force, Portland, 1989; tchr., counselor Bridge Bible Club, Mt. Sinai Cmty. Bapt. Ch., 1990-94; coord. Bridge Gang Transition, 1993-94. Mem. Oreg. Mediation Assn., Portland Urban League. Home: 836 N Holland St Portland OR 97217-1334

HELD, NANCY B., perinatal nurse, lactation consultant; b. Winchester, Mass., Sept. 4, 1957; d. Ann and Laurence Babine; m. Lew Held, May 22, 1976; children: David, Jessica. BSN, NYU, 1979; MS, U. Calif., San Francisco, 1992. Cert. lactation and childbirth educator, Am. Soc. Psychoprophylaxis Obstetrics. Labor/delivery nurse Pascack Valley Hosp., Westwood, N.J., 1979-83; obstetrics educator Drs. Pinski, Wiener & Grasso, Westwood, N.J., 1982-85; ob/gyn office nurse Drs. Power Hagbom Holter & Clark, San Francisco, 1986-87; asst. to dir. maternity svcs. Women's Health Assn., Greenbrae, Calif., 1987-89; perinatal edn. and lactation ctr. clin. coord. Calif. Pacific Med. Ctr., San Francisco, 1989—; owner North Bay Lamaze, 1988—; speaker in field. Recipient Founders Day award, NYU. Fellow Am. Coll. Childbirth Educators; mem. Assn. Women's Health Obstetric and Neonatal Nursing (spkr. nat. con. 1993, nat. rsch. utilization team 1993), Am. Soc. Psychoprophylaxis (chpt. co-pres.), Nurses Assn. of Am. Coll. Ob/Gyn, Internat. Childbirth Educators Assn., Internat. Lactation Cons. Assn., Sigma Theta Tau.

HELDER, DAVID ERNEST, artist, educator; b. Seattle, Feb. 4, 1947; s. Reinard Wright and Maxine Edda (Spiva) H.; m. Sallye Ann Giles, Aug. 7, 1976; 1 child, Julian Oliver. AA, Yuba Coll., Marysville, Calif., 1966; BA in Sculpture, Calif. Coll. Arts and Crafts, Oakland, 1969, MFA, 1971; MA in Aesthetic Edn., Stanford U., 1975. Aesthetic edn. and art direction cons. U. Mpls. Super Computer Inst., 1988—. San Francisco Arts Festival, 1980, Stamford (Conn.) Art Assn., 1988, Exhibited in solo shows at Wake Gallery, Cape Town, South Africa, 1972, Margaret Jensen Gallery, San Francisco, 1976, Park Gallery, San Francisco, 1977, Lyle Tuttle Gallery, San Francisco, 1979, Jaymark Gallery, San Francisco, 1981; group shows include San Diego Art Inst., 1988, Alligator Gallery, San Francisco, 1988, Helio Gallery, N.Y.C., 1991, Rayco Gallery, San Francisco, 1991, North East Juried Exposition, Mass., 1993. Home: 644 Stanyan St San Francisco CA 94117-1807 Studio: 636 Stanyan St San Francisco CA 94117-1807

HELFERT, ERICH ANTON, management consultant, author, educator; b. Aussig/Elbe, Sudetenland, May 29, 1931; came to U.S., 1950; s. Julius and Anna Maria (Wilde) H.; m. Anne Langley, Jan. 1, 1983; children: Claire L., Amanda L. BS, U. Nev., 1954; MBA with high distinction, Harvard U., 1956, DBA, 1958. Newspaper reporter, corr., Neuburg, Fed. Republic of Germany, 1948-52; rsch. asst. Harvard U., 1956-57; asst. prof. bus. policy San Francisco State U., 1958-59; asst. prof. fin. and control Grad. Sch. Bus. Adminstrn., Harvard U., 1959-65; internal cons., then asst. to pres., dir. corp. planning Crown Zellerbach Corp., San Francisco, 1965-78, asst. to chmn., dir. corp. planning, 1978-82, v.p. corp. planning, 1982-85; mgmt. cons., San Francisco, 1985—; co-founding dir. Modernsoft, Inc.; mem. Dean's adv. coun. San Francisco State Bus. Sch., sch. fin. Golden Gate U.; bd. dirs., past chmn. and pres. Harvard U. Bus. Sch. No. Calif.; trustee Saybrook Inst. Author: Techniques of Financial Analysis, 1963, 8th edit., 1994, Valuation, 1966, (with others) Case Book on Finance, 1963, Controllership, 1965; contbr. articles to profl. jours. Exch. student fellow U.S. Inst. Internat. Edn., 1950; Ford Found. doctoral fellow, 1956. Mem. Assn. Corp. Growth (past pres., bd. dirs. San Francisco chpt.), Inst. Mgmt. Cons., Commonwealth Club, Phi Kappa Phi. Roman Catholic. Home: 111 W 3rd Ave # 401 San Mateo CA 94402-1521 Office: 1777 Borel Pl Ste 508 San Mateo CA 94402-3514

HELFFERICH, MERRITT RANDOLPH, geophysical research administrator; b. Hartford, Conn., Aug. 10, 1935; s. Reginald Humphrey and Virginia (Merritt) H.; m. Carla Anne Ostergren, July 11, 1959 (div. 1977); children: Deirdre Alida, Tryntje Bronwyn; m. April Evalyn Crosby, Aug. 24, 1985. BA, U. Alaska, 1966; MPA, Harvard U., 1990. Surveyor Golden Valley Electric Assn., Fairbanks, Alaska, 1965-66; engring. technician Geophys. Inst., U. Alaska, Fairbanks, 1966-69, field technician, meteorologist Poker Flat Rsch. Range, 1969-76, head tech. svcs., 1976-83, asst. dir., 1986-88, assoc. dir., 1988-93; ice technician Humble Oil Co./U. Alaska, S.S. Manhattan, Northwest Passage Voyage, 1969; assoc. v.p. human resource devel. U. Alaska, Fairbanks, 1983, asst. to chancellor, 1983-86, assoc. v.p. human resource devel., 1993, dir. Elvey addition project, 1994—; exec. v.p. U. Alaska Tech. Devel. Corp., Fairbanks, 1994—; legis. liaison U. Alaska, Fairbanks, 1983-86; adv. bd. NSF Polar Ice Coring Office, Fairbanks, 1989-94; bd. dirs. Internat. Small Satellite Orgn., Washington, Snedden Parks Found., Northern Alaska Environ. Ctr. Mem. editl. bd. U. Alaska Press, Fairbanks, 1986-94. Commr. Alaska Women's Commn., Juneau, 1988-89; mem., co-chair Main St. Fairbanks, 1990-94; mem. Fairbanks Native Cultural Ctr. Com., 1991-93; chair Fairbanks North Star Borough Riverfront Commn., 1992—; bd. dirs. Suedden Parks Found., 1993—, No. Alaska Environ. Ctr., 1994—. Helfferich Glacier named in his honor U.S. Bd. Geographic Names, 1971; recipient Antarctic Svc. medal NSF, 1971, Nick Begich Scholarship Fund award, 1989, Alumni Achievement award U. Alaska Alumni Assn., 1993. Fellow Explorers Club (chair exploration com. Alaska Yukon chpt. 1991—); mem. AAAS, Soc. Rsch. Adminstrs., Am. Geophys. Union, Assn. Univ. Tech. Mgrs., Rotary Club of Fairbanks. Democrat. Home: PO Box 80769 Fairbanks AK 99708-0769 Office: U Alaska Tech Devel Corp PO Box 81370 Fairbanks AK 99708

HELFINSTINE, KELLY ANN, financial planner, securities company executive; b. Salt Lake City, Nov. 4, 1957; d. James William Helfinstine and Jan Elaine (Bragg) Marshall. BA, U. Ariz., 1979. Cert. fin. planner. Mgmt. trainee The Ariz. Bank, Phoenix, 1980-81; mktg. rep. The Ariz. Lottery, Phoenix, 1981; pvt. practice fin. planning Phoenix, 1983-86; divisional v.p. Jones Internat. Securities, Phoenix, 1986—. Mem. Internat. Assn. Fin. Planners, Inst. Cert. Fin. Planners (cert.). Home: 2423 E Taxidea Way Phoenix AZ 85048-9074 Office: Jones Internat Securities 9697 E Mineral Ave Englewood CO 80112-3408

HELFORD, PAUL QUINN, communications educator, academic administrator; b. Chgo., June 27, 1947; s. Norman and Eleanor (Kwin) H.; m. Leslie Gale Weinstein, July 11, 1971; children: Ross Michael, Benjamin Keith. BA, U. Ill., 1969; MA, Northeastern Ill. U., 1977. Cert. tchr., Ill., Oreg., Ariz. Tchr. John Hersey High Sch., Arlington Heights, Ill., 1969-73; freelance writer Mill Valley, Calif., 1973-75; mgr., program dir. Sta. KOZY-TV, Eugene, Oreg., 1976-88, mktg., sales, and program dir. Group W Cable, 1984-88; producer, with mktg. Northland Broadcasting, Flagstaff, Ariz., 1989-91; lectr. cinema and broadcasting No. Ariz. U., 1989—, acad. coord. for instrnl. TV, 1995—; dir. Native Am. Video Workshops, 1991—, Flagstaff Festiva. of the Arts Film Festival, 1992, No. Ariz. U. Instrnl. TV Programming, 1994—; writer New Times, Phoenix, 1992. Writer, producer Paul Helford's Hollywood Oldies, 1976-81, In Review, 1981, Live from the Fair, 1981-85, Group W Cable Minutes, 1984-85, Bad Horror and Sci. Fiction, 1985 (Award for Cable Excellence 1986), KOZY movie promotional spots 1976-88 (Award for Cable Excellence 1984, 88, CLIO award nomination 1988, 1989); contbr. articles to profl. jours. Recipient CLIO award 1984, 86, Cable Mktg. Grand award, 1981, 85. Mem. Nat. Assn. Cable Programmers. Home: 5152 Hickory Dr Flagstaff AZ 86004-7389 Office: Northland Broadcasting PO Box 3421 Flagstaff AZ 86003-3421

HELGESON, DUANE MARCELLUS, retired librarian; b. Rothsay, Minn., July 2, 1930; s. Oscar Herbert and Selma Olivia (Sateren) H.; B.S., U. Minn., 1952. Librarian, Chance-Vought Co., Dallas, 1956-59, System Devel. Corp., Santa Monica, Calif., 1959-62, Lockheed Aircraft, Burbank, Calif., 1962-63, C.F. Braun Co., Alhambra, Calif., 1963-74; chief librarian Ralph M. Parsons Co., Pasadena, Calif., 1974-79; pres. Mark-Allen/Brokers-in-Info., Los Angeles, 1976-80; phys. scis. librarian Calif. Inst. Tech., Pasadena, 1980-84; corp. librarian Montgomery Watson, Pasadena, 1985-94, ret. 1994. mem. adv. bd. Los Angeles Trade Tech. Coll., 1974-79, U. So. Calif. Library Sch., 1974-79. Served with USAF, 1952-54. Mem. Spl. Libraries Assn. (chmn. nominating com. 1974). Co-editor: (with Joe Ann Clifton) Computers in Library and Information Centers, 1973. Home: 2706 Ivan Hill Ter Los Angeles CA 90039-2717

HELLE, JOHN HAROLD (JACK HELLE), fishery research biologist; b. Williston, N.D., Apr. 26, 1935; s. Harold Cliford and Alice (Linquist) H.; m. Marilyn D. Matthews, Dec. 27, 1959; children: Jeanmarie Helle Davis, Joanna. BS, U. Idaho, 1958, MS, 1961; PhD in Fishery Sci., Oreg. State U., 1979. Fishery rsch. biologist U.S. Fish and Wildlife Svc., Auke Bay, Alaska, 1960-70, Nat. Marine Fisheries Svc., Auke Bay, 1971—; hon. rsch. fellow Marischal Coll., U. of Aberdeen, Scotland, 1964-65. Fellow Am. Inst. Fishery Rsch. Biologists (pres. 1990-92); mem. AAAS, Am. Fisheries Soc. (cert. fisheries scientist), Pacific Fishery Biologists. Office: Auke Bay Fisheries Lab 11305 Glacier Hwy Juneau AK 99801-8626

HELLER, ANTHONY FERDINAND, electronics engineer; b. N.Y.C., Oct. 6, 1944; s. Louis Richard and Alma Gunda (Schauer) H. BA in Psychology, Hofstra U., 1967; MS in Indsl. Psychology, San Diego State U., 1971. Rsch. analyst Navy Med. Neuropsychiat. Rsch. Unit, San Diego, 1967-71; prin. Montessori Internat. Youth U., Stonybrook, N.Y., 1971-72; mgr. Pacific Stereo, L.A., 1972-80; owner, operator Heller Automotive Security Systems, Lawndale, Calif., 1981-85; nat. dir. tng. Anes Electronics, Marina del Rey, Calif., 1985-90, Directed Electronics, San Marcos, Calif., 1990-91; engr. AudiovoxWest Corp., Cerritos, Calif., 1991—; instr. Fred Kennedy Assocs., San Pedro, Calif., 1991—; owner, operator Tng. Cons. Internat., Redondo Beach, Calif., 1990—. Assoc. editor: Autosound and Communications, 1987-89, C.A.R.S. Mag., 1989—. Active Am. Brotherhood Aimed Toward Edn., Torrance, Calif., 1992. Recipient Cert. of Recognition Calif. Crime Prevention Officers Assn., 1989, City of Newport Beach, 1990. Mem. So. Calif. Confedn. of Clubs, 5th Chpt. Motorcycle Club (road capt. 1981-83, v.p. 1983-84), Port Royal Yacht Club (charter), Chosen Few Motorcycle Club (pres. San Gabriel Valley chpt.), Hermosa Beach Alano Club (bd. dirs., spl. events coord. 1992—). Home: Vessel Gypsy Boy, Port Royal Marina 555 N Harbor Dr Slip 5 Redondo Beach CA 90277-2076

HELLER, DEAN, state official. Sec. of state State of Nev., Carson City. Home: 1520 Andorra Dr Carson City NV 89703-2308 Office: Sec of State Capitol Complex Carson City NV 89710

HELLER, JULES, artist, writer; b. N.Y.C., Nov. 16, 1919; s. Jacob Kenneth and Goldie (Lassar) H.; m. Gloria Spiegel, June 11, 1947; children: Nancy Gale, Jill Kay. AB, Ariz. State Coll., 1939; AM, Columbia U., 1940; PhD, U. So. Calif., 1948; DLitt, York U., 1985. Spl. art instr. 8th St. Sch., Tempe, Ariz., 1938-39; dir. art and music Union Neighborhood House, Auburn, N.Y., 1940-41; prof. fine arts, head dept. U. So. Calif., 1946-61; vis. asso. prof. fine arts Pa. State U., summers 1955, 57; dir. Pa. State U. (Sch. Arts), 1961-63; founding dean Pa. State U. (Coll. Arts and Architecture), 1963-68; founding dean Faculty Fine Arts York U., Toronto, 1968-73; prof. fine arts Faculty of Fine Arts, York U., 1973-76; dean Coll. Fine Arts, Ariz. State U., Tempe, 1976-85; prof. art Coll. Fine Arts, Ariz. State U., 1985-89; prof. emeritus, dean emeritus, 1990—; vis. prof. Silpakorn U., Bangkok, Thailand, 1974, Coll. Fine Arts, Colombo, Sri Lanka, 1974, U. Nacional de Tucumán, Argentina, 1990, U. Nacional de Cuyo, Mendoza, Argentina, 1990; lectr., art juror; Cons. Open Studio, 1975-76; mem. vis. com. on fine arts Fisk U., Nashville, 1974. Printmaker; exhibited one man shows, Gallery Pascal, Toronto, U. Alaska, Fairbanks, Alaskaland Bear Gallery, Visual Arts Center, Anchorage, Ariz. State U., Lisa Sette Gallery, 1990, Centro Cultural de Tucumán, San Miguel de Tucumán, 1990; exhibited numerous group shows including Canadian Printmaker's Showcase, Pollack Gallery, Toronto, Mazelow Gallery, Toronto, Santa Monica Art Gallery, L.A. County Mus., Phila. Print Club, Seattle Art Mus., Landau Gallery, Kennedy & Co. Gallery, Bklyn. Mus., Cin. Art Mus., Dallas Mus. Fine Arts, Butler Art Inst., Oakland Art Mus., Pa. Acad. Fine Arts, Santa Barbara Mus. Art, San Diego Gallery Fine Arts, Martha Jackson Gallery, N.Y.C., Yuma Fine Arts Assn., Ariz., Toronto Dominion Centre, Amerika Haus, Hannover, Fed. Rep. Germany, U. Md., Smith-Andersen Galleries, Palo Alto, Calif., Grunewald Ctr. Graphic Arts, L.A., Univ. So. Fla., Tampa, Sheldon Meml. Gallery, Lincoln, Nebr., Santa Cruz (Calif.) Mus., Drake U., Iowa, Bradley U., Ill., Del Bello Gallery, Toronto, Honolulu Acad. Fine Arts; represented in permanent collections, Nat. Mus. Am. Art Smithsonian Instn., Washington, Long Beach Mus. Art, Library of Congress, York U., Allan R. Hite Inst. of U. Louisville, Ariz. State U., Tamarind Inst., U. N.Mex., Zimmerli Mus. Rutgers U., N.J., Can. Council Visual Arts Bank, also pvt. collections; author: Problems in Art Judgment, 1946, Printmaking Today, 1958, revised, 1972, Papermaking, 1978, 79; co-editor: North American Women Artists of the Twentieth Century, 1995; contbg. artist: Prints by California Artists, 1954, Estampas de la Revolucion Mexicana, 1948; illustrator: Canciones de Mexico, 1948; author numerous articles. Adv. bd. Continental affairs com. Americas Soc., 1983-86. With USAAF, 1941-45. Can. Coun. grantee; Landsdowne scholar U. Victoria; Fulbright scholar, Argentina, 1990. Mem. Coll. Art Assn. (Disting. Teaching of Art award 1995), Authors Guild, Internat. Assn. Hand Papermakers (steering com. 1986—), Nat. Found. Advancement in the Arts (visual arts panelist 1986-90, panel chmn. 1989, 90), Internat. Assn. Paper Historians, Internat. Coun. Fine Arts Deans (pres. 1968-69). Home: 6838 E Cheney Dr Paradise Valley AZ 85253-3525

HELLER, PHILIP, lawyer; b. N.Y.C., Aug. 12, 1952; s. Irving and Dolores (Soloff) H.; divorced; 1 child, Howard Philip. BA summa cum laude, Boston U., 1976, JD, 1979. Bar: Mass. 1979, N.Y. 1980, U.S. Ct. Appeals (1st and 9th cirs.) 1980, U.S. Supreme Ct. 1983, Calif. 1984, U.S. Dist. Ct. (all dists.) Calif., U.S. Dist. Ct. (ea. and so. dists.) N.Y., U.S. Dist. Ct. Mass. Law clk. to judge Cooper U.S. Dist. Ct. (so. dist.) N.Y., N.Y.C., 1979; assoc. Zevnik, Horton, Guibard & McGovern, P.C., L.A., 1994—; litigation ptnr. Williams and Zevnik, L.A. Legis. aid Senator Edward M. Kennedy, Boston, Washington, 1969-71; mem. staff Gov. Michael S Dukakis, Boston, 1974-75. Mem. ABA (litigation sect.), Calif. Bar Assn., L.A. County Bar Assn. Democrat. Home: 9950 Durant Dr Beverly Hills CA 90212 Office: Zeunik Horton Guibard & McGovern, PC 633 W 5th St 22d Fl 663 W 5th St 22nd Fl Los Angeles CA 90071

HELLMAN, F(REDERICK) WARREN, investment advisor; b. N.Y.C., July 25, 1934; s. Marco F. and Ruth (Koshl) H.; m. Patricia Christina Sander, Oct. 5, 1955; children: Frances, Patricia H., Marco Warren, Judith. BA, U. Calif., Berkeley, 1955; MBA, Harvard U., 1959. With Lehman Bros., N.Y.C., 1959-84, ptnr., 1963-84; exec. mng. dir. Lehman Bros., Inc., N.Y.C., 1970-73; pres. Lehman Bros., Inc., 1973-75; ptnr. Hellman Ferri Investment Assocs., 1981-89, Matrix Ptnrs., 1981—; gen. ptnr. Hellman & Friedman, San Francisco; bd. dirs. DN & E Walter, Am. Pres. Cos., Lt., Levi Strauss & Co., Williams-Sonoma, Inc., Il Fornaio (Am.) Corp., Franklin Resources, Inc., Mobile Media, Falcon Bldg Products, Inc.; trustee The Brookings Inst. Bd. dirs. Children Now. Mem. Bond Club, Piping Rock Club, Century Country Club, Pacific Union Club.

HELLMAN, ROBERT BARRY, JR., venture capitalist; b. Waterloo, Iowa, Nov. 6, 1959; s. Robert Barry Sr. and Roberta Anne (Hill) H.; m. Reneé Christine Michelis, Dec. 31, 1992. BA in Econs., Stanford U., 1982; MS in Econs., London Sch. Econs., 1985; MBA, Harvard U., 1987. Assoc. cons. Bair & Co., Tokyo, 1982-85; assoc. Farley Industries, Chgo., 1986; ptnr. McCown DeLeeuw & Co., Menlo Park, Calif., 1987—; bd. dirs. BMC West, Boise, Idaho, Vans, Inc., Orange, Calif., Graphic Arts Ctr., Portland, Oreg., Dimac, Inc., St. Louis. Recipient Baker scholarship Harvard Bus. Sch., 1987. Mem. Harvard Bus. Sch. Assn. (No. Calif. pres. 1992—), The Guardsmen, Assn. for Corp. Growth, Harvard Ctr. for Housing Studies. Office: McCown DeLeeuw and Co 3000 Sand Hill Rd # 3-290 Menlo Park CA 94025-7116

HELLMAN, URSULA SYLVIA See RADHA, SIVANANDA

HELLREICH, PHILIP DAVID, dermatologist; b. Bklyn., Sept. 19, 1941; s. Emanuel and Sophie (Kopplemann) H.; m. Carolyn Heilbrunn, Nov. 3, 1965 (div. 1972); 1 child, Jennifer Bliss; m. Janice Mirian Wills, Sept. 28, 1974. BA, Hamilton Coll., 1962; MD, SUNY, Syracuse, 1966. Resident in dermatology USPHS, S.I., N.Y., 1967-69; fellow in dermatology Columbia U./Presbyn. Hosp., N.Y.C., 1969-70; dep. chief dept. dermatology USPHS, S.I., 1970-71; asso. clin. prof. medicine U. Hawaii, Honolulu, 1984—; clin. dermatologist Honolulu Med. Group, 1971-72, Windward Med. Group, 1972-73; clin. dermatologist in pvt. practice Kailua Dermatology Assocs. Ltd., Hawaii, 1973—; cons. VA Outpatient Clinic, Honolulu, 1972-79. County chair Honolulu County Rep. Party, 1988-91; 3d vice chair Rep. Party State of Hawaii, Honolulu, 1992. Recipient 1st prize Fred Wise Meml. Lectureship, N.Y. Acad. Medicine, 1969. Fellow Am. Acad. Dermatology; mem. AMA, Internat. Soc. Dermatologists, Hawaii Med. Assn., Hawaii Fed. Physicians and Dentists (pres. 1984-88, chmn. legis. com. 1988—). Office: Kailua Dermatology Assocs 40 Aulike St Ste 311 Kailua HI 96734-2753

HELLWARTH, ROBERT WILLIS, physicist, educator; b. Ann Arbor, Mich., Dec. 10, 1930; s. Arlen Roosevelt and Sarah Matilda (Townsend) H.; m. Abigail Gurfein, Sept. 20, 1957 (div. 1979); children: Benjamin John, Margaret Eve, Thomas Abraham; m. Theresia deVroom, Dec. 20, 1985; 1 child, William Albert Detroit. B.S., Princeton U., 1952; D.Phil. (Rhodes scholar), St. John's Coll., Oxford (Eng.) U., 1955. Sr. scientist, mgr. Hughes Research Labs., Malibu, Calif., 1956-70; vis. assoc. prof. elec. engring. and physics U. Ill., Urbana, 1964-65; research assoc., sr. research fellow Calif. Inst. Tech., Pasadena, 1966-70; NSF sr. postdoctoral fellow Clarendon Lab.-St. Peter's Coll., Oxford (Eng.) U., 1970-71; George Pfleger prof. elec. engring., prof. physics U. So. Calif., Los Angeles, 1970—. Author monograph, articles in field; asso. editor: IEEE Jour. Quantum Electronics, 1964-76. Grantee NSF; Grantee Dept. Energy; Grantee Air Force Office Sci. Research; Grantee U.S. Army Research Office. Fellow IEEE (Quantum Electronics award), Am. Phys. Soc., AAAS, Optical Soc. Am. (Charles Hard Townes award); mem. Nat. Acad. Engring., Nat. Acad. Scis., AAUP, Phi Beta Kappa, Sigma Xi, Eta Kappa Nu. Home: 711 16th St Santa Monica CA 90402-3005 Office: U So Calif Physics Dept SSC 303 Los Angeles CA 90089-0484

HELLYER, CONSTANCE ANNE, communications executive, writer; b. Puyallup, Wash., Apr. 22, 1937; d. David Tirrell and Constance (Hopkins) H.; m. Peter A. Corning, Dec. 30, 1963 (div. 1977); children: Anne Arundel, Stephanie Deak; m. Don W. Conway, Oct. 12, 1980. BA with honors, Mills Coll., 1959. Grader, researcher Harvard U., Cambridge, Mass., 1959-60; researcher Newsweek mag., N.Y.C., 1960-63; author's asst. Theodore H. White and others, N.Y.C., 1964-69; freelance writer, editor Colo., Calif., 1969-75; writer, editor Stanford (Calif.) U. Med. Ctr., 1975-79; communications dir. No. Calif. Cancer Program, Palo Alto, 1979-82; comm. dir. Stanford Law Sch., Palo Alto, 1982—. Founding editor (newsletters) Insight, 1978-80, Synergy, 1980-82, Stanford Law Alum, 1992—; editor (mag.) Stanford Lawyer, 1982—; contbr. articles to profl. jours. and mags. Recipient silver medal Coun. for Advancement and Support Edn., 1985, 89, award of distinction dist. VII, 1994. Mem. No. Calif. Sci. Writers Assn. (co-founder, bd. dirs. 1979-93), Phi Beta Kappa. Democrat. Home: 2080 Louis Rd Palo Alto CA 94303-3451 Office: Stanford Law Sch Stanford CA 94305-8610

HELM, GEORGE NEVILLE, III, finance and mortgage banking company executive; b. Union City, Tenn., Nov. 4, 1954; s. George Neville and Nancy Lee (Stokes) H.; m. Lana A. Smirnov; children: Nicholas Aaron, Jonathan Grant. BS in Bus., Ark. State U., 1976. Cert. fin. planner; registered investment advisor; profl. pub. speaker. Mktg. rep. Equitable Life Assurance Soc.of U.S., Lowell, Ark., 1976-77; dist. asst. Equitable Life Assurance Soc.of U.S., 1977-80; sales mgr. John Hancock Fin. Svcs., Little Rock, 1980-82; reg. mgr. John Hancock Fin. Svcs., 1982-84; dir. agencies John Hancock Fin. Svcs., Boston, 1984-86; pres., mortgage banking and real estate fin. specialist Helm & Assocs, Las Vegas, Nev., 1986—. Contbr. articles to profl. jours. Mem. Internat. Assn. Fin. Planners, Internat. Bd. Stds. &

Practices for Cert. Fin. Planners, Greater Boston Soc. of Inst. Cert. Fin. Planners. Mem. Ch. of Christ. Office: 1005 S 3rd St Las Vegas NV 89101-6803

HELMBOLD, WILLIAM ROSS, lawyer, educator; b. Cin., Mar. 17, 1947; s. William Wallace and Muriel Mary (Washington) H.; m. Nancy Earle Franklin, Jan. 7, 1968; 1 child, Jonathan Ross. BS cum laude, Calif. Luth. U., 1972; JD, Calif. Western Sch. Law, 1975. Bar: Calif. 1976, U.S. Dist. Ct. (so. dist.) Calif. 1977, U.S. Dist. Ct. (cen. dist.) Calif. 1982, U.S. Supreme Ct. 1980. Dep. pub. defender Ventura County, Calif., 1977-80; pvt. practice Ventura, Victorville, and Westlake Village, Calif., 1980-93; prof. MBA dept. Calif. Luth. U., Thousand Oaks, 1977-88; adv. dir. Calif. Fed. Savs. and Loan, Ventura, 1987-88; judge pro tempore Ventura County Superior and Mcpl. Ct., 1980-93. Mem. staff Calif. Western Sch. Law Internat. Law Jour., 1973-75. Founding trustee Amyotrophic Lateral Sclerosis Assn., bd. dirs. Ventura County chpt., 1987-92, pres. 1989-92. Named Boss of Yr., Ventura County Legal Secs., 1980, Outstanding Trial Atty., Ventura County Pub. Defenders Office, 1977-80. Mem. ABA, Ventura County Bar Assn., Ventura County Lawyer Referral, Ventura County Criminal Def. Assn. (bd. dirs. 1984-85, 88-92), Briarwood Golf Club. Republican.

HELMER, DAVID ALAN, lawyer; b. Colorado Springs, May 19, 1946; s. Horton James and Alice Ruth (Cooley) H.; m. Jean Marie Lamping, May 23, 1987. BA, U. Colo., 1968, JD, 1973. Bar: Colo. 1973, U.S. Dist. Ct. Colo. 1973, U.S. Ct. Claims, 1990, U.S. Ct. Appeals (10th cir.) 1993, U.S. Supreme Ct. 1991. Assoc., Neil C. King, Boulder, Colo., 1973-76; mgr. labor rels., mine regulations Climax Molybdenum Co., Inc. div. AMAX, Inc., Climax, Colo., 1976-83; prin. Law Offices David A. Helmer, Frisco, Colo., 1983—; sec., bd. dirs. Z Comm. Corp., Frisco, 1983-90. Editor U. Colo. Law Rev., 1972-73; contbr. articles to legal jours. Bd. dirs. Summit County Council Arts and Humanities, Dillon, Colo., 1980-85, Advisor Advocates for Victims of Assault, Frisco, 1984—; legal counsel Summit County United Way, 1983—, v.p., bd. dirs., 1983-88; bd. dirs., legal counsel Summit County Alcohol and Drug Task Force, Inc., 1984—, Pumpkin Bowl Inc./Children's Hosp. Burn Ctr., 1989—. Chmn. Summit County Reps., 1982-89; chmn. 5th Jud. Dist. (Colo.) Rep. Com., 1982-89; chmn. resolutions com. Colo. Rep. Conv., 1984, del. Rep. Nat. Com., 1984; chmn. reaccreditation com. Colo. Mountain Coll., Breckenridge, 1983; founder, bd. dirs. Dillon Bus. Assn., 1983-87, Frisco Arts Coun., 1989—; atty. N.W. Colo. Legal Svcs. Project, Summit County, 1983—; mcpl. judge Town of Dillon, Colo., 1982—, Town of Silverthorne, Colo., 1982—. Master sgt. USAR, 1968-74. Mem. ABA, Colo. Bar Assn. (bd. govs. 1991—, mem. exec. com. 1995—), Continental Divide Bar Assn. (pres. 1991-95, v.p. 1995—), Summit County Bar Assn. (pres. 1990—), Dillon Corinthian Yacht Club (commodore local club 1987-88, 95—, vice commodore, 1994, club champion 1989-91, Winner of Colo. Cup, Colo. State Sailing Championships 1991), Phi Gamma Delta. Lutheran. Home: PO Box 30 352 Snake River Dr Dillon CO 80435-0300 Office: PO Box 868 619 Main St Frisco CO 80443-0868

HELMICH, PAMELA PENCE, architect; b. Weiser, Ida., Feb. 7, 1945; d. James William and Helen Elizabeth (Clough) P.; m. David Michael Helmich, June 3, 1978; children by previous marriage—Nicholas Byron Jodar, Willow Susan Jodar. B.A., U. Calif.-Berkeley, 1972. Intern architect U.S. Gen. Services Adminstrn., San Francisco, 1972-76; architect U.S. Customs Service, San Francisco, 1976-78; designer Environ. Planning & Research, San Francisco, 1978-79; owner GHI Arch. & Design, San Francisco, 1979—; referee Calif. Bar Ct., Los Angeles, 1982-83; designer Rugh House, 1980; lectr. in field. Mem. AIA, Found. for San Francisco Archtl. Heritage, Nat. Trust for Historic Preservation. Republican. Christian.

HELMINIAK, CLARE, public health service officer; b. Woodruff, Wis., Mar. 12, 1956; d. Harry H. and Catherine (Specht) H.; m. Gene Carnicom; children: Whitney Alexis, Heath Britten, J. Kirk. BS in Zoology summa cum laude, U. Wis., 1978; MD, Med. Coll. Wis., 1982. Intern Edward W. Sparrow Hosp., Lansing, Mich., 1982-83; gen. med. officer Mescalero (N.Mex.) IHS Hosp., 1983-84; gen. med. officer dept. pediatrics Alaska Native Med. Ctr., Anchorage, 1984-85; adminstr. hepatitis B program Alaska Native Health Bd., Anchorage, 1985-88; asst. dir. hepatitis B program Alaska Area Native Health Svc., Anchorage, 1985-88; med. officer Parker (Ariz.) IHS Hosp., 1989—; diabetes com. officer Parker Indian Health Svc. Hosp., intermittent acting clin. dir., Phoenix area pharmacy and therapeutics com., Phoenix area Patient Care Component physician trainer, 1989—; preceptorship in radiology St. Bincent's Hosp., Dublin, Ireland, 1981; preceptorship in internal medicine and rural medicine Nat. Health Svc. Corps., Appalachian Regional Hosp., Hazard, Ky., 1981; externship in family medicine Wis. Acad. Family Physicians, Kaukauna (Wis.) Clinic and Cmty. Hosp., 1979. Treas. Parker Piranha Swim Team, 1994—; active La Paz County 4H, 1994—. Decorated Bronze Star; recipient Phoenix Area Exceptional Performance award, 1992, Outstanding Svc. award Intertribal Coun. Ariz., 1992. Mem. AAUW, Am. Soc. for Circumopolar Health, MUMPS Users Group, Assn. Mil. Surgeons the U.S. (Ribbon award), Commd. Officers Assn. USPHS (Ribbon award), Res. Officers Assn. (Ribbon award), Mo. Foxtrotting Horse Assn. Democrat. Roman Catholic. Office: USPHS/IHS RR 1 Box 12 Parker AZ 85344-9703

HELMUTH, PHILIP ALAN, tax consultant; b. Alhambra, Calif., Dec. 29, 1965; s. Melvin I. and Elsie (Borkholder) H. Student, MiraCosta Coll., 1985-89, Palomar Coll., 1989-90. Data entry operator Melco Bus. Svc., Vista, Calif., 1980-83, bookkeeper, 1983-91; ptnr., tax cons. Melco Bus. Svc., Vista, 1992—; bookkeeper Underwater Schs. of Am., Oceanside, 1985-86; owner, notary pub. Vista, 1987—. Mem. Nat. Notary Assn. (com. mem. editl. adv. com. 1990-93, pub. image com. 1990-93), Nat. Assn. Enrolled Agts., Calif. Soc. Enrolled Agts. (Palomar chpt. dir. 1995-96), Escondido Grad. Spokesman Club (sec. 1991-92, pres. 1992-93, treas. 1993-95). Office: Melco Bus Svc 410 S Santa Fe Ave Ste 102 Vista CA 92084-6163

HELPRIN, BENSON RAIMON, fine arts educator; b. Bklyn., July 11, 1933; s. Benjamin Edel and Shirley (Levine) H.; m. Mary Lovejoy Pierce, 1958 (dec. 1987); children: Cathryn Eldridge, Pamela, Heather Sydney; m. Tekla Coleman Valley, July 6, 1991. BPA, BFA, Art Ctr. Coll. Design, Pasadena, Calif., 1963, MFA, 1965. Asst. prof. Calif. State U., L.A., 1969-72; advt. photographer L.A., 1972-79; co-dir. The Rollei Internat. Seminar on Photography, London, 1977-79; contbg. editor Petersen's Photographic Mag., L.A., 1975-86; prof. fine art San Jose (Calif.) State U., 1980—. Author: Photo Lighting Techniques, Self-Assignments in Photography; contbr. articles on photography to profl. jours. Named Outstanding Prof. San Jose State U., 1984, award L.A. Art Dirs., 1975, 76, 77. Mem. Mensa. Home: 1072 El Solyo Ave Campbell CA 95008-3304 Office: San Jose State U 1 Washington Sq San Jose CA 95112-3613

HELSELL, ROBERT M., construction executive; b. Seattle, Mar. 29, 1937; s. Frank P. and Ellen (Bringloe) H.; m. Linda M. Clark, Dec. 19, 1961; children—Kristina, Ingrid, Spencer, Alexa. B.A., Dartmouth Coll., 1959, M.B.E., 1960. C.P.A., Wash. With Haskins & Sells, 1961-64; treas. Cascade Natural Gas Co., 1964-68; successively sec.-treas., exec. v.p., pres. and chief exec. officer Howard S. Wright Constrn. Co., Seattle, 1974-84; pres., chief exec. officer Wright Schuchart, Inc., 1980-84, Sprague Resources Corp., 1984-89; vice chmn. bd. Schuchart & Assocs., 1980-87; pres., chief exec. officer Wilder Constrn. Co., Bellingham, Wash., 1989—; dir. Ranier Bancorp. and Security Pacific Bank, Seafirst Corp., 1992. Bd. dirs. Virginia Mason Hosp., 1984-89, Lakeside Sch., 1969-73, 93—, Seattle Children's Home, 1968-77, pres., 1972-75, Corp. Council for Arts, 1981—, pres., 1984, chmn., 1985, Washington Roundtable, 1988—; trustee Seattle Art Mus., 1973-88, Western Washington U., 1994—; mem. men's adv. com. Children's Orthopedic Hosp., 1980-89, Western Found., 1992. Lt. comdr. USCG, 1961-68. Mem. Assoc. Gen. Contractors. Republican. Episcopalian. Clubs: Univ., Rainier, Seattle Tennis, Seattle Yacht, Wash. Athletic (Seattle), Bellingham Yacht Club. Office: Wilder Constrn Co 2006 N State St Bellingham WA 98225-4218

HELSPER, JAMES T., surgical oncologist, researcher, educator; b. Mpls., Mar. 29, 1924; s. Salvius John and Gretchen Louise (Gleissner) H.; m. Mildred Ann Belinsky, June 11, 1951 (div. Aug. 1972); children: James Thomas Jr., Richard Scott, Paige Carla; m. Carolyn Marie Harrison, Dec. 26, 1975; 1 child, Brian Harrison Helsper. BS, St. Vincent Coll., 1945; MD, Jefferson Med. Coll., 1947; postgrad., U. Pa., 1949-50. Diplomate Am. Coll. Surgeons, Am. Bd. Surgery, 1956; lic. Calif., N.Y., N.J., Fla., Mass. Intern Med. Ctr., Jersey City, N.J., 1947-48, residency, 1948-49; resident surgery U.S. Naval Hosp., Portsmouth, Va., 1951-52; chief resident surgery Queens Gen. Hosp., N.Y., 1952-53; asst. resident surgery Med. Ctr. for Cancer and Allied Diseases, N.Y., 1953-54, spl. fellow head and neck svc., 1954, sr. resident surgery, 1955-57; mem. surg. staff Huntington Meml. Hosp., Pasadena, Calif., Kenneth Norris Jr. Cancer Hosp.; attending surgeon L.A. County USC Med. Ctr.; emeritus assoc. clin. prof. surgery U. So. Calif. Sch. Medicine, L.A.; head melanoma site team U. So. Calif. Comprehensive Cancer Ctr., L.A.; mem. head and neck site team U. So. Calif. Comprehensive Cancer Ctr.; asst. clin. prof. surgery Loma Linda (Calif.) U. Sch. Medicine; chmn. tumor bd. L.A. County Gen. Hosp., 1963, 70, 81-82; cancer liaison fellow Am. Coll. Surgeons L.A. County/USC Med. Ctr., Norris Cancer Hosp.; from student and corpsman to capt. USNR, 1943-84. Mem. AMA, ACS (bd. govs. 1994), Am. Cancer Soc. (Calif. divsn., L.A. county unit chmn. profl. edn. com., 1965-67, v.p. for program 1967-69, 84—. pres. elect 1969-70, 85-86, pres. 1970-71, 86-87, chmn. nom. com. 1971-72, Calif. divsn. chmn. profl. edn com. 1974-75, mem. profl. edn. com. 1971-76, mem. bd. dirs. 1967—, mem. pub. info. com. 1969-71, mem. Macomber Legacy Com. 1975-82, mem. rsch. com. 1987-88, named Man of The Year 1991), Am. Fedn. Clin. Oncologic Socs., Am. Radium Soc., Am. Soc. Clin. Oncology, Calif. Med. Assn. (mem. com. on cancer), Calif. Med. Assn. (mem. com. on cancer), N.Y. Acad. Medicine, L.A. County Med. Assn. (mem. com. on cancer, jr. sect. pres. 1966), L.A. Surg. Soc., L.A. Acad. Medicine, Pasadena Med. Soc., Internat. Union Against Cancer (mem. sci. com.), Pan-Pacific Surg. Assn., Soc. Surg. Oncology (James Ewing Soc.), Soc. Head and Neck Surgeons (pres. 1988-89), Flying Physicians Assn., The Adventurer's Club, Quiet Birdmen. Home: 580 Arbor St Pasadena CA 91105-1536 Office: 50 Bellefontaine St Ste 301 Pasadena CA 91105-3132

HELTON, THOMAS JOE, computer scientist, writer; b. Ft. Wayne, Ind., Aug. 15, 1944; s. Vernon L. and Isabelle E. (Price) H.; m. Karen Sue Andersen, Dec. 21, 1965 (div. Apr. 1978); children: Thomas Vernon, Heather Lea; m. Mary Elizabeth Martin, Feb. 12, 1979; children: Amity Rae, Sara May, Duane Thomas, Thomas Joe, Benjamin Samuel. AB, Ind. U., 1968, MBA, 1970; postgrad., U. Chgo., 1972. CPA Ill., 1973, Mo., 1977. Supr. Touche Ross & Co., Chgo., 1970-74; asst. controller Federated Dept. Stores, Dallas, 1975-76; dir., fin. pub. rels. May Dept. Stores Co., St. Louis, 1977-79; contr. Cole Nat. Corp., Richmond Hts., Ohio, 1980-83; pres. Thinc, Bremerton, Wash., 1983-84; lectr. Grays Harbor Coll., Aberdeen, Wash., 1984-85; systems mgr. Southwestern Bell Telephone Co., St. Louis, 1985-92; mgr. arch. R & D Group Health Coop. of Puget Sound, Seattle, Wash., 1993—; columnist John Wiley & Sons, N.Y.C., 1990-92; pres. Sybase N.W. User Group, Seattle, 1994—. Contbr. articles to profl. jours. Mem. Borland Internat. Exec. Adv. Bd., Scotts Valley, Calif., 1987-90; v.p. Protect Our Pets, Bridgeton, Mo., 1989-92. Walter E. Heller fellow, 1969. Mem. ACM, AAAI, Internat. Neural Network Soc., Level 5 Users Group (exec. v.p. 1988-92), Beta Gamma Sigma. Home: 104 NW 47th St Seattle WA 98107 Office: Group Health Cooperative Puget Sound 521 Wall St Seattle WA 98121-1524

HEMANN, RAYMOND GLENN, aerospace company executive; b. Cleve., Jan 24, 1933; s. Walter Harold Marsha Mae (Colbert) H.; BS, Fla. State U., 1957; postgrad. U.S. Naval Postgrad. Sch., 1963-64, U. Calif. at Los Angeles, 1960-62; MS in Systems Engring., Calif. State U., Fullerton, 1970, MA in Econs., 1972, cert. in tech. mgmt. Calif. Inst. Tech., 1990; m. Lucile Tinnin Turnage, Feb. 1, 1958; children: James Edward, Carolyn Frances; m. Pamela Lehr, Dec. 18, 1987. Aero. engring. aide U.S. Navy, David Taylor Model Basin, Carderock, Md., 1956; analyst Fairchild Aerial Surveys, Tallahassee, 1957; research analyst Fla. Rd. Dept., Tallahassee, 1957-59; chief Autonetics div. N.Am. Rockwell Corp., Anaheim, Calif., 1959-69; v.p., dir. R. E. Manns Co., Wilmington, Calif., 1969-70; mgr. Avionics Design and Analysis Dept. Lockheed-Calif. Co., Burbank, 1970-72, mgr. Advanced Concepts div., 1976-82; gen. mgr. Western div. Arinc Research Corp., Santa Ana, 1972-76; dir. Future Requirements Rockwell Internat., 1982-85; dir. Threat Analysis, Corp. Offices, Rockwell Internat., 1985-89; pres., chief exec. officer Advanced Systems Rsch., Inc., 1989—; adj. sr. fellow Ctr. Strategic and Internat. Studies, Washington, 1987—; bd. dir. Fla. State U. Rsch. Found., 1994—; cons. various corps. U.S. govt. agys.; sec., bd. dirs. Calif. State U., Fullerton, Econs. Found. ; mem. naval studies bd. panels Nat. Acad. Scis., 1985—, Arms Control Working Group; asst. prof. ops. analysis dept. U.S. Naval Postgrad. Sch., Monterey, Calif., 1963-64, Monterey Peninsula Coll., 1963; instr. ops. analysis Calif. State U., Fullerton, 1963, instr. quantitative methods, 1969-72; program developer, instr. systems engring. indsl. rels. ctr. Calif. Inst. Tech., 1992—; lectr. Brazilian Navy, 1980, U. Calif., Santa Barbara, 1980, Yale U., 1985, Princeton U., 1986, U.S. Naval Postgrad. Sch., 1986, Ministry of Def., Taiwan, Republic of China, 1990; Calif. Inst. Tech., 1992; mem. exec. forum Calif. Inst. Tech., 1991—. Chmn. comdr.'s adv. bd. CAP, Calif. Wing, 1990-94, nat. adv. bd., 1994—; reader Recording for the Blind, 1989—. With AUS, 1950-53. Syde P. Deeb scholar, 1956; recipient honor awards Nat. Assn. Remotely Piloted Vehicles, 1975, 76; named to Hon. Order Ky. Cols., 1985. Comml., glider and pvt. pilot. Fellow AAAS, AIAA (assoc.); mem. IEEE, Ops. Rsch. Soc. Am., Air Force Assn., Nat. Coalition for Advanced Mfg. (adv. bd. 1990—), N.Y. Acad. Scis., Assn. Old Crows, L.A. World Affairs Coun., Phi Kappa Tau (past pres.). Episcopalian. Contbr. articles to profl. jours. and news media.

HEMINGWAY, W(ILLIAM) DAVID, banker; b. L.A., Apr. 28, 1947; s. Donald William and Donna (Laws) H.; m. Gay Etta Jorgensen, Apr. 15, 1977; children: Ryan, Jonathan, Jamon. BA, Brigham Young U., 1971; MBA, U. Utah, 1973. Sr. v.p. Zions First Nat. Bank, Salt Lake City, 1982-84, exec. v.p., 1984—; pres. Internat. TV Network, 1986-88, bd. dirs. Nev. State Bank, Las Vegas, Murdock Travel, Inc., Salt Lake City. Candidate Utah Legislature, Salt Lake City, 1972; mem. Electorial Coll., Salt Lake City, 1976, Utah adv. bd. to U.S. Civil Rights Commn., Salt Lake City, 1976—. Mem. Utah State Money Mgmt. Coun. (elected chmn. 1991), Utah Bankers Assn. (bd. dir. 1992-94, vice chmn., 1994-95, chmn., 1995—). Republican. Mormon. Office: Zions First Nat Bank 1 S Main St Salt Lake City UT 84111-1909

HEMION, DWIGHT ARLINGTON, television producer, director; b. New Haven, Mar. 14, 1926; s. Dwight Arlington and Bernice Ruby (Berquist) H.; m. Katherine Bridget Morrissy, Sept. 1, 1973; children—Katherine, Dwight Gustav. Student pub. schs., Verona, N.J. Asso. dir. ABC-TV, N.Y.C., 1946-49; TV dir. Tonight Show, NBC-TV, N.Y.C., 1950-60; dir. Perry Como TV show, N.Y.C., 1960-67; producer/dir. Yorkshire Prodns., N.Y.C., 1967-70; producer/dir. TV spls. in assn. with ATV, London; producer/dir. Smith-Hemion Prodns., Los Angeles, 1975-90. Dir.: Frank Sinatra: A Man and His Music, 1965 (Emmy award TV Acad. Arts and Scis.); The Sound of Burt Bacharach, 1969, Singer Presents Burt Bacharach, 1970, Barbra Streisand and Other Musical Instruments, 1973, Steve and Eydie-Our Love is Here to Stay, 1975, America Salutes Richard Rodgers: The Sound of His Music, 1976, Bette Midler-Ol' Red Hair is Back, 1977, Ben Vereen ... His Roots, 1977, Steve and Eydie Celebrate Irving Berlin, 1978, IBM Presents Baryshnikov on Broadway, 1979 (Emmy award), Goldie and Kids ... Listen to Us!, 1982 (Emmy award), Sheena Easton...Act I, 1983 (Emmy award), Anne Murray's Winter Cranival...From Quebec, 1984, 4 Emmy Award Shows, 5 Christmas in Washington shows, 6 TV Acad. Hall of Fame shows, 50th Presdl. Inaugural Gala, Neil Diamond Hello Again, opening ceremonies Liberty Weekend, Barbra Streisand One Voice, We The People Constitutional Gala, Julie Andrews The Sound of Christmas, All Star Salute to Our Troops, and many others. Served in AC U.S. Army, 1944-46. Named Dir. of Year in TV Dirs. Guild Am., 1965. Mem. Purcival Country Club. Office: Smith-Hemion Prodns PO Box 15 1438 N Gower Los Angeles CA 90053-0015

HEMMERS, OLIVER ANDREAS, physicist; b. Berlin, Aug. 23, 1963; s. Hans-Joachim and Margot Erna (Laskowski) H. Diploma, Tech. U. Berlin, 1988, postgrad., 1988-92, Dr.rer.nat. in Physics, 1993. Rsch. assoc. Fritz-Haber-Inst. Max Planck Gesellschaft, Berlin, 1993-94; rsch. assoc. U. Las Vegas, 1994—. Mem. Am. Phys. Soc., German Phys. Soc., Chess Club. Office: U Las Vegas Dept Chemistry Box 454003 4505 S Maryland Pky Las Vegas NV 89154-9900

HEMMINGS, PETER WILLIAM, orchestra and opera administrator; b. London, Apr. 10, 1934; s. William and Rosalind (Jones) H.; m. Jane Frances Kearnes, May 19, 1962; children—William, Lucy, Emma, Rupert, Sophie. Grad. Gonville and Caius Coll., Cambridge, 1957; LL.D. (hon.), Strathclyde U., Glasgow, 1978. Clk., Harold Holt Ltd., London, 1958-59; planning mgr. Sadlers Wells Opera, London, 1959-65; gen. adminstr. Scottish Opera, Glasgow, 1962-77; gen. mgr. Australian Opera, Sydney, 1977-79; mng. dir. London Symphony Orch., 1980-84; gen. dir. Los Angeles Music Ctr. Opera Assn., 1984—; gen. mgr. New Opera Co., London, 1956-65, dir. Royal Acad. Music; gen cons. Compton Verney Opera Project. Served to lt. Brit. Signal Corps, 1952-54; Fed. Republic Germany. Fellow Royal Scottish Acad. Music, Royal Acad. Music (hon.); mem. Am. Friends of Sadeer Wells (pres. 1994—), Internat. Assn. Opera Dirs., 1977-79, Opera Am. (v.p.). Anglican. Club: Garrick (London). Home: 775 S Madison Ave Pasadena CA 91106-3831 Office: LA Music Ctr Opera 135 N Grand Ave Los Angeles CA 90012-3013

HEMMY, MARY LOUISE, social work administrator; b. Mpls., Nov. 14, 1914; d. Albert H. and Mary (Scott) H. BS, U. Minn., 1936, MA in Social Wk., 1941. Caseworker Washington U. Med. Ctr., St. Louis, 1937-40, Ill. Svcs. for Crippled Children, Springfield, 1941-42; instr., asst. prof. Sch. Social Wk., Washington U., 1942-45; dir. social wk. dept. Washington U. Med. Ctr., 1945-52; assoc. prof., dir. social wk. Coll. Medicine, U. Ill., Chgo., 1952-53; exec. dir. Am. Assn. Med. Social Workers, Washington, 1953-55; prof. sch. medicine sch. social work U. Pitts., 1956-59; exec. dir. Benjamin Rose Inst., Cleve., 1959-77; mem. spl. med. adv. group VA, 1963-68; mem. Ohio Bd. Examiners Nursing Home Adminstrs., 1973-77. Mem. Nat. Assn. Social Workers (bd. dirs. 1961-63), Am. Assn. Homes for Aging (bd. dirs. 1963-70). Home: 13505 SE River Rd Portland OR 97222-8038

HEMPHILL, ALAN POLK, management consultant; b. Montgomery, Ala., Aug. 22, 1933; s. Alan Polk and Elizabeth Evans (Orr) H.; m. Jean Tilden Baker, June 8, 1957; children: Elizabeth, Alan, Laurie. BSEE, U.S. Naval Acad., 1957; MA in Mgmt., Nat. U., 1987. Commd. ensign U.S. Navy, 1957, advanced through grades to lt. comdr., 1977; various assignments, San Diego, 1957-77; mgr. Prestige Properties, Poway Calif., 1977-80; founder Orion Bus. Systems, San Diego, 1980-82; pres., chief exec. officer Sta. KBSC-TV, Glendale, Calif. (sta. received 12 Emmy awards), 1982-83; chmn., bd. dirs. Oak Broadcasting Systems, Glendale, 1983-84; pres. Community Bus. Cons., San Diego, 1984-85; prof. computer sci. Nat. U., Vista, Calif., 1984—; trustee Sta. KBSC-TV Stock of Oak Industries, San Diego, 1982-84; panelist TV series On Edge, 1986-88; cons. Oak Industries, San Diego, 1984; bd. dirs. Community Bus. Cons., San Diego, 1984; sr. v.p. Orion Network Solutions, 1990-91. Contbr. articles and columns to profl. jours. and Commnunity News Network, Inc., chpts. to books. Gen. mgr. Remember the Pueblo, San Diego, 1968; pres., chmn. bd. Green Valley Civic Assn., Poway, 1974-75; pres., bd. dirs. North County Bd. of Jr. Achievement, 1979. Mem. Nat. U. Alumni Assn. (pres. 1991-92, dir. alumni 1992-94), Kiwanis (pres. Rancho Bernardo chpt. 1980-81).

HEMPHILL, NORMA JO, special event planning and tour company executive; b. Enid, Okla., Nov. 25, 1930; d. Wyatt Warren and Wanda Markes (Parker) Stout; m. Benjamin Robert Hemphill, June 21, 1952; children: Susan Colleen, Robert Gary. Student, Okla. State U.; BA, U. Calif., Berkeley, 1955. Former acct. Better Bus. Bookkeeping, Lafayette, Calif.; tchr., Head Start tchr. Chino (Calif.) Elem. Sch., 1966-68; pres., founder Calif. Carousel and Carousel Tours, Lafayette, 1972—; mem. adv. com. The William Penn Mott, Jr. Vis. Ctr., San Francisco, 1995—; speaker in field; cons., dir. various orgns. Past bd. dirs. PTA, Moraga, Calif., Lafayette; bd. dirs. Children's Home Soc., Upland, Calif., 1965-69; past demonstation tchr. Presbytery of Bay Area, San Francisco; past supt. 1st Presbyn. Ch., Oakland, Calif., elder, 1977—, trustee, 1980; mem. hon. adv. com. Festival of Lake, Oakland, 1982; bd. govs. Goodwill Industries, 1978-79; founder, chmn. Joint Svc. Clubs Foster Children's Ann. Christmas Party; mem. adv. com. for William Penn Mott Jr. Visitors Ctr., Presidio of San Francisco Nat. Park, 1995—. Named Person of Yr. award Advt.-Mktg. Assn. East Bay, 1978; co-recipient Event of Yr. award, Am. Pub. Rels. Assn., 1984. Mem. Lake Merritt Breakfast Club (Oakland, spl. events com., bd. govs., named Citizen of Community 1992), Lake Merritt Inst. (hon.), Soroptomist (very important women honor roll Diablo Valley 1990, keynote speaker 1991), Pi Beta Phi (bd. dirs., spl. events com. Contra Costa County chpt., Founder's Day speaker at U. Calif.-Berkeley, 1993). Office: Calif Carousel & Carousel Tours PO Box 537 Lafayette CA 94549-0537

HEMPHILL-HALEY, EILEEN, micropaleontologist, geologist; b. Ft. Bragg, N.C., July 30, 1959; d. John Allen and Margaret Rose (Scollin) Hemphill; m. Mark Allen Haley. BS, Humboldt State U., 1982; PhD, U. Calif., Santa Cruz, 1992. Cert. geologist. Cons. micropaleontologist Daniel McKeel Consulting, Inc., Lincoln City, Okla., 1982-83; rsch. geologist U.S. Geol. Survey, Menlo Park, Calif., 1983—. Mem. Am. Geophys. Union, Geol. Soc. Am. (Student Rsch. grant 1988), Internat. Soc. for Diatin Rsch., Soc. Econ. Paleontologists/Mineralogists, N.W. Sci. Assn. Office: US Geol Survey Univ Oreg c/o 1272 Geol Scis Eugene OR 97403-1272

HEMRY, LARRY HAROLD, immigration inspector; b. Seattle, Jan. 4, 1941; s. Harold Bernard and Florence Usborne (Achilles) H.; m. Nancy Kay Ballantyne, July 10, 1964 (div. Apr. 1976); children: Rachel Dalayne, Aaron Harold, Andrew LeRoy. BA, Seattle Pacific Coll., 1963; postgrad., Western Evang. Sem., Portland, Oreg., 1969, 70. Ordained to ministry Free Meth. Ch., 1968. Clergyman Free Meth. Ch., Vancouver, B.C., Can., 1963-64, Mt. Vernon, Wash., 1968-69; clergyman Colton (Oreg.) Community Ch., 1969-71; edit clk. Moody Bible Inst., Chgo., 1964-66; pres., founder Bethel Enterprises, Colton, 1969-71; immigration insp. U.S. Immigration and Naturalization Svc., Sumas, Wash., 1972—. Author, historian: Some Northwest Pioneer Families, 1969, The Hemry Family History Book, 1985; author: An Earnest Plea to Earnest Christians, 1969. chmn. com. to establish and endow the James A. Hemry meml. scholarship fund Seattle Pacific U., 1975. Fellow Seattle Pacific U. (Centurians Club); mem. The Nature Conservancy, The Sierra Club. Office: US Immigration and Naturalization Svc PO Box 99 Sumas WA 98295-0099

HEMSLEY, DAVID LEE, computer company executive; b. Salzburg, Austria, Oct. 19, 1950; came to U.S., 1953; s. Glen Merrill and Arlene Lofthouse (Pulsipher) H.; m. Donna Elizabeth Hoover, Aug. 10, 1973; children: Richard, Melody, Jill, Teresa, Ryan, Amy, Justin, Darren. BA in Math., San Jose State U., 1976, MS in Math., 1983. Software engr. CSC, Mountain View, Calif., 1976-77, Link Flight Simulation, Sunnyvale, Calif., 1977-82, Ford Aerospace, Palo Alto, Calif., 1982-84, Kaiser Electronics, San Jose, Calif., 1984-89, Prodata, Inc., Citrus Heights, Calif., 1991-92, Jones Futurex, Rocklin, Calif., 1993-94; pres. System Design Automation, Placerville, Calif., 1989—. Inventor software, 1989. Mem. IEEE Computer Soc., Nat. Coun. Systems Engring. Republican. Mem. LDS Ch. Office: System Design Automation PO Box 2171 Placerville CA 95667-2171

HENAGER, CHARLES HENRY, civil engineer; b. Spokane, Wash., July 11, 1927; s. William Franklin and Mary Agnes (Henry) H.; m. Dorothy Ruth Parker, May 6, 1950; children: Charles Henry, Jr., Donald E., Roberta R. BS in Civil Engring., Wash. State U., 1950. Registered profl. engr., Wash. Instrumentman Wash. State Dept. Hwys., Yakima, 1950-52; engr. Gen. Electric Co., Richland, Wash., 1952-62; shift supr., reactor GE, Richland, Wash., 1962-63, sr. engr., 1963-65; sr. devel. engr. Battelle Pacific N.W. Labs., Richland, 1965-68, sr. rsch. engr., 1968—. Contbr. articles to profl. jours.; patentee in field. With USN, 1945-46. Fellow Am. Concrete Inst. (tech. activities com. 1987-89, Del Bloem award 1986), ASTM (subcom. 1980-92), ASCE (pres. Columbia sect. 1961-62); mem. Kennewick Swim Club (pres. 1962-63), Sigma Tau, Tau Beta Pi, Phi Kappa Phi. Republican. Methodist. Home: 1306 N Arthur Pl Kennewick WA 99336-1545 Office: Battelle Pacific NW Labs Battelle Blvd Richland WA 99352

HENCH, PHILIP KAHLER, physician; b. Rochester, Minn., Sept. 19, 1930; s. Philip Showalter and Mary Genevieve (Kahler) H.; m. Barbara Joan Kent, July 10, 1954; children: Philip Gordon, John Kahler, Amanda Kent. BA, Lafayette Coll., 1952; MD, U. Pitts., 1958; MSc in Medicine, U. Minn., 1965. Intern U. Colo. Med. Ctr., 1958-59; fellow in medicine and rheumatology Mayo Graduate Sch., Rochester, Minn., 1959-63; with Inst. for Arthritis and Metabolic Diseases, NIH, Bethesda, Md., 1963-64; asst. div. rheumatology Scripps Clinic and Rsch. Found., La Jolla, Calif., 1965-66, assoc., 1966-70, assoc. mem., 1970-74, mem., head, 1974-82, sr. cons.,

1982—, adj. asst. mem. dept. neuropharmacology, mem. dept. acad. affairs; asst. clin. prof. U. Calif. Sch. Medicine, San Diego; cons. to pharm. cos.; mem. People to People Mission to China on study of Aging. Contbr. articles on rheumatic diseases, pain and sleep disorders to profl. jours.; mem. editorial com. Rheumatism Revs., 1974-84; editorial reviewer Arthritis and Rheumatism, Jour. Rheumatology, 1985—; bd. spl. cons. Patient Care mag., 1987—. Mem. bd. advisors San Diego Opera. Recipient Arthritis Found. award (6), San Diego chpt., 1971-80; Philip S. Hench scholar Mayo Grad. Sch. Medicine, 1965. Fellow ACP, Am. Coll. Rheumatology (chmn. nonarticular rheumatism study group 1975-82, com. on preventive and rehab. medicine 1984-85, com. on rheumatologic practice 1975-77); mem. AMA, Nat. Soc. Clin. Rheumatologists, Am. Pain Soc., Calif. Med. Assn., Internat. Assn. for Study Pain, La Jolla Acad. Medicine (pres. 1994-96), Arthritis Found. (bd. govs. San Diego chpt., Best Doctors in Am. award 1992-93, 94-95), San Diego Hist. Soc., San Diego Mus. Fine Arts, San Diego Opera (bd. advisors). Republican. Home: 7856 La Jolla Vista Dr La Jolla CA 92037-3530 Office: Scripps Clinic & Rsch Found 10666 N Torrey Pines Rd La Jolla CA 92037-1027

HENCH, ROBERT IRVING, architect; b. E. Hampton, N.Y., June 17, 1928; s. Lee Owen and Esther (Sanford) H.; m. Ann Darling Dwinelle, Aug. 18, 1956; children—Brian, Barry, Sandra. B.Arch., Syracuse U., 1957. Registered architect, Calif. Architect, Dan Dworsky & Assoc., Los Angeles, 1959-60, William Blurock & Assoc., Newport Beach, Calif., 1960-73; ptnr. Wm. Blurock & Ptnrs., 1973-82; sr. ptnr. The Blurock Partnership, 1982—. Prin. works include Dana Hills H.S., Calif., Capistrano Valley H.S., Temecula Valley H.S., Temescal Canyon H.S., Orange Coast Coll., Costa Mesa, Calif., Coastline Administrn. Ctr., Fountain Val, Calif., Student Svcs. Bldgs. Fullerton Coll., Saddleback Coll., Irvine Valley Coll., Santa Ana-Orange County Transp. Ctr.; campus arch. Citrus Coll.; project mgr. Vocat. Tech. Ctr. Compton Coll. Served to 1st lt. C.E., U.S. Army, 1945-49, 53-54 (ETO). Mem. AIA (sec. 1978). Republican. Presbyterian. Club: Balboa Yacht. Home: 1020 Madison Pl Laguna Beach CA 92651-2805 Office: The Blurock Partnership 2300 Newport Blvd Newport Beach CA 92663-3702

HENDERSON, ARTHUR JAMES, business educator; b. Denver, May 19, 1947; s. Marshall Woodrow and Pauline (Lauk) H.; m. Cynthia Lou Brauer, Jan. 28, 1968 (div. Sept. 1989); children: Marshall W., James Scott; m. Carole Starr, Oct. 17, 1990. BS in Bus. Mgmt. and Mktg., Nat. Coll., 1990. cert. c.c. tchr., Ariz. Enlisted USAF, 1965, advanced through grades to sgt., 1979; petroleum, oils and lubricants specialist USAF, Clovis, N.Mex., 1965-67, adminstrv. specialist, 1967-71; liaison to Moroccan Air Force USAF, Kinitra, Morocco, 1971-72; spl. asst. to ctr. comdr. USAF, San Antonio, 1972-73; chief Atlantic postal ops. USAF, Kokaa, Thailand, 1973-74; 1st sgt. 522d tactical fighter squadron USAF, Clovis, 1974-79; 1st sgt. 822d supply squadron USAF, Tacoma, 1979-80; instr. leadership and mgmt. tng. 15th Air Force USAF, Ellsworth AFB, 1980-85; ret. USAF, 1985; owner/operator Henderson's Upholstery, Rapid City, S.D., 1981-89; instr. bus. Park's Coll., Tucson, 1990—. Scoutmaster Boy Scouts Am., Clovis, 1969-71, cubmaster, 1974-79, scoutmaster, Rapid City, 1981-88; packmaster Cub Scouts Am., Kinitra, 1971-72, Tacoma, 1979-80. Decorated Commendation medal. Mem. Disabled Am. Vets., Christian Businessmen's Assn., Toastmasters Internat. (1st Pl. award Area II Humorous Speech Contest 1987, Best Spkr. of Yr. 1987). Home: 5326 E 7th St Tucson AZ 85711-2351 Office: Park's Coll 6992 E Broadway Blvd Tucson AZ 85710-2803

HENDERSON, GEORGE MILLER, foundation executive, former banker; b. Indpls., Aug. 19, 1915; s. Ben Wymond and Verlinda (Miller) H.; m. Janice Himmelwright, Sept. 2, 1952; children: Donna, Bonnie, Heather, Randall, Darcy. Student, Harvard U., 1960. With S.H. Kress & Co., 1933-36; fire control supr. U.S. Forest Svc., Zig Zag, Oreg., 1936-42; asst. mgr. fgn. trade dept. Portland C. of C., 1946-47; with 1st Nat. Bank Oreg., Portland, 1947-80, v.p., 1953-62, sr. v.p., 1962-71, exec. v.p., 1971-80; pres. Oreg. Ind. Coll. Found., 1980-94. Chmn. Portland Aviation Commn., 1950-51, Oreg. Pks. Commn., 1956-86, Columbia Basin Export-Import Conf., 1961-62; pres. Rose Festival Assn., 1953-54, Family Counseling Svc., 1959-60, Pacific Internat. Livestock Exposition, 1965-67; chmn. woorld brotherhood banquet NCCJ, 1963; bd. dirs. Ind. Coll. Funds Am., 1980-94, Nature Conservancy, 1987-90. Mem. Oreg. Bankers Assn. (pres. 1962), Assn. Res. City Bankers, Pacific Northwestern Ski Assn. (pres. 1947-48), Pacific N.W. Trade Assn. (pres. 1964-65), Arlington Club, Multnomah Club, Cascade Club. Home: 18000 SW Bany Rd Beaverton OR 97007-5735

HENDERSON, HOLLIS ALLEN, transportation consultant, railway executive; b. Decatur, Ala., Nov. 11; s. Roy C. and Alice M. (Johnson) H.; m. Gean, Aug. 2, 1945 (dec. 1965); m. JoAnn Wessel, Feb. 25, 1967; children: Hollis, Mike, Candice, Richard, Kathy. AAME, U. Ga. Tech., 1942; BSEE, U. Utah, 1959; Degree in Transp. Mgmt., Stanford U., 1962. Cert. Railway Engr. Advanced to chief mechanical officer So. Pacific Transp. Co., San Francisco, 1946-72, chief mechanical officer, 1972-77; v.p. equipment Consolidated Rail Corp., Phila., 1977-83; v.p. ops. CSX Corp., Alexandria, Va., 1983-87; prin. Henderson Cons., San Diego, 1987—. Author in field. With USN, 1942-45. Mem. Assn. Am. Railroads, N.Y. Railway Assn. (pres. 1980), Pacific Railway Assn. (v.p. 1959). Republican. Protestant. Home and Office: 18575 Lancashire Way San Diego CA 92128-1033

HENDERSON, JANE WHALEN, travel company executive; b. Fort Dodge, Iowa, June 24, 1913; d. William L. and Blanche (Tremaine) Whalen; m. Lon St. Clair Henderson, Oct. 16, 1946 (div.); children: Thomas, Clare, Anne. Student Fort Dodge Jr. Coll., Iowa, 1931-32, Fort Dodge Bus. Coll., 1932-33, Armstrong Coll., 1937-38. Travel cons. Capwells Travel, 1938-42, Peck Judah Travel Bur., San Francisco, 1942-48; mgr. World Travel Bur., Anaheim, Calif., 1955-56, Fullerton, Calif., 1958-60; mgr. Travel Advisers, Santa Ana, Calif., 1964-65; internat. travel adviser Anaheim Travel, 1960-64; v.p. sales Orange Empire Travel Bur., Anaheim, 1965-70; owner, pres. Jane Henderson Travel, Orange, Calif., 1970-88, cons., 1988—; cons N.Am. Sch. Travel, Newport Beach, Calif., 1968—; chmn. travel com. and trip coord. Continuous Learning Experience Calif. State U., Fullerton, 1993—; mem. adv. bd. Orange (Calif) Nat. Bank, 1982—. Gold sponsor Miss Orange Pageant, 1976-86; mem. street naming com. City of Orange, 1985-91, mem. sister city program, 1985—. Named Orange Citizen of Yr., 1983. Mem. Am. Soc. Travel Agts. (scholarship in her name Washington), Pacific Area Travel Assn., Orange County Travel Agts. (pres. 1978), Cruise Lines Internat., Orange C. of C. Roman Catholic. Lodge: Soroptimists Internat. Office: Jane Henderson Travel 633 S Brea Blvd Brea CA 92621

HENDERSON, JOHN DREWS, architect; b. St. Louis, July 30, 1933; s. Russell Dewey and Hazel Agnes (Drews) H.; m. Barbara Lee Beckman, June 25, 1955; children: Susan Lee, John Beckman. BArch, U. Ill., 1956. Registered architect, Calif., Nat. Council Archtl. Registration Bds. With Delawie, Macy & Henderson, San Diego, 1966-77, Macy, Henderson & Cole, AIA, San Diego, 1977-86; pres. John D. Henderson, FAIA, 1986— . Mem. San Diego Hist. Sites Bd., 1972-78, Gaslamp Quarter Task Force, 1976-78, Gaslamp Quarter Council, 1984-86; mem. City Mgr.'s Com. for Seismic Retrofit for Older Bldgs., 1986-92; bd. dirs. Historic Am. Bldgs. Survey Found., 1984-86; Calif. Hist. Bldgs. Code Safety Bd., 1976—; apptd. by Gov. of Calif. to State Hist. Resources Commn., 1990-95, reapptd., 1995—, chmn., 1992-93; Calif. advisor Nat. Trust Historic Preservation, 1975-78; chmn. adv. bd. Historic Am. Bldgs. Survey, 1976-78; bd. dirs. Gaslamp Quarter Found., 1984-86. Lt. USN, 1956-59. Recipient hist. preservation awards from City San Diego, San Diego Hist. Soc., San Diego chpt. and Calif. Council AIA, La Jolla Women's Club, Am. Assn. State and Local History. Am. Inst. Planners, Save Our Heritage Orgn. Fellow AIA (officer, dir. local chpt., 1969-73, chpt. pres. 1972, editor guidebooks 1970, 76, state bd. dirs. 1971-73, nat. hist. resources com. 1974, 76, 78, Calif. regional rep. 1976-78); mem. San Diego Archtl. Found. (bd. dirs. 1984-86, 89-91), San Diego Hist. Soc. (officer, bd. dirs. 1975, pres. 1975), San Diego History Campaign (exec. com. 1981-86), Coronado Men's Golf Club. Republican. Presbyterian.

HENDERSON, LAVELL MERL, retired biochemistry educator; b. Swan Lake, Idaho, Sept. 9, 1917; s. George Merl and Nellie Marie (Gambles) H.; m. Maurine Criddle, Aug. 16, 1939; children: Janet Louise, Jeanne, Linda Marie. BS, Utah State U., 1939; MS, U. Wis., 1941, PhD, 1947. Instr. U. Wis., Madison, 1947-48; asst. prof. U. Ill., Urbana, 1948-57; prof., head Okla. State U., Stillwater, 1957-63; prof., head U. Minn., St. Paul, 1963-74, prof, assoc. dean, 1974-84, prof. emeritus, 1984—; mem. food and nutrition bd. NAS, Washington, 1965-71; mem. nutrition study sect. NIH, Washington, 1973-77, nutrition sci. tng. com. Nat. Inst. Gen. Med. Sci., Washington, 1965-69. Editor: Advances in Nutrition Research, 1976-84; editorial bd. Jour. Nutrition, 1965-68, 83-86; contbr. articles to profl. jours. Bd. dirs. Hormel Inst., Austin, Minn., North Star Rsch. & Devel., Mpls.; site visitor U.S. Office Edn., Title II, Washington, 1964-65. Grantee NIH, 1951-84; recipient Borden award Am. Inst. Nutrition, 1970. Mem. Am. Chem. Soc., Am. Soc. Biochemistry & Molecular Biology, Am Inst. Nutritin (pres. 1977, fellow 1986). Home: 8612 Mt Majestic Rd Sandy UT 84093-1833

HENDERSON, NANCY GRACE, marketing and systems executive; b. Berkeley, Calif., Oct. 23, 1947; d. John Harry and Lorraine Ruth (Johnson) H. BA, U. Calif., Santa Barbara, 1969; MBA, U. Houston, 1985; teaching credential, U. Calif., L.A., 1971. Chartered Fin. Analyst. Tchr. Keppel Union Sch. Dist., Littlerock, Calif., 1969-72, Internat. Sch. Prague, Czechoslovakia, 1972-74, Sunland Luth. Sch., Freeport, Bahamas, 1974-75; tchr., dept. head Internat. Sch. Assn., Bangkok, Thailand, 1975-79; exec. search Diversified Human Resources Group, Houston, Tex., 1979-82; data processing analyst Am. Gen. Corp., Houston, 1982-83, personnel and benefits dept., 1983-85, investment analyst, 1985-86, equity security analyst/quantitative portfolio analyst, 1986-87; dir. mktg. and communications Vestek Systems Inc., San Francisco, 1987—; tchr. English as Second Language program Houston Metro. Ministries, 1980-81. Pres., bd. dirs. Home Owners Assn., Walnut Creek, Calif., 1988-90; tchr. English to refugees Houston Metro Ministries, 1982; exec. dir. Internat. Child Abuse Prevention Found., 1989; ch. choir, coun., fundraising and com. chmn. Presbyn. Ch.; active Crisis Hotline, 1978-79, 92-93; dir. project Working in Networks for Good Shelter, 1993-95. Named a Notable Woman of Tex., 1984-85. Mem. Assn. for Investment Mgmt. and Rsch., Toastmasters (pres. Houston chpt. 1983, v.p. 1982-83). Office: Vestek Systems 388 Market St Ste 700 San Francisco CA 94111-5314

HENDERSON, RICKEY HENLEY, professional baseball player; b. Chgo., Dec. 25, 1958. With minor league baseball clubs, 1976-79; with Oakland Athletics, 1979-84, 89-93, N.Y. Yankees, 1985-89, Toronto Blue Jays, 1993-94, Oakland Athletics, 1994—. Winner Am. League Gold Glove, 1981; named Most Valuable Player, American League, 1990, Am. League All-Star team, 1980, 82-88, 90-91. Sporting News Am. League All-Star Team, 1981, 85, 90, Sporting News Am. League Silver Slugger Team, 1981, 85, 90, Sporting News Silver Shoe award, 1982, Sporting News Golden Shoe award, 1983, Am. Championship Series MVP, 1989. Office: Oakland As Oakland Coliseum Oakland CA 94621*

HENDERSON, SARAH ALLAN, English language educator; b. St. Louis, June 10, 1951; d. William Douglass Jr. and Margaret Allan (Houk) H.; m. George Philip Ramirez, Nov. 28, 1975; children: Emily, James. MA in Teaching, Lewis & Clark Coll., 1988. Cert. tchr., Oreg. Instr. Portland (Oreg.) C.C., 1989; instr. English dept. U. Portland, 1989-93; instr. Learning Assessment Ctr. Marylhurst (Oreg.) Coll., 1993—; presenter in field. Editor (with S. Dreyfuss): Marylhurst PLA Portfolio Development Guide, 2d edit. 1994, Writing Successful PLA Essays: What Evaluators Want, 1994; contbr. articles to profl. jours. Bd. dirs. Oreg. Am. Coll. Testing Program. Mem. MLA, Coun. on Adult and Exptl. Learning, Nat. Coun. Tchrs. English. Democrat. Presbyterian. Office: Marylhurst Coll Learning Assessment Ctr Marylhurst OR 97036

HENDERSON, THELTON EUGENE, federal judge; b. Shreveport, La., Nov. 28, 1933; s. Eugene M. and Wanzie (Roberts) H.; 1 son, Geoffrey A. B.A., U. Calif.-, Berkeley, 1956, J.D., 1962. Bar: Calif. 1962. Atty. U.S. Dept. Justice, 1962-63; assoc. firm FitzSimmons & Petris, 1964, assoc., 1964-66; directing atty. San Mateo County (Calif.) Legal Aid Soc., 1966-69; asst. dean Stanford (Calif.) U. Law Sch., 1968-76; ptnr. firm Rosen, Remcho & Henderson, San Francisco, 1977-80; judge, now chief judge U.S. Dist. Ct. (no. dist.) Calif., San Francisco, 1980—; asso. prof. Sch. Law, Golden Gate U., San Francisco, 1978-80. Served with U.S. Army, 1956-58. Mem. ABA, Nat. Bar Assn., Charles Houston Law Assn. Office: US Dist Ct PO Box 36060 16700 Valley View Ave Ste 300 La Mirada CA 90638-5841*

HENDERSON, THOMAS JAMES, construction company executive; b. 1931. BS, MS, MIT, 1954. From project mgr. to exec. asst. J.L. Simmons Co., Decatur, Ill., 1958-61; with Guy F. Atkinson Co., South San Francisco, Calif., 1961—, various mgmt. positions, 1961-75, v.p., gen. mgr. Lake Ctr. Industries, 1975-83, sr. v.p., 1983-85, group v.p., 1985-86, exec. v.p., 1986-87, pres., chief oper. officer, 1987-88, pres., chief exec. officer, 1988-89, chmn., pres., chief exec. officer, from 1989, chmn., chief exec. officer, also bd. dirs. Served to Lt. USN, 1955-58. Office: Guy F Atkinson Const Co 10 W Orange Ave South San Francisco CA 94080-3315

HENDERSON, WILLIAM DARRYL, army officer, writer; b. Trail, B.C., Can., Aug. 26, 1938; came to U.S., 1953; s. William Roland and Flora (McCallum) H.; m. Marilyn Jean Rapp, Nov. 1964 (div. 1981); children: Gregory, Timothy; m. Mary Ann Gutman, Dec. 6, 1985. Student, U. Vienna, Austria, 1959-60; BA in Polit. Sci., Stanford U., 1961; PhD in Internat. Rels. and Comparative Politics, U. Pitts., 1970; honor grad., Comd. and Gen. Staff Coll., 1974; postgrad., Nat. War Coll., 1982. Commd. 2d lt. U.S. Army, 1961, advanced through grades to col., 1988; writer San Francisco Examiner, 1990; writer, cons. Can. Govt., Ottawa, 1991-92; appointed presdl. commr. Women in the Armed Forces, Washington, 1992—; asst. prof. U.S. Mil. Acad., West Point, N.Y., 1972; mil. corr. San Francisco Examiner, 1991. testified Senate and House Armed Svcs. Com., 1993. Author: Why the Viet Cong Fought, 1979, Cohesion, The Human Element in Combat, 1985, The Hollow Army, 1990; included in book of Best Newspaper Editorials for 1990-91; contbr. articles to profl. jours. Decorated Legion of Merit, Bronze Star, Purple Heart, Combat Infantryman's Badge. Home and Office: 19880 Lark Way Saratoga CA 95070

HENDERSON-DIXON, KAREN SUE, psychologist; b. Bloomington, Ill., Mar. 25, 1946; d. Charles Lewis and Faye Lanore (Wantland) Henderson; m. David Thomas Biggs, Dec. 2, 1967 (div. 1972); m. Dean Eugene Dixon Jr., Jan. 13, 1973; children: Christopher, Matthew. BA, U. Calif., Berkeley, 1966; MS, San Jose (Calif.) State Coll., 1971; PhD, Union Inst., 1991. Lic. clin. psychol., Alaska; cert. community coll. tchr. Clin. psychologist pvt. practice, Anchorage, 1980—; pvt. practice, 1980—; adj. prof. U. Alaska, Anchorage, 1994—; cons. Alaska Youth and Parent Found., Anchorage, 1989—, Kenai Peninsula Counseling Svcs., 1995—, Parents United, Anchorage, 1989; mental health cons. Rural Alaska Community Action Program, Anchorage, 1988; cons., mem. adolescent treatment team Charter North Hosp., Anchorage, 1985-88; cons. Infant Impaired Hearing Program, Anchorage, 1984-85, Parent Tng. Ctr., Anchorage, 1980-82; psychiat. social worker Langdon Psychiat. Clinic, Anchorage, 1976-80; instr. in psychology U. Alaska Community Coll., Anchorage, 1974-81; parole agt. narcotic outpatient program State Dept. Corrections, Oakland, Calif., 1972-74; group counselor II, caseworker Alameda County Probation Dept., Oakland, Calif., 1971-72; cons. psychologist Alviso (Calif.) Econ. Devel. Program, 1971-72; instr. psychology Coll. of Alameda, 1973; faculty adv. for coop. edn. U. Alaska C.C., 1975-76. Sec., liaison to bd. Susitna Sch. PTA, Anchorage, 1983-84; co-chmn. optional bd. Susitna Sch., 1984-85, chmn., 1985-86, vol. coord., 1988-89; mem. adv. bd. Steller Alternative Sch., 1992—. Mem. APA, Alaska Psychol. Assn. Democrat. Office: 2550 Denali St Ste 1608 Anchorage AK 99503-2737

HENDLER, GORDON LEE, curator; b. N.Y.C., Dec. 11, 1946; s. Jack and Charlotte Hendler. BS, Rutgers U., 1968; PhD, U. Conn., 1973. Postdoctoral fellow Woods Hole (Mass.) Oceanographic Instn., 1973-74, Smithsonian Inst., 1974-75; dir. Galeta Marine Lab., Panama, 1976-78; marine biologist Smithsonian Oceanographic Sorting Ctr., Washington, 1978-85; curator, head invertebrate zool. sect. Natural History Mus., Los Angeles, 1985—; adj. asst. prof. U. So. Calif., 1988—. Mem. adv. bd. Jour. Diseases of Aquatic Organisms, 1985—. Mem. AAAS, Am. Soc. Zoologists, Western Soc. Naturalists, Soc. Systematic Zoology. Home: 19790 Grand View Dr Topanga CA 90290-3312 Office: Natural History Mus 900 Exposition Blvd Los Angeles CA 90007-4057

HENDLEY, ASHLEY PRESTON, JR., clinical social worker; b. Tyler, Tex., Sept. 15, 1938; s. Ashley Preston Sr. and Theresa Marie (Parenti) H.; m. Vivian Janis Rodriguez, June 24, 1960 (div. Jan. 1977); children: Gerald Michael, Ashley Preston III, William Loy, Brian Matthew; m. Ann Louise Cherry, Dec. 29, 1984. BA in Comparative Sociology, U. Puget Sound, 1979; MSW, U. Wash., 1983. Cert. social worker, Wash. Clin. instr. U. Wash., Seattle, 1985—; cons., bd. dirs. Pierce County AIDS/HIV Adv. Bd., Tacoma, Wash., 1989—. Contbr. articles to profl. jours. Cons., bd. dirs. Children's Indsl. Home, Tacoma, 1989—; cons. City of Tacoma Sr. Svcs., 1983—; guardian ad Litem Superior Ct. State of Wash., County of Pierce, Tacoma, 1990-92. With U.S. Army, 1956-76, Vietnam. Mem. Am. Assn. Spinal Cord Injury Psychologists and Social Workers (assoc. editor 1988-94). Roman Catholic. Home: 10501 Idlewild Rd SW Tacoma WA 98498-5608 Office: VA Med Ctr American Lk Tacoma WA 98493

HENDREN, DEBRA MAE, critical care nurse; b. Belle Fourche, S.D., Apr. 27, 1959; d. Clyde Leslie and Kathryn Ann (Daughters) F.; m. Anthony Ray Martinez, May 21, 1983 (div.); m. Cecil B. Hendren, Nov. 21, 1992. AD, Casper Coll., 1987, cert. EMT, 1990. RN, Colo., Wyo.; CCRN. Nurse Wyo. Med. Ctr., Casper, North Suburban Med. Ctr. (formerly Humana Hosp. Mountain View), Thornton, Colo.; nurse Swedish Med. Ctr., Englewood, Colo., charge nurse ICU, 1993—. Mem. Wyo. Nurses Assn., Colo. Nurses Assn., AACN. Home: 5168 E 126th Ct Thornton CO 80241-3001

HENDREN, MERLYN CHURCHILL, investment company executive; b. Gooding, Idaho, Oct. 16, 1926; d. Herbert Winston and Annie Averett Churchill; student U. Idaho, 1944-47; B.A. with honors, Coll. of Idaho, 1986. m. Robert Lee Hendren, June 14, 1947; children—Robert Lee, Anne Aleen. With Hendren's Furniture Co., Boise, 1947-69; co-owner, v.p. Hendren's Inc., Boise, 1969-87, pres. 1987—. Bd. dirs. Idaho Law Found., 1978-84; chmn. Coll. of Idaho Symposium, 1977-78, mem. adv. bd., 1981—; bd. dirs. SW Idaho Pvt. Industry Council, 1984-87; pres. Boise Council on Aging, 1959-60, mem. adv. bd., 1986—; mem. Gov.'s Commn. on Aging, 1960, Idaho del. to White House Conf. Aging, 1961; trustee St. Luke's Regional Hosp., 1981-92; mem. adv. bd. dirs. Boise Philharm. Assn., Inc., 1981—, Ballet Idaho; bd. dirs. Children's Home Soc. Idaho, 1988; founding pres. Idaho Congl. Award Program, 1993—; sustaining mem. Boise Jr. League. Mem. Boise C. of C. (bd. dirs. 1984-87), Gamma Phi Beta. Episcopalian. Home: 3504 Hillcrest Dr Boise ID 83705-4503 Office: 1109 Main St Ste 230 PO Box 9077 Boise ID 83702

HENDREN, ROBERT LEE, JR., academic administrator; b. Reno, Oct. 10, 1925; s. Robert Lee and Aleen (Hill) H.; m. Merlyn Churchill, June 14, 1947; children: Robert Lee IV, Anne Aleen. BA magna cum laude, Coll. Idaho, LLD (hon.); postgrad., Army Univ. Ctr., Oahu, Hawaii. Owner, pres. Hendren's Inc., 1947—; pres. Albertson Coll. Idaho, Caldwell, 1987—; bd. dirs. 1st Interstate Bank Idaho. Trustee Boise (Idaho) Ind. Sch. Dist., chmn. bd. trustees, 1966; chmn. bd. trustees Coll. Idaho, 1980-84; bd. dirs. Mountain View coun. Boy Scouts Am., Boise Retail Merchants, Boise Valley Indsl. Found., Boise Redevel. Agy., Ada County Marriage Counseling, Ada County Planning & Zoning Com., Blue Cross Idaho. Recipient Silver and Gold award U. Idaho. Mem. Boise C. of C. (pres., bd. dirs.), Idaho Sch. Trustees Assn., Masons, KT, Shriners, Rotary (Paul Harris fellow). Home: 3504 Hillcrest Dr Boise ID 83705-4503 Office: Albertson Coll Idaho 2112 Cleveland Blvd Caldwell ID 83605-4432

HENDRICK, HAL WILMANS, human factors educator; b. Dallas, Mar. 11, 1933; s. Harold Eugene and Audrey Sarah (Wilmans) H.; m. Mary Francis Boyle; children: Hal L., David A., John A. (dec.), Jennifer G. BA, Ohio Wesleyan U., 1955; MS, Purdue U., 1961, PhD, 1966. Cert. profl. ergonomist; registered psychologist, Tex. Asst. prof. U. So. Calif., L.A., assoc. prof., 1979-86; exec. dir. Inst. of Safety and Systems Mgmt., U. So. Calif., L.A., 1986-87; prof., dean Coll. of System Sci., U. Denver, 1987-90; prof. U. So. Calif., 1986—; pres. Bd Cert. of Profl. Ergonomists, 1992-94. Author: Behavioral Research and Analysis, 1980, 2d edit., 1989, 3rd edit., 1990; editor seven books; contbr. articles to profl. jours. Lt. col. USAF, 1956-76. Fellow APA, Human Factors Soc. (pres. L.A. chpt. 1986-87, pres. Rocky Mountain chpt. 1989-90, pres. elect 1994-95), Am. Psychol. Soc.; mem. Internat. Ergonomics Assn. (pres. Geneva 1990-94, immediate past pres. 1994-97, sec. gen. 1987-89, exec. com. 1984-87, U.S. rep.), Ergonomics Soc. (U.K.), Soc. for Indsl. and Orgnl. Psychology. Democrat. Home: 7100 E Crestline Ave Englewood CO 80111-1600 Office: Inst Safety & System Mgmt U So Calif Los Angeles CA 90089-0021

HENDRICKS, BRIAN JAMES, insurance company executive, consultant; b. Idaho Falls, ID, Aug. 18, 1948; s. James Andrew and Zelta (Walker) H.; m. Cora Lee Jones, June 5, 1970; children: Brian J. II, Todd J., Berkley J. BA, ID State U., 1973; CLU, Am. Coll., 1981, ChFC, 1983. Chartered Fin. Cons. Tchr. Ch. Jesus Christ Latter Day Saints, Veracruz, Mex., 1968-70; shipping Roger Bros. Seed Co., Pocatello, Idaho, 1970-73; field underwriter Mut. N.Y., Boise, Idaho, 1973-77; agt., owner Hendricks Ins. Agy., Soda Springs, Idaho, 1977—; ptnr. South Main Partnership, Soda Springs, 1989—; fin. cons. Hendricks Ins. Agy., Soda Springs, Idaho, 1985—; owner Chile-Mex.-U.S.A. Cons. and Fin., 1990—; pres. Caribou Internat. Cons. Assn., 1991—. Pres. Ida-North Carol Missionary Fund, 1992-94; scout mater Boy Scouts Am., Pocatello, Idaho, 1983-90, instr. Univ. Scouting, 1992; asst. lodge advisor Order of the Arrow, 1984-91, asst. sect. advisor, 1992—; planning and zoning commr. City of Soda Springs, 1992—;. Recipient Merit award Boy Scouts Am., Pocatello, Idaho, 1989, Founders award Boy Scouts Am., 1992. Mem. C. of C., State Farm Ins. Millionare Club, State Farm Legion Honor, Kiwanis Club. Mem. LDS Ch. Office: Hendricks Ins Agy 240 S Main St Soda Springs ID 83276-1657

HENDRICKS, DELOY G., nutrition educator; b. Pocatello, Idaho, Dec. 18, 1938; s. Gerald Kenneth and Jennie Rachael (Bloxham) H.; m. Cora Jean Wood, June 13, 1962; children: Judy Lee, LaLee, Jolene, Janet Sue, Jerrae, Joy Marie, Clint Elwin. BS, U. Idaho, 1961; PhD, Mich. State U., 1967. Asst. prof. Utah State U., Logan, 1967-72, assoc. prof., 1972-77, prof., 1977—. Co-inventor for method for improving meat quality, 1988; author: (book chpt.) Introduction to Chemical Analysis of Food, 1994. Councilman City Coun., Providence, Utah, 1982-86. Lt. U.S. Army, 1961-63. Mem. Am. Inst. Nutrition (grad. edn. com. 1980-84), Sigma Xi. Office: Utah State U Dept Nutrition UMC 8700 Logan UT 84322-8700

HENDRICKS, GLENN RICHARD, publishing executive; b. Galesburg, Ill., Oct. 6, 1964; s. Richard Dean Hendricks and Barbara Joan (Turner) Hendricks Hepner; m. Ann Frances Coatney, Aug. 20, 1988. BS, Ill. State U., 1986. Art dir. Greenville (N.C.) Printing Co., 1986-87; asst. night mgr. The Gap, L.A., 1987-88; creative dir. O.S.P. Pub., Monterey Park, Calif., 1988-89, v.p. licensing, 1989—; cons. G.R.H., Inc., L.A., 1994—; speaker in field. Author mags. The Licensing Book, 1993, The Licensing Directory, 1994. Mem. Licensing Industry Merchandizers Assn. (bd. dirs. 1993—). Office: OSP Pub Inc 1001 Monterey Pass Rd Monterey Park CA 91754

HENDRICKS, KATHERINE, lawyer; b. Logan, Utah, Apr. 12, 1949; d. Charles Durrell and Leah Grace (Funk) H.; m. O. Yale Lewis, Jr., Sept. 7, 1985. BS, MS, MIT, 1972; JD, Boston U., 1975. Bar: Mass. 1976, Colo. 1982, Wash. 1984, U.S. Dist. Ct. Mass. 1979, U.S. Dist. Ct. (no. dist.) N.Y., U.S. Dist. Ct. Colo., U.S. Dist. Ct. Wash., U.S. Ct. Appeals (1st cir.), 1978, U.S. Ct. Appeals (9th cir.), 1984. Assoc. Palmer & Dodge, Boston, 1975-81, Garfield & Hecht, Aspen, Colo., 1981-84, Wickwire, Lewis, Goldmark & Schorr, Seattle, 1984-86; ptnr. Hendricks & Lewis, Seattle, 1986—. Mem. ABA, Wash. State Bar Assn. (chmn. intellectual property sect. 1991—), Wash. Vol. Lawyers of Arts (bd. dirs. 1988—, pres. 1991—), MIT Enterprise Forum of N.W. (bd. dirs. 1988—, chmn. 1993—), Seattle-King County Bar Assn. Office: Hendricks & Lewis 2675 1st Ave Seattle WA 98121-1304

HENDRICKS, MARK KENNETH, animator, artist; b. Detroit, Feb. 20, 1952; s. Burton Neal and Shirley Elizabeth (Cochrane) H.; m. Debra Sue Harbourne, June 17, 1972 (div. Sept. 1984); children: Deirdra Isis, Dustin Quake; m. Brenda Kae Cooper, Sept. 22, 1986. BFA, Ea. Mich. U., 1975; BA in Psychology, Sonoma State U., 1978; postgrad., Laney Coll., 1978-80, U. Calif., Berkeley, 1980-82. Illustrator Brown and Caldwell, Walnut Creek, Calif., 1981-84; animator Fed. Res. Bank, San Francisco, 1984—; mem. Sta. KQED-TV, San Francisco, 1986, KETH-TV, San Jose, Calif., 1990, KCET, San Mateo, Calif., 1992; cons. Lockheed Aerospace, Sunnyvale, Calif., 1986—, Journalism dept. U. Calif., Berkeley, 1987—, Wells Fargo Bank, San Franciso, 1987—, Opta Imaging, Sunnyvale, 1991—; mem. Modern Mus., San Franciso, 1988, Folk Art Mus., San Francisco, 1990, Smithsonian Instn.,

1990. Animator: (ednl. videos) Signs of the Times, 1986, How Banks Create Money, 1987, Velocity, 1988, Striking a Balance, 1989, Grass Roots, 1990, The FED Our Central Bank, 1991, Capacity, 1992, Money, 1993, Trade in Action, 1994. Mem. ASIFA, Spl. Interest Group on Computer Graphics. Home: 2448 Monticello Ave Oakland CA 94601-5543 Office: Fed Res Bank 101 Market St San Francisco CA 94105-1530

HENDRICKSEN, HOLMES G., hotel executive; b. Holyoke, Colo., Apr. 22, 1933; s. Fred Willard and Esther Irene Hendricksen; m. Christine Lee Dishman, May 26, 1979. BS, U. Utah, 1956. With Harrah's, Tahoe, Nev., 1957—; gen. mgr. Harrah's Tahoe, 1968-71; v.p. entertainment Harrah's Reno/Tahoe, 1971-76, exec. v.p. entertainment and pub. relations, 1977—; pres. AIR Corp. Clubs: Hidden Valley Country, Friars. Office: Harrah's PO Box 10 Reno NV 89504-0010

HENDRICKSON, DAVID CALVIN, political science educator; b. Oklahoma City, Okla., Mar. 22, 1953; s. Calvin Wesley and Frances (Hewitt) H.; m. Clelia de Moraes; children: Whitney, Wesley, Marina. BA in History, Colo. Coll., 1976; MA in Polit. Sci., Johns Hopkins U., 1981, PhD in Polit. Sci., 1982. Coord. undergrad. internat. rel. program Johns Hopkins U., Balt., 1979-81; legis. asst. Daniel P. Moynihan, Washington, 1981; asst. prof. polit. sci. Colo. Coll., Colorado Springs, 1983-89, assoc. prof. polit. sci., 1989—; book rev. editor Fgn. Affairs Jour., N.Y.C., 1994; presenter The Lehrmann Inst., 1983, 84, 85; chair panel Internat. Studies Assn., Air Force Acad., 1984, Anaheim, 1986, Washington, 1987, U.S. Inst. of Peace, Washington, 1988, The Ethikon Inst., Mont St. Michel, France, 1989, India Internat. Ctr., New Delhi, 1989; participant Conf. on the Rule of Law, Liberty Fund, The Broadmoor, Colorado Springs, 1985, Conf. on Ethics and Nuclear Deterrence, Aspen, Colo., 1985; lectr. Air Force Acad., 1988. Author: The Future of American Strategy, 1987, Reforming Defense: The State of American Civil-Military Relations, 1988; author: (with Robert W. Tucker): The Fall of the First British Empire: Origins of the War of American Independence, 1982, Empire of Liberty: The Statecraft of Thomas Jefferson, 1990, The Imperial Temptation: The New World Order and America's Purpose, 1992; contbr. articles to profl. jours. Grantee NEH, 1990; Rsch. fellow The Lehrmann Inst., 1984-85, John M. Olin Found. fellow, 1986-87; recipient Burlington No. Faculty Achievement award Colo. Coll., 1989. Mem. Am. Polit. Sci. Assn., Coun. on Fgn. Rels. (Whitney Shepardson fellow 1991-92). Democrat. Unitarian. Office: Colo Coll Dept Polit Sci 14 E Cache La Poudre St Colorado Springs CO 80903-3243

HENDRICKSON, ELIZABETH ANN, secondary education educator; b. Bismarck, S.D., Oct. 21, 1936; d. William Earl and Hilda E. (Sauter) Hinkel; m. Roger G. Hendrickson, Apr. 18, 1960; 1 child, Wade William. BA, Jamestown Coll., 1958; postgrad., U. Calif., Davis, 1962, Calif. State U., Sacramento, 1964, U. San Diego, 1985-88, Ottawa U., 1986-88. Cert. tchr., Calif. Tchr. Napoleon (N.D.) High Sch., 1958-59, Kulm (N.D.) High Sch., 1959-61, Del Paso Jr. High Sch., Sacramento, 1961, Mills Jr. High Sch., Rancho Cordova, Calif., 1961—. Mem. NEA, AAUW, Calif. Assn. for Gifted, Calif. Edn. Assn., Sacramento Area Gifted Assn., Soroptimists (news editor Rancho Cordova club 1985, sec. 1986). Democrat. Lutheran. Home: 2032 Kellogg Way Rancho Cordova CA 95670-2435

HENDRICKSON, ROBERT J., educational administrator; b. West Chester, Pa., Dec. 3, 1935; s. Carl W. Sr. and Ethel A. (Butler) H.; m. Barbara M. Nale, June 18, 1960; children: Robert J., Jr., Susan E. Hendrickson Landers. BS, West Chester State U., 1957; MEd, Seton Hall U., 1963. Tchr., adminstr. Newark Acad., Livingston, N.J., 1957-79; v.p. Internat. Trading and Commodities, N.Y.C., 1979-80; athletic dir. The Hun Sch., Princeton, N.J., 1980-84; regional dir. of sales and mktg. Aramis, St. Louis and N.Y.C., 1984-87; dean of students Phoenix Country Day Sch., Paradise Valley, Ariz., 1987—; cons., Phoenix, 1991—. Chmn. edn. com. Youth Vol. Assn., Maricopa County, Ariz., 1993-94. Named to Hall of Fame, Newark Acad., 1984; honored by Newark Police Dept. for svc. to youth, 1975. Mem. Ariz. Coaches Assn., Ariz. Assn. Sch. Coun. Advs., others. Home: 4256 E Rosemonte Dr Phoenix AZ 85024-3344 Office: Phoenix Country Day Sch 3901 E Stanford Dr Paradise Valley AZ 85253-7500

HENDRICKSON, WILLIAM LEE, French language educator; b. Denver, Feb. 13, 1936; s. William Francis and Virginia Maria (Maloney) H.; m. Ruth Suzanne Bader, Dec. 29, 1976; 1 child, Matthew Lee. BA, Ariz. State U., 1959; postgrad., U. Strasbourg, France, 1959-60; MA, U. Kans., 1962; PhD, Princeton U., 1969. Asst. instr. U. Kans., Lawrence, 1960-62, Princeton (N.J.) U., 1963-64; instr., then asst. prof. Brown U., Providence, 1965-72; asst. prof. Washington U., St. Louis, 1972-76; asst. prof. Ariz. State U., Tempe, 1976-78, assoc. prof., 1978—. Co-author: Quinze Lecons de francais, 1972; co-editor: Jean Misrahi Memorial Volume, 1977, Studies on Seven Sages of Rome, 1978; editor: Contrastes: Contrastive Studies, 1989. Mem. Balsz Sch. Dist. Planning Assessment Com., Phoenix, 1992-94. Fulbright grantee, 1959-60, NEH grantee, 1973-74; fellow Camargo Found., Cassis, France, 1983. Mem. MLA, Soc. Rencesvals, Internat. Arthurian Soc., Am. Assn. Tchrs. of French (v.p. 1979-81, co-pres., 1989-93, exec. com. 1986-89), Cen. Ariz. Consortium on Internat. Edn., Phi Kappa Phi. Democrat. Roman Catholic. Home: 2422 N 56th St Phoenix AZ 85008-2626 Office: Ariz State U Dept Langs and Lit Tempe AZ 85287-0202

HENDRIX, LOUISE BUTTS, retired educator, author; b. Portland, Tenn., June 16, 1911; d. Luther Edward and Johnny Henrietta (McNeill) B.; m. Edwin Alonzo Hendrix, Aug. 1, 1934 (dec. May 1991); children: Lynette Louise, Edwin Alonzo Jr. AB, Chico (Calif.) State Coll., 1932; postgrad., Sacramento State U., 1934-62, Coll. Pacific, 1934-62; Diploma of merit, U Delle Arti, Parma, Italy, 1982. Tchr. jr. high sch. Rio Vista, Calif., 1932-34; newspaper worker Chico Enterprise, 1930-32; tchr. jr. high sch. Alpaugh, Calif., 1944-45; newspaper corr. Sacramento Bee, Marysville Appeal Dem., Live Oak, Calif., 1945-52, Oroville Mercury Register Marysville Appeal Dem., Biggs, Calif., 1935-40; tchr. jr. high sch. Live Oak, 1952-69; ret., 1969. Author: Better Reading and Writing with Journalism, 1974, Sutter Buttes-Land of Histum Yani, 1980, 6th edit., 1992, Petals and Blossoms, 1983, Squaw Man, 1987; contbr. poetry to profl. jours. Mem. Sutter County Parks and Recreation Commn., Yuba City, 1977-80; founder Save Sutter Buttes Assn., Inc., Yuba City, 1978, sec., treas., 1978-90. Recipient Poet of Yr. award World Congress Poets, Orlando, Fla., 1986, Gold Poet award World of Poetry Conv., Anaheim, Calif., 1988. Fellow Internat. Poetry Soc.; mem. AAUW, Calif. Retired Tchrs. Assn., Sierra Club (Conservationist of Yr. 1974), Woman's Club (pres. Yuba City chpt. 1978-79). Democrat. Roman Catholic. Home: 1354 Geneva Ave Yuba City CA 95991-6711

HENDRIX, TIMOTHY DALE, highway construction company manager; b. Poplar Bluff, Mo., Dec. 7, 1954; s. Ralph Alexander Jr. and Bernice Ann (Nadeau) H.; m. Linda Lee Savage, Mar. 6, 1982; children: Christopher Michael, Jeremy Raymond, Brian James. BSCE, Worcester Poly. Inst., 1975; MSCE, Stanford U., 1976. Registered profl. engr., Calif., Oreg. Estimator, constrn. engr. Wildish Corvallis (Oreg.) Constrn. Co., 1976-77; estimator, project engr. Wildish Constrn. Co., Eugene, Oreg., 1977-78; project mgr. Wildish Constrn. Co., Bend, Oreg., 1979; mgr. Wildish Corvallis Cos., 1979-81; chief estimator Wildish Cos., Eugene, 1981-84, project mgr., 1983-86; project mgr. Wildish Standard Paving Co., Eugene, 1986-88, mgr., 1989—. Mem. AGC (Columbia chpt. bd. dirs. 1992-94), Downtown Athletic Club. Office: Wildish Standard Paving Co 3600 County Farm Rd Eugene OR 97408-4616

HENDRY, JOHN EASTON, III, physician, surgeon; b. San Jose, Calif., Oct. 21, 1943; s. John Easton Jr. and Katherine E. Hendry. BA cum laude, Stanford U., 1966; MD, McGill U., Montreal, Can., 1970. Diplomate Am. Bd. Ob-Gyn., Nat. Bd. Med. Examiners. Inter Santa Clara Valley Med. Ctr., San Jose, Calif., 1969-70; resident in ob-gyn. Wash. U.-Barnes Hosp., St. Louis, 1972-75, chief resident, 1974-75; mem. sr. active staff Mercy San Juan Hosp., Carmichael, Calif., 1975—, Mercy Am. River Hosp., Carmichael, Calif., 1975—; mem. courtesy staff Roseville (Calif.) Cmty. Hosp., 1975—; mem. Sacramento Physicians Network, Inc., 1989—, Hill Physicians Med. Group, 1991-92; peer reviewer Med. Bd. Calif., Blue Shield HMO, CorCare Ind. Med. Evaluation; mem. panel of arbitrators Am. Arbitration Assn.; mem. panel Physicians for Quality. Fellow ACOG; mem. AMA, Calif. Med. Assn., No. Calif. Obstet. and Gynecol. Soc., Am. Assn. Gynecologic Laparoscopists, Sacramento-El Dorado Med. Soc. Office: 5525 Dewey Dr Ste 104 Fair Oaks CA 95628-3130

HENELY, JOANN HOUSH, real estate company owner; b. Sparta, Wis., May 29, 1928; d. Herman F. and Merle E. (Owen) Housh; m. Michael Floyd Henely, Sept. 9, 1947; children: Michael William, John Richard, Robert Martin, Donald Roger. Student, Drake U., 1945-47; BA in Travel Industry Mgmt., Hawaii Pacific U., 1981. Owner Henely Wholesale, Omaha, 1965-67; owner Red Carpet Real Estate, Danville, Alamo, Calif., 1968-73, Henely Assocs., San Diego, Honolulu, 1973—. Contbr. travel and real estate articles to publs. Pres., founder State of Hawaii Independent Travel Agts., Honolulu, 1986-88; past pres. Little League, Pony League, Newcomers, Hosp. Guild, Woman's Club, Church Woman's Guild, Omaha, 1958-64, Newcomers, Woman's Club, Hosp. Guild, Orinda, Calif., 1964-67; mem. Republican Women, Honolulu, LWV, Honolulu, A.S.H., abortion rights-pro-choice groups, Honolulu; ways and means chair Honolulu Symphony, 1987-88. Mem. AAUW (treas. Hawaii chpt. 1987-88, chmn. Friends Around the World Hawaii chpt. 1986-88), DAR (chpt. chmn. TV and Movies, Calif., 1988-91, state chmn. TV and movies, Calif., 1987, officer and membership chmn. 1988, Hawaii del. to nat. conv. 1987, state chmn. Americanism 1994-95, state flag chmn. 1993-95, chmn. constrn. com. to meet Am. Disabilities Act Aloha chpt. 1994, 95), Ind. Travel Agts., Computer Geneaology Soc. San Diego (rep. to Assn. Pers. Computers Users Group), Sandwich Islands Geneaology and Computer Soc. Republican. Unity. Home: 2727 De Anza Rd Spc Sd6 San Diego CA 92109-6825 Office: Henely Assocs 2161 Kalia Rd Apt 1212 Honolulu HI 96815-1944

HENG, STANLEY MARK, military officer; b. Nebraska City, Nebr., Nov. 4, 1937; s. Robert Joseph Sr. and Margaret Ann (Volkmer) H.; m. Sharon E. Barrett, Oct. 10, 1959; children: Mark, Nick, Lisa. Student, Command and Gen. Staff Coll., 1969, Nat. Def. U., 1979; BA, Doane Coll., 1987. Commd. adj. Nebr. N.G., 1966, advanced through grade to major gen., 1966-87; adj. Nebr. Mil. Dept., Lincoln, 1966-77, adminstrv. asst., 1978-86; adj. gen., civil def. dir. State of Nebr., Lincoln, 1987—. Mem. N.G. Assn. U.S., N.G. Assn. Nebr. (exec. sec. 1967-71, Svc. award 1970), Adj. Gens. Assn., Am. Legion. Democrat. Mem. United Ch. of Christ. Office: Mil Dept 1300 Military Rd Lincoln NE 68508-1090

HENKEL, CATHY, newspaper sports editor. Office: The Seattle Times Fairview Ave N & John St PO Box 70 Seattle WA 98111-0070

HENKIN, WILLIAM ASHER, psychotherapist; b. Bklyn., July 17, 1944; s. William Ascher and Ethel (Novick) H. BS, Northwestern U., 1965, MA, 1967; MA, Calif. Inst. Internat. Studies, 1985; PhD, Inst. Advanced Study Sexuality, 1993. Instr. Northwestern U., Evanston, Ill., 1967-69; editor various publs., Chgo., 1970-73, N.Y.C., 1970-73, San Francisco, 1970-73; freelance writer San Francisco, 1973—; psychotherapist pvt. practice, San Francisco, 1987—; adj. prof. Profl. Sch. Psychology, San Francisco, 1992—; faculty Advanced Mgmt. Inst., San Francisco, 1994—. Author: The Spiral Tapestry, 1981, co-author: The Physic Healing Book, 1978, Bodywise, 1985. Fellow Am. Acad. Clin. Sexuality; mem. Calif. Assn. Marraige & Family Therapists, Soc. Scientific Study of Sex (past pres., San Francisco chpt.ú, Harry Benjamin Internat. Gender Dysphoria Assn. Office: 1801 Bush St Ste 111 San Francisco CA 94109-5239

HENLEY, ERNEST MARK, physics educator, university dean emeritus; b. Frankfurt, Germany, June 10, 1924; came to U.S., 1939, naturalized, 1944; s. Fred S. and Josy (Dreyfuss) H.; m. Elaine Dimitman, Aug. 21, 1948; children: M. Bradford, Karen M. B.E.E., CCNY, 1944; Ph.D., U. Calif. at Berkeley, 1952. Physicist Lawrence Radiation Lab., 1950-51; research assoc. physics dept. Stanford U., 1951-52; lectr. physics Columbia U., 1952-54; mem. faculty U. Wash., Seattle, 1954—; prof. physics U. Wash., 1961-95; prof. emeritus, 1995—; chmn. dept. U. Wash., 1973-76, dean Coll. Arts and Scis., 1979-87, dir. Inst. for Nuclear Theory, 1990-91; rschr., author numerous publs. on symmetries, nuclear reactions, weak interactions and high energy particle interactions; chmn. Nuclear Sci. Adv. Com., 1986-89. Author: (with W. Thirring) Elementary Quantum Field Theory, 1962, (with H. Frauenfelder) Subatomic Physics, 1974, 2nd edit. 1991, Nuclear and Particle Physics, 1975. Bd. dirs. Pacific Sci. Ctr., 1984-87, Wash. Tech. Ctr., 1983-87; trustee Associated Univs., Inc., 1989—, chmn. bd., 1993—. Recipient sr. Alexander von Humboldt award, 1984, T.W. Bonner prize Am. Physics Soc., 1989, Townsend Harris medal CCNY, 1989; F.B. Jewett fellow, 1952-53, NSF sr. fellow, 1958-59, Guggenheim fellow, 1967-68, NATO sr. fellow, 1976-77. Fellow Am. Phys. Soc. (chmn. div. nuclear physics 1979-80, pres. elect. 1991, pres. 1992), AAAS (chmn. physics sect. 1989-90); mem. Nat. Acad. Scis., Sigma Xi. Office: U Wash Physics Dept FM 15 Seattle WA 98195

HENLEY, JEFFREY O., restaurant executive; b. Phoenix, Nov. 6, 1948; s. Justin Oniel and Jane Ellen (Rice) H.; children—Amy, Julie, Todd. B.A., U. Calif.-Santa Barbara, 1966; M.B.A., UCLA, 1967. Cost acctg. supr. Hughes Aircraft Co., Culver City, CA, 1967-70; div. controller Tridair Industries, Redondo Beach, Calif., 1970-72, Fairchild Camera & Instrument, Mountain View, Calif., 1972-75; dir. fin. Memorex Corp., Santa Clara, Calif., 1975-79; v.p., controller Saga Corp, Menlo Park, Calif., 1979-82, exec. v.p., 1982—; pres. Fast Service Restaurant Group, Menlo Park, Calif., 1985—. Bd. dirs. Herbert Hoover Boys' & Girls' Club, Menlo Park, Calif., 1983, pres., 1984—. Mem. Fin. Exec. Inst., Sigma Phi Epsilon. Republican. Presbyterian. Home: 107 Puesta Del Sol Los Gatos CA 95030-1131

HENLEY, PRESTON VANFLEET, former banker, financial consultant; b. Fort Madison, Iowa, July 7, 1913; s. Jesse vanFleet and Ruth (Roberts) H.; m. Elizabeth Artis Watts, Mar. 31, 1940 (div. June 1956); children: Preston Edward VanFleet, Stephen Watts, John vanFleet; m. 2d, Helena Margaret Greenslade, Nov. 29, 1964; 1 adopted son, Lawrence D. Student Tulane U., 1931-34, Loyola U., New Orleans, 1935-36; A.B., Calif. State Coll. at Santa Barbara, 1939; postgrad. U. Wash., 1939-40, N.Y. U., 1943, 46. Teaching fellow U. Wash., 1939-40; sr. credit analyst, head credit dept. Chase Nat. Bank, 45th St. br. N.Y.C., 1942-49; Western sales rep. Devoe & Raynolds, Inc., N.Y.C., 1949-51; v.p., comml. loan officer, mgr. credit dept. U.S. Nat. Bank, Portland, Oreg., 1951-72; loan adminstr. Voyageur Bank Group, Eau Claire, Wis.; v.p. Kanabec State Bank, Mora, Minn., Montgomery State Bank (Minn.), Park Falls State Bank (Wis.), Montello State Bank (Wis.), 1972; v.p., mgr. main office, sr. credit officer So. Nev. region Nev. Nat. Bank, Las Vegas, 1973-75; bus. and fin. cons., 1975—; loan cons. Continental Nat. Bank, Las Vegas, 1983-89; instr. Am. Inst. Banking, Portland, 1952-65, Multomah Coll., Portland, 1956-62, Portland State U., 1961-72, Mt. Hood Community Coll., 1971-72, Clark County Community Coll., 1979-83; adv. dir. Vita Plus, Inc., 1979-83; exec. dir. Nev. Minority Purchasing Council, 1979-80; dir., treas. Consumer Credit Counselling Service of Oreg. 1965-72. Treas., Ore. chpt. Leukemia Soc., 1965-66; mem. Menninger Found. 1965-67; trustee, exec. com. St. Rose delima Hosp. Found., 1982-87;dir. So. Nev. chtp. Assn. Part-Time Profls., 1985-87. Served with USNR, 1943-45. Mem. Oreg. Bankers Assn., Robert Morris Assos. (pres. Oreg. chpt. 1959-60, nat. dir. 1961-64), Nat., Oreg. assns. credit mgmt., Credit Research Found., Inst. Internal Auditors, S.A.R., Beta Mu, Leaf and Scarab, Alpha Phi Omega, Portland C. of C., Oreg. Retail Council. Republican. Episcopalian. Mason (32 deg., Shriner). Contbr. articles to profl. jours. Home and Office: 7778 Locke Haven Dr Las Vegas NV 89123-0734

HENNESSEY, ALICE ELIZABETH, forest products company executive; b. Havenhill, Mass., May 24, 1936; d. H. Nelson and Elizabeth E. (Johnson) Pingree; A.B. with honors, U. Colo., 1957; cert. with distinction Harvard-Radcliffe Program in Bus. Adminstrn., 1958; m. Thomas M. Hennessey, June 13, 1959; children—Shannon, Sheila, Thomas N. With Boise Cascade Corp. (Idaho), 1958—, sec. to pres., 1958-60, adminstrv. asst. to pres., 1960-61, 65-71, corp. sec., 1971—, v.p., 1974-82, sr. v.p., 1982—. Dir. First Interstate Bank of Idaho. Bd. dirs. Boise Pub. Libr. Found., U. Idaho Found.; sustaining mem. Boise Jr. League; mem. exec. bd. U S WEST Communications, Idaho. Mem. Am. Soc. of Corp. Secs., Nat. Investor Relations Inst., Pub. Relations Soc. of Am., Phi Beta Kappa, Alpha Chi Omega. Office: Boise Cascade Corp 1 Jefferson Sq Boise ID 83728-0001

HENNESSY, BARBARA ROSE, city controller; b. Passaic, N.J., Sept. 18, 1948; d. Euro Francis Eusebi and Rosaria J. (Botta) Hecathorn; m. Glenn Wayne Hennessy, Feb. 23, 1980; stepchildren: Diana Hennessy Hanley, Scott Allan. AA, Long Beach City Coll., 1968; BS summa cum laude, Calif. State U., 1971. CPA. Auditor Arthur Andersen & Co., L.A., 1971-73; controller Atomic Disposer Co., Westminster, Calif., 1973-74; chief acct. Monogram Industries, Redondo Beach, Calif., 1974-77; from acct. to city controller City of Long Beach, 1977—; tchr. govt. acct. Calif. Soc. Mcpl. Fin. Officers, 1986-92. Mem. Govt. Fin. Officers Assn. (tchr. 1988-89, spkr. nat. confs. 1986—, chair spl. review exec. com. 1991-94, com. on acct., auditing & fin. reporting 1988—, chair popular reporting task force 1991—), Sweet Adelines Internat. (asst. dir., choreographer Golden Sands chpt. 1977—), Alpha Gamma Sigma. Office: City of Long Beach - Fin 333 W Ocean Blvd Fl 6 Long Beach CA 90802-4604

HENNIGAN, JAMES MICHAEL, lawyer; b. Tucson, Nov. 2, 1943; s. James Edward and Alice Elizabeth (Boehm) H.; m. Phyllis Lynn Rothkopf, Aug. 26, 1973; children: Amanda Michelle, Cassandra Asch. BA, U. Ariz., 1966, JD with distinction, 1970. Bar: Ariz. 1970, Calif. 1974. Trial atty. U.S. Dept. of Justice, Washington, 1970-72; assoc. Snell & Wilmer, Phoenix, 1972-73; ptnr. Lovitt, Hannan & Hennigan, San Francisco, 1973-75, Martori, Meyer, Hendricks & Victor, Phoenix, 1975-77, Howrey & Simon (formerly Hennigan & Mercer), 1983—; lectr. U. Ariz., 1973—, The Am. Law Inst., 1993—; law rep. 9th Cir. Judicial Conf., 1993—. Author law rev. article The Essence of Standing: The Basis of a Constitutional Right to be Heard, 1969. Founder, chmn., Dir.'s Roundtable, L.A. County Mus. of Art, 1982—; bd. of visitors U. Ariz., Coll. of Law. Mem. Am. Bd. Trial Advs., Am. Law Inst., L.A Bar Assn. (bd. dirs. litigation sect.), State Bar of Ariz., State Bar of Calif., Order of Coif. Office: 550 S Hope St Ste 1400 Los Angeles CA 90071-2635

HENNING, MARTHA LOUISE, English language educator; b. Monterey, Calif., Nov. 14, 1948; d. Robert J. and Ruth J. (Udden) H.; m. Peter M. Stock; children: Nathan C. Hamilton, Sarah L. Hamilton. AB in English, Stanford U., 1970; MA in Humanities, SUNY, Buffalo, 1972; PhD in Rhetoric and Composition, U. Louisville, 1993. Lectr. U. Ind. S.E., New Albany, 1985, U. Louisville, 1987, Jefferson C.C., Louisville, 1989-90, Bellarmine Coll., Louisville, 1990-91; prof. English Portland (Oreg.) C.C., 1991—; bd. dirs., mem. adv. com. Young Rhetoricians' Conf., Monterey, Calif., 1991—. Contbr. articles to profl. publs. Mem. MLA, Assn. Profl. Writing Cons., Internat. Soc. for History of Rhetoric, Nat. Coun. Tchrs. English, Rhetoric Soc. Am., Stanford Alumnae Assn. (life). Home: 7430 SW 76th Ave Portland OR 97223-7489 Office: Portland CC PO Box 19000 Portland OR 97280-0990

HENNINGS, DOROTHY ANN, financial planner; b. Spokane, Wash., Mar. 23, 1937; d. Theodore Baza LaRue and Florence Irene (Jaeger) Innes; m. Peter L. Sbarbaro Sr., May 16, 1959 (div. 1973); children: Peter L. Jr., David A., John E. AS in Acctg., Napa Valley Coll., 1974; BS, Calif. State U., Sacramento, 1977. Cert. fin. planner. Acctg. asst. Napa (Calif.) County Counsel for Econ. Opportunity, 1972-73; owner, cons. Dash Enterprises, American Canyon, Calif., 1973-78; owner, bookkeeper Reliable Meats, American Canyon, 1973-74; fin. planner IDS Fin. Svcs., Napa, 1983-94, Am. Express Fin. Advisors, Napa, 1995—. Vol. Boy Scouts Am., Am. Canyon PTA, Little League, Pop Warner Football; sponsor T-ball and Babe Ruth Bambino and Babe Ruth League Teams; tax preparer Vita, Napa, 1973-74. Mem. Toastmasters, Soroptimist Club, Order Ea. Star, Women of Moose, Greater Napa Valley Lions. Republican. Office: Am Express Fin Advisors 3033 California Blvd Napa CA 94558-3304

HENNION, CAROLYN LAIRD (LYN HENNION), investment executive; b. Orange, Calif., July 27, 1943; d. George James and Jane (Porter) Laird; m. Reeve L. Hennion, Sept. 12, 1964; children: Jeffrey Reeve, Douglas Laird. BA, Stanford U., 1965; grad. Securities Industry Inst., U. Pa., 1992. CFP, fund specialist; lic. ins. agt.; registered gen. securities prin. Portfolio analyst Schwabacher & Co., San Francisco, 1965-66; adminstrv. coord. Bicentennial Commn., San Mateo County Calif., 1972-73; dir. devel. Crystal Springs Uplands Sch., Hillsborough, Calif., 1973-84; tax preparer Household Fin. Corp., Foster City, Calif., 1982, freelance, 1983-87; sales promotion mgr. Franklin Distbrs., Inc., San Mateo, 1984-86, v.p. and regional sales mgr. of N.W., 1986-91, Mid-Atlantic, 1991-94; v.p. Viatech, Inc., 1986-92; v.p. Keypoint Svcs. Internat., 1992—; pres. Brock Rd. Corp., 1993—; v.p. Strand, Atkinson, Williams & York, Medford, Oreg., 1994—. Editor: Lest We Forget, 1975. Pres. South Hillsborough Sch. Parents' Group, Calif., 1974-75; sec. Vol. Bur. of San Mateo County, Burlingame, Calif., 1975; chmn. Community Info. Com., Town of Hillsborough, 1984-86, mem., sub-com. chmn. fin. adv. com., 1984-86; mem. coun. Town of Buncom, Oreg., 1990—; bd. dirs. Pacific N.W. Mus. Natural History, 1995—; chmn. Jackson County Applegate Trail Sesquicentennial Celebration, 1995—. Recipient awards Coun. for Advancement and Support of Edn., 1981, Exemplary Direct Mail Appeals Fund Raising Inst., 1982, Wholesaler of Yr. Shearson Lehman Hutton N.W Region, 1989, Golden Mic award Frederic Gilbert Assocs., 1993. Mem. Securities Industry Assn. (chmn. state membership 1989-91), Internat. Assn. Fin. Planners (sec. Oreg. chpt. 1988-89, bd. dirs.), Inst. Cert. Fin. Planners, Bond Club Phila., Buncom Hist. Soc., Oreg. Shakespeare Festival, Britt Festivals, So. Oreg. Hist. Soc., Arts Coun. So. Oreg., Jr. League. Republican. Home: 3232 Little Applegate Rd Jacksonville OR 97530-9303 Office: Strand Atkinson Williams & York 1 North Holly Medford OR 97501

HENRICKSEN, LISA ALAINE, development director; b. Tallahassee, Fla., Dec. 12, 1964; d. Gerhard Chester Jr. and Linda (Smith) H. BA in Bus. Adminstrn. and music, Chatham Coll., 1986; MBA in Mktg., Drexel U., 1990. Adminstrv. intern Pitts. Symphony, 1984; publicity intern theater dept. U. Pitts., 1985-86; personal banker Commonwealth Fed. Savs. and Loan, Malvern, Pa., 1988; adminstrv. asst. Phila. Orch., 1988-90, vol. coord., 1990-93; devel. dir. St. Barnabas Sr. Svcs., L.A., 1993—. Vol. U. So. Calif. Sch. Music, L.A. Baroque Orch.; singer various chs. and choir. Mem. Nat. Soc. Fundraising Execs., Jr. League of L.A. Democrat. Lutheran. Office: St Barnabas Sr Svcs 675 S Carondelet St Los Angeles CA 90057-3309

HENRICKSON, EILER LEONARD, geologist, educator; b. Crosby, Minn., Apr. 23, 1920; s. Eiler Clarence and Mabel (Bacon) H.; m. Kristine L. Kuntzman; children: Eiler Warren, Kristin, Kurt Eric, Ann Elizabeth. BA, Carleton Coll., 1943; PhD, U. Minn., 1956. Geologist U.S. Geol. Survey, Calif., 1943-44; instr. Carleton Coll., 1946-47, 48-51, asst. prof., 1951-53, 54-56, assoc. prof., 1956-62, prof., 1962-70, Charles L. Denison prof. geology, 1970-87, chmn. dept., 1970-78, wrestling coach, 1946-58, 83-87; prof. geology, chmn. dept. Colo. Coll., 1987—; instr. U. Minn., 1947-48, 53-54; vis. lectr. numerous univs., Europe, 1962; cons. Jones & Laughlin Steel Corp., 1946-58, Fremont Mining Co., Alaska, 1958-61, G.T. Schieldahl Co., Minn., 1961-62, Bear Creek Mining Co., Mich., 1965-66, U. Minn. Messenia Expdn., 1966-75, Exxon Co., 1977-78, Cargill Corp., Mpls., 1983-84, Leslie Salt Co., San Francisco, 1985-86, various other cos.; research scientist, cons. Oak Ridge (Tenn.) Nat. Lab., 1985-86; cons. Argonne Nat. Lab., 1966-78, research scientist, summers, 1966-67; field studies metamorphic areas, Norway and Scotland; dir. young scholars program NSF, 1988-90. Author: Zones of Regional Metamorphism, 1957. Dir. Northfield Bd. Edn., 1960-63; steering com. Northfield Community Devel. Program, 1966-67. Served as 1st lt. USMCR, 1943, AUS, 1944-46. Fulbright research scholar archeol. geology, Greece, 1966-87. Mem. AAAS, Mineral Soc. Am., Nat. Assn. Geology Tchrs., Minn. Acad. Sci (vis. lectr.), Am. Geol. Inst., Geol. Soc. Am., Soc. Econ. Geologists, Rocky Mountain Assn. Geologists, Nat. Wrestling Coaches and Ofcls. Assn., Archaeol. Inst. Am. (vis. lectr.), Sigma Xi. Home: 19560 Four Winds Way Monument CO 80132-9309 Office: Colo Coll Dept Geology Colorado Springs CO 80903

HENRIKSEN, MELVIN, mathematician, educator; b. N.Y.C., N.Y., Feb. 23, 1927; s. Kaj and Helen (Kahn) H.; m. Lillian Viola Hill, July 23, 1946 (div. 1964); children—Susan, Richard, Thomas; m. Louise Levitas, June 12, 1964. B.S., Coll. City N.Y., 1948; M.S., U. Wis., 1949, Ph.D. in Math, 1951. Asst. math., then instr. extension div. U. Wis., 1948-51; asst. prof. U. Ala., 1951-52; from instr. to prof. math. Purdue U., 1952-65; prof. math., head dept. Case Inst. Tech., 1965-68; research assoc. U. Calif. at Berkeley, 1968-69; prof., chmn. math. dept. Harvey Mudd Coll., 1969-72, prof., 1972—; mem. Inst. Advanced Study, Princeton, 1956-57, 63-64; vis. prof. Wayne State U., 1960-61; rsch. assoc. U. Man., Winnipeg, Can., 1975-76; vis. prof. Wesleyan U., Middletown, Conn., 1978-79, 82-83, 86-87, 93-94. Author: (with Milton Lees) Single Variable Calculus, 1970; assoc. editor: Algebra Universalis, 1993—; contbr. articles to profl. jours. on algebra, rings of functions, gen. topology. Sloan fellow, 1956-58. Mem. Am. Math. Soc., Math. Assn. Am. (assoc. editor Am. Math. monthly 1988-91, assoc. editor

Algebra Universalis 1993—). Home: 504 W Bowling Green Dr Claremont CA 91711-2716

HENRIKSSON, THOMAS MARTIN, chemist, researcher; b. Kristofta, Sweden, Dec. 13, 1951; came to U.S., 1980; s. Hjalmar Valfrid and Hildur Linnea (Almer) H.; m. Diana Marie Lander, Mar. 15, 1980; children: Sarah, Kristofer. BS, U. Lund, Sweden, 1973; PhD, U. Lund, 1982. Postdoctoral fellow U. Calif., Berkeley, 1982-85; rsch. chemist Sclavo, Inc., Sunnyvale, Calif., 1985-88; scientist Athena Neuroscis. Inc., South San Francisco, 1988-89, Cetus Corp., Emeryville, Calif., 1989-91; prin. scientist Chiron Corp., Emeryville, Calif., 1991—. Contbr. articles to sci. jours. Pvt. Army, 1973-74, Sweden. Mem. Am. Chem. Soc., Am. Assn. for Clin. Chemistry, AAAS. Roman Catholic. Office: Chiron Corp 4560 Horton St Emeryville CA 94608-2916

HENROTTE, GAYLE ALLEN, linguistics educator and musicologist; b. Long Beach, Calif., Nov. 20, 1935; d. Frank Joseph Henrotte and Barbara (Allen) Wright. AB in Music, Vassar Coll., 1958; MLS in Libr. Sci., U. Ala., 1981; PhD in Musicology, U. N.C., 1967; PhD in Linguistics, U. Calif., Berkeley, 1988. Instr. music Rosary Coll., River Forest, Ill., 1965-66; asst. prof. Miss. U. for Women, Columbus, 1966-82; teaching asst. U. Calif., Berkeley, 1982-88; asst. prof. German Cleve. State U., 1988-90; adj. prof. U. La Verne, Calif., 1990—, Mt. San Antonio Coll., Walnut, Calif., 1993—; adj. prof. Calif. State Polytechnic U., Pomona, 1995—. Author: Music, Language, and Linguistics, 1995. Music cons. Roman Cath. Diocese of Natchez, Miss., 1966-70. Recipient fellowship U. Vienna, Rotary Internat., 1962-63, NEH, U. Mo., 1989. Mem. TESOL, Rocky Mountain MLA, Philol. Assn. of Pacific Coast (sessions organizer 1985—), Medieval Congress (sessions organizer 1988—). Roman Catholic. Office: Mount San Antonio Coll 1100 N Grant Ave Walnut CA 91789

HENRY, DAVID ALLEN, advertising executive; b. Cedar Rapids, Iowa, Apr. 16, 1950; s. Don Albert and Anna Mae (Manwiller) H.; m. Elise Marie Cohen, June 7, 1981 (div. Apr. 1988); children: Lauren, Erica, Sylvia. BBA, U. Iowa, 1972. V.p. mktg. Movie Systems, Inc., Denver, 1975-77; chmn., chief exec. officer Henry Gill Advt., Denver, 1977—; mem. bd. advisors Entrepreneurial Inst. Denver, 1989. Bd. dirs. Direction 2,000 Found., Littleton, Colo., 1990-93, Littleton Pub. Schs. Found.; nat. advisor White House Conf. for Drug-Free Am., Washington, 1988. Recipient Award of Merit, United Way Mile High Child Care, Denver, 1988, Cert. of Appreciation, Communities for Drug-Free Colo., 1989, Sch. Restructuring Program, Gov. of Colo., 1990, Cert. of Merit, Keep Denver Beautiful, 1990. Mem. Am. Mktg. Assn., Am. Assn. Advt. Agys. (mem. western bd. govs. 1988-92, chmn. bd. dirs. Rocky Mountain Coun. 1988), Denver Advt. Fedn. (bd. dirs. 1987-91), Denver Press Club, Greater Denver C. of C. (mem. bd. advisors 1990, Cert. of Appreciation 1989). Office: Henry Gill Advt 1225 17th St Ste 2500 Denver CO 80202-5525

HENRY, GARY NORMAN, flight test and astronautical engineer, educator; b. Fort Wayne, Ind., Nov. 3, 1961; s. Norman Thomas and Elaine Cathrine (Schabb) H. BS in Astro. Engring. with distinction, USAF Acad., 1984; MS in Aero./Astronautical Engring., Stanford U., 1988; grad., USAF Test Pilot Sch., 1994. CFP. Commd. 2d lt. USAF, 1984, advanced through grades to maj., 1995; project engr. USAF Weapons Lab., Kirtland AFB, N.Mex., 1984-87; asst. prof. astronautics USAF Acad., Colorado Springs, 1989-93; flight test engr. 418 Flight Test Squadron, Edwards AFB, Calif., 1993-94, chief flight dynamics br., 1994—. Editor: (textbook) Space Propulsion Analysis and Design, 1995; contbr. articles to profl. jours. Mem. AIAA (sr. mem., hybrid rocket tech. com. 1993-94, Young Engr. of Yr. Rocky Mountain region 1993), Soc. Flight Test Engrs., Am. Soc. Engring. Edn., Nat. Endowment for Fin. Edn. Office: 418 Flight Test Squadron Edwards CA 93523

HENRY, HOLLY JEAN, nutritionist, researcher; b. St. Paul, Jan. 4, 1948; d. Walter Ralph and Clarice Viola (Parkin) Holmstrom; m. Ted Alan Henry, June 14, 1970; 1 child, Shelley Brooke. BS, Oreg. State U., 1970, MS, 1980. Rsch. dietitian Oreg. Health Scis. U., Portland, 1979-84; clin. dietitian Children's Orthopedic Hosp., Seattle, 1984-85; rsch. nutritionist Group Health Coop., Redmond, Wash., 1985-88; lead rsch. nutritionist Fred Hutchinson Cancer Rsch. Ctr., Seattle, 1984—; lectr. Portland (Oreg.) State U., 1981; spkr. Am. Cancer Soc., Seattle, 1990—. Contbr. articles to profl. jours. Mem. Am. Dietetic Assn. (registered dietitian), Wash. State Dietetic Assn., Greater Seattle Dietetic Assn. (spkr. 1990—), Toastmasters Internat. (sec. 1988, treas. 1993, Able Toastmaster award 1993). Office: Fred Hutchinson Cancer Rsch Ctr 1124 Columbia MP 1002 Seattle WA 98104

HENRY, HOWARD WARD, court reporter; b. Dodge City, Kans., Jan. 5, 1927; s. Edwin Ruthvan and Grace Louisa (Meeks) H.; m. Zona Gail Ehret, Sept. 11, 1955; children: Sharon Kay, Daniel Kent. AA, Dodge City (Kans.) Jr. Coll., 1948; student, Cain-Powell Bus. Coll., Dodge City, 1948, Profl. Sec. Sch., San Francisco, 1949; BA, U. N.Mex., 1960. Cert. shorthand reporter. Ct. reporter 6th Jud. Dist. Ct., Deming, N.Mex., 1951-57, Howard W. Henry & Co., Albuquerque, 1957-92, U.S. Dist. Ct., Albuquerque, 1965-82. Pub. 5 vols. on surname indexing for geneal. studies. With USN, 1944-46, 50-51, PTO. Mem. VFW, Am. Legion, U.S. Ct. Reporters, Nat. Shorthand Reporters, N.Mex. Shorthand Reporters. Democrat. Home: 1500 Cliffside Ct NW Albuquerque NM 87105-1015

HENRY, KAREN HAWLEY, lawyer; b. Whittier, Calif., Nov. 5, 1943; d. Ralph Hawley and Dorothy Ellen (Carr) Hawley; m. John Dunlap, 1968; m. Charles Gibbons Henry, Mar. 15, 1975; children: Scott, Alexander, Joshua; m. Don H. Phemister, June 21, 1991; children: Justin Phemister, Jonathan Phemister, Keith Phemister. BS in Social Scis., So. Oreg. Coll., 1965; MS in Labor Econs., Iowa State U., 1967; JD, U. Calif., 1976. Instr., Medford (Oreg.) Sch. Dist., 1965-66; rsch. asst. dept. econs. Iowa State U., Ames, 1966-67; dir. rsch. program Calif. Nurses Assn., San Francisco, 1967-72; labor rels. coord. Affiliated Hosps. of San Francisco, 1972-79; ptnr. Littler, Mendelson, Fastiff & Tichy, San Francisco, 1979-86; mng. ptnr. labor and employment law Weissburg and Aronson, Inc., San Francisco, 1986-90; prin. Karen H. Henry, Inc., Sacramento, 1991—. Author: Health Care Supervisor's Legal Guide, 1984, Nursing Administration Law Manual, 1986, ADA: Ten Steps to Compliance, 1992, 3rd edit., 1995; edit. bd. Health Care Supervisor; contbr. articles on employment law issues to profl. jours. Mem. Calif. Soc. Healthcare Attys. (bd. dirs. 1986-87, pres. 1987-88), Am. Hosp. Assn. (ad hoc labor atty. com.), State Bar of Calif., Sacramento Bar Assn., Thurston Soc., Order of Coif. (law jour.). Office: Karen H Henry Inc Senator Hotel Office Bldg 1121 L St Ste 1000 Sacramento CA 95814-3926

HENRY, KEITH DOUGLAS, architect; b. Winnipeg, Man., Can., Oct. 25, 1957; s. Charles Eric and Ruth Elva (McDonald) H.; m. Elizabeth Anne McNulty, June 19, 1993. B of Environ. Studies, U. Man., Winnipeg, 1978, MArch, 1982. Design architect Ferguson Folstad Friggstad Architects, Saskatoon, Regina, Sask., Can., 1982-86; assoc. ptnr. Folstad & Friggstad Architects, Saskatoon, 1986-92; ptnr. Friggstad Downing Henry Architects-Wilson Bailey Tech., Saskatoon, 1992—. Prin. works include John Paul II Collegiate (Award of Merit Sask. Assn. Architects 1991), Bedford Rd. Collegiate, Can. Nat. Inst. Blind Svc. Ctr. (Award of Excellence Sask. Masonry Inst. 1993). Recipient Marion M. Graham Collegiate award Am. Assn. Sch. Adminstrs./AIA, 1985. Mem. Royal Archtl. Inst. Can., Sask. Assn. Architects (registered, mem. coun. 1993—, 1st v.p. 1994-95, pres. 1995—), North Saskatoon Bus. Assn., Aurum Club. Office: Friggstad Architects, 2233 Avenue C North, Saskatoon, SK Canada S7L 5Z2

HENRY, PHILIP LAWRENCE, marketing professional; b. Los Angeles, Dec. 1, 1940; s. Lawrence Langworthy and Ella Hanna (Martens) H.; m. Claudia Antonia Huff, Aug. 9, 1965 (div. 1980); children: Carolyn Marie, Susan Michelle; m. Carrie Katherine Hoover, Aug. 23, 1985. BS in Marine Engring., Calif. Maritime Acad., 1961. Design engr. Pacific Telephone Co., San Diego, 1963-73; service engr. Worthington Service Corp., San Diego, 1973-78; pres. Realmart Corp., San Diego, 1978-81; dir. mktg. Orbit Inn Hotel and Casino, Las Vegas, 1981-84; pres. Comml. Consultants, Las Vegas, 1984—, Gray Electronics Co., Las Vegas, 1986—. Inventor electronic detection device, 1986. Served to lt. (j.g.) USNR, 1961-67. Republican. Mem. Christian Sci. Ch. Home: 1843 Somersby Way Henderson NV 89014-3876

HENRY, WILLIAM RADER, mechanical engineering consultant; b. Conover, N.C., Feb. 27, 1943; s. William Huit and Madolyn Floy (Rader) H.; m. Violeta Belen Mercado, Sept. 30, 1969; children: Michelle Lynn, Thomas Vincent. AA, Allan Hancock Jr. Coll., 1966; BS in Mech. Engring., U. Mo., 1969. Registered profl. engr., N.Y., Calif. Engr. B.F. Goodrich, Akron, Ohio, 1969-70; sr. engr. B.F.G. Internat., Akron, 1971-73; area maintenance engr. B.F.G. Tire Co., Oaks, Pa., 1974-75; area maintenance mgr. B.F.G. Tire Co., Miami, Okla., 1978-79; maintenance mgr. Tropical do Brazil, Fieria de Santana, 1976-77; project engr. GE, Schenectady, N.Y., 1980-81; project mgr. Kinetic Systems, Inc., Santa Clara, N.Y., 1982-84; v.p. Facilitech, Inc., Santa Clara, 1985-91; prin. Facilities Tech. Inc., Santa Clara, 1992—. With USAF, 1962-66. Mem. ASME, ASHRAE. Republican. Roman Catholic. Home: 5918 Silver Leaf Rd San Jose CA 95138-1811 Office: Facilities Tech Inc 2370 Walsh Ave # B Santa Clara CA 95051

HENSEL, JEFFREY, geologist, consultant; b. Detroit, Nov. 15, 1962; s. Manfred Karl and Liane Bertha (Freuck) H.; m. Kimberly Ann Habel, Sept. 6, 1986; children: Rachael Anna, Kayla Marie. BS in Geology, Wayne State U., 1984; MS in Environ. Studies, Calif. State U., Fullerton, 1992. Registered geologist, Wyo., Calif., Ky.; registered environ. assessor, Calif. Geologist GMC Assocs. Inc., Northville, Mich., 1985-86, BCL Assocs. Inc., Long Beach, Calif., 1986-89; sr. geologist Radian Corp., Irvine, Calif., 1989—; advisor environ. affairs dept. and environ. studies bd. Calif. State U., Fullerton, 1990-92. Mich. Indsl. Soc. grantee, 1984. Mem. Nat. Water Well Assn., Ducks Unltd. Republican. Roman Catholic. Office: Radian Corp 16845 Von Karman Ave # 100 Irvine CA 92714-4920

HENSLEY, DOROTHY SUE, elementary educator; b. Louisville, Ky., Apr. 30, 1946; d. Vincent and Dorothy Mae (Staab) H. BA, U. Louisville, 1968; MA, U. Denver, 1972. Tchr. Louisville Pub. Schs., 1968-71, Jefferson County Pub. Schs., Golden, Colo., 1972—. Pres. of bd. Denver Mus. of Miniatures Dolls and Toys, Denver, 1992-94, bd. dirs., 1988-92. Mem. NEA, Jefferson County Edn. Assn., Colo. Edn. Assn., Colo. Coun. of Internat. Reading Assn., Nat. Assn. of Miniature Enthusiasts, Mile High Minature Club.

HENSLEY, JACKSON MOREY, artist; b. Portales, N.Mex., Sept. 6, 1940; s. E.T. Jr. and E.M. Hensley; m. Carolyn Brown Hensley, Aug. 5, 1961 (dec. 1989); children: Michael M., Janet M.; m. Tresa Vorenberg Hensley; Aug. 14, 1989; 1 child, Morika Rose Hensley. Student, Nat. Acad. Design, N.Y.C. Prin. works exhibited in numerous group shows including Knickerbocker Artist Exhibit, N.Y.C., Hudson River Artist Exhibit, White Plains, N.Y., IBM Gallery, Washington, Salmagundi Club, N.Y.C., Stamford (Conn.) Mus., Nat. Arts Club, N.Y.C., La. State Mus., many others; paintings represented in numerous collections including Madewood Plantation House Mus., New Orleans, Desert Caballeros Mus., Wickensburg, Ariz., Diamond T. Found. Mus., Tex., Arabian Horse Trust Mus., Denver, L.A. Mus. West Collection, others. Mem. Salmagundi Club, Cliff Dwellers Club, Arts and Letters Club, Arts Club (Montreal, Washington), Nat. Arts Club, Royal British Club, Savage Club, Chelsea Art Club, Art et Amicite, Providence Art Club. Home: 10 Highview Ln Santa Fe NM 87505

HENSON, PAMELA JANE CARLIN, air force official; b. Dayton, Ohio, May 15, 1957; d. Ralph Eugene and Beatrice Anne (Tedrow) C.; m. Donald Fred Henson, July 10, 1976. BS in Fin., Wright State U., 1980; MBA, U. Dayton, 1984; grad., USAF Air War Coll., 1990; postgrad., Harvard U., 1992. Fin. mgr. aeronaut. systems div. Wright Patterson AFB, Dayton, 1978-84, chief cost estimating B-2 Program, 1984-87, chief cost analysis div. Air Force Logistics Command, 1987-89; spl. asst., fin. mgr. Sec. of Air Force, Fin. Mgmt. Br. The Pentagon, Washington, 1990-91; dep. dir. fin. mgnt. Space Systems div., L.A. AFB, 1991—. Harvard sr. exec. fellow, 1992. Mem. Am. Soc. Mil. Comptrollers, Inst. Cost Analysis (Dayton chpt. dir. policy 1988, co-dir. publicity 1987), Nat. Wildlife Fedn., Phi Eta Sigma, Alpha Lambda Delta. Republican. Methodist.

HENTZ, VINCENT R., surgeon; b. Jacksonville, Fla., Aug. 29, 1942. MD, U. Fla., 1968. Intern Stanford (Calif.) Hosp., 1968-69, resident in plastic surgery, 1969-74, now hand surgeon; fellow in hand surgery Roosevelt Hosp., N.Y.C., 1974-75. Office: 900 Blake Wilbur Dr Palo Alto CA 94304-2205*

HEPLER, KENNETH RUSSEL, manufacturing executive; b. Canton, Ohio, Mar. 31, 1926; s. Clifton R. and Mary A. (Sample) H.; m. Beverly Best, June 9, 1945; 1 child, Bradford R. Student, Cleve. Art Inst., 1946-47, Case Western Res. U., 1948-50. V.p., adminstr. A. Carlisle and Co., San Francisco, 1954-67; pres. K.R. Hepler and Co., Menlo Park, Calif., 1968-73, Paramount Press., Jacksonville, Fla., 1974-75; pvt. practice printing broker, 1976-80; chmn. Hickey and Hepler Graphics Inc., San Francisco, 1981—; instr. printing prodn., San Francisco City Coll. With USAAC, 1943-45. Mem. San Francisco Litho Club (pres. 1972), Phila. Litho Club (sec. 1975-76), Newtown Exchange Club (pres. 1976), Elks. Republican. Presbyterian. Office: Hickey & Hepler Graphics Inc 1485 Bay Shore Blvd San Francisco CA 94124-3002

HEPLER, MERLIN JUDSON, JR., real estate broker; b. Hot Springs, Va., May 13, 1929; s. Merlin Judson and Margaret Belle (Vines) H.; m. Lanova Helen Roberts, July 25, 1952; children: Nancy Andora, Douglas Stanley. BS in Bus., U. Idaho, 1977; grad., Realtors Inst., 1979. Cert. residential specialist. Enlisted USAF, 1947, advanced through grades to sgt., 1960, ret., 1967; service mgr. Lanier Bus. Products, Gulfport, Miss., 1967-74; sales assoc. Century 21 Singler and Assn., Troy, Idaho, 1977-79; broker B&M Realty, Troy, 1979—. Mem. Nat. Assn. Realtors, Am. Legion, U. Idaho Alumni Assn., Air Force Sgts. Assn. Republican. Lodge: Lions. Home: 1081 Driscoll Ridge Troy ID 83871-9605 Office: B&M Realty W 102 A St PO Box 187 Troy ID 83871-0187

HEPLER, OVID MANSFIELD, minister; b. Englewood, Colo., Jan. 25, 1922; s. Edgar W. and Evalyn (Parks) H.; m. Marian A. Milburn, Jan. 6, 1941; 1 child, Judith Anne. BA, U. Colo., 1966; DD, Faith Sem., Elkins Park, Pa., 1988. Various clerical positions Denver & Rio Grande RR, Denver, 1939-44; editor 1st Bapt. Ch. and Western Voice Pubs., Englewood, Colo., 1945-55; pvt. contractor Littleton, Colo., 1956-66; pastor Haven Bapt. Ch., Denver, 1967—; bd. dirs. Rocky Mt. Evangel. Assn., 1948-68; exec. com. Internat. Coun. Christian Chs., 1983—; pres. Coun. Bible Believing Chs., USA, 1987—. Editor: Western Voice, 1950-55, 85—. Home and Office: Haven Bapt Ch 6600 S Windermere St Littleton CO 80120-3204

HERB, EDMUND MICHAEL, optometrist, educator; b. Zanesville, Ohio, Oct. 9, 1942; s. Edmund G. and Barbara R. (Michael) H.; divorced; children—Sara, Andrew; m. Jeri Herb. O.D., Ohio State U., 1966. Pvt. practice optometry, Buena Vista, Colo., 1966—; past prof. Timberline campus Colo. Mountain Coll. Mem. Am. Optometric Assn., Colo. Optometric Assn. Home: 16395 Mt Princeton Rd Buena Vista CO 81211-9505 Office: 115 N Tabor St Buena Vista CO 81211 also: Leadville Colorado Med Ctr Leadville CO 80461

HERB, FREDERICK WILLIAM, hotel executive; b. Berkeley, Calif., Feb. 28, 1964; s. Michael David and Marion (Athearn) H. Dir. sales Harbor View Inn, Santa Barbara, Calif., asst. gen. mgr.; gen. mgr. Sandman Inn, Santa Barbara, Calif.; tourism coun. Greater Santa Barbara Lodging Assn. Mem. Beachside Merchants Assn. Home: PO Box 90101 Santa Barbara CA 93190-0101

HERBAUGH, ROGER DUANE, computer and software company executive; b. Mt. Vernon, Wash., May 20, 1957; s. Donald Lloyd and Kathleen Joyce (Anderson) H.; m. Anne Louise Finlayson, May 8, 1993; children: Andrew David Miller, Celeste Jane Miller, Trevor Allan Miller, Vanessa Anne Miller, Deirdre Rose Miller. AA, Skagit Valley Coll., 1984; BA, Western Wash. U., 1986. Cert. Microsoft profl. Computer programmer Stockmar Northwestern, Mt. Vernon, 1986-87; chief exec. officer, computer cons. Herbaugh & Assocs., Inc., Mt. Vernon, 1987—, also pres. bd. dirs.; cons. Shell Oil Co., Anacortes, Wash., 1986—, BP Oil Co., Ferndale, Wash., 1986-93, ARCO, Blaine, Wash., 1989—, Tosco, Ferndale, Wash., 1993—, Tosco, Seattle, 1993—; Microsoft Solutions provider; bd. dirs., pres. Software Plus, Inc., Mt. Vernon, 1991—. Sgt. U.S. Army, 1975-81. Mem. Burlington C. of C., Mt. Vernon C. of C., Kiwanis (sec., bd. dirs. Mt. Vernon chpt.). Republican. Mem. LDS Ch. Office: Herbaugh & Assocs Inc 1686 S Burlington Blvd Ste 201 Burlington WA 98233-3208

HERBERT, CHESLEY C., psychiatrist; b. Charlotte, N.C., June 7, 1943; m. Marie Genevieve Groszko, Aug. 10, 1975; Rachel G., Andrew G. AB in History, Duke U., 1961-65; MD, Columbia U., 1965-69. Diplomate Am. Bd. Psychiatry and Neurology; lic. physician and surgeon, Calif., Nat. Bd. Med. Examiners, DEA. Intern Harlem Hosp. Ctr., N.Y.C., 1969-70; resident in psychiatry U. Calif., San Francisco, 1970-73, fellow in social psychiatry, 1973-75; pvt. practice San Francisco, 1973—; asst. clin. prof. psychiatry U. Calif., San Francisco, 1975-83, assoc. clin. prof., 1983—; staff psychiatrist On Lok Sr. Health Svcs., San Francisco, 1980—; cons. Psychopathic divsn. Superior Ct., San Francisco, 1974-78, North of Market Sr. Alcohol Program, San Francisco, 1979-80; psychiatrist srs. unit N.E. Mental Health Ctr., San Francisco, 1975-79; chief divsn. psychiatry dept. medicine Davies Med. Ctr., San Francisco, 1988—; courtesy staff mem. St. Francis Meml. Hosp., Calif. Pacific Med. Ctr., Chinese Hosp. Contbr. articles to profl. jours. Mem. Am. Assn. Geriatric Psychiatry, Am. Psychiat. Assn., No. Calif. Psychiat. Soc., Calif. Med. Assn., San Francisco Med. Soc. Office: 45 Castro St Ste 302 San Francisco CA 94114-1010

HERBERT, CHRISTOPHER JAY, marketing professional, management consultant; b. Flint, Mich., May 8, 1953; s. Clarence LaVern and Doris Julia (Potter) H.; m. Nancy Ellen Welch, Dec. 19, 1987. BA, Lewis and Clark Coll., 1975; MBA, Ariz. State U., 1984. Cert. neuro-linguistic programming practitioner. Planner Maricopa Employment and Tng. Adminstrn., Phoenix, 1977-78; asst. dir. for planning and program devel. Maricopa County Human Resources Dept., Phoenix, 1978-81, CETA adminstr., 1981; v.p. Cons. Assocs., Inc., Phoenix, 1981-82; pres. C.J. Herbert & Co. Inc., Scottsdale, Ariz., 1982-85; v.p. Behavior Rsch. Ctr., Inc., Phoenix, 1985-89; pres. The Insight Group Inc., Phoenix, 1989—; mem. mktg. com. Phoenix Symphony, 1988-90. Bd. dirs. Grand Canyon Assn., 1992—, pres., 1994—; bd. dirs. The Phoenicians, 1994. Mem. Qualitative Rsch. Cons. Assn. (chair professionalism com. 1992—, conv. speaker 1993, 94, bd. dirs. 1995—), Am. Assn. Polit. Cons., Am. Assn. Pub. Opinion Rsch., Am. Inst. Wine and Food (chmn. Ariz. chpt. 1993, mem. nat. membership com. 1994), Brotherhood of Knights of the Vine (Master Knight, bd. dirs. Phoenix chpt. 1991—), Phoenix C. of C. (bd. dirs. 1987-89, chmn. small bus. coun. 1986-87, mem. health care coun. 1993—). Office: The Insight Group Inc 311 W Lynwood St Phoenix AZ 85003-1206

HERBERT, GAVIN SHEARER, health care products company executive; b. Los Angeles, Mar. 26, 1932; s. Gavin and Josephine (D'Vitha) H.; children by previous marriage Cynthia, Lauri, Gavin, Pam; 2d. m. Ninetta Flanagan, Sept. 6, 1986. B.S., U. So. Calif., 1954. With Allergan, Inc., Irvine, Calif., 1950—; v.p. Allergan, Inc., 1956-61, exec. v.p., pres., 1961-77, chmn. bd., CEO, 1977-91, chmn. bd., 1992—; pres. Eye and Skin Care Products Group Smith Kline Beckman Corp., 1981-89; exec. v.p. Smith Kline Beckman Corp., 1986-89; bd. dirs. Beckman Instruments, Inc., Calif. Healthcare Inst. Mem. Rsch. to Prevent Blindness (bd. dirs.), Big Canyon Country Club, Newport Harbor Yacht Club, Pacific Club, Beta Theta Pi. Republican. Office: Allergan Inc PO Box 19534 2525 Dupont Dr Irvine CA 92715-1531

HERBERT, MARY KATHERINE ATWELL, freelance writer; b. Grove City, Pa., Dec. 9, 1945; d. Stewart and Luella Irene (Brown) Atwell; m. Roland Marcus Herbert; children: Stephen Todd, Amy Elizabeth, Jill Anne. BA, Ariz. State U., 1968, MA, 1973; film cert., U. So. Calif., 1978. Film writer Scottsdale Daily Progress, 1976-79; dir. pub. relations Phoenix Theatre, 1980-85; script analyst, 1985-86; exec. asst. to v.p. prodn. De-Laurentiis Entertainment Group, 1986; producer's assoc. film TRAXX, 1986-87; devel. dir. Devin/DeVore Prodns., 1988-89; free-lance script analyst and writer Glendale, Calif., 1989—. Script writer: (TV shows) Trial By Jury, Dick Clark Prodn., Dry Heat, Blind Desire, others; author: Writing Scripts Hollywood Will Love, 1994. Mem. Encanto Homeowners Assn., Phoenix, 1976-80; bd. mgrs. Hollywood-Wilshire YMCA. Mem. Women in Comms., Artists Rights Found., Kappa Delta Pi, Pi Lambda Theta.

HERDECK, DONALD ELMER, publishing executive, retired humanities educator; b. Chgo., Nov. 19, 1924; s. Elmer and Violet (Cotter) H.; m. Margaret L. Herdeck. BA, MA, U. Chgo., 1948; PhD, U. Pa., 1968. Tchr. French and English Girard Coll., Phila., 1952-54; fgn. svc. officer U.S. Dept. State, Washington, 1955-64; assoc. prof. humanities Georgetown U., Washington, 1965-87; pub., chmn., pres. Three Continents Press, Colorado Springs, 1973—. Author: African Authors: A Bio-Critical Bibliographical Ency., 1971, Caribbean Writers: A Bio-Critical Bibliographical Ency., 1974; editor, contbr. Three Dynamity Authors: Derek Walcott, Naguib Mahfouz, Wole Soyinka, 1995. Pres. Cabin John Citizens Assn., Bethesda, Md., 1969-70. With U.S. Army, 1943-46, ETO. Mem. African Lit. Assn., 103d Infantry Assoc.

HERDEG, HOWARD BRIAN, physician; b. Buffalo, Oct. 14, 1929; s. Howard Bryan and Martha Jean (Williams) H.; m. Beryl Ann Fredricks, July 21, 1955; children: Howard Brian III, Erin Ann Kociela. Student Paul Smith's Coll., 1947-48, U. Buffalo, 1948-50, Canisius Coll., 1949; DO, Phila. Coll. Osteopathic Medicine, 1954; MD, U. Calif.-Irvine Coll. Medicine, 1962. Diplomate Am. Acad. Pain Mgmt. Intern, Burbank (Calif.) Hosp., 1954-55; practice medicine specializing in gen. medicine, surgery and pain mgmt., Woodland Hills, Calif., 1956—; chief med. staff West Park Hosp., Canoga Park, Calif., 1971-72, trustee, 1971-73; chief family practice dept. West Hills Regional Med. Center (formerly Humaua Hosp. West Hills, 1982-83, 84-85, 88-89), mem. exec. com., 1984-85, 88-89, Mem. Hidden Hills (Calif.) Pub. Safety Commn., 1978-82; bd. dirs. Hidden Hills Community Assn., 1971-73, pres., 1972; bd. dirs. Hidden Hills Homeowners Assn., 1973-75, pres., 1976-77; bd. dirs. Woodland Hills Freedom Season, 1961-67, pres., 1962; mem. Hidden Hills City Council, 1984—, mayor pro tem, 1987-90, mayor, 1990-92. Recipient disting. service award Woodland Hills Jr C. of C., 1966. Mem. Woodland Hills C. of C. (dir. 1959-68, pres. 1967), Theta Chi, Gamma Pi. Republican. Home: 24530 Deep Well Rd Hidden Hills CA 91302-1210 Office: 22600 Ventura Blvd Woodland Hills CA 91364-1414

HERDRICH, NORMAN WESLEY, magazine editor; b. Spokane, Wash., July 17, 1942; s. Fred N. and Florice J. (Birchill) H.; m. Mary Susan Webb, Aug. 16, 1975; children: Megan Marie, Heidi Susan, Kristin Ruth. B.S., Wash. State U., 1969. Field editor Northwest Unit Farm Mags., Spokane, 1969-78; prodn. editor Western Farmer-Stockman Mags., Spokane, 1978—. Served with USNR, 1963-65. Mem. Wash. State Grange, Soc. Profl. Journalists, Nat. Rifle Assn., Spokane Editorial Soc. (sec.-treas. 1974-77, 1st v.p. 1977-78, pres. 1978-79), Wash. Wool Growers Assn., Soc. Profl. Journalists. Methodist. Club: Spokane Press (dir. 1978, treas. 1979). Home: 12711 E Saltese Ave Spokane WA 99216-0373 Office: Rev Tower 999 W Riverside Ave Spokane WA 99201-1010

HEREMAN, WILLY ALOIS MARIA, mathematics educator; b. Lokeren, Belgium, Sept. 17, 1954; came to U.S. 1983; s. Achiel Emma and Mariette Irma (Tijdgat) H. BS in Math., U. Ghent, Belgium, 1974, MS in Math., 1976, PhD in Math., 1982. Rsch. asst. State U. Ghent, 1976-82; NATO rsch. fellow U. Iowa, Iowa City, 1983-84, 85-86; rsch. assoc. State U. Ghent, 1984-85; asst. prof. math. U. Wis., Madison, 1986-89; assoc. prof. math. Colo. Sch. Mines, Golden, 1989—. Contbr. numerous articles to profl. jours. Laureate, Royal Acad. Scis., Lit. and Fine Arts of Belgium, 1985. Mem. Am. Math. Soc., Soc. Indsl. and Applied Math. Home: 2225 Bluff St Boulder CO 80304-3715 Office: Col Sch Mines Dept of Math Golden CO 80401

HERENDEEN, DAVID LOUIS, software company executive; b. Niagara Falls, N.Y., July 12, 1946; s. Donald George and Lois Irene (Stewardson) H.; m. Carol Ann Coulter, Dec. 3, 1966 (div. Dec. 1980); 1 child, Melissa Ann; m. Lenora May Linabury, Dec. 21, 1980. AS in Math., Niagara County C.C., 1966; BS in Computer Sci., UCLA, 1975. Assoc. engr. Bell Aerospace Corp., Buffalo, N.Y., 1966-72; mng. Hughes Aircraft Co., El Segundo, Calif., 1972-73, 78-79, MacNeal-Schwedler Corp., Pasadena, Calif., 1979-82; v.p. Universal Analytics, Inc., Torrance, Calif., 1973-77, 82—; bd. dirs. Universal Analytics, Inc. Contbr. articles to profl. jours. Recipient Douglas Michel Nastran Achievement award NASA, 1993. Mem. AIAA,

IEEE Computer Sci., Assn. for Computing Machinery. Office: Universal Analytics Inc 3625 Del Amo Blvd Ste 370 Torrance CA 90503-1689

HERGER, WALLY W., congressman; b. Yuba City, Calif., May 20, 1945. Formerly mem. Calif. State Assembly; mem. 100th-102d Congresses from 2d Calif. dist., 1987—; mem. agr., mcht. marine and fisheries coms. 100th-103rd Congresses from 2d Calif. dist.; mem. budget com., mem. ways and means com.; owner Herger Gas, Inc. Office: US House of Representatives 2433 Rayburn Bldg Washington DC 20515-0005*

HERGERT, RICHARD GARY, government official, property tax assessment executive; b. Seattle, Aug. 9, 1949; s. Wilfred Adam and Beatrice Stella (Bergseth) H.; m. Patricia Jaclyn McDougall, Sept. 11, 1971; children: Elizabeth Anne, Thomas Scott, Gary James. BA, U. Wash., 1972. Cert. assessor, Wash. Alcoholism worker Seattle/King County Dept. Health, 1972-74; systems analyst King County Dept. Assessments, Seattle, 1974-83, sect. supr., 1983-91, supr. comml. appraisal sect., 1991—; data processing sect. chief, Wash. Army NG, Seattle, 1976-82; data processing instr. USAR, Tacoma, 1982-85; data processing technician USAR, Seattle, 1985—; cons. for proposed city incorporations Renton, Wash., Fed. Way, Wash., 1987-88. Bd. dirs., b.p. Northshore youth Basketball Assn., Woodinville, 1986-89, 1994—; founder Northshore Spirit Girls Basketball Asns.; basketball coach Bothell high Sch., 1989-93; bd. dirs. City of Woodinville Inc., Yes! com., 1986-89. Mem. Internat. Assn. of Assessing Officers (King County chpt.). Home: 16231 194th Ave NE Woodinville WA 98072-9265 Office: King County Dept Assessment King County Adminstrn Rm 853 Seattle WA 98104

HERHAHN, FRANK T., plastic surgeon; b. Scottsbluff, Nebr., Oct. 17, 1937. MD, U. Nebr., 1962. Plastic surgeon Presbyn. Hosp., Albuquerque; adj. asst. prof. plastic surgery U. N.Mex. Office: 1700 Rio Grande Blvd NW #4 Albuquerque NM 87107-3042*

HERING, WILLIAM MARSHALL, medical organization executive; b. Indpls., Dec. 26, 1940; s. William Marshall and Mary Agnes (Clark) H.; m. Suzanne Wolfe, Aug. 10, 1963. BS, Ind. U., 1961, MS, 1962; PhD, U. Ill., Urbana, 1973. Tchr. Indpls. pub. schs., 1962-66; asst. dir. sociol. resources project Am. Sociol. Assn., 1966-70; dir. social sci. curriculum Biomed. Interdisciplinary Project, Berkeley, Calif., 1973-76; staff assoc. Tchrs. Ctrs. Exchange, San Francisco, 1976-82; dir. research Far West Lab. Ednl. Research and Devel., San Francisco, 1979-82, sr. research assoc., 1982-85; mgr. human resource devel. Bank Am., San Francisco, 1985-94; dir. programs Am. Acad. Ophthalmology, San Francisco, 1994—; mem. Nat. Adv. Bd. Educ. Resource Info. Ctr.; cons. U.S. Dept. Edn.; pres. Social Sci. Educ. Consortium, 1981-82, bd. dirs., 1979-81; bd. dirs. San Francisco Chamber Orch., 1986—. Nat. Inst. Educ. grantee, 1979-82. Mem. Am. Soc. Tng. and Devel. (v.p. 1986), Golden Gate Soc., Nat. Audubon Soc., Phi Delta Kappa. Republican. Episcopalian. Contbr. over 100 articles on social studies edn., staff devel., ednl. research and evaluation to profl. jours. Home: 731 Duboce Ave San Francisco CA 94117-3214 Office: 655 Beach St San Francisco CA 94109-1336

HERLIHY, THOMAS MORTIMER, lawyer; b. N.Y.C., Apr. 8, 1953; s. John Wilfred and Mary Frances (O'Sullivan) H.; m. Janice Anne Lazzaro, Aug. 26, 1978; children: Carolyn Jane, John Wilfred II. BA in History, Columbia U., 1975; JD, Fordham U., 1978. Bar: Calif. 1978, U.S. Dist. Ct. (no. dist.) Calif. 1978, U.S. Dist. Ct. (ea. and so. dists.) Calif. 1979, U.S. Dist. Ct. (cen. dist.) Calif. 1984, U.S. Ct. Appeals (9th cir.) 1979. Assoc. Pettit & Martin, San Francisco, 1978-82; ptnr. Kornblum, Kelly & Herlihy, San Francisco, 1982-88, Kelly, Herlihy & Bane, San Francisco, 1988—; lectr. Rutter Group, trial skills program Calif. Continuing Edn. of Bar, 1983-86, 87, 88. Mem. ABA (litigation sect., torts and ins. practice sect.), Calif. Bar Assn., San Francisco Bar Assn., Calif. Def. Counsel, Def. Research Inst. Republican. Roman Catholic. Clubs: Olympic, Commonwealth (San Francisco); Columbia. Home: 1424 Cortez Ave Burlingame CA 94010-4711 Office: Kelly Herlihy & Bane 44 Montgomery St Ste 2500 San Francisco CA 94104-4712 also: 500 N State College Blvd Ste 4 Orange CA 92668-1604

HERLINGER, DANIEL ROBERT, hospital administrator; b. Boskovice, Czechoslovakia, Oct. 27, 1946; came to U.S., 1950, naturalized, 1956; s. Rudolf and Ingeborg (Gessler) H.; m. Susanne Reiter, June 1, 1969; children: Lisa, Rebecca, Joanna. BS, Loyola U., Chgo., 1968; MBA, George Washington U., 1971. Asst. adminstr. Michael Reese Hosp., Chgo., 1971-73; v.p. Mercy Hosp., Chgo., 1973-84; pres. St. John's Regional Med. Ctr., Oxnard, Calif., 1984-94, Mercy Healthcare Ventura County, 1994—. Fellow Am. Coll. Hosp. Adminstrs.; mem. Young Pres. Orgn., Rotary. Jewish. Home: 1648 Aspenwall Rd Westlake Vlg CA 91361-1704 Office: Mercy Healthcare Ventura County 1600 N Rose Ave Oxnard CA 93030-3722

HERMAN, ANDREA MAXINE, newspaper editor; b. Chgo., Oct. 22, 1938; d. Maurice H. and Mae (Baron) H.; m. Joseph Schmidt, Oct. 28, 1962. BJ, U. Mo., 1960. Feature writer Chgo.'s Am., 1960-63; daily columnist News Am., Balt., 1963-67; feature writer Mainichi Daily News, Tokyo, 1967-69; columnist Iowa City Press-Citizen, 1969-76; music and dance critic San Diego Tribune, 1976-84; asst. mng. editor features UPI, Washington, 1984-86, asst. mng. editor news devel., 1986-87; mng. editor features L.A. Herald Examiner, 1987-91; editor/culture We/Mbl Newspaper, Washington, 1991—. Recipient 1st and 2d prizes for features in arts James S. Copley Ring of Truth Awards, 1982, 1st prize for journalism Press Club San Diego, 1983. Mem. Soc. Profl. Journalists, Am. Soc. Newspaper Editors, AP Mng. Editors, Women in Communications. Office: We/Mbl Newspaper 1350 Connecticut Ave NW Washington DC 20036-1701

HERMAN, DAVID JAY, orthodontist; b. Rome, N.Y., Oct. 4, 1954; s. Maurice Joseph and Bettina S. (Stiener) H.; m. Mary Beth Appleberry, Apr. 11, 1976; children: Jeremiah D., Kellin A. BA in Biology, San Jose State U., 1976; DDS, Emory U., 1981; MS in Orthodontics, U. N.C., 1992, MPH, 1992. Comdr. USPHS, 1990; advanced gen. practice resident Gallup (N. Mex.) Indian Med. Ctr., 1983-84; clin. service specialist Ames Co., Santa Clara, Calif., 1976-77; service unit dental chief Keams Canyon (Ariz.) Service Unit USPHS Indian Health Service, 1981-82; staff dental officer Crownpoint (N. Mex.) Service Unit, 1982-83; service unit dental program chief Winslow (Ariz.) Service Unit, 1984-86; Navajo area dental br. chief Window Rock, Ariz., 1986-89; mem. grad. residency com. U. N.C., Chapel Hill, 1990-91; Navajo area orthodontic specialist Shiprock, N. Mex., 1992—; mem. health adv. bd. Navajo Reservation Headstart, 1986-89; health promotion/disease prevention cons. USPHS-Indian Health Svc. Navajo Area, Window Rock, 1986-89; cons. Ariz. IHS Periodontal Health Task Force, 1986-90. Asst. wrestling coach Winslow (Ariz.) H.S., 1984-86, Gallup High Sch., 1987-89, Chapel Hill H.S., 1991-92, Farmington H.S., 1992—; mem. Farmington Youth Wrestling Program, 1992—. Recipient Healthy Mothers/Healthy Babies Disease Prevention award, 1988, USPHS Achievement medal, 1985, Headstart Achievement award, 1989, Ariz. Pub. Health Assn. Hon. award, 1989; Nat. Health Svc. Corp. scholar Emory U., 1977-81. Mem. ADA, Am. Assn. Pub. Health Dentists, Commd. Officers Assn., Am. Assn. Orthodontists, Rocky Mountain Soc. Orthodontists, Navajo Area Dental Soc. (pres. 1985), Am. Assn. Dental Rsch., Am. Assn. Mil. Orthodontists (sec.-treas. 1992, v.p. 1993-94, pres. 1995—).

HERMAN, FREDERICK FLINT, allergist; b. L.A., 1955. MD, St. Louis U., 1982. Allergist Roseville (Calif.) Cmty. Hosp.; clin. assoc. prof. Med. Ctr. U. Calif., Davis. Office: 729 Sunrise Ave Roseville CA 95661-4565*

HERMAN, GEORGE ADAM, writer; b. Norfolk, Va., Apr. 12, 1928; s. George Adam and Minerva Nevada (Thompson) H.; m. Patricia Lee Glazer, May 26, 1955 (div. 1989); children: Kurt, Erik, Karl, Lisa, Katherine, Christopher, Jena, Amanda; m. Patricia Jane Piper Dubay, Aug. 25, 1989; children: Lizette, Paul, Kirk, Victoria. PhB, Loyola Coll., 1950; MFA, Cath. U., 1954; cert. fine arts, Boston Coll., 1951,52,53. Asst. prof. Clarke Coll., Dubuque, Iowa, 1955-60, Villanova (Pa.) U., 1960-63; asst. prof., playwright in residence Coll. St. Benedict, St. Joseph, Minn., 1963-65; chmn. theatre dept. Coll. Great Falls, Mont., 1965-67; media specialist Hawaii State Dept. Edn., Honolulu, 1967-75, staff specialist, 1975-83; sr. drama critic Honolulu Advertiser, 1975-80; artistic dir. Commedia Repertory Theatre, Honolulu, 1978-80; freelance writer, lectr. Portland, Oreg., 1983—; lectr. Portland State U., 1985—; film actor SAG, L.A., 1975—. Author: (plays) Company of Wayward Saints, 1963 (McKnight Humanities award 1964), Mr. Highpockets, 1968, A Stone for Either Hand, 1969, Tenebrae, 1984, (novels) Carnival of Saints, 1994 (finalist Oreg. Book Awards 1994), A Comedy of Murders, 1994, Tears of the Madonna, 1995. Pres. local chpt. Nat. Sch. Pub. Rels. Assn., Honolulu, 1981-83; bd. dirs. Honolulu Community Theatre, 1981-82, Hawaii State Theatre Coun., Honolulu, 1981. With U.S. Army, 1950-52. Named Genesian Jewel Nat. Cath. Theatre Conf., 1949; recipient Hartke Playwrighting award Cath. U., 1954, Excellence award Am. Security Coun., 1967. Mem. Am. Legion, Amnesty Internat., Ednl. Theatre Assn. (bd. dirs. 1990—).

HERMAN, JAMES JEROME, electrical engineer, lawyer; b. Sheboygan, Wis., July 23, 1929; s. Jacob and Amalia (Biel) H.; m. Lynn R. Willis, Sept. 8, 1951; children: Mark, Julie, Matthew. BA, Ripon (Wis.) Coll., 1952; BS in Elec. Engring., MIT, 1952; MS, U. Wis., 1956; JD, U. Santa Clara, 1979. Electronics engr. Raytheon, Waltham, Mass., 1952; grad. sch. rsch. asst. U. Wis., Madison, 1955-56; sr. electronics engr. Convair divsn. Gen. Dynamics, San Diego, 1956-59; prin. engr. Link Divsn. Gen. Precision Corp., Palo Alto, Calif., 1959-60; rsch. specialist, staff engr., sr. staff engr., tech. cons. Lockheed Missiles & Space Co., Sunnyvale, Calif., 1960-90; vol. atty. Sr. Citizens Legal Svcs., Santa Cruz, Calif., 1994. 1st lt. USAF, 1953-55. Recipient Pub. Svc. Group Achievement award NASA, 1981. Mem. AIAA, IEEE, Calif. State Bar. Republican. Lutheran. Home: 3040 Wisteria Way Aptos CA 95003-3318

HERMAN, JUDITH AXELROOD, marketing research consultant; b. Boston, Dec. 4, 1931; d. Irving and Beatrice (Gottlieb) Axelrood; m. Bertrand Ian Herman, Oct. 20, 1957; children: Lydia Beatrice Herman Lazar, Roger Michael. BA in Liberal Arts, Boston U., 1952; MBA, Columbia U., 1955. Project mgr. Gen. Foods, White Plains, N.Y., 1970-73, Audits & Surveys, N.Y.C., 1973-76; dir. rsch. Saks Fifth Ave., N.Y.C., 1976-78, Bobbie Brooks, Cleve., 1978-80; mgr. multi divsnl. rsch. Levi Strauss & Co., San Francisco, 1980-84; pres. Info. & Strategy, Oakland, Calif., 1984—; rsch. assoc. grad. faculty CUNY, 1974-75. Mem. Am. Mktg. Assn., Bus. Mktg. Assn. Office: Info & Strategy 9469 Skyline Blvd Oakland CA 94611-1738

HERMAN, MICHAEL HARRY, physicist, researcher; b. Hartford, Conn., June 8, 1954; s. Richard Allen and Barbara Jane (Weinstein) H.; m. Susan Barbara Blum, Apr. 5, 1981; children: Edward, Beth, Andrea, Eva. BA in Physics, Grinnell Coll., 1976; PhD in Physics, Pa. State U., 1982. Sr. engr., materials tech. Intel Corp., Santa Clara, Calif., 1982-84; sr. device physicist, tech. devel. Intel Corp., Santa Clara, 1984-87; staff scientist Charles Evans & Assocs., Redwood City, Calif., 1987-89; sr. scientist Charles Evans & Assocs., Redwood City, 1989-91; head of characterization Power Spectra, Inc., Sunnyvale, Calif., 1991-93, program mgr., 1993—. Contbr. chpt. to Analysis of Microelectronic Materials and Devices, 1991; contbr. articles to Jour. Electronic Materials, Jour. Applied Physics. Mem. IEEE, Am. Phys. Soc., Materials Rsch. Soc., Soc. Photometric Instrumentation Engrs., Phi Beta Kappa, Phi Kappa Phi. Home: 1331 Belleville Way Sunnyvale CA 94087-3821 Office: Power Spectra 919 Hermosa Ct Sunnyvale CA 94086-4103

HERMANN, JAMES RAY, management executive; b. Richmond, Calif., Dec. 25, 1946; s. R. Ray and Jimmie (Ball) H.; m. Jacqueline Ferrari Feusier, Dec. 22, 1970; children: Nicole Alison, Ivette Alison. BA, San Francisco State U., 1968; JD, U. Calif., San Francisco, 1972. Bar: Calif. 1972, U.S. Dist. Ct. (no. dist.) Calif. 1972, U.S. Ct. Appeals (9th cir.) 1972, U.S. Tax Ct. 1973, U.S. Supreme Ct. 1978; CPA, Calif.; cert. fin. planner, real estate appraiser, real estate broker, life and disability ins. broker; lic. series 7 and 22 Nat. Assn. Securities Dealers. Dean Sch. of Acctg. Armstrong Coll., Berkeley, Calif., 1975-77; mng. atty. Yanello & Flippen Law Offices, Oakland, Calif., 1977-79; chief operating officer Bus. Fin. Group, Walnut Creek, Calif., 1979-81; prin. Antonini Profl. Corp., San Francisco, 1981-86; CEO Rolex Mgmt. Group, Orinda, Calif., 1985-93; dir. Heald Colls. of Calif., San Francisco, 1992—; chmn. Wall St. Capital Mgmt., Orinda, 1987-91, J.R. Hermann Prodns., Inc., Orinda, 1985-91; arbitrator Am. Arbitration Assn., San Francisco, 1987—; pres. Nova Images, Inc., Orinda, 1992—; cons. Geneva Corp., Irvine, Calif., 1987-89, 94—, Strategic M/A Internat. Inc., Reading, pa., 1989-90, GVA Fin. Group, Inc., Phoenix, 1990-91; lectr. Fund Raising Sch., Ind. U., 1992—; lectr. fin. seminars numerous orgns., 1984—. Author: Adding Financial Planning to Your Practice, 1984, Case Studies in Financial Planning, 1985, Accountant's Guide to Financial and Estate Planning for Business Owners, 1990; columnist Outlook Mag., 1986-88; contbr. articles to profl. jorus. Capt. spl. forces U.S. Army, 1970-72. Mem. ABA, AICPA, Internat. Biog. Ctr. (adv. coun. 1988—), Calif. Soc. CPAs (chmn. fin. planning com. 1985-87), Univ Club (mem. com. 1987-89), Assn. for Corp. Growth. Office: PO Box 2218 Orinda CA 94563-6618

HERMOSILLO, CARLOS J., plastic surgeon; b. Stockton, Calif., 1945. MD, Loyola U., Maywood, Calif., 1971. Plastic surgeon Hoag Meml. Hosp., Newport Beach, Calif. Office: PO Box 9395 South Laguna CA 92677-0395*

HERNANDEZ, JO FARB, museum and curatorial consultant; b. Chgo., Nov. 20, 1952. BA in Polit. Sci. & French with honors, U. Wis., 1974; MA in Folklore and mythology, UCLA, 1975; postgrad., U. Calif., Davis, 1978, U. Calif., Berkeley, 1978-79, 81. Registration Mus. Cultural History UCLA, 1974-75; Rockefeller fellow Dallas Mus. Fine Arts, 1976-77; asst. to dir. Triton Mus. Art, Santa Clara, Calif., 1977-78, dir., 1978-85; adj. prof. mus. studies John F. Kennedy U., San Francisco, 1978; grad. advisor arts adminstrn. San Jose (Calif.) State U., 1979-80; dir. Monterey (Calif.) Peninsula Mus. Art, 1985-93, cons. curator, 1994—; prin. Curatorial and Mus. Mgmt. Svcs., Watsonville, Calif., 1993—; lectr., panelist, juror, panelist in field USIA, Calif. Arts Coun., others; vis. lectr. Am. Cultural Ctr., Jerusalem, 1989, Binat. Ctr., Lima, Peru, 1988, Daytona Beach Mus. Art, 1983, Israel Mus., 1989, U. Chgo., 1981, others; guest on various TV and radio programs. Contbr. articles to profl. publs.; author: (mus. catalogs) The Day of the Dead: Tradition and Change in Contemporary Mexico, 1979, Three from the Northern Island: Contemporary Sculpture from Hokkaido, 1984, Crime and Punishment: Reflections of Violence in Contemporary Art, 1984, The Quiet Eye: Pottery of Shoji Hamada and Bernard Leach, 1990, Alan Shepp: The Language of Stone, 1991, Wonderful Colors: The Paintings of August Francois Gay, 1993, Jeannette Maxfield Lewis: A Centennial Celebration, 1994, Armin Hansen, 1994, Jeremy Anderson: The Critical Link/A Quiet Revolution, 1995, among others. Bd. dirs. Bobbie Wynn and Co. of San Jose, 1981-85, Santa Clara Arts and Hist. Consortium, 1985; bd. dirs. Non-Profit Gallery Assn., 1979-83, v.p., 1979-80. Recipient Golden Eagle award Coun. Internat. Nontheatrical Events, 1992, Leader of Decade award Arts Leadership Monterey Peninsula, 1992. Mem. Am. Assn. Mus. (mus. assessment program surveyor 1990, 94, lectr. 1986, nat. program com. 1992-93), Calif. Assn. Mus. (chair ann. meeting 1990, chair nominating com. 1988, 90, 93, bd. dirs. 1985-94, v.p. 1987-91, pres. 1991-92), Artable, Am. Folklore Soc., Western Mus. Conf. (bd. dirs., exec. com. 1989-91, program chair 1990), Nat. Coun. for Edn. in Ceramic Arts, Phi Beta Kappa. Office: Curatorial and Mus Mgmt Svcs 345 White Rd Watsonville CA 95076-0429

HERNANDEZ, LILLIAN A., health facility administrator; b. Inglewood, Calif., May 12, 1959; d. John Erling and Lillian Alice (Hastings) Johnson; m. David Robert Hernandez, Aug. 11, 1979; children: Linda Marie, Amber Michelle, Christine Lee. AA, Cerritos Jr. Coll., 1981; BS in Bus., Calif. State U., Long Beach, 1986. Cert. quality circle facilitator. Note teller Bank of Am., Bellflower, Calif., 1978-79; computer operator Piping Products West, Vernon, Calif., 1981; counselor/asst. mgr. Zoe Employment Agy., Los Alamitos, Calif., 1981-82; pers. asst./quality circle facilitator Hazel of Calif. Inc., Santa Fe Springs, 1982-86; employment coord. PARTNERS Nat. Health Plans, San Bernardino, Calif., 1987-89; owner Cream Whippeeze, Riverside, Calif., 1989-91; Riverside County media coord. William Dannemeyer for U.S. Senate, 1991-92; human resources dir. Manor Care Nursing Ctr., Hemet, Calif., 1993—; Interview panalist City of Riverside, Calif., 1990. Chmn. Citizens' Adv. Affirmative Action Com., Riverside, Calif., 1990; founding mem. Riverside Citizens for Responsible Behavior, 1990—; bd. dirs. Greater Riverside Hispanic Chamber, 1989-91; mem. Community Rels. Commn., 87-94; chmn. recreation and culture, 1989-90, parliamentarian, 1988-90; assoc. mem. Calif. Rep. State Cen. Com., 1989-92; mem. Calif. Rep. State Com., Riverside County Ctrl. Com.; vice-chair 2d supervisoral dist.; adv. com. law enforcement policy, Calif. Rep. State Party, 1989-92, del., 1992—; founding mem. v.p. Riverside Citizens for Responsible Behavior, 1990—; mem. Cmty Rels. Commn., 1987-89. Mem. Personnel and Indsl. Rels. Assn. Republican. Office: Manor Care Nursing Ctr 1717 W Stetson Ave Hemet CA 92545

HERNANDEZ, SAM, sculptor, educator; b. Hayward, Calif., Jan. 23, 1948; s. Ferdinand Rudolph and Martha (Pelaez) H.; m. Jo Farb, Sept. 5, 1976; 1 child, Larissa Anne. BA in Art, Calif. State U., Hayward, 1970; diploma (hon.), U. Sonora, Mexico, 1972; MFA in Art, U. Wis., 1974. Dir. sculpture program East Tex. State U., Commerce, 1974-77; asst. prof. Santa Clara (Calif.) U., 1977-83, assoc. prof., 1983—, chair art dept., 1980-86; vis. lectr. U. Wis., Madison, 1980; artist in residence Skopje (Macedonia) U., 1986; vis. artist Honolulu (Hawaii) Acad. Arts, 1992; vis. instr. Anderson Ranch, Snowmass Village, Colo., 1994, 95, Haystack Sch., Deer Isle, Maine, 1994. One man shows include Palm Springs Desert Mus., Oakland Mus., San Jose Mus. Art, Gresno Art Mus., Honolulu Acad. Arts, U. Oreg. Mus. Art.; group shows include San Francisco Mus. Art, Crocker Art Mus., Sacramento, Am. Craft Mus., Philbrook Mus. Art, Tulsa, Mexican Mus., San Antonio, Contemporary Mus., Honolulu, Contemporary Art Ctr., Cin., Mus. of Macedonia, Skopje, New Orleans Mus. Art; co-author: The Day of the Dead: Tradition and Change in Contemporary Mexico, 1979. Individual Artist fellow Cultural Coun. Santa Clara (Calif.) County, 1983, Visual Artist fellow Nat. Endowment for the Arts, Washington, 1984, Sr. Fulbright fellow Fulbright Program, 1986; Individual Artist grantee No. Calif. Grantmakers/NEA, Santa Cruz, 1989. Office: Santa Clara U Art Dept Bellomy at the Alameda Santa Clara CA 95053

HERNANDEZ, SERGIO JOSEPH, investigator; b. L.A., Oct. 29, 1948; s. Emidio Delgado and Juanita (Villalobos) H.; m. Diane Corrine Velarde, July 27, 1977; children: Corina, Natalie, Jenna. Student, E.L.A. Jr. Coll., Monterey Park, Calif., 1967-69; BA, Calif. State U., Northridge, 1977. Probation officer L.A. (Calif.) County Probation, 1975-85; investigator II L.A. (Calif.) County Pub. Defender, 1985—; art dir. Con Safos Mag., L.A., 1968-72. Polit. cartoonist Vanguard News, 1989; illustrations have appeared in various publs. Mem. Calif. Def. Investigators Assn., Elks. Roman Catholic. Home: 31317 Indian Oak Rd Acton CA 93510-2137 Office: LA County Pub Defender 210 W Temple St Los Angeles CA 90012-3210

HERNRIED, LUCY S., physician; d. H. Peter Hernreid (dec. Mar. 1987); 2 sons. BA, Swarthmore Coll., 1953; MD, N.Y. Med. Coll., 1957. Pediat. assoc. dir. pulmonary sect. Good Samaritan Hosp., Phoenix, 1970-74, dir. pediat. pulmonary sect., 1974-82; sect. chief pediat. pulmonology Phoenix Children's Hosp., 1982-87, mem. pulmonary sect., 1987—, dir. Cystic Fibrosis Ctr., 1974—, chmn. dept. medicine, 1986-88, 92-94; sr. clin. lectr. in pediats. U. Ariz., Tucson, 1987—. Fellow Am. Acad. Pediats. (chest sect.); mem. Am. Thoracic Soc., Maricopa County Pediat. Soc., Ariz. Pediat. Soc. Office: Phoenix Childrens Hosp 909 E Brill St Phoenix AZ 85006-2513

HEROLD, RALPH ELLIOTT, motion picture arts educator; b. L.A., Dec. 5, 1919; s. Henry Danelle and Isabelle (Baker) H. BS, St. Andrews Coll., 1951; PhD in Mgmt. Sci., Clayton U., 1978. Instr. media sci. L.A. City Schs., 1949-56; staff asst. flight ops. Hughes Aircraft Co., Culver City, Calif., 1955-57; mgr. logistics & program control N.Am. Aviation, L.A., Canoga Park, Downey, Calif., 1957-67; mgr. quality assurance McDonnell Douglas Astronautics, Huntington Beach, Calif., 1967-70; dir. motivational sci. Systematix, Fullerton, Calif., 1970-74; pers. dir. Chapman U., Orange, Calif., 1974-75; instr. Am. film heritage Rancho Santiago Coll., Santa Ana, Calif., 1976—. Contbr. numerous articles to profl. jours.; prodr. film-to-video Objective Kobe, own color footage of Kobe, Japan in WWII. Lt. col. U.S. Army Signal Corps, 1940-63. Mem. Theater Hist. Soc. Am., Ret. Officers Assn., Cinecon, Hollywood Stuntman's Assn. Home: 161 Avenida Majorca Unit N Laguna Hills CA 92653-4112

HERON, DAVID WINSTON, librarian; b. Los Angeles, Mar. 29, 1920; s. Charles Morton and Elizabeth (Atsatt) H.; m. Winifred Ann Wright, Aug. 24, 1946; children—Holly Winston, James, Charles. A.B., Pomona Coll., 1942; B.L.S., U. Calif. at Berkeley, 1948; M.A., U. Calif. at Los Angeles, 1951. Reference asst. U. Calif. at Los Angeles Library, 1948-52; librarian Am. embassy, Tokyo, Japan, 1952-53; staff asst. to librarian Grad. Reading Room U. Calif. at Los Angeles, 1953-55; asst. to dir. Stanford Libraries, 1955-57, asst. dir., 1959-61; asst. librarian Hoover Instn., Stanford, 1957-59; dir. libraries U. Nev., Reno, 1961-68, U. Kans., Lawrence, 1968-74; univ. librarian U. Calif. at Santa Cruz, 1974-78, emeritus librarian, 1979—; sr. lectr. Sch. Library and Info. Studies, 1978-79; head reader services Hoover Instn., 1980-86; library adviser U. Ryukyus, Naha, Okinawa, 1960-61; mem. Kans. Library Adv. Commn., 1973-74. Author: Forever Facing South, 1991; editor: A Unifying Influence, 1981; mem. editorial bd. Coll. and Rsch. Librs.; contbr. articles to gen. and profl. jours. Served as 1st lt. AUS, 1942-46, ETO. Mem. ALA (exec. bd.), Kans. Library Assn., Nev. Library Assn. (pres. 1963-65), Assn. Research Libraries (bd. dirs. 1974), ACLU, Assn. Coll. and Research Libraries (editor monographs; chmn. U. libraries sect. 1970-71). Democrat. Home: 120 Las Lomas Dr Aptos CA 95003-3221

HERPIN, WILLIAM BERNARD, JR., deputy program manager; b. St. Petersburg, Fla., Aug. 16, 1943; s. William Bernard Herpin Sr. and Mary Louise (Johnston) Murrah; m. Linda Elaine Bjornerud, June 6, 1965; children: Tiffany, Nikki, Kari. BS in Aerospace Engring., U. Kans., 1973; MA in Computer Resource Mgmt., Webster U., 1985. Comm. officer USS John Marshall, Vallejo, Calif., 1974-75; asst. weapons officer USS John Marshall, Pearl Harbor, Hawaii, 1975-77; tng. support officer Naval Submarine Tng. Ctr. Pacific, Pearl Harbor, Hawaii, 1977-79; ops. officer USS Robert E Lee, Pearl Harbor, Hawaii, 1979-80; br. chief Air Force Space Command, Colorado Springs, 1980-85; task leader Nat. Systems & Rsch. Co., Colorado Springs, 1985-94, dep. program mgr., 1994—; mem. accountability com. Sch. Dist. 11, Colorado Springs, 1984-85. V.p. Pikes Peak Chpt. MADD, Colorado Springs, 1983-86; sr. victim asst. team caseworker Colorado Springs Police Dept., 1987—, handicap parking enforcement officer, 1993—; pres. Our Savior Luth. Ch., Colorado Springs, 1989-94. Lt./Capt. USN/USAF, 1965-85. Named Colo. lifesaver Colo. Dept. Hwy. Safety, 1986, Outstanding vol. Colorado Springs Police Dept. Traffic, 1988. Mem. The Ret. Officers Assn., Law Enforcement Alliance of Am., Pikes Peak Computer Application Soc. (treas. Sysop 1980—), NRA, Pikes Peak Chpt. MADD (v.p. treas. 1984—). Republican. Lutheran. Home: 532 Potter Ct Colorado Springs CO 80909-5427 Office: Nat Systems & Rsch Co 5475 Mark Dabling Blvd Ste 200 Colorado Springs CO 80918-3848

HERRERA, FRANCISCO RAFAEL, political advisor; b. Salvatierra, Mex., Nov. 11, 1943; came to U.S., 1944; s. Jess and Josephine (Rodriguez) H. BA, St. John's Coll., Camarillo, Calif., 1965; MS, San Diego State U., 1975; MPA, Harvard U., 1986. City coun. rep. City Mgr.'s Office, San Diego, 1978-80; sr. com. cons. Office of Mayor, San Diego, 1980-83; dir. intergovtl. rels. U.S. Senator Pete Wilson, Washington, 1983-85; dir. Dept. Binational Affairs City of San Diego, 1986-88; cons. San Diego, 1988-89; sr. policy advisor U.S. Senator Pete Wilson, San Diego, 1989-91; asst. to gov. for internat. affairs Gov. of Calif., Sacramento, 1991-93; internat. rels. dir. San Diego Gas & Electric, 1993—; presenter profl. confs., orgns. including Am. Planning Assn., Am. Gas Assn., Border Trade Alliance, Nat. Assn. Pub. Adminstrs. Bd. govs. Arthritis Found., San Diego, 1987-90; founding mem. Border Trade Alliance, 1986; bd. dirs. San Diego Arthritis Found. Recipient Outstanding Pub. Svcs. award Oxnard Harbor Dist., 1985, Outstanding Appointed Official award Calif. Hispanic C. of C., 1992. Mem. San Diego County Internat. Trade Commn. (commr. 1986-90), Harvard U. Alumni Assn. (exec. coun. Kennedy Sch. Govt., past pres. 1989-92). Roman Catholic. Office: San Diego Gas & Electric 101 Ash St Ste Eb-1612 San Diego CA 92101-3017

HERRERA, JOHN, professional football team executive; married; 7 children. BA in History, U. Calif., Davis. Tng. camp asst. L.A. Raiders, 1963-68, pub. rels. asst., 1968, pub. rels. dir., 1978-80, sr. exec., 1985—; dir. player pers. B.C. Lions, 1981-82; gen. mgr. Sask. Roughriders, 1983-84; with scouting depts. Tampa Bay Buccaneers, 1975-76, Washington Redskins, 1977. Office: Los Angeles Raiders 332 Center St El Segundo CA 90245-4047

HERRERA, ROBERT BENNETT, retired mathematics educator; b. L.A., July 24, 1913; s. Royal Robert and Rachel (Mix) H.; AA, L.A. City Coll., 1934; AB, UCLA, 1937, MA, 1939; m. Agnes Mary MacDougall, May 18,

1941; children: Leonard B., Mary Margaret, William R. Tchr. high sch., Long Beach, Calif., 1939-41; statistician U.S. Forest Survey, Berkeley, Calif., 1941-45; faculty L.A. City Coll., 1946-79, prof. math., 1966-79, chmn. math. dept., 1975-79, ret., 1979; lectr. math. UCLA, 1952-75; cons. Ednl. Testing Svc., Princeton, 1965-68, Addison Wesley Pub. Co., 1966-68, Goodyear Pub. Co., 1970-76. Mem. AAAS, Math. Assn. Am. (past sec. So. Calif. sect., past gov.), Am. Math. Soc., Internat. Oceanic Soc., Phi Beta Kappa, Pi Mu Epsilon. Democrat. Author: (with C. Bell, C. Hammond) Fundamentals of Arithmetic for Teachers, 1962. Home: 2737 S Kihei Rd # 159 Kihei HI 96753-9609 Office: PO Box 134 Kihei HI 96753-0134

HERRERA, SANDRA JOHNSON, school system administrator; b. Riverside, Calif., June 21, 1944; d. William Emory Johnson and Mildred Alice (Alford) Wimer; m. Wynn Neal Huffman, Feb. 19, 1962 (div. May 1967); 1 child, Kristen Lee; m. Steven Jack Herrera, June 21, 1985. AA in Purchasing Mgmt., Fullerton Coll., 1983; BSBA, U. Redlands, 1985, MA in Mgmt., 1988. Sr. purchasing clk Fullerton (Calif.) Union High Sch. Dist., 1969-77, buyer, 1977-79, coord. budgets and fiscal affairs, 1979-83; asst. dir. fin. svcs. Downey (Calif.) Unified Sch. Dist., 1983-85; dir. acctg. Whittier (Calif.) Union High Sch. Dist., 1985-89; asst. supt. bus. Whittier City Sch. Dist., 1989-91, Oxnard Elem. Sch. Dist., 1991—; cons. Heritage Dental Lab., El Toro, Calif, 1981—. Spl. dep. sheriff Santa Barbara (Calif.) County Sheriff's Mounted Posse, 1986-90; spl. dep. marshal U.S. Marshals Posse, Los Angeles, 1987-95. Mem. Calif. Assn. Sch. Bus. Ofcls. (treas. S.E. sect. 1985, mem. acct. R & D com. 1983-89, mem. chief bus. officials com. 1989—), So. Calif. Paraders Assn. (exec. sec. 1976—), Calif. State Horsemens Assn. (regional v.p. 1986-87, sec. 1988), Alpha Gamma Sigma. Home: 5688 La Cumbre Rd Somis CA 93066-9783 Office: Oxnard Elem Sch Dist 1051 S A St Oxnard CA 93030-7442

HERRERA, SHIRLEY MAE, personnel and security executive; b. Lynn, Mass., Apr. 5, 1942; d. John Baptiste and Edith Mae Lagasse; m. Christian Yanez Herrera, Apr. 30, 1975; children: Karen, Gary, Ivan, Iwonne. AS in Bus., Burdette Bus. Coll., Lynn, 1960; student, Wright State U., 1975-78. Cert. facility security officer, med. asst. in pediatrics. Med. asst. Christian Y. Herrera, M.D., Stoneham, Mass., 1972-74; human resource adminstr. MTL Systems, Inc., Dayton, Ohio, 1976-79; dir. pers. and security Tracor GIE, Inc., Provo, Utah, 1979—; cons. on family dynamics family enrichment program Hill AFB, Utah, 1980-82; cons. on health care memt. Guam 7th Day Adventist Clinic, 1983; cons. on basic life support and CPR, Projecto Corazon, Monterrey, Mex., 1987—; faculty mem. Inst. for Reality Therapy, 1991—. Contbg. editor Inside Tractor, 1991—. Chmn. women's aux. YMCA Counselling Svcs., Woburn, Mass., 1970; chmn. youth vols. ARC, Wright-Patterson AFB, Dayton, 1974-76; trustee Quail Valley Homeowner's Assn., Provo, 1988-89; rep. A Spl. Wish Found., Provo, 1989. Recipient James S. Cogswell award Def. Investigative Svc., Dept. Def., 1987. Mem. Soc. for Human Resource Mgmt., Inst. for Realty Therapy (cert.), Pers. Assn. Ctrl. Utah, Women in Mgmt. (coun. mem. 1991—), Nat. Classification Mgmt. Soc. (chairperson Intermountain chpt. 1992-94), Provo/Orem C. of C. (gov. rev. coun.). Republican. Home: 3824 Little Rock Dr Provo UT 84604-5234

HERRICK, SYLVIA A., health service administrator; b. Minot, N.D., Oct. 5, 1945; d. Sylvester P. and Ethelina (Harren) Theis; m. Michael M. Herrick, Nov. 8, 1989; children: Leo J., Mark A. BSN, U. N.D., 1967; MS in Pub. Health Nursing, U. Colo., Denver, 1970; sch. nurse credential, San Jose State U., 1991; postgrad., Golden Gate U. RN, Calif.; cert. pub. health nursing, health svc. Pub. health nurse Dept. Pub. Health City of Mpls.; instr. nursing San Francisco State U.; cons. exec. search Med-Power Resources, Alameda; coord. health svcs. Alameda Unified Sch. Dist.; team mgr. home care nursing and program devel. coord. Vis. Nurse Assn. and Hospice of No. Calif.; speaker Bay Area Scoliosis Assn., 1990. Mem. Nat. Nurses Bus. Assn., Calif. Sch. Nurses Orgn. (bd. dirs., chair edn Bay Coast sect.), Delta Kappa Gamma. Home: 1711 Encinal Ave Alameda CA 94501-4020

HERRICK, TRACY GRANT, fiduciary; b. Cleve., Dec. 30, 1933; s. Stanford Avery and Elizabeth Grant (Smith) H.; B.A., Columbia U., 1956, M.A., 1958; postgrad. Yale U., 1956-57; M.A., Oxford U. (Eng.), 1960; m. Maie Kaarsoo, Oct. 12, 1963; children—Sylvi Anne, Alan Kalev. Economist, Fed. Res. Bank, Cleve., 1960-70; sr. economist Stanford Research Inst., Menlo Park, Calif., 1970-73; v.p., sr. analyst Shuman, Agnew & Co., Inc., San Francisco, 1973-75; v.p. Bank of Am., San Francisco, 1975-81; pres. Tracy G. Herrick, Inc., 1981—; lectr. Stonier Grad. Sch. Banking, Am. Bankers Assn., 1967-76; commencement speaker Memphis Banking Sch., 1974; bd. dirs. Jefferies Group, Inc., Jefferies & Co., Inc., Anderson Capital Mgmt., Inc. Fellow Fin. Analysts Fedn.; mem. Assn. Investment Mgmt. Rsch., Sacramento Security Analysts Soc., San Francisco Soc. Security Analysts, Com. for Monetary Rsch. and Edn., Inc. Republican. Congregationalist. Author: Bank Analyst's Handbook, 1978; Timing, 1981; Power and Wealth, 1988; contbr. articles to profl. jours. Home: 1150 University Ave Palo Alto CA 94301-2238

HERRINGER, FRANK CASPER, diversified financial services company executive; b. N.Y.C., Nov. 12, 1942; s. Casper Frank and Alice Virginia (McMullen) H.; m. Maryellen B. Cattani; children: William, Sarah, Julia. A.B. magna cum laude, Dartmouth, 1964, M.B.A. with highest distinction, 1965. Prin. Cresap, McCormick & Paget, Inc. (mgmt. cons.), N.Y.C., 1965-71; staff asst. to Pres., Washington, 1971-73; adminstr. U.S. Urban Mass Transp. Adminstrn., Washington, 1973-75; gen. mgr., chief exec. officer San Francisco Bay Area Rapid Transit Dist., 1975-78; exec. v.p., dir. Transamerica Corp., San Francisco, 1979-86, pres., 1986—, chief exec. officer, 1991—; bd. dirs. Unocal Corp., Pacific Telesis, Occidental Life Ins. Co., Transam. Fin. Group, Transam. Leasing. Trustee Calif. Pacific Med. Ctr. Mem. Phi Beta Kappa. Clubs: San Francisco Golf, Olympic, Pacific Union, Villa Taverna. Office: Transam Corp 600 Montgomery St San Francisco CA 94111-2702

HERRMAN, MARCIA KUTZ, child development specialist; b. Boston, June 16, 1927; d. Cecil and Sonia (Schneider) Kutz; m. Bayard F. Berman, July 23, 1949 (div. 1960); m. William H. Herrman, June 23, 1961; 1 child, Fred. BA, Smith Coll., 1949; MA, Pacific Oaks Coll., 1974. Cert. tchr., Calif. NIMH intern Cedars-Sinai Med. Ctr., L.A., 1966-67; ednl. therpist L.A. Child Guidance Clinic, 1967-69, Child and Family Study Ctr., Cedars-Sinai Med. Ctr., 1969-71; dir. tng., asst. project dir. handicapped early edn. program Dubnoff Ctr., North Hollywood, Calif., 1972-76; child devel. cons. various schs., agys. and families, Studio City, Calif., 1969—; cons. L.A. Child Guidance Clinic, Head Start, Child Care and Devel. Svcs., 1969-73; profl. expert L.A. Unified Sch. Dist., 1976-80; vis. faculty mem. Pacific Oaks Coll., Pasadena, Calif., 1970-76. Vol. Alliance for Children's Rights, 1992-94, Child Advocate's Office, Superior Ct., L.A., 1983—; active polit. campaigns, 1950's and 1960's; mem. Dependency Ct. Com., 1988-92, Task Force on Rep. of Children in Dependency, 1994, Children's Commn., L.A. County, 1988-93, L.A. Foster Care Network, 1987-94, L.A. County MacLaren Children's Ctr. Task Force, 1990—; mem. cmty. adv. com. St. Joseph's Ctr., 1992—. Recipient Vol. of Yr. award L.A. County Bd. Suprs., 1986, Commendation for Dedicated Svc. to Community, 1991, Recognition award for Outstanding Svc. to Children L.A. County Inter-Agy. Coun. on Child Abuse, 1991; Sophia Smith scholar, 1949. Fellow Am. Orthopsychiat. Assn.; mem. N.Y. Acad. Scis., Assn. Child Devel. Specialists, Nat. Ct. Appointed Spl. Advocate Assn. Democrat. Jewish. Home and Office: 3919 Ethel Ave Studio City CA 91604-2204

HERRMANN, GEORGE, mechanical engineering educator; b. USSR, Apr. 19, 1921. Diploma in Civil Engring., Swiss Fed. Inst. Tech., 1945, PhD in Mechanics, 1949. Asst., then asso. prof. civil engring. Columbia, 1950-62; prof. civil engring. Northwestern U., 1962-69; prof. applied mechanics Stanford, 1969—; cons. SRI Internat., 1970-80. Contbr. 260 articles to profl. jours.; editl. bd. numerous jours. Fellow ASME (hon. mem. 1990, Centennial medal 1980); mem. ASCE (Th. v. Karman medal 1981), Nat. Acad. Engring., AIAA (emeritus). Office: Stanford U Div Applied Mechanics Durand Bldg 281 Stanford CA 94305-4040

HERRMANN, WALTER, retired laboratory administrator; b. Johannesburg, Republic of South Africa, May 2, 1930; came to U.S., 1953; s. Gottlob Friedrich and Gertrud Louise (Retzlaff) H.; m. Betty Allard (div.); children: Peter Friedrich, Inga Louise; m. Ednarae B. Gross. BSc in Engring. cum laude, U. Witwatersrand, Republic South Africa, 1950; PhD in Mech. Engring., U. Witwatersrand, 1955. Rsch. engr. MIT, Boston, 1953-55, sr. rsch. engr., 1957-64; lectr. U. Cape Town, Rep. South Africa, 1955-57; div. supr. Sandia Nat. Labs., Albuquerque, 1964-67, dept. mgr., 1967-82, dir. engring. scis., 1982-90, dir. shock physics rsch., 1990-93; retired Sandia Nat. Labs., 1993; W.W. Clyde prof. U. Utah, Salt Lake City, 1971-72. Contbr. articles to profl. jours. Mem. ASME, Am. Phys. Soc., Nat. Acad. Engring.

HERRON, CAROL CHRISTINE, financial planner, home economist; b. Lebanon, Oreg., Dec. 17, 1944; d. Ralph Elwood and Mary Mabel (Morris) H. BS, Oreg. State U., 1967, MS, 1971. Cert. home economist; CFP. Home economist W.F. West High Sch., Chehalis, Wash., 1968-69; extension agt. Wash. State U., Bellingham, 1971; extension specialist Wash. State U., Pullman, 1972-74; coord., instr. Portland (Oreg.) Community Coll., 1974-83; energy cons. Energy Counselors, Beaverton, Oreg., 1983-86; dir. devel. Coll. Home Econs. Oreg. State U., Corvallis, 1986-88; registered rep. Waddell and Reed Fin. Svcs., Beaverton, Oreg., 1988—. Mem. fin. coun. St. Anthony's Ch., 1994—. Mem. Internat. Assn. for Fin. Planning, Am. Assn. Family and Consumer Scis. (nominating com. 1988-90, cert. chair 1992—, sewing fair facilities chair 1990, 92, 94, ex-officio fin. com. 1993—), Oreg. Home Econs. Assn. (bd. dirs., pres.1986-89), Oreg. State U. Coll. Home Econs. Alumni Assn. (bd. dirs. 1984-87). Democrat. Roman Catholic. Office: Waddell and Reed Fin Svcs 8625 SW Cascade Ave Ste 290 Beaverton OR 97008-7180

HERRON, ELLEN PATRICIA, retired judge; b. Auburn, N.Y., July 30, 1927; d. David Martin and Grace Josephine (Berner) Herron; A.B. Trinity Coll., 1949; M.A., Cath. U. Am., 1954; J.D., U. Calif.-Berkeley, 1964. Asst. dean Cath. U. Am., 1952-54; instr. East High Sch., Auburn, 1955-57; asst. dean Wells Coll., Aurora, N.Y., 1957-58; instr. psychology and history Contra Costa Coll., 1958-60; dir. row Stanford, 1960-61; assoc. Knox & Kretzmer, Richmond, Calif., 1964-65. Bar: Calif., 1965. Ptnr. Knox & Herron, 1965-74, Knox, Herron and Masterson, 1974-77 (both Richmond, Calif.); judge Superior Ct. State of Calif., 1977-87; pvt. judge, 1987-90; pvt. judge Jud. Arbitration and Mediation Svc., Inc. (JAMS- Endispute), 1990—; ptnr. Real Estate Syndicates, Calif., 1967-77; owner, mgr. The Barricia Vineyards, 1978—. Active numerous civic orgns. Democrat. Home: 51 Western Dr Richmond CA 94801-4011

HERRON, SIDNEY EARL, sales executive; b. Aberdeen, Wash., May 25, 1952; s. Marshall Elbie and Martha Elizabeth (Nicholson) H.; m. Gloria Annette Hanson, Mar. 17, 1973 (div. Mar 1983); children: Jason, Angela; m. Alison Marie Young, Oct. 12, 1985; children: Jeff, Amanda, Shane. Student, U. Washington, Seattle, Grays Harbor Coll., 1970-71, Northwest Coll., 1971-72. Field service engr. Teltone Corp., Kirkland, Wash., 1973-77, sales engr., 1977-80, area sales mgr. component products, 1980-81, area sales mgr. data products, 1981-83, nat. accounts mgr. pvt. label div., 1983-84, western regional sales mgr., 1985-86; product mgr. data products Teltone Corp., Kirkland, 1986-89; western regional sales mgr. Teltrend, Inc., Kirkland, Wash., 1989-90; with mktg. and sales Rapcom Corp., Bellevue, Wash., 1990-91; pres., founding ptnr. Avicom, Inc., Bothell, Wash., 1991—; mgmt. cons. TRC Systems Corp., Federal Way, Wash., 1986-87. Author, editor and actor videotaped tech. tng., 1976; author sales tng. manual for Teltone Corp., 1983. Mem. Internat. Airline Passangers' Assn. Republican. Club: Columbia Athletic (Kirkland, Wash.). Home and Office: Avicom Inc 2506 171st Pl SE Bothell WA 98012-6512

HERSCHER, URI DAVID, academic administrator, history educator, rabbi; b. Tel Aviv, Mar. 14, 1941; s. Joseph and Lucy (Strauss) H.; m. Eleanor Grant, June 15, 1969 (div. 1983); children: Joshua, Gideon; m. Myna Meshul, Oct. 14, 1990. BA, U. Calif., Berkeley, 1964; MA in Hebrew Lit., Hebrew Union Coll., Cin., 1970; DHL, Hebrew Union Coll., L.A., 1973. Dir. admissions Hebrew Union Coll., Cin., 1970-72, asst. to pres., 1972-75; exec. v.p., prof. Am. Jewish history Hebrew Union Coll., Cin., N.Y.C., L.A. and Jerusalem, 1975—. Author: Jewish Agricultural Utopias in America, 1981; co-author: On Jews, America and Immigration, 1980; editor: A Century of Memories, 1983; co-editor: Queen City Refuge, 1989; contbr. articles to profl. jours. Mem. Cen. Conf. Am. Rabbis, Am. Jewish Com., Assn. Reform Zionists Am., L.A. Jewish Fedn. (bd. dirs). Office: Hebrew Union Coll 3077 University Ave Los Angeles CA 90007-3717

HERSCHLER, LESLIE NORMAN, elementary education educator; b. Hollywood, Calif., Dec. 22, 1958; s. Melvin H. and Ruth Celia (Pianko) H.; m. Jill Belman Gottfried, June 26, 1988. BA in Psychology, U. Calif., Irvine, 1979; cert. teaching, Calif. State U., Long Beach, 1985; MS, Nat. U., 1988. Educator Lynwood (Calif.) Unified Sch. Dist., 1985—; leadership team Will Rogers Elem. Sch., Lynwood, 1990-91. Crisis listener Hotline So. Calif., 1978—. Democrat. Jewish. Home: 6762 Acacia Ave Garden Grove CA 92645-3020 Office: Lynwood Unified Sch Dist 11321 Bullis Rd Lynwood CA 90262-3600

HERSHMAN, JEROME MARSHALL, endocrinologist; b. Chgo., July 20, 1932; s. Maurice and Gertrude (Zemel) H.; m. Fleurette Kram, Dec. 22, 1957; children: Daniel, Michael, Jeffrey. BS, Northwestern U., 1952; MS, Calif. Inst. Technology, 1953; MD, U. Ill., 1957. Diplomate Am. Bd. Internal Medicine, Endocrinology & Metabolism. Fellow in endocrinology New England Ctr. Hosp., Boston, 1961-63; clin. investigator Northwestern U. Med. Sch., Chgo., 1964-67; chief clin. nuclear medicine Birmingham (Ala.) VA Hosp., 1967-71, chief endocrine sect., 1971-72; prof. Sch. Medicine U. Ala., Birmingham, 1967-72, UCLA, 1972—; chief endocrinology and metabolism West L.A. VA Med. Ctr., 1972—. Editor: Thyroid, 1991; mem. editorial bd. Am. Jour. of Medicine, 1989—; editor: Practical Endocrinology, 1981, Endocrine Pathophysiology, 2d edit., 1982, 3d edit., 1988, Syllabus of 38th Annual Postgraduate Assembly of the Endocrine Soc., 1986. Capt. USAF, 1959-61. Mem. Am. Thyroid Assn. (dir. 1989—, pres. 1992-93). Jewish. Home: 15970 Meadowcrest Rd Sherman Oaks CA 91403-4714 Office: West LA VA Med Ctr 11301 Wilshire Blvd Los Angeles CA 90073-1003

HERSHMAN, LYNN LESTER, artist; b. Cleve.; 1 dau., Dawn. B.S., Case-Western Res. U., 1963; M.A., San Francisco State U., 1972. Prof. U. Calif., Davis, 1984—; Vis. prof. art U. Calif., Berkeley, Calif. Coll. Arts and Crafts, San Jose State U., 1974-78; assoc. project dir. Christo's Running Fence, 1973-76; founder, dir. Floating Mus., 1975-79; ind. film/video producer and cons., 1979—. Author works in field; one-man shows include Santa Barbara Mus. Art, 1970, Univ. Art Mus., Berkeley, Calif., 1972, Mills Coll., Oakland, Calif., 1973, William Sawyer Gallery, 1974, Nat. Galleries, Melbourne, Australia, 1976, Mandeville Art Gallery, U. Calif., San Diego, 1976, M.H. de Young Art Mus., 1978, Pallazo dei Diamonte, Ferrara, Italy, 1978, San Francisco Art Acad., 1980, Portland Center Visual Arts, 1980, New Mus., New Sch., N.Y.C., 1981, Inst. Contemporary Art, Phila., 1981, Anina Nosai Gallery, N.Y.C., 1981, Contemporary Art Center, Cin., 1982, Toronto, Los Angeles Contemporary Exhibits, 1986, Univ. Art Mus. Berkeley, 1987, Madison (Wis.) Art Ctr., 1987, Intersesction for the Arts, San Francisco, Pacific Film Archive, A. Space, "Guerilla Tactics" Toronto, Can., Venice Bienalle Global Village; group exhbns. include Cleve. Art Mus., 1968, St. Paul Art Ctr., 1969, Richmond (Calif.) Art Ctr., 1970, 73, Galeria del Sol, Santa Barbara, Calif., 1971, San Francisco Art Inst., 1972, Richard Demarco Art Gallery, Edinburgh, Scotland, 1973, Laguna Beach (Calif.) Art Mus., 1973, Univ. Art Mus., Univ. Calif., Berkeley, 1974, Bronx (N.Y.) Mus., 1975, Linda Ferris Gallery, Seattle, 1975, Madenville Art Gallery, San Diego, Contemporary Arts Mus., Houston, 1977, New Orleans, 1977, Ga. Mus. Art, Athens, 1977, New Mus., N.Y., 1981, Calif. Coll. Arts and Crafts, 1981, San Francisco Mus. Modern Art, 1979, 80, 90, Art-Beaubourg, Paris, 1980, Ars Electronica, 1989, Am. Film Inst., 1989, Mus. Moving Image Internat. Ctr. for Photography, 1989, Kitchen Ctr. for Video-Music, N.Y., 1990, Robert Koch Gallery, San Francsico, 1990, Inst. Contemporary Art, London, 1990, Frankfurt (Germany) Art Fair, 1990, Inst. Conteporary Art, Boston, 1991, Oakland (Calif.) Mus., 1991, La Cite des Arts et des Nouvelles Technologies, Montreal, 1991, Richard F. Brush Art Gallery, Canton, N.Y., 1992, Jack Tilton Gallery, N.Y., 1992, Southeastern Ctr. for Contemporary Art, Winston-Salem, N.C., 1992, Bonner Kunstverein, Bonn, Germany, 1992, Chgo. Ave. Armory, 1992, Retrospective, Tribute, 1994, Nelson Gallery, Paris, 1994, Hess Collection, 1994. Bd. dirs. San Francisco Art Acad., Spectrum Found., Motion a Performance Collective. Western States Regional fellow (film/video), 1990; grantee Nat. Endowment for the Arts, (2) Art Matters Inc., San Francisco Found., N.Y. State Coun. for the Arts, Zellerbach Family Fund, Inter Arts of Marin, Gerbode Found., The Women's Project; recipient Dirs. Choice award San Francisco Internat. Film Festival, 1987, tribute 1987 Mill Valley Video Festial, Exptl. Video award 1988, 1st prize Montbelliard, France, 1990, 2d prize, Vigo, Spain, 1992, 1993 Ars Electronica, Austria, WRO Poland, Nat. Film Theatre, London, Gerber award Seattle Art Mus., 1994, ZKM/Siemans award, 1995. Mem. Assn. Art Pubs. (dir., Annie Gerber award 1995). Office: 1935 Filbert St San Francisco CA 94123-3503

HERSKER, SUSAN CATHERINE UTKE, interior designer; b. Fairborn, Ohio, July 28, 1954; d. Ronald Dean and Catherine Lenore (Stunz) Utke; m. Michael Conrad Hersker, Oct. 8, 1977; children: Jason Michael, Steven Ryan. BFA, Ariz. State U., 1976. Interior designer Baker Bros. Interiors, Phoenix, 1975-77, Barrows Furniture, Phoenix, 1978-90; interior designer/owner Design Directives, Scottsdale, Ariz., 1990-94; interior designer Interior Studio Group, LLC, Scottsdale, 1990—. Mem. Jr. League of Phoenix, 1990—; com. chair Orpheum Theater Restoration, Phoenix, 1990—; instr. Art Masterpiece Program, Tempe, Ariz., 1989—; spkr./instr. Phoenix Honors Cotillion, 1980—. Mem. Am. Soc. Interior Designers (bd. dirs. 1987-92, 1st place award 1989). Republican. Lutheran. Office: Design Directives 7633 E Acoma Dr Ste 104 Scottsdale AZ 85260-3401

HERSMAN, MARION FRANK, professional administrator, lawyer; b. Huntington, W.Va., Nov. 12, 1932; s. Marion Rockefeller and Frances Mae (Peabody) H.; m. Carole Anne Birthright, Oct. 1960 (div.); 1 child, Frank Eric Birthright; m. Nina Claire Mohay, Dec. 24, 1976 (div.); 1 child, Alicia Claire; m. Eleonora Georgi Hivrina, April 11, 1995. B.S. in Chemistry, Physics and Math, Ohio State U., 1953; Ph.D. in Chemistry (Victor Chem. fellow, Colgate Palmolive-Peet fellow, Univ. fellow), U. Ill., 1956; J.D., George Washington U., 1958, LL.M., 1960; M.A., New Sch. for Social Research, 1964. Bar: Va. 1958, N.Y. 1959, D.C. 1960, U.S. Supreme Ct. 1960, U.S. Ct. Appeals (D.C. cir.) 1960. Teaching fellow U. Ill.; patent examiner U.S. Patent Office, Washington, 1956-57; assoc. firm Burns Doane, Benedict & Irons, Washington, 1957-59, Arthur, Dry & Dole, N.Y.C., 1959-60, Fish, Richardson & Neave, N.Y.C., 1960-64; staff assoc. office sci. resources planning NSF, Washington, 1964-67; office of planning and policy studies NSF, 1967-69, head office intergovtl. sci. programs, 1969-72, dir. office intergovtl. sci. and research utilization, 1972-75; exec. dir. Colo. Planning Coordinating Council, 1976; spl. asst., sci. and tech. advisor to Gov. Colo., 1976; sci. and tech. advisor Fedn. Rocky Mountain States, Denver, 1977; dir. Rocky Mountain Tech. Sharing Task Force, 1977; dir. Div. Water Resources Hillsborough County, Tampa, Fla., 1977, dir. Div. Pub. Utilities, 1977-78; dir. Office of Planning and Intergovtl. Relations Hillsborough County, Tampa, 1978-79; asst. county adminstr. Hillsborough County (Fla.) Div. Pub. Utilities, 1978-79; vice chmn. Hillsborough Intergovtl. Resource Recovery Mgmt. Com.; mem. Fla. Community Conservation Com., 1978-80, Urban Consortium, 1978-80; spl. asst. to pres. U. South Fla., 1979-80; atty. NSF, 1980-82; dir. com. on hazardous materials Fed. Emergency Mgmt. Agy., 1981-83; vis. disting. prof. Nova U., 1982, spl. asst. to pres. for program devel., 1982; asst. city mgr. for health and human services City of Austin, (Tex.), 1982-84; exec. v.p. Lawyers Title of Ky., 1983-85; ptnr. LTK Enterprises, 1983-85; exec. v.p., chief operating officer Automation Telecommunications and Management Inc., Austin, Tex., 1984-85; dir. research and state services The Council of State Govts., Lexington, Ky., 1985-87; town mgr. Town of Snow Hill, Md., 1988; county mgr. Nye County, Nev., 1988-90; pres. RH Mgmt. Assocs., 1990—; speaker in field. teaching assoc. George Washington U., 1957-59; chmn., exec. dir. com. on intergovtl. sci. relations Fed. Council Sci. and Tech., Exec. Office of Pres., 1969-73; mem. Agrl. Yearbook adv. bd. U.S. Dept. Agr., 1969, mem. tech. adv. bd. nat. rural communities facilities assessment, 1978; chmn. com. on policy mgmt. and assistance U.S. Office Mgmt. and Budget, Washington, 1974-75; mem. com. on tech. sharing President's Office Sci. and Tech., 1972-74; chmn. So. Nev. Rural Health Fair, 1991; prof. urban engring. Nat. U. Mex., Mexico City, 1975; vis. faculty CSC, Kings Point, N.Y., 1975, Fed. Exec. Inst., Charlotteville, Va., 1977, Golden Gate U., 1979-80; vis. prof. U. Colo. Grad. Sch. Pub. Affairs, 1976-77, U. South Fla., 1978, Martin Sch., U. Ky., 1986-88; spl. asst. to dir. NSF, 1976-80; cons. Office Sci. and Tech., Exec. Office of Pres., 1976-80, Western Govs.' Task Force on Regional Policy Mgmt., 1976-77; cons. USDA, 1978; mem. Subcom. on Research Utilization Transp. Research Bd.-NRC-Nat. Acad. Scis., 1981-82; adminstr. Pahrump Valley Med. Ctr., 1991-92; pres. Nev. Health and Med. Found., 1991-92; U.S. exec. advisor mayor and city coun., City of Narva, Estonia, 1994; U.S. exec. advisor City of Tartur, Estonia, 1994, Internat. Exec. Svc. Corps, 1994; U.S. trade rep. City of Narva, Estonia, 1994—. Contbg. author: Science and Technology Policies, 1973; bd. editors and consultants: Scholar and Educator, 1977; mem. editorial bd.: Jour. Edn. and Scholar, 1977-87; contbr. articles to profl. jours. Bd. dirs. Warwick Assn., 1980-81;hmn. consumers and bus. affairs com. D.C. Area Neighborhood Council; mem. Washington Mayor's Planning and Budget Adv. Com., 1980-82; vol. exec. Internat. Exec. Svcs. Corps., 1994—; Pahrump Arts Coun., 1994—. Recipient Pub. Service award states of Ga., La., Ala., Pa., Okla., N.C., Pub. Service award So. Interstate Nuclear Bd., Pub. Service award Nat. Conf. State Legislatures; Picatinny Arsenal grantee; U.S. Govt. grantee. Mem. Va., D.C., Fed. bar assns., Am. Chem. Soc., Am. Soc. Pub. Adminstrn. (chmn. sect. on intergovtl. adminstrn. and mgmt. 1977-79, Public Service award), AAAS, Sigma Xi, Phi Lambda Upsilon, Delta Theta Phi (chmn. scholarships), Alpha Chi Sigma, Kappa Sigma. Home and Office: PO Box 3434 2070 S Page St Pahrump NV 89041-3434

HERSON, MICHAEL K., physician, educator; b. Manchester, Eng., Sept. 20, 1954; m. Janice Carol Brooks, Aug. 8, 1982; children: Alison, Matthew. BA, Pomona Coll., 1976; MD, Chgo. Med. Sch., 1981. Endocrinologist Cigna Health Plans, L.A., 1986-90, chief of medicine, 1988-90; endocrinologist Northwest Permanente, Portland, Oreg., 1990—; asst. clin. prof. medicine Oreg. Health Scis. U., 1990—. Fellow Am. Coll. Endocrinology; mem. Am. Diabetes Assn., The Endocrine Soc.

HERTE, MARY CHARLOTTE, plastic surgeon; b. Milw., May 31, 1951; chief of surgery Humana Sunrise, Las Vegas, 1989-92; chief of plastic surgery Humana Children's Hosp., Las Vegas, 1990—. BS, Mt. Mary Coll., Milw., 1973; MD, U. Wis., 1977. Diplomate Am. Bd. Plastic Surgery. Research fellow in plastic surgery Grad. Sch. Medicine Ea. Va. U., Norfolk, 1978; resident in gen. surgery Univ. Hosps., Madison, Wis., 1978-81, resident in plastic surgery, 1981-83; practice medicine specializing in plastic surgery Las Vegas, Nev., 1983—; chief of surgery Humana Sunrise, Las Vegas, 1989-92; chief of plastic surgery Sunrise Children's Hosp., Las Vegas, 1990—. Recipient Woman of Promise award Good Housekeeping Mag., 1985. Fellow ACS, Am. Acad. Pediatrics; mem. Am. Cleft Palate Assn., Assn. Women Surgeons, Am. Med. Women's Assn., Am. Soc. Plastic and Reconstructive Surgeons, Nev. State Med. Soc. (del. 1986-88), Clark County Med. Soc. (trustee 1986-88), Nev. Soc. Women Physicians (v.p. 1991-93, pres. 1994—), Soroptimist Internat. (treas., fin. sec. Greater Las Vegas chpt. 1985-87). Office: 3006 S Maryland Pky Ste 415 Las Vegas NV 89109-2235

HERTEL, HOWARD JAY, photographer; b. Oakland, Calif., Apr. 25, 1924; s. Elmer Joseph and Lillian Ruth (Hultberg) H.; m. Laverne Wilson, June 1949 (div. June 1965); children: Douglas Jay (dec.), Kenneth Bruce. Grad. H.S., Lafayette, Calif. Comml. photographer Waters and Hainlin Studio, Oakland, 1942-43; photographer, photo lab. tech. Army Air Forces, 1943-45; photographer Stanford Rsch. Inst., Menlo Park, Calif., 1950-53; freelance photographer San Francisco; faculty mem. Stanford (Calif.) U., 1950-53; market rsch. interviewer Field Rsch. Corp., San Francisco, 1994. Pres. Young Reps., Sacramento. Staff sgt. USAFR, 1964; active Sr. Ctr.-Aquatic Park San Francisco, 1994. Named assoc. Royal Photographic Soc., Bath, Eng., 1955. Mem. Air Force Assn. (life).

HERTLEIN, FRED, III, industrial hygiene laboratory executive; b. San Francisco, Oct. 17, 1933; s. Fred and Herta (Komning) H.; m. Clara Kam Fung Tse, Apr. 1958 (div. Apr. 1982); children: Fritz, Hans Wernher, Lisa Marie, Gretel Marga. BS in Chemistry, U. Nev., 1956; postgrad., U. Hawaii, Manoa, 1956-58. Cert. profl. chemist, indsl. hygienist, safety profl., hazard control mgr., bldg. insp. and mgmt. planner, biol. safety profl. Grad. teaching ast. in chemistry U. Hawaii, Honolulu, 1956-58; air pollution sampling sta. operator Truesdail Labs., Honolulu, 1957; chemist oceanographical research vessels Dept. Interior, 1957-59; with Bechtel-Hawaiian

Dredging, 1959; co-owner marine survey co. Honolulu, 1959-60; radiochemist Pearl Harbor (Hawaii) Naval Shipyard, 1959-62, indsl. hygienist med. dept., 1962-69, head indsl.hygiene br., 1969-72; indsl. hygiene program mgr. Naval Regional Med. Clinic, Pearl Harbor Naval Sta., 1972-78; pres., dir. lab. and indsl. hygiene, co-owner Indsl. Analytical Lab., Inc., Honolulu, 1978--; pres. F. Hertlein & Assocs., 1970-78; asst. clin. prof. U. Hawaii Sch. Pub. Health, 1973—. Contbr. articles to profl. jours. Named Outstanding Male Fed. Employee, Honolulu Fed. Exec. Council, 1967, Citizen of Day citation Sta. KGU76, Honolulu, 1972, cert. of achievement Toastmasters Internat., 1974, expression of appreciation U. Hawaii Sch. Pub. Health, 1985. Fellow Am. Inst. Chemists (life); mem. AAAS, Am. Acad. Indsl. Hygiene, Am. Chem. Soc., Am. Indsl. Hygiene Assn., Gesellschaft fü Aerosolforschung, Gesellschaft Deutscher Chemiker, Profl. Assn. Diving Instrs. (instr. emeritus), Tubists Universal Brotherhood Assn. (life). Home: 1493 Kaweloka St Pearl City HI 96782-1513 Office: Indsl Analytical Lab Inc 3615 Harding Ave Ste 305 Honolulu HI 96816-3759

HERTLING, G. H., Germanics educator; b. Pasadena, Calif., June 14, 1930; m. Darlene M. Hertling; children: Sonja, Dieter. BA, U. Calif., Berkeley, MA, PhD. From instr. to asst. prof. to assoc. prof. U. Wash., Seattle, 1961-74, prof., 1974—; mem. senate U. Wash., Seattle. Author books and articles on 18th, 19th and 20th century German lit. Mem. MLA, Am. Assn. Tchrs. German, Pacific Ancient and Modern Lang. Assn. (v.p. 1994, pres. 1995). Office: Dept Germanics U Wash Box 353130 Seattle WA 98195-3130

HERTNEKY, RANDY LEE, optometrist; b. Burlington, Colo., Jan. 9, 1955; s. Harry Francis and Darleen Mae (Walters) H.; m. Laura Ann Ciaccio, Nov. 28, 1981; children: Lisa Kay, Erin Elizabeth. BA, U. Colo., 1977; OD, So. Calif. Coll. Optometry, Fullerton, 1981. Pvt. practice optometry Yuma, Colo., 1982—. Precinct committeeman Yuma County Reps., 1986—; mem. bd. rev. Boy Scouts Am., Yuma, 1982—; chmn. Yuma High Sch. Bldg. Com., 1987-89; bd. dirs. Yuma Hosp. Found., 1990—; chmn. Yuma Sch. Curriculum Com., 1993. Mem. APHA, Colo. Optometric Assn. (trustee 1989-90), Lions (treas. 1987-88, pres. 1991-92, Lion of Yr. 1991-92), Coll. of Optometrists in Vision Devel. (assoc.), KC (sec. 1990—). Roman Catholic. Office: 107 S Main St Yuma CO 80759-1913

HERTWECK, ALMA LOUISE, sociology and child development educator; b. Moline, Ill., Feb. 6, 1937; d. Jacob Ray and Sylvia Ethel (Whitt) Street; m. E. Romayne Hertweck, Dec. 16, 1955; 1 child, William Scott. A.A., Mira Costa Coll., 1969; B.A. in Sociology summa cum laude, U. Calif.-San Diego, 1975, M.A., 1977, Ph.D., 1982. Cert. sociology instr., multiple subjects teaching credential grades kindergarten-12, Calif. Staff research assoc. U. Calif.-San Diego, 1978-81; instr. sociology Chapman Coll., Orange, Calif., 1982-87; instr. child devel. MiraCosta Coll., Oceanside, Calif., 1983-87, 88-89; instr. sociology U.S. Internat. U., San Diego, 1985-88 ; exec. dir., v.p. El Camino Preschools, Inc., Oceanside, 1985—. Author: Constructing the Truth and Consequences: Educators' Attributions of Perceived Failure in School, 1982; co-author: Handicapping the Handicapped, 1985. Mem. Am. Sociol. Assn., Am. Ednl. Research Assn., Nat. Council Family Relations, Nat. Assn. Edn. Young Children, Alpha Gamma Sigma (life). Avocations: foreign travel; sailing; bicycling. Home: 2024 Oceanview Rd Oceanside CA 92056-3104 Office: El Camino Preschs Inc 2002 California St Oceanside CA 92054-5673

HERTWECK, E. ROMAYNE, psychology educator; b. Springfield, Mo., July 24, 1928; s. Garnett Perry and Nova Gladys (Chowning) H.; m. Alma Louise Street, Dec. 16, 1955; 1 child, William Scott. BA, Augustana Coll., 1962; MA, Pepperdine U., 1963; EdD, Ariz. State U., 1966; PhD, U.S. Internat. U., 1978. Cert. sch. psychologist, Calif. Night editor Rock Island (Ill.) Argus Newspaper, 1961; grad. asst. psychology dept. Pepperdine Coll., L.A., 1962; counselor VA, Ariz. State U., Tempe, 1963; assoc. dir. Conciliation Ct., Phoenix, 1964; instr. Phoenix Coll., Phoenix, 1965; prof. Mira Costa Coll., Oceanside, Calif., 1966—, mem. senate coun., 1968-70, 85-87, 89-91, chmn. psychology-counseling dept., 1973-75, chmn. dept. behavioral sci., 1976-82, 87-88, 90-91; part-time lectr. dept. bus. adminstrn. San Diego State U., 1980-84, Sch. Human Behavior U.S. Internat. U., 1984-89; prof. psychology Chapman Coll. Mem. World Campus Afloat, 1970; pres. El Camino Preschs., Inc., Oceanside, Calif., 1985—. Bd. dirs. Lifeline, 1969, Christian Counseling Center, Oceanside, 1970-82; mem. City of Oceanside Childcare Task Force, 1991—; mem. City of Oceanside Community Rels. Commn., 1991—, vice chair, 1994; mem. steering com. Healthy Cities Project City of Oceanside, Calif., 1993—. Mem. Am., Western, North San Diego County (v.p. 1974-75) psychol. assns., Am. Assn. for Counseling and Devel., Nat. Educators Fellowship (v.p. El Camino chpt. 1976-77), Am. Coll. Personnel Assn., Phi Delta Kappa, Kappa Delta Pi, Psi Chi, Kiwanis (charter mem. Carlsbad club, dir. 1975-77). Home: 2024 Oceanview Rd Oceanside CA 92056-3104 Office: Mira Costa Coll PO Box 586312 Oceanside CA 92058-6312 also: El Camino Preschs Inc 2002 California St Oceanside CA 92054-5673

HERWIG, KARL ROBERT, physician; b. Phila., Nov. 12, 1935; s. Louis and Elizabeth Frances (Myers) H.; m. Barbara K. Bosscher, Oct. 26, 1963; children: Susan Elizabeth, K. Robert. BS, Ursinus Coll., 1957; MD, Jefferson Med. Coll., 1961. Diplomate Am. Bd. Urology. Intern U. Mich., Ann Arbor, 1961-62, resident gen. surgury, 1962-64; fellow Peter Sent Brigham Hosp., Boston, 1964; urology resident U. Mich., Ann Arbor, 1964-67; staff urologist U.S. Naval Medical Ctr., Bethesda, Md., 1967-69; urology faculty U. Mich., 1969-77; staff urologist Scripps Clinic, La Jolla, Calif., 1977—; instr., assoc. prof. U. Mich., 1969-77; urology div. head Scripps Clinic, 1977—, sr. cons., 1994; clinical assoc. prof. U. Calif., San Diego, 1977—. Contbr. articles to profl. jours. With U.S. Navy, 1967-69. Recipient Faculty Achievement award U. Mich., 1972. Fellow Am. Coll. Surgeons; mem. Am. Urological Assn., Cen. Surgical Soc., Am. Assn. Endocrine Surgeons, Collier Surgical Soc., Am. Med. Soc., Rotary. Republican. Presbyterian. Office: Scripps Clinic 10666 N Torrey Pines La Jolla CA 92037

HERZ, MICHAEL JOSEPH, marine environmental scientist; b. St. Paul, Aug. 12, 1936; s. Malvin E. and Josephine (Daneman) H.; m. Joan Klein Levy, Feb. 3, 1962 (div. 1982); children: David M., Daniel J., Ann K.; m. Naomi Brodie Schalit, Aug. 21, 1984; children: Nathaniel B., Hallie R. BA, Reed Coll., 1958; MA, San Francisco State U., 1962; PhD, U. So. Calif., 1966. Program coord. postdoctoral tng. program U. Calif., San Francisco, 1969-73, asst. prof., 1969-73, assoc. prof. in residence, 1973-74; exec. dir., dir. water quality tng. program San Francisco Bay. chpt. Oceanic Soc., 1974-77; nat. exec. v.p., nat. co-dir. rsch. and policy Oceanic Soc., San Francisco, 1977-84; sr. rsch. scientist San Francisco State U., 1984-88; exec. dir. and baykeeper San Francisco Bay-Delta Preservation Assn., 1989-95; pvt. cons. Alna, Maine, 1995—; chmn. bd. govs. Tiburon Ctr. Environ. Studies, San Francisco State U., 1985-86; NRC com. mem. Effectiveness of Oil Spill Disperants, Washington, 1985-87; mem. com. on ocean disposal of radwaste Calif. Dept. Health, Sacramento, 1985-92; mem. tech. adv. com. Calif. Office of Oil Spill Prevention and Response, 1992-95; bd. dirs. Friends of the Earth, Washington, 1989—, Aquatic Habitat Inst., 1986-89; mem. Alaska Oil Spill Commn., 1989-90. Author, co-editor: (books) Memory Consolidation, 1972, Habituation I & II, 1973; contbr. reports to profl. publs. Chmn. community adv. bd. Sta. KQED (Pub. Broadcast System affiliate), 1979-85, San Francisco, citizens adv. com. San Francisco Bay Conservation and Devel. Commn., 1979—, chmn. 1984; mem. tech. adv. com. San Francisco Bay Regional Water Quality Control Bd., Oakland, Calif., 1979-82, Assn. Bay Area Govts., Oakland, 1983-84; mem. bay area adv. com. Sea Grant Marine Adv. Program, San Francisco, 1983-89; mem. com. Bur. Land Mgmt., Pacific States Regional Tech. Working Group, 1979-83. Served with U.S. Army, 1958-59. Predoctoral fellow NIMH, U. So. Calif., 1963-64; postdoctoral fellow NIMH, UCLA Brain Research Inst., 1966-68. Mem. AAAS, Calif. Acad. Scis., San Francisco Bay and Estuarine Assn., San Francisco Oceanic Soc., Oceanic Soc. (bd. dirs. 1984-89), Sigma Xi. Home and Office: PO Box 274 Alna ME 04535-0274

HERZBERG, DOROTHY CREWS, middle school educator; b. N.Y.C., July 8, 1935; d. Floyd Houston and Julia (Lesser) Crews; m. Hershel Zelig Herzberg, May 22, 1962 (div. Apr. 1988); children: Samuel Floyd, Laura Jill, Daniel Crews. AB, Brown U., 1957; MA, Stanford U., 1964; JD, San Francisco Law Sch., 1976. Legal sec. various law firms, San Francisco, 1976-78; tchr. Mission Adult Sch., San Francisco, 1965-66; tchr. secondary and univ. levels Peace Corps, Nigeria, 1961-63; investigator Office of Dist. Atty., San Francisco, 1978-80; sr. adminstr. Dean Witter Reynolds Co., San Francisco, 1980-83; registered rep. Waddell and Reed, 1983-84; fin. services rep. United Resources, Hayward, Calif., 1984-86; tax preparer H&R Block, 1987; revenue officer IRS, 1987-89; now tchr. ESL, West Contra Costa Sch. Dist., El Cerrito, Calif., 1989—. Editor: (newsletters) Coop. Nursery Sch. Council, 1969-71, Miraloma Life, 1976-82, Dem. Women's Forum, 1980-81, Stanford Luncheon Club, 1984-85. Bd. dirs. LWV, San Francisco, 1967-69, mem. speakers bur., 1967-80; pres. Council Coop. Nursery Schs., San Francisco, 1969-71; bd. dirs. Miraloma (Calif.) Improvement Club, 1977-88, pres., 1980-81; alt. for supr. San Francisco Mayor's Commn. on Criminal Justice, 1978. Democrat. Unitarian. Home: 1006 Richmond St El Cerrito CA 94530-2616

HERZBERG, GERHARD, physicist; b. Hamburg, Germany, Dec. 25, 1904; emigrated to Can., 1935, naturalized, 1945; s. Albin and Ella (Biber) H.; m. Luise H. Oettinger, Dec. 29, 1929 (dec.); children: Paul Albin, Agnes Margaret; m. Monika Tenthoff, Mar. 21, 1972. Dr. Ing., Darmstadt Inst. Tech., 1928; postgrad., U. Goettingen, U. Bristol, 1928-30; D.Sc. hon causa, Oxford U., 1960; D.Sc., U. Chgo., 1967, Drexel U., 1972, U. Montreal, 1972, U. Sherbrooke, 1972, McGill U., 1972, Cambridge U., 1972, U. Man., 1973, Andhra U., 1975, Osmania U., 1976, U. Delhi, 1976, U. Bristol, 1975, U. Western Ont., 1976; Fil. Hed. Dr., U. Stockholm, 1966; Ph.D. (hon.), Weizmann Inst. Sci., 1976, U. Toledo, 1984; LL.D., St. Francis Xavier U., 1972, Simon Fraser U., 1972; Dr. phil. nat., U. Frankfurt, 1983, others. Lectr., chief asst. physics Darmstadt Inst. Tech., 1930-35; research prof. physics U. Sask., Saskatoon, 1935-45; prof. spectroscopy Yerkes Obs., U. Chgo., 1945-48; prin. research officer NRC Can., Ottawa, 1948, dir. div. pure physics, 1949-69, disting. research scientist, 1969-94, emeritus; Bakerian lectr. Royal Soc. London, 1960; holder Francqui chair U. Liege, 1960. Author books including: Spectra of Diatomic Molecules, 1950; Electronic Spectra and Electronic Structure of Polyatomic Molecules, 1966, The Spectra and Structures of Simple Free Radicals, 1971, (with K.P. Huber) Constants of Diatomic Molecules, 1979. Appt. to Queen's Privy Coun. for Can., 1992. Recipient Faraday medal Chem. Soc. London, 1970, Nobel prize in Chemistry, 1971; named companion Order of Can., 1968, academician Pontifical Acad. Scis., 1964. Fellow Royal Soc. London (Royal medal 1971), Royal Soc. Can. (pres. 1966, Henry Marshall Tory medal 1953), Hungarian Acad. Sci. (hon.), Indian Acad. Scis. (hon.), Am. Phys. Soc. (Earle K. Plyler prize 1985), Chem. Inst. Can.; mem. Internat. Union Pure and Applied Physics (past v.p.), Am. Acad. Arts and Scis. (hon. fgn. mem.), Am. Chem. Soc. (Willard Gibbs medal 1969, Centennial fgn. fellow 1976), Nat. Acad. Sci. India, Indian Phys. Soc. (hon.), Japan Acad. (hon.), Chem. Soc. Japan (hon.), Royal Swedish Acad. Scis. (fgn., physics sect.), Nat. Acad. Sci. (fgn. assoc.), Faraday Soc., Am. Astron. Soc., Can. Assn. Physicists (past pres., Achievement award 1957), Optical Soc. Am. (hon., Frederic Ives medal 1964). Home: 190 Lakeway Dr Rockcliffe Pk, Ottawa, ON Canada K1L 5B3 Office: Nat Rsch Coun, Ottawa, ON Canada K1A 0R6

HERZER, RICHARD KIMBALL, franchising company executive; b. Ogden, Utah, June 2, 1931; s. Arthur Vernon and Dorothy (Cortez) H.; m. Phyllis Ann McCullough, Mar. 29, 1958; children: Diane E., Mark V., Craig K. BS, UCLA, 1958. Vice-pres., contr. United Rent All, Inc., L.A., 1967-71; dir. fin. planning Internat. Industries Inc., North Hollywood, Calif., 1971-73, v.p., controller, 1973-75, v.p. fin., 1975-79, pres., 1979—, chmn. bd., CEO, 1983—; bd. dirs. IHOP Corp., 1979—. Trustee So. Calif. chpt. Multiple Sclerosis, 1984—. 1st lt. U.S. Army, 1953-56. Mem. Calif. Restaurant Assn. (dir. 1985-94), Phi Delta Theta. Republican. Home: 4411 Woodleigh Ln La Canada Flintridge CA 91011-3542 Office: IHOP Corp 525 N Brand Blvd Glendale CA 91203-1903

HERZING, ALFRED ROY, computer executive; b. Kitchener, Ont., Can., June 23, 1958; naturalized, 1982; s. Alfred Georg and Kaethe (Binder) H.; m. Marjorie, Aug. 20, 1983; 1 child, Adam. BSEE, Calif. Poly. Inst., 1981. Telecom. engr. Union Oil Co., L.A., 1982-84; computer planning analyst Union Oil-UNOCAL, 1984-86; supr. facilities mgmt. UNOCAL Corp. Info. Svcs., Anaheim, Calif., 1986-89, bus analyst, 1989, mgr. planning and analysis, 1989-91, mgr. tech. & bus. assessment, 1991—; speaker ENTELEC, Dallas, San Antonio, 1983, 85. Host athletic tournament Alfred Roy Herzing Invitational Frisbee Golf Tournament, 1980—. Mem. IEEE, Toastmasters (L.A. chpt. pres. 1986-87, gov. area 12 1987-88, arminstrv. lt. gov. dist. 52 1988-89, ednl. lt. gov. dist. 52 1989-90, dist. gov. 1990-91, Toastmaster of Yr. 1990, region II conf. edn. presenter 1992, 93, chmn. dist. 52 1992-93, 93-94, pres. speakers forum club 1993-94, CTM/ATY.DTM chmn. founder's dist. 1993-94, 94-95), Yorba Linda Achievers Club (charter mem., pres. 1993-94). Republican. Home: 20365 Via La Vieja Yorba Linda CA 92687-3211 Office: UNOCAL 5460 E La Palma Ave Anaheim CA 92807-2074

HERZOG, WHITEY (DORREL NORMAN ELVERT HERZOG), former professional baseball team executive; b. New Athens, Ill., Nov. 9, 1931. Infielder, outfielder Washington Senators, 1956-58, Kansas City Athletics, 1958-60, Balt. Orioles, 1961-62, Detroit Tigers, 1963; scout Kansas City Athletics, 1964, coach, 1965; coach N.Y. Mets, 1966, dir. player devel., 1967-72; mgr. Tex. Rangers, 1973; coach Calif. Angels, 1974-75, interim mgr., 1974; mgr. Kansas City Royals, 1975-79; mgr. St. Louis Cardinals, 1980-90, v.p., 1990; sr. v.p., dir. player pers. Calif. Angels, 1991-94; retired, 1994. Named Sporting News Man of Yr., 1982, Nat. League Mgr. of Yr., 1982, 85, 87, A.L. Mgr. of Yr., 1976, UPI Exec. of Yr., 1981-82.

HESS, ANN MARIE, systems specialist, electronic data processing specialist; b. Grants Pass, Oreg., Mar. 29, 1944; d. Wilbur Lill and Esther Elaine Groner; m. William Charles Hess, July 25, 1969; children: David William, William Albert. BSEE, BS in Math., Oregon State U., 1968. Engr. Lawrence Livermore Lab., Livermore, Calif., 1968-69; mgr., owner RBR Scales, Inc., Anaheim, Calif., 1969-84; lead engr. Rockwell Internat., Seal Beach, Calif., 1984-86, '87-88; software engr. Hughes Aircraft Co., Fullerton, Calif., 1986-87; sr. engr. Logican Eagle Tech., Inc., Eatontown, N.J., 1988-91; owner Holistic Eclectic Software Svc., Orange, Calif., 1991-93; database adminstr. Jacobs Engring Group, 1993—. Active Calif. Master Chorale, Santa Ana, 1990-92. Mem. IEEE, Am. Soc. Quality Control, Phi Kappa Phi, Eta Kappa Nu, Tau Beta Pi. Lutheran. Office: JEG/PEP 251 S Lake Ave Pasadena CA 91101-3003

HESS, CATHERINE MARY, museum curator; b. L.A., Mar. 27, 1957; d. Harry Joseph and Myrtle (Klein) H.; m. Laurence Bradley Frank, Dec. 31, 1988; 1 child, Julian Guthrie. BA, UCLA, 1979, MA cum laude, 1983. Curatorial asst. J. Paul Getty Mus., Malibu, Calif., 1984-86, asst. curator, 1987-90, assoc. curator, 1991—; guest lectr. L.A. County Mus. Art, 1987, 90, 94, Calif. State U., Long Beach, 1990, George R. Gardiner Mus., Toronto, Ont., Can., 1988, 89, Pescara, Italy, 1989, San Diego Mus. Art, 1994, St. Louis Art Mus., 1994. Author: Italian Maiolica: Catalogue of the Collections J. Paul Getty Museum, Malibu, 1988; co-author: Looking at European Ceramics 1400-1900, 1993, Decorative Arts: An Illustrated Summary Catalogue J. Paul Getty Museum, Malibu, 1993. Office: J Paul Getty Museum 17985 Pacific Coast Hwy Malibu CA 90265-5708

HESS, CHARLES EDWARD, environmental horticulture educator; b. Paterson, N.J., Dec. 20, 1931; s. Cornelius W. M. and Alice (Debruyn) H.; children: Mary, Carol, Nancy, John, Peter; m. Eva G. Carroad, Feb. 14, 1981. BS, Rutgers U., 1953; MS, Cornell U., 1954, PhD, 1957; DAgr (hon.), Purdue U., 1983; DSc (hon.), Delaware Valley Coll., Doylestown, Pa., 1992. Asst. prof. Purdue U., West Lafayette, Ind., 1958-61, assoc. prof., 1962-64, prof., 1965; rsch. prof., dept. chmn. Rutgers U., New Brunswick, N.J., 1966, assoc. dean, dir. N.J. Agrl. Exptl. Sta., 1970, acting dean Coll. Agrl. and Environ. Sci., 1971, dean Cook Coll., 1972-75; assoc. dir. Calif. Agrl. Exptl. Sta., 1975-89; asst. sec. sci. and edn. USDA, Washington, 1989-91; dean Coll. Agrl. and Environ. Scis. U. Calif., Davis, 1975-89, prof. dept. environ. horticulture, 1991—, dir. internat. programs Coll. Agrl. and Environ. Scis., 1992—; cons. U.S. AID, 1965, Office Tech. Assessment, U.S. Congress, 1976-77; chmn. study team world food and nutrition study NAS, 1976; mem. Calif. State Bd. Food and Agriculture, 1984-89; mem. Nat. Sci. Bd., 1982-88, 92—, vice chmn., 1984-88; co-chmn. Joint Coun. USDA, 1987-91; bd. dirs. Asian Vegetable R & D Ctr., Taiwan. Mem. West Lafayette Sch. Bd., Ind., 1963-65, sec., 1963, pres., 1964; mem. Gov.'s Commn. Blueprint for Agr., 1971-73; bd. dirs. Davis Sci. Ctr., 1992-94; trustee Internat. Svc. for Nat. Agrl. Rsch., The Hague, Netherlands, 1992—. Served with AUS, 1956-58. Mem. U.S. EPA (biotechnology sci. adv. com. 1992—), AAAS (chmn. agriculture sect. 1989-90), Am. Soc. Hort. Sci. (pres. 1973), Internat. Plant Propagators Soc. (pres. 1973), Agrl. Research Inst., Phi Beta Kappa, Sigma Xi, Alpha Zeta, Phi Kappa Phi. Office: U Calif Coll Agrl & Environ Scis Dept Environ Horticulture Davis CA 95616

HESS, DOROTHY HALDEMAN, college official; b. Bareville, Pa., July 2, 1941; d. Titus Myer and Anna Mae (Haldeman) H. BA, Elizabethtown Coll., 1965. Tchr. French and German, Millville (N.J.) Jr. High Sch., 1965-67; tchr., dir. Full Day Head Start, Lancaster, Pa., 1967-72; ednl. cons. and trainer Day Care Ctrs. Inc., Harrisburg, Pa., 1972-74; supr. database Architectron Ltd., Newport Beach, Calif., 1980-83; info. specialist Woodbury U., L.A., 1983-85; asst. dir. adminstrv. computing Scripps Coll., Claremont, Calif., 1985-87, dir. info. systems and computing, 1987—. Contbg. author: CWIS and Networks, 1992, Administrative Systems, 1993. Mem. Internat. POISE Users Group Inc. (founding, bd. dirs. 1987-91, pres.-elect 1992-93, pres. 1993-94), Assn. for Mgmt. of Info. in Higher Edn. (speaker 1991), Inst. for Ednl. Computing. Office: Scripps Coll 1030 Columbia Ave Claremont CA 91711-3905

HESS, FREDERICK SCOTT, artist; b. Balt., July 12, 1955; s. Charles Stevens and Katherine Ruth Hess; m. Gita Tabatabai, Dec. 28, 1989; 1 child, Ava Katarina. BS, U. Wis., 1977; postgrad., Vienna Acad. Fine Art, 1979-84. artist in residence Bahman Cultural House, Tehran, Iran, 1992, Cité Internat. des Arts, Paris, 1993. Solo exhibitions include Gallery Herzog, Vienna, Austria, 1979, Galerie im Tabak Museum, Vienna, Austria, 1982, Ousey Gallery, L.A., Calif., 1985, 86, 88, 89, 90, 92, 94, U. So. Calif. Fisher Art Gallery, 1987-88, Santa Clara U. de Saisset Mus., Santa Clara, Calif., 1987-88, Mt. San Jacinto Coll., San Jacinto, Calif., 1989, Fresno Art Mus., Fresno, Calif., 1991, Underground Exhibition, Tehran, Iran, 1993; exhibited in group shows at Taipei (Taiwan) Fine Arts Mus., 1987, U. So. Calif., L.A., 1987-88, Laguna Art Mus., Laguna Beach, Calif., 1988, Henry Art Gallery, U. Washington, Seattle, 1988, Fresno (Calif.) Art Mus., 1988-89, Flint (Mich.) Inst. Art, 1991, San Diego Mus. Art, 1991, Triton Mus., Santa Clara, Calif., 1992, Oakland (Calif.) Mus., 1992. Recipient Theodor Koerner award Austrian Min. Culture, Vienna, 1981, WESTAF award Nat. Endowment for the Arts, 1990; fellow J. Paul Getty Trust, 1991, Nat. Endowment for the Arts, 1991. Mem. The Artists' Group.

HESS, HELEN ELIZABETH, retired secondary school educator, musician; b. Elkader, Iowa, Feb. 22, 1930; d. James Dale and Helen Louise (Wahl) Welsch; m. Roger Merle Hess, Dec. 18, 1966. BA, U. So. Miss., 1952, MA, 1955. Tchr. Natchez (Miss.) Pub. Schs., 1952-54; tchr. Bakersfield (Calif.) City Schs., 1955-89, ret., 1989; staff mem. Bakersfield Symphony Orch., 1989—. Life mem. Washington Jr. H.S.; mem. Assistance League Bakersfield, 1990—, active in resource devel.; bd. dirs. Bakersfield Masterworks Chorale; pres. area ballroom dance club. Named Outstanding Classroom Tchr., Bakersfield Rotary Club, 1970. Mem. Local and State Ret. Tchrs. Assn. Republican. Presbyterian. Office: Bakersfield Symphony Orch 1401 19th St Ste 130 Bakersfield CA 93301-4400

HESS, IVAN EDWARD, set designer, educator; b. Pasadena, Calif., Aug. 3, 1945; s. Robert Edward and Virginia (Yerxa) H.; div.; 1 child, Jedediah Nathaniel. BA, Calif. State U., Hayward, 1967; MFA in Theatrical Design, Stanford U., 1971; postgrad. spl. masters class J. Svoboda, San Francisco, 1973; postgrad., Lindisfarne Inst., N.Y.C., 1977-82. Designer, tech. dir. Hayward (Calif.) Cmty. Theatre, 1965; staff tech. dir. Mills Coll., 1967-68; designer, tech. dir. Calif. Theatre Arts, 1969; designer, instr. Calif. State U., Hayward, 1970; assoc. prof., designer Humboldt State U., Arcata, Calif., 1971-78, 80-81; prof., designer Humboldt State U., Arcata, 1983—; substitute instr. San Joes State U., 1968, part time designer Calif. State U., Hayward, 1964-67; designer Oakland Repertory Theatre, 1968. San Mateo (Calif.) Light Opera, 1968, Santa Rosa Repertory Theatre, 1978; vis. artist, Tufts U., Boston, 1978-80, faculty, site architect, Lindiafarne Inst., 1981-82; prof., designer London U. Goldsmiths, 1982-83; instr., designer Hartnell Coll., 1990, Cypress Coll., 1990-91; cons. Minor Theatre, 1988-93, Pier Two, San Francisco, 1987, other Ednl. theatres. Set designs include Son of the Wilderness, Caucasion Chalk Circle, Penny for a Song, The Physicist, Caligula, The Magic Hand, Marat/Sade, Ballad of an Outcast, The Time of Your Life, What the Butler Saw, Il Travotore, Blythe Spirit, Beaux Strategem, Cyrano de Bergerac, Flea in her Ear, Rimers of Eldritch, The Tooth of Crime, The Ghost Sonata, Vanities, Good Woman of Szechuan, Too True To Be Good, Vinegar Tom, The Bacchae, The Road Not Taken, Annie Get Your Gun, Hair, Two Sisters on the Old Road, One Man's Hero, Mr & Mrs Coffee, Echo Location, Song of Hydrogen, Schwyek in the Second World War, I, Lionel, Sheetrock and the Piano Tuner, Architect and the Emperor of Assyria, Taking Leave, Heidi Chronicles; tech. dir. The Hostage, Arms and the Man, The Visit, A Little Night Music, Cabaret; lighting design Chopin in Space. Mem. AAUP, U.S. Inst. Theatre Tech., Calif. State Employees Assn., Lindisfarne Assn., Western Mining Coun., Calif. Faculty Assn., Am. Coll. Theatre Festival (chmn. region XIII, past regional chair Kennedy Ctr.), New Dramatists (N.Y.C.), Calif. Ednl. Theatre Assn., Assn. for Theatre in Higher Edn., Calif. Ednl. Theatre Assn., Am. Theatre in Higher Edn. Home: 1190 Tilley Ct Arcata CA 95521-6720 Office: Humboldt State U Theatre Arts Dept Arcata CA 95521

HESS, RICHARD NEAL, plastic surgeon; b. Phila., June 16, 1957. MD, U. Ariz., 1983. Chmn. plastic surgery Northwest Hosp., Tucson. Office: Aesthetic Surg of Tucson 5585 N Oracle Rd Tucson AZ 85704-3821*

HESS, ROBERT, JR., ambulance service executive; b. East Cleveland, Ohio, Oct. 22, 1957; s. Robert and Patricia Lou Hess; m. Susan Hole, Jan. 28, 1983; children: Christine Renee, Robert III, Jessica Marie. Student Cuyahoga C.C., 1977-78; MBA Case Western Reserve U., 1992. With Physician's Ambulance Svc., South Euclid, 1972-94, v.p. in charge fin., data processing, med. assurance, 1978-86, sr. v.p., COO, 1986-94; pres., CEO PhysMed, Inc., Inc., South Euclid, Ohio, 1986-94; sr. v.p., COO Physician's/Medic Transport, Inc., Columbus, Ohio, 1990-94; EMS project mgr. Rural/Metro Corp., Scottsdale, Ariz., 1994—; bd. dirs. Hess Enterprises, Inc.; adj. faculty Cuyahoga C.C., vice chmn. Emergency Med. Technician Tng. Dept., 1986-90, mem. paramedic admissions com. Dir. rsch. U.S. Emergency Med. Technician Assn., 1981. Instr. advanced cardiac life support Am. Heart Assn., 1981-88; mem. Ohio Bd. Regents Paramedic Adv. Com., 1980-86; alternate mem. emergency med. svc. adv. com. Ohio Bd. Edn., 1986-92; mem. United Way Cleve., eagle com., 1987; paramedic adv. coun. Hillcrest Hosp.; mem. Ohio EMS Bd Ohio Dept. Edn., 1986-88; bd. dir. Commn. on Accreditation of Ambulance Svcs., 1990—, vice chair, 1990-94; mem. golf tournament com. March of Dimes, 1990-94; bd. dirs. March of Dimes Birth Defects Found., No. Ohio Chpt., 1993-94, chmn. campaign com. March of Dimes Metro Divsn., 1993-94; mem. exec. com. March of Dimes, 1993-94; mem. Ohio Ambulance Assn. (pres. 1981-82, trustee 1980-81, chmn. govtl. affairs com. 1985-87), Am. Ambulance Assn. (dir. 1980-83, 90-94, fin. com. 1987, govtl. affairs com., accreditation com., bd. dirs. 1990—, vice chmn. industry image com. 1993—), Am. Ambulance Assn. Found. (exec. dir.), Nat. Assn. Emergency Med. Technicians, Ohio Assn. Emergency Med. Services. Republican. Roman Catholic. Office: 8401 E Indian School Rd Scottsdale AZ 85251-2855

HESSE, CHRISTIAN AUGUST, mining and tunneling industries consultant; b. Chemnitz, Germany, June 20, 1925; s. William Albert and Anna Gunhilda (Baumann) H.; B. Applied Sci. with honors, U. Toronto (Ont., Can.), 1948; m. Brenda Nora Rigby, Nov. 4, 1964; children: Rob Christian, Bruce William. Registered profl. engr., Can.; chartered engr., U.K. In various mining and constrn. positions, Can., 1944-61; jr. shift boss N.J. Zinc Co., Gilman, Colo., 1949; asst. layout engr. Internat. Nickel Co., Sudbury, Ont., 1949-52; shaft and tunnel engr. Perini-Walsh Joint Venture, Niagara Falls, Ont., 1952-54; constrn. project engr. B. Perini & Sons (Can.) Ltd., Toronto, Ottawa, and New Brunswick, 1954-55; field engr. Aries Copper Mines Ltd., No. Ont., 1955-56; instr. in mining engring. U. Toronto, 1956-57; planning engr. Stanleigh Uranium Mining Corp. Ltd., Elliot Lake, Ont., 1957-58, chief engr., 1959-60; subway field engr. Johnson-Perini-Kiewit Joint Venture, Toronto, 1960-61; del. Commonwealth Mining Congress, Africa, 1961; with U.S. Borax & Chem. Corp., 1961-90; mng. dir. Yorkshire Potash, Ltd., London, 1970-71, gen. mgr., pres. Allan Potash Mines Ltd., Allan, Sask., Can., 1974, chief engr. U.S. Borax & Chem. Corp., L.A., 1974-77, v.p.

engring., 1978-81, 87-90, v.p. and project mgr. Quartz Hill molybdenum project, 1981-90; v.p. Pacific Coast Molybdenum Co., 1981-90, v.p. mining devel., 1984-90. Sault Daily Star scholar, Sault Sainte Marie, Ont., Can., 1944. Fellow Inst. Mining and Metallurgy; mem. SME/AIME (chmn. So. Calif. mining sect. 1994-95), Can. Inst. Mining and Metallurgy (life), Assn. Profl. Engrs. Ont., Prospectors and Developers Assn., N.W. Mining Assn., Alaska Miners Assn., L.A. Tennis Club. Lutheran.

HESSLER, CURTIS ALAN, newspaper publishing company executive; b. Berwyn, Ill., Dec. 27, 1943; s. Robert A. and Ruth T. (Teeter) H.; m. Christine Mary Cocker, Dec. 14, 1968; children: Alexander, Francesca. BA, Harvard U., 1966; postgrad. (Rhodes scholar), Oxford U., 1966-69; JD, Yale U., 1973; MA in Econs, U. Calif., Berkeley, 1976. Exec. asst. to Sec. Treasury, Dept. Treasury, Washington, 1977-79, asst. sec. for econ. policy, 1980; assoc. dir. Office Budget and Mgmt., Washington, 1979; ptnr. Paul Weiss Rifkind Wharton & Garrison, 1981-82; exec. v.p. Sears World Trade, Inc., 1982-84; exec. Unisys Corp., 1985-90; exec. v.p. Times-Mirror Co., 1991—. Home: 570 Bradford St Pasadena CA 91105-2409 Office: The Times Mirror Co 220 W 1st St Los Angeles CA 90012*

HESTER, RANDOLPH THOMPSON, JR., landscape architect, educator; b. Danville, Va., Dec. 12, 1944; s. Randolph Thompson and Virginia (Green) H.; m. Marcia Jeanne McNally, Mar. 17, 1983; 1 child, Nathaniel Christopher. BA, N.C. State U., 1969, BS in Landscape Architecture, 1968; M in Landscape Architecture, Harvard U., 1969. Registered landscape architect, N.C. Prof. Pa. State U., State Coll., 1969-70; prof. N.C. State U., Raleigh, 1970-80, city univ. coord., 1972-75; prof. U. Calif., Berkeley, 1981—, chmn. dept. landscape architecture, 1987-92; assoc. dir. Ctr. Environ. Design Rsch., Berkeley, 1982-85; designer community devel. sect., Cambridge, Mass., 1969-72. Author: Rural Housing Site Planning, 1974 (award 1975), Neighborhood Space, 1975 (Am. Soc. Landscape Architects. Merit award 1986), Community Goal Setting, 1982, Planning Neighborhood Space with People, 1984, The Meaning of Gardens, 1990, Community Design Primer, 1990; founder planning process Goals for Raleigh , 1972-76 (All Am. City award 1976); designer urban wilderness Runyon Canyon, 1986 (Am. Soc. Landscape Architect Honor award 1987); mem. editorial bd. Places mag., 1985—. Chmn. Five Points Citizens Adv., Coun., Raleigh, 1973, Georgetown-Roanoke Neighborhood Assn., Raleigh, 1979; councilman City of Raleigh, 1975-77; commr. Parks and Recreation Bd., Berkeley, 1982-86; bd. dirs. Ctr. for Environ. Change, 1985—; trustee Small Town Inst., 1988—. Recipient Outstanding Extension Svc. award N.C. State U., 1974, Virginia Dare award City of Manteo, N.C., 1981. Mem. Am. Soc. Landscape Architects (Nat. Merit award 1976, Nat. Honor award 1984, Honor award 1991, numerous other awards). Democrat. Methodist. Office: U Calif Dept Landscape Architecture 202 Wurster Hall Berkeley CA 94720

HETLAND, JOHN ROBERT, lawyer, educator; b. Mpls., Mar. 12, 1930; s. James L. and Evelyn (Lundgren) H.; m. Mildred Woodruff, Dec. 1951 (div.); children: Lynda Lee Catlin, Robert John, Debra Ann Allen; m. Anne Kneeland, Dec. 1972; children: Robin T., Willcox, Elizabeth J. Pickett. B.S.L., U. Minn., 1952, J.D., 1956. Bar: Minn. 1956, Calif. 1962, U.S. Supreme Ct, 1981. Practice law Mpls., 1956-59; assoc. prof. law U. Calif., Berkeley, 1959-60, prof., 1960—; prin. Hetland & Kneeland, PC, Berkeley, 1959—; vis. prof. law Stanford U., 1971, 80, U. Singapore, 1972, U. Cologne, Fed. Republic Germany, 1988. Author: California Real Property Secured Transactions, 1970, Commercial Real Estate Transactions, 1972, Secured Real Estate Transactions, 1974, 1977; co-author: California Cases on Security Transactions in Land, 2d edit., 1975, 3d edit., 1984, 4th edit., 1992; contbr. articles to legal, real estate and fin. jours. Served to lt. comdr. USNR, 1953-55. Fellow Am. Coll. Real Estate Lawyers, Am. Coll. Mortgage Attys., Am. Bar Found.; mem. ABA, State Bar Calif., State Bar Minn., Order of Coif, Phi Delta Phi. Home: 20 Red Coach Ln Orinda CA 94563-1112 Office: 2600 Warring St Berkeley CA 94704-3415

HETT, JOAN MARGARET, civic administrator; b. Trail, B.C., Can., Sept. 8, 1936; s. Gordon Stanley and Violet Thora (Thors) Hett; B.Sc., U. Victoria (B.C., Can.), 1964; M.S., U. Wis., Madison, 1967, Ph.D., 1969. Ecologist, Eastern Deciduous Forest Biome, Oak Ridge Nat. Lab., 1969-72; coor. sites dir. Coniferous Forest Biome, Oreg. State U., Corvallis and U. Wash., Seattle, 1972-77; ecol. cons., Seattle, 1978-84; plant ecologist Seattle City Light, 1984-86; supr. Rights-of-Way, Seattle City Light, 1986-91, vegetation mgmt. mgr., Seattle City Light, 1991—. Mem. Ecol. Soc. Am., Brit. Ecol. Soc., Am. Inst. Biol. Scis., Am. Forestry Assn., Sigma Xi. Contbr. articles to profl. jours.; research in plant population dynamics, land use planning, forest sucession.

HETTER, GREGORY PAULSON, plastic surgeon; b. Lakehurst, N.J., Sept. 8, 1936. MD, U. Wash., 1963. Plastic surgeon Sunrise Hosp., Las Vegas; clin. asst. prof. plastic surgery U. Nev. Office: Rocky Mountain Soc Pl Recon 3017 W Charleston Blvd Ste 80 Las Vegas NV 89102-1928*

HETZEL, FREDRICK WILLIAM, biophysicist, educator; b. Toronto, June 28, 1946; came to U.S., 1974; BS, U. Waterloo, Ont., Can., 1970, MS, 1971, PhD, 1974; JD, Wayne State U., 1994. Sr. CA rsch. scientist Radiation Med. Dept. Div. Radiology, Buffalo, N.Y., 1976-78; asst. prof. Biophysics Dept. SUNY, Buffalo, N.Y., 1977-78; rsch. prof. Grad. Div. Niagra (N.Y.) U., 1978; sr. radiation biologist Therapeutic Radiology, Henry Ford Hosp., Detroit, 1978-82; adjunct asst. prof. Biology Dept. Wayne State U., Detroit, 1979-85; clin. assoc. prof. Physics Dept. Oakland U., Rochester, Mich., 1982-85; assoc. prof. Physics Dept. Oakland U., Rochester, 1985-87; dir. radiobiology Neurology Dept. Henry Ford Hosp., Detroit, 1982-90; prof. Physics Oakland U., Rochester, Mich., 1987-93, dir. radiation oncology rsch., 1991-93; dir. R & D Presbyn./St. Luke's Med. Ctr., Denver, 1993—; co-organizer, guest faculty Hyperthermia and Cancer Therapy, Seattle, 1984, Madison, Wis., 1985, Durham, N.C., 1987; profl. cons. hyperthermia FDA Regulations, Protocol Design, 1986; mem. med. staff bylaws com. Henry Ford Hosp., 1989; mem. radiation study sect. DHHS/NIH/DRG, 1989-93. Assoc. editor: Radiation Rsch., 1987-91. Grantee NIH, 1979-88, 86-90 (2), 87-90, 92—. Mem. N.Am. Hyperthermia Group (memberhsip com. 1987-88, sec.-treas. 1989-91), Am. Assn. Physicians in Medicine (chmn. task group), Am. Soc. Clin. Oncology, Am. Coll. Med. Physics. Home: 1969 Monaco Pky Denver CO 80220-1647 Office: Presbyn/St Luke's Med Ctr Dept Rsch Develop 1850 High St Denver CO 80218-1308

HEUMAN, DONNA RENA, lawyer; b. Seattle, May 27, 1949; d. Russell George and Edna Inez (Armstrong) H. BA in Psychology, UCLA, 1972; JD, U. Calif., San Francisco, 1985. Cert. shorthand reporter, 1978—; owner, Heuman & Assocs., San Francisco, 1978-86; real estate broker, Calif., 1990—. Mem. Hastings Internat. and Comparative Law Rev., 1984-85; bd. dirs. Saddleback, 1987-89. Jessup Internat. Moot Ct. Competition, 1985, N. Fair Oaks Mcpl. Adv. Coun., vice chair, sec., 1993-95. Mem. ABA, NAFE, ATLA, Nat. Shorthand Reporters Assn., Women Entrepreneurs, Calif. Shorthand Reporters Assn., Calif. State Bar Assn., Nat. Mus. of Women in the Arts, Calif. Lawyers for the Arts, San Francisco Bar Assn., Commonwealth Club, World Affairs Coun., Zonta (bd. dirs.). Home: 750 18th Ave Menlo Park CA 94025-2018 Office: Superior Ct Calif Hall Of Justice Redwood City CA 94063

HEUSCHELE, WERNER PAUL, veterinary researcher; b. Ludwigsburg, Federal Republic of Germany, Aug. 28, 1929; came to U.S., 1932, naturalized, 1951; s. Karl August and Margarete Anna (Wagner) H.; m. Carolyn Rene Bredeson, Jan. 1, 1983; children: Eric W.K., Mark R. (dec.), Jennifer M. Student, San Diego State Coll., 1947-50; BA in Zoology, U. Calif., Davis, 1952, DVM, 1956; student, NIH, Bethesda, Md., 1966; PhD in Med. Microbiology, Virology, Immunology, U. Wis., 1969. Diplomate Am. Coll. Vet. Microbiologists, Am. Coll. Zoological Medicine. Mgr. veterinary hosp. Zool. Soc. San Diego, 1956-61, head, microbiology/virology, 1981-86, dir. research, 1986—; research veterinarian Plum Island Animal Disease Lab., Orient Point, N.Y., 1961-70; tng. resident in vet. pathology Armed Forces Inst. Pathology, Washington, 1965-66; assoc. prof. infectious disease Kansas State U., Manhattan, 1970-71; head, virology, research and devel. Jensen-Salsbery Labs., Kansas City, Kans., 1971-76; prof. vet. preventive medicine Ohio State U., Columbus, 1976-81; cons. Syntro Corp., San Diego, 1985-88, SIBIA, San Diego, 1983-90, UN-FAO-UNDP, Maracay, Venezuela, 1979, 80; grant rev. panelist USDA, Washington; mem. com. on bovine tuberculosis eradication, com. on animal health and vet. medicine, bd. on agrl. NRC, 1992—. Contbr. articles to profl. jours. Recipient U. Calif.-Davis Sch. of Vet. Medicine Alumni Achievement award, 1991. Mem. USDA (VS adv. blue-ribbon panel 1987-91), Am. Assn. Zool. Pks. and Aquariums (profl. fellow), Am. Assn. Zoo Veterinarians (life, pres. 1958-59, sec., treas. 1959-61), Am. Vet. Med. Assn., Wildlife Disease Assn. (v.p. 1985-87), Internat. Union for Conservation of Nature and Natural Resources Vet. Specialist Group (species survival com.), Columbus Zoo Assn. (bd. dirs. 1977-81), Am. Coll. Vet. Microbiologists (bd. govs. 1984-87), Am. Coll. Zool. Medicine (hon.), U.S. Animal Health Assn., Sigma Xi, Phi Zeta. Home: 4690 59th St San Diego CA 92115-3830 Office: Zool Soc San Diego PO Box 551 San Diego CA 92112-0551

HEUVING, JEANNE DIANE, literature educator; b. Seattle, July 31, 1951; d. Ralph and M. Yvonne (Loe) H. BA in English, Stanford U., 1973; MA in Creative Writing, U. Wash., 1982, PhD in English, 1988. Instr. Cornish Coll. of the Arts, Seattle, 1981-88; asst. prof. Beloit (Wis.) Coll., 1988-90; asst. prof. U. Wash., Bothell, 1990-95, assoc. prof., 1995—. Author: Omissions Are Not Accidents: Gender in the Art of Marianne Moore, 1992; contbr. articles and poems to profl. jours. Faculty rsch. grantee U. Wash., 1993. Mem. MLA. Home: 1816 N 38th St Seattle WA 98103-8326 Office: Univ Wash/Bothell Campus 22011 26th Ave SE Bothell WA 98021-4900

HEWITT, EDWIN, mathematician, educator; b. Everett, Wash., Jan. 20, 1920; s. Irenaeus Prime and Margaret (Guthrie) H.; m. Carol Blanchard, Mar. 4, 1944 (div. Apr. 1962); children: Margaret, Elizabeth; m. Pamela Jones Meyer, May 28, 1964 (div. Oct. 1973). A.B., Harvard, 1940, M.A., 1941, Ph.D., 1942. Ops. analyst USAAF, 1943-45; Guggenheim fellow, mem. Inst. Advanced Study, 1945-46, 55-56; asst. prof. math. Bryn Mawr Coll., 1946-47; lectr. U. Chgo., 1947-48; mem. faculty U. Wash., Seattle, 1948—, prof. math., 1954-86, prof. math. emeritus, 1986—; vis. prof. U. Uppsala, Sweden, 1951-52, Australian Nat. U., Canberra, 1963, 70, 76, U. Tex., 1972-73, Math. Inst. of Acad. Scis., USSR, 1969-70, 73, 76, U. New S. Wales, 1976, 78, 82, U. Erlangen-Nürnberg, 1975-76, 86, U. Hokkaido (Japan), 1982, U. Passau, (Fed. Republic Germany), 1986, U. Fairbanks, Ala., 1983; Mem. div. math. NRC, 1957-69, exec. com, 1960-62, 67-69; mem. U.S. Nat. Com. for Math., 1973-77, chmn., 1975-77. Author: Theory of Functions of a Real Variable, 1961, (with Kenneth A. Ross) Abstract Harmonic Analysis I, 1963, Vol. II, 1970, (with Karl R. Stromberg) Real and Abstract Analysis, 1965; also research papers. Recipient Alexander von Humboldt Found. prize, 1975, 86. Mem. Am. Math. Soc. (council 1955-65), Math. Assn. Am., Phi Beta Kappa, Sigma Xi. Home: 10706 Lakeside NE Seattle WA 98125 Office: U of Wash Dept Mathematics GN 50 Seattle WA 98195

HEWITT, JERENE CLINE, English language educator; b. Chinook, Mont., Dec. 25, 1917; d. Charles G. and Dorothy Elizabeth (Strother) Grobee; m. Ronald A. Cline, 1938 (dec.); children: Alan, Scott, Mike; m. William F. Hewitt, June 25, 1977 (dec.). BA, U. Calif., Irvine, 1966, MFA, 1968, PhD, 1981. Mgr. dept. correspondence Dun & Bradstreet, L.A., 1939-41; statistician Lockheed, 1941-44; freelance writer, editor, 1948—; teaching asst. U. Calif., Irvine, 1966-67, teaching assoc., 1967-68; asst. prof. English Calif. State U., L.A., 1968-71; assoc. prof. Pasadena (Calif.) City Coll., 1971-80, prof., 1980-83, dir. creative writing program dept. English, 1973-83, prof. emerita, 1983—; owner Words, Inc., Whittier, Calif. Author: Selected Poems, 1968, Essentials, 1972, The Epigram in English, 1981; contbr. poetry, articles and short stories to publs. Mem. AAUP, MLA, Acad. Am. Poets, Writers' Club Whittier (pres. 1962-64, bd. dirs.), UCLA Whittier Bruins. Home: 13713 Philadelphia St Whittier CA 90601-4423

HEWITT, JOHN CHARLES, political and computer consultant; b. Tucson, Sept. 8, 1967; s. Jeruel George and Dorothy Marie (Bradshaw) H. AA in Gen. Studies, Pima C.C., Tucson, 1987; BA in Creative Writing, U. Ariz., 1990. Editor in chief Aztec Press, Tucson, 1986; instl. asst. U. Ariz., Tucson, 1989-91; prodn. asst. Harte-Hankes Pubs., Tucson, 1991-92; polit. cons. Pub. Policy Assocs., Tucson, 1992-95; computer cons. pvt. practice, Tucson, 1993—, notary pub., State of Ariz., Tucson, 1993—. Asst. editor (literary jour.) Sonora Rev., 1984; editor: (literary jour.) Spectrum, 1984; author: (teleplay) Gulliver, 1992. Vol. Salvation Army, 1992; vol. writer Am. Lung Assn. of Ariz., 1992-94; Rep. precinct committeeman, Pima County, 1993-94; dep. campaign mgr. Barbara Barrett for Gov., Ariz., 1993-94. Recipient Honors scholarship Pima C.C., 1985-86, U. Ariz., 1987-88. Mem. Pub. Rels. Soc. Am., Writers at Risk (founder). Home: 8431 E Malvern Pl Tucson AZ 85710-4242 Office: PO Box 65989 Tucson AZ 85728

HEWITT, WILLIAM JAMES, municipal official; b. Apr. 29, 1944; m. Sharon Hewitt; 3 children. BS, Brandon (Can.) U.; cert. in adult edn., Red River C.C., Winnipeg, Can.; cert. in pub. adminstrn., Assiniboine Coll., Brandon; cert. in fire svc. mgmt., Internat. City Mgmt. Assn. cert. fire fighter, fire prevention officer, fire svc. instr., Can. Vol. fire fighter Virden Vol. Fire Dept., 1964-68; fire fighter City of Brandon Fire Dept., 1968-73; asst. fire commr. Office Manitoba Fire Commr., 1973-78, mgr. field svcs. sect., 1978-86; fire chief City of Saskatoon, Can., 1986—; developer Manitoba Fire Coll., apptd. prin., 1978; past chair Manitoba Fire Svcs. Mobile Radio Comm. Com., Manitoba Fire Coll. Protection Tech. Adv. Com., Manitoba Pub. Fire Safety Edn. Com. Contbr. articles to profl. jours.; presenter confs. in Boston, Memphis, Cin., Toronto, Regina, Yellowknife, Winnipeg, Ottawa, others; speaker in field. Mem. Internat. Soc. Fire Svc. Instrs. (bd. dirs. 1976-92), Internat. City Mgmt. Assn. (instr. firesvc. adminstrn. program), Internat. Fire Svcs. Tng. Assn. (fire svc. instr. textbook and fire dept. ops. textbook coms. 1976-81), Internat, Assn. Fire Chiefs (1st v.p. Can. divsn.), Nat. Fire Protection Assn., Can. Fire Chief's Assn. (bd. dirs.), Sask. Fire Chief's Assn. (pres.), Sask. Profl. Qualifications and Standards Bd. (chmn. 1986-92), Sask. C. of C., N.D. State Fireman's Assn. (hon. life). Office: Fire Depart, City Hall, Saskatoon, SK Canada S7K 0J5*

HEWLETT, WILLIAM (REDINGTON), manufacturing company executive, electrical engineer; b. Ann Arbor, Mich., May 20, 1913; s. Albion Walter and Louise (Redington) H.; m. Flora Lamson, Aug. 10, 1939 (dec 1977); children: Eleanor Hewlett Gimon, Walter B., James S., William A., Mary Hewlett Jaffe; m. Rosemary Bradford, May 24, 1978. BA, Stanford U., 1934, EE, 1939; MS, MIT, 1936; LLD (hon.), U. Calif., Berkeley, 1966, Yale U., 1976, Mills Coll., 1983, Marquette U., 1994; DSc (hon.), Kenyon Coll., 1978, Poly. Inst. N.Y., 1978; LHD (hon.), Johns Hopkins U., 1985; EngD (hon.), U. Notre Dame, 1980, Utah State U., 1980, Dartmouth Coll., 1983; PhD, Rand Grad. Inst.; D Electronic Sci. (hon.), U. Bologna, Italy, 1989; HHD (hon.), Santa Clara U., 1991. Electromedical researcher, 1936-39; co-founder Hewlett-Packard Co., Palo Alto, Calif., 1939, ptnr., 1939-46, exec. v.p., dir., 1947-64, pres., 1964-77, chief exec. officer, 1969-78, chmn. exec. com., 1977-83, vice chmn. bd. dirs., 1983-87, emeritus dir., 1987—; mem. internat. adv. council Wells Fargo Bank, 1986-92; trustee Rand Corp., 1962-72; trustee Carnegie Inst., Washington, 1971-90, trustee emeritus, 1990—, chmn. bd. 1980-86; dir. Overseas Devel. Council, 1969-77; bd. dirs. Inst. Radio Engrs. (now IEEE), 1950-57, pres. 1954; coord. chpt. on rsch. in industry for 5-Yr. Outlook Report, NAS, 1980-81; mem. adv. coun. on edn. and new techs. The Tech. Ctr. of Silicon Valley, 1987-88; past bd. dirs. Chrysler Corp., FMC Corp., Chase Manhattan Bank, Utah Internat. Inc. Contbr. articles to profl. jours.; patentee in field. Trustee Stanford U., 1963-74, Mills Coll., Oakland, Calif., 1958-68; mem. Pres.'s Gen. Adv. Com. on Fgn. Assistance Programs, Washington, 1965-68, Pres.'s Sci. Adv. Com., 1966-69; mem. San Francisco regional panel Commn. on White House Fellows, 1969-70, chmn., 1970; pres. bd. dirs. Palo Alto Stanford Hosp. Ctr., 1956-58, bd. dirs., 1958-62; dir. Drug Abuse Council, Washington, 1972-74, Kaiser Found. Hosp. & Health Plan Bd., 1972-78; chmn. The William and Flora Hewlett Found., 1966—; bd. dirs. San Francisco Bay Area Council, 1969-81, Inst. Medicine, Washington, 1971-72, The Nat. Acads. Corp., 1986—, Monterey Bay Aquarium Rsch. Inst., 1987—, Univ. Corp. for Atmospheric Rsch. Found., 1986-88. Lt. col. AUS, 1942-45. Recipient Calif. Mfr. of Yr. Calif. Mfrs. Assn., 1969, Bus. Statesman of Yr. Harvard Bus. Sch. No. Calif., 1970, Medal of Achievement Western Electronic Mfrs. Assn., 1971, Industrialist of Yr. (with David Packard) Calif. Mus. Sci. and Industry and Calif. Mus. Found., 1973, Award with David Packard presented by Scientific Apparatus Makers Assn., 1975, Corp. Leadership award MIT, 1976, Medal of Honor City of Boeblingen, Germany, 1977, Herbert Hoover medal for disting. service Stanford U. Alumni Assn., 1977, Henry Heald award Ill. Inst. Tech., 1984, Nat. Medal of Sci. U.S. Nat. Sci. Com., 1985, Laureate award Santa Clara County BUs. Hall of Fame Jr. Achievement, 1987, World Affairs Coun. No. Calif. award, 1987, Degree of Uncommon Man award Stanford U., 1987, Laureate award Nat. Bus. Hall of Fame Jr. Acievement, 1988; Decorated Comdr.'s Cross Order of Merit Fed. Republic Germany, 1987, John M. Fluke Sen. Meml. Pioneer award, Electronics Test Mag., 1990, Silicon Valley Engring. Hall of Fame award Silicon Valley Engrng. Coun., 1991, Exemplary Leader award Am. Leadership Forum, 1992, Alexis de Tocqueville Soc. award United Way, Santa Clara County, 1991, Nat. Inventors Hall of Fame award Nat. Inventors Hall of Fame Found. Akron, 1992, Howard Vollum Leadership award Oreg. Grad. Inst. Sci. and Tech., 1993, Internat. Citizens award World Forum of Silicon Valley, 1994, Lifetime Achievement award Lemelson-MIT prize, 1995; named to Lowell H.S. Alumni Assn. Wall of Fame, 1995. Fellow NAE (Founders award 1993), IEEE (life fellow, Founders medal with David Packard 1973), Franklin Inst. (life, Vermilye medal with David Packard 1976), Am. Acad. Arts and Scis.; mem. NAS (panel on advanced tech. competition 19, president's circle 1989—), Instrument Soc. Am. (hon. life), Am. Philos. Soc., Calif. Acad. Sci. (trustee 1963-68), Assn. Quadrato della Radio, Century Assn. N.Y.C. Office: Hewlett-Packard Co 3000 Hanover St Palo Alto CA 94304-1112

HEXT, KATHLEEN FLORENCE, regulatory compliance consultant; b. Bellingham, Wash., Oct. 7, 1941; d. Benjamin Byron and Sarah Debell (Youngquist) Gross.; m. George Ronald Hext, June 13, 1964 (div. 1972); m. William H. Lewis, Nov. 14, 1992. BA magna cum laude, Lewis & Clark Coll., Portland, Oreg., 1963; MA, Stanford U., 1964; MBA, UCLA, 1979. CPA; chartered bank auditor; cert. info. systems auditor. Chief exec. officer Internat. Lang. Ctr., Rome, 1970-77; sr. auditor Peat, Marwick, Mitchell & Co., L.A., 1979-81; mgr. fin. audit Lloyds Bank, L.A., 1981-83, mgr. EDP audit, 1983-85; dir. corp. audit First Interstate Bancorp, L.A., 1985-89, sr. v.p., gen. auditor, 1989-91, sr. v.p., chief compliance officer, 1991-94; compliance cons. Proactive, Inc., 1993—; treas., Arcadia H.O. Assoc., El Monte, Calif., 1982-84, 86-88, pres., 1985. Recipient Edward W. Carter award UCLA, 1979. Mem. AICPA, Calif. Soc. CPA. Republican. Avocations: photography, microcomputers, reading. Home and Office: Proactive Inc 1226 Upland Hills Dr S Upland CA 91786-9173

HEYCK, THEODORE DALY, lawyer; b. Houston, Apr. 17, 1941; s. Theodore Richard and Gertrude Paine (Daly) H. BA, Brown U., 1963; postgrad. Georgetown. U., 1963-65, 71-72; JD, N.Y. Law Sch., 1979. Bar: N.Y. 1980, Calif. 1984, U.S. Ct. Appeals (2nd cir.) 1984, U.S. Supreme Ct. 1984, U.S. Dist. Ct. (so. and ea. dists.) N.Y. 1980, U.S. Dist. Ct. (we. and no. dists.) N.Y. 1984, U.S. Dist. Ct. (cen. and so. dists.) Calif. 1984, U.S. Ct. Appeals (9th cir.) 1986. Paralegal dist. atty. Bklyn., 1975-79; asst. dist. atty. Bklyn. dist., Kings County, N.Y., 1979-85; dep. city atty., L.A., 1985—; bd. dirs. Screen Actors Guild, N.Y.C., 1977-78. Mem. ABA, AFTRA, NATAS, SAG, Bklyn. Bar Assn., Assn. Trial Lawyers Am., N.Y. Trial Lawyers Assn., N.Y. State Bar Assn., Calif. Bar Assn., Fed. Bar Council, L.A. County Bar Assn., Actors Equity Assn. Home: 2106 E Live Oak Dr Los Angeles CA 90068-3639 Office: Office City Atty City Hall E 200 N Main St Los Angeles CA 90012-4110

HEYER, CAROL ANN, illustrator; b. Cuero, Tex., Feb. 2, 1950; d. William Jerome and Merlyn Mary (Hutson) H. BA, Calif. Lutheran U., 1974. Freelance artist various cos., Thousand Oaks, Calif., 1974-79; computer artist Image Resource, Westlake Village, Calif., 1979-81; staff writer, artist Lynn-Davis Prodns., Westlake Village, Calif., 1981-87; art dir. Northwind Studios Internat., Camarillo, Calif., 1988-89; illustrator Touchmark, Thousand Oaks, 1989—; cons. art dir., writer Lynn-Wenger Prodns., 1987-89; guest speaker Thousand Oaks Libr., Author's Faire, Calif. Luth. U.; guest artist/speaker Oxnard Libr.; booksignings/appearances Anaheim Conv. Ctr., L.A. Conv. Ctr., Am. Booksellers Assn. Illustrator (children's books) A Star in the Pasture, 1988, The Dream Stealer, 1989, The Golden Easter Egg, 1989, All Things Bright and Beautiful, 1992, Rapunzel, 1992, The Christmas Carol, 1995, Prancer, Gift of the Magi, Dinosaurs, (adult book) The Artist's Market, also L.A. Times, Daily News, The Artist's Mag., News Chronicle; also cover art for Dragon mag., Dungeon mag., Aboriginal Sci. Fiction mag. and various novels, books and games; illustrator Bugs Bunny Coloring Book, Candyland Work Book, The Dragon Sleeps Step Ahead Workbook, Dark Harvest, City of Sorcerers; interior art for various publs. including (mags.) Amazing Stories two covers, Interzone, Aboriginal Sci. Fiction Mag., Alfred Hitchcokcs Mystery Mag., Ideals mag., Realms of Fantasy mag., (book) Tome of Magic (also art for game cards); writer (screenplay) Thunder Run, 1986; illustrator, writers (children's books) Beauty and the Beast, 1989, The Easter Story, 1989, Excalibur, Robin Hood, 1993; paintings for line of Fantasy Art Prints, Scafa/Tornabene, religious art prints; rep. by Every Picture Tells a Story Gallery, Worlds of Wonder; one-woman show Adventures for Kids Gallery; illustrator poster for motion picture and TV fund; writer Disney ednl. prodns., others. Recipient Lit. award City of Oxnard Cultural Arts Commn. and Carnegie Art Inst., 1992, Best Cover Art Boomerang award, 1989, Cert. of Merit, Career Achievement award Calif. Luth. U., 1993, Cert. of Excellence Alumni Career Achievement award, 1993, Print's Regional Design Ann. award, 1992, Best Paper Backs award Internat. Reading Assn./Children s Book Coun. Joint Com., 1994. Mem. Soc. Children's Book Writers (judge 1990, Mag. Merit award 1988), Assn. Sci. Fiction and Fantasy Artists, Soc. Illustrators (Cert. of Merit 1990-92). Home and Office: Touchmark 925 Ave Arboles Thousand Oaks CA 91360

HEYL, ALLEN VAN, JR., geologist; b. Allentown, Pa., Apr. 10, 1918; s. Allen Van and Emma (Kleppinger) H.; student Muhlenberg Coll., 1936-37; BS in Geology, Pa. State U., 1941; PhD in Geology, Princeton U., 1950; m. Maxine LaVon Hawke, July 12, 1945; children: Nancy Caroline, Allen David Van. Field asst., govt. geologist Nfld. Geol. Survey, summers 1937-40, 42; jr. geologist U.S. Geol. Survey, Wis., 1943-45, asst. geologist, 1945-47, assoc. geologist, 1947-50, geologist, Washington and Beltsville, Md., 1950-67; staff geologist, Denver, 1968-90; cons. geologist 1990—; disting. lectr. grad. coll. Beijing, China and Nat. Acad. Sci., 1988; disting. invited lectr. Internat. Assn. Genesis Ore Deposits 9th Symposium, Beijing, 1994; chmn. Internat. Commn. Tectonics of Ore Deposits. Fellow Instn. Mining and Metallurgy (Gt. Brit.), Geol. Soc. Am., Am. Mineral. Soc., Soc. Econ. Geologists; mem. Inst. Genesis of Ore Deposits, Geol. Soc. Wash., Colo. Sci. Soc., Rocky Mountain Geol. Soc., Friends of Mineralogy (hon. life), Evergreen Naturalist Audubon Soc., Sigma Xi, Alpha Chi Sigma. Lutheran. Contbr. numerous articles to profl. jours., chpts. to books. Home: PO Box 1052 Evergreen CO 80439-1052

HEYMAN, THERESE THAU, curator, art historian; b. N.Y.C., Sept. 22, 1930; d. Morris and Mathilda H.; m. Ira Michael Heyman; 1 child, James N. heyman. BA, Smith Coll., Northampton, Mass., 1951; MA, Yale U., 1958. Cert. Mus. Mgmt. Inst., 1981. Curatorial asst. Yale U., New Haven, Conn., 1963; sr. curator Oakland (Calif.) Mus., 1963-93; guest curator Nat. Mus. Am. Art, Washington, 1993—; guest curator Santa Barbara (Calif.) Mus. Art, 1991—. Exhibited in group shows Oakland Mus., 1972, Oakland Mus., 1973, 74, 78, 82, 85, Calif. Prints, 1975. Bd. dirs. Alameda County Art Commn., Oakland, 1970-79. Mem. Print Coun. Am., Oracle-Photography Group. Office: The Oakland Museum 1000 Oak St Oakland CA 94607-4820

HEYNS, ROGER WILLIAM, retired foundation executive and educator; b. Grand Rapids, Mich., Jan. 27, 1918; s. Garrett and Rosa (Klooster) H.; m. Esther Gezon, Sept. 20, 1941; children—Michael, John, Daniel. Student Hope Coll., 1936-37; A.B., Calvin Coll., 1940; M. Clin. Psychology, U. Mich., 1942, Ph.D., 1948. Instr. psychology U. Mich., 1947-48, asst. prof., 1948-55, assoc. prof., 1955-57, prof., 1957-65; dean Coll. Lit., Sci. and Arts, 1958-62; v.p. acad. affairs, 1962-65, prof. psychology and edn., 1971; chancellor U. Calif. at Berkeley, 1965-71; pres. Am. Council on Edn., Washington, 1972-77, William and Flora Hewlett Found., 1977-92; mem. Nat. Sci. Bd., 1967-76. Bd. dirs. SETI Inst., World Affairs Coun.; mem. Coun. of Fgn. Rels., 1978—. Capt. USAF, 1942-46. Recipient outstanding tchr. award U. Mich., 1952, faculty distinguished service award, 1958; Clark Kerr award for outstanding service to edn., 1967; Benjamin Ide Wheeler award as Berkeley's Most Useful Citizen, 1969; Robert C. Kirkwood award for greatest service to N. Calif., 1969. Fellow Am. Psychol. Assn.; mem. Phi Beta Kappa, Sigma Xi, Phi Kappa Phi. Office: 84 Clay Dr Atherton CA 94027-5420

HEYNSSENS, JULIE B., electrical engineer; b. Augusta, Ga., May 31, 1965; d. Vernon Broadus and Dorothy May (Sheffield) Bodenheimer; m. Paul B. Heynssens, June 27, 1987; children: Gwendolyn May, Ian Paul. BSEE, Auburn U., 1987; MSEE, Ariz. State U., 1991. Elec. engr. Motorola, Cellular, Arlington Heights, Ill., 1990-92; engr. Nat. Optical Astron. Observatories, Tucson, 1992—. Mem. exec. com. Lamar County Republican Party, Hattiesburg, Miss., 1982-84; pres. Dunwoody Young Republicans, Atlanta, 1981-82. Mem. IEEE, Women in Astronomy, Eta Kappa Nu. Home: PO Box 40067 Tucson AZ 85717-0067 Office: NOAO PO Box 26732 Tucson AZ 85726-6732

HEYWOOD, THOMAS KAY, physical education educator, coach; b. Salt Lake City, Mar. 19, 1959; s. Joseph Fred and Rita (Heywood) H.; m. Sherri Lynnette Garbett, May 9, 1981; children: Joseph Jack, Alisha Ann, Kirt Thomas, Spencer Allen. AAS, Ricks Coll., Rexburg, Idaho, 1981; BA, Weber U., 1984; MS, Brigham Young U., 1987. Sales mgr. Utah Jazz, 1980-81; transformer mgr. Utah Power and Light, 1981-83; profl. basketball player (drafted) Golden State Warriors, 1983; profl. basketball player Francana Brazil Basketball, 1983-84, C.B.A. Basketball, Casper, Wyo., 1984-85; tchr., coach Morgan H.S. Sem. (LDS Ch.), Utah, 1985-86; admissions coord., asst. coach Ricks Coll., Rexburg, Idaho, 1986-92; dir. assistantships Ricks Coll., Rexburg, 1987-92, dir. selective recruitment, 1989-92; athletic acad. coord., head women's basketball coach, asst. men's basketball coach Coll. Northwestern C.C., 1992-94; head men's basketball, baseball, cross-country, track coach Bryce Valley H.S., Tropic, Utah, 1994-95, tchr. English, health, history, phys. edn., 1994-95; head women's basketball coach, asst. men's basketball coach Snow Coll., Ephraim, Utah, 1995—; chmn. Utah R.E. Tchr. Asst. scoutmaster Boy Scouts Am., Rexburg, 1987, scout explorer basketball coach, 1987; mem. Make-a-Wish Found., 1991. Recipient Basketball award Big Sky Athletic All Conf., 1983, West Valley City 1st Athlete of Yr. award West Valley C. of C., 1985. Mem. LDS Ch. Home: PO Box 91 Tropic UT 84776-0091

HIATT, KARL BRINTON, plastic surgeon; b. Winston-Salem, N.C., Apr. 23, 1956. MD, Duke U., 1983. Plastic surgeon Mesa (Ariz) Lutheran Hosp. Office: 3418 E Encanto St Mesa AZ 85213-6216*

HIATT, PETER, library educator; b. N.Y.C., Oct. 19, 1930; s. Amos and Elizabeth Hope (Derry) H.; m. Linda Rae Smith, Aug. 16, 1968; 1 child, Holly Virginia. B.A., Colgate U., 1952; M.L.S., Rutgers U., 1957, Ph.D., 1963. Head Elmora Br. Library, Elizabeth, N.J., 1957-59; instr. Grad. Sch. Library Service Sci. Rutgers U., 1960-62; library cons. Ind. State Library, Indpls., 1963-70; asst. prof. Grad. Library Sch., Ind. U., 1963-66, assoc. prof., 1966-70; dir. Ind. Library Studies, Bloomington, 1967-70; dir. continuing edn. program for library personnel Western Interstate Commn. for Higher Edn., Boulder, Colo., 1970-74; dir. Grad. Sch. Library and Info. Sci., U. Wash., Seattle, 1974-81, prof., 1974—; prin. investigator Career Devel. and Assessment Center for Librarians, 1979-83, 90-93; dir. library insts. at various colls. and univs.; adv. project U.S. Office Edn.-ALA, 1977-80; bd. dirs. King County Libr. Sys., pres., 1991, 95, sec., 1993-94; prin. investigator Career Devel. and Assessment Ctrs. for Librs.: Phase II, 1990-93. Author: (with Donald Thompson) Monroe County Public Library: Planning for the Future, 1966, The Public Library Needs of Delaware County, 1967, (with Henry Drennan) Public Library Services for the functionally Illiterate, 1967 (with Robert E. Lee and Lawrence A. Allen) A Plan for Developing a Regional Program of Continuing Education for Library Personnel, 1969, Public Library Branch Services for Adults of Low Education, 1964; dir., gen. editor: The Indiana Library Studies, 1970; author: Assessment Centers for Professional Library Leadership, 1993; mem. editorial bd. Coll. and Rsch. Librs., 1969-73; co-editor Leads: A Continuing Education Newsletter for Library Trustees, 1973-75, Octavio Noda; author chpts., articles on library continuing edn., staff devel. and libr. adult svcs. Mem. ALA (officer), Pacific N.W. Libr. Assn., Assn. Libr. and Info. Sci. Educators (officer, Outstanding Svc. award 1979), ACLU. Home: 19324 8th Ave NW Seattle WA 98177-3023 Office: U Wash Grad Sch Libr and Info Sci Seattle WA 98195

HIBBARD, CHARLES GUSTIN, historian; b. Climax, Mich., May 14, 1925; s. Byron C. Hibbard and B. Todd; m. Shirley Van Drunen, Nov. 29, 1952 (div. Mar. 1976); children: Elizabeth, Catherine, Rebecca, Robert; m. Mavis Hardy, Dec. 22, 1979. BS, U. Utah, 1960, PhD, 1980; MA, U. So. Calif., 1969. Cert. secondary tchr., Utah. Enlisted USAF, 1949, advanced to chief master sgt., air traffic contr., air traffic contr., 1949-70; historian USAF, various locations, 1982-89; postal clk. U.S. Postal Svc., Salt Lake City, 1972-77; pres. Ft. Douglas (Utah) Mil. Mus. Assn., 1993—; bd. dirs. Hill AFB (Utah) Mus., 1986-89. Author: 509th Composite Group Trains at Wendover, 1995 Fall Air Power History; editor, contbr. to book History of Hill AFB, Utah, 1988; contbr. to Ency. of Am. West, 1994, Hist. Dictionary of USAF, 1992. Decorated Bronze Star. Mem. Utah Hist. Soc., Wasatch Westerners (pres. 1991-92), Oreg.-Calif. Trails Assn., Western History Assn. Office: Ft Douglas Mus Assn 32 Potter St Salt Lake City UT 84113-5046

HIBBARD, RICHARD PAUL, industrial ventilation consultant, lecturer; b. Defiance, Ohio, Nov. 1, 1923; s. Richard T. and Doris E. (Walkup) H.; BS in Mech. Indsl. Engring., U. Toledo, 1949; m. Phyllis Ann Kirchoffer, Sept. 7, 1948; children: Barbara Rae, Marcia Kae, Rebecca Ann, Patricia Jan, John Ross. Mech. engr. Oldsmobile div. Gen. Motors Corp., Lansing, Mich., 1950-56; design and sales engr. McConnell Sheet Metal, Inc., Lansing, 1956-60; chief heat and ventilation engr. Fansteel Metall. Corp., North Chicago, Ill., 1960-62; sr. facilities and ventilation engr. The Boeing Co., Seattle, 1962-63; ventilation engr. environ. health div. dept. preventive medicine U. Wash., 1964-70, lectr. dept. environ. health, 1970-82, lectr. emeritus, 1983—; prin. Indsl. Ventilation Cons. Svcs., 1983—; chmn. Western Indsl. Ventilation Conf., 1962; mem. com. indsl. ventilation Am. Conf. Govtl. Indsl. Hygienists, 1966—; mem. staff Indsl. Ventilation Conf., Mich. State U., 1955—. With USAAF, 1943-45, USAR, 1946-72. Recipient Disting. Svc. award Indsl. Ventilation Conf., Mich. State U., 1975, 93. Mem. Am. Soc. Safety Engrs. (R.M. Gillmore Meml. award Puget Sound chpt.), ASHRAE, Am. Inst. Plant Engrs., Am. Indsl. Hygiene Assn. (J.M. Dallevalle award 1977), Am. Foundryman's Soc. Lodges: Elks, Masons. Contbr. articles on indsl. hygiene and ventilation to profl. jours. Home: 41 165th Ave SE Bellevue WA 98008-4721

HIBBS, JOHN DAVID, software executive, engineer, business owner; b. Del Norte, Colo., Jan. 26, 1948; s. Alva Bernard and Frances Ava (Cathcart) H.; m. Ruthanne Johnson, Feb. 28, 1976. BSEE, Denver U., 1970. Elec. engr. Merrick and Co., Denver, 1972-73; lighting engr. Holophane div. Johns Manville, Denver, 1973-79; lighting products mgr. Computer Sharing Svcs., Inc., Denver, 1979-83; pres., owner Computer Aided Lighting Analysis, Boulder, Colo., 1983-86, Hibbs Sci. Software, Boulder, 1986—; co-founder Sport Sail, Inc. Author CALA, CALA/Pro and PreCALA lighting programs. With USNR, 1970-72. Recipient 1st prize San Luise Valley Sci. Fair, 1963. Mem. IEEE, Illuminating Engring. Soc. North Am. (chmn. computer com. 1988-91), Computer Soc. IEEE (chmn. computer problem set com. 1991—). Home: 5105 Independence Rd Boulder CO 80301-3024 Office: 2888 Bluff St Ste 515 Boulder CO 80301-1227

HIBLER, JUDE ANN, photojournalist; b. Portland, Oreg., Apr. 6, 1943; d. William Eliot and Myrtle Winifred (Johnson) Henderson; m. Jeffrey Charles Hibler, Jan. 27, 1962; 1 child, Beth Karen. Student, Portland State Coll., 1960-61, Pima C.C., 1980, U. Colo., Boulder, 1982, Antioch U. West, 1981-82. Exec. sec., office mgr. Campus Christian Ctr., Tucson, 1979-80; alcohol counselor Whole Person Health Ctr., Boulder, 1984; adminstrv. mgr. Nordstrom, San Diego, 1985-88; publ., editor, owner Jazz Link Mag., San Diego, 1988-91; co-owner, photojournalist Jazz Link Enterprises, Longmont, Colo., 1991—; cons. El Cajon (Calif.) Jr. High Sch., 1989, Long Beach (Calif.) High Sch., 1990. Co-author: Joe Pass: Improvising Ideas, 1994, (biography) Joe Pass, 1995, Encyclopedia of Jazz, 1995, The Dale Bruning Jazz Guitar Series Vol. 1: Phrasing & Articulation, 1995; publ./editor: Jazz Link Mag., 1988 (best jazz pub. 1988); editor The Gift of Jazz Connection mag., 1995—; photographer: (book covers) Joe Pass Note by Note, 1994, Improvising Ideas, 1994; photojournalist Jazzscene of Oreg., JazzNow Mag., 1992-94, Concord Jazz. Named Outstanding Svc. Nat. Assn. Jazz Educators, 1989, First Friend of Jazz Dr. Billy Taylor's Soundpost, 1991. Mem. San Diego Musicians Union (hon. mem.). Democrat.

HICK, KENNETH WILLIAM, business executive; b. New Westminster, B.C., Can., Oct. 17, 1946; s. Les Walter and Mary Isabelle (Warner) H. BA in Bus., Eastern Wash. State Coll., 1971; MBA (fellow), U. Wash., 1973, PhD, 1975. Regional sales mgr. Hilti, Inc., San Leandro, Calif., 1976-79; gen. sales mgr. Moore Internat., Inc., Portland, 1979-80; v.p. sales and mktg. Phillips Corp., Anaheim, Calif., 1980-81; owner, pres., chief exec. officer K.C. Metals, San Jose, Calif., 1981-87; owner, pres., chief exec. officer Losli Internat. Inc., Portland, Oreg., 1987-89; pres. Resources N.W. Inc., 1989—; communications cons. Asso. Pub. Safety Communication Officers, Inc., State of Oreg., 1975-93; numerous cons. assignments, also seminars, 1976—. Contbr. to numerous publs., 1976—. Mem. Oreg. Gov.'s Tax Bd., 1975-76; pres. Portland chpt. Oreg. Jaycees, 1976; bd. fellows U. Santa Clara, 1983—. Served with USAF, 1966-69. Decorated Commendation medal. Mem. Am. Mgmt. Assn., Am. Mktg. Assn., Assn. M.B.A. Execs., Assn. Gen. Contractors, Soc. Advancement Mgmt., Home Builders Assn. Roman Catholic. Home: 17627 Kelok Rd Lake Oswego OR 97034-6655 Office: Resources N/W Inc PO Box 1909 Lake Oswego OR 97035-0209

HICKCOX, LESLIE KAY, health educator, counselor; b. Berkeley, Calif., May 12, 1951; d. Ralph Thomas and Marilyn Irene (Stump) H. BA, U. Redlands, 1973; MA, U. Pacific, 1975; MEd, Columbia U., 1979; MEd, EdD, Oreg. State U., 1986, 88, 91. Cert. state C.C. instr. (life), Calif. Instr. health curriculum and supervision Concordia Coll., Portland, Oreg.; health and phys. edn. instr. Portland (Oreg.) C.C.; instr. human studies and comm. Marylhurst (Oreg.) Coll.; edn. supr., instr. Oreg. State U., Corvallis; phys. edn. instr., dir. intramurals SUNY, Stony Brook; founder Experiential Learning Inst., 1992—. Contbr. articles to profl. jours. Mem. Nat. Ctr. for Health Edn., Assn. for Advancement of Health Edn., Coun. for Curriculum Instrn., Higher Edn. Rsch. and Devel. Soc. Australasia, Coun. for Adult and Exptl. Learning, Kappa Delta Phi, Phi Delta Kappa. Office: Maryhurst Coll Dept Human Studies Marylhurst OR 97036

HICKEL, WALTER JOSEPH, investment firm executive, forum administrator; b. nr. Claflin, Kans., Aug. 18, 1919; s. Robert A. and Emma (Zecha) H.; m. Janice Cannon, Sept. 22, 1941 (dec. Aug. 1943); 1 son, Theodore; m. Ermalee Strutz, Nov. 22, 1945; children: Robert, Walter, Jr., Jack, Joseph, Karl. Student pub. schs., Claflin; D.Eng. (hon.), Stevens Inst. Tech., 1970, Mich. Tech. U., 1973; LL.D. (hon.), St. Mary of Plains Coll., St. Martin's Coll., U. Md., Adelphi U., U. San Diego, Rensselaer Poly. Inst., 1973, U. Alaska, 1976, Alaska Pacific U., 1991; D.Pub. Adminstrn. (hon.), Willamette U. Founder Hickel Investment Co., Anchorage, 1947—; gov. State of Alaska, 1966-69, 90-94; sec. U.S. Dept. Interior, 1969-70; sec. gen. The Northern Forum, 1994—; former mem. world adv. council Internat. Design Sci. Inst.; former mem. com. on sci. freedom and responsibility AAAS; nominated for pres. at 1968 Republican Nat. Convention; co-founder Yukon Pacific Corp. Author: Who Owns America?, 1971; contbr. articles to newspapers. Mem. Rep. Nat. Com., 1954-64; bd. regents Gonzaga U.; bd. dirs. Salk Inst., 1972-79, NASA Adv. Coun. Exploration Task Force, 1989-91; mem. Gov.'s Econ. Com. on North Slope Natural Gas, Alaska, 1982. Named Alaskan of Year, 1969, Man of Yr. Ripon Soc., 1970; recipient DeSmet medal Gonzaga U., 1969, Horatio Alger award, 1972, Grand Cordon of the Order of Sacred Treasure award His Imperial Majesty the Emperor of Japan, 1988. Mem. Pioneers of Alaska, Alaska C. of C. (former chmn. econ. devel. com.), Equestrian Order Holy Sepulchre, Knights Malta, KC, Capitol Hill. Home: 1905 Loussac Dr Anchorage AK 99517-1225 Office: PO Box 101700 Anchorage AK 99510-1700

HICKERSON, GLENN LINDSEY, leasing company executive; b. Burbank, Calif., Aug. 22, 1937; s. Ralph M. and Sarah Lawson (Lindsey) H.; m. Jane Fortune Arthur, Feb. 24, 1973. B.A. in Bus. Adminstrn, Claremont Men's Coll., 1959; M.B.A., N.Y. U., 1960. Exec. asst. Douglas Aircraft Co., Santa Monica, Calif., 1963; sec., treas. Douglas Fin. Corp., Long Beach, Calif., 1964-67, regional mgr. customer financing, 1967; exec. asst. to pres. Universal Airlines, Inc., Detroit, 1967-68, v.p., treas., asst. sec., 1968-69, pres., 1969-72; v.p., treas., asst. sec. Universal Aircraft Service, Inc., Detroit, 1968-69, chmn. bd., 1969-72; v.p., treas. Universal Airlines Co., Detroit, 1968-69, pres., 1969-72; group v.p. Marriott Hotels, Inc., Washington, 1972-76; dir. sales Far East and Australia Lockheed Calif. Co., 1976-78, dir. mktg. Americas, 1978-79, dir. mktg. Internat., 1979-81, v.p., internat. sales, 1981-83; v.p. comml. mktg. internat. Douglas Aircraft Co., McDonnell Douglas Corp., 1983-89; mng. dir. GPA Asia Pacific, El Segundo, Calif., 1989-90; exec. v.p. GATX Air, San Francisco, 1990—. Bd. govs. Keck Ctr. for Internat. Strategic Studies; mem. Calif. Export Adv. Council. Served to lt. (j.g.) USCGR, 1960-62. H.B. Earhart Found. fellow, 1962. Mem. Internat. Assn. Charter Airlines (exec. com. 1971), Pacific Union Club. Home: 3225 Jackson St San Francisco CA 94118-2016 Office: GATX Air 4 Embarcadero Ctr San Francisco CA 94111-4106

HICKEY, JOHN MILLER, lawyer; b. Cleve., June 4, 1955; s. Lawrence Thomas and Margaret (Miller) H.; m. Sharon Salazar, Aug. 4, 1984; children: Theodore James, John Salazar, Margaret Maureen. Student, U. Wales, U.K., 1975-76; BA, Tulane U., 1977; JD cum laude, Calif. We. Sch. Law, 1981; LLM, NYU, 1982. Bar: Calif. 1981, N.Mex. 1983, U.S. Dist. Ct. N.Mex. 1983, U.S. Tax Ct. 1983, U.S. Ct. Appeals (10th cir.) 1983. Prodn. control mgr. Randall-Textron, Inc., Wilmington, Ohio, 1977-78; assoc. Montgomery & Andrews, Santa Fe, 1983-88; shareholder, dir. Compton, Coryell, Hickey & Ives, Santa Fe, 1988-93, Hickey & Ives, Santa Fe, 1993—. Bd. dirs. Los Alamos (N.Mex.) Econ. Devel., Hospice Ctr., Inc., Santa Fe; sec. Inst. Water Policy Studies, Santa Fe. Republican. Roman Catholic. Home: 806 Camino Zozobra Santa Fe NM 87505-6101 Office: Hickey & Ives 300 Paseo De Peralta Ste 101 Santa Fe NM 87501-5501

HICKEY, WINIFRED E(SPY), former state senator, social worker; b. Rawlins, Wyo.; d. David P. and Eugenia (Blake) Espy; children: John David, Paul Joseph. BA, Loretto Heights Coll., 1933; postgrad. U. Utah, 1934, Sch. Social Service, U. Chgo., 1936; LLD (hon.) U. Wyo., 1991. Dir. Carbon County Welfare Dept., 1935-36; field rep. Wyo. Dept. Welfare, 1937-38; dir. Red Cross Club, Europe, 1942-45; commr. Laramie County, Wyo., 1973-80; mem. Wyo. Senate, 1980-90; dir. United Savs. & Loan, Cheyenne; active Joint Powers Bd. Laramie County and City of Cheyenne. Pub. Where the Deer and the Antelope Play, 1967. Pres., bd. dirs. U. Wyo. Found., 1986-87; pres. Meml. Hosp. of Laramie County, 1986-88, Wyo. Transp. Mus., 1990-92; chmn. adv. council div. community programs Wyo. Dept. Health and Social Services; pres. county and state mental health assn., 1959-63; trustee, U. Wyo., 1967-71, St. Mary's Cathedral, 1986—; active Nat. Council Cath. Women, Gov. Residence Found., 1991—, Wyo. Transp. Mus., 1993—; chair Am. Heritage Assocs. of U. Wyo., 1992—. Named Outstanding Alumna, Loretto Heights Coll., 1959, Woman of Yr. Wyo. Commn. for Women, 1988, Legislator of Yr. Wyo. Psychologists Assn., 1988. Mem. Altrusa Club (Cheyenne).

HICKLIN, RONALD LEE, music production company executive; b. Burlington, Wash., Dec. 4, 1937; s. Wendell C. and Theodora (Van Voorhis) H.; children: Jennifer Lynn, Mark Allan; m. Trudi Takamatsu, Oct. 23, 1994. Student, U. Wash., 1956-57. Pres. S.A.T.B. Inc., L.A., 1979—, Killer Music, Inc., Hollywood, Calif., 1982—, T.T. B.B., Inc., Hollywood, 1989—; ptnr. Killer Tracks, Primat Am., Hollywood, 1990—. Lead tenor The Eligibles, 1958-62; vocal dir., singer Piece of Cake Inc., 1968-81; arranger, producer Calif. Raisin Adv. Bd., 1982 (recipient 2 Clios 1983); producer/co-writer Wheaties, 1983 (Clio award); producer/composer Gatorade, 1983; producer/performer Levi's 501 Blues, 1984. With USAF, 1959-65. Mem. NARAS (MVP award 1973, 75), AFTRA (nat. bd. dirs. 1970-85, local bd. dirs. 1968-85), Screen Actors Guild (nat. bd. dirs. 1975), Am. Fedn. Musicians, Hollywood C. of C. Home: 30 Kewen Pl San Marino CA 91108-1104 Office: Killer Music Inc 6520 W Sunset Blvd Los Angeles CA 90028-7202

HICKMAN, BERT GEORGE, JR., economist, educator; b. Los Angeles, Oct. 6, 1924; s. Bert George and Caroline E. (Douglass) H.; m. Edythe Anne Warshauer, Feb. 9, 1947; children: Wendy Elizabeth, Paul Lawrence, Alison Diane. B.S., U. Calif.-Berkeley, 1947, Ph.D., 1951. Instr. Stanford U., 1949-51; research asso. Nat. Bur. Econ. Research, 1951-52; asst. prof. Northwestern, 1952-54; mem. sr. staff Council Econ. Advisers, 1954-56; research asso. Brookings Instn., 1956-58, mem. sr. staff, 1958-66; prof. Stanford U., 1966—; vis. prof. U. Calif. at Berkeley, 1960, London Grad. Sch. Bus Studies, 1972-73, , Inst. Advanced Studies, Vienna, Austria, 1974, 1975, Kyoto U., 1977; NSF fellow Netherlands Econometric Inst., Rotterdam, 1964-65; Ford Found. Faculty research fellow, 1968-69; mem. com. econ. stability Social Sci. Research Council, 1959-61, chmn., 1962—; hon. prof. U. Vienna, 1985—; chmn. Energy Modeling Forum working group on macroecon. impacts of global modeling Stanford U., 1982-83; Am. coord. US-USSR program on econ.-math. macromodeling Am. Coun. Learned Socs., 1988-90. Author: Growth and Stability of the Postwar Economy, 1960, Investment Demand and U.S. Economic Growth, 1965, (with Robert M. Coen) An Annual Growth Model of the U.S. Economy, 1976; Editor: Quantitative Planning of Economic Policy, 1965, Econometric Models of Cyclical Behavior, 1972, Global International Economic Models, 1983, International Monetary Stabilization and the Foreign Debt Problem, 1984, International Productivity and Competitiveness, 1992; co-editor: Global Econometrics, 1983, Macroeconomic Impact of Energy Shocks, 1987; contbr. articles to profl. jours. Served with USNR, 1943-46. Vis. fellow Internat. Inst. Applied Systems Analysis, 1979, 80; resident fellow Rockefeller Found., 1989; named Hon. Prof. U. Vienna, Austria. Fellow Econometric Soc.; mem. Am. Econ. Assn. (chmn. census adv. com. 1968-71, tech. subcom. to rev. bus. cycle devels. 1962-68, nominating com. 1978-79, chmn. seminar on global modeling, conf. on econometrics and math. econs. 1975-83), Phi Beta Kappa, Phi Eta Sigma. Home: 904 Lathrop Dr Stanford CA 94305-1060 Office: Stanford U Dept Econs Stanford CA 94305

HICKMAN, CRAIG RONALD, author; b. Borger, Tex., Dec. 5, 1949; s. Winston Whitehead and Verla (Bingham) H.; m. Pamela Lewis, Nov. 17, 1972; children: Jared Winston, Kimberly Michelle, Leigh Megan. BA in Econs. cum laude, Brigham Young U., 1974; MBA with honors, Harvard U., 1976. Cons. Ernst & Ernst (now Ernst & Young), L.A., 1976-77; sr. planning analyst Dart Industries, L.A., 1977-79, campaign mgr. Wright for Gov., Salt Lake City, 1980; mgr. cons. svcs. Arthur Young & Co. (now Ernst & Young), 1980-83; pres. Bennett Info. Group, Salt Lake City, 1983-85; chmn., pres. Mgmt. Perspectives Group, Provo, Utah, 1985-91; author, cons. Provo, 1985—; cons. Frito-Lay, Dallas, 1985, Procter & Gamble, Cin., 1986, AT&T, ea. U.S., 1986, Fla. Power & Light, 1987, Systematic Mgmt. Svcs., Phila., 1988, Geneva Steel, Vineyard, Utah, 1989, Found. Health Corp., Sacramento, 1990, Centex, Dallas, Am. Express, N.Y.C., 1994; keynote speaker numerous corp. confs., U. Md., Notre Dame, Head Start Program, Dalhousie U., numerous assns. and USIA, India, Israel, Egypt, Saudi Arabia, 1985-94; bd. dirs. Am. Parts sys. Co-author: Creating Excellence, 1984 (nat. bestseller paperback 1986), The Future 500, 1987; author: Mind of a Manager, Soul of a Leader, 1990 (internat. bestseller paperback 1992), Practical Business Genius, 1991, The Strategy Game, 1993, The Oz Principle, The Organization Game, 1994, The Productivity Game, 1995; contbr. articles and commentaries to profl. jours. Mem. ASTD. Republican. Mem. LDS Ch. Home: 3751 Little Rock Dr Provo UT 84604-5288

HICKMAN, DONN MICHAEL, plastic surgeon; b. Tampa, Fla., 1951. MD, U. Miami, 1976. Plastic surgeon Meml. Med. Ctr., Long Beach, Calif. Office: 4401 Atlantic Ave Ste 101 Long Beach CA 90807-2239*

HICKMAN, GRACE MARGUERITE, artist; b. Reno, Nev., Nov. 7, 1921; d. Charles Franklin and Jeannie (McPhee) Wolcott; m. Robert Frederick Hickman, Apr. 10, 1943; children—John Charles, Carol Ann Hickman Harp, David Paul. Student Emily Griffiths Opportunity Sch., Denver, 1968-71, Red Rocks Community Coll., Golden, Colo., 1974-75, Loretto Heights Coll., Denver, 1983-85. Tchr. art Aurora Parks & Recreation, Colo., 1979-81; instr. paint workshop Marine Resource Ctr., Atlantic Beach, N.C., 1981, 82; lectr. color theory Aurora Artists Club, 1985; instr. creative color Acapulco Art Workshops, 1987, 88; tchr. color theory and art fundamentals Colo. Free U., 1991-92. One woman shows include Internat. House, Denver, 1974, Foothills Art Ctr., Golden, Colo., 1975, Greek Market Place, Denver, 1976, Marine Resource Ctr., Atlantic Beach, N.C., 1983, Depot Art Ctr., Littleton, Colo., 1984, Sheraton DTC, Women's Bank Denver, 1986, NYU Sch. Environmental Medicine, Tuxedo, 1987, Studio Paul Kontny, Denver, 1988. group shows include: Wellshire Presbyn. Ch., Denver, 1975, Brass Cheque Gallery, Denver, 1978, Colo. Women in Arts, Denver, 1979, Garelick's Gallery, Scottsdale, Ariz., 1982; Bold Expressions, Littleton, Colo., 1983. represented in permanent collections: Augustana Luth. Ch., Denver, South Shores Ins. Agy., Huntington Beach, Calif., Texon Gen. Partnership, Englewood, Colo., others. Coordinator figure study Bicentennial Art Ctr., Aurora, 1986; pres. Depot Art Ctr., Littleton, Colo., 1980-82. Mem. Nat. Mus. for Women in the Arts, Artists Equity Assn., Colo. Artists Equity Assn. (chmn. publicity Colo. 1% for Art 1976-77), Pastel Soc. Am., Littleton Fine Arts Guild (pres. 1976-77), Art Students League, Colo. Speakers Bur. (coordinator), Nat. Mus. Women in Arts. Democrat. Lutheran. Club: Aurora Athletic. Avocations: swimming; reading; art history. Home: 12361 E Bates Cir Aurora CO 80014-3311

HICKMAN, MAXINE VIOLA, social services administrator; b. Louisville, Miss., Dec. 24, 1943; d. Everett and Ozella (Eichelberger) H.; m. William L. Malone, Sept. 5, 1965 (div. 1969); 1 child, Gwendolyn. BA, San Francisco State U., 1966; MS, Nova U., 1991; postgrad., Calif. Coast U., 1991—. Lic. State of Calif. Dept. Social Svcs. IBM profl. mechanic operator Wells Fargo Bank, San Francisco, 1961-65; dept. mgr. Sears Roebuck & Co., San Bruno, Calif., 1966-77; adminstr. Pine St. Guest House, San Francisco, 1969-88; fin. planner John Hancock Fin. Svcs., San Mateo, Calif., 1977-81; chief exec. officer Hickman Homes, Inc., San Francisco, 1981—; cons. BeeBe Meml. Endowment Found., Oakland, Calif., 1990—, Calif. Assn. Children's Home-Mems., Sacramento, 1989—. Mem. NAACP, San Francisco. Named Foster Mother of Yr., Children's Home Soc. Calif., 1985, Woman of Yr., Gamma Nu chpt. Iota Phi Lambda, 1991. Mem. Foster Parents United, Calif. Assn. Children's Homes, Nat. Bus. League, Order of Ea. Star, Masons (worthy matron), Alpha Kappa Alpha. Democrat. Baptist. Office: Hickman Homes Inc 67 Harold Ave San Francisco CA 94112-2331

HICKS, BETHANY GRIBBEN, lawyer, commissioner; b. N.Y., Sept. 8, 1951; d. Robert and DeSales Gribben; m. William A. Hicks III, May 21, 1982; children: Alexandra Elizabeth, Samantha Katherine. AB, Vassar Coll., 1973; MEd, Boston U., 1975; JD, Ariz. State U., 1984. Bar: Ariz. 1984. Pvt. practice Scottsdale and Paradise Valley, Ariz., 1984-91; law clk. to Hon. Kenneth L. Fields Maricopa County Superior Ct. (S.E. dist.), Mesa, 1991-93, judge pro tem, 1993—, commr., 1994—; magistrate Town of Paradise Valley, Ariz., 1993-94; commn., judge, 1995—. Mem. Jr. League of Phoenix, 1984-91; bd. dirs. Phoenix Children's Theatre, 1988-90; parliamentarian Girls Club of Scottsdale, Ariz., 1985-87, 89-90, bd. dirs., 1988-91; mem. exec. bd., sec. All Saints' Episcopal Day Sch. Parents Assn., 1991-92, pres., 1993-94; mem. Nat. Charity League, 1995—. Mem. ABA, State Bar Ariz., Maricopa County Bar Assn. Republican. Episcopalian. Club: Paradise Valley Country.

HICKS, DAVID EARL, author, inventor; b. Indpls., Jan. 1, 1931; s. John Arthur and Marguerite (Barnes) H.; m. Shirlene Lavan Barlow, Jan. 22, 1958 (div. June 1973); children: Sharon Lynn, Brenda Kay; m. Margaret Leigh Payne, Feb. 17, 1977; children: David Bradley, Leslie Ann, Brian Patrick. Grad., Nat. Radio Inst., 1953; student, Purdue U., 1959-60, Miami-Dade Community Coll., 1971-72. Cert. advanced paramedic. Tech. writer, editor Howard W. Sams, Inc., Indpls., 1958-64; tech. writer Systems Engring. Labs. Inc., Ft. Lauderdale, Fla., 1964-67; publs. mgr. Novatronics, Inc., Pompano Beach, Fla., 1967-69; pres. Datatek, Inc., Ft. Lauderdale, 1969-71; tech. writer Systems Devel. Corp., Colorado Springs, Colo., 1973-74, Ford Aerospace Corp., Colorado Springs, 1974-76; pres. Nutronics Corp., Colorado Springs, 1982-87; tech. writer Digital Equipment Corp., Colorado Springs, 1978-88; pres. Innovation USA Mag., Colorado Springs, 1989; tech. cons., inventor pvt. practice, Colo. Springs, 1964-65, 75-92; novelist Colo. Springs, 1992—; tech. cons. Japan Electronics, Tokyo, 1962-63, Nutronics Corp., Longmont, Colo., 1987. Author of eight tech. books (two made best seller list) including: Citizens Band Radio Handbook, 1961, Amateur Radio-VHF and Above, 1965, CB Radio Operating Procedures, 1976; contbr. articles to electronics jours.; inventor of new electric charging system, 1978, awarded U.S. patent, 1981; lectr. numerous sci. and invention seminars, 1978—. Communications officer CD, Indpls., 1962-63; judge sci. fair Pub. Sch. System, Colorado Springs, 1986-87. Served with USN, 1948. Recipient Red Cross Hall of Fame, Indpls., 1963; grantee U.S. Dept. of Energy, 1984; recipient Nat. Energy Resources Tech. Innovation award, 1989, Disting. Leadership award Am. Biog. Inst. 1990, cert. of merit Internat. Biog. Ctr., 1990. Mem. Soc. of Am. Inventors (bd. dirs., Pres. award 1989), Am. Radio

Relay League, Author's Guild, Author's League of Am. Republican. Office: PO Box 25053 Colorado Springs CO 80936-5053

HICKS, JAMES B(RADLEY), lawyer; b. L.A., Mar. 28, 1959; s. John and Liane (Wolker) H.; m. Natalia A. Huryn, Oct. 15, 1983. BA, MA, Yale U., 1978; MBA, JD, Harvard U., 1982. Bar: Calif. 1982, U.S. Dist. Ct. (ctrl. dist.) Calif. 1982, U.S. Dist. Ct. Colo. 1987, U.S. Ct. Appeals (3d cir.) 1985, U.S. Ct. Appeals (9th and 10th cirs.) 1988, U.S. Ct. Appeals (1st cir.) 1993, U.S. Supreme Ct. 1988. Assoc. Sullivan & Cromwell, N.Y.C., 1982, Paul, Hastings, Janofsky & Walker, Santa Monica, Calif., 1983-84, Loeb and Loeb, L.A., 1984-87, White & Case, L.A., 1987-91; ptnr. Andrews & Kurth L.L.P., L.A., 1991—. Contbr. articles to profl. jours. Mem. ABA (appellate advocacy com. 1991—, bus. torts litigation and intellectual property coms. 1992—), L.A. County Bar Assn. (bench and bar rels. com. 1986—, moot ct. com. 1987—), Calif. Bar (history law in Calif. com. 1986-88, chmn. Calif. Supreme Ct. Soc. subcom. 1987-88, appellate com. 1994—), U.S. Supreme Ct. Hist. Soc., 9th Jud. Cir. Hist. Soc., Harvard Club N.Y.C., Pandits Club New Haven. Office: Andrews & Kurth LLP Ste 4200 601 S Figueroa St Los Angeles CA 90017-5704

HICKS, JAMES KENNETH, entertainment industry executive; b. Pierre, S.D., July 31, 1964; s. Harold Kenneth and Priscila Marie (Haberer) H.; m. Kimberly Ann Mattis, July 28, 1984; children: Melissa Ann, Spencer James. BS in Mech. Engring., S.D. Sch. Mines and Tech., 1986; MBA, Pacific Luth. U., 1991. Mgr. Albertson's Food & Drug, Rapid City, S.D., 1983-87; engr. Boeing Co., Seattle, 1987-94; pres. Splty. Entertainment, Inc., Mercer Island, Wash., 1992—. Mem. Am. Mktg. Assn., Internat. Family Entertainment Ctr. Assn. Republican. Lutheran. Office: Splty Entertainment Inc 7683 SE 27th St Ste 315 Mercer Island WA 98040-2826

HICKS, MORRIS ALVIN, dentist; b. Scottville, Ill., Aug. 31, 1936; s. Charles Alvin and LaFern (Watkins) H.; m. Marlene Elizabeth Henerhoff, June 3, 1956 (div. 1983); children: Melinda, Murray, Myron; m. Linda Lee Giller, Mar. 26, 1983; children: Teri, Joe, Traci, Curt. BS, Western Ill. U., 1958, U. Ill., 1963; DDS, U. Ill., Chgo., 1965; MEd, U. Tex., 1966. Sci. tchr. Roodhouse (Ill.) High Sch., 1958-60; commd. officer dentist U.S. Pub. Health Svc., 1965-69; pvt. practice dentist Tucson, 1969—. Pres. Sertoma, 1974; gov. Sertoma Ariz. dist., 1975. Major USPHS, 1965-69. Fellow Acad. Gen. Dentistry; mem. ADA (alt. del. 1987—), So. Ariz. Dental Assn. (pres. 1981-82), Ariz. Dental Assn. (pres. 1989-90), Am. Coll. Dentists, Internat. Coll. Dentists, Pierre Fauchard Acad., Am. Equilibrium Soc., Masons, Scottish Rite, Shriners. Republican. Home: 9392 N Calle Buena Vis Tucson AZ 85737-4904 Office: 7040 N Oracle Rd Tucson AZ 85704-4330

HICKS, NORM, airport operations executive; b. 1941. BBA, Golden Gate U., 1964; postgrad., U.S. Naval Postgrad. Sch., 1971. Exec. dir., COO Mohave County Airport Authority, Bullhead City, Ariz. Office: Mohave County Airport Auth 2750 Locust Blvd Bullhead City AZ 86430*

HICKS, PHILIP STANLEY, psychiatrist; b. St. Louis, May 25, 1928; s. Thomas Ross and Mabel Louise (Kinnecome) H.; m. Marilyn Fenton, Apr. 15, 1951 (div. Sept. 1973); children: Catherine, Elizabeth, John, Sara; m. Penny Linda Harris, Nov. 17, 1979; 1 child, Michael Harris. BA in Chemistry, U. N.D., 1948; MD, Boston U., 1948-52. Diplomate Am. Bds. Medical Examiners, Psychiatry and Neurology; lic. physician and surgeon, Calif. Intern Boston City Hosp., 1952-53; resident neuropsychiatry Michael Reese Hosp., Chgo., 1953-55; resident psychiatry The Langley Porter Clinic, San Francisco, 1955-56; candidate, clin. assoc. The San Francisco Psychoanalytic Inst., 1956-65; med. dir. The Family Rehab. Ctr., San Rafael, Calif., 1965-68; asst. clin. prof. dept. psychiatry Univ. Calif., San Francisco, 1968—; med. dir. Cowell Treatment Ctr. of Sacramento Childrens Home, 1968-69, Lane Childrens Ctr., Sebastopol, 1969-75; chief dept. psychiatry and neurology 5th Gen. Hosp., Bad Cannstatt, West Germany, 1975-77; asst. chief dept. psychiatry Leyterman Army Med. Ctr., San Francisco, 1977-79; chief dept. psychiatry Silas B. Hays Army Community Hosp., Fort Ord, Calif., 1979-81; chief med. officer Correctional Tng. Facility, Soledad, Calif., 1981-83; chief psychiatrist Natividad Med. Ctr., Salinas, Calif., 1983-84, Calif. State Prison, San Quentin, Calif., 1986-91; pvt. practice, 1991—; pvt. practice San Rafael, 1956-75; clin. instr. U. Calif., San Francisco, 1956-68; psychiatric Calif. State Prison, San Quentin, Calif., 1956-57, San Francisco Gen. Hosp., 1957-58, Clearwater Ranch Childrens Home, Philo, Calif., 1957-64, Correctional Tng. Facility, Soledad, 1984-86, Forensic Program Napa (Calif.) State Hosp., 1991-94, Contra Costa County Mental Health Svcs., 1994—; faculty Letterman Army Med. Ctr., San Francisco, 1977-79, dir. forencis module, 1987-91; vis. faculty residency tng. program, Tripler Army Med. Ctr., Honolulu, 1982-92; faculty residency tng. program, Calif. Pacific Med. Ctr., San Francisco, 1992-94; cons. Contra Costa County Cmty. Mental Health Activity, 1956-60, Marin County Health Dept., San Rafael, 1957-58, Family Svc. Agy. of Marin, San Rafael, 1957-58, Atascadero (Calif.) State Hosp., 1978-81, Aetna Fed. Health Programs, 1994—, Med. Bd. Calif. Author, presenter and lectr. in field. With USNR, 1945052; Col. Med. Corps USAR, 1975-81, reserve duty, 1981—. Mem. Am. Acad. Psychiatry and the Law, Am. Psychiatric Soc. (life), No. Calif. Psychiatric Soc. (life), Forensic Mental Health Assn. Calif., Marin Psychiatric Soc. (pres. 1960-75), Begg Soc. Boston U. Honor Med. Soc., Alpha Omega Alpha Honor Med. Soc. Home and Office: 26 Mount Rainier Dr San Rafael CA 94903-1078

HICKS, ROBERT ALVIN, psychology educator; b. San Francisco, July 25, 1932; s. James B. and Vera L. (Brand) H.; m. Maralee Jeffries, June 15, 1957; 1 child, Gregory J. BA, U. Calif., Santa Barbara, 1955; MA, San Jose State U., 1960; PhD, U. Denver, 1964. Psychometrist San State (Calif.) U., 1957-61, prof., 1966—, NIH-MBRS program dir., 1980—; lectr., asst. prof. U. Denver, 1961-66; exec. officer Western Psychol. Assn., San Jose, 1985—. Contbr. articles to profl. jours. Fellow APA, Am. Psychol. Soc., Western Psychol. Assn.; mem. Psychonomic Soc., Sleep Rsch. Soc., Sigma Xi. Office: San Jose State U Dept Psychology San Jose CA 95192-0189

HICKSON, ERNEST CHARLES, financial executive; b. L.A., July 14, 1931; s. Russell Arthur and Marilyn Louise (Mambert) H.; m. Janice Beleal, Sept. 5, 1959; children: Arthur, Jennifer, Barton. BS, U. So. Calif., 1961; postgrad., UCLA Grad. Sch. of Bus. Admin., 1961-63. Lic. real estate broker, Calif., 1986. Credit supr. ARCO (Richfield Oil), L.A., 1955-60; asst. v.p. Union Bank L.A., 1960-64; v.p. County Nat. Bank (now Wells Fargo), Orange, Calif., 1964-67; v.p., sr. loan ofcr. City Bank, Honolulu, 1967-70; pres., CEO Shelter Corp., 1968-72; exec. v.p., dir. U.S. Fin., Inc., San Diego, 1970-73; pres., CEO USF Investors, 1971-73; exec. v.p. Sonnenblick Goldman, L.A., 1973-76; pres., CEO First Hawaiian Devel., Honolulu, 1976-82; CEO TMH Fin. Corp. (merged into Wall Street Fin. Corp., 1994), Santa Ana, Calif., 1982-94, exec. v.p., pres. divsn. fin. svcs., 1994—, also bd. dirs. Author: (novel) The Developers, 1978; editor: (monthly newsletter) Financial Marketing, 1978-83. Staff sgt. USAF, 1950-53. Recipient Exec. award Grad. Sch. of Credit and Fin. Mgmt., Stanford U., 1964, Assocs. award The Nat. Inst. of Credit, UCLA, 1959. Mem. U. So. Calif. Assocs., U. So. Calif. Pres.'s Circle, Urban Land Inst., Town Hall, Center Club (Costa Mesa), Pacific Club (Honolulu), Outrigger Canoe Club (Honolulu), Phi Gamma Delta. Office: Wall Street Fin Griffin Towers 6 Hutton Centre Dr Santa Ana CA 92707-5707

HICKSON, ROBIN JULIAN, mining company executive; b. Irby, Eng., Feb. 27, 1944; s. William Kellett and Doris Matilda (Martin) H.; m. P. Anne Winn, Mar. 28, 1964; children: Richard, Sharon, Nicholas, Steven. BS in Mining Engring. with honors, U. London, 1965; MBA, Tulane U., 1990. Mining engr. N.J. Zinc Co., Austinville, 1965-70; divisional mgr. N.J. Zinc Co., Jefferson City, Tenn., 1970-71; spl. project engr. Kerr McGee Corp., Grants, N.Mex., 1971-72; gen. mgr. Asarco, Inc., Vanadium, N.Mex., 1972-78; gen. mgr. Gold Fields Mining Corp., Ortiz, N.Mex., 1978-83, Mesquite, Calif., 1982-86; v.p. Freeport Mining Co., New Orleans, 1986-91, Freeport Indonesia Inc., Irian Jaya, 1991-92; pres. Freeport Rsch. and Engring. Co., New Orleans, 1992-93; sr. v.p. Cyprus Climas Metals Co., Tempe, Ariz., 1993-94; pres. Cyprus Amax Engring. and Project Devel. Co., Tempe, 1994—; officer Cyprus Amax Minerals Co., 1994—. Author: (with others) Interfacing Technologies in Solution Mining, 1981. Mem. Instn. Mining and Metallurgy, Am. Inst. Mining and Metallurgy, Mining and Metall. Soc., N.Mex. Mining Assn. (bd. dirs. Santa Fe, N.Mex. chpt. 1975-83), Calif. Mining Assn. (bd. dirs. Sacramento chpt. 1982-86), Beta Gamma Sigma. Episcopalian. Home: 12246 S Honah Lee Ct Phoenix AZ 85044-3455 Office: PO Box 22015 1501 W Fountainhead Pky Tempe AZ 85282-1846

HIDALGO, MIGUEL, transportation company executive; b. Detroit, Nov. 10, 1958; s. Manuel and Ann (Molina) H.; m. Rausdha Nelly Cachoa, Nov. 14, 1992; children: Jesahel, Monica Natasha. BA in Communications, Pepperdine U., 1981; MBA in Internat. Bus., Nat. U., 1991, MS in Aero. Mgmt., 1991, postgrad., 1992. Owner Pacific Trans Service, Los Angeles, 1981-83; legal adminstr. Hidalgo & Assocs., Los Angeles, 1985-90; ops. and customs Aero Calif. Airlines, San Diego, 1990-91; pres. AeroCargo, San Diego, 1992—; owner AeroCargo, Inc., Baja AirWest Express, Nelly's Oil Co., Nelly's Pilot/Aircraft Supply, Brown Field Rental Car Svc. Author: Baja Nelly's Flightguide to Mexico, 1994; contbr. articles to profl. jours. Active S.W. Rep. Project; advisor Polit. Edn. Project. With USN, mem. Res., ret., 1985-91. Mem. Pepperdine Assocs., Huntington Libr. Republican. Roman Catholic. Office: AeroCargo Brown Field Airport 1424 Continental St San Diego CA 92173-1717

HIDDLESTON, RONAL EUGENE, drilling and pump company executive; b. Bristow, Okla., Mar. 21, 1939; s. C.L. and Iona D. (Martin) H.; m. Marvelene L. Hammond, Apr. 26, 1959; children: Michael Scott, Mark Shawn, Matthew Shane. Student, Idaho State U., 1957-58. With Roper's Clothing and Bishop Redi-Mix, Rupert, Idaho, 1960-61; pres., chmn. bd., gen. mgr. Hiddleston Drilling, Rupert, 1961-66, Mountain Home, Idaho, 1966—; bd. dirs. Ground Water Pub. Mem. Mountain Home Airport Adv. Bd., 1968—; hon. mem. Idaho Search and Rescue. Mem. Nat. Ground Water Assn. (dir., past pres., chmn. fund raising new hdqrs.), Idaho Ground Water Assn. (dir., past pres.), Pacific N.W. Water Well Assn. (dir.), N.W. Mining Assn., Nat. Fedn. Ind. Businessmen, Ground Water Inst. (bd. dirs.), Aircraft Owners and Pilots Assn., Ducks Unltd., Nat. 210 Owners Club, Optimists, Masons, Shriners. Home: 105 Goodall St Mountain Home ID 83647-1629 Office: RR 3 Box 610D Mountain Home ID 83647-9206

HIGDON, BERNICE COWAN, retired elementary education educator; b. Sylva, N.C., Feb. 26, 1918; d. Royston Duffield and Margaret Cordelia (Hall) Cowan; m. Roscoe John Higdon, Aug. 12, 1945; children: Ronald Keith, Rodrick Knox, Krista Dean. BS, Western Carolina U., 1941; cert. tchr., So. Oreg. Coll., 1967; student, Chapman Coll., 1971. Cert. tchr., Calif. Prin., tchr. Dorsey Sch., Bryson City, N.C., 1941-42; expeditor Glenn L. Martin Aircraft Co., Balt., 1942-45; tchr. elem. sch. Seneca, S.C., 1945-46, Piedmont, S.C., 1946-47; tchr. elem. sch. Columbia, S.C., 1950-51, Manteca, Calif., 1967-68; kindergarten tchr. 1st Bapt. Ch., Medford, Oreg., 1965-67; tchr. elem. sch. Marysville (Calif.) Unified Sch. Dist., 1968-83; tchr. Headstart, Manteca, 1968. Past counselor Youth Svc. Bur., Yuba City, Calif.; troop leader Girl Scouts U.S.A., Medford, 1962-63; past Sunday sch. tchr. 1st Bapt. Ch., Medford; bd. dirs. Christian Assistance Network, Yuba City, 1984-85; aux. vol. Fremont Med. Ctr., Yuba City, 1984-94; deaconess Evang. Free Ch., Yuba City, 1991-93. Recipient cert. of appreciation Marysville Unified Sch. Dist., 1983, Christian Assistance Network, 1985; cert. of recognition Ella Elem. Sch., Marysville, 1983. Mem. Calif. Ret. Tchrs. Assn., Nat. Ret. Tchrs. Assn., Sutter Hist. Soc., AAUW, Am. Assn. Ret. Persons. Home: 1264 Charlotte Ave Yuba City CA 95991-2804

HIGGINBOTHAM, LLOYD WILLIAM, mechanical engineer; b. Haydentown, Pa., Nov. 24, 1934; s. Clarence John and Nannie Mae (Piper) H.; m. Genevieve Law, Oct. 17, 1953 (div.); 1 child, Mark William; m. Mary Bannaian, July 23, 1966; 1 child, Samuel Lloyd. With rsch. and devel. TRW Inc., Cleve., 1953-57; pres. Higginbotham Rsch., Cleve., 1957-64, Higginbotham Assocs., Woodland Hills, Calif., 1964—; founder, CEO Engrs. of World, Woodland Hills, Calif., 1993—; founder, pres., CEO Enhance Engring. Edn. Found., Inc., Woodland Hills, 1994—, Engrs. of the World, Woodland Hills, 1994—; pres., CEO Engrs. Coun., 1992—; cons. grad. engring. programs UCLA., Calif. State U., L.A., U. So. Calif.; pres. adv. com. Pierce Coll., L.A.; adv. com. So. Calif. Productivity Ctr.; cons. various Calif. legislators; founder, pres., CEO Enhance Engring. Edn. Found. Inc., 1994—, Engrs. of the World, Inc., 1994—. Mem. Town Hall Calif. Recipient Community Svc. award City of Downey, Calif, 1974, Archimedes award NSPE, Outstanding Contbr. Recognition, 1986, Outstanding Leadership Recognition, 1987, William B. Johnson Meml. Internat. Interprofl. award, 1992. Fellow Inst. Advancement of Engring. (exec. dir. 1984-93); mem. Soc. Carbide and Tool Engrs. (chmn. 1974-76), Soc. Mfg. Engrs. (chmn. San Fernando Valley chpt. 1977-79, numerous awards), San Fernando Valley Joint Coun. Engrs. (now Engrs. Coun., Inc., advisor, pres. 1981-82, 92-94), San Fernando Valley Engrs. Coun. (pres., CEO 1992—), Profl. Salesmen's Assn., Am. Soc. Assn. Execs., L.A. Coun. Engrs. and Scientists (exec. mgr. 1984-93), L.A. Area C. of C., Toastmasters, Masons. Republican. Office: Higginbotham Assocs 24300 Calvert St Woodland Hills CA 91367-1113

HIGGINS, CORNELIUS J., engineering executive; b. 1941. PhD, U. N.Mex., 1964. Assoc. divsn. dir. Mechanics Rsch. Inc., Albuquerque, 1969-73; v.p. Civil Nuclear Sys. Corp., Albuquerque, 1973-75; chief rsch. engr. U. N.Mex., Albuquerque, 1975-79; with Applied Rsch. Assoc. Inc., Albuquerque, 1979—, now pres, CEO. With USAF, 1964-69. Office: Applied Research Assoc Inc 4300 San Mateo Blvd NE Albuquerque NM 87110-1260*

HIGGINS, JAMES BRADLEY, dentist; b. Richmond, Ind., July 3, 1941; s. James Randall and Mildred Ethel (White) H.; m. Dorothy Campbell, Dec. 29, 1964; children: Kimberly, Amy, Michaelle Ann, James. DDS, Ind. U., Bloomington, 1966. Resident dentist Ind. State Mental Hosp., Richmond, 1966; pvt. practice dentistry San Jose, Calif., 1968—; lectr. hypnosis Calif. Dental Assts. Assn., 1974-88; cons. Calif. State Bd. Dental Examiners, 1978-80; co-chmn. Santa Clara County Dentist Peer Rev. Com., 1982-84; dental lectr. San Jose Unified Sch. Dist. Bd. dirs. Santa Clara County Health Dept., San Jose, 1986-90, Noble Sch. Parent Tchr. Adv. Bd., San Jose. Capt. Dental Corp, USAF, 1966-68. Mem. ADA, NAACP (life), Nat. Dental Assn., Calif. Dental Assn., Santa Clara County Dental Soc., 100 Black Men of San Jose Assn. (charter). Democrat. Office: 4600 Alum Rock Ave San Jose CA 95127-2463

HIGGINS, RUTH ANN, social worker, family therapist; b. Rock Valley, Iowa, Sept. 23, 1944; d. Neal and Tillie (Feekes) Vonk; m. 1972 (div. Sept. 1986); children: Ashlie Kay, Steven Grant. BA, Northwestern Coll., 1966; MA, U. Colo., 1978; LCSW, U. Denver, 1983. Cert. profl. tchr., Colo., social worker, Colo. Tchr. Adams County Dist. 12, Northglenn, Colo., 1967-69, Dept. Def., Clark AFB, The Philippines, 1969-70, Jefferson County Schs., Lakewood, Colo., 1970-75; social worker Boulder (Colo.) County Mental Health Ctr., 1977, Boulder Community Counseling Ctr., 1979-81, Columbine Counseling Ctr., Broomfield, Colo., 1981—; sch. social worker Adams County Sch. Dist. 12, Northglenn, Colo., 1985—; part time social worker Hospice of Metro Denver, 1984-85, Boulder Valley Pub. Schs., 1985, Lutheran Hospice Care, Wheatridge, Colo., 1985. Author, editor: Nothing Could Stop the Rain, 1976. Recipient Hon. Mention Counselor of Yr. award Colo. Sch. Counselors Assn., 1994. Mem. Nat. Assn. Social Workers. Democrat.

HIGGINS, SHAUN O'LEARY, media executive; b. Princeton, Ind., Mar. 22, 1948; s. John Frank and Laura Dorothea (Thompson) H.; m. Ann Glendening, Nov. 23, 1975; children: Flannery Maeve, Ian Dashiell. BA in Comm., DePauw U., 1971. Reporter, city editor Lu-Mar Newspapers, Inc., Bloomington, Ind., 1967-69; mng. editor The Times, Brazil, Ind., 1969-72; congl. cand. 7th Dist. Ind. Dem., Brazil, 1972; cons. Keep's Creek Assocs., Indpls., 1972-73; wire editor Times & Times World, Roanoke, Va., 1973-74; freelance writer, editor self-employed, N.Y.C., 1974-75; news editor, state bur. chief Lee Newspapers, Inc., Billings, Helena, Mont., 1975-79; asst. mng. editor Cowles Pub. Co., Spokane, Wash., 1973-83; mktg. dir. Cowles Pub. Co., Spokane, 1983-88, dir. mktg. and sales, 1988—; pres., COO New Media Ventures, Inc., Cowles Pub. Co., Spokane, 1993—; cons. in field; instr. in field; owner The Oxalis Group, Spokane, 1979—. Co-producer "Good Paper" TV commercial, 1986 (Telly award, 1988; 2 Emmy awards, 1987); dir. "The Arts Can Change Your Life, 1988 (MAX award, 1988); author: Review Tower, 1985 (MAX award, 1985), Toward Greater Understanding, 1989, Database Marketing Applications for Newspapers, 1993. Bd. dirs., trustee Wash. Commn. for Humanities, Seattle, 1988-93, United Way of Spokane County, 1988-91, Spokane Regional Conv. and Visitors Bur., 1991-94, Spokane Symphony Orch., 1991—, Community Devel. Bd., Spokane, 1986-88; trustee, chmn. Spokane Area Econ. Devel. Coun., 1983-91, chair, 1990; chmn. Festival of Four Cultures. Recipient Emmy(s) N.A.T.A.S., 1987, Telly award Cin. Broadcasters, 1988, MAX Best of Show award Spokane Advt. Fedn., 1988, Best of Show award Internat. Newspaper Mktg. Assn., 1987, Silver Strand award INMA-West, 1993; named Spokane Advt. Profl. of Yr., 1988, Media, Inc. Northwest Print Media Person of the Year, 1992. Mem. Spokane Advt. Fedn. (pres. 1988-89), Direct Mktg. Assn., Pub. Rels. Soc. Am., Soc. Profl. Journalists, Internat. Newspaper Mktg. Assn. (trustee, internat. pres. 1993—), Newspaper Assn. Am. (retail coun., bus. devel. com., chair nat. polit. task force), Fedn. Internationale des editeurs des Journaux (exec. mem., dir.), Chautauqua Soc. of Ea. Wash. U. Home: 428 W 27th Ave Spokane WA 99203-1854 Office: Cowles Pub Co 999 W Riverside Ave Spokane WA 99201-1010

HIGGS, TIMOTHY GERALD, environmental engineer; b. Wayne, Mich., Apr. 18, 1960; s. Gerald David and Ethelyn Marie (Dishnow) H.; m. Melanie Sue Hartwig, Mar. 16, 1991; 1 child, Matthew Eric. BSChemE, Mich. State U., 1983. Registered profl. engr., Ariz. Facilities, environ. engr. Intel Corp., Livermore, Calif., 1984-87; staff environ. engr. Intel Corp., Chandler, Ariz., 1987-94, corp. environ. engr., 1994—; mem. Maricopa County Air Quality Rule's Workgroup, Maricopa County, Phoenix, 1993, pollution prevention grants com. Ariz. Dept. Environ. Quality, Phoenix, 1993-94. Contbr. articles and papers to profl. publs. Vol. Babbit for Pres. Campaign, Phoenix, 1988, Intel-Adopt A Family Christmas Program, Chandler, 1990-94, Intel-Stree or Dreams Project, Chandler, 1991. Mem. Ariz. Assn. Industries (environment com. 1990-94). Office: Intel Corp 145 S 79th St MS:C10-22 Chandler AZ 85226

HIGH, THOMAS W., utilities company executive; b. Oakland, Calif., Dec. 7, 1947; s. William A. and Vera D. (Blumann) H.; m. Nancy J. Hughes, June 8, 1969. B.A., U. Calif., Berkeley, 1968; grad. advanced mgmt. program, Harvard U., 1992. Dir. legis. services Pacific Gas and Electric Co., San Francisco, 1982-84, asst. sec., 1984-85, corp. sec., 1985-86, v.p., corp. sec., 1986-91, chmn., 1991-94, v.p., asst. to CEO, 1994-95, sr. v.p. corp. svcs., 1995—. Trustee Am. Conservatory Theatre, 1991—; mem. coun. Friends of the Bancroft Libr. Office: Pacific Gas and Electric Co B 32 PO Box 770000 San Francisco CA 94177-0001

HIGHBERGER, WILLIAM FOSTER, lawyer; b. Suffern, N.Y., May 15, 1950; s. John Kistler and Helen Stewart (Foster) H.; m. Carolyn Barbara Kuhl, July 12, 1980; children: Helen Barbara, Anna Mary. AB, Princeton U.; JD, Columbia U. Bar: Calif. 1976, U.S. Dist. Ct. (cen. dist.) Calif. 1976, U.S. Ct. Appeals (2d cir.) 1976, U.S. Ct. Appeals (9th cir.) 1977, U.S. Dist. Ct. (so. and ea. dists.) Calif. 1979, U.S. Supreme Ct. 1980, D.C. 1981, U.S. Dist. Ct. (no. dist.) Calif. 1981, U.S. Dist. Ct. D.C. 1982, U.S. Ct. Appeals (D.C. cir.) 1982, U.S. Ct. Appeals (3d cir.) 1983, N.Y. 1984, U.S. Dist. Ct. (so. dist.) N.Y. 1984, U.S. Dist. Ct. (ea. dist.) N.Y. 1985. Law clk. to judge U.S. Ct. Appeals (2d cir.), Bridgeport, Conn., 1975-76; assoc. Gibson, Dunn & Crutcher, Washington and L.A., 1976-82, ptnr., 1983—. Notes and comments editor Columbia U. Law Rev., 1974. Mem. Nat. Trust for Hist. Preservation, Washington, 1980—, Nature Conservatory, Calif., 1981—, Pacific Palisades (Calif.) Presbyn. Ch., 1987—. James Kent scholar Columbia U., 1973. Mem. ABA (com. on individual rights and repsonibilities in workplace, labor sect., litigation sect.), Indsl. Relations Research Assn., Am. Judicature Soc., Internat. Soc. for Social Security and Labor Relations Law. Republican. Clubs: Princeton (N.Y.C.); Univ. Cottage (Princeton, N.J.). Office: Gibson Dunn & Crutcher 333 S Grand Ave Los Angeles CA 90071-1504

HIGHLANDER, RICHARD WILLIAM, communications executive; b. Beckley, W.Va., Feb. 17, 1940; s. Ronald William and Lucille Bernice (Bland) H.; m. Ida Mae Canterbury, June 26, 1965; one child, Alison Renee. BA, Rutgers U., 1963; MA, U. Ga., 1972. Commd. 2d lt. U.S. Army, 1963, advanced through grades to lt. col., 1979, ret., 1984; dir. communications, def. systems group FMC Corp., Santa Clara, Calif., 1984-94; v.p. comm. United Def. LP, Santa Clara, 1994—. Contbr. articles to profl. jours., Freedom Found. award 1966, 81. Trustee San Jose Repertory Co., 1985. Decorated Legion of Merit with bronze oak leaf cluster, Bronze Star with two bronze oak leaf clusters, Purple Heart. Mem. PRSA (accredited), Assn. U.S. Army, Internat. Assn. Bus. Communicators, Calif. Mfrs. Assn. (bd. dirs. 1985, chmn. bd. 1993), Aerospace Industries Assn. (comm. coun.), Rotary, San Jose Met. C. of C. (bd. dirs.), Chi Psi. Republican. Methodist. Home: 1486 Oak Canyon Dr San Jose CA 95120-5711

HIGHT, HAROLD PHILIP, retired security company executive; b. Crescent City, Calif., Apr. 17, 1924; s. Vernon Austin and Mary Jane (Gontau) H.; m. Margaret Rose Edelman, Nov. 19, 1945 (div. 1949); children: Linda Marie, Beverly Sue; m. Doris Louise Dunn, June 20, 1982. Student police sci., Coll. of Redwoods, 1969. With Pan Am. World Airways, South San Francisco, Calif., 1945-51, 52; officer Richmond (Calif.) Police Dept., 1952-54; aircraft electrician Internat. Atlas Svc., Oakland, Calif., 1954-56; security officer radiation lab. AEC, Livermore, Calif., 1956-58; chief police Port Orford (Oreg.) Police Dept., 1958-61; dep. sheriff, sgt., evidence technician Del Notre County Sheriff's Dept., Crescent City, 1961-85; security officer, sgt. Del Notre Security Svc., Crescent City, 1985. With USN, 1941-45, 51-52. Mem. Internat. Footprint Assn. (sec., treas. bd. dirs. Crescent City 1985—), Navy League U.S. (2d v.p. Crescent City 1984—), Tin Can Sailors, Masons, Scottish Rite (32d degree), Elks, Grange. Republican. Roman Catholic. Home: 110 Lafayette Way Crescent City CA 95531-8351

HIGLEY, DEBRA KAY, geologist; b. Scotia, Calif., Apr. 16, 1954; d. Floyd and Charlotte E. (Abbott) H. BS in Geology, Mesa State Coll., 1977; MS in Geochemistry, Colo. Sch. Mines, 1983, PhD in Geology, 1994. Geologist Nuclear Assurance Corp., Grand Junction, Colo., 1976-81, N.Am. Exploration, Kaysville, Utah, 1981, U.S. Geol. Survey, Lakewood, Colo., 1982—. Cartoonist: Geology and Wildflowers of Western Colorado, 1977; contbr. articles to profl. jours. Mem. Am. Assn. Petroleum Geologists, Soc. Luminescent Microscopy and Spectroscopy, Rocky Mountain Assn. Geologists, Soc. for Sedimentary Geology (pres. Rocky Mountain sect. 1994). Republican. Office: US Geol Survey MS 940 Bldg 25 DFC Lakewood CO 80225

HILBERT, ROBERT BACKUS, county water utility administrator; b. Pleasant Grove, Utah, Jan. 4, 1929; s. Rudy and Sarah M. (Whitecar) H.; m. Dora Jean Davis, Aug. 26, 1949; children—Susan Jean (Mrs. Barry Bernards), Robert Jeffrey, Richard Wayne, Robert Layne. Student, U. Utah at Salt Lake City, 1946-47. Engring. aide U.S. Bur. Reclamation, Salt Lake City, 1947-52; field engr. Templeton, Linke & Alsup (cons. engrs.), Salt Lake City, 1952-54; gen. mgr., sec.-treas. Salt Lake County Water Conservancy Dist., Salt Lake City, 1954-89, ret., 1989; pres., chmn. bd. dirs. Central Utah Water Conservancy Dist., Orem, 1964-91; chmn. State of Utah Drinking Water Bd., 1979—; sr. cons. Montgomery-Watson Cons. Engrs., Salt Lake City, 1990—. Mem. water policy task force of nat. resource com. Utah State Legislature, 1974—. Served with AUS, 1950-52. Named Water Utility Man of the Year Intermountain sect. Am. Water Works Assn., 1969; named Am. Water Works Assn. leader to Goodwill People to People Tour of Iron Curtain Countries, 1972, Led Water Industry Tour of Soviet Union, 1989. Mem. Am. Water Works Assn. (dir. 1969-72, pres. 1974-75), Utah Water Users Assn. (pres. 1970-73), Salt Lake County Water and Wastewater Assn. (pres. 1971-72). Democrat. Mem. Ch. of Jesus Christ of Latter-day Saints. Home: PO Box 21721 Salt Lake City UT 84121-0721

HILBERT, STEPHANIE MAYER, actress, director, producer; b. Detroit, Mar. 28, 1943; d. Zygmunt S. and Florence (Bart) Mayer; m. Morton Shelly Hilbert, July 3, 1972; 1 child, Stephen Bart. BFA, U. Conn., 1965, MA, 1967. Assoc. Conn. Commn. on the Arts, Hartford, 1967-69; Caribbean cons. Nat. Endowment for Arts, Washington, 1969-70; project dir. Environ. Awareness Film Project U.S. Virgin Islands Govt., St. Thomas, 1969-70; rsch. assoc. U. Mich., Ann Arbor, 1970-73; comm. cons. Commn. on Profl. and Hosp. Activities, Ann Arbor, 1973-74; pres. video prodn. and program devel. Comm. Cons. Co., Ann Arbor, 1974-76, Hilbert Prodns. Co., Ann Arbor, 1974-86, Environ. Cons. Co., Bellevue, Wash., 1992—; prodr. East Shore Readers Theatre, 1992—; comm. cons. Nile River Project, Cairo and Aswan, Egypt, 1974, 75, 76, Pan Am. Health Orgn., San Jose, Costa Rica, 1977; performing arts cons. U.S. Mil., Bangkok, Thailand, 1972. Pres.

Internat. Study Group, Brussels, 1989-91; bd. mem. Am. Theatre Co., Brussels, 1987-92; performing arts cons. Internat. Festival, Brussels, 1987-92; entertainment producer Am. Club, Brussels, 1989-91. Recipient Alexander Barnes Meml. Scholarship Adelphi (N.Y.)U., 1961-63, Victor Borge Scholarship U. Conn., 1963-65, Appreciation awards Charlotte Amalie Inter-Island Film Co., 1970, Am. Podiatry Assn. Aux., 1976; U. Conn. acting fellow, 1965-67. Mem. Actors' Equity. Unitarian. Home: 14635 NE 13th Pl Bellevue WA 98007-4008

HILBRECHT, NORMAN TY, lawyer; b. San Diego, Feb. 11, 1933; s. Norman Titus and Elizabeth (Lair) H.; m. Mercedes L. Sharratt, Oct. 24, 1980. B.A., Northwestern U., 1956; J.D., Yale U., 1959. Bar: Nev. 1959, U.S. Supreme Ct. 1963. Assoc. counsel Union Pacific R.R., Las Vegas, 1962; ptnr. Hilbrecht & Jones, Las Vegas, 1962-69; pres. Hilbrecht, Jones, Schreck & Bernhard, 1969-83, Hilbrecht & Assocs, 1983—, Mobil Transport Corp., 1970-72; gen. counsel Bell United Ins. Co., 1986-94; mem. Nev. Assembly, 1966-72, minority leader, 1971-72; mem. Nev. Senate, 1974-78; asst. lectr. bus. law U. Nev., Las Vegas. Author: Nevada Motor Carrier Compendium, 1990. Mem. labor mgmt. com. NCCJ, 1963; mem. Clark County (Nev.) Dem. Ctrl. Com., 1959-80, 1st vice chmn., 1965-66; del. Western Regional Assembly on Ombudsman; chmn. Clark County Dem. Conv., 1966, Nev. Dem. Conv., 1966; pres. Clark County Legal Aid Soc., 1964, Nev. Legal Aid and Defender Assn., 1965-83; assoc. for justice Nat. Jud. Coll., 1993, 94. Capt. AUS, 1952-67. Named Outstanding State Legislator Eagleton Inst. Politics, Rutgers U., 1969. Mem. ABA, ATLA, Am. Judicature Soc., Am. Acad. Polit. and Social Sci., State Bar Nev. (chmn. adminstrv. law com. 1991-94, chmn. sect. on adminstrv. law 1995—), Nev. Trial Lawyers (state v.p. 1966), Am. Assn. Ret. Persons (state legis. com. 1991-94), Elks, Phi Beta Kappa, Delta Phi Epsilon, Theta Chi, Phi Delta Phi. Lutheran. Office: 723 S Casino Center Blvd Las Vegas NV 89101-6716

HILDE, REUBEN LYNN, plastic surgeon; b. L.A., 1943. Plastic surgeon, Loma Linda U., 1971. Plastic surgeon Presbyn. Inter. Comm Hosp., Whittier, Calif. Office: 7957 Painter Ave Whittier CA 90602-2414*

HILDEBRAND, CAROL ILENE, librarian; b. Presho, S.D., Feb. 15, 1943; d. Arnum Vance and Ethel Grace (Cole) Stoops; m. Duane D. Hildebrand, Mar. 21, 1970. BA, Dakota Wesleyan U., Mitchell, S.D., 1965; M in Librarianship, U. Wash., 1968. Tchr. Watertown (S.D.) H.S., 1965-67; libr. dir. Chippewa County Libr., Montevideo, Minn., 1968-70, The Dalles (Oreg.)-Wasco County Libr., 1970-72; libr. Salem (Oreg.) Pub. Libr., 1972-73; libr. dir. Lake Oswego (Oreg.) Pub. Libr., 1973-82; asst. city libr. Eugene (Oreg.) Pub. Libr., 1982-91, acting city libr., 1991-92, libr. dir., 1993—; cons., condr. workshops in field. Vice chmn. LWV, Lane County, 1987; bd. dirs. People for Oreg. Librs. Polit. Action Com., 1986—; sec. Citizens for Lane County Libr., 1985-88. Mem. ALA (chpt. councilor 1990-94), AAUW (bd. dirs. 1986), Pacific N.W. Libr. Assn. (pres. 1989-90), Oreg. Libr. Assn. (pres. 1976-77), Rotary, Phi Kappa Phi. Methodist. Office: Eugene Public Library 100 W 13th Ave Eugene OR 97401-3433

HILDEBRAND, MILTON, zoology educator, retired; b. Phila., June 15, 1918; s. Joel Henry and Emily J. (Alexander) H.; m. Viola Memmler, Aug. 11, 1943; children: Ross, Kern, Joan. AB, U. Calif., Berkeley, 1940, MA, 1948, PhD, 1951. Lectr. U. Calif., Davis, 1948-52, asst. prof., 1952-56, assoc. prof., 1956-62, prof., 1962-86, prof. emeritus, 1986—; mammalogist expdn. to Ctrl. Am., U. Calif., Berkeley, 1941-42. Author: Anatomical Preparations, 1968, Analysis of Vertebrate Structure, 1974, Laugh and Love, 1979; contbr.: Functional Vertebrate Morphology, 1985. Recipient Disting. Teaching award Acad. Senate of U. Calif., Davis, 1973. Mem. Am. Soc. Zoologists (sec. div. vertebrate morphology 1963-68, chair 1968-70).

HILDEBRANDT, DARLENE MYERS, information scientist; b. Somerset, Pa., Dec. 18, 1944; d. Kenneth Geary and Julia (Klim) Myers; m. Peter Anton Hildebrandt, May 26, 1983; 1 child, Robin Adaire. BA, U. Calif., Riverside, 1969; MA, U. Wash., 1970. Info. specialist U. Wash. Acad. Computer Ctr., Seattle, 1970-73, library assoc., 1974-75, mgr. computing info. services adminstr., 1976-85, adminstr. computing info. services, 1986-91; head sci. librs. Wash. State U., Seattle, 1991—. Editor: (newsletter) Points Northwest (Elaine D. Kaskela award 1973, 75, Best ASIS 1974); compiler and editor Computing Inof. Directory, 1985—. Recipient Civitan award, 1963. Mem. Am. Soc. for Info. Sci. (founding mem. Pacific Northwest chpt. 1971, chairperson 1975, 76, bd. dirs. 1980, 83, chpt. award 1978). Office: Wash State U Owen Sci & Engring Libr Pullman WA 99164-3200

HILDEBRANDT-WILLARD, CLAUDIA JOAN, banker; b. Inglewood, Calif., Feb. 12, 1942; d. Charles Samual and Clara Claudia (Palumbo) H.; m. I. LeRoy Willard, Nov. 5, 1993. BBA, U. Colo. Head teller First Colo. Bank & Trust, Denver, 1969-70; asst. cashier First Nat. Bank, Englewood, Colo., 1975-79, asst. v.p., 1979-83, v.p., 1983-92; owner CJH Enterprises, Inc., Breckenridge, Colo., 1980—, Garden Tea Shop, Georgetown, Colo., Laudiac, Inc., Breckenridge, 1993—. Mem. Nat. Assn. Bank Women, Fin. Women Internat. (pres. elect. 1989-92), Am. Soc. for Pers. Adminstrn., Am. Inst. Banking, Mile High Group. Roman Catholic. Home: PO Box 5714 Breckenridge CO 80424-5714 also: PO Box 665 Georgetown CO 80444-0665 Office: 612 A 6th St Georgetown CO 80444

HILDEBRANT, ANDY MCCLELLAN, retired electrical engineer; b. Nescopeck, Pa., May 12, 1929; s. Andrew Harmon and Margaret C. (Knorr) H.; m. Rita Mae Yarnold, June 20, 1959; children: James Matthew, David Michael, Andrea Marie. Student, State Tchrs. Coll., Bloomsburg, Pa., 1947-48, Bucknell U., 1952-54, UCLA, 1955-57, Utica Coll., 1965-70. Rsch. analyst Douglas Aircraft Co., Santa Monica, Calif., 1954-57; specialist engring. GE, Johnson City, N.Y., 1957-58, Ithaca, N.Y., 1958-64; elec. engr. GE, Utica, N.Y., 1964-70, Sylvania Electro Systems, Mountain View, Calif., 1970-71, Dalmo-Victor Co., Belmont, Calif., 1971-72, Odetics/Infodetics, Anaheim, Calif., 1972-75, Lear Siegler, Inc., Anaheim, 1975-78, Ford Aerospace, Newport Beach, Calif., 1978-79, THUMS Long Beach Co., Long Beach, Calif., 1979-94; ret., 1994; elec. engring. cons. Perkin-Elmer, Auto Info. Retrieval, Pi-Gem Assn., Pasadena, Calif., Palo Alto, Calif., 1971-73. Patentee AC power modulator for a non-linear load. Juror West Orange County Mpcl. Ct., Westminster, Calif., 1979, U.S. Dist. Ct., L.A., 1991-92. With USN, 1948-52. Recipient Cert. Award in Indsl. Controls Tech., Calif. State U., Fullerton, 1991-92. Mem. Orange County Chpt. Charities (sec. 1988), KC (past grand knight 1987-88). Republican. Roman Catholic. Home: 20392 Bluffwater Cir Huntington Beach CA 92646-4723

HILDERBRAND, JOHN ORMAND, real estate agent, retired rancher; b. Portland, Oreg., Apr. 10, 1927; s. Ormand George and Lois Marion (Barnett) H.; m. Wanda Fay Tucker, June 11, 1950; children: Ormand, Jill, Jeff. BS, Oreg. State U., 1950. Ranch owner, operator Sherman County, Oreg., 1950—; real estate agt. J. Freedman Realtor, Bend, Oreg., 1987—; mem. Sherman County Co-op bd. dirs., bd. dirs. soil conservation, Sherman County. Bd. edn. Wasco Grade Sch., Sherman Union High Sch.; charter mem. Sherman Rd. Adv. Bd. With U.S. Navy, 1945-46. Mem. Sherman County Wheat Growers (pres.), Masons (master, pres. Mid-Columbia Shrine Club 1994), Elks. Home: 96247 Hilderbrand Ln Wasco OR 97065-3043 Office: J Freedman & Co Realtor 15 SW Colorado Ave Bend OR 97702-1150

HILER, EMERSON GARD, psychiatrist; b. Passaic, N.J., July 9, 1919; s. Edward Everett and Pauline Chatfield (Gard) H.; m. Carolyn Alice Montgomery, 1944 (div. 1971); children: Beth Swanson, Craig Hiler, Wendy Hewitt, Ellen Ruona; m. Sara Louise Spriggs, Jan. 14, 1973; stepchildren: Laura Schroeder, Alice Regan. BS, Stanford U., 1942, MD, 1945. Diplomate Am. Bd. Psychiatry and Neurology in Psychiatry. Rotating intern Orange County (Calif.) Hosp., 1945-46; psychiat. resident Brentwood Neuropsychiat. Hosp./VA Ctr., L.A., 1948-51; pvt. practice psychiatry Ontario, Calif., 1951-52; various to unit chief Brentwood Neuropsychiat. Hosp./VA Ctr., L.A., 1964-66; asst. chief psychiatry svc., chief consultation sect. VA Hosp., Long Beach, Calif., 1966-70, chief psychiatry svc., 1970-71, chief consultation sect., 1972-77; psychiatrist Orange County Mental Health Svcs., Santa Ana, Calif., 1977-84; forensic psychiatrist Riverside County Dept. Mental Health/Pub. Guardian's Office, Riverside, Calif., 1984—; clin. instr. dept. psychiatry, Stanford U., Sch. of Medicine, Palo Alto, Calif., 1954-56; asst. clin. prof. psychiatry, Loma Linda Sch. of Medicine, L.A., 1960-64; assoc. clin. prof. psychiatry, UCLA Sch. of Medicine, L.A., 1964-66; asst. clin. prof. of psychiatry and human behavior, U. Calif., Irvine, 1966—. Contbr. articles to profl. jours. Capt. U.S. Army, 1946-48. Recipient Disabled Am. Vets. Nat. award 1974. Fellow APA (life); mem. So. Calif. Psychiat. Soc. Office: Riverside Cty Mental Health PO Box 1446 Riverside CA 92502-1446

HILGAR, MARIE-FRANCE, educator, foreign language; b. St. Palais, France, June 19, 1933; d. Edouard Cherubin and Marie-Andrée (Théodon) Srabian; m. Lawrence Henry Hilgar, July 5, 1954 (dec. Dec. 1992); children: John, Andrew, Marie-Florence, Grace. BA, Ind. U. Pa., 1963; MA, San Francisco State U., 1966; PhD, U. Calif., Davis, 1971. Tchr. East Brady (Pa.) Area High Sch., 1963-64; lectr. San Francisco State U., 1967; instr. Peace Corps, San Francisco, 1966-71; asst. prof. U. Nev., Las Vegas, 1971-75, assoc. prof., 1975-80, prof., 1980-89, disting. prof. French, 1989—. Author: la Mode des Stances, 1974; editor: Etudes autour d' Alcools, 1985, Transactions of Samuel Johnson Society, 1990, Actes de Las Vegas, 1991. Pres. French Alliance, Southern Nev., 1975—; v.p. Ladies Aux. Fleet Reserve, Assn., Las Vegas, 1981; coord. Our Lady Victory Traditional Cath. Ch., Las Vegas, 1987—. Mem. Philological Assn. Pacific Coast (pres.-elect 1994-95), Northwest Soc. Eighteenth Century Studies (pres. 1988, 91), N.Am. Soc. Seventeenth Century (pres. 1977, 90, 91), Phi Sigma Iota (internat. pres. 1986—). Home: 1760 Carlos Dr Las Vegas NV 89123-1410 Office: U Nev Las Vegas NV 89154

HILKER, WALTER ROBERT, JR., lawyer; b. L.A., Apr. 18, 1921; s. Walter Robert and Alice (Cox) H.; children: Anne Katherine, Walter Robert III. BS, U. So. Calif., 1942, LLB, 1948. Bar: Calif. 1949. Sole practice Los Angeles, 1949-55; ptnr. Parker, Milliken, Kohlmeier, Clark & O'Hara, 1955-75; of counsel Pacht, Ross, Warne, Bernhard & Sears, Newport Beach, Calif., 1980-84. Trustee Bella Mabury Trust; bd. dirs. Houchin Found. Served to lt. USNR, 1942-45. Decorated Bronze Star. Mem. ABA, Calif. Bar Assn., Orange County Bar Assn. Republican. Clubs: Spring Valley Lake Country (Apple Valley, Calif.); Balboa Bay (Newport Beach, Calif.). Home and Office: 151 Stonecliffe Aisle Irvine CA 92715-5700

HILL, ALICE LORRAINE, history, geneology, and social researcher, educator; b. Moore, Okla., Jan. 15, 1935; d. Robert Edward and Alma Alice (Fraysher) H.; children: Debra Hrboka, Pamela Spangler, Eric Shiver, Lorraine Smith. Grad., Patricia Stevens Modeling Sch., Orlando, Fla., 1963; student, Draughton Sch. Bus., Oklahoma City, 1968-69, Troy State U., 1970-71, Ventura Coll., 1974; AA in Gen. Edn., Rose Coll., Midwest City, Okla.; BS in Bus. and Acctg., Central State U., 1977; student, U. Okla., 1977-78. Accredited tchr. Calif.; ordained min. Gospel Ministry, 1982; lic. realtor. Former model; with L.A. Unified Sch. Dist.; founder A. Hill & Assocs., Oxnard, Calif., 1993—; co-founder Law of Moses Common Law Legal Assn., Kingfisher, Okla.; rschr. Americana 2000. Author: America, We Love YOu (Congressional Record Poem), 1975; ghost writer of Book for Shafenberg Research Found., 1981; contbr. various articles and poems to profl. publs. Named hon. grad. Patricia Stevens Modeling Sch. (Fla.); recipient scholarship Leadership Enrichment Program, Okla., 1977, Hon. recognition Okla. State Bd. of Regents for Higher Edn., 1977, Presdl. citations from Pres. Ford, 1975, 76, Admired Woman of the Decade award, 1994, Life Time Achievement award, 1995, Most Gold Record award, 1995, Key award for Rsch., Internat. Cultural Diploma of Honor, 1995, Woman of Yr. award, 1995. Mem. NAFE, NEA, AAUW, Internat. Platform Assn. Home: 1646 Lime Ave Oxnard CA 93033-6897

HILL, ANDREW WILLIAM, jazz musician, composer; b. Chgo., June 30, 1937; s. William Robert and Hattie (Mathews) H.; m. La Verne Bradford, Jan. 8, 1963 (dec. Jan. 1989). MusB, New Coll. Calif., San Francisco, 1980. Performer with Charlie Parker Detroit; accompanist with Dinah Washington, Johnny Hartman, others, 1954-60, performer Roland Kirk Band, 1954-60, rec. artist with Roland Kirk, 1960-62; rec. artist Blue Note Records, 1961-63, 63-70; composer in residence Colgate U., Hamilton, N.Y., 1963-70; Heritage touring fellow Smithsonian Instn., 1970-72; mus. dir. New Coll. Calif., San Francisco, 1971-76; mus. panelist Calif. Arts Coun., 1984-89. Compositions include Bobby's Tune, 1989, Golden Sunset, 1989, Spiritual Lover, 1989, Pinnacle, Tail Feathers, Monk's Glimpse, Tripping, Chilly Mac, Ball Square, Domani, La Verne, Verona Rag, Tinkering, Retrospect, Refuge, New Monastery, Flight 19, Spectrum, Dedication, Point of Departure, 1965. Home and Office: JAZZFUND 940 NW Front Ave Unit L-5 Portland OR 97209-3767*

HILL, ANNA MARIE, manufacturing executive; b. Great Falls, Mont., Nov. 6, 1938; d. Paul Joseph and Alexina Rose (Doyon) Ghekiere. AA, Oakland Jr. Coll., 1959; student, U. Calif., Berkeley, 1960-62. Mgr. ops. OSM, Soquel, Calif., 1963-81; purchasing agt. Arrow Huss, Scotts Valley, Calif., 1981-82; sr. buyer Fairchild Test Systems, San Jose, Calif., 1982-83; materials mgr. Basic Test Systems, San Jose, 1983-86; purchasing mgr. Beta Tech., Santa Cruz, Calif., 1986-87; mgr. purchasing ICON Rev., Carmel, Calif., 1987-88; materials mgr. Integrated Components Test System, Sunnyvale, Calif., 1988-89; mfg. mgr. Forte Comm., Sunnyvale, 1989-94; sr. buyer Cisco Systems, San Jose, Calif., 1994—; cons., No. Calif., 1976—. Counselor Teens Against Drugs, San Jose, 1970, 1/2 Orgn., Santa Cruz, 1975-76. Mem. Am. Prodn. Invention Control, Nat. Assn. Female Execs., Nat. Assn. Purchasing Mgmt., Porsche Club Am., Am. Radio Relay League. Democrat. Club: Young Ladies Radio League. Home: 733 Rosedale Ave # 4 Capitola CA 95010-2248 Office: Cisco Systems 110 W Tasman Dr San Jose CA 95134-1700

HILL, ANTHONY WHITING, electronic sales engineer; b. Boston, Aug. 5, 1930; s. Philip Cushing and Marie Teresa (Whiting) H.; m. Sandra Shepherd, Aug. 17, 1952; children: Darcelle Sisley Hill Cooper, Donald Coby. BSEE, U. Calif., Berkeley, 1958. Owner Hill's Sch. of Danse, Hayward, Calif., 1958-74; electronic sales engr. Anthem Electronics, San Jose, Calif., 1974-94; pvt. cons. in computers, trainer Castro Valley, Calif., 1994—. With USNR, 1952-54. Home and Office: 18938 Walnut Rd Castro Valley CA 94546-2006

HILL, APRIL LEE See **HARRIS, APRIL LEE**

HILL, CLAUDIA ADAMS, tax consultant; b. Long Beach, Calif., Oct. 14, 1949; d. Claude T. Adams and Geraldine (Jones) Crosby; m. W. Eugene Hill, Sept. 14, 1968 (div. Oct. 1983); children: Stacia Heather, Jonathan Eugene; m. Larry C. Enoksen, June 4, 1988. BA, Calif. State U., Fullerton, 1972; MBA, San Jose State U., 1978. Systems analyst quality assurance group United Technology Ctr., 1972-73; with Commrs. Adv. Group IRS, 1987; prin., owner Tax Mam, Inc., 1974—; noted lectr. in field of taxation; tax advisor to Rsch. Inst. Am., also pubs., Nev., tax analysts, Va. Contbr. articles to profl. jours. Mem. Nat. Soc. Pub. Accts. (accredited tax advisor, liaison to profl. assns. IRS, Franchist Tax Bd., v.p. tax standards bd. accreditation coun. acctg. and taxation), Nat. Assn. Enrolled Agts., Calif. Soc. Enrolled Agts. Republican. Office: TAX MAM Inc 10680 S De Anza Blvd Cupertino CA 95014-4446

HILL, DALE RICHARD, military officer; b. Charleston, W.Va., Dec. 20, 1939; s. Cecil Thomas Jr. and Frances Eileen (Gillespie) H.; m. Linda Lee Ergeson, Apr. 20, 1962 (dec. 1971); m. Debbie Kay Hildebrant, Feb. 19, 1972; children: Mark, Bret, Lara, Dale, Adam. BS, W.Va. State Coll., 1967; MA, Cen. Mich. U., 1977; grad., USA Command and Gen. Staff Coll., 1982. Commd. 2d lt. U.S. Army, Ft. Benning, Ga., 1968; advanced through grades to lt. col. U.S. Army, 1984; aide-de-camp USA Operational Test and Evaluation Agy., Falls Church, Va., 1976-80; ops. officer Hdqrs. 3 Bde, 2 Infantry divsn., Camp Howze, Republic of Korea, 1980-81; emergency action officer Hdqr. Readiness Command, MacDill AFB, Fla., 1981-82; plans tng. officer Hdqrs. Multinat. Force & Observers Sinai, El Gorah, 1982-83; chief current ops. Hdqr. I Corps., Ft. Lewis, Wash., 1983-86; commdr. Yakima (Wash.) Firing Ctr., 1986-89. Democrat. Home: 1588 N River Rd Prosser WA 99350

HILL, DAVID ALLAN, electrical engineer; b. Cleve., Apr. 21, 1942; s. Martin D. and Geraldine S. (Yoder) H.; m. Elaine C. Dempsey, July 9, 1971. BSEE, Ohio U., 1964, MSEE, 1966; PhD in Elect. Engring., Ohio State U., 1970. Vis. fellow Coop. Inst. for Rsch. Environ. Sci., Boulder, Colo., 1970-71; rsch engr. Inst. for Telecommunication Scis., Boulder, 1971-82; sr. scientist Nat. Inst. Standards and Tech., Boulder, 1982—; adj. prof. U. Colo., Boulder, 1980—. Editor Geosci. and Remote Sensing Jour., 1980-84, Antennas and Propagation Jour., 1986-89; contbr. over 100 articles to profl. jours., chpt. to book. Recipient award for best paper Electromagnetic Compatability Jour., 1987. Fellow IEEE (chpt. chmn. 1975-76, editor 1986-89); mem. Electromagnetic Soc. (bd. dirs. 1980-86), Internat. Union Radio Sci. (nat. com. 1986-89), Colo. Mountain Club (Boulder), Sierra Club. Office: Nat Inst Standards & Tech 813-07 325 Broadway St Boulder CO 80303-3337

HILL, DEBRA LEE, school counselor, educator; b. Flint, Mich., Feb. 22, 1955; d. Charles Lynn and Barbara Hattie (Kerr) Bugbee; m. Randy Steve Hill, Sept. 2, 1978; children: Heather Leigh, Christopher Thomas. BA, Olivet Nazarene U., 1977; postgrad., Memphis State, 1987-88; MA, Gov.'s State, 1987; MS, Nat. U., 1992. Emergency rm. crisis specialist Riverside Hosp., Kankakee, Ill., 1976-77; coord. adult program Riverside Mental Health Unit, Kankakee, 1977-85; psychotherapist Eastwood Mental Health Unit, Memphis, 1986-88; with Beginning Alcohol and Addictions Basic Edn. Studies alcohol/drug edn. Ctr. Creative Alternatives, Huntington Beach, 1988-90; dir./counselor intervention program Westminster (Calif.) Sch. Dist., 1990—; with counseling ministries Cmty. Ch., Westminster, 1988—; mem. sch. attendance rev. bd. Westminster Sch. Dist., 1992—; peer leadership advisor City of Westminster/Westminster Sch. Dist., 1993—. Vol. phone counselor Suicide Crisis Ctr., Memphis, 1987-88; coord. religious cmty. Red Ribbon Steering Com., Huntington Beach, 1992-93. Recipient Golden Bell award Calif. Sch. Bd. Assn., 1994; Leadership scholar Nat. U., 1991. Mem. Am. Counseling Assn., Am. Sch. Counselor Assn., Am. Assn. Christian Counselors, Assn. Specialists Group Work, Assn. Counseling, Edn. and Supervision, Assn. Spiritual, Ethical Values Counseling. Home: 8812 Tamarisk Cir Westminster CA 92683-6840 Office: Westminster Sch Dist Intervention Program 14171 Newland St Westminster CA 92683-1503

HILL, DONALD WAIN, education accreditation commission executive; b. Montfort, Wis., June 14, 1924; s. Victor Charles and Emma Grace (Carr) H.; m. Phyllis Kay Hogan, July 2, 1949; children: Leslie Scott Hill Barnett, Lance Howlett Hill, Lawson Wain Hill. BBA, U. Wis., 1949, MBA, 1953. Budget analyst City of Milw., 1950-53; adminstrv. analyst State of Wis., Madison, 1953-54; bus. mgr. U. Wis., Milw., 1954-56; mem. joint staff Coord. Comm. for Higher Edn., Madison, 1956-59; asst. supt. schs. Chgo. Pub. Schs., 1959-66; exec. vice chancellor City Colls. of Chgo., 1966-84; ednl. cons. Hill Assocs., Carlsbad, Calif., 1984-86; asst. dir., sr. accreditation specialist for western U.S. Accreditation Commn. of Career Sch. and Colls. of Tech., Washington, 1986—; chmn. fin. com. Ill. Task Force on Edn., Springfield, 1965-66; mem. Ill. Higher Edn. Master Plan Com., Urbana, 1963-64; chmn. facilities com. Task Force to Form U. of Wis.-Milw., 1956; mem. fin. study com. U.S. Office Edn., Washington, 1963. Contbr. articles to profl. jours. Mem. ednl. credentials and credit rev. team Am. Coun. on Edn., Abu Dhabi, 1987; mem. task force on collective bargaining Carnegie Found., N.Y.C., 1975-76. With U.S. Infantry, 1942-46, ETO. Mem. Wis. Acad. Scis., Arts and Letters (higher edn. rep. for Wis. Acad. Rev. 1957—), Econ. Club Chgo. Presbyterian. Home: 3459 Pontiac Dr Carlsbad CA 92008-2135 Office: Accreditation Commn Career Schs and Colls Tech 2101 Wilson Blvd Ste 302 Arlington VA 22201

HILL, EARL MCCOLL, lawyer; b. Bisbee, Ariz., June 12, 1926; s. Earl George and Jeanette (McColl) H.; m. Bea Dolan, Nov. 22, 1968; children: Arthur Charles, John Earl, Darlene Stern, Tamara Fegert. BA, U. Wash., 1960, JD, 1961. Bar: Nev. 1962, U.S. Ct. Clms. 1978, U.S. Ct. Apls. (9th cir.) 1971, U.S. Sup. Ct. 1978. Law clk. Nev. sup. ct., Carson City, 1962; assoc. Gray, Horton & Hill, Reno, 1962-65, ptnr. 1965-73; ptnr. Marshall Hill Cassas & de Lipkau (and predecessors), Reno, 1974—, Sherman & Howard, Denver, 1982-91; judge pro tem Reno mcpl. ct., 1964-70; lectr. continuing legal edn.; mem. Nev. Commn. on Jud. Selection 1977-84; trustee Rocky Mountain Mineral Law Found. 1976-95, sec. 1987-88. Mem. ABA, State Bar Nev. (chmn. Com. on Jud. Adminstrn. 1971-77), Washoe County Bar Assn., Nev. Trial Lawyers Assn., Am. Judicature Soc., Lawyer Pilots Bar Assn., Soc. Mining Law Antiquarians (sec./treas. 1975—). Club: Prospectors. Contbr. articles to profl. publs. Office: Holcomb Profl Ctr 333 Holcomb Ave Ste 300 Reno NV 89502-1648

HILL, ERNEST ELWOOD, nuclear engineer; b. Oakland, Calif., May 15, 1922; s. George Leslie and Ollie Isis (Moreland) H.; m. Bettejean Schaegelen, Mar. 27, 1942; children: Eric Evan, Steven Richard, Lawrence Martin. BSME, U. Calif., Berkeley, 1943, MS in Nuclear Engring., 1959. Registered profl. engr., Calif. Prodn. supr. Fed. Pacific Electric, San Francisco, 1947-55; reactor supr. Lawrence Livermore Nat. Lab., Livermore, Calif., 1955-64; br. chief AEC, Berkeley, 1964-67; engring. div. leader Lawrence Livermore Nat. Lab., Livermore, 1967-82; pres. Hill Assocs., Danville, Calif., 1982—; bd. dirs. Hill Assocs., Danville; adminstrv. judge U.S. Nuclear Regulatory Commn., Washington, 1972—. Contbr. articles to profl. jours. Capt. USAAF, 1943-46, PTO. Mem. Am. Nuclear Soc. (sect. chair 1967). Office: Hill Assocs 210 Montego Dr Danville CA 94526-4815

HILL, EUGENE DUBOSE, JR., consulting engineer; b. Louisville, Aug. 22, 1926; s. Eugene DuBose and Lila Perrin (Robinson) H.; m. Margaret Preston Hodges, Feb. 18, 1950; children: Eugene DuBose III, Margaret Hill Hilton, Virginia Hill Martinson. BS in Engring., Princeton U., 1948. Asst. chemist Devoe & Raynolds Co., Louisville, 1948-50; rschr., salesman, asst. sec. Louisville Cement Co., 1950-59; sales rep., spl. masonry rep., asst. v.p. sales tech. svcs., dir. product quality and devel. Ideal Cement Co. (later divsn. of Ideal Basic Industries), 1959-85; assoc. Openaka Corp., Inc., Denver, 1985—. Lt. (j.g.) USNR, 1944-46. Fellow Am. Concrete Inst. (bd. dirs. 1981-84, tech. activities com. 1987-93); mem. ASTM. Episcopalian. Home and Office: 3910 S Hillcrest Dr Denver CO 80237-1110

HILL, GEOFFREY WILLIAM, publisher; b. Cirencester, Eng., Oct. 7, 1941; came to the U.S., 1947; s. Ceril Hill and Olive Dora (Belcher) Colburn; m. Vicki Lynn Hill; children: Kari, Kelli, Kimi. Grad. H.S., Portland, Oreg. Journeyman's cert. in typography. Delivery boy Paul O. Giesey, Adcrafters, Portland, 1958-61, typography apprentice, 1962-66, typography journeyman, 1967-69, typography dept. head, 1970-71; ptnr. advt. prodn. Feiring & Hill Ad Agy., Bend, Oreg., 1972-73; owner advt. prodn. Geoff Hill Advt., Bend, 1974-90; owner Sun Pub., Bend, 1976—; entertainer and singer, Oreg., 1960-74. Editor: (quar. mag.) Cascades East Mag., 1976, (book) Fishing Central Oregon, 1994. Mem. Bend C. of C., Sisters C. of C., Redmond C. of C. Home: PO Box 5784 Bend OR 97708-5784

HILL, GORDON R., purchasing executive; b. Burbank, Calif., Apr. 7, 1950; s. Frank H. and Leah S. Hill; m. Chaluay K. Hill, May 14, 1976; children: Brenda, David, Michael. BS, U. So. Calif., 1972; MBA, Ariz. State U., 1983. Cert. Purchasing Mgr. Assoc. buyer Procter and Gamble, Cinn., 1977-79; sr. buyer Armour-Dial, Inc., Phoenix, 1979-84; sr. buyer Sperry Corp., Phoenix, 1984-86, subcontract adminstrn., 1986-87; purchasing mgr. Honeywell, Inc., Phoenix, 1987-92; dir. purchasing Anacomp, Inc., San Diego, 1992-94; purchasing mgr. Solar Turbines Inc., San Diego, 1994—. Bd. dirs. Rancho Bernardo H.S. Bronco Booster Club, 1995—. Comdr. USNR, 1972—. Decorated Joint Svc. Commendation medal; Trustee scholar U. So. Calif., 1969, Calif. State scholar, 1969. Mem. Nat. Assn. Purchasing Mgrs. (bd. dirs. San Diego 1995—). Office: Solar Turbines Inc PO Box 85376 San Diego CA 92186-5376

HILL, GREG, newspaper bureau chief. San Francisco bur. chief Wall St. Jour. Office: Wall St Jour 201 California St Ste 1350 San Francisco CA 94111-5002

HILL, HARRY DAVID, city official, human resources professional; b. Whittier, Calif., Oct. 29, 1944; s. Harry Boreman and Winifred Nell (Purvis) Hill; m. Linda Mae Price, Nov. 8, 1969; 1 child, Jon Ryan. AA, Los Angeles Harbor Coll., Wilmington, Calif., 1964; BA in Polit. Sci., UCLA, 1966; M of Pub. Adminstrn. in Human Resources, U. So. Calif., 1972. Personnel aide City of Anaheim, Calif., 1966-67, personnel analyst, 1967-71, sr. personnel analyst, 1971-75, personnel services mgr., 1975-83, asst. human resources dir., 1983-88, asst. labor rels. dir., 1988-94, dir. human resources, 1994—; chmn. supervisory com. Anaheim Area Credit Union, 1981-89, bd. dirs., 1989-95. Mem. So. Calif. Pub. Labor Coun. (treas. 1986-87, pres. 1988), Internat. Pers. Mgmt. Assn. (pres. western region 1983-84), So. Calif. Pers. Mgmt. Assn. (pres. 1978-79), Coop. Pers. Svcs. (bd. dirs. 1987—).

Democrat. Office: City of Anaheim 200 S Anaheim Blvd Fl 3 Anaheim CA 92805-3820

HILL, JAMES EDWARD, insurance company executive; b. Chgo., Mar. 3, 1926; s. George and Mary Luella (Hutchens) H.; m. Jessie Mae Birmingham, Jan. 29, 1949; children: James R., Ellen M. Student Denver U., 1947, MS in Fin. Svcs., Am. Coll., Bryn Mawr, Pa., 1980. CLU; chartered fin. cons.; cert. fin. planner. Office mgr., purchasing agt., acct. Steve Tojek Co., Milw., 1948-54; office mgr., acct. Oreg. Athletic Equipment Co., Portland, 1954-56; spl. agt. Prudential Ins. Co., Portland, 1956-58, div. mgr., 1958-70; gen. agt. Gt. Am. Res. Ins. Co., Portland, 1970—; v.p. Robert A. Amey Co. Inc., mfrs. reps., 1971-75; pres. Diversified Plans, Inc., 1979-89, v.p., 1989—. V.p. Multnomah County Young Republicans, 1957-58; vice chmn. Washington County Parks Adv. Bd., 1978, chmn., 1979-83; local sch. committeeman Beaverton, Or. Sch. Dist., 1993 (elected), instr. Life Underwriter Tng. Coun.; mem. task force for curriculum and instrn. Oreg. Sch. Dist., Beaverton; dir. Citizens for Pub. Edn. Inc., 1991—; treas. Evergreen Presbyn. Ch., 1993—. With U.S. Army, 1944-47. Recipient Edgar M. Kelly award Prudential, 1967. Mem. Oreg. Life Underwriters Assn. (edn. chmn. 1981-82, pres.-elect 1982-83, pres. 1983-84), Port'and Life Underwriters Assn. (dir. 1978-80, chmn. edn. com. 1978-80, pres. 1980-81, Am. Soc. C.L.U.s, (C.L.U. of Yr. award Portland chpt.; instr.), Am. Family Assn. (Oreg. state dir. 1993—). Home and Office: 12980 NW Saltzman Ct Portland OR 97229-4668

HILL, JIM, state official; 1 child, Jennifer. BA in Econs., Mich. State U., 1969; MBA, Indiana U., 1971, JD, 1974. Asst. atty. gen. Oreg. Dept. of Justice, 1974-77; hearing referee Oreg. Dept. of Revenue, 1977-81; personnel specialist and cons. State Farm Ins., 1984-86; elected mem. Oreg. House of Reps., 1983-87, Oreg. State Sen., 1987-93; dir. mktg. PEN-NOR, Inc., Portland Gen. Contractors, 1986-88; corp. accts. mgr. for Latin Am. Mentor Graphics, 1988-93. Office: Oreg State Treasury 159 State Capital Salem OR 97310

HILL, JOHN EARL, mechanical engineer; b. Ely, Nev., July 18, 1953; s. Earl M. and Florence (Lagos) H.; m. Terry Lynn Biederman, Oct. 3, 1981; 1 child, Felicia Biederman. BA in Social Psychology, U. Nev., 1974, BSME, 1981. Cert. engr. in tng. Machinist B&J Machine and Tool, Sparks, Nev., 1977-78; designer, machinist Screen Printing Systems, Sparks, Nev., 1978, Machine Svcs., Sparks, 1978-81; computer programmer U. Nev., Reno, 1980-81; design engr. Ford Aerospace and Communications Corp., Palo Alto, Calif., 1981-82, 86-88; contract design engr. Westinghouse Electric Corp., Sunnyvale, Calif., 1982-83; contract project engr. Adcotech Corp., Milpitas, Calif., 1983-84; sr. engr. Domain Tech., Milpitas, 1984-85; project engr. Exclusive Design Co., San Mateo, Calif., 1985-86; automation mgr. Akashic Memories Corp., San Jose, Calif., 1988-94; Seagate Magnetics, Fremont, Calif., 1994—; ptnr. Automated Bus. Svcs., San Jose; engr. Seagate Magnetics, Fremont, Calif., 1994—. Mem. Robotics Internat. of Soc. Mfg. Engrs., Tau Beta Pi, Pi Mu Epsilon, Phi Kappa Phi. Home: 147 Wildwood Ave San Carlos CA 94070-4516 Office: Seagate Magnetics 47010 Kato Rd Fremont CA 94538-7332

HILL, JUDITH DEEGAN, lawyer; b. Chgo., Dec. 13, 1940; d. William James and Ida May (Scott) Deegan; children: Colette M., Cristina M. BA, Western Mich. U., 1960; JD, Marquette U., 1971; cert. U. Paris, Sorbonne, 1962; postgrad. Harvard U., 1984. Bar: Wis. 1971, Ill. 1973, Nev. 1976, D.C. 1979. Tchr., Kalamazoo (Mich.) Bd. Edn., 1960-62, Maple Heights (Ohio), 1963-64, Shorewood (Wis.) Bd. Edn., 1964-68; corp. atty. Fort Howard Paper Co., Green Bay, Wis., 1971-72; sr. trust adminstr. Continental Ill. Nat. Bank & Trust, Chgo., 1972-76; atty. Morse, Foley & Wadsworth Law Firm, Las Vegas, 1976-77; dep. dist. atty., criminal prosecutor Clark County Atty., Las Vegas, 1977-83; atty. civil and criminal law Edward S. Coleman Profl. Law Corp., Las Vegas, 1983-84; pvt. practice law, 1984-85; atty. criminal div. Office of City Atty., City of Las Vegas, 1985-89, pvt. practice law, 1989—. Bd. dirs. Nev. Legal Services, Carson City, 1980-87, state chmn., 1984-87; bd. dirs. Clark County Legal Services, Las Vegas, 1980-87; mem. Star Aux. for Handicapped Children, Las Vegas, 1986—; Greater Las Vegas Women's League, 1987-88; jud. candidate Las Vegas Mcpl. Ct, 1987, Nev. Symphony Guild, Variety Club Internat., 1992-93, Las Vegas Preservation Group. Recipient Scholarship, Auto Specialties, St. Joseph, Mich., 1957-60, St. Thomas More Scholarship, Marquette U. Law Sch., Milw., 1968-69; juvenile law internship grantee Marquette U. Law Sch., 1970. Mem. Nev. Bar Assn., So. Nev. Assn. Women Attys., Ill. Bar Assn., Children's Village Club (pres. 1980) (Las Vegas, Nev.). Home: 521 Sweeney Ave Las Vegas NV 89104-1436 Office: Ste 211 726 S Casino Center Blvd Las Vegas NV 89101-6700

HILL, KEITH ROLAND, financial planner, insurance broker; b. Tyler, Tex., June 14, 1951; s. Emmett Hill and Willie Mae (Campbell) Hill-Wilson; m. Augusta Louise Barfield, Dec. 26, 1980; children: Kellus R. Kerrun R. Student, U. Abilene, Tex., 1970-72, U. of Sam Houston, 1972-74; BS in Biology, U. Tex., 1977. Cert. tchr. Sr. program dir. C.E.T.A. Govt. Agy., Tyler, 1977-78; entrepreneur exec. Oxford Group, Ltd., Aurora, Colo., 1978—. chief judge City of Aurora Mcpl. Elections, 1985—; basketball ofcl. YMCA, Aurora, 1990—. Recipient award Rotary, 1966, Optimist, 1966, Pacesetter award Merril-Dow Corp., 1979; named Colo. Outstanding Leader Western Image Publs., 1989. Mem. Am. Mgmt. Assn., Nat. Life Underwriters Tng. Coun., Colo. Cert. Life & Health Underwriters Assn. (cert. life underwriter). Home: PO Box 441410 Aurora CO 80044-1410 Office: Oxford Group Ltd PO Box 441410 Aurora CO 80044-1410

HILL, MICHAEL JOHN, newspaper editor; b. Joliet, Ill., Dec. 28, 1954; s. Elton John and Dolores Congetta (Romano) H.; m. Mary Louise Bergin, June 6, 1981 (div. 1993). BS in Journalism, No. Ill. U., 1977. Reporter gen. Muncie (Ind.) Star newspaper, 1977-78; reporter police-courts Oshkosh (Wis.) Northwestern newspaper, 1978-80; reporter govt. Messenger-Inquirer newspaper, Owensboro, Ky., 1980-82, Jour. Times newspaper, Racine, Wis., 1982-87; reporter capitol Capital Times, Madison, Wis., 1987-89, city editor, 1989-93; asst. city editor Las Vegas Rev. Jour., Las Vegas, 1993—. Contbr. articles to publs. Recipient 1st place investigative reporting Wis. Newspaper Assn., 1990, Wis. Am. Legion Auxiliary Assn. best stories on youth issues award, 1986, Wis. Press Assn. honorable mention investigative reporting, 1985, Inland Daily Press Assn. honorable mention, investigative, interpretive and background reporting, 1984, Wis. Press Assn., 3rd place, investigative reporting, 1983, 2d pl. freedom of info. Ky. Press Assn., 1982, 3rd place, best news story, 1982. Mem. ACLU, Investigative Reporters and Editors. Office: Las Vegas Rev Jour PO Box 70 Las Vegas NV 89125-0070

HILL, NATHAN SCOTT, art organization executive, cultural consultant, lecturer; b. Fremont, Calif., Jan. 6, 1962; s. N. Eugene and Patricia (Yeager) H.; m. Laura S. Weir, Aug. 19, 1984. BA in Polit. Sci., George Washington U., 1985; MA in Govt., U. Va., 1988; postgrad., U. Calif.-Davis. Co-dir. Calif. Art Rsch., Davis, 1991—; rsch. and policy analyst Calif. Sch. Bds. Assn., West Sacramento, 1993—. Author, editor, presenter articles, chpts., papers on art history, cultural policy and planning, polit. sci., and edn. Commr. City of Davis Peace & Justice Commn. 1990-92, chmn., 1991-92; commr. City of Davis Civic Arts Commn., 1992-93; bd. dirs. Napa County Legal Assistance Agy., Napa, Calif., 1995—; mem. policy adv. bd. U. Calif. Calif. Alliance for Math. and Sci., Oakland, 1995—. World Affairs Coun. scholar U. Calif.-Davis, 1983; du Pont fellow U. Va., 1985-86; adminstrn. fellow Nat. Endowment for Arts, Washington, 1991; rsch. fellow U. Calif. Washington Ctr., 1992-93. Mem. Am. Edn. Rsch. Assn. Home: 1136 Stonybrook Dr Napa CA 94558-5243 Office: Calif Sch Bds Assn PO Box 1660 West Sacramento CA 95691-6660

HILL, NORBERT S., JR., professional society executive; b. Warren, Mich., Nov. 26, 1946; s. Norbert S. Hill and Eileen Johnson; m. Mary Anne Hill, Mar. 25, 1972; children: Melissa, Megan , Norbert III. BS in Sociology/Anthropology, U. Wis., 1969, MS in Guidance and Counseling, 1971; PhD (hon.), Cumberland Coll., 1994. Asst. dean students U. Wis., Green Bay, 1972-77; edn. policy fellow Inst. for Ednl. Leadership, Washington, 1980-81; dir. native Am. ednl. opportunity program U. Colo., Boulder, 1977-83; exec. dir. Am. Indian Sci. & Engring. Soc., Boulder, Colo., 1983—; bd. dirs. George Bird Grinnell Am. Indian Children's Edn. Fdn., 1990—; mem. Blue Ribbon Adv. Panel Am. Chem. Soc., 1993—, Nat. Sci. Fdn.'s "Project Mosaic" Adv. Com., 1992—, Math. Scis. Edn. Bd. NAS, 1990-93, Com. on Opportunities in Sci. AAAS, 1986-93; leadership coun. Nat. Action Coun. for Minorities in Engring, N.Y.C., 1986—; chmn. Smithsonian Inst.'s Nat. Mus. of the Am. Indian, 1991—. Author: (book) Words of Power Voices from Indian America, 1994; contbr. articles to profl. jours.; publisher: Winds of Change Mag., 1986— (Ozzie award,1994). Adv. bd. Spelman Coll, 1994—, Technos Quarterly (Editl.), 1993—; bd. dirs. Colo. Endowment for the Humanities, Environ. Def. Fund, Women and Fdns./Corp. Philanthoropy, Four Worlds Fdn., Minority Grad. End. Com. ETS/GRE Bd., George Washington U. Nat. Ctr. for Native Am. Studies & Policy Devel., Career Coun. for the Devel. of Minorities; pres. Dr. Rosa Minoka Hill Fdn., 1982—; mem. Coun. of Advs. to President Elect Clinton's Transition Team for Edn., 1992, EPA's Environ. Edn. Adv. Coun., 1991-94, Fact Finding Team Nat. Insts. of Health Office of Minority Programs, 1991, Task Force Indian Nats. at Risk, 1990-91, Parent Adv. Com. Boulder Valley Sch. Dist., Colo., 1977-90, Edn. Com. and Oneida Tribe Trust Com. Gt. Lakes Intertribal Coun., Wis., 1975-77; trustee St. George's Sch., Newport, R.I., 1990-93, Heye Fdn., 1988-90; chmn. Oneida Film Project, Wis., 1976, Oneida Tribal Edn. Com., Wis., 1970-74, Native Am. Career Exposition, Denver, Colo., 1978-79. EPDA fellow Counselor Grad. Tng. Inst., 1970-71, Edn. Policy fellow Inst. for Ednl. Leadership, Washington, 1981, Indian Grant scholarship, 1964-68, Young Alumni award, U. Wis., 1979, Reginald H. Jones Disting. Svc. award Nat. Action Coun. for Minorities Engring., 1988, Chancellor's award U. Wis., 1988, Boulder Cmty. Action Multicultural award for Edn., 1994. Home: 2817 La Grange Cir Boulder CO 80303-6314 Office: Am Indian Sci and EngringSoc 1630 30th St Ste 301 Boulder CO 80301-1014

HILL, PHILIP RICHARDSON, management consultant; b. Boston, Aug. 5, 1930; s. Philip Cushing and Marie Teresa (Whiting) H.; m. Lenita Lillian Patronelle Louise Quiroz del Campos, Nov. 1954 (div. Nov. 1965); children: Gregory Richardson, David Cushing, Christopher Whiting; m. Gudrun Randolph, June 1966 (div. Feb. 1974); children; Derek Peter, Marc Alan; m. Hatsue Akimoto, Mar. 27, 1977. BS, Calif. State U., L.A., 1957; MS, Calif. State U., Northridge, 1962. Dir. corp. planning Litton Industries GmbH, Bonn, Germany, 1963-65, Levitt & Sons, Lake Success, N.Y., 1966-68; v.p. BRC, L.A., 1968-71; pres. IIT-Bldg. System Far East, Tokyo, 1971, ESI Japan, Tokyo, 1971-73, Am. Wirewrap, San Jose, Calif., 1979-90, Micon Industries, Oakland, Calif., 1980-81, Philip R. Hill & Co., Inc., Corvallis, Oreg., 1970—. Author: The Apartment Management Guide, 1977, Planning for Company Growth, 1979, Smart Management, 1980, The Peter Hill Family in Americas from 1663, 1992; contbr. articles to profl. jours. Served with U.S. Army, 1953-55. Republican. Office: Philip R Hill & Co Inc 3558 NW Fillmore Ave Corvallis OR 97330-4941

HILL, RALPH HAROLD, wholesale grocery company executive; b. Miller, Mo., Dec. 22, 1914; s. Richard Henry and Geneva Gertrude (Woodard) H.; m. Velma Lee Friar, Sept. 20, 1937; children: James Ralph, Richard Lee, Janice Louise. Student pubs. schs. With San Diego div. Alfred M. Lewis, Inc., Riverside, Calif., from 1935, mgr. dept. frozen food, 1953-56; mgr. Ariz. div. Alfred M. Lewis, Inc., Phoenix, 1956-63; pres., chief exec. officer Alfred M. Lewis, Inc., Riverside, 1963-82, 83-86, chmn. bd., from 1980; v.p., bd. dirs. Orange Empire Fin. Inc., Riverside; pres. Alfred M. Lewis Properties, Inc., Riverside; pres., chief exec. officer Lewis Retail Foods, Inc., Riverside, 1988—; dir. M&M, L.A., Riverside. Served with USNR, 1943-45. Mem. So. Calif. Grocers Assn., Pres. Assn., Am. Mgmt. Assn., Riverside C. of C. (bd. dirs. 1970-76, pres. 1974-75). Lodge: Rotary (pres. 1972-73). Home: 1891 Fairview Ave Riverside CA 92506-1643 Office: Alfred M Lewis Inc 3021 Franklin Ave Riverside CA 92507-3337

HILL, ROBERT BRYANT, chiropractor; b. Lynch, Nebr., July 12, 1952; s. Robert Walton and Elise Naomi (Rohde) H.; m. Donna Kay Hankins, Feb. 11, 1971; children: Karri Dawn, Donald Brent. AS, Bakersfield (Calif.) C.C., 1972; Grad., L.A. Police Acad., 1973; BS in Biology, L.A. Coll. Chiropractic, 1991, D of Chiropractic, 1993. Diplomate Nat. Bd. Chiropractic Examiners. Police officer L.A. Police Dept., 1972-81; intern Thie Chiropractic Clinic, Pasadena, Calif., 1992-93; physician Hill Chiropractic, Bakersfield, 1993—; guest lectr. Bakersfield Adventist Acad., 1993-94. Mem. Calif. Chiropractic Assn., Kern County Chiropractic Soc., Am. Pub. Health Assn., L.A.C.C. Alumni Assn., Bakersfield Adventist Mens Assn. Republican. Seventh-Day Adventist. Office: All Star Chiropractic Hill Chiropractic 4646 Wilson Rd Ste 104 Bakersfield CA 93309-5895

HILL, ROBERT GILBERT, aeronautical engineer; b. N.Y.C., Oct. 30, 1934; s. Walter Henry and Catherine (Ebbrell) H.; m. Elizabeth York Grimes, Oct. 5, 1957; children: Connie, Deborah, Jennifer. BS in Aero. Engring., Rensselaer Poly. Inst., 1957. Aerodynamicist Republic Aviation, N.Y., 1957; with Lockheed Missile and Space Co., Sunnyvale, Calif., 1960—, mgr., 1984—. Vol. Big Bros./Big Sisters, San Jose, Calif., 1986—. Lt. USAF, 1958-60. Mem. Nat. Mgmt. Assn., Oakland Yacht Club, Sigma Alpha Epsilon. Republican. Baptist. Home: 1188 Cypress Trace Dr Melbourne FL 32940-1619

HILL, ROBERT MARTIN, police detective, consultant, lecturer; b. Hammond, Ind., Dec. 10, 1949; s. Donald Edwin and Norma Jeanne (Beal) H.; m. Connie Carolina Nordquist, Dec. 19, 1970. BA, U. Minn., 1974; postgrad., U. Phoenix; cert. in fin. fraud, IRS, Glynco, Ga., 1984; cert. in questioned documents, U.S. Secret Service, Glynco, Ga., 1986. Cert. police officer, Ill., Minn., Ariz.; cert. fraud examiner. Police officer Rolling Meadows (Ill.) Police Dept., 1970-72, St. Paul Police Dept., 1972-79; police officer Scottsdale (Ariz.) Police Dept., 1980-81, police fraud detective, 1981—; com. mem. Fraud Ariz. Banker's Assn., 1985-86; lectr. various colls. and orgns. Recipient Dirs. Commendation U.S. Secret Svc., Washington, 1986, Commendation, Dept. Defense, 1993; named Investigator of Yr. Econ. Crime Investigators, 1991. Mem. Internat. Assn. Credit Card Investigators (v.p. 1985-86, pres., bd. dirs. 1986-88, Nat. Law Enforcement Officer of the Yr. award 1986, Ariz. chpt. Police Officer of the Yr. 1984, 86, 93), Internat. Assn. Auto Theft Investigators, Internat. Police Assn., Assn. Cert. Fraud Examiners. Republican. Baptist. Office: 9065 E Via Linda Scottsdale AZ 85258-5400

HILL, ROGER WENDELL, sugar company executive; b. Torrington, Wyo., Aug. 4, 1939; s. Harold Henry and Vivian Lois (Haas) H.; m. Barbara Jean Clark, July 15, 1962; children—Roger Scott, Robert Clark. B.S., U. Wyo., 1961; A.A., Ft. Lewis A&M, Durango, Colo., 1959. Asst. county agt. Wyo. Extension Service, Cheyenne, 1961-63; with Holly Sugar Corp., 1963—, various positions in Wyo., Colo., 1963-70, agrl. mgr., Worland, Wyo., 1970-73, Brawley, Calif., 1973-78, gen. mgr. cane div., Santa Ana, Calif., 1978-79, gen. agrl. mgr., Colorado Springs, 1979-81, v.p. agriculture, Colorado Springs, 1981-84, sr. v.p. agr., 1984—. Contbr. articles to agrl. publs. Mem. Am. Soc. Sugarbeet Technologists (program chmn. 1982), Riverton Jaycees, Worland C. of C., Alpha Zeta. Republican. Presbyterian. Lodges: Rotary, Elks. Home: 2245 Oak Hills Dr Colorado Springs CO 80919-3477 Office: Holly Sugar Corp PO Box 1052 Colorado Springs CO 80901-1052

HILL, RONALD GREGORY, library director; b. Corona, Calif., Mar. 17, 1952; s. Robert Edward and Marcella (Dunlap) H.; m. Clare Kevin Thurmond; children: Hannah, Gabriel, Leah, Mariam. BA, Austin Coll., 1974; postgrad., Am. U., 1975, U. Tex., 1976; MLS, U. Tex., 1983. Fgn. affairs specialist USAID, Washington, 1975-76; legis. aide Tex. Legis., Austin, 1977-81; ref. libr. Legis. Ref. Libr., Austin, 1982-83; head bus. dept. Ector County Libr., Odessa, Tex., 1983-84; dir. Seguin (Tex.)-Guadalupe County Pub. Libr., 1984-87, Corsicana (Tex.) Pub. Libr., 1987-90, Fairbanks (Alaska) North Star Borough Libr., 1990—. State del. Alaska Dem. Party, Fairbanks, 1992. Mem. Alaska Libr. Assn. (continuing edn. com. chair 1991-94, v.p./pres.-elect 1994-95). Office: Noel Wein Libr 1215 Cowles St Fairbanks AK 99701-4313

HILL, RUTH BEEBE, author, editor; b. Cleve., Apr. 26, 1913; d. Herman C. and Flora M. (Frantz) Beebe; m. Borroughs R. Hill, Oct. 17, 1940 (dec. 1982); 1 child, B. Reid. AB, Case Western Res. U., 1935, MA, 1937; HHD (hon.), Oglethorpe U., 1993. Lectr. dept. geology U. Miss., Oxford, 1937-39; head bridal cons. May Co., Denver, 1940-41, Filene's, Boston, 1941-43; founder, owner Gull Hill Elem. Sch., New Orleans, 1946-49; mag. columnist Horse and Rider, L.A., 1967-68; freelance editor, lectr. L.A., 1979—; lectr. Leigh Bur., L.A., 1979-82. Author: Hanta Yo, 1979 (Pulitzer prize nominee, Overseas award 1979, Ohioana award 1979, Booksellers award for excellence in writing 1979, Nat. Heritage award 1979, honoree Am. Acad. Achievement 1979). Mem. DAR (San Juan Islands chpt.), Nat. Writers (bd. dirs.), Nat. PEN Women. Republican. Presbyterian. Home: PO Box 788 Friday Harbor WA 98250-0788

HILL, STEVEN RICHARD, business executive; b. Oakland, Calif., May 17, 1947; s. Ernest Ellwood and Bettyjean (Schaegelen) H.; m. Sandra Ann Logan, Sept. 7, 1968; children: Heather Dawn, Tessa Michelle. BS in Forest Mgmt., U. Calif., Berkeley, 1969; MBA, UCLA, 1971. Planning analyst Weyerhaeuser Co., Wash. and N.C.; mgr. corp. raw material allocation Weyerhaeuser Co., Tacoma, 1974-78, dir. human resource planning, 1979-82, dir. benefits, compensation, health, 1982-86, v.p. employee relations, 1986-90, sr. v.p. human resources, 1990—; staff asst. U.S. Dept. Energy, Washington, 1978-79. Commr. Wash. State Hosp. Rate Setting Commn., Olympia, 1985-89; mem. Pres.' Commn. on White House Fellows, 1989-90, pres., 1989-90. White House fellow Pres.' Commn. on White House Fellows, Washington, 1978. Democrat. Congregationalist. Home: 5326 Hyada Blvd NE Tacoma WA 98422-1618 Office: Weyerhaeuser Co Tacoma WA 98477

HILL, SUSAN HOLMES, library director; b. July 31, 1949; d. Walter C.D. and Mildred G. (Holdren) Holmes; m. Steven Lloyd Hill, Nov. 27, 1984; 1 child, Jennifer Denise. BS cum laude, Brigham Young U., 1972, MLS, 1977. Media aide Prince Georges Sch. Dist., 1972-73; in tech. svcs. Utah State Libr., 1977-80, reference libr., 1980-84, reference libr. Info. Svcs., 1985-91; substitute libr. Salt Lake County Libr. System, 1985-91; dir. Brigham City Libr., 1991—. Author: Book Selection for Children, 1986, Books: Your Own Adventure! A Librarian's Planning Manual, 1986, Children's Storytime At the Library, 1986, Programming for Your Library, 1987, others. Vol. dir. 151 mission support Utah Air N.G. Family Support, 1990—. Recipient Utah Humanities Merit award. Mem. Utah Libr. Assn. (past chair adult and reference svcs. sect., past chair spl. libr. sect., chair pub. sect.). Mormon. Office: Brigham City Libr 26 E Forest St Brigham City UT 84302-2112

HILL, WALTER EDWARD, JR., geochemist, extractive metallurgist; b. Moberly, Mo., June 4, 1931; s. Walter Edward and Louise Katherine (Sours) H.; m. Beverly Gwendolyn Kinkade, Sept. 8, 1951; children: Walter III, Michele, Janet, Sean, Christopher. BA in Chemistry, U. Kans., 1955, MA in Geology, 1964. Cert. safety instr., Mine Safety and Health Adminstrn. Mgr. standards div. Hazen Rsch. Inc., Golden, Co., 1974-79; lab dir. Earth Scis. Inc., Golden, Colo., 1979-80; tech. svcs. supr. Texasgulf Inc., Cripple Creek, Colo., 1980-82; gen. mgr. Calmet, Fountain, Colo., 1983; tech. svs. mgr. Marathon Gold, Craig, Colo., 1984-85; cons., 1985-86; chief chemist Nev. Gold Mining, Winnemucca, 1987-88; ops. mgr. Apache Energy & Minerals, Golden, Colo., 1989-91; cons., 1991—; speaker in field. Contbr. 28 articles to profl. jours. Sgt. U.S. Army, 1950-52. Fellow Am. Inst. Chemists (life); mem. Assn. Exploration Geochemists, Kans. Geol. Soc., Denver Mining Club. Republican. Roman Catholic. Home and Office: 1486 S Wright St Lakewood CO 80228-3857

HILLBERG, RONALD WILLIAM, lawyer; b. Turlock, Calif., May 27, 1952; s. Carl Evald and Merlyn Jean (Miner) H.; m. Aila Maxine Tietjen, Sept. 20, 1986; children: Joel Reagan, Daniel Reagan. BA in Econs. with honors, Stanford U., 1974; JD, UCLA, 1977. Cert. specialist in estate planning, probate and trust law. Atty. Chief Counsel, IRS, Washington, 1977-78; assoc. Robert E. Triebskh, Turlock, Calif., 1978-79, Griffith & Masuda, Turlock, 1979-80; pvt. practice Turlock, 1981—; judge protem Stanislaus Mcpl. Ct., Turlock, 1992-93. Pres. Stanislaus County Econ. Devel. Corp., Modesto, Calif., 1984-85; planning commr. City of Turlock, Calif., 1985-88, coun. mem., 1988—, mayor protem, 1994—; mem. Stanislaus Area Assn. Govts., Modesto, 1988—. Mem. Calif. State Stanislaus Found. (sec. 1990-94, trustee), Turlock Rotary Club, Turlock C., of C. (pres. 1983-85), Turlock High Sch. Auditorium Restoration (sec. 1986-94). Republican. Lutheran. Office: PO Box 506 Turlock CA 95381-0506

HILLESTAD, CHARLES ANDREW, lawyer; b. McCurtain, Okla., Aug. 30, 1945; s. Carl Oliver and Aileen Hanna (Sweeney) H.; m. Ann Ramsey Robertson, Oct. 13, 1973. BS, U. Oreg., 1967; JD, U. Mich., 1972. Bar: Colo. 1972, U.S. Dist. Ct. Colo. 1972, U.S. Ct. Appeals (10th cir.) 1972, Oreg. 1993; lic. real estate broker, Colo. Law clk. to presiding justice Colo. Supreme Ct., Denver, 1972-73; ptnr. DeMuth & Kemp, Denver, 1973-83, Cornwell & Blakey, Denver, 1983-90, Scheid & Horlbeck, Denver, 1990-93, Gablehouse & Epel, Denver, 1993-94; solo practice Cannon Beach, Oreg., 1994—; co-developer award winning Queen Anne Inn Co., Capitol Hill Mansion and Cheyenne Canyon Inn hotels; mem. ad hoc com. Denver Real Estate Atty. Specialists. Co-author: Annual Surveys of Real Estate Law for Colo. Bar Assn.; contbr. articles to profl. jours.; assoc. editor of Inn Times Travel Writer. Former coun. mem. Denver Art Mus.; former chmn. Rocky Mountain chpt. Sierra Club; former bd. dirs. Hist. Denver, Inc.; former mem. Com. for Denver Arts, Am. Assn. Arbitrators Panel, Denver Ptnrship., Denver Visitor's Bur., Audubon Soc., Nat. Trust for Hist. Preservation, Friends of Photography, Leadership Denver Assn., Denver Metro Conv. and Visitors Bur., Leadership Seaside. Served to staff sgt. U.S. Army, 1968-70, Vietnam. Recipient Colo. Co. of Yr. award Colo. Bus. Mag., Award of Honor Denver Ptnrship., Newsmaker of Yr. and Outstanding Achievement awards Am. Assn. Hist. Inns, Tourism Person of Yr. award Denver Conv. and Visitor's Bur., Rocky Mountain Spectacular Inn award B&B Rocky Mountains Assn., Best Inns of Yr. awards County Inns Mag. and Adventure Rd. Mag., Best of Denver award Westward newspaper. Mem. ABA, Colo. Bar Assn., Denver Bar Assn., Colo. Lawyers for the Arts, POETS. Office: PO Box 1065 1347 S Hemlock Cannon Beach OR 97110

HILLIARD, KARYN JEAN, accountant; b. Portsmouth, Va., July 5, 1964; d. Eugene Carl and Carlene Ellen (Rossy) Young; m. Brent Allison Hilliard, Nov. 16, 1986 (div. Oct. 1991). BBA in Acctg., U. Tex., Arlington, 1986. CPA, Tex. Sr. tax acct. Ernst & Young, Dallas, 1986-90; acctg. mgr. Convex Computer Corp., Richardson, Tex., 1990-94; internat. tax acct. McKesson Corp., San Francisco, 1994; internat. tax software devel. Computer Lang. Rsch., Carrollton, Tex., 1995—. Mem. AICPA, Tex. Soc. CPA's, Dallas Mus. Art, World Wildlife Fund, Delta Zeta Alumnae Soc. Lutheran.

HILL-JONES, KATHLEEN LOIS, performing art school executive; b. Denver, Sept. 11, 1955; d. James Jenkins and Elaine (Marcella) Hill; m. Clinton Daniel Jones, Feb. 14, 1982; 1 child, Terrence Drake. BA, Colo. Women's Coll., 1977. Choreographer Fashion Bar TV Comml., Denver, 1981, Pure Gold Cheerleaders USFL, Denver, 1985, Kenny Rodgers Western Wear, Denver, 1990; exec., art dir. Hill Acad. of Dance and Dramatics, Denver, 1976—; bd. dirs. Colo. Dance Alliance, Denver, 1986-89; guest judge I Love Dance, Portland, Oreg., 1991-93. Performer Met. Troupers Charity Entertainers, Colo., 1970-76. Named Young Careerist, Bus. and Profl. Women of Am., 1978; recipient Scholastic scholarships Colo. Women's Coll., 1973-77. Mem. Colo. Dance Alliance (bd. dirs. 1986-89), Colo. Dance Festival, Internat. Tap Assn. Democrat. Roman Catholic. Office: Hill Acad Dance/Dramatics 1338 S Valentia St Ste 110 Denver CO 80231-2167

HILLMAN, MILTON HENRY, ophthalmologist, lawyer; b. Bklyn., Dec. 10, 1929; s. Nathan William Hillman and Esther (Deutsch) Waller; m. Mia Muriel Larsgaard, July 4, 1969; 1 child, Joseph Dana (dec.). BS, U. Miami, Fla., 1951, MD, 1956; JD, Glendale U., 1990. Bar: Calif. 1990; diplomate Am. Bd. Ophthalmology, Nat. Bd. Med. Examiners. Intern L.A. County Gen. Hosp., 1956-57; staff physician Rancho Los Angeles Hosp., Downey, Calif., 1958; flight surgeon USAF, U.S and Japan, 1958-61; pvt. practice medicine Santa Cruz, Calif., 1962-66; resident in ophthalmology Hollywood Presbyn. Hosp., L.A., 1966-69; pvt. practice ophthalmology Hollywood, Calif., 1970-91; pvt. practice law Pasadena, Calif., 1991—; sr. instr. ophthalmology Hollywood Presbyn. Hosp., L.A., 1970—. Capt. USAF, 1958-61. Fellow ACS, Am. Soc. Cataract & Refractive Surgery, Am. Bd. Ophthalmology, Am. Coll. Legal Medicine; mem. ABA, AMA, L.A. Soc. Ophthalmology, Calif. Med. Assn., L.A. County Med. Assn., Calif. Bar Assn., L.A. County Bar Assn. Home and Office: 1200 S Oak Knoll Ave Pasadena CA 91106-4443 Office: 5525 Etiwanda Ave Ste 311 Tarzana CA 91356-3646 Office: 4418 Vineland Ave Ste 218 North Hollywood CA 91602-2159

HILLMER, ROBIN LYNN, critical care, medical/surgical nurse; b. Fairmont, Minn., Jan. 12, 1958; d. Walter Herman and Marilyn Ruth

(Hughes) H. BSN, U. Wis., 1981; M. Nursing, U. Wash., 1990, postgrad., 1993-94. Cert. specialist; CCRN, BLS, ACLS. Staff nurse St. Joseph's Hosp., Milw., 1981-87, Harborview Med. Ctr., Seattle, 1987, Providence Med. Ctr., Seattle, 1987-90; clin. faculty Seattle Pacific U., 1990; clin. faculty/lectr. Seattle U., 1990-91; clin. nurse specialist Providence Med. Ctr., Seattle, 1991—. Bd. dirs. Home for Unwed Mothers, Resurrection Luth. Ch., Seattle, 1989-91; sec. Luths. for Life, Seattle, 1992-94, v.p., 1994-95, pres., 1995—; mem. ch. coun. Resurrection Luth. Ch., 1992—. Recipient Humanitarian award U. Wash. Sch. Nursing, 1990. Mem. AACN (Greater Milw. area chpt. sec. 1984-85, v.p. 1985-86, Puget Sound chpt. sec. 1992-93, edn. coord. 1993-95), Sigma Theta Tau, Phi Kappa Phi. Republican. Home: 22020 9th Ave S Des Moines WA 98198-6309 Office: Providence Med Ctr PO Box 34008 500 17th Ave Seattle WA 98124-1008

HILLS, LINDA LAUNEY, advisory systems engineer; b. New Orleans, June 21, 1947; d. Edgar Sebastien and Isabel (James) Launey; m. Marvin Allen Hills Sr. Jan. 29, 1977 (div. July 1982); 8 stepchildren. Student, Navy Avionics Schs., Memphis and San Diego, 1979-89; certs. in IBM Tech. Tng., System Mgmt. Schs., Chgo. and Dallas. Cert. disaster recovery planner. Sec. Calhoun and Barnes Inc. Co., New Orleans, 1965; clk. typist Social Security Adminstrn., New Orleans, 1965-67, U.S. Marshal's Office, New Orleans, 1967-69; supr. U.S. Atty.'s Office, New Orleans, 1969; with clk.'s office U.S. Dist. Ct. (ea. dist.) La., New Orleans, 1969-73; steno, sr. sec. Kelly Girl and Norrell Temp Services, New Orleans, 1974; aviation electronic technician, PO2 USN, Memphis and San Diego, 1974-78; customer engr. trainee IBM, Dallas, 1979; customer engr., systems mgmt. specialist IBM, San Diego, 1979-84; system ctr. rep. NSD Washington System Ctr. IBM, Gaithersburg, Md., 1984-87; ops. specialist mktg. dept. IBM, San Diego, 1987—, adv. systems engr., 1988-91; lectr., cons. in field. Author 5 books. Vol. Touro Infirmary, Dialysis Unit, New Orleans, 1965-67, New Orleans Recreation Dept. 1964-68, PALS-Montgomery County Mental Health Orgn., Bethesda, Md., 1984-87, various polit. candidates, 1963—; mem. Calif. Gov.'s Subcom. on Disaster Preparedness. Mem. NAFE, ACP, DAV, Info. System Security Assn., Women Computer Profls. San Diego, Data Processing Mgmt. Assn., San Diego Zoolog. Soc., Assn. System Mgmt., Smithsonian Instn. (resident assoc.), Nat. Trust Hist. Preservation. Office: PO Box 261806 San Diego CA 92196-1806

HILLS, REGINA J., journalist; b. Sault Sainte Marie, Mich., Dec. 24, 1953; d. Marvin Dan and Ardithanne (Tilly) H.; m. Vincent C. Stricherz, Feb. 25, 1984. B.A., U. Nebr., 1976. Reporter UPI, Lincoln, Nebr., 1976-80, state editor, bur. mgr., 1981-82; state editor, bur. mgr. UPI, New Orleans, 1982-84, Indpls., 1985-87; asst. city editor Seattle Post-Intelligencer, 1987—; panelist TV interview show Face Nebr., 1978-81; vis. lectr. U. Nebr., Lincoln, 1978, 79, 80; columnist weekly feature Capitol News, Nebr. Press Assn., 1981-82. Recipient Outstanding Coverage awards UPI, 1980, 82. Mem. U. Nebr. Alumni Assn., Zeta Tau Alpha. Office: Seattle Post-Intelligencer 101 Elliott Ave W Seattle WA 98119-4220

HILLYARD, LYLE WILLIAM, lawyer; b. Logan, Utah, Sept. 25, 1940; s. Alma Lowell and Lucille (Rosenbaum) H.; m. Alice Thorpe, June 24, 1964; children: Carrie, Lisa, Holly, Todd, Matthew. BS, Utah State U., 1965; JD, U. Utah, 1967. Bar: Utah 1967. Pres. Hillyard, Anderson & Olsen, Logan, 1967—; senator State of Utah, Salt Lake City, 1985—. Rep. chmn. Cache County, Logan, 1970-76; Utah State Rep., 1981-84; pres. Cache County C. of C., 1977. Named one of Outstanding Young Men of Am., Utah Jaycees, 1972; recipient Disting. Svc. award, Logan Jaycees, 1972, Merit award Cache Valley coun. Boy Scouts Am., 1981. Mem. ABA, Utah State Bar Assn., Cache County Bar Assn., Assn. Trial Lawyers Am., Am. Bd. Trial Advocates. Mormon. Club: Big Blue (Logan). Lodge: Kiwanis. Office: Hillyard Anderson & Olsen 175 E 1st N Logan UT 84321-4601

HILMAS, DUANE EUGENE, toxicologist; b. Virginia, Minn., Jan. 6, 1938; s. Eugene A. and Hilma M. (Luoma) H.; m. Barbara Louise Heldman, Dec. 30, 1961; children: Natalie L., Gregory E., Kenneth D., Aric T., Corey J. AS, Virginia Jr. Coll., 1956; BS, U. Minn., 1959, DVM, 1961; MSPH, U. N.C., 1964; PhD, Colo. State U., 1972. Diplomate Am. Coll. Vet. Preventive Medicine. Veterinarian in pvt. practice Cloquet, Minn., 1961; commd. 1st lt. U.S. Army, 1962, advanced through grades to col., 1985, retired, 1985; sr. program mgr. Battelle, Columbus, Ohio, 1985; health effects dir. EG&G Rocky Flats, Golden, Colo., 1991. Patentee in field; contbr. articles to profl. jours. Mem. Am. Vet. Med. Assn., Am. Coll. Vet. Preventive Medicine (continuing edn. chair 1988-89), Soc. Exptl. Biology and Medicine, Health Physics Soc., Radiation Rsch. Soc., Soc. Risk Analysis. Home: 7523 Estate Cir Longmont CO 80503-7260

HILTON, BARRON, hotel executive; b. Dallas, 1927; s. Conrad Hilton. Founder, pres. San Diego Chargers, Am. Football League, until 1966; v.p. Hilton Hotels Corp., Beverly Hills, Calif., 1954; pres., chief exec. officer Hilton Hotels Corp., Beverly Hills, 1966—, chmn., 1979—, also dir.; chmn., pres., dir. Hilton Equipment Corp, Beverly Hills, Calif; mem. gen. adminstrv. bd. Mfrs. Hanover Trust Co., N.Y.C. Office: Hilton Hotels Corp 9336 Civic Center Dr Beverly Hills CA 90210-3604*

HILTON, ERIC MICHAEL, hotel industry executive; b. Dallas, July 1, 1933; s. Conrad N. and Mary (Barron) H.; m. Patricia Skipworth, Aug. 14, 1954; children: Eric Michael, Beverly, Linda, Joseph B. Student, U. Tex., 1950-51, Cornell Hotel Sch., 1953-54. Various exec. position Dallas Statler Hilton, 1955-59; resident mgr. Dreshler Hilton, Columbus, Ohio, 1959-60; gen. mgr. Aurora Hilton, Ill., 1960-61; resident mgr. Shamrock Hilton, Houston, 1961-66; SW sales mgr. Hilton Hotels Corp., Houston, 1966-69; SW regional mgr. Hilton Inns, Inc., Houston, 1969-72, divisional v.p., 1972; sr. v.p. internat. real estate devel. Hilton Hotels Corp., Beverly Hills, Calif.; dir. Greenspoint Bank, Houston. Pres. N. Braes Bayou Little League, 1963; exec. v.p. Houston Trade and Travel Fair, 1963; chmn. Sponsors Club, PineOak Horse Show, 1964; bd. dirs. Harris County Cancer Soc., Tex., 1964, Houston Livestock Show and Rodeo, 1964, Conrad N. Hilton Found., Beverly Hills, Calif., 1968—, Fun Football, 1963, Lifemark Corp., 1978—; bd. dirs. Am. Contract Bridge League, 1973, pres. dist. 16, 1974; trustee Allen Acad., Bryan, Tex., 1970—, Little League Found., 1977—. Served with U.S. Army, 1953-55. Mem. Airline Passengers Assn. (nat. adv. bd. 1970—), Future Bus. Leaders Assn., Phi Beta Lambda. Office: Hilton Hotels Corp 9336 Civic Center Dr Beverly Hills CA 90210-3604

HILTON, EVA MAE (EVE HILTON), banker; b. Long Beach, Calif., Jan. 19, 1950; d. Albert Martin Wennekamp and Eva Geraldine (Hughes) Wennekamp Johnson; m. Charles H. Hilton, Jr., Nov. 30, 1968 (Div. 1982). Sr. teller Bank of Hawaii, Kailua, 1969-70; asst. mgr. ops. Ariz. Bank, Tucson, 1970-79; teller Valley Nat. Bank, Salome, Ariz., 1979-80; asst. v.p., mgr. Citiphone sales Citibank (Ariz.), Phoenix, 1980-93, v.p., br. mgr Norwest Bank Ariz., Phoenix, 1993—; instr. Am. Inst. Banking, Tucson, 1981. Mem. NAFE. Avocations: racquetball, water sports, reading. Home: 13233 N 25th Dr Phoenix AZ 85029-1441 Office: Norwest 3300 N Central Ave Phoenix AZ 85014-3039

HILYARD, DAVID FRANKLIN, optician; b. Hartland, Maine, Mar. 16, 1949; s. Clarence Emery and Glenda Irene (Doughty) H.; m. Darrie Jean Young, Sept. 28, 1984; children: Lisa, Chad, Wyatt, Spenser. Student, Norwalk Tech. Inst., 1968-69. Optical technician Laser Optics, Inc., Danbury, Conn., 1966-69, 71-76; radio team chief, sgt. U.S. Army, 1969-71; master optician, supr. Zygo Corp., Middlefield, Conn., 1976-85; specialist, chief optician UCO/Lick Observatory, U. Calif., Santa Cruz, 1985—. Author: (manual) Conventional Optical Polishing Procedures, 1982, Keck Telescope High Resolution Spectograph Optical Components, 1993; co-author: (technical report) University of California Tech. Report #49 Mosaic Project, 1988, Keck Telescope High Resolution Spectograph Design Review, 1990, UCO/Lick Tech. Report #75, 1994. Mem. Am. Inst. of Physics, Optical Soc. of Am., Soc. of Photo-Optical Instrumentation Engrs. Home: 255 Cottini Way Santa Cruz CA 95060-9467 Office: Univ of California Lick Observatory 1156 High St Santa Cruz CA 95064-1077

HIMMELBERG, BARBARA TAYLOR, controller; b. Schenectady, N.Y., Aug. 17, 1951; d. Robert Arthur and Maureen (Balhoff) Taylor; m. Jerome Paul Himmelberg Jr., Feb. 14, 1985. BS in Math., U. Mass., 1973. Account rep. GE Info. Svc. Co., Schenectady, 1973-78; fin. mgr. GE, Bridgeport, Conn., 1978-79, Dallas, 1979-80, Rome, Ga., 1980-81, Portland, Oreg., 1982-83; fin. mgr. Tektronix Inc., Portland, 1983-88; chief fin. officer Am. Guarantee Fin. Corp., Portland, 1988-89; contr. Lasco Shipping Co., Portland, 1990—. Treas. Mothers Against Drunk Driving, Portland Bradley-Angle House Shelter, Portland; bd. dirs. Komen Breast Cancer Found., Portland, Cascade AIDS Project, Portland. Office: Lasco Shipping Co 3200 NW Yeon Ave Portland OR 97210-1524

HIMMERICH Y VALENCIA, ROBERT THERON, historian, farmer; b. Ipswich, S.D., Dec. 13, 1932; s. Fred and Florence Lucille (Angel-Barnard) Himmerich; m. Eva Margaret Valencia, Sept. 24, 1953; 1 child, Marc Valencia Himmerich. BA, Calif. State U., Fullerton, 1970, MA, 1975; PhD, UCLA, 1984. Enlisted U.S. Marine Corps, 1950, commd. 2d lt., 1953, advanced through grades to maj., 1967, served in Korea, Vietnam, Hawaii among others, 1950-73, ret., 1973; owner Himmerich Trucks, Tustin, Calif., 1973-75; v.p. Jaskulski, Himmerich & Horan Brokerage Inc., Costa Mesa, Calif., 1975-91; vis. asst. prof. dept. history U. N.Mex., Albuquerque, 1985-90, assoc. dir. acad. programs Latin Am. Inst., 1990-92, assoc. prof. dept. history, 1994—; lectr. dept. history UCLA, 1985; editor N.Mex. Hist. Rev., Albuquerque, 1992—; farmer, Pena Blanca, N.Mex., 1985—. Author: Encomenderos of New Spain, 1991. Bd. dirs. Santa Fe Fiesta Found., 1989—, N.Mex. Endowment for the Humanities, Albuquerque, 1993—; mem. Santa Fe Rodeo Assn., 1991—. Mem. We. History Assn., Rocky Mountain Coun. on Latin Am. History, Marine Corps Assn. Libertarian. Roman Catholic. Office: U NMex Dept History Albuquerque NM 87131

HINCH, STEPHEN WALTER, manufacturing engineer; b. Seattle, July 13, 1951; s. Harlan Delmer and Ivy Roslyn (Thrush) H.; m. Nicolette Constance Obritsch, Sept. 11, 1976; children: Gregory P., Juliana G. BS, MS in Engring., Harvey Mudd Coll., 1974. Mfg. engr. Hewlett-Packard Co., Santa Rosa, Calif., 1974-78; mfg. engring. mgr. Hewlett-Packard Co., Rohnert Park, Calif., 1978-84; corp. SMT program mgr. Hewlett-Packard Co., Palo Alto, Calif., 1984-88, Santa Rosa, Calif., 1988—; rsch. and devel. mgr. Hewlett-Packard Co., Santa Rosa, 1988—; instr. Inst. Interconnection and Packaging of Electronic Circuits, Lincolnwood, Ill., 1985-93. Author: Handbook of Surface Mount Technology, 1988; contbr. chpts. to books, tech. articles to profl. jours. Mem. Bennett Valley Sch. Bd. Trustees, 1994. Mem. Telecomms. Industries Assn., Optical Soc. Am. Office: Hewlett-Packard Co 1412 Fountain Grove Pky Santa Rosa CA 95403-1738

HINCH, WILLIAM HARRY, retired consulting engineer; b. Amity, Colo., June 16, 1919; s. William Harry and Eleanor H. (Hargreaves) H.; m. Josephine Ann Benedeck, June 26, 1940: 1 child, William Harry Jr. BSEE, U. Denver, 1940; postgrad., U. Chgo., U. Denver, Los Alamos U., 1941-47. Registered profl. engr., Colo. V.p., gen. mgr., co-founder Engring. Cons., Inc., Denver, 1958-71; projects include Yanhee Multipurpose Project, Thailand, Kremasta Hydroelectric Project, Greece, Brahmaputra Multipurpose Project, East Pakistan, Uda Walawe Irrigation and Power Project, Ceylon, Power System Study, Yugoslavia; indsl. fellow Cen. Sci. Co., Chgo., 1940-41; jr. engr. Pub. Svc. Co. Colo., 1941; rsch. asst. U. Chgo.; inst. engr. Hanford (Wash.) Engring. Works; head health physics, Manhattan Project U. Calif., Los Alamos, N.Mex., 1942-46; design and supervisory engr. U.S. Bur. Reclamation, 1941-42, 46-57; instr. engring. physics U. Denver, 1946-47; lectr. on nuclear radiation numerous schs., socs., med. and mil. groups, 1955-65; investor since 1971. Editor Feasibility Studies, 1953-70; contbr. articles to profl. jours. Mem. Mayor's Commn. on Civil Def., 1948-50; bd. dirs. U. Denver Alumni Bds., 1950-59; trustee Colo. Acad., Denver, 1973-79. Recipient Engring. Innovation awards U.S. Bur. Reclamation, Denver, 1953-57, Bronze medal Am. Nuclear Soc., Washington, 1962, Outstanding Alumnus award U. Denver, 1969, Cert. Recognition, Soc. Nuclear Medicine, Chgo., 1977. Mem. IEEE, NSPE, Internat. Conf. on Large Electric High Tension Systems, Cons. Engrs. Coun., U.S. Com. on Large Dams, Colo. Soc. Engrs., Colo. Engring Coun., Reclamation Tech. Club, Sigma Pi Sigma. Club: Pinehurst Country. Home: 3922 S Chase Way Denver CO 80235-3133

HINCHEY, BRUCE ALAN, environmental engineering company executive; b. Kansas City, Mo., Jan. 24, 1949; s. Charles Emmet and Eddie lee (Scott) H.; m. Karen Adele McLaughlin, Nov. 27, 1969 (div. Nov. 1983); children: Scott Alan, Traci Denise, Richard Austin; m. Karen Robitaille, Apr. 10, 1993. Student, U. Mo., Rolla, 1967-71. Source testing crew chief Ecology Audits, Inc., Dallas, 1971-76; lab. mgr. Ecology Audits, Inc., Casper, Wyo., 1976-78; mgr. ops. Ecology Audits, Inc., Dallas, 1978-79; v.p. Kumpe & Assoc. Engrs., Casper, 1979-81; pres. Western Environ. Svcs. and Testing, Inc., Casper, 1981—; pres. Mining Assocs. Wyo., Cheyenne, 1986-87. Mem. Wyo State Ho. of Reps., Cheyenne, 1989—, majority floor leader, mgmt. coun., rules com., energy coun.; active Natrona County Rep. precinct, Casper, 1986—, Am. Legis. Exch. Coun., 1989—; chair Natrona County Rep. Party, 1988-89. 1st lt. C.E., U.S. Army NG, 1971-79. Mem. Am. Inst. Mining Engrs., Nat. Fedn. Ind. Bus. (Guardian award), Air Pollution Control Assn., Casper C. of C., Rotary, Shriners, Masons. Baptist. Office: Western Environ Svcs and Testing Inc 913 N Foster Rd Casper WY 82601-1640

HINCKLEY, GORDON B., church official; s. Bryant S. and Ada (Bitner) H.; m. Marjorie Pay, Apr. 29, 1937; children: Kathleen Hinckley Barnes, Richard G., Virginia Hinckley Pearce, Clark B., Jane Hinckley Dudley. Asst. to Council of Twelve Apostles, Church of Jesus Christ Latter Day Saints, 1958-61, mem. council, 1961-81, Counselor of the First Presidency, 1981-82, Second Counselor of the First Presidency, 1982-85, First Counselor to the First Presidency, 1985-95; pres. of ch., 1995—. Office: First Presidency LDS Ch 47 E South Temple Salt Lake City UT 84150 also: Bonneville Internat Corp Broadcast House 55 E 3rd Ave # D Salt Lake City UT 84107-4722

HIND, HARRY WILLIAM, pharmaceutical company executive; b. Berkeley, Calif., June 2, 1915; s. Harry Winham and B.J. (O'Connor) H.; m. Diana Vernon Miesse, Dec. 12, 1940; children—Leslie Vernon Hind Daniels, Gregory William. B.S., U. Calif., Berkeley, 1939; LL.D., U. Calif.-Berkeley, 1968; D.Sc. (hon.), Phila. Coll. Pharmacy, 1982. Founder Barnes-Hind Pharms., Inc., Sunnyvale, Calif., 1939—; now chmn. emeritus Pilkington/Barnes-Hind, Inc.; pres. Hind Health Care, Inc. Contbr. articles to profl. jours.; designer ph meter and developer of ophthamic solutions. Mem. chancellor's assocs. U. Calif.; trustee emeritus U. Calif.-San Francisco Found. Recipient Ebert award for pharm. research, 1948, Eye Research Found. award, 1958, Helmholtz Ophthalmology award for research, 1968, Carbert award for sight conservation, 1973, Alumnus of Yr. award U. Calif. Sch. Pharmacy, 1965, Disting. Service award U. Calif. Proctor Found., 1985, Commendation by Resolution State of Calif., 1987, Pharmaceutical Achievements commendation State of Calif. Assembly, Hon. Recognition award Contact Lens Mfrs. Assn., 1990. Fellow AAAS; mem. Am. Pharm. Assn. (Man of Yr. Pharmacist's Planning Svc. 1987), Am. Optometric Assn. (Man of Yr. award, 1987), Contact Lens Soc. Am. (Hall of Fame 1989), Am. Assn. Pharm. Scientists, Am. Chem. Soc., Calif. Pharm. Assn., N.Y. Acad. Scis., Los Altos Country Club, Sigma Xi, Rho Chi, Phi Delta Chi. Office: 165 Gibraltar Ct Sunnyvale CA 94089-1301

HINDS, ELIZABETH JANE, humanities educator; b. Alpena, Mich., Dec. 20, 1960; d. Kenneth William and Jean Gertrude (Hill) Wall; m. André Louis Hinds, Aug. 11, 1982 (div. July 1992). BA, U. Okla., 1982; MA, U. Tulsa, 1984, PhD, 1989. Asst. prof. Howard U., Washington, 1989-92; asst. prof. U. No. Colo., Greeley, 1992-94, assoc. prof., 1994—. Contbr. articles to profl. jours. Faculty Rsch. grantee Howard U., 1990, Faculty Devel. grantee U. Colo., 1992. Mem. MLA, Am. Lit. Assn., Popular Culture Assn. Office: Univ No Colo Dept of English Greeley CO 80631

HINER, ALLEGRA BROUGHTON, business manager; b. San Francisco, Feb. 9, 1956; d. Nicholas Ohlandt and Marjorie Sybil (Lipski) Broughton; m. Samuel Page Hiner, Apr. 20, 1984. BA in Psychology and Expressive Arts, Sonoma State U., 1982. Bus. mgr. Novato (Calif.) Inst. for Somatic Rsch. and Tng., 1979—; adv. bd. mem. Napa (Calif.) Valley Music Festival, 1993—. Author, musician: Love and Desire, 1992, Stand Up For Love, 1990, Across the River, 1988, Slow Fire, 1984. Recipient New Folk Showcase award Kerrville Music Festival, 1988. Mem. Folk Alliance N.Am., No. Calif. Songwriters Assn. Democrat. Home: PO Box 733 Penngrove CA 94951-0733 Office: Novato Inst 1516 Grant Ave Ste 212 Novato CA 94945-3146

HINERFELD, SUSAN HOPE SLOCUM, writer, editor; b. N.Y.C., Aug. 6, 1936; d. Milton Jonathan and Belle Esther (Gibralter) Slocum; m. Robert Elliot Hinerfeld, June 27, 1957; children: Daniel Slocum, Matthew Ben. BA, Wellesley Coll., 1957. Co-author: Manhattan Country Doctor, 1986; editor: Wellesley After-Images, 1974; contbr. book revs. to various publs. Mem. Authors Guild, Nat. Book Critics Cir. Democrat. Home: 131 S Cliffwood Ave Los Angeles CA 90049-3821

HINES, MELISSA, neuroscientist; b. Moline, Ill., Nov. 27, 1951; d. William Joseph and Janice Ethel (Sersig) H.; m. Richard Green; 1 child, Adam Hines-Green. BA, Princeton (N.J.) U., 1973; PhD, UCLA, 1981. Lic. clin. psychologist, Calif. Postdoctoral scholar U. Calif., Anatomy and Brain Rsch. Inst., L.A., 1981-84; vis. scientist St. Bartholomews Hosp., U. of London Endocrinology, 1992, Wis. Primate Ctr., U. Wis., Madison, 1981-82; rsch. scientist dept. psychiatry and anatomy UCLA, 1984-89, asst. prof. dept. psychiatry, 1989-93, assoc. prof., 1993—; pvt. practice psychology L.A., 1989—; reviewer, site visitor Pub. Health Svc., Washington, 1989—. Contbr. articles to profl. jours. Rsch. grantee NIH, 1981—; fellowship grant Giannini Found., 1983-84. Mem. Brain Rsch. Inst., Internat. Acad. of Sex Rsch., Am. Psychol. Soc., Sigma Xi. Office: UCLA Dept Psychiatry 760 Westwood Plaza Los Angeles CA 90095

HINES, WILLIAM EVERETT, publisher, producer, cinematographer, writer; b. San Bernardino, Calif., Apr. 2, 1923; s. Everett Ellsworth and Etta Elvira (Gillard) H. Student, UCLA, 1941-43, 46; BA, U. So. Calif., L.A., 1950, MA, 1951. Cameraman, film editor N.Am. Aviation, Inc., L.A. and Downey, Calif., 1951-53; founder, pres. Ed-Venture Films, L.A., 1954—; sec., treas. Sampson Prodns., S.A., Panama, 1956-60; v.p. Intro-Media Prodns., Inc., L.A., 1971-75; pres., pub. Ed-Venture Films/Books, L.A., 1985—; cons., expert witness, L.A., 1965—; lectr., instr., L.A., 1958—. Author: Job Descriptions...For Film & Video, 4 edits., 1961-84, Operating Tips for Film and Video, 1993; writer Operating Tips column for Internat. Photographer mag., 1987—; contbr. numerous features to profl. jours.; producer: (edn]. film) Running For Sheriff, 1954 (Merit award 1955, 56); producer films., commls. Mem. profl. adv. bd. Calif. State U., Long Beach, 1973—, Northridge, 1974—; chmn. bd. trustees Producers and Film Craftsmen Pension and Health Plans, L.A., 1965-79. Sgt. USAAF, 1943-46. Recipient Spl. citation City of L.A., 1966. Mem. Nat. Assn. Broadcast Employees and Technicians, Internat. Photographers Guild, Internat. Alliance Theatrical Stage Employees (exec. bd. dirs. 1989—, dir. tng. 1992—), Soc. Oper. Cameramen (charter, sec. 1984—, corp. liaison 1991—), Am. Film Inst., Publishers Mktg. Assn., Nat. Geog. Soc., Assn. Film Craftsmen (pres., mem. exec. bd. 1957-79), Masons, Shriners, Ephebian Soc., Sigma Nu (Epsilon Pi chpt.). Office: Ed-Venture Films/Books 1122 Calada St Los Angeles CA 90023-3115

HINES, WIRT A., plastic surgeon; b. Paris Island, S.C., Jan. 18, 1943. MD, U. Miami, 1968. Plastic surgeon Aita View Cottonwood Hosp., Utah. Office: 1151 E 3900 S Ste B115 Salt Lake City UT 84124-1216*

HING, LAWRENCE STEWART, lawyer, stock exchange official; b. Englewood, N.J., Mar. 4, 1963; s. Jin Hing and Lily Cheng Goon; m. Denise Marie Kieszkowski, Sept. 5, 1992. BA, Yale U., 1985; JD, NYU, 1988. Bar: Calif. 1988, D.C. 1990. Assoc. Orrick, Herrington & Sutcliffe, San Francisco, 1988-90; atty. Securities and Exchange Commn., San Francisco, 1990-94; sr. counsel Securities and Exch. Commn., San Francisco, 1994—. Recipient Scottish Univ. Internat. Summer Schs. grant U. Edinburgh, Scotland, 1984; U.K.-Berkeley MBA scholarBritish Consulate-Gen., 1995. Mem. Phillips Exeter Alumni Assn. Northern Calif., Yale Alumni Assn. Home: 1200 Francisco St Apt 7 San Francisco CA 94123-2318

HINMAN, FRANK, JR., urologist, educator; b. San Francisco, Oct. 2, 1915; s. Frank and Mittie (Fitzpatrick) H.; m. Marion Modesta Eaves, Dec. 3, 1948. AB with great distinction, Stanford U., 1937; MD, Johns Hopkins U., 1941. Diplomate Am. Bd. Urology (trustee 1979-85). Intern Johns Hopkins Hosp., 1941-42; resident Cin. Gen. Hosp., 1942-44, U. Calif. Hosp., 1945-47; pvt. practice medicine specializing in urology San Francisco, 1947-85; assoc. clin. prof. urology U. Calif., San Francisco, 1954-62, clin. prof., 1962—; urologist-in-chief Children's Hosp., 1957-85; mem. adv. council Nat. Inst. Arthritis, Diabetes, Digestive and Kidney Diseases, 1983-86. Served to lt. USNR, 1944-46. Fellow ACS (regent 1972-80, vice-chmn. 1978-79, v.p. 1982-83), Royal Coll. Surgeons (hon., Eng.); mem. Am. Urol. Assn. (hon.), Am. Assn. Genito-Urinary Surgeons (hon., pres. 1981), Clin. Soc. Genito-Urinary Surgeons (pres. 1979), Internat. Urol. Soc. (pres. Am. sect. 1980-84), Am. Assn. Clin. Urologists, Am. Fedn. Clin. Research, Soc. Pediatric Urology (founder, pres. 1971), Soc. Univ. Urologists (founding mem., pres. 1973), Am. Acad. Pediatrics (pres. urology sect. 1986), Urodynamics Soc. (founding mem., pres. 1980-82), Genito Urinary Reconstructive Soc. (founding mem.), Pan Pacific Surg. Assn. (v.p. 1980-83), Internat. Continence Soc., Brit. Assn. Urologic Surgeons (hon.) (St. Paul Medalist 1991), Société Française d'Urologie, Australasian Soc. Urologic Surgeons (hon.), Phi Beta Kappa, Alpha Omega Alpha. Clubs: Bohemian, St. Francis Yacht, San Francisco Yacht, Tahoe Yacht. Home: 1000 San Francisco St San Francisco CA 94109 Office: U Calif Med Ctr San Francisco CA 94143-0738

HINMAN, GEORGE BURKE, lawyer; b. Lincoln, Nebr., Apr. 29, 1949; s. Jack Leroy and Margaret Isabella (Burke) H. BA, U. Nebr., 1976; JD, Calif. Western Sch. Law, 1980. Bar: Calif. Assoc. Milberg Weiss Bershad Hynes & Lerach, San Diego, 1980-82; assoc. Sullivan Cummins Wentz McDade & Wallace, San Diego, 1983-87, ptnr., 1987—. Editor-in-chief Calif. Western Internat. Law Jour., 1980. Mem. Calif. Bar Assn., San Diego County Bar Assn. Democrat. Episcopalian. Office: Sullivan Cummins Wertz McDade & Wallace 945 Fourth Ave San Diego CA 92101

HINRICHS, EDGAR NEAL, retired geologist; b. New York, N.Y., Dec. 14, 1922; s. Edgar Gerhard and Lucile (Cazier) H.; m. Gertrude Elaine Verstegen, Sept. 30, 1950; children: Daniel Karl, Richard Neal, Jeffrey Andrew. BA, Oberlin Coll., 1947; MS, Cornell U., 1950. Geologist U.S. Geol. Survey, Denver, Colo., 1948-86; vol. geologist U.S. Geol. Survey, 1987—. Vol. driver ARC, 1990-93; vol. swim instr. YMCA, 1993—. Lt. (j.g.) USNR, 1944—. Fellow Geol. Soc. of Am.; mem. Colo. Sci. Soc. (sec. 1953-55).

HINRICHS, MARK CHRISTIAN, electrical engineer; b. Decatur, Ill., May 30, 1953; s. Edmund Carl and Dorothy Clara (Keller) H.; m. Marlene Elaine Krommenhoek, Apr. 24, 1976; children: Jeffrey Mark, Peter Eugene, Benjamin Paul. AA, Bethany Luth. Coll., 1973; BSEE, U. Minn., 1975; MSEE, Ga. Inst. Tech., 1991. Registered profl. engr., Iowa, N.Mex. Engring. mgr. N.W. Iowa Power Coop., LeMars, 1975-84; staff mem. Los Alamos (N.Mex.) Nat. Lab., 1984—; frequency coord. Utilities Telecommunications Coun., LeMars, 1976-78; cons. in field. Mem. POW/MIA League of Families, Washington, 1984—, Am. Radio Relay League, Newington, Conn., 1970—. Mem. IEEE (local bd. dirs. 1982-84), IEEE Power Engring. Soc. (local chpt. chmn. 1995—), IEEE Power Electronics Soc. Republican. Lutheran. Home: 406 Catherine Ave Los Alamos NM 87544-3565 Office: Los Alamos Nat Lab PO Box 1663 Los Alamos NM 87544-0600

HINSHAW, DAVID B., SR., hospital administrator; b. 1923. Grad., Loma Linda U., 1947, post grad., 1947-48. Intern White Meml. Hosp., L.A., 1946-47; resident gen. and vascular surgery VA Hosp., U. Oreg., 1950-54; pvt. practice, 1954—; instr. Sch. Medicine, Loma Linda U., Calif., 1954-83; pres. Loma Linda Faculty Med. Group, 1973—, Adventist Health System Loma Linda Inc., Loma Linda, Calif., 1982—, Loma Linda U. Med. Ctr., Calif., 1983—, Loma Linda Mecantile Inc., Loma Linda, Calif., 1988—. With U.S. Army, 1948-50. Office: Loma Linda U Med Ctr PO Box 2000 Loma Linda CA 92354-0200

HINSHAW, HORTON CORWIN, physician; b. Iowa Falls, Iowa, 1902; s. Milas Clark and Ida (Bushong) H.; m. Dorothy Youmans, Aug. 6, 1924; children: Horton Corwin, Barbara (Mrs. Barbara Baird) (dec.), Dorothy (Mrs. Gregory Patent). A.B., Coll. Idaho, 1923, D.Sc., 1947; A.M., U. Calif., 1926, Ph.D., 1927; M.D., U. Pa., 1933. Diplomate Am. Bd. Internal Medicine, Nat. Bd. Med. Examiners. Asst. prof. zoology U. Calif., 1927-28; adj. prof. parasitology and bacteriology Am. U., Beirut, Lebanon, 1928-31; instr. bacteriology U. Pa. Sch. Medicine, 1931-33; fellow, 1st asst. medicine.

Mayo Found., U. Minn., 1933-35, asst. prof., 1937-46, assoc. prof., 1946-49; cons. medicine Mayo clinic, 1935-49, head sec. medicine, 1947-49; clin. prof. medicine, head divsn. chest diseases Stanford Med. Sch., 1949-59; clin. prof. medicine U. Calif. Med. Sch., 1959-79, emeritus prof., 1979—; chief thoracic disease svc. So. Pacific Meml. Hosp., 1958-69; dir. med. svcs.and chief staff Harkness Community Hosp. and Med. Ctr., San Francisco, 1968-75; Dir. med. ops. Health Maintenance No. Calif., Inc.; mem. Calif. Com. Regional Med. Programs, 1969-75. Author: Diseases of the Chest, rev. edit., 1980; co-author: Streptomycin in Tuberculosis, 1949; contbr. over 215 articles to med. publs.; co-discoverer antiTB chemotherapy, exptl. and clin., with several drugs. Del. various internat. confs., 1928-59. Recipient Disting. Alumnus award Mayo Found., 1990. Fellow A.C.P., Am. Coll. Chest Physicians; hon. mem. Miss. Valley Med. Assn.; mem. AMA, Nat. Tb Assn. (bd. dirs., chmn. com. therapy, v.p. 1946- 47, 67-68, rsch. com.), Am. Thoracic Soc. (pres. 1948-49, hon. life 1979), Am. Clin. and Climatol. Soc., Minn. Med. Assn., Am. Bronchoesophalogical Assn., Am. Soc. Clin. Investigation, Cen. Soc. Clin. Rsch., Soc. Exptl. Biology and Medicine, Aero-Med. Assn., Am. Lung Assn. (hon., Hall of Fame 1980), Minn. Soc. Internal Medicine, Sigma Xi, Phi Sigma, Gamma Alpha. Mem. Soc. of Friends. Home: 400 Deer Valley Rd Apt 4L San Rafael CA 94903-5515

HINSHAW, MARK LARSON, architect, urban planner; b. Glendale, Calif., Aug. 17, 1947; s. Lerner Brady and Alice Elaine (Larson) H.; m. Caryl Ann Kunsemuller, Dec. 21, 1968 (div. 1982); 1 child, Erica; m. Marilyn Kay Smith, June 18, 1983; children: Lindsay, Christopher. B.Arch. magna cum laude, U. Okla., 1970; M. Urban Planning, CUNY, 1972. Registered architect, Wash. Sr. planner Planning Dept., Anchorage, 1976-77; project planner TRA, Seattle, 1977-82; urban designer, City of Bellevue, Wash., 1982-90; ind. cons., 1991—; architect-in-the-sch., Seattle Sch. Dist., 1979. Columnist on architecture, urban design Seattle Times, 1993—; contbr. articles to profl. publs. and books. Mem. Urban Beautification Commn., Anchorage, 1975, Design Jury, Hemet (Calif.) Civic Ctr. Competition, Seattle Design Commn., 1990-91. Served to 1st lt. USAF, 1972-76. NEA grantee, 1975; recipient Merit award for Hist. Preservation, City Seattle, 1983. Fellow AIA (pres. Seattle chpt. 1992-93); mem. Am. Planning Assn. (sec. Wash. chpt. 1982, v.p. 1983-85, pres. 1987-89), Am. Inst. Cert. Planners (mem. nat. bd. 1994—). Office: 911 Western Ave Ste 203 Seattle WA 98104-1031

HINSVARK, DON GEORGE, social services agency professional; b. Helena, Mont., Mar. 27, 1934; s. Almer Burton and Carmen Christine (Houston) H.; m. Jacqueline Rica Sarfati, July 10, 1958; children: Jon Felix, Timothy Joel, Michael David, Symone Hinsvark Sass. BA, U. So. Calif., 1956; MA in Tchg. and Counseling, San Diego State U., 1967; postgrad., sch. adminstrn. cert., U. La Verne, 1984-86; Cert. Career Counseling/Legal Asst., U. Calif.-San Diego, 1994. Cert. tchr. gen. elem. and jr. high edn., sch. adminstrn., sch. counselor, Calif. Tchr. San Diego (Calif.) City Schs., 1962-65, dist. counselor, 1965-85, dist. counselor team leader, 1985-91, chmn. sch. attendance rev. bd., 1992; career counselor Dyasayd Consultation, San Diego, 1993; supr. and acting dir. Voices for Children, San Diego, 1994—; mem. San Diego Commn. on Children, Youth and Families, 1994—, adv. bd. San Diego State U. Sch. Social Work, 1993—; adv. bd., instr. U. La Verne (Calif.), Edn. Dept., 1984-88; presenter in field. Joint author: Crisis Team Handbook, 1988; contbr. articles to profl. jours. Coach Age Group Swim Team, Coronado, Calif., 1962, Pop Warner Football, Coronado, 1970-71; coach and mgr. Little League Baseball, Coronado, 1970-75, Sr. Little League Baseball, Coronado, 1976-77. Lt. USN, 1956-61, Atlantic and Pacific; capt. USNR. Recipient NROTC scholarship USN, 1952-56; scholar Nat. Def. Edn. Inst., U.S. Govt. 1966, 68. Mem. Calif. Sch. Social Workers Assn. (pres. San Diego chpt. 1972, state area rep. 1979), San Diego City Student Svcs. Assn. (pres. 1983-84, 86-87), Calif. Sch. Counselors Assn. (area rep. 1982-83, 92-93, Area Counselor of Yr. 1992), Calif. Assn. for Counseling and Devel. (pres. San Diego chpt. 1992-93), Kiwanis (v.p., sec. San Diego chpt. 1987, Educator of Yr. 1991), Am. Counseling Assn. Home: 720 Country Club Ln Coronado CA 92118-2038 Office: Voices for Children 2851 Meadow Lark Dr San Diego CA 92123

HINTON, LESLIE FRANK, media executive; b. Bootle, Lancashire, Eng., Feb. 19, 1944; came to U.S., 1976, naturalized, 1985; s. Frank Arthur and Lilian Amy (Bruce) H.; m. Mary Christine Weadick, Mar. 30, 1968; children: Martin Frank, Thomas Adam, William Daniel, James Arthur, Jane Amy. Reporter Adelaide News, South Australia, 1960-65; desk editor Brit. United Press, London, 1965-66; reporter The Sun, London, 1966-69, 71-76; writer, editor Adelaide News, South Australia, 1969-70; U.S. corr. News Internat., N.Y.C., 1976-78; news editor The Star, N.Y.C., 1978-80, mng. editor, 1980-82; assoc. editor Boston Herald, 1982-85; editor-in-chief Star Mag., 1985-87; exec. v.p. Murdoch Mags., N.Y.C., 1987-90, pres., 1990-91; pres., chief exec. officer News Am. Pub., Inc., N.Y.C., 1991-93; chmn., CEO Fox TV Stations Inc, Fox News Inc., L.A., 1993-94; exec. v.p. strategic planning Fox TV Group, Beverly Hills, Calif., 1994—. Office: Fox TV Group 10201 W Pico Rd Beverly Hills CA 90213*

HINTZ, CHARLES RAY, television engineer; b. Reno, Nev., Jan. 1, 1948; s. Raymond Edgar and Hilda Ida (Daily) H.; m. Hisako Endo, Sept. 29, 1984. AS, Sierra Coll., Rocklin, Calif., 1968; BA, Chico (Calif.) State U., 1970; MS in Edn., Calif. State U., Hayward, 1993. Electronics instr. Heald Inst. Tech., San Francisco, 1974; studio engr. ABC-Hollywood, L.A., 1975; asst. chief engr. KOLO, Reno, Nev., 1976-78; TV engr. KRON, San Francisco, 1979-82; mgr. curriculum devel. Sony Broadcast P.C., San Jose, 1982-88; sr. engr. KTVU/Cox Enterprise, Inc., Oakland, Calif., 1988—. Author: Magnetic Recording for Television Engineers, 1992. Active mem. curriculum com. Napa Valley (Calif.) Coll., 1979—. Mem. ASCD, Soc. of Motion Picture and TV Engrs. (mgr. SFO sect. 1992-94, sec./treas. 1995—). Democrat. Buddhist. Office: KTVU-TV 2 2 Jack London Sq Oakland CA 94607-3727

HIRANO, IRENE ANN YASUTAKE, museum director; b. L.A., Oct. 7, 1948; d. Michael S. and Jean F. (Ogino) Yasutake; 1 child, Jennifer. BS in Pub. Adminstrn., U. So. Calif., 1970, MPA in Pub. Adminstrn., 1972. Project adminstr. U. So. Calif., 1970-72; assoc. dir. Asian Women's Ctr., 1972-73; nat. project coord., Japanese site supr. Nat. Asian Am. Field Study, L.A., 1973-75; cons. U.S. Dept. Health, Edn. and Welfare, Adminstn. on Aging, San Francisco, 1975; exec. dir. T.H.E. Clinic for Women, Inc., L.A., 1975-88; exec. dir., pres. Japanese Am. Nat. Mus., L.A., 1988—; lectr., spkr. in field. Mem. L.A. Ednl. Alliance for Restructuring Now, 1993—, Pres's. Com. on Arts & Humanities, 1994—, Commn. on Future of Smithsonian Inst., 1993—, L.A. Coalition, 1993—; trustee Malborough Sch., 1993—; co-founder Leadership Edn. for Asian Pacifics, 1983, pres. 1983-86, v.p. 1986-90; pres., bd. dirs. Asian Pacific Am. Support Group, U. So. Calif., 1984-88; bd. dirs. Liberty Hill Found., 1984-88, community funding bd., 1981-84, chairperson Calif. Commn. on the Status of Women, 1981-82, commn. mem., 1976-83, many others. Recipient Nat. Outstanding Asian/Pacific Islander award NEA, 1983, Outstanding Women of the '90's, Robinson's Corp., 1992, Outstanding Svc. award Nat. Women's Polit. Caucus, 1986, Nat. Inst. Women of Color, 1984, Outstanding Alumni award U. So. Calif., 1994, So. Calif. Hist. Soc. Cmty. award, 1995. Office: Japanese Am Nat Mus 369 E 1st St Los Angeles CA 90012-3901

HIROHATA, DEREK KAZUYOSHI, air force reserve officer; b. Dos Palos, Calif., June 26, 1963; s. Vincent Yoshinobu and Gertrude Sumiko (Kimura) H. BA in Polit. Sci., Calif. State U., Fresno, 1987; MA in Aerospace Sci., Embry Riddle U., 1992; postgrad., So. Ill. U., Carbondale; grad., Italian Mil. Jump Sch., 1989, USAFE Command & Control Sch., 1990, Brit. Army Jump Sch., 1990. Commd. 2d lt. U.S. Air Force, advanced through grades to capt., 1991; ground launched cruise missile launch control officer Italy and U.K., 1988-90; emergency actions officer 501 Tactical Missile Wing, RAF Greenham Common, U.K., 1989-90; chief force mgmt. 513 Svcs. Squadron, RAF Mildenhall, U.K., 1990-92; billeting & food svc. coord., laison officer Air Fete, Eng.; treaty inspector escort Conventional Forces Europe; USAFR, 1993—, 932 SVS ops. officer. Contbr. to poetry anthologies Am. Poetry Soc., 1993, Poets Pen Quarterly, 1993, Memories Anthology, 1994, Delta. Coord. peer support network Sch. Law So. Ill. U., Carbondale, founder, capt. trial advocacy competition team, 1994-95; mem. Jessup Internat. Moot Ct. team. Mem. ABA, ATLA (founder So. Ill. U.-Carbondale chpt.), Christian Legal Soc., Internat. Law Soc., So. Ill. U.-Carbondale Student Bar Assn., So. Ill. U.-Carbondale Law & Medicine Soc., Air and Space Smithsonian, Officers' Christian Fellowship, Airforce Assn., Air Force Edn. Soc., U.S. Capitol Hist. Soc., Calif. State U.-Fresno Alumni Orgn., West Coast Karate Assn., Assn. Air Force Missileers (assoc.), Sigma Nu (alumni advisor So. Ill. U.-Carbondale chpt., dist. commdr.). Republican. Methodist. Home: PO Box 243 South Dos Palos CA 93665-0243

HIROHATA, LAURIE ANN, state agency official; b. Merced, Calif., Sept. 29, 1958; d. Lawrence T. and Carolyn (Yamamoto) H. BA in Psychology, BS in Human Devel., U. Hawaii, 1980; MSW, U. Kans., 1983; EdM, U. Ill., 1988. Adminstrv. asst. Cath. Social Svcs. Individualized Svcs. to the Elderly, Honolulu, 1983-84; family and community svcs. specialist Easter Seal Soc. Hawaii, Honolulu, 1984-85; rural groups coord. Honolulu Gerontology Program, 1986; program specialist Hawaii State Coun. on Vocat. Edn., Honolulu, 1986-87; rsch. asst. U. Ill. Transition Inst., Champaign, 1987-88; planner Hawaii Dept. Human Svcs., Honolulu, 1988-90, Office of State Planning, Honolulu, 1990—; part time lectr. Honolulu Community Coll. Human Svcs. Dept., 1990—; project dir. Hawaii Assistive Tech. Svcs. Project, Honolulu, 1991-93; pvt. practice, educator Nihon Fukushi U. Internat. Ctr., 1993—; part time pvt. practice cons./trainer vocat. counseling spl. needs, 1990—; part time lectr. dept. human resources U. Hawaii, 1993. Editor reference guide Kans. Bds. and Commns., 1988. Vol. Community Svc. Sentencing Program, Honolulu, 1985; advocate Palolo Residents to Stop Hillside Devel., 1987. Mem. Am. Assn. for Counseling Devel., Nat. Assn. Social Workers, Health and Community Svcs. Coun. of Hawaii, Young Dems., Phi Delta Kappa, Kappa Delta Pi, Phi Upsilon Omicron (Beta Alpha chpt.). Office: Internat Ctr Nihon Fukushi U, Okuda Mihama-cho, Aichi-Ken 470-32 Chita-gun Japan

HIROTA, DENNIS ISAO, engineering executive, civil engineer; b. Honolulu, Apr. 4, 1940; s. Sam O. and Yukino (Yamane) H.; m. Kathryn Ennis, Jan. 6, 1968; children: Maile Marie, Dan. H. BSCE, U. Mich., 1963, MS, 1964, PhD, 1970. Profl. engr., Hawaii. Exec. v.p. Sam O. Hirota, Inc., Honolulu, 1971-86, pres., 1986—; bd. dirs. Ctrl. Pacific Bank, Honolulu, CPB, Inc., Honolulu. Capt. USAF, 1968-71. Mem. Pacific Club, Mid-Pacific Country Club. Home: 706 Puuikena Dr Honolulu HI 96821-2509 Office: Sam O Hirota Inc 864 S Beretania St Honolulu HI 96813-2502

HIRSCH, ANTHONY T., physician; b. N.Y.C., Jan. 29, 1940; s. Robert S. and Minna Hirsch; m. Barbara Hershan, July 8, 1961; children: Deborah, Kenneth, Steven. BS cum laude, Tufts U., 1961, MD, 1965. Diplomate Am. Bd. Pediatrics, Am. Bd. Allergy-Immunology. Pvt. practice pediatrics Children's Med. Group, L.A., 1973-84; chair dept. pediatrics, dir. residency tng. program in pediatrics White Meml. Med. Ctr., L.A., 1984—. Capt. USAF, 1969-71. Fellow Am. Acad. Pediatrics (chair access task force Calif. br., mem. nat. access task force, chair coun. on pediatric practice), Am. Acad. Allergy-Immunology. Office: White Meml Med Ctr Dept Pediatrics 414 N Boyle Ave Los Angeles CA 90033-2410

HIRSCH, BETTE G(ROSS), college administrator, foreign language educator; b. N.Y.C., May 5, 1942; d. Alfred E. and Gladys (Netburn) Gross; m. Edward Raden Silverblatt, Aug. 16, 1964 (div. Feb. 1975); children: Julia Nadine, Adam Edward; m. Joseph Ira Hirsch, Jan. 21, 1978; stepchildren: Hillary, Michelle, Michael. BA with honors, U. Rochester, 1964; MA, Case Western Res. U., 1967, PhD, 1971. Instr. and head French dept. Cabrillo Coll., Aptos, Calif., 1973-90, div. chair fgn. langs. and communications div., 1990—; mem. steering com. Santa Cruz County Fgn. Lang. Educators Assn., 1981-86; mem. liaison com. fgn. langs. Articulation Coun. Calif., 1982-84, sec., 1983-84, chmn., 1984-85; workshop presenter, 1982—; vis. prof. French Mills Coll., Oakland, Calif., 1983; mem. fgn. lang. model curriculum stds. adv. com. State Calif., 1984; instr. San Jose (Calif.) State U., summers 1984, 85; reader Ednl. Testing Svc. Advanced Placement French Examination, 1988, 89; peer reviewer for div. edn. programs, NEH, Washington, 1990, 91, 93; grant evaluator, NEH, 1995; mem. fgn. lang. adv. bd. The Coll. Bd., N.Y.C., 1986-91. Author: The Maxims in the Novels of Duclos, 1973, co-author: (with Chantal Thompson) Ensuite, 1989, 93, Moments Litteraires, 1992, (with Chantal Thompson and Elaine Phillips) Mais Ou! Workbook, Lab. Manual, Video Manual; contbr. revs. and articles to profl. jours. Pres. Loma Vista Elem. Sch. PTA, Palo Alto, Calif., 1978-79; bd. dirs. United Way Stanford, Palo Alto, 1985-90, mem. allocations com., 1988. Grantee NEH, 1980-81, USIA, 1992; Govt. of France scholar, 1982. Mem. Am. Coun. on Teaching of Fgn. Langs., Am. Assn. Tchrs. French (exec. coun. No. Calif. chpt. 1980-85), Assn. Calif. Community Coll. Adminstrs., Assn. Depts. Fgn. Langs. (exec. com. 1985-88, pres. 1988), Modern Lang. Assn. (mem. adv. com. on fgn. langs. and lits. 1995—). Democrat. Jewish. Home: 4149 Georgia Ave Palo Alto CA 94306-3813 Office: Cabrillo College 6500 Soquel Dr Aptos CA 95003-3119

HIRSCH, JOEL GIDEON, lawyer; b. Oakland, Calif., July 8, 1951; s. Werner Zvi and Hilde Esther (Zwirn) H.; m. Bonnie Ivy Bogin, Feb. 14, 1994; 1 child, Bennett Walker Bogin. AB summa cum laude, UCLA, 1973; JD, U. Calif., Berkeley, 1976. Bar: Calif. 1976. Assoc. Cox, Castle & Nicholson, Century City, Calif., 1976-79; gen. counsel bus. Carlsberg Corp., L.A., 1979-85; ptnr. Shea & Gould, L.A., 1988; pvt. practice Century City, Calif., 1988—. Contbr. articles to profl. jours. Mem. State Bar Calif.

HIRSCH, WALTER, economist, researcher; b. Phila., Apr. 21, 1917; s. Arnold Harry and Ann Belle (Feldstein) H.; m. Leanore Brod, Feb. 12, 1939 (dec. 1985); stepchild, Stephen M. Gold; children: Jeffrey A., Robert A.; m. June Freedman Gold Clark, Dec. 16, 1986. BS in Econs., U. Pa., 1938; LLD (hons.), Chapman Coll., 1968. Economist U.S. Bur. Stats., Washington and N.Y.C, 1946-50, Dept. USAF, Washington, 1950-51, Nat. Prodn. Auth., Washington, 1952-53; dir. indsl. mobilization Bur. Ordnance Dept. USN, Mechanicsburg, Pa., 1954-56; ops. rsch. analyst Bur. Supplies and Accts. Dept. USN, Arlington, Va., 1956-58; economist, ops. rsch. analyst Internat. Security Affairs Office Sec. of Def., Arlington, 1958-61; chief ops., rsch. analyst Gen. Svcs. Adminstrn., Washington, 1961-63; ops. rsch. analyst Spl. Projects Office Sec. of Def., Arlington, 1963-67; dir. ednl. rsch. U.S. Office Edn., San Francisco, 1967-72; cons. on loan to Office of Dean Acad. Planning, San Jose (Calif.) State U., 1972-74. Author: Unit Man-Hour Dynamics for Peace or War, 1957, Internal Study for Office Secretary of Defense: Sharing the Cost of International Security, 1961. Vol. De Young Mus., San Francisco, 1981-84, Calif. Palce of Legion of Honor, Phila. Mus. Art, 1984-86; pres. Met. Area Reform Temples, Washington, Nat. Fedn. Temple Brotherhoods; supporter Phila. Orch., San Francisco Symphony, San Francisco Conservatory Music, Curtis Inst. With USAAF, 1942-46. Recipient Meritorious Civilian Svc. award Navy Dept., 1956. Mem. Pa. Athletic Club, Commonwealth Club of Calif., World Affairs Council, Press Club of San Francisco, Phi Delta Kappa.

HIRSCH, WERNER ZVI, economist, educator; b. Linz, Germany, June 10, 1920; came to U.S., 1946, naturalized, 1955; s. Waldemar and Toni (Morgenstern) H.; m. Hilde E. Zwirn, Oct. 30, 1945; children: Daniel, Joel, Ilona. BS with highest honors, U. Calif., Berkeley, 1947, PhD, 1949. Instr. econs. U. Calif., 1949-51; econ. affairs officer UN, 1951-52; economist Brookings Instn., Washington, 1952-53; asst. research dir. St. Louis Met. Survey, 1956-57; prof. econs. Washington U., St. Louis, 1953-63, dir. Inst. of Urban and Regional Studies; economist Resources for Future, Inc., Washington, 1958-59; dir. Inst. Govt. and Pub. Affairs UCLA, 1963-73, prof. econs., 1963—; mem. senate acad. coun. U. Calif., 1985-87, 89-91; mem. acad. senate faculty welfare com. U. Calif., 1984—, chair, 1985-87, 89-91, mem. restructure task force, 1993—; scholar in residence Rockefeller Study Ctr., 1978; cons. Rand Corp., 1958—, U.S. Senate Com. on Pub. Works, 1972, Calif. Senate Select Com. on Structure and Adminstrn. Pub. Edn., 1973, Joint Econ. Com. of Congress, 1975-76, OECD, 1977-80; mem. com. to improve productivity of Govt. Com. Econ. Devel., 1975-76; chmn. L.A. City Productivity Adv. Com., 1982-85; active Transit Rsch. Panel of NRC, 1993—. Author: Introduction to Modern Statistics, 1957, Analysis of the Rising Costs of Education, 1959, Urban Life and Form, 1963, Elements of Regional Accounts, 1964, Regional Accounts for Public Decisions, 1966, Inventing Education for the Future, 1967, The Economics of State and Local Government, 1970, Regional Information for Government Planning, 1971, Fiscal Crisis of America's Central Cities, 1971, Program Budgeting for Primary and Secondary Public Education, 1972, Governing Urban America in the 1970s, 1973, Urban Economic Analysis, 1973, Local Government Program Budgeting: Theory and Practice, 1974, Recent Experiences with National Planning in the United Kingdom, 1977, Law and Economics: An Introductory Analysis, 1979, 2d rev. edit., 1988, Higher Education of Women: Essays in Honor of Rosemary Park, 1978, Social Experimentation and Economic Policy, 1981, The Economics of Municipal Labor Markets, 1983, Urban Economics, 1984, Economist's Role in Government at Risk, 1989, Public Finance and Expenditures Under Federalism, 1990, Privatizing Government Services, 1991; mem. editl. bd. Pakistani Jour. Applied Econs., 1980—, Internat. Rev. Law and Econs., 1985-88, Urban Affairs Quar., 1991-94. Bd. dirs. Calif. Coun. Environ./Econ. Balance, Calif. Found. on Economy, 1979-89, U. Calif. Retirement Sys., 1986-94, Wilstein Inst.,; bd. govs. Edmund G. Brown Inst., 1981-86; mem. UCLA Bldg. Authority, 1984-87, Acad. Senate Restructure Task Force, 1993—, UCLA Coun. on Planning and Budget; pres. Am. Friends Wilton Park, 1983-85, Friends Graphic Arts, 1974-79; exec. com. regional bd. Anti-Defamation League, 1986—; trustee U. Art Mus., Berkeley, 1991—; gov. U. Calif. Faculty Ctr., 1992-94; chair U. Judaism acad. bd. Mem. Am. Econ. Assn., Am. Farm Econs. Assn., Western Region Sci. Assn. (bd. dirs., pres. 1978-80), Town Hall West (pres. 1978-79), L.A. World Affairs Coun., Phi Beta Kappa, Sigma Xi. Home: 11601 Bellagio Rd Los Angeles CA 90049-2112 Office: U Calif Dept Econs Los Angeles CA 90024-1477

HIRSCHE, BLAYNE LYNN, plastic surgeon; b. Lethbridge, Alta., Can., Feb. 27, 1942; s. Lynn Alfred and Hortense Florence (Lybbert) H.; m. Sandra Lee Baird, June 20, 1965; children: Leslie Serre, Blayne Lynn II, Nicole, Lexy, Cyril, Kristina. BS, U. Alta., Edmonton, Can., MD. Intern Foothills Hosp., Calgary, Alta., Can.; resident Mayo Grad. Sch., Rochester, Minn., fellow, sr. resident, chief resident; sr. resident Peter Bent Brigham Hosp., Boston; chief resident Children's Hosp., Boston; pvt. practice Provo, Utah; v.p. Assn. Fellows, Mayo Clinic, Rochester, 1974-75; gen. surgeon Adams Clinic, Hibbing, Minn., 1975. Recipient Benson Inst. Humanitarian Svc. award Brigham Young U., 1992. Mem. Utah State Plastic Surgeons Soc. (pres. 1992), Collegium Aesculapium (pres. 1993). Republican. Mem. LDS Ch. Home and Office: 4157 Imperial Way Provo UT 84604

HIRSCHFELD, A. BARRY, publishing executive; b. Denver, Aug. 18, 1942; m. Arlene Friedman; 2 children. BS, Calif. State Poly. U., 1964; MBA, U. Denver, 1966. Pres. A.B. Hirschfeld Press, Denver, 1966—. Mem. Colo. Concern; past bd. chmn. Denver Art Mus.; past chmn., exec. com. Denver Met. Conv. and Visitors Bur., life trustee; bd. dirs. Pub. Svc. Co. of Colo.; bd. govs. 9Who Care; mem. endowment com., past bd. Allied Jewish Fedn.; bd. dirs. Boettcher Found., Boy Scouts Am., Colo. Bus. Com. for Arts, Mountain States Employers Coun., pres. 1995—, Nat. Conf. Christians and Jews, Rocky Mountain Multiple Sclerosis Ctr.; mem. Mayor's Adv. com., Denver, many others. Recipient U. Denver Founders Day Award for cmty. svc., 1991, Humanitarian of Yr. award Nat. Jewish Ctr., 1988, Martin Luther King Jr. Social Responsibility award, 1987. Mem. Met. Denver Exec. Club (past pres., past bd. dirs.), Mile Hi Stadium Club (v.p.), One Hundred Club of Denver. Home: 5200 Smith Rd Denver CO 80216

HIRSCHFELD, ARLENE F., civic worker, homemaker; b. Denver, Apr. 6, 1944; d. Hyman and Gertrude (Schwartz) Friedman; m. A. Barry Hirschfeld, Dec. 17, 1966; 2 children. Student, U. Mich., 1962-64; BA, U. Denver, 1966. English tchr. Abraham Lincoln High Sch., Denver, 1966-70. Pres. Jr. League of Denver 1986-87, v.p. ways and means, 1985-86, v.p. mktg., 1982-83, chmn. Colo. Cache mktg. com., 1978-79, chair holiday mart 1981, 1985-87, participant in Nat. Jr. League Mktg. Conf.; trustee Graland Country Day Sch., 1988—, bd. sec. 1990—, chmn. edn. com., 1989-95, chmn. parent coun. nominating com., 1984-85, pres. parent coun., 1982-83, auction chmn., 1980, 81; bd. dirs. Allied Jewish Fedn., 1988—; co-chmn. collector's choice event Denver Art Mus., 1989, 94; co-chmn. benefit luncheon Pub. Edn. Coalition, 1990, mini grants selection com., 1985-87; mem. bd. Minoru Yasui Community Vol. award, 1986-87; mem. Greater Denver C. of C. Leadership Denver, class of 1987-88; bd. dirs. Women's Found. Colo. 1992—, Anti-Defamation League, 1994—, Colo. Spl. Olympics, 1994—;bd. trustees Denver Art Mus., 1995—; mem. dean's coun. Harvard Divinity Sch., 1992—; exec. com. Children's Diabetes Found. Denver. Named Humanitarian of Yr. Nat. Jewish Ctr., 1988, named to Colo. Women's Econ. Devel. Coun. by Gov. of Colo., 1989—, Sustainer of Yr. Jr. League, 1992; recipient Nat. Women's Mus. of the Arts. Colo. Chpt. award, 1991, U. Denver Founder's Day Alumni Community Svc. award; recipient Woman of Distinction award Rocky Mtn. News and Hyatt Beaver Creek, 1993, Colo. I Have A Dream Found. award, 1994. Mem. Colo. Women's Forum. Office: 5200 Smith Rd Denver CO 80216-4525

HIRSCHFELD, GERALD JOSEPH, cinematographer; b. N.Y.C., Apr. 25, 1921; s. Ralph and Kate (Zirker) H.; m. Sarnell Ogus, June 5, 1945 (div. June 1972); children—Alec, Marc, Eric, Burt; m. Julia Warren Tucker, July 28, 1981. Student, Columbia U., 1938-40. Dir. photography Signal Corps Photog. Ctr. U.S. Army, 1945-47; cinematic instr. New Inst. for Film, Bklyn., 1947-49; freelance dir. photography for TV and Film N.Y.C., 1949-54; dir. photography, v.p. MPO Videotronics, Inc., N.Y.C., 1954-72; freelance dir., cameraman, cinematographer N.Y.C., Hollywood (Calif.), 1972—; cinema instr. Am. Film Inst., L.A., 1980, Tahoe Film and Video Workshop, Lake Tahoe, Nev., 1984, Washington Film and Video Assn., 1987; staff mem. Internat. Film and Video Workshops, Rockport, Maine, 1995. Cinematographer for films including: Young Frankenstein, My Favorite Year, Diary of a Mad Housewife, The Neon Empire (ACE award nomination 1990); author: Image Control, 1992 (Kraszna-Krausz Internat. Book Award 1994). With Signal Corps U.S. Army, 1941-45. Mem. Internat. Photographer's Union, Am. Soc. Cinematographers. Home and Office: 361 Scenic Dr Ashland OR 97520-2623

HIRSCHFIELD, ALAN J., entrepreneur. B.S., U. Okla.; M.B.A., Harvard U. V.p. Allen & Co., Inc., 1959-67; v.p. fin., dir. Warner Bros. Seven Arts, Inc., 1967-68; with Am. Diversified Enterprises, Inc., 1968-73; pres., chief exec. officer Columbia Pictures Industries, N.Y.C., 1973-78; vice chmn., chief operating officer 20th Century-Fox Film Corp., L.A., 1979-81; chmn. bd., chief exec. officer 20th Century-Fox Film Corp., 1981-85; cons., investor entertainment industries, L.A., 1985-89; mng. dir. Wertheim Schroder & Co., L.A., 1990-92; co-CEO Data Broadcasting Corp., 1990—; bd. dirs. Cantel Internat., Inc. Bd. dirs. Conservation Internat., Trout Unltd. Office: PO Box 7443 Jackson WY 83001-7443

HIRSH, DWIGHT CHARLES, III, microbiologist; b. L.A., Oct. 5, 1938; s. Dwight Charles and Elizabeth Curtice H.; m. Lucy M. Tuschak; children: Dwight C. IV, Elizabeth M. BS, Loyola U., L.A., 1960; DVM, U. Calif., Davis, 1966; PhD, Stanford U., 1972. Asst. prof. microbiology U. Mo., Columbia, 1972-74; from asst. to assoc. prof. microbiology U. Calif., Davis, 1974-83, prof. microbiology, 1983—. Recipient Norden Disting. Tchr. award U. Calif. Sch. Vet. Med., 1980, 90, Disting. Tchr. award U. Calif. Acad. Senate, 1994. Mem. K.C. (fin. sec. 1990—). Republican. Roman Catholic. Office: Univ Calif Sch Vet Med Davis CA 95616

HIRSH, NORMAN BARRY, management consultant; b. N.Y.C., Apr. 20, 1935; s. Samuel Albert and Lillian Rose (Minkow) H.; m. Christina M. Poole, Sept. 21, 1957 (div. 1967); children: Richard Scott, Lisa Robin; m. Sharon Kay Girot, Dec. 29, 1973; 1 child, Sharon Margaret. BSME, Purdue U., 1956; cert. in mgmt., UCLA, 1980. Mech. engr. Ford Motor Co., Dearborn, Mich., 1956-58; design engr. Gen. Dynamics, San Diego, 1958-62; mech. engr. aircraft divsn. Hughes Tool Co., Culver City, Calif., 1962-65, project engr. aircraft divsn., 1965-69, engr. mgr. aircraft divsn., 1969-72; dep. program dir. Hughes Helicopters, Culver City, 1972-79, v.p., 1979-84; v.p., gen. mgr. Hughes Helicopters, Mesa, Ariz., 1984-85; exec. v.p. McDonnell Douglas Helicopter Co., Mesa, 1986-90; pres. Rogerson Hiller Corp., Port Angeles, Wash., 1990-93, Rogerson Aircraft Corp. Flight Structures Group, Port Angeles, 1990-93; cons. in field. Served with U.S. Army. Recipient Disting. Engring. Alumnus award Purdue U., 1990, Outstanding Mech. Engring. Alumnus award, 1991. Hon. fellow Am. Helicopter Soc. (chmn. 1986-87); mem. Assn. U.S. Army, Army Aviation Assn. Am., Am. Def. Preparedness Assn., Nat. Aeronautic Assn., Helicopter Assn. Internat.

HIRSHEN, SANFORD, architect, educator; b. N.Y.C., Feb. 6, 1935; s. Harry and Mildred (Zaidman) H.; m. Vivian Ann Greenberg, June 2, 1957; children: Richard K., Julie M. A.B., Columbia Coll., 1957; B.Arch., Columbia U., 1959. Lic. architect. With various archtl. firms, 1960-65; ptnr. Hirshen Trumbo & Assocs., Architects, Berkeley, 1965-91; dir. Sch. Architecture U. B.C., Vancouver, 1991—; prof. emeritus U. Calif., Berkeley. Served with U.S. Army, 1959-60. Recipient Guggenheim fellowship, 1984-

85. Fellow AIA, RAIC, MAIBC. Democrat. Jewish. Home: 2002 Prince St Berkeley CA 94703-2519 Office: U BC Sch Architecture, 6333 Memorial Rd, Vancouver, BC Canada

HIRSON, ESTELLE, retired school educator; b. Bayonne, N.J.; d. Morris and Bertha (Rubinstein) Hirson; student UCLA, U. So. Calif., summers 1949-59, San Francisco, summer 1955, U. Hawaii, 1955; B.E., San Francisco State U., 1965. Tchr. High St. Homes Sch., Oakland, Calif., 1949-54, Prescott Sch., 1955-60, Ralph Bunche Sch., 1960-72; owner Puzzle-Gram Co., Los Angeles, 1946-49; pres. Major Automobile Co., 1948-60. Chpt. v.p. City of Hope, San Francisco, 1962-63; bd. dirs. Sinai-Duarte Nat. Med. Center, 1946-50, also parliamentarian, life mem. Mem. NEA, Calif., Oakland, Los Angeles tchrs. assns., Sigma Delta Tau. Democrat. Mem. Order Eastern Star; Scottish Rite Women's Assn. (v.p. L.A. 1982, fin. sec. 1989). Rights to ednl. arithmetic game Find the Answer 1948, 51. Home: 8670 Burton Way Apt 328 Los Angeles CA 90048-3953

HIRST, WILMA ELIZABETH, psychologist; b. Shenandoah, Iowa; d. James H. and Lena (Donahue) Ellis; m. Clyde Henry Hirst (dec. Nov. 1969); 1 child, Donna Jean (Mrs. Alan Robert Goss). AB in Elementary Edn., Colo. State Coll., 1948, EdD in Ednl. Psychology, 1954; MA in Psychology, U. Wyo., 1951. Lic. psychologist, Wyo. Elem. tchr., Cheyenne, Wyo., 1945-49, remedial reading instr., 1949-54; assoc. prof. edn., dir. campus sch. Nebr. State Tchrs. Coll., Kearney, 1954-56; sch. psychologist, head dept. spl. edn. Cheyenne (Wyo.) pub. schs., 1956-57, sch. psychologist, guidance coordinator, 1957-66, dir. rsch. and spl. projects, 1966-76, also pupil personnel, 1973-84; pvt. cons., 1984—; vis. asst. prof. U. So. Calif., summer 1957, Omaha U., summer 1958, U. Okla., summers 1959, 60; vis. assoc. prof. U. Nebr., 1961, U. Wyo., summer 1962, 64, extension divsn., Kabul, Afghanistan, 1970, Cath. U., Goias, Brazil, 1974; investigator HEW, 1965-69; prin. investigator effectiveness of spl. edn., 1983-84; participant seminar Russian Press Women and Am. Fedn. Press Women, Moscow and Leningrad, 1973. Sec.-treas. Laramie County Coun. Community Svcs., 1962; mem. speakers bur., mental health orgn.; active Little Theatre, 1936-60, Girl Scout Leaders Assn., 1943-50; mem. Adv. Coun. on Retardation to Gov.'s Commn.; mem., sec. Wyo. Bd. Psychologist Examiners, 1965-71 vice chmn., 1971-74; chmn. Mayor's Model Cities Program, 1969; mem. Gov.'s Com. Jud. Reform, 1972; adv. council Div. Exceptional Children, Wyo. Dept. Edn., 1974; mem. transit adv. group City of Cheyenne, 1974; bd. dirs. Wyo. Children's Home Soc., 1968, treas., 1978-84; rsch. on women's prisons State of Wyo., 1989; bd. dirs. Goodwill Industries Wyo., chmn., 1981-83; mem. Wyo. exec. com. Partners of Americas, 1970-86; del. Internat. Conv. Ptnrs. of Ams., Jamaica, 1987; del., moderator pers. com. Presbytery of Wyo., 1987-90, mem. mission program com., 1991—, spl. gifts com. 1994—; bd. dirs. workforce opportunities adv. com. AARP, 1992-94; Friendship Force ambassador to Honduras, 1979; chmn. bd. SE Wyo. Mental Health Center, 1969; elder 1st Presbyn. Ch., Cheyenne, 1978—, also bd. deacons; chmn. adv. assessment com. Wyo. State Office Handicapped Children, 1980, 81; mem. allocations com. United Way of Laramie County, active People to People Internat., Child Welfare Project, 1992; participant People to People Internat. Citizen Amb. Program, child welfare project assist Lithuania, Latvia, Estonia, 1992. Named Woman of Year, Cheyenne Bus. and Profl. Women, 1974. Diplomate Am. Bd. Profl. Psychology. Fellow Am. Acad. Sch. Psychology; mem. APA, ASCD, Internat. Council Psychologists (chmn. Wyo. div. 1980-85), AAUP, Am. Assn. State Psychology Bds. (sec.-treas. 1970-73), Wyo. Psychol. Assn. (pres. 1962-63), Laramie County Mental Health Assn. (bd. mem., corr. sec. 1963-69, pres.), Wyo. Mental Health Assn. (bd. mem.), Internat. Platform Assn., Am. Ednl. Research Assn., Assn. for Gifted (Wyo. pres. 1964-65), Am. Personnel and Guidance Assn., Am. Assn. Sch. Adminstrs., NEA (life, participant seminar to China 1978), AAUW, Cheyenne Assn. Spl. Personnel and Prins. (pres. 1964-65, mem. exec. bd. 1972-76), Nat. Fedn. Press Women (dir. 1979-85), DAR (vice regent Cheyenne chpt. 1975-77), AARP (state coordinator 1988-92, preretirement planning specialist 1986-88, state coord. work force program, 1992—, leadership coun., state del. nat. conv. 1990, pilot project Wyo. state delivery for retirement planning 1990—, AARP Works, op. project state govt. edn. assn. and AARP work force vols. video for retirement planning statewide 1993, master trainer retirement planning 1993—, employment planning master trainer, 1994—, planning com. Area 8 Conf., leadership meeting 1994), Psi Chi, Kappa Delta Pi, Pi Lambda Theta, Alpha Delta Kappa (pres. Wyo. Alpha 1965-66). Presbyn. Lodge Soc. Colonial Dames XVII Century, Order Eastern Star, Daus. of Nile. Clubs: Wyo. Press Women, Zonta (pres. Cheyenne 1966-66, treas. dist. 12 1974). Author: Know Your Schoolgist, 1963; Effective School Psychology for School Administrators, 1980. Home and Office: 3458 Green Valley Rd Cheyenne WY 82001-6124

HIRSTEL, ROBERT, labor relations consultant; b. Portland, Oreg., Oct. 10, 1917; s. Edward and Pearl (Jacob) H.; m. Aida Dibar, June 14, 1944; children: Coco, Denise Hirstel Shaughnessy. BS, Oreg. State U., 1941; MS, NYU, 1942. Supt., pers. dir. Dept. Store Lipman North, Portland, Oreg., 1947-55; cons. Seattle and Portland, 1955—. Capt. U.S. Army, 1942-47, ETO. Mem. Met. Opera Nat. Coun., Wash. Athletic Club, Rainzer Club, Seattle Opera Assn. (bd. dirs. 1975-90). Home: 9228 SE 59th St Mercer Island WA 98040-5021 Office: 1218 3rd Ave Ste 2101 Seattle WA 98101

HIRT, CYRIL WILLIAM, physicist; b. Flushing, N.Y., Dec. 20, 1936; s. Cyril W. and Margret E. (Plumb) H.; m. Virginia L. Warren, June 22, 1968; children: Heather, Amber. BS, U. Mich., 1958, MS, 1959, PhD, 1963. Staff scientist Los Alamos (N.Mex.) Nat. lab., 1963-72, group leader, 1973-80; chief scientist Sci. Applications Inc., La Jolla, Calif., 1972-73; pres. Flow Sci. Inc., Los Alamos, 1980—. Contbr. numerous articles to profl. jours. Mem. AAAS. Office: Flow Sci Inc 1325 Trinity Dr Los Alamos NM 87544-3217

HISAKA, ERIC TORU, plastic surgeon; b. Stockton, Calif., 1951. MD, U. Calif., Davis, 1977. Plastic surgeon Valley Care Hosp., Pleasanton, Calif.; also with Tri Valley Surgical Ctr., Pleasanton, Calif. Office: 5720 Stoneridge Mall Rd # 13 Pleasanton CA 94588-2828*

HISE, MARK ALLEN, dentist; b. Chgo., Jan. 17, 1950; s. Clyde and Rose T. (Partipilo) H. AA, Mt. San Antonio Coll., Walnut, Calif., 1972; BA with highest honors, U. Calif., Riverside, 1974; MS, U. Utah, 1978; DDS, UCLA, 1983. Instr. sci. NW Acad., Houston, 1978-79; chmn. curriculum med. coll. prep program UCLA, 1980-85; instr. dentistry Coll. of Redwoods, Eureka, Calif., 1983; practice dentistry Arcata, Calif., 1983—; participant numerous radio and TV appearances. Editor: Preparing for the MCAT, 1983-85; contbr. articles to profl. jours.; speaker in field. Henry Carter scholar U. Calif., 1973, Calif. State scholar 1973, 74, Rgents scholar U. Calif., 1973; Calif. State fellow, 1975, NIH fellow, 1975-79. Mem. AAAS, ADA, Calif. Dental Assn., Acad. Gen. Dentistry, Nat. Soc. for Med. Research, Norht Coast Scuba Club (Eureka, Calif.). Roman Catholic. Home and Office: 1225 B St Arcata CA 95521-5936

HISLOP, KARE ELIZABETH, music director, educator; b. Calif., Aug. 20, 1948; m. Donald Lindsay Hislop, Sept. 9, 1967; children: Victoria, Laurel. BA, Chico State Coll., 1969; MA, Calif. State U., Chico, 1976. Cert. elem. and secondary tchr., Calif. Tchr. Red Bluff (Calif.) H.S., 1971-89, Evergreen Sch. Dist., Cottonwood, Calif., 1980, Elkins Sch., Paskenta, Calif., 1989-93; music dir. First United Meth. Ch., Red Bluff, 1980—. Author: Recipies From the Adobe, 1993. Facilitator Tehama County Child Assault Prevention, Red Bluff, 1990-92; leader, trainer, cons. Sierra Cascade Girl Scout Coun., Red Bluff, 1971—; dir. Christie Hill Ch. Camp, Red Bluff, 1979—. Mem. IDE Adobe Interpretive Assn. (pres. 1991—), Am. Lung Assn. (murder mystery chair 1990—), Kappa Delta Pi. United Methodist.

HISLOP, MERVYN WARREN, health advocate administrator, psychologist; b. Vancouver, B.C., Apr. 26, 1937; s. George and Freda (Wickenden) H.; m. Marilyn Gail Johnson, July 24, 1965; children: Lawren Nyall, Mylene Lorelle. B.A. with honors, U. B.C., 1965; M.A., McMaster U., 1967, Ph.D., 1970. Cert. psychologist, Ont., B.C. cert. health adminstr. Dir. behaviour mgmt. services Surrey Place Centre, Ministry of Health, Toronto, Ont., 1970-73; dir. psychol. services Woodlands Ministry of Human Resources, New Westminster, B.C., 1973-78; coordinator life edn. program New Westminster, 1975-77; exec. dir. Riverview Hosp., Port Coquitlam, B.C., 1978-85, Valleyview Hosp., Port Coquitlam, B.C., 1985-86; dir. legis. and regulatory affairs Mental Health Services Div., B.C. Ministry of Health, 1986-89; psychiat. adv. Govt. Alberta, Can., 1989—; research proposal submission cons. Can. Council, 1973; mem. edn. adv. com. Douglas Coll., 1983-86. Demonstration model grantee Province Ont., 1971; province Ont. grad. fellow McMaster U., 1969; recipient David and Jean Bolocan Meml. prize U. B.C., 1965; Nat. Rsch. Coun. Can. scholar, 1965, 66, 67, 68. Mem. Can. Coll. Health Service Execs. (cert.), Can. Inst. Law and Medicine, Coll. Psychologists B.C., Coll. Psychologists Ont. Home: 17203-57 Ave, Edmonton, AB Canada T6M 1B8

HITCHCOCK, VERNON THOMAS, farmer, lawyer; b. Selma, Ind., Feb. 21, 1919; s. Lucian Elmer and Loda Alice (King) H.; m. Betty Kathryn Orr, May 24, 1949; children: Brenda, Linda, Nancy, Debra, Randolph. BS in Agr., Purdue U., 1940; JD, Stanford U., 1953. Bar: Calif. 1954, U.S. Supreme Ct. 1961. Pilot Southwest Airways, San Francisco, 1946, TWA, Kansas City, Mo., 1947-51; pvt. practice Healdsburg, Calif., 1954-55; dep. atty. gen. State of Calif., Sacramento, 1956; dep. county counsel Sonoma County, Santa Rosa, Calif., 1957-65; exec. dir. Libyan Aviation Co., Tripoli, 1966-67; legal counsel Sonoma County Schs., 1967-82; farm mgr. Selma, Ind., 1975—; originator Freedom Under Law program. Author: The Airline to Infinity. Active Am. Security Council, 1965—. Served to comdr. USNR, 1941-79. Mem. Res. Officers Assn., Naval Order U.S., Commonwealth Club San Francisco, Quiet Birdmen, Odd Fellows. Republican. Episcopalian.

HITCHENS, DAVID WILLIAM, health facility administrator; b. Evanston, Ill., Oct. 16, 1955; s. Matthew Eugene and Annamae (De Caluwe) H.; m. Barbara Steiner, Apr. 26, 1980; children: Sharon, Collette. BA, Marquette U., 1977. Dir. materials mgmt. The Children's Hosp., Denver, 1983-88; materials mgr. Nat. Jewish Ctr. Immunology and Respiratory Medicine, Denver, 1988—. Roman Catholic. Home: 6800 S Sherman St Littleton CO 80122-1000 Office: Nat Jewish Ctr 1400 Jackson St Denver CO 80206-2761

HITE, CATHARINE LEAVEY, orchestra manager; b. Boston, Oct. 1, 1924; d. Edmond Harrison and Ruth Farrington Leavey; m. Robert Atkinson Hite, Aug. 28, 1948; children: Charles Harrison, Patricia Hite Barton, Catharine Hite Dunn. BA, Coll. William and Mary, 1945. Restoration guide Williamsburg Restoration, 1944-45; asst. edn. dept. Honolulu Acad. Arts, 1945-46; sec., tour guide edn. dept. office chief curator Nat. Gallery Art, 1946-48; opera liason/coord. Honolulu Symphony, 1972-73, asst. to gen. mgr., 1973-75, community devel. dir./opera coord., 1975-77, dir. ops./opera prodn. coord., 1977-79, orch. mgr., 1979-84, mem. exec. com., 1965-69, pres. women's assn., 1965-66; com. chmn., opera assn. chmn. Hawaii Opera Theatre, 1966-69. Mem. W. R. Farrington Scholarship Com., 1977-94, chmn., 1982-94; mem. community arts panel State Found. Culture and the Arts, 1982, State Found. Music and Opera, 1984; docent Iolani Palace, 1990—. Mem. Jr. League, Alliance Français, Hawaii Watercolor Soc. Mem. Phi Beta Kappa. Episcopalian.

HIXON, ROBIN RAY, food service executive, writer; b. Vancouver, Wash., May 4, 1954; s. Charles Donovan and Leona Margaret (Teske) Hixson. Exec. chef, Am. Culinary Fedn., 1972-77. Cert. Am. Restaurant Assn., 1992. Apprentice Redlion Inns, Vancouver, 1972-77, exec. chef, 1977-80; exec. chef Hilton Hotel, Baton Rouge, 1981; chief steward Delta Queen Steamboat Co., New Orleans, 1981-86, gen. mgr., 1986-88; exec. chef Icicle Seafoods Inc., Seattle, 1989-92, Sea Spirit Cruise Lines, Inc., 1992—, Petersburg Fisheries, Inc., Alaska, 1993—; cons. RSVP Travel Prodns., Inc., Mlps., 1992—. Author: American Regional Cuisines, 1987; contbr. articles to profl. jours. Mem. Nat. Trust for Hist. Preservation, 1982-92, Wash. Hist. Preservation, 1990-92, Oreg. Pub. Broadcasting, 1990-92, N.Y. Met. Opera, 1973-80; performer Peruvian Singers, 1972-74. Mem. Am. Culinary Fedn. (writer 1985-91), Chefs De Cuisine Soc. Oreg. (sgt. at arms 1974-80). Democrat. Home: 1701 Broadway St # 262 Vancouver WA 98663-3436 Office: PO Box 1147 Petersburg AK 99833-1147

HJELMSTAD, WILLIAM DAVID, lawyer; b. Casper, Wyo., Apr. 4, 1954; s. Alvin Gordon and A. Thecla (Walz) H.; m. Jenny M. Osmon, Nov. 27, 1993; children: Jennifer Ashley, Allison Caitlin. AA in Social Sci., Casper Coll., 1974; BS in Psychology, U. Wyo., 1976, JD, 1979. Bar: Wyo. 1979, U.S. Dist. Ct. Wyo. 1979. Dept. county pros. atty. Hot Springs County, Thermopolis, Wyo., 1979-80; asst. pub. defender Natrona County, Casper, Wyo., 1980-82; sole practice, Casper, 1981—. Mem. ATLA, ABA (mem. family law com. 1983-84, adoption com. 1983-84), Wyo. State Bar Assn. (mem. alcohol and substance abuse com., lawyers assistance com. 1988—), Natrona County Bar Assn., Wyo. Trial Lawyers Assn., Am. Judicature Soc., Acad. Family Mediators, Wyo. Cowboy Shootout Com. Lodges: Elks, Kiwanis. Home: PO Box 90001 Casper WY 82609-1001

HJORTSBERG, WILLIAM REINHOLD, author; b. N.Y.C., Feb. 23, 1941; s. Helge Reinhold and Anna Ida (Welti) H.; m. Marian Souidee Renken, June 2, 1962 (div. 1982); children—Lorca Isabel, Max William.; m. Sharon Leroy, July 21, 1982 (div. 1985). BA, Dartmouth Coll., 1962; postgrad., Yale U., 1962-63, Stanford U., 1967-68. Ind. author, screenwriter, 1969—; adj. prof. media and theatre arts Mont. State U., 1991—. Author: Alp, 1969, Gray Matters, 1971, Symbiography, 1973, Toro! Toro! Toro!, 1974, Falling Angel, 1978, Tales & Fables, 1985, Nevermore, 1994, films: Thunder and Lightning, 1977, Legend, 1986; co-author TV film: Georgia Peaches, 1980; contbg. editor Rocky Mountain Mag., 1979; contbr. fiction to Realist, Playboy, Cornell Rev., Penthouse, Oui, Sports Illustrated; contbr. criticism to N.Y. Times Book Rev. Recipient Playboy Editorial award, 1971, 78; Wallace Stegner fellow, 1967-68; Nat. Endowment Arts grantee, 1976. Mem. Authors Guild, Writers Guild Am. Home and Office: Main Boulder RT Mc Leod MT 59052

HO, ANNA SHAO-FU, lawyer; b. Chung King, China, Nov. 5, 1946; came to U.S., 1964; d. Lung-King and Shih Wei (Shu) H.; m. Thomas Tam, Jan. 26, 1967 (div. 1979); children: Alena, Stanley; m. Kurt Patt, Apr. 16, 1988. BA, Brigham Young U., 1967; JD, U. West L.A., 1976. Bar: Calif. 1983, U.S. Dist. Ct. (cen. dist.) Calif. 1983. Paralegal Otto Frank Swanson, Esq., Marina del Rey, Calif., 1977; adminstrv. asst. to U.S. Magistrate L.A., 1977-79; paralegal Tarlow & Tarlow, Torrance, Calif., 1979-80; pvt. practice criminal def. Torrance, 1983—; instr. Calif. State U. at Dominguez Hills, Carson, 1980-85. Active Human Resources Commn., Torrance, 1985-88. Recipient Cmty. Svc. award City of Torrance, 1988. Democrat. Office: Anna Ho Atty at Law 1601 N Sepulveda Blvd # 511 Manhattan Beach CA 90266-5111

HO, IWAN, research plant pathologist; b. Souzhou, Jiangsu, China, Apr. 15, 1925; came to U.S., 1956; m. Mei-Chun Chang, Nov. 29, 1975; 1 child, Tomur M. BS, Nat. Shanghai U., 1946; MS, La. State U., 1958; PhD, Oreg. State U., 1984. Microbiologist Seattle Pub. Health Dept., 1962-66; research plant physiologist Forestry Scis. Lab., Corvallis, Oreg., 1970—; courtesy asst. prof. Coll. Forestry, Oreg. State U. Mem. Mycol. Soc. Am., Am. Soc. Plant Physiologists, Internat. Soc. Plant Molecular Biology, Sigma Xi. Democrat. Episcopalian. Home: 1686 SW Bullevard St Philomath OR 97370-9538 Office: Forestry Sci Lab Pacific NW Rsch Sta 3200 SW Jefferson Way Corvallis OR 97331-8550

HO, KATY, dietitian, real estate broker; b. Shanghai, China, Oct. 11, 1948; came to U.S., 1969; d. Chien-Sheng and Mai-Yeng (Shu) H.; m. Kuang-Tsan Kenneth Chiang; children: Christina, Jamie. BS, U. Mo., 1972, MS, 1974. Clin. dietitian St. Joseph's Hosp., Ft. Wayne, Ind., 1974-76, New Eng. Med. Ctr., Boston, 1976-78; dir. food service St. John of God Hosp., Brighton, Mass., 1978; clin. dietitian Worcester (Mass.) City Hosp., 1979, U. Mass. Med. Ctr., Worcester, 1979-80, Allegheny Gen. Hosp., Pitts., 1981, VA Med. Ctr., Lebanon, Pa., 1985-86, Santa Clara Valley Med. Ctr., San Jose, 1987-89, Mission Oak Hosp., Los Gato, 1987-89. Vol. Cupertino Community Service. Mem. Am. Dietetic Assn., Calif. Dietetic Assn., Asian-Am. Club, Omicron Nu, Gamma Sigma Delta, Phi Upsilon. Democrat. Office: Century 21 Adobe 5609 Kanan Rd Agoura Hills CA 91301-3358

HO, OWEN MATTHEW, store planning consultant, caterer/event planner; b. Honolulu, Feb. 24, 1946; s. Frank Stephen and Matilda (Pomroy) H. Store designer/planner Sears, Roebuck and Co., 1965-70, Liberty House, 1970-73, Duty Free Shoppers Ltd. Partnership Group, 1973-90; visual merchandise dir. DFS Ltd. Partnership, Hong Kong, Hawaii; owner Imagery Visual Design Group, 1990—; cons. Mayor's Com., Honolulu, 1986, 90; theme planner, decorator for head of state events Former Gov. George Ariyoshi, 1976-84, Sen. Spark matusnaga, Pres. George Bush, 1990, Gov. John Waihee, 1984-92, Mayor Frank Fasi; state rep. PATA Conv., Hong Kong, 1992. Designer Hawaii Pavilion and Grand Finale party. Designer City Hall Christmas decorations, Honolulu, 1984—; active charity events Boy Scout of Yr. Dinner, 1993, First Night, Carole Kai Bedrace and others. Recipient Grand Prize float designer Aloha Week Festival Floats and Kamehameha Day Festival, 1979, 89. Home: 2825 S King St Apt 1003 Honolulu HI 96826-3534

HO, PHUONG MINH, software engineer; b. Hai Phong, Vietnam, Oct. 13, 1954; came to U.S., 1979; s. Phu Dac and Nga Tue (Tran) H.; m. Victoria Hoaithu Nguyen, Sept. 15, 1975; children: Lily Bichngoc, Alexander Anhnam. BS in Elec. and Computer Engring., Oreg. State U., 1983; MS in Elec. and Computer Engring., Portland State U., 1989. Teaching asst. Portland State U., 1983-84; design engr. II Morrow Inc., Salem, Oreg., 1984-86, software engr. II, 1986-89, software engr. III, 1989-92, sr. software engr., 1992—. Mem. IEEE, Inst. of Navigation, Eta Kappa Nu. Republican. Buddhism. Office: II Morrow Inc 2345 Turner Rd SE Salem OR 97302-2059

HO, RODNEY JIN YONG, educator, medical researcher; b. Rangoon, Burma, May 21, 1959; came to U.S., 1977; s. David Shoon-Khat and Po-Kin (Paw) H.; m. Lily S. Hwang, July 10, 1988; children: Beatrice Eirene, Martin Theodore. BS, U. Calif., Davis, 1983; MS, U. Tenn., 1985, PhD, 1987. Teaching asst. U. Tenn., Knoxville, 1984-85, rsch. asst., 1985-87; postdoctoral fellow, assoc. investigator Stanford (Calif.) U. Sch. Medicine, 1987-90, asst. prof. pharmaceutics Sch. Pharmacy U. Wash., Seattle, 1990—; affiliate investigator of pharmacology Fred Hutchinson Cancer Rsch. Ctr., Seattle, 1991—. Author: Liposomes as Drug Carriers, 1988, Topics in Vaccine Adjuvant Research, 1991, Trophoblast Research, Vol. 8, 1994, Placental Toxicology, 1995; patentee immunoliposome assays, composition and treatment for herpes simplex; contbr. numerous articles on infectious diseases, pharmaceutical sciences, virology, immunology band biochemistry to sci. jours. Mem. AAAS, Am. Assn. Coll. Pharmacy, Am. Assn. Pharm. Scientists, Am. Chem. Soc., Biophys. Soc., Internat. Soc. Antiviral Rsch., N.Y. Acad. Sci. Office: U Wash Sch Pharmacy Dept Pharms Box 357610 Seattle WA 98195

HO, STUART TSE KONG, investment company executive; b. Manila, Nov. 18, 1935; came to U.S., 1936; s. Chinn and Betty (Ching) H.; m. Mary Lois Lee, June 17, 1961; children: Peter, Cecily, Heather. BA, Claremont (Calif.) McKenna, 1957; JD, U. Mich., 1963. Bar: Hawaii. Asst. sec. to chmn. bd. Capital Investment of Hawaii, Honolulu, 1965—; chmn. bd. Gannett Pacific Corp., 1987—; trustee Coll. Retirement Equities Fund, N.Y.C.; bd. dirs. Bancorp Hawaii, Inc., Honolulu, Gannett Co., Inc., Rosslyn, Va., Aloha Airgroup, Inc., Honolulu. Representative Hawaii Ho. of Reps., Honolulu, 1966-70, majority fl. leader, 1968-70; del. Constnl. Conv. of 1968, Honolulu, 1968; regent U. Hawaii, Honolulu, 1971-74. 1st lt. U.S. Army, 1958-60, ETO. Democrat. Office: Capital Investment Hawaii 733 Bishop St Ste 1700 Honolulu HI 96813-4019

HO, VINCENT BOK, diagnostic radiologist; b. Boston, Aug. 9, 1963; s. Shui and Kean Yue (Chung) H. BS, U. Mich., 1985, MD, 1987. Diplomate Am. Bd. Radiology, Nat. Bd. Med. Examiners. Intern Walter Reed Army Med. Ctr., Washington, 1987-88, resident in diagnostic radiology, 1988-92; chief body/cardiovasc. MRI Svc. Madigan Army Ctr., Tacoma, 1992—, chief uroradiology, 1992—, dir. radiol. rsch., 1993—; asst. clin. prof. Sch. Medicine, U. Wash., Seattle, 1993—; program chmn. Wash.-Oreg. Radiology Residents' Rsch. Symposium, Tacoma, 1994. Served to maj. U.S. Army, 1987—. Mem. Radiol. Soc. N.Am. (Cum Laude Sci. Exhibit award 1991), Soc. Magnetic Resonance, Am. Soc. Neuroradiology (Cum Laude Sci. Exhibit award 1991), Am. Roentgen Ray Soc., Am. Coll. Radiology, Pacific N.W. Radiol. Soc. Office: Madigan Army Med Ctr Dept Radiology (MCHJ-R) Tacoma WA 98431

HO, WAN CHUEN, plastic surgeon; b. Hong Kong, China, 1933. MD, U. Hong Kong, 1958. Plastic surgeon Kaiser Permanente Hosp., Bellflower, Calif.; also vol. hand surgeon U. So. Calif. County Hosp. Office: Kaiser Permanente Hosp 9400 Rosecrans Ave Bellflower CA 90706-2217*

HOAG, JOHN ARTHUR, retired bank executive; b. Freeport, N.Y., Sept. 29, 1932; s. John Hoag and Viola (Babcock) Hobson; m. Jeanette Makaio, Dec. 5, 1959; children: Steve, Vanessa, Kanani. BS, U. Mo., 1955; grad., Pacific Coast Banking Sch., Wash., 1970; MBA, U. Hawaii, 1977. Account exec. Walston & Co., N.Y.C., 1960; mgmt. trainee 1st Hawaiian Bank, Honolulu, 1960, br. mgr., Hilo, 1968, Island v.p., 1970-76, sr. v.p., mgr., 1976, exec. v.p. loan group, 1979, pres., 1989-94, also bd. dirs.; vice chmn. bd. dirs., 1994; retired 1st Hawaiian Bank, 1995; pres. 1st Hawaiian Inc., Honolulu, 1991-95, also bd. dirs.; vice chm. 1st Interstate Bank Hawaii, Honolulu, 1991—; vice chmn. of bd., 1994—, ret., 1995; pres., chmn. bd. Hawaii Reserves, Inc.; vice chmn. Pioneer Fed. Savs. Bank. Bd. regents Tokai Internat. Coll., 1992; bd. dirs. Hawaii Med. Svc. Assn., 1981-93, Honolulu Polynesian Cultural Ctr., 1990-93, Kapiolani Med. Ctr. for Women and Children, Honolulu, 1989—. Capt. USMC, 1955-60. Mem. Pres.' Club U. Hawaii, C. of C. of Hawaii (chmn. bd. 1992-93). Mem. LDS Ch. Office: 1st Hawaiian Bank 1132 Bishop St Ph Honolulu HI 96813-2830 also: First Hawaiian Bank PO Box 3200 Honolulu HI 96847-0001

HOAG, PAUL STERLING, architect; b. Spokane, Aug. 7, 1913; s. Percival Doane and Emma Imogen (Rusk) H.; m. Nancy Jean Lawrence, Oct. 21, 1967. Student, Washington State Coll., Pullman, 1930-31, Stanford U., 1932-33. Lic. architect, Calif., Colo., Tex., Wash. Gen. mgr. Hoag X-Ray Co., Spokane, 1933-42; designer various war industry cos., 1942-45; architect apprentice Richard Neutra, L.A., 1945-46, Paul Robinson Hunter and others, L.A., 1946-48; prin. Paul Sterling Hoag, L.A., 1948-87, Crane Island, Wash., 1987—; intr. advanced design So. Calif. Inst. Architecture; entire body of archtl. design drawings placed in archives U. Calif. Art History Dept. Prin. works include Falcon Plastics Factory, Oxnard, Calif. (Top Plan of 1970 award Modern Mfg.), Old Ranch Country Club, Seal Beach, Calif., Huntington Harbor (Calif.) Beach Club, Happy Valley Sch., Ojai, Calif., Adobe Hotel, Yachats, Oreg., Sterling Holloway residence, Laguna Beach, Calif., Beatrice Wood studio and residence, Ojai; monthly columnist The Listener, L.A. Architect; contbr. articles to profl. jours. and newspapers. Architect mem. Bel-Air Archtl. Com., L.A., 1982-88, San Vicente Design Rev. Bd., 1980-86; design cons. San Juan County (Wash.) for Eastsound town redesign, 1990-94. Fellow AIA. Home and Office: PO Box 124 Deer Harbor WA 98243-0124

HOAGLAND, ALBERT JOSEPH, JR., psychotherapist, hypnotherapist, minister; b. Clayton, N.J., July 2, 1939. Cert. psychiat. tech., Ancora State Hosp., 1958; RN, Monmouth Med. Ctr., 1961; BS, Monmouth Coll., 1964; MSW, Rutgers U., 1966; M.Div., Fuller Theol. Sem., 1978; D in Ministry, Boston U., 1981; PhD, Am. Inst. Hypnotherapy, 1989, D.C.H., 1991; MS in Oriental Medicine, Samra U. of Oriental Medicine, 1995. Ordained to ministry Disciples of Christ, 1978; lic. clin. social worker, Calif., marriage, family and child counselor, Calif.; cert. sch. counselor, anger therapist, eating disorders therapist. Pvt. practice counseling, 1959-69; psychiat. technician, RN N.J. State Hosp., 1958-66; instr., cons. Los Angeles County Dept. Probation, 1972-75; instr. psychology Calif. Grad. Inst., 1973; instr. Chapman Coll., 1972-74; instr. psychology Calif. State U., Dominguez Hills, 1974; instr. Torrance (Calif.) Adult Sch., 1977-79, 81-85; pastor Ariz., 1984-85, Calif., 1978-79, 81-84, Mass., 1979-81; subs. tchr. Marana (Ariz.) Sch. Dist., 1985; instr. Beverly Hills Adult Sch., 1984—; exec. dir. Personal Counseling Svcs. and Hypnotherapy Ctr. (name changed to Hoagland Healing Arts Complex), San Pedro, 1986—; instr. Samra U. of Orienta Medicine, 1994-95; religious educator various retreats, programs, summer camps, etc., 1975—. Author: Anger to Intimacy, 1988; editor Jonestown Collection, 1978, Professional Papers from the Desert, 1970, What's Your Problem?, 1989; producer (film) Gestalt Art Therapy, 1974. Mem. Congress of Disciples Clergy, Disciples of Christ Hist. Soc., Disciples Peace Fellowship; trainer, cons. L.A. Coun. Exploring divsn. Boy Scouts Am., 1971-73, 88—, explorer post advisor, 1988—; coach Palos Verdes (Calif.) Soccer Program, basketball and soccer Torrance City Sports Program; dir. YWCA Delinquency Prevention Program, San Pedro, 1986-89; chair cmty. adv. coun. San Pedro High Sch.; campaigned for mayor of San Pedro, 1988.

Recipient Adult God and Svc award, 1989. Mem. Nat. Tchrs. Assn., Nat. Assn. Social Workers, Am. Assn. Marriage and Family Therapists, Am. Osteo. Assn., Nat. Assn. Christians in Social Work, Harbor Area Police Clergy Coun. (pres.), Am. Bd. Hypnotherpaists, Nat. Assn. Clergy Hypnotherapists, World Fedn. Mental Health, Clowns of Am., San Pedro Rotary (sec.), Phi Delta Kappa. Democrat. Home: 3318 Torrance Blvd Torrance CA 90503-5011 Office: Hoagland Healing Arts Complex PO Box 367 San Pedro CA 90733-0367

HOAGLAND, SAMUEL ALBERT, lawyer, pharmacist; b. Mt. Home, Idaho, Aug. 19, 1953; s. Charles Leroy and Glenna Lorraine (Gridley) H.; m. Karen Ann Mengel, Nov. 20, 1976; children: Hiliary Anne, Heidi Lynne, Holly Kaye. BS in Pharmacy, Idaho State U., 1976; JD, U. Idaho, 1982. Bar: Idaho 1982, U.S. Dist. Ct. Idaho 1982, U.S. CT. Appeals (9th cir.) 1984. Lectr. clin. pharmacy Idaho State U., Pocatello, 1976-78, lectr. pharmacy law, 1985-86, dean's adv. council Coll. Pharmacy, 1987-92; hosp. pharmacist Mercy Med. Ctr., Nampa, Idaho, 1978-79; retail pharmacist Thrifty Corp., Moscow, Idaho, 1980-82; assoc. Dial, Looze & May, Pocatello, 1982-89, Prescott & Foster, Boise, Idaho, 1989-90; pvt. practice, 1990—; gen. counsel Design Innovations and Rsch. Corp., 1991—; chmn. malpractice panel Idaho Bd. Medicine, Boise, 1983-92, adminstrv. hearing officer, 1989-92. Contbr. to law publs. Bd. dirs. Cathedral Pines Camp, Ketchum, Idaho. Mem. ABA, Idaho State Bar Assn., Idaho Pharm. Assn., Idaho Trial Lawyers Assn., Boise Bar Assn., Capital Pharm. Assn., Am. Pharm. Assn., Idaho Soc. Hosp. Pharmacists (bd. dirs.), Am. Soc. Pharmacy Law, Flying Doctors Am. (Atlanta) (bd. dirs.). Home: 11901 W Mesquite Dr Boise ID 83713-0813 Office: 2309 Mountain View Dr Ste 205 Boise ID 83706-1065

HOANG, DUC VAN, theoretical pathologist, educator; b. Hanoi, Vietnam, Feb. 17, 1926; came to U.S. 1975, naturalized 1981; s. Duoc Van and Nguyen Thi (Tham) H.; m. Mau-Ngo Thi Vu, 7 children. M.D., Hanoi U. Sch. Medicine, Vietnam, 1953; DSc, Open Internat. U., Sri Lanka, 1989. Dean Sch. Medicine Army of the Republic of Vietnam, Saigon, 1959-63; dean Minh-Duc U. Sch. Medicine, Saigon, 1970-71; clin. prof. theoretical pathology U. So. Calif. Sch. Medicine, L.A., 1978—; adj. prof. Emperor's Coll. Traditional Oriental Medicine, Santa Monica, Calif., 1988—, sci. and med. dir. Author: Towards an Integrated Humanization of Medicine, 1957; The Man Who Weights the Soul, 1959; Eastern Medicine, A New Direction?, 1970; also short stories; translator: Pestis, introduction to the work of Albert Camus, Vietnamese translation of La Peste; editor: The East (co-founder); jour. Les Cahiers de l'Asie du Sud-Est. Founder, past pres. Movement for Fedn. Countries S.E. Asia; co-founder, past v.p. Movement for Restoration Cultures and Religions of Orient; active Vo-Vi Meditation Assn. Am.; mem. The Noetic Inst., 1988—, Internat. Found. for Homeopathy, 1987; founder, pres. Intercontinental Found. for Electro-Magnetic Resonance Rsch., 1989—; coord. Unity and Diversity World Health Coun., 1992—. Named hon. dean The Open Internat. U. of Complementary Medicines, Sri Lanka, 1989; Unity-and-Diversity World Coun. fellow, 1990—. Mem. AAUP, Assn. Clin. Scientists, Am. Com. for Integration Eastern and Western Medicine (founder), Assn. Unitive Medicine (founder, pres.). Republican. Roman Catholic. Clubs: U. So. Calif. Staff, U. So. Calif. Faculty Members (Los Angeles). Home: 3630 Barry Ave Los Angeles CA 90066-3202 Office: LAC-USC Med Ctr Los Angeles CA 90033-1084

HOAR, WARREN THOMAS, automotive executive, consultant; b. Paterson, N.J., Jan. 30, 1927; s. Henry Alfred and Lucille (Thomas) H.; m. Marian A. Duhaime, Aug. 20, 1949 (div. June 1969); children: Richelle, Christopher, Kevin, Peter, Shawn, Julie; m. Anne Steward Pollock, June 14, 1984. BS, Purdue U., 1949. Advt. IBM, N.Y.C., 1949-51; pres. Warren T. Hoar Agy., Inc., Bristol, Conn., 1952-84, Vintage Mercedes Cars, Inc., various, 1984—. Sgt. USAF, 1945-47, ETO. Mem. Mercedes Benz Club Am., Classic Car Club Am. (vice dir. S.E. region, 1966-67), Mercedes Veteranen Club Germany. Republican. Baptist. Home and Office: Vintage Mercedes Cars Inc 921 Sleeping Indian Rd San Luis Rey CA 92068-2118

HOARE, TYLER JAMES, sculptor; b. Joplin, Mo., June 5, 1940; s. Melvin James and Dorotha Maude (Beadle) H.; m. Kathy Joyce Quinn, Mar. 9, 1963; 1 dau., Janet Elaine. Student, U. Colo., 1959-60, Sculpture Center, N.Y.C., 1960-61; BFA, U. Kan., 1963; postgrad., Calif. Coll. Arts and Crafts, 1965-67. instr. extension U. Calif. at Berkeley, 1973—; guest lectr. San Francisco Art Inst., San Francisco State Coll. Exhibited one man shows, New Center U.S. Art Gallery, Kansas City, Mo., 1964, Jewish Community Center Gallery, Kansas City, Studio C, Berkeley, Calif., 1965, Derby Gallery, Berkeley, Lucien Labaudt Gallery, San Francisco, 1966, U. Calif.-Berkeley, 1966, 67, 93, Free U. Berkeley Gallery, Fredric Hobb's San Francisco Art Center, 1967, Green Gallery, San Francisco, 1968, St. Mary's Coll., 1969, John Bolles Gallery, San Francisco, 1969, 71, San Francisco State Coll., 1970, Camberwell Sch. Art, London, Eng., 1971, SUNY, Albany, Atherton Gallery, Menlo Park, Calif., 1972, Stanford, 1973, Richmond (Calif.) Art Ctrs., 1983, Calif. State U. Hayward, Keokuk (Iowa) Art Ctr., Olive Hyde Art Ctr., Fremont, Calif., John Bolles Gallery, San Francisco, Cen. Sch. Art & Design, London, 1974, Daly City (Calif.) Civic Ctr., San Mateo (Calif.) Arts Coun./Sunshine Gallery, County of San Mateo Hall of Justice, 1975, Purdue U. Gallery 1, 1976, Spiva Art Ctr., Mo. So. State Coll., 1977, Manner of Speaking, San Franciso, Stuart Gallery, Berkeley, 1978, Studio 718, San Francisco, 1980, Geotrope Gallery, Berkeley, 1981, Studio Nine, Benicia, Calif., Marin County Civic Ctr., San Rafael, 1982, Solano Community Coll., Suison City, Calif., 1983, Oakland Art Assn. Gallery, 1986, Coastal Art League Mus., Half Moon Bay, Calif., 1989, U. Art Gallery, Calif. State U., Hayward, 1993, A.C.C.I. Gallery, Berkeley, 1993, Ctr. for Visual Arts, Oakland, Calif., 1993, 94, Art Rsch. Ctr., Budapest, 1993, Steering Wheel West Art Gallery, San Francisco, 1993, Photocopier Art, Ace Art, Winnipeg, Can., 1993, Irvine Arts Ctr., 1993, U. Tex., Dallas, 1993, 10, 000 Humans Edicions, Barcelona, 1993, Culver City, Calif., 1993, Monroe C.C., Rochester, N.Y., 1993, Hockey 100, Calgary, Alta., 1993, Fresno Art Mus., 1993, Luther Coll., Decorah, Iowa, 1993, 94, Corridor Gallery Tex. Tech U., Lubbock, 1993, Ctr. d'Art de Baie, St. Paul, Quebec, 1993, AUA Gallery, Lebanon, N.H., 1993, Artists Book Works, Chgo., 1993, Les Vraies Folies Bergeres, Paris, 1993, Arlington (Va.) Art Ctr., 1993, Barrett Art Gallery, Utica Coll. Syracuse U., 1993, Bedford Gallery, Ctr. for Arts, Walnut Creek, Calif., 1994, Copy Art, Barcelona, 1994, Mus. Artpool, Budapest, 1994, CopyArt, Berlin, 1994, Gallery Without Walls, Australia, 1994, LeSabord Exchange, Quebec, 1994, Internat. MailArt Exposition, Paris, 1994, Xantus Janos Mus., 1994, Group A-Z Vasarely Mus. Budapest, 1994, Santa Barbara Mus. Art, 1994, Artists Stamps, Dallas, 1994, A.I.M. Internat., Seattle, Wash., 1994, Bunnell St. Gallery, Homer, Alaska, 1994, Madrid, Spain, 1994, Osaka, Japan, 1994, Internat. Archive, Piza, Italy, 1994, U. Calif., San Francisco, 1994, Oakland City Hall, 1994, Tarragona Spain, 1994, Galerie Arts Technologiques, Montreal, 1994; exhibited in numerous group shows 1963, The Trading Co. II, U. Calif., Berkeley, 1989, Western Wash. U. Bellingham, 1989, Calif. Mus. of Photography, 1989, U. Calif., Riverside, 1989, Eye Tahoe, Venice, Calif., 1989, Holsum Roc Gallery, Chgo., 1989, Cleve. Inst. of Art, 1989, Sonoma State U. Art Gallery, 1989, Rohnert Park, Calif., 1989, Gallery 25, Fresno, Calif., 1989, The Art Store Gallery, L.A., 1989, Art-Pool, Buda-Ray U. Budapest, Hungary, 1989, Jr. Coll. Albany, N.Y., 1989, Ohlone Coll. Art Gallery, Fremont, Calif., 1990, Alcorcon Culture Office, Madrid, N.Y., 1990, Corr. Sch., N.Y.C., Balley Art Gallery, Walnut Creek, Calif., 1990, Mercer Gallery, 1990, Monroe Community Coll. Rochester, N.Y., 1990, Acad. of Art Coll. Gallery, San Francisco, 1990, Sonama State U., 1990, Can. Union, Scarborough, Ont., Can., 1990, Sangamon State U., Springfield, Ill., 1990, Jr. Coll. of Albany, 1990, Adirondack Community Coll., Glen Falls, N.Y., 1990, Contemporary Tech. Art, Museo Internat. De Electrografia, 1990, Monroe Community Coll., Mercer Gallery, Rochester, N.Y., 1991, Wilder Gallery, Los Gatos, Calif., 1991, Buda-Ray U., 1991, Guy Bleus Archives, Belgium, 1991, Art Electro-Images, Paris, 1991, Action Art Internat., Chgo., 1991, Goodwill, Kent, Wash., 1991, Electrografia Museo Internat., Spain, 1991, Contemporary Art Gallery, Aono, Japan, 1991, Shadow Archive, Kenosha, Wis., 1991, Oakland Mus., Calif., Pasadena Mus., Calif., Calif. Palace of Legion of Honor, San Francisco, San Francisco Mus., Library of Congress, Pratt Graphics Center, Los Angeles County Mus., Cin. Mus.; represented in permanent collections, USIA, Washington, SUNY-Albany, Oakland Mus., Calif. Coll. Arts and Crafts, others. Address: 30 Menlo Pl Berkeley CA 94707-1533

HOBART, BILLIE, education educator, consultant; b. Pitts., Apr. 19, 1935; d. Harold James Billingsley and Rose Stephanie (Sladack) Green; m. W.C.H. Hobart, July 20, 1957 (div. 1967); 1 child, Rawson W. BA in English, U. Calif., Berkeley, 1967, EdD, 1992; MA in Psychology, Sonoma State U., 1972. Cert. tchr., Calif. Asst. prof. Coll. Marin, Kentfield, Calif., 1969-78; freelance cons., writer, 1969—; asst. prof. Contra Costa Coll., San Pablo, Calif., 1986—. Author: (cookbook) Natural Sweet Tooth, 1974, (non-fiction) Expansion, 1972, Purposeful Self: Coherent Self, 1979; contbr. articles to profl. jours. Served with WAC, 1953-55. Mem. NAFE, Mensa, Phi Delta Kappa, Commonwealth Club San Francisco. Home and Office: PO Box 1542 Sonoma CA 95476-1542

HOBART, WILLIS LEE, editor; b. Corvallis, Oreg., Sept. 15, 1942; s. Irvin Edwin and Lillian Lucille (Wilson) H.; children: Todd, Ryan, Bradley. BS in Fish and Wildlife Mgmt., Oreg. State U., 1965. Reporter Lincoln County Leader, Toledo, Oreg., 1966; editor Sandy (Oreg.) Post, 1967; editor edn. and agr. Daily Courier, Grants Pass, Oreg., 1967-68; asst. dir. conservation dept. NRA, Washington, 1968-73; mng. editor Marine Fisheries Rev. U.S. Nat. Marine Fisheries Svc., Seattle, 1973-76, editor Marine Fisheries Rev., 1977—, office dir. sci. publs., 1991—; freelance outdoor writer and photographer, 1965—. Author, editor: Conservation Action Handbook, 1968; co-editor: Our Living Oceans, 1991; editor: (jour.) Marine Fisheries History, 1988. Mem. Am. Fisheries Soc., Outdoor Writers Assn. Am., Wildlife Soc., Northwest Outdoor Writers Assn. Office: Nat Marine Fisheries Svc Sci Publ Office 7600 Sand Point Way NE Seattle WA 98115-6349

HOBBS, C. D., utilities executive; b. Indpls., Sept. 29, 1943; s. Morris Fitz and Edla Elizabeth (Hedberg) H.; m. Linda Louise Mulder, Sept. 10, 1988; 1 child, Keynan. BSBA, U. Fla., 1966, MBA, 1968. Instr. sch. bus. adminstrn. U. Fla., Gainsville, Fla., 1970-72; asst. prof. fin. U.S. Internat. U., San Diego, 1972-75; asst. prof. Whittier (Calif.) Coll., 1976-77; sr. fin. analyst Portland (Oreg.) Gen. Electric. Co., 1977-80, v.p., controller, 1980-82, v.p., planning, 1982-85; v.p., treas. Portland Gen. Corp., 1986; v.p., chief fin. officer Columbia Willamette Devel. Co., Portland, 1987; chief operating officer CW Real Estate Investments, Portland, 1988; sr. v.p. Portland Gen. Corp., 1988—. Trustee Marylhurst Coll., Portland, 1984-87; chmn. bd. dirs. Jr. Achievement, Portland, 1986-87. With U.S. Army, 1968-70. Recipient Silver Award Jr. Achievement, 1988; U.S. Office Edn. NDEA Title IV Fellow, 1967-69. Mem. Urban Land Inst., Fin. Mgmt. Assn., Fin. Execs. Inst., Northwest Electric Light and Power Inst. (div. chmn. 1985-86), City Club (Portland). Republican. Office: Portland Gen Corp World Trade Ctr Bldg 121 SW Salmon St Portland OR 97204-2901

HOBBS, GUY STEPHEN, financial executive; b. Lynwood, Calif., Feb. 23, 1955; s. Franklin Dean and Bette Jane (Little) H.; m. Laura Elena Lopez, Jan. 6, 1984; 1 child, Mariah Amanda. BA, U. Calif., Santa Barbara, 1976; MBA, U. Nev., 1978. Sr. rsch. assoc. Ctr. for Bus. and Econ. Rsch., Las Vegas, Nev., 1978-80; pvt. practice mgmt. cons. Las Vegas, 1979-82; mgmt. analyst Clark County, Las Vegas, 1980-81, sr. mgmt. analyst, 1981-82, dir. budget and fin. planning, 1982-84, comptroller, dir. fin., chief fin. officer, 1984—; lectr. in mgmt. Coll. Bus. and Econs., U. Nev., Las Vegas, 1977-88; pres. Pacific Blue Ent., 1991—; mem. Interim Legis. Com. Infrastructure Fin., 1993-94. Author publs. in field. Chmn. com. Panasonic/Las Vegas Invitational Golf Tournament, 1983, 84, 85; mem. exec. bd. Community Action for Lake Mead, Las Vegas, 1990. Mem. Am. Assn. Budget and Program Analysts, Am. Soc. Pub. Adminstrn. (Pub. Adminstr. of Yr. 1987), Govt. Fin. Officers Assn. (Fin. Reporting Achievement award 1984-94, Disting. Budget Presentation award 1993, 94, 95), Math. Assn. Am., Internat. City Mgmt. Assn., Ops. Mgmt. Assn. Republican. Office: Clark County 225 Bridger Ave Las Vegas NV 89101-6112

HOBBS, KENNETH BURKETT, foundation administrator, consultant; b. Appalachia, Va., Dec. 18, 1930; s. Earl Kaylor and Mary Katherine (Horner) H.; m. Faye Rollins, Oct. 28, 1950; 1 child, George Bradford. BS in Pharmacy, Auburn U., 1956, MS in Ednl. Adminstrn., 1959; postgrad., Ohio State U., U. Wash., 1960, 69; D Comml. Sci. (hon.), London Inst. Applied Rsch., Eng., 1973. Exec. dir. Ohio Acad. Sci., Columbus, 1959-61; chief, TV and Radio NASA, Washington, 1961-63; adminstrv. asst. Battelle Columbus Labs., Ohio, 1963-66; exec. officer Battelle Seattle Rsch. Ctr., 1966-73; exec. v.p. John Young Sci. Cen., Orlando, Fla., 1973-80; pres. Rollins-Hobbs Assocs., Inc., Winter Park, Fla., 1980-89; CEO Kadlec Med. Ctr. Found., Richland, Wash., 1990—; pres. bd. dirs. Neurological Ctr., Richland, 1990—; instr. Auburn U., 1956-59. Producer-dir. TV programs, exec. producer (motion picture) The John Glenn Story, 1963; art editor Literary Mag., U. N.C. Pres. bd. dirs. Friends of the (Richland) Libr.; mem. bd. visitors Winthrop Coll., rock HIll, S.C., 1981-82; fund devel. worker Citizens for a Progressive Richland, 1990; rschr. John H. Glenn senatorial campaign, 1965. Comdr. USN, 1956-59. Disting. Wash. State Citizen, one of 10 Outstanding Young Men of Columbus. Fellow Ohio Acad. Sci., AAAS; mem. Soc. Rsch. Adminstrs. (pres. 1968), Seattle Salvation Army Adv. Bd. (chmn. 1967), Assn. Healthcare Philanthropy, Explorers Club, Tri-City Country Club, Rotary, Phi Kappa Tau, Alpha Phi Omega, Phi Delta Kappa. Republican.

HOBBS, STEPHEN CRAIG, management consultant; b. Monroe, Wis., Jan. 8, 1950; s. Howard W. and Mayme (Terry) H.; m. Leila B. Paulson, Oct. 22, 1989. BS in Labor and Indsl. Rels., Mich. State U., 1972, BA in Econs., 1972; postgrad., U. Colo., 1976-78. Cert. mgmt. acct. Mgr. Saunders Leasing Systems, Inc., Denver, 1972-74; ops. mgr. Best Brands, Inc., Denver, 1974-76; contr., purchasing mgr. R & L Distbg. Co., Denver, 1976-80; contr. Ctr. Equipment Co., Denver, 1980-87; cons. C & S Assocs., Denver, 1987-90; CFO Bell Plumbing & Heating Co., Denver, 1990-94; ptnr. Telesis Cons. Co., Englewood, Colo., 1994—; small bus. cons. South Met. Denver C. of C., Littleton, 1992—, bus. issues com., 1992—. Mem. Inst. Mgmt. Accts. (nat. com. mem. 1993—, past pres. coun. Centennial chpt. 1992—, chpt. pres. 1991-92, v.p. 1988-91), Constrn. Fin. Mgmt. Assn., Am. Fin. Assn. Office: Telesis Cons 7500 E Arapahoe Rd Ste 250 Englewood CO 80112-1277

HOBERG, MICHAEL DEAN, management analyst, educator; b. Pipestone, Minn., Feb. 27, 1955; s. Dennis Edwin and Beverly Ann (Voss) H.; divorced; 1 child, Heather; m. Janet Lee Freeman, Mar. 5, 1995. BS in Park Adminstrn., Calif. State U., Sacramento, 1977; MPA, Calif. State U., Turlock, 1982; grad., Law Enforcement Mgmt. Ctr., Stanton, Calif., 1988; PhD in Pub. Adminstrn., Greenwich U., 1993. Ranger naturalist Nat. Park Svc., Three Rivers, Calif., 1977; park ranger San Joaquin County, Stockton, Calif., 1977-82, park svcs. specialist, 1983-86, mgmt. analyst, 1986—; park ranger State of Calif., Perris, 1982-83; adj. instr. Delta Coll., Stockton, 1987-90; dir. Hoberg Mgmt. and Consulting, Stockton, 1987—. Mem. com. Stockton Asparagus Festival, 1985; mem. Quail Lakes Bapt. Ch., Stockton, 1986—. Recipient cert. Calif. Peace Officers Assn., 1994, Fencing Champion foil No. Calif. Intercollegiate Athletic Conf., 1977. Mem. AAUP, ASPA, Acad. Criminal Justice Scis. (student affairs com. 1993-94), U.S. Fencing Assn. (9th pl. Nat. Championships award 1988). Democrat. Home: 2209 Meadow Ave Stockton CA 95207-1428 Office: San Joaquin County 7000 S Canlis Blvd French Camp CA 95231

HOBGOOD, E(ARL) WADE, college dean; b. Wilson, N.C., June 28, 1953; s. Max Earl and Mary (Carpenter) H.; m. Dianne Bland, Apr. 24, 1977; children: Courtney, Heather. BFA, E. Carolina U., 1975, MFA, 1977. Asst. prof. art Ark. State U., Jonesboro, 1977-78; design dir. and asst./assoc. prof. art Western Carolina U., Cullowhee, N.C., 1978-84; chmn., assoc. to full prof. art and design Winthrop U., Rock Hill, S.C., 1984-88, acting chmn. dept. music, 1991-92, assoc. dean and prof. Sch. Visual and Performing Arts, 1988-92; dean Coll. of Fine Arts Stephen F. Austin State U., Nacogdoches, Tex., 1992-93, Calif. State U., Long Beach, 1993—; faculty cons. Ednl. Testing Svcs., 1993—; field reader/evaluator, field-initiated studies grants U.S. Dept. Edn., 1992—; sr. evaluator Nat. Assn. Schs. of Art and Design, 1987; chair grants rev. panel Pub. Corp. for Arts, 1994; mem. cultural planning com. City of Long Beach; evaluator/cons. Arts Edn. Partnership Grants, Ky. Arts Coun., 1992; evaluator/panelist Challenge grants, NEA, 1991, correspondent/cons. Arts Edn. Rsch. Briefing, 1991; cons. in field. One-person exhibit Limestone Coll., 1985; group shows include SFA Art Faculty Exhbn., 1992, Black Mountain Invitational, 1981, High Point Invitational, 1980, State of S.C. Traveling Exhbn., 1984-85, others. Mem. selection com. Pub. Corp. for the Arts, Long Beach, 1993; bd. dirs. Rock Hill Arts Coun., 1985-89; mem. planning com. Cultural/City of Rock Hill, 1988-92, County of York, S.C., 1989-92; mem. Long Beach Mus. of Art, 1993—, Univ. Art Mus., 1993—, KLON Jazz Radio, 1993—. Recipient medallion in arts edn. Kennedy Ctr. for Performing Arts, Washington, 1988, 1st place award U.S. Bicentennial Com., Keep America Beautiful mural design, 1976, A&M Records Advt. award, 1975, R.J. Reynolds Permanent Collection purchase, 1975, 1st place Southern Visions Photography, 1984, others. Mem. Internat. Coun. Fine Arts Deans, Coll. Art Assn., Long Beach C. of C., Japan Am. Soc., Greater L.A. World Trade Assn., Long Beach Mus. Art, Phi Kappa Phi. Office: Calif State Univ Coll of the Arts 1250 N Bellflower Blvd Long Beach CA 90840-0006

HOBSON, DONNIS STACY, plastic surgeon; b. 1948. MD, U. Chgo., 1974. Plastic surgeon Children's Hosp., Oakland, Calif. Office: 4351 Bridgeview Dr Oakland CA 94602-1910*

HOBSON, WAYNE K., humanities educator; b. Moscow, Idaho, July 1, 1941; s. Karl and Dorothy Hobson; m. Nancy Robinson, Aug. 20, 1966; children: Jeffrey, Emily. BA, U. Oreg., 1965; MAT, Reed Coll., 1966; MA, Stanford U., 1969, PhD, 1977. From asst. to assoc. prof. Calif. State U., Fullerton, 1973-86; prof. Calif. State U. Fullerton, Fullerton, 1986—. Author: American Legal Profession and the Organizational Society, 1890-1930, 1986. Mem. Am. Studies Assn., Orgn. Am. Historians, Am. Soc. for Legal History. Democrat. Home: 915 Miramar St Laguna Beach CA 92651 Office: Dept Am Studies Calif State Univ Fullerton CA 92634

HOCH, ORION LINDEL, corporate executive; b. Canonsburg, Pa., Dec. 21, 1928; s. Orion L.F. and Ann Marie (McNulty) H.; m. Jane Lee Ogan, June 12, 1952 (dec. 1978); children: Andrea, Brenda, John; m. Catherine Nan Richardson, Sept. 12, 1980; 1 child, Joe. BS, Carnegie Mellon U., 1952; MS, UCLA, 1954; PhD, Stanford U., 1957. With Hughes Aircraft Co., Culver City, Calif., 1952-54; with Stanford Electronics Labs., 1954-57; sr. engr., dept. mgr., divsn. v.p., divsn. pres. Litton Electron Devices div., San Carlos, Calif., 1957-68; group exec. Litton Components divsn., 1968-70; v.p. Litton Industries, Inc., Beverly Hills, Calif., 1970, sr. v.p., 1971-74, pres., 1982-88, chief exec. officer, 1986-93, chmn., 1988-94, also dir.; pres. Intersil, Inc., Cupertino, Calif., 1974-82; chmn. exec. com., dir. Western Atlas, Inc., Beverly Hills, 1994—; bd. dirs. Measurex Corp., Litton Industries, Inc. Trustee Carnegie-Mellon U. Served with AUS, 1946-48. Mem. IEEE, Sigma Xi, Tau Beta Pi, Phi Kappa Phi. Office: Western Atlas Inc 360 N Crescent Dr Beverly Hills CA 90210-4802*

HOCH, WILLIAM HENRY, surgeon, urologist; b. N.Y.C., Feb. 22, 1944; s. Saul and Dorothy Louise (Edelson) H.; children: Jeffrey Stewart, Laura Elizabeth. AB, Ohio State U., 1965; MD, Johns Hopkin's U., 1969. Diplomate Am. Bd. Urology. Intern, then resident Case Western Res. U., Cleve., 1969-74; urologist Woodland (Calif.) Clinic Med. Group, 1976-90; pvt. practice urologist Davis, Calif., 1991—; sec., treas. Sutter Davis Hosp., chief of staff, 1993—. Author: (chpt.) Campbell's Urology, Lewis Textbook of Surgery; contbr. articles to profl. jours. With USAF, 1974-76. Fellow ACS; mem. Am. Urologic Assn. Office: 1105 Kennedy Pl Ste 2 Davis CA 95616-1272

HOCHSCHILD, ARLIE RUSSELL, sociology educator; b. Boston, Jan. 15, 1940; d. Francis Henry and Ruth (Libbey) Russell; m. Adam M. Hochschild; children: David R., Gabriel R. BA, Swarthmore Coll., 1962, LittD, 1993; MA, U. Calif., Berkeley, 1965, PhD, 1969. Asst. prof. sociology U. Calif., Santa Cruz, 1969-71; asst. prof. sociology U. Calif., Berkeley, 1971-75, assoc. prof., 1975-83, prof., 1983—; E.M. Lang vis. prof. Swarthmore Coll., fall 1992; advisor Ford Found. Work Family Collaborative Rsch. Project, 1991—; mem. adv. com. Inst. for Study of Social Change, U. Calif., Berkeley, 1984-86, 93-94. Author: The Managed Heart, 1983, The Second Shift: Working Parents, 1989; mem. bd. editors The Am. Prospect, Gender and Society. Recipient award for Notable Book of Yr. in Social Scis., N.Y. Times Book Rev., 1983, 89; Alfred P. Sloan Found. grantee, 1993-95; Ford Found. grantee, 1990-91; Ctr. for Advanced Study in Behavioral Studies fellow Stanford U. Mem. Sociol. Rsch. Assn., Internat. Assn. for Rsch. on Emotion, Am. Sociol. Assn., Sociologists for Women in Society. Office: U Calif Berkeley Dept Sociology Berkeley CA 94720

HOCHSCHILD, CARROLL SHEPHERD, medical equipment and computer company executive, educator; b. Whittier, Calif., Mar. 31, 1935; d. Vernon Vero and Effie Corinne (Hollingsworth) Shepherd; m. Richard Hochschild, July 25, 1959; children: Christopher Paul, Stephen Shepherd. BA in Internat. Rels., Pomona Coll., 1956; Teaching credential U. Calif., Berkeley, 1957; MBA, Pepperdine U., 1985; cert. in fitness instrn., U. Calif., Irvine, 1988. Cert. elem. tchr., Calif. elem. tchr. Oakland (Calif.) Pub. Schs., 1957-58, San Lorenzo (Calif.) Pub. Schs., 1958-59, Pasadena (Calif.) Pub. Schs., 1959-60, Huntington Beach (Calif.) Pub. Schs., 1961-63, 67-68; adminstrv. asst. Microwave Instruments, Corona del Mar, Calif., 1968-74; co-owner Hoch Co., Corona del Mar, 1978—. Rep. Calif. Tchrs. Assn., Huntington Beach, 1962-63. Mem. AAUW, P.E.O. (projects chmn. 1990-92, corr. sec. 1992-94, chpt. pres. 1994-95), Internat. Dance-Exercise Assn., NAFE, ASTD (Orange County chpt.), Assistance League Newport-Mesa. Republican. Presbyterian. Clubs: Toastmistress (corr. sec. 1983), Jr. Ebell (fine arts chmn. Newport Beach 1966-67).

HOCHSCHILD, RICHARD, medical instruments executive, researcher; b. Berlin, Germany, Aug. 28, 1928; came to U.S., 1939; s. Paul and Ann Ida (Schosstag) H.; m. Carroll Corinne Shepherd, July 25, 1959; children: Christopher Paul, Stephen Shepherd. BA in Physics, Johns Hopkins U., 1950; MA in Physics, U. Calif., Berkeley, 1957. Tech. adv. U.S. Atomic Energy Commn., N.Y.C., 1951-53; chief 300 area U.S. Atomic Energy Commn., Hanford, Wash., 1953-54; pres. Metrol, Inc., Pasadena, Calif., 1957-60; asst. to v.p. Budd Co., Phoenixville, Pa., 1960-61; pres. Microwave Instruments Co., Corona del Mar, Calif., 1962-74; chief exec. officer Hoch Co., Corona del Mar, 1975—; cons. in field. Patentee and author in field. Office: Hoch Co 2915 Pebble Dr Corona Del Mar CA 92625-1518

HOCK, DELWIN D., utilities company executive; b. 1935. BS in Bus. Adminstrn., U. Colo., 1956. Acct. Gen. Electric Co., 1956-57, Arthur Young & Co., 1957-62; with Pub. Service Co. of Colo., Denver, 1962—, various mgmt. positions, 1962-79, v.p. acctg., 1979, v.p., asst. sec., 1979-80, sr. v.p., 1980-86, pres., COO, 1986-88, pres. CEO, 1988-89, chmn. bd., pres., CEO, 1989—, also bd. dirs. Office: Pub Svc Co Colo PO Box 840 Denver CO 80201

HOCKETT, LORNA DEE, elementary education educator; b. Portland, Oreg., Aug. 14, 1954; d. Wallace Loren and Ava Dee (Thomas) Johnson; m. John Bennett, June 15, 1975; children: Tara Dianne, Bryan Nathan, Kevin Loren. BS, Oreg. State U., 1976, MEd, 1986. Cert. elem. tchr., Oreg. Tchr. Waldport Elem. Sch., Waldport, Oreg., 1978—; trainer, ombudsman Drug Edn. Ctr., Charlotte, N.C., 1990-92; trainer developing capable people Sunrise Assocs., Provo, Utah, 1990-95. Mem. NEA (adv. panel profl. libr., mem. task force 1992, trainer Nat. Diversity Cadre), Oreg. Edn. Assn. (del. 1984-93, chair ins. claims rev. com. 1986-92, bd. dirs. 1993-96), Lincoln County Edn. Assn. (Tchr. of Yr. award 1991, treas. 1985-95, bargaining team 1992-96), Delta Kappa Gamma. Democrat. Home: PO Box 1388 Waldport OR 97394-1388 Office: Waldport Elem Sch 265 Bay St Waldport OR 97394

HOCKFELD, MARLA GAIL GERECHT, advertising and public relations executive; b. St. Louis, Aug. 22, 1965; d. Harold and Susan Kay (Krashine) Gerecht; m. Randy Allen Hockfeld, Jan. 16, 1993. BA in Communication, U. Ala., Tuscaloosa, 1986. Pub. rels. intern U. Ala. U. Rels., Tuscaloosa, 1985-86; credit hostess Bullock's Dept. Store, Las Vegas, Nev., 1985-88; publicity dir., editor The Jewish Reporter newspaper Jewish Fedn. of Las Vegas, 1987-93, leadership coord., 1989-92; owner So. Nev. Advt. and Pub. Rels., Henderson, Nev., 1993—; mktg. coord. Fitzgeralds Casino/Hotel, Las Vegas, 1993—; newsletter editor Bryce Hosp., Tuscaloosa, spring 1986; pub. rels. intern R & R Advt. Ltd. of Las Vegas, summer 1986. Mem. Women in Comms.

HOCKING, PHOENIX JEANNE (SANDRA J. HOCKING), writer; b. Santa Barbara, Calif., Dec. 1, 1948; d. Sioux Jay and L. Geneva (Ball) Dupont; m. Cobert Raymond Patton; m. Paul Chester Day; children: Cora Lynn Patton, Heather Ruth Day Crowley; m. Frank Benham Hocking Jr.,

Feb. 14, 1980; stepchildren: Donald Hocking, Dennis Hocking. Client svcs. coord. Shasta County Women's Refuge, Redding, Calif.; vol. prison visitor Prisoner Visitation and Support, Phila. Author: Living With Your Selves, 1992, Someone I Know Has Multiple Personalities, 1994, 37 To One-Living As An Integrated Multiple, 1995. Coord. Sleeping Bag Project, Shasta County, 1993-94. Democrat. Mem. Soc. of Friends. Home: PO Box 5305 Cottonwood CA 96022-5305

HOCKMUTH, JOSEPH FRANK, physicist, psychotherapist; b. Buffalo, N.Y., Mar. 6, 1942; s. Joseph Frank and Gertrude Marie (Merkley) H.; m. Sharon Louise Van Deusen Tiernan, June 30, 1965 (div.); children: Joseph Fess, Catherine Marie; m. Katherine Nancy Genco, June 1, 1991 (div.). BS in Physics, Calif. State U., 1965; MA in Psychology, Norwich U., 1992. Cert. substance abuse counselor, Ariz. Bd. Behavioral Health Examiners; cert. coll. instr., Ariz. State Bd. Rsch. engr. Westinghouse Astroelectronics, Newbury Park, Calif., 1965-66; rsch. engr. Lockheed Missile & Space Co., Sunnyvale, Calif., 1966-69, sr. rsch. engr., 1972-78; radiation effects engr. IRT Corp., San Diego, 1969-72, staff scientist, 1984-87; addictions counselor Charter Hosp., Glendale, Ariz., 1992-93; prin. staff engr. Motorola Govt. Sys. & Tech. Group, Scottsdale, Ariz., 1978-84; tech. staff engr. Motorola GSTG, Scottsdale, Ariz., 1987—, divsn. cons. for radiation effects, 1987—; psychotherapist Fountain Hills, Ariz., 1992—. Contbr. Awakenings mag., 1992—. Funds coord. United Way, Scottsdale, 1988-90; class sponsor Wounded Knee (Wyo.) Tribal Elem. Sch., 1992—. Sgt. Calif. NG, 1960-68. Fellow Am. Counseling Assn., Ariz. Counselors Assn., Noetic Scis. Inst.; mem. ASTM (com. 1985—), IEEE (ofcl. tech. paper reviewer 1993). Roman Catholic. Home: 15024 E Windyhill Rd Fountain Hls AZ 85268-1323 Office: Motorola GSTG 8201 E Mcdowell Rd # H2550 Scottsdale AZ 85257-3812

HOCKNEY, DAVID, artist; b. Bradford, Yorkshire, Eng., July 9, 1937; s. Kenneth and Laura H. Attended, Bradford Coll. Art, 1953-57, Royal Coll. Art, London, 1959-62; D (hon.), U. Oxford, Eng., 1995; hon. degree, U. Aberdeen, 1988, Royal Coll. Art, London, 1992; U. Oxford, Eng., 1995. Lectr. U. Iowa, 1964, U. Colo., 1965, U. Calif. Berkeley, 1967; lectr. UCLA, 1966, hon. chair of drawing, 1980. One-man shows include Kasmin Gallery, 1963-89, Mus. Modern Art, N.Y.C., 1964, 68, Stedelijk Mus., Amsterdam, Netherlands, 1966, Whitechapel Gallery, London, 1970, Andre Emmerich Gallery, N.Y.C., 1972—, Musee des Arts Decoratifs, Paris, 1974, Museo Tamayo, Mexico City, 1984, L.A. Louver, Calif., 1986, 89—, Nishimura Gallery, Tokyo, 1986, 89, 90, 94, Met. Mus. Art, 1988, L.A. County Mus. Art, 1988, Tate Gallery, London, 1988, 92, others; designer: Rake's Progress, Glyndebourne, Eng., 1975; sets for Magic Flute, Glyndebourne, 1978, Parade Triple Bill, Stravinsky Triple Bill, Met. Opera House, 1980-81, Tristan und Isolde, Los Angeles Music Ctr. Opera, 1987; Turandot Lyric Opera, Chgo., 1992—, San Francisco Opera, 1993, Die Frau Ohne Schatten, Covent Garden, London, 1992, L.A. Music Ctr.Opera, 1993; author: David Hockney by David Hockney, 1976, David Hockney: Travels with Pen, Pencil and Ink, 1978, Paper Pools, 1980, David Hockney Photographs, 1982, Cameraworks, 1983, David Hockney: A Retrospective, 1988, Hockney Paints the Stage, 1983, That's the Way I See It, 1993; illustrator: Six Fairy Tales of the Brothers Grimm, 1969, The Blue Guitar, 1977, Hockney's Alphabet, 1991. Recipient Guinness award and 1st prize for etching, 1961, Gold medal Royal Coll. Art, 1962, Graphic prize Paris Biennale, 1963, 1st prize 8th Internat. Exhbn. Drawings Lugano, Italy, 1964, 1st prize John Moores Exhbn. Liverpool, Eng., 1967, German award of Excellence 1983, 1st prize Internat. Ctr. of Photography, N.Y., 1985, Kodak photography book award for Cameraworks, 1984, Praemium Imperiale Japan Art Assn., 1989, 5th Ann. Gov. Calif. Visual Arts award, 1994. Office: 7508 Santa Monica Blvd Los Angeles CA 90046-6407

HODES, ABRAM, pediatrician; b. Jeannette, Pa., Mar. 2, 1922; s. Samuel and Rachel (Gross) H.; m. Mildred Rose Hodes, June 22, 1947; children: Alan Eliot, Jay Michael. BS, Pa. State U., 1942; BM, Northwestern U., 1945, MD, 1946. Sch. pub. health physician San Bernardino (Calif.) County Health Dept., 1950-51; pvt. practice San Bernardino, 1950—. Chmn. San Bernardino Israel Bond Assn., 1967, United Jewish Appeal, 1981, 90-93. Fellow Am. Acad. Pediatrics; mem. Am. Med. Soc., Calif. Med. Soc., San Bernardino County Med. Soc., Optimists (life), B'nai B'rith (pres. 1991-95), Jewish War Vets, Phi Beta Kappa, Phi Delta Epsilon. Republican. Home: 604 Avery St San Bernardino CA 92404-1708

HODGDEN, HUGH JERRY, geological consulting executive; b. Manhattan, Kans., July 12, 1931; s. Frank Burton and Emily Elizabeth (Bennett) H.; 1 adopted child, Dewey L. Pleake. BS in Geol. Engring., U. Kans., 1953, MS in Geology, 1960. Archtl. draftsman Hercules Powder Co., Sunflower Ord Works, Kans., 1951-53; asst. instr. geology U. Kans., Lawrence, 1953-54; geologist Continental Oil Co., Colo., Wyo. and La., 1957-63; western regional mgr. Info. Handling Svcs., Chgo. and L.A., 1963-67; nat. sales mgr. Share Rsch. Corp., Santa Barbara, Calif., 1967-68; asst. to pres., geologist Internat. Nuclear Corp., Denver and Calgary, Can., 1968-70; pres., CEO Rangeland Resources, Inc., Denver, 1970-72; owner Hodgden & Assocs., Denver, 1972—; owner, pres., CEO Hodgden Oil Co., Denver and Golden, Colo., 1980—; founder, pres., CEO Alaska Platinum Ltd., Golden and Platinum, Alaska, 1992—; mem. Kans. U. Geol. Assocs. Bd., 1993—. Contbr. articles to profl. jours. Active various civic orgns., Golden, 1978—; mem. All Breed Rescue, Denver, 1992—. Capt. USAF, 1954-56. Mem. Am. Assn. Petroleum Geologists (cert. petroleum geologist), Soc. Ind. Profl. Exploration Scientists (cert. profl. geologist), Rocky Mountain Assn. Geologists, Kans. Geol. Soc., Denver Internat. Petroleum Soc. Office: Hodgden Oil Co 408 18th St Golden CO 80401-2433

HODGDON, LINWOOD L., sociology educator; b. Plainfield, Vt., Mar. 19, 1917; married; 3 children. BA, Am. Internat. Coll., 1941; MA, Mich. State U., 1947, PhD, 1952. From asst. prof. to prof. dept. econ. and sociology Kans. State U., Manhattan, 1949-58; Fulbright prof. sociology/anthropology Inst. Social Scis., Agra (India) U., 1958-59; acting dir. Cmty. Devel. Br. U.S. Ops. Mission, Seoul, Korea, 1061-62, cons. cmty. devel., 1960-62; cons. cmty. devel. Ford Found., New Delhi, 1962-64; dir. Office Internat. Programs Colo. State U., Ft. Collins, 1964-68, prof. sociology, 1968-82, prof. sociology emeritus, 1982—; cons. Australian govt., 1964, State Dept./AID, India, 1978, Malaysian govt./Asian Devel. Bank, 1979-80; mem. planning team Consortium for Study of Nigerian Rural Devel., AID/Govt. Nigeria, 1965, 66, 67, vice chmn. consortium coun., 1966-67; seminar participant Am. Assn. Colls. for Tchr. Edn., Egypt, 1973; Fulbright prof. sociology of devel. Nat. U., Bangi, Malaysia, 1985-86; sociology prof. Semester at Sea, U. Pitts., fall 1990; papers presented at numerous internat. profl. confs. Contbr. chpts. to books, papers to conf. procs. and profl. jours. Pres. Lesher Jr. High Sch. PTA, 1968-69; pres. Ft. Collins Poudre Golden K Kiwanis Club, 1988-89; bd. dirs. Ft. Collins Kiwanis Club, 1966-69, 76-78, South Coll. Cmty. Assn., 1965-68. Lt. USNR, 1942-46, PTO. Grantee Mich. Med. Soc. and pvt. founds., 1947-48, Kans. Acad. Sci., 1953, AID, 1960-61, 62, Ford Found., 1963-64, Colo. State U. Faculty Coun. Rsch. Com., 1973. Mem. Alpha Kappa Delta, Gamma Sigma Delta, Sigma Xi, Phi Kappa Delta, Phi Kappa Phi. Home: 1121 Robertson St Fort Collins CO 80524-3924

HODGEN, MAURICE DENZIL, financial development administrator, educator; b. Timaru, New Zealand, Aug. 7, 1929; s. William Arnold and Lindsey Frances (Neill) H.; m. Rhona Brandstater, June 20, 1951; children: Philip Denzil, Victoria Anne. Student, Avondale Coll., Cooranbong, Australia, 1948-50; B.S., Pacific Union Coll., 1953; M.A., Columbia U., 1956, Ed.D., 1958. Asst. prof. La Sierra Coll., Riverside, Calif., 1958-64; lectr. Solusi Coll., Bulawayo, Zimbabwe, 1964-66; dir. tchr. edn. Helderberg Coll., Somerset W., S. Africa, 1966-68; assoc. prof. Sch. Edn. Loma Linda (Calif.) U., 1968-72, prof., 1972—, dean grad. sch., 1978-87; adminstr. fin. devel. Claremont (Calif.) U. Ctr., 1987-93. Exec. dir. Riverside Community Found., 1993—. Served with U.S. Army, 1953-55. Office: 3800 N Orange St Ste 230 Riverside CA 92501-3622

HODGES, JOSEPH GILLULY, JR., lawyer; b. Denver, Dec. 7, 1942; s. Joseph Gilluly Sr. and Elaine (Chanute) H.; m. Jean Todd Creamer, Aug. 7, 1971; children: Ashley E., Wendy C., Elaine V. BA, Lake Forest Coll., 1965; JD, U. Colo., 1968. Bar: Colo. 1968, U.S. Dist. Ct. Colo. 1969, U.S. Ct. Mil. Appeals 1969. Assoc. Hodges, Kerwin, Otten & Weeks, Denver, 1969-73; assoc. Davis, Graham & Stubbs, Denver, 1973-76, ptnr., 1976-86; pvt. practice lawyer Denver, 1986—. Bd. dirs. Arapahoe Colo. Nat. Bank, Littleton, Colo., 1971-90, Cherry Creek Improvement Assn., Denver, 1979-91; bd. trustees Lake Forest (Ill.) Coll., 1977-87; pres. Colo. Arlberg Club, Winter Park, Colo., 1984-85; treas. St. Johns Episcopal Cathedral, Denver, 1981—. Capt. USAR, 1969-74. Named Best Lawyers in Am., Woodward/White, N.Y.C., 1994-95. Fellow Am. Coll. Trust and Estate Counsel (state chmn. 1991—); mem. ABA (chmn. probate sec. G-2 Tech. 1990—), Am. Judicature Soc., Colo. Bar Assn. (chair probate coun. 1981-82), Denver Bar Assn., Denver Estate Planning Coun., Colo. Planned Giving Roundtable (bd. 1991-94), Rotary Club Denver, Kappa Sigma, Phi Alpha Delta. Republican. Office: 3300 E 1st Ave Ste 600 Denver CO 80206-5809

HODGES, ROSE MARIE, secondary education educator; b. Ft. Plain, N.Y., Mar. 10, 1927; d. Leo John Cosman Smith and Marion Louise Smith (Dingman) Powers; m. Edward Joseph Doyle, Sept. 4, 1948 (div. Oct. 1963); children: Stephen E. Doyle, Michael W. Doyle, Sharon M. Doyle; m. John H. Hodges, Aug. 25, 1979. BS, Ithaca Coll., 1949. Tchr. drama and English Bainbridge (N.Y.) H.S., 1956-58, Cortland (N.Y.) H.S., 1958-60; tchr. drama and English Vista (Calif.) Unified Sch. Dist., 1961-87, asst. to psychologist, 1987-88. Author: Rosie's Treasures, Books 1-4, 1993, My Diary Books, 1994. Mem. DAR. Home: 1751 W Citracado Pky # 265 Escondido CA 92029-4141

HODGES, VERNON WRAY, mechanical engineer; b. Roanoke, Va., Dec. 26, 1929; s. Charlie Wayne and Kathleen Mae (Williams) H.; m. Lorraine Patricia Smart, Apr. 1, 1955 (div. 1966); children: Vernon Wray Jr., Gregory Elmer, MIchelle Lynn; m. Linda Lou Wall, Feb. 3, 1967; children: Kenneth Wray, Kelly Dianne. BS in Mech. Engring., Va. Poly. Inst. and State U., 1951; MS in Systems Mgmt., U. So. Calif., 1979. Registered profl. engr., Kans., Wash., Calif. Commd. 2d lt. USAF, 1951, advanced through grades to major, 1964, ret., 1965; flight test engr. Boeing Co., Wichita, Kans., 1966-71; sr. engr. Boeing Co., Seattle, 1971-76; systems test engr. Rockwell Internat., Edwards AFB, Calif., 1976-77; sr. engr. Rockwell Internat., Palmdale, Calif., 1981-90, Hughes Helicopters, Inc., Culver City, Calif., 1977-81, Computer Scis. Corp., Edwards AFB, 1990-93; pvt. comml. pilot, Lancaster, Calif., 1953—; asst. prof. air sci. Boston U., 1958-61. Elder, deacon Presbyn. Ch. USA, Lancaster, 1966—; active Calif. Rep. Cen. Com., Sacramento, 1977—, Rep. Cen. Com., Washington, 1977—. Recipient Letter of Commendation, USAF. Mem. ASME, NSPE (sec. 1972-75), Air Force Assn., Masons, Shriners. Home: 2731 West Ave J-8 Lancaster CA 93536

HODGINS, JACK STANLEY, author; b. Comox Valley, Vancouver Island, B.C., Can., Oct. 3, 1938; s. Stanley H. and Reta A. (Blakely) H.; m. Dianne Child, Dec. 17, 1960; children: Shannon, Gavin, Tyler. B.Ed., U. B.C., 1961, D Litt., 1995. Tchr. high sch. English and creative writing Nanaimo, B.C., 1961-79; tchr. workshops, cons. and speaker in field, 1976—; writer-in-residence Simon Fraser U., Vancouver, 1977, U. Ottawa (Ont.), 1979; prof. U. Victoria. Author: fiction Spit Delaney's Island, 1976 (B.C. Eaton's Book award 1977), The Invention of the World, 1977 (Gibson's First Novel award 1978), The Resurrection of Joseph Bourne, 1979 (Gov. Gen. Can. award fiction 1980), The Honorary Patron, 1987 (Can.-Carribean Region Commonwealth Lit. prize), The Barclay Family Theatre, 1981, Innocent Cities, 1990; (travel book) Over Forty in Broken Hill, 1992; (children's novel) Left Behind in Squabble Bay, 1988; textbook Teaching Short Fiction, 1978, (nonfiction) A Passion for Narrative: A Guide for Writing Fiction, 1993; editor: textbook The Frontier Experience, 1976, The West Coast Experience, 1976; co-editor: textbook Voice and Vision, 1971; contbr. articles mags., newspapers. Recipient President's medal U. Western Ont., 1973, Periodical Distbrs. award, 1979, Can.-Australia award, 1986; grantee Can. Council, 1973, 80. Mem. Writers Union Can., PEN. Address: 2640 MacDonald, Victoria, BC Canada V8N 1X9

HODGSON, GREGORY BERNARD, software systems engineer; b. Chgo., July 17, 1946; s. John George and Lucille (Nass) H.; m. Kathleen Patricia, Aug. 11, 1972 (div. July 1974); m. Kathryn Marie Maytum, Feb. 14, 1976. BS in Computer Engring., U. Ill., 1972. Computer programmer specialist Lockheed Missiles and Space Co., Sunnyvale, Calif., 1972-81, software systems engr., 1981-89; software sys. cons. Lockheed Missiles and Space Co., Sunnyvale, 1989-95; engr./scientist Hewlett-Packard Co., Sunnyvale, Calif., 1995—; cons. in field. Served with U.S. Army, 1966-69. State of Ill. VA scholar, 1970-72. Mem. Ill. VA Assn. (coord. fed. and state affairs 1970-72). Republican. Roman Catholic. Home: 469 1/2 Curie Dr San Jose CA 95123-4925

HODGSON, LYNN MORRISON, marine biologist; b. Atlanta, July 30, 1948; d. Fred Grady Jr. and Florence Kimball (Morrison) H. BS, Coll. of William and Mary, 1970; MS, U. Wash., 1972; PhD, Stanford U., 1979. Asst. rsch. scientist U. Fla., Gainesville, 1979-81; vis. asst. prof. U. Ark., Fayetteville, 1981-82; asst. rsch. scientist Harbor Br. Found., Ft. Pierce, Fla., 1982-85; asst. prof. biology Northern State U., Aberdeen, S.D., 1985-88, chair dept. math. and natural scis., 1988-92, assoc. prof. biology, 1989-92; assoc. prof. biology U. Hawaii at West Oahu, Pearl City, 1992—. Contbr. articles to Botanica Marina, Marine Biology, Jour. of Phycology and others. Grantee S.D. Dept. of Water and Natural Resources, 1987-88, Hawaii Natural Areas Reserves, 1990-91, Ednl. Improvement Fund, 1992-93, Hawaii Dept. of Health, 1993-94. Mem. Internat. Phycological Soc., Brit. Phycological Soc., Phycological Soc. of Am. (nominations chair 1986-87), S.D. Acad. Scis. (pres. 1992), Sigma Xi, Kappa Mu Epsilon. Office: U Hawaii at West Oahu 96-043 Ala Ike St Pearl City HI 96782-3366

HODGSON, STEVEN SCOTT, educational administrator; b. Cadillac, Mich., Mar. 14, 1954; s. Bruce Rodney and Helen Marie (Girven) H.; m. Laurie Ann Vriesman, Aug. 6, 1977; children: Brianne Rae, Chelsea Marie, Brock Aaron. AA, Grace Bible Coll., 1975; BS in Edn., Ctrl. Mich. U., 1977. Cert. tchr., spl. edn. tchr., adminstr., supr., Colo. Classroom tchr. Hastings (Mich.) Pub. Schs., 1977-81; coord. planning, monitoring, data collection Barry Intermediate Schs., Hastings, 1981-82; ins. agt. Nat. Health, Dallas, 1982-84; mortgage loan officer BankPlus Mortgage, San Antonio, 1985-90; fin. planner Prin. Fin. Group, Des Moines, 1990-91; interim elem. prin. Evangelical Christian Acad., Colorado Springs, Colo., 1990-91, dir. devel., 1991—; fin. cons. Sunbelt Energy Corp., Huntsville, Ala., 1982. Chmn. bd. dirs. Village Seven Share, Colorado Springs, 1992—; team leader fundraising Boy Scouts Am., Colorado Springs, 1989-90; guest lectr. BBB, Colorado Springs, 1988. Grantee Covenant Coll., 1993-94. Mem. ASCD, Assn. Christian Schs. Internat. (accreditation team mem. 1993-94). Republican. Presbyterian. Home: 5238 Borrego Dr Colorado Springs CO 80918-2412 Office: Evangelical Christian Acad 4050 Nonchalant Cir S Colorado Springs CO 80917-2921

HODKIEWICZ, MELINDA JANE, maintenance engineer; b. London, Jan. 3, 1964; came to U.S., 1987; d. Keith Arthur Bertram and Gloria Ann (Leyden) R.; m. Paul Hodkiewicz, June 1994. MA in Metallurgy with honors, Oxford U., Eng., 1985. Grad. trainee Consol. Gold Fields PLC, London, 1985-86; metallurgist Goldsworthy Mining Ltd., Australia, 1986-87; asst. to mng. dir. Consol. Gold Fields PLC, London, 1987; metallurgist Gold Fields Chimney Creek, Winnemucca, Nev., 1987-89; mill metallurgist Barrick Goldstrike Mines, Inc., Elko, Nev., 1989-90, sr. maintenance engr., 1990—. Recipient Strakosch scholarship, Oxford U., 1984. Mem. AIME, Inst. Mining and Metallurgy, Western Mill Maintenance Assn. (v.p. 1994), London Bus. Sch. Alumni Assn., Oxford U. Alumni Assn. Office: Barrick Goldstrike Mines PO Box 29 Elko NV 89803-0029

HODSON, CHRISTINE ANN, psychologist; b. Chgo., Oct. 19, 1951; d. Roger Mithoff and Patricia Ann (Hill) H.; m. Gerard Fischer Jr., May 10, 1986; 1 child, Nathan David. BA, U. Calif., Santa Cruz, 1974; MS, Calif. State U., 1976; PhD, U. Md., 1982. Lic. psychologist, Calif. Therapist U. Md. Parent/Child Svc., College Park, 1978-80; psychometrist Prince George's Sch. Dist., Prince George's County, Md., 1979-80; trainee Alameda County Mental Health, Oakland and Fremont, Calif., 1980-82; pvt. practice Oakland and Fremont, 1983—; family ct. counselor Alameda County Family Ct. Svcs., 1982—; cons. to schs. and shelters, 1980-93; presenter at profl. confs. and to profl. orgns. Contbr. to profl. publs. NIMH fellow, 1976. Mem. APA, No. Calif. Soc. Clin. Hypnosis, No. Calif. Mediation Assn. Office: Alameda County Family Ct Svcs 1221 Oak St Oakland CA 94612

HODSON, NANCY PERRY, real estate agent; b. Kansas City, Mo., Nov. 19, 1932; d. Ralph Edward Perry and Juanita (Youmans) Jackman; m. William K. Hodson, Oct. 4, 1974 (div. Jan. 1985); children: Frank Tyler, Lisa Thompson, Suzanne Desforges, Robert Hodson. Student, Pine Manor Jr. Coll., 1950-51, Finch Coll., 1951-53. Cert. real estate agt., Calif.; cert. interior designer. Owner Nancy Perry Hodson Interior Design, L.A. and Newport Beach, Calif., 1974-82; agt. Grubb and Ellis, Newport Beach, 1990, Turner Assocs., Laguna Beach, Calif., 1990-92. Founder U. of Calif. Arboretum, Irvine, 1987, Opera Pacific, Costa Mesa, Calif., 1987; mem. U. of Calif. Rsch. Assocs., Irvine, 1986; pres. Big Canyon Philharm., Newport Beach, 1990; bd. dirs. Jr. Philharm., L.A., 1975-78. Mem. Big Canyon Country Club, L.A. Blue Ribbon 400 (1975-78), Jr. League Garden Club (pres. 1990-91), Big Canyon Garden Club (pres. 1989-91), Inst. of Logopedics (chmn. 30th Anniversary 1965), Guilds of Performing Arts Ctr. Presbyterian.

HODSON, SARA SUZANNE, manuscripts curator; b. Whittier, Calif., June 3, 1949; d. C. Hartley and Elizabeth M. (Holland) H.; m. Peter J. Blodgett, Mar. 26, 1988. BA with honors, Whittier Coll., 1971, MA in English, 1977; MLS, UCLA, 1979. Libr. asst. The Huntington Libr., San Marino, Calif., 1973-77, curator of lit. manuscripts, 1979—; adv. bd. DuPlessis Archives, Fuller Sem., Pasadena, Calif., 1994-95; adj. instr. Claremont (Calif.) Grad. Sch., 1994; mem. faculty Western Archives Inst., Pomona, Calif., 1994, Pasadena, 1995. Contbr. essays to Conrad Aiken: A Priest of Consciousness, 1989, Dictionary of Literary Biography Yearbook, 1992, Pre-Raphaelites in Context, 1992; editor: Guide to Literary Manuscripts, 1979; contbr. articles to profl. jours. Recipient scholarship Calif. Scholarship Fedn., 1967. Mem. Am. Libr. Assn., Soc. Am. Archivists (chair manuscripts repositories sect. 1994-95, vice chair/chair elect privacy and confidentiality roundtable, 1994-95), Soc. Calif. Archivists (treas. 1986-88, v.p. 1990-91, pres. 1991-92), Jack London Soc., Renaissance Conf. of So. Calif.

HOEFER, GREGORY ALLEN, banker; b. Seattle, Wash., Aug. 15, 1952; s. Roland Glen and Joyce Marwite (Pearson) H.; m. Gail Jean Anderson, Aug. 25, 1973 (div. Dec. 1986); m. Maryn Lyn Jacobson, Nov. 12, 1992; children: Jedidiah, Anna. BS, Seattle Pacific U., 1974; MTh, Freelandia Inst., Fredonia, Mo., 1978; PhD, Clayton Sch. Theology, California, 1979. Fellow Seattle Pacific U., 1976; mgr. Western Appraisal Co., Seattle, 1975-82; chief appraiser State of Wash., Olympia, 1982-84; chief appraiser, west region U.S. Treasury/Banks & Thrifts, Seattle, 1984-92; regional mgr., comml. appraisal Bank of Am., Las Vegas, 1992—; cons. Hoefer Corp., Seattle, 1980-90; tchr. Appraisal Inst., USA, 1982—; preacher Evangel. Ch. Alliance, Olympia, 1982-84. Co-author publs. in field. Recipient award of Excellence Fed. Fin. Instns. Examination Coun., 1990. Mem. Nat. Soc. Appraisers. Office: Bank of America 5781 West Sahara Las Vegas NV 89102

HOEFFLIN, RICHARD MICHAEL, lawyer, judicial administrator, contractor; b. L.A., Oct. 20, 1949; s. David Greenfield and Gloria (Harrison) H.; m. Susan J. Amoroso, Mar. 29, 1969; children: Alyssa, Jennifer, Richard, II. BS in Acctg. cum laude, Calif. State U.-Northridge, 1971; JD, Loyola U., Los Angeles, 1974. Bar: Calif. 1974, U.S. Dist. Ct. (cen. dist.) Calif. 1974, U.S. Tax Ct. 1976, U.S. Dist. Ct. (no. and so. dists.) Calif. 1976, U.S. Supreme Ct. 1982. With Lewitt, Hackman, Hoefflin, Shapiro, Marshall & Harlan, 1974—, ptnr., 1977—; judge pro tem L.A. Superior Ct., 1982—, family law mediator, 1982-86; judge pro tem, Ventura County, Superior Ct., 1991—; arbitrator Am. Arbitration Assn., Fee Dispute Resolution Svcs. For L.A. County Bar. Co-founder Ventura County Homeowners For Equal Taxation, Westlake Village, Calif., 1978-79; pres. counsel Westlake Hills Homeowners Assn., 1975-77; chmn. celebrity Love Match Tennis Tour. for John McEnroe United Cerebral Palsy/Spastic Children Found., 1990—. Mem. ABA, L.A. Bar Assn., Ventura County Bar Assn., San Fernando Valley Bar Assn., Westlake North Ranch Tennis Assn. (pres. 1977-78), North Ranch Country Club (pres. tennis assn. 1984-85). Republican. Roman Catholic. Office: Lewitt Hackman Hoefflin Shapiro Marshall & Harlan 16633 Ventura Blvd Ste 1100 Encino CA 91436-1870

HOEFFLIN, STEVEN M., plastic surgeon; b. Seattle, Wash., 1946. MD, UCLA, 1972. Plastic surgeon Santa Monica (Calif.) Hosp.; also clin. prof. UCLA. Office: 1530 Arizona Ave Santa Monica CA 90404-1208*

HOEHN, RAYMOND PHILIP, JR., map librarian; b. Poplar Bluff, Mo., Oct. 23, 1941; s. Raymond Philip and Florentine Jeanne (Lesniak) H. AB, UCLA, 1963; MLS, U. Calif., Berkeley, 1967. Reference libr. U. Calif. Libr., Berkeley, 1967-69, map libr., 1969—. Author: Union List of Sanborn Fire Insurance Maps Held by Institutions in the U.S. and Canada, Vol. 1, 1976. Mem. ALA (Honors award Map and Geography Round Table 1994), We. Assn. Map Librs. (hon. life; pres. 1976-77), Calif. Map Soc., Am. Congress on Surveying and Mapping, Am. Fedn. Tchrs., Sierra Club. Home: 51 Levant St San Francisco CA 94114-1409 Office: U Calif Earth Sci and Map Libr 230 Earth Sci Bldg Berkeley CA 94720-6000

HOEHN, ROBERT J., plastic surgeon, educator; b. East St. Louis, Ill., 1929; m. Margaret M. Guest Maier (div. Oct. 1987); children: Robert Anthony Till, Margaret Eve; m. Nancy Ruth Vincent Baum. MD, Washington U., St. Louis, 1956. Diplomate Am. Bd. Plastic Surgery. Intern Vancouver Gen. Hosp., Can., 1956-57; resident McGill U., Montreal, 1960-61; fellow in hand surgery N.Y. Hosp.-Cornell, 1962-63, resident in plastic surgery, 1963-65; clin. prof. plastic surgery U. Colo., 1978—; with Aurora Presbyn. Hosp., 1978—, Aurora Regional Med. Ctr., 1978—, Denver Children's Hosp., 1978—, Porter Meml. Hosp., 1982—, Swedish Hosp., 1982—; pvt. practice. Fellow ACS; mem. AAPS, Am. Soc. Plastic and Reconstructive Surgeons, Plastic Surgery Rsch. Coun. Home: 2601 S Quebec St # 3 Denver CO 80231 Office: # 205 3535 Cherry Cr N Dr Denver CO 80209

HOEHNE, JOHN H., allergist; b. Omaha, Nebr., 1940. MD, U. Nebr. Allergist Marin Gen. Hosp., Greenbrae, Calif.; also asst. clin. prof. U. Calif. Office: 901 Nevin Ave Richmond CA 94801-3143*

HOELL, NOEL LORAINE, psychiatrist; b. Helena, Mont., July 31, 1939; s. Edward J. and Bessie P. (Laramie) H.; children: Geoffrey K., Andrea B. MD, U. Chgo., 1964. Cert. psychiatrist. Intern U. Oreg., 1964-65; resident in pscyhiatry U. Colo., 1965-69; asst. prof. U. Calif. Davis Med. Sch., Sacramento, 1972-77; staff psychiatrist Western Mont. Regional Community Mental Health Ctr., Missoula, 1977-78; pvt. practice Missoula, 1978—. Maj. U.S. Army Med. Corps, 1969-72. Mem. Am. Psychiat. Assn., Mont. Psychiat. Assn. (legis. rep., sec., pres., dep. rep. 1979—), Western Mont. Med. Soc. Office: 554 W Broadway St Missoula MT 59802-4008

HOERNER, MICHAEL DUANE, beauty salon executive; b. Spokane, May 31, 1957; s. John Valentine and Maxine W. (Moffit) H.; m. Monya J. Patterson, Sept. 8, 1990. Lic. in Cosmetology, M'Lady Sch. of Beauty, Spokane, 1978; Lic. in Ins. Sales, Combined Ins. Sch., Portland, Oreg., 1981. Lic. in securities sales. Stylist Laurel & Hardys, Spokane, 1978-79, Trimmers-The Crescent, Spokane, 1979-80; bookkeeper Stratton Electronics, Spokane, 1980-81; sales mgr., acct. exec. Combined Ins., Spokane, 1981-84; shift mgr., stylist Supercuts, Spokane, 1984-86; sales dir., broker Allied Capital Group, Spokane, 1986-88; asst. mgr., stylist Cutter's Edge Hair Design, Spokane, 1988-90; mgr., founder Shear Satisfaction Salon, Seattle, 1990-93; pres., CEO Shear Satisfaction Salons, Inc., Seattle, 1993—. Mem. Civitan, Palm Beach, Fla., 1988. Ship serviceman USN, 1975-76. Office: Shear Satisfaction Salons 19505 44th Ave W Ste H Lynnwood WA 98036-5658

HOFERT, JACK, consulting company executive, lawyer; b. Phila., Apr. 6, 1930; s. David and Beatrice (Schatz) H.; m. Marilyn Tukeman, Sept. 4, 1960; children: Dina, Bruce. BS, UCLA, 1952, MBA, 1954, JD, 1957. Bar: Calif. 1957; CPA, Calif. Tax supr. Peat, Marwick Mitchell & Co., L.A., 1959-62, tax mgr., 1974-77; v.p. fin. Pacific Theaters Corp., L.A., 1962-68; freelance cons. L.A., 1969-74; tax mgr. Lewis Homes, Upland, Calif., 1977-80; pres. Di-Bru, Inc., L.A., 1981-87, Scolyn, Inc., L.A., 1988-95; bus. cons., 1995—; dir. Valley Fed. Savs. and Loan Assn., 1989-92. Mem. UCLA Law Rev., 1956-57; contbr. articles to tax, fin. mags. Served with USN, 1948-49. Home and Office: 2479 Roscomare Rd Los Angeles CA 90077-1812

HOFF, BERNADINE RYAN, management consultant; b. Creighton, Nebr., Aug. 29, 1926; d. Ralph Russell and Ella Helma (Boysen) Ryan; m. Edwin J.

Hoff, Jan. 15, 1962 (div. June 1973); 1 child, Denise Kelly. BA in Secondary Edn., Northeastern Ill. U., 1970; MA in Diversified Edn., U.S. Internat. U., 1974, PhD in Mgmt., 1979. Ops. asst. Spiegel, Inc., Chgo., 1957-64; dir. off-campus grad. program U.S. Internat. U., San Diego, 1973-76; cons. pvt. practice, San Diego, 1973—; dir. program devel. Pepperdine U., Santa Ana, Calif., 1976-77; program dir., continuing mgmt. edn. U. Minn., Mpls., 1977-80; dir. continuing edn. San Diego State U., 1980-81; pres., CEO Nat. Cons. Referrals, Del Mar, Calif., 1980-85; v.p. acad. affairs LaJolla U., San Diego, 1992-93; adj. faculty Nat. U., San Diego, 1981—; mktg. advisor, cons. Link Data Corp., San Diego, 1992—, Saddleback Coll., Mission Viejo, Calif., 1982-83, others. Mem. NAt. Mgmt. Assn. (pres., v.p.). Home and Office: 3710 Balboa Dr Oceanside CA 92056

HOFF, RENAE, magistrate; b. Caldwell, Idaho, Feb. 23, 1951; d. Edwin Herbert Hoff and Agnes Mary (Stoltz) Feiling; m. Craig L. Gibson. BA, Coll. of Idaho, 1979; JD, Southwestern U., 1981. Bar: Idaho 1981, U.S. Dist. Ct. Idaho 1981, U.S. Ct. Appeals (9th cir.) 1986. Assoc. Gunn & Hoff, Caldwell, 1981-90; magistrate judge Third Jud. Dist. of Idaho, 1990—; referral atty. pro bono panel Idaho State Bar, 1983-90 (vol. lawyers policy coun. 1989—, coun. chair 1992, Equal Access to Justice award 1988, 93); staff atty. Indsl. Spl. Indemnity Fund, 1986-90; city atty. Marsing, Idaho, 1987-90; prosecutor Homedale City, Idaho, 1987-90; bd. dirs. Mercy House. Mem. ABA, Nat. Assn. Women Judges, 3d Jud. Bar Assn., Assn. Trial Lawyers Am., Idaho Trial Lawyers Assn. , Idaho Women Lawyers, Canyon County Lawyers Club (pres. 1990). Office: Canyon County Ct Annex 120 9th Ave S Nampa ID 83651-3825

HOFFENBLUM, ALLAN ERNEST, political consultant; b. Vallejo, Calif., Aug. 10, 1940; s. Albert A. and Pearl Estelle (Clarke) H. BA, U. So. Calif., 1962. Mem. staff L.A. County Rep. Com., 1967-71; staff dir. Rep. Assembly Caucus Calif. legislature, Sacramento, 1973-75; polit. dir. Rep. Party of Calif., L.A., 1977-78; owner Allan Hoffenblum & Assocs., L.A., 1979—. Capt. USAF, 1962-67, Vietnam. Decorated Bronze Star medal. Mem. Internat. Assn. Polit. Cons., Am. Assn. Polit. Cons. Jewish. Office: 9000 W Sunset Blvd Ste 406 West Hollywood CA 90069-5804

HOFFLUND, PAUL, lawyer; b. San Diego, Mar. 27, 1928; s. John Leslie and Ethel Frances (Cline) H.; m. Anne Marie Thalman, Feb. 15, 1958; children: Mark, Sylvia. BA, Princeton (N.J.) U., 1950; JD, George Washington U., 1956. Bar: D.C. 1956, U.S. Dist. Ct. D.C. 1956, U.S. Ct. Appeals (D.C. cir.) 1956, Calif. 1957, U.S. Dist. Ct. (so. dist.) Calif. 1957, U.S. Ct. Mil. Appeals 1957, U.S. Ct. Claims 1958, U.S. Ct. Appeals (9th cir.) 1960, U.S. Supreme Ct. 1964, U.S. Tax Ct. 1989. Assoc. Wencke, Carlson & Kuykendall, San Diego, 1961-62; ptnr. Carlson, Kuykendall & Hofflund, San Diego, 1963-65, Carlson & Hofflund, San Diego, 1965-72; Christian Sci. practitioner San Diego, 1972-84; arbitrator Mcpl. Cts. and Superior Ct. of Calif., San Diego, 1984—; pvt. practice San Diego, 1985—; adj. prof. law Nat. U. Sch. Law, San Diego, 1985-94; judge pro tem Mcpl. Ct. South Bay Jud. Dist., 1990—; disciplinary counsel to U.S. Tax Ct., 1989—; asst. U.S. atty. U.S. Dept. of Justice, L.A., 1959-60, asst. U.S. atty. in charge, San Diego, 1960-61, spl. hearing officer, San Diego, 1962-68; asst. corp. counsel Govt. of D.C., 1957-59. Author: (chpt. in book) Handbook on Criminal Procedure in the U.S. District Court, 1967; contbr. articles to profl. jours. Treas. Princeton Club of San Diego; v.p. Community Concert Assn., San Diego; pres. Sunland Home Found., San Diego, Trust for Christian Sci. Orgn., San Diego; chmn. bd. 8th Ch. of Christ, Scientist, San Diego. With USN, 1950-53, comdr. JAGC, USNR, 1953-72, ret. Mem. ABA, San Diego County Bar Assn., Inst. Global Ethics, World Affairs Coun., Phi Delta Phi. Democrat. Home and Office: 6146 Syracuse Ln San Diego CA 92122-3301

HOFFMAN, CHARLES FENNO, III, architect; b. Greenwich, Conn., May 28, 1958; s. Harrison Baldwin Wright and Louise Elkins (Sinkler) H.; m. Pia Christina Ossorio, Dec. 27, 1980; children: Wilhelmina C. L., Frederic W. S., Henry F. BA in Environ. Design, U. Pa., 1983; MArch, U. Colo., 1986. Designer Fenno Hoffman & Assocs., Boulder, Colo., 1983—; pvt. practice designer Boulder, 1985; assoc. William Zmistowski Assoc. Architects, 1987—, Pellecchia-Olson Architects, Boulder, 1989—; prin. Fenno Hoffman Architects PC, Boulder, Colo., 1991—; cons. Summit Habitats, Inc., 1984—; design cons. The Denver Partnership, 1985, Downtown Denver, Inc., 1985; guest critic U. Colo., 1990—, guest lectr., 1991-92, 94, 95. Prin. works include Ca'Venier Mus. for Venice Bienalle, 1985, Cleveland Pl. Connestion, Denver, 1985 (1st prize 1985), hist. renovated house, Boulder, 1986, 3 Gates 3 Squares, Denver, 1986, Geneva Ave. House, 1992, Jarrow Montessori Sch. master plan, 1994; numerous residential and multi-family projects, 1991-94; Northwest Classroom, 1995; author: Urban Transit Facility, A Monorail for Downtown Denver, 1985. Mem. Am. Planning Assn., Architects & Planners ofBoulder. Democrat. Episcopalian. Clubs: Rallysport Racquet (Boulder). Office: 505 Geneva Ave Boulder CO 80302-7139

HOFFMAN, DARLEANE CHRISTIAN, chemistry educator; b. Terril, Iowa, Nov. 8, 1926; d. Carl Benjamin and Elverna (Kuhlman) Christian; m. Marvin Morrison Hoffman, Dec. 26, 1951; children: Maureane R., Daryl K. BS in Chemistry, Iowa State U., 1948, PhD in Nuclear Chemistry, 1951. Chemist Oak Ridge (Tenn.) Nat. Lab., 1952-53; mem. staff radiochemistry group Los Alamos (N.Mex.) Sci. Lab., 1953-71, assoc. leader chemistry-nuclear group, 1971-79, divsn. leader, chem.-nuclear divsn., 1979-82, div. leader isotope and nuclear chem. div., 1982-84; prof. chemistry U. Calif., Berkeley, 1984-91, prof. emerita, 1991-93, prof. grad. sch., 1993—; faculty sr. scientist Lawrence Berkeley (Calif.) Lab., 1984—; dir.'s fellow Los Alamos Nat. Lab., 1990—; dir. G.T. Seaborg Inst. for Transactinium Sci., 1991—; panel leader, speaker Los Alamos Women in Sci., 1975, 79, 82; rschr. Guggenheim Found., 1978-79; mem. subcom. on nuclear and radiochemistry NAS-NRC, 1978-81, chmn. subcom. on nuclear and radiochemistry, 1982-84; titular mem. commn. on radiochem. and nuclear techniques Internat. Union of Pure and Applied Chem., 1983-87, sec., 1985-87, chmn., 1987-91, assoc. mem. 1991-93; mem. com. 2d Internat. Symposium on Nuclear and Radiochemistry, 1988; planning panel Workshop on Tng. Requirements for Chemists in Nuclear Medicine, Nuclear Industry, and Related Fields, 1988, radionuclide migration peer rev. com., Las Vegas, 1986-87, steering com. Advanced Steady State Neutron Source, 1986-90, steering com., panelist Workshop on Opportunities and Challenges in Research with Transplutonium Elements, Washington, 1983; mem. energy rsch. adv. bd. cold fusion panel, Dept. Energy, 1989-90; mem. NAS separations subpanel of separations tech. and transmutation systems panel, 1992-94, NAS-NRC Bd. on Radioactive Waste Mgmt., 1994—; lectr. Japan Soc. Promotion Sci. Contbr. numerous articles in field to profl. jours. Recipient Alumni Citation of Merit Coll. Scis. and Humanities, Iowa State U., 1978, Disting. Achievement award Iowa State U., 1986; Sr. postdoctoral fellow NSF, 1964-65. Fellow Am. Inst. Chemists (pres. N.Mex. chpt. 1976-78), Am. Phys. Soc., AAAS; mem: Am. Chem. Soc. (chmn. nuclear chemistry and technology div. 1978-79, com. in sci. 1986-88, exec. com. div. nuclear chem. and tech. 1987-90, John Dustin Clark award Cen. N.Mex. sect. 1976, Nuclear Chemistry award 1983, Francis P. Garvan-John M. Olin medal 1991), Am. Nuclear Soc. (co-chmn. internat. conf. Methods and Applications of Radioanalytical Chemistry 1987), Norwegian Acad. Arts and Scis, Sigma Xi, Phi Kappa Phi, Iota Sigma Pi (nat. hon.), Pi Mu Epsilon, Sigma Delta Epsilon, Alpha Chi Sigma. Methodist. Home: 2277 Manzanita Dr Oakland CA 94611-1135 Office: Lawrence Berkeley Lab MS70A-3307 NSD Berkeley CA 94720

HOFFMAN, DAVID WAYNE, III, real esate appraiser; b. Sarra Polichie, Luciana, Italy, Sept. 22, 1955; came to U.S., 1959; s. Desurondro Augustine Cozza and Hazel Annabelle (Rosenthal) Ankley; m. Janie Louise Charbonal, May 6, 1974 (div. Sept. 1974). MA in Econs., Gonzaga U., 1979; BA, Wash. State U., 1983; cert. in property mgmt., Spokane C.C., 1986. Lic. real estate appraiser, Wash. Rep. Gus J. Cozza Constrn. Co., Spokane, Wash., 1973-75; regional rep. Broumer, Gottlieb, Inc., SEattle, 1975-80; v.p., sec.-treas. Washco Corp., Spokane, 1980—; property mgr., ptnr. real estate sales Diversified Apt. Reality Co., Inc., Seattle, 1989—; ptnr. Girtz Bakery, Spolane, 1985-87. Mem. Spokane Club, Wash. Athletic Club, Athletic Round Table, Seattle Tennis Club, Manito Country Club, Moose, Brotherhood of Friends Lodge. Republican. Roman Catholic. Home: 9900 Spain NE Ste H0-1041 Albuquerque NM 87111 Office: D A R C O Inc 420 E Howell Seattle WA 98122

HOFFMAN, DONALD DAVID, cognitive and computer science educator; b. San Antonio, Dec. 29, 1955; s. David Pollock and Loretta Virginia (Shoemaker) H.; m. Geralyn Mary Souza, Dec. 13, 1986; 1 child from previous marriage, Melissa Louise. BA, UCLA, 1978; PhD, MIT, 1983. MTS and project engr. Hughes Aircraft Co., El Segundo, Calif., 1978-83; rsch. scientist MIT Artificial Intelligence Lab, Cambridge, Mass., 1983; asst. prof. U. Calif., Irvine, 1983-86, assoc. prof., 1986-90, full prof., 1990—; cons. Fairchild Lab. for Artificial Intelligence, Palo Alto, Calif., 1984; panelist MIT Corp. vis. com., Cambridge, 1985, NSF, Washington, 1988; conf. host IEEE Conf. on Visual Motion, Irvine, 1989; conf. host Office of Naval Rsch. Conf. on Vision, Laguna Beach, Calif., 1992. Co-author: Observer Mechanics, 1989; contbr. articles to profl. jours. Vol. tchr. Turtle Rock Elem. Sch., Irvine, 1988-90. Recipient Distinguished Scientific award, Am. Psychol. Assn., 1989, Troland Rsch. award U.S. Nat. Acad. Scis., 1994; grantee NSF, 1984, 87. Mem. AAAS. Office: U Calif Dept Cognitive Sci Irvine CA 92717

HOFFMAN, DONALD JAMES, management consultant; b. Urbana, Ill., Nov. 20, 1948; s. Harold L. and Dorothy P. (McCarty) H.; m. Susan L. Hoffman, Mar. 20, 1971. BSBA, Biola U., 1970; MBA, Calif. State Poly. U., Pomona, 1974. Cert. in mgmt. acctg. Contr. Biola U., La Mirada, 1970-75; area contr. Calif. ops. Internat. Paper Co., 1975-77, project mgr. Calif. ops., 1977-78, mng. planning western ops., 1978-80, product mgr. wood products, 1980-81, timber and wood products, 1981-83, mng. lumber and plywood, 1983-85; pres., CEO Hudson Group, Inc., 1985-88; prin. The Crest Co., 1989—; bd. dirs. Kewennaw Land Assn., Ltd., Ironwood, Mich. Commr. Wasco County Planning Commn., 1994. Named Outstanding Young Men of Am. U.S. Jaycees, 1980. Baptist. Office: The CREST Co 2080 State Rd Mosier OR 97040-9781

HOFFMAN, GARY ALLAN, retail executive; b. Jacksonville, Fla., Aug. 31, 1949; s. Louis A. and Myrna H.; m. Silvia Patricia Biscar, Oct. 14, 1979; children: Andrea, Brooks. BA in Polit. Sci. magna cum laude, Calif. State U., San Francisco, 1971. No. Calif. regional dir. St. Jude Children's Rsch. Hosp. Found., Memphis, Tenn., 1972-74; program devel. specialist Calif. Credit Union League, Pomona, 1975-77; sr. tng. specialist Crocker Nat. Bank, San Francisco, 1977-78; program coord. Inst. for Profl. Devel., San Jose, Calif., 1978-79; mgr., sr. acct. exec. Sales Cons., San Mateo, Calif., 1979-86; pres., CEO Serramonte Candle Co., Inc., Daly City, Calif., 1986-93, Lumiere, San Bruno, Calif., 1993—; chpt. v.p. ASTD, L.A., 1974. Campus coord. Dem. Nat. Com., San Mateo, 1968, precinct chairperson, 1972. Mem. Green Hills Country Club, Anti-Defamation League. Democrat. Home: 231 Bridgeport Dr Half Moon Bay CA 94019-4238 Office: Lumiere PO Box 97 Moss Beach CA 94038-0097

HOFFMAN, GEORGE ALAN, consulting company executive; b. Albany, N.Y., May 16, 1937; s. Irving Marshall and Margaret (Coyne) H.; m. Kim Thi Nguyen, Oct. 10, 1971; children: Caroline, Christine. AB, U. Calif., Berkeley, 1980, MBA, 1982. Mgmt. analyst Am. Can Co., N.Y.C., 1966-69; cons. Vietnamese Air Force, Bien Hoa, Vietnam, 1970-74, Puslitbang, Jakarta, Indonesia, 1974-75; v.p. Union Bank, Oakland, Calif., 1987—. Author: Indonesian Production-sharing Oil Contracts, 1982. Mem. Mensa. Club: Commonwealth (San Francisco). Office: 460 Hegenberger Rd Oakland CA 94621-1423

HOFFMAN, JUDY GREENBLATT, preschool director; b. Chgo., June 12, 1932; d. Edward Abraham and Clara (Morrill) Greenblatt; m. Morton Hoffman, Mar. 16, 1950 (div. Jan. 1983); children: Michael, Alan, Clare. BA summa cum laude, Met. State Coll., Denver, 1972; MA, U. No. Colo., 1976. Cert. tchr., Colo. Pre-sch. dir. B.M.H. Synagogue, Denver, 1968-70, Temple Emanuel, Denver, 1970-85, Congregation Rodef Shalom, Denver, 1985-88; tchr. Denver Pub. Schs., 1988—; bilingual tchr. adults in amnesty edn. Denver Pub. Schs., 1989-90. Author: I Live in Israel, 1979, Joseph and Me, 1980 (Gamoran award), (with others) American Spectrum Single Volume Encyclopedia, 1991. Coord. Douglas Mountain Therapeutic Riding Ctr. for Handicapped, Golden, Colo., 1985—; dir. Mountain Ranch Summer Day Camp for Denver Pub. Schs., 1989-91. Mem. Nat. Assn. Temple Educators. Democrat.

HOFFMAN, MARIANNE MACINA, nonprofit organization administrator; b. N.Y.C., Apr. 29, 1951; d. Vito William Jr. and Frances (Florio) Macina; m. Neil Richard Hoffman, April 29, 1995. BS in Journalism, U. Fla., 1973; postgrad., U. London, 1973; AA in Advt. ARt, Inst. Atlanta, 1975. Writer Clearwater (Fla.) Sun, 1965-69; pub. rels., graphics specialist Hensley-Schmidt Engts., Atlanta, 1975-76; creative dir. Mackey Green & Assocs., Atlanta, 1976; assoc. editor So. Banker Mag., Atlanta, 1977-78; managing editor Pension World Mag., Atlanta, 1978-79; communications writer No. States Power Co., Mpls., 1979-80; advt. dir. Carlton Celebrity Dinner Theater, Bloomington, Minn., 1980-82; coord., mktg. svcs. St. Paul Cos. Inc., 1982-87; regional mgr. Western Ins. Info. Svc., Portland, Oreg., 1987—; bd. dirs. Ins. Edn. Found. Oreg., Portland, 1989—. Exec. prodr.: (consumer videos) Preventing Home Burglary, 1988 (Gold medal 1990), Don't Give a Thief a Free Ride: Preventing Auto Theft, 1990, Bon Voyage: Tips for a Safe Vacation, 1993. Mem. task force Oreg. Juvenile Firesetter Edn., Salem, 1988-92; mem. Oreg. Coun. Against Arson, 1988—, v.p., 1994, 95; mem. exec. bd. Crime Prevention Assn. Oreg., 1992-94, treas., 1995—; bd. dirs. Oreg. Traffic Safety NOW, 1988-91. Recipient Merit award Ins. Info. Inst., N.Y.C., 1989, Commendation award Oreg. Coun. Against Arson, 1989, Crime Prevention award Crime Prevention Assn. Oreg., 1990, Media award, 1989. Mem. Soc. Chartered Property Casualty Underwriters (Oreg. chpt. bd. dirs. 1990-92, new designee rep. we. region 1989-90, cert.). Republican. Roman Catholic. Office: Western Ins Info Svc 11855 SW Ridgecrest Dr Ste 107 Beaverton OR 97008-6356

HOFFMAN, NEIL EUGENE, cell biologist; b. N.Y.C., Jan. 9, 1956; s. Edward Martin and Aza H.; m. Setsuko Tsukamoto, Dec. 11, 1981; children: Aaron, Masa. BS, Cornell U., 1978; PhD, U. Calif., Davis, 1982. Postdoctoral fellow Mich. State U., East Lansing, Mich., 1983-86, Rockefeller U., N.Y.C., 1986-87, U. Pa., Phila., 1987-88; staff scientist Carnegie Instn., Stanford, Calif., 1988—. Contbr. articles to profl. jours. Recipient First award NIH, 1989-95; postdoctoral fellow NSF, 1986-88. Mem. Am. Soc. Plant Physiology, Am. Chem. Soc., Internat. Soc. Plant Molecular Biology, Am. Soc. Cell Biology. Office: Carnegie Inst Washington 290 Panama St Stanford CA 94305-4101

HOFFMAN, RODNEY JOSEPH, computer scientist; b. San Antonio, Oct. 10, 1950; s. Herbert Irving and Jewel (Greenberg) H. BA, Rice U., 1972; MS, U. So. Calif., L.A., 1974. Rsch. asst., teaching asst. U. So. Calif., L.A., 1972-78; tech. staff mem. Xerox Corp., El Segundo, Calif., 1979-92, Jet Propulsion Lab., Pasadena, Calif., 1992—; instr. Occidental Coll., L.A., 1978—; reader Edni. Testing Svc., Princeton, N.J., 1987-92. Contbr. articles to profl. jours. Bd. dirs. Nat. Orgn. Gay and Lesbian Scientists and Tech. Profls., Pasadena, 1989-92; mem. cmty. adv. bd. Sta. KCET-TV, L.A., 1986-93. Mem. IEEE, Computer Profls. for Social Responsibility (nat. treas. 1988-92), Assn. for Computing Machinery. Office: PO Box 77076 Los Angeles CA 90007-0076

HOFFMAN, WAYNE MELVIN, retired airline official; b. Chgo., Mar. 9, 1923; s. Carl A. and Martha (Tamillo) H.; m. Laura Majewski, Jan. 26, 1946; children—Philip, Karen, Kristin. B.A. summa cum laude, U. Ill., 1943, J.D. with high honors, 1947. Bar: Ill. bar 1947, N.Y. bar 1958. Atty. I.C. R.R., 1948-52; with N.Y.C. R.R. Co., 1952-67, exec. asst. to pres., 1958-60, v.p. freight sales, 1960-61, v.p. sales, 1961-62, exec. v.p., 1962-67; chmn. bd. N.Y. Central Trans. Co., 1960-67, Flying Tiger Line, Inc. and Tiger Internat., Inc., 1967-86; trustee Aerospace Corp., 1975-86, 87—; bd. dirs. Rohr Industries; chmn. Hoffman Pacific Corp., 1985—. Trustee McCallum Theatre, Palm Desert, Calif., Eisenhower Med. Ctr., Rancho Mirage, Calif. Served to capt. inf. AUS, World War II. Decorated Silver Star, Bronze Star with oak leaf cluster, Purple Heart with oak leaf cluster; Fourragere (Belgium). Mem. Bohemian Club (San Francisco), Vintage Club (Indian Wells), Phi Beta Kappa. Home: 74-435 Palo Verde Dr Indian Wells CA 92210-7367 Office: 2450 Montecito Rd Ramona CA 92065-1619

HOFFMAN, WILLIAM YANES, plastic surgeon; b. Rochester, N.Y., 1952. MD, U. Rochester, 1977. Plastic surgeon U. Calif. San Francisco Med. Ctr.; also prof. plastic surgery U. Calif., San Francisco. Office: UC San Fran Plastic Surgery 350 Parnassus Ave Ste 509 San Francisco CA 94117-3608*

HOFFMANN, JON ARNOLD, aeronautical engineer, educator; b. Wausau, Wis., Jan. 13, 1942; s. Arnold D. and Rita J. (Haas) H.; m. Carol R. Frye. BSME, U. Wis., 1964, MSME, 1966. Register profl. engr., Calif. Research engr. Trane Co., 1966-68; prof. aeronautical engring. Calif. Poly. State U., San Luis Obispo, 1968—; research engr. Stanford U. NSF Program, 1970; research fellow Ames Research Ctr. Ctr. NASA/ASEE, 1974-75; tech. cons. NASA/AMES Research Ctr., 1977; design engr. Cal/ Poly ERDA contract, 1976-77; prin. investigator NASA-ARC Cooperative Agreement, 1983. Contbr. articles to profl. jours. Grantee NASA, NSF. Mem. ASME. Home: 1044 Via Chula Robles Arroyo Grande CA 93420-4915 Office: Calif Poly State U Dept Aero Engring San Luis Obispo CA 93407

HOFFMANN, KATHRYN ANN, humanities educator; b. Rockville Centre, N.Y., Oct. 26, 1954; d. Manfred and Catherine (Nanko) H.; m. Brook Ellis, Nov. 25, 1987. BA summa cum laude, SUNY Buffalo, 1975; MA, The Johns Hopkins U., 1979, PhD, 1981. Asst. prof. French lit. and lang. U. Wis.-Madison, 1981-88, U. Hawaii-Manoa, Honolulu, 1992—; mng. ptnr. Yuval Design Partnership, Chgo., 1988-92. Assoc. editor Substance, 1982-87; contbr. articles to profl. jours.; designer clothing accessories. Grantee NEH, 1993, 95; fellow Inst. Rsch. in Humanities, 1984-85, Am. Coun. Learned Socs., 1984-85. Mem. MLA, Hawaii Assn. Lang. Tchrs., N.Am. Soc. for 17th Century French Literature, S.E. Am. Soc. for 17th Century Studies, Soc. for Interdisciplinary Study of Social Imagery, Phi Beta Kappa. Home: 2640 Dole St Apt C-6 Honolulu HI 96822-2331 Office: U Hawaii Manoa Dept European Languages & Lit 1890 E West Rd # 483 Honolulu HI 96822-2318

HOFFMANN, TIMOTHY JAY, computer networking executive; b. Milw., Aug. 2, 1958; s. Thomas R. and Lorna G. Hoffmann. B in Computer Sci., U. Minn., 1980. Analyst United Computing Svcs., Kansas City, Mo., 1980-84; sr. analyst Control Data Corp., Kansas City, 1984-89; sr. network analyst Power Computing, Dallas, 1989-93; prin. network engr. Infonet Svcs. Co., El Segundo, Calif., 1993—. Co-author: (textbook) Fortran: A Structured, Disciplined Style, 1st, 2d, 3d edits., 1980—. Office: Infonet Svcs Co 2100 E Grand Ave El Segundo CA 90245-5024

HOFFMEISTER, GERHART, German language educator; b. Giessen, Germany, Dec. 17, 1936; came to U.S., 1966, naturalized citizen, 1993; s. Johannes and Inge Caecilie (Johannsen) H.; m. Margaret von Poletika, May 28, 1966 (div. Dec. 1988); 1 child, George A. Degree, U. Bonn, Fed. Republic Germany, 1963, U. Cologne, Fed. Republic Germany, 1966; PhD, U. Md., 1970. Student tchr. U. Cologne, 1964-66; instr. U. Md., 1966-70; asst. prof. U. Wis., Milw., 1970-74; assoc. prof. Wayne State U., Detroit, 1974-75; assoc. prof. U. Calif., Santa Barbara, 1975-79, prof., 1979—, bd. dirs. Comparative Lit. program, 1991—. Author: (with others) Germany 2, 000 Years III, 1986; editor: Goethe in Italy, 1988, French Revolution, 1989, European Romanticism, 1989. Recipient award Am. Philos. Assn., 1974, Max Kade Found., 1986, 88. Mem. MLA, Am. Assn. Tchrs. German, Goethe Soc. N.Am. Home: 117 Calle Alamo Santa Barbara CA 93105-2818 Office: U Calif Dept German Santa Barbara CA 93106

HOFFORD, HARRY, marketing professional; b. 1924. Market planning mgr. Nat. Brewing Co., Miami, Fla., 1960-68; dir. of mktg. Nat. Brewing Co., Phoenix, Ariz., 1968-80; gen. mgr. Polar Beverage divsn. Circle K. Corp., Phoenix, 1980-82; v.p. Promotional Mktg. Svcs., Phoenix, 1981—. Office: Promotional Marketing Services 4105 N 20th St Ste 190 Phoenix AZ 85016-6039*

HOFFORD, NANCY, marketing professional; b. 1928. Freelance promotional person Hollywood, Calif. and Phoenix, Ariz., 1960-81; pres. Promotional Marketing Svc., Phoenix, 1981—. *

HOFGARD, KURT CHRISTOPHER, lawyer, insurance executive; b. Boulder, Colo., Nov. 5, 1966; s. William Glenn and Edna Blanche (Hampton) H. BA with honors, Stanford U., 1989; JD, Lewis and Clark Coll., 1993. Bar: Oreg. 1993, Colo. 1994. Tech. editor Sci. Applications Internat. Corp., Washington, 1989-90; v.p., gen. mgr. Hofgard & Co., Boulder, Colo., 1994—; corp. subagt. N.Y. Life Ins. Co., Boulder, 1994. Current materials editor (jour.) Environ. Law, 1992—. contbr. 1993—. Congressional intern U.S. Ho. of Reps., Washington, 1989. Mem. ABA, Oregon State Bar, Colo. Bar Assn., Boulder County Bar Assn. Office: Hofgard & Co 1871 Folsom St Boulder CO 80302-5702

HOFMAN, EDMOND JOHN, secondary school educator, police official; b. Monterey Park, Calif., Sept. 10, 1945; s. Siegfried Hector and Anna Maria (van Hall) H.; m. Michele Teri Butrum, May 15, 1969 (div. Feb. 1989); children: Jason Stuart, Edmond Ryan, Jodi Nicole; m. Diana Jeanne Tuttle, Aug. 1, 1990. AA in Police Sci., Orange Coast Coll., 1966; AA in Anthropology, Social Sci., Fullerton Coll., 1989; BA in Anthropology with honors, Calif. State U., Fullerton, 1990. Advanced cert. police officer standards and tng. Police officer Anaheim (Calif.) Police Dept., 1969-85; edn. asst. Anaheim Union H.S. Dist., 1986-89; tchr. Perris (Calif.) Union H.S. Dist., 1989-91, Murrieta Valley (Calif.) Unified Sch. Dist., 1991—. Coach, asst. coach Am. Soccer Assn., 1977-84; reserve park ranger Orange County Harbors, Beaches and Parks, 1988-93; cub scout master Boy Scouts Am., Orange County, 1977-84; wildlife rehabilitator State of Calif. Fish and Game, 1989—. Corp. USMC, 1966-68, Vietnam. Decorated Nat. Defense Medal, Vietnam Svc. Medal with 2 stars, Vietnam Campaign Medal, Presdl. Unit Citation. Mem. PTA, Murrieta Tchrs. Assn. (site rep. 1991—), Anaheim Police Assn. Home: PO Box 1105 Murrieta CA 92564-1105 Office: Murrieta Valley Unified Sch Dist 24515 Lincoln Ave Murrieta CA 92562-5807

HOFMAN, ELAINE D., state legislator; b. Sacramento, Sept. 20, 1937; d. Willard Davis and Venna (Gray) Smart; m. Cornelius Adrianus Hofman, Dec. 14, 1956; children: Catharina, John, Casie, Cornelius. BA, Idaho State U., 1974. Tchr. music edn. Sch. Dist. 25, Pocatello, Idaho, 1977-84; spl. asst. to Gov. Evans State of Idaho, Pocatello, 1984-87; field rep. to Congressman Stallings 2d Dist. Congressional Office, Pocatello, 1987-89; mem. Idaho Ho. of Reps., Pocatello, 1990—. Recipient Elect Lady award Lambda Delta Sigma, 1991; named Idaho Mother of Yr., Am. Mother's Assn., 1992, S.E. Idaho Family of the Yr., 1980. Democrat. Mem. Ch. of Jesus Christ of Latter-day Saints. Home: 216 S 16th Ave Pocatello ID 83201-4003

HOFMANN, ALAN FREDERICK, biomedical educator, researcher; b. Balt., May 17, 1931; s. Joseph Enoch and Nelda Rosina (Durr) H.; m. Marta Gertrud Pettersson, Aug. 15, 1969 (div. 1976); children: Anthea Karin, Cecilia Rae; m. Helga Katharina Aicher, Nov. 3, 1978. BA with honors, Johns Hopkins U., 1951, MD with honors, 1955; PhD, U. Lund, Sweden, 1965; MD honoris causis, U. Bologna, Italy, 1988. Intern, then resident dept. medicine Columbia Presbyn. Med. Ctr., N.Y.C., 1955-57; clin. assoc. clin. ctr. Nat. Heart Inst., NIH, Bethesda, Md., 1957-59; postdoctoral fellow, dept. physiol. chemistry U. Lund, Sweden, 1959-62; asst. physician Hosp. of the Rockefeller U., N.Y.C., 1962-64; outpatient physician N.Y. Hosp., N.Y.C., 1963-64; assoc. physician Hosp. of the Rockefeller U., N.Y.C., 1964-66; cons. in medicine, assoc. dir. gastroenterology unit Mayo Clinic, Rochester, Minn., 1966-77; attending physician Med. Ctr. U. Calif.-San Diego, 1977—; asst. prof. dept. medicine Rockefeller U., N.Y.C., 1964-66; assoc. prof. medicine and biochemistry U. Minn. Mayo Grad. Sch., 1966-69, assoc. prof. medicine and physiology, 1969-70, prof. medicine and physiology, 1970-73; prof. medicine and physiology Mayo Med. Sch., 1973-77; cons. physiology Mayo Clinic, Rochester, 1975-77; prof. medicine U. Calif., San Diego, 1977—, adj. prof. pharmacy, U. Calif., San Francisco, 1986—; vis. prof. pharmacy U. Mich., Ann Arbor, 1980-85. Patentee solvent for direct dissolution of cholesterol gallstones, breath test for pancreatic exocrine function, bile acid replacement therapy; contbr. numerous articles to profl. jours., books, films. Recipient Travel award Wellcome Trust, 1961-63, Travel award NSF, 1964, Sr. Scientist award Humboldt Found., Fed. Republic of Germany, 1976, 91 (shared prize) Eppinger Prize, Falk Found., 1976, Disting. Achievement award Modern Medicine mag., 1978 Chancellor's Rsch. Excellence award U. Calif., 1986; Nat. Fedn. fellow, 1959-61, USPHS fellow, 1962-63, Fogarty Internat. Sr. fellow NIH, 1986; Rockefeller Found. scholar, Bellagio, Italy, 1980. Fellow AAAS, Royal Soc. Medicine; mem. Am. Assn. Study of Liver Disease (numerous coms., pres. 1984), Swedish Soc. for Gastroenterology (hon.), Soc. Gastrointestinal Radiology (hon.), Gastroent. Soc. Australia (hon.), Chilean Soc. Gastroent. (hon.), Brit. Soc. Gastroent. (hon.), Royal Flemish Acad. for Medicine Belgium (hon., fgn. corr. mem.), German Soc. for Gastroenterology (hon.), Am. Soc. Clin. Investigation, Am. Assn. Physicians, Am. Liver Found. (chmn. sci. adv. bd. 1986-91), Am. Physiol. Soc., Am. Gastroent. Assn. (chmn. biliary diseases coun. 1991-92, Disting. Achievement award 1970, co-winner Beaumont prize 1979, Friedenwald medal 1994), Am. Physiol. Soc., Phi Beta Kappa, Sigma Xi, Alpha Omega Alpha, Omicron Delta Kappa. Home: 5870 Cactus Way La Jolla CA 92037-7069

HOFMANN, FRIEDER KARL, biotechnologist, consultant; b. Eppstein, Hessen, Fed. Republic of Germany, June 15, 1949; came to U.S., 1984; s. Friedrich Karl and Anna Johannette (Heist) H.; m. Sigrid Marianne Thomae, Sept. 5, 1975. MS, J.W. Goethe U., Frankfurt, Fed. Republic of Germany, 1977, PhD, 1981. Staff scientist, asst. prof. J.W. Goethe U., Frankfurt, 1977-81; sci. mgr. Brunswick Corp., Eschborn, Fed. Republic of Germany, 1982-84; tech. dir. Biotechnetics, San Diego, 1984-90; pres. Hofmann & Co., Oceanside, Calif., 1990—, Ctr. for Continuous Edn., Oceanside, Calif., 1992—. Author: (with others) Scale-Up and Downstream Processing of rDNA Products, 1991, GMP Production of Monoclonal Antibodies, 1991; contbr. over 40 articles to profl. jours. Recipient Senckenberg prize Senckenberg Rsch. Soc., Frankfurt, Fed. Republic of Germany, 1977; Kirkpatrick Chem. Engring. Achievement Honor award, Chem. Engring., 1989, Parenteral Drug Assn. Jour. award, Parenteral Drug Assn., Pa., 1985. Mem. Am. Chem. Soc., Am. Inst. Chem. Engrs., Tissue Culture Assn., European Soc. for Animal Cell Tech. Office: Hofmann & Co 2360 Autumn Dr Ste C Oceanside CA 92056-3528

HOFMANN, PAUL BERNARD, health care consultant; b. Portland, Oreg., July 6, 1941; s. Max and Consuelo Theresa (Bley) H.; m. Lois Bernstein, June 28, 1969; children: Julie, Jason. BS, U. Calif., Berkeley, 1963, MPH, 1965, DPH, 1994. Research assoc. in hosp. adminstrn. Lab. of Computer Sci., Mass. Gen. Hosp., Boston, 1966-68; asst. dir. Lab. of Computer Sci., Mass. Gen. Hosp., 1968-69; asst. adminstr. San Antonio Community Hosp., Upland, Calif., 1969-70; assoc. adminstr. San Antonio Community Hosp., 1970-72; dep. dir. Stanford (Calif.) U. Hosp., 1972-74, dir., 1974-77; exec. dir. Emory U. Hosp., Atlanta, 1978-87; exec. v.p., chief ops. officer Alta Bates Corp., Emeryville, Calif., 1987-91; cons. Alta Bates Corp., Emeryville, 1991-92, Alexander & Alexander, San Francisco, 1992-94; disting. vis. scholar Stanford (Calif.) U. Ctr. for Biomed. Ethics, 1993—; sr. fellow Stanford (Calif.) U. Hosp., 1993-94; sr. cons. stragetic healthcare practice Alexander & Alexander Cons. Group, Moraga, Calif., 1994—; instr. computer applications Harvard U., 1968-69; lectr. hosp. adminstrn. UCLA, 1970-72, Stanford U. Med. Sch., 1972-77; assoc. prof. Emory U. Sch. Medicine, Atlanta, 1978-87. Contbr. articles to profl. jours. Served with U.S. Army, 1959. Fellow Am. Coll. Hosp. Adminstrs. (recipient Robert S. Hudgens meml. award 1976); mem. Am. Hosp. Assn., Assn. Univ. Programs in Health Adminstrn., U. Calif. Alumni Assn.

HOFMANN, TIMOTHY ALAN, mental health, marital and family counselor; b. Mishawaka, Ind., Dec. 10, 1955; s. Stanley Rex and Clarice (Van Paris) H.; m. Linda Marie Harvey, June 8, 1978; children: Katrina, Adam. AA, Scottsdale (Ariz.) C.C., 1977; BS, Ariz. State U., 1981; M of Counseling, U. Phoenix, 1993. Cert. assoc. counselor, Ariz., master practitioner of neuro-linguistic programming. Systems programmer Garrett Turbine, Phoenix, 1978, Ariz. State U., Tempe, 1979-84; mgr. Ramada Inns, Inc., Phoenix, 1984; systems engr./mgr. Hitachi Data Systems, Phoenix, 1985-94; counseling intern Tri-City Behavioral Svcs., Tempe, 1992-93; counselor, owner, pres. Personal Dynamics, Chandler, Ariz., 1988—. Mem. APA (assoc.), ACA (profl.), Am. Mental Health Counselors Assn., Mesa C. of C. Home: 530 W Summit Pl Chandler AZ 85224-1515 Office: Personal Dynamics 813 W Elliot Rd Ste 5 Chandler AZ 85224-1904

HOFSTETTER, JANE ROBINSON, artist, educator; b. Oakland, Calif., Feb. 23, 1936; d. Thomas O. and Fern (Worstell) Robinson; m. William R. Hofstetter, Aug. 3, 1958; children: David, Glen. Student, U. Calif., Berkeley, San Francisco Sch. of Design, Chouinard Art Inst., L.A. lectr. in field. Represented in permanent collections State of Calif. Collection, Asilomar, San Ramon and Santa Clara City Halls, Kayser Hosp., Calif., IBM Hdqs. and Gen. Facilities, Gould Inc., No. Calif. Savings and Loan, Systems Control Inc., Zerox Corp., Finance Am. Recipient over 200 awards. Mem. Nat. Watercolor Soc., Watercolor West Soc., Midwest Watercolor Soc., Soc. Western Artists. Studio: 308 Dawson Dr Santa Clara CA 95051-5806

HOGAN, CLARENCE LESTER, retired electronics executive; b. Great Falls, Mont., Feb. 8, 1920; s. Clarence Lester and Bessie (Young) H.; m. Audrey Biery Peters, Oct. 13, 1946; 1 child, Cheryl Lea. BSChemE, Mont. State U., 1942, Dr. Engring. (hon.), 1967; MS in Physics, Lehigh U., 1947, PhD in Physics, 1950, D in Engring. (hon.), 1971; AM (hon.), Harvard U., 1954; D in Sci. (hon.), Worcester Poly. U., 1969. Rsch. chem. engr. Anaconda Copper Mining Co., 1942-43; instr. physics Lehigh U., 1946-50; mem. tech. staff Bell Labs., Murray Hill, N.J., 1950-51, sub-dept. head, 1951-53; assoc. prof. Harvard U., Cambridge, Mass., 1953-57, Gordon McKay prof., 1957-58; gen. mgr. semi-conductor products divsn. Motorola, Inc., Phoenix, 1958-60, v.p., 1960-66, exec. v.p., dir., 1966-68; pres., chief exec. officer Fairchild Inst., Mt. View, Calif., 1968-74, vice chmn. bd. dirs., 1974-85; gen. chmn. Internat. Conf. on Magnetism and Magnetic Materials, 1959, 60; mem. materials adv. bd. Dept. Def., 1957-59; mem. adv. coun. dept. electrical engring. Princeton U.; mem. adv. bd. sch. engring. U. Calif., Berkeley, 1974—, adv. bd. dept. chem. engring. Mont. State U., 1988—; mem. nat. adv. bd. Desert Rsch. Inst., 1976-80; mem. vis. com. dept. electric engring. and computer sci. MIT, 1975-85; mem. adv. coun. div. electrical engring. Stanford U., 1976-86; mem. sci. and ednl. adv. com. Lawrence Berkeley Lab., 1978-84; mem. Pres.'s Export Coun., 1976-80; mem. adv. panel to tech. adv. bd. U.S. Congress, 1976-80. Patentee in field; inventor microwave gyrator, circulator, isolator. Chmn. Commn. Found. Santa Clara County, Calif., 1983-85; mem. vis. com. Lehigh U., 1966-71, trustee, 1971-80, also life trustee; trustee Western Electronic Edn. Fund; mem. governing bd. Maricopa County Jr. Coll.; bd. regents U. Santa Clara. Lt. (j.g.) USNR, 1942-46. Recipient Community Svc. award NCCJ, 1978, Medal of Merit Am. Electronics Assn., 1978, Berkeley Citation U. Calif., 1980; named Bay Area Bus. Man of Yr. San Jose State U., 1978, One of 10 Greatest Innovators in Past 50 Yrs. Electronics Mag., 1980. Fellow AAAS, IEEE (Frederick Philips gold medal 1976, Edison silver medal Cleve. Soc. 19078, Pioneering medal for microwave theory and tech. 1993), Inst. Elec. Engrs. (hon.); mem. NAE, Am. Phys. Soc., Menlo Country Club, Masons, Sigma Xi, Tau Beta Pi, Phi Kappa Phi, Kappa Sigma. Democrat. Baptist. Home: 36 Barry Ln Atherton CA 94027-4023

HOGAN, CURTIS JULE, union executive, industrial relations consultant; b. Greeley, Kans., July 25, 1926; s. Charles Leo and Anna Malene (Rousello) H.; m. Lois Jean Ecord, Apr. 23, 1955; children: Christopher James, Michael Sean, Patrick Marshall, Kathleen Marie, Kerry Joseph. BS in Indsl. Rels., Rockhurst Coll., 1950; postgrad., Georgetown U., 1955, U. Tehran, Iran, 1955-57. With Gt. Lakes Pipeline Co., Kansas City, Mo., 1950-55; with Internat. Fedn. Petroleum and Chem. Workers, Denver, 1955-85; gen. sec. Internat. Fedn. Petroleum and Chem. Workers, 1973-85; pres. Internat. Labor Rels. Svcs., Inc., 1976—; cons. in field; lectr. Rockhurst Coll., Kansas City, 1951-52. Contbr. articles to profl. publs. Served with U.S. Army, 1945-46. Mem. Internat. Indsl. Rels. Assn., Indsl. Rels. Rsch. Assn., Oil Chem. and Atomic Workers Internat. Union. Home: 435 S Newport Way Denver CO 80224-1321 Office: Internat Fed Petroleum Chem Workers 435 S Newport Way Denver CO 80224-1321

HOGAN, EDDY, librarian; b. San Antonio, May 26, 1952; s. Robert and Susie (Morales) H. BA in English, U. Houston, 1976; MLS, U. Tex., 1978, postgrad., 1979. Reference libr. Main Libr. U. Colo. Univ. Libr., Boulder, 1979-84, U. Calif. Gen. Libr., Berkeley, 1984-87; data & info. svcs. libr. Cecil H. Green Libr. Stanford (Calif.) U. Univ. Librs., 1987-90; electronic info. svcs. libr. Calif. State U. Univ. Libr., Sacramento, 1990—; presenter, keynote spkr. in field. Mem. bd. editors Jour. Acad. Librarianship, 1993—; contbr. articles to profl. jours. H.E.A. Title II-B minority fellow U. Tex., 1977-78; grantee Calif. State U., Sacramento Hornet Found., 1992; Microsoft CD-ROM Libr. scholar, 1989. Mem. ALA (mgm.-at-lg., systems and svcs. sect. 1990-93, libr. adminstrn. and mgmt. assn. 1994-97, current topics planning com., chmn. Assn. Coll. and Rsch. Librs. univ. librs. sect. 1990-92, chmn. publs. com., libr. instrn. roundtable 1983-84, chmn. com. libr. svcs. to Spanish-speaking), Calif. State U. Librs.-North (pres. 1992—). Home: 5801 Elk Spring Way Elk Grove CA 95758-6163 Office: Calif State U Libr 2000 Jed Smith Dr Sacramento CA 95819-2640

HOGAN, MERVIN BOOTH, mechanical engineer, educator; b. Bountiful, Utah, July 21, 1906; s. Charles Ira and Sarah Ann (Booth) H.; m. Helen Emily Reese, Dec. 27, 1928; 1 son, Edward Reese. B.S., U. Utah, 1927, M.E., 1930; M.S., U. Pitts., 1929; Ph.D., U. Mich., 1936, postgrad.; Sterling fellow, Yale U., 1937-38. Registered profl. engr., Conn., Mich., N.Y., Utah, Va. chartered engr., U.K. Design engr. Westinghouse Electric Corp., East Pittsburgh, Pa., 1927-31; asst. prof. mech. engring. U. Utah, Salt Lake City, 1931-36, asso. prof., 1936-39, prof., 1939-56, chmn. dept. mech. engring., 1951-56, prof., 1971-76, prof. emeritus, 1976—; mgr. product design engring. GE, Syracuse, N.Y., 1956-65; mgr. design assurance engring. GE, Phoenix, 1965-70; cons. engr. GE, Waynesboro, Va., 1970-71; cons. Chgo. Bridge & Iron, 1950-56. Author: Mormonism and Freemasonry: The Illinois Episode, 1977, The Origin and Growth of Utah Masonry and Its Conflict with Mormonism, 1978, Mormonism and Freemasonry under Covert Masonic Influences, 1979, Freemasonry and the Lynching at Carthage Jail, 1981, Freemasonry and Civil Confrontation on the Illinois Frontier, 1981, The Involvement of Freemasonry with Mormonism on the American Midwestern Frontier, 1982; contbr. articles to engr. jours., numerous articles to Masonic publs. Recipient Merit of Honor award U. Utah, 1981. Fellow ASME, Inst. Mech. Engrs. (London), Yale Sci., Engring. Assn.; mem. IEEE (sr.), Nat. Eagle Scout Assn., DeMolay Legion of Honor, S.R. in State N.Y., Utah Soc. SAR (pres. 1983-84), Aztec Club, Timpanogos Club, Elfun Soc., Rotary, Masons (33 deg.), Shriners, Prophets, KT, DeMolay, Quatuor Coronati Lodge 2076, Sigma Xi, Phi Kappa Phi, Tau Beta Pi, Pi Tau Sigma, Sigma Nu, Theta Tau, Alpha Phi Omega, Phi Lambda Epsilon. Home: Douglas Park 921 Greenwood Terr Salt Lake City UT 84105 Office: U Utah 3008 Merrill Engring Bldg Salt Lake City UT 84112

HOGAN, MICHAEL R(OBERT), federal judge; b. Oregon City, Oreg., Sept. 24, 1946; married; 3 children. A.B., U. Oreg. Honors Coll., 1968; J.D., Georgetown U., 1971. Bar: Oreg. 1971, U.S. Ct. Appeals (9th cir.) 1971. Law clk. to chief judge U.S. Dist. Ct. Oreg., Portland, 1971-72; assoc. Miller, Anderson, Nash, Yerke and Wiener, Portland, 1972-73; magistrate judge U.S. Dist. Ct. Oreg., Eugene, 1973-91, dist. judge, 1991—, chief judge, 1995—; bankruptcy judge U.S. Dist. Oreg., Eugene, 1973-80. Mem. ABA, Oreg. State Bar Assn. Office: US Courthouse 211 E 7th Ave Eugene OR 97401-2722

HOGAN, RICHARD FRANKLIN, sales executive, marketing professional; b. Lompoc, Calif.; s. Richard Franklin and Jewel Earlene (Miller) H.; m. Alice Geralyn Hyne, Nov. 6, 1982. Retail div. mgr. CVMC, Inc., Gardnerville, Nev., 1977-79; fin. dir. CVMC, Inc., Gardnerville, 1980-81, gen. mgr., 1982-87; pres., corp. exec. officer Alrich Corp., Gardnerville, 1987-88; state sales mgr. TCI Cablevision of Nev., Reno, 1988-90; sales, mktg. dir. Toppo Mfg., 1990-92, First Hybrid Corp., 1993-95; CEO Alrich Corp., 1995—; dir. Alrich Corp., Gardnerville, 1987—. Bd. dir. Nev. State FFA Found., Carson City, Nev., 1988—. Mem. Am. Mktg. Assn. (v.p. adminstrn. no. Nev. 1993-94, pres.-elect 1994—). Home: 871 W Bonanza Dr Carson City NV 89706-8105 Office: Alrich Corp PO Box 30029 # 221 Reno NV 89520

HOGARTH, BURNE, cartoonist, illustrator; b. Chgo., Dec. 25, 1911; s. Max and Pauline H.; m. Constance Holubar, June 27, 1953; children: Michael, Richard, Ross. Student Art Inst. Chgo., 1925-27, Chgo. Acad. Fine Arts, 1926-29, Crane Coll., 1928-30, U. Chgo., 1930-32, Northwestern U., 1931-32, Columbia U., 1956-57. Asst. cartoonist to Lyman Young, Tim Tyler's Luck, N.Y.C., 1934; cartoonist Pieces of Eight, McNaught Syndication, N.Y.C., 1935; free lance artist King Features, N.Y.C., 1935-36; staff artist Johnstone Agy., N.Y.C., 1936-37; cartoonist Sunday Color Page, Tarzan, United Feature Syndication, N.Y.C., 1937-50, Sunday page Drago, Post-Hall Syndication, N.Y.C., 1946, Miracle Jones, United Features, N.Y.C., 1948; founder Sch. Visual Arts, N.Y.C., 1947-70, v.p., coord. curriculum, instr., 1947-70; author Watson-Guptill, N.Y.C., 1958-89; instr. Parsons Sch., N.Y.C., 1976-79; pres. Pendragon Press Ltd., N.Y.C., 1975-79; with Art Ctr. Coll. Design, Pasadena, Calif., 1982—, Otis Art Inst., Parsons Sch. Design, L.A., 1981—; seminar presenter U. Colo., Boulder; spl. guest German Comics Fair, Cologne, Berlin, 1990; participant traveling exhbn. Sites 1990-92, U.S.; hosted by U.S. Embassy cultural staff, guest and pres. Tarzan Exhibit Am. Cultural Ctr., Brussels, 1995; numerous exhbns. worldwide including Musee des arts decoratives, Louvre, Paris, 1968, 69, Smithsonian Inst., 1990—, Gallery Karikatury, Warsaw, 1990; one man show Paris, 1967, Bibliotheque Municipale, 1985, Palais de Longchamps, Marseille, France, 1985; group show Gallery Karikatury, Warsaw, Poland, 1990; represented in permanent collections: Smithsonian Instn., Mus. Cartoon Art, U. Colo., U. Wyo., Mus. Art, Gijon, Spain, others. Author: Dynamic Anatomy, 1958, Drawing the Human Head, 1965, Dynamic Figure Drawing, 1970, Drawing Dynamic Hands, 1977, Dynamic Light and Shade, 1981, Dynamic Wrinkles and Drapery, 1991, The Arcane Eye of Hogarth, 1992; creator graphic novels Tarzan of the Apes, 1972, Jungle Tales of Tarzan, 1976, Golden Age of Tarzan, 1979, Life of King Arthur, 1984, The Arcane Eye of Hogarth, 1992; creator, illustrator (with Harry Hurwitz) Morphos the Shapechanger, 1995; author (videocassette) Draw The Human Head, 1989. Trustee NCS Milt Gross Fund., 1980; active 43d Ann. Conf. on World Affairs, Boulder, 1990. Named Best Illustration Cartoonist, Nat. Cartoonists Soc., 1974, 75, 76, Artist of Yr., Pavilion of Humour, 1975; recipient Premio Emilio Freixas Silver plaque V-Muestra Internat. Conv., 1978, Pulcinella award V-Mostra Internat. del Fumetto, 1983, Caran D'Ache Silver plaque Internat. Comics Conv., 1984, Adamson Silent Sam award Comics '85 Internat. Conv., 1985, Golden Palms award Cesar Illustration Group, Paris, 1988, Premio Especial award 7th Internat. Salon of Humor, Barcelona, Spain, 1989, Golden Lion award Burroughs Bibliophiles, U. Louisville, 1990, Bronze trophy German Comics Fair, Cologne, Fed. Republic Germany, 1990, L'Age D'Or award Cesar Illustration Group, 1992, Lifetime Achievement award Kansas City Comic Conv., 1992. Mem. Nat. Cartoonists Soc. (pres. 1977-79, Reuben Silver plaque 1993-94), Mus. of Cartoon Art, Am. Soc. Aesthetics, Nat. Art Edn. Assn., WHO, Graphic Arts Soc., Internat. Assn. Authors of Comics and Cartoons. Address: 6026 Lindenhurst Ave Los Angeles CA 90036-3217

HOGARTH, CHRISTOPHER GRANT, documentation specialist; b. Vancouver, B.C., Aug. 7, 1960; came to U.S., 1987.; s. Gordon Lauder and Margaret Anne (Grant) H. BA, U. B.C., 1983; MA, Ohio State U., 1989; MS, Rensselaer Poly., 1990. Applications assoc. Oracle Corp., Redwood Shores, Calif., 1990; tech. writer Frame Tech. Inc., San Jose, Calif., 1990-91; tech. writer/Sysadmin Autodesk Inc., Sausalito, Calif., 1991-92; sr. compositor Women Writers Project, Brown Univ., Providence, 1992-93; prodn. mgr. TSS Ltd., Westport, Conn., 1992-94; mgr. tech. svcs. group Onyx Graphics Corp., Midvale, Utah, 1994—; founder Dramatech Cons., Vancouver, 1980-87. Author: (chapbook) Moon Tears, 1978, Shadows and Vampires, 1989. Co-chair Stonewall Ctr. Support Group, Salt Lake City, 1994. Tchg. fellow Ohio State U., Columbus, 1987-88, rsch. fellow, 1988-89. Mem. Am. Mgmt. Assoc., MLA, Soc. Tech. Communicators, Nat. Coun. Tchrs. English, West Vancouver Yacht Club, Nat. Assn. Desktop Pubs., sr. mem. Soc. Tech. Comms.

HOGE, ROBERT WILSON, museum curator; b. Wilmington, Del., Jan. 5, 1947; s. George Lee and Rosalie Jessie (Colton) H.; m. Laura Lee Brown, June 20, 1980 (div. Mar. 1991). BA, U. Colo., 1969. Cert. tchr., Colo., Iowa. Dir. Sanford Mus., Cherokee, Iowa, 1976-81; curator Am. Numismatic Assn., Colorado Springs, Colo., 1981—. Contbg. editor The Numismatist, 1989—; columnist The Numismatist. Named one of Outstanding Young Men in Am., 1981. Mem. Am. Assn. Museums (Internat. Mus. Ptnr. award 1989), Am. Numismatic Soc., Royal Numismatic Soc., Mountain-Plains Mus. Assn., Colo.-Wyo. Assn. Museums, Numismatics Internat., Phi Beta Kappa. Office: Am Numismatic Assn 818 N Cascade Ave Colorado Springs CO 80903-3208

HOGENHOUT, FRANK PAUL, accounting manager; b. Geldrop, The Netherlands, Dec. 6, 1943; came to U.S., 1957; s. Frank and Christine (Brons) H.; m. Hyang Pae Lee, Jan. 30, 1972 (div. Aug. 1985); children: Joanne, Constance, Mark; m. Nancy Lee Dent, Nov. 12, 1988; children: Lisa, Luke. BA in Philosophy, St. Thomas Seminary, Kenmore, Wash., 1968; BA in Accounting, U. Puget Sound, 1977; MBA, City Univ., Seattle, 1978. Staff accountant, revenue agt., acctg. mgr. Boeing Co., IRS and Internat. Care Ctrs., Inc., 1973-80; chief acct., asst. contr. McCann Constrn. Co., Inc., Seattle, 1980-83; gen. mgr., contr. Controlled Power, Inc., Bothell, Wash., 1990-91; clk., treas. City of Woodland, Wash., 1992-94; owner, acct. Accountax, Kirkland, Wash., 1983-92. 1st lt. U.S. Army, 1969-71; maj. USAR, 1971-90. Roman Catholic. Office: Assn of Washington Bus 1414 Cherry Olympia WA 98507

HOGGATT, CLELA ALLPHIN, English language educator; b. Des Moines, Sept. 9, 1932; d. Addison Edgar and Frances (Buckallew) Philleo; m. Charles Allphin; children: Beverly, Valerie, Clark, Arthur, Frances; m. John Hoggatt. AA, Grand View Jr. Coll., 1952; BA summa cum laude, U. No. Iowa, 1954; MA, Tex A&I U., 1961. Cert. life tchr. Iowa, Tex.; permanent life community coll. credential, Calif. Tchr. social studies Los Fresnos (Tex.) Jr. High Sch., 1954-55; tchr. English Cummings Jr. High Sch., Brownsville, Tex., 1956-59, Fickett Jr. High Sch., Tucson, 1963-66, Portola Jr. High Sch., L.A., 1956-59; instr. speech Tex. Southmost Jr. Coll., Brownsville, 1959; tchr. history and English Ysleta High Sch., El Paso, Tex., 1963-66; prof. English L.A. Trade-Tech. Coll., 1969-75, L.A. Mission Coll., 1975—. Author: Women in the Plays of Henrik Ibsen, 1975, The Writing Cycle, 1986, Good News for Writers, 1990; contbr. to Words, Words, Words, 1981, Emily Dickinson: A Centennial Celebration, 1890-1990, In the West of Ireland, John Trumball: An Anthology in Memoriam. Grand View Jr. Coll. scholar, 1951-52, U. No. Iowa scholar, 1953-54. Mem. Am. Mensa, Pi Gamma Mu. Democrat. Office: LA Mission Coll 13356 Eldridge Ave Sylmar CA 91342-3200

HOGLE, ANN MEILSTRUP, painter, art educator; b. San Francisco, Sept. 23, 1927; d. Carlton Fredrick Meilstrup and Lillian (Hackney) Meilstrup Willer; m. Richard Raymond (div.); children—Timothy, Megan, Catherine; m. George H. Hogle, Aug. 29, 1966. Student U. Oreg., 1945-47, Marylhurst Coll., 1949-50; B.F.A., Calif. Coll. of Arts and Crafts, 1976, M.F.A., 1978. One-person shows include Stanford U., Calif., 1966, Palo Alto Cultural Ctr., Calif., 1976, William Sawyer Gallery, San Francisco, Butters Gallery, Portland, 1993; exhibited in group shows at Portland Art Mus., Janus Gallery, Los Angeles, Richmond Art Ctr., William Sawyer Gallery, San Francisco, 84, Purdue U., Ind., Penninsula Mus., Monterey, Calif., 1993; represented in permanent collections Kemper Ins. Cos., St. Francis Meml. Hosp., Dysan Corp., First Interstate Bank. Portland Mus. Recipient Phelan awards exhibit Legion of Honor, 1965.

HOGLUND, JOHN ANDREW, lawyer; b. Cleve., July 19, 1945; s. Paul Franklin and Louise (Anderson) H.; m. Patricia Olwell, May 27, 1972; children: Britt Hannah, Maeve Olwell, Marc Paul-Joseph. BA, Augustana Coll., 1967; JD, George Washington U., 1972. Bar: Wash. 1973, U.S. Dist. Ct. (we. dist.) Wash. 1973, U.S. Ct. Appeals (9th cir.) 1973. Law clk. Wash. State Supreme Ct., 1973-74; assoc. Mooney, Cullen & Holm, Olympia, 1973-75; ptnr. Cullen, Holm, Hoglund & Foster, Olympia, 1975-81; pvt. practice Olympia, 1981—; pres. Hoglund Enterprises, 1987—; adj. prof. law sch. U. Puget Sound, Tacoma, Wash., 1989-90, trustee, 1984-92. Co-author: SKYCYL Practicing Law Manual, 1986—, WSBA Book Automobile Negligence Law, 1988. Vice chmn. Group Health Coop., Olympia, 1978, Thurston County Dem. Cen. Com., Olympia, 1980; chmn. bd. dirs. S.W. Wash. Health Sys. Agy., 1979; alumni bd. dirs. George Washington U. Nat. Law Ctr., 1994—. With U.S. Army, 1967-69. Named Boss of Yr. Thurston County Legal Secs. Assn., 1985. Mem. ABA, Thurston County Bar Assn. (trustee 1988-90, Svc. awards 1987, 90), Assn. Trial Lawyers Am. Wash. State Trial Lawyers Assn. (pres. 1983-84, Brandeis award 1980), Wash. State Trial Lawyers Found. (pres. 1985-87), Wash. State Bar Assn. (chmn. UPL com. 1979, CPR com., pub. rels. com.), Nat. Law Ctr. George Washington U. (alumni bd. 1994—), Kiwanis (Disting. Pres. award 1980). Mem. United Ch. Christ. Office: PO Box 7877 Olympia WA 98507-7877

HOGOBOOM, WILLIAM PERRY, judge, arbitrator, mediator; b. Pasadena, Calif., Oct. 31, 1918; s. William Coryell and Grace Wise (Hogsett) H.; m. Betty Cornwell, June 30, 1944 (dec. Jan. 1991); children: William, Christian, Katherine, Lissa. BA, Occidental Coll., 1939; MPA, U. So. Calif., L.A., 1941, JD, 1949, LLD (hon.), 1978; LLD (hon.), W. L.A. Sch. Law, 1977. Bar: Calif. 1949, U.S. Ct. Appeals (9th cir.) 1950, U.S. Dist. Ct. (so. dist.) Calif. 1949, U.S. Supreme Ct. 1967. Ptnr. Iverson & Hogoboom, L.A., 1950-68; judge Superior Ct. of Calif., L.A., 1968-83; v.p., gen. counsel U. So. Calif., L.A., 1983-91; arbitrator, mediator L.A., 1993—. Author: California Family Law Practice, 1979. Lt. USN, 1944-46. Fellow Internat. Acad. Trial Judges; mem. L.A. County Bar Assn. (trustee 1975-77), Calif. Judges Assn., Order of Coif, Phi Beta Kappa. Home and Office: 192 Annandale Rd Pasadena CA 91105

HOGUE, BONNIE MARIE KIFER GOSCIMINSKI, child care educator, consultant; b. Niagara Falls, N.Y., May 31, 1947; d. Ralph Henry and Emogene Viola (Severance) Kifer; m. Conrad S. Gosciminski, Aug. 9, 1969; children: Steven, Heidi, Jason; m. William R. Hogue, Nov. 15, 1994. BEd, Mansfield (Pa.) State U., 1969; MS in Human Svcs., Murray (Ky.) State U., 1995. Tchr. Col-Mont Area Vocat. Tech., Bloomsburg, Pa., 1969-70, Coatesville (Pa.) Area Sch. Dist., 1971-72, Bradford (Pa.) Area Schs., 1972-76, Christian County Schs., Hopkinsville, Ky., 1976-82; with supply and pers. depts. U.S. Army Law Enforcement Command, Ft. Campbell, Ky., 1983-87; tng. specialist Blanchfield Army Community Hosp., Ft. Campbell, 1987-91; sch. age latch key specialist Child Devel. Svcs., Ft. Campbell, 1991-92; Family Child Care outreach Child Devel. Svcs., Ft. Richardson, Alaska, 1992—. Officer, bd. dirs. Christian County Assn. for S.P.M.D., Hopkinsville, 1978-92; mem. Hopkinsville Human Rels. Commn., 1989-92; parent advisor Title I com. Christian County High Sch., 1989-90. Recipient Outstanding Performance award Dept. Army, 1983-92, Sustained Performance award, 1989, 93; Vol. of Yr. award Christian County Assn. Dyslexia, 1981. Mem. NAFE, NAYCC, NAEYC, AFCCA, Ky. Coalition for Sch.-Age Child Care. Home: 2200 Grizzly Bear Cir Wasilla AK 99654-2728

HOGUE, TERRY GLYNN, lawyer; b. Merced, Calif., Sept. 23, 1944; s. Glynn Dale and Lillian LaVonne (Carter) H.; m. Joanne Laura Sharples, Oct. 3, 1969; children: Morgan Taylor, Whitney Shannon. BA, U. Calif., Fresno, 1966, postgrad., 1967; JD, U. Calif., San Francisco, 1972. Bar: Calif. 1972, Idaho 1975, U.S. Dist. Ct. (cen. dist.) Calif. 1973, U.S. Dist. Ct. Idaho 1975, U.S. Supreme Ct. 1976. Assoc. Reid, Babbage & Coil, Riverside, Calif., 1972-75; pvt. practice, Hailey, Idaho, 1975-77; ptnr. Campion & Hogue, Hailey, 1977-80; Hogue & Speck, Hailey and Ketchum, Idaho, 1980-82, Hogue, Speck & Aanestad, Hailey and Ketchum, Idaho, 1982—. Bd. dirs. Blaine County Med. Ctr., Hailey, 1975-91. Sgt. U.S. Army, 1969-71. Mem. ABA, Calif. Bar Assn., Idaho Bar Assn. (hearing panel of profl. conduct bd. 1991—, chmn. profl. conduct bd. 1994-95), 5th Jud. Dist. Bar Assn. (magistrate com. 1991-93, ethics com. 1991-93), Idaho Trial Lawyers Assn. (bd. dirs. 1982-93, treas. 1985-86, sec. 1986-87, v.p. 1988-89, pres. 1989-90), Assn. Trial Lawyers Am. (sec. coun. of pres. 1989-90, Atla Weideman Wisocki award 1990), Am. Inns. of Ct. (charter Master Bench chpt.), Hailey C. of C. (bd. dirs. 1975-83), Rotary. Home: PO Box 1259 500 Onyx Dr Ketchum ID 83340-1259 Office: Hogue Speck & Aanestad Box 987 120 E Ave Ketchum ID 83340

HOHENSTEIN, HENRY JOHN, land use planner, educator; b. Cohoes, N.Y., Sept. 28, 1931; s. Charles Henry and Ann Mildred (Eldon) H.; m. Mary Arline Kennedy, Aug. 29, 1953 (div. May 1974); children: Anne, Henry, Ellen, Elizabeth, Frederick; m. Susan Natalie Carroll, Oct. 2, 1988. BS, Rutgers U., 1953; M in City and Regional Planning, Calif. Poly. State U., 1985. Owner 7-H Co., Atascadero, Calif., 1974-84; redevel. dir. City of Desert Hot Springs, Calif., 1984-86; assoc. planner City of Indio, Calif., 1986-88; cmty. devel. dir. City of Indio, 1992-94; dir. planning Interactive Design, Palm Springs, Calif., 1988-92; adj. faculty Coll. of the Desert, Palm Desert, 1986-94. Author: IRS Conspiracy, 1974. Planning commr. Planning Commn., City of Desert Hot Springs, 1987-91. Maj. USMC, 1953-56. Home: 9090 Calle Escorial Desert Hot Springs CA 92240-1647

HOHING, FREDERICK WILLIAM, humanities educator; b. Audobon, N.J., Feb. 13, 1945; s. Frederick William Sr. and Emily Barbara (Platig) H.; 1 child, Sophia Angela. BA in English, Suffolk U., 1967; MA in English, U. Wis., Milw., 1971, PhD in Lit., 1983. Vol. Peace Corps, Washington, 1967-69; teaching asst. U. Wis., Milw., 1969-75; instr. Upward Bound Program,

Milw., 1970-73; instr. English Bir Zeit U., West Bank, Israel, 1975-76; Pace prof. Chapman Coll., Orange, Calif., 1977-79; edn. specialist Dept. U.S. Navy, Cubi Point, Philippines, 1979-85; dir. Pace Hawaii City Colls. Chgo., Pearl Harbor, 1985-87; asst. prof. English and humanities Hawaii Pacific U., Honolulu, 1987-90, assoc. prof., 1990—. Author: (story) North Dakota Quarterly, 1986, Ice River, 1987; (play) Michael Cassio, 1994. Mem. Am. Philatelic Soc., The Planetary Soc. Office: Hawaii Pacific U 1060 Bishop St Honolulu HI 96813

HOHNER, KENNETH DWAYNE, retired fodder company executive; b. St. John, Kans., June 24, 1934; s. Courtney Clinton and Mildred Lucile (Forrester) H.; m. Sherry Eloi Anice Edens, Feb. 14, 1961; children: Katrina, Melissa, Steven, Michael. BS in Geol. Engring., U. Kans., 1957. Geophysicist Mobil Oil Corp., New Orleans, Anchorage, Denver, 1957-72; sr. geophysicist Amerada Hess Corp., Houston, 1972-75, ARAMCO, London, 1975-79; far east area geophysicist Hamilton Bros., Denver, 1979-83; owner Hohner Poultry Farm, Erie, Colo., 1979—; pres. Hohner Custom Feed, Inc., Erie, Colo., 1982—. Mem. Soc. Exploration Geophysicists. Home: 823 Weld County Rd 7 Erie CO 80516

HOILAND, ANDREW CALVIN, architect; b. Great Falls, Mont., Aug. 3, 1926; s. Andrew C. and Ida (Mohondro) H.; m. Patricia Ruth Willits, Aug. 13, 1950; children: William H., Richard C., Diana Ruth. B.S. in Architecture, Mont. State Coll., 1949. Draftsman A.V. McIver (architect), Great Falls, 1949-52; prin. A. Calvin Hoiland (architect), Great Falls, 1952-54; partner Hoiland & Lund (architects), Great Falls, 1953-63, Hoiland-Zucconi (architects), Great Falls, 1964-74, A. Calvin Hoiland (Architect), 1974—; Pres. Mont. Bd. Archtl. Examiners, 1968. Assoc. editor Am. Architects Directory, 1969-70; mem. editorial adv. bd. Symposia mag., 1968-78, Northwest Archtl. mag., 1983-85; important works include: Great Falls swimming pools, 1963, Mountain View Sch., Great Falls, 1968-69, Great Falls fire stas., 1969-71, Gregson Hot Springs swimming pools, 1972, Great Falls PCA-FLBA Office, 1978, I.F.G. Leasing Bldg, Great Falls, 1980, Heritage Inn, French Quarter, Great Falls, 1979-80, Giant Springs Trout Hatchery, Great Falls, 1984, Midgetman Launcher Facility, Malmstron AFB, 1988. Chmn. charity ball for Great Falls Rehab. Center, 1961-62; chmn. master plan com. Great Falls Swimming Pool, 1962-65; chmn. adv. council Great Falls chpt. DeMolay; bd. dirs. Great Falls Camp Fire Girls. Served with USAAC, World War II. Named to Legion of Honor Order DeMolay, 1956, Cross of Honor, 1976. Mem. AIA (pres. Mont. 1961-62, editor Mont. publ. 1965-71), Great Falls Soc. Architects (charter pres. 1953), Mont. Tech. Council (charter pres. 1960-61), Sigma Chi. Methodist (chmn. bd. trustees, mem. bldg. com. Wesley Center, mem. Mont. bd. missions). Lodges: Masons (master 1979), Scottish Rite (master 1980), Royal Order of Scotland, York Rite, Shriners, Kiwanis (pres. Great Falls 1964). Home and Office: 2826 3rd Ave S Great Falls MT 59405-3110

HOIVIK, THOMAS HARRY, military educator, international consultant; b. Mpls., June 6, 1941; s. Tony Horace and Helen Lenea (Carlsen) H.; m. Judith Lisa Kohn; children: Todd, Gregory. BA, U. Minn., 1963; grad. with distinction, Naval Test Pilot Sch., 1969; MS with distinction, Naval Postgrad. Sch., 1973; grad. with distinction, Naval War Coll., 1976; MA, Salve Regina U., 1988. Cert. exptl. test pilot, air transport pilot, jet aircraft, helicopter, glider single and multi-engine. Commd. ensign USN, 1963, advanced through grades to capt., 1963-91; test pilot Naval Air Test Ctr., Patuxent River, Md., 1968-71; program mgr. H-53 aircraft Naval Air Systems Command, Washington, 1976-78; comdg. officer Helicopter Mine Countermeasure Squadron 14, Norfolk, Va., 1978-80; dir. U.S. Naval Test Pilot Sch., Patuxent River, 1980-82; fed. exec. fellow Ctr. for Strategic and Internat. Studies, Washington, 1982-83; chair tactical analysis Naval Postgrad. Sch., Monterey, Calif., 1983-85; comdg. officer Naval Air Sta., Willow Grove, Pa., 1985-87; ret. USN, 1991; chair applied systems analysis Naval Postgrad. Sch., Monterey, 1987-91, prof. acquisition mgmt., 1991—; ret. capt. USN, 1991; dir. test and evaluation sr. level curriculum Defense Acquisition U., 1993—; mem. U.S. Congrl. Study Group on Nat. Strategy, Washington, 1982-83, World Economy, 1982-83; cons. U.S., Internat. Govt. Orgns., 1990—; founder, pres. Lysonics Rsch. Internat., 1993; flight demonstration pilot Paris Internat. Air Show, 1967. Contbr. articles to profl. jours. Bd. dirs. Vocat. Edn. Bd., Montgomery County, Pa., 1985-87, Congrl. Svc. Acad. Appointment Bd., Phila., 1985-87; youth leader, counselor YMCA, St. Paul, 1955-61. Recipient Legion of Merit Pres. of U.S., 1987, Outstanding Youth Leadership award YMCA, 1960; established U.S. Helicopter Speed Record, 1966. Mem. AIAA, Soc. of Exptl. Test Pilots, Internat. Test and Evaluation Assn., Nat. Contract Mgmt. Assn., Ops. Rsch. Soc. Am., Mil. Ops. Rsch. Soc., U. Minn. "M" Club, Disable Am. Vets (life), Sigma Alpha Epsilon. Office: Naval Postgrad Sch Monterey CA 93943

HOKANA, GREGORY HOWARD, engineering executive; b. Burbank, Calif., Nov. 24, 1944; s. Howard Leslie and Helen Lorraine (Walker) H.; m. Eileen Marie Youell, Apr. 29, 1967; children: Kristen Marie, Kenneth Gregory. BS in Physics, UCLA, 1966. Design engr. Raytheon Co., Oxnard, Calif., 1967-74; staff engr. Bunker Ramo Corp., Westlake Village, Calif., 1974-84; mgr. analog engring. AIL Systems, Inc., Westlake Village, 1984-91; mgr. product devel. Am. Nucleonics Corp., Westlake Village, 1991-93; tech. mgr. Litton Data Sys., Agoura Hills, Calif., 1994—. Mem. IEEE, Assn. Old Crows. Democrat. Methodist. Home: 3485 Farrell Cir Newbury Park CA 91320-4333 Office: Litton Data Systems PO Box 6008 Agoura Hills CA 91376-6008

HOKE, JUDY ANN, physical education educator; b. Mesa, Ariz., May 3, 1951; d. Jewell Juett and Margaret Lucille (Gibson) H. BA, Ariz. State U., 1973, MS, 1976. Cert. tchr. Ariz. Tchr., coach womens Tennis Temple Union High Sch. Dist., Tempe, Ariz., 1973—, chmn. Phys. Edn., 1978—; former co-chmn. sch. improvement com.; chmn. East Valley Women's Tennis Region; mem. Nat. Honor Soc. selection com., scholarship com. Mem. First Christian Ch., Phoenix Zoo. Named Outstanding Secondary Phys. Edn. Tchr. Yr. State of Ariz., 1991. Mem. NEA, AAHPERD, Ariz. Alliance Health Phys. Edn. Recreation and Dance, Tempe Secondary Edn. Assn., Women's Internat. Tennis Assn., U.S. Tennis Assn. Republican. Office: Marcos de Niza High Sch 6000 S Lakeshore Dr Tempe AZ 85283-3049

HOLABIRD, TIMOTHY MARSHALL, real estate appraiser; b. L.A., Aug. 5, 1915; s. Harry Gilette and Cora (Evans) H.; m. Mary Leslie Holabird, Nov. 25, 1939; children: Timothy Marshall Jr., Dennis W., Frederick N., Christopher E. Student, Pasadena City Coll., 1933-34, U. Calif., Berkeley, 1935-36. Asst. appraiser Harry G. Holabird Co., L.A., 1936-42; ind. appraiser Timothy M. Holabird & Son, Pasadena, Calif., 1946—; past arbitrator City of Pasadena, pvt. industry orgns.; expert witness various legal procs. Lt. comdr. USNR, 1942-46, WWII. Mem. Internat. Real Estate Inst., Soc. Subdivsn. Appraisers (formerly Soc. Fed. Fee Appraisers, pres. 1961-63, treas. 1956-60), Nat. Assn. Rev. Appraisers (cert.), Nat. Assn. Real Estate Appraisers (cert.). Home: 1205 Garfield Ave South Pasadena CA 91030-3921 Office: Timothy M Holabird & Son 127 N Madison Ave Pasadena CA 91101-1750

HOLBECK, HERBERT JOHN, mechanical engineer; b. Duluth, Minn., Aug. 23, 1928; s. John Ingwall and Laura Rebecca (Gates) H.; m. Betty Louise Hall, Sept. 12, 1953; children: Susan Lauranne, John Herbert. BSCE, Oreg. State U., 1951, MSCE, 1955; MSME, U. So. Calif., 1963. Registered profl. engr., Oreg., Calif. Instr. engring. Oreg. State U., Corvallis, 1953-56; sr. engr. Jet Propulsion Lab., Pasadena, Calif., 1956-62, supr. engring. group, 1963-69, mem. tech. staff, 1970-85, tech. mgr., 1986—. Lay speaker United Meth. Ch., Altadana, Calif., 1965—; coach Little League, Altadena, 1968-70, Pony League, Pasadena, 1971-72; asst. scoutmaster Boy Scouts Am., Pasadena, 1970-74. 1st lt. U.S. Army, 1951, 53, PTO. Fellow AIAA (assoc.); mem. ASCE (life). Home: 3560 Hollyslope Rd Altadena CA 91001 Office: Jet Propulsion Lab 4800 Oak Grove Dr Pasadena CA 91109-8001

HOLBROOK, ANTHONY, manufacturing company executive; b. 1940; married. With Advanced Micro Devices Inc., Sunnyvale, Calif., 1973—, former exec. v.p., chief operating officer, pres., chief operating officer, 1986-90, vice chmn., chief tech. officer, 1990—, also bd. dirs. Office: Advanced Micro Devices Inc Box 3453 915 DeGuigne St Sunnyvale CA 94088

HOLBROOK, JAMES RUSSELL, lawyer; b. Kansas City, Mo., Sept. 24, 1944; s. Newell James and Martha Inez (Russell) H.; m. Meghan Zanolli, Feb. 12, 1983. Student, MIT, 1962-63; BA, Grinnell (Iowa) Coll., 1966; MA, Ind. U., 1968; JD, U. Utah, 1974. Bar: Utah 1974, U.S. Ct. Appeals (10th cir.) 1977, U.S. Supreme Ct. 1980, U.S. Dist. Ct. Utah. Law clk. to chief judge U.S. Dist. Ct. Utah, Salt Lake City, 1973-75; pvt. practice Salt Lake City, 1975-78, asst. U.S. Atty. of Utah, 1978-80; ptnr. Giauque & Williams, Salt Lake City, 1980-82; gen. counsel Intermountain Power Agy., Murray, Utah, 1982-83; ptnr. Callister Nebeker & McCullough, Salt Lake City, 1983—; mem. adv. com. on revisions to local rules of practice U.S. Dist. Ct. Utah, 1989—, mem. alt. dispute resolution subcom., 1991—; mem. alt. dispute resolution com. Utah Jud. Coun., 1993—; adj. prof. U. Utah Coll. Law, Salt Lake City, 1984-88, 90—. Articles editor Jour. Contemporary Law, 1973-74; contbr. articles to profl. jours. Mem. bd. Internat. Visitors Utah Coun., Salt Lake City, 1984—; mem. exhbns. coun. Utah Mus. Fine Arts, Salt Lake City, 1986-92, 94—; bd. govs. Salt Lake Found., Salt Lake City, 1987-92. With U.S. Army, 1968-70, Vietnam. Decorated Bronze Star, Army Commendation medal; NSF fellow, 1966-68, Woodrow Wilson Found. fellow, 1966. Mem. ABA, Utah Bar Assn. (commr. 1988-90), Fed. Bar Assn. (pres. Utah chpt. 1984-85), Sutherland Inn of Ct. (master of the bench 1984—), Alta Club, Phi Beta Kappa, Sigma Phi Epsilon. Democrat. Home: 775 Hilltop Rd Salt Lake City UT 84103-3311 Office: Callister Nebeker & McCullough 900 Kennecott Bldg Salt Lake City UT 84133

HOLBROOK, MICHAEL EDWARD, communications company executive; b. Sycamore, Ill., Nov. 1, 1958; s. George Paulette Nd Verna Mae (Haeffner) H.; m. Joci L. Campbell, Nov. 20, 1976 (div. June 1983); 1 child, Michael Edward; m. Joyce Ann Borninkhof. AA, Kishwaukee Coll., Malta, Ill., 1980; BA, No. Ill. U., 1983. Asst. dir. Providence Med. Ctr., Seattle, 1983-85; real estate broker Wallace & Wheeler, Kirkland, Wash., 1986-89; pres., CEO Landmark Comms. Group, Kirkland, 1989—. Contbr. articles to Seattle Times, Petersons PhotoGraphic, Garden mag., others. Office: Landmark Comms Group 11410 NE 124th St Ste 604 Kirkland WA 98034-4305

HOLBROOK, PETER GREENE, artist; b. N.Y.C., Apr. 13, 1940; s. Richard Greene and Margaret Primrose (Henderson) H.; children: Acacia, Sean. BA, Dartmouth Coll., 1961; Cert., Bklyn. Mus. Art Sch., 1963. Tchr. Oxbow Summer Sch. Painting, Saugatuck, Mich., 1968, U. Ill., Chgo., 1968-70, North Shore Art League, Winnetka, Ill., 1968, Calif. State U., Hayward, 1970-71, Ctr. for Arts and Humanities, Sun Valley, Idaho, 1988. One-man shows include Carpenter Galleries, Hanover, N.H., 1960, Richard Gray Gallery, Chgo., 1964, 66, 67, 69, 70, 73, 76, Unitarian Ch., Chgo., 1968, Indpls. Mus. Art, 1970, William Sawyer Gallery, San Francisco, 1975, Nautilus Gallery, Arcata, Calif., 1976, ADI Gallery, San Francisco, 1977, 78, Frumkin Struve Gallery, Chgo., 1980, 82, Mattingly-Baker Gallery, Dallas, 1982, Kauffman Gallery, Houston, 1983, Struve Gallery, Chgo., 1985, Larry Munson Gallery, Santa Fe, 1986, Capricorn Galleries, Bethesda Md., 1987, 89, 90, 92, Lewis Newman Galleries, Beverly Hills, Calif., 1988, 89, 90, Bell Gallery, Woodstock, N.Y., 1988, Shaklee Terrace Gallery, San Francisco, 1991, Jan Cicero Gallery, Chgo., 1991, John Pence Gallery, San Francisco, 1991, Equitable Life Gallery, San Francisco, 1992; exhibited in group shows at Frumkin Struve Gallery, Chgo., 1980, Kauffman Galleries, Houston, 1981, Cultural Ctr., Eureka, Calif., 1981, Frumkin Struve Gallery, Chgo., 1982, Hamline U., St. Paul, 1983, Scottsdale (Ariz.) Ctr. for Arts, 1984, Coll. Redwoods, Eureka, 1985, Bell Gallery, Rhinebeck, N.Y., 1986, John Pence Gallery, San Francisco, 1987, 88, 89, 90, Sun Valley Art Ctr., Idaho, 1987, Payne Gallery Moravian Coll., Bethlehem, Pa., 1988, Atlee and Atlee Fine Arts, Eureka, 1989, Jan Cicero Gallery, Chgo., 1989-90, 90, Internat. Art Expo Navy Pier, Chgo., 1990, and more; mus. exhbns. include Civic Arts Gallery, Walnut Creek, Calif., 1980, Pa. Acad. Fine Art, Phila., 1982, U. Wis. and Ill. State U., 1982, Springfield (Mo.) Art Mus., 1982, 86, Ft. Wayne (Ind.) Mus. Art, 1983, Rahr-West Mus., Manitowoc, Wis., 1984, San Francisco Mus. Modern Art, 1985, Nat. Mus. Art, Washington, 1987, Butler Inst., Youngstown, Ohio, 1987, Mesa (Ariz.) Southwest Mus., 1987, 94, Hunter Art Mus., Chattanooga, 1994; represented in permanent mus. collections Ind. State U., Indpls., Nat. Collection Fine Arts Smithsonian, Washington, No. Ill. U., De Kalb, Bklyn. Mus., N.Y.C., Art Inst. Chgo., Cornell Coll., Mt. Vernon, Iowa, Mus. S.W., Midland, Tex., U. Nebr., Lincoln, Boise Art Mus., Springfield Art Mus., Achenbach Collection Palac of Legion of Honor, San Francisco, Oakland (Calif.) Mus.; represented in permanent corp. collections Am. Fedn. Arts, N.Y.C., Bank of Am., San Francisco, Dolby Labs., San Francisco, Gulf Pipeline, Houston, Ill. Bell Telephone, Chgo., Koffler Found., Chgo., Minn. Mining & Mfg., St. Paul, Western Electric, N.Y.C., H.J. Heinz Co., Pitts., Continental Bank, Singapore, FMC Corp., Chgo., Kemper Ins. Co., Chgo., Shaklee Corp., San Francisco, Plz. of Ams., Dallas, Clorox Co., Oakland, Stroud & Waller, Chgo., R.J. Reynolds Co., Winston-Salem, N.C., Frito-Lay Corp, Dryers Corp., Oakland. Recipient Walter H. Stevens award Watercolor USA, 1981, Raffael prize for watercolor Cultural Ctr., 1981, Max Beckman Meml. fellowship Bklyn. Mus. Sch., 1962-63, James B. Reynold Fgn. Study fellowship, Paris, 1961-62, Marcus Heiman award for creative arts Dartmouth Coll., 1960; recipient Emily L. Wild prize Art Inst. Chgo., 1968, Bartels prize, 1967, James Clark prize, 1965.

HOLCOM, FLOYD EVERETT, international business consultant; b. Astoria, Oreg., Jan. 19, 1964; s. Edward Everett and Esther Jean (Wilkinson) H. BA in Bus. Adminstrn., Oreg. State U., 1989; MBA, Portland State U., 1991. Sr. spl. ops. engr. Joint Spl. Forces Commd. Dept. Def.; dir. internat. trade field study program Internat. Trade Inst., Portland, Oreg.; internat. dir. The IBIS Group, 1991—; spl. envoy State of Oreg. rep. to Fujian Provincial Govt., China, 1990; ind. retail co. with Unocal, 1979-89. Responsible for 1st U.S. comml. shipment to Vietnam since 1975, 1992. Mem. adv. coun. Internat. Bus. Degree program Linfield Coll.; mem. adv. bd. Open U. of Ho Chi Minh City, Vietnam. Served with U.S. Army, 1981-86, spl. forces res., 1986-94, spl. forces N.G., 1994-95. Mem. Assn. Internat. Trade Specialists (former v.p., bd. dirs.), Japan-Am. Soc. Oreg., Pacific N.W. Internat. Trade Assn., Suzhou-Portland Sister City Assn. (bd. dirs.), N.W. Regional China Coun. (former chmn. fgn. hospitality com.), World Affairs Coun. Oreg., World Trade Ctr. Portland. Republican. Episcopalian. Home: 4925 Birch St Astoria OR 97103

HOLCOMBE, WILLIAM JONES, manufacturing company executive; b. 1925. Group v.p. De Laval Turbine Inc., 1960-65, pres., chief exec. office, 1965-72; group v.p. Transamerica Corp., 1972-75; chmn. bd. dirs., CEO, pres. Teton Inc., 1976-86; chmn., CEO, pres. Imo Industries, Inc., Lawrenceville, N.J., 1986-92; chmn. bd. Imo Industries, Lawrencevile, N.J., 1992-93; ret., 1993; cons. in field Norco, Calif., 1993—.

HOLDCROFT, LESLIE THOMAS, clergyman, educator; b. Man., Can., Sept. 28, 1922; s. Oswald Thomas and Florence (Waterfield) H.; student Western Bible Coll., 1941-44; BA, San Francisco State Coll., 1950; MA, San Jose State Coll., 1955; postgrad. Stanford, 1960, 63, U. Cal., 1965-67; DDiv., Bethany Bible Coll., 1968; m. Ruth Sorensen, July 2, 1948; children: Cynthia Ruth, Althea Lois, Sylvia Bernice. Instr. Western Bible Coll., 1944-47; instr. Bethany Bible Coll., 1947-55, dean edn., 1955-68, v.p., 1967-68; pres. Western Pentecostal Bible Coll., 1968-87; acad. cons., researcher, Clayburn, B.C., 1991—; pastor Craig Chapel, 1959-68; dir. Can. Pentecostal Corr. Coll., Clayburn, 1985-90. Pres., Assn. Canadian Bible Colls., 1972-76. Author: The Historical Books, 1960, The Synoptic Gospels, 1962, The Holy Spirit, 1962, The Pentateuch, 1951, 95, Divine Healing, 1967, The Doctrine of God, 1978, The Four Gospels, 1988, 94, Anthropology: A Biblical View, 1990, Soteriology: Good News in Review, 1990, Ecclesiology: Christ's Treasure on Earth, 1992. Home: 34623 Ascott Ave, Abbotsford, BC Canada V2S 5A3 Office: Box 700, Abbotsford, BC Canada V2S 6R7

HOLDEN, GEORGE FREDRIC, brewing company executive, public policy specialist, consultant; b. Lander, Wyo., Aug. 29, 1937; s. George Thiel Holden and Rita (Meyer) Zulpo; m. Dorothy Carol Capper, July 5, 1959; children: Lorilyn, Sherilyn, Tamilyn. BSChemE, U. Colo., 1959, MBA in Mktg., 1974. Adminstr. plastics lab. EDP, indsl chems. plant, prodn. process engring., tool control supervision, aerospace (Minuteman, Polaris, Sparrow), Parlin, N.J., Salt Lake City, Cumberland, Md., 1959-70; by-product sales, new market and new product devel., resource planning and devel. and pub. rels. Adolph Coors Co., Golden, Colo., 1971-76; dir. econ. affairs corp. pub. affairs dept., 1979-84, dir. pub. affairs rsch., 1984-86; owner Phoenix Enterprises, Arvada, 1986—; mgr. facilities engring. Coors Container Co., 1976-79; instr. brewing, by-products utilization and waste mgmt. U. Wis.; cons., speaker in field. Mem. bd. economists Rocky Mountain News, 1990—; mem. Heritage Found. Ann. Guide to Pub. Policy Expert, 1987—, Speakers Bur., Commn. on the Bicentennial U.S. Constitution, 1991-93; del. Colo. Rep. Conv., 1976—; adv. Cost of Govt. Day; bd. dirs. Colo. Pub. Expenditures Coun., 1983-86, Nat. Speakers Assn., Colo. Speakers Assn. (bd. dirs. 1987-90, 91-93), Nat. Assn. Bus. Economists, Colo. Assn. Commerce and Industry Ednl. Found. Sr. fellow budget policy Independence Inst. Colo. "ThinkTank". Mem. U.S. Brewers Assn. (chmn. by-products com., Hon. Gavel, 1975), Am. Inst. Indsl. Engrs. (dir. 1974-78), Washingtons Am. for Tax Reform Found. Co-author: Secrets of Job Hunting, 1972; The Phoenix Phenomenon, 1984, Total Power of One in America, 1991; contbr. articles to Chem. Engring. mag., 1968-76, over 400 published articles, white papers in field; over 900 speeches, 455 appearances on radio talk shows nationwide. Home: 6463 Owens St Arvada CO 80004-2732 Office: Phoenix Enterprises PO Box 1900 Arvada CO 80001-1900

HOLDEN, HEIDI JOYCE RUMMEL, dietitian; b. L.A., Feb. 26, 1958; d. William Dean and Helene Adaline Cecelia (Thorstenson) Rummel; m. Terry Holden, Sept. 9, 1978; children: Jaclyn Beth, Joshua Taylor. BS with honors, Calif. State U., Northridge, 1992, postgrad., 1992—. Coord. peer nutrition program Calif. State U., Northridge, 1991-92; pvt. practice Santa Clarita, Calif., 1994—; supr. Woman, Infant and Children, Santa Clarita, 1994—; dietetics cons. Santa Clarita Pregnancy Ctr., 1994. Leader Girl Scouts U.S., Santa Clarita, 1993-94. Mem. SAG, Am. Dietetic Assn. (registered dietitian), Calif. Dietetic Assn., L.A. Dietetic Assn., Sports, Cardiovascular and Wellness Nutritionists, Consulting Nutritionists, Kappa Omicron Nu. Democrat. Lutheran. Home: 27903 Dexter Dr Santa Clarita CA 91350-3670 Office: 23504 Lyons Ave Santa Clarita CA 91321-2500

HOLDEN, JAMES TODD, publishing executive; b. Phila., Mar. 7, 1964; s. James Minshall II and Joan Ann (Weaver) H. BA, Mich. State U., 1986; JD, DePaul U., 1989. Bar: Calif. 1989. Assoc. atty. Ely, Fritz, Hogan & DiPinto, Santa Ana, Calif., 1989-91, Coppo & Cosgrove, San Diego, 1991-93; prin. Law Offices of James T. Holden, Cardiff, Calif., 1992; sec., gen. counsel Marcoa Pub., Inc., San Diego, 1992—; legal cons. Vehicle Systems Analysis, Clarkston, Mich., 1987—. Vol., Vols. in Parole, San Diego, 1991, St. Vincent DePaul Ctr., San Diego, 1993. Recipient Am. Jurisprudence award Lawyers Co-op Pub., 1987. Mem. ABA (planning bd. 1990—), Def. Rsch. Inst. (vice chair com. 1991—), Am. Corp. Counsel Assn., State Bar Calif., Mich. Tech. Presidents Club. Republican. Episcopalian. Home: 387 Broadmoor Ave Pittsburgh PA 15228-2585 Office: Marcoa Pub Inc 5960 Cornerstone Ct W San Diego CA 92121-3711

HOLDEN, WILLIAM WILLARD, insurance executive; b. Akron, Ohio, Oct. 5, 1958; s. Joseph McCullem and Lettitia (Roderick) H.; m. Kim Homan, Aug. 31, 1985; 1 child, Jennifer Catharine. BA, Colgate U., 1981. Crime ins. trainee Chubb & Son, Inc., N.Y.C., 1981-82; exec. protection dept. mgr. Chubb & Son, Inc., San Jose, Calif., 1982-85, Woodland Hills, Calif., 1986-91; v.p., mgr. Fin. Svcs. Group, Inc., Rollins, Hudig, Hall, L.A., 1991—; tng. analyst Chubb & Son, Inc., Warren, N.J., 1985-86. Co-author manual: Chubb Claims Made Training, 1985; contbr. articles to Colgate alumni mag. Mgr., coach Campbell (Calif.) Little League, 1983-85; pres. Le Parc Homeowners Assn., Simi Valley, Calif., 1987-89; mem. Community Assn. Inst., L.A., 1986—. Mem. Profl. Liability Underwriting Soc. (L.A. steering com.). Republican. Office: Rollins Hudig Hall of So Calif Universal City CA 91608

HOLDER, FRANK, agricultural products executive; b. 1926. With Griffin-Holder Co., 1960—. Office: Griffin-Holder Co 20445 Us Highway 50 Rocky Ford CO 81067-9407*

HOLDER, J. HAL, food products executive; b. 1954. With Griffin-Holder Co., Rocky Ford, Colo., 1972—, now pres. Office: Griffin-Holder Co 20445 Us Highway 50 Rocky Ford CO 81067-9407*

HOLDER, THOMAS JAY, art educator; b. Kansas City, Mo., Jan. 21, 1940; s. Ward Leonard and Olive (Henrie) H.; m. Martha H. Hofmann, 1961 (div. 1971); children: Barbara L., Sheridan W.; m. Jacqueline E. Jacobs, Dec. 27, 1991; children: Rachel C., Kiersten N. BA in Painting, San Diego State U., 1965; MFA, U. Wash., 1969. Part-time instr. San Diego City Coll., Mesa Coll., 1965-67; teaching asst. San Diego State U., 1967; part-time instr. Highline Coll., 1968-69; instr. U. Wash., 1969-70; prof. art U. Nev., Las Vegas, 1971—, chair dept. art, 1972-74, 82-86; dir. Donna Beam Fine Art Gallery, 1984-91; founding dir. Nev. Inst. for Contemporary Art, 1985-91. Paintings represented in numerous collections including Brenau Coll., 1991, Bank of Am., Nev., 1977-89, First Interstate Bank, Las Vegas, 1987, Internat. Athletic Club, Kansas City, 1984, Nev. Mus. Art, Reno, 1983, others; exhibited in numerous one-person and group shows incuding William Traver Gallery, Seattle, 1990, Nev. Inst. Contemporary Art, 1993, Brendan Walter Gallery, Santa Monica, Calif., 1992, No. Ariz. U. Art Mus., Flagstaff, 1992. Visual arts fellow Nev. State Coun. on Arts, 1992, grantee, 1991; recipient Best in Show award Brenau Coll. Nat. Invitational, 1989, 1st place award 23d S.W. Ann., 1989. Mem. Coll. Art Assn. Home: 740 N Magic Way Henderson NV 89015 Office: U Nev 4505 S Maryland Pky Las Vegas NV 89154-9900

HOLDERMAN, JOHN LORAN, financial broker; b. Dixon, Ill., Mar. 5, 1944; s. Donald Kenneth and E.J. (Huggins) H.; divorced; 1 child, Angela Dyan. Student, East Moline (Ill.) Jr. Coll., 1983. Gen. mgr. Progressive Graphics, Oreg., Ill., 1972-76; with Storm Printing, Dallas, 1976-81; owner resale shop Rockford, Ill., 1981-90; pres. JLHInterprises, Inc., San Ysidro, Calif., 1992—. With USN, 1969-72, Vietnam. Recipient Golf Record of Achievement ABI, 1994. Democrat. Roman Catholic. Home: 416 W San Ysidro Blvd # L-530 San Diego CA 92173-2443

HOLDING, CAROL PIERSON, market positioning consultant; b. St. Louis, Feb. 4, 1956; d. Emery Lancaster and Joan Marcia (Godwin) Pierson; m. Reynolds Walker Holding, June 7, 1986; 1 child, Carolyn Walker. AB in Econs., Smith Coll., 1976; MBA, Harvard U., 1980. V.p. Ally & Gargard, N.Y.C., 1980-86, Citibank, N.Y.C., 1986-88; sr. v.p. Siegel-Gale, N.Y.C., 1988-91, McCann-Erickson, San Francisco, 1991; pres. Holding Assocs., San Francisco, 1992—. Bd. dirs. Planned Parenthood, San Francisco, 1993—, Bill T. Jones/Arnie Zane and Co., N.Y.C., 1986-91, Rocking Horse Sch., N.Y.C., 1989-91; head planning com. Swedenborgian Ch., San Francisco, 1993—. Mem. San Francisco Ad Club, Commonwealth Club. Office: Holding Assocs 65 Carmelita St San Francisco CA 94117-3312

HOLDSWORTH, JANET NOTT, women's health nurse; b. Evanston, Ill., Dec. 25, 1941; d. William Alfred and Elizabeth Inez (Kelly) Nott; children: James William, Kelly Elizabeth, John David. BSN with high distinction, U. Iowa, 1963; M of Nursing, U. Wash., 1966. RN, Colo. Staff nurse U. Colo. Hosp., Denver, 1963-64, Presbyn. Hosp., Denver, 1964-65, Grand Canyon Hosp., Ariz., 1965; asst. prof. U. Colo. Sch. Nursing, Denver, 1966-71; counseling nurse Boulder PolyDrug Treatment Ctr., Boulder, 1971-77; pvt. duty nurse Nurses' Official Registry, Denver, 1973-82; cons. nurse, tchr. parenting and child devel. Teenage Parent Program, Boulder Valley Schs., Boulder, 1980-88; bd. dirs., treas. Nott's Travel, Aurora, Colo., 1980—; instr., nursing coord. ARC, Boulder, 1979-90, instr., nursing tng. specialist, 1980-82. Mem. adv. bd. Boulder County Lamaze Inc., 1980-88 ; mem. adv. com. Child Find and Parent-Family, Boulder, 1981-89; del. Rep. County State Congl. Convs., 1972-94, sec. 17th Dist. Senatorial Com., Boulder, 1982-92; vol. Mile High ARC, 1980; vol. chmn. Mesa Sch. PTO, Boulder, 1982-92, bd. dirs., 1982—, v.p., 1983—; elder Presbyn. ch. Mem. ANA, Colo. Nurses Assn. (bd. dirs. 1975-76, human rights com. 1981-83, dist. pres. 1974-76), Coun. Intracultural Nurses, Sigma Theta Tau, Alpha Lambda Delta. Republican. Home: 1550 Findlay Way Boulder CO 80303-6922 Office: Teenage Parent Program 3740 Martin Dr Boulder CO 80303-5448

HOLL, WALTER JOHN, architect, interior designer; b. Richardton, N.D., May 14, 1922; s. John and Rose Mary (Raskop) H.; m. Eleanor Mary Triervieler, Jan. 23, 1943; children—Mark Walter, Michael John, Randall Gregory, Linda Michelle, Timothy James, John Walter. Student in architecture Internat. Corr. Schs., 1946-47, structural engring., 1959; student in interior design U. Nebr., 1976; student in photography Clarke Coll., 1981. Licensed architect, Calif., interior designer, Ill. Steel detailer, estimator E.J.

Voggenthaler Co., Dubuque, Iowa, 1941-43; engr., also methods developer Marinship Corp. Sausalito, Calif., 1942-44; ptnr. Holl & Everly, Dubuque, 1946-47; prin. Holl Designing Co., also W. Holl & Assocs., Dubuque and San Francisco, 1947-87; prin. Walter J. Holl, Burlingame, Calif, 1987, 89, San Diego, 1989—; mem. convoy USCG Ofcl. Presdl. Security Patrol, 1979-86; cons. Clarke Coll. Art Students, Dubuque, 1953-61; commd. architect, interior designer and constructor renovations Dubuque County Couthouse, 1978-85; oral exam commr. Calif. Bd. Archtl. Examiners, 1994—; cert. mem. Calif. State Office Emergency Svc. Patentee castered pallet. Chmn. Dubuque Housing Rehab. Commn., 1976-77. Served with AUS, 1944-46. Recipient Nat. Bldg. Design awards, 1968, 69, 73, 94. Mem. AIA (pres.-elect north county sect. San Diego chpt. 1995, bd. dirs. 1995—), USCG Aux. (comdr. 1975-78), Am. Soc. Interior Designers (profl.), Am. Arbitration Assn. (panel arbitrators), Inst. Bus. Designers (profl. Chgo. chpt.). Roman Catholic. Clubs: Dubuque Golf and Country, Julien Dubuque Yacht (commodore 1974-75), Mchts. and Mfrs. (Chgo.). Home: 11255 Tierrasanta Blvd San Diego CA 92124-2888 Office: Walter J Holl AIA ASID Architect PO Box 420823 San Diego CA 92142-0823

HOLLADAY, KELLY GAYLE, science educator; b. Hobbs, N.Mex., Sept. 27, 1958; d. William Dallas Holladay and Robbie Geane (Barton) Eason. A in liberal arts, Tarrant County Jr. Coll., Ft. Worth, 1981; student, Tex. Tech. U., 1982-83; BS in geology, U. Tex., 1985; M in sci. edn., Tex. Women's U., 1990. Sales Zales Jewelers, Hobbs, 1976-77; clerical Ft. Worth Nat. Bank, Ft. Worth, 1978-79; sales Century 21 Loughty, Benbrook, Tex., 1980-81; technician Overland Exploration, Denver, 1985-86; tchr. Arlington (Tex.) Ind. Schs., 1987-89, Hobbs Pub. Sch., 1989-90; prof. New Mex. Jr. Coll, Hobbs, 1990—; conf. coord. New Mex. Adult Edn. Assn., Albuquerque, N.Mex., 1994—; mem. N.Mex. Jr. Coll. faculty senate, 1991—; staff development Project 353, Albuquerque, 1993—. VIP vol. Nat. Pks., Carlsbad Cavers, N. Mex., 1994—; literacy tutor N.Mex. Literacy Vol., Hobbs, 1991-92, coord., 1991-92. Mem. N.Mex. Adult Edn. Assn. (bd. dirs. 1989—), Assn. Tex. Pub. Educators, Am. Assn. Petroleum Geologist, Ft. Worth Bd. Realtors, Gamma Sigma Sigma. Democrat. Baptist. Home: 106 W Coyote Hobbs NM 88240

HOLLAN, CAROL ANGELA, plastic surgeon; b. Decatur, Ala., 1946. MD, U. Fla., 1973. Plastic surgeon Sharp Meml. Hosp., San Diego; also asst. prof. U. Calif., San Diego. Office: 8010 Frost St Ste 503 San Diego CA 92123-4222*

HOLLAND, GARY NORMAN, ophthalmologist, educator; b. Long Beach, Calif., July 30, 1953; s. Richard L. and Edith (Hewson) H. MD, UCLA, 1979. Diplomate Am. Bd. Ophthalmology, Nat. Bd. Med. Examiners; lic. MD, Calif., Ga. Intern in internal medicine UCLA, 1979-80; resident in ophthalmology Jules Stein Eye Inst., L.A., 1980-83; fellowship in uveitis rsch. Proctor Found. U. Calif. San Francisco, 1983-84; cornea fellowship Emory U. Med. Sch., Atlanta, 1984-85; prof. ophthalmology Jules Stein Eye Inst. UCLA, 1985—. Assoc. editor Am. Jour. of Ophthalmology, 1993-96. Mem. Assn. Rsch. in Vision and Ophthalmology (chmn. immunology and microbiology sect. 1994-95), Am. Uveitis Soc. (chmn. edn. and rsch. com. 1994-95). Office: UCLA Jules Stein Eye Inst 100 Stein Plz Los Angeles CA 90095-7003

HOLLAND, H. RUSSEL, federal judge; b. 1936; m. Diane Holland; 3 children. BBA, U. Mich., 1958, LLB, 1961. With Alaska Ct. System, Anchorage, 1961, U.S. Atty.'s Office, Dept. Justice, Anchorage, 1963-65; assoc. Stevens & Savage, Anchorage, 1965-66; ptnr. Stevens, Savage, Holland, Erwin & Edwards, Anchorage, 1967-68; sole practice Anchorage, 1968-70; ptnr. Holland & Thornton, Anchorage, 1970-78, Holland, Thornton & Trefry, Anchorage, 1978, Holland & Trefry, Anchorage, 1978-84, Trefry & Brecht, Anchorage, 1984; judge U.S. Dist. Ct. Alaska, Anchorage, 1984—. Mem. ABA, Alaska Bar Assn., Anchorage Bar Assn. Office: US Dist Ct 222 W 7th Ave Unit 54 Anchorage AK 99513-7504*

HOLLAND, HENRY NORMAN, marketing consultant; b. Norfolk, Va., Oct. 13, 1947; s. Henry Norman and Edith Leigh (O'Bryan) H.; m. Linda Diane Eggerking, June 1, 1968 (div. 1983); 1 child, Steven Frederick; m. Jane Elizabeth Bond, Dec. 27, 1983. BA, Chaminade Coll., 1972; MBA, U. Hawaii, 1977. Lic. ins. broker, Calif. Mgr. Chevron USA, Honolulu, 1965-75; dealer Dillingham Chevron, Honolulu, 1975-82; gen. mgr. Barcat Enterprises, San Francisco, 1982-85; counselor E.K. Williams of San Francisco, 1985; gen. mgr. Woodside (Calif.) Oil Co., 1985-88; cons. Holland Bus. Mgmt., San Francisco, 1989—; dir. Chevron Fed. Credit Union, Honolulu, 1971-75. Author Make Yours Service tng. seminars, newsletter, safety programs; contbr. articles to profl. jours. Loaned mgr. United Way, Honolulu, 1972; nation chief YMCA Indian Guides, Kailua, Hawaii, 1976-79. With U.S. Army, 1967-69, Vietnam. Mem. English Speaking Union, Met. League San Francisco Symphony, Golden Gate Nat. Parks Assn., Nat. Trust for Historic Preservation, San Francisco Mus. Soc., Chevron Adv. Coun., Nat. Assn. Enrolled Agts., Calif. Assn. Enrolled Agts., Sovereign Order of Saint John of Jerusalem Knights Hospitaller, VFW. Republican. Presbyterian. Office: 1700 Broadway Apt 506 San Francisco CA 94109-2450

HOLLAND, MICHAEL JAMES, computer services administrator; b. N.Y.C., Nov. 20, 1950; s. Robert Frederick and Virginia June (Wilcox) H.; Anita Garay, Jan. 5, 1981 (Aug. 1989); 1 child, Melanie. BA in Comparative Lit., Bklyn. Coll., 1972. Enlisted USN, 1975, advanced to CPO, 1989; field med. technician 3rd Marine Divsn., Okinawa, Japan, 1976-77, 1st Marine Divsn., Camp Pendleton, Calif., 1978-79; clin. supr. Naval Hosp. Subic Bay, Philippines, 1979-81; dept. head Tng. Ctr. USMCR, Johnson City, Tenn., 1981-84; clin. supr. No. Tng. Area, Okinawa, 1984-85, 3rd Marine Air Wing, Camp Pendleton, 1985-88; cons. Naval Regional Med. Command, San Diego, 1988-90; system analyst Naval Med. Info. Mgmt. Ctr. Detachment, San Diego, 1990-92; computer svcs. adminstr. U.S. Naval Hosp., Guam, 1993—. Mem. Fleet Res. Assn., Nat. City C. of C. (com. 1989-91), Assn. for Computing Machinery.

HOLLAND, ROBIN JEAN, personnel company executive; b. Chgo., June 22, 1942; d. Robert Benjamin and Dolores (Levy) Shaeffer; 1 child, Robert Gene. BA in Pub. Rels. magna cum laude, U. So. Calif., 1977. Account exec., pub. rels. firm, 1977-79, Mgmt. Recruiters, 1979; owner, operator Holland Exec. Search, Marina Del Rey, Calif., 1979—; pres. Bus. Communications, 1983—; cons. on outplacement to bus.; condr. seminars on exec. search; guest lectr. and instr. on exec. recruiting at community colls. Active Ahead with Horses, Audubon Soc., conservation orgns. Recipient numerous local honors. Mem. Am. Coaster Enthusiasts, LK.A. Can., Mensa, Peruvian Paso Horse Owners and Breeders N.Am. Office: Holland Exec Search 4748 Admiralty Way Ste 9774 Marina Del Rey CA 90292

HOLLATZ, SARAH SCHOALES, rancher, business owner; b. N.Y.C., Sept. 1, 1944; d. Dudley Nevison and Virginia Jocelyn (Vanderlip) Schoales; m. David Earl Hollatz, Jan. 27, 1968 (div. June 1985); children: Melissa Virginia, Peter David. BS, U. Wis., 1966; postgrad., U. So. Calif., L.A., 1966. Copywriter Max W. Becker Advt., Long Beach, Calif., 1966-67; advt. dir. officers news USN, Coronado, Calif., 1968-70; with syndicate dept. Morgan Stanley & Co., N.Y.C., 1970-72; lay-out asst. North Castle News, Armonk, N.Y., 1972-75; performer, writer Candy Band, Pound Ridge, N.Y., 1975-82; owner, mgr. Circle Bar Guest Ranch, Utica, Mont., 1983—; bd. dirs. Park Inn, Lewistown, Mont. Artist, composer: Play Me a Song, 1978, Going Home, 1980; composer: (mus. play) Elsie Piddock, 1979, Secret Garden, 1981, Windows, 1989. Soloist Hobson (Mont.) Meth. Ch., 1983—; founder What the Hay, Utica, 1990—. Mem. Mont. Emergency Med. Assn. (bd. dirs. 1990—), Dude Rancher's Assn. (bd. dirs. 1989—). Episcopalian. Home and Office: Circle Bar Guest Ranch Utica MT 59452

HOLLENBACH, DAVID JOHN, astrophysicist; b. Kirksville, Mo., Oct. 10, 1942; s. John William and Winifred (Lohman) H.; m. Jane Elizabeth Rosenthal, July 31, 1971; 1 child, Anna Elizabeth. AB, Hope Coll., 1964; PhD, Cornell U., 1969. Vis. asst. prof. Colo. Coll., Colorado Springs, 1971-73; asst. prof. U. Colo., Colorado Springs, 1973-75; rsch. scientist U. Calif., Berkeley, 1975-79; Nat. Rsch. Coun. assoc. NASA Ames, Moffett Field, Calif., 1979-80; rsch. scientist NASA Ames, Moffett Field, 1980—. Editor: Interstellar Processes, 1988; contbr. articles to profl. jours. Fellow Harvard U., 1968-70, Woodrow Wilson, 1965, Danforth, 1965-68, NSF, 1965-68. Mem. Internat. Astron. Union, Am. Astron. Soc. (councilor 1992-95). Office: NASA Ames Rsch Ctr MS 245-3 Moffett Field CA 94035

HOLLENBECK, DOROTHY ROSE, special education educator; b. Yakima, Wash., May 8, 1941; d. George Milford and Blance Mary (McCarthy) Hollenbeck; BS in Speech and Lang. Therapy, Marquette U., 1964; MA in Spl. Edn., San Francisco State U., 1969; m. Thomas M. Chambers, Aug. 14, 1971; adopted children—David, Monique, Christopher, George, Elizabeth. Speech pathologist Mpls. Pub. Schs., 1964-65, Milbrae (Calif.) Sch. Dist., 1965-68; reading specialist Dept. Def., Landstuhl, Germany, 1970-71; tchr. children with extreme learning problems Portland (Oreg.) Public Schs., 1971-80, dept. chmn. spl. edn., 1980-84, program specialist program devel., 1984-86, diagnostic specialist assessment program spl. edn., 1986-94, speech and lang. pathologist, 1994-95; spch. and lang. pathologist, spl. edn. tchr., Chinacum, Washington Sch. Dist. 1995 —; cert. instr. develop. therapy U. Ga., 1982; instr. Portland State U., D.C.E., 1982, 83. HEW Dept. Rehab. fellow, 1969. Mem. Am. Speech and Hearing Assn. (cert. in clin. competence), Common Cause, Cousteau Soc., NEA, Oreg. Edn. Assn., Nat. Council Exceptional Children (presenter nat. conv. 1984). Democrat. Roman Catholic. Author: PEACHES (Pre-Sch. Ednl. Adaptation for Children Who Are Handicapped), 1978. Home: 524 Pierce Port Townsend WA 98368 Office: Chinacum Pub Schs P O Box 278 Chimacum WA 98325

HOLLERAN, DONNA MARIE, nurse; b. Oregon City, Oreg., June 19, 1952; d. Delbert Wayne and Esther Marie (Grim) Moshberger; m. Patrick Anthony Holleran, Apr. 6, 1974; children: Jill Marie, Benjamin Patrick. BA in English, Oreg. State U., 1974; cert. in nursing, Lane C.C., 1989; ADN, Cabrillo Coll., 1991. RN, Calif. Staff nurse Watsonville (Calif.) Community Hosp., 1991—; mem. profl. performance com. Watsonville Hosp., 1992—. Disaster relief nurse ARC, Santa Cruz, Calif. Mem. ANA, Calif. Nurses Assn. Democrat. Home: 277 Spreading Oak Dr Scotts Valley CA 95066-4606

HOLLEY, ELIZABETH SHELBY, educational therapist; b. Lennox, Calif., Dec. 4, 1926; d. Guy Sheldon and Bessie Edna (Humphreys) Bedwell; m. Erwin Dale Thomson, Apr. 26, 1943 (dec. Feb. 1963); m. Kenneth Gunnar Holley, Apr. 10, 1963; children: Edward, Evonne, Fiona, Luana, Raymond, Jean, Kevin. AA, L.A. City Coll., 1959; BA, L.A. State Coll., 1961, MA, 1963. Lic. marriage, family and child counselor. Ednl. therapist Marianne Frostig Ctr., L.A., 1959-64, West Valley Ctr. for Ednl. Therapy, Canoga Park, Calif., 1964-80; dir. Studio for Acad. Achievement, Sherman Oaks, Calif., 1980-87; vol. Peace Corps, Jamaica, 1987-89; ednl. therapist in pvt. practice Woodland Hills, Calif., 1990—; cons. Kaiser/Permanente, Woodland Hills, Calif., 1992—. Author: A Practical Parents Handbook on Teaching Children with Learning Disabilities, 1994. Bd. dirs. Orton Dyslexia Soc., L.A., 1980-87; vol. Juvenile Justice Connection, Van Nuys, Calif. Mem. Assn. of ednl. Therapists (founding mem., bd. dirs. 1979-87). Democrat. Home: 5656 Manton Ave Woodland Hills CA 91367-3028

HOLLEY, JACK K., journalist; b. Denver, Jan. 2, 1937; s. W. Jack and Grace H. (Hood) H.; m. Mary B. Holley; children: Richard T., Laura A., Michael D. BA in Journalism, U. Colo., 1960. Reporter The Chieftain, Pueblo, Colo., 1959; copy editor The World-Herald, Omaha, 1961-63, reporter, columnist, 1963-67, urban affairs reporter, 1967-70, asst. city editor, 1970-72, city editor, 1972-74, asst. to exec. editor, 1974-76, news editor, 1976-79, day mng. editor, 1979-81, mng. editor for adminstrn., 1981-82; asst. prof.Medill Sch. Journalism Northwestern U., 1982-90; news editor The Press-Enterprise, Riverside, Calif., 1990-91, asst. mng. editor news, 1991—; dir. undergraduate studies Northwestern U., 1983-85, dir. Evanston Program, 1985-86; mem. mgmt. com. conf. on newsroom tech. AP Mng. Editors, 1986; moderator regional job seminar Am. Soc. Newspaper Editors, 1985; mem. 1st amendment watchdog group instrumental in Stuart vs. Nebr. Press Assn., Media of Nebr.; participant in continuing edn. seminars Inland Press Assn. Small Newspaper Conf., Itasca, Ill., Poyntner Inst. for Media Studies Program in Media Mgmt., St. Petersburg, Fla., Am. Press Inst., Reston, Va., ABA Fair Trial-Free Press Seminar, Reno, Nev., among others. Ford Found. fellow, 1967, Fellow Inst. for Modern Comm., Northwestern U., 1986-87. Mem. Soc. Profl. Journalists, Calif. Soc. Newspaper Editors (instr. 1993, 94), Am. Assn. Pub. Opinion Rsch. (panelist 1988-90), Midwest Assn. Pub. Opinion Rsch., Sigma Delta Chi. Office: The Press-Enterprise 3512 14th St Riverside CA 92501-3814

HOLLINGSWORTH, MARGARET CAMILLE, financial services administrator, consultant; b. Washington, Feb. 20, 1929; d. Harvey Alvin and Margaret Estelle (Head) Jacob; m. Robert Edgar Hollingsworth, July 14, 1960 (div. July 1980); children: William Lee, Robert Edgar Hollingsworth Jr., Barbara Camille, Bradford Damion. AA, Va. Intermont Coll., 1949. Bookkeeper Fred A. Smith Real Estate, Washington, 1949-53; adminstrv. mgr. Airtronic, Inc., Bethesda, Md., 1953-61; pers. adminstr. Sears Roebuck, Washington, 1973-74; adminstrv. mgr., communication mgr. Garvin GuyButler Corp., San Francisco, 1980-88, exec. sec., pers. mgr., 1989—; assoc. Robert Hollingsworth Nuclear Cons., Walnut Creek, Calif., 1975-79. Mem., bd. dirs. Civic Arts, Walnut Creek, 1975. Recipient Spl. Recognition award AEC, 1974. Mem. Internat. Platform Assn., Commonwealth Club, Beta Sigma Phi (pres. 1954). Democrat. Presbyterian. Home: 1108 Limeridge Dr Concord CA 94518-1923 Office: Garvin GuyButler Corp 456 Montgomery St Ste 1900 San Francisco CA 94104-1252

HOLLINGSWORTH, MEREDITH BEATON, enterostomal therapy clinical nurse specialist; b. Danvers, Mass., Oct. 5, 1941; d. Allan Cameron and Arlene Margaret (Jerue) Beaton; m. William Paul Hollingsworth, Nov. 19, 1983; stepchild, Brendon R. Diploma, R.I. Hosp. Sch. Nursing, Providence, 1968; BS in Nursing, U. Ariz., 1976; MS in Human Resource Mgmt., Golden Gate U., 1984; postgrad., U. Tex., 1988, U. N.Mex., 1989—. Cert. enterostomal therapy nurse, health edn. specialist. Commd. ensign USN, 1968, advanced through grades to lt. comdr., 1979; charge nurse USN, USA, PTO, 1968-88; command ostomy nurse, head ostomy clinic Naval Hosp. Portsmouth, Va., 1985-88; pres., chief exec. officer Enterostomal Therapy Nursing Edn. and Tng. Cons. (ETNetc), Rio Rancho, N.Mex., 1989-90; mgr. clin. svcs. we. area Support Systems Internat., Inc., Charleston, S.C., 1990-92; pres., CEO Paumer Assocs. Internat., Inc., Rio Rancho, N.Mex., 1992—; enterostomal therapy nurse, clin. nurse specialist, educator Presbyn. Health Care Svcs., Albuquerque, 1993—. Mem. adminstrv. bd. Baylake United Meth. Ch., Virginia Beach, 1980-83; chmn. bd. deacons St. Paul's United Ch., Rio Rancho; active Am. Cancer Soc. Mem. Wound, Ostomy and Continence Nurses Soc. (nat. govt. affairs com., govt. affairs com. Rocky Mountain region, pub. rels. com., regional pres. 1989-93, nat. sec. 1994—), United Ostomy Assn., World Coun. Enterostomal Therapists, N.Mex. Soc. Healthcare Edn. and Tng. of Am. Hosp. Assn., N.Mex. Health Care Assn., Care Star Network. Republican. Office: PO Box 44395 Rio Rancho NM 87174-4395

HOLLIS, SUSAN TOWER, college dean; b. Boston, Mar. 17, 1939; d. James Wilson and Dorothy Parsons (Moore) Tower; m. Allen Hollis, Nov. 10, 1962 (div. Feb. 1975); children: Deborah Durfee, Harrison. AB, Smith Coll., 1962; PhD, Harvard U., 1982. Asst. prof. Scripps Coll., Claremont, Calif., 1988-91; prof. Coll. of Undergrad. Studies The Union Inst., L.A., 1991-93; dean of the college and prof. humanities Sierra Nev. Coll.-Lake Tahoe, Incline Village, Nev., 1993-95. Author: The Ancient Egyptian "Tale of Two Brothers", 1990; asst. editor: Working With No Data, 1987; co-editor: Feminist Theory and the Study of Folklore, 1994; mem. adv. bd. KMT, A Modern Jour. of Ancient Egypt, 1991—; contbr. articles to profl. publs. Music vol. Open Readings, Belmont, Mass., 1982-88; vol. Sierra Club, 1988—; problem capt. Odyssey of the Mind, Nev., 1994, 95. Mem. Am. Acad. Religion, Am. Assn. Higher Edn., Am. Folklore Soc., Am. Oriental Soc., Am. Rsch. Ctr. Egypt, Internat. Egyptology Soc., Soc. Biblical Lit., Appalachian Mountain Club (co-leader 1987—), N.Y. Acad. Scis., Incline Village/Crystal Bay C. of C. (sec. and bd. dirs. 1994—). Democrat. Home: PO Box 7284 866 Northwood Blvd #29 Incline Village NV 89452 Office: Sierra Nevada Coll PO Box 4269 800 College Dr Incline Village NV 89450

HOLLISON, ROBERT VICTOR, JR., physician, medical executive; b. Honolulu, Nov. 9, 1947; s. Robert Victor and Gladys (Yamanoha) H.; children: Renee, Keith, Dawn. BA, U. Hawaii, 1969; MD, U. Wash., 1973. Diplomate Am. Bd. Internal Medicine, Am. Bd. Family Practice, Am. Bd. Geriatric Medicine, Am. Bd. Sports Medicine; cert. FAA flight examiner, FAA med. rev. officer for drug screening. Various to chief resident Madigan Army Med. Ctr., Ft. Lewis, Wash., 1975-76; dir. residency tng. Madigan Army Med. Ctr., Ft. Lewis, 1980-82; clin. asst. prof. of family medicine U. Wash. Sch. Medicine, Seattle, 1980-82; chief Hawaii Kai Straub Clinic, Honolulu, 1982-84; pvt. practice Univ. Family Medicine, Honolulu, 1983—; med. dir., cons. Hawaii Job Corps, Honolulu, 1983-92; med. dir. Comprehensive Home Svcs. of Hawaii, Honolulu, 1991—; comdr. Tripler USAR Hosp. Augmentation, Honolulu, 1991—; med. dir. The Queen's Health Care Plan, Inc./Island Care, Honolulu, 1991-94; asst. prof. internal medicine, family medicine, and pub. health U. Hawaii Sch. Medicine, 1982—; med. dir. Island Nursing Home/Oahu Care Facility, Honolulu, 1987—, Occupational Medicine-Kapiolani Med. Ctr. for Women and Children, Honolulu, 1990—. Contbg. author: Family Medicine: Principles and Practices, 1983, Hawaii's Unfinished Health Agenda: Primary and Specialty Healthcare, 1994. Mem. community rels. coun. Hawaii Job Corps, Honolulu, 1985—; mem. Am. Cancer Soc., Honolulu, 1984-86, Hawaii Kai Neighborhood Bd. # 1, Honolulu, 1983-86, chmn. health and safety com., 1983-85. Col. U.S. Army, 1970—. Named to Outstanding Young Men of Am., 1978, 84. Fellow Am. Coll. Physicians, Am. Acad. Family Physicians; mem. Hawaii Acad. Family Physicians (pres. 1992-93, pres.-elect 1991-92), Am. Coll. Physician Execs., Hawaii Med. Assn. (coun., county bd. govs. 1994—), Res. Officer Assn., Phi Beta Kappa. Office: Univ Family Medicine 1904 University Ave Honolulu HI 96822-2403

HOLLMANN, MARTIN, aircraft design engineer; b. Berlin, Germany, Dec. 6, 1940; s. Hans Erich and Gisella (Schimmelbusch) H.; married; children: Eric Matthew, Christian. BS in Aeronautical Ops., Calif State U., San Jose, 1969; MS in Mech. Engring., U. Cen. Fla., 1974. Design engr. Convair Aerospace/Divsn. of Gen. Dynamics, Inc., San Diego, Calif., 1969-72; sr. engr. Martin Marietta Corp., Orlando, Fla., 1972-74; sr. design engr. Lockheed Missiles and Space Co., Inc., Palo Alto, 1974-78; program engr. Ford Aerospace and Comms. Corp., Palo Alto, Calif., 1978-80; sr. engr. Westinghouse Electric Corp., Sunnyvale, Calif., 1980-82; sr. project engr. FMC Corp., San Jose, 1982-84; prin. engr. Kaiser Electronics Corp., San Jose, Calif., 1984-86; pres. Aircraft Designs, Inc., Monterey, Calif., 1986—; projects include all graphite MX-missile canister, world's first composite armored personnel carrier, Star Kraft six-passenger aircraft, Lancair series of aircraft, structural design and anlysis of the hydrofoil for Catalina Flyer, 1991, others; clientele include Lockheed, DuPont, NASA, Beechcraft, TASK Rsch., Inc., Westfoil Internat., Westinghouse, Universal Studios, NEICO Aviation, Hughes Aircraft, California Microwave, others. Author: (books) Modern Aircraft Design, Vol. 1, Vol. 2, Composite Aircraft Design, Modern Gyroplane Design, Flying the Gyroplane, Succeed in Aviation, Modern Aerodynamic Flutter Analysis, Modern Aircraft Drafting, ABCs of Desktop Finite Element Analysis, others. Mem. AIAA. Republican. Lutheran.

HOLLOWAY, CINDY, mortgage company executive; b. Queens, N.Y., Aug. 8, 1960; d. Richard Stephen and Beverly Bunny (Harris) Tannenbaum; m. David Milton Holloway (div. Mar. 1986); 1 child, Benjamin Jerome. BA, Calif. State U., Fullerton, 1981. Lic. real estate broker. Waitress Bob's Big Boy, San Bernardino, Calif., 1984-85; receptionist RNG Mortgage Co., San Bernardino, 1985; loan processor Quality Mortgage Co., Colton, Calif., 1985-88, loan officer, 1988-91; loan officer RNG Mortgage, 1991-92; v.p., br. mgr. Mountain West Fin., 1992—. Mem. San Bernardino Bd. Realtors (spl. events com. 1988—, comm. com. 1990—), Nat. Trust for Hist. Preservation, San Bernardino Execs. Assn., Assn. Profl. Mortgage Women (bd. dirs. 1989-90, v.p. 1992-93, Affiliate of Yr. award 1990), San Bernardino Execs. Group (bd. dirs. 1994—). Home: PO Box 3187 Crestline CA 92325-3187

HOLLOWAY, ROBERT WESTER, radiochemist; b. Morrilton, Ark., Jan. 3, 1945; s. Otho and Bessie Vance (Woolverton) H.; m. Mary Ella Hamel, Dec. 31, 1970; children: David, Jason. BS, Harding Coll., 1967; postgrad., U. Okla., 1968; PhD, U. Ark., 1977. Asst. prof. U. Ark., Pine Bluff, 1976-79; research chemist DuPont Corp., Aiken, S.C., 1979-81; supervisory chemist EPA, Las Vegas, 1981-94; pres. Nev. Tech. Assocs., Inc., 1994—. Contbr. articles to profl. jours. Served to capt. USAF, 1967-72. Mem. Am. Chem. Soc., Health Physics Soc., Toastmasters, Optimists. Republican. Home: 311 E Desert Rose Dr Henderson NV 89015-8107 Office: Nev Tech Assocs Inc PO Box 90748 Henderson NV 89009-0748

HOLM, AUDREY CHRISTINE, health care organization administrator; b. Spokane, Wash., July 27, 1929; d. A.O. Marcus and Gunda Marie (Myhre) H. BSBA, U. Denver, 1958; MPH, U. Calif., Berkeley, 1966. RN, Calif. Asst. adminstr. Maricopa County Med. Ctr., Phoenix, 1974-78, Tex. Tech Teaching Hosp., Lubbock, 1976-78, Herrick Hosp. and Health Ctr., Berkeley, Calif., 1978-83; assoc. adminstr. Booth Meml. Med. Ctr., Flushing, N.Y., 1983-90, Booth Silvercrest S.N.F., Jamaica, N.Y., 1990-91; adminstr. Salvation Army Retirement Community, Asbury Park, N.J., 1991-94. Commd. officer, Salvation Army, 1948; bd. dirs., officer Soroptimist Internat. Fellow Am. Coll. Healthcare Execs. (examiner); mem. Am. Coll. Healthcare Adminstrs. Office: Salvation Army 222 E Indiana Ave Spokane WA 99207-2318

HOLMAN, JOHN FOSTER, investment banker; b. Chgo., Dec. 11, 1946; s. William Judson and Evelyn Mae (Foster) H.; m. Paula Susan Anderson, Aug. 1, 1970 (div. Oct. 1978). BS, Ariz. State U., 1969, MBA, 1971, JD, 1975; Cert. Fin. Planner, Coll. for Fin. Planning, 1991. Bar: Ariz. 1975; cert. fin. planner; registered investment advisor; lic. fed. securities. Congl. legis. intern, 1971; trial atty. Johnson, Tucker, Jessen & Dake, Phoenix, 1975-78, Holman, Meador and Hergott, Phoenix, 1978-80; nat. mktg. dir. Franchise Fin. Corp. Am., Phoenix, 1980-87; mng. dir. Fin. Resource Group, Sausalito, Calif., 1987-89; pres. Holman Internat. Group, Phoenix, 1990—; CEO, Internat. Salvage Corp., 1992—; pres. Fin. Freedom Assocs., Ltd., Phoenix, 1992—; v.p. retail and instnl. mktg. McKee Securities, 1993-94; mktg. dir. McKinley Capital Mktg., 1994—; prin. John F. Holman, P.C., 1981—. Founder Am. Wellness Assn., 1989—; mem. camp com. YMCA, Phoenix, 1968—; life mem. Rep. Senatorial Inner Circle, 1984—, Senatorial Commn., 1991; mem. Rep. Presdl. Task Force, 1989—; elder Presbyn. Ch., 1970—; mem. Ariz. Acad. Town Halls, 1969—. Capt. U.S. Army, 1968-76. Recipient Presdl. Order of Merit, 1991. Mem. Fed. Bar Assn., State Bar Ariz., Sales and Mktg. Execs. Phoenix, Ariz. State U. Alumni Assn. (bd. dirs. 1975-81), Internat. Platform Assn., World Record Setting Am. Transcontinental Relay Team, Mt. Kenya Safari Club, Capitol Hill Club, Delta Sigma Pi, Pi Sigma Epsilon.

HOLMAN, KAREN MARIE, purchasing agent; b. Anchorage, Sept. 6, 1962; d. Joseph Willie and Rose Millicent (Watson) Anderson; m. Robert L. Holman Jr., Nov. 27, 1982. AA in Bus. Adminstrn., Anchorage Community Coll., 1984; BA in Orgnl. Adminstrn., Alaska Pacific U., 1991. Sr. office clk. Bur. of the Census, Anchorage, 1980; premium audit clk. Providence Wash. Ins., Anchorage, 1981-82; info. systems clk. G.A Ltd., Anchorage, 1982-83; purchasing agt. State of Alaska, Anchorage, 1984-89, U. Alaska, Anchorage, 1989-92, ATU Telecommunications, 1992—. Del. Dem. Group State Caucuses, Anchorage, 1989; mem. Greater Friendly Temple Ch. of God in Christ; bd. dirs. Alaska Women's Resource Ctr., 1989-91. Home: 3722 Randolph St Anchorage AK 99508-4529

HOLMAN, PAUL DAVID, plastic surgeon; b. Waynesboro, Va., Mar. 13, 1943; s. Wallace D. and Rosalie S. Holman. BA, U. Va., 1965; MD, Jefferson Med. Coll., 1968. Intern, George Washington U. Hosp., Washington, 1968-69, resident in gen. surgery, 1969-70, 72-74; resident in plastic surgery Phoenix Plastic Surgery Residency, 1974-76; practice medicine specializing in plastic surgery, Phoenix, 1977—; mem. staff Good Samaritan Hosp., Phoenix, St. Joseph's Hosp., Phoenix, Phoenix Children's Hosp. Served to lt. comdr. USNR, 1970-72. Diplomate Am. Bd. Surgery, Am. Bd. Plastic Surgery. Mem. AMA, ACS, Am. Soc. Plastic and Reconstructive Surgeons, Phi Beta Kappa. Office: 2111 E Highland Ave Ste 105 Phoenix AZ 85016-4732

HOLMES, BARBARA ANN KRAJKOSKI, secondary education educator; b. Evansville, Ind., Mar. 21, 1946; d. Frank Joseph and Estelle Marie (DeWeese) Krajkoski; m. David Leo Holmes, Aug. 21, 1971; 1 child, Susan Ann Sky. BS, Ind. State U., 1968, MS, 1969, specialist cert., 1976; postgrad. U. Nev., 1976-78. Acad. counselor Ind. State U., 1968-69, halls dir., 1969-73;

dir. residence halls U. Utah, 1973-76; sales assoc. Fidelity Realty, Las Vegas, Nev., 1977-82. cert. analyst Nev. Dept. Edn., 1981-82; tchr. Clark County Sch. Dist., 1982-87, computer cons., adminstrv. specialist instructional mgmt. systems, 1987-91, chair computer conf., 1990-92, adminstrv. specialist K-6, 1990-93, dean of students summer sch. site adminstr. Eldorado H.S., 1991—. Named Outstanding Sr. Class Woman, Ind. State U., 1969; recipient Dir's. award U. Utah Residence Halls, 1973, Outstanding Sales Assoc., 1977; Tchr. of Month award, 1983, Dist. Outstanding Tchr. award, 1984, Dist. Excellence in Edn. award, 1984, 86, 87, 88. Mem. Nev. Assn. Realtors, AAUW, Am. Assn. Women Deans, Adminstrs. and Counselors, Am. Personnel and Guidance Assn., Am. Coll. Personnel Assn., Nevadans for Equal Rights Amendment, Alumnae Assn. Chi Omega (treas. Terre Haute chpt. 1971-73, pres., bd. officer Las Vegas 1977-81), Clark County Panhellenic Alumnae Assn. (pres. 1978-79), Computer Using Educators So. Nev. (sec. 1983-86, pres.-elect 1986-87, pres. 1987-88, state chmn. 1988-89, conf. chmn. 1989-92, sec. 94—, Hall of Fame 1995), Job's Daus. Club (guardian sec. 1995—), Order Ea. Star, Phi Delta Kappa (Action award 1990-91, 1992-93, 93-94, newspaper editor 1992-93). Developed personal awareness program U. Utah, 1973-76. Home: 2531 E Oquendo Rd Las Vegas NV 89120-2413 Office: Eldorado High Sch 1139 Linn Ln Las Vegas NV 89110-2628

HOLMES, DORIS LEE, nursing administrator; b. Yuma, Colo., Mar. 15, 1937; d. Wenzel and Cora (Miller) Dreher; m. James Kelly Holmes, May 20, 1958 (div. Aug. 1980); children: Brian Kelly, Teresa Galye. AA in Nursing Arts, Denver U., 1958; AA in Gen. Edn., LACC, L.A., 1972. RN, Calif. I.V. therapist Cedars-Sinai Med. Ctr., L.A., 1969-71, nigh nursing supr., 1971-73, night charge nurse MICU, 1973-76, asst. coord. MICU, 1976-78, hemodialysis staff nurse, 1978-82, primary home dialysis nurse, 1982-83; asst. headnurse for home dialysis Ushawl Cedars-Sinai Dialysis Unit, L.A., 1983-85; DON L.A. Dialysis Tng. Ctr., 1985—; lectr., in-svc. trainer hosp., nursing homes, nursing seminars, So. Calif., 1982—. Author articles on peritoneal dialysis. Office: LA Dialysis Tng Ctr 10780 Santa Monica Blvd # 480 Los Angeles CA 90025-4749

HOLMES, MICHAEL, oil and gas consultant; b. London, Oct. 6, 1936; came to U.S., 1963, naturalized, 1975; s. Norman Edward and Iris I. (Fisher) H.; m. Francoise J. Charlet, July 14, 1962 (div.); children: Antony I., Dominic M.; m. Sally Haven, July 13, 1973. (div.). B.S.C., U. London, 1957, Ph.D., 1961; M.S., Colo. Sch. Mines, 1973. Geologist, Brit. Petroleum, London, 1960-66, Shell Can., Edmonton, Alta., 1966-68; research scientist Marathon Oil, Denver, 1968-73; exploration mgr. Berry Wiggins, London, 1973-74; v.p. H.K. Van Poollen, Denver, 1974-78; prin. Michael Holmes, Denver, 1978—; dir. Cibola Energy Corp., Albuquerque. Author: (with others) Reservoir Economics and Engineering Manual, 1973. Bd. dirs. English Speaking Union, Denver, 1970-73. Mem. Arapahoe C. of C. (bd. dirs. 1970-73), Am. Assn. Petroleum Geologists, Soc. Petroleum Engrs., Soc. Profl. Well Log Analysts, Rocky Mountain Assn. Geologists, Am. Inst. Profl. Geologists.

HOLMES, MICHAEL GENE, lawyer; b. Longview, Wash., Jan. 14, 1937; s. Robert A. and Esther S. Holmes; children: Helen, Peyton Robert. AB in Econs., Stanford U., 1958, JD, 1960. Bar: Oreg. 1961, U.S. Dist. Ct. Oreg. 1961, U.S. Ct. Appeals (9th cir.) 1961, Temp. Emergency Ct. Appeals 1976, U.S. Supreme Ct. 1976. Assoc. Spears, Lubersky, Bledsoe, Anderson, Young & Hilliard, Portland, 1961-67, ptnr., 1967-90; ptnr. Lane Powell Spears Lubersky, Portland, 1990—; mem. Oreg. Joint Com. of Bar, Press & Broadcasters, 1982-85, sec., 1983-84, chmn. 1985. Author Survey of Oregon Defamation and Privacy Law, ann. 1982—. Trustee Med. Research Found. Oreg., Portland, 1985-94, exec. com., 1986-94; trustee Portland Civic Theatre, 1962-66. Mem. ABA (antitrust law sect., labor and employment law sect.), Oreg. Bar Assn., Phi Beta Kappa, Arlington Club.

HOLMES, PAUL LUTHER, political scientist, educational consultant; b. Rock Island, Ill., Mar. 7, 1919; s. Bernt Gunnar and Amanda Sophia (Swenson) H.; m. Ardis Ann Grunditz, Nov. 1, 1946; children: Mary Ann, David Stephen. BA, U. Minn., 1940; MA, Stanford U., 1949, EdD, 1968; MA, George Washington U., 1964. Career officer U.S. Navy, 1941-64, ret. as capt.; adminstr. Laney Coll., Oakland, Calif., 1965-70; dean Contra Costa Coll., San Pablo, Calif., 1970-71; pres. Coll. of Alameda (Calif.), 1971-75, prof. polit. sci., 1975-80; dir. doctoral studies program No. Calif., Nova U., 1975-80; cons. in higher edn., Gig Harbor, Wash., 1981—; regent Calif. Luth. U., 1973-76. Decorated Navy Air, Joint Service medals. Mem. AAUP, Am. Polit. Sci. Assn., Navy League, Stanford Univ. Alumni Assn., Phi Delta Kappa. Lutheran. Club: Rotary (Gig Harbor).

HOLMES, RALPH EDWARD, plastic surgeon; b. San Diego, Calif., Dec. 8, 1943. MD, Boston U., 1967. Plastic surgeon U. Calif.San Diego Med. Coll. Office: UC San Diego MC 200 W Arbor Dr San Diego CA 92103-1911*

HOLMES, RICHARD ALBERT, software engineer, consultant; b. Santa Barbara, Calif., May 7, 1958; m. Janet M. Dunbar; children: Brian D., Kevin M. AA in Music summa cum laude, City Coll. San Francisco, 1987; BS in Computer Sci. summa cum laude, Nat. U., 1991; postgrad., Stanford U., 1993—. Ind. software cons. San Francisco, 1986-88; software quality assurance contractor Oxford & Assocs., Mountain View, Calif., 1988-89; microkernel diagnostics engr. Apple Computer, Cupertino, Calif., 1990-93, file system engr., 1994—. CCSF tchr. & faculty scholar, 1986, 87, Alpha Gamma Sigma scholar, 1987. Mem. IEEE, Assn. for Computing Machinery, Alpha Gamma Sigma (treas. 1986-87). Office: Apple Computer Inc MS 302-40Z 20525 Mariani Ave Cupertino CA 95014

HOLMES, RICHARD BROOKS, mathematical physicist; b. Milw., Jan. 7, 1959; s. Emerson Brooks Holmes and Nancy Anne (Schaffter) Winship. BS, Calif. Inst. Tech., 1981; MS, Stanford (Calif.) U., 1983. Sr. systems analyst Comptek Rsch., Vallejo, Calif., 1982-83; staff scientist Western Rsch., Arlington, Va., 1983-85; sr. scientist AVCO Everett (Mass.) Rsch. Lab., 1985-88; prin. rsch. scientist North East Rsch. Assocs., Woburn, Mass., 1988-90; sr. mem. tech. staff Rocketdyne div. Rockwell Internat., Canoga Park, Calif., 1990—; cons. North East Rsch. Assocs., 1990. Contbr. Matched Asymptotic Expansions, 1988; contbr. articles to Phys. Rev. Letters, Phys. Rev., Jour. of the Optical Soc. Am. and IEEE Jour. of Quantum Electronics. Mem. No. Calif. Scholarship Founds., Oakland, 1977; mem. Wilderness Soc., Washington, 1989. Stanford fellow Stanford U., 1982; fellow MIT, 1990; recipient Presdl. Medal of Merit, 1992. Mem. AAAS, Am. Phys. Soc., Optical Soc. Am. Office: Rockwell Internat Rocketdyne Div 6633 Canoga Ave # Fa40 Canoga Park CA 91303-2703

HOLMES, ROBERT C., securities trader; b. 1936. With Liberty Fin. Inc., Irvine, Calif., 1966-92; with Liberty Capital Markets, 1983—, now chmn. bd. dirs.; chmn. bd. dirs. Liberty Realty Capital Asset Mgmt. and Liberty Capital Asset Mgmt. Inc., Irvine, 1991—. Office: Liberty Capital Markets Inc 4 Park Plz Ste 2000 Irvine CA 92714-8559*

HOLMES, ROBERT EUGENE, state legislative consultant, journalist; b. Shelbyville, Ind., June 5, 1928; s. Eugene Lowell and Sarah Lucinda (Hughes) H.; m. Retha Carolyn Richey, June 27, 1955 (div. Sept. 1966); children: Enid Adair Offley, William Houstoun (dec.), Holly Ann Holmes. BA in Polit. Sci., DePauw U., 1950; MA in Journalism, Ind. U., 1953; MA in Communs. and Urban Affairs, Stanford U., 1976. Staff reporter Elkhart, Ind. Truth, 1954-57; city editor, investigative editor Press-Enterprise, Riverside, Calif., 1957-70; sr. cons. Calif. State Senate Dem. Caucus, Sacramento, 1971-74, dep. dir., 1978-79; press sec. Lt. Gov. of Calif., Sacramento, 1975-77; project dir. Border Area Devel. Study, U.S. Econ. Devel. Adminstrn., Sacramento, 1978; staff dep. dir. Calif. Senator Robert Presley, Sacramento, 1979-83; chief cons. Joint Legis. Ethics Com., Calif. Legislature, Sacramento, 1981-82; staff dir. Joint Com. on Prison Constrn. and Ops., Calif. Legislature, Sacramento, 1983-94; rsch. cons. Calif. Rsch. Bur., Calif. State Libr., Sacramento, 1991-92. Author, editor rschr. legis. reports; contbg. editor creative writing quar. Noah's Hotel, Inverness, Calif., 1991—; contbr. articles to mags., short stories, 1961—. Pres., Golden Bear Dem. Club, Sacramento, 1972-74; media dir. Lt. Gov. Campaign, Sacramento and L.A., 1974. Sgt. USMC, 1951-53. Recipient Silver Gavel award ABA, 1969, 1st Place media award Calif. State Bar Assn., 1968, 1st Place award Calif. Newspaper Pubs. Best Series, 1969, 70, 71, Jack Anderson award for excellence in journalism Calif. Correctional Peace Officers Assn., 1993; Am. Polit. Sci. Assn. Ford Found. fellow Stanford U., 1970. Mem. NAACP, ACLU, Calif. Writers Club, Common Cause. Democrat. Home: 416 Florin Rd Sacramento CA 95831-2007

HOLMES, THOMAS LEROY, small business owner; b. Vancouvr, Wash., Apr. 14, 1953; s. Clifford Leroy and Dorothy Ann (Predeek) H.; m. Patricia Lynn Blake, Apr. 12 (div.); 1 child, Blake Leroy. BS in Bus., Oreg. State U., 1975. Outside salesman Empire Pacific Industries, 1975-82; owner, treas. NW Door and Supply, Inc., Tigard, Oreg., 1982—. Office: NW Door and Supply Inc PO Box 68 Tualatin OR 97062-0068

HOLMES, WILLARD, art gallery director; b. Saskatoon, Sask., Canada. Grad. in art history, U. B.C., 1972. With Fine Arts Gallery, U. B.C.; head of exhbns. Nat. Gallery of Can.; curator Vancouver Art Gallery; dir. Pender St. Gallery, from 1975; chief curator, dir. Charles Scott Gallery, head curatorial studies program Emily Carr Coll., 1976-87; chief curator, interim dir., then dir. Vancouver Art Gallery, 1987-93. Office: Vancouver Art Gallery, 750 Hornby St, Vancouver, BC Canada V6Z 2H7

HOLMES-CALVERT, JACQUELIN ANN, workers compensation administrator; b. Balt., Sept. 5, 1947; d. Paul Chester and Ethel Marie (Parker) Bianchi; m. Larry Lee Lockman, Nov. 29, 1963 (div. Oct. 1972); children: Carole Jean, Gregory Stephen; m. John Stephen Holmes, July 27, 1974 (div. May 1993); m. Stephen W. Calvert, May 19, 1995. AA in Psychology, Community Coll. of Denver, 1975; BSBA, Regis Coll., 1988; postgrad., U. Colo., Denver, 1991—. Cert. personnel classification, examinations and rules interpretation, Colo.; lic. claims adjuster. With staff support/counseling div. Community Coll. of Denver North Campus, 1973-74, asst. to dir. community services div., 1974-77; claims adjuster State Compensation Ins. Fund, Denver, 1978-80, 82-84; owner day care ctr. Littleton, Colo., 1980-82; personnel analyst Colo. Dept. Labor & Employment, Denver, 1984-88; adminstr. EEO and affirmative action Colo. Dept. Natural Resources, Denver, 1988-90; adminstr. spl. funds Colo. Div. Labor, Denver, 1990-91; dep. dir. Colo. Div. Workers Compensation, Denver, 1991—; mem. adv. bd. Colo. Health Elec. Data Interchange. Student govt. rep. Community Coll. of Denver, 1973-74; organizer Classified Employees Council, Denver, 1975; vol. orgn. support Arapahoe County Family Day Care, Littleton, 1981-82; coach Teen Quiz Team (Champions 79-83), Littleton, 1979-83; marriage enrichment cons. Littleton Ch. of the Nazarene, 1986-87; Sunday sch. tchr., 1980-87. Named an Outstanding Employee Gov.'s Office Colo. State Govt., 1986. Mem. Internat. Pers. Mgrs. Assn., Internat. Assn. Accident. Bds. and Commns. (electronic data interchange med. subcom.), Colo. EEO and AF-firmative Action Coalition, Colo. Coun. Mediators Assn., Pilot Club. Home: 1551 Larimer St Apt 2603 Denver CO 80202-1638 Office: Colo Div of Workers Compensation 1515 Arapahoe St Tower 2 Ste 640 Denver CO 80202

HOLMES-SMITH, DAVID MICHAEL, computer engineer, consultant, priest, dean; b. Whittier, Calif., Nov. 25, 1955; s. Norman Kenneth Smith and Joanne Sherwood (Jackman) Chace; m. Kathleen Martha Holmes, Apr. 15, 1989; 1 child, Kelly Leilani Holmes-Smith. BA in Performing Arts, U. Hawaii, 1990, MEd, 1992; MS in Info. Sys., Hawaii Pacific U., 1993; postgrad., Internat. Grad. Sch. Theology, Honolulu, 1994—. Ordained Anglican priest Episcopal Ch., 1993. Instr. Hawaii Pacific U., Honolulu, 1990-94; owner, designer Holmes-Smith Engring., Honolulu, 1992—; instr. Mid-Pacific Inst., Honolulu, 1994—; priest St. Michaels Mission, Honolulu, 1994—; dean Holy Order of the Culdee, 1995—; cons. edn., computer tech., 1992—. Author/producer: (musical) Forgotten Legend, 1988, Tabernacle Liturgy, 1990. Chair edn. and comm. com. Anglican Episcopal Diocese of Okla., 1993—; mem. Rutherford Inst., Honolulu, 1992. Iona Inst. rsch. fellow. Mem. Internat. Soc. for Teaching in Edn., Epsilon Delta Phi, Phi Eta Sigma, Delta Mu Delta. Home and Office: 1914 University Ave Apt 209 Honolulu HI 96822-2473

HOLMGREN, RICHARD S., JR., environmental engineering executive; b. 1928. BS in Civil Engring., MIT, 1950; MS in Sanitary Engring., U. Calif., Berkeley, 1957. With Montgomery Watson, 1958—, now chmn. Office: Montgomery Watson Ams 200 N Lake Ave # 1200 Pasadena CA 91101-1829*

HOLMSTROM, DAVID EDWIN ARTHUR, mortgage banking executive, consultant; b. Seattle, Sept. 3, 1943; s. Earl A. and Linnea Sanders (Bystedt) H.; m. Pamela Waite, Sept. 11, 1965 (div. Dec. 1974); m. Elaine Monfils, Feb. 18, 1977; children: Todd Gunnar, Brett David. BSBA, U. Wash., 1966. Asst. v.p. Rainier Nat. Bank, Seattle, 1966-77; pres. Am. Money Investments, Lynnwood, Wash., 1977-80; v.p. Rainier Credit Co., Seattle, 1980-84; v.p., mgr. Nat. Bank of Can. (Laurentide), Seattle, 1984-88, Bank of Calif., Seattle, 1988-91; mng. ptnr. HRM Capital, Inc., Mill Creek, Wash., 1991—. With USAR, 1961-64. Named Jaycee of Yr., 1970. Mem. Mill Creek Country Club (men's chmn. 1989). Office: HRM Capital Inc Ste 100 16000 Bothell Everett Hwy Mill Creek WA 98012-1515

HOLO, SELMA REUBEN, museum director, educator; b. Chgo., May 21, 1943; d. Samuel and Ghita (Hurwitz) Reuben; children from previous marriage: Robert, Joshua; m. Fred Croton, June 18, 1989. BA, Northwestern U., 1965; MA, Hunter Coll., 1972; PhD, U. Calif., Santa Barbara, 1980; postgrad., Mus. Mgmt. Inst., 1985. Lectr. Art Ctr. Coll. of Design, Pasadena, Calif., 1973-77; curator of acquisitions Norton Simon Mus., Pasadena, 1977-81; dir. Fisher Gallery and mus. MA art history/mus. studies program U. So. Calif., L.A., 1981—; guest curator, cons. Getty Mus., Malibu, Calif., 1975-76, 81; guest curator Isetan Mus., Tokyo, 1982; cons. Nat. Mus. for Women in Arts, Washington, 1984; reviewer grants Inst. Mus. Svcs., Washington, 1986, 87, Getty Grant Program, 1988-90; panel chmn. Internat. Com. on Exhbn. Exch., Washington, 1984; panelist NEA, Washington, 1985, 91, 92, 93, Idaho Commn. on the Arts; mem. admission panel Mus. Mgmt. Inst., 1990; hon. curator Tokyo Fuji Mus.; lectr. museology IVAM, Valencia, Spain, 1994, Compultense U. Masters in Museology, 1994, Universidad Castilla La Mancha in Museology, 1995. Author: (catalogues) Goya: Los Disparates, 1976; co-author: La Tauromaquia: Goya, Picasso and the Bullfight, 1986; editor: Keepers of the Flame, The Unofficial Artists of Leningrad, 1990; guest editor New Observations, 1990; contbr. articles to profl. jours. Fellow La Napoule Art Found., 1988, Fulbright Found., 1994; Kress Found. grantee, N.Y., 1979, Internationes Fed. Repubic of Germany grantee, 1985, 92; recipient Fuj Fine Art award, 1990, Grant Com. for Cooperation Between U.S. Univs. and Spanish Govt. Mem. ICOM, Coll. Art Assn. (survey com. mus. studies programs 1986), Am. Assn. Mus., Art Table. Office: U So Calif Fisher Gallery 823 Exposition Blvd Los Angeles CA 90007-4005

HOLST, SANFORD, strategic consulting executive, author; b. Batavia, N.Y., Nov. 4, 1946; s. William Walker and Catherine (Loggie) H.; children: Suzanne, Kristina. BS in Aero., Astronautics, MIT, 1968; MBA, UCLA, 1970. Engr. advanced design group Lockheed Aircraft Corp., Los Angeles, 1968-71; analyst UCLA, Los Angeles, 1972-73, So. Calif. Assn. Govts., Los Angeles, 1973-78; systems analyst Northwest Industries, Los Angeles, 1978-80; v.p. computer systems dept. Parsons Corp., Pasadena, Calif., 1980-93; pres. The Holst Group, L.A., 1993—. Author: Kombucha Phenemenon, 1995; editor Taurus mag., 1971-72; contbr. articles to profl. jours. Vice chmn. Beverly Hills (Calif.) Bicentennial Com., 1976. Mem. Phi Kappa Sigma (pres. Alpha Mu chpt. 1967-68). Office: Holst Group 14755 Ventura Blvd Ste 413 Sherman Oaks CA 91403-3669

HOLST, WENDELL, marketing professional, consultant, writer; b. Edgar, Nebr., Sept. 15, 1920; s. Gustav Adolph and Johanna Rebecca Maria (Rahmann) H.; m. Imogene Perkins, Oct. 18, 1947; children: Mark W. Holst, Marilyn J. Holst Thore. Student, Northwestern Coll. Law, 1946-47; grad., Ins. Inst., 1951. Payroll auditor U.S. Dept. Interior, Portland, Oreg., 1941-43, social security adminstr., 1946-47; acct. sys. specialist to intermountain mgr. Oreg. Mutual Ins. Co., McMinnville, 1947-53; asst. sec., exec. v.p. Western Pacific Ins. Co., Seattle, 1953-70; exec. v.p. Groninger & Co., Seattle, 1970-72; pres. Consumers United Ins. Co., Seattle, 1972-75, Forest Industries Ins., Albany, Oreg., 1975-77, Timber-Line Gen. Agy., McMinnville, 1975-77, Inter-West Ins. Co., McMinnville, 1979-85; mktg. cons. various cos., Oreg., 1985—. Author: Getting Most Out of Small Business, 1993, Getting Most Out of Your Insurance, 1993, Getting Most Out Of Your Travels, 1993, Getting Most Out of Just Thinking, 1993, Getting Most Out of Your Retirement, 1995, Getting Ahead? Oh Yes You Can, 1995; inventor short-cut endorser. Del. Indsl. Conf. Bd., Seattle, 1955-70; campaign mgr. Ins. Commr. Cand., Seattle, 1970-74; sec. Little League Baseball, Seattle, 1959-64; chmn. bd. YMCA, Seattle; com. chmn. Boy Scouts Am., Seattle, 1957. With USN, 1942-46. Mem. Ins. Acctg. and Sys. Assn. (nat. pres. 1972-73), Masons, Shriners, Elks. Presbyterian. Home and Office: 2205 Saint Andrews Dr Mcminnville OR 97128-2455

HOLT, DENNIS F., media buying company executive. Student, U. So. Calif. Salesman RKO, L.A.; founder, pres. chief exec. officer Western Internat. Media Corp., L.A. Office: Western Internat Media Corp 8544 W Sunset Blvd West Hollywood CA 90069-2310

HOLT, STEVEN HAMILTON SKOV, strategic design company executive, educator; b. Hartford, Conn., Sept. 24, 1957; s. John Nicholas Holt and Alice Claire (Humphrey) Lund; m. Mara Elizabeth Skov, Aug. 27, 1994. AB in Cognitive Sci., Brown U., 1982; MFA in Design Studies, Stanford U., 1992. Celia Siegel fellow Cooper-Hewitt Mus., N.Y.C., 1982; editor I.D. Mag., N.Y.C., 1983-85; designer Smart Design, N.Y.C., 1986; dir. product design studies Parsons Sch. Design, N.Y.C., 1986-90; ptnr. Zebra Design, Cologne, Germany, 1987-90; visionary Frogdesign, Sunnyvale, Calif., 1992—; chmn. indsl. design dept. Calif. Coll. Arts & Crafts, San Francisco, 1995—. Contbg. editor: Axis Mag., Tokyo, 1986—, Indsl. Ontwerpen Mag., Rotterdam, The Netherlands, 1989-93; contbg. editor, columnist Met. Home Mag., N.Y.C., 1988-91, Graphis Mag., N.Y.C., 1993—; contbr. articles to profl. jours. Mem. Indsl. Design Soc. Am., Soc. Archtl. Historians. Office: Frog Design 1327 Chesapeake Ter Sunnyvale CA 94089

HOLTMAN, WILLIAM J., railroad company executive; b. 1921; married. Grad. in Metall. Engring., Colo. Sch. Mines, 1943, Met.E., 1947. With The Denver and Rio Grande Western R.R. Co., 1958—, chief mech. officer, to 1966, div. supt., 1966-68, v.p. exec. dept., 1968-69, exec. v.p., gen. mgr., 1969-76, pres., chief operating officer, 1976-78, chmn., pres., chief exec. officer, 1978—, dir.; pres., dir. Rio Grande Industries, Inc.; dir. 1st Nat. Bank of Denver. Served to 1st lt. USAF, 1943-46. Office: Rio Grande Western RR 1 Market Plz San Francisco CA 94105 also: St Louis Southwestern RY Co 1 Market Plz San Francisco CA 94105

HOLTON, WILLIAM CHESTER, engineer, consultant; b. Caldwell, Idaho, May 2, 1939; s. Chester Clayton and Margaret Ann (MacLaren) H.; m. Rhoberta Phaigh Romo, June 1, 1958 (div. Sept. 1976); children: William Lee, Robert Charles, Ronald Clayton. AS, Regents Coll., 1986. lic. FCC. Electronic technician Litton Industries, L.A., 1963-66; applications engr. 3M Co., Camarillo, Calif., 1966-74; program analyst USN, Port Magu, Calif., 1974-75; video supr. U. Calif., Santa Barbara, 1975-77; cons. Great Am. Tech. Services, L.A., 1977—. Creator digitally controlled screenings theater for Steven Spielberg at Universal Studios, first high speed sound-on-film editing suite in People's Republic of China, variable speed projection control system for Eddie Murphy. Mem. Soc. Motion Picture TV Engrs. (voting). Office: Great Am Tech Svcs 6711 Rohnerville Rd Hydesville CA 95547

HOLTORF, SUSAN CAROLINE, dietitian; b. Sunnyside, Wash., Oct. 21, 1955; d. David Alexander Strausz and Caroline Bressler (Gannon) Cerrillo; m. Paul Christian Holtorf, June 15, 1975; children: Ashley Caroline, Alexander Miles. BS in Home Econs., Wash. State U., 1977. Clin. dietitian Mercy Med. Ctr., San Diego, 1977-79; nutrition support team dietitian VA Med. Ctr., Salt Lake City, 1979-85; clin. dietitian VA Med. Ctr., Portland, Oreg., 1985—; instr. Oreg. Health Scis. U., Portland, 1985-93, sr. instr., 1993—. Mem. nutrition edn. com. Am. Heart Assn., Salt Lake City, 1983-85; nutrition com. Oreg. Diabetes Assn., Portland, 1986-88. Mem. Am. Dietetic Assn. (registered), Utah Dietetic Assn. (handbook com. 1980-85), S.W. Wash. Dietetic Assn., Portland Dietetic Assn. (pub. rels. com. 1988-90). Episcopalian. Office: VA Med Ctr 120-NH PO Box 1035 Portland OR 97207

HOLTZ, JOSEPH NORMAN, marketing executive; b. Matawan, N.J., Oct. 11, 1930; s. Joseph Antone and Catherine Martina (Crosby) H.; m. Irene Strano, July 15, 1951; children: Joseph Jr., Karl, Gary, Robert, Eric. AA, De Vry Tech. Inst., 1954; student, Monmouth Coll., 1955-56; BBA, Nat. U., 1988, MBA, 1989; grad., Realtor Inst. Lic. real estate agent Nat. Assn. Realtors, Cert. Factoring Specialist designation Internat. Factoring Inst., Cert. Mortgage Investor designation Nat. Mortgage Investors Inst. Engr. Bendix Aviation, Red Bank, N.J., 1952-56, Hughes Aircraft Co., L.A., 1956-73; pres. Jo-Rene Assocs., Orange, Calif., 1973-86; asst. v.p. Builders Sales Corp., Santa Ana, Calif., 1986-87; exec. v.p. The Lehnert Group, Irvine, Calif., 1987-88; pres. J.N. Holtz Assocs., Orange, 1988—; CEO Holtz Funding Group, Orange, 1994—; v.p., corp. broker Mortgage Outlet Corp., 1992-94; corp. broker Shancie Real Estate Corp., 1992-94. Com. mem. United Way, Santa Ana, 1987—. Mem. IEEE, Inst. Residential Mktg., Sales and Mktg. Coun., Nat. Assn. Factoring Profls., Nat. Real Estate and Mortgage Investors Assn., Phoenix Club, Am. Soc. for Quality Control. Republican. Home: 5045-2 E Almond Ave Orange CA 92669 Office: J N Holtz Assocs PO Box 10014 Santa Ana CA 92711-0014

HOLTZ, TOBENETTE, aerospace engineer; b. Rochester, N.Y., June 20, 1930; d. Marcus and Leah (Cohen) H.; m. Joseph Laurinovics, Dec. 25, 1964. BS in Aeronautical Engring., Wayne State U., 1958; MS in Aero/Astro Engring., Ohio State U., 1964; PhD, U. So. Calif., L.A., 1974. Sr. engr. North Am. Aviation, Columbus, Ohio, 1954-59; rsch. assoc. Ohio State U., Columbus, 1959-60; sr. engr. U. So. Calif. Rsch. Found., Pt. Mugu, 1960-62, Northrop Corp., Hawthorne, Calif., 1962-67; engring. specialist McDonnell Douglas Corp., Huntington Beach, Calif., 1967-75; staff engr. Acurex Corp., Mountain View, Calif., 1975-76; project mgr. Aerospace Corp., El Segundo, Calif., 1976-82; tech. mgr. TRW, Inc., San Bernardino, Calif., 1982—. Contbr. articles to profl. jours. Assoc. fellow AIAA (sect. vice chair 1980-82, 91-92, nat. tech. com. 1991-95, organizer nat. tech. confs. 1979, 86, 88, 94, Disting. Svc. award 1983). Office: TRW Inc PO Box 1310 San Bernardino CA 92402

HOLTZAPFEL PESANTE, PATRICIA KELLY, health facility executive; b. Madison, Wis., Jan. 29, 1948; d. Raymond Michael and Laura Margaret (Stegner) Kelly; m. Robert Adrian Bunker, Oct. 4, 1975 (div. June 1979); m. Raymond Paul Holtzapfel, Mar. 12, 1983 (div. Feb. 1992); m. Jose Patrick Pesante, June 19, 1993. RN, Ariz.; cert. pub. health nurse. Staff nurse Madison Gen. Hosp., 1970-72; bloodmobile staff nurse ARC, Madison, 1972-73; pub. health nurse Dane County Pub. Health Dept., Madison, 1973-75; field health nurse CIGNA Health Plan, Phoenix, 1975-84; dir. nursing Olsten Health Care, Phoenix, 1984-85; mgr. bus. Holtzapfel Phys. Therapy and Pain Control Clinic, Phoenix, 1985-89, bus. cons., 1989-92; supr. CIGNA Healthplan Ariz., Phoenix, 1989-92. Bd. dirs. Deer Valley Vocat. Arts Adv. Coun., Phoenix, 1986-89. Mem. The Exec. Female Assn., Ariz. Networking Council.

HOLYER, ERNA MARIA, adult education educator, writer, artist; b. Weilheim, Bavaria, Germany, Mar. 15, 1925; d. Mathias and Anna Maria (Goldhofer) Schretter; AA, San Jose Evening Coll., 1964; student San Mateo Coll., 1965-67, San Jose State U., 1968-69, San Jose City Coll., 1980-81; DLitt, World U., 1984; DFA (hon.), The London Inst. Applied Rsch., 1992; m. Gene Wallace Holyer, Aug. 24, 1957. Freelance writer under pseudonym Ernie Holyer, 1960—; tchr. creative writing San Jose (Calif.) Met. Adult Edn., 1968—; artist, 1958—. Exhibited in group shows Crown Zellerbach Gallery, San Francisco, 1973, 74, 76, 77; I.B.C. Gallery, San Francisco, 1978 (medal of Congress, 1988, 89, 92, 94, Congress Challenge trophy, 1990), L.A., 1981, Cambridge, Eng., 1992, Cambridge, Mass., 1993, San Jose, Calif., 1993, Edinburgh, Scotland, 1994. Recipient Woman of Achievement Honor cert. San Jose Mercury-News, 1973, 74, 75, Lefoli award for excellence in adult edn. instrn. Adult Edn. Senate, 1972, Women of Achievement awards League of Friends of the Santa Clara County Commn., San Jose Mercury News, 1987, various art awards. Mem. Nat. League Am. Pen Women Inc., Calif. Writers Club, World Univ. Roundtable (doctoral). Author: Rescue at Sunrise, 1965; Steve's Night of Silence, 1966; A Cow for Hansel, 1967; At the Forest's Edge, 1969; Song of Courage, 1970; Lone Brown Gull, 1971; Shoes for Daniel, 1974; The Southern Sea Otter, 1975; Sigi's Fire Helmet, 1975; Reservoir Road Adventure, 1982; Wilderness

Journey, 1985. Contbr. articles to various mags., newspapers, and anthologies. Home and Office: 1314 Rimrock Dr San Jose CA 95120-5611

HOLZBERLEIN, KURT W., cablevision news director; b. Meeker, Colo., July 14, 1962; s. John Monte and Sally Anne (Mohar) H. BA in Am. Studies, U. Notre Dame, 1985. Announcer Sta. KMKR, Meeker, 1980-86; vol. prodr. Sta. KBDI-TV, Denver, 1986-88; bur. reporter, anchor Sta. KREX-TV Network, Grand Junction, Colo., 1988-89; reporter, anchor Columbine Cablevision, Ft. Collins, Colo., 1989-91, news dir., 1991—. Recipient Cableace award for newscast Nat. Acad. Cable Programmers, 1993, 94, gen. reporting award for newscast AP, Denver, 1993. Mem. Soc. Profl. Journalists (award for gen. reporting and series Denver 1992), Radio and TV News Dirs. Assn. Office: Columbine Cablevision 1201 University Ave Fort Collins CO 80521-4554

HOLZBOG, THOMAS JERALD, architect, planner; b. Milw., Oct. 25, 1933; s. Walter Charles and Dorothy (Van Holten) H.; divorced; children: Jessica Jane, Arabella Laura. BArch, Yale U., 1960; M Urban Design, Harvard U., 1968. Registered architect, N.Y., Mass., Calif., Wis. Nev. Field supr. Walter C. Holzbog, Wis.; draftsman Paul Rudolph, New Haven, 1958-59; rschr., draftsman Candilis, Josic & Woods, Paris, 1960; deisgner draftsman Sir Leslie Martin, Cambridge, Eng., 1960-61; project designer Sir Denys Lasdun & Ptnrs., London, 1961-64; job capt. I. M. Pei & Ptnrs., N.Y.C., 1965-67; pres. T. J. Holzbog Architect, L.A. and Boston, 1967—; speaker, educator in field; adj. prof., lectr. Harvard U., Columbia U., Pratt Inst., R.I. Sch. Design, Tufts U., Calif. Poly. State U., UCLA; vis. critic various univs. Work exhibited and pub. in profl. publs. Co-founder, mem. Westwood Design Rev. Bd., 1989-91; mem. bd. advisors UCLA Extension, 1987-88; past chmn. Design Adv. Com., Lexington, Mass.; past mem. Hist. Dist. Commn., Lexington; past bd. dirs. Interfaith Housing Corp., Lexington; past mem. edn. and urban design com. Boston Soc. Architects; past mem. Mayor's Task Force on Urban Design, N.Y.C. Capt. U.S. Army, 1954-56. Recipient numerous design awards; Fulbright scholar, 1960. Mem. AIA (past chmn., co-founder L.A. Found., past chmn., co-founder student affiliate com.), Am. Inst. Cert. Planners, Am. Soc. Landscape Architects, Nat. Coun. Archtl. Registration Bds., Archtl. Assns. London, Nat. Inst. Archtl. Edn., Scarab, Sigma Chi. Home and Office: 1301 Warnall Ave Los Angeles CA 90024-5355

HOLZER, ERIC ROLAND, plastic surgeon; b. Switzerland, 1947. MD, Med. U. Geneve, 1977. Plastic surgeon Dameron Hosp., Stockton, Calif. Office: 4118 Donaldson Dr Stockton CA 95219*

HOLZER, THOMAS LEQUEAR, geologist; b. Lafayette, Ind., June 26, 1944; s. Oswald Alois and Ruth Alice (Lequear) H.; children: Holly Christine, Elizabeth Alice. BSE, Princeton U., 1965; MS, Stanford U., 1966, PhD, 1970. Asst. prof. geology U. Conn., Storrs, 1970-75; adj. environmentalist Griswold & Fuss, Manchester, Conn., 1973-75; research geol. U.S. Geol. Survey, Menlo Park, Calif., 1975-82, rsch. geologist, 1984-88, 93—; dep. asst. dir. rsch. U.S. Geol. Survey, Reston, Va., 1982-84, chief br. engring. seismology and geology, 1989-93; cons. assoc. prof. geology and environ. sci. Stanford U., 1994-95. Contbr. numerous articles to profl. jours. Coach Am. Youth Soccer Orgn., Palo Alto, Calif., 1979-82. Recipient Superior Svc. award U.S Geol. Survey, 1981, Outstanding Pub. Svc. award U.S. Geol. Survey, 1991. Fellow Geol. Soc. Am. (chmn. engring. geology divsn. 1988-89, councilor 1995-97, Disting. Svc. award 1995); mem. AAAS, Am. Geophys. Union, Assn. Groundwater Scientists and Engrs., Sigma Xi. Republican. Presbyterian. Home: PO Box 851 Palo Alto CA 94302-0851 Office: US Geol Survey 345 Middlefield Rd Menlo Park CA 94025-3561

HOM, RICHARD YEE, research engineer; b. Phoenix, July 26, 1950; s. Tommy Look and Betty (Mah) H.; BS in Engring. Sci. and Aero. and Aerospace Tech., Ariz. State U., 1973; m. Kathleen Chien; 1 child, Matthew Thomas Yee. Asst. engr. Sperry Flight System, Phoenix, 1973; sr. engr., composite tool engring. Boeing Comml. Airplane Co., Seattle, 1973-84; specialist engr. 1984-88, sr. specialist engr. R & D, metall. processing and advanced projects Boeing Aerospace Co., 1984-90, also automation tech.; with customer svcs. and airline support Boeing Comml. Airplane Group, 1990-91; prin. rsch. engr. metallics rsch. and devel. Boeing Def. and Space Group, 1991—. Mem. AIAA, SMA, Air Force Assn., Soc. Mfg. Engrs., Aircraft Owners and Pilots Assn., ASM Internat. Home: 28704 15th Ave S Federal Way WA 98003-3161 Office: Boeing Def and Space Group M/S 8J-74 PO Box 3999 # 74 Seattle WA 98124-2499

HOMAN, RALPH WILLIAM, finance company executive; b. Wilkes-Barre, Pa., June 7, 1951; s. Norman Ryan and Adelaide Bernice (Sandy) H.; m. Donna Marie Webb, Jan. 25, 1975. BS in Acctg., Wheeling Coll., 1977; MBA in Mktg., Nat. U., 1986. Paymaster Dravo Corp., Pitts., 1974-75; tax preparer H&R Block, Wheeling, W.Va., 1977; fin. services exec. NCR Credit Corp., Sacramento, 1977-84; leasing exec. CSB Leasing, Sacramento, 1984-85; pres. Convergent Fin. Svcs., Colorado Springs, Colo., 1985—; bd. dirs. Concord Coalition, Colorado Springs. Sponsor Harrison High Sch. Key Club; cons. Jr. Achievement, 1990—. Co-winner Name the Plane Contest Pacific Southwest Airlines, 1984. Mem. The 30/40 Something Social Club (founder, pres. Sedonna chpt.), Am. Assn. of Boomers (pres. Pikes Peak chpt. 1992-93), Toastmasters (treas. Oak Creek chpt. 1988-89), Kiwanis (sec. 1988-89, founder, chmn. adult soccer league), Concord Coalition (bd. dirs., pres. Colorado Springs chpt.). Home and Office: Convergent Fin Svcs 5720 Escapardo Way Colorado Springs CO 80917-3340

HOMAN, RICH, magazine editor. Exec. editor Road & Track, Newport Beach, Calif. Office: Road & Track 1499 Monrovia Ave Newport Beach CA 92663-2752

HOMESTEAD, SUSAN E. (SUSAN FREEDLENDER), psychotherapist; b. Bklyn., Sept. 20, 1937; d. Cy Simon and Katherine (Haas) Eichelbaum; m. Robert Bruce Randall, 1956 (div. 1960); 1 child, Bruce David; m. George Gilbert Zanetti, Dec. 13, 1962 (div. 1972); m. Ronald Eric Homestead, Jan. 16, 1973 (div. 1980); m. Arthur Elliott Freedlender, April, 1, 1995. BA, U. Miami-Fla., 1960; MSW, Tulane U., 1967. Diplomate Am. Bd. Clin. Social Work; Acad. Cert. Social Workers, 1971, LCSW, Va., Calif. Psychotherapist, cons., Richmond, Va., 1971—, Los Altos, Calif.; pvt. practice, cons. Piedmont Psychiatric Ctr., P.C. (formerly Psychol. Evaluation Rehab. Cons., Inc.), Lynchburg, Va., 1994—; cons. Family and Children's Svcs., Richmond, 1981—, Richmond Pain Clinic, 1983-84; Health Internat. Va., P.C., Lynchburg, 1984-86, Franklin St. Psychotherapy & Edn. Ctr, Santa Clara, Calif., 1988-90; pvt. practice, 1971—; Santa Clara County Children's Svc., 1973-75, 86-88; co-dir. asthma program Va. Lung Assn., Richmond, 1975-79, Loma Prieta Regional Ctr.; chief clin. social worker Med. Coll. Va., Va. Commonwealth U., 1974-79; field supr. 1980 Census, 1981-87. Contbr. articles to profl. jours. Active Peninsula Children's Ctr., Morgan Ctr., Coun. for Community Action Planning, Community Assn. for Retarded, Comprehensive Health Planning Assn. Santa Clara, Mental Health Commn., Children and Adolescent Target Group Calif., Women's Com. Richmond Symphony, Va. Mus. Theatre, mem. fin. com. Robb for Gov.; mem. adv. com. Va. Lung Assn.; mem. steering com. Am. Cancer Soc.(Va. div.), Epilepsy Found., Am. Heart Assn. (Va. div.), Cen. Va. Guild for Infant Survival. Mem. NASW, Va. Soc. Clin. Social Work, Inc. (charter mem., sec. 1975-78), Internat. Soc. Communicative Psychoanalysis & Psychotherapy, Am. Acad. Psychotherapists, Internat. Soc. for the Study of Multiple Personality and Dissociation, Am. Assn. Psychiatric Svcs. for Children.

HONAKER, JIMMIE JOE, lawyer; b. Oklahoma City, Jan. 21, 1939; s. Joe Jack and Ruby Lee (Bowen) H.; children: Jay Jimmie, Kerri Ruth. BA, Colo. Coll., 1963; JD, U. Wyo., 1966; MA, U. No. Colo., 1991; MS, U. Wyo., Laramie, 1995. Bar: Colo. 1966, U.S. Dist. Ct. Colo. 1966-94, U.S. Ct. Appeals (10th cir.) 1982. Sole practice Longmont, Colo., 1966-91. Incorporator Longmont Boys Baseball, 1969; chmn. Longmont City Charter Commn., 1973; chmn. ch. bd. 1st Christian Ch., Longmont, 1975, 76; chmn. North Boulder County unit Am. Cancer Soc., 1978, 79. Recipient Disting. Svc. award Longmont Centennial Yr., 1971; named Outstanding Young Man, Longmont Jaycees, 1973. Mem. Colo. Bar Assn. (interprofl. com. 1972-91), Christian Legal Soc., Nat. Wheelchair Basketball Assn. (cert.), Internat. Assn. Approved Basketball Ofcls. (cert.), Nat. Eagle Scout Assn., Ecol. Soc. Am., Colo. Mountain Club, Phi Alpha Delta. Address: PO Box 7 Laramie WY 82070-0007

HONAKER, RICHARD HENDERSON, lawyer; b. Laramie, Wyo., Mar. 10, 1951; s. Hayward E. and Faola I. (Henderson) H.; m. Shannon Kathleen Casey, Dec. 24, 1978; children: Heather, Harmony, Dustin. BA cum laude, Harvard U., 1973; JD, U. Wyo., 1976. Bar: Wyo. 1976, U.S. Dist. Ct. Wyo., 1976, U.S. Ct. Appeals (10th cir.) 1977, U.S. Supreme Ct. 1989. Asst. atty. gen. State of Wyo., Cheyenne, 1976-78, state pub. defender, 1979-81; ptnr. Honaker, Hampton & Newman, Rock Springs, Wyo., 1981—. Press sec. to Gov. of Wyo., 1978; mem. Wyo. State Ho. of Reps., Sweetwater County, 1986-93. Mem. Wyo. Bar Assn., Wyo. Trial Lawyers Assn. (v.p. 1985-86, pres. 1986), Assn. Trial Lawyers Am., Am. Bd. Trial Advocates (charter), Christian Legal Soc. Office: Honaker Hampton & Newman PO Box 1000 Rock Springs WY 82902-1000

HONDA, YOSHIO, computer company executive; b. 1945. With Fujitsu Am., Inc., San Jose, Calif., 1966—, Fujitsu Computer Packing Tech., San Jose, 1991—. Office: Fujitsu Computer Packing Tech 3811 Zanker Rd San Jose CA 95134-1402*

HONDL, EDELTRAUD A., retired psychiatrist; b. Cèsky Trêbova, Czech Republic, Jan. 8, 1939; came to the U.S., 1961; d. Josef and Emma (Blaschke) H.; m. Arthur A. Murray, Nov. 19, 1972; six stepchildren. AA, Holy Ghost Coll., 1962; BS, DePaul U., 1965; MD magna cum laude, Marquette U., 1968. Diplomate Am. Bd. Psychiatry. Resident in gen. psychiatry and child psychiatry U. Wash. Hosps., Seattle, 1969-73; med. dir. Mental Health North, Seattle, 1973-83; pvt. practice adult and child psychiatry Harvard Psychiat. Group, Seattle, 1983-95; cons. Child Devel. Ctr. Program, Seattle, 1974-80; med. dir. Luther Child Ctr., Everett, Wash., 1990-93. Regional dir. AMWA, Pacific N.W., 1979-90. Fellow Am. Psychiat. Assn. (treas. 1978-93), Wash. State Psychiat. Assn., Seattle Chpt. Psychiat. Assn., Am. Med. Women's Assn. (life), Wash. State Med. Assn. Democrat. Roman Catholic.

HONEYCHURCH, DENIS ARTHUR, lawyer; b. Berkeley, Calif., Sept. 17, 1946; s. Winston and Mary Martha (Chandler) H.; m. Judith Ann Poliquin, Oct. 5, 1969; children: Sean, James, Thomas. BA, UCLA, 1968; JD, U. Calif., San Francisco, 1972. Bar: Calif. 1972, U.S. Dist. Ct. (no. dist.) Calif. 1972, U.S. Ct. Appeals (9th cir.) 1972. Dep. pub. defender Sacramento County Calif., Sacramento, 1973-75; supervising asst. pub. defender Solano County, Fairfield, Calif., 1975-78; ptnr. Honeychurch & Finkas and predecessor firm, Fairfield, 1978—. Bd. dirs. Fairfield-Suisun Unified Sch. Dist., Fairfield, 1979-83, Solano Community Coll., Fairfield, 1985—; chmn. bd. dirs. Downtown Improvement Dist., Fairfield, 1980-82; active Dem. Ctrl. Com. Solano County, 1992—. Mem. ABA, Assn. Trial Lawyers Am., Nat. Assn. Criminal Def. Lawyers, Calif. Trial Lawyers Assn., Calif. Attys. Criminal Justice, Calif. Pub. Defenders Assn., Solano County Bar Assn. (pres. 1991), Calif. Bd. Legal Specialization (cert.), Nat. Bd. Trial Advocacy (cert.). Democrat. Office: Honeychurch & Finkas 823 Jefferson St Fairfield CA 94533-5513

HONEYCUTT, VAN B., computer services company executive; b. 1945. With Computer SciencesCorp., El Segundo, Calif., 1975—, past v.p., past pres. industry svcs. group, now pres., CEO, COO. Office: Computer Scis Corp 2100 E Grand Ave El Segundo CA 90245-5024

HONG, NORMAN G. Y., architect; b. Honolulu, May 5, 1947; s. Kwai Ing and Patricia Y.S. (Dye) H.; m. Lorna Sachiko Yano, Aug. 11, 1973; 1 child, Christopher. T.S.C. BArch, U. Hawaii, 1969. Registered architect, Hawaii. Designer, John Tatom Architect, Honolulu, 1969-71; assoc. Group 70 Inc., Honolulu, 1971-77, prin., 1977-80, ptnr., 1980-84, mng. ptnr., 1984-88, pres., chief operating officer, 1989-90, vice chmn., 1990—. Bd. dirs. Manpower Planning Agy. Honolulu, 1972; com. mem. Ann. Gov./Mayor's Prayer, Honolulu, 1984; mem. Mayor's Adv. Com. on Chinatown Gateway, 1987, mem. adv. bd. spl. design dists., 1989—; mem. Epephany Epis. Sch. Bd., 1989-91; mem. Haleiwa Spl. Design Adv. Com., 1986-87, Gov's Congress on Hawaii's Future, 1988; vice chmn., commr. Commn. on Culture and Arts, Honolulu, 1991—. Recipient C.W. Dickey award U. Hawaii, 1967, Cert. Exemplary Performance, Dept. Navy Pacific Divsn., 1984, Chief Engrs. Design Merit award, 1991. Mem. Constrn. Specifications Inst., AIA, Hawaii Soc. AIA (v.p. Hawaii 1987, pres. 1988, sec. Hawaii 1984-86, chmn. long range plan com. 1987, chmn. state conv., 1983, Design award Oahu chpt. 1993), Plaza Club, Honolulu Country Club, Rotary. Mem. Kaimuki Christian Church. Office: Group 70 Inc 925 Bethel St # 5 Honolulu HI 96813-4307

HONG, PATRICIA ANNE, nursing educator; b. Honolulu, Apr. 16, 1950; d. Samuel Kyung Sook and Mariko (Kutsunai) H.; m. Michael Grandinetti, June 30, 1979. BSN, U. Md., 1972; MA in Nursing, U. Wash., 1976. CCRN, AACN, clin. specialist ANCC. Instr. U. Wash., Seattle, 1976-79; office nurse Pulmonary Med. Assoc., Sacramento, 1979-80; mgr., statewide ADN Anchorage C.C., 1983-84; asst. prof. ADN program U. Alaska, Anchorage, 1984-91, assoc. prof., 1991—; nursing cons. Delaney, Wiles, Hayes, Reitman and Brubaker, Anchorage, 1990-91, Anderson, Holman and Houghton, Tacoma, 1989; mem. policy transition team for human svcs. State of Alaska, 1995. Contbr. author: Cardiac Care Nursing, 1981. Officer nurse corps USNR, 1972-79; officer USAFR, 1980—. Named Individual Mobilization Augmentee of Yr., Nurse Corp, ARPC, USAFR, Denver, 1990; recipient traineeship for grad. study USPHS, Seattle, 1974. Mem. AACN, Alaska Nurses Assn. (pres. 1989-93), Sigma Theta Tau. Democrat. Presbyterian. Office: U Alaska 3211 Providence Dr Anchorage AK 99508-4614

HONGO, FLORENCE MAKITA, educational association administrator; b. Cressey, Calif., Nov. 21, 1928; d. Haruzo and Shizu M.; m. Andrew Yoshiwara, Oct. 28, 1950 (div. May 1974); children: Janice Lee, Kim Ann, Jon Noel, Sue Ellen, J. Paul; m. Masanori Hongo, Dec. 25, 1981. BA in History, San Francisco State U., 1972. Gen. mgr. Asian Am. Curriculum Project, Inc., San Mateo, Calif., 1970—; instr. humanities & ethnic studies dept. Coll. San Mateo, 1978-92; adv. specialist title IV San Mateo City Elem. Sch. Dist., 1969-72; cons., lectr. and presenter in field. Contbr. chpts. to books and articles to profl. jours. Office: AACP Inc 234 Main St PO Box 1587 San Mateo CA 94401

HONGSERMEIER, MARTIN KARL, software and systems architect, consultant; b. Grand Island, Nebr., Aug. 13, 1953; s. Leo Albert and Ingeborg Albine Hongsermeier; m. Fana Renē Gudde, Oct. 10, 1990; 1 child, Karl. BS in Geophys. Engring., Colo. Sch. Mines, Golden, 1978. Well log computer programmer Birdwell div. Seismograph Svc. Corp., Tulsa, 1979-85; prin. programmer analyst Teledyne Brown Engring., Lawton, Okla., 1985-90; sr. mem. tech. staff Nichols Rsch. Corp., Huntsville, Ala., 1990-91; sr. software engr. Codar Tech., Inc., Longmont, Colo., 1991—; rschr. Bit$mith, Lawton, Colo., 1982-92; advisor U.S. Army Field Artillery Tactical Data Sys., 1985—. Bd. dirs. Oak Ridge Property Owners Assn., Kingston, Okla., 1985-86. Mem. IEEE Computer Soc., Assn. for Computing Machinery. Home: PO Box 1461 Longmont CO 80502-1461 Office: Codar Tech Inc 2405 Trade Center Ave Longmont CO 80503-7602

HONIG, BILL, state educational administrator; b. San Francisco, Apr. 23, 1937; s. Louis and Miriam (Anixter) H.; m. Nancy Catlin, June 2, 1973; children: Michael, Carolyn, Steven, Jonathan. BA, U. Calif., Berkeley, 1958, JD, 1963; MA, San Francisco State U., 1972. Bar: Calif. 1964; cert. tchr., Calif. Clk. Calif. Supreme Ct., 1963-64; atty. Calif. Dept. Fin., 1964-67; assoc. Pettit & Martin, San Francisco, 1967-71; tchr. San Francisco Unified Sch. Dist., 1972-76; dir. Staff Devel. Project, San Francisco, 1977-79; supt. Reed Union Elem. Sch. Dist., Tiburon, Calif., 1979-82; supt. pub. instrn. State of Calif., Sacramento, 1983—; mem. Calif. State Bd. Edn., 1975-82, past officer, pres. exec. sec. 1982; regent U. Calif., 1983—; trustee Calif. State Colls. and Univs., 1983—. Author: (with others) Handbook for Planning an Effective Reading Program, 1983; Last Chance for Our Children: How You Can Help Save Our Schools, 1985; contbr. articles to profl. jours. Mem. Carnegie Forum on Edn., PTA, YMCA, Nat. Commn. on Children. 2d lt. U.S. Army, 1958-59. Mem. C. of C. (state edn. com.), Order of Coif. Jewish. Office: Sch Edn San Francisco State U 1100 Holloway Ave San Francisco CA 94132-2728

HONNING, BENGT EUGENE, chiropractic physician, consultant, biochemist; b. Sundsvall, Sweden, Sept. 8, 1927; came to U.S., 1931; s. Walfrid Eugen and Julia Margareta (Vestine) H.; m. Mary Lou Neely, Feb. 7, 1948; children: Sharon Ann, Dale Eldred. BS, Calif. State U., 1964; MS, Wm. Darren U., 1965, PhD in Biochemistry, 1967; LLB, Blackstone Sch. Lab., 1978; DC, L.A. Coll. Chiropractic, 1969. Diplomate Nat. Bd. Chiropractic Examiners. Biochemist Am. Med. Labs., L.A., 1956-69; chiropractor, neurologist Long Beach, Calif., 1969—; biochemist Biochem. Consultants, Long Beach, 1967-88; prof. biochemistry L.A. Coll. Chiropractic, 1967-69. Author: Self Winding Clock Company, 1980; contbr. articles to profl. jours. Chief libr. Self Winding Clock Assn., Long Beach, 1979—. Served with USN, 1945-47. Mem. Am. Chem. Soc., Am. Soc. Clin. Pathologists, Am. Astron. Soc., Nat. Assn. of Watch and Clock Collectors (cert. of merit 1993, pres. 1980-84). Lutheran. Home: 1161 E Marcellus St Long Beach CA 90807-1609 Office: 1165 E San Antonio Dr Ste A Long Beach CA 90807-2374

HOOD, EDWARD, data processing executive; b. L.A., Nov. 5, 1954; s. Thomas Leslie and Mary (Jewell) H. AA in Adminstrn. of Justice, L.A. City Coll., 1977; BA in Phys. Edn., Calif. State U., L.A., 1980. Ordained to ministry, Bapt. Ch., 1983. Dir. pub. rels. and fin. Greater Revelation Bapt. Ch., L.A., 1979-83, assoc. minister, 1981-92; assoc. minister Gospel Truth Ch., L.A., 1981-84; owner Compusys, L.A., 1989—; chmn. and pres. Video Documentary, L.A., 1988—; asst. prin. and tchr. Grace Luth. Christian Elem. Sch., L.A., 1990-91; pastor Bright and Morning Star Cmty. Christian Ch., San Bernardino, 1992—; athletic and audio-visual equip. person Nat. Youth Sports Program, summers 1983-90; athletic equip. attendant II, Calif. State U., L.A., 1981-90, part-time lectr., 1989-90; substitute instructional aide San Bernardino County, Calif., 1992—. Author: The Philosophy "Paradoxism:; creator "Black Jesus or Compassion collection". Pres. Menlo Ave. Block Club Neighborhood Watch, L.A., 1984-87; asst. coach "B" football, instr. K-coll., Manual Arts High Sch., 1979. With USMC, 1972-74. Democrat. Home: N75 8505 Mulberry Ave Apt L Fontana CA 92335-2935

HOOD, GARY ALLEN, curator, arts consultant; b. Wichita, Kans., Oct. 22, 1943; s. H. Leroy and Avie Emeline (Harris) H.; m. Linda Lee Boose, April 8, 1966; children: Bethina, Carina, Denae, Allen. BAE, Wichita State U., 1967, MA, 1972, MFA, 1975. Curatorial asst. Walker Art Ctr., Mpls., 1972-73; from asst. curator to sr. curator Wichita State U., 1973-90; arts & exhibits dir. Mus. Southwest, Midland, Tex., 1990-93; curator of exhibits Inst. Am. Indian Arts Mus., Santa Fe, 1993-95; writer, arts cons., 1995—; arts cons. Kans. Arts Commn., Topeka, 1974-77, 89, U. Santa Clara Seminars, 1974-76, Kans. City (Mo.) Artists Coalition, 1986, Indian Ctr., Wichita, 1980, 89, Anderson DeBartoco Pan, Tucson, 1994-95, No. Navajo Med. Ctr., Shiprock, N.Mex., 1994-95. Author: (catalogues) 20th Century Sculpture, 1984, Majesty in Motion: Waugh, 1988, Paintings of Eisenhower, 1989, Silent Partner: Schmidt, 1993; (books) Plains Indian Art, 1995, Southwest Indian Art, 1995. Capt. U.S. Army, 1966-69. Recipient fellow Ford Found., 1973-75, NEPDA, USDE, 1971-72; grantee Ford Found., 1972-73; scholar Internat. Order of the King, 1970-71. Mem. Am. Assn. Mus., Nat. Art Edn. Assn., Choctaw Nation of Okla. Home: 1857 Camino Lumbre Santa Fe NM 87505-5631

HOOD, MICHAEL JAMES, theatre educator; b. San Bernardino, Calif., Nov. 29, 1946; s. Howell Badley and Bette B. (Cole) H.; m. Katherine Elizabeth Shryock, Aug. 4, 1968; children: Molly Lorraine, Cole Southford. BA in Theatre, Ariz. State U., 1972; MA in Drama and Communications, U. New Orleans, 1975, MFA in Drama and Communications, 1975. Cert. tchr. of stage combat. Asst. prof. theatre and speech U. Alaska, Anchorage, 1976-80, chair, assoc. prof. theatre and speech, 1980-84, assoc. dean Coll. Art and Scis., 1984-87, chair, prof. theatre and dance, 1987—; pres. N.W. Drama Conf. Inc., Monmouth, Oreg.,1988-92; pres. Alaska Theatre of Youth, Anchorage, 1989—. Contbr. articles to profl. jours. With USN, 1964-67. Recipient Outstanding Direction awards Am. Coll. Theater Festival, 1982, 84, 88, 92; N.W. Drama Conf. Pres.'s award. 1994. Mem. Soc. Am. Fight Dirs., Assn. Theatre in Higher Edn., Assn. for Canadian Studies in U.S. Home: 1942 N Salem Dr Anchorage AK 99508-5181 Office: U Alaska 3211 Providence Dr Anchorage AK 99508-4614

HOOD, PAUL, reservoir engineer; b. Barton-on-Sea, Hants., Eng., Mar. 18, 1948; came to U.S., 1987; s. Robert James and Olga Margaret (Lark) H.; m. Gillian Patricia Eisele, Nov. 30, 1974 (div. May 1979); 1 child, Miriam Eleanor Eisele; m. Linda Dee Stafford, Oct. 27, 1989 (div. Oct. 1991); children: Sonya Ray, Tasha Marie; m. Mary Jane Saxton, June 28, 1992. BSc in Math. Physics, Birmingham (Eng.) U., 1969; MSc in Civil Engring., Swansea (Wales) U., 1972, PhD in Civil Engring., 1974. Rsch. asst. U. Wales, Swansea, 1972-74; rsch. fellow U. Reading, U.K., 1974-75; rsch. programmer Seismograph Svc. Ltd., Keston, Kent, U.K., 1975-77; rsch. geophysicist British Petroleum, London, 1978-80; staff reservoir engr. British Petroleum, various locations, 1980-89; prin. cons. British Petroleum, Houston, 1990-92; mgr. reservoir engring. Sci. Software Intercomp, Denver, 1992-95; ind. reservoir engring. cons., 1995—. Contbr. articles to profl. jours., chpts. to books. G.B. rep. NATO CIOR Competition, Oslo, 1973, Athens, Greece, 1974. Capt. Brit. Army Res., 1968-83. Mem. Soc. Petroleum Engrs., Soc. Exploration Geophysicists, European Assn. Exploration Geophysicists (Van Weelden award 1978).

HOOD, ROBERT H., JR., aircraft manufacturing company executive. P-res.McDonnell Douglas Missile Systems Co. unit McDonnell Douglas Corp., Long Beach, Calif., until 1989, pres. Douglas Aircraft Co. unit, 1989—. Office: McDonnell Douglas Corp Douglas Aircraft Co Unit 3855 N Lakewood Blvd Long Beach CA 90846-0003

HOOK, RALPH CLIFFORD, JR., business educator; b. Kansas City, Mo., May 2, 1923; s. Ralph Clifford and Ruby (Swanson) H.; m. Joyce Fink, Jan. 20, 1946; children—Ralph Clifford III, John Gregory. BA, U. Mo., 1947, MA, 1948; PhD, U. Tex., 1954. Instr. U. Mo., 1947-48; asst. prof. Tex. A&M U., 1948-51; lectr. U. Tex., 1951-52; co-owner, mgr. Hook Buick Co., also Hook Truck & Tractor Co., Lee's Summit, Mo., 1952-58; assoc. prof. U. Kansas City, 1953-58; dir. Bur. Bus. Research and Services, Ariz. State U., 1958-66, prof. mktg., 1960-68; dean Coll. Bus. Adminstrn., U. Hawaii, 1968-74; prof. mktg. U. Hawaii, 1974—; vis. Disting. prof. N.E. La. U., 1979; dir. Hook Bros. Corp., Hilo Coast Processing Co. Ltd., Pan Pacific Inst. Ocean Scis., Mauna Loa Macadamia Ptnrs., ltd. partnerships; mem. Nat. Def. Exec. Res., Dept. Commerce. Author: (with others) The Management Primer, 1972, Life Style Marketing, 1979, Marketing Service, 1983; contbr. (with others) monograph series Western Bus. Roundup; founder, moderator monograph series Western Bus. Roundup radio series, 1958-68. Bd. dirs. Jr. Achievement Hawaii; trustee Tokai U. Honolulu Ctr., 1987—. Served to 1st lt. F.A. AUS, 1943-46; col. Res. Recipient alumni citation of merit U. Mo. Coll. Bus. and Pub. Adminstrn., 1969; Distinguished Service award Nat. Def. Transp. Assn., 1977, God and Service award United Meth. Ch./Boy Scouts Am., 1986; named to Faculty Hall Fame Ariz. State U. Coll. Bus. Assn., 1977, Hawaii Transp. Hall of Fame, 1986. Fellow Internat. Coun. for Small Bus. (pres. 1963); mem. Hawaii World Trade Assn. (pres. 1973-74), Am. Mktg. Assn. (v.p. 1965-67, pres. Central Ariz. chpt. 1960-61, pres. Honolulu chpt. 1991-92), Western Assn. Collegiate Schs. Bus. (pres. 1972-73), Sales and Mktg. Execs. Internat. (life mem.), Acad. Internat. Bus., Nat. Def. Transp. Assn. (Hawaii v.p. 1978-82), Newcomen Soc. N. Am. (Hawaii chmn.), Pi Sigma Epsilon (v.p. for edn. programs 1990-94), Mu Kappa Tau (sec.-treas. 1991-94, v.p. 1994—), Beta Gamma Sigma, Omicron Delta Kappa, Beta Theta Pi, Delta Sigma Pi (gold coun.). United Methodist. Home: 311 Ohua Ave Apt 1104D Honolulu HI 96815-3658 Office: U Hawaii Coll Bus Adminstrn 2404 Maile Way Bldg C Honolulu HI 96822-2223

HOOKER, JO, interior designer; b. Evanston, Ill., Dec. 13, 1932; d. Armand Francis and Josephine Margaret (Daus) Conto; m. Donald E. Hooker, Feb. 11, 1956 (div. 1975); children: Elizabeth Ann Hooker Gilbertson, Kathryn Maura Hooker. BFA, U. Ill., 1955; postgrad., Ariz. State U., 1972-76. Cert. Nat. Coun. for Interior Design. Interior designer Barrows Design Studio, Phoenix, 1976-94; interior designer, owner Jo Hooker Design Assocs., Scottsdale, Ariz., 1994—. Designer showcases for Phoenix Home and Garden, 1986, 87, 91. Mem. Am. Soc. Interior Designers (profl.; Model Home award Ariz. North chpt. 1985). Office: Jo Hooker Design Assocs 6615 N Scottsdale Rd Scottsdale AZ 85250-4421

HOOPER, CATHERINE EVELYN, developmental engineering senior; b. Bklyn., Nov. 10, 1939; d. Frederick Charles Jr. and Catherine Veronica (Heaney) Podeyn; m. Melvyn Robert Lowney, Nov. 30, 1957 (div. 1970); children: Denise Lowney Andrade, Michele Lowney Budris; m. William White Hooper, Sept. 21, 1974. Student, San Jose (Calif.) City Coll., 1969, De Anza Coll., 1980. Insp. Amelco Semiconductor, Mountain View, Calif., 1966-68; lab. technician Fairchild R & D, Palo Alto, Calif., 1968-73; sr. lab. technician Varian Cen. Rsch., Palo Alto, 1973-84; sr. devel. engr. Hughes Rsch. Labs., Malibu, 1984—. Contbr. articles to profl. jours. Pres. Conejo Valley chpt. Nat. Women's Polit. Caucus., 1994—. Mem. Am. Vacuum Soc., Materials Rsch. Soc., Grad. Women in Sci. (L.A. pres. 1990-92), Internat. Soc. Optical Engrs., Sigma Xi (sec. 1987-90, 94). Office: Hughes Rsch Labs 3011 Malibu Canyon Rd Malibu CA 90265-4737

HOOPER, ROGER FELLOWES, architect; b. Southampton, N.Y., Aug. 18, 1917; s. Roger Fellowes and Justine Van Rensselaer (Barber) H.; m. Patricia Bentley, Aug. 10, 1946; children: Judith Bayard Teresi, Rachel Bentley Zingg, Roger Fellowes III. AB, Harvard U., 1939, MArch, 1948. Registered architect, Calif., Wash. Ptnr. Malone & Hooper, San Francisco, 1949-60; ptnr., pres. Hooper Olmsted & Emmons, San Francisco, 1964-79; chmn. Hooper Olmsted & Hrovat, San Francisco, 1980—. Bd. mgr. Marin YMCA, San Rafael, Calif.; bd. dirs., pres. Marin Conservation League, San Rafael. Lt. comdr. USNR, 1941-45, WWII. Mem. AIA. Office: Hooper Olmsted & Hrovat 77 Water St San Francisco CA 94133-1813

HOOPES, SIDNEY LOU, educational association administrator; b. Monterey, Calif., Oct. 24, 1944; d. Jack Sidney Wayne Combs and Alta Virginia (Lane) Combs-Snow; m. Dan Fredrick Hoopes, Oct. 11, 1969; children: Rachel Virginia, Sarah Elizabeth. BSBA in Mktg., U. Ark., 1964. Market rschr. Procter & Gamble, Cin., 1964-65; asst. press sec. U.S. Senator J. W. Fulbright, Washington, 1966-68; adminstr. regional office Tex. Chapparal Basketball Team, Lubbock, 1970-71; office adminstr., sec. Tex. Tech. U., Lubbock, 1971-72; office adminstr. Hoopes Law Office, Idaho Falls, Idaho, 1973-82; cons. mktg. and advt. Idaho Falls, 1983—; field rep. to Richard H. Stallings U.S. Congressman; exec. dir. Edn. Found., Idaho Falls, 1994—. Environ. educator Sch. Dist. #91, Idaho Falls, 1982-86; treas. Bonneville County Dem. Party, 1975-76, sec., 1988—; chief fund raiser Yellowstone Nat. Park Inst., 1983-84; bd. dirs. Idaho Falls Opera Theatre, 1984—; dist. field. mgr. U.S. Ho. of Reps. in 2d Congl. Dist. of Idaho. Named One of Outstanding Young Women Dems. in Idaho, 1975; proclaimed Sidney Hoopes Appreciation Day, Idaho Falls Opera Theatre, 1989. Mem. Greater Yellowstone Coalition (charter). Episcopalian. Home: 1950 Alan St Idaho Falls ID 83404-5722

HOOPS, HERM, park ranger, educator. BS in Edn., U. Vt., 1964-68. Public use specialist U.S. Fish and Wildlife Svc. Charels Russell Refuge, Lewiston, Mont., 1977-80; environ. edn. specialist Gateway Nat. Recreation Area Nat. Park System, N.Y.C., 1980-84; interpretive specialist Rocky Mt. Region Office Nat. Park System, Denver, 1984-87; dist. naturalist Dinosaur Nat. Monument Nat. Park System, Jansen, Utah, 1987-94; planner Wayside Exhibits, 1987—; leader Environ. Prlgrams, 1970—; river runner W Wild Rivers, 1964—. Author of park visitor information and materials, contbr. articles to profl. jours. Office: Dinosaur Nat Monument PO Box 128 Jensen UT 84035-0128

HOOPS, WILLIAM JAMES, clergyman; b. Welch, Okla., June 10, 1957; s. Paul Raymond and Bertha Lue (Stillwell) H.; m. Susan Denise Towers, May 12, 1983; 1 child, Robert Paul. BA, Okla. Bapt. U., 1983; MDiv, Golden Gate Sem., 1987. Ordained to ministry So. Bapt. Ch., 1987. Ministerial intern 1st Bapt. Ch., Concord, Calif., 1984-87; pastor 1st Bapt. Ch., Marina, Calif., 1987-91; chaplain USAFR, Travis AFB, Calif., 1975—, Fed. Bur. Prisons, Lompoc, Calif., 1991—. Producer TV documentary Insights, 1986-87. Bible tchr. 1st So. Bapt. Ch., Lompoc, 1991—. Capt. USAFR, 1975—. Mem. Calif. So. Bapt. Conv. (revival steering com. 1988-90), Cen. Coast Bapt. Assn. (vice moderator 1987-88, dir. evangelism 1988-91), Pacific Coast Bapt. Assn., Air Force Assn., Res. Officers Assn., Lompoc Fed. Correctional Instn. Employees Club (sec. 1991-92), Cen. Coast Ministerial Alliance (pres. 1988-89).

HOOVER, DONALD BRUNTON, geophysicist, gemologist; b. Cleve., June 17, 1930; s. Paul Leslie and Florence (Brunton) H.; m. Lucille Elizabeth Smith, Jan. 22, 1977. BS, Case Inst. Tech., Cleve., 1952; MSE, U. Mich., 1953; DSc, Colo. Sch. Mines, Golden, 1966. Registered profl. engr., Ohio. Seismic trainee Gulf Rsch. & Devel. Co., Harmarville, Pa., 1953; engr. Gulf Rsch. & Devel. Co., 1956-58; geophysicist U.S. Geol. Survey, Denver, 1960—; advisor geophysics Departmento Nacional de Producao Mineral, Rio de Janeiro, 1969-72; U.S. rep. in geophysics Pan Am. Inst. Geography and History, Mexico City, 1988-90. Author: Topaz; contbr. articles to profl. jours. With U.S. Army, 1954-56. Recipient U.S. Geol. Survey superior performance award, 1990. Fellow Gemmological Assn. Gt. Britain; mem. AAAS, Soc. Exploration Geophysicists (workshop organizer 1989), Assn. Exploration Geochemists, Colo. Soc. for Natural Hazards Rsch. (pres. 1976), Mineral. Soc. Am., Gemmological Assn. (U.K.), Colo. Gemmological Assn. (pres. 1984, 93), Gemmological Inst. Am. Alumni Assn. Office: US Geol Survey PO Box 25046 Denver CO 80225-0046

HOOVER, GEORGE SCHWEKE, architect; b. Chgo., July 1, 1935; s. George Milton and Antoinette (Schweke) H.; children: Sandra Jean, Ranya Sue; m. Mary Elizabeth Benoit, June 6, 1987. B.Arch., Cornell U., 1958. Registered architect, Colo., Calif., Tex., Minn., Ala., Tenn. Draftsman Holabird Root and Burgee, Chgo., 1957; Designer James Sudler Assocs., Denver, 1961-62; architect Ream, Quinn Assocs., Denver, 1962-65, Muchow Assocs., Denver, 1965-76; prin. Hoover Berg Desmond, Denver, 1976—; tenured prof. architecture, coll. Architecture and Planning, U. Colo.; vis. lectr. U. N.Mex., Okla. State U., Harvard U. Principal works include: Douglas County Adminstrn. Bldg., Light of the World Cath. Ch., U. Colo. Bldg., Denver, Denver Diagnostic and Reception Ctr., Labs. for Atmospheric and Space Physics, U. Colo., Boulder, Colo., Colo. Acad. Master Plan, U. Ariz. Engrng. Complex Master Plan, Multipurpose Arena, Nat. Western Stockshow, Nat. Wild Animal Rsch. Ctr., Colo. State U., Conf. Ctr.; Storage Tech. Corp., Aerospace & Mechanical Engrng. Bldg. U. Az., Environ. and Natural Resources Bldg. U. Az., Master Plan Cummins Power Generation Group Hdqs., Fridley, Minn., Master Plan Fleetguard and Mfg. Plant, Cookeville, Tenn.; finalist Denver Cen. Libr. Competition, 1991; exhbn. first ten yrs. of work Gund Hall Gallery, Grad. Sch. Design, Harvard U., 1986; mem. editorial bd. Avant Garde. Served to lt. (j.g.) USN, 1958-61. Recipient 1st design award Progressive Architecture, 1972, citation, 1974, design award, 1984, 87, Charles Goodwin Sands Medal for Excellence in design Tau Beta Pi; named An Outstanding Young Architect, Archtl. Record, 1974, Fed. Design Achievement award, 1984, Honor award Interfaith Forum on Religion, Art, and Arch., 1986; Tau Sigma Delta medal, 1991. Fellow AIA (steering com., Pitts. Corning award 1989, nat. honor award 1975, 83, 90, Firm of Yr. award Colo. chpt. 1991, Regional Firm of Yr. award 1992, Architect of Yr. award Colo. chpt. 1995); Nat. Acad. Design; mem. Nat. Com. Design (steering com., chmn. awards task group 1989-92), Nat. Com. Archtl. Edn. (steering com. 1990-92). Episcopalian. Home: 320 Humboldt St Denver CO 80218-3934 Office: Hoover Berg Desmond 1645 Grant St Denver CO 80203-1601

HOOVER, PEARL ROLLINGS, nurse; b. LeSueur, Minn., Aug. 24, 1924; d. William Earl and Louisa (Schickling) Rollings; m. Roy David Hoover, June 19, 1948 (dec. 1987); children: Helen Louise, William Robert (dec.). Grad. in nursing, U. Minn., 1945, BS in Nursing, 1947; MS in Health Sci., Calif. State U., Northridge, 1972. Dir. affiliate nursing sch. Mooselake (Minn.) State Hosp., 1948-49; nursing instr. Anchor Hosp., County Hosp., St. Paul, 1949-51; student nurse supr. and instr. Brentwood VA Hosp., L.A., 1951-52; sch. nurse L.A. Unified City Schs., 1963-91, substitute sch. nurse, 1991-95; part-time sch. nurse L.A. Unified City Schs., 1991-95, Van Nuys (Calif.) Mid. Sch., 1992-93. Camp nurse United First Meth. Ch., winter and summer past 35 yrs. Mem. L.A. Coun. Sch. Nurses, Calif. Sch. Nurses Orgn. Democrat. Methodist. Home: 17851 Lull St Reseda CA 91335-2237

HOOVER, ROBERT CLEARY, retired bank executive; b. Highland Park, Ill., July 26, 1928; s. Howard Earl and Dorothy (Higgs) H.; m. Beatrice Leona Borroughs, June 21, 1949 (div.); children: Catherine, Robert C. II, Holly; m. Nancy Ellen Pitman, July 25, 1959 (div.); children: John, Elizabeth, Courtney; m. Cecilia Susan Flournoy, July 3, 1981; 1 child, Whitney Suzanne. BA, U. Calif., Berkeley, 1950. Asst. advt. mgr. Hoover Co., North Canton, Ohio, 1951-54; v.p., asst. gen. mgr. Golden State Linen Svc., Oakland, Calif., 1954-61; asst. mgr. Wells Fargo Bank, San Francisco, 1961-66; v.p. Bank Calif. Assn., San Francisco, 1966-84, v.p., spl. asst. to chmn. bd. and chief exec. officer, 1984-94; ret. Bd. mem. Providence Hosp., Oakland, 1985-91, Bay Area Tumor Inst., 1975—. Mem. Am. Inst. Banking, Naval War Coll. Found. (life), Navy League United States (life), Naval Order U.S. (life), Bohemian Club, Claremont Country Club, Pacific Union Club. Republican. Episcopalian. Home: 46 Sotelo Ave Piedmont CA 94611-3535

HOOVER, WILLIAM R(AY), computer service company executive; b. Bingham, Utah, Jan. 2, 1930; s. Edwin Daniel and Myrtle Tennessee (McConnell) H.; m. Sara Elaine Anderson, Oct. 4; children—Scott, Robert, Michael, James, Charles. B.S., M.S., U. Utah. Sect. chief Jet Propulsion Lab., Pasadena, Calif., 1954-64; v.p. Computer Scis. Corp., El Segundo, Calif., 1964-69, pres., 1969-94, chmn. bd., 1972-95, also former CEO. *

HOPE, DOUGLAS OLERICH, newspaper editor; b. Chgo., Aug. 31, 1934; s. Daniel Kelly and Islea Margaret (Olerich) H.; m. Suzanne Edwina Boehm, 1954 (div. May 1963); 1 child, Douglas A.; m. Eileen G. Turney, June 29, 1963; children: Ruthann G., Francesca C. BA in Communications, U. Wash., 1958, BA in Russian Area Studies, 1959. City editor, asst. mng. editor San Gabriel Valley Daily Tribune, W. Covina, Calif., 1965-67; editor Oxnard Press-Courier, Oxnard, Calif., 1967-69; asst. mng. editor Sacramento Bee, 1977-80; night mng. editor Virginian-Pilot, Norfolk, 1980-82; asst. mng. editor San Diego Union, 1984-86; exec. editor Santa Barbara (Calif.) News Press, 1986-87; deputy mng. editor San Diego Union, 1987-92; mng. editor San Diego Union-Tribune, 1992-95, sr. editor adminstrn., 1995—. Mem. Am. Soc. Newspaper Editors, Calif. Soc. Newspaper Editors, Phi Beta Kappa. Office: Union Tribune Pub Co 350 Camino De La Reina San Diego CA 92108-3003

HOPE, FRANK LEWIS, JR., retired architect; b. San Diego, Apr. 10, 1930; s. Frank Lewis and Marion (Bullock) H.; m. Barbara Lee Prichard, Dec. 20, 1952; children—Gretchen Lynn, Gail A. Metzger, Carolyn Hoffos, Frank Leland, Jacqueline. B. Arch., U. Calif., Berkeley, 1952. Registered architect, Calif. Pres. Frank L. Hope & Assocs., San Diego, 1955-78; chmn. Hope Cons. Group, San Diego, 1978—; owner, pres., chief exec. officer Hope Design Group, San Diego; dir. Security Pacific Nat. Bank, Los Angeles, 1978. Chmn. San Diego Unified Port Dist., 1975; bd. dirs. San Diegans Inc., 1975; regent U. Calif.-Berkeley, 1984—. Served to 1st lt. U.S. Army, 1953-55. Fellow AIA (pres. San Diego council 1968, Calif. council, 1972); mem. Nat. Inst. Architecture (bd. dirs.), San Diego C. of C. (bd. dirs., pres. 1981). Republican. Roman Catholic. Clubs: San Diego Yacht (commodore), San Diego Country. Office: Hope Architects & Engineers 3938 Santa Nella Pl San Diego CA 92130-2288

HOPE, GERRI DANETTE, telecommunications management executive; b. Sacramento, Feb. 28, 1956; d. Albert Gerald and Beulah Rae (Bane) Hope. AS, Sierra Coll., Calif., 1977; postgrad. Okla. State U., 1977-79. Instructional asst. San Juan Sch. Dist., Carmichael, Calif., 1979-82; telecomm. supr. Delta Dental Svc. of Calif., San Francisco, 1982-85; telecomm. coordinator Farmers Savs. Bank, Davis, Calif., 1985-87; telecomm. officer Sacramento Savs. Bank, 1987-95; owner GDH Enterprises, 1993—; telecomm. analyst II dept. ins. State Calif., 1995—. founder Custom Label Designer, Sacramento; mem. telecomm. adv. panel Golden Gate U., Sacramento; lectr. in field. Mem. NAFE, Telecomm. Assn. (v.p. membership com. Sacramento Valley chpt., 1993), Am. Philatelic Soc., Sacramento Philatelic Assn., Errors, Freaks and Oddities Club, Philatelic Collectors. Republican. Avocations: writing, computers, philately, animal behavior, participating in Christian ministry. Home: 3025 U St Antelope CA 95843-2513

HOPKIN, JOHN BARTON, publisher, editor; b. Evanston, Ill., Mar. 23, 1952; s. Arthur McMurrin and Jean (Delaney) H.; m. Janet Dawn Gillies, Apr. 30, 1987; 1 child, Shane. BA magna cum laude, Harvard U., 1974; BA in Music Edn., San Francisco State U., 1981. Tchr. Holy Trinity Secondary Sch., Kingston, Jamaica, 1974-76; tchr., performing musician pvt. practice, Port Reyes Station, Calif., 1976-78; instr. Jamaica Sch. Music, Kingston, 1978-79; tchr. Millbrook (N.Y.) Sch., 1981-83; publisher, editor Experimental Musical Instruments, Nicasio, Calif., 1984—. Home and Office: Experimental Musical Instruments PO Box 784 Nicasio CA 94946

HOPKINS, CECILIA ANN, business educator; b. Havre, Mont., Feb. 17, 1922; d. Kost L. and Mary (Manaras) Sofos; B.S., Mont. State Coll., 1944; M.A., San Francisco State Coll., 1958, M.A., 1967; postgrad. Stanford U.; Ph.D., Calif. Western U., 1977; m. Henry E. Hopkins, Sept. 7, 1944. Bus. tchr. Havre (Mont.) High Sch., Mateo, Calif., 1942-44; sec. George P. Gorham, Realtor, San Mateo, 1944-45; escrow sec. Fox & Cars 1945-50; escrow officer Calif. Pacific Title Ins. Co., 1950-57; bus. tchr. Westmoor High Sch., Daly City, Calif., 1958-59; bus. tchr. Coll. of San Mateo, 1959-63, chmn. real estate-ins. dept., 1963-76, dir. div. bus., 1976-86, coord. real estate dept., 1986-91; cons. to commr. Calif. Div. Real Estate, 1963-91, mem. periodic rev. exam. com.; chmn. C.C. Adv. Com., 1971-72, mem. com., 1975-91; projector direction Calif. State Chancellor's Career Awareness Consortium, mem. endowment fund adv. com., c.c. real estate edn. com., state c.c. adv. com.; mem. No. Calif. adv. bd. to Glendale Fed. Savs. and Loan Assn.; mem. bd. advisors San Mateo County Bd. Suprs., 1981-82; mem. real estate edn. and rsch. com. to Calif. Commr. Real Estate, 1983-90; mem. edn., membership, and profl. exchange coms. Am. chpt. Internat. Real Estate Fedn., 1985-92. Recipient Citizen of Day award KABL, Outstanding Contbns. award Redwood City-San Carlos-Belmont Bd. Realtors, Nat. Real Estate Educators Assn. award emeritus, 1993; named Woman of Achievement, San Mateo-Burlingame br. Soroptimist Internat., 1979. Mem. AAUW, Calif. Assn. Real Estate Tchrs. (state pres. 1964-65, life hon. dir. 1962—, Outstanding Real Estate Educator of Yr. 1978-79), Real Estate Cert. Inst. (Disting. Merit award 1982), Calif. Bus. Edn. Assn. (certificate of commendation 1979), San Francisco State Coll., Guidance and Counseling Alumni, Calif. Real Estate Educators' Assn. (dir. emeritus, hon. dir. 1990), Real Estate Nat. Educators Assn. (award emeritus for outstanding contributions, 1993), San Mateo-Burlingame Bd. Realtors (award emeritus Outstanding Contbrs. to Membership), Alpha Delta, Pi Lambda Theta, Delta Pi Epsilon (nat. dir. interchpt. rels. 1962-65, nat. historian 1966-67, nat. sec. 1968-69), Alpha Gamma Delta. Co-author: California Real Estate Principles; contbr. articles to profl. jours. Home: 504 Colgate Way San Mateo CA 94402-3206

HOPKINS, DAVID MOODY, geologist; b. Nashua, N.H., Dec. 26, 1921; s. Donald Wheeler and Henrietta (Moody) H.; m. Joan Prewitt, Dec. 27, 1949 (dec. Sept. 1955); children: Dana, Chindi Ann; m. Martha Bryant, Sept. 25, 1957 (div. June 1970); 1 child, Alexander Carrier Hopkins; m. Rachel Chouinard Stanley, Aug. 23, 1970. BS, U. N.H., 1942; MS, Harvard U., 1948, PhD, 1955. From geologist to sr. rsch. geologist U.S. Geol. Survey, Washington, 1942-55, W.S. Geol. Survey, Menlo Park, Calif., 1955-84; disting. prof. U. Alaska, Fairbanks, 1985-94; ret., 1994; cons. U.S. Nat. Park Svc., Anchorage, 1986—. Editor, contbr. The Bering Land Bridge, 1967; co-editor, contbr. Paleoecology of Beringia, 1982; contbr. articles to profl. jours. With USAF, 1945-47. Recipient Franklin Burr award Nat. Geographic Soc., 1993. Fellow Geol. Soc. Am. (chmn. Geomorphology and Quarternary Geol. divsn. 1969-70, Archaeol. Geology divsn. 1984-85, Kirk Bryan award 1968, Career award in Geoarcheology 1990), Arctic Inst. N.Am. (editl. bd. 1979—), Calif. Acad. Sci.; mem. Am. Quarternary Assn. (pres. 1974), Soc. Am. Archaeology (Fryxell award 1988). Democrat. Home: 40 Steelhead Rd Fairbanks AK 99709-3201 Office: U Alaska Dept Geology and Geography Fairbanks AK 99709-5780

HOPKINS, GLENN ERNEST, artist, educator; b. Washington, May 19, 1949; s. Wilford Clyde and Dorothy Mary (Ruffner) H.; m. Phyllis Goodwin, Oct. 7, 1972 (div. 1980); 1 child, Gary Buckminster. BS, Western Md. Coll., 1971; MFA, UCLA, 1979. Cert. tchr., Calif. Dir. acting program Buck's Rock Camp, New Milford, Conn., 1969-73; producer, dir. Mootney Theatre Co., Venice, Calif., 1975—; advisor Calif. State Adult Curriculum, 1977—; instr. divsn. career and continuing edn. L.A. Unified Sch. Dist., 1977—; guest lectr. numerous orgns. Bd. dirs. Nomenus, Inc.; active Santa Monica Meth. Ch., Com. to Monitor Poppers; convener Westside Greens, Indian Springs Com. Mem. Dramatists Guild Am., Va. Ctr. Creative Arts, Ragdale Inst. Office: Venice Mootney Theatre 11882 Texas Ave Los Angeles CA 90025

HOPKINS, HENRY TYLER, art educator, university gallery director; b. Idaho Falls, Idaho, Aug. 14, 1928; s. Talcott Thompson and Zoe (Erbe) H.; children—Victoria Anne, John Thomas, Christopher Tyler. BA, Sch. of Art Inst., Chgo., 1952, MA, 1955; postgrad., UCLA, 1957-60; PhD (hon.), Calif. Coll. Arts and Crafts, 1984, San Francisco Art Inst., 1986. Curator exhbns., publs. Los Angeles County Mus. of Art, 1960-68; dir. Fort Worth Art Mus., 1968-74, San Francisco Mus. of Modern Art, 1974-86; chmn., art dept. Univ. Calif., Los Angeles, 1991—; dir. F.S. Wight Gallery, UCLA, 1991—, UCLA/Armand Hammer Mus. Art & Cultural Ctr., 1994—; lectr. art history, extension U. Calif. at Los Angeles, 1958-68; instr. Tex. Christian U., Fort Worth, 1968-74; dir. U.S. representation Venice (Italy) Bienniel, 1970; dir. art presentation Festival of Two Worlds, Spoleto, Italy, 1970; co-commr. U.S. representation XVI São Paulo (Brazil) Biennale, 1981; cons. NEA, mem. mus. panel, 1979-84, chmn., 1981; cons., mem. mus. panel NEH, 1976. Contbr. numerous articles to profl. jours., also numerous mus. publs. Served with AUS, 1952-54. Decorated knight Order Leopold II, Belgium); recipient special internat. award, Art L.A., 1992. Mem. Assn. Art Mus. Dirs. (pres. 1985-86), Coll. Art Assn., Am. Assn. Museums, Western Assn. Art Museums (pres. 1977-78). Home: 939 1/2 Hilgard Ave Los Angeles CA 90024-3032 Office: UCLA/Armand Hammer Mus Art 10899 Wilshire Blvd Los Angeles CA 90024-4314

HOPKINS, JAMES WILLIAM, career officer, educator; b. Ft. Worth, Sept. 19, 1949; s. Donald Lawrence and Frances (Kuban) H.; m. Mary Laura Helbing, Nov. 6, 1971; children: Elizabeth, Emily, Steve, Paul. BA in English, U. Tex., Arlington, 1971; MA in English, Midwestern State U., 1977; M Libr. and Info. Sci., U. Tex., 1986; grad. distinguished, Officer Tng. Sch. Commd. 2d lt. USAF, 1971, advanced through grades to lt. col., 1989; Titan II Inter Continental Ballistic Missile launch officer, instr. launch officer USAF, Davis-Monthan AFB, Ariz., 1972-73; Titan II Inter Continental Ballistic Missile launch officer instr., squadron comdr. USAF, Sheppard AFB, Tex., 1974-77; instr., asst. prof. English, asst. dir., acting dir. acad. librs. USAF Acad., Colo., 1977-82; flight comdr., squadron comdr., wing exec. officer USAF Officer Tng. Sch., Lackland AFB, Tex., 1982-85; asst. dir., exec. officer acad. librs., assoc. prof. English USAF Acad., Colo., 1986-88, comdr., dean faculty squadron, dir. faculty support, assoc. prof., 1989-92; dir. acad. librs., assoc. prof. USAF Acad., Colorado Springs, Colo., 1992—; mem. tenure coun. USAF Acad., 1990-94, mem. meml. bd., 1992-94, mem. faculty coun.; mem. Air Force Librs. Steering Com., 1992-94, Colo. Acad. Libr. Com., 1992-94; presenter in field. Co-editor: Resource book for the Teaching of English Composition, 1978; contbr. articles to profl. jours. Bd. dirs. Friends of Air Force Acad. Libr., 1992-94. Decorated Air Force Achievement medal with 1 oak leaf cluster; recipient Orgnl. Excellence award with 2 oak leaf clusters, Meritorious Svc. medal with 3 oak leaf clusters. Mem. ALA, Colo. Libr. Assn., Colo. Coun. Acad. Librs. (chmn. 1993-94), Assn. Coll. and Rsch. Librs., Libr. Adminstrn. and Mgmt. Assn., Beta Phi Mu. Office: USAF Academy Library U S A F Academy CO 80840

HOPKINS, LEE WALLACE, writer; b. L.A., June 30, 1934; s. Leon Wallace and Eva (Bong) H.; m. Barbara Franklin, Aug. 15, 1958 (div. 1963); m. Carol Porter, Sept. 15, 1970 (div. 1984); children: Alison Christina, Carolyn Alexandra. BA with honors, UCLA, 1957. Dir. pub. rels. and advt. Calif. Blue Shield, San Francisco, 1959-67; account exec. Doremus & Co., San Francisco, 1967-70; pres. Lee Hopkins Pub. Rels., San Francisco, 1970-90, Task Force 2000 Communications, San Francisco, 1990—. Contbr. book revs. to profl. jours. and newspapers; author: After They Learn to Dance, 1974, The Origin of Design, 1986, The Dream of Regulus, 1988, The Feast of Tantalus, 1991. Sgt. U.S. Army, 1957-59. Mem. Marines' Meml. Club. Democrat. Episcopalian. Office: Task Force 200 Comm 69 Whitney St Ste C San Francisco CA 94131-2769

HOPKINS, PAMELA WITHERS, architect; b. Fort Sheridan, Ill., Aug. 17, 1947; d. William Price and Jacqueline (McElvain) Withers; m. Thomas Hollis Hopkins, July 1, 1972; children—Hollis McTaggart, Whitney Price. B.Arch., U. Colo., 1970. Registered architect, Colo. Architect Stephenson & Turner, Sydney, Australia, 1970-71, Odonnell Wicklund & Pigozzi, Chgo., 1972-77; architect, ptnr. Snowdon & Hopkins, Vail, Colo., 1977—. Mem. Planning and Environ. Commn., Town of Vail; trustee Vail Mt. Sch. Mem. AIA (jury Nat. AIA/ALA library design competition 1987, Western Mountain region award of merit for Vail Pub. Library). Episcopalian.

HOPKINS, PHILIP JOSEPH, journalist, editor; b. Orange, Calif., Dec. 10, 1954; s. Philip Joseph and Marie Elizabeth H.; m. Susan Lisa Ingman Hopkins, Oct. 5, 1991; 1 child, Robin Genevieve Hopkins. BA in Journalism, San Diego State U., 1977. Cert. tissue therapist Center for Decubitis Ulcer Research, 1981. Reporter, La Jolla Light & Journal (Calif.), 1973; editorial cons. San Diego Union, 1974; asst. producer Southwestern Cable TV, San Diego, 1974; corr. Mission Cable TV, San Diego, 1975; photojournalist United Press Internat., San Diego, 1976; editor Rx Home Care mag., L.A., 1981, Hosp. Info. Mgmt. mag., 1981; editor, assoc. pub. Arcade mag., 1982; mng. editor Personal Computer Age, L.A., 1983-84; bur. chief Newsbytes syndicated column, 1985-86; v.p. Humbird Hopkins Inc., L.A., 1978-88; personal fin. writer Hume Pub. Co., 1987-89; writer, editor and researcher Ind. Rsch. and Info. Svc., 1988-90; writer, analyst Geneva Bus. Rsch., 1990; sci. writer, The Cousteau Soc., 1990; pub. cons. U. So. Calif., 1989; lead programmer analyst Kaiser Permanente, 1991—. Recipient 1st and 4th place awards Nikon, Inc., Photo Contest, 1974; 3rd prize Minolta Camera Co. Creative Photography awards, 1975; Best Feature Photo award Sigma Delta Chi Mark of Excellence contest, 1977. Pres. Ind. Writers of So. Calif., 1988. Mem. Computer Press Assn. (life, hon.). Co-author: The Students' Survival Guide, 1977, 78; photographs have appeared in Time and Omni mags., The Mythology of Middle Earth, Parenting Your Aging Parents, Beginners Guide to the SLR, NBC-TV's Saturday Night Live. Office: PO Box 40939 Pasadena CA 91114-7939

HOPKINS, RICHARD LEE, educator, writer; b. Oklahoma City, June 30, 1927; s. Famos Richard and Veva Lee (Helms) H.; m. Eleanor Bellamy, June 22, 1952 (div. June 1965); m. Judith Ada Gots, Aug. 10, 1965 (div. Oct. 1982); children: Ruthann, Melissa, David, Rachel, Jenny; m. Lucy Young Noyes, Dec. 23, 1983. BA, U. Okla., 1950; MA, Ohio State U., 1952; EdD, Boston U., 1980. Editl. writer Des Moines Register, 1954-61; pres., gen. mgr. New Direction Broadcasting, Des Moines, 1961-62; dir. Latin Am. Tng. Ctr. U.S. Peace Corps, Arecibo, P.R., 1963-67; dep. dir. tng. U.S. AID, Washington, 1967-68; v.p., dir. Westinghouse Learning Corp., N.Y.C. and Washington, 1968-71; sr. cons. Arthur D. Little, Inc., Washington and Cambridge, Mass., 1972-74; dean Coll. Profl. Edn. Clark U., Worcester, Mass., 1974-78; pres., dir. Sch. for Internat. Tng., Brattleboro, Vt., 1979-83; dir. Sandia Foothills Ctr. Exptl. Learning., Placitas, N.Mex., 1983—; vis. prof. ednl. founds. and comm. U. N.Mex., Albuquerque, 1986-92; mem. White House Conf. on Children and Youth, Washington, 1971. Author: Narrative Schooling: Experiential Learning and the Transformation of American Education, 1994; contbr. articles to profl. jours. Bd. dirs. N.Mex. Civil Liberties Union, 1989-92. Cpl. USMC, 1944-46, PTO. Recipient Douglas McGregor Meml. award, 1967. Democrat. Home: 20 Ridge Rd Placitas NM 87043-9526

HOPKINS, ROBERT ARTHUR, retired industrial engineer; b. Youngstown, Ohio, Dec. 14, 1920; s. Arthur George and Margaret Viola (Brush) H.; m. Mary Madelaine Bailey, Apr. 6, 1946; 1 child, Marlaine Hopkins Kaiser. BBA, Case Western Reserve U., 1949; cert. loss control engr., U. Calif., Berkeley, 1969. Ins. agt. Nat. Life and Accident Ins. Co., Lorain, Akron, Ohio, 1951-56, San Mateo, Calif., 1951-56; ins. agt., engr. Am. Hardware Mt. Ins. Co., San Jose, Fresno, Calif., 1956-60; loss control engr. Manhattan Guarantee-Continental Ins. Co., Calif., 1967-77. Organizer Operation Alert DC, Lorain, 1951-52; prin. spkr. DC, Fresno, 1957; active Pleasant Hill (Calif.) Civil Action Com., 1981-83; civilian coord. Office Emergency Svcs., Pleasant Hill, 1983-85; advisor, coord. airshows and warbird aircraft, 1980—; chmn. bd. Western Aerospace Mus., Oakland, Calif., 1988; ops. asst. for tower and ops. 50th Anniversary Golden Gate Bridge, San Francisco, 1987; advisor, coord. Travis AFB Air Expo '90, 1990, NAS Alameda (Calif.) 50th Anniversary, 1990; advisor NAS Moffett Field

Air Show, 1990, 92, Calif. Coast Air Show, Half Moon Bay, 1993-94, Dixon May Fair honoring WWII 50th anniversary, 1995; warbird coord. Port of Oakland Airshow, 1987; warbird advisor/coord. Beale AFB, 1993—; mem. Smithsonian Mus, Smithsonian Air & Space Mus; charter mem. Nat. Mus. of Am. Indian. Recipient Letter of Appreciation Fresno DC, 1957, cert. of appreciation City of Pleasant Hill, 1986, cert. of recognition and spl. citizenship award Calif. State Senate, 1995. Mem. No. Calif. Safety Engrs. Assn. (v.p., pres., chmn. 1974-77), Confederate Air Force (mem. staff, leader Pacific wing 1980—), Nat. Aero. Assn., Aero. Club No. Calif., Hamilton Field Assn. (dir. ops. Wings of Victory Air Show 1987, coord. 1988, 89—, asst. to pres. 1989—, advisor contr. 1990—), VFW (life, state civil disaster chmn. Area 5 Calif. 1991), Air Force Assn., Kiwanis (chpt. sec.-treas.). Republican. Roman Catholic. Home: 48 Mazie Dr Pleasant Hill CA 94523-3310

HOPKINS, STEPHEN DAVIS, mining company executive; b. N.Y.C., Oct. 31, 1907; s. Louis Davis and Margaret Hall (Daly) H.; m. Hildegarde Lupprian, 1942 (dec. 1983). BA, Yale U., 1935. Page N.Y. Stock Exch., 1928; specialist clk. N.Y. Stock Exch., N.Y.C., 1929-31; teller 1st Nat. Bank, Greenwich, Conn., 1935-37; editor Commerce & Fin. mag., 1938-41; chief adminstrv. officer Jensvold Mfg. Co., Olympia, Wash., 1945-46; account exec. Conrad, Bruce & Co., Seattle, 1947-48; investment counsel Pacific Rsch. & Mgmt. Co., Seattle, 1949-63; gen. mgr. plywood coop., Tacoma, 1951-52; writer nat. media on domestic currency consumer point view Deer Lodge, Mont., 1962—; CFO placer mining Yukon ter., $D, Can., 1994—; advisor, cons. to U.S. currency mgrs., 1962—; advisor to currency mgrs. Republic of Russia, 1992, 93, placer mining, Dawson/Klondike area, Yukon Territory, Can., 1994—. Editor: U.S. Coin and Currency Laws from 1775 , Inflation Watch (registered trademark), 1978-83. Head usher St. George's Episcopal Ch., N.Y.C., 1975-76; mem. western Wash. enrollment and scholarship com. Yale U., 1948-52. 1st lt. C.E., U.S. Army, 1942-45. Mem. Mil. Order World Wars (officer Seattle chpt. 1950). Home and Office: 525 W 3rd Ave Anchorage AK 99501-2240

HOPKINSON, SHIRLEY LOIS, library science educator; b. Boone, Iowa, Aug 25, 1924; d. Arthur Perry and Zora (Smith) Hopkinson; student Coe Coll., 1942-43; AB cum laude (Phi Beta Kappa scholar 1944), U. Colo., 1945; BLS, U. Calif., 1949; MA (Honnold Honor scholar 1945-46), Claremont Grad. Sch., 1951; EdM, U. Okla., 1952, EdD, 1957 Tchr. pub. sch. Stigler, Okla., 1946-47, Palo Verde High Sch., Jr. Coll., Blythe, Calif., 1947-48; asst. librarian Modesto (Calif.) Jr. Coll., 1949-51; tchr., librarian Fresno, Calif., 1951-52, La Mesa, Cal., 1953-55; asst. prof. librarianship, instructional materials dir. Chaffey Coll., Ontario, Calif., 1955-59; asst. prof. librarian ship, San Jose (Calif.) State Coll., 1959-64; assoc. prof., 1964-69, prof., 1969—; bd. dirs. NDEA Inst. Sch. Librs., summer 1966; mem. Santa Clara County Civil Service Bd. Examiners. Recipient Master Gardner cert. Oreg. State U. Extension Svc. Book reviewer for jours. Mem. ALA, Calif. Library Assn., Audio-Visual Assn. Calif., NEA, AAUP, AAUW (dir. 1957-58), Bus. Profl. Women's Club, Sch. Librs. Assn. Calif. (com. mem., treas. No. sect. 1951-52), San Diego County Sch. Librs. Assn. (sec. 1945-55), Calif. Tchrs. Assn., LWV (bd. dirs. 1950-51, publs. chmn.), Phi Beta Kappa, Alpha Lambda Delta, Alpha Beta Alpha, Kappa Delta Pi, Phi Kappa Phi (disting. acad. achievement award 1981), Delta Kappa Gamma (sec. 1994—). Author: Descriptive Cataloging of Library Materials; Instructional Materials for Teaching the Use of the Library. Contbr. to profl. publs. Editor: Calif. Sch. Libraries, 1963-64; asst. editor: Sch. Library Assn. of Calif. Bull., 1961-63; book reviewer profl. jours. Office: 1340 Pomeroy Ave Apt 408 Santa Clara CA 95051-3658

HOPPE, ARTHUR WATTERSON, columnist; b. Honolulu, Apr. 23, 1925; s. Arthur Scrivner and Margaret Elizabeth (Watterson) H.; m. Gloria Mary Nichols, Apr. 27, 1946; children—Leslie, Andrea, Arthur, Prentiss. B.A. cum laude, Harvard U., 1949. Reporter San Francisco Chronicle, 1950-60, columnist, 1960—. Author: The Love Everybody Crusade, 1960, Dreamboat, 1962, The Perfect Solution to Absolutely Everything, 1968, Mr. Nixon and My Other Problems, 1971, Miss Lollipop and the Doom Machine, 1973, The Tiddling Tennis Theorem, 1977, The Marital Arts, 1985, Having a Wonderful Time, 1995. Served with USNR, 1942-46, PTO. Office: Chronicle Pub Co 901 Mission St San Francisco CA 94103-2905

HOPPENSTEADT, JON KIRK, law librarian; b. Milw., Feb. 24, 1959; s. George Arthur and Sheila Ann (Doyle) H. BA, U. Nev., 1980, '81; MA, Denver U., 1984; JD, U. Minn., 1989. Rschr., abstractor TrendTrack, Boulder, Colo., 1983; reference libr. intern Denver U., Englewood (Colo.) Pub. Libr., 1984; indexer, abstractor Info. Access Co., Foster City, Calif., 1984-86; pub. libr. intern Mpls. Pub. Libr., 1987-88; student dir. Legal Assistance to Minn. Prisoners, Mpls., 1988-89; reference libr. Univ. Minn. Law Libr., Mpls., 1988-91; victims' rights advocate unaffiliated, Rohnert Park, Calif., 1992—. Cataloger Westlaw Legal Database Catalog, 1991. Mem. Nat. Orgn. for Victim Assistance, Washington, 1992; founder Profls. for Access, Santa Rosa, Calif., 1993; mem. Nat. Victim Ctr., Ft. Worth, 1993. Mem. Am. Assn. Law Librs. Democrat. Lutheran. Home and Office: 4889 Fairway Dr Rohnert Park CA 94928-1306

HOPPER, SALLY, state legislator; widowed; children: Nancy, Joan, Caroline, Anne. BA, U. Wyo., 1956. Mem. Colo. Senate, Denver, 1987—; chair Senate Health, Environ., Welfare and Insts. com.; chair Criminal Justice Commn, mem. Judiciary com. Mem. nat. bd. Physically Challenged Access to the Woods; mem., past chair bd. Spalding Rehab. Hosp.; bd. dirs. Bayard Industries. Mem. Kappa Kappa Gamma. Republican. Episcopalian. Home: 21649 Cabrini Blvd Golden CO 80401-9487

HOPPER, WILBERT HILL, retired oil industry executive; b. Ottawa, Ont., Can., Mar. 14, 1933; s. Wilbert Clayton and Eva (Hill) H.; m. Patricia Marguerite Walker, Aug. 12, 1957; children: Sean Wilbert, Christopher Mark. Student, Scots Coll., Sydney, Australia, Wellington (New Zealand) Coll.; BSc in Geology, Am. U.; MBA, U. Western Ont., London; LLD (hon.), Wilfrid Laurier U. Petroleum geologist Imperial Oil, 1955-57; petroleum economist Foster Assocs., 1959-61; sr. energy economist Nat. Energy Bd., Ottawa, 1961-64; sr. petroleum cons. Arthur D. Little, Inc., Cambridge, Mass., 1964-73; asst. dep. min. energy policy Dept. of Energy, Mines and Resources, Ottawa, 1973-75; pres., chief exec. officer Petro-Can., 1976-79, now dir., 1979-93; chmn., bd. dirs. Westcoast Energy Inc.; vice-chmn., bd. dirs. Panarctic Oils Ltd.; bd. dirs. Can.-China Trade Coun., ICG Propane Inc., Bi-Provincial Upgrader Joint Venture. Mem. bd. govs. Oxford Inst. for Energy Studies, Ottawa; mem. internat. adv. coun. Centre for Global Energy Studies; mem. adv. com. Sch. Bus. Adminstrn., U. Western Ont. Decorated officer Order of Can. Mem. Can. Econ. Assn., Am. Econ. Assn., Can. Soc. Petroleum, Am. Assn. Petroleum Geologists, Can. Inst. for Advanced Rsch., Can. Inst. Mining and Metallurgy, Soc. Petroleum Engrs., Ont. Petroleum Inst. Inc. Office: Petro-Canada, 150-6th Ave SW PO Box 2844, Calgary, AB Canada T2P 3E3*

HOPPING, WILLIAM RUSSELL, hospitality industry consultant and appraiser; b. Balt., May 3, 1947; s. Russell Leroy and Janet Louise (Cloud) H.; m. Catherine Wilson. BS in Hotel Adminstrn., Cornell U., 1969; MBA, U. Denver, 1978. Mgr. Sylvania (Ohio) Country Club, 1972-77; sr. cons. Pannell Kerr Forster, Denver, 1978-82; cons. Ginther Wycoff Grp., Denver, 1982-85; pres. W.R. Hopping & Co., Inc., Denver, 1985—. Vol., Big Bros., Inc., Denver, 1990—; chmn. adv. bd. U. Denver Profl. Career Devel. Prog., 1987-88, chmn. task force, Career and Placement Ctr., 1989. 1st lt. U.S. Army, 1970-72. Mem. Appraisal Inst., Internat. Soc. Hospitality Cons. (pres. 1990-91, chmn. 1991-93, chmn. emeritus, 1993—), Cornell Soc. Hotelmen (pres. Rocky Mountain chpt. 1984-85). Office: W R Hopping & Co Inc 6334 S Yates Ct Littleton CO 80123-6738

HORAN, ADEL EDWARD, sociology and psychology educator; b. Salt Lake City, Sept. 17, 1943; s. Awad and Martha (Neshweiwat) H.; m. Samira A., May 11, 1966; 1 child, Marsha. BFA, Da Vinci Art Acad., 1964; MFA, Sussex Coll., 1981; MA in Psychology, Liberty U., 1981; PhD in Human Svcs., Walden/Ind. U., 1994. Art dir. Nesco Advt., Jordan, 1960-65, Kuwait Oil Co., 1965-71, Samira Advt., Toronto, Can., 1971-76, Readers Digest, Pleasantville, N.Y., 1976-79, Yonkers (N.Y.) Gazette, 1979-82; fine artist Horan Art Studio, Phoenix, 1982-85; instr. Rio Salado Coll., Phoenix, 1985-88, Horan Art Sch., Phoenix, 1988-94; counselor St. John of the Desert, Phoenix, 1990-93; prof. sociology and psychology Ariz. Inst. Bus. and Tech., 1995—. Author: Orogins and Early Egyptian Art, 1982, Art in the Middle East, 1982; publisher (mag.) The Immigrant, 1978, The Arab World, 1978. Mem. Am. Assn. Counseling Devel., Am. Assn. Christian Counseling, Am. Assn. Family Therapists, Am. Assn. of Aged, Am. Multicultural Assn., Am. Portrait Soc., Phoenix Guild, Calif. Reference, Firebirds League, Scottsdale Artists League, Paradise Valley (Ariz.) C. of C., Gibran Khalil Gibran Scholar Found N.Am. Republican. Roman Catholic.

HORAN, MARY ANN THERESA, nurse; b. Denver, July 4, 1936; d. John Paul and Lucille (Somma) Perito; m. Stephen F. Horan, Sr., Dec. 28, 1957; children: Seanna, Dana, Michelle, Annette, Stephen Jr., Christine, David. BSN, Loretto Heights Coll., Denver, 1958; postgrad, Pima Community Coll., 1982. RN, Ala. Staff nurse Med. Ctr. Hosp., Huntsville, Ala., 1978-79, Crestwood Hosp., Huntsville, 1980-81, St. Joseph Hosp. Eye Surgery, Tucson, 1981—; v.p. Success Achievement Ctr., Tucson, 1987—; Amway distbr. Horan and Assocs., 1992—. Contbr. articles to nursing jours. Republican. Roman Catholic. Home: 8311 E 3rd St Tucson AZ 85710-2550

HORLER, BRIAN LESLIE, controller; b. Wells, Somerset, Eng., Aug. 23, 1935; s. George Thomas and Gertrude Amanda (Bailey) H.; m. Virginia Louise Palmer, Sept. 4, 1965; 1 child, Jennifer Ann. BSBA, John F. Kennedy U., 1983, MBA in Acctg., 1984. Acct./office mgr. Fountain Forestry Ltd., Wells, 1959-62; acct. South London Elec., 1962-65; asst. to dirs. Sawyer Tanning Co., Napa, Calif., 1965-66; cost acct. Kawneer Inc., Richmond, Calif., 1967-69; contr. Far West Lab., San Francisco, 1970-87; corp. contr. Calif. Med. Rev., Inc., San Francisco, 1987-89; contr. Foster Engring. Inc., San Francisco, 1990—. Mem. aquatics bd. YMCA, Pinole, Calif., 1981-85, chmn. silent auction, 1983, 85. Mem. Inst. Mgmt. Accts. (dir. profl. edn. 1986-87, dir. manuscripts 1987-88). Republican. Home: 1837 Saint Andrews Dr Moraga CA 94556-1056

HORN, CHRISTIAN FRIEDRICH, venture capital company executive; b. Dresden, Germany, Dec. 23, 1927; came to U.S., 1954, naturalized, 1959; s. Otto Hugo and Elsa H.; m. Christa Winkler, Feb. 13, 1954; 1 child, Sabrina. M.S., Technische Hochschule, Dresden, 1951; Ph.D., Technische Hochschule, Aachen, Germany, 1958. Rsch. scientist German Acad. Sci., Berlin, 1951-53, Farbwerke Hoechst, Germany, 1953-54; research mgr. Union Carbide, N.Y.C., 1954-65; pres. Polymer Tech. Inc., N.Y.C., 1965-74; v.p. W.R. Grace & Co., N.Y.C., 1974-81, sr. v.p., 1981—, bd. dirs., 1985-89; pres. Grace Ventures Corp., Cupertino, Calif., 1983—; mng. ptnr. Horn Venture Ptnrs, Cupertino, 1987—; bd. dirs. Hometown Buffet, Inc., ASI Ctrls., Inc., Roasters Corp., Timothy's Coffees of the World, Roadhouse Grill, Inc. Patentee in field. Served with German Army, 1944-45. Decorated Iron Cross. Mem. Am. Chem. Soc. Lutheran. Home: 27827 Via Feliz Los Altos CA 94022-2421 Office: Grace Horn Ventures 20300 Stevens Creek Blvd Cupertino CA 95014-2240

HORN, DENIS RICHARD, airport executive; b. Bklyn., June 4, 1932; s. John and Lenore Marguirite (Johnson) H.; m. Claire Capitanio Horn, Sept. 5, 1955; children: Jeffrey Douglas, Erica Jeanne. BS, Ithaca (N.Y.) Coll., 1955; MPA, Calif. State U., Fullerton, 1973. Cert. airport exec. USMC, 1955-75; Mgr. Ops. and Facilities John Wayne Airport Orange County, Santa Ana, Calif., 1976-88; gen. mgr., CEO Monterey (Calif.) Peninsula Airport Dist., 1988—; past chmn. Aviation tech. Adv. Com., So. Calif. Assn. Govt.'s, 1987, L.A.; past pres. Calif. Assn. Airport Execs., 1988; adj. faculty mem. Sch. Pub. Adminstrn. U. So. Calif., L.A., 1976-78, Embry Riddle Aero. U., San Bernardino, 1986-88; exec. asst., chmn. Orange County, bd. supervisers 1976-78; past chmn. Calif. Tech. Adv. Com. on Aero., Sacramento, 1989-92. Dir. Mission Viejo Cmty. Svcs. Dist., Calif., 1986-87. Mem. ASPA, Airport Operators Coun. Internat., Am. Assn. Airport Execs., Civil Air Patrol, Rotary. Democrat. Home: 25390 Quail Smt Monterey CA 93940-6615 Office: Monterey Peninsula Airport PO Box 550 Monterey CA 93942-0550

HORN, JOHN HAROLD, lawyer; b. Eugene, Oreg., Mar. 4, 1927; s. Harold William and Mildred A. (Truesdale) H.; m. Deloris Eileen Davis, Aug. 22, 1948; children: Lorraine, Deborah, Lisa, Darren. BS, U. Oreg., 1949, JD, 1951. Bar: Oreg. 1951, U.S. Dist. Ct. Oreg. 1957. Ptnr. Horn & Slocum, Roseburg, Oreg., 1961-65, Riddlesbarger, Pederson, Young & Horn, Eugene, 1970-74, Young, Horn, Cass & Scott, Eugene, 1974-82; pvt. practice Roseburg, 1965-70; pvt. practice, Eugene, 1982—. Chmn. fund raising Douglas County unit ARC, 1966, county chmn., 1968; exec. bd., legal advisor Eugene Mission, 1979—; pres. bd. dirs. Jubilee Ministries, Eugene, 1980—; v.p., bd. dirs. His Word Broadcasting, 1989-91, pres. bd. dirs., 1991—. Recipient Outstanding Svc. award ARC, 1968. Mem. ABA, Oreg. Bar Assn., Douglas County Bar Assn. (pres. 1960, chmn. grievance com. 1961-62), Lions. Republican. Home: 640 Elwood Ct Eugene OR 97401-2235 Office: 875 Country Club Rd Eugene OR 97401-2255

HORN, KENNETH PORTER, aeronautical/astronautical engineering administrator; b. Ft. Worth, Dec. 10, 1937; s. John Melton and Hilda Marjorie (Teitelbaum) H.; m. Ann Harper, July 28, 1979. BA in Mech. Engring., Rice U., 1960, MS in Mech. Engring., 1962; PhD in Aeronautics/Astronautics, Stanford U., 1966. Engr. NASA Manned Spacecraft Ctr., Houston, 1961; rsch. engr. Aerospace Corp., El Segundo, Calif., 1966-72, sect. head, 1972-75; assoc. program dir. Rand Corp., Santa Monica, Calif., 1978-85, project leader, 1975—, dept. head, 1988-90, program dir., 1985—. Contbr. articles to profl. jours. Recipient fellowship Ford Found., 1964-66, scholarship Mission Mfg., 1961. Fellow AIAA (assoc.); mem. Am. Phys. Soc., Sigma Tau, Sigma Xi. Office: Rand Corp 1700 Main St Santa Monica CA 90401-3208

HORN, ROBERT ELDON, university researcher, think-tank executive, entrepreneur; b. Webster City, Iowa, Aug. 24, 1933; s. Ralph Oscar and Esther Frieda (Timm) H.; m. Niela Miller; 1 child, Jennifer Kren (dec.); 1 stepchild, Andrea Halleck Adams. V.p. Meridian Internat. Inst., San Francisco, 1993—; chmn. Info. Mapping, Inc. Author: Developmental Testing, 1965, Language: Change and Communication, 1967, Writing Reports, 1977, 3d edit., 1980, Mapping Hypertext: Analysis, Linkage and Display of Knowledge for the Next Generation of On-Line Text and Graphics, 1989, others; editor: Trialectics: Toward a Practical Logic of Unity, 1983, others. Served with U.S. Army, 1955-57. Woodrow Wilson fellow, 1956; World Acad. of Art and Sci. fellow, 1992. Office: Meridian Internat Inst One Sansome St San Francisco CA 94104

HORN, (JOHN) STEPHEN, congressman, political science educator; b. San Juan Bautista, Calif., May 31, 1931; s. John Stephen and Isabelle (McCaffrey) H.; m. Nini Moore, Sept. 4, 1954; children: Marcia Karen Horn Yavitz, John Stephen. AB with great distinction, Stanford, 1953, postgrad., 1953-54, 55-56, PhD in Polit. Sci, 1958; M in Pub Adminstrn., Harvard, 1955. Congl. fellow, 1958-59; adminstrv. asst. to sec. labor Washington, 1959-60; legislative asst. to U.S. Senator Thomas H. Kuchel, 1960-66; sr. fellow The Brookings Instn., 1966-69; dean grad. studies and research Am. U., 1969-70; pres. Calif. State U., Long Beach, 1970-88, Trustee prof. polit. sci., 1988-93; mem. 103rd Congress from 38th Calif. dist., 1993—; sr. cons., host The Govt. Story on TV, The Election Game (radio series), 1967-69, vice chmn. U.S. Commn. on Civil Rights, 1969-80 (commr. 1980-82); chmn. Urban Studies Fellow Adv. Com., U.S. Dept. HUD, 1969-70; mem. Law Enforcement Ednl. Prog. Adv. Com., U.S. Dept Justice, 1969-70; adv. bd. Nat. Inst. Corrections, 1972-88 (chmn. 1984-87),. Author: The Cabinet and Congress, 1960, Unused Power: The Work of the Senate Committee on Appropriations, 1970, (with Edmund Beard) Congressional Ethics: The View from the House, 1975. Active Pres.-elect Nixon's Task Force on Orgn. Exec. Br., 1968, Kutak Found.; vice chmn. Long Beach Area C. of C., 1984-88; cofounder Western U.S. Com. Arts and Scis. for Eisenhower, 1956; chmn. Am. Assn. State Colls. and Univs., 1985-86; mem. Calif. Ednl. Facilities Authority, 1984-93. USAR, 1954-62. Fellow John F. Kennedy Inst. Politics Harvard U., 1966-67. Fellow Nat. Acad. Pub. Adminstrn.; mem. Stanford Assocs., Stanford Alumni Assn. (pres. 1976-77), Phi Beta Kappa, Pi Sigma Alpha. Republican. Office: 1023 Longworth House Office Bldg Washington DC 20515*

HORNACEK, JEFFREY JOHN, professional basketball player; b. Elmhurst, Ill., May 3, 1963. Student, Iowa State. With Phoenix Suns, 1986-92; guard Phila. 76ers, 1992-94, Utah Jazz, 1994—. Named NBA All-Star, 1992. Office: Utah Jazz 5 Delta Ctr Salt Lake City UT 84101*

HORNADAY, ALINE GRANDIER, publisher, independent scholar; b. San Diego, Sept. 14, 1923; d. Frank and Lydia Landon (Weir) Grandier; m. Quinn Hornaday, Oct. 9, 1965. BA, Union of Experimenting Colls., San Diego, 1977; PhD, U. Calif., San Diego, 1984. Pub. San Diego Daily Transcript, 1952-72, columnist, 1972-74; dir. San Diego Ind. Scholars, 1985-87, 94-95; co-pub. Jour. Unconventional History, Cardiff, Calif., 1989—; vis. scholar U. Calif., San Diego, 1984—; speaker at profl. confs. Co-author: The Hornadays, Root and Branch; contbr. articles to profl. jours. Commr. San Diego City Libr. Commn., 1964-70. Mem. San Diego Ind. Scholars, Nat. Coalition Ind. Scholars, Med. Assn. of Pacific, Am. Hist. Assn., Medieval Acad. Am., Nat. Soc. Colonial Dames of Am., Wed. Club (pres. 1964-65). Home and Office: 6435 Avenida Cresta La Jolla CA 92037-6514

HORNBEIN, VICTOR, architect; b. Denver, Oct. 26, 1913; s. Samuel and Rose (Frumess) H.; m. Ruth Kriesler, Mar. 20, 1947; children: Victoria Ann, Peter. Student, Atelier Denver, Beaux-Arts Inst. Design, 1930-35. Practice as Victor Hornbein, architect, 1940-60; with firm Victor Hornbein and Edward D. White, Jr., Denver, 1960-76; partner Victor Hornbein and Edward D. White, Jr., 1960-76; prin. Victor Hornbein & Assos., Denver, 1976-80; partner Victor Hornbein & John James, 1980-82; prin. Victor Hornbein, Architect, 1982—; vis. lectr. U. Denver, 1949-52, U. Colo., 1958-59, 68, 75, mem. design rev. bd., 1969-73; design adv. panel region 8 Gen. Services Adminstrn., 1967-70; vol. faculty U. Colo. Sch. Architecture, 1989-90. Major works include: conservatory and edn. bldg. Denver Bot. Gardens, 1966-71, conservatory and edn. bldg. Porter Library, Colo. Women's Coll., Denver, 1962, Bethesda Hosp., Denver, 1970, René Spitz Children's divsn. Ft. Logan Mental Health Center, Denver, 1965, housing for elderly, 1973, Sanctuary Wellshire Presbyn. Ch., 1980, Orchid and Bromeliad House, Denver Bot. Gardens, 1980, Wellshire Presbyn. Ch., 1985. Pres. Met. Council Community Services, 1957; bd. advisors Wright-Ingraham Inst., 1972—, trustee, 1974—, chmn. bd. trustees, 1975-82. Served with AUS, 1942-45. Decorated Bronze Star; recipient Modern Architecture Preservation League 1st Ann. Lifetime Achievement award, 1995. Fellow AIA (pres. Colo. Central chpt. 1971, Silver medal Western Mountain region 1981). Home and Office: Victor Hornbein Architect 266 Jackson St Denver CO 80206-5525

HORNE, RALPH SHELDON, JR., manufacturing executive, management consultant, newspaper columnist; b. Evanston, Wyo., Aug. 28, 1935; s. Ralph Sheldon Sr. and Emma DeEtte (Hilton) H.; m. Deann Gayle Taylor, Mar. 24, 1961; children: Gayle Brenda, Scott Sheldon, Carrie Louise. Student, U. Utah, 1959; AA in Comml. Sci., Stevens Henager Coll., 1961; student, Riverside (Calif.) City Coll., 1963-64, Ea. Wash. State U., 1977. R.R. telegrapher Union Pacific R.R., Evanston, 1953-58; pub. acct. James Horne Jr., PA, Evanston, 1962; bookkeeping supr. Security Title Ins. Co., Riverside, 1963-65; acct. Crane Enterprises, Inc., Riverside, 1965-66; acctg. supr. Alumax Mill Products, Inc., Riverside, 1967-70; acctg. mgr. Alumax Bldg. Products, Inc., Perris Valley, Calif., 1970-72; div. controller Alumax Irrigation Products, Inc., Spokane, Wash., 1972-80, div. gen. mgr., 1980-85; br. gen. mgr. Sailor Div. Alumax Door Products, Inc., Clarksville, Tex., 1985-90; newspaper columnist weekly humor column Uinta County Herald, Evanston, Wyo., 1994-95; pres. Am. Leadership Devel. Group, Paris, Tex., 1989-92. With U.S. Army, 1954-57, Korea. Mem. Red River Valley Indsl. Mgrs. Assn. (pres. 1985-90), Leadership Lamar County (cert. 1986), Inst. Mgmt. Accts., Great Music West (bd. mem. 1993-94). Republican. Mormon. Home: PO Box 1515 105 Navajo Circle Evanston WY 82931-1515

HORNER, ALTHEA JANE, psychologist; b. Hartford, Conn., Jan. 13, 1926; d. Louis and Celia (Newmark) Greenwald; children: Martha Horner Hartley, Anne Horner Benck, David, Kenneth. BS in Psychology, U. Chgo., 1952; PhD in Clin. Psychology, U. So. Calif., 1965. Lic. psychologist, N.Y., Calif. Tchr. Pasadena (Calif.) City Coll., 1965-67; from asst. to assoc. prof. Los Angeles Coll. Optometry, 1967-70; supr. Psychology interns Pasadena Child Guidance Clinic, 1969-70; pvt. practice specializing in psychoanalysis and psychoanalytic psychotherapy. N.Y.C., 1970-83; supervising psychologist dept. psychiatry Beth Israel Med. Ctr., N.Y.C., 1972-83, coordinator group therapy tng., 1976-82, clinician in charge Brief Adaptation-Oriented Psychotherapy Research Group, 1982-83; assoc. clin. prof. Mt. Sinai Sch. Medicine, N.Y.C., 1977-91, adj. assoc. prof., 1991—; mem. faculty Nat. Psychol. Assn. for Psychoanalysis, N.Y.C., 1982-83; sr. mem. faculty Wright Inst. Los Angeles Postgrad. Inst., 1983-85; pvt. practice specializing in psychoanalysis and psychoanalytic psychotherapy L.A., 1983—; clin. prof. dept. Psychology UCLA, 1985—. Author: (with others) Treating the Oedipal Patient in Brief Psychotherapy, 1985, Object Relations and the Developing Ego in Therapy, 1979, rev. edit., 1984, Little Big Girl, 1982, Being and Loving, 1978, 3d edit. 1990, Psychology for Living (with G. Forehand), 4th edit., 1977, The Wish for Power and the Fear of Having It, 1989, The Primacy of Structure, 1990, Psychoanalytic Object Relations Therapy, 1991; mem. editorial bd. Jour. of Humanistic Psychology, 1986—, Jour. of the Am. Acad. of Psychoanalysis; contbr. articles to profl. jours. Mem. AAAS, Am. Psychol. Assn., Calif. State Psychol. Assn., Am. Women Sci., Nat. Psychol. Assn. for Psychoanalysis, Am. Acad. Psychoanalysis (sci. assoc.), So. Calif. Psychoanalytic Soc. and Inst. (hon.). Office: 638 W Duarte Rd Arcadia CA 91007-7616

HORNER, ANTHONY ADAM, pediatrician, educator; b. N.Y.C., May 24, 1960; s. Harry and Joan Ruth (Frankel) H. BA in Biochemistry, U. Calif. San Diego, 1983; MD, St. Louis U., 1987. Diplomate Am. Bd. Pediatrics, Am. Bd. Allergy and Immunology. Resident in pediatrics UCLA Med. Ctr., 1990; fellow in pediatric immunology Boston Children's Hosp., 1994; asst. prof. pediatrics med. sch. U. Calif. San Diego, San Diego, 1994—; dir. pediatric allergy and immunology med. ctr. U. Calif. San Diego, 1994—; co-principle investigator Children's Asthma Mgmt. Program, San Diego, 1994—. Fellow Am. Acad. Pediatrics, Am. Acad. Allergy and Immunology. Office: U Calif San Diego Sch Medicine 9500 Gilman La Jolla CA 92093-0609

HORNER, HARRY CHARLES, JR., sales executive, theatrical and film consultant; b. Pitts., Oct. 30, 1937; s. Harry Charles and Sara Marie (Hysong) H.; m. Patricia Ann Hagarty, June 15, 1965 (div. 1981); m. Sharon Kae Wyatt, Dec. 30, 1983; children: Jeffrey Brian, Jennifer Leigh, Mark Gregory. BFA, U. Cin., 1963; postgrad., Xavier U., Cin., 1963-64. Mgr. Retail Credit Co., Atlanta, 1964-68; ops. mgr. Firestone Tire and Rubber Co., L.A., 1968-80; exec. v.p. Romney/Ford Enterprises Inc., Scottsdale, Ariz., 1980-85; sales mgr. Environ. Care Inc., Calabassas, Calif., 1985-93; ops. v.p. Albuquerque (N.Mex.) Grounds Maintenance, Inc., 1993—; pres., chief exec. officer The Cons. Group Cos. Ltd., Palm Desert, Calif., 1984—; pres. E. Valley Theatre Co., Chandler, Ariz., 1984-86. Cons. Ariz. Commn. on Arts, Phoenix, 1983-84. Republican. Mem. LDS Ch. Office: Albuquerque GroundsMaintenance Inc 8442 Washington Pl NE Albuquerque NM 87113

HORNER, JENNIE LINN, retired educational administrator, nurse; b. Memphis, Tex., Feb. 27, 1932; d. Lester C. and Cecil T. (Knight) Linn; m. Billy A. Gooch, June 4, 1951 (dec.); children: Brenda Michael, Patricia Lynn Magneson, Robert Allen; m. 2d Donald M. Horner, July 26, 1975. RN, U. Tex., 1955; BS, No. Ariz. U., 1977, MA, 1978, EdD, 1984. Cert. tchr., registered nurse, Ariz., Tex. Indsl. nurse Lipton Tea Co., Galveston, Tex., 1955-56; head nurse U. Tex. Med. Br., Galveston, 1956-58; sch. nurse Wash. Sch. Dist., Phoenix, 1970-77; tchr. middle sch., 1977-80; asst. prin. Murphy Sch. Dist., Phoenix, 1980-82; assoc. prin. middle sch. Madison Sch., Phoenix, 1982-84; lang. arts coordinator Madison Sch. Dist., Phoenix; prin. Dysart Unified Sch. Dist., Phoenix, 1984-87; adminstr. for ednl. svcs., 1987-91; med. cons. Medahab, Phoenix. Mem. Assn. Supervision and Curriculum Devel., Sch. Nurses Orgn. Ariz. (past pres.), Am. Vocat. Assn., Nat. Assn. Sch. Nurses, Nat. Assn. Elem. Sch. Prins., Ariz. Sch. Health Assn. (bd. dirs.), Ariz. Adminstrs. Assn., Aware West, Phi Delta Kappa. Democrat. Home: 14239 N 50th Ln Glendale AZ 85306-4447

HORNER, LEE, foundation executive, speaker, consultant, computer specialist; b. Sault Ste. Marie, Ont., Can., Mar. 18, 1944; came to U.S., 1976; d. William E. and Gladys (Boomhower) H.; m. Claude Lavallee, Jan. 21, 1960 (div. Sept. 1969); children—Kevin Lauren Lavallee/Petalos, Cynthia

Lee Lavallee; m. James G. Petalos, Jan. 9, 1970 (dec. Jan. 1977). Student Concordia U., Montreal, Que., Can., 1975-76, U. Nev.-Las Vegas, 1977, 90. Pres., LHP Investments, Inc., Las Vegas, 1978—; v.p. Casa Mobile Corp., real estate, San Francisco, 1979—; founder, chmn. bd. PMS Research Found., Las Vegas, 1982—; pub. speaker Premenstrual Syndrome, health, wellness, cycles. Author: How to Chart Your Course to Freedom, 1983; Mini-Nutrition and Exercise Manual, 1983; PMS Minder, 1983; PMS Wellness Workbook, 1985, PMS Support Group Manual, 1985. Mem. Am. Soc. Fund Raising Execs., Am. Bus. Women's Assn., Nat. Speakers Assn. (founding pres. Las Vegas chpt. 1984-85, 88—). Club: Windjammer, Toastmasters (ednl. v.p. 1980, adminstrv. v.p. 1983, 88, pres. 1989—). Home: 2754 El Toreador St Las Vegas NV 89109-1710 Office: LHP Investments Inc/ PMS Research Found PO Box 14574 Las Vegas NV 89114-4574

HORNING, ROBERT ALAN, securities broker; b. Bristol, Tenn., Jan. 8, 1954; s. Sanford Lee and Pauline Stern (Marks) H.; m. Phyllis Ann Bockian, Apr. 12, 1981; children: Aaron Marks, Rachel Michelle. BA, U. Tenn., 1976, MA, 1979. Edn. specialist Knoxville (Tenn.) Police Dept., 1979-80; security cons. Sonitrol of Knoxville, 1980-81; sales rep. Guardsmark, Inc., Charleston, W.Va., 1981-84; mgr. in charge Guardsmark, Inc., L.A., 1984-88; v.p. mktg.-western region Fed. Armored Express, L.A., 1988-92; ptnr. Upton Affiliates, L.A., 1993—. Bd. dirs. B'Nai Tikvah Congregation, L.A., 1989—, v.p. membership, 1991. Mem. Am. Soc. Indsl. Security (chmn. L.A. chpt. 1990), Internat. Platform Assn., Phi Beta Kappa, Omicron Delta Kappa. Democrat. Jewish. Home: 7072 W 85th St Los Angeles CA 90045-2625 Office: Upton Affiliates 7072 W 85th St Los Angeles CA 90045-2625

HOROWITZ, BEN, medical center executive; b. Bklyn., Mar. 19, 1914; s. Saul and Sonia (Meringoff) H.; m. Beverly Lichtman, Feb. 14, 1952; children: Zachary, Jody. BA, Bklyn. Coll., 1940; LLB, St. Lawrence U., 1940; postgrad. New Sch. Social Rsch., 1942. Bar: N.Y. 1941. Dir. N.Y. Fedn. Jewish Philanthropies, 1940-45; assoc., ea. regional dir. City of Hope, 1945-50, nat. exec. sec., 1950-53, exec. dir., 1953-85, gen. v.p., bd. dirs., 1985—, bd. dirs. nat. med. ctr., 1980—; bd. dirs. Beckman Rsch. Inst., 1980—. Mem. Gov.'s Task Force on Flood Relief, 1969-74. Bd. dirs., v.p. Hope for Hearing Found., UCLA, 1972—; bd. dirs. Forte Found., 1987-92, Ch. Temple Housing Corp., 1988-93, Leo Baeck Temple, 1964-67, 86-89, Westwood Property Owners Assn., 1991—. Recipient Spirit of Life award, 1970, Gallery of Achievement award, 1974, Profl. of Yr. award So. Calif. chpt. Nat. Soc. Fundraisers, 1977; Ben Horowitz chair in rsch. established at City of Hope, 1981. City street named in his honor, 1986. Jewish. Formulated the role of City of Hope as pilot ctr. in medicine, sci., and humanitarianism, 1959. Home: 221 Conway Ave Los Angeles CA 90024-2601 Office: City of Hope 208 W 8th St Los Angeles CA 90014-3208

HOROWITZ, JED H., plastic surgeon, reconstructive surgeon; b. N.Y.C., Dec. 29, 1952; s. Bernard Joseph Horowitz and Ruth Zimmerman; m. Joanne Harrington Mayers, Dec. 19, 1980; children: Jamie, Jessica. BS summa cum laude, SUNY, Stony Brook, 1973; MD, SUNY, Buffalo, 1977. Diplomate Am. Bd. Plastic Surgery. Categorical surgical internship Boston U. Affiliated Hosps., 1977-78; gen. surgical resident Grady Meml. Hosp. & Emory U. Sch. of Medicine, Atlanta, 1978-79, 1980-82; gen. surgical rsch. fellow clinical rsch. facility Emory U. Hosp. and Sch. of Medicine, 1979-80; fellowships in craniofacial, microsurgery and hand surgery dept. Plastic and Maxillofacial Surgery U. Va. Med. Ctr., Charlottesville, 1982-83; resident plastic and maxillofacial surgery U. Va. Med. Ctr., 1983-84; chief resident dept. Plastic and Maxillofacial Surgery U. Va. Med. Ctr., 1984-85; clin. asst. prof. divsn. plastic surgery; clin. instr. dept. plastic and maxillofacial surgery U. Va. Med. Ctr., 1984-85; emergency room cons. Boston U. Hosp., 1977-78, Grady Meml. Hosp. Surgical Emergency Clinic, Atlanta, 1978-79. Contbr. articles to profl. jours.; speaker in field. Mem. ACS, Am. Soc. Plastic and Reconstructive Surgeons, Am. Cleft Palate Assn., L.A. County Med. Assn., Calif. Med. Assn., Calif. Soc. Plastic Surgery, Long Beach Surgical Soc., Orange County Med. Assn. Home: 16911 Coral Cay Ln Huntington Beach CA 90720 Office: Plasticos Inst for Plastic Reconstruction Surgeons 1441 Avocado Ave Newport Beach CA 92660 also: 3801 Katella Ave Ste 402 Los Alamitos CA 90720

HOROWITZ, MYER, retired university president, education educator; b. Montreal, Que., Can., Dec. 27, 1932; s. Philip and Fanny Cotler H.; m. Barbara Rosen, 1956; children: Carol Anne, Deborah Ellen. BA, Sir George Williams U., 1956; MEd, U. Alta., 1959; EdD, Stanford U., 1965; LLD (hon.), McGill U., 1979, Concordia U., 1982, Athabasca U., 1989, U. B.C., 1990, U. Alta., 1990. Tchr. elem. and high schs., Montreal, Que. area, 1952-60; lectr. in edn. McGill U., 1960-62, asst. prof., 1963-65, assoc. prof., 1965-67, prof., 1967-69, asst. dean, 1965-69; prof., chmn. dept. elem. edn. U. Alta., 1969-72, dean of edn., 1972-75, v.p. (acad.), 1975-79, pres., 1979-89, prof. emeritus, 1990—. Contbr. articles to profl. jours. Decorated officer Order of Can. Fellow Can. Coll. Teachers. Jewish. Office: U of Alta, 845B Edn Centre, Edmonton, AB Canada T6G 2G5

HOROWITZ, ZACHARY I., entertainment company executive; b. N.Y.C., Apr. 27, 1953; s. Ben and Beverly (Lichtman) H.; m. Barbara J. Natterson. BA summa cum laude, Claremont Mens Coll., 1975; JD, Stanford U., 1978. Bar: Calif. 1978. Assoc. Kaplan, Livingston, Goodwin, Berkowitz & Selvin, Beverly Hills, Calif., 1978; sr. atty. CBS Records, Los Angeles, 1978-80, dir. bus. affairs West Coast, 1980-83; v.p. bus. and legal affairs MCA Records, Universal City, Calif., 1983-84, sr. v.p. bus. and legal affairs, 1984-88; sr. v.p. bus. and legal affairs MCA Music Entertainment Group, Universal City, 1986-89; exec. v.p. MCA Music Entertainment Group, 1989-94; COO MCA Music Entertainment Group, Universal City, 1994—; bd. dirs. MCA Victor Japan; mem. op. com. Motown Recording Co., L.A., 1988-93. Mem. bd. editors Stanford Law Rev., 1977-78. Nat. bd. dirs. City of Hope, 1989—, vice chmn. Music Industry chpt., 1985-86, chmn. maj. gifts com., 1986-90, nat. campaign co-chmn., 1990-91, pres., 1991-92, chmn., 1993-95, endowment chair, 1995—; mem. adv. bd. City of Hope Nashville Celebrity Baseball Challenge, 1995—. Mem. Record Industry Assn. Am. (bd. dirs. 1990—, budget com. 1993—). Office: MCA Records Inc 70 Universal City Plz Universal City CA 91608

HORROCKS, JOHN CHARLES, chemical engineer; b. Middlebury, Vt., May 3, 1960; s. Harold Hart and Jeanne Shirley (Williams) H.; m. Pamela Jean Byrne, July 31, 9182; children: Hillary Rose, Samantha Jeanne. B-SChemE, U. N.H., 1982, MSChemE, 1987. Registered profl. engr., Calif. Commd. 2d lt. USAF, 1983, advanced through grades to capt., 1987; space shuttle engr. USAF, Vandenberg AFB, Calif., 1983-85; design engr. USAF, McClellan AFB, Calif., 1987-92; laser design engr. USAF, Kirtland AFB, N.Mex., 1992—. Contbr. articles to profl. publs. Mem. AIChE. Republican. Episcopalian. Home: 4540 Samara Rd NW Albuquerque NM 87120-5245 Office: Phillips Lab Bldg 619 Kirtland AFB NM 87117

HORSLEY, PAULA ROSALIE, accountant; b. Smithfield, Nebr., Sept. 7, 1924; d. Karl and Clara Margaret (Busse) Fenske; m. Phillip Carreon (dec.); children—Phillip, James, Robert, David, Richard; m. Norby Lumon, Apr. 5, 1980. Student AIB Bus. Coll., Des Moines, 1942-44, YMCA Coll., Chgo., 1944-47, UCLA Extension, 1974. Acctg. mgr. Montgomery Ward & Co., Denver, 1959-62; acct. Harman & Co., C.P.A.s, Arcadia, Calif., 1962-67; controller, officer G & H Transp., Montebello, Calif., 1967-78; comptroller Frederick Weisman Co., Century City, Calif., 1978-80; chief fin. officer Lutheran Shipping, Madang, Papua, New Guinea, 1980-82; prin. Village Bookkeeper, acctg. cons., Monreno Valley, Calif., 1982—; chief fin. officer Insight Computer Products and Tech., Inc., Carlsbad, 1988—. Vol. crises counselor, supr. and instr. Melodyland Hotline, Anaheim, Calif., 1976-79. Mem. NAFE, Riverside Tax Cons., Nat. Soc. Tax Profls., Internat. Platform Assn. Republican. Lutheran. Avocations: church activities, reading, cooking, phys. fitness. Home: 1440 Brentwood Way Hemet CA 92545-7774 Office: Insight Computer Products and Techs Inc 4604 Vinyard St Oceanside CA 92057-5127

HORSTMAN, CAROL BELLHOUSE, lawyer; b. Brantford, Ont., Can., Oct. 14, 1953; came to U.S., 1960, naturalized, 1980; d. Gerald LaVerne and Irma (Vansickle) Bellhouse; m. James K. Horstman, July 2, 1980 (div.); children: Whitney Sarah, Michael Andrew. B.A., Wesleyan U., 1976; J.D., Washington U., St. Louis, 1980. Bar: Ill. 1981, U.S. Dist. Ct. (cen. dist.) Ill. 1981, Colo. 1991. Assoc., Costello, Young & Metnik, Springfield, Ill., 1980-82; sole practice, Springfield, 1982—; Mem. Ill. Bar Assn., Cen. Ill. Bar Assn., Nat. Assn. Women Bus. Owners, Sangamon County Bar Assn. Office: PO Box A Leadville CO 80461-1017

HORTON, EDWARD CARL, military officer; b. Syracuse, N.Y., Sept. 5, 1950; s. Carl and Marjorie Lucille (Clark) H.; m. Chong Sun Kim, Aug. 23, 1980; children: Paul E., David S. BA, U.S. Mil. Acad., 1972; MS in Pers. Mgmt., Troy State U., 1980; MPA, U. Mont., 1983. Commd. 2d lt. U.S. Army, 1972, advanced through grades to lt. col., 1990; platoon leader, exec. officer Co B, 1-506 Infantry, 101st Airborne divsn., Ft. Campbell, Ky., 1973-74, scout platoon leader, support platoon leader, 1974-75; detachment comdr. 2d Replacement Detachment, 2d Infantry divsn., Camp Casey, Korea, 1975-76; co. comdr., instr., asst. chief Benning Ranger divsn. U.S. Army Ranger Sch., Ft. Benning, Ga., 1977-80; asst. prof. mil. sci. U. Mont., Missoula, 1980-83; with 193d Infantry Brigade, Ft. Clayton, Panama, 1983-86; staff officer Office Tech. Advisor and Army Initiatives Group, Washington, 1987-90; comdr. 5th Battalion, 87th Infantry, 193d Infantry Brigade, Ft. Davis, Panama, 1990-92, Yakima (Wash.) Tng. Ctr., 1992—; mem. policy com. Cultural and Natural Resources Fed. Adv. Panel, Yakima, Wash., 1992—. Mem. Assn. of U.S. Army, Ellensburg C. of C., Greater Yakima C. of C. (ex officio bd. dirs. 1992—), Rotary. Home: 7712 Cashland Ct Alexandria VA 22315-5934

HORTON, GWENDOLYN, nursing educator emeritus; b. Moose Jaw, Sask., Can., June 7, 1914; came to U.S., 1919; d. Orville A. and Myrtle (King) H. AA, L.A. City Coll.; BS, Calif. State U., L.A., 1968, MS, 1974. RN; cert. pub. health. Policewoman L.A. Police Dept., 1940-45; prof. nursing L.A. City Coll., Trade Teck Coll., East L.A. Coll., Harbor Coll.; prof. nursing L.A. Pierce Coll., 1972-83, prof. emeritus, 1983—. Mem. Descanso Gardens Guild, LaCanada, Calif., 1953-56, San. Fernando Valley Bd. Realtors, Van Nuys, Calif., 1980-91; bd. dirs. Owners of Subsidized Housing; pres. L.A. Garden Club, 1988-90. Mem. Water and Power Assocs. L.A. (bd. dirs. 1989-94), Apt. Assn. Greater L.A. (v.p. 1990-91, bd. dirs.), Calif. Nurses Assn., L.A. Cinema Club, L.A. Breakfast Club (emergency aid com.), Los Feliz Rep. Women Federated, So. Calif. Rep. Women, Calif. Rep. Women. Home: 2041 N Vermont Ave Los Angeles CA 90027-1952

HORTON, JODI, healthcare executive; b. Lake Village, Ark., Dec. 2, 1943; d. Joseph E. and Laurette (Ralph) Russell; m. Christopher Wyman Horton; children: Kristin Wyman Horton, Edward Ezra Horton. Student, Coll. of William and Mary, 1961-63; BFA, U. Ga., 1965. Regional coord. Easter Seal Soc., White Plains, N.Y., 1978-79; community rels. coord. United Hosp., Port Chester, N.Y., 1979-82; dir. pub. rels. and devel. St. Joseph's Med. Ctr., Yonkers, N.Y., 1982-86, v.p. pub. rels. and devel., 1986-92; pub. affairs mgr. FHP Health Care, Tucson, 1993—; bd. dirs. Codac Behavioral Health Svcs., 1995—. Pres. Rye (N.Y.) Hist. Soc., 1989-92; bd. govs. St. Michael's Parish Day Sch., Tucson, 1992-95; mem. vestry St. Michael All Angels Ch., 1993—; mem. Time for Tucson, 1994—; mem. campaign cabinet United Way of Greater Tucson, 1995—; bd. dirs. Am. Heart Assn., Pima County, 1995—. Mem. Assn. Devel. Officers (pres. Westchester County, N.Y. chpt. 1989-92), Pub. Rels. Soc. Am. (bd. dirs. Westchester/Fairfield chpts. 1987-92, So. Ariz. chpt. 1993—, pres.-elect 1995—). Democrat. Episcopalian. Office: FHP Health Care 6245 E Broadway Blvd Tucson AZ 85711-4009

HORTON, JOHN MICHAEL, psychoanalyst; b. Boston, Feb. 13, 1946; s. William Donald and Cecilia Frances Horton; m. Jane Ellen Howell, Sept. 2, 1973; 1 child, Jesse Ellen. BA, U. Wash., 1968, MD, 1972. Diplomate Am. Bd. Psychiatry and Neurology. Intern Mt. Zion Hosp., San Francisco, 1972-73, resident, 1973; asst. clin. prof. psychiatry U. Calif. Sch. Medicine, San Francisco, 1975-86, U. Wash. Sch. Medicine, Seattle, 1987—; pvt. practice psychiatry and psychoanalysis San Francisco, 1978-86, Seattle, 1986—. Mem. Am. Psychiat. Assn., Am. Psychoanalytic Assn. Roman Catholic. Office: John M Horton MD 4033 E Madison St Seattle WA 98112-3117

HORTON, JONATHAN CHARLES, neuroscientist, neuro-ophthalmologist; b. Edmonton, Alberta, Can., Nov. 16, 1954; came to U.S., 1960; s. George Klaus and Pamela (Fairbrother) H.; m. Lidia Mucia, Dec. 22, 1984; children: Nathanael Carroll, Matthew David, Christina Ixmukane. AB in History, Stanford U., 1976; MD, Harvard U., 1984, PhD, 1984. Diplomate Am. Bd. Ophthalmology. Med. intern Mass. Gen. Hosp., Boston, 1984-85, neurology resident, 1985-86; ophthalmology resident Georgetown U. Hosp., Washington, 1986-89; neuro-ophthalmology/ pediatric ophthalmology fellow U. Calif., San Francisco, 1989-90, asst. prof. of ophthalmology and neurology, 1990—. Contbr. articles to profl. jours. Grantee: N. Calif. Soc. to Prevent Blindness, San Francisco, 1990, Nat. Eye Inst., Washington, 1993. Fellow N. Am. Neuro-Ophthalmology Soc., Am. Acad. Ophthalmology; mem. AAAS, Soc. for Neurosci., Assn. for Rsch. in Vision and Ophthalmology, Cordes Eye Soc., Phi Beta Kappa. Home: 2230 Sheraton Pl San Mateo CA 94402 Office: U C San Francisco Dept Ophthalmology 10 Kirkham St # K301 San Francisco CA 94122-3815

HORTON, LAWRENCE STANLEY, electrical engineer, apartment developer; b. Hanston, Kans., July 25, 1926; s. Gene Leigh and Retta Florene (Abbott) H.; m. Margaret Ann Cowles, Nov. 26, 1946 (dec. 1964); children: Craig, Lawrence Stanley, Steven J.; m. Julia Ann Butler Wirkkula, Aug. 15, 1965; stepchildren: Charles Wirkkula Horton, Jerry Higginbotham Horton. BSEE, Oreg. State U., 1949. Elec. engr. Mountain States Power Co., Calif. Oreg. Power Co., Pacific Power and Light Co., 1948-66; mgr. Ramic Corp., 1966-69; cons. elec. engr. Marquess and Assocs., Medford, Oreg., 1969-85, sec., bd. dirs.; pres., owner Medford Better Housing Assn., 1985—; ptnr. Eastwood Living Group, Jackson St. Properties, T'Morrow Apts., Lake Empire Apts., Johnson Manor, Fountain Pla., Champion Pk.; bd. dirs. Valley of Rogue, developer various apt. complexes, 1969—, Horton Plz.; bd. dirs. Medford Hist. Commn. Active Medford Planning Commn., Archtl. Review Commn., Housing Authority; bd. govs. State of Oreg. Citizens Utility; pres. United Fund, 1963-64. With USN, 1945-46. Named Rogue Valley Profl. Engr. of Yr., 1969. Mem. IEEE, Nat. Soc. Profl. Engrs., Profl. Engrs. of Oreg., So. Oreg. Rental Owners Assn. (pres.), Rogue Valley Geneol. Soc. (pres.), Medford C. of C. (dir.), Rogue Valley Country Club, Rogue Valley Yacht Club (commodore 1974-75, dir., local fleet capt., champion), Rogue Valley Knife and Fork (past pres.), San Juan 21 Fleet Assn. (western vice commodore, Top Ten San Juan Sailor West Coast, 1980), Jackson Toastmasters (founder 1957), Univ. Club, Medford Rotary, Kiwanis (life, pres. Crater Golden 1990-91). Republican. Methodist. Grad. instr. Dale Carnegie course, 1955, 56; contbr. elec. articles to profl. assns., 1956-61. Office: Medford Better Housing Assn 1118 Spring St Medford OR 97504-6272

HORTON, MICHAEL L., mortgage company executive, publishing executive; b. Pasadena, Calif., Oct. 19, 1961; s. Jerry S. and Mary L. Horton. BA in Bus. Econs., Claremont McKenna Coll., 1983. Lic. real estate broker. Gen. mgr. I.W.S., Pasadena, 1976-80; proprietor NBB Svcs. Orgn., Upland, Calif., 1980-85; regional mgr. Sycamore Fin. Group Inc., Rancho Cucamonga, Calif., 1984-87; CEO, pres. Boulder Fin. Corp., Rancho Cucamonga, 1987—, M.C.M. Pub. Corp., Rancho Cucamonga, 1992—; pres., CEO Sandstone Realty Group, Inc., 1995—. Author: A Real Estate Professional's Guide to Mortgage Finance, 1985; author Mortgage Fin. Newsletter, 1984—; author fin. workshop. Mem. Rep. State Ctrl. Com., Calif., 1980—, Bldg. and Industry Assn., Rancho Cucamonga, 1988—, Res Publica Soc., Claremont, Calif., 1986—; donor mem. L.A. World Affairs Coun., 1988—. Claremont McKenna Coll. scholar, 1981-83; recipient Dons D. Lepper Meml. award Exec. Women Internat., 1981, So. Calif. Edison Bus. Competition award, 1979, 81. Mem. Nat. Assn. Realtors, Inland Empire West Bd. Realtors.

HORVITZ, ERIC JOEL, computer scientist, decision theorist; b. N.Y.C., Apr. 14, 1958; s. David and Florence (Blank) H. BA in Biophysics, SUNY, Binghamton, 1980; PhD in Med. Informatics, Stanford U., 1990, MD, 1993. Rsch. scientist Stanford Knowledge Systems Lab., 1986-90; prin. investigator Rockwell Sci. Ctr., Palo Alto, Calif., 1990-93; sr. rschr. Decision Theory group Microsoft Rsch., Redmond, Wash., 1993—; founder, chmn. Knowledge Industries, Palo Alto, 1988—; fellow Stanford Ctr. for Internat. Security and Arms Control, 1985-86; founder, bd. dirs. Ctr. for Innovative Diplomacy, Palo Alto, 1983-88. NASA grad. rsch. fellow, 1987-90. Mem. IEEE, AMA, Am. Assn. for Artificial Intelligence, Am. Med. Informatics Assn. Office: Decision Theory Group Microsoft Rsch Redmond WA 98052-6399

HORWICH, FRANKLIN M., software company executive; b. Chgo., Sept. 12, 1960; s. Norman and Marcia (Morris) H.; m. Margaret Ann Webb, May 20, 1990. BS, So. Ill. U., 1979; MBA, Wharton U., 1992. Programmer, analyst TenMan Systems, Chgo., 1978-79; dir. data processing Transaction Svcs., Chgo., 1979-83; dir. product devel. Perle Ltd., Chgo., 1983-85; pres. Frank Horwich & Assocs., Chgo., 1985-87; v.p. Secutron Corp., Denver, 1987—; dir. data processing RAF Fin. Corp., Denver, 1988-92. Inventor in field. Vol. Colo. for Clinton, Denver, 1992. Mem. Colorado Mountain Club, Sierra Club. Office: Secutron Corp 3773 Cherry Creek North Dr Denver CO 80209-3804

HORWIN, LEONARD, lawyer; b. Chgo., Jan. 2, 1913; s. Joseph and Jennie (Fuhrmann) H.; m. Ursula Helene Donig, Oct. 15, 1939; children—Noel Samuel, Leonora Marie. LLB cum laude, Yale U., 1936. Bar: Calif. 1936, U.S. Dist. Ct. (cen. dist.) Calif. 1937, U.S. Ct. Appeals (9th cir.) 1939, U.S. Supreme Ct. 1940. Assoc., Lawler, Felix & Hall, 1936-39; ptnr. Hardy & Horwin, Los Angeles, 1939-42; counsel Bd. Econ. Warfare, Washington, 1942-43; mem. program adjustment com. U.S. War Prodn. Bd., 1942-43; attache, legal advisor U.S. Embassy, Madrid, Spain, 1943-47; sole practice, Beverly Hills, Calif., 1948—; dir., lectr. Witkin-Horwin Rev. Course on Calif. Law, 1939-42; judge pro tempore Los Angeles Superior Ct., 1940-42; instr. labor law U. So. Calif., 1939-42. U.S. rep. Allied Control Council for Ger., 1945-47; councilman City of Beverly Hills, 1962-66, mayor, 1964-65; chmn. transp. Los Angeles Goals Council, 1968; bd. dirs. So. Calif. Rapid Transit Dist., 1964-66; chmn. Rent Stabilization Com., Beverly Hills, 1980. Fellow Am. Acad. Matrimonial Lawyers; mem. ABA, State Bar Calif., Order Coif. Clubs: Balboa Bay, Aspen Inst. Author: Insight and Foresight, 1990; contbr. articles to profl. jours. Office: 121 S Beverly Dr Beverly Hills CA 90212-3002

HORWITZ, BARBARA ANN, physiologist, educator, consultant; b. Chgo., Sept. 26, 1940; d. Martin Horwitz and Lillian (Knell) Bloom; m. John M. Horowitz, Aug. 17, 1970. BS, U. Fla., 1961, MS, 1962; PhD, Emory U., 1966. Asst. rsch. physiologist U. Calif., Davis, 1968-72, asst. prof. physiology, 1972-75, assoc. prof., 1975-78, prof., 1978—, chair animal physiology, 1991-93, chair neurobiology, physiology and behavior dept., 1993—; cons. Am. Inst. Behavioral Rsch., Palo Alto, Calif., 1980, Am. Inst. Res., Washington, 1993—, NSF, Washington, 1981-84, NIH, Washington, 1995—. Contbr. articles to profl. jours. Recipient prize for teaching and scholarly achievement U. Calif., Davis, 1991, Disting. Teaching award, 1992, Pres's. award for Excellence in Fostering Undergrad. Rsch., 1995; USPHS postdoctoral fellow, 1966-68. Fellow AAAS; mem. Am. Physiol. Soc. (edn. & program coms., coun. 1993—), Am. Soc. Zoologists, N.Y. Acad. Scis., N.Am. Assn. for the Study of Obesity (exec. coun. 1988-92), Soc. Exptl. Biol. Medicine (exec. coun. 1990-94), Phi Beta Kappa (pres. Davis chpt. 1991-92), Sigma Xi (pres. Davis chpt. 1980-81), Phi Kappa Pi, Phi Sigma (v.p. Davis chpt. 1983—, nat. v.p. 1989—). Office: U Calif Dept Neurobiology Phys Davis CA 95616

HORWITZ, KAMALA MARIE, sales professional; b. Fort Ord, Calif., Dec. 7, 1967; d. William and Bonnie (Blackorby) Kaufman; m. Gary Horwitz, Aug. 15, 1993. BS in Biology, U. Calif., Irvine, 1989; MBA, U. So. Calif., L.A., 1994. Hosp. rep. Merck Human Health Divsn., Orange, Calif., 1989-94; region vaccine sales mgr. Merck Vaccine Divsn., Manhattan Beach, Calif., 1994—; acct. leader Astra Merck, Woodland Hills, Calif., 1995—. Mem. Am. Mktg. Assn. Home: 645 33rd St Manhattan Beach CA 90266-3423

HOSACK, KATHLEEN ELIZABETH, art consultant, artist; b. Portland, Oreg.; d. Harold Ferdinand and Elizabeth Magdalene (Ramser) Jacobsen; m. Charles Weeks Hosack, June 20, 1973; children: Geoffrey, Cameron. BA, Boise State U., 1974; MA, U. Idaho, 1987. Tchr. Lake Hazel Elem., Boise, 1974-77; comm. cons. Shasta Pacific, Portland, 1979-80; pub., editor arts and entertainment guide, Coeur d'Alene, Idaho, 1981-83; dir. Downtown Bus. and Profl. Assn., Coeur d'Alene, 1982-83; coord. Community Concepts, Coeur d'Alene, 1984-85; arts writer, corr. The Spokesman-Review, Spokane, 1989-90; drawing instr. North Idaho Coll. Community Educ., Coeur d'Alene, 1989-92; cons. Idaho Arts Adv. Network, Coeur d'Alene, 1991—; artist in residence Citizens Coun. for the Arts, Coeur d'Alene Pub. Schs., 1988-90. Exhibited in group shows including Western Women's Art Showcase, 1985, 1986, Cheney Cowles Art Mus., 1988, Art on the Green Juried Exhbn. (Holmberg award 1987, Jurors award 1986, 88, 89, Pres. award 1991), Blake Gallery, Seattle, 1990, Inland Artists Invitational Exhbn., Coeur d'Alene, 1990. Pres. Coeur d'Alene Cultural Ctr., 1988-90, mem. adv. bd., 1992—; arts commr. City of Coeur d'Alene, 1989-91; Cultural Ctr. chairperson, Kootenai County Centennial, Coeur d'Alene, 1989-90; bd. dirs. Performing Arts Alliance Com., Citizens Coun. for the Arts. Recipient Upbeat Citizen award Coeur d'Alene C. of C., 1983, Golden "K" award Kiwanis, Coeur d'Alene, 1985, Career Excellence award in Arts and Culture Women's Forum, 1990. Mem. Am. Counseling Assn., U. Idaho Grad. Rehab. Assn., Tau Kappa Sigma. Home: 1020 E Mountain Coeur D Alene ID 83814

HOSHI, KATSUO KAI, international business executive; b. Satomimura, Kujigun, Ibaraki, Japan, Aug. 28, 1933; s. Takeyasu and Take H.; m. Yukiko Imajima, Mar. 24, 1959; children: Manami Hoshi Hunt, Naomi Hoshi Diebenow, Brian D. BA in Fgn. Study, Sophia U., Tokyo, Japan, 1959; MS in Mktg., Calif. State U., 1969; Doctrem honoris causa Econs. & Commerce, U. Internat. Speriorum Pro-Deo, 1994. Internat. liaison Nihon Clary Register, Tokyo, 1959-61; nat. A/C sales mgr. Olivetti Corp. of Japan, Tokyo, 1961-67; v.p. Kubota Tractor Corp., Compton, Calif., 1969-83, Auburn (Nebr.) Consol. Industries, 1978-83; sr. v.p. Transport Mgmt. Svc., Inc., N.Y.C., 1983-85; exec. v.p. Merzario USA, Inc., N.Y.C., 1985-86; pres. Canon Italia SpA, Verona, Italy, 1986-91, Canon Milano SpA, Milan, Italy, 1988-91, Canon Trading USA, Inc., Irvine, Calif., 1992—; bd. dirs. Kubota Tractor Corp., Compton, Calif., 1972-83, Auburn (Nebr.) Consol. Industries, 1978-83, Merzario Singapore, 1984, Merzario Hong Kong, 1984, Merzario USA, Inc., N.Y.C., 1985-86, Canon Italia SpA, Verona, 1986-91, Canon Trading USA, Inc., Irvine; mem. global adv. coun. Am. Grad. Sch. Internat. Mgmt., 1994—. Recipient Nebr. Citizenship award, 1978, Baton Rouge Citizenship award, 1979, scholarship Japan-Am. Soc., 1967. Mem. Japan Am. Soc. of So. Calif. (co-chair, 1995—). Home: 54 Club Vis Dove Canyon CA 92679-3747 Office: Canon Trading USA Inc Irvine CA 92718

HOSICK, HOWARD LAWRENCE, cell biology educator, academic administrator; b. Champaign, Ill., Nov. 1, 1943; s. Arthur Howard and Eunice Irma (Miller) H.; m. Cynthia Ann Jacobson, June 15, 1968; children: Steven Cameron, Anna Elise, Rachel Victoria. BA, U. Colo., 1965; PhD, U. Calif., Berkeley, 1970. Postdoctoral fellow Karolinska Inst., Stockholm, 1970-72; asst. research biochemist U. Calif., Berkeley, 1972-73; asst. prof. Wash. State U., Pullman, 1973-78, assoc. prof., 1978-83, prof. cell biology, 1983—, chmn. dept. zoology, 1983-87, chmn. dept. genetics and cell biology, 1987-91; vis. scientist U. Reading, Eng., 1978; disting. scientist Aichi Cancer Ctr., Nagoya, Japan, 1986; vis. scholar Cambridge U., 1994; rsch. com. Am. Heart Assn., 1989; grant rev. com. Nat. Cancer Inst., 1993—. Rev. editor In Vitro Cellular and Molecular Biology, 1986—; contbr. articles to profl. jours. Bd. govs. Internat. Assn. Breast Cancer Rsch., 1993—. Recipient H.S. Boyce award, 1981, Shell Faculty Devel. award, 1984, Cancer Rsch. award Eagles Club, 1989, G. and L. Pfeiffer Rsch. Found. award, 1992; fellow NIH, NSF, Am. Cancer Soc., Damon Runyan-Walter Winchell Cancer Fund, Fogarty Internat. Ctr., 1968—; grantee NIH, NSF, Am. Cancer Soc., Am. Inst. Cancer Rsch., Pfeiffer Found., 1973—. Mem. Am. Soc. Cell Biology, Tissue Culture Assn., Am. Assn. Cancer Research, Internat. Assn. Breast Cancer Research. Democrat. Buddhist. Lodge: Rotary. Home: 1185 NE Lake St Pullman WA 99163-3869 Office: Wash State U Dept Zoology Pullman WA 99164-4236

HOSKINS, THOMAS RICHARD, JR., corporate securities agent; b. Wichita, Kans., Mar. 21, 1959; s. Thomas Richard and Doris Jewell (Riddle) H. AA of Applied Bus. in Acctg., U. Cin., 1980; BS in Bus. Adminstrn., U. Nev., Reno, 1984. Tax examiner IRS, Covington, Ky., 1979-82; asst. mgr. MGM Grand Hotel and Casino, Reno, 1985-86; sales analyst Internat. Game Technol., Reno, 1987-90; investigative agt. Nev. Gaming Control Bd., Carson City, Nev., 1990-95, corp. securities agent, 1995—. Named Dean's

List U. Nev., Reno, 1984. Mem. U. Cin. Alumni Assn. Republican. Office: State of Nevada Gaming Control Board 1150 E William St Carson City NV 89710

HOSLER, LADDIE, editor; b. Allentown, Pa., June 13, 1926; d. Edwin William Cheesbrough and Evelyn (Lilly) Foster; children: Sharon, Lynn, David, Peter. BA, Pa. State U., 1948, BS, 1967, MEd, 1968; MS in Counseling, San Diego State U., 1988. Tchr. fine arts/crafts Bellefonte (Pa.) Jr. High Sch., 1969-71; editor pub. a contact svc. for women "The Wishing Well" (Laddie's Ventures II), San Diego, 1974—. Office: The Wishing Well PO Box 713090 Santee CA 92072-3090

HOSLEY, EDWARD HOWARD, career development organization executive; b. Oakland, Calif., Nov. 12, 1930; s. Howard Herman and Grace Marguerite (Swim) H.; m. Harriet Esther Howells, Apr. 27, 1958. BA in Geology, U. Calif., Berkeley, 1956; MA in Anthropology, UCLA, 1962, PhD in Anthropology, 1966. Instr. El Camino Coll., Torrance, Calif., 1964-65; asst. prof. Calif. State U., Fullerton, 1965-66, U. Alaska, Fairbanks, 1966-68; assoc. prof. Eastern Oreg. State Coll., LaGrande, 1968-71; prof., assoc. dean Eisenhower Coll., Seneca Falls, N.Y., 1971-78; prof., assoc. v.p. acad. affairs SUNY, Potsdam, 1978-90; pres. Career Devel., Beaverton, Oreg., 1990—. Author: Alaska Natives, 1968, The Kolchan, 1968, Eskimo Prehistory, 1969; contbr. articles to profl. jours. and chpts. in books. With U.S. Army, 1952-54. Research fellow NSF, 1962, NEH, 1968; grantee Nat. Mus. Can., 1966; recipient McConnell Found., 1975. Fellow Am. Anthrop. Assn., Soc. for Applied Anthropology; mem. ACA, Assn. for Psychol. Type, Nat. Assn. Practicing Anthropologists. Episcopalian. Home: 4401 Wagon Wheel Cir Forest Grove OR 97116-3328 Office: Career Devel PO Box 850 Forest Grove OR 97116-0850

HOSMER, BRADLEY CLARK, retired military officer, educational consultant; b. San Antonio, Oct. 8, 1937; s. Clark L. and Elynor (Hendrickson) H.; m. Zita Vlavianos, Jan. 4, 1964; children: Basil, Caitlin, Andrew. BS, USAF Acad., 1959; MA, Oxford U., 1962; grad., Squadron Officer Sch., 1965, Naval War Coll., 1969, Nat. War Coll., 1975. Commd. 2nd lt. USAF, 1959, advanced through grades to lt. gen., 1986; supt. USAF Acad., North Colorado Springs, Colo., 1991-94; ret. USAF, 1994; ind. cons. edn. and strategic leadership Alexandria, Va., 1994—. Office: HQ USAFA/SUPT 2304 Cadet Dr Ste 342 U S A F Academy CO 80840*

HOSSLER, DAVID JOSEPH, lawyer, educator; b. Mesa, Ariz., Oct. 18, 1940; s. Carl Joseph and Elizabeth Ruth (Bills) H.; m. Gretchen Anne, Mar. 2, 1945; 1 child, Devon Annagret. BA, U. Ariz., 1969; JD, 1972. Bar: Ariz. 1972, U.S. dist. ct. Ariz. 1972, U.S. Supreme Ct. 1977. Legal intern to chmn. FCC, summer 1971; law clk. to chief justice Ariz. Supreme Ct., 1972-73; chief dep. county atty. Yuma County (Ariz.), 1973-74; ptnr. Hunt, Stanley and Hossler, Yuma, Ariz., 1974—; instr. in law and banking, law and real estate Ariz. Western Coll.; instr. in bus. law, mktg. Webster U; co-chmn. fee arbitration com. Ariz. State Bar, 1990—. Mem. precinct com., Yuma County Rep. Cen. Com., 1974—, vice chmn., 1982; chmn. region II Acad. Decathalon competition, 1989; bd. dirs. Yuma County Ednl. Found., Yuma County Assn. Behavior Health Svcs., also pres., 1981; coach Yuma High Sch. mock ct. team, 1987—; bd. dirs. Friends of U. Med. Ctr. With USN. Recipient Man and Boy award Boys Clubs Am., 1979, Freedoms Found. award Yuma Chpt., 1988, Demolay Legion of Honor, 1991; named Vol. of Yr., Yuma County, 1981-82. Mem. Assn. Trial Lawyers Am., Am. Judicature Soc., Yuma County Bar Assn. (pres. 1975-76), Navy League, VFW, Am. Legion, U. Ariz. Alumni Assn. (nat. bd. dirs., past pres.), Rotary (pres. Yuma club 1987-88, dist. gov. rep. 1989, dist. gov. 1992-93). Editor-in-chief Ariz. Adv., 1971-72. Episcopalian (vestry 1978-82). Home: 2802 S Fern Dr Yuma AZ 85364-7909 Office: Hunt Stanley & Hossler 330 W 24th St Yuma AZ 85364-6455

HOSTETLER, JEFF W., professional football player; b. Johnstown, Pa., Apr. 22, 1961; m. Vicky Nehlen; children: Jason, Tyler, Justin. Attended, Pa. State U.; grad. in fin., W.Va. U. Cert. fin. planner. Player N.Y. Giants, 1984-92; quarterback Superbowl XXV championship team, 1991; with L.A. Raiders, 1993—. Named to Acad. All Am. Season, 1983-84. Address: care LA Raiders 332 Center St El Segundo CA 90245-4047*

HOSTICKA, CARL JOSEPH, academic administrator, educator, legislator; b. Oak Park, Ill., June 21, 1944; s. Harold E. and Marilyn (Simons) H.; 1 child, Anna Tamura. BA, Brown U., 1965; PhD, MIT, 1976. Assoc. dir. Peace Corps India, 1968-71; prof. U. Oreg., Eugene, 1977—, assoc. v.p., 1989—. State rep. Oreg. Ho. of Reps., Salem, 1983-95, majority leader, 1990. Democrat. Home: PO Box 3236 Eugene OR 97403-0236 Office: U Oreg Dept Planning & Pub Policy Eugene OR 97403

HOSTLER, CHARLES WARREN, international affairs consultant; b. Chgo., Dec. 12, 1919; s. Sidney Marvin and Catherine (Marshall) H.; 1 son, Charles Warren, Jr. B.A., U. Calif. at Los Angeles, 1942; M.A., Am. U., Beirut, Lebanon, 1955, Georgetown U., 1950; Ph.D., Georgetown U., 1956. Commd. 2d lt. U.S. Air Force, 1942, advanced through grades to col., 1963; ret., 1963; dir. internat. ops. McDonnell Douglas Corp., Middle East, N.Africa, Beirut, 1965-67; mgr. internat. ops. McDonnell Douglas Corp., Paris, 1963-65; mgr. internat. mktg., missiles and space McDonnell Douglas Corp., 1967-69; pres. Hostler Investment Co., Newport Beach, Calif., 1969-74; chmn. bd. Irvine (Calif.) Nat. Bank, 1972-74; dir. Wynn's Internat., Inc., Fullerton, Calif., 1971-74; dep. asst. sec. for internat. commerce, dir. Bur. Internat. Commerce, U.S. Dept. Commerce, Washington, 1974-76; regional v.p. Mid-East and Africa, E-Systems Inc., Cairo, Egypt, 1976-77; pres. Pacific SW Capital Corp., San Diego, 1977-89; ambassador U.S. Govt., Bahrain, 1989-93; hon. consul gen. State of Bahrain, 1993—; adj. prof. Sch. Internat. Svc., Am. U., Washington, 1955-63. Author: Turkism and the Soviets, 1957, The Turks of Central Asia, 1993; contbr. articles to econ., comml. and mil. jours. Chmn. Calif. Contractors State License Bd., 1973-79, San Diego County Local Agy. Formation Commn., 1979-89; chmn. Calif. State Park and Recreation Commn., 1983-89. Decorated Legion of Merit; recipient Fgn. Affairs award for pub. svc. U.S. State Dept. Mem. Am. Polit. Sci. Assn., Am. Ordnance Assn., Middle East Inst. (bd. govs. 1962-80, 93—). Office: # 302 1101 First St Coronado CA 92118-1474

HOSTNIK, CHARLES RIVOIRE, lawyer; b. Glen Ridge, N.J., Apr. 8, 1954; s. William John and Susan (Rivoire) H.; m. Gail J. Martinolich, Aug. 23, 1980; children: Katherine M., James M. AB, Dartmouth Coll., 1976; JD, U. Puget Sound, 1979. Bar: Wash. 1980, U.S. Dist. Ct. (we. dist.) Wash. 1980, U.S. Dist. Ct. (ea. dist.) Wash. 1982, U.S. Ct. Appeals (9th cir.) 1983, Hoh Tribal Ct. 1984, Nisqually Tribal Ct. 1984, Puyallup Tribal Ct. 1984, Shoalwater Bay Tribal Ct. 1984, Skokomish Tribal Ct. 1984, and others. Asst. atty. gen. Atty. Gen.'s Office State of Wash., Olympia, 1980-84; assoc. Kane, Vandeberg, Hartinger & Walker, Tacoma, 1984-87; ptnr. Anderson, Burns & Hostnik, Tacoma, 1988—; trial and appellate judge N.W. Regional Tribal Supreme Ct., Edmonds, Wash., 1986—. Author: (chpt.) Washington Practice, 1989. Mem. com. to re-elect Justice R. Guy, Olympia and Tacoma, 1990. Mem. N.W. Tribal Ct. Judges Assn., NAm. Indian Ct. Judges Assn. Office: Anderson Burns & Hostnik 4041 Ruston Way Ste 2A Tacoma WA 98402-5392

HOTCHKISS, VIVIAN EVELYN, employment agency executive; b. Fulda, Germany, May 5, 1956; came to U.S., 1957; d. Fred Roy and Rosemary (Wehner) Krug. Student, Pierce Coll., 1974-75, Calif. State U., Northridge, 1976, UCLA, 1991-92. Adminstrv. sec. Taurus Fin. Corp., Hollywood, Calif., 1976-79; adminstrv. asst. Peoples Fin. Corp., Encino, Calif., 1979-81, Thor Employment Agy., L.A., 1981-83, Creative Capital Corp., L.A., 1983-85; owner, pres. Bus. Systems Staffing & Assocs., L.A., 1985—; exec. dir. Edn., Counseling & Placement Program, L.A., 1990—. Author: (newsletter) The Leader; contbr. articles to newspaper, 1990. Mem. Execs. Assn. L.A. (membership dir. 1989—, Member of Yr. 1990), Calif. Assn. Pers. Cons., Pers. and Indsl. Rels. Assn. Office: Bus Sys Staffing & Assocs Inc 10680 W Pico Blvd Ste 210 Los Angeles CA 90064-2223

HOTLE, JACKIE LEE, credit union executive; b. Waco, Tex., Aug. 21, 1939; d. Charles Fredrick William and Neva Jean (Jennings) Steffen; m. Tommy Joe Jackson, Nov. 29, 1956 (div. 1970); 1 child, Steven Wade; m. Ronald V. Hotle, Nov. 23, 1974; 1 child, Randel Keith. Student, Durham Bus. Coll., 1958, U. Wis., Madison, 1985. Pres. Waco Telco Fed. Credit Union, 1960-70, Simmons Fed. Credit Union, Dallas, 1970-72, PIA Fed. Credit Union, Dallas, 1972-74, Natrona County Sch. Employee Credit Union, 1981—; v.p., bd. dirs. Wyo. Cen. Fed. Credit Union, Casper, 1986-87; supervisory com. System United Corp. Fed. Credit Union, 1988—; judge Distbv. Edn. Clubs Am., Casper, 1986, 89. Mem. Wyo. Credit Union League, Casper, 1987-93. Mem. Pioneer Chpt. Credit Unions (pres. 1990, 91), Soroptimist Internat. (treas. Cen. Wyo. chpt. 1987-88, pres. 1990, bd. dirs. 1992, treas. children's nutrition svcs. 1991-93). Republican. Episcopalian. Home: 1730 S Spruce St Casper WY 82601-4539 Office: Natrona County Sch Employee Fed Credit Union 900 Werner Ct Ste 100 Casper WY 82601-1327

HOTZ, HENRY PALMER, physicist; b. Fayetteville, Ark., Oct. 17, 1925; s. Henry Gustav and Stella (Palmer) H.; m. Marie Brase, Aug. 22, 1952; children: Henry Brase, Mary Palmer, Martha Marie. B.S., U. Ark., 1948; Ph.D., Washington U., St. Louis, 1953. Asst. prof. physics Auburn U., Ala., 1953-58, Okla. State U., Stillwater, 1958-64; assoc. prof. Marietta Coll., Ohio, 1964-66; physicist, scientist-in-residence U.S. Naval Radiol. Def. Lab., San Francisco, 1966-67; assoc. prof. U. Mo., Rolla, 1967-71; physicist Qanta Metrix div. Finnigan Corp., Sunnyvale, Calif., 1971-74; sr. scientist Nuclear Equipment Corp., San Carlos, Calif., 1974-79, Envirotech Measurement Systems, Palo Alto, Calif., 1979-82, Dohrmann div. Xertex Corp., Santa Clara, Calif., 1982-86; sr. scientist Rosemount Analytical Div. Dohrmann, 1983-91; cons. Burlingame, Calif., 1991—; cons. USAF, 1958-62; mem. lectr. selection com. for Hartman Hotz Lectrs. in law, liberal arts U. Ark. Served with USNR, 1944-46. Mem. Am. Phys. Soc., Am. Assn. Physics Tchrs., AAAS, Phi Beta Kappa, Sigma Xi, Sigma Pi Sigma, Pi Mu Epsilon, Sigma Nu. Methodist. Lodge: Masons. Home: 290 Stilt Ct Foster City CA 94404-1323 Office: Hotz Assocs 525 Almer Rd Apt 201 Burlingame CA 94010-3955

HOUCHIN, KENNETH WAYNE, ophthalmologist, neuro-opthalmologist, educator; b. Phoenix, Apr. 19, 1958; s. Merle Cleo and Mildred Elizabeth (Knittle) H. BA with highest honors, Union Coll., 1981; MD, Loma Linda U., 1985. Intern in internal medicine Loma Linda (Calif.) U. Med. Ctr., 1985-86, resident in neurology, 1986-89, resident in ophthalmology, 1990-93; fellow in neuro-ophthalmology U. Minn., Mpls., 1989-90; asst. prof., neuro-ophthalmologist Inland Eye Inst. Loma Linda U. Sch. Medicine, 1993—; gen. ophthalmologist Inland Eye Inst., Colton, Calif., 1993—; lectr., presenter in field; clk. in third-world ophthalmology Maluti Adventist Hosp., Lesotho, Africa. Contbr. articles to profl. publs., photographs to NBC Today Show, 1979-80, book Kansas in Color, 1982, also greeting cards and calendar. Mem. AMA, Adventist Internat. Eye Soc., Am. Acad. Neurology, Am. Acad. Ophthalmology (subcom. internat. ophthalmology com. 1991-93), Assn. for Rsch. in Vision and Opthalmology, Calif. Med. Assn., N.Am. Neuro-Ophthalmology Soc., San Bernardino County Med. Soc., Tri-County Eye Soc. (pres. Riverside, San Bernardino, Ea. L.A. Counties). Office: Loma Linda U Inland Eye Inst FMO # 1800 11370 Anderson St Loma Linda CA 92354

HOUGAN, TOM MCKAY, advertising executive; b. Colfax, Wash., June 23, 1935; s. Melvin C. and Laura (McKay) H.; m. Lois Jean McBride, Jan. 4, 1958; children: Debra, Scott, Mark. BA, Wash. State U., 1957; postgrad., U. Kans., 1957, Portland State U., 1968. Sr. copywriter Gen. Electric Corp., Schenectady, 1960-65; chmn. bd. dirs. Gerber Advt., Portland, Oreg., 1965-95; dir., exec. com. Assn. Oreg. Industries, Salem, 1983-94; Western regional chmn. Am. Advt. Fedn., Washington, 1978-80; pres. Portland Advt. Fedn., 1975-76. Pub. rels. chmn. United Way Portland, 1976; trustee Citizens for a Drug-Free Oreg., Wash. State Univ. Found., 1990—; chmn. adv. bd. Edward R. Murrow Sch. Communication, Wash. State U.; trustee Wash. State U. Found. Served to 1st lt. U.S. Army, 1958-60. Recipient Advt. Pres. of Yr. Silver Medal award, Am. Advt. Fedn., 1976; named Advt. Prof. of Yr., Portland. Advt. Fedn., 1976, Clark County Vol. Yr. United Way, 1995; Mayor's Corp. Citizen award Volunteer Council, Portland, 1984. Mem. Am. Assn. Advt. Agys. (gov. Oreg. coun.), Utility Communicators Internat., Ducks Unlimited, Tau Kappa Epsilon (pub. rels. chmn.). Republican. Presbyterian. Home: 27212 NE Bjur Rd Ridgefield WA 98642-9756 Office: Gerber Advt Agy 209 SW Oak St Portland OR 97204-2714

HOUGH, J. MARIE, vocational education educator; b. Trenton, N.J., Oct. 15, 1940; d. Michael J. and Evelyn M. (Klink) Mazur; m. Gary T.M. Hough, Apr. 7, 1990. Degree in bus. adminstrn., Rider Bus. Coll., 1964; AA, L.A. City Coll., 1967; B of Edn., Cin. Coll., 1970; MEd, Azusa Pacific U., 1982. Cert. tchr., Calif. Vocat. tchr. Papua New Guinea Inst., 1972-80; adminstrv. asst. Princeton (N.J.) U., 1980-82; bus. instr. Criss Coll., Anaheim, Calif., 1983-87; instr. office occupations Regional Occupational Program, Santa Ana, Calif., 1987-90; bus. instr. Somos Hermandas Unidas, Anaheim, 1991-92; office tech. instr. United Cambodian Community Vocat. Ctr., Long Beach, Calif., 1992-93; bus. mgr. Hough Enterprises, San Clemente, Calif., 1993-95; realtor First Team Real Estate, Mission Viejo, Calif., 1995—. Mem. Am. Vocat. Assn. Home: 913 Avenida Presidio San Clemente CA 92672-2217 Office: First Team Real Estate Inc 24166 Alicia Pkwy Mission Viejo CA 92691

HOUGH, MICHAEL JAMES, sculptor, educator; b. Anaheim, Calif., Jan. 20, 1960; s. Richard Guy Hough and Barbara Jean (Dierberger) Moody; m. Ronelle Bingham, July 28, 1984; m. Tracy Lee Watts, Mar. 23, 1991; 1 child, Timothy Michael Enke. BA in Art, Calif. State U., Sacramento, 1983, MA in Art, 1989; MFA in Ceramic Sculpture, RISD, 1993. Graphic designer J.K. Bonum, Sacramento, Calif., 1980-86; mem. TV prodn. staff Sta. KVIE Channel 6, Sacramento, Calif., 1983-89; art tchr. El Sereno H.S., Fair Oaks, Calif., 1987-90; ceramics instr. RISD, Providence, 1991-93; art tchr. Snake River Correctional Facilities, Ontario, Oreg., 1993—, Boise (Idaho) State U., 1994—, Treasure Valley C.C., Ontario, 1994—; ceramic artist Weiser (Idaho) Sculpture Works, 1983—; vis. artist Foresthill and Auburn Union Sch. Dists., Calif., 1984-91; mural painter Taylor Studios, Sacramento, South Lake Tahoe, and Carson City, Nev., 1988—; presenter Raku demonstrations Sacramento Open Studio Tours, 1989, 90; fin. dir., mem. 750 Gallery, Sacramento, 1987-89; dir. Witt Gallery, Calif. State U., Sacramento, 1985-86; kiln rm. mgr. RISD, 1991-93. One-man shows include 750 Gallery, Sacramento, 1987, ArtWorks Gallery, Fair Oaks, Calif., 1987, 89, Michael Himovitz Gallery, Sacramento, 1990, 93, 95, Himovitz Pavillions, Sacramento, 1991, Habatat/Shaw Gallery, Farmington Hills, Mich., 1994, Gallery at Glendeven, Mendocino, Calif., 1994; group shows include Thesis Exhbn. RISD Roitman Gallery, Providence, Rhode Island, Grad. Exbhn., 1993, Habatat/Shaw Gallery, Mich., 1993, Farrell Collection, Washington, 1993, Holmes Fine Art Gallery, San Jose, Calif., 1993, Cafe au Clay Cup Invitational Lincoln Arts, Calif., 1994, Contemporary Crafts Gallery, Portland, 1994, The Potters Ctr., Boise, 1994, Michael Himovitz Gallery, 1994; represented in permanent collections at Faviana Olivier, Boston, Pac-Tel Corp., Calif., Embassy Suites Hotel, South Lake Tahoe, Calif., Sacramento First Nat. Bank, Tower Corp., Sacramento, Hewlett Packard Co., Roseville, Calif.; author: (books) Raku Pottery, 1991, Raku: A Practical Approach, 1991; contbr articles to profl. jours. Invitational-promotion fundraiser Sta. KXJZ, Sacramento, 1991. Avocations: collecting, gardening, cooking, traveling. Home and Studio: 527 E Court St Weiser ID 83672-2214

HOUGHTON, ROBERT CHARLES, secondary education educator; b. Dover, N.H., Apr. 12, 1958; s. Raymond David and Barbara Jean (Lyle) H. Student, USCG Acad., New London, Conn., 1976-77; BA with honors, U. Calif., Riverside, 1987, postgrad., 1987-89. Teaching credential, Calif. Various teaching positions, 1977-80; pharmacy technician Anaheim (Calif.) Meml./Brea (Calif.) Cmty., 1980-85; teaching asst. U. Calif., Riverside, 1988-90; instr. Mt. San Jacinto (Calif.) Coll., 1989-90; tchr. Desert Sands Unified, Indio, Calif., 1990—; counselor Chem. Awareness Network, Indio, Calif., 1990—; computer cons. Desert Sands Unified Sch. Dist., Indio, 1994—; resident tchr. Calif. State U., San Bernardino, 1994-95; asst. tour dir. Lakeland Tours, Washington, 1991-95. Mem. NEA, Nat. Coun. Social Studies, Nat. Geographic Soc., Calif. Tchrs. Assn., Nat. Trust Historic Preservation, Civil War Trust. Republican. Home: 72600 Fred Waring Dr Apt 407 Palm Desert CA 92260-5223 Office: 81195 Miles Ave Indio CA 92201-2807

HOUK, KENDALL NEWCOMB, chemistry educator; b. Nashville, Tenn., Feb. 27, 1943; s. Charles H. and Janet Houk; 1 child, Kendall M.; m. Robin L. Garrell. AB, Harvard U., 1964, MS, 1966, PhD, 1968. Asst. prof. chemistry La. State U., Baton Rouge, 1968-72, assoc. prof., 1972-75, prof., 1975-80; prof. U. Pitts., 1980-86; prof. UCLA, 1986-91, chmn. dept. chemistry and biochemistry, 1991-94; dir. chemistry div. nat. Sci. Found., 1988-90. Contbr. numerous articles to profl. jours. Recipient Cope Scholar award Am. Chem. Soc., 1988. Mem. AAAS, Am. Chem. Soc. (Cope Scholar award 1988, James Flack Norris award in physical organic chemistry 1991). Office: UCLA Dept Chemistry and Biochemistry 405 Hilgard Ave Los Angeles CA 90095

HOULE, JOSEPH ADRIEN, orthopaedic surgeon; b. Ft. Saskatchewan, Alta., Can., Nov. 3, 1928; came to U.S., 1978; s. Adelard Houle and Bertha (Durocher) Guay; divorced; children: Valerie, Diane, Lorraine, Louis, Doreen, Ludmilla, Virginia; m. Marjorie Elizabeth Tuhy. BSc, cert. in premed., U. Ottawa, 1955; MD, Laval U., 1960, Licentiate Med. Council of Can., 1960. Cert. specialist orthopaedic surgery, Quebec, Can. Intern Hotel Dieu Hosp., Quebec City, Can., 1959-60; resident in gen. surgery St. Vincent de Paul Hosp., Sherbrooke, Que., Can., 1960-61, St. Vincent's Hosp., Bridgeport, Conn., 1961-62; resident in orthopaedic surgery Montreal Children's Hosp., Montreal Gen. Hosp. and Queen Mary's Vet. Hosp., 1962-65; practice medicine specializing in orthopaedic surgery Montreal, Can., 1965-78; chief of orthopaedic surgery Thomas Davis Med. Ctr., Tucson, 1978—. Produced film Mechanical Knee, 1969. Mem. Bd. Med. Examiners of Ariz., 1978. Served to capt. Royal Can. Forces, 1956-67. Mem. AMA, Can. Orthopaedic Assn., Ariz. Orthopaedic Assn., Pima County Med. Soc. Roman Catholic. Home: 3715 N Pantano Rd Tucson AZ 85715-2348 Office: Thomas Davis Med Ctrs 707 N Alvernon Way Tucson AZ 85711-1801

HOUPIS, HARRY LOUIS FRANCIS, research physicist; b. Johnson City, N.Y., Jan. 18, 1954; s. Louis Harry and Annamarie Houpis.; m. Carole Lynn Turner, Jan. 28, 1984; children: Demetrius Vesalius, Carissa Selena. BS in Math., MIT, 1976, BS in Physics, 1976; MS in Physics, U. Calif. San Diego, La Jolla, 1978, PhD in Physics, 1981. Asst. rsch. physicist U. Calif. San Diego, La Jolla, 1981-87; vis. rsch. physicist Max Planck Inst. for Aeronomie, Katlenburg-Lindau, Fed. Republic Germany, 1985, Cen. Rsch. Inst. for Physics, Budapest, Hungary, 1986, Supercomputer Computations Rsch. Inst. Fla. State U., Tallahassee, 1986-87; vis. and assoc. rsch. physicist Space Physics Rsch. Lab. U Mich., Ann Arbor, 1987-88; tech. staff Mission Rsch. Corp., Monterey, Calif., 1988-90; dir. we. region Ctr. for Remote Sensing, Missoula, Mont., 1990-94; pres. EnviroSens, Inc., Missoula, Mont., 1995—; lectr. in physics Hartnell C.C., Salinas, Calif., 1989-90; proposal refree NASA, NSF, Washington, 1985—; manuscript referee Jour. Geophys. Rsch. and Icarus, 1981-92. Author: The Physics of Comets; contbr. numerous articles to profl. jours. Pub. lectr. San Diego Speakers Bur., 1979-86. Fulbright sr. scholarship Coun. for Internat. Exch. of Scholars, 1985-86; Max Planck Soc. fellowship, Max Planck Inst., 1983, 85. Mem. Am. Geophys. Union, Am. Phys. Soc. Home: 3509 Norman Dr Missoula MT 59801-3001 Office: EnviroSens Inc 415 N Higgins Ave Ste 124 Missoula MT 59802-4522

HOURANI, LAUREL LOCKWOOD, epidemiologist; b. Carmel, Calif., Sept. 10, 1950; d. Eugene Franklin and Katherine Ruth (Miller) Betz; m. Ghazi Fayez Hourani, Feb. 28, 1984; children: Nathan, Danna, Lisa. BA, Chico State U., 1977; MPH, Am. Univ. Beirut, 1983; PhD, U. Pitts., 1990. Prog. evaluator Community Hosp. Monterey Peninsula, Carmel, Calif., 1978-81; instr./researcher Am. Univ. Beirut, 1981-85; predoctoral fellow U. Pitts., 1985-89; researcher, cons. V.A. Med. Ctr., Pitts., 1988-90; dir., tumor registry Med. Ctr. U. Calif. Irvine, Orange, 1990-92, head divsn. health scis. Med. Ctr.; head, divsn. of health scis. Naval Health Rsch. Ctr., San Diego, Calif., 1993—; cons. Nat. Devel. Commn. South Lebanon, 1981-83. Author: No Water, No Peace, 1985; contbr. articles to profl. jours. Bd. dirs. Am. for Justice in Middle East, Beirut, 1982-85, Nat. Devel. Com., South Lebanon, 1983-85. Recipient grant V.A., Pitts., 1989, rsch. grant U. Rsch. Bd., Beirut, 1985. Mem. Am. Psychol. Assn., Am. Pub. Health Assn., Soc. for Epidemiologic Rsch. Office: Naval Health Rsch Ctr Divsn Epidemiology PO Box 85122 San Diego CA 92186-5122

HOUSE, DAVID L., electronics components company executive; b. 1943. With Raytheon, 1965-69, Honeywell, 1969-72, Microdata, 1972-74; v.p., gen. mgr. Intel Corp., 1974—, now sr. v.p. Office: Intel Corp 3065 Bowers Ave Santa Clara CA 95054-3202*

HOUSE, EDWARD BRILEY, JR., librarian; b. Newport News, Va., June 21, 1948; s. Edward Briley and Susie Marie (Davenport) H.; m. Jeanne Elizabeth Agren, Nov. 8, 1975; children: Sarah Elizabeth, Caitlin Marie. AA in Social Scis., Canal Zone Coll., 1968; BS in Secondary Edn., U. Nebr., 1970; MLS, U. Wash., 1983. Painter Clair Davis Painting, Phoenix, Oreg., 1972-75; owner Ed House Housepainting, Central Point, Oreg., 1975-81; dir. G.H. and L.E. Brown Pub. Libr., Washington, N.C., 1983-85; supervising libr. Albany (Oreg.) Pub. Libr., 1985-90, dir., 1990—. Mem. budget com. Linn-Benton Cmty. Coll., Albany, 1992-94. Mem. ALA, Oreg. Libr. Assn. (v.p./pres. elect 1995—, chair pub. libr. divsn. 1993-94), Greater Albany Rotary Club (sec. 1990-94). Home: 2005 NW Bloom Ln Albany OR 97321-1024 Office: Albany Pub Libr 1390 Waverly Dr SE Albany OR 97321-6945

HOUSE, GEORGE MICHAEL, museum curator; b. Silver City, N.Mex., Apr. 2, 1955; s. William Winfrey House and Ruth Lestra (Williams) Billings; m. Maria Cedillo Enriquez, Dec. 24, 1983; children: Vanessa Yvette, Joshua Michael, Benjamin Alexander. BA in History and Social Sci., Western N.Mex. U., 1984, MA in History, 1985. With forest svc. USDA, Silver City, N.Mex., 1973, Kingston, N.Mex., 1976; museum curator Space Ctr., Alamogordo, N.Mex., 1985—; cons., instr., rschr., lectr. Space Ctr., Alamogordo, 1985—. Contbr. articles to publs. Sunday sch. tchr. Ch. of Christ, Bayard, N.Mex., 1976-85, Alamogordo, 1985—; juror Otero County Courthouse, Alamogordo, 1990. With USN, 1973-76. Dean Caulkins Meml. scholar Western N.Mex. U., 1983, Bd. of Regents scholar Western N.Mex., 1983. Mem. Pi Gamma Mu (Cert. of Merit 1984). Home: PO Box 382 Alamogordo NM 88311-0382 Office: Space Ctr PO Box 533 Top of NM Hwy 2001 Alamogordo NM 88311-0533

HOUSE, KAREN SUE, nursing consultant; b. San Francisco, July 16, 1958; d. Mathas Dean and Marilyn Frances (Weigand) H. Casa Loma Coll., 1985; AS in Nursing, SUNY at Albany, 1987. Psychiat. charge nurse Woodview Calabasas (Calif.) Hosp., 1985-87, Treatment Ctrs. Am., Van Nuys, Calif., 1987-88; cons., RN Valley Village Devel. Ctr., Reseda, Calif., 1988; plastic surg. nurse George Sanders, M.D., Encino, Calif., 1986—; nurse New Image Found., 1989—, Mid Valley Youth Ctr., 1991—; dir. nursing Encino Surgicenter (Sanders), 1992—; dir. nursing Devel. Tng. Svcs. for Devel. Disabled, 1988—; nurse cons. New Horizons for Developmentally Disabled, 1993. Recipient Simi Valley Free Clinic Scholarship. Mem. Encino C. of C. Home: 29748 Saguaro St Santa Clarita CA 91384-3567 Office: 16633 Ventura Blvd Ste 110 Encino CA 91436-1834

HOUSEMAN, KIMBERLY LYNN, special education educator, counselor; b. Omaha, Oct. 16, 1966; d. Ronald William and Lynn Etta (Keeler) Swassing; m. Richard D. Houseman, Aug. 20, 1994. BA in Elem. Edn., Deaf Edn. K-12, Fontbonne Coll., St. Louis, 1988; MA in Counseling Psychology, Lewis & Clark Coll., Portland, Oreg., 1994. Cert. tchr. elem. edn., deaf edn. K-12. Houseparent St. Joseph Inst. for Deaf, St. Louis, 1984-88, tchr. deaf, 1987-88, learning ctr. supr., 1987-88; tchr. deaf Tucker Maxon Oral Sch. for Deaf, Portland, 1988-90; restaurant mgr. Godfather's Pizza, Portland, 1989—; sch. counselor K-8 Stafford Elem. Sch., Portland, 1994—. Mem. Am. Counseling Assn. Roman Catholic. Home: 18080 NW Cornell Rd E Beaverton OR 97006

HOUSEWORTH, DEREK EUGENE, software test engineer; b. Nacodoches, Tex., Jan. 25, 1969; s. Donald Eugene and Vera Jean (Draper) H. BS in Bus. with high honors, Mont. State U., 1992. Systems software analyst Applied Systems Tech., Kalispell, Mont., 1988-89; computer operator II Mont. State U., Bozeman, 1990; software tng. cons. Bozeman, 1990-92; lead software test engr. Microsoft Corp., Redmond, Wash., 1992—. Named SBI Case of Yr., Undergrad., U.S. SBA, Washington, 1993. Mem. Assn. Computing Machinery, Phi Kappa Phi, Beta Gamma Sigma. Office: Microsoft Corp One Microsoft Way Redmond WA 98052

HOUSEWORTH, LAURA JENNINGS, lawyer; b. Kansas City, Kans., Mar. 22, 1927; d. Frank Harvey and Lucile (Pollock) Jennings; m. Richard Court Houseworth, Nov. 1, 1952; children: Louise, Lucile, Court II. BA magna cum laude, Lake Forest Coll., 1949; MEd, U. Mo., 1951; JD, Ariz. State U., 1974. Bar: Ariz. 1975, D.C. 1989. Nat. rep. Chi Omega, Cin., 1949-50; asst. dean women U. Kans., Lawrence, 1951-52; dep. county atty. Maricopa County, Phoenix, 1975-88, juvenile div., 1979—, sr. trial atty., asst. supr. juvenile div., 1985—, extradition atty., 1987—, grand jury, 1987—; lectr. Nat. Family Support Assn., San Diego, 1977; arbitrator Superior Ct., 1986; judge pro tem Ariz. Ct. Appeals, 1986. Founding bd., pres. Vol. Bur., Tucson, 1969; founding bd. Girl's Club Tucson, 1970; founding bd., 1st v.p. Crisis Nursery, Phoenix, 1978; exec. bd. United Way, Legal Aid, Family Svc.; nat. trustee Lake Forest Coll., 1992—. Mem. ABA, ATLA, Maricopa County Bar Assn., Ariz. Women's Lawyers Assn., Ariz. Acad. Republican. Episcopalian. Club: Jr. League Phoenix. Home: Colonia Miramonte # 83 Paradise Valley AZ 85253

HOUSEWORTH, STEVEN MICHAEL, court counselor; b. St. Cloud, Minn., Mar. 19, 1951; s. John Leman Houseworth and Lovina Francis (Sand) Bystrom; m. Joanne Marie Winterroth, Dec. 31, 1994; children: Sherry Lynn, Lisa Lynn, Bradley Steven. BS, Portland State U., 1974; postgrad., Lewis and Clark Coll., 1991—. Ct. counselor Clackamas County Juvenile Ctr., Oregon City, Oreg., 1975—; exec. dir. Theft Talk Counseling Svc., Portland, Oreg., 1983—; instr. Clackamas C.C., Oregon City, 1983—, Portland C.C., 1990—; dep. sheriff Clackamas County Sheriff, Oregon City, 1983—. Author: (manual) Teacher's Manual-Stealing, 1989. Mem. Toastmasters, Canby, Oreg., 1984-92; sustaining mem. Rep. Nat. Com., Washington, 1994. Mem. APA (affiliate). Republican. Office: Theft Talk Counseling Svcs 3530 SE 52nd Portland OR 97206

HOUSEWRIGHT, ALFRED NEIL, religious organization executive; b. Ft. Worth, Sept. 22, 1930; s. Chester Roy and Marion Edna (Kinder) H.; divorced; children: Elizabeth Ann, Joseph Neil. BA, Tex. Christian U., 1952; MDiv, Vanderbilt U., 1962; D Cert., St. Andrews Scotland, 1968. Asst. prof., assoc. dean Vanderbilt Div. Sch., Nashville, 1964-74; v.p. Grad. Theol. Union, Berkeley, Calif., 1974-83, acting pres., 1981-82; pres. Cogswell Coll., San Francisco, 1983-86; exec. dir. Nat. Conf. Christians and Jews, San Francisco, 1986-92, Ecumenical Ministries No. Calif., San Francisco, 1993—. Democrat. Home: 1645 Fulton St San Francisco CA 94117-1318

HOUSLEY, PHIL F, professional hockey player; b. St. Paul, Mar. 9, 1964. Mem. USA hockey team World Cup Tournament, 1982; with Buffalo Sabers, 1982-90; defenseman Winnipeg Jets, St. Louis Blues, 1993, Calgary Flames, 1994—; player NHL All-Star game, 1984, 89-93. Named to NHL All-Rookie Team, 1982-83. Office: Calgary Flames, P O Box 1540 Station M, Calgary, AB Canada T29 3B9

HOUSMAN, RICHARD J., custom house broker; b. Chgo., Sept. 4, 1948; s. Richard Jacob and Gertrude Catherine (Zeilenga) H.; m. Rosa Lee Pappenheim, June 21, 1975. BA, Hope Coll., 1970; MA, U. Denver, 1975. Lic. custom house broker. Import specialist U.S. Customs Svc., Chgo., 1970-72; customs broker Charles M. Schayer & Co., Denver, 1973-74, McClary, Swift & Co., San Francisco, 1975-79, Ted L. Rausch & Co., Portland, Oreg., 1979-85, George S. Bush & Co., Portland, 1985-92, James J. Boyle & Co., Portland, 1992—; instr. import classes Columbia River Brokers Assn., Portland, 1987—, World Trade Ctr., Portland, 1991—. Mem. Columbia Rivers Brokers Assn. (bd. mem. 1993—, chair edn. com. 1994—, chair membership com. 1993—), Portland C. of C. (chmn. Europe subcom. 1991—), German-Am. C. of C. (founding mem. Portland chpt. 1994). Democrat. Home: 5440 SE Lincoln St Portland OR 97215-3938 Office: James J Boyle & Co 7505 NE Ambassador Pl Portland OR 97220-1377

HOUSTON, C(LARENCE) STUART, radiologist, educator; b. Williston, N.D., Sept. 26, 1927; s. Clarence Joseph and Sigridur (Christianson) H.; m. Mary Isabel Belcher, Aug. 12, 1951; children: Stanley, Margaret, David, Donald. MD, U. Man., Winnipeg, Can., 1951; DLitt, U. Sask., Saskatoon, Can., 1987. Demonstrator in anatomy U. Sask., 1960-61, teaching fellow in radiology, 1963-64, lectr., 1964-65, asst. prof., 1965-67, assoc. prof., 1967-69, prof., 1969-95, emeritus prof., 1995—, head dept. med. imaging, 1982-87. Author: To the Arctic by Canoe, 1974, Pioneer of Vision, 1980, Arctic Ordeal, 1984, R.G. Ferguson, Crusader, 1991, Arctic Artist, 1994; editor Jour. Can. Assn. Radiologists, 1976-81. Recipient Roland Michener Conservation award Can. Wildlife Fedn., 1986, Douglas H. Pimlott Conservation award Can. Nature Fedn., 1988, Ralph D. Bird award Man. Naturalists' Soc., 1989, Doris Huestis Speirs award Soc. Can. Ornithologists, 1989, Eugene Eisenmann medal Linnean Soc. N.Y., 1990, Sask. Order of Merit, 1992, Officer of Order of Can., 1993. Mem. Can. Soc. for History of Medicine (pres. 1987-89), Royal Coll. Physicians and Surgeons (mem. coun. 1984-90, chmn. specialty com. 1984-88), Am. Ornithologists' Union (mem. coun. 1978-80, mem. memorials com. 1984—, v.p. 1990-91). Home: 863 University Dr, Saskatoon, SK Canada S7N 0J8 Office: U Hosp Dept Med Imaging, 103 Hospital Dr, Saskatoon, SK Canada S7N 0W8

HOUSTON, ELIZABETH REECE MANASCO, county education official, consultant; b. Birmingham, Ala., June 19, 1935; d. Reuben Cleveland and Beulah Elizabeth (Reece) Manasco; m. Joseph Brantley Houston; 1 child, Joseph Brantley Houston III. BS, U. Tex., 1956; MEd, Boston Coll., 1969. Cert. elem. tchr., Calif., cert. spl. edn. tchr., Calif., cert. community coll. instr., Calif. Tchr., elem. Ridgefield (Conn.) Schs., 1962-63; staff, spl. edn. Sudbury (Mass.) Schs., 1965-68; staff intern Wayland (Mass.) High Sch., 1972; tchr., home bound Northampton (Mass.) Schs., 1972-73; program dir. Jack Douglas Ctr., San Jose, Calif., 1974-76; tchr. specialist spl. edn., coord. classroom svcs., dir. alternative schs. Santa Clara County Office Edn., San Jose, Calif., 1976-94; instr. San Jose State U., 1980-87, U. Calif., Santa Cruz, 1982-85, Santa Clara U., 1991—; cons. Houston Rsch. Assocs., Saratoga, Calif., 1981—. Author: (manual) Behavior Management for School Bus Drivers, 1980, Classroom Management, 1984, Synergistic Learning, 1988, Learning Disabilities in Psychology for Correctional Education, 1992. Recipient President's award Soc. Photo-Optical Instrumentation Engrs., 1979, Classroom Mgmt. Program award Sch. Bds. Assn., 1984, Svc. to Youth award, Juvenile Ct. Sch. Adminstrs. of Calif., 1989, 90. 91, 92; grantee Santa Clara County Office Edn. Tchr. Advisor Program U.S. Sec. Edn., 1983-84. Mem. Coun. Exceptional Children, Juvenile Ct. Sch. Adminstrs. Calif.,. Home: 12150 Country Squire Ln Saratoga CA 95070-3444

HOUSTON, HARRY ROLLINS, retired obstetrician, gynecologist; b. Bangor, Maine, Mar. 2, 1928; s. Howard Raymond and Ethel Elizabeth (Rollins) H.; m. Bett Grierson, Dec. 17, 1950; children: Susan, James, Barbara. Student, Bates Coll., 1948-51; MD, Tufts U., 1955; postgrad., Hebrew U., Jerusalem, 1993—. Diplomate, Am. Bd. Ob-Gyn. Enlisted USN, 1946, served in PTO, 1946-48, commd. ensign, 1951, advanced through grades to capt., 1970; intern, then resident U.S. Naval Hosp., Chelsea, Mass., 1955-60; chief ob.-gyn. Naval Sta. Hosp., Kodiak, Alaska, 1960-62; chief ob.-gyn. various U.S. Naval Hosps., 1966-76; ret. USN, 1976; pvt. practice Bremerton, Wash., 1976-93; chief ob.-gyn., Harrison Meml. Hosp., Bremerton, 1978-80. Comdr. Peninsula Squadron, CAP, Bremerton, 1966-70. Fellow Am. Coll. Ob.-Gyn.; mem. AMA, Kitsap County Med. Assn., Washington State Med. Assn., Yokosuka (Japan) Lodge, Masons, Naval Coun., Shriners, Scottish Rite. Republican. Presbyterian.

HOUSTON, JANE HUNT, retired educator; b. Upper Montclair, N.J., Dec. 22, 1919; d. MacLean and Mary Hunt (Young) H. BA, Duke U., 1941; MEd, U. Wyo., 1960. Cert. tchr., Wyo. Field worker Glendale (Calif.) coun. Girl Scouts U.S., 1941-45; exec. dir. Sacramento coun. Girl Scouts U.S., 1945-46, Cheyenne (Wyo.) coun. Girl Scouts U.S., 1946-56; tchr. Laramie County Sch. Dist. # 1, Cheyenne, 1956-79; ret., 1979. Co-author: Centennial, Wyoming 1876-1976-the Real Centennial. Bd. dirs. Carbon Power and Light Inc., Saratoga, Wyo., 1983—, Centennial Water and Sewer Dist., 1988—. Mem. LWV, Centennial Valley Hist. Assn. (sec. 1975—), Wyo. State Hist. Soc. (charter), Laramie County Ret. Tchrs. (com. chmn. 1980-95). Republican. Office: Centennial Valley Hist Soc PO Box 200 Centennial WY 82055

HOUSTON, JOHN ALBERT, political science educator; b. Spokane, Dec. 24, 1914; s. John Alexander and Ethel (Robinson) H.; m. Marjorie Anne Robinson, Aug. 14, 1939 (dec. Sept. 1968); children: Alexandra Louise (Mrs. Lee Benham), John Alexander II (dec. Aug. 1979), Ann Celeste; m. Pollyanna Turner, Nov. 1, 1969. A.B. in Econs, Stanford, 1936, M.A. in Internat. Relations, 1947; Ph.D. in polit. sci, U. Mich., 1951. Ins. broker Johnson & Higgins, San Francisco, 1936-37; case aide Calif. Relief Adminstrn., 1938-40; asst., then asso. prof. polit. sci. U. Miss., 1949-54; faculty Knox Coll., Galesburg, Ill., 1954—; prof. polit. sci. Knox Coll., 1957-80, prof. emeritus, 1980—, Philip Sydney Post disting. prof., 1961-80; sec.-treas. Midwest Collegiate Athletic Conf., 1961-67. Author: Latin America in the United Nations, 1956, Book; rev. editor: Midwest Jour. Polit. Sci, 1962-65. Mem. Galesburg Planning Commn., 1956-57. Served to lt. comdr. USNR, 1941-45. Social Sci. Research Council fellow, 1956. Mem. Am. Polit. Sci. Assn., Midwest Conf. Polit. Scientists, Omicron Delta Kappa, Pi Sigma Alpha, Scabbard and Blade, Sigma Alpha Epsilon. Home: 565 Henley Way Ashland OR 97520-3119

HOVENGA, TRENT LAVERN, surgeon; b. Estherville, Iowa, July 29, 1958; s. LaVern Bernard and Jeradine Marian (Laidig) H.; m. Lisa Marie Borkowski, May 20, 1983; children: Bard Parker, Claire Marie, Hunter Halsted, Madeline Kay. AB, Washington U., St. Louis, 1980; MD, U. Iowa, 1984. Commd. 2d lt. U.S. Army, 1980, advanced through grades to maj., 1990; gen. surgery resident Fitzsimons Army Med. Ctr., Aurora, Colo., 1984-89; staff surgeon Landstuhl (Germany) Army Regional Med. Ctr., 1989—, Evans Army Community Hosp., Fort Carson, Colo., 1992—. Fellow ACS. Republican. Presbyterian. Home and Office: 110 Rugely Ct Colorado Springs CO 80906-5954

HOVERSTAD, RONALD ALAN, marketing educator; b. Rochester, Minn., July 27, 1951; s. Norval Andreason and Juanita (Benson) H.; m. Annella Kay Bernard, June 25, 1977; children: Anna, Sara. BA, Augsburg Coll., 1974; MBA, St Cloud State U., 1981; PhD, U. Minn., 1986. Asst. prof. Tex. Christian U., Ft. Worth, 1985-90; asst. prof. U. Pacific, Stockton, Calif., 1990-92, assoc. prof., dir. MBA Program, 1992—. Contbr. articles to profl. jours. Recipient Rsch. fellowship, U. Minn., Mpls., 1984-85. Mem. Am. Mktg. Assn., Assn. for Consumer Rsch., Southern Mktg. Assn. (best paper promotion and pricing 1987), Southwestern Mkgt. Assn., Am. Assn. for Advances in Health Care, Beta Gamma Sigma, Phi Kappa Phi. Democrat. Roman Catholic. Home: 2112 Piccardo Cir Stockton CA 95207-7870 Office: U Pacific 3601 Pacific Cir Stockton CA 95211-0110

HOVEY, LESLIE MORRIS, plastic surgeon, educator; b. Anaheim, Calif., Aug. 6, 1936; s. Morris and Georgia M. (Guss) H.; m. Loretta (Szluk) Hovey, June 8, 1963; children: Kevin A., Christopher A., Jason D., Justin D. BA in Physiology, U. Calif., Berkeley, 1959; MD, George Washington U., 1963. Diplomate Am. Bd. Surgery, Am. Bd. Plastic Surgery. Intern Tripler Army Med. Ctr., Hawaii, 1963-64, surgery resident, 1964-68; commdg. officer 43rd Surgical Hosp., Korea, 1968-69; fellow head & neck surgery Walte Reed Army Med. Ctr., Washington, 1969-70; resident plastic surgery U. Miami Sch. of Medicine, Fla., 1971-72; plastic surgeon U.S. Army, 1972-76; pvt. practice San Francisco, 1977-87; clinical assoc. prof. plastic surgery Stanford U., Palo Alto, Calif., 1987—; chief of staff St. Francis Med. Hosp., San Francisco, 1985-87; bd. dirs. Plastic Surgery Ednl. Found., Chgo., 1986-92. Mem. of surgical teams to fgn. countries Reconstructive Surgery Found., 1977—. U.S. Army Res. Fellow ACS; mem. Am. Soc. Plastic & Reconstructive Surgery, Am. Burn Assn., Calif. Soc. Plastic Surgery, Soc. Head & Neck Surgeons, Santa Clara County Med. Assn. Office: Santa Clara Vly Med Ctr Divsn Plastic Surgery 751 S Bascom Ave San Jose CA 95128

HOVIND, DAVID J., manufacturing company executive; b. 1940. BA, U. Wash., 1964; postgrad., Stanford U., 1984. With PACCAR Inc., Bellevue, Wash., 1964—, sr. v.p., 1986-87, exec. v.p., 1987-93; now pres. PACCAR Inc., 1993—. Office: PACCAR Inc PO Box 1518 777 106th Ave NE Bellevue WA 98004-5001*

HOVIS, JAMES BRUNTON, federal judge; b. Yakima, Wash., Dec. 15, 1922; Bar: Wash. 1950, U.S. Dist. Ct. (ea. dist.) Wash. 1952, U.S. Dist. Ct. (we. dist.) Wash. 1971, U.S. Ct. Claims 1968, U.S. Tax Ct. 1977, U.S. Ct. Appeals (9th cir.) 1963, U.S. Supreme Ct. 1956. BS, U. Wash., 1949, JD, 1950; student, Wash. State Coll., Ctrl. Wash. Coll. Bar: Wash. 1950, U.S. Dist. Ct. (ea. dist.) Wash. 1952, U.S. Dist. Ct. (we. dist.) Wash. 1971, U.S. Claims Ct. 1968, U.S. Tax Ct. 1977, U.S. Ct. Appeals (9th cir.) 1963, U.S. Supreme Ct. 1956. Assoc. Velikanje & Velikanje, Yakima, Wash., 1950-52; pvt. practice Zillah, Wash., 1950-52; ptnr. Hovis & Kaiser, Yakima, Wash., 1952-54, Brown, Hovis & Cockrill, Yakima, Wash., 1954-64, Hovis, Cockrill & Roy, Yakima, Wash., 1965-82, Hovis, Cockrill, Weaver & Bjur, Yakima, Wash., 1982-87; U.S. Magistrate judge U.S. Dist. Ct. (ea. dist.), Spokane, Wash., 1987-91, Yakima, Wash., 1991-95. Mem. Wash. State Parks & Recreation Commn., 1961-66, chmn., 1962-65, Wash. State Racing Commn., 1983-84; dir. Sundown M Ranch, 1967-87, pres., 1987, Yakima Valley Regional Libr., 1986-87. Office: US Dist Ct 25 S 3rd St Yakima WA 98901-2715*

HOVSEPIAN, ABRAHAM, metal products executive; b. Windsor, Ont., Canada, Feb. 4, 1926; came to the U.S., 1926, naturalized, 1945; s. Minas and Sophia (Apelian) H.; children: Paul George, Carol Grace. BS, Wayne State U., 1949; postgrad., U. So. Calif., 1960-61, Calif. State U., 1962-63. cert. mfg. engr. Engr. Ford Motor Engring. Rsch., Dearborn, Mich., 1949-51, carboloy divsn. Gen. Electric, Detroit, 1951-54; pres. Sci. Platters Inc., Alhambra, Calif., 1954—; dir. Progressive Savings & Loan Assn., 1967-74; founder, dir., treas. Diversified Industries, L.A., 1968—; dir., treas. Diversified Ins. Svcs., L.A., 1970—; dir. Continental Bank, Alhambra, 1973-81, Comco Inc., Sun Valley, Calif., Tokai Bank of Calif., 1981—; chmn. bd. dirs. Ingleside Psychiatric Mental Health Ctr., Rosemead, Calif.; chmn. bd. trustees Alhambra Cmty. Hosp.; pres. Alhambra CSC; mem. Pasadena Tournament of Roses Assn. Served with USN, 1944-46. Recipient Outstanding Citizenship award Civitan Club, 1968, cert. of honor Alhambra City Coun., 1968, Alhambra Redevelopment Agy., 1969, Ingleside Psychiat. Mental Health Ctr., 1970, Alhambra Cmty. Hosp., 1972. Mem. Nat. Assn. Metal Finishers, Soc. Mfg. Engrs., Metal Finishing Assn. So. Calif., Alhambra C. of C. (pres. 1969). Clubs: Rotary Internat. (pres.), Mason (Alhambra). Republican. Congregationalist. Home: 317 La France Ave Apt 3 Alhambra CA 91801-1757 Office: 318A S Palm Ave Alhambra CA 91803-1524

HOVY, EDUARD H., computational linguist; b. Johannesburg, South Africa, Feb. 20, 1956; came to the U.S., 1981; BS, Rand Afrikaans U., 1977; MS, Yale U., 1983, PhD, 1987. Project leader Info. Scis. Inst., Marina Del Rey, Calif., 1987—; asst. rsch. prof. U. So. Calif., L.A., 1989—. Author: Generating Natural Language, 1988; co-editor: Aspects of Automated Language Generation, 1992; mem. editorial bd.: Jour. Computational Linguistics, 1991-93. Recipient Scientiae prize Rand Afrikaans U., 1977. Mem. Assn. Computational Linguistics (exec. com. 1994—), Am. Assn. Artificial Intelligence, Cognitive Sci. Assn. Office: U So Calif Info Scis Inst 4676 Admiralty Way Marina Del Rey CA 90292

HOWARD, BRADFORD REUEL, travel company executive; b. Honolulu, Aug. 6, 1957; s. Joseph DeSylva and Marguerite Evangeline (Barker) H.; m. Marcia Andresen, June 23, 1985; 1 child, Evan DeSilva Andresen. BS in Bus., U. Calif., Berkeley, 1979. Owner, operator Howard Janitorial Svcs., Oakland, Calif., 1970-80; prodn. mgr. Oakland Symphony Orch., 1976-80; brand mgr. The Clorox Co., Oakland, 1980-85; gen. mgr., corp. sec. Howard Tours, Inc./Howard Enterprises, Oakland, 1985—; co-owner Howard Mktg. Cons., Oakland, 1985—; cons. Marcus Foster Found., Oakland, 1984-85; pres., gen. mgr. Piedmont (Calif.) Community Theater, 1976-92. Mem. Calif. Alumni Assn. (bd. dirs. 1991—), U. Calif. Bus. Alumni Assn. (v.p. 1986-88, pres. 1988-89, Bay Area chpt. 1983-84), U. Calif. Devel. Coun., Oakland-Sunrise Rotary (sec. 1985-87, pres. 1987-88), Lake Merrit Breakfast Club. Office: Howard Tours Inc 526 Grand Ave Oakland CA 94610-3515

HOWARD, CHRISTOPHER PHILIP, business consultant; b. N.Y.C., Aug. 6, 1947; s. Murray and Hope (McGurn) H.; m. Danina Mary Hill, June 29, 1987; children: Sean, Stephen, Coby, Katherine, Sasa. BA in Econs., Stanford U., 1968; MBA, Santa Clara U., 1970. Cert. mgmt. acct., mgmt. cons., documented advisor to bus. Cons. Ernst & Ernst, CPAs, Phoenix, 1972-74; ops. mgr. Jensen Tools & Alloys Inc., Phoenix, 1974-77; CFO Pioneer Industries, Inc., Phoenix, 1977-80; sr. v.p. Health-Tech Mgmt., Inc., Phoenix, 1980-84; mng. prin. Howard and Assocs., Inc., Phoenix, 1984-87; consulting mgr. Grant Thornton, CPAs, Reno, 1987-89; mng. ptnr. Howard Consulting Group, Reno, 1989—; faculty mem. U. Nev., Reno, 1991-95. 1st lt. USAF, 1970-72. Mem. Inst. Cert. Mgmt. Accts., Inst. Cert. Mgmt. Cons., Inst. Bus. Appraisers, Stanford U. Alumni Assn. Episcopalian. Office: Howard Consulting Group 6880 S McCarran A-10 Reno NV 89509

HOWARD, DARCIE SHEILA, special education educator; b. Kingston, Ont., Can., Aug. 20, 1946; came to U.S., 1964; d. Gard Shaw Forrester and Mary Elizabeth (Nunn) Pike; m. Norman D. Howard, Sept. 18, 1966; children: Aaron, Matthew. BA, U. Calif., Berkeley, 1968; edn. credential, Calif. State U., Hayward, 1969; paralegal degree, Rancho Santiago Coll., 1987. Cert. tchr., Calif. Svc. rep. Pacific Bell Telephone Co., Berkeley, 1966; tchr. Oakland (Calif.) Pub. Schs., 1969-73; tchr., tutor Calvary Christian Sch., Santa Ana, Calif., 1980-86; owner ABCaDE Computers, Santa Ana, 1986-93; spl. edn. tchr. Orange (Calif.) Unified Sch. Dist., 1990—; owner Calif. Sweet-Briar, 1991-93. Republican. Home: 1513 E Franzen Ave Santa Ana CA 92701-1641

HOWARD, GEORGE HARMON, management consultant; b. St. John, Wash., Nov. 14, 1934; s. George Philip and Corrinne Cadwallader (Rippeteau) H.; m. Elizabeth Ann Ogden, Dec. 22, 1956 (dec. July 1991); children: Debra Ann Leming, Keith Philip, Corrie Lou Govostis, Stacia Elizabeth. BA, Wash. State U., 1957; MBA, Harvard U., 1967. Sales rep. Burroughs Corp., Spokane, Wash., 1957; various positions USAF, Kirtland AFB, 1958-77; vice commdr. AF Contract Mgmt. Div., Kirkland AFB, N.Mex., 1978; mgr. corp. devel. Leisure Dynamics, Evergreen, Colo., 1978-80; pres. HBK Assocs., Inc., Evergreen, 1981-87; dir. ops. ILX Lightwave Corp., Bozeman, Mont., 1988-89; sr. cons. Matrix Mgmt. Group, Seattle, 1990-94; owner HBK Assocs., Auburn, Wash., 1994—; pres. Howard Farms, Inc., St. John, Wash., 1986—. Co-author: TFX Acquisition, 1966. Instr. Red Rocks Community Coll., Denver, 1986-87; del. Colo. Rep. Conv., Denver, 1984. Recipient Outstanding Sr. award Wash. State U., 1957, Legion of Merit award USAF, 1978, Bronze star USAF, 1968. Mem. Shrine, York Rite Bodies, Masonic Lodge, Order of Eastern Star, Wheatland Grange, Air Force Assn., The Ret. Officers Assn. Republican. Episcopalian. Home: 6358 S 298th Pl Auburn WA 98001-3040 Office: HBK Assocs 6358 S 298th Pl Auburn WA 98001-3040

HOWARD, JAMES WEBB, investment banker, lawyer, engineer; b. Evansville, Ind., Sept. 17, 1925; s. Joseph R. and Velma (Cobb) H.; m. Phyllis Jean Brandt, Dec. 27, 1948; children: Sheila Rae, Sharon Kae. B.S. in Mech. Engring, Purdue U., 1949; postgrad., Akron (Ohio) Law Sch., 1950-51, Cleve. Marshall Law Sch., 1951-52; M.B.A., Western Res. U., 1962; J.D., Western State Coll. Law, 1976. Registered profl. engr., Ind., Ohio. Jr. project engr. Firestone Tire & Rubber Co., Akron, 1949-50; gen. foreman Cadillac Motor Car div. GM, 1950-53; mgmt. cons. M.K. Sheppard & Co., Cleve., 1953-56; plant mgr. Lewis Welding & Engring. Corp., Ohio, 1956-58; underwriter The Ohio Co., Columbus, 1959; chmn. Growth Capital, Inc., Chgo., 1960—; pvt. practice law San Diego, 1979-85; pres. Meister Brau, Inc., Chgo., 1965-73, The Home Mart, San Diego, 1974-82; mng. agt., fin. instn. specialist FDIC/RTC, 1985-90; specialist in charge Office of FDIC-DOL, Portland, Oreg., 1986-87; pres. Creative Mgmt. Group, Scottsdale, Ariz., 1991—. Developer of "Lite" beer. Co-chmn. Chgo. com. Ill. Sesquicentennial Com., 1968. Served with AUS, 1943-46. Decorated Bronze Star, Parachutist badge, Combat Inf. badge. Mem. ASME, Nat. Assn. Small Bus. Investment Cos. (past pres.), State Bar Calif., Grad. Bus. Alumni Assn. Western Res. U. (past gov.), Masons, Tau Kappa Epsilon, Pi Tau Sigma, Beta Gamma Sigma. Methodist.

HOWARD, JANE OSBURN, educator; b. Morris, Ill., Aug. 12, 1926; d. Everett Hooker and Bernice Otilda (Olson) Osburn; B.A., U. Ariz., 1948; M.A., U. N.Mex., 1966, Ph.D., 1969; m. Rollins Stanley Howard, June 5, 1948; children—Ellen Elizabeth, Susan (Mrs. John Karl Nuttall). Instr. U. N.Mex. Sch. Medicine, Albuquerque, 1968-70, mem. staff pediatrics, deaf blind children's program, Albuquerque, 1971-72, asst. dir. N.Mex. programs for deaf blind children, 1972—, instr. psychiatry, instr. pediatrics, coordinator deaf-blind children's program, 1972-76, edn. cons., 1976—, publicity and pub. relations cons., 1983—; Cons. Mountain-Plains Regional Ctr. for Services to Deaf-Blind Children, Denver, 1971-74, Bur. Indian Affairs, 1974. Active Cystic Fibrosis, Mother's March, Heart Fund, Easter Seal-Crippled Children. Recipient fellowships U. N.M., 1965, 66, 66-67, 67-68, U. So. Calif. John Tracy Clinic, 1973. Fellow Royal Soc. Health; mem. Council Exceptional Children, Am. Assn. Mental Deficiency, Nat. Assn. Retarded Children, AAUW, Pi Lambda Theta, Zeta Phi Eta, Alpha Epsilon Rho. Republican. Methodist. Home: 615 Valencia Dr SE Albuquerque NM 87108-3742

HOWARD, JERALD JAMES, software engineer; b. Santa Clara, Calif., Nov. 19, 1964; s. Kenneth Gordon and Shirley Ann (Howard) Marseilles; m. Sheryl Lynn Sundquist, Aug. 11, 1990. BS in Computer Engring., Calif. State U., Long Beach, 1988; MS in Computer Sci., San Diego State U., 1994. Software engr. R & D Unisys Corp., 1988; assoc. engr. flight scis. Lockheed Aero. Systems Co., 1989-90; sr. tech. graphics analyst Template Graphics Software, 1990—; sr. software engr. Hewlett Packard, Oreg., 1995—; tutorial asst. SIGGRAPH-93; tutorial speaker XHibition-93. Mem. Assn. Computing Machinery, Tau Beta Pi.

HOWARD, JO ANN, business owner; b. L.A., Nov. 22, 1937; d. John George and Lucile Anne (Farish) Heinzman; m. William Harold Howard, Dec. 2, 1958; children: Teri Lynn Wilson, Tracey Ann Currie, Randall William, Richard John. Student, Mt. San Antonio Coll., 1957. Escrow officer, mgr. So. Cities Escrow, Hemet, Calif., 1970-75; escrow officer Hemet Escrow, 1975-76; ptnr. Ramona Escrow, Hemet, 1976-79; pres., supr. Howard Escrow, Hemet, 1979—; pres. Recon Enterprises, Inc., Hemet, 1976—, Chaparral Accomodators, Inc., Hemet, 1990—. Pres. Sorpotimists Internat., San Jacinto-Hemet Valley, Calif., 1979. Named one of Disting. Pres.'s, Soroptimists, 1978-80; recipient Woman of Distinction award Soroptimist Internat. (San Jacinto-Hemet Valley 1990). Mem. Women's Coun. Bd. Realtors (affiliate, treas.), Hemet-San Jacinto Bd. Realtors (affiliate), San Jacinto C. of C., Hemet C. of C., Calif. Escrow Assn. (pres. Calif. chpt. 1991), Riverside County Escrow Assn. (bd. dirs. 1985—), Escrow Inst. of Calif. (bd. dirs. 1992—). Republican. Presbyterian. Office: Howard Escrow 3292 E Florida Ave Ste D Hemet CA 92544-4941

HOWARD, JOHN MAURICE, III, chemistry educator; b. El Paso, Tex., Nov. 13, 1969; s. John Maurice Jr. and Nancy Lee (Dwyer) H. BS in Chemistry, Met. State Coll., 1994. Counselor Singing Waters Ranch, Holden, La., 1987-89; chemistry tutor Met. State Coll., Denver, 1993—. Mem. Concord Coalition, Washington, 1993—; sponsor Sta. KRMA-TV, Denver, 1993—; founding mem. United We Stand, Am., Denver, 1993—. Mem. Am. Chem. Soc. (treas. student affiliate 1991-92).

HOWARD, KATSUYO KUNUGI, counselor, educator, consultant; b. Kushigata, Yamanashi, Japan, Apr. 9, 1945; came to U.S., 1972; m. John P. Howard, Feb. 14, 1976; children: Shinichi, Keiko. BS, Chiba (Japan) U., 1968; MA in Linguistics, Calif. State U., Fresno, 1976, MA in Counseling, 1979. Lic. marriage, family and child counselor, Calif.; cert. tchr., community coll. credential, adult edn., Calif. Instr. Fresno City Coll., 1976-80; advisor Internat. Student Counseling, Calif. State U., Fresno, 1978-80, counselor, 1980-86; coord. SE Asian Student Svcs., Calif. State U., Fresno, 1986—; pvt. practice and cons., Fresno, Calif., 1992—; presenter in field. Author: Passages: An Anthology of the Southeast Asian Refugee Experience, 1990; producer: (video) Pathfinders: Hmong Refugees in Higher Education, 1987. Bd. dirs. The East-/west Ctr. Assn. East-West Community Svcs. Mem. Soc. for Intercultural Edn., Tng. and Rsch., Nat. Assn. for Fgn. Student Affairs, Cen. Valley Asian Pacific Women (bd. dirs.), Japanese Am. Citizen League, Calif. Assn. Marriage and Family Therapists, Cen. Valley Refugee Forum, Am. Assn. for Counseling and Devel., Am. Coll. Pers. Assn., Hmong Am. Women Assn., Asian & Pacific Americans in Higher Edn. Office: Calif State U Fresno Student Union # 306 Fresno CA 93740

HOWARD, MEL, film producer, educator; b. Bklyn., Feb. 17, 1935. AB, Bklyn. Coll., 1955; postgrad., Columbia U., N.Y.C., 1956. Assoc. dir. Am. Film Inst., 1967-69; head grad. div. Inst. Film & TV NYU, 1974-76; chmn. broadcast and film Boston U., 1990-93; pres. New Voices/New Visions

Films; bd. dirs. Planet Ctrl., TV. Co-assoc. prodr. (films) Night of the Generals, Quackser Fortune Has A Cousin In The Bronx, Renaldo and Clara, Washington Affair, Snapshots (also dir.), The Chosen, The Goodbye People, Beat Street, He Makes Me Feel Like Dancing, Rented Lips, The Boost, (theatre) Plough And The Stars, Raisin In The Sun (Broadway), Once There Was A Russian (Broadway); prodn. exec. (films) Twelve Chairs, Night Visitor, First Love, Ice, Switch, The Pawnbroker, Glen and Randa, The Swimmer, THe Happening, The Group, A Thousand Clowns, 5 Heartbeats; actor in films and theatre including leads in Hester Street and Snapshots; head european prodn. for UMC Pictures, Horizon Pictures, Sam Spiegel. Fellow Sundance Inst.; mem. Actors Studio, Dirs. Unit.

HOWARD, ROBERT STAPLES, newspaper publisher; b. Wheaton, Minn., Oct. 23, 1924; s. Earl Eaton and Helen Elizabeth (Staples) H.; m. Lillian Irene Crabtree, Sept. 2, 1945; children: Thomas, Andrea, William, David. Student, U. Minn., 1942, 45. Pub. various daily, weekly newspapers, 1946-55; pub. Chester, Pa. Times, 1955-61; Pres. Howard Publs. (18 daily newspapers), 1961—. With AUS, 1942-43; 2d lt. USAAF, 1944-45. Home: PO Box 1337 Rancho Santa Fe CA 92067-1337 Office: PO Box 570 Oceanside CA 92049-0570

HOWARD, SHERWIN WARD, theatre educator; b. Safford, Ariz., Feb. 19, 1936; s. Fred Pack and Beatrice Sarah (Ward) H.; m. Annette Mina Shoup, June 30, 1961; children: Andrea Lynne, John Stanley, Stephen Ward, David Stowell. BS, Utah State U., 1960, MA, 1963; MFA, Yale U., 1966; PhD, U. Wis., 1980. Asst. to provost, asst. prof. Ohio U., Athens, 1966-69; asst. to pres., assoc. prof. Lawrence U., Appleton, Wis., 1969-80; prof. theatre arts, dean Coll. Arts and Humanities Weber State U., Ogden, Utah, 1980—; pres. Deep Springs Coll., Dyer, Nev., 1992-95. Author: (poems) Sometime Voices, 1988 (Utah Poet of Yr.), also plays and poems. 1st lt. U.S. Army, 1960-62. Mem. Dramatists Guild, Phi Sigma Iota, Pi Lambda Theta. Home: Deep Springs Coll 5150 Shawnee Ave Ogden UT 84403

HOWARD, VICTOR, management consultant; b. Montreal, Que., Can., Aug. 12, 1923; s. Thomas and Jean (Malkinson) H.; BA, Sir George Williams U., 1947; BSc, 1948; PhD, Mich. State U., 1954; m. Dorothy Bode, Dec. 25, 1953. Mech. design engr. Canadian Vickers Ltd., Montreal, 1942-46; with Aluminum Co. Can., 1946-48, E.B. Badger Co., Boston, 1948-50; asst. prof. Mich. State U., 1952-56; social scientist Rand Corp., 1956-58; staff exec., personnel dir. System Devel. Corp., Santa Monica, Calif., 1958-66; staff cons. Rohrer, Hibler & Replogle, San Francisco, 1966-69; mng. dir. Rohrer, Hibler & Replogle Internat., London and Brussels, 1969-74, ptnr. 1974, mgr. San Francisco, 1974-88, dir., 1979-88; pres. V. Howard and Assocs., 1988—, The Inst. on Stress and Health in the Work Place, 1988—; vice chair State Bd. Psychology, 1989-93. Fellow Brit. Inst. Dirs.; mem. Am. Psychol. Assn., Western Psychol.Assn., U.S. Power Squadrons (comdr. Sequoia Squadron 1981, dist. comdr. 1987), Calif. State Mil. Res. (col. 1984), Reform Club, Hurlingham (London) Club, Thames Motor Yacht Club (Molesey, Eng.), Order of St. John of Jerusalem (chevalier)Sovereign Mil. Order of the Temple, Masons (33 degree), Shriners, Sigma Xi. Office: 1350 Old Bayshore Hwy Ste 610 Burlingame CA 94010

HOWARD, WILLIAM MATTHEW, lawyer, business executive, arbitrator, author; b. Oak Park, Ill., Dec. 16, 1934; s. William and Martha Geraldine (Herlock) H.; m. Linda Marie Eckelkamp, Dec. 30, 1991; children from previous marriage: Matthew William, Stephanie Sue. BSBA, U. Mo., 1956, JD, 1958; postgrad., U. Nice, France, 1976, U. London, 1977; PhD, Ariz. State U., 1995. Bar: Mo. 1958, U.S. Supreme Ct. 1986. Jr. ptnr. Bryan, Cave, McPheeters & McRoberts, St. Louis, 1958-66; asst. to pres. Granite City (Ill.) Steel Co., 1966-69; pres. Thomson Internat. Co., Thibodaux, La., 1969-70; founder, pres., chmn. bd. The Catalyst Group, Phoenix, Ariz., 1970—; adj. faculty U. Mo., Columbia, 1956-58, St. Louis U., 1958-61, Ariz. State U., 1994—; chmn. unauthorized practice law com. Mo. Bar, St. Louis, 1964-65; chmn. bd. N.V. Vulcaansoord, Terborg, The Netherlands, 1975-78, E. Chalmers Holdings, Ltd., Glasgow, Scotland, 1977-78; exec. cons. Chem. Bank, Irvine, Calif., 1985-90; vis. lectr. UCLA, 1987; arbitrator Am. Arbitration Assn., N.Y.C., 1987—, N.Y. Stock Exch., 1987—, Nat. Assn. Securities Dealers, Chgo., 1987—, Nat. Futures Assn., Chgo., 1988—, Am. Stock Exch., N.Y.C., 1988—; hearing officer Mo. Dept. Natural Resources, Jefferson City, 1987-89, Internat. Ct. Arbitration, 1993, Inter-Am. Comml. Arbitration Commn., 1993; bd. dirs. Xeric Corp., Denver. Editor newsletter Extras, 1970—; exec. producer: (motion picture) Twice a Woman, 1979; contbr. numerous articles and revs. to various jours. Bd. dirs. U. Mo. Alumni Assn., 1986, Breckenridge (Colo.) Film Festival, 1989, Actors Theatre Phoenix, 1990; mem., pres.' club adv. bd. Phoenix Art Mus., 1990; dir. Scottsdale Cultural Coun., 1991. Mem. Am. Arbitration Assn. (regional adv. com.), Soc. Profls. in Dispute Resolution, Phoenix C. of C., Mensa, Order of Coif. Office: Catalyst Group 2619 E Beekman Pl Phoenix AZ 85016-7483

HOWATT, SISTER HELEN CLARE, human services director; b. San Francisco, Apr. 5, 1927; d. Edward Bell and Helen Margaret (Kenney) H. BA, Holy Names Coll., 1949; MS in Libr. Sci., U. So. Calif., 1972; cert. advanced studies Our Lady of Lake U., 1966. Joined Order Sisters of the Holy Names, Roman Cath. Ch., 1945. Life teaching credential, life spl. svcs. credential, prin. St. Monica Sch., Santa Monica, Calif., 1957-60, St. Mary Sch., L.A., 1960-63; tchr. jr. high sch. St. Augustine Sch., Oakland, Calif., 1964-69; tchr. jr. high math St. Monica Sch., San Francisco, 1969-71, St. Cecilia Sch., San Francisco, 1971-77; libr. dir. Holy Names Coll., Oakland, Calif., 1977-94; activities dir. Collins Ctr. Sr. Svcs., 1994—. Contbr. math. curriculum San Francisco Unified Sch. Dist., Cum Notis Variorum, publ. Music Libr., U. Calif., Berkeley. Contbr. articles to profl. jours. NSF grantee, 1966, NDEA grantee, 1966. Mem. Cath. Libr. Assn. (chmn. No. Calif. elem. schs. 1971-72), Calif. Libr. Assn., ALA, Assn. Coll. and rsch. Librs. Home and Office: 2550 18th Ave San Francisco CA 94116-3005

HOWD, ROBERT ALLEN, toxicologist; b. McMinnville, Oreg., Nov. 19, 1944; s. Leland Ernest and Dorothy (Capps) H.; m. Sherry Lea Rock, Dec. 23, 1966; 1 child, Jennifer. BA, Linfield Coll., 1966; PhD, U. Wash., 1973. Chemist FDA, Seattle, 1966-68; postdoctoral fellow MIT, Cambridge, 1973-75; biochem. pharmacologist SRI Internat., Menlo Park, Calif., 1975-88; toxicologist, Toxic Substances Control Prog. Calif. Dept. Health Svcs., Sacramento, 1988-91; toxicologist pesticide & environ. toxicology sect. Office of Environ. Health Hazard Assessment, Calif. EPA, Berkeley, 1991—. Contbr. articles to profl. jours.; inventee in field. NIH fellow MIT, 1973-75. Mem. AAAS, Am. Soc. for Pharmacology and Exptl. Therapeutics, Soc. Risk Analysis, Soc. of Toxicology. Office: Calif EPA Office of Environ Health Hazard Assessment 2151 Berkeley Way # 11 Berkeley CA 94704-1011

HOWE, ADRIAN CLARENCE, state agency administrator; b. Greybull, Wyo., July 16, 1953; s. Walter Clarence and Luella Kathleen (Trumbull) H.; m. Nena Rea Fisher, June 5, 1974; children: Travis Walter, Destinee Adrianne, Shawndra Marie. AAS, C.C. of Air Force, Lackland AFB, Tex., 1979. Staff tech., angiography and spl. procedures supr. USAF, Lackland AFB, Tex., 1972-79; spl. procedures and angiography supr. Billings (Mont.) Deaconess Hosp., 1979-82; health physicist, coord. x-ray inspection program Mont. Dept. Health and Environ. Scis., Helena, 1982-87, bur. chief, occupl. and radiol. health bur., 1987—; chmn. Mont. Bd. Radiol. Techs., Helena, 1982-87, Mont. Lead Adv. Com., Helena, 1994; mem. high level waste com. Western Interstate Energy Bd., Denver, 1990—; com. mem. Western Interstate Compact for Mgmt. of Low-level Radioactive Waste, Olympia, Wash., 1990—; active Conf. Radiation Control Program Dirs. Sgt. USAF, 1972-79. Recipient Spl. Achievement award EPA, 1986, Exec. Bd. award for outstanding achievement in radiation protection Conf. Radiation Control Program Dirs., Inc., 1988, Region VIII Achievement award EPA, 1994. Mem. Am. Registry Radiologic Technologists. Office: Mont Dept Health & Environ Scis 1400 Broadway Helena MT 59620

HOWE, BRYANT RICHARD, legislative staff member; b. Salt Lake City, Mar. 28, 1956; s. Richard Cuddy and Juanita (Lyon) H.; m. Sandra Kay Swander, Aug. 7, 1981; children: Alicia, Taylor, Megan, Miquelle, Alexander. BA with honors, U. Utah, 1980; MPA, Brigham Young U., 1982. Rsch. and pub. policy analyst Utah Legis., Salt Lake City, 1982—. Recipient Outstanding History Student award Utah State Hist. Soc., 1980. Mem. Nat. Conf. State Legis. Health Policy Staff Network (staff chair children and family svcs. com. 1994-95). Mem. LDS Ch. Office: Office Legis Rsch 436 State Capitol Building Salt Lake City UT 84114-1202

HOWE, DRAYTON FORD, JR., lawyer; b. Seattle, Nov. 17, 1931; s. Drayton Ford and Virginia (Wester) H.; m. Joyce Arnold, June 21, 1952; 1 son, James Drayton. A.B., U. Calif.-Berkeley, 1953; LL.B., Hastings Coll. Law, 1957. Bar: Calif. 1958, C.P.A. Calif. Atty. IRS, 1958-61; tax dept. supr. Ernst & Ernst, San Francisco, 1962-67; ptnr. Bishop, Barry, Howe, Haney & Ryder, San Francisco, 1968—; lectr. on tax matters U. Calif. extension, 1966-76. Mem. Calif. Bar Assn., San Francisco Bar Assn. (chmn. client relations com. 1977). Calif. Soc. C.P.A.s.

HOWE, JOSEPH WILLIAM, radiologist; b. Galeton, Pa., May 27, 1930; s. Lawrence Evered and Mabel Jane (Howe) H.; m. Mary Dolores Rathfon, May 9, 1953; children: Hollie D. Martin, Daniel W., Steven L., Nancy D. Rawson, Melinda G. Shillig, Jaynan Lotts. Student, Pa. State U., 1949-50, Elizabethtown (Pa.) Coll., 1950; DC, Palmer Coll. Chiropractic, Davenport, Iowa, 1952; cert. in Roentgenology, Nat. Coll. Chiropractic, 1959. Diplomate Am. Chiropractic Bd. Radiology, Nat. Bd. Chiropractic Examiners; lic. chiropractor, Pa., Ohio, Ill., Calif. Pvt. practice New Cumberland, Pa., 1952-54, 56-68; dir. radiology and rsch. Assocs. Diagnostic Ctr., Tallmadge, Ohio, 1968-72; prof., chmn. Roentgenology dept. Nat. Coll. Chiropractic, Lombard, Ill., 1972-76, dir. clin. sci. div., 1976-78; prof., chmn. radiology dept. L.A. Coll. Chiropractic, Whittier, Calif., 1978-87, prof. radiology, dir. radiology residency program, 1987-89; pvt. practice Sylmar, Calif., 1978-87, West Las Angeles, 1989—. Contbr. articles to profl. jours. With U.S. Army, 1954-56. Fellow Am. Chiropractic Coll. Radiology; mem. Am. Chiropractic Assn., Coun. Diagostic Imaging, Calif. Chiropractic Assn., Am. Pub. Health Assn. Republican. Mormon. Home and Office: 13403 Lochrin Ln Sylmar CA 91342-1855 also: 10474 Santa Monica Blvd # 202 Los Angeles CA 90025-6929

HOWE, LEE MARTIN, electronics marketing executive, army officer; b. Oakland, Calif., Nov. 7, 1952; s. Nate Houghton and Helen J. (Martin) H.; m. Donna G. Keuper, June 6, 1976; children: Christine Ann, Kenneth Martin. BA in Bus. and Pub. Adminstrn., U. San Francisco, 1974, MA in Mktg. and Internat. Rels., 1976; MA in Mil. Sci. and Strategy, Command and Gen. Staff Coll., 1988. Lic. comml. pilot. Storekeeper, buyer Officers Open Mess, Nas Alameda, Calif., 1968-70; computer systems operator Bank of Am., San Francisco, Calif., 1970-74; dist. salesman Clairol Corp., San Mateo, Calif., 1974-76; reconnaissance officer 2d Mil. Intelligence Bn., Europe, 1979-82; dist. sales mgr. Rockbestos Wire & Cable Co., New Haven, 1984-85; sr. govt. account mgr., regional specialist Gould Computer Systems, Santa Clara, Calif., 1985-86; mgr. internat. sales and mktg. Walkins-Johnson Co., Palo Alto, Calif., 1986-92; pres. ID. Internat. Mktg., Redwood City, Calif., 1992—. Author: Aerial Reconnaissance Handbook, 1981; editor (area studies) Tech. Transfer into the Pacific Rim, 1988. Mem. spl. com. on youth employment City and County of San Francisco, 1974-75; mem. spl. com. Assn. Bay Area Govts., Berkeley, Calif., 1974-76; active U.S. Little League, Fremont, Calif., 1988—; spokesperson Nat. Crime Prevention Coun., San Francisco Bay Area, Calif., 1994; vol. World Cup Soccer USA, 1994. Lt. col. USAR, 1984—. Decorated 3 Army Commendation medals, 2 Meritorious Svc. medals, Presdl. Award Excellence. Mem. Assn. Old Crows (chpt. rep. 1986-88), Alumni Assn. U. San Francisco (chmn.), Animal Rescue Found., Nat. Crime Prevention Coun. (spokesperson 1994—). Office: ID Internat Mktg 1647 Kentfield Ave Redwood City CA 94061-2746

HOWE, RICHARD CUDDY, state supreme court justice; b. South Cottonwood, Utah, Jan. 20, 1924; s. Edward E. and Mildred (Cuddy) H.; m. Juanita Lyon, Aug. 30, 1949; children: Christine Howe Schultz, Andrea Howe Reynolds, Bryant, Valerie Howe Winegar, Jeffrey, Craig. B.S., U. Utah, 1945, J.D., 1948. Bar: Utah. Law clk. to Justice James H. Wolfe, Utah Supreme Ct., 1949-50; judge city ct. Murray, Utah, 1951; individual practice law Murray, 1952-80; justice Utah Supreme Ct., 1980—; mem. Utah Constitutional Revision Commn., 1976-85. Chmn., original mem. Salt Lake County Merit Coun.; mem. Utah Ho. of Reps., 1951-58, 69-72, Utah Senate, 1973-78. Named Outstanding Legislator Citizens' Conf. State Legislatures, 1972. Mem. ABA, Utah Bar Assn., Sons of Utah Pioneers. Mem. LDS Ch. Office: Utah Supreme Ct 332 State Capitol Building Salt Lake City UT 84114-1202

HOWE, WARREN BILLINGS, physician; b. Jackson Heights, N.Y., Oct. 25, 1940; s. John Hanna and Francelia (Rose) H.; m. Hedwig Neslanik, Aug. 7, 1971; children: Elizabeth Rose, Sarah Billings. BA, U. Rochester, 1962; MD, Washington U., St. Louis, 1965. Diplomate Am. Bd. Family Practice with CAQ in Sports Medicine, Nat. Bd. Med. Examiners. Intern Phila. Gen. Hosp., 1965-66; resident physician Highland Hosp./U. Rochester, 1969-71; family physician Family Medicine Clinic of Oak Harbor (Wash.), Inc., PS, 1971-92; student health physician, univ. team physician We. Wash. U., Bellingham, 1992—; team physician Oak Harbor High Sch., 1972-92; head tournament physician Wash. State High Sch. Wrestling Championships, Tacoma, 1989—; attending physician Seattle Goodwill Games, 1990; clin. asst. prof. U. Wash. Sch. Medicine, 1975-82. Contbr. articles to profl. jours. and chpts. to books. Bd. dirs. Oak Harbor Sch. Dist. #201, 1975-87; chmn. Oak Harbor Citizen's Com. for Sch. Support, 1988-90. Lt. comdr. USN, 1966-69, Vietnam. Recipient Disting. Svc. award City of Oak Harbor, 1984; Paul Harris fellowship Oak Harbor Rotary Club. Fellow Am. Coll. Sports Medicine (chair membership com.), Am. Acad. Family Physicians; mem. AMA, Wash. State Med. Assn., Am. Med. Soc. for Sports Medicine, Am. Coll. Health Assn. Presbyterian. Home: 4222 Northridge Way Bellingham WA 98226-7804 Office: WWU Student Health Ctr 25 High St Bellingham WA 98225-5942

HOWELL, DONNA MURRAY, brokerage executive; b. Opa Locka, Fla., May 19, 1958; d. William Clifton and Paula Anne (Thuot) Williams; m. John Murray, May 25, 1990. BA in Econs., U. Calif., Davis, 1981. Clk. Merrill Lynch Pierce Fenner & Smith, San Francisco, 1982-87, mgr., 1987; asst. mgr. Donaldson, Lufkin & Jenrette, San Francisco, 1988-91; compliance officer Hambrecht & Quist, San Francisco, 1991-93; chief investment officer Capital Network Svcs., San Francisco, 1993—. Fundraiser, vol., tutor Project Read-Adult Literacy, San Francisco, 1984-91, Haight Ashbury Cmty. Svcs., 1992—. Mem. AAUW. Democrat. Episcopalian. Office: Capital Network Svcs 1 Bush St Fl 11 San Francisco CA 94104-4425

HOWELL, MARY ELIZABETH, small business owner; b. Galesburg, Ill., Feb. 19, 1942; d. John A. Shaner and Elizabeth N. (Bowen) Knowles; m. Murrell D. Howell, Dec. 22, 1969; children: Cherie, Thomas, Dean, Murrell. Cert., Alamo Beauty Coll., 1961; grad., Jane Grace Sch. Dress Design, 1973; BS in Bus. Adminstrn., U. Redlands, 1985; cert. in mgmt., U. Calif., Irvine, 1991; D in Internat. Bus., Internat. Cultural Corr. Inst., Madras, India, 1994. Owner, operator Howell's Acctg., Minot, N.D., 1972-78; gen. mgr. Gravel Products, Inc., Minot, 1978-80; controller Bluebird Internat., Inc., Denver, 1981-83; owner, pres. Magnetic Power Systems, Huntington Beach, Calif., 1984—; free-lance cons. Huntington Beach, 1984—; acctg. and budget cons. for mfg., health care, real estate, electronics, academia and personal svcs.; owner Cosmetics For Me, Huntington Beach, 1987—. Copyright Thin Graille of Insanity etching; patentee rail system, pitch control ground effect vehicle; designer needlework, costumes and hairstyles for amateur theater groups; developer cosmetic cream. Leader Girl Scouts USA, Minot, 1973-75, den mother Boy Scouts Am., Minot, 1974, fund raiser Minot AFB Little League and Youth Orgn., 1975; active Hadassah, 1975—, Temple Sharon sisterhood, Costa Mesa, Calif., 1986—. Mem. NAFE, Inst. Mgmt. Accts. Orange Coast (dir. 1982, 93, v.p. edn. and profl. devel. 1984, 86, sec. 1985, v.p. adminstrn. 1987, pres. 1988, nat. community svc. com. 1989-90, nat. dir. 1992—), Toastmasters (cert., pres. 1989). Republican. Jewish. Office: Magnetic Power Systems PO Box 1115 Huntington Beach CA 92647-1115

HOWITT, DAVID ANDREW, human resources executive; b. N.Y.C., Feb. 11, 1953; s. George and Naomi Doris (Rubenstein) H.; m. Leigh Ann Louise Kulp, Jan. 31, 1976; children: Jennifer Elizabeth, Caitlin Rachel. BS in Bus. and Econs., Lehigh U., 1975. Cert. sr. profl. in human resources. Pers. rep. Mutual Benefit Life Ins. Co., Newark, 1975-80; mgr. human resources C-E Lummus, The Lummus Co., Bloomfield, N.J., 1980-83; dir. human resources Pubrs. Phototype, Inc., Carlstadt, N.J., 1983-85; asst. v.p. human resources Fireman's Fund Ins. Co., Novato, Calif., 1985—. Mem. of corp. United Way of Morris County, Cedar Knolls, N.J., 1986-89; pres. Boy Area Outreach and Recreation Program, 1993—; bd. dirs. Edn. Found. Orinda, 1994—. Mem. Soc. for Human Resources Mgmt., No. Calif. Human Resources Coun., Assn. Human Resources Systems Profls. Democrat. Office: Fireman's Fund Ins Co 777 San Marin Dr Novato CA 94998-0001

HOWLAND, PETER MCKINNON, academic administrator; b. Corvallis, Oreg., Apr. 2, 1956; s. James Chase and Ruth Louise (Meisenhelder) H. BA, Linfield Coll., 1978; postgrad., Boise State U., 1981-82; MA in Interdisciplinary Studies, Oreg. State U., 1985. Travel agt. Sather Tours and Travel, Salem, Oreg., 1979-81; office asst. then devel. asst. Linfield Coll., McMinnville, Oreg., 1985-90, devel. asst. for rsch., 1990-94, dir. of rsch. and records, 1994—. Mem. Pi Sigma Alpha. Republican. Mormon. Office: Linfield Coll Office Coll Rels 900 S Baker St Mcminnville OR 97128

HOWLETT, JOHN DAVID, urban planner, consultant; b. Akron, Colo., July 16, 1952; s. John Butler and Reavis Lavina (Smith) H. BA, U. Nebr., 1975, M in Urban and Regional Planning, 1977. Urban and regional planner Oblinger-McCaleb, Denver, 1979-80; staff project mgr. Greater Denver C. of C., 1980-83; dir. econ. devel. City of Littleton, Colo., 1983-87; dir. civic and econ. devel., interim pres. The Denver Partnership, Denver, 1987-91; mng. assoc. Linton, Mields, Reisler & Cottone, Inc., Denver, 1991—; mem. Arapahoe/Douglas Pvt. Industry Coun., Englewood, Colo., 1984-87; mem. steering com. New Bus. and Industry Coun., Denver, 1985-87; mem. exec. com. Met. Denver Network, 1987-91. Mem. profl. adv. coun. Coll. Arch. U. Nebr., Lincoln, 1980—; vice chmn. C-470 Inter-Camber Task Force, Denver, 1984-87; trustee AMC Cancer Rsch. Ctr., Lakewood, Colo., 1985-87; mem. exec. bd. Friends Auraria Libr., Denver, 1989-90; mem. vocat. adv. com. Mental Health Corp., 1990-94. Mem. Am. Planning Assn. (pres. Colo. chpt. 1985-87, Karen Smith Chpt. award 1987), City Club Denver (pres. 1984-85). Democrat. Presbyterian. Home: 3026 W Prentice Ave Apt L Littleton CO 80123-7785 Office: Linton Mields Reisler & Cottone 410 17th St Ste 1345 Denver CO 80202-4426

HOWSLEY, RICHARD THORNTON, lawyer, regional government administrator; b. Medford, Oreg., Jan. 31, 1948; s. Calvin Nevil and Arvilla Constance (Romine) H.; m. Susan Erma Johnson, Oct. 23, 1971; children: James Denver, Kelly Ann. BA, Willamette U., 1970; MS, Va. Poly. Inst. and State U., 1974; JD, Lewis and Clark Law Sch., 1984. Bar: Oreg. 1984, Wash. 1985, U.S. Dist. Ct. (we. dist.) Wash., 1985. Tech. editor U.S. Bur. Mines, Arlington, Va., 1971-72; program mgr., sr. planner KRS Assos., Inc., Reston, Va., 1972-74; exec. dir. Rogue Valley Council Govts., Medford, 1974-78; exec. dir. Regional Planning Council of Clark County, Vancouver, Wash., 1978-84; pres. Landerholm, Memovich, Lansverk & Whitesides, Vancouver, 1985-92; pvt. practice, Vancouver, 1992—; vice chmn. Oreg. Council of Govts. Dirs. Assn., 1976-77, chmn., 1977-78; mem. regional adv. com. So. Oreg. State Coll., 1975-78. Mem. Medford-Ashland Air Quality Adv. Com., 1977-78. Carpenter Found. scholar, 1966-70, Leonard B. Mayfield Meml. scholar, 1966-67, Albina Page Found. scholar, 1966-70. Mem. ABA, Oreg. State Bar Assn., Wash. State Bar Assn., Am. Planning Assn., Am. Inst. Cert. Planners, Internat. City Mgmt. Assn. (10-yr. service award), Nat. Assn. Regional Councils (10-yr. service award). Democrat. Methodist. Home: 1616 NW 79th Cir Vancouver WA 98665-6626 Office: Richard T Howsley PS 1400 Washington St Ste 200 Vancouver WA 98660-2968

HOYE, WALTER BRISCO, retired college administrator; b. Lena, Miss., May 19, 1930; s. William H. and LouBertha (Stewart) H.; m. Vida M. Pickens, Aug. 28, 1954; children—Walter B. II, JoAnn M. B.A., Wayne State U., 1953. Sports/auto editor Detroit Tribune, 1958-65; sports editor Mich. Chronicle, 1965-68; assoc. dir. pub. relations San Diego Chargers Football Co., 1968-76; media liason NFL, 1972-75; community services officer San Diego Coll. Dist., 1976-78; placement officer Ednl. Cultural Complex, San Diego, 1978-80, info. officer, 1980-82, placement officer, adminstrv. asst., 1982-83, placement/program support supr., 1983-91, supr. program support svcs., 1989—; cons. in field. Bd. dirs. San Diego County ARC; active San Diego Conv. and Tourist Bur., Joint Ctr. Polit. Studies, Am. Cancer Soc., San Diego Urban League, Neighborhood Housing Assn., Public Access TV. Named San Diego County Citizen of Month, May, 1979; recipient United Way Award of Merit, 1974. Mem. Internat. Assn. Auditorium Mgrs., Am. Personnel and Guidance Assn., San Diego Career Guidance Assn., Nat. Mgmt. Assn., Assn. Calif. Community Coll. Adminstrs., Calif. Community Coll. Placement Assn., Rocky Mountain Assn. Student Fin. Aid Adminstrs. Home: 6959 Ridge Manor Ave San Diego CA 92120-3146

HOYT, ANTHONY ROSS, mechanical engineer; b. Cedar City, Utah, Jan. 23, 1952; s. Ross Norman and Wanda (Bringhurst) H.; m. Mary Ann Seamands, May 6, 1972; children: Michael, Joseph. BS, U. Wyo., 1979; MS, U. N.Mex., 1981. Rsch. aide U. Wyo., Laramie, 1977-79; rsch. engr. Lockheed Missiles & Space Co., Albuquerque, 1986-89; cons. Klingsporn Engring., Lander, Wyo., 1989-90; mech. engr. DH Print, Riverton, Wyo., 1990-94; air quality engr. Dept. Environ. Quality, Lander, 1994—; cons. Toma Engring., Lander, 1994—. Scoutmaster Boy Scouts Am., Albuquerque, 1979-84, Lander, 1989-91. Capt. USAF, 1979-86. Decorated Meritorious Svc. Medal with oak leaf cluster; NSF fellow, 1977. Mem. Vols. in Tech. Assistance, Tau Beta Pi, Phi Kappa Phi. Republican. LDS. Office: Toma Engring 904 W Main St Lander WY 82520-3040

HOYT, BRADLEY JAMES, account executive; b. Spokane, Wash., Sept. 26, 1949; s. Delmar W. and Katherine (Bjerke) H.; m. Carolyn Nirk (div.); 1 child, Bret; m. Christine M. Loomis, Nov. 28, 1977 (div.); 1 child, Harley. BA in Bus. Adminstrn., Eastern Wash. U., 1976; cert., Coll. Fin. Planning, 1987. Adminstrv. asst. Boise Cascade Homes, Post Falls, Idaho, 1976-77, dealer, coordinator, 1977-78; direct sales rep. Boise Cascade Homes, Boise, 1978-80, territorial sales mgr., 1980-81; v.p., office mgr. Cascade Homes, Post Falls, 1981-82; registered rep. Waddell & Reed, Spokane, 1982-84, sr. acct. exec., 1984—; mem. Pres.'s Coun., Waddell & Reed, 1990-92; pres. Hoyt Ranch, Inc., Spokane, 1978—. Mem. N.W. Natural Resources Bd., 1993—. Mem. Inst. CFPs, Spokane C. of C. (mem. prodn. com. 1987—, 1st v.p. 1988, pres. Ag Expo 1989, chairperson Ag bur. 1994-95). Office: Waddell & Reed 9016 E Indiana Ave Spokane WA 99212-2464

HOYT, DIANA VAUGHN, fundraising executive; b. Denver, Jan. 26, 1945; d. Michael and Virginia Rose (Barnes) Grega; m. Michael Lee, Dec. 1967 (div. Dec. 1973); m. Roy Alan Flegenheimer, July 28, 1974 (div. Jan. 1992); m. Robert L. Hoyt, Jan. 9, 1994; children: Elon Michael, Rachel Anne; m. Robert Hoyt, Jan. 1994. AA, Hutchinson (Kans.) Jr. Coll., 1965; BS, Kans. U., 1967; MA, Ariz. State U., 1972. Cert. high sch. tchr., Ariz., cert. fundraising, Nat. Soc. of Fund Raising Exec. Math tchr. various high schs., Ariz. and Mo., 1967-75; devel. officer Ariz. Mus. Sci. and Tech., Phoenix, 1986-88, Desert Bot. Garden, Phoenix, 1988-89, Actors Theatre, Phoenix, 1989-91, TERROS Behavioral Health Svcs., Phoenix, 1991-95, Ariz. Cactus Pine Girl Scout Coun., Phoenix, 1995—. Mem. Samaritans, 1987—; women's campaign chmn. United Jewish Appeal, 1984-86; mem. Valley Leadership, 1986-87. Recipient Lee Amada Young Leadership award Jewish Fedn. Greater Phoenix, 1981, Golda Meir award, 1990. Mem. Nat. Soc. Fund Raising Execs. (bd. dirs. Greater Ariz. chpt., pres. 1995), Jewish Bus. and Profl. Women's Nat. Coun., Coun. for Jews with Special Needs (pres.), Beta Gamma Sigma, Phi Lambda Theta, Phi Theta Kappa. Democrat. Jewish. Home: 4929 E Laurel Ln Scottsdale AZ 85254-4640 Office: Ariz Cactus Pine Girl Scout Coun PO Box 21776 Phoenix AZ 85036

HOYT, EARL WESLEY, materials scientist, accelerator technologist; b. Chgo., July 28, 1927; s. Wesley Henry Hoyt and Elsa Bernice Plank; m. Virginia L. Rocco, Nov. 12, 1949 (div. July 1974); children: Noelle R., Randall C., Wayne W., Mark W.; m. Dorothy J. Franklin, July 1, 1984. Student, Wilson Coll., Chgo., 1947-50, Ill. Inst. Tech., Chgo., 1950-52, U. Chgo., 1952-54. Assoc. staff. Argonne Nat. Lab., Lemont, Ill., 1947-57; metallurgist, ceramist Gen. Electric Lab., Pleasanton, Calif., 1957-63; materials scientist Stanford (Calif.) Linear Accelerator Ctr., 1963—; cons. Stanford U., 1970—. Author more than 100 tech. publs., reports and jour. articles in fields of nuclear and accelerator tech. Served with USMCR, 1945-47. Home: 3655 Kentucky Ave Riverbank CA 95367-2911 Office: Stanford U PO Box 4349 Palo Alto CA 94309-4349

HOYT, JACK WALLACE, engineering educator; b. Chgo., Oct. 19, 1922; s. Claire A. and Fleta M. (Wheeler) H.; B.S., Ill. Inst. Tech., 1944; M.S., UCLA, 1952, Ph.D., 1962; m. Helen Rita Erickson, Dec. 27, 1945; children: John A., Katheryn M. (Mrs. Richard Everett), Annette M. (Mrs. Walter Butler), Denise M. (Mrs. Paul Kruesi). Research engr. gas turbines Cleve. Lab., NACA, 1944-47; mem. staff Naval Ocean Systems Center, Navy Dept., DOD, San Diego, 1948-79, asso. for sci. fleet engring. dept., 1967-79, now cons.; vis. prof. mech. engring. Rutgers U., New Brunswick, N.J., 1979-81; Benjamin Meaker vis. prof. U. Bristol (Eng.), 1987; prof. mech. engring. San Diego State U., 1981-94; active in research, 1994—. Fellow ASME (Freeman scholar 1971); mem. N.Y. Acad. Scis., Soc. Naval Architects and Marine Engrs. Author, patentee in fieldSpl. rsch. propulsion and hydrodynamics. Home: 4694 Lisann St San Diego CA 92117-2441

HOYT, LEEZA LEE, public relations and advertising firm executive; b. Cairo, Egypt, Nov. 27, 1955; (parents Am. citizens); d. Harry Grant and Lucille H. BA cum laude in Pub. Relations, U. So. Calif., 1977; MBA, Loyola U., L.A., 1983. Lic. in real estate sales, Calif. Real estate salesperson Ladera Realty, L.A., 1976-78; account coordinator/jr. account exec. Lewis & Assocs., L.A., 1978-79; jr. account exec. Ayer Jorgensen Macdonald (now N.W. Ayer, ABH Internat.), advt. firm, Los Angeles, 1979; recruitment adminstr. Lawler, Felix & Hall, L.A., 1980-81; account exec. Clive Hoffman Assocs., L.A., 1981-83; sr. account exec. Rifkind, Pondel & Parsons, L.A., 1983-84; founder, pres. Hoyt Orgn., Torrance, Calif., 1984—. Fund-raising chmn. for 1980 Spl. Olympics, L.A. Jr. C. of C.; mem. L.A. Hdgrs. City Assn., Archtl. Guild U. S.C. Named to Outstanding Young Women Am., U.S. Jaycees, 1980. Mem. Pub. Rels. Soc. Am., Soc. Mktg. Profl. Svcs., L.A. C. of C., Torrance C. of C., U. So. Calif. South Bay Young Alumni (2d v.p. bd. dirs. 1982), Trojan Jr. Aux. (dir. 1978-80), Trojan Fourth Estate (bd. dirs.), Town and Gown Jrs., Alpha Gamma Delta Alumni (exec. coun. 1983-84), Internat. Coun. of Shopping Ctrs. Office: 22750 Hawthorne Blvd Ste 230 Torrance CA 90505-3651

HOYT, ROSEMARY ELLEN, trust officer; b. Iowa City, Iowa, Apr. 12, 1949; d. Joseph Asa Hoyt and Mary Jane (Brobst) Vandermark; m. Louis O. Scott, Oct. 16, 1965 (div. Nov. 1968); children: Wayne L. Lawson, Jo Anna Jane Kollasch; m. David K. Duckworth, July 23, 1983 (div. Dec. 1994); 1 child, Mary Rose. Cert. in applied banking/consumer credit, Am. Inst. Banking, 1988; cert. in trust adminstrn., Cannon Fin. Inst., 1989, cert. trust ops. specialist, 1991; BBA, So. Calif. U., 1992. Teller Community Bank of Fla., St. Petersburg, 1973-75; bookkeeper Chevron Svc. Sta., St. Petersburg, 1975-77, Landmark Bank, St. Petersburg, 1977-80; teller First Nat. Bank of Ely, Nev., 1981, Nev. Bank and Trust, Ely, 1982; asst. v.p. and trust officer First Nat. Bank Farmington, N.Mex., 1983—; pres., founder Day Camp Southside, St. Petersburg, 1976-77. Planning chmn. terr. 5 ann. meeting ARC, Farmington, 1990-91, babysitting instr., 1990—, basic aid tng. instr., 1992, Project Read instr., 1994. Recipient Appreciation award ARC, 1991. Mem. Fin. Women Internat. (by-laws com. 1990-91, treas. 1993-94), Nat. Assn. Trust Ops. Specialists (bd. dirs. 1992), Am. Bus. Women's Assn. (v.p. 1991, pres. 1992, Appreciation award 1989, Woman of Yr. 1995). Republican. Baptist. Home: 1710 E 23d St # 4 Farmington NM 87401 Office: First Nat Bank Farmington PO Box 4540 Farmington NM 87499-4540

HRDY, SARAH BLAFFER, anthropology educator; b. July 11, 1946; m. Daniel B. Hrdy; 3 children. AB summa cum laude, Radcliffe Coll., 1969; PhD in Anthropology, Harvard U., 1975. Instr. in anthropology U. Mass., Boston, 1973; lectr. in biol. anthropology Harvard U., Cambridge, Mass., 1975-76, postdoctoral fellow in biology, 1977-78; assoc. in biol. anthropology Peabody Mus., Harvard U., 1979; sr. fellow Am. Inst. Indian Studies, New Delhi, India, 1980-81; vis. assoc. prof. Rice U., Houston, 1981-82; prof. in anthropology U. Calif., Davis, 1984—; presenter workshops in field; tchr. hygiene to Spanish-speaking adults El Paraiso, Honduras, 1967; mem. adv. bd. Primates, 1984-90; mem. editorial Cultural Anthropology, 1984—; cons. editor Am. Jour. Primatology, 1980—; assoc. editor Human Evolution, 1985-88, Numan Nature, 1989. Author: The Black-man of Zinacantan: A Central American Legend, 1972, The Langurs of Abu: Female and Male Strategies of Reproduction, 1977, The Woman that Never Evolved, 1981 (Notable Book of Yr., N.Y. Times), Infanticide Comparative and Evolutionary Perspectives, 1984; contbr. articles, revs. to profl. publs.; producer various films in field. Guggenheim fellow, 1987-88; grantee Wenner-Gren Found., 1982, 85, Miller Found., 1971, Smithsonian Instn., 1979, NSF, 1979, U. Calif., 1985, Rockefeller Found., 1985. Fellow Am. Acad. Arts and Scis.; mem. NAS, Am. Soc. Naturalists, Am. Soc. Primatologists, Animal Behavior Soc., Am. Anthropol. Soc., Internat. Primatolog. Soc., Calif. Acad. Scis., Phi Beta Kappa. Office: U Calif Dept Anthropology Young Hall Davis CA 95616

HRUT, CHRISTOPHER BOLESLAW, sales and marketing executive; b. Szczecin, Poland, Apr. 18, 1958; came to U.S. 1986; s. Zdzislaw and Halina (Maj) H. MSc, Gdansk U., Poland, 1982; Dipl.Eng., Tech. U. Gdansk, 1983; MSc, MIT, 1987; MBA, Harvard U., 1989. Sr. supr. Gdansk Shipyard, 1983-86; exec. asst. Fuji-Xerox, Tokyo, 1988; mng. exec. Network Equip. Technologies, 1989-90; dir. Trimble Navigation & Navigation Techs., Sunnyvale, Calif., 1991—; gen. ptnr. Renaissance Capital, Boston, 1993—; gen. ptnr. European Renaissance Ptnrs.; cons. in field. Contbr. articles to profl. jours. MIT grantee, Harvard Bus. Sch. fellow, Kosciuszko Found. grantee. Mem. Harvard Bus. Sch. Club No. Calif., MIT Club No. Calif., Commonwealth Club of Calif., Harvard U. Club No. Calif., Churchill Club, Kosciuszko Found., Harvard U. Club of Poland (founding chmn. 1991—), Harvard U. Club of Hungary (founding chmn. 1990—), Harvard U. Club of Czechoslovakia (founding chmn. 1990—). Office: Navigation Techs 740 E Arques Ave Sunnyvale CA 94086-3833 also: Zaruskiego 26, PL-80-299 Gdansk-Osowa Poland

HSIA, CHI-CHENG, finance educator; b. Nanking, China, May 28, 1928; came to U.S., 1978; s. Yu-Shu and Yi-Ching (Tai) H.; m. Yi-Huang, July 15, 1957; children: Janice, Joan. BA, Taiwan U., 1951; MS, UCLA, 1971, PhD, 1974. Assoc. prof. Taiwan U., Taipei, 1974-78; from asst. prof. to assoc. prof. Wash. State U., Pullman, 1979-87; assoc. prof. Portland (Ore.) State U., 1987-89, prof., 1989—; vis. asst. prof. UCLA, 1978-79; cons. Willamette Mgmt. Assocs., Portland, 1992—. Mem. Am. Fin. Assn., Am. Acad. Acct. & Fin., Fin. Mgmt. Assn., Western Am. Fin. Assn., Eastern Am. Fin. Assn., Southern Am. Fin. Assn. Office: Sch Bus Portland State U Portland OR 97207-0751

HSIAO, CHIE-FANG, neuroscientist; b. Chi-Yei, Taiwan, Jan. 15, 1945; came to U.S., 1983; s. Zu-Chin and Chiao (Ching) H.; m. Shu-Lan Lin, Jan. 29, 1976; children: Kathryne, Amy. BS in Pharmacology, Taipei (Taiwan) Med. Coll., 1976; PhD in Med. Sci., Osaka (Japan) U., 1983. Rsch. assoc. SUNY, Stony Brook, 1983-85, U. Colo., Boulder, 1985-89; rsch. instr. U. Mo., Kansas City, 1989-92; neuroscientist U. Calif., L.A., 1992—; lectr. U. Mo., Kansas City, 1988-89; rsch. instr. Osaka U. Med. Sch., 1981-83, U. Calif., L.A., 1992—. Advisor Taipei Med. Sch. Alumni, Calif., 1993, Taiwanese Assn., Colo., 1985. Recipient Nat. Rsch. Svc. award NIH, 1992, fellowship Fight for Sight Inc., 1984, scholarship Japan Rotary, 1982. Mem. AAAS, Soc. for Neurosci., Naturalistic Soc. USA. Home: 1437 S Westgate Ave Apt 12 Los Angeles CA 90025-2250 Office: Univ Calif 405 Hilgard Ave Los Angeles CA 90024-1301

HSIEH, MICHAEL THOMAS, venture capitalist; b. Hong Kong, Mar. 9, 1958; came to U.S., 1968; s. Ching Chi and Za Za (Suffiad) H.; m. Tonia Chao, Sept. 6, 1987. BA, Harvard U., 1980, MBA, 1984. Analyst Merrill Lynch Capital Markets, N.Y.C., 1980-81; assoc. Sun Hung Kai Securities, N.Y.C., 1981-82; asst. v.p. Chappell and Co., San Francisco, 1984-86; pres. LF Internat. Inc., San Francisco, Calif., 1986—; bd. dirs. Millworks Trading Co., Ltd., N.Y.C., Wilke Rodriguez, N.Y.C., Li & Fung (Trading) Ltd., Hong Kong, The Original San Francisco Toymakers. Exec. dir. Ctr. for Pacific Rim, U. San Francisco. Mem. Harvard Club, San Francisco Tennis Club. Office: LF Internat Inc 360 Post St Ste 705 San Francisco CA 94108-4903

HSIEH, RUDY RU-PIN, banker; b. Taipei, Taiwan, July 6, 1950; came to U.S., 1976; s. Yu-Fu and Lan-Ying (Wu) H. B.S., Fu-Jen Catholic U., Taiwan, 1973; M.B.A., Long Island U., 1978. Credit officer Cathay Bank, Los Angeles, 1979; asst. v.p., Monterey Park, Calif., 1979-81, asst. v.p., asst. mgr., 1981-84, v.p., mgr., 1984-86 ; legislator, Republic of China, 1987-90; bd. dirs. Yong Chang Securities Co, Taiwan, 1988-92; exec. v.p. United Nat. Bank, L.A., 1992—. Pres. Taiwan Benevolent Assn. of Calif., Monterey Park, 1983; bd. dirs. Taiwan Benevolent Assn. of Am., Bethesda, Md., 1982, v.p., 1983, pres., 1984. Mem. Chinese Am. Profl. Soc., Overseas Chinese Commn. Office: United Nat Bank 855 S Atlantic Blvd Monterey Park CA 91754-4735

HSIEH, YOU-LO, fiber and polymer scientist, educator; b. Taipei, Taiwan, Republic of China, Feb. 16, 1953; came to U.S., 1975; d. Men-Chu and Tze-hue (Hsiao) Hsieh; m. A. Bruce Playle, May 11, 1980; children: Arlo, Alma. BS, Fu-Jen U., Taipei, 1975; MS, Auburn (Ala.) U., 1977; PhD, U. Md., 1981. Asst. prof. U. Calif., Davis, 1981-88, assoc. prof., 1988-94, prof. div. textiles and clothing, 1994—. Author rsch. papers. Recipient German Acad. Exch. Svcs. award, N.Y.C.; NSF grantee; Cotton Inc. grantee. Mem. Am. Chem. Soc., Am. Phys. Soc., Am. Textile Chemists and Colorists Soc., The Fiber Soc. Office: U Calif Davis Div Textiles and Clothing Davis CA 95615-8722

HSU, APO, conductor; b. Keelung, Taiwan, Rep. China, Oct. 7, 1956; came to U.S., 1981; d. Ying-Shyr and Yueh-Shur (Lin) H. BA, Nat. Taiwan Normal U., Taipei, Taiwan, 1980; MusM, Hartt Sch. Music, 1984, artist diploma, 1985. Music dir. St. Cloud State U. Orchestra, Minn., 1986-91, Heartland Symphony Orchestra, Little Falls, Minn., 1988-91, Ctrl. Minn. Youth Symphony, St. Cloud, 1989-91; conductor in residency Peter Britt Festivals, Jacksonville, Oreg., 1990; affiliate artist, NEA conductor Oreg. Symphony, Portland, 1991-94; music dir. Oreg. Mozart Players, Eugene, 1991—. Chamber Orchestra Series grantee Ctrl. Minn. Arts Coun., 1989. Mem. Am. Symphony Orchestra League, Conductors Guild, Am. String Tchrs. Assn., Pi Kappa Lambda. Home: 2935 NE 15th Ave Portland OR 97212 Office: Oregon Mozart Players 30 E Broadway Ste 100 Eugene OR 97401

HSU, CHARLES, venture capitalist; b. N.Y.C., Oct. 31, 1957; s. Chichang and Ujjala (Deb) H. AB in Biochemistry magna cum laude, Harvard U., 1979; PhD in Genetics, Stanford U., 1984, MBA, 1990. Tchg. fellow Harvard U., Cambridge, 1978-79; postdoctoral fellow Stanford U., 1984; staff scientist Creative Biomolecules, San Francisco, 1984-85, Invitron Corp., Redwood City, Calif., 1985-87; sr. scientist Invitron Corp., Redwood City, 1987-88; ind. cons. Comm-Tech Internat., Menlo Park, Calif., 1989; investment mgr. Advent Internat. Corp., Boston, 1990-92, ptnr., 1992—; membership sales and program advisor Summit Orgn., Foster City, Calif., 1987-88; cons. Stanford Bus. Sch. Alumni Consulting Team, 1993—. Contbr. articles to profl. jours. Presdl. scholar, 1975. Mem. AAAS. Democrat. Office: Advent Internat Corp 2180 Sand Hill Rd Menlo Park CA 94025

HSU, CHIEH SU, applied mechanics engineering educator, researcher; b. Soochow, Kiangsu, China, May 27, 1922; came to U.S., 1947.; s. Chung yu and Yong Feng (Wu) H.; m. Helen Yung-Feng Tse, Mar. 28, 1953; children—Raymond Hwa-Chi, Katherine Hwa-Ling. BS, Nat. Inst. Tech., Chungking, China, 1945; MS, Stanford U., 1948, PhD, 1950. Project engr. IBM Corp., Poughkeepsie, N.Y., 1951-55; assoc. prof. U. Toledo, 1955-58; assoc. prof. Univ Calif.-Berkeley, 1958-64, prof., 1964—, chmn. div. applied mechanics, 1969-70; mem. sci. adv. bd. Alexander von Humboldt Found. of Fed. Republic Germany, Bonn, 1985—; mem. U.S. nat. com. theoretical and applied mechanics U.S. Nat. Acad. Scis., 1985-90. Author: Cell-to-Cell Mapping, 1987; contbg. author: Thin-Shell Structures, 1974, Advances in Applied Mechanics, vol. 17, 1977; tech. editor: Jour. Applied Mechanics, N.Y.C., 1976-82; assoc. editor profl. jours.; author of over 105 tech. papers. Recipient Alexander von Humboldt award Fed. Republic Germany, 1986; Guggenheim Found. fellow, 1964-65; Miller research prof., U. Calif.-Berkeley, 1973-74. Fellow ASME (Centennial award 1980) Am. Acad. Mechanics; mem. Acoustical Soc. Am., Soc. Indsl. and Applied Math., U. S. Nat. Acad. Engring., Acad. Sinica, Sigma Xi. Office: U Calif Dept Mech Engring Berkeley CA 94720-1740

HSU, JOHN Y., computer scientist; b. Republic of China, Mar. 17, 1938; came to U.S., 1962; s. James and Margaret (Yen) H.; m. Sheryl L. Hsu, Dec. 18, 1965; children: Mary, David. BSEE, Nat. Taiwan U., 1959; MSEE, U. Calif., Berkeley, 1964, PhD, 1969. Cons. Ames Rsch. Ctr., Mountain View, Calif., 1973-74, Federic Electric/ITT, Vandenberg, Calif., 1971-79, Inst. for Info. Industry, Taipei, 1979-80, Control Data Corp., Campbell, Calif., 1981-82, IBM Corp., San Jose, Calif., 1987-89; prof. Calif. Poly., San Luis Obispo, Calif., 1970—. Mem. IEEE (sr.), Assn. for Computing Machinery. Office: Calif Poly San Luis Obispo CA 93407

HSU, SHU-DEAN, hematologist, oncologist; b. Chiba, Japan, Feb. 21, 1943; came to U.S., 1972; s. Tetzu and Takako (Koo) Minoyama; m. San-San Hsu, Mar. 3, 1973; children: Deborah Te-Lan, Peter Jie-Te. MD, Taipei (Taiwan) Med. Coll., 1968. Diplomate Am. Bd. Internal Medicine, Am. Bd. Hematology, Am. Bd. Med. Oncology. Asst. in medicine Mt. Sinai Sch. Medicine, N.Y.C., 1975-77; asst. instr. medicine U. Tex., Galveston, 1977-78; lectr. in medicine Tex. A&M U., Temple, 1978-80; asst. prof. medicine U. Ark., Little Rock, 1980-83; practice medicine specializing in hematology-oncology Visalia (Calif.) Med. Clinic, 1983—; chief hematology and oncology VA Med. Ctr., Temple, Tex., 1978-80. Contbr. articles to profl. jours. Fellow ACP; mem. N.Y. Acad. Scis., Am. Soc. Clin. Oncology, Am. Soc. Hematology, Calif. Med. Assn., Tulare County Med. Soc. Club: Visalia Racquet. Home: 3500 W Hydeway Visalia CA 93291 Office: Visalia Med Clinic PO Box 3347 Olympic Valley CA 96146

HU, CHI YU, physicist, educator; b. Szchwan, China, Feb. 12, 1933; came to U.S., 1956, naturalized, 1974; s. T.C. and P.S. (Yang) H.; children—Marica, Mark, Albert, Han Chin. B.S., Nat. Taiwan U., 1955; Ph.D., M.I.T., 1962. Research asso. St. John's U., Jamaica, N.Y., 1962-63; asst. prof. physics Calif. State U., Long Beach, 1963-68; asso. prof. Calif. State U., 1968-72, prof., 1972—; NSF vis. prof. UCLA, 1988-90. Contbr. articles to profl. jours. NSF summer fellow, 1965, 76; grantee NSF, 1969-70, 86-88, 88-90, 90—, Calif. State U. Long Beach Found., 1965, 66, 70, 72, Dept. Energy, 1986-88. Mem. Am. Phys. Soc., AAUP, United Profs. Calif. Office: Calif State U Dept Physics Long Beach CA 90840

HU, JOHN CHIH-AN, retired chemist, research engineer; b. Nanzhang, Hubei, China, July 12, 1922; came to U.S., 1954, naturalized, 1965; s. Qi-Qing and Zhao-Xian (Zeng) H.; BS in Chemistry, Nat. Central U., Nanjing, China, 1946; MS in Organic Chemistry, U. So. Calif., 1957, postgrad., 1957-61; PhD (hon.) Marquis Giuseppe Scicluna Internat. Univ. Foundation, 1985; m. Betty Siao-Yung Ho, Oct. 26, 1957; children: Arthur, Benjamin, Carl, David, Eileen, Franklin, George. Dir. rsch. dept. Plant 1, Taiwan Fertilizer Mfg. Co., Chilung, 1947-54; rsch. assoc. chemistry dept. U. So. Calif., L.A., 1957-61; rsch. chemist Chem Seal Corp. Am., Los Angeles, 1961-62; rsch. chemist Products Rsch. & Chem. Corp., Glendale, Calif., 1962-66; sr. rsch. engr., materials and tech. unit, Boeing Co., Seattle, 1966-71, specialist engr. Quality Assurance Labs., 1971-90, ret., 1990; cons. UN; lectr., China, profl. confs. Fellow Am. Inst. Chemists; mem. Am. Chem. Soc. (chmn. Puget Sound sect. 1988, councilor 1989-92), Royal Soc. Chemistry (London), N.Y. Acad. Sci., Phi Lambda Upsilon. Patentee Chromatopyrography; contbg. author: Analytical Approach, 1983, Advances in Chromotography, vol. 23, 1984; contbr. articles on analytical pyrolysis, gas chromatography, mass spectrometry, polymer characterization, chemistry and tech. of sealants and adhesives to profl. publs. in Chinese and English; editor Puget Sound Chemist, 1984-92; referee profl. jours. Analytical Chemistry, Analytica Chimica Acta, Am. Chem. Soc. short courses. Home: 2813 Whitworth Ave S Renton WA 98055-5008

HU, TEH-WEI, economics educator; b. Shanghai, Oct. 10, 1937; came to U.S., 1961; married. PhD, U. Wis., 1967. Statis. analyst World Bank, Washington, 1962-63; asst. prof. Pa. State U., University Park, 1966-70, assoc. prof., 1970-72, prof., 1972-86; prof. U. Calif., Berkeley, 1986—, chmn., 1990-93; cons. World Bank, 1985-93, Ford Found., 1983-88, Ministry of Health, People's Rep. of China, 1990—. Named Disting. in Social Svcs., Pa. State Alumni Assn., 1985, Disting. Alumni, Econs. Inst., U. Colo., 1992. Mem. Am. Econs. Assn., N.Am. Chinese Econs. Assn. (pres. 1987-89). Office: U Calif Sch Pub Health 412 Warren Hall Berkeley CA 94720

HUANG, ALVIN SHIH-AN, food science educator; b. Ping Tung, Taiwan, Apr. 25, 1955; came to U.S., 1980; s. Chia and Hsui Min (Chiang) H.; m. Joyce Chaoyong Luh, June 14, 1981; children: Joanne J. Huang, Daniel R. Huang. BS, Nat. Taiwan U., 1977, MS, 1979; PhD, U. Wis., 1985. Sr. scientist Hansen's Lab., Milw., 1986-87; prin. investigator NutraSweet, Mt. Prospect, Ill., 1987-89; asst. prof. U. Hawaii, Honolulu, 1989-94, assoc. prof., 1994—; v.p. KaiGo Inc., Honolulu, 1992—; cons. HPC Foods, Honolulu, 1994—. Author: Fundamentals of Biodegradable Polymer, 1993; contbr. articles to profl. jours. Patentee in field. Recipient Turn-of-Yr. award State of Hawaii, 1994, Biodegradable Packaging award USDA, 1991. Mem. Inst. Food Technologists (sect. chmn. 1993-95). Baptist. Home: 541 Kealahou St Honolulu HI 96825-2943 Office: U Hawaii 1800 E West Rd Honolulu HI 96822-2318

HUANG, CHIEN CHANG, electrical engineer; b. Nanking, Peoples Republic of China, Feb. 16, 1931; came to U.S., 1957; s. Ling-Kuo Huang and Yi-Ching Liu; m. Li-May Tsai, June 2, 1962; children: Frederick G., Lewis G. BSEE, Taiwan Coll. Engring., Tainan, 1954; MSEE, U. Ill., 1959; postgrad., U. Pa., 1960-62. Engr. Burrough Corp., Paoli, Pa., 1960-64; sr. staff engr. Unisys Corp., San Diego, 1974—; sr. engr. Philco Ford Corp., Blue Bell, Pa., 1965-69; staff engr. Fairchild Semiconductor, Mountain View, Calif., 1969-71; sr. staff engr. Am. Micro Systems, Santa Clara, Calif., 1971-74. Contbr. articles to profl. jours. Home: 14481 Maplewood St Poway CA 92064-6446 Office: Unisys Corp 10850 Via Frontera San Diego CA 92127-1705

HUANG, FRANCIS FU-TSE, mechanical engineering educator; b. Hong Kong, Aug. 27, 1922; came to U.S., 1945, naturalized, 1960; s. Kwong Set and Chen-Ho (Yee) H.; m. Fung-Yuen Fung, Apr. 10, 1954; children: Raymond, Stanley. BS, San Jose State Coll., 1951; MS, Stanford U., 1952; Profl. M.E., Columbia U., 1964; Cultural Doctorate in Energy Sci. (hon.), World U., Ariz., 1990. Design engr. M.W. Kellogg Co., N.Y.C., 1952-58; faculty San Jose (Calif.) State U., 1958—, assoc. prof. mech. engring., 1962-67, prof., 1967-91, prof. emeritus, 1991, chmn. dept., 1973-81; hon. prof. heat power engring. Taiyuan (People's Republic of China) U. Tech., 1981—. Author: Engineering Thermodynamics—Fundamentals and Applications, 1976, 2d edit., 1988. Capt. Chinese Army, 1943-45. Recipient Disting. Teaching award Calif. State Coll. System, 1968-69; named Outstanding Prof. of Yr., Tau Beta Pi, 1967, 76, Prof. of Yr., Pi Tau Sigma, 1985; NSF faculty fellow, 1962-64. Mem. AAAS, ASME, AIAA, AAUP, Am. Soc. Engring. Edn., N.Y. Acad. Scis., Sigma Xi. Home: 1259 Sierra Mar Dr San Jose CA 95118-1235 Office: San Jose State U Dept Mech Engring San Jose CA 95192

HUANG, JEN-TZAW, pharmaceutical executive; b. Taipei, Taiwan, Oct. 8, 1938; s. C.W. Huang; m. Grace Huang; 1 child, George. BS, Nat. Taiwan U., 1962; MS, U. Houston, 1969; PhD, U. Tex., Houston, 1972. Sr. rsch. scientist Inst. of Neurochemistry, Wards Island, N.Y., 1975-80; assoc. mem. Va. Mason Rsch. Ctr., Seattle, 1980-86; dir. scientific affairs JBC, Inc. Gifu Rsch. Lab., Kaizu, Gufu, Japan, 1986-88; mgr. JBC Inc., USA br., Thousand Oaks, Calif., 1988-91; v.p. FASA Co., Thousand Oaks, 1991—. Contbr. articles to profl. jours. Grantee NIH, 198-, 83. Mem. Regulatory Affairs Profl. Soc., Am. Assn. Lab. Animals Sci. Office: 1378 Oakridge Ct Thousand Oaks CA 91362-1923

HUANG, KUN LIEN, software engineer, scientist; b. Nantou, Taiwan, Jan. 20, 1953; came to U.S., 1984; S. Chai-Chang and Fei-Chei (Chi) H.; m. Sue Hui Lee, Mar. 24, 1981; 1 child, Wayne. BS, Nat. Taipei Inst. Tech., Taiwan, 1973, N.D. State U., 1986; MS, U. Mo., 1988. Mech. engr. Ta Tung Aluminum Co., Taipei, 1975-76; rsch. mgr. Ta Tung Aluminum Co., Tapei, 1976-77, prodn. tech. mgr., 1977-79, quality control mgr., 1979-84; computer programmer U. Mo., Columbia, 1988; systems analyst, programmer NCR Corp., San Diego, 1989-92; database cons. Gamma-Metrics, 1992-93; software engr. Science Applications Internat. Corp., 1993—; cons. Computing Ctr., U. Mo., Columbia, 1987-88. Recipient Nat. scholarship Republic China Jaycees, Taipei, 1972. Mem. AAAS, San Diego Taiwanese Cultural Assn. Republican. Home: 8939 Adobe Bluffs Dr San Diego CA 92129-4400

HUANG, LINDA CHEN, plastic surgeon; b. Ithaca, N.Y., July 24, 1952. MD, StanfordU, 1979. Chmn. plastic surgery St. Joseph Hosp., Denver. Office: 1578 Humboldt St Denver CO 80218-1638*

HUANG, SHI, molecular biologist; b. Da Lian, China, Oct. 26, 1961; came to U.S., 1984; s. Ce and Jingmin (Peng) H.; m. Ruoping Chen, Apr. 28, 1989; children: Matthew, Samuel. BS, Fudan U., 1983; PhD, U. Calif., Davis, 1988. Postdoctoral fellow U. Calif., San Diego, 1989-92; asst. staff scientist La Jolla (Calif.) Rsch. Found., 1992—. Pew Charitable Trusts scholar in biomed. sci., Phila., 1993—; Am. Heart Assn. postdoctoral fellow, 1992. Office: La Jolla Cancer Rsch Found 10901 N Torrey Pines Rd La Jolla CA 92037-1005

HUANG, SUNGRUNG, engineer; b. Taipei, July 26, 1960; came to U.S., 1987; s. Wanliang and Cheh (Lee) H.; m. Tsaefen Yang, Sept. 7, 1983; children: Jeffrey, Vickie, Diane. BSEE, Nat. Taiwan U., Taipei, 1982, MSEE, 1985; PhDEE, U. Rochester, 1990. Ultrasound scientist Bio-Imaging Rsch. Inc., Lincolnshire, Ill., 1990-92; image analysis engr. Acuson Computed Sonography, Mountain View, Calif., 1992—. Inventor sonoelasticity imaging, blood loss monitoring system, needle tip position monitoring system. Mem. IEEE, Am. Inst. of Ultrasound, Acoustical Soc. of Am. Office: Acuson PO Box 7393 Mountain View CA 94039

HUANG, XUEDONG DAVID, senior reseacher; b. Wuhan, Hubei, China, Oct. 20, 1962; came to U.S., 1989; s. Heqing and Jiansong (Ling) H.; m. Yingzhi Zhou, Oct. 4, 1986; 1 child, Angela. BS, Hunan U., Chanagsha, China, 1982; MS, Tsinghua U., Beijing, 1984; PhD, U. Edinburgh, U.K., 1989. Rsch. assoc. Tsinghua U., Beijing, 1984-87; fellow, vis. scientist U. Edinburgh, 1987-89; rsch. computer scientist Carnegie Mellon U., Pitts., 1989-93; mgr., sr. rschr. Speech Rsch. group, Microsoft Corp., Redmond, Wash., 1993—. Author: Hidden Markov Models for Speech Recognition, 1990; inventor in field; assoc. editor IEEE Trans. on Speech and Audio Processing, 1992—. Mem. IEEE (sr. mem., Paper award 1994). Home: 10026 177th Ave NE Redmond WA 98052-3289 Office: Microsoft Corp Redmond WA 98052

HUANG, ZHIJIAN, biochemist; b. Shaxian, Peoples Republic of China, Oct. 7, 1963; came to the U.S., 1989; s. Zhaoxiang and Dexun (Zhang) H.; m. Weimin You, Dec. 9, 1988; 1 child, Peter M. BS, Zheijiang U., 1983; PhD, Med. U. Beijing, 1988. Staff scientist II Molecular Probes, Inc., Eugene, Oreg., 1990—. Contbr. articles to profl. jours. Mem. Am. Soc. for Cell Biology, Biophys. Soc. Home: 2125 W 27th Ave Eugene OR 97405-1421 Office: Molecular Probes Inc 4849 Pitchford St Eugene OR 97402-9144

HUBBARD, CHARLES RONALD, engineering executive; b. Weaver, Ala., Feb. 4, 1933; s. John Duncan Hubbard and Athy Pauline (Lusk) Thorpe; m. Betty Lou McKleroy, Dec. 29, 1951; 1 son, Charles Ronald Hubbard II. BSEE, U. Ala., 1960. Mktg. mgr. Sperry Corp., Huntsville, Ala., 1969-71, head engring. sect., 1971-74; sr. staff engr. Honeywell Inc., Clearwater, Fla., 1974-76, mgr., 1976-79, chief engr., West Covina, Calif., 1979-83, assoc. dir. engring., 1983-84, assoc. dir. advanced systems, 1984-87, assoc. dir. programs, 1987-88; v.p. govt. systems div. Integrated Inference Machines, Anaheim, Calif., 1988-91; pres. Synergy Computer Systems, Anaheim, 1991—. Served as staff sgt. USAF, 1953-57. Recipient Outstanding Fellow award U. Ala., 1991. Mem. IEEE (sect. chmn. 1972-73). Methodist. Home: 5460 E Willowick Cir Anaheim CA 92807-4642 Office: Synergy Computer Systems Ste 3060 5753-G East Santa Ana Canyon Rd Anaheim CA 92807

HUBBARD, DAVID ALLAN, minister, educator, religious association administrator; b. Stockton, Calif., Apr. 8, 1928; s. John King and Helena (White) H.; m. Ruth Doyal, Aug. 12, 1949; 1 child, Mary Ruth. BA, Westmont Coll., Calif., 1949; BD, Fuller Theol. Sem., Pasadena, Calif., 1952, ThM, 1954; PhD, St. Andrews U., Scotland, 1957; DD (hon.), John Brown U., 1975; LHD (hon.), Rockford Coll., 1975, Hope Coll., 1990; DLitt (hon.), King Sejong U., Korea, 1985; EdD (hon.), Friends U., 1990; DD (hon.), North Park Coll. & Theol. Sem., 1993. Ordained to ministry Conservative Bapt. Assn., 1952, Am. Bapt. Chs. in the U.S.A., 1984. Lectr. Old Testament studies St. Andrews U., 1955-56; asst. prof. Bibl. studies Westmont Coll., 1957, chmn. dept. Bibl. studies and philosophy, 1958-63; interim pastor Montecito (Calif.) Community Ch., 1960-62; pres., prof. Old Testament Fuller Theol. Sem., 1963-93, pres. emeritus, prof. emeritus Old Testament, 1993—; exec. v.p. Fuller Evangelistic Assn., 1969-92; Tyndale Old Testament lectr., Cambridge, Eng., 1965, Soc. Old Testament Studies lectr., London, 1971, lectr. numerous U.S. univs., 1973—. Speaker: internat. radio broadcast The Joyful Sound, 1969-80; author: With Bands of Love, 1968, (with others) Is God Dead?, 1966, Is Life Really Worth Living?, 1969, What's God Been Doing All This Time?, 1970, What's New?, 1970, Does the Bible Really Work?, 1971, Psalms for All Seasons, 1971, Is The Family Here To Stay?, 1971, The Practice of Prayer, 1972, Spanish edit., 1974, Chinese edit., 1979, How To Face Your Fears, 1972, The Holy Spirit in Today's World, 1973, Church—Who Needs It?, 1974, They Met Jesus, 1974, More Psalms for All Seasons, 1975, An Honest Search for a Righteous Life, 1975, Colossians Speaks to the Sickness of Our Time, 1976, Happiness: You Can Find the Secret, 1976, Beyond Futility, 1976, Chinese edit., 1982, Themes from the Minor Prophets, 1977, Strange Heroes, 1977, Galatians: Gospel of Freedom, 1977, Thessalonians: Life That's Radically Christian, 1977, Why Do I Have to Die?, 1978, How to Study the Bible, 1978, What We Evangelicals Believe, 1979, Book of James: Wisdom That Works, 1980, Right Living in a World Gone Wrong, 1981, German edit., 1982, Parables Jesus Told, 1981, (with Bush and LaSor) Old Testament Survey, 1982, The Practice of Prayer, 1982, The Second Coming, 1984, Proclamation 3: Pentecost 1, 1985, Unwrapping Your Spiritual Gifts, 1985, Holy Spirit in Today's World, 1986, Tyndale Commentary: Joel, Amos, 1987, Tyndale Commentary: Hosea, 1989, Communicator's Commentary: Proverbs, 1989, Ecclesiastes, Song of Solomon, WORD 1991; contbg. editor: Eternity mag.; mem. editl. bd. The Ministers' Permanent Library, 1976-92; adv. bd. Evang. Book Club, 1977-86; contbr. articles to dictionaries, mags. Chmn. Pasadena Urban Coalition, 1968-71; mem. Calif. Bd. Edn., 1972-75; bd. dirs. Nat. Inst. Campus Ministries, 1974-78. Personal tribute - festschrift Studies in Old Testament Theology, Word, Inc., 1992. Mem. Catholic Biblical Assn., Nat. Assn. Bapt. Profs. Religion, Nat. Assn. Profs. Hebrew, Am. Acad. Religion, Soc. Bibl. Lit., Soc. for Old Testament Study, Inst. Bibl. Rsch., Assn. Theol. Schs. in U.S. and Can. (exec. com. 1972-80, pres. 1976-78), Fuller Evang. Assn. (trustee 1969-92, exec. v.p. 1969-82). Home and Office: 658 Chelham Way Santa Barbara CA 93108-1060

HUBBARD, DAVID RICHARDSON, neurologist; b. Hartford, Conn., Feb. 25, 1948; s. David Richardson and Margaret (Acherly) H.; m. Arlene Hubbard; children: Devin, Alexandria. BA, Yale U., 1970; MA, Stanford U., 1971; MD, U. Conn., 1977. Diplomate Am. Bd. Neurology and Psychiatry. Intern Yale-Waterbury Hosp., 1978; resident in neurology Albert Einstein Coll. Medicine, 1978-80, chief resident neurology, 1981; asst. prof. Cornell Med. Sch., N.Y.C., 1981-83; assoc. prof. U. Calif. San Diego Med. Sch., 1983—; neurologist Sharp Hosp. Pain Ctr., San Diego, 1991—. Recipient Scholastic Excellence award U. Conn. Med. Sch., 1977, Beyond the Call of Duty award Scripps Hosp., 1990. Mem. Calif. Med. Assn., Am. Pain Soc., Internat. Assn. Study of Pain. Office: Sharp Pain Rehab 2999 Health Center Dr San Diego CA 92123-2762

HUBBARD, DONALD, marine artist, writer; b. Bronx, N.Y., Jan. 15, 1926; s. Ernest Fortesque and Lilly Violet (Beck) H.; student Brown U., 1944-45; A.A., George Washington U., 1959, B.A., 1958; student Naval War Coll., 1965-66; m. Darlene Julia Huber, Dec. 13, 1957; children: Leslie Carol, Christopher Eric, Lauren Ivy, Carmeron C. McNall. Commd. ensign U.S. Navy, 1944, advanced through grades to comdr., 1965; served naval aviator, ret., 1967; founder Ocean Ventures Industries, Inc., Coronado, Calif., 1969, operator, 1969-77; marine artist; founder, operator Sea Eagle Pubs., Coronado, 1988; lectr. on marine art; SCUBA instr. Author: Ships-in-Bottles, 2d edition, 1988, A How to Guide to a Venerable Nautical Craft, 1971; Buddleschiffe: Wie Macht Man Sie, 1972; The Complete Book of Inflatable Boats, 1979; Where to Paddle in San Diego County and Nearby Mexico, 1992, Days of You: Rhymes & Other Writings, 1995; editor: The Bottle Shipwright; works featured in Am. Artist of the Bookplate, 1970-90, Cambridge Bookplate Press, 1990; contbr. articles in field to publs. Decorated Air Medal. Mem. Ships-in-Bottles Assn. (pres. N.Am. div. 1982—), Nature Printing Soc., Am. Soc. Bookplate Collectors adn Designers, San Diego Watercolor Soc. (bd. dirs. 1981-82), Marine Hist. Soc., San Diego Maritime Assn. Home and Office: 1022 Park Pl Coronado CA 92118-2822

HUBBARD, GREGORY SCOTT, physicist; b. Lexington, Ky., Dec. 27, 1948; s. Robert Nicholas and Nancy Clay (Brown) H.; B.A., Vanderbilt U., 1970; postgrad. U. Calif., Berkeley, 1975-77; m. Susan Artimissa Ruggeri, Aug. 1, 1982. Lab. engr. physics dept. Vanderbilt U., Nashville, 1970-73; staff scientist Lawrence Berkeley Lab. Dept. Instrument Techniques, Berkeley, Calif., 1974-80; dir. research and devel. Canberra Industries, Inc., Detector Products Div., Novato, Calif., 1980-82; v.p., gen. mgr. Canberra Semicondr., Novato, Calif., 1982-85; cons., owner Hubbard Cons. Services, 1978—; cons. SRI Internat., Menlo Park, Calif., 1979-86, sr. rsch. physicist, 1986-87; div. staff scientist space exploration projects office Ames Rsch. Ctr., NASA, Moffett Field, Calif., 1987-90, chief space instrumentation and studies br. NASA Ames Rsch. Ctr., Moffett Field, 1990-92; deputy chief space projects divsn., NASA Ames Rsch. Ctr., Moffett Field, 1992—; lectr. in field. Recipient Founders Scholarship, Vanderbilt U., 1966, Exceptional Achievement medal NASA, 1994. Mem. AIAA, IEEE, Nuclear Sci. Soc., Am. Phys. Soc., Commonwealth Club Calif., Hon. Order Ky. Cols.

HUBBARD, KENDALL BRUCE, educational administrator; b. Seattle, Jan. 30, 1945; s. Harry F. and Ruth (Merrithew) H.; m. Joy Ellen Fox (div. Feb. 1978); m. Virginia Green, Aug. 19, 1984; children: Kira Alison, Raina. BA, Moravian Coll., 1967. Cert. tchr., Wash. Tchr. Holland Twp. Schs., Milford, N.J., 1968-76; owner, CEO Daedalus Image Works, Seattle, 1977-83; adminstrv. asst. Chinook Learning Ctr., Clinton, Wash., 1984-90; adminstr. Whidbey Island Waldorf Sch., Clinton, 1991—. NSF teaching intern, 1973. Home: PO Box 10 Clinton WA 98236-0010

HUBBARD, RICHARD WARD, clinical biochemist; b. Battle Creek, Mich., Dec. 24, 1929; s. Ralph Martin and Myrtle (Ward) H.; m. Constance Mae Hubbard, Nov. 18, 1951; children: Robert John, Jeffrey Allen, Karen Ann. BA, Pacific Union Coll., 1951; MS, Purdue U., 1959, PhD, 1961. Analytical chemist Willard Storage Battery Co., East L.A., 1951-53; med. tech. trainee L.A. County Gen. Hosp., 1953-54; instr. biochemistry Dept. Dermatology, U. Mich., Ann Arbor, 1960-63; sr. rsch. chemist Spinco div. Beckman Instruments, Palo Alto, Calif., 1963-67; project leader biochemistry NASA/SRI, Biosatellite Primate Pr., Menlo Park, 1967-70; asst. prof. biochemistry Depts. Pathology and Biochemistry, Loma Linda (Calif.) U., 1970-73, assoc. prof. biochemistry, 1973-89, assoc. prof. pathology, 1989—; cons., tchr. Beckman Instruments, Palo Alto, 1967-69; cons. biochemistry NASA/Standford Rsch. Inst., Menlo Park, Fla., 1970-72; cons. chromatology Lab. Data Control, Riviera Beach, Calif., 1978-79; scientific advisor Spinco div. Beckman Instruments, Palo Alto, 1986—. Author: Preservation of Biol. Sp., 1972; (with others) Amino Acid Connection, 1988, Monographs on Atherosclerosis, 1990. Mem. Am. Inst. Nutrition, Am. Inst. Clin. Nutrition, Am. Assn. Clin. Chemists (sec. 1980-84), Am. Chem. Soc., Am. Soc. Med. Tech. (chpt. pres. 1983), N.Y. Acad. Sci., Calif. Soc. Med. Tech. (stud bowl dir. 1979-92, Outstanding Mem. 1989), Omicron Sigma, Phi Lambda Upsilon, Sigma Xi. Republican. Seventh-Day Adventist. Home: 1906 Verde Vista Dr Redlands CA 92373-7322

HUBBS, DONALD HARVEY, foundation executive; b. Kingman, Ariz., Jan. 3, 1918; s. Wayne and Grace Lillian (Hoose) H.; m. Flora Vincent, June 14, 1945; children: Donald Jr., Susan Tyner, Diane Schultz, Wayne, David, Adrienne Busk. BA in Edn., Ariz. State U., 1940; JD, Southwestern U., 1956. Bar: Calif., 1956; CPA. Acct. Wright and Hubbs, L.A., 1945-67; pvt. practice atty. L.A., 1956-81; pres., dir. Conrad N. Hilton Found., L.A., 1981—; bd. dirs. Trans World Airlines, 1977; regent Mt. St. Mary's Coll., 1983—; bd. councilors U. So. Calif. Law Sch., 1992—. 1st lt. (inf.) U.S. Army. Mem. State Bar of Calif., So. Calif. Assn. for Philanthropy (pres. 1985-86), Riviera Country Club, L.A. Country Club. Home: 1658 San Onofre Dr Pacific Palisades CA 90272-2735 Office: Conrad N Hilton Found 10100 Santa Monica # 740 Los Angeles CA 90067

HUBER, ARTHUR FRANCIS, II, military officer; b. Miami Beach, Fla., May 17, 1960; s. Arthur Francis Sr. and Amalia (Navarro) H. BA in Govt. and Internat. Rels., U. Notre Dame, 1983, BS in Aero. Engring., 1983, MS in Aero. Engring., 1985; grad., USAF Test Pilot Sch., 1990. Commd. 2d lt. USAF, 1983, advanced through grades to maj., 1994; astronautical engr. Air Force Space Tech. Ctr., Kirtland AFB, N.Mex., 1985-87, program mgr., 1987-88, exec. officer, 1988-89; flight test engr. 46th Test Wing, Eglin AFB, Fla., 1990-94; RAND rsch. fellow, 1994—; presenter in field. Lector, eucharistic minister Roman Cath. Ch., 1978—. Decorated Air Force Achievement medal with Oak Leaf Cluster, Meritorious Svc. medal with oak leaf cluster, Nat. Def. Svc. medal. Sr. mem. AIAA; mem. Soc. Flight Test Engrs., Air Force Assn., Sigma Xi, Tau Beta Pi, Pi Sigma Alpha, Sigma Gamma Tau. Republican. Home: 2450 20th St Apt E Santa Monica CA 90405-2715 Office: AFELM RAND PO Box 2138 1700 Main St Santa Monica CA 90407-2138

HUBER, NORMAN KING, geologist; b. Duluth, Minn., Jan. 14, 1926; s. Norman and Hedwig Marie (Graessner) H.; m. Martha Ann Barr, June 2, 1951; children: Steven K., Richard N. BS, Franklin and Marshall Coll., 1950; MS, Northwestern U., 1952, PhD, 1956. Registered geologist, Calif. Geologist U.S. Geol. Survey, Menlo Park, Calif., 1954—; authority geology of Sierra Nev. Contbr. articles to profl. jours. With U.S. Army, 1944-46, Europe and Japan. S.F. Emmons fellow Soc. Econ. Geologists, 1953-54. Fellow Geol. Soc. Am. Home: 220 Diablo Ave Mountain View CA 94043-4117 Office: US Geol Survey M/S 975 345 Middlefield Rd Menlo Park CA 94025-3561

HUBER, WAYNE CHARLES, engineering educator; b. Shelby, Mont., Aug. 2, 1941; s. Hubert Henry and Lois Marion (Hendrickson) H.; m. Catherine Ann Forster, June 22, 1968; 1 child, Lydia Ann. BS, Calif. Inst. Tech., Pasadena, 1963; MS, MIT, 1965, PhD, 1968. Registered profl. engr., Fla. Asst. prof. Dept. of Environ. Engring. Scis., U. Fla., Gainesville, 1968-73, assoc. prof., 1973-79, prof., 1979-91; prof., head Dept. of Civil Engring., Oreg. State U., Covallis, 1991—; cons. Nat. Oceanic and Atmospheric Adminstrn., Rockville, Md., 1990-91, Internat. Inst. for Hydraulic and Environ. Engring., Delft, Netherlands, 1988-91, U.S. EPA, Washington, 1978-83. Co-author: Hydrology and Floodplain Analysis, 1992; contbr. articles to profl. jours. Recipient Lorenz G. Straub award U. Minn., 1969, Outstanding Tech. Achievement award Fla. Engring. Soc., 1985. Mem. ASCE (com. chair 1990-92, Hilgard Hydraulic prize 1973), Internat. Assn. for Hydraulic Rsch., Am. Geophys. Union, Am. Water Resources Assn., Sigma Xi, Tau Beta Pi. Democrat. Home: 3310 NW Crest Dr Corvallis OR 97330-1809 Office: Oreg State U Dept Civil Engring Corvallis OR 97331-2302

HUBERT, HELEN BETTY, epidemiologist; b. N.Y.C., Jan. 22, 1950; d. Leo and Ruth (Rosenbaum) H.; m. Carlos Barbaro Arostegui, Sept. 11, 1976 (div. May 1987); 1 child, Joshua Daniel Hubert. BA magna cum laude, Barnard Coll., 1970; MPH, Yale U., 1973, MPhil, 1976, PhD, 1978. Rsch. assoc. Yale U., New Haven, 1977-78; rsch. epidemiologist Nat. Heart, Lung and Blood Inst., Bethesda, Md., 1978-84; rsch. dir. Gen. Health, Inc., Washington, 1984-87; sr. rsch. scientist Stanford (Calif.) U., 1988—. Peer rev. Am. Jour. Epidemiology, Am. Jour. Pub. Health, Chest, Jour. AMA (JAMA), Archives Internal Medicine; contbr. articles to profl. jours., chpts. to books. Mem. APHA, Am. Heart Assn. (Coun. on Epidemiology), Am. Coll. Epidemiology, Soc. Epidemiol. Rsch., Arthritis Health Profls. Assn., Phi Beta Kappa, Sigma Xi (grant-in-aid for rsch. 1978). Office: Stanford Univ Med Ctr Dept Health Rsch and Policy Rm T210 Stanford CA 94305

HUCK, LARRY RALPH, manufacturers representative, sales consultant; b. Yakima, Wash., Aug. 10, 1942; s. Frank Joseph and Helen Barbara (Swalley) H.; 1 child, Larry Ralph II. Student Wash. Tech. Inst., 1965-66, Seattle Community Coll., 1966-68, Edmonds Community Coll., 1969-70. Salesman, Kirby Co., Seattle, 1964-68, sales mgr., 1968-69; saleman Sanico Chem. Co., Seattle, 1968-69; salesman Synkoloid Co., Seattle, 1970-71; tech. sales rep. Vis Queen div. Ethyl Corp., Seattle, 1971-75; Western sales mgr. B & K Films, Inc., Belmont, Calif., 1975-77; pres. N.W. Mfrs. Assocs., Inc., Bellevue, Wash., 1977-86; pres. combined sales group, 1984 ; nat. sales mgr. Gazelle, Inc., Tomah, Wis., 1979-81; dir. sales J.M.J. Mktg. E.Z. Frame div., 1984-85; pres. Combined Sales Group, Seattle, 1984; nat. accounts mgr. Upnorth Plastics, St. Paul, 1984-87; pres. Combined Sales Group, Inc., Redmond, Wash., 1987—. V.p. Bellevue Nat. Little League; basketball coord. Cath. Youth Orgn., Sacred Heart Ch.; head baseball coach Pierce Coll., Tacoma. With USMC, 1959-64. Mem. Nat. Coun. Salesmen's Orgns., Mfrs. Agts. Nat. Assn., Am. Hardware Mfrs. Assn., Northwest Mfrs. Assn. (pres.), Hardware Affiliated Reps., Inc., Door and Hardware Inst., Internal Conf. Bldg. Ofcls., Am. Baseball Coaches Assn., Marine Corps Assn., 1st Marine Div. Assn., 3d Marine Div. Assn. (life, v.p.). Roman Catholic. Office: 14925 NE 40th St Redmond WA 98052-5326

HUCKABEE, PHYLLIS, gas industry professional; b. Andrews, Tex., Aug. 11, 1963; d. Tommie Jack and Sylvia (Wingo) H. BBA in Fin., Tex. Tech U., 1984, MBA, 1986. Clk. loan escrow 1st Fed. Savs. Bank, Lubbock, Tex., 1984; mgmt. trainee El Paso (Tex.) Nat. Gas Co., 1986-87, analyst rate dept., 1987-88, specialist Calif. affairs, 1988-91, rep. Calif. affairs, 1991-92; asst. dir. Cambridge Energy Rsch. Assocs., Oakland, Calif., 1992-93; regulatory rels. mgr. So. Calif. Gas Co., San Francisco, 1994—; mem. adj. faculty No. Calif. campus U. Phoenix, San Francisco, 1994—. Bd. dirs. El Paso Community Concert Assn., 1988, bd. dirs. Performing Arts Workshop, 1991-92, mem. adv. bd., 1992—; vol. Bus. Vols. for Arts, San Francisco, 1989, East Bay Habitat for Humanity, 1993; tutor, fundraiser Project Read, San Francisco, 1990. Mem. Women Energy Assocs. (bd. dirs. 1990—), Berkeley Archtl. Heritage Assn., Pacific Coast Gas Assn. Methodist. Democrat. Home: 1721 Mcgee Ave Berkeley CA 94703-1225 Office: So Calif Gas Co 601 Van Ness Ave Ste 2014 San Francisco CA 94102-6310

HUCKEBY, KAREN MARIE, graphic arts executive; b. San Diego, June 4, 1957; d. Floyd Riley and Georgette Laura (Wegimont) H. Student Coll. of Alameda, 1976; student 3-M dealer tng. program, St. Paul, 1975. Staff Huck's Press Service, Inc., Emeryville, Calif., 1968—, v.p., 1975—. Mem. Rep. Nat. Task Force, 1984—; bd. dirs. CitiArts Benefactors, Concord, Calif., 1990-93, v.p., treas., 1991-93. Recipient service award ARC, 1977. Mem. East Bay Club of Printing House Craftsman (treas. 1977-78), Oakland Mus. Soc., Nat. Trust Historic Preservation, Smithsonian Inst., San Francisco Mus. Soc., Internat. Platform Assn., Am. Film Inst., Commonwealth Club. Home: 1054 Hera Ct Hercules CA 94547 Office: Staff Huck's Press Svc Inc 691 S 31st St Richmond CA 94804-4022

HUCKSTEAD, CHARLOTTE VAN HORN, retired home economist, artist; b. Garwin, Iowa, Jan. 13, 1920; d. George Loren and Esther Olive (Carver) Van Horn; m. Lowell Raine Huckstead (dec.); children: Karen C., Roger H., Martha E., Paul R., Sarah S. BS, U. Wisc., 1942; BFA, Boise (Idaho) State U., 1989. Merchandising Montgomery Ward, Chgo. and Santa Monica, Calif., 1941-42; "Rosie the Riveter" WWII, Chgo. and Beloit, Wis., 1942-46; woman's editor Dairyland News, Milw., 1950-54; interior designer, cons., tchr. South Bend, Marshfield, Wis., Merced, Calif., 1952-69; extenion home economist U. Minn., Rochester, 1973-78; dir. food svcs. Milton (Wisc.) Sch. Dist., 1978-85; artist, 1952—. Painting and sculpture. Bd. dirs. Rock County Hist. Soc., Janesville, Wis., 1979-84, Milton Hist. Soc., 1979-85; vol. Idaho Geneaoclogy Libr., 1994-95; treas. Wis. Food Svc. Assn., 1980-85; leader/mem. Girl Scouts Am., 1934-78. Mem. AAUW, NOW, Idaho Hist. Soc. (vol. 1985-94), Idaho Centennial Art Group (sec. 1991, show chmn. 1992, historian 1993-95), Idaho Water Color Soc., Morrison Ctr. Aux. (vol. 1986-94, bd. dirs. 1992-93, Audubon Soc., Ch. Women United (editor 1985-86), Sierra Club, Boise Art Mus., Wis. Alumni Assn., Friends of Hist. Mus. Boise, Boise Art Alliance. Republican. Protestant. Home: 10507 Irving Ct Boise ID 83704-8054

HUD, NICHOLAS VINCENT, biophysicist; b. L.A., June 8, 1964; s. Joseph Anton and Helen Mary (Kern) H.; m. Mona Gonzalez, Oct. 5, 1987; children: Nicholas Xavier, Antony Alexander. BS in physics cum laude, Loyola Marymount U., 1986; MS in applied physics, U. Calif., Davis, 1988, PhD in applied physics, 1992. Physicist Lawrence Livermore Nat. Lab., Livermore, Calif., 1987-95; with dept. of chemistry UCLA, 1995—. Contbr. articles to profl. jours. Ahmanson Found. fellow, L.A., 1984-86, NIH postdoctoral fellowship, 1995—. Mem. Biophys. Soc. Office: Dept of Chemistry Univ Calif at Los Angeles Los Angeles CA 90095

HUDGINS, CHRISTOPHER CHAPMAN, English educator; b. Richmond, Va., Mar. 22, 1947; s. William Jesse and Cathryn (Turner) H.; m. Marsha Lee Huffman, Aug. 22, 1970 (div. Dec. 1986); 1 child, Caitlin Crawford. AB, Davidson Coll., 1968; MA, Emory U., 1969, PhD, 1976. Univ. fellow Emory U., Atlanta, 1968-69; instr. English Old Dominion U., Norfolk, Va., 1969-71; teaching asst. Emory U., Atlanta, 1971-74, lectr., 1974-75; asst. prof. English U. Nev., Las Vegas, 1976-82; assoc. prof. English U. Nev., 1982—, chair English, 1984-93; cons. in field. Contbr. articles to profl. jours.; editorial bd. Harold Pinter Rev., 1986—. Dir., lectr. Humanities Com. and Allied Arts Coun., Las Vegas, 1980—; bd. dirs. faculty devel. seminars NEH, 1987, 88; gov.'s appointee Nev. Humanities Commn., exec. bd. Mem. MLA, Soc. for Cinema Studies, Harold Pinter Soc. (v.p.), David Mamet Soc. (v.p., treas.). Office: U Nevada 4505 S Maryland Pky Las Vegas NV 89154-9900

HUDGINS, LOUANNE, pediatrician, educator; b. Leavenworth, Kans., Nov. 17, 1957. BA, U. Kans., 1980; MD, U. Kans., Kansas City, 1984. Diplomate Am. Bd. Pediatrics, Am. Bd. Med. Genetics. Asst. prof. pediatrics U. Ariz., Tucson, 1990-93, U. Wash., Seattle, 1993—. Fellow Am. Acad. Pediatrics; mem. Am. Soc. Human Genetics. Office: Children's Hosp & Med Ctr 4800 Sand Point Way CH-25 Seattle WA 98105-0371

HUDSON, CHRISTOPHER JOHN, publisher; b. Watford, Eng., June 8, 1948; s. Joseph Edward and Gladys Jenny Patricia (Madgwick); m. Lois Jeanne Lyons, June 16, 1979; children: Thomas, Ellen, Ronald, Timothy. BA with honors, Cambridge U., Eng., 1969, MA with honors, 1972. Promotion mgr. Prentice-Hall Internat., Eng., 1969-70; area mgr. Prentice-Hall Internat., Eng., France, 1970-71; mktg. mgr. Prentice-Hall Internat., Englewood Cliffs, N.J., 1971-74, dir. mktg., 1974-76, asst. v.p., 1976; group internat. dir. I.T.T. Pub., N.Y.C., 1976-77; pres. Focal Press, Inc., N.Y.C., 1977-82; v.p., pub. Aperture Found. Inc., N.Y.C., 1983-86; head publs. J. Paul Getty Trust, L.A., 1986—. Author: Guide to International Book Fairs, 1976; pub. Aperture, 1983-86, J. Paul Getty Mus. Jour., 1986—. Mem. adv. coun. Nat. Heritage Village, Kioni, Greece; mem. trade with eastern Europe com. Assn. Am. Pubs., N.Y., 1976-79, internat. fairs com., 1986-88. Mem. Internat. Assn. Mus. Publs. (Frankfurt, Fed. Republic Germany, chmn. 1992—), U.S. Mus. Publ. Group (chmn. 1989—), Internat. Pubs. Assn., Hellenic Soc. (London), Oxford & Cambridge Club (London), Internat. Assn. Scholarly Pubs. (sec.-gen. 1994-97, chmn. internat. contracts com.). Office: J Paul Getty Trust 17985 Pacific Coast Hwy Malibu CA 90265-5708

HUDSON, EDWARD VOYLE, linen supply company executive; b. Seymour, Mo., Apr. 3, 1915; s. Marion A. and Alma (Von Gonten) H.; student Bellingham (Wash.) Normal Coll., 1933-36, also U. Wash.; m. Margaret Carolyn Greely, Dec. 24, 1939; children—Edward G., Carolyn K. Asst. to mgr. Natural Hard Metal Co., Bellingham, 1935-37; partner Met. Laundry Co., Tacoma, 1938-39; propr., mgr. Peerless Laundry & Linen Supply Co., Tacoma, 1939—; propr. Independent Laundry & Everett Linen Supply Co., 1946-74, 99 Cleaners and Launderers Co., Tacoma, 1957-79; chmn. Tacoma Public Utilities, 1959-60; trustee United Mut. Savs. Bank; bd. dirs. Tacoma Better Bus. Bur., 1977—. Pres., Wash. Conf. on Unemployment Compensation, 1975-76; pres. Tacoma Boys' Club, 1970; v.p. Puget Sound USO, 1972-91; elder Emmanuel Presbyn. Ch., 1974—; past campaign mgr., pres. Tacoma-Pierce County United Good Neighbors. Recipient Disting. Citizen's cert. U.S. Air Force Mil. Airlift Com., 1977; U.S. Dept. Def. medal for outstanding public service, 1978. Mem. Tacoma Sales and Mktg. Execs. (pres. 1957-58), Pacific NW Laundry, Dry Cleaning and Linen Supply Assn. (pres. 1959, treas. 1965-75), Internat. Fabricare Inst. (dir. dist. 7 treas. 1979, pres. 1982), Am. Security Council Bd., Tacoma C. of C. (pres. 1965), Air Force Assn. (pres. Tacoma chpt. 1976-77, v.p. Wash. state 1983-84, pres. 1985-86), Navy League, Puget Sound Indsl. Devel. Council (chmn. 1967), Tacoma-Ft. Lewis-Olympia Army Assn. (past pres.) Republican. Clubs: Elks (vice chmn. bd. trustees 1984, chmn. 1985-86), Shriners (potentate 1979), Masons, Scottish Rite, Tacoma, Tacoma Country and Golf, Jesters, Rotary (pres. Tacoma chpt. 1967-68), Tacoma Knife and Fork (pres. 1964). Home: 3901 N 37th St Tacoma WA 98407-5636 Office: Peerless Laundry & Linen Supply Co 2902 S 12th St Tacoma WA 98405-2539

HUDSON, GARY MICHAEL, corporate executive; b. Lander, Wyo., July 28, 1946; s. Frank L. and Sarah Elizabeth (Jones) H.; m. Linda Ann Shaw, July 5, 1985; 1 child, Zachary Michael. BA, U. Wyo., 1968; MA, Western Ky. U., 1970. Tchr. Hopkinsville (Ky.) Pub. Schs., 1968-69; tchr., counselor Warren County Sch., Hadly, Ky., 1969-70; counselor, social worker Wyo. State Tng. Sch., Lander, 1970-72; counselor, adminstr. Cen. Wyo. Coll., Riverton, 1972-75; chief exec. officer Community Entry Svcs., Riverton, 1975—. Contbr. articles and revs. to profl. jours., mem. editorial adv. bd. Sta. KTRZ-TV, Riverton, 1989-90. Mem. adv. bd. Cen. Wyo. Coll. Trades and Industry, Riverton, 1989—, Human Devel. Svcs. Program, 1990—, Wyo. Dept. Health, 1991—, Pineridge Hosp., Lander, 1986-88; chairperson employer com. Rocky Mountain Regional Head Injury Ctr., 1991—; chairperson Regional Svcs. Providers Wyo., 1990-92; bd. dirs. Riverton Bicentennial Com., 1976, Wyo. Assn. Retarded Citizens, Cheyenne, 1983-86, Nat. Assn. Devel. Disability Couns., Washington, 1980-81, Rocky Mountain Brain Injury Ctr., 1991—. Recipient Regional Dir.'s award Region 8 HEW, 1977. Mem. Wyo. Assn. Rehab. Facilities (chmn. 1984-85, sec. 1985-87), Fremont County Assn. Retarded Citizens, Lions, Masons (master 1984-85), Hugh de Payne Commandry (comdr. 1985-86). Republican. Episcopalian. Home: 2980 Sinks Canyon Rd Lander WY 82520-9714 Office: Community Entry Svcs 2441 Peck St Riverton WY 82501-2272

HUDSON, HEATHER ELIZABETH, telecommunications educator, consultant, lawyer; b. Vancouver, B.C., Can., Jan. 4, 1947; came to U.S., 1968; d. Bruce Earl and Beulah May (Ashton) Hudson. BA with honors, U. B.C., 1968; MA, Stanford U., 1969, PhD, 1974; JD, U. Tex., 1987. Bar: Calif. Cons. Can. Dept. Comms., Ottawa, Ont., 1970-74, State of Alaska, Anchorage, 1976-77; dir. telecomms. Acad. for Ednl. Devel., Washington, 1977-81; assoc. prof. U. Tex., Austin, 1981-87; prof., dir. telecomms. program McLaren Sch. Bus., U. San Francisco, 1987—; pres. Keewatin Comms., Ottawa, 1980—; mem. adv. bd. NRC, FCC, OTA, Washington, 1990—, Privacy Rights Clearinghouse, San Diego, 1992—. Author: When Telephones Reach the Village, 1984, Rural America in the Information Age, 1989, Communication Satellites, 1990, Electronic Byways, 1995; mem. editorial bd. Telecommunications Policy. Recipient Electronic Media Book of Yr. award Nat. Assn. Broadcasters, 1990; East-West Ctr. sr. fellow, Honolulu, 1991, CIRCIT sr. fellow, Melbourne, 1992, Asia-Pacific Disting. Lectureship Fulbright fellowship, 1995—. Mem. ABA, Bar Assn. San Francisco, Internat. Comm. Assn., Pacific Telecomms. Coun., Bay Area Telecomms. Forum. Stanford Alumni Assn. (life), City Club of San Francisco, Sierra Club, World Wildlife Fund, Amnesty Internat., Commonwealth Club, World Affairs Coun. Office: U San Francisco 2130 Fulton St San Francisco CA 94117-1080

HUDSON, JERRY E., university president; b. Chattanooga, Mar. 3, 1938; s. Clarence E. and Laura (Campbell) H.; m. Myra Ann Jared, June 11, 1957; children: Judith, Laura, Janet, Angela. B.A., David Lipscomb Coll., 1959; M.A., Tulane U., 1961, Ph.D., 1965; LL.D. (hon.), Pepperdine U., 1983. Systems engr. IBM, Atlanta, 1961; prof. Coll. Arts and Scis., Pepperdine U., 1962-75; provost, dean Coll. Arts and Scis., Malibu Campus, Pepperdine U., 1971-75; pres. Hamline U., St. Paul, 1975-80, Willamette U., Salem, Oreg., 1980—; dir. Portland Gen. Co., E.I.I.A. Mem. Nat. Assn. Ind. Colls. (bd. dirs.), Phi Alpha Theta. Office: Willamette U Office of Pres 900 State St Salem OR 97301-3930

HUDSON, JOHN IRVIN, retired marine officer; b. Louisville, Oct. 12, 1932; s. Irvin Hudson and Elizabeth (Reid) Hudson Hornbeck; m. Zetta Ann Yates, June 27, 1954; children—Reid Irvin, Lori Ann, John Yates, Clark Ray. B.S. in Bus. Mgmt., Murray State U., 1971. Commd. 2d lt. USMC, 1954, advanced through grades to lt. gen., 1987; comdg. officer Marine Fighter Attack Squadron 115, Vietnam, 1968, Marine Corps Air Sta., Yuma, Ariz., 1977-80; asst. wing comdr. 2d Marine Air Wing, Cherry Point, N.C., 1980-81; comdg. gen. LFTCLANT 4th Marine Amphibious Brigade, Norfolk, Va., 1981-83, 3d Marine Aircraft Wing, El Toro, Calif., 1985-87; dep. chief staff for manpower Hdqrs. USMC, Washington, 1987-89; dir. U.S. Marine Corps Edn. Ctr., Quantico, Va., 1983-85; ret. active duty Hdqrs. USMC, Washington, 1989. Apptd. to Ariz. State Transp. Bd., 1994—. Decorated DFC, DSM, Bronze Star, Air medals, Silver Hawk; flew 308 combat missions in Vietnam in F-4 Phantom. Mem. VFW, Marine

Corps Aviation Assn. (life), Marine Corps Assn., Marine Corps Hist. Soc., Order of Daedalians. Home: 12439 E Del Rico Yuma AZ 85367-7366

HUDSON, LEE (ARLENE HUDSON), environmental activist; b. Oakland, Calif., Apr. 17, 1936; d. Clyde Edward and Helen Therese (Cerutti) McIrvin; m. James Joseph Coté, Mar. 28, 1958 (div. 1963); 1 child, Steven Michael. BA in Psychology, Calif. State U., Sacramento, 1976, postgrad., 1977-78. Exec. field dir. Dem. State Cen. Com., Sacramento, 1967-68; mem. staff Calif. Legis., Sacramento, 1967-72; founder, chmn., editor newsletter The Group for Alternatives to Spreading Poisons, Nevada City, Calif., 1983—; non-chem. advocate on adv. com. to Calif. Dept. Transp. Roadside Vegetation Mgmt. Com., 1993—. Vol. various state, fed. and local campaigns or initiatives, 1967—; founding mem. Toxics Coordinating Project, San Francisco, 1985-90; co-founder Calif. Coalition for Alternatives to Pesticides, Arcata and Eureka, 1983—, pres., chmn. bd. dirs., 1989—; mem. Com. for Sustainable Agriculture, 1986—, mem. mktg.-order subcom., 1986-89; bd. dirs. NW Coalition for Alternatives to Pesticides, Eugene, 1987-93; mem., chmn. tech. writing com. Nevada County Adv. Com. on Air Pollution, 1988-93; mem. Hazardous Waste Transfer Facility Siting Com. for Nevada County, 1989-90; mem. Nevada County Hazardous Waste Task Force, 1987—, chair tech. sub-com., 1988-90; mem. Cen. Valley Hazardous Waste Minimization Com., 1990-91. Mem. Sierra Club (chmn. toxic sub-com. Sierra Nevada group 1985-88), Amnesty Internat. Better World Soc., Cascade Holistic Econ. Cons., Coun. for Livable World, Nat. Peace Inst. Found., People's Med. Soc., Earth First, Nat. Resources Def. Coun., Nevada County C. of C., Greenpeace, Planning and Conservation League, Nevada County Greens Alliance, North Columbia Schoolhouse Cultural Ctr., South Yuba River Citizen's League, Siskiyou Mountains Resource Coun. (life), Rural Def. League. Mem. Universal Life Ch. Home and Office: 10984 Ridge Rd Nevada City CA 95959-8751

HUDSON, MICHAEL ELLIOTT, SR., human resource specialist; b. L.A., Jan. 15, 1955; s. Joe Sr. A. and Dorothy (Elliott) H.; m. June Maria Grundy, Dec. 23, 1978; children: Michael Jr., April. BA, Pacific U., 1977; MBA, Loyola Marymount U., 1981. Coord. broadcast ops. St. KLCS-TV, L.A., 1977-88; pers. analyst L.A. Unified Sch. Dist., 1988-89, supr. employment office, 1989-92, personnel analyst, 1992—; with career awareness program Dorsey High Sch., L.A, 1986—; with bus. adv. com. San Pedro (Calif.) Wilmington Skills Ctr., 1989—, Harbor Occupational Ctr., San Pedro, 1989—. Bd. dirs. Consumer Credit Counselors, L.A., 1985-88; mem. Calif. Afro-Am. Mus. Found., L.A., 1988—; mem. Westchester (Calif.) YMCA Men's Club, 1986—. Named Campaign Goal-Buster Weingart Urban Ctr. YMCA, L.A., 1983, 84, 85; recipient Shining Example award ARC, L.A., 1985. Mem. Radio and TV Ednl. Soc. (pres. 1987-88, v.p. 1985-87), Pers. Testing Coun., So. Calif. Pers. Mgmt. Assn., Pers. and Indsl. Rels. Assn. Loyola Marymount U. MBA Alumni Assn., Pacific U. Alumni Assn., Alpha Phi Alpha (career awareness program 1980-83). Home: 5514 Deane Ave Los Angeles CA 90043-2353 Office: L A Unified Sch Dist Employee Rels Office Dept L PO Box 3307 Los Angeles CA 90051

HUDSON, PATRICK A., plastic surgeon; b. Blickling, Eng., July 4, 1948. MD, London U., 1972. Diplomate Am. Bd. Plastic Surgery. Intern St. Stephens-Hillingdon, London, 1972-73; resident Danbury Hosp., 1973-74; resident U. N.Mex. Hosp., Albuquerque, 1974-78, fellow in hand surgery, 1978; with Presbyn. Hosp., St. Joseph Hosp., Albuquerque; pvt. practice; preceptor U. N.Mex. Fellow ACS; mem. BMA, NMMS, Am. Assn. Hand Surgery, Am. Soc. Plastic and Reconstructive Surgeons. Office: 4273 Montgomery Blvd NE # 230-E Albuquerque NM 87109-1103

HUDSON, STEVEN REX, accountant; b. Portales, N.Mex., Feb. 1, 1956; s. Rex Don and Dolly Pauline (Skinner) H.; m. Tina Marie Campbell, June 25, 1983 (div. July 1990); children: Whitney Beth, Tyler Payne. BBA, Ea. N.Mex. U., 1980. CPA, N.Mex. Bookkeeper McKay & Co., P.C., Clovis, N.Mex., 1977-80, acct., 1980-86, acct., shareholder, 1986-91; pvt. practice acctg., pvt. practice, Portales, 1991—. Bd. dirs. Curry County United Way, Clovis, 1985-90; trustee Clovis Campus, Ea. N.Mex. U., 1989, Plains Regional Med. Ctr., Clovis and Portales, 1990—. Mem. AICPA, N.Mex. Soc. CPA's, Roosevelt County C. of C. (bd. dirs. 1992-94). Republican. Home: 124A Yucca Dr Portales NM 88130-7155 Office: 712 W 1st St Portales NM 88130-5930

HUDSON, VINSON JENE, market research executive; b. Sparta, Ga., Feb. 24, 1938; s. Eugene and Reola M. (Johnson) H.; m. Jewel C. Boswell, Sept. 7, 1963; children: Vinson J. II, Victor B., Vinessa J. BSEE, San Jose State U., 1970; MSEE and Med. Electronics, Stanford U., 1973. Pres., industry analyst Jewson Enterprises, Redwood City, Calif., 1973—. Author, pub.: The POMIS U.S. Analysis Report, 1973— (sales awards), (directory) Satisfaction Rating Directory of POMIS Vendors, 1992 (sales awards). Mentor Stanford Alumni Mentor Program, 1993. With USAF, 1956-60. Republican. Baptist. Office: Jewson Enterprises PO Box 1331 Menlo Park CA 94026-1331

HUELSBECK, JULIE MARIE, librarian; b. Appleton, Wis., Apr. 12, 1957; d. Richard John and Phyllis Jean (Flanagan) H. BA in Spanish, BA in Libr. Sci., U. Wis., Oshkosh, 1979; MLS, U. Wis., Milw., 1980. Info. libr. El Paso Pub. Libr., 1981-86; asst. coord., interlibr. loan libr. Tex. Trans.-Pecos Libr. System, El Paso, 1986-92; libr. Mohave County Libr. Dist., Bullhead City, Ariz., 1992—; participant Internetworking Rural Librs. Inst., U. Wis.-Milw./Dept. Edn., 1994. Mem. Friends of the Bullhead City Libr., 1992—; sec. Workplace, Edn. and Literacy Coalition of Mohave County, 1994—; bd. rep. Mohave Libr. Alliance, 1994—. Mem. Ariz. State Libr. Assn. Roman Catholic. Office: Bullhead City Libr 1170 E Hancock Rd Bullhead City AZ 86442

HUETER, JAMES WARREN, painter, sculptor; b. San Francisco, May 15, 1925; m. Alabelle M. Hunter, 1948. BA, Pomona Coll., 1948; MFA, Claremont (Calif.) Grad. Sch., 1951. One-man shows include Pasadena (Calif.) Art Mus., 1955, Heritage Gallery, L.A., 1961, 62, 64, 67, Tobey C. Moss Gallery, L.A., 1984, 86, 88, 91, 93, U. Calif., Davis, 1986, Claremont Grad. Sch., 1989; exhibited in group shows Pasadena Art Mus., 1950-59, L.A. County Mus., 1952, 54-59, 38th Corcoran Biennial, Washington, 1983-84, Albuquerque Mus., 1984, Bklyn. Mus., 1984, San Francisco Mus. Modern Art, 1984. Recipient 1st Prize Purchase award Pasadena Art Mus., 1952, Long Beach (Calif.) State U., 1961, 1st Prize award L.A. County Fair award 1951, L.A. County Mus., 1955, Frye Mus., 1957. Home: 190 E Radcliffe Dr Claremont CA 91711-2832 Office: Tobey C Moss Gallery 7321 Beverly Blvd Los Angeles CA 90036-2503

HUEY, CONSTANCE ANNE BERNER, mental health counselor; b. Tacoma, Wash., Jan. 20, 1938; d. Julian Boyd Berner and Beatta Kathryn (Day-Berner) Schoel; m. Donn R. Huey, July 26, 1961 (dec. June 1990); 1 child, Jennifer Anne. BA, U. Wash., 1959, MEd, 1976; cert. alcohol studies, Seattle U., 1980. Speech, Eng. tchr. Pub. H.S., Seattle, 1959-68; tchr., supr., adminstr. U. Wash., Seattle, 1968-82; instr. in alcohol studies program Seattle U., Seattle, 1980-86; pvt. practice, 1980—; cons. Contbg. author: We Did the Best We Could, 1993; guest on radio talk shows; presenter in workshops and seminars. Mem. Am. Counseling Assn., Seattle Counseling Assn., Women's Mental Health Assn., Nat. Assn. Alcoholism and Drug Abuse Counselors, Washington Assn. Alcoholism and Drug Abuse Counselors. Home: 1800 Taylor Ave N #10 Seattle WA 98109

HUFF, DALE EUGENE, environmental services executive; b. Windsor, Colo., Nov. 1, 1930; s. Floyd Eugene and Katherine Oleva (Parsons) H.; m. Flossie Leone Moses, Nov. 18, 1951; children: Clifford Allen, Herbert Eugene, Dalene Faye, Linda Reneé. BA, Pacific Union Coll., 1963, MA, 1968. Tchr. Pleasant Hill (Calif.) Jr. Acad., 1963-66; prin. Ukiah (Calif.) Jr. Acad., 1966-71; tchr. Paradise (Calif.) Adventist Acad., 1971-80; acct. Loma Linda (Calif.) U., 1980-86, environ. svcs. exec., 1986—. With U.S. Army, 1946-49. Mem. Nat. Exec. Housekeeping Assn. (exec. bd. 1987-90). Republican. Home: 10961 Desert Lawn Dr # 145 Calimesa CA 92320-2242 Office: Loma Linda U Dept Environ Svcs Loma Linda CA 92350

HUFF, JANET HOUSE, special education educator; b. Kansas City, Mo., Sept. 5, 1947; d. Arthur William and Juanita Joan (Cook) House; m. William Earl Huff, Dec. 20, 1975; children: Ryan, Anesi. BS in Edn., Emporia State U., 1970; postgrad., U. Kans., 1973, U. No. Colo., 1975-76, 83, Calif. State U., Bakersfield, 1986-89, U. Phoenix, 1992—. Cert. specialist in learning handicapped, Calif.; cert. psychology, educationally handicapped and spl. tchr. I, Colo. Tchr.'s aide Lyon County, Emporia, Kans., 1968-70; tchr. spl. edn. Kansas City (Kans.) Unified Sch. Dist., 1970-73; learning prescription specialist S.W. Bd. Coop. Svcs., Cortez, Colo., 1973-74; tchr. spl. edn. Mesa County Valley Sch. Dist. 51, Grand Junction, Colo., 1974-86; resource specialist Bakersfield (Calif.) City Schs., 1986-89, Fresno (Calif.) Unified Sch. Dist., 1989-90; tchr. spl. edn. Cherry Creek Sch. Dist. 5, Aurora, Colo., 1990-92; ednl. cons. Jefferson County Sch. Dist. 1, 1992—. City chmn. March of Dimes, Grand Junction; bd. dirs. Mesa Little League, Grand Junction, 1975, Westminster Little League, Denver, 1990-92; chmn. silent auction Am. Cancer Soc., Bakersfield, 1986-88, dist. chmn., Denver, 1990-92. Mem. NEA, Coun. for Exceptional Children, Internat. Reading Assn., Colo. Edn. Assn. Lutheran.

HUFF, KENNETH O., oilfield executive, geologist; b. Daleville, Ind., Dec. 17, 1926; s. George Byron and Mary Ethel (Smith) H.; m. Donna Mae Zimmerschied, Mar. 25, 1957; children—John, Robert, Donald, Patricia. Student Purdue U., 1944-45, Ball State U., 1947-48; B.S. in Geology, Ind. U., 1956. Well logging engr. Core Labs., Inc., Williston, N.D. and Farmington, N.Mex., 1956-64, lab. mgr., sales engr. Farmington and Casper, Wyo., 1964-67, supr. Rocky Mountain dist., Casper, 1967-69, cons. geologist, 1969-72; pres. cons. geologist Adventures, Inc., Casper, 1972—; mem. dist. export council U.S. Dept Commerce, Wyo., 1977-83. Patentee in field. Served as sgt. U.S. Army, 1944-46, 50-51; Korea. Mem. Soc. Petroleum Engrs., Am. Assn. Petroleum Geologists, Wyo. Geol. Assn. Republican. Club: Petroleum (Casper). Home: 1106 Payne Ave Casper WY 82609-2639 Office: Adventures Inc 535 N Lennox St Casper WY 82601-2144

HUFF, MARILYN L., federal judge; b. 1951. BA, Calvin Coll., Grand Rapids, Mich., 1972; JD, U. Mich., 1976. Assoc. Gray, Cary, Ames & Frye, 1976-83, ptnr., 1983-91; judge U.S. Dist. Ct. (so. dist.) Calif., San Diego, 1991—. Contbr. articles to prof. jours. Mem. adv. coun. Calif. LWV, 1987—, Am. Lung Assn.; bd. dirs. San Diego and Imperial Counties, 1989—; mem. LaJolla Presbyn. Ch. Named Legal Profl. of Yr. San Diego City Club and Jr. C. of C., 1990; recipient Superior Ct. Valuable Svc. award, 1982. Mem. ABA, San Diego Bar Found., San Diego Bar Assn. (bd. dirs. 1986-88, v.p. 1988, chmn. profl. edn. com. 1990, Svc. award to legal profession, 1989, Lawyer of Yr. 1990), Calif. State Bar Assn., Calif. Women Lawyers, Am. Bd. Trial Advs., Libel Def. Resource Ctr., Am. Inns of Ct. (master 1987—, exec. com. 1989—), Lawyers' Club San Diego (adv. bd. 1989-90, Belva Lockwood Svc. award 1987), Univ. Club, Aardvarks Lt. Office: US Dist Ct US Courthouse 940 Front St San Diego CA 92101-8994*

HUFF, WELCOME REX ANTHONY, chemical researcher; b. Indpls., Mar. 26, 1967; s. Welcome Charles and Judith Kathleen (Payton) H. BS in Chemistry with honors, Ind. U., 1989. Undergrad. researcher G.E. Ewing Group, Ind. U., Bloomington, 1988-89; grad. researcher D.A. Shirley Group, U. Calif., Berkeley, 1989—. Fundraiser Multiple Sclerosis Soc., Monterey, Calif., 1990. H.G. Day Summer Rsch. scholar Ind. U. Chemistry Dept., 1988, H.G. Day Acad. Yr. Rsch. scholar Ind. U. Chemistry Dept., 1988. Mem. AAAS, NRA, Am. Chem. Soc., Am. Phys. Soc., Alpha Chi Sigma. Home: 25 Neva Ct Oakland CA 94611-1826 Office: Lawrence Berkeley Lab MS 2-300 1 Cyclotron Rd Berkeley CA 94720

HUFFER, KARIN DIANNE, marriage and family therapist, writer; b. Pocatello, Idaho, Oct. 18, 1941; d. Adolph Rayner and Jane Ann Pearson; m. James Darwin Huffer, July 21, 1976; children: Jason Darwin, Jordan Dwight. BS, U. Idaho, 1963; MS, U. Nev., 1972. Cert. marriage and family therapist, Nev.; cert. counselor, Nev. Tchr. Clark County Sch. Dist., Las Vegas, Nev., 1963-76; dir. family life edn. Family Counseling Svc., Las Vegas, Nev., 1976-79; counselor at risk students Clark County Sch. Dist., Las Vegas, Nev., 1986—; pvt. practice therapist Las Vegas, Nev., 1972—; seminar speaker on Legal Abuse Syndrome, 1990—. Author: Legal Abuse Syndrome, 1994, (workbook) The Winning Woman, 1983, (workbook) Beyond Rage and Back, 1994. Founder VICTRE (project to assist victims recovery and restoration), Las Vegas, 1992. Mem. NEA, Am. Assn. Marriage and Family Therapists (clin. mem. 1972—), Nev. Guidance Assn., Phi Delta Kappa. Office: Bridge Counseling Assocs 1701 W Charleston Blvd Bldg Las Vegas NV 89104-1303

HUFFEY, VINTON EARL, clergyman; b. Luana, Iowa, July 7, 1915; s. Walter Angus and Tilda Boleta (Olson) H.; m. Lillian Bertha Crouse, June 22, 1942; children: Naomi, Rhoda, Stephen, Deborah. Student, Ctrl. Bible Coll., Springfield, Mo., 1936-38, North Ctrl. Bible Coll., Mpls., 1938-40. Ordained to ministry Assembly of God Ch., 1942. Pastor Assembly of God, Oelwein, Iowa, 1940-43, LeMars, Iowa, 1943-47; evangelist Assembly of God, Iowa and Mo., 1947-48; pres. youth Assembly of God, Iowa and North Mo., 1948-52, editor News of West Ctrl., 1948-52; pastor Assembly of God, Ames, Iowa, 1952-58, Monrovia, Calif., 1958-78; crusader inner-city evangelism Assembly of God, 1978-93; pastor Assembly of God, South Pasadena, Calif., 1993—; motivation lectr. Assemblies of God, 1980-92; originator inner-city revolving loan fund So. Calif. Dist. Assemblies of God, Springfield, Mo., 1982. Author: (pamphlet) The Church and America's Inner-cities, 1981. Mem. Think Am. Com. City Coun., Duarte, Calif., 1962, lit. rev. com., 1965; chmn. What About Duarte? L.A. County Dept. Human Rels. City of Hope, Duarte, 1963. Recipient Decade of Harvest award So. Calif. Dist. Coun. Assemblies of God Ch., Irvine, Calif., 1994. Republican. Home and Office: 161 N Mayflower Ave Monrovia CA 91016-2005

HUFFINE, CHARLES WALTER, psychiatrist, child psychiatrist; b. Seattle, May 25, 1941; s. Charles Walter and Helen Olive (Challiss) H.; m. Lucy Hoague, Sept. 6, 1960 (div. July 1964); m. Constance Lee Simmers, Dec. 28, 1967; children: Mason, Jessica. BS, U. Wash., 1963, MD, 1963. Pvt. practice Seattle, 1975—; psychiat. cons. Seattle Mental Health Inst., 1975-94, Luther Child Ctr., Everett, Wash., 1975-78, Children's Home Soc. Wash., Seattle, 1977-93, Youth Advs., Seattle, 1980—, Friends of Youth, Renton, Wash., 1993—, King County Div. Mental Health, Seattle, 1993—; rsch. therapist dept. psychology U. Wash., Seattle, 1988-91, 94—. Maj. U.S. Army, 1971-73. Mem. Am. Assn. Community Psychiatrists (sec. 1990—), Wash. State Assn. Community Psychiatrists (pres. 1995), Am. Soc. for Adolescent Psychiatry (N.W. Soc. rep. ho. of dels. 1985—), N.W. Soc. for Adolescent Psychiatry, Am. Psychiat. Assn., Am. Acad. Child and Adolescent Psychiatry. Democrat. Office: Lake Union Psychiat Group 3123 Fairview Ave E Seattle WA 98102-3051

HUFFMAN, DAVID GEORGE, electrical engineer; b. Fresno, Calif., Apr. 13, 1965; s. Fred Norman and Sharon (Richardson) H.; m. Johnnie Ann Valtierra, Sept. 21, 1991; children: Matthew Christopher Kenerly, Makenna Francisca-Elise. BSEE, Fresno State U., 1988. Field engr. Power Systems Testing Co., Fresno, Calif., 1988-93, dir. engring., 1993—, mgr., 1994—. Mem. Internat. Electronic and Electrical Engrs. Assn., Eta Kappa Nu. Office: Power Systems Testing Co 4688 W Jennifer Ave Ste 108 Fresno CA 93722-6418

HUFFMAN, KEVIN WAYNE, non-commissioned army officer; b. Offutt AFB, Nebr., Sept. 26, 1956; s. Eugene Max and MaryAnn (Cox) H.; m. Jeanette Louise Hall, June 9, 1989; children: Terri Huffman Smiley, Shawn Edward, Ricky Allen. Assoc. in Gen. Studies, Ctrl. Tex. Coll., 1994. Enlisted U.S. Army, 1974; graves registration specialist 16th Field Svc. Co., 240th QM Battalion, Ft. Lee, Va., 1974-78, 553d Field Svc. Co., 70th Ordinance Battalion, Ft. Bliss, Tex., 1979-82; mortuary NCOIC U.S. Army Mortuary Affairs Activities EUR, Frankfurt, Fed. Republic Germany, 1982-84, 305th S&S Co., Yongsan, Korea, 1985-86; graves registration NCO and histologist William Beaumont Army Med. Ctr., Ft. Bliss, 1984-85; graves registration non-commd. officer A Co., 48th Fwd Spt. Bn. 2AD, Ft. Hood, Tex., 1986-90; graves registration non-commissioned officer A Co., 502d Fwd Spt. Battalion 2AD, Ft. Hood, 1990-91; mortuary affairs non-commd. officer A Co. 215 Fwd Spt. Bn. 1CD, Ft. Hood, 1991-94; ret. U.S. Army, 1994; cemetery mgr. Ft. Hood, 1992-94; osteologist various law enforcement agys., 1992-94; anthropologist, osteologist Mariah and Assocs., Killeen, Tex., 1993-94. Author: The Complete Directory of Cemeteries at Ford Hood, Texas, 1994. Mem. Four Winds Inter-Tribal Soc., Killeen, 1993-94. Mem. Masons. Republican.

HUFFMAN, LINDA RAE, artist, educator, cartoonist; b. Pitts., Mar. 5, 1946; d. Raymond Charles and Elizabeth Rose (Kress) Miller; m. James Joseph Short, July 4, 1964 (div. 1978); children:Janine Marie, James Raymond; m. Charles Daryl Huffman, Feb. 14, 1987. Grad. high sch., Chgo.; student, Orange Coast & Golden W Colls., 1969-70. Pvt. oil painting instr. San Diego, 1975-80, Spokane, Wash., 1980-86, Seattle, 1986—. Exhibited in group shows at Simic Galleries, Calif., Queen Elizabeth II Gallery and Mus. Mem. Internat. Platform Assn. Home: 5014 S 3rd Ave Everett WA 98203-4133

HUFFMAN, NONA GAY, financial consultant, retirement planning specialist; b. Albuquerque, June 22, 1942; d. William Abraham and Opal Irene (Leaton) Crisp; m. Donald Clyde Williams, Oct. 20, 1961; children: Debra Gaylene, James Donald. Student pub. schs. Lawndale, Calif. Lic. ins., securities dealer, N.Mex. Sec. City of L.A., 1960, L.A. City Schs. 1960-62, Aerospace Corp., El Segundo, Calif., 1962-64, Albuquerque Pub. Schs., 1972-73, Pub. Service Co. N.Mex., Albuquerque, 1973; rep., fin. planner Waddell & Reed, Inc., Albuquerque, 1979-84; broker Rauscher Pierce Refsnes, Inc., 1984-85; rep., investment and retirement specialist Fin. Network Investment Corp., 1985-89, John Hancock Fin. Svcs., 1989-90; account exec. Eppler, Guerin & Turner, Inc., 1990-91, Fin. Network Investment Corp., Albuquerque, 1991—; instr. on-site corp. training in fin. strategies for retirement, instr. fin. strategies for successful retirement U. N.Mex. Continuing Edn., instr. employee retirement seminars Fed. Exec. Bd. Mem. Profl. Orgn. Women (co-chmn.), Women in Bus. (Albuquerque chpt.), Internat. Assn. Fin. Planners. Office: Fin Network Investment Corp 8500 Menaul Blvd NE # 195B Albuquerque NM 87112-2298

HUFFMAN, RUSSELL LLOYD, energy, economics and computer consultant; b. Long Beach, Calif., Dec. 28, 1945. Radar and electronic cert., Sch. Applied Aerospace Scis., 1972; BA in Econs., Calif. State U., Sacramento, 1977; AS in Math., AA in Bus. Adminstrn., Coll. of the Desert, 1992. rschr. in quantum thermodynamics and natural econs. Home: PO Box 1301 Twentynine Palms CA 92277

HUFSCHMIDT, MAYNARD MICHAEL, resources planning educator; b. Catawba, Wis., Sept. 28, 1912; s. John Jacob and Emma Lena (Von Arx) H.; m. Elizabeth Louise Leake, July 5, 1941; children: Emily Ann, Mark Andrew. BS, U. Ill., 1939; MPA, Harvard U., 1955, DPA, 1964. Planner Ill. State Planning Commn., Chgo., 1939-41; engr. U.S. Nat. Resources Planning Bd., Washington, 1941-43; budget examiner U.S. Bur. Budget, Washington, 1943-49; program staff mem. Office of Sec., Dept. Interior, Washington, 1949-55; research asso. Grad. Sch. Public Adminstrn., Harvard U., 1955-65; prof. depts. city and regional planning, environ. scis. and engring. U. N.C., Chapel Hill, 1965—; fellow Environ. and Policy Inst., East-West Center, Honolulu, 1979-85, acting dir., 1985-86, sr. cons., 1986-89, sr. fellow, 1990-94; cons. U.S. Bur. Budget, 1961, Council Econ. Advisers, 1965-67, Nat. Acad. Scis., 1967, 69-70, Pan-Am. Health Orgn., 1967, 70, WHO, 1970, 71, 76, 77, Resources for Future, 1955, 56, 72-74. Author: (with Arthur Maass and others) Design of Water-Resource Systems, 1962, (with Myron B. Fiering) Simulation Techniques for Design of Water-Resource Systems, 1966; Editor: Regional Planning—Challenge and Prospects, 1969; editor: (with Eric L. Hyman) Economic Approaches to Natural Resource and Environmental Quality Analysis, 1982, (with David E. James and others) Environment, Natural Systems and Development: An Economic Valuation Guide, 1983, (with John A. Dixon) Economic Valuation Techniques for the Environment, 1986, (with K. William Easter and John A. Dixon) Watershed Resources Management, 1986, (with Janusz Kindler) Approaches to Integrated Water Resources Management in Humid Tropical and Arid and Semiarid Zones in Developing Countries, 1991, (with Michael Bonell and John S. Gladwell) Hydrology and Water Management in the Humid Tropics, 1993. Recipient Clemens Herschel award Boston Soc. Civil Engrs., 1958, Pub. Svc. award U.S. Dept. Interior, 1994; named Friend of Univs. Coun. on Water Resources, 1990; sr. postdoctoral rsch. fellow NSF, 1971.

HUG, PROCTER RALPH, JR., federal judge; b. Reno, Mar. 11, 1931; s. Procter Ralph and Margaret (Beverly) H.; m. Barbara Van Meter, Apr. 4, 1954; children: Cheryl Ann, Procter James, Elyse Marie. B.S., U. Nev., 1953; LL.B., J.D., Stanford U., 1958. Bar: Nev. 1958. With firm Springer, McKissick & Hug, 1958-63, Woodburn, Wedge, Blakey, Folsom & Hug, Reno, 1963-77; U.S. judge 9th Circuit Ct. Appeals, Reno, 1977—; chmn. 9th Cir. Edn. Com., 1984-89, chmn. long range planning com., 1992-93; chmn. Nev. State Bar Com. on Jury Inst.; dep. atty. gen. State of Nev.; v.p. dir. Nev. Tel. & Tel. Co., 1958-77. V.p. Young Dems. Nev., 1960-61; chmn. bd. regents U. Nev.; bd. visitors Stanford Law Sch.; mem. Nev. Humanities Commn., 1988-94; vol. civilian aid sect. U.S. Army, 1977. Lt. USNR, 1953-55. Recipient Outstanding Alumnus award U. Nev., 1967, Disting. Nevadan citation, 1982; named Alumnus of Yr. U. Nev., 1988. Mem. ABA (bd. govs. 1976-78), Am. Judicare Soc. (bd. dirs. 1975-77), Nat. Judicial Coll. (bd. dirs. 1977-78), Nat. Assn. Coll. and Univ. Attys. (past mem. exec. bd.), U. Nev. Alumni Assn. (past pres.), Stanford Law Soc. Nev. (pres.). Office: US Ct Appeals 9th Cir 50 W Liberty St Ste 800 Reno NV 89501-1948

HUGEN, MICHAEL FRANK, journalist, publisher; b. Oskaloosa, Iowa, Jan. 11, 1955; s. Leonard Paul Hugen and Madonna Hope (Agan) Hugen-Bender; m. Maryann Deanie Robinson, Jan. 11, 1986. Grad. high sch., Lompoc, Calif. Copywriter B & B Ad Agy., Lompoc, Calif., 1975-77; columnist Slick Mag., Lompoc, Calif., 1977-79; freelance writer Lone Wolf Prodns., Lompoc, 1984—; news announcer, writer Radio Sta. KRQK-FM, Lompoc, 1985-88; lifestyles editor Santa Ynez Valley News, Solvang, Calif., 1988-89; copy editor Lompoc Record, 1989-91; sports editor Los Padres Sun, Lompoc, 1991-92; co-owner, editor Castle Island Pub., Lompoc, 1993—; co-owner Infinity Media Group, Lompoc, 1994—; pub., editor Lompoc Free Press, 1994—; writing instr. Lompoc Parks & Recreation, 1990—; cons. Image Prodns., Lompoc, 1993—. Editor: Paragon, 1993. Prodr., writer, dir. Lompoc Civic Theatre, 1991; dir. Masque Theatre Troupe, Argentia, Nfld., Can., 1983; dir. Lompoc Christian Youth, 1977-79, lay min., 1977-79; prodr. City Youth Drama Day, Lompoc, 1977; active Leadership Lompoc Valley, 1992. With USN, 1979-85. Recipient best short story award 9th Quadrant Sci. Fiction Mag., 1983, cert. of appreciation Optimists Club, 1986, French Festival, 1990-91, Lompoc Parks and Recreation Dept., 1977. Mem. Lompoc Valley Bus. Assn., Lompoc C. of C. Democrat. Office: Infinity Media Group 8450 Cedros Ave Panorama City CA 91402

HUGH, GEORGE M., pipeline company executive. COO TransCan. Pipelines Ltd., Calgary, Alta.; bd. dirs. Great Lakes Gas Transmission Co., Detroit, Trans. Que. and Maritimes, Montreal, Foothills Pipe Lines (Sask.) Ltd., Calgary, Alberta Nat. Gas, Calgary. Office: TransCan Pipelines Ltd, PO Box 1000 Sta M, Calgary, AB Canada T2P 4K5 Home: 111 -5th Ave SW, Calgary, AB Canada T2P 3Y6

HUGH, MICHAEL YOUNG, allergist; b. Korea, 1958. MD, Med. Coll. Ga., 1984. Allergist Walter Reed AMC, Washington. Office: Ste 7235 8889 Caminto Plz Centro San Diego CA 92122*

HUGHES, BESSIE, nursing administrator; b. Tuscaloosa, Ala., Aug. 27, 1939; d. David and Sufronia B. Williams; m. Willie D. Hughes, Dec. 23, 1961 (div.); 1 child, Yvette D. Diploma, Grady Meml. Sch. Nursing, Atlanta, 1959; AA, S.W. Coll., L.A., 1980; BS, Pacific Christian Coll., Fullerton, Calif., 1985; postgrad., Calif. State U., L.A. RN, Calif. Head nurse L.A.C. U.S.C. Med. Sch., L.A.; nursing supr. Martin Luther King Drew Med. Ctr., L.A., epidemiologist, assoc. nursing dir.; active social workers dept. Martin Luther King Drew Med. Ctr. Mem. L.A. County Bd. Suprs., L.A. City Bd. Edn. Recipient Asst. Sec. of Health award U.S. Dept. Health & Human Svcs., 1990, Svc. for Humanity award Chi Eta Phi, 1991, Spl. Achievement award King/Drew Med. Ctr., 1991. Mem. ANA, Nat. Black Nurses Assn., Am. Practitioners Infection Control. Home: 3 Mejorana Rancho Santa Margarita CA 92688

HUGHES, BRADLEY RICHARD, marketing executive; b. Detroit, Oct. 8, 1954; s. John Arthur and Nancy Irene (Middleton) H.; m. Linda McCants, Feb. 14, 1977; children: Bradley Richard Jr., Brian Jeffrey. AA, Oakland Coll., 1974; BS in Bus., U. Colo., 1978, BJ, 1979, MBA in Fin. and Mktg., 1981, MS in Telecommunications, 1990. Cert. office automation profl., cert. systems profl. Buyer Joslins Co., Denver, 1979; mktg. adminstr. Mountain Bell, Denver, 1980-82; ch. cons. AT&T Info. Systems, mktg. exec. AT&T,

Denver, 1983-86, acct. exec., 1986-87; mktg. mgr. U.S. West, Denver, 1987—; dir. govt. program U. Colo. Bd. dirs. Brandychase Assn.; state del., committeeman Republican Party Colo. Mem. IEEE, Assn. MBA Execs., U.S. Chess Fedn., Internat. Platform Assn., Mensa, Intertel, Assn. Telecommunications Profls., Am. Mgmt. Assn., Am. Mktg. Assn., Info. Industry Assn., Office Automation Soc. Internat., World Future Soc., Triple Nine Soc., Internat. Soc. Philos. Inquiry, Assn. Computing Machinery. Republican. Methodist. Home: 5759 S Jericho Way Aurora CO 80015-3653 Office: US West 188 Inverness Dr W # 600 Englewood CO 80112-5207

HUGHES, EDWARD JOHN, artist; b. North Vancouver, B.C., Feb. 17, 1913; s. Edward Samuel Daniell and Katherine Mary (McLean) H.; m. Fern Rosabell Irvine Smith, Feb. 10, 1940 (dec. 1974). Grad., Vancouver Sch. Art, 1933. Exhbns. include retrospective, Vancouver Art Gallery, 1967, Surrey Art Gallery, Art Gallery of Greater Victoria, Edmonton Art Gallery, Calgary Glenbow Gallery, 1983-85, Nat. Gallery Can., Beaverbrook Gallery, Fredericton, 1983-85; represented in permanent collections, Nat. Gallery Can., Ottawa, Art Gallery Ont., Toronto, Vancouver Art Gallery, Montreal Mus. Fine Art, Greater Victoria Art Gallery; ofcl. Army war artist, 1942-46. Served with Can. Army, 1939-46. Recipient Can. Council grants, 1958, 63, 67, 70. Mem. Royal Can. Acad. Arts. Presbyterian. Address: 2449 Heather St, Duncan, BC Canada V9L 2Z6

HUGHES, EUGENE MORGAN, university president; b. Scottsbluff, Nebr., Apr. 3, 1934; s. Ruby Melvin and Hazel Marie (Griffith) H.; m. Margaret Ann Romeo; children: Deborah Kaye, Greg Eugene, Lisa Ann, Jeff, Mark, Christi. Diploma, Neb. Western Coll., 1954; BS in Math. magna cum laude, Chadron State Coll., 1956; MS in Math., Kans. State U., 1958; PhD in Math., George Peabody Coll. for Tchrs., Vanderbilt U., 1968. Grad. asst. dept. math. Kans. State U., Manhattan, 1956-57; instr. math. Nebr. State Tchrs. Coll. at Chadron, 1957-58; asst. prof. math., head dept. Chadron State Coll., 1958-66, assoc. prof., 1966-69, prof. math., 1969-70, dir. rsch., 1965-66, asst. to the pres., 1966-68, dean adminstrn., 1968-70; grad. asst. dept. math. George Peabody Coll. for Tchrs., Nashville, 1962-63, 64-65; asst. to undergrad. dean George Peabody Coll. for Tchrs., 1964, asst. to pres., 1964-65; instr. Peabody Demonstration Sch., 1963-64; prof. math. No. Ariz. U., Flagstaff, 1970-93; dean No. Ariz. U. (Coll. Arts and Scis.), 1970-71, provost univ. arts and sci. edn., 1971-72, acad. v.p., 1972-79, pres., 1979-93, pres. emeritus, 1993—; pres. Wichita State U., 1993—; cons. Nebr. Dept. Edn., 1966-70; mem. adv. bd. United Bank Ariz., 1980-82; mem. nat. adv. bd. Ctr. for Study of Sport in Society, 1990; bd. dirs. Ariz. Bank; mem. adv. bd. Bank IV, 1993—. Mem. staff bd. trustees Nebr. State Colls., Lincoln, 1969-70; co-dir. workshop tchr. edn. North Cen. Assn. U. Minn., 1968-70; officer fed. ednl. programs, Nebr., Ariz., 1966-93; mem. Ariz. Commn. Post-secondary Edn.; bd. fellows Am. Grad. Sch. Internat. Mgmt., 1980-93; mem. Gov.'s Com. Quality Edn., Chadron Housing Authority, 1968-70, Pres.' Commn. NCAA; pres. bd. dirs. Ariz. State Bd. Edn., 1991, Flagstaff Summer Festival, Ariz. Coun. Humanities and Pub. Policy, Mus. No. Ariz., Grand Canyon coun, Boy Scouts Am.; chair Ariz. Leadership Adv. Coun., 1990-93; mem. Ariz. Town Hall, 1991; commr. Western Interstate Commn. for Higher Edn., 1992-93; mem. Gov.'s Strategic Partnership for Econ. Devel., 1992; mem. Christopher Columbus Quincentenary Commn., 1990—; sec., mem. Wichita/Sedgwick Partnership for Growth, 1993—, Wichita/Sedgwick County Employment Tng. Bd., 1993—. Ariz. Acad. NSF fellow, 1963, 64; recipient Chief Manuelito award Navajo Tribe, 1976, Disting. Svc. award Chadron State Coll., 1982, Flagstaff Citizen of Yr., 1988, Disting. Math. Grad. award Kans. State U., 1990, Cmty. Svc. award, 1994; named Hon. Chmn. black Bd. Dirs., 1989. Mem. NEA, Am. Assn. State Colls.and Univs. (past chmn. & mem. com. on grad. studies 1979—, bd. dirs., mem. com. on accreditation, 1980—), Math. Assn. Am. (vis. lectr. secondary schs. Western Nebr. 1962), Ariz. Edn. Assn., North Cen. Assn. Colls. and Secondary Schs. (coord. 1968-72, cons./evaluator 1977—), Nat. Coun. Tchrs. of Math., Wichita Area C. of C., Flagstaff C. of C., Blue Key, Masons, Elks, Rotary (past pres.), Pi Mu Epsilon, Phi Delta Kappa, Kappa Mu Epsilon, Phi Kappa Phi.

HUGHES, GETHIN B., bishop. Bishop Episcopal Diocese of San Diego, 1992—. Office: Episcopal Diocese of San Diego 2728 6th Ave San Diego CA 92103-6397*

HUGHES, HERBERT HOWARD, public administrator; b. Roy, N.Mex., Sept. 15, 1930; s. Herbert Perry and Katherine Ruth (Hill) H.; m. Nancy Wagnet, Sept. 28, 1957; children: Katerine Ellen, H. W. Bryn. BS, U. N.Mex., 1956; MS, Fla. State U., 1958, PhD, 1960. Prof. U. No. Colo., Greeley, 1960-66; dir. N.Mex. edn. rsch. com. State of N.Mex., Santa Fe, 1966-67, state budget dir., 1967-68; prof. U. N.Mex., Albuquerque, 1968-70; health and edn. bus. cons. Albuquerque, 1970-73; v.p. Fidelity Nat. Bank, Albuquerque, 1973-75; state banking commr. State of N.Mex., Santa Fe, 1975-77; dir. evaluation N.Mex. cancer program U. N.Mex. Med. Sch., Albuquerque, 1977-78; mgr. adminstrn. BDM Corp., Albuquerque, 1978-80; dir. fin. and adminstrn., pub. safety and adminstrv. svcs. Bernalillo County, Albuquerque, 1980—; part-time city councillor City of Albuquerque, 1987—. Sr. author: (booklet) State Responsibility for Public Edn. in N.Mex., 1967. V.p. State Constl. Conv., State of N.Mex., 1969—; mem. steering com. Energy, Environment and Natural Resources, Nat. League of Cities, 1994, 95. Mem. APA, Am. Soc. Pub. Adminstrn. (pres. 1980—), Am. Edn. Rsch. Assn. (N.Mex. br. 1960—), Nat. Conf. State Bank Suprs., Assn. Mil. Surgeons U.S., Naval Res. Assn. Home: 7112 Lantern Rd NE Albuquerque NM 87109-2915 Office: City County Bldg 1 Civic Plz 10th Fl Albuquerque NM 87102

HUGHES, JAMES ARTHUR, electrical engineer; b. Wayne, Nebr., Feb. 15, 1939; s. James Wallace and Ruth Genevieve H.; m. Judy Lorraine Gaskins, July 18, 1967; children: Robert Linn, Benjamin Reed, Barnaby James. BSEE, U. Nebr., 1967. Electronic technician, space tech. labs. TRW, Redondo Beach, Calif., 1963-67, mem. tech. staff systems group, 1967-80, sect. mgr. electronics and def. div., 1980-82, systems engr. space and electronics group, 1982-93, sub-project mgr., 1993—. Designer solid state thermostat, pn generator. Deacon First Bapt. Ch. Lakewood, Long Beach, Calif., 1975-76, 78-80, 87-89; mem. exec. bd. parent-tchr. fellowship, Grace Sch., Rossmoor, Calif., 1981-87. With USN, 1959-63. Mem. AAAS, IEEE, Nat. Soc. Profl. Engrs. Republican. Office: TRW Space and Electronics Group 1 Space Park Blvd # 1869 Redondo Beach CA 90278-1001

HUGHES, (ROBERT) JOHN, journalist, educator; b. Neath, Wales, Apr. 28, 1930; s. Evan John and Dellis May (Williams) H.; m. Vera Elizabeth Pockman; children: Wendy Elizabeth, Mark Evan; m. Peggy Janeane Jordan; 1 child, Evan Jordan. Student stationers cos. sch., trade sch., London, 1941-46; student, Harvard U., 1961-62; LLD (hon.), Colby Coll. African corr. Christian Sci. Monitor, Boston, 1955-61, asst. fgn. editor, 1962-64, Far East corr., 1964-70, mng. editor, 1970, editor, 1970-79, editor, mgr., pub., 1976-79; assoc. dir. USIA, Washington, 1981-82; dir. Voice of Am., Washington, 1982; asst. sec. of state Dept. of State, Washington, 1982-85; columnist Christian Sci. Monitor, Boston, 1985—; prof. journalism Brigham Young U., Provo, Utah, 1991—; U.S. del. to Maui conf. on future of U.S.-Japan Rels., 1988; mem. Joint Coun. Fgn. Rels./Asia Soc. task force to South Korea, 1986-87; bd. dirs. Pulitzer Prize bd., Luce Asian Fellows selection com., Nieman Fellows selection com., Harvard U.; chmn. Elijah Parish Lovejoy selection com. Colby Coll., Maine; judge Sigma Delta Chi awards in journalism; dir., cons. News-Jour. Co., Wilmington, Del., 1975-78; adj. prof. journalism Boston U., 1986-87; pres., editor, pub. Concord Comm., Maine, 1989-91; chmn. Pres. Bush's Task Force US Govt. Internat. Broadcasting, 1991; chmn. Presdl./Congl. Commn. Broadcasting to People's Republic of China, 1992; mem. Corp. Pub. Broadcasting Adv. Commn., 1993; asst. sec.-gen., dir. comm. UN, 1995. Author: The New Face of Africa, 1962, Indonesian Upheaval, 1966; dir. radio broadcasting Christian Sci. Monitor, prodr. MonitoRadio, 1987-89. Recipient Pulitzer Prize for internat. reporting, 1965, Best Newspaper Reporting from Abroad award Overseas Press Club, 1967; Nieman fellow Harvard U., 1961-62. Mem. Am. Soc. Newspaper Editors (past pres.), Pacific Comms. Rsch. Coun., Fgn. Corr. Club Hong Kong (pres.). Office: Brigham Young U Dept Comms Provo UT 84604

HUGHES, JOHN WILLARS, police officer; b. Jacksonville, Fla., Oct. 24, 1940; s. C.R. and Helen B. Hughes; m. Karen A. Chibante, Mar. 17, 1962 (div. Nov. 1987); children: Amanda Marie, Shaughnan Lee; m. Kathleen Prentice, Apr. 7, 1989. Grad., Calif. Hwy. Patrol Acad., 1966. Enlisted USAF, 1958, resigned, 1966; state traffic officer Calif. Hwy. Patrol, Sacramento, 1966-76; owner Am. Brassmiths, Concord, Calif., 1976-87; police officer Dist. Police Svc., Concord, Calif., 1987—; law enforcement instr. Criminal Justice Tng. Ctr., Pittsburg, Calif., 1989; subject matter expert Commn. on Peace Officer State of Tng., Sacramento, 1992. Author: Square Peg for a Round Hole: A 20 Year Investigation into the Assassination of President John F. Kennedy, 1992, If I Only Had an Eraser, 1992, Law Enforcement FA/CPR, 1992, No Sir I Didn't Kill Anybody, 1994. Instr. ARC, Contra Costa, Calif., 1978, Am. Heart Assn., Contra Costa, 1970. Mem. Calif. Police Officers Assn., Police Officers Rsch. Orgn., Calif. Assn. Hwy. Patrol. Baptist. Home: 2195 Toronto Ln Concord CA 94520-1548

HUGHES, JUDITH MARKHAM, history educator; b. N.Y.C., Feb. 20, 1941; d. Sanford H. and Sylvia (Kovner) Markham; m. H. Stuart Hughes, Mar. 26, 1964; 1 child, David. BA with high honors, Swarthmore Coll., 1962; MA, Harvard U., 1963, PhD, 1970. Teaching fellow Harvard U., Cambridge, Mass., 1965-66, 67-70, asst. prof. social studies, 1970-75; assoc. prof. history U. Calif., San Diego, 1975-84, prof. history, 1984—. Author: To the Maginot Line: The Politics of French Military Preparation in the 1920s, 1971, Emotion and High Politics: Personal Relations at the Summit in Late 19th-Century Britain and Germany, 1983, Reshaping the Psychoanalytic Domain: The Work of Melanie Klein, W.R.D. Fairbairn, and D.W. Winnicott, 1989, From Freud's Consulting Room: The Unconscious in a Scientific Age, 1994; mem. editl. bd. Diplomatic History, 1976-78, Psychohistory Rev., 1993—; also articles and book revs. Woodrow Wilson Found. fellow, 1962-63, Nat. Endowment Humanities fellow, 1974. Mem. Am. Hist. Assn., N.Am. Conf. Brit. Studies, Group for Use of Psychology in History, Am. Psychoanalytic Assn. (affiliate), Western Assn. Women Historians (article prize com. 1985), Phi Beta Kappa. Office: U Calif Dept History 0104 9500 Gilman Dr La Jolla CA 92093-0104

HUGHES, LAUREL ELLEN, psychologist, educator, writer; b. Seattle, Oct. 30, 1952; d. Morrell Spencer and Eleanore Claire (Strong) Chamberlain; m. William Henry Hughes Jr., Jan. 27, 1973; children: Frank, Ben, Bridie. BA in Psychology, Portland State U., 1980, MS in Psychology, 1986; D in Clin. Psychology, Pacific U., 1988. Lic. psychologist, Oreg. Counselor Beaverton (Oreg.) Free Meth. Ch., 1982-85; psychotherapist Psychol. Svc. Ctr., Portland, Oreg., 1986, Psychol. Svc. Ctr. West, Hillsboro, Oreg., 1987-89; pvt. practice Beaverton, 1990—; adj. mem. faculty Portland C.C., 1990-91, U. Portland,1992—, CU/Seattle. 1993—; vis. asst. prof. U. Portland, 1991-92; psychol. cons. children's weight control group St. Vincent's Hosp., Portland, 1991. Author: How To Raise Good Children, 1988, How To Raise a Healthy Achiever, 1991; contbr. articles to profl. jours. Tchr. Sunday sch. Beaverton Free Meth. Ch., 1983-88; mother helper Walker Elem. Sch., Beaverton, 1988-90, 92-93; foster parent Washington County, Oreg., 1976-77, 79-80; vol. disaster mental health svcs. ARC, 1993—. Mem. APA, Oreg. Psychol. Assn. (bd. dirs. 1990-91, editor jour. 1990-91). Office: 4320 SW 110th Ave Beaverton OR 97005-3009

HUGHES, LINDA J., newspaper publisher; b. Princeton, B.C., Can., Sept. 27, 1950; d. Edward Rees and Madge Preston (Bryan) H.; m. George Fredrick Ward, Dec. 16, 1978; children: Sean Ward, Kate Ward. BA, U. Victoria (B.C.), 1972. With Edmonton Jour., Alta., Can., 1976—, from reporter to asst. mng. editor, 1984-87, editor, 1987-92, pub., 1992—. Southam fellow U. Toronto, Ont., Can., 1977-78. Office: Edmonton Journal, 10006 101st St PO Box 2421, Edmonton, AB Canada T5J 2S6

HUGHES, MARVIS JOCELYN, poet, photographer; b. Ft. Worth, May 17, 1942; d. C.H. and Bobbye Etta (Harrell) H.; m. Rodolfo J. Broullon, May 1972 (div. 1980); 1 child (dec.). Student, UCLA, 1960-65, NYU, 1968-72. Poet-in-residence Brockman Gallery, L.A., 1980-81, Calif. State Mus. African-Am. Culture and History, L.A., 1984, William Grant Still Art Ctr., City of L.A., 1981-85; photographer, videographer Dept. HEW, Washington, 1971-72, 75-77; photography instr. Internat. Children's Sch., L.A., 1980-81; media producer Broadcast Media Prodns., U. So. Calif., L.A., 1980; videographer, libr. L.A. Inst. Contemporary Art, 1979. Author: Vis-a-Vis and Other Poems, 1960s, The Time Traveller Variations, 1980s, Bones and Eyes, 1990s, (film) Ciné-Poém #1. . .n, 1970s. Named Golden Poet of Yr., World of Poetry, 1987, 91, 92; anthologized in Greates Poems of the 20th Century, World of Poetry, 1979. Mem. PEN West, Calif. Poets in the Schs., L.A. Poetry Festival, Nat. Coun. Negro Women, Assn. for Study of African-Am. Life and History, NAACP. Methodist. Office: Marvis Hughes/The Book Fund 5020 Rodeo Rd # 1 Los Angeles CA 90016

HUGHES, MARY KATHERINE, lawyer; b. Kodiak, Alaska, July 16, 1949; d. John Chamberlain and Marjorie (Anstey) H.; m. Andrew H. Eker, July 7, 1982. BBA cum laude, U. Alaska, 1971; JD, Willamette U., 1974; postgrad. Heriot-Watt U., Edinburgh, Scotland, 1971. Bar: Alaska 1975. Ptnr., Hughes, Thorsness, Gantz, Powell & Brundin, Anchorage, 1974-95, mem. mgmt. com., 1991-92; mcpl. atty. Municipality of Anchorage, 1995—. trustee Alaska Bar Found., pres., 1984—; bd. visitors Willamette U., Salem, Oreg., 1980—; bd. dirs. Alaska Repertory Theatre, 1986-88, pres., 1987-88; commr. Alaska Code Revision Commn., 1987-94; mem. U. Alaska Found., 1985—, trustee, 1990—; bd. dirs. Anchorage Econ. Devel. Corp., 1989-94, chmn. 1994; mem. adv. bd. Providence Hosp., 1993—. Fellow Am. Bar Found.; mem. Alaska Bar Assn. (bd. govs. 1981-84, pres. 1983-84), Anchorage Assn. Women Lawyers (pres. 1976-77), AAUW, Delta Theta Phi. Republican. Roman Catholic. Club: Soroptimists (v.p. 1986-87, pres. 1986-87). Home: 2240 Kissee Ct Anchorage AK 99517-1003 Office: Municipality Anchorage PO Box 196650 Anchorage AK 99519-6650

HUGHES, PAUL LUCIEN, art gallery owner; b. N.Y.C., Apr. 8, 1938; s. Paul Joseph and Yvonne (DeVoluy) H.; m. Nancy Souther, Dec. 16, 1961; children—Danielle, Amy. Student Kenyon Coll., Gambier, Ohio, 1956-57, Army Lang. Sch., Monterey, Calif., 1958-59; B.A., NYU, 1967; postgrad. Sch. Visual Arts, N.Y.C., 1968-69. Russian interpreter U.S. Army, Berlin, 1960-61; assoc. buyer J.C. Penney, N.Y.C., 1961-65: sales rep. Knoll Internat., N.Y.C., 1965-71, regional mgr., Denver, 1971-75; prin. Inkfish Gallery, Denver, 1975—. Office: Inkfish Gallery 949 Broadway Denver CO 80203-2705

HUGHES, ROBERT LACHLAN, newspaper executive; b. Regina, Saskatchewan, Can., June 1, 1944; s. Robert Wesley and Helen Elizabeth (MacLachlan) H.; m. Barbara Elaine Barootes, June 28, 1980; children: Geoffrey Robert, Ryan Stewart Gordon. Office boy, gen. reporter, police reporter, sports reporter Regina (Sask.) Leader-Post, 1962-69; sports columnist Saskatoon (Sask.) Star-Phoenix, 1969-70, Calgary Albertan, Can., 1970-72; sports editor, columnist Regina Leader-Post, 1972-88, mng. editor, news columnist, 1988-94, exec. v.p., 1994—. Dir. George Reed Found. for Handicapped; founding dir. Gord Currie Youth Devel. Fund, Brad Hornung Found. Recipient Can. 125 medal Govt. of Can., 1992; named to Hall of Fame Can. Football Football Reporters of Can., 1990. Mem. Can. Mng. Editors Assn. (bd. dirs. 1989-94), Can. Daily Newspapers Assn., Royal United Svcs. Inst., Regina Golf Club. Office: The Leader-Post, 1964 Park St, Regina, SK Canada S4P 3G4

HUGHES, ROBERT MERRILL, control system engineer; b. Glendale, Calif., Sept. 11, 1936; s. Fred P. and Gertrude G. (Merrill) H.; AA, Pasadena City Coll., 1957; 1 child, Tammie Lynn Cobble. Engr. Aerojet Gen. Corp., Azusa, Calif., 1957-64, 66-74; pres. Automatic Electronics Corp., Sacramento, 1964-66; specialist Perkin Elmer Corp., Pomona, Calif., 1974-75; gen. mgr. Hughes Mining Inc., Covina, Calif., 1975-76; project mgr. L&A Water Treatment, City of Industry, Calif., 1976-79; dir. Hughes Industries Inc., Alta Loma, Calif., 1979—; pres. Hughes Devel. Corp., Carson City, Nev.; chmn. bd. Hughes Mining Inc., Hughes Video Corp. Registered profl. engr., Calif; lic. gen. bld. contractor. Mem. AIME, Nat. Soc. Profl. Engrs., Instrument Soc. Am., Am. Inst. Plant Engrs. Republican. Patentee in field. Home: 10009 Banyan St Alta Loma CA 91737-3603 Office: PO Box 915 Carson City NV 89702

HUGHES, TERESA P., state legislator; b. N.Y.C., Oct. 3, 1932; m. Frank E. Staggers; children: Vincent, Deidre. BA, Hunter Coll.; MA, NYU; PhD, Claremont Grad. Sch. Prof. edn. Calif. State U., L.A.; social worker; mem. Calif. Senate, 1975—; chair edn. com., mem. pub. employees and retirement com., mem. housing and cmty. devel. and local govt. coms.; bd. trustees L.A. County H.S. for Arts and Edn. Coun. Music Ctr., Calif.; active Mayor Bradley Edn. Com. Founder Aware Women. Mem. Nat. Coalition 100 Black Women, Calif. State Employees Assn., Calif. Tchrs. Assn., Coalition Labor Union Women. Democrat. Home: 1906 W 22nd St Los Angeles CA 90018-1644 Office: Calif Senate 4035 State Capitol Sacramento CA 95814 Office: 1 W Manchester Blvd Ste 401 Inglewood CA 90301-1750

HUGHES, TRAVIS HUBERT, geologist; b. Rapid City, S.D., Feb. 21, 1937; s. Frank Lyon and Jane (Brown) H.; m. Suzy Hatcher, Dec. 22, 1957; children: Travis Jr., Tracy. BA, Vanderbilt U., Nashville, 1959, MS, 1960; PhD, U. Colo., 1967. Registered profl. geologist, Ind., Tenn., Ga., Fla., N.C., S.C., Ark., Wyo., Ky., Oreg. Chief geologist Oman Constrn. Co., Nashville, 1960-62; prof. geology U. Ala., Tuscaloosa, 1966-82; v.p. P.E. LaMoreaux & Assocs., Inc., Tuscaloosa, 1982-92; prin. Hydraulic Cons., Inc., Lakewood, Colo., 1992—; chmn. dept. geology U. Ala., 1978-81; sr. staff scientist Environ. Inst. for Waste Mgmt. Studies, U. Ala., 1984-88; mem. sr. rev. group Waste Mgmt. of North Am.; mem. com. on onshore oil and gas leasing Nat. Acad. Scis., 1989-90. Contbr. over 40 articles to profl. jours. Recipient Waldemar Lindgren award for excellence in rsch. Soc. Econ. Geologists,, 1968, NASA Citation for Innovative Rsch., 1978, Dist. Achievement in Earth Sci., Fedn. Lapidary and Mineralogical Socs., 1979. Mem. Geol. Soc. Am., Geochem. Soc., Nat. Assn. Geology Tchrs., Am. Geol. Inst., Assn. Ground Water Scientists and Engrs., Am. Inst. Profl. Geologists (pres. 1986). Home: 512 N Jackson St Golden CO 80403-1326 Office: Hydrologic Consultants Inc 143 Union Blvd Ste 525 Lakewood CO 80228-1827

HUGHES, W. JAMES, optometrist; b. Shawnee, Okla., Oct. 15, 1944; s. Willis J. and Elizabeth Alice (Nimohoyah) H. B.A. in Anthropology, U. Okla., 1966, M.A. in Anthropology, 1972; O.D., U. Houston, 1976; M.P.H., U. Tex., 1977. Lic. Optometrist, Okla., Tex., W. Va. commd. med. officer USPHS, 1966; advanced through the grades to capt./optometrist, USPHS, 1993; physician's asst., Houston, Dallas, 1969-70; teaching asst. in clin. optics U. Houston, 1973-74, contact lens research asst., 1974; Wesley Jessen Contact Lens Rep., 1974-76; extern eye clinic Tuba City Indian Hosp., 1975; teaching fellow pub. health optometry U. Houston, 1975-76; Indian Health Service optometrist, Eagle Butte, S.D., 1976; optometrist vision care project Crockett Ind. Sch. Dist., 1977; vision care program dir. Bemidji Area Indian Health Service, 1977-78; optometrist Navajo Area Indian Health Service, Chinle Health Ctr., 1978-79; adj. prof. So. Calif. Coll. of Optometry, Los Angeles, U. Houston Coll. of Optometry, 1978—, So. Coll. Optometry, Memphis, 1980—; optometrist Shiprock USPHS Indian Hosp., 1979—; chief vision care program Northern Navajo Med. Ctr., 1994—; dir. eye clinic USPHS Northern Navajo Med. Ctr., Shiprock, N.Mex.; Navajo area Indian Health Service rep. to optometry career devel. com. USPHS. Sgt. U.S. Army, 1966-69, Capt. USPHS 1993—. Decorated Bronze Star, Purple Heart. Recipient House of Vision award 1974; Community Health Optometry award 1976; Better Vision scholar, 1973-76. Mem. Am. Pub. Health Assn., Am. Optometric Assn., Tex. Optometric Assn. Commd. Officers Soc., Assn. Am. Indian Physicians, Beta Sigma Kappa. Democrat. Roman Catholic. Contbr. articles to profl. jours.

HUGHS, MARY GERALDINE, accountant, social service specialist; b. Marshalltown, Iowa, Nov. 28, 1929; d. Don Harold, Sr., and Alice Dorothy (Keister) Shaw; A.A., Highline Community Coll., 1970; B.A., U. Wash., 1972; m. Charles G. Hughs, Jan. 31, 1949; children: Mark George, Deborah Kay, Juli Ann, Grant Wesley. Asst. controller Moduline Internat., Inc., Chehalis, Wash., 1972-73; controller Data Recall Corp., El Segundo, Calif., 1973-74; fin. adminstr., acct. Saturn Mfg. Corp., Torrance, Calif., 1974-77; sr. acct., adminstrv. asst. Van Camp Ins., San Pedro, Calif., 1977-78; asst. adminstr. Harbor Regional Ctr., Torrance, Calif., 1979-87; active bookkeeping svc., 1978—; instr. math. and acctg. South Bay Bus. Coll., 1976-77. Sec. Pacific N.W. Mycol. Soc., 1966-67; treas., bd. dirs. Harbor Employees Fed. Credit Union; mem. YMCA Club. Recipient award Am. Mgmt. Assn., 1979. Mem. Beta Alpha Psi. Republican. Methodist. Author: Iowa Auto Dealers Assn. Title System, 1955; Harbor Regional Center Affirmative Action Plan, 1980; Harbor Regional Center - Financial Format, 1978—; Provider Audit System, 1979; Handling Client Funds, 1983. Home and Office: 18405 Haas Ave Torrance CA 90504-5405

HUGO, JOAN LYALL, academic administrator, art critic, curator; b. Weehawken, N.J., Jan. 12, 1930; d. Thomas Lyall and Bertha (Agnus) Dowey; m. Michel Hugo, May 2, 1952 (div.); children: Alan, Peter. BS in Libr. Sci., Simmons Coll., 1951. Libr. Am. Libr. Paris, 1952-53; cataloguer Bklyn. Mus. Libr., 1954, libr. dir. Otis Art Inst., L.A., 1957-80; So. Calif. editor Artweek, Oakland, Calif., 1980-90; westcoast editor New Art Examiner, Chgo., 1990-94; asst. to provost Calif. Inst. Arts, Valencia, 1990—; instr. Otis Art Inst., 1978-90, UCLA Ext., 1982-90; curator numerous exhbns. Contbr. reviews to profl. jours., catalogue essays. Bd. dirs. L.A. Contemporary Exhbns., L.A., 1980-84, Woman's Bldg., L.A., 1986-89, Cactus Found., L.A., 1988—; mem. bd. advisors Found. Art Resources, L.A., 1986—. Recipient Vesta award Woman's Bldg., 1990. Mem. Coll. Art Assn., Art Table, Assn. Internat. des Critiques D'Art. Office: Calif Inst Arts 24700 Mcbean Pky Valencia CA 91355-2340

HUGO, NANCY, county official, alcohol and drug addiction professional; b. Cedar Rapids, Iowa, May 4, 1944; d. Roger S. and Phyllis Anita (Wenger) Conrad; m. Marshall G. Hugo, Apr. 5, 1968; 1 child, Andrea. BS, Drake U., 1966; MS, Pepperdine U., 1987; adminstrn. credential, U. Calif., Irvine, 1989. Cert. adminstr., middle sch. educator, Calif. Tchr., adminstrv. asst. Ocean View Sch. Dist., Huntington Beach, Calif., 1966-90; coord. alcohol and drug prevention edn., program mgr. juvenile ct. schs. drug and alcohol programs Orange County Dept. Edn., Costa Mesa, Calif., 1990—, coord. phys. edn., 1991-93, coord. bus. edn. partnership, 1993—. Mem. ASCD, NEA, Assn. Calif. Sch. Adminstrs., Calif. Edn. Assn., Calif. Assn. Health Phys. Edn. Recreation and Dance, Calif. Tchrs. Assn. Home: 4606 Cortland Dr Corona Del Mar CA 92625-2707 Office: Orange County Dept Edn 200 Kalmus Dr Costa Mesa CA 92626-5922

HUI, KENNETH CHI-WAN, surgeon; b. Hong Kong, Dec. 22, 1955; s. Kenneth K.L. and Ada S.H. (Wong) H.; m. Anna Hui, Nov. 21, 1981; children: Kenneth Jr., Eric. MD, BS, U. London, England, 1979. Diplomate Am. Bd. Plastic Surgery. Asst. prof. Stanford U. Med. Ctr., Palo Alto, Calif., 1991; staff surgeon VA Med. Ctr., Palo Alto, Calif., 1991, sect. chief divsn. plastic surgery, 1992—; chmn. care review com. Stanford U. Med. Ctr. Divsn. Plastic Surgery, Calif., 1992. Contbd. articles to profl. jours. Recipient Basic Sci. Rsch. prize N.J. Chpt. Am. Coll. Surgeons, 1987. Fellow Royal Coll. Surgeons, Am. Coll. Surgeons; mem. Stanford Asian Am. Med. Faculty Assn., Am. Soc. Plastic and Reconstructive Surgery, Calif. Soc. Plastic Surgeons, Am. Soc. for Reconstructive Microsurgery, Pan Pacific Surgical Assn. Office: Stanford U Med Ctr Divsn Plastic Surgery NC-104 Stanford CA 94305

HUIGENS, DANIEL DEAN, dentist; b. Osmond, Nebr., May 16, 1953; s. Mickey Helen (White) H.; m. Linda Sue Wilbourn, May 19, 1982 (div. 1991); 1 child, Matthew Blake. BA, U. LaVerne, 1975; BS, U. Okla., 1979, DDS with honors, 1982. EMT Community Ambulance Svc., San Dimas, Calif., 1971-74; emergency room technician San Dimas Community Hosp., San Dimas, Calif., 1974-77; physician assoc. Muskogee Bone and Joint Clinic, 1979-82; dentist Drs. Huigens and Hanawalt, LaVerne, Calif., 1986—; mem. part time staff UCLA Coll. Dentistry. Mem. ADA, Acad. Gen. Dentistry, Calif. Dental Assn., Tri County Dental Soc., Pomona Valley Amatuer Astronomers Assn., LaVerne C. of C., Omicron Kappa Upsilon. Office: Dr Dan Huigens 2187 Foothill Blvd Ste E La Verne CA 91750

HULICK, DIANA EMERY, museum director, art historian, photographic consultant, educator; b. Boston, 1950. A.B. in English cum laude, Bryn Mawr Coll., 1971; M.F.A. in Photography, Ohio U., 1973; M.F.A. in Modern Art, Princeton U., 1978, Ph.D., 1984. Mem. faculty Stephens Coll., Columbia, Mo., 1973-76, U. Man., summer 1975, N.S. Coll. Art and Design, summer 1979, U. Del., part-time 1980, U. Wis.-Milw., 1981; gallery dir. U. Denver, 1982-83; dir. galleries, curator art collection, asst. prof. U. Maine, Orono, 1983-86; asst. prof. dept. photography and cinema Ohio State U., 1986-88, Ariz. State U. 1988-95; adjudicator Nat. Found. Advancement in the Arts, 1983-87; photographic cons. Sabbathday Lake Shakers, 1985-86, cons. 1986—. One-woman shows include: Photoworks, Boston, 1975, U.

Man., 1975, Middle Tenn. State U., 1976, Stephens Coll., 1976, Utah State U., 1976, Polaroid Bldg., Boston, 1976, Carleton Coll., 1980; group shows: U. Fla., Gainesville, 1972, Smithsonian Instn., Washington, 1973, U. Mo., 1974, U. Iowa Mus., 1976, Kansas City Art Inst., 1976, R.I. Sch. Design, 1979, Temple U., Phila., 1980, U. Denver, 1983, U. Maine, 1984, 85, Ohio U., 1984; represented in permanent collections: Carleton Coll., Princeton U., Ohio U., Stephens Coll. Kress grantee, 1977; Spears grantee, 1978, 79; McCormick fellow, 1979; Woodrow Wilson grantee, 1980; Dayton Hudson Disting. Vis. artist Carleton Coll., 1980. Office: 805 N Robson Mesa AZ 85201

HULL, GRANT WARREN, music educator, composer; b. Ely, Nev., Aug. 29, 1928; s. Helen Teresa (Bauman) Hull; m. Carol Ellen Beckwith, Aug. 29, 1949; children: Terry Beckwith, Holli Rae, Helen Brooke, Carol Lisa. BA, Pomona Coll., 1950; MA, Claremont Grad. Sch., 1951. Music tchr. Ft. Jones (Calif.) H.S., 1951-53, Stockton (Calif.) Unified Sch. Dist., 1953-83, U. Pacific Music Camp, Stockton, Calif., 1960-67; assoc. editor Wynn Music, Orinda, Calif., 1971—; performing musician, 1953—. Composer more than 50 published works for sch. bands and orchs. Bd. dirs. Stockton Symphony, 1971, Stockton Musicians Assn., 1992. Mem. Swingaires, Masons. Home: 2456 W Alpine Ave Stockton CA 95204-2731

HULL, JANE DEE, state official, former state legislator; b. Kansas City, Mo., Aug. 8, 1935; d. Justin D. and Mildred (Swenson) Bowersock; m. Terrance Ward Hull, Feb. 12, 1954; children: Jeannette Shipley, Robin Hillebrand, Jeff, Mike. BS, U. Kans., 1957; postgrad., U. Ariz., 1972-78. Spkr. pro tem Ariz. Ho. of Reps., Phoenix, 1993, chmn. ethics com., chmn. econ. devel., 1993, mem. legis. coun., 1993, mem. gov.'s internat. trade and tourism adv. bd., 1993, mem. gov.'s strategic partnership for econ. devel., 1993, mem. gov.'s office of employement implementation task force, 1993, spkr. of house, 1989-93, house majority whip, 1987-88; now secretary of state State of Arizona, Phoenix. Bd. dirs. Morrison Inst. for Pub. Policy, Beatitudes D.O.A.R., 1992, Ariz. Town Hall, Ariz. Econs. Coun.; mem. dean's coun. Ariz. State U., 1989-92; assoc. mem. Heard Mus. Guild, Cactus Wren Rep. Women, ; mem. Maricopa Med. Aux., Ariz. State Med. Aux., Freedom Found., Valley Citizens League, Charter 100, North Phoenix Rep. Women, 1970, Trunk 'N Tusk Legis. Liaison Ariz. Rep. Party, 1993; Rep. candidate sec. of state, 1994. Recipient Econ. Devel. award Ariz. Innovation Network, 1993. Mem. Nat. Orgn. of Women Legislators, Am. Legis. Exch. Coun., Nat. Rep. Legislators Assn. (Nat. Legislator of Yr. award 1989), Soroptimists (hon.). Republican. Roman Catholic. Home: 10458 N 9th St Phoenix AZ 85020-1585

HULL, JANE LAUREL LEEK, retired nurse, administrator; b. Ontario, Calif., July 4, 1923; d. William Abram and Susan Bianca (Pethick) Leek; R.N., Columbia Presbyn. Sch. Nursing, 1944; B.A., Redlands U., 1977; ; m. James B. Hull, Oct. 10, 1944 (dec.); children—James W., William P., Kenneth D. Supr. obstetrics Mid-Valley Hosp., Peckville, Pa., 1945-46; sch. and surg. nurse acute nursing Scranton (Pa.) State Hosp., 1947-52; nurse San Antonio Community Hosp., Upland, Calif., 1953-55; office nurse H.L. Archibald, Upland, 1965; vis. nurse Pomona West End Inc., continuity of care coordinator, Claremont, Calif., 1968-73, exec. dir., 1973-92 (named pres. 1991); tchr. ARC nursing course to high sch. students; cons. Livingston Meml. Vis. Nurse Assn. Ventura, Calif. Recipient Woman Achiever award, Pomona Valley, 1983, Excellence in Edn. award Nat. Assn. Home Care, 1988. Treas. PTA, Pomona, Calif.; vol. exec. dir. Inland Hospice Assn., 1979-80, accreditation commn., 1988-89. Nat. Found. for Hospice/Home Care, 1988. Mem. Am. Assn. Retired Persons (local coord.), Calif. Nurses Assn. (pres. dist. 53 1958), Calif. Assn. for Health Services at Home (dir.), Calif. League Nursing, Nat. Homecaring Council (dir.). Home Care Aide Assn. Am. (chmn.), bd. mem. Nat. Assn. of Home Care. Republican. Club: Zonta (Ontario, Upland, pres., 1976). Organizer Homemaker Dept. in Vis. Nurse Assn., 1972, pres., 1991; developer (with Don Baxter Corp.) plugs for in-dwelling Foley catheters, 1963. Home: 543 W F St Ontario CA 91762-3117

HULL, JOSEPH POYER DEYO, geologist, consultant; b. Tulsa, Okla., Jan. 21, 1931; s. Joseph Poyer Deyo and Mary Ethel (Sanders) H.; m. Renate Kranz, May 27, 1962; children—Thomas Deyo, Karen Sanders. A.B., Hamilton Coll., 1952; M.A., Columbia U., 1953, Ph.D., 1955. Dist. Subsurface geologist Humble Oil & Refining Co., Midland, Tex., 1955-58; mgr. Can. exploration Kerr-McGee Corp., Calgary, Alta., Can., 1959-75; pres., chief exec. officer Impel Energy Corp., Denver, 1975-80, Page Petroleum Inc., Denver, 1980-81; v.p. exploration Ensource Inc., Denver, 1981-84; v.p. div. mgr. Sabine Corp., Denver, 1984-86; v.p. exploration Wolf Energy Co., 1987-90; cons., 1990—. NSF fellow, 1952-55. Fellow Geol. Soc. Am.; mem. Am. Assn. Petroleum Geologists (life), Soc. Econ. Mineralogists and Paleontologists, Soc. Econ. Geologists, Rocky Mountain Assn. Geologists (pres. 1982), Phi Beta Kappa, Sigma Xi. Democrat. Unitarian. Home and Office: 64 S Flora Way Golden CO 80401-5330

HULL, MAURY LANE, mechanical engineering educator; b. Washington, July 18, 1947; s. Maury Isaac and Marguerite Fern (Lane) H.; m. Karen Slakey, Sept. 15, 1984. BSME, Carnegie-Mellon U., 1969; MSME, U. Calif., Berkeley, 1970, PhD in Mech. Engring., 1975. Asst. specialist in mech. engring. U. Calif., Berkeley, 1975; from asst. prof. to assoc. prof. mech. engring. U. Calif., Davis, 1976-88, prof. mech. engring., 1988—; cons. Tyrolia Corp., Vienna, Austria, 1985—, Shimano Corp., Osaka, Japan, 1988—. Mem. editl. bd. Internat. Jour. Sport Biomechanics, 1989-92, Jour. Biomechanics, 1993—; contbr. numerous tech. articles to sci. jours. and procs. Fellow ASME; mem. Internat. Soc. Skiing Safety, Internat. Soc. Biomechanics, Am. Soc. Biomechanics (Giovanni Borelli award 1989), Orthopedic Rsch. Soc. Home: 8565 Olive School Ln Winters CA 95694-9652 Office: U Calif Dept Mech Engring Davis CA 95616

HULL, MCALLISTER HOBART, JR., retired university administrator; b. Birmingham, Ala., Sept. 1, 1923; s. McAllister Hobart and Grace (Johnson) H.; m. Mary Muska, Mar. 23, 1946; children: John McAllister, Wendy Ann. B.S. with highest honors, Yale, 1948, Ph.D. in Physics, 1951. From instr. to asso. prof. physics Yale U., 1951-66; prof. physics, chmn. dept. Oreg. State U., 1966-69; prof. physics, chmn. dept. State U. N.Y. at Buffalo, 1969-72, dean Grad. Sch., 1972-74, dean. grad. and profl. edn., 1974-77; provost U. N.Mex., 1977-85, counselor to pres., 1985-88, prof. emeritus physics, 1988—; adviser to supt. schs., Hamden, Conn., 1958-65. Author papers, books, chpts. in books, articles in encys. Bd. dirs. Western N.Y. Reactor Facility, 1970-72; trustee N.E. Radio Obs. Corp., 1971-77; pres. Western Regional Sci. Labs., 1977; chmn. tech. adv. com. N.Mex. Energy Research Inst., 1981-83, mem., 1983-88; co-chmn. Nat. Task Force on Ednl. Tech., 1984-86. Served with AUS, 1943-46. Faculty fellow Yale U., 1964-65. Fellow Am. Phys. Soc.; mem. Am. Assn. Physics Tchrs. (chmn. Oreg. sect. 1967-68). Office: U NMex Dept Physics and Astronomy Univ Of New Mexico NM 87131

HULL, ROGER KERMIT, military officer; b. Chattanooga, Tenn., Apr. 19, 1946; s. George Fletcher and Dorothy Helen (Suddarth) H.; m. Mary Alison Welter Hull, Dec. 21, 1981; children: Nathan Kyle, Rachel Rebecca. BS in Aviation Mgmt., Auburn U., Ala., 1968; MS in Ops. Rsch., Naval Postgrad. Sch., Monterey, Calif., 1977. Cert. flight instr. fixed wing and hot air balloon, airline transport pilot, designated acquisition profl., USN. Flight student Naval Aviation Sch. Command, Pensacola, Fla., 1968-69; advanced jet flight instructor Naval Aviation Training Command, Kingsville, Tex., 1969-71; combat attack pilot Attack Squadron 146, Lemoore Calif., Vietnam, 1971-74; student Naval Postgrad. Sch., Monterey, Calif., 1974-77; competition parachutist U.S. Parachute Team, Pope Valley, Calif., 1977; dept. head Attack Squadron 56, Yokosuka, Japan, 1977-81; chief operation test dir. Air Test & Eval. Squadron Five, China Lake, Calif., 1981-84; air ops. officer Cruiser Destroyer Group One, San Diego, 1984-87; program mgr. Space & Naval Warfare Systems Command, Washington, 1987-90; commanding officer Naval Weapons Eval. Facility, Albuquerque, N.Mex., 1990-93; small bus. owner "Copy To:", Hanford, Calif., 1975-77; pvt. computer cons., MacPro, Washington, 1987-90; cons. ops. analyst, San Diego, 1984-87. Author: United We Fall, 1977; contbr. articles to profl. jours. Mem. Gov.'s Disting. Pub. Svc. awards Coun., 1991. Capt., USN, 1968—. Recipient World Champion Parachutist, Fed. Aeronautics Internat., Gatton, Autralia, 1977; Indiv. Overall Nat. Champion Parachutist, U.S. Parachute Assn., Talequah, Okla., 1977; Proven Subspecialist Ops. Rsch., USN., 1981; Proven Subspecialist Command & Control, USN, 1988. Mem. U.S. Parachute Assn., Fed. Exec. Bd., Mensa, Mil. Ops. Rsch. Soc., Omicron Delta Kappa. Office: Vice Commdr Naval Air Warfare Ctr Weapons Divsn Point Mugu NAWC CA 93042

HULL, SUZANNE WHITE, retired cultural institution administrator, writer; b. Orange, N.J., Aug. 24, 1921; d. Gordon Stowe and Lillian (Siegling) White; m. George I. Hull, Feb. 20, 1943 (dec. Mar. 1990); children: George Gordon, James Rutledge, Anne Elizabeth. BA with honors, Swarthmore Coll., 1943; MSLS, U. So. Calif., 1967. Mem. staff Huntington Libr., Art Gallery and Bot. Gardens, San Marino, Calif., 1969-86, dir. adminstrn. and pub. svcs., 1972-86, also prin. officer. Author: Chaste, Silent and Obedient, English Books for Women, 1475-1640, 1982, 88; editor: State of the Art in Women's Studies, 1986. Charter pres. Portola Jr. H.S. PTA, L.A., 1960-62; pres. Children's Svc. League, 1963-64, YWCA, L.A., 1967-69; mem. alumni coun. Swarthmore Coll., 1959-62, 83-86, mem.-at-large, 1986-89; mem. adv. bd. Hagley Mus. and Libr., Wilmington, Del., 1983-86, Betty Friedan Think Tank, U. So. Calif., 1985-93; hon. life mem. Calif. Congress Parents and Tchrs.; bd. dirs. Pasadena Planned Parenthood Assn., 1978-83, mem. adv. com., 1983—; founder-chmn. Swarthmore-L.A. Connection, 1984-85, bd. dirs., 1985-92; founder Huntington Women's Studies Seminar, 1984, mem. steering com., 1984-91, mem. adv. bd., 1991—; bd. dirs. Pasadena Girls Club, 1988-91; mem. organizing com. Soc. for Study of Early Modern Women, 1993-94; adv. bd. The Early Modern Englishwoman: A Facsimile Libr. of Essential Works, 1995—. Mem. Monumental Brass Soc. (U.K.), Renaissance Soc., Brit. Studies Conf., Western Assn. Women Historians, Soc. Study of Early Modern Women, Authors Guild, Beta Phi Mu (chpt. dir. 1981-84). Home: 1465 El Mirador Dr Pasadena CA 91103-2727 Office: 1151 Oxford Rd San Marino CA 91108-1218

HULLAR, THEODORE LEE, environmental educator; b. Mar. 19, 1935; m. Joan J. Miller, Aug. 2, 1958; children: Theodore W., Timothy E. BS with high distinction, U. Minn., 1957, PhD in Biochemistry, 1963. Asst. prof. medicinal chemistry SUNY, Buffalo, 1964-69, assoc. prof., 1969-75, assoc. dean grad. sch., 1969-71; dep. commr. programs and research N.Y. State Dept. Environ. Conservation, 1975-79; assoc. dir. Cornell U. Agrl. Experiment Sta., 1979-81, dir., 1981-84; assoc. dir. research N.Y. State Coll. Agriculture and Life Scis., Cornell U., 1979-81; dir. N.Y. State Coll. Agriculture and Life Scis. Cornell U., 1981-84; adj. prof. natural resources, prof. natural resources Cornell U., 1981-84; chancellor, prof. biochem. U. Calif., Riverside, 1985-87; prof. environ. toxicology U. Calif., Davis, 1987—, chancellor, 1985-94; chmn. hazardous waste mgmt. com. So. Calif. Assn. Govs., 1986-87, chmn. air quality task force, 1985-87, mem. regional adv. coun., 1985-87; chmn. con. on environment nat. Assn. State Univs. and Land Grant Colls., 1985-93, com. on biotech., 1982-88, chmn. program devel. subcom., 1982-88, coord. Agr. Rsch. Initiative; chn. Gov. Deukmejian's Task Force on Toxics, Waste and Tech., 1985-86; chmn. bd. agr. Nat. Rsch. Coun., 1988-93; co-founder, chmn. Calif. Coun. on Sci. and Tech., 1988-93; mem. gov. bd. Internat. Irrigation Mgmt. Inst., 1991—; bd. dirs. Boyce Thompson Inst. for Plant Rsch., 1985—; chair univ. rev. and accreditation coms., 1990—; lectr. various orgns. Contbr. articles to profl. jours. Commr. Environ. Quality Erie County, N.Y., 1974-75; alternate to Gov. N.Y. on Delaware and Susquehanna River Basin Commns., 1975-79; mem. N.Y. State Agrl. Resources Commn., 1974-75; mem. Arlington Heights Greenbelt Study Com., 1986-87; mem. Monday Morning Group, 1985-87; active various community orgns. NSF postdoctoral fellow SUNY Buffalo, 1963-64. Mem. Am. Chem. Soc., AAAS, Chem. Soc. London, Regional Inst. So. Calif., Greater Riverside C. of C., (bd. dirs. 1985-87), Sigma Xi. Home: PO Box 1606 Davis CA 95617-1606 Office: U Calif Davis Office of Chancellor Davis CA 95616*

HULSE, JERRY, journalist; b. Grand Junction, Colo., Sept. 5, 1924; s. Leslie and Elena (Bates) H.; m. Helene Carr, Oct. 20, 1945; children: Richard, Robert. AA, L.A. City Coll., 1947. Newspaper reporter San Fernando Valley Times, Calif., 1948-52; gen. news reporter L.A. Times, 1952-60, travel editor, 1960-90, writer syndicated travel column On The Go, 1961-92, travel columnist, 1990—; syndicated travel columnist. Author: Jody, 1976, also paperback and publ. in 15 countries (Reader's Digest Book of Month); over 600 mag. articles in Saturday Evening Post, Saturday Rev., Reader's Digest, New Yorker, Esquire, Popular Sci., Good Houskeeping, other popular mags.; contbg. editor Avenues Mag. With USNR, World War II. Decorated Legion of Honor (France), 1987; recipient 2 Pulitzer Prize nominations, Strebin-Dobben award for journalism excellence, 1972, Henry Burroughs Meml. writing award, 1973, 1st place award Aviation Space Writers Assn., 1975, Golden Pen award Am. Soc. Travel Agts., 1980, Can. travel award, 1980, 1st pl. Silver Pen award Mexico, 1982, 88; Lowell Thomas Travel Journalism award Soc. Am. Travel Writers, 1987, Gold award Pacific Area Travel Assn., 1987, Lowell Thomas best article award, 1988, Melva C. Pederson award, 1988, Hawaii Visitors Bur. award, 1989, Lowell Thomas grand award, 1990, Gold medal Pacific Area Travel Assn., 1992. Republican. Office: 4525 Camellia Ave North Hollywood CA 91602-1907

HULSE, JOHN EDWARD, former telephone company executive; b. Hannibal, Mo., June 11, 1933; s. Giles and Edythe (Watt) H.; B.S., U.S.D., 1955; m. Mary Jean Pfeiffer, Aug. 21, 1954; children: Celine, Michelle, Christi, Mary Pat, Michael. Gen. comml. and mktg. mgr. Northwestern Bell Telephone Co., Omaha, 1968-72, dir. mktg. sales project AT&T, N.Y.C., 1972-74, v.p., chief exec. officer, Sioux Falls, S.D., 1974-75, v.p., chief exec. officer, Mpls., 1975-79, sr. v.p., Omaha, 1979-81; exec. v.p., chief fin. officer Pacific Telesis Group (formerly Pacific Tel. & Tel.), San Francisco, 1981-82, vice-chmn. bd., chief fin. officer, 1983-92. Trustee San Francisco Ballet Assn. Mem. Fin. Execs. Inst. (pres. San Francisco chpt. 1986, dir. western area 1987-90), Telephone Pioneers Am. (sr. v.p., 1990, pres. 1991), San Francisco C. of C. (dir., treas.), World Affairs Council No. Calif, Pvt. Sector Council. Clubs: San Francisco Bankers, Commonwealth, Blackhawk Country. Office: Pacific Telesis Group 140 New Mountgomery St Ste 1824 San Francisco CA 94105*

HULSE, RALPH ROBERT, management consultant; b. St. Joseph, Mo., Jan. 14, 1935; s. Ralph Raymond and Eva Laduska (Hatfield) H.; m. Gwen Lea Bartosh, May 21, 1956 (div. 1959); m. Jutta-Beaujean, Jan. 14, 1961. AB, Cen. Meth. Coll., 1957; MEd, U. Mo., 1965. Continuing edn. programmer U. Mo., Columbia, 1969-71; dir. edn. tng. North Kansas City (Mo.) Meml. Hosp., 1971-74; mgmt. cons. Lawrence-Leiter, Kansas City, 1974-77; adminstr. U.S. Congress, 6th dist., Mo., 1977-78; bus. cons. Hulse & Assocs., Kansas City, 1978-88; adminstr. Sales Tng. Inst. div. Mile Hi Bus. Coll., Denver, 1988-89; bus. cons., pres. Crystal Devel. Systems, Inc, Denver, 1989-95; agent Bankers Life & Casualty Ins., 1994—; founder, bd. dirs. Opportunity Industry Inc., St. Joseph, 1965-71; pres. State Adult Edn. Assn., Mo., 1978-79. Contbr. articles to profl. jours. (Nat. Pub. award 1974, 75). Served with U.S. Army, 1959-61. Mem. Colo. Cons. Assn. (founder, pres. 1985-87). Republican. Methodist. Home and Office: 5202 Union Ct #2 Arvada CO 80002-1934

HUMBER, PHILIP RICHARD, plastic surgeon; b. Milw., Wis., Jan. 19, 1950. MD, Med. Coll. Wis., 1976. Plastic surgeon Scripps Encinitas Hosp., Calif.; also with Tri-City Med. Ctr., Calif. Office: 320 Santa Fe Dr Ste 107 Encinitas CA 92024-5139*

HUME, DARRELL J., retail executive; b. 1948. Student, U. Wash. With Nordstrom, Inc., Seattle, 1969—, corp. merchandizer men's sportswear, 1991—. Office: Nordstrom Inc 1501 5th Ave Seattle WA 98101-1603*

HUME, STEPHEN, writer, editor; b. Blackpool, Lancashire, Eng., Jan. 1, 1947; came to Can. 1948; s. James and Joyce (Potter) H.; m. Susan Winifred Mayse, July 29, 1970. B.A., U. Victoria, B.C., 1971. Reporter Victoria Times, B.C., Can., 1968-71; Arctic corr. Edmonton Jour., Yellowknife, NWT, Can., 1971-73; city editor Edmonton Jour., Edmonton, Alta., Can., 1975-77; weekend editor Edmonton Jour., Edmonton, Alta., 1977-79; editor Edmonton (Alta.) Jour., 1981-87, gen. mgr., 1987-89; columnist-at-large The Vancouver Sun, 1989—. Author: (poetry, essays) Signs Against An Empty Sky, 1980, And the House Sank Like a Ship in the Long Prairie Grass, 1987, Ghost Camps: Memory and Myth on Canada's Frontier, 1989 (Alta. Writers' Guild lit. prize 1989). Recipient So. Pres.'s award for commentary, 1990, citation for column writing Nat. Newspaper Awards, 1990, 93. Office: Vancouver Sun, 2250 Granville St, Vancouver, BC Canada V6H 3G2

HUMES, CHARLES WARREN, counselor, educator; b. Cambridge, Mass.; s. Charles W. and Alice E. Humes; m. Marilyn A. Harper, Aug. 7, 1965; children: Rebecca Ellyn, Malinda Maye. MA, NYU, 1952; EdM, Springfield Coll., 1956; EdD, U. Mass., 1968. Lic. profl. counselor, Va.; cert. profl. counselor, Ariz. Sch. psychologist Westfield Pub. Schs. (Mass.), 1955-62; dir. guidance Westfield Pub. Schs. (Mass.), 1962-70; assoc. prof. Springfield Coll. (Mass.), 1968-70; dir. pupil svc. and spl. edn. Greenwich Pub. Schs. (Conn.), 1970-80; assoc. prof. No. Va. Grad. Ctr., Va. Tech. U., Falls Church, 1980-88, prof. 1988-93, prof. emeritus, 1993—; pvt. practice, Vienna, Va. and Phoenix, 1985—. V.p. Westfield Area Child Guidance Clinic, 1963-65, pres., 1965-66; mem. Greenwich Hosp. Nursing Coun., 1970-75. Mem. APA, Conn. Assn. Counselor Edn. & Supervision (pres. 1979-80), Am. Counseling Assn. (cons.), InterAm. Soc. Psychology, Phi Delta Kappa (v.p. Va. Tech. 1982-83), Phi Kappa Phi. Author: Pupil Services: Development, Coordination, Administration, 1984; Contemporary Counseling: Services, Applications, Issues, 1987. Book rev. editor Sch. Counselor, 1984-93. Contbr. over 60 articles on counseling to profl. jours. Home and Office: 15038 E Palomino Blvd Fountain Hls AZ 85268-4813

HUMES, EDWARD, journalist, writer. Author: Buried Secrets, 1992, Good Cop, Bad Cop, 1992. Recipient Pulitzer prize for beat reporting, 1989. *

HUMMEL, FRED ERNEST, architect; b. Sheridan, Wyo., Jan. 10, 1927; s. Fred Edward and Glenna Ruth (Horton) H.; m. Sue Anne Estep, May 11, 1970; children: Jessica, Rebecca and Amber (triplets); children by previous marriage: Glenn, Mark, Shaun and Lindsay (twins). B.A., U. Calif.-Berkeley, 1951. Pvt. practice architecture Ventura, Calif., 1951-68, Sacramento, 1973—; state architect, State of Calif., Sacramento, 1968-73; instr. architecture UCLA, 1966-67, Davis, 1974; mem. adv. panel for archtl. services GSA, 1974; cons. State of Ark. Capitol Outlay Study, 1975; chmn. Calif. Bldg. Standards Coordination Council, 1970-71; ex-officio mem. Calif. Bldg. Standards Commn., 1969-73, Field Act Adv. Group, 1968-72; archtl. cons. Mich. Gov.'s Commn. on Architecture, 1972; mem. Calif. Gov.'s Earthquake Council, 1972-73, Calif. Affirmative Action Implementation Com., 1971-72, Calif. Ad Hoc Commn. on Energy Conservation, 1973, Capitol Mall Adv. Planning Com., 1970-71, Calif. Gov.'s Task Force on Capitol Outlay Projects, 1970-71; mem. adv. com. on environ. design and urban studies to Calif. Coordinating Council for Higher Edn., 1970-71; mem. adv. group on engring. and earthquake scis. to Calif. Joint Legis. Com. on Seismic Safety, 1972-73; mem. Commn. of the Californias, 1972-82; mem. adv. bd. Nat. Park System, 1981-84; mem. Sacramento County Sheriff's Air Squadron, 1981; apptd. by Pres. Reagan to bd. dirs. Nat. Inst. Bldg. Scis., 1986-90; apptd. project mgr. Ronald Reagan Presdl. Library, 1986-91, Del Mar Racetrack, 1991-93. Served to 1st lt. inf. U.S. Army, 1945-47, 51, Korea. Recipient award of honor Chico State U., 1974, Hon. award Cons. Engrs. Assn. of Calif., 1969, presentation Ann. Architects and Engrs. Forum, Los Angeles, 1969, Calif. Senate and Assembly resolutions of commendation, 1973. Fellow AIA (pres., dir. Santa Barbara, Calif. chpt. 1962, dir. Calif. council 1961-63, mem. Calif. profl. practice com. 1969, mem. exec. com. Calif. council, state treas. 1961-62, AIA Disting. Service Citation Calif. council 1973, v.p. edn. Calif. council 1978, mem. nat. govtl. relations com. 1974-76, nat. capitol com. 1973-74, dir. Central Valley chtp. 1973-74, mem. nat. architects in govt. com. 1971-72, chmn. Calif. council architects in govt. com. 1970-73, mem. Calif. govt. relations com. 1964-67, dir. Ventura County chpt. 1964-66, mem. Calif. evaluation bd. 1964). Republican. Home: 5007 Sugar Ln Carmichael CA 95608-3128

HUMMEL, JOSEPH WILLIAM, hospital administrator; b. Vinton, Iowa, Dec. 7, 1940; married. BA, Calif. State U., 1965; M Health Adminstrn., U Calif., 1966. Adminstrv. instr. Merrithew Meml. Hosp., Martinez, Calif., 1965; adminstrv. res. Mt. Zion Hosp. and Med. Ctr., San Francisco, 1966-67, adminstrv. pat. care, 1967-68, adminstrv. asst., 1968-70; assoc. adminstr. Valley Med. Ctr., Fresno, Calif., 1970-74; CEO Kern Med. Ctr., Bakersfield, Calif., 1974-86; adminstr. Kaiser Found. Hosp., L.A., 1987—. Mem. Calif. Hosp. Assn. (bd. dirs. 1983-89). Home: 2050 Maginn St Glendale CA 91202-1128 Office: Kaiser Found Hosp 4867 W Sunset Blvd Los Angeles CA 90027-5969

HUMPHERYS, A. RICH, state police administrator; b. Boise, Idaho, July 14, 1933; s. Rich and Evaline (Liggett) H.; m. Shirley Ann Evans, Aug. 20, 1956; children: Robert Rich, Randy Ray. Student, U. Idaho, 1973, Idaho State U., 1973-74. Roving port Idaho State Police, Boise, 1958-61; from patrolman to sgt. Idaho State Police, Lewiston and Pocatello, 1961-78; lt. Idaho State Police, Pocatello, 1978-83; capt. Idaho State Police, Boise, 1983-86, supt., 1986—; mem. Idaho Traffic Safety Commn., 1986—, Peace Officers Standards and Tng. Council, Boise, 1986-87. V.p. PTA, Lewiston, 1964, pres., 1965. With USN, 1950-54, Korea. Cited for Disting. Service Gov. Idaho, 1976. Mem. Internat. Assn. Chiefs of Police, Idaho Chiefs' Assn., Idaho Peace Officers Assn., Elks. Democrat. Mem. LDS Ch. Office: Idaho State Police 3311 W State St PO Box 55 Boise ID 83707

HUMPHREY, JOHN JULIUS, university program director, historian, writer; b. Booneville, Miss., Jan. 22, 1926; s. George Duke and Josephine (Robertson) H.; m. Mary Margaret Ryan, Jan. 19, 1949; children: George Duke II, Laurie Ann. BS, Miss. State U., 1945; BA, U. Wyo., 1946, MA, 1964, postgrad., 1964-68; postgrad., U. Ariz., 1969-71. Pres. J.J. Humphrey Co. Inc., Laramie, Wyo., 1947-68; lectr. History U. Ariz., Tucson, 1969-71, asst. dir. placement, 1969-70, dir. scholarships, awards, 1970-72, dir. office of scholarships and fin. aid, 1972-84, dir. scholarship devel., 1970-91; asst. to pres. western area Cumberland Coll., Williamsburg, Ky., 1991; v.p. bus. affairs Tucson Coll. Arts and Scis., 1992. Sec. Baird Found., Tucson, 1970—; bd. dirs. Bendalin Fund, Phoenix, 1976—, Cacioppo Found., Tucson, 1986—; cons. DeMund Found., St. Louis, 1970—; mem. Pres. Club U. Ariz. Found.; mem. Ariz. Assn. Fin. Aid Officers, 1970-91, pres., 1973-74; pres. Ariz. Coll. & Univ. Faculty Assn., 1972-73. Ivinson Meml. Hosp. Bd., Laramie, 1964-68. Recipient Spl. award U. Ariz. Black Student Govt., 1983, Black Alumni, 1990; Study grantee U. Ariz., 1993—. Mem. Am. Indian Alumni Assn. (Spl. Appreciation for Svc. in Scholarships Native Ams. award 1982), Mormon History Assn., Masons (32 degree, Knight York Cross of Honor), Shriners. Methodist. Home: 6901 E Potawatami Dr Tucson AZ 85715-3246

HUMPHREY, PHYLLIS A., writer; b. Oak Park, Ill., July 22, 1929; d. Richard William and Antoinette (Chalupa) Ashworth; m. Herbert A. Pihl, Sept. 13, 1946 (div. 1957); children: Christine Pihl Gibson, Gary Fraizer Pihl; m. Curtis H. Humphrey, June 21, 1965; 1 child, Marc. AA, Coll. San Mateo, Calif., 1972; postgrad., Northwestern U., 1945-47. Ptnr. Criterion House, Oceanside, Calif., 1972—. Author: Wall Street on $20 a Month, 1986, Golden Fire, 1986; author radio scripts Am. Radio Theatre, 1983-84; contbr. short storis and articles to popular mags. Recipient 2d prize award Readers Digest Mag., 1980. Mem. Mensa. Republican. Christian Sci. Ch. Office: Criterion House PO Box 586295 Oceanside CA 92058-6295

HUMPHREY, SHIRLEY JOY, state representative, education consultant; b. Cheyenne, Wyo., May 26, 1937; d. Verlan E. and Inez M. (Tanner) R.; m. John E. Humphrey, Aug. 9, 1959; children: Michael Scott, Marci Lynne. BS in HOme Econs., Wyo. U., 1960. High sch. tchr. dist. #2 Laramie Sch. Dist., Albin, Wyo., 1964-75; high sch. tchr. dist. #1 Laramie Sch. Dist., Cheyenne, 1975-80; coll. instr. Laramie County Community Coll., Cheyenne, 1980-85; civil rights coord. Wyo. State Dept. Edn., Cheyenne, 1987-89; mem. Wyo. State Legislature, Cheyenne, 1983—; nutritionist food and nutrition program USDA; pres. Wyo. Home Econs. Tchrs., 1964-70. Bd. dirs. Laramie County Fair, Cheyenne, 1975-85; mem. Women's Civic League, Cheyenne, 1970—, Sr. Citizens Adv. Coun., Cheyenne, 1985—. Recipient Distg. Svc. award Future Homemakers Am., 1988; named Hon. State Farmer Future Farmers Am., 1982. Mem. Kappa Kappa Gamma Alumna (pres. 1974-75). Democrat. Presbyterian.

HUMPHREY, WILLIAM ALBERT, mining company executive; b. Potrerillos, Chile, Jan. 12, 1927; s. Thomas Z. and Ethel K. (Kolbe) H.; m. Edna Lillian Joule, Dec. 20, 1947; children: Patricia Ann, Nancy Joule, Katherine Elisabeth, William Albert. B.S., U. Ariz., 1950. Registered mining engr.,

Ariz. From jr. engr. to supervisory positions Cananea Consol. Copper Co., Sonora, Mex., 1950-68, v.p., asst. gen. mgr., 1968-71, exec. v.p., gen. mgr., dir., 1971-75; v.p. planning Anaconda Butte Ops., Butte, Mont., 1975; v.p. ops. Newmont Mining Corp., N.Y.C., 1975-81; exec. v.p. ops., dir. Homestake Mining Co., San Francisco, 1981-91, pres., COO, 1991-92, vice chmn., bd. dirs., 1992—; bd. dirs. Homestake Gold of Australia Ltd., Adelaide. Mem. Western Regional Coun., Salt Lake City, 1981—, trustee, 1992—; bd. dirs. Nat. Mining Hall of Fame and Mus., YMCA of San Francisco. Mem. AIME, Am. Mining Congress, World Trade Club, Tau Beta Pi. Republican. Home: 2469 Biltmore Dr Alamo CA 94507-2305 Office: 500 Ygnacio Valley Rd Walnut Creek CA 94596-3840

HUMPHREYS, JOSEPH ROY, consultant; b. San Francisco, Apr. 14, 1938; s. Roy William and Vera Josephine (Lyon) H.; m. Joan Ann Budz, July 17, 1965; children: Josephine, Wendy Lyon, Joseph S. BA, St. Patrick's Coll., Menlo Park, Calif., 1959; MA, U. San Francisco, 1965. Various staff positions Social Security Adminstrn., Balt. and Santa Rosa, Calif., 1965-68; specialist in social legis. Congl. Rsch. Svc., Libr. of Congress, Washington, 1968-73; profl. staff mem. Com. on Fin., U.S. Senate, Washington, 1973-91; ind. cons. San Francisco, 1991—. Mem. Nat. Acad. Social Ins. Democrat. Roman Catholic. Home: 20 Knollview Way San Francisco CA 94131-1216

HUMPHRIES, STEPHEN EDWARD, writer; b. Camden, N.J., Oct. 14, 1950; s. Edward W. and Dolores (Weaver) H.; m. Elsa Schroeder, Oct. 30, 1977 (div. Oct. 1983); m. Ruth Ivy Frishman, Sept. 27, 1992. AA with honors, Broward Community Coll., 1970; student, U. Colo., 1972-74, Colo. Sch. Mines, 1981-84, Met. State Coll., 1986-88. Engring. tech., tech. writer Enviro-Test Ltd., Denver, 1975-77; asst. editor Am. Water Works Assn., Denver, 1977; assoc. project scientist TRC Environ. Cons., Denver, 1978-82; geol. asst., writer Colo. Sch. Mines, Golden, 1983-84; reporter, editor High Timber Times, Conifer, Colo., 1984-88; reporter Aspen (Colo.) Times/Times Daily, 1988-89; copy editor The Leader Newspapers, Houston, 1989; mng. editor S. Coast Community Newspapers, Santa Barbara, Calif., 1989-90; freelance writer Houston, 1989-91; editor Tahoe World, Tahoe City, Calif., 1991-93; freelance writer Truckee, Calif., 1993—. Trustee Tahoe Forest Hosp. Found., Truckee Donner Land Trust; vol. U.S. Geol. Survey; adv. bd. Tahoe Truckee Housing Devel. Corp. Recipient 2d place feature photography for weeklies award Colo. Press Assn., 1985, hon. mention news stories for weeklies, 1987, sweepstakes winner feature stories for weeklies, 1989; hon. mention serious columnist for weekly Nat. Newspaper Assn., 1987, hon. mention editorial pages for weeklies, 1989; award Met. Water Providers, 1987, Meritorious Svc. award VFW, 1988. Mem. Internat. Soc. Weekly Newspaper Editors, Soc. Profl. Journalists.

HUMPHRIES, WILLIAM R., state land commissioner; b. Hot Springs, N.Mex., Dec. 19, 1946; s. William A. and Charlta Arletta (Coleman) H.; m. Carol A. Curry, June 14, 1969; children: Heidi K., Chery L. Student, Ft. Lewis Coll., 1964-67; BS, N.Mex. State U., 1971. Ranch owner, operator Lindrith, N.Mex., 1963—; instr. Largo Canyon Sch., Counselor, N.Mex., 1971-73; v.p., br. mgr. First State Bank, Cuba, N.Mex., 1974-78; pres. Security Bank, Ruidoso, N.Mex., 1978; gen. mgr. N.Mex. State Fair, Albuquerque, 1980-82, Santa Fe Racing, Inc., 1983; commr. State Land Office, Santa Fe, 1987—; vice-chmn. State Investment Coun., Santa Fe, 1987—; mem. Oil Conservation Commn., Santa Fe, 1987—. Mem. coun. on agrl. rsch., extension and teaching Nat. Univ. Support Group, 1986—; regent N.Mex. State U., Las Cruces, 1972-84; bd. trustees Manzano Day Sch., Albuquerque, 1981-82; chmn. HUB Resource and Devel. Coun., Albuquerque, 1975-80; supr. Cuba Soil and Water Conservation Dist., 1976-80. Recipient Excellence in Grazing award Am. Soc. Range Mgmt., 1976, Pres.'s award N.Mex. State U., 1984; named one of Outstanding Young Men. Am., 1974. Mem. N.Mex. Cattlegrower's Assn., N.Mex. Farm Bur. (Outstanding Service to Agr. award 1978). Republican. Methodist. Home: PO Box 108 Lindrith NM 87029-0108 Office: State Land Office 310 Old Santa Fe Trail PO Box 1148 Santa Fe NM 87504

HUMPHRY, DEREK, association executive, writer; b. Bath, Somerset, Eng., Apr. 29, 1930; came to U.S., 1978; s. Royston Martin and Bettine (Duggan) H.; m. Jean Edna Crane, May 5, 1953 (dec. Mar. 1975); children: Edgar, Clive, Stephen; m. Ann Wickett Kooman, Feb. 16, 1976 (div. 1990); m. Gretchen Crocker, 1991. Student pub. schs. Reporter, Evening News, Manchester, Eng., 1951-55, Daily Mail, London, 1955-63; editor Havering Recorder, Essex, Eng., 1963-67; sr. reporter Sunday Times, London, 1967-78; spl. writer L.A. Times, 1978-79; founder, exec. dir. Hemlock Soc. N.Am., L.A., 1980-92, pres. 1988-90. Author: Because They're Black, 1971 (M.L. King award 1972), Police Power and Black People, 1972; Jean's Way, 1978, Let Me Die Before I Wake, 1982, The Right to Die, 1986, Final Exit, 1991, Dying With Dignity, 1992, Lawful Exit, 1993. With Brit. Army, 1948-50. Mem. World Fedn. Right-to-Die Socs. (newsletter editor 1979-84, 1992-94, sec.-treas. 1983-84, pres. 1988-90), Ams. Death with Dignity (v.p. 1993), Hemlock Soc. No. Calif. (v.p. 1994), Euthanasia Rsch. and Guidance Orgn. (pres. 1993—). Home: 24829 Norris Ln Junction City OR 97448-9559

HUNDAHL, SCOTT ALFRED, oncologic surgeon; b. Omaha, Jan. 2, 1956; s. Robert E. and Mariann Berg (Hundahl) Appley; m. Conchita Leilani Siri, May 13, 1986 (div. Dec. 1992). BA magna cum laude, Harvard U., 1977; MD, Yale U., 1981. Diplomate Am. Bd. Surgery, Am. Bd. Med. Examiners. Resident in general surgery U. Hawaii, Honolulu, 1981-86; fellow Meml. Sloan-Kettering Cancer Ctr., N.Y.C., 1986-88; asst. prof. surgery U. Hawaii, Honolulu, 1988—; rsch. staff Cancer Rsch. Ctr. Hawaii, Honolulu, 1993—; mem. Commn. on Cancer, Chgo., 1993—; regional chmn. Commn. on Cancer Liaisons, 1993—; assoc. chief surgery Queen's Med. Ctr., Honolulu, 1993-95, chief of surgery, 1995—; pvt. practice surgical oncology, Honolulu, 1988—; co-founder, bd. dirs. Comprehensive Home Svcs. Hawaii, 1986—. Pres. Honolulu unit Am. Cancer Soc., 1992-93, v.p. 1993—; vice chair Nat. Cancer Data Com., 1994—. Recipient best presentation award WHO Collaborating Ctrs. for Gastric Cancer, Munich, Germany, 1993. Fellow Soc. Surgical Oncology, Am. Coll. Surgeons (exec. com. Hawaii chpt. 1991—, state chmn. 1991—); mem. AMA, AAAS, Pacific Club, Hawaii Wado Kai (pres. 1989—), Hawaii Med. Assn. (continuing med. edn. com. 1992—, bd. councilors 1992—), Assn. Harvard Chemists, Hawaiian Surgical Assn., Honolulu County Med. Soc., Soc. Head & Neck Surgeons, Soc. Surgical Oncology, Internat. Cancer Data Com. Republican. Episcopalian. Office: Cancer Rsch Ctr Hawaii 1236 Lauhala St Honolulu HI 96813-2424

HUNDLEY, PATRICK DAVID, college program administrator; b. Jackson, Tenn., Feb. 26, 1948; s. Cecil Turner and Frances Verdi (Odell) H.; m. Janice Lynn Shelton Norton, Mar. 26, 1970 (div. Sept. 1974); 1 child, David Shelton Norton; m. Susan Lynn Child, May 10, 1975; children: Sarah Ruth, Patrick Daniel. BA, Tenn. Wesleyan Coll., 1970; MA, Mid. Tenn. State U., 1975; postgrad., Okla. State U., 1975-78. Asst. dist. exec. Boy Scouts Am., Chattanooga, 1970-71; program analyst Tenn. Dept. Mental Health, Nashville, 1973-75; grad. teaching asst. Okla. State U., Stillwater, 1975-78; asst. prof. U. Ark., Little Rock, 1978-80; dir. devel. Phillips U., Enid, Okla., 1980-83; dir. devel.-engring. Wash. State U., Pullman, 1983-87; dir. devel. Southeastern Mass. U., North Dartmouth, 1987-88; v.p. St. Andrews Presbyn. Coll., Laurinburg, N.C., 1988-90; dir. devel.-pharmacy Oreg. State U., Corvallis, 1990-95; asst. chancellor for univ. advancement U. Wis., Platteville, 1995—. Editor: The Magic of Names, 1978; contbr. articles to profl. jours. Mem. Nat. Soc. Fund Raising Execs., Coun. for Advancement and Support of Edn., Am. Assn. Colls. of Pharmacy. Democrat. Mem. Evang. Luth. Ch. Am. Home: 720 Heer St Platteville WI 53818 Office: U Wis Office Univ Advancement Kaarmann Libr Platteville WI 53818

HUNG, JENNY, development specialist; b. Taipei, Taiwan, Mar. 2, 1962; d. You Tsai and Yueh Chin (Yuan) H. BA, U. Calif., Riverside, 1983; MAS, Johns Hopkins U., 1987. Devel. specialist Modern Irrigation, Upland, Calif.; tech. writer City Nat. Bank, L.A.; researcher in field. Mem. Johns Hopkins U. Alumni Assn. Home: 1285 Clark St Upland CA 91784-1733

HUNG, SAMMY T., physician; b. Swatow, China; s. Phillip H. and Sou-Mui (Wong) H.; m. Patricia A. Hung, Aug. 22, 1970 (div. July 1988); children: Erick, Kevin, David, Mailee. BA, Amherst Coll., 1968; PhD, U. Calif., Berkeley, 1972; MD, U. Calif., San Francisco, 1976. Diplomate Am. Bd. Internal Medicine. Intern then resident VA Med. Ctr., Martinez, Calif., 1976-79, pulmonary fellow, 1979-81; med. dir. dept. cardiopulmonary St. Rose Hosp., Hayward, Calif., 1981—; cons. in field. Fellow Am. Coll. Chest Physicians; mem. ACP. Office: 27001 Calaroga Ave Ste 4 Hayward CA 94545-4345

HUNING, DEBORAH GRAY, actress, dancer, audiologist, photographer/video producer-editor; b. Evanston, Ill., Aug. 23, 1950; d. Hans Karl Otto and Angenette Dudley (Willard) H.; divorced; 1 child, Bree Alyeska. BS, No. Ill. U., 1981, MA, 1983. Actress, soloist, dancer, dir. various univ. and community theater depts., Bklyn., Chgo. and Cranbrook, B.C., Can., 1967—; ski instr. Winter Park (Colo.) Recreation Assn., 1975-79; house photographer C Lazy U Ranch, Granby, Colo., 1979; audiologist, ednl. programming cons. East Kootenay Ministry of Health, Cranbrook, 1985-89; ind. video prodn./asst., 1991—; owner Maxaroma Espresso and Incredible Edibles, 1993-95; pres. The Network Connection, 1995—, Sound Comm., 1989—; master of ceremonies East Kootenay Talent Showcase, EXPO '86, Vancouver B.C., Can., 1986; creator, workshop leader: A Hearing Impaired Child in the Classroom, 1986. Producer, writer, dir., editor (video) Down With Decibels, 1992; author: Living Well With Hearing Loss: A Guide for the Hearing-Impaired and Their Families, 1992. Sec., treas. Women for Wildlife, Cranbrook, 1985-86; assoc. mem. adv. bd. Grand County Community Coll., Winter Park, Colo., 1975-77; assoc. mem. bd. dirs. Boys and Girls Club of Can., Cranbrook, 1985. Mem. Internat. Marine Animal Trainers Assn.

HUNKINS, RAYMOND BREEDLOVE, lawyer, rancher; b. Culver City, Calif., Mar. 19, 1939; s. Charles F. and Louise (Breedlove) H.; m. Mary Deborah McBride, Dec. 12, 1968; children: Amanda, Blake, Ashley. BA, U. Wyo., 1966, JD, 1968. Ptnr. Jones, Jones, Vines & Hunkins, Wheatland, Wyo., 1968—; spl. counsel U. Wyo., Laramie, State of Wyo., Cheyenne; faculty Western Trial Adv. Inst., 1993—; owner Thunderhead Ranches (Albany & Platte Counties, Wyo.); gen. ptnr. Split Rock Land & Cattle Co. Chmn. Platte County Reps., Wheatland, 1972-74, Adv. Coun. Coll. of Commerce & Industry, 1978-79; Governor's Crime commn., 1970-78; pres. Wyo. U. Alumni Assn., 1973-74, commr. Wyo. Aeronautics Commn., 1987—. With USMC, 1955-57. Fellow Am. Coll. Trial Lawyers, Internat. Soc. Barristers, Am. Bd. Trial Advs.; mem. ABA (aviation com. 1980—, litigation sect., forum com. on constrn. industry), Wyo. Bar Assn. (chmn. grievance com. 1980—, U.S. Dist. and local rules com. 1990—), Wyo. Trial Lawyers Assn. (past pres., bd. dirs. 1995—), Lions, Elks. Office: Jones Jones Vines & Hunkins PO Drawer 189 9th and Maple Wheatland WY 82201

HUNNICUTT, RICHARD PEARCE, metallurgical engineer; b. Asheville, N.C., June 15, 1926; s. James Ballard and Ida (Black) H.; B.S. in Metall. Engring., Stanford, 1951, M.S., 1952; m. Susan Haight, Apr. 9, 1954; children—Barbara, Beverly, Geoffrey, Anne. Research metallurgist Gen. Motors Research Labs., 1952-55; sr. metallurgist Aerojet-Gen. Corp., 1955-57; head materials and processes Firestone Engring. Lab., 1957-58; head phys. scis. group Dalmo Victor Co., Monterey, 1958-61, head materials lab., 1961-62; v.p. Anamet Labs., Inc., 1962-82, exec. v.p., 1982—; partner Pyrco Co. Author: Pershing, A History of the American Medium Tank T20 Series, 1971, Sherman, A History of the American Medium Tank, 1978, Patton, A History of the American Main Battle Tank, vol. 1, 1984, Firepower, A History of the American Heavy Tank, 1988, Abrams, A History of the American Main Battle Tank, vol. 2, 1990, Stuart, A History of the American Light Tank, Vol. 1, 1992, Sheridan, A History of the American Light Tank Vol. 2, 1995. Served with AUS, 1943-46. Mem. Electrochem. Soc., AIME, Am. Soc. Metals, ASTM, Am. Welding Soc., Am. Soc. Lubrication Engrs. Research on frictional behavior of materials, development of armored fighting vehicles. Home: 2805 Benson Way Belmont CA 94002-2938 Office: 3400 Investment Blvd Hayward CA 94545-3811

HUNNICUTT, ROBERT WILLIAM, engineer; b. Pauls Valley, Okla., Aug. 12, 1954; s. James Warren Hunnicutt. BS, N.Mex. State U., 1980. Sr. assoc. engr. IBM, Tucson, 1980-94. Mem. Ariz.-Sonora Desert Mus. Republican. Home: 8383 S Pistol Hill Rd Tucson AZ 85747-9161

HUNSAKER, FLOYD B., accountant; b. Collinston, Utah, Sept. 6, 1915; s. Allen G. and Mary Ann (Bowcutt) H.; grad. high sch.; m. Zella D. Hepworth, Mar. 3, 1943; children: Marcia (Mrs. Marvin Bahr), Charlene (Mrs. Abelino Ancira), Sonia (Mrs. Val Fisher), Rhonda (Mrs. Kim Veigel), Tamara (Mrs. Randy Beardall). Lic. ins. salesman, security dealer, notary pub., Lincoln County, Wyo. Owner, operator dairy farm, Bedford, Wyo., 1946-70; acct., Afton, Wyo., 1959—; owner Credit Bur. Star Valley, Afton, 1967-87; mcpl. judge Town of Afton, 1967-77; local office claimstaker Wyo. Unemployment Compensation Dept., 1975-85. Pres., Holdaway Sch. PTA, 1960; active Boy Scouts Am., 1946-49, 58-67; chmn. Cub Scouts com., 1987—; bd. dirs. Star Valley Sr. Citizens, 1981-83, 84-88; pres. Lower Valley 4-H council, 1961-62, leader, 1959-63; chmn. Star Valley chpt. Am. Revolution Bicentennial Adminstrn., 1975-76, Star Valley chpt. ARC, 1976—; ward pres. Sunday Sch., 1985-87; mem. Wyo. Centennial Com., 1990; subdivider Fertile Acres 1981-88; archtl. designer Star Valley Vets. Meml. Monument, 1990; mem. Lincoln County Selective Svc. Bd., 1984—. Pub. Star Valley Bus. Directory, 1990—. Recipient 50 Yr. Vol. award ARC, 1992. Served with Devils Brigade, 1941-45; ETO. Mem. Farm Bur. (exec. sec. Lincoln County 1961-66), Internat. Platform Assn., Afton C. of C. (dir. 1973-74), Star Valley C. of C. (dir. 1988—, exec. sec. 1989-90, treas. 1991—, Outstanding Cmty. Svc. award 1994), VFW (post svc. officer 1949—, post quartermaster 1959—, dist. comdr. Wyo. 1974-75, 77-78, state dept. jr. vice comdr. 1978-79, sr. vice comdr. 1979-80, state comdr. 1980-81, dist. comdr. 1982-83, 86-88, chmn. state audit com. 1985-94), Am. Legion (post svc. officer, adj. treas. 1975—). Mem. Ch. of Jesus Christ of Latter-day Saints. Home: PO Box 516 323 Adams St Afton WY 83110 Office: 498 Washington St Afton WY 83110

HUNSBERGER, CHARLES WESLEY, library director; b. Elkhart, Ind., Sept. 25, 1929; s. Charles August and Emma Edna (Zimmerman) H.; m. Hilda Carol Showalter, July 3, 1949 (div.); children: Jonathan Wesley, Jerald Wayne, Jane Wannette. BA, Bethel Coll., Mishawaka, Ind., 1952; MLS, Ind. U., 1967. Mem. Ft. Wayne (Ind.) Libr. Staff, 1960-62; dir. Columbia (Ind.) City Libr., 1962-64, Monroe County Libr., Bloomington, Ind., 1964-71, Clark County Libr. Dist., Las Vegas, Nev., 1971-93; owner Las Vegas Libr. Cons. Svcs., 1993—, Las Vegas, Nev. cons. sch., pub. librs., 1968-70; lectr. libr. schs. Ind. U., 1970-71, U. Ariz., 1974, U. Nev., Reno, 1976; mem. Nev. Coun. on Librs., 1973-81, chmn., 1980-81. Mem. Calif. Libr. Assn., ALA, Nev. Libr. Assn. (named Libr. of Yr. 1988), Internat. Assn. of Met. City Librs. (sec./treas., 1992—), Rotary (pres. 1979-80, Las Vegas-Paradise chpt.). Democrat. Home: 1501 Crestview Dr Las Vegas NV 89124-9135 Office: Las Vegas Libr Cons Svcs PO Box 73221 Las Vegas NV 89170-3221

HUNSBERGER, ROBERT EARL, mechanical engineer, manufacturing executive; b. San Diego, Nov. 9, 1947; s. Arnold and Edith Mae (Miller) H.; m. Charlotte Louise Herr, Mar. 30, 1968; children: David Arnold, Allen Robert. BS in Mech. Engring., San Diego State Coll., 1969, MBA, 1975. Project engr. Gen. Atomic Co., San Diego, 1970-75; pvt. practice commodity mktg. specialist San Diego, 1975-77; devel. engr. Solar Turbines, Inc., San Diego, 1977-82, project engr., 1982-84, project mgr., 1984-89, mgr. pub. svcs., 1989-92, sourcing mgr., 1992—. Contbr. articles to profl. jours. Leader local Webelos, 1981-82; com. chmn. Boy Scouts Am., Ramona, Calif., 1982-83, cub master, 1983-84, com. mem., 1982—, com. chmn., 1985-86. Recipient Spirit of Courage award San Deigo Inst. Burn Medicine, 1979, Cert. Commendation Calif. Hwy. Patrol, 1979, B.S.A. Dist. Unit award, 1992. Republican. Club: Model A Restorers.

HUNT, BARNABAS JOHN, priest, religious order administrator; b. Sayre, Pa., Jan. 6, 1937; s. Clarence Elmer and Margarite Frances (Bennett) H. BS in Edn., Pa. State U., 1958; postgrad., Elmira Coll., 1960-61, Portland (Oreg.) State U., 1969-70, Clackamas Community Coll., 1970-71, Mt. Hood Community Coll., 1973-74. Ordained priest Episcopal Ch., 1984, joined Soc. St. Paul, Episcopal Ch. Headmaster St. Luke's Sch., Soc. St. Paul, Gresham, Oreg., 1961-64; lic. adminstr. St. Jude's Nursing Home, Inc., Portland and Sandy, Oreg., 1964-73; assoc. rector Soc. St. Paul, Palm Desert, Calif., 1975-89, rector, 1989—; brother-in-charge St. Paul's Press, Sandy, 1969-76. Pres. adv. bd. The Carlotta, 1985-92. Mem. Tri-County Bd., Oreg. Agy. on Aging, 1971-76; pres. Sandy C. of C., 1972; mem. Sandy City Coun., 1975-76, candidate for City Coun., City of Palm Desert, 1986; pres. St. Jude's Home, Inc., Palm Desert, 1989—. Fellow Am. Coll. Health Care Adminstrs. (pres. Coll. Found. 1984-87); mem. Nat. Guild Churchmen (pres. 1982—), Conf. on Religious Life in Anglican Communion (v.p. 1992—). Episcopalian. Home and Office: PO Box 14350 Palm Desert CA 92255-4350

HUNT, CHARLES AMOES, librarian; b. Montclair, N.J., Jan. 21, 1950; s. William Henry Hunt and Juliet Adele (Carter) Bey. Cert. computer programing, MTI Bus. Coll., 1968; BA in English Lit., tchg. cert., Doane Coll., 1973; MSLS, Syracuse U., 1975. Cert. librarianship. Asst. br. libr., br. libr. The Chgo. (Ill.) Pub. Libr., 1975-78; tech. libr. Atlantic Richfield Co., L.A., 1978-79; reference libr. Calif. State U., Fullerton, 1979; English tchr., libr. Kiddy Coll. English Sch., Mishima City, Japan, 1979-81; adult svcs. libr., br. libr. Stockton (Calif.)-San Joaquin County Pub. Libr., 1981-90, supervising libr., br. mgr., 1991—; cons. Office for Libr. Outreach Svcs. Adv. Com., ALA, Chgo., 1977-79. Editor: Information and Referral Promotional Samples, 1988. Judge Yosemite Forensic League, Stockton, 1986-88; fund distbn. reviewer, mem. recertification com. United Way of San Joaquin County, Stockton, 1994-95; sec. San Joaquin chpt. ACLU, 1995. Scholar Turrell Fund, East Orange, N.J., Doane Coll., Crete, Nebr., 1969-73; fellow Syracuse (N.Y.) U., 1974-75. Mem. NAACP, ALA (com. chair, sect. pres.), Pub. Libr. Assn., Social Responsibilities Round Table, Black Caucus, Freedom to Read Found., Calif. Libr. Assn. (com. mem.), Calif. Librs. Black Caucus, Manteca (Calif.) Kiwanis (newsletter editor 1985-89). Democrat. Baptist. Home: 1209 W Downs St Stockton CA 95207-6913 Office: Manteca Libr Stockton-San Joaquin County Pub Libr 320 W Center St Manteca CA 95336

HUNT, DENNIS, public relations executive. BA in English, Notre Dame U.; MA in Edn. Adv. mgr., contbg. editor San Francisco Bus. Mag.; v.p. Deaver & Hannaford; mng. ptnr. Hunt/Marmillion Assocs., 1983-88; exec. v.p., gen. mgr. Ogilvy Adams &Rinehart, 1988-92; sr. exec. v.p., coo Stoorza, Siegaus & Metzger, Sacramento, 1992—; adj. instr. Santa Monica (Calif.) Coll. Office: Stoorza Ziegaus & Metzger 555 Capitol Mall # 600 Sacramento CA 95814

HUNT, DONALD R., retired librarian; b. Richmond, Ind., Nov. 5, 1921; s. Ronald Gilbert Hunt and Mildred Rorena (Lathrop) Warfield; m. Virginia Clark, June 24, 1947; children: Cynthia Hatch, Jeffrey, Kristin E. Bentz. BA, U. Colo., 1950, MS, 1951; postgrad., Stanford U., 1951-53; MALS, U. Mich., 1954. Reference librarian Wash. State U., Pullman, 1954-55; head reference Oreg. State U., 1956-62, asst. librarian, head pub. service, 1962-65, assoc. dir. libraries, 1965-72; library dir. San Jose (Calif.) State U., 1972-76; dean libraries U. Tenn., Knoxville, 1976-88. Served with USNR, 1943-46. Mem. ALA, Southeastern, Tenn. library assns., Phi Kappa Phi, Omicron Delta Kappa. Home: 2526 NW Kinderman Dr Corvallis OR 97330-2250

HUNT, FRANK BOULDIN, architect, water color artist; b. Morrill County, Nebr., July 19, 1915; s. Frank Neal and Sylvia Sybil (Ball) H.; m. Isabel Jean Phillips, Sept. 6, 1950; m. Donna Henderson Thomas, Dec. 27, 1955. Student, U. Nebr., 1934-35, U. Calif., Berkeley, 1937-38. Draftsman and designer firms in Calif., 1938-42, 46-48; partner Kitchen and Hunt (Architects), San Francisco, 1948-62; pres. Kitchen and Hunt (Architects), 1962-73, Hunt and Co. (Architects), San Francisco, 1973-75; dir. Hunt and Co. (Architects), 1975-81; v.p., dir. Kennedy/Jenks Engrs., San Francisco, 1975-86, Ecker Co., San Francisco, 1966-82. Prin. works include library expansion, residence halls, Crocker Nuclear Lab. at U. Calif., Davis, 1954-65, facilities for VIII Olympic Winter Games, Squaw Valley, Calif., 1956-60; cons.: U.S. Olympic Tng. Center, 1978-80; facilities for Pacific No. Region Eastman Kodak Co., San Francisco, 1956-58, water treatment plants, Marin County (Calif.) Municipal Water Dist., 1957-73; F.B. Hunt Residence, 1958-60; mausoleums at Mountain View Cemetery, Oakland, Calif., 1958-60, 74-76, 80-81; Donner Animal Bioradiol. Lab, Lawrence Berkeley (Calif.) Lab, 1961-64, 76; music classroom bldg., Calif. State U., Hayward, 1963-66, Reno-Sparks (Nev.) Joint Water Pollution Control plant, 1965-67, 77-82, San Francisco Bay Area Rapid Transit Dist. stas. at North Berkeley, Oakland West, South Hayward, Union City, Fremont, 1965-73, Santa Clara County (Calif.) water treatment plants and related facilities, 1966-73, Maintenance and Ops. Center, United Air Lines, San Francisco Internat. Airport, 1969-72, 76-86, Pacific No. Region distbn. center, Eastman Kodak Co., San Ramon, Calif., 1967-69, Kern County (Calif.) water treatment plant, 1973-76, Central Marin San. Agy. Treatment Plant, San Rafael, Calif., 1980-84, Palace Hotel rehab., San Francisco, 1979-85. Served to lt. USNR, 1942-46. Recipient numerous design awards; archtl. models of Blyth Olmpic Arena, F.B. Hunt residence, related material at Mus. Calif., Oakland. Fellow AIA; mem. Eastbay Watercolor Soc., Phi Gamma Delta. Studio: 56 Roble Rd Berkeley CA 94705-2838

HUNT, GEORGE ANDREW, lawyer; b. Salina, Utah, Mar. 5, 1949; s. Loyd G. and Inez Hunt; m. Elizabeth Jean Brandise, July 28, 1973 (div.); children: Rachael, Rinaldo, Andrew, Geoffrey. BS in Internat. Relations cum laude, U. Utah, 1971, JD, 1974. Bar: Utah 1974, U.S. Dist. Ct. Utah 1974, U.S. Ct. Appeals (10th cir.) 1976, U.S. Supreme Ct. 1978, U.S. Ct. Appeals (9th cir.) 1984. Assoc. Snow, Christensen & Martineau, Salt Lake City, 1974-78, ptnr., 1978-90; founding ptnr. Williams & Hunt, Salt Lake City, 1991—. Pres. U. Utah Coll. of Law, Salt Lake City, 1974. Mem. Utah Bar Assn. (bar examiner 1976-80, chmn. constrn. law sect. 1985-88), Salt Lake County Bar Assn. (mem. exec. com. 1979—, treas. 1984. sec. 1985, v.p. 1986-87, pres. 1987-88), U. Coll. of Law (bd. trustees 1993—). Republican. Roman Catholic. Clubs: Ft. Douglas Country. Office: Williams & Hunt PO Box 45678 Salt Lake City UT 84145-0678

HUNT, HOLLY, elementary education educator; b. Mesa, Ariz., July 24, 1963; d. Albert Lufkin and Mary Louise (Schneider) H. BA in Edn., No. Ariz. U., 1987. Cert. spl. edn. and elem. tchr., Ariz. Elem. tchr. Deer Valley Pub. Schs., Phoenix, 1988—; reading specialist Chpt. One, Phoenix, 1993-94. Mem. LDS Ch. Home: 3631 W Charleston Ave Glendale AZ 85308-2808 Office: Desert Winds Elem Sch 19825 N 15th Ave Phoenix AZ 85027-4305

HUNT, JACK, animal breeder; b. 1945. Grad., Harvard U. CEO Taylor Co. of Tex., Amarillo, 1975-81; with Tejon Ranch Co., 1981—, now pres. Office: Tejon Ranch Co 4436 Lebec Rd Lebec CA 93243*

HUNT, JOHN JOSEPH, state agency administrator; b. Miami, Fla., Sept. 10, 1952; s. John J. and Marjori (Kern) H. BS in Social Studies Edn., Fla. Internat. U., 1977, MPA, 1991. Cert. profl. pub. buyer Nat. Inst. Govtl. Purchasing. Gen. mgr. Nat. Screen Mfg. Corp., Miami, 1975-81; asst. to utilities dir. City of North Miami Beach, Fla., 1982-93; grant coord. State of Hawaii Dept. Health, Lihue, 1993—; data processing com. City North Miami Beach, 1992-93. City councilman code enforcement Village El Portal, Fla., 1987, city councilman pub. safety, 1988. Recipient Resolution of Appreciation, Village Coun., Village of El Portal; Outstanding scholar Fla. Internat. U., Sch. Pub. Adminstrn., North Miami, 1992. Mem. Assn. for Info. and Imaging Mgmt., Fla. Water Pollution Control Operators Assn. (co-editor Pipeline Mag. 1991-92), Miami Chpt. Nat. Inst. Govt. Purchasing, Deja-Brews Homebrew Club. Democrat. Home: PO Box 86 Anahola HI 96703-0086 Office: State Hawaii DOH Inike Recovery 4370 Kukui Grove St Ste 109 Lihue HI 96766-2002

HUNT, MARY LOU, counselor, small business owner; b. Bell, Calif., Apr. 23, 1932; d. David Allen and Ruth Irene (Bolton) Smith; m. Earl Busby Hunt, Dec. 20, 1954; children: Robert David, Susan Mary, Alan James, Steven Thomas. BA in Psychology, Stanford U., 1954, MA in Psychology, 1954. Tchr., counselor Women's Guidance Ctr. U. Wash., Seattle, 1972; from sec. to pres., cons. counselor Individual Devel. Ctr. Inc., Seattle, 1972-86, pres., dir., 1986—, also bd. dirs. Contbr. chpt. to book Management Preparation for Women, 1978. Bd. dirs. Seattle Day Nursery Assn., 1974-76, Together in Employment, Seattle, 1976, Focus on Part-Time Employment, Seattle, 1982-85, Classical Music Supporters, 1987-93. Mem. ASTD (bd. dirs. Seattle 1979-82, membership dir. 1980-82), Am. Counseling Assn., Wash. Counseling Assn., Nat. Career Devel. Assn., Puget Sound Career Devel. Assn. (pres. 1988-89), Wash. Career Devel. Assn. (pres. 1990-91, co-pres. 1989-90). Office: Individual Devel Ctr 1020 E John St Seattle WA 98102-5740

HUNT, PETER HULS, director, theatrical lighting designer; b. Pasadena, Calif., Dec. 16, 1938; s. George Smith and Gertrude (Ophuls) H.; m. Virginia

Osborn, Jan. 19, 1965 (div. Jan. 1972); m. Barbette Tweed, Feb. 6, 1972; children: Max, Daisy, Amy. BA, Yale U., 1961, MFA in Drama, 1963. Free-lance lighting designer N.Y.C., 1959-69, free-lance theatre dir., 1969—; free-lance motion picture dir. Los Angeles, 1972—; artistic dir. Williamstown Theatre Festival, 1989—. Dir.: (plays) "1776," 1969 (Tony award 1970), Give 'Em Hell Harry, 1975; (TV movie) Skeezer, 1981 (Peabody award 1982); (cable TV play) Bus Stop, 1982 (ACE award 1983). Recipient Christopher award, 1972, Edgar award, 1982. Office: Creative Artists Agy 9830 Wilshire Blvd Beverly Hills CA 90212-1804

HUNT, PETER ROGER, film director, writer, editor; b. London, Mar. 11, 1925; came to U.S., 1975; s. Arthur George and Elizabeth H.; widowed; 1 child, Nicholas Constantine. Student, London Sch. Music. Actor English Repertory Theater, London. Camera asst., asst. editor various documentaries; asst. editor various feature films. London Film Co.; scriptor various films; editor (films): Hill in Korea, Admirable Crichton, Cry From the Streets, Greengage Summer (Am. title: Loss of Innocence), Ferry to Hong Kong, H.M.S. Defiant (Am. title: Damn the Defiant), Sink the Bismarck; supervising editor, 2d unit dir.: Dr. No, Call Me Bwana, From Russia with Love, Goldfinger, Ibcress File, Thunderball, You Only Live Twice, Desperate Hours; assoc. producer: Chitty Chitty Bang Bang; dir.: On Her Majesty's Secret Service, Gullivers Travels (film and animated), Gold, Shout at the Devil, Death Hunt, Wild Geese II, Assassination, Hyper Sapien, (TV episodes) Marlowe, Shirley's World, Persuaders; (NBC-TV movie) Beasts in the Streets, (ABC-TV mini-series) Last Days of Pompeii, (CBS-TV special) Eyes of a Witness. Mem. Assn. Cinematic Technicians Great Britain, Dirs. Guild of Am., Motion Picture Acad. Arts, Acad. Television. Office: 2337 Roscomare Rd #2-145 Los Angeles CA 90077-1851

HUNT, ROBERT WILLIAM, theatrical producer, data processing consultant; b. Seattle, June 8, 1947; s. William Roland and Margaret Anderson (Crowe) H.; m. Marcie Loomis, Aug. 24, 1968 (div. Dec. 1975); 1 child, Megan; m. Susan Moyer, June 17, 1989; children: Donovan, Jillian. BA, U. Wash., 1969. CPA, Wash. Data processing cons Arthur Andersen & Co., Seattle, 1968-78; owner, cons. Robert W. Hunt & Assocs., Seattle, 1978—; exec. producer Village Theatre, Issaquah, Wash., 1979—; developer Francis J. Gaudette Theatre, Issaquah, Wash., 1994; cons. San Francisco Mus. Modern Art, 1981-90, Mus. of Flight, Seattle, 1983-90, Met. Mus. N.Y.C., 1984-85. Creator arts computer software; prodr. (mus.) Eleanor, 1987, Heidi, 1989, Charlie and the Chocolate Factory, 1989, Book of James, 1990, Funny Pages, 1991, Jungle Queen Debutante, 1991, Glimmerglass, 1995, City Kid, 1995; creator, writer (pop group music and video) The Shrimps, 1984. Chmn. com. Seattle Arts Commn., 1975-78; treas. Arts Resource Svcs., Seattle, 1976-78; gen. mgr. Musicomedy Northwest, Seattle, 1977-79. Grantee Seattle Arts Commn., 1978-79, Wash. State Arts Commn., 1980—, King County Arts Commn., 1980—, Nat. Endowment for the Arts, 1992—. Mem. Wash. Soc. CPAs., Nat. Alliance of Mus. Theatre Producers (treas., bd. dirs.). Office: Village Theatre 120 Front St N Issaquah WA 98027-3234

HUNT, WILLIAM E., SR., state supreme court justice; b. 1923. B.A., LL.B., Univ. Mont. Bar: 1955. Justice Mont. Supreme Ct., Helena. Office: Mont Supreme Ct Justice Bldg Helena MT 59620*

HUNTEN, DONALD MOUNT, planetary scientist, educator; b. Montreal, Que., Can., Mar. 1, 1925; came to U.S., 1963, naturalized, 1979; s. Kenneth William and Winnifred Binnmore (Mount) H.; m. Isobel Ann Rubenstein, Dec. 28, 1949; children: Keith Atherton, Mark Ross. B.Sc., U. Western Ont., 1946; Ph.D., McGill U., 1950. From research asso. to prof. physics U. Sask. (Can.), Saskatoon, 1950-63; physicist Kitt Peak Nat. Obs., Tucson, 1963-77; sci. adv. to asso. adminstr. for space sci. NASA, Washington, 1976-77; prof. planetary scis. U. Ariz., Tucson, 1977-88, Regents prof., 1988—; cons. NASA, 1964—. Author: Introduction to Electronics, 1964; (with J.W. Chamberlain) Theory of Planetary Atmospheres, 1987; contbr. articles to profl. jours. Recipient Pub. Svc. medal NASA, 1977, 85, medal for exceptional sci. achievement, 1980. Mem. Am. Phys. Soc., Can. Assn. Physicists (editor 1961-63), Am. Geophys. Union, Am. Astron. Soc. (chmn. div. planetary scis. 1977), Internat. Astron. Union, Internat. Union Geodesy and Geophysics, Internat. Assn. Geomagnetism and Aeronomy, AAAS, Nat. Acad. Scis., Explorers Club. Club: Cosmos (Washington). Home: 3445 W Foxes Den Dr Tucson AZ 85745-5102 Office: U Ariz Dept Planetary Scis Tucson AZ 85721

HUNTER, ANNARAE, mental health counselor; b. Davao, Philippines, Oct. 10, 1936; came to U.S., 1945; d. Walter Curtis and Margaret Louise (Whitfield) T.; m. Alan Martin Cohen, June 22, 1959 (div. Jan. 1972); children: Jonathan Miles, Rachel; m. Robert Earl Hunter, Aug. 19, 1973. BS, Skidmore Coll., 1958; MA, Antioch New Eng., Keene, N.H., 1988. Art tchr. pub. schs. Mass., Ohio, N.H., 1958-85; chem. dependency counselor Beech Hill Hosp., Dublin, N.H., 1987-90; mental health clinician Ea. Aleutian Tribes, Inc., Sand Point, Alaska, 1991-94. Named Mental Health Clinician of Yr. Dept. Social Svcs., State Alaska, 1992.

HUNTER, DUNCAN LEE, congressman; b. Riverside, Calif., May 31, 1948; m. Lynne Layh, 1973; children: Robert Samuel, Duncan Duane. J.D., Western State U., 1976. Bar: Calif. 1976. Practiced in San Diego; mem. 97th Congress from 42d Dist. Calif., 98th-102nd Congresses from 45th Dist. Calif., 103rd Congress from 52nd Dist. Calif.; mem. nat. security com., subcom. mil. installations and facilities, chmn. subcom. on mil. procurement, subcom. on mil. pers. Served with U.S. Army, 1969-71, Vietnam. Decorated Air medal, Bronze Star. Mem. Navy League. Republican. Baptist. *

HUNTER, JUDY ARLENE, pediatrician; b. Detroit, Dec. 24, 1956; d. Arthur Charles Sr. and Nancy Azalee (Burgess) Kirkland; m. Solomon Morris Davis, Sept. 26, 1992. BS with distinction, U. Mich., 1978; MD, Wayne State U., 1983. Diplomate Am. Acad. Pediatrics. Coord. VA Nursing Aid Program, Ann Arbor, Mich., 1977-78; v.p. Black Med. Assn. Wayne State Sch. Medicine, Detroit, 1979-80; resident in pediatrics Children's Hosp. Mich., Detroit, 1983-86, chief resident in pediatrics, 1986-87; pediatrician Bridgeton (N.J.) Area Health Svcs., 1987-91; asst. chief pediatrics Bridgeton div. South Jersey Hosp. System, 1990-91; pediatrician Bay Shore Med. Group, Torrance, Calif., 1990-91. Program dir. Cumberland Teenshop Inc., Bridgeton, 1990-91, west coast regional dir., 1993—; com. mem. African Am. Unity Festival Com., Bridgeton, 1991, Black Hall of Fame-Cumberland County, Bridgeton, 1987-91; mem. A.M.E. Ch. Missionary Soc., 1980-91. Recipient Alumni Acad. scholarship U. Mich., 1975-76. Fellow Am. Acad. Pediatrics; mem. AMA, Am. Med. Student Assn., Nat. Med. Assn., Washington Dubois Investment Group (founding), LIRRA Investment Group (pres., founding mem. 1994—), Phi Beta Pi, Theta Kappa Psi. Democrat. Home: 30437 Rhone Dr Palos Verdes Peninsula CA 90275-5740 Office: Bay Shore Med Group 3565 Del Amo Blvd Torrance CA 90503-1637

HUNTER, KENNETH A., plastic surgeon; b. Manchester, Eng., 1941. MD, Loma Linda U., 1971. Plastic surgeon Redlands Cmty. Hosp. Office: 1150 Brookside Ave Ste K Redlands CA 92373-6303*

HUNTER, LYNN (KOENIG), reporter, historian; b. Artesia, N.Mex., Mar. 4, 1950; d. William Samuel and Betty (Angle) H. BS in Journalism, Ea. N.Mex. U., 1972. Reporter Roswell (N.Mex.) Daily Record, 1972-75; reporter, news editor Clovis (N.Mex.) News-Jour., 1978-80; mng. editor The Pampa (Tex.) News, 1980-82; reporter, news editor Artesia Daily Press, 1983—. Contbr. articles to profl. jours. Recipient Nat. Citation, AP Mng. Editors Assn., 1978, 1st pl. AP Mng. Editors N.Mex., 1987, E.H. Shaffer award N.Mex. Press Assn.; named Hon. Chpt. Farmer, Artesia FFA, 1989, and others. Mem. Lincoln County Hist. Soc. (asst. editor newsletter 1992-94), Friends of Lincoln County Heritage Trust. Home: 1007 W Centre Ct Artesia NM 88210-2603 Office: Artesia Daily Press 503 W Main St Artesia NM 88210-2067

HUNTER, R. HAZE, state legislator; b. Cedar City, Utah, Oct. 5, 1924; m. Betty B. Hunter. Student, U. Utah. Chmn. bd. North East Furniture; pres. NEFCO Fin.; owner B&H Family Ptnr.; Utah state legislator, 1980—; mem. State and Local Affairs standing com., 1981-82, 85-86, 87-88; chmn. Bus. and Consumer Consumer Concerns standing com., 1983-84, mem. 1981-82, 85-86; chmn. Gen. Govt. and Capitol Facilities appropriations com., 1988-89, mem. 1983-84; mem. Bus. Labor and Agriculture appropriations com., 1981-82, 85-86, Bus. Labor and Econ. Devel. standing com., 1987-88, constl. revision com., law and justice adv. com. Bishop, high councilman Ch. of Latter Day Saints. Mem. Iron Mission Park C. of C. (past pres., mem. Southern Utah devel. com.), Lions (past pres. Cedar City chpt., past dist. gov.). Office: 295 S Ridge Rd Cedar City UT 84720-2905

HUNTER, RICHARD WILLIAM, educational director; b. Long Beach, Calif., Aug. 26, 1954; s. Lloyd Lawson and Margaret Elizabeth (Upjohn) H. AA, Chemeketa Community Coll., Salem, Oreg., 1972; BS in Sociology, Willamette U., 1976; MSW, Portland (Oreg.) State U., 1978. Researcher Oreg. Gov.'s Commn. on Youth, Salem, 1973-74; counseling coord. Comprehensive Youth Svcs. Ctr., Salem, 1978-79; social worker Salem Pub. Sch. Dist., 1979-81, Oreg. Children's Svcs. Div., Dallas, 1981-85; social worker supr. Oreg. Children's Svcs. Div., Corvallis, 1985-87; dir. tng. rsch. and tng. ctr. on family support and children's mental health Portland State U., 1987-94, asst. prof. grad. sch. social workers, 1994—; field instr. Western Oreg. State Coll., Monmouth, 1979-81, Portland State U., 1984-85, instr., 1988—. Author: (monograph) Changing Roles, Changing Relationships: Parent-Professional Collaboration on Behalf of Children with Emotional Disabilities, 1988, Parents as Policy Makers, 1994. Mem. adv. com. Oreg. Justice Juvenile, Salem, 1976-80, Salem Youth Commn., 1972-73; chmn. Oreg. Human Resoures Opportunities Coalition, Salem, 1974-75, Oreg. Alliance Social Svc. Workers, Portland, 1981-83, Coalition in Oreg. for Parent Edn. Bd. Dirs.; mem. adv. bd. Oregon Family Support Network. Mem. NASW, Nat. Fedn. Families for Children's Mental Health, Bertha Capen Reynolds Soc. Democrat. Office: Portland State U Grad Sch Social Workers P O Box 751 Portland OR 97207

HUNTER, TIM BRADSHAW, radiologist, educator; b. Balt., Aug. 15, 1943; s. Leo Lauren and Naomi (Bradshaw) H. BA, DePauw U., 1966; MD, Northwestern U., Chgo., 1968; BS, U. Ariz., 1980. Diplomate Am. Bd. Radiology. Fellow, Dept. Radiology, Coll. Medicine U. Ariz., Tucson, 1975, from asst. prof. to prof. radiology, 1975-87, prof., 1987—, dir. Tucson Breast Ctr., 1986-90, dir. Div. of Abdominal Imaging, 1993-94; chief of staff Univ. Med. Ctr., Tucson, Ariz., 1993—; chmn. Soc. for Computer Applications in Radiology, Harrisburg, Pa., 1989; pres. Ariz. Radiological Soc., 1982. Editor: The Computer in Radiology, 1986; sr. editor: Radiologic Guide to Medicial Devices and Foreign Bodies, 1994. Pres. Internat. Dark-Sky Assn., Tucson, 1988—, Tucson Amateur Astronomy Assn., 1989-91. Lt. USN, 1961-71, Vietnam. Am. Coll. Radiology fellow, 1991. Mem. Phi Beta Kappa, Alpha Omega Alpha. Republican. Office: U Ariz Dept Radiology Ahsc 1501 N Campbell Ave N Tucson AZ 85724

HUNTER, TONY (ANTHONY REX HUNTER), molecular biologist, educator; b. Ashford, Kent, Eng., Aug. 23, 1943; came to U.S., 1971; s. Ranulph Rex and Nellie Ruby Elsie (Hitchcock) H.; m. Philippa Charlotte Marrack, July 19, 1969 (div. 1974); m. Jennifer Ann Maureen Price, June 8, 1992; 1 son, Sean Alexander Brocas. BA, U. Cambridge, Eng., 1965, MA, 1966, PhD, 1969. Rsch. fellow Christ's Coll., U. Cambridge, 1968-71, 73-75; rsch. assoc. Salk Inst., San Diego, 1971-73, asst. prof., 1975-78, assoc. prof., 1978-82, prof., 1982—, Am. Cancer Soc. Rsch. Prof., 1992—; adj. prof. biology U. Calif. San Diego, La Jolla, 1982—. Contbr. articles to sci. jours. Recipient award Am. Bus. Found. for Cancer Rsch., 1988, Katharine Berkan Judd award Meml. Sloan-Kettering Cancer Ctr., 1992, Internat. award Gairdner Found., 1994, Hopkins Meml. award Biochem. Soc., 1994, Mott prize GM Cancer Rsch. Found., 1994. Fellow Am. Acad. Arts and Scis., Royal Soc. London, Royal Soc. for Arts, Mfrs. and Commerce; mem. European Molecular Biology Orgn. (assoc.). Home: 4578 Vista De La Patria Del Mar CA 92014 Office: Salk Inst Biol Studies Molecular Biology & Virology Lab 10010 N Torrey Pines Rd La Jolla CA 92037-1002

HUNTER, WILLIAM JAMES, microbiologist; b. N.C., Oct. 12, 1946; s. Fred Sample and Mattie Louise (Strong) H.; m. Shirley Wu, Jan. 15, 1977; 1 child, Christopher. BA, East Carolina U., 1968; PhD, N.C. State U., 1974. Rsch. assoc. N.C. State U., Raleigh, 1974-77; microbiologist USDA-ARS, Ft. Collins, Colo., 1977—. Contbr. chpts. to books and numerous articles to profl. jours.; co-patentee in field. Mem. Am. Soc. Microbiology, Plant Physiology Soc. Am. Office: USDA-ARS 1701 Centre Ave Fort Collins CO 80526-2081

HUNTLEY, ALICE MAE, manufacturing executive; b. Atoka, Okla., May 9, 1917; d. Joseph LaHay and Lula May (Stapp) Howe; BA U. Okla., 1939; m. Loren Clifford Huntley, Nov. 7, 1942; children—Loren Lee, Marcia Lynn. Reporter, McAlester (Okla.) News Capital, 1939-41; sec., asst. to pres. and chmn. bd. N.Am. Aviation, L.A., 1941-63; sec., co-owner Tubular Specialties Mfg., Inc., L.A., 1966-90; retired 1990; Former sec. 1st Baptist Ch. of Westchester; sec. Westchester-Del Rey Republican Women, 1959-60; assoc. mem. Rep. State Cen. Com., 1973. Cert. profl. sec.; named Outstanding Sec. in So. Calif., So. Calif. chpt., 1954, Internat. Sec. of Yr., 1955 (both Nat. Secs. Assn.). Home: 1645 San Pablo Dr San Marcos CA 92069-4715 Office: 13011 S Spring St Los Angeles CA 90061-1633

HUNTLEY, MARK EDWARD, biological oceanographer; b. Seattle, May 7, 1950; s. James Robert Huntley and Patricia Mary (Barricklow) Kissel; m. Patricia Darlene McFarlane, June 21, 1973 (div. 1980); children: Seth, Timothy; m. Kimberly Batcheller Brown, Sept. 19, 1981 (div. 1992); children: Swan Fairchild, Flannery Elizabeth, Zara Eldrith, Fletcher Wells. BSC with honors, U. Victoria, B.C., Can., 1976; PhD, Dalhousie U., Halifax, N.S., Can., 1980. Postdoctoral fellow Inst. Marine Resources, Scripps Instn. Oceanography, U. Calif. San Diego, La Jolla, Calif., 1980-82, asst. rsch. biologist, 1982-84; adj. lecturer Scripps Instn. Oceanography, U. Calif. San Diego, La Jolla, 1984—; asst. rsch. biologist marine biology rsch. div. Scripps Instn. Oceanography, La Jolla, 1984-87, assoc. rsch. biologist, 1987—; pres. Aquasearch, Inc., San Diego, 1984-88, chief oper. officer, 1988-93, CEO, 1993—, also chmn. bd. dirs., 1988—; deputy coord. water rsch. project U. Calif. San Diego, La Jolla, 1988-90; chmn. bd. dirs. Aquasearch, Inc., San Diego, 1984—; chief scientist Rsch. Antarctic Coastal Ecosystem Rates, La Jolla, 1986-87, 89, 91-92; exec. and steering com. mem. Global Ocean Ecosystem Dynamics, Washington, 1989—. Editor: Biological Treatment of Agricultural Wastewater, 1989; inventor Aquasearch Growth Module, 1989. Grantee Nat. Sci. Found. Office Naval Rsch., 1980—. Mem. Am. Soc. Limnology and Oceanography, Oceangraphy Soc. Office: Scripps Instn Oceangraphy 0202 La Jolla CA 92093

HUNTSMAN, EDWARD LOYD, business consultant, marketing executive; b. Farmington, N.Mex., Dec. 19, 1951; s. Arral B and Ann McFarland (Viles) H.; m. Debbie J. Komadina, Aug. 21, 1976; 1 child, Steven Christopher. Student, U. N.Mex., 1973-75; BS in Bus. Adminstrn., Pacific Western U., L.A., 1991, MBA in Mgmt., 1993. Staff instr. U. N.Mex., Gallup, 1976-78; sta. mgr., staff mgr. Frontier Airlines, Denver and Durango, Colo., 1977-85; corp. sales mgr. Tamarron Inn and Country Club, Durango, 1985-86; dir. mktg. Royal West Airlines, Las Vegas, 1986-88; mgr. sales and svc. Am. West Vacations, Tempe, Ariz., 1988-91; bus. and mktg. cons. Total Resource Network, Tempe, 1991—; mktg. cons. Huntsman Graphic Design, Phoenix, 1988—; call ctr. dir. Maxserv, Inc., Scottsdale, Ariz., 1993—. Photographer: Graphic Art Collateral, 1983. Bd. dirs. McKinley County United Way, Gallup, 1976-78; mem. exec. bd. Boy Scouts Am., Las Vegas, 1986-87; staff instr. Police Athletic League, Albuquerque, 1978-80; mem. Durango Area Mktg. Group, 1985-86; elder Presbyn. Ch. U.S.A., Durango, 1985. Sgt. U.S. Army, 1969-73, Viet Nam and Germany. Decorated Army Commendation medal; recipient Outstanding Leadership award Albuquerque Police Athletic League, 1976, Cert. of Merit for stopping a hijacking attempt Air Transp. Assn. Am./FAA, 1983; col., aide-de-camp to Gov. of N.Mex., 1976; named to Outstanding Young Men of Am., 1987. Office: Total Resource Network 2850 S Roosevelt St Tempe AZ 85282-2021

HUNTTING, CYNTHIA COX, artist; b. San Francisco, Sept. 2, 1936; d. E. Morris and Margaret (Storke) Cox; m. Edward Tyler Huntting Jr., Mar. 8, 1969 (div. 1974). BA, Smith Coll., 1958; San Francisco Art Inst., 1959. Artist Emporium White House, San Francisco, 1958-61; artist, staff Pace Program Stanford U., 1962-64; artist World Affairs Council No. Calif., San Francisco, 1964-67; artist pvt. practice San Francisco, 1968—; mem. Modern Art Council Bd. San Francisco Mus. Modern Art, 1970-78. Active Jr. League San Francisco, Inc. Republican. Episcopalian. Clubs: Town and Country, Metropolitan, Calif. Tennis. Home and Office: 2720 Lyon St San Francisco CA 94123-3815

HUPP, HARRY L., federal judge; b. L.A., Apr. 5, 1929; s. Earl L. and Dorothy (Goodspeed) H.; m. Patricia Hupp, Sept. 13, 1953; children: Virginia, Karen, Keith, Brian. AB, Stanford U., 1953, LLB, 1955. Bar: Calif. 1956, U.S. Dist. Ct. (cen. dist.) Calif. 1956, U.S. Supreme Ct. Pvt. practice law Beardsley, Hufstedler and Kemble, L.A., 1955-72; judge Superior Ct. of Los Angeles, 1972-84; appointed fed. dist. judge U.S. Dist. Ct. (cen. dist.) Calif., L.A., 1984—. Served with U.S. Army, 1950-52. Mem. Calif. Bar Assn., Los Angeles County Bar Assn. (Trial Judge of Yr. 1983), Order of Coif, Phi Alpha Delta. Office: US Dist Ct 312 N Spring St Los Angeles CA 90012-4701*

HUPPERT, MERLE CECIL, mechanical engineer; b. Dysart, Iowa, June 29, 1917; s. Edwin Alvertis and Rosa (Gulick) H.; m. Leslie Barbara Little, June 17, 1942; children: Judith, Daniel, Frederick. BSME, Iowa State U., 1942; postgrad., Case Inst. Tech., 1944-47, UCLA, 1957, 62. Mech. engr. NASA Lewis Rsch. Ctr., Cleve., 1942-56, Rocketdyne divsn. Rockwell Internat., Caonga Park, Calif., 1956-70; mgr. turbopump analysis sect. Aerojet Nuclear Sys. Co., Sacramento, 1970-72; surface effects ship performance supr. Aerojet Gen. Corp., Tacoma, 1972-74; mem. R&D staff, mech. engr. Aerojet-Gen. Corp., Liquid Rocket Co., Sacramento, 1974-83; pvt. practice cons. El Dorado Hills, Calif., 1984—. Patentee in field; contbr. articles to profl. publs. Recipient Apollo Achievement award NASA, 1969. ASME (sr.), AIAA, Sons in Retirement. Home: 3535 Mesa Verdes Dr El Dorado Hills CA 95762

HURABIELL, JOHN PHILIP, SR., lawyer; b. San Francisco, June 2, 1947; s. Emile John and Anna Beatrice (Blumenauer) H.; m. Judith Marie Hurabiell, June 7, 1969; children—Marie Louise, Michele, Heather, John Philip Jr. J.D., San Francisco Law Sch., 1976. Bar: Calif. 1977. Sole practice, San Francisco, 1977-86; ptnr. Huppert & Hurabiell, San Francisco, 1985—; pres. San Francisco S.A.F.E., Inc., 1983-88, pres. emeritus 1988—. Treas. Rep. election coms.; 1st v.p. Bling Babies Found., 1989-91, bd. dir., sec., 1995—; bd. dirs. Calif. State Mining and Mineral Mus., 1990-93. With USN, Vietnam. Decorated Navy Commendation Medal. Mem. Calif. Bar Assn., Assn. Trial Lawyers Am., San Francisco Trial Lawyers Assn., Lawyers Club San Francisco, St. Thomas More Soc., St. Francis Hook & Ladder Soc. (trustee). Roman Catholic. Clubs: The Family Ferrari Club Am., Golden Gate Breakfast Club. Lodge: KC, Alhambra (organizing regional dir. 1983-85). Editor, primary author: C.A.L.U. Business Practices Guidelines, rev. edit., 1980. Avocation: racing vintage automobiles. Office: Huppert & Hurabiell 1355 Market St Ste 417 San Francisco CA 94103-1317

HURD, JAMES DANIEL, software and product designer; b. Washington, Jan. 17, 1955; s. James Douglas and Nancy (Schwartz) H. BFA, George Washington U., 1981. Pres. Jim Hurd Design, Washington, 1982-85, San Francisco, 1986-93; pres. Up Software, San Francisco, 1993—. Author: Software: Achieveing Your Career, 1993; co-author software: Jump Start Your Job Skills, 1994; author: Presents Alice, 1990. Recipient nat. graphic design awards in Am. Corp. Identity 5 and 8, Coll. Choice award Insider Mag., 1994. Democrat. Office: Up Software Inc 722 Lombard St Ste 204 San Francisco CA 94133-2300

HURD, PAUL GEMMILL, lawyer; b. Salt Lake City, Nov. 23, 1946; s. Melvin Erskine and Marjorie (Gemmill) H. BS, Portland State U., 1968; JD, Lewis and Clark Coll., 1976. Bar: Oreg. 1976, Wash. 1984, U.S. Dist. Ct. Oreg. 1980, U.S. Ct. Appeals (9th cir.) 1981, U.S. Supreme Ct. 1988. Sr. dep. dist. atty. Multnomah County Dist. Atty., Portland, Oreg., 1976-80; trial counsel Burlington No. R.R., Portland, 1980-84; asst. gen. counsel Freightliner Corp., Portland, 1984-89, assoc. gen. counsel, 1989—. Trustee Leukemia Assn. of Oreg., Portland, 1984-90. Mem. ABA, Oreg. Bar Assn., Wash. Bar Assn., Multnomah Bar Assn., Am. Corp. Counsel Assn. (bd. dirs. N.W. chpt.), Nat. Inst. for Trial Adv. (diplomate 1982). Republican. Presbyterian. Office: Freightliner Corp Legal Dept PO Box 3849 Portland OR 97208-3849

HURLBERT, ROGER WILLIAM, information service industry executive; b. San Francisco, Feb. 18, 1941; s. William G. and Mary (Greene) H.; m. Karen C. Haslag, Nov. 6, 1982; children: Sage, Mica, Chula, Monk, Morris. BS in Community Devel., So. Ill. U., 1965. Newspaper editor and reporter various, San Francisco Bay Area, 1958-62; pvt. practice investigation Ill., 1963-65; advisor San Francisco Planning Urban Rsch. Assn., 1969-87; pres. Sage Info. Svcs., San Francisco, 1988—. Compiler Western States Land Data Base, 1972—. Pres. Haight-Ashbury Neighborhood Coun., San Francisco, 1959-61. With U.S. Army, 1966-68, Vietnam. Recipient Cert. of Merit San Francisco Coun. Dist. Merchants Assn., 1972. Mem. Info. Industry Assn., Direct Mktg. Assn., Mail Advt. Svc. Assn. Internat., League of Men Voters (v.p. 1959—). Democrat. Office: Sage Info Svcs 414 Clement St # 5 San Francisco CA 94118-2367

HURLEY, BRUCE PALMER, artist; b. Tacoma, May 9, 1944; s. Gerald Baynton and Donna Ray (Whealey) H.; m. Ivy Jane Partridge; 1 child, Paul George. BS in Edn., Oreg. Coll. Edn., 1968. Cert. secondary edn. tchr. One-man shows include Goldberg's, 1966, Hillsboro Pub. Libr., 1969, 71, Valley Art Assn., Forest Grove, 1971, 74; group shows include Portland Art Mus., 1970, Northwest Artist Workshop, 1979, Sun Bird Gallery, 1986, Sunriver Juried Show, 1986, 92, Beaverton Arts Showcase, 1990, 91, 92, 93; represented in permanent collections Oreg. Coll., Oriental Medicine, David Wheeler, D.C., Schools Med. Plz., Tigard, Oreg.; author: Planet Ploob Vacation, 1992, Divine Soliloquy, 1994; inventor; numerous paintings, drawings and sculptures. Recipient Cmty. Svc. award Beaverton Arts Commn., 1993, Royal Patronage award Hutt River, Australia, 1995. Mem. Theosophical Soc.

HURLEY, FRANCIS T., archbishop; b. San Francisco, Jan. 12, 1927. Ed., St. Patrick Sem., Menlo Park, Calif., Catholic U. Am. Ordained priest Roman Cath. Ch., 1951; with Nat. Cath. Welfare Conf., Washington, asst. sec., 1958-68; assoc. sec. Nat. Cath. Welfare Conf., now U.S. Cath. Conf., 1968-70; consecrated bishop, 1970; titular bishop Daimlaig and aux. bishop Diocese of Juneau, Alaska, 1970-71; bishop of Juneau, 1971-76, archbishop of Anchorage, 1976—. Office: Archdiocese of Anchorage Chancery Office 225 Cordova St Anchorage AK 99501-2409*

HURLEY, MARK JOSEPH, bishop; b. San Francisco, Dec. 13, 1919; s. Mark J. and Josephine (Keohane) H. Student, St. Joseph's Coll., Mountain View, Calif., 1939, St. Patrick's Sem., Menlo Park, Calif., 1944; postgrad., U. Calif., Berkeley, 1943-45; PhD, Cath. U. Am., 1947; JCB, Lateran U., Rome, 1963; LLD, U. Portland, 1971. Ordained to priest Roman Cath. Ch., 1944. Asst. supt. schs. Archdiocese, San Francisco, 1944-51; tchr. Serra High Sch., San Mateo, Calif., 1944; prin. Bishop O'Dowd High Sch., Oakland, Calif., 1951-58, Marin Cath. High Sch., Marin County, Calif., 1959-61; supt. schs. Diocese, Stockton, Calif., 1962-65; chancellor, diocesan counsultor Diocese, 1962-65; asst. chancellor Arcdiocese, San Francisco, 1965-67; vicar gen. Arcdiocese, 1967-69; titular bishop Thunusuda; aux. bishop Thunusuda, San Francisco, 1967-69; bishop Santa Rosa, Cal., 1969—; pastor St. Francis Assisi Ch., San Francisco, 1967—; prof. grad. schs. Loyola U., Balt., 1946, U. San Francisco, 1948, San Francisco Coll. Women, 1949, Dominican Coll., San Rafael, Calif., 1949, Cath. U. Am., 1954; prof. theology Beda Coll. Rome, 1987—, Angelicum U., Rome, 1989—; Del. Conf. Psychiatry and Religion, San Francisco, 1957; mem. bd. Calif. Com. on Study Edn., 1955-60; cons. Congregation for Cath. Edn., 1986—; del.-at-large Cal., White House Conf. on Youth, 1960; Cath. del., observer Nat. Council Chs., Columbus, Ohio, 1964; del. edn. conf. German and Am. educators, Nat. Cath. Edn. Assn., Munich, Germany, 1960; mem. commns. sems., univs. and schs. II Vatican Council, Rome, 1962-65; mem. commn. Christian formation U.S. Cath. Conf. Bishops, 1968; asst. archdiocesan coordinator Campaign on Taxation Schs. Calif., 1958, Rosary Crusade, 1961; adminstr. Cath. Sch. Purchasing Div., 1948-51, St. Eugene's Ch., Santa Rosa, Calif., 1959, St. John's Ch., San Francisco, 1961; mem. U.S. Bishops' Press Panel, Vatican Council, 1964-65, U.S. Bishops' Com. on Laity, 1964, U.S. Bishops' Com. Cath.-Jewish Relationships, 1965—, U.S. Bishops' Com. on Ecumenical and Interreligious Affairs, 1970, Conf. Maj. Superiors of Men, 1970; chmn. citizens Com. for San Francisco State Coll., 1968—; mem. adminstrn. bd. Nat. Council Cath. Bishops, 1970, mem. nominating com., 1971; mem. Internat.

Secretariat for Non-Believers, Vatican, 1973; chmn. Secretariat for Human Values, Nat. Conf. Cath. Bishops, Washington, 1975; mem. Secretariat for Non-Believers, Vatican, 1986—; Vatican del. World Intellectual Properties Orgn., Washington, 1990; adj. prof. philosophy Grad. Theol. Union, Berkeley, Calif., 1994. Syndicated columnist San Francisco Monitor, Sacramento Herald, Oakland Voice, Yakima (Wash.) Our Times, Guam Diocesan Press, 1949-66, TV speaker and panelist, 1956-67; author: Church State Relationships in Education in California, 1948, Commentary on Declaration on Christian Education in Vatican II, 1966, Report on Education in Peru, 1965, The Church and Science, 1982, Blood on the Shamrock, 1989, The Unholy Ghost, 1992. Trustee N.Am. Coll., Rome, 1970, Cath. U. Am., 1978—, Cath. Relief Services, 1979; cons. Congregation for Edn.; mem. Secretariat for Non-Belief, Vatican City; bd. dirs. Overseas Blind Found. Address: 273 Ulloa St San Francisco CA 94127

HURLEY, REBECCA JOHNSON, marketing professional; b. East Moline, Ill., June 24, 1950; d. Raymond Harold and Alberta (Powell) Ifft; m. James Patrick Hurley, June 7, 1989; stepchildren: James Patrick II, Adrienne. BA in Social Scis. cum laude, Colo. State U., 1972. Dir. pub. rels. Gates Land Co., Colorado Springs, Colo., 1977-88; dir. media rels. U.S. Space Found., Colorado Springs, 1988-89, Concept Comm., Inc., Colorado Springs, 1989-92; rsch. devel. dir. Colorado Springs Cablevision, Colorado Springs, 1992-94; regional mktg. devel. mgr. Century Comm. Corp., Colorado Springs, 1994—; mem. task force EDC Pub. Rels. and Comm., 1986-88, 94. Author: Everyone's Complete Astrology & Horoscope, 1971, Astrology for Men, 1972, Astrology For Women, 1972. Bd. dirs. El Paso County Fair, 1975-78, Pikes Peak Ctr. Bd., 1988 94; adv. bd. Colorado Springs Park and Recreation, 1979-82; active mem. Jr. League of Colorado Springs, 1981-87, Am. Cancer Soc., 1990-93. Recipient Women's Life Festival Woman of Spirit and Note award, 1990. Home: 1817 Pine Grove Ave Colorado Springs CO 80906-2929 Office: Century Comm Corp 100 E Saint Vrain St Ste 100 Colorado Springs CO 80903-1143

HURLEY, THOMAS JEREMIAH, psychiatrist; b. Mpls., July 28, 1922; s. Jeremiah and Louise (Daskoski) H.; m. Etta Lorraine Emery, Oct. 29, 1943; children: Thomas, George, Pamela, Deborah, Linda. BS in chem., U. Oreg., 1947, MD, 1949. Diplomate Am. Bd. Psychiatry & Neurology. Rotating intern Mpls. Gen. Hosp., 1949-50; resident Army Medical Corps., 1950-52; resident psychiatrist Inst. of Living and Yale, 1952-54; assoc. psychiatrist Emory John Brady Hosp., 1954-57; pvt. practice, 1957-85; chief psychiatrist St. Francis Hosp., Colo. Springs, Colo., 1958-68; clinical dir. after care program El Paso County, 1959-70; pvt. practice part-time, 1985—; cons. Internat. Union Printers Home and Hosp., 1976—; active staff Meml. Hosp., Colorado Springs. Capt. U.S. Army, 1950-51. Decorated Bronz Star medal U.S. Army, 1951. Fellow Acad. of Psychosomatic Medicine. Republican. Lutheran. Home and Office: 2008 Crest Haven Cir Colorado Springs CO 80909-2903

HURLOW, RANDAL THOMAS, communications executive; b. Tacoma, July 14, 1962; s. Edward James and Marilyn Ann (Fansler) H. BA in Speech Comms., Western Wash. U., 1986. Comms. asst. Pub. Info. Office Western Wash. U., 1986-88, resident dir. Office Residence Life, 1986-88; dist. exec. dir. S.W. Area Office Am. Cancer Soc., 1986-90, media rels. coord. Washington divsn. Office, 1990-91, dir. comms. Washington divsn. Office, 1991-94; pub. rels. specialist Virginia Mason Med. Ctr., Seattle, 1994—. Mem. Pub. Rels. Soc. Am. (mem. Puget Sound chpt., chmn. pub. rels. primer seminar 1989, chmn. membership com. 1995, participant Totem Awards com., long range planning com., 2 Totem awards 1993, Outstanding New Mem. of Yr. 1989), Kiwanis. Home: 1119 1st Ave # 205 Seattle WA 98101-2934

HURNEY, JEANNE MURACO, public relations executive; b. Cleve., Jan. 8, 1959; d. James Michael and JoAnne Evelyn (Chahulski) Muraco; m. Martin Russell Hurney, Jan. 23, 1988. BA in Polit. Sci., U. Cin., 1981; MA in Journalism and Pub. Affairs, The Am. Univ., 1982. Legis. asst. Rep. Edward F. Feighan, Washington, 1982-83; asst. to dir. internat. affairs Hill and Knowlton, Washington, 1983; comms. specialist AARP, Washington, 1984; editor, reporter The Washington Times, 1985-89; pres. JMH, San Diego, Washington, 1989-93; dir. mktg. and pub. rels. Helen Woodward Animal Ctr., Rancho Santa Fe, Calif., 1993—. Mem. Pub. Rels. Soc. Am., Profl. Ski Instrs. Am. Office: Helen Woodward Animal Ctr. PO Box 64 Rancho Santa Fe CA 92067-0064

HURST, C. GRANT, bank executive, state agency administrator; m. Lucille; children: Heidi Hurst Richards, Jason, Jeff. Various pos. Valley State Bank, 1961-71, v.p., cashier, 1971-80, branch adminstr., 1980-88, with comml. dept., 1988—; sr. v.p. Bank One. Active Sandy City Coun., The Salt Lake Water Conservancy Bd.; past chmn. State Bd. Edn., 1991—, bishop 1978-83, high councilor 1983-89; singer, actor in cmty. and regional theaters. Office: State Office of Edn 250 E 500 S Salt Lake City UT 84111-3204*

HURT, CHARLIE DEUEL, III, library school director, educator; b. Charlottesville, Va., Sept. 20, 1950; s. Charlie Deuel Jr. and Timie Oletta (Young) H.; m. Susan Edith Scudamore, May 15, 1981. BA, U. Va., 1971; MLS, U. Ky., 1975; PhD, U. Wis., 1981. Engring. librarian U. Va., Charlottesville, 1975-78, automation librarian, 1977-78; asst. prof. McGill U., Montreal, Que., Can., 1981-84, assoc. prof., 1984; assoc. prof. Simmons Coll., Boston, 1984-86; dir., prof. lib. sch. U. Ariz., Tucson, 1986—; prin. Info. Prime, Montreal, 1984—; cons. Scudamore & Assocs. Montreal, 1984-85. Author: Information Sources in Science and Technology, 1994; co-author: Scientific and Technical Literature, 1990; contbr. articles to profl. jours. Hollowell grantee Simmons Coll., 1984. Mem. ALA, IEEE, Am. Math Soc., Assn. Library and Info. Sci. Edn., History Sci. Soc., N.Y. Acad. Sci. Home: 1820 W Wimbledon Way Tucson AZ 85737-9070 Office: U Ariz Sch Libr Sci 1515 E 1st St Tucson AZ 85719-4505

HURVITZ, JAMES S., plastic surgeon; b. Santa Monica, Calif., Feb. 21, 1947. MD, U. So. Calif., 1973. Instr., plastic surgeon L.A. County U. So. Calif. Med. Ctr. Office: 724 E 2021 Santa Monica Blvd Santa Monica CA 90404-2208*

HURWITZ, GEORGE K., allergist; b. San Francisco, Calif., 1931. MD, U. Calif., San Francisco, 1954. Allergist John Muir Hosp., Walnut Creek, Calif.; also prof. U. San Francisco. Office: 85 Southwind Cir Richmond CA 94804-7405*

HURWITZ, LAWRENCE NEAL, investment banking company executive; b. Austin, Tex., Mar. 21, 1939; s. John and Sarah Ruth (Blumenthal) H.; m. Kathleen O'Day, Feb., 1977 (div. Dec. 1935); 1 child, Kimberlee Colleen; m. Mynette Lee, Nov., 1989; 1 child, Jonathan Lee. Student, U. Tex., 1957-59; MBA with distinction, Harvard U., 1961. With rsch. dept. Harvard U., 1961-62; asst. to v.p. Atlantic Rsch. Corp., 1962-65; comptr. TelAutograph Corp., 1965; dir. Gen. Artists Corp., 1965-69; pres. Sprayregen & Co., N.Y.C., 1969-83; chmn. Country Junction, Inc., 1969-82; mktg. dir. Beneflex, Inc., 1985-86; v.p. Tech. Liberation Capital, Inc., Houston, 1986-89, Amex Systems, Houston, 1986-89; v.p., chief fin. officer Intile Designs, Inc., Houston, 1989; pres. Lawrence Fin. Ptnrs., Newport Beach, Calif., 1990—; vice chmn., mem. exec. com. Empire Life Ins. Co. Am.; dir., mem. exec. com. Old Town Corp., Stratton Group Ltd., Sayre & Fisher Co., Tech. Tape, Inc., DFI Communications Inc., Columbia Gen. Corp., Cal. Data Systems Corp.; dir. Indsl. Electronic Hardware Corp., Bloomfield Bldg. Industries, Inc., Apollo Industries, Inc., Aberdeen Petroleum Corp., Investors Book Club, Inc., Ling Fund, Am. Land Co., Terrific Nutrient & Chem. Corp., N. Lake Corp., Datatronics, Inc., Merada Industries, Inc., AK Electric Corp., Aerocon, Inc., Hallmark Communications, Inc., Detroit Gray Iron & Steel Foundries, Inc., Fin. Tech., Inc., Wid's Films & Film Folks, Investors Preferred Life Ins. Co., Langdon Group, Inc., Essex Systems Corp., Chelsea Nat. Bank, Newport Chem. Industries, Inc. Editor: How to Invest in Letter Stock, 1970, Spin-Offs and Shells, 1970. Mem. Harvard Bus. Sch. Club, Bay Area Execs. Club, B'nai Brith (pres. W. Houston lodge), Harvard Club (v.p. Orange County). Jewish. Home: 701 Teakwood Rd Los Angeles CA 90049-1327 Office: PO Box 491773 Los Angeles CA 90049-8773

HUSEIN, FIROZ, airport terminal executive; b. 1946. Student, U. Bombay, 1965-69; MS, Brigham Young U., 1971. With Varco-Pruden, Holbrook, Mass., 1970-77, Varco-Pruden Builder, Fresno, Calif., 1977-79; pres. Span Constrn. & Engring. Inc., Madera, Calif., 1979—. Office: Corp Aircraft Inc 4885 E Shields Ave Fresno CA 93726-6420*

HUSIC, FRANK, management consultant; b. 1948. Tchr. bus. Wharton Sch., 1969-74; sr. v.p. Alliance Capital Mgmt., San Francisco, 1974-86; also bd. dirs. Alliance Capital Mgmt.; with Husic Capital Mgmt., 1986—. Office: Husic Capital Management 555 California St San Francisco CA 94104-1502*

HUSKEY, HARRY DOUGLAS, information and computer science educator; b. Whittier, N.C., Jan. 19, 1916; s. Cornelius and Myrtle (Cunningham) H.; m. Velma Elizabeth Roeth, Jan. 2, 1939 (dec. Jan. 1991); children: Carolyn, Roxanne, Harry Douglas, Linda; m. Nancy Grindstaff, Sept. 10, 1994. BS, U. Idaho, 1937; student, Ohio U., 1937-38; MA, Ohio State U., 1940, PhD, 1943. Temp. prin. sci. officer Nat. Phys. Labs., Eng., 1947; head machine devel. lab. Nat. Bur. Standards, 1948; asst. dir. Inst. Numerical Analysis, 1948-54; asso. dir. computation lab. Wayne U., Detroit, 1952-53; asso. prof. U. Calif., Berkeley, 1954-58, prof., 1958-68, vice chmn. elec. engring., 1965-66; prof. info. and computer sci. U. Calif., Santa Cruz, 1968-85, prof. emeritus, 1985—; dir. Computer Center, 1968-77, chmn. bd. info. sci., 1976-79, 82-83; vis. prof. Indian Inst. Tech., Kanpur; (Indo-Am. program), 1963-64, 71, Delhi U., 1971; cons. computer div. Bendix, 1954-63; vis. prof. M.I.T., 1966; mem. computer sci. panel NSF, Naval Research Adv. Com.; cons. on computers for developing countries UN, 1969-71; chmn. com. to advise Brazil on computer sci. edn. NAS, 1970-72; project coord. UNESCO/Burma contract, 1973-79; mem. adv. com. on use microcomputers in developing countries NRC, 1983-85. Co-editor: Computer Handbook, 1962. Recipient Disting. Alumni award Idaho State U., 1978, Pioneer award Nat. Computer Conf., 1978, IEEE Computer Soc., 1982; U.S. sr.scientist awardee Fulbright-Alexander von Humboldt Found., Mathematisches Institut der Tech. U. Munich, 1974-75, 25th Ann. medal ENIAC; inducted into U. Idaho Alumni Hall of Fame, 1989. Fellow AAAS, ACM, IEEE (edit. bd., editor-in-chief computer group 1965-71, Centennial award 1984), Brit. Computer Soc.; mem. Am. Math. Soc., Math. Assn. Am., Assn. Computing Machinery (pres. 1960-62), Am. Fedn. Info. Processing Socs. (governing bd. 1961-63), Sigma Xi. Home: 102 Gristmill Ter Spartanburg SC 29307 Office: U Calif Computer & Info Sci Santa Cruz CA 95064

HUSS, CHARLES MAURICE, municipal building official; b. Chgo., Nov. 11, 1946; s. Charles Maurice and June Pierce (Bailey) H.; m. Winifred Louise Traughber, Dec. 24, 1973; children: Amber Elaine, Ra Ja Lorraine, Micah Alexander, Gabriel Joe, Cameron M., Jordan Charles. AA, Kendall Coll., 1984; student Chukchi Community Coll., 1978-83, Oregon State U., 1985, Western Oreg. State Coll., 1984-89, U. Cin., 1985—, U. Alaska, Western Ill. U., 1987, City U., 1986, Nat. Fire Acad., 1986-88, Ohio U., 1989—. Traffic mgr. The Harwald Co., Evanston, Ill., 1966-67, asst. v.p., 1968-69; traffic mgr. Northwestern U. Press, Evanston, 1969-71; fire chief City of Kotzebue, Alaska, 1971-76, asst. city mgr., 1973-76; dir. maintenance USPHS Hosp., Kotzebue, 1976-79; pres., gen. mgr. Action Builders, Inc., Kotzebue, 1979-82; gen. mgr. Husky Maintenance Svcs., 1982—; chief bldg. insp. City of Kotzebue, 1985—; adj. faculty Nat. Fire Acad., Emmitsburg, Md. Guest essayist Seven Days and Sunday (Kirkpatrick), 1973; contbr. to Alaska Craftsman Home Building Manual. Chmn. Kotzebue Planning Commn., 1978-82, Kotzebue Sch. Bd., 1974-79, 83—; founding vice chmn. Kotzebue chpt. ARC; mem. Alaska Criminal Code Revision Commn., 1976-78; mem. Fire Marshal's Sprinkler Task Force; mem. Alaska Fire Fighter Tng. Commn.; mem. Arctic Fire Mitigation Code Task Force, Statewide Bldg. Code Task Force, Alaska Housing Fin. Corp. Bldg. Inspector Standards Task Force; asst. chief Kotzebue Vol. Fire Dept., 1972-76, 82—; bd. dirs, instr. Alaska Craftsman Home Program 1986—; instr. Kotzebue Regional Fire Tng. Ctr., 1982—. Pullman Found. scholar, 1964-65, Blackburn Coll. scholar, 1964-65, Ill. State scholar, 1964-66. Mem. ASHRAE, Am. Constrn. Inspectors Assn. (registered constrn. inspector, engring. divsn., bldg. divsn., mech., elec., med. gas divsns.), Alaska Assn. for Computers in Edn., Constrn. Specifications Inst., Internat. Soc. Fire Svc. Instrs., Fire Marshals Assn. N.Am., Bldg. Ofcls. and Code Adminstrs. Internat., Alaska Firefighters Assn., Internat. Assn. Fire and Arson Investigators, Assn. Fire Protection Designers, Western Fire Chiefs Assn., Internat. Conf. Bldg. Ofcls. (cert. bldg. ofcl., fire, plumbing, elec., combination dwelling and mech. insp.; accessibility specialist, sprayed fireproofing and plan rev. inspector), Am. Soc. Safety Engrs., Internat. Assn. Plumbing and Mech. Ofcls., Internat. Assn. Elec. Insps., Internat. Assn. Fire Chiefs, Bldg. Officials and Code Adminstrs. Internat., So. Bldg. Code Cong. Internat., Earthquake Engring. Rsch. Inst., Home Builders Assn. Alaska, Nat. Fire Protection Assn., Soc. Nat. Fire Acad. Instrs., Coalition for Home Fire Safety, Masonry Soc., Kotzebue C. of C. Home and Office: PO Box 277 Kotzebue AK 99752-0277

HUSSAIN, SHAKEELA FATIMA, internist; b. Hyderabad, India; came to U.S., 1977; d. Arif Husain and Rasheeda (Fatima) Arastu; m. Mukarram Hussain, Jan. 7, 1981. AA, Glendale C.C., 1981; BS in Biochemistry, UCLA, 1982; MD, Wayne State U., 1988. Diplomate Am. Bd. Internal Medicine, Nat. Bd. Med. Examiners; lic. physician, Calif. Rsch. ssoc. tissue typing lab. UCLA Sch. Medicine, 1984-88; fellow in tranfusion medicine dept. physiology Sch. Medicine Wayne State U., Detroit, 1985; resident in internal medicine Primary Care Track, Henry Ford Hosp., Detroit, 1988-91; internist Buenaventura Med. Clin., Camarillo, Calif., 1991—. Ednl. vol. Am. Cancer Soc., Glendale, Calif., 1979-82. Recipient Ernestine Rose Meml. award, 1979, 80, Bank of Am. award for sci., 1980; Calif. State scholar, 1980-82. Mem. AMA, ACP. Office: Buenaventura Med Clinic 86 Daily Dr Camarillo CA 93010-5803

HUSTON, HARRIETTE IRENE OTWELL (REE HUSTON), retired county official; d. Harry C. Otwell and Fannie (Mitchell) Otwell Geffert; m. Dan E. Huston, Jan. 21, 1951; children: Terry Dane, Dale Curtis, Ronald William, Randall Philip. BS, Kans. State Coll., 1951. Cert. life ins. agt., Wash.; cert. wastewater operator in tng., Wash. Tchr. Kans., Ill., 1955-68; assoc. home economist McCall's Patterns Co., N.Y.C., 1959-62; counselor, owner Dunhill of Seattle Personnel, 1968-75; enrollment officer, trainer, adminstrv. sec. Teller Tng. Insts., Seattle, 1975-76; life and health ins. agt. Lincoln Nat. Sales, Seattle, 1976-77; office mgr., adminstrv. sec. ARA Transp. Group, Seattle, 1977-78; asst. to the pres. Pryde Corp., Bellevue, Wash., 1978-80; sr. sec. Municipality of Met. Seattle, 1980-92, project asst., 1992-93; adminstrv. specialist II King County Dept. Met. Svcs. (formerly Municipality of Met., 1993-95; ret., 1995. Co-author: Homemaking textbook, 1956; contbr. articles to profl. jours.. Sec. exec., mem. gen. bd. Bellevue Christian Ch., Disciples of Christ, 1976-77, 86-87, chmn. flowers com., 1978-83, elder, 1978, deacon, 1987; bd. dirs., sec. Surrey Downs Comty. Club, Bellevue, 1983-85; mem. choir Sequim Presbyn. Ch., 1994—; vol. leader, coord. Linking Home and Sch. Through the Workplace, 1992-93. Recipient Clothing award check McCall's Patterns Co., N.Y.C., 1962, Certs. of Merit Metro Hdqrs., Seattle, 1981, 82, 83, 86, 89. Mem. Bellevue Bridge Club. Home: 1783 E Sequim Bay Rd Sequim WA 98382-8675

HUSTON, MARK LOUIS, economics educator; b. San Francisco, Dec. 5, 1951; s. ARthur Robert and Doris June (Crouch) H.; m. Anne Beyer (div. 1980); 1 child, Lauren Suzanne; m. Edel Corla Savage, Sept. 30, 1982; 1 child, Mardel Leyland. BA in Bus., U. San Francisco, 1977; MA in Econs., U. Pitts., 1979; MBA in Bus. Adminstrn., Calif. Coast U., 1987, PhD in Bus. Adminstrn., 1994. Med. adminstrn. specialist USAF, 1970-74; supr. data processing Pacific Mut. Ins. Co., Curte Madra, Calif., 1974-77; asst. fellow U. Pitts., 1977-79; sr. forecast analyst General Tire & Rubber, Akron, Ohio, 1979-81; supr., mgmt. cons. Arabian Bechtel, Jubail, Saudi Arabia, 1981-83; sr. cons., pres. Bus. and Econ. Svcs., San Rafael, Calif., 1983-89; regional v.p. IMPAC, Litchfield, Calif., 1989-90; assoc. prof. econs. San Diego-Mesa Coll., San Diego, 1990—. Author: Executive Computer Literacy, 1986, Drug Abuse-Client-Pay Programs: Insurance Billing Intake and Billing Handbook, 1986, Economic Principles and Course Notes, 1st edit., 1992, 2d edit., 1993; producer World War II Film series, 1993. Sgt. USAF, 1970-74. Mem. Am. Fedn. Tchr., Am. Legion. Republican. Home: 2750 Wheatstone St # 146 San Diego CA 92111-5447 Office: Mesa Coll 7520 Mesa College Dr San Diego CA 92111-5000

HUSZCZUK VEL HUSZCZA, ANDREW RICHARD, physiologist; b. Wilno, Poland, Oct. 7, 1939; came to U.S., 1979; s. Leon and Jadwiga (Oladowska) H.; m. Teresa Lada, June 7, 1973 (div. June 1983); 1 child, Paulina; m. Beata Brzezinski, July 21, 1990, 1 child, Agata. MSc, Warsaw (Poland) Poly., 1964; PhD, Polish Acad. Scis., Warsaw, Poland, 1972. Rsch. asst. Polish Acad. Scis., Warsaw, Poland, 1964-66, sr. rsch. asst., 1967-69, chief designer, 1970-72, asst. prof., 1973-79; vis. scientist Harbor-UCLA Med. Ctr., Torrance, Calif., 1979-82, rsch. assoc., 1982-88, assoc. rschr., 1988-93; dir. R & D Vacumetrics, Ventura, Calif., 1993—; vol. rsch. prof. Calif. State U., Long Beach, 1993—; rsch. fellow U. Oxford, U.K., 1968-69; dir. Medipan Sci. Instruments, Warsaw, 1972-73; postdoctoral rsch. fellow Charring Cross Hosp. Med. Sch., London, 1973-74. Contbr. numerous articles to Jour. of Physiology, Jour. of Applied Physiology and others; patentee in field. Recipient Sci. award of the Yr., Polish Acad. Scis., 1970; grantee Am. Lung Assn., 1982-83, Am. Heart Assn., 1982-84, NIH, 1985-88. Mem. Am. Physiol. Soc., Am. Heart Assn. Office: Vacumetrics 4483 Mcgrath St Ventura CA 93003-7737

HUTCHENS, JOHN GREGORY, engineering/management consultant; b. Denver, June 16, 1960; s. John Raymond and Delores Marie (Schoepf) H.; m. Carol Lynn Zanmiller, Aug. 10, 1991; 1 child, Zoe Elizabeth. BS in Electronic Engring. Tech., DeVry Tech. Inst., 1982; MS in Mgmt., Boston U., 1991. Registered profl. engr., Colo. Mem. tech. staff Hughes Aircraft Space and Comm., Elsegundo, Calif., 1982-88; sr. rsch. engr. Lockheed Missiles and Space, Eng., 1988-94; assoc., cons. Booz-Allen & Hamilton, Colorado Springs, Colo., 1994—. Mem. IEEE. Home: 3940 Regency Dr Colorado Springs CO 80906-4319 Office: Booz Allen & Hamilton 1050 S Academy Blvd Colorado Springs CO 80910-3924

HUTCHERSON, CHRISTOPHER ALFRED, marketing, recruiting, and educational consultant; b. Memphis, June 13, 1950; s. Wayne Alfred Hutcherson and Loretta (Morris) Kindsfather; m. Glenda Ann Champ, May 22, 1971. BS, U. Houston, 1972, MA in Adminstrn., 1977, postgrad., 1977-79. Cert. tchr. and adminstr., Tex. Pvt. music instr. Spring Br. and Pasadena Ind. Sch. Dists., Tex., 1968-75; jr. high and high sch. band dir. Deer Park (Tex.) Ind. Schs., 1972-80; recruiter M. David Lowe Personnel, Houston, 1981; sales dir. Instl. Financing Svcs., Benicia, Calif., 1982-85; sales mgr. Instl. Financing Svcs., Benicia, 1985-87; nat. tng. dir. Champion Products and Svcs., San Diego, 1987-88, west coast and midwest sales mgr., 1988-89; pres. Camelot, Inc., Auburn, Calif., 1989-91; pres., CEO Camelot Telephone Assistance Program, Inc., Folsom, Calif., 1991-92; nat. dir. sales and mktg. edn. and devel. Nat. Scrip Ctr., Inc., 1992—; fund raising cons. non-profit orgns., 1982—; speaker in field. Judge Tex. jr. high and high sch. bands, 1974-81, regional band chmn. 1973-77; choir dir. St. Hyacinth Ch., Deer Park, 1979-81; vice chmn. Ch. Coun. St. Hyacinth Ch., 1980; founder Tex. Region XIX Jr. High Band Competition, 1973 (Spl. Achievement award 1979); 1st chair Clarient Tex. All-State Band, 1968. Mem. Kappa Kappa Psi (v.p. Outstanding Mem. award 1970). Republican. Roman Catholic. Home: 14105 Lodestar Dr Grass Valley CA 95949-8362

HUTCHESON, JERRY DEE, manufacturing company executive; b. Hammon, Okla., Oct. 31, 1932; s. Radford Andrew and Ethel Mae (Boulware) H.; B.S. in Physics, Eastern N. Mex. U., 1959; postgrad. Temple U., 1961-62, U. N.Mex., 1964-65; m. Lynda Lou Weber, Mar. 6, 1953; children—Gerald Dan, Lisa Marie, Vicki Lynn. Research engr. RCA, 1959-62; sect. head Motorola, 1962-63; research physicist Dikewood Corp., 1963-66; sr. mem. tech. staff Signetics Corp., 1966-69; engring. mgr. Litton Systems, Sunnyvale, Calif., 1969-70; engring. mgr. Fairchild Semiconductor, Mountain View, Calif., 1971; equipment engr., group mgr. Teledyne Semiconductor, Mountain View, 1971-74; dir. engring. DCA Reliability Labs., Sunnyvale, 1974-75; founder, prin. Tech. Ventures, San Jose, Calif., 1975—; chief exec. officer VLSI Research, Inc., 1981—. Democratic precinct committeeman, Albuquerque, 1964-66. Served with USAF, 1951-55. Registered profl. engr., Calif. Mem. Nat. Soc. Profl. Engrs., Profl. Engrs. Pvt. Practice, Calif. Soc. Profl. Engrs., Semiconductor Equipment and Materials Inst., Soc. Photo-Optical Instrumentation Engrs., Am. Soc. Test Engrs., Presbyterian. Club: Masons. Contbr. articles to profl. jours. Home: 5950 Vista Loop San Jose CA 95124-6562 Office: VSLI Rsch 1754 Technology Dr Ste 117 San Jose CA 95110-1308

HUTCHINGS, DALE, realtor; b. Bakersfield, Calif., Mar. 23, 1954; s. Cleave and Effie Letha (Wheeler) H.; m. Mary Georgette Coder, Oct. 11, 1975; children: Christina Renee, Cheryl Anne. AA, Bakersfield Jr. Coll., 1982; diploma, Universal Tech. Inst., 1983; BA, Calif. State U., Bakersfield, 1990, MA, 1992. Sales rep. Am. Nat. Ins., Bakersfield, 1976-80; claim adjuster Gen. Adjustment Bureau Bus. Svcs., Ind., Bakersfield, 1985; dist. office adjuster Auto Club of So. Calif., Bakersfield, 1985-87; internrisk mgmt. dept. Am. Soc. Pub. Administrs., Bakersfield, 1990-91; grad. intern County Adminstrv. Office, Bakersfield, 1991-93; realtor Prudential Am. West, Bakersfield, 1993-95, Watson Realty Co., Bakersfield, 1995—. Vol. fundraiser Kern County Shrine Club, Bakersfield, 1989. Mem. ASPA (bd. dirs. 1991-92, scholar 1990-91), Internat. City Mgrs. Assn., Pub. Risk Mgmt. Assn., Masons (jr. deacon 1989, marshall 1990, 32 degree), Knights Templar Calif. (Sir Knight), Al Malaikah Temple (Noble, fundraiser 1988). Republican. Mem. Religious Sci. Ch. Home: 6808 Caswell Ave Bakersfield CA 93309-3408 Office: Watson Realty Co 5501 Stockdale Hwy Bakersfield CA 93309

HUTCHINGS, LEANNE VON NEUMEYER, communications executive, research consultant, writer; b. L.A.; d. F. Louis and Greta Catherine (Clifford) von Neumeyer; children: Marc Lane, Kristin LeAnne, Michael Lane, Jamie Laird, Jeremy Leif, Breton Louis. Student Brigham Young U., 1962. Rschr., writer, owner Heritage Tree, Arcadia, Calif., 1970—; internat. bd. advisors, dir. protocol, mem. scholarship grant review com. Neeley Scholarship Found., 1988-89; dir. pub. communications Ch. of Jesus Christ of Latter-day Saints, Foothill and Glendale regions, Calif., 1975-92, dir. cmty. rels., 1984-92, asst. dir. area coun., 1984; adminstrv. asst. dir. grant propsal review com. Calif. Pub. Affairs Dept., L.A., 1990—; seminar coord. R.E.D.I., Inc., L.A., 1982-91, corp. rels. dir., 1984-91; design cons. H.M.J. Time & Eternity Collection, L.A., 1985—; dir. Rexall Internat., 1995—; mem. nat. adv. coun. motion picture studio Brigham Young U., Provo, Utah, 1986-89; adminstrv. dir. Pasadena Geneal. Libr., Calif., 1977-82; writer, co-producer KBIG, Sideband Div. Radio, L.A., 1979-80; exec. assoc adminstr. Calif. Bicentennial Found. for the U.S. Constitution, 1987; regional cons. Latter-Day Sentinel Newspaper, L.A., 1985-89; mem. Scholarship Found., L.A., 1985-89, exec. dir., 1988-89; mem. Brigham Young U. Marriott Sch. Bus. Mgmt. Soc., L.A., 1990—; mem. com. on child pornography legis. chmn. pub. info. portfolio com., 1988-91, L.A. County Commn. on Obscenity & Pornography, 1988-91, artist. Author: Honored Heritage, 1975, Woman's Place of Honor, 1976, Prologue and Tapestry, 1976, Moments with the Prophets, 1977, Southern California: The Earthquake Threat, 1981, Quake!: Preparing Home, Family and Community, 1982, The Peregrine Papers, 1986; columnist HeritageTree Foothill Intercity News, Knight-Ridder Pub., 1977-79; contbg. writer Women's Exponent Southern Calif. edit.; Sentinel; journalism series, 1978-80; also articles, collected works, stage trilogy; art exhibits include Wilshire Alma Exhibit, 1985, The Grand Artists Hall, 1986-88. Pres. Daus. Utah Pioneers-Los Angeles County, 1983-85; dir. protocol L.A. County Law Enforcement Conf., 1990; dir. recept. protocol State of Calif. Law Enforcement Conf. of Child Porngraphy, 1990; chmn. So. Calif. Task Force on Pornography, 1989-92; instr. earthquake preparedness and survival Arcadia chpt. ARC, L.A., 1983-85; mem. Cmty. Coordinating Coun., Arcadia, 1983-86; mem. exec. bd. Calif. Utah Women, L.A., 1977-79, 85-86, chmn. L.A. County Commn. Pub. Rels. Portfolio, 1988; exec. dir. Neeley Scholarship Found., 1989-91; coord. planning com. California '96: One Hundred Fifty Years LDS Sequicentennial, 1994—; display coord. L.A. Temple Hill Visitors Ctr., 1994—; lineage rsch. dir. von Neumeyer-Burches & Assocs., 1992—. Recipient Best of Exhibit award Sculptor's West Workshop, 1982, cert. of recognition L.A. County, 1989, cert. appreciation L.A. County, 1990. Mem. Assn. Latter-Day Media Artists (assoc. editor Voice of ALMA 1978-83, exec. bd. 1977-81, chmn. spl. events, 1985-90, internat. bd. govs. fellow 1981-83), Am. Film Inst., LDS Bookseller's Assn., Deseret Bus. and Profl. Assn., Marriott Bus. Mgmt. Soc. (L.A. chpt.), Assn. L.D.S. Pub. Rels. Profls., Pub. Rels. Soc. Am. (L.A. chpt.), Nat. Mus. Women in the Arts (charter), Arcadia Tournament of Roses Assn., Arcadia C. of C. (chmn. industry commn. of women's div. 1983-85, mem. exec. bd. 1985-86), Internat. Platform Assn. Republican. Mem. Ch. of Jesus Christ of Latter-Day Saints. Avocations: sculpting, oil painting. Office: 1591 E Temple Way Los Angeles CA 90024-5801

HUTCHINS, EARL LEROY, retired school system administrator; b. Deer Park, Wash., Nov. 26, 1908; s. Harry Merton and May Edith (Burroughs) H.; m. Helen Lucile Weeks, Aug. 27, 1934 (dec. May 1978); children: Linda Mary, Stephen Weeks, Patrick Earl; m. Betty Soule Hazen, June 11, 1979. BA in Edn., Western Wash. U., 1941; MA, Stanford U., 1951. Program dir. State of Wash., Longview, 1957-59; adminstrv. asst. Longview Pub. Schs., 1959-61, asst. supt., 1961-74; retired, 1974. Chmn. publicity com. Longview Sr. Ctr., 1986-88; pres. Longview Kiwanis Club, 1957. Wash. Edn. Assn. (pres. Skamokawa, Wash. chpt. 1937-38). Home: 575 Peardale Ln # 9 Longview WA 98632-3255

HUTCHINS, JEFFREY CARLTON, protective services official; b. Coronado, Calif., May 28, 1959; s. Carlton Leroy and Lucille (Cash) H.; m. Patricia Lynn Palmer, Feb. 16, 1980; children: Ashleigh Lynne, Emily Erin, Glenell Renee, Kendall Marie. AS in Criminal Justice, Southwestern Calif. Coll., Chula Vista, 1983. Dispatcher City of Coronado Police Dept., 1977-80, police officer, 1980-86, police investigator, 1986-89, police sgt., 1989—; rep. City of San Diego County Disaster Coun., 1986-89; mem. So. Calif. Emergency Svcs. Assn., 1986-89. Cons.: (book) Emergency Planning Guidelines for Local Law Enforcement, 1989. Mem. Calif. Police Officers Assn., Coronado Police Officers Assn. (sec., treas. 1977-80), Fraternal Order of Police, Amateur Radio League, Coronado Kiwanis. Republican. Methodist. Office: Coronado Police Dept 578 Orange Ave Coronado CA 92118-1827

HUTCHINS, JOHN MILTON, lawyer; b. Washington, Dec. 5, 1950; s. Edward John and Majorie Dolores (Wiegert) H.; m. Dale Denise Ockl; 1 child, Adam Edward. BA, U. Colo., 1973, JD, 1976. Bar: Colo. 1976, Tex. 1980, U.S. Ct. Mil. Appeals 1978, U.S. Supreme Ct. 1983. Asst. city atty. City of El Paso, Tex., 1982; asst. Colo. atty. gen. Colo. Office of Atty. Gen., Denver, 1982-84, 1st asst. Colo. atty. gen., 1984-90; asst. U.S. atty. dist. of Colo. U.S. Atty.'s Office, Denver, 1990—. Contbr. articles to profl. publs. Mem. Northglenn (Colo.) City Charter Commn., 1975, Northglenn City Coun., 1976-77; grand juror Adams County, Colo. Grand Jury, Brighton, 1988. Maj. U.S. Army, 1977—. Mem. Denver Posse of Westerners (sec. 1989-90, v.p. 1992—), State Bar of Tex., Colo. Bar Assn. Republican. Presbyterian. Office: Office of US Atty 1961 Stout St Denver CO 80294-0101

HUTCHINS, ROBERT BRUCE, lawyer; b. Audubon, Iowa, Nov. 22, 1953; s. Leslie D. and Carma I. (Hogueisson) H.; m. Marla A. Nelson, Aug. 20, 1988; 1 child, Grant N. BA, Yale U., 1975; JD, UCLA, 1988. Bar: Calif. 1988, U.S. Dist. Ct. (ctrl. dist.) Calif. 1989, U.S. Dist. Ct. (so. dist.) Calif. 1992, U.S. Tax Ct. 1990, U.S. Ct. Appeal (9th cir.) 1992. Asst. editor Anchor Press/Doubleday, N.Y.C., 1976-79; editor Facts on File, N.Y.C., 1979-82; atty. Jeffer, Mangels, Butler & Marmaro, L.A., 1988—. Mem. ABA, State Bar Calif., Los Angeles County Bar Assn., Assn. Bus. Trial Lawyers. Democrat. Office: Jeffer Mangels Butler & Marmaro 2121 Avenue Of The Stars Los Angeles CA 90067-5010

HUTCHINSON, CHARLES SMITH, JR., book publisher; b. Topeka, Oct. 17, 1930; s. Charles S. and Cecil Marguerite (Weidenhamer) H.; m. Elizabeth Dunbar Hall, June 16, 1956; children: Amy Elizabeth, Todd Charles. B.A., Principia Coll., 1952. Editor-in-chief, sec., dir. Burgess Pub. Co., Mpls., 1955-65; editor-in-chief coll. and profl. books Reinhold Book Corp., N.Y.C., 1965-68; editor-in-chief profl. and reference books Van Nostrand Reinhold Co., N.Y.C., 1968-70; pres., chmn. bd. Dowden, Hutchinson and Ross, Inc., Stroudsburg, Pa., 1970-78, v.p., sec., 1978-80; v.p. Hutchinson Ross Pub. Co., Stroudsburg, 1980-83; sci. pub. Van Nostrand Reinhold Co., N.Y.C., 1984-86; mng. dir. Hutchinson Assocs., Prescott, Ariz., 1987-91; pres. Geosci. Press, Inc., Phoenix, 1989—, Harbinger House, Inc., Tucson, 1992-94; mng. ptnr. Picacho Peak Press, L.L.C., Tucson, 1994—. Bd. dirs. Hist. Farms Assn., pres., 1985-87. With C.E., U.S. Army, 1952-55. Recipient NuJay award Mpls. Jaycees, 1957. Fellow Geol. Soc. Am.; mem. Rocky Mountain Books Pubs. Assn., Kiwanis (treas. Stroudsburg chpt. 1977-78, v.p. 1978-80, pres. 1980-81, Disting. Pres. award 1981). Home: 5520 N Camino Arenosa Tucson AZ 85718-5416

HUTCHINSON, EDWARD PAUL, air force officer; b. Tucson, May 19, 1961; s. Willard Lafayette and Dorothy Jean (Ellis) H. AAS in Security Adminstrn., C.C. of the Air Force, Montgomery, Ala., 1989; AAS in Electronic Sys. Tech., C.C. of the Air Force, 1994. Cert. peace officer, Ariz.; emergency med. technician. Enlisted U.S. Air Force, 1978, served in U.S., Europe, Asia, Africa, 1978—; Elite Guard flight chief 7001st Spl. Security Squadron, Ramstein Air Base, West Germany, 1983-86; non-commd. officer in charge secure communication 53d Combat Communications Squadron, Robins AFB, Ga., 1987-90; aircraft security flight chief 836th Security Police Squadron, Davis-Monthan AFB, Ariz., 1990-91, non-commd. officer in charge, confinement, 1991; shift comdr. 355th Security Police Squadron, Davis-Monthan AFB, 1991-95; ret. USAF, 1995; quality advisor, 1992—; res. officer Tucson Police Dept., 1991—; mil. customs insp. U.S. Customs Svc., Nogales, Ariz., 1991—. Troop com. mem. Boy Scouts Am., Robins AFB, 1988-89; vol. emergency med. technician USAF Clinic, Spangdahlem Air Base, West Germany, 1982-83. Decorated Air Force Commendation medal, two Air Force Achievement medals, Air Force Meritorious Svc. medal; named to Outstanding Young Men in Am., 1987. Christian. Office: 355th Security Police Sqdn Davis Monthan AFB AZ 85707

HUTCHINSON, JOSEPH CANDLER, retired foreign language educator; b. Hazelhurst, Ga., Jan. 10, 1920; s. George Washington and Lillie Arizona (Rowan) H.; m. June Cruce O'Shields, Aug. 12, 1950 (div. 1980); children: Junie O'Shields, Joseph Candler. BA, Emory U., 1940, MA, 1941; PhD, U. N.C., 1950; postgrad. U. Paris, summers 1951, 53. Tchr., Tech. High Sch., Atlanta, 1941-42; instr. French, German, Italian, Emory U., Atlanta, 1946-47; instr. U. N.C., Chapel Hill, 1947-50, asst. prof., 1954, assoc. prof., to 1957; asst. prof. Sweet Briar (Va.) Coll., 1950-51, 53-54; assoc. prof. Tulane U., New Orleans, 1957-59; fgn. lang. specialist U.S. Office Edn., Washington, 1959-64; acad. adv. hdqrs. Def. Lang. Inst., Washington, 1964-74, Monterey, 1974-77, dir. tng. devel. Def. Lang. Inst. Fgn. Lang. Ctr., Monterey, Calif., 1977-82, asst. acad. dean, 1982-85; dean of policy, from 1985-88; vis. prof. U. Va., Charlottesville, 1966, Arlington, 1970, Georgetown U., 1968, Am. U., 1971; cons. Council of Chief State Sch. Officers, 1960, U. Del., 1966, U. Colo., 1968, U. Ill., 1968; U.S. del. Bur. Internat. Lang. Coordination, NATO, 1964-79, 81-82, 86-87. Author: Using the Language Laboratory Effectively: School Executive's Guide, 1964, The Language Laboratory: Equipment and Utilization in Trends in Language Teaching, 1966, others; editor Dialog on Language Instruction, 1986-88; contbr. articles to profl. jours. Served with U.S. Army, 1942-46, 51-53. Decorated Bronze Star. Mem. Am. Council on Edn. (task force on internat. edn. 1973), NEA (sec. dept. fgn. langs. 1961-64), AARP/VOTE (17th Congl. dist. team), Higher Edn. Assn. Monterey Peninsula, Am. Council on Teaching of Fgn. Lang., MLA, Am. Mgmt. Assn., Am. Soc. Tng. and Devel., Nat. Assn. Ret. Fed. Employees (v.p. Monterey chpt. 1990, pres. 1991-92), Monterey Choral Soc., Camerata Singers, Presidio of Monterey Officers and Faculty, Washington Linguistics Club (v.p. 1970-72). Episcopalian.

HUTCHISON, JAMES DONALD, retired engineer, historian; b. Lafayette, Colo., Jan. 15, 1921; s. John Porter and Hazel Jane (Hood) H.; m. Elizabeth May Marion, Dec. 9, 1945; children: John William, Daniel James, Janet May (Mrs. Gerald Lee Morrell), Ronald Raymond. Student, U. Colo.; BA, U. No. Colo., 1974. Registered profl. engr., Colo.; land surveyor, Colo. Telegraph operator Colo. and So. R.R., Denver, 1945-46; rodman Colo. Dept. Hwys., Denver, 1949-51; cryogenic technician Cambridge Corp., Boulder, 1953-54; project engr. Colo. Dept. Hwys., Boulder, 1954-82; engr. cons. Lafayette, Colo., 1982—; mus. dir. Lafayette Miner's Mus., 1987—. Author: Survey and Settlement Lafayette Colorado, 1994; editor: The War Years 50th Anniversary Album Lafayette Colorado, 1994. Unit leader Boy Scouts Am., Lafayette, 1956-82; dir. Lafayette Centennial History Book, 1990. With USMC, 1942-45. Recipient Silver Beaver award Long Peak Coun. Boy Scouts Am., 1968, Person of the Yr. award Lafayette News, 1990. Mem. VFW (life), Lafayette Hist. Soc., Colo. Hist. Soc., Assn. No. Front Range Mus. Assn. (v.p.), Lafayette Lions Club (pres. 1993-94, zone chmn. 1994-95), Scottish Clan Donald (Colo. eastern convener 1995—). Methodist. Home: 778 Applewood Dr Lafayette CO 80026-8908

HUTCHISON, JOHN NELSON, correspondent; b. Arlington, Iowa, May 1, 1911; s. Orson Ray and Lulu Olive (Webber) H.; m. Sarabel Roberts, Dec. 24, 1937 (dec. June 1990); children: Judith, Susan; m. Vivienne Audrey Barnett, Aug. 15, 1991. BA, U. Ark., 1937. Reporter Cin. Post and Memphis Comml. Appeal, 1937-41, San Francisco News, 1946-48; fgn. svc. officer European Coop. Adminstrn., Paris, 1948-52; dir. Press & Publs., U.S. Info. Agy., Washington, 1952-55; pub. rels. officer United Fund of Bay Area, San Francisco, 1955-59; dir. info. Am. Nat. Red Cross, Washington, 1959-60; fgn. svc. officer U.S. Info. Agy., Washington, London, Manila, Wellington; corr. New Zealand Herald, Christchurch Press, Auckland, Christchurch, 1973—. Co-author: Gods, Men and Wine, 1965, Wines of the World, 1967, The Book of California Wine, 1984; contbg. editor Wines and Vines Mag., 1973—; contbr. more than 1000 articles to newspapers and mags. Lt. col. U.S. Army, 1941-46. Decorated Bronze Star. Mem. Savile Club London. Democrat. Home and Office: 441 Zimpher Dr Sebastopol CA 95472

HUTCHISON, LOYAL DWAYNE, pharmacist; b. Stockton, Calif., Jan. 3, 1933; s. Lester and Muriel (Van Nortwick) H.; m. Jean E. McColl, Jan. 26, 1961; children: Michael, Donald. BS in Pharmacy, U. Pacific, 1966. Pharmacist Fifth St. Pharmacy, Stockton, 1966-76, prin., 1976—; prin. Hutchison Pharmacies Inc., Stockton, 1976—, McKinley Pharmacy, Stockton, 1976—, Lathrop (Calif.) Pharmacy, 1976—. Served with U.S. Army, 1957-59. Fellow Am. Coll. Apothecary; mem. Calif. Pharmacists Assn. (Pac Silver Circle), Am. Pharmacists Assn. Home: PO Box 1737 Stockton CA 95201-1737 Office: Hutchison Pharmacies Inc 1839 S El Dorado St Stockton CA 95206-2025

HUTCHISON, MERRILL DEAN, recreation facility professional; b. Pocatello, Idaho, Jan. 28, 1948; s. William Merrill and Cleo Jean (Flint) H.; m. Erma LuDean Young, July 14, 1973; children: Merrill, Daniel, David, Janae, Mark, Bryan, Brent. BS, Brigham Young U., 1971. Maintenance worker I Provo (Utah) City Parks, 1974-78, maintenance worker II, 1978-82, park maintenance supr., 1982-93, project mgr., 1993—; master gardener USU Exention Svc., 1988—. Hunter safety instr. Utah State Divsn. of Wildlife Resource, Provo, 1982—; scoutmaster Boy Scouts Am., Provo, 1991—; del. to state polit. conv. Rep. Party, Provo, 1984, 94, 95. Mem. NRA, Pacific State Rifle Club (treas. 1974-94), Utah State Rifle and Pistol Assn. (chmn. rifle chpt. 1982-89). Office: Provo City Parks/Recreation 351 W Center St Provo UT 84601-4338

HUTCHISON, RICHARD LOUIS, plastic surgeon; b. Elgin, Ill, Jan. 31, 1956. MD, U. Chgo., 1983. Plastic surgeon Fairbanks Meml. Hosp., Batavia, Ak., 1994—. Office: 1919 Lathrop St Fairbanks AK 99701-5930*

HUTNER, HERBERT L., financial consultant, lawyer; b. N.Y.C.; s. Nathan M. and Ethel (Helhor) H.; m. Juli Reding, Nov. 28, 1969; children by previous marriage: Jeffrey J., Lynn M. Colwell; 1 stepson, Christopher D. Taylor. B.A., Columbia U., 1928, J.D., 1931. Bar: N.Y. 1932. Ptnr., Osterman & Hutner, mem. N.Y. Stock Exch., N.Y.C., 1945-57; successively pres. N.E. Life Insurance Co., N.Y.C.; chmn. bd. Sleight & Hellmuth Inc., N.Y.C.; chmn. bd. Pressed Metals of Am., Port Huron, Mich.; chmn. bd. Struthers Wells Corp., Warren, Pa., Plateau Mining Co. Inc., Oak Ridge, Tenn.; investor, cons., L.A., 1963—; dir. United Artists Communications, Inc., 1965-87, Todd AO-Glen Glen, 1987—, L.A. Rams, 1972-75, mem. adv. bd., 1991—; chmn. bd. Cellvent, Inc., 1991—. Chmn. pres.'s adv. com. on arts, Kennedy Ctr., 1982-90; founder L.A. Music Ctr.; chmn. profl. sports com. United Way; corporator Eye Rsch. Inst., Boston; mem. internat. adv. com. Up With People. Decorated title DATO, Sultan of Johore, Malaysia, Highest Order of the Crown, 1981. Mem. ASCAP, Deepdale Golf Club (Manhasset, N.Y.). Composer: The Super Bowl Song, Go Rams Go, others.

HUTTER, JAMES RISQUE, retired lawyer; b. Spokane, Wash., Mar. 20, 1924; s. James R. and Esther (Nelson) H.; m. Patricia Ruth Dunlavy, Aug. 12, 1951 (dec.); children: Bruce Dunlavy, Gail Anne, Dean James, Karl Nelson; m. Elizabeth Brown Ruess, Mar. 10, 1990. B.S., UCLA, 1947; J.D., Stanford U., 1950. Bar: Calif. 1951, U.S. Supreme Ct. 1965. Assoc. Gibson, Dunn & Crutcher, L.A. and Beverly Hills, Calif., 1950-58, ptnr., 1959-89; dir. Fifield Manors, Los Angeles, 1955—, v.p., 1964-85, pres., 1985—. Bd. dirs., chmn. fin. com. Congl. Found. for Theol. Studies, Nat. Assn. Congl. Christian Chs., 1961-67; mem. San Marino (Calif.) City Planning Commn., 1968-90, chmn., 1976-90. With 104th inf. div. AUS, 1943-46. Decorated Purple Heart. Mem. State Bar Calif. (com. on corps. 1973-76, exec. com. bus. law sect. 1976-78), ABA, Los Angeles County Bar Assn., Beverly Hills Bar Assn. (bd. govs. 1968-70), Am. Judicature Soc., Town Hall, City Club on Bunker Hill, Valley Hunt Club, Phi Delta Phi, Beta Gamma Sigma, Phi Kappa Psi. Home: 1400 Circle Dr San Marino CA 91108-1003 Office: Gibson Dunn & Crutcher 333 S Grand Ave Fl 48 Los Angeles CA 90071-1504

HUTTON, PAUL ANDREW, history educator, writer; b. Frankfurt, Germany, Oct. 23, 1949; naturalized citizen; s. Paul Andrew and Louise Katherine (Johnson) H.; m. Vicki Lynne Bauer, 1972 (div. 1985); 1 child, Laura; m. Lynn Terri Brittner, Dec. 31, 1989; children: Lorena, Paul. BA, Ind. U., 1972, MA, 1974, PhD, 1981. Editorial asst. Jour. Am. History, Bloomington, Ind., 1973-77; instr. history Utah State U., Logan, 1977-80, asst. prof., 1980-84; asst. prof. U. N.Mex., Albuquerque, 1984-86, assoc. prof., 1986—. Author: Phil Sheridan and His Army, 1985; editor: Ten Days on the Plains, 1985, Soldiers West, 1987, The Custer Reader, 1992, (series) Eyewitness to the Civil War, 1991-93; assoc. editor Western Hist. Quar., 1977-84; editor N.MEx. Hist. Rev., 1985-91. Recipient Evans Biography award Brigham Young U., 1986; Mead disting. rsch. fellow Huntington Libr., 1988. Mem. Orgn. Am. Historians (Ray A. Billington award 1986), Western Hist. Assn. (exec. dir. 1990—), Soc. for Mil. History, Western Writers Am. (Spur award 1985), Writers Guild Am. West. Home: 29 Encantado Loop Santa Fe NM 87505-8275 Office: U NMex Dept History Albuquerque NM 87131

HUYGHE, JACQUES M., manufacturing executive; b. Lille, Nord, France, Nov. 29, 1943; came to the U.S., 1981; s. Marcel and Jacqueline (Jeandaud) H.; m. Evelyne Vanackere, July 10, 1968; children: Julien, Jerome. B in Engring., Pub. Works, Paris, 1968; MS, Laval U., Quebec, 1976. Program mgr. Dept. Energy and Resources, Quebec, 1969-72; dep. gen. mgr. AerоPhoto, Inc., Quebec, 1972-76; gen. mgr. Quebec Mapping Co., 1976-79; v.p. U.S. ops. Matra Tech., Inc., Santa Clara, Calif., 1979-89; v.p. internat. mktg. Fairchild Def., Germantown, Md., 1990-92; v.p. mktg. Internat. Imaging Sys., a Datron Co., Milpitas, Calif., 1992—. Contbr. articles to profl. jours. Mem. Armed Forces Communications and Electronics, Assn. Old Crows, Assn. for Unmanned Vehicles, Am. Soc. for Photogrammetry. Office: Datron Transco Inc 1500 Buckeye Dr Milpitas CA 95035-7418

HWANG, CORDELIA JONG, chemist; b. N.Y.C., July 14, 1942; d. Goddard and Lily (Fung) Jong; m. Warren C. Hwang, Mar. 29, 1969; 1 child, Kevin. Student Alfred U., 1960-62; BA, Barnard Coll., 1964; M.S., SUNY-Stony Brook, 1969. Rsch. asst. Columbia U., N.Y.C., 1964-66; analytical chemist Veritron West Inc., Chatsworth, Calif., 1969-70; asst. lab. dir., chief chemist Pomeroy, Johnston & Bailey Environ. Engrs., Pasadena, Calif., 1970-76; chemist Met. Water Dist. So. Calif., Los Angeles, 1976-79, rsch. chemist 1980-91, sr. chemist 1992—; mem. Joint Task Group on Instrumental Identification of Taste and Odor Compounds, 1983-85, instr. Citrus Coll., 1974-76; chair Joint Task Group on Disinfection by-products: chlorine, 1990. Mem. Am. Chem. Soc., Am. Water Works Assn. (cert. water quality analyst level 3, Calif.-Nev.), Am. Soc. for Mass Spectrometry. Office: Met Water Dist So Calif 700 Moreno Ave La Verne CA 91750-3303

HWANG, DAVID GENPAI, ophthalmologist, educator; b. Carbondale, Ill., Aug. 22, 1963. Student, Northwestern U., 1978-80; BS, U. Calif., San Francisco, 1982, MD, 1984. Diplomate Am. Bd. Ophthalmology, Nat. Bd. Med. Examiners; cert. physician and surgeon, Calif. Intern U. Calif. San Franciso Hosps., 1984-86, resident in internal medicine, 1985-86, resident in ophthalmology, 1986-89; fellow in cornea, external disease and uveitis U. So. Calif./Doheny Eye Inst., L.A., 1989-90; clin. instr. ophthalmology U. So. Calif. Sch. Medicine, L.A., 1989-90; asst. prof. ophthalmology U. Calif. San Francisco Sch. Medicine, 1990—; co-dir. cornea svc. U. Calif., San Francisco, 1990—, med. dir. Eye Bank, 1990—, rsch. assoc. Francis I. Proctor Found., 1992—. Contbr. numerous articles to profl. jours. Heed fellow, 1989-90; NIH grantee, 1989, others. Mem. ACS, AAAS, AMA, Calif. Med. Assn., Am. Acad. Ophthalmology, Contact Lens Assn. Ophthalmologists, Assn. for Rsch. in Vision and Ophthalmology, Am. Soc. Cataract and Refractive Surgery, Internat. Soc. Refractive Keratoplasty, Am. Soc. Microbiology, Paton Soc., Alpha Omega Alpha. Office: U Calif San Francisco Dept Ophthalmology 10 Kirkham St Rm K301 San Francisco CA 94122-3815

HWANG, KOU MAU, pharmaceutical executive; b. Kaoshiung, Taiwan, Sept. 5, 1940; came to U.S., 1966; s. Tien C. and Zui C. (Yu) H.; m. Sue H. Cheng, Sept. 5, 1969; children: Sandy, Carol, Nancy. BS, Kaohsiung Med. Coll., 1964; MS, Ohio State U., 1969, PhD, 1972; postgrad., Yale U., 1974. Teaching asst. Duquesne U., Pitts., 1965-66, Ohio State U., Columbus, Ohio, 1967-71; rsch. fellow Yale Med. Sch., New Haven, 1972-76; asst. prof. M.D. Anderson Hosp./Univ. Tex., Houston, 1976-77, U. So. Calif., L.A., 1977-79; sr. investigator Nat. Cancer Inst., Frederick, Md., 1980-83; sr. scientist Cetus Inc., San Francisco, 1984; sr. dir. Genelabs Inc., Redwood City, Calif., 1985-93; pres. Sintong Pharm. U.S. Inc., Hayward, Calif., 1993—; vis. prof. Rutger U., Piscataway, N.J., 1985-88; educator Internat. AIDS Confs., U.S., China, 1989; cons., lectr. Kaushiung Med. Coll., Taiwan, 1991-92. Patentee AIDS Therapy, 1989, New Therapy for Herpes Simplex, 1992; inventor in field; contbr. numerous articles to profl. jours. Cultural exch. person Taiwanese Prof. Assn., 1990—. 2nd lt. Taiwanese Army, 1964-65. Rsch. grantee Welch Found., Houston, 1977, Am. Cancer Soc., L.A., 1977-80; sml. bus. grantee U.S. Govt., San Carlo, Calif., 1987-88; recipient Nat. Drug Discovery grants NIAID, Redwood City, 1988-91. Mem. Am. Assn. Cancer Rsch., Am. Chem. Soc., AAAS, Rho Chi. Home: 220 Stanbridge Ct Danville CA 94526-2630 Office: Sintong Pharm US Inc 3401 Investment Blvd Hayward CA 94545-3801

HYAMS, HAROLD, lawyer; b. Bklyn., May 19, 1943; s. Frank Charles and Celia (Silverstein) H.; m. Simone Elkeharrat, Nov. 18, 1973; children: Gabriel, Galite, Emilie, Jonathan. BA, U. Vt., 1965; MA in Latin Am. Studies, Georgetown U., 1966; JD, Syracuse U., 1970. Bar: N.Y. 1971, Ariz. 1974, U.S. Dist. Ct. Ariz. 1974, U.S. Ct. Appeals (9th cir.) 1974. Asst. to the gen. counsel Am. Express Co., N.Y.C., 1970-72; atty. Legal Aid Soc., Bklyn., 1973; ptnr. Harold Hyams and Assocs., Tucson, 1974—; mem. panel of arbitrators Am. Arbitration Assn., N.Y.C., 1971-73. Bd. dirs. Chafetz Chaim Congregation, Tucson, 1985-90, Tucson Hebrew Acad., 1985-86; mem. Commn. on Ariz. Environ., 1988. Mem. Am. Bd. Trial Advs., Ariz. Trial Lawyers Assn., Pima County Bar Assn., Assn. Trial Lawyers Am. (adv. bd. trial advocates 1990, cert. specialist in personal injury and wrongful death 1991). Home: 3175 N Elena Maria Tucson AZ 85715-2915 Office: 680 S Craycroft Rd Tucson AZ 85711-7108

HYATT, LAURA, healthcare company executive; b. L.A.. V.p. C.V.S.C., Culver City, Calif. Author 1 book; contbr. articles to profl. jours. Recipient Golden Advocate award HPRMA, 1990. Mem. ASCA (exec. dir., exec. dir. quarterly, ACRM legis., CMSA legis., lobbyist).

HYBIL, JAMES J., insurance agency executive; b. Cleve., Oct. 1, 1944; s. James J. and Helen A. (Jakobonski) H.; m. Gayle M. Kubit, Nov. 16, 1968; 1 child, Rebecca M. AB, John Carroll U., University Heights, Ohio, 1967. CLU, ChFC. Ins. agt./broker Prudential Ins. of Am., Cleve., 1975-85; pres. Hybil-Kugler-Balint Ins., North Royalton, Ohio, 1985—. Paul Harris fellow, Rotary, 1988. Mem. Internat. Assn. Fin. Planning, Cleve. Assn. Life Underwriters, Nat. Assn. Health Indemnifiers, North Royalton C. of C., Soc. of CLUs and ChFCs (chpt. trustee 1989—), Rotary (pres. 1981-82). Roman Catholic. Home: 12800 N Star Dr Cleveland OH 44133-5943 Office: Hybil Kugler Balint 3505 E Royalton Rd # 205 Cleveland OH 44147-2998*

HYBL, WILLIAM JOSEPH, lawyer, foundation executive; b. Des Moines, July 16, 1942; s. Joseph A. and Geraldine (Evans) H.; m. Kathleen Horrigan, June 6, 1967; children: William J. Jr., Kyle Horrigan; BA, Colo. Coll., 1964; JD, U. Colo., 1967. Bar: Colo. 1967. Asst. dist. atty. 4th Jud. Dist., El Paso and Teller Counties, 1970-72; pres., exec. v.p., dir. Garden City Co., 1973—; dir. Broadmoor Hotel, Inc., 1973—, also vice-chmn., 1987—; chmn., CEO, trustee El Pomar Found, Colorado Springs, Colo., 1973—; pres. U.S. Olympic Com. 1991-92; bd. dirs. USAA, San Antonio, KN Energy Inc., Lakewood, Colo., FirstBank Holding Co. of Colo., Lakewood; mem. Colo. Ho. Reps., 1972-73; spl. counsel The White House, Washington, 1981. Trustee, vice chmn. Colo. Coll., 1978—; pres., trustee Air Force Acad. Found.; sec., trustee Nat. Jr. Achievement; vice chmn. bd. U.S. Adv. Commn. on Pub. Diplomacy, 1990—; civilian aide to sec. of army, 1986—. Capt. U.S. Army, 1967-69. Republican.

HYLAND, PENELOPE, writer, artist; b. Columbus, Ohio, Sept. 19, 1953; d. John Roth Hyland and Martha Ann (Burger) Shipman; m. Charles David Moore (div. 1989); children: Jacquetta Nicole, Tara, Chad David, Shaun Dai. BS, U. So. Colo., 1987; MA, Adams State Coll., 1989; D of Clin. Hypnotherapy, Am. Inst. Hypnotherapy, 1990. Cert. hypnotherapist, Edu-Kinesthetics. Neuropsychiat. technician Assocs. for Psychotherapy, Pueblo, Colo., 1987-88; clin. therapist Parkview Anxiety and Depression Unit, Pueblo, Colo., 1990; counselor U. So. Colo., Pueblo, Colo., 1988, acad. advisement coord., 1988-89, psychotherapist, tchr., writer, 1988—; founder, exec. dir. Stop Abusive Family Environments, Pueblo, 1986—; speaker in field. Author: (booklet) A Survival Guide for Battered Women, 1985. Adv. coun. Pueblo County Sheriff Dept., 1992; crisis counselor YWCA Crisis Shelter, Pueblo, 1981-86; leadership com. Bus. Women's Network, Pueblo, 1989-92; campaign advisor Dem. Candidate for Commr., Pueblo, 1990. Named Outstanding Coll. Student, 1989, Outstanding Woman of Yr., U. So. Colo., 1985-86; recipient Honors and Spl. Distinction, U. So. Colo., 1987, Vol. Svc. award YWCA, 1983. Mem. Bus. Women's Network, Psi Chi, Alpha Chi.

HYLKO, JAMES MARK, health physicist; b. Detroit, Sept. 11, 1961; s. James John and Frances Rose (Gorski) H. BS in Biochemistry, Ea. Mich. U., 1984; MPH in Health Physics, U. Mich., 1986. Lab. tech. dept. chemistry Ea. Mich. U., Ypsilanti, 1980-84; environ. radiochemist Argonne (Ill.) Nat. Lab., 1984; radiochemist U. Mich., Ann Arbor, 1984-86; health physics tech. Monticello (Minn.) Nuclear Sta., 1985; rsch. scientist U. Va., Charlottesville, 1986-88; health physicist Fluor Daniel Inc., Chgo., 1988-92, Roy F. Weston, Inc., Albuquerque, 1992—; instr. dept. chem. and nuclear engring. U. N.Mex., fall 1993, fall 1994; mem. nuclear/ednl. planning com. Am. Power Conf., Chgo., 1989-91; guest lectr. Purdue U., 1991; invited speaker Inst. Atomic Energy, Swierk-Otwock, Poland, 1991. Contbr. over 40 articles to Jour. Radiation Protection Mgmt., Nuclear Tech., and book revis.; contbr. over 50 conf. presentations including internat. confs. in Berlin, Germany and Versailles, France, 1995. Judge N.Mex. Regional and State Sci. and Engring. Fair, 1993, 94, 95. Fellow Inst. Nuclear Power Ops., 1986. Mem. Health Physics Soc. (history com. Rio Grande chpt. 1993—), Am. Nuclear Soc. (exec. bd.), Toastmasters (pres. Fluor Daniel chpt. 1990). Office: Roy F Weston Inc 6501 Americas Pky NE Ste 800 Albuquerque NM 87110-5372

HYMAN, KEVIN MICHAEL, communications executive; b. Dallas, Mar. 8, 1950; s. Joseph Raymond and Mary Angela (Dwyer) H.; m. Marjanna Mercer, July 17, 1983; children: Colleen, Chasen, Katelynn. BA in Econs., U. No. Colo., 1972; MA in Econs., U. R.I., 1974. Asst. prof. econs. Nasson Coll., Springvale, Maine, 1974-78; v.p. Boettcher & Co., Colorado Springs, Colo., 1978-85; chief exec. officer, pres. Citizens' Cable, Colorado Springs, Colo., 1985-89; also bd. dirs. Citizens' Cable, Colorado Springs; gen. mgr. Cablevision, Colorado Springs, 1989—. Bd. dirs. Better Bus. Bur., pres., 1993; bd. dirs. Pikes Peak Amateur Hockey Assn., Colorado Springs, coach, 1987-88, rep., 1991—, pres. 1993; trustee Bob Johnson Ice Hickey Found.; coord. West El Paso Little League, Colorado Springs; dir. Profile Theatre, Portland, Maine, 1974-76. Mem. Colo. Cable TV Assn. (bd. dirs. 1994), Colo. C. of C., Colo. Amateur Hockey Assn., Country Club of Colo. Roman Catholic. Office: Cablevision 213 N Union Blvd Colorado Springs CO 80909-5705

HYNDS, FRANCES JANE, communications management consultant; b. Martin, Tenn., Oct. 27, 1929; d. Loyd Orion and Hunter Elizabeth (Goad) H. BS in Journalism, McMurry Coll., 1951; MA in Telecommunications, U. So. Calif., 1961, PhD in Communications, 1984. Dir. pub. info., instr. journalism McMurry Coll., Abilene, Tex., 1951-53; dir. pub. relations Oklahoma City U., 1953-55; acct. exec., corp. sec. Joe Leighton & Assocs. Inc., Hollywood, Calif., 1956-65; prin. Hynds Co., Los Angeles, 1965—; pres., sole owner Matrix Works, Inc., L.A., 1987—; sr. lectr., adj. faculty, dir. pub. relations program for mgmt. U. So. Calif. Sch. Journalism, Grad. Sch. Bus. Mem. Pub. Relations Soc. Am. (dir. 1975-77, nat. assembly del., pub. rels. counselor), Women in Communications Inc. (dir. 1967-72; Far West region Woman of Achievement 1980, Los Angeles chpt. Freedom of Info. award, Nat. Founders award, 1982, pres. scholarship and edn. found. 1992—). Recipient LULU award for the Best Corporate Pub. Rels. in the We. U.S., L.A. Advtg. Women, 1975. Author (with Norma L. Bowles): Psi Search, The New Investigation of Psychic Phenomena that Separates Fact from Speculation, 1978; transl. French, 1983; contbr. articles to profl. jours.

HYNEK, FREDERICK JAMES, architect; b. Minot, N.D., May 24, 1944; s. Frederick Frank and Esther Irene (Hermanson) H.; m. Jane Rebecca Lowitz, June 9, 1966; children: Tyler James, Scott Anthony. BArch, N.D. State U., 1967. Intern archtl. firms in Bismarck, N.D., 1967-72; architect Gerald W. Deines, Architect, Casper and Cody, Wyo., 1972-73; v.p. Gerald Deines and Assos., 1973-77; propr. Fred J. Hynek, AIA/Architect, Cody, 1977-80; pres. Design Group, P.C., Architects/Planners, Cody, 1980-86; pres. CHD Architects, Cody, 1986-94; CEO Cathexes, Inc., Reno, 1994-95; project mgr. Merrick and Co., Denver, 1995—; mem. cert. of need rev. bd. State of Wyo., 1984-87, selection com. for archtl. students for Western Interstate Commn. for Higher Edn. Profl. Student Exchange Program, U. Wyo., 1979—; chmn. archtl. adv. commn. City of Cody. Bd. dirs. Cody Stampede, Inc., 1977-82, Cody Nordic Ski Found., Park County Libr. Found.; chmn. Cody Econ. Devel. Council, 1982-84; coach Absaroka Ski Assn., Bill Koch Youth Ski League, 1990—. Served with USAR, 1967-68. Mem. AIA (dir. Wyo. chpt. 1976-83, pres. 1980, 81, sec./treas., 1990-91; conf. chmn. Western Mountain region 1977, mem. awards jury 1981, 92, treas. 1982-86; chmn. design awards jury N.D. 1981, 2 awards for Excellence in Archtl. Design Wyo. chpt.), U.S. Ski Assn., U.S. Ski Coaches Assn., Cody County C. of C. (dir., pres. 1982). Republican. Presbyterian. Clubs: Cody Country Amb. (Amb. of Yr. 1990). Mem. editorial adv. bd. Symposia mag., 1981-82. Home: 227 S Jasper Cir Aurora CO 80017 Office: 2450 S Peoria St Aurora CO 80014

HYSON, MORTON ISAAC, neurologist, vocalist; b. Detroit, July 10, 1949; s. Aaron Hyson and Betty (Berman) Ellias; m. Nicole Claire Baillargeon, June 6, 1982; 1 child, Kimberley. MD, Wayne State U., 1979. Diplomate Am. Bd Psychiatry and Neurology; lic. physician Nev., N.Y., Tex. Intern McGill U./Montreal (Quebec, Can.) Neurol. Hosp., 1980-81, resident in neurology, 1982-83; pvt. practice Arlington Tex., 1983-90, Las Vegas, 1990—; weekend coord. emergency rm. Potsdam (N.Y.) Gen. Hosp., 1981-83; clin. assoc. prof. dept. neurology U. Tex. Southwestern Med. Sch., Dallas. appeared in Tosca, Nev. Opera Theatre, 1994, Butterfly, 1993, Amahl, 1993, The Marriage of Figaro, 1991, Il Turco in Italia, Opera Piccola Bremen, Germany, 1991, The Gondoliers, The Lyric Opera, 1990. Cleve. Inst. Music scholar, 1969. Mem. AMA, Am. Assn. Neurologists, Clark County Med. Soc., Nev. State Med. Assn., Muscular Dystrophy Assn. (med. dir. Las Vegas 1991—). Office: 2020 Goldring Ave Ste 402 Las Vegas NV 89106-4000

IACANGELO, PETER AUGUST, actor; b. Bklyn., Aug. 13, 1948; s. Peter and Mary Rose (Bordini) I.; m. Melody Rose Marzola, Apr. 5, 1975; children: Peter August III, Perique Ashly, Paxton Aaires. AA in Marine Biology, Suffolk County Community Coll., 1968; BFA, Hofstra U., 1971. Actor South Bronx (N.Y.) Repertory Co., 1971, The Fifteen Cent Token Improvisation, N.Y.C., 1971; actor off-Broadway One Flew Over The Cuckoo's Nest, 1972, Moon Children, 1972-74; actor off-Broadway and N.Y. Shakespeare Festival Comedy of Errors, 1975; actor on-Broadway Three Penny Opera, 1976-77; actor Blood Brothers Warner Bros., N.Y.C. and Hollywood, Calif., 1977; actor Hoodlums Nai Bonet Entertainment, N.Y.C., 1977; ind. actor, 1978—; actor on Broadway Filumena, N.Y.C., 1979-80, Passione, N.Y.C., 1980; tchr. Upward Bound Program, Brunswick, Maine, 1968; owner, tchr., coach Conflict Workshop, N.Y.C., 1971-74; tchr., acting coach Learning Tree U., Northridge, Calif., 1985-86. Contbr. short stories and poems to various mags., 1965—; appeared in numerous prodns. including Tattoo, 1978, Times Square, 1979, Spittoon, 1980-81, Hanky Panky, 1981, Hero at Large, 1979, Archie Bunkers Place, 1981, Hill Street Blues, 1981, St. Elsewhere, 1981, The A Team, 1981, 86, Taxi, 1981, 82, Cagney & Lacey, 1982, Over Here, Mr. President, 1982, The Jeffersons, 1982, 85, Carpool, 1982, Gimmie a Break, 1982, Hardcastle & McCormick, 1983, The Phoenix, Falcon Crest, 1983, Masquerade, 1984, Cheers, 1984, Night Court, 1984, The Fall Guy, 1984, Knots Landing, 1985, Amazing Stories, Who's the Boss, 1985, Our Family Honor, 1985, The Return of Mickey Spillane's Mike Hammer, 1986, The New Mike Hammer, 1986, Easy Street, 1986, The Tortellis, 1986, Santa Barbara, 1986, On The Edge, 1987, Amen, 1987, Valerie's Family, 1988, Over the Edge, 1988, Nitti, 1988, Killer Instinct, 1989, Gangsters, 1989, Freddy's Nightmares, 1989, Brothers, 1989, Alf, 1989, Mr. Belvedere, 1989, Wolf, 1989, Capital News, 1990, Singer & Sons, 1990, Best Intentions, 1990, Strong Man's Weak Child at L.A.T.C., 1990, (TV shows) They Came From Outer Space, 1991, Babes, 1991, Life Goes On, 1991, Murphy Brown, 1991, Dream On, 1991, Dear John, 1991, Good & Evil, 1991, Walter & Emily, 1991, Quantum Leap, 1992, Down the Shore, 1992, Good Advice, 1992, Love and War, 1993, (feature film) We're Talking Serious Money, 1991, Addams Family II, 1993, The Night of the Running Man, 1994 (TV) Wild Oats, 1994. Vol. Better Horizons Program, Selden, N.Y., 1967-68, Nat. Fedn. of the Blind, N.Y.C., 1971-73, Spl. Olympics, So. Calif., 1981—; actor benefit performance for N.Y.C. and Mayor John V. Lindsey, 1972; celebrity participant St. Jude's Children's Hosp. Fun Shoot. Recipient certificate Mayor John V. Lindsey, 1972. Mem. AFTRA, NRA, SAG, Actors Equity Assn., Actors Fund Am. (life), West Coast Ind. Chess Masters (pres.), The Universal Coterie of Pipe Smokers, Pipe Collectors Internat. (life). Roman Catholic.

IACOBELLIS, SAM FRANK, aerospace company executive; b. Fresno, Calif., Aug. 17, 1929; s. Frank and Mary (Ceppaglia) I.; m. Helene Myers, June 11, 1954; children: Sam F. II, Lee Ann. B MechE, Calif. State U., Fresno, 1952; M in Engring., UCLA, 1963. Registered profl. mech. and nuclear engr., Calif. Design engr. N.Am. Aircraft div. Rockwell Internat., Los Angeles, 1952-53, engring. supr., 1953-57; v.p. Rocketdyne div. Rockwell Internat., Canoga Park, Calif., 1957-73; pres. Atomics Internat. div. Rockwell Internat., Canoga Park, Calif., 1973-78, Energy Systems Group div. Rockwell Internat., Canoga Park, Calif., 1978-81; exec. v.p., B-1B program mgr. N.Am. Aircraft Ops. div. Rockwell Internat., El Segundo, Calif., 1981-84, pres., B-1B program mgr., corp. v.p., 1984-88; pres. Aerospace Ops. Rockwell Internat., El Segundo, Calif., 1988-89, exec. v.p., chief oper. officer, 1989-93; exec. v.p., dep. chmn. major programs Rockwell Internat., Seal Beach, Calif., 1993—; co-founder, chmn. bd. Warner Ctr. Bank, 1981-90; bd. dirs. Rohr, Inc., U.S. Space Found. Patentee turbomolecular vacuum pump, rocket engine design. Mem. engrs. council Calif. State U., Fresno, 1983, UCLA Sch. Engring., 1983; trustee UCLA Found., 1985; bd. dirs. Calif. State U. Found., 1988. Named Engring. Alumnus of Yr., UCLA, 1980, Calif. State U., Fresno, 1982, Engr. of Yr., San Fernando Valley Engrs. Council, Los Angeles; recipient Indsl. Tech. Mgmt. award Region II, Soc. Mfg. Engrs. Fellow AIAA. Club: Bel Air (Calif.) Country. Home: 5585 Wellesley Dr Calabasas CA 91302-3112 Office: Rockwell Internat 2201 Seal Beach Blvd Seal Beach CA 90740-5603

IAMELE, RICHARD THOMAS, law librarian; b. Newark, Jan. 29, 1942; s. Armando Anthony and Evelyn (Coladonato) I.; m. Marilyn Ann Berutto, Aug. 21, 1965; children: Thomas, Ann Marie. BA, Loyola U., L.A., 1963; MSLS, U. So. Calif., 1967; JD, Southwestern U., L.A., 1976. Bar: Calif. 1977. Cataloger U. So. Calif., L.A., 1967-71; asst. cataloger L.A. County Law Libr., 1971-77, asst. ref. libr., 1977-78, asst. libr., 1978-80, libr. dir., 1980—. Mem. ABA, Am. Assn. Law Librs., Calif. Libr. Assn., So. Calif. Assn. Law Librs., Coun. Calif. County Law Librs. (pres. 1981-82, 88-90). Office: Los Angeles County Law Libr 301 W 1st St Los Angeles CA 90012-3100

IBERALL, ARTHUR SAUL, physicist, publisher; b. N.Y.C., June 12, 1918; s. Benjamin and Anna (Katz) I.; m. Helene Rubenstein, Jan. 28, 1940; children: Eleanora Iberall Robbins, Pamela Iberall Rubin, Althea, Valerie Iberall O'Connor. B.S., CCNY, 1940, postgrad., 1940-41; postgrad., George Washington U., 1942-45; hon. degree, Ohio State U., 1976. Gen. physicist Nat. Bur. Standards, Washington, 1941-53; research dir. ARO Equipment Corp., Cleve., 1953-54; chief physicist Rand Devel. Corp., Cleve., 1954-65; chief scientist, pres. Gen. Tech. Services, Inc., Upper Darby, Pa., 1965-81; editor, pub. CP2: Commentaries-Physical and Philosophical, 1990—; vis. scholar UCLA, 1981-92; grad. teaching U. Calif., Irvine, 1993. Author: Toward a General Science of Viable Systems, 1972, On Pulsatile and Steady Arterial Flow, 1973, Physics of Membrane Transport, 1973, Bridges in Science: From Physics to Social Science, 1974, On Nature, Life, Mind and Society, 1976, What's Wrong with Evolution, 1989, How to Run a Society, 1991, Foundations for Social and Biological Evolution, 1993; editor: (with J. Reswick) Technical and Biological Problems of Control; A Cybernetic View, 1970, (with A. Guyton) Regulation and Control in Physiological Systems, 1973; assoc. editor: Am. Jour. Physiology, Integrative and Comparative Physiology, 1976-90; contbr. tech. articles to profl. jours. Fellow ASME (chmn. auto. control div. 1973); mem. Am. Phys. Soc., N.Y. Acad. Scis., Biomed. Engring. Soc. (Alza Disting. lectr. 1975), Am. Cybernetic Soc., Microcirculation Soc., Instrument Soc. Am., Biophys. Soc., Sigma Xi. Democrat. Jewish. Club: Cosmos. Home: 5070 Avenida Del Sol Laguna Hills CA 92653-1876

ICE, RICHARD EUGENE, retired minister, retirement housing company executive; b. Ft. Lewis, Wash., Sept. 25, 1930; s. Shirley and Nellie Rebecca (Pedersen) I.; m. Pearl Lucille Daniels, July 17, 1955 (dec. June 7, 1992); children: Lorinda Susan, Diana Laurene, Julianne Adele. AA, Centralia Coll., 1950; BA, Linfield Coll., 1952, LHD (hon.), 1978; MA, Berkeley Bapt. Div. Sch., 1959, DD (hon.), 1995; grad. advanced mgmt. program Harvard U., 1971. Ordained to ministry Am. Bapt. Ch., 1954; pastor Ridgecrest Community Bapt. Ch., Seattle, 1955-59; dir. ch. extension Wash. Bapt. Conv., 1959-61; dir. loans Am. Bapt. Extension Corp., Valley Forge, Pa., 1961-64; assoc. exec. minister Am. Bapt. Chs. of West, Oakland, Calif., 1964-67, dep. exec. sec., treas. Am. Bapt. Home Mission Socs., Valley Forge, 1967-72; pres. Am. Bapt. Homes of the West, Oakland, 1972-95, pres. emeritus, 1995—; dir. Minister's Life Ins. Co., Mpls., 1975-87, chmn. bd. dirs. 1986-87; bd. dir. Bapt. Life Assn., Buffalo, 1988—; pres. Am. Bapt. Homes and Hosps. Assn., 1978-81. v.p. Am. Bapt. Chs. U.S.A., 1990-91; Ministers and Missionaries Benefit Bd., 1982-89; mem. Bapt. Joint Com. on Pub. Affairs; trustee Linfield Coll., 1972—, chmn. bd. trustees, 1994—; trustee Calif./Nev. Methodist Homes, 1975—, Bacone Coll., 1968-77, Grad. Theol. Union, Berkeley, Calif., 1982—; trustee Am. Bapt. Sem. of West, Berkeley, 1975—, chmn. bd. trustees, 1987-95. Recipient Disting. Baconian award Bacone Coll., 1977, Disting. Alumnus award Centralia Coll., 1981, Meritorious Service award Am. Assn. Homes for Aging, 1982, Merit citation Am. Bapt. Homes and Hosp. Assn., 1985, Award of Honor Calif. Assn. Homes for the Aging, 1988. Mem. U.S. Assn. for UN, Am. Assn. Homes and Svcs. for Aging (Award of Honor 1994), Calif. Assn. Homes for Aging, Harvard Bus. Sch. Assn. No. Calif., The Oakland 100, Pi Gamma Mu. Democrat. Clubs: Harvard of San Francisco, Bellevue, Oakland. Office: Am Baptist Homes of West 400 Roland Way Oakland CA 94621-2012

ICENOGLE, RONALD DEAN, physical chemist, writer; b. Bismarck, N.D., May 5, 1951; s. Grover Donald and Mary Adeline (Parks) I.; m. Maria Cecilia Co., Apr. 26, 1987; children: Paul Steven, James Andrew. BS, Mich. State U., 1974; MS, Cornell U., 1977, PhD, 1981; postgrad., Ea. Washington U., 1994—. Rsch. chemist Shell Devel. Co., Houston, 1980-85; writer on philosophy and sci. Spokane, Wash., 1985-87; sr. devel. engr. Teknor Apex Co., Pawtucket, R.I., 1987-89; writer Spokane, Wash., 1990—; agt. N.Y. Life Ins. Co., Spokane, 1991; ind. ins. mktg. agt. Spokane, 1991-92. Author: Science and Moral Choice, 1995; co-inventor, 5 U.S. patents low-smoke polypropylene insulation compounds, also fgn. patents granted; contbr. articles to profl. jours. Mem. Am. Chem. Soc., N.Y. Acad. Scis., Internat. Platform Assn., Phi Beta Kappa, Phi Kappa Phi, Kappa Delta Pi. Republican. Roman Catholic. Home and Office: 2303 W Mission Ave Spokane WA 99201-2926

ICERMAN, LARRY, advanced technology business consultant, research and development administrator; b. Muncie, Ind., Sept. 22, 1945; s. Charles and Janelyn (Mock) I. BS in Aeronautics and Astronautics, MIT, 1967; MS in Applied Mechanics, U. Calif., San Diego, 1968, PhD in Engring. Sci., 1976; MBA in Fin., San Diego State U., 1976. Asst. prof. Washington U., St. Louis, 1976-79, assoc. prof., 1979-80; dir. N.Mex. Energy Inst., Las Cruces, N.Mex., 1980-81, N.Mex. State U. Energy Inst., Las Cruces, 1982-83, N.Mex. Energy R&D Inst., Santa Fe, 1984-86, N.Mex. R&D Inst., Santa Fe, 1986-89; pres. Icerman & Assocs., Santa Fe, 1989—; bd. dirs. Permacharge Corp., Albuquerque, Coronado Ventures Forum Sante Fe. Co-author: Energy: Demands, Resources, Impact, Technology, and Policy, 1974, 76,2d edit., 78, 3d edit., 81, revised edit., Energy: Non-Nuclear Energy Technologies, 1975, 77, 2d revised edit., 84, revised and enlarged edit., Renewable Resource Utilization for Development, 1981; mem. editorial bd. Energy: The Internat. Jour., 1979-90. Bd. dirs. Tri-Area Assn. for Econ. Devel., Pojoaque, N.Mex., 1990—; mem. edl. coun. MIT, Cambridge, Mass., 1981—. Spl. Recognition for Energy Innovation award U.S. Dept. Energy, 1985, Energy Innovation awards, 1986, 88. Mem. AAAS, AIAA, Am. Chem. Soc., Am. Mgmt. Assn., N.Mex. Entrepreneurs Assn. (bd. dirs. 1990-93), Geothermal Resources Coun., Internat. Assn. for Hydrogen Energy, Internat. Solar Energy Soc. Home and Office: 2999 Calle Cerrada Santa Fe NM 87505-5393

ICHELSON, DAVID LEON, physician; b. San Francisco, Oct. 12, 1921; s. Maury Moses and Selene Diane (Jones) I.; m. Jean Pearch, June 14, 1946 (div.); m. Patricia Badali, Sept. 26, 1958; children: Suzanne, Kathryn, David Jr., Nancy, Mary Jane, Beth Ann; m. Katherine E. Shippey, Dec. 26, 1981. AB, Stanford U., 1943; MD, Bowman Gray U., 1950. Intern L.A. County Hosp., 1950-51; resident Tulare County Hosp., 1951-53; pvt. practice Calif., 1953-86, Sacramento, 1986—; chmn. gen. practice dept. Stanford Hosp., Palokto, Calif., 1976, Sequoia Hosp., Redwood City, Calif., 1979; chief staff Corning (Calif.) Meml. Hosp., 1987. Patent on athletic bra and hair clip for repairing scalp lacerations. Inf. U.S. Army, 1944-46. Mem. Am. Acad. Family Practice. Home: 6825 Steamboat Way Sacramento CA 95831-2513

ICHIKAWA, WAYNE, oral and maxillofacial surgeon; b. Palo Alto, Calif., July 25, 1954; s. Thomas Toshiaki and June Haruko (Jofuku) I.; m. Kathryn Linda Ito, Aug. 22, 1987; 1 child, Matthew Paul. AA, Foothill Coll., 1974; BA, U. Calif., Berkeley, 1976; DDS, U. Calif., Los Angeles, 1981; MS, U. Ill., Chgo., 1986. Diplomate Am. Bd. Oral and Maxillofacial Surgery. Practice medicine specializing in oral and maxillofacial surgery San Leandro, Calif., 1985-86, San Jose, Calif., 1986-88, Campbell, Calif., 1988—; intern, then resident in oral and maxillofacial surgery U. Ill. Med. Ctr./VA Hosp., Chgo., 1981-85; adj. asst. prof. dept. oral and maxillofacial surgery U. Pacific, San Francisco, 1987. Contbr. articles to profl. jours. Fellow Am. Assn. Oral and Maxillofacial Surgeons, Am. Coll. Oral and Maxillofacial Surgeons; mem. ADA, Am. Dental Soc. Anesthesiology, Calif. Assn. Oral and Maxillofacial Surgeons, Calif. Dental Assn., No. Calif. Soc. Oral and Maxillofacial Surgeons, Santa Clara County Dental Soc., Western Soc. Oral and Maxillofacial Surgeons. Buddhist. Office: 1580 Winchester Blvd Ste 101 Campbell CA 95008-0519

IDEMAN, JAMES M., federal judge; b. Rockford, Ill., Apr. 2, 1931; s. Joseph and Natalie Ideman; m. Gertraud Erika Ideman, June 1, 1971. BA, The Citadel, 1953; JD, U. So. Calif., 1963. Bar: Calif. 1964, U.S. Dist. Ct. (cen. dist.) Calif. 1964, U.S. Ct. Mil. Appeals 1967, U.S. Supreme Ct. 1967. Dep. dist. atty. Los Angeles County, 1964-79; judge Los Angeles County Superior Ct., 1979-84; appointed judge U.S. Dist. Ct. (Cen. Dist.) Calif., Los Angeles, 1984—. Served to 1st lt. U.S. Army, 1953-56, col. AUS Ret. Republican. Office: US Dist Ct 312 N Spring St Los Angeles CA 90012-4701

IDOURAINE, AHMED, researcher; b. Souk El-Had, Algiers, Algeria, Jan. 22, 1948; came to U.S., 1983; s. Mohamed Idouraine and Fatma Kennoud; 1 child, Melissa-Sara. BS in Food Tech., Nat. Inst. Agronomy, Algiers, 1977; MS in Food Scis., U. Ariz., 1987, PhD in Nutritional Scis., 1993. Rsch. team leader Sonatrach, Algiers, 1977-81; instr. food sci. dept. Nat. Inst. Light Industries, Boumerdes, Algeria, 1981-83; rsch./tchg. asst. dept. nutrition & food sci. U. Ariz., Tucson, 1985-93; post-doctorate rsch. fellow Harrington Arthritis Rsch. Ctr., Phoenix, 1994—. Contbr. over 15 articles to profl. jours.; also over 20 abstracts and presentations. McClelland scholar U. Ariz., 1991, Food Sci. scholar, 1992. Mem. Inst. Food Technologists, Am. Assn. Cereal Chemists, Ariz. Soc. Food Technologists, Sigma Xi, Gamma Sigma Delta. Office: Harrington Arthritis Rsch Ctr 1800 E Van Buren St Phoenix AZ 85006

IDURY, RAMANA MURTHY, computer scientist; b. Bhimavaram, India, Jan. 24, 1962; s. Kesavarama Murthy and Savitri Devi (Kallakuri) I.; m. Radha Modukuri, Aug. 15, 1988; 1 child, Ramya Mala. B of Tech., Indian Inst. Tech., 1984, M of Tech., 1985; MS in Computer Sci., Rice U., 1992, PhD in Computer Sci., 1993. Rsch. asst. I.I.T., India, 1985; teaching asst. Rice U., Houston, 1988-90, rsch. asst., 1990-92; systems engr. rsch. & devel. CMC Ltd., India, 1986-88; researcher Keck Ctr., Houston, 1992; rsch. assoc. in computational biology U. So. Calif., L.A., 1993-95; biocomputational scientist Sequana Therapeutics, Inc., San Diego, 1995—; presenter in field. Contbr. articles to profl. jours. W.M. Keck Found. fellow; Nat. Merit scholar. Mem. Assn. Computing Machinery, Telugu Assn. So. Calif.

IGNAT, STEVEN JOHN, aerospace company executive; b. Painesville, Ohio, June 20, 1958; s. Elmer Henry and Margret Mary (Lipovich) I.; m. Maria Eugenia Yanez, Oct. 29, 1994. BS in Engring., West Point (N.Y.) Acad., 1980; postgrad., U. Ariz., 1995—. Project mgr., rsch. engr. air defense systems divsn. Gen. Dynamics Corp., Pomona, Calif., 1987-91; program devel. mgr. Hughes Missile Systems Co., Tucson, 1991—. Capt. U.S. Army, 1980-87. Recipient Bausch & Lomb Sci. award, 1977. Republican. Roman Catholic. Home: 1261 W Sandtrap Way Tucson AZ 85737-6909

IGO, GEORGE JEROME, physics educator; b. Greeley, Colo., Sept. 2, 1925; s. Henry J. and Ida J. (Danielsen) I.; m. Nancy Tebonn, May 12, 1953; children: Saffron, Peter Alexander. AB, Harvard Coll., 1949; MS, U. Calif., Berkeley, 1951, Phd, 1953. Postdoctoral Yale Univ., 1954, Brook Haven Nat. Lab., Upton, N.Y., 1955-57; instr. Stanford Univ., Palo Alto, Calif., 1957-59; guest prof. Univ. Heidelberg, Germany, 1960; staff mem. Lawrence Berkeley (Calif.) Lab., 1961-66, Los Alamos (N.Mex.) Nat. Lab., 1966-68; prof. UCLA, 1969—. With U.S. Army, 1944-46. Recipient Fulbright Travel award, 1960, Saclay, France, 1970, Sr. Scientist award Alexander von Humboldt Found., 1991. Fellow Am. Phys. Soc. Office: UCLA Dept Physics 405 Hilgard Ave Los Angeles CA 90024-1301

II, JACK MORITO, aerospace engineer; b. Tokyo, Mar. 20, 1926; s. Iwao and Kiku Ii; came to U.S., 1954, naturalized, 1966; BS, Tohoku U., 1949; MS, U. Washington, 1956; M in Aero. Engring., Cornell U., 1959; PhD in Aero. and Astronautics, U. Wash., 1964; PhD in Engring., U. Tokyo, 1979; children: Keiko, Yoshiko, Mutsuya. Reporter, Asahi Newspaper Press, Tokyo, 1951-54; aircraft designer Fuji Heavy Industries Ltd. Co., Tokyo, Japan, 1956-58; mem. staff structures rsch. Boeing Co., Seattle, 1962—. Mem. AIAA, Japan Shumy and Culture Soc. (pres. 1976—), Sigma Xi. Mem. Congregational Ch. Contbr. numerous articles on aerodyns. to profl. jours. Office: The Boeing Co M S 67-HC Seattle WA 98124

IJAMS, JAN ALLISON, lighting technician; b. Morenci, Ariz., Apr. 29, 1944; s. Mel Allison and Era Dardenella (Hickey) I.; m. Cindy Casey, 1974 (div. 1982). BFA in Lighting, U. Ariz., 1975; MFA, Ohio U., 1977. Dir. theatre Waynesburg (Pa.) Coll., 1977-79; staff dir., tech. dir. Meadows Playhouse, Las Vegas, 1979-82; stage electrician IATSE # 720, Las Vegas, 1983-90; light operator Desert Inn Hotel, Las Vegas, 1991-93, Starlight Express Hilton Hotel, Las Vegas, 1993—; actor Theatre West, Las Vegas, 1988—; lighting designer Clark County C.C., Las Vegas, 1982—. Dir.: (film) The Auction, 1973. Sgt. U.S. Army, 1969-72, Vietnam. Named one of Outstanding Young Men Am., 1976-77. Home and Office: 3895 Las Vegas Blvd N Las Vegas NV 89115-1505

IKEDA, CLYDE JUNICHI, plastic and reconstructive surgeon; b. Kobe, Japan, 1951; s. Paul Tamotsu and Kazu (Murayama) I. BA, SUNY, Binghamton, 1973; MD, N.Y. Med. Coll., Valhalla, 1979. Chmn. residency tng. program St. Francis Meml. Hosp., San Francisco, 1991—, med. dir. burn ctr., 1992—, med. examiner, 1993—, med. dir. wound healing ctr., 1994—. Fellow Am. Coll. Surgeons. Office: 1199 Bush St Ste 640 San Francisco CA 94109-5999

IKEDA, DONNA RIKA, state senator; b. Honolulu, Aug. 31, 1939; d. William G. and Lillian (Kim) Yoshida; div.; children: Rika, Aaron, Julie. BA in Speech, U. Hawaii. Substitute tchr., 1969-71; legis. rschr. Hawaii Rep. Rsch. Office, 1971-74; asst. v.p. Grand Pacific Life Ins. Ltd., Honolulu, 1989—; mem. Hawaii Ho. of Reps., 1974-86, Hawaii Senate, 1987—. Office: Hawaii Senate Hemmeter Bldg Rm 503 235 S Beretania St Honolulu HI 96813

IKEDA, MOSS MARCUS MASANOBU, state education official, lecturer, consultant; b. Los Angeles, Sept. 11, 1931; s. Masao Eugene and Masako (Yamashina) I.; m. Shirley Yaeko Okimoto; children: Cynthia Cecile Ikeda Tamashiro, Mark Eugene, Matthew Albert. BE, U. Hawaii, 1960, MEd, 1962; postgrad. Stanford U., 1961-62; M in Mil. Art and Sci., U.S. Army Command and Gen. Staff Coll., 1975; grad. U.S. Army War Coll., 1976; EdD, U. Hawaii, 1986. Tchr., Farrington H.S., Honolulu, 1962-64; vice-prin. Kailua Intermediate Sch. 1964-65; adminstrv. intern Central Intermediate Sch., Honolulu, 1965-66; vice-prin. Kaimuki H.S., Honolulu, 1966-67; prin. Kawananakoa Intermediate Sch., Honolulu, 1967-68, Kailua H.S., 1969-71, Kalaheo H.S., Kailua, 1972-77; ednl. specialist Hawaii Dept. Edn., Honolulu, 1977-79, ednl. adminstr., 1979-95; frequent spkr. on edn.; lectr. U. Hawaii, 1987—. Served with AUS, 1951-57, 68-69, col. U.S. Army ret. Decorated Legion of Merit, Army Commendation medal. Mem. Nat. Assn. Secondary Sch. Prins., Western Assn. Schs. and Colls. (past bd. dirs., pres., chair), Accrediting Commn. for Sch's. (immediate past chair), Network for Outcome-Based Schs., Commonwealth Coun. for Ednl. Adminstrn., Assn. U.S. Army, Res. Officers Assn., Go For Broke Assn., Army War Coll. Alumni Assn., Hawaii Govt. Employees Assn., Phi Delta Kappa, Phi Kappa Phi. Home and Office: 47-494 Apoalewa Pl Kaneohe HI 96744-4565

IKEDA, TSUGUO (IKE IKEDA), social services center administrator, consultant; b. Portland, Oreg., Aug. 15, 1924; s. Tom Minoru and Tomoe Ikeda; m. Sumiko Hara, Sept. 2, 1951; children: Wanda Amy, Helen Mari, Julie Ann, Patricia Kiyo. BA, Lewis & Clark Coll., 1949; MSW, U. Wash., 1951. Social group worker Neighborhood House, Seattle, 1951-53; exec. dir. Atlantic St. Ctr., Seattle, 1953-86; pres. Urban Partnerships, Seattle, 1986-88, Tsuguo "Ike" Ikeda and Assoc., Seattle, 1988—; cons. Seattle, 1988—; cons. Commn. on Religion and Race, Washington, 1973, North Northeast Mental Health Ctr., Portland, 1985; affirmative action cons. NASW, Washington, 1977; cons./trainer various other orgns.; conf. coord. Beyond the Mask of Denial Wash. State Conf. on Drug/Alcohol/Substance Abuse in the Asian/Pacific Islander Cmtys., 1993; coord. Minority Mental Health Colloquium in Wash., 1994-95; coord. Asian Pacific Islander Coming Home Together Summit-95, Tacoma, Asian Pacific Bi-Ann. Leadership Conf., 1995-96; Tsuguo "Ike" Ikeda, Pub. Svc. ann. award established in 1987. Mem. Nat. Task Force to develop standards and goals for juv. delinquency, 1976; mem. Gov.'s Select Panel for social and health svcs., Olympia, Wash., 1977; chmn. Asian Am. Task Force, Community Coll., Seattle dist., 1982, King County Coordinated Health Care Initiative Client Edn., Mktg. Subcom., 1993; div. chmn. social agys. Seattle United Way campaign, 1985; vice-chmn. Wash. State Com. on Vocat. Edn., Olympia, 1985-86, chmn. 1986-87; chmn. regional adv. com. Dept. Social and Health Svcs., 1990-91; mem. Gov. Mike Lawry's Commn. on Ethics Govt., Campaign Practices, 1993—. With Mil. Intelligence Lang. Sch., 1945-46. Recipient cert. appreciation U.S. Dept. Justice, Washington, 1975-76, Am. Dream award Community Coll. Dist., Seattle, 1984, Asian Counseling & Referral Svc., 1991, 95, Wing Luke Mus., 1991-92, Atlantic St. Ctr., 1992, Seattle Chines Post, 1992, Bishop's award, PNW Conf., U. Meth. Ch., Tacoma, Wash., 1984, community service award Seattle Rotary Club, 1985, Outstanding Citizen award Mcpl. League, Seattle and King County, 1986, Outstanding Leadership award Dept. Social and Health Svcs., 1993, community service award South Pacific Islander Program Seattle Pub. Schs., 1993, Pasasalmat award Filipino Youth Activities, 1993, Tsuguo "Ike" Ikeda Park, 1995, numerous others. Mem. Nat. Assn. Social Workers (chpt. pres., Social Worker of Yr. 1971), Vol. Agy. Exec. Coalition (pres., Outstanding Community Svc. award 1979), Ethnic Minority Mental Health Consortium (chmn., Outstanding Ldr. 1982, David E. "Ned" Skinner Community Svc. award 1990), Minority Exec. Dirs. Coalition (organizer, mem. chmn. 1980-86). Democrat. Methodist.

ILKIW, JANET ELIZABETH, veterinary science educator; b. Wahroonga, NSW, Australia, June 14, 1949; d. Albert George and Laura Margheritta (Kerz) Wright; m. William John Ilkiw, 1970 (div.). BVS, U. Sydney, 1972, PhD, 1980. Diplomate Bd. of Veterinary Surgeons, NSW. Tutor, vet anaesthetist U. Sydney/Vet. Clin. Studies, NSW, 1976-79, lectr., 1979-82, sr. lectr., head dept., 1983-87; asst. prof. dept. surgery U. Calif., Davis, 1987-91, assoc. prof., 1992—, assoc. prof, head dept. surgery, 1994—. Mem. Assn. Vet. Anaesthetists, Australian Coll. Vet. Surgeons. Office: Univ Calif Davis CA 95616

ILLMAN, DEBORAH LOUISE, chemist; b. Seattle, Jan. 15, 1955; d. Robert Ware and Patricia Ann (Wyman) I.; m. Michael Lloyd Brown, June 30, 1976 (div. Jan. 1983). BS in Chemistry, U. Wash., 1976; PhD in Chemistry, UNICAMP, Campinas, Brazil, 1981. High sch. tchr. Am. Sch. Campinas, 1977-79; grad. research fellow UNICAMP, 1978-81; postdoctoral lectr. chemistry U. Wash., Seattle, 1982-84, assoc. dir., 1984-93; assoc. editor Chem. & Engring. News, Seattle, 1993—; cons. Infometrix, Inc., Seattle, 1982—. Author: (textbook) Chemometrics, 1986. Candidate for State Legislature 46th dist., Seattle, 1986. NSF travel award to attend NATO Advance Study Inst., Italy, 1983. Mem. AAAS, Chemometrics Soc., Am. Chem. Soc. (editor Puget Sound Chemist 1983-84). Office: Chem & Engring News 4715 NE 100th St Seattle WA 98125-8133

IMAD, AZMI PHILIP, environmental health and safety engineer; b. Dhour Shweir, Lebanon, Nov. 12, 1942; came to U.S., 1976; s. Philip Khattar and Zakieh (Hanna Beshara) Emad; m. Sana'a Rahbany. BS, Am. U., Beirut, 1963; MSc, U. London, 1966. Registered profl. safety engr. Dir. safety ctr. Am. U., Beirut, 1966-76; environ. protection specialist U. Md., College Park, 1976-79; dir. environ. health and safety, radiation safety officer U. Colo., Boulder, 1979—; safety cons. NIH, Bethesda, Md., 1976-77; developed and presented nationwide tng. seminars on hazardous materials and safety; produced a video tng. program on lab. safety. Contbr. articles to profl. publs. Internat. Atomic Energy Agy. fellow, 1964-66. Mem. Am. Soc. Safety Engrs., Health Physics Soc., Campus Safety Assn. (pres. 1988-89, outstanding svcs. award 1983, outstanding leadership awards 1987, 90, 94). Office: U Colo Campus Box 375 Boulder CO 80309-0375

IMAMURA, DANIEL TATSUYA, computer programmer, consultant; b. Honolulu, July 17, 1964; s. Takeshi and Sachiyo (Hayashi) I. BS in Math. and Computer Sci., U. Hawaii, 1986. Computer programmer Rsch. Corp. of U. Hawaii, Honolulu, 1987-89, computer specialist, 1989—; ptnr. HIT Computing Svcs., Honolulu, 1992-94. Mem. IEEE, Assn. for Computing Machinery. Office: IBSNAT Project 2500 Dole St # 117 Honolulu HI 96822-2303

IMAMURA, EUGENE HACHIRO, osteopathic physician, surgeon; b. Waipahu, Hawaii. BS, U. Hawaii, 1943; DO, Kansas City Coll. Osteopath, 1953. Intern Waldo Gen. Hosp., Seattle, 1953-54; pvt. practice Seattle, 1955-86, Terrace, 1986—; pres. of staff Waldo Gen. Hosp., Seattle, 1957-58. Life patron Edmonds Art Festival. With U.S. Army, 1944-46. Mem. Am. Osteo. Assn. (life mem.), UHS Coll. of Oseteo. Med., Wash. Osteo. Med. Assn. (life), Am. Coll. Gen. Practitioners, Am. Coll. Osteo. Family Physicians. Home: 16024 75th Pl W Edmonds WA 98026-4524 Office: 5707 244th St SW Mountlake Terrace WA 98043-5449

IMANA, JORGE GARRON, artist; b. Sucre, Bolivia, Sept. 20, 1930; s. Juan S. and Lola (Garron) I.; grad. Fine Arts Acad., U. San Francisco Xavier, 1950; cert. Nat. Sch. for Tchrs., Bolivia, 1952; came to U.S., 1964, naturalized, 1974; m. Cristina Imana; children—George, Ivan. Prof. art Nat. Sch. Tchrs., Sucre, 1954-56; prof. biology Padilla Coll., Sucre, 1956-60; head dept. art Inst. Normal Simon Bolivar, La Paz, Bolivia, 1961-62; propr., mgr. The Artists Showroom, San Diego, 1973—. Over 90 one-man shows of paintings in U.S., S. Am. and Europe, 1952—, including: Gallery Banet, La Paz, 1965, Artists Showroom, San Diego, 1964, 66, 68, 74, 76, 77, San Diego Art Inst., 1966, 68, 72, 73, Contrast Gallery, Chula Vista, Calif., 1966, Central Public Library, San Diego, 1969, Universidad de Zulia, Maracaibo, Venezuela, 1969, Spanish Village Art Center, San Diego, 1974, 75, 76, La Jolla Art Assn. Gallery, 1969, 72-93, Internat. Gallery, Washington, 1976, Galeria de Arte L'Atelier, La Paz, 1977, Museo Nacional, La Paz, 1987, Casa del Arte, La Jolla, Calif., 1987, Museo Nacional, La Paz, Bolivia, 1988, Simon Patino Found., Bolivia, 1994; numerous group shows including: Fine Arts Gallery, San Diego, 1964, Mus. of Modern Art, Paris, 1973, exhibits in galleries of Budapest (Hungary), 1975, Moscow (USSR), 1975, Warsaw (Poland), 1976; represented in permanent collections: Museo Nacional, La Paz, Bolivia, Museo de la Universidad de Potosi, Bolivia, Muse Nacional de Bogota, Colombia, S. Am., Ministerio de Edn., Managua, Nicaragua, Bolivian embassy, Moscow and Washington, also pvt. collections in U.S., Europe and Latin Am.; executed many murals including: Colegio Padilla, Sucre, Bolivia, 1958, Colegio Junin, Sucre, Bolivia, 1959, Sindicato de Construccion Civil, Lima, Peru, 1960. Hon. consul of Bolivia, So. Calif., 1969-73. Served to lt. Bolivian Army, 1953. Recipient Mcpl. award Sucre, Bolivia, 1958. Mem. San Diego Art Inst., San Diego Watercolor Soc., Internat. Fine Arts Guild, La Jolla Art Assn. Home: 3357 Caminito Gandara La Jolla CA 92037-2907

IMBER, WAYNE EVAN, allergist; b. N.Y.C., 1954. MD, St. Louis U., 1979. Allergist Valley Presbyn. Hosp., Van Nuys, Calif. Office: 16861 Ventura Blvd Ste 305 Encino CA 91436-1706*

IMMKEN, LA DONNA L., medical geneticist; b. St. Louis, Jan. 27, 1950. MD, U. Mo., 1977. Med. geneticist Valley Children's Hosp., Fresno, Calif. Office: Vly Childrens Hosp Dept Med Genetics Prenatal 3151 N Millbrook Ave Fresno CA 93703-1425*

IMPERIAL, JOHN VINCE, management information engineer, consultant; b. Honolulu, Feb. 5, 1958; s. Filomeno and Vicenta (Lapinig) I.; m. Lynn Sau-Mee Ching, Aug. 13, 1988. BSEE, U. Hawaii, 1982; MBA with distinction, Hawaii Pacific U., 1993, MS in Info. Scis., 1994. Rsch. engr. Lockheed Missiles and Space Co., Sunnyvale, Calif., 1982-86; design engr. SECON Inc., Redondo Beach, Calif., 1986; mem. tech. staff TRW Def. Systems Group, Redondo Beach, 1986-88; systems engr. SAIC Comsystems, Hickam AFB, Hawaii, 1988-89; sr. systems engr. Computer Scis. Corp., Honolulu, 1989-92, Camp Smith, Hawaii, 1992-93; sr. systems engr. I-Net, Inc., Wheeler Army Airfield, Hawaii, 1993-94; cons. EDS Mgmt. Consulting Svcs., Mililani, Hawaii, 1994—; cons. to various orgns., Honolulu, 1990-94. Coach, referee Am. Youth Soccer Orgn., Pearl City, Hawaii, 1990—; bd. dirs., coach SAY Soccer, Honolulu, 1991. Mem. IEEE, Soc. Photooptical and Instrumentation Engrs., Computer Measurement Group, Assn. for Computing Machinery, Delta Mu Delta, Epsilon Delta Pi. Home and Office: 94-294 Lupua Pl Mililani HI 96789-2151

IMPROTA, ROBERT STEPHEN, plastic surgeon; b. Brklyn., 1943. MD, SUNY, 1969. Plastic surgeon Pleasant Valley Hosp., Camarillo, Calif. Office: 2460 N Ponderosa Dr # A 117 Camarillo CA 93010-2375*

IMRE, JOHN VANARSDALE, quality improvement consultant; b. N.Y.C., Sept. 23, 1937; s. Raymond Paul and Elisabeth (Muir) I. B in Elec. Engring., Cornell U., 1962; BA in English Lit., U. Wash., 1975, MA in English Lit., 1979; MA in Whole Sys. Design, Antioch U., 1990. Quality improvement pubs. cons., author Volt Tech. Boeing Aerospace, Seattle, 1984-86; author, editor, writer, instr. Quality Improvement Ctr. Boeing Commercial Airplane Group, Renton, Wash., 1986-88; process improvement methods cons., mgr. Everett (Wash.) Divsn. Boeing Commercial Airplane Group, 1988—; cons., instr. in field; presenter papers. AUthor: Canyon Racer's Pocket Guide, 1983, Managing Quality Guide, 1985 (Excellence award Soc. Tech. Comm. 1986), Guide to Total Quality, 1987; co-author: Total Quality Improvement, 1987 (Disting. award Soc. Tech. Comm. 1988); contbr. newsletters. Recipient Achievement award Soc. Tech. Comm., 1987, Merit award Internat. Assn. Bus. Communicators, 1988. Mem. ASTD (chpt. bd. dirs.), Enological Soc. (Seattle chpt. bd., regional bd. sec. 1990—, chmn. many coms.), Profl. Ski Instrs. Am. (cert. level 3), Orgnl. Devel. Network (chpt. bd. dirs., planning com. 1995, conf. 1994—), Assn. Quality and Participation, Mensa. Home: 344 18th Ave E Seattle WA 98112-5109

INABA, LAWRENCE AKIO, educational director; b. Honolulu, May 19, 1932; m. Violet C. Oki, Mar. 19, 1955; 1 child, Lori. BEd, U. Hawaii, 1960, MEd, 1963; PhD, Ohio State U., 1970; EdD, Ashiya U., Japan, 1980. Cert. tchr., Hawaii. Electronics instr. Roosevelt High Sch., Honolulu, 1959-68; rsch., teaching assoc. Ohio State U., Columbus, 1968-70; program specialist vocat. edn. Dept. Edn., Honolulu, 1970-75, adminstr. vocat. edn., 1975-76, ednl. dir., 1976-85; state dir. vocat. edn. U. Hawaii, Honolulu, 1985-90; dir. Ashiya U. Rsch. Ctr., Honolulu, 1991—; cons. in field. Author: Analysis of Job Tasks, 1973, Effective Use of Advisory Committee, 1975, Content Identification and Vaildation, 1974, Trends and Developments in Vocational Education, 1984. NDEA fellow, 1967. Mem. Hawaii Vocat. Assn., Am. Vocat. Assn. (Guidance Divsn. Svc. award 1991), Hawaii Electronics Assn., Am. Tech. Educators Assn., Epsilon Pi Tau (Disting. Svc. award 1988, Laureate citation 1978), Phi Delta Kappa. Home: 3791 Pukalani Pl Honolulu HI 96816-3813 Office: 1117 Kapahulu Ave Honolulu HI 96816-5811

INAMA, CHRISTOPHER ROY, lawyer; b. Burbank, Calif., Apr. 4, 1952; s. Leo H. Inama and Jeanne (Bauer) Truax; m. Colleen J. Deal, Dec. 30, 1986. BA, U. Calif., Santa Barbara, 1974; JD, Hastings Coll. Law, San Francisco, 1977. Bar: Calif. 1977, U.S. Dist. Ct. (no. dist.) Calif. 1977. Atty. Law Office of Christopher R. Inama, San Carlos, Calif., 1978—; chief of security San Francisco Giants, 1974-89. County chair Calif. Libertarian Party, San Mateo County, 1990-92; candidate Calif. State Assembly, Dist. 21, 1990, Calif. State Senate, Dist. 11, 1992. With USCGR, 1987—. Mem. MENSA, Hastings Old Boys Rugby Club, St. Thomas More Soc., Native Sons of Golden West #66. Libertarian. Roman Catholic. Office: Law Office of C R Inama 790 Laurel St San Carlos CA 94070-3114

INCAUDO, GARY ARNOLD, allergist; b. Mount Clemers, Mich., 1945. MD, U. Calif., Irvine, 1971. Allergist U. Hosp., Sacramento; with Enloe Hosp., Chico Cmty. Hosp.; clin. prof. U. Calif., Davis. Office: 270 Cohasset Rd Ste 100 Chico CA 95926-2210*

INCAUDO, JOSEPH AUGUST, engineering company executive; b. 1940. MA, UCLA; MBA, Harvard U., 1964. CPA, Calif. Cons., auditor Touche Ross & Co., L.A., 1964-68; contr. Bullocks, L.A., 1969-76; v.p. ops. May Co., L.A., 1976-78; v.p. fin. Tobias Kotzin Corp., L.A., 1978-80; v.p., CFO Vinnell Corp., Alhambra, Calif., 1980-83; sr. v.p., CFO Aecom Tech. Corp., L.A., 1983—; bd. dirs. Resource Scis. of Arabia Ltd., Inst. of Social and Econ. Policy in the Middle East, John F. Kennedy Sch. Govt., Harvard U. Office: Aecom Tech Corp 3250 Wilshire Blvd # 5 Los Angeles CA 90010-1502

INDIEK, VICTOR HENRY, finance corporation executive; b. Spearville, Kans., Nov. 15, 1937; s. Ben W. and Helen Ann (Schreck) I.; m. Marlene Gould, June 2, 1962; children: Kathy, Kevin. Student, U. Nebr., 1955-57; BS in Bus., U. Kans., 1959; postgrad., U. Nebr., 1955-57. CPA, Kans. Audit mgr. Arthur Andersen & Co., Kansas City, Mo., 1961-70; pres., chief exec. officer Fed. Home Loan Mortgage Corp., Washington, 1970-77; pres., dir. Builders Capital Corp., Los Angeles, 1977-84; chief fin. officer, exec. v.p. Fin. Corp. of Am., Irvine, Calif., 1984-88; pres., chief exec. officer FarWest Savs. and Loan Assn., Newport Beach, Calif., 1988—; v.p. and pres. regional Assn. Small Businesses Investment Cos., 1979-81, bd. govs. nat. assn., 1982. Mem. Selective Service Bd., Santa Monica, Calif., 1978; capt. United Fund, Kansas City, 1968. Served with USN, 1959-61. Republican. Roman Catholic. Office: FarWest Savs & Loan Assn 4001 Macarthur Blvd Newport Beach CA 92660-2510

INFANTE, CHRISTINE MARIE, communications consultant; b. Pitts., May 3, 1952; d. Umbert Rocco and Elizabeth Ann Infante; m. Paul Henrie Levy, June 9, 1980; children: Aaron, Alexia. BA, Carnegie-Mellon, 1974. Pub. relations supr. Jones & Laughlin Steel Corp., Pitts., 1974-79; communications cons. Christine M. Infante Communications, San Diego, 1979-83; editor Pacific Bell/Pacific Telesis, San Francisco, 1984-86; communications cons. Wm. M. Mercer Meidinger Hansen, Boston, 1986-89; cons. Christine Infante Advt. Publs., Exec. & Mktg. Communications, 1989-91, Towers Perrin, San Diego, 1992—. Copywriter Dimensions: The Business of Humor, 1986 (Andy award 1987); editor CONSULT Mag., 1989, PACIFIC Mag. 1984-86. Recipient Merit award Pub. Rels. Soc. Am., 1985, Merit award Bell Ringer Publicity Club, Boston, 1989. Office: Towers Perrin 7676 Hazard Center Dr Ste 100 San Diego CA 92108-4504

ING, MALCOLM ROSS, eye surgeon, educator; b. Honolulu, Oct. 31, 1934; s. Edmund T.K. and Audrey Helen (Dunseath) I.; m. Audrey Anne Regut, Dec. 22, 1955; children: Karen, Debra, Sandra. MD, Yale U., 1959. Chief ophthalmology Queen's Hosp., Honolulu, 1970-73, 83-85, 87-88; chief ophthalmology U. Hawaii Sch. Med., Honolulu, 1983—, prof. ophthalmology, 1988—; chief ophthalmology Kapiolani Med. Ctr., Honolulu, 1988—. Capt. USMC, 1966-68. Mem. AMA, Am. Assn. Pediat. Ophthalmology and Strabismus (charter, Honor award 1993), Am. Ophthalmol. Soc., Am. Bd. Ophthalmology (diplomate, assoc. examiner), Hawaii Med. Assn., Hawaii Ophthalmol. Soc. (pres. 1983-85). Office: Kapiolani Med Ctr 1319 Punahou St # 1110 Honolulu HI 96826

ING, ROBERT YUN KWIN, allergist; b. Hong Kong, 1933. MD, Tulane U., 1961. Allergist Inland Valley Med. Ctr. Hosp., Wildomar, Calif. Office: 25485 Med Center Dr Ste 104 Murrieta CA 92562*

INGALLS, JEREMY, poet, educator; b. Gloucester, Mass., Apr. 2, 1911; d. Charles A. and May E. (Dodge) Ingalls. AB, Tufts Coll., 1932, AM, 1933; student, U. Chgo., 1938-39; LHD, Rockford Coll., 1960; LittD, Tufts U., 1965. Asst. prof. English Lit. Western Coll., Oxford, Ohio, 1941-43; resident poet, asst. prof. English lit. Rockford (Ill.) Coll., 1948-50, successively assoc. prof. English and Asian studies, prof., chmn. div. arts, chmn. English dept., 1950-60; Fulbright prof. Am. lit., Japan, 1957; Rockefeller Found. lectr. Kyoto Am. Studies seminar, 1958. Author: A Book of Legends, 1941, The Metaphysical Sword, 1941, Tahl, 1945, The Galilean Way, 1953, The Woman from the Island, 1958, These Islands Also, 1959, This Stubborn Quantum, 1983, Summer Liturgy, 1985, The Epic Tradition and Related Essays, 1989; translator (from Chinese) A Political History of China, 1840-1928 (Li Chien-Nung), 1956, The Malice of Empire (Yao Hsin-Nung), 1970, (from Japanese) Tenno Yugao (Nakagawa), 1975. Recipient Yale Series of Younger Poets prize, 1941, Shelley Meml. award, 1950, and other awards for poetry; apptd. hon. epic poet laureate United Poets Laureate Internat., 1965; Guggenheim fellow, 1943, Chinese classics rsch. fellow Republic of China, 1945, 46, Am. Acad. Arts and Letters grantee, 1944, Ford Found. fellow Asian studies, 1952, 53. Fellow Internat. Inst. Arts and Letters; mem. MLA (chmn. Oriental-western lit. rels. conf.), Assn. Asian Studies (life), Authors Guild, Poetry Soc. Am., New Eng. Poetry Soc., Dante Soc. Am. (life), Phi Beta Kappa, Chi Omega. Episcopalian. Home: 6269 E Rosewood St Tucson AZ 85711-1638

INGBER, BETH, intuitive practitioner/counselor; b. N.Y.C., Feb. 28, 1945; d. Frank and Lillian Ingber. BA, Bklyn. Coll., 1970; MA, UCLA, 1978. Cert. in intuitive cons., counseling, teaching and learning body and kinetic intervention. Spiritual dir. and founder The Stream, L.A., 1980-86; ptnr., co-founder The Healing Partnership, L.A. and Ramona, 1986-90; spiritual dir. and founder The Triple Eye Found., Escondido, Calif., 1990-93; intuitive practitioner, counselor, cons. and tchr. Ramona, 1980—; spiritual activist, co-founder Rising Mountains Setting Suns, Ramona, 1993—; co-founder Spiritual Activist Movement, L.A. and Ramona, 1993—. Author: The Autobiography of Mary Magdalene, 1988; tapes include: The Healing of God, The Alienation of Love, Spirituality: The Last Block to Freedom; videotapes include Breaking the "I" Barrier, 1992. West Coast coord. Wages for Housework Campaign, L.A., 1974-78; co-founder The Looseleaf Directory: Linking Bodies, Minds and Spirits in the Healing Arts, 1994. Mem. Ptnrs. for Planetary Recovery (svc. com. mem. 1994). Office: Rising Mountains Setting Suns PO Box 1607 Ramona CA 92065

INGERMAN, MICHAEL LEIGH, realtor; b. N.Y.C., Nov. 30, 1937; s. Charles Stryker and Ernestine (Leigh) I.; m. Madeleine Edison Sloane; Nov. 24, 1984; children by previous marriage: Shawn Marie, Jenifer Lyn. BS, George Washington U., 1963. Health planner, Marin County, Calif., 1969-72; regional cons. Bay Area Comprehensive Health Coun., San Francisco, 1972-73; hosp. cons. Booz, Allen & Hamilton, San Francisco, 1974; health planning coord. Peralta Hosp., Oakland, Calif., 1975-76; pres. Discern, Inc., mgmt. cons., Nicasio, Calif., 1976-93; prin. Human Resources Mgmt. Group, San Francisco, 1991-93; sales assoc. Frank Howard Allen Realtors, Greenbrae, Calif., 1993—; instr. Golden Gate U., 1981-88. Bd. dirs. Nicasio Land Owners Assn., 1989-91, pres., 1990; coord. Nicasio Disaster Com., 1988-89; nat. bd. dirs. Am. Friends Svc. Com., 1980-81, bd. dirs. John Woolman Sch., 1980-87, 90-94, bd. chmn., 1991, Hospice of Marin, 1983-89, pres. bd. dirs., 1988-89; bd. dirs. Vol. Ctr. Marin, 1991—, Friends Assn. Svc. for the Elderly, 1984-89, pres. 1988-89; mem. Marin County Civil Grand Jury, 1977-78, Nicasio Design Rev. Com., 1979-83; mem. allocation com. Marin County United Way, 1993—, campaign com., 1994—. Office: Frank Howard Allen Realtors 505 Sir Francis Drake Blvd Greenbrae CA 94904-2305

INGERSOLL, ANDREW PERRY, planetary science educator; b. Chgo., Jan. 2, 1940; s. Jeremiah Crary and Minneola (Perry) I.; m. Sarah Morin, Aug. 27, 1961; children: Jeremiah, Ruth Ingersoll Wood, Marion, Minneola, George. BA, Amherst Coll., 1960; PhD, Harvard U., 1965. Rsch. fellow Harvard U., Cambridge, Mass., 1965-66; mem. staff summer study program Woods Hole (Mass.) Oceanographic Inst., 1965, 70-73, 1976, 80, 92; asst. prof. Calif. Inst. Tech., Pasadena, 1966-71, assoc. prof., 1971-76, prof., 1976—; prin. investigator Pioneer Saturn Infrared Radiometer Team, NASA; mem. Voyager Imaging Team, NASA, Cassini Imaging Team; interdisciplinary scientist, Mars Observer Project, Galileo Project, NASA. Bd. trustees Poly. Sch., Pasadena. Fellow AAAS, Am. Geophys. Union; mem. Am. Astron. Soc. (vice chmn. div. planetary sci. 1988-89, chmn. 1989-90). Office: Calif Inst Tech # 170-25 Pasadena CA 91125

INGERSOLL, JOHN GREGORY, physicist, energy specialist, educator; b. Athens, Greece, July 25, 1948; came to U.S., 1971; s. Gregory and Catherine (Asteris) I.; m. Sally Lynn Roberts, Apr. 7, 1984. BS, Nat. Tech. U., Athens, 1970; MS, Syracuse U., 1973; PhD, U. Calif., Berkeley, 1978. Instr. physics U. Calif., 1974-75, research asst. Lawrence Berkeley Lab., 1975-77, from asst. research prof. to assoc. research prof. Lawrence Berkeley Lab., 1978-82; sr. staff scientist Hughes Aircraft Co., Los Angeles, 1983—; staff mem., advisor USN Energy Office, Washington, 1988—; cons. Calif. Energy Commn., Sacramento, 1981-82, U.S. Dept. Energy, Washington, 1981-83, Bldg. Industry, N.Y. and Calif., 1982—; prin. investigator Energy Tech. Group UCLA, 1983—; mem. tech. team for devel. of a comml. passenger electric vehicle GM, 1990—. Contvr. over 70 articles on nuclear sci., renewable energy sources, indoor air quality, efficient utilization of energy in bldgs., passive solar systems and solar elec. energy to profl. jours.; contbg. author to 3 books on energy mgmt. in bldgs.; patentee heat pipe devels., non-freon low power air conditioner for electric vehicles and buses. Mem. Rep. Presdl. Task Force, Calif., 1981-83. Served as lt. USNR, 1982—. Recipient 2d Pl. award Edison Electric Inst., Gen. Motors, and Dept. Energy, 1993; fellow Democritus Nuclear Research Ctr., Athens, 1970, Syracuse U., 1972, Rockefeller Found., 1974. Mem. Gen. Motors team (tasked with development, production, mktg. of passenger electric vehicle). Presbyterian. Home: 21315 Lighthill Dr Topanga CA 90290-4442 Office: Hughes Aircraft Co PO Box 902 El Segundo CA 90245-0902

INGERSOLL, RICHARD KING, lawyer; b. Algoma, Wis., Aug. 13, 1944; s. Robert Clive and Bernice Eleanore (Koehn) I.; m. Caroline Soi-Keu Yee, Aug. 31, 1968; children: Kristin Paula Juk-Yee, Karin Eleanor Juk-Ling. BBA, U. Mich, 1966; JD, U. Calif.-Berkeley, 1969. Bar: Ill. 1969, Hawaii 1973. Asst. prof. U. Ill.-Champaign, 1969-70; assoc. Sidley & Austin, Chgo., 1970-73; ptnr. Rush, Moore, Craven, Kim & Stricklin, Honolulu, 1973-88; prin. Gelber, Gelber, Ingersoll & Klevansky, Honolulu, 1989—; speaker tax law seminars; bd. dirs. MacFarms of Hawaii, Inc., Honolulu. Mem. ABA (Taxation, Bus., and Internat Law coms.), Waialae Country Club (mem. finance com.). Democrat. Home: 944 Waiholo St Honolulu HI 96821-1226

INGLE, JAMES CHESNEY, JR., geology educator; b. Los Angeles, Nov. 6, 1935; s. James Chesney and Florence Adelaide (Geldart) I.; m. Fredricka Ann Bornholdt, June 14, 1958; 1 child, Douglas James. B.S. in Geology, U. So. Calif., 1959, M.S. in Geology, 1962, Ph.D. in Geology, 1966. Registered geologist, Calif. Research assoc. Univ. So. Calif., 1961-65; vis. scholar Tohoku U., Sendai, Japan, 1966-67; asst., assoc. to full prof. Stanford U., Calif., 1968—; W.M. Keck prof. earth scis. Stanford U., 1984—, chmn. dept. geology, 1982-86; co-chief scientist Leg 31 Deep Sea Drilling Project, 1973, co-chief scientist Leg 128 Ocean Drilling Program, 1989; geologist U.S. Geol. Survey W.A.E, 1978-81. Author: Movement of Beach Sand, 1966; contbr. articles to profl. jours. Recipient W.A. Tarr award Sigma Gamma Epsilon, 1958; named Disting. lectr. Am. Assn. Petroleum Geologists, 1986-87, Joint Oceanographic Institutions, 1991; A.I. Leverson award Am. Assn. Petroleum Geologists, 1988. Fellow Geol. Soc. Am., Calif. Acad. Scis.; mem. Cushman Found. (bd. dirs. 1984-91), Soc. Profl. Paleontologists and Mineralogists (Pacific sect. 1958—, pres. 1993-94), Am. Geophys. Union.

INGLE, JOHN IDE, dental educator; b. Colville, Wash., Jan. 19, 1919; s. John James and Jessie Belle (Ide) I.; m. Joyce Ledgerwood, July 11, 1940; children: John Geoffrey, Leslie Ide Ingle Moxley, Schuyler Neal. Student, Wash. State U., 1936-38; D.D.S., Northwestern U., 1942; M.S.D., U. Mich., 1948. Diplomate: Am. Bd. Endodontics, Am. Bd. Periodontology. Asst. Northwestern U., 1942-43; asst. prof. endodontics and periodontology Sch. Dentistry, U. Wash., 1948-51, assoc. prof., 1951-59, prof., 1959-64, exec. officer dept., 1956-64; dean Sch. Dentistry, U. So. Calif., Los Angeles, 1964-72; dir. div. internat. health, sr. profl. assoc. Inst. Medicine Nat. Acad. Scis., 1973-78; pres. Palm Springs Seminars, 1978-92; sr. lectr. UCLA, 1979; vis. lectr. Loma Linda U., 1983; attending staff exec. com. Los Angeles County/ U. So. Calif. Med. Center, 1964-72; cons. Nat. Bd. Dental Examiners, 1964-68; endodontics, asst. surgeon gen. U.S. Army, 1969-70, Nat. Naval Med. Center, 1973; mem. adv. com. dental health Office Sec. HEW, 1970-72; mem. rev. com. on dental edn. NIH, 1970; mem. adv. panel on nat. health ins. U.S. Ho. of Reps. Ways and Means Com., 1975. Author: (with others) Endodontics, 1965, 2d edit. (with E.E. Beveridge) 1976, 3d edit., 1985, 4th edit. (with L.K. Bakland), 1994, (with A.L. Ogilvie) An Atlas of Pulpal and Periapical Biology, 1965; editor: (with P. Blair) International Dental Care Delivery Systems, 1978. Bd. dirs. Los Angeles United Way Crusade, 1967-69. Served with Dental Corps AUS, 1943-46. Recipient Northwestern U. Alumni Merit award, 1966. Fellow AAAS, Internat., Am. colls. dentists; mem. Internat. Assn. Dental Research, Am. Assn. Endodontists (past pres., Ralph F. Sommer research award 1987), Am. Acad. Periodontology, Am. Dental Assn. (cons. dental therapeutics), Los Angeles Dental Soc. (sec. 1968-71), Am. Assn. Dental Schs., Alpha Omega (hon. mem., Achievement medal 1985). Club: Cosmos (Washington). Home: 255 Skate Creek Rd Ashford WA 98304-9738

INGLE, ROBERT D., newspaper editor, newspaper executive; b. Sioux City, Iowa, Apr. 29, 1939; s. Walter J. and Thelma L (McCoy) I.; m. Martha N. Nelson, Sept. 12, 1964 (div. 1984); 1 child, Julia L.; m. Sandra R. Reed, Mar. 2, 1985. B.A. in Journalism and Polit. Sci., U. Iowa, 1962. Various positions Miami Herald, 1962-75, asst. mng. editor, 1975-77, mng. editor, 1977-81; exec. editor San Jose (Calif.) Mercury News, 1981-93, pres., exec. editor, 1993-95; v.p. new media Knight-Ridder Inc., San Jose, Calif., 1995—. Pres. Calif. First Amendment Coalition, 1990-92. Mem. AP Mng. Editors Assn., Am. Soc. Newspaper Editors. Office: Knight Ridder New Media Ctr 981 Ridder Park Dr San Jose CA 95131

INGOLDSBY, WILLIAM POWER, realtor; b. L.A., June 20, 1947; s. Arthur William and Elizabeth M. (Power) I. BA, U. Calif., Riverside, 1969; MA, U. Wales, Cardiff, 1970; MLitt, Oxford (Eng.) U., 1972. Real estate salesman William Wilson Co., Pasadena, Calif., 1981-88; office mgr. Jon Douglas Co., Pasadena, 1988-90, estates dir. Douglas Properties, 1990-92; real estate salesman French and French Fine Properties, Santa Fe, 1993—. Mem. Santa Fe Assn. Realtors. Office: French and French Fine Prop 231 Washington Ave Santa Fe NM 87501-1926

INGRAM, ARTONYON S., mental health professional, therapist; b. Fremont, N.C., Dec. 2, 1962; s. Gliffie and Doris Ingram. BS, Atlantic Christian Coll., 1985; cert. in drugs and alcohol abuse, Pierce Coll., Steilacoom, Wash., 1993, AA, 1993; MEd, City U., Bellevue, Wash., 1995; cert. parent educator, Clover Pk. Tech. Coll., 1995. Teaching parent Onslow Mental Health Ctr., Jacksonville, N.C., 1987-89; social svcs. asst. Rainer Vista Health Care, Puyallup, Wash., 1990-91, Lakewood Health Care,

Tacoma, Wash., 1990-91; group life counselor Jessie Dyslin Boys Ranch, Tacoma, Wash., 1991-92; case mgr. Puget Sound Ctr., Tacoma, Wash., 1991; counselor intern Dotters Counseling Ctr., Puyallup, Wash., 1992-93, Cross Rd. Treatment Ctr., Tacoma, 1993; instr. Clover Pk. Tech. Coll., Tacoma, 1993—. Counselor First Bapt. Ch., Jacksonville, N.C. With USNG, 1981-88. Army Nat. Guard scholar, 1978-81, L.N. Forbes scholar, Boeing Engrng. scholar, 1993. Mem. Nat. Assn. Alcoholism and Drug Abuse Counselors, Chem. Dependency Profls. Home: 3910 B 70th Ave NW Gig Harbor WA 98335 Office: Clover Park Tech Coll 4500 Steilacoom Blvd Tacoma WA 98498

INGRAM, CECIL D., accountant, state legislator; b. Blackfoot, Idaho, Dec. 27, 1932; s. Orval Otto and Mary Marjorie (Evans) I.; m. Lois Ann Glenn, Dec. 28, 1952; children: Cynthia, William, Christopher. BBA, U. Oreg., 1962. Contr. transp. & distbn. divsn. Boise (Idaho) Cascade Corp., 1962-91; senator Idaho State Legislature, Boise, 1993—. Capt. U.S. Army, 1953-58, Korea. Mem. Masons. Republican. Baptist. Home: 7025 El Caballo Dr Boise ID 83704-7320

INGRAM, PEGGY JOYCE, secondary education educator; b. Wichita Falls, Tex., Feb. 15, 1943; d. Albert Cronjie and Esther (Wiist) Weiss; m. Darwin Keith Ingram, Aug. 19, 1972; 1 child, Lindsey Michelle. Student, Midwestern U., 1961-62; BS, West Tex. State U., 1966; MNS, U. Okla., 1972; postgrad., Ea. N.Mex. U., 1975. Cert. secondary sci. tchr. Tchr. Palo Duro High Sch., Amarillo, Tex., 1966-72, Texico (N.Mex.) High Sch., 1972-73; tchr., chair sci. dept. Clovis High Sch., 1973—; tchr. Ea. N.Mex. U., Clovis, 1981-82; participant NASA Honors Workshop, Jet Propulsion Lab., 1990. Mem. NEA, Clovis Edn. Assn., Nat. Sci. Tchrs. Assn., N.Mex. Acad. of Sci., Delta Kappa Gamma. Democrat. Methodist. Home: 2501 Williams Ave Clovis NM 88101-3330 Office: Clovis High Sch 1900 N Thornton St Clovis NM 88101-4555

INGRAM, WILLIAM AUSTIN, federal judge; b. Jeffersonville, Ind., July 6, 1924; s. William Austin and Marion (Lane) I.; m. Barbara Brown Lender, Sept. 18, 1947; children: Mary Ingram Mac Calla, Claudia, Betsy Ingram Friebel. Student, Stanford U., 1947; LL.B., U. Louisville, 1950; LLD honoris causas, Santa Clara U., 1994. Assoc., Littler, Coakley, Lauritzen & Ferdon, San Francisco, 1951-55; dep. dist. atty. Santa Clara (Calif.) County, 1955-57; mem. firm Rankin, O'Neal, Luckhardt & Center, San Jose, Calif., 1955-69; judge Mcpl. Ct., Palo Alto-Mountain View, Calif., 1969-71, Calif. Superior Ct., 1971-76; judge U.S. Dist. Ct. (no. dist.) Calif., San Jose, 1976-88, chief judge, 1988-90; sr. judge, 1990—. Served with USMCR, 1943-46. Fellow Am. Coll. Trial Lawyers. Republican. Episcopalian. Office: US Dist Ct 280 S First St Rm 5198 San Jose CA 95113

INLOW, RUSH OSBORNE, chemist; b. Seattle, July 10, 1944; s. Edgar Burke and Marigale (Osborne) I.; BS, U. Wash., 1966; PhD, Vanderbilt U., 1975; m. Gloria Elisa Duran, June 7, 1980. Chemist, sect. chief U.S. Dept. Energy, New Brunswick Lab., Argonne, Ill., 1975-78, chief nuclear safeguards br. Albuquerque ops., 1978-82, sr. program engr. Cruise missile systems, 1983-84, program mgr. Navy Strategic Systems, 1984-85, dir. weapon programs div., 1985-88, dir. prodn. ops. div., 1988-90, asst. mgr. safeguards and security, 1990-94, asst. mgr. nat. def. programs, 1994—; apptd. Fed. Sr. Exec. Svc., 1985. Served with USN, 1966-71. Tenn. Eastman fellow, 1974-75; recipient President's Meritorious Exec. award, 1994. Mem. Am. Chem. Soc., Sigma Xi. Republican. Episcopalian. Contbr. articles to profl. jours.

INMAN, CLAUDIA JEAN, banker; b. Portland, Oreg., Oct. 23, 1942; d. Claude John and Dorothy Caroline (Svarvari) Forrette; m. Charles Dibert, June 28, 1970 (div. Dec. 1977); m. Robert Willard Inman, Apr. 12, 1980; 1 child, Brian Dibert. Student, Portland State Coll., 1970-88, Lewis & Clark Coll., 1979; banking degree, U. Wash., 1983. Proof transit clk. Bank of Calif., Portland, 1960-62, 68-69; proof and transit clk. LaSalle Nat. Bank, Chgo., 1963-65; with computer payroll and ops. Bank of Calif., Portland, 1969, ops. officer, 1974-75, liaison officer, 1975-79, credit officer, 1979-80, corp. loan officer, asst. v.p., 1980-86, asst. v.p. real estate loans, 1986-89, v.p. real estate loans, 1990-93; v.p. comml. loans Bank of Vancouver, Wash., 1993—; bd. dirs. Machinists and Boilermakers Fed. Credit Union, 1983-88. Vol. Oreg. Art Mus. Rental Sales Gallery, Portland, 1987—; participant women in pvt. sector Am. bus.-culture class Internat. Devel. Ctr. Japan, Williamette U., Salem, 1988-91; mem. Women in Action, 1993—. Mem. Oreg. Mortgage Bankers Assn. (com. 1988-91), Oreg. Bankers Assn. (com. 1980—), Robert Morris Assocs. (bd. dirs. Oreg. 1991), Bank Adminstrn. Inst. (bd. dirs. 1984-87), Fin. Women Internat. (nat. bd. dirs. 1985-86), Women in Action, Robert Morris Assocs., Vancouver C. of C., Rotary. Democrat. Roman Catholic. Home: 4660 SW Ormandy Way Portland OR 97221-3116 Office: Bank of Vancouver 109 E 13th St Vancouver WA 98660-3229

INNES, KENNETH FREDERICK, III, lawyer; b. San Francisco, May 15, 1950; s. Kenneth F. Jr. and Jean I.; m. Patricia Ann Graboyes, May 12, 1973; children: Kenneth F. IV, Julia Christine. BA, San Francisco State U., 1972, JD, 1984. Bar: Calif. 1984, U.S. Dist. Ct. (no. dist.) Calif. 1987, U.S. Dist. Ct. (ea. dist.) Calif. 1988. Tchr. secondary schs. Red Bluff, Calif., 1973-74; postal clk. U.S. Postal Svc., Vallejo, Calif., 1977-84; postal insp. U.S. Postal Svc., Denver, 1984-87; regional atty. U.S. Postal Inspection Svc., Memphis, 1987-90, fin. auditor, 1990-92, regional atty., 1992—. Capt. USMCR, 1974-77. Mem. ABA, Calif. Bar Assn., Mensa, Elks. Democrat. Roman Catholic. Home: 157 Heartwood Ct Vallejo CA 94591-5638 Office: US Postal Insp Svc 7717 Edgewater Dr Ste 202 Oakland CA 94621-3013

INOUYE, DANIEL KEN, senator; b. Honolulu, Sept. 7, 1924; s. Hyotaro I. and Kame Imanaga; m. Margaret Shinobu Awamura, June 12, 1949; 1 child, Daniel Ken. A.B., U. Hawaii, 1950; J.D., George Washington U., 1952. Bar: Hawaii 1953. Asst. pub. prosecutor Honolulu, 1953-54, pvt. practice, 1954—; majority leader Territorial Ho. of Reps., 1954-58, Senate, 1958-59; mem. 86th-87th U.S. Congresses from Hawaii, U.S. Senate from Hawaii, 1963—; sec. Senate Dem. Conf., 1978-88; chmn. Dem. Steering Com., Senate Com. on Appropriations; chmn. subcom. def., mem. Commerce Com.; chmn. subcom. on communications Select Com. on Intelligence, 1976-77, ranking mem. subcom. budget authorizations, 1979-84; former chmn. Select Com. Indian Affairs; mem. Select Com. on Presdl. Campaign Activities, 1973-74; chmn. Sen. select com. Secret Mil. Assistance to Iran and Nicaraguan Opposition, 1987; ranking minority mem. Appropriations subcom. on defense, Commerce, Sci., & Transp. subcom on surface transp. & merchant marine; mem. Indian Affairs Com., Rules & Adminstrn. Com. Joint Com. on the Libr. & Congl. Intern Program, Dem. Steering & Coordination Com. Author: Journey to Washington. Active YMCA, Boy Scouts Am. Keynoter; temporary chmn. Dem. Nat. Conv., 1968, rules com. chmn., 1980, co-chmn. conv., 1984. Pvt. to capt. AUS, 1943-47. Decorated D.S.C., Bronze Star, Purple Heart with cluster; named 1 of 10 Outstanding Young Men of Yr. U.S. Jr. C. of C., 1960; recipient Splendid Am. award Thomas A. Dooley Found., 1967 Golden Plate award Am. Acad. Achievement, 1968. Mem. DAV (past comdr. Hawaii), Honolulu C. of C., Am. Legion (Nat. Comdr.'s award 1973). Methodist. Clubs: Lion. (Hawaii), 442d Veterans (Hawaii). Home: 469 Ena Rd Honolulu HI 96815-1749 Office: US Senate 722 Hart Senate Bldg Washington DC 20510*

INSLEE, JAY R., congressman, lawyer; b. Feb. 9, 1951; s. Frank and Adele Inslee; m. Trudi Anne Inslee; children: Jack, Connor, Joe. BA in Econs., U. Wash., 1973; JD magna cum laude, Willamette U., 1976. Atty. Peters, Fowler & Inslee, Selah, Wash., 1976-92; city prosecutor City of Selah, 1976-82; mem. from 14th dist. Wash. State Ho. of Reps., 1988-92; mem. 100th-103d Congresses from 4th Dist. State of Wash., 1992—. Chair Selah Sch. Bond Com., 1980; bd. dirs. New Valley Osteopathic Hosp., 1978-86. Mem. Wash. State Trial Lawyers Assn. (bd. dirs. 1984-88). Democrat. Office: US Ho of Reps Office of Ho Mems Washington DC 20515*

INTRIERE, ANTHONY DONALD, physician; b. Greenwich, Conn., May 9, 1920; s. Rocco and Angelina (Belcastro) I.; m. Carol A. Yarmey, Aug. 1, 1945; children: Sherry Showmaker, Michael, Nancy M., Lisa A. MD, U. Mich., 1944. Intern, New Rochelle (N.Y.) Hosp., 1944-45; pvt. practice, Greenwich, Conn., 1947-53, Olney, Ill., 1956-61, Granite City, Ill., 1961-74, San Diego, 1975—; fellow in internal medicine Cleve. Clinic, 1953-55; fellow in gastroenterology Lahey Clinic, Boston, 1955-56. Capt. M.C., AUS, 1945-47. Fellow Am. Coll. Gastroenterology (assoc.); mem. AMA, ACP (assoc.), Am. Soc. Internal Medicine. Home: 9981 Caminito Chirimolla San Diego CA 92131-2001

INTRILIGATOR, DEVRIE SHAPIRO, physicist; b. N.Y.C.; d. Carl and Lillian Shapiro; m. Michael Intriligator; children: Kenneth, James, William, Robert. BS in Physics, MIT, 1962, MS, 1964; PhD in Planetary and Space Physics, UCLA, 1967. NRC-NASA rsch. assoc. NASA, Ames, Calif., 1967-69; rsch. fellow in physics Calif. Inst. Tech., Pasadena, 1969-72, vis. assoc., 1972-73; asst. prof. U. So. Calif., 1972-80; mem. Space Scis. Ctr., 1978-83; sr. rsch. physicist Carmel Rsch. Ctr., Santa Monica, Calif., 1979—; dir. Space Plasma Lab., 1980—; cons. NASA, NOAA, Jet Propulsion Lab.; chmn. NAS-NRC com. on solar-terrestrial rsch., 1983-86, exec. com. bd. atmospheric sci. and climate, 1983-86, geophysics study com., 1983-86; U.S. nat. rep. Sci. Com. on Solar-Terrestrial Physics, 1983-86; mem. adv. com. NSF Divsn. Atmospheric Sci. Co-editor: Exploration of the Outer Solar System, 1976; contbr. articles to profl. jours. Recipient 3 Achievement awards NASA, Calif. Resolution of Commendation, 1982. Mem. AAAS, Am. Phys. Soc., Am. Geophys. Union, Cosmos Club. Home: 140 Foxtail Dr Santa Monica CA 90402-2048 Office: Carmel Rsch Ctr PO Box 1732 Santa Monica CA 90406-1732

INTRILIGATOR, MICHAEL DAVID, economist, educator; b. N.Y.C., Feb. 5, 1938; s. Allan and Sally I.; m. Devrie; children: Kenneth, James, William, Robert. SB in Econs., MIT, 1959; MA, Yale U., 1960; PhD, MIT, 1963. Asst. prof. econs. UCLA, 1963-66, assoc. prof., 1966-72, prof., 1972—, prof. dept. polit. sci., 1981—, prof. dept. policy studies, 1994—, dir. Ctr. Internat. and Strategic Affairs, 1982-92; dir. Jacob Marschak Interdisciplinary Coll. 1977—; cons. Inst. Def. Analysis, 1974-77, ACDA, 1968, Rand Corp., 1962-65. Author: Mathematical Optimization and Economic Theory, 1971, also Taiwanese, Spanish and Russian edits., Econometric Models, Techniques and Applications, 1978, also Greek and Spanish edits., (with others) A Forecasting and Policy Simulation Model of the Health Care Sector, 1979; mem. adv. editorial bd. Math. Social Scis., 1983—; assoc. editor Jour. Optimization Theory and Applications, 1979-91, Conflict Mgmt. and Peace Sci., 1980—; co-editor: (series) Handbooks in Economics, 1980—, Advanced Textbooks in Economics, 1972—; editor: (with Kenneth J. Arrow) Handbook of Mathematical Economics, 3 vols., 1981-85; (with Zvi Griliches) Handbook of Econometrics, 3 vols., 1983-86, (with B. Brodie and R. Kolkowicz) National Security and International Stability, 1983, (with H.A. Jacobsen) East-West Conflict: Elite Perceptions and Political Opinions, 1988, numerous others; contbr. articles to profl. jours. Woodrow Wilson fellow, 1959-60; MIT fellow, 1960-61; recipient Disting. Teaching award UCLA, 1966; Ford fellow, 1967-68; Warren C. Scoville disting. teaching award UCLA, 1976, 79, 82, 84. Fellow Econometric Soc.; mem. Internat. Inst. Strategic Studies, Council Fgn. Relations, others. Office: UCLA Dept Econs Los Angeles CA 90024-1477

INVERSO, MARLENE JOY, optometrist; b. Los Angeles, May 10, 1942; d. Elmer Encel Wood and Sally Marie (Sample) Hirons; m. John S. Inverso, Dec. 16, 1962; 1 child, Christopher Edward. BA, Calif. State U., Northridge, 1964; MS, SUNY, Potsdam, 1975; OD, Pacific U., 1981. Cert. doctor optometry, Wash., Oreg. English tchr. Chatsworth (Calif.) High Sch., 1964-68, Nelson A. Boylen Second Sch., Toronto, Ont., Can., 1968-70, Gouverneur (N.Y.) Jr.-Sr. High Sch., 1970-74, 76-77; reading resource room tchr. Parishville (N.Y.) Hopkinton Sch., 1974-75; coordinator learning disability clinic SUNY, Potsdam, 1975-77; optometrist and vision therapist Am. Family Vision Clinics, Olympia, Wash., 1982—; mem. adv. com. Sunshine House St. Peter Hosp., Olympia, 1984-86, Pacific U. Coll. Optometry, Forest Grove, Oreg. 1986. Contbr. articles to profl. jours. Mem. Altrusa Svc. Club, Olympia, 1982-86; tchr. Ch. Living Water, Olympia, 1983-88, Olympia-Lacey Ch. of God, 1989—, sec. women's bd., 1990; bd. advisors Crisis Pregnancy Ctr., Olympia, 1987-89; den mother Cub Scouts Am. Pack 202, Lacey, Wash., 1987-88; vol. World Vision Countertop ptnr., 1986—. Fellow Coll. Optometrists in Optometric Devel.; mem. Am. Optometric Assn. (sec. 1983-84), Assn. Children and Adults with Learning Disabilities, Optometric Extension Program, Sigma Xi, Beta Sigma Kappa. Home: 4204 Timberline Dr SE Olympia WA 98503-4443

IORIO, JOHN EMIL, retired education educator; b. Bklyn., Dec. 20, 1932; s. Frederick and Helen (Grandillo) I.; m. Helen Capobianco, Dec. 20, 1958; children: Frederick Joseph, John Richard. BS in Polit Sci., Manhattan Coll., 1954; MS in Elem. Edn., Bklyn. Coll., 1967; profl. diploma Adminstrn, Supervision, Fordham U., 1984. Cert. elem. tchr., adminstr., prin. supt. N.Y.S., N.Y.C. Elem. tchr. N.Y.C., 1965-72; adminstrv. asst. P.S. 214K, Dist. 19, N.Y.C., 1972-74, asst. prin., 1974-75; adminstr. Office of Fed. and State Reimbursable Programs, N.Y.C., 1975-76; asst. prin. Ps. 153Q, Dist. 24, N.Y.C., 1976; asst. prin., head of sch. PS 128Q Dist. 24, Queens, N.Y., 1976-79; prin. PS 128Q Dist. 24, Queens, 1979-87; community supt. Dist. 24, Queens, 1987-90; presenter at many ednl. confs. and workshops. 1983-90. Contbr. articles to profl. jours. Recipient Builder of Brotherhood award, Nat. Conf. Christians and Jews, 1981, Arts in Edn. Programs award, Young Audiences of N.Y., 1989, Project Innovation Spl. Merit award, Education mag., 1990, others; named Educator of Yr. Assn. Tchrs. of N.Y., 1988; grantee Nat. Endowment for Humanities, 1981. Home: 3928 Edgemoor Way Las Vegas NV 89121-4829

IPPOLITI, RALPHINE ANN, program manager; b. Schenectady, N.Y., Apr. 8, 1954; d. George Valletta and Norma Joan Goram; m. Del Weather, May 28, 1993; stepchildren: Erik Weathers, Kathleen Weathers. BS, U. Md., 1979. Sr. tech. asst. RCA, Greenbelt, Md., 1972-73; sr. software engr. Computer Scis. Corp., Greenbelt, 1973-80; sr. engr., specialist Ford Motor Co., Houston, 1980-86, Palo Alto, Calif., 1986-87, Reston, Va., 1987-92; sr. program mgr. Loral, Palo Alto, 1992—. Recipient NASA awards, 1981, 83, 87, 88, 89. Address: 18817 Martha Ave Saratoga CA 95070-4641

IPSEN, GRANT RUEL, insurance and investments professional; b. Malad, Idaho, Nov. 6, 1932; s. Nephi Ruel and Ada (Hughes) I.; m. Edna Wayne Hughes, July 27, 1956; children: Edna Gaye, LeAnn, Garin Grant, Shawna Lee, Wayne Ruel. BA, Brigham Young U., 1961. CPA Idaho; CLU, ChFC. Acct. Ernst & Ernst, Boise, Idaho, 1961-64; with sales dept. Mut. of N.Y., Boise, 1964—; mem. Idaho State Senate, 1992—. Active Boy Scouts Am., 1945—; co-convener Boise Religious Freedom Com., 1991-94. With U.S. Army, 1956-58. Named Agt. of Yr., Boise Assn. Life Underwriters, 1978, Man of Yr., Mut. of N.Y., 1982. Mem. Million Dollar Round Table (life), Brigham Young Univ. Alumni (bd. dirs. 1987-93). Republican. LDS.

IRAGUI-MADOZ, VICENTE J., neurologist, neurosciences educator; b. Pamplona, Spain, Oct. 27, 1946; s. Miguel and Marce (Madoz) Iragui; m. Evelyn S. Tecoma, July 4, 1992. MD, U. Navarra, Pamplona, Spain, 1969; PhD, U. Calif., San Diego, 1977. Intern U. Hosp., Pamplona, Spain, 1969-70, resident neurology, 1971-72; intern U. Calif. Med. Ctr., San Diego, 1976-77, resident neurology, 1977-80; instr. in neurology Sch. Medicine, U. Navarra, Spain, 1972-73; instr. neuroanatomy Sch. Medicine, U. Calif., San Diego, 1973-75; staff neurologist U. Calif. and VA Med. Ctr., San Diego, 1980—, dir. clin. neurophysiology, 1982—; dir. Epilepsy Ctr. U. Calif., San Diego, 1984—, prof. dept. neuroscis., 1992—; cons. Speech, Health and Neurosensory Ctr., Children's Hosp., San Diego, 1981-84. Fulbright fellow, 1973-75, Ministry Fgn. Affairs fellow French Govt., 1973, A.P. Sloan Found. fellow U. Calif., 1975-76. Mem. Am. Neurol. Assn., Am. Acad. Neurology, Am. Electroencephalographic Soc., Am. Epilepsy Soc., San Diego Neurol. Soc., Sociedad Española de Neurologia, Western EEG Soc. (pres. 1989-90). Office: U Calif Med Ctr Mail Code 8740 200 W Arbor Dr San Diego CA 92103-1911

IRANI, MEHRABOON S., pathologist; b. Bombay, Nov. 12, 1958; came to U.S., 1984; s. Shapoor Ardeshir and Khorshed S. (Panthaki) I. BA, Cambridge U., 1980, MB BChir, 1982, MA, 1984. Diplomate in anat. pathology, clin. pathology, blood banking hematopathology Am. Bd. Pathology. Resident in anat. and clin. pathology Baylor Coll. Medicine, Houston, 1984-88, fellow in hematopathology, 1989-90; fellow in transfusion medicine U. Ariz., Tucson, 1988-89; physician-in-charge Hematology/blood bank VA Med. Ctr., Houston, 1990-93; pathologist Pathology Assocs. of Albuquerque, 1993—; pathologist, dir. coagulation lab. Presbyn. Hosp., Albuquerque/. Fellow Coll. Am. Pathologists, Am. Soc. Clin. Pathologists; mem. AMA, Am. Assn. Blood Banks. Parsee (Zoroastrian). Office: Presbyn Hosp Lab 1100 Central SE Albuquerque NM 87106

IRANI, RAY R., oil, gas and chemical company executive; b. Beirut, Lebanon, Jan. 15, 1935; came to U.S., 1953, naturalized, 1956; s. Rida and Naz I.; children: Glenn R., Lillian M., Martin R. BS in Chemistry, Am. U. Beirut, 1953; PhD in Phys. Chemistry, U. So. Calif., 1957. Rsch. scientist, then sr. rsch. scientist Monsanto Co., 1957-67; assoc. dir. new products, then dir. research Diamond Shamrock Corp., 1967-73; with Olin Corp., 1973-83, pres. chems. group, 1978-80; corp. pres., dir. Olin Corp., Stamford, Conn., 1980-83, COO, 1981-83; chmn. Occidental Petroleum Corp. subs. Occidental Chem. Corp., Dallas, 1983-94; CEO Occidental Petroleum Corp., subs. Occidental Chem. Corp., Dallas, 1983-91; chmn. Can. Occidental Petroleum Corp. Ltd., Calgary, 1987—; exec. v.p. Occidental Petroleum Corp., L.A., 1983-84, pres., chief operating officer, 1984-91, chmn., pres., chief exec. officer, 1991—, also bd. dirs.; bd. dirs. Am. Petroleum Inst., Oxy Oil and Gas USA Inc., Occidental Oil and Gas Corp., Occidental Petroleum Investment Corp. Author: Particle Size; also author papers in field; numerous patents in field. Trustee U. So. Calif., Am. U. Beirut, St. John's Hosp. and Health Ctr. Found., Natural History Mus. Los Angeles County; bd. govs. Los Angeles Town Hall, Los Angeles World Affairs Coun. Mem. Nat. Petroleum Coun., Am. Inst. Chemists, Am. Chem. Soc., Sci. Rsch. Soc. Am., Indsl. Rsch. Inst., The Conf. Bd., Calif. Bus. Roundtable, The Calif. C. of C., Nat. Assn. Mfrs. (bd. dirs.), Am. Petroleum Inst. (bd. dirs.). Office: 10889 Wilshire Blvd Los Angeles CA 90024 also: Oxy Petrochem Inc 5005 Lyndon B Johnson Fwy Dallas TX 75244-6119

IRBY, PAMELA JO, family practice physician; b. Spokane, Wash., Sept. 8, 1964; d. Donald Clifford and Joline Audrey (Brett) Board; m. Denny Mark Irby, Aug. 15, 1987. AB, Stanford U., 1987, MD, 1993. Rsch. asst. Stanford (Calif.) Ctr. for Rsch. & Disease Prevention, 1986-92; resident physician Merced (Calif.) County Hosp., 1993—. Mem. Am. Acad. Family Physicians, Calif. Acad. Family Physicians. Home: 3635 9th Ave Merced CA 95340-3101 Office: Family Practice Residency Program 315 E 13th St Merced CA 95340

IRISH, THOMAS JUDSON, plastic surgeon; b. Forest City, Iowa, May 23, 1936; m. Sandra. BS, Iowa State Coll., 1958; MD, State U. of Iowa, 1962. Pvt. practice Plastic Surgeons NW, Tacoma, Wash., 1972—. Fellow ACS; mem. Am. Soc. Plastic and Reconstructive Surgery, Alpha Omega Alpha. Office: Plastic Surgeons NW 1802 S Yakima Ave Ste 208 Tacoma WA 98405-5304

IRONS, GEORGE BENTON, plastic surgeon; b. Lewisburg, W.Va., Oct. 14, 1933; s. George Benton Sr. and Anna Ruth (Christie) I.; m. Sudelle Kiser, June 6, 1958; children: Andrew, Susan, Stesha. BA, W.Va. U., 1954, BS, 1956; MD, Med. Coll. Va., 1958. Head divsn. plastic surgery Mayo Clinic, Scottsdale, Ariz., 1987—. Office: Mayo Clinic Scottsdale 13400 E Shea Blvd Scottsdale AZ 85259-5404

IRSFELD, JOHN HENRY, English language educator, novelist; b. Bemidji, Minn., Dec. 2, 1937; s. Hubert Louis and Mary Lillian (McKee) (dec. Nov. 1992) I.; m. Margaret Elizabeth Drushel, Aug. 29, 1965 (div. Feb. 1978); 1 child, Hannah Christine; m. Janet Elizabeth Jones, May 5, 1984. BA, U. Tex., 1959, MA, 1966, PhD, 1969. Tchr. Spanish and English Calallen, Tex., 1959-60; teaching asst. U. Texas, Austin, 1960-61, 64-68, teaching assoc., 1968-69; from asst. prof. to assoc. prof. English U. Nev., Las Vegas, 1969-73, prof., 1977—, dep. to pres., 1987, v.p., dep. to pres., 1990-94. Author: (novels) Coming Through, 1975, Little Kingdoms, 1976, 89, Rats Alley, 1987. Sgt. inf. U.S. Army, 1961-64. Democrat. Office: U Nev 4505 S Maryland Pky Las Vegas NV 89154-9900

IRVINE, DONALD WILLIAM, telecommunications company executive; b. Kissimmee, Fla., Nov. 12, 1948; s. William Thomas and Violet Helen (Menapace) I.; m. Patricia Ann Holland, Nov. 14, 1970; children: William Preston, Richard Neil. AAS, Seminole C.C., 1980; BS, Rollins Coll., 1984. Advance to PBX engr. Fla. Tel. Corp., Leesburg, 1970-79; from product administr. to PBX engring. mgr. United Tel. of Fla., Winter Park, 1979-81; ops. mgr. United Telecom, Winter Park, 1981-84; product mgr. Vodavi Technology Corp., Scottsdale, Ariz., 1984-88; dir. product mgmt. Executone Info. Sys., Scottsdale, 1988-94; v.p. product devel. Vodavi Comms., Scottsdale, 1994—. V.p. CWA Local 3176, Leesburg, 1973-74. Served in U.S. Navy, 1966-70. Named boss of yr. 1977 Eustis (Fla.) Jaycees. Mem. Ind. Tel. Pioneer Assn., Seabee Veterans of Am., Ariz. Software Assn. Republican. Baptist. Home: 5731 E Acoma Dr Scottsdale AZ 85254-2403 Office: Vodavi Comms Sys Inc 8300 E Raintree Dr Scottsdale AZ 85260-2537

IRVINE, VERNON BRUCE, accounting educator, administrator; b. Regina, Sask., Can., May 31, 1943; s. Joseph Vern and Anna Francis (Phillip) I.; m. Marilyn Ann Craik, Apr. 29, 1967; children: Lee-Ann, Cameron, Sandra. B. Commerce, U. Sask., 1965; MBA, U. Chgo., 1967; PhD, U. Minn., 1977. Cert. mgmt. acct. Researcher, Sask. Royal Commn. on Taxation, Regina, 1964; lectr. acctg. Coll. Commerce, U. Sask., Saskatoon, 1967-69, asst. prof., 1969-74, assoc. prof., 1974-79, prof., 1979—, head dept. acctg., 1981-84; profl. program lectr. Inst. Chartered Accts., Regina, 1982-84, Soc. Mgmt. Accts., Saskatoon, 1982-84, 94—. Co-author: A Practical Approach to the Appraisal of Capital Expenditures, 1981; Intermediate Accounting: Canadian Edition, 1982, 4th edit., 1994; contbr. articles to acctg. jours. Grantee John Wiley & Sons, Ltd., 1981, 85, 87, 88, 92, 93, Soc. Mgmt. Accts. Can., 1979, Pres.'s Fund, U. Sask., 1978, Nelson Can. grantee, 1990. Bd. dirs. Big Sisters of Sask., 1987-90. Fellow Soc. Mgmt. Accts. Can. (bd. dirs. 1979-82, 85-87, 89-92, chmn. Nat. Edn. Svcs. com.); mem. Can. Acad. Acctg. Assn. (pres. 1994-95, pres.- elect 1993-94, sec. 1992-93, exec. com., chmn. mem. com. 1989-91), Internat. Acctg. Standards Com. (Can. rep. 1984-87), Internat. Fedn. Accts. Council (tech. advisor 1988-90), Soc. of Mgmt. Accts. of Sask. (pres. 1980-81). Clubs: Sutherland Curling (treas. 1979-83), Saskatoon Golf and Country (bd. dirs. 1988-90). Home: 45 Cantlon Crescent, Saskatoon, SK Canada S7J 2T2 Office: U Sask, Commerce Bldg 25 Campus Dr, Saskatoon, SK Canada S7N 5A7

IRWIN, CHARLES DENNIS, JR., geological consultant; b. Rushville, Nebr., Oct. 10, 1930; s. Charles Dennis and Elsie Gladys (Prell) I.; m. Patricia Jean Riley, Apr. 18, 1959; children: Laurie, Christy, David. BA, U. Colo., 1952; PhD, U. N.Mex., 1969. Jr. computer analyst Robert H. Ray Co., Dickinson, N.D., 1952; jr. geologist Gulf Oil Co., Salt Lake City, 1955, Ardmore, Okla., 1956; project geologist Carter Oil Co., Durango, Colo., 1957-60; project and dist. geologist Tenneco Oil Co., Durango, Casper, Colo., Wyo., 1960-66; area exploration mgr. Wolf Ridge Minerals Corp., Albuquerque, 1968-69; regional explorationist Walter Duncan Oil Properties, Denver, 1970-73; cons. geologist Boulder, Colo., 1973—. Editor: Geological Cross-Sections of Colorado, 1977; contbr. articles to profl. jours. With USN, 1953-54, Korea. Mem. Am. Assn. Petroleum Geologists (adv. coun. 1994—, sec. ho. of dels. 1981-82), Rocky Mountain Assn. Geologists (pres. 1990, councilor 1987, 2 v.p. 1984, sec. 1976), Four Corners Geol. Soc. (1st v.p. 1965, sec. 1960-61), Wyo. Geol. Assn., Computer Oriented Geol. Scientists, Assn. Petroleum Geochem. Explorationists, Soc. Ind. Profl. Earth Scientists. Presbyterian. Home and Office: 220 Cimmaron Way Boulder CO 80303-4204

IRWIN, CHARLES EDWIN, JR., pediatrics educator; b. Medford, Mass., Dec. 15, 1945; s. Charles Edwin and Molly Esther (Rosenberg) I.; m. Nancie Noel Kester, Apr. 21, 1979. BS, Hobart Coll., 1967; BMS, Dartmouth Med. Sch., 1969; MD, U. Calif., 1971. Asst. prof. pediatrics U. Calif. Med. Ctr., San Francisco, 1977-84, dir. div. of adolescent med., 1977—, assoc. prof. pediatrics, 1984-90; prof. pediatrics, 1990—; bd. dirs. Nat. Adolescent Health Info. Ctr. Mem. editorial bd: jour. Adolescent Health Care, 1982, Internat. jour. Adolescent Medicine, 1984, Pediatrican jour., 1984. R. W. Johnson Found. clin. scholar, 1974; W. T. Grant Found. grantee, 1985; recipient APA Teaching award, 1990, Nat. Ctr. Youth Law award, 1987. Fellow Am. Acad. Pediatrics (exec. committeeman 1982-85); mem. AAAS, Soc. Pediatric Rsch., Am. Pediatric Soc., Soc. Adolescent Medicine (exec. council mem. 1985—, rsch. award 1985), Am. Pub. Health Assn. Office: U Calif Med Ctr 400 Parnassus Ave San Francisco CA 94122-2721

IRWIN, MILDRED LORINE WARRICK, library consultant, civic worker; b. Kellerton, Iowa, June 21, 1917; d. Webie Arthur and Bonnie Lorine (Hyatt) DeVries; m. Carl Wesley Warrick, Feb. 11, 1937 (dec. June 1983); children: Carl Dwayne, Arthur Will; m. John B. Irwin, Feb. 1, 1994. BS in Edn., Drake U., 1959; M of Librarianship, Kans. State Tchrs. Coll., 1970. Cert. tchr., libr., Iowa. Elem. tchr. Monroe Ctr. Rural Sch., Kellerton, Iowa, 1935-37, Denham Rural Sch., Grand River, Iowa, 1945-48, Grand River Ind. Sch., 1948-52, Woodmansee Rural Sch., Decatur, Iowa, 1952-55, Centennial Rural Sch., Decatur, 1955-56; elem. tchr., acting libr. Cen. Decatur Sch., Leon, Iowa, 1956-71, media libr. jr. and sr. high sch., 1971-79; libr. Northminster Presbyn. Ch., Tucson, 1985-93, advisor, 1994—; media resource instr. Graceland Coll., Lamoni, Iowa, 1971-72; lit. dir. S.W. Iowa Assn. Classroom Tchrs., 1965-69. Editor (media packet) Mini History and Quilt Blocks, 1976, Grandma Lori's Nourishing Nuggets for Body and Soul, 1985, As I Recall (Loren Drake), 1989, Foland Family Supplement III, 1983; author: (with Quentin Oiler) Van Der Vlugt Family Record, 1976; compiler, editor Abigail Specials, 1991; compiler Tribute to Ferm Mills 1911-1992, 1992; co-editor: (with Dorothy Heitlinger) Milestones and Touchstones, 1993; contbr. articles to publs. Leader Grand River 4-H Club for Girls, 1954-58; sec. South Ctrl. Iowa Quarter Horse Assn., Chariton, 1967-68; chmn. Decatur County Dems., 1981-83, del., 1970-83; pianist Salvation Army Amphi League of Mercy Rhythm Noters, 1984-90; pianist, dir. Joymakers, 1990—; Sunday Sch. tchr. Decatur United Meth. Ch., 1945-54, 80-83, lay speaker, 1981-83, dir. vacation Bible sch., 1982, 83. Named Classroom Tchr. of Iowa Classroom Tchrs. Assn., 1962, Woman of Yr., Leon Bus. and Profl. Women, 1978, Northminster Presbyn. Ch. Women, 1990; English and reading grantee Nat. Dept. Edn., 1966. Mem. NEA (life), AAUW (chmn. Tucson creative writing/cultural interests 1986-87, 89-93, historian, 1994—, Honoree award for ednl. found. programs Tucson br., Svc. award 1991), Internat. Reading Assn. (pres. Clarke-Ringgold Decatur chpts. 1967-68), Cen. Community Tchrs. Assn. (pres. 1961-62), Pima County Ret. Tchrs. Assn. (pres. 1989-90), Decatur County Assn. (pres. 1961-63), Decatur County Ret. Tchrs. Assn. (historian 1980-83), Iowa Edn. Assn. (life), Presbyn. Women (hon. life 1990—), Luth. Ch. Libr. Assn. (historian Tucson area chpt. 1991-92, v.p. 1993-94, pres. 1994-95), Delta Kappa Gamma (pres. Iowa Beta XI chpt. 1974-76, sec. 1984-85, historian Ariz. Alpha Gamma chpt. 1986-89). Democrat. Presbyterian. Home: 2879 E Presidio Rd Tucson AZ 85716-1539

IRWIN, R. ROBERT, lawyer; b. Denver, July 27, 1933; s. Royal Robert and Mildred Mary (Wilson) I.; m. Sue Ann Scott, Dec. 16, 1956; children—Lori, Stacy, Kristi, Amy. Student U. Colo., 1951-54, B.S.L., U. Denver, 1955, LL.B., 1957. Bar: Colo. 1957, Wyo. 1967. Asst. atty. gen. State of Colo., 1958-66; asst. div. atty. Mobil Oil Corp., Casper, Wyo. 1966-70; prin. atty. No. Natural Gas Co., Omaha 1970-72; sr. atty. Coastal Oil & Gas Corp., Denver 1972-83, asst. sec. 1972-83; ptnr. Baker & Hostetler, 1983-87; pvt. practice 1987—. Mem. Colo. Bar Assn., Arapahoe County Bar Assn., Rocky Mountain Oil and Gas Assn. Republican. Clubs: Los Verdes Golf, Petroleum, Denver Law (Denver). Office: 9960 E Chenango Ave Englewood CO 80111-3606

ISAAC, ROBERT MICHAEL, mayor, lawyer; b. Colorado Springs, Colo., Jan. 27, 1928; s. Isaac Albert and Sigrid Elvira (Oksa) I.; children from previous marriage: Leslie Ann Isaac Williams, Julia Hermine Isaac Harrington, Melissa Sue Isaac Denton, Tiffany Ann, Chance Robert. Student, U. Colo., 1945-46; BS, U.S. Mil. Acad., 1951; JD, U. So. Calif., 1962. Sales engr. Trane Co., Los Angeles, 1957-62; practice law and dep. city atty. City Colorado Springs, 1962-64; asst. dist. atty. 4th Jud. Dist. Colo., Colorado Springs, 1965-66; judge Colorado Springs Mcpl. Ct., 1966-69; ptnr. Trott, Kunstle, Isaac & Hughes, Colorado Springs, 1969-72, Isaac, Walsh & Johnson, Colorado Springs, 1972-74, Isaac, Johnson & Alpern, 1974-88; councilman City of Colorado Springs, 1975-79, mayor, 1979—; past pres. U.S. Conf. Mayors; mem. adv. bd. Nat. League Cities; mem. adv. commn. Ingergovtl. Rels. Gen. chmn. YWCA/YMCA/USO fund dr., past pres. Pikes Peak Y/USO; past pres. El Paso County Soc. Crippled Children and Adults; past mem. Nat. USO Council; chmn. Pikes Peak Area Council Govts., 1976-78. Served as officer inf. U.S. Army, 1951-57. Mem. El Paso County Bar Assn. Episcopalian. Office: Office of the Mayor PO Box 1575 30 S Nevada Ave Ste 401 Colorado Springs CO 80903-1825

ISAACS, CAROLINE MARIE, geologist; b. Portland, Oreg., July 7, 1946; d. John Dove and Mary Carol (Zander) I. A.B., U. Calif.-Berkeley, 1970; Ph.D., Stanford U., 1980. Geophys. tech. asst. Chevron Overseas, San Francisco, 1972-74; phys. sci. tech. U.S. Geol. Survey, Menlo Park, Calif., 1974-77, geologist, 1977—; project leader. Author: Guide to the Monterey Formation in the California Coastal Area, Ventura to San Luis Obispo, 1981; editor, contbg. author Petroleum Generation and Occurrence in the Miocene Monterey Formation, California, 1983; editor Procs. of 11th Ann. Pacific Climate Workshop, 1995. Contbr. articles to sci. jours. Mem. Am. Assn. Petroleum Geologists (assoc. editor bull. 1994—), Soc. Econ. Paleontologists and Mineralogists, Am. Mus. Natural History, Sigma Xi, Phi Beta Kappa, Am. Geophys. Union. Office: US Geol Survey 345 Middlefield Rd # 999 Menlo Park CA 94025-3561

ISAACS, JONATHAN WILLIAM, oil company executive; b. Chgo., Apr. 9, 1957; s. Kenneth Sidney and Ruth Elizabeth (Johnson) I.; m. Marcia Eileen Gresback, Jan. 2, 1979 (div. Feb. 1986). BA, Lake Forest Coll., 1980. Prin. Kenisa Oil Co., Northbrook, Ill., 1980—, Kenisa Drilling Co., Denver, 1986—. First to utilize Diamonium Phosphate Drilling Mud in Denver Julesburg Basin biodegradable into fertilizer, (HN4) 2 HPO 4; inventor downhole non-metalic oil well tubing system. Mem. NRA, Nat. Skeet Shooting Assn., Ind. Petroleum Assn., Denver Assn. Petroleum Landmen, Rep. Mens Club, Denver Athletic Club, Exmoor Country Club, Alpha Nu Chi Psi. Republican. Office: Kenisa Drilling Co 410 17th St Denver CO 80202-4402

ISAACSON, GENE LESTER, fine arts educator; b. Rugby, N.D., June 14, 1936; s. Lester O. and Sybil J. (Strandness) I. BA in Art and Music, Concordia Coll., Moorhead, Minn., 1958; MFA, U. No. Colo., 1962. Lic. tchr., Calif., Oreg., Iowa, Minn. Supr. art Mt. Pleasant (Iowa) Pub. Schs., 1960-62; chmn. dept. art Willamette U., Salem, Oreg., 1962-64; art historian, chair Rancho Santiago Coll., Santa Ana, Calif., 1964—, Orange Coast Coll., Costa Mesa, Calif., 1975—; asst. prof. art history Chapman Coll., 1970-71; advisor/cons. City Arts Programs, Calif.; art/archtl. advisor various orgns. Editor Art Forum Newsletter, 1982-92; contbr. articles to profl. jours. Bd. trustees Orange County Ctr. for Contemporary Art, Santa Ana, 1984-94; advisor High Sch. Performing Arts, Calif., 1989-93. Lutheran. Home: PO Box 6157 Huntington Beach CA 92615-6157 Office: Rancho Santiago Coll 17th & Bristol Sts Santa Ana CA 92706

ISAACSON, JOSEPH MORRIS, allergist; b. Omaha, May 10, 1949. MD, U. Mich., 1975. Allergist Good Samaritan Hosp., San Jose, Calif., 1981—; with Cmty. Hosp., Los Gatos, Calif., 1982—; allergist O'Connor Hosp., 1993—; clin. asst. prof. Stanford U., 1985—. Office: 3002 Leigh Ave San Jose CA 95124-2222*

ISAACSON, ROBERT LOUIS, investment company executive; b. Chgo., Apr. 21, 1944; s. Abe B. and Laverne (Skolka) I. BS, Mich. State U., 1966. Mktg. mgr. Florasynth, Inc., San Francisco, 1966-69; br. mgr. Florasynth, Inc., Lincolnwood and Palo Alto, Calif., 1969-72; br. office mgr. Geldermann, Palo Alto, 1972-76; founder, pres. Commodity Investment Cons., Los Altos, Calif., 1976—, Future Funding Cons., Menlo Park, Calif., 1976—; co-founder, co-chmn. Nat. Assn. Futures Trading Advisors; bd. dirs. Futures Industry Assn. Edn. and Tng., Williams & Clarissa, Inc.; bd. dirs., exec. com., membership com. Nat. Futures Assn.; membership Nat. Futures Assn. Regional Bus. Conduct Com.; v.p. Lind-Waldock Co., Chgo.; pres. Interalliance U.S.A. Contbr. articles to mags and profl. jours. Founder Fun for Lunch Bunch. With U.S. Mil., 1966-72. Recipient Doncheon award Managed Accounts Report, 1984. Mem. San Francisco Futures Soc., Managed Futures Assn. (past co-chmn., bd. dirs.), Asian Pacific Managed Futures Assn. (bd. dirs., founding mem.), Peninsula Commodities Club, Elks, Kiwanis. Home: 380 La Questa Way Woodside CA 94062-2428 Office: Commodity Investment Cons Future Funding Cons 380 La Questa Way Woodside CA 94062-2428

ISAUTIER, BERNARD FRANÇOIS, oil and gas executive; b. St.-Symphorien, Indre et Loire, France, Sept. 19, 1942; s. Francois and Genevieve (Roy) I.; m. Charlotte Roche, July 22, 1968; children: Anne-Caroline, Armelle, Francois. Grad., Ecole Polytechnique, Paris, 1963, Ecole des Mines, Paris, 1966, Institute d'Etudes Politiques, Paris, 1968. Advisor on uranium to Pres. Rep. of Niger, 1968-70; Head dept. mining exploration French Ministry of Industry, Paris, 1970-73, adviser to minister of industry for energy and raw materials, 1973-75; gen. mgr. SEREPT (subs. Elf-Aquitaine Group), Tunis, Tunisia, 1976-78; pres. Aquitaine Co. of Can. Ltd., Calgary, Alta., 1978-81; pres., CEO Canterra Energy Ltd., Calgary, Alta., 1981-86, Polysar Energy & Chem. Corp., Toronto, Ont., from 1986; formerly chmn., CEO Thomson Consumer Electronics, Paris; now pres., CEO Can. Occidental Petroleum Ltd., Calgary, Alta., Can.; bd. dirs. Credit Lyonnais Can., Lafarge Coppee, France. Served to lt. Res. Army of France, 1961-64. Decorated Order of Nat. Mesite. Office: Can Occidental Petroleum Ltd, 1500, 635 8th Ave SW, Calgary, AB Canada T2P 3Z1

ISBELL, ALAN GREGORY, editor, writer, publisher; b. Denver, June 7, 1951; s. Morris Leroy Isbell and Ida Belle (Lanyon) Whittemore; m. Sherry Ann Meiers, July 8, 1972; children: Zane Michael, Evan Kele. AA with honors, Coll. Alameda, 1975; BS, U. Colo., 1978. Reporter Douglas County News Press, Castle Rock, Colo., 1978-80; bur. chief Glenwood Post, Glenwood Springs, Colo., 1980-83; news editor Sun Press, Kaneohe, Hawaii, 1984-86; editor Mauian mag., Lahaina, Hawaii, 1986-87, South Maui Times, Kihei, Hawaii, 1988-93, Haleakala Times, Makawao, Hawaii, 1994, Maui Inc. Mag., Makawao, 1994, Today Mag., Kihei, Hawaii, 1994; pub., editor Maui Tribune, Wailuku, Hawaii, 1994—; contbg. editor Colorado River Jour., 1981-83; regional correspondent AP, 1981-83; Hawaii correspondent World News, N.Y.C., 1986-88; freelance writer, Maui, 1987-88; Maui news correspondent KGMB-TV, Honolulu, 1987-88, Honolulu Star Bulletin, 1989-90. Recipient award Colo. Press Assn., 1983. Mem. Hawaii Pubs. Assn. (awards 1990, 92-93, 95), Soc. Profl. Journalists, Maui Assn. Reporters and Editors. Home: 2751 Kauhale St Kihei HI 96753-9633

ISBELL, HAROLD M(AX), writer, investor; b. Maquoketa, Iowa, Sept. 20, 1936; s. H. Max and Marcella E. I.; BA cum laude (scholar), Loras Coll., 1959; MA (fellow), U. Notre Dame, 1962; grad. U. Mich. Grad. Sch. Bank Mgmt., 1982; m. Mary Carolyn Cosgriff, June 15, 1963; children: Walter Harold, Susan Elizabeth, David Harold, Alice Kathleen. Instr., U. Notre Dame, South Bend, Ind., 1963-64; assoc. prof. St. Mary's Coll., 1969-72; asst. prof. San Francisco Coll. for Women, 1964-69; with Continental Bank & Trust Co., Salt Lake City, 1972-83, v.p., 1977-83, comml. credit officer, 1978-83, also dir. Trustee Judge Meml. Cath. High Sch., Salt Lake City, 1977-84; mem. Utah Coun. for Handicapped and Developmentally Disabled Persons, 1980-81; bd. dirs. Ballet West, 1983-90, emeritus, 1990—, Story Line Press, 1994—, Smuin Ballets, San Francisco, 1994—; founder Cath. Found. Utah, pres. 1984-86, trustee, 1984-89. Mem. MLA, Mediaeval Acad. Am., Am. Assn. for the Advancement of Sci. Democrat. Roman Catholic. Club: Alta. Editor and translator: The Last Poets of Imperial Rome, 1971, Ovid: Heroides, 1990; contbr. to publs. in field of classical Latin lit. and contemporary Am. Lit.

ISBERG, REUBEN ALBERT, radio communications engineer; b. Chugwater, Wyo., Dec. 11, 1913; s. Albert Gust and Laura Carolina (Thun) I.; m. Dorothe Louise Hall, Feb. 23, 1936; children: Jon Lewis, Barbara Louise Isberg Johnson, Edward Russel. AB in Phys. Sci., U. No. Colo., 1935. Registered profl. engr., Calif. Radio and TV engr. W2XBS/WNBT-NBC, N.Y.C., 1939-42; electronic devel. engr. div. war rsch. Columbia U., Mineola, N.Y., 1942-46; chief engr. KRON-TV, San Francisco, 1946-52; ind. cons. TV engr. various locations, 1952-54; sr. engr. Ampex Corp., Redwood City, Calif., 1954-60; statewide communications engr. U. Calif., Berkeley, 1960-67; ind. cons. radio communications engr. Berkley, 1967—; chair subcom. for FM radio stereo standards NSRC, Washington,1 960-61; mem. com. for establishing 2500 MHz instrnl. TV svc., FCC, 1965-67. Contbr. to profl. publs. Named Honored Alumnus, U. No. Colo., 1993. Fellow IEEE (chair awards com. vehicular tech. soc. 1984-90, Avant Garde medal and cert. 1991), Audio Engring. Soc., Soc. Motion Picture and TV Engrs., Radio Club Am.; mem. Acoustical Soc. Am., Soc. Cable TV Engrs., Inst. Radio Engrs. (chair San Francisco sect. 1951). Republican. Congregationalist. Home: Apt B127 32200 SW French Prairie Dr Wilsonville OR 97070-7466

ISELY, BARBARA J., sociologist, consultant; b. Winfield, Kans., Dec. 28, 1941; d. Lyman S. and S. Elise (Isely) Johnson; m. Charles C. Langford, 1968. BM, Southwestern Coll., 1964; M in Music Edn., North Tex. State U., 1967; MA in Sociology, U. Oreg., 1975, PhD in Sociology, 1981. Asst. prof. sociology Oreg. State U., 1980-90, adminstr. women in internat. devel. coord., 1984-85; affiliated rschr. Gandhigram Rural U. and Tamil U., India, 1987-93; sociologist PKM Campus, Kathamandu, Nepal, 1993; lectr. in field; cons. on World Bank funded project, Lagos, Nigeria, 1995. Contbr. articles to profl. jours. Vol. condr. profl. devel. workshops for faculty members various univs. and colls., India, 1991-94. Recipient Servant Leadership award Southwestern Coll., Winfield, 1993. Mem. APHA, Am. Sociol. Assn., Internat. Fedn. for Women in Agr. (founding), Rural Sociol. Soc., Assn. for Women in Devel., Population Assn. Am., Women in Soc. of the Internat. Sociol. Assn. (rsch. com.).

ISELY, HENRY PHILIP, association executive, integrative engineer, writer, educator; b. Montezuma, Kans., Oct. 16, 1915; s. James Walter and Jessie M. (Owen) I; m. Margaret Ann Sheesley, June 12, 1948; children: Zephyr, LaRock, Lark, Robin, Kemper, Heather Capri. Student South Oreg. Jr. Coll., Ashland, 1934-35, Antioch Coll., 1935-37. Organizer, Action for World Fedn., 1946-50, N.Am. Coun. for People's World Conv., 1954-58; organizer World Com. for World Constl. Conv., 1958, sec. gen., 1959-66; sec. gen. World Constn. and Parliament Assn., Lakewood, Colo., 1966—, organizer worldwide prep. confs., 1963, 66, 67, 1st session People's World Parliament and World Constl. Conv. in Switzerland, 1968, editor assn. bull. Across Frontiers, 1959—; co-organizer Emergency Coun. World Trustees, 1971, World Constituent Assembly at Innsbruck, Austria, 1977, Colombo, Sri Lanka, 1978-79, Troia, Portugal, 1991; organizer Provisional World Parliament 1st session, Brighton, Eng., 1982, 2d Session New Delhi, India, 1985, 3d Session Miami Beach, Fla., 1987, mem. parliament, 1982—; sec. Working Commn. to Draft World Constn., 1971-77; pres. World Svc. Trust, 1972-78; ptnr. Builders Found., Vitamin Cottages, 1955—, chmn. bd. dirs, 1985—; pres. Earth Rescue Corps, 1984—; sec.-treas. Grad. Sch. World Problems, 1984—, prof. world problems, 1990—; cabinet mem. Provisional World Govt., 1987—; pres. World Govt. Funding Corp., 1986—; co-organizer Global Ratification and Elections Network, 1991—, sec., 1992—. Author: The People Must Write the Peace, 1950, A Call to All Peoples and All National Governments of the Earth, 1961, Outline for the Debate and Drafting of a World Constitution, 1967, Strategy for Reclaiming Earth for Humanity, 1969, Call to a World Constituent Assembly, 1974, Proposal for Immediate Action by an Emergency Council of World Trustees, 1971, Call to Provisional World Parliament, 1981, People Who Want Peace Must Take Charge of World Affairs, 1982, Plan for Emergency Earth Rescue Administration, 1985, Plan for Earth Finance Credit Corporation, 1987, Climate Crisis, 1989, Handbook for Planet Earth, 1993, Technological Breakthroughs for A Global Energy Network, 1991, Bill of Particulars: Why The U.N. Must Be Replaced, 1994, Manifesto for the Inauguration of World Government, 1994, Call to the Fourth Session of the Provisional World Parliament, 1995, Critique of the Report of the Commission on Global Governance, 1995; co-author, editor: A Constitution for the Federation of Earth, 1974, rev. edit., 1991, also author several world legis. measures adopted at Provisional World Parliament. 1968-77; co-author Plan for Collaboration in World Constituent Assembly for 1991; creator treatment for screen drama History Hangs by a Thread; designer prefab modular panel system of constrn., master plan for Guacamaya project in Costa Rica. Candidate for U.S. Congress, 1958. Hon. rsch. doctorate in edn., 1989; recipient Honor award Internat. Assn. Educators for World Peace, 1975, Gandhi medal, 1977. Mem. ACLU, Fellowship of Reconciliation, World Union, World Federalist Assn., World Future Soc., Earth Island Inst., Internat. Soc. for Ecol. Econs., Internat. Assn. for Hydrogen Energy, Friends of Earth, Wilderness Soc., Solar Energy Soc., Sierra Club, Amnesty Internat., World Resoures Inst., Human Rights Watch, Nat. Nutritional Foods Assn., Environ. Def. Fund, Greenpeace, Internat. Studies Assn., Ctr. for Study of Democratic Instns., War Resistors League, Audubon Soc., Worldwatch Inst., Internat. Assn. Constl. Law, Earth Regeneration Soc., Internat. Soc. Universalism (Honor award 1993), Zero Population Growth, Mt. Vernon Country Club. Home: Lookout Mountain 241 Zephyr Ave Golden CO 80401 Office: 1480 Hoyt St Ste 31 Lakewood CO 80215-4755

ISEMAN, MICHAEL DEE, medical educator; b. St. Paul, Mar. 3, 1939; s. Manuel Wessel and Eileen Catherine (Croghan) I.; m. Joan Marie Christensen, Aug. 31, 1963; children: Thomas Michael, Matthew Charles. BA in History, Princeton U., 1961; MD, Columbia U., 1965. Intern, jr. resident in medicine Columbia Svc., Bellevue Hosp., N.Y.C., 1965-67; sr. resident in medicine Columbia Svc., Harlem Hosp., N.Y.C., 1969-70; fellow pulmonary medicine Harlem Hosp., N.Y.C., 1970-72; assoc. dir. pulmonary svc. Denver Gen. Hosp., 1972-82; chief clin. mycobacteriology svc. Nat. Jewish Ctr. for Immunology and Respiratory Medicine, Denver, 1982—; asst. prof. medicine U. Colo. Sch. Medicine, Denver, 1973-79, assoc. prof. medicine, 1979-89, prof., 1989—. Assoc. editor Am. Rev. Respiratory Diseases, N.Y., 1984-89. Pres. Am. Lung Assn. Colo., Denver, 1982-83; alumni trustee Princeton U., 1981-85. Lt. comdr. USN, 1967-69. Prin. investigator devel. and evaluation of drugs for treatment of mycobacterium avium in AIDS, NIH, 1984-1992. Fellow ACP, Am. Coll. Chest Physicians; mem. Am. Thoracic Soc. (v.p. 1983-84). Presbyterian. Office: Nat Jewish Ctr Immunology & Respiratory Medicine 1400 Jackson St Denver CO 80206-2761

ISENBERG, HAROLD, physician; b. Chgo., Oct. 28, 1938; s. Morton Joseph and Helen (Pruzansky) I.; divorced 1982; children: Gerard, Warren. BS in Zoology, U. Ill., 1959; BS in Pharmacy, U. Ill., Chgo., 1963, BS in Dentistry, 1966, DDS, 1968; MD, U. of East, Quezon City, Philippines, 1976. Diplomate Am. Bd. Family Practice. Pharmacist Urban's Pharmacy, and Budlong Drugs, Chgo., 1963-64, Stite's Pharmacy, Macomb, Ill., 1969-72; dentist Barkley Dental Group Ltd., Macomb, 1969-72; intern U. Ill. Coll. Medicine, Peoria, 1977-78, resident in family practice, 1978-80; part-time emergency rm. physician Meth. Med. Ctr., Peoria, Ill., 1977-80; family practice physician Hawthorne Community Med. Group, Torrance, Calif., 1980-91, Cigna Staff Model, Torrance, 1991—; asst. instr. U. Ill., Chgo., 1968-69, Peoria, 1977-80; vol. clin. instr. Harbor UCLA, Torrance, 1983—. Contbg. author: American Academy of Family Practice, 1982; investigator Practical Cardiology jour., 1990. Mem. Simon Wiesenthal Ctr., L.A., 1983—, Music Ctr., L.A., 1986—. Partial Acad. scholar U. of the East, 1973. Fellow Am. Acad. Family Practice; mem. AMA, ADA, Ill. Dental Soc., Prairie Valley Dental Soc., Calif. Med. Soc., Los Angeles County Med. Assn., Rho Chi. Jewish. Office: CIGNA 3333 Skypark Dr Torrance CA 90505-5020

ISENBERG, PHILLIP L., state legislator; b. Gary, Ind., Feb. 25, 1939; s. Walter M. and Violet R. (Phillips) I.; m. Marilyn Y. Araki, July 13, 1963. B.A., Calif. State Coll., Sacramento, 1961; J.D., U. Calif., Berkeley, 1967. Bar: Calif. 1967. Practice law Sacramento; mem. Sacramento City Council, 1971-75; mayor City of Sacramento, 1975-82;; mem. Calif. Assembly, 1982—. Mem. Calif. Bar Assn. Democrat. Office: 6005 State Capital Sacramento CA 95814

ISENOR, LINDA DARLENE, grocery retailer, marketing professional; b. Calgary, Alta., Can., Oct. 3, 1955; d. Frank Carl and Mavis Ella (Jarnett) Kachmarski; m. Larry Douglas Isenor, Oct. 13, 1973. Diploma in mktg., So. Alta. Inst. Tech., Calgary, 1988. Cert. travel cons. Calgary Bd. Edn. Cashier to asst. mgr. G&S Restaurants Balmoral Ltd., Calgary, 1972-74; cashier, supr. Calgary Coop. Assn. Ltd., 1974-75, supr., 1975-78, head cashier, 1978-80, asst. grocery merchandiser, 1980-81, grocery merchandising specialist, 1981-82, grocery procurement specialist, 1982-83, grocery mktg. supr. for pricing and costing, 1983-93, grocery mktg. mgr., 1993—. Office: Calgary Coop Assn Ltd, 200 S 8500 MacLeod Trail SE, Calgary, AB Canada T2H 2N1

ISHIGURO, TOYOSUKE, international business consultant, educator; b. Nagaya, Japan, Aug. 9, 1929; came to U.S., 1958; S. Kusuo and Hanae (Nakashima) I.; m. Aiko Kuroki, Aug., 1984. BA with honors, Kwansai Gakuin U., Japan, 1957; BA in Polit. Sci., Pasadena U., 1962; MA in Polit. Sci., U. So. Calif., 1964; JD, Loyola U., 1976. Instr. dept. Asian studies USC, L.A., 1962-64; legal asst. Fredrick W. Hill Law Office, L.A., 1973-77; assoc. Iwasaki, Thomas and Sheffield, 1977-87; pres. Ishiguro & Assocs., Beverly Hills, Calif., 1988—; adj. prof. law Loyola U., L.A., 1979—; lectr. for Japan External Trade Orgn.. to Japanese Bus. Orgns.; speaker to various groups includeing Calif. Bar Assn. Author: 4 books based on his lectrs. on Am. Law pub. in Japanese. Mem. Phi Delta Phi (life), Phi Sigma Sipha. Home: 2042 Ajax Cir West Covina CA 91792-1501 Office: Ishiguro & Assocs. 9250 Wilshire Blvd Beverly Hills CA 90212-3352

ISHII, CLYDE HIDEO, plastic surgeon; b. Lihue, Hawaii, Mar. 29, 1952. MD, Jefferson Med. Coll. Plastic surgeon Queens Med. Ctr., Honolulu; chief plastic surgery Shriners Hosp., Honolulu, 1993—. Office: 1380 Lusitana St Ste 702 Honolulu HI 96813-2449*

ISHIKAWA-FULLMER, JANET SATOMI, psychologist, educator; b. Hilo, Hawaii, Oct. 17, 1925; d. Shinichi and Onao (Kurisu) Saito; m. Calvin Y. Ishikawa, Aug. 15, 1950; 1 child, James A.; m. Daniel W. Fullmer, June 11, 1980. BE, U. Hawaii, 1950, MEd, 1967; MEd, U. Hawaii, 1969, PhD, 1976. Diplomate Am. Acad. Pain Mgmt. Instr. Honolulu Bus. Coll., 1953-59; instr., counselor Kapiolani Community Coll., Honolulu, 1959-73; prof., dir. counseling Honolulu Community Coll., 1973-74, dean of students, 1974-77; psychologist, v.p., treas. Human Resources Devel. Ctr., Inc., Honolulu, 1977—; cons. United Specialties Co., Tokyo, 1979, Grambling (La.) State U., 1980, 81, Filipino Immigrants in Kalihi, Honolulu, 1979-84, Legis. Ref. Bur., Honolulu, 1984-85, Honolulu Police Dept., 1985; co-founder Waianae (Hawaii) Child and Family Ctr., 1979-92. Co-author: Family Therapy Dictionary, 1991, Manabu: The Diagnosis and Treatment of a Japanese Boy with a Visual Anomaly, 1991; contbr. articles to profl. jours. Commr. Bd. Psychology, Honolulu, 1979-85; co-founder Kilohana United Meth. Ch. and Family Ctr., 1993—. Mem. APA, ACA, Hawaii Psychol. Assn., Pi Lambda Theta (sec. 1967-68, v.p. 1968-69, pres. 1969-70), Delta Kappa Gamma (sec., v.p., scholarship 1975, Outstanding Educator award 1975, Thomas Jefferson award 1993, Francis E. Clark award 1993). Home: 154 Maono Pl Honolulu HI 96821-2529 Office: Human Resources Devel Ctr 1750 Kalakaua Ave Apt 809 Honolulu HI 96826-3725

ISHIMATSU, EIJI, investment company executive; b. 1951. With Hazama-Gumi Ltd., Tokyo, 1972-87; pres., sec. Hazama USA Corp., Gardena, Calif., 1987—. Office: Hazama USA Corp 1045 W Redondo Beach Blvd Gardena CA 90247-4128*

ISHLER, MICHAEL WILLIAM, structural engineer; b. Cleve., Dec. 21, 1952; s. William Edward and Elizabeth (Swift) I.; m. Kathleen Ann Abell, Sept. 6, 1975; children: Stephanie Ann, Matthew Scott. BArch, U. Cin., 1977, MS, 1979; SM, MIT, 1981. Sr. engr. Owens Corning Fiberglas, Toledo and Granville, Ohio, 1981-86; assoc. Ove Arup & Ptnrs., London, 1987-88, L.A., 1988-93; prin. consulting structural engr. Ishler Design & Engring. Assocs., Santa Monica, Calif., 1993—. Inventor double hexagonal mesh air supported fabric roof structure, 1985, parallel compression ring fabric roof structure, 1986. Mem. ASCE (sec.-treas. Toledo chpt. 1983-85, Outstanding Engr. 1985), Structural Engrs. So. Calif., Alpha Rho Chi. Home: 2314 Pearl St Santa Monica CA 90405-2830

ISHMAEL, WILLIAM EARL, land use planner, civil engineer; b. Mt. Sterling, Ky., Mar. 11, 1946; s. Charles William and Alice Clay (Trimble) I. BSCE, Duke U., 1968; MA in Urban Planning, U. Mich., 1975. Registered civil engr., Calif., Ky.; registered planner Am. Inst. Cert. Planners. Petroleum engr. Humble Oil (now Exxon), New Orleans, 1968-69; dep. dir. Richmond Regional Planning Commn., Richmond, Va., 1975-78; sr. planner Nolte and Assocs., Sacramento, 1978—, assoc. of the corp., 1984-90, v.p., mng. prin., Sacramento, 1990—; cons. So. Pacific RR . Mem. City Planning Commn., Sacramento, 1983-89, vice chmn., 1985, chmn. 1986; bd. dirs. Sacramento Heritage, 1983-88, chmn., 1985-86; chmn. Urban Design Task Force for Downtown Sacramento, 1986; active Big Bros., 1978-83. Served to lt. USN, 1969-72. Named Mover and Shaper Heir Apparent, Exec. Pl. Mag., 1986. Mem. Am. Planning Assn. (dir. pro tem 1981-83, Disting. Service award 1983), Chi Epsilon. Office: Nolte & Assocs 1750 Creekside Oaks Dr Ste 200 Sacramento CA 95833-3640

ISIDORO, EDITH ANNETTE, horticulturist; b. Albuquerque, Oct. 14, 1957; d. Robert Joseph and Marion Elizabeth (Miller) I. BS in Horticulture, N.Mex. State U., 1981, MS in Horticulture, 1984; postgrad., U. Nev., Reno, 1992—. Range conservationist Soil Conservation Service, Estancia, Grants, N.Mex., 1980-82; lab. aide N.Mex. State U. Dept. Horticulture, Las Cruces, 1982, 83-84; technician N.Mex. State U. Coop. Extension Service, Las Cruces, 1983-84, county agrl. extension agt., 1985; area extension agr. U. Nev., Reno, Fallon, 1985—; hay tester Nev. Agrl. Services, Fallon, 1988-92. Mem. AAUW, Am. Soc. Hort. Sci., Am. Horticulture Soc., Am. Botany Soc., Am. Horticulture Therapy Assn., Alpha Zeta, Pi Alpha Psi. Home: 3900 Sheckler Rd Fallon NV 89406-8202 Office: Churchill County Coop Extension 1450 Mclean Rd Fallon NV 89406-8880

ISMACH, ARNOLD HARVEY, journalism educator; b. N.Y.C., Dec. 28, 1930; s. Louis and Augusta (Lacher) I.; m. Judy Daniels, June 20, 1959 (div. 1975); children: Richard, Theresa. BA, U. Okla., 1951; MA, UCLA, 1970; PhD, U. Wash., 1975. News editor Union-Bulletin, Walla Walla, Wash., 1954-56; reporter, editor Sun-Telegram, San Bernardino, Calif., 1956-69; prof. journalism U. Minn., Mpls., 1973-85; dean journalism U. Oreg., Eugene, 1985-94, prof. journalism, 1994—; cons. Pub. Relations Ctr., Los Angeles, 1970-75; pres. Communications Research Ctr., Mpls., 1973-85. Co-author: (textbooks) New Strategies, 1976, Enduring Issues, 1978, Reporting Processes, 1981. Served to sgt. U.S. Army, 1951-54. Mem. Soc. Profl. Journalists, Assn. for Edn. in Journalism, Am. Assn. Pub. Opinion Rsch. Democrat. Home: 5326 Tahsili St Eugene OR 97405-4021 Office: Sch Journalism and Comm Univ Oreg Eugene OR 97403

ISRAEL, DAVID, journalist, screenwriter, producer; b. N.Y.C., Mar. 17, 1951; s. Hyman and Edith Oringer I.; m. Lindy De Koven, Aug. 8, 1987. B.S. in Journalism, Northwestern U., 1973. Reporter Chgo. Daily News, 1973-75; columnist Washington Star, 1975-78, Chgo. Tribune, 1978-81, Los Angeles Herald Examiner, 1981-84; chmn., pres. Big Prodns., Inc., Los Angeles; producer, writer OCC Prodns., Los Angeles, 1985-88; exec. prodr., writer Lorimar Television, L.A., 1988-92, Paramount Pictures, Hollywood, 1992-93; writer, exec. prodr. Stephen J. Cannell Prodns., Inc., Hollywood, 1993—; dir. office of Pres., Los Angeles Olympic Organizing Com., 1984. Writer: Bay City Blues, 1983; prodr., writer: A Comedy Salute to Baseball, NBC, 1985; supervising prodr., writer: Fast Copy, NBC, 1985-86; co-creator, supervising prodr.: Crimes of the Century, 1987-88; co-exec. prodr., writer: Midnight Caller, NBC, Lorimar TV, 1988-91, The Untouchables, Paramount TV, 1992-93; exec. prodr., writer: Jake Lassiter: Justice on the Bayou, NBC, Stephen J. Cannell Prodns., 1995. Mem. AFTRA, Writers Guild Am., Chgo. Athletic Assn. Office: Cannell Studios 7083 Hollywood Blvd Hollywood CA 90028-8901

ISRAEL, JOAN, social worker; b. Bklyn., July 19, 1943; d. Joseph Israel and Irene (Solon) Kansey; m. Ronald Jerome Janesh, June 28, 1980 (div. Feb. 1985); 1 child, Ariel Naomi. BA, Bklyn. Coll., 1965; MSW, U. Mich., 1974. Lic. clin. social worker, Nev. Social worker Alameda County Welfare Dept., Oakland, Calif., 1965-72; group therapist Pacific Ctr. for Human Growth, Berkeley, Calif., 1975-77; individual and group therapist, bd. dir. Bi-Ctr., San Francisco, 1976-78; clin. social worker, supr. Audrey L. Smith Devel. Ctr., San Francisco, 1977-78; psychiat. social worker South Nev. Adult Mental Health Dept., Las Vegas, 1978-84, part-time clin. social worker, 1988—; pvt. practice clin. social worker Las Vegas, 1984—. Contbr. articles to profl. publs. Organizer Drug/Alcohol Abuse Task Force, Las Vegas, 1983-84, Task Force on AIDS, Las Vegas, 1985-86. Mem. NASW (chair nominating com. 1978-80, 82-84, sec. 1984-86, chair com. on inquiry 1988—, legis. chair 1982-84, diplomate clin. social work), Sierra Club. Democrat. Jewish. Office: 3180 W Sahara Ave Ste 25C Las Vegas NV 89102-6005

ISRAEL, MARK A., pediatrics and neurological surgery educator; b. Newburgh, N.Y., Aug. 12, 1946; m. Susan Jean Israel; children: Joshua, Rebecca, Samuel. BA, Hamilton Coll., 1968; MD, Yeshiva U., 1973. Intern, resident Children's Hosp., Boston, 1973-75; postdoctoral fellow Nat. Inst. Allergy and Infectious Disease, Bethesda, Md., 1975-77; fellow in pediatric oncology Nat. Cancer Inst., Bethesda, 1978-82, investigator, 1982-84, chief molecular genetic sect., 1984-89; prof. pediatrics and neurol. surgery U. Calif., San Francisco, 1989—. Editor: Molecular Biology of Cancer, 1994; contbr. more than 100 articles to profl. jours. Trustee Marin Acad., San Raphael, Calif., 1992—; mem. citizens adv. com. San Quentin (Calif.) Prison, 1993—. Served with USPHS, 1975-89. Recipinet USPHS commendation, 1985, 87, Heinz Karger Found. award, Geneva, 1988. Mem. Am. Soc. Clin. Investigation, Soc. Pediatric Rsch., Am. Assn. Cancer Rsch., Am. Assn. Clin. Oncologists, Alpha Omega Alpha. Office: U Calif 513 Parnassus Ave Rm HSE722 San Francisco CA 94143-0520

ISRAEL, PAUL NEAL, computer design engineer, author; b. Balt., Apr. 22, 1959; s. Sheldon Leonard and Sheila Lee (Goldmacher) I. BS in EECS, U. Calif., Berkeley, 1981. Project mgr. computer sci. dept. U. Calif., Berkeley, 1981-82; design engr. Electronic Signature Lock Corp., Berkeley, 1983; staff engr. Qantel Bus. Systems, Hayward, Calif., 1983-89; sr. hardware design engr. SBE, Inc., Concord, Calif., 1989-90; engring. contractor Renegade Systems, Sunnyvale, Calif., 1990-92; prin. engr. Unisys Corp., San Jose, Calif., 1992-95. Mem. IEEE, Assn. Computing Machinery, Bay Area Sci. Fiction Assn. Office: 434 S Bernardo Ave #2 Sunnyvale CA 94086

ISRAEL, RICHARD STANLEY, investment banker; b. Oakland, Calif., Sept. 27, 1931; s. Sybil Noble, July 29, 1962; children: Richard Lee, Lynne, Lawrence. BA, U. Calif., Berkeley, 1953, MA, 1953. Copy editor San Francisco Chronicle, 1953-59; publicist CBS TV Network, L.A., 1959-62; sr. v.p. Rogers & Cowan, Beverly Hills, Calif., 1962-69; v.p. Cantor, Fitzgerald, Beverly Hills, 1969-73; pres. Sponsored Cons. Svcs., L.A., 1973—. Pres. North Beverly Dr. Homeowners Assn., Beverly Hills, 1986-88; v.p. Temple Emanuel, Beverly Hills, 1988-93, L.A. chpt. Juvenile Diabetes Found. Internat, 1987—. With U.S. Army, 1956-58. Recipient Alumni citation U. Calif. Alumni Assn., Berkeley, 1984. Mem. L.A. Venture Assn. (pres. 1987), Assn. for Corp. Growth (bd. dirs. L.A. chpt.). Democrat. Office: Sponsored Cons Svcs 8929 Wilshire Blvd Ste 214 Beverly Hills CA 90211-1951

ISSARI, M(OHAMMAD) ALI, film producer, educator, consultant; b. Esfahan, Iran, Oct. 3, 1921; s. Abbas Bek and Qamar (Soltan) I.; m. Joan Gura Aamodt, 1953; children: Scheherezade, Katayoun, Roxana. B.A., U. Tehran, Iran, 1963; M.A., U. So. Calif., 1968; Ph.D., 1979. Films officer Brit. Embassy, Brit. Council Joint Film Div., Tehran, 1944-50; asst. motion picture officer USIS, 1950-65; cons. to various Iranian Govt. ministries on film and TV devels., 1950-77; liaison officer Am. and Iranian govt. ofcls., 1950-65; prof. cinema Coll. Communication Arts and Scis. Mich. State U., East Lansing, 1969-81; also dir. instructional film and multimedia prodn. Mich. State U., 1969-78; mass media cons., 1981—; pres. Multimedia Prodn. Svcs., Thousand Oaks, Calif., 1989—; film, public relations adviser to Iranian Oil Operating Cos. in, Iran, 1963-65; spl. cons. on edn. and instructional TV Saudi Arabian Ministry of Info., 1972; tchr. Persian lang. Iran-Am. Soc., Tehran, 1949-59; introduced audio-visual edn. in Iran, 1951; established first film festivals in Iran. Producer, dir. over 1000 ednl., instructional and documentary films, 1956-78; freelance film reporter: Telenews, UPI, Iran, 1959-61; project dir., exec. producer: Ancient Iran Film Series, 1974-78; dir. film prodn. workshops, Cranbrook Inst., Detroit, 1973-74; author: (with Doris A. Paul) A Picture of Persia, 1977, What is Cinema Vérité?, 1979, Cinema in Iran, 1900-1979, 1989; contbr. articles on ednl. communication and audio-visual instruction to periodicals and profl. jours. Founder, exec. sec. Youth Orgn. of Iran, 1951-52; v.p. Rugby Football Fedn., Iran, 1952-53, pres., 1954-55. Recipient Cine Golden Eagle award, 1975, Meritorious Honor award USIA, 1965; decorated Order of Magnum Cap Ord: S.F. Danaie M. Sigillum, King of Denmark, 1960, Order of Cavalieres Italy, 1958, Order of Oranje Nassau Queen Juliana of Holland, 1959, Orders of Kooshesh and Pas HIM Shah of Iran, 1951, 57, Order of Esteghlal King Hussein of Jordan, 1960, Order of Ordinis Sancti Silvestri Papae Pope John 23d, 1959. Mem. Anglo-Iranian Dramatic Soc. (bd. dirs. 1943-50), Mich. Film Assn. (co-founder 1972, bd. dirs. 1972-73), Mid. East Studies Assn., N.Am. Soc. Motion Picture and TV Engrs. (life), Ancient Studies Inst. (co-founder, pres. 1989-93), Bashgahe Iran, Inc. (co-founder, pres. 1990-95), Assn. Ednl. Comm. and Tech., Delta Kappa Alpha (v.p. 1967). Office: Multimedia Prodn Svcs 982 Golden Crest Ave Newbury Park CA 91320-5814

ISSE, NICANOR G., plastic surgeon; b. Tucuman, Argentina, 1947. MD, U. Nacional de Tucuman, San Miguel, 1964. Plastic surgeon Huntington Meml. Hosp., Pasadena, Calif. *

ISTEL, JACQUES ANDRE, mayor; b. Paris, Jan. 28, 1929; came to U.S., 1940, naturalized, 1951; s. Andre and Yvonne Mathilde Cremieux I.; m. Felicia Juliana Lee, June 14, 1973; 1 dau. by previous marriage, Claudia Yvonne. A.B., Princeton, 1949. Stock analyst Andre Istel & Co., N.Y.C., 1950, 55; pres. Parachutes Inc., Orange, Mass., 1957-87, Intramgmt. Inc., N.Y.C., 1962-80; chmn. Pilot Knob Corp., 1982—; mayor Town of Felicity, Calif., 1986—; curator Ctrl. Point for Memories, Calif., 1992—; pres. VI World Parachuting Championships, 1962; capt. U.S. Parachuting team, 1956, capt., team leader, 1958; chmn. Mass. Parachuting Commn., 1961-62; lifetime hon. pres. Internat. Parachuting Commn., Fedn. Aero. Internat., 1965—; chmn. Hall of Fame of Parachuting, 1973—; founder Nat. Collegiate Parachuting League, 1957. Author: Coe the Good Dragon at the Center of the World, 1985, Coe le Bon Dragon au Centre du Monde, 1985. Contbr. articles to encys., profl. publs. Trustee Inst. for Man and Sci., 1975-82; bd. dirs. Marine Corps Scholarship Found., 1975-85. Served with USMC, 1952-54; lt. col. Res. Recipient Leo Stevens award, 1958, Diplome Paul Tissandier, 1969. Mem. Nat. Aero. Assn. (bd. dirs. 1965-68), Fedn. Internat. des Centres (pres. 1990—), Cercle de l'Union Interalliée (Paris), Marine Corps Res. Officers Assn., DAV (life), Racquet and Tennis Club (N.Y.C.), Princeton Club (N.Y.C.). Home: Northview Felicity CA 92283 also: 10 rue Galilée, 75116 Paris France Office: 1 Center Of The World Plz Felicity CA 92283-7777

ITTNER, PERRY MARTIN, sales and marketing consultant; b. Anaheim, Calif., June 14, 1961; s. Franklin Glenn and Delina (Martin) I.; m. Sylvia Marie Garcia, May 16, 1987; children: Kristina Nicole, Amber Delayne. Student, Cerritos Coll., 1979-82. Purchasing agt. Shield Healthcare, Inc., Van Nuys, Calif., 1979-85; gen. mgr. Propak div. of Devco Med. Co., Santa Fe Springs, Calif., 1985-86; materials mgr. Reliable Med. Supply, Brea, Calif., 1986-87; dir. sales and mktg. Telesis Rsch. Group, La Crescenta, Calif., 1985-90; mktg. product specialist Interhealth Corp., Whittier, Calif., 1988-89; prin. Psi Healthcare Assocs., Hacienda Heights, Calif., 1990—; v.p. sales and mktg. Health Industry Resources, 1994—. Mem. Health Industry Reps. Assn., The Planetary Soc. Office: Psi Healthcare Assocs 2332 S Peck Rd Ste 270 Whittier CA 90601

IVERSON, PETER JAMES, historian, educator; b. Whittier, Calif., Apr. 4, 1944; s. William James and Adelaide Veronica (Schmitt) I.; m. Kaaren Teresa Gonsoulin, Mar. 7, 1983; children: Erika, Jens, Tim, Scott. BA in History, Carleton Coll., 1967; MA in History, U. Wis., 1969, PhD in History, 1975. Vis. asst. prof. Ariz. State U., Tempe, 1975-76; from asst. prof to prof. U. Wyo., Laramie, 1976-86; coordinator div. social and behavioral scis. Ariz. State U., Phoenix, 1986-88; prof. history Ariz. State U., Tempe, 1988—; vis. prof. Carleton Coll., 1991; Panelist, reviewer Nat. Endowment Humanities, Washington, 1986—. Author: The Navajos: A Critical Bibliography, 1976, The Navajo Nation, 1981, Carlos Montezuma, 1982, The Navajos, 1990, When Indians Became Cowboys: Native Peoples and Cattle Ranching in the American West, 1994; editor: The Plains Indians of the 20th Century, 1985; co-editor: Major Problems in American Indian History, 1994; assoc. editor The Historian, 1990-95; mem. editl. bd. Pacific Hist. Rev., 1986-88, Jour. Ariz. History, 1987-89, Social Sci. Jour., 1988—, Montana: The Magazine of Western History, 1993—. Acting dir. McNickle Ctr. for History of Am. Indian Newberry Libr., 1994-95, mem. adv. bd., 1993—; bd. dirs. Ariz. Humanities Coun., 1993—; chmn. Wyo. Coun. Humanities, 1981-82; mem. Mus. No. Ariz. Flagstaff, 1984—, Heard Mus., Phoenix, 1986—, Desert Bot. Garden, Phoenix, 1986—. Recipient Chief Manuelito Appreciation award Navajo Nation, 1984; Newberry Libr. fellow, Chgo., 1973-74, Nat. Endowment Humanities fellow, 1982-83, Leadership fellow Kellogg Found., Battle Creek, Mich., 1982-85, Disting. Achievement award Carleton Coll. Alumni Assn., 1992. Mem. Am. Soc. Ethnohistory (coun. 1991-93, chmn. program com. 1994, chmn. prize com. 1987), Western Social Sci. Assn. (pres. 1988-89), Orgn. Am. Historians, Western History Assn. (chmn. prize com. 1991, co-chmn. program com. 1995). Office: Ariz State U Dept History Tempe AZ 85287

IVERSON, RONALD E., plastic surgeon; b. Hailey, Idaho, 1938. MD, UCLA, 1965. Plastic surgeon Eden Hosp., Castro Valley, Calif.; clin. prof. Stanford U. Office: Plas Surg Ctr 1387 Santa Rita Rd Pleasanton CA 94566-5643*

IVERSON, WAYNE DAHL, landscape architect, consultant; b. Mt. Horeb, Wis., Oct. 27, 1931; s. Inman Oliver and Anna Mathilda (Dahl) I.; m. Barbara Ruth Lusk, May 17, 1958; children: David, Ann, Caroline. BS, U. Wis., 1955, MS, 1956. Landscape architect Nat. Pk. Svc., San Francisco, 1956-58, Inyo Nat. Forest, Bishop, Calif., 1958-66; regional landscape architect, So. region U.S. Forest Svc., Atlanta, 1966-67, Calif. region, 1967-86; prin. Scenic Resource Mgmt., Sedona, Ariz., 1987—. Author: (handbook) National Forest Landscape Management, (with others) Landscape Assessment, 1975, (with others) American Landscape Architecture, 1989. co-founder No. Ariz. Trust Lands, Sedona, 1988 mem. bd. adjustment City of Sedona, 1989; mem. pks. and recreation com. Coconino County, Flagstaff, Ariz., 1989—; bd. dirs. Keep Sedona Beautiful, Inc., 1988—. Cpl. U.S. Army, 1952-54, Korea. Recipient 1st Alumni award Landscape Architecture dept., U. Wis., Madison, 1981, Award of Excellence, Nat. Soc. for Pk. Resources, 1982, Presdl. Design award Nat. Endowment for Arts, 1984, 1st Arthur Hawthorne Carhart award U.S. Forest Svc., 1992. Fellow Am. Soc. Landscape Architects. Office: Scenic Resources Mgmt 115 Highland Rd Sedona AZ 86336-6152

IVES, JOHN DAVID (JACK IVES), geography and environmental sciences educator; b. Grimsby, Eng., Oct. 15, 1931; came to U.S., 1967; s. Harry and Ellen May (McKay) I.; m. Pauline Angela H. Cordingley, Sept. 11, 1954; children: Nadine Elizabeth, Anthony Ragnar, Colin Harry, Peter Robert. BA in Gen. Geography/Geology, U. Nottingham, 1952, BA in Geography, 1953; PhD, McGill U., Montreal, Que., Can., 1956. Postdoctoral rsch. asst. Arctic Inst. N.Am., 1956-57, dir. McGill Subarctic Rsch. Lab.; asst. prof. geography dept. McGill U., 1957-60; asst. dir. geog. br. Canadian Fed. Dept. Mines and Tech. Surveys, chief div. phys. geography, 1960-64; dir. geog. br. Canadian Fed. Dept. Energy, Mines and Resources, Ottawa, Ont., 1964-67; dir. Inst. Arctic and Alpine Rsch.; prof. geography U. Colo., Boulder, 1967-79, prof. mountain geography, 1980-89; prof., chmn. dept. geography U. Calif., Davis, 1989-93, prof. mountain geoecology divsn. environ. studies, 1994—; guest prof. U. Bern, Switzerland, 1976-77; chmn. internat. working group UNESCO Man and the Biosphere Project 6; chmn. IGU Commn. on Mountain Geoecology and Sustainable Devel., 1972-80, 88—; mem. adv. com. program natural resources UN U., 1978-85, coord. project on mountain ecology and sustainable devel., 1979—, official univ. del. to Rio de Janeiro Earth Summit, UN Conf. on Environment and Devel., 1992; chmn. Canadian Nat. Adv. Com. on Geog. Research, 1964-67; mem. subcom. snow and ice NRC of Can., 1964-67; mem. commn. on ecology Internat. Union for Conservation Nature and Natural Resources. Co-author: The Himalayan Dilemma: Reconciling Development and Conservation, 1989; co-editor: Arctic and Alpine Environments, 1974; founder, chmn. editorial bd.; Arctic and Alpine Research, 1967-81; contbr. articles to profl. jours. U. Colo. Coun. on Rsch. and Creative Work grantee for Nunatak study in Arctic Norway, 1973; rsch. grantee NASA, 1971-82; rsch. grantee NSF, 1969-79; Guggenheim Meml. fellow, 1976-77; hon. academician Yunnan Acad. of Social Sci., China, 1994—. Fellow Geol. Soc. Am., Arctic Inst. N.Am. (bd. govs.); mem. Glaciological Soc., Internat. Mountain Soc. (founding pres. 1980, editor Mountain R & D quar. 1981—), Am. Assn. Geographers, Chinese Glaciological Soc., Ctrl. Himalayan Environ. Assn., World Mountain Network Newsletter, 1990. Home: 233 Huerta Pl Davis CA 95616-0272 Office: U Calif Divsn Environ Studies Davis CA 95616

IVIE, EVAN LEON, computer science educator; b. American Fork, Utah, May 15, 1931; s. Horace Leon and Ruth (Ashby) I.; m. Betty Jo Beck, Mar. 29, 1957; children—Dynette, Mark, Joseph, Robert, Ann, Rebecca, John, James, Mette, Emily, Peter. B.S., Brigham Young U., 1956, B.E.S., 1956; M.S., Stanford U., 1957; Ph.D., MIT, 1960. Instr., MIT, Cambridge, 1960-66; mem. tech. staff Bell Labs., Murray Hill, N.J., 1966-79; prof. computer sci. Brigham Young U., Provo, Utah, 1979—; pres. Ivie Computer Corp., Provo, 1979—. Inventor: Data Base Computers, 1972; Programmer's Workbench, 1975; Electronic Yellow Pages, 1978; Reader's Workbench, 1984. Leader, Boy Scouts Am., 1954-83; mem. Warren Sch. Bd., N.J., 1975-78. Served to 1st lt. USAF, 1957-60. Stanford U. fellow, 1956-57; NSF fellow, 1960-63; Fullbright Scholar Kiev Polytechnic Inst., Ukraine, 1992-93. Mem. Assn. Computing Machinery, IEEE (sr.). Republican. Mormon. Home: 1131 Dover Dr Provo UT 84604-5255 Office: Brigham Young U 2232 Tmcb Provo UT 84602-1044

IVY, BENJAMIN FRANKLIN, III, financial and real estate investment advisor; b. Bremerton, Wash., May 18, 1936; s. Edward Byron Ivy and Ada Josephine (Anderson) Steele; m. Karen Yvonne Thompson, July 14, 1961 (div. June 1979); children: Britt Annemarie Ivy, Zenah Blair; m. Emily Cecile Rawlins, Apr. 18, 1982 (div. June 1992). BME, Cornell U., 1959; MBA, Stanford U., 1961. CFP. Purchasing agent U. Calif., Berkeley, 1960-62; contract adminstr. Lockheed Missiles and Space div., Sunnyvale, Calif., 1962-64; asst. to pres. Tridea subsidiary McDonnell Douglas, Pasadena, Calif., 1964-68; v.p. Mitchum, Jones & Templeton, Inc., Palo Alto, Calif., 1968-74, Paine Webber, Palo Alto, 1974; pres. Morgan Investment Svcs., Inc., Palo Alto, 1974-84; v.p. Morgan, Olmstead, Kennedy & Gardner, Inc., 1974-84; pres., chmn. Ivy Fin. Enterprises, Inc., Palo Alto, 1984—; pres. Ivy Fin. Svcs., Palo Alto; bd. dirs., v.p. and registered prin. Assoc. Group, Inc., L.A. Founder Found. to Eliminate the Nat. Debt, Palo Alto, 1992. Mem. Palo Alto Masons, Palo Alto Elks, Sharon Heights Golf and Country Club, Internat. Assn. of Fin. Planners (charter mem., bd. dirs. 1972-73), Pacific Stock Exch. (assoc.), Cornell U. Alumni Assn., Stanford Alumni Assn. (life), Stanford Bus. Sch. Alumni Assn. (life), Kappa Sigma. Office: Ivy Fin Enterprises Inc 525 University Ave Fl 6 Palo Alto CA 94301-1903

IWAI, WILFRED KIYOSHI, lawyer; b. Honolulu, Aug. 21, 1941; s. Charles Kazuo and Michiko (Sakimoto) I.; m. Judy Tomiko Yoshimoto, Mar. 1, 1963; children: Kyle K., Tiffany Seiko. BS in Bus., U. Colo., 1963, JD, 1966. Bar: Hawaii 1966, Colo. 1966, U.S. Dist. Ct. Hawaii 1966, U.S. Ct. Appeals (9th cir.) 1966. Dep. corp. counsel State of Hawaii, Honolulu, 1966-71; assoc. Kashiwa & Kanazawa, Honolulu, 1971-75; ptnr. Kashiwa, Iwai, Motooka & Goto, Honolulu, 1975-82, also bd. dirs.; ptnr. Iwai, Goto & Morris, Honolulu, 1982—; also bd. dirs. Iwai Goto & Morris, Honolulu. Mem. ABA, Hawaii Bar Assn., Assn. Trial Lawyers Am., Bldg. Industry Assn., Bldg. Owners & Mgrs. Assn. Hawaii. Club: Draftsmen's (Honolulu) (pres.). Office: Iwai Goto & Morris 820 Mililani St Ste 502 Honolulu HI 96813-2935

IWASAKI, KOUICHI, molecular geneticist; b. Yokosuka, Kanagawa, Japan, Jan. 10, 1961; came to U.S., 1986; s. Yukio and Mayako Iwasaki. BS, Kyoto (Japan) U., 1984, MS, 1986; PhD, U. Wis., 1991. Rsch. assoc. Washington U., St. Louis, 1991-94, U. Wash., Seattle, 1994—. Contbr. articles to profl. jours. Recipient Keck award W. Keck Found., 1992. Mem. AAAS, Soc. for Neurosci. Office: U Wash Dept Genetics Mail Stop SK-50 Seattle WA 98195

IZADI, PARVIN, medical technologist; b. Kashan, Iran, Aug. 17, 1942; came to U.S., 1963; d. Mehdi and Zivar (Tootoonchi) Firoozbakht; m. Reza Izadi, Sept. 28, 1968; children: Kayvon, Cameron. BS in Biology, Fresno State U., 1968. Cert. med. tech., Calif. Med. technologist I Children's Hosp. L.A., 1968-69, 71-72, rsch. technologist, 1968-71, rsch. specialist III, 1972-82, supr., instr., 1982—. Author: Megakaryocytes in Vitro, 1981; contbr. articles to profl. jours. Mem. Am. Soc. Clin. Pathologists (cert. technologist in hematology, cert. specialist in hematology), Calif. Assn. Med. Lab. Technologists. Republican. Home: 2819 Pine Lawn Dr La Crescenta CA 91214-1349 Office: Children's Hosp Mail # 54 Los Angeles CA 90027

IZENOUR, CHRISTINE, lighting designer; b. San Antonio, Jan. 22, 1949; d. Charles Stevens and Elizabeth Christine (Lien) I. AA in Fine Arts, Pensacola (Fla.) Jr. Coll., 1970; BA in Metaphysics, Am. Nat. Inst., Calabasas, Calif., 1986; B Ind. Studies, U. South Fla., 1983. Sr. stage operator Walt Disney World, Orlando, Fla., 1971-74; lighting designer Ch. St. Sta., Orlando, 1974-76; prodn. asst. Quinn Martin Prodns., Hollywood, Calif., 1977-79; lighting designer Walt Disney Prodns., Epcot, Fla., 1979-83; design engr. Hubert Wilke, Inc., North Hollywood, Calif., 1984-86; researcher, writer Am. Nat. Inst., 1986-87; freelance designer, writer Glendale, Calif., 1986-88, Santa Monica Mountains Conservancy, Malibu, Calif., 1988-89; sr. designer Francis Krahe & Assocs., Newport Beach, Calif., 1989; freelance designer, prin. Christine Izenour Assocs., 1989—; mem. adv. bd. dept. interior design Am. Nat. Coll., Westwood, Calif., 1991-92. Columnist Westar Courier newspaper, 1986. Water safety instr. ARC, Ft. Walton Beach, Fla., 1966-76; vol. Cerebral Palsy Telethons, Orlando, 1974-75; co-founder Cathedral Players, Orlando, 1975; Marshal Olympic Torch Run, Los Angeles, 1984. Fellow Nat. Thespian Soc., 1967. Mem. Nat. Assn. Female Execs., Phi Kappa Phi. Republican. Home: PO Box 94 San Simeon CA 93452-0094

IZUEL, LEEANNA, lawyer; b. Pasadena, Calif., Feb. 23, 1967; d. Anthony George and Roberta Lee (Border) I. Bachelor's degree, UCLA, 1988, JD, 1991. Bar: Calif. 1991, U.S. Dist. Ct. (ctrl. dist.) Calif. 1992. Assoc. atty. Mudge Rose Guthrie Alexander & Ferdon, L.A., 1991—. Editor UCLA Law Rev., 1990-91. Active Town Hall, L.A., 1994. Mem. Nat. Assn. Bond Lawyers, State Bar Calif., L.A. County Bar Assn., UCLA Alumni Assn., Mortar Bd., Phi Alpha Delta, Sigma Kappa. Home: 6480 E Bixby Hill Rd Long Beach CA 90815-4709 Office: Mudge Rose Guthrie Alexander & Ferdon 333 S Grand Ave Los Angeles CA 90071-1504

IZZO, JOHN B(APTIST), management consultant; b. Waterbury, Conn., Dec. 22, 1957; s. John B. and Irene M. (Turpel) I.; m. Susan C. Duerksen, May 9, 1992; 1 child, Lena C. BA in Sociology, Hofstra U., 1979; MDiv, McCormick Theol. Sem., Chgo., 1981; PhD in Speech Comm., Kent State U., 1993. Assoc. minister First Presbyn. Ch., Norwalk, Ohio, 1981-84; sr. minister Brownlee Presbyn. Ch., Youngstown, Ohio, 1984-87; pres. Tiva Assocs., San Deigo, 1987-89; sr. cons. Kaiser Permanente, San Diego, 1989-92; v.p. Einstein Cons. Group, Phila., 1992—; adj. faculty San Diego State U., 1990-92; cons. in field. Contbr. articles to profl. jours. Mem. Nat. Speakers Assn., Orgn. Devel. Network (chair nat. conf. 1989, bd. dirs. 1992), San Diego Coalition for Cairo (b. dirs. 1993—), Bayside Settlement House (bd. dirs. 1991—), Sierra Club (chair population com. 1994), Phi Beta Kappa. Democrat. Office: Einstein Cons PO Box 34188 San Diego CA 92163-4188

IZZO, MARY ALICE, real estate broker; b. Mesa, Ariz., Aug. 5, 1953; d. Edward Lee and Evangeline Lauda (Gorraiz) Meeker; m. Michael David Izzo, Dec. 26, 1971; children: Michael Wade, Clinton Jarred, Antoinette Marie. Student, Pioneer Coll., 1977, Yavapai Coll., 1984-93. Cert. realtor, Ariz. Sales agt. Babbit Bros., Flagstaff, Ariz., 1970-76; owner Cottonwood (Ariz.) Tees, 1978-84; realtor Weston Realty, Cottonwood, 1985-86, Coldwell Banker Mabery Real Estate, Cottonwood, 1986-89; sales agent, assoc. broker The Glenarm Land Co., Cottonwood, 1989-94; office mgr., sec. Izzo & Sons Contracting, 1985—, Wilhoit Water Co., 1991-93. Auhtor: Current Customer Cook Book, 1984. Bd. dirs. cub scouts Boy Scouts Am., 1984, 87; bd. dirs. AYSO Soccer, Verde Valley, Ariz., 1984-87, 92—, coach tournament all girls' traveling team, 1993—; leader youth group, Cottonwood. Democrat. Roman Catholic. Home: PO Box 2002 Cottonwood AZ 86326-2002 Office: The Glenarm Land Co 408 S Main St Cottonwood AZ 86326-3903

JABARA, MICHAEL DEAN, investment banker; b. Sioux Falls, S.D., Oct. 26, 1952; s. James M. and Jean Marie (Swiden) J.; m. Gundula Beate Dietz, Aug. 26, 1984; children: James Michael, Jenna Mariel. Student, Mich. Tech. U., 1970-72; BSBA, U. Calif., Berkeley, 1974; MBA, Pepperdine U., 1979. Mgr. original Sprint project team So. Pacific Communications Corp., 1976-78; network product mgr. ROLM Corp., 1978-81; cons. McGraw Hill Co., Hamburg (Fed. Republic of Germany) and London, 1982-83; founder, chief exec. officer Friend Techs. Inc. (merger VoiceCom Systems, Inc.), San Francisco, 1984-88; pres. VoiceCom Ventures, San Francisco, 1988-93; mng. dir. Telecom, EMS Group Ltd., London, 1993—; owner Jabara & Co., Glenbrook, Nev., 1993—. Patentee in field. Active Tahoe-Douglas C. of C. Mem. Infor. Industry Assn. (conf. program chair 1995), Assn. for Corp. Growth, Caribbean Cable TV Assn., Satellite Broadcasters & Comms. Assn., Pepperdine Bus. Alumni, U. Calif. Berkeley Bus. Alumni, The Classic Cars of the Candy Store, Reno Jaguar Club, Tahoe-Douglas Rotary, Lighting W

Ranch Golf Club. Office: Jabara & Co PO Box 568 Glenbrook NV 89413-0568

JABLECKI, CHARLES K., clinical neurologist; b. Providence, Dec. 17, 1943; m. Elizabeth; 1 child, Michael. BA magna cum laude, Harvard U., 1965, MD cum laude, 1969. Bd. cert. Am. Bd. Psychiatry and Neurology, Am. Bd. Electrodiagnostic Medicine. Intern internal medicine Presbyn. St. Luke's Hosp., Chgo., 1969-70; resident clin. neurology Mayo Grad. Sch., Mayo Clinic, Rochester, Minn., 1972-76; instr. in neurology Mayo Med. Sch., U. Minn., Rochester, 1975-76; asst. clin. prof. neurosciences U. Calif., San Diego, 1976-82, assoc. clin. prof. neurosciences, 1982—; co-dir. Clin. Neurophysiology Lab. U. Calif. Med. Ctr., San Diego, 1978-82, dir. Neurology Outpatient Clinics, 1979-82; staff assoc. Lab. of Neurochemistry, NIMH, Bethesda, Md., 1970-72; neurology cons. U. Hosp., San Diego, 1976—, Sharp Hosp., San Diego, 1982—, Mercy Hosp., San Diego, 1982—; cons. Muscular Dystrophy Assn., San Diego, 1978—; cons. electromyographer EMG Lab., Children's Hosp., San Diego, 1978—; examiner Am. Assn. Electromyography and Electrodiagnosis, 1979-89, Am. Bd. Psychiatry and Neurology, 1982—, Am. Bd. Electrodiagnostic Medicine, 1990—; qualified med. evaluator State of Calif., 1992—. Contbr. chpts. to books and articles to profl. jours. Asst. surgeon USPHS, 1970-72. Scholar Harvard Coll., 1961-65, Charles H. Smith scholar Harvard Med. Sch., 1965-69. Fellow Am. Acad. Neurology, Am. Assn. Electrodiagnostic Medicine (pres. 1995-96, nomenclature com. 1975-76, chair membership com. 1976-80, equipment and material com. 1978-80, bd. dirs. 1979-82, profl. standards com., others), Am. Acad. Disability Evaluating Physicians; mem. AMA, San Diego Neurol. Assn. (sec.-treas. 1992—), Assn. Qualified Med. Evaluators. Office: 550 Washington St Ste 221 San Diego CA 92103-2227

JACISIN, JOHN JAMES, psychiatrist; b. Ironwood, Mich., June 30, 1942; s. Frank Anthony and Amelia Lucy J.; m. Hoa Thi Hyunh, Feb. 27, 1971; children: Ann, Tina, Kim. Student Mich. Tech. U., 1960-61; BS in Psychology, U. Mich., 1964, MD, 1968. Diplomate Am. Bd. Psychiatry and Neurology. Intern, Mt. Carmel Hosp., Columbus, Ohio, 1968-69; resident in psychiatry U., Mich., Ann Arbor, 1971-74; dir. inpatient psychiatry Riverwood Cmty. Mental Health Ctr., St. Joseph, Mich., 1974-75; dir. psychiat. inpatient svcs. Henry Ford Hosp., Detroit, 1975-81, acting dept. chmn., 1976-77, dir. psychiat. residency tng. program., 1977-87, dept. vice chmn., 1984-87, dir. psychiat. services Fairlane Ctr., 1981-84; clin. instr. U. Mich. Med. Sch., 1977-87; dir. inpatient svc., Modesto Psychiat. Ctr., Calif., 1987-91, assoc. med. dir., 1991-93; Psychiat. Med. Group, Modesto, 1987—; mem. adj. faculty U. Pacific, 1991-94. Served to capt. USAF, 1969-71. Decorated Bronze star. Fellow Am. Psychiat. Assn.; mem. AMA, Am. Coll. Clin. Psychiatrists, Anxiety Disorder Assn. Am., Ctrl. Calif. Psychiat. Soc., Obsessive Compulsive Disorder Found. Office: Psychiat Med Group 3425 Coffee Rd Ste 2A Modesto CA 95355-1582

JACK, MINTA SUE, hospital department head; b. Huntsville, Tex., Aug. 24, 1935; d. Clinton Orrin and Dorris Eugenia (Pierce) Bunn; m. Samuel Garred Jack, Jr., June 8, 1957 (div. 1984); children: Samuel Garred III, Paul Alan. BA with distinction, U. N.Mex., 1957. Cert. secondary educator. High sch. tchr. Albuquerque Pub. Schs., 1957-58; bd. dirs. Delta Delta Delta, Reno, 1962-63; com. chmn. Tustin (Calif.) Sch. Dist. PTO, 1965-70, Red Hill Luth. Sch., Tustin, 1970-74; bd. dirs. Assistance League of Tustin, 1972-83, Performing Arts Ctr. Guilds, Orange County, Calif., 1983-88; bd.d irs. Delta Delta Delta, Orange County, Calif., 1987-91; dir., vol. Western Med. Ctr., Santa Ana, Calif., 1986—. Vol. leader Boy Scouts/Little League, Tustin, 1966-72; vol. Olympic Organizing Com., L.A., 1984; assoc. Mexican Am. Nat. Women, Santa Ana, 1988-90; mem. Freedom Found./Valley Forge, Santa Ana, 1988-90. Recipient Writing award, 1989, Newsletter award, 1991, Community Svc. award Disneyland, 1981, Amelia Earhart award U. Calif., 1989, Ernestine Grigsby award Delta Delta Delta, 1989; named Woman of Yr. nominee Panhellenic Assn., 1989. Mem. AAUW, So. Calif. Assn. Dirs. of Vol. Svcs. (bd. dirs. 1987-91), Am. Soc. Dirs. Vol. Svcs. (membership com. 1989), Assistance League of Tustin (pres. 1980-81), Westmed Gold Club (membership com. 1986-92), Chapman Univ. Music Assocs. (bd. dirs. 1987-92), Mortar Bd., Delta Delta Delta (pres. 1988-89, bd. dirs. 1988-91), Dirs. Vols. in Agencies, Phi Kappa Phi, Phi Alpha Theta, Pi Lambda Theta. Episcopalian. Home: 7634 Appaloosa Trail Orange CA 92669 Office: Western Med Ctr 1001 N Tustin Ave Santa Ana CA 92705

JACKLIN, DOYLE, food products executive. With Vaughan Jacklin Corp., Coeur d'Alene, Idaho, 1965-83; v.p. Jacklin Seed Co., Post Falls, Idaho, 1983—. With USN, 1962-65. Office: Jacklin Seed Co 5300 W Riverbend Rd Post Falls ID 83854*

JACKLIN, DUANE, agricultural products executive; b. 1945. With Vaughan Jackin Corp., Coeur d'Alene, Idaho, 1968-83; pres., treas. Jacklin Seed Co., Post Falls, Idaho, 1983—. With USN, 1966-68. Office: Jacklin Seed Co 5300 W Riverbend Rd Post Falls ID 83854*

JACKMAN, JAY M., psychiatrist; b. Bklyn., June 4, 1939; s. James Jeremiah and Dora (Emmer) J.; m. Judith Gail Meisels, Nov. 23, 1963 (div. Sept. 1987); children: Tenaya, Rashi, Jason Scott; m. Myra Hoffenberg Strober, Oct. 21, 1990. BA, Columbia U., 1960; MD, Harvard U., 1964. Diplomate Am. Bd. Psychiatry and Neurology. Rotating intern San Francisco County Gen. Hosp., 1965; psychiat. resident Stanford U., 1969; asst. dir. community psychiatry Mt. Zion Hosp., San Francisco, 1969-70; dir. drug treatment programs Westside Community Mental Health Ctr., San Francisco, 1970-74; pvt. practice San Francisco, 1969-74; dir. Lanakila Clinic Kalihi-Palama Community Mental Health Ctr., Honolulu, 1974-75; pvt. practice specializing in forensic psychiatry, Honolulu, 1975-90, Stanford, Calif., 1990—; cons. Salvation Army Addiction Treatment Facility, Honolulu, 1974-81; chmn. Task Force on Drugs, Nat. Coun. Community Mental Health Ctrs., 1971-75; chmn. no. sect. Calif. Assn. Methodone Programs, 1973-74. Contbr. articles on substance abuse to profl. jours. Trustee Foothill-DeAnza C.C. Bd., 1993—; active Mayor's Adv. Com. on Drug Abuse, Honolulu, 1975-77. Mem. Am. Psychiat. Assn. (commn. on drugs 1973-77), Am. Acad. Psychiatry and Law, No. Calif. Psychiat. Soc., Santa Clara County Bar Assn. (vol., lay mem. fee arbitration com. 1992), Calif. Attys. for Criminal Justice. Democrat. Jewish.

JACKSON, ALBERT SMITH, electronics engineer; b. Sylvia, Kans., Feb. 2, 1927; s. Oliff Harold and Nellie Blanche (Dewhurst) J.; m. Solace Patricia Smith, June 9, 1951; (div. Aug. 1978); children: Linda Michelle, Jill Sharon, Theresa Louise, Steven Thomas, Craig Michael; m. Elaine Sonia Spontak, Sept. 1, 1978. AA, John Muir Coll., 1948; BSEE, MSEE, Calif. Inst. Tech., 1952; PhDEE, Cornell U., 1956. From instr. to asst. prof. Cornell U., Ithaca, N.Y., 1952-59; dept. mgr. TRW Computers Co., Canoga Park, Calif., 1959-61; pres. Control Tech., Inc., Long Beach, Calif., 1961-65, 71-72; chief scientist Milgo Electronic Corp., Miami, Fla., 1965-71; pres. Opto Logic Corp., Long Beach, 1972-75; engrng. mgr. Motorola, Inc., Orange, Calif., 1975—; cons. Naval Research Lab., Washington, 1964-69, Gen. Electric Corp., Ithaca, 1953-59; lectr. UCLA, 1972-77, U. Calif., Irvine, 1965—. Author: Analog Computation, 1960; contbr. articles to profl. jours.; inventor in field. Active Redevel. Agy., Seal Beach, Calif., 1972-74. Served with USN, 1945-46. Named Outstanding Mem. of Extension Faculty, U. Calif.-Irvine, 1985. Mem. IEEE (chmn. profl. group on human factors in engrng. 1953-64, regional ednl. coordinator 1984-86). Republican. Office: Motorola Inc 101 Pacifica Ste 300 Irvine CA 92718-3330

JACKSON, ALLEN KEITH, museum administrator; b. Rocky Ford, Colo., July 22, 1932; s. Monford L. and Leliah Jean (Hipp) J.; m. Barbara May Hollard, June 13, 1954; children: Cary Vincent, Deborah Kay and Edward Keith (twins), Fredrick James. B.A., U. Denver, 1954; Fulbright fellow, Cambridge (Eng.) U., 1955; Th.M. (Elizabeth Iliff Warren fellow), Iliff Sch. Theology, 1958; Ph.D. (Honor fellow), Emory U., 1960. Meth. student minister Erie, Colo., 1955-58; ordained elder Meth. Ch., 1958; instr. sociology Emory U., 1958-60; chaplain, asst. prof. religion and sociology Morningside Coll., Sioux City, Iowa, 1960-62; dean coll. Morningside Coll., 1962-67; pres. Huntingdon Coll., Montgomery, Ala., 1968-93; ret., 1993; dir. Idaho Mus. Natural History Idaho State U., Pocatello, 1993—. Contbr. articles to profl. jours. Past pres. Montgomery Area United Appeal. Mem. Ala. Assn. Ind. Colls. and Univs. (pres. 1969-71), Ala. Council Advancement Pvt. Colls. (pres. 1975-81), Phi Beta Kappa, Omicron Delta Kappa, Beta Theta Pi. Club: Rotarian. Home: 6353 Old Ranch Rd Pocatello ID 83204-3841 Office: Mus Natural History Idaho State U Pocatello ID 83204

JACKSON, BETH ANN, nursing administrator; b. Boulder, Colo., Nov. 8, 1950; d. James Madison and Lillian Lucille (Hoy) J. BS in Edn., N.Mex. State U., 1971; BSN, Loretto Heights, 1975; MBA, U. Phoenix, 1986. Unit adminstr. U. Colo. Health Scis. Ctr., Denver, 1975-87; DON St. Vincent Hosp., Santa Fe, 1987-88; v.p. nursing St. Mary's Health Svcs., Grand Rapids, Mich., 1989—. Bd. mem. Cherry St. Svcs., Grand Rapids. Named Johnson and Johnson Wharton fellow Wharton Sch. Bus., Phila., 1990. Mem. ANA, AONE/MONE, ACHCE, Lakeshire Nurses Assn. (bd. mem. 1991—), West Ctrl. Orgn. Nurse Exec. (pres. 1992—), Sigma Theta Tau. Republican. Methodist. Home: PO Box 370485 Denver CO 80237-0485 Office: St Marys Health Svcs 200 Jefferson Ave SE Grand Rapids MI 49503-4502

JACKSON, BETTY EILEEN, music and elementary school educator; b. Denver, Oct. 9, 1925; d. James Bowen and Fannie (Shelton) J. MusB, U. Colo., 1948, MusM, 1949, MusB in Edn., 1963; postgrad. Ind. U., 1952-55, Hochschule für Musik, Munich, 1955-56. Cert. educator Colo., Calif. Tchr., accompanist, tchr. H.L. Davis Vocal Studios, Denver, 1949-52; teaching assoc. U. Colo., Boulder, 1961-63, vis. lectr., summers 1963-69; tchr. Fontana Unified Sch. Dist., Calif., 1963-92, pvt. studio, 1966—; lectr. in music Calif. State U., San Bernardino, 1967-76; performer, accompanist, music dir. numerous musical cos. including performer, music dir. Fontana Mummers, 1980—, Riverside Community Players, Calif., 1984—; performer Rialto Community Theatre, Calif., 1983—; head visual and performing arts com. Cypress Elem. Shc., 1988-92. Performances include numerous operas, musical comedies and oratorios, Cen. City Opera, Denver Grand Opera, Univ. Colo., Ind. Univ. Opera Theater (leading mezzo), 3 tours of Fed. Republic Germany, 1956-58; oratorio soloist in Ind., Ky., Colo., and Calif., West End Opera (lead roles), Riverside Opera (lead roles). Judge, Inland Theatre League, Riverside, 1983-92; mem. San Bernardino Cultural Task Force, 1981-83. Fulbright grantee, Munich, 1955-56; named Outstanding Performer Inland Theatre League, 1982-84; recipient Outstanding Reading Tchr. award, 1990, Tchr. of Yr. nominations, 1990, 91, Honorary Svc. award 1992. Mem. AAUW (bd. dirs., cultural chair 1983-86), NEA, Nat. Assn. Tchrs. Singing (exec. bd. 1985-89), Internat. Reading Assn., Music Educators Nat. Conf., Calif. Tchrs. Assn., Calif. Elem. Educators Assn., Fontana Tchrs. Assn., Music Tchrs. Assn., Arrowhead Reading Coun., San Bernardino Valley Concert Assn. (bd. dirs. 1977-83), Internat. Platform Assn., Nat. Assn. for Preservation and Perpetuation of Storytelling (1990—), Order Eastern Star, Kappa Kappa Iota (v.p. 1982-83), Sigma Alpha Iota (life), Chi Omega. Avocations: community theater and opera, travel, collecting Hummels and plates. Home: PO Box 885 Rialto CA 92377-0885

JACKSON, BEVERLEY JOY JACOBSON, columnist, lecturer; b. L.A., Nov. 20, 1928; d. Phillip and Dorothy Jacobson; student U. So. Calif., UCLA; m. Robert David Jackson (div. Aug. 1964); 1 child, Tracey Dee. Daily columnist Santa Barbara (Calif.) News Press, 1968-92, Santa Barbara Independent, 1992—; nat. lectr. Santa Barbara History, History of China Recreated, Chinese Footbinding, Shoes for Bound Feet, China Today; free lance writer, fgn. corr. Bd. dirs. Santa Barbara br. Am. Cancer Soc., 1963—; mem. art mus. coun. L.A. Mus. Art, 1959—, mem. costume coun., 1983—; docent L.A. Mus. Art, 1962-64; mem. exec. bd. Channel City Club (formerly Channel City Women's Forum), 1969—; mem. adv. bd. Santa Barbara Mus. Natural History, Coun. of Christmas Cheer, Women's Shelter Bldg., Direct Relief Internat., Nat. Coun. Drug and Alcohol Abuse, Am. Oceans Campaign; mem adv. bd. Hospice of Santa Barbara, 1981—, Stop AIDS Coun., Arthritis Found.; bd. dirs. So. Calif. Com. for Shakespear's Globe Theatre; chmn. Santa Barbara Com. for Visit Queen Elizabeth II, 1982—; founder costume guild Santa Barbara Hist. Soc.; curator Chinese collections Santa Barbara Hist. Mus.; adv. bd. Santa Barbara Choral Soc.; hon. bd. Santa Barbara Salvation Army, Ensemble Theatre Santa Barbara; adv. bd. Storyteller Sch. Homeless Children. Author: Dolls and Doll Houses of Spain, 1970, (with others) I'm Just Wild About Harry, 1979, Spendid Slippers: The History of Chinese Footbinding and Lotus Shoes, 1995. Home: PO Box 5118 Santa Barbara CA 93150-5118

JACKSON, BO (VINCENT EDWARD JACKSON), professional baseball, former football player; b. Bessemer, Ala., Nov. 30, 1962; m. Linda Jackson. Student, Auburn U. Baseball player Kansas City Royals, 1986-91; football player L.A. Raiders, 1987-90; baseball player Chicago White Sox, 1991-93, California Angels, 1994-95. Recipient Heisman Trophy, 1985, All-Star Game MVP, 1989; mem. NFL Pro Bowl Team, 1990; mem. A.L. All-StarTeam, 1989, named Comeback Player of Yr., Sporting News, 1993. Office: care California Angels 2000 E Gene Autry Way Anaheim CA 92806-6100*

JACKSON, BRUCE GEORGE, lawyer; b. Portland, Oreg., July 15, 1942; s. George William and Sally Marie (Dorner) J.; m. Jane Jackson, Sept. 8, 1972; children: Yvette, Scott. BS cum laude, U. Oreg., 1966; JD, U. Calif.-Berkeley, 1970. Bar: Hawaii 1971, U.S. Dist. Ct. Hawaii 1971. Assoc. Case, Kay & Lynch, Honolulu, 1970-74; ptnr. Curtis W. Carlsmith, Honolulu, 1974-76; sole practice, Honolulu, 1977-94; ptnr. Gilbert, Jackson & Godbey, Honolulu, 1995—. speaker on real property law, land trusts, estate planning, 1977—. Served with N.G., 1960-68. Mem. ABA (chmn. real property and fin. svcs. sect.), Hawaii Bar Assn., Hawaii Estate Planning Coun., Historic Hawaii Found., Sigma Phi Epsilon (life). Democrat. Clubs: Honolulu, Kailua Racquet. Student editor: Kragen & McNulty on Federal Income Taxation, 1970. Office: Pauahi Tower Ste 2300 1001 Bishop St Honolulu HI 96813-3429

JACKSON, DAWNA DARLENE, mental health counselor, educator; b. Livingston, Mont., July 14, 1946; d. Donald William and Eva Mae (Boyer) Nelson; m. Gary F. Jackson, Aug. 9, 1969. BA, Idaho State U., 1969, M in Counseling, 1982. Lic. profl. tchr., Idaho; cert. secondary sch. tchr., Idaho. Sch. tchr. phys. edn. Sch. Dist. # 55, Blackfoot, Idaho, 1968-70; juvenile probation officer Ada County Juvenile Ctr., Boise, Idaho, 1971-77, 81-82; clinic dir. Weight Loss Clinic of Am., Boise, 1978-81; facility dir. Idaho Youth Ranch, Boise, 1983-85; psychotherapist, pvt. practice Family Comm. Counseling Boise, 1983—; mem. adj. faculty Albertson Coll. of Idaho, Caldwell, 1988—; mental health cons. Malheur County Head Start Program, Ont., Oreg., 1992—; cons. Migrant Indian Coalition, Ont. and Hermaston, Oreg., 1992-93; active Idaho Licensed Profl. Counselors Licensing Bd., 1994—. Bd. dirs. Parents and Youth Against Drug Abuse, Boise, 1986-88; pres., bd. dirs. Idaho Arthritis Found., Boise, 1987-89; active Shepherd of the Valley Luth. Ch., Boise. Mem. ACA, Idaho Counselors Assn. (Disting. Svc. award 1989), Idaho Mental Health Counselors Assn. (Counselor of Yr. 1988-89), Internat. Assn. Marriage & Family Counselors. Office: Family Comm Counseling 1084 N Cole Rd Boise ID 83704-8642

JACKSON, DEBORAH TONGE, dietitian, consulting nutritionist; b. Tacoma, Aug. 1, 1951; d. Harry Warren and Sarah Lou (Miller) Tonge; m. Frank William Jackson, May 25, 1974; children: Garth Maury, Brittany Ann. BS, U. Wash., 1973, MEd, 1983. Registered dietitian; cert. diabetes educator. Clin. dietitian St. Joseph Hosp., Tacoma, 1976-80, 82-84, head clin. dietitian, 1980-82; diabetes nutrition educator Good Samaritan Hosp., Puyallup, Wash., 1987-92; cons. nutritionist Sound Nutrition, Vashon, Wash., 1982—. Mem. Am. Dietetic Assn., Am. Diabetes Assn. (v.p. Wash. affiliate 1992-93, pres. of bd. Wash. affiliate 1993-94), Wash. Assn. Diabetes Educators, Wash. State Dietetic Assn., Greater Seattle Dietetic Assn. (chair legis. com. 1994-95), Vashon Women's Rowing Club (treas. 1991—). Office: Sound Nutrition PO Box 13091 Burton WA 98013-0091

JACKSON, DORIS ANN, public relations professional; b. Corpus Christi, Tex., Mar. 24, 1947; d. Frederick Joseph and Lucille Lois (Hickstein) J. BA, Okla. State U., 1974; MA, Webster U., 1982. With Security Pacific Nat. Bank, Goleta, Calif., 1969-71; commd. 2d lt. USAF, 1971, advanced through grades to capt., 1978, with human resources dept., 1974-86, with pub. rels. dept., 1986—. Contbr. numerous articles to newspapers and mags. Mem. Pub. Rels. Soc. Am., Ret. Officers Assn., NAFE. Republican. Lutheran. Office: 58 Spl Ops Wing Pub Affairs 4249 Hercules Way SE Kirtland AFB NM 87117

JACKSON, FRANK THOMAS, engineering manager; b. Union City, N.J., Jan. 16, 1934; s. Frank T. Sr. and Ruth Ann (Broulatour) J.; m. Alice L. Stewart, Aug. 5, 1951; children: Frank T. Jr., John A., Alisa D., Michael P. B in Engring., Long Beach (Calif.) Coll., 1960; JD, Orange Coast Coll., 1987; LLB, Citrus Belt Law Sch., 1985. Engrng. mgr. Indsl. Electronic Engrng., Van Nuys, Calif., 1966-71; owner, mgr. Lincoln Pub., Anaheim, Calif., 1971-82; sr. design engr. Ford Aerospace, Newport Beach, Calif., 1982-84; engrng. mgr. Hartwell Corp., Placenta, Calif., 1984—; cons. Tech Star Co., Anaheim, 1989—, Modern Graphics, Anaheim, 1980—. Author: Military Hardware Handbook, 1974, Engine Specification Manual, 1980, Material & Finishes Handbook, 1980; inventor missile latch; 8 patents in field; contbr. articles to profl. jours. Office: Hartwell Corp 900 S Richfield Rd Placentia CA 92670-6732

JACKSON, GENE, food products executive; b. 1931. Mgr. Duda & Sons, Belle Glade, Fla., 1953-79; pres. Gene Jackson Farms Inc., Oxnard, Calif., 1979—. Office: Gene Jackson Farms Inc 195 Victoria Ave Oxnard CA 93030-8796*

JACKSON, HARRY ANDREW, artist; b. Chgo., Apr. 18, 1924; s. Harry and Ellen Grace J.; m. Theodora Rehard DuBois, 1946 (div.); m. Grace Hartigan, 1948 (div.); m. Claire Rodgers, 1950 (div.); m. Joan Hunt, 1951 (div.); m. Sarah Mason, Sept. 10, 1962 (div.); children: Matthew, Molly; m. Tina Lear, Aug. 11, 1973 (div.); children: Jesse, Luke, Chloe. Diploma, H.S., 1945; LLD (hon.), U. Wyo., 1986. Founder fine art foundry Camaiore, Italy, 1964—, Wyo. Foundry Studios di Harry Jackson, Italy, 1965—; CEO Harry Jackson Studios (formerly Wyo. Foundry Studios, Inc.), Cody, Wyo., 1971—; founder Western Arts Found., 1974—; foundry ptnr. Jackson-Mariani Fine Art Foundry, Camaiore, Italy, 1985—; founder Harry Jackson Art Mus., Cody, Wyo., 1994. Author: Lost Wax Bronze Casting, 1972; one man exhbns. include Ninth St. Show, N.Y.C., 1951, Tibor de Nagy Gallery, N.Y.C., 1952, 53, Martha Jackson Gallery, N.Y.C., 1956, M. Knoedler & Co., N.Y.C., 1960, Amon Carter Mus., Fort Worth, 1961, 68, Kennedy Galleries, N.Y.C., 1964, 68, Smithsonian Instn., Washington, 1964, Whitney Gallery Western Art, Cody, 1964, 81, Mont. Hist. Soc., 1964, NAD, 1965, 68, Nat. Cowboy Hall of Fame, Oklahoma City, 1966, XVII Mostra Internazionale d'Arte, Premio del Fiorino, Florence, Italy, 1966, Pennational Artists Ann., Pa., 1967, Mostra de Arte Moderna, Convento di S. Lazzaro, Camaiore, 1968, Am. Artists Profl. League, N.Y., 1968, Cowboy Artists Am., 1971-76, S.W. Mus., L.A., 1979, Smith Gallery, N.Y.C., 1981, 85; major retrospective exhbns. include Buffalo Bill Hist. Ctr., 1981, Palm Springs Desert Mus., 1981, Mpls. Inst. Art, 1982, Camaiore, Italy, 1985, Met. Mus. Art, N.Y.C., 1987; represented in permanent collections Met. Mus. Art, NAD, Nat. Mus. Am. Art, Nat. Portrait Gallery, Washington, Her Majesty Queen Elizabeth II, Sandringam Castle, Eng., Am. Mus. of Gt. Britain, Bath, Eng., U.S. State Dept., Washington, Lyndon Baines Johnson Meml. Libr., Austin, Tex., Ronald Reagan Meml. Libr., Santa Barbara, Calif., Whitney Gallery Western Art, Plains Indian Mus., Buffalo Bill Hist. Ctr., Cody, Wyo., Wadsworth Atheneum, Hartford, Conn., Alberta Glenbow Mus., Calgary, Can., Univ. So. Calif., Stanford (Calif.) Univ., Love Libr. Univ. Nebr., Lincoln, Portsmouth (R.I.) Abbey, S.W. Mus., Gene Autrey Mus., L.A., Nat. Cowboy Hall of Fame, Oklahoma City, Gilcrease Mus., Tulsa, Fort Pitts Mus., Pitts., Amon Carter Mus., Pro Rodeo Cowboy Hall of Fame, Colorado Springs, Colo., Eiteljorg Mus., Indpls., Shelburne (Vt.) Mus., Columbus (Ga.) Mus. Arts & Scis., Oreg. Hist. Soc., Portland, Salt Lake City Art Ctr., Norfolk (Nebr.) Arts Ctr., Aspen (Colo.) Art Mus., Woolaroc Mus., Bartlesville, Okla., U. Wyo. Art Mus., Laramie, Mont. Hist. Soc., Helena, Norton Mus., Shreveport, La., Columbia U., N.Y.C., Trout Gallery Dickinson Coll., Carlisle, Pa., Ctrl. Wyo. Coll., Riverton, N.W. C.C., Powell, Wyo., Baylor Sch., Chattanooga, Orme Sch., Mayer, Ariz., others; commd. works include (sculpture) William R. Coe Commn., 1959, 60, Fort Pitt Mus., 1964, 73, Plains Indian Mus., Cody, Wyo., Ctrl. Wyo. Coll., Riverton, 1978, 81, Piazza della Chiesa, Capezzano, Pianore, Italy, 1985, Great Western Savs. & Loan, Santa Barbara, Calif., 1985, John Wayne monumental sculpture Beverly Hills, Calif, 1981, 84, (portrait busts) Met. Mus. Trustees, C. Douglas Dillon, 1985, 87, (portrait) "John Wayne" TIME cover, Aug. 8, 1969 (Nat. Best Cover Art award Am. Inst. Graphic Arts 1969), (paintings) Whitney Gallery Western Art, Cody, 1960, 66, (mural) R.K. Mellon. Served with USMC, 1942-45. Decorated Purple Heart with gold star; recipient Gold medal NAD, 1968; grantee Fulbright, 1954, Italian Govt., 1956, 57. Fellow NAD (academician), RISD, Nat. Acad. Western Art, Nat. Sculpture Soc., Am. Artists League; mem. Bohemian Club (San Francisco). Office: PO Box 2836 Cody WY 82414-2836 also: Via Montegiori, 55040 Camaiore Lucca, Italy

JACKSON, ISAIAH, conductor; b. Richmond, Va., Jan. 22, 1945; s. Isaiah Allen and Alma Alverta (Norris) J.; m. Helen Tuntland, Aug. 6, 1977; children: Benjamin, Katharine, Caroline. B.A. cum laude, Harvard U., 1966; M.A., Stanford U., 1967; M.S., Juilliard Sch. Music, 1969, D.M.A., 1973. Founder, condr. Juilliard String Ensemble, N.Y.C., 1970-71; asst. condr. Am. Symphony Orch., N.Y.C., 1970-71, Balt. Symphony Orch., 1971-73; assoc. condr. Rochester (N.Y.) Philharmonic Orch., 1973-87; music dir. Flint (Mich.) Symphony Orch., 1982-87, Dayton (Ohio) Philharm. Orch., 1987—; prin. condr. Royal Ballet, Covent Garden, London, 1986, music dir., 1987-90; prin. guest condr. Queensland (Australia) Symphony Orch., 1993—; guest condr. N.Y. Philharm. Orch., 1978, Boston Pops Orch., 1983, 90-94, Cleve. orch., 1983-84, 86-87, 89-92, Detroit Sympohny Orch., 1983, 85, San Francisco Symphony, 1984, Toronto Symphony, 1984, 90, Orch. de la Suisse Romande, 1985, 88, BBC Consert Orch., 1987, Berlin Symphony, 1989-94, Dallas Symphony, 1993; numerous recordings for Koch, Australian Broadcating Corp. Recipient First Gov.'s award for arts in Va., Commonwealth Va., 1979, Signet Soc. medal for the arts Harvard U., 1991. Office: care United Arts 3906 Sunbeam Dr Los Angeles CA 90065-3551

JACKSON, JANE W., interior designer; b. Asheville, N.C., Aug. 5, 1944; d. James and Willie Mae (Stoner) Harris; m. Bruce G. Jackson; children: Yvette, Scott. Student, Boston U., 1964; BA, Leslie Coll., 1967; postgrad., Artisan Sch. Interior Design, 1980-82. Tchr. Montessori, Brookline, Mass., 1969-72; interior designer, owner Nettle Creek Shop, Honolulu, 1980-88; owner Wellesley Interiors, Honolulu, 1988—. Active Mayor's Com. for Small Bus., Honolulu, 1984. Mem. Honolulu Club. Democrat. Office: Wellesley Interiors PO Box 1662 Kaneohe HI 96744

JACKSON, JESS S., vintner. JD, U. Calif. Practice San Francisco; now pres. Kendall-Jackson Winery Ltd., Santa Rosa, Calif., chmn. bd. dirs. Mem. Calif. Bar Assn. Office: Kendall-Jackson Winery Ltd 421 Aviation Blvd Santa Rosa CA 95403-1069*

JACKSON, JEWEL, retired state youth authority executive; b. Shreveport, La., June 3, 1942; d. Willie Burghardt and Bernice Jewel (Mayberry) Norton; children: Steven, June Kelly, Michael, Anthony. With Calif. Youth Authority, 1965—, group supr., San Andreas and Santa Rosa, 1965-67, youth counselor, Ventura, 1967-78, sr. youth counselor, Stockton, 1978-81, parole agt., 1986, treatment team supr., program mgr., Whittier and Ione, 1981-91; retired, 1991; pres. Valley Paralegal Svc., Stockton. Avocations: reading, horseback riding, interior design, fabric painting, stamp collecting. Home: 2416 Hall Ave Stockton CA 95205-8422

JACKSON, JOSEPH BRIAN, physician, health facility administrator; b. Brunswick, Ga., Dec. 23, 1946; s. J. A. and M. J. (Ross) J.; m. Cathleen Ann Goddard, Feb. 17, 1969 (div. 1982); children: Tracy Rene, Brian Eric. BS in Chemistry, San Diego State U., 1969; MD, Loma Linda U., 1973. Criminalist San Bernardino County (Calif.) Sheriff's Dept., 1969-70; intern, resident Santa Clara Valley Med. Ctr., San Jose, Calif., 1973-74; emergency medicine specialist Sharp Cabrillo Med. Ctr., San Diego, 1975-82, dep. dir. emergency rm., 1980-82; med. dir. East County Community Clinic, El Cajon, Calif., 1982-91; pvt. practice Ramona, Calif., 1991-92; chief adult medicine Logan Heights Family Health Ctr., San Diego, Calif., 1992—; investigator CODA trial Phizer Inc., 1991. Mem. Area 5 Emergency Planning Com., San Diego, 1976-78; mem. Robert Wood Johnson Pilot Health Ins. Program, San Diego, 1986-88. Nat. Merit scholar UpJohn Co., 1964. Lutheran. Office: Logan Heights Family Health Ctr 1809 National Ave San Diego CA 92113-2113

JACKSON, KEITH DOUGLAS, police captain; b. Vallejo, Calif., Sept. 19, 1950; s. Douglas Eugene and Lavada (Wallace) J.; m. Carolyn Lee Mangione, Dec. 30, 1972; children: Jeffrey Keith, Kevin Joseph. BS, San Jose State U., 1972; MS, Calif. State Poly. U.-Pomona, 1991. Police officer Fremont (Calif.) Police Dept., 1975-80, police detective, 1980-82, police sgt., 1982-83, police lt., 1983-88, police capt., 1988—. Bd. dirs. Am. Heart Assn., Alameda County, Calif., 1991. Capt. USMC, 1969-79. Recipient Leatherneck award USMC, 1969. Mem. Calif. Peace Officers Assn., Command Coll. Alumni Assn., Marine Corps Res. Officers Assn., Rotary (pres. Club of Mission San Jose 1987—). Republican. Office: Fremont Police Dept 39710 Civic Center Dr Fremont CA 94538-2359

JACKSON, MARY TALLMADGE, obstetrician/gynecologist; b. Hollywood, Calif., Sept. 14, 1950; d. Matthew Tallmadge and Mary Elizabeth (Morrill) Moorehead. BA in English, U. Hawaii, Hilo, 1973; MD, Loma Linda U., 1980. Diplomate Am. Coll. Obstetrics/Gynecology, Nat. Bd. Med. Examiners. Intern in integrated internal medicine U. Hawaii, 1980-81; 543d gen. dispensary U.S. Army Med. Corps, Taegu, Korea, 1981-83; resident in obstetrics & gynecology Letterman Army Med. Ctr., Presidio San Francisco, 1983-86; Ireland Army Cmty. Hosp. U.S. Army Med. Corps, Ft. Knox, Ky., 1986-88; ob-gyn Straub Clinic and Hosp., Honolulu, 1988—; clin. instr. John Burns Sch. Medicine U. Hawaii, Honolulu, 1989—. Bd. dirs. Planned Parenthood Hawaii, 1989-94. Decorated commendation medal U.S. Army, 1983, 88, svc. ribbon, 1982, overseas ribbon, 1983, res. medal, 1987. Fellow Am. Coll. Obstetrics & Gynecology; mem. AMA (physician's recognition 1987, 89, 93), Am. Med. Women's Assn., Honolulu Athletic Club. Office: Straub Clinic & Hosp Dept Ob-Gyn 888 S King St Honolulu HI 96813-3009

JACKSON, MICHAEL VINCENT, physician, medical educator; b. Buffalo, N.Y., May 10, 1952; s. Vincent S. and Joan Marie (Guest) J.; m. Virginia Marie Hanson; children: Brian, Christopher. BS, Boston Coll., 1974; MD, Tufts U., 1978. Cert. internal medicine, pulmonary medicine and critical care Am. Bd. Internal Medicine. Intern and resident in internal medicine U. Mich., Ann Arbor, 1978-81; fellow in pulmonary and critical care medicine U. Pa., Phila., 1981-83; physician Pulmonary Medicine Assocs., Reno, 1983—; pres., CEO Pulmonary Medicien Assocs., Reno, Nev., 1995—; assoc. clin. prof. U. Nev., Reno, 1983—; co-dir. ICU, Washoe Med. Ctr., Reno, 1992—; dir. ICU No. Nev. Med. Ctr., Sparks, Nev., 1993—. Fellow Am. Coll. Chest Pysicians; mem. ACP, AMA, Am. Thoracic Soc., Soc. for Critical Care Medicine, Nev. State Med. Soc., Nev. Soc. for Repiratory Care (med. dir. 1992—), Med. Group Mgmt. Assn., Soc. Physicians in Adminstrn. Office: Pulmonary Medicine Assocs 236 W Sixth St Ste 100 Reno NV 89503-4517

JACKSON, MILES MERRILL, university dean; b. Richmond, Va., Apr. 28, 1929; s. Miles Merrill and Thelma Eugertha (Manning) J.; m. Bernice Olivia Roane, Jan. 7, 1954; children: Miles Merrill III, Marsha, Muriel, Melia. BA in English, Va. Union U., 1955; MS, Drexel U., 1956; postgrad., Ind. U., 1961, 64; PhD, Syracuse U., 1974. Br. libr. Free Libr., 1955-58; acting libr. C.P. Huntington Meml. Libr., Hampton (Va.) U., 1958-59, libr., 1959-63, asst. prof. libr. sci., 1958-62; territorial libr. Am. Samoa, 1962-64; chief libr. Trevor Arnett Libr., Atlanta U., 1964-69; also lectr. Sch. Libr. Sci.; assoc. prof. State U. N.Y., Geneseo, 1969-75; prof. U. Hawaii, 1975—, dean, 1983—, chmn. interdisciplinary program in communication and info. scis., 1985-89; Fulbright lectr. U. Tehran, Iran, 1968-69; libr. cons. Fiji, Samoa, Papua New Guinea, Micronesia; USIA cons. India, 1983, Pakistan, 1985; chmn. bd. Hawaii Lit., Inc., 1985-88. Editor: A Bibliography of Materials on Negro History and Culture for Young People, 1968, Comparative and International Librarianship, 1971, International Handbook of Contemporary Developments in Librarianship, 1981, Pacific Island Studies: Review of the Literature, 1986, Linkages Over Space and Time, 1993; mem. editl. bd. Internat. Jour. Info. Mgmt., Internat. Libr. Rev., 1982-87; founder, editor Pacific Info. and Libr. Svcs. Newsletter; contbr. articles to profl. jours.; book reviewer. Bd. dirs. Cen. YMCA, 1986—, Hawaii Gov.'s Coun. on Literacy, 1986—, Hawaii ACLU, 1990-94, office holder in Dem. party of Hawaii, 1992—. With USNR, 1946-48. Recipient Outstanding Alumnus award Va. Union U., 1987; Rsch. grantee Am. Philos. Soc., 1966; Coun. on Libr. Resources fellow, 1970, vis. fellow Republic of China, 1986; Harold Lancour fgn. travel awardee Beta Phi Mu, 1976. Mem. ALA (chmn. Internat. Rels. Roundtable 1988-89), Assn. for Libr. and Info. Sci. Edn. (pres. 1989-90), Coll. Lang. Assn. (hon. mention poetry 1954, 2d prize award short story 1955). Democrat. Office: U Hawaii Sch Library & Info Studies 2550 The Mall Honolulu HI 96822-2233

JACKSON, PATRICK GAIL, sociology and criminology educator, researcher, consultant; b. Escalon, Calif., May, 7, 1951; s. Harper James and Marjorie Lou (Nelson) J.; m. Cindy A. Stearns, Jan. 1, 1985. AB summa cum laude, Calif. State U.-Fresno, 1973; MA, U. Calif.-Davis, 1975, PhD, 1980. Grad. student asst. Calif. Youth Authority, Sacramento, 1977-80; postgrad. researcher Ctr. Adminstrn. Criminal Justice, U. Calif. Sch. Law, Davis, 1980-83; lectr. U. Calif., Davis 1982-85; asst. prof. dept. sociology U. of Mo., St. Louis, 1985—; sr. assoc. Nat. Council on Crime and Delinquency, San Francisco, 1982-83; cons. in field. Author: The Paradox of Control: Parole Supervision of Youthful Offenders, 1983 (Outstanding Acad. Book award, 1984); contbr. articles to profl. jours. Law Enforcement Assistance Adminstrn. fellow, 1978-79, fellow nominee U.S. Supreme Ct., 1984, Nat. Inst. Justice summer fellow, 1984, Calif. Atty. Gen.'s fellow, 1986. Mem. Am. Sociol. Assn., Am. Soc. Criminology, Law and Soc. Assn., Soc. Study Social Problems, Acad. Criminal Justice Scis., Western Soc. Criminology, Pacific Sociol. Assn. Democrat. Office: Sonoma State U Rohnert Park CA 94928

JACKSON, PATRICK JOSEPH, insurance executive; b. Minn., Mar. 31, 1942; s. Paul Arthur and Lucille Margaret (Cummings) J.; m. Barbara Ann Simpson, July 19, 1964 (div. Apr. 1980); m. Shirley Ann Wellman, Sept. 12, 1982; children: Patricia Ann, Laura Kathleen, Katherine Lucille, Stacy Lynn. BS, Portland State U., 1968. Bank loan officer First Nat. Bank of Oreg., Portland, 1964-68; credit mgr. Meier & Frank Corp., Portland, 1968-70; agt., mgr. Aetna Life, San Jose, Calif., 1970-75; dist. mgr. Calif. Casualty, San Jose, 1975-78; gen. agt. Great So. Life, San Jose, 1978-82; account agt., agy. mgr. Allstate Ins., San Jose, 1982—; instr. Santa Clara (Calif.) U., 1974-76. Author: (monograph) The Affairs of, 1978; newspaper columnist, 1978-82. Mem. ins. subcom. Calif. State Senate, San Jose, 1978; officer Los Gatos (Calif.) Police Res., 1970-78, treas., 1974-78; mem. Sch. Site Coun., Saratoga, Calif., 1978-80; mem. City Coun., Discovery Bay, Calif., 1991-95, mauyor, 1993-94. Named Man of Yr., Los Gatos Youth Unltd., 1978. Mem. San Jose Life Underwriters (bd. dirs. 1974-76), No. Calif. Tollycraft Assn. (sec. 1995—), Discovery Bay Yacht Club. Republican. Lutheran. Office: Allstate Ins Co 2923 The Villages Pky San Jose CA 95135-1442

JACKSON, PETER VORIOUS, III, retired association executive; b. Butte, Mont., May 18, 1927; s. Peter V. and Besse Portia (McLean) J.; m. Johnneta Pierce, Apr. 29, 1949; children: Ward, Michelle (Mrs. Jerry Vanhour), Johnathan. Wheat and cattle rancher, 1949—; mem. Mont. Ho. of Reps., 1971-72; chief Grass Conservation bur. Mont. Dept. Natural Resources, Helena, 1972-74; supr. Conservation Dist. Madison County, Ennis, Mont., from 1957; past exec. dir. Western Environ. Trade Assn., Helena.; exec. v.p. Soc. for Range Mgmt., Denver, 1983-92; ret., 1992; vol. to develop and implement grazing lands conservation initiative Soil Conservation Svc., USDA, 1992—; mem. Nat. Steering Com. of Grazing Land Conservation Initiative, 1993. Author: Montana Rangeland Resources Program, 1970. Mem. Madison County Fair Bd.; pres. Grazing Lands Forum, 1988. Recipient Renner award Soc. Range Mgmt., 1971, Conservation award Mont. Wildlife Fedn., 1966. Mem. Nat. Assn. Conservation Dists. (bd. dirs.), Mont. Assn. Conservation Dists. (exec. v.p. 1974), Soc. for Range Mgmt. (nat. pres., spl. award for outstanding achievement 1992). Lodges: Masons, Elks. Home and Office: PO Box 174 Harrison MT 59735-0174

JACKSON, RICHARD H., geography educator, writer; b. Orem, Utah, Apr. 22, 1941; s. John Henry and Nan Ennice (Ellsworth) J.; m. Mary Wadley, June 3, 1965; children: Joel, John, Mark, Mariah Lynne. BS, Brigham Young U., Provo, Utah, 1965, MS, 1966; PhD, Clark U., Worcester, Mass., 1970. Instr. geography Brigham Young U., 1969-70, asst. prof., 1970-75, assoc. prof., 1975-78, prof., 1979—; cons. Bur. Land Mgmt., Provo, 1976-78. Author: Mormon Role in Settlement of the West, 1978 (award Mormon Hist. Assn. 1979), Land Use in America, 1981, World Regional Geography, 1982, 3d edit., 1990, Cultural Geography, 1990; contbr. numerous articles to profl. jours. Bd. appeals Utah County, 1976-82; councilman City of Orem, 1979-87; bd. dirs. Redd Ctr. for Western History, Brigham Young U., 1978—, Utah Transit Authority, Salt Lake City, 1990—. Recipient Disting. Univ. Svc. award Utah Acad. Scis., Arts and Letters, Salt Lake City, 1985. Mem. Assn. Am. Geographers (Outstanding Tchr. award 1986), Am. Planning Assn., Utah History Assn. (Outstanding Scholarly Article award 1985). Home: 356 S Palisades Dr Orem UT 84058-5740 Office: Brigham Young U 690E Swkt Provo UT 84602-1130

JACKSON, RICKEY, professional football player; b. Pahokee, Flor., Feb. 20, 1958. Student, U. Pittsburgh. Linebacker New Orleans Saints, 1981-94, San Francisco 49ers, 1994—. Office: San Francisco 49ers 4949 Centennial Blvd Santa Clara CA 95054-1229

JACKSON, ROBERT BRADLEY, ecologist, educator; b. London, Eng., Sept. 26, 1961; came to the U.S., 1967; s. David Edward and Elinor W.G. Jackson; m. Sally Graves; children: Robert Graves, David Alexander. BS in Chem. Engring., Rice U., 1983; MS in Plant Ecology, Utah State U., 1989, MS in Stats., PhD in Plant Ecology, 1992. Tech. sales and svc. staff Dow Chem. Co., L.A., 1983-87; global change fellow Stanford (Calif.) U., 1993-94; asst. prof. dept. botany U. Tex., Austin, 1995—. Contbr. articles to profl. jours. Disting. Postdoctoral fellow for global change Dept. Energy, 1992. Mem. AAAS, Brit. Ecol. Soc., Ecol. Soc. Am. (Buell award 1990), Soc. for Range Mgmt., Soc. for Conservation Biology. Office: U Tex Dept Botany Austin TX 78713

JACKSON, ROBERT LORING, science and mathematics educator, academic administrator; b. Mitchell, S.D., June 8, 1926; s. Olin DeBuhr and Edna Anna (Hanson) J.; m. Elizabeth Denise Koteski; children: Charles Olin, Catherine Lynne, Cynthia Helen. BS, Hamline U., 1950; MA, U. Minn., 1959; PhD, 1965. Tchr. math. and sci., pub. schs., Heron Lake, Minn., 1950-52; tchr. math. Lakewood (Colo.) Sr. High Sch., 1952-53, Nouassuer Air Force Sch. Casablanca, Morocco, 1953-54, Baumholder (Germany) Elem. Sch., 1954-55, U. Minn. Univ. Lab. Sch., Mpls., 1955-60; asst. prof. sci. and math. edn. U. Minn., Mpls., 1965-66, assoc. prof., 1966-70, prof., 1970-94; emeritus prof. 1994—, head sci. and math. edn., 1980-84, assoc. chmn., dir. undergrad. studies, curriculum and instrn., 1984-88, assoc. chmn., 1989-92; vis. prof. Hamline U., St. Paul, 1958, Mont. State U., Bozeman, 1981, Bethel Coll., St. Paul, 1981, No. Mich. U., Marquette, 1983-84; cons. math. Minn. Dept. Edn., St. Paul, 1960-62. Bd. dirs. Oratorio Soc. Minn., Minn. Chorale, Mpls., 1973-88, pres., 1978-80. With U.S. Army, 1944-46. Decorated Purple Heart; recipient First Alumni award 1988, Disting. Teaching award Coll. Edn., U. Minn., 1984. Mem. Minn. Coun. Tchrs. Math., Nat. Coun. Tchrs. Math., Math. Assn. Am., Internat. Platform Assn. Methodist. Co-author: (book/man series) Laboratory Mathematics, 1975-76. Home: 810 Purple Sage Ter Henderson NV 89015-5692 Office: U Minn 159 Pillsbury Dr SE Minneapolis MN 55455-0208

JACKSON, RONALD EDWARD, SR., small business owner; b. San Diego, Calif., Apr. 17, 1957; s. Ollie and Marksene Elizabeth (Fields) J.; children: Shameka Machell, Ronald Edward Jr. Student, San Diego City Coll. Owner Jani-King Comml. Cleaning Svc., Honolulu. Inventor Jackson Personal Compact Solution Ctr., 1994. Office: Jani-King Comml Cleaning 3 Waterfront Pl Ste 100 Honolulu HI 96813

JACKSON, SALLY, location casting director; b. Lubbock, Tex., June 2, 1950; d. Francis Marion and Dorothy (Kelly) J. Location casting dir.: (films) Koyannisquatsi, 1975, Red Dawn, 1983, Silverado, 1985, The Milagro Beanfield War, 1986, Young Guns, 1988, Indiana Jones and the Last Crusade, 1988, Young Guns II, 1990, City Slickers, 1990, White Sands, 1991, Natural Born Killers, 1993, Wyatt Earp, 1993, others, (TV) Dress Gray, 1986, Gambler III, 1987, Desperado II and III, 1987, The Hunters, 1989, Unsolved Mysteries, 1990, To Save a Child, 1991, America's Most Wanted, 1992, Revenge on the Highway (Overdrive), 1992, The Last Outlaw, 1993, others; set prodn. coord. Silverado, 1985. Coun. mem. moving image arts adv. coun. Coll. Santa Fe, 1993-94. Mem. SAG. Home: 286 Calle Loma Norte Santa Fe NM 87501

JACKSON, SHARON JUANITA, management consultant; b. Modesto, Calif., Sept. 21, 1938; d. H. Edward and Beatrice C. (Wright) Melin; m. John L. George, Apr. 27, 1956 (div. 1974); children: Terri A., Tami L., Timothy J., Tobin E. BS in Edn. magna cum laude, Calif. State U., Hayward, 1965; MEd Guidance and Counseling, Hardin-Simmons U., 1976; MBA in Mgmt., Golden Gate U., 1984. Cert. elem. edn., Calif., elem., secondary counseling, Tex. Tchr. elem. Hayward (Calif) Unified Sch. Dist., 1965-73; tchr. diagnostics, group therapist Tex. Youth Coun., Brownwood, 1974-75; assoc. dir. New Directions Psychiat. Half Way House, Abilene, Tex., 1975-77; exec. dir. Mental Health Assn., Abilene, 1977-78, San Francisco, 1979-84; pres. Health Mktg. & Mgmt., San Francisco, 1983—; exec. dir., cons. Vision of Am. At Peace, Berkeley, Calif., 1984, Oakes Children's Ctr., San Francisco, 1985-87; mktg. dir. Mental Health Providers of Calif., 1987-90; prin., v.p. health care devel. Sakhalin region, Russia Health Marketing and Mgmt., 1990-92; instr. managed care U. San Francisco, 1994; sr. assoc. Behavioral Health Alliance dir. nat. practice 1991-92; founding exec. dir., v.p. adminstrn. Planet Live Earthbeat TV, Inc.; bd. dirs. PL Enterprises, Inc.; vis. lectr. McMurry Coll., Abilene, 1976-78; cons. Dyess AFB, Abilene, 1976-78, Abilene Youth Ctr., 1976-78; speaker in field, 1979—. Chair Commn. on Status of Women of Marin County, Calif., 1985—; mem. adv. com. Displaced Homemaker Project, Sacramento, 1985-90; founder, Children's Mental Health Policy Bd., 1984-90; pres. Artisans Gallery, Mill Valley, Calif., 1984—. Grantee Fed. Dept. Justice, Brownwood, 1975, pvt. community founds., Calif., 1979-87. Mem. NAFE, Council of Calif. Mental Health Contractors, Am. Soc. Profl. Exec. Women. Avocations: travel, gourmet cooking, hiking, public speaking. Home and Office: PO Box 2392 Mill Valley CA 94942-2392

JACKSON, STANLEY MARTIN, plastic surgeon; b. Bay City, Tex., 1947. MD, La. State U., 1973. Plastic surgeon Puget Sound Med. Ctr., Tacoma, Good Samaritan Hosp., Puyallup, Wash., 1984—. Office: 105 27th Ave SE Puyallup WA 98374-1150*

JACKSON, STEVEN ALAN, telecommunications professional; b. Canyon, Tex., Dec. 25, 1946; s. Billy J. and Amy Jean (Walker) J.; m. Allison Margaret Wintz, Feb. 10, 1972 (div. Jan. 1976); m. Diana Dee Blair, Nov. 17, 1979. BA, Rice U., 1971. V.p., pres. Exec. Income Analysis, Houston, 1972-74; chief fin. officer J.H. Rose Truck Line, Inc., Houston, 1974-76; CEO Jackson, Houser & Assocs., Houston, 1976-79; chief fin. officer, CEO Kelly Constrn. Co., San Antonio, Tex., 1979-80; chief fin. officer Cloud Corp., San Antonio, 1980-82; CEO, owner Jackson and Kelly Enterprises, San Antonio and Austin, 1982-87, Jackson Enterprises, Horseshoe Bay, Tex., 1987-89; v.p. Am. Tel Group, Inc., Albuquerque, 1989—; lectr., class coord. Rice U., Houston, 1971-72; subject of documentary Eyes of Tex. mag., 1976, Houston Bus. Jour., 1976. Recipient Man of Yr. award Houston-Galveston Area Mgmt., 1971, two Addy awards Nat. Advt. Assn., San Antonio, 1982. Office: Am Tel Group Inc 5850 Eubank Blvd NE # 16 Albuquerque NM 87111-6132

JACKSON, SUZANNE FITZALLEN, painter, poet, scenographer; b. St. Louis, Jan. 30, 1944; d. Roy Dederick and Ann Marie (Butler) Jackson; 1 child, Rafiki C.D. Smith-Mhunzi. BA, San Francisco State U., 1966; MFA, Yale U., 1990. Tchr. Watts Towers Art Ctr., Stanford U., Elliott-Pope Preparatory Sch., Idyllwild, Calif.; asst. prof., scenographer St. Mary's Coll. Md.; owner and dir. Gallery 32, L.A., 1968-70; dir. Sunflower-Seed Prodns., 1978—; artist-in-residence Normal Edits. Workshop, Ctr. for Visual Arts, Ill. State U., Normal, 1977, Savannah (Ga.) Coll. Art and Design, Gibbs Mus. Art Gallery, Charleston, S.C., U. S.C. Idyllwild Sch. Music and Arts, 1981, 82; vis. lectr. San Francisco State U., 1986. One woman shows include San Jose Art League, 1972, U. Pacific, Stockton, Calif., 1972, Fresno Art Ctr., 1972, Ankrum Gallery, L.A., 1972-74, 76, 78, Fashion Moda, N.Y.C., 1984, Ingber Gallery, N.Y.C., 1984, Sargent Johnson Gallery, San Francisco, 1985; exhibited in group shows at Oakland Mus., 1971, Carnegie Inst., Pitts., 1971-72, San Diego Mus. Art, 1972, 74, Santa Barbara Mus. Art, 1973, Pioneer Mus., Haggin Art Galleries, Stockton, Calif., 1975, Studio Mus. Harlem, N.Y.C., 1977, Calif. Mus. African-Am. History and Culture, L.A., 1981, 89, Mus. African Am. Art, L.A., 1985, others; works in collections at Indpls. Mus. Art, UCLA, Palm Springs Desert Mus., Ankrum Gallery, L.A., many others. Bd. dirs. L.A. Black Arts Coun., 1969-70, San Francisco Arts Commn., Brockman Gallery Artists; mem. Calif. Arts Commn.; vice chmn. Calif. Arts Coun., 1976-78, Century City Cultural Commn., 1978-79; project dir. cultural exch. program Lagos (Nigeria)-Wajumbe Cultural Instn., San Francisco, 1985-86; costume, scenic designer for theatre, dance and film United Scenic Artists, 1960—. Scholar Internat. Found. for Humane Soc. and Kindness to Animals, 1961; fellow Idyllwild Assocs., 1982-84. Mem. Actor's Equity Assn. (dancer, choreographer, actress 1966—), Costume Soc. Am., Ctr. for the Study of Beadwork, Internat. Women's Writing Guild. Home and Studio: PO Box 5038 Saint Mary's City MD 20686-5038

JACKY, PETER B., medical geneticist; b. Madison, Wis., July 18, 1947. PhD, U. Brit. Columbia. Geneticist Kaiser Permanente, Clackmas, Oreg., 1983—; adj. prof. Wash. State U., Pullman, 1990—. Office: Kaiser Permenente NW-RLAB Dir Cyto/Molecular Genet 10220 SE Sunnyside Rd Clackamas OR 97015-9764*

JACOB, MARY, nutritional biochemistry educator, researcher; b. Chngannur, Kerala, India, May 28, 1933; came to U.S., 1964; d. K. Chacko and Susannah (Ittyerah) J. BS, U. Madras, 1953, MS, 1958; MS, U. London, 1963; PhD, U. Ill., 1969. Lectr. Western Australian Inst. Tech., Perth, 1976-77; asst. prof. Ariz. State U., Tempe, 1977-80; prof. Calif. State U., Long Beach, 1980—; speaker Orange County Nutrition Coun., Santa Ana, Calif., 1986. Contbr. numerous articles to profl. jours. Mem. N.Y. Acad. Scis., Am. Inst. Nutrition, Am. Coll. Nutrition, AAAS, Gerontol. Soc. Am. Office: Calif State U Dept Family Consumer Sci 1250 N Bellflower Blvd Long Beach CA 90840-0006

JACOB, STANLEY WALLACE, surgeon, educator; b. Phila., 1924; s. Abraham and Belle (Shulman) J.; m. Marilyn Peters; 1 son, Stephen; m. Beverly Swarts; children—Jeffrey, Darren, Robert; m. Gail Brandis; 1 dau., Elyse. M.D. cum laude, Ohio State U., 1948. Diplomate: Am. Bd. Surgery. Intern Beth Israel Hosp., Boston, 1948-49; resident surgery Beth Israel Hosp., 1949-52, 54-56; chief resident surg. service Harvard Med. Sch., 1956-57, instr., 1958-59; asso. vis. surgeon Boston City Hosp., 1958-59; Kemper Found. research scholar A.C.S., 1957-60; asst. prof. surgery U. Oreg. Med. Sch., Portland, 1959-66; asso. prof. U. Oreg. Med. Sch., 1966—; Gerlinger prof. surgery Oreg. Health Scis. U., 1981—. Author: Structure and Function in Man, 5th edit, 1982, Laboratory Guide for Structure and Function in Man, 1982, Dimethyl Sulfoxide Basic Concepts, 1971, Biological Actions of DMSO, 1975, Elements of Anatomy and Physiology, 1989; contbr. to: Ency. Brit. Served to capt. M.C. AUS, 1952-54; col. Res. ret. Recipient Gov.'s award Outstanding N.W. Scientist, 1965; 1st pl. German Sci. award, 1965; Markle scholar med. scis., 1960. Mem. Phi Beta Kappa, Sigma Xi, Alpha Omega Alpha. Home: 1055 SW Westwood Ct Portland OR 97201-2708 Office: Oreg Health Scis U Dept Surgery 3181 SW Sam Jackson Park Rd Portland OR 97201

JACOBS, ALICIA MELVINA, account executive; b. Newark, June 24, 1955; d. Alvin and Melvina (McKinney) J. BA, Oberlin Coll., 1977. Caseworker Essex County Welfare Bd., Newark, 1977-78; sr. audit analyst N.J. Blue Cross, Newark, 1978-80; fin. analyst N.Y. State Office of the Spl. Cont., N.Y.C., 1980-81; account exec. Fortune Temporary Personnel, N.Y.C., 1981-84; sales mgr. Wall St. Temporary, N.Y.C., 1984-85; account exec. Maxwell Macmillan, N.Y.C., 1985-90; account exec. Rsch. Inst. Am., Newark, 1990-91, Westfield, 1992-93, Century City, Calif., 1993—. Fund-raising chmn. The Africa Project, N.Y.C., 1989—; sec. We Are Family, Newark, 1989—; mentor, tutor Welcome Bapt. Ch., Newark, 1991—; vol. Scott-Krueger Cultural Ctr., Newark, 1991—. Recipient Heroine award Montclair (N.J.) High Sch., 1990, Participant award Madison Ave. Sch., Newark. Mem. NAACP, N.J. Law Librs. Assn., Coalition of 100 Black Women. Home: 4617 Maytime Ln Culver City CA 90230-5070

JACOBS, ARTHUR DIETRICH, educator, researcher, health services executive; b. Bklyn., Feb. 4, 1933; s. Lambert Dietrich and Paula Sophia (Knissel) J.; m. Viva Jane Sims, Mar. 24, 1952; children: Archie (dec.), David L., Dwayne C., Dianna K. Hatfield. BBA, Ariz. State U., 1962, MBA, 1966. Enlisted USAF, 1951, commd. 2d lt., 1962, advanced through grades to maj., 1972, ret., 1973; indsl. engr. Motorola, Phoenix, 1973-74; mgmt. cons. state of Ariz., 1974-76; mgmt. cons. Productivity Internat., Tempe, Ariz., 1976-79; faculty assoc. Coll. Bus. Adminstrn., Ariz. State U., Tempe, 1977-94; productivity advisor Scottsdale (Ariz.) Meml. Health Services Co., 1979-84; researcher U.S. internment of European-Am. aliens and citizens of European ancestry during World War II. Bd. dirs. United Way of Tempe, 1979-85. Mem. Am. Soc. Quality Control, Ariz. State U. Alumni Assn. (bd. dirs. 1973-79, pres. 1978-79), Inst. Indsl. Engrs. (pres. Central Ariz. chpt. 1984-85), Ops. Research Soc. Am., Sigma Iota Epsilon, Beta Gamma Sigma, Delta Sigma Pi. Club: Optimist (life) (Tempe). Co-editor: The World War Two Experience-The Internment of German-Americans: Documents, vol. IV; contbr. articles to profl. jours.

JACOBS, BRUCE MARRIN, lawyer; b. Oakland, Calif., July 21, 1926; s. Allen Walter and Celia Teresa (Marrin) J.; m. Jane Gray, June 26, 1954; children: Tracy Ann, Brian G., Nancy C. Fleming. AB, U. Calif., Berkeley, 1947; JD, U. San Francisco, 1953. Bar: Calif. 1953. Assoc. Law Office Robert K. Byers, Gilroy, Calif., 1953-56; ptnr. Byers & Jacobs, Gilroy, 1957-67, Jacobs & Biafore, Gilroy, 1967-74, Jacobs & McDonald, Gilroy, 1974—; dir. Nat. Fiberglass, Gilroy. Bd. pres. Gavilan Community Coll., Gilroy, 1963, trustee, 1963-73; city atty. City of Gilroy, 1968-91. Lt. (j.g.) USN, 1944-49, PTO. Mem. State Bar Calif., Gilroy C. of C. (pres. 1958), Gilroy Rotary (pres. 1957, 59), Gilroy Elks. Republican. Presbyterian. Home: 7820 Santa Theresa Dr Gilroy CA 95020-4923 Office: Jacobs & McDonald PO Box 458 Gilroy CA 95021-0458

JACOBS, DONALD PAUL, architect; b. Cleve., Aug. 8, 1942; s. Joseph W. and Minnie Mae (Grieger) J.; m. Sharon Daugherty, Apr. 14, 1963 (dec. Feb. 1992); m. Julie Brinkerhoff, Apr. 24, 1993. B.S., U. Cin., 1967. Registered architect, Calif., Tex. Draftsman, intern Skidmore, Owings & Merrill, San Francisco, 1967-70; pvt. practice architecture Sea Ranch, 1970-86, chmn. design com., 1975-79; prin. Dorius Archs., Corona del Mar, Calif., 1986-94; pres. JBZ Dorius Arch. & Planning, Irvine, 1994—. Prin. works represented to numerous newspapers and magazines. Co-chair Project Playhouse, Homeaid, 1993-95. Mem. AIA (2 awards 1973-74, 77-78, Bay Area Honor Design Excellence award 1974, Homes for Better Living Merit award 1976, Housing Merit award 1978, vice chair nat. housing com., 1995), Sr. Housing Coun. (Orange County chpt. bd. dirs. 1993-94). Republican. Home: 309 Poppy Ave Corona Del Mar CA 92625-3024 Office: JBZ Dorius Arch & Planning 2415 Campus Dr Ste 200 Irvine CA 92715

JACOBS, HENRY STEPHEN, computer engineer; b. N.Y.C., Oct. 9, 1950; s. Leonard Irving and Shirley Ruth J.; m. Phylis Lee Papurt, Aug. 12, 1979; children: Sabrina, Rebecca. BS in Systems Engring., Case Western Reserve U., 1972; MS in Systems Engring., UCLA, 1976. Mem. tech. staff TRW Defense & Space Systems, Redondo Beach, Calif., 1972-74; rsch. asst. UCLA-Biotech. Lab., L.A., 1974-76; sr. microprocessor engr. Beckman Instruments, Inc., Fullerton, Calif., 1976-84; sr. software engr. Comtal Divsn. 3M, Pasadena, Calif., 1984-87, Archive Corp., Costa Mesa, Calif., 1987-91; prin. software engr. CalComp, Anaheim, Calif., 1991—. Mem. Acad. Magical Arts, Inc., Toastmasters Internat. Home: 17 Whistling Isle Irvine CA 92714-5459 Office: CalComp 2411 W La Palma Ave Anaheim CA 92801-2610

JACOBS, JOANNE LEE, journalist; b. Chgo., Mar. 31, 1952; d. Alan Joseph and Phyllis (Leaf) Jacobs; m. Colin Bowman Hunter, June 18, 1977 (div. 1985); 1 child, Allison Sarah Hunter. BA in English and Creative Writing, Stanford U., 1974. Copy editor, reporter Suburban Newspapers, Cupertino, Calif., 1974-76; assoc. editor Super 8 Filmaker, San Francisco, 1976-78; copy editor San Jose (Calif.) Mercury News, 1978-80, editorial writer, 1980-84, columnist, editorial writer, 1984—; bd. dirs. Stanford Daily. Bd. dirs. Women's Freedom Network, Washington, 1993—. Mich. Journalism fellow U. Mich., 1990-91.

JACOBS, JOHN HOWARD, association executive; b. Phila., June 7, 1925; s. Howard Elias and Elizabeth Pauline (Dresel) J.; m. Shirley Elizabeth Salini, Apr. 21, 1960. BS in Econs., N.Mex. State U., 1950; LLD (hon.),

Golden Gate U., 1985. Adminstrv. officer U.S. Fgn. Service (NATO), London, Paris, 1951-53; gen. mgr. Vis-a-Pack Corp., Beverly, N.J., 1953-58; exec. dir. Red. Agy., City of Stockton, Calif., 1958-66, San Francisco Planning and Urban Research, 1966-81; exec. dir. San Francisco C. of C., 1981-88, pres., 1988-89; chmn. Pacific Region Nat. Assn. Housing and Redevel. Ofcls., Stockton, 1965-66, mem. nat. bd. govs., San Francisco, 1966-70. Trustee emeritus Fine Arts Mus. San Francisco; bd. dirs. Point Reyes Bird Obs., San Francisco, World Affairs Coun. No. Calif., San Francisco State U. Found.; chmn. pres.'s adv. coun. San Francisco State U.; v.p. San Francisco Devel. Fund. Home: 2823 Octavia St San Francisco CA 94123-4305

JACOBS, KENT FREDERICK, dermatologist; b. El Paso, Tex., Feb. 13, 1938; s. Carl Frederick and Mercedes D. (Johns) J.; m. Sallie Ritter, Apr. 13, 1971. BS, N.Mex. State U., 1960; MD, Northwestern U., 1964; postgrad., U. Colo., 1967-70. Dir. service unit USPHS, Laguna, N.Mex., 1966-67; pvt. practice specializing in dermatology Las Cruces, N.Mex., 1970—; cons. U.S. Army, San Francisco, 1968-70, cons. NIH, Washington, 1983, Holloman AFB, 1972-77; research assoc. VA Hosp., Denver, 1969-70; preceptor U. Tex., Galveston, 1976-77; mem. clin. staff Tex. Tech U., Lubbock, 1977—; asst. clin. prof. U. N.Mex., Albuquerque, 1972—; bd. dirs. First Nat. Bank of Dona Ana County, Las Cruces, N.Mex., 1987—. Novelist; contbr. articles to profl. jours. and popular mags. Trustee Mus. N.Mex. Found., 1987—, mem. bd. regents Mus. N.Mex., 1987—, pres. ,1989-91; bd. dirs. Dona Ana Arts Coun., 1992-93; bd. dirs. N.Mex. State U. Found., 1993—. Invitational scholar Oreg. Primate Ctr., 1968; Acad. Dermatology Found. fellow, 1969; named Disting. Alumnus N.Mex. State U., 1985. Fellow Am. Acad. Dermatology, Royal Soc. Medicine, Soc. Investigative Dermatology; mem. AMA, Fedn. State Med. Bds. (bd. dirs. 1984-86), N.Mex. Med. Soc., N.Mex. Bd. Med. Examiners (pres. 1983-84, N.Mex. State U. Alumni Assn. (bd. dirs. 1975-79), Mil Gracias Club (pres. 1972-74) Pres.'s Assocs., Univ. Ambs., Rotary, Phi Beta Kappa, Beta Beta Beta. Democrat. Presbyterian. Home: 3610 Southwind Rd Las Cruces NM 88005-5556 Office: 2525 S Telshor Blvd # 15-106 Las Cruces NM 88011-5071 also: Mus NM PO Box 2087 Santa Fe NM 87504-2087

JACOBS, LAURENCE WILE, marketing educator; b. Cin., May 26, 1939; s. Arthur Leonard and Josephine (Yuster) J.; m. Susan Stone, Aug. 1, 1965; children: Andrew Wile, Julie Bridget. BS, U. Pa., 1961; MBA, Ohio State U., 1963, PhD, 1966. Mgmt. trainee F&R Lazarus Co., Columbus, Ohio, 1961-62; research assoc. Mktg. Sci. Inst., Phila., 1965-66; asst. prof. mktg. U. Hawaii, Honolulu, 1966-69, assoc. prof., 1969-73, prof. mktg., 1973—. Author: Advertising and Promotion for Retailing, 1972; computer mgmt. game TIMSIM, 1967. Mem. Am. Mktg. Assn. (pres. 1970-71). Home: 1474 Kamole St Honolulu HI 96821-1422 Office: U Hawaii 2404 Maile Way Honolulu HI 96822-2223

JACOBS, PETER ALAN, artist, educator; b. N.Y.C., Jan. 31, 1939; s. Peter A. and Elsie Katherine (Hirchi) J.; m. Nanci Gardner, Apr. 1, 1961; children: Christopher P.D., Cathi Kottenstette. BS, SUNY, New Paltz, 1960, MS, 1962; EdD, Vanderbilt U., 1965. Assoc. prof. art SUNY, New Paltz, 1961-62; prof. art and dept. chair U. Wis., Whitewater, 1965-70, No. Ariz. U., Flagstaff, 1970-74, Ctrl. Mich. U., Mt. Pleasant, 1975-76; prof. art and dept. chair Colo. State U., Ft. Collins, 1976-86, prof. art, 1988—; vis. prof. and dept. head U. Wyo., Laramie, 1987-88; pres. The Douglas Soc., Native Arts Dept., Denver Art Mus., 1994—. Over 65 one-artist exhbns. in 14 states including Nicolaysen Art Mus., Casper, Wyo., 1991, Wyo. State Mus., Cheyenne, 1991, Julliet Denious Gallery, Carnegie Ctr. for Arts, Dodge City, Kans., 1990, Banares Hindu U., Varanasi, India, Gallery Bog, Boulder, Colo., Scottsdale (Ariz.) Fine Arts Ctr., Port Huron (Mich.) Mus. of Art, Ohio State U., Columbus, Northwestern U., Evanston, Ill.; exhbns. in Italy, India, Poland, Germany, Can., Bulgaria; numerous juried exhbns. Bd. dirs. Nightwalker Enterprises, Ft. Collins, Colo., 1985—, One-West Contemporary Art Ctr., Ft. Collins, 1979-86, Artists' Adv. Com., 1994-95. Fulbright scholar, India, 1981-82. Mem. Coll. Art Assn., Native Am. Art Study Assn., Artist Adv. Coun. One-West Contemporary Art Ctr. Lutheran. Office: Colo State U Dept Art Fort Collins CO 80523

JACOBS, RANDALL BRIAN, lawyer; b. N.Y.C., July 8, 1951; s. John and Evelyn Jacobs; 1 child, Jillian. BA, Coll. of Idaho, 1972; JD, U. West L.A., 1978. Bar: Calif., D.C., Wis. Lawyer B. Randall Jacobs Law Corp., Brentwood, Calif., 1978—; real estate broker Morgan Reed & Co., Brentwood, 1979—; pvt. investigator Randy Brian Assocs., Brentwood, 1976—. Reserve deputy sheriff, L.A. County Sheriff, L.A., 1979—. Mem. Shom Rim Soc., Nat. Rifle Assn., Masons, Shriners. Office: Law Offices R B Jacobs 522 S Sepulveda Blvd Ste 110 Los Angeles CA 90049-3539

JACOBS, ROBERT COOPER, political scientist, consultant; b. N.Y.C., Jan. 23, 1939; s. Max and Paula (Glotzer) J.; m. Barbara Linda Lax (div.); children: Michael, Deborah; m. Mollie Jenks Edson; children: Elliot, Madeleine, Eleanor. AB, CCNY, 1959; AM, Columbia U., 1961, PhD, 1970. Instr. Colby Coll., Waterville, Maine, 1965-68, asst. prof., 1968-70; from asst. prof. to prof. Cen. Wash. U., Ellensburg, 1970—, dir. law and justice, 1974-88, prof., 1982—; vis. prof. criminal justice Temple U., 1988-89. Contbr. articles to profl. jours. and encyclopedias. Mem. Kittitas County Juvenile Accountability Bd., Ellensburg, 1975—. N.Y. State Regents scholar, 1955-59; State of N.Y. teaching fellow, 1962-63. Mem. Am. Polit. Sci. Assn., Wash. Assn. Criminal Justice Educators (past pres.), Supreme Ct. Hist. Soc. Democrat. Home: 111 E 10th Ave Ellensburg WA 98926-2909 Office: Cen Wash U Dept Polit Sci Ellensburg WA 98926

JACOBS, ROBERT NEIL, meat industry executive; b. L.A., Jan. 27, 1938; s. Donald Henry and Bertha Amanda (Reeves) J.; m. Patricia Ann Dickinson, June 23, 1955 (div. May 28, 1983); children: Mary Patricia, Debra Elaine, Robert Neil Jr., Jeffrey David, George William, John Harold, Michael James, Michelle Elizabeth; m. Geraldine Yoko Pennell, Oct. 8, 1983. Salesperson H. Shenson, Inc., San Francisco, 1958-70; gen. mgr. Wing-Lee Valley Meat Co., Sacramento, 1970-78; owner Horatio's Restaurant, Sacramento, 1979-82; sales mgr. Luce & Co., Inc., San Francisco, 1983-84; dir. meat ops. Bi-Rite Food Svc., San Francisco, 1988-90; gen. sales mgr. Facciola Meat Co., Palo Alto, Calif., 1984-88, 90-93; pres. RNJ Assocs., San Francisco, 1991—; dir. sales No. Calif. Durham Meat Co., San Jose, Calif., 1994—. Pres. Little League, Sacramento, 1969-71. Mem. Pacific Coast Chefs Assn. (assoc.). Republican. Baptist. Office: RNJ Associates PO Box 281482 San Francisco CA 94128-1482

JACOBS, SALLIE RITTER, painter, sculptor; b. Las Cruces, N.Mex., May 9, 1947; d. John Barnes Ritter and Billie Ruth (Carter) Simpson; m. Kent Frederick Jacobs, Apr. 13, 1971. Student, U. Rome Coll. Art History, 1965, Edinburgh (Scotland) Coll. Art, 1967-68; BA, Colo. Coll., 1969. One-woman shows include Lubbock (Tex.) Art Ctr., 1970, N.Mex. Arts Commn., Santa Fe, 1974, Las Cruces Cmty. Ctr., 1975, Aldridge Fine Arts, Albuquerque, 1980, Woodrow Wilson Fine Arts, Santa Fe, 1989, Adobe Patio Gallery, Mesilla, N.Mex., 1991, 93; exhibited in group shows at El Paso (Tex.) Mus. Art, 1988, Colorado Springs (Colo.) Fine Arts Ctr., 1995, Laguna Gloria Mus., Austin, Tex., 1979, Santa Fe Festival of the Arts, 1979, 83, The Governor's Gallery, Santa Fe, 1987, 94, Pioneer's Mus., Colo. Springs, 1985, 86, 88, N.Mex. State U., Las Cruces, 1988, 89, Dona Ana Arts Coun., Las Cruces, 1992, Tucson Mus. Art, 1995, Tex. Commn. Arts, Austin, 1987; represented in permanent collections U. Tex. Sch. of Law, Phelps Dodge Corp., Sunwest Bank, Albuquerque, N.Mex. State U.; featured in Contemporary Women Artists mag., 1984,Contemporary Western Artists mag., 1985. Bd. dirs. Women's Bd., Mus. N.Mex., Santa Fe, 1987—, Dona Ana Arts Coun., Las Cruces, 1990—. Mem. Internat. Sculpture Ctr. Episcopalian. Home and Studio: 3610 Southwind Rd Las Cruces NM 88005-5556

JACOBS, WILBUR RIPLEY, writer, history educator; b. Chgo.; s. Walter Ripley and Nona Isabel (Deutsch) J.; divorced; children: Elizabeth Shirley Jacobs Hayden, Catherine Elaine,; m. Priscilla Beth Dehmel, Dec. 20, 1982; children: William Ripley, Emily Marilyn. BA with honors, UCLA, MA with honors, PhD; postgrad., Johns Hopkins U. Prof. history U. Calif., Santa Barbara, 1965-88, chmn., dean of students; apt. rsch. scholar Huntington Libr., San Marino, Calif., 1989—; vis. prof. U. Calif., Berkeley, Claremont Grad. Sch., UCLA, Ind. U., U. Mich.; Fulbright prof. Australian Nat. U., Canberra; Am. studies lectr. U. Sidney, Melbourne U., U. Papua New Guinea, U. Queensland; lectr. U. Calif. Alumni Camps; U.s. Dept. State Cultural Exch. Program Yugoslavia, rep. for vis. historians fron USSR. Author: Wilderness Politics and Indian Gifts, 1968, (Pacific Coast Am.-Hist. Assn. prize), The Historical World of Frederick Jackson Turner, 1968, Dispossessing the American Indian, 1985, Francis Parkman, The Historian As Hero, 1991, On the Trail of Turner, 100 Years of Writing Western History, 1994; co-author: Turner Bolton and Webb, Three Historians of the Frontier, 1965, Survey of American History, 1949; editor: The Paxton Riots and The Frontier Theory, 1958, Letters of Francis Parkman, 1960 (runner up Pulitzer prize in history 1961), Indians of the Southern Colonial Frontier, 1969, Benjamin Franklin, Philosopher-Statesman or Materialist, 1972; contbr. numerous articles, essays to profl. jours., newspapers, Encyc. Britannica. L.A. County Smog Testamony. Mem. exec. bd. dirs. Econ. Roundtable of So. Calif., Get Oil Out, Santa Barbara, Throop Unitarian Ch. Grantee Stanford U., Rockefeller Found., Ford Found., Am. Philos. Soc., Huntington Libr. Mem. Am. Hist. Assn. (Pacific coast br., pres.), Am. Soc. Ethnohistory (pres.), Am. Soc. Environ. History (pres.), Am. Studies Assn. (pres. Calif. br.), Humane Soc. U.S. (nat. bd.), Assocs. Calif. Inst. Tech., Mass. Hist. Soc.

JACOBSEN, GERALD BERNHARDT, biochemist; b. Spokane, Wash., Nov. 25, 1939; s. Hans Bernhardt and Mabel Grace (Swope) J.; m. Sally-Ann Heimbigner, June 7, 1961 (div. 1976); children: Claire Elise, Hans Edward; m. Jean Eva Robinson, Dec. 5, 1976. BA, Whitman Coll., 1961; MS, Purdue U., 1965, PhD, 1970. Postdoctoral fellow Oreg. State U., Corvallis, 1970-73; rsch. chemist Lamb-Weston, Inc., Portland, Oreg., 1973-85, sr. rsch. chemist, 1985—; presenter at profl. confs. Contbr. articles to profl. jours. Grantee NSF, 1960; NIH grad. fellow, 1965; Herman Frasch postdoctoral fellow Oreg. State U., 1970. Mem. AAAS, Am. Oil Chemists Soc., Am. Chemistry Soc., Assn. Ofcl. Analytical Chemists, Sigma Xi. Home: 1204 Knollwood Ct Richland WA 99352-9448 Office: Lamb Weston Tech Ctr 2005 Saint St Richland WA 99352-5302

JACOBSEN, LAREN, programmer, analyst; b. Salt Lake City, June 15, 1937; s. Joseph Smith and Marian (Thomas) J.; B.S., U. Utah, 1963; m. Audrey Bartlett, July 29, 1970 (div.); children—Andrea, Cecily, Julian. Programmer, IBM Corp., 1963-70; systems programmer Xerox Computer Services, 1970-79; pres. Prescient Investments Co., 1975-82; sr. systems analyst Quotron Systems, Los Angeles, 1979-86; programmer/analyst Great Western Bank, 1987-92. Served with USAR, 1961. Mem. Am. Guild Organists (dean San Jose chpt. 1967), Mensa. Home: PO Box 91174 Los Angeles CA 90009-1174

JACOBSEN, MICHAEL ANTHONY, art historian, educator; b. Pasadena, Calif., June 4, 1942; s. Lars P. and Dorothy (Stuart) J.; m. Rebecca Hanson, Sept. 25, 1970; 1 child, Leif Peter. BA, U. Calif., Santa Barbara, 1965, MA, 1970; PhD, Columbia U., 1976. Asst. prof. Cleve. State U., 1973-77; assoc. prof., chair art history dept. U. Ga., Athens, 1979-86; vis. assoc. prof. Stanford U., Palo Alto, Calif., 1987, U. Calif., Riverside, 1988; lectr. Calif. State Poly. U., Pomona, 1989—. Contbr. articles to profl. publs. Rsch. grantee, 1968-82; S. H. Kress Found. fellow, 1971-72. Mem. Coll. Art Assn., So. Calif. Art Historians. Office: Calif State Poly U 3801 W Temple Ave Pomona CA 91768-2557

JACOBSEN, PAMELA, special education director, consultant, counselor; b. Cleve., June 25, 1947; d. Michael Antony and Mary (Pappas) Hoty; m. William Henry Jacobsen, Aug. 21, 1971 (div. 1982). BS in Elem. Edn., Baldwin-Wallace Coll., 1969; postgrad. in learning disabilities, Akron U., 1971-72; MA in Educating Handicapped, Adams State Coll., 1976, Cert. assessor. Tchr. Strongsville Schs., Ohio, 1969-71, lang. disabilities tchr., 1971-73; educationally handicapped itinerant tchr. Dist. 60, Pueblo, Colo., 1973-74, educationally handicapped lab. educator, 1974-77, educationally handicapped resource tchr., 1977-79, emotional/behavior disorder educator, 1979-86, child study team specialist, 1986-92, dir. spl. edn.; educator Summer Champ Camp for Asthmatics, Woodland Park, Colo., 1983-86. Author: Correct and Effective Use of Placement and Procedures for Emotionally Disordered Students, 1985. Active Pueblo Nature Ctr., 1981—; area chmn. Channel 8 Pub. TV Auction, 1982-87; bd. dirs. Altrusa Club of Pueblo, 1986, sec., 1990-91, v.p., 1992—; nominating com. Columbine Coun. Girl Scouts U.S., 1984-86. Recipient Hon. Mention award Gov. Colo., 1985; Service award Champ Camp Program, 1984, 85; IDEA fellow, 1987-95. Mem. NAFE, Colo. Assn. Sch. Execs. (div. ednl. specialists 1989—, bd. dirs. 1991-93), Nat. Assn. Secondary Sch. Prins. (cert. assessor 1992), Bus. and Profl. Women, Phi Delta Kappa (v.p. 1985-87, pres. 1987-89), Delta Kappa Gamma. Greek Orthodox. Club: Pueblo Athletic, Pueblo Country Club. Avocations: golf, hiking, reading, swimming. Home: 1100 W 26th St Pueblo CO 81003-1722 Office: Pueblo Sch Dist #60 315 W 11th St Pueblo CO 81003-2804

JACOBSEN, RICHARD T., mechanical engineering educator; b. Pocatello, Idaho, Nov. 12, 1941; s. Thorleif and Edith Emily (Gladwin) J.; m. Vicki Belle Hopkins, July 16, 1959 (div. Mar. 1973); children: Pamela Sue, Richard T., Eric Ernest; m. Bonnie Lee Stewart, Oct. 19, 1973; 1 child, Jay Michael; stepchild: Erik David Lustig. BSME, U. Idaho, 1963, MSME, 1965; PhD in Engring. Sci., Wash. State U., 1972. Registered profl. engr., Idaho. Instr. U. Idaho, 1964-66, asst. prof. mech. engring., 1966-72, assoc. prof., 1972-77, prof., 1977—, chmn. dept. mech. engring., 1980-85, assoc. dean engring., 1985-90, assoc. dir. Ctr. for Applied Thermodynamic Studies, 1975-86, dir., 1986—, dean engring., 1990—. Author: International Union of Pure and Applied Chemistry, Nitrogen-International Thermodynamic Tables of the Fluid State-6, 1979; Oxygen-International Thermodynamic Tables of the Fluid State-9, 1987, Ethylene-International Thermodynamic Tables of the Fluid State-10, 1988, ASHRAE Thermodynamic Properties of Refrigerants (2 vols.), 1986; numerous reports on thermodynamic properties of fluids, 1971—; contbr. articles to profl. jours. NSF sci. faculty fellow, 1968-69; NSF rsch. and travel grantee, 1976-83; Nat. Inst. Standards and Tech. grantee, 1974-91, Gas Rsch. Inst. grantee, 1986-91, 1992—, Dept. Energy grantee, 1991—. Fellow ASME (faculty advisor 1972-75, 78-84, chmn. region VIII dept. heads com. 1983-85, honors and awards chmn. 1985-91, K-7 tech. com. thermophys. properties 1985—, chmn. 1986-89, 92-95, rsch. tech. com. on water and steam in thermal power systems, 1988—, gen. awards com. 1985-91, chmn. 1988-91, com. on honors 1988—, mem. bd. on profl. practice and ethics, 1991—), N.W. Coll. and Univ. Assn. for Sci. (bd. dirs. 1990-93), Idaho Rsch. Found. (bd. dirs. 1991—), Soc. Automotive Engrs. (Ralph R. Teetor Edn. award, Detroit 1968), ASHRAE (co-recipient Best Tech. Paper award 1984), Internat. Energy Agy. (Annex 18 thermophys. properties environ. acceptable refrigerants 1991—), Sigma Xi, Tau Beta Pi, Phi Kappa Phi (Disting. Faculty award 1989). Office: U Idaho Coll Engring Office of Dean Janssen Engring Bldg 125 Moscow ID 83844

JACOBSMEYER, JAY MICHAEL, electrical engineer; b. Okaloosa County, Fla., Mar. 13, 1959; s. John Henry and Patricia Ann (McDonough) J.; m. Joyce Ann Deem, June 20, 1981; children: Abigail Ann, Brian James. BS magna cum laude, Va. Poly. Inst. & State U., 1981; MS, Cornell U., 1987. Registered profl. engr., Colo. Commd. 2nd lt. USAF, 1981-90, advanced through grades to capt., 1985; elec. engr. 3397 Tech. Tng. Squadron, Biloxi, Miss., 1981-82; comm. engr. 1st Combat Comm. Group, Wiesbaden, Germany, 1982-85; communications engr. HQ Air Force Space Command, Colorado Springs, 1987-90; resigned USAF, 1990; staff engr. ENSCO, Inc., Colorado Springs, 1990-91, sr. staff engr., 1991-93; co-founder, chief tech. officer Pericle Comm. Co., 1992—. Patent pending wireless data modem; contbr. articles to profl. publs. Maj. USAFR. Decorated Meritorious Svc. medal, Air Force Commendation medal; named Man of Yr., Va. Poly. Inst. and State U., 1981; rsch. grantee, NSF, USN. Mem. IEEE (sr.), Armed Forces Comm. and Electronics Assn. (v.p. 1989-90), Air Force Assn., Omicron Delta Kappa, Eta Kappa Nu. Home: 2475 Edenderry Dr Colorado Springs CO 80919-3876

JACOBSON, ALBERT DALE, pediatrician, accountant; b. Portland, Oreg., Mar. 28, 1942; s. Leonard Dale and Allice Cleo (Wiesendanger) J.; m. Donna Marie Shaw, Aug. 8, 1964; children: Heidi, Craig, Bryan and Chad. BS in acctg., Ariz. State U., 1964; MD, U. Oreg., Portland, 1969. CPA, Oreg.; diplomate Am. Bd. Pediatrics, Am. Bd. Nephrology. Pub. acct. Winn & Co., Eugene, Oreg., 1964-65; intern Good Samaritan Hosp., Phoenix, Ariz., 1970; residency in pediatrics and pediatric nephrology fellowship Naval Hosp., San Diego, 1972, U. Calif., San Diego, 1972; chief pediatrics Naval Regional Med. Clinic, Pearl Harbor, Hawaii, 1972-75; sect. chief pediatric nephrology Tripler Army Hosp., Honolulu, 1972-75; attending staff pediatrician, clin. asst. prof. pediatrics U. Hawaii Med. Sch., Honolulu, 1972-75; pediatrician Health Maintenance Assocs., Phoenix, Ariz., 1975-77; v.p. Health Maintenance Assocs., Inc., Phoenix, Ariz., 1976-77; adminstrv. staff pediatrician, sect. head pediatric nephrology Maricopa County Gen. Hosp., 1977-78; chief pediatric rehab. Barrows Neurological Institution, 1986-88, Children's Med. Ctr., St. Joseph's Hosp., 1986-88; pvt. practice Pediatric Assocs., P.C., Phoenix, Ariz., 1977—; divsn. chmn. Emergency Dept. Children's Hosp., Honolulu, 1972-75; cons. Waimano State Institution for the Retarded, 1972-75, Children's Hosp., Honolulu, 1972-75; advisor Poision Contro Ctr. State of Hawaii, 1972-75; chief of pediatrics Naval Regional Med. Clinics, 1972-75; navy chmn. child abuse com. Tripler Army Hosp., 1972-75; mem. gov.'s adv. bd. Child Protection Soc., 1972-75; media rep., TV appearances on children's health Phoenix Pediatric, 1981-92; host weekly radio program, KTAR Speaking of Kids, 1982-84. Contbr. to profl. jours. Coach Phoenix Little League, 1975-93. Comdr. U.S. Navy, 1970-75. Oreg. State Heart Assn. fellow, 1966; Nat. Pharm. and Drug Mfg. Rsch. fellow, 1968. Fellow Am. Acad. Pediatrics (tech. advisor third party payments, 1972-75, state chmn. child health planning com., 1975-77, sec. Ariz. chpt. 1980-82, advisor com. of pediatric practice, 1983-92, chmn. child health finance, 1986-89), Am. Spinal Injury Assn.; mem. AMA, Internat. Soc. Pediatrics, Honolulu and State Hawaii Pediatric Soc. (state chmn. on third party payments), Phoenix Pediatric Soc., Ariz. Med. Assn., Maricopa County Med. Assn., Maricopa County Pediatric Soc. (pres. elect. 1981-82, pres. 1982-83, com. for the formation of Phoenix Children's Hosp., 1979-83). Office: Pediatric Assocs PC Pointe Corridor Ctr II 7600 N 15th St Ste 130 Phoenix AZ 85020-4330

JACOBSON, DEAN MARTIN, marine biology educator, researcher; b. Edwards AFB, Calif., Nov. 7, 1957; s. Robert Herbert and Virginia Ann (Peterson) J.; m. Paula Anne Yup, May 4, 1985. AB, Occidental Coll., 1979; PhD, Mass. Inst. Tech./Woods Hole Oceanographic Inst., 1987. NATO postdoctoral fellow U. B.C., Vancouver, Can., 1988; assoc. rschr., electron microscopist Howard Hughes Med. Inst., MIT, 1989-90; curator Provasoli Guillard Ctr. Culture of Marine Phytoplankton, Bigelow Lab., Boothbay Harbor, Maine, 1990-93; asst. prof. biology Whitworth Coll., Spokane, Wash., 1994—. Contbr. articles to profl. jours. Mem. Phycological Soc. Am., Soc. Protozoologists. Democrat. Office: Whitworth Coll Hawthorne Rd Spokane WA 99251

JACOBSON, DONALD THOMAS, management consultant; b. Powers Lake, N.D., June 5, 1932; s. Martin I. and Gladys E. (Thronson) J.; BA, Whitman Coll., 1954; MBA, Stanford U., 1956; m. Andrea Marie Moore, Aug. 14, 1954 (dec.); 1 child, Kathryn E. Hanson. Sales and mktg. mgmt. Guy F. Atkinson Co., Portland, Oreg., 1959-63; sales control mgr. Boise Cascade Corp., Portland, 1964-66; v.p. and dir. rsch. Lund, McCutcheon, Jacobson, Inc., Portland, 1966-74; pres. Mgmt./Mktg. Assocs., Inc., Portland, 1974—; mem. Oreg. Rep. Club, 1960-64, mem. bd. dirs., v.p. 1960, pres. 1961; mem. County Rep. Cen. Com., 1962-64; chmn. Oreg. Bus. Workshops, 1974-76; exec. com., dir. Full-Circle, Inc., 1971-77. Lt. U.S. Army, 1956-59. Decorated commendation ribbon; recipient Oreg. Econ. Devel. award, 1973; Mem. Am. Mktg. Assn. (pres. Oreg. chpt. 1972-73, bd. dirs. 1967-74, 89-93, Oreg. Marketer of Yr. award 1991, chair Internat. Outreach Com., 1992-93), Inst. Mgmt. Cons. (cert.; founding mem., founding pres. Pacific N.W. chpt. 1980-81), Mktg. Rsch. Assn., Nat. Assn. Bus. Economists, Portland Metro. C. of C. (bd. dirs. 1987-90, chmn.'s award Outstanding Svc., 1987), Met. Chambers Econ. Devel. Coun. Portland Area (chmn. mktg. task force 1983-85, emerging issues com., 1987-89, labor policy com. 1988-91, chmn. Tri-Met Task Force 1985-88, chmn. transpn. com. 1987-88), The Planning Forum (v.p. Oreg. chpt. 1986-87, bd. dirs., 1986-90), U.S. Dept. Commerce (nat. def. exec. res. 1966—), (chmn. Oreg.-Idaho assn. 1969-70), Oregonians for Cost-Effective Govt. (bd. dirs. 1986-90, bd. advisor 1991-92), Econ. Roundtable (coord. 1982—), Whitman Coll. Alumni Assn. (bd. dirs. 1971-75, pres. 1975-77), Stanford U. Bus. Sch. Assn. (founding pres. Portland chpt. 1971-72), Phi Beta Kappa. Republican. Lutheran. Contbr. articles on mgmt. and mktg. to profl. jours.

JACOBSON, EDWIN JAMES, medical educator; b. Chgo., June 27, 1947; s. Edwin Julius and Rose Josephine (Jirinec) J.; m. Martha Shanks; 1 child, Emily. BA, U. So. Calif., 1969; MD, UCLA, 1976. Diplomate Nat. Bd. Med. Examiners, Am. Bd. Internal Medicine; lic. physician, Calif. Intern in medicine UCLA Hosp., 1976-77, resident in medicine, 1977-79, fellow in nephrology, 1979-81, chief resident in medicine, 1979-81; asst. clin. prof. of medicine UCLA, 1981-88, assoc. clin. prof. medicine, 1988-94, clin. prof. medicine, 1994—; adj. asst. prof. medicine, UCLA, 1980-81; mem. med. sch. admissions com. UCLA, 1981—, med. staff credentials com., 1984—, med.staff exec. com., 1990-94, med. staff/hosp. adminstrn. liaison com. 1991-94, hosp./med. sch. faculty rels. com., 1991—, nat. kidney found., 1991—, med. adv. bd., 1991—; prin. investigator A/M Group Grant, UCLA Med. Ctr., 1993, Peter Langer Meml. Fund Award, 1993; lectr. in field. Author: Medical Diagnosis: An Algorithmic Approach, 1989; co-author: (with P. Healy) Il Proceso Decisionale nella Diagnosi Medica, 1992; manuscript rev. bd.: Bone Marrow Transplantation, 1988—, Jour. Am. Geriatrics Soc., 1989—; editor for symposia in field; contbr. articles to profl. jours.; editor book chpts. Recipient Upjohn Achievement award, 1977. Mem. ACP, Alpha Omega Alpha. Office: UCLA 100 UCLA Medical Plz # 690 Los Angeles CA 90024

JACOBSON, JACOB G., psychoanalyst; b. N.Y.C., June 17, 1928; s. Max and Jeanne (Schatz) J.; married; children: Carol Wright, Beth Smith, Matthew Jacobson. BS in Psychology, U. Mich., 1948, MD, 1952. Diplomate Am. Bd. Psychiatry and Neurology. Clin. asst. prof. to assoc. prof. psychiatry U. Colo., Denver, 1958-86, clin. prof., 1986—; faculty Denver Inst. Psychoanalysis, 1972—, tng. and supr. analyst, 1977—. Contbr. articles to profl. jours. Life fellow APA. Mem. Am. Psychoanalytic Assn. (chmn. com. on insts. 1986-91). Office: 1636 16th St Boulder CO 80302-6356

JACOBSON, JAY ANDREW, physician; b. Spartanburg, S.C., Sept. 19, 1945; s. Abraham Irving and Doris (Barbanell) J.; m. Julie Evelyn Taylor, May 4, 1969; 1 son, Aaron Robert. BS in Chemistry, U. Mich., 1967; MD with honors, U. Fla., 1971. Diplomate Am. Bd. Internal Medicine, sub-bd. infectious diseases. Resident in internal medicine U. Fla., Gainesville, 1971-73; epidemiologist CDC, Atlanta, 1974-75; fellow in infectious diseases U. Utah, Salt Lake City, 1976-78, mem. faculty, 1978—, prof. internal medicine, 1990—; chief div. med. ethics, mem. div. infectious diseases LDS Hosp./U. Utah Sch. Medicine, Salt Lake City, 1989—; vis. scholar U. Chgo. Ctr. for Clin. Med. Ethics, 1988-89; chmn. instl. rev. bd. U. Utah Sch. Medicine, 1994—. Contbr. articles to med. jours. Pres. Congregation Kol Ami, Salt Lake City, 1990-92. Lt. comdr. USPHS, 1974-76. Fellow ACP, Infectious Diseases Soc. Am.; mem. Soc. for Health and Human Values, Am. Soc. for Law, Medicine and Ethics, Utah Med. Assn. (task force of HIV/AIDS 1987-95, Disting. Svc. award 1990). Democrat. Office: LDS Hosp Divsn Med Ethics 8th Ave And C St Salt Lake City UT 84143

JACOBSON, LOWELL STEVEN (JAKE JACOBSON), railroad executive; b. Riley, Kans., Sept. 17, 1940; s. Myron A. and Irene (Anderson) J.; m. Patricia L. Boyce, Feb. 2, 1963; children: Michael W., Jacqulin D. Steel bridge worker Union Pacific R.R., Frankfort, Kans., 1958-64; indsl. foreman Union Pacific R.R., Salina, Kans., 1964-69; indsl. supt. Union Pacific R.R., Kansas City, Mo., 1969-73; trainmaster Union Pacific R.R., Topeka, 1973-85; supt. Union Pacific R.R., Kans., Nebr., Mo., Colo., 1985; railroad cons. S.W. U.S., 1986-87; gen. supt., gen. mgr., v.p. Copper Basin Ry., Hayden, Ariz., 1987—. Sgt. USAF, 1963-66. Named Railroader of the Yr., Rlwy. Age Mag., 1994. Office: Copper Basin Ry Highway 177 Hayden AZ 85235

JACOBSON, LYNN, newspaper editor; b. Seattle, May 22, 1961; d. Paul Edward and Anne Louise (Mosher) J.; m. Stuart Hebb McFeely, Sept. 16, 1989; 1 child, Liam Givan. BA in Comm., U. Wash., 1984; MA in Performance Studies, NYU, 1989. Asst. editor TDR, N.Y.C., 1987-89, Am. Theatre, N.Y.C., 1989-91; mng. editor Mirror/Seattle Times, 1992—; writer Variety, Seattle Weekly, Am. Theatre, Stagebill, N.Y. Press, 1986—. Vol. KUOW pub. radio, Seattle, 1992-94; co-dir. Fellowship Activities, Inc., Seattle, 1992-94. Mem. ACLU, Soc. of Profl. Journalists. Democrat. Office: Mirror 1100 Denny Way Seattle WA 98109-5309

JACOBSON, PHILLIP LEE, architect, educator; b. Santa Monica, Calif., Aug. 27, 1928; s. Allen Wilhelm and Greta Percy (Rohde) J.; m. Effie Laurel Galbraith, Nov. 6, 1954; children: Rolf Wilhelm, Christina Lee, Erik Mackenzie. B. Archtl. Engring. with honors, Wash. State U., 1952; postgrad. (Fulbright scholar), U. Liverpool, Eng., 1952-53; M.Arch., Finnish Inst. Tech., Helsinki, 1969. Field supr. Gerald C. Field Architect, 1950; designer, draftsman John Maloney Architect, 1951, 53-55; designer, project mgr. Young, Richardson, Carleton & Detlie Architects, 1955-56; designer, project architect John Carl Warnecke Architect, San Francisco, Calif., 1956-58; ptnr., design dir. TRA, Seattle, 1958-92; prof. architecture/urban design and planning U. Wash., Seattle, 1962—; pres. TRA Alaska Inc. Author: Housing and Industrialization in Finland, 1969, The Evolving Architectural Design Process, 1969; contbr. articles to profl. jours.; major archtl. works include Aerospace Research Lab., U. Wash., Seattle, 1969, McCarty Residence Hall, 1960, Highway Adminstrn. Bldg., Olympia, Wash., 1970, Sea-Tac Internat. Airport, 1972, Issaquah (Wash.) High Sch., 1962, State Office Bldg. 2, Olympia, 1976, Sealaska Corporate Hdqrs. Bldg., Juneau, Alaska, 1977, Group Health Hosp., Seattle, 1973, Metro Shelter Program, Seattle, 1977, N.W. Trek Wildlife Preserve, 1976, Rocky Reach/Rock Island Recreation Plan, 1974, master plan mouth of Columbia River, 1976, U. Wash. Biol. Sci. Bldg., 1981, Wegner Hall, Wash. State U., 1982, Wash. Conv. Ctr., 1988, King County Aquatics Ctr., 1990, Albuquerque Airport, 1989, U. Wash. Health Scis. H Wing, 1993. Mem. Seattle Planning and Redevel. Council, 1959-69, v.p., 1966-67; mem. Seattle Landmark Preservation Bd., 1976-81; trustee Pilchuck Sch., Northwest Trek Found., AIA/Seattle Archtl. Found. With U.S. Army, 1946-47. Fulbright-Hays Sr. Research fellow Finland, 1968-69; named to Order of White Rose, Govt. Finland, 1985; recipient numerous design awards including Silver plaque Finnish Soc. Architects, 1992; mem. numerous design awards juries. Fellow AIA (pres. Wash. state council 1965, dir. Seattle chpt. 1970-73, sr. council 1970—, Seattle chpt. medal 1994); mem. Am. Inst. Cert. Planners, Phi Kappa Phi, Tau Beta Pi, Tau Sigma Delta, Scarab, Sigma Tau (outstanding alumnus 1967). Home: 3935 51st Ave NE Seattle WA 98105-5243 Office: TRA 215 Columbia St Seattle WA 98104-1551

JACOBSON, RAYMOND EARL, electronics company executive; b. St. Paul, May 25, 1922; s. Albert H. and Gertrude W. (Anderson) J.; BE with high honors, Yale U., 1944; MBA with distinction, Harvard U., 1948; B.A. (Rhodes scholar), Oxford U., 1950, M.A., 1954; m. Margaret Maxine Meadows, Dec. 22, 1959 (div. 1986); children: Michael David, Karl Raymond, Christopher Eric. Asst. to gen. mgr. PRD Electronics, Inc., Bklyn., 1951-55; sales mgr. Curtiss-Wright Electronics Div., Carlstadt, N.J., 1955-57; dir. mktg. TRW Computers Co., Los Angeles, 1957-60; v.p. ops. Electro-Sci. Investors, Dallas, 1960-63; pres. Whitehall Electronics, Inc., Dallas, 1961-63, dir., 1961-63; chmn. bd. Gen. Electronic Control, Inc., Mpls., 1961-63, Staco, Inc., Dayton, Ohio, 1961-63; pres. Maxson Electronics Corp., Gt. River, N.Y., 1963-64, Jacobson Assocs., San Jose, Calif., 1964-67; co-founder, pres., chmn., chief exec. officer Anderson Jacobson, Inc., San Jose, 1967-88; chmn. Anderson Jacobson, SA, Paris, 1974-88; chmn. Anderson Jacobson, Ltd., London, 1975-85; chmn. Anderson Jacobson Can., Ltd./Ltée, Toronto, 1975-85, Anderson Jacobson, GmbH, Cologne, 1978-83, CXR Corp., San Jose, 1988-94; bd. dirs. Tamar Electronics, Inc., L.A., Rawco Instruments, Inc., Dallas, 1960-63, Micro Radionics, Inc., L.A., 1964-67; lectr. engring., UCLA, 1958-60; mem. underwriting Lloyd's London, 1975—. Committeeman, Eagle Scout Boy Scouts Am., 1968-80. Lt. (j.g.) USNR, 1943-46. Mem. Assn. Am. Rhodes Scholars, Harvard Bus. Sch. Assn., Oxford Soc., Yale Club, Sigma Xi, Tau Beta Pi. Republican. Lutheran. Clubs: Courtside Tennis, Seascape Swim and Racquet. Home: 1247 Montcourse Ln San Jose CA 95131-2420

JACOBSON, SIDNEY, editor; b. N.Y.C., Oct. 20, 1929; s. Reuben and Beatrice (Edelman) J.; m. Ruth Allison, July 4, 1957 (div. Feb. 1975); children: Seth, Kathy; m. Maggi Silverstein, Feb. 26, 1975. BA, NYU, 1950. Exec. editor Harvey Comics, N.Y.C., 1952-83, Marvel Comics, N.Y.C., 1983-89; v.p., editor in chief Harvey Comics Entertainment, L.A., 1989—. Author: Streets of Gold, 1985, Another Time, 1989; writer (comic books) Captain Israel, 1972, The Black Comic Book, 1973, (TV animation series) Johnny Cypher in Dimension Zero, 1975, (TV series) Felix the Cat, 1982, (monthly) You Can't Do That in Comics, 1986; lyricist various popular songs. Mem. Am. Soc. Composers, Authors and Pubs., Am. Guild Authors and Composers, Authors Guild. Home: 2276 S Beverly Glen Blvd Los Angeles CA 90064-2464 Office: Harvey Comics Entertainment 100 Wilshire Blvd Santa Monica CA 90401-1110

JACOBSON, STEPHEN RICHARD, geologist, geochemist, researcher; b. N.Y.C., Sept. 25, 1944; s. Reuben and Anne J.; m. Rosemary Anne Askin Jacobson, Jan. 17, 1981; 1 child, Ruth Anne. BS in Geology, Dickinson Coll., Carlisle, Pa., 1969; AM in Geol. Scis., Harvard U., 1972; PhD in Geology and Mineralogy, Ohio State U., 1978. Lectr. CUNY, 1972-73; part time faculty Calif. State U., Long Beach, 1989—; geologist to sr. geologist Chevron USA, Denver, 1978-86; sr. rsch. geologist Chevron Oil Field Rsch. Co., La Habra, Calif., 1986-90, sr. rsch. assoc., 1990-92; sr. rsch. assoc. Chevron Petroleum Tech. Co., La Habra, Calif., 1993—. Contbr. numerous scientific articles. Mem. Am. Assn. Petroleum Geologists, Am. Assn. Stratigraphic Palynologists, Ohio State U. Alumni Soc. (v.p. geol. scis. dept.). Office: Ohio State U 155 S Oval Mall Columbus OH 43210

JACOBSON, STEVE EVAN, production company executive; b. St. Louis, May 8, 1955; s. Leonard and June Annette (Groff) J. BA, U. So. Calif., L.A., 1977. Prodn. asst. on-air promotion ABC, L.A., 1978; writer Walt Disney Prodns., Burbank, Calif., 1978-79; freelance producer on-air promotion NBC, Burbank, 1979-81, writer, producer on-air promotion, 1981-83, mgr. on-air promotion, 1983-88; v.p. on-air promotion CBS, L.A., 1988-93; pres. Pittard-Sullivan-Fitzgerald, Inc. and Nu Pictures, Inc., 1993—. Co-producer (film) Junior High School, 1978 (over 40 internat. awards 1978-79). Recipient Bronze award Broadcast Designers Assn., 1988, 90, 93, Finalist award Internat. Film & TV Festival, N.Y., 1988. Mem. Broadcast Promotion & Mktg. Execs., U. So. Calif.-Cinema/TV Alumni Assn. Office: Pittard Sullivan Fitzgerald 6430 W Sunset Blvd Ste 200 Los Angeles CA 90028-7905

JACOBSON, STUART NEIL, biotechnology company executive, consultant; b. N.Y.C., Aug. 28, 1953; s. Roy and Shirley (Roth) J.; m. Gretchen Marion Haupt, June 5, 1977; children: Jesse, Eli, Taimi. BS, CCNY, 1974; MS, Cornell U., 1978, PhD, 1981. Rsch. technician Sloan Kettering Inst., N.Y.C., 1974-75; sci. script cons. Chris Jeans Prodns., N.Y.C., 1980; owner, mgr. The Upper Crust, Salt Lake City, 1982-88; founder, mgr. S. J. Biologics, Camarillo, Calif., 1989—; microbiol. cons. various orgns., 1986—.

JACOBSON, SVERRE THEODORE, retired minister; b. Loreburn, Sask., Can., Sept. 20, 1922; s. Sverre and Aline Tomina (Joel) J.; m. Phyllis Lorraine Sylte, Sept. 14, 1948; children—Katherine Ann, Paul Theodore. B.A., U. Sask., 1946; B.D., Luther Theol. Sem., Sask., 1947; postgrad., Luther Theol. Sem., St. Paul, Minn., 1952-53; Th.D., Princeton Theol. Sem., 1959. Ordained to ministry Evang. Luth. Ch., 1947. Pastor Lomond, Alta., 1947-53; lectr. Luther Theol. Sem., Saskatoon, Sask., 1956-57; pastor Torquay, Sask., 1958-63; asst. to pres. Evang. Luth. Ch. Can., Saskatoon, 1963-70; pres. Evang. Luth. Ch. Can., 1970-85; interim parish pastor Calgary, Alta., Saskatoon, Weyburn, Elbow and Loreburn, Sask., 1987—; lectr. Luth. Theol. Sem., Saskatoon, 1987-88. Home: 53 Moxon Crescent, Saskatoon, SK Canada S7H 3B8

JACOBY, RUSSELL, history educator; b. N.Y.C., Apr. 23, 1945. BA, U. Wis., 1967; MA, U. Rochester, 1968; student, Ecole Pratique Hautes Etudes, Paris, 1970; PhD in History, U. Rochester, 1974. Lectr. Boston U., Boston, 1974-75; scholar in residence Brandeis U., 1975-76; lectr. dept. History U. Calif., L.A., 1976-79; vis. asst. prof. History U. Calif., Irvine, 1979-80; vis. assoc. prof. Humanities Simon Fraser U., Vancouver, B.C., Can., 1983-84; vis. scholar, assoc. prof. Lonergan U. Coll./Liberal Arts Coll. Concordia U., Montreal, Can., 1985-86; vis. sr. lectr. U. Calif., San Diego, 1986-87; vis. assoc. prof. history U. Calif., Riverside, 1988-91; vis. assoc. prof. history UCLA, 1992-94, adj. prof. history, 1995—. Author: Social Amnesia: A Critique of Conformist Psychology from Adler to Laing, 1975, Dialectic of Defeat: Contours of Western Marxism, 1981, The Repression of Psychoanalysis: Otto Fenichel and the Political Freudians, 1983, The Last Intellectuals: American Culture in the Age of Academe, 1987, Dogmatic Wisdom: How the Culture Wars Divert Education and Distract America, 1994; co-editor: The Bell Curve Debate, 1995; contbr. articles to profl. jours.; lectr. in field. Mellon Post-doctoral fellow, 1976-77, NEH grantee, 1976, Guggenheim fellow, 1980-81. Office: U Calif Dept History Los Angeles CA 90024

JACQUES, MICHAEL LOUIS, artist, educator; b. Barre, Vt., Apr. 12, 1945; s. Louis and Verna Netti (Fleck) J.; m. Rose Yesu, Aug. 1967 (div. Jan. 1981); m. Karen Eckler, July 7, 1983; 1 child, M. Tyler Jacques; 1 stepchild, Sebastian O'Brien. BFA, Boston U., 1967; MFA, U. Hartford, 1971. Tchg. fellow U. Hartford (Conn.), 1967-69; art instr. Montserrat Sch. Visual Art, Beverly, Mass., 1971-88; prof. art Emmanuel Coll., Mass., 1971-87, Saddleback Coll., Calif., 1989-93, Art Inst. So. Calif., 1993—, Miracosta Coll., Oceanside, Calif., 1994—; illustrator U.S. Army, Alexandria, Va., 1969-71; artist-in-residence Abt Assocs., Inc., Cambridge, Mass., 1980-81, Va. Mus., Richmond, 1981-82; co-dir. Laguna Fine Art Group, Fashion Island, Newport Beach, Calif., 1990-92; dir. Michael Jacques Fine Art, Laguna Beach, 1989—. One-man exhbns. include Athenaeum Mus., Alexandria, Va., Framemakers Gallery, Mass., Ghent Galleries, Norwalk, Va., Jacques Gallery, Laguna Beach, Calif., Mills Gallery, Boston, Springfield (Mass.) Mus. Fine Arts, U. Mass., Worcester, numerous others; more than 125 nat. exhbns. including Am. Acad. Inst. Arts and Letters, Hudson Valley Art Assn., Mus. Am. Art; represented in permanent collections at Amherst (Mass.) Coll., Ark. Art Ctr., Bridgewater (Mass.) State Coll., Brockton (Mass.) Art Mus., Brown U., R.I., Chesterfield Land and Timber Corp., Mass., Chrysler Mus., Va., Computer Scis. Corp., Va., DeCordova Mus., Mass., DelLand Mktg. Corp., Va., Duxbury Art Complex, Mass., First Nat. Bank of Boston, Greensborough Agr. and Tech. Coll., N.C., Harbor Capital Mgmt., Mass., Holy Cross Coll., Mass., Ho. of Reps., Washington, Nat. Collection Fine Arts, Smithsonian, Nat. Collection, Peking, China, Phila. Mus. Art, Phillip Morris Collection, Springfield Mus. Fine Arts, Tufts U., Mass., U. Mass. Med. Ctr., Vt. State Courthouse, Va. Mus. Fine Arts, Wm. Nelson Rockhill Mus., Mo., Worcester (Mass.) Art Mus., others; Author, illustrator: Images of Age, 1980 (Desi award graphic design 1981, Desi award book cover 1981, Distinctive Merit award book design Art Dirs. Club Boston 1981, Merit award book jacket design Art Dirs. Club Boston 1981). Recipient Am. Book award nomination for book illustration/original art, 1982. Mem. Acad. Artists Assn. (coun. 1972-76), Boston Printmakers Assn., Copley Soc. (Copley Master 1981), L.A. Printmakers Soc., Audubon Artists Assn., Boston Visual Artists Union. Home: 933 Meadowlark Dr Laguna Beach CA 92651-2832

JADUS, MARTIN ROBERT, cellular immunologist; b. Girardville, Pa., Jan. 10, 1953; s. Albert Joseph and Mary Margaret (Sokol) J.; m. Yolanda Yong-Chan. MS in Biology, Fla. Inst. Tech., 1978; PhD in Pathology, U. Fla., 1983. Postdoctoral fellow Children's Hosp. of L.A., 1983-85; vis. prof. U. S. Fla., Tampa, 1985-86; staff scientist Biotherapeutics Inc., Franklin, Tenn., 1986-88; sr. scientist Marrow Tech., Inc., San Diego, 1988-90; health rsch. specialist Vets. Affairs Med. Ctr., Long Beach, Calif., 1990—. Contbr. articles to profl. jours. Mem. AAAS, Am. Assn. Hematologists, Internat. Soc. Hematology, Soc. for Biol. Therapeutics, Am. Assn. Immunologists, Leukocyte Biology Soc. Office: VA Med Ctr 5901 E 7th St Long Beach CA 90822

JAEGER, DAVID ARNOLD, aerospace company executive; b. Hanford, Calif., Oct. 16, 1938; s. Charles Arnold and Kathryn (Barthuli) J.; m. Cynthia Diana Malone, Aug. 24, 1963; 1 child, Jennifer Hilary. BS, Fresno State U., 1963; MBA, U. Calif., Berkeley, 1965. Asst. treas. Boeing Co., Seattle, 1975-87, v.p., treas., 1987—; dir. Pvt. Export Funding Corp. Mem. Fin. Execs. Inst. Republican. Lutheran. Office: The Boeing Co PO Box 3707 Stop 10-20 Seattle WA 98124-2207

JAEGER, JEFF TODD, professional football player; b. Tacoma, Wash., Nov. 26, 1964. Student, Wash. Coll. With Cleve. Browns, 1987; kicker L.A. Raiders, 1989—. Office: LA Raiders 332 Center St El Segundo CA 90245-4047*

JAFFE, CHARLES J., allergist; b. Phila., Feb. 3, 1946. MD, Duke U., 1971, PhD, 1972. Allergist Scripps Meml. Hosp., Encinitas, Calif.; prof. allergy and immunology U. Calif., San Diego. Office: 477 N El Camino Real Ste A308 Encinitas CA 92024-1329*

JAFFE, F. FILMORE, judge; b. Chgo., May 4, 1918; s. Jacob Isadore and Goldie (Rabinowitz) J.; m. Mary Main, Nov. 7, 1942; children: Jo Anne, Jay. Student, Southwestern U., 1936-39; J.D., Pacific Coast U., 1940. Bar: Calif. 1945, U.S. Supreme Ct. 1964. Practiced law Los Angeles, 1945-91; ptnr. Bernard & Jaffe, Los Angeles, 1947-74, Jaffe & Jaffe, Los Angeles, 1975-91; apptd. referee Superior Ct. of Los Angeles County, 1991—, apptd. judge pro tem, 1991—; mem. L.A. Traffic Commn., 1947-48; arbitrator Am. Arbitration Assn., 1968-91; chmn. pro bono com. Superior Ct. Calif., County of Los Angeles, 1980-86; lectr. on paternity. Served to capt. inf. AUS, 1942-45. Decorated Purple Heart, Croix de Guerre with Silver Star, Bronze Star with oak leaf cluster; honored Human Rights Commn. Los Angeles, Los Angeles County Bd. Suprs.; recipient Pro Bono award State Bar Calif., commendation State Bar Calif., 1983. Mem. ABA, Los Angeles County Bar (honored by family law sect. 1983), Los Angeles Criminal Ct. Bar Assn. (charter mem.), U.S. Supreme Ct. Bar Assn., Masons, Shriners. Office: Superior Ct LA County 111 N Hill St Los Angeles CA 90012-3117

JAFFER, ADRIAN MICHAEL, physician; b. Cape Town, S. Africa, Aug. 24, 1943; came to U.S., 1969; s. George Daniel Jaffer and Theresa (Kourie) Binsted; children: Brendan, Terence. MBChB, U. Cape Town Med. Sch., 1966. Diplomate Am. Coll. Physicians. Intern Loyola Univ. Hosp., Maywood, Ill., 1969-70; resident Northwestern U., Chgo., 1970-72; fellow Harvard U., Boston, 1972-73, Scapps Clinic & Rsch., LaJolla, Calif., 1973-75, Northwestern U., Chgo., 1975-76; pvt. practice LaJolla, 1976—; assoc. clin. prof. U. Calif. San Diego, LaJolla, 1976—. Contbr. articles to profl. jours. Mem. AMA, Am. Coll. Rheumotology, Am. Acad. Allergy. Office: 9850 Genesee Ave Ste 860 La Jolla CA 92037-1219

JAGER, MERLE LEROY, aerospace engineer; b. Eugene, Oreg., Sept. 22, 1942; s. Earl Christian and Alma Marie (Jensen) J.; m. Shannon Kay Jacobsen, Mar. 18, 1967; children: Holly, Peter, Melanie, Marissa,. BS in Mech. Engring., Oreg. State U., 1965; MS in Aeronautical Engring., U. So. Calif., 1967. Aerodynamicist Lockheed-Calif. Co., Burbank, 1965-68; rsch. engr. The Boeing Co., Seattle, 1968-70; aerodynamics engr. Gates Learjet Corp., Torrance, Calif., 1970; project engr. Irvin Industries, Inc., Gardena, Calif., 1971-73; aerodynamics mgr. Northrop Corp., Hawthorne, Calif., 1973-91; mgr. flight mechanics Northrop Corp., Pico Rivera, Calif., 1991—. Patentee in field. Treas. Goldenwest Assn., Westminster, Calif., 1976-78; tribal chief YMCA Indian Princess Program, Huntington Beach, Calif., 1986-87; bishopric counselor Mormon Ch., Westminster, 1986—. Mem. AIAA, Tau Beta Pi, Pi Tau Sigma, Sigma Tau. Republican. Home: 15282 Notre Dame St Westminster CA 92683-6117 Office: Northrop Corp Aircraft Div Advanced Tech/Design Ctr 8900 E Washington Blvd Pico Rivera CA 90660

JAGNOW, DAVID HENRY, petroleum geologist; b. Dubuque, Iowa, Nov. 24, 1947; s. Albert August and Ardath Helen (Goettsch) J.; divorced; children: Daniel David, Robert Carl, Beth Laura. BA in Geology, U. Iowa, 1970; MS in Geology, U. N.Mex., 1977. Exploration geologist Shell Oil Co., Houston, 1973-77; staff geologist Energy Reserves Group, Denver, 1977-78; exploration mgr. Donald C. Slawson Oil Producer, Oklahoma City, 1978-82; consulting geologist pvt. practice, Edmond, Okla., 1982-87, Los Alamos, N.Mex., 1987—; venture capitalist Venture Calital Info., Edmond, 1986-87, Los Alamos, 1987—; dir. Pure Water Technologies, Albuquerque, 1991-93; caves & karst task force Bur. Land Mgmt., Carlsbad, N.Mex., 1991-93, Guadalupe caverns geology panel Nat. Park Svc., Carlsbad, 1993. Author: Cavern Development in the Guadalupe Mountains, 1979, Stories From Stones, 1992. Conservation chair, v.p. Pajarito Grotto, Los Alamos, 1993-94. Recipient Gov.'s Dist. Svc. award Gov. Iowa, 1970, W.A. Tarr award Sigma Gamma Epsilon, 1970, Lowden prize Geology U. Iowa, 1970. Fellow Nat. Speleological Soc.; mem. Am. Assn. Petroleum Geologists, N.Mex. Entrepreneurs Assn. (bd. dirs. 1988-89), Cave Rsch. Found. (chief scientist 1988-89), Omicron Delta Kappa. Lutheran. Office: Venture Capital Info Inc 901 18th St # 11300 Los Alamos NM 87544-4001

JAHN, E. MARK, research specialist; b. Evanston, Ill., Apr. 24, 1955; s. Richard g. and Lois (Koenig) J.; m. Joanne Musselwhite, Sept. 15, 1979 (div. Aug. 1993); children: Jenna P., Janelle A. AAS, Harper Coll., Palatine, Ill., 1978; BS, Calif. Poly. State U., 1982; MA, San Diego State U., 1992. Mfg. engr. Storage Tech., Louisville, 1982-84; mfg. rsch. engr. Rohr Industries, Inc., Chula Vista, Calif., 1984-86; sr. quality engr. Info. Magnetics, San Diego, 1986-87; engring. supr. Johnson & Johnson, ACO, San Diego, 1987-89; rsch. specialist Rohr, Inc., Chula Vista, Calif., 1990—; prin. Mfg. Methods Cons., Jamul, Calif., 1989—; adj. prof. mech. engring. San Diego State U., 1987-90. Inventor method of manufacturing laminated plastic tooling and tooling produced thereby. Advisor Nat. U., San Diego, 1987-88. Mem. Soc. for the Advancement of Material and Process Engring. Office: Rohr Inc 850 Lagoon Dr Chula Vista CA 91910-2001

JAIN, ARVIND, engineer; b. New Delhi, India, Mar. 10, 1965; came to U.S., 1989; s. Harbanslal Loonkarandas and Shakuntala (Kishorilai) J.; m. Pavana Padmarajiah Adhikari, Dec. 6, 1990. Diploma in electronis, D.I.M.S., Bombay, India, 1982; BME, Gulbarga (India) U., 1987; diploma in computer sci., Zodiac Computer Acad., 1988; MS, U. South Miss., 1990. Project coord. (Divsn. of West Germany) Heiza, Bombay, 1988-89; rsch. asst. U. South Miss., Hattiesburg, 1989-90; design engr. Nordskog Ind. Inc., Van Nuys, Calif., 1990, structural strength engr., 1990-92, sr. stress engr., 1992-93; pres. Pacific Hope Program Inc., Irvine, Calif., 1993—; sr. stress engr. Aircraft Products Co., Delray Beach, Fla., 1993—; dir. Pacific Hope Program Inc., Irvine, 1993—; cons. engr., 1994—. Author: Static Test Methods for - Sandwich Composites, 1994; inventor parametric design system; contbr. articles to profl. jours. Mem. ASME (affiliate), SME (chmn. 1989-90), Am. Soc. of Quality Control (student mem. 1989-90). Home: 105 Chatham Ct Boynton Beach FL 33436-2851 Office: Nordskog Ind Inc PO Box 130 Delray Beach FL 33447-0130

JALAL, MAHBUBUL A.F., research chemist; b. Sylhet, Bangladesh, Dec. 31, 1948; came to U.S., 1982; s. Muhammad Nasibur Rahman and Kamrun Nesa Khanam; m. Ayesha Shirin Majumdar, Jan. 4, 1973; children: Adib Adnan, Niaz Ahsan, Sahel Afsan. BS with honors, U. Dhaka, Bangladesh, 1968, MS, 1969; PhD, U. Liverpool, Eng., 1977; MIBiol., CBiol. (hon.), Inst. of Biology, London, 1981. Chartered biologist, Eng. Lectr. plant scis. U. Dhaka, 1970-73, U. Chittagong, Bangladesh, 1973; postdoctoral assoc. dept. chemistry U. Glasgow, Scotland, 1977-78; postdoctoral assoc. depts. chemistry and botany U. Sheffield, Eng., 1978-82; rsch. scientist dept. chemistry U. Okla., Norman, 1982-88; scientist Plant Cell Rsch. Inst., Dublin, Calif., 1988-91; sr. rsch. chemist Pan-Agrl. Labs., Madera, Calif., 1991-94; rsch. chemist Valent USA Corp., 1995—. Contbr. chpts. to books, more than 30 articles to profl. jours.; patentee microbial method. Mem. Am. Chem. Soc., Inst. of Biology (London). Home: 1421 E Salem Ave Fresno CA 93720-2240 Office: Pan-Agrl Labs 6560 Trinity Ct Dublin CA 94568

JALLINS, RICHARD DAVID, lawyer; b. L.A., Mar. 21, 1957; s. Walter Joshua and Elaine Beatrice (Youngerman) J.; m. Katherine Sue Pfeiffer, June 12, 1982; children: Stephen David, Rachel Marie. BA, U. Calif., Santa Barbara, 1978; JD, Calif. Western Sch. Law, 1981. Bar: Calif. 1988, U.S. Dist. Ct. (so. dist.) Calif. 1988. Panel atty. Bd. Prison Terms, Sacramento, 1989—, Appellate Defenders, Inc., San Diego, 1989-91, Calif. Dept. Corrections, Parole Hearings Divsn., Sacramento, 1992-94. Mem. ABA, Calif. Prisoners Rights Union, San Diego County Bar Assn., Phi Alpha Delta. Home: 11857 Via Hacienda El Cajon CA 92019-4096

JAMAR, PETER NORTON, urban planner; b. Duluth, Minn., Jan. 4, 1957; s. Norton and Joan Helen (Hanson) J. BA, Gustavus Adolphus Coll., 1979; postgrad., U. Colo., 1979-81. Town planner Town of Vail, Colo., 1980-83; dir. planning Berridge Assocs., Inc., San Francisco, 1983-87; pres. Peter Jamar Assoc., Inc., Vail, 1987—; cons. in field. Mem. Urban Land Inst., Am. Planning Assn., Am. Inst. Cert. Planners (cert.), Coldstream Assn. (bd. dirs. 1987-90), Cascade Club. Office: Peter Jamar Assocs Inc 108 S Frontage Rd W Vail CO 81657-5053

JAMES, ANTHONY AMADÉ, molecular biologist, educator; b. Ypsilanti, Mich., Nov. 16, 1951; s. Bernard Benedict and Florence (Fitzgerald) J. BSc in Biology, U. Calif., Irvine, 1973, PhD in Developmental Genetics, 1979. Postdoctoral fellow in biol. chemistry Harvard U., Boston, 1979-83, asst. prof. Tropical Pub. Health, 1985-89; postdoctoral fellow in biology Brandeis U., Waltham, Mass., 1983-85; asst. prof. molecular biology and biochemistry U. Calif., Irvine, 1989-93, assoc. prof. molecular biology and biochemistry, 1993—. Author: (with others) Tropical and Geographical Medicine, 2d edit., 1990; editor Insect Molecular Biology, 1991—; contbr. articles to profl. jours. Fellow Med. Found., Inc., 1982-84, Am. Cancer Soc., 1980-81. Fellow Royal Entomol. Soc. (Burroughs-Wellcome Fund scholar award in Molecular Parsitology, 1994), AAAS; mem. Am. Soc. Tropical Medicine and Hygiene, Am. Com. on Vector Entomology, Entomol. Soc. Am., Genetics Soc. Am. Office: U Calif Dept Molecular Biology Irvine CA 92717

JAMES, BARRY ALAN, import-export consultant; b. Detroit, July 12, 1941; s. Frank Szydlowski and Genivieve (Nienaltowski) James; m. Patricia martha Springer, Dec. 1, 1961; children: Patrick B., Kelly A. BA in Bus., Wayne State U., 1965; M Mktg., Mich. State U., 1969. Dist. mgr. Intermetro Industries, Wilkes Barre, Pa., 1971-78; v.p. mktg. Candie Corp. Am., Chgo., 1979-82; pres., CEO Meridian (USA) Ltd., Englewood, Colo., 1983-92; pres. James Assocs. (USA) Ltd., Englewood, 1993—; cons. World Tableware Internat., Wallingford, Conn., 1993-94. Patentee interlocking plastic shelving system. With USN, 1957-61. Mem. Jaycees (pres. 1970-72), Chinese C. of C. (bd. dirs. 1993-94). Republican. Roman Catholic. Home: 1228 Oakwood Ave Daytona Beach FL 32114-5755

JAMES, DARYL NORMAN, environmental engineer; b. Culver City, Calif., Feb. 2, 1946; s. Warren and Alayne (Meistral) Smith; m. June Alice McClow, June 24, 1978; children: Matthew Dwayne, Andrew David. A of Engring., El Camino Coll., 1966; BSME, Calif. State U., Long Beach, 1969. Registered profl. engr., Nev., Calif. Structural design engr. Northrup Corp., Hawthorne, Calif., 1969-70; mech. engr. Long Beach (Calif.) Naval Shipyard, 1970-73; recreation supr. City of Manhattan Beach, Calif., 1975-79; engring. technician Spink Corp., Reno, 1979-80; civil engr. Nev. Dept. Transp., Carson City, 1980-86, prin. engr., 1986-92, chief environ. svcs., 1992—. Appointed mem. Parks & Recreation Commn., Carson City, Nev., 1993-94. Home: 3782 Prospect Dr Carson City NV 89703-7529 Office: Nev Dept Transp 1263 S Stewart St Carson City NV 89701-5229

JAMES, DON, university athletic coach; m. Carol Hoobler; children: Jeff, Jill, Jeni. M.Ed., U. Kans., 1957. Grad. asst. U. Kans., 1956-57; tchr., coach Southwest Miami (Fla.) High Sch., 1957-59; asst. coach Fla. State U., 1959-66, U. Mich., 1966-68, U. Colo., 1968-70; head football coach Kent State U., 1971-74; head football coach U. Wash. Huskies, 1974-92, head coach Divsn. 1A football champions (tied with U. Miami), 1991; coach North-South Shrine Game, Miami, 1973, Ohio Shrine Game, 1973, 74, Am. Bowl, 1976, East-West Shrine Game, San Francisco, 1979, Japan Bowl, 1979. Served with Transp. Corps U.S. Army, 1954-56. Named Coach of Yr. Mid Am. Conf., 1972, Ohio Coach of Yr. Coll. Football Coaches Assn., 1972, Coach of Week UPI, 1977, Nat. Coach of Yr. Am. Football Coaches Assn., 1978, Nat. Coach of Yr. Athlon Publs., 1981, Pre-Season Coach of Yr. Playboy Mag., 1982; U. Wash. Rose Bowl Champions, 1978, 82, Sun Bowl Champions, 1979, Pac-10 Champions, 1980, 81, Aloha Bowl Champions, 1982, Orange Bowl Champions, 1985, Freedom Bowl Champions, 1985. Mem. Omega Delta Kappa. Lodge: Rotary. Office: U Wash Athletic Dept Graves Bldg Seattle WA 98195

JAMES, DOT (DOROTHY ANN JAMES), researcher, writer, fund-raiser, editor; b. San Antonio, Sept. 14, 1938; d. Royal Percy and Eloise (Ohlen) J. BA in History, So. Meth. U., 1960; MA in Edn., Stanford U., 1962; postgrad., U. San Francisco, 1984-85, U. Santa Cruz, 1987-88. Cert. in secondary edn., Calif., human svcs. counseling. Mgmt. analyst Dept. of Navy, Treasure Island, Calif., 1963-65; tchr. pub. high sch. Gilroy, Calif., 1965-69, Caldwell, Idaho, 1969-71; editor in chief Venus mag., Palo Alto, Calif., 1973-75; ptnr., chief exec. officer F.S. Button Mfg. Co., San Jose, Calif., 1975-83; exec. dir. AIDS Found. of Santa Clara County, San Jose, Calif., 1983-84; free-lance mgmt. cons. and writer San Jose, 1984—; office mgr. Adult Independence Devel. Ctr., Santa Clara, Calif., 1987; dir. vols. Emergency Housing Consortium, San Jose, 1987-88; coord. community devel. Shelter Against Violent Environments (S.A.V.E.), Fremont, Calif., 1988; with devel. office Santa Clara U., 1988-90; prin. Paladin Editorial Svcs., San Jose, 1990—. Designer/mfr. feminist slogan buttons housed in Women's Collection, Smithsonian Inst., Washington; contbr. monographs and articles to profl. pubs. Active various women's rights, environ., animal welfare, orgns. for developmentally and physically disabled, gay rights, pub. health groups, 1962—; bd. dirs. Aris Project, Campbell, Calif., 1987-88; crisis intervention counselor Suicide Crisis Svc. of Santa Clara County, San Jose; commr. City of San Jose Human Rights Commn. Grantee Nat. Def. Edn. Act, 1967, Coe Found., 1969; Nonprofit Orgn. Mgmt. Inst. scholar, 1984. Mem. Stanford Bay Area Profl. Women, Nat. Soc. of Fundraising Execs., Santa Clara County Hist. and Geneal. Soc. Democrat.

JAMES, FRANKLIN JOSEPH, JR., public policy educator; b. Tampa, Fla., Nov. 11, 1946; s. Franklin Joseph Sr. and Eve (Keene) J.; m. Melanie Anne Lee, Sept. 9, 1967 (dec. Dec. 1987); children: Charles, Philip. BA in Econs. with honors, U. Ga., 1967; MPhil in Econs., Columbia U., 1976, PhD in Econs., 1976. Rsch. asst. Nat. Bur. Econ. Rsch., N.Y.C., 1969-71; sr. rsch. economist Rutgers U., Ctr. for Urban Policy, New Brunswick, N.J., 1971-74; rsch. assoc. The Urban Inst., Washington, 1974-77; dir. urban policy staff U.S. Dept. Housing and Urban Devel., Washington, 1977-81; prof. pub. policy U. Colo., Denver, 1981—; dir. doctoral studies U. Colo. Grad. Sch. Pub. Affairs, Denver; mem. rsch. adv. com. Fed. Nat. Mortgage Assn., Washington; mem. adv. com. Ctr. Cmty. Devel., N.Y.C. Co-author: President's National Urban Policy Report, 1980, Minorities in the Sunbelt, 1984; co-editor: Future of National Urban Policy, 1990. Staff dir. Colo. Pub. Pvt. Housing State Task Force, Denver; rsch. Gov.'s Task Force on the Homeless, Denver; mem. Mayor's Disbursement Com. for Ryan White Fund, Denver. Mem. Phi Beta Kappa. Democrat. Episcopalian. Home: 546 E Nichols Dr Littleton CO 80122-2838

JAMES, FREBURN LEROY, pathologist, retired; b. Battle Creek, Mich., Mar. 11, 1921; s. Freburn Watson and Aelola Adelaide (Clark) J.; m. Nina Wilanna Johnson, Apr. 11, 1946; children: Cherelyn Yvette, Karyl Susan, Donald Freburn. BA, W.Va. U., 1944; MD, Loma Linda U., 1949. Diplomate Am. Bd. Pathology. Instr. pathology for nurses Glendale Sanitarium and Hosp., 1948-50; instr. histology extension course Camp Roberts U. Calif., Santa Barbara, 1952; pathologist, dir. labs. Boulder Colo. Sanitarium and Hosp., 1953-55; pathologist Boulder County Hosp., 1953-54; instr. pathology U. Colo. Med. Sch., Denver, 1954-55; asst. pathologist, dir. sch. of med. tech. St. Joseph's Hosp., Denver, 1955; pathologist, dir. labs., dir. sch. med. tech. Port Huron (Mich.) Hosp., 1955-62; pathologist, dir. labs. Westminster (Calif.) Community Hosp., 1962-67; dir. Clin. Lab. Freburn L. James, M.D., Huntington Beach, Calif., 1963-69; pathologist Orange (Calif.) County Med. Ctr., 1967-69; asst. clin. prof. pathology U. Calif., Irvine, 1969, Grand Valley State Coll., Allendale, Mich., 1982-83; pathologist, dir. various labs. ICN Med. Labs. (formerly United Med. Labs.), Portland, Oreg., 1969-80; pathologist, dir. Reese-James Pathology Lab., Portland, 1969-75, Officer Histology Assocs. Lab., P.C., Portland, 1975-80, Heritage Hosp. Lab., Muskegon Heights, Mich., 1980-86, Visitors Hosp. (formerly Unity Hosp. Lab.), Buchanan, Mich., 1981-87, Continental Bio-Clin. Lab. Svcs., Inc., Grand Rapids, Mich., 1980-88, Reed City (Mich.) Hosp. Lab., 1986-88, Three Rivers (Mich.) Area Hosp. Lab., 1986-88; locum tenens, pathologist Kennewick (Wash.) Gen. Hosp., 1990—, Sunnyside (Wash.) Hosp., 1990—, Our Lady of Lourdes Hosp., Pasco, Wash., 1990—, Western Labs., Yakima, Wash., 1990—; part-time worker Reed City Hosp. Lab., Three Rivers Area Hosp. Lab., Bio-Clin. Lab. Svcs., Inc., 1988-89. Capt., USAR, 1951-53. Fellow Am. Soc. Clin. Pathology, Coll. Am. Pathologists; mem. AMA, Am. Soc. Cytology.

JAMES, GARRY, executive editor; b. L.A., Jan. 24, 1944; s. Gerald Jerry and Betty Jane J.; m. Adrianna Wenda, Aug. 10, 1971 (div. Sept. 1989); 1 child, Alexandria Alice; m. Susan James, Nov. 3, 1990. BA, Calif. State U., Northridge, 1966. Newsman UPI, L.A., 1971; assoc. editor Petersen Pub., L.A., 1971-73, exec. editor, 1982—, editor, 1974-76; expert Sotheby-Parke Bennet, L.A., 1973-74; editor Calif. Real Estate mag., L.A., 1976; assoc. editor Architectural Digest, L.A., 1976-78; freelance writer L.A., 1978-82. Contbr. articles on antique firearms and military history to numerous jours. Bd. dirs. U.S. Firearms Mus., Washington, 1992—. Capt. U.S. Army, 1966-71, U.K. Republican. Office: Petersen Pub 6420 Wilshire Blvd Los Angeles CA 90048

JAMES, GEORG LEROY, broadcasting executive; b. Colorado Springs, Colo., June 10, 1942; s. Cecil H. and Madeline (Dillon) J.; m. Joanne P. James, Aug. 18, 1986; children from previous marriage, Kevin, Brandon James. Student, Pueblo Jr. Coll. Former gen. mgr., owner KPIK, Colorado Springs, announcer, chief engr., sales, mktg. and pub. rels. staff; mktg. dir. Security Pacific Indsl. Bank, 1980; v.p. engring. and devel. KIQX Radio Sta., Durango, Colo., 1982-85; announcer personality KKCS Radio Sta., Colorado Springs, 1985; owner, operator motel bus. Dillon Motel, Manitou Springs, 1987—; part-time co-host talk show Kvor Radio Sta., Colorado Springs, 1989-91. Mem. Fiesta and Rodeo Com., Snowdown Com.; mem. Manitou Springs Park and Recreation Adv. Bd., 1991; mem. Ambassadors Com., Mktg. Com., Manitou Springs; chmn. Accommodations Com. and Intergovtl. Affairs Com., Manitou Springs; mem. Colo. Springs City Coun., 1977-81; chmn. Ambulance Svc. Tech. Adv. Bd., Colorado Springs; mem. regional plumbing com. Regional Bldg. Dept.; bd. dirs. Nat. Little Britches Rodeo; mem. Pikes Peak Area Coun. Govts., 1977-81; chmn. gov. front range project El Paso County. Mem. Manitou Springs C. of C. (bd. dirs. 1993). Home and Office: 134 Manitou Ave Manitou Springs CO 80829-2427

JAMES, GEORGE BARKER, II, apparel industry executive; b. Haverhill, Mass., May 25, 1937; s. Paul Withington and Ruth (Burns) J.; m. Beverly A. Burch, Sept. 22, 1962; children: Alexander, Christopher, Geoffrey, Matthew. AB, Harvard U., 1959; MBA, Stanford U., 1962. Fiscal dir. E.G. & G. Inc., Bedford, Mass., 1963-67; fin. exec. Am. Brands Inc., N.Y.C., 1967-69; v.p. Pepsico, Inc., N.Y.C., 1969-72; sr. v.p., chief fin. officer Arcata Corp., Menlo Park, Calif., 1972-82; exec. v.p. Crown Zellerbach Corp., San Francisco, 1982-85; sr. v.p., chief fin. officer Levi Strauss & Co., San Francisco, 1985—; bd. dirs. Pacific States Industries, Inc., Basic Vegetable Products, Inc., Canned Foods Inc., Fibreboard Corp. Author: Industrial Development in the Ohio Valley, 1962. Mem. Andover (Mass.) Town Com., 1965-67; mem. Select Congl. Com. on World Hunger; mem. adv. coun. Calif. State Employees Pension Fund; chmn. bd. dirs. Towle Trust Fund; trustee Nat. Corp. Fund for the Dance, Cate Sch., Levi Strauss Found., Stern Grove Festival Assn., Zellerbach Family Fund, San Francisco Ballet Assn., Com. for Econ. Devel.; bd. dirs. Stanford U. Hosp., World Affairs Coun.; mem. San Francisco Com. on Fgn. Rels. With AUS, 1960-61. Mem. Pacific Union Club, Family Club, Bohemian Club, Menlo Circus Club, Harvard Club, N.Y. Athletic Club. Home: 207 Walnut St San Francisco CA 94118-2012 Office: Levi Strauss & Co Levi's Pla 1155 Battery St San Francisco CA 94111-1230

JAMES, HELEN ANN, plastic surgeon; b. Palmerston North, New Zealand, May 5, 1940; came to U.S., 1977; d. George Headley and Betty Beatrice (McDonald) J.; married (dec. Apr. 1993). MB, ChB, U. Otago, Dunedin, New Zealand, 1964; Fellow, Royal Coll. Surgeons, London, England, 1972. Diplomate Am. Bd. Plastic Surgery. Internship Palmerston North Hosp., New Zealand, 1965-66; residency plastic surgery Brdg Earn Hosp., Perthshire, England, 1973-74, St. Lukes Hosp., Bradford, England, 1975-77; fellow plastic surgery Mount Sinai Med. Ctr., Miami Beach, 1977-79; residency plastic surgery N.C. Meml. Med. Ctr., Chapel Hill, 1979-81; St. Joseph Hosp., Bellingham, Wash.; pvt. practice Bellingham, Wash. Mem. AMA, Am. Soc. Plastic and Reconstructive Surgeons, Wash. State Med. Assn. Office: 3001 Squalicum Pky Ste 5 Bellingham WA 98225-1932

JAMES, HERB MARK (JAY JAMES), foundation and insurance executive, free trade consultant; b. Trail, B.C., Can., Jan. 30, 1936; s. George William and Violet Ethyl (Corbin) J. Student, bus. adminstrn. Simon Fraser U., 1965-69; m. Patricia Helen Boyd, Nov. 1, 1958; 1 child, Brad Mark. Founder Internat. Sound Found., Ottawa, Can., 1967—, Blaine, Wash., 1975—; cons. Fed. Bus. Dev. Bank; mem. bus. adv. bd. U.S. Senate, 1981—; pres. Bus. Navigator Svcs.; cons. Can. Internat. Devel. Agy.; founder Better Hearing Better Life projects, Fiji, Kenya, Cayman Islands, Nepal, Costa Rica, Pakistan, Guatemala, Mex., Canada-Panama Assist Group, 1995—. Musician B. Pops Orch., South Pacific N.G.O. Group, Ctrl. European Enterprise Devel. Group, North-South Free Trade Adjustment Group. Govt. of Can. grantee, 1973-83. Mem. Christian Bus. Men's Assn., Can.-Philippines Soc. (co-founder), UN Armed Forces Assn. (regional dir.), Conbrio Soc. (hon. dir.), Blaine C. of C., Masons, Shriners, Demolay. Office: Am Bldg PO Box 1587 Blaine WA 98231-1587

JAMES, JEFFREY ALAN, military chaplain; b. Heidelberg, Germany, Feb. 21, 1962; came to the U.S., 1962; s. Robert Lowell and Pauline Dorothy (Erskine) J.; m. Mary Frances McLaren, July 25,1984 (dec. May 1992); m. Jerrie G. Lim, June 4, 1994. BA, Northwest Bible Coll., 1984; MDiv, Ch. of God Sch. Theology, 1987. Ordained minister Ch. of God, 1990. Youth min. Ch. of God, Lemmon, S.D., 1987-88; pastor Ch. of God, Mobridge, S.D., 1988; commd. 2d lt. USAF, 1988, advanced through grades to capt., 1988; chaplain USAF, Castle AFB, Calif., 1988-89, Travis AFB, Calif., 1989-93; chaplain FE Warren AFB, Fe Warren AFB, Wyo., 1993—; counselor Prepare/Enrich, Mpls., 1989—. Chaplain USAFR, 1987-88. Mem. Soc. for Pentecostal Studies. Republican. Home: 3200 Thomas Rd Cheyenne WY 82009-4553 Office: 90 MW/HC 7000 Randall Ave Fe Warren AFB WY 82005-2974

JAMES, MARION RAY, magazine founder, editor; b. Bellmont, Ill., Dec. 6, 1940; s. Francis Miller and Lorraine A. (Wylie) J.; m. Janet Sue Tennis, June 16, 1960; children: Jeffrey Glenn, David Ray, Daniel Scott, Cheryl Lynne. BS, Oakland City Coll., Ind., 1964; MS, St. Francis Coll., Fort Wayne, Ind., 1978. Sports and city editor Daily Clarion, Princeton, Ind., 1963-65; English tchr. Jac-Cen-Del High Sch., Osgood, Ind., 1965-66; indsl. editor Whirlpool Corp., Evansville and LaPorte, Ind., 1966-68, Magnavox Govt. and Indsl. Electronics Co., Fort Wayne, 1968-79; editor, pub., founder Bowhunter mag., Fort Wayne, Ind., 1971-88; editor Bowhunter mag., Kalispell, Mont., 1989—; instr. Ind.-Purdue U., Ft. Wayne, 1980-88. Author: Bowhunting for Whitetail and Mule Deer, 1975, Successful Bowhunting, 1985, My Place, 1991; editor: Pope and Young Book World Records, 1975, 2nd edit., 1993, Bowhunting Adventures, 1977. Recipient Best Editorial award United Community Svc. Publs., 1970-72; named Alumnus of Yr., Oakland City Coll., 1982, to Hall of Fame, Mt. Carmel High Sch., Ill., 1983. Mem. Outdoor Writers Assn. Am., Fort Wayne Assn. Bus. Editors (Fort Wayne Bus. Editor of Yr. 1969, pres. 1975-76), Toastmasters (Able Toastmaster award), Alpha Phi Gamma, Alpha Psi Omega, Mu Tau Kappa. Home: 600 Bayou Rd Kalispell MT 59901-6561

JAMES, MARK WILLIAM, cameraman; b. L.A., Nov. 10, 1954; s. William Dean J. and Barbara Elizabeth (Lyon) Harrison; m. Christine Marie McGarry, Mar 3, 1990; 1 child, William Scott. BA in Anthropology, Claif. State U., L.A., 1978; postgrad., UCLA, 1987. News cameraman KNBC-TV, 1987, 88, 90; freelance cameraman, 1987-88, 88-89, 1989-90, 90—; judge ATAS nat. and local Emmy, ACE awards. Mem. Nat. Press Club, Nat. Press Photographers Assb., L.A. Press Club (cert. merit 1992), L.A. Press Photographers Assn. Home: 2420 Los Olivos Ln La Crescenta CA 91214-3130

JAMES, MATTHEW CRAIG, programmer, analyst; b. San Diego, Mar. 13, 1967; s. Charles S. and Lenna S. (Mortti) J.; m. Traci Rieckmann, June 23, 1990. BSBA in MIS, Oreg. State U., 1990. Cert. computing profl. Programmer, analyst Safeco Life Ins. Co., Redmond, Wash., 1990-91; sr. programmer, analyst Blue Cross Blue Shield of Utah, Salt Lake City, 1991—. Mem. Assn. System Mgrs., Data Processing Mktg. Assn. Democrat. Office: Blue Cross Blue Shield Utah 2455 Parleys Way Salt Lake City UT 84109-1217

JAMES, NORMAN JOHN, plastic and reconstructive hand surgeon; b. Milw., Nov. 25, 1938. BA, Lawrence Coll., 1960; MD, U. Chgo., 1964. cert. gen. surgery, plastic surgery, hand surgery. Office: E235 Rowan St Ste 206 Spokane WA 99207-1240

JAMES, SONDRA MAE MARGARET, nurse; b. Lincoln, Nebr., July 30, 1944; d. James Henry Anthony and Mae (Rucksdashel) Croghan. RN, St. Mark's Hosp. Sch. Nursing, 1965; BA in Social Psychology, U. Nev., 1990, MA in Counseling & Ednl. Psychology, 1994. RN St. Mark's Hosp., Salt Lake City, 1965-68, Dr. Charles D. Behrens, Salt Lake City, 1968-71, Valley West Hosp., Salt Lake City, 1971-73, William B. Ririe Hosp., Ely, Nev., 1973-77, White Pine Care Ctr., Ely, 1978-82, Washoe Med. Ctr., Reno, 1982—; pvt. practice marriage and family therapy intern Reno, 1994—. Crisis line vol. Suicide Crisis Line, Reno, 1987-88. Mem. ACA, Internat. Assn. Marriage and Family Counselors, Am. Assn. Marriage and Family Therapists, Nev. Assn. Marriage and Family Therapists. Office: 248 W 1st St Ste 106 Reno NV 89501

JAMES, STAN LAWRENCE, surgeon; b. Kalona, Iowa, July 2, 1931; s. Thomas R. and Alice A. (Welsh) J.; divorced; children: Heather A., Brett A., Blake T.; m. Julie Carol Keller. BA, U. Iowa, 1953, MD, 1962. Intern Emanuel Hosp., Portland, Oreg., 1962-63; resident U. Iowa, Iowa City, 1963-64, resident in orthopaedic surgery, 1964-67; pvt. practice Eugene, Oreg., 1967—; clin. assoc. prof. surgery Oreg. Health Scis. U., Portland; orthopedic cons. U.S. Nordic Ski Team, 1982; courtsey prof. dept. exercise and movement sci. U. Oreg., Eugene, adv. bd. internat. inst. for health and sport scis., 1993-94; team physician Athletics West Track and Field Club, Eugene, 1978-85; med. dir. U.S. Olympic Trials, Eugene, 1976, 80; sports medicine cons. Korean Nat. Sports Program, Seoul, 1983; rsch. cons. Nike, Inc., Beaverton, Oreg., 1976-83. Contbr. articles to profl. jours. Capt. U S. Army, 1953-56. Fellow Am. Acad. Orthopaedic Surgeons, Am. Coll. Sports Medicine; mem. North Pacific Orthopaedic Soc., AMA, Phi Beta Kappa, Phi Epsilon Kappa, Alpha Kappa Kappa. Home: 2895 Arline Way Eugene OR 97403-2527 Office: Orthopedic & Fracture Clinc 1200 Hilyard St Ste 600 Eugene OR 97401-8131

JAMES, VIRGINIA LYNN, contracts executive; b. March AFB, Calif., Feb. 6, 1952; d. John Edward and Azella Virginia (Morrill) Anderson; children: Raymond Edward, Jerry Glenn Jr. Student, Sinclair Community Coll., 1981-83, U. Tex., San Antonio, 1980, Redlands U., 1986, San Diego State U., 1994. With specialized contracting USAF, Wright-Patterson AFB, Ohio, 1973-77; with logistics contracting USAF, Kelly AFB, Tex., 1977-81; contract specialist USAF, Wright-Patterson AFB, Ohio, 1981-84; spl. asst. Peace Log, Tehran, Iran, 1977; acting chief of contracts cruise missile program Gen. Dynamics/Convair, San Diego, 1984-86; contracts mgr. VERAC, Inc., San Diego, 1986-90, Gen. Dynamics, San Diego, 1990-92; mgr. contracts Scientific-Atlanta, San Diego, 1992-93; dir. contracts GreyStone, San Diego, 1993—; cons. Gen. Dynamics, San Diego, 1985, Efratrom, 1986. Mem. Nat. Assn. Female Execs., Nat. Mgmt. Assn., Nat. Contract Mgmt. Assn. Republican. Office: GreyStone Tech 15010 Avenue Of Science Ste 200 San Diego CA 92128-3422

JAMES, WAYNE EDWARD, electrical engineer; b. Racine, Wis., Apr. 2, 1950; s. Ronald Dean James and Arlene Joyce (Mickelsen) Dawson; m. Bertie Darlene Tague, July 18, 1972; children: Terry Scott, Kevin Arthur. BS in Electronic Engring. Tech., U. So. Colo., 1976. Electronic technician Lawrence Livermore (Calif.) Nat. Lab., 1976-80; electronic technician Inmos Corp., Colorado Springs, Colo., 1980-86, CAD engr., 1986-87; CAD engr. United Techs. Microelectronics Ctr., Colorado Springs, 1988—. Sec.-treas. Stratmoor Hills Vol. Fire Dept., Colorado Springs, 1983, 84, lt., 1985, capt., 1986. Served with USN, 1968-72. Named Fireman of Yr., Stratmoor Hills Vol. Fire Dept., 1983. Lutheran. Office: United Techs Microelectronics Ctr 1575 Garden Of The Gods Rd Colorado Springs CO 80907-3415

JAMES, WILLIAM LANGFORD, aerospace engineer; b. Southampton, Va., Jan. 13, 1939; s. Leroy and Worthie (Murphy) J.; m. Elaine Cecilia Reed; children: William Jr., Terri Lynne. Student, Va. State Coll., 1956, Hampton Inst., 1958; BS, Calif. State U., Los Angeles, 1962, MS, 1964; postgrad., U. Nev., Reno, 1984; spl. engring. studies, UCLA, 1970-82. Rsch. engr. non-metallic materials lab. N.Am. Aviation, L.A., 1960-67; rsch. analyst tech. staff The Aerospace Corp., El Segundo, 1967-75, materials engr., 1975-85; project engr. program mgmt. office space launch ops. The Aerospace Corp., El Segundo, Calif., 1985—. Contbr. numerous articles and reports to profl. publs.; patentee in field. Recipient numerous awards for USAF space contributions. Mem. AAAS, Soc. Advancement Material and Process Engring. (vice-chmn. 1987-89). Home: PO Box 19735 Los Angeles CA 90019-0735 Office: Aerospace Corp M5 712 M5 712th Los Angeles CA 90009

JAMESON, DAVID LEE, evolutionary biologist; b. Ranger, Tex., June 3, 1927; s. Aubrey Murl and Gertrude (Harwood) J.; m. Marianne Mayo, June 11, 1949; children: Roy Alan, David Laurence, Robert Carey, Carol Lee. Student, So. Meth. U., 1948, U. Tex., 1952. Asst. prof. biology Pacific U., Forest Grove, Oreg., 1952-53, U. Oreg., Eugene, 1953-57; prof. biology San Diego State U., 1957-67; prof. biology U. Houston, 1967-91, dean grad. sch., 1971-74; sr. rsch. fellow Calif. Acad. Scis., San Francisco, 1989—. Editor Am. Soc. Ichthyologists & Herpetologists, 1960-65; author: Genetics of Speciation, 1977, Evolutionary Genetics, 1977; contbr. more than 85 articles to profl. jours. With USN, 1944-46, PTO. Grantee A.E.C., O.N.R., NSF, NIH. Fellow AAAS; mem. Soc. for the Study of Evolution (sec. 1970-76). Home: 634 El Pintado Danville CA 94526-1405 Office: Calif Acad of Sci Golden Gate Park San Francisco CA 94118

JAMIESON, DALE WALTER, philosophy and biology educator; b. Sioux City, Iowa, Oct. 21, 1947; s. Dale Walter and Betty Jo (Smith) J.; m. Toby Carlin Jacober, Sept. 23, 1988. BA, San Francisco State U., 1970; MA, U. N.C., 1972, PhD, 1976. Instr., asst. prof. N.C. State U., Raleigh, 1975-78; asst. prof. SUNY, Fredonia, 1978-80; asst. prof. U. Colo., Boulder, 1980-85, assoc. prof., 1985-92, prof. environmental philosophy and philosophy biology, 1992—. Co-editor: Interpretation and Explanation in the Study of Animal Behavior, 1990, Reflecting on Nature, 1994. Office: U Colorado Dept Philosophy CB 232 Boulder CO 80309

JAMIESON, JAMES BRADSHAW, foundation administrator; b. L.A., June 10, 1931; s. Charles Cameron and Ruth (Bradshaw) J.; m. Perry McNaughton, Dec. 27, 1959; children: Jeffrey McNaughton, Dalton Charles. AA, Citrus Coll., 1950; BA, Claremont Men's Coll., 1955; MA, Claremont Grad. Sch., 1958; PhD, Brown U., 1966. Assoc. prof. polit. studies Pitzer Coll. and Claremont Grad. Sch., 1968-75; rsch. polit. scientist UCLA, 1972-73; v.p. for devel. Pitzer Coll., 1968-72, v.p., 1973-78, prof. polit. studies, 1975-83, exec. v.p., 1979-83, acting pres., 1978-79; prof. govt. Claremont Grad. Sch., 1975-87; v.p. for rsch. Claremont McKenna Coll., 1983-87; exec. dir. Found. for Performing Art Ctr., San Luis Obispo, Calif., 1987—; commr. Calif. Postsecondary Edn. Commn., Sacramento, 1987-92; dir. Global Village, Seattle, 1989—. Contbr. articles to profl. jours. Staff, sec. Ctrl. Coast Performing Arts Ctr. Commn., San Luis Obispo, 1993—. Sgt. USAF, 1950-52. Fellow Brown U., 1960, 63, teaching fellow, 1962, fellow Resources for the Future, 1964; rsch. grantee U.S. Dept. Interior, 1972-73. Mem. Santa Lucia Flyfishers (bd. dirs. 1988—), Trout Unltd. (bd. dirs. Calif. coun. 1989-94, bd. dirs. nat. bd. 1986-90), Marine's Meml. Club. Office: Found for Performing Arts 1160 Marsh St Ste 302 San Luis Obispo CA 93401-3312

JAMIESON NICHOLS, JILL, journalist; b. Denver, Sept. 20, 1956; d. Paul Clark Jr. and Dorothy Marie (Pulley) Jamieson; m. Kevin Shawn Nichols, July 9, 1953; 1 child, Holly Marie Nichols. BA in Mass Comms., U. So. Colo., 1979. Reporter, photographer Bent County Democrat, Las Animas, Colo., 1979-81, Valley Courier, Alamosa, Colo., 1981-83; assoc. editor Canyon Courier, Evergreen, Colo., 1983-87, Golden (Colo.) Transcript, 1987—. Mem. Jeffco Local Emergency Planning Com., Golden, 1988-89. Recipient Cmty. Svc. award Colo. Press Assn., 1986, 94, Sweepstakes Best News Story award, 1989, Shining Star award, 1993, Best Feature Story award, 1994. Republican. Home: 2014 Washington Cir Golden CO 80401-2363 Office: Golden Transcript 1000 10th St Golden CO 80401-1028

JAMIN, MATTHEW DANIEL, lawyer, magistrate judge; b. New Brunswick, N.J., Nov. 29, 1947; s. Matthew Bernard and Frances Marie (Newburg) J.; m. Christine Frances Bjorkman, June 28, 1969; children: Rebecca, Erica. BA, Colgate U., 1969; JD, Harvard U., 1974. Bar: Alaska 1974, U.S. Dist. Ct. Alaska 1974, U.S. Ct. Appeals (9th cir.) 1980. Staff atty. Alaska Legal Svcs., Anchorage, 1974-75; supervising atty. Alaska Legal Svcs., Kodiak, Alaska, 1975-81; contract atty. Pub. Defender's Office State of Alaska, Kodiak, 1976-82; prin. Matthew D. Jamin, Atty., Kodiak, 1982; ptnr. Jamin & Bolger, Kodiak, 1982-85, Jamin, Ebell, Bolger & Gentry, Kodiak, 1985—; part-time magistrate judge U.S. Cts., Kodiak, 1984—. Part-time instr. U. Alaska Kodiak Coll., 1975—; active Theshold Svcs., Inc., Kodiak, 1985—, pres., 1985-92; active Kodiak Alliance for Mentally Ill, 1993—. Mem. Alaska Bar Assn. (Professionalism award 1988), Kodiak Bar Assn. Office: US Dist Ct 323 Carolyn Ave Kodiak AK 99615-6348

JAMPOL, JEFFREY, music industry executive; b. L.A., Sept. 16, 1958; s. Richard Alan and Sylvia X. (Levine) J. Student, Sonoma State U., 1974-76; BA, San Francisco State U., 1978. Retail mgmt. CBS, Inc., San Francisco, 1976-78; local promotion CBS, Inc. Epic Records, San Francisco, 1978-79, WEA, Inc. Atlantic Records, San Francisco, 1979-81; exec. producer Polymedia, Inc., Beverly Hills, Calif., 1981-83; nat. advt./promotion mgr. Music Connection Mag., Hollywood, Calif., 1983-84; nat. advt. dir. Gold Trade Publ., Inc., Encino, Calif., 1984-89; v.p., assoc. publisher Coast Media, Inc., Culver City, Calif., 1990-94; sr. v.p., ptnr. Brentwood News Group, Inc., Westwood, Calif., 1990; prin. Jampol Artist Mgmt., L.A., 1993—. Mem. Nat. Acad. Rec. Arts and Scis. (bd. dirs. L.A. chpt. 1983-85, voting mem. 1985—), Westchester/LAX C. of C. (bd. dirs. 1992-93), Culver City Jaycees, Santa Monica Jaycees. Democrat. Office: 2546 Westwood Blvd Los Angeles CA 90064-3240

JAMSHIDIPOUR, YOUSEF, bank executive, economist, financial planner; b. Arak, Iran, July 7, 1935; came to U.S., 1991; s. Hossein and Kobra (Sohrabi) J.; m. Aghdas Jalaifar, 1938; children: Ramin, Lily, Katia. BA, Tehran U., 1959, MBA, 1961; MA, The Am. U., 1963; MPA, Harvard U., 1973; postgrad., U. Mich., U. Colo. Dir. gen. Bank Markazi Iran, Tehran, 1963-76; v.p. Iranian Inst. of Banking, Tehran, 1973-78; exec. v.p., mem. exec. bd. Bank Melli Iran, Tehran, 1976-80; exec. v.p. D.M.I., Geneva, Switzerland, 1981-88; sr. fin. advisor Hill Samuel Investment Svc., London, 1988-91; fin. cons. 1st Affiliated Securities, Irvine, Calif., 1991-93; fin. planner IDS Fin. Svcs., Irvine, 1993-95; financial advisor Am. Express Fin. Advisors Inc., Irvine, 1995—; lectr. U. Tehran, 1973-78. Contbr. articles to profl. jours. Home: 26541 Laurel Crest Dr Laguna Hills CA 92653-7550 Office: Am Express Fin Advisors 2 Park Plz Irvine CA 92714

JANDA, JOHN MICHAEL, microbiologist, researcher; b. Burbank, Calif., Nov. 4, 1949; s. Bernard Frederick and Mary Ellis (Alexopoulos) J.; m. Claudia Beth Kissling, June 2, 1979; children: John Michael Jr., Matthew David, Jennifer Megan. BS in Biology, Loyola U., Westchester, Calif., 1971; MS in Microbiology, Calif. State U., L.A., 1975; PhD in Microbiology and Immunology, UCLA, 1979; postdoctoral studies, The Mt. Sinai Med. Ctr., N.Y.C., 1979-81. Diplomate Am. Bd. Med. Microbiology and Pub. Health; cert. pub. health microbiologist, Calif.; lic. clin. microbiologist, Calif. Asst. dir., prof. The Mt. Sinai Hosp. and Med. Ctr., N.Y.C., 1981-84, assoc. dir., prof., 1984-86; rsch. microbiologist Microbial Diseases Lab., Berkeley, Calif., 1986-90, rsch. scientist, 1990—, chief enterics and spl. pathogens sect., 1994—; lectr. ASM Found. for Microbiology, 1994—. Mem. editl. bd. European Jour. Clin. Microbiology and Infectious Diseases; contbr. articles to profl. jours. and newsletters, chpts. to books. Recipient Disting. Alumni award Calif. State U. L.A., 1993; NIH predoctoral fellow, 1977-79; species Aeromonas jandaei named in honor of sci. contributions, 1991. Mem. Am. Soc. Microbiology (subcom. facultative anaerobic gram negative rods 1987-90), Phi Kappa Phi. Roman Catholic. Office: Microbial Diseases Lab 2151 Berkeley Way Berkeley CA 94704-1011

JANDA, KIM D., chemist; b. Cleve., Aug. 23, 1958; married; children: Nikole, Christopher. BS, U. South Fla., 1980; MS, U. Ariz., 1983, PhD, 1984. Adj. asst. mem. dept. molecular biology Rsch. Inst. Scripps Clinic, La Jolla, Calif., 1987-88, asst. prof. dept. molecular biology, 1989-90, assoc. prof. dept. molecular biology and chem., 1991-92, assoc. prof., 1993—; cons. Procter and Gamble, Unilever Rsch., Inc.; sci. adv. bd. mem. Catalytic Antibodies, Inc., Found. CombiChem.; lectr. in field. Contbr. numerous articles to profl. jours. Named Scholar Athlete of Yr. U. South Fla., 1979-80; recipient Alfred P. Sloan fellowship, 1993-95, NIH First award, 1990-95, Carl S. Marvel fellowship U. Ariz., 1984; numerous other grants. Fellow Am. Inst. Chemists; mem. Am. Chem. Soc., Themis Honor Soc., Sigma Phi

Epsilon. Office: The Scripps Rsch Inst 10666 N Torrey Pines Rd La Jolla CA 92037-1027

JANES, ROBERT ROY, museum director, archaeologist,; b. Rochester, Minn., Apr. 23, 1948; m. Priscilla Bickel; children: Erica Helen, Peter Bickel. Student, Lawrence U., 1966-68, BA in Anthropology cum laude, 1970; student, U. of the Ams., Mexico City, 1968, U. Calif., Berkeley, 1968-69; PhD in Archaeology, U. Calgary, Alta., Can., 1976. Postdoctoral fellow Arctic Inst. N.Am., U. Calgary, 1981-82; adj. prof. archaeology U. Calgary, 1990—; founding dir. Prince of Wales No. Heritage Centre, Yellowknife, N.W.T., 1976-86, project dir. Dealy Island Archaeol. and Conservation Project, 1977-82; founding exec. dir. Sci. Inst. of N.W.T.; sci. advisor Govt. of N.W.T., Yellowknife, 1986-89; dir., chief exec. officer Glenbow Mus., Calgary, 1989—; adj. prof. anthropology U. Calgary, 1990—. Author manuscripts, monographs, book chpts.; contbr. articles to profl. jours. mem. First Nations/CMA Task Force on Mus. and First Peoples, 1989-92. Recipient Nat. Pks. Centennial award Environment Can., 1985, Can. Studies Writing award Assn. Can. Studies, 1989, Disting. Alumni award Alumni Assn. of U. Calgary, 1989, L.R. Briggs Disting. Achievement award Lawrence U., 1991; Can. Coun. doctoral fellow, 1973-76; rsch. grantee Govt. of Can., 1974, Social Scis. and Humanities Rsch. Coun. Can., 1988-89. Fellow Arctic Inst. N.Am. (bd. dirs. 1983-90, vice chmn. bd. 1985-89, hon. rsch. assoc. 1983-84, chmn. priorities and planning com. 1983-84, mem. exec. com. 1984-86, adv. editor Arctic jour. 1987—), Am. Anthrop. Assn. (fgn. fellow); mem. Soc. for Am. Archaeology, Can. Archaeol. Assn. (v.p. 1980-82, pres 1984-86, co-chmn. fed. heritage policy com. 1986-88), Current Anthropology (assoc.), Can. Mus. Assn. (hon. life mem., cert. accreditation 1982, Outstanding Achievement award in Mus. Mgmt. 1992), Am. Assn. Mus., Alta. Mus. Assn. (moderator seminars 1990, Merit award 1992), Internat. Coun. Mus., Can. Art Mus. Dirs. Orgn. (mem.-at-large bd. dirs.), Mus. West (bd. dirs.), Ranchmen's Club, Calgary Philharmonic Soc., Sigma Xi. Home: Box 32 Site 32, RR 12, Calgary, AB Canada T3E 6W3 Office: Glenbow Mus-AB Inst, 130 9 Ave SE, Calgary, AB Canada T2G 0P3

JANIGIAN, BRUCE JASPER, lawyer, educator; b. San Francisco, Oct. 21, 1950; s. Michael D. Janigian and Stella (Minasian) Amerian; m. Susan Elizabeth Frye, Oct. 4, 1986; children: Alan Michael, Alison Elizabeth. AB, U. Calif., Berkeley, 1972; JD, U. Calif., San Francisco, 1975; LLM, George Washington U., 1982. Bar: Calif. 1975, U.S. Supreme Ct. 1979, D.C. 1981. Dir. Hastings Rsch. Svcs., Inc., San Francisco, 1973-75; judge adv. in Spain, 1976-78; atty. advisor AID U.S. State Dept., Washington, 1979-84; dep. dir., gen. counsel Calif. Employment Devel. Dept., Sacramento, 1984-89; Fulbright scholar, vis. prof. law U. Salzburg, Austria, 1989-90; chmn. Calif. Agrl. Labor Rels. Bd., 1990-95; v.p. Europe, resident dir. Salzburg (Austria) Seminar, 1995—; prof. law McGeorge Sch. Law, U. Pacific, Sacramento, 1986—, Inst. on Internat. Legal Studies, Salzburg, summer 1987, London Inst. on Comml. Law, summers 1989, 92, 93; vis. scholar Hoover Inst. War, Revolution and Peace, Stanford U., 1991-92; dir. Vienna-Budapest East/West Trade Inst., 1993; vis. prof. law U. Salzburg, 1995—. Editor: Financing International Trade and Development, 1986, 87, 89, International Business Transactions, 1989, 92, International Trade Law, 1993, 94. Coordinating fund raiser March of Dimes, Sacramento, 1987. Capt. USNR, JAGC, 1975-79, mem. Res. Fulbright scholar, 1989-90; decorated Meritorious Achievement medal; recipient USAID Meritorious Honor award. Mem. Calif. Bar Assn., D.C. Bar Assn., Sacramento Bar Assn. (exec. com. taxation sect. 1988-89), Sacramento Met. C. of C. (award for program contbns. and community enrichment 1989), Nat. Rep. Lawyers Assn., Naval Res. Officers Assn., Marine Meml. Assn., Fulbright Assoc. (life), Knights of Vartan, Phi Beta Kappa. Home: 1631 12th Ave Sacramento CA 95818-4146 Office: Schloss Leopoldskron, Box 129, A-5010 Salzburg Austria

JANIGRO, DAMIR, physiologist, educator; b. Zagreb, Croatia, Mar. 16, 1957; came to the U.S., 1984; s. Antonio and Neda (Cihlar) J.; m. Kim Ann Conklin, Dec. 20, 1989; 1 child, Mattia Antonio. PhD, U. Milan, Italy, 1982. Project leader FIDIA Rsch. Labs., Abano, Italy, 1982-84; postdoctoral assoc. U. Wash., Seattle, 1984-87; rsch. assoc. U. Milan, Italy, 1987-89; asst. prof. U. Wash., Seattle, 1990—. Recipient First award NIH, 1994. Mem. Am. Heart Assn., A. Physiol. Soc., Internat. Brain Rsch. Orgn., Soc. for Neurosci.

JANKOVITZ, JOSEPH EDWARD, psychologist, educator, nurse; b. N.Y.C., Oct. 24, 1943; s. Joseph George and Theresa (Wrbal) J.; m. Joann Coulbourn O'Boyle, Aug. 6, 1976; children: Joseph G., Robert O'Boyle, Suzan O'Boyle, Joseph K. O'Boyle. AA in Nursing, Glendale C.C., 1972; BS in Rehab. Counseling, U. Ariz., 1974, MEd in Counseling, 1975; PhD in Clin. Psychology, La Jolla U., 1992. RN, Ariz.; cert. in clin. and med. Ericksonian hypnosis, substance abuse counseling, neuro linguistic programming (master practitioner and trainer), eye movement desensitization and reprocessing. Staff nurse U. Ariz. Hosp., Tucson, 1972-73; charge nurse psychiat. unit St. Mary's Hosp. and Health Ctr., Tucson, 1973-74, Pima County Hosp., Tucson, 1974-77; owner, clin. dir. Horizons Unltd Counseling Svcs., Tucson, 1977-80; charge nurse Posada Del Sol, Tucson, 1980-81; asst. DON Desert Hosp., Palm Springs, Calif., 1981-83; assoc. DON Indio (Calif.) Cmty. Hosp., 1983; mental health unit supr. Victor Valley Hosp., Victorville, Calif., 1984-86; clin. intern, psychiat. RN Horizons Unlimited Counseling Svc., Joshua Tree, 1986-91; post-doctoral intern, clin. therapist Dept. Mental Health San Bernadino County, 1993—; adj. prof. psychology Chapman U., Copper Mountain Campus of Coll. of Desert. Bd. dirs. Joshua Basin Water Dist., 1986-90. With USN, 1960-68, Vietnam. Decorated Cross of Galantry (Vietnam). Mem. Masters and Wardens Assn. (pres. 1979), Masons (32d degree, master 1979), Shriners, Kappa Delta Pi, Phi Delta Kappa.

JANKOWSKI, THEODORE ANDREW, artist; b. New Brunswick, N.J., Dec. 14, 1946; s. Theodore Andrew and Lois (Amarescu) J.; m. Rebecca Buck, July 23, 1983; 1 child, Tito Henry. Student, McMurrough Sch. Art, Indialantic, Fla., 1956-58, 74-75, R.I. Sch. Design, 1972, Cape Sch. of Art, Provincetown, Mass., 1975-76, 79-87, Cen. Fla. U., 1976-77. One-man shows include Eye of Horus Gallery, Provincetown, 1985; exhibited in group shows at Provincetown Art Assn. Mus., 1984, Bethlehem (Pa.) City Hall, 1988, Michael Ingbar Gallery, N.Y.C., 1988, 91; represented in permanent collections at State Mus. at Palace of Peter the Gt., Leningrad, USSR, Mishkan Olemanut Mus. Art, Israel, CIGNA Mus., Phila., Johns Hopkins U., Balt., Holyoke (Mass.) Mus. Art, McGill U., Montreal, Que., Can., Downey (Calif.) Mus. Art, Ark. Art Ctr., Little Rock, others. Mem. Copley Soc. Boston, Internat. Platform Assn. Home: PO Box 791 Kapaau HI 96755-0791

JANKURA, DONALD EUGENE, hotel executive, educator; b. Bridgeport, Conn., Dec. 20, 1929; s. Stephen and Susan (Dirga) J.; m. Elizabeth Deborah Joynt, June 20, 1952; children: Donald Eugene Jr., Stephen J., Daria E., Diane E., Lynn M. BA in Hotel Adminstrn., Mich. State U., 1951. Asst. sales mgr. Pick Fort Shelby Hotel, Detroit, 1951-53; steward Dearborn Inn and Colonial Homes, Dearborn, Mich., 1953-54, sales mgr., 1954-60, resident mgr., 1960-62; gen. mgr. Stouffer's Northland Inn, Southfield, Mich., 1962-64; staff adviser Stouffer Motor Inns, Cleve., 1964-66, v.p., 1966-68; v.p. Assoc. Inns & Restaurants Co. Am., Denver, 1968-76, exec. v.p., 1976-81, sr. v.p., 1981-91; pres. Waverly Hospitality Assocs., Parker, Colo., 1991-94; dir. Sch. Hotel and Restaurant Mgmt. U. Denver, 1988-91; disting. spl. lectr. hospitality U. New Haven, Conn.; pres. Am. Hotel Assn. Directory Corp., 1986; guest lectr. Mich. State U., 1964, Fla. Internat. U., 1968, Cornell U., 1983, Denver U., 1986-87; mem. industry adv. bd. U. Denver, Mich. State U.; mem. adv. bd. Acad. Travel and Tourism-Nat. Acad. found., Denver, 1991—; commr. Accreditation Commn. Programs in Hospitality Adminstrn., 1995—. Commr. Commn. on Accreditation for Hospitality Mgmt., 1994—; pres. Evergreen Homeowner's Assn., 1994—; mem. USAF Innkeeper Evaluation Team, 1993, 95. Named to Hall of Fame Colo. Hotel and Lodging Assn., 1992, Mich. State U. Sch. Hotel, Restaurant and Instl. Mgmt., 1995; named Alumnus of Yr. Mich. State U. Hotel Sch., 1986; recipient Ednl. Inst. Am. Hotel and Motel Assn. CHA designation, 1979, emeritus award, 1995. Mem. Am. Hotel and Motel Assn. (dir. 1978-80, vice chmn. industry adv. coun. 1980-81, sec.-treas. 1985, v.p. 1986, pres. 1987—, chmn. host com. 1994), Colo./Wyo. Hotel and Motel Assn. (dir., bd. dirs. 1984—, Disting. Svc. award 1983), Pinery Country Club, Pres.'s Club, Masons, Phi Kappa Tau. Episcopalian. Home and Office: 7445 E Windlawn Way Parker CO 80134-5941

JANNETTE, MARCY, rehabilitation nurse, consultant; b. St. Paul, Feb. 25, 1951; d. L.J. and Marie Jannette. BSN, Calif. State U., Fresno, 1973; MBA, Nat. U., Fresno, 1989. Cert. med.-surg. nurse, rehab. nurse. Nurse case mgr. Fremont (Calif.) Comp Ins. Co.; rehab. cons., owner MJ Med. Rehab., Clovis, Calif. Mem. Assn. Rehab. Nurses, Alumni Assn. Calif. State U.-Fresno, Alumni Assn. Nat. U., Case Mgrs. Soc. Am. Office: Fremont Comp Ins 1690 W Shaw Ave Ste 110 Fresno CA 93711-3516

JANSEN, GUSTAV RICHARD, food science educator; b. N.Y.C., May 19, 1930; s. Gustav Enoch and Ruth Miriam (Olson) J.; m. Coerene Miller, July 5, 1953; children: Norman, Barbara, Kathryn, Ellen. Student, Wagner Coll.; BA, Cornell U., 1950, PhD, 1958. Assoc. chemist Am. Cyanamid, Stamford, Conn., 1953-54; rsch. biochemist E.I. DuPont De Nemours, Wilmington, Del., 1958-62; rsch. fellow Merck Inst., Rahway, N.J., 1962-69; prof., dept. head Colo. State U., Ft. Collins, 1969-90, prof. emeritus, 1990—; mem. human nutrition bd. for sch. counselors USDA, Washington, 1986-91; mem. com. on mil. nutrition rsch. Inst. Medicine. 2d lt. USAF, 1950-53. Fellow Inst. Food Technologists (exec. com. 1989-91); mem. AAAS, Am. Inst. Nutrition, Am. Soc. for Biochemistry and Molecular Biology, Nat. Assn. Scholars. Republican. Methodist. Home: 1804 Seminole Dr Fort Collins CO 80525-1536 Office: Colo State U Dept Food Sci & Human Nutrition Fort Collins CO 80523

JANSON, RICHARD ANTHONY, plastic surgeon; b. Passaic, N.J., Nov. 30, 1945; m. Mary Ann Janson, 1971; children: Sarah, Matthew. BA, Rice U., 1967; MD, Med. Coll. Wis., 1971. Intern St. Joseph Hosp., Denver, resident in gen. surgery; resident in plastic surgery U. Tex. Med. Branch, Galveston, 1976-79; pvt. practice Grand Junction, Colo., 1979—. Fellow ACS, Am. Soc. Plastic & Reconstructive Surgeons; mem. Colo. Soc. Plastic & Reconstructive Surgeons. Office: 1120 Wellington Ave Grand Junction CO 81501-6129

JANSSEN, EUNICE CHARLENE, healthcare facility administrator; b. Urania, La., Mar. 23, 1948; d. Luther Clarence and Eunice Bobby (Pendarvis) Smith. BS in Nursing, Humboldt State U., 1970; MS in Nursing, Calif. State U., Fresno, 1980. Dir. nurses, asst. adminstr., coord. patient care svcs. Mad River Community Hosp., Arcata, Calif.; nursing supr. Fresno (Calif.) Community Hosp. Mem. Am. Soc. Healthcare Risk Mgmt., CANA (region 9 nurses interest group). Home: 1220 Winchester Ave Mckinleyville CA 95521-8803

JANSSEN, JAMES ROBERT, consulting software engineer; b. Frederick, Md., June 14, 1959; s. Robert James and Kathryn Doris (Randolph) J.; m. Deborah June Dellwo, Mar. 15, 1986 (div. Sept. 20, 1988). BSEE, Stanford U., 1981, MSEE, 1982. Simulation technician Varian Assocs., Palo Alto, Calif., 1981; hardware design engr. Fairchild Test Systems, San Jose, Calif., 1982-86, Factron Test Systems, Latham, N.Y., 1986-87; software, sys. designer Schlumberger Technologies Labs., Palo Alto, 1988; software engr. Photon Dynamics, Inc., San Jose, 1989-90, ADAC Labs., Milpitas, Calif., 1990-92; software, system designer ADAC Labs., Aalborg, Denmark, 1992, Milpitas, 1992-94; consulting software engr. self-employed, Sunnyvale, Calif., 1994—; pres., founder Digital Studio Systems, Inc., Sunnyvale, 1990-93. Patentee multiple timing signal generator. Civic vol. City of Sunnyvale, 1993. Mem. Tau Beta Pi. Home and Office: 107 S Mary Ave Apt 47 Sunnyvale CA 94086-5816

JANTZEN, J(OHN) MARC, retired education educator; b. Hillsboro, Kans., July 30, 1908; s. John D. and Louise (Janzen) J.; m. Ruth Patton, June 9, 1935; children: John Marc, Myron Patton, Karen Louise. A.B., Bethel Coll., Newton, Kans., 1934; A.M., U. Kans., 1937, Ph.D., 1940. Elementary sch. tchr. Marion County, Kans., 1927-30, Hillsboro, Kan., 1930-31; high sch. tchr., 1934-36; instr. sch. edn. U. Kans., 1936-40; asst. prof. Sch. Edn., U. of Pacific, Stockton, Calif., 1940-42; assoc. prof. Sch. Edn., U. of Pacific, 1942-44, prof., 1944-78, prof. emeritus, 1978—, also dean sch. edn., 1944-74, emeritus, 1974—, dir. summer sessions, 1940-72; condr. overseas seminars; mem., chmn. commn. equal opportunities in edn. Calif. Dept. Edn., 1959-69; mem., chmn. Commn. Tchr. Edn. Calif. Tchrs. Assn., 1956-62; mem. Nat. Coun. for Accreditation Tchr. Edn., 1969-72. Bd. dirs. Ednl. Travel Inst., 1965-89. Recipient Hon. Service award Calif. Congress of Parents and Tchrs., 1982; Paul Harris fellow Rotary Found., 1980; named Outstanding Rotarian of the Yr. North Stockton, Calif. Rotary Club, 1989-90. Mem. NEA, Am. Edn. Rsch. Assn., Calif. Edn. Rsch. Assn. (past pres. 1954-55), Calif. Coun. for Edn. Tchrs., Calif. Assn. of Colls. for Tchr. Edn. (sec., treas. 1975-85), Phi Delta Kappa. Methodist. Lodge: Rotary. Home: 117 W Euclid Ave Stockton CA 95204-3122

JAOUEN, RICHARD MATTHIE, plastic surgeon. MD, U. Autonoma de Guadalajara, Jalisco, Mexico, 1975. Intern St. Joseph Hosp., Denver, 1976-77, surgeon, 1977-81; plastic surgeon Ind. U. Med. Sch., Indpls., 1981-83, North Colo. Med. Ctr., Greeley, Colo., 1983—. Office: 1640 25th Ave Greeley CO 80631-4957*

JAQUITH, GEORGE OAKES, ophthalmologist; b. Caldwell, Idaho, July 29, 1916; s. Gail Belmont and Myrtle (Burch) J.; BA, Coll. Idaho, 1938; MB, Northwestern U., 1942, MD, 1943; m. Pearl Elizabeth Taylor, Nov. 30, 1939; children: Patricia Ann Jaquith Mueller, George, Michele Eugenie Jaquith Smith. Intern, Wesley Meml. Hosp., Chgo., 1942-43; resident ophthalmology U.S. Naval Hosp., San Diego, 1946-48; pvt. practice medicine, specializing in ophthalmology, Brawley, Calif., 1948—; pres. Pioneers Meml. Hosp. staff, Brawley, 1953; dir., exec. com. Calif. Med. Eye Council, 1960—; v.p. Calif. Med. Eye Found., 1976—. Sponsor Anza council Boy Scouts Am., 1966—. Gold card holder Rep. Assocs., Imperial County, Calif., 1967-68. Served with USMC, USN, 1943-47; PTO. Mem. Imperial County Med. Soc. (pres. 1961), Calif. Med. Assn. (del. 1961—), Nat., So. Calif. (dir. 1966—, chmn. med. adv. com. 1968-69) Soc. Prevention Blindness, Calif. Assn. Ophthalmology (treas. 1976—), San Diego, Los Angeles Ophthal. Socs., Los Angeles Research Study Club, Nathan Smith Davis Soc., Coll. Idaho Assocs., Am. Legion, VFW, Res. Officers Assn., Basenji Assn., Nat. Geneal. Soc., Cuyamaca Club (San Diego), Elks, Phi Beta Pi, Lambda Chi Alpha. Presbyterian (elder). Office: PO Box 511 665 S Western Brawley CA 92227-0511

JARCHO, LEONARD W., retired neurology educator; b. N.Y.C., Aug. 12, 1916; s. Julius and Susana (Wallenstein) J.; m. Ann Elizabeth Adams, Apr. 11, 1956; children: John Adams, Daniel Gordon, William Stephen. AB, Harvard U., 1936; MA, Columbia U., 1937, MD, 1941. Intern in medicine Beth Israel Hosp., Boston, 1942; asst. resident medicine Mt. Sinai Hosp., N.Y.C., 1946-47; fellow in medicine Johns Hopkins Sch. Medicine, Balt., 1946, 47-52; instr. medicine Johns Hopkins Sch. Medicine, 1952; clin. clk. neurology Nat. Hosp. Queen Sq., London, 1958; fellow in neuropathology Mass. Gen. Hosp., Boston, 1959; from asst. prof. to prof. neurology U. Utah, Salt Lake City, 1959-81, prof. emeritus, 1981—. With U.S. Army, 1943-46.

JARDIN, MATTHEW ROBERT, aerospace engineer; b. Salinas, Calif., July 30, 1968; s. Robert William Jardin and Anne Lynn (Gamboa) Fox. Aerospace engr., Boston U., 1988; BS in Aeros. and Astronautics, U. Wash., 1990, MS in Aeros. and Astronautics, 1992. Chief ops. Kirsten Wind Tunnel U. Wash., Seattle, 1988-90; rsch. asst. Aerospace & Energetics Rsch. Program, Seattle, 1990-92; programmer, analyst Sterling Software, NASA Ames Divsn., Palo Alto, Calif., 1993-94; aerospace engr. NASA Ames Rsch. Ctr., Moffett Field, Calif., 1994—. Recipient Aerospace Design award Rockwell Internat., U. Wash., 1990. Mem AIAA (young members dir. 1994—, Abe Zarem award 1995). Office: NASA Ames Rsch Ctr MS 210-9 Moffett Field CA 94035

JARECKE, KENNETH JOHN, photojournalist; b. Fairfax, Mo., May 9, 1963; s. Bernard Harry and Melissa Lou (Fulkerson) J.; m. Souad Tamer Michael, July 4, 1992; 1 child, Shadya Elizabeth. Student, U. Nebr., Omaha, 1981-83. Photographer, stringer AP, Omaha, 1982-85; assoc. photographer Contact Press Images, N.Y.C., 1984-86, mem. photographer, 1986—; contract photographer Time Mag., N.Y.C., 1990—. Author: Just Another War, 1992, (with others) Game Day USA, 1990, Children of the Dragon, 1990, A Day in the Life Series, 1989—, among others. Recipient numerous awards World Press Photo, Amsterdam, 1989, 90, 92, Nat. Press Photographers Assn., 1989—. Home and Office: RR 1 Box 351 Joliet MT 59041-9722

JARED, DANIEL WADE, telecommunications company executive; b. Denver, Dec. 19, 1925; s. D. Wade and Lennie E. (Miller) J. BS, U. Houston, 1947; postgrad., Utah State U., 1961-62. Assoc. engr. Boeing Airplane Co., Seattle, 1959; mathematician Wasatch div. Thiokol Chem. Corp., Brigham City, Utah, 1960-63; project engr. aerospace div. Amphenol-Borg Electronics Corp., Chatsworth, Calif., 1963-64; field project engr. Bendix Field Engring Corp., Barstow, Calif., 1964; sci. programmer Air Force Rocket Propulsion Lab., Edwards AFB, Calif., 1965-68; sr. field engr. Singer-Gen. Precision, inc., Edwards AFB, Calif., 1968-69; tech. programmer Singer-Gen. Precision, Inc., Glendale, Calif., 1969-70; spl. tech. cons. System Devel. Corp., Santa Monica, Calif., 1970, spl. programming cons., 1970; sr. engring. tech. County of San Bernardino (Calif.) Pub. Works Adminstrn., 1971-74; adminstrv. analyst County of San Bernardino (Calif.) Environ. Improvement Agy., 1974-75; planner I County of El Paso, Colorado Springs, Colo., 1977-79; tech. cons. Westrans Corp., Colorado Springs, Colo., 1982; pres. Neptune Telecommunications, Barstow, 1984—; cons. pipe organ design. Contbr. articles to profl. jours. Mem. AAAS, Congress on Surveying and Mapping, AIAA, Am. Guild of Organists, Galactic Soc. (pres., exec. dir.).

JARMAN, DONALD RAY, public relations professional, minister, retired; b. Benton Harbor, Mich., May 6, 1928; s. Ray Charles and Grace Marie (Timanus) J.; m. Bo Dee Foster, July 7, 1950 (div. 1985); children: Mark, Katharine Law, Luanne Miller; m. Sharon Lee Becker, Feb. 16, 1991. BA, Chapman U., 1950; MDiv, Lexington Theol. Sem., 1953; DMin, Sch. of Theology, Claremont, 1970. Ordained min. Disciples of Christ, 1950; cert. fundraising exec. Nat. Soc. Fundraising Execs., 1980-89. Pastor Sharpsberg (Ky.) Christian, 1950-53, First Christian Ch., Santa Maria, Calif., 1953-58, St. Claire St. Ch. of Christ, Kirkcaldy, Scotland, 1958-61, So. Bay Christian, Redondo Beach, Calif., 1961-71; dir. human value in health care Eskaton, Charmichael, Calif., 1971-73; exec. dir. Northwestern NBA Svc., Portland, Oreg., 1973-85; dir. pub. relations and mktg. Retirement Housing Found., Long Beach, Calif., 1985-89; part time minister Pico Rivera Christian Ch., 1986-87; dir. community rels. Coscan Davidson Homes, Signal Hill, Calif., 1989—; interim min. Southgate First Christian Ch., 1994-95; pres. So. Calif. Mins., 1967; chmn. Pacific S.W. Region Christian Ch., 1968; mem. gen. bd. Disciples of Christ, 1969-70; exec. dir. Signal Hill Econ. Devel. Bd., 1992—. Editor: Reachout, 1973-84, Hill Street News, 1992-95; editor-in-chief: December Rose, 1985-89; columnist NW Senior News, 1980-84. Pres. Signal Hill C. of C., 1992-93; treas. Hist. Soc., Signal Hill, 1990-94; commr. L.A. County Commn. on Aging, 1994—. Recipient Master Make-up Technician award Portland Opera, 1983, Outstanding Older American award City of Signal Hill, Calif., 1993. Mem. Rotary (pres. Progress, Oreg. 1983-84, pres. Signal Hill 1993-94, Paul Harris fellow), Chapman Univ. Alumni Assn. (pres.-elect 1993-94, pres. 1994-95, bd. trustees 1994—), Los Alamitos Cmty. Art League, LA. Pastel Soc., Masons. Democrat. Home: 1923 Molino Ave Unit 101 Signal Hill CA 90804-1028 Office: Coscan Davidson Homes 2501 Cherry Ave Ste 160 Signal Hill CA 90806-2034

JARMON, LAWRENCE, developmental communications educator; b. L.A., Nov. 7, 1946; s. Robert and Movella (Young) J. BA, Calif. State U., 1969, MA in Adminstrn. Health and Safety, 1988; MS, U. Wash., 1972; EdD in Edn. Adminstrn., Wash. State U., 1975; MA, Calif. State U., L.A., 1988. Cert. alcohol and drug problems specialist. Athletic dir., instr. dept. phys. edn. L.A. SW Coll., 1975-85, agy. dir. summer programfor disadvantaged youth, 1975-94, asst. dean instruction, 1976, project adminstr. NCAA, 1977-79; instr. health edn. Golden West Coll., Huntington Beach, Calif., 1978; instr. dept. English Calif. State U., L.A., 1986; instr. dept. edn. Nat. U., L.A., 1986-88; prof. developmental comm. L.A. S.W. Coll., 1988-92, prof. dept. devel. comm., staff devel. coord. and dir., dir. nat. youth sports program, 1993—. Author numerous booklets, manuscripts and manuals on sports programs and edn. qualifications and policies. Bd. advisors Scholastic Placement Orgn. for Student Athlete, Mount Laurel, N.J.; bd. dirs. Black Edn. Commn., L.A. Unified Sch. Dist., Calif. State U., L.A. Alumni Assn., Involvement for Young Achievers, L.A., L.A. Police Dept. Football Centurions, Paradise Ch. Found., Inc., L.A., Pop Warner Little Scholars, Inc., Phila.; employee assistance program liaison officer L.A. Cmty. Dist. Named one of Outstanding Young Men of Am., 1980, 81. Mem. Am. Alliance Health, Phys. Edn. and Recreation, Am. Alliance Health Edn., Am. Assn. Sch. Adminstrs., Calif. State Alumni Assn., U. Wash. Alumni Assn., Wash. State Alumni Assn., Calif. Assn. Health, Phys. Edn. and Recreation, Calif. State Athletic Dirs. Assn., L.A. Jr. C. of C., Kappa Alpha Psi, Nat. Interscholastic Athletic Adminstrs. Assn., Phi Delta Kappa. Office: LA SW Coll 1600 W Imperial Hwy Los Angeles CA 90047-4810

JAROS, DEAN, university official; b. Racine, Wis., Aug. 23, 1938; s. Joseph and Emma (Kotas) J. B.A., Lawrence Coll., Appleton, Wis., 1960; M.A., Vanderbilt U., 1962, Ph.D., 1966. Asst. prof. polit. sci. Wayne State U., Detroit, 1963-66; from asst. prof. to prof. polit. sci. U. Ky., 1966-78, assoc. dean Grad. Sch., 1978-80; dean Grad. Sch. No. Ill. U., DeKalb, 1980-84; dean Grad. Sch. Colo. State U., Ft. Collins, 1984-91, assoc. provost, 1991—. Author: Socialization to Politics, 1973, Political Behavior: Choices and Perspectives, 1974, Heroes Without Legacy, 1993, also articles.; Mem. editorial bds. profl. jours. Mem. Exptl. Aircraft Assn. Office: Colo State U Grad Sch Fort Collins CO 80523

JARRETT, JOHN R., plastic surgeon; b. Grand Forks, N.D., 1939. MD, Northwestern U., 1965. Intern Milw. County Gen. Hosp., 1965-66; surgeon Marquette Hosp., 1966-69; plastic surgeon St. Louis U., 1969-71; now plastic surgeon Sacred Heart Hosp., Eugene, Oreg., 1971—. Office: 655 E 11th Ave Eugene OR 97401-3621*

JARRETT, RONALD DOUGLAS, nurse, lawyer; b. Oceanside, Calif., Oct. 31, 1952; s. William Douglas and Francia Elizabeth (Ladd) J.; m. Lois Ellen Shurmaster, Dec. 23, 1984; 1 child, Emily Rose. ASN, Cabrillo Coll., 1981; student, SUNY, Albany, 1984-88; JD, Lincoln Law Sch. Sacramento, 1993. Bar: Calif. 1993; RN, Calif. Hosp. corpsman USN, 1970-74; psychiat. technician County Mental Health Dept., Santa Cruz, Calif., 1974-81; staff nurse ICU/CCU Watsonville (Calif.) Community Hosp., 1981-84; RN, ICU, CCU Dominican Santa Cruz Hosp., Santa Cruz, Calif., 1983-85; staff nurse ICU U. Calif.-Davis Med. Ctr., Sacramento, 1986-87; staff nurse ICU/emergency room Calif. Healthcare Cons., Sacramento, 1987-90; nurse ICU, critical care unit, emergency room Yolo Gen. Hosp., Woodland, Calif., 1990-91; with Nursing Svcs. Internat., 1991-92; law clk. Klauschie & Shannon, 1993-94; assoc. Eggleston & O'Brien, Sacramento, 1994—; affiliate faculty Am. Heart Assn., Salinas, Calif., 1979-84; assoc. faculty Cabrillo Coll. nursing dept., Aptos, Calif., 1983-85; med. record rev. Cigna. Served to HM3 USN, 1970-73. Fellow Ancient Mystical Order Rose Crucis; mem. ABA, Sacramento County Bar Assn. Republican. Home: 9400 Marcola Ct Sacramento CA 95826-5221 Office: PO Box 796 100 Estates Dr Roseville CA 95678-0796

JARVIK, GAIL PAIRITZ, medical geneticist; b. Evanston, Ill., Feb. 8, 1959; d. Lawrence Alan and Lenore Mae P.; m. Jeffrey Gil Jarvik, Aug. 22, 1992. PhD in Human Genetics, U. Mich., 1986; MD, U. Iowa, 1987. Sr. rsch. fellow U. Washington, Seattle; affiliate mem. Fred Hutchinson Cancer Rsch. Ctr., Seattle, 1994—. Contbr. to profl. jours. Howard Hughes Rsch. fellow, 1992—. Mem. Am. Soc. Human Genetics, Internat. Genetic Epidemiology Soc.

JARVIS, DONALD BERTRAM, judge; b. Newark, N.J., Dec. 14, 1928; s. Benjamin and Esther (Golden) J.; BA, Rutgers U., 1949; JD, Stanford U., 1952; m. Rosalind C. Chodorcove, June 13, 1954; children: Nancie, Brian, Joanne. Bar: Calif. 1953. Law clk. Justice John W. Shenk, Calif. Supreme Ct., 1953-54; assoc. Erskine, Erskine & Tulley, 1955; assoc. Aaron N. Cohen, 1955-56; law clk. Dist. Ct. Appeal, 1956; assoc. Carl Hoppe, 1956-57; adminstrv. law judge Calif. Pub. Utilities Commn., San Francisco, 1957-91, U.S. Dept. of Labor, 1992—. mem. exec. com. Nat. Conf. Adminstrv. Law Judges, 1986-88, sec. 1988-89, vice-chair, 1990-91, chair-elect, 1991-92, chair 1992-93; pres. Calif. Adminstrv. Law Judges Coun., 1978-84; mem. faculty Nat. Jud. Coll., U. Nev., 1977, 78, 80. Chmn. pack Boy Scouts Am., 1967-69, chmn. troop, 1972; class chmn. Stanford Law Sch. Fund, 1959, mem. nat. com., 1963-65; dir. Forest Hill Assn., 1970-71. Served to col. USAF Res., 1949-79. Decorated Legion of Merit. Mem. ABA (mem. ho. of dels. 1993—), State Bar Calif., Bar Assn. San Francisco, Calif. Conf. Pub. Utility Counsel (pres. 1980-81), Air Force Assn., Res. Officers Assn., De Young

Museum Soc. and Patrons Art and Music, San Francisco Gem and Mineral Soc., Stanford Alumni Assn., Rutgers Alumni Assn., Phi Beta Kappa (pres. No. Calif. 1973-74), Tau Kappa Alpha, Phi Alpha Theta, Phi Alpha Delta. Home: 530 Dewey Blvd San Francisco CA 94116-1427 Office: 211 Main St San Francisco CA 94105-1905

JARVIS, LOVELL STUBER, economist, educator; b. Halstead, Kans., June 18, 1941; s. Laurence Fredonia and Virginia Francis (Moore) J.; m. Nancy Anne Beall, June 10, 1968 (div. Dec. 1975); 1 child, Hope Oriana; m. Maria Isabel Rivas, Dec. 29, 1979; children: Lucas Sebastian, Daniel Christopher, Amalia Pilar. BA in Econs., U. Kans., 1964; PhD in Econs., MIT, 1969. Rsch. assoc. Guayana Project Harvard-MIT Joint Ctr. for Urban Studies, Caracas, Venezuela, 1965; vis. rschr. Ctr. for Econ. Rsch., Torcuato Di Tella Inst., Buenos Aires, 1968; asst. prof. dept. econs. U. Calif., Berkeley, 1969-77, vis. lectr. dept. econs., 1978-83; prof. dept. agrl. econs. U. Calif., Davis, 1984—, chair grad. program internat. agrl. devel., 1987-90; program advisor in econs. The Ford Found., Santiago, 1972-73; vis. prof. dept. industry Faculty of Phys. Scis. and Math., U. Chile, 1973; cons. The World Bank, 1974—, Ministry Agriculture and Fisheries, Uruguay, 1976, 77, Programa Regional del Empleo para Am. Latina y el Caribe, Santiago, Chile, 1978, 79, others; vis. prof. Corporacion de Investigaciones Econs. para Latinoamerica, Santiago, 1991-92. Contbg. editor: Handbook for Latin American Studies, 1974-75; editorial adv. bd.: East Africa Economic Review, 1985—; contbr. book revs. and articles to profl. jours. Recipient Fulbright award for rsch., 1991, Social Sci. Rsch. Coun. award, 1991-92. Office: U Calif Dept Agrl Econs Davis CA 95616

JASINEK, GARY DONALD, newspaper executive; b. Champaign, Ill., Sept. 17, 1950; s. William Gerald and Doris Margaret (Brethorst) J.; m. Carole Riggs, Nov. 9, 1974; children: Andrea Sarah, Adam Christopher. Student, San Diego State U., 1968-74. Reporter The Daily Californian, El Cajon, 1975-76, city editor, 1976-79; editor Red Oak (Iowa) Express, 1979-81; editor Los Alamos (N.Mex.) Monitor, 1981-83, editor, gen. mgr., 1983-87; asst. metro editor Tacoma (Wash.) Morning News Tribune, 1987-88, metro editor, 1988-91, columnist, 1991. Mem. N.Mex. AP Mng. Editors (bd. dirs. 1984, pres. 1986, 1st Pl. Column award and 2d Pl. Editorial award 1982, 2d Pl. Editorial award 1984, 1st Pl. Editorial award 1985, 86), Calif. Newspaper Pubs. (1st Pl. award 1979), Iowa Press Assn. (3d Pl. award 1981), N.Mex. Press Assn. (1st Pl. award 1982). Home: 10121 Crescent Valley Dr NW Gig Harbor WA 98332-9576 Office: Tacoma News Tribune PO Box 11000 Tacoma WA 98411-0008

JASON, DEBRA ANN, copywriter; b. Flushing, N.Y., Dec. 1, 1954. BA, Queens Coll., 1975; MA, U. Colo., 1977. Prodn. dir., copywriter Krupp Mail Order, Boulder, Colo., 1983-87; prodn. mgr. Mellow Mail, N.Y.C., 1987-88; acct. coord., jr. copywriter Grey Direct, N.Y.C., 1988; owner, copywriter The Write Direction, Boulder, Colo., 1989—; tchr. continuing edn. program U. Colo., Boulder; presenter seminar Boulder County Bus. Expo., 1993. Contbr. articles to bus. publs. Participant Leadership Boulder XI, 1991-92; bd. dirs. YWCA, Boulder, 1992-93. Recipient Outstanding Accomplishment citation Boulder C. of C. and City of Boulder, 1991. Mem. Denver Advt. Fedn. (pub. rels. com. 1991-92), Boulder C. of C. (chair bus. women's leadership group 1991-92, program com. 1992-93, small bus. support coun. 1993-94, bd. dirs. 1994—, Vol. of Yr. 1993), Rocky Mt. Direct Mktg. Assn. (newsletter editor 1993—, bd. dirs. 1995—), Art Dirs. Club of Denver (newsletter editor 1990-91, Bronze award of excellence 1991). Office: The Write Direction Ste B 1920 13th St Boulder CO 80302

JAUME, JUAN CARLOS, physician, educator; b. Buenos Aires, Dec. 27, 1959; came to U.S., 1986; s. Juan Antonio and Hebe Teresa J.; m. Maria Alejandra Alfonso, June 1, 1987. MD, Nat. U. Buenos Aires, Buenos Aires, 1985. Intern U. Hosp. Nat. U. Buenos Aires, 1985-86; vis. postdoctorate in Surgery SUNY, Stony Brook, 1986-87, resident in Surgery, 1987-88; resident in Internal Medicine Albert Einstein Coll. of Medicine, Bronx, 1988-91; fellow in endocrinology/metabolism U. Calif., San Francisco, 1991-94, asst. prof. medicine, endocrinology and metabolism, 1994—. Contbr. articles to profl. jours. Office: VA Med Ctr U Calif Thyroid Molecular Biology Unit 4150 Clement St San Francisco CA 94121-1598

JAUREQUI, LETICIA LÓPEZ, English language educator; b. La Mirada, Calif., Nov. 21, 1958; d. Martin and Teresa (Robles) Lopez; m. Robert R. Jauequi, June 23, 1990; 1 child, Lena G. BA, Yale U., 1980; TESOL cert., Calif. State U., Fullerton, 1992, MA, 1992. Asst. prodr. Interam. Commn., L.A., 1984-85; assoc. prodr./writer Sta. KCET-TV, L.A., 1985; mktg. dir./assoc. prodr. Glendon Assn., L.A., 1986-89; instr. ESL Saddleback Coll., Mission Viejo, Calif., 1992, Cypress (Calif.) Coll., 1992-93; instr. Spanish Cerritos Coll., Norwalk, Calif., 1992-94; instr. ESL Fullerton (Calif.) Coll., 1993-94, Rancho Santiago Coll., Santa Ana, Calif., 1994—; pres. Translation Svcs., La Mirada, 1992—. Co-author: Psychological Defenses of Everyday Life, The Workbook. Mentor Puente program Fullerton Coll., 1990-94; recruiter, presenter Yale U., 1989—; mem. Hispanic Acad. of Media Arts and Scis., L.A., 1983-89, League of United Latino Am. Citizens, Norwalk, 1990—. Recipient Emmy award NATAS, L.A., 1986; Minority scholar Calif. State U., 1991-92. Democrat. Roman Catholic. Home: 13145 San Felipe St La Mirada CA 90638-3451 Office: Rancho Santiago Coll 1530 W 17th St Santa Ana CA 92706-3315

JAWAD, SAID TAYEB (SAID TAYEB DJAWAD), paralegal, political commentator, writer; b. Kandahr, Afghanistan, Feb. 27, 1958; came to U.S., 1986; s. Mir Hussain and zakia Shah; m. Shamin Rahman, Nov. 16, 1986. Student, Kabul (Afghanistan) U., 1976-80; postgrad., Wilhelms U., Muenster, Germany, 1984-86, Long Island U., 1986. Paralegal Lehnardt & Bauman, N.Y.C., 1988-89, Steefel, Levitt & Weiss, San Francisco, 1989—; polit. commentator various radio and TV stas. Editor weekly newspaper OMAID; pub. Modern Dictatorship, Occupation of Wakhan, Soviets Expansion to the South, Fundamentalism in Central Asia; contbr. articles to profl. jours. throughout world. Bd. dirs. Afghanistan Cultural Soc., San Francisco, 1990—; mem. Internat. Soc. for Human Rights, Frankfort, Germany, 1986—; mem. nat. adv. bd. Info. Am., Atlanta, 1991—; active Amnesty Internat., N.Y.C., 1987—. Home: 4279 Merced Cir Antioch CA 94509-8227

JAY, DAVID JAKUBOWICZ, management consultant; b. Danzig, Poland, Dec. 7, 1925; s. Mendel and Gladys Gitta (Zalc) Jakubowicz; came to U.S., 1938, naturalized, 1944; BS, Wayne State U., 1948; MS, U. Mich., 1949, postgrad., 1956-57; postgrad. U. Cin., 1951-53, MIT, 1957; m. Shirley Anne Shapiro, Sept. 7, 1947; children: Melvin Maurice, Evelyn Deborah. Supr. man-made diamonds GE Corp., Detroit, 1951-56; instr. U. Detroit, 1948-51; asst. to v.p. engring. Ford Motor Co., Dearborn, Mich., 1956-63; project mgr. Apollo environ. control radiators N.Am. Rockwell, Downey, Calif., 1963-68; staff to v.p. corporate planning Aerospace Corp., El Segundo, Calif., 1968-70; founder, pres. PBM Systems Inc., 1970-83; pres. Cal-Best Hydrofarms Coop., Los Alamitos, 1972-77; cons. in field, 1983—. Pres., Community Design Corp., Los Alamitos, 1971-75; life master Am. Contract Bridge League. Served with USNR, 1944-46. Registered profl. engr., Calif., Mich., Ohio. Fellow Inst. Advancement Engring.; mem. Art Stamp and Stencil Dealers Assn. (pres. 1993—), Inst. Mgmt. Sci. (chmn. 1961-62), Western Greenhouse Vegetable Growers Assn. (sec.-treas. 1972-75), Tau Beta Pi. Jewish. Patentee in air supported ground vehicle, others. Home: 13441 Roane Santa Ana CA 92705-2271 Office: 13882 Newport Ave # E Tustin CA 92680-4666

JAY, DEBORAH, marketing professional. BA in Psychology and Polit. Sci., UCLA, 1972; MA in Polit. Sci., U. Calif., Berkeley, 1973, PhD in Polit. Sci., 1981. Survey rsch. analyst Survey Rsch. Ctr. U. Calif., Berkeley, 1973-77; cons. various firms including Teknekron and Pub. Sector, 1978-81; survey rsch. specialist, rsch. social scientist SRI Internat., Menlo Park, Calif., 1981-88, program dir., 1989; mgr. mgmt. consulting group KPMG Peat Marwick, San Francisco, 1988; with Field Rsch. Corp., San Francisco, 1991—, v.p., rsch. dir., pres., 1993—. Office: Field Research Corp 550 Delancy St Ste 900 San Francisco CA 94107-1401*

JAY, MARTIN EVAN, historian, educator; b. N.Y.C., May 4, 1944; s. Edward and Sari Toby (Sidel) J.; m. M. Catherine Gallagher, July 6, 1974; 1 child, Rebecca Erin; 1 stepchild, Margaret Shana Gallagher. BA, Union Coll., Schenectady, N.Y., 1965; PhD, Harvard U., 1971. Prof. history U. Calif., Berkeley, 1971—. Author: The Dialectical Imagination, 1973, Marxism and Totality, 1984, Adorno, 1984, Downcast Eyes, 1993, Force Fields, 1993; sr. editor Theory and Society, 1977—; columnist Salmagundi, Saratoga Springs, N.Y., 1987—; editor Cultural Critique, Berkeley, 1990—. Guggenheim fellow, 1973; NEH fellow, 1979; Rockefeller Found. fellow, 1984; Am. Coun. Learned Socs. fellow, 1989. Mem. Am. Hist. Assn. Home: 718 Contra Costa Ave Berkeley CA 94707-1918 Office: U Calif Dept History Berkeley CA 94720

JAY, NORMA JOYCE, artist; b. Wichita, Kans., Nov. 11, 1925; d. Albert Hugh and Thelma Ree (Boyd) Braly; m. Laurence Eugene Jay, Sept. 2, 1949; children: Dana Denise, Allison Eden. Student Wichita State U., 1946-49, Art Inst. Chgo., 1955-56, Calif. State Coll., 1963. Illustrator Boeing Aircraft, Wichita, Kans., 1949-51; co-owner Back Door Gallery, Laguna Beach, Calif., 1973-88. One-woman shows include Milcir Gallery, Tiburon, Calif., 1978, Newport Beach City Gallery, 1981; group shows include Am. Soc. Marine Artists ann. exhbns., N.Y.C., 1978-86, Peabody Mus., Salem, Mass., 1981, Mystic Seaport Mus. Gallery, Conn., 1982-95, Grand Cen. Galleries, N.Y., 1979-84, The Back Door Gallery, Laguna Beach, Calif., 1973-88, Mariners' Mus., Newport News, Va., 1985-86, Nat. Heritage Gallery of Fine Art, Beverly Hills, Calif., 1988—, Md. Hist. Mus., 1989, Kirsten Gallery, Seattle, 1991-93, R.J. Schaefer Gallery Mystic (Conn.) Seaport Mus., 1992, Vallejo Gallery, Newport Beach, Calif., 1992, Caswell Gallery, Troutdale, Oreg., 1994-95, Columbia River Maritime Mus., Astoria, Oreg., 1994, Coos Art Mus., Coos Bay, Oreg., 1994-95, Arnold Art Gallery, Newport, Conn., 1994; represented in permanent collections including James Irvine Found., Newport Beach, Niguel Art Assn., Laguna Niguel, Calif., Deloitte, Haskins & Sells, Costa Mesa, Calif., M.J. Brock & Sons Inc., North Hollywood, Calif., others. Recipient Best of Show award Ford Nat. Competition, 1961, First Pl. award Traditional Artists Exhbn., San Bernadino County Mus., 1976, Artist award Chriswood Gallery Invitational Exhbn., Rancho California, Calif., 1973. Fellow Am. Soc. Marine Artists (charter); mem. Niguel Art Assn. (first pres. 1968, hon. life mem. 1978), Artists Equity, Am. Artists Profl. League. Republican.

JAYME, WILLIAM NORTH, writer; b. Pitts., Nov. 15, 1925; s. Walter A. and Catherine (Ryley) J.; student Princeton, 1943-44, 47-49. With Young & Rubicam Advt., Inc., 1949, Charles W. Gamble & Assos., 1949-50; asst. circulation promotion mgr. Fortune mag., 1950-51, Life mag., 1951-53, copy dir., sales and advt. promotion CBS Radio Network, N.Y.C., 1953-55; sr. copywriter McCann-Erickson, Inc., 1955-58; established own advt. creative service, 1958-71; pres. Jayme, Ratalahti, Inc., 1971—; lectr. direct mktg. Stanford U., Radcliffe Coll., worldwide mktg. confs. Producer U.S. Army radio program Music Motorized, 1945-46; editor, producer Time, Inc. TV programs Background for Judgment, 1951, Citizen's View of '52; script editor CBS Radio-UPA motion picture Tune in Tomorrow, 1954; creator promotions that launched Smithsonian, New York, Bon Appetit, Food & Wine, California, American Health, Air & Space, other nat. mags.; author script adaptations for Studio One and other TV programs, articles and stories in periodicals. Served as sgt., 2d Armored Div., AUS, 1944-46. Democrat. Episcopalian. Club: Century Assn.,(N.Y.C.). Author: (with Roderick Cook) Know Your Toes and Other Things to Know, 1963; (with Helen McCully, Jacques Pepin) The Other Half of the Egg, 1967; (opera libretto, with Douglas Moore) Carry Nation. Address: 1033 Bart Rd Sonoma CA 95476-4707

JEBENS, ARTHUR BERTRAM, management consultant, lawyer; b. Davenport, Iowa, Mar. 30, 1916; s. Gus and Anna Marie (Bertram) J.; m. Genett Herrick, June 25, 1940; children: Jennifer Herrick, Arthur Herrick, Holly Ann Herrick. BA, U. Iowa, 1937, JD, 1939; MA in pub. adminstr., U. Minn., 1941. Mcpl. analyst U. Minn., Mpls., 1940-41; rsch. asst. Am. Mcpl. Assn., Chgo., 1941; legislative rsch. analyst Dept. Agri., Washington, 1942-47; adminstrn. analyst Fed. Pub. Housing, Washington, 1942-47; mgmt. analyst Office of Sec. Interior Dept., Washington, 1947-52; dir. mgmt. rsch. U.S. Dept. Interior, Washington, 1952-70; vice chancelor adminstrn. U. Calif., Riverside, 1970-73; mgmt. cons. U. Calif., San Diego, 1973-76; cons. U.S. Bureau of Budget, Washington, 1968; awards com. U.S. Dept. Interior, Washington, 1952-70. Contbr. articles to profl. jours. Pres. Parent Teachers Assn., Bethesda, Md., 1954, Mohican Hills Civic Assn., Bethesda, 1956, Interagency Mgmt. Analyst Assn., Washington, 1962. With U.S. Army, 1943-45, Germany. Decorated Bronze Star, POW medal, Combat Infatryman badge, U.S. Army; Rockefellow grant Stillman Found., U. Minn., 1939-40, congressional fellow Am. Pol. Sci. Assn., Washington, 1966. Mem. Am. Assn. Advancement Sci., Audubon Soc., Wilderness Soc., Iowa Bar, Am. Soc. Pub. Adminstrn. (v.p. 1965). Democrat. Home: 956 Santa Queta Solana Beach CA 92075-1527

JEDENOFF, GEORGE ALEXANDER, steel consultant; b. Petrosovodsk, Russia, July 5, 1917; came to U.S., 1923, naturalized, 1928; s. Alexander N. and Barbara Vacilivna (Sepiagina) J.; m. Barbara Jane Cull, Feb. 27, 1943; children: Nicholas, Nina. A.B. in Mech. Engring. magna cum laude, Stanford, 1940, M.B.A., 1942. With U.S. Steel Corp., 1942-74; indsl. engr. U.S. Steel Corp. (Columbia-Geneva Steel div.), Pittsburg, Calif., 1942-43; gen. foreman U.S. Steel Corp. (Columbia-Geneva Steel div.), 1946-52, asst. supt. sheet finishing, 1952-53, cold reduction, 1953-54, supt. cold reduction, 1954, asst. gen. supt., 1955-58, gen. supt., 1959; gen. supt. U.S. Steel Corp. (Geneva Works), Utah, 1960-67, Gary, Ind., 1967-69; gen. mgr. heavy products U.S. Steel Corp., Pitts., 1969-70; v.p. (Western Steel ops.), 1970-73; pres., dir. USS Engrs. & Cons., Inc. (subsidiary), Pitts., 1974; pres., chief operating officer, dir. Kaiser Steel Corp., Oakland, Calif., 1974-77; dir. Kaiser Internat. Shipping Corp., Kaiser Resources Ltd. (Can.), Hamersley Holdings (Melbourne), Australia, Kaiser Industries, 1974-77; now cons. steel industry and gen. mgmt. Active Boy Scouts Am., 1960—; pres. Utah Valley United Fund, 1966, N.W. Ind., 1968; co-chmn. Urban Coalition, Gary, 1968; mem. health and med. com. Am. Bur. Med. Aid to China, 1974; Bd. dirs. Mercy Hosp., Gary, 1967-69; mem. adv. council Brigham Young U., 1965-73; bd. dirs. Keep Am. Beautiful; chmn. East Bay major gifts com. Stanford U., 1978.; bd. govs. Stanford Assocs., 1984-86. Served to lt. USNR, 1943-46. Recipient Jesse Knight Indsl. Citizenship award Brigham Young U., 1966; Disting. Service award Stanford Bus. Sch. Alumni Assn., 1978; named Man of Year Utah Harvard Club, 1967. Mem. Iron and Steel Inst., Assn. Iron and Steel Engrs. (pres. 1977), Western Pa. Safety Coun. (exec. com. 1970-74), Bituminous Coal Operators Assn. (dir. 1974-77), Am. Assn. Engring. Socs. (commn. internat. rels.), Oakland C. of C. (dir. 1976-79), Ind. C. of C. (dir. 1967-69), Stanford U. Bus. Sch. Alumni Assn. (nat. pres. 1956-57), Phi Beta Kappa, Tau Beta Pi. Clubs: Alta (Salt Lake City); Claremont (Oakland); Pacific-Union (San Francisco).

JEFFERDS, MARY LEE, environmental education executive; b. Seattle, July 16, 1921; d. Amos Osgood and Vera Margaret (Percival) J.; AB, U. Calif. at Berkeley, 1943, gen. secondary teaching cert., 1951; MA, Columbia U., 1947; cert. Washington and Lee U., 1945. Sec. Fair Play Com. Am. Citizens Japanese Ancestry, 1943-44; adminstrv. asst. U.C. Alumni Assn. book Students at Berkeley, 1949; dir. Student Union Monterey Jr. Coll., 1949-50; mgr. Nat. Audubon Soc. Conservation Resource Ctr., Berkeley, 1951-66; dir. Nat. Audubon Soc. Bay Area Ednl. Svcs., 1966-71; curriculum cons. Project WEY, U. Calif. Demonstration Lab. Sch., Berkeley, 1972-83. Cons. Berkeley Sch. Dist., Alameda County Schs. Mem. land- use com. Environ. Edn. com. East Bay Mcpl. Utility Dist., 1986-87; mem. steering com. Nat. Sci. Guild, Oakland Mus., 1970-76; community adviser Jr. League of Oakland, 1972-76. Mem. Berkeley Women's Town Coun., 1970-91; mem. NAACP.; bd. dirs. East Bay Regional Park Dist., 1972-91, pres., 1978-80, 88-90; bd. dirs. Save San Francisco Bay Assn., 1969-91, People for Open Space, 1977-86, Calif. Natural Areas Coordinating Coun., 1968-90, Living History Ctr., 1982-85; mem. steering com. Bay Area Environ. Edn. Alliance, 1982-85, regional planning com. Assn. of Bay Area Govts., 1988-91, exec. com. Citizens for Eastshore State Park, 1985—; v.p. Friends of Bot. Garden, U. Calif., Berkeley, 1976-80, trustee, 1986—. With USAAF, 1944-46. Recipient Merit award Calif. Conservation Coun., 1953; Woman of Achievement award Camp Fire Girls, 1976; Merit award Am. Soc. Landscape Architects, 1979, Conservation award Golden Gate Audubon Soc., 1985, Benjamin I. Wheeler medal, 1991; mem. Am. Farmland Trust. Mem. AAUW (Calif. com. 1970-73), Prytanean Alumnae, Inc. (pres. 1969-71, chmn. adv. coun. 1971-73, adv. com. Urban Creeks Coun. 1986-91), Nature Conservancy (chmn. no. Calif. chpt. 1970-71), LWV, Regional Parks Assn. (citizens com. to complete the refuge), Nat. Women's Polit. Caucus, Golden Gate Audubon Soc., Sierra Club (environ. edn. com. No. Calif. chpt. 1973-77), U. Calif. Alumni Assn., Inst. Calif. Man in Nature, Calif. Assn. Recreation and Park Dists. (v.p. 1978-81, 1988-90, Oustanding Bd. Mem. award 1989), Preserve Area Ridgelands, Calif. Native Plant Soc., Planning and Conservation League, Urban Ecology, Cousteau Soc., Soroptomists, Pi Lambda Theta, Mortar Board, Gavel (pres.). Democrat. Mem. adv. com. Natural History Guide Series U. Calif. Press, 1972-91. Home: 2932 Pine Ave Berkeley CA 94705-2349

JEFFERIES, JOHN TREVOR, astronomer, astrophysicist, observatory administrator; b. Kellerberrin, Australia, Apr. 2, 1925; came to U.S., 1956, naturalized, 1967; s. John and Vera (Healy) J.; m. Charmian Candy, Sept. 10, 1949; children: Stephen R., Helen C., Trevor R. MA, Cambridge (Eng.) U., 1949; DSc, U. Western Australia, Nedlands, 1962. Sr. research staff High Altitude Obs., Boulder, Colo., 1957-59, Sacramento Peak Obs., Sunspot, N.Mex., 1957-59; prof. adjoint U. Colo., Boulder, 1961-64; prof. physics and astronomy U. Hawaii, Honolulu, 1964-83, dir., Inst. Astronomy, 1967-83; dir. Nat. Optical Astronomy Obs., Tucson, 1983-87; astronomer Nat. Optical Astronomy Obs., 1987-92; cons. Nat. Bur. Stds., Boulder, 1960-62; disting. vis. scientist Jet Propulsion Lab., 1991-94. Author: (monograph) Spectral Line Formation, 1968; contbr. articles to profl. jours. Guggenheim fellow, 1970-71. Mem. Internat. Astron. Union, Am. Astron. Soc. Home: 1652 E Camino Cielo Tucson AZ 85718-1105 Office: Nat Optical Astronomy Obs PO Box 26732 Tucson AZ 85726-6732

JEFFERS, GENE, association executive; b. Canton, Ohio, Oct. 30, 1948; s. Eugene Leroy, Jr. and Ann Elizabeth (Eberhart) J.; m. Carol Saile, Aug. 21, 1971; children: Jessica Ann, Jane Elizabeth. BA in Psychology, U. Md., 1971, MA in Journalism/Pub. Rels., 1983. Mgr., retail Sun Radio, Washington, 1971-72; mgr., photo studio Vicar Photography, Silver Spring, Md., 1972-73; freelance photojournalist Washington, 1973-78; staff photographer ARC, Washington, 1978-82, spl. projects asst., 1982-83, asst. dir. pub. affairs, 1983-85, media rels. assoc., 1985-87, mgr. media rels., 1986-88; v.p. pub. affairs Nat. Assn. Broadcasters, Washington, 1988-94; exec. dir. Western Ins. Info. Svc., L.A., 1994—. Recipient Gold "Cindy" award Indsl. Photography, 1981. Mem. Pub. Rels. Soc. Am. (Silver Anvil award 1987). Home: 330 E Cordova St Apt 358 Pasadena CA 91101-4608 Office: 3530 Wilshire Blvd # 1610 Los Angeles CA 90010-2328

JEFFERS, IDA PEARLE, management consultant, volunteer; b. Houston, Tex., Sept. 5, 1935; d. Stanford Wilbur and Ida Pearle (Kinkead) Oberg; m. Samuel Lee Jeffers, Aug. 29, 1956; children: John Laurence (dec.), Julie Elizabeth Flynn, Melinda Leigh. Student, U. Colo., 1953-56; BA in History, U. N.Mex., 1957. Asst. to mayor City of Albuquerque, 1978, dir. capital improvements, 1979-81; pres. Orgn. Plus, 1988—; guest lectr. U. N.Mex. Albuquerque Pub. Sch., 1968-71. Chmn. Comprehensive Plan Rev., Bond Issue, various coms., Albuquerque, 1968—; mem. Middle Rio Grand Coun. Govts., Albuquerque, 1972-74; mem. Environ. Planning Commn., Albuquerque, 1972-77, chmn. 1975-76; chmn. Citizen Adv. Group, Community Devel., Albuquerque, 1974-75; mem. Jr. League, Albuquerque, 1966—, bd. dirs. 1970-76; mem. N. Mex. Architect, Engrs. Joint Practice Bd. 1978-85, chmn. 1983-85; treas. St. Mark's Episcopal Ch., 1983-86; pres. Eldorado High Sch. Parents, Albuquerque, 1985-86; pres. Regional Conservation Land Trust, Albuquerque, 1987-91; trustee Found., Study and Care of Organic Brain Damage, Houston, 1972-82, pres. 1982-94; mem. Urban Transp. Planning Policy Bd., 1972-74; chmn. community advisors Albuquerque Youth Symphony, 1985-91; founder, chair Friends of Sandia (N.Mex.) Sch., 1965-68, chmn. devel. pre-sch. bd., 1974; mentor Leadership Albuquerque, 1987-91; bd. dirs. Good Govt. Group, Albuquerque, 1988-92, treas. 1988-92; mem., treas. Albuquerque Arts Alliance, 1988-91; mem. Albuquerque All Faiths, All Faith's Receiving Home Aux., 1964-68, sec. 1966, Jr. Women Club, 1963-66, Chaparral Coun. Girl Scouts leaders, 1971-73, selections chmn., 1973-74, Albuquerque Tutorial Coun., 1967-69; foundation bd. Albuquerque Youth Symphony, 1995—. Recipient Disting. Pub. Svc. award, State of N. Mex., 1975, Disting. Woman of N. Mex. award, N.Mex. Women's Polit. Caucus, 1976, Golden Talon award Eldorado High Sch., Albuquerque, 1985, Panhellenic Coun. Disting. Alumnae award 1979. Mem. Rotary, Delta Gamma (pres. 1963-67, chmn. collegiate adv. bd. 1968-71, Cable and Shield awards 1970, 77). Republican. Episcopalian.

JEFFERY, JAMES NELS, protective services official; b. Torrance, Calif., May 16, 1944; s. Daryl Fredrick and Mildred Evelyn (Sogard) J. AA, Long Beach City Coll., 1964; student, Calif. State U., Long Beach, 1964-65, Calif. State U., Sacramento, 1979-80. Capt., firefighter L.A. Fire Dept., 1965-87; dir. Long Beach (Calif.) Search & Rescue Unit, 1968—; asst. chief fire div. Calif. Office Emergency Svcs., Riverside, 1987—; rep. Firescope Communications, Riverside, 1979—. Co-author emergency plans. Chmn. svc. com. Boy Scouts Am., Long Beach, 1979-81, tng. com., 1982—; bd. dirs. Long Beach Community Episepsy Clinic, 1971-72. Recipient Disting. Svc. award Long Beach Jaycees, 1977, Community Svc. award Long Beach Fire Dept., 1978, Silver Beaver award Boy Scouts Am., 1983, Commendation Mayor City of L.A., 1985. Mem. Calif. State Firemen's Assn., Calif. Fire Chiefs Assn., Nat. Coord. Coun. on Emergency Mgmt., Nat. Eagle Scout Assn., So. Calif. Assn. Foresters and Fire Wardens, Lions, Elks. Republican. Lutheran. Home: 3916 Cerritos Ave Long Beach CA 90807-3608 Office: Office Emergency Svcs PO Box 92257 Long Beach CA 90809-2257

JEFFREDO, JOHN VICTOR, aerospace engineer, manufacturing company executive, inventor; b. Los Angeles, Nov. 5, 1927; s. John Edward and Pauline Matilda (Whitten) J.; m. Elma Jean Nesmith, (div. 1958); children: Joyce Jean Jeffredo Ryder, Michael John; m. Doris Louise Hinz, (div. 1980); children: John Victor, Louise Victoria Jeffredo-Warden; m. Gerda Adelheid Pillich, 1980. Grad. in Aeronautical Engring. Cal-Aero Tech. Inst., 1948; AA in Machine Design, Pasadena City Coll., 1951; grad. in Electronics The Ordnance Sch. U.S. Army, 1951; AA in Am. Indian Studies, Palomar Coll., 1978; postgrad. U. So. Calif., 1955-58; MBA, La Jolla U., 1980, PhD in Human Rels., 1984. Design engr. Douglas Aircraft Co., Long Beach and Santa Monica, Calif., 1955-58; devel. engr. Honeywell Ordnance Corp., Duarte, Calif., 1958-62; cons. Honeywell devel. labs., Seattle, 1962-65; supr. mech. engr. dept. aerospace div. Control Data Corp., Pasadena, Calif., 1965-68; project engr. Cubic Corp., San Diego, 1968-70; supr. mech. engring. dept. Babcock Electronics Co., Costa Mesa, Calif., 1970-72; owner, operator Jeffredo Gunsight Co., Fallbrook, Calif., 1971-81; chief engr. Western Designs, Inc., Fallbrook, Calif., 1972-81, exec. dir., 1981-88, CEO, 1988—; owner, operator Western Designs, Fallbrook, 1981-87, Western Design Concepts, Inc., 1987-94; exec. dir. JXJ, Inc., San Marcos, Calif., 1981-88, CEO, 1988—; mgr. Jeffredo Gunsight div., 1981-94; chief engr. JXJ, Inc., 1987-92, (merger JXJ, Inc. and Western Design Concepts, Fallbrook, Calif.), prin., 1992—; owner, mgr. Energy Assocs., San Diego, 1982-86; pres. Jeffredo Internat., 1984-88; founder, chief exec. officer John-Victor Internat., San Marcos, Calif., Frankfurt, Fed. Republic Germany, 1988—; engring. cons. Action Instruments Co., Inc., Gen. Dynamics, Alcyon Corp., Systems Exploration, Inc. (all San Diego), Hughes Aircraft Co., El Segundo, Allied-Bendix, San Marcos; bd. dirs. Indian World Corp., JXJ., Inc., John-Victor Internat. Author: Gabrieleño, The Ocean People, Wildcatting. Contbr. articles to trade jours. and mags.; guest editl. writer Town Hall, San Diego Union; narrator: (film) The Sacred Desert, 1994; patentee agrl. frost control, vehicle off-road drive system, recoil absorbing system for firearms, telescope sight mounting system for firearms, breech mech. sporting firearm, elec. switch activating system, 37 others, others pending. Mem. San Diego County Border Task Force on Undocumented Aliens, 1979-80, 81-82; chmn. Native Californian Coalition, 1982—; bd. dirs. Nat. Geog. Soc., 1968. With U.S. Army, 1951-53. Recipient Superior Svc. Commendation award U.S. Naval Ordnance Test Sta., Pasadena, 1959. Mem. AIAA (sr. mem.), Soc. Automotive Engrs., Nat. Rifle Assn. (life), San Diego Zool. Soc., Sierra Club (life), The Wilderness Soc. Avocations: sculpture, chess, music, archaeology, conservation, travel. Home: 1629 Via Monserate Fallbrook CA 92028-9305 Office: PO Box 669 San Marcos CA 92079-0669

JEFFREY, JOHN ORVAL, lawyer; b. Portsmouth, Va., Aug. 6, 1963; s. Orval L. and Mary L. (Coakley) J. BA, U. Dayton (Ohio), 1985; diploma internat. legal studies, U. San Diego, Paris, 1987; JD, Southwestern U., L.A., 1988. Bar: Calif. 1988, U.S. Dist. Ct. (cen. dist.) Calif. 1988. Assoc. Shield & Smith, L.A., 1989-90, Hewitt, Kaldor & Prout, L.A., 1990-93; mgr. bus. and legal affairs fx subs. Fox TV. Campaign worker John Glenn Campaign for Pres., N.H., 1984; vol. Amnesty Internat. Mem. ABA (internat. law sect., litigation sect., entertainment/sports law sect.), Internat. Bar Assn.,

Los Angeles County Bar Assn. (mem. evaluation profl. standards com., mem. legis. activity com., mem. artists and the law com.), Phi Alpha Delta, Alpha Nu Omega. Democrat. Office: fx Fox TV Business Affairs PO Box 900 Beverly Hills CA 90213-0900

JEFFREY, RONALD JAMES, youth director, educator; b. Cheyenne, Wyo., Mar. 11, 1949; s. John Thomas and Lillian Leola (Carter) J.; m. Marilyn Mansell, Dec. 10, 1977; children: Keeya, Kaylee. BS, Chardon St. Coll., 1972; MS, U. No. Colo., 1976. Dir. Office of Youth Alterntives, Cheyenne, 1971—; cons. various human svc. groups, Cheyenne, 1972—, Title IV Sch. Adminstrn. State of Colo., 1973-74; instr. Laramie County Community Coll., Cheyenne, 1973-85, U. Wyo., Laramie, 1977-90; bd. dir. Rocky Mountain Fed. Bank, Cheyenne; guest speaker various group, 1980—. Author: A Guide for the Family Therapist, 1984; co-author: The Family: A Living Kaleidoscope, 1981; editor (manual) "We Care" Volunteer Training, 1981. Mem. Wyo. Youth Initiative, Cheyenne, Wyo. African/Am. Hist. Com., Cheyenne, Adult Learning Ctr. Adv. Bd.; bd. dir. United Way, Cheyenne, 1987—. Recipient George Washington Honor medal Feedom Found., 1977, Jefferson award Jefferson Com., 1980. Mem. Wyo. Assn. of Marriage and Family (past pres. 1987-89), Phi Delta Kapp. Democrat. Methodist. Office: Office Youth Alternatives 1328 Talbot Ct Cheyenne WY 82001-2648

JEFFRIES, RUSSELL MORDEN, communications company official; b. Carmel, Calif., July 15, 1935; s. Herman M. and Louise (Morden) J.; m. Barbara Jean Borcovich, Nov. 24, 1962; 1 child, Lynne Louise. AA, Hartnell Coll., 1971. Sr. communications technician AT&T, Salinas, Calif., 1955-91; mayor City of Salinas, 1987-91. Pres. El Gabilan Sch. PTA, Salinas, 1971-74, Salinas Valley Council PTA, 1975-76; mem. Salinas City Sch. Bd., 1975-81; mem. Salinas City Council, 1981-87; bd. dirs. Community Hosp. Salinas Found., 1987—, Salinas-Kushikino Sister City, 1987—, pres. 1992-93, John Steinbeck Ctr. Found., 1987—, Food Bank for Monterey County, 1992—; hon. bd. dirs. Monterey Film Festival, 1987, Calif. Rodeo Assn., 1987; mem. ctrl. bd. Calif. Regional Water Quality, 1992—. Recipient hon. service award PTA, Salinas, 1976; cert. of appreciation Calif. Dept. Edn., 1980, Salinas City Sch. Dist., 1981, Calif. Sch. Bds. Assn., 1981, Steinbeck Kiwanis, Salinas, 1987; named hon. mem. Filipino community Salinas Valley, 1988. Mem. Salinas C. of C., Native Sons Golden West, K.C., Rotary, Moose. Republican. Roman Catholic. Home: 204 E Curtis St Salinas CA 93906-2804

JELLINEK, ROGER, editor; b. Mexico City, Jan. 16, 1938; came to U.S., 1961; s. Frank Louis Mark and Marguerite Lilla Donne (Lewis) J.; m. Margherita DiCenzo, Dec. 22, 1963 (div. 1984); children: Andrew Mark, Claire; m. Eden-Lee Murray, 1984; 1 child, Everett Peter Murray. Student, Bryanston Sch., Dorset, Eng., 1951-56; MA, Cambridge U., Eng., 1961. Assoc. editor Random House, 1963-64; editor Walker & Co., 1964-65; editor N.Y. Times Book Rev., 1966-70, dep. editor, 1970-73; editor in chief Times Books, Quadrangle/N.Y. Times Book Co., 1974-78, sr. editor, 1978-81, editor Lamont newsletter and yearbook, 1981-91; pres. Clairemark, Ltd., 1981—, Jellinek & Murray Literary Agy. Editor Atlantic Realm Project, 1983-93; publisher Hawaii map series. With Royal Marines, 1956-57; 2d lt. Brit. Intelligence Corps., 1957-58. Mellon fellow Yale, 1961-63. Home and Office: 980 Kaahue St Honolulu HI 96825-1341

JEMMOTT, ELIZABETH JOY, real estate broker; b. Montego Bay, Jamaica, Feb. 21, 1941; d. William Arden and Sheila Cameron (Branch) J. Lic. real estate broker. Assoc. Vaughan's Real Estate, Montego Bay, 1962-67, Graham Assocs., Montego Bay, 1967-71; property mgr. Spanish Trace Apts., Altamonte Springs, Fla., 1972-76; pres. Shoes by Claude, Naples, Fla., 1976-78; assoc. Mueller Co., Naples, 1978-81; pres. E. Joy Jemmott Inc. (domestic and fgn. investors in comml. property), Winter Park, Fla., 1981—; v.p. Overseas Adminstrn. Services Inc., Orlando, Fla., 1983-86. Mem. Orlando Area Bd. Realtors, Kona Bd. Realtors. Republican. Episcopalian.

JENES, THEODORE GEORGE, JR., retired military officer; b. Portland, Oreg., Feb. 21, 1930; s. Theodore George and Mabel Marie (Moon) J.; m. Beverly Lorraine Knutson, Jan. 29, 1953; children—Ted, Mark. BS, U. Ga., 1956; MS, Auburn U., 1969; grad., Army Command and Gen. Staff Coll., Armed Forces Staff Coll., Air War Coll.; LLD (hon.), U. Akron, 1986. Enlisted U.S. Army, 1951, commd. 2d lt., 1953, advanced through grades to lt. gen., 1984, various assignments, 1953-75; comdr. 3d Brigade, 2d Inf. Div., Republic of Korea, 1975-76, 172d Inf. Brigade, Ft. Richardson, Alaska, 1978-81; dep. commdg. gen. U.S. Army Tng. Ctr., Ft. Dix, N.J., 1976-78; comdr. 4th Inf. Div., Ft. Carson, Colo., 1982-84; dep. commdg. gen. U.S. Army Combined Arms Combat Devel. Activity, Ft. Leavenworth, Kans., 1981-82; comdg. gen. 3d U.S. Army, Ft. McPherson, Ga., 1984-87; commander U.S. Army Forces Ctrl. Command, Ft. McPherson, Ga., 1984-87; dep. comdg. gen. hdqrs. U.S. Army Forces Command, Ft. McPherson, Ga., 1984-87, ret., 1987; cons. Burdeshaw and Assocs., 1987-88; gen. mgr. Seattle Tennis Club, 1988-94. Decorated D.S.M., Legion of Merit, Bronze Star, Meritorious Service medal, Air medal, Army Commendation medal, Vietnamese Cross of Gallantry with Silver Star. Mem. Assn. of U.S. Army, Rotary. United Methodist. Home: 809 169th Pl SW Lynnwood WA 98037-3307

JENKINS, BILLIE BEASLEY, film company executive; b. Topeka, June 27, 1943; d. Arthur and Etta Mae (Price) Capelton; m. Rudolph Alan Jenkins, Nov. 1, 1935; 1 child, Tina Capirce. Student, Santa Monica City Coll., 1965-69. Exec. sec. to v.p. prodn. Screen Gems, L.A., 1969-72; exec. asst. Spelling/Goldberg Prodns., 1972-82; dir. adminstrn. The Leonard Co./Mandy Films, 1982-85, v.p., 1985-87; exec. asst. to pres. and chief oper. officer 20th Century Fox Film Corp., L.A., 1986-87, dir. adminstrn., 1987-90, dir. prodn. svcs. & resources Fox Motion Pictures div., 1990-92; program coord. Am. Film Inst. Gary Hendler Minority Filmmakers Program, 1990-93; pres., CEO Masala Prodns., Inc., 1991—. Asst. to exec. producer: (films) War Games, 1984, Spacecamp, 1986; (movies for TV) Something about Amelia, 1984, Alex, The Life of a Child, 1985; (series) Paper Dolls, 1985, Cavanaughs, 1987, Charlie's Angels, Rookies, others. Commr. L.A. City Cultural Heritage Commn., 1992-93. Named 1991 Woman of Excellence, Boy Scouts Am. Mem. NAFE, Women in Film Assn. (pres. 1991, 92, advisor to exec. bd.), Black Women's Network, Am. Film Inst., Ind. Feature Prodns./West, Motivating Our Students Through Experience (exec. bd. mem.).

JENKINS, BRUCE, sportswriter; b. Oct. 4, 1948; s. Gordon Jenkins; m. Martha Jane Stanton; 2 children. Degree in Journalism, U. Calif., Berkeley, 1971. With San Francisco Chronicle, 1973—, sports columnist, 1989—. Author: Life After Saberhagen, 1986, North Shore Chronicles, 1990. Recipient nat. awards AP, UPI, Basketball Writers Assn.; nominated Pulitzer Prize for columns Barcelona Olympics, 1992. Office: San Francisco Chronicle 901 Mission St San Francisco CA 94103-2905

JENKINS, BRUCE STERLING, federal judge; b. Salt Lake City, Utah, May 27, 1927; s. Joseph and Bessie Pearl (Iverson) J.; m. Margaret Watkins, Sept. 19, 1952; children—Judith Margaret, David Bruce, Michael Glen, Carol Alice. B.A. with high honors, U. Utah, 1949, LL.B., 1952, J.D., 1952. Bar: Utah 1952, U.S. Dist. Ct. 1952, U.S. Supreme Ct. 1962, U.S. Circuit Ct. Appeals 1962. Pvt. practice law Salt Lake City, 1952-59; assoc. firm George McMillan, 1959-65; asst. atty. gen. State of Utah, 1952; dep. county atty. Salt Lake County, 1954-58; bankruptcy judge U.S. Dist. Ct., Dist. of Utah, 1965-78; judge U.S. Dist. Ct. of Utah, 1978—, chief judge, 1984-93; adj. prof. U. Utah, 1987-88. Research, publs. in field; contbr. essays to Law jours.; bd. editors: Utah Law Rev, 1951-52. Mem. Utah Senate, 1959-65, minority leader, 1963, pres. senate, 1965, vice chmn. commn. on orgn. exec. br. of Utah Govt., 1965-66; Mem. adv. com. Utah Tech. Coll., 1967-72; mem. instl. council Utah State U., 1976. Served with USN, 1945-46. Mem. Utah State Bar Assn., Salt Lake County Bar Assn., Am. Bar Assn., Fed. Bar Assn., Order of Coif, Phi Beta Kappa, Phi Kappa Phi, Phi Eta Sigma, Phi Sigma Alpha, Tau Kappa Alpha. Democrat. Mormon. Office: US Dist Ct 251 US Courthouse 350 S Main St Salt Lake City UT 84101-2106*

JENKINS, CREED HAROLD, writer; b. Springville, Utah, July 25, 1926; s. Chester William and Sara Elisa (Finch) J.; m. Eleanor Walker, Sept. 6, 1994; children: Eric (dec.), Diane, Bart, Marcia. AA in Bus. Mgmt., Compton Coll.; BS in Bus. Mgmt., U. So. Calif., MS in Bus. Edn. Nat. mgr. trucking and warehousing Kaiser Aluminum and Chem. Co., Oakland, Calif.; pres., chmn. bd. dirs., founder Consol. Distbn. Co., Union City, Calif.; freelance writer; sr. cons. Calif. Task Reduction Task Force, Sacramento. Author: (textbooks) Modern Warehouse Management, 1975, Complete Guide to Modern Warehouse Management, 1992. Credit mgr. Credit Union, Torrance, Calif., 1950. With USN, 1944-46, PTO. Mem. Commonwealth Club of Calif. Home: 38235 Ashford Way Fremont CA 94536-5278

JENKINS, GENI LOUISE EVANS, home health nurse; b. Chula Vista, Calif., Sept. 26, 1954; d. Howard Eugene and Gladys Louise (Phinney) Evans; m. Larry Joseph Jenkins, May 24, 1985; children: Gretchen Dawn, Thomas Glenn. ADN, Walla Walla (Wash.) C.C., 1984; BSN, Lewis Clark State Coll., 1992. RN, Wash., Idaho, Oreg.; cert. home health nurse ANA. Staff oncol. nurse St. Joseph's Regional Med. Ctr., Lewiston, Idaho, 1984-86; office nurse Southway Internists, Lewiston, 1986-90; office urol. nurse D.A. Shrader, MD, Lewiston, 1990-91; home health nurse St. Joseph's Regional Med. Ctr., Lewiston, 1991-93; DON Able Home Health Svcs., Inc., Lewiston, 1993—; speaker in field. Mem. ANA, Idaho Nurses Assn., Nat. League of Nursing. Home: 2856 Mayfair Dr # B Lewiston ID 83501-4212

JENKINS, LOREN B., publisher, writer; b. New Orleans, Oct. 26, 1938; s. Stephen B. Jenkins and Lorena (Lackey) Dabney; m. Nancy Harmon, June 1964 (div. 1985); children: Sara, Nicholas; m. Laura Thorne, May 15, 1986. BA in Polit. Sci., U. Colo., 1961; postgrad., Columbia U., 1963-64. Ski instr. Aspen (Colo.) Ski Sch., 1958-61; tchr. Peace Corps., Sierra Leone, West Africa, 1961-63; reporter Port Chester (N.Y.) Dayly Item, 1964-65; newsman UPI, N.Y., London, Madrid, Paris, 1965-69; corr. Newsweek, Madrid, Hong Kong, Beirut, Saigon, Rome, 1969-79, The Washington Post, Rome, 1979-89; publisher, editor The Aspen Times, 1992—. Edward R. Murrow fellow Coun. Fgn. Rels., 1988-89; recipient Pulitzer Prize for Internat. Reporting The Washington Post, 1983, Overseas Press Club award Newsweek, 1976. Office: The Aspen Times 310 E Main St Aspen CO 81611-1930

JENKINS, ROYAL GREGORY, manufacturing executive; b. Springville, Utah, Dec. 11, 1936; s. Chester W. and Sarah E. (Finch) J.; m. Donna Jeanne Jones, Aug. 3, 1957; children: Brad, Kent. BS in Engring., San Jose State U., 1959; MBA, U. Santa Clara, 1968. With Lockheed Corp., Sunnyvale, Calif., 1959-64; contr. ICORE Industries, Sunnyvale, 1964-68; div. v.p. fin. Dart Industries, Los Angeles, 1968-74; dir. planning, div. v.p. Avery Label Group, Avery Internat., Los Angeles, 1974-81, group v.p. Materials Group, Painesville, Ohio, 1981-87, sr. v.p. tech. and planning, Pasadena, Calif., 1987-88, sr. v.p. fin., 1988—; CFO, Avery Dennison Corp. Republican. Avocation: golf. Office: Avery Dennison 150 N Orange Grove Blvd Pasadena CA 91103-3534

JENKINS, SPEIGHT, opera company executive, writer; b. Dallas, Jan. 31, 1937; s. Speight and Sara (Baird) J.; m. Linda Ann Sands, Sept. 6, 1966; children: Linda Leonie, Speight. B.A., U. Tex.-Austin, 1957; LL.B., Columbia U., 1961; DMus (hon.), U. Puget Sound, 1992; HHD, Seattle U., 1992. News and reports editor Opera News, N.Y.C., 1967-73; music critic N.Y. Post, N.Y.C., 1973-81; TV host Live from the Met, Met. Opera, N.Y.C., 1981-83; gen. dir. Seattle Opera, 1983—; classical music editor Record World, N.Y.C., 1973-81; contbg. editor Ovation Mag., N.Y.C., 1980—, Opera Quar., Los Angeles, 1982—. Served to capt. U.S. Army, 1961-66. Recipient Emmy award for Met. Opera telecast La Boheme TV Acad. Arts and Scis., 1982. Mem. Phi Beta Kappa Assocs. Presbyterian. Home: 903 Harvard Ave E Seattle WA 98102-4561 Office: Seattle Opera Assn PO Box 9248 Seattle WA 98109-0248*

JENKINS, WILLIAM WALTER, psychologist, consultant; b. Phila., Sept. 10, 1943; s. William and Emily Elizabeth (Bachman) J.; m. Doreen Gayle Meyers, may 30, 1976; children: Eran Scott, Joshua Ian, Tracey Lynn. BS, Temple U., 1968; MEd, Pa. State U., 1974, PhD, 1982. Lic. psychologist, Ariz. Commd. 1st lt. USAF, 1970; advance through grades to lt. col. USNG, 1993; program coord. psychology dept. Phila. State Hosp., 1975-78; psychologist base svc. unity MH/MR, Bellefonte, Pa., 1978-82; program dir. Stress Control Svcs., Inc., Middletown, Pa., 1982-84; sr. staff psychologist Deveraux Ctr., Scottsdale, Ariz., 1985-87; clin. dir. Alamo Juvenile Instn., Phoenix, 1987-88; program dir. children's treatment unit Ariz. State Hosp., Phoenix, 1988-91; pvt. practice cons. psychology Scottsdale, Ariz., 1985—; cons. psycholgist Community Care Network, Scottsdale, 1990-92, Prehab of Mesa (Ariz.), 1990—, Maricopa Clin. Mgmt., 1992-93, Comcare, 1993—; cons. Therapy Rehab. Svcs., 1992—, Desert Vista Hosp., Mesa, Ariz., 1995—; cons. Sta. WITF-PBS, Harrisburg, Pa., coord. community responses TV series on grief and loss Begin with Goodbye, 1982; cons. Continuing Porfl. Edn. Devel. Project, University Park, Pa., GE, Phila, Ariz. Dept. Corrections, Phoenix, Charter counseling Ctr., Phoenix; lectr. personality devel. and disorders in children Psychiat. Technician Tng. Program, 1988-91. Contbr. articles to profl. jours. Facilitator support group for parents of young head injured children St. Joseph's Hosp., 1986-87. Diplomate Am. Bd. Vocat. Experts; mem. APA, N.G. Assn., Pa. State U. Alumni Assn., Phi Kappa Phi. Jewish. Home: 15233 N 62nd Pl Scottsdale AZ 85254-2505

JENNER, BRUCE, sportscaster, former Olympic athlete; b. Mt. Kisco, N.Y., Oct. 28, 1949; s. William and Ester Jenner; m. Chrystie Crownover (div.); children: Burt, Casey, Brandon, Brody; m. Kris Jenner; children: Kourtney, Kimberly, Khloe, Robert. Grad., Graceland Coll., Lamoni, Iowa, 1973. Mem. U.S. Olympic Team, Munich, 1972, Montreal, 1976; founder, pres. 8634 inc., 1976—; pres. Fitness Coun. for FXTV; nat. spokesperson Gen. Aviation Task Force, 1991, Neo-Life health care products; lectr. at colls. and univs., bus. and indsl. convs.; motivational speaker, sports commentator, entrepreneur, commercial spokesperson. Author: (with Philip Finch) Decathlon Challenge: Bruce Jenner's Story, 1977, Bruce Jenner's Guide to Family Fitness, 1978, Bruce Jenner's Viewers Guide to the Olympics, 1980, 84, The Teenage Guide To Fitness, 1984; actor: (film) Can't Stop the Music, 1980; prodr., actor: (TV film) Grambling's White Tiger, 1981, The Steeler and the Pittsburgh Kid; guest star: (TV series) CHiPS, 1981, The Fall Guy, Murder She Wrote; guest host: ABC's Good Morning America, 1988, ABC's Home Show; host: Star Games; sports commentator: ABC Sports, NBC Sports; creator health videos, including (with Kris Jenner) Women's Defense and Fitness Program; TV infomercials: Superstep, StairClimber Plus, Super Fit, The Best Health and Fitness with Kris and Bruce Jenner, (with Gary Player) Rhythum Golf, Minimax; appeared in commls. for Wheaties, Minolta, London Fog. Active Special Olympics, Gov. Coun. Physical Fitness. Won Olympic Gold medal in decathlon, 1976; named Male Athlete of Yr., AP Poll, 1976, one of Ten Outstanding Young Men in Am., U.S. Jaycees, Outstanding Internat. Spokesperson of Yr., 1978; recipient James E. Sullivan trophy as Outstanding Amateur Athlete of Yr., 1976, Track and Field Performer of Yr. award Sport mag., 1976, Celebrity Outreach award, 1993; inducted into Olympic Hall of Fame, 1986, Bay Area Hall of Fame, 1993. Office: PO Box 11137 Beverly Hills CA 90213-4137

JENNERICH, ELAINE, librarian; b. New Castle, Pa., Apr. 17, 1947; d. C. Paul and Regina Anna (Wajert) Zaremba; m. Edward John Jennerich, May 27, 1972; children: Ethan Edward, Emily Elaine. AB, Syracuse U., 1968; MSLS, Drexel U., 1970; PhD, U. Pitts., 1974. Ref. libr. CarLow Coll., Pitts., 1971-74; head ref. svc. Baylor U., Waco, Tex., 1974-83; libr. bond investment Aetna Life and Casualty, Hartford, Conn., 1983-84; ref./media libr. Va. Intermont Coll., Bristol, Va., 1984-85; libr. dir. Emory & Henry Coll., Emory, Va., 1985-87; circulation libr. U. Wash., Seattle, 1988-89; constrn. coord. U. Wash. Librs., Seattle, 1989-91, staff devel. coord., 1991—. Co-author: Reference Interview As Creative Art, 1989. Mem. ALA, Phi Beta Mu, Chi Omega. Roman Catholic. Office: Univ of Washington RM-25 FM-25 Suzzallo Libr Seattle WA 98195

JENNERJAHN, WARREN P., artist, educator; b. Milw., June 15, 1922; s. Ervin Henry and Helen (Krewshewski) J.; m. Elizabeth M. Schmitt, Mar. 14, 1947; children: Hans, Ann. BS in Art Edn., Milw. State Tchrs. Coll., 1946; MS in Art Edn., U. Wis., 1947. Instr. Black Mountain (N.C.) Coll., 1949-51, Cooper Union, N.Y.C., 1952-54, Hunter Coll., N.Y.C., 1953; prof. Adelphi U., Garden City, N.Y., 1954-87; instr. Sedona (Ariz.) Art Ctr., 1990—. Illustrator: (album cover) Choral Music From Five Centuries, 1973, (books) Respect for Life, 1974, Laboratory Investigations in Human Physiology, 1978. Active Sedona (Ariz.) Art Ctr., 1991—. 1st lt. U.S. Army Air Corps, 1941-45, ETO. Grantee Louis Comfort Tiffany grant, N.Y.C., 1952, Adelphi U., Garden City, 1961-87. Home: 707 Rainbow Trl Sedona AZ 86351-9204

JENNESS, VALERIE, sociologist, educator; b. San Antonio, Mar. 7, 1963; d. Terrell Hayes Jenness and Lassie May (Martin) Bonner. BS in Sociology, Ctrl. Wash. U., 1985; MA in Sociology, U. Calif., Santa Barbara, 1987, PhD in Sociology, 1991. Asst. prof. sociology Wash. State U., Pullman, 1991—. Author: Making It Work: The Prostitutes' Rights Movement in Perspective, 1993; contbr. articles and book revs. to profl. jours.; author chpt. in Modern Homosexualities: Fragments of Lesbian and Gay Experience, 1992; adv. editor Social Problems, 1993—, Race, Sex and Class, 1994—, Criminology, 1994—; lectr., presenter in field. Recipient teaching grants U. Calif.-Santa Barbara, 1986, 88, 89, Wash. State U., 1995; recipient rsch. grants Radcliffe Coll., 1989, U. Calif.-Santa Barbara, 1990, Wash. State U., 1992, 93. Mem. Am. Sociol. Assn., Soc. for Study of Social Problems (vice-chair law & soc. divsn. 1994—, chair sexual behavior, communities & politics divsn. 1992-94, mem. nominating com. 1992-94), Am. Soc. Criminology, Sociologists for Women in Society, Pacific Sociol. Assn. (com. on teaching 1994—, com. on status of women in sociology 1991-92), Law and Soc. Assn., Wash. State Sociol. Assn., Nat. Coun. for Rsch. on Women. Democrat. Office: Wash State U Dept Sociology Pullman WA 99163

JENNETT, SHIRLEY SHIMMICK, hospice executive, nurse; b. Jennings, Kans., May 1, 1937; d. William and Mabel C. (Mowry) Shimmick; m. Nelson K. Jennett, Aug. 20, 1960 (div. 1972); children: Jon W., Cheryl L.; m. Albert J. Kukral, Apr. 16, 1977 (div. 1990). Diploma, Rsch. Hosp. Sch. Nursing, Kansas City, Mo., 1958. RN, Mo., Colo., Tex., Ill. Staff nurse, head nurse Rsch. Hosp., 1958-60; head nurse Penrose Hosp., Colorado Springs, Colo., 1960-62, Hotel Dieu Hosp., El Paso, Tex., 1962-63; staff nurse Oak Park (Ill.) Hosp., 1963-64, NcNeal Hosp., Berwyn, Ill., 1964-65, St. Anthony Hosp., Denver, 1968-69; staff nurse, head nurse, nurse recruiter Luth. Hosp., Wheat Ridge, Colo., 1969-79; owner, mgr. Med. Placement Svcs., Lakewood, Colo., 1980-84; vol., primary care nurse, admissions coord., team mgr. Hospice of Metro Denver, 1984-88, dir. patient and family svcs., 1988, exec. dir., 1988-94; mem. adv. com. Linkages Assn. for Older Adults, Denver, 1989-90. Community liaison person U. Phoenix, 1988-90. Mem. NAFE, Nat. Hospice Orgn. (bd. dirs. 1992-95), Colo. Hospice Orgn. (bd. dirs., pres. 1991-93). Republican. Mem. Ch. of Religious Sci. Office: Hospice of Metro Denver 3955 E Exposition Ave Ste 500 Denver CO 80209-5033

JENNINGS, CHARLES RAYMOND, music educator, bands director; b. Oakland, Calif., Oct. 21, 1955; s. Charles Raymond and Ann V. Jennings; m. Heather Lane Owen, June 20, 1987; children: Emily Ann, Catherine Michelle, Robert Weston. AA, Santa Rosa (Calif.) Jr. Coll., 1975; BA in Music, Calif. State U., Chico, 1976, MA in Music, 1983; D of Mus. Arts, U. So. Calif., 1995. Music tchr., dir. bands, chmn. dept. Sonoma Valley H.S., Sonoma, Calif., 1978-85; music instr., acting dir. bands Santa Rosa Jr. Coll., 1985-86, Modesto (Calif.) Jr. Coll., 1986-87; music instr. Kings River C.C., Reedley, Calif., 1987-88; music tchr., dir. instrumental music, dist. arts facilitator Tamalpais Union H.S. Dist., Mill Valley, Calif., 1989—; prof. music, dir. bands San Joaquin Delta Coll., Stockton, Calif., 1989—. Condr. various honor bands in Calif. Mem. NEA, Internat. Assn. Jazz Educators, Music Educators Nat. Conf., Coll. Band Dirs. Nat. Assn., Music Assn. Calif. C.C.s (pres. 1992-94), Pi Kappa Lambda. Democrat. Lutheran. Office: San Joaquin Delta Coll Dept Music 5151 Pacific Ave Stockton CA 95207-6304

JENNINGS, EMMIT M., surgeon; b. Tucumcari, N.Mex., Oct. 12, 1922; s. Felix Carlow and Rose (Wich) J.; m. Laura-Jean Cameron. Sept. 23, 1950; children: Katherine, John, Patrick, Teresa, Margaret, Colleen, Maureen. BS, Notre Dame, 1945; MD Sch. of Medicine, St. Louis U., 1946. Diplomate Am. Bd. Surgery, Am. Coll. Surgeons. Physician family practice, Tucumcari, 1950-51; chief of surgery U.S. Army, Ft. Huachuea, 1951-53; fellowship thoraci surgery, L.A., 1953-54; pvt. practice Gen. Surgery, Roswell, N. Mex., 1954-93; pres. N. Mex. Med. Soc., 1967-68, N. Mex. Physicians Liability Co., Albuquerque, 1986-93; del. from N. Mex. AMA, 1968-76. Mem. City Coun. of Roswell, 1960-64; commr. Chaves County, 1989-92; senator State of N.Mex., Santa Fe, 1993—. Capt. U.S. Army, 1943-46, 51-53. Recipient A.H. Robbins award for Community Svc., 1980; named Man of the Yr. Jaycees, Roswell, 1957. Mem. Am. Legion, Knights of Columbus, Elks. Republican. Roman Catholic. Home: 2001 Biazos Roswell MN 88201 Office: 212 W 1st St Roswell NM 88201-4602

JENNINGS, JESSE DAVID, anthropology educator; b. Oklahoma City, July 7, 1909; s. Daniel Wellman and Grace (Cruce) J.; m. Jane Noyes Chase, Sept. 7, 1935; children: Jesse David, Herbert Lee. B.A., Montezuma Coll., 1929; Ph.D., U. Chgo., 1943; D.Sc., U. Utah, 1980. Anthropologist Nat. Park Service, 1937-42, 45-48; mem. faculty U. Utah, 1948—, prof. anthropology, 1949-86, prof. emeritus, 1986—, disting. research prof., 1970—, disting. prof. anthropology, 1975—; Mem. anthropology-psychology div. Nat. Acad. Sci.-NRC, 1954-56; vis. prof. anthropology Northwestern U., 1960, U. Minn., 1961, U. Hawaii, 1965, 67-68; adj. prof. U. Oreg., 1980—; lectr. summer inst. anthropology U. Colo., 1961, Fairmont Coll., 1962; lectr. semi-centennial symposium Am. archeology Rice U., 1962; Reynolds lectr. U. Utah, 1962, Leigh lectr., 1975; dir. Glen Canyon Archeol. Salvage Project, 1957-66, Utah Mus. Natural History, 1965-73; cons. instl. studies NSF, 1964-66. Author: (with A.V. Kidder and E.M. Shook) Excavations at Kaminal Juyu, Guatemala, 1946, (with E.A. Hoebel) Readings in Anthropology, 3d edit, 1972, The Archeology of the Plains: An Assessment, 1956, Danger Cave, 1957, also numerous articles, reports, papers.; editor: (with Edward Norbeck) Prehistoric Man in the New World, 1964, (with Robert F. Spencer) Native Americans, 1965, 2d edit., 1977, Prehistory of North America, 1968, 2d edit., 1974, 3d edit., 1989, Accidental Archaeologist: Memoirs of Jesse D. Jennings, 1994, Warner Modular Publs. in Anthropology, 1972-74, (with others) Pacific Anthrop. Records No. 25, 1976, No. 32, 1980, (with others) Ancient Native Americans, 1978, Prehistory of Utah and the Eastern Great Basin, 1978, Prehistory of Polynesia, 1979, Cowboy Cave, 1980, Bull Creek, 1981, Ancient North Americans, Ancient South Americans, 1983; editor for: (with others) N.Am., Atlas of Archaeology, Rainbird Reference Books, 1972. Served to comdr. USNR, 1942-45. Recipient Viking medal in archaeology Wenner Gren Found. Anthrop. Research, 1958. Mem. AAAS (nat. v.p., chmn. sect. H 1961, 69), NAS, Soc. Am. Archaeology (editor bull. 1950-54, pres. 1958-59, Disting. Service award 1982), Am. Anthrop. Assn. (exec. bd. 1953-56), Phi Beta Kappa, Sigma Xi, Phi Kappa Phi. Home: 21801 Siletz Hwy Siletz OR 97380-9721

JENNINGS, JUDITH MADRONE, city official; b. Teaneck, N.J., May 21, 1949; d. Frank Gouverneur and Ethel Kathleen (Richards) J. BA, CUNY, N.Y.C., 1971. Cert. elec. inspector. Electrician Internat. Brotherhood of Elec. Workers, Oakland, Calif., 1978-86; elec. inspector City of Oakland, Calif., 1986—. Mem. Internat. Assn. Elec. Inspectors (cert.), Internat. Brotherhood of Elec. Workers. Office: City of Oakland 1330 Broadway Oakland CA 94612-2503

JENNINGS, MARCELLA GRADY, rancher, investor; b. Springfield, Ill., Mar. 4, 1920; d. William Francis and Magdalene Mary (Spies) Grady; student pub. schs.; m. Leo J. Jennings, Dec. 16, 1950 (dec.). Pub. relations Econolite Corp., Los Angeles, 1958-61; v.p., asst. mgr. LJ Quarter Circle Ranch, Inc., Polson, Mont., 1961-73, pres., gen. mgr., owner, 1973—; dir. Giselle's Travel Inc., Sacramento; fin. advisor to Allentown, Inc., Charlo, Mont.; sales cons. to Amie's Jumpin' Jacks and Jills, Garland, Tex. Investor. Mem. Internat. Charolais Assn., Los Angeles County Apt. Assn. Republican. Roman Catholic. Home and Office: 509 Mt Holyoke Ave Pacific Palisades CA 90272-4328

JENNINGS, MAX, newspaper editor; b. Mesa, Ariz., Aug. 3, 1941; s. Garland E. and Irma Louise Jennings; m. Carol A. Trickett; children: John, Jason. BA, Tex. Tech U., 1963; MA, Ariz. State U., 1974; postgrad. U. Ariz. Staff corr. UPI, Cheyenne, Wyo., 1963-64, bur. chief, 1964-65, regional exec., Albuquerque, 1965-67, fgn. desk, N.Y.C., 1967, fgn. corr., Peru and Bolivia, 1968-70; asst. prof. dept. journalism Ariz. State U., 1971-78; exec. editor Mesa Tribune, Ariz., 1979-88; editor Dayton Daily News, 1988—. Author: I'll Take Tomorrow, The Mary Gohlke Story, 1985. Contbr. articles to women's mags. and profl. jours. Served to 2d lt. U.S. Army, 1963-64. Named

Journalism Educator of Yr., Western Newspapers Found., Phoenix, 1977. Mem. NCCJ, Am. Soc. Newspaper Editors, AP Mng. Editors Assn., Rotary, Sigma Delta Chi. Methodist.

JENNINGS, M(YRON) KENT, political science educator; b. Chowchilla, Calif., June 4, 1934; s. Talmadge Aldine and Ethel Lulabelle (Dodd) J.; m. Holly Lucille Phillips, Sept. 1, 1956; children: James Steven, Cynthia Diane, Larkin Kent. BA magna cum laude, U. Redlands, 1956; PhD, U. N.C., 1961. Research assoc. Brookings Instn., Washington, 1960-63; from asst. prof. to prof. polit. sci. U. Mich., Ann Arbor, 1963-84, 1985—; prof. polit. sci. U. Calif.-Santa Barbara, 1982—; vis. research assoc. U. Oreg., Eugene, 1969-70; vis. prof. U. Tilburg, (Netherlands), 1971-72, UCLA, 1980. Author: Community Influentials, 1964, (with others) The Image of the Federal Service, 1964, The Political Character of Adolescence, 1974, Governing American Schools, 1974, Generations and Politics, 1981, Parties in Transition, 1986, Continuities in Political Action, 1989; editor: (with others) The Electoral Process, 1966, Comparative Political Socialization, 1970, Elections at Home and Abroad, 1994. Guggenheim fellow, 1977-78; fellow Ctr. for Advanced Studies in Behavioral Scis., 1977-78, Am. Acad. Arts and Scis., 1982; Netherlands Inst. for Advanced Study in Humanities and Social Scis., 1989. Mem. Am. Polit. Sci. Assn. (coun. 1976-77), Midwest Polit. Sci. Assn. (v.p. 1980-81), Western Polit. Sci. Assn., Internat. Soc. Polit. Psychology (coun. 1982-84, pres. 1989-90), Phi Beta Kappa. Office: Ctr for Polit Studies 4030 Isr Bldg 426 Thompson Ann Arbor MI 48109

JENNINGS, PAUL CHRISTIAN, civil engineering educator, academic administrator; b. Brigham City, Utah, May 21, 1936; s. Robert Webb and Elva S. (Simonsen) J.; m. Millicent Marie Bachman, Aug. 28, 1981; m. Barbara Elaine Morgan, Sept. 3, 1960 (div. 1981); children: Kathryn Diane, Margaret Ann. BSCE, Colo. State U., 1958; MSCE, Calif. Inst. Tech., 1960, PhD, 1963. Prof. civil engring., applied mechanics Calif. Tech. Inst., Pasadena, 1966—, chmn. divsn. engring., 1985-89, v.p., provost, 1989-95, acting v.p. for bus. and fin., 1995—; mem. faculty bd. Calif. Tech. Inst., 1974-76, steering com., 1974-76, chmn. nominating com., 1975, grad. studies com., 1978-80; cons. in field. Author: (with others) Earthquake Design Criteria. Contbr. numerous articles to profl. jours. 1st lt. USAF, 1965-66. Recipient Achievement in Academia award Coll. Engring. Colo. State U., 1992; Erskine fellow U. Canterbury, New Zealand, 1970, 85. Fellow AAAS, New Zealand Soc. Earthquake Engring.; mem. ASCE (Walter Huber award 1973, Newmark medal 1992), Seismol. Soc. Am. (pres. 1980), Earthquake Engring. Rsch. Inst. (pres. 1981-83), Athenaeum Club. Home: 516 S Catalina Ave Pasadena CA 91106-3307 Office: Calif Inst Tech Mail Code 212-31 Pasadena CA 91125

JENNINGS, REBA MAXINE, critical care nurse; b. Gainesville, Mo., Oct. 28, 1936; d. William Claude and Osa Marie (Whillock) Loftis; m. Robert Wayne Jennings, Nov. 10, 1953; children: Sherry Anita, Robert Allen, Lalia Marie. Diploma, Burge Sch. Nursing, Springfield, Mo., 1983. ACLS; RN, Mo., Alaska. Med-surg. staff nurse AMI-Springfield Community Hosp., 1983-84; pvt. duty nurse Western Med. Svcs., Springfield, 1984; staff nurse in CCU, ICU, emergency dept. Tri-County Sisters of Mercy Hosp., Mansfield, Mo., 1984-85; cardiac telemetry staff nurse St. John's Regional Health Ctr., Springfield, 1985-93; nurse obs. unit Valley Hosp., Palmer, Alaska, 1993-94; nurse PCU Alaska Regional Hosp., Anchorage, 1994; PCU nurse Providence Alaska Med. Ctr., Anchorage, 1995—.

JENNISON, BRIAN L., environmental specialist; b. Chelsea, Mass., June 13, 1950; s. Lewis L. and Myra S. (Piper) J. BA, U. N.H., 1972; PhD, U. Calif., Berkeley, 1977; cert. hazardous materials mgr., U. Calif., Davis, 1986. Teaching, rsch. asst. U. Calif., Berkeley, 1972-77; staff rsch. assoc. Dept. of Molecular Biology, Berkeley, 1978-80; instr. dept. biology Calif. State U. Hayward, 1977; sr. biologist San Francisco Bay Marine Rsch. Ctr., Emeryville, Calif., 1980-81; inspector I Bay Area Air Quality Mgmt.Dist., San Francisco, 1981-83, inspector II, 1983-88; enforcement program specialist Bay Area Air Quality Mgmt. Dist., San Francisco, 1988-92; dir. air quality mgmt. div. Washoe County Dist. Health Dept., Reno, Nev., 1992—; cons. U.S. Army Corps of Engrs., L.A., 1980, San Francisco, 1981; instr. U. Calif., Berkeley ext., 1990-93, Assoc. Bay Area Govs., 1990-92; adj. prof. U. Nev., Reno, 1994—. Contbr. articles to profl. jours. Sustaining mem. Rep. Nat. Com., Washington. Postdoctoral fellow, Harbor Br. Found., 1977-78. Mem. AAAS, Air and Waste Mgmt. Assn. (chmn. Ea. Sierra chpt. 1994—), Navy League of U.S. (life), Phi Beta Kappa. Republican. Office: Washoe County Dist Health Dept PO Box 11130 Reno NV 89520

JENSEN, ARTHUR ROBERT, psychology educator; b. San Diego, Aug. 24, 1923; s. Arthur Alfred and Linda (Schachtmayer) J.; m. Barbara Jane DeLarme, May 6, 1960; 1 child, Roberta Ann. B.A., U. Calif., Berkeley, 1945; Ph.D., Columbia U., 1956. Asst. med. psychology U. Md., 1955-56; research fellowInst. Psychiatry U. London, 1956-58; prof. ednl. psychology U. Calif., Berkeley, 1958-94; prof. emeritus, 1994—. Author: Genetics and Education, 1972, Educability and Group Differences, 1973, Educational Differences, 1973, Bias in Mental Testing, 1979, Straight Talk about Mental Tests, 1981; Contbr. to profl. jours., books. Guggenheim fellow, 1964-65, fellow Ctr. Advanced Study Behavioral Scis., 1966-67. Fellow AAAS, Am. Psychol. Assn., Eugenics Soc., Am. Psychol. Soc.; mem. Psychonomic Soc., Am. Soc. Human Genetics, Soc. for Social Biology, Behavior Genetics Assn., Psychometric Soc., Sigma Xi. Office: U Calif Sch Edn Berkeley CA 94720

JENSEN, BARBARA REBECCA, English language educator; b. Tracy, Calif., Feb. 26, 1955; d. William Raymond and Rebecca Katherine (Boyes) Lewis; m. Truman Ray Jensen, Mar. 8, 1985; children: Aubrey Rebecca Rhodes, Luke Franklin Jensen. BA in Liberal Studies, Calif. State U., Stanislaus, Turlock, 1982, BA in English, 1982, MA in English Writing Theory, 1990, postgrad. Cert. jr. coll. tchr., Calif. Teaching asst., grad. teaching asst. Calif. State U., Stanislaus, 1987-90, asst. dir. Writing Ctr., 1989-90; edn. coord. Phoenix Houst/Tuum Est, Turlock, 1987-91; instr. English Modesto (Calif.) Jr. Coll., 1987—, dir. Writing Ctr., 1992—. Contbr. articles to profl. jours.; newsletter editor Sons of Norway, Modesto, 1989. Named Woman of Distinction, Modesto Jr. Coll., 1993-94. Mem. MLA, NEA, AAUW, Nat. Coun. Tchrs. English. Republican. Episcopalian. Home: 358 N Minaret Ave Turlock CA 95380-4162 Office: Modesto Jr Coll 435 College Ave Modesto CA 95350-5808

JENSEN, C. NEIL, association executive, lobbyist; b. Laramie, Wyo., July 8, 1939; s. George Taylor and Sylvia (Schmucker) J.; m. Linda L. Jensen, June 30, 1960; children: Cyneil, Colleen, Rick. BS, BYU, 1961. Cert. pharmacy patient counselor. Office adminstr., sales rep. Lakeside Labs., Milw., 1961-72; nat. sales mgr. Dental Div. Warner Lambert, Morris Plains, N.J., 1972-77; pres. J&J Bus. Cons., Provo, Utah, 1977-80; exec. dir. Utah Pharm. Assn., Salt Lake City, 1980—; lobbyist Utah Pharm. Assn., 1980—; adj. prof. U. Utah, 1984-88. Writer, editor: Utah Pharmacy Digest. Scout master, Boy Scouts of Am., Provo, 1978-84 (named Scoutmaster of Yr. 1983). Mem. Am. Pharm. Assn. (com. mem. 1980—), Nat. Assn. Retail Druggists, Nat. Assn. Pharm. Execs. (holder various offices 1980—), Salt Lake C. of C. Republican. Mormon. Home: 2800 Kalmia Ave Apt C101 Boulder CO 80301-1582

JENSEN, CAROLYN JEAN, marketing and public relations researcher; b. Visalia, Calif., Nov. 7, 1947; d. Charles Thomas and Bette Jean (Williamson) Madden; m. Robert Laurits Jensen, Apr. 6, 1968 (div. Dec. 1980); children: Francene Ann, Christene Ann, Jeanne Marie. AA, Coastline Coll., 1978, cert, 1982; BSBA in mktg., fin., U. Phoenix, 1992, MA in Orgnl. Mgmt., 1995. Conservation rep. Southern Calif. Edison, Santa Ana, 1978-80; conservation, load mgmt. cons. Southern Calif. Edison, Rosemead, Calif., 1980-81; energy svcs. cons. Southern Calif. Edison, Santa Ana, 1981-89, sales and mktg. supr., 1989-91; project mgr. Southern Calif. Edison, Rosemead, 1991-92, program mgr., 1992-93, adminstrv., 1993-95; adminstrv. K.L. Geans Co., 1994—; corp. speaker Southern Calif. Edison; tech. cons. Urban Rail, Orange County Urban Trail, 1992. Contb. articles to profl. jours. Adv. Rails for Trails, Laguna Beach, 1992-94, Urban Design for Mass Transit, Orange County, 1991-93; exec. com. Parent Teacher Orgns. 1980-90, exec. vol. 1985. Recipient Nat. Maglev Initiative award, Fed. Railroad Adminstrn, Washington, 1992, Mktg. award Edison Elec. Inst., Washington, 1988, 89, Exemplary Vol. award Carnation Co. and Vol. Ctr. for Orange County, 1985, 86. Mem. Wycliffe Assocs. (Cornerstone award 1986, 87), Women in Engring. Advocates, NAFE, Am. Soc. Heating, Refrigerating & Air Conditioning Engrs. (tech. energy com. 1993-94, Energy award 1989, 90, 91, Gov. affairs com. 1990, 91). Republican. Presbyterian. Home: 14451 Pinewood Rd Tustin CA 92680 Office: KL Geans Co 2809 Woodbine Ave Fullerton CA 92635

JENSEN, D. LOWELL, federal judge, lawyer, government official; b. Brigham, Utah, June 3, 1928; s. Wendell and Elnora (Hatch) J.; m. Barbara Cowin, Apr. 20, 1951; children: Peter, Marcia, Thomas. A.B. in Econs, U. Calif.-Berkeley, 1949, LL.B., 1952. Bar: Calif. 1952. Dep. dist. atty. Alameda County, 1955-66, asst. dist. atty., 1966-69, dist. atty., 1969-81; asst. atty. gen. criminal div. Dept. Justice, Washington, 1981-83, assoc. atty. gen., 1983-85, dep. atty. gen., 1985-86; judge U.S. Dist. Ct. (no. dist.) Calif., San Francisco, 1986—; mem. Calif. Council on Criminal Justice, 1974-81; past pres. Calif. Dist. Atty.'s Assn. Served with U.S. Army, 1952-54. Fellow Am. Coll. Trial Lawyers; mem. Nat. Dist. Atty.'s Assn. (victim/witness commn. 1974-81), Boalt Hall Alumni Assn. (past pres.). Office: US Dist Ct 1301 Clay St Oakland CA 94612-5217

JENSEN, DAVID WARREN, structural, aerospace and civil engineering educator; b. LaChappelle, France, Jan. 23, 1956; came to U.S., 1958; s. Warren Edgar and Verla B. (Muir) J.; m. GayLynn Brady, June 27, 1980; children: Joshua, Brady, Mark, Lisa, Spencer. BS cum laude, Brigham Young U., 1980; SM, MIT, 1981, PhD, 1986. Engring. aid Bur. Reclamation, Provo, Utah, 1978-79; research asst. MIT, Cambridge, Mass., 1980-86; asst. prof. aerospace engring. Pa. State U., University Park, 1986-91, assoc. prof., 1991-95, civil engring Brigham Young U., 1993—. Pres. MIT Grad. Student Coun., Cambridge, 1983-84. Recipient Spl. Achievement award Bur. Reclamation, Provo, 1978; USN-Am. Soc. for Engring. Edn. summer faculty research fellow, 1987, Air Force Office Sci. Rsch.-Universal Energy Systems fellow, 1988, Boeing Faculty fellow, 1995. Mem. AIAA, ASCE, Am. Soc. Engring. Edn., Am. Soc. Composites, Phi Kappa Phi, Tau Beta Pi, Sigma Xi. Republican. Mormon. Avocations: camping, horses, basketball, computers, racquetball. Home: 525 W 3050 S Mapleton UT 84664 Office: Brigham Young U 24066 CB-368 Provo UT 84602

JENSEN, DOUGLAS BLAINE, lawyer; b. Fresno, Calif., Feb. 10, 1943; s. Rodger Blaine and Margaret Mae J.; m. Lesley S. Smith, Sept. 4, 1967 (div.); children—Clayton B., Kelly E.; m. Patty Stocking Telles, Aug. 5, 1988. AB, Stanford U., 1964, JD, 1967. Bar: Calif. 1967, U.S. Dist. Ct. (ea. dist.) Calif., U.S. Dist. Ct. (no. dist.) Calif., U.S. Ct. Appeals (9th cir.). Clk. to judge U.S. Ct. Appeals 9th Cir., Fresno and San Francisco, 1967-68; Internat. Legal Ctr. fellow, Santiago, Chile, 1968-70; assoc. Miller, Groezinger, Pettit, Evers & Martin, San Francisco, 1970-72, Baker, Manock & Wanger, Fresno, Calif., 1972-74; ptnr. Baker, Manock & Jensen, Fresno, 1974—; adj. prof. water law San Joaquin Coll. Law, 1980-83. Chmn. Valley Children's Hosp., 1976-93 . Mem. ABA, State Bar Calif., Fresno County Bar Assn. (pres. 1982-83). Club: Rotary (pres. 1992-93). Contbr. article to legal publ. Office: 5260 N Palm Ave Ste 421 Fresno CA 93704-2217

JENSEN, EDMUND PAUL, bank holding company executive; b. Oakland, Calif., Apr. 13, 1937; s. Edmund and Olive E. (Kessell) J.; m. Marilyn Norris, Nov. 14, 1959; children: Juliana L., Annika M. BA, U. Wash., 1959; postgrad., U. Santa Clara, Stanford U., 1981. Lic. real estate broker, Oreg., Calif. Mgr. fin. plan and evaluation Technicolor, Inc., Los Angeles, 1967-69; group v.p. Nat. Industries & Subs, Louisville, 1969-72; v.p. fin. Wedgewood Homes, Portland, 1972-74; various mgmt. positions U.S. Bancorp, Portland, 1974-83; pres., COO U.S. Bancorp, Inc., Portland, 1983-93; vice chmn., COO U.S. Bancorp, Inc., Portland, 1993-94; pres., CEO Visa Internat., 1994—; bd. dirs. U.S. Nat. Bank of Oreg., U.S. Bank Washington. Chmn. United Way, 1986, N.W. Bus. Coalition, 1987; bd. dirs. Saturday Acad., Portland, 1984—, Visa U.S.A., Visa Internat., Marylhurst Coll., Oreg. Bus. Coun., Oreg. Downtown Devel. Assn., Oreg. Ind. Coll. Found., 1983—, treas., 1986—, chmn., 1988—; bd. dirs. Portland Art Mus., 1983—, vice chmn., 1989—. Mem. Portland C. of C. (bd. dirs. 1981—, chmn. 1987), Assn. Res. City Bankers, Assn. for Portland Progress (pres. 1988), Waverly Country Club, Multnomah Athletic Club, Arlington Club. Office: US Bancorp PO Box 8837 Portland OR 97208-8837

JENSEN, GERALD RANDOLPH, editor, graphics designer; b. Kalispell, Mont., Aug. 12, 1924; s. Hans Clemen and Mabel (Everson) J.; m. Helen Jeanne Levine, Dec. 11, 1943; 1 child, Marjorie Jeanne. MA, Union U., 1976, PhD, 1978; LittD, Internat. Acad. World Frat. of Scholars, London. Regional and nat. dir. Youth & Christian Edn. Internat., Four Square Los Angeles, 1946-54; dir. San Francisco Youth for Christ, San Francisco, 1955-60; v.p. Sacred Records, Whittier, Calif., 1960-63; dir. pub. Full Gospel Bus. Men's Fellowship, Los Angeles, 1962-69; pres. Triangle Prodns., Burbank, Calif., 1970-79, Claiborne-Jensen Advt., Arcadia, Calif., 1980-82, Jerry Jensen & Assoc., Santa Fe Springs, Calif., 1982-85; editor Full Gospel Bus. Men's Fellowship, Costa Mesa, Calif., 1985—; bd. dirs. High Adventure Ministries, Van Nuys, Calif., 1970-94, Found. for Airborne Relief, Long Beach, Calif., 1986-89, Ambassadors of Aid, Vancouver, British Columbia, 1978-94, Friends in the West, Seattle, 1969-94, Internat. Bible Inst., Santa Fe Springs, Calif., 1982-94. Bd. regens Golden State U., Los Angeles, 1979-89; advt. & pub. relations Orange County Jesus Rally, Anaheim, Calif., 1980-81. Recipient Award of Merit Golden State U., 1986. Mem. Evang. Press Assn., Am. Mgmt. Assn. Republican. Home: 5772 Garden Grove Blvd # 48 Westminster CA 92683-1817 Office: 3150 Bear St Costa Mesa CA 92626-2926

JENSEN, HELEN, musical artists management company executive; b. Seattle, June 30, 1919; d. Frank and Sophia (Kantosky) Leponis; student pub. schs., Seattle; m. Ernest Jensen, Dec. 2, 1939; children: Ernest, Ronald Lee. Co-chmn., Seattle Community Concert Assn., 1957-62; sec. family concerts Seattle Symphony Orch., 1959-61; hostess radio program Timely Topics, 1959-60; gen. mgr. Western Opera Co., Seattle, 1962-64, pres. 1963-64; v.p., dir., mgr. pub. rels. Seattle Opera Assn., 1964-83, preview artists coord., 1981-84; bus. mgr. Portland (Oreg.) Opera Co., 1968, cons., 1967-69; owner, mgr. Helen Jensen Artists Mgmt., Seattle, 1970-92. First v.p. Music and Art Found., 1981-84, pres. 1984-85. Recipient Cert., Women in Bus in the Field of Art, 1973, award Seattle Opera Assn., 1974, Outstanding Svc. award Music and Art Found., 1984, Women of Achievement award Women in Communications, 1992. Mem. Am. Guild Mus. Artists, Music and Art Found. (life), Seattle Opera Guild (life, bd. dirs. 1988-92, pres., award of distinction 1983, parliamentarian 1987-89), Ballard Symphony League (sec.), Portland Opera Assn., Portland Opera Guild, Seattle Civic Opera Assn. (pres. 1981—), 200 Plus One, Aria Preview, Lyric Preview Group (chmn. 1988-92), Past Pres. Assembly (pres. 1977-79, parliamentarian 1987-89), Pres.'s Forum (1st v.p. 1990-91, program vice chmn. 1987-88, pres. 1991-92), North Shore Performing Arts Assn. (pres. 1981), Women of Achievement (past pres's. assembly, chmn.), Pres.'s Forum (pres. 1991-92), Woman's Century Club (chmn. art, drama, music dept. 1992-93), Helen Jensen Hiking Club. Home: 19029 56th Ln NE Seattle WA 98155-3156

JENSEN, JAKKI RENEE, retail company executive; b. Eugene, Oreg., Mar. 1, 1959; d. Philip William Jensen and Mary Katherine (Sommers) Henderson; m. Johnny Claiborne Hawthorne, May 7, 1983. Student, Oreg. State U., 1977-78; student (hon.), Portland State U., 1978-81. With Nordstrom Inc., Beaverton, Oreg., 1981—; mgr. cosmetics Nordstrom Inc., Beaverton, 1984; mgr. cosmetics Nordstrom Inc., Walnut Creek, Calif., 1984-86, buyer cosmetics, 1986-88; buyer cosmetics Nordstrom Inc., San Francisco, 1988-93; area mdse. mgr. Nordstrom Own Product, San Francisco, 1993—. Affiliate, vol. San Francisco Soc. for Prevention of Cruelty to Animals, 1990—. Mem. No. Calif. Cosmetic Assn. Republican. Home: 118 Costanza Dr Martinez CA 94553-6600 Office: 865 Market St San Francisco CA 94103-1900

JENSEN, JAMES LESLIE, chemistry educator, dean; b. Tulare, Calif., Oct. 17, 1939; s. Lester Eugene and Mabel Irene (Brown) J.; m. Nancy Ruth Peterson, Aug. 13, 1960; children: Randall Mark, Linda Suzanne. BA in Chemistry, Westmont Coll., 1961; MA in Chemistry, U. Calif., Santa Barbara, 1963; PhD in Organic Chemistry, U. Wash., 1967. Instr. chemistry Westmont Coll., Santa Barbara, Calif., 1962-64, U. Wash., Seattle, 1968; from asst. prof. to prof. Calif. State U., Long Beach, 1968—, assoc. dean Sch. Natural Scis., 1983-93, dean Coll. Nat. Scis. and Math., 1993—; vis. scientist Brandeis U.-W.P. Jencks Lab., Waltham, Mass., 1974-75; vis. prof. U. Calif. Irvine, 1981-82; chmn. various univs. and schs. dept. coms.; lectr. over 40 univs. and profl. confs., U.S., U.K., France, Italy, Sweden. Reviewer NSF, Jour. Am. Chem. Soc., Jour. Organic Chemistry; contbr. 25 articles to profl. jours. Weyerhauser fellow, U. Wash., 1966-67; scholar Westmont Coll., 1957-58, 60-61; recipient Merit award Long Beach Heart Assn., 1970, Disting. Service award Am. Heart Assn., 1971; grantee: NSF, NIH. Mem. AAAS, Am. Sci. Affiliation, Internat. Union of Pure and Applied Chemistry, Am. Chem. Soc. (organic div.), Royal Soc. Chemistry (organic chemistry div., fast reactions groups), Nat. Assn. for Sci., Tech., Soc., Sigma Xi, Phi Beta Kappa, Phi Lambda Upsilon. Republican. Office: Calif State U Dept Chemistry Long Beach CA 90840

JENSEN, JOHN MICHAEL, mathematics educator, consultant; b. Bklyn., Feb. 4, 1949; s. John Adolph and Katherine Mary (O'Sullivan) J.; m. Joyce Ann Janiga, Jan. 3, 1981. BA, Fordham U., 1970; MA, Ariz. State U., 1978. Math. tchr. Shea Mid. Sch., Phoenix, 1971-73, Paradise Valley High Sch., Phoenix, 1973-74; math. tchr., dept. head Shadow Mountain High Sch., Phoenix, 1974-80, Horizon High Sch., Scottsdale, Ariz., 1980—; cons. The Coll. Bd., San Jose, Calif., 1988—; adj. instr. Ottawa U., Phoenix, 1987-91, Maricopa County C.C., Phoenix, 1978-93. Woodrow Wilson Inst. fellow Princeton U., 1985; named Tchr. of Yr. Ariz. Assn. Engr. & Sci. Soc., 1987; recipient Presdl. Award in Math., Pres. of U.S., 1987. Mem. NEA, Ariz. Edn. Assn., Paradise Valley Edn. Assn. (treas. 1976), Nat. Coun. Tchrs. Math., Mensa.

JENSEN, JON NORMAN, clinical child psychologist; b. Richmond, Calif., Jan. 20, 1950; s. Viggo Norman and Florene Pearl (Wilson) J.; m. Theresa Marie Lazaneo, Mar. 25, 1972 (div. May 1977). BA in Exptl. Psychology, U. Calif., Santa Barbara, 1977; MS in Clin. Psychology, Auburn U., 1981, PhD in Clin. Psychology, 1989. Lic. psychologist, Calif. Fellow in child/adolescent psychology U. Tex. Med. Br., Galveston, 1989; child psychologist Madison Ctr., South Bend, Ind., 1989-90, Humboldt County Mental Health, Eureka, Calif., 1990-92; pvt. practice Eureka, Calif., 1991—; adj. prof. psychology Humboldt State U., Arcata, Calif., 1992-93. Active ACLU, No. Calif., 1992—, Sierra Club, 1992—, Amnesty Internat., Arcata, 1993—; mem. Leadership Coun.-So. Poverty Law Ctr. Mem. APA, Calif. Psychol. Assn., Calif. Assn. Psychol. Providers. Mem. Green Party. Office: 930 Third St Ste 201 Eureka CA 95501

JENSEN, JUDY DIANNE, psychotherapist; b. Portland, Oreg., Apr. 8, 1948; d. Clarence Melvin and Charlene Augusta (Young) J.; m. Frank George Cooper, Sept 4, 1983; stepchildren: Pamela Cooper, Brian Cooper. BA in Sociology and Anthropology with honors, Oberlin Coll., 1970; MSW, U. Pitts., 1972; postgrad., U. Wis., 1977. Lic. clin. social worker, marriage and family therapist, Oreg. Social worker Day Hosp. Western Psychiat. Inst. and Clinic, Pitts., 1972-73, South Hills Child Guidance Ctr., Pitts., 1973-74; mem. drug treatment program Umatilla County Mental Health Clinic, Pendleton, Oreg., 1975-77; social worker Children's Services Div. State of Oreg., Pendleton, 1978-80, therapist intensive family services project, 1980—, dir. intensive family services project, 1986—; pvt. practice Pendleton, 1980—. NIMH grantee, 1970-72; NDEA fellow 1977; Gen. Motors scholar Oberlin Coll., 1966-70. Mem. Am. Assn. Marriage and Family Therapists (clin.), Nat. Assn. Social Workers. Home: 325 NW Bailey Ave Pendleton OR 97801-1604 Office: PO Box 752 Pendleton OR 97801-0752

JENSEN, LAWRENCE ROBERT, lawyer; b. Oakland, Calif., Apr. 7, 1959; s. Robert Johan and Dolores Fawn (Freeland) J.; m. Susan Kim McShane, Aug. 23, 1983 (div. 1986); m. Terry Ann Hutson, July 29, 1989 (div. 1993). BA in Psychology with honors, U. Calif., Santa Cruz, 1984; JD cum laude, Santa Clara U., 1987. Bar: Calif. 1987, U.S. Dist. Ct. (no. dist.) Calif. 1987, U.S. Ct. Appeals (9th cir.) 1991. Assoc. Howell & Hallgrimson, San Jose, 1987-89, Law Offices of Joseph DiCiuccio, San Jose, 1989-90, Hallgrimson, McNichols, McCann & Inderbitzen, San Jose, 1990-92, Liccardo, Rossi, Sturges & McNeil, San Jose, 1992-94; pvt. practice San Jose, 1994—. Bd. dirs. ACLU, No. Calif. Affiliate, 1987-89, 92-94, Santa Clara Valley chpt., 1986-89, 92-95, chair, 1993-95; bd. dirs. San Jose Northside Neighborhood Assn., 1992—, v.p. 1993-95. Recipient Cert. of Recognition State Bar Bd. Govs., 1989. Mem. Santa Clara County Bar Assn., Calif. Trial Lawyers Assn., Santa Clara County Trial Lawyers Assn. Office: 95 S Market St 3d Fl San Jose CA 95113

JENSEN, MARVIN O., national park superintendent; b. Mapleton, Utah, Aug. 25, 1940; s. Ruel W. and Ethel Josepha (Otte) J.; m. Mary Lynn Blackett, Dec. 17, 1960; children: Russel M., Mary Kay. BA in Range Mgmt., Utah State U., 1963. Range mgmt. specialist Bureau of Land Mgmt., Kanab, Utah, 1963-65, area mgr., 1965-69; area mgr. Bureau of Land Mgmt., Moab, Utah, 1969-74, river mgmt. specialist, 1975-76; unit mgr. Nat. Park Svc., Grand Canyon, Ariz., 1976-81; mgmt. asst. Nat. Park Svc., Sequoia Kings Canyon, Calif., 1982-87; supt. Nat. Park Svc., Kenai Fjords Nat. Park, Alaska, 1987, Glacier Bay Nat. Park, Alaska, 1988—; charter mem. interagy. whitewater com., Moab, 1973-81; N.Am. chmn. No. Lattitudes Biosphere Res. Commn., Glacier Bay, 1992—. Contbr. articles to profl. jours. Mem. Am. Cetacean Soc., Assn. Nat. Park Rangers, Nat. Park Svc. Alumni Assn. Office: Glacier Bay Nat Park & Preserve PO Box 140 Gustavus AK 99826-0140

JENSEN, RICHARD DENNIS, librarian; b. Payson, Utah, Oct. 20, 1944; s. Ruel Whiting and Ethel Josepha (Otte) J.; m. Maxine Swasey, Apr. 21, 1966; children: Shaun, Craig, Todd, Jana, Brad, Kristine, April, Lynne. BS in Zoology, Brigham Young U., 1971, MLS, 1976. Asst. sci. libr. Brigham Young U., Provo, Utah, 1971-76, life sci. libr., 1976-84, dept. chair sci. and tech. libr., 1985—. Co-author: Agricultural and Animal Sciences Journals and Serials: An Analytical Guide, 1986, (indexes) Great Basin Naturalist, 50 Year Index, 1991, BYU Geology Studies, Cumulative Index, vol. 1-37, 1954-1991, 1992. Mormon. Office: Brigham Young U Sci & Tech Dept 2222 Hbll Provo UT 84602-1035

JENTZSCH, RICHARD ALLEN, city manager; b. Salt Lake City, Utah, Oct. 4, 1938; s. Carl Eugene and Garda (Webb) J.; m. Gale Patricia Hammond, Dec. 15, 1967; 1 child, Charles Edward. Student adult edn., Salt Lake City Pub. Schs., 1958-60; student, U. Utah, 1960-61, Portland State U., 1971, Chemeketa Community Coll., 1971. Asst. county planner/surveyor Davis County Planning and Engring. Depts., Farmington, Utah, 1957-65; planner Lorain County Regional Planning Commn., Elyria, Ohio, 1965-68; prin. planner Ind. State Planning Svcs. Agy., Indpls., 1968-70; local govt. coord. Intergovernmental Rels. div. Exec. Dept. State of Oreg., Salem, 1970-77, acting asst. adminstr., 1974-75, acting adminstr., 1975; exec. dir. Lincoln-Uinta Assn. Govts., Kemmerer, Wyo., 1977-79, Ind. Heartland Coord. Commn., Indpls., 1979-81; city adminstr. City of Myrtle Point, Oreg., 1981-83; exec. dir. Mid-Columbia Coun. Govts., The Dalles, Oreg., 1983-89; planning and devel. dir. City of Page, Ariz., 1989-90; asst. city mgr. for planning and devel. CIty of Page, Ariz., 1990—. Mem. Jefferson City (Oreg.) Planning Commn. and Budget Com., elected to city coun., 1977, chmn. coun. fin. com., ex-officio mem. planning commn.; sec. Myrtle Point (Oreg.) C. of C. Devel. Com., 1981-83; mem. The Dalles C. of C., 1984-88, mem. child care task force, 1988; mem. Wasco County Jail Task Force, 1987-88; mem. Page/Lake Powell C. of C., 1989—. Mem. Internat. City Mgmt. Assn., Am. Planning Assn., No. Ariz. Coun. Govts. (regional coun. 1992—, transp. tech. sub-com. 1989—, transp. com. 1992—, co-chair overall econ. devel. dist. adv. com. 1992—), Rural Ariz. Econ. Devel. Adv. Com. Home: PO Box 484 Page AZ 86040-0484 Office: City of Page PO Drawer HH Page AZ 86040

JERISON, HARRY JACOB, psychology educator; b. Bialystok, Poland, Oct. 13, 1925; came to U.S., 1929; m. Irene Landkof, Dec. 17, 1950. BS in Biol. Scis., U. Chgo., 1947, PhD in Psychology-Biol. Scis., 1954. Lectr. in psychology U. Ind., South Bend, 1951-52; rsch. psychologist Aero Medi. Lab., Dayton, Ohio, 1949-57; from assoc. prof. to prof., dir. behavior rsch. lab. Depts. Psychology and Biology Antioch Coll., Yellow Springs, Ohio, 1957-69; prof. biobehavioral scis. and psychology UCLA, 1969-92, prof. emeritus, 1993—; vis. scientist Applied Psychology Unit Med. Rsch. Coun., Cambridge, Eng., 1978-79; acad. visitor Dept. Zoology Oxford U., 1986; vis. prof. Istituto de Antropologia Universita di Firenza, Italy, 1986-87, Dept. Psychology U. Hawaii, 1987, Max-Planck-Inst. f. Biologische Kybernetik, Tubingen, Fed. Republic of Germany, 1989, Dept. Psychology Univ. Coll., London, 1993—; dir. Evolutionary Biology Intelligence NATO ASI, 1986-87; James Arthur lectr. Am. Mus. Natural History, N.Y.C., 1989. Fellow

Ctr. Advanced Study Behavioral Scis., Stanford, Calif., 1967-68; scholar in residence Rockefeller Found. Study and Conf. Ctr., Bellagio, Italy, 1983. Home: 503 W Rustic Rd Santa Monica CA 90402-1115 Office: UCLA Psychiat Dept Los Angeles CA 90024

JERMANN, JERRY, administrator; b. Vancouver, Wash., July 16, 1947; s. Julius Benjamin and Anne Lou (Smith) J.; m. Kathleen Ethel Sharp, Feb. 14, 1968 (div.); 1 child, Andrea Christisem. BS in Ceramic Engring., U. Wash., 1970, BA in Anthropology with honors, 1971, MA in Anthropology, 1973, PhD in Anthropology, 1981. Dir. Office of Pub. Archaeology, U. Wash., Seattle, 1974-82; cultural resources mgr. URS Cons., San Bernardino, Calif., 1983-85; cultural resources URS Cons., Sacramento, Calif., 1985-87; sr. archaeologist Dames & Moore, San Diego, 1987-88; tech. data svcs. mgr. URS Cons., Sacramento & Long Beach, Calif., 1988-92; prin. scientist Brown & Caldwell, Seattle, 1992-94, Pleasant Hill, Calif., 1992-94; proposal mgr. Bechtel Nat., Inc., San Francisco, 1994—; adv. bd. Wash. Archaeological Rsch. Coun., Pullman, Wash., 1976-82. NSF fellow, 1963, Nat. Lead Co. fellow, 1970-71; Longview Fibre Co. scholar, 1965, 66, Interpace Co. scholar, 1969. Office: Bechtel Nat Inc 50 Beale St San Francisco CA 94105-1813

JERMINI, ELLEN, educational administrator, philosopher; b. Krefeld, Germany, Aug. 25, 1939; came to U.S., 1986.; d. Maximilian and Mathilde (Wachtberger) Wilms; m. Helios Jermini, 1961 (div. June 1989); children: Mariella Arnoldi, Diego Jermini. PhB, U. Healing, 1984, M in Healing Sci., 1985, PhD, 1986; PhB, U. Philosophy, 1992. Sec. Germany, Switzerland, 1962; pub. translator, 1984—; seminar organizer Europe, 1983—; dir. U. Philosophy/European Found., 1986—; pres. U. Healing, Campo, Calif., 1986—, U. Philosophy, Campo, 1986—; abbot Absolute Monastery, Campo, 1986—. Editor: (newsletter Italian) Absolute, (newsletter German) Absolute; co-author: Practitioner's Manual. Spkr. various univs. and orgns. in Calif. and N.Y., 1989-92, St. Petersburg, Moscow, 1991, Africa, 1994, Egypt, 1995, various seminars and workshops, Ghana, Nigeria. Home and Office: Univ of Healing 1101 Far Valley Rd Campo CA 91906-3213

JERNIGAN, EARL WESLEY, archaeologist, museum director; b. Alhambra, Calif., June 1, 1940; s. Harvey Richard and Jeanne Jernigan; m. Gisela Evelyn Brashear, June 8, 1968; children: Marcus, Kevin, Thomas, Alan. BA, U. Ariz., 1968, MA, 1970, PhD, 1973. Asst. prof. anthropology U. Ariz., Tucson, 1978-86; sign designer various Tucson firms, 1986-89; dir. mus. Ea. Ariz. Coll., Thatcher, 1989—. Author: Jewelry of the Prehistoric Southwest, 1978, White Metal Universe, 1980; illustrator: (children's) One Green Mesquite Tree (Best Juvenile Book of Yr. 1988), Agave Blooms Just Once (co-recipient Author of Yr. 1990). Office: Ea Ariz Coll Thatcher AZ 85552-0769

JERNSTEDT, KENNETH ELLIOTT, lawyer; b. Rockeville Center, N.Y., Feb. 27, 1944; s. Kenneth Allen and Laura Jean (Elliott) J.; m. Sandra Reece, Aug. 20, 1967; children: Erik, Matt, Kaitlin. BA in History, Stanford U., 1966; JD, U. Calif., Berkeley, 1969. Bar: Calif. 1970, Oreg. 1970, U.S. Dist. Ct. Oreg., U.S. Ct. Appeals (9th cir.), U.S. Supreme Ct. 1977. Assoc. Spears, Lubersky, Campbell, Bledsoe & Young, Portland, Oreg., 1970-75; ptnr. Spears, Lubersky, Campbell, Bledsoe & Young, Portland, 1975-80; ptnr., exec. com. Bullard, Korshoj, Smith & Jernstedt, Portland, 1980—. Bd. dirs. Vis. Nurses Assn., Portland, 1973-82; mem. Oreg. Fish and Wildlife Commn., 1987-92, chmn., 1988-90; basketball coach Sellwood Boys Club, Portland, 1981-87, West Sylvan Sch., Portland, 1987-90; coach S.E. Soccer Assn., Portland, 1981-90; coach Lake Oswego Soccer Assn. 1992; coach youth basketball YMCA, 1992-93. Mem. ABA (labor sect.), Calif. Bar Assn., Oreg. State Bar Assn. (exec. bd. labor sect. 1975), Multnomah Athletic Club, Stanford Club (pres. 1974-75). Republican. Office: Bullard Korshoj Smith & Jernstedt 1000 SW Broadway Ste 1900 Portland OR 97205

JERRITTS, STEPHEN G., computer company executive; b. New Brunswick, N.J., Sept. 14, 1925; s. Steve and Anna (Kovacs) J.; m. Audrey Virginia Smith, June 1948; children: Marsha Carol, Robert Stephen, Linda Ann; m. 2d, Ewa Elizabet Rydell-Vejlens, Nov. 5, 1966; 1 son, Carl Stephen. Student, Union Coll., 1943-44; B.M.E., Rensselaer Poly. Inst., 1947, M.S. Mgmt., 1948. With IBM, various locations, 1949-58, IBM World Trade, N.Y.C., 1958-67, Bull Gen. Electric div. Gen. Electric, France, 1967-70, merged into Honeywell Bull, 1970-74; v.p., mng. dir. Honeywell Info. Systems Ltd., London, 1974-76; group v.p. Honeywell U.S. Info. Systems, Boston, 1977-80; pres., chief operating officer Honeywell Info. Systems, 1980-82, also bd. dirs.; pres., chief exec. officer Lee Data Corp., 1983-85; with Storage Tech. Corp., 1985-88, pres., chief operating officer, 1985-87, also bd. dirs., vice-chmn. bd. dirs., 1988; pres., chief exec. officer NBI Corp., 1988-92, also bd. dirs.; corp. sr. v.p., pres. Lat. Am. Wang Labs, Inc.; bd. dirs. Scully Signal Co., Wang Labs. Inc.; cons. mgmt. corp. turnarounds. Bd. dirs. Guthrie Theatre, 1980-83, Charles Babbage Inst., 1980-92, Minn. Orch., 1980-85; trustee Rensselaer Poly. Inst., 1980-85. With USNR, 1943-46. Mem. Computer Bus. Equipment Mfrs. (dir. exec. com. 1979-82), Assoc. Industries Mass. (dir. 1978-80). Home and Office: 650 College Ave Boulder CO 80302-7136

JERRYTONE, SAMUEL JOSEPH, trade school executive; b. Pittston, Pa., Mar. 21, 1947; s. Sebastian and Susan Teresa (Chiampi) J.; children: Sandra, Cheryl, Samuel, Sebastian. Assoc. in Bus., Scranton (Pa.) Lackawanna Jr. Coll., 1966. Mgr. House of Jerrytone Beauty Salon, West Pittston, Pa., 1967-68; regional sales dir. United Republic Life Ins., Harrisburg, Pa., 1970-76; night instr. Wilkes-Barre (Pa.) Vo-Tech High Sch., 1976-78; spl. sales agt. Franklin Life Ins. Co., Wilkes-Barre, 1978-80; instr. Jerrytone Beauty Sch., Pittston, Pa., 1968-69, supr., 1969—; prof. sch. evaluator Nat. Accrediting Com. Arts and Scis., Washington, 1984—; mem. adv. craft com. Wiles-Barre Vo-Tech High Sch., 1988—. Mem. com. Rep. Presdl. Task Force, Washington, 1984. Mem. Pa. Hairdressers Assn., Nat. Accrediting Com. Cosmetology, Am. Coun. Cosmetology Educators, Masons (3d degree award 1983, 32d degree award Lodge Coun. chpt. consistory 1984), Shriners (Irem temple). Roman Catholic. Office: JTC Tng Schs 953 E Sahara Ave Ste 24A Las Vegas NV 89104-3005

JERSIN, EDWARD ANTHONY, lawyer; b. Pueblo, Colo., Oct. 12, 1920; s. Anthony and Frances (Nolan) J.; children: K. Suzanne Lambdin, Robert A., Anthony A., Mary F. BA, U. Denver, 1942, JD, 1946. Bar: Colo. 1946. Sole practice, Denver, 1946—. Commr., Jud. Selection of County Judges, Denver County, 1977-82; commr. Community Rels. Commn., Denver County, 1962-83. Served as spl. agt. CIC, U.S. Army, 1943-45. Mem. Colo. Bar Assn. (bd. govs. 1971-74), Denver Bar Assn. (1st v.p. 1976-77), Colo. Bar Found., ABA. Democrat. Roman Catholic. Clubs: Denver Athletic, Petroleum. Lodges: KC, Rotary. Office: 1430 First Interstate Tower S 621 17th St Denver CO 80293-9303

JERSKY, BRIAN, statistician; b. Johannesburg, Transvaal, South Africa, Oct. 13, 1957; came to U.S., 1988; s. Jechiel and Hannah (Skudowitz) J. BS, U. Witwatersrand, Johannesburg, South Africa, 1986, BS with honors, 1988; MS, Cornell U., 1990, PhD, 1992. Asst. prof. Sonoma State U., Rohnert Park, Calif., 1992—; rsch. asst. U. of the Witwatersrand, 1986-87. Jewish. Office: Sonoma State U Darwin Hall Dept Math 1801 E Cotati Ave Rohnert Park CA 94928

JERVIS, JANE LISE, academic administrator, science historian; b. Newark, N.J., June 14, 1938; d. Ernest Robert and Helen Jenny (Roland) J.; m. Kenneth Albert Pruett, June 20, 1959 (div. 1974); children: Holly Jane Pruett, Cynthia Lorraine Pruett; m. Norman Joseph Chonacky, Dec. 26, 1981; children: Philip Joseph Chonacky, Joseph Norman Chonacky. AB, Radcliffe Coll., 1959; MA, Yale U., 1974, MPhil, 1975, PhD in History of Sci., 1978. Freelance sci. editor and writer, 1962-72; edn. advisor, adminstr. U. Md. Program/USAF, France, 1964-65; lectr. in history Rensselaer Poly. Inst., 1977-78; dean Davenport Coll., lectr. in history of sci. Yale U., 1978-82; dean students., assoc. prof. history Hamilton Coll., 1982-87; dean coll., lectr. in history Bowdoin Coll., 1988-92, acting pres., 1990; pres. Evergreen State Coll., Olympia, Wash., 1992—. Author: Cometary Theory in 15th Century Europe; contbr. articles to profl. jours.; book reviewer; presenter in field. Trustee Maine Hist. Assn., 1991-92; chair Maine selection com. Rhodes Scholarship Trust, 1990-92, chair N.W. selection com., 1992-93; commr. N.W. Assn. Schs. and Colls. Commn. on Colls., 1994—. Office: Evergreen State Coll Office of President Olympia WA 98505

JERVIS, WILLIAM HORACE, plastic and reconstructive surgeon; b. Vicksburg, Miss., Dec. 7, 1934; s. William H. Jr. and Margaret Elizabeth (Bates) J.; children: Vincent H., Helga J., Hans W. BA, Occidental Coll., 1957; MD, McGill U., Montreal, Can., 1961. Diplomate Am. Bd. Plastic Surgery, Nat. Bd. Med. Examiners; lic. physician and surgeon, Calif. Internship L.A. County Gen. Hosp., 1961-62; flight surgeon Brooks AFB, San Antonio, 1963; capt. Evreux (France) AFB and Lockbourne AFB, 1963-65; gen. surgery Pacific Med. Ctr., San Francisco, 1965-66, Kaiser Found. Hosp., Oakland, Calif., 1969-71; gen. practice residency Contra Costa County Hosp., Martinez, Calif., 1968-69; plastic surgery residency U. Tex. Southwestern Med. Sch., Dallas, 1972-74; pvt. practice plastic and reconstructive surgery Walnut Creek, Calif., 1974—; vol. reconstructive surgery La Familia Found. Hosp., Nuevo Progresso, Guatemala, 1983, 84, 85, 86, 87, 88, 89, 90, 93; clin. instr. plastic surgery Sch. of Medicine U. Calif., Davis, 1979-92; chief sect. plastic surgery John Muir Med. Ctr., Walnut Creek, 1982-85. Contbr. articles to profl. jours. Fellow Am. Coll. Surgeons; mem. AMA, Calif. Med. Assn., Alameda-Contra Costa Med. Soc., Am. Soc. Plastic and Reconstructive Surgeons, Calif. Soc. Plastic Surgeons, Am. Soc. for Aesthetic Plastic Surgery.

JESKE, KEITH WILLIAM, real estate and mortgage executive; b. Milw., June 16, 1950; s. Gilbert F. and Betty A. (Langdon) J.; children: KC William, Camie Sloan; m. Christy Sue Bynum, Feb. 12, 1993. AA, San Bernardino Valley Coll., 1971; BA, Point Loma, San Diego, 1973; JD, U. West Los Angeles, 1976. Chmn. bd., CEO Keith Jeske Realty, Las Vegas, Nev., 1976—; CEO Levin Mortgage, Las Vegas, 1991—; pres., CEO Echelon Group, 1994—; pres. Fred Sands Las Vegas Properties, 1995—; CEO United Fin. Mortgage Corp.; cons. Consumer Credit Counselors, L.A., 1974-78, Culver City (Calif.) Planning Commn., 1975-77. Author: Goal Mind, 1988; contbr. articles to profl. jours. Mediator Community Mediation of San Diego, 1990; educator, aribitrator Alternative Dispute Resolutions, Las Vegas, 1992. Named Sales Person of Yr., Beverly Hills, 1973, Mgr. of Yr., Bd. of Realtors, L.A., 1979. Mem. Nat. Assn. Realtors, Calif. Assn. Realtors, L.A. Bd. Realtors, Culver City Bd. Realtors, Las Vegas Bd. Realtors, Mortgage Brokers Assn., Mortgage Bankers Assn. Home: 1101 Broadmoor Ave Las Vegas NV 89109-1556

JESSUP, W. EDGAR, JR., lawyer; b. L.A., Sept. 9, 1922; s. Walter E. and Marian (Moses) J.; m. Audrey B. Vail; children: Bryn W., Holden D. ScB in Engring. magna cum laude, Brown U., 1943; JD, U. So. Calif., L.A., 1949. Bar: Calif. 1950, U.S. Dist. Ct. (cen. dist.) Calif. 1950, U.S. Claims Ct. 1976, U.S. Tax Ct., 1952. Founding ptnr. Ervin, Cohen & Jessup, Beverly Hills, Calif., 1953—; lectr. Sch. Engring. U. So. Calif., 1950-58, Sch. Law, 1965-76; bd. dirs. Logicon, Inc., L.A., Magnetika, Inc., L.A. Author: Law & Specifications for Engineers & Scientists, 1963; contbr. articles to profl. jours. Bd. dirs. Assn. Alumni Brown U., Providence, 1985-89, Westside Family YMCA, West Los Angeles, Calif., chmn., 1988-93; bd. dirs. Brentwood (Calif.) Westwood Symphony, 1953-93; bd. mgrs. L.A. Metro YMCA, 1988-93. Lt. USNR, 1943-46, ETO, PTO. Mem. ABA, State Bar Calif., L.A. Bar Assn., Beverly Hills Bar Assn., Brown U. Club So. Calif. (pres. 1984-91), Calif. Yacht Club (former flag officer), Order of Coif, Tau Beta Pi, Phi Kappa Phi, Phi Alpha Delta. Office: Ervin Cohen & Jessup 9401 Wilshire Blvd Beverly Hills CA 90212-2928

JESTE, DILIP VISHWANATH, psychiatrist, researcher; b. Pimpalagaon, India, Dec. 23, 1944; came to U.S., 1974; naturalized Feb., 1980; m. Sonali D. Jeste, Dec. 5, 1971; children: Shafali, Neelum. B in Medicine & Surgery, U. Poona, India, 1966; D. Psychiat. Medicine, Coll. Physicians and Surgeons, 1970; MD, U. Bombay, 1970. Cer. Am. Bd. Psychiatry and Neurology, 1979; lic. physician, D.C., Md., Calif. Hon. asst. prof. KEM Hosp., G.S. Med. Coll., Bombay, 1971-74; staff psychiatrist St. Elizabeth's Hosp., Washington, 1977-82, chief movement disorder unit, 1982-86; clin. assoc. prof. psychiatry Walter Reed Med. Ctr., Bethesda, Md., 1981-84; assoc. clin. prof. psychiatry and neurology George Washington U., Washington, 1984-86; prof. psychiatry and neurosci. U. Calif., San Diego, 1986—; chief psychiatry svc. San Diego VA Med. Ctr., San Diego, 1989-92; dir. geriatric psychiatry clin rsch ctr. U. Calif. and VA Med. Ctr., San Diego, 1992—; vis. scientist dept. neuropathology Armed Forces Inst. of Pathology, Washington, 1984-86; co-dir. Med. Students' Psychiatry Clerkship Program, 1987-91; ad-hoc mem. Vets. Adminstrn. Neurobiology Grant Rev. Bd., 1984—; participant numerous meeting and confs.; lectr. in field. Co-author: Understanding and Treating Tardive Dyskinesia, 1982; editor: Neuropsychiatric Movement Disorders, 1984, Neurpsychiatric Dementias, 1986, Psychosis and Depression in the Elderly, 1988; contbr. articles to numerous profl. jours, reviewer numerous profl. jours. Mem. Acad. Geriatric Resource Com., U. Calif., 1986-87, mem. com. on joint doctoral program in clin. psychology, 1986-87, mgmt. com. faculty compensation fund com., 1988-89, chmn. Psychiat. Undergrad. Edn. Com., 1987. Recipient Merit award NIMH, 1988; recipient numerous grants in field. Fellow Indian Psychiatric Soc. (recipient Sandoz award 1973), Am. Psychiatric Assn. (co-chmn. Tardive Dyskinesia task force 1984-92), Am. Coll. Neuropsychopharm. (co-chmn. fin. com. 1988-89); mem. Soc. for Neurosci., Internat. Brain Rsch. Orgn., Soc. Biolog. Psychiatry (A.E. Bennett Neuropsychiatric Rsch. award 1981), Am. Acad. Neurology, Am. Geriatrics Soc., Calif. Psychiatric Soc., Am. Assn. Geriatric Psychiatry, West Coast Coll. Biolog. Psychiatry, San Diego Soc. Psychiatric Physicians, Assn. Scientists of Indian Origin in Am. (pres. neurosci. chpt. 1988—, named Outstanding Neuroscientist 1988). Office: Vets Affairs Med Ctr 3350 La Jolla Village Dr V116A San Diego CA 92161

JEWELL, EDWARD WILLIAM, career officer, radiologist, health facility administrator; b. N.Y.C., Oct. 21, 1954; s. Edward W. and Pauline Anne (Renier) J. BA, U. Pa., 1977; MD, Georgetown U., 1981. Diplomate Am. Bd. Radiology. Advanced through ranks to comdr. USN; intern U.S. Naval Hosp., Oakland, Calif., 1981-82, dept. head, residency dir., 1992—; resident in radiology U.S. Naval Hosp., San Diego, 1985-89; dept. head, residency dir. U.S. Naval Hosp., Okinawa, Japan, 1989-92; flight surgeon New River USMC, Jacksonville, N.C., 1983-85. Active mem. Nature Conservancy, Washington, Habitat for Humanity, Americus, Ga., World Wildlife Fund, Washington, Wilderness Soc., Washington. Mem. Am. Roentgen Ray Soc., Radiologic Soc. North Am. Roman Catholic.

JEWELL, NICHOLAS PATRICK, statistics educator; b. Paisley, Scotland, Sept. 3, 1952; came to U.S., 1979; s. Brian McCalmont and Phyllis Mary (Large) J.; m. Debra Jean Cederborg, June 27, 1980; 1 child, Britta Lisa. BSc, U. Edinburgh, 1973, PhD, 1976. Asst. prof., dir. statis. libr. Princeton (N.J.) U., 1979-81; asst. prof. Biostats., Sch. Pub. Health U. Calif., Berkeley, 1981-83, assoc. prof., 1982-87, co-chair group in Biostats., 1986-94, prof., 1987—, vice provost, 1994—; mem. core faculty program U. Calif., San Francisco, 1985—, prof. Biostats., 1987—; reviewer manuscripts Wiley, Oxford U. Press, Marcel Dekker, reviewer proposals NSF, NIH, Nat. Sci. Engring. Rsch. Coun. Can.; speaker numerous confs. Author: (with K. Dietz and V. Farewell): AIDS Epidemiology, Methodological Issues, 1992; editor: Lifetime Data Analysis; assoc. editor: International Statistical Review; referee numerous jours. including Jour. Applied Probability, Annals of Statistics, Jour. Business and Economic Statistics, Jour. Statistical Planning and Inference, Jour. AIDS, Advances in Applied Mathematics; contbr. articles to profl. jours., chpts. to books. Carnegie scholar, 1971, Sir David Baxter scholar, U. Edinburgh, 1973-76; Thouron fellow U. Pa., 1976, postdoctoral Harkness fellow U. Berkeley, 1976-77, Stanford U., 1977-79, rsch. fellow U. Edinburgh, 1978-79, Regents jr. faculty fellow U. Calif., Berkeley, 1982; grantee Scottish Home and Health Dept., 1978-79, N.J. Dept. Health, 1979-81, NSF, 1980-82, NIMH, 1982-86, NIH/HHS, 1983-85, Nat. Inst. Aging, 1986-89, 86-92, 89-91, Nat. Inst. Allergy and Infectious Diseases, 1987—, 1989-93, 1992—. Fellow Am. Statis. Assn. (v.p. biostats. San Fransisco Bay Area chpt., 1982-84, pres. elect., 1984-85, pres. 1985, chair nominating com. Dist. 7 Rep. 1985, chair, 1987, mem. 1988, 91, assoc. editor Annals of Stats., Statis. Sci.), Biometric Soc. (judge student paper competition, 1986-87, chair 1988, pres. elect. WNAR region 1990, pres. 1991, past pres. 1992), Inst. Math. Stats. (treas. 1985-88, mgmt. com. Current Index. Stats. 1985-88, nominating com. 1988-89), Bernoulli Soc. Office: Univ Calif Sch Pub Health Dept Biostatistics Berkeley CA 94720

JEWETT, DON LEE, medical researcher; b. Eureka, Calif., Jan. 28, 1931. AB, San Francisco State U., 1953; postgrad., U. Calif., Berkeley, 1954-56; MD, U. Calif., San Francisco, 1960; DPhil, Oxford U., 1963. Lic. physician and surgeon, Calif. Intern Kaiser Found. Hosp., San Francisco, 1960-61; NIH postdoctoral fellow Oxford U. and Yale U., 1961-64; asst. prof. depts. physiology and neurosurgery U. Calif. San Francisco, 1964-72, resident orthopaedic tng. program, 1972-75, clin. instr. dept. orthopaedic surgery, 1972-75, assoc. prof., 1975-89, prof., 1990-91, mem. med. staff, 1975-91, med. dir. dept. phys. and occupational therapy, 1981-91; dir. rsch. Abratech Corp., Sausalito, Calif., 1991—. Author: (with M.D. Rayner) Basic Concepts of Neuronal Function, 1984; contbr. articles to profl. jours., chpts. to books. Office: Abratech Corp 475 Gate 5 Rd Ste 255 Sausalito CA 94965

JHINGAN, ANIL KUMARI, chemist, molecular biologist; b. New Delhi, June 16, 1955; came to U.S., 1985; d. O.P. and Shanti D. (Jhingan) H.; m. Aslam M. Ansari. BSc in Chemistry with honors, Delhi U., 1974, MSc in Organic Chemistry, 1976, PhD in Chemistry, 1982. Chemistry lectr. Delhi U., 1981-86; postdoctoral rschr. in chemistry U. Calif., Berkeley, 1985-86; postdoctoral rschr. in pharmacy U. Calif., San Francisco, 1986-89; project leader in biotech. Pioneer Hi-Bred Internat., Johnston, Iowa, 1989-92; rsch. investigator Roche Molecular Sys., Alameda, Calif., 1992-93; cons. Alameda, Calif., 1994—. Contbr. articles to profl. jours.; patentee in field. Recipient scholarship Ministry of Edn., Govt. of India, 1984. Mem. AAAS, Am. Soc. for Microbiology, Am. Chem. Soc. (Tech. Paper award 1992). Home and Office: 1575 5th Ave Apt 201 San Francisco CA 94122-3831

JIANG, TIEFENG, artist; b. Ningbo, Zhejiang, China, Oct. 3, 1938; s. Dazhi Jiang and Jian Hu; m. Zhaolin Jiang, Mar. 19, 1989. BA with honors, Ctrl. Inst. Fine Arts, Beijing, 1964. Artist Fingerhut Group Pubs., Golden Valley, Minn., 1983—; instr., prof. Yunnan Art Acad., 1978-83. Exhibited in traveling shows in U.S. including Everson Mus., N.Y., Springfield (Ohio) Art Mus., others, 1983—; illustrator (books) Secret of Jinchun Tree, 1978, A Shi Ma, 1981, Two Little Peacock, 1976, Little Red Riding Hood, 1980, The Ugly Duckling, 1980; design animated cartoon Two Little Peacock, 1976; executed mural Stone Forest, Great Hall of the People, Beijing, 1979. Recipient 1st pl. award Teen-Ager's Pub. House of China, Beijing, 1978, 2d pl. award UN Competition, Japan, 1980, 1st pl. Illustrated Books award Jiangsu Province, 1979. Office: Fingerhut Group Pubs Inc 400 N Lilac Dr Golden Valley MN 55422

JIMÉNEZ, FRANCISCO, academic administrator; b. San Pedro Tlaquepaque, Mexico, June 29, 1943; came to U.S., 1947; s. Francisco and Maria (Hernandez) Gonzalez J.; m. Laura Catherine Facchini, Aug. 17, 1968; children: Francisco Andres, Miguel Antonio, Tomas Roberto. BA, Santa Clara (Calif.) U., 1966; MA, Columbia U., 1969, PhD, 1973; postgrad., Harvard U., 1989. Preceptor Columbia U., N.Y.C., 1969-70, assoc. of Spanish, 1971-72, asst. prof., 1972-73; asst. prof. Santa Clara U., 1973-77, assoc. prof., 1977-81; prof. San Filippo Univ., 1981—; instr. ctr. for continuing edn. Santa Clara U., Mexico City, 1975-77; assoc. v.p. for acad. affairs Santa Clara U., 1990—; vis. prof. U. Mexico, 1987; mem. Accrediting Commn. for Sr. Colls. and Univs., 1989—; bd. dirs. Western Assn. of Schs. and Colls. Accrediting Commn. Author: Los episodios nacionales, 1974, Viva la lengua, 1975, 87, Mosaico de la Vida, 1981, several short stories which have been reprinted in numerous anthologies of Am. Lit.; editor: The Identification and Analysis of Chicano Literature, 1979, The Bilingual Review, 1973—, Poverty and Social Justice, 1987, (with others) Hispanics in the United States: An Anthology of Creative Literature, 1980, 82; contbr. numerous articles to profl. jours. Chmn. Calif. Commn. on Tchr. Credentialing, 1976-86; vice chair Calif. Coun. for Humanities, 1987—; bd. dirs. Far West Lab. Ednl. R&D, 1988—, elected chair, 1991—; bd. dirs. Western Assn. Schs. and Colls. Accrediting Commn., 1992—; mem. accrediting commn. Sr. Colls. and Univs., 1989—; bd. trustees Mitty H.S., San Jose, Calif., 1993—. Woodrow Wilson fellow, 1966. Mem. Am. Assn. for Higher Edn., MLA, Nat. Chicano Coun. Higher Edn., Assn. Calif. Tchrs. Fgn. Langs., Pacific Coast Coun. Latin Am. Studies, Am. Assn. Tchrs. Spanish and Portuguese, Nat. Assn. Chicano Studies, Western Assn. Schs. and Colls. (bd. dirs. 1992—). Democrat. Roman Catholic. Home: 624 Enos Ct Santa Clara CA 95051-6207 Office: Santa Clara U Office Acad Affairs Santa Clara CA 95053

JIMENEZ, JOSEPHINE SANTOS, portfolio manager; b. Lucena, Quezon, Philippines, June 6, 1954; came to U.S., 1972; d. Jose Hirang and Virginia Villapando (Santos) J. BS, NYU, 1979; MS, MIT, 1981. Securities analyst Mass. Mut. Life Ins. Co., Springfield, 1982-83; investment officer One Fed. Asset Mgmt., Boston, 1984-87; sr. analyst, portfolio mgr. Emerging Markets Investors Corp., Washington, 1988-91; mng. dir., portfolio mgr. Montgomery Asset Mgmt., San Francisco, 1991—; founding ptnr. Montgomery Emerging Markets Fund. Mem. Inst. Chartered Fin. Analysts. Office: Montgomery Asset Mgmt 600 Montgomery St San Francisco CA 94111-2702

JIMMINK, GLENDA LEE, retired elementary school educator; b. Lamar, Colo., Feb. 13, 1935; d. Harold Dale and Ruth Grace (Ellenberger) Fasnacht; m. Gary Jimmink, Oct. 24, 1964 (div. 1984); 1 child, Erik Gerard. BA, U. LaVerne, Calif., 1955. Tchr. elem. grades Pomona (Calif.) Unified Sch. Dist., 1955-61, Palo Alto (Calif.) Unified Sch. Dist., 1961-65, San Rafael (Calif.) Sch. Dist., 1966-95; ret.; mem. curriculum coun. San Rafael Sch. Dist., 1983-90, 94-95, mentor tchr., 1989-90, mem. social studies steering com., 1990-95; charter mem. Marin County Curriculum Connection, 1991—. Artist, pub. (calendar) Dry Creek Valley, 1987; author: World Geography Resource Handbook for Tchrs., 1990, others. Mem. Marin Arts Coun., San Rafael, 1988—, Big Bros.-Big Sisters, San Rafael, 1986-93, PTA, San Rafael, 1988—, Earthwatch, 1990—. Mem. NEA, Calif. Tchrs. Assn., San Rafael Tchrs. Assn., Nat. Wildlife Soc., Sierra Club, Gualala Arts Assn.

JINDRICH, ERVIN JAMES, coroner, medical and legal consultant; b. Chgo., June 5, 1939; s. Ervin James and Lydia Renata (Ahrens) J.; m. Denise Lobeth Fowler, Mar. 4, 1970; children: Devin Logan, Antonia Elizabeth. Student, U. Ill., 1957-60; BS, Northwestern U., 1961, MD, 1964. Diplomate Am. Bd. Anatomic, Clin. and Forensic Pathology. Intern Charity Hosp., New Orleans, 1967-68; resident in anatomic and clin. pathology Kaiser Hosp., San Francisco, 1968-72; resident in forensic pathology U. Calif. Med. Sch., San Francisco, 1972-73; clinic and emergency rm. physician Contra Costa County, Richmond and Martinez, Calif., 1967-68; chief med. examiner, coroner City and County of San Francisco, 1973-74; coroner Marin County, San Rafael, Calif., 1975—; forensic pathology cons. Medico-Legal Consultations, Mill Valley, Calif., 1975—. Contbr. articles to profl. jours. Trustee Suicide Prevention and Cmty. Counseling of Marin, San Rafael, 1977—. Capt. U.S. Army, 1965-67. Fellow Am. Acad. Forensic Scis.; mem. Nat. Assn. Med. Examiners. Home: 9 Heuters Ln Mill Valley CA 94941-2701 Office: Marin County Coroner Office Civic Ctr Rm 154 San Rafael CA 94903

JOAQUIM, RICHARD RALPH, hotel executive; b. Cambridge, Mass., July 28, 1936; s. Manuel and Mary (Marrano) J.; m. Nancy Phyllis Reis, Oct. 22, 1960; 1 child, Vanessa Reis. BFA, Boston U., 1955, MusB, 1959. Social dir., coord. summer resort, Wolfeboro, N.H., 1957-59; concert soloist N.H. Symphony Orch., Vt. Choral Soc., Choral Arts Soc., Schenectady Chamber Orch., 1957-60; coord. performance functions, mgr. theatre Boston U., 1959-60, asst. program dir., 1963-64, dir. univ. programs, 1964-70; gen. mgr. Harrison House of Glen Cove; dir. Conf. Svc. Corp., Glen Cove, N.Y., 1970-74, sr. v.p., dir. design and devel.; v.p. Arltec, also mng. dir. Sheraton Internat. Conf. Ctr., 1975-76; v.p., mng. dir. Scottsdale (Ariz.) Conf. Ctr. and Resort Hotel, 1976—; pres. Internat. Conf. Resorts, Inc., 1977, chmn. bd., 1977—; pres. Western Conf. Resorts; concert solist U.S. Army Field Band, Washington, 1960-62. Creative arts cons., editorial cons., concert mgr. Commr. recreation Watertown, Mass., 1967—; mem. Spl. Study Com. Watertown, 1967—, Glen Cove Mayor's Urban Renewal Com., Nat. Com. for Performing Arts Ctr. at Boston U., Jacob K. Javits Fellows Program Fellowship Bd. Bd. dirs. Nat. Entertainment Conf.; trustee Boston U., 1983—, Hotel and Food Adminstrn. Program Adv. Bd., Boston U., 1986—, Ariz. Opera Co. With AUS, 1960-62. Recipient Disting. Alumni award Boston U., 1991. Mem. Assn. Coll. and Univ. Concert Mgrs., Am. Symphonic League, Am. Fedn. Film Socs., Assn. Am. Artists, Am. Pers. and Guidance Assn., La Chaine des Rotisseurs, Knights of the Vine, Order of St. John, Nat. Alumni Council Boston U. Clubs: The Lotos (N.Y.). Office: Scottsdale Conf Ctr & Resort Hotel 7700 E Mccormick Pky Scottsdale AZ 85258-3431

JOCHIM, MICHAEL ALLAN, archaeologist; b. St. Louis, May 31, 1945; s. Kenneth Erwin and Jean MacKenzie (Keith) J.; m. Amy Martha Waugh, Aug. 12, 1967; children: Michael Waugh, Katherine Elizabeth. BS, U. Mich., 1967, MA, 1971, PhD, 1975. Lectr. anthropology U. Calif., Santa Barbara, 1975-77, asst. prof., 1979-81, assoc. prof., 1981-87, prof., 1987—, dept. chmn., 1987-92; asst. prof. Queens Coll. CUNY, Flushing, 1977-79; mem. archaeology rev. panel NSF, Washington, 1988-90. Author: Hunter-gatherer Subsistence and Settlement, 1976, Strategies for Survival, 1981; editor (series) Interdisciplinary Contributions to Archaeology, 1987—. Chmn. Community Adv. Com. for Spl. Edn., Santa Barbara County, 1980-82. Grantee NEH, 1976, NSF, 1980, 81, 83, 89, 91, 94, Nat. Geog. Soc., 1987. Fellow Am. Anthrop. Assn.; mem. Soc. for Am. Archaeology, Sigma Xi. Office: Univ of Calif Dept Anthropology Santa Barbara CA 93106

JOCHUM, LESTER H., dentist; b. Chgo., Nov. 19, 1929; s. J. Harry and Hilma O. (Swanson) J.; m. Anne Elizabeth Cannon, Sept. 20, 1952 (div. Apr. 1983); 1 child, David S. Student U. Wyo., 1947-48; BS in Bus. Adminstrn. with honors, Oreg. State U., 1952; pre-dental student Portland State Coll., 1959-60; B.S. with honors in Sci., U. Oreg., 1963, D.M.D., 1964. Staff acct. Pacific Telephone and Telegraph Co., San Francisco, 1952-59; gen. practice dentistry, San Jose, Calif., 1965-83; dental cons. Delta Dental Plan of Calif., Sacramento, 1983—; ptnr. Trinity Imports, 1985-93. Contbr. articles Calif. Wine Press; also others. Asst. chief Santa Clara Reserve Police Dept., Calif., 1976-83. Active No. Calif. diocese Episc. Ch. Served with U.S. Army, 1952-54. Mem. Sacramento Dist. Dental Soc., Calif. Dental Assn., ADA, Phi Kappa Phi, Psi Omega, Alpha Phi Omega, Lambda Chi Alpha (ritual chmn. 1951, soc. chmn. 1952). Republican. Office: Delta Dental Plan of Calif 7667 Folsom Blvd Sacramento CA 95826-2618

JOFFE, BARBARA LYNNE, software developer; b. Bklyn., Apr. 12, 1951; d. Lester L. and Julia (Schuelke) J.; m. James K. Whitney, Aug. 25, 1990; 1 child, Nichole. BA, U. Oreg., 1975; MFA, U. Mont., 1982. Applications engr. So. Pacific Transp., San Francisco, 1986-93; computer fine artist Barbara Joffe Assocs., San Francisco, 1988-92; instr. computer graphics Ohlone Coll., Fremont, Calif., 1990-91; adv. programme project mgr. ISSC/IBM So. Pacific, Denver, 1994—. Group exhibits include Calif. Crafts XIII, Sacramento, 1983, Rara Avis Gallery, Sacramento, 1984, Redding (Calif.) Mus. and Art Ctr., 1985, Euphrat Gallery, Cupertino, Calif., 1988, The Computer Mus., Boston, 1989, Siggraph Traveling Art Show, Europe and Australia, 1990, 91, 7th Nat. Computer Art Invitational, Cheney, Wash., 1994, Visual Arts Mus., N.Y.C., 1994. Mem. Assn. Computing Machinery. Home: 7271 S Jersey Ct Englewood CO 80112-1512

JOFFE, BENJAMIN, mechanical engineer; b. Riga, Latvia, Feb. 23, 1931; came to U.S., 1980, naturalized, 1985; s. Alexander and Mery (Levenson) J.; m. Frida Erenshteyn, Aug. 6, 1960; children: Alexander, Helena. ASME, Mech. Tech. Sch., Krasnoyarsk, USSR, 1951; BSME, Polytechnic Inst. Moscow, 1959; MSME, Polytechnic Inst. Riga, 1961; PhD, Acad. Scis., Riga, 1969. Design engr. Electromachine Mfg. Corp., Riga, 1955-59, head engring. dept., 1959-62; sr. design engr. Acad. Scis., Riga, 1962-67; sr. scientist Inst. Physics, Riga, 1967-78; chief design engr. Main Design Bur., Riga, 1978-80; sr. design engr. Elec-Trol, Inc., Saugus, Calif., 1980-81; sr. design engr. VSI Aerospace div. Fairchild, Chatsworth, Calif., 1981-85; mech. engring. mgr. Am. Semiconductor Equipment Tech., Woodland Hills, Calif., 1985-90; mem. tech. staff Jet Propulsion Lab. Calif. Inst. Tech., Pasadena, 1991—. Author: Mechanization and Automatization of Punching Presses at the Plants of the Latvian SSR, 1963, Mechanization and Automatization of Processes of Plastic Parts Production at the Plants of the Latvian SSR, 1964, Mechanization and Automatization of Control and Measuring Operations, 1966, and 5 sci. engring. books; contbr. numerous articles to profl. jours. Recipient Honored Inventor award Latvian Republic, Riga, 1967, 1st prize Latvian Acad. Scis., 1972, Latvian State award in engring. scis., 1974. Mem. ASME (dir. exec. bd.). Republican. Home: 22314 James Alan Cir Chatsworth CA 91311-2054 Office: Calif Inst Tech Jet Propulsion Lab 4800 Oak Grove Dr Pasadena CA 91109-8001

JOHANNSEN, DAVID CHARLES, physicist, aerospace engineer; b. Pasadena, Calif., Oct. 3, 1957; s. Charles Edward and Mary Jane (Boies) J. BS with honor, Calif. Inst. Tech., 1979; MS, U. Calif., Riverside, 1981, PhD, 1983. Mem. tech. staff Hughes Aircraft Co., El Segundo, Calif., 1982-83; rsch. physicist Allied Corp., Westlake Village, Calif., 1983-84; engring. specialist Northop Electronics Div., Hawthorne, Calif., 1984-87; project engr. Aerospace Corp., El Segundo, 1987—; vis. asst. prof. Loyola Marymount U., L.A., 1982. Author: (with others) Tunable Solid State Lasers, 1985. Mem. L.A. Conservancy, Pasadena Hist. Soc., Pasadena Heritage. Mem. AIAA, Optical Soc. Am., Soc. Archtl. Historians (So. Calif. chpt.), Assn. Lit. Scholars and Critics. Republican.

JOHANOS, DONALD, orchestra conductor; b. Cedar Rapids, Iowa, Feb. 10, 1928; s. Gregory Hedges and Doris (Nelson) J.; m. Thelma Trimble, Aug. 27, 1950; children—Jennifer Claire, Thea Christine, Gregory Bruce (dec.), Andrew Mark, Eve Marie; m. Corinne Rutledge, Sept. 28, 1985. Mus.B., Eastman Sch. Music, 1950, Mus.M., 1952; D.F.A. (hon.), Coe Coll., 1962. Tchr. Pa. State U., 1953-55, So. Meth. U., 1958-62, Hockaday Sch., 1962-65; now condr. laureate Honolulu Symphony Orch. Mus. dir., Altoona (Pa.) Symphony, 1953-56, Johnstown (Pa.) Symphony, 1955-56, asso. condr., Dallas Symphony Orch., 1957-61, resident condr., 1961-62, mus. dir., 1962-70, assoc. condr., Pitts. Symphony, 1970-79, mus. dir., Honolulu Symphony Orch., 1979—, artistic dir., Hawaii Opera Theater, 1979-83, guest condr., Phila. Orch., Amsterdam Concertgebouw Orch., Pitts. Symphony, Rochester Philharm., New Orleans Philharm., Denver Symphony, Vancouver Symphony, Chgo. Symphony, San Francisco Symphony, Netherlands Radio Philharm., Swiss Radio Orch., Mpls. Symphony, Paris Opera, Boston Symphony, San Antonio Symphony, Orchestre Nat. de Lyon, others; recordings for Marco Polo, Naxos, Turnabout, Candide, others. Advanced study grantee Am. Symphony Orch. League and Rockefeller Found., 1955-58. Mem. Am. Fedn. Musicians Internat. Congress of Strings (dir.). Office: Honolulu Symphony Orch 1441 Kapiolani Blvd Ste 1515 Honolulu HI 96814-4407

JOHANSON, DONALD CARL, physical anthropologist; b. Chicago, Ill., June 28, 1943; s. Carl Torsten and Sally Eugenia (Johnson) J. ; m. Lenora Carey, 1988. BA, U. Ill., 1966; MA, U. Chgo., 1970, PhD, 1974; DSc (hon.), John Carroll U., 1979; D.Sc. (hon.), Coll. of Wooster, 1985. Mem. dept. phys. anthropology Cleve. Mus. Natural History, 1972-81, curator, 1974-81; pres. Inst. Human Origins, Berkeley, Calif., 1981—; prof. anthropology Stanford U., 1983-89; adj. prof. Case Western Res. U., 1978-81, Kent State U., 1978-81. Co-author: (wht M.A. Edey) Lucy: The Beginnings of Humankind, 1981 (Am. Book award 1982), Blueprints: Solving the Mystery of Evolution, 1989, (with James Shreeve) Lucy's Child: Discovering a Human Ancestor, 1989, (with Kevin O'FArrell) Journey from the Dawn: Life With the World's First Family, 1990, (with Lenora Johanson and Blake Edgar) Ancestors: In Search of Human Origins, 1994; host PBS Nature series; prodr.: (films) Lucy in Disguise, 1982; host, narrator NOVA series In Search of Human Origins, 1994; contbr. numerous articles to profl. jours. Recipient Jared Potter Kirtland award for outstanding sci. achievement Cleve. Mus. Natural History, 1979, Profl. Achievement award U. Chgo., 1980, Gold Mercury Internat. ad personem award Ethiopia, 1982, Humanist Laureate award Acad. of Humanism, 1983, Disting. Svc. award Am. Humanist Assn., 1983, San Francisco Exploratorium award, 1986, Internat. Premio Fregene award, 1987, Alumni Achievement award U. Ill., 1995; grantee Wenner-Gren Found., NSF, Nat. Geog. Soc., L.S.B. Leakey Found., Cleve. Found., George Gund Found., Roush Found. Fellow AAAS, Calif. Acad. Scis., Rochester (N.Y.) Mus., Royal Geog. Soc.; mem. Am. Assn. Phys. Anthropologists, Internat. Assn. Dental Research, Internat. Assn. Human Biologists, Am. Assn. Africanist Archaeologists, Soc. Vertebrate Paleontology, Soc. Study of Human Biology, Societe de l'Anthropologie de Paris, Centro Studi Ricerche Ligabue (Venice), Founders' Coun., Chgo. Field Mus. Natural History (hon.), Assn. Internationale pour l'etude de Paleontologie Humaine, Mus. Nat. d'Histoire Naturelle de Paris (corr.), Explorers Club (hon. dir.), Nat. Ctr. Sci. Edn. (supporting scientist). Office: Inst Human Origins 1288 9th St Berkeley CA 94710-1501

JOHANSON, JERRY RAY, company executive; b. Murray, Utah, Aug. 29, 1937; s. Albert F. and Elizabeth (Cox) J.; m. Harlean Marie Shepherd, July 12, 1957; children: Kerry, Bryan, Michael, Cynthia, Elizabeth. PhD, U. Utah, 1962. Registered profl. engr., Calif., Mass. Sr. technologist U.S. Steel Applied Rsch. Lab., Monroeville, Pa., 1962-66; pres. Jenike & Johanson, Inc., North Billerica, Mass., 1966-85, JR Johanson, Inc., San Luis Obispo, Calif., 1985—. Contbr. 150 papers and 20 patents in field. Mem. ASME (exec. com. 1972-73, Henry Hess award 1966), Am. Soc. Chem. Engrs., Inst. Briquetting and Agglomeration (Neal Rice award 1989). Mormon. Office: JR Johanson Inc 712 Fiero Ln Ste 37 San Luis Obispo CA 93401-7979

JOHN, YVONNE MAREE, artist, interior designer; b. Leeton, New South Wales, Australia, Sept. 8, 1944; came to U.S., 1966; d. Percy Edward and Gladys May (Markham) Thomas; m. Michael Peter John, Aug. 20, 1966; children: Michael Christian, Stephen Edwin Dennis. Student, Buenaventura Coll., 1969, U. Calif., Santa Barbara, 1975; cert., United Design Guild, 1975; AA, Interior Design Guild, 1976; Diploma, Internat. Correspondence Sch., 1976. Designer Percy Thomas Real Estate, Leeton, 1960-66; cosmetologist, artist Bernard's Hair Stylists, Ventura, Calif., 1966-67, 74-73; cosmetologist Banks Beauty Salon, Chgo., 1968-69; owner, mgr. Yvonne Maree Designs, Ventura and Olympia, Wash., 1978—; owner, cosmetologist Mayfair Salon, Leeton, 1962-66; owner, mgr. Y.M. Boutique, Griffith, Australia, 1965-66. Contbr. numerous short stories and poems to newspapers; artist numerous pen and ink drawings; exhibited one-person show Royal Mus. Sydney, Australia, 1954; exhibited group shows Ventura County Courthouse, 1970, Wash. Women in Art, Olympia, 1990, Timberland Libr., Olympia, 1990, Maska Internat. Gallery, Seattle, 1991, Nat. Hqrs. of Am. Soc. Interior Designers, Washington, 1992, Michael Stone Collection, Washington, 1992, Mus. Modern Art, Bordeaux, France, 1993, UN Fourth World Conf. on Women, Beijing, China, 1995, others; 1st release of ltd. edit. prints, 1992; exhibited oil painting and drawing Hargis Unique Gallery, Pomona, Calif., 1994; works collected in Royal Mus. of Sydney, O'Toole Coll., Melbourne, Nat. Mus. of Women in Arts, Washington, Patterson Collection, Mich., Witherow Collection, Washington, Samaniego Collection, Calif., Ronald Reagon Collection, Calif. Artist Ventura County Gen. Hosp., 1970's. Recipient Cash and Cert. awards Sydney Newspapers, 1950's, Ribbon awards Sydney County Fairs, 1950's, 1st round winner painting Hathaway Competition, Ventura, Calif., 1970's. Mem. Am. Platform Assn. Office: Yvonne Maree Designs PO Box 2143 Olympia WA 98507-2143

JOHNS, DAVID M., conservationist; b. Portland, Oreg., Mar. 26, 1951; m. Carol E. Jones, 1992. BS, Portland State U., 1976; MA, Columbia U., 1978, JD, 1981. Bar: N.Y. Asst. downtown planning and devel. Office of Mayor, City of Portland, 1975-76; atty. advisor Office of Sec., U.S. Dept. Transp., 1980-81; asst. mgr. Portland Bur. Gen. Svcs., 1981-85; mgr. urban svcs. program, legis. affairs Portland Bur. Water Works, 1985-92; with reforestation project Inst. Forestry and Natural Resources, Nicaragua, 1987; advisor Environ. Law Ctr., Can., Can. Fed. Govt. Environ. and External Affairs Dept., 1990-91; pres., exec. dir. The Wildlands Project, 1992—; vis. instr. Inst. Policy Studies, 1981; vis. prof. polit. sci. Oreg. State U., 1989; adj. asst. prof. polit. sci. Portland State U., 1981—; bd. dirs. Wild Earth Mag., edit. advisor, 1990—. Contbr. articles to profl. jours. Internat. fellow Columbia U.; Harlan Fiske Stone scholar Columbia Law Sch., Portland U. scholar. Mem. N.Y. State Bar Assn., Soc. Ecological Restoration and Mgmt., Soc. Conservation Biology. Office: The Wildlands Project PO Box 1276 Mcminnville OR 97128

JOHNS, RICHARD SETH ELLIS, lawyer; b. Eugene, Oreg., Apr. 23, 1946; s. Frank Errol Jr. and Emily Elizabeth (Ellis) J.; m. Eleanor Lee Kuntz, Mar. 8, 1981. BA in English, U. Calif., Santa Barbara, 1968; JD, U. Calif., San Francisco, 1971. Bar: Calif. 1971, Ill. 1972. Instr. law U. Chgo., 1972-73; assoc. Atchison, Topeka & Santa Fe RR, Chgo., 1973-75, Furth, Fahrner, Bluemle & Mason, San Francisco, 1975-84; of counsel Maier, Dimitriou & Ross, San Francisco, 1984; ptnr. Rubenstein, Bohachek & Johns, San Francisco, 1985-88, Kipperman & Johns, San Francisco, 1988—. Contbr. articles to Calif. Law Rev. Bd. dirs. Congregation Beth Shalom, San Francisco, 1982-92, Bay Area sect. Am. Jewish Com., 1984—; leader Family Policy Task Force, 1987-88; guest of Christian Dem. Union, Konrad Adenhauer Stiftung-German-Am. Jewish Exchange Program, Fed. Republic Germany, 1985. 1st lt. U.S. Army, 1972-75. Mem. ABA, Calif. Bar Assn., Concordia-Argonaut Club. Office: Kipperman & Johns 456 Montgomery St Ste 1200 San Francisco CA 94104-1245

JOHNS, ROY (BUD JOHNS), publisher, author; b. Detroit, July 9, 1929; s. Roy and Isabel Johns; m. Judith Spector Clancy, 1971 (dec. 1990); m. Frances Moreland, 1992. BA in English and Econs., Albion (Mich.) Coll., 1951. Various editorial positions Mich. and Calif. daily newspapers, 1942-60; bur. chief Fairchild Pubs., 1960-69; dir. corp. communications Levi Strauss & Co., 1969-81, corp. v.p., 1979-81; pres. Synergistic Press, Inc., San Francisco, 1968—; bd. dirs. Apple-Wood Books, Bedford, Mass., Documentary Rsch., Inc., Buffalo; founder, ptnr. Apple Tree Press, Flint, Mich., 1954-55; cons. on communications, publishing and related areas. Author: The Ombibulous Mr. Mencken, 1968, What is This Madness?, 1985; co-editor, author: Bastard in the Ragged Suit, 1977; scriptwriter, exec. producer: What is This Madness?, 1976; exec. producer: The Best You Can Be, 1979 (CINE Golden Eagle award 1980); editor: Old Dogs Remembered, 1993; free-lance writer numerous mag. articles. Mem. Nat. Coun. of Mus. of Am. Indian, N.Y.C., 1980-90; dir. The San Francisco Contemporary Music Players, 1981—, Greenbelt Alliance, San Francisco, 1982—, pres., 1990-95. Home and Office: 3965 Sacramento St San Francisco CA 94118-1627

JOHNSON, ALAN BOND, federal judge; b. 1939. BA, Vanderbilt U., 1961; JD, U. Wyo., 1964. Pvt. practice law Cheyenne, Wyo., 1968-71; assoc. Hanes, Carmichael, Johnson, Gage & Speight P.C., Cheyenne, 1971-74; judge Wyo. Dist. Ct., 1974-85; judge U.S. Dist. Ct. Wyo., 1986—, part-time fed. magistrate, 1971-74; substitute judge Mcpl. Ct., Cheyenne, 1973-74. Served to capt. USAF, 1964-67, to col. Wyo. Air N.G., 1973-90. Mem. ABA, Wyo. State Bar, Laramie County Bar Assn. (sec.-treas. 1968-70), Wyo. Jud. Conf. (sec. 1977-78, chmn. 1979), Wyo. Jud. Council. Office: O'Mahoney Fed Ctr Rm 2242 2120 Capitol Ave Cheyenne WY 82001-3633

JOHNSON, ALICE ELAINE, retired academic administrator; b. Janesville, Wis., Oct. 9, 1929; d. Floyd C. and Alma M. (Walthers) Chester; m. Richard C. Johnson, Sept. 25, 1948 (div. 1974); children: Randall S., Nile C., Linnea E. BA, U. Colo., 1968. Pres., administrator Pikes Peak Inst. Med. Tech., Colorado Springs, Colo., 1968-88; mem. adv. com. to Colo. Commn. on Higher Edn., 1979-80, State Adv. Coun. on Pvt. Occupational Schs., Denver, 1978-86; mem. tech. adv. com. State Health Occupations, 1986-88; bd. dirs. All Souls Unitarian Ch., Colorado Springs, 1990—, mem. celebration team, 1990-91, pres. bd. trustees, 1991-93. Mem. Colo. Pvt. Sch. Assn. (pres. 1981-82, bd. dirs. 1976-88, Outstanding Mem. 1978, 80), Phi Beta Kappa. Democrat. Unitarian.

JOHNSON, ARNOLD GORDON, clergyman; b. Albert Lea, Minn., June 30, 1936; s. Arnold Clifford and Georgia (Godtland) B.; m. Mary Lou Zemke, Mar. 26, 1960; children: Dawn Marie, Eric Blair, Tanya Leigh, Mija Leah. BA, St. Olaf U., Northfield, Minn., 1958; MDiv., Luther Sem., St. Paul, 1968; MA, Liberty U., 1990. Ordained to ministry, Luth. Ch. Commd. 2d lt. USAF, 1958, pilot, 1959-65, pilot Minn. Air N.G., 1965-68, chaplain, 1968, advanced through grades to col., 1981, ret., 1984; parish evangelist The Am. Luth. Ch., Seattle, 1978—; stewardship counselor Evang. Luth. Ch., Spokane, 1984—; interim pastor Luth. Ch. of The Master, Coeur d' Alene, Idaho, 1991, First Luth. Ch., Kennewick, Wash., 1991-92, Richland (Wash.) Luth. Ch., 1992-93. Author: The Chaplain's Role as a Transcendant Symbol in the Military, 1974. Fundraiser United Way, Lubbock, Tex., 1979. Mem. Red River Valley Fighter Pilots Assn., Rotary, Lions (v.p. 1985—), Daedalians (v.p. 1985-86). Home: 1815 S Koren St Spokane WA 99212-3264 Office: Richland Luth Church Richland WA 99352

JOHNSON, ARTHUR WILLIAM, JR., planetarium executive; b. Steubenville, Ohio, Jan. 8, 1949; s. Arthur William and Carol (Gilcrest) J.; B.Mus., U. So. Calif., 1973. Lectr., Griffith Obs. and Planetarium, 1969-73; planetarium writer, lectr. Mt. San Antonio Coll. Planetarium, Walnut, Calif., 1970-73; dir. Fleischmann Planetarium, U. Nev., Reno, 1973—. Organist, choirmaster Trinity Episcopal Ch., Reno, 1980—; bd. dirs. Reno Chamber Orch. Assn., 1981-87 , 1st v.p., 1984-85. Nev. Humanities Com., Inc. grantee, 1979-83; apptd. Nev. state coord. N.S.T.A./NASA Space Sci. Student Involvement Program, 1994. Mem. Am. Guild Organists (dean No. Nev. chpt. 1984-85), Internat. Planetarium Soc., Cinema 360, Inc. (treas. 1985-90, pres. 1990—), Pacific Planetarium Assn. (pres. 1980), Lions (pres. Reno Host Club 1991-92), Reno Advt. Club (dir. Sheep Dip Show 1988, 90, 92). Republican. Episcopalian. Writer, producer films: (with Donald G. Potter) Beautiful Nevada, 1978, Riches: The Story of Nevada Mining, 1984. Office: Fleischmann Plantarium U Nev 1650 N Virginia St Reno NV 89503-1738

JOHNSON, BONNIE JEAN, dietitian, diabetes educator; b. Albion, Mich., Apr. 26, 1940; d. William Emil Albert and Esther L. (Towns) Stark; m. Dennis N. Johnson, Aug. 28, 1965; children: Denene Johnson Huff, Brent Michael, Troy Matthew. BS in Home Econs., Valparaiso U., 1962; cert., U. Mich., 1963. Cert. diabetes educator, registered and lic. dietitian. Clin. dietitian E.W. Sparrow Hosp., Lansing, Mich., 1963-66; univ. dietitian No. Mich. U., Marquette, Mich., 1966; cons. dietitian Upjohn Cmty. Nursing Homes, Kalamazoo, Mich., 1967-68, Tuscola County Med. Care Facility, Caro, Mich., 1970-75, Caro (Mich.) Cmty. Hosp., 1972-76; staff dietitian Caro (Mich.) Regional Mental Health Inst., 1969-70; cons. dietitian Hills & Dales Gen. Hosp., Cass City, Mich., 1974-77, clin. dietitian, 1978-89; diabetes educator, dietitian St. Luke's Hosp., Saginaw, Mich., 1989-91; clin. dietitian Terry Reilly Health Svcs., Nampa, Idaho, 1991-94; diabetes educator Humphreys Diabetes Ctr., Boise, Idaho, 1994—. Health promotion grantee W.K. Kellogg Found., 1986. Mem. Am. Dietetic Assn. (mem. diabetes care and edn. splty. group 1994—, mem. practice stds. com.), Am. Assn. Diabetes Educators, Idaho Dietetic Assn., Treasure Valley Dietetic Assn., Snake River Assn. Diabetes Educators (mem. nominations com., newsletter editor 1991—), Valparaiso U. Alumni Assn. (mem. Idaho chpt., initiator 1993—, pres. univ. guild 1993—). Home: 12227 W Hickory Dr Boise ID 83713-1433 Office: St Alphonsus/Humphreys Diabetes Ctr 5257 Fairview Ave Ste 100 Boise ID 83706

JOHNSON, BYRON JERALD, state supreme court judge; b. Boise, Idaho, Aug. 2, 1937; s. Arlie Johnson and V. Bronell (Dunten) J.; children: Matthew, Ethan, Elaine, Laura; m. Paticia G. Young, 1984. AB, Harvard U., 1959, LLB, 1962. Bar: Idaho, 1962. Justice Idaho Supreme Ct., Boise, 1988—. Office: Supreme Ct Idaho PO Box 83720 Boise ID 83720-0002

JOHNSON, CATHY, accountant; b. L.A., Apr. 18, 1953; d. Grover Cleveland and Naomi Esther (Johnson) Williams; 1 child, Milton Clyde JOrdan, Jr. AA, Sacramento City Coll., 1984; BS, Calif. State U., Sacramento, 1987. Acctg. clerk Texaco Oil Co., L.A., 1973-75; bookkeeper Nichols Inst., San Juan Capistrano, Calif., 1980, Matsukas Bros. Paper Co., L.A., 1981; acct. 1st Nationwide Bank, Sacramento, 1988; bookkeeper Calif. Optometric Credit Union, Sacramento, 1989-90; acct. Planning and Conservation League, Sacramento, 1990-91; prin. Budget Bookkeeping, Rancho Cordova, Calif., 1991—. Contbr. United Negro Coll. Fund, N.Y.C., 1988; Christmas vol. Salvation Army Outreach Svc., Sacramento, 1990, Iraq relief vol. St. Ignatius Parish, Sacramento, 1991; big sister The Birthing Project, Sacramento, 1990-91. Marion Muddox scholar Calif. State U., 1986. Mem. Nat. Assn. Accts., Calif. State U. Alumna, Sacramento Bus. Chpt. Office: Budget Bookkeeping PO Box 2904 Rancho Cordova CA 95741-2904

JOHNSON, CHARLES HENRY, JR., lawyer; b. New Haven, May 24, 1946; s. Charles Henry Sr. and Helen (Taylor) J. BA, Yale U., 1968, JD, 1972. Bar: Pa. 1972, U.S. Dist. Ct. (ea. and mid. dists.) Pa., Supreme Ct. Assoc. Montgomery, McCracken, Walker & Rhoads, Phila., 1972-75; asst. chief counsel FDA, Washington, 1975-78; supr. trial atty. EEOC, Washington, 1978-79; atty. Conn. Gen. Life Ins. Co., Bloomfield, Conn., 1979-82; counsel New Eng. Mutual Life Ins. Co., Boston, 1982-93; pvt. practice Venice, Calif., 1993—; prof. Whittier Law Sch., L.A., 1995—. Bd. dirs. Roxbury Youthworks, Inc., 1989-92; mem. The Partnership, Inc., Boston, 1987-92; minority initiative task force Greater Boston Conv. and Visitors Bur., 1988-92. Boston fellow, 1988. Mem. ABA, Nat. Bar Assn. Democrat. Baptist. Office: 4050 Buckingham Rd Ste 200 Los Angeles CA 90008-2349

JOHNSON, CHARLES ROBERT, television news anchor, reporter; b. Olivia, Minn., Apr. 6, 1954; s. Robert George and Dorothy Jean (Warner) J.; m. Karen Marie Langager, Sept. 4, 1976; children: Robert, Elizabeth. BA, U. Minn., 1976. Air personality, promotions dir. Sta. KQIC-FM Radio, Willmar, Minn., 1976-78; air personality, program dir. Sta. WJJY-FM Radio, Brainerd, Minn., 1978-79; air personality, community affairs dir. Sta. KFOR Radio, Lincoln, Nebr., 1979-80; anchor, reporter WDIO-TV, Duluth, Minn., 1980-82, KSTW-TV, Seattle-Tacoma, 1982—. Writer, producer, host pub. affairs TV program Johnson's Jour., 1984-85. Vol. University Place Sch. Dist., Tacoma, 1988-89. Lutheran. Office: Sta KSTW-TV PO Box 11411 Tacoma WA 98411-0411

JOHNSON, CHARLES WILLIAM, state supreme court justice; married. BA in Econs., U. Wash., 1973; JD, U. Puget Sound, 1976. Pvt. practice law Pierce County, Wash., 1977-90; judge Supreme Ct. of Wash., Olympia, 1991—; pub. defender for indigent criminal defendants; prosecutor, defender in superior ct. hearings; pro tem judge in Pierce County. Mem. Wash. State Bar Assn., Tacoma-Pierce County Bar Assn. Office: Wash Supreme Ct Temple of Justice PO Box 40929 Olympia WA 98504

JOHNSON, CHRIS ALAN, ophthalmology educator; b. Roseburg, Oreg., Oct. 1, 1949; s. Carl John and Violet Marian (Bloomquist) J.; m. Debra Pauline Johnson, Dec. 18, 1971; children: Kristin Patricia, Matthew Carl. BA, U. Oreg., 1970; MSc, Pa. State U., 1972, PhD, 1974. Postdoctoral rsch. fellow U. Fla., Gainesville, 1975-76; from postdoctoral rsch. fellow to assoc. prof. U. Calif., Davis, 1977-89, prof., 1989—; ophthalmology rep. Calif. Dept. Motor Vehicles Med. Adv. Bd., Sacramento, 1990—; chmn. visual fields subcom. eye care tech. forum Nat. Eye Inst., Bethesda, Md., 1992—; cons. in field. Patentee apparatus and method for visual field testing, real-time interactive optimized test sequence; contbr. articles to profl. jours. Chief coach Am. Youth Soccer Assn., Davis, 1988-90. Recipient Sr. Sci. Investigator award Rsch. to Prevent Blindness, 1992, Glenn Fry award Am. Optometric Assn., 1994. Mem. Optical Soc. Am., Am. Acad. Opthalmology (Honor award 1988, Disting. Svc. award 1987), Assn. for Rsch. in Vision and Ophthalmology, Internat. Perimetric Soc. (bd. dirs. 1980-84), Calif. Alta Ophthalmol. Soc. Avocations: fishing, hiking, jazz piano. Office: U Calif Dept Ophthalmology 1603 Alhambra Blvd Sacramento CA 95816-7051

JOHNSON, CIRI DIANE, graphic design firm owner; b. Ann Arbor, Mich., Aug. 19, 1956; d. Paul Christian and Genevieve Ruth J. Student, U. Ariz., 1974-76, U. Oreg., 1976-78; BFA, San Francisco Art Inst., 1980; MA, NYU, 1982. Artist asst. Lucio Pozzi, N.Y.C., 1983-85; editor, art dir. New Observations Mag., N.Y.C., 1985-91; owner Ciri Johnson Design, Bklyn, 1988-91, Tucson, 1991—; asst. tchr. Parson's Sch. Design, N.Y.C., 1985-86; instr. NYU, 1982. Prin. works published in The National Poetry Magazine of Lower East Side, 1988-90; designed promotional piece for Elisa Monte Dance Co. chosen for reproduction in 1991 Artist's Market. Mem. Resources for Women, Tucson Ad Club (Bronze Addy award for mag. advt. campaign, Merit cert. 1992, 94, Gold Addy award for art exhbn. catalog, Bronze Addy for self-promotion 1993). Democrat.

JOHNSON, CONOR DEANE, mechanical engineer; b. Charlottesville, Va., Apr. 20, 1943; s. Randolph Holaday and Louise Anna (Deane) J.; m. Laura Teague Rogers, Dec. 20, 1966; children: William Drake, Catherine Teague. BS in Engring. Mechanics, Va. Poly. Inst., 1965; MS, Clemson U., 1967, PhD in Engring. Mechanics, 1969. Registered profl. engr., Calif. With Anamet Labs., Inc., 1973-82; sr. structural analyst Anamet Labs., Inc., Dayton, Ohio, 1973-75; prin. engr. Anamet Labs., Inc., San Carlos, Calif., 1975-81, v.p., 1981-82; program mgr. Aerospace Structures Info. and Analysis Ctr., 1975-82; co-founder, pres. CSA Engring., Inc., Palo Alto, 1982—; tech. dir. damping conf., exec. com. N.Am. Conf. on Smart Materials and Structures. Contbr. articles to profl. jours. Capt. USAF, 1969-73. Mem. AIAA, ASME (structures and materials award 1981), N.Am. Smart Sturctures and Materials Conf. (exec. com., tech. chmn. Damping confs. 1991, 93, 95), Gourmet Cooking Club, Sigma Xi. Methodist. Home: 3425 Lodge Dr Belmont CA 94002-1210 Office: CSA Engring Inc 2850 W Bayshore Rd Palo Alto CA 94303-3843

JOHNSON, CURTIS LEE, real estate executive and broker; b. Medford, Oreg., Oct. 20, 1956; s. Edward Lee and Anne Virginia (Christensen) J.; m. Bonita Sue Maddox, May 22, 1982 (June 1987); m. Karen Jean

MacLauchlan, Apr. 29, 1989; children: Jamie Lyn, Justin Robert. BS, Oreg. State U., 1978. Cert. realtor. Chief lobbyist Assoc. Students of Oreg. State U., Salem, 1977-78, Mont. Student Lobby, Helena, 1979-80; real estate owner, mgr. Jackson County Fed. Savs. and Loan Assn., Medford, Oreg., 1980-87; real estate mgr. Eugene F. Burrill Lumber Co., Medford, Oreg., 1987—; v.p., broker Burrill Real Estate Co., Medford, Oreg., 1988—; mem. adv. bd. Bear Creek Valley Sanitary, Medford, 1990—, Jackson County Urban Renewal, White City, 1992—; mem. 2050 Medford Water Commn., 1992—. Bd. dirs. United Way of Jackson County, Medford, 1985; bd. dirs., pres. Kiwanis Club and Found., Medford, 1988-86; bd. dirs., treas. Rogue Coun. Campfire, Medford, 1986. Mem. Medford/Jackson County C. of C. (bd. dirs.), Rogue Valley Country Club, Moose. Home: 1528 Ridge Way Medford OR 97504-6681

JOHNSON, D. ARLO, artist; b. San Antonio, Mar. 13, 1952; s. Duane Arlo and Sammy Budge (Tubbs) J.; m. Janice Bradshaw, June 7, 1973; children: Morgan, Yvonne, Peter, Tolon, Melanie, Bryce. AA, Salt Lake C.C., West Valley City, Utah, 1990. Tour guide Grey Line Motor Tours, Salt Lake City, 1971-78; bus. mgr. Skaggs Drug Ctr., Salt Lake City, 1978-80; mgr. Skaggs Telecom., Salt Lake City, 1980-82; purchasing supr. Am. Express, Salt Lake City, 1982-90; artist, owner Arlo's Oils, Salt Lake City, 1990—. One-man shows include West Valley City Arts Coun., 1990; group shows include Eidlejory Mus., Indpls., 1994; represented in permanent collections West Valley City Hall. With Army N.G., 1970—. Recipient mayor's art award City of West Valley City, 1993; grantee West Valley Arts Coun., 1990—. Mem. Intermountain Soc. Artists, Gt. Basin Artists. Mem. LDS Ch. Home and Studio: 5570 Karma Ave West Valley City UT 84120-4418

JOHNSON, DALE FREDRICK, chemist; b. Pittsburg, Calif., Oct. 3, 1957; s. Neil Henry and Betty Louise (Bray) J.; m. Deborah Ann Walker, Mar. 11, 1978 (div. Dec. 1981); 1 child, Joseph Andrew; m. Susan Marie Valienzi, July 25, 1992. BS in Chemistry, N.C. State U., 1980; MS in Indsl. Chemistry, U. Ctrl. Fla., 1984; PhD in Phys. Chemistry, Calif. Inst. Tech., 1994. Instr. chemistry Monterey (Calif.) Peninsula Coll., 1985-86; grad. rsch. asst. Cal Inst. Tech., Pasadena, 1986-89, U. Calif., Santa Barbara, 1990-93; rsch. chemist Dasibi Environ. Corp., Glendale, Calif., 1993-94, Norton Co., Irvine, Calif., 1994—; instr. math., physics and chemistry Nuclear Power Sch., Orlando, Fla., 1980-84, divsn. dir. math., 1983-84; cons. Dasibi Environ. Corp., 1993. Co-patentee in field; contbr. articles to profl. jours. Pres., v.p., bd. dirs. Rosalind Pl. Homeowners Assn., Pasadena, Calif., 1987-89, 91—. Lt. USN, 1980-84. Mem. AAAS, Am. Vacuum Soc. of Am. Inst. Physics, Am. Chem. Soc., Materials Rsch. Soc. Episcopalian. Home: 222 S Catalina Ave Apt 7 Pasadena CA 91106-3283

JOHNSON, DAVID GEORGE, Chinese history educator; b. Webster, S.D., July 15, 1938; s. George Andrew and Elizabeth Caroline (Herrlinger) J.; m. In Ja Rhee, June 6, 1976; 1 child, Caroline. AB, Harvard U., 1960; PhD, U. Calif., Berkeley, 1970. Asst. prof. dept. East Asian langs. and cultures Columbia U., N.Y.C., 1970-79; assoc. prof. dept. history U. Calif., Berkeley, 1983-87, prof., 1987—; dir. Chinese Popular Culture Project, Berkeley, 1987—; mem. Am. Coun. Learned Socs.-Social Sci. Rsch. Coun. Joint Com. on Chinese Studies, N.Y.C., 1984-89. Author: Medieval Chinese Oligarchy, 1977, (with others) Domesticated Deities and Auspicious Emblems, 1992; editor, contbr.: Ritual Opera, Operatic Ritual, 1989, Ritual and Scripture in Chinese Popular Religion, 1995; co-editor, contbr. Popular Culture in Late Imperial China, 1987; mem. editl. bd. Studies in Chinese Ritual, Theatre and Folklore. Grantee ACLS, 1978, 81, 83, NEH, 1987-91, Rockefeller Found., 1987-91, Com. on Scholarly Comm. with the Peoples Republic of China, 1984. Mem. Assn. for Asian Studies (China and Inner Asia Coun. 1988-91). Office: U Calif Dept History Dwinelle Hall Berkeley CA 94720

JOHNSON, DAVID SELLIE, civil engineer; b. Mpls., Apr. 10, 1935; s. Milton Edward and Helen M. (Sellie) J. BS, Mont. Coll. Mineral Sci. Tech., 1958. Registered profl. engr., Mont. Trainee Mont. Dept. Hwys., Helena, 1958-59, designer, 1959-66, asst. preconstrn. engr., 1966-68, regional engr., 1968-72, engring. specialities supr., 1972-89, preconstrn. chief, 1989-93, forensic engr., 1965—, traffic accident reconstructionist, 1978—; consulting engr., 1985—. Contbr. articles on hwy. safety to profl. jours. Adv. bd. mem. Helena Vocat.-Tech. Edn., 1972-73. Fellow Inst. Transp. Engrs. (expert witness coun.); mem. NSPE, Nat. Acad. Forensic Engrs. (diplomate), Mont. Soc. Profl. Engrs., Transp. Rsch. Bd. (geometric design com., tort liability com.), Wash. Assn. Tech. Accident Investigators, Corvette Club, Treasure State Club (pres. Helena 1972-78, sec. 1979-82), Shriners. Home and Office: 1921 E 6th Ave Helena MT 59601-4766

JOHNSON, D'ELAINE ANN HERARD, artist; b. Puyallup, Wash., Mar. 19, 1932; d. Thomas Napoleon and Rosella Edna (Berry) Herard; m. John Laffette Johnson, Dec. 22, 1956. B.F.A., Central Wash. U., 1954; M.F.A., U. Wash., 1958, postgrad. U. London, 1975—; postgrad U. Wash., 1975—. Instr. art Seattle Pub. Schs., 1954-78, Mus. History and Industry, Seattle, 1954-56; dir. Mt. Olympus Estate, Edmonds, Wash., 1971; cons. art groups, Wash. State, 1954—. lectr. Cen. Wash. State U., Seattle PTA, Creative Arts Assn., Everett, Everett Community Coll., Women's Caucus for Art, Seattle, numerous others; served as art juror for numerous shows. Founder Mt. Olympus Preserve for Arts, Edmonds, Wash., 1971, sponsor art events, 1971—; active Wash. Coalition Citizens with Disabilities. Exhibited in group shows: Fry Art Mus., Seattle, 1964, Seattle Art Mus., 1959, Henry Art Gallery, Seattle, Vancouver Maritime Mus., B.C., Can., 1981, N.S. Art Mus., Can., 1971, Whatcom Mus., Bellingham, Wash., 1975, State Capitol Mus., Olympia, Wash., 1975, Corvallis State U., Oreg., 1982, Newport Mus., Oreg., Nat. Artist Equity, 1972, Belluvue Art Mus., Seattle, 1989, Rosicrusian Egyption Mus., San Jose, Calif., 1990, St. Mark's Cathedral, Seattkem 1991, Sidney Mus. and Arts Assn., Port Orchard, Wash., 1991, Bellvue Art Mus., 1992, Pacific Arts Ctr. Hauberg Gallery, Seattle, 1992, Bon Marche Gallery, Seattle, 1992, Northeast Trade and Exbn. Hall, 1993, Edmonds (Wash.) Art Mus., 1993, Ilwaco (Wash.) Heritage Mus., 1993, Robert Frey Gallery, Seattle, 1994; over 300 exhibits 1950—, over 1200 paintings through 1970; Illustrator: The Bing Crosby Family Music Books for Children, 1961; TV art instr. TV-9 U. Wash., 1968. Elected to Wash. State Art Commn. Registry, Olympia, 1982; recipient numerous awards. Mem. Nat. Artist Equity, Internat. Soc. Artists, The Cousteau Soc., Am. Council for Arts, Nat. Women's Studies Assn., Assn. Am. Culture, Internat. Platform Assn., Nat. Pen Women Assn., Kappa Delta Pi, Kappa Pi. Avocations: scuba diving, camping, travel, violin, writing. Home and Office: 16122 72d St Ave W Edmonds WA 98206-4517

JOHNSON, DORIS ANN, educational administrator; b. Marinette, Wis., Dec. 4, 1950; d. Jerome Louis and Jean Fern (Henry) La Plant; m. Daniel Lee Leonard, June 10, 1972 (div. June 1987); children: Jeremiah Daniel, Erica Leigh, Wesley Cyril; m. Paul Robert Johnson, Oct. 21, 1989; stepchildren: Kindra Michelle, Tanya Mari. Student, U. Wis., Oshkosh, 1969-70; BA in Edn., U. Wis., Eau Claire, 1973; MS in Edn., U. Wis., Whitewater, 1975; postgrad., Oreg. State U., 1988—. Reading specialist Brookfield (Wis.) Cen. High Sch., 1975-79; lead instr. N.E. Wis. Tech. Coll., Marinette, 1979-87; dir. adult basic edn. Umpqua C.C., Roseburg, Oreg., 1987-95, dir. developmental edn., 1995—; founding bd. dirs. Project Literacy, Umpqua Region, Roseburg, 1989—; mem. adv. bd. Umpqua Cmty. Action Network, Roseburg, 1987-94; mem. State Dirs. of Adult Edn., Oreg., 1987—, vice chair, 1992-93, chair, 1993-94; mem. Adminstrn. Assn., Roseburg, 1989—, chair, 1993-94, 94-95; bd. dirs. Greater Douglas United Way, 1994—; adv. bd. Oreg. Literacy Line, 1994—. Co-author literacy module Communication Skills, 1988; author ednl. curriculum. Bd. dirs. St. Joseph Maternity Home, Roseburg, 1987-90, founding mem.; mem. Literacy Theater, Roseburg, 1988—, Greater Douglas United Way Bd., 1994—; mem. Project Leadership, Roseburg, 1988-89; mem. adv. bd. Oregon Literacy Line, 1994—; mem. Roseburg Valley Rep. Women, 1994—. State legalizatoin assistance grantee Fed. Govt., 1988-93, homeless literacy grantee Fed. Govt., 1990-91, family literacy grantee Fed. Govt., 1991-93, intergenerational literacy grantee State of Oreg., 1991, literacy expansion grantee Fed. Govt., 1992-95, literacy outreach grantee Fed. Govt., 1992—, staff devel. spl. projects grantee Fed. Govt., 1992-93. Fellow Nat. Inst. Leadership Devel., Am. Assn. Adult and Continuing Edn., Oreg. Assn. Disabled Students, Oreg. Developmental Edn. Studies, Oreg. Assn. for Children with Learning Disabilities, Tchrs. of English to Spkrs. of Other Langs., Western Coll. Reading and Learning Assn., Am. Assn. Women in Coll. and Jr. Coll., Roseburg Valley Rep. Women, Altrusa Internat. Club of Roseburg (chair literacy com. 1993-94, 94-95), Rep. Women. Republican. Lutheran. Home: 761 Garden Grove St Roseburg OR 97470-9511 Office: Umpqua CC PO Box 967 Roseburg OR 97470

JOHNSON, DOUGLAS SCOTT, writing educator; b. Joplin, Mo., May 14, 1964; s. Lee W. and Betty L. (Maupin) J.; m. Mary Alice Hartley, Jan. 30, 1993. BA in English, Pittsburgh (Kans.) State U., 1989, MA in English, 1992. Writing instr. Pittsburgh State U., 1989-90, Highline C.C., Des Moines, 1993—, Green River C.C., Auburn, Wash., 1993—. Author: Transformations, 1994, Between Earth and Angels, 1994. Home: PO Box 772 Auburn WA 98071-0772

JOHNSON, DOUGLAS WALTER, artist; b. Portland, Oreg., July 8, 1946; s. Herbert Walter Johnson and Barbara Elizabeth (Speer) Hall. Student, San Jose (Calif.) State Coll. Artist Jamison Gallery, Santa Fe, 1971-77, Horwich Gallery, Santa Fe, 1977-86, Gerald Peters Corp., Santa Fe, 1986—. Executed mural El Dorado Hotel, 1986; exhibited in numerous group shows.

JOHNSON, E. ERIC, insurance executive; b. Chgo., Feb. 7, 1927; s. Edwin Eric and Xenia Alice (Waisanen) J.; m. Elizabeth Dewar Brass, Sept. 3, 1949; children: Christal L. Johnson Neal, Craig R. BA, Stanford U., 1948. Dir. group annuities Equitable Life Assurance Soc., San Francisco, 1950-54; div. mgr. Equitable Life Assurance Soc., L.A., 1955-59; v.p. Johnson & Higgins of Calif., L.A., 1960-67, dir., 1968-87, chmn., 1986-87; chmn. TBG Fin., L.A., 1988—; bd. dirs. Am. Mutual Fund; exec. v.p. Johnson & Higgins, N.Y.C., 1984-87. Bd. dirs. Sta. KCET, pub. TV, L.A., 1977-95, chmn., 1992-94; mem. adv. bd. UCLA Med. Ctr., 1983—, chmn. 1995—; bd. dirs. Johnson Comprehensive Cancer Ctr., UCLA, 1985—, Stanford U. Grad Sch. Bus., 1986-91; trustee Nuclear Decommissioning Trust, Rosemead, Calif., 1986-94. Mem. Calif. Club, L.A. Country Bluc, Vintage Club, Riviera Tennis Club, Links Club N.Y.C., Beach Club, So. Calif. Tennis Assn. (treas.). Office: TBG Fin 2029 Century Park E Los Angeles CA 90067-2901

JOHNSON, EARL, JR., judge, author; b. Watertown, S.D., June 10, 1933; s. Earl Jerome and Doris Melissa (Schwartz) J.; m. Barbara Claire Yanow, Oct. 11, 1970; children: Kelly Ann, Earl Eric, Agaarn Yanovitch. B.A. in Econs., Northwestern U., 1955, LL.M., 1961; J.D., U. Chgo., 1960. Bar: Ill. 1960, U.S. Ct. Appeals (9th cir.) 1964, D.C. 1965, U.S. Supreme Ct. 1966, Calif. 1972. Trial atty., organized crime sect. Dept. Justice, Washington, Miami, Fla. and Las Vegas, Nev., 1961-64; dep. dir. Neighborhood Legal Services Project, 1964-65; dep. dir. OEO Legal Services Program, 1965-66, dir., 1966-68; vis. scholar Center for Study of Law and Soc., U. Calif., Berkeley, 1968-69; assoc. prof. U. So. Calif. Law Center, Los Angeles, 1969-75, dir. clin. programs, 1970-73; prof. law U. So. Calif. Law Center, 1976-82, dir. Program Study Dispute Resolution Policy, Social Sci. Research Inst., 1975-82; assoc. justice Calif. Ct. Appeal, 1982—; co-dir. Access to Justice Project, European U. Inst., 1975-79; vis. scholar Inst. Comparative Law, U. Florence, Italy, 1973, 75; Robert H. Jackson lectr. Nat. Jud. Coll., 1980; adv. panel Legal Services Corp., 1976-80; legis. impact panel Nat. Acad. Scis., 1977-80; faculty Asian Workshop on Legal Services to Poor, 1974; mem. Internat. Legal Ctr., Legal Services in Developing Countries, 1972-75; Founder, bd. mem. Action for Legal Rights, 1971-74; pres., trustee Western Ctr. on Law and Poverty, 1972-73, 76-80; v.p., chmn. exec com. Calif. Rural Legal Assistance Corp., 1973-74; exec. com. Nat. Sr. Citizens Law Ctr., 1980-82; sec. Nat. Resource Ctr. for Consumers of Legal Services, 1974-82; chair Nat. Equal Justice Libr. Com., 1989-92; pres., bd. dirs. Consortium for Nat. Equal Justice Libr., Inc., 1992—; chair Calif. Access to Justice Working Group, 1993-95. Author: Justice and Reform: The Formative Years of the American Legal Services Program, 1974, 2d edit., 1978, Toward Equal Justice: A Comparative Study of Legal Aid in Modern Societies, 1975, Outside the Courts: A Survey of Diversion Alternatives in Civil Cases, 1977, Dispute Processing Strategies, 1978, Dispute Resolution in America, 1985, California Trial Guide, 7 vols., 1986, Texas Trial Guide, 6 vols., 1989, New York Trial Guide, 5 vols., 1990, Florida Civil Trial Guide, 5 vols., 1990, Ill. Civil Trial Guide, 5 vols., 1991, Fed. Trial Guide, 5 vols., 1992, Indiana Civil Trial Guide, 5 vols., 1992, California Family Law Trial Guide, 5 vols., 1992, Pennsylvania Civil Trial Guide, 5 vols., 1992, Mich. Trial Guide, 5 vols., 1993, N.C. Civil Trial Guide, 5 vols., 1993, California Criminal Trial Guide, 3 vols., 1994; editor: U. Chgo. Law Rev, 1960; mem. editorial bd. Am. Bar Found. Rsch. Jour., 1987—; contbr. articles to books and periodicals. Bd. dirs. Beverly Hills Bar Found., 1972-73, Nat. Legal Aid and Defenders Assn., 1987-91; trustee Los Angeles Legal Aid Found., 1969-71; mem. Los Angeles County Regional Planning Commn., 1980-81; bd. visitors U. San Diego Law Sch., 1983-86. Served with USNR, 1955-58. Recipient Dart award for acad. innovation U. So. Calif., 1971, Loren Miller Legal Services award Calif. State Bar, 1977, Appellate Justice of the Yr. award Los Angeles Trial Lawyers Assn., 1989, Outstanding Jud. Achievement award Calif. Trial Lawyers Assn., 1991; named So. Calif. Citizen of Week, 1978; Ford Found. fellow, 1960; Dept. State lectr., 1975; grantee Ford Found.; grantee Russell Sage Found.; grantee Law Enforcement Assistance Adminstrn.; grantee NSF. Fellow Am. Bar Found. (rsch. adv. com. 1995—); mem. ABA (com. chmn. 1972-75, spl. com. resolution minor disputes 1976-83, coun. sect. of individual rights and responsibilities 1990-91, consortium on legal svcs. and the pub. 1991-94), Calif. Bar Assn., L.A. Bar Assn. (neighborhood justice ctr. com. 1976-81), Law and Soc. Assn., Nat. Legal Aid and Defender's Assn. (bd. dirs. 1968-74), Am. Acad. Polit. and Social Sci., Calif. Judges Assn. (appellate cts. com. 1983-87, 93—, ethics com. 1985-89), Internat. Assn.ocedural Law, Order of Coif. Democrat. Office: Ct Appeals Calif 2d Appellate Dist 300 S Spring St Los Angeles CA 90013-1230

JOHNSON, EARVIN (MAGIC JOHNSON), professional sports team executive, former professional basketball coach; b. Lansing, Mich., Aug. 14, 1959; s. Earvin and Christine Johnson; m. Cookie Kelly; 1 son, Earvin. Student, Mich. State U., 1976-79. Basketball player L.A. Lakers, 1979-91; sportscaster NBC-TV, 1993-94; head coach L.A. Lakers, 1994, v.p., co-owner, 1994—; gold medalist, U.S. Olympic Basketball Team, 1992. Author: (autobiography) Magic, 1983; (autobiography, with Roy S. Johnson) Magic's Touch, 1989; What You Can Do to Avoid AIDS, 1992; My Life, 1992. Mem. NCAA Championship Team, 1979, Nat. Basketball Assn. All-Star Team, 1980, 82-92, Nat. Basketball Assn. Championship Team, 1980, 82, 85, 87, 88; named Most Valuable Player, Nat. Basketball Assn. Playoffs, 1980, 82, 87, Nat. Basketball Assn., 1987, 89, 90, All-Star Game, 1990, 92, Player of the Year, Sporting News, 1987; recipient Schick Pivotal Player award, 1984; holder NBA rec. most career assists. Office: Great Western Forum 3900 W Manchester Blvd PO Box 10 Inglewood CA 90306*

JOHNSON, EINAR WILLIAM, lawyer; b. Fontana, Calif., Apr. 6, 1955; s. Carl Wilbur and Judith Priscilla (Orcutt) J.; m. Cynthia Jeanne Bailey, Oct. 9, 1976; children: Brian Mark (dec.), Carl Einar, Gregory Daniel, Christopher James, Shaun Curtis, Bradford Keith. BA in Speech Communications, Brigham Young U., 1980; JD, J. Reuben Clark Law Sch., Provo, Utah, 1983. Bar: Calif. 1983, U.S. Dist. Ct. (cen. dist.) Calif. 1984, U.S. Ct. Appeals (9th cir.) 1986, U.S. Supreme Ct. 1987. Asst. debate coach Brigham Young U., Provo, Utah, 1979-80; fin. committeeman Jed Richardson for Congress, Provo, 1980; sales mgr./salesman Ortho Mattress, Orem, Utah, 1979, 81; law clk. Acret & Perrochet, L.A., 1982; jud. clk. U.S. Cts., Salt Lake City, 1983-84; litigation atty. Smith & Hilbig, Torrance, Calif., 1984-90; litigation ptnr. Smith & Hilbig, 1990-93; owner, founder Johnson and Assocs., 1993—; editor Moot Ct. program J. Reuben Clark Law Sch., 1982-83. Contbr. articles to profl. jours. Missionary, leader Ch. of Jesus Christ of Latter Day Saints, Denver, 197476, Sunday sch. tchr., L.A., 1986-89, stake high counselor, 1989-92, 1st counselor ward bishopric, 1992-93, pres. elders quorum, 1993-94, high counselor, 1994—. Recipient A.H. Christensen award, Am. Jurisprudence awards Bancroft-Whitney, 1981. Mem. ABA, Calif. Bar Assn., L.A. County Bar Assn., Assn. Trial Lawyers Am., Internat. Platofrm Assn., Order Barristers, Kappa Tau Alpha. Republican. Mormon. Office: Smith & Hilbig 21515 Hawthorne Blvd Torrance CA 90503-6501

JOHNSON, ELIZABETH HILL, foundation administrator; b. Ft. Wayne, Ind., Aug. 21, 1913; d. Harry W. and Lydia (Buechner) Hill; m. Samuel Spencer Johnson, Oct. 7, 1944 (dec. 1984); children: Elizabeth Katharine, Patricia Caroline. BS summa cum laude, Miami U., Oxford, Ohio, 1935; MA in English Lit., Wellesley Coll., 1937; postgrad., U. Chgo., 1936. Cert. tchr., Ohio. Pres., co-founder S.S. Johnson Found., Calif. Corp., San Francisco, 1947—. Mem. Oreg. State Bd. Higher Edn., Eugene, 1962-75, Oreg. State Edn. Coord. Com., Salem, 1975-82, Assn. Governing Bds., Washington, 1970-80, chairperson, 1975-76; mem. Oreg. State Tchr. Standards and Practices Commn., Salem, 1982-89; bd. dirs. Lewis and Clark Coll., Portland, Oreg., 1985—, Pacific U., Forest Grove, Oreg., 1982—, Sunriver Prep. Sch., 1983-92, Oreg. Hist. Soc., Portland, 1985—, Cen. Oreg. Dist. Hosp., Redmond, 1982—, Oreg. High Desert Mus., 1984—, Bend, Oreg., Health Decisions, 1986-92, Ctrl. Oreg. Coun. Aging, 1991—. Lt. USNR, 1943-46. Named Honoree March of Dimes White Rose Luncheon, 1984; recipient Aubrey Watzek award Lewis and Clark Coll., 1984, Cen. Oreg. 1st Citizen award, Abrams award Emanuel Hosp., 1982, Pres. award Marylhurst Coll., 1991, Thomas Jefferson award Oregon Historical Soc., 1993. Mem. Am. Assn. Higher Edn., Am. Assn. Jr. Colls., ASCD, Soroptimists (hon.), Francisca Club, Town Club, Univ. Club, Waverley Club, Beta Sigma Phi, Phi Beta Kappa, Phi Delta Kappa, Delta Gamma. Republican. Lutheran. Home: 415 SW Canyon Dr Redmond OR 97756-2028 Office: S S Johnson Found 441 SW Canyon Dr Redmond OR 97756-2028

JOHNSON, ELLWOOD GERD, English language educator; b. McCall, Idaho, Nov. 4, 1924; s. Orlando Bennett and Hilkea (Jenssen) J.; m. Diane Louise Ostrom, Aug. 25, 1983; children: Wendy, Helen, Karen, Michael. PhD in English, U. Wash., 1969. Prof. Am. lit. Western Wash. U., Bellingham, 1963—. Contbr. articles to profl. jours. Mem. Modern Lang. Assn. Office: Western Wash U Dept English Bellingham WA 98226

JOHNSON, F. BRENT, microbiologist, educator; b. Monroe, Utah, Mar. 31, 1942; s. Horace Jay and Ida (Christiansen) J.; m. Paula Dawn Forbush, June 18, 1965; children: Brian, Matthew, Christopher, Wesley, Stephanie. Student, Coll. So. Utah, 1960-61; BS, Brigham Young U., 1966, MS, 1967, PhD, 1970. NIH predoctoral fellow Brigham Young U., Provo, Utah, 1966-70, asst. prof. microbiology, 1972-75, assoc. prof., 1975-80, prof., 1980—; postdoctoral fellow NIH, Bethesda, Md., 1970-72; lab. dir. Richards Lab., Inc., Pleasant Grove, Utah, 1986—; lab. dir. MicroVir Labs., Inc., Orem, Utah, 1989—, also pres., chmn. bd.; pres., chmn. bd. Johnson Biorsch. & Devel. Corp., Orem. Contbr. articles to profl. jours. USAF fellow, 1977, rsch. grantee, 1978-82, NIH, 1973-76. Mem. Am. Soc. for Microbiology, AAAS, Sigma Xi, Phi Kappa Phi. LDS Ch. Office: Brigham Young U 887 Widb Provo UT 84602-1049

JOHNSON, FRANK, state official, educator; b. Ogden, Utah, Mar. 12, 1928; s. Clarence Budd and Arline (Parry) J.; m. Maralyn Brewer, Aug. 15, 1950; children: Scott, Arline, Laurie, Kelly, Edward. BS, U. Utah, 1955; MS, U. Ill., 1958, PhD, 1960. Instr. U. N.D., Grand Forks, 1955-56; teaching asst. U. Ill., Urbana, 1956-59; rsch. asst. prof. U. Del., Newark, 1959-60; prof. U. Utah, Salt Lake City, 1960-93, assoc. dean, 1970-77; dir. divsn. pub. utilities State of Utah, Salt Lake City, 1989-95; cons. Gen. Foods, Sears, Magnavox, Albertsons, Zion Bank, Nat. Food Brokers Assn., others. Legis. Utah House of Reps., Salt Lake City, 1982-88. Republican. Home: 2373 E Dayspring Ln Salt Lake City UT 84124

JOHNSON, FRANK EDWARD, newspaper editor; b. Pekin, Ill., July 1, 1920; s. Frank Ellis and Margaret (Pitner) J.; m. Louise Marguerite Beall, Sept. 16, 1945; children—Frank Edgar, Christia Louise Gibbons, John Jeffrey (dec.). U. Ariz., Tucson, 1946-47. Reporter Galion Inquirer, Galion, Ohio, 1945; reporter News-Journal, Mansfield, OH, 1945; reporter Ariz. Daily Star, Tucson, 1946-47, city editor, 1948-61, asst. mng. editor, 1961-67, mng. editor, 1967-82, exec. editor, 1983-85; contbg. editor Ariz. Daily Star, 1986-87, ret., 1987. Bd. dirs. Fan Kane Fund for Brain-Damaged Children, Tucson, 1950-91, Ariz. Daily Star Sportsman's Fund, Tucson, 1966—. Served as 1st sgt. U.S. Army, 1940-45. Named Tucson's Newsman of Yr., Tucson Press Club, 1966; recipient Disting. Service to Journalism award, Ariz. Press Club, 1981, Freedom of Info. award Valley of the Sun chpt. Soc. Profl. Journalists, 1986; named Master editor-pub., Ariz. Newspapers Assn., 1982. Mem. Am. Soc. Newspaper Editors, AP Mng. Editors Assn. (bd. dirs. 1981-83, regent 1985—), Ariz. Newspapers Assn. (pres. 1976-77), Soc. Profl. Journalists, Tucson Press Club (pres. 1969).

JOHNSON, FRANKLIN MCBEE, wholesale distribution executive; b. Seattle, Feb. 26, 1927; s. Leonard Franklin and Hazel Elisabeth (McBee) H.; m. Colleen Margaret Seiling, Sept. 10, 1956; children: Cappi Willey, Kerri McCaul. Student, U. Wash., 1945-57, 79. Owner retail grocery store, Seattle, 1947-62; v.p. sales Secoma Distbg. Co., Seattle, 1962-71; gen. mgr. gen. mdse. Assoc. Grocers Inc., Seattle, 1971-76, v.p. mktg., 1976-87, sr. v.p. mktg., 1987—; bd. dirs. Wash. State Food Distbrs. Assn., Seattle, 1987-93; pres. Gen. Merchandisers Assn., Seattle, 1975; frequent speaker in field. Contbr. articles to trade publs. Bd. dirs. Edmonds (Wash.) Community Coll., 1989-92; mem. Edmonds City Planning Group, 1975; bd. dirs. Husky Fever Com., Seattle, 1985—. Mem. We. Assn. Food Chains, N.W. Planning Group, Food Mfrs. Inst., Masons. Republican. Methodist. Office: Assoc Grocers Inc 3301 S Norfolk St Seattle WA 98118-5648

JOHNSON, GARY EARL, governor; b. Minot, N.D., Jan. 1, 1953; s. Earl W. and Lorraine B. (Bostow) J.; m. Dee Simms, Jan. 27, 1976; children: Seah, Erik. BA in Polit. Sch., U. N.Mex., 1975. Pres., CEO Big J Enterprises, Albuquerque, 1976—; gov. State of N.Mex., 1995—. Bd. dirs. Entrepreneurship Studies at U. N.Mex., 1993-95. Named to list of Big 50 Remodelers in the USA, 1987; named Entrepreneur of Yr., 1995. Mem. LWV, C. of C. Albuquerque (bd. dirs. 1993-95). Republican. Lutheran. Office: Office of Gov State Capitol Santa Fe NM 87503*

JOHNSON, GARY KENT, management education company executive; b. Provo, Utah, Apr. 16, 1936; s. Clyde LeRoy and Ruth Laie (Taylor) J.; m. Mary Joyce Crowther, Aug. 26, 1955; children: Mary Ann Johnson Harvey, Gary Kent, Brent James, Jeremy Clyde. Student Brigham Young U., 1954-55, U. Utah, 1955-58, 60-61, U. Calif.-Berkeley, 1962. Sales rep. Roche Labs., Salt Lake City, 1958-61, sales trainer, Denver, 1962, sales trainer, Oakland, Calif., 1962, div. mgr., Seattle, 1962-69; sec.-treas. Western Mgmt. Inst., Seattle, 1969-71; pres. WMI Corp., Bellevue, Wash., 1971—, Provisor Corp., 1983-86; speaker, cons. various nat. orgns. Bd. dirs. Big Bros.; del. King County Republican Com. Served with U.S. N.G., 1953-61. Walgreen scholar, 1955-58; Bristol scholar, 1958. Mem. Am. Soc. Tng. and Devel., Internat. Platform Assn., Bellevue Athletic Club. Phi Sigma Epsilon. Mem. LDS Ch. Author: Select the Best, 1976; Antitrust Untangled, 1977; The Utilities Management Series, 1979; Performance Appraisal, A Program for Improving Productivity, 1981, QSE Quality Service Everytime, 1990, Continuous Performance Improvement, 1993. Office: WMI Corp 1416 W Lake Sammamish Pky SE Bellevue WA 98008

JOHNSON, GERALDINE ESCH, language specialist; b. Steger, Ill., Jan. 5, 1921; d. William John Rutkowski and Estella Anna (Mannel) Pietz; m. Richard William Esch, Oct. 12, 1940 (dec. 1971); children: Janet L. Sohngen, Daryl R., Gary Michael; m. Henry Bernard Johnson, Aug. 23, 1978 (dec. 1988). BSBA, U. Denver, 1955, MA in Edn., 1958, MA in Speech Pathology, 1963; vocat. credential, U. No. Colo., 1978, postgrad.; postgrad., Metropolitan State Coll., U. Colo., Colo. State U., Colo. Sch. of Mines. Cert. speech therapist, Colo.; cert. tchr., Colo. Tchr. music Judith St. John Sch. Music, Denver, 1946-52; tchr. West High Sch., Denver, 1955-61, chmn. bus. edn. dept., 1958-61, reading specialist, 1977-78; speech therapist, founder South Denver Speech Clinic, 1965-71; tchr. Educationally Handicapped Resource Rm., Denver, 1971-74, Diagnostic Ctr., The Belmont Sch., Denver, 1974-77; speech-lang. specialist elem. and jr. high schs., Denver, 1978-86; itinerant speech-lang. specialist various elem. and jr. high schs., Denver, 1978—; ret. Denver Pub. Sch. System, 1986; home lang tchr. Early Childhood Edn., Denver, 1975; mem. Ednl. TV Adv. com., Colo.; sec. Cen. Bus. Edn. Com., Colo; tchr. letter writing clinics, local bus., Denver, 1960—. Former judge Colo. State Speech Festivals; demonstrator, lectr. Speech-Lang. and Learning Disabilities area Colo. Edn. Assn., 1971-73; vol. communications and prereading skills tchr. YMCA. Recipient Spl. Edn. award Denver Pub. Schs., 1986. Mem. Speech-Lang.-Hearing Assn. (cert.), U. Denver Sch. Bus. Alumni Bd., Beta Gamma Sigma, Kappa Delta Pi, Delta Pi Epsilon. Home: 14050 E Linvale Pl Apt 502 Aurora CO 80014-3735

JOHNSON, GERI ANN, consultant, economist; b. Pasadena, Calif., May 15, 1955; d. Jack L. and Charlene Joann (Hay) J.; m. Lawrence Brook Alderfer, June 13, 1987. Student, U. Granada, Spain, 1974; BS in Econs., U. Calif., Irvine, 1980, M of Systems Analysis, 1984. Mgr. consulting Deloitte & Touche, L.A., 1984-93; prin. XD Consulting, San Diego, 1993—; cons.

Pima County Recorder, Tucson, 1989, L.A. County Grand Jury, 1989-90, San Diego County, 1991-92, Puerto Rico Govt., 1992-94. Active in Surfrider Found., Long Beach, 1993, Calvary Ch., Seal Beach, Calif., 1993. Mem. Internat. Assn. Assessing Officers (Outstanding Appraisal Project 1994), Calif. Assessors' Assn., Calif. Recorders' Assn. (info. com.).

JOHNSON, GLORIA LEE, publisher, writer; b. Fruitland, Idaho, Feb. 16, 1931; d. Clayton Everett and Norma May (Doty) Anderson; m. Robert Lee Johnson, June 28, 1948; children: Randall, Dann, Kim, Brigette, Jauna. Office staff Voght Transfer, Ontario, Oreg., 1946-47; dental asst. Daniels DMD, Ontario, 1948-49; receptionist, asst. Peffley MD, Arco, Idaho, 1960-61; asst., x-ray technician Hodge MD, Blackfoot, Idaho, 1963-64; floral designer Vonnie's Flowers, Newberg, Oreg., 1968-69; mgr. breeding farm, trainer Stature Arabians, Dayton, Oreg., 1969-89; exec., owner Color Photo Ads Inc., Dayton, 1984-89; editor, pub. Kingsong Pubs., Salem, Oreg., 1990—. Charter mem., sec. Snake River Valley Art Assn., Ontario, 1956; chmn. mother's march Crippled Children's Fund, Butte County, Idaho, 1960; sec. Humane Soc., Yamhill County, Oreg., 1974; charter mem., publicity Beauty Pageant, Butte County, 1960; dir. Women's Ministries, Christian Ctr. of Salem, 1995. Recipient Cert. Recognition award Blue Book Arabian Industry, 1983. Mem. Oreg. Assn. Christian Writers, Internat. Platform Assn. Office: Kingsong Pubs 3160 Windsor Ave NE Salem OR 97301-1766

JOHNSON, GREGORY HAROLD, experimental test pilot, fighter pilot; b. Upper Ruislip, Middlesex, England, May 12, 1962; came to the U.S., 1964; s. Harold Cumings and Marion Joyce (Frye) J.; m. Cari Michele Harbaugh Johnson, July 8, 1989; children: Matthew, Joseph. BS, U.S. Air Force Acad., 1984; MS, Columbia U., 1985. cert. USAF pilot, F-15E fighter pilot, test pilot. T-38 instr. pilot 54 Flying Training Squadron, Reese AFB, Tex., 1986-89; F-15E fighter pilot 335 Fighter Squadron, Seymour Johnson AFB, N.C., 1990-93; test pilot USAF F-15 Combined test Force, Edwards AFB, Calif., 1994—; Desert Storm fighter pilot 335 Fighter Squadron, Seymour Johnson AFB, N.C., 1991. Decorated DFC, Saudi Arabia, 1991; Guggenheim fellow Columbia U., 1984; Eagle Scout, Boy Scouts Am., 1978. Mem. AIAA, Planetary Soc., Optimist Club. Republican. Methodist. Home: 6821 Spaatz Dr Edwards CA 93523-2113 Office: Test Pilot Sch EDA Edwards CA 93523

JOHNSON, GWENAVERE ANELISA, artist; b. Newark, S.D., Oct. 16, 1909; d. Arthur E. and Susie Ellen (King) Nelson; m. John Wendell Johnson, Dec. 17, 1937; 1 child, John Forrest. Student, Mpsl. Sch. Art, 1930; BA, U. Minn., 1937; MA, San Jose State U., 1957. Cert. gen. elem., secondary, art tchr., Calif. Art tchr., supr. Austin (Minn.) Schs., 1937-38; art tchr. Hillbrook Sch., Los Gatos, Calif., 1947-52; art tchr., supr. Santa Clara (Calif.) Pub. Schs., 1952-55; art tchr., dept. chmn. San Jose (Calif.) Unified Schs., 1955-75; owner Tree Tops studio, San Jose, 1975—. Juried shows: Los Gatos Art Assn., 1976-79, 85-88, Artist of Yr., 1988 (1st and 2d awards), 83, 84 (Best of Show awards), Treeside gallery, 1991, Los Gatos, 1980, 81 (1st awards); Livermore Art Assn., 1977 (2d award), Los Gatos Art Mus., 1981 (1st award), 82 (2d award), 91 (best of show award), Rosicrucean Mus., 1983, Centre d'Art Contemporian, Paris, 1983; creator Overfelt portrait Alexian Bros. Hosp., San Jose, Calif., 1977; exhibited in group shows ann. Garden Art Show, 1981-95, Triton Art Mus., 1983-95. Recipient Golden Centaur award Acad. Italia, 1982, Golden Album of prize winning Artists, 1984, Golden Flame award Academia Italia, 1986, others. Mem. San Jose Art League, Santa Clara Art Assn., Los Gatos Art Assn. (Artist of Yr. 1988, 2d, 3d awards), Santa Clara Art Assn. (Artist of Yr. 1983, 3 First awards 1989, 2d award in spl. merit achiever's exhbn. 1992, 3 First awards in merit achiever's exhbn. 1993), Soc. Western Artists, Nat. League Am. Penwomen (corr. sec., Merit Achiever award), Los gatos Art Assn., Santa Clara Art Assn., San Jose Art League. Home and Office: 2054 Booksin Ave San Jose CA 95125-4909

JOHNSON, HEIDI SMITH, science educator; b. Mpls., June 1, 1946; d. Russell Ward and Eva Ninette (Holmquist) Smith; m. Alan C. Sweeney, Dec. 21, 1968 (div. 1977); m. Robert Allen Johnson, July 17, 1981. BA, U. Calif., Riverside, 1969; MA, No. Ariz. U., 1992. Park ranger U.S. Nat. Parks Svc., Pinnacles Nat. Monument, 1972-73; aide Petrified Forest Mus. Assn., Ariz., 1973-75; dispatcher police dept. U. Ariz., Tucson, 1975-76; communications operator II dept. ops. City of Tucson, 1976-78; dispatcher Tucson Police Dept., 1978-82, communications supr., 1982-85, communications coord., 1985; substitute tchr. Bisbee (Ariz.) Pub. Schs., 1985-91; instr. English Cochise Community Coll., Douglas, Ariz., 1990-92; tchr. English/creative writing Bisbee H.S., 1992-93; tchr. phys. sci. and geology Lowell Mid. Sch., Bisbee, 1993—; GEd tchr. Cochise County Jail, 1988-89; owner Johnson's Antiques and Books, Bisbee, 1990—. Assoc. editor Ariz. Fossil Record. Trustee Bisbee Coun. on Arts and Humanities, 1986-88; pres. Cooper Queen Libr. Bd., Bisbee, 1988-91; book sales chmn. Shattuck Libr., Bisbee Mining Mus., 1987-92. Mem. Mid-Am. Paleontol. Soc., Sierra Club (nat. wilderness survey com. 1968-72), Zero Population Growth (founder Riverside, Calif. chpt. 1969), Ariz. Geol. Soc., Paleontol. Soc. So. Ariz., So. Calif. Palentol. Soc. Roman Catholic. Home: PO Box 1221 Bisbee AZ 85603-2221

JOHNSON, HERMAN LEONALL, research nutritionist; b. Whitehall, Wis., Apr. 1, 1935; s. Frederick E. And Jeanette (Severson) J.; m. Barbara Dale Matthews, July 3, 1960 (dec. May 1971); m. Barbara Ann Badger, Apr. 3, 1976. BA in Chemistry, North Cen. Coll., Naperville, Ill., 1959; MS in Biochemistry & Nutrition, Va. Poly. Inst. and State U., 1961, PhD in Biochemistry and Nutrition, 1963. Rsch. biochemist S.R. Noble Found., Ardmore, Okla., 1963-65; nutrition chemist U.S. Army Med. Rsch., Denver, 1965-74; nutrition physiologist Letterman Army Rsch., Presidio San Francisco, 1974-80, Western Human Nutrition Rsch. Ctr. USDA, Presidio San Francisco, 1980—. Contbr. numerous articles to profl. jours. Trustee 1st Meth. Ch., Ronnert Park, Calif., 1985-94, mem. fin. com., 1994—. With Med. Svc. Corps U.S. Army, 1954-56. Named one of Outstanding Young Men of Am., 1975; NIH traineeship Va. Poly. Inst. and State U., Blacksburg, 1961-63. Mem. AAAS, Am. Inst. Nutrition, Am. Soc. Clin. Nutritionists, Am. Coll. Nutritionists, Am. Coll. Sports Medicine, Sebastopol Spinners, Sigma Xi, Phi Lambda, Phi Sigma. Republican. Home: 256 Alden Ave Rohnert Park CA 94928-3704 Office: USDA Western Human Nutrition Rsch Ctr PO Box 29997 San Francisco CA 94129-0997

JOHNSON, HOLLY ROUILLARD, public relations executive; b. Norwood, Mass., Dec. 19, 1960; d. Lawrence Hadley Rouillard and Carol Hyde (Sreenan) Rouillard-Wolff; m. Perry Brian Johnson, Nov. 28, 1960. BS, U. Denver, 1983. Asst. dir. pub. rels. Colo. Ski Country USA, Denver, 1983-87; news bur. mgr. Colo. Tourism Bd., Denver, 1987-90; group mgr. travel, tourism, consumer mktg. JohnstonWells Group, Denver, 1990-94; pres. Johnson Comms., 1994—; mem. tourism adv. coun. Denver Conv. and Visitors Bur., 1993—; mem. mktg. adv. coun. Downtown Denver Partnership, 1991—. Mem. N.Am. Ski Journalists Assn., Travel and Tourism Rsch. Assn. Democrat. Episcopalian. Home: 4098 Surrey Ct Lafayette CO 80026 Office: Johnson Comms 4098 Surrey Ct Lafayette CO 80026

JOHNSON, JACQUELINE DOLORES, community health nurse; b. N.Y.C., Apr. 28, 1948; d. Thomas Frank and Geraldine Louise (Riddick) J. BSN, L.I. U., 1974; MPH, Johns Hopkins U., 1985. RN, N.Y.; cert. community health nurse, ANCC. Pub. health nursing supr. Vis. Nurse Assn. N.Y., N.Y.C., 1974-76; commd. U.S. Army, 1976, advanced through grades to lt. col., 1988; med./surg. nurse Brooke Army Med. Ctr., Ft. Sam Houston, Tex., 1976, community health nurse, 1976-78; chief preventive medicine U.S. Army Med. Dept. Activity, Aberdeen Proving Ground, Md., 1979-80; community health nurse U.S. Army Med. Dept. Activity, Ft. Irwin, Calif., 1980-81, Ft. Irwin, 1981-82, Ft. Belvoir, Va., 1982-84; dir. preventive medicine U.S. Army Med. Dept. Activity, Ft. Drum, N.Y., 1988-92; chief community health nurse Med. Dept. Activity, Ft. Carson, Colo., 1992-93; chief pub. health and safety dept. U.S. Med. Dept. Activity, Ft. Carson, Colo., 1993—; mem. minority human immunodeficiency virus adv. group Office of Surgeon Gen., Washington, 1990—. Mem. ANA, APHA. Office: Pub Health & Safety Dept US Army MEDDAC Fort Carson CO 80913

JOHNSON, JAMES DANIEL, theoretical physicist; b. Toledo, Mar. 21, 1944; s. James Elmer and Gwendolin (Dale) J.; m. Suzanne Darling, June 11, 1966; 1 child, Ian Christopher. B.S., Case Inst. Tech., 1966; M.A., SUNY-Stony Brook, 1968, Ph.D., 1972. Research assoc. Rockefeller U., N.Y.C., 1972-74; research assoc. Los Alamos Nat. Lab., Los Alamos, N.Mex., 1974-76, staff mem., 1976-89, acting head Sesame Library, 1982-85, project mgr. carbon project, 1984-89, dep. group leader, 1989—; head Sesame Libr., 1989—. Contbr. articles to profl. jours. Adult advisor Gt. S.W. Area council Boy Scouts Am., 1980-83; adult advisor sr. high youth group United Ch. of Los Alamos, 1982-85; active Los Alamos Light Opera Orgn., Los Alamos Little Theater; mem. U.S. Del. to Nuclear Testing Talks, 1988-89. Recipient Disting. Performance award Los Alamos Nat. Lab, 1988; NSF fellow 1966-71; Air Force grantee, 1980-82. Mem. Am. Phys. Soc., AAAS. Democrat. Club: Los Alamos Ski. Home: 321 Manhattan Loop Los Alamos NM 87544-2918 Office: Los Alamos Nat Lab T-1 MS B221 Los Alamos NM 87545

JOHNSON, JAMES DAVID, concert pianist, educator; b. Greenville, S.C., Aug. 7, 1948; s. Theron David and Lucile (Pearson) J.; m. Karen Elizabeth Jacobson, Feb. 1, 1975. MusB, U. Ariz., 1970, MusM, 1972, D of Mus. Arts, 1976; MusM, Westminster Choir Coll., 1986. Concert pianist, organist Pianists Found. Am., Boston Pops Orch., Royal Philharm., Nat. Symphony Orch., Leningrad Philharmonic, Victoria Symphony, others, 1961—; organist, choirmaster St. Paul's Episcopal Ch., Tucson, 1968-74, First United Meth. Ch., Fairbanks, Alaska, 1974-89, All Saints Episc. Ch., Omaha, 1995—; prof. music U. Alaska, Fairbanks, 1974-91, chair music dept., 1991; Isaacson prof. of music U. Nebr., Omaha, 1994—; organist, choirmaster All Sts. Episcopal Ch., Omaha, 1995—. Recordings include Moszkowski Etudes, 1973, Works of Chaminade Dohnanyi, 1977, Mendelssohn Concerti, 1978, Beethoven First Concerto, 1980, Beethoven, Reinecke, Ireland Trios with Alaska Chamber Ensemble, 1988, Kabalevsky Third Concerto, Muczynski Concerto, Muczynski Suite, 1990, Beethoven Third Concerto, 1993. Recipient Record of Month award Mus. Heritage Soc., 1979, 80; finalist mus. amb. program USIA, 1983. Mem. Music Tchrs. Nat. Assn., Phi Kappa Phi, Pi Kappa Lambda. Episcopalian. : Office: U Nebr Dept Music Omaha NE 68182

JOHNSON, JAMES GIBSON, JR., community recycling specialist; b. Flagstaff, Ariz., Feb. 26, 1938; s. James Gibson and Inga Anette J.; m. Faye Bodian, Aug. 23, 1973; children: Jill Johnson, Ginger Johnson, Jonathan Johnson. BA, U. Colo., 1960. Editor, pub. Town and Country Rev., Boulder, Colo., 1963-78; owner James G. Johnson and Assocs., Boulder, Colo., 1978-87; exec. dir. Eco Cycle Recycling, Boulder, Colo., 1987-89; community recycling specialist Office of Energy Conservation, State of Colo., Denver, 1989—. Mem. Open Space Bd. Trustees, Boulder, 1980-85, chmn., 1984-85; mem. Boulder County Pks. and Open Space Bd., 1985-93; chmn., 1987-89; mem. Boulder County Planning Commn., 1993—. Democrat. Home: 630 Northstar Ct Boulder CO 80304-1021 Office: Colo Office of Energy Conservation 1675 Broadway Ste 1300 Denver CO 80202-4613

JOHNSON, JAMES LAWRENCE, clinical psychologist, writer; b. Devils Lake, N.D., Sept. 17, 1953; s. Lawrence Tillman and Irene (Fah) J.; m. Paula Lou Sechler, Aug. 28, 1981; children: Daniel, Michael, Alisha. BA, U. N.D., 1975; MA, Azusa Pacific U., 1980; PhD, U.S. Internat. U., San Diego, 1990. Lic. marriage, family, child counselor and psychologist. Writer, editor Campus Crusade for Christ, San Bernardino, Calif., 1975-77; marriage, family, child counselor Foothill Community Mental Health Ctr., Glendora, Calif., 1978-81; social worker Le Roy Boys Home, LaVerne, Calif., 1981-83; counselor Creative Counseling Ctr., Pomona and Claremont, Calif., 1983—, Covina (Calif.) Psycholog. Group, 1981—; freelance writer, 1977-78, 90—; counselor trainer Stephen Ministries, Covina, 1985-86. Contbr. numerous articles to profl. and popular jours. Editor, advisor 1st Bapt. Ch., Covina, 1988, cabinet leader singles ministries, 1980-82. Mem. APA (clin.), Calif. Assn. Marriage and Family Therapists (clin.), Christian Writers' Fellowship, Psi Chi. Office: Creative Counseling Ctr 250 W 1st St Ste 214 Claremont CA 91711-4743

JOHNSON, JAMES RALPH, artist, writer; b. Fort Payne, Ala., May 20, 1922; s. James Andrew and Vera Sue (Small) J.; m. Betty Ann Johnson, Dec. 24, 1942 (div. Oct. 1961); children—JoAnn Johnson Harrell, Glen, David; m. Burdetta Fay Beebe, Oct. 11, 1961. BS in Econs., Howard Coll., Birmingham, Ala., 1943. Instr. art workshop, Santa Fe and Albuquerque, 1972—. Author: Animals and Their Food, 1972; Zoos of Today, 1971; Photography for Young People, 1971; Southern Swamps of America, 1970; Everglades Adventure, 1970; Animal Paradise, 1969; Moses' Band of Chimpanzees, 1969; Ringtail, 1968; Blackie-The Gorilla, 1968; Pepper, 1967; Advanced Camping Techniques, 1967; The Wolf Cub, 1966; Anyone Can Backpack in Comfort, 1965; Anyone Can Camp in Comfort, 1964; Camels West, 1964; Utah Lion, 1962; Anyone Can Live Off the Land, 1961; Best Photos of the Civil War, 1962; Wild Venture, 1961; Horsemen Blue & Gray, 1960; Big Cypress Buck, 1957; The Last Passenger, 1956; Lost on Hawk Mountain, 1954; Mountain Bobcat, 1953; (with B. F. Beebe) American Bears, 1965; American Wild Horses, 1964; contbr. articles to profl. jours. Served to maj. USMC, 1942-64. Recipient Jr. Book award cert. Boys Clubs Am., 1965. Mem. Am. Indian and Cowboy Artists, Nat. Western Artists Assn., Artists Equity, Outdoor Writers Am., Western Writers Am., Western Writers Assn., Santa Fe Artists Soc., Travelers' Century Club, Seven Continents Club. Home: PO Box 5295 Santa Fe NM 87502-5295

JOHNSON, JAMES WILLIAM, III, journalism educator; b. Flushing, N.Y., Feb. 6, 1938; s. James William Jr. and Edith C. (Horne) J.; m. Marilyn Dale Moyer, May 26, 1967; 1 child, Thayer Jay. BA, U. Ariz., 1961. Editor, reporter Oakland (Calif.) Tribune, 1961-79; assoc. prof. U. Ariz., Tucson, 1979—; cons. Contra Costa Times, Walnut Creek, Calif., 1989. Contbr. numerous articles to mags. Bd. dirs. Ariz. Humanities Coun. Recipient Nat. Teaching award Poynter Inst. for Media Studies, 1983, Ariz. Journalism Tchr. of Yr. Ariz. Newspapers Assn., 1983. Mem. Soc. Profl. Journalists (pres. Southern Ariz. chpt. 1989, nat. health and welfare com.), Contra Costa Press Club (pres. 1968), Sigma Chi. Republican. Methodist. Home: 1454 E Allen Rd Tucson AZ 85719-1419 Office: U Ariz Dept Journalism Franklin Building Rm 101M Tucson AZ 85721

JOHNSON, JANET KAY, nurse; b. Atlanta, Nov. 15, 1957; d. Karell and Georgia Lucille (Houtz) G.; m. Charles E. Kelly Jr., Jan. 16, 1986 (div. 1989); m. Michael A. Johnson, July 11, 1992. Diploma, Ga. Bapt. Sch. Nursing, Atlanta, 1978; BS in Health Arts, Coll. St. Francis, Joliet, Ill., 1989. CEN, ACLS, EMT-I, EMT-II; cert. flight nurse, trauma nurse care, advanced burn life support, basic trauma life support, pediatric advanced life support, advanced pediatric life support, emergency nurse pediat. provider. Staff nurse Northside Hosp., Atlanta, 1978; staff nurse, clin. mgr. emergency medicine, cardiology St. Joseph's Hosp., Atlanta, 1978-91; staff nurse North Fulton Med. Ctr., Atlanta, 1982; asst. surgical nurse R. Zaworski M.D., Roswell, Ga., 1980-81; flight nurse Providence Hosp., Anchorage, 1991-93; mgr. emergency dept. Ctrl. Peninsula Gen. Hosp., Soldotna, Alaska, 1993—; provider, instr. basic cardiac life support, Atlanta, 1978—, trauma nursing care, Atlanta, 1990; lectr. local sch. career programs; vol., lectr. Eastern Mercy Med., Inc.; state Medevac instr., 1991—; mem. women's resource task force, sexual assault lectr. Local Emergency Planning Com. Mem. Nat. Emergency Nurses Assn. (seminar chair 1990, govt. affairs chair 1990, state coun. rep. 1988, 90, pres. Metro Atlanta 1991, Alaska del. 1994). Baptist. Office: Ctrl Peninsula Gen Hosp Emergency Dept 250 Hospital Pl Soldotna AK 99669-7559

JOHNSON, JEFFREY PAUL, systems engineer; b. Columbus, Ohio, Jan. 10, 1945; s. Samuel and Joyce Eileen (Lockary) J.; m. Rita Rae Rapino, Dec. 1, 1973; children: Jeffrey Paul Jr., Margaret Joyce. BS in Physics, Ohio U., 1967; MS in Sys. Engring., Wright State U., 1978. Nuclear rsch. officer air force weapons lab. USAF, Kirtland AFB, Ohio, 1967-69; optical physical fgn. tech. divsn. USAF, Wright-Patterson AFB, Ohio, 1971-73; dep. missile combat crew cmdr. USAF, McConnell AFB, Kans., 1973-74; rsch. physicist Sys. Rsch. Labs., Dayton, Ohio, 1974-79; tech. staff Rockwell Internat., Anaheim, Calif., 1979-84; sr. staff scientist Photon Rsch. Assocs., La Jolla, Calif., 1984—. Mem. Internat. Soc. Optical Enring. Optical Soc. Am. Home: 12825 War Horse St San Diego CA 92129-2221 Office: Photon Rsch Assocs 10350 N Torrey Pines Rd # 300 La Jolla CA 92037-1020

JOHNSON, JEROME LINNÉ, cardiologist; b. Rockford, Ill., June 19, 1929; s. Thomas Arthur and Myrtle Elizabeth (Swanson) J.; m. Molly Ann Rideout, June 27, 1953; children: Susan Johnson Nowels, William Rideout. BA, U. Chgo., 1951; BS, Northwestern U., 1952, MD, 1955. Diplomate Nat. Bd. Med. Examiners. Intern U. Chgo. Clinics, 1955-56; resident Northwestern U., Chgo., 1958-61; chief resident Chgo. Wesley Meml. Hosp., 1960-61; mem., v.p. Hauch Med. Clinic, Pomona, Calif., 1961-88; pvt. practice cardiology and internal medicine Pomona, 1988—; clin. assoc. prof. medicine, U. So. Calif., L.A., 1961—; mem. staff Pomona Valley Hosp. Med. Ctr., chmn. coronary care com. 1967-77; mem. staff L.A. County Hosp. Citizen ambassador, People to People; mem. Town Hall of Calif., L.A. World Affairs Coun. Lt. USNR, 1956-58. Fellow Am. Coll. Cardiology, Am. Geriatrics Soc., Royal Soc. Health; mem. Galileo Soc., Am. Heart Assn. (bd. dirs. L.A. County div. 1967-84, San Gabriel div. 1963-89), Am. Soc. Internal Medicine, Inland Soc. Internal Medicine, Pomona Host Lions. Home: 648 Delaware Dr Claremont CA 91711-3457

JOHNSON, JOAN BRAY, insurance company consultant; b. Kennett, Mo., Nov. 19, 1926; d. Ples Green and Mary Scott (Williams) Bray; m. Frank Johnson Jr., Nov. 6, 1955; 1 child, Victor Kent. Student, Drury Coll., 1949-51, Cen. Bible Inst. and Coll., 1946-49. Staff writer Gospel Pub. Co., Springfield, Mo., 1949-51; sec. Kennett Sch. Dist. Bd. Edn., 1951-58; spl. features corr. Memphis Press-Scimitar, 1959-60; sec. to v.p. Cotton Exchange Bank, Kennett, Mo., 1959-60; proposal analyst Aetna Life Ins. Co., El Paso, Tex., 1960-64, pension adminstr., 1964-71; office mgr. Brokerage div. Aetna Life Ins. Co., Denver, 1971-78; office adminstr. Life Consol. div. Aetna Life Ins. Co., Oakland, Calif., 1979-82; office adminstr. PFSD div. Aetna Life Ins. Co., Walnut Creek, Calif., 1983-86; office adminstr. PFSD-Health Mktg. div. Aetna Life Ins. Co., Sacramento, Calif., 1986-89; regional adminstr. Aetna Life Ins. Co., Hartford, Conn., 1989-91; cons. Aetna Life Ins. Co., Riverside, Calif., 1991—. Officer local PTA, 1964-71; pres. Wesley Service Guild, 1968-71; den mother Boy Scouts Am. Recipient Life Service award PTA, 1970. Fellow Life Office Mgmt. Assn. (instr. classes); mem. DAR (regent Silver State Nev. chpt. 1994-96), Assn. Bus. and Profl. Women, Life Underwriters Assn., Clark County Heritage Mus. Build, Nev., 1993—, Last Monday Club, Opti-Mrs., Allied Arts Club. Democrat. Methodist. Home: 2415 La Estrella St Henderson NV 89014-3608 Office: 1677 N Main St Ste 250 Santa Ana CA 92701-2324

JOHNSON, JOHN DAVID, pediatrician; b. Palo Alto, Calif., Sept. 14, 1938; s. Willis Hugh and Elizabeth Ann (Schma) J.; m. Margaret Jane Grider, June 19, 1960; children: William Todd, Timothy Hugh, Kelly Lynn. AB, Wabash Coll., 1960; MD, Stanford U., 1965. Diplomate Am. Bd. Pediatrics, Am. Bd. Neonatal and Perinatal Medicine. Intern in pediatrics Johns Hopkins Hosp., 1965-66, resident in pediatrics, 1966-67; resident in pediatrics Stanford U. Hosp., 1969-70; asst. prof. pediatrics Stanford (Calif.) U. Sch. Medicine, 1970-77, assoc. prof., 1977-79; assoc. prof. pediatrics and ob-gyn U. N.Mex. Sch. Medicine, Albuquerque, 1979-83, prof. pediatrics and ob-gyn, 1983—, chmn. pediatrics, 1986-93; chief staff U. N.Mex. Med. Ctr., Albuquerque, 1989-91. Contbr. articles to profl. jours. Lt. col. UPHS, 1967-69. Rsch. grant NIH, 1983-90. Mem. Soc. for Pediatric Rsch. (pres. 1984, sec. treas. 1977-82), Am. Pediatric Soc., Am. Acad. Pediatrics, Western Soc. Pediatric Rsch. (pres. 1987), Perinatal Rsch. Soc. (pres. 1989-90), N.Mex. Pediatrics Soc. (exec. com. 1989-91), N.Mex. Med. Soc. Office: U NMex Sch Medicine Dept Pediatrics ACC-3 Albuquerque NM 87131

JOHNSON, JOHN PHILIP, geneticist, researcher; b. Wabash, Ind., June 6, 1949; s. Melvin Leroy and Cleo Pauline (Aldrich) J.; m. Sheryl Kay Kennedy, June 3, 1978; children: Craig Eric, Lindsay Sara. BS, U. Mich., 1971, MD, 1975. Diplomate Am. Bd. Pediatrics, Am. Bd. Med. Genetics. Intern, 2d-yr. resident Children's Hosp. Los Angeles, 1975-77; 3d yr. resident in pediatrics U. Utah, Salt Lake City, 1977-78, fellow in genetics, 1980-82, asst. prof. pediatrics, 1982-85; pediatrician Family Health Program, Salt Lake City, 1978-80; assoc. dir. med. genetics, attending/active staff physician Children's Hosp. Oakland, Calif., 1985-92; dir. med. genetics, attending/active staff physician Children's Hosp., Oakland, 1992-94; dir. med. genetics Shodair Children's Hosp., Helena, Mont., 1994—, active mem. staff, 1995—; clinic physician Utah State Tng. Sch., American Fork, 1982-85; attending and staff physician Primary Children's Med. Ctr., Salt Lake City, 1978-80. Contbr. articles to med. jours. Recipient William J. Branstrom award U. Mich., 1967. Fellow Am. Acad. Pediatrics; mem. Am. Soc. Human Genetics, Soc. for Pediatric Rsch., Alpha Omega Alpha. Home: 2604 Gold Rush Ave Helena MT 59601-5625 Office: Shodair Children's Hosp PO Box 5539 Helena MT 59604-5539

JOHNSON, KATHERINE HOLTHAUS, health care marketing professional; b. Denver, Mar. 19, 1961; d. William Philip and Barbara Kristine (Nielsen) Holthaus; m. Robert Scott Johnson; children: Katie Maree, Brian David. B in Applied Math. Engring., U. Colo., 1983; MBA, U. Denver, 1992. Acctg. intern Cooper, Haugen & Co., CPAs, Englewood, Colo., 1982-84; market analyst mktg. dept. Porter Meml. Hosp., Denver, 1985-88; account exec. Tallant LaPointe & Ptnrs., Inc., Englewood, 1988-92; advt. mgr. Micromedex, Inc., Denver, 1992-93; mktg. cons. Highlands Ranch, Colo., 1993—. Judge, vol. 4-H Clubs, Met. Denver, 1979—; supt. Sunday sch. Ascension Luth. Ch., Littleton, Colo., 1985-87. Recipient 2 Advantage awards Adventist Health System, 1987. Mem. Soc. for Healthcare Planning and Mktg., Am. Hosp. Assn., Acad. for Health Svcs. Mktg., Am. Mktg. Assn., Alpha Chi Omega. Republican.

JOHNSON, KEITH RONALD, obstetrician/gynecologist; b. Chgo., Mar. 19, 1929; s. Clarence Albert and Alma Alice (Semrad) J.; m. Esther Louise Rieve, June 26, 1954; children: Robert, Jeffrey, Cynthia. BS, U. Ill., 1950; MD, U. Ill., Chgo., 1954. Diplomate Am. Bd. Obstetrics and Gynecology. Intern L.A. City Hosp., 1954-55; resident in ob/gyn San Diego County Gen. Hosp./Mercy Hosp., 1957-60; pvt. practice specializing in ob/gyn. La Mesa, Calif., 1960—. Lt. USNR, 1955-57. Fellow Am. Coll. Obstetricians and Gynecologists, Internat. Coll. Surgeons; mem. Calif. Med. Assn., San Diego Med. Assn., Am. Assn. Gynecol. Laparoscopists, Rotary. Republican. Office: 8881 Fletcher Pky Ste 285 La Mesa CA 91942-3135

JOHNSON, KENNETH LOUIS, education marketing specialist; b. Blackfoot, Idaho, Dec. 22, 1957; s. Stuart Paul and Afton (Dance) J.; m. Stacy Rae Siirila, Sept. 29, 1989; children: Rachel Garrett, Patrick Garrett, Lisa Johnson. BA cum laude, Brigham Young U., 1982; MBA in Health Svcs. Adminstrn., U. Utah, 1988, postgrad., 1995—. Dir. pub. rels. Bingham Meml. Hosp., Blackfoot, Idaho, 1982; pub. rels. specialist U. Utah Health Scis., Salt Lake City, 1982-89; dir. mktg. Lakeview Hosp., Bountiful, Utah, 1989-90, asst. adminstr., 1990-92; mktg. adminstr. Weber State U., Ogden, Utah, 1992-95, dir. rsch., 1995—; mktg. cons. Sport Cove Scuba Diving, Salt Lake City, 1984-88, U. Utah Small Bus., Salt Lake City, 1986; pub. rels. cons. Springville (Utah) World Folkfest, 1986. Cub master, den leader, explorer advisor Boy Scouts Am., Utah, 1986—; coun. mem. United Way, Davis County, Utah, 1990-91; mem. Ogden/Weber Leadership Acad., 1994. Mem. Internat. Assn. Bus. Communicators, Am. Coll. Healthcare Execs., Utah Soc. for Hosp. Planning, Mktg. & Pub. Rels. (pres. 1990-91, past pres. 1991-92), Rotary Internat. (Layton, Utah). LDS. Home: 3090 N 1150 E Ogden UT 84414-1894 Office: Weber State U Univ Rels Univ Cir Ogden UT 84408

JOHNSON, KEVIN MAURICE, professional basketball player; b. Sacramento, Calif., Mar. 4, 1966. Student, U. Calif. Basketball player Cleveland Cavaliers, 1987-88, Phoenix Suns, 1988—. Named to Dream Team II, 1994, NBA Most Improved Player, 1989, All-NBA Second Team, 1989-91, 94, All-NBA Third Team, 1992. Office: care Phoenix Suns 2910 N Central Ave Phoenix AZ 85012-2704

JOHNSON, KIM, customer account representative; b. Indpls., June 2, 1959; s. Broderick Hanna and Kathryn Elenore (Parker) J.; married, June 13, 1982; children: Joshua, Chelsea, Jennifer. BS, Ariz. State U., 1981; MA of Mgmt., U. Phoenix, 1989. Cert. Ariz. C.C. Bd. in Bus. Receiver, leader govt. electronics group Motorola, Inc., Tempe, Ariz., 1979-83; analyst material ctonrol govt. electronics group Motorola, Inc., Scottsdale, Ariz., 1983-89, supr. material control, 1989-90; customer account rep. semicondr. product sector Motorola, Inc., Chandler, Ariz., 1990—. Cubmaster pack 285 Cub Scouts, Chandler, 1991-94; mentor Ariz. Bus. Leaders for Edn., Phoenix, 1992. With U.S. Army, 1986. Republican. Methodist. Home: 2526 W Orchid Ln Chandler AZ 85224-3930 Office: Motorola Inc SPS 1300 N Alma School Rd Chandler AZ 85224-2939

JOHNSON, LAWRENCE M., banker; b. 1940. Student, U. Hawaii. With Bank of Hawaii, Honolulu, 1963—, exec. v.p., 1980-84, vice chmn., 1984-89, pres., 1989—, now chmn. bd., CEO; pres. Bancorp Hawaii, Inc. Office: Bancorp Hawaii Inc PO Box 2900 Honolulu HI 96813 Office: Bancorp Hawaii Inc 130 Merchant St Honolulu HI 96813-4408*

JOHNSON, LAYMON, JR., utility marketing analyst; b. Jackson, Miss., Sept. 1, 1948; s. Laymon and Bertha (Yarbrough) J.; m. Charlene J. Johnson, Nov. 13, 1982. B in Tech., U. Dayton, 1970; MS in Systems Mgmt., U. So. Calif., 1978. Mem. tech. staff Rockwell Internat., Canoga Park, Calif., 1975-77; sr. dynamics engr. Gen. Dynamics, Pomona, Calif., 1978-83; fin. systems specialist Northrop Corp., Pico Rivera, Calif., 1983-90; utility mktg. analyst dept. water and power City of L.A., 1991—. Lt. comdr. USNR, 1970-92. Mem. Naval Res. Assn., Assn. Mil. Surgeons U.S., Los Angeles County Mus. Art, Music Ctr. L.A., Smithsonian Assocs., Nat. Hist. Soc., ISSM Triumvirate, Tau Alpha Pi. Democrat. Roman Catholic.

JOHNSON, LEAYN HUTCHINSON, nursing educator, mental health nurse; b. Elizabeth, Pa., June 3, 1936; d. Ernest Eba and Edna (Caley) Hutchinson; m. Donald E. Johnson, Mar. 10, 1959; children: Donna Lynn, Donald E. Diploma, McKeesport Hosp. Sch. Nursing, 1957; BSN cum laude, Wright State U., 1975; MS, Ohio State U., 1977; PhD in Psychology, U.S. Internat. U., 1987. RN, Calif. From lectr. to asst. prof. U. Hawaii, Honolulu; prin. Ourself Counseling Ctr., Newport Beach, Calif.; asst. prof. Calif. State U., Long Beach; assoc. prof. Mem. ANA, Calif. Nurses Assn., Sigma Theta Tau. Home: 16932 Edgewater Ln Huntington Beach CA 92649-4206 Office: 1400 Quail St Ste 235 Newport Beach CA 92660

JOHNSON, LEE CARROLL, electronics company executive; b. Monroe, Ind., Sept. 29, 1933; s. Thetus Jesse and Vida Louise (Ward) J.; m. Donna Lee Heald, Nov. 25, 1951; children: Marga Lynn Johnson Cullumber, Shelon Lee. BEE, Purdue U., 1953; LLB, LaSalle U., Chgo., 1966. V.p., dir. bus. devel. ITT Aerospace, Ft. Wayne, Ind., 1952-74; v.p., gen. mgr. govt. electronics group Motorola Corp., Scottsdale, Ariz., 1974-88; cons. Motorola U., Schaumburg, Ill. Patentee in field. Mem. fin. com. Devereux Found., Scottsdale, 1981-88. Mem. IEEE, Air Force Assn., Navy League, Assn. of U.S. Army, NRA (life), Aircraft Owners and Pilots Assn., Assn. Old Crows. Republican. Methodist. Home and Office: 9090 N 86th Pl Scottsdale AZ 85258-1934

JOHNSON, LEONA MINDELL, librarian, educator; b. Bremerton, Wash., Sept. 18, 1946; d. Edward and Adene Mindell (Lynum) Vig; m. James David Stein, Nov. 27, 1969 (div. 1977); 1 child: Korin Nicole; m. Paul Wallace Johnson, May 21, 1977; children: Gunnar, Turi, Ole-Paul. BA in Psychology, Western Wash. U., 1969; forest technician cert., Peninsula Coll., 1975; MEd, Central Wash. U., 1994. Cert. tchr. K-8, Wash. Forest engr. Crown Zellerbach, Sekiu, Wash., 1975-77; forest tech. U.S. Forest Svc., Cle Elum, Wash., 1978; libr. Roslyn (Wash.) Pub. Libr., 1978—, Carpenter Meml. Libr., Cle Elum, 1980-81; libr. II Clallam Bay (Wash.) Correctional Ctr., 1990; grad. asst. Ctrl. Wash. U., Ellensburg, Wash., 1992-93; substitute tchr. Cle Elum (Wash.)-Roslyn Sch., 1994—. Scholar AAUW, 1992. Mem. Internat. Reading Assn., Kappa Delta Pi, Psi Chi. Office: Roslyn Pub Libr 201 S 1st St Roslyn WA 98941

JOHNSON, LEONIDAS ALEXANDER, optometrist; b. Chgo., Jan. 16, 1959; s. Leon and Dolores J.; m. Crystal Dwaun Ellington, June 23, 1990. BA in Biology, Ill. Wesleyan U., 1981; BS in Visual Sci., So. Calif. Coll. of Optometry, Fullerton, 1983, OD, 1985; student, Grace Theol. Sem., Long Beach, Calif., 1986-89, Biola U., La Mirada, Calif., 1991—. Registered Optometrist. Optometrist Larry Gotlieb, O.D., Redondo Beach, Calif., 1985-86, James Moses, O.D., Inglewood, Calif., 1986-87, Eyecare U.S.A., Montclair, Calif., 1987-89, Pearle Visioncare, Brea, Calif., 1989-94, Watt's Health Found., Inc., L.A., 1994—; quality assurance com. mem. Eyecare U.S.A., 1988-89; investigator Ocular Hypertension Treatment Study. Contbr. article to profl. jour. Deacon Friendship Bapt. Ch., Yorba Linda, Calif. Fellow Am. Acad. Optometry; mem. Am. Optometric Assn., Calif. Optometric Assn., Nat. Optometric Assn. Home: PO Box 4434 Diamond Bar CA 91765-0434 Office: Watts Health Ctr 10300 Compton Ave Los Angeles CA 90002-3628

JOHNSON, LEROY FRANKLIN, chemist; b. Seattle, Feb. 4, 1933; s. LeRoy F. and Anna C. (Amdahl) J.; m. Margaret L. Lindsley, Sept. 8, 1956; children: Noel L., Brett N. BS, Oreg. State U., 1954, MS, 1956. NMR applications chemist Varian Assocs., Palo Alto, Calif., 1957-72; v.p. rsch. Nicolet Magnetics Corp., Mountain View, Calif., 1972-83; sr. scientist GE NMR Instruments, Fremont, Calif., 1983-92; analytical NMR mgr. Bruker Instruments, Fremont, 1992-94; cons. NMR, 1994—; NMR short course tchr. Am. Chem. Soc., 1966—. Author: Carbon-13 NMR Spectra, 1972; contbr. articles to tech. jours. Mem. Am. Chem. Soc. (exceptional achievement award 1992), Internat. Soc. Magnetic Resonance.

JOHNSON, LLOYD WARREN, artist, real estate investor; b. N.Y.C., June 5, 1941; Carl Gustave and Edna Lillian (Klein) J. BS, N.Y. Inst. Tech., 1964. Paintings in many group exhibitions including Pietrantonio Gallery, Interchurch Ctr., Union Carbide Gallery, Artists Equity Gallery, Brooklyn Union Gas Co. Gallery, also colls., librs. and regional mus. Treas. Anna Meltzer Art Soc., N.Y.C., 1970-74, pres. 1974-75. Mem. Artists Equity of N.Y.

JOHNSON, LOIS JEAN, music educator; b. L.A., Jan. 13, 1950; d. Kenneth Franklin and Iona Jean (Miller) J. BA, Brigham Young U., 1971, MusM, 1975; postgrad., Ind. U. Grad. teaching asst. Brigham Young U., Provo, Utah, 1972-75, instr. voice, 1975—; instr. music study Vienna, Austria, 1978; chief registrar vital stas. City-County Health Dept., Provo, 1979-85; mus. dir. Utah Valley Choral Soc., Provo, 1980—, trustee, 1983—; mus. dir. Promised Valley Playhouse, Salt Lake City, 1984; dir. choral activities, chair Fine Arts Dept. American Fork (Utah) High Sch., 1985—, chmn. fine arts dept., 1986—; mem. coll. bd. adv. placement Devel. Com. for Music Theory, 1993—; recitalist, soloist Mormon Tabernacle Choir, Salt Lake City, 1972-91. Mem. NEA, Am. Choral Dirs. Assn. (pres. Utah chpt. 1991-93), Nat. Assn. Tchrs. Singing (v.p. local chpt. 1983-84), Utah Edn. Assn., Music Educators Nat. Conf., Utah Music Educators Assn. Republican. Mormon. Home: 835 N 750 W Provo UT 84604-3213 Office: Am Fork High Sch 510 N 600 E American Fork UT 84003-1914

JOHNSON, M. EARL, clergyman, administrator; b. Kandiohy, Minn., Feb. 11, 1928; s. Alvin Victor Emmanuel and Rose Evangeline (Peterson) J.; m. Darliene Joyce Morken, June 7, 1949; children: Billy Bryant, Jacque Lynn, Robert Anthony, Wendi Lee. Diploma, North Ctrl. Bible Coll., Mpls., 1950; postgrad., U. Oreg., 1954-58. Ordained to ministry Assemblies of God Ch., 1950. Pastor Assemblies of God Ch., Pelican Rapids, Minn., 1950-52, Granada, Minn., 1952-54; coll. tchr. Open Bible Standard, Eugene, Oreg., 1954-58; min. of music Bethel Temple, Assemblies of God, Sacramento, 1958-65; pastor Assemblies of God, Downey, Calif., 1965-68, Bethel Ch. Assemblies of God, Redding, Calif., 1968-82; exec. officer No. Calif./Nev. Dist. Coun., Inc. Assemblies of God, Santa Cruz, Calif., 1982—. Trustee Bethany Coll., Santa Cruz, 1978—, Am. Indian Bible Coll., Phoenix, 1983—; chmn. bd. trustees Asian Pacific Bible Sch., L.A., 1989—. Republican. Office: No Calif and Nev Dist Coun Assemblies of God 125 Bethany Dr Santa Cruz CA 95066-2803

JOHNSON, MAGIC See **JOHNSON, EARVIN**

JOHNSON, MARIAN ILENE, education educator; b. Hawarden, Iowa, Oct. 3, 1929; d. Henry Richard and Wilhelmina Anna (Schmidt) Stoltenberg; m. Paul Irving Jones, June 14, 1958 (dec. Feb. 1985); m. William Andrew Johnson, Oct. 3, 1991. BA, U. La Verne, 1959; MA, Claremont Grad. Sch., 1962; PhD, Ariz. State U., 1971. Cert. tchr., Iowa, Calif. Elem. tchr. Cherokee (Iowa) Sch. Dist., 1949-52, Sioux City (Iowa) Sch. Dist., 1952-56, Ontario (Calif.) Pub. Schs., 1956-6l, Reed Union Sch. Dist., Belvedere-Tiburon, Calif., 1962-65, Columbia (Calif.) Union Sch. Dist., 1965-68; prof. edn. Calif. State U., Chico, 1972-91. Home: 26437 S Lakewood Dr Sun Lakes AZ 85248-7246

JOHNSON, MARY BETTINA BLACK, physical education educator, athletic trainer; b. Salt Lake City, Mar. 2, 1952; d. Wayne Lythgoe and Bettina Loewen (Rothrock) Black; m. Carl Lowell Johnson, July 26, 1974; 1 child, Robert Wayne Rå. BS, U. Utah, 1974, MS, 1984, PhD, 1990. Cert. tchr., Utah. Phys. edn. tchr. Mt. Jordan Jr. High Sch., Sandy, Utah, 1974-78, Alta High Sch., Sandy, Utah, 1978-84; adj. faculty U. Utah, Salt Lake City, 1986-89; assoc. athletic trainer U.S. Olympic Com., Colorado Springs, Colo., 1986; athletic trainer Salt Lake Sports Medicine, 1987-89; grad. asst. athletic trainer U. Utah Athletics, Salt Lake City, 1985-89; asst. prof. athletic tng./pre-phys. therapy San Diego State U., 1989-93; asst. prof., dir. athletic tng. dept. human performance Met. State Coll. Denver, 1993—. contbr. articles to profl. jours. Named one of Outstanding Young Women of Am., 1979; Affirmative Action grantee, Rsch. scholar and Creative Arts grantee San Diego State Univ. Mem. AAHPERD, Nat. Athletic Trainers Assn. (cert., grad. student scholarship 1984, membership rsch. grant 1991), Far West Athletic Trainers Assn., Rocky Mountain Athletic Trainers Assn., Colo. Athletic Trainers Assn., Calif. Athletic Trainers Assn., Utah Athletic Trainers Assn. Democrat. Office: Met State Coll Denver Dept HPSL Campus Box 25 Po Box 173362 Denver CO 80217-3362

JOHNSON, MARYANN ELAINE, educational administrator; b. Franklin Twp., Pa., Nov. 1, 1943; d. Mary I. Sollick; BS in Elementary Edn., Mansfield State U., Pa., 1964; MS in Elementary Edn., U. Alaska, College 1973; EdD, Wash. State U., Pullman, 1981; married. Tchr. Nayatt Sch., Barrington, R.I., 1964-66, North Sch., North Chicago, Ill., 1966-67, Kodiak (Alaska) On-Base Sch., 1967-71, Eastmont Sch. Dist., 1971-74, reading coord., East Wenatchee, Wash., 1974-77, adminstrv. asst., 1977-82, asst. supt. Sec. Parent Advisory Com., 1982-93; asst. supt. South Kitsap Sch. Dist., Port Orchard, Wash., 1993-95; curriculum dir. Clarkston Sch. Dist., Wash.; chair Wash. State Discover Card Scholarship, 1993—. Active Ctrl. Wash. Hosp. Bd., 1991-93, Ctrl. Wash. Hosp. Found. Bd., 1993—. Mem. Assn. Supervision and Curriculum Devel. (review coun. 1993-99), Wash. State Assn. Supervision and Curriculum Devel. (bd. dirs. 1986-89, pres. elect 1989-90, pres. 1990-91, Educator of Yr. 1981), NEA, Wash. Assn. Sch. Adminstrs. (bd. dirs., chmn. curriculum and instrn. Job-Alike, profl. devel. com., Project Leadership, pres. elect 1986-87, pres. 1987-88, leadership award, 1986, award of merit, 1992, Exec. Educator 100 1988, 93, chmn. WASA 21st century scholarship com. 1988—, leadership acad. 1993), Am. Assn. Sch. Adminstrs. (resolutions com. 1988-89, com. for advancement of sch. adminstrs. 1989-92), East Wenatchee C. of C. (bd. dirs. 1990-93, chair edn. com. 1990-91), Delta Kappa Gamma (pres. 1982-84), Phi Delta Kappa, Phi Kappa Phi. Named Eastmont Tchr. of the Yr., 1973-74. Office: Clarkston Sch Dist 847 5th St PO Box 70 Clarkston WA 99403-0070

JOHNSON, MARYANNA MORSE, business owner; b. Oxford, Miss., Dec. 21, 1936; d. Hugh McDonald and Anna Sullivan (Virden) Morse; children: Julianna, Hunter, Cynthia, Capp. Student, Miss. U. for Women, 1957; BSN cum laude, Tex. Woman's U., 1986. RN, Tex. Owner MJM & Assocs., Boulder, Colo., 1968—; health promotion cons., 1986—. Mem. Sigma Theta Tau. Home: 3102 Bell Dr Boulder CO 80301-2277

JOHNSON, MARYANNE ELIZABETH, private school educator; b. Caribou, Maine, Oct. 16, 1962; d. Bernard Michael and Ardele Louise (Ostrom) Russik; m. William Robert Johnson Jr., Sept. 22, 1989. A, Ctrl. Piedmont C.C., Charlotte, N.C., 1982; BA in English, U. N.C., Charlotte, 1985. Cert. tchr., Ariz. Tchr., asst. Tutoring Svcs., Inc., Charlotte, 1985-89; asst. dir., tchr. The Learning Lab, Tucson, Ariz., 1990—; cons. Cholla High Sch., Tucson, 1993—. Co-author newsletter The Learning Lab, 1991—; contbr. articles to newspapers. Docent Tohono Chul Park, Tucson, 1993—. Mem. U.S. Fencing Assn. (sec.-treas. Ariz. divsn. 1992-93), Sigma Tau Delta. Office: 231 W Giaconda Way # 129 Tucson AZ 85704-4341

JOHNSON, MILDRED IRENE, retired business educator; b. Oakland, Iowa, Feb. 27, 1924; d. Roy McKinley and Erna Emma (Klopping) F.; m. Robert Douglas Johnson, July 14, 1945; children: Douglas Wells, Lynn Anne. BSBA, Colo. State U., 1965, MS in Bus. Adminstr., 1968. Instr. Colo. State U., Fort Collins, 1967-78, asst. prof., 1979-82, lectr., 1983-85, asst. prof. emeritus, 1986—; cons. numerous firms and orgns. including Bell Telephone Labs., Murray Hill, N.J., 1983-85, Houghton Mifflin Co., Allyn and Bacon, Scott Foresman and Co., Boston, 1985, We. Temporary Svcs., Ft. Collins, 1982, Colo. Pub. Health Assn., Denver, 1983, Poudre R-1 Schs., Ft. Collins, 1983-84, Colo. Vocat. Edn. Assn., Denver, 1977, Colo. Civil Svc. Assn., Ft. Collins C. of C. Co-producer: (videotape) Computer Text Analysis, 1983, (film) Administrative Office Mng. and Bus. Tech. Edn., 1980; co-author: (computer manual) Business Report Computer Manual, 1983; contbr. articles to profl. jours.; speaker in field. Vol. Salvation Army, Ft. Collins, 1981-86, Girl Scouts U.S.A., Arvada, Colo., 1961, 4-H Clubs, Ft. Collins, 1965, March of Dimes, Denver, Boy Scouts Am., Denver, 1957-60, ARC, Denver, 1951, Am. Cancer Soc., Ft. Collins; bd. dirs. 1st Presbyn. Ch. Found., Ft. Collins, 1990—, v.p., 1992-93, pres., 1993—; pres. Kimberling Charitable Trust, 1993—; bd. dirs., com. chmn. Ft. Collins Audubon Soc., 1982-85; com. mem. United Way, Ft. Collins, 1977-84; rec. sec. Ft. Collins Symphony Guild, 1988-89, 2d v.p., bd. dirs., 1989-92, 1st v.p., 1994—; trustee Ft. Collins Symphony Assn., 1992—, bd. dirs.; patron Ft. Collins Symphony and Lincoln Ctr. Performing Arts, 1979-80, 92, 93. Mem. Assn. for Bus. Comms., Colo. State U. Alumni Assn., Colo. State U. Faculty Club (bd. dirs., pres. 1979-83), Quota Internat. (sec. 1981, bd. dirs. 1981-86, cons. 1983-84, dist. 9 sec., treas. 1982), Questers Internat. (bd. dirs., treas. Ft. Collins club 1991-92), Rotary (chmn. bull. com. 1992-94, chmn. club svc. com. 1992-95, pres.-elect 1995-96, chmn. and pres. Ft. Collins Breakfast Rotary Charitable Found., 1995—), Phi Omega Pi, Beta Epsilon, Delta Pi Epsilon (sec. 1983-85, bd. dirs. 1983-85), Beta Gamma Sigma, Phi Kappa Phi (historian 1974, treas. 1975, sec. 1976, 77, v.p. 1978, pres.-elect 1979, pres. 1980, bd. dirs. 1974-80, regional v.p. 1983-89, nat. regent 1989-92, nat. found. trustee 1983-92, nat. dir. 1983-92, nat. v.p. Phi Kappa Phi Found. 1986-89). Republican. Presbyterian. Home: 1330 Calabasas Ct Fort Collins CO 80525-2886 Office: Colo State U Mgmt Dept Fort Collins CO 80523

JOHNSON, MIRIAM MASSEY, sociology educator; b. Atlanta, Jan. 12, 1928; d. Herbert Neal and Leola (Paullin) Massey; m. Guy Benton Johnson Jr., July 21, 1951; children: Frank Shannon, Rebekah Paullin. PhD, Harvard U., 1955. Instr. U. Oreg., Eugene, 1959-63, 73-75, asst. prof., 1975-80, assoc. prof., 1980-88, prof., 1988—, retired emerita, 1993; acting dir. Ctr. for Study of Women in Soc., U. Oreg., 1986-88, 91. Author: (with Jean Stockard) Sex Roles: Sex Inequality and Sex Role Development, 1980, Gender and Society, 1991; author: Strong Mothers Weak Wives, 1988. Rockefeller Found. grantee, 1988-89. Office: U Oreg Dept Sociology Eugene OR 97403

JOHNSON, NICHOLAS LEROY, scientist; b. Mpls., Jan. 31, 1950; s. Francis LeRoy and Marjory Madeline J.; m. Mary Elizabeth Proter, Apr. 5, 1969; 1 child, Kevin LeRoy. BS in Physics, Memphis State U., 1974. Adv. scientist Teledyne Brown Engring., Colorado Springs, 1979-92; prin. scientist Kaman Scis. Corp., Colorado Springs, 1992—; mem. Nat. Rsch. Coun. Com. on Space Debris, 1993-94, Nat. Rsch. Coun. Com. on Space Station, 1993—. Author: The Soviet Year in Space, annually 1981-90, Handbook of Soviet Lunar and Planetary Exploration, 1979, Handbook of Soviet Manned Space Flight, 1980, 88, Soviet Space Programs, 1980-1985, 1987, Artificial Space Debris, 1987, 2d edit., 1991, Soviet Military Strategy in Space, 1987, Europe and Asia in Space, 1991-1992, 1994, The Soviet Reach for the Moon, 1994, also more than 80 articles. Served to staff sgt. USAF, 1969-72, to lt. USN, 1975-79. Recipient Disting. Alumni award Memphis State U., 1989. Fellow AIAA (assoc.), Brit. Interplanetary Soc.; mem. Nat. Rsch. Coun. (com. on space debris 1993-94, com. on space sta. 1995—). Office: Kaman Scis Corp 1500 Garden Of The Gods Rd Colorado Springs CO 80907-3416

JOHNSON, P. ANNA, publishing executive; b. Niagara Falls, N.Y., July 18, 1938; d. Walter Sherman and Laura Ann (Wiseman) J.; children: Arlo Eugene Rodieck, Jorma Leonard Rodieck. BA, Colby Coll., 1960; postgrad., Nat. Art Sch., Sydney, Australia, 1963-64, George Washington U., 1983. Counselor Boston Ctr. for Blind Children, 1960-61; dance tchr. Pennshurst Girls High Sch., Sydney, 1962; rsch. asst. Sydney U., 1963; artist, potter Sydney, 1966-78; pub. Open Hand Pub. Inc., Seattle, 1981-83, Washington, 1983-88, Seattle, 1988—; bd. dirs. Multicultural Pubs. Exch., Madison Wis., Book Pubs. N.W., 1991-93. Pub., editor: Habari Gani? What's the News, 1992; pub.: The Black West, 1985, High Tide of Black Resistance, 1994, Stone on Stone/Piedra sobre Piedra, 1994. Bd. dirs. Kinma Sch., Sydney, 1974-78; sec. Unemployed and Poverty Action Coun., Washington, 1984-87. Grantee Nat. Coun. for Arts, Australia, 1975, Nat. Endowment for the Arts, 1994. Office: Open Hand Pub Inc PO Box 22048 Seattle WA 98122-0048

JOHNSON, PAMELA KAY, counselor, educator, farmer; b. Great Falls, Mont., Sept. 28, 1959; d. David George and Lorraine Jeanne (Preputin) J.; m. Royce Roman McDunn, Nov. 19, 1988 (div. June 1993). BS in Elem. Edn., Eastern Mont. Coll., 1982; M in Profl. Counseling, Coll. Great Falls, 1994. Cert. tchr., Mont. 4th grade tchr. St. Peter and Paul Sch., Great Falls, 1982-85; Chpt. 1 reading tchr. Lady of Lourdes Sch., Great Falls, 1985-86; reading resource tchr. Great Falls Pub. Sch. Dist. 1, 1986-87, Chpt. 1 reading tchr., 1987-92; owner, farmer Brady, Mont., 1986—; intern Spectrum Learning, Great Falls, 1994-95, counselor, 1995—; faculty rep. Mountain View Sch. PTA, Great Falls, 1988-90; chem. awareness response edn. team leader Great Falls Pub. Sch. Dist. 1, 1987-92, jr. varsity girls basketball coach, 1990-92. Parenting facilitator Cascade County Ext. Office, Great Falls, 1992-94, Cascade County Headstart, 1993. Mem. ACA, Phi Delta Kappa. Roman Catholic. Office: Spectrum Learning 1101 15 North Great Falls MT 59401

JOHNSON, PATRICIA GAYLE, corporate communication executive, writer; b. Conway, Ark., Oct. 23, 1947; d. Rudolph and Frances Modene (Hayes) J. Student U. Calif., Irvine, 1965-68. Advance rep. Disney on Parade, Los Angeles, 1971-75; mktg. dir., dir. field ops. Am. Freedom Train, 1975-77; publ. rels. mgr. Six Flags, Inc., Los Angeles, 1977-81; mgr. corp. communications Playboy Enterprises, Inc., Los Angeles, 1981-82; external rels. mgr. Kal Kan Foods, Inc., Los Angeles, 1982-86; v.p. Daniel J. Edelman, Inc., 1986-88; sr. v.p. Amies Advt. and Pub. Rels., Irvine, 1988-89; dir. pub. rels. World Vision, Monrovia, Calif., 1989-92; v.p. The Bohle Co., L.A., 1992—; lectr. U. So. Calif., UCLA, Calif. State U., Northridge, Calif. State U., Dominguez Hills. Bd. dirs. Jeopardy Youth Gang Intervention Program. Mem. Pub. Rels. Soc. Am. (past officer), Pub. Affairs Council, Delta Soc. (advisor). Mem. Foursquare Gospel Ch. Collaborator TV scripts; contbr. articles to various consumer and profl. mags. Office: The Bohle Co 1999 Avenue Of The Stars Los Angeles CA 90067-6022

JOHNSON, PETER, pharmaceutical executive; b. 1946. MA in Philosophy, U. Calif., San Diego. Rsch. assoc. U. Calif., 1971-76; with Johnson-Henry & Co., Encinitas, Calif., 1977-82, Agouron Inst., La Jolla, Calif., 1982—; with Agouron Pharms., Inc., 1984—, now pres. Office: Agouron Pharmaceuticals Inc 10350 N Torrey Pines Rd La Jolla CA 92037-1020*

JOHNSON, PHYLLIS ELAINE, chemist; b. Grafton, N.D., Feb. 19, 1949; d. Donald Gordon and Evelyn Lorraine (Svaren) Lanes; m. Robert S.T. Johnson, Sept. 12, 1969; children: Erik, Sara. BS, U. N.D., 1971, PhD, 1976. Instr. chemistry Mary Coll., Bismarck, N.D., 1971-72; postdoctoral rsch. fellow U. N.D., Grand Forks, 1975-79, chemist, 1977-79; rsch. chemist USDA Human Nutrition Rsch. Ctr., 1979-87, rsch. leader for nutrition, biochemistry and metabolism, 1987-91; assoc. dir. Pacific West Area USDA-ARS, 1991—. Editor: Stable Isotopes in Nutrition, 1984; mem. editorial bd. Jour. Micronutrient Analysis, 1988-91; contbr. articles to profl. jours. Chmn. Parents of Gifted and Talented, 1984-86. Recipient Arthur S. Flemming award Outstanding Sci. Achievement, 1989, Women in Sci. and Engring. award, 1993. Mem. Am. Soc. for Clin. Nutrition, Am. Chem. Soc., Am. Inst. Nutrition, Internat. Soc. for Trce Element Rsch. in Humans (sec. 1992-95), Exec. Women in Govt., Sr. Exec. Assoc., Soc. Exptl. Biology and Medicine, Phi Beta Kappa, Sigma Xi. Lutheran. Lodge: Sons of Norway (dist. v.p. 1984-86, dist. pres. 1986-88, internat. bd. dirs. 1988-92). Avocations: cooking, skiing, needlework, camping. Home: 828 Dorset Way Benicia CA 94510-3609 Office: USDA 800 Buchanan St Berkeley CA 94710-1105

JOHNSON, QULAN ADRIAN, software engineer; b. Great Falls, Mont., Sept. 17, 1942; s. Raymond Eugene and Bertha Marie (Nagengast) J.; m. Helen Louise Pocha, July 24, 1965; children—Brenda Marie, Douglas Paul, Scot Paul, Mathew James. B.A. in Psychology, Coll. Gt. Falls, 1964. Lead operator 1st Computer Corp., Helena, Mont., 1966-67; v.p., sec.-treas. Computer Corp. of Mt., Great Falls, 1967-76, dir., 1971-76; sr. systems analyst Mont. Dept. Revenue, Helena, 1976-78; software engr. Mont. Systems Devel. Co., Helena, 1978-80; programmer/analyst III info. systems div. Mont. Dept. Adminstrn., Helena, 1980-82; systems analyst centralized services Dept. Social and Rehab. Services State of Mont., 1982-87, systems and programming mgr. info systems, Blue Cross and Blue Shield of Montana, Helena, 1987—. Mem. Assn. for Systems Mgmt., Data Processing Mgmt. Assn., World Future Soc., Mensa. Club: K.C. (rec. sec. 1975-76). Home: 2231 8th Ave Helena MT 59601-4841 Office: Blue Cross & Blue Shield Info Systems 404 Fuller Ave Helena MT 59601-5006

JOHNSON, RANDALL DAVID (RANDY JOHNSON), professional baseball player; b. Walnut Creek, Calif., Sept. 10, 1963. Student, U. So. Calif. With Montreal (Can.) Expos, 1985-89; pitcher Seattle Mariners, 1989—. Named to All-Stars, 1990, 93, 94. Office: Seattle Mariners 411 1st Ave S PO Box 4100 Seattle WA 98104-2860*

JOHNSON, RAYMOND A., apparel executive; b. 1942. Grad., Western Wash. U. With Nordstrom Inc., 1969—; co-chmn. Nordstrom Inc., Seattle, 1995—. Office: Nordstrom Inc 1501 5th Ave Seattle WA 98101-1603*

JOHNSON, RICHARD GREENE, physician, psychiatrist, psychoanalyst; b. Louisville, June 3, 1921; s. Greene Johnson and Anne Wood Stout; m. Agnes Campbell Johnson, Nov. 2, 1945; children: Carole, Richard Jr., Craig, Holly. Student, Centre Coll. Ky.; BA, U. Louisville, 1943, MD, 1946; PhD, So. Calif. Psychoanalytic Inst., 1956. Diplomate Am. Bd. Psychiatry and Neurology. Rotating internship Met. Hosp. N.Y.C. Dept. Hosp., 1946-47; residency Emory U./Walter Reed Army Hosp.; pvt. practice, 1955—; clin. faculty dept. psychiatry UCLA, 1954—; asst. clin. prof. dept. psychiatry UCLA; cons. dept. dermatology UCLA; organizer, med. dir., chmn. bd. dirs. Westwood Psychiatric Hosp., 1959-70; organizer Mental Health Clinic Westwood Cmty. Meth. Ch., 1955; cons. LA County Dept. Mental Health, 1968-73, LA Protestant Cmty. Svcs., 1957-73; area chmn. Acad. of Religion and Mental Health; mem. rsch. com. Nat. Assn. Psychiatric Hosps., 1964. Capt. U.S. Army, 1948-54. Mem. LA County Med. Assn. (com. mental health and clergy, chmn. mental health com. of Bay dist. branch, pres. section on psychiatry 1975—). Republican. Office: 12301 Wilshire Blvd Ste 310 Los Angeles CA 90025

JOHNSON, RICHARD KARL, hospitality company executive; b. Gaylord, Minn., May 27, 1947; s. Karl S. and Mildred (Tollefson) J.; m. Eva Margaret Wick, Oct. 12, 1973; children: Michelle, Richard, Ryan. BA, Gustavus Adolphus U., St. Peter, Minn., 1969. Gen. mgr. Green Giant Restaurants, Inc., Mpls., 1969-71, Mpls. Elks Club, Mpls., 1971-73; dir. concept devel. Internat. Multifoods, Mpls., 1972-75; v.p. concept devel. A&WFood Svcs. Can., North Vancouver, B.C., 1975-81; dir. food and beverages Ramada, Reno, 1981-82; pres., owner R.K. Johnson & Assoc., Reno, 1981—; owner D.J. Mgmt., 1990—; asst. gen. mgr. Gold Dust West Casino, Reno, 1983-85; gen. mgr. P&M Corp., Reno, 1985-86; v.p. ops. C.P.S.W. Inc., Reno and Tempe, Ariz., 1986-87, Lincoln Fairview, Reno, 1987-89; v.p. corp. affairs Myers Realty, 1991—. Mem. Aircraft Owners and Pilots Assn., Nat. Restaurant Assn., Nev. Realtor, Elks Club. Lutheran. Home and Office: RK Johnson & Assoc 825 Meadow Springs Dr Reno NV 89509-5913

JOHNSON, RICHARD LUMUS, systems analyst; b. Key West, Fla., Mar. 28, 1964; s. Larry R. and Jeanie R. (Mitchell) J.; m. Caroline S. Daybell, Dec. 16, 1989; 1 child, Drew M. BS in Computer Sci., Calif. State U., Fullerton, 1986. Network adminstr., software developer Hughes Aircraft, Ground Sys. Group, Fullerton, Calif., 1985-90; network/sys. adminstr. Gen. Dynamics, Air Def. Sys. Divsn., Rancho Cucamonga, Calif., 1990-91; computer ops. mgr. CIGNA Corp., Fin. Instn. Risk Svcs. & Techs., Irvine, Calif., 1991—; dir., support svcs. Relational Data Sys., Irvine, 1992—. Author of software. Mem. IEEE (affiliate), Assn. Computing Machinery. Home: 7377 Hinsdale Pl Rancho Cucamonga CA 91730-6736 Office: Relational Data Systems 30 Executive Park Ste 260 Irvine CA 92714-6741

JOHNSON, ROBERT BRITTEN, geology educator; b. Cortland, N.Y., Sept. 24, 1924; s. William and Christine (Hofer) J.; m. Garnet Marion Brown, Aug. 30, 1947; children: Robert Britten, Richard Karl, Elizabeth Anne. Student, Wheaton (Ill.) Coll., 1942-43, 46-47; AB summa cum laude, Syracuse U., 1949, MS, 1950; PhD, U. Ill., 1954. Asst. geologist Ill. Geol. Survey, 1951-54; asst. prof. geology Syracuse U., 1954-55; sr. geologist and geophysicist C.A. Bays & Asso., Urbana, Ill., 1955-56; from asst. prof. to prof. engring. geology Purdue U., 1956-66, head, engring. geology dept., 1964-66; prof. geology DePauw U., 1966-67, head, dept. geology, 1966-67; prof. geology Colo. State U., 1967-88, acting chmn. dept. geology, 1968, chmn. dept., 1969-73, prof. in charge geology programs, dept. earth resources, 1973-77, acting head dept. earth resources, 1979-81, prof. emeritus, 1988—; geologist U.S. Geol. Survey, 1976-88; cons. in field, 1957—; instr. Elderhostel programs, 1991—. Active local Boy Scouts Am., 4-H Club, Sci. Fair, dist. schs. Served with USAAF, 1943-46. Fellow Geol. Soc. Am. (E.B. Burwell Jr. Meml. award 1989); mem. Assn. Engring. Geologists (Claire P. Holdredge Outstanding Publ. award 1990), Internat. Assn. Engring. Geology, Phi Beta Kappa. Republican. Home: 2309 Moffett Dr Fort Collins CO 80526-2122

JOHNSON, ROBERT HERSEL, journalist; b. Colorado City, Tex., May 28, 1923; s. Robert Hersel and Leah (Sikes) J.; m. Luise Putcamp, Jr., Feb. 24, 1945; children: Robert Hersel, III, Luise Robin, Jan Leah, Stephanie Neale, Jennifer Anne. B.S. in Journalism, So. Methodist U., 1947. Reporter Phoenix Gazette, 1940-42; asst. sports editor Ariz. Republic, Phoenix, 1942-43; newscast writer Sta. KOY, Phoenix, 1943; reporter Dallas Times-Herald, 1946; with AP, 1946-88, Utah-Idaho bur. chief, 1954-59, Ind. bur. chief, 1959-62, Tex. bur. chief, 1962-69, gen. sports editor, 1969-73, mng. editor, 1973-77, asst. gen. mgr., spl. asst. to pres., 1977-84, N.Mex. bureau chief, 1984-88; prof. journalism N.Mex. State U., Las Cruces, 1988, U. N.Mex., Albuquerque, 1989; exec. dir. N.Mex. Found. for Open Govt., Albuquerque, 1989—; mem. Newspaper Readership Coun., 1977-82. Mem. N. Mex. Hist. Records Adv. Bd., 1993—. Capt. USMCR, 1943-46, 51-52. Home: 2740 Tramway Cir NE Albuquerque NM 87122-1205

JOHNSON, ROBERT LELAND, lawyer; b. Denver, May 1, 1933; m. Pamela Gay Stearns, June 6, 1964; children: Mary Morris (dec.), Anthony Morris. BA, Yale U., 1955; JD, U. Denver, 1958, BA in English, 1962. Bar: Colo. 1959, U.S. Dist. Ct. Colo. 1959, U.S. Ct. Appeals (10th cir.), 1959, U.S. Supreme Ct. 1959. Pvt. practice law Denver, 1962—; asst. regional svcs. counsel region 8 U.S. Gen. Svcs. Adminstrn.; law clk. Colo. Supreme Ct.; lectr. U. Colo., 1978-83. Author: The Newspaper Accounts of B.F. Wright, Esq., and Others of Louisa County, Iowa, 1967, Trial Handbook for Colorado Torts Lawyers, 1967, Matrimonial Practice in Colorado Courts, 1969, The American Heritage of James Norman Hall, 1970, Colorado Mechanic's Liens, 1970, A Geneaological Excursion Through Historic Philadelphia, 1976 (with Pamela Gay Johnson) A Mother's Love, 1977, Letters to Glenn Doman: A Story on Enriched and Accelerated Childhood Development, 1980, Super Babies, 1982, Super Kids & Their Parents, 1986, The Ancestry of Anthony Morris Johnson, vols. 1 and 2, 1989, vol. 3, 1991, vol. 4, 1994, Corriegenda to Ancestry of Anthony Morris Johnson vol. 3, 1991, The King Arthur Book or Second Corriegenda to Supplement to Ancestry of Anthony Morris Johnson vol. 3, 1991. Mem. ABA, Am. Judicature Soc., Colo. Trial Lawyers Assn., Denver Bar Assn. (legal aid and pub. defender com., family law com., interprofl. com.). Democrat. Mem. Soc. of Friends. Home: 534 Pearl St Apt 306 Denver CO 80203-3881 Office: 705 W 8th Ave Denver CO 80204-4329

JOHNSON, RODNEY DALE, law enforcement officer, photographer; b. Montebello, Calif., May 14, 1944; s. Albert Gottfreid and Maxine Elliot (Rogers) J.; m. Karen Rae Van Antwerp, May 18, 1968; 1 child, Tiffany Nicole. AA, Ela Community Coll., 1973; postgrad. Law Enforcement Spl., FBI, Acad., 1976; BA, U. of La Verne, 1978. Cert. tchr. police sci., Calif. Dep., Los Angeles County Sheriff, 1969-75, dep. IV, 1976-78, sgt., 1978—; fire arms inst., Hacienda Heights, Calif., 1975—; photographer Weddings and Portraits, 1983-94; photography instr., Hacienda Heights, 1983-94; pres. Wheelhouse Enterprises, Inc., Whittier, 1971-86; instr. State Sheriff's Civil Procedural Sch. Los Medanos Coll., Concord, Calif., 1985-88. Creator and actor, Cap'n Andy, 1973-80; song writer for Cap'n Andy theme, 1972. Sgt. USMC, 1965-69, Vietnam, master gunnery sgt. Res., 1969-94, ret.; intelligence chief, Persian Gulf. Recipient Service award Trinity Broadcasting Network, 1979. Mem. Profl. Peace Officers Assn., Sheriff's Relief Assn., Assoc. Photographers Internat., Marine Corps. Intelligence Assn., Inc. Republican. Mem. Assembly of God. Club: Faithbuilders (pres. 1981-87), (Pomona).

JOHNSON, RONALD DOUGLAS, business executive; b. Klamath Falls, Oreg., Sept. 16, 1949; s. Clifford Douglas and Anna Elizabeth (Fine) J.; m. Wendi Susan Brown, Aug. 20, 1972; children: Bryan Douglas, Timothy Christopher, Michael Casey. BA in Polit. Sci., Wash. State U., 1975, MA in Pub. Adminstrn., 1976, MA in Agrl. Econs., 1981. Rsch. asst. Wash. Water Rsch. Ctr., Pullman, 1974-75; mgmt. trainee Potlatch Corp., 1971-74; intern Gov. Daniel J. Evans, Olympia, Wash., 1975; rsch. asst. Wash. State U., Pullman, 1976-79; asst. mgr. Reardan Grain Gowers Assn., Wash., 1980-82; gen. mgr. Bean Growers Warehouse Assn., Twin Falls, Idaho, 1982-84; dry bean group mgr. Rogers NK Seed Co., Boise, Idaho, 1984-95; owner Agraplus, Inc., 1995—; cons. Rogers Seed Co., Basic Am. Foods, Sunspiced Inc., 1994—; bd. dirs. Consolidated Agrl. Inc., Twin Falls. With U.S. Army, 1968-70, Viet Nam. Commn. Econ. Assistance grantee Oreg. State U., 1978, Washington Water Rsch. grantee, Wash. State U., 1976. Home: 4190 N Jones Ave Boise ID 83704-2700 Office: Rogers Seed Co 1755 Westgate Dr Boise ID 83704-7174

JOHNSON, RUTH EILEEN, dietitian, researcher, home economics educator; b. Hot Springs, S.D., July 23, 1927; d. George Ernest and Eva Mae Lebo; m. James H. Johnson Jr., Aug. 7, 1948; children: Kenneth L., Gary S. BS, U. Nebr., 1947, postgrad., 1950-51; MA, Calif. State U., 1971. Rsch. asst. food and nutrition rsch. dept. U. Nebr., Lincoln, 1947-51; rsch. technician Scripps Coll., Claremont, Calif., 1969; instr., collaborating investigator men's phys. edn. Calif. State U.-Long Beach, 1970-71, instr. home econs., 1970-72; asst. prof. home econs. Calif. State U.-Los Angeles, 1971-75; chief nutritionist Mr. Fit Ctr., 1974-79; sr. nutritionist, clin. coord. atherosclerosis rsch. U. So. Calif. Sch. Medicine, 1979-87, asst. clin. prof. medicine, 1987—; cons. in field. Author, co-author numerous text and reference materials. Editor Calif. Home Economist, 1964-75. Founding com. mem. Meals on Wheels, Whittier, Calif., 1969; Calif. Congress Parents and Tchrs., 1961-72; pres. Lowell High Sch., 1968-69; Dental health chmn. Macy and Starbuck Schs., 1962-68. Mem. Am. Heart Assn. (fellow council of epidemiology; Los Angeles Affiliate Vol. of Yr. 1981-82, Heart of Gold award, 1991, Achievement award 1995), Am. Home Econs. Assn., Calif. Home Econs. Assn. (Outstanding Home Economist 1979, 83), Am. Dietetics Assn., Calif. Dietetics Assn., Nutrition Today Soc. Am. Soc. Testing and Materials, Greater Los Angeles Nutrition Council, Calif. Nutrition Council, Orange County Nutrition Council, AAUW (Las Distinguidas award 1985), Iota Sigma Pi, Phi Delta Gamma, Kappa Omicron Nu. Avocations: needlepoint, piano, bridge, travel. Home: 10110 Pounds Ave Whittier CA 90603-1649

JOHNSON, RUTH FLOYD, secondary education educator, consultant; b. Plateau, Ala., Apr. 19, 1935; d. Nathan Daniel and Ora Anna (Ellis) Floyd; children: Anthony, Walter, Camille. Student, Tuskegee Inst., 1951-53; BS in History, Bowie (Md.) State U., 1970; MEd in Counseling, U. Md., 1977; PhD in Human Svcs. Adminstrn., Univ. for Humanistic Studies, San Diego, 1982. Cert. tchr., counselor. Radio personality Sta. WMOZ, 1953-56; owner, dir. Azalea Sch. Dance, 1954-56; numerous posts for fed. govt., 1957-69; tchr., adminstr. Pub. Schs. of Prince George's County, Md., 1970-78; tchr.-counselor Dunbar S.T.A.Y. Sch., Washington, 1974-75; instr. child and youth study divsn. U. Md., 1977-78; CEO Diametron Corp., 1979-81; tchr. L.A. Unified Sch. Dist., 1980-82, Pasadena (Calif.) Unified Sch. Dist., 1982-83, Rialto (Calif.) Unified Sch. Dist., 1984—. Author: Remediating Mass Poverty: Development of a Model Program, 1982, Pep Squad handbook, 1991, (with others: Government/Contemporary Issues: A Curriculum Guide, 1976. Active PTAs; mem. organizing com. Peppermill Village Civic Assn., 1966; vol. Boy Scouts Am., 1968-72, Sr. Citizens of Prince George's County, 1974-76; bd. dirs.Mill Point Improvement Assn., 1975-78, Combined Communities in Action, 1976-78; mem. Prince George's County Hosp. Commn., 1978; mem. Altadena Town Coun., 1983; founder Rialto Freedom and Cultural Soc., 1988; mem. Calif. 36th Dist. Bicentennial Adv. Com., 1989; mem. exec. com. Rialto Police/Community Rels. Team, 1993. Recipient Outstanding Svc. to Children and Yourh award Md. Congress PTA, 1969, Services to Boy Scouts Am. award, 1969, Svcs. to Sr. Citizens award, 1975, Community Svc. award Rialto Freedom and Cultural Soc., 1993, others. Mem. NEA, NAACP, Nat. Assn. Univ. Women, Nat. Coun. Negro Women, Zeta Phi Beta, Gamma Phi Delta. Home: PO Box 1946 Rialto CA 92377-1946

JOHNSON, SCOTT, architect; b. Salinas, Calif., Feb. 1, 1951; s. Russell and Louise (Haynie) J.; m. Margaret E. Bates, June 22, 1974; children: Maxwell Bates Johnson, Zoe Cristina Bates Johnson. Student, Stanford U., 1970-71; AB in Architecture magna cum laude, U. Calif., Berkeley, 1972; MArch, Harvard U., 1975. Registered architect, Calif., N.Y., Guam, No. Mariana Islands. Prin. designer Skidmore Owings & Merrill, L.A., 1976, San Francisco, 1977; design assoc. Philip Johnson, John Burgee Architects, N.Y.C., 1978-83; design ptnr. Johnson Fain & Pereira Assocs., L.A., 1983—; vis. lectr. UCLA Grad. Sch. Architecture & Urban Planning, UCLA Ext., U. So. Calif. Sch. Architecture & Inst. for Profl. Devel., SCI-ARC, So. Calif. Inst. Architecture, New Sch. Architecture, San Diego. Prin. works include Fox Plaza, L.A., 1987, Andrex Point, Torrance, Calif., 1989, Paradise Restaurant, L.A., 1989, Rincon Ctr., San Francisco, 1990, Nestle USA Hdqrs., Glendale, Calif., 1991, 1999 Avenue of the Stars, L.A., 1992, Opus One Winery, Oakville, Calif., 1992, LeoPalace Resort, Manenggon Gills, Guam, 1993, Pasadena Towers, Calif., 1993, SunAm. Corp. Hdqrs., L.A. mem. Mus. of Architecture com. Chgo. Athenaeum; mem. UCLA dean's coun. UCLA Grad. Sch. Architecture & Urban Planning; founding mem. Restoration Assocs. of the Freeman House; founder Mus. of Contemporary Art, L.A., mem. architecture & design coun. Mem. AIA (Design award L.A. chpt. 1984, Citation Honor award 1984, Design award Orange County chpt. 1984), Urban Land Inst., L.A. Forum for Architecture and Urban Design, Westside Urban Forum, USC Archtl. Guild, L.A. Conservancy, Nat. Trust for Historic Preservation, Phi Beta Kappa. Office: Johnson Fain & Pereira Assocs 6100 Wilshire Blvd Ste 500 Los Angeles CA 90048-5112

JOHNSON, STEPHEN ALDEN, computer programmer; b. Houston, June 19, 1974; s. Dean Alden and Karen Jean (Smith) J. Grad. H.S., Chula Vista, Calif. Gardener White Water, Oklahoma City, 1991; bus boy IU Sports Grill, Oklahoma City, 1991; assembler Mesa Ridge Techs., Inc., San Diego, 1991-92; salesman Vector Mktg. Corp., La Mesa, Calif., 1992; lab. asst. Biola Univ., La Mirada, Calif., 1993; programmer, analyst Biola Univ., La Mirada, 1993—, in-charge-of world wide web site, 1993-95. Mem. Assn. Computing Machinery. Republican. Baptist. Address: Box 1705A 13800 Biola Ave La Mirada CA 90639-0002

JOHNSON, STEVE MICHAEL, flower essence researcher, educator; b. Idaho Falls, Idaho, May 13, 1953; s. Robert and Gail Jean (Bateman) J. Student, U. Idaho, 1971, Utah State U., 1972-73, Western Wash. State U., 1974. Forestry technician U.S. Forest Svc., Idaho and Calif., 1971-76; forestry technician Bur. Land Mgmt., U.S. Dept. Interior, Oreg., 1977, Alaska, 1978-91; owner, founder Alaskan Flower Essence Project, Homer, 1984—. Author: Flower Essences of Alaska, 1992. Democrat. Home and Office: Alaskan Flower Essence Project PO Box 1369 Homer AK 99603

JOHNSON, STEWART WILLARD, civil engineer; b. Mitchell, S.D., Aug. 17, 1933; s. James Elmer Johnson and Grace Mahala (Erwin) Johnson Parsons; m. Mary Anis Giddings, June 24, 1956; children: Janelle Chiemi, Gregory Stewart, Eric Willard. BSCE, S.D. State U., 1956; BA in Bus. Adminstrn. and Polit. Sci., U. Md., 1960; MSCE, PhD, U. Ill., 1964. Registered profl. engr., Ohio. Commd. 2d lt. USAF, 1956, advanced through grades to lt. col.; prof. mechs. and civil engring. Air Force Inst. Tech. USAF, Dayton, Ohio, 1964-75; dir. civil engring. USAF, Seoul, Republic of Korea, 1976-77; chief civil engring. research div. USAF, Kirtland AFB, N.Mex., 1977-80; ret. USAF, 1980; prin. engr. BDM Corp., Albuquerque, 1980-94, Johnson and Assocs., Albuquerque, 1994—; cons. space sci., lunar basing NASA, U. N.Mex., N.Mex. State U., Los Alamos Nat. Labs., 1986—; adj. prof. civil engring. U. N.Mex., 1987—; prin. investigator devel. concepts for lunar astron. obs. U. N.Mex., N.Mex. State U., NASA, 1987—; tech. chmn. Space '88 and Space '90 Internat. Confs.; gen. chair Space '94 Internat. Conf., Albuquerque; vis. lectr. Internat. Space U., Japan, 1992, Huntsville, Ala., 1993, Barcelona, Spain, 1994, Stockholm, 1995; mem. panel on siting lunar base European Space Agy., 1994. Editor Engineering, Construction, and Operations in Space, I and II; contbr. articles to profl. jours. Pres. ch. coun. Ch. of Good Shepherd United Ch. of Christ, Albuquerque, 1983-85, chmn. bd. deacons, 1991-93; S.W. Conf. (United Ch. Christ) del. to Gen. Synod XIX, St. Louis, 1993, Gen. Synod XX, Oakland, Calif., 1995; trustee Lunar Geotech. Inst., 1990—; mem. adv. bd. Lab. for Extraterrestrial Structures Rsch., Rutgers U., 1990—. Fellow Nat. Acad. Scis. NRC, 1970-71. Mem. AIAA (space logistics com., Engr. of Yr. region IV 1990), ASCE (chmn. exec. com. aerospace divsn. 1979, tech. activities com. 1984, chmn. com space engring. and constrn. 1987—, mem. nat. space policy com. 1988—, chmn. 1990—, Outstanding News Corr. award 1981, Aerospace Scis. and Tech. Applications award 1985, 90, Edmund Friedman Profl. Recognition award 1989), Soc. Am. Mil. Engrs., Am. Geophys. Union, Sigma Xi, Pi Sigma Alpha. Republican. Mem. United Ch. of Christ.

JOHNSON, SYLVIA SUE, university administrator, educator; b. Abiline, Tex., Aug. 10, 1940; d. SE Boyd and Margaret MacGillivray (Withington) Smith; m. William Ruel Johnson; children: Margaret Ruth, Laura Jane, Catherine Withington. BA, U. Calif., Riverside, 1962; postgrad., U. Hawaii, 1963. Elem. edn. credential, 1962. Mem. bd. regents U. Calif.; mem. steering com. Citizens Univ. Com., chmn., 1978-79; bd. dirs., charter mem. U. Calif.-Riverside Found., chmn. nominating com., 1983—; pres., bd. dirs. Friends of the Mission Inn, 1969-72, 73-76, Mission Inn Found., 1977—, Calif. Bapt. Coll. Citiznes Com., 1980—; bd. dirs. Riverside Comty. Hosp., 1980—, Riverside Jr. League, 1976-77, Nat. Charity League, 1984-85; mem. chancellors blue ribbon com., devel. com. Calif. Mus. Photography. Named Woman of Yr., State of Calif. Legislature, 1989, 91, Citizen of Yr., C. of C., 1989. Mem. U. Calif.-Riverside Alumni Assn. (bd. dirs. 1966-68, v.p. 1968-70).

JOHNSON, THOMAS EUGENE, biology educator; b. Denver, June 19, 1948; s. Albert L. Johnson and Barbara J. (Bickle) Lloyd; m. Victoria J. Simpson, Apr. 24, 1982; children: Ariel Rene, Paul Andrew, Katherine Elizabeth. BS, MIT, 1970; PhD, U. Wash., 1975. Research assoc. Cornell U., Ithaca, N.Y., 1975-77, U. Colo., Boulder, 1977-82; fellow Inst. Behavioral Genetics U. Colo., Denver, 1981-82; asst. prof. U. Calif., Irvine, 1982-88; assoc. prof. U. Colo., Boulder, 1988—; organizer UCLA Symposium on Molecular Biology of Aging, 1989, Keystone Symposium on Molecular Biology of Aging, 1988, 91; chair Gordon Conf. on Biology on Aging, 1992. Editor: Handbook of the Biology of Aging; assoc. editor Jour. of Gerontology Biol. Sci. Grantee USPHS, Washington, 1978, 85, 88, 91, 92, 95, NSF, Washington, 1982; USPHS fellow, 1977, AFAR, 1986, 87; recipient Busse award for biomed. gerontology, 1993, Nathan Shock award Gerontology Rsch. Ctr. Fellow Gerontology Soc. of Am. (chair biol. sci. 1991-92), Am. Fedn. for Aging Rsch.; mem. AAAS, Nat. Inst. Aging, Genetics, Soc. Am., Am. Aging Assn. (bd. dirs. 1990-95), Nat. Inst. Health (biological and clin. aging rev. subcom. A 1992-96). Democrat. Unitarian. Office: U Colo Inst Behavioral Genetics PO Box 447 Boulder CO 80309-0447

JOHNSON, TORRENCE VAINO, astronomer; b. Rockville Centre, N.Y., Dec. 1, 1944; s. Vaino Oliver and Priscilla Welch (Sneed) J.; m. Mary Eleanor Zachman, Mar. 31, 1967; children: Aaron Torrence, Eleanor Nancy. B.S. with honors, Washington U., St. Louis, 1966; Ph.D., Calif. Inst. Tech., 1970. Research assoc. Planetary Astronomy Lab., MIT, 1969-71; resident research assoc. NRC, Jet Propulsion Lab., Pasadena, 1971-73, sr. scientist, mem. tech. staff, 1973-74; group supr. Optical Astronomy Group, 1974-85, project scientist Project Galileo, 1977—, research scientist, 1980-81, sr. research scientist, 1981—; vis. assoc. prof. Calif. Inst. Tech., 1981-83; cons. Jet Propulsion Lab., Pasadena, 1971. NASA trainee Calif. Inst. Tech., 1966-69, Exceptional Svc. medal NASA, 1991; recipient Exceptional Achievement medal NASA, 1980, 81. Fellow Explorers Club, Am. Geophys. Union (pres. planetology sect. 1990-92); mem. AAAS, Am. Astron. Soc. (sec.-treas. divsn. planetary sci. 1977-80), Internat. Astron. Union, Planetary Soc. (founding mem.), Internat. Acad. Astronautics (corres.), Sigma Xi. Office: California Inst Tech 183-501 Jet Propulsion Lab 4800 Oak Grove Dr Pasadena CA 91109-8001

JOHNSON, VILIA JOCELYN, perfume company executive; b. Bamberg, S.C., Dec. 21, 1953; d. John Franklin and Mary Elizabeth (Covington) J. BA in Lang. and Lit., BA in Social and Behavioral Scis., U. S. Fla., 1974. Sales clk. Sandcastle Swimwear, N.Y.C., 1975-76; market rep. Allied Stores Mktg., N.Y.C., 1976; retail buyer Mabley and Carew, Cin., 1977-78, Richman Gordman, Omaha, 1978-84; account exec. Cosmair Inc., Kansas City, Kans., 1984-85, Dallas, 1985; regional sales mgr. Cosmair Inc., St. Louis, 1986-87; asst. v.p., mgr. field sales Cosmair Inc., Dallas, 1987-89, L.A., 1990—. Office: Cosmair Designer Fragrances 575 5th Ave New York NY 10017-2422

JOHNSON, W. CEDRIC, computer company executive; b. 1952. Degree in Applied Math., Claremont (Calif.) Coll., 1974. Ops. rsch., sys. integration Rockwell Internat., L.A., 1975-77; pres., CEO ETA Techs. Corp., L.A., 1978—; cons. Honeywell, Sperry, Westinghouse, Gen. Dynamics. Office: ETA Technologies Corp 5220 Pacific Concourse Dr Los Angeles CA 90045-6277*

JOHNSON, WALTER EARL, geophysicist; b. Denver, Dec. 16, 1942; s. Earl S. and Helen F. (Llewellyn) J.; Geophys. Engr., Colo. Sch. Mines, 1966; m. Ramey Kandice Kayes, Aug. 6, 1967; children—Gretchen, Roger, Aniela. Geophysicist, Pan. Am. Petroleum Corp., 1966-73; seismic processing supr. Amoco Prodn. Co., Denver, 1973-74, marine tech. supr., 1974-76, div. processing cons., 1976-79, geophys. supr. No. Thrust Belt, 1979-80; chief geophysicist Husky Oil Co., 1981-82, exploration mgr. Rocky Mountain and Gulf Coast div., 1982-84; geophys. mgr. ANR Prodn. Co., 1985—; pres. Sch. Lateral Ditch Co.; cons. engr. Bd. dirs. Rocky Mountain Residence, nursing home. Registered profl. engr., cert. geologist, Colo. Mem. Denver Geophys. Soc., Soc. Exploration Geophysicists. Republican. Baptist. Office: 600 17th St Ste 800 Denver CO 80202

JOHNSON, WARREN LYLE, educator; b. Mpls., Oct. 14, 1939; s. Paul A. and Irene (Lazorik) Wilson; m. Lana-Jean Cole, June 24, 1967; 1 child, Kenneth Lee. BS, Ea. N.Mex., 1962; MA, Boston U., 1984; postgrad., Air War Coll., 1976; diploma, Def. Systems Coll., 1989; student, Royal Mil. Coll., Swindon, Eng., 1989. Polit. intern State of N.Mex., Santa Fe, 1962-63; commd. 2d lt. USAF, 1964, advanced through grades to major, 1976, ret., 1984; educator State of N.H., Concord, 1984-85; analyst U.S. Govt., Boston, 1985-86, U.S. Govt., U.S. Embassy, Bonn, Germany, 1986-88; reQ officer U.S. Govt., USAF Hqrs. Europe, 1988-90; educator Albuquerque Pub. Sch., 1991—; head negotiator U.S. Govt., Germany, 1986-90, with spl. projects, Washington, 1990; selected to work with Josephson Inst. of Ethics in Character Issues in Pub. Edn., 1994; established 1st U.S. Civil Air Patrol Cadet in Pub. Schs. in U.S., 1994. Editor concept paper. V.p. Shenandoah Neighborhood Assn., Albuquerque, 1991—; mem. Mayors Adv. Bd. ram, Albuquerque, 1991-92. Decorated Cross of Gallantry, Bronze Star, Meritorious Svc; NAS grantee, 1993-94. Mem. Am. Polit. Sci. Soc., Ret. Officers Assn., U.S. Naval Inst. and Nimitz Mus., Vietnam Vets. Am. (state rep. 1986-94, v.p. 1994—, state edn. chmn.), DAV, Masons (32d degree). Democrat. Lutheran.

JOHNSON, WAYNE EATON, writer, editor, former drama critic; b. Phoenix, May 9, 1930; s. Roscoe and Marion (Eaton) J.; children: Katherine, Jeffrey. BA, U. Colo., 1952; postgrad., Duke U., 1952-53; postgrad. (KLM polit. reporting fellow 1957), U. Vienna, Austria, 1955-56; MA, UCLA, 1957. Reporter Internat. News Service, Des Moines, 1958, Wheat Ridge (Colo.) Advocate, 1957, Pueblo (Colo.) Chieftain, 1959; reporter Denver Post, 1960, editorial writer, music critic, 1961-65; arts and entertainment editor Seattle Times, 1965-82, drama critic, 1980-92; instr. journalism Colo. Woman's Coll., 1962. Author: show: A Concert Program for Actor and Orchestra, 1971, America! A COncert of AMerican Images, Words and Music, 1973, From Where the Sun Now Stands: The Indian Experience, 1973; editor, co-publisher: Secrets of Warmth, 1992, Footprints on the Mountains, 1994, The Burgess Book of Lies, 1994. Served with CIC AUS, 1953-55, Korea. Home: 11303 Durland Pl NE Seattle WA 98125-5926

JOHNSON, WAYNE HAROLD, librarian, county official; b. El Paso, Tex., May 2, 1942; s. Earl Harold and Cathryn Louise (Greeno) J.; m. Patricia Ann Froedge, June 15, 1973; children: Meredith Jessica (dec.), Alexandra Noëlle Victoria. BS, Utah State U., 1968; MPA, U. Colo., 1970; MLS, U. Okla., 1972. Circulation libr. Utah State U., Logan, 1968, adminstrv. asst. libr., 1969; with rsch. dept. Okla. Mgmt. and Engring. Cons., Norman, 1972; chief adminstrv. svcs. Wyo. State Libr., Cheyenne, 1973-76, chief bus. officer libr. archives and hist. dept., 1976-78, state libr., 1978-89; county grants mgr. Laramie County, Wyo., 1989—. Trustee Bibliog. Ctr. for Rsch., Denver, pres., 1983, 84; mem. Cheyenne dist. Longs Park coun. Boy Scouts Am., 1982-86; active Cheyenne Frontier Days, 1975—; mem. admissions and allocation com. United Way, 1991-94; mem. Ho. of Reps., Wyo. Legislature, 1993—. Served with USCG, 1960-64. Mem. Aircraft Owners and Pilots Assn., Cheyenne C. of C. (chmn. transp. com. 1982, 83, military affairs com. 1994—), Am. Legion. Republican. Presbyterian. Club: No. Colo. Yacht. Lodges: Masons, Kiwanis (bd. dirs. 1986, 87). Office: County Bldg 19th St & Carey Ave Cheyenne WY 82001

JOHNSON, WILLIAM HARRY, international management consultant; b. Ridley Park, Pa., Oct. 1, 1941; s. Harry Brown and Florence Lydia (Round) J.; m. Anna Marie Castellanos, Oct. 19, 1984. BS, Drexel U., Phila., 1963; MBA, Drexel U., 1967. Mgmt. exec. DuPont Co., Wilmington, Del., 1963-69; bus. analysis mgr. Imperial Chem. Ind., Wilmington, 1970-76; mgr. analysis and acquisitions Fluor Daniel Corp., Irvine, Calif., 1976-78; fin. analysis mgr. Alexander Proudfoot, Chgo., 1978-79; exec. v.p., chief fin. officer Sego Internat., Niagara Falls, Ont., Can., 1980-82; exec. v.p., gen. mgr. Sci. Mgmt. Corp., Basking Ridge, N.J., 1982-87; exec. mgr. McDonnell Douglas Corp., Long Beach, Calif., 1987—; bd. dirs. CRA, Inc., Clariton, Pa., Madden Assocs., Buffalo Grove, Ill., KABB Inc., El Segundo, Calif., Sego Intenat., Productivity Cons., Inc., Montreal, Que., Can., Commonwealth Cons., London. Contbr. articles to profl. jours.; author: Explosives Distributors, 1967. Mem. Rep. Nat. Com., Washington, El Segundo Residents Assn. Recipient Presdl. Achievement award, Rep. Nat. Com., 1988, Outstanding Achievement award, Sego Internat., 1981. Mem. Inst. Indsl. Engrs., Am. Mgmt. Assn., Nat. Productivity Assn. of Can. (dir. 1980-85), Nat. Assn. Accts., Nat. Petroleum Refinery Assn., Am. Mktg. Assn., Internat. Productivity Orgn., Drexel U. Alumni Assn. (bd. dirs.), Highlander Clan, Lions (Kowloon, Hong Kong), K & C Clans Assn. (Hong Kong), Internat. Bus. Assocs. (Sydney, Australia). Republican. Presbyterian. Home: 807 Hillcrest St El Segundo CA 90245-2025 Office: McDonnell Douglas 3855 N Lakewood Blvd Long Beach CA 90846-0003

JOHNSON, WILLIAM HUGH, JR., hospital administrator; b. N.Y.C., Oct. 29, 1935; s. William H. and Florence P. (Seinsoth) J.; m. Gloria C. Stube., Jan. 23, 1960; children: Karen A., William H. III. B.A., Hofstra U., 1957; M.Ed., U. Hawaii, 1969. Commd. 2d lt. U.S. Army, 1957, advanced through grades to lt. col., 1972, health adminstr., world wide, 1957-77, health adminstr., world wide, ret., 1977; chief exec. officer U. N. Mex. Hosp., Albuquerque, 1977—; asst. prof. U.S. Mil. Acad., West Point, N.Y., 1962-65; mem. clin. faculty U. Minn., Mpls., 1980-83; preceptor Ariz. State U., Tempe, 1982-83; pres. Albuquerque Area Hosp. Council, 1980; bd. dirs. Bank Am. of N.Mex. Vice pres. Vis Nurse Service, Albuquerque, 1979; mem. exec. bd., Albuquerque Com. on Devel.; pres. Magnifico Arts Fiesta; bd. dirs. Good Will N.Mex. Decorated Army Commendation Medal with 2 oak leaf clusters, Order of Merit (Rep. of Vietnam), Legion of Merit. Mem. Am. Hosp. Assn. (governing bd. met. hosp. sect. 1982-86, chmn. com. AIDS, mem. regional policy bd. 1982-86, 88—), Am. Coll. Hosp. Adminstrs., Coun. Tchg. Hosps. (bd. dirs.), N.Mex. Hosp. Assn. (bd. dirs. 1983, chmn.), Nat. Assn. Pub. Hosps., Greater Albuquerque C. of C. (bd. dirs., econ. planning coun., v.p.), N.Mex. Assn. Commerce and Industry (treas.), Albuquerque Conv. and Visitors Bur. (bd. dirs.). Roman Catholic. Home: 7920 Sartan Way NE Albuquerque NM 87109-3128 Office: Univ N Mex Hosp 2211 Lomas Blvd NE Albuquerque NM 87106-2745

JOHNSON, WILLIAM LEWIS, materials science educator; b. Bowling Green, Ohio, July 26, 1948; s. Melvin Carl and Martha Maxine (Roller) J.; m. Rachel Marie Newman, Jan. 21, 1984. B.A., Hamilton Coll., 1970; Ph.D.,

Calif. Inst. Tech., 1974. Staff IBM Watson Research Ctr., Yorktown Heights, N.Y., 1975-77; asst. prof. materials sci. Calif. Inst. Tech., Pasadena, 1977-80, assoc. prof., 1980-84, prof., 1984—; R.F. Mettler Prof. materials sci., 1989— ; cons. Lawrence Livermore Lab., 1979—, Dresser Industries, Irvine, Calif., 1978—, Gen. Motors Research, Warren, Mich., 1983—, Hughes Research Ctr., Malibu, Calif., 1981—. Co-author: Glassy Metals I, 1981; Properties of Amorphous Metals, 1983; Physical Metallurgy, 1983, ASM Metals Handbook-Metallic Glasses, 1990. U.S. Steel fellow, 1971; Alexander von Humboldt fellow, 1988; recipient Rothery award Am. Metals Soc., 1995—. Mem. Metals Soc. of AIME, Am. Phys. Soc., AAAS, Materials Rsch. Soc., Phi Beta Kappa, Sigma Xi. Lutheran. Home: 3546 Mountain View Ave Pasadena CA 91107-4616 Office: Calif Inst of Tech Div Engring & Applied Scis Mail Code 138 78 Pasadena CA 91125

JOHNSON, WILLIAM LEWIS, information science eduator; b. Ft. Worth, June 8, 1957; s. Larry Claud and Rhoda Ann (Brown) J.; m. Kimberly Gallaway Hale, Jan. 2, 1982. AB in Linguistics summa cum laude, Princeton U., 1978; MS in Computer Sci., Yale U., 1980, PhD in Computer Sci., 1985. Programmer Princeton U., 1974-78, Max-Planck-Institut, Munich, 1975; sr. programmer Computer Data Access, Inc., 1980-81; rsch. asst. Yale U., 1979-80, 82-85; rsch. scientist Info. Scis. Inst., U. So. Calif., Marina del Rey, 1985—, project leader, rsch. asst. prof., 1987—; cons. Andersen Cons., Inc., 1988-91, NASA Jet Propulsion Lab., 1993. Editor-in-chief Automated Software Engring.; contbr. numerous articles to profl. publs. Mem. Special Interest Group for Artificial Intelligence (sec./treas., former editor in chief bull., conf. chair 7th Knowledge-Based Software Engring. Conf., also several program coms.), Soc. Artificial Intellingence in Edn. (exec. com., Soc. Artificial Intelligence in Edn. 93 tutorial/workshop chair-world conf. on artificial intelligence edn., also steering and program coms.), Am. Assn. for Artificial Intelligence (chair automating software design workshop, co-chair 1991 spring symposium on design composite systems, program com. AAAI-88);. Office: U So Calif Info Scis Inst 4676 Admiralty Way Marina Del Rey CA 90292

JOHNSON, WILLIAM POTTER, newspaper publisher; b. Peoria, Ill., May 4, 1935; s. William Zweigle and Helen Marr (Potter) J.; m. Pauline Ruth Rowe, May 18, 1968; children: Darragh Elizabeth, William Potter. AB, U. Mich., 1957. Gen. mgr. Bureau County Rep., Inc., Princeton, Ill., 1961-72; pres. Johnson Newspapers, Inc., Sebastopol, Calif., 1972-75, Evergreen, Colo., 1974-86, Canyon Commons Investment, Evergreen, 1974—; pres., chmn. bd. dirs. Johnson Media, Inc., Winter Park, Colo., 1987—. Author: How the Michigan Betas Built a $1,000,000 Chapter House in the '80s. Alt. del. Rep. Nat. Conv., 1968. Lt. USNR, 1958-61. Mem. Colo. Press Assn., Nat. Newspaper Assn., Maple Bluff Country Club, Beta Theta Pi. Home: 5302 Lighthouse Bay Dr Madison WI 53704-1114 Office: PO Box 409 Winter Park CO 80482-0409

JOHNSON, WILLIAM STEWART, cultural arts administrator; b. Spring Lake, Mich., Jan. 3, 1933; s. Howard Kenneth Johnson and Dorothy Irene (Cooper) Van Den Heuvel; m. Luanna Hughes, Sept. 1, 1964. Student, Howe (Ind.) Mil. Sch., 1948-51; BA, Mich. State U., 1955. Dir. govt. rels. IBM Corp., Washington, 1978-88; chmn. Inst. Am.-Indian Arts, Santa Fe, 1988—. Bd. dirs. YMCA, Washington, 1980-82, Mary Baldwin Coll., Staunton, Va., 1980-86. 1st lt. U. S. Army, 1956-64. Mem. Am. Soc. Personnel Adminstrs. Home: 740 Calle Del Resplendor Santa Fe NM 87501-5987 Office: Inst Am Indian Arts Cathedral Pl PO Box 1836 Santa Fe NM 87504-1836

JOHNSTON, ANDREA RUTH, writer, educator; b. N.Y.C., Nov. 25, 1944; d. Stephen Emul and Kathryn Mary (Countis) Senecka; m. William R. Johnston, Feb. 29, 1972 (div. Apr. 1984); 1 child, Jesse William. BA, CUNY, 1966; JD, Empire Coll., 1984. Cert. tchr., N.Y., Calif. Tchr. N.Y.C. Bd. Edn., 1964-72; founding pres. Nat. Assn. for Edn. Young Children, N.J., 1973-75; founding dir. R.R. Rainbow Sch., Guerneville, Calif., 1978-83; founding owner The Learning Tree, Sussex, N.J., 1973-76; writer, critic The Paper, Freestone, Calif., 1981-94, The Independent, Santa Rosa, Calif., 1994; tchr. Sonoma County Office of Edn., Santa Rosa, 1984-94; cons. Ms. Found. for Women, Guerneville, Calif., 1995—; co-founder (with Gloria Steinem) Talks for Girls, nationwide project on consciousness raising and feminism for young girls, 1994. Author: Living on the Farm, 1976; theatre reviews, 1992. Mem. NEA, Nat. Assn. for Gifted (Calif. bd. dirs. 1988-92). Democrat. Home: 18200 Sweetwater Springs Rd Guerneville CA 95446-8915 Office: Talks for Girls PO 01799 Guerneville CA 95446

JOHNSTON, BERNARD FOX, foundation executive; b. Taft, Calif., Nov. 19, 1934; s. Bernard Lowe and Georgia Victoria (Fox) J.; m. Audrey Rhoades, June 9, 1956 (div. Sept. 1963); 1 child, Sheldon Bernard. BA in Creative Arts, San Francisco State U., 1957, MA in World Lit., 1958. Lectr. philosophy Coll. of Marin, Kentfield, Calif., 1957-58; lectr. humanities San Francisco State U., 1957-58, 67-68; instr. English Contra Costa Coll., San Pablo, Calif., 1958-63; Knowles Found. philosophy fellow, 1962; fellow Syracuse (N.Y.) U., 1964-66; freelance writer Piedmont, Calif., 1966-77; pres. Cinema Repertory, Inc., Point Richmond, Calif., 1978-89, Athena Found., Tiburon-Truckee, Calif., 1990—; exec. prodr. (TV series) The Heroes of Time. Author: (screenplay) Point Exeter, 1979, Ascent Allowed, 1988 (award); author, editor: Issues in Education: An Anthology of Controversy, 1964, The Literature of Learning, 1971. Mem. Coun. for Basic Edn., Wilson Ctr. Assocs., Smithsonian Instn., Donner Land Trust, San Francisco State Alumni Assn. Office: Athena Found 14036 Ramshorn St Truckee CA 96161-7157

JOHNSTON, CHARLES, protective services official. BA in Law Enforcement Adminstrn., San Jose State U.; MPA, U. No. Colo.; grad., Nat. Acad. FBI; attended, Harvard U., Northwestern U., U. Denver, U. Colo. Police officer Salinas (Calif.) Police Dept.; police officer Lakewood (Calif.) Police Dept., 1970-80, acting chief of police, 1980-81, chief of police, 1981—; active Colo. Peace Officer Stds. and Tng. Bd., Justice Assistance Act Adv. Bd. Mem. Jefferson County coun. ARC; chmn. steering com. Law Enforcement Torch Run; active Colo. Spl. Olympics. Decorated Bronze star (4), Purple Heart, Army Air medal; recipient Man of Yr. award Lakewood Sentinel, 1984, Hall of Fame award Lakewood/South Jefferson County C. of C., 1989; named Vol. of Yr., Colo. Spl. Olympics Hall of Fame, 1990. Office: Lakewood Police Dept 445 S Allison Pky Lakewood CO 80226-3105*

JOHNSTON, GAIL LIRAGIS, laboratory director; b. Atlantic City, N.J., Sept. 3, 1951; d. William and Mary Agnes (Cathcart) Liragis; m. R.C. Johnston, Jan. 14, 1984. B.A./B.S., U. Calif.-Santa Cruz, 1974, postgrad. 1978; Cert. U. Calif.-Los Angeles, 1976. Pub. info. officer Calif. State Parks, Santa Cruz, 1974-75; paralegal Berliner, Cohen & Flaherty, San Jose, 1976-78; tchr. Pajaro Unified, Watsonville, Calif., 1978-80; asst. to dir. Moss Landing Marine Labs., Calif., 1980—; adv. panel U. Santa Clara's Paralegal Program, 1976-78. Contbg. author: Central Calif. Coastal Conservation Commn.'s Coastal Land Environment, 1974; K-12 Environmental Edn. Handbook, 1979. Greek Orthodox. Address: Moss Landing Marine Labs PO Box 450 Moss Landing CA 95039-0450

JOHNSTON, GWINAVERE ADAMS, public relations consultant; b. Casper, Wyo., Jan. 6, 1943; d. Donald Milton Adams and Gwinavere Marie (Newell) Quillen; m. H.R. Johnston, Sept. 26, 1963 (div. 1973); children: Gwinavere G., Gabrielle Suzanne; m. Donald Charles Cannalte, Apr. 4, 1981. BS in Journalism, U. Wyo., 1966; postgrad., Denver U., 1968-69. Editor, reporter Laramie (Wyo.) Daily Boomerang, 1965-66; account exec. William Kostka Assocs., Denver, 1966-71, v.p., 1969-71; exec. v.p. Slottow, McKinlay & Johnston, Denver, 1971-74; pres. The Johnston Group, Denver, 1974-92; chair, CEO The Johnston-Wells Group, Denver, 1992—; adj. faculty U. Colo. Sch. Journalism, 1988-90. Bd. dirs. Leadership Denver Assn., 1975-77, 83-86, Mile High United Way, 1989-95, Colo. Jud. Inst., 1991—, Denver's 2% Club. Fellow Am. Pub. Rels. Soc. (pres. Colo. chpt. 1978-79, bd. dirs. 1975-80, 83-86, nat. exec. com. Counselor's Acad. 1988-93, sec.-treas. 1994, pres.-elect 1995, profl. award Disting. Svc. award 1992); mem. Colo. Women's Forum, Rocky Mountain Pub. Rels. Group (founder), Denver Athletic Club, Denver Press Club. Republican. Home: 717 Monaco Pky Denver CO 80220-6040 Office: The Johnston Wells Group 1512 Larimer St Ste 720 Denver CO 80202-1622

JOHNSTON, MARILYN ELAINE (GREENE), nonprofit organization executive director; b. Richmond, Va., June 26, 1947; d. William Joseph and Theresa (Davis) Greene; m. Carroll Deane Johnston, July 24, 1976; children: Heather Danielle, Pamela Nicole. BA, Longwood Coll., 1968; MEd, Va. Commonwealth U., 1970; EdD, Oreg. State U., 1978. Tchr. Richmond (Va.) City Schs., 1968-69; counselor, fgn. student advisor Balt. City Schs. and Inver Hill C.C., Minn., 1970-76; ednl. cons., 1978-89; com. adminstr. Oreg. Legis., Salem, 1989, 93; exec. dir. Oreg. Gov.'s Sch., Salem, 1994—; commr. Oreg. Gov.'s Commn. for Women, 1990-93, Salem Human Rights Commn., Salem, 1985-90. Author: So You Were Successful in Getting a Proposal Funded - Now What?, 1980, (manual) Career and Vocational Guidance for Special Needs Students, 1981; co-author: Building a Community Business/Education Partnership, 1988. Chair Local Sch. Adv. Com., 1985-87; Sunday sch. dir., 1994—. Recipient Community Sch. award, 1986. Mem. Internat. Vocat. Edn. and Tng. Assn., Am. Vocat. Assn., Nat. Assn. of Ptnrs. in Edn., Bus. and Profl. Women, Chemeketan Hiking Group, Phi Kappa Phi. Democrat. Office: Oreg Govs Sch Willamette Univ 900 State St # D241 Salem OR 97301-3930

JOHNSTON, PATRICIA KATHLEEN, college dean; b. Seattle, May 21, 1936; d. Robert Leonard and Dorothy Evelyn (Crow) Pearson; m. Edward Paul Johnston, Sept. 3, 1955; children: Linda Suzanne Johnston Murosako, Martin Edward. BA, Walla Walla Coll., 1958; MPH, Loma Linda U., 1978; MS, U. Wash., 1979; DrPH, UCLA, 1987. Registered dietitian. Instr. Loma Linda (Calif.) U., 1979-81, asst. prof., 1981-88, assoc. prof., 1988-94, prof., 1994—, dir. DrPH program, 1987-90, chmn. nutrition dept., 1990—, assoc. dean Sch. Pub. Health, 1990—; chmn. program 2d Internat. Congress on Vegetarian Nutrition, Washington, 1992, editor proc.; speaker in field. Contbr. articles to profl. jours.; editor jour. Vibrant Life, 1988-95. Recipient Danforth Found. award Auburn Acad., 1953, Honored Student award L.A. Nutrition Coun., 1985, G. Emmerson award UCLA, 1985. Mem. APHA, Am. Dietetic Assn., Am. Soc. Bone and Mineral Rsch., Calif. Nutrition Coun., Soc. Nutrition Edn., Assn. Grad. Faculties in Pub. Health Nutrition, Calif. Dietetic Assn. (v.p. 1993-95), Omicron Nu, Delta Omega (nat. merit award 1981). Seventh Day Adventist. Office: Loma Linda U Sch Pub Health Loma Linda CA 92350

JOHNSTON, RITA MARGARET, Canadian provincial government official; b. Melville, Sask., Can., Apr. 22, 1935; d. John R. and Annie Chyzzy L. Leichert; m. George Johnston, Apr. 28, 1951; children: Darlene, Colleen, Rock. Stenographer, mgr. Bell Fin. Ltd.; alderman Dist. of Surrey, until 1983; mem. Legis. Assembly, from 1983; min. mcpl. affairs, recreation and culture B.C. Govt., 1986-89, min. transp. and hwys., 1989-91, dep. premier, then premier, 1991. Mem. Surrey Bus. and Profl. Women, Surrey C. of C. Home: 6595 King George Hwy, Surrey, BC Canada V3W 4Z2

JOHNSTON, ROBIN REYNOLDS, cardiologist; b. Chgo., Apr. 10, 1932; s. Dallas Reynolds and Elizabeth (Kern) Johnston; m. Dorothy True Jameson, Apr. 27, 1957; children: Scot Jameson, Susan Elizabeth, Emily Evelyn, Caroline Kern. BA in Chemistry, U. Ill., 1954, MD, 1957. Diplomate Am. Bd. Cardiology. Intern Mpls. Gen. Hosp., 1957-58; resident in internal medicine U. Minn. Hosp., Mpls., 1958-60; resident in internal medicine U. Wash. Hosp., Seattle, 1960-61, cardiology fellow, 1961-62; instr. medicine U. Tex. Southwestern, Dallas, 1964-65; cardiologist Va. Mason Clinic, Seattle, 1965—; dir. heart catheterization lab. Va. Mason Hosp., Seattle, 1965—. Contbr. articles to profl. jours. Bd. govs. Va. Mason Med. Ctr. Fellow ACP, Am. Coll. Cardiology; mem. Am. Heart Assn. (bd. dirs. Washington chpt. 1986), Phi Beta Kappa, Alpha Omega Alpha. Republican. Episcopalian. Office: Va Mason Clinic 1100 9th Ave Seattle WA 98101-2756

JOHNSTON, THOMAS ALIX, artist, educator; b. Oklahoma City, June 4, 1941; s. Elmer Arthur and Madelyn Leona (Norton) J.; m. Kathleen Lord, Feb. 17, 1962 (div. 1971); children: Steven Thomas, Scott Randall; m. Ann Gail Friedman, Sept. 27, 1980. AA, San Diego City Coll., 1963; BA, San Diego State U., 1965; MFA, U. Calif., Santa Barbara, 1967. Prof. art Western Wash. U., Bellingham, 1967—; dir. Western Gallery Western Wash. U., 1983-87; artist Atelier Lacourière et Frélaut, Paris, 1981, 82, 88, 93, Atelier Rudolf Broulim, Zwijndrecht, Belgium, 1988, Santa Reparata Graphic Arts Ctr., Florence, Italy, 1981, Atelier 17, Paris, 1980; artist in residence Chateau Suduiraut, Preignac, France, 1993. Numerous one-man and group shows, including Galerie Jean-Claude Riedel, Paris, 1989, Tacoma Art Mus., 1990, Ctr. on Contemporary Art, Seattle, 1990, Dart Gallery, Chgo., 1992, Seattle Art Mus., 1992, Davidson Galleries, Seattle, 1993, Louisa McIntosh Gallery, Atlanta, 1993, SAGA, Paris, 1993, Chateau Suduiraut, 1994, Atelier Lacourière, Frèlaut, 1994; represented in permanent collections, including Beaufour Collection, Paris. Office: Western Wash U 518 High St Bellingham WA 98225-5946

JOHNSTON, THOMAS JOHN, management consultant; b. Oak Park, Ill., Nov. 2, 1922; s. John J. and Helen J. (Gilmore) J.; m. Elaine Berger, Feb. 16, 1946; children—Elene Johnston Kapp, Molly, Anne Johnston Gardner, Karen, John. B.S., St. Marys Coll., 1943; Postgrad., Columbia U., 1943. Personnel analyst Western Electric Co. Inc., Chgo., 1946-49; retail personnel mgr. Montgomery Ward & Co., Chgo., 1949-54; dir. personnel Panellit Inc., Chgo., 1954-56; assoc. Heidrick & Struggles Inc., Chgo., 1956-60, dir. in charge West Coast ops., 1960-70; pres., chief exec. officer Heidrick & Struggles Inc., San Francisco, Calif., 1970-91; 1978-91; chair emeritus Heidrick & Struggles Inc., Calistoga, 1991—; bd. dirs. Chalone, Inc. Mem. U. Redland's Pres.'s Adv. Council, 1968-73; mem. Pres.'s Commn. on White House Fellows, 1971-76; trustee Robert Louis Stevenson Sch., Pebble Beach, Calif., 1977—, chmn. bd. dirs., 1984—. Served to lt. USNR, 1942-46, PTO. Republican. Roman Catholic. Clubs: Calif., University, Annandale Golf, San Francisco Yacht. Lodge: Knights of Malta.

JOHNSTON, VIRGINIA EVELYN, editor; b. Spokane, Wash., Apr. 26, 1933; d. Edwin and Emma Lucile (Munroe) Rowe; student Portland C.C., 1964, Portland State U., 1966, 78-79; m. Alan Paul Beckley, Dec. 26, 1974; children: Chris, Denise, Rex. Proofreader, The Oregonian, Portland, 1960-62, teletypesetter operator, 1962-66, operator Photon 200, 1966-68, copy editor, asst. women's editor, 1968-80; spl. sects. editor (UPDATE), 1981-83, 88-95; editor FOODday, 1982—; pres. Matrix Assos., Inc., Portland, 1975—, chmn. bd., 1979—; pres. Bones & Brew Inc.; bd. dir. Computer Tools Inc. Cons. Dem. Party Oreg., 1969, Portland Sch. Dist. No. 1, 1978. Mem. Eating and Drinking Soc. Oreg. (past pres.), We. Culinary Inst. (mem. adv. bd.), Portland Culinary Alliance (mem. adv. bd.), Internat. Food Media Conf. (mem. adv. bd.). Democrat. Editor Principles of Computer Systems for Newspaper Mgmt., 1975-76. Home: 4140 NE 137th Ave Portland OR 97230-2624 Office: Oregonian Pub Co 1320 SW Broadway Portland OR 97201-3469

JOHNSTONE, CLINT, electric power industry executive. Sr. v.p., bd. dirs. Bechtel Nat. Inc., San Francisco. Office: Bechtel Nat Inc 50 Beale St # 3965 San Francisco CA 94105-1813*

JOHNSTONE, IAIN MURRAY, statistician, educator, consultant; b. Melbourne, Victoria, Australia, Dec. 10, 1956; s. Samuel Thomas Murray and Pamela Beatrice (Kriegel) J. BS with honors, Australian Nat. U., Canberra, 1978, MS, 1979; PhD, Cornell U., 1981. Asst. prof. stats. Stanford (Calif.) U., 1981-85, assoc prof. stats., 1986-92, assoc. prof. biostatistics, 1987-92, prof. stats., biostatistics, 1992—, dept. chmn., 1994—. Assoc. editor (jours.) Annals of Stats., 1987-91, 95—; contbr. articles to profl. jours. Alfred P. Sloan Rsch. fellow, 1988-90; named Presdl. Young Investigator, NSF, 1985-92. Fellow Royal Statis. Soc. (Guy bronze medal 1995), Inst. Math. Stats. (program sec. 1991-94), Am. Statis Assn.; mem. AAAS, Am. Math. Soc. Office: Stanford U Dept Stats Sequoia Hall Stanford CA 94305-4065

JOHNSTONE, KENNETH ERNEST, electronics and business consultant; b. L.A., Sept. 13, 1929; s. John Ernest and Lorena Hayes (Patterson) J.; m. Edna Mae Iverson, Aug. 20, 1950; children: Bruce, Kent, Anita, Christian, Daniel, Carol, Karen. BSEE, U. Wash., 1966. Registered profl. engr., Wash. Electronics technician The Boeing Co., Seattle, 1955-66, engr., 1966-75; engring. mgr. Boeing Aerosystems Internat., Seattle, 1975-85; ptnr. North Creek Engring., Lynnwood, Wash., 1985-87; pres. SensorLink Corp., Lynnwood, 1987-90; electronics and bus. cons. Bellingham, Wash., 1991—; internat. lectr. in field. Mem. IEEE (sr.), Tau Beta Pi. Home and Office: 3765 E Smith Rd Bellingham WA 98226-9573

JOHNSTONE, PATRICK C., food products executive; b. 1924. Chief exec. Spokane Seed Co., 1947—, pres., gen. mgr., chmn. bd. dirs., pres. Office: Spokane Seed Co 6015 E Alki Ave Spokane WA 99212-1019*

JOINER, DENNIS ASHLEY, personnel management consultant; b. Reno, Mar. 20, 1953; s. Virgil Lafayette and Rebecca Elizabeth (Moon) J.; m. Sharon Corinne Dunn, Jan. 26, 1980. BA in Psychology, Calif. State U., Sacramento, 1975, MS in Counseling, 1978. Pers. analyst Calif. State Pers. Bd., Sacramento, 1977-80; cons., owner Dennis A. Joiner & Assocs., Fair Oaks, Calif., 1980—. Contbr. numerous articles to profl. jours. Mem. Internat. Pers. Mgmt. Assn. Assessment Coun. (dir. 1987-92, pres. 1990-91), Pers. Testing Coun. No. Calif. (bd. dirs. 1988, 89, pres. 1987). Home and Office: Dennis A Joiner & Assocs 4975 Daru Way Fair Oaks CA 95628-5452

JOKLIK, GÜNTHER FRANZ, mining company executive; b. Vienna, Austria, May 30, 1928; came to U.S., 1953; s. Karl Friedrich and Helene (Giessl) J.; m. Pamela Mary Fenton, Dec. 22, 1962; children: Carl Duncan, Katherine Pamela, Paul Richard. B.Sc. with 1st class honors, U. Sydney, Australia, 1949, Ph.D., 1953; DSc (hon.), U. Utah, 1994. Exploration geologist Kennecott Corp., N.Y.C., 1954-62; exploration mgr. Australia div. AMAX, Inc., Greenwich, Conn., 1963-71, v.p., 1972-73; v.p. Kennecott Corp., 1974-79, pres., CEO, 1980-93; ret., 1993; sr. v.p. metals Std. Oil Co. (parent), Cleve., 1982-89; dir. First Security Corp., Salt Lake City, Cleve. (Ohio)-Cliffs, Inc.; mem. Nat. Strategic Materials Adv. Com., 1984-89; hon. consul for U.K., Salt Lake City, 1995. Chmn. Salt Lake City Olympic Organizing Com. for Winter Games of 2002. Fulbright scholar Columbia U., 1953-54; recipient Giant In Our City award Salt Lake Area C. of C., 1994. Mem. Nat. Acad. Engring, Copper Club (Man of Yr. 1989), Alta Club (Salt Lake), The Country Club. Office: Eagle Gate Tower # 700 60 E South Temple Salt Lake City UT 84111-1004

JONAITIS, ALDONA CLAIRE, museum administrator, art historian; b. N.Y.C., Nov. 27, 1948; d. Thomas and Demie (Genaitis) J. BA, SUNY, Stony Brook, 1969; MA, Columbia U., 1972, PhD, 1977. Chair art dept. SUNY, Stony Brook, 1983-85, assoc. provost, 1985-86, vice provost undergrad. studies, 1986-89; v.p. for pub. programs Am. Mus. Natural History, N.Y.C., 1989—. Author: From the Land of the Totem Poles, 1988; editor, author: Chiefly Feasts: The Enduring Kwakiutl Potlatch, 1991. Mem. Native Am. Art Studies Assn. (bd. dirs. 1985—). Office: Univ of AK Mus 907 Yukon Dr Fairbanks AK 99775

JONASSEN, JAMES O., architect; b. Aberdeen, Wash., July 23, 1940; s. James E. and Marjorie E. (Smith) J.; m. Patricia E. Glen, June 9, 1958 (div. Oct. 1975); m. Marilyn Joan Kampa, June 11, 1977; children—Christian A., Steven E. B.Arch., U. Wash., 1964; M.S. in Architecture, Columbia U., 1965. Registered architect, Ala., Alaska, Ariz., Calif., Colo., Fla., Ga., Idaho, Ill., Kans., La., Minn., Mo., Mont., Nebr., Nev., N.Mex., N.D., N.C., Ohio, Okla., Oreg., S.D., Tex., Wash., Utah, Wis., D.C., Del., Mass., Miss., N.H., N.Y., R.I., Vt., P.R., British Columbia, Can. Designer NBBJ Group, Seattle, 1965-70, ptnr., 1970-83, chief exec. officer, 1983—. Prin. works include Battelle Meml. Lab., Richland, Wash., 1965, (lab. of year award, 1968), Heath Profl. Bldg., 1970, Children's Orthopedic Hosp., Seattle, 1972, (AIA Honor award 1976), St. Mary's Hosp. Surg. Pavilion, Rochester, Minn., 1982, St. Vincent Med. Office Bldg., Portland, Oreg., 1983, Scottsdale Meml. Hosp. N., Ariz., 1984, Seattle VA Hosp., 1985, Stanford U. Hosp., 1986, St. Joseph Hosp. Med. Ctr., 1988, Providence Med. Ctr., Seattle, 1990 (AIA Merit award), David Grant Med. Ctr., Fairfield, Calif., 1986 (USAF Honor award 1989, Spl. citation DOD 1988, Type 1 Honor award USAF 1989, Excellence in Design award DOD 1991). Bd. dirs. Health Facilities Rsch. and Edn. Project, 1991—, Swedish Med. Ctr. Found., 1993, Sch. Zone Inst., 1990—; pres. bd. Architecture and Children Project, 1990-92. Naramore Found. fellow, 1969; Columbia U. scholar, 1964; Recipient Seattle Newsmaker Tomorrow award Time Mag., 1978. Fellow AIA (chmn. steering com. 1983-85, nat. com. architecture for health, mem. Nat. Life Cycle Task Force 1977, bd. dirs. Seattle chpt. 1985-87); mem. Am. Hosp. Assn., Western Hosps. Assn. (chmn. architects sect. 1973), Wash. Athletic Club, Columbia Tower Club, Rotary. Office: NBBJ 111 S Jackson St Seattle WA 98104-2820

JONES, ALAN C., grocery company executive; b. 1942; married. BS, Portland State U., 1967. Computer operator United Grocers Inc., Portland, Oreg., 1964-66, buyer, 1966-72, inventory control mgr., 1972-74, mktg. dept. mgr., 1974-82, asst. gen. mgr., 1982-83, pres., 1983—, formerly chief exec. officer, sec., treas. Served with USAF, 1960-64. Office: United Grocers Inc PO Box 22187 Milwaukie OR 97269-2187

JONES, AMELIA GWEN, art history educator, curator; b. Durham, N.C., July 14, 1961; d. Edward Ellsworth and Virginia (Sweetnam) J.; m. Anthony Joseph Sherin, Mar. 7, 1987; 1 child, Evan Ellsworth Sherin-Jones,. BA, Harvard U., 1983; MA, U. Pa., 1987; PhD, UCLA, 1991. Curator Univ. Art Gallery, Riverside, Calif., 1991-92, Calif. Mus. Photography, Riverside, Calif., 1993-94, Hammer Mus., L.A., 1993—; art writer Art Forum, Art Issues, N.Y., L.A., 1987—; instr., advisor Art Cen. Coll. Design, Pasadena, Calif., 1990-91; art history, art instr. U. Southern Calif., L.A., 1992; art history prof. U. Calif., Riverside, 1991—; adv. Workshop on Visual Culture U. Calif., Irvine, 1994—; cons. J. Paul Getty Mus., Malibu, Calif., 1986. Author: Postmodernism and the En-Gendering of Marcel Duchamp, 1994; contbr. articles to profl. jours. Bd. dirs. L.A. Cen. of Photographic Studies, 1994—, Teachers for a Dem. Culture, 1993—, Women's Action Coalition, 1992-93. Recipient Disting. Humanist Achievement award U. Calif., 1994, postdoctoral fellowship Am. Coun. of Learned Societies, N.Y., 1994-95, Dickson fellowship UCLA, 1989-91, Dean's fellowship U. Pa., 1986-87, Harvard Coll. fellowship Harvard U., 1980-82. Mem. Coll. Art Assn., Internat. Assn. of Art Critics. Home: 339 S Orange Dr Los Angeles CA 90036-3008 Office: U Calif Dept Art History Riverside CA 92521

JONES, ANN AKRIDGE, hospital administration executive; b. Dallas, June 1, 1945; d. Frank O. and Mary Virginia (Touchstone) Akridge; m. M. Douglas Jones Jr., May 25, 1968; children: Monica Akridge, Tobin Laurence. BA, U. Tex., 1967; MA, U. Colo., 1971, PhD, 1977. From spl. asst. to pres. to v.p. planning and devel. Johns Hopkins Hosp., Balt., 1979-84; v.p. ops. Zamoiski Co., Balt., 1984-85; adminstr. Johns Hopkins Med. Inst., Balt., 1986-89; exec. dir. Spiegel & McDiarmid, Washington, 1989-90; asst. vice chancellor U. Colo. Health Sci. Ctr., Denver, 1990-91; dir. facilities Univ. Hosp., Denver, 1991-94, assoc. v.p., 1994—; cons. St. Vincent's Hosp., N.Y.C., 1982—. Contbr. articles to profl. jours. Advisor pub. affairs Planned Parenthood, Denver, 1992-94; bd. dirs. Md. Com. for Children, 1985-89, Balt. City Ct. Appointed Spl. Advocates, 1990, Colo. Children's Campaign, Denver, 1994—. Recipient Gov. citation State of Md., 1982, Leadership award House of Ruth, 1984, Recognition cert., 1985, Citizen citation Balt. Mayor's Task Force, 1987. Mem. Am. Soc. Hosp. Engrs., Am. Assn. Med. Colls. Home: 734 Spring Ranch Dr Golden CO 80401-9749 Office: Univ Hosp 4200 E 9th Ave Denver CO 80220-3706

JONES, ARTHUR FRANCIS, surgeon; b. Utica, N.Y., May 13, 1946; s. Arthur Hywel and Ellen Joanna (Burke) J.; m. Patricia Ann Barton, Aug. 24, 1968 (div. Apr. 1981); children: David A., Eric W.; m. Wanda Lea Stewart, June 4, 1983; 1 child, Christopher. AB, Hamilton Coll., 1967; MD cum laude, Yale U., 1971. Diplomate Am. Bd. Surgery. Intern U. Colo., Denver, 1971-72, resident in surgery, 1972-73, 75-79; ptnr., surgeon Foothills Surg. Assocs., Wheat Ridge, Colo., 1979—; chmn. dept. surgery Luth. Med. Ctr., Wheat Ridge, 1989-90. Maj. U.S. Army, 1973-75. Fellow ACS (pres. Colo. chpt. 1991); mem. Denver Acad. Surgery (program dir. 1994-95), Southwestern Surg. Soc., Alpha Omega Alpha. Unitarian. Office: Foothills Surg Assocs 8550 W 38th Ave Ste 308 Wheat Ridge CO 80033-4355

JONES, BARBARA DEAN, substance abuse counselor; b. Taunton, Mass., Dec. 11, 1931; d. Laurance Franklin and Amy Laura (Harrington) Dean; m. Rial Cooper Jones, Aug. 31, 1957 (div. July 1987); children: Dean Michael, Mark Jackson, Amy Winifred. Student, Duke U., 1952; BA, U. Mass., 1953; MEd in Human Svcs., Boston U., 1983. Cert. in alcohol education and prevention, Fla., 1981; lic. real estate agt., Va., 1979, Calif., 1984. Psychiat. social worker Alcohol Rehab. Ctr., Butner, N.C., 1953-55; social case worker Granville County Dept. Pub. Welfare, Oxford, N.C., 1955-56; dist. dir. Bright Leaf Girl Scout Coun., Durham, N.C., 1956-57; kindergarten tchr. Sasebo, Japan, 1961; social worker Assn. for the Blind, Charleston, S.C., 1962-63; tchr. Am. Studies Ctr., Naples, Italy, 1980-82; alcohol rehab. counselor Navy Regional Med. Ctr., Naples, 1982-83; family counselor Parkside Recovery Ctr., Oceanside, Calif., 1987-89; human rels. cons. Decorating Den, Anaheim, Calif., 1989-90; alcohol facilitator Navy Alcohol Safety Action Program, Naples, 1980-83. Bd. dirs. Fairfax (Va.) Ballet Co., 1978, YWCA, Glendora, Calif., 1972; pres. Naval Officers Wives Club, Charleston, 1964; chmn. alcohol and drug abuse com. Self Esteem Task Force of San Diego County, 1990. Recipient cert. of appreciation U.S. Navy, 1983; Yale U. Summer Sch. of Alcohol Studies fellow, 1955. Mem. AAUW, Women's Internat. Ctr. Republican. Episcopalian. Home and Office: 3421 Summerset Way Oceanside CA 92056-3208

JONES, BEVERLY ANN MILLER, nursing administrator, patient services executive; b. Bklyn., July 14, 1927; d. Hayman Edward and Eleanor Virginia (Doyle) Miller. BSN, Adelphi U., 1949; m. Kenneth Lonzo Jones, Sept. 5, 1953; children: Steven Kenneth, Lonnie Cord. Chief nurse regional blood program ARC, N.Y.C., 1951-54; asst. dir., acting dir. nursing M.D. Anderson Hosp. and Tumor Inst., Houston, 1954-55; asst. dir. nursing Sibley Meml. Hosp., Washington, 1959-61; assoc. dir. nursing svc. Anne Arundel Gen. Hosp., Annapolis, Md., 1966-70; asst. adminstr. nursing Alexandria (Va.) Hosp., 1972-73; v.p. patient care svcs., Longmont (Colo.) United Hosp., 1977-93; pvt. cons., 1993—; instr. ARC, 1953-57; mem. adv. bd. Boulder Valley Vo.-Tech Health Occupations Program, 1977-80; chmn. nurse enrollment com. D.C. chpt. ARC, 1959-61; del. nursing adminstrs. good will trip to Poland, Hungary, Sweden and Eng., 1980. Contbr. articles to profl. jours. Bd. dirs. Meals on Wheels, Longmont, Colo., 1978-80, Longmont Coalition for Women in Crisis, Applewood Living Ctr., Longmont; mem. Colo. Hosp. Assn. Task Force on Nat. Commn. on Nursing, 1982; mem. utilization com. Boulder (Colo.) Hospice, 1979-83; vol. Longmont Police Bur., Colo.; mem. coun. labor rels. Colo. Hosp. Assn., 1982-87; mem.-at-large exec. com. nursing svc. adminstrs. Sect. Md. Nurses' Assn., 1966-69; mem. U. Colorado Task Force on Nursing, 1990; vol. Champs program St. Vrain Valley Sch. Dist.; vol. Longmont Police Dept. Mem. Am. Orgn. Nurse Execs. (chmn. com. membership svcs. and promotions, nominee recognition of excellence in nursing adminstrn.), Colo. Soc. Nurse Execs. (dir. 1978-80, 84-86, pres. 1980-81, mem. com. on nominations 1985-86). Home: 853 Wade Rd Longmont CO 80503-7017

JONES, BOB GORDON, bishop; b. Paragould, Ark., Aug. 22, 1932; s. F.H. and Helen Truman (Ellis) J.; m. Judith Munroe, Feb. 22, 1963; children: Robert Gordon, Timothy Andrew. B.B.A., U. Miss., 1956; M.Div., Episcopal Sem. S.W., 1959, D.D. hon., 1978. Asst. to dean Trinity Cathedral, Little Rock, 1959-62; vicar St. George-in-Arctic, Kotzebue, Alaska, 1962-67; rector St. Christopher's Ch., Anchorage, 1967-77; bishop Episcopal Diocese Wyo., Laramie, 1977—; chmn. bd. Cathedral Home Children, Laramie, 1977—; mem. exec. com. Provence N.W., Helena, Mont., 1980-83, Coalition 14, Phoenix, 1982-84. Pres. Arctic Circle C. of C., Kotzebue, 1966; mem. exec. com. Alaska C. of C., Juneau, 1967; chmn. allocations com. United Way, Anchorage, 1973-75; pres. United Way Anchorage, 1975-76. Served with USN, 1950-55, Korea. Republican. Lodges: Lions; Elks. Home: 104 S 4th St Laramie WY 82070-3162 Office: Episcopal Diocese of Wyo PO Box 1007t Laramie WY 82070-3162*

JONES, BRENDA GAIL, school district administrator; b. Winnipeg, Man., Can., Nov. 5, 1949; d. Glen Allen and Joyce Catherine (Peckham) McGregor. BA, San Francisco State U., 1972; MA, U. San Francisco, 1983. Cert. tchr., sch. adminstr., Calif. Tchr. Lakeport (Calif.) Unified Sch. Dist., 1973-82, asst. prin., 1982-88, dir. ednl. svcs., 1988—; instr. English Mendocino Coll., Ukiah, Calif., 1977-82. Mem. Assn. Calif. Sch. Adminstrs. (past pres. 1987, Lake County charter), Order Ea. Star (worthy matron Clear Lake chpt. 1995). Democrat. Episcopalian. Home: 1315 20th St Lakeport CA 95453-3051 Office: Lakeport Unified Sch Dist 100 Lange St Lakeport CA 95453-3297

JONES, CHARLES IRVING, bishop; b. El Paso, Tex., Sept. 13, 1943; s. Charles I. Jr. and Helen A. (Heyward) J.; m. Ashby MacArthur, June 18, 1966; children: Charles I. IV, Courtney M., Frederic M., Keith A. BS, The Citadel, 1965; MBA, U. N.C., 1966; MDiv, U. of the South, 1977, DD, 1989. CPA. Pub. acctg. D.E. Gatewood and Co., Winston-Salem, N.C., 1966-72; dir. devel. Chatham (Va.) Hall, 1972-74; instr. acctg. U. of the South, Sewanee, Tenn., 1974-77; coll. chaplain Western Ky. U., Bowling Green, 1977-81; vicar Trinity Episcopal Ch., Russelville, Ky., 1977-85; archdeacon Diocese of Ky., Louisville, 1981-86; bishop Episcopal Diocese of Mont., Helena, 1986—; bd. dirs. New Directions Ministries, Inc., N.Y.C.; mem. standing com. Joint Commn. on Chs. in Small Communities, 1988-91, Program, Budget and Fin., 1991-94; v.p. province VI Episcopal Ch., 1991-94, mem. Presiding Bishop's Coun. Advice, 1991-94. Author: Mission Strategy in the 21st Century, 1989, Total Ministry: A Practical Approach, 1993; bd. editors Grass Roots, Luling, Tex., 1985-90; contbr. articles to profl. jours. Founder Concerned Citizens for Children, Russelville, 1981; bd. dirs. St. Peter's Hosp., Helena, 1986—. With USMCR, 1961-65. Mem. Aircraft Owners and Pilots Assn. Office: Diocese Mont 515 N Park Ave Helena MT 59601-2703

JONES, CHARLES J., consultant; b. Marshfield, Oreg., Jan. 29, 1940; s. Charles J. Cotter and Lois C. (Smith) Meltebeke; m. Sharon S. Madsen, Mar. 29, 1969; children: Mary E., Judith A., Kari C., April M., Autumn C. AS in Fire Sci. Tech., Portland Community Coll., 1974; BS in Fire Adminstrn., Eastern Oreg. State Coll., 1983; diploma, Nat. Fire Acad., 1983, 85; MPA, Lewis and Clark Coll., 1989. Cert. class VI fire officer, Oreg., hazardous materials instr., fire instr. I; lic. real estate agt., Oreg. From firefighter to capt. Washington County Fire Dist., Aloha, Oreg., 1964-74, battalion chief, 1974-81, dir. comms., dir. research and devel., 1981-85, dir. strategic planning, 1986-88; cons. Tualatin Valley Fire & Rescue, Aloha, 1989-90; pres., CEO Jones Transp., 1989—; basic and advanced 1st aid instr. ARC, 1965-80; cons. Washington County Consol. Communications Agy., 1983-86, chmn. 9-1-1 mgmt. bd., 1982-83; mem. adv. bd. Washington County Emergency Med. Svcs., 1981-83; owner/instr. Internat. Vocat. Inst. and Family Tree Learning Ctrs. Jones Internat., Ltd., 1990-95. Editor local newsletter Internat. Assn. Firefighters, 1970; contbr. articles on fire dept. mgmt. to jours. Active Community Planning Orgn., Washington County, 1979-90, chmn. 1988-89. With USAF, 1957-59. Mem. Oreg. Fire Chiefs Assn. (chmn. seminar com. 1982-83, 89, co-chmn. 1981, 84, 86, 87, 88). Republican. Mem. Infinity Universal Ch. Office: Jones Transp PO Box 7206 Aloha OR 97007-7206

JONES, CHARLIE, television sports announcer; b. Ft. Smith, Ark.; m. Ann; children: Chuck, Julie. JD, U. Ark., 1953. Play-by-play broadcaster Am. Football League, ABC-TV, 1960-64, NFL, 1965—, Cin. Reds TV Network, 1973-74, USC Basketball, 1974-75, Seattle Seahawks preseason football, Sta. KING-TV, 1985-89; commentator for Wide World of Sports ABC, 1961-64; sports dir. Sta. WFAA-TV, Dallas, 1962-65, Sta. WMAQ-TV, Chgo., 1974; sports commentator NBC-TV, 1965—; play-by-play broadcaster Colo. Rockies TV Network, 1993—. Television broadcasting firsts include Super Bowl I, first Am. Football League Championship game, first Am. Football League nationally televised game, first NBC SportsWorld, first World Cup Gymnastics, first World Cup Marathon, first World Championships of Track and Field, Helsinki, 1983, first World Indoor Championships of Track and Field, Indpls., 1987, first Sr. Skins Game, Hawaii, 1988; hosted TV shows: Seahawks Insider, Almost Anything Goes, Pro-Fan; appeared in TV series: Ironside, McMillan and Wife, Columbo, The Dick Van Dyke Show, Rich Man, Poor Man; appeared in several Movies of the Week and motion pictures Personal Best, Return of the Killer Tomatoes, and Killer Tomatoes Strike Back. Recipient Emmy award for documentary Is Winning the Name of the Game, 1982, Outstanding Achievement award Freedoms Found. of Valley Forge, 1982, Bronze medal for co-producing, co-hosting, co-writing The American Frontier, PBS-TV, Internat. TV Festival of N.Y., 1982, Headliner of Yr. award for outstanding contbns. in field of TV San Diego Press Club, 1986, Disting. Alumnus award U. Ark., 1989. Mem. Confrerie des Chevaliers du Tastevin. Office: 8080 El Paseo Grande La Jolla CA 92037-3228

JONES, CLARK DAVID, restaurant executive, accountant; b. Wells, Nev., May 12, 1935; s. Waldo LeRoy and Beatrice (Bollschweiler) J.; m. LaRue Morrison, Nov. 20, 1953 (div. 1985); children: Debra, Pam, David, Diane, Christy; m. Pam James. BS in Acctg., U. Nev., 1957; postgrad. U. Utah, 1964-65. CPA, Nev. Mgr., Al Huber, CPA, Elko, Nev., 1960-62; ptnr. Main Hurdman CPAs, Salt Lake City, 1962-70; v.p. fin. JB's Restaurants, Inc., Salt Lake City, 1970-81, pres., 1981—; bd. dirs. JB's Restaurant Inc., MDT Inc., Hometown Buffer, Inc. Chmn. Utah Opera. 1st lt. U.S. Army, 1958-60. Mem. AICPA, Utah Soc. CPAs, Nat. Restaurant Assn., Rotary. Republican. Mormon. Home: 9717 Ruskin Cir Sandy UT 84092-3573 Office: JB's Restaurants Inc 1010 W 2610 S Salt Lake City UT 84119-2434

JONES, CLEON BOYD, research engineer; b. Norwalk, Calif., Nov. 9, 1961; s. Cleon Earl and Marjorie Helen (McDade) J. BS in Math., Biola U., 1983. Rsch. libr. Christian Rsch. Inst., San Juan Capistrano, Calif., 1981-84; flight control engr. Leading Systems, Inc., Irvine, Calif., 1984-90; rsch. engr. Dynamic Rsch., Inc., Torrance, Calif., 1990—. Recipient NASA Group Achievement award Pilot Project Team, 1994. Republican. Home: 12464 Fallcreek Ln Cerritos CA 90703-2075

JONES, D. MICHAEL, banker; b. Tacoma, June 25, 1942; s. Delbert Edward and Marilyn Maurine (Myers) J.; m. Linda R. Lavigne, June 7, 1964; 1 child, Karee Michele. BA in Econs., Wash. State U., 1964. CPA, Wash. Acct. Deloitte Haskins & Sells, Seattle, 1964-68, princ., 1968-72; treas. Old Nat. Bancorp., Spokane, Wash., 1973-76, exec. v.p., 1976-81, pres., 1982-87; pres. Moore Fin. Group Inc. (now West One Bancorp), Boise, ID, 1987—; bd. dirs. Columbia Paint Co., Spokane. Bd. dirs. Spokane City Libraries, 1974-78, Leadership Spokane, 1982-84; sec. treas., bd. dirs. Spokane Unltd., 1980-86. Recipient Outstanding Alumnus award, Wash. State U., 1986. Mem. Am. Inst. CPA's, Wash. Soc. CPA's, Spokane C. of C. (sec. treas. 1985-86). Episcopalian. Clubs: Spokane (pres. 1984-85); Hayden Lake (Idaho) Country (pres. 1982-83). Office: West One Bancorp PO Box 8247 Boise ID 83733-8247*

JONES, DANIEL LEE, software development company executive; b. Sterling, Colo., Feb. 17, 1954; s. Gerald Dean and Joyce Elaine (Pyle) J.; m. Laurie Elaine Ganong, Sept. 6, 1975; 1 child, Jonathon Alexander. AB cum laude, Dartmouth Coll., 1976; MA in Physics, U. Calif., Davis, 1977, PhD in Physicis, 1979. Assoc. in physics U. Calif., Davis, 1976-79; physicist Argonne (Ill.) Nat. Lab., 1979-82; mem. tech. staff TRW, Inc., Redondo Beach, Calif., 1982-84; chief scientist, co-founder Affine Scis. Corp., Newport Beach, Calif., 1984-85; chief scientist Peripheral Systems, Inc., Van Nuys, Calif., 1985-89; dir. info. systems Jones & Jones, Sterling, Colo., 1989—; v.p., co-founder Jones Techs. Inc., Sterling, 1991-92, also bd. dirs.; dir. info. sys. Sykes Enterprises, Inc., Sterling, 1992—; sec. Jones Techs. Inc., Sterling, 1991—; cons. Davis Polk & Wardwell, N.Y.C., 1987-91. Author (newspaper column) Your Computer, 1991—; contbr. articles to profl. jours. Dist. accountability com. RE-1 Valley Schs., Sterling, 1991—, dist. tech. com., 1991—. Recipient Rufus Choate scholar Dartmouth Coll., 1972, Outstanding Contbrn. Inst. of Internal Auditors, 1987-88; tech. transfer grantee TRW, Inc., 1982. Mem. IEEE, IEEE Computer Soc., Assn. for Computing Machinery, Soc. for Indsl. and Applied Math., Uni-Forum. Republican. Methodist. Home: 510 Glenora St Sterling CO 80751-4642 Office: Sykes Enterprises Inc 777 N 4th St Sterling CO 80751-3244

JONES, DARYL EMRYS, university administrator, English educator; b. Washington, July 26, 1946; s. William Emrys and Willa Jean (Hibbard) J.; m. Martha Ann Bilton, June 11, 1979. BA, Mich. State U., 1968, MA, 1970, PhD, 1974. Prof. English Tex. Tech U., Lubbock, 1973-86, chmn. English dept., 1982-86; prof. English, dean Coll. Arts and Scis. Boise (Idaho) State U., 1986-91, interim exec. v.p., 1991-93; writer-in-residence State of Idaho, 1992, 93; provost, v.p. for acad. affairs Boise (Idaho) State U., 1993—. Author: The Dime Novel Western, 1978, Someone Going Home Late, 1990; author numerous poems and book revs. NDEA fellow, 1969-71, Creative Writing fellow NEA, 1985. Mem. Tex. Assn. Creative Writing Tchrs. (pres. 1984-86), Tex. Joint Coun. Tchrs. of English (pres. South Plains area coun. 1983-84), Tex. Inst. Letters (Natalie Ornish Poetry award 1990), Coun. Colls. Arts and Scis., Internat. Coun. Fine Arts Deans, Idaho Humanities Coun., Phi Beta Kappa, Phi Kappa Phi. Home: 1375 E Monterey Dr Boise ID 83706-5078 Office: Boise State U Provost 1910 University Dr Boise ID 83725-0001

JONES, DAVID, artist; b. Columbus, Ohio, Feb. 26, 1948. Student, Ohio State U., 1967; BFA, Kansas City Art Inst., 1970; MA, U. Calif., Berkeley, 1971, MFA, 1973. One-man shows include Braunstein/Quay Gallery, 1984, 87, 91-92, San Jose State U., 1971, Daniel Weinberg Gallery, 1973, Michael Walls Gallery, 1975; exhibited in group shows at San Diego State U., 1971, U. Santa Clara, 1971, San Francisco Art Festival, 1971-72, Pasadena Mus. Art, 1972, San Francisco Art Inst., 1973, 75, Whitney Mus. Am. Art, 1975, Huntsville Mus. Art, 1977, San Francisco Mus. Modern Art, 1976, Nat. Collection Fine Arts Smithsonian Instn., 1976, Art Inst. and Calif. State U., 1982, Richard/Bennett Gallery, 1989, Chgo. Internat. Art Exposition, 1989, Oakland Mus., 1994, U. Calif., Berkeley, 1994. Marian Davies fellow U. Calif., Berkeley, 1972; recipient Eisner prize U. Calif., Berkeley, 1971, 1st Painting prize Richmond Art Ctr., 1971, Group Show award Oakland Mus., 1971, Purchase award San Francisco Art Festival, 1971, 1st Purchase award in sculpture DeSaisset Mus., Santa Clara, Calif., 1971; Nat. Endowment Arts Artists grantee, 1974. Home: PO Box 8872 Emeryville CA 94608

JONES, DONALD FORSYTH, food equipment company executive; b. Chgo., Mar. 28, 1942; s. H. Carter and Dorothy S. (Simons) J.; m. Jeri Lynn Riha, July 3, 1965; children: Marcus, David. BS in Indsl. Engring., Calif. State Poly. U., 1965. Test engr. Boeing Co., Seattle, 1965-70; plant mgr. Western Kraft Corp., Portland, Oreg., 1970-78; gen. mgr. Spear & Jackson, Ltd., Eugene, Oreg., 1978-80; pres. J.V. Northwest, Inc., Portland, 1980—. Contbr. articles to mags. Republican. Mem. Christian Ch. (Disciples of Christ). Home: 17405 Wren Ct Lake Oswego OR 97034-6670 Office: JV Northwest Inc 28120 SW Boberg Rd Wilsonville OR 97070-9205

JONES, DONNA MARILYN, real estate broker, legislator; b. Brush, Colo., Jan. 14, 1939; d. Virgil Dale and Margaret Elizabeth (McDaniel) Wolfe; m. Donald Eugene Jones, June 9, 1956; children: Dawn Richter, Lisa Shira, Stuart. Student, Treasure Valley Community Coll., 1981-82; grad., Realtors Inst. Cert. residential specialist. Co-owner Parts, Inc., Payette, Idaho, 1967-79; dept. mgr., buyer Lloyd's Dept. Store, Payette, Idaho, 1979-80; sales assoc. Idaho-Oreg. Realty, Payette, Idaho, 1981-82; mem. dist. 13 Idaho Ho. of Reps., Boise, 1987-90, mem. dist. 10, 1990—; assoc. broker Classic Properties Inc., Payette, 1983-91; owner, broker ERA Preferred Properties Inc., 1991—. Co-chmn. Apple Blossom Parade, 1982; mem. Payette Civic League, 1968-84, pres. 1972; mem. Payette County Planning and Zoning Commn., 1985-88, vice-chmn. 1987; field coordinator Idaho Rep. Party Second Congl. Dist., 1986; mem. Payette County Rep. Cen. Com. 1978—; precinct II com. person, 1978-79, state committeewoman, 1980-84, chmn. 1984-87; outstanding county chmn. region III Idaho Rep. Party Regional Hall of Fame, 1985-86; mem. Payette County Rep. Women's Fedn., 1988—, bd. dirs., 1990-92; mem. Idaho Hispanic Commn., 1989-92, Idaho State Permanent Bldg. Adv. Coun., 1990—; bd. dirs. Payette Edn. Found., 1993—, Western Treasure Valley Cultural Ctr., 1993—; nat. bd. dirs. Am. Legis. Exchange Coun., 1993—; mem. legis. adv. coun. Idaho Housing Agy., 1992—; committeeperson Payette County Cen.; chmn. Ways and Means Idaho House of Reps., 1993—; Idaho chmn. Am. Legis. Exchange Coun., 1991—. Recipient White Rose award Idaho March of Dimes, 1988; named Payette/Washington County Realtor of Yr., 1987. Mem. Idaho Assn. Realtors (legis. com. 1984-87, chmn. 1986, realtors active in politics com. 1982—, polit. action com. 1986, polit. affairs com. 1986-88, chmn. 1987, bd. dirs. 1984-88), Payette/Washington County Bd. Realtors (v.p. 1981, state dir. 1984-88, bd. dirs 1983-88, sec. 1983), Bus. and Profl. Women (Woman of Progress award 1988, 90, treas. 1988), Payette C. of C., Fruitland C. of C., Wiesr C. of C.. Republican. Home: 1911 1st Ave S Payette ID 83661-3003 Office: ERA Preferred Properties 1610 6th Ave S Payette ID 83661-3348

JONES, DOUGLAS CLYDE, author; b. Winslow, Ark., Dec. 6, 1924; s. Marvin Clyde and Bethel Mae (Stockburger) J.; m. Mary Arnold, Jan. 1, 1949; children: Mary Glenn, Martha Claire, Kathryn Greer, Douglas Eben. B.A. in Journalism, U. Ark., 1949; M.S. in Mass Communications, U. Wis., Madison, 1962. Commd. U.S. Army, 1949, advanced through grades to lt. col., 1968; service in W. Ger. and Korea; chief armed forces news br. Dept. Def., 1966-68, ret., 1968; prof. U. Wis. Sch. Journalism, Madison, 1968-74. Painter of plains Indians, 1974-75; novelist, 1976—; author: Treaty of Medicine Lodge, 1966, Court Martial of G.A. Custer, 1976 (Spur award Western Writers Am. 1976), Arrest Sitting Bull, 1977, Creek Called Wounded Knee, 1978, Winding Stair, 1979, Elkhorn Tavern, 1980 (Friends of Am. Writers award 1980), Weedy Rough, 1981, The Barefoot Brigade, 1982, Season of Yellow Leaf, 1983, Gone the Dreams and Dancing, 1984 (Spur award Western Writers Am. 1985), Roman, 1986 (Spur award 1986); (short stories) Hickory Cured, 1987, Remember Santiago, 1988, Come Winter, 1989, The Search for Temperance Moon, 1991, This Savage Race, 1993. Served with U.S. Army, 1943-45, World War II, PTO. Decorated Commendation medal (3) Legion of Merit. Recipient Chancellor's award U. Wis., 1987, Owen Wister award for body of work Western Writers Am., 1993. Home: 1424 Harold St Fayetteville AR 72703-3823

JONES, DOUGLAS RAYMOND, farming executive, state legislator; b. Twin Falls, Idaho, Mar. 24, 1949; s. Leslie Raymond and Charlotte Baine (Miller) J.; m. Mary Elizabeth Morris, June 11, 1976; children: Jennifer, Heather, Douglas Jr. BS in Agr., U. Idaho, 1972. V.p. Leslie R. Jones, Inc., Twin Falls, 1972-86, pres., 1986—; rep. Idaho Ho. of Reps., Boise, 1985—; vice chmn. edn. com. Nat. Conf. of State Legislators, Washington, 1992-94. Mem. Gov.'s Task Force on Agr., Boise, 1979-08-; mem. exec. com. Agrl. Consulting Coun., U. Idaho, Moscow, 1984-94; pres. Twin Falls County Farm Bur., 1980-82; bd. dirs. young farmers Idaho Farm Bur., Boise, 1978-80; troop fin. chmn. Boy Scouts Am., Twin Falls, 1972-94; v.p. Twin Falls Zoning and Planning Bd., 1984-85. Recipient Golden Apple award Idaho Edn. Assn., 1988, Terry Reilly Dedication to Young Children with Disabilities award Assn. for Early Childhood Learning, 1989, Friends of Coops. award, Idaho Coop. Coun., 1992. Mem. Twin Falls C. of C. (chmn. agrl. com. 1982-85), Rotary (Blue Lakes chpt.), Alpha Zeta. Republican. Office: Leslie R Jones Inc 3653 Highway 93 Twin Falls ID 83301-0237

JONES, EBON RICHARD, retail executive; b. Oak Park, Ill., Aug. 23, 1944; s. Ebon Clark and Marilyn B. (Dow) J.; m. Sally Samuelson, Jan. 27, 1968; children: Stephanie Blythe, Heather Denise. B.A., Priceton U., 1966; M.B.A., Stanford U., 1968. Adminstrv. asst. Nat. Air Pollution Control Adminstrn., Washington, 1968-70; cons. McKinsey & Co., San Francisco and Paris, 1970-83; exec. v.p. Safeway Stores Inc., Oakland, Calif., 1983-86, group v.p., 1986-88, exec. v.p., 1988—. Bd. dirs. San Francisco Zool. Soc., 1979—, chmn. bd., 1979-85, pres., 1985-90, 94; mem. bd. govs. Uniform Code Coun., 1984-93; trustee Crystal Springs Uplands Sch., 1986-93. Mem. Phi Beta Kappa. Home: 58 Chester Way San Mateo CA 94402-1043 Office: Safeway Inc Supply Ops 2800 Ygnacio Valley Rd Walnut Creek CA 94598-3534

JONES, EDWARD LOUIS, historian, educator; b. Georgetown, Tex., Jan. 15, 1922; s. Henry Horace and Elizabeth (Steen) J.; m. Dorothy M. Showers, Mar. 1, 1952 (div. Sept. 1963); children: Cynthia, Frances, Edward Lawrence; Lynne Ann McGreevy, Oct. 7, 1963; children Christopher Louis, Teresa Lynne. BA in Philosophy, U. Wash., 1952, BA in Far East, 1952, BA in Speech, 1955, postgrad., 1952-54; JD, Gonzaga U., 1967. Social worker Los Angeles Pub. Assistance, 1956-57; producer, dir. Little Theatre, Hollywood, Calif. and Seattle, 1956-60; research analyst, cons. to Office of Atty. Gen., Olympia and Seattle, Wash., 1963-66; coordinator of counseling SOIC, Seattle, 1966-68; lectr., advisor, asst. to dean U. Wash., Seattle, 1968—; instr. Gonzaga U., Spokane, Wash., 1961-62, Seattle Community Coll., 1967-68; dir. drama workshop, Driftwood Players, Edmonds, Wash., 1975-76. Author: The Black Diaspora: Colonization of Colored People, 1988, Tutankhamon: Son of the Sun, King of Upper and Lower Egypt, 1978, Black Orators' Workbook, 1982, Black Zeus, 1972, Profiles in African Heritage, 1972, From Rulers of the World to Slavery, 1990, President Zachary Taylor and Senator Hamlin: Union or Death, 1991, Why Colored Americans Need an Abraham Lincoln in 1992, Forty Acres and a Mule: The Rape of Colored Americans, 1994; editor pub. NACADA Jour. Nat. Acad. Advising Assn., more. V.p. Wash. Com. on Consumer Interests, Seattle, 1966-68. Served to 2d lt. Fr. Army, 1940-45. Recipient Outstanding Teaching award U. Wash., 1986, Tyee Inst. Yr. U. Wash., 1987, appreciation award Office Minority Affairs, 1987, acad. excellence award Nat. Soc. Black Engrs., 1987, Appreciation award Fla. chpt. Nat. Bar Assn., 1990; Frederick Douglass scholar Nat. Coun. Black Studies, 1985, 86. Mem. Nat. Assn. Student Personnel Adminstrs., Smithsonian Inst. (assoc.), Am. Acad. Polit. and Social Sci., Nat. Acad. Advising Assn. (bd. dirs. 1979-82, Cert. of Appreciation 1982, editor Jour. 1981—, award for Excellence 1985), Western Polit. Sci. Assn. Democrat. Baptist. Office: U Wash Seattle WA 98195

JONES, GAIL KATHLEEN, educational administrator; b. Oklahoma City, June 28, 1935; d. Lloyd Clifton Jones and Cleo Kathleen (Shackelford) Ahlstedt; m. Jerry Lynn Jones, Aug. 8, 1954; children: Kathleen DeVaughan, Jerry Clifton, Gregory Taylor. BA in English, Cen. Wash. U., 1971. Coordinator outreach program Ellensburg City Library, Wash., 1971-77; dir. alumni affairs and community rels. Cen. Wash. U., Ellensburg, 1977-95, ret., 1995, now disting. emeriti adminstr.; Pub. newsletter Central Today, 1977—. Mem. Wash. Gov.'s com. for Handicapped, 1978-83; officer United Way Bd., Ellensburg, 1982-86; mem. Beautification Commn., Ellensburg, 1980-83, Distributive Edn. Adv. Council, Ellensburg, 1978-82, chair, Ctrl. Wash. U. Centennial, 1990-92. Mem. Council Advancement and Support Edn., AAUW, LWV, Ellensburg C. of C. Presbyterian. Lodge: Soroptimists (charter pres. Kittitas County (Wash.) club 1986-88, dist. dir. 1990-92). Home: 405 N Anderson St Ellensburg WA 98926-3145

JONES, GALEN RAY, physician assistant; b. Salt Lake City, Feb. 1, 1948; s. Leonard Ray and Veda (Whitehead) J.; m. Patricia Ann Poulson, Jan. 21, 1972; children: Brian, Marci, Natalie. Grad., Med. Field Svc. Sch. Ft. Sam Houston, San Antonio, 1971; BS, U. Utah, 1982. Missionary Ch. of Jesus Christ of Latter Day Saints, Alta., Sask., Can., 1967-69; asst. mgr. Cowan's Frostop Hamburger Stand, Salt Lake City, 1969-70; with Safeway Stores, Inc., Salt Lake City, 1970; o.r. tech. Latter Day Saint Hosp., Salt Lake City, 1973-75; physician asst. Lovell Clinic Inc., Lovell, Wyo., 1975-77, Family Health Care, Inc., Tooele, Utah, 1977-86, West Dermatology and Surgery Med. Grp., Redlands, Calif., 1986-95; maturation lectr. Tooele Sch. Dist., 1978-86; course dir., instr. EMT, North Big Horn Coutny Search and Rescue, 1976; instr. EMT, Grantsville Ambulance Inc., 1979-85; lectr. on skin care and changes to sr. citizen groups, hosp. auxs., health fairs, 1986—; high sch. sophomore sem. tchr. religion, 1991-95. Author: (with others) The P.A. Medical Handbook, 1995. Chmn. County Health Teen Pregnancy Prevention Project, Tooele, 1980-81; adv. bd. State Dept. Health-Rural Health Network, Salt Lake City, 1985-86; health lectr. County Health & Edn. Dept. Progs., Tooele, 1977-86; mormon bishop/pastor Lakeview Ward, Latter Day Saints Ch., Tooele, 1982-86; mem. Utah Acad. Physician Assts. (pres. 1980-81, editor newsletter 1979-80). With U.S. Army, 1971-73. U. Utah grantee, 1966, 67, 69. Fellow Am. Acad. Physician Assts., Calif. Acad. Physicians Assts. Republican. Mem. LDS Ch. Home: 101 Channing St Redlands CA 92373-4862

JONES, GARTH NELSON, public administration educator; b. Salt Lake City, Feb. 25, 1925; s. Harry H. and Sophronia Dubois (Nelson) J.; m. Verda Marie Clegg, Sept. 29, 1950; children: Edward Hood, Garth Kevin, Drew Luke. B.S., Utah State U., 1947; M.S., U. Utah, 1948, Ph.D., 1954. Mem. faculty Brigham Young U., Provo, Utah, 1953-56; with AID, Indonesia, 1957-61, Pakistan, 1967-69; mem. faculty U. So. Calif., 1961-67; sr. scholar East-West Center, Hawaii, 1969-70; mem. faculty Colo. State U., 1970-72; with UN, N.Y.C., 1972-73; mem. faculty U. Alaska, Anchorage, 1973—; former dean Sch. Bus. and Public Adminstrn. U. Alaska; vice chmn. Alaska Coun. Edn.; cons. to govt. and industry World Bank, UN Population Program, Ford Found. Rural Devel., U.S. Dept. State; mem. citizen's adv. bd. Bur. Land Mgmt., 1989-93; bd. dirs. Alaska World Affairs Coun.; mem. faculty U. Gadah Mada, Indonesia, U. Punjab, Pakistan, Nat. Chengci U., Taiwan. Mem. bd. editors profl. jours.; contbr. articles to profl. jours. Chmn. Anchorage Mayor's Ad Hoc Govtl. Rev. Commn., 1978, Anchorage Urban Obs.; Anchorage Mayor-elect's transition team, 1987. Fulbright-Hayes scholar, Taiwan, 1982-83. Mem. LDS Ch. Office: U Alaska 3221 Providence Dr Anchorage AK 99508-4614

JONES, GAYLE CLAUSSE, secretary; b. Ogden, Utah, June 22, 1947; d. Joseph James and Helen Jean (Blackinton) Clausse; m. Robert Scott Jones,

May 22, 1971 (div. Oct. 1979); 1 child, Marie Jones. BBA, Steven Henagers Bus. Coll., 1969; AS, Weber State U., 1991, BS, 1993. Sec. Ogden Iron Works, 1970-75, Weber County Sch. Dist., 1977—. Chorister Daus. of Utah Pioneers; mem. Utah Hist. Soc., Weber County Hist. Soc. Mem. LDS Ch.

JONES, GERRE LYLE, marketing and public relations consultant; b. Kansas City, Mo., June 22, 1926; s. Eugene Riley and Carolyn (Newell) J.; m. Charlotte Mae Reinhold, Oct. 30, 1948; children: Beverly Anne Jones Putnam, Wendy S. Jones Stout. BJ, U. Mo., 1948, postgrad., 1953-54. Exec. sec. Effingham (Ill.) C. of C., 1948-50; field rep. Nat. Found. Infantile Paralysis, N.Y.C., 1950-57; dir. pub. relations Inst. Logopedics, Wichita, Kans., 1957-58; owner Gerre Jones & Assocs., Pub. Relations, Kansas City, Mo., 1958-63; info. officer Radio Free Europe Fund, Munich, Federal Republic of Germany, 1963-65, spl. asst. to dir. pub. relations, 1965-66; exec. asst. pub. affairs Edward Durell Stone, 1967-68; dir. mktg. and communications Vincent G. Kling & Ptnrs., Phila., 1969-71; mktg. cons. Ellerbe Architects, Washington, 1972; v.p. Gaio Assocs., Ltd., Washington, 1972-73, exec. v.p., 1973-76; exec. v.p. Bldg. Industry Devel. Services, Washington, 1973-76; pres. Gerre Jones Assocs. Inc., Albuquerque, 1976-89, ret., 1989; sr. v.p. Barlow Assocs., Inc., Washington, 1977-78; lectr. numerous colls. and univs. Author: How to Market Professional Design Services, 1973, 2d edit., 1983, How to Prepare Professional Design Brochures, 1976, (with Stuart H. Rose) How to Find and Win New Business, 1976, Public Relations for the Design Professional, 1980; contbr. articles to profl. jours. Served with USAAF, 1944-45, maj. USAF (ret.). Mem. Internat. Radio and TV Soc., Nat. Assn. Sci. Writers, AIA (hon.), Sigma Delta Chi, Alpha Delta Sigma, Phi Delta Phi, Overseas Press Club, Masons. Republican.

JONES, GLENN ROBERT, cable systems executive; b. Jackson Center, Pa., Mar. 2, 1930. BS in Econs., Allegheny Coll.; JD, U. Colo.; diploma exec. program, Stanford U.; LHD (hon.), Allegheny Coll. Author: (poetry) Briefcase Poetry of Yankee Jones, vol. I, 1978, vol. II, 1981, vol. III, 1985, Jones: Dictionary of Cable Television Terminology, 1973, 2d edit., 1976, 3d edit., 1987. Mem. World Future Soc., Nat. Cable TV Assn. Office: Jones Intercabel Inc 9697 E Mineral Ave Englewood CO 80112-3408

JONES, GRANT RICHARD, landscape architect, planner; b. Seattle, Aug. 29, 1938; s. Victor Noble and Iona Bell (Thomas) J.; m. Ilze Grinbergs, 1965 (div. 1983); 1 child, Kaija. Student, Colo. Coll., 1956-58; B.Arch., U. Wash., 1962; M.Landscape Architecture, Harvard U., 1966, postgrad. (Frederick Sheldon fellow), 1967-68. Draftsman Jones Lovegren Helms & Jones, Seattle, 1958-59; assoc. Richard Haag Assocs., Seattle, 1961-65; research asso. landscape architecture research office Harvard U., 1966-67; land planner Eckbo Dean Austin & Williams, Honolulu, 1968-69; prin. Jones & Jones, Seattle, 1969—; lectr. in field. chmn. landscape archtl. registration bd., State of Wash., 1974-79; mem. council Harvard U. Grad. Sch. Design, 1978-82, 91-96, vis. com. Harvard U. Grad. Sch. , 1993-96, U. Wash. Coll Arch., 1990—, mem. bd. Scenic Am. 1994—, Waterfront Ctr. 1990—. Author: The Nooksack Plan: An Approach to the Investigation and Evaluation of a River System, 1973, (with B. Gray and J. Burnham) A Method for the Quantification of Aesthetic Values for Environmental Decision Making, 1975, Design as Ecogram, 1975, (with J. Coe and D. Paulson) Woodland Park Zoo: Long Range Plan, Development Guidelines and Exhibit Scenarios, 1976, Landscape Assessment. . .Where Logic and Feelings Meet, 1978; major landscape archtl. and planning works include Nooksack River Plan, Bellingham, Wash.; Yakima River Regional Greenway, Yakima, Wash., Union Bay Teaching and Research Arboretum, U. Wash., Seattle, Newhalem Campground, North Cascades Nat. Park, Woodland Park Zool. Gardens, Seattle, Washington Park Arboretum, U. Wash., Seattle, zoo master plans for Kansas City, Roanoke, Va., Detroit and Honolulu, Dallas Arboretum and Bot. Garden, Wash. State Capitol lake plan, Toledo Zoo African Savannah Complex. Recipient nat. award Am. Assn. Zoos and Pub. Aquaria, 1981, 82, 83, 84. Fellow Am. Soc. Landscape Architects (chmn. Wash. chpt. 1972-73, trustee 1979—, v.p., 1988-90, Merit award in community design 1972, Honor award in regional planning 1974, Merit award in regional planning 1977, Merit award in park planning 1977, Merit award in instnl. planning 1977, Pres.'s award of excellence 1980, merit award in landscape planning 1982, 84, 86)Nature Conservancy, Am. Hort. Soc., Am. Assn. Bot. Gardens and Arboreta, Wash. Environ. Council, Phi Gamma Delta. Office: Jones & Jones 105 S Main St Seattle WA 98104-2535

JONES, J. GILBERT, research consultant; b. San Francisco, June 1, 1922; s. Enoch Roscoe L. Sr. and Remedios (Ponce de Leon) J.; student U.S. Mcht. Marine Acad., 1942-44, San Francisco City Coll., 1942-44, 46-47; AB, U. Calif., Berkeley, 1949, MA, 1952. Lic. pvt. investigator. Ins. insp. Ins. Cos. Insp. Bur., San Francisco, 1959-62; pub. rels. cons., San Francisco, 1962-67; ins. insp. Am. Svc. Bur., San Francisco, 1967-72; propr., mgr. Dawn Universal Internat. San Francisco, 1972—, Dawn Universal Security Svc., San Francisco, 1983—. Mem. SAR, Sons. Spanish-Am. War Vets. Soc., World Affairs Coun. N. Calif., U. Calif. Alumni Assn., Commonwealth Club of Calif. Republican. Office: PO Box 424057 San Francisco CA 94142-4057

JONES, JAMES DAVID, health care executive; b. Harrison, Ark., Jan. 14, 1948; s. James Andrew and Thelma (Rogers) J.; m. Judith Ann Salzman, Feb. 10, 1968 (div. Apr. 1983); 1 child, Kirk Anthony; m. Cherryl Lynn Walker, Mar. 3, 1984; 1 child, Callie Ann. BBA, Nat. U., 1985. Pro. lt. USCG, 1977, retired, 1987; exec. dir. Big Valley Med. Ctr., Bieber, Calif., 1987—; instr. Lassen C.C., Susanville, Calif., 1990—; mem. exec. com. primary care clinics adv. com. State of Calif., Sacramento, 1988-91; pres. Associated Calif. Health Ctrs. Benefit Trust, Sacramento, 1989-92. Treas. Big Valley Sports Assn., 1992—; sports announcer Big Valley High Sch., 1990—. Named Honorary Okie Gov. Okla., Oklahoma City, 1978. Mem. Nat. Rural Health Assn., Calif. Primary Care Assn., Bieber C. of C., Fall River Golf & Country Club. Republican. Office: Big Valley Med Ctr 554-850 Med Ctr Dr Bieber CA 96009

JONES, JAMES HENRY, physiology educator, researcher; b. Phoenix, Oct. 23, 1952; s. Loyal Herbert and Marjorie Lois (McHenry) J.; m. Kim Elizabeth Longworth, Sept. 22, 1990. BS, BA, U. Ariz., 1974, MS, 1976; PhD, Duke U., 1979; DVM, Colo. State U., 1983. Park ranger, naturalist U.S. Natural Park Svc., Yellowstone Nat. Park, 1973-76, Glacier Nat. Park, 1981-82; sr. rsch. officer U. Cape Town, South Africa, 1980; biology lectr. Dept. Organismic and Evolutionary Biology Harvard U., Cambridge, Mass., 1983-86; asst. assoc. prof. Sch. Vet. Medicine U. Calif., Davis, 1986—, chair physiology grad. group, 1992—, chair animal use and care com., 1993—; vis. prof. anatomy U. Berne, Switzerland, 1986; vis. prof. physiology U. São Paulo, 1990. Author, editor: Comparative Vertebrate Exercise Physiology, Vols. A and B, 1994; contbr. articles to profl. jours. With USN, 1970-72. Grantee NIH, 1987, NASA, 1989, Am. Heart Assn., 1992. Mem. Am. Physiol. Soc. (Scholander award 1986), Am. Soc. Zoologists. Office: U Calif Dept Surg and Radiol Scis Sch Vet Medicine Davis CA 95616

JONES, JAN LAVERTY, mayor. Grad. Stanford Univ. Mayor, City of Las Vegas. Office: Office of Mayor City Hall 10th Fl 400 Stewart Ave Las Vegas NV 89101-2942

JONES, JANET DULIN, writer, film producer; b. Hollywood, Calif., Sept. 6, 1957; d. John Dulin and Helen Mae (Weaver) J. BA, Calif. State U., Long Beach, 1980. Developer mini-series and TV series Embassy Communications, Los Angeles, 1981-84; assoc. to producer Hotel Aaron Spelling Prodns., Los Angeles, 1984-85; writing intern Sundance Film Inst., Los Angeles, 1985; feature film story analyst Carson Prodns., Los Angeles, 1985-86; freelance screenplay and play writer Los Angeles and N.Y.C., 1986—. Author (screenplays) Fade Away, 1986, Alone in the Crowd, 1987, Story of the Century, 1988, The Long Way Home, 1989, (play) Cousin Judy, 1989, The Set-Up, 1990, Roommates, 1991, Local Girl, 1991, Dickens and Crime, 1992, (books) Little Bear Books, Vols. 1-5, A Weighty, Waity Matter—My Adventures with India, 1992, Coming and Going,. 1993, Watching the Detectives, 1994, The Ambassadors, 1994. Bd. dirs. Sterling Cir. of Aviva Ctr. for Girls, 1990; bd. dirs., recording sec., steering com. The Creative Coalition, 1991-92. Mem. ACLU, Earth Communication Office (TV and film coms.), Writers Guild Am., Ind. Feature Project, Am. Film Inst., Sundance Film Inst. (pre-selection com. 1985-87), People for Am. Way, Habitat for Humanity, Amnesty Internat., Delta Gamma.

JONES, JEANNE RAE, art director; b. Washington, June 25, 1948; d. Richard Carlyle and Eleanor Mary (Raia) J. BA in Art, Calif. State U., Northridge, 1973. Assoc. editor TL Enterprises, Inc., Agoura, Calif., 1983-90; asst. art dir. TL Enterprises, Inc., Agoura, 1986-90; art dir. TL Enterprises, Inc., Camarillo, Calif., 1990—; illustrator Trailer Life, Agoura, 1987-94; designer Vineyard Christian Fellowship, Thousand Oaks, Calif., 1993-94. Scholar Chinard Art Inst., 1963. Mem. Nat. Geographic Soc., Sierra Club, Amnesty Internat., Calif. State U. Northridge Alumni Assn., Conejo Valley Mac User Group. Republican. Office: TL Enterprises Inc 3601 Calle Tecate Camarillo CA 93012

JONES, JEFFREY DEAN, interior designer; b. L.A., May 12, 1960; s. Philip Brent and Karin Myrial (Kavelin) J.; m. Sharon Kay Wanerus, Feb. 29, 1992; 1 child, Casey Matthew. BFA with honors, Chapman U., 1992. Cert. interior designer, Calif. Pres. Brentwood Contract Interiors, Palm Desert, Calif., 1994—. Contbr.: The Desert Sun, 1994. Recipient Cert. Merit Lightolier, 1988. Mem. AIA (affiliate), Am. Soc. Interior Designers (exec. bd. 1991, Presdl. Citation 1992), Internat. soc. Interior Designers (profl. mem.), Internat. Soc. Lighting Designers (assoc.); media spokesperson for Calif. Coun. for Interior Design Cert.

JONES, JERVE MALDWYN, construction company executive; b. Los Angeles, Sept. 21, 1918; s. Oliver Cromwell and Zola (Hill) J.; m. Alice Castle Holcomb, Apr. 12, 1942; children—Jay Gregory, Janey Lee Matt, Joel Kevin. B.S. in Civil Engring., U. So. Calif., 1939. Registered profl. engr., Calif. Stress analyst Northrop Aircraft, L.A., 1940-43; ptnr. Jones Bros. Constrn. Co., Beverly Hills, Calif., 1946-56; pres., chief exec. officer Peck/Jones Constrn. Corp. (formerly Jones Bros. Constrn. Co.), Beverly Hills, Calif., 1956—, cons. Jerve M. Jones Assocs., Beverly Hills, 1970—; chmn. Jones Constrn. Mgmt., Beverly Hills, 1983—. Bd. dirs. Huntington Library, San Marino, Calif., 1984—, Pepperdine U., Malibu, Calif., Boy Scouts Am., L.A., Santa Monica Hosp. Found., YMCA Met. L.A.; chmn. L.A. Music Ctr., United Fund Campaign; life mem. Town Hall Calif., L.A., adv. bd. UCLA Med. Ctr.; mem. State Calif. Strong Motion Instrumentation Program, Dept. Mines and Geology. With USNR, 1943-46, PTO. Recipient Civil Engring. Alumnus of Yr. award U. So. Calif., 1985, Bronze Hat award United Contractors Assn., 1985, Disting. Scout award, 1989. Mem. Constrn. Mgmt. Assn. Am. (nat. pres. 1984, Founders award 1985), Archtl. Guild, Archimedes Circle, Constrn. Industry Commn. (chmn. 1980-84), Assoc. Gen. Contractors Am., Los Angeles Area C. of C. (dir.). Republican. Episcopalian. Clubs: Los Angeles Country, California. Lodge: Rotary (dir. 1962-68). Office: Peck/Jones Constrn Corp 10866 Wilshire Blvd Fl 7 Los Angeles CA 90024-4300

JONES, JOANNA PATRICIA, education educator, college official, consultant; b. Chgo., Dec. 23, 1935; d. John Edward Payne and O'Deal Pauline (Dammann) Fear; m. Leon Koenen (div.); 1 child, Diana Suzanne; m. Paul Jones, Nov. 19, 1972; children: Glenn, Randy, Bonnie, Paula. BA, Colgate U., 1958; BS, Pacific Oaks Coll., 1959, MA, 1971; MA, Claremont Grad. Sch., 1969, PhD, 1981. Mem. staff, tchr. Pacific Oaks Coll., Pasadena, Calif., 1959-71; dir. edn. Orange County Head Start, Orange, Santa Ana, Calif., 1965-71; instr. Mt. Sac Coll., Walnut, Calif., 1966-70, 89—; prof. Chaffey Coll., Rancho Cucamonga, Calif., 1971-94; mem. edn. staff Claremont (Calif.) Grad. Sch., 1972-74; trainer child devel. assoc. Los Angeles County Head Start, 1980-85; instr. Fontera (Calif.) Woman's Prison, 1985-88; staff devel. mgr. Chaffey Coll., Rancho Cucamonga, Calif., 1994—; cons. on child devel.; cons. Far West Lab for Edn. Rsch., San Francisco, 1965-71. Contbr. articles to profl. jours.; presenter in field, Taiwan, Japan, Australia. Co-founder Prevention of Child Abuse, Pomona, Calif., 1983; chair Cultural Arts Com., Pomona, 1988—. Mem. Assn. for Childhood Edn. Internat., Nat. Assn. Edn. Young Children, Internat. Play Assn., UCLA Alumni Assn., Pi Lambda Theta. Home: 1295 Loma Vista St Pomona CA 91768-1437 Office: Faculty Senate Chaffey Coll 5885 Haven Ave Rancho Cucamonga CA 91737-3002

JONES, JOE W., educational research laboratory executive; b. 1932. BS, Stanford U., 1954, MS, 1958. With Arthur Andersen & Co., Seattle, 1958-71; dir. fin. Northwest Regional Ednl. Lab., Portland, Oreg., 1972—. Office: Northwest Regional Ednl Lab 101 SW Main St Ste 500 Portland OR 97204*

JONES, JOEL MACKEY, educational administrator; b. Millersburg, Ohio, Aug. 11, 1937; s. Theodore R. and Edna Mae (Mackey) Jones; children: Carolyn Mae, Jocelyn Corinne. BA, Yale U., 1960; MA, Miami U., Oxford, Ohio, 1962; PhD, U. N.Mex., 1966. Dir. Am. studies U. Md., Balt., 1966-69; chmn. Am. studies U. N.Mex., Albuquerque, 1969-73, asst. v.p. acad. affairs, 1973-77, dean faculties, assoc. provost, prof. Am. studies, 1977-85, v.p. adminstrn., 1985-88; pres. Ft. Lewis Coll., Durango, Colo., 1988—. Contbr. numerous essays, articles and chpts. to books. Founder Rio Grande Nature Preserve Soc., Albuquerque, 1974—; bd. dirs., mem. exec. com., United Way, Albuquerque, 1980-83; nat. bd. cons. NEH, 1978—; bd. dirs. Mercy Hosp., 1990-94, 1st Nat. Bank; mem. ACE Commn. on Leadership. Farwell scholar Yale U., New Haven, 1960; Sr. fellow NEH, 1972, Adminstrv. fellow Am. Coun. Edn., Washington, 1972-73. Mem. Am. Studies Assn., Am. Assn. Higher Edn., Am. Assn. State Colls. and Univs. (chair com. on cultural diversity, Colo. state rep., 1994—). Home: 35 Lewis Mountain Ln Durango CO 81301-6531 Office: Ft Lewis Coll Office of Pres Durango CO 81301-3999*

JONES, JOHN HARDING, photographer; b. Pitts., Apr. 28, 1923; s. John F. and Emma E. (West) J.; m. Shirley M.; children: Blair H., Dawn M. Merewood. BA, Rochester Inst. Tech., 1949; MBA, Pepperdine U., 1978; PhD, London U., 1983; PhD in Edn., St. John's U., 1976. Chief photographer U.S. Steel Corp., Pitts.; mgr. art & photo dept. Magnavox Corp., Urbana, Ill.; chief photographer rehab. medicine sect. U.S. Vet. Adminstrn., L.A.; coord. rehab. medicine domiciliary sect. Wadsworth VA Hosp., L.A.; tchr. Carnegie Mellon Inst., Pitts., Earl Wheeler Schs., Pitts., Seattle U., Art Inst. Pitts.; dir., owner The Little Studio, Panorama City, Calif., 1989—, The Little Studio West, Panorama City, 1994—. Author: Photography, 1972, The Correspondence Educational Directory, 1976, 79, 84, 94, Correspondence Courses for High School Credit & GED Preparation, 1994. Comdr. USNR, ret. Mem. Profl. Photographers Am., Masons, Shriners, Order of the Eastern Star. Presbyn. Home and Office: 8774 Tyrone Ave Panorama City CA 91402-2539

JONES, JOHN WESLEY, entrepreneur; b. Wenatchee, Wash., Nov. 15, 1942; s. Richard F. and Hazel F. (Hendrix) J.; m. Melissa L. Meyer, June 22, 1968 (div. 1982); children: John E., Jennifer L.; m. Deborah G. Matthews, Apr. 24, 1993. BA in Bus./Econs., Western Wash. U., Bellingham, 1966. Trainee Jones Bldg., Seattle, 1967-69; mgr. Jones Bldg., 1969-78; owner/mgr. N.W. Inboards, Bellevue, Wash., 1974-78, Jones Bldg., Seattle, 1978-86; pvt. investor Bellevue, 1987—; owner/mgr. J. Jones Enterprises, 1994—; trustee BOMA Health & Welfare Trust, 1982-86, chmn. 1986; mem. Seattle Fire Code Adv. Bd., 1979-86. With USMCR, 1966-72. Mem. Seattle Bldg. Owners and Mgrs. Assn. (trustee 1979-86), Bldg. Owners & Mgrs. Internat., N.W. Marine Trade Assn., Am. Assn. Individual Investors, Seattle Yacht Club, NRA, Internat. Show Car Assn., Nat. Street Rod Assn. Republican. Home: 61 Skagit Key Bellevue WA 98006-1021 Office: 12819 SE 38th St # 288 Bellevue WA 98006-1326

JONES, JOHNPAUL, architect. BArch, U. Oreg., 1967. Registered architect, Wash., Calif., Oreg., Idaho, Hawaii, Ariz., N.Mex., Fla.; nat. cert. architect, NCARB. With Paul Thiry, Architect, Seattle, Oda/McCarty Architects, Hilo, Hawaii; sr. prin. Jones & Jones, Architects and Landscape Architects, Seattle, 1972—; lectr. in field. Prin. works include Cedar River Visitor Facility, Seattle, Dea'ht Tribal Elders Ctr., Neah Bay, Wash., Edn. Pavilion and Children's Zoo, Honolulu, Longhouse Cultural Edn. Ctr., Olympia, Washington, Mercer Slough Nature Ctr., Bellevue, Wash., Overlake Blueberry Farm, Bellevue, Seattle Children's Mus., Stimson Green Hist. Gardens, Seattle, Ctr. Urban Horticulture Bldgs. and Douglas Rsch. Conservatory U. Wash., Seattle, rsch. lab. and support greenhouses U. Alaska, Fairbanks, Tilikum Pl. Urban Pub. Sq., Seattle, Eagle Island State Pk. Bldgs., Boise, Idaho, Gene Coulon Meml. Beach Pk. Bldgs., Renton, Washington (Honor award AIA 1982, 1st Honor award Am. Steel Assn. 1982, Excellence on the Water Honor award Waterfront Ctr. 1987, The Inhabited Landscape award Archtl. League N.Y. Exhbn. 1987), Newcastle Beach Pk. Bldgs., Bellevue (Merit award AIA 1988, Best Design of 1988 Times Mag., Excellence on the Water Honor award Waterfront Ctr. 1988, Honor award regional AIA 1990), Newhalem ranger sta. and campground bldg. North Cascades Nat. Pk., Washington (1st Honor award Am. Wood Coun. 1981), Nat. Pk. Svc. Skagway (Alaska) Maintenance Facility, Hertz Administrn. Maintenance and Regional Facility, SeaTac Airport, Washington, others, (landscape designs) Zool. Soc. San Diego, Woodland Pk. Zoo and Zool. Gardens (Pres.'s Award of Excellence Am. Soc. Landscape Architects 1980), Seattle, City of Honolulu Dept. Pks. and Recreation, N.Mex. State Pks., Carlsbad, Dallas Zoo, Point Defiance Zoo & Aquarium (Merit award Wash. chpt. Am. Soc. Landscape Architects 1981), Tacoma, Ariz.-Sonora Desert Mus., Tucson, San Diego Zoo (Best Exhibit award Am. Assn. Zool. Pks. & Aquariums 1989), others, (historic preservation) Icicle Canyon Arts Ctr., Leavenworth, Washington, Icicle Canyon Guest Lodges, Klondike Goldrush Nat. Hist. Pk. Maintenance Facility, Skagway. Chmn. Pioneer Sq. Hist. Preservation Bd., Seattle; former bd. dirs. King County United Way. Fellow AIA (mem. Seattle chpt.); mem. Nat. Assn. Indian Architects & Engrs. Office: Jones & Jones 105 S Main St Seattle WA 98104-2535

JONES, JORDAN DOUGLAS, writer, publisher; b. Van Nuys, Calif., Nov. 10, 1963; s. Carl Lawrence and Alice May (Hill) J. BA (hons.) in Eng., Calif. State U., Northridge, 1987; diploma, L'Universite Catholique, Angers, France, 1989; MA in Eng., U. Calif., Davis, 1991. Tech. writer Teradyne, Inc., Agouna Hills, Calif., 1989-93, MICOM Communications Corp., Simi Valley, Calif., 1993—; mem. grad. studies com. Eng. dept. U. Calif., Davis, 1990-91, speakers com., 1990-91, creative writing com., 1990-91. Author: Sand and Coal: Poems, 1993; co-editor Northridge Review, 1987, poetry editor: California Quarterly, 1989-91; editor, publisher Bakunin, 1990 [illegible] Com. mem. Citizens Helping Pielaet, Simi Valley, 1982; founding mem. Students Against Apartheid, Northridge, Calif., 1986-87. Recipient Merit award Soc. Tech. Communication, 1992. Mem. Soc. Tech. Communications, Coun. Literacy Mags. and Presses, COSMEP: The Internat. Assn. Small Press Publishers, Sigma Tau Delta (charter). Office: Bakunin PO Box 1853 Simi Valley CA 93062-1853

JONES, LEONARD DALE, facilities engineer; b. Cheyenne, Wyo., Feb. 21, 1948; s. Clifford Dale and Mary Mauverine (Hardin) J.; m. Sheila Rae Lansberry, Aug. 14, 1971; children: Shannon Marie, Meghan Anne. BS, Colo. Sch. of Mines, 1971; MBA, Nova U., 1985. Registered profl. engr., Va., Colo. Powerhouse engr. Stauffer Chem. Co., Green River, Wyo., 1978-81, plant svcs. supt., 1981-85; supr. customer svc. engr. Wis. Natural Gas Co., Racine, 1985-87; facilities mgr. Nat. Renewable Energy Lab., Golden, Colo., 1987—; cons. engr. LSJ Assocs., Littleton, Colo., 1991—; adj. instr. Gateway Tech. Inst., Kenosha, 1986. Conty del. Wyo. Rep. Conv., Jackson, 1984; precinct chair Sweetwater County Rep. Party, Green River, 1983-85; mem. Deer Creek Housing task force, Jefferson County Sch. Dist., Littleton, 1988; chmn., mem. Parks and Recreation Bd., Green River, 1980-84; ruling elder Genesis Presbyn. Ch., Littleton, 1990—; mem. ch. extension com. Presytery of Denver, 1989-92. Recipient Pres. award for Exceptional Performance Midwest Rsch. Inst., 1990. Mem. Assn. of Energy Engrs., Masons, Lakewood Foothills Rotary Club, Cheyenne Consistory, AASR. Home: 28 Mesa Oak Littleton CO 80127-3555 Office: Nat Renewable Energy Lab 1617 Cole Blvd Golden CO 80401

JONES, LILLIE AGNES, retired elementary education educator; b. Leroy, Iowa, Nov. 25, 1910; d. Oraz Wesley and Lorena Floy (Buffum) Davis; m. John Hammond Jones, May 27, 1938 (dec. Aug. 1994); children: John Harry, Mary Agnes Jones Edwards. BA, Colo. State Coll. Edn., 1937. Cert. elem. tchr., Colo. Elem. tchr. Weld County Sch. Dist. 8l, Kersey, Colo., 1930-34, Weld County Sch. Dist. 12l, Erie, Colo., 1934-38, Longmont (Colo.) Pub. Schs., 1955-59, Adams County Sch. Dist. 12, Thornton, Colo., 1959-67, Littleton (Colo.) Pub. Schs., 1967-69; Farmington (N.Mex.) Pub. Schs., 1969-76, ret., 1976; cataloger Longmont Pub. Libr., 1953-55. Kersey High Sch. scholar, 1928. Mem. AAUW (life, past treas. Longmont), Nat. Ret. Tchrs. Assn., N.Mex. Ret. Tchrs. Assn. (life), Pub. Employees Retirement Assn., Colo. Ret. Sch. Employees Assn., Alpha Delta Kappa (rec. sec. Farmington 1975-76, sec. Sun City, Ariz. 1980, historian 1982). Democrat. Home: Sun Grove Resort Village 10134 W Mohawk Ln Apt 1017 Peoria AZ 85382-2251

JONES, LOUISA ELSA, medical association executive; b. Watertown, N.Y., Nov. 18, 1940; d. Emlen Howell and Elsa (Singer) J. BS, Fordham U., 1962. Programmer Dillon Read & Co., N.Y.C., 1965-67; editor research publs. dept. anesthesiology U. Wash., Seattle, 1968-82; exec. officer Internat. Assn. for the Study of Pain, Seattle, 1978—. Recipient La Médaille de la Ville de Paris, 1993. Mem. Am. Soc. Assn. Execs., Am. Pain Soc., Can. Pain Soc. Democrat. Roman Catholic. Office: Internat Assn for Study of Pain 909 NE 43d St Ste 306 Seattle WA 98105

JONES, MARK ALAN, broadcast technician; b. San Francisco, 1957; m. Stephanie Phillips, 1983. BA in Communication Studies, Calif. State U., 1979. Chief operator Sta. KXPR, Sacramento, 1979-80, with ops./prodn.dept., 1980-95. Recipient pub. radio program award for Excellence, Corp. Pub. Broadcasting, 1981. Office: Stas KXPR/KXJZ Inc 3416 American River Dr Ste B Sacramento CA 95864-5715

JONES, MARK LOGAN, educational association executive, educator; b. Provo, Utah, Dec. 16, 1950; s. Edward Evans and Doris (Logan) J. BS, Ea. Mont. Coll., 1975; postgrad. in labor rels., Cornell U.; postgrad., SUNY, Buffalo. Narcotics detective Yellowstone County Sheriff's Dept., Billings, Mont., 1972-74; math tchr. Billings (Mont.) Pub. Schs., 1975-87; rep. Nat. Edn. Assn. of N.Y., Buffalo, Jamestown, 1987-91, Nat. Edn. Assn. Alaska, Anchorage, 1991—. Photographs featured in 1991 N.Y. Art Rev. and Am. Artist. Committeeman Yellowstone Dem. Party, Billings, 1984-87; exec. com. Dem. Cen. Com., Billings, 1985-87; bd. dirs. Billings Community Ctr., 1975-87; concert chmn. Billings Community Concert Assn., 1980-87; bd. dirs. Chautauqua County Arts Coun.; bd. dirs. Big Brothers and Big Sisters Anchorage. With U.S. Army, 1970-72. Recipient Distinguished Svc. award, Billings Edn. Assn., 1985, Mont. Edn. Assn., 1987. Mem. Billings Edn. Assn. (bd. dirs. 1980-82, negotiator 1981-87, pres. 1982-87), Mont. Edn. Assn. (bd. dirs. 1982-87), Ea. Mont. Coll. Tchr. Edn. Project, Accreditation Reviewer Team Mont. Office Pub. Edn., Big Sky Orchard, Masonic, Scottish Rite. Home: PO Box 102904 Anchorage AK 99510-2904

JONES, NANCY LANGDON, financial planner, investment advisor; b. Chgo., Mar. 24, 1939; d. Lewis Valentine and Margaret (Seese) Russell; m. Lawrence Elmer Langdon, June 30, 1962 (div. 1970); children: Laura Kimberley, Elizabeth Ann; m. Claude Earl Jones, Jan. 1, 1973. BA, U. Redlands, Calif., 1962; MS, Coll. for Fin. Planning, 1991. CFP; registered investment advisor; accredited tax advisor. Bookkeeper Russell Sales Co., Santa Fe Springs, Calif., 1962-70; office mgr. Reardon, McCallum & Co., Upland, Calif., 1970-77; broker, assoc. ERA Property Ctr., Upland, 1977-84; registered rep. Fin. Network Investment Corp., Pasadena, Calif., 1984-92; pvt. practice fin. planning Upland, 1984—; ptnr. Jones, Graham & Assocs., Registered Investment Advisors, Upland, Calif., 1994; adj. faculty Coll. Fin. Planning, Denver, 1986-94; mem. nat. comprehensive exam. question writing com. CFP Bd. Stds., 1994-95; del. U.S. fin. and investment leaders study mission to the People's Rep. of China and Hong Kong, 1993. Leader Spanish Trails coun. Girl Scouts U.S., 1974-81; mem. exec. com. Corp. 2000 Coun., San Antonio Cmty. Hosp. Recipient Hon. Svc. award Valencia Elem. Sch., 1978. Mem. SAG, Inland Soc. of Tax Cons., Estate Planning Coun., Internat. Assn. Fin. Planners (pres. San Gabriel Valley chpt. 1987-88, mem. exec. bd. So. Calif. conf. 1992—), Am. Bus. Women's Assn. (pres. Upland chpt. 1989-90, gen. chmn. 1995 Pacific Spring conf., Woman of Yr. award 1988), Inst. CFPs San Gabriel Valley Soc. (pres. 1992-93, chmn. 1993-94, bd. dirs. 1990—), Nat. Coun. Exchangers (sec. 1986-87), Inland Soc. Tax Cons., Estate Planning Coun. Pomona Valley (bd. dirs. 1995—), Women's Bus. Network (pres. 1987-88), Registry of Fin. Planning Practitioners, Inland Valley Profl. Aux. (charter, bd. dirs. 1991-92), Assistance League of Upland, Upland C. of C. Home and Office: 2485 Mesa Ter Upland CA 91784-1078

JONES, NATHANIEL, bishop. Bishop Ch. of God in Christ, Barstow, Calif. Office: Ch of God in Christ 630 Chateau Way Barstow CA 92311-5721

JONES, NEIL FORD, surgeon; b. Merthyr Tydvil, Wales, England, Nov. 30, 1947; s. John Robert and Kathleen Mary (Ford) J.; m. Barbara Rose

Unterman, Feb. 18, 1978; 1 child, Nicholas Huw. B of Medicine, B of Surgery, MA, Oxford (Eng.) U., 1975. Registrar N.E. Thames Regional Plastic Surgery Centre, Billericay, Eng., 1982; fellow in hand microsurgery Mass. Gen. Hosp. Harvard U., Boston, 1983; asst. prof. surgery U. Pitts., 1984-89, assoc. prof. surgery, 1989-93, dir. fellowship tng. in hand and microsurgery, 1987-93; prof., chief of hand surgery UCLA Med. Ctr. dept. orthopedic surgery divsn. plastic and reconstructive surgery, 1993—. Contbr. articles to profl. jours. Fellow Royal Coll. Surgeons Eng., Am. Coll. Surgeons; mem. Am. Soc. Plastic and Reconstructive Surgeons, Am. Soc. Surgery of the Hand, Am. Soc. Reconstructive Microsurgery, Internat. Soc. Reconstructive Microsurgery. Home: 532 N Bonhill Rd Los Angeles CA 90049-2326 Office: UCLA Med Ctr 200 UCLA Med Plz # 140 Los Angeles CA 90055

JONES, PENN HOLTER, advertising executive; b. Dallas, Dec. 18, 1961; s. Gordon Lee Jr. and Marilyn Christine (Holter) J.; m. Erin Gail Dettling, May 30, 1987; 1 child, Hayley McConnell. Student, U. So. Calif., 1979-84. Press box intern L.A. Express/U.S. Football League, 1983; mid-day news intern KTTV, Hollywood, Calif., 1983; intern L.A. (Calif.) Dodgers, 1984, asst. pub. rels. staff, 1984-86; affiliate rels. mgr. Harmon Cove Prodns./Dodgervision, Hollywood, 1986-87; account exec. Popular Mechanics/Hearst Corp., Santa Monica, Calif., 1987-88; account exec. Cosmopolitan/Hearst Corp., Santa Monica, 1988-89, L.A. mgr., 1989-90, west coast mgr., 1990-94; west coast advt. dir. Time/In Style, L.A., 1994—. Bd. dirs. U. So. Calif. Cardinal & Gold, life mem. Mem. Jr. C. of C. (dir. L.A. open, traffic control 1988-90, Best Performance award 1989), Sigma Alpha Epsilon (pres., Order of Phoenix award 1983-84). Home: 2260 24th St Santa Monica CA 90405-1811

JONES, RICHARD THEODORE, biochemistry educator; b. Portland, Oreg., Nov. 9, 1929; s. Lester Tallman and Olene (Johnson) J.; m. Marilyn Virginia Beam, June 20, 1953; children: Gary Richard, Alan Donald, Neil William. Student, Calif. Inst. Tech., 1948-51, Ph.D., 1961; B.S., U. Oreg., 1953, M.S., M.D., 1956. Student asst. dept. physiology U. Oreg. Med. Sch., Portland, 1953-56; asst. prof. med. sch. U. Oreg., 1961-64, assoc. prof. exptl. medicine and biochemistry, 1964-67, prof., 1967-95; prof. emeritus U. Oreg., 1996—; chmn. dept. biochemistry and molecular biology med. sch. U. Oreg., 1967-93; acting pres. U. Oreg. Health Scis. Center, 1977-78; intern Hosp. U. Pa., 1956-57; rsch. asst. dept. chemistry Calif. Inst. Tech., 1959-60; mem. biochemistry tng. com. Nat. Inst. Gen. Med. Scis., NIH, 1968-73, med. sci. tng. com., 1971-74; comprehensive sickle cell centers ad hoc rev. com. Nat. Heart, Lung and Blood Inst., 1974-77; biochemistry test com. Nat. Bd. Med. Examiners, 1968-74, FLEX com., 1982-94. Contbr. articles to profl. jours. Mem. Am. Soc. Biochem. and Molecular Biology, AAAS, Sigma Xi, Alpha Omega Alpha, Tau Beta Pi. Home: 2634 SW Fairmount Blvd Portland OR 97201-1433 Office: 3181 SW Sam Jackson Park Rd Portland OR 97201-3011

JONES, ROBERT ALONZO, economist; b. Evanston, Ill., Mar. 15, 1937; s. Robert Vernon and Elsie Pierce (Brown) J.; m. Ina Turner Jones; children: Lindsay Rae, Robert Pierce, Gregory Alan, William Kenneth. AB, Middlebury Coll., 1959; MBA, Northwestern U., 1961, LLD (hon.) Middlebury (Vt.) Coll., 1992. Economist Hahn, Wise & Assoc., San Carlos, Calif., 1966-69; sr. rsch. officer Bank of Am., San Francisco, 1969-74; v.p., dir. fin. forecasting Chase Econometrics, San Francisco, 1974-76; chmn. bd. Money Market Svcs., Inc., Belmont, Calif., 1974-86; chmn. bd. MMS Internat., Redwood City, Calif., 1986-89, chmn. emeritus, 1989—; chmn. bd. dirs. Market News Svc., N.Y.C.; chmn. emeritus Geonomics Inst., Middlebury, 1995—, chmn. bd., 1986-95; chmn. bd. Jones Internat., 1989—; chmn. bd. Market News Svc., Inc., N.Y.C., 1993—; chmn. bd. Market Broadcasting Corp., Incline Village, N.Y.; dean coun. Harvard U. Div. Sch., Cambridge, Mass., 1991—; mem. Kellogg Alumni Adv. Bd., Northwestern U., 1993—; instr. money and banking, Am. Inst. Banking, San Francisco, 1971, 72; councilman, City of Belmont (Calif.), 1970-77, mayor, 1971, 72, 75, 76; dir. San Mateo County Transit Dist., 1975-77; chmn. San Mateo County Coun. of Mayors, 1975-76; trustee Incline Village Gen. Improvement Dist., Nev., 1984-85, trustee, Carlmont United Meth. Ch., 1978-81. Author: U.S. Financial System and the Federal Reserve, 1974, Power of Coinage, 1987. 1st lt. USAR, 1961-68. Named Hon. Life Mem. Calif. PTA, ordo honorum Kappa Delta Rho Nat. Fraternity; recipient Ernst & Young Entrepreneur of the Yr. award, 1986. Mem. Nat. Assn. Bus. Economists, San Francisco Bond Club. Republican. Methodist. Office: Jones Internat Inc PO Box 7498 Incline Village NV 89452-7498

JONES, ROBERT EDWARD, federal judge; b. Portland, Oreg., July 5, 1927; s. Howard C. and Leita (Hendricks) J.; m. Pearl F. Jensen, May 29, 1948; children—Jeffrey Scott, Julie Lynn. BA, U. Hawaii, 1949; JD, Lewis and Clark Coll., 1953; LLD (hon.), City U., Seattle, 1984, Lewis and Clark Coll., 1995. Bar: Oreg. 1953. Trial atty. Portland, Oreg., 1953-63; judge Oreg. Circuit Ct., Portland, 1963-83; justice Oreg. Supreme Ct., Salem, 1983-90; judge U.S. Dist. Ct. Oreg., Portland, 1990—; mem. faculty Nat. Jud. Coll., Am. Acad. Jud. Edn., ABA Appellate Judges Seminars; former mem. Oreg. Evidence Revision Commn., Oreg. Ho. of Reps.; former chmn. Oreg. Commn. Prison Terms and Parole Stds.; adj. prof. Northwestern Sch. Law, Lewis and Clark Coll., 1963—, Willamette Law Sch., 1988—. Bd. overseers Lewis and Clark Coll. Served to capt. JAGC, USNR. Recipient merit award Multnomah Bar Assn., 1979; Citizen award NCCJ, Legal Citizen of the Yr. award Law Related Edn. Project, 1988; Service to Mankind award Sertoma Club Oreg.; James Madison award Sigma Delta Chi; named Disting. Grad., Northwestern Sch. Law. Mem. State Bar Oreg. (past chmn. CLE), Oreg. Cir. Judges Assn. (pres. 1967—), Oreg. Trial Lawyers (pres. 1969). Office: US Dist Ct House 620 SW Main St Portland OR 97205-3037

JONES, ROBERT THOMAS, aerospace scientist; b. Macon, Mo., May 28, 1910; s. Edward Seward and Harriet Ellen (Johnson) J.; m. Megan Lillian More, Nov. 23, 1964; children: Edward, Patricia, Harriet, David, Gregory, John. Student, U. Mo., 1928; Sc.D. (hon.), U. Colo., 1971. Aero. research scientist NACA, Langley Field, Va., 1934-46; research scientist Ames Research Center NACA-NASA, Moffet Field, Calif., 1946-62; sr. staff scientist Ames Research Center, NASA, 1970-81, research assoc., 1981—; scientist Avco-Everett Research Lab., Everett, Mass., 1962-70; cons. prof. Stanford U., 1981. Author: (with Doris Cohen) High Speed Wing Theory, 1960, Collected Works of Robert T. Jones, 1976, Wing Theory, 1987; contbr. (with Doris Cohen) articles to profl. jours. Recipient Reed award Inst. Aero. Scis., 1946, Inventions and Contbns. award NASA, 1975, Prandtl Ring award Deutsche Gesellschaft für Luft and Raumfahrt, 1978, Pres.'s medal for disting. fed. service, 1980, Langley medal Smithsonian Instn., 1981, Excalibur award U.S. Congress, 1981, Aeronautical Engring. award NAS, 1990. Fellow AIAA (hon.); mem. NAS (award in aero. engring. 1989), NAE, Am. Acad. Arts and Scis. Home: 25005 La Loma Dr Los Altos CA 94022

JONES, ROBERT TRENT, JR., golf course architect; b. Montclair, N.J., July 24, 1939; s. Robert Trent J. and Ione (Davis) J. B.A., Yale U., 1961; postgrad. in law, Stanford U. Pres., prin. designer Robert Trent Jones II, Palo Alto, Calif., Robert Trent Jones II Internat., Internat. assoc. SRI Internat., 1983; amateur golfer numerous tournaments, speaker in field. Author: Golf By Design, 1993. Chmn. Calif. Parks and Recreation Commn., 1983; mem. San Francisco Com. on Fgn. Relations, 1983. Recipient Family of the Yr. award Met. Golf Writers and Golf Owners Assn., award Am. Acad. Achievement, 1989. Mem. Am. Soc. Golf Course Architects (exec. com.), Urban Land Inst. (exec. com.), Am. Soc. Golf Course Architects (pres. 1989—). Democrat. Clubs: Bohamian Golf, San Francisco Golf; Royal and Ancient Golf (St. Andrews, Scotland); Spyglass Hill Golf, Pine Valley Golf. Office: 705 Forest Ave Palo Alto CA 94301-2102

JONES, ROGER CLYDE, retired electrical engineering educator; b. Lake Andes, S.D., Aug. 17, 1919; s. Robert Clyde and Martha (Albertson) J.; m. Katherine M. Tucker, June 7, 1952; children: Linda Lee, Vonnie Lynette. B.S., U. Nebr., 1949; M.S., U. Md., 1953; Ph.D. U. Md., 1963. With U.S. Naval Research Lab., Washington, 1949-57; staff sr. engr. to chief engr. Melpar, Inc., Falls Church, Va., 1957-58; cons. project engr. Melpar, Inc., 1958-59, sect. head physics, 1959-64, chief scientist for physics, 1964; prof. dept. elec. engring. U. Ariz., Tucson, 1964-89; dir. quantum electronics lab. U. Ariz., 1968-88, adj. prof. radiology, 1978-86, adj. prof. radiation-oncology, 1986-88, prof. of radiation-oncology, 1988-89, prof. emeritus, 1989—; tech. dir. H.S.C. and A., El Paso, 1989—; guest prof. in exptl. oncology Inst. Cancer Research, Aarhus, Denmark, 1982-83. Patentee in field. Served with AUS, 1942-45. Mem. Am. Phys. Soc., Optical Soc. Am., Internat. Soc. Optical Engring., Bioelectromagnetics Soc., IEEE, AAAS, NSPE, Am. Congress on Surveying and Mapping, Eta Kappa Nu, Pi Mu Epsilon, N.Mex. Acad. Sci. Home: 5809 E 3rd St Tucson AZ 85711-1519

JONES, ROGER WAYNE, electronics executive; b. Riverside, Calif., Nov. 21, 1939; s. Virgil Elsworth and Beulah (Mills) J.; m. Sherill Lee Bottjer, Dec. 28, 1975; children: Jerrod Wayne, Jordan Anthony. BS in Engring., San Diego State U., 1962. Br. sales mgr. Bourns, Inc., Riverside, 1962-68; sales and mktg. mgr. Spectrol Electronics, Industry, Calif., 1968-77, v.p. mktg., 1979-81; mng. dir. Spectrol Reliance, Ltd., Swindon, England, 1977-79; sr. v.p. S.W. group Kierulff Electronics Corp., L.A., 1981-83; v.p. sales and mktg. worldwide electronic techs. div. Beckman Instruments, Fullerton, Calif., 1983-86; pres., ptnr. Jones & McGeoy Sales, Inc., Newport Beach, Calif., 1986—. Author: The History of Villa Rockledge, A National Treasure in Laguna Beach, 1991. Republican. Home: 4 Royal St George Newport Beach CA 92660 Office: 5100 Campus Dr Newport Beach CA 92660-2101

JONES, RONALD CHARLES, hospital administrator; b. Panaca, Nev., Jan. 20, 1937; s. Charles Russell and Margaret Leona (Heaps) J.; m. Nancy Christensen, Dec. 23, 1955; children: Linda Diane, Jackie Lynn, Karen Kaye, Ronald Brent, Patricia Marie, Bryan David, Brandon Lee. BS, U. nev., Reno, 1955; M in Healthcare Adminstrn., Baylor U., 1970. Commd. 2d lt. U.S. Army, 1959, advanced through grades to col., 1980; comdr. 47th Field Hosp., Ft. Sill, Okla., 1979; dep. comdr. for adminstrn. MEDDAC and Reynolds Army Hosp., Ft. Sill, 1979-84, 2d Gen. Hosp., Langstuhl, Germany, 1984-87; dep. post comdr., chief staff, dep. comdr. for adminstrn. Fitzsimmons Army Med. Ctr., 1987-89; ret. U.S. Army, 1989; dir. mil. rels. LDS Ch., 1989-91; asst. adminstr. Utah Valley Regional Med. Ctr., Provo, 1991—. Decorated Silver Star, Legion of Merit with oakleaf cluster, Disting. Flying Cross, Bronze Star, Meritorious Svc. medal with 3 oakleaf clusters, Air medal with 30 oak leaf clusters, Army Commendation medal with oakleaf cluster, others. Fellow Am. Coll. Healthcare Execs.; mem. Am. Hosp. Assn., Assn. U.S. Army, Utah Hosp. Assn. Home: 2636 W Jody St West Jordan UT 84088 Office: Utah Valley Regional MC 1034 N 500 W Provo UT 84604-3380

JONES, RONALD H., computer information systems executive; b. San Diego, Feb. 11, 1938; s. Henry G. and Geneva H. (Hodges) J.; m. Carol Sue Carmichael, Dec. 9, 1967. BS, San Diego State Coll., 1959, MS, 1961. Project mgr. UNIVAC, San Diego, 1961-67, Computer Scis. Corp., San Diego, 1967-75; v.p. Interactive, Inc., San Diego, 1975-92; owner Consulting Co., San Diego, 1992—; ind. cons., programmer various mfg. & distbg. cos., San Diego, 1992—. Contbr. articles to profl. jours; tech. advisor to Internat. Spectrum Mag. Advisor San Diego State Univ.; Rep. nat. committeeman, 1979—. Mem. AARP, Am. Prodn. and Inventory Control Soc., Assn. for Computing Machinery, Calpirg and Ucan. Presbyterian. Home and Office: 2484 Pine St San Diego CA 92103-1042 Office: Johnstone Supply 4320 Pacific Hwy San Diego CA 92110-3106

JONES, SALLY LEWIS, healthcare administrator; b. Enterprise, Oreg., Nov. 26, 1943; d. Edgar Vance adn Effie Jewell (Silver) Lewis; m. Charles Cabel Jones, Jan. 12, 1968 (div. Nov. 1984); children: Vance H., Nova C. BS, U. Oreg., 1966; MS, U. Hawaii, 1987. Staff nurse Barnes Vet.'s Hosp., Vancouver, Wash., 1966; asst. head nurse Martin Army Hosp., Ft. Benning, Columbus, Ga., 1966-67, Tripler Army Med. Ctr., Honolulu, 1967-69; staff nurse The Queen's Med. Ctr., Honolulu, 1980-87, clin. nurse specialist, 1987-89, acting dir., 1989-90, dir., 1990—; cons. U. Hawaii, Honolulu, 1987-88, Edu-Center, Honolulu, 1988-89. Adminstr. Nat. Head and spinal Cord Injury Prevention, Honolulu, 1987-91; mem. Am. Women's Aux., Oreg., 1944—. Capt. U.S. Army, 1965-68. Scholar Nat. Health Found., 1962-66; decorated Vietnam Svc. medal. Mem. Am. Orgn. Nurse Execs. (corr. sec. Hawaii chpt. 1991—), Nat. League for Nursing, Hawaii/Pacific Head Injury Assn., Nat. Spinal Cord Injury Assn., Sigma Theta Tau, Alpha Tau Delta. Democrat. Office: The Queens Med Ctr 1301 Punchbowl St Honolulu HI 96813-2413

JONES, SANDRA LOU, college program director; b. Golden, Colo., July 13, 1944; d. John R. and Evelyn M. (Anderson) Hampton; m. Jerry Schloffman, June 29, 1963 (div. 1980); children: Jerry Jon, Heather Nicole; m. Stuart A. Jones, May 15, 1982. Student, Colo. State U., 1962-63. Sec. Adams State Coll., Alamosa, Colo., 1963-65; adminstrv. sec. Met. State Coll., Denver, 1965-75, adminstrv. officer, 1975-80, asst. dir. Contract Personnel, 1980-82, dir. Contract Personnel, 1982-87, dir. Personnel, Payroll, 1987—. Bd. dirs. Cardinals Aurora (Colo.) Youth League, 1978-84, Hinkley High Athletic Boosters, Aurora, 1985-90; mem. adminstrv. bd. Burns Meml. United Meth. Ch., Aurora, 1984—, mem. fin. com., 1993—. Recipient Colo Cupa Roadrunner award, 1993. Mem. Colo. Coll. and Univ. Assn. (pres. 1994-95), Coll. and Univ. Pers. Assn. (human resources exec. com. 1991-93, 95—). Methodist. Home: 684 Dearborn St Aurora CO 80011-6917

JONES, SCOTT AUSTIN, software developer, microcomputer consultant; b. Phoenix, Aug. 22, 1962; s. Travis Hayhurst and Mary Louise (Coy) J. BA, U. Ariz., Tucson, 1988. Sr. programmer analyst Alpha Therapeutic Corp., L.A., 1988-90; owner Austin Software Design, L.A., Grand Junction, 1989—; cons., Austin Software Design, L.A., Grand Junction; software reviewer, Assn. of Shareware Profls. Author: Recursive Realm, 1989, 90, 91. Mem. Assn. of Shareware Profls. Office: Austin Software Design PO Box 30133 Grand Junction CO 81503-3200

JONES, STANLEY BELMONT, counselor; b. Newport News, Va., Aug. 7, 1961; s. Stanley Brown and Irma Virginia (Owens) J.; m. LaRita Yvonne Ross, June 21, 1986; 1 child, Alanah Yvonne. BA in Speech Comm., U. Richmond, 1983; MEd in Guidance and Counseling, City U., 1995. Commd. officer U.S. Army, 1983, advanced through grades to capt., 1988; various positions 542nd Maintenace Co., Ft. Lewis, Wash., 1984-87; plans and policy officer 593rd Area Support Group, Ft. Lewis, 1987-88; logistics officer 1st Maintenance Battalion, Boblingen, Germany, 1989-90; co. comdr. 22nd Maintenance Co., Heilbronn, Germany, 1990-91; maintenance officer 44th Support Bat., Ft. Lewis, 1992; ret. U.S. Army, 1992; counselor, football coach A.G. Hudtloff Jr. H.S., Tacoma, 1993—; planner earthquake preparedness A.G. Hudtloff Jr. H.S., Tacoma, 1993—, cons. sch. adv. bd, 1993—, dir. student conflict mediation program, 1993—. Named Outstanding Young Men in Am., 1984. Mem. ACA, NEA, Wash. Edn. Assn., Phi Beta Sigma (sec. Mu Omicron chpt. 1981-82, v.p., 1982-83), Phi Beta Sigma (Epsilon Epsilon Sigma chpt.). Baptist. Office: AG Hudtloff Jr HS 7702 Phillips Rd SW Tacoma WA 98498-6344

JONES, THERESE ANN, humanities educator; b. Pitts., June 9, 1954; d. Tony Patrick and Jane Elizabeth (Hall) Misasi; m. W. Christopher Jones III, Aug. 16, 1974; 1 child, Sara Elizabeth. BA in Theater Arts, Pitts. State U., 1980, MA in English, 1982; PhD in English, U. Colo., 1990. Instr. humanities dept. U. Colo., Boulder, 1990-94; postdoctoral fellow human values in medicine program Northeastern Ohio U. Coll. Medicine, Rootstown, 1994—; HIV/AIDS peer educator U. Colo., Boulder, 1992-94. Author: Feminist Literary Theory Dictionary, 1994; editor: Sharing the Delirium, 1994. Prodr., fundraiser Wardenburg Student Health & Boulder County AIDS Project, U. Colo., 1994, prodr., creator interdisciplinary performance on AIDS Farrand Acad. Program, 1993. Outstanding grad. scholar Pitts. State U., 1982; grad. fellow U. Colo. Coll. Arts and Sci., 1985, 87, James Folsom Dissertation fellow dept. English U. Colo., 1988. Mem. MLA, Rocky Mount MLA (chair women and lit. com.), Artists Confronting AIDS.

JONES, THOMAS ROBERT, social worker; b. Escanaba, Mich., Jan. 3, 1950; s. Gene Milton and Alica Una (Mattson) J.; m. Joy Sedlock. BA, U. Laverne, 1977; MSW, U. Hawaii, 1979. Social work assoc. Continuing Care Svcs., Camarillo, Calif., 1973-78; psychiat. social worker Camarillo State Hosp., 1980-84; psychotherapist Terkensha Child Treatment Ctr., Sacramento, Calif., 1984-86; psychiat. social worker Napa (Calif.) State Hosp., 1986-87, Vets. Home Calif., Yountville, 1987—. Mem. Nat. Assn. Social Workers, Soc. Clin. Social Work, Am. Orthopsychiat. Assn., Acad. Cert. Social Workers, Assn. for Advancement Behavior Therapy. Home: PO Box 1095 Yountville CA 94599-1095 Office: Vets Home Calif Yountville CA 94599

JONES, THOMAS WILLIAM, artist; b. Lakewood, Ohio, Aug. 13, 1942; s. Robert W. and Roberta P. (Poske) J.; m. Carrie Pemberton, July 21, 1973. Diploma of Art, Cleve. Inst. Art, 1964. Selected exhbns. include Hubbard Mus., Ruidoso Downs, N.Mex. (Art Award of Excellence), Colo. Heritage Ctr. Mus., Denver, Henry Gallery Invitation, Seattle, Nat. Acad. Western Art, Oklahoma City, 154th Nat. Acad. Design, N.Y.C., Springfield (Mo.) Art Mus., Butler Inst. Am. Art, Youngstown, Ohio, Seattle Art Mus., Frye Art Mus., Seattle; commd. to paint ofcl. White House Christmas card for Pres. and Mrs. Ronald Reagan, 1985-88. Works in permanent collections at Frye Art Mus., Seattle, Gen. Telephone Co. of N.W., Seattle First Nat. Bank, Western Internat. Hotels, Carlton House, Pitts., St. Francis Hotel, San Francisco, Eddie Bauer, Inc., Redmond, Wash., Wash. Mut. Savs. Bank, Seattle, City of Seattle Selects II, Safeco, Seattle, Pacific Car and Foundry, Seattle, USN, Rainier Bank, Seattle, Reed, McClure, Moceri and Thonn, P.S., Seattle; contbr. articles to profl. jours. Recipient Ted Kautzky Meml. award Am. Watercolor Soc. 108th Ann., 1975, 112th Ann. Bronze Medal, 1979, Nat. Acad. Western Art Gold Medal, 1987, Silver Medal, 1984, 93, others. Mem. Nat. Acad. Western Art, Fedn. Can. Artists (hon.).

JONES, THORNTON KEITH, research chemist; b. Brawley, Calif., Dec. 17, 1923; s. Alfred George and Madge Jones; m. Evalee Vestal, July 4, 1965; children: Brian Keith, Donna Eileen. BS, U. Calif., Berkeley, 1949, postgrad., 1951-52. Research chemist Griffin Chem. Co., Richmond, Calif., 1949-55; western product devel. and improvement mgr. Nopco Chem. Co., Richmond, Calif., 1955; research chemist Chevron Research Co., Richmond, 1956-65, research chemist in spl. products research and devel., 1965-1982; product quality mgr. Chevron USA, Inc., San Francisco, 1982-87, ret. Patentee in field. Vol. fireman and officer, Terra Linda, Calif., 1957-64; mem. adv. com. Terra Linda Dixie Elem. Sch. Dist., 1960-64. Served with Signal Corps, U.S. Army, 1943-46. Mem. Am. Chem. Soc., Forest Products Research Soc., Am. Wood Preservers Assn., Alpha Chi Sigma. Republican. Presbyterian.

JONES, VERNON QUENTIN, surveyor; b. Sioux City, Iowa, May 6, 1930; s. Vernon Boyd and Winnifred Rhoda (Bremmer) J.; student UCLA, 1948-50; m. Rebeca Buckovecz, Oct. 1981; children: Steven Vernon, Gregory Richard, Stanley Alan, Lynn Sue. Draftsman III Pasadena (Calif.) city engr., 1950-53; sr. civil engring. asst. L.A. County engr., L.A., 1953-55; v.p. Treadwell Engring. Corp., Arcadia, Calif., 1955-61, pres., 1961-64; pres. Hillcrest Engring. Corp., Arcadia, 1961-64; dep. county surveyor, Ventura, Calif., 1964-78; propr. Vernon Jones Land Surveyor, Riviera, Ariz., 1978—; city engr. Needles (Calif.), 1980-87; instr. Mohave Community Coll., 1987—. Chmn. graphic tech. com. Ventura Unified Sch. Dist., 1972-78, mem. career adv. com., 1972-74; mem. engring. adv. com. Pierce Coll., 1973; pres. Mgmt. Employees of Ventura County, 1974. V.p. Young Reps. of Ventura County, 1965. Pres., Marina Pacifica Homeowners Assn., 1973. Mem. League Calif. Surveying Orgns. (pres. 1975), Am. Congress on Surveying and Mapping (chmn. So. Calif. sect. 1976), Am. Soc. Photogrammetry, Am. Pub. Works Assn., County Engr. Assn. Calif. Home: 913E San Juan Ct Bullhead City AZ 86442-5618

JONES, WALT, food executive; b. 1938. Ptnr. Sun Valley Packing, Del Rey, Calif., 1962—. Office: Sun Valley Packing 5469 Portola Ave Del Rey CA 93616*

JONES, WANDA CAROL, nurse; b. Riverside, Calif., Jan. 2, 1956; d. Wallace Campbell and Erma Frances (Elliott) Wendelstadt; m. Rodney Jay Shelton, Feb. 16, 1980 (dec.); 1 child from previous marriage, Wendy Mae Cox; m. Jimmy L. Jones, July 30, 1992. Cert. in voc. nursing, United Health Careers, 1982; AS, San Bernardino Valley Coll., 1987. RN, Calif. Tchr. piano Fontana, Calif., 1969-75; underwriter Prudential Ins. Co., San Bernardino, Calif., 1977; newspaper editor Allied Constrn. Ind., San Bernardino, 1979-82; nursing asst. San Bernardino County Med. Ctr., 1982-83; voc. nurse Remedy Health Svcs., San Bernadino, 1983; voc. nurse Kaiser Permanente, Fontana, 1983-87, RN, 1987—. Active Oasis Christian Fellowship. Mem. NAFE, United Nurses Assn. Calif., Grange Club, Order of Rainbow for Girls, Piano and Organ Club, Clinkers Organ Club, Alpha Gamma Sigma.

JONES-EDDY, JULIE MARGARET, librarian; b. Hayden, Colo., Feb. 20, 1942; d. Hugh A. and Margaret E. (Tagert) J.; m. John H. Eddy Jr., June 3, 1965; 1 child, Mark. BA, U. Colo., 1964; MLS, U. Okla., 1976. Cert. libr. Art tchr. Fort Collins (Colo.) Pub. Schs., 1964-65, Gunnison (Colo.) Pub. Schs., 1965-66; govt. documents libr. Tutt Libr., Colo. Coll., Colorado Springs, 1977—; presenter in field of oral history project on women, 1984—. Author: (videotape) Women of Northwestern Colorado, 1890-1940: Glimpses of Our Lives, 1984; author: Homesteading Women: An Oral History of Colorado, 1890-1950, 1992. Grantee Colo. Endowment for the Humanities, 1984, 89. Mem. ALA, Colo. Libr. Assn., Oral History Assn. Office: Colorado Coll Tutt Library 1021 N Cascade Ave Colorado Springs CO 80903

JONGEWARD, GEORGE RONALD, systems analyst; b. Yakima, Wash., Aug. 9, 1934; s. George Ira and Dorothy Marie (Cronk) J.; m. Janet Jeanne Williams, July 15, 1955; children: Mary Jeanne, Dona Lee, Karen Anne. BA, Whitworth Coll., 1957; postgrad., Utah State U., 1961. Sr. systems analyst Computer Scis. Corp., Honolulu, 1969-71; cons. in field Honolulu, 1972-76; prin. The Hobby Co., Honolulu, 1977-81; sr. systems analyst Computer Systems Internat., Honolulu, 1981—, asst. v.p., 1994—; instr. EDP Hawaii Pacific U., Honolulu, 1982—. Mem. car show com. Easter Seal Soc., Honolulu. 1977-82; active Variety Club, Honolulu, 1978-81. Mem. Mensa (local pres. 1967-69), Triple-9. Republican. Presbyterian. Home: 400 Hobron Ln Apt 2611 Honolulu HI 96815-1206 Office: Computer Systems Internat 841 Bishop St Ste 501 Honolulu HI 96813-3905

JONISH, ARLEY DUANE, retired bibliographer; b. Walker, Minn., June 18, 1927; s. Howard Florian and Mabel Pauline (Rinde) J.; m. Thelma O. Ofstedal, Aug. 13, 1955 (dec. May 1988); children—Eleanor Ann, David Paul. B.S., Bemidji State U., 1949; M.A., U. Minn., 1962. Tchr., librarian Pub. Schs., Red Lake Falls, Minn., 1949-55, Mahnomen, Minn., 1955-60; instr. library sci. U. No. Iowa, Cedar Falls, 1960-62; circulation librarian U. N.Mex., Albuquerque, 1962-63; ref. librarian Western Oreg. Coll., Monmouth, 1963-66; dir. Penrose Meml. Library Whitman Coll., Walla Walla, Wash., 1966-87, bibliographer, 1987-89, ret., 1989; cons. to librs. Walla Walla, 1990—; mem. Wash. Govs. Conf. on Libraries and Info. Sci., Olympia, 1977-80, Wash. State Adv. Council on Libraries, Olympia, 1975-80. Precinct committeeman Republican Party, Walla Walla County, 1980-82. Served with USN, 1945-46, PTO. Mem. ABA, Wash. Library Assn., Pacific Northwest Library Assn., AAUP, NEA, Northwest Assn. Pvt. Colls. and Univs. (chmn. library sect. 1970, 80), Assn. Coll. and Research Libraries (pres. Wash. state chapter 1987). Lodge: Elks. Home: 253 NE Cedar St College Place WA 99324-2130

JONKER, PETER EMILE, gas company executive; b. The Hague, The Netherlands, Sept. 15, 1948; came to U.S., 1966, naturalized, 1985; s. Jacob and Jurrina (Wories) J.; m. Janet Lynn Gotfredson, Sept. 6, 1974; children: Jeffrey, Annelies. BSChemE cum laude, U. So. Calif., 1971, MSChemE, 1972; JD with honors, Western State U., Fullerton, Calif., 1979. Bar: Calif. 1979. Research engr. Union Oil Co., Los Angeles, 1972-75; regulations coordinator Union Oil Co., L.A., 1975-79, atty., 1979; mgr. govtl. and pub. affairs Western Liquefied Nat. Gas, L.A., 1979-81; mgr. environ. permitting Tosco Corp., L.A., 1981-83; mgr. regional pub. affairs So. Calif. Gas. Co., L.A., 1983-85, mgr. rate design, demand forecast and analysis, 1986-88, mgr. fed. energy affairs, 1988-90, mgr. support svcs., 1990-92; mgr. policy and planning So. Calif. Gas Co., L.A., 1992-94, mgr. external affairs, 1994-95, dir. govtl. affairs, 1995—; mem. So. Coast Air Quality Mgmt. Dist. Adv. Coun., L.A., 1983-85; mem. Fed. Clean Air Act Adv. Com.; dir. Calif. Coun. for Environ. and Econ. Balance, 1994—. Editor Western State Law Rev., 1976-79; contbr. articles to profl. jours. Trustee, deacon San Marino (Calif.) Presbyn. Community Ch., 1980—; councilman U. So. Calif. Engring. Student Council, Los Angeles, 1971-72, dir. Engring. Alumni Assn., 1971-72; fgn. del. White House Conf., Washington, 1971. Mem. Am. Gas Assn., Air and Waste Mgmt. Assn. (v.p. West Coast chpt. 1984, 85, dir. West Coast sect. 1993—), Fed. Energy Bar Assn., Pacific Coast Gas Assn., Tau Beta Pi (pres., v.p. Calif. Delta chpt. 1970-71). Republican. Home: 2450 Melville Dr San

Marino CA 91108-2616 Office: So Calif Gas Co 555 W 5th St Los Angeles CA 90013-1010

JONSSON-DEVILLERS, EDITH, foreign language educator; b. Marseille, France; came to U.S., 1969; married: Erik Jonsson, Mar. 29, 1959; children: Sylvia, Irline. Diploma of English Studies, Cambridge (U.K.) U., 1954; Lic. in Letters, The Sorbonne, Paris, 1957; PhD in Comparative Lit., U. Calif., San Diego, 1976. Cert. interpreter Spanish/French, Calif. Free-lance interpreter, 1960—; free-lance translator San Diego, 1970—, ct. interpreter, 1986—; asst. prof. U. Calif., San Diego, 1970-76, 87—, Occidental Coll., L.A., 1976-79; lectr. U. San Diego, 1969-70, 82-86, San Diego State U., 1981-87, 91; founding dir. Alliance Francaise Sch., San Diego, 1989-93. Contbr. articles to profl. jours. Fulbright travel grantee, 1954-55; U. Calif.-San Diego Dissertation fellow, 1975. Mem. MLA, Am. Lit. Translators Assn., Calif. Ct. Interpreters Assn. (v.p. 1994—), Am. Translators Assn., U.S. Mexico Border Health Assn. Instituto Internacional de Literatura Iberoamericana. Office: French-Spanish Lang Svcs PO Box 17644 San Diego CA 92177-7644

JOOST-GAUGIER, CHRISTIANE L., art history educator; b. Ste. Maxime, France; d. Louis Clair and Agnes Larsen Gaugier; children: Leonarda A. Joost, Nathalie P. Joost. BA, Radcliffe Coll., 1955; MA, Harvard U., 1959, PhD, 1973. Lectr. U. Mich., Ann Arbor, 1960; asst. prof. Mich. State U., East Lansing, 1961-62, Tufts U., Medford, Mass., 1968-73; assoc. prof. to prof., dept. chmn. N.Mex. State U., Las Cruces, 1975-85; prof., dept. chmn. U. N.Mex., Albuquerque, 1985-87, prof. art history, 1987—; bd. dirs. Nat. Coun. Art Adminstrs. Author: Selected Drawings of Jacopo Bellini, 1980; contbr. articles to profl. jours. Grantee Delmas, Am. Philos. Soc.; Fulbright fellow, ACLS fellow, Vassie James Hill fellow AAUW. Mem. Coll. Art Assn. Am. (bd. dirs.), Renaissance Soc. Am. (bd. dirs.), Soc. for the Classical Tradition, Am. Assn. for Italian Studies, The Sixteenth Century Soc. Office: Univ NMex Dept Art & Art History Albuquerque NM 87131

JOPLIN, ALBERT FREDERICK, transportation executive; b. Victoria, B.C., Can., Feb 22, 1919; s. Albert Edward and Emily Eliza (Norford) J.; m. Margaret Brigid McMorragh-Kavanaugh, May 26, 1947 (dec.); 1 child, Mary Lynn Barbara; m. Dorothy Anne Cook, July 29, 1977. BASc in Civil Engring., U. B.C., 1948. With Can. Pacific Ltd., 1947-87, spl. engr., Calgary, 1962-65, devel. engr., Vancouver, 1965-66, mgr. spl. projects, 1966-68, system mgr. planning and devel., Montreal, Que., 1968-69, dir. devel. planning, 1969-71, v.p. mktg. and sales CP Rail, 1971-74, v.p. operation and maintenance, 1974-76; gen. mgr. Marathon Realty, 1965-66; pres., chief exec. officer Canadian Pacific (Bermuda) Ltd., 1976-84; chmn., bd. dirs. Leaders Equity Corp., Vancouver, Advanced Smelters Tech. Inc.; pres., chief exec. officer Cen. Ocean Industries Ltd. Commr., gen. dir. Can. Pacific Pavilion Expo '86, 1984-87; assoc. mem. Boy Scouts Can. Served with RCAF, 1941-45. Mem. Assn. Profl. Engrs. B.C. (life), Engring. Inst. Can. (life), Can. Soc. Civil Engrs. (life), Can. Maritime Law Assn., Vancouver Maritime Arbitrators Assn., Inst. Corp. Dirs. Can., Air Force Officers Assn., Indian Ocean Flying Boat Assn., Terminal City Club (Vancouver), Jericho Officers' Mess Club (Vancouver), Royal Montreal Golf Club, Traffic Club, Mount Stephen Club (Montreal), Canadian Railway Club, Western Canada Railway Club, Bermuda Maritime Museum (life), Vancouver Maritime Mus., Nat. Trust (Bermuda), Rotary (Vancouver, B.C., Paul Harris fellow), Order of St. John, Beta Theta Pi. Home: 4317 Staulo, Vancouver, BC Canada V6N 3S1 Office: PO Box 43, 200 Granville St, Vancouver, BC Canada V6C 2R3

JORDAHL, GEIR ARILD, photographer, educator; b. Kristiansund, Norway, Jan. 27, 1957; came to U.S., 1961; s. Sigurd and Solveig Ingvarda (Pedersen) J.; m. Kathleen Patricia O'Grady, Sept. 24, 1983. BA, Calif. State U., Hayward, 1979; MFA, Ohio U., 1983. Life C.C. teaching credential, Calif. Teaching assoc. Ohio U., Athens, 1980-82; instr. photography Chabot Coll., Hayward, Calif., 1983—; owner, mgr. Geir & Kate Jordahl, Photography, Hayward, 1983—; ind. curator, Hayward, 1984—; coord. PhotoCen. Photography Programs, Hayward, 1983—; artist-in-residence Yosemite (Calif.) Nat. Park, 1993; mem. curatorial com. Hayward Forum for Arts/Sun Gallery, 1992. Exhibited in numerous shows including Kansas City (Mo.) Art Inst., 1987, Ohio State Art Gallery, Newark, 1987, Mus. Art U. Oreg., Eugene, 1988, Mus. for Photography, Braunschweig, Germany, 1988, Ansel Adams Gallery, Yosemite, 1989, Mus. Modern Art, Tampere, Finland, 1989, Trenton (N.J.) Mus. Art, 1991, Ansel Adams Ctr. for Photography, San Francisco, 1990, Photo Forum Gallery, Pitts., 1993, Yosemite Nat. Park Mus., 1994, Ansel Adams Gallery, 1995, Bibliotheque Nat. de France, and other pvt. and pub. collections; contbr. to profl. publs.; photographer various catalogues. Precinct capt. Hayward Dem. Com., 1992. Recipient purchase award Hayward Area Forum Arts, 1986, Ohio State U., 1987, Yosemite Nat. Park and Curry Co., 1992, award of excellence Calif. State Fair, 1987, 89, One of Top 100 New Photographers award Maine Photog. Workshops and Kodak Corp., 1987, Innovative New Program award Calif. Parks and Recreation Soc., 1990; scholar Calif. State U., 1975, Ohio U., 1981, Oslo Internat. Summer Sch., 1982, exch. scholar U. Trondheim, Norway, 1983, Peder P. Johnsen scholar Sons of Norway, 1983. Mem. Soc. Photog. Edn., Internat. Assn. Panoramic Photographers, Friends of Photography, San Francisco Camerawork. Home and Studio: PO Box 3998 144 Medford Ave Hayward CA 94540

JORDAN, CHARLES MORRELL, retired automotive designer; b. Whittier, Calif., Oct. 21, 1927; s. Charles L. and Bernice May (Letts) J.; m. Sally Irene Mericle, Mar. 8, 1951; children: Debra, Mark, Melissa. BS, MIT, 1949; PhD (hon.), Art Ctr. Coll. Design, 1992. With GM, Warren, Mich., 1949—, chief designer Cadillac Studio, 1957-61, group chief designer, 1961-62, exec. in charge automotive design, 1962-67, dir. styling Adam Opel A.G., 1967-70, exec. in charge Cadillac, Oldsmobile, Buick Studios, 1970-73, exec. in charge Chevrolet, Pontiac and Comml. Vehicle Studios, 1973-77, dir. design, 1977-86, v.p. design staff, 1986-92; retired, 1992. Bd. trustees Ctr. for Creative Studies. 1st lt. USAF, 1952-53. Recipient First Nat. award Fisher Body Craftsman's Guild, 1947, disting. svc. citation Automotive Hall of Fame, 1993. Mem. Calif. Scholastic Fedn. (life), Ferrari Club Am. Address: PO Box 8330 Rancho Santa Fe CA 92067-8330

JORDAN, ELLEN RAUSEN, law educator, consultant; b. Denver, Feb. 6, 1943; d. Joseph and Sarah (Ratner) Rausen; m. Carl Parsons Jordan, Aug. 20, 1967; children: Daniel Victor, Timothy Julian. BA, Cornell U., 1964; JD, Columbia U., 1972. Bar: Md. 1972. Analyst Nat. Security Agy., Ft. Meade, Md., 1964-66; programmer Bankers Trust Co., N.Y.C., 1966-69; sole practice, Cumberland, Md., 1972-75; asst. prof. law U. Ga., Athens, 1976-79, assoc. prof., 1980-85, prof., 1985-91, assoc. dean Sch. of Law, 1983-86; dean Sch. of Law, U. Calif., Davis, 1991-92; prof. of law, 1992—; vis. asst. prof. U. Va., Charlottesville, 1979-80; cons. U.S. Dept. Justice, Washington, 1980-81, Adminstrv. Conf. of U.S., Washington, 1982-83; acting assoc. v.p. academic affairs, U. Ga., 1986-88. Contbr. articles to profl. jours. Legal History fellow U. Wis., 1983. Mem. ABA, Assn. Am. Law Schs (exec. com. 1986-89), Am. Law Inst., Phi Beta Kappa, Phi Kappa Phi. Home: 2 Sequoia Pl Woodland CA 95695-4435 Office: UC Davis School of Law King Hall Davis CA 95616

JORDAN, FRANK M., mayor; b. San Francisco, Calif.; m. Wendy Paskin; children: Jim Jordan, Frank J. Jordan, Thomas Jordan. Former chief of police, San Francisco, 1986-1990; mayor City of San Francisco, 1992—. Office: Office of Mayor 401 Van Ness Ave Rm 336 San Francisco CA 94102-4603*

JORDAN, GLENN, theater director; b. San Antonio, Apr. 5, 1936. B.A., Harvard U., 1957; postgrad., Yale U. Drama Sch., 1957-58. Dir. regional and stock theatre, including Cafe La Mama, late 1950s; N.Y. directorial debut with Another Evening With Harry Stoones, 1961; other plays include A Taste of Honey, 1968; Rosencrantz and Guildenstern Are Dead, 1969, A Streetcar Named Desire at Cin. Playhouse in the Park, 1973, All My Sons at Huntington Hartford Theatre, 1975; founder, N.Y. TV Theater, 1965, dir. various plays, including Paradise Lost and Hogan's Goat; dir. mini-series Benjamin Franklin, CBS, 1974 (Emmy award 1975, Peabody award); Family, ABC-TV series, 1976-77, including segment Rights of Friendship (Dirs. Guild Am. award); numerous TV plays for public TV, including Eccentricities of a Nightingale, 1976; The Displaced Person, 1976; TV movies including Shell Game, 1975, One Of My Wives Is Missing, 1975, Delta County U.S.A, 1977, In The Matter of Karen Ann Quinlan, 1977, Sunshine Christmas, 1977, Les Miserables, 1978, Son-Rise, A Miracle of Love, 1979, The Family Man, 1979, The Women's Room, 1980, Lois Gibbs and the Love Canal, 1982, Heartsounds, 1984 (Peabody award), Toughlove, 1985, Dress Gray, 1986, Something in Common, 1986, Promise, 1986 (2 Emmy awards for producing, directing, Peabody award, Golden Globe award), Echoes in the Darkness, 1987, Jesse, 1988, Home Fires Burning, 1988, Challenger, 1989, The Boys, 1990, Sarah Plain and Tall, 1990, Aftermath, 1990, O Pioneers!, 1991, Barbarians at the Gate, 1992 (Emmy award Outstanding Made for TV Movie, 1993, Golden Globe award, Best Mini-series or movie made for TV, 1994), To Dance with the White Dog, 1994, Jane's House, 1994, My Brother's Keeper, 1994, A Streetcar Named Desire, 1995; dir: feature film Only When I Laugh (Neil Simon), 1981, The Buddy System, 1983, Mass Appeal, 1984. Recipient Emmy awards for N.Y. TV Theater Plays, 1970, Actors Choice, 1970. Office: care Bill Haber Creative Artists Agy 9830 Wilshire Blvd Beverly Hills CA 90212-1804 Office: Creative Artists Agy 9401 Wilshire Blvd Ste 700 Beverly Hills CA 90212-2920

JORDAN, ISOLDE JAHNCKE, Spanish and Portuguese language educator; b. Lisbon, Sept. 16, 1942; came to U.S., 1982; d. Bernhard and Grete (Durholt) Jahncke; m. William Thomas Warren III, July 7, 1967 (div. Feb. 1973); children: Alex Warren, John Warren; m. Sandoe Quarton Jordan, Feb. 2, 1987. Cert. in teaching, U. Bonn, Germany, 1965; PhD, U. Paris, 1966; PhD in Spanish, U. Colo., 1987. Lectr. Portuguese U. Ill., Urbana, 1967-69, U. Freiburg, Germany, 1972-73; lectr. Spanish and Portuguese U. Colo., Boulder, 1987-94, sr. instr., 1994—. Author: Introduccion al analisis linguistico del discurso, 1994; editor: El inmovilismo existencial en la narrativa de Julio Ricci; contbr. articles to profl. jours. Mem. MLA, Am. Assn. Tchrs. Spanish and Portuguese. Home: 3243 4th St Boulder CO 80304-2155 Office: U Colo Dept Spanish CB278 Boulder CO 80309

JORDAN, JAMES DOUGLAS, JR., chemical dependency consultant; b. Bklyn., Oct. 1, 1965; s. James Douglas Sr. and Vergia (Kemp) J. BS, Coll. of Notre Dame, Belmont, Calif., 1987, MA in Psychology, 1993. Leadership devel. specialist Regional Leadership, Menlo Park, Calif., 1986-88; counselor Community Living Ctrs., Redwood City, Calif., 1987-89, client program coord., 1989-90; juvenile group supr. San Mateo Probation Dept., Belmont, Calif., 1988-93; supervising case mgr. Community Living Ctrs., Redwood City, 1990-92; exec. cons. Chem. Dependency Cons. and Mktg. Group, San Jose, Calif., 1992—. Author papers. Rschr. Congl. Election Com., Sunnyvale, Calif., 1988-91; dir. pub. rels. Omega Youth Club, East Palo Alto, Calif., 1991—. Mem. Coll. of Notre Dame Alumni Assn. (bd. dirs. 1988-91), Delta Epsilon Sigma, Kappa Gamma Pi. Office: Chem Dependency Consulting & Mktg Group 5339 Prospect Rd # 409 San Jose CA 95129-5033

JORDAN, JEFFREY GUY, foodservice marketing executive; b. Oshkosh, Wis., May 21, 1950; s. Berwin Russell and Delores Suzanne (Tomlitz) J. BS, U. Wis., Oshkosh, 1973; postgrad., UCLA, 1978. Analyst corp. planning and rsch. May Co. Dept. Store, L.A., 1973-77; dir. mktg. svcs. DJMC Advt., L.A., 1977-80; dir. mktg. Wienerschnitzel, Internat., Newport Beach, Calif., 1980-84, York Steakhouse Restaurants (Gen. Mills), Columbus, Ohio, 1984-85, Paragon Restaurant Group, San Diego, 1985-87; v.p. mktg. Paragon Steakhouse Restaurants, Inc., San Diego, 1987—; cons., presenter U.S. Internat. U., San Diego, 1989. Mem. Conv. and Visitors Bur., San Diego; vol. Boys' Club of Am., Oshkosh, 1973-74; fundraising coord. Am. Cancer Soc., L.A., 1976. Mem. Am. Mktg. Assn., Multi Unit Foodservice Operators Assn., San Diego Advt. Assn. (creative exec. 1986-88), San Diego C. of C. Republican. Lutheran. Office: 6620 Convoy Ct San Diego CA 92111-1009

JORDAN, JOHN EMORY, language professional, educator; b. Richmond, Va., Apr. 8, 1919; s. Emory DeShazo and Magdalene (Yarbrough) J.; m. Marie Estelle Keyser, June 14, 1943 (dec. Sept. 1986); children: John Craig, Leigh Keyser, Hugh DeShazo; m. Katherine Lee Lyle, Dec. 4, 1987. BA, U. Richmond, 1940; MA, Johns Hopkins U., 1942, PhD, 1947. Jr. instr. English Johns Hopkins U., 1946-47; mem. faculty U. Calif. at Berkeley, 1947—, prof. English, 1959-85, prof. emeritus, 1986—, vice chmn. dept., 1960-69, chmn. dept., 1969-73, acad. asst. to chancellor, 1962-65, acad. asst. v.p. acad. affairs and personnel, 1974-75; Mem. Calif. Adv. Com. English Framework, 1964-67. Author: Thomas de Quincey, Literary Critic, 1952, reprinted 1972, Stevenson's Silverado Journal, 1954, De Quincey to Wordsworth, 1962, Using Rhetoric, 1965, Why The Lyrical Ballads?, 1976; co-author: English Romantic Poets and Essayists, 2d edit, 1966, English Language Framework, 1968; editor: (Thomas de Quincey) Confessions of an English Opium Eater, 1960, English Mail Coach, 1960, Reminiscences of the English Lake Poets, 1961, (Shelley and Peacock) Defence of Poetry and the Four Ages of Poetry, 1965, Questions of Rhetoric, 1971, Sackville West, A Flame in Sunlight, 1974, Peter Bell (Cornell Wordsworth), 1985; co-editor: Some British Romantics, 1966. Served with USNR, 1942-46. Recipient Honors citation U. Calif.-Berkeley, 1986; Ford fellow, 1954-55, Guggenheim fellow, 1958-59, Humanities rsch. fellow, 1967-68, 73-74; Gayley lectr., 1964. Mem. MLA (chmn. sect. 9 1963-64, contbr. Romantic Bibliography 1965—), Nat. Council Tchrs. English (dir. 1965-68), Phi Beta Kappa, Phi Gamma Delta, Tau Kappa Alpha, Pi Delta Epsilon, Omicron Delta Kappa. Home: 834 Santa Barbara Rd Berkeley CA 94707-2018

JORDAN, LAWRENCE WILLIAM, engineering educator; b. Lakewood, Ohio, Mar. 8, 1931; s. Lawrence William and Virginia Lee (Little) J.; m. Donna Faye Craig, June 15, 1957; children: Craig Robert, Juli Claire, Lori Elaine. BChemE, Ohio State U., 1956, MSc, 1957, PhD, 1959; JD, UCLA, 1971. Bar: Calif. 1972, U.S. Ct. Appeals (9th cir.) 1973, U.S. Supreme Ct. 1981; registered profl. engr., Ohio, Calif., Oreg. Research engr. Calif. Research, La Habra, 1959-67; research chemist Aerojet-Gen., Downey, Calif., 1967-68; assoc. Bullivant, Wright et al, Portland, Oreg., 1971-74, Norman Stoll, Portland, 1974-77; city atty. Lake Oswego, Oreg., 1977-79; asst. adminstr. Oreg. Dept. Commerce, Salem, 1979-81; pres. SITEC, Salem, 1981-89; prof. of engring., dept. chair Coll. of Marin, Kentfield, Calif., 1989—. Author: Azeotropy: The Binary Systems, 1961, Continuing Legal Education Family Law, 1973 (award 1974). Mem. Orange (Calif.) City Council, 1964-72; mem. Salem Planning Commn. 1984-86. Fellow Proctor & Gamble Co., 1957, Dow Chem. Corp., 1958, Ford Found., 1970; Wilson scholar UCLA, 1968. Mem. State Bar Calif., Salem C. of C. (greeter, com. chmn. 1984-85), Tau Beta Pi, Pi Mu Epsilon, Sigma Xi, Phi Lambda Upsilon. Home: PO Box 176 Kentfield CA 94914-0176 Office: Coll of Marin 835 College Ave Kentfield CA 94904-2551

JORDAN, LOYD EDWARD, county sheriff; b. Ft. Collins, Colo., July 15, 1950; s. Lloyd Ross and Norma Shirleen (Tuescher) J.; children: Loyd Ross II, Andrew Trenton Jordan, Claire Cereen. BA, U. Northern Colo., 1972. Laborer Western States Constrn., Loveland, Colo., 1972-73; adjuster Gen. Adjustment Bur., Stochton, Calif., 1972-76; dep. sheriff Weld County (Colo.) Sheriff's Office, Greeley, 1976-87, sheriff, 1987—. founding mem. Weld Svc. Abuse Team, Greeley, 1979-84; mem. Colo. Juvenile Justice and Delinquency Council, Denver, 1987—; dist. capt. Weld County Rep. Party, Greeley, 1980-86. Mem. County Sheriff's of Colo., Am. Jail Assn., Nat. Sheriff's Assn., Northeastern Colo. Peace Assn., Colo. State Sheriff's Posse Assn., Shriner (2d v.p. 1988), South Platte Lions, Masons. Home: 1714 11th Ave Greeley CO 80631-5508 Office: Weld County Sheriff's Office 910 10th Ave # 759 Greeley CO 80631-3873

JORDAN, MICHAEL AYTCH, accounts manager; b. Lewiston, Idaho, July 22, 1948; s. Aytch Jordan and Betty Jean (Petrie) Jordan Nestor; m. Nancy Loraine Lewis, sept. 27, 1972 (div. June 1990); m. Betsy Jane Conant, Dec. 27, 1990; children: Leatha, Sarah, Joshua, Michael. BBA magna cum laude, Nat. U., 1978, MBA, 1979. Human resource rep. Westinghouse, Richland, Wash., 1980; wardrobe cons. S.L. Sterling, Kennewick, Wash., 1980-84; med. ctr. acct. mgr. Wyeth-A-Lerst Labs., Phila., 1984—; study adv. bd. N.W. Pharmacy Rsch. Network, Seattle, 1993—. With USN, 1968-79, Vietnam. Mem. Nat. Bus. Womens Assn. Home: 23620 219th Pl SE Maple Valley WA 98038-8593

JORDAN, RAYMOND ALAN, forensic engineer, consultant; b. Haldimand County, Ont., Can., Dec. 18, 1942. B Engring. Sci., U. Western Ont., 1966; MS, Tex. A&M U., 1974. Registered profl. engr., Ariz., Ont.; cert. safety profl. Commd. 2d lt. Can. Armed Forces, 1966, advanced through grades to maj., served as aerospace engr., 1966-83, ret., 1983; co-founder, v.p. Microstar Software Ltd., Nepean, Ont., 1983-85; engring. cons. Arndt and Assocs., Tempe, Ariz., 1985-87; pres. Jordan Cons. Svcs., Phoenix, 1987—; prin. Jordan Fine Arts, Phoenix, 1987—; chief exec. officer The Jordan Group, Phoenix, 1991—; aerospace engring. adv. bd. Can. Armed Forces, 1975-77; cons. Ambon Internat., Phoenix, 1991—; mem. First Circle bd. dirs. Atlatl, 1994—. Contbr. articles to profl. publs. Mayor Community Coun., Medley, Alta., Can., 1977; mem. minister's adv. com. on further edn., Province of Alta., 1978. Recipient Can. Merit award Govt. of Can., 1978, Cert. of Merit, Aerospace Engring. Test Establishment, Cold Lake, Alta., 1978. Mem. Am. Soc. Safety Engrs., Nat. Forensics Ctr., Internat. Soc. Air Safety Investigators, Alpha Pi Mu. Office: The Jordan Group 9402 S 43rd Pl Phoenix AZ 85044-5545

JORDAN, ROBERT LEON, lawyer, educator; b. Reading, Pa., Feb. 27, 1928; s. Anthony and Carmela (Votto) J.; m. Evelyn Allen Willard, Feb. 15, 1958; children—John Willard, David Anthony. BA, Pa. State U., 1948; LLB, Harvard U., 1951. Bar: N.Y. 1952. Assoc. White & Case, N.Y.C., 1953-59; prof. law UCLA, 1959-70, 75-91, prof. law emeritus, 1991—, assoc. dean Sch. Law, 1968-69; vis. prof. law Cornell U., Ithaca, N.Y., 1962-63; co-reporter Uniform Consumer Credit Code, 1964-70, Uniform Comml. Code Articles 3, 4, 4A, 1985-90; Fulbright lectr. U. Pisa, Italy, 1967-68. Co-author: (with W.D. Warren) Commercial Law, 1983, 3d edit., 1992, Bankruptcy, 1985, 3d edit., 1993, 4th edit., 1995. Lt. USAF, 1951-53. Office: UCLA Sch Law 405 Hilgard Ave Los Angeles CA 90024-1301

JORDAN, WILLIAM W., food executive; b. 1928. Controller Bistrin's Dept. Store, Eureka, Calif., 1959-69, Arnel of Calif., San Francisco, 1969-70; with Naturipe Berry Growers, Watsonville, Calif., 1970—. Office: Naturipe Berry Growers 305 Industrial Rd Watsonville CA 95076-5118*

JORGENSEN, DONALD ALLAN, health facility administrator, immunologist; b. Omaha, Feb. 6, 1952; s. Allan Herbert and Virginia (Vance) J.; m. Mary Patricia Simpson, Sept. 5, 1975; children: Jason Allan, Katherine Marie, Jacob John. BS in Biology, George Mason U., 1974. From lab. technician to v.p. Kent Labs., Redmond, Wash., 1974—. Contbr. articles to profl. jours. Office: Kent Labs 23404 NE 8th St Redmond WA 98053-7227

JORGENSEN, ERIK HOLGER, lawyer; b. Copenhagen, July 19, 1916; s. Holger and Karla (Andersen) J.; children: Jette Friis, Lone Olesen, John, Jean Ann. JD, San Francisco Law Sch., 1960. Bar: Calif. 1961. Pvt. practice law, 1961-70; ptnr. Hersh, Hadfield, Jorgensen & Fried, San Francisco, 1970-76, Hadfield & Jorgensen, San Francisco, 1976-88 . Pres. Aldersly, Danish Retirement Home, San Rafael, Calif., 1974-77, Rebild Park Soc. Bay Area chpt., 1974-77. Fellow Scandinavian Am. Found. (hon.); mem. ABA, San Francisco Lawyers Club, Bar Assn. of San Francisco, Calif. Assn. Realtors (hon. life bd. dirs.). Author: Master Forms Guide for Successful Real Estate Agreements, Successful Real Estate Sales Agreements, 1995; contbr. articles on law and real estate law to profl. jours.

JORGENSEN, GORDON DAVID, engineering company executive; b. Chgo., Apr. 29, 1921; s. Jacob and Marie (Jensen) J.; BS in Elec. Engring., U. Wash., 1948, postgrad. in bus. and mgmt., 1956-59; m. Nadina Anita Peters, Dec. 17, 1948 (div. Aug. 1971); children: Karen Ann, David William, Susan Marie; m. Barbara Noel, Feb. 10, 1972 (div. July 1976); m. Ruth Barnes Chalmers, June 15, 1990. With R.W. Beck & Assos., Cons. Engrs., Phoenix, 1948—, ptnr., 1954-86; pres. Beck Internat., Phoenix, 1971—. Served to lt. (j.g.) U.S. Maritime Service, 1942-45. Recipient Outstanding Service award Phoenix Tennis Assn., 1967; Commendation, Govt. Honduras, 1970. Registered profl. engr., Alaska, Ariz., Calif., Colo., Nev., N.Mex., N.D., Utah, Wash., Wyo. Mem. IEEE (chmn. Wash.-Alaska sect. 1959-60), Nat. Soc. Profl. Engrs., Am. Soc. Appraisers (sr. mem.), Ariz. Cons. Engrs. Assn., Ariz. Soc. Profl. Engrs., Internat. Assn. Assessing Officers, Southwestern Tennis Assn. (past pres.), U.S. Tennis Assn. (pres. 1987-88, chmn. U.S. Open com.); chmn. U.S. Davis Cup com.; chmn. Internat. Tennis Fed., Davis Cup com. Presbyterian (elder). Project mgr. for mgmt., operation studies and reorgn. study Honduras power system, 1969-70. Home: 74-574 Palo Verde Dr Indian Wells CA 92210-7314 Office: RW Beck & Assocs 3003 N Central Ave Phoenix AZ 85012-2902

JORGENSEN, JUDITH ANN, psychiatrist; b. Parris Island, S.C.; d. George Emil and Margaret Georgia Jorgensen; BA, Stanford U., 1963; MD, U. Calif., 1968; m. Ronald Francis Crown, July 11, 1970. Intern, Meml. Hosp., Long Beach, 1969-70; resident County Mental Health Services, San Diego, 1970-73; staff psychiatrist Children and Adolescent Services, San Diego, 1973-78; practice medicine specializing in psychiatry, La Jolla, Calif., 1973—; staff psychiatrist County Mental Health Services of San Diego, 1973-78, San Diego State U. Health Services, 1985-87; psychiat. cons. San Diego City Coll., 1973-78, 85-86; asst. prof. dept. psychiatry U. Calif., 1978—, assoc. prof. dept. psychiatry, 1991—; chmn. med. quality rev. com. Dist. XIV, State of Calif., 1982-83. Mem. Am. Psychiat. Assn., San Diego Soc. Psychiat. Physicians (chmn. membership com. 1976-78, v.p. 1978-80, fed. legis. rep. 1985-87, fellowship com. 1989), Am. Soc. Adolescent Psychiatry, San Diego Soc. Adolescent Psychiatry (pres. 1981-82), Calif. Med. Assn. (former alternate del.), Soc. Sci. Study of Sex, San Diego Soc. Sex Therapy and Edn. (cert. sex therapist), San Diego County Med. Soc. (credentials com. 1982-84). Club: Rowing. Office: 470 Nautilus St Ste 211 La Jolla CA 92037-5970

JORGENSEN, LELAND HOWARD, aerospace research engineer; b. Rexburg, Idaho, Nov. 1, 1924; s. Leland Maeser and Anne Molyneaux (Howard) J.; m. Lynone Watkins, Mar. 24, 1949; children: Leland Ronald Jorgensen, Paul Victor Jorgensen, Jonathan Arthur Jorgensen, Sara Anne Jorgensen. BS in Mech. Engring. with honors, U. Utah, 1948; MS in Mech. Engring. with honors, Stanford U., 1949; PhD in Mech. Engring. with high honors, Calif. Coast U., 1977. Rsch. engr. NACA-Ames Aero. Lab., Moffett Field, Calif., 1949-59; rsch. scientist NASA-Ames Rsch. Ctr., Moffett Field, Calif., 1959-66, tech. asst. chief thermo and gas dynamics div., 1966-68, tech. asst. chief aeronautics div., 1968-71, aerospace rsch. scientist, 1971-80; aerospace cons. Sandy, Utah, 1980—; mem. aerodyn. panel for space shuttle NASA, 1978-80; cons. on Agile missile USN, 1972; cons. on air-slew missile USAF, 1973. Contbr. over 50 articles on aerodyns. of missiles and aircraft at subsonic, transonic, supersonic and hypersonic speeds to profl. jours. Trustee Saratoga (Calif.) Sch. Dist., 1977-81; v.p. Eagle Scout Assn. Santa Clara (Calif.) coun. Boy Scouts Am., 1962-72; pres. Neighborhood 5 Granite Cmty., Sandy, 1990-93; high priest LDS Ch. Lt. USNR, 1944-46, PTO. Fellow AIAA (assoc.); mem. SAR (pres. Salt Lake City chpt. 1989, pres. Utah Soc. 1992, chaplain 1994-96), Sons of the Utah Pioneers (life), Freedoms Found. at Valley Forge, Tau Beta Pi, Pi Tau Sigma, Sigma Nu, Theta Tau. Office: Aerospace Cons 3 La Montagne Ln Sandy UT 84092

JORGENSEN, LOU ANN BIRKBECK, social worker; b. Park City, Utah, May 14, 1931; d. Robert John and Lillian Pearl (Langford) Birkbeck; student Westminster Coll., 1949-51; B.S., U. Utah, 1953, M.S.W., 1972, D.S.W., 1979; grad. Harvard Inst. Ednl. Mgmt., 1983; m. Howard Arnold Jorgensen, June 9, 1954; children: Gregory Arnold, Blake John, Paul Clayton. Social work adminstr. nursing home demonstration project, dept. family and community medicine U. Utah Med. Ctr., Salt Lake City, 1972-74; mental health ednl. specialist Grad. Sch. Social Work, U. Utah, 1974-77, 77-80, asst. prof., 1974-80, assoc. prof., 1980-94, prof., 1994—, dir. doctoral program, 1984-89, assoc. dean, 1986-94; regional mental health cons. Bd. dirs. Info. and Referral Ctr., 1975-82, United Way of Utah, 1976-82, Pioneer Trail Parks, 1977-83, Rowland Hall-St. Marks Sch., 1980-86; Salt Lake County housing commr., 1980-86, Utah State Health Facilities Bd., 1991—, chair, 1994; pres. Human Svcs. Conf. for Utah, 1979-80; bd. dirs. Alzheimer Assn., Utah chpt., 1990—, Salt Lake County Coalition Bus. and Human Svcs., 1990-94, Town Club 1990-93, Valley Mental Health Bd., 1990—. Mem. Coun. on Social Work Edn., Commn. Women in High Edn., Nat. Assn. Social Workers (pres. Utah chpt. 1978-79), Adminstrs. of Public Agys. Assn., Human Svcs. Assn. Utah, Jr. League of Salt Lake City, Phi Kappa Phi. Republican. Episcopalian. Clubs: Town. Author: Explorations in Living, 1978, Social Work in Business and Industry, 1979; Handbook of the Social Services, 1981; contbr. articles to profl. jours. Home: 1458 Kristianna Cir Salt Lake City UT 84103-4221 Office: U Utah Grad Sch Social Work Social Work Building Bldg 324 Salt Lake City UT 84112-1182

JORGENSEN, PAUL ALFRED, English language educator emeritus; b. Lansing, Mich., Feb. 17, 1916; s. Karl and Rose Josephine (Simmons) J.; m. Virginia Frances Elfrink, Jan. 3, 1942; children: Mary Catherine, Elizabeth Ross Jorgensen Howard. A.B., Santa Barbara State Coll., 1938; M.A., U.

Calif. at Berkeley, 1940, Ph.D., 1945. Instr. English Bakersfield (Calif.) Jr. Coll., 1945-46, U. Calif., Berkeley, summer 1946, U. Calif., Davis, 1946-47; mem. faculty UCLA, 1947—, prof. English, 1960-81, prof. emeritus, 1981—; vis. prof. U. Wash., summer 1966; mem. editorial com. U. Calif. Press, 1957-60; mem. Humanities Inst. U. Calif., 1967-69; mem. acad. adv. council Shakespeare Globe Ctr. N.Am. Author: Shakespeare's Military World, 1956, (with Frederick B. Shroyer) A College Treasury, rev. edit, 1967, (with Shroyer) The Informal Essay, 1961, Redeeming Shakespeare's Words, 1962; editor: The Comedy of Errors, 1964, Othello: An Outline- Guide to the Play, 1964, (with Shroyer) The Art of Prose, 1965, Lear's Self-Discovery, 1967, Our Naked Frailties: Sensational Art and Meaning in Macbeth, 1971, William Shakespeare: The Tragedies, 1985; mem. bd. editors Film Quar, 1958-65, Huntington Library Quar, 1965-83, Coll. English, 1966-70; mem. adv. com. Publs. of MLA of Am, 1978-82. Guggenheim fellow, 1956-57; Regents' Faculty fellow in humanities, 1973-74. Mem. Modern Lang. Assn., Shakespeare Assn. Am. (bibliographer 1954-59), Renaissance Soc. Am., Philol. Assn., Pacific Coast (exec. com. 1962-63), Internat. Shakespeare Assn. Episcopalian. Home: 234 Tavistock Ave Los Angeles CA 90049-3229

JOSE, SHIRLEY ANN, nurse, critical care educator; b. Pueblo, Colo., Mar. 26, 1934; d. William Henry and Mildred Dorothy (Sanders) Priest; m. Laurent A. Jose, June 13, 1958; children: Steven William, Lauren Michele. BSN, Loma Linda U., 1957; MS, U. Colo., 1969. RN Colo. Staff nurse White Meml. Hosp., L.A., 1957-58, West Covina (Calif.) Hosp., 1958-59; sr. instr. Colo. State Hosp., Pueblo, 1960-62; charge nurse Swedish Med. Ctr., Englewood, Colo., 1965-68; asst. prof. Union Coll., Lincoln, Nebr., 1969-74; nursing coord. Porter Meml. Hosp., Denver, 1974-77; critical care nurse Dept. Vets. Affairs Med. Ctr., Denver, 1977-80, nursing instr., 1980-91, critical care educator, 1991-95, clin. coord., 1995—; asst. clin. prof. Sch. Nursing, U. Colo. Health Sci. Ctr., 1984—, mem. access com., 1987-88; reviewer Critical Care Nurse, 1986—; instr. ACLS, Am. Heart Assn., Denver, 1989—. Author of poems. Mem. citizens adv. com. Denver C.C., 1981—, chmn., 1991. Recipient Golden Poet award, 1991, Editor's Choice award Oustanding Achievement in Poetry, 1994. Mem. AACN, NNSDO, Hosp. Staff Devel. Network (program planning com. 1990-91), Sigma Theta Tau. Office: Dept VA Med Ctr 1055 Clermont St Denver CO 80220-3808

JOSEFF, JOAN CASTLE, manufacturing executive; b. Alta., Can., Aug. 12, 1922; naturalized U.S. citizen, 1945; d. Edgar W. and Lottie (Coates) Castle; BA in Psychology, UCLA; widowed; 1 son, Jeffrey Rene. With Joseff-Hollywood, jewelry manufacture and rental, Burbank, Calif., 1939—, chmn. bd., pres., sec.-treas., 1948—; exec. aircraft components mfg. co. Numerous TV appearances including CBS This Morning, Australia This Morning, Am. Movie Channel. Mem. Burbank Salary Task Force, 1979—, L.A. County Earthquake Fact-Finding Commn., 1981— ; bd. dirs. San Fernando Valley area chpt. Am. Cancer Soc., treas., Genesis Energy Systems, Inc., 1993—; mem. Rep. Cen. Com.; del. Rep. Nat. Conv., 1980, 84, 88, 92; voting mem. Calif. Rep. Party; chmn. Women Legis.; active Beautiful People Award Com. Honoring John Wayne Carcer Clinic; appointed by Gov. Wilson to Barber and Cosmotology Bd; appointed br Pres. Clinton to Selective Svc. System. Recipient Women in Achievement award Soroptomist Internat., 1988. Mem. Women of Motion Picture Industry (hon. life), Nat. Fedn. Rep. Women (bd. dir., Caring for Am. award 1986), Calif. Rep. Women (bd. dir., treas. 1986-90), North Hollywood Rep. Women (pres. 1981-82, parliamentarian), Nat. Fedn. of Rep (voting mem., program chair, 1994—), Calif. Fedn. of Rep. Women (chaplain, Americanism chmn. so. div., regent chmn. Women in Achievement award 1988), L.A. County Fedn. of Rep. Women (scholarship chmn.), Home: 10060 Toluca Lake Ave Toluca Lake CA 91602-2924 Office: 129 E Providencia Ave Burbank CA 91502-1922

JOSEPH, CONRAD, home health care executive; b. London, Mar. 10, 1946; came to U.S., 1947; s. William and Jane Joseph (Rothschild) J.; children: Colleen, Samantha, Sabrina. BBA, U. Detroit; MBA, London U.; PhD in Econs., Am. U. Commodity trader IMF Group, Nassau; CFO McFarlane Hazel Park Race Track; CEO/CFO St. Clair Group HMO, Grosse Pointe, Mich.; bd. Nassua Invest Pension Ltd., 1985-90, AP Bahamas Fund Ltd., 1980-90, Bahamas Marine Group, Nassau, 1980-90. Pres. Young Reps., Grosse Pointe, 1964-80; pres. Jr. Achievement, Grosse Pointe; rep. A.A. With USN, 1965-67. Mem. Mortgage Bankers Assn. (pres. 1975-80), Commodity Trader Assn. (treas. 1970-80), Commodity Pool Ops. (v.p.), Nursing Home Owners, Govs. Home Com. (v.p.). Republican. Jewish. Office: Conrad Joseph Commodity Grp 509 E Mcwilliams Ave Ste C Las Vegas NV 89101-2019

JOSEPH, EZEKIEL (ED JOSEPH), manufacturing company executive; b. Rangoon, Burma, June 24, 1938; s. Joe E. Joseph and Rachel Levi; m. Sheila G. Rabinovitch, Feb. 17, 1963; children: Renah, Heather, Jerald. Mktg. mgr. Gen. Electric Corp., Waynesboro, Va., 1968-75; dir. Actron div. McDonnell Douglas Corp., Monrovia, Calif., 1975-78; pres. Joseph Machinery Inc., Huntington Beach, Calif., 1978-84, Xtalite Display Systems Inc.), Huntington Beach, 1985-88, Secure Optical Systems Inc., Anaheim, Calif., 1992—; pres. Retract-a-Roof Inc., Huntington Beach. Pres. Temple Beth David, Huntington Beach, 1990—. Mem. Austin Healey Assoc. Democrat. Home: 16242 Typhoon Ln Huntington Beach CA 92649-2542 Office: Chemtek Co 16835 Algonquin St Ste 366 Huntington Beach CA 92649-3810

JOSEPH, GEORGE MANLEY, retired judge; b. Caldwell, Idaho, Aug. 31, 1930; s. Ben Manley and Mabel Gertrude (Newburn) J.; m. Elizabeth Lyle Starr, dec. 21, 1954; children: Sarah Katherine, Amy Elizabeth, Abigail Serena, Benjamin Manley, Jonathan Lyle. BA, Reed Coll., 1951; JD, U. Chgo., 1955; LLM, NYU, 1959. Law clk. Oreg. Supreme Ct., Salem, Oreg., 1955-56; law prof. Ohio No. U., Dickinson Sch. Law, U. Ark., 1956-63; dep. dist. atty. Multnomah County, Portland, Oreg., 1963-66; pvt. practice Portland, 1966-74; county counsel Multnomah County, Portland, 1975-77; judge Oreg. Ct. of Appeals, Salem, 1977-80; chief judge Ct. of Appeals Oreg., Salem, 1981-92. Alumni trustee Reed Coll., Portland, 1972-75, trustee, 1975-80; chmn. City-Coun ty Charter Commn., Portland, 1971-74; bd. vis. Willamette U. Sch. Law, Salem, 1980-92; vis. com. mem. Oriental Inst. U. Chgo., 1986—. Mem. Oreg. State Bar Assn., ABA, Multnomah Bar Assn., Council of Chief Judges (exec. com. vice-chmn. 1983-84, chmn. 1984-85). Home: 7110 SE 29th Ave Portland OR 97202-8730

JOSEPH, GREGORY NELSON, media critic; b. Kansas City, Mo., Aug. 25, 1946; s. Theodore Leopold and Marcella Kathryn (Nelson) J.; m. Mary Martha Stahler, July 21, 1973; children: John, Jacqueline, Caroline. AA, Met. C.C., Kansas City, 1967; BA with honors, U. Mo., Kansas City, 1969. Intern, cub reporter Kansas City Star-Times, 1965-67; feature writer, asst. city editor The Pasadena (Calif.) Union, 1971-73; investigative reporter The Pasadena Star-News, 1973-75; bus. writer The Riverside (Calif.) Press Enterprise, 1975-76; reporter, consumer writer, feature writer, TV critic The San Diego Tribune, 1976-90; TV columnist The Ariz. Republic, Phoenix, 1990-94; media critic, 1994—. Recipient various writing awards Copley Newspapers, Pasadena and San Diego, 1971-73, 83, Pub. Awareness award San Diego Psychiat. Physicians, cert. of appreciation Epilepsy Soc. San Diego County, 1989. Mem. SAG, NATAS (bd. govs. 1990-92), TV Critics Assn., Internat. Platform Assn. Roman Catholic. Home: 4864 W Alice Ave Glendale AZ 85302-5107

JOSEPH, JAMES EDWARD, engineering technician; b. Napa, Calif., Sept. 24, 1946; s. Wilbur Raymond and Lois Grace (Pouget) J.; m. Deborah Dianne Horvath, June 5, 1971; children: Brian Christopher, Stacy Lynn Joseph Holster. Diploma, N. Am. Sch. Drafting, 1974, hon. grad. cert., 1977; AA, Napa Valley Coll., 1976; BS, So. Ill. U., 1986. Naval archtl. aide Mare Island Naval Shipyard, Vallejo, 1967-70; naval archtl. technician Mare Island Naval Shipyard, Vallejo, Calif., 1974-77, 77-89; naval architect tech. supr. Mare Island Naval Shipyard, Napa, 1989-91, project leader, 1991-92, material control mgr., 1992-94, engrng. technician, 1994—; refinery operator Union Oil Co. Calif., 1971-74; designer, draftsman Morris Guralnick Assocs., Inc., 1974, propulsion technician, 1977; designer, draftsman, owner, operator Joseph's Drafting & Design Svc., 1984-88; engrng. technician Puget Sound Naval Shipyard, Bremerton, Wash., 1994—; designer, draftsman Napa Babe Ruth Baseball League, 1986. Author: (material control program) Navyshipydmareinst, 1993, Desk Notes for Ocean Engineering Subsafe Re-Entry Control Group, 1994. Chair citizen adv. panel Dept. Motor Vehicles, Napa; bd. dirs. Youth Adv. Bd. Oleum Fed. Credit Union, Rodeo, Calif., 1971-74; coach Young Am. Bowling Assn., Napa, 1980-3, 93-94, T-Ball and Babe Ruth Baseball, 1979-80, 85-86; auditor West Park Elem. Sch. PTA, parent vol., outdoor edn. vol. trips. Mem. Am. Bowling Congress. Republican. Office: Puget Sound Naval Shipyard Engring Code 126 Bremerton WA 98314-5000

JOSEPH, JOYCE MARIE See AMIN, JAMILLAH MAARIJ

JOSEPHSON, HAROLD ALLAN, real estate developer; b. Montreal, Que., Can., July 21, 1944; s. Joseph and Edith (Marco) J.; m. Sheila Gloria Laing, July 4, 1966 (div. July 1976); children: Daniel, Robert.; MBA with distinction, Harvard U., 1971. V.p. Marcil Mortgage Corp., Montreal, 1976-78; prin. Josephson Properties, Montreal, 1978-83, Los Angeles, 1983—. Mem. Urban Land Inst., Nat. Assn. Indsl. and Office Parks, Internat. Council Shopping Ctrs. Jewish. Club: Beverly Hills Country (Los Angeles), Regency (Los Angeles).

JOSHI, SATISH DEVDAS, organic chemist; b. Bombay, Maharashtr, India, Sept. 29, 1950; came to U.S., 1982; s. Devdas Ganesh and Premlata (Prabhu) J.; m. Shima Janakimohan Bhadra, May 2, 1974; children: Shruti, Shilpa. BS, Bombay U., 1970, MS, 1972; PhD in Chemistry, Bombay U., Bombay, 1977. Rsch. fellow State U. Gent, Belgium, 1979-81, Louvain Med. Sch., Brussels, Belgium, 1981-82; rsch. assoc. Mt. Sinai Sch. Medicine, N.Y.C., 1982-85; group leader Bachem, Inc., Torrance, Calif., 1985-87; dir. Bachem Biosci. Inc., Phila., 1987-89; pres., chief exec. officer Star Biochems., Torrance, 1989-91; tech. dir. Mallinckrodt Inc., St. Louis, 1991—. Mem. AAAS, ACS, Am. Peptide Soc., Torrance C. of C. Home: 1928 Via Estudillo Palos Verdes Estates CA 90274

JOST, RICHARD FREDERIC, III, lawyer; b. N.Y.C., Sept. 25, 1947; s. Richard Frederic Jr. and Gertrude (Holoch) J.; m. Sally Ann Galvin, July 29, 1972; children: Jennifer, Richard IV. BA, Dickinson Coll., 1969; JD, Syracuse U., 1975. Bar: N.Y. 1976, Nev. 1978, U.S. Dist. Ct. Nev. 1979, U.S. Supreme Ct. 1984. Dep. dist. atty. Elko (Nev.) County Dist. Atty.'s Office, 1976-80; dep. atty. gen. Nev. Atty. Gen.'s Office, Carson City, 1980-83; ptnr. Jones, Jones, Close & Brown, Las Vegas, Nev., 1983—. Trustee United Meth. Ch., Carson City, Nev., 1982-83; bd. dirs. Ormsby Assn. Retarded Citizens, Carson City, 1982-83. Served to lt. USNR, 1970-74. Mem. ABA (urban, state and local govt. law sect.), Clark County Bar Assn., Nat. Assn. Bond Lawyers. Democrat. Home: 2840 S Monte Cristo Way Las Vegas NV 89117-2951 Office: Jones Jones Close & Brown 300 S 4th St Ste 700 Las Vegas NV 89101-6014

JOW, PAT See KAGEMOTO, PATRICIA JOW

JOY, CARLA MARIE, history educator; b. Denver, Sept. 5, 1945; d. Carl P. and Theresa M. (Lotito) J. AB cum laude, Loretto Heights Coll., 1967; MA, U. Denver, 1969, postgrad., 1984—. Instr. history Community Coll. Denver; prof. history Red Rocks Community Coll., Lakewood, Colo., 1970—; cons. for innovative ednl. programs; reviewer fed. grants, 1983-89; mem. adv. panel Colo. Endowment for Humanities, 1985-89. Contbr. articles to profl. publs. Instr. vocat. edn. Mile High United Way, Jefferson County, 1975; participant Jefferson County Sch. System R-1 Dist., 1983-88; active Red Rocks Community Coll. Speakers Bur., 1972-89, strategic planning com., 1992—; chair history discipline The Colo. Core Transfer Consortium Project, 1986—; Colo. Dept. of Edn. (mem. history, geography, civics stds. and geography frameworks adv. com. 1995—). Cert. in vocat. edn. Colo. State Bd. Community Colls. and Occupational Edn., 1975; mem. evaluation team for Colo. Awards, edn. and civic achievement for Widefield Sch. Dist. #3, 1989; mem. Red Rocks Community Coll.-Clear Creek Sch. System Articulation Team, 1990-91. Ford Found. fellow, 1969; recipient cert. of appreciation Kiwanis Club, 1981, Cert. of Appreciation Telecommunication Coop. for Colo's. Community Colls., 1990-92; Master Tchr. award U. Tex. at Austin, 1982. Mem. Am. Hist. Assn., Am. Assn. Higher Edn., Nat. Council for Social Studies, Nat. Geog. Soc., Inst. Early Am. History and Culture, Nat. Edn. Assn., Colo. Edn. Assn., Colo. Council for Social Studies, The Smithsonian Nat. Assocs., Denver Art Mus., Denver Mus. of Nat. Hist., Community Coll. Humanities Assn., Orgn. Am. Historians, The Colo. Hist. Soc., Colo. Endowment for the Humanities, Colo. Geographic Alliance, Soc. History Edn., Phi Alpha Theta. Home: 1849 S Lee St Apt D Lakewood CO 80232-6252 Office: Red Rocks Community Coll 13300 W 6th Ave Golden CO 80401-5398

JOYCE, CASEY JOHN, grant development specialist, consultant; b. Ft. Benton, Mont., June 15, 1959; s. Edwin Joseph and Verda Agnus (McMahon) J.; m. Lenny Jean Proefrock, May 17, 1986. BS, Mont. State U., Billings, 1983. Recreation therapist Butte (Mont.) Pk. Royal Convalescent Ctr., 1983-84; project dir., grant writer Dist. VII Human Resources Devel. Coun., Billings, Mont., 1984-90; grant devel. specialist Mont. Tradeport Authority, Billings, 1990—. Pres. Billings Coun. for Nat. Coun. for Prevention of Child Abuse, 1993-94. Mem. Nat. Soc. Fund Raising Execs. (program chair 1993-94, treas. 1994-95). Office: Mont Tradeport Authority Ste 300W 2722 3rd Ave N Billings MT 59101

JOYCE, CLAUDE CLINTON, data processing executive; b. Lordsburg, N.Mex., May 10, 1931; s. William Claude and Minnie Merline (Gibson) J.; m. Wanda Cliftine Land, Dec. 7, 1951; children: Claude Clifton, Lani Caprice. BS in Acctg., San Diego State U., 1956. Supr. tabulator machines USN Supply Depot, San Diego, 1952-55; sales rep. Service Bur. Corp. subs. IBM, San Diego and San Francisco, 1955-59; dir. Mgmt. Adv. Services Price Waterhouse, San Francisco, 1959-68; sr. v.p. mgmt. info. systems Albertsons Inc., Boise, Idaho, 1968-90; ret., 1990; exec. v.p. Dubl-Click Software Corp., Bend, Oreg., 1984—. Served with USN, 1948-52. Recipient Achievement award Carnegie Melon U. and AMS, 1987. Mem. Assn. Systems Mgmt. (pres. 1972-73, Dist. Service award 1976). Republican. Lodges: Shriners (pres. 1979), Rotary, Mason. Home and Office: 9400 W Pebble Brook Ln Boise ID 83703-1760

JOYCE, JOHN DAVID, art educator, artist; b. Kindersley, Sask., Can., Jan. 7, 1946; came to U.S., 1970; m. Katharine Clark Smith, Aug. 22, 1970; 1 child, Anna Clark. BA in Liberal Arts and Humanities, Carleton U., 1969; MA in Broadcast Comm., U. Oreg., 1972, MFA in video, film and design, 1975. Asst. prof. Loyola U., Montreal, Can., 1975-76; instr. art and media arts Lane C.C., Eugene, Oreg., 1978—. One-man shows include Mayer Gallery, Marylhurst Coll., Lake Oswego, Oreg., 1981, Lane C.C. Gallery of Art, Eugene, Oreg., 1981, Gallery of Art, Chemeketa C.C., Salem, Oreg., 1982, Buckley Gallery, U. Portland, Oreg., 1982, Centre Eye Gallery Photography, Calgary, Can., 1982, Western Oreg. State Coll., Monmouth, 1983, Triton Mus. Art, Santa Clara, Calif., 1983, Benton County Mus., Philomath, Oreg., 1984, N.W. Artists Workshop, Portland, 1985, U. Oreg. Mus. Art, Eugene, 1985, 93, Maryhill Mus. Art, Goldendale, Wash., 1986, Marcuse Pfeifer Gallery, N.Y.C., 1987, 89, others; group exhbns. include Pratt Inst., N.Y.C., 1981, Ctrl. Wash. U., 1980, 82, 83, Meml. Gallery Ariz. State U., Tempe, 1982, Calif. Inst. Arts, Valencia, 1982, L.A. Ctr. Photographic Studies, 1983, Friends of Photography, Carmel, Calif., 1983, Galveston Arts Ctr., 1984, U. Calif. Berkeley, 1984, Alvin Gallery, Hong Kong, 1984, Pub. Image Gallery, N.Y.C., 1984, McIntosh/Drysdale Gallery, Washington, 1987, Boise Gallery of Art, 1986-87, Kohler Arts Ctr., Sheboygan, Wis., 1988, 90, Laura Russo Gallery, Portland, 1988, Clark Coll., Vancouver, 1989, Houston Ctr. Photography, 1990, Portland Art Mus., 1992, Walkers Pt. Ctr. Arts, Mpls., 1994; represented in collections Peninsula Coll., Port Angeles, Wash., Nike World Hdqrs., Portland, U. Oreg. Mus. Art; subject of profl. articles. Artist in Residence grantee NEA, Open Gallery, Eugene, Oreg., 1981, Can. Coun. Short-Term Support grantee, 1982; recipient Best of Show award Oreg./Wash. Juried Exhbn., Maryhill Mus. Art, 1985; Oreg. Artist's fellow Oreg. Arts Commn., 1986; named Top 100 New Photographers of 1987, Maine Photographic Workshops, 1987; participant Western States Art Fedn. Collectors' Resource Project, 1991. Home: 990 Madison Eugene OR 97402

JOYCE, MARILYN SCHMIDT, consulting company executive; b. Covington, Ky., Sept. 3, 1942; d. Robert Andrew and Rita Marie (Stadtmiller) S.; m. Clayton Robert Joyce, Nov. 29, 1975; stepchildren—David Joyce, Kathryn Joyce Keehn, Robert Joyce. B.A., Thomas More Coll., 1964; M.Ed., Xavier U., 1968. Tchr., Colerain High Sch., Cin., 1964-68; tchr. N.E. High Sch., Ft. Lauderdale, Fla., 1968-69; chmn. dept. curriculum devel. Henderson High Sch., Atlanta, 1969-75; trainer, mgr. URS Corp., Seattle, 1977-80; founder, pres. Joyce Inst., Seattle, 1981-95, dir.; ergonomics tng. cons. Textron, Inc., Washington Post, U.S. Postal Svc.; speaker Internat. Ergonomics Conf., 1986, 89, 90, 94, 95, Nat. Safety Coun. Conf., 1986, 91. Editor tng. courses: Dataspan, 1981, Datahealth, 1985. Author: Ergonomics: Humanizing the Automated Office, 1989; co-author tng. manual: Practical Office Ergonomics, 1986, Pro-Read, 1972. Mem. Am. Soc. Safety Engrs., Human Factors Soc., Am. Soc. Tng. and Devel., Internat. Safety & Ergonomics Soc., Seattle C. of C. (trustee 1988), Columbia Tower Club. Democrat. Roman Catholic. Home: 2220 40th Ave E Seattle WA 98112-2406

JOYCE, STEPHEN FRANCIS, human resource executive; b. Pitts., Nov. 24, 1941; s. John F. and Anna May (Boyle) J.; children: Autumn, Shannon. BSBA, Youngstown U., 1964. Asst. employment mgr. Collins div. Rockwell Internat., Newport Beach, Calif., 1967-70; pers. mgr. Hyland div. Baxter Labs., Inc., Costa Mesa, Calif., 1970-76; dir. indsl. rels. Pertec Computer Corp., Irvine, Calif., 1976-83; v.p. human resources Denny's, Inc., La Mirada, Calif., 1983-88; sr. v.p. human resources Ross Stores, Inc., Newark, Calif., 1988—. Mem. exec. bd. Pres.'s Com. on Employment of People with Disabilities. With U.S. Army NG, 1965-71. Mem. Am. Compensation Assn., Coll. Placement Coun., Employment Mgmt. Assn., Soc. Human Resource Mgmt. Republican. Home: 685 High St Palo Alto CA 94301-1626 Office: Ross Stores Inc 8333 Central Ave Newark CA 94560-3433

JOYCE, STEPHEN MICHAEL, lawyer; b. Los Angeles, Mar. 19, 1945; s. John Rowland and Elizabeth Rose (Rahe) J.; m. Bernadette Anne Novey, Aug. 18, 1973; children: Natalie Elizabeth, Vanessa Anne. BS, Calif. State U., Los Angeles, 1970; JD, U. San Fernando, 1976. Bar: Calif. 1976, U.S. Dist. Ct. (cen. dist.) Calif. 1977, U.S. Ct. Claims 1981. Pvt. practice Beverly Hills, Calif., 1976-93; ptnr. Gold & Joyce, Beverly Hills, 1982-84; personal atty. to Stevie Wonder and various other celebrities, 1977—. Contbr. articles to profl. jours. Served to pvt. USAR, 1963-69. Mem. ABA, Calif. Bar Assn., Los Angeles County Bar Assn., Beverly Hills Bar Assn., Los Angeles Trial Lawyers Assn. Democrat. Roman Catholic. Club: Calabasas (Calif.) Athletic. Home: 4724 Barcelona Ct Calabasas CA 91302-1403 Office: 16530 Ventura Blvd Ste 600 Encino CA 91436-2006

JOYNER, DARLA JEAN, trade association executive; b. Sioux Falls, S.D., Dec. 4, 1947; d. John Jay and Darlene Dorothy (Loe) Anderberg; m. John A. Joyner, Dec. 7, 1968; children: Jay Arthur, Amy Renee, Evan James. AA, Arapahoe Community Coll., 1974; postgrad., Met. State Coll., Denver, 1974-78; cert., Inst. Organizational Mgmt., Boulder, Colo., 1986. Layout artist JC Penney, Denver, 1973-74; gen. mgr. Bozeman (Mont.) Area C. of C., 1978-83, exec. v.p., chief exec. officer, 1983—; state adv. coun. Mont. Small Bus. Administrn.; S.W. Mont. adv. bd. Horizon Airlines. Editor Ignacio Chieftain mag., 1971-72, Beverage Analyst Mag., 1972-73. Trustee Belgrade (Mont.) City-County Planning Bd., 1986—, Belgrade Sch. Dist., 1990—, vice chair, 1990-93; bd. dirs. Big Bros. and Sisters, Bozeman; bd. dirs., steering com. Mike Mansfield Found. Sgt. USMC, 1966-69. Mem. Am. C. of C. Execs (del. 1989-90), Mountain States Assn. C. of C. (pres. bd. dirs. 1990-91), Mont. Assn. Chamber Execs. (pres. 1987-88), Bus. Profl. Women (v.p. Bozeman chpt. 1982-83, Outstanding Young Woman award 1983, Woman of Achievement award 1985), Gallatin Performing Art Ctr. (sec., bd. dirs. 1989—), Mont. SBA (adv. coun. 1992—), Mont. State Rural Devel. Coun. (exec. com.), Mus. Rockies, Rotary.

JOYNER, JOHN BROOKS, museum director; b. Balt., Nov. 24, 1944; s. Joseph Brooks and Majel Ethel (Sanichas) J.; m. Marcia Lee Perkins, Apr. 5, 1966 (div. 1979); 1 child, Shelly Lyn; m. Georgina Louise Davis, May 1, 1982; 1 child, Jonathan Burgess. BA, U. Md., 1966, MA, 1969; postgrad., NYU, 1968-71. Teaching asst. U. Md., College Pk., 1966-68, mus. fellow, 1969-70; adj. lectr. Hunter Coll., CUNY, N.Y.C., 1970-71; curator Towson State U. Art Gallery, Towson, MD., 1972-74; dir., curator Nickle Arts Mus./U. Calgary, Alta., Can., 1975-80; lect. U. Alta., Edmonton, Can., 1980-83; exec. dir. South Bend (Ind.) Art Ctr., 1983-87; dir. Montgomery (Ala.) Mus. Fine Arts, 1987-93, Vancouver Art Gallery, 1993—; grants reviewer Inst. Mus. Svcs., Washington, 1988-89; project dir. George Rickey in South Bend, 1983-85; founder/dir. Brooks Joyner Art Cons. Ltd., Calgary, Alta., Can., 1980-83. Author: Marion Nicol R.C.A., 1979, (exbn. catalogue) The Drawings of Arshile Gorky, 1969; contbr. articles to art mags. Sec. Cottage Hill Found., Montgomery, 1989; adv. Jr. League of Montgomery, 1988-89. Recipient fellowship NYU, 1969, Smithsonian Instn., Washington, 1972. Mem. Assn. Art Mus. Dirs., Am. Assn. Museums (small mus. adminstrs. com., accreditation reviewer 1989), Can. Art Mus. Dirs. Orgn., Internat. Coun. Museums. Republican. Home: 1732 Bewicke Ave, North Vancouver, BC Canada V7M3C4

JOYNER, SETH, professional football player; b. Spring Valley, NY, Nov. 18, 1964. Student, U. Texas, El Paso. Linebacker Phila. Eagles, 1986-94; with Arizona Cardinals, 1994—. Office: Arizona Cardinals PO Box 888 Phoenix AZ 85001-0888*

JU, JINGFANG, biochemist; b. Chifeng, Peoples Republic of China, June 18, 1967; came to U.S., 1990; s. Guang Zhu and Xiufeng Xiu Ju; m. Jing Yu. BS, Northeastern U., Shenyang, Liaoning, 1989; MS, N.Mex. Highlands U., 1992; postgrad., U. So. Calif., 1994—. Tchg. asst. N.Mex. Highlands U., Las Vegas, 1990-91, rsch. asst., 1991-92; rsch. asst. U. So. Calif., L.A., 1992—. Recipient scholarship Northeastern U., 1985-87, fellowship Los Alamos Nat. Lab., 1991-92. Mem. AAAS, Am. Assn. Cancer Rsch. (assoc.). Home: 1225 Benito Ave Apt E Alhambra CA 91803-2310

JUAREZ, MARETTA LIYA CALIMPONG, social worker; b. Gilroy, Calif., Feb. 14, 1958; d. Sulpicio Magsalay and Pelagia Lagotom (Viacrusis) Calimpong; m. Henry Juarez, Mar. 24, 1984. BA, U. Calif., Berkeley, 1979; MSW, San Jose State U., 1983. Lic. clin. social worker; cert. in eye movement desensitization and reprocessing. Mgr. Pacific Bell, San Jose, Calif., 1983-84; revenue officer IRS, Salinas, Calif., 1984-85; social worker Santa Cruz (Calif.) County, 1985, Santa Clara County, San Jose, 1985—; co-chair Inter-Agy. Coun. of South Santa Clara County. Recipient award Am. Legion, 1972. Mem. NASW, Nat. Coun. on Alcoholism, Assn. Play Therapists. Democrat. Roman Catholic.

JUAREZ, MARK ANDREW, computer analyst; b. Whittier, Calif., Dec. 26, 1960; s. Andrew Ralph Juarez and Rosa de la Rosa; m. Teresa Ann Messina, July 12, 1986; children: Christopher Mark, Kathleen Rose. BA, Calif. State Polytechnic U., 1985; MA, Calif. State U., Dominguez Hills, Calif., 1988. Cert. adult edn. tchr., Calif. Owner Archtl. Hardware and Electronics, Alhambra, Calif., 1988—; personnel rep. Allstate Ins., Glendale, Calif., 1985-86; electronic sales rep., buyer Constrn. Hdwre. Co., Pomona, Calif., 1986-89; regional rep. U.S. JVC, Cypress, Calif., 1989-90; adminstr./computer cons. San Gabriel (Calif.) Valley Constrn., 1990-91; programmer analyst Ralphs Grocery Co., Compton, Calif., 1991—. Pres. Planning Commn., Alhambra, 1988—. Mem. IEEE. Home: 425 N Chapel Ave Apt B Alhambra CA 91801-2571 Office: Ralphs Grocery Co 1100 W Artesia Blvd Compton CA 90220

JUBERG, RICHARD KENT, mathematician, educator; b. Cooperstown, N.D., May 14, 1929; s. Palmer and Hattie Noreen (Nelson) J.; m. Janet Elisabeth Witchell, Mar. 17, 1956 (div.); children: Alison K., Kevin A., Hilary N., Ian C.T.; m. Sandra Jean Vakerics, July 8, 1989. BS, U. Minn., 1952, PhD, 1958. Asst. prof. U. Minn., Mpls., 1958-65; sci. faculty fellow Universita di Pisa, Italy, 1965-66; assoc. prof. U. Calif., Irvine, 1966-72, U. Sussex, Eng., 1972-73; prof. U. Calif., Irvine, 1974-91, prof. emeritus, 1991—; vis. prof. U. Goteborg, Sweden, 1981; mem. Courant Inst. Math. Scis., NYU, 1957-58. Contbr. articles to profl. jours. With USN, 1946-48, Guam. NSF Faculty fellow, Univ. Pisa, Italy, 1965-66. Mem. Am. Math. Soc., Tau Beta Pi. Democrat. Office: U Calif Math Dept Irvine CA 92717

JUDD, BRUCE DIVEN, architect; b. Pasadena, Calif., Sept. 28, 1947; s. David Lockhart and Martha Leah (Brown) J.; m. Diane Reinbolt, Feb. 4, 1976 (div. Oct. 1985); 1 child, Ian David. BArch, U. Calif., Berkeley, 1970, MArch, 1971. Registered arch., Calif., Nev.; cert. Nat. Coun. Archtl. Registration Bds. Designer Ribera and Sue Landscape Archs., Oakland, Calif., 1968-70, Page Clowdsley & Baleix, San Francisco, 1971-75; v.p. Charles Hall Page Assocs., San Francisco, 1975-80; ptnr. Archtl. Resources Group, San Francisco, 1980—; mem. adv. bd. fed. rehab. guidelines program Nat. Inst. Bldg. Scis., HUD, 1978-80; mem. city-wide survey planning com. City of Oakland, Calif., 1979-80; cons. Nat. Main St. Program, Washington. Bd. dirs., co-founder Oakland Heritage Alliance, 1980-85; mem. Calif. Hist. Resources Commn., 1982-86, chmn., 1983-85; bd. dirs. Preservation Action, Washington, 1982-85, 90—, Friends of Terra Cotta, 1981-86, Berkeley Archtl. Heritage Assn., 1993—; mem. bd. advisors Nat. Trust for Hist. Preservation, Washington, 1981-90, advisor emeritus, 1990—; bd. trustees Calif. Preservation Found., San Francisco, 1985—, v.p., 1990-92, trustee, 1990—; active Calif. State Hist. Bldg. Safety Bd., 1991-93, also others. Recipient Excellence Honor award State of Calif., Excellence award in archtl. conservation, Spl. Restoration award Sunset Mag.; named Preservationist of Yr., Calif. Preservation Found., 1993. Fellow AIA (preservation officer No. Calif. chpt. 1978-81, hist. resources com. Calif. coun. 1979-80, nat. hist. resources com. 1981—, chmn. 1981-82); mem. Internat. Assn. for Preservation Tech. (bd. dirs. 1983-85), Park Hills Homes Assn. (chmn. archtl. com. 1992—), U.S./Internat. Coun. Monuments and Sites. Office: Archtl Resources Group Pier 9 The Embarcadero San Francisco CA 94111

JUDD, DENNIS L., lawyer; b. Provo, Utah, June 27, 1954; s. Derrel Wesley and Leila (Lundquist) J.; m. Carol Lynne Chilberg, May 6, 1977; children: Lynne Marie, Amy Jo, Tiffany Ann, Andrew, Jacquelyn Nicole. BA in Polit. Sci. summa cum laude, Brigham Young U., 1978, JD, 1981. Bar: Utah 1981, U.S. Dist. Ct. Utah 1981. Assoc. Nielson & Senior, Salt Lake City and Vernal, Utah, 1981-83; dep. county atty. Uintah County, Vernal, 1982-84; ptnr. Bennett & Judd, Vernal, 1983-88; county atty. Daggett County, Utah, 1985-89, 91—; pvt. practice Vernal, 1988—; county atty. Daggett County, 1991—; mem. governing bd. Uintah Basin applied Tech. Ctr., 1991-95, v.p., 1993-94, pres., 1994-95. Chmn. bd. adjustment Zoning and Planning Bd., Naples, 1982-91, 94—; mem. Naples City Coun., 1982-91; mayor pro tem City of Naples, 1983-91; legis. v.p. Naples PTA, 1988-90; v.p. Uintah Dist. PTA Coun., 1990-92; mem. resolution com. Utah League Cities and Towns, 1985-86, small cities com., 1985-86; trustee Uintah Sch. Dist. Found., 1988—, vice chmn., 1991-93; mem. Uintah County Sch. Dist. Bd. Edn., 1991-95, v.p., 1991-92, pres., 1992-95. Hinkley scholar Brigham Young U., 1977. Mem. Utah Bar Assn., Uintah Basin Bar Assn., Statewide Assn. Prosecutors, Vernal C. of C. Republican. Mormon. Home: 402 E 1500 S Vernal UT 84078-4471 Office: 319 W 100 S Ste B Vernal UT 84078-2517

JUDD, THOMAS ELI, electrical engineer; b. Salt Lake City, Apr. 12, 1927; s. Henry Eli Judd and Jennie Meibos; m. Mary Lu Edman, June 21, 1948; children: Shauna, Kirk E., Blake E., Lisa. BSEE, U. Utah, 1950. Registered profl. engr., Utah. Mech. engr. Utah Power & Light Co., Salt Lake City, 1950-55; chief engr. Electronic Motor Car Corp., Salt Lake City, 1955-56, Equi-Tech Corp., Salt Lake City, 1978-79; hydraulic devel. engr. Galigher Co., Salt Lake City, 1956-58; pres. Toran Corp., Salt Lake City, 1958-71, T M Industries, Salt Lake City, 1971-78; chief exec. officer, mgr. Ramos Corp., Salt Lake City, 1979—; project cons. Eimco Corp., Salt Lake City, 1966; design cons. to tech. cos. Patentee in field in U.S. and fgn. countries; contbr. editor U.S. Rail News, 1982—. Cons. Nat. Fedn. Ind. Bus., 1983—. With USNR, 1945-46, PTO. Mem. Tau Beta Pi. Republican. Mormon. Home: 956 Elm Ave Salt Lake City UT 84106-2330 Office: Ramos Corp 125 Harris Ave Salt Lake City UT 84115-5204

JUDELSON, HOWARD SETH, plant pathology educator; b. N.Y.C., Oct. 12, 1958; s. Norman and Lila (Sachs) J. BS in Biochemistry, Cornell U., 1980; PhD in Molecular Biology, U. Wis., 1985. Postdoctoral fellow U. Calif., Davis, 1986-90, asst. geneticist, 1990-94; asst. prof. U. Calif., Riverside, 1994—. Fellow NIH, 1980-84, McKnight Found., 1988-90. Office: Dept Plant Pathology Univ Calif Riverside CA 92521

JUDGE, GEORGE GARRETT, economics educator; b. Carlisle, Ky., May 2, 1925; s. William Everett and Etna (Perkins) J.; m. Sue Dunkle, Mar. 17, 1950; children: Lisa C., Laura S.; m. Margaret C. Copeland, Oct. 8, 1976. BS, U. Ky., 1948; MS, Iowa State U., 1949, PhD, 1952. Asst. prof. U. Conn., Storrs, 1951-55; prof. U. Okla., Stillwater, 1955-58; vis. prof. Yale U., New Haven, 1958-59; prof. econs. U. Ill., Urbana, 1959-86; prof. U. Calif., Berkeley, 1986—; vis. disting. prof. U. Ga., 1977-79; cons. Internat. Wool Secretariat, London, 1976-77. Author: Learning and Practicing Econometrics, 1993, Improved Methods of Inference, 1986, Introduction to the Theory and Practice of Econometrics, 1982, 88, Theory and Practice of Econometrics, 1980, 85, Pre-Test and Stein Rule Estimators, 1978, Allocation Over Space and Time, 1975, Spatial Equilibrium, 1972; Markov Processes, 1970. Served with USAAF, 1943-45; PTO. Fellow Social Sci. Research Council, 1958-59, NSF, 1965-66; NSF grantee, 1976-87. Fellow Econometric Soc.; mem. Am. Statis. Assn., Am. Econ. Assn. Club: Dial. Avocations: golf, sailing. Office: U Calif 207 Giannini Berkeley CA 94720

JUDSON, CHERYL JEAN, college administrator, management consultant; b. Mpls., Mar. 6, 1947; d. Peter Joseph and Eileen Clair (Smith) Lynch; divorced. BA, U. Minn., Duluth, 1969; MA, Mich. State U., 1972; PhD, Oreg. State U., 1981. Dir. admissions St. Martins Acad., Rapid City, S.D., 1972-75; vets. coord. Oreg. Inst. Tech., Klamath Falls, 1975-77; asst. dir. fin. aid Oreg. State U., Corvallis, 1978-84; dir. fin. aid Met. State Coll. of Denver, 1984-92, asst. v.p. fin. aid, 1993—; mem. nat. adv. bd. Am. Coll. Testing, Iowa City, Iowa, 1987-89, mem. regional adv. bd., 1984-87. Author monograph. Title IX coord. LWV, Klamath Falls, Oreg., 1975. Named to Outstanding Young Women of Am., 1982. Mem. Nat. Assn. Fin. Aid Adminstrs. (editorial bd. 1981-88, assoc. editor 1988-89), Colo. Assn. Fin. Aid Adminstrs., Rocky Mt. Assn. Student Affairs Adminstrs., Rocky Mountain Dressage Soc. (treas. 1990-92), N.Am. Trail Ride Conf. Home: 10955 Gray Cir Westminster CO 80030 Office: Met State Coll Denver PO Box 2 Denver CO 80210

JUERGENSMEYER, MARK KARL, sociology educator. BA in Philosophy with distinction, U. Ill., 1962; MDiv, Union Theol. Sem., 1965; MA in Polit. Sci. with honors, U. Calif., Berkeley, 1968, PhD in Polit. Sci., 1974. Instr. in polit. sci. U. R.I., 1968; lectr. in South Asian studies U. Calif., Berkeley, 1970-71, vis. assoc. prof. religious studies, 1977-84, vis. prof., 1984-87, adj. prof., 1988-89; prof. ethics Grad. Theol. Union, 1974-89; prof. religious studies U. Hawaii, 1989-93, affiliate prof. polit. sci., 1990-93, dean Sch. Hawaiian, Asian and Pacific Studies, 1989-93, asst. to pres. internat. programs, chair pres.'s com., 1989-93; prof. sociology, chair Global Peace and Security program U. Calif., Santa Barbara, 1993—; chair Systemwide Peace Rsch. program Systemwide Pacific Rim Rsch. program, Santa Barbara; cons., presenter, lectr., conf. organizer in field; appeared in radio and TV programs, San Francisco, 1975-89, Seattle, 1986, St. Louis, Washington, Boston, N.Y., 1984-87, Honolulu, 1989-93, Chgo., N.Y., L.A., 1993; mem. internat. working group on religion, ideology and peace U.S. Inst. of Peace, Washington, 1990—; mem. goals and mission rev. com. East-West Ctr., 1990-91; exec. bd. Vox Prodns., Inc., 1982-89; chair Asia Bur., 1976-80; vis. prof. Punjab U., Chandigarh, 1966-67, 70-71. Author: Religion as Social Vision: The Movement Against Untouchability in 20th Century Punjab, 1982, Religious Rebels in the Punjab, 1988, Fighting With Gandhi, 1984, Fighting Fair: A Nonviolent Strategy for Resolving Everyday Conflicts, 1986, The New Cold War? Religious Nationalism Confronts the Secular State, 1994; editor: Imagining India: Essays on Indian History, 1989, Teaching the Introductory Course in Religious Studies: A Sourcebook, 1991, Violence and the Sacred in the Modern World. Mem. adv. bd. Internat. Soc. for Ethics and Animals, 1985—; mem. radio series exec. bd. Calif. Coun. for Humanities, 1984-86. Grantee U.S. Dept. Edn., 1972-74, U.S. Dept. HEW, 1972-74, Henry W. Luce Found., 1974, 79-81, 82-84, NEH, 1976-79, 79-83, 85-87, 88-89, 88-91, 93, Sikh Found., 1985, MacArthur Found., 1987, Harry Frank Guggenheim Found., 1988-90, others. Mem. Nat. Assn. State and Land Grand Univs. and Colls., Assn. Internat. Edn. Adminstrs. (conf. speaker 1991, nat. exec. com. 1993), Am. Acad. Religion (chair nominating com. 1983-85, pres. western region 1983-84, exec. com. religion in modern India group 1979-83, panel organizer), Assn. for Asian Studies (exec. com., rsch. com. on Punjab 1979—, panel organizer). Office: U Calif Dept Sociology Santa Barbara CA 93106

JUHASZ, SUZANNE, English language educator; b. Chgo., Apr. 12, 1942; d. Philip Julius and Janet Carol (Rosenthal) Hecht; m. Joseph B. Juhasz, June 18, 1963 (div. Apr. 1980); children: Alexandra, Jennifer, Antonia. BA, Bennington Coll., 1963; MA, U. Calif., Berkeley, 1967, PhD, 1970. Instr. San Jose (Calif.) State U., 1973-74; from asst. to assoc. prof. English U. Colo., Boulder, 1974-84, prof. English, 1984—. Author: Naked and Fiery Forms: Modern American Poetry by Women, A New Tradition, 1976, The Undiscovered Continent: Emily Dickinson and the Space of the Mind, 1983; (with C. Miller and M.N. Smith) Comic Power in Emily Dickinson, 1993; Reading from the Heart, 1994. Martha Clifford fellow AAUW, 1981-82, Faculty Rsch. fellow U. Colo., 1987-88. Mem. MLA, Emily Dickinson Internat. Soc. (bd. dirs. 1988—, editor The Emily Dickinson Jour. 1990—). Office: Univ Colo Dept English CB226 Boulder CO 80304

JUKKOLA, GEORGE DUANE, obstetrician, gynecologist; b. Aliquippa, Pa., Feb. 28, 1945; s. Waino Helmer and Bedlia (Pyle) J.; m. Gretchen Louise Strom, Feb. 14, 1970 (div. 1984): children: David, Jeffrey; m. Wendee Leigh Bookhart, Apr. 23, 1988 (div. 1993). BA in Psychology, U. Calif., Berkeley, 1970; MD, U. Pitts., 1975. Diplomate Am. Bd. Ob-Gyn., Am. Bd. Quality Assurance Utilization Rev. Physicians. Caseworker Pa. Dept. Welfare, Rochester, 1971; resident in ob.-gyn. Akron (Ohio) Med. Ctr., 1975-78; pvt. practice Riverside, Calif., 1978—; co-founder Family Birthing Ctr. Riverside, 1981-87; mng. ptnr. Parkview Profl. Ctr., Riverside, 1984-93; chief dept. ob-gyn. Parkview Cmty. Hosp., Riverside, 1986-91, vice-chief of staff, 1992-93, chief of staff, 1994—; chmn. ob-gyn. dept. Moreno Valley Med. Ctr., 1991-93, dir. perinatal svcs., 1992-94; guest lectr. Riverside Cmty. Coll., 1984, 85; health care adv. com. 43rd Congl. Dist., Calif., 1994—; mem. Riverside County Fetal-Infant Mortality Com., 1994—. With USAF, 1965-69. Decorated Air medal with 4 oak leaf clusters. Fellow Am. Coll. Ob.-Gyn.; mem. AMA, Am. Coll. Physican Execs., Calif. Med. Assn. (mem. survey team), Riverside County Med. Assn., Am. Assn. Individual Investors, Victoria Club Riverside, Inland Physicians Med. Group (v.p. 1987-88), Mensa. Republican. Unitarian-Universalist. Home: 10252 Victoria Ave Riverside CA 92503-6100 Office: 3900 Sherman Sr Ste F Riverside CA 92503-4062

JULANDER, PAULA FOIL, association administrator; b. Charlotte, N.C., Jan. 21, 1939; d. Paul Baxter and Esther Irene (Earnhardt) Foil; m. Roydon Odell Julander, Dec. 21, 1985; 1 child, Julie McMahan Shipman. Diploma, Presbyn. Hosp. Sch. Nursing, Charlotte, N.C., 1960; BS magna cum laude, U. Utah, 1984; MS in Nursing Adminstrn., Brigham Young U., 1990. RN, Utah. Nurse various positions Fla. and S.C., 1960-66; co-founder, office mgr. Am. Laser Corp., 1970-79; gen. staff nurseoper. rm. Salt Lake Surg. Ctr., Salt Lake City, 1976-79; self employed Salt Lake City; teaching asst. U. Utah, Salt Lake City; rep. Utah State Legislature Coms., 1989-92; demo. nominee lt. gov., 1992; adj. faculty Brigham Young U. Coll. Nursing, 1987—; bd. dirs. Block Fin. Svcs.; mem. Utah state exec. bd. U.S. West Comm., 1993—; bd. regents Calif. Lutheran U., 1994. Pres. Utah Nurses Found., 1986-88; mem. Statewide Task Force on Child Sexual Abuse, 1989-90, Utah Nursing Resource Study, 1985—, State Feasibility Task Force for Nurses, 1985—, Women's Polit. Caucus, Statewide Abortion Task Force, 1990; bd. dirs. Community Nursing Svc. Home Health Plus, 1992-94; trustee Westminster Coll., 1994—, HCA-St. Mark's Hosp., 1994. Mem. ANA (del. conv. 1986-90), LWV, Utah Nurses Assn. (legis. rep. 1987-88, pres.), Nat. Orgn. Women Legislators, Sigma Theta Tau, Phi Kappa Phi (Susan Young Gates award 1991). Home: 1467 Penrose Dr Salt Lake City UT 84103-4466 Office: Utah Nurses Assn 455 E 400 S Ste 402 Salt Lake City UT 84111-3008

JUMAO-AS, ALEX BARONDA, engineer; b. Surigao City, The Philippines, June 12, 1961; came to U.S., 1982; s. Gaudencio Tamosa and Adelaida (Baronda) J.; m. Remedios Panoncillo, Jan. 28, 1981; children: Real James, Rylan Justin. BS in Indsl. Engring. with high honors, U. San Jose Recoletos, Cebu City, Philippines, 1982; grad. mech. and elec. tech. with high honors, U. Alaska, 1988, AAS in Archtl. and Engring. with honors, 1989, BS in Civil Engring. with high hons., 1989. Drafter Dept. Interior Bur. Land Mgmt., Anchorage, 1983-84, Raj Bhargava Assocs., Anchorage, 1984; asst. engr., drafter Unicom, Inc., Anchorage, 1984-93; civil engr. Raytheon Svc Co., Anchorage, 1993—; adj. instr. U. Alaska, 1989-91; v.p. Unicom, Inc. Anchorage Employee Svc. Assn., 1985-86. Mem. Metro Cebu Jaycees, Am. Inst. Design and Drafting, Pundok Bisaya (Cebuano Filipino Assn. Alaska) (v.p.), Bisayans of Alaska (mem. bd. dirs. 1993-94). Roman Catholic. Home: 8412 Barnett Dr Anchorage AK 99518-2900 Office: Raytheon Svc Co 801 B St Ste 201 Anchorage AK 99501-3657

JUMONVILLE, FELIX JOSEPH, JR., physical education educator, realtor; b. Crowley, La., Nov. 20, 1920; s. Felix Joseph and Mabel (Rogers) J.; m. Mary Louise Hoke, Jan. 11, 1952; children: Carol, Susan. BS, La. State U., 1942; MS, U. So. Calif., 1948, EdD, 1952. Assoc. prof. phys. edn. Los Angeles State Coll., 1948-60; prof. phys. edn. Calif. State U., Northridge, 1960-87, emeritus prof. phys. edn., 1987—; owner Felix Jumonville Realty, Northridge, 1974-82, Big Valley Realty, Inc., 1982-83, Century 21 Lamb Realtors, 1983-86, Cardinal Realtors, 1986-87; varsity track and cross-country head coach L.A. State Coll., 1952-60, Calif. State U., Northridge, 1960-71. Served with USCGR, 1942-46. Mem. Assn. Calif. State Univ. Profs., AAHPER, Pi Tau Pi, Phi Epsilon Kappa. Home: 2001 E Camino Parocela Apt 98N Palm Springs CA 92264-8229

JUN, JONG SUP, public administration educator; b. Sunsan, Korea, July 26, 1936; s. Myung D. and Jeum S. (Pai) J.; m. Soon Y. Jun, Sept. 16, 1964; children: Eugene, Amy. LLB, Yeungnam U., Taegu, Korea, 1960; MA, U. Oreg., 1964; PhD, U. So. Calif., 1969. Prof. Calif. State U., Hayward, 1968—; vis. prof. Hosei U., Tokyo, 1992-93; coord. Pub. Adminstrn.Theory Network, 1993—. Author: Public Administration: Design and Problem Solving, 1986, Philosophy of Administration, 1994; editor: Development in the Asia Pacific, 1994; editor Internat. Rev. Adminstrv. Sci., 1991; co-editor Adminstrn.Theory and Praxis, 1993—. Recipient Rsch. Grant award Social Rsch.Coun., N.Y., 1979, Outstanding Acad. Achievement award Am. Soc. Pub. Adminstrn., San Francisco, 1982. Home: 18698 Mount Lassen Ct Castro Valley CA 94552-1955 Office: Calif State U Hayward CA 94552

JUNDIS, ORVY LAGASCA, writer, consultant, educator; b. Bato, Leyte, Philippines, Sept. 30, 1943; s. Andrew Acenas and Aurora Fernandini (Lagasca) J.; m. Edna Claire Salaver, Mar. 15, 1971 (div. June 1983); children: Elrik Mikhael, Maya Rebecca, Franz Gilchrist; m. Editha Erlina Diez, Feb., 9, 1993. Inf. tng., U.S. Army, 1965, med. tng., 1966; AA in Liberal Arts, cert. social work, City Coll. San Francisco, 1983; BA in Humanities, New Coll. Calif., San Francisco, 1984; cert. of Ministry, Jesus Christ is Lord Ch., 1993; studied with grandmaster, Antonio Ilustrisimo, Jose Mena, Ondo Caburnay, Ernesto Presas, Ed Farris. Cert. Black Belt in Lapunti, Arnis de Abanico, 3rd degree Black Belt in Doblete Rapilon. Free-lance writer San Francisco, 1968—; writer, editorial cartoonist Mabuhay Republic Newspaper, San Francisco, 1970-88; art advisor Top Illustrators and Cartoonists, various locations, 1971—; promotional writer Fine Art Painters, various locations, 1971—; fgn. corr. Philippine Press, Manila, 1971—; contbg. editor Chelsea House Pub., N.Y.C., 1976; sr. writer Witty World Internat. Mag., North Wales, Pa., 1987—; cons. Philippine Kommix Industry, 1971—, Marvel Comics, N.Y.C., 1973-79, Japanese Comic Book Industry, Tokyo, 1973—; bd. dirs. Philippine Am. Hist. Archives, San Francisco; founder XArt, Xperimental Artspaces, 1990; founder Bayanihan Arts for the Cmty., 1994; lectr. U. Calif., Berkeley, Skyline Coll., San Mateo, Calif., U. of The Philippines, Siliman, Calif. State U., Davis, San Francisco State U., San Francisco Art Inst. Author, editor: Liwanag, 1975, World Ency. of Comics, 1976; exhbns. include Cultural Ctr. Philippines, Manila, Capricorn Asunder Gallery, San Francisco, Otis Art Inst., L.A.; contbr., mem. editl. bd. Without Names, 1985; contbr. articles to profl. jours. Coord. Philippine Am. Cmty. Endeavor, 1968—; co-founder Sch. Ethnic Studies, San Francisco State Coll., 1968; sponsor, founder Pace Youth Basketball Team, Bago Bantay, Quezon City, Philippines, 1971; educator Chinese Cultural Ctr., San Francisco, 1984; advisor anti-drugs comic book Pilipino Early Intervention Project, San Francisco, 1987; designer AIDS edn. poster Westbay Pilipino Multi Svc. Ctr., San Francisco, 1989; instr. Kaesar Pilipino-Am. Martial Arts/Dagatan Silat to diabetics, San Francisco. Recipient Commendation Philippine Consulate, San Francisco, 1970, Oakland (Calif.) Mus., 1982, Mayor of San Francisco, 1990, cert. recognition Acad. Am. Poets, City Coll. San Francisco, 1984. Mem. Kearny St. Workshop, Poetry for the People, Liwanag Artists, Kommix Barkada, Bay Area Pilipino Am. Writers (editl. bd.), Manilatown Oral Historians (advisor), Philippine Silat Assn., Lapunti Arnis De Abanico, Ilustrisimo Kombat Arts, Modern Arnis, Bago Bantay Warrior Arts, Tondo Arnis Club, Miguelin Martial Arts, Tulisan Alimpus Self-Def. Soc. Democrat. Office: Philippine Am Hist Archives PO Box 12174 San Francisco CA 94112-0174

JUNE, ROY ETHIEL, lawyer; b. Forsyth, Mont., Aug. 12, 1922; s. Charles E. and Elizabeth F. (Newnes) J.; m. Laura Brautigam, June 20, 1949; children—Patricia June, Richard Tyler. B.A., U. Mont., 1948, B.A. in Law, 1951, LL.B., 1952. Bar: Mont. 1952, Calif. 1961. Sole practice, Billings, Mont., 1952-57, Sanders and June, 1953-57; real estate developer, Orange County, Calif., 1957-61; ptnr. Dugan, Tobias, Tornay & June, Costa Mesa, Calif., 1961-62; city prosecutor, Costa Mesa, 1962-63, asst. city atty., 1963-67, city atty., 1967-78; sole practice, Costa Mesa, 1962—. Atty. Costa Mesa Hist. Soc., Costa Mesa Playhouse Patron's Assn., Red Barons Orange County, Costa Mesa Meml. Hosp. Aux., Harbor Key, Child Guidance Ctr. Orange County, Fairview State Hosp. Therapeutic Pool Vols., Inc.; active Eagle Scout evaluation team, Harbor Area Boy Scouts Am., YMCA; atty. United Fund/Community Chest Costa Mesa and Newport Beach; bd. dirs. Boys' Club Harbor Area, bd. dirs. Mardan Ctr. Ednl. Therapy, United Cerebral Palsy Found. Orange County. Served with USAF, World War II. Decorated Air medal with oak leaf cluster, D.F.C. Mem. Mont. Bar Assn., Calif. Bar Assn., Orange County Bar Assn., Harbor Bar Assn., Costa Mesa C. of C. (bd. dirs.). Clubs: Masons, Scottish Rite, Shriners, Santa Ana Country, Amigos Viejos, Los Fiestadores.

JUNG, DONALD T., pharmacokineticist; b. L.A., Apr. 10, 1953; s. Benson and Betty T.Y. (Dear) J.; m. Young Mi Lee, Mar. 31. 1984; children: Stacy T., Brian P. BS in Biochemistry, U. Calif., Davis, 1974; MS in Pharm. Chemistry, U. Calif., San Francisco, 1978; PhD Pharm. Sci., U. Ariz., 1980. Teaching asst. Sch. Pharmacy U. Calif., San Francisco, 1975-77; rsch. and teaching asst. Coll. Pharmacy U. Ariz., Tucson, 1979-80; asst. prof. Coll. Pharmacy U. Ill., Chgo., 1981-87, coord. Clin. Pharmacokinetics Lab. Coll. Pharmacy, 1987, adj. prof. pharmacodynamics Coll. Pharmacy, 1987—; vis. prof. BioFarmasi, Fakultas Farmasi U. Gadjah Mada, Yogyakarta, Indonesia, 1985; assoc. dir. Syntex Rsch., Palo Alto, Calif., 1987—; cons. Hoechst-Roussel Pharms. Inc., Somerville, N.J., 1980, FDA, 1986-87. Contbr. articles to profl. jours. Calif. Heart Assn. fellow, 1974, U. Calif. San Francisco Regent's fellow, 1974-75; U. Ariz. Grad. Academic scholar, 1979-80. Mem. Am. Pharm. Assn., Am. Assn. Pharm. Scientists, Acad. Pharm. Scis., Phi Kappa Phi, Rho Chi.

JUNG, HENRY HUNG, mechanical engineer; b. Hong Kong, Aug. 3, 1957; s. Cheuk-Sun and Siu-Kuen (Ma) J.; m. Mi-Ying Miranda, Mar. 28, 1986. BS MechE, Ariz. State U., 1980; MS MechE, U. Ill., 1983; MBA, Santa Clara U., 1994. Engr. Lockheed Aircraft, Burbank, Calif., 1981-82; researcher U. Ill., Champaign-Urbana, 1982-83; engr. Pratt & Whitney Aircraft, West Palm Beach, Fla., 1983-84; sr. scientist Lockheed Missiles & Space Co., Palo Alto, Calif., 1984-94; engr. Sun Microsystems Co., Mountain View, Calif., 1994—. Mem. ASME, AIAA, N.Y. Acad. Scis., Sigma Xi, Tau Beta Pi, Pi Tau Sigma. Home: 21486 Holly Oak Dr Cupertino CA 95014-4928 Office: Sun Microsys 2550 Garcia Ave Mountain View CA 94043-1100

JUNG, KWAN YEE, artist; b. Toisun, Kwang Tung, China, Nov. 25, 1932; came to U.S., 1963; s. Fred Hing and Shun Tong (Lee) J.; m. Yee Wah Yip, Sept. 10, 1962; children: Jeanne, Kathy, Laura. BA, New Asia Coll., Hong Kong, 1961. Comml. artist advt. dept. Hong Kong Soy Bean Products Co., 1961-63; owner Jung's Gallery, La Jolla, Calif., 1976-78; freelance artist, instr., demonstrator San Diego, 1978—; jury panelist African-Am. Mus. Art, San Diego, 1994—. Exhibns. include 170th annual exhibn. Nat. Acad. Design, 1995, The Am. Fine Art Connection Poway Ctr. for the Performing Arts, Calif., 1995, Water to Women Margaret Cross Gallery, Old Pasadena, Calif., 1995, May Show Kim's Art Gallery, Rowland Heights, Calif., 1995. Recipient First Place award San Diego Watercolor Soc., 1973, Best of Show award Sumi-E Soc. Am., 1974, Purchase award Springville Mus. Art, 1974. Mem. Nat. Acad. Design (Merit award 1992, nat. academician), Am. Watercolor Soc., Nat. Watercolor Soc., Asiatic Art Guild (pres. 1992—). Home: 5468 Bloch St San Diego CA 92122-4010

JUNG, TIMOTHY TAE KUN, otolaryngologist; b. Seoul, Korea, Dec. 1, 1943; came to U.S., 1969; s. Yoon Yong and Helen Chung-Hyuk (Im) J.; m. Lucy Moon Young, Sept. 10, 1972; children: David, Michael, Karen. BS, Seoul Nat. U., 1966, Loma Linda U., 1971; MD, Loma Linda U., 1974; PhD, U. Minn., 1980. Diplomate, Am. Bd. Otolaryngology. Med. intern Loma Linda (Calif.) U. Med. Ctr., 1974-75; resident in surgery U. Minn. Med. Sch., Mpls., 1975-76; resident in otolaryngology U. Minn. Med. Sch., 1976-80, asst. prof. otolaryngology, 1980-84, clin. asst. prof., dir. prostaglandin lab., 1984-85; assoc. prof., dir. otolaryngology rsch. Loma Linda U., 1985-90, prof., dir. otolaryngology rsch., 1990-92, clin. prof., assoc. dir. otolaryngology rsch., 1992—; mem. deafness and communications disroders rev. com. Nat. Inst. Deafness and Communications, NIH, 1989-92. Contbr. numerous chpts. to med. books, over 100 articles and abstracts to med. jours. Sgt. Korean army, 1966-69. Recipient Edmund Price Fowler award. Fellow ACS, Triological Soc., Am. Acad. Otolaryngology (honor award 1990); mem. AMA, Am. Otol. Soc., Am. Neurol. Soc., Soc. Univ. Otolaryngologists, Assn. Rsch. in Otolaryngology, Centurions, Collegium Otorhinolaryngogicum Amicetiae Sacrum, Alpha Omega Alpha. Seventh-day Adventist. Home: 11790 Pecan Way Loma Linda CA 92354-3452 Office: 3975 Jackson St Ste 202 Riverside CA 92503-3947

JUNG, YEE WAH, artist; b. Canton, Kwang Tung, China, Sept. 4, 1936; came to U.S., 1963; d. Yeun Tsin and Shiu Fung (Poon) Yip; m. Kwan Yee Jung, Sept. 10, 1962; children: Jeanne, Kathy, Laura. Student, Chung Nam Art Sch., Wupei, China, 1954-58, New Asia Coll., Hong Kong, 1958-62. Art instr. Shiu Fung Art Studio, Hong Kong, 1958-63; art tchr. Chi-Ching Mid. Sch., Hong Kong, 1962-63; freelance artist San Diego, 1963—; owner Jung's Gallery, La Jolla, Calif., 1976-78; solo juror Clairemont Art Guild Annual, San Diego, 1989. Exhbns. include Am. Fine Art Connection Exhbn., Poway (Calif.) Ctr. for the Performing Atts, 1995, Watercolor USA, Knoxville (Tenn.) Mus. of Art, 1995. Recipient First prize So. Calif. Expo, 1970, Watercolor USA Cash award Calif. Nat. Watercolor Soc., 1973, First Place award 25th Annual Art Festival, San Diego, 1989, Three King award Advent Fine Art 7th Annual, San Diego, 1990. Mem. Nat. Watercolor Soc., Watercolor Honor Soc., Asiatic Art Guild (panel juror 1993). Home: 5468 Bloch St San Diego CA 92122-4010

JUNGBLUTH, CONNIE CARLSON, senior tax compliance specialist; b. Cheyenne, Wyo., June 20, 1955; d. Charles Marion and Janice Yvonne (Keldsen) Carlson; m. Kirk E. Jungbluth, Feb. 5, 1977; children: Tyler, Ryan. BS, Colo. State U., 1976. CPA, Colo. Sr. acct. Rhode Scripter & Assoc., Boulder, Colo., 1977-81; mng. acct. Arthur Young, Denver, 1981-85; asst. v.p. Dain Bosworth, Denver, 1985-87; v.p. George K. Baum & Co., Denver, 1987-91; acct. Ariz. Luth. Acad., 1994-95; sr. tax acct. Ernst & Young, LLP, Phoenix, 1995—. Active Denver Estate Planning Coun., 1981-85; organizer Little People Am., Rocky Mountain Med. Clinic and Symposium, Denver, 1986; adv. bd. Children's Home Health, Denver, 1986-89; fin. adv. bd. Gail Shoettler for State Treas., Denver, 1986; campaign chmn. Kathi Williams for Colo. State Legislature, 1986; mem. Sch. dist. 12 Colo. Edn. Found. Bd., 1991, Napa Sch. Dist. Elem. Site Com., 1992-94. Named one of 50 to watch, Denver mag., 1988. Mem. AICPA, Colo. Soc. CPAs (strategic planning com. 1987-89, instr. bank 1983, trustee 1984-87, pres. bd. trustees 1986-87, bd. dirs. 1987-89, chmn. career edn. com. 1982-83, pub. svc. award 1985-87), Colo. Mcpl. Bond Dealers, Metro North C. of C. (bd. dirs. 1987-90), Denver City Club (bd. dirs. 1987-88), Phi Beta Phi. Office: Ernst & Young LLP 40 N Central Ste 90 Phoenix AZ 85004

JUNGBLUTH, KIRK E., real estate appraiser, mortgage banking executive; b. Lima, Ohio, Apr. 5, 1949; s. Harold A. and Marjorie J. (Brown) J.; m. Connie Carlson, Feb. 5, 1977; children: Tyler, Ryan. Student, Mesa Coll., Grand Junction, Colo., Regis Coll., Denver. Cert. gen. real estate appraiser, Calif., Ariz. Loan officer, real estate appraiser Home Fed. Savs. & Loan, Ft. Collins, Colo., 1973-76; real estate appraiser Jungbluth & Assocs., Ft. Collins, 1976-83; pres., bd. dirs. Security Diamond Corp., Denver, 1982-90; nat. sales dir. InfoAm. Computers, Denver, 1982-90; chmn. bd. dirs., CEO U.S. Capital Lending Corp., Denver, 1987-90; ct.-appointed receiver Dist. Ct.

State of Colo., 1990; mgr. real estate appraisal World Savs. & Loan Assn., Walnut Creek, 1992—, Pleasanton, Calif., 1992—. Sec.-treas. St. Peters Luth. Ch., Ft. Collins, Colo., 1980-81, pres., 1982-84. Sgt. USMC, 1969-71. Republican.

JUNGKIND, WALTER, design educator, writer, consultant; b. Zurich, Switzerland, Mar. 9, 1923; came to Can., 1968; s. Oskar and Frieda (Leuthold) J.; m. Jenny Voskamp, 1953; children—Christine, Stefan, Brigit. Nat diploma, Kunstgewerbeschule, Zurich, 1943; nat diploma, Regent Street Poly tech., London, 1953. Freelance designer London, 1955-68; lectr. London Coll. Printing and Graphic Arts, 1960-65, sr. lectr., 1965-68; assoc. prof. dept. art and design U. Alta., Edmonton, Can., 1968-72, prof., 1972-90, prof. emeritus, 1990—; Design cons. pub. works Province of Alta., 1972-75; chmn. Canadian Adv. Com. Standards Council Can., 1978—. Initiator and curator internat. exhbn. Graphic Design for Pub. Service, 1972, Language Made Visible, 1973. Recipient Design Can. award Nat. Design Council Can., 1979, 1984; Chmns. award Nat. Design Council Can., 1982. Fellow Soc. Chartered Designers Gt. Britain, Soc. Graphic Designers Can. (pres. 1978-82); mem. Internat Council Design Assns. (pres. 1974-76, Design for Edn. award 1972.). Home: 6304-109th Ave, Edmonton, AB Canada T6A 1S2

JURA, JEAN-JACQUES, English language and literature educator; b. Amarillo, Tex., May 5, 1950; s. Edmond and Adrienne Marie (Flagothier) J.; m. Lisette marguerite Masse, Sept. 13, 1980; 1 child, Chantal Lisette. BA, U. Calif., Riverside, 1972; MA, Calif. State U., 1983; PhD, U. Calif., Irvine, 1988. Cert. secondary tchr., Calif. Instr. French Saddleback C.C., Mission Viejo, Calif., 1985-86, Golden West Coll., Huntington Beach, Calif., 1987-94; instr. English El Camino Coll., Torrance, Calif., 1993—; assoc. in French, teaching asst. U. Calif., Irvine, 1984-88; lectr. comparative lit. Calif. State U., Long Beach, 1989-90, lectr. French, 1989—; translator Tri-Town Prodns., Burbank, Calif., 1991-92, Walton Tool Co., Inc., Long Beach, 1992—, Waksul Assocs., Inc., Long Beach, 1993-94; translator, proofreader The Designory, Inc., Long Beach, 1993—. Contbr. articles to profl. jours. Rsch. grantee U. Calif., 1988. Mem. MLA, Calif. Tchrs. Assn., Philol. Assn. Pacific Coast (presiding officer 1989—), Phi Beta Kappa, Phi Kappa Phi. Republican. Roman Catholic. Home: 3565 Linden Ave Apt 337 Long Beach CA 90807-4541 Office: Long Beach State U Dept Romance/German/Russian 1250 N Bellflower Blvd Long Beach CA 90840-0006

JURY, DEBRA E. (DEBBIE JURY), emergency nurse, consultant, author, educator; b. Las Cruces, N.Mex., Mar. 22, 1957; d. Robert Charles and Elois (Awalt) Aylett; m. Jeffrey Paul Jury, Mar. 29, 1986; children: Dana Renee, Travis Adair, Zane William. ADN, N.Mex. State U., 1977; postgrad., Calif. State U., Carson, 1990—. CEN; trauma nurse course cert. Staff nurse Meml. Gen. Hosp., Las Cruces, 1977-78, team leader, 1978, asst. charge nurse, 1978-79, asst. IV therapist/chemotherapist, 1979-80, asst. charge nurse, 1983; office RN Richard H. Higgs M.D., Las Cruces, 1980-83; staff nurse Clovis (Calif.) Community Hosp., 1983-84, staff triage nurse, 1984-94; emergency med. svcs. specialist, tng. officer Fresno County Dept. Health, Fresno, Calif., 1994—; lectr., cons. PACE symposia, 1995—; cons. RN preceptor, lectr., nurse educator Genentech, San Francisco, 1985-95. Contbr. articles to profl. jours. Voting mem. Community Hosps. of Ctrl. Calif., Fresno, 1987—. Named Emergency Nurse of the Yr., Mid-Valley Emergency Nurses, 1990, scholarship, 1993. Mem. Emergency Nurses Assn. (fundraising chair 1989, pres.-elect 1990, pres. 1991, past pres. 1992, chair emergency nurse of yr. com. 1993, 94), Am. Trauma Soc., Calif. Emergency Nurses Assn. (co-chair membership 1994, chair 1995, mem. prehospital com. 1994—), Calif. Nurses Assn. (co-chair program com. region 5 RN of Yr. Com. 1993-94), Safety Belt Safe, Scottish Soc. Ctrl. Calif. Democrat. Office: Emergency Med Svcs PO Box 11867 Fresno CA 93775-1867

JUSTICE, JAMES WALCOTT, physician, research scientist; b. N.Y.C., Dec. 16, 1932; s. Frederick Emerson and Eleanor Gertrude (Haddock) J.; m. M. Ann Haight, Feb. 11, 1961; children: Sean, Wade, Kathleen, Scott. BA, Bucknell U., 1954; MD, N.Y. Med. Coll., 1958; MPH, Johns Hopkins U., 1962. Diplomate gen. preventive medicine Am. Bd. Preventive Medicine and Pub. Health. Intern Stanford U., San Francisco, 1958-59; resident pub. health U. Okla., Oklahoma City, 1963-65; commd. officer USPHS, 1959-85; med. dir. State Alaska Dept. Corrections, Anchorage, 1985-87; rsch. scientist Native Am. Rsch. and Tng. Ctr. Ariz. Health Sci. Ctr., U. Ariz., Tucson, 1987—. Author: Bibliography Health and Disease Native America, 1988; contbr. chpts. to books and articles to profl. jours. Pres. Family/Faculty Assn., Tucson, 1974-75; chmn. Home Owner's Assn., Tucson, 1975, 89-90. Col. USPHS, 1959-85. Decorated Meritorious medal USPHS-DHHS, 1973; recipient Group Achievement award NASA, 1977, Fgn. Svc. award USPHS-DHHS, 1981, Nat. Recognition award Nat. Indian Health Bd., 1982. Fellow Am. Coll. Preventive Medicine; mem. APHA, Ariz. Pub. Health Assn., Physicians for Social Responsibility, Ctr. for Creative Photography, So. Ariz. Water Color Guild. Office: Native Am Rsch Ctr Univ Ariz 1642 E Helen St Tucson AZ 85719

JUTAMULIA, SUGANDA, electro-optic scientist; b. Muara Enim, Indonesia, July 11, 1954; s. Harris Intankusuma (dec.) and Conny (Julian) J.; m. Xiaoye Sherry Li, June 9, 1990. BS, Bandung Inst. Tech., Indonesia, 1977; PhD, Hokkaido U., Sapporo, Japan, 1985. Rsch. assoc. Pa. State U., University Park, 1985-87, instr., 1988; sr. scientist Quantex Corp., Rockville, Md., 1988-91; mgr. prodn. devel. Kowa Co. Ltd., San Jose, Calif., 1991-93, gen. mgr. R&D, 1994—. Editor: Selected Papers on Optical Correlators, 1993, Selected Papers on Optical Neural Networks, 1994; co-author: Optical Signal Processing Computing and Neural Networks, 1992; guest editor Optical Memory and Neural Networks jour., 1994, Optical Engring. jour., 1995. Indonesian Min. Edn. Sci. scholar, 1973-77, Japanese Min. Edn. Monbusho scholar, 1980-85. Mem. IEEE, Soc. Photo-Optical Instrumention Engrs., Optical Soc. Am., Japan Applied Physics Soc. Roman Catholic. Home: 38730 Lexington St Apt 274 Fremont CA 94536-6242 Office: Kowa Co Ltd 1731 Technology Dr Ste 595 San Jose CA 95110

JUVET, RICHARD SPALDING, JR., chemistry educator; b. Los Angeles, Aug. 8, 1930; s. Richard Spalding and Marion Elizabeth (Dalton) J.; m. Martha Joy Myers, Jan. 29, 1955 (div. Nov. 1978); children: Victoria, David, Stephen, Richard P.; m. Evelyn Raeburn Elthon, July 1, 1984. B.S., UCLA, 1952, Ph.D., 1955. Research chemist Dupont, 1955; instr. U. Ill., 1955-57, asst. prof., 1957-61, assoc. prof., 1961-70; prof. analytical chemistry Ariz. State U., Tempe, 1970—; vis. prof. UCLA, 1960, Cambridge (Eng.) U., 1964-65, Nat. Taiwan U., 1968, Ecole Poly., France, 1976-77, U. Vienna, Austria, 1989-90; mem. air pollution chemistry and physics adv. com. EPA, HEW, 1969-72; mem. adv. panel on advanced chem. alarm tech., devel. and engring. directorate, def. sys. divsn. Edgewood Arsenal, 1975; mem. adv. panel on postdoctoral associateships NAS-NRC, 1991-94. Author: Gas-Liquid Chromatography, Theory and Practice, 1962; Editorial advisor to: Jour. Chromatographic Sci., 1969-85, Jour. Gas Chromatography, 1963-68, Analytica Chimica Acta, 1972-74, Analytical Chemistry, 1974-77, biennial reviewer in, 1962-76. NSF sr. postdoctoral fellow, 1964-65; recipient Sci. Exch. Agreement award to Czechoslovakia, Hungary, Romania and Yugoslavia, 1977. Fellow Am. Inst. Chemists; mem. AAAS, Am. Chem. Soc. (nat. chmn. divsn. analytical chemistry 1972-73, nat. sec.-treas. divsn. analytical chemistry 1969-71, divsn. com. on chem. edn., subcom. on grad. edn. 1988—, councilor 1978-79, coun. com. analytical reagents 1985-95, chmn. U. Ill. sect. 1968-69, sec., 1962-63, co-author Reagent Chenicals 7th edit. 1986, 8th edit. 1993, directorate divsn. officers' caucus 1987-90), Internat. Platform Assn., Internat. Union Pure and Applied Chemistry, Am. Radio Relay League, Sigma Xi, Phi Lambda Upsilon, Alpha Chi Sigma (profl. rep.-at-large 1989-94, chmn. expansion com. 1990-92, nat. v.p. grand collegiate alchemist 1994—). Presbyn. (deacon 1960—, ruling elder 1972—, commr. Grand Canyon Presbytery 1974-76). Home: 4821 E Calle Tuberia Phoenix AZ 85018-2932 Office: Ariz State U Dept Chemistry and Biochemistry Tempe AZ 85287-1604

KABAT, HUGH, pharmacy educator; b. Manitowoc, Wis., Oct. 3, 1932; s. Frank William and Norene Mary (McCorkle) K.; m. Rita Catherine Laboe, Sept. 15, 1956 (div. Oct. 1977); children: Edward Michael, Patrick William, James Robert; m. Sally Phoebe Gutteridge, Aug. 16, 1980. BS in Pharmacy, U. Mich., 1954, MS in Hosp. Pharmacy, 1956; PhD in Pharm. Adminstrn., U. Colo., 1961. Cert. pharmacist, Mich., N.Mex. Instr. U. Colo., Boulder, 1959-61; from asst. prof. to prof., assoc. dean U. Minn., Mpls., 1961-86; prof. U. N.Mex., Albuquerque, 1984—; cons. AID, USPHS, 1984—, Project HOPE, 1988, HHS Ctrs. Excellence, 1988; Dorothy Dillon Meml. lectr. N.Mex. Soc. Hosp. Pharmacists, 1990. Author: Drug-Induced, 1968, Clinical Pharmacy Handbook, 1968. Capt. USPHS, 1956-58. Fellow Acad. Pharm. Scis., 1974; recipient disting. service award, Minn. Epilepsy League, 1971; Hallie Bruce Meml. lectr., Minn. Soc. Hosp. Pharmacists, 1969; Fulbright scholar, 1977. Fellow Am. Pharm. Assn., 1953—; mem. Am. Assn. Colls. Pharmacy, Am. Soc. Hosp. Pharmacists, Am. Pharm. Assn., Fulbright Assn. Office: U NMex Coll Pharmacy Albuquerque NM 87131

KADDEN, BRUCE JAY, rabbi; b. Berkeley, Calif., Nov. 7, 1954; s. Paul Emanuel and Shirley Janice (Hertzberg) K.; m. Barbara Ellen Binder, Sept. 2, 1978; children: Alana Sharon, Micah Benjamin. AB in Religious Studies, Stanford (Calif.) U., 1976; MA in Hebrew Letters, Hebrew Union Coll., L.A., 1979. Ordained rabbi, 1981. Rabbi Mount Zion Temple, St. Paul, 1981-84; Jewish chaplain Correctional Tng. Facility, Soledad, Calif., 1987—; rabbi Temple Beth El, Salinas, Calif., 1984—. Co-author: Teaching Tefilah: Insights and Activities on Prayer, 1994, Teaching Mitzvot: Concepts, Values and Activities, 1988. Bd. dirs. Ctr. for Community Advocacy, Salinas, 1993—, Planned Parenthood, Monterey County, 1985-92. Mem. Pacific Asn. of Reform Rabbis. Democrat. Office: Temple Beth El 1212 Riker St Salinas CA 93901-2111

KADEL, RICHARD WILLIAMS, physicist; b. Richmond, Calif., Nov. 11, 1951; s. Edward E. and Marian A. (Halsted) K. BA, Yale U., 1973; MS, Princeton U., 1975, PhD, 1977. Assoc. scientist MIT, Boston, 1977-80; scientist I Fermi Nat. Accelerator Lab., Batavia, Ill., 1980-89; sr. staff scientist Lawrence Berkeley (Calif.) Lab., 1989—; mem. CDF Collaboration, Fermi Lab., Batavia, 1980—. Wilson fellow Fermi Lab., Batavia, 1980-85. Mem. Am. Phys. Soc. Office: Lawrence Berkeley Lab 1 Cyclotron Rd MS 50-137 Berkeley CA 94720

KADNER, CARL GEORGE, biology educator emeritus; b. Oakland, Calif., May 23, 1911; s. Adolph L. and Otilia (Pecht) K.; m. Mary Elizabeth Moran, June 24, 1939; children: Robert, Grace Wickersham, Carl L. BS, U. San Francisco, 1933; MS, U. Calif., Berkeley, 1936, PhD, 1941. Prof. biology Loyola Marymount U., Los Angeles, 1936-78, prof. emeritus, 1978—; trustee Loyola U., Los Angeles, 1970-73. Served to maj. U.S. Army, 1943-46. Mem. Entomol. Soc. Am. (emeritus), Sigma Xi, Alpha Sigma Nu. Republican. Roman Catholic. Home: 8100 Loyola Blvd Los Angeles CA 90045-2639

KADOTA, MARK FUMIO, artist; b. L.A., Dec. 27, 1951; s. Hayao and Shizuko (Tokuda) K. Ceramics tchr. Carpinteria (Calif.) Craft Ctr., 1970-73; art tchr. de Young Mus. Art Sch., San Francisco, 1979-83, Art Reach Program, San Francisco, 1979-83, Youth in Arts, Marin, Calif., 1981-82, San Francisco Mus. Modern Art, 1982; mus. asst. Fine Arts Mus., San Francisco, 1979-80; art instr. Honolulu Acad. Arts, 1984-85, Artist in the Sch., Honolulu, 1984-89. One man shows include Art Works Gallery, Honolulu, 1974, Bishop Mus., Honolulu, 1975, de Young Mus. Art Sch., 1979, 80, 82, Humboldt State U., Calif., 1980, Ramsay Gallery, Honolulu, 1985, 86, Bishop Sq. Gallery, Honolulu, 1988, 90, Robyn Buntin Gallery, Hawaii, 1991, 92; exhibited in group shows at The Honolulu Acad. Arts, 1976, Contemporary Arts Ctr., Honolulu, 1976, 77, Fine Arts Mus., San Francisco, 1980, Jehu Gallery, San Francisco, 1980, Artisans Guild Fine Arts Competition, Marin, Calif., 1981, San Mateo Internat. Art Competition, Marin, Calif., 1981, 82, 22d Annual Art Exhibition, HAFA, Hayward, Calif., 1983, Hawaii Artist League, Honolulu, 1984, 85, Honolulu Acad. Arts, 1986, 88, 92, Honolulu Japanese C. of C., 1987, The Contemporary Mus., Honolulu, 1990, 91, 92, The Stones Gallery, Kauai, Hawii, 1991, Mashrabia Gallery, Cairo, 1993; represented in permanent collections The Contemporary Arts Ctr., The Honolulu Culture and Arts, The Mus. Het Toreke, Tienen, Belgium, The Honolulu Advertiser, The Stedelijk Inst., Genk, Belgium, Junta De Freguesia De Monchique, Almada, Portugal, The State Found. on Culture and Arts, Haw., The Contemporary Mus., Fedn. Des Oeuvres Laiques De La Manche, France. Recipient Marion Stinton award, 1981, 2d place award Honolulu Japanese C. of C., 1991, Hon. Mention award Assn. Honolulu Artist, 1992, 1st place award Honolulu Japanese C. of C., 1992. Home: 87 530 Hakimo Rd Waianae HI 96792

KAEMPFER, WILLIAM HUTCHISON, economics educator; b. West Chester, Pa., Mar. 4, 1951; s. John Henry and Jane McFarlane (Hutchison) K.; m. Suzanne Hearne, July 17, 1976 (div. Mar. 1983); m. Mary Gerilyn Arnberg Pecchio, Dec. 30, 1992; 1 child, Jenna Marie. BA, Coll. Wooster, 1973; MA, Duke U., 1975, PhD, 1979. Instr. Coll. Wooster, Ohio, 1975-76; asst. prof. U. N.C., Greensboro, 1978-79, U. Wash., Seattle, 1979-81; asst. prof. U. Colo., Boulder, 1981-88, assoc. prof., 1988-94, prof., 1994—; asst. prof. Claremont (Calif.) McKenna Coll., 1985-88; assoc. prof. Claremont Grad. Sch., 1990. Author: International Economic Sanctions, 1992; contbr. articles to profl. jours. Mem. Am. Economic Assn. Office: Univ Colo PO Box 256 Boulder CO 80309-0256

KAFENTZIS, JOHN CHARLES, journalist, educator; b. Butte, Mont., Aug. 18, 1953; s. Christian and Betty Ann (Gaston) K.; m. Teresa Marie Nokleby, June 5, 1976; children: Kathryn Anne, Christian John. BA in Journalism, U. Mont., 1975. Reporter The Missoulian, Missoula, Mont., 1974-76, The Hardin (Mont.) Herald, 1976; reporter The Spokesman-Rev., Spokane, Wash., 1976-80, copy editor, 1980-83, chief copy desk, 1983-89, news editor, 1989-94, news designer, 1994—; mem. adj. faculty Ea. Wash. U., Cheney, 1982—. Greek Orthodox. Office: The Spokesman-Rev W999 Riverside Spokane WA 99210

KAFOURY, ANN GRAHAM, psychotherapist; b. Spokane, Wash., Mar. 27, 1945; d. William Matheson and Gladys Irene (Swift) Graham; m. David Kafoury; children: Trevor, Kenan, Stephanie. BA, U. Oreg., 1967; MAT, Portland State U., 1976; MA in Counseling and Psychology, Lewis and Clark Coll., 1982. Tchr. U.S. Peace Corps, Ghana, West Africa, 1967-69, Tigard (Oreg.) Sr. H.S., 1970-74, Portland (Oreg.) C.C., 1976-79; cons. Oreg. Fitness & Health Ctr., Good Samaritan Hosp., Portland, 1982-83; alcohol and drug counselor, co-dependency group leader Cedar Hills Hosp., Portland, 1989-93, outpatient coord., 1990-93; pvt. practice psychotherapist Portland, 1982—; Oreg. network coord. Eye Movement Desensitization and Reprocessing, Portland, 1992—; intensive family therapist, Portland, 1993—. Chairperson Hillside Park Bd., Portland, 1977-80; mem. Friends of West Women's Hotel, Portland, 1983-88; officer, bd. mem. Burnside Cmty. Coun., Portland, 1984-87; sponsor Oreg. Counselors Polit. Action Com., Oreg., 1988—. Mem. ACA, Oreg. Counseling Assn., Nat. Bd. Cert. Counselors. Home: 804 NW Culpepper Ter Portland OR 97210-3125 Office: 10490 SW Eastridge St Ste 130 Portland OR 97225-5030

KAGAN, STEPHEN BRUCE (SANDY KAGAN), travel agency executive; b. Elizabeth, N.J., Apr. 27, 1944; s. Herman and Ida (Nadel) K.; m. Susan D. Kaltman, July 3, 1966; children—Sheryl, Rachel. B.S. in Econs., U. Pa., 1966; M.B.A. in Fin., Bernard Baruch Coll., 1969. Chartered fin. analyst. Security analyst Merrill Lynch Pierce Fenner & Smith, N.Y.C., 1966-68; dir. research Deutschmann & Co., N.Y.C., 1968-70; v.p. Equity Sponsors, Inc., N.Y.C., 1970-72; v.p., investment counselor Daniel H. Renberg & Assocs., Inc., Los Angeles, 1972-78; regional v.p. Carlson Travel Network, Van Nuys, Calif., 1978—. Vice pres. bd. Temple Beth Hillel, North Hollywood, Calif., 1976-83. Mem. Inst. Cert. Fin. Analysts, Beta Gamma Sigma. Home: 13952 Weddington St Van Nuys CA 91401-5751 Office: Carlson Wagonlit Travel 7100 Hayvenhurst Ave Ste 310 Van Nuys CA 91406-3804

KAGAN, YISHAI, electronics engineer; b. Haifa, Israel, Dec. 22, 1952; came to U.S., 1988; s. Dov and Erna (Rabinovitz) K.; m. Zohara Sherer, Mar. 13, 1978; children: Niv, Tomer. BSEE, Technion, Haifa, 1975. Electronics group leader IDF, Israel, 1975-80; mem. tech. staff Armament Devel. Authority, Israel, 1980-82, group leader, 1982-84, chief project engr., 1984-88; sr. engr. Harmonic Lightwaves, Santa Clara, Calif., 1988-90, mgr. electronics, 1990-91, dir. electronics, 1991—. Inventor in field. Served to maj. Israeli Navy, 1975-80. Mem. IEEE, Soc. Cable TV Engrs. Home: 1386 Enderby Way Sunnyvale CA 94087 Office: Harmonic Lightwaves 3005 Bunker Hill Ln Santa Clara CA 95054-1106

KAGEMOTO, PATRICIA JOW (PAT JOW), artist, printmaker; b. N.Y.C., Feb. 20, 1952; d. Tong Fook and Toy Kuen (Lee) Jow; m. Haro Kagemoto, Sept. 21, 1991. BFA, SUNY, New Paltz, 1975. Printmaking workshop asst. SUNY, New Paltz, 1974-75, print shop asst., 1975; printmaking cons. Comm. Village, Ltd., Kingston, N.Y., 1975-84; arts and crafts tchr. Neighborhood Svc. Orgn., Poughkeepsie, N.Y., 1976; printmaking instr., adminstrv. asst. Comm. Village, Ltd., Kingston, 1977-79; exhbn. auditor N.Y. State Coun. on Arts, N.Y.C., 1984-87; gallery asst. Watermark/Cargo Gallery, Kingston, 1988-91; vis. artist N.Y. State Summer Sch. of Visual Arts, Fredonia, 1978, SUNY, New Paltz, 1983-84; cons. printer Printmaking Workshop, N.Y.C., 1984; children's printmaking workshop dir. Woodstock (N.Y.) Libr., 1989. One-woman shows Woodstock Libr., 1989, Watermark/Cargo Gallery, 1991, also others; ; 2-person shows Catherine Street Gallery, N.Y.C., 1983, 84, Cinque Gallery, N.Y.C., 1984, Watermark/Cargo Gallery, 1989; exhibited in numerous group shows, including Schenectady Mus., 1977, Albany (N.Y.) Inst. History and Art, 1978, Keane Mason Gallery, N.Y.C., 1982, Aaron Faber Gallery, N.Y.C., 1984, Printmaking Workshop, N.Y.C., 1984, Woodstock Artists' Assn., 1985, 91, Watermark/Cargo Gallery, 1989. Recipient grant Am. the Beautiful Fund, 1976, Ulster County Decentralization grant N.Y. State Coun. on Arts, 1989. Studio: 2806 Truman Ave Oakland CA 94605-4847

KAGIWADA, REYNOLD SHIGERU, advanced technology manager; b. L.A., July 8, 1938; s. Harry Yoshifusa and Helen Kinue (Imura) K.; m. Harriet Hatsune Natsuyama, Aug. 19, 1961; children: Julia, Conan. BS in Physics, UCLA, 1960, MS in Physics, 1962, PhD in Physics, 1966. Asst. prof. in residence physics UCLA, 1966-69; asst. prof. physics U. So. Calif., 1969-72; mem. tech. staff TRW, Redondo Beach, Calif., 1972-75, scientist, sect. head, 1975-77, sr. scientist, dept. mgr., 1977-83, lab. mgr., 1984-87, project mgr., 1987-88, MIMIC chief scientist, 1988-89, asst. program mgr., 1989-90; advanced technology mgr. TRW, Redondo Beach, 1990—. Presenter papers at numerous profl. meetings, co-author more than 40 articles; patentee eight solid state devices. Recipient Gold Medal award TRW, 1985, Ramo Tech. award, 1985, Transfer award. Fellow IEEE (v.p. IEEE MTT-S Adminstrn. Com. 1991, pres. 1992); mem. Assn. Old Crows, Sigma Pi Sigma, Sigma Xi. Home: 3117 Malcolm Ave Los Angeles CA 90034-3406 Office: TRW-SEG Bldg M5 Rm 1470 One Space Park Bldg Redondo Beach CA 90278

KAHAN, SHELDON JEREMIAH, musician, singer; b. Honolulu, Mar. 5, 1948; s. Aaron Kahan and Marianne (Royjiczek) Sann. Student, Tel Aviv U., 1967-69, Merritt Coll., 1972-74. Guitarist The Grim Reapers, Miami Beach, Fla., 1965-66; bassist The Electric Stage, Jerusalem, 1969-71; music dir., musician Fanfare, L.A., 1974-75, Jean Paul Vignon & 1st Love, L.A., 1975-76; musician Jenny Jones & Co., L.A., 1976; musician, vocalist Fantasy, L.A., 1977-79; leader, musician, vocalist Fortune, L.A., 1980-83; bassist Johnny Tillotson Show, Nev., 1983; ptnr., musician, vocalist Heartlight, L.A., 1983-84; leader, musician, vocalist The Boogie Bros., L.A., 1984—; arranger, conductor L.A. Rock Chorus, 1988; musician, vocalist Jeremiah Kahan, L.A., 1988; bass player LIX, L.A., 1990—; solo act Sheldon Kahan, L.A., 1990—; spokesman Moore Oldsmobile & Cadillac, Valencia, Calif., 1987. Compiled musical work copyrighted in Libr. of Congress: "Sheldon Jeremiah Kahan The Early Years-Vol.I"; producer/disc jockey Kaleidoscope Radio Mag., Am. Radio Network; one-man show El Capitan, Irvine, Calif., 1990, Sagebrush Cantina, Calabassas, Calif., 1990, Don Jose, Artesia, Calif., Pineapple Hill, Tustin, Calif, 1991, The Fling, Tustin, 1992, Beverly Garland, N. Hollywood, Calif., Brian Patch, Garden Grove, Calif., Sugar Suite, Granada Hills, Calif, 1993; albums include "Out of the Shadows", 1992, "City Lights", 1993. Mem. AFTRA, Am. Fedn. Musicians. Democrat. Jewish. Home: 3915 1/2 Fredonia Dr Los Angeles CA 90068-1213

KAHANEY, PHYLLIS SHERMAN, humanities educator; b. New Orleans, Nov. 4, 1948; d. Moss Dumar and Evelyn (Jackson) Sherman; m. Alan Kahaney, June 23, 1978; children: Cory, Jeanne, Amelia. BA, U. Iowa, 1971; MA, San Diego State U., 1981; PhD, NYU, 1991. Dir. Writing Across the Curriculum Program U. San Diego, 1986-93; asst. prof., dir. writing program U. Hawaii, Hilo, 1993—. Author: (with others) Interdisciplinary Handbook of Adult Lifespan Learning, 1994; co-editor: Theoretical and Critical Perspectives on Teacher Change, 1993. Mem. MLA, Nat. Coun. Tchrs. English, Coun. of Coll. Composition and Communication, Associated Writing Programs, Legal Writing Inst. Home: 84 Pukihae St Apt 505 Hilo HI 96720-2404 Office: 200 W Kawili St Hilo HI 96720-4075

KAHLE, LYNN RICHARD, psychology and marketing educator; b. Hillsboro, Oreg., Dec. 6, 1950; s. Walter Raymond and Dorothea Elizabeth (Schaus) K.; m. Debra Claire Eisert, Aug. 19, 1978; children: Kevin, Kurt. AA, Concordia Coll., Portland, Oreg., 1971; BA with distinction, Concordia Coll., Ft. Wayne, Ind., 1973; MA, Pacific Luth. U., 1974; PhD, U. Nebr., 1977; postdoctoral study, U. Mich., 1978-80. Asst. prof. U. Nebr., Lincoln, 1977-78; postdoctoral fellow U. Mich., Ann Arbor, 1978-80; asst. prof. U. N.C., Chapel Hill, 1980-83; from asst. prof. to chair and James Warsaw prof. Dept. Mktg. U. Oreg., Eugene, 1983—. Author: Attitudes and Social Adaptation, 1984, Marketing Management, 1990; author, editor Social Values and Social Change, 1983; assoc. editor Psychology and Marketing, 1983-85; contbr. articles to profl. jours. Pres. Commn. on Rights of Aging, Eugene, 1987-91, Human Rights Pres.'s Coun., Eugene, 1988-91; bd. dirs. Orgn. Econ .Initiatives, Eugene, 1988—. Recipient Nat. Research Svc. award U. Mich., 1978-80. Fellow Am. Psychol. Assn.; mem. Am. Mktg. Assn., Assn. For Consumer Rsch., Soc. Consumer Psychology. Democrat. Lutheran. Home: 2685 Bowmont Dr Eugene OR 97405-5906 Office: University of Oregon Dept Marketing Eugene OR 97403-1208

KAHN, EARL LESTER, market research executive; b. Kansas City, Mo., May 30, 1919; s. Samuel and Sarah (Kaufman) K. BA, Harvard U., 1940; MA, U. Chgo., 1947. Pres. Social Research, Inc., Chgo., 1946-74; chmn. bd. KPR Assocs., Inc., Scottsdale, Ariz., 1974-88. Contbr. articles to profl. jour. Served to capt. USAF, 1942-46. Mem. Am. Mktg. Assn, Am. Sociol. Assn. Home: 5608 N Scottsdale Rd Paradise Valley AZ 85253-5912

KAHN, IRWIN WILLIAM, industrial engineer; b. N.Y.C., Feb. 3, 1923; s. Milton and Clara (Clark) K.; B.S., U. Calif.-Berkeley, 1949; student Cath. U., 1943-44; m. Mildred Cross, May 14, 1946 (dec. May 1966); children: Steven Edward, Michael William, Evelyn Ruth, Joanne Susan; m. 2d, Marajayne Smith, Oct. 9, 1979. Chief indsl. engr. Malsbary Mfg. Co., Oakland, Calif., 1953-57, Yale & Towne Mfg. Co., San Leandro, Calif., 1957-60; sr. indsl. engr. Eitel McCulloch, San Carlos, Calif., 1961-62, Lockheed, Sunnyvale, Calif., 1962-69; v.p. Performance Investors, Inc., Palo Alto, 1969-74; with Kaiser-Permanente Services, Oakland, 1974-76; nat. mgr. material handling Cutter Labs., Berkeley, Calif., 1976-83; sr. mgmt. engr. Children's Hosp. Med. Ctr., Oakland, 1983; sr. indsl. engr. Naval Air Rework Facility, Alameda, Calif., 1983-85, Naval Supply Ctr., Oakland, 1985-88; vis. lectr. U. Calif., Berkeley, 1986; tchr. indsl. engring. Laney Coll., Oakland, 1967—, Chabot Coll., Hayward, Calif.; pres. East Bay Table Pad Co., 1990. Chmn. Alameda County Library Adv. Commn., 1965—. Served with AUS, 1943-46. Registered profl. engr., Calif. Mem. Am. Inst. Indsl. Engrs. (chpt. pres. 1963-64, chmn. conf. 1967 nat. publ. dir. aerospace div. 1968-69), Calif. Soc. Profl. Engrs. (pres. chpt.). Club: Toastmasters (dist. gov. 1960-61).

KAHN, JEFFREY HAY, retired investment banker; b. Evanston, Ill., Jan. 13, 1939; s. Harry James and Helen Barbara (Neubrech) K.; m. Maurine C. Frank, June 24, 1961; children: Jeffrey H., Heather Fay, Jennifer Girard. BA, Yale U., 1960. Sales rep. H.J. Kahn Co., Chgo., 1960-65; with Smith Barney, Harris, Upsham & Co., Inc. and predeccesors, Chgo., 1965-68; mgr. Smith Barney, Harris/Upham & Co., Inc. and predecessors, L.A., 1968-71; nat. salesman Smith Barney, Harris/Upham & Co., Inc. and predecessors, N.Y.C., 1971-76; N.E. regional dir. Smith Barney, Harris, Upsham & Co., Inc. and predeccesors, N.Y.C., 1976-83, dir. svcs. group, 1983-89, exec. v.p., 1989; pres. Prescott, Ball & Turben, Inc., Cleve., 1990-91; sr. exec. v.p. Kemper Securities, Chgo., 1991-92; ret., 1992. Trustee Iona Coll., New Rochelle, N.Y., 1975—, Miss Hall's Sch., Pittsfield, Mass., 1985—, St. Vincent Hosp., Harrison, N.Y. Decorated Knight of Malta, 1982. Mem. Westchester Country Club (gov. 1981-90). Clubs: Westchester Country (chmn. 1985), Desert Highlands (Scottsdale, Ariz.), Met. Club (N.Y.C.), Desert Mountain (Scottsdale). Home: 10040 E Happy Valley Rd Scottsdale AZ 85255

KAHN, JOEL SHELDON, physician; b. Washington, Sept. 27, 1956; s. Werner David and Gladys (Homer) K.; m. Ann Reimers, Feb. 6, 1982; 1 child, Ashley Elizabeth. BS, George Washington U., 1977; MD, U. Md., 1981. Diplomate Am. Bd. Emergency Medicine. Surg. resident physician Cedars-Sinai Med. Ctr., L.A., 1981-83; pvt. practice, emergency physician Calif., 1983—. Editor (newspaper) The Aesculapian, 1979-81. Chmn. Second Undergrad. Conf. on Bioethics, Washington, 1977. Mem. Am. Coll. Emergency Physicians, Phi Beta Kappa, Alpha Chi Sigma. Democrat. Jewish. Home: 4 Delamesa W Irvine CA 92720-1839

KAHN, KEVIN COMERFORD, software engineering executive; b. N.Y.C., Dec. 8, 1950; s. Arthur L. and Eileen M. (Comerford) K.; m. Suzanne Louise Schmitt, May 22, 1976. BS in Math., Manhattan Coll., 1972; MS in Computer Sci., Purdue U., 1973, PhD in Computer Sci., 1976. Sr. software engr. Intel Corp., Santa Clara, Calif., 1976-77, Aloha, Oreg., 1977-79, software project leader, 1979-82, dept. mgr., Hillsboro, Oreg., 1982-83, software engring. mgr., 1983-86, engring. mgr., 1986—, dir. systems architecture BiiN, Hillsboro, 1988—, lab. mgr., 1990-93; Intel fellow, dir. Software Arch., 1994-95, dir. comm. infrastructure lab., 1995—. Contbr. articles to profl. jours. Patentee in field. NSF fellow, 1972. Mem. Assn. Computer Machinery, Spl. Interest Group Operating Systems (sec., treas. 1983-85), Phi Beta Kappa. Home: 3324 SW Sherwood Pl Portland OR 97201-1461 Office: Intel Corp JFZ-52 5200 NE Elam Young Pky Hillsboro OR 97124-6463

KAHN, LINDA MCCLURE, maritime industry executive; b. Jacksonville, Fla.; d. George Calvin and Myrtice Louise (Boggs) McClure; m. Paul Markham Kahn, May 20, 1968. BS with high honors, U. Fla.; MS, U. Mich., 1964. Actuarial trainee N.Y. Life Ins. Co., N.Y.C., 1964-66, actuarial asst., 1966-69, asst. actuary, 1969-71; v.p., actuary US Life Ins., Pasadena, Calif., 1972-74; mgr. Coopers & Lybrand, Los Angeles, 1974-76, sr. cons., San Francisco, 1976-82; dir. program mgmt. Pacific Maritime Assn., San Francisco, 1982—. Bd. dirs. Pacific Heights Residents Assn., sec.-treas., 1981; trustee ILWU-PMA Welfare Plan, SIU-PD-PMA Pension and Supplemental Benefits Plans, 1982-90, Seafarers Med. Ctr., 1982-90, others. Fellow Soc. Actuaries (chmn. com. on minority recruiting 1988-91, chmn. actuary of future sect. 1993—); mem. Internat. Actuarial Assn., Internat. Assn. Cons. Actuaries, Actuarial Studies Non-Life Ins., Am. Acad. Actuaries, Western Pension and Benefits Conf. (newsletter editor 1983-85, sec. 1985-88, treas. 1989-90), Actuarial Club Pacific States, San Francisco Actuarial Club (pres. 1981), Met. Club, Commonwealth Club, Soroptimists Club (v.p. 1973-74). Home: 2430 Pacific Ave San Francisco CA 94115-1238 Office: Pacific Maritime Assn 550 California St San Francisco CA 94104-1006

KAHN, MARIO SANTAMARIA, international marketing executive; b. Manila, Jan. 16, 1956; came to U.S., 1980; s. Rene L. and Dolores (Santamaria) K.; m. Maria Victoria Legaspi, Dec. 28, 1987; 1 child, Marc Daniel. AB in Mktg. & Comm., De La Salle U., Manila, 1977; MA in Comm. Mgmt. cum laude, U. So. Calif., 1982; postgrad., Stanford U., 1989. Assoc. prof. De La Salle U., Manila, 1978-80; account mgr. McCann-Erickson, Manila, 1977-80; teaching asst. U. So. Calif., L.A., 1980-82; ops. mgr. Dayton-Hudson Corp., Mpls., 1982-85; regional mgr. Europe/Middle East/Australasia and Sunkist Soft Drinks Internat. Sunkist Growers, Inc., Ontario, Calif., 1986—; bd. dirs. Sunkist Soft Drink Internat. Mem. Am. Mktg. Assn., Am. Mgmt. Assn., Stnaford Alumni Assn., Annenberg Alumni Assn., De La Salle Alumni Assn., SunKist Soft Drink Internat. Bd. Office: Sunkist Growers Inc 720 E Sunkist St Ontario CA 91761-1861

KAHN, MERLE DEBORAH, lawyer; b. Chgo., Dec. 2, 1961; d. Kalvin Harvey and Evelyn (Henry) K. BA with high distinction in English lit., U. Ill., 1983; JD, George Washington U., 1987. Bar: Ill. 1988, D.C. 1989, Calif. 1992, U.S. Dist. Ct. (no. dist.) Calif. 1992, U.S. Ct. Appeals (9th cir.) 1992. Counsel Atty. Registration and Disciplinary Commn., Chgo., 1989-91; pvt. practice San Francisco, 1991-94; assoc. Nervo & Bean, San Francisco, 1994—; guest speaker Immigrant Legal Resource Ctr., San Francisco, 1993—. Active Calif. Abortion Rights Action League, San Francisco, 1992—. Mem. Calif. State Bar Assn., D.C. Bar Assn., Am. Immigrant Lawyers Assn., Keizai Soc. Democrat. Jewish. Home: 562 University Dr Menlo Park CA 94025-5158 Office: Nervo & Bean 235 Montgomery St Ste 629 San Francisco CA 94104-2909

KAHN, MIRIAM, anthropology educator; b. N.Y.C., Mar. 30, 1948; d. Ludwig Werner and Tatyana (Uffner) K.; m. Richard Lee Taylor, Oct. 26, 1985; 1 child, Rachel Kahn Taylor. BA, U. Wis., 1970; MA, Bryn Mawr (Pa.) Coll., 1974, PhD, 1980. Asst. to Margaret Mead Am. Mus. of Natural History, N.Y.C., 1970-71; exhibit researcher and designer Field Mus. of Natural History, Chgo., 1973; asst. prof. Vanderbilt U., Nashville, 1980-81, The New Sch. of Music, Phila., 1985-86; asst. prof., curator Asian and Pacific ethnology Burke Mus. U. Wash., Seattle, 1986—, assoc. prof., 1991—; cons. Seattle Art Mus., 1988—. Author: Always Hungry, Never Greedy, 1986; co-editor: Continuity and Change in Pacific Foodways, 1988; contbr. articles to profl. jours. Inst. for Intercultural Studies grantee, 1970, 76, Field Mus. of Natural History grantee, 1973, Nat. Mus. of Can. grantee, 1974, Bryn Mawr Coll. grantee, 1974, Werner-Gren Found. for Anthopol. Rsch., 1976, 79, NIMH grantee, 1976, Am. Friends Svc. Com. grantee, 1979, NSF grantee, 1981, 88, Wash. Commn. for the Humanities grantee, 1988, U. Wash. grantee, 1990, Jewish Communal Fund grantee, 1994, Am. Philos. Soc. grantee, 1994, NEH grantee, 1994; Fulbright fellow, 1995. Home: 2806 NW 60th St Seattle WA 98107-2508 Office: U Wash Dept Of Anthropology Seattle WA 98195

KAHN, PAUL MARKHAM, actuary; b. San Francisco, May 8, 1935; s. Sigmund Max and Alexandrina K. (Strauch) K.; m. Linda P. McClure, May 20, 1968. BS, Stanford U., 1956; MA, U. Mich., 1957, PhD, 1961. Asst. actuary Equitable Life Assurance Soc., N.Y.C., 1961-71; v.p., life actuary Beneficial Standard Life, Los Angeles, 1971-75; v.p., actuary Am. Express Life Ins. Co., San Rafael, Calif., 1975-77, P.M. Kahn & Assocs., 1977—; adj. prof. actuarial math. San Francisco State U. Editor Dictionary of Actuarial and Life Ins. Terms, 1972, 2d edit., 1983, Credibility: Theory and Practice, 1975, Computational Probability, 1980. Fellow Soc. Actuaries (Triennial prize 1961-64), Can. Inst. Actuaries, Conf. of Cons. Actuaries; mem. Am. Acad. Actuaries, Internat. Actuarial Assn., Inst. Actuaries (Eng.), Spanish Actuarial Inst., Swiss Actuarial Assn., German Actuarial Assn., Italian Actuarial Inst., Am. Antiquarian Soc., Grolier Club (N.Y.C.) Zamorano Club (L.A.), Roxburghe Club, Concordia-Argonaut Club (San Francisco), Pacific Club (Honolulu). Address: 2430 Pacific Ave San Francisco CA 94115

KAHN, SEYMOUR, air transportation executive; b. 1927. Student, UCLA, Southwest U. Prin. Seymour Kahn, Westwood, Calif., 1947-66; asst. to pres. Bell Electronics Corp., Gardena, Calif., 1966-69; pres. IPM Tech. Inc., L.A., 1969—, Maytag Aircraft Corp. Office: Maytag Aircraft Corp 3939 E San Miguel St Colorado Springs CO 80909-3409*

KAHN, VIVIAN, urban planner; b. N.Y., Mar. 16, 1944; d. Elmer Albert and Lillian (Kahn) Neumann; m. Robert Tim Brown, Aug. 23, 1963 (div. Nov. 1968); m. Larry J. Mortimer, April 1, 1986; 1 child, Aaron C. Kahn-Mortimer. BA, CUNY, 1965; attended, Pratt Inst. Sch. Architecture, 1969-71, Columbia U. Sch. Journalism, 1965-66. Reporter Ridgewood (N.J.) Newspapers, 1966-67, N.Y. Times, 1967-69; sr. planner Assn. Bay Area Govts., Oakland, Calif., 1972-76; chief cmty. assist. State Office of Planning and Rsch., Sacramento, Calif., 1976-78; exec. dir. No. Calif. Assn. Non-Profit Housing, San Francisco, 1983-84; prin., ptnr. Kahn/Mortimer Associates, Oakland, Calif., 1979—; planning mgr., zoning officer City of Berkeley, Calif., 1987-95; mem. bd. dirs. Jubilee West, Inc., Oakland, 1993—, Am. Planning Assn., Washington, 1994—. Contbr. articles to profl. jours. Trustee Calif. Preservation Found., Oakland, 1987-90; pres., mem bd. dirs. Metro-Greater Oakland Dem. Club, 1989—; chair 37th Dist. Dem., Seattle, 1982-83; treas. seattle Housing Resources Group, 1980-83. Recipient Alumni scholar Columbia U. Sch. Journalism, N.Y., 1965. Mem. AICP, Phi Beta Kappa. Home: 4623 Davenport Ave Oakland CA 94619

KAIDA, TAMARRA, art and photography educator; b. Lienz, Austria, July 6, 1946; came to U.S., 1950; d. Ivan and Matrona (Bratasuk) K.; m. Paul S. Knapp; 1 child, Krister. BA, Goddard Coll., 1974; MFA, SUNY, Buffalo, 1979. Tutor photography Empire State Coll., 1977-79; asst. dir. dept. edn. Internat. Mus. Photography, George Eastman House, 1976-79; vis. lectr. Ariz. State U., Tempe, 1979-80, asst. prof., 1980-85, assoc. prof., 1985-92, prof., 1992—; represented by Etherton Gallery, Tucson, Califia Books, San Francisco; mem. faculty Internat. Sommerakademie fur Bildende Kunst, Salzburg, Austria, 1985, Friends of Photography Summer Workshop, Carmel, Calif., 1989, vis. photographers program R.I. Sch. Design, 1989, guest artist lecture and lazer print transfer demonstration Photography Studies in France, Paris, 1991; panelist NEA S.W. Regional Photography Task Force, 1980; juror nat. photography competition Calif. Inst. Arts, Valencia, 1981; curator, lectr., cons. in field. Author: (with Rita Dove) The Other Side of the House, 1988; Tremors from the Faultline, 1989; contbr. articles to profl. jours.; author short stories; many one-woman shows including Scottsdale (Ariz.) Ctr. Arts, 1987, Fine Arts Gallery RISD, 1989, OPSIS Found. Gallery, N.Y.C., 1990, Fyerweather Gallery U. Va., Charlottesville, 1991, Photography Gallery, Fine Art Ctr., U. R.I., Kingston, R.I., 1992, Kharkov (Ukraine) Regional Mus. Art, 1993, Sky Harbor Airport, Phoenix, Ariz., 1994; numerous nat. and internat. group shows including Coconino Ctr. Arts, Flagstaff, Ariz., 1985, Frankfurt Art Soc., Germany, 1985, Mus. Art and Trade, Hamburg, Germany, 1985, Boulder (Colo.) Ctr. Visual Arts, 1985, Art Inst. Chgo., Mpls. Coll. Art & Design, 1986, Hood Mus. Art Dartmouth Coll., Hanover, N.H., 1987, Lawrence (Kans.) Art Ctr., 1987, Miller's Studio, Zurich, Switzerland, 1987, Palazzo Braschi, Rome, 1987, Sante Fe Ctr. Photography, 1987, Dinnerware Gallery, Tucson, 1987, Sante Fe Ctr. Arts (purchase award), 1987, Rockwell Mus., Corning, N.Y., 1987, Grand Canyon Coll., Phoenix, 1987, Tucson Mus. Art, 1988, Halsey Gallery Coll. of Charleston, S.C., 1988, Long Beach (Calif.) Coll. Fine Arts, 1988, Atrium Gallery U. Conn. Storrs, 1988, Gallery of Kans. City (Mo.) Artists Coalition (1st prize, fellowship award) 1989, Lieberman and Saul Gallery, N.Y.C., 1989, Downey (Calif.) Mus. Art, 1989, Anderson Ranch Arts Ctr., Aspen, Colo., 1989, San Francisco Camerawork, 1990, Phoenix Mus. Art, 1990, Ctr. for Photography, Cin., 1991, Mus. Art U. Okla., 1991, Rockford (Ill.) Coll., 1991, Ctr. for Creative Photography, Tucson, 1991-92; Huntington Gallery, Mass. Coll. Art, Boston, 1992, Ariz. State Capital, Phoenix, 1992, Barbara Zusman Art and Antiques Gallery, Santa Fe, N.Mex., 1992; internat. traveling exhbns.; represented in permanent collections Union Russian Art Photography, Moscow, U. Calif. Santa Cruz, Kennedy Ctr. Performing Arts, Washington, L.A. County Mus. Art, Internat. Mus. Photography George Eastman House, Rochester, N.Y., N.Y. Pub. Libr., SUNY Buffalo, Libr. Congress, Polaroid Corp., Cambridge, Mass., Sante Fe Mus. Fine Arts, Scottsdale Ctr. Art, Snell and Wilmer, Phoenix, Valley Nat. Bank, Phoenix, others; photographs featured various works. Judge spring art show Scottsdale C.C., 1980; organizer Artist Against Hunger money and food drive Ariz. State U. Sch. Art, 1984; juror New Times Newspaper, 1985, Tempe Fine Arts Ctr., 1989, Yavapai Coll., Prescott, Ariz., 1989. Recipient Faculty Grant-in-Aid, 1982, 85, 93, Current Works 1989 Excellence award Soc. Contemporary Photography, Visual Artists fellowship grant Nat. Endowment for Arts, 1986, rsch. grant Coll. Fine Arts, 1987, 93, grant Arts/Social Svcs./Humanities, 1989, Sch. Art Assistance to Faculty, 1990, Visual Arts fellowship grant Ariz. Commn. Arts, 1989-90, Inst. for Studies in Arts, 1992, materials grant Polaroid Corp., 1992, Gov.'s Arts award, 1992, Women's Studies Summer Rsch. award., 1992. Mem. Coll. Arts Assn., Soc. PhotographicEdn. (co-chair, organizer West/S.W. Regional Conf. 1983), Friends of Photography (Ferguson award 1983). Democrat. Russian Orthodox. Home: 534 N Orange Mesa AZ 85201-5609

KAIL, JOSEPH GERARD, computer sales executive, marketing executive; b. Cin., Dec. 23, 1946; s. Henry Thomas and Cosma (Contadino) K.; m. Patricia Lynne Riedel, June 28, 1969; children: Robert, Daniel, Joseph. BS, Xavier U., Cin., 1969, MEd, 1973. Tchr., athletic coach Alter High Sch., Kettering, Ohio, 1969-77; sales rep. Philips Bus. Systems, Inc., Cin., 1977-78, Hewlett-Packard Co., Dayton, 1978-81; dist. sales mgr. Hewlett-Packard Co., Pitts., 1981-83; sales mgr. Rocky Mountain area Hewlett-Packard Co., Denver, 1983-87, western regional sales mgr. bus. computer systems, 1988-91, western regional mktg. mgr. computer systems, 1991-92, am. mktg. mgr. computer systems organization, 1992-93, nat. sales mgr., home products, 1994—. Com. mem. troop 986, Boy Scouts Am., Denver, 1984-88, Highlands Ranch High Sch. Boosters, Denver, 1988. Republican. Roman Catholic. Office: Hewlett-Packard Co 24 Inverness Dr E Englewood CO 80112-5624

KAISCH, KENNETH BURTON, psychologist, priest; b. Detroit, Aug. 29, 1948; s. Kenneth R. Kaisch and Marjorie F. (Howe) Bourke; m. Suzanne Carol LePrevost, Aug. 31, 1969; 1 child, Samuel. BA, San Francisco State U., 1972; MDiv, Ch. Divinity Sch. Pacific, 1976; MS, Utah State U., 1983, PhD in Clin. Psychology, 1986. Ordained deacon Episcopal Ch., 1976, priest, 1977; lic. clin. psychologist, Calif. Intern local parish, 1973-76; ordinand tng. program Ch. of the Good Shepherd, Ogden, Utah, 1976-77; pastor St. Francis' Episc. Ch., Moab, Utah, 1977-80, St. John's Episc. Ch., Logan, Utah, 1980-84; psychol. asst. Peter Ebersole, Ph.D., Fullerton, Calif., 1984-86; intern in clin. psychology Patton State Hosp., Calif., 1985-86; psychol. asst. Ronald Wong Jue, Ph.D., Fullerton and Newport Beach, Calif., 1986-88; pvt. practice clin. psychologist Calif., 1988—; clin. dir. Anxiety Clinic, Fullerton, 1993—; exec. dir. Contemplative Congress, Fullerton, 1988-91; founder, pres. OneHeart, Contemplative Visions, Fullerton, 1990—; supply priest Episc. Diocese of L.A.; invited lectr. Acad. Sch. Profl. Psychology, Moscow, 1992, 93. Co-author: Fundamentals of Psychotherapy, 1984; author: Finding God: A Handbook of Christian Mediation, 1994; contbr. numerous articles to profl. jours. Mem. St. Andrew's Episc. Ch., Fullerton. Mem. APA, Calif. Psychol. Assn., Assn. of Transpersonal Psychology, Anxiety Disorders Assn. Am., Nat. Register of Health Svc. Providers in Psychology, Phi Kappa Phi, Rotary (bd. dirs., past officer). Episcopalian. Office: 2555 E Chapman Ave Ste 617 Fullerton CA 92631-3621

KAKFWI, STEPHEN, Canadian government official. Mem. Legis Assembly, 1987-95; Min. Justice, Intergovernmental and Aboriginal Affairs; former pres. Dene Nation. Office: Min Justice Intergovtl & Aboriginal Affairs, PO Box 1320, Yellowknife, NT Canada X1A 2L9

KALAPACS, ILDIKO, visual artist, dancer; b. Szeged, Hungary, June 13, 1965; came to U.S., 1987; d. Janos and Maria (Molnar) K.; m. Miklos Frech, Mar. 31, 1984 (div. Oct. 1988); m. Wayne Kraft, Dec. 28, 1988. BA in Studio Art, Ea. Wash. U., Spokane, 1992. Stone carver Városgazdálkodási Vállalat, Szeged, 1984-85, Maroti Lajos, Budapest, Hungary, 1986; instr. art Corbin Art Ctr., Spokane, 1993—; bd. dirs. mem. coms. Corbin Art Ctr., 1993-94; mem. Davenport Arts Dist., 1993-94; dir., choreographer Erdely Dance Ensemble, 1988-94. Executed mural Raw Energy of Spokane, 1992; choreographer numerous Hungarian folk dance suites, 1988—; designer modern dance choregoraphy backgrounds Namaste Modern Dance Group, 1991. Ea. Wash. U. scholar, 1989-91; Am. Bus. Women's Assn. scholar, 1990-91. Home and Office: 804 W 12th Ave Spokane WA 99204-3712

KALAT, STEPHEN SALMAN, psychologist; b. Jersey City, Apr. 16, 1950; s. Harry and Molly (Sondak) K.; m. Linda Susan Gang, Aug. 25, 1990; 1 child, Harris. BA, The Am. U., 1971, PhD in Counseling, 1977. Lic. psychologist, Colo. Ind. practice psychology Denver, 1980—; v.p. bd. dirs. Washington (D.C.) Free Clinic, 1974-77; cons. psychologist Mercy Med. Ctr., Denver, 1979-89, Care Unit Colo., Aurora, 1988-90, Mediplex Rehab. Hosp., Thorton, Colo., 1992, 93; chair profl. adv. bd. U. Denver Sch. Profl. Psychology, 1985-86; dir. psychology Charter Hosp., Aurora, 1989-90, Denver, 1990-92; pres. Denver divsn. Colo. Soc. Clin. Hypnosis, Denver, 1991-94. Bd. dirs. Colo. Head Injury Found., 1994-95. Mem. APA, Nat. Acad. Neuropsychology, Colo. Psychol. Assn. (chmn. profl. practice 1988-94, Disting. Svc. to Psychology award 1993). Office: Rehab Diagnostics & Treatment 360 S Monroe St #350 Denver CO 80209

KALB, BENJAMIN STUART, television producer, director; b. L.A., Mar. 17, 1948; s. Marcus and Charlotte K. BS in Journalism, U. Oreg., 1969. Sportswriter, Honolulu Advertiser, 1971-76; traveled with tennis profl. Ilie Nastase; contbr. articles N.Y. Times, Sport Mag. and Tennis U.S.A., 1976; editor Racquetball Illustrated, 1978-82; segment producer PM Mag. and Hollywood Close-Up, 1983-86; exec. producer Ben Kalb Prodns., 1986—; instr. sports in soc. U. Hawaii, 1974-75. Producer (video) The Natural Way to Meet the Right Person, 1987; producer, dir. (video) Casting Call: Director's Choice, 1987, The Natural Way to Meet The Right Person (Best Home Videos of Yr. L.A. Times), (TV pilot and home video) Bizarro, 1988, (infomercial) How To Start Your Own Million Dollar Business, 1990, The Nucelle Promise, 1993-94; segment dir. (home video) Movie Magic, 1990, (TV show) Totally Hidden Video; writer-segment dir. (home video) Making of The American Dream Calendar Girl, 1991; producer, host (cable TV show) Delicious Sports, 1987-88; segment dir. Totally Hidden Video (Fox TV Network), 1991-92; prodr., dir. short feature film Love Match, 1995. Served with Hawaii Army N.G., 1970-75. Named Outstanding Male Grad. in Journalism, U. Oreg., 1969. Mem. Sigma Delta Chi (chpt. pres. 1968). Democrat. Jewish. Contbr. articles to mags. and newspapers. Home: 1429 S Bundy Dr # 4 Los Angeles CA 90025-2108 Office: Ben Kalb Prodns 1341 Ocean Ave Ste 160 Santa Monica CA 90401-1066

KALENSCHER, ALAN JAY, surgeon; b. Bklyn., July 9, 1926; s. Abraham and Julia (Horwitz) K.; BS, Union Coll., Schenectady, 1945; MD, N.Y. U., 1949; m. Hannah Blaufox, June 18, 1949; children: Judith Lynne, Mark Robert. Intern Morrisania City Hosp., N.Y.C., 1949-50; surg. resident Maimonides Med. Ctr., Bklyn., 1950-51, 54; asst., then chief resident Bronx Mcpl. Hosp. Ctr., 1954-56; mem. faculty surgery dept. Albert Einstein Coll. Medicine, 1956-59; practice medicine specializing in surgery, Sacramento, 1959-84; chief med. officer Disability Evaluation Div. Calif. State Dept. Soc. Svcs., 1984—; attending surgeon Sacramento Med. Ctr.; commr. Bd. Med. Quality Assurance Calif.; clin. faculty dept. surgery U. Calif. Coll. Medicine, Davis, 1970-75 . Served with USNR, 1943-45, 51-53; ETO, Korea. Recipient citation N.Y.C. Cancer Com., 1959. Diplomate Am. Bd. Surgery, Nat. Bd. Med. Examiners (examiner 1957-59). Fellow Am. Soc. Contemporary Medicine and Surgery; mem. AAAS, Calif. Med. Assn., Sacramento County Med. Soc., Am. Diabetes Assn., Am. Mensa Ltd.

KALIHER, MICHAEL DENNIS, historian, book seller; b. Santa Monica, Calif., Nov. 7, 1947; s. Eugene Charles and Phyllis Joan (McClary) K. BA, U. Ariz., 1990. Pres. Klamath County (Oreg.) Hist. Soc., 1985; founder Native Am. History Week, Klamath County Mus., 1985-86. Contbr. articles to various hist. jours. Mem. Thoreau Soc., Pi Lambda Theta, Phi Alpha Theta. Roman Catholic. Home: PO Box 634 Winslow AZ 86047-0634

KALIS, MURRAY, advertising agency executive, writer; s. Bernard and Bernis Kalis. B.S. in Communications, U. Ill.; postgrad. Drake U., U. Iowa. Former chmn. art dept. Midwestern Coll., Denison, Iowa; creative dir., v.p. Leo Burnett Advt., Chgo.; exec. creative dir., sr. v.p. Young & Rubicam Advt. Joint Ventures, L.A.; pres. Kalis Advt., L.A., 1989—. Served to 1st lt. U.S. Army. Recipient cert. of merit N.Y. Art Dirs. One Show; Bronze Lion, Cannes Festival, gold medal Chgo. Film Festival, Clio award, Best in West, Belding, Spl. award UN for Pub. Svc. Advt., intaglio art in permanent collection Phila. Mus. Art. Author: Candida by Amy Voltaire, 1979; Love in Paris, 1980; Are You Experienced? The Jimi Hendrix Story, 1984, (play) Single Scene, 1989. Clubs: Creative, Los Angeles Advt.

KALKBRENNER, EDWARD JOSEPH, JR., pilot, consultant; b. Belleville, Ill., Dec. 8, 1942; s. Edward Joseph Sr. and Bessie Marie (Johnston) K.; m. Mary Susan Kenny, Aug. 21, 1965 (div. Sept. 1981); children: Melissa Jane, Cynthia Marie Buschmann; m. Karen Kathleen Moore, June 12, 1982; stepchildren: Dawn Marie Hilterbrand, Tiffany Anne Boehm. BSEE, St. Louis U., 1964, MBA, 1982. Elec. engr. IBM, Owego, N.Y., 1969-70; mktg. rep. IBM, St. Louis, 1970-73; systems mgr. Chemtech Industries, Inc., St. Louis, 1973-75, Rueckert Meat Co., Littleton, Colo., 1975-76; chief pilot Southwestern Bell Telephone Co., Littleton, Colo., 1976-84; corp. pilot U.S. West, Inc., Englewood, Colo., 1984—; v.p. Kalkbrenner & Assocs., Inc., Aurora, Colo., 1985—, Mgmt. Synergy, Inc., Denver, 1986—; v.p. Customers First, Inc., Littleton. Active in ch. and fundraising orgns. Capt. USAF, 1964-69, Vietnam. Roman Catholic. Home: 15941 Sampson Rd Littleton CO 80127-9525

KALLAY, MICHAEL FRANK, II, medical devices company official; b. Painesville, Ohio, Aug. 24, 1944; s. Michael Frank and Marie Francis (Sage) K.; BBA, Ohio U., 1967; m. Irma Yolanda Corona, Aug. 30, 1975; 1 son, William Albert. Salesman, Howmedica, Inc., Rutherford, N.J., 1972-75, Biochem. Procedures/Metpath, North Hollywood, Calif., 1975-76; surg. specialist USCI div. C. R. Bard, Inc., Billerica, Mass., 1976-78; western and central regional mgr. ARCO Med. Products Co., Phila., 1978-80; Midwest regional mgr. Intermedics, Inc., Freeport, Tex., 1980-82; Western U.S. mgr. Renal Systems, Inc., Mpls., 1982—; pres. Kall-Med, Inc., Anaheim Hills, Calif., 1982—. Mem. Am. Mgmt. Assn., Phi Kappa Sigma. Home and Office: PO Box 17248 7539 E Bridgewood Dr Anaheim CA 92817-7248

KALLENBERG, JOHN KENNETH, librarian; b. Anderson, Ind., June 10, 1942; s. Herbert A. and Helen S. K.; m. Ruth Barrett, Aug. 19, 1965; children: Jennifer Anne, Gregory John. A.B., Ind. U., 1964, M.L.S., 1969. With Fresno County Library, Fresno, Calif., 1965-70, dir., 1976—; librarian Fig Garden Pub. Library br., 1968-70; asst. dir. Santa Barbara (Calif.) Pub. Library, 1970-76; mem. Calif. Libr. Svcs. bd., 1990—, v.p. 1992—; Beth Ann Harnish lectr. com., 1988-91, chmn., 1989-90. Mem. Calif. Libr. Assn. (councilor 1976-77, v.p., pres. 1987), Calif. County Librs. Assn. (pres. 1977), Calif. Libr. Authority for Sys. and Svcs. (chmn. authority adv. coun. 1978-80), Kiwanis (pres. Fresno 1981-82, lt. gov. divsn. 5 1991-92, co-editor Cal-Nev-Ha News 1993-94). Presbyterian. Office: Fresno County Free Libr 2420 Mariposa St Fresno CA 93721-2204

KALMANSOHN, ROBERT BRUCE, physician, consultant, lecturer; b. Sioux City, Iowa, June 20, 1924. Student, Creighton U., 1942-43, U. Vt., 1943-44, Washington U., St. Louis, 1943-45; MD, U. Nebr., 1948. Diplomate Am. Bd. Internal Medicine. Intern Mt. Zion Hosp., San Francisco, 1948-49, resident in cardiology, 1949-50; fellow in cardiology Harvard Med. Svc., Beth Israel Hosp., Boston, 1950-51; pvt. practice internal medicine and cardiology, 1953—; attending cardiologist VA; attending physician in cardiology Cedars Sinai Med. Ctr.; assoc. clin. prof. medicine UCLA Med. Sch.; cardiac cons. L.A. City Sch. System, State of Calif., Dept. Vocat. Rehab.; mem. speakers bur. Los Angeles County Heart Assn.; lectr. in field. Mem. editorial staff Circulation, Exec. Health Letter; sr. editor, mem. editorial staff, editor-in-chief Jour. of Angiology; contbr. numerous articles to profl. jours. Chair subcom. on lit. and films Los Angeles County Heart Assn. Served to 1st lt. M.C., U.S. Army, 1951-53. Fellow ACP, Am. Coll. Cardiology, Am. Coll. Angiology (v.p., pres.-elect), Am. Coll. Chest Physicians, Internat. Coll. Angiology; mem. AMA, Calif. Med. Assn., Am. Heart Assn., L.A. County Med. Assn., Alpha Omega Alpha. Jewish. Office: Kalmansohn Med Corp 852 S Robertson Blvd Los Angeles CA 90035

KAM, THOMAS KWOCK YUNG, accountant educator; b. Honolulu, Nov. 12, 1955; s. William Kwock Yung and Mae S. M. (Yee) K.; m. Sally Ben Huai, July 9, 1983; children: Tiffany L. M., Stephen C. M. BBA, U. Hawaii, 1975, MBA, 1978, postgrad., 1993—. CPA, Hawaii; CMA. Intern Coopers & Lybrand, Honolulu, 1975-76; instr. Beckers CPA Rev. Course, Honolulu, 1982-83; statis. asst. Hawaiian Elec. Co., Inc., Honolulu, 1976-78, assoc. budget analyst, 1978-86; adult edn. tchr. Farrington Cmty. Sch., Honolulu, 1978-84, McKinley Cmty. Sch., Honolulu, 1978-86; lectr. West Oahu Coll., Honolulu, 1986; asst. prof. acctg. and fin. Hawaii Pacific U., Honolulu, 1984—. Mem. Neighborhood Bd. (Liliha-Kapalama), 1980-83; treas., fin. com. chmn. Neighborhood Bd. (Pearl City), 1985-88, vice chair health, edn. and welfare com. 1985, chmn., 1988-93, chmn. devel., planning and zoning com. 93—; auditor Kams' Soc., 1984-89, third v.p. 1990-91, second v.p. 1992-93, first v.p. 1994—); loan com. mem. Native Hawaiian Revolving Loan Fund, 1989-91; co-facilitator Pearl City Highlands Elem. Sch. SCBM Coun., 1992-93, 95—; dir. Pearl City Highlands Elem. Sch., Kokua Hui, 1992-93, treas., 1993—. Named Co-Adult Edn. Tchr. of Yr., Hawaii Adult Edn. Assn., 1988. Mem. AICPA, Hawaii Adult Edn. Assn. (dir. 1978-79, treas. 1979-81, pres. 1981-83), Hawaii Bus. Educators Assn., Inst. Mgmt. Accts., Hui Luna Club (dir. 1978, 85, auditor 1979, treas. 1980, 81), Friends of the Libr. of Hawaii, Toastmasters (Kam 720 Club treas. 1981, 82, Disting. Toastmaster 1985, Dist. 49 audit com. chmn. 1981-82, treas. 1982-84, speechcraft chmn. 1984-85). Office: Hawaii Pacific Univ 1188 Fort Street Mall Ste 252 Honolulu HI 96813-2713

KAMADA, ALAN KATSUKI, pharmacology educator; b. Sacramento, Sept. 22, 1964; s. Kenneth Katsuki and Hazel Masae (Hayase) K. D in Pharmacy, U. So. Calif., 1988. Lic. pharmacist, Calif., Colo., Nev. Intern in pharmacy Medi-Val Drugs, Lomita, Calif., 1985-88; resident in pharmacy VA Med. Ctr., Denver, 1988-89; clin. pharmacy fellow Nat. Jewish Ctr. Immunology and Repiratory Medicine, Denver, 1989-92, asst. prof. clin.

pharmacology, 1993—; staff pharmacist Dept. Veterans Affairs Med. Ctr., Denver, 1989; lectr. in field. Author: (with others) Handbook of Pediatrics, 17th edit., 1993, Asthma and Rhinitis, 1994; mem. editoril bd. Annals of Pharmacotherapy, 1994—; ad hoc reviewer jours.; contbr. numerous articles and abstracts to profl. jours. Grantee Miles, Inc., 1989, Upjohn Co., 1989, 91, Muro Pharm., 1992. Mem. Am. Acad. Allergy and Immunology, Am. Coll. Clin. Pharmacy (grantee 1991), Colo. Soc. Hosp. Pharmacists. Office: Nat Jewish Ctr Immunology & Respiratory Medicine 1400 Jackson St Denver CO 80206-2762

KAMEENUI, JAMES ANDREW, accountant; b. Honolulu, Apr. 2, 1963; s. Alexander Andrew and Barbara Ann (Daniel) K. AD, Heald Bus. Coll., Hayward, Calif., 1990. Gen. mgr. Shell Food Marts, Fremont, Calif., 1982-86, 87-89; technician Gnu Comms., Milpitas, Calif., 1986-87; clerical asst. Calif. State U., Hayward, 1989; pers. specialist Pedcom, Inc., Fremont, 1989-90; wardrobe cons. J.C. Penney Co., Hayward, Calif., 1990-91; jr. acct., purchase agt. Westech Comms., Inc., Hayward, 1991—; pres. James Alexander & Assocs., Hayward, 1993—; analyst Fed. Tax Assn., Newark, Calif., 1993—. Mem. Nat. Assn. Federated Tax Preparers, Am. Numis. Assn., Highlander Club. Republican. Christian. Office: James Alexander & Assocs 27911 Industrial Blvd Ste 137 Hayward CA 94545

KAMEGAI, MINAO, physicist, consultant; b. Koshu, Korea, July 7, 1932; came to U.S., 1952; s. Kuwasaburo and Cho (Kaneko) K.; children: Stephanie Marie, Sharon Akemi; m.Meera McCraig Blattner, June 22, 1985. BA, U. Hawaii, 1957; MS, U. Chgo., 1960, PhD, 1963. Lic. tech. transfer and commercialization specialist. Sr. physicist Knolls Atomic Power Lab., Schenectady, N.Y., 1963-66, Lawrence Livermore (Calif.) Nat. Lab., 1966-93; cons. Kamegai and Assocs., Livermore, 1994—. Bd. dirs. U. Chgo. Alumni Assn., San Francisco, 1980-92, Livermore-Yotsukaido Sister City Orgn., Livermore, 1988-90. Mem. World Affairs Coun. No. Calif., Japan Soc. No. Calif., Keizai Soc., Tech. Transfer Soc. No. Calif., Asian Am. Mfrs. Assn., Sigma Xi, Phi Beta Kappa. Home and Office: Kamegai and Assocs 908 Florence Rd Livermore CA 94550-5541

KAMEMOTO, GARETT HIROSHI, reporter; b. Honolulu, Oct. 30, 1966; s. Fred I. and Alice T. (Asayama) K. BA, U. Hawaii, 1989. Reporter Sta. KHVH, Honolulu, 1989-92, 93-94; Sta. KGMB-TV, Honolulu, 1992-93, 94—. Home: 3664 Waaloa Way Honolulu HI 96822-1151 Office: Sta KGMB-TV 1534 Kapiolani Blvd Honolulu HI 96814-3715

KAMILLI, ROBERT JOSEPH, geologist; b. Phila., June 14, 1947; s. Joseph George and Marie Emma (Clauss) K.; m. Diana Ferguson Chapman, June 28, 1969; children: Ann Chapman, Robert Chapman. BA summa cum laude, Rutgers U., 1969; AM, Harvard U., 1971, PhD, 1976. Geologist Climax Molybdenum Co., Empire, Colo., 1976-79, asst. resident geologist, 1979-80; project geologist Climax Molybdenum Co., Golden, Colo., 1980-83; geologist U.S. Geol. Survey, Saudi Arabian Mission, Jeddah, 1983-87, mission chief geologist, 1987-89; rsch. geologist U.S. Geol. Survey, Tucson, Ariz., 1989—; adj. prof. U. Colo., Boulder, 1981-83. Mem. editorial bd. Econ. Geology; contbr. articles to profl. jours. Henry Rutgers scholar Rutgers U., 1968-69. Fellow Gol. Soc. Am., Soc. Econ. Geologists; mem. Ariz. Geol. Soc., Sigma Xi, Phi Beta Kappa. Home: 5050 N Siesta Dr Tucson AZ 85715-9652 Office: US Geol Survey Tucson Field Office U Ariz Gould-Simpson Bldg # 77 Tucson AZ 85721

KAMIN, AVIVA, sports association administrator. BS in Phys. Edn. and Health Edn. & Psychology, U. Ariz., 1954; MA in Clin. Psychology, Calif. State U., 1963; PhD in Clin. Psychology, Human Behavior, Higher Edn. Leadership, U.S. Internat. U., San Diego, 1976. Phys. edn. instr., coach El Camino Coll., 1961-70, athletic dir., 1968-72, coord. student activities, 1970-72, dean of students, 1972-76; pres. Matchmaker Realty, Inc., Long Beach, Calif., 1980—; commr. Western State Athletic Conf., 1981—; chair of grants and project com. Beach Cities Health Dist., 1992—, pres. bd. dirs., 1994—. Named to Athletic Hall of Fame U. Ariz., 1985, Commr. of the Yr. City Manhattan Beach Parks and Recreation Commn., 1992-93, Hall of Fame El Camino Coll., 1994, State Athletic Hall of Fame Adminstrv. Divsn. Cmty. Coll., 1995. Office: Western State Conf 812 6th St Manhattan Beach CA 90266-5821*

KAMIN, SCOTT ALLAN, lawyer; b. Portland, July 1, 1948; s. Lloyd F. and Edith G. (Goldstein) K.; m. Susan Jo Whitlock, Mar. 12, 1978; children: Sarah R., Leah R. BS, U. Oreg., 1971; JD, Lewis & Clark Coll., 1976. Bar: Oreg. 1976, U.S. Dist. Ct. Oreg. 1976, U.S. Tax Ct. 1976. Assoc. atty. Douglas H. Stearns, P.C., Portland, Oreg., 1976-79; atty., ptnr. Weatherhead & Kamin, Portland, 1979-81; atty., shareholder Scott A. Kamin, P.C., Portland, 1981—; IRS liaison Oreg. State Bar, Lake Oswego, 1989—, tax sect. seminar, 1992. Mem. Mensa. Office: 1020 SW Taylor St Ste 550 Portland OR 97205-2510

KAMINE, BERNARD SAMUEL, lawyer; b. Oklahoma City, Dec. 5, 1943; s. Martin and Mildred Esther Kamine; m. Marcia Phyllis Haber, Sept. 9, 1982; children: Jorge Hershel, Benjamin Haber, Tovy Haber. BA, U. Denver, 1965; JD, Harvard U., 1968. Bar: Calif. 1969, Colo. 1969, U.S. Supreme Ct. 1973. Dep. atty. gen. Calif. Dept. Justice, L.A., 1969-72; asst. atty. gen. Colo. Dept. Law, Denver, 1972-74; assoc. Shapiro & Maguire, Beverly Hills, Calif., 1974-76; ptnr. Kamine, Steiner & Ungerer (and predecessor firms), L.A., Calif., 1976—; instr. Glendale (Calif.) U. Coll. Law, 1971-72; judge pro tem Mcpl. Ct., 1974—, Superior Ct., 1989—; arbitrator Calif. Pub. Works Contract Arbitration Com., 1990—, Am. Arbitration Assn., 1976—; mem. adv. com. legal forms Calif. Jud. Coun., 1978-82; lectr. Calif. Continuing Edn. of the Bar Programs, 1979-95. Contbr. chpts. to legal texts, articles to profl. jours. Mem. L.A. County Dem. Cen. Com., 1982-85; mem. Pacific S.W. Regional Bd. Anti-Defamation League, 1982—, exec. com., 1988—, treas., 1990-92, sec. 1992-94. Lt. col. USAR, 1969—. Mem. ABA, Calif. State Bar Assn. (chair conf. dels. calendar coordinating com. 1991-92), L.A. County Bar Assn. (chair Superior Cts. com. 1977-79, chair constrn. law subsect. of real property sect. 1981-83), Engring. Contractors' Assn. (bd. dirs. 1985—, rep. Am. Pub. Works Assn.-Associated Gen. Contractors Joint Coop. Com. that pubs. Standard Specifications for Pub. Works Constrn. 1984—, affiliate chair 1992-93), Bd. Registered Constrn. Insps., Res. Officers Assn. (pres. chpt. 1977-78), Omicron Delta Kappa. Office: 350 S Figueroa St Ste 250 Los Angeles CA 90071-1201

KAMINSKI, CHARLES ANTHONY, portfolio manager; b. Norwich, Conn.; m. Elizabeth Carbery Wick, Oct. 19, 1985; children: Catherine, Ian, Charles. BEE, MIT, 1970, MEE, 1972; MBA, Harvard U., 1974. Chartered fin. analyst. Assoc. John Barry and Assocs., Newport Beach, Calif., 1974-75; sales mgr. N.Am. Video, Acton, Mass., 1975-79; v.p. mktg. Creare Innovations, Hanover, N.H., 1979-82; pres. Commtech, Cambridge, Mass., 1982-84; group mktg. mgr. Instrumentation Lab. (Allied), Lexington, Mass., 1983-84; dir., portfolio mgr. Baring Am. Asset Mgmt., Boston, 1984-92; sr. v.p. investments GNA, Seattle, 1992—; bd. dirs. Wash. State Investment Bd., GE Capital Assurance Co., Great Northern Insured Annuity Corp., First GNA Life Ins. Co., Fed. Home Life Ins. Co., PHF Life Ins. Co. Mem. Inst. CFA, Boston Econ. Club, Sigma Xi, Eta Kappa Nu, Tau Beta Pi. Home: 7224 W Mercer Way Mercer Island WA 98040-5534 Office: GNA Two Union Square Seattle WA 98101

KAMINSKY, GLENN FRANCIS, deputy chief of police retired, business owner, teacher; b. Passaic, N.J., Apr. 29, 1934; s. Francis Gustave and Leona Regina (Tubach) K.; m. Janet Lindesay Strachan (div. June 1985); childrenn: Lindesay Anne, Jon Francis; m. Melanie Sue Rhamey, Mar. 11, 1989. BS in Police Sci., San Jose (Calif.) State Coll., 1958; MS in Adminstrn., San Jose State U., 1975. Cert. tchr., Alaska, N.Y., Calif., Colo., Fla., N.Mex., Oreg., Wyo., Va., Oreg., also others. Police officer San Jose Police Dept., 1957-65, sgt., 1965-75, lt., 1975-81; dep. chief Boulder (Colo.) Police Dept., 1981-92; ret.; pres. Kaminsky & Assocs., Inc., Longmont, Colo. 1981—. Author, editor: textbook Implementing the FTO Program, 1981—; contbr. articles to profl. jours. Exec. dir. Nat. Assn. Field Tng. Officers Assn. Sgt. U.S. Army, 1957-61, Korea. Mem. Police Mgmt. Assn. (sec. 1983-88), Calif. Assn. Police Tng. Officers, Internat. Assn. Women Police, Calif. Assn. Adminstrn. of Justice Educators, Internat. Assn. Chiefs of Police (use of deadly force com.). Republican. Episcopalian. Home and Office: 8965 Sage Valley Rd Longmont CO 80503-8885

KAMM, HERBERT, journalist; b. Long Branch, N.J., Apr. 1, 1917; s. Louis and Rose (Cohen) K.; m. Phyllis I. Silberblatt, Dec. 6, 1936; children: Laurence R., Lewis R., Robert H. Reporter, sports editor Asbury Park (N.J.) Press, 1935-42; with AP, 1942-43; with N.Y. World-Telegram and Sun, 1943-66, successively rewrite man, picture editor, asst. city editor, feature editor, mag. editor, 1943-63, asst. mng. editor, 1963, mng. editor, 1963-66; exec. editor N.Y. World Jour. Tribune, 1966-67; editorial cons. Scripps Howard Newspapers, 1967-69; assoc. editor Cleve. Press, 1969-80, editor, 1980-82, editor emeritus, 1982; edit. dir. Sta. WJW-TV, Cleve., 1982-85; instr. journalism Case Western Res. U., 1972-75, Calif. Poly., San Luis Obispo, 1991—. Radio and TV news commentator and panelist, 1950-85, TV talk show host, 1974-85; freelance writer, 1985—; author: A Candle for Popsy, 1953; editor: Junior Illustrated Encyclopedia of Sports, 1960. Bd. overseers Case Western Res. U., 1974-78. Herb Kamm scholarship in journalism established Kent State U., 1983, Calif. Poly., 1995; inducted Cleve. Journalism Hall of Fame, 1986. Mem. AFTRA, Soc. Profl. Journalists (pres. Calif. Missions chpt. 1986-87). Clubs: City of Cleve. (pres. 1982), Silurians. Home: 147 River View Dr Avila Beach CA 93424-2307

KAMPFER, JOHN BRENNAN, data processing administrator; b. Albany, N.Y., May 10, 1939; s. Franklyn Fredrick and Jeanne Marie (Fleming) K.; m. Joyce Elizabeth Boiser, Dec. 6, 1963 (div. Feb., 1990); children: Valerie (dec.), Robert, Regina, Elizabeth. BS, U.S. Military Acad., 1961; MS Computer Systems Mgmt., U.S. Naval Postgrad. Sch., 1969; MBA, U. S. Fla., 1976. Cert. CDP, CSP, Inst. for Certification of Computer Profls. Commd. 2d. lt. U.S. Army, 1961, adv. through ranks to Lt. Col., 1977; 25th Inf. Divsn. U.S. Army, Hawaii, 1962-66; 3d Bde 25th Inf. Divsn., 4th Inf. Divsn. U.S. Army, 1967-68, Hdqs. DA, 1969-71; mgr. pers. actions divsn. U.S. Army, Long Binh, Vietnam, 1971-72; data processing staff officer U.S. Readiness Command, Tampa, Fla., 1972-76; mgr. programming 25th Data Processing Unit Persinscom., Heidelberg, Germany, 1976-78; mgr. computer ops. 25th Data Processing Unit Persinscom., Heidelberg, 1978-79, mgr. plans and devel., 1979-80; data processing mgr. Rapid Deployment Joint Task Force (ctrl. command), Tampa, 1979-80; from mgr. planning to asst. mgr. facilities, data security Data Processing Divsn. Bank of Hawaii, Honolulu, 1981-87; mgr. facilities, data security Data Processing Divsn. Bank Hawaii, Honolulu, 1987-91;. Elected mem. Wahiawa Neighborhood Bd., 1985—, chmn. 1992—; mem. ctrl. com. Hawaii Dems., 1986—, treas., 1990-94; mem. Hawaii election adv. com., Honolulu, 1987-94; pres. catechetical bd. Our Lady of Sorrows Ch., 1994—. Decorated Bronze Star medal (2), U.S. Army. Mem. Data Processing Mgmt. Assn. (v.p. , exec. v.p., pres. Hawaii chpt.), Info. Systems Security Assn. (founding pres. 1990—), Lions Club (v.p., bd. dirs., pres. Wahiawa chpt., Dist. 50 zone chmn. 1992-93, region chmn. 1993-94). Office: Bank of Hawaii IS 309 PO Box 2900 Honolulu HI 96846

KAMRANY, NAKE MOHAMMAD, educator of economics and law; b. Kabul, Afghanistan, Aug. 29, 1934; came to U.S., 1955; s. Shair M. Kamrany and Farukh (Sultan) Sidiqi; m. Barbara Helen Gehlke, Dec., 1957 (div.); children: Michael Shair John, Lily Joy; m. Sajia Walizada, Nov. 12, 1978; children: Dennis Wali, Michelle Nazo. BS, UCLA, 1959; MA, U. So. Calif., L.A., 1962, PhD, 1962; JD, U. West L.A., Culver City, 1981. Sr. economist Battelle Inst., Columbus, Ohio, 1962-65, System Devel. Corp., Santa Monica, Calif., 1965-69; country economist World Bank, Washington, 1969-71; chief economist Info. Scis. Inst. U. So. Calif., L.A., 1971-73; dir., rsch. assoc. Ctr. for Policy Alternative, MIT, Cambridge, Mass., 1973-76; dir. program in law and econs. Dept. Econs. U. So. Calif., 1976—, prof., sr. lectr., 1976—; econ. cons. for law firms, 1986—; expert economist UN, Lebanon, 1980-82; bd. dirs. Ocean Towers Corp., Santa Monica, 1989—. Author; Internat. Econ. Reform, 1977, Econ. Issues of the Eighties, 1979, The New Economics of Less Developed Countries, 1978; editor Econ. Directions, 1989—. Active numerous community organizations. Grantee Advanced Project Agy., NSF, Sloan Found., Agy. of Internat. Devel. for Sahel Project; recipient Assocs. award U. So. Calif. Mem. Am. Econ. Assn., Soc. for Internat. Devel., Newport Found. (bd. dirs.), Afghanistan Studies Assn. (founder). Home: 1106 Kagawa St Pacific Palisades CA 90272-3837 Office: U So Calif Dept Econs Los Angeles CA 90089

KANANACK, MICHAEL JESSE, lawyer; b. Newark, June 3, 1947; s. Harry and Regina Helen (Jacobs) K.; m. Annie Broussard, June 19, 1991; children: Travis André, Quinn Hébert. BA, U. Md., Balt., 1969; JD, U. Balt., 1972. Bar: Calif. 1973, U.S. Dist. Ct. (ctrl. dist.) Calif. 1973, U.S. Ct. Claims 1980, U.S. Tax Ct. 1980, U.S. Ct. Appeals (9th cir.) 1980, U.S. Supreme Ct. 1980. Ptnr. Kananack, Murgatroyd, Baum & Hedlund, L.A., 1973-92, of counsel, 1992-95; ret., 1995. Editor U. Balt. Law Rev., 1971-72. Office: Kananack Murgatroyd Baum & Hedlund 12100 Wilshire Blvd Ste 650 Los Angeles CA 90025-7106

KANCHIER, CAROLE, psychologist; b. Winnipeg, Manitoba, Can.; came to U.S., 1993; d. Michael and Mary (Dyma) K. BA in Social Scis., U. Manitoba, Winnipeg, Can., BEd in Guidance and Counseling, MEd in Guidance and Counseling; PhD in Counseling Psychology, U. Calgary, Alberta, Can., 1981. Registered psychologist; cert. tchr. Dir. arts and crafts Winnipeg Parks Bd.; dir. women's phys. edn. Daniel McIntyre Collegiate, Winnipeg; dir. publicity Royal Winnipeg Ballet; dir. guidance and counseling Kelvin H.S., Winnipeg; dir. rsch. Thomson and Lightstone, Calgary, 1981-82; instr. edn. psychology U. Calgary, 1981-82; edn. and psychology cons. Vogue Bus. Svcs., Calgary, 1981-82; faculty edn. psychology and adult edn. U. Alta., Edmonton, 1983-92; pres. Questers Consulting, Mountain View, Calif., 1983—; vis. fellow Inst. Transpersonal Psychology, Palo Alto, Calif., 1990; chair career change Nat. Career Devel. Assn., Alexandria, Va., 1989-93; exec. bd. Life Plan Ctr., San Francisco, 1993—; instr., advisor adult edn. credentialing program U. Calif, Santa Cruz, 1994—. Author: Dare to Change Your Job--And Your Life, 1995 (Best Can. popular book 1989); contbr. articles to profl. jours. including Encyclopedia of Career Decisions and Work Issues, The Career Devel. Quarterly, Internat. Jour. for Advancement of Counseling, Jour. Employment Counseling, Am. Counselor, etc. Mem. ASTD, Am. Psychol. Assn., Am. Counseling Assn., Inst. Noetic Scis., Can. Assn. Adult Edn., Canadian Psychol. Assn. Home and Office: 555 W Middlefield Rd # 206 Mountain View CA 94043-3543

KANDELL, MARSHALL JAY, public relations counselor; b. Bklyn., Dec. 5, 1937; s. Harry and Mollie Rebecca (Remstein) K.; m. Judith Ann Zeve, May 28, 1961; children: Paul Bryon, Robin Pilar. AA in Journalism, Los Angeles City Coll., 1958; student Calif. State U., Los Angeles, 1963-65. Cert. tchr. community colls., Calif. Pub. rels. staff City of Hope (Calif.) Nat. Med. Ctr., 1966-68; v.p. Roger Beck Pub. Rels., Sherman Oaks, Calif., 1968-71; account supr. Laurence Laurie & Assoc., L.A., 1971-72; community rels. dir. St. Mary Med. Ctr., Long Beach, Calif., 1972-75; dir. pub. rels. Cedars-Sinai Med. Ctr., L.A., 1975; founder Marshall Jay Kandell Pub. Rels., Huntington Beach, Calif., 1976-91; pub. rels. dir. Housing Authority City of L.A., 1991-94, owner Marshall Jay Kandell Pub. Rels., Eugene, Oreg., 1994—; vis. faculty mem. Calif. State U., Long Beach; mem. founding faculty Coastline Community Coll. Pres. Encino Jaycees, 1970-71; pres. Community Vol. Office, Long Beach, 1975-76; bd. dirs. Long Beach chpt. ARC, 1974-75, Civic Ctr. Barrio Housing Corp., Santa Ana, Calif., 1985-93, Big Brother-Big Sister of Mid-Oreg., 1994—; mem. Citizen's Adv. Commn. 1984 Olympic Games, adv. panel Jewish Family Svc. of Orange County, Calif.; v.p. Irvine Jewish Community, 1973; founding mem., v.p. Congregation B'nai Tzedek, Fountain Valley, Calif., 1976. Served in USAF, 1958-63. Recipient Disting. Svc. award Encino Jaycees, 1972; MacEachern award Acad. Hosp. Pub. Relations, 1973-74; Best written story award Press Club Greater Los Angeles, 1965, also writing, photojournalism, pubs., pub. rels. awards Pacific Coast Press Club, 1973-82, Acad. Hosp. Pub. Rels., 1973-74, Internat. Assn. Bus. Comm. Orange County, 1984, Nat. Assn. Housing & Redevel. Officials, 1993-94. Mem. Pub. Relations Soc. Am. (accredited). Democrat. Jewish.at. Jewish. Home: 3401 Agate St Eugene OR 97405-4395

KANDLER, JOSEPH RUDOLPH, financial executive; b. Vienna, Austria, Dec. 13, 1921; came to Can., 1952; s. Franz and Maria Franziska (Stanzel) K.; m. Lubomyra-Melitta Melnechuk, June 15, 1963. D.Rerum Commercialium, Sch. Econs., Vienna, 1949; Chartered Acct., Inst. Chartered Accts. Alta., 1965. Sales exec. Philips, Vienna, 1951; acct. Brown & Root, Ltd. Edmonton, Alta., Can., 1952-54, 56, chief acct., 1957-64; v.p. fin. Healy Ford Ctr. and Assoc. Cos., Edmonton, 1964-89; pres. Sentha Investments, Ltd., Edmonton, 1978—. Bd. dirs. Edmonton Symphony, 1969-72, Alta. Cultural Heritage Council, 1973-81, Edmonton Opera, 1982-84, Tri-Bach Festival, 1982-84; founder Johann Strauss Found., Alta., bd. dirs. 1975-84, pres. 1975-78, founder, pres. B.C. chpt., 1985—; bd. govs. U. Alta., 1982-86, mem. senate, 1973-79, 82-86; mem. adv. com. on cultural and convention ctr. City of Edmonton, 1974-78, vice-chmn., 1976-78. Recipient Achievement award for svc. to community Govt. Alta., 1975, Johann Strauss medal in gold Vienna Tourist Bd., 1989, Knight's Cross of Honor 1st Class Republic of Austria, 1990, Golden Emblem of Honor City of Vienna, 1991, Golden Emblem of Honor Sch. Econs., Vienna, 1995. Mem. Inst. Chartered Accts. Alta. Address: Sentha Investments Ltd, 392 Langs Rd, Salt Spring Island, BC Canada V8K 1N3

KANE, BARTHOLOMEW ALOYSIUS, state librarian; b. Pitts., Nov. 2, 1945; s. Bartholomew A. and Ruth M. (Loerlein) K.; m. Elaine Murphy; 1 child, Leah. BA in Journalism, Pa. State U., 1967; MLS, U. Pitts., 1971; cert., Modern Archives Inst., 1987. Cert. Preservation Inst. Nat. Archives, 1990. Dir. Bradford Meml. Library, El Dorado, Kans., 1972-74; researcher Hawaii Dept. Planning and Econ. Devel., Honolulu, 1974-75, state librarian, 1982—; librarian Hawaii State Library System, Lanai City, 1975-79, Honolulu, 1979-82; adj. faulty mem. U. Hawaii, Manoa, 1986, 88, 92. Mem. Gov.'s Coun. on Literacy, 1985—. Hazel McCoy fellow Friends of Library of Hawaii, 1971. Mem. ALA, Hawaii Libr. Assn. Democrat. Home: 44-130 Puuohalai Pl Kaneohe HI 96744-2545 Office: Hawaii State Pub Libr System 465 S King St Rm B-1 Honolulu HI 96813-2911

KANE, KAREN MARIE, public affairs consultant; b. Colorado Springs, Colo., Mar. 7, 1947; d. Bernard Francis and Adeline Marie (Logan) K. Student, Mills Coll., Oakland, Calif., 1965-66; BA, U. Wash., 1970, MA, 1973, PhC, 1977, postgrad. Pub. affairs cons., housing subcom. Seattle Ret. Tchrs. Assn., 1981-84; pub. affairs cons. 1st U.S. Women's Olympic Marathon Trials, 1982-83, Seattle, 1985—. Contbr. articles to newsletters and mags. Vol. various polit. campaigns, Seattle; bd. dirs. Showboat Theatre Found./Bravo (formerly Showboat Theatre Found.), 1984—; hist. preservation chmn. LWV, Seattle, 1989—; hist. preservation chmn. sec. bd. trustees, mem. exec. com. Allied Arts of Seattle, 1987—; mem. Mayor's Landmark Theatre Adv. Group, 1991-93; mayoral appointee as commr. on Pike Pl. Market Hist. Commn., Seattle, 1992—. Recipient Award of Honor Wash. Trust for Hist. Preservation, 1990, Recognition award Found. for Hist. Preservation and Adaptive Reuse, Seattle, 1991; Am. Found. grantee, 1989, 91. Mem. Am. Assn. Univ. Women, Mills Coll. Alumnae Assn., U. Wash. Alumni Assn., Nat. Trust for Hist. Preservation, Hist. Hawai'i Found., Found. for San Francisco's Archtl. Heritage, Internat. Platform Assn. Office: Allied Arts of Seattle 105 S Main St Seattle WA 98104-2535

KANE, KATHLEEN LILLIAN, university administrator, lawyer; b. Whittier, Calif., Aug. 13, 1950; d. Wallace Edwin and Harriet M. (Burch) K. BA, Whittier Coll., 1971; JD, U. San Francisco, 1976. Bar: Calif. 1976. Atty. in pvt. practice, Lafayette, Calif., 1976-83; dir. planned giving U. Calif., San Francisco, 1983-87; v.p. U. Calif. San Francisco Found., 1987—. Mem. Am. Assn. Med. Colls., Coun. for Advancement and Support of Edn., Met. Club, City Club. Presbyterian. Office: U Calif San Francisco Found 44 Montgomery St San Francisco CA 94104-4602

KANE, THOMAS JAY, III, orthopaedic surgeon, educator; b. Merced, Calif., Sept. 2, 1951; s. Thomas J. Jr. and Kathryn (Hassler) K.; m. Marie Rose Van Emmerik, Oct. 10, 1987; chidlren: Thomas Keola, Travis Reid, Samantha Marie. BA in History, U. Santa Clara, 1973; MD, U. Calif., Davis, 1977. Intern U. Calif. Davis Sacramento Med. Ctr., 1977-78, resident in surgery, 1978-81; resident in orthopaedic surgery U. Hawaii, 1987-91; fellowship adult joint reconstruction Rancho Los Amigos Med. Ctr., 1991-92; ptnr. Orthop. Assocs. of Hawaii, Inc., Honolulu, 1992—; asst. prof. surgery U. Hawaii, Honolulu, 1993—, chief divsn. implant surgery, 1993—. Contbr. articles to profl. jours. Mem. AMA, Hawaii Med. Assn., Hawaii Orthop. Assn., Am. Acad. Orthop. Surgery, Alpha Omega Alpha, Phi Kappa Phi. Office: Orthopaedic Assocs Hawaii 1380 Lusitana St Ste 608 Honolulu HI 96813-2442

KANE, THOMAS REIF, engineering educator; b. Vienna, Austria, Mar. 23, 1924; came to U.S., 1938, naturalized, 1943; Ernest Kanitz and Gertrude (Reif) K.; m. Ann Elizabeth Andrews, June 4, 1951; children: Linda Ann, Jeffrey Thomas. BS, Columbia U., 1950, MS, 1952, PhD, 1953; D Tech. Scis. (hon.), Tech. U. Vienna, Austria, 1990. Asst. prof., assoc. prof. U. Pa., Phila., 1953-61; prof. Sch. Engring. Stanford U., Calif., 1961—; cons. NASA, Harley-Davidson Motor Co., AMF, Lockheed Missiles and Space Co., Vertol Aircraft Corp., Martin Marietta Co., Kellet Aircraft Co. Author: (vol. 1) Analytical Elements of Mechanics, 1959, (vol. 2), 1961, Dynamics, 1972, Spacecraft Dynamics, 1983; Dynamics: Theory and Applications, 1985; contbr. over 150 articles to profl. jours. Served with U.S. Army, 1943-45, PTO. Recipient Alexander von Humboldt prize, 1988. Fellow ASME, Am. Astronautical Soc. (Dirk Brouwer award 1983); mem. Sigma Xi, Tau Beta Pi. Office: Stanford U Dept Mech Engring Durand Bldg 265 Stanford CA 94305

KANEGIS, ARTHUR L.D., film producer, screenwriter; b. Washington, Nov. 4, 1947; s. Leon and Lillian (Hayman) K.; m. M. Susan Grabill, Sept. 2, 1967 (div.); 1 child, Robin Aura; m. Molly Post. BA, Earlham Coll., Richmond, Ind., 1969. Audio-visual documentary producer, writer Am. Friends Svc. Com., Phila., 1969-77; media dir. Ctr. for Def. Info., Washington, 1977-85; pres. Future Wave Inc., Santa Fe, 1985—; producer 2020 Prodns., Inc., Santa Fe, 1987—; audio-visual producer, speechwriter McGovern for Pres., Washington, 1972; juror Cine Film Festivals, 1984-88. Produced several documentaries including The Automated Airwar, 1970, Sharing Global Resources, The Post War War, War Without Winners II, 1982, The Weapons Bazaar, 1985, (feature film) OOOPS!, 1991; author: The Bully Proof Shield, 1991; contbr. articles to profl. jours. Recipient 1st place blue ribbon Am. Film Festival, 1980. Mem. Ind. Feature Film Producers, World Federalist Assn., World Future Soc. Quaker. Office: 2020 Prodns Inc 105 Camino Teresa Santa Fe NM 87505-4703

KANEHIRO, KENNETH KENJI, insurance educator, risk analyst, consultant; b. Honolulu, May 10, 1934; s. Charles Yutaka and Betty Misako (Hoshino) K.; m. Eiko Asari, June 23, 1962; 1 child, Everett Peter. B in Counseling Psychology, U. Hawaii, 1956, grad. cert. in Counseling Psychology, 1957; grad. cert. in ins., The Am. Inst., 1971. Chartered property and casualty underwriter. Claims adjustor Cooke Trust Co., Honolulu, 1959-62, underwriter, 1962-66; account supr. Alexander & Baldwin, Honolulu, 1966-68; spl. risk exec. Hawaiian Ins. & Guaranty, Honolulu, 1968-71; br. mgr. Hawaiian Ins. & Guaranty, Hilo, Hawaii, 1971-72, Marsh & McLennan, Inc., Hilo, 1972-78; sr. mktg. rep. Occidental Underwriters, Honolulu, 1978-87; pvt. practice Honolulu, 1987—; coord. Ins. Sch. of Pacific, Honolulu, 1978—; lectr. ins. Hawaii Dist. Cts., 1986—; cons. Dai Tokyo Royal State Ins. Co., 1992—; mem. arbitration panel, ct. observer panel Hawaii Family Ct., 1993—, Hawaii Criminal Ct., 1994—. Adult leader Boy Scouts Am., Hilo and Honolulu, 1956—, risk mgr. Aloha coun., Honolulu, 1980—; edn. chmn. Gen. Ins. Assn., Hawaii, Hilo, 1971-77; bd. dirs. The Children's House, Pearl City, Hawaii, 1987—; ins. cons. Arcadia Retirement Residence, Honolulu, 1987—; bd. govs. U. Hawaii Founders Alumni Assn., Honolulu, 1993—, scholarship chmn., 1993—. With U.S. Army, 1957-59. Recipient First Lady's Outstanding Vol. award First Lady/State of Hawaii, 1990. Mem. Soc. Chartered Property and Casualty Underwriters (pres. 1986-87, Continuing Profl. Devel. award 1988, 92, 95), Soc. Ins. Trainers and Educators. Home: 1128 Ala Napunani St Apt 705 Honolulu HI 96818-1606

KANENAKA, REBECCA YAE, microbiologist; b. Wailuku, Hawaii, Jan. 9, 1958; d. Masakazu Robert and Takako (Oka) Fujimoto; m. Brian Ken Kanenaka, Nov. 10, 1989; 1 child, Kent Masakazu. Student, U. Hawaii, Manoa, 1976-77; BS, Colo. State U., 1980. Lab. asst. Colo. State U., Ft. Collins, 1979-80; microbiologist Foster Farms, Livingston, Calif., 1980-81; microbiologist Hawaii Dept. Health, Lihue, 1981-86, Honolulu, 1986—. Mem. Am. Soc. Microbiology (Hawaii chpt.), Nat. Registry of Microbiologists, Am. Soc. Microbiology. Clubs: Brown Bag (Lihue) (pres. 1985-86); Golden Ripples (4-H leader). Home: 1520 Liholiho St Apt 502 Honolulu HI 96822-4093 Office: Hawaii Dept Health Lab 1250 Punchbowl St Honolulu HI 96813-2416

KANER, CEM, lawyer, computer software consultant; b. Detroit, July 8, 1953; s. Harry and Wilma Kaner; 1 child, Virginia Rose. Student, U. Windsor (Ont., Can.), 1971-72; BA, Brock U., St. Catharines, Ont., 1974; postgrad., York U., Toronto, Ont., 1975-76; PhD, McMaster U., Hamilton, Ont., 1984; JD, Golden Gate U., 1993. Cert. quality engr.; Bar: Calif., 1993. Asst. mgr. Gallenkamp Shoes, Toronto, 1975; systems analyst Kaners and 1 plus 1, Windsor, 1981-83; lectr. McMaster U., 1981-83; software testing supr. MicroPro (WordStar), San Rafael, Calif., 1983-84; human factors analyst, software engr. Telenova, Los Gatos, Calif., 1984-88; software testing mgr. creativity div. Electronic Arts, San Mateo, Calif., 1988; software devel. mgr., documentation group mgr., dir. of documentation and software testing Power Up Software, San Mateo, 1989-94; pvt. practice Calif., 1994—; sr. assoc. Psylomar Orgn. Devel., San Francisco, 1983-85. Author: Testing Computer Software, 1988, (with Jack Falk and Hung Q Nguyen) Testing Computer Software, 2d edit., 1993 (recipinet award of excellence No. Calif. Tech. Publ. Competition 1993); contbr. articles to profl. publs. Cons. Dundas (Ont.) Pub. Library, 1982-83; vol. Santa Clara County Dept. Consumer Affairs, San Jose, 1987-88; alt. mem. San Mateo County Dem. Central Com., 1988-89; chmn. Foster City Dem Club, 1989; vol. dep. dist. atty. County of Santa Clara, Calif., 1994; grievance handler, intellectual property, book contract advisor Nat. Writers Union, San Francisco, Calif., 1994—; bd. dir. No. Calif. Hemophilia Found., Oakland, Calif., 1995—. Scholar, Can. Nat. Rsch. Coun., 1977-78, Can. Natural Scis. and Engring. Rsch. Coun., 1979, Golden Gate U. Tuition scholar, 1989-93. Mem. ABA, ATLA, APA, ACLU, Assn. Computing Machinery, Am. Soc. Quality Control, Consumer Attys. Assn. Calif., Human Facotrs and Econs. Soc., Soc. for Tech. Comm. Jewish. Office: 1060 Highland Ct Apt 4 Santa Clara CA 95050-5899

KANIECKI, MICHAEL JOSEPH, bishop; b. Detroit, Apr. 13, 1935; s. Stanley Joseph and Julia Marie (Konjora) K. BA, Gonzaga U., 1958, MA in Philosophy, 1960; MA in Theology, St. Mary's, Halifax, Can., 1966. Ordained priest, 1965; consecrated bishop, 1984. Missionary Alaska, 1960-83; coadjutor bishop Diocese of Fairbanks, Alaska, 1984-85, bishop, 1985—. Address: 1316 Peger Rd Fairbanks AK 99709-5168*

KANNENBERG, IDA MARGUERITE, writer; b. West Liberty, Iowa, Oct. 28, 1914; d. Ernest John and Vera Ella (Smith) Green; m. David Harold Murdach, Nov. 30, 1934 (div. Aug. 1956); 1 child, Lee Rae Murdach Kirk; m. William Paul Kannenberg, June 26, 1969 (dec. Mar. 1988). Student, Multnomah C.C. Sec. various civil svc. and legal orgns. Portland, Oreg., 1955-69; owner antique shops Eugene and Portland, Oreg., 1969-89. Author: UFOs and the Psychic Factor, 1992, Alien Book of Truth, 1993, Project Earth From The E.T. Perspective, 1995. Mem. Soc. for Investigation of The Unexplained, Mensa. Home and Office: Hartmut Jager Art Ltd 415 Brae Burn Dr Eugene OR 97405-4941

KANNER, EDWIN BENJAMIN, electrical manufacturing company executive; b. N.Y.C., July 2, 1922; s. Charles and Grace (Edelson) K.; m. S. Barbara Penenberg, Aug. 3, 1944; children: Jaimie Sue, Richard, Keith. BBA, CCNY, 1943; MBA, Harvard U., 1947. Asst. West Coast mgr. Fairchild Publs., N.Y.C. and L.A., 1948-50; gen. mgr. Dible Enterprises, L.A., 1951-53; sales mgr., gen. mgr., prs. Western Insulated Wire Co. div. Teledyne, L.A., 1954-68; pres. Carol Cable Co. West div. Avnet, L.A., 1969-79; exec. v.p., COO Avnet Inc., N.Y.C., 1980-83; pres. Pacific Electricord and Am. Ins. Wire Co., L.A., also Providence, 1948—. Lt. comdr. USNR, 1943-47, PTO. Office: Pacific Electricord 747 W Redondo Beach Blvd Gardena CA 90247-4203

KANNER, RICHARD ELLIOT, physician; b. Bklyn., Oct. 1, 1935; s. William W. and Elsie Alice (Karpf) K. AB, U. Mich., 1958; MD, SUNY, Bklyn., 1962. Diplomate Am. Bd. Internal Medicine, sub-bd. pulmonary disease. Intern then resident in internal medicine U. Utah Hosps., Salt Lake City, 1962-65; fellow pulmonary medicine Columbia Presbyn. Med. Ctr., N.Y.C., 1965-66, U. Utah Med. Ctr., 1968-70; from instr. to assoc. prof. medicine U. Utah Sch. Medicine, Salt Lake City, 1970-90, instr. medicine, 1970-71, asst. prof. medicine, 1971-77, assoc. prof. medicine, 1977-91, prof. medicine, 1991—; vis. assoc. prof. medicine Harvard Med. Sch., Boston, 1980-81. Mem. air quality bd. Dept. Environ. Quality, State of Utah, 1988—, chmn., 1995—. Served to lt. comdr. USNR, 1966-68, Vietnam. Fellow Am. Coll. Chest Physicians (chmn. coun. of govs. 1991), mem. Am. Thoracic Soc. Office: U Utah Sch Medicine 701 Wintrobe Bldg Salt Lake City UT 84132

KANNER, STEVEN BRIAN, immunologist; b. Miami, Fla., Oct. 2, 1958; s. Ben and Sylvia Ruth (Naness) K. BA, U. Calif., Berkeley, 1980; PhD, U. Miami, 1986. Post-doctoral fellow U. Va., Charlottesville, 1986-90; sr. scientist Bristol-Myers Squibb, Seattle, 1990-93, sr. rsch. investigator, 1993—. Contbr. articles to profl. jours. Recipient Presdl. scholarship U. Miami, 1981-86, post-doctoral fellowship NIH, 1987-90. Mem. Am. Soc. Microbiology, Am. Assn. Immunologists.

KANTEN, STEVEN CRAIG, communications company executive; b. Marshfield, Wis., Aug. 15, 1952; s. Glen Charles and Viola Dorothy (Friberg) K.; m. Karen Wheelock Malm, July 15, 1985; children: Christopher Brooks, Bethany James. BS, U. Utah, 1979, MS, 1982, PhD, 1984. Instr. skiing Alta (Utah) Ski Lifts, 1974-88; cons. Shipley Assocs., Bountiful, Utah, 1985-90, sr. cons., 1988-90; pres. Kanten Comm. Internat., Park City, Utah, 1990—. Author: Listener-Based Presentations, 1991, Reader-Based Writing, 1991, Conducting Problem Solving Meetings, 1993. Mem. ASTD. Office: 3697 Wagon Wheel Way Park City UT 84060-5340

KANTER, MICHAEL HOWARD, pathologist; b. Chgo., Mar. 21, 1956; s. Morton Lee and Audrey Lee (Wilsey) K.; m. Sandra May Spitzer, May 15, 1983; children: Melanie, Robert. BS in Cybernetics, UCLA, 1976; MD, U. Calif., San Francisco, 1980. Diplomate Am. Bd. Anatomic and Clin. Pathology and Transfusion Medicine. Resident in pathology Harbor-UCLA Med. Ctr., Torrance, 1980-83, chief resident in pathology, 1983-84; pathologist, dir. blood bank So. Calif. Kaiser Permanente Med. Group, L.A., 1984—. Contbr. articles to profl. publs.; mem. editorial bd. TransFusion. Grantee Kaiser Permanente Rsch. Program, 1988. Mem. Coll. Am. Pathologists, L.A. Soc. Pathologists, Am. Assn. Blood Banks (inspector 1984-90), Nat. Blood Found. (grant review com.). Office: Kaiser Permanente Med Group 5601 De Soto Ave Woodland Hills CA 91367-6701

KANTOR, IGO, film and television producer; b. Vienna, Austria, Aug. 18, 1930; came to U.S., 1947; s. Samuel and Miriam (Sommerfreund) K.; m. Enid Lois Dershewitz, June 24, 1962; children: Loren, Mark, Lisa. AA, UCLA, 1950, BS, 1952, MS in Polit. Sci., 1954. Fgn. corr. Portuguese Mag. Flama, L.A., 1949-57; music supr., editor Screen Gems, Columbia, L.A., 1954-63; post-prodn. supr. various ind. cos. L.A., 1963-64; music supr.-editor Universal-MCA, L.A., 1964-66; pres., film editor Synchrofilm, Inc., L.A., 1966-74; pres., producer Duque Films, Inc., L.A., 1971-78; ind. producer Jerry Lewis Films, Film Ventures, L.A., 1979-84; pres., producer Laurelwood Prodns. Inc., L.A., 1984-87, Major Arts Corp., L.A., 1987—; pres. Jubilee Holding Co., L.A., 1988—. Producer Legends of the West with Jack Palance (TV spl. series), 1992, United We Stand, 1988, Act of Piracy, 1987, The Golden Eagle Awards, 1986, It's A Wonderful World, 1986, The Grand Tour, 1985, Shaker Run, 1984, From Hawaii with Love, 1983, Night Shadows, 1983, Kill and Kill Again, 1981, Hardly Working, 1980, Good Luck, Miss Wyckoff, 1979, Holiday Classic Cartoons, 1994, many others. Named Emmy nominee, 1967, 68, 69, 70. Mem. Acad. Motion Picture Arts & Scis. (exec. sound bd. 1969-71), Dirs. Guild Am. (assoc. dir.). Democrat. Jewish. Home: 11501 Duque Dr Studio City CA 91604-4279 Office: Major Arts Corp 144 S Beverly Dr Beverly Hills CA 90212

KAO, CHENG CHI, electronics executive; b. Taipei, Taiwan, Republic of China, Aug. 3, 1941; s. Chin Wu and Su Chin (Wu) K.; m. Susan Lin, July 4, 1970; children: Antonia Hueilan, Albert Chengwei, Helen Siaolan. BS, Taiwan U., 1963; AM, Harvard U., 1965, PhD, 1969. Research fellow Harvard U., Cambridge, Mass., 1969-70; scientist Xerox Corp., Webster, N.Y., 1970-75; mgr. Internat. Materials Research, Inc., Santa Clara, Calif., 1976-78; exec. v.p. President Enterprises Corp., Tainan, Taiwan, 1979-85; pres. Kolyn Enterprises Corp., Los Altos, Calif., 1979—. Contbr. articles to profl. jours. Bd. dirs. Taipei Am. Sch., 1980-82. Mem. IEEE, Chinese Inst. Elec. Engring. (bd. dirs. 1982-85), Sigma Xi. Club: Am. in China (Taipei), Palo Alto Hills Golf and Country. Office: Kolyn Enterprises Corp 4962 El Camino Real Ste 119 Los Altos CA 94022-1410

KAO, FA-TEN, education researcher; b. Hankow, Peoples Republic of China, Apr. 20, 1934; came to U.S., 1956; s. Ling-mai and Hang-seng (Feng) K.; m. Betty Chia-mai Tang, Dec. 17, 1960; 1 child, Alan. PhD, U. Minn., 1964. Instr. U. Colo. Med. Ctr., Denver, 1965-67, asst. prof., 1967-70, assoc. prof., 1970-81; prof. Health Scis. Ctr, Denver, 1981—; sr. fellow Eleanor Roosevelt Inst. for Cancer Rsch., Denver, 1965—; vis. scientist Oxford U., Eng., 1973-74; rsch. scientist European Molecular Biology Lab., Heidelberg, Fed. Republic of Germany, 1985; World Bank spl. cons. on Chinese Provincial Univs. Devel. Project; hon. prof. Harbin Med. U., 1987, Tongji Med. U., Wuhan, People's Republic of China, 1988. Contbr. articles to profl. jours. Mem. AAAS, Genetics Soc. Am., Am. Soc. Human Genetics, Am. Soc. Cell Biology, Am. Assn. Cancer Rsch., Soc. for in Vitro Biology. Home: 305 Leyden St Denver CO 80220-5994 Office: Eleanor Roosevelt Inst Cancer Rsch 1899 Gaylord St Denver CO 80206-1210

KAO, LILY CHING-CHIUNG, neonatologist; b. Hong Kong, Hong Kong, Aug. 4, 1951; came to U.S., 1970; d. Eugene Wei-yu and Yun-Ling (Chiang) K.; m. Wen Hsien Hsu, July 2, 1983; children: Davina, Christina, Sarena, Edmund. BA, Temple U., 1974; MD, U. Pa., 1978. Intern, resident in pediat. Pitts. Children's Hosp., 1978-81; neonatology and respiratory disease fellow L.A. Children's Hosp., 1981-82; neonatologist Children's Hosp., Oakland, Calif., 1983—. Fellow Am. Acad. Pediat.; mem. Am. Thoracic Soc., Western Soc. Pediat. Rsch., Soc. Pediat. Rsch. Office: Children's Hosp Oakland CA 94609

KAO, PHILIP MIN-SHIEN, software consultant; b. L.A., Dec. 16, 1963; s. Donald and Jennie (Chen) Kao; m. Lori Suzanne Wilson, June 25, 1989; 1 child, Rachel Su-Ying, Nicholas Andrew. BA, U. Calif., San Diego, 1985. Student engr. Hughes Aircraft Co., Fullerton, Calif., 1983-85; rsch. asst. Hybritech Inc., San Diego, 1986; rsch. assoc. Salk Inst. Biotech. Ind. Assocs., La Jolla, Calif., 1986-90; analytical chemist Alliance Pharm. Corp., San Diego, 1990-91; network adminstr. Ligand Pharms., Inc., San Diego, 1991-94; customer software support Artecon Inc., Carlsbad, Calif., 1994—. Contbr. articles to profl. jours. Mem. Am. Chem. Soc., AAAS, Assn. Am. Clin. Chemistry. Office: Artecon Inc 6305 El Camino Real Carlsbad CA 92009-1606

KAO, YASUKO WATANABE, library administrator; b. Tokyo, Mar. 30, 1930; came to U.S., 1957; d. Kichiji and Sato (Tanaka) Watanabe; m. Shih-Kung Kao, Apr. 1, 1959; children: John Sterling, Stephanie Margaret. B.A., Tsuda Coll., 1950; B.A. in Lit., Waseda U., 1955; M.S.L.S., U. So. Calif., 1960. Instr., Takinogawa High Sch., Tokyo, 1950-57; catalog librarian U. Utah Library, 1960-67, Marriott Library, 1975-77, head catalog div., 1978-90; dir. libr. Teikyo Loretto Heights U., 1991-95. Contbr. articles to profl. jours. Vol., Utah Chinese Am. Community Sch., 1974-80, Asian Assn. Utah, 1981-90. Waseda U. fellow, 1958-59. Mem. ALA, Asian Pacific Librs. Assn., Assn. Coll. and Research Libraries, ALA Library and Info. Tech. Assn., Colo. Library Assn., Utah Coll. Libr. Coun., Beta Phi Mu. Home: 2625 Yuba Ave El Cerrito CA 94530

KAPELOVITZ, LEONARD HERMAN, psychiatrist; b. Dickinson, N.D., Aug. 22, 1939; s. Ignace and Ethel Rose (Grouse) K.; m. Abbey Carol Poze, June 10, 1965; children: Mara Ilise, Daniel Ignace. SB, U. Chgo., 1961; MD, Harvard U., 1965; grad., Denver Psychoanalytic Inst., 1980. Diplomate Am. Bd. Psychiatry and Neurology. Chief resident in psychiatry U. Colo., Denver, 1968-69; asst. prof. psychiatry U. Colo. Med. Sch., Denver, 1971-75, clin. asst. prof. psychiatry, 1975—; pvt. practice psychiatry and psychoanalysis Englewood, Colo., 1975—; med. dir. psychiatry St. Anthony Hosp, Westminster, Colo., 1991—; vice chair psychiatry Provenant Health Systems, Denver, 1993—; mem. faculty Colo. Soc. for Psychology and Psychoanalysis, Denver, 1990—; mem. continuing med. edn. faculty Denver Psychoanalytic Soc., 1990—, Denver Psychoanalytic Inst., 1990—. Author: To Love and To Work, 1976, 2d edit., 1987; contbr. articles to profl. jours. Pres. bd. dirs. Denver Mental Health Ctr., 1983-85; candidate Colo. Ho. of Reps., 1972. Served as capt. USAF, 1969-71. Fellow Am. Psychiat. Assn.; mem. Colo. Psychiat. Soc., Denver Psychoanalytic Soc., Colo. Soc. for Psychology and Psychoanalysis, Maimonides Soc. Democrat. Jewish. Office: 8095 E Prentice Ave Englewood CO 80111-2705

KAPERICK, JOHN ANTHONY, information specialist; b. Tacoma, Wash., July 11, 1964; s. Victor Raymond and Billie Ann (Carlson) K.; m. Dawn Marie Canfield, Aug. 5, 1989; 1 child, Amanda Jeanne Kaperick. Cert., Bates Vocat. Tech. Inst., Tacoma, Wash., 1985; cert., Boeing Computer Svcs., Seattle, 1990. Apprentice cabinetmaker Custom Craft Fixtures, Tacoma, 1986-87; computer operator Vic's Enterprises, Tacoma, 1987-90; info. specialist NOAA (U.S. Dept. Commerce), Seattle, 1990—. Mem. Spl. Librs. Assn., Environment and Resource Mgmt. Divsn. Office: NOAA Hazmat 7600 Sand Point Way NE Seattle WA 98115-6349

KAPLAN, DONALD SHELDON, real estate developer and rehabilitator, property management company executive; b. L.A., Aug. 1, 1938; s. Adolph Iven and Ruth Janet (Rose) K.; m. Marsha Lynn Le Van, June 12, 1960 (div. July 1980); children: Lisa Ann, Drew Jason; m. Joanne Natalie Cossu, Apr. 19, 1981; children: Alyson Ilene, Tara Ruth. Student, L.A. City Coll., 1957-58, Pacific State U., 1959-60. Pres. DSK Devel. Co., Inc., 1964--, Advanced Maintenance Corp., Inc., 1974--, DSK Mgmt. Co., Inc., 1983--, New Renaissance Investments, Inc., 1986--, Kaplan Enterprises, Inc., L.A., 1986--; pres. Telephony Worldwide Enterprises, 1989—, Voice Telephone Co., 1993—, Fin. Svcs. of Am., 1993—, Western Fin. Investments, 1992—. Home and Office: Kaplan Enterprises Inc 5699 Kanan Rd Apt 234 Agoura Hills CA 91301-3358

KAPLAN, GARY, executive recruiter; b. Phila., Aug. 14, 1939; s. Morris and Minnie (Leve) K.; m. Linda Ann Wilson, May 30, 1968; children: Michael Warren, Marc Jonathan, Jeffrey Russell. BA in Polit. Sci., Pa. State U., 1961. Tchr. biology N.E. High Sch., Phila., 1962-63; coll. employment rep. Bell Telephone Labs., Murray Hill, N.J., 1966-67; supr. recruitment and placement Unisys, Blue Bell, Pa., 1967-69; pres. Electronic Systems Personnel, Phila., 1969-70; staff selection rep. Booz, Allen & Hamilton, N.Y.C., 1970-72; mgr. exec. recruitment M&T Chems., Rahway, N.J., 1972-74; dir. exec. recruitment IU Internat. Mgmt. Corp., Phila., 1974-78; v.p. personnel Crocker Bank, Los Angeles, 1978-79; mng. v.p. ptnr. western region Korn-Ferry Internat., Los Angeles, 1979-85; pres. Gary Kaplan & Assocs., Pasadena, Calif., 1985—. Mgmt. columnist, Radio and Records newspaper, 1984-85. Chmn. bd. dirs. Vis. Nurse Assn., L.A., 1985-87; bd. dirs. The Wellness Community-Nat. Capt. Adj. Gen. Corps., U.S. Army, 1963-66. Mem. Calif. Exec. Recruiters Assn. (bd. dirs.), Am. Compensation Assn. Home: 1735 Fairmont Ave La Canada Flintridge CA 91011-1632 Office: Gary Kaplan & Assocs 201 S Lake Ave Pasadena CA 91101-3004

KAPLAN, GEORGE WILLARD, urologist; b. Brownsville, Tex., Aug. 24, 1935; s. Hyman J. and Lillian (Bennett) K.; m. Susan Gail Solof, Dec. 17, 1961; children: Paula, Elizabeth, Julie, Alan. BA, U. Tex., 1955; MD, Northwestern U., 1959, MS, 1966. Diplomate Am. Bd. Urology. Intern Charity Hosp. of La. at New Orleans, 1959-60; resident Northwestern U., 1963-68; instr. Med. Sch. Northwestern U., Chgo., 1968-69; clin. prof., chief pediatric urology Sch. Medicine U. Calif., San Diego, 1970—; trustee Children's Hosp. and Health Ctr., San Diego, 1978-90, Am. Bd. Urology, Bingham Farms, Mich., 1991—; del. Am. Bd. Med. Specialties, Evanston, Ill., 1992—. Author: Genitourinary Problems in Pediatrics; asst. editor Jour. Urology, Balt., 1982-89; assoc. editor Child Nephrology and Urology, Milan, Italy, 1988—; contbr. articles to profl. publs. Pres. med. staff Children's Hosp., San Diego, 1980-82. Lt. USN, 1960-63. Recipient Joseph Capps prize Inst. of Medicine, 1967. Fellow ACS (pres. San Diego chpt. 1980-82), Am. Acad. Pediatrics (chmn. sect. on urology 1986); mem. AMA, Soc. for Pediatric Urology (pres. 1993), Am. Urol. Assn., Soc. Internat. Urologie, Soc. Univ. Urologists. Republican. Jewish. Office: Pediatric Urology Assocs 7930 Frost St Ste 407 San Diego CA 92123-2741

KAPLAN, HENRY GEORGE, oncologist, educator; b. Staten Island, N.Y., Feb. 3, 1947; s. Alfred H. and Dorothy (Avins) K.; m. Susan V. Dorfman, June 29, 1969; 1 child, Elizabeth. AB in Chemistry, U. Rochester, 1968, MD, 1972. Intern U. Wash., Seattle, 1972-73, resident, 1973-74; chief resident medicine U. Wash., Seattle, Md., 1976-77; asst. prof. medicine U. Wash., Seattle, 1979-81, clin. asst. prof., 1981-88, clin. assoc. prof., 1988—; clin. assoc. oncology Nat. Cancer Inst., Bethesda, Md., 1974-76; asst. prof. Med. Sch. Brown U., Providence, 1979-80; chief oncology Swedish Hosp. Med. Ctr., Seattle, 1986-94. Surgeon USPHS, 1974-76. Mem. ACP, APHA, Am. Fedn. Clin. Rsch., Am. Assn. Cancer Rsch., Am. Soc. Clin. Oncology, Alpha Omega Alpha. Office: Swedish Hosp Tumor Inst 1221 Madison St Seattle WA 98104-1360

KAPLAN, JONATHAN, psychiatrist, educator; b. N.Y.C., Sept. 5, 1943; s. Milton A. and Marian W. Kaplan; m. Lynna M. Gay, Oct. 25, 1980; 1 child, Daniel Aaron. BA, Swarthmore Coll., 1964; MD, U. Pa., 1968. Diplomate Am. Bd. Psychiatry and Neurology. Straight med. intern U. Wis. Hosp., Madison, 1968-69; resident in psychiatry U. Pa. Hosp., Phila., 1969-72; sr. investigator NIMH, Washington, 1971-74; unit chief VA Hosp., Palo Alto, Calif., 1974-78; pvt. practice Menlo Park, Calif., 1979—; clin. assoc. prof. dept. psychiatry Stanford (Calif.) U., 1980—. Contbr. articles to profl. jours. Surgeon USPHS, 1971-74. Mem. Am. Psychiat. Assn., No. Calif. Psychiat. Assn. Office: 1225 Crane St Ste 106 Menlo Park CA 94025-4253

KAPLAN, LAURENCE SCOTT, computer engineer; b. Englewood, N.J., Sept. 23, 1962; s. Leonard and Vivian (Hacker) K. BA cum laude, Dartmouth Coll., 1984; MS, NYU, 1988. Software engr. Compugraphics Corp., Wilmington, Mass., 1984-86; rsch. asst. Ultracomputer Rsch. Project, N.Y.C., 1986-88; unix devel. engr. BBN Advanced Computers, Cambridge, Mass., 1988-91; computer engr. operating systems Tera Computer Co., Seattle, 1991—. Courant Inst./NYU fellow, 1986, Army Rsch. Org./NYU fellow, 1987. Mem. IEEE Computer Soc. Democrat. Jewish.

KAPLAN, MARJORIE ANN PASHKOW, school district administrator; b. Bronx, N.Y., Apr. 10, 1940; d. William B. and Laura (Libov) Pashkow; m. Marvin R. Kaplan, Aug. 16, 1962 (dec. 1980); children: Eliot, Mara; m. Timothy Sweeney, 1985 (div. 1986). BA, Smith Coll., 1962; MA, Ariz. State U., 1974, PhD, 1979. Presch. dir., tchr. Temple Beth Israel, Phoenix, 1967-72; tchr. Washington Sch. Dist., Phoenix, 1972-74, coord., 1974-75, prin., 1975-81; asst. supt. Paradise Valley Unified Sch. Dist., Phoenix, 1981-83, supt., 1984-92; supt. Shawnee Mission Unified Sch. Dist., Overland Park, Kans., 1992—. Named Supt. of Yr., Ariz. Sch. Bd. Assn., 1987-88, 92; named to Top 100 Educators, Exec. Educator mag., 1986. Mem. Am. Assn. Sch. Adminstrs. Office: Shawnee Mission Unified Sch Dist 512 7235 Antioch Rd Shawnee Mission KS 66204-1758

KAPLAN, MARTIN HAROLD, writer, producer; b. Newark, N.J., Aug. 21, 1950; m. Susan R. Estrich, Nov. 26, 1986; children: Isabel, James. AB summa cum laude, Harvard Coll., 1971; MA, Cambridge (Eng.) U., 1973; PhD, Stanford (Calif.) U., 1975. Program exec. Aspen (Colo.) Inst. for Humanistic Studies, 1975-76; exec. asst. to the commr. U.S. Office of Edn., HEW, Washington, 1977-78; chief speechwriter to the v.p. The White House, Washington, 1978-80; columnist, editor Washington Star, 1981; guest scholar Brookings Instn., Washington, 1982; dep. campaign mgr., chief speechwriter Mondale Presdl. campaign, Washington, 1983-84; v.p. prodn. Walt Disney Studios, Burbank, Calif., 1985-88, writer, producer, 1989—. Screenwriter Noises Off, 1992; screenwriter, exec. prodr. The Distinguished Gentleman, 1992 (Environ. Media award). Marshall scholar Brit. Govt., 1971; Danforth fellow Danforth Found., 1973. Office: Walt Disney Studios 500 S Buena Vista St Burbank CA 91521-0001

KAPLAN, MIKE, film and video producer, director, and distributor, marketing executive; b. Providence, Mar. 16, 1943; s. Julius and Ida (Rabinovitz) k. BA, U. R.I., 1964. Assoc. editor Ind. Film Jour., N.Y.C., 1964-65; publicist MGM, N.Y.C., 1965-68, publicity coord., 1968, nat. publicity dir., 1968-71; v.p. Polaris Prodns., London, 1971-73; internat mkgt. exec. Warner Bros., L.A., London, 1973-74; pres. Circle Assocs. Ltd., U.S., London, 1973—, Lion's Gate Distbn., 1975-80; mktg. v.p. Lion's Gate Films (Robert Altman), 1975-80; producer, pres. Circle Assoc. Ltd., L.A., 1978—; v.p. mktg. Northstar Internat., Hal Ashby, L.A., 1981-83; pres. mktg. Alive Films, L.A., 1985-87. Producer: (Film) The Whales of August, 1987; (video) Oak Grove Sch., 1988; assoc. prodr.; (film) Short Cuts, 1992; prodr., dir. (documentary) Luck, Trust and Ketchup: Robert Altman in Carver Country, 1994; actor: Buffalo Bill and The Indians, Welcome To L.A., Choose Me, The Player. Recipient Best Film award Nat. Media Awards, Retirement Rsch. Found., 1987, Key Art award Hollywood Reporter, 1976, 87. Mem. Acad. Motion Picture Arts and Scis., Screen Actors Guild, Publicists Guild. Office: Circle Assocs PO Box 5730 Santa Monica CA 90409-5730

KAPLAN, MILTON EMANUEL, retired accountant, tax consultant; b. N.Y.C., Oct. 5, 1914; s. Meyer and Ida K.; m. Lillian Nathanson, Aug. 31, 1937 (dec. Sept. 1990). BBA, CCNY, 1937. CPA, N.Y. Acct. Schnur, Jaffe & Co., N.Y.C., 1937-38, City of N.Y., 1938-41; pvt. practice N.Y.C., 1953-60; internal revenue agt. U.S. Dept. Treasury, N.Y.C., 1941-53, 60-63; internat. examiner U.S. Dept. Treasury, Washington, 1963-71; strike force rep. U.S. Dept. Justice and U.S. Dept. Treasury, Washington and N.Y.C., 1971-74; large case examiner U.S. Dept. Treasury, Mineola, N.Y., 1974-77, ret., 1977. Treas. Israel Ctr., Flushing, N.Y., 1950-74, Congregation Sholom, Seal Beach, Calif., 1977—, Golden Rain Found., Seal Beach, 1987—; mem. appeals bd. City of Seal Beach, 1980—; pres. Mut. 7 Bd., Seal Beach, 1983-87; fin. cons. Leisure World Emergency Meals, 1982—. Recipient Outstanding Svc. award U.S. Dept. Justice Organized Crime and Racketeering Sect., 1974, Albert Gallatin award U.S. Sec. Treasury, 1977, Merit award U. Judaism, 1993. Mem. B'nai Brith (pres. 1982-84, Akiba award 1988, 50 Yr. Recognition award 1994), KP (life), Am. Red Mogen David for Israel.

KAPLAN, ROBERT B., linguistics educator, consultant, researcher; b. N.Y.C., Sept. 20, 1929; s. Emanuel B. and Natalie K.; m. Audrey A. Lien, Apr. 21, 1951; children—Robin Ann Kaplan Gibson, Lisa Kaplan Morris, Robert Allen. Student, Champlain Coll., 1947-48, Syracuse U., 1948-49; B.A., Willamette U., 1952; M.A., U. So. Calif., 1957, Ph.D., 1962. Teaching asst. U. So. Calif., Los Angeles, 1955-57, instr. coordinator, asst. prof. English communication program for fgn. students, 1965-72, assoc. prof., dir. English communication program for fgn. students, 1972-76, assoc. dean continuing edn., 1973-76, prof. applied linguistics, 1976-95, prof. emeritus, 1995—, dir. Am. Lang. Inst., 1986-91; instr. U. Oreg., 1957-60; cons. field service program Nat. Assn. Fgn. Student Affairs, 1964-84; pres.-elect faculty senate U. So. Calif., 1988-89, pres., 1989-90; adv. bd. internat. comparability study of standardized lang. exams. U. Cambridge Local Exams. Syndicate. Author: Reading and Rhetoric: A Reader, 1963; (with V. Tufte, P. Cook and J. Aurbach) Transformational Grammar: A Guide for Teachers, 1968; (with R.D. Schoesler) Learning English Through Typewriting, 1969; The Anatomy of Rhetoric: Prolegomena to a Functional Theory of Rhetoric, 1971; On the Scope of Applied Linguistics, 1980; The Language Needs of Migrant Workers, 1980; (with P. Shaw) Exploring Academic English, 1984; (with U. Connor) Writing Across Languages: Analysis of L2 Text, 1987; (with W. Grabe) Introduction To Applied Linguistics, 1991, Writing Around the Pacific Rim, 1995; editorial bd. Jour. Asian Pacific Communication, Internat. Educator, BBC English Dictionary, Second Lang. Instruction/Acquisition Abstracts, Jour. of Second Lang. Writing, Forensic Linguistics; contbr. articles to profl. jours., U.S. Australia, Brazil, Can., Chile, Germany, Holland, Japan, Mexico, N.Z., Philippines and Singapore; mem. editorial bd. Oxford Internat. Encyclopedia Linguistics; editor in chief Ann. Rev. Applied Linguistics, 1980-91, editorial bd., 1991—; contbr. notes, revs. to profl. jours. U.S. and abroad. Bd. dirs. Internat. Bilingual Sch. L.A., 1986-91, Internat. Edn. Rsch. Found., 1986-94. Served with inf. U.S. Army, Korea. Fulbright sr. scholar, Australia, 1978, Hong Kong, 1986, New Zealand, 1992. Mem. Am. Anthrop. Assn., AAAS, Am. Assn. Applied Linguistics (v.p., pres. 1992-94), AAUP, Assn. Internationale de Linguistique Appliquee, Assn. Internationale Pour La Researche et La Diffusion Des Methodes Audio-Visuelles et Structuro-Globales, Assn. Tchrs. English as Second Lang. (chmn. 1968-69), Calif. Assn. Tchrs. English to Speakers Other Langs. (pres. 1970-71), Can. Council Tchrs. English, Nat. Assn. Fgn. Student Affairs (nat. pres. 1983-84), Linguistics Soc. Am., Tchrs. English to Speakers of Other Langs. (1st v.p., pres. 1989-91). Office: U So Calif Dept Linguistics Los Angeles CA 90089

KAPLAN, SAMUEL, pediatric cardiologist; b. Johannesburg, South Africa, Mar. 28, 1922; came to U.S., 1950, naturalized, 1958; s. Aron Leib and Tema

K.; m. Molly Eileen McKenzie, Oct. 17, 1952. MB, BcH., U. Witwatersrand, Johannesburg, 1944, MD, 1949. Diplomate: Am. Bd. Pediatrics. Intern Johannesburg, 1945; registrar in medicine, 1946; lectr. physiology and medicine U. Witwatersrand, 1946-49; registrar in medicine U. London, 1949-50; fellow in cardiology, research assoc. U. Cin., 1950-54, asst. prof. pediatrics, 1954-61, assoc. prof. pediatrics, 1961-66, prof. pediatrics, 1967-87, asst. prof. medicine, 1954-67, assoc. prof. medicine, 1967-82, prof. medicine, 1982-87; prof. pediatrics UCLA, 1987—; cons. NIH; hon. prof. U. Santo Tomas, Manila. Mem. editl. bd. Circulation, 1974-80, Am. Jour. Cardiology, 1976-81, Am. Heart Jour., 1981—, Jour. Electrocardiology, 1977-94, Clin. Cardiology, 1979—, Jour. Am. Coll. Cardiology, 1983-87, Progress Pediat. Cardiology, 1990—. Cecil John Adams fellow, 1949-50; grantee Heart, Lung and Blood Inst. of NIH, 1960—. Mem. Am. Pediatric Soc., Am. Soc. Pediatric Research, Am. Heart Assn. (med. adv. bd. sect. circulation), Am. Fedn. Clin. Research, Am. Coll. Cardiology, Internat. Cardiovascular Soc., Am. Acad. Pediatrics, Am. Assn. Artificial Internal Organs, Midwest Soc. Pediatric Research (past pres.), Sigma Xi, Alpha Omega Alpha; hon. mem. Peruvian Soc. Cardiology, Peruvian Soc. Angiology, Chilean Soc. Cardiology, Burma Med. Assn. Office: UCLA Sch Medicine Dept Pediatric Cardiology Los Angeles CA 90024

KAPLAN, SIDNEY JOSEPH, sociologist, educator; b. Malden, Mass., Feb. 1, 1924; s. Harry and Rena (Chernoff) K.; m. Shirley Taugher, Aug. 22, 1978; children: Carter, Cydney Rena. B.A. magna cum laude, Boston U., 1949, M.A., 1950; Ph.D., Wash. State U., 1953. From instr. to assoc. prof. sociology U. Ky., 1953-62; prof. sociology U. Toledo, 1962-89, prof. emeritus, 1989—, chmn. dept. sociology and anthropology, 1962-66, 69-82; assoc. dean Coll. Arts and Scis., 1962-68. Served with USAAF, 1946-47. Mem. N. Central Sociol. Soc. (v.p. 1964-65), Phi Beta Kappa. Home: 84 Calle Aragon Unit R Laguna Hills CA 92653-3925

KAPLINSKI, BUFFALO, artist; b. Chgo., May 25, 1943; s. Jacob Kaplinski and Genevive Stryczek; m. Vicky Jeanine Smith, June 10, 1944; 1 child, Tiaja Karenina. Student, Chgo. Art Inst., 1964, Am. Acad. Art, 1965. lectr. Foothills Art Ctr., Golden, Colo., Denver Art Mus., Jewish Comty. Ctr., Denver; master instr. Art Students League, Denver. One-man shows include Am. Water Color Soc., N.Y.C., Nat. Acad. Design, N.Y.C., U. Portland, Oreg., Berger Sandzen Mus., Lindsberg, Kans., Southwestern Biennial-Mus. N.Mex., Santa Fe, Denver Art Mus., Mus. Natural History, Denver, Contemporary S.W., Potsdam (N.Y.) Coll.; exhibited in group shows Denver Art Mus., 1993, Nat. Cowboy Hall of Fame, Oklahoma City, 1993, Pioneer Mus., Colorado Springs, Colo., 1993, Pikes Peak Ctr., Colorado Springs, 1993, Opicka Gallery, Denver, 1994, Loveland (Colo.) Mus., 1994; represented in pvt. and pub. collections. Home: PO Box 44 Elizabeth CO 80107-0044

KAPLOWITZ, KAREN (JILL), lawyer; b. New Haven, Nov. 27, 1946; d. Charles Cohen and Estelle (Gerber) K.; m. Alan George Cohen, Aug. 17, 1980; children: Benjamin, Elizabeth. BA cum laude, Barnard Coll., 1968; JD, U. Chgo., 1971. Bar: Calif. 1971, U.S. Dist. Ct. (cen. dist.) Calif. 1971. Assoc. O'Melveny & Myers, L.A., 1971-74; ptnr. Bardeen, Bersch & Kaplowitz, L.A., 1974-80, Alschuler, Grossman & Pines, L.A., 1980—. Contbr. articles to profl. jours. Mem. vis. com. U. Chgo. Law Sch., 1990-93. Mem. Assn. Bus. Trial Lawyers (bd. govs.), Calif. Women Lawyers (Fay Stender award 1982), Women Lawyers Assn. L.A. Home: 244 Euclid St Santa Monica CA 90402-2116 Office: Alschuler Grossman & Pines 2049 Century Park E # 39 Los Angeles CA 90067-3101

KAPOOR, ASHOK KUMAR, engineer; b. Allahabad, Uttar Pradesh, India, Feb. 7, 1952; s. Ram Nate and Sarla Kapoor; m. Nisha Malhotra, May 9, 1984; 1 child, Shweta. BTech, Indian Inst. Tech., 1973; MS, U. Cin., 1979, PhD, 1981. Illumination engr. Philips India Ltd., Bombay, 1973-76; with Fairchild Rsch. Ctr., Palo Alto, Calif., 1981-87; mgr. tech. devel. ASIC div. Nat. Semicondr., Santa Clara, Calif., 1987-88; sr. mem. tech. staff HP Labs., Palo Alto, 1988-91; mgr. device tech. LSI Logic, Santa Clara, 1991—; co-chair exec. tech. adv. bd. Semiconductor Rsch. Corp., 1995. Editor: Polysilicon Bipolar Transistors; contbr. tech. articles to profl. jours.; patentee in field. Mem. IEEE (sr.), IEEE Electron Devices Soc. (pres. Santa Clara Valley chpt. 1991-92), Sigma Xi. Hindu. Home: 1056 Amarillo Ave Palo Alto CA 94303-3705

KAPOOR, SANDRA A., restaurant management educator; b. Madison, S.D., Sept. 10, 1952; d. Curt and Harriette (Ochs) Kaiser; m. Tarun Kapoor. BS in Nutrition and Food Sci., S.D. State U., 1974; M. Pub. Health Nutrition, U. Minn., 1976, PhD, 1986. Food svc. dir./chef Project Newgate, St. Paul, 1974-75; cons. dietitian Tracy (Minn.) Hosp., 1978-79; instr. Culinary Inst. Am., Hyde Park, N.Y., 1979-80; coord. continuing edn. programs and adj. faculty instr. Dept. of Vocat. and Tech. Edn., U. Minn., St. Paul, 1981-83; cons./seminar dir./trainer Pomona, Calif., 1976—; assoc. prof. hotel, restaurant and instnl. mgmt. S.W. State U., Marshall, Minn., 1976-86; owner/operator Kebabi Restaurant and Bar, Kebabi Cafe, The Caterers, Mpls., 1984-91; asst. prof. hotel, restaurant and instnl. mgmt. Mich. State U., East Lansing, 1986-88; prof. Sch. Hotel and Restaurant Mgmt. Calif. State Poly. U., Pomona, 1988—; cook SAGA Foodsvc., Brookings, S.D., 1970-74; food svc. dir./chef Elks Youth Camp, Brainerd, Minn., summers 1974-75; gen. mgr., exec. chef Minnesouri Club and Resort, Alexandria, Minn., summers 1976-77; dir. nutrition Weight Reduction Resort, Camp Camelot, South Hampton, N.Y., summer 1980; lectr. in field. Author: Bulimia: A Program for Friends and Family Members, 1988, Professional Healthy Cooking, 1995, Healthy & Delicious: 400 Professional Recipes, 1995; contbr. numerous articles to profl. jours. Named to Outstanding Young Women in Am., 1981; grantee S.W. State U., 1977, 78, 79, 84, 85, Calif. State Poly. U., 1988, 89, 90, 91, Calif. Restaurant Assn., 1991; Maternal and Child Health fellow Dept. Pub. Health, U. Minn., Mpls., 1975-76, Nat. Inst. Foodsvc. Industry fellow, 1983. Mem. Am. Dietetic Assn. (registered), Calif. Dietetic Assn., Am. Culinary Fedn., Chefs de Cuisine, Nat. restaurant Assn., Calif. Restaurant Assn., Hospitality and Tourism Educators, Pacific Hospitality and Tourism Educators, Roundtable for Women in Foodsvc. (Pace Setter award 1991). Office: Calif Poly State Univ Sch Hotel/Restaurant Mgmt 3801 W Temple Ave Pomona CA 91768-2557

KAPP, ELEANOR JEANNE, impressionistic artist, writer, researcher; b. Hagerstown, Md., Oct. 16, 1933; d. James Norman and Nellie Belle (Welty) Weagley; m. Alan Howard Kapp, Sept. 25, 1972. Cert., L.A. Interior Design, 1969; student, U. Utah, 1976-82. Artist Farmers Ins. Group, L.A., 1960-63; interior designer W&J Sloane, Beverly Hills, Calif., 1965-70; ski resort exec. Snowpine Lodge, Alta, Utah, 1970-84; dir. mktg. and pub. rels. Alta Resort Assn., 1979-84; free-lance photographer Alta, 1979—; bus. owner Creative Art Enterprises, Sandy, Utah, 1984-85; artist-resident Collector's Corner Art Gallery, San Ramon, Calif., 1991—; owner Art of Jeanne Kapp, Lafayette, Calif., 1985—; artist-resident St. Germain Gallery, Tiburon, Calif., 1993—, Regional Art Ctr. Gift Store, Walnut Creek, Calif., 1994—, Valley Art Ctr., Walnut Creek, 1995—. Author, pub.: The American Connection, 1985, 91; author, prodr. (documentary) A Look at China Today, 1981; photographer: Best of the West, 1983. Promotion liaison Alta Town Coun., 1980-84; floral decorator Coun. State Govts., Snowbird, Utah, 1976; photographer Utah Dems., Salt Lake City, 1981; exhibit curator Salt Lake County Libr. System, 1982, founder Alta Br. Libr., 1982; fundraiser Friends of Libr., Alta, 1982; mem. Alta Town-Libr. Adv. Bd., 1983. Recipient Cert. of Appreciation, Salt Lake County Libr. System, 1981, Cert. of Recognition, Gov. Cal Rampton, Salt Lake City, 1972-74, Calendar Cover award Utah Travel Coun., 1981, Internat. Invitational Art Exhibit, Centre Internat. D'Art Contemporain, Paris, 1983. Mem. Internat. Platform Assn., Diablo Art Assn. (pub. rels. chmn. 1987, Hon. Mention award 1989), Concord Art Assn. (1st pl. award 1991), Alamo and Danville Artist's Soc. (cir. leader 1990—, Hon. Mention award 1991, chmn. art exhbn. 1993, chmn. art program 1994), Las Junas Artist Assn. (juror's asst. 1992, 2d pl. award 1992, curator art exhbn. 1995). Home: 411 Donegal Way Lafayette CA 94549-1707

KAPPY, MICHAEL STEVEN, pediatrics educator; b. Bklyn., Feb. 8, 1940; s. Jack and Lilyan (Banchefsky) K.; children: Douglas Bruce, Gregory Louis. BA, Johns Hopkins U., 1961; MD, PhD, U. Wis., 1967. Asst. prof. U. Ariz. Med. Sch., Tucson, 1975-78; fellow pediatric endocrinology Johns Hopkins Hosp., Balt., 1978-80; assoc. prof. U. Fla. Med. Sch., Gainesville, 1980-85; clin. prof. U. Ariz. Med. Sch., Tucson, 1985-94; med. dir. Children's Health Ctr., Phoenix, 1985-94; prof. pediatrics U. Colo. Health Sci. Ctr., Denver, 1994—; chief pediatric endocrinology The Children's Hosp., Denver, 1994—. Editor: (jour.) Today's Child, 1985, (book) Wilkins-The Diagnosis and Treatment of Endocrine Disorders in Children and Adolescents, 1994. Med. advisor Am. Diabetes Assn., Phoenix, 1985-94; bd. dirs. Ronald McDonald House, Phoenix, 1987-94. Mem. Assn. Pediatric Program Dirs. (pres. 1992-94), Soc. for Pediatric Rsch., Endocrine Soc., Am. Acad. Pediatrics, Physicians for Social Responsibility, Alpha Omega Alpha. Home: 483 Josephine St Denver CO 80206-4208 Office: The Childrens Hosp B-265 1056 E 19th Ave # B-265 Denver CO 80218-1007

KARABAY, ADNAN SAMI, artist; b. Ankara, Turkey, Jan. 4, 1957; came to the U.S., 1960; s. Vecihi and Sylvia (Catala) K. BA in Econs., UCLA, 1976. Tchr. Am. Acad. Interior Design, Seattle, 1979-82; interior designer L'Ermitage Hotels Internat., L.A., 1985-92; costume designer Noel Taylor, L.A., 1986-94; pvt. practice artist L.A., 1990—. Works exhibited 8 times in Tiffany & Co. window displays, at Entre-Nous Gallery, Vancouver, B.C., Can., 1992, Dyansen Gallery, Beverly Hills, Calif., 1992, C.F.M. Gallery, N.Y.C., 1993-95, Stricoff Fine Arts, N.Y.C., 1994, Edith Lambert Gallery, Santa Fe, 1995, Mus. of Miniatures, L.A., Rosalie Whyel Mus. Doll Art, Seattle, Demi Moore Mus. Doll Art, Sun Valley, Utah, Musée de Neuilly, Paris; subject of numerous articles on doll art. Named Boy of the Yr., YMCA, Manhattan, 1967. Mem. Am. Soc. Interior Design (cert.). Home and Office: 1414 N Fairfax Ave Apt 204 Los Angeles CA 90046-3928

KARABELA, LEDA, public relations and fund raising executive; b. Thessaloniki, Greece, Dec. 8, 1957; came to U.S., 1980; m. George Triadafilopoulos, May 31, 1980 (div. Apr. 1991); children: Thano, Julie. LLB in Jurisprudence, Aristotelian U. Law Sch., Greece, 1970; MS in Pub. Rels. with honors, Boston U., 1988; negotiation program for sr. execs., Inter U. Consortium, Harvard, MIT, Tufts U., 1991. Dir. alumni rels. Anatolia Coll. Office of Trustees, Boston, 1983-87; cons. to dir. mktg., client rels. Sullivan & Worcester Law Office, Boston, 1987-88; dir. ops. BBB, Inc., Boston, 1988-89; account exec. BBK Advt., Pub. Rels., Chestnut Hill, Mass., 1989-90; dir. mktg., and comms., annual giving Alta Bates Med. Ctr. Found., Berkeley, Calif., 1990—. Mem. Pub. Rels. Soc. Am. (accredited pub. relations professional). Nat. Soc. Fund Raising Execs. (cert.), Assn. of Healthcare Philanthrophy. Office: Alta Bates Found 2450 Ashby Ave Berkeley CA 94705-2067

KARAKEY, SHERRY JOANNE, financial and real estate investment company executive, interior designer; b. Wendall, Idaho, Apr. 16, 1942; d. John Donald and Vera Ella (Frost) Kingery; children: Artist Roxanne, Buddy (George II), Kami JoAnne, Launi JoElla. Student, Ariz. State U., 1960. Corp. sec., treas. Karbel Metals Co., Phoenix, 1963-67; sec. to pub. Scottsdale (Ariz.) Daily Progress, 1969-72; with D-Velco Mfg. of Ariz., Phoenix, 1959-62, dir., exec. v.p., sec., treas., 1972-87; mng. ptnr. Karitage, Ltd., Scottsdale, 1987—.

KARALIS, JOHN PETER, computer company executive, lawyer; b. Mpls., July 6, 1938; s. Peter John and Vivian (Deckas) K.; m. Mary Curtis, Sept. 7, 1963; children: Amy Curtis, Theodore Curtis. BA, U. Minn., 1960, JD, 1963. Bar: Minn. 1963, Mass. 1972, Ariz. 1983, N.Y. 1986, Pa. 1986. Pvt. practice Mpls., 1963-70; assoc. gen. counsel Honeywell Inc., Mpls., 1970-83, v.p., 1982-83; pvt. practice Phoenix, 1983-85; sr. v.p., gen. counsel Sperry Corp., N.Y.C., 1985-87; v.p. gen. counsel Apple Computer Inc., Cupertino, Calif., 1987-89; of counsel Brown and Bain, Phoenix, 1989-92; v.p. corp. devel. Tektronix, Inc., Portland, 1992—; bd. dirs. Sony/Tektronix Corp., Merix Corp.; mem. bd. advisors Ctr. for Study of Law, Sci. and Tech. Ariz. State U., Temps, 1983—, adj. prof. Coll. Law, 1990-91. Author: International Joint Ventures, A Practical Guide, 1992. Recipient Disting. Achievement award Ariz. State U., Tempe, 1985. Mem. Met. Club (N.Y.C.), Gainey Ranch Golf Club.

KARASA, NORMAN LUKAS, home builder, geologist; b. Balt., June 10, 1951; s. Norman and Ona K.; m. Lois J. Hansen, Jan. 4, 1974; children: Andrew, Jane. AB in Geology, Rutgers Coll., 1973; MS in Geophysics, U. Wyo., 1976; MBA in Fin., U. Colo., Colorado Springs, 1990. Systems mgr. Brit. Petroleum, N.Y.C., 1973-74; seismic processing leader Phillips Petroleum, Bartlesville, Okla., 1976-79; geophysicist Phillips Petroleum, Houston, 1979-80; internat. spl. project geophysicist Marathon Oil, Findlay, Ohio, 1980-82; internat. exploration geophysicist Marathon Oil, Houston, 1982-85, internat. reservoir geologist/geophysicist, 1985-86; home builder, designer, owner D'signer Inc., Monument Homes, Colo., 1986—, developer, hydrologist, 1992—; lic. stock broker, ins. advisor Prin. Group, Colo., 1987—. Active Boy Scouts Am., Colo., 1987—. Mem. Home Builder Assocs. Presbyterian. Office: Monument Homes PO Box 1423 Monument CO 80132-1423

KARATZ, BRUCE E., business executive; b. Chgo., Oct. 10, 1945; s. Robert Harry and Naomi Rae (Goldstein) K.; m. Janet Louise Dreisen, July 28, 1968; children: Elizabeth, Matthew, Theodore. BA, Boston U., 1967; JD, U. So. Calif., 1970. Bar: Calif. 1971. Assoc. Keatinge & Sterling, Los Angeles, 1970-72; assoc. corp. counsel Kaufman and Broad, Inc., Los Angeles, 1972-73; dir. forward planning Kaufman and Broad, Inc., Irvine, Calif., 1973-74; pres. Kaufman and Broad Provence, Aix-en-Provence, France, 1974-76, Kaufman and Broad France, Paris, 1976-80, Kaufman and Broad Devel. Group, Los Angeles, 1980-86; pres., chief exec. officer Kaufman and Broad Home Corp., Los Angeles, 1986—, also bd. dirs.; bd. dirs. MacFrugal's Bargains, Close-Outs, Inc., Honeywell Corp. Mem. bd. govs. Cedars Sinai Med. Ctr., L.A., 1983—; founder Mus. Contemporary Art, L.A., 1981; trustee Pitzer Coll., Claremont, Calif., 1983—; bd. dirs. Coro Found., 1981; trustee, pres. Wilshire Blvd. Temple. Mem. Young Pres.' Orgn. Democrat. Office: Kaufman & Broad Home Corp 10877 Wilshire Blvd Los Angeles CA 90024-4341*

KARAYIORGOU, MARIA, geneticist; b. Athens, Greece, Apr. 23, 1963; came to U.S., 1988; d. Stefanos and Efstathia (Krokou) K.; m. Joseph A. Gogos, Apr. 15, 1988. MD, U. Athens, 1987. Registered Eng. Gen. Med. Coun. Rsch. fellow MIT, Cambridge, 1988-93; staff scientist Fred Hutchinson Cancer Rsch. Ctr., Seattle, 1993—. Contbr. articles to profl. jours. Scottish Rite Schizophrenia grantee, 1993-95. Mem. AAAS, Am. Soc. Human Genetics, Rsch. Soc. N.Am., Sigma Xi. Home: 2874 30th Ave W Seattle WA 98199-2714 Office: Fred Hutchinson Cancer Rsch Ctr 1124 Columbia St A3 023 Seattle WA 98104

KARELITZ, RAYMOND, secondary school educator and writer; b. Fontainebleau, France, Nov. 11, 1952; came to U.S., 1957; s. Mitchell and Gabriella (Kaiser) K. BA cum laude, U. Hawaii, 1974, MA, 1975, Profl. Diploma, 1992. Tchr. St. Louis Sch., Honolulu, 1984-85, 89-90, 1994—; tchr. Farrington High Sch., Honolulu, 1990—; pres., instr. Verbal and Math (SAT) Program, Honolulu, 1986—; pub. Hi-Lite Pub. Co., Honolulu, 1991—; pres. Golden Memories Cookies, Inc., Honolulu, 1983-84, Goin' Back Enterprises, Honolulu, 1976-84; lectr. Leeward C.C., Honolulu, 1976-78; tutor Verbal and Math Enrichment Program, Honolulu, 1984-93; condr. workshops in field. Author: Understanding the SAT in 10 Easy Lessons, 1991, Rock Lyrics Trivia Quiz Book, 1993, Hi-Lite Series Vocabulary Program, 1993, The New SAT in 10 Easy Steps, 1994, Rock Lyrics Quiz Book, 1994, Karelitz Dictionary of One-Word Definitions, 1994, (novels) Fear None But the Innocent, From the Other Side, Even Odds, 1994. Office: Hi-Lite Publishing Co PO Box 240161 Honolulu HI 96824-0161

KARI, DAVEN MICHAEL, humanities educator; b. Hot Springs, S.D., Sept. 24, 1953; s. John Nelson and Corinna Nicolls (Morse) K.; m. Priya Perianayakam, Apr. 4, 1988; children: David Prem, Daniel Michael, Dante Gabriel. BA in English, Bibl. Studies, History, Fresno Pacific Coll., 1975, BA in Music, 1977; MA in English, Baylor U., 1983; MA, PhD in English, Purdue U., 1985, 86; MDiv, PhD, So. Bapt. Theol. Sem., 1988, 91. Lic. to ministry, 1971. Photography studio technician Johnson's Studio, Manteca, Calif., 1975-77; grad. teaching asst. Baylor U., Waco, Tex., 1978-79; minister of music Calvary Bapt. Ch., West Lafayette, Ind., 1984-85; grad. teaching asst. Purdue U., West Lafayette, Ind., 1979-85; lectr. in English Jefferson C.C., Louisville, 1987-90, Spalding U., Louisville, 1986-90, U. Louisville, 1986-90; asst. prof. English Mo. Bapt. Coll., St. Louis, 1991; assoc. prof. English Calif. Bapt. Coll., Riverside, 1991—. Author: T. S. Eliot's Dramatic Pilgrimage, 1990, Bibliography of Sources in Christianity and the Arts, 1994. Founder, co-dir. local Boys Brigade, Linden, Calif., 1969-71; asst. pastor Linden (Calif.) First Bapt. Ch., 1971; chair transp. com. Calvary Bapt. Ch., West Lafayette, 1982-83, dir. singles ministry, 1983-85; moderator Scholar's Bowl Quiz Contest, Riverside, 1993-94. Recipinet Lit. Criticism award Purdue U., 1983; named to Outstanding Young Men of Am., 1985; named Faculty Mem. of Yr., Calif. Bapt. Coll., 1993. Mem. MLA, Nat. Coun. Tchrs. English, Am. Acad. Religion, Conf. on Christianity and Lit. Democrat. Baptist. Home: 23878 Bouquet Canyon Pl Moreno Valley CA 92557-2956

KARIMI, SIMIN, linguist, educator; b. Tehran. BA in German Lang. and Lit., U. Tehran, 1973, MA in Gen. Linguistics, 1976; PhD in Linguistics, U. Wash., 1989. Instr. linguistics Calif. State U., Dominguez Hills, 1989-90; mem. linguistics and anthropology joint degree program U. Ariz., Tucson, 1991—, asst. prof. linguistics, Persian lang., 1991—; mem. numerous acad. coms.; lectr. and cons. in field; presenter workshops. Contbr. articles to profl. publs. Recipient scholarship Ministry of Higher Edn. in Iran, 1976, Grad. Sch. Tuition scholar U. Wash., 1986, SBS Rsch. Professorship, 1994; Travel grantee U. Ariz., 1993. Mem. Soc. Iranian Studies, Linguistic Soc. Am., MId. Ea. Studies Assn. Office: Dept Linguistics Univ Ariz Tucson AZ 85721

KARIPINENI, SHAKIRA BAIG, obstetrician, gynecologist; b. Hyderabad, India, Oct. 21, 1950; came to the U.S., 1974; d. Hamid Ali and Basheer-Unnisa (Khan) Baig; m. Ramesh Chander Karipineni, Dec. 30, 1976; children: Reshma, Farah. MBBS, Gandhi Med. Coll., Hyderabad, 1970; MD, Albert Einstein Coll., 1979, specialist in ob-gyn., 1988. Intern Albert Einstein Coll. Medicine, Bronx, N.Y., 1975-76, resident in ob-gyn., 1976-79; cons., attending La Guardia Med. Group, Cornell U., 1979-80; pvt. practice, Fremont, Calif., 1980—; pres. Universal Unity, Fremont, 1991—. Author, editor: (jour.) Times of Universal Unity, 1991, (book) Times of Universal Unity, 1992; pub.: Quran-Final Testament, 1993, Jesus Myths and Messages, 1993. Fellow ACOG; mem. AMA, Calif. Med. Assn., Alameda Contra Costa Med. Assn. Republican. Office: Universal Unity #400 1860 Mowry Ave Ste 400 Fremont CA 94538-1730

KARKIA, MOHAMMAD REZA, energy engineer, educator; b. Tabriz, Iran, Sept. 12, 1949; came to the U.S., 1979; s. Mohammad Taghi and Safieh M. Karkia; m. Mehran Karkia, June 20, 1981 (div. 1988); 1 child, Leila; m. Mojgan M. Karkia, Sept. 12, 1990; 1 child, Amir-Ali. BS in Engring., Sussex U., 1976; MS, U. Pitts., 1981; DBA, Newport U., 1990. V.p. W.F. Ryan & Assocs., Inc., Pitts., 1981-87; systemwide energy and utilities engr. Chancellor's Office Calif. State U., Los Alamitos, 1987—; mem. Calif. State Energy Policy Adv. Com., Sacramento, 1989—. Contbr. articles to Critical Issues in Facilities Mgmt. Mem. ASHRAE, Assn. Energy Engrs. (sr., Energy Engr. of Yr. 1985-86), Assn. Phys. Plant Adminstrs. Home: 12781 Chase St Garden Grove CA 92645-2641 Office: Calif State U 4665 Lampson Ave Los Alamitos CA 90720-5139

KARKOSKI, JOSEPH, environmental engineer; b. Ft. Wayne, Ind., Apr. 3, 1966; s. Joseph and Eve Marie (Sandor) K.; m. Lisa Destro, Nov. 16, 1991; 1 child, Francesca Destro. BSChemE with honors, Mich. State U., 1988. Assoc. engr. IBM Corp., San Jose, Calif., 1988-89, 90; environ. engr. U.S. EPA, San Francisco, 1990-92; water resources control engr. State of Calif./U.S. EPA, Sacramento, 1992—. Author reports, article in field. Active Union Concerned Scientists, Sacramento, 1994; chair ecol. action task force Unitarian Universalist Soc., Sacramento, 1994. Nat. Merit scholar, 1984, GM scholar, 1986. Office: Calif Regional Water Quality Control Bd 3443 Routier Rd Ste A Sacramento CA 95827-3003

KARL, GEORGE, professional basketball coach; b. Penn Hills, Pa., May 12, 1951; m. Cathy Karl; children—Kelci Ryanne, Coby Joseph. Grad., U. N.C., 1973. Guard San Antonio Spurs, NBA, 1973-78, asst. coach, head scout, 1978-80; coach Mont. Golden Nuggets, Continental Basketball Assn., 1980-83; dir. player acquisition Cleve. Cavaliers, 1983-84, coach, 1984-86; head coach Golden State Warriors, Oakland, Calif., from 1986, Albany (N.Y.) Patrons, 1988-89, 90-91, Real Madrid, Spain, 1991-92, Seattle Supersonics, 1992—. Named Coach of Yr., Continental Basketball Assn., 1981, 83. Mem. Continental Basketball Assn. Office: care Seattle Supersonics 190 Queen Anne Ave N Ste 200 Seattle WA 98109-9711*

KARLEN, PETER HURD, lawyer, writer; b. N.Y.C., Feb. 22, 1949; s. S. H. and Jean Karlen; m. Lynette Ann Thwaites, Dec. 22, 1978. BA in History, U. Calif., Berkeley, 1971; JD, U. Calif., Hastings, 1974; MS in Law and Soc., U. Denver, 1976. Bar: Calif. 1974, U.S. Dist. Ct. (so. dist.) Calif. 1976, U.S. Dist. Ct. (no. dist.) Calif. 1983, Hawaii 1989, U.S. Supreme Ct. 1990, Colo. 1991. Assoc. Sankary & Sankary, San Diego, 1976; teaching fellow Coll. of Law U. Denver, 1974-75; lectr. Sch. of Law U. Warwick, United Kingdom, 1976-78; pvt. practice La Jolla, Calif., 1979-86; prin. Peter H. Karlen, P.C., La Jolla, 1986—; adj. prof. U. San Diego Sch. of Law, 1979-84; mem. adj. faculty Western State U. Coll. of Law, San Diego, 1976, 79-80, 88, 92. Contbg. editor Artweek, 1979-95, Art Calendar, 1989—, Art Cellar Exch. mag., 1989-92; mem. editl. bd. Copyright World, 1988—; contbr. numerous articles to profl. jours. Mem. Am. Soc. for Aesthetics, Brit. Soc. Aesthetics. Office: 1205 Prospect St Ste 400 La Jolla CA 92037-3613

KARLER, HENRY, agricultural products executive. Various positions Karler Packing Co., Albuquerque, 1951—, now exec. v.p. Office: Karler Packing Co Inc 9111 Broadway Blvd SE Albuquerque NM 87105-7485*

KARLER, JESS, agricultural products executive; b. 1913. With Karler Packing Co., Inc., 1950—, now pres. Office: Karler Packing Co Inc 9111 Broadway Blvd SE Albuquerque NM 87105-7485*

KARLSON, SCOTT JAY, audio book publishing company sales executive; b. Evanston, Ill., Aug. 2, 1958; s. John Albert Karlson and Ruth Hazel (Peterson) Cleek; m. Linda Kay Long, Sept. 20, 1980; 1 child, Danielle Lee. BA in Comm. Arts, Loyola U., Chgo., 1980. Nat. buyer VSI, Inc., Northrook, Ill., 1982-84, nat. sales tng. mgr., 1984-85, gen. mgr., 1985-86; nat. buyer Chgo. Tape Authority, Northrook, 1986-89; v.p. ops. Enttec, Santa Fe, 1989-91; mgr. sales and ops. Sunset Prodns., Inc., Santa Fe, 1991—. Author: 'Cause an Otter Told Me, 1992; editor The Texan, 1991, Return of the Texan, 1992, Roger Zelazny's Chronicles of Amber, 10 vols., 1992-94; co-prodr., engr. audiobook American Indian Myths and Legends, also 9 others, 1991-92. Methodist. Home: 5 Conchas Loop Santa Fe NM 87505-8805 Office: Sunset Prodns Inc 369 Montezuma Ave Ste 416 Santa Fe NM 87501-2626

KARLSTROM, PAUL JOHNSON, art historian; b. Seattle, Jan. 22, 1941; s. Paul Isadore and Eleanor (Johnson) K.; m. Ann Heath, Dec. 29, 1964; 1 dau., Clea Heath. BA in English Lit, Stanford U., 1964; MA, UCLA, 1969, PhD (Samuel H. Kress fellow), 1973. Asst. curator Grunwald Center for Graphic Arts, UCLA, 1967-70; Samuel H. Kress fellow Nat. Gallery Art, Washington, 1970-71; instr. Calif. State U., Northridge, 1972-73; West Coast regional dir. Archives Am. Art, Smithsonian Instn. at De Young Mus., San Francisco, 1973-91, Huntington Libr., 1991—. Guest curator Hirshhorn Mus., Washington, 1977; author: Louis M. Elishemius, 1978, Los Angeles in the 1940's Post-Modernism and the Visual Arts, 1987, The Visionary Art of James M. Washington, Jr., 1989, Fletcher Benton, 1990, Turning the Tide: Early Los Angeles Modernists, 1920-1956, 1990; video producer David Hockney, 1984, 93, George Tsutakawa in Japan, 1988; contbr. articles to profl. jours.; mem. editorial bd. Calif. Hist. Soc. Mem. adv. bd. Humanities West, Jacob Lawrence Catalogue Raisonni Project; b. dirs. Bay Area Video Coalition, S.W. Art History Coun., Virginia Steele Scott Found. Office: Archives Am Art Huntington Libr 1151 Oxford Rd San Marino CA 91108-1218

KARLTON, LAWRENCE K., federal judge; b. Bklyn., May 28, 1935; s. Aaron Katz and Sylvia (Meltzer) K.; m. Mychelle Stiebel, Sept. 7, 1958 (dec.). Student, Washington Sq. Coll., 1952-54; LL.B., Columbia U., 1958. Bar: Fla. 1958, Calif. 1962. Acting legal officer Sacramento Army Depot, Dept. Army, Sacramento, 1958-60; civilian legal officer Sacramento Army Depot, Dept. Army, 1960-62; individual practice law Sacramento, 1962-64; mem. firm Abbott, Karlton & White, 1964, Karlton & Blease, 1964-71, Karlton, Blease & Vanderlaan, 1971-76; judge Calif. Superior Ct. for Sacramento County, 1976-79, U.S. Dist. Ct. (ea. dist.) Calif., Sacramento, 1979—; formerly chief judge U.S. Dist. Ct., Sacramento, 1983-90. Co-chmn. Central Calif. council B'nai B'rith Anit-Defamation League Commn., 1964-65; treas. Sacramento Jewish Community Relations Council, chmn., 1967-68; chmn. Vol. Lawyers Commn. Sun Valley ACLU, 1964-76. Mem. Am. Bar Assn., Sacramento County Bar Assn., Calif. Bar Assn., Fed. Bar Assn., Fed. Judges Assn., 9th Cir. Judges Assn. Club: B'nai B'rith (past pres.). Office: US Dist Ct 2012 US Courthouse 650 Capitol Mall Sacramento CA 95814-4708*

KARNIK, AVINASH RAMKRISHNA, electronics engineer; b. Bombay, May 31, 1940; came to U.S., 1964; s. Ramkrishna W. and Ashalata R. K.; m. Aruna A. Wadhavkar, Jan. 12, 1969; children: Jwala, Prachi. BE, U. Bombay, 1961; M Tech., Indian Inst. Tech., Bombay, 1963; PhD, U. Rochester, 1969. Rsch. scientist Xerox Corp., Webster, N.Y., 1969-71, devel. engr., 1972-74, mgr. systems, 1976-81; mgr. process rsch. Rank Xerox, Eng., 1974-76; project mgr. Electrosystems div. Aerojet, Azusa, Calif., 1981-82, mgr. electronics, 1982-84, chief engr. for design, 1984-86, chief engr. for systems, 1986-91; instrument mgr. jet propulsion lab, 1991. Contbr. articles to profl. jours.; inventor blade for metering liquid devel. Founder Rochester chpt. Assn. Indians in Am., 1976; mem. conv. exec. com. Brihan Maharashtra Mandal, L.A., 1991. Mem. Sigma Xi. Office: Jet Propulsion Lab 4800 Oak Grove Dr Pasadena CA 91109-8001

KARPAN, KATHLEEN MARIE, former state official, lawyer, journalist; b. Rock Springs, Wyo., Sept. 1, 1942; d. Thomas Michael and Pauline Ann (Taucher) K. B.S. in Journalism, U. Wyo., 1964, M.A. in Am. Studies, 1975; J.D., U. Oreg., 1978. Bar: D.C. 1979, Wyo. 1983, U.S. Dist. Ct. Wyo., U.S. Ct. Appeals (D.C. and 10th cirs.). Asst. news editor Cody Enterprise, Wyo., 1964; press asst. to U.S. Congressman Teno Roncalio U.S. Ho. of Reps., Washington, 1965-67, 71-72, adminstrv. asst., 1973-74; asst. news editor Wyo. Eagle, Cheyenne, 1967; free-lance writer, 1968; teaching asst. dept. history U. Wyo., 1969-70; desk editor Canberra Times, Australia, 1970; dep. dir. Office Congl. Relations, Econ. Devel. Adminstrn. U.S. Dept. Commerce, Washington, 1979-80, atty. advisor Office of Chief Counsel, Econ. Devel. Adminstrn., 1980-81; campaign mgr. Rodger McDaniel for U.S. Senator, Wyo., 1981-82; asst. atty. gen. State of Wyo., Cheyenne, 1983-84, dir. Dept. Health and Social Services, 1984-86, sec. of state, 1987-94. Del. Dem. Nat. Conv., San Francisco, 1984, Atlanta, 1988, N.Y.C., 1992; mem. bd. govs. Nat. Dem. Leadership Coun., drafting com. Dem. Nat. Platform, Santa Fe, 1992. W.R. Coe fellow, 1969. Mem. Wyo. Bar Assn., Bus. and Profl. Women, Rotary, Zonta. Roman Catholic. Home: 410 W 2nd Ave Cheyenne WY 82001-1211 Office: Wyo Sec of State State Capital Cheyenne WY 82002

KARPELES, DAVID, museum director; b. Santa Barbara, Calif., Jan. 26, 1936; s. Leon and Betty (Friedman) K.; m. Marsha Mirsky, June 29, 1958; children: Mark, Leslie, Cheryl, Jason. BS, U. Minn., 1956, postgrad., 1956-59; MA, San Diego State U., 1962; postgrad., U. Calif., Santa Barbara, 1965-69. Founder Karpeles Manuscript Libr. Mus., Montecito, Calif., 1983—; dir., founder Karpeles Manuscript Libr. Mus., Santa Barbara, Calif., 1988—, N.Y.C., 1990—, Tacoma, Wash., 1991—, Jacksonville, Fla., 1992—, Duluth, Minn., 1993—, Charleston, S.C., 1995—; established the 1st cultural literacy program, presented to schs. by respective mus. staffs, 1993—. Creator program to provide ownership of homes to low-income families, 1981. Recipient Affordable Housing Competition award Gov. Edmund G. Brown Jr., State of Calif., Dept. Housing and Community Devel., 1981. Jewish. Home: 465 Hot Springs Rd Santa Barbara CA 93108-2029

KARPENKO, VICTOR NICHOLAS, mechanical engineer; b. Harbin, China, Jan. 23, 1922; s. Nicholas Stephan and Sophia Andrea (Kootas) K.; came to U.S., 1941, naturalized, 1943; student San Francisco State Coll., 1941-42, Oreg. State Coll., 1943; B.S. in Mech. Engring., U. Calif., Berkeley, 1948; m. Lydia Kamotsky, June 23, 1950; children—Victor, Mark, Alexandra. Staff engr. Atomic Products Equipment div. Gen. Electric Co., San Jose, Calif., 1956-57; project engr. nuclear explosives engring. Lawrence Livermore (Calif.) Lab., 1957-65, sect. leader nuclear explosives engring., 1965-66, div. leader Nuclear Test Engring. div., 1966-76, project mgr. Mirror Fusion Test Facility, 1976-85; div. head Magnet System Superconducting Super Collider, Univ. Research Assn., Berkeley, Calif., 1986-87, cons. tech. and mgmt., 1987—; ptnr. devel. cryogenic equipment PHPK Tech. Inc., Columbus, Ohio, 1992—; mem. fusion reactor safety com. Dept. Energy; mem. Containment Evaluation Panel, ERDA. Dist. chmn. U. Calif. Alumni Scholarship Program, 1976-80; com. mem. U. Calif. Alumni Scholarship Program, 1972-76; pres. San Ramon AAU Swim Club, 1964. Served with AUS, 1943-46. Registered profl. mech. and nuclear engr., Calif. Mem. Am. Nuclear Soc., Calif. Alumni Assn. Republican. Greek Orthodox. Home: 613 Bradford Pl Danville CA 94526-2357

KARPILOW, CRAIG, physician; b. San Francisco, Oct. 23, 1947; s. David and Babette (David) K.; BSc, U. Alta. (Can.), 1967; MA, U. So. Calif., 1970; MD, Dalhousie U., 1974. Diplomate Canadian Coll. of Family Practice. Intern, Dalhousie U., Halifax, N.S., Can., 1974-75; resident in family practice medicine Meml. U. Nfld., St. John's, 1975-77; practice medicine specializing in family medicine and occupational medicine, 1978-95; practice occupational medicine, Snohomish, Wash., 1981-83; med. health officer Storey County, Nev., 1978-80; med. dir. Med. Ctr., Dayton, 1978-81; pres. Internat. Profl. Assocs. Ltd., 1978—; med. dir./clin. N.W. Occupational Health Ctrs., Seattle, 1983-84; ptnr. physician, co-dir. CHEC Med. Ctr., Seattle, 1984-85; head dept. occupational and diagnostic medicine St. Cabrini Hosp., Seattle, 1984-86; med. dir. N.W. Indsl. Health Svcs., 1985-86, Queen Anne Med. Ctr., Seattle, 1985-95, Travel Med. and Immunization Clinic of Seattle, 1986-94; ptnr. Clin. Assocs., 1990-95. Diplomate Am. Bd. Family Practice; licenciate Med. Coll. Can. Author: Occupational Medicine in The International Workplace, 1991, Handbook of Occupational Medicine, 1994. Fellow Am. Acad. Family Practice, Am. Coll. Occupational & Environmental Medicine, Royal Soc. Tropical Medicine, Am. Coll. Occupational Medicine (recorder Ho. of Dels./bd. dirs. 1990-91); mem. AMA, Am. Soc. Tropical Medicine and Hygiene, Wash. State Med. Assn. King County Med. Soc., Wash. Acad. Family Physicians (rsch. collaborative, Com. on Rsch.), Am. Coll. Occupational and Environ. Medicine (chmn. internat. occupational medicine sect.), N.W. Occupational Med. Assn. (bd. dirs. 1985-92, 95—, pres. 1990-91), Can. Soc. for Internat. Health, Can. Pub. Health Assn., Am. Com. Clin., Tropical and Travel Medicine, Can. Soc. of Northwest, Marimed Found. Pacific N.W. (adv. bd.), Seattle Swiss Soc., Finnish Soc., Corinthian Yacht Club, Nature Conservancy, Rotary (bd. dirs., chmn. internat. rels. com., chmn. Hepatis Project, chmn. Malaria Project), U. So. Calif. Alumni assn., Kappa Sigma. Office: 525 First Ave W Seattle WA 98119

KARPISEK, MARIAN ELLEN, librarian; b. Dover, Ohio, May 8, 1938; d. Samuel C. and Ruth E. (Meese) Ream; m. Robert L. Karpisek, Aug. 13, 1960; children: Kristine L., Jennifer L. Karpisek Storie. BS in Elem. Edn., Miami U., 1960; MS in Edn., U. Utah, 1975, adminstrv. cert., 1984. Cert. tchr. 3rd grade tchr. Lower Twp. Consolidated Schs., Cape May, N.J., 1960-61; 1st grade tchr. Denver Pub. Schs., 1961-64; 6th grade tchr. Mayfield Hts. (Ohio) Sch. Dist., 1968-69; libr. media specialist Riley Elem. Sch., Salt Lake City, Utah, 1970-72, E. High Sch., Salt Lake City, 1972-81; supr. libr. media svcs. Salt Lake City Sch. Dist., 1981—; adj. faculty Brigham Young U., 1985-92; mem. Utah Libr. Svcs. and Constrn. Act Bd., 1985-92, Utah Govs. Conf. on Libr. and Info. Svcs., 1990-91; grant reviewer Coll. Libr. Tech. and Coop. Grants Program, 1988-91, 93. Contbr. Utah sect. Reading for Young People, 1980, Making Self-Teaching Kits for Library Skills, 1983, Policy Making for School Library Media Programs, 1989; contbr. articles to profl. jours. Recipient Ralph D. Thomson scholarship U. Utah, 1975. Mem. Am. Libr. Assn. (active numerous coms. Am. Assn. Sch. Librs., John Cotton Dana Libr. Pub. Rels. award 1984), Utah Libr. Assn. (pres. 1993-94, Libr. of Yr. 1991), Utah Libr. Media Suprs. Assn. (chair 1986-89, 93-94), Utah Ednl. Libr. Media Assn. (Disting. Svc., award 1990), Phi Delta Kappa (treas. 1984-88, Outstanding Svc. award 1988). Home: 57 San Rafael Ct West Jordan UT 84088-9508 Office: Dist Media Ctr Salt Lake City Sch Dist 1430 Andrew Ave Salt Lake City UT 84104-3449

KARPMAN, ROBERT RONALD, orthopedic surgeon; b. Phila., Nov. 18, 1952; s. Sol H. and Tillie C. (Ginsburg) K.; m. Laurel Ann Brody, May 29, 1977; children: Hannah Elizabeth, Jodi Gayle. BA magna cum laude, LaSalle Coll., Phila., 1973; MD, U. Pa., Phila., 1977; MBA, U. Phoenix, 1992. Diplomate Am. Bd. Orthopedic Surgeons. Intern U. Ariz. Health Scis. Ctr., Tucson, 1977-78, resident in orthopedic surgery, 1978-81; gen. surgery intern U. Ariz., Tucson, 1977-78; pvt. practice Phoenix, 1981-86; resident in orthopedic surgery U. Ariz., Tucson, 1978-81; dir. acad. affairs Maricopa Med. Ctr., Phoenix, 1992—; adj. prof. dept. biomed. engring. Ariz. State U., Phoenix, 1991—; clin. assoc. prof. surgery Coll. Medicine U. Ariz., Tucson, 1989—. Editor: Musculoskeletal Disorders in Aging, 1989; contbr. 25 articles to profl. jours., 1981. Fellow ACS, Royal Soc. Medicine, Am. Acad. Orthopedic Surgeons; mem. Am. Orthopedic Foot and Ankle Soc., Gerontol. Soc. Am., Acad. Orthopedic Soc. (2d pres.-elect), Ariz. Geriatrics Soc. (pres. 1990-91). Jewish. Office: Maricopa Med Ctr 2601 E Roosevelt St Phoenix AZ 85008-4973

KARR, CHERYL LOFGREEN, film producer, consultant; b. Norco, Calif., Oct. 6, 1954; d. Ted Lee and Charlotte Dorae (Mackinga) Lofgreen; m. Paul Michael James Karr, Apr. 21, 1977. AA, Brigham Young U., 1975, BA, 1978, MA, 1983. Instr. radio and TV prodn. Brigham Young U., Provo, Utah, 1976-77; writer, dir. Paul S. Karr Prodns., Phoenix, 1978-80; mng. editor Weeknight TV News Mag., Provo, 1981-82; gen. mgr. CCN Cable Network, Provo, 1982-83; news reporter The Daily Herald, Provo, 1984; v.p. prodn. Alpine Film and Video Exchange, Inc., Orem, Utah, 1984-86; producer, dir. Sta. KBYU-TV, Provo, 1984—; instr. English, Utah Valley Community Coll., Orem, 1986—; pres. SEEN-BY-SCENE PRODNS., Orem, 1987—; cons. Film Video Services, Phoenix, 1985-87, Producers Consortium, Orem, 1986—, Skaggs Retail Inst., Provo, 1987—; producer, dir. hdqrs. USMC, Washington, Count Me In, Spl. Svcs. Media Campaign, 1989; producer, dir., writer State of Utah, Earthquake Awareness Media Campaign, 1989; assoc. producer feature film Rockwell, 1990. Writer documentary Escape from Ground Zero, 1983; producer, writer documentary Tonga: A King and Its People, 1987; writer Yue Sai Kan, Inc., CCTV, 1986—; writer, dir. documentary Islands of Love: People of Faith, 1992; producer feature films Into the Paradise, 1994, Summer of the Eagle, 1994. Recipient Prodn. Excellence award Phototec, 1978, Nat. TV award Women in Communications, 1983, Golden Microphone award Brigham Young U., 1984, Cine Golden Eagle, 1993, Gold Camera award, 1993, Angel award, 1993, Emmy award, 1993, Houston Internat. Film Festival Worldfest Gold award., 1995. Mem. Am. Film Inst. Republican. Mormon. Home: 1045 N 300 E Orem UT 84057-3324 Office: Seen-By-Scene Prodns PO Box 1254 Orem UT 84059-1254

KARR, DAVID DEAN, lawyer; b. Denver, Sept. 3, 1953; s. Dean Speece and Jean (Ransbottom) K.; m. Laura A. Foster, Apr. 10, 1982; children: Emily Ann, Bradley Foster. BA, U. Puget Sound, 1975; JD, Loyola U., 1979. Bar: Colo. 1979, U.S. Dist. Ct. 1979, U.S. Ct. Appeals (10th cir.) 1981, U.S. Supreme Ct. 1983. Assoc. Pryor Carney & Johnson, P.C., Englewood, Colo., 1979-84, ptnr., 1984—. Mem. ABA (lead atty. pro bono team death penalty project Tex. chpt. 1988—), Colo. Bar Assn. (interprofl. com. 1990—), Denver Bar Assn., Def. Rsch. Inst. Home: 5474 E Hinsdale Cir Littleton CO 80122-2538 Office: Pryor Carney & Johnsonn PC 6200 S Syracuse Way Ste 400 Englewood CO 80111-4741

KARRAS, DONALD GEORGE, tax administrator; b. Sioux City, Iowa, Dec. 23, 1953; s. George D. and Mary T. (Kyriakos) K.; m. Donna Lynn Ciripompa, Mar. 6, 1982; children: Dane Anthony, Dillon James. BA, Augustana Coll., 1977; MBA, U. S.D., 1980, JD, 1981. CPA, S.D. Bar: S.D. 1981. Instr. U. S.D. Sch. Bus., Vermillion, 1980-81; tax sr. acct. Deloitte Haskins & Sells, Denver, 1981-84; tax mgr. The Anschutz Corp., Denver, 1984-87; dir. taxes Kennecott Corp., Salt Lake City, 1988-92; v.p. Taxes Newmont Mining Corp., Denver, 1992—. Mem. Colo. Pub. Expenditure Coun. Mem. ABA, S.D. Bar Assn., Am. Hellenic Ednl. Progressive Assn., Tax Execs. Inst. (v.p. region VIII), Am. Mining Congress (tax com.), Rocky Mountain Mineral Law Found., Colo. Mining Assn., Internat. Fiscal Assn., Nev. Mining Assn. Republican. Greek Orthodox. Home: 7100 W Princeton Ave Denver CO 80235-3036 Office: Newmont Mining Corp One Norwest Ctr 1700 Lincoln St Denver CO 80203-4501

KARRAS, NOLAN ELDON, investment advisor; b. Ogden, Utah, Dec. 30, 1944; s. Orien John and Afton Elaine (Green) K.; m. Lynda Francel Purrington, Nov. 22, 1967; children: Brett N., Jodie Lynn, Darrin O. BS, Weber State U., 1970; MBA, U. Utah, 1970; HHD (hon.), Coll. of E. Utah, 1990. CPA, Colo., Utah; registered investment adv., Utah. Acct. Arthur Andersen & Co., Denver, 1970-72, Peat, Marwick & Mitchell, Salt Lake City, 1972-75, Schmitt, Griffiths & Smith, Ogden, 1975-79; fin. v.p. Jack B. Parson Cos., Ogden, 1979-93; registered rep. Investment Mgmt. & Rsch., Roy, Utah, 1985—; pres. Superior Air Handling Corp., Cldarfield, Utah, 1990-91; bd. dirs. Pacificorp, Utah Power & Light. Mem. Utah Ho. of Reps., Salt Lake City, 1981-90, majority leade, 1987-88, spkr., 1989-90; adv. om. Salt Lake City Olympic Bid Com., 1989-90. With USAR, 1963-69. Recipient Outstanding Legislator award AFL-CIO, 1986, Disting. Alumnus award Weber State U., 1990, Outstanding Alumnus award Beta Alpha Psi, 1988-89. Mem. AICPA (Pub. Svc. award 1987), Utah Assn. CPAs (Disting. Svc. award 1987), Ogden/Weber C. of C. (bd. dirs. 1989-93). Republican. Mormon. Home: 4096 S 2275 W Roy UT 84067-2065 Office: 4695 S 1900 W # 3 Roy UT 84067-2669

KARROS, ERIC PETER, professional baseball player; b. Hackensack, N.J., Nov. 4, 1967. BA in Econs., UCLA, 1993. 1st baseman L.A. Dodgers, 1988—. Named Nat. League Rookie of the Year, 1992. Office: Dodger Stadium 1000 Elysian Park Ave Los Angeles CA 90012-1112

KARSON, CATHERINE JUNE, computer programmer, consultant; b. Salt Lake City, Jan. 26, 1956; d. Gary George and Sylvia June (Naylor) Anderson; m. Mitchell Reed Karson, June 14, 1987; 1 child, Rhonda. A in Gen. Studies, Pima C.C., Tucson, 1989, AAS in Computer Sci., 1990. Night supr. F.G. Ferre & Son, Inc., Salt Lake City, 1973-76, exec. sec., 1977-79; operating room technician Cottonwood Hosp., Salt Lake City, 1976-77; customer svc. rep., System One rep. Ea. Airlines, Inc., Salt Lake City and Tucson, 1979-88; edn. specialist Radio Shack Computer Ctr., Tucson, 1988-89; programmer/analyst Pinal County DPIS, Florence, Ariz., 1989-90; systems analyst Carondelet Health Svcs., Tucson, 1990; programmer/analyst Sunquest Info. Sys., Tucson, 1990-94, sr. tech. proposal specialist, 1994-95; software developer, 1995—; cons. Pinal County Pub. Fiduciary, Florence, 1990, UBET, Barbados, W.I., 1990—, numerous clients, Tucson, 1990-93. Mem. bus. adv. coun. Portable Practical Ednl. Preparation, Inc., Tucson, 1990-91. Mem. Nat. Sys. Programmer Assn. Republican. Jewish. Home: 6066 N Serendipity Ln Tucson AZ 85704-5322

KASAMA, HIDETO PETER, accountant, real estate consultant; b. Tokyo, Nov. 21, 1946; came to U.S., 1969; s. Toshiyoshi and Hamako (Yoshioka) K.; m. Evelyn Patricia Cruz (div. Apr. 1990); children: Jennifer, Nicole, Leona; m. Heidi W. Snare, June 29, 1991. BABA, Seattle U., 1971, MBA, 1973. CPA. Mgmt. trainee Security Pacific Bank, Seattle, 1972-74; audit supr. Ernst & Young, Seattle, 1974-79; pres. KASPAC Corp., Seattle, 1979-89; mng. ptnr. Kasama & Co., Seattle, 1980—. Contbr. articles to newspapers. Mem. AICPA, Wash. Soc. CPA's, Columbia Tower Club (founder). Home: 725 9th Ave S Edmonds WA 98020-3311 Office: Kasama & Co 3147 Fairview Ave E Ste 110 Seattle WA 98102-3041

KASARI, LEONARD SAMUEL, quality control professional, concrete consultant; b. Los Angeles, Sept. 22, 1924; s. Kustaa Adolph and Impi (Sikio) K.; m. Elizabeth P. Keplinger, Aug. 25, 1956; children: Lorraine Carol, Lance Eric. Student, Compton Coll., 1942-43, UCLA, 1964-70. Registered profl. engr., Calif. Gen. construction Los Angeles, 1946-61; supr. inspection service Osborne Labs., Los Angeles, 1961-64; mgr. customer service Lightweight Processing, Los Angeles, 1965-77; dir. tech. service Crestlite Aggregates, San Clemente, Calif., 1977-78; quality control mgr. Standard Concrete, Santa Ana, Calif., 1978-92. Camp dir. Torrance YMCA, High Sierras, Calif., 1969-80, mem. bd. mgrs., 1970—. Served with USN, 1943-46. Recipient Sam Hobbs Svc. award ACI-So. Calif., 1992; named Hon. Life Mem. Calif. PTA, 1983. Mem. Am. Concrete Inst., So. Calif. Structural Engrs. Assn. Democrat. Lutheran. Office: 2450 W 233rd St Torrance CA 90501-5730

KASHAP, SURAJNAYAN PAUL, philosophy educator; b. Jalalpur, Punjab, India, July 1, 1929; came to U.S., 1960; s. Gurdayal and Maya Devi (Bedi) K.; m. Nancy Sherry Kashap, Nov. 1, 1957; children: Ashwin Philip, Christopher Sanjiv, Andrew Deven. BA with honors, MA, U. Bombay, India, 1953; MA with honors, U. Edinburgh, Scotland, 1956; BLitt, Oxford (Eng.) U., 1960. Asst. prof. Wheaton Coll., Norton, Mass., 1961-63, Brown U., Providence, 1963-69; prof. philosophy U. Calif., Santa Cruz, 1969—. Author: Spinoza and Moral Freedom, 1987; editor: Studies in Spinoza, 1972; contbr. articles to profl. jours. Fellow Cowell Coll., U. Calif., Santa Cruz. Mem. Am. Philos. Assn., N.Am. Spinoza Soc. (exec. bd.), Gray's Inn. Office: U Calif Cowell Coll Santa Cruz CA 95064-1099

KASKEL, NEAL T., financial services executive; b. Buffalo, Oct. 6, 1943; s. David and Bertha (Perlmuter) K.; m. Geraldine Slutsky, Apr. 3, 1966; children: Amy Melissa, Robert Jason. BS, DePaul U., 1966; MBA, Northwestern U., 1972. Market rsch. analyst D'Arcy Advt., Chgo., 1965-67; rsch. supr. Foote, Cone & Belding, Chgo., 1967-72; market rsch. mgr. Armour-Dial, Phoenix, 1972-74, Hunt-Wesson Foods, Fullerton, Calif., 1974-79; dir. mktg. svcs. FHP, Fountain Valley, Calif., 1979-81; mktg. mgr. TCM div. Smith Internat., Tustin, Calif., 1981-83; v.p. Geneva Cos., Irvine, Calif., 1983—; adj. prof. Calif. State U., Fullerton, 1975—, U. LaVerne, Fountain Valley, 1990—, U. Phoenix, Fountain Valley, 1990—. Bd. mem. Jewish Family Svc., Orange County, Calif., 1980-84; exec. bd. mem. Jewish Fedn., Orange County, 1984—; pres. Congregation B'Nai Tzedek, Fountain Valley, 1984-87; trustee Sch. Assets Mgmt. Inc., Fountain Valley, 1989-91. Lt. USNR, 1968-74. Home: 18880 Mount Morgan Cir Fountain Vly CA 92708-6517 Office: Geneva Cos 5 Park Plz Irvine CA 92714-5995

KASMER, IRENE, fashion and textile executive; b. Bilky, Czechoslovakia, Sept. 24, 1926; came to the U.S., 1948; d. Izidor and Malvina Amalia (Klein) Markovic; m. Gerald Stuart Kasmer, Aug. 29, 1954; children: Jeff Anthony, Bruce Neal, Lauren Michele. AA in Art, LATTI Coll., L.A., 1953. Designer Bell Sportswear, L.A., 1948-50; prof. costume design, lectr. L.A. Trade Tech. Coll., 1951-54; chief designer, dir. Ardee Sportswear, L.A., 1951-66; pres. Irene Kasmer Inc., L.A., 1966—; founder, pres. Modac Mus. Fashion Designers and Creators, L.A., 1994—, also bd. dirs.; cons., designer, 1951—; pres. Mus. Fashion Designers and Creators, L.A., 1991—. Fashion adv. com. to mayor, L.A., 1970—. Recipient Young Designer award Calif. Stylist, 1957, Mayda award May Co., 1960, Trend Setting Toby award, 1962, Designer award Monsanto and DuPont, 1960-65. Mem. Fashion Group Internat. (bd. dirs. 1960—), Textile Group Internat. (bd. dirs. 1987—). Home: 315 S Bedford Dr Beverly Hills CA 90212-3724 Office: 910 S Los Angeles St Ste 302 Los Angeles CA 90015-1726

KASPER, CHRISTINE ELEANA, nursing educator, researcher; b. Chgo., Mar. 16, 1953; d. John Michael and Olga (Kozor) K.; m. Ramiro G. Iturralde, June 25, 1978; children: Alexandra Vitoria Iturralde, Gabrielle Augusta Iturralde. BSN, U. Evansville (Ind.), 1975; MSN, Rush U., Chgo., 1976; PhD, U. Mich., 1982. RN, Ill., Mich., Wis., Calif. Tchr./practitioner Rush Presbyn.-St. Luke's Hosp., Chgo., 1976-77; predoctoral fellow U. Mich., Ann Arbor, 1978-82; teaching asst. U. Mich., 1978-81; postdoctoral fellow Rush Med. Coll., Chgo., 1982-84; asst. prof. nursing U. Wis., Madison, 1984-88, UCLA, 1988—. Contbr. articles to profl. jours. Grantee NASA, NIH; recipient Rackman Dissertation/Thesis award, 1980, Nat. Rsch. Svc. award DHHS, 1978-81. Fellow Am. Acad. Nursing, Am. Coll. Sports Medicine; mem. Am. Nurses Assn., Biophys. Soc., Midwest Nurses Rsch. Soc., N.Y. Acad. Sci., Am. Soc. Gravitational and Space Biology, Sigma Theta Tau. Russian Orthodox. Office: UCLA Sch Nursing 10833 Le Conte Ave Los Angeles CA 90024

KASS, JEFFREY ROBERT, journalist; b. L.A., Sept. 29, 1968; s. George Harold and Judi Margo (Margolis) K. BA, U. Calif., Santa Barbara, 1990; MA, NYU, 1992; cert. Spanish, U. Madrid, 1990. Freelance writer various periodicals, N.Y., 1991-92; reporter Thomson Newspapers, Ventura, Calif., 1992-94, L.A. Times, 1994—; mem. bd. dirs. Ventura County Press Club, 1992-94. mem. Bilingual Toastmasters, Oxnard, Calif., 1993-94. Office: L A Times 23133 Hawthorne Blvd Ste 200 Torrance CA 90505-3729

KASS, JEROME ALLAN, writer; b. Chgo., Apr. 21, 1937; s. Sidney J. and Celia (Gorman) K.; children from previous marriage: Julie, Adam; m. Delia Ephron, May 21, 1982. BA, NYU, 1958, MA, 1959. Playwright: Monopoly, 1965, Saturday Night, 1968, (mus.) Ballroom, 1978 (Tony nomination), (TV) A Brand New Life, 1973, Queen of the Stardust Ballroom, 1975 (Writers Guild Am. award, Emmy nomination), My Old Man, 1979, The Fighter, 1982, Scorned and Swindled, 1984, Crossing to Freedom (aka Pied Piper), 1989, Last Wish, 1991, The Only Way Out, 1993, Secrets, 1995; screenwriter: The Black Stallion Returns, 1981, (miniseries) Evergreen, 1985; author: Four Short Plays by Jerome Kass, 1966, Saturday Night, 1969. Mem. Dramatists Guild, Writers Guild Am., Am. Film Inst. (instr.), Phi Beta Kappa. Home: 2211 Broadway New York NY 10024

KASS, PHILIP HOWARD, epidemiology educator; b. L.A., Aug. 19, 1958; s. Leonard and Zita (Dunn) K.; m. Jan Carmikle, Oct. 14, 1961; children: Lauren, Alexander. DVM, U. Calif., Davis, 1983, M of Preventive Veterinary Medicine, 1984, MS in Stats., 1988, PhD in Epidemiology, 1990. Asst. prof. epidemiology U. Calif., Davis, 1990—. Mem. Am. Coll. Vet. Preventive Medicine (sec. epidemiology specialty 1993-95), Am. Statis. Assn., Biometrics Soc., Am. Vet. Med. Assn., Soc. Epidemiologic Rsch., Calif. Acad. Vet. Medicine (bd. dirs. 1994-95). Home: 2760 Ottowa Ave Davis CA 95616-2928 Office: U Calif Sch Vet Medicine Dept Population Health & Reproduction Davis CA 95616

KASSABIAN, ANAHID, media theorist; b. N.Y.C., Oct. 12, 1959; d. Richard P. and Iris Stephanie (Noorian) K.; m. Leo Gulvad Svendsen, Dec. 31, 1986; 1 child, Maral Kassabian Svendsen. BA in Media Studies, Fordham U., 1986; MA in Modern Thought and Lit., Stanford U., 1988, PhD in Modern Thought and Lit., 1993. Grad. fellow Stanford (Calif.) U., 1986-92; freelance writer Redwood City, Calif., 1987—; instr. Stanford (Calif.) U., 1992-93; devel. dir. The Women's Philharmonic, San Francisco, 1993-94; lectr. cinema dept. San Francisco State U., 1994; lectr. U. Calif., Berkeley, 1995; assoc. scholar Inst. Rsch. on Women and Gender, Stanford U., 1995—; pres., bd. dirs. Aunt Lute Found., San Francisco, 1994—. Editor spl. issue Stanford Humanities Rev., 1993. Steering com. mem. Voice for Choice, San Mateo, Calif., 1993. Recipient travel grant Kaltenborn Found., 1988, Am.-Scandinavian Found., 1988, Whiting fellowship Whiting Found., 1990-91. Mem. Internat. Assn. for Study of Popular Music (exec. com. 1992—), Midwest Sociol. Soc., MLA, Speech Comm. Assn., Nat. Assn. Armenian Scholarship and Rsch. Home: 391 Belmont Ave Redwood City CA 94061-3416

KASSEBAUM, GENE GIRARD, sociology educator; b. St. Louis, June 24, 1929; s. John G. and Flora (Girard) K.; m. Gayathri Rajapur, Aug. 1966; 1 child, Krishna. AB, U. Mo., 1951; MA, Harvard U., 1955, PhD, 1958. Rsch. asst. Harvard U., Cambridge, Mass., 1954-57; rsch. assoc. Cornell U. Med. Ctr., N.Y. Hosp., N.Y.C., 1957-60, Sch. Pub. Health, UCLA, L.A., 1960-65; assoc. prof. Am. U. in Cairo, Egypt, 1965-68; prof. sociology U. Hawaii, Honolulu, 1968—, dir. ctr. youth rsch., 1993—. Author: Delinquency and Social Policy, 1974; co-author: Women's Prison, 1965, Prison Treatment Parole Survival, 1971; contbr. articles to profl. jours. Cpl. U.S. Army, 1951-53. Sr. Fulbright scholar U.S. Dept. State, India, 1974, 81. Mem. Am. Soc. Criminology, Am. Sociol. Assn., Phi Beta Kappa. Office: Univ Hawaii 2424 Maile Way Honolulu HI 96822-2223

KASSNER, MICHAEL ERNEST, materials science educator, researcher; b. Osaka, Japan, Nov. 22, 1950; (parents Am. citizens); s. Ernest and Clara (Christa) K.; m. Marcia J. Wright, Aug. 19, 1972 (div. Dec. 1976). BS, Northwestern U., 1972; MS, Stanford U., 1979, PhD, 1981. Metallurgist Sargent and Lundy Engrs., Chgo., 1977; metallurgist Lawrence Livermore (Calif.) Nat. Lab., 1981-90, head phys. metallurgy and joining sect., 1988-90; lectr. San Francisco State U., 1983; prof. Naval Postgrad. Sch., Monterey, Calif., 1984-86; prof., dir. grad. program in materials sci. Oreg. State U., Corvallis, 1990—, program dir. grad. materials sci., 1995—; temporary assignment as project mgr. Office Basic Energy Scis., U.S. Dept. Energy, 1991—; vis. scholar dept. physics U. Groningen, Netherlands, 1985-87; vis. scholar dept. materials, sci. and engring. Stanford U., 1981-83. Author over 100 sci. articles; editor various sci. jours. Lt. USN, 1972-76; lt. comdr. USNR, 1976-81. Fulbright scholar, The Netherlands, 1983-84. Mem. ASME, Am. Soc. Metals, The Metall. Soc., Materials Research Soc., Sigma Xi. Roman Catholic. Home: PO Box 269 Otter Rock OR 97369-0269

KASTEN, BETTY LOU, state legislator; b. Sharon, Pa., Apr. 6, 1938; d. Louis and Betty Todut; m. David Kasten; children: Tod Louis, Elaine Katherine. BA, U. Denver, MS. Rancher, farmer; mem. Mont. Ho. of Reps., 1989—; past bd. trustees Mid River Telephone; past mem. Mont. Health Sys. Agy., Ea. Sub-Area Coun. Kellogg fellow Mont. State U. Mem. Mont. Farm Bur., Mont. Stockgrowers, Mont. Woolgrowers, Mont. Grain Growers, McCone County Cowbelles, Brockway Homemakers. Republican. Home: HC 77 Box A-14 Brockway MT 59214-9701 Office: Mont Ho of Reps State Capitol Helena MT 59620-0001

KASTRUL, JEROME JOE, geriatrician; b. Chgo., Dec. 14, 1934; s. Sam and Gladys (Lipschitz) K.; m. Patricia Ann Gillis, May 19, 1967; children: Sterling, Jenifer, Stephen, Patrick, Tamara, Michelle, David, Lisa. AB, U. Chgo., 1954; MD, Northwestern U., 1958. Diplomate Am. Bd. Internal Medicine. Med. dir. Phoenix (Ariz.) Geriatric Inst., 1964-93; staff physician Family and Sr. Care, Peoria, Ariz., 1993—; med. dir. Kivel Geriatric Ctr., Phoenix, 1982-90, Nova Home Health Care, Phoenix, 1989-93, Tempe (Ariz.) Adult Day Health Ctr., 1991—, Glendale (Ariz.) Adult Day Health Ctr., 1992—. Mem. Gov.'s Adv. Coun. on Aging, Phoenix, 1989-93, Gov.'s Alzheimer Adv. Com., Phoenix, 1991-93. Mem. ACP, Am. Geriatrics Soc., Ariz. Med. Soc. Home: 12014 N 60th Ave Glendale AZ 85304

KASULKA, LARRY HERMAN, aerospace company executive; b. Wagner, S.D., Apr. 5, 1940; s. Alfred E. and Lillian J. (Gasper) K.; m. Susan A. Smart, Sept. 8, 1962; children: Shawn L., Christine A. BS in Electronics, Northrop U., 1961; grad. cert. in bus. adminstrn., UCLA, 1969; grad. cert., Brookings Inst., 1986, Harvard U., 1989. Registered profl. engr., Calif. Electronic engr. Douglas Aircraft Co., 1962-77; unit chief avionics McDonnell Douglas Astronautics Co., 1977-81, br. chief avionics, 1981-84; dir. design engr. McDonnell Douglas Electronic Systems Co., 1984-87, dir. program mgmt., 1987-89, dir. new bus., 1989-91; spl. asst. U.S. Dept. Commerce, Office of the Dep. Sec., 1990-91; v.p., dep. gen. mgr. Kennedy Space Ctr. McDonnell Douglas Space Systems Co., 1991-93; v.p., gen. mgr. McDonnell Douglas Aerospace N.Mex. Ops., 1993-94; presenter in field. Contbr. articles to profl. jours. Bd. dirs. Brevard Achievement Ctr., Rockledge, Fla., 1991-93; mentor Sci. Engrin. and Rsch. Career Help; mem. Pres. Commn. Exec. Exch. Alumni U. Calif.-L.A. Alumni. Recipient Commendation White Ho. Pres. Bush, 1990, Instrumentation Soc. of Am., 1983, Sr. Exec. Svc. award Dept. Commerce, Sec. Mosbacher, 1990; named Outstanding Cadet, CAP-Internat. Aviation Cadet Exch.; named to Hon. Order of Ky. Cols. Fellow AIAA (assoc.); mem. Armed Forces and Comm. Elec. Assn., Nat. Man. Assn., Assn. for Quality Participation, Am. Soc. Quality Control. Office: McDonnell Douglas Aerospace 5301 Bolsa Ave Huntington Beach CA 92647-2048

KASZNIAK, ALFRED WAYNE, neuropsychologist; b. Chgo., June 2, 1949; s. Alfred H. and Ann Virginia (Simonsen) K.; B.S. with honors, U. Ill., 1970, M.A., 1973, Ph.D., 1976; m. Mary Ellen Beaurain, Aug. 26, 1973; children: Jesse, Elizabeth. Instr. dept. psychology Rush Med. Coll., Chgo., 1974-76, asst. prof. dept. psychology, 1976-79; from asst. prof. to assoc. prof. dept. psychiatry U. Ariz. Coll. Medicine, Tucson, 1979-82, assoc. prof. dept. psychology and psychiatry, 1982-87; prof. depts. psychology, neurology and psychiatry, 1987—; chmn. U. Ariz. Commn. on Gerontology, 1990-93, acting head U. Ariz. dept. psychology, 1992-93 ; dir. U. Ariz. Coordinated Clin. Neuropsychology Program; staff psychologist Presbyn.-St. Luke's Hosp., Chgo., 1976-79, Univ. Hosp., Tucson, 1979—; mem. human devel. and aging study sect. div. research grants NIH, 1981-86. Trustee So. Ariz. chpt. Nat. Multiple Sclerosis Soc., 1980-82; mem. med. and sci. adv. bd. Nat. Alzheimer's Disease and Related Disorders Assn., 1981-84; mem. VA Geriatrics and Gerontology Adv. Com., 1986-89, Ariz. Gov.'s Adv. Com. on Alzheimer's Disease, 1988-92; mem. med. adv. bd. Fan Kane Fund for Brain-Injured Children, Tucson, 1980-92. Grantee Nat. Inst. Aging, 1978-83, 89-94, NIMH, 1984-94, Robert Wood Johnson Found., 1986-89. Fellow Am. Psychol. Assn. (Disting. Contbr. award div. 20 1978, pres. clin. geropsychology sect. 1995); mem. Internat. Neuropsychol. Soc., Soc. for Neurosci., Gerontol. Soc. (rsch. fellow 1980). Author 2 books; editorial cons. Jour. Gerontology, 1979-92; mem. editorial bd. Psychology and Aging, 1984-87; The Clin. Neuropsychologist, 1986—, Clin. Geropsychology, 1994—, Jour. Clin. and Exp. Neuropsychol., 1987-90, Jour Gerontology, 1988-92, Neuropsychology, 1992-93; contbr. articles to profl. jours. Home: 2327 E Hawthorne St Tucson AZ 85719-4944 Office: U Ariz Dept Psychology Tucson AZ 85721

KATANO, MARC, artist; b. Tokyo, July 17, 1952 (father Am. citizen); m. Nicole Henkin. B.F.A. with distinction, Calif. Coll. Arts and Crafts, 1975. One-man shows include: Stephen Wirtz Gallery, 1980, 83, 94, Calif. State U., 1982, Hodges/Banks Gallery, Seattle, 1984, Richard Green Gallery, N.Y.C., 1988, Sharon Traux Fine Art, Venice, Calif., 1993, Gallery Fresca, Tokyo, Japan, 1994; exhibited in group shows at Stephen Wirtz Gallery, San Francisco, 1981, Berkeley Arts Ctr., Calif., 1980, E.B. Crocker Art Mus., Sacramento, Calif., 1981, San Francisco Mus. Modern Art, 1981, St. Paul Companies Hdqrs., Minn., Amfac Ctr. Plaza, Honolulu-Japanese C. of C., 1983, Sheldon Meml. Art Gallery, U. Nebr., 1985, Palo Alto Cultural Ctr., 1988, Maruzen Gallery, Sensai, Japan, 1991, Gallery Finarte, Nagoya, Japan, 1992, Gallery IV, L.A., 1993, Korean Cultural Ctr., L.A., 1994, L.A. Artcore, L.A., 1994, Elizabeth Leach Gallery, Portland, 1994, others. Recipient KQED-Crown Zellerbach Exhbn. award, 1980; Soc. Encouragement Contemporary Art award, 1981. Office: 49 Geary St San Francisco CA 94108-5705

KATCHATAG, STANTON OSWALD, civic and political worker; b. Unalakleet, Alaska, Nov. 9, 1917; s. Joseph H. and Helga (Muktuk) K.; m. Irene Unal Benjamin, Sept. 27, 1940; children: Pearl, Shirley, Sheldon, Vernita, Virgil, Helga, Paul. Student pub. schs., Unalakleet. Various positions U.S. Postal Svc., until 1970, mail carrier, 1970-75; journeyman carpenter, 1975-86. Pres. Native Village Unalakleet; chmn. bd. Kawerak, Inc., Bering Straits Native Assn.; mem., former chmn. Western Alaska Tribal Coun.; mem. Eskimo Walrus Commn.; bd. dirs. Norton Sound Health Corp., Rural Alaska Cmty. Action Program; mem. exec. bd. dirs., co-founder Alaska Inter-Tribal Coun.; mem. dels. from Alaska to Inuit Circumpolar Conf. With U.S. Army, 1945-46. Recipient recognition of esteemed elder Unalakleet Native Corp., 1973; Elder of Yr. award Kawerak, Inc., Nome, Alaska, 1987, Bd. Mem. of Yr. award, 1993; Citizen of Yr. award City of Unalakleet, 1992. Democrat. Home: PO Box 268 Unalakleet AK 99684 Office: Native Village of Unalakleet PO Box 270 Unalakleet AK 99684-0270

KATCHEN, CAROLE LEE, writer, artist; b. Denver, Jan. 30, 1944; d. Samuel and Gertrude (Levin) K.; m. Philip Goldhammer, 1967 (div. 1970). BA, U. Colo., 1965. Freelance journalist, 1964—; corr. Life Mag., 1989-92; columnist Dance Action Mag., 1989-90 ; columnist, mem. editorial rev. bd. Colo. Woman Mag., 1976-80; cons. children's literature Volt Tech. Corp., 1971; presenter in field. Author: I Was a Lonely Teenager, 1965, The Underground Light Bulb, 1969, Promoting and Selling Your Art, 1978, Figure Drawing Workshop, 1985, Painting Face and Figures, 1986, Planning Your Paintings Step-by-Step, 1988 (Dutch edit. 1990), Your Friend, Annie, 1990, Creative Painting with Pastel, 1990, Watercolor, Oil, Acrylic, 1991, Dramatize Your Paintings with Tonal Values, 1993, Painting with Passion, 1994; script writer, co-prodr. Screamplay, 1991; script writer (comml. audio tape) Let the Games Begin!, 1991, (video) Cafe Talk, 1986; contbg. editor Artist's Mag., 1985—, Today's Art & Graphics, 1980-81; editor, pub. Trip Mag., 1967-68; editor, copywriter Tempo Mag., 1964-65; one-woman shows include Denver Art Gallery, 1972, Denver Women's Press Club, 1974, Centro Colombo-Americano, Bogota, Colombia, 1974, Valhalla Gallery, Witchita, Kans., 1978, 1st Nat. Bank Denver, 1980, Cynthia Madden Gallery, Denver, 1981, Gerhard Wurzer Gallery, Houston, 1981, Gallery of S.W., Taos, N.Mex., 1981, Savageau's Gallery, Denver, 1984, Hooks-Epstein Gallery, Houston, 1985, Saks Galleries, Denver, 1993, Taylor's Contemporanea Art Gallery, Hot Springs, Ark., 1995; represented in permanent collections Mus. Outdoor Art, Englewood, Colo., Northwest Community Hosp., Arlington Heights, Ill., AGIP, Houston, Tex., Petro Lewis Corp., Denver, Cherry Creek Nat. Bank, Denver, Rotan Mosle Corp., Denver, Denver Symphony Orch., Denver Women's Press Club, Penrose Community Hosp., Colorado Springs. Recipient Outstanding Achievement in Art award West Valley Coll., 1970, Outstanding Working Woman award U.S. Dept. Labor and Colo. Coun. on Working Women, 1982, Spl. Recognition award Women in Design, 1988, Better Price Store award Okla. Art Workshops Ann. Exhibit, 1993; nominated Internat. Women of Yr., London, 1992-93. Mem. Pastel Soc. Am. (Kans. Pastel Soc. award 1990, Avelyn Goldsmith award 1993, Holbein award 1994), Internat. Assn. Pastel Socs. (mem. bd. dirs.).

KATHER, GERHARD, retired air force base administrator; b. Allenstein, Germany, Jan. 30, 1939; came to U.S., 1952, naturalized, 1959; s. Ernst and Maria (Kempa) K.; m. Carol Anne Knutsen, Aug. 18, 1962; children: Scott T., Cynthia M., Tracey S., Chris A.; m. Mary Elsie Frank, Oct. 25, 1980. BA in Govt., U. Ariz., 1964; MPA, U. So. Calif., 1971; cert. in personnel adminstrn., U. N.Mex., 1987. Tchr. social studies, Covina, Calif., 1965-67; tng. officer Civil Personnel, Ft. MacArthur, Calif., 1967-70; chief employee tng. and devel. Corps Engrs., L.A., 1970-72; chief employee tng. and devel. Frankfurt Area Army Personnel Office, 1972-73; chief employee rels. and tng. brs. Corps Engrs., L.A., 1973-74; chief employee devel. and tng. Kirtland AFB, N.Mex., 1974-87; labor relations officer, Kirtland AFB and detachments in 13 U.S. cities, 1987-90; ret., 1990; project coord., adv. Protection and Advocacy System, 1991—. Mem. adv. com. Albuquerque Tech.-Vocat. Inst., 1982-92, U. N.Mex. Valencia Campus, 1985-92; mem. Coalition for Disability Rights, 1988—; chmn. Comprehensive Accessibility Network, 1990—; adv. coun. N.Mex. Disability Prevention, 1992—; recording sec. N.Mex. Commn. Blind State Rehab. Adv. Coun., 1993—. Served with USAF, 1958-64. Named Prominent Tng. and Devel. Profl., H. Whitney McMillan Co., 1984; Outstanding Handicapped Fed. Employee of Yr., all fed. agys., 1984; recipient Govt. Employees Ins. Co. GEICO Pub. Svc. award for work in phys. rehab., 1988. Mem. Am. Soc. Tng. and Devel. (treas. chpt. 1984-85), Paralyzed Vets. Am. (bd. dirs. 1986-87, pres. local chpt. 1986-87, 1990-92), Toastmasters Internat. (chpt. treas., v.p., pres. 1967-70), Vietnam Vets. of Am., Phi Delta Kappa. Democrat. Roman Catholic. Office: 1720 Louisiana Blvd NE Ste 204 Albuquerque NM 87110-7070

KATHKA, DAVID ARLIN, director educational services; b. Columbus, Nebr.; s. Arlin Arthur and Edith Ferne (Wilcox) K.; m. Anne Condon Butler, Aug. 15, 1965. BA, Wayne (Nebr.) State Coll., 1964, MA, 1966; PhD in History, U. Mo., 1976. Tchr. Ravenna (Nebr.) Pub. Schs., 1964-65; instr. Midwestern Coll., Denison, Iowa, 1966-68; prof. history Western Wyo. Coll., Rock Springs, 1972-87, dean acad. affairs, 1980-84, interim pres., 1984-85, v.p. acad. affairs, 1985-87; dir. State Parks and Cultural Resources Div., State of Wyo., Cheyenne, 1987-94, Sweetwater Bd. Coop. Ednl. Svcs., Wyo., 1994—; adj. prof. U. Wyo., Laramie, 1976—; vis. instr. U. Mo., St. Louis, 1971-72; cons. various Wyo. govt. agys.; mem. gov.'s Blue ribbon Task Force on Cultural Resources, Wyo. Trails adv. com. Author hist. papers; contbr. hist. articles to mags. Bd. dirs. Sweetwater Mus. Found., Wyo. Territorial Park, 1987-94, Tracks Across Wyo., Wyo. Hist. Found.; mem. Wyo. Centennial Commn., 1986-87, Rock Springs Libr. Bd.,1 984-87, Gov.'s Com. on Hist. Preservation, 1982; v.p. Rocky Mountain Region Kidney Found., Denver, 1976-77. Recipient Wyo. Humanities award for exemplary svc., 1990. Mem. Orgn. Am. Historians, Wyo. State Hist. Soc. (pres. 1984-85). Democrat. Office: Sweetwater Bd Coop Ednl Svcs Box 428 Rock Springs WY 82902-0428

KATHOL, ANTHONY LOUIS, finance executive; b. San Diego, June 12, 1964; s. Cletus Louis and Regina Antoinette (Ellrott) K.; m. Kathleen Marie Moore, Jan. 23, 1988; children: Nicole Kathleen, Natalie Antoinette, Holly Rose. BS, U. So. Calif., 1986; MBA, U. San Diego, 1988. Fin. aid analyst U. San Diego, 1986-87; bookkeeper Golden Lion Tavern, San Diego, 1987-88; fin. and budget coord. Santa Fe Pacific Realty Corp. (name now Catellus Devel. Corp.), Brea, Calif., 1988-91; mgr. fin. analysis SW U.S. Catellus Devel. Corp., Anaheim, Calif., 1992-93; mgr. leasing Pacific Design Ctr., West Hollywood, Calif., 1994-95, dir. fin. and policy, 1995—. Calif. Bldg. Industry Assn. fellow, 1986, U. San Diego fellow, 1987. Mem. U. San Diego Grad. Bus. Students Assn., K.C. (fin. sec. 1990-91), Tau Kappa Epsilon. Republican. Roman Catholic. Home: 3805 Maxon Ln Chino CA 91710-2073 Office: Pacific Design Ctr #M-60 8687 Melrose Ave West Hollywood CA 90069-5701

KATHREN, RONALD LAURENCE, health physicist; b. Windsor, Ont., Can., June 6, 1937; s. Ben and Sally (Forman) K.; m. Susan Ruth Krafft, Dec. 24, 1964; children: SallyBeth, Daniel, Elana (dec.). BS, UCLA, 1957; MSc, U. Pitts., 1962. Diplomate Am. Bd. Health Physics (bd. dirs. 1982-84, sec.-treas. 1984); Am. Acad. Environ. Engrs., Am Bd. Med. Physics; registered profl. engr., Calif. Health physicist Lawrence Radiation Lab. U. Calif., Livermore, 1962-67; mgr. external dose evaluation, Battelle Pacific N.W. Labs., Richland, Wash., 1967-70, sr. rsch. scientist, 1970-72, staff scientist, program mgr., 1978-89; dir. U.S. Transuranium and Uranium Registries Hanford Environ. Health Found., 1989-92, prof., dir. U.S. Transuranium and Uranium Registries, Wash. State U., 1992—; U.S. expert Internat. Atomic Energy Agy., Caracas, Venezuela, 1977; affiliate assoc. prof. U. Wash., 1978-94, prof., 1994, program coordinator in radiol. scis., 1980-82, 86-88; cons. Adv. Com. Reactor Safeguards, Washington, 1979-89; cons. adv. com. Nuc. Waste, 1988-94; mem. adv. com. Richland City Schs., 1985-87; bd. dirs. Mid-Columbia Symphony, 1987-92, Nuc. Medicine Rsch. Working Group, 1994—; chmn. Nat. Coun. Radiation Protection and Measurements Sci. Com. on Collective Dose, 1991-95; mem. Nat. Coun. of Examiners for Engring. and Surveying Com. on Examinations for Profl. Engrs., 1993—. Author: Ionizing Radiation: Tumorigenic and Tumoricidal Effects, 1983; Radioactivity in the Environment, 1984; Radiation Protection, 1985, The Plutonium Story, 1994. Editor: (with others) Health Physics: A Backward Glance, 1980; Computer Applications in Health Physics, 1984, Environmental Health Physics, 1993. Contbr. numerous articles to profl. jours., tech. reports, and chpts. in books. USPHS fellow, 1961-62; recipient Arthur Humm award Nat. Registry Radiation Protection Technologists, 1988; named Hartman Orator Radiology Centennial, 1995. Mem. Health Physics Soc. (life fellow, pres. 1989-90, pres. Columbia chpt. 1971, dir. 1973-76, Elda E. Anderson award 1977, founders award 1985, Herbert M. Parker award 1994), Am. Assn. Physicists in Medicine, Am. Acad. Health Physics (bd. dirs. 1984-86, 93—), AAAS, Soc. Radiol. Protection (cert. in applied health physics). Home: 137 Spring St Richland WA 99352-1651 Office: Wash State Univ 100 Sprout Rd Richland WA 99352-1641

KATO, NORMAN SCOTT, cardiac surgeon, educator; b. Chgo., Dec. 30, 1955; s. Walter Yoneo and Anna Chieko (Kurata) K.; m. Nancy Jane Douts, July 20, 1985; children: Nicole Anna-Marie, Natalie Gene Yoneko. BA with distinction, Swarthmore Coll., 1977; MD, U. Pa., 1981. Diplomate Am. Bd. Med. Examiners, Am. Bd. Surgery with subspecialty in surg. critical care, Am. Bd. Thoracic Surgery. Intern in surgery U. Pa. Hosp., Phila., 1981-82, resident in surgery, 1982-86, chief resident in surgery, 1986-87; postdoctoral fellow in physiology U. Pa., Phila., 1987-89; resident in cardiothoracic surgery NYU, 1989-90, chief resident in cardiothoracic surgery, 1990-91; asst. prof. surgery UCLA Med. Ctr., 1991—; dir. GHCH/UCLA Heart Ctr., Granada Hills, 1993—; cons. Interqual, Boston, 1994—. Contbr. articles to profl. jours. Pfizer postdoctoral fellow Pfizer Pharms., 19[illegible]; grantee Am. Heart Assn., 1993. Mem. Phi Beta Kappa, Alpha Omega Alpha. Home: 10218 Briarwood Dr Los Angeles CA 90077-2522 Office: UCLA Med Ctr Divsn Cardiothoracic Surgery 10833 Le Conte Ave Los Angeles CA 90024

KATONA, ROBERT ROY, artist, sculptor; b. Athens, Ohio, Mar. 16, 1947; s. Arthur and Verna (Wendelin) K.; m. Jo Laverne Bell, 1980; children: Katherine Day, John Darren. Student, U. Colo., 1965. Numerous one-man shows, including Gallery One, Denver, 1985, 90, 91, Grace Harkin Gallery, N.Y., 1989, Chabot Gallery, San Jose, Calif., 1990, 93, C. Anthony Gallery, Dallas, 1990, 91, Fillmore Plaza Gallery, Denver, 1993; exhibited in group shows Denver Art Mus., 1968, 73-74, Munich Mus. Art, 1982, Taipei Mus. Fine Arts, 1983, Arabian Internat. Art Exhbn., 1982-85, Salmagundi Club, N.Y.C., 1983, Fine Arts Mus. of Long Island, N.Y., 1989, New Yorkers in Barcelona, Spain, 1990, also others; represented in permanent collections USAF Acad., also corp. and pvt. collections. Recipient Jenkins award Gilpin County Arts Assn., 1970, 74, 1st prize for book illustration Soc. Illustrators, 1976, 1st prize for graphics Grolla D'Oro Internat., Treviso, Italy, 1982.

KATSONIS, MICHAEL GEORGE, pharmacist; b. Harrisburg, Pa., Nov. 7, 1951; s. George Manuel and Doris Virginia (Geise) K. BS in Pharmacy, U. Pitts., 1974. Lic. pharmacist, Pa., Fla., Colo., Utah. Lift opr. Breckenridge (Colo.) Ski Area, 1985-86, 87-88; asst. mgr. Checker Auto Parts, Denver, 1986-87; staff pharmacist Pharmacy Mgmt. Svcs., Inc., Tampa, Fla., 1988-90, U. Fla. Student Health Ctr., Gainesville, 1990-92; pharmacy mgr. Winn-Dixie, Kissimmee, Fla., 1992-93; with Payless Drug Stores, 1993; staff pharmacist K-Mart Pharmacy, Orem, Utah, 1993-94; pharmacy mgr. K-Mart Pharmacy, Farmington, Utah, 1994—. Mem. United Way Chmn.'s Leadership Club, Gainesville, 1990-91, Rep. Nat. Com., Washington, 1991, Pres.'s Club, Washington, 1992, Campaign Coun., Washington, 1992—, Presdl. Roundtable, Washington, 1992—; life mem. Rep. Senatorial Inner Circle, Washington, 1992, Rep. Presdl. Task Force, Washington, 1992. Republican Senatorial medal of Freedom 1994. Fellow Nat. Cath. Pharmacists guild; mem. Am. Pharm. Assn., Am. Soc. Pharmacy Law, Fla. Pharmacy Assn. (orgnl. affairs coun. 1990-92), Alachua County Assn. Pharmacists (sec. 1991-92), Ctrl. Fla. Pharmacy Assn. (v.p.-elect 1992), Utah Pharmacy Assn. (life), Utah Elephant Club, Olympus-Crossroads Kiwanis Club Salt Lake City, Gold Spike Leadership Circle (bronze mem. 1992), Mystic Shrine El Kalah Temple (noble 1994, 95). Home: 147 Plumtree Ln Apt 7F Midvale UT 84047-1128

KATZ, ALAN ROY, public health educator; b. Pitts., Aug. 21, 1954; s. Leon B. and Bernice Sonia (Glass) K.; m. Donna Marie Crandall, Jan. 19, 1986. BA, U. Calif., San Diego, 1976; MD, U. Calif., Irvine, 1980; MPH, U. Hawaii, 1987; postgrad., U. So. Calif., 1980-81, U. Hawaii, 1982-83. Staff physician emergency medicine L.A. County U. So. Calif. Med. Ctr., 1981-82; staff physician, med. dir. Waikiki Health Ctr., Honolulu, 1983-87; dir. AIDS/STD prevention program Hawaii State Dept. of Health, Honolulu, 1987-88; asst. prof. dept. pub. health scis. U. Hawaii, Honolulu, 1988-94, assoc. prof., 1994—, dir. preventive medicine residency program, 1994—; bd. dirs. Hawaii AIDS Task Group; mem. Chlamydia control workgroup USPHS, 1985-87. Me. Leptospirosis ad hoc com. Hawaii State Dept. Health, Honolulu, 1988—, mem. prenatal screening adv. com., 1992—; mem. com. human subjects U. Hawaii, 1989—. USPHS Chlamydia Prevalence Survey grantee, Hawaii, 1986, Tuberculosis Survey grantee U. Hawaii, 1991; recipient presdl. citation for meritorious teaching, U. Hawaii, 1989, regents medal excellence in teaching U. Hawaii, 1992. Fellow Am. Coll. Preventive Medicine; mem. Am. Pub. Health Assn., Soc. Epidemiologic Rsch., Delta Omega. Office: U Hawaii Sch Pub Health Dept Pub Health Sci 1960 E West Rd Honolulu HI 96822-2319

KATZ, BARRETT, neuro-ophthalmologist; b. New York, June 8, 1949; m. Deborah Ann Borrelli, Sept. 23, 1981; children: Matthew, Jacob. AB, Colgate U., 1969; MD, Western Res. Sch. Medicine, 1973. Intern Parkland Meml. Hosp., Dallas, 1973-74; staff assoc. NIH, Bethesda, Md., 1974-75; resident in neurology Harvard Med. Sch., Boston, 1975-78; resident in ophthalmology Tufts-New Eng. Med. Ctr., Boston, 1978-81; fellow in neuro-ophthalmology U. Calif., San Francisco, 1981; asst. prof. depts. ophthalmology, neurology, neurosurgery U. Ariz., Tucson, 1982-84; asst. prof. depts. ophthalmology and neuroscis. U. Calif. San Diego, La Jolla, 1984-88, assoc. prof. depts. ophthalmology and neuroscis., 1988-89; prof., sr. scientist dept. ophthalmology Calif. Pacific Med. Ctr. and Smith-Kettlewell Eye Rsch. Inst., San Francisco, 1989—; The Wayne and Gladys Valley prof., vice-chmn. dept. ophthalmology Calif. Pacific Med. Ctr. and Smith-Kettlewell Eye Rsch. Inst, San Francisco, 1990—; sci. reviewer Investigative Ophthalmology and Visual Sci., Ophthalmology, Archives of Ophthalmology, Am. Jour. Ophthalmology, Jour. Clin. Neuro-Ophthalmology, Psychopharmacology, Survey of Ophthalmology, Archives of Neurology, Neuro-Ophthalmology. Contbr. over 140 articles to profl. jours. and conf. procs. Rsch. grantee VA Med. Ctr., The Arthur N. Pack Found., Found. Glaucoma Rsch., NIH, No. Calif. Soc. to Prevent Blindness. Office: Calif Pacific Med Ctr Smith-Kettleman Eye Rsch Inst 2340 Clay St San Francisco CA 94115

KATZ, ILLANA PAULETTE, writer; b. N.Y.C., May 30, 1946; d. Emanuel and Alice (Reich) Schear; m. David Arthur Katz, July 31, 1966; children: Heather, Todd, Ethan, Seth. BA in Anthropology, Calif. State U., 1977, postgrad. Pres., pub. Real Life Storybooks, Northridge, Calif., 1992—; mini-course instr. L.A. Unified Sch. Dist., 1985, 93; lectr. State Autism Conv., 1994, Nat. Autism Conv., 1994. Author: Joey and Sam, 1993 (award 1994), Show Me Where It Hurts, 1993, Uncle Jimmy, 1994, Sarah, 1994, Sunshine, Sit Down, Steven!, Hungry-Mind-Hungry-Body; (audio-cassette) Was Einstein Autistic?, 1994. Head of Israeli affairs United Synagogue, Beverly Hills, 1988; aliyah councelor Jewish Fedn., L.A., 1991—. Mem. Authors and Celebrities Forum (Award of Excellence 1994), Soc. of Children's Book Writers, Book Publicists Assn. Home: 8370 Kentland Ave West Hills CA 91304-3329 Office: Real Life Storybooks 8370 Kentland Ave Canoga Park CA 91304-3329

KATZ, JERI BETH, lawyer; b. Washington, Nov. 6, 1964; d. Stanley J. and Paula (Goldberg) K.; m. Daniel Alan Ezra, June 19, 1988 (div. Dec. 1990). BA, U. Md., 1987; JD, Cath. U., Washington, 1990. Bar: Md. 1990, D.C. 1991, U.S. Ct. Appeals (6th cir.) 1991, U.S. Ct. Internat. Trade 1992, Colo. 1994. Assoc. Winston & Strawn, Washington, 1990; ptnr. Law Offices Royal Daniel, Washington, 1990-94, Daniel & Katz, L.L.C., Breckenridge, Colo., 1994—. Home: PO Box 6602 Breckenridge CO 80424-6602 Office: Daniel & Katz LLC 130 Ski Hill Rd Ste 160 P O Box 567 Breckenridge CO 80424

KATZ, JERRY PAUL, corporate executive; b. L.A., Jan. 24, 1944; s. Samuel and Dorothy Rose (Solovay) K.; m. Judy Simmering, Sept. 10, 1985 (div. 1988); m. Julie Stacey, Aug. 26, 1990. AA, East L.A. Coll., 1964; BS, BA, Calif. State U., 1970. Registered sanitarian, Calif. Sanitarian L.A. County Health Dept., L.A., 1971-73; dir. Compton (Calif.) Model Cities Vector Control, 1973-74; health officer Lynwood (Calif.) City, 1974-76; pres., chief exec. officer Associated Industries, L.A., 1976—; cons., bd. dirs. All Am. Fire Protection, L.A., 1987—. Founding mem. Moore St. Homeowners Assn., Monterey Park, Calif., 1989—; mem. Nature Conservancy, World Wildlife Fund. Recipient World Record (2) hang gliding Nat. Assn. Aeronautics, 1977; named for Distance-Altitude Gain, Guinness Book of World Records, London, 1977. Mem. Native Am. Rights Fund, Green Peace, Surfrider Found., U.S. Hangliding Assn., Sea Shepard Soc. Office: Associated Industries 5140 Via Corona St Los Angeles CA 90022-2007

KATZ, JOHN W., lawyer, state official; b. Balt., June 3, 1943; s. Leonard Wallach and Jean W. (Kane) K.; m. Joan Katz, June 11, 1969 (div. 1982); 1 child, Kimberly Erin. BA, Johns Hopkins U., 1965; JD, U. Calif., Berkeley, 1969; DDL (hon.) U. Alaska, 1994. Bar: Alaska, Pa., U.S. Dist. Ct. D.C. 1971, U.S. Ct. Appeals (D.C. cir.), U.S. Tax Ct., U.S. Ct. Claims, U.S. Ct. Mil. Justice, U.S. Supreme Ct. Legis. and adminstrv. asst. to Congressman Howard W. Pollock of Alaska, Washington, 1969-70; legis. asst. to U.S. Senator Ted Stevens of Alaska, Washington, 1971; assoc. McGrath and Flint, Anchorage, 1972; gen. counsel Joint Fed. State Land Use Planning Commn. for Alaska, Anchorage, 1972-79; spl. counsel to Gov. Jay S. Hammond of Alaska, Anchorage and Washington, 1979-81; commr. Alaska Dept. Natural Resources, Juneau, 1981-83; dir. state fed. relations and spl. counsel to Gov. Bill Sheffield of Alaska, Washington and Juneau, 1983-86; dir. state-fed. relations, spl. counsel to Gov. Steve Cowper of Alaska, Washington, 1986-90, Gov. Walter J. Hickel of Alaska, Washington, 1990-94, Gov. Tony Knowles, 1994—; mem. Alaska Power Survey Exec. Adv. Com. of FPC, Anchorage, 1972-74; mem. spl. com. hard rock minerals Govs. Council of Sci. and Tech., Anchorage, 1979-80; guest lectr. on natural resources U. Alaska, U. Denver. Contbr. articles to profl. jours.; columnist Anchorage Times until 1991. Acad. supr. Alaska Externship Program, U. Denver Coll. Law, 1976-79; mem. Reagan-Bush transition team for U.S. Dept. Justice, 1980. Recipient Superior Sustained Performance award Joint Fed. State Land Use Planning Commn. for Alaska, 1978, Resolution of Commendation award Alaska Legis., 1988. Republican. Office: State of Alaska Office of Gov 444 N Capitol St NW # 336 Washington DC 20001-1512

KATZ, MAURICE HARRY, lawyer; b. N.Y.C., Jan. 18, 1937; s. Milton and Florence (Davies) K.; m. Margery Rosenberg, May 5, 1962; children: Brian, Bradley, Andrew. AB cum laude, Columbia U., 1958; JD, Harvard U., 1961. Bar: N.Y. 1962, U.S. Ct. Appeals N.Y. 1962, U.S. Supreme Ct. 1962, Calif. 1963. Assoc. Loeb & Loeb, L.A., 1962-64, Freshman, Marantz et al., Beverly Hills, Calif., 1964-66; ptnr. Grobe, Reinstein & Katz, Beverly Hills, 1966-76, Katz and Weisman, 1976-78; pvt. practice L.A., 1978—; prof. law U. San Fernando, L.A., 1965-76, U. West L.A., 1976-83; judge pro tem Beverly Hills Mcpl. Ct., 1968-70, L.A. Mcpl. Ct., 1985-88; hearing officer Los Angeles CSC, 1976-79; arbitrator L.A. County Superior Ct., 1980—,

Am. Assn. Arbitration, 1987—. Program chmn. Am. Art Coun., L.A. County Mus. Art, 1983-86, chmn., 1988-91; chmn. acquisition fine arts com. Skirball Mus., Hebrew Union Coll., L.A., 1985-86; trustee Ennis-Brown House, 1980-84, Archives Am. Art-Smithsonian Instn., 1991-94; sec. L.A.-Bordeaux Sister City Com., 1981—; judge L.A. County Wine Fair, 1981-84; overseer Huntington Libr., Art Collections and Bot. Gardens, 1993—. Served with USMCR, 1961-62. Mem. Calif. Bar Assn., L.A. County Bar Assn., Century City Bar Assn., Beverly Hills Bar Assn., Wine and Food Soc. Hollywood (chmn. 1984-85), Chaîne des Rôtisseurs, Phi Beta Kappa. Jewish.

KATZ, MICHAEL JEFFERY, lawyer; b. Detroit, May 11, 1950; s. Wilfred Lester and Bernice (Ackerman) K. BE with honors, U. Mich., 1972; JD, U. Colo., 1976; cert. mgmt., U. Denver, 1985, cert. fin. mgmt., 1990. Bar: Colo. 1978. Rsch. atty., immigration specialist Colo. Rural Legal Svcs., Denver, 1976-77, supervising atty. migrant farm lab., 1977-78; ind. contractor Colo. Sch. Fin., Denver, 1978-79; sole practice Denver, 1978-86; assoc. Levine and Pitler, P.C., Denver, 1986-88; gen. counsel, sec. Grease Monkey Internat., Inc., Denver, 1988-92; prin. Katz & Co., Denver, 1992—; exec. v.p. Nat. Network Exchange, Inc., Denver, 1992—; lectr. on incorporating small bus. and real estate purchase agreements Front Range Coll., 1986—, condr. various seminars on real estate and landlord/tenant law, 1980—; of counsel Levine and Pitler, P.C., Englewood, Colo., 1985—. Contbr. Action Line column Rocky Mountain News; contbr. articles to profl. jours. Mem. Assn. Trial Lawyers Am., Am. Arbitration Assn. (mem. panel of arbitrators 1989), Denver Bar Assn. (mem. law day com. 1985—, mem. real estate com. 1980—, mem. pro bono svcs. com. 1984—), U.S. Yacht Racing Assn., Dillon Yacht Club. Office: Nat Network Exchange Inc 820 16th St Mall Ste 720 Denver CO 80202-2913

KATZ, RICHARD EMANUEL, photographer, educator; b. Montreal, June 14, 1960; came to the U.S., 1988; s. Abe and Carman Josie (Ingelrelst) K. BA, McGill U., 1985; postgrad., Antioch U. Tchr. Laurenval Sch. Bd., Laval, Canada, 1982-85; tchr. Alexander Moss High Sch., Tel Aviv, 1986-87; photojournalist Jerusalem, 1985-88; tchr. Spring Creek Cmty., Thompson Falls, Mont., 1988-89; photojournalist Sanders County Herald, Thompson Falls, 1989-90, Pierce County Herald, Puyallup, Wash., 1992-93; counselor YouthCare, Seattle, 1991-94; tchr. Temple Beth Am, Seattle, 1991—; photographer, tchr. Seattle. Recipient numerous awards Soc. Profl. Journalists, 1992, 93, 2d place awardWash. Newspaper Pubs. Assn., 1993. Mem. Nat. Press Photographers Assn. Jewish. Home: 512 N 73d St Seattle WA 98103

KATZ, ROBERT IRWIN, retired physician; b. Springfield, Mass., Dec. 16, 1924; s. Julius Louis and Florence (Greenburg) K. Student, Tufts Coll., 1942-44; MD, Tufts U., 1948. Diplomate Am. Bd. Surgery, Am. Bd. Thoracic Surgery, Nat. Bd. Med. Examiners. Intern Charity Hosp. of La., New Orleans, 1948-49, resident in pathology, 1949-50; resident in gen. surgery Boston City Hosp., 1953-56; resident in surg. oncology Anderson Cancer Ctr. U. Tex., Houston, 1956-57; resident in thoracic surgery VA Hosp., L.A., 1960-61, Children's Hosp., L.A., 1961; chief thoracic surgery V.A. Hosps., Sepulveda/San Fernando, Calif., 1962-70; pvt. practice general and thoracic surgery L.A., 1970-86; head gen. surgery Naval Hosp., Corpus Christie, Tex., 1987; head dept. surgery Naval Hosp., Cherry Point, N.C., 1988-90; surgeon USS New Jersey WES PAC, 1986, 88; ret., 1990; clin. asst. prof. UCLA Med. Ctr., 1969-89, U. So. Calif., L.A., 1964-91. Contbr. articles to profl. jours. Tournament ofcl. So. Calif. Tennis Umpires Assn., L.A., 1972—; commr. Calif. Bd. Medicine, Sacramento, Calif., 1980—. With USN, 1944-45, surgeon USMC, 1950-52, US Merchant Marines, 1953. Recipient clin. fellowship Am. Cancer Soc., Houston, 1957-58. Fellow Am. Coll. Chest Physicians; mem. AAAS, Soc. Thoracic Surgeons, So. Med. Assn., So. Assn. Oncologists, Assn. Mil. Surgeons of U.S., Marine Corps Hist. Soc., Nat. Wildlife Fedn. (life), U.S. Tennis Assn. (life), Naval Res. Assn., M.D. Anderson Assocs. Republican. Jewish. Home and Office: 1733 Centinela Ave Santa Monica CA 90404-4238

KATZ, ROGER, pediatrician, educator; b. Menominee, Mich., Feb. 23, 1938; s. Peter W. and Mae C. (Chudacott) K.; m. Barbara Morquelan, Feb. 5, 1966; children: Carl, Gary, Robyn. BS, U. Wis., 1960; MD, U. Louisville, 1965. Diplomate Am. Bd. Allergy and Immunology, Am. Bd. Pediatric Allergy, Am. Bd. Pediatrics. Clin. prof. pediatrics UCLA, 1978—; speaker in field. Author and editor sci. books and manuscripts. Maj. U.S. Army, 1970-72. Fellow Am. Acad. Allergy, Asthma and Immunology, Am. Coll. Allergy, Asthma and Immunology (bd. regents 1990-93), Am. Acad. Pediat., Am. Coll. Chest Physicians, Joint Coun. Allergy and Immunology (pres. 1986-90). Office: 100 UCLA Med Plz 552 Los Angeles CA 90095-6970

KATZ, STEVEN JOSEPH, school counselor; b. Springfield, Ohio, June 2, 1946; s. Robert and Mildred (Popov) K. BA in Econs., Oberlin Coll., 1968; MEd in Elem. Edn., Antioch Coll., Yellow Springs, Ohio, 1971; MS in Anthropology, U. Oreg., 1979, MS in Counseling, 1980. Cert. Nat. Bd. Cert Counselors, Nat. Bd. Cert. Sch. Counselors. Psychiat. aide Lincoln (Nebr.) State Hosp., 1967; elem. tchr. Phila. Pub. Schs., 1979-72; firefighter U.S. Forest Svc., Trout Lake, Wash., 1975-77; cultural resource archaeologist U.S. Forest Svc./Bur. Land Mgmt., Oreg., 1978-87; elem. sch. counselor, tchr. Bethel Sch. Dist., Eugene, Oreg., 1986—; mem. at risk team Bethel Sch. Dist., Eugene, 1986-89, mem., chair counselor adv. com., 1990-94, co-founder family advocacy cmty. team, 1993-94, mem. leadership team, 1992-94. Co-author: An Assessment of Mental Health Svcs. for Native Americans in Aouthwest Oregon SW Oreg. Indian Health Project & Oreg. State Dept. Human Resources, 1981, (presentation) Effective Classroom, Group and Individual Guidance, 1994; program host KLCC-FM, Eugene, 1979—. Mem. Oreg. Tuba Ensemble Oreg. Tuba Assn., Eugene, 1979—; bd. mem. Eugene Symphonic Band, Eugene, 1991-94. Mem. ACA, Oreg. Counseling Assn., Oreg. Soc. Individual Psychology. Office: Bethel Sch Dist 4640 Barger Dr Eugene OR 97402

KATZ, TONNIE, newspaper editor. BA, Barnard Coll., 1966; MSc, Columbia U., 1967. Editor, reporter newspapers including The Quincy Patriot Ledger, Boston Herald Am., Boston Globe; Sunday/projects editor Newsday; mng. editor Balt. News Am., 1983-86, The Sun, San Bernardino, Calif., 1986-88; asst. mng. editor for news The Orange County Register, Santa Ana, Calif., 1988-89, mng. editor, 1989-92, editor, v.p., 1992—. Office: Freedom Newspapers Inc Orange County Register 625 N Grand Ave Santa Ana CA 92701-4347

KATZ, VERA, mayor, former college administrator, state legislator; b. Dusseldorf, Germany, Aug. 3, 1933; came to U.S., 1940; d. Lazar Pistrak and Raissa Goodman; m. Mel Katz (div. 1985); 1 child, Jesse. BA, Bklyn. Coll., 1955, postgrad., 1955-57. Market research analyst TIMEX, B.T. Babbitt, N.Y.C., 1957-62; mem. Oreg. Ho. of Reps., Salem; former dir. devel. Portland Community Coll., from 1982; mayor City of Portland, Oreg., 1993—; mem. Gov.'s Council on Alcohol and Drug Abuse Programs, Oreg. Legis., Salem, 1985—; mem. adv. com. Gov.'s Council on Health, Fitness and Sports, Oreg. Legis., 1985—; mem. Gov.'s Commn. on Sch. Funding Reform; mem. Carnegie task Force on Teaching as Profession, Washington, 1985-87; vice-chair assembly Nat. Conf. State Legis., Denver, 1986—. Recipient Abigail Scott Duniway award Women in Communications, Inc., Portland, 1985, Jeanette Rankin First Woman award Oreg. Women's Polit. Caucus, Portland, 1985, Leadership award The Neighborhood newspaper Portland, 1985, Woman of Achievement award Commn. for Women, 1985, Outstanding Legis. Advocacy award Oreg. Primary Care Assn., 1985, Service to Portland Pub. Sch. Children award Portland Pub. Schs., 1985. Fellow Am. Leadership Forum (founder Oreg. chpt.); mem. Dem. Legis. Leaders Assn., Nat. Bd. for Profl. Teaching Standards. Democrat. Jewish. Office: Office of the Mayor City Hall Rm 303 1220 SW 5th Ave Portland OR 97204-1913*

KATZBECK, KAREN LYNN, accounting executive; b. Chgo., Aug. 11, 1951; d. Frank A. and Lorraine S. (Williams) K.; m. Carl A. Petersen, June 17, 1972 (div. June 1975); m. Jack L. Shishido, Dec. 10, 1982 (div. Oct. 1991). BS, U. Ill.-Chgo., 1976. CPA. Mem. tax staff Price Waterhouse, Chgo., 1977-78, tax sr./mgr., Tokyo, 1978-82, tax mgr., L.A., 1982-83, sr. mgr., 1984-85; mgr. internat. tax Walt Disney Co., Burbank, Calif., 1985-88; chief fin. officer Santiago Air Conditioning, 1988-89; v.p. fin., adminstrn. Houlihan, Lokey, Howard & Zukin, Inc., L.A., 1989-93; exec. dir. Cox, Castle and Nicholson, L.A., 1993, pvt. practice, 1994—. Active Asia Pacific Coun. Am. Chambers, Tokyo, 1979-82. Recipient Pres.'s Leadership award Am. C. of C. in Japan, 1980. Mem. AICPA, Calif. CPA Soc., Am. Soc. Women CPAs, Japan-Am. Soc., Glendale C. of C. Office: 2041 Parkmount Dr Ste 201 Glendale CA 91206-1746

KATZUNG, BERTRAM GEORGE, pharmacologist; b. Mineola, N.Y., June 11, 1932; m. Alice V. Camp; children: Katharine Blanche, Brian Lee. BA, Syracuse U., 1953; MD, SUNY, Syracuse, 1957; PhD, U. Calif., San Francisco, 1962. Prof. U. Calif., San Francisco, 1958—. Author: Drug Therapy, 1991, Basic and Clinical Pharmacology, 1995, Pharmacology, Examination and Board Review, 1995; contbr. to profl. jours. Markle scholar. Mem. AAAS, AAUP, Am. Soc. Pharmacology and Exptl. Therapeutics, Biophysical Soc., Fed. Am. Scientists, Internat. Soc. Heart Rsch., Soc. Gen. Physiologists, Western Pharmacology Soc., N.Y. Acad. Sci., Phi Beta Kappa, Alpha Omega Alpha, Golden Gate Computer Soc. Office: UCSF Dept Pharmacology PO Box 0450 San Francisco CA 94143

KAUFFMAN, GEORGE BERNARD, chemistry educator; b. Phila., Sept. 4, 1930; s. Philip Joseph and Laura (Fisher) K.; m. Ingeborg Salomon, June 5, 1952 (div. Dec. 1969); children: Ruth Deborah (Mrs. Martin H. Bryskier), Judith Miriam (Mrs. Mario L. Reposo); m. Laurie Marks Papazian, Dec. 21, 1969; stepchildren: Stanley Robert Papazian, Teresa Lynn Papazian Baron, Mary Ellen Papazian Yoder. BA with honors, U. Pa., 1951; PhD, U. Fla., 1956. Grad. asst. U. Fla., 1951-55; rsch. participant Oak Ridge Nat. Lab., 1955; instr. U. Tex., Austin, 1955-56; rsch. chemist Humble Oil & Refining Co., Baytown, Tex., 1956, GE, Cin., 1957, 59; asst. prof. chemistry Calif. State U., Fresno, 1956-61; assoc. prof. Calif. State U., 1961-66, prof., 1966—, guest lectr. coop. lecture tours Am. Chem. Soc., 1971; vis. scholar U. Calif., Berkeley, 1976, U. Puget Sound, 1978; dir. undergrad. rsch. participation program NSF, 1972. Author: Alfred Werner—Founder of Coordination Chemistry, 1966, Classics in Coordination Chemistry, Part I, 1968, Part II, 1976, Part III, 1978, Werner Centennial, 1967, Teaching the History of Chemistry, 1971, Coordination Chemistry: Its History through the Time of Werner, 1977, Inorganic Coordination Compounds, 1981, The Central Science: Essays on the Uses of Chemistry, 1984, Frederick Soddy (1877-1956): Early Pioneer in Radiochemistry, 1986, Aleksandr Porfirevich Borodin: A Chemist's Biography, 1988, Coordination Chemistry: A Century of Progress, 1994; contbr. numerous articles to profl. publs.; contbg. editor: Jour. Coll. Sci. Teaching, 1973—, The Hexagon, 1980—, Polyhedron, 1983-85, Industrial Chemist, 1985-88, Jour. Chem. Edn., 1987—, Today's Chemist, 1989-91, The Chemical Intelligencer, 1994—; guest editor: Coodination Chemistry Centennial Symposium (C3S) issue, Polyhedron, 1994; editor tape lecture series: Am. Chem. Soc, 1975-81. Named Outstanding Prof. Calif. State U. and Colls. System, 1973, recipient Exceptional Merit Service award, 1984, Meritorious Performance and Profl. Promise award, 1986-87, 88-89; recipient Coll. Chemistry Tchr. Excellence award Mfg. Chemists Assn., 1976, Chugaev medal, 1976, Kurnakov medal, 1990, Chernyaev medal, 1991 USSR Acad. Sci., George C. Pimentel awd. in Chemical Education, Am. Chemical Soc., 1993, Dexter award in history of chemistry, 1978, Marc-Auguste Pictet medal, Société de Physique et d'Histoire Naturelle de Genève, 1992, Pres.'s medal of Distinction Calif. State U., Fresno, 1994 ; Research Corp. grantee, 1956-57, 57-59, 59-61, Am. Chem. Soc. Petroleum Research Fund grantee, 1962-64, 65-69, Am. Philos. Soc. grantee, 1963-64, 69-70, NSF grantee, 1960-61, 63-64, 67-69, 76-77, NEH grantee, 1982-83; John Simon Guggenheim Meml. Found. fellow, 1972-73; grantee, 1975; Strindberg fellow Swedish Inst., Stockholm, 1983. Mem. AAAS, AAUP, Assn. Univ. Pa. Chemists, History of Sci. Soc., Soc. History Alchemy and Chemistry, Am. Chem. Soc. (chmn. divsn. history of chemistry 1969, mem. exec. com. 1970, councilor 1976-78, George C. Pimentel award in Chem. Edn., 1993), Mensa, Sigma Xi, Phi Lambda Upsilon, Phi Kappa Phi, Alpha Chi Sigma, Gamma Sigma Epsilon. Home: 1609 E Quincy Ave Fresno CA 93720-2309 Office: Calif State U Dept Chemistry Fresno CA 93740

KAUFMAN, ALBERT I., lawyer; b. N.Y.C., Oct. 2, 1936; s. Israel and Pauline (Pardes) K.; m. Ruth Feldman, Jan. 25, 1959; 1 son, Michael Paul. AA, L.A. City Coll., 1957; BA, U. San Fernando Valley, 1964, JD, 1966. Bar: Calif. 1967, U.S. Ct. Appeals (9th cir.) 1968, U.S. Supreme Ct. 1971, U.S. Dist. Ct. (cen. dist.) Calif. 1967, U.S. Tax Ct. 1971, U.S. Ct. Internat. Trade 1981. Sole practice, Encino, Calif., 1967—; judge pro tem L.A. Mcpl. Ct., 1980—, L.A. Superior Ct., 1991—; family law mediator L.A. Superior Ct., 1980—. Mem. Pacific S.W. regional bd. Anti-Defamation league of B'nai B'rith, 1970-91. Served with USAF, 1959-65, to col. CAP, 1956—. Recipient Disting. Svc. award B'nai B'rith, 1969; Exceptional Svc. award CAP, 1977. Mem. ABA, L.A. County Bar Assn., San Fernando Valley Bar Assn., Consumer Atty. Assn. of Calif., Consumer Atty. Assn. L.A. Republican. Clubs: Toastmasters, Westerners 1117 (pres. 1969), B'nai B'rith (pres. 1971-72), Santa Monica Yacht (judge adv.) Office: 17609 Ventura Blvd Ste 201 Encino CA 91316-3825

KAUFMAN, CHARLES DAVID, controller; b. N.Y.C., Apr. 17, 1931; s. M. Laurence Kaufman; m. Elvira Sampere Camps, Mar. 1, 1955; children: John, Janet. BS, Northwestern U., 1952; MBA, NYU, 1958. CPA, N.Y. Fin. analyst Nestle Co., Stamford, Conn., 1958-61; area contr. IBM World Trade Corp., Mexico City, 1967-69; dir. fin. controls ITT Corp., Brussels and N.Y.C., 1974-85, controller, 1985-94; ret., 1994. Cpl. U.S. Army, 1952-54. Mem. AICPAs, N.Y. Soc. CPAs, Ariz. Soc. CPAs.

KAUFMAN, DAVID GRAHAM, construction company executive; b. North Canton, Ohio, Mar. 20, 1937; s. DeVere and Josephine Grace (Graham) K.; student Kent State U., 1956; grad. Internat. Corr. Schs., 1965; grad. N.Y. Inst. Photography, 1983; postgrad. Calif. Coast U.; m. Carol Jean Monzione, Oct. 5, 1957 (div. Aug. 1980); children—Gregory Allan, Christopher Patrick. Machinist apprentice Hoover Co., North Canton, Ohio, 1955-57; draftsman-designer Goodyear Aircraft Corp., Akron, Ohio, 1957-60, Boeing Co., Seattle, 1960-61; designer Berger Industries, Seattle, 1961-62, Puget Sound Bridge & Drydock, Seattle, 1963, C.M. Lovsted, Seattle, 1963-64, Tracy, Brunstrom & Dudley, Seattle, 1964, Rubens & Pratt Engrs., Seattle, 1965-66; founder, owner, Profl. Drafting Svcs., Seattle, 1965, Profl. Take-Off Svcs., Seattle, 1966, Profl. Representation Svcs., Seattle, 1967, pres. Kaufman Inc., Seattle, 1967-83, Kaufman-Alaska Inc., Juneau, 1975-83 , Kaufman-Alaska Constructors, Inc., Juneau, 1975-83. Trustee, advisor Kaufman Internat., The Kaufman Group, Kaufman Enterprises; constrn. mgr. U. Alaska, 1979-84; constrn. cons. Alaskan native and Eskimo village corps., 1984—; prin. Kaufman S.W. Assocs., N. Mex., 1984—, Graham Internat., 1992—. Mem. Constrn. Specifications Inst., Associated Gen. Contractors Seattle Constrn. Council, Producers Council Oreg., Wash., Idaho, Hawaii, Alaska, Portland C. of C., Nat. Eagle Scout Assn. Republican. Roman Catholic. Club: Toastmasters (past gov.). Lodge:Lions. Home: PO Box 1781 Santa Fe NM 87504-1781 Office: PO Box 458 Haines AK 99827-0458

KAUFMAN, EDWARD REDDING, psychiatrist, educator. BA, Temple U., 1956; MD, Jefferson Med. Coll., 1960. Intern L.A. County Hosp., 1960-61; resident N.Y. State Psychiat. Inst., Columbia Presbyn. Med. Ctr., N.Y.C., 1961-64; med. dir. chem. dependency progrm Capistrano by the Sea Hosp., Dana Point, Calif., 1991—; psychiatrist N.Y. State Psychiat. Inst., 1966-67, St. Lukes Hosp., 1967-70; dir. N.Y.C. Prison Mental Health Svcs., 1970-72; pvt. practice N.Y.C., 1972-77, Irvine, Calif., 1977—; clin. prof. U. Calif., Irvine, 1992—; examiner Am. Bd. Psychiatry and Neurology, 1980—; E. Pumpian-Mindlin Ann. Vis. professorship U. Okla., 1988. Author: Substance Abuse and Family Therapy, 1985; author: (with others) Substance Abuse: Clin. Problems and Perspectives, 1981, Adolescent and Family Therapy: A Handbook of Theory and Practice, 1985, Alcohol Abuse Treatment Research, 1985, Psychotherapy of Addicted Persons, 1994; editor-in-chief Am. Jour. Drug and Alcohol Abuse, 1974—; exec. editor: Internat. Jour. Addictions, 1980—; editorial bd. Advances in Alcohol and Substance Abuse, 1980—, Clin. Textbook of Addictive Disorders, 1990; editor: Drug Abuse: Modern Trends, Issues and Perspective, 1978, Critical Concerns in the Field of Drug Abuse, 1979, Family Therapy of Drug and Alcohol Abuse, 1979, 2d edit. 1992, Encyclopedic Handbook of Alcoholism, 1982, Familientherpie Bei Alkohol und Drogenabhaniegkeit, 1983, Power to Change: Family Case Studies in The Treatment of Alcoholism, 1984; contbr. articles to profl. jours. Fellow USPHS, 1959; grantee NIH, 1965, Van Ameringen Found., 1968-70, Lower East Side Svc. Ctr., 1972-76, U. Calif., Irvine, 1980-94, NIMH, 1983-86, Calif. Dept. Mental Health, 1985-88, Beverly Lowry Rsch. Endowment, 1986. Fellow Am. Psychiat. Assn. Home: 31105 Holly Dr Laguna Beach CA 92677-2620 Office: Capistrano by the Sea Hosp 34000 Capistrano by Sea Dr PO Box 398 Dana Point CA 92629

KAUFMAN, HERBERT MARK, finance educator; b. Bronx, N.Y., Nov. 1, 1946; s. Henry and Betty (Fried) K.; m. Helen Laurie Fox, July 23, 1967; 1 child, Jonathan Hart. BA, SUNY, Binghamton, 1967; PhD, Pa. State U., 1972. Economist Fed. Nat. Mortgage Assn., Washington, 1972-73; asst. prof. Ariz. State U., Tempe, 1973-76; econs. prof. Ariz. State U., 1980-88; fin. prof. Ariz. State U., Tempe, 1988—, chair dept. fin., 1991—; exec. dir. Ctr. for Fin. System, chmn. dept. fin. Ariz. State U., 1988—; cons. World Bank, Washington, 1985-86, Gen. Acctg. Office, Washington, 1985, Congl. Budget Office, Washington, 1980. Author: Financial Markets, Financial Institutions and Money, 1983, (with others) The Political Economy of Policy Making, 1979, Money and Banking, 1991; contbr. articles to profl. jours. Mem. Am. Econ. Assn., Am. Fin. Assn., Nat. Assn. of Bus. Economists. Home: 1847 E Calle De Caballos Tempe AZ 85284-2505 Office: Ariz State U Dept Fin Tempe AZ 85287

KAUFMAN, IRVING, retired engineering educator; b. Geinsheim, Germany, Jan. 11, 1925; came to US., 1938, naturalized, 1945; s. Albert and Hedwig Kaufmann; m. Ruby Lee Dordek, Sept. 10, 1950; children—Eve Deborah, Sharon Anne, Julie Ellen. B.E., Vanderbilt U., 1945; M.S., U. Ill., 1949, Ph.D., 1957. Engr. RCA Victor, Indpls., Ind. and Camden, N.J., 1945-48; instr., research assoc. U. Ill., Urbana, 1949-56; sr. mem. tech. staff Ramo-Wooldridge & Space Tech. Labs., Calif., 1957-64; prof. engrng. Ariz. State U., 1965-94, ret., 1994; founder, dir. Solid State Research Lab., 1968-78; collaborator Los Alamos Nat. Lab., 1989, 91; vis. scientist Consiglio Nazionale delle Ricerche, Italy, 1973-74; vis. prof. U. Auckland, N.Z., 1974; liaison scientist U.S. Office Naval Rsch., London, 1978-80; lectr. and cons. elec. engrng. Contbr. articles to profl. jours. Recipient Disting. Research award Ariz. State U. Grad. Coll., 1986-87; Sr. Fulbright research fellow Italy, 1964-65, 73-74, Am. Soc. for Engrng. Edn./Naval Rsch. Lab. fellow, 1988. Fellow IEEE (life, Phoenix sect. leadership award 1994); mem. Electromagnetics Acad., Gold Key (hon.), Sigma Xi, Tau Beta Pi, Eta Kappa Nu, Pi Mu Epsilon. Jewish. Office: Ariz State U Dept Elec And Engring Tempe AZ 85287

KAUFMAN, JUDITH DIANE, English language educator, consultant; b. Boston, Feb. 10, 1947; d. David G. and Shirley Bernice (Goodman) K. BA in Russian Lang. and Lit., U. Chgo., 1970, MA in Russian Lit., 1972, PhD in Comparative Lit., 1978. Editl. asst. Acta Cytologica, Chgo., 1977-79; vis. asst. prof. English Eastern Wash. U., Cheney, 1979-82, dir. tech. comm. program, 1980—, asst. prof. English, 1982-85, assoc. prof. English, 1985-92, prof. English, 1992—; cons. tech. writing, editing St. Martin's Press, N.Y.C., 1983-85, Little, Brown, Boston, 1986, Holt, Rinehart & Winston, N.Y.C., 1986, Harper & Row, N.Y.C., 1988, Scott, Foresman, Glenview, Ill., 1989-90, Blair Press, Boston, 1991, Harper Collins, N.Y.C., 1992, Harcourt Brace Jovanovich, Ft. Worth, 1992-93, Intercollegiate Ctr. Nursing Edn., Spokane, Wash., 1990-92. Assoc. editor: Differential Social Impacts of Rural Resource Development, 1986; contbr. articles to profl. jours. Mem. planning com. Wash. Ctr. for Improving the Quality of Undergrad. Edn., 1992—. Woodrow Wilson fellow, 1970-71, Nat. Def. Edn. Act Title VI fellow, 1972-74, Josephine de Karman fellow, 1974-75. Mem. AAUP, MLA, Nat. Coun. Tchrs. English, Soc. Tech. Comm. (sr., chpt. employment mgr. 1990—), Assn. Tchrs. Tech. Writing, Coun. Programs in Tech. and Sci. Comm., Rocky Mountain Modern Lang. Assn., U. Chgo. Alumni (schs. com.), Phi Beta Kappa. Jewish. Office: Eastern Wash U MS-25 526 5th St Cheney WA 99004-2431

KAUFMAN, JULIAN MORTIMER, broadcasting company executive, consultant; b. Detroit, Apr. 3, 1918; s. Anton and Fannie (Newman) K.; m. Katherine LaVerne Likins, May 6, 1942; children: Nikki, Keith Anthony. Grad. high sch., Newark. Pub. Elizabeth (N.J.) Sunday Sun, Inc., 1937-39; account exec. Tolle Advt. Agy., San Diego, 1947-49; pub. Tucson Shopper, 1948-50; account exec. ABC, San Francisco, 1949-50; mgr. Sta. KPHO-TV, Phoenix, 1950-52; gen. mgr., v.p. Bay City TV Corp., San Diego, 1952-85; v.p. Jai Alai Films, Inc., San Diego, 1961—; TV cons. Julian Kaufman, Inc., San Diego, 1985—; dir. Spanish Internat. Broadcasting, Inc., L.A. Contbr. articles to profl. jours.; producer (TV show) Pick a Winner. Mem. Gov.'s adv. bd., Mental Health Assn., 1958—; bd. dirs. Francis Parker Sch., San Diego Better Bus. Bur., 1979-84, San Diego Conv. and Visitors Bur., World Affairs Coun., Pala Indian Mission. Served with USAAF, 1942-46. Recipient Peabody award, 1975, Emmy award, 1980. Mem. San Diego C. of C., Advt. and Sales Club, Sigma Delta Chi. Republican. Clubs: San Diego Press, University (San Diego). Home: 3125 Montesano Rd Escondido CA 92029-7302 Office: 8253 Ronson Rd San Diego CA 92111-2004

KAUFMAN, STEPHAN, news director. AA, San Bernardino Valley Coll., 1967; BS, San Diego State U., 1970; postgrad., U. Denver, 1978. News dir. Sta. KCKC, San Bernardino, 1970-71, Sta. WORC, Worchester, Mass., 1971-72; newsman Sta. WAVZ, New Haven, Conn., 1972-73; asst. news dir. Sta. WHK, Cleve., 1973-74, Sta. KLAK, Denver, 1974-75; newsman Sta. KIMN/KYGO, Denver, 1975-81; news dir. Sta. KSLQ, St. Louis, 1981-82; news anchor Sta. KSD-FM, St. Louis, 1982; news dir. Sta. KVET/KASE, Austin, 1983, Sta. KNIX FM/KCWW AM, Phoenix, 1983-91; midday news anchor Sta. KTAR, Phoenix, 1991-93; news dir. Sta. KGA, Spokane, Wash., 1993—. Home: 32122 N Elk-Chattaroy Rd Chattaroy WA 99003 Office: KGA Radio PO Box 30013 Spokane WA 99223-3026

KAUNE, JAMES EDWARD, ship repair company executive, former naval officer; b. Santa Fe, N.Mex., Mar. 4, 1927; s. Henry Eugene and Lucile (Carter) K.; B.S., U.S. Naval Acad., 1950; Naval Engr. degree Mass. Inst. Tech., 1955; B.S. in Metallurgy, Carnegie-Mellon U., 1960; m. Pauline Stamatos, June 24, 1956; children: Bradford Scott, Audrey Lynn, Jason Douglas. Commd. ensign U.S. Navy, 1950, advanced through grades to capt., 1970; asst. gunnery officer U.S.S. Floyd B. Parks, 1950-52; project officer U.S.S. Gyatt, Boston Naval Shipyard, 1955-57; main propulsion officer U.S.S. Tarawa, 1957-58; asst. planning officer Her Majesty's Canadian Dockyard, Halifax, N.S., Can., 1960-62; repair officer U.S.S. Cadmus, 1962-64; fleet maintenance officer Naval Boiler and Turbine Lab., 1964-68; various shipyard assignments, 1968-70, material staff officer U.S. Naval Air Forces Atlantic Fleet, 1971-74; production officer Phila. Naval Shipyard, 1974-79; comdr. Long Beach Naval Shipyard, Calif.; exec. v.p. Am. Metal Bearing Co., Garden Grove, Calif., from 1979; gen. mgr. San Francisco div. Topp Shipyards, Alameda, Calif., v.p. engrng. Point Richmond Shipyard, Calif., 1983-84; v.p. engrng., mktg. Service Engrng. Corp, San Francisco, 1984-92; CEO Am. Modular Power Systems, San Francisco, 1992—. Mem. Am. Soc. Naval Engrs., Am. Soc. Quality Control, Soc. Naval Architects and Marine Engrs., U.S. Naval Inst., Am. Soc. Metals. Episcopalian. Club: Masons. Contbr. articles to profl. jours. Home: 403 Camino Sobrante Orinda CA 94563-1844 Office: Am Modular Power Systems Russ Bldg 235 Montgomery St Ste 820 San Francisco CA 94104-2906

KAUNE, WILLIAM TYLER, physicist; b. Everett, Wash., Aug. 31, 1940; s. Tyler and Mary (Beuttler) K.; m. Gayle Rogers, May 6, 1972; children: Lauren E., Amelia A. BS in Physics, U. Wash., 1966; PhD in Physics, Stanford U., 1973. Asst. prof. physics Loyola Marymount U., L.A., 1973-75; staff engr. Battelle-N.W., Richland, Wash., 1980-87; physicist Nat. Bur. Standards, Boulder, Colo., 1987-88; sr. scientist, v.p. Enertech Cons., Campbell, Calif., 1988-91; chief scientist, pres. EM Factors, Richland, Wash., 1991—; organizer and chmn. workshops. Author: (with others) Biological Effects of Extremely Low-Frequency Electromagnetic Fields, 1970; contbr. numerous chpts. to books and articles to profl. jours. Fellow IEEE (sr., founding chmn. 1979-82, mem. working group coms.), Am. Inst. Biol. Scis., Bioelectro Magnetic Soc. (bd. dirs. 1980-83, mem. coms., editl. bd. jours. 1981-87). Office: EM Factors 530 Lee Blvd Richland WA 99352-4225

KAUNITZ, JONATHAN DAVIDSON, physician; b. N.Y.C., Nov. 6, 1950; s. Paul Ehrlich and Rita (Davidson) K.; m. Christine Lee, July 31, 1983; children: Justin Lee, Genevieve Jung. BA in Molecular Biology, Columbia Coll., 1972, MD, 1976. Diplomate Am. Bd. Internal Medicine, Am. Bd. Gastroenterology. Intern in medicine Presbyn. Hosp., N.Y.C., 1976-77, resident in medicine, 1977-79; gastroenterology fellow U. Calif., San

Francisco, 1979-80, gastrointestinal rsch. fellow, 1980-81; gastrointestinal rsch. fellow U. Calif., L.A., 1981-82; asst. prof. medicine U. Calif. L.A. Sch. Medicine, 1983-91; assoc. investigator VA Career Devel. Series, 1984-85, rsch. assoc., 1985-88, clin. investigator, 1990-95; assoc. dir. UCLA Integrated Tng. Program in Digestive Diseases, 1986-90; assoc. prof. dept. medicine Sch. Medicine UCLA, 1991—; assoc. chief med. svc. gastrointestinal sect. Wadsworth VA Med. Ctr., 1993—; mem. legis. assembly UCLA, 1991-94, com. on appointments and promotions, alternate 1991-92, mem. 1992—; dir. acad. career devel. UCLA Divsn. of Digestive Diseases Ctr., 1993—; assoc. dir. UCLA Integrated Tng. Program in Digestive Diseases, 1986-90, exec. com., 1986-90, dir. fellow evaluation, 1986-89, curriculum adv. bd., 1988-89, curriculum coord., 1984-88, applicant screening com., 1984-89; investigator Ctr. for Ulcer Rsch. and Edn., 1986—, many other coms. Editl. bd. Am. Jour. of Physiology; ad hoc reviewer Gastroenterology, Am. Jour. Physiology, Jour. of Membrane Biology, Jour. of Clin. Investigation, Pfluger's Archiv, Can. Jour. of Physiology and Pharmacology. Recipient numerous rsch. grants. Mem. Columbia Coll. of Physicians and Surgeons (alumni dir. 1976—, alumni day scientific com. 1991), Soc. for Auditory Integration Tng. (bd. dirs. 1993—), Am. Gastroenterol. Assn. (abstract selection com., intestinal disorders sect. 1994, abstract reviewer molecular and cell biology sect. 1988, 89), Western Soc. for Clin. Investigation, 1987, 89), West Coast Salt and Water Club (program chmn. ann. meeting, session co-chair 1992), Alpha Omega Alpha.

KAUPINS, GUNDARS EGONS, education educator; b. Mpls., Dec. 29, 1956; s. Alfreds and Skaidrite (Akots) K. BA, Wartburg Coll., 1979; MBA, U. No. Iowa, 1981; PhD, U. Iowa, 1986. Grad. asst. U. No. Iowa, Cedar Falls, 1979-81; employee rels. asst. Norand Corp., Cedar Rapids, 1983; grad. asst. Univ. Iowa, Iowa City, 1981-86; assoc. prof. Boise (Idaho) State U., 1986—; cons. in field. Contbr. articles to profl. jours. Recipient rsch. grants Boise State U., 1987-89, Ponder scholarship U. Iowa, 1983-85; named Adv. of the Yr., Boise State U., 1989. Mem. Soc. for Human Resource Mgmt. (sec., v.p. 1982-83), ASTD (sec. 1989), Assn. of Mgmt., Acad. of Mgmt., Am. Psychol. Assn. Home: 1829 W Boise Ave Apt F Boise ID 83706-3403 Office: Boise State U Dept Mgmt Boise ID 83725

KAUZLARICH, SUSAN MARY, chemistry educator, researcher; b. Worcester, Mass., Sept. 24, 1958; d. James Joseph and Sally Ann (Smith) K.; m. Peter Klavins, May 7, 1988; children: Lukas, Anna, Paul. BS, Coll. William and Mary, 1980; PhD, Mich. State U., 1985. Postdoctoral researcher Ames Lab., Iowa State U., 1985-87; asst. prof. solid state chem. U. Calif., Davis, 1987-92, assoc. prof., 1992—. Contbr. articles to profl. jours. Mem. AAAS, Am. Chem. Soc., Materials Rsch. Soc., Sigma Xi, Iota Sigma Pi. Office: Univ Calif Dept Chemistry Davis CA 95616

KAVISH, KIMBERLY LAYNE, art director, photographer; b. L.A., Sept. 7, 1951; d. Robert Michael and Vera Elaine (Howell) K. BA of Art, U. Calif. Davis, 1973; cert., Brooks Inst. Photography. Photographer, designer, 1973-82; photo editor Photo Forum mag., Santa Barbara, Calif., 1982-89; art dir. Santa Barbara mag., Pasadena mag., Santa Barbara, 1986—. Com. mem. Santa Barbara Mus. of Art, 1990—. Democrat. Office: 226 E Canon Perdido St Ste H Santa Barbara CA 93101-2234

KAWACHIKA, JAMES AKIO, lawyer; b. Honolulu, Dec. 5, 1947; s. Shinichi and Tsuyuko (Murashige) K.; m. Karen Keiko Takahashi, Sept. 1, 1973; 1 child, Robyn Mari. BA, U. Hawaii, Honolulu, 1969; JD, U. Calif., Berkeley, 1973. Bar: Hawaii 1973, U.S. Dist. Ct. Hawaii 1973, U.S. Ct. Appeals (9th cir.) 1974, U.S. Supreme Ct. 1992. Dep. atty. gen. Office of Atty. Gen. State of Hawaii, Honolulu, 1973-74; assoc. Padgett, Greeley & Marumoto, Honolulu, 1974-75, Law Office of Frank D. Padgett, Honolulu, 1975-77, Kobayashi, Watanabe, Sugita & Kawashima, Honolulu, 1977-82; ptnr. Carlsmith, Wichman, Case, Mukai & Ichiki, Honolulu, 1982-86, Bays, Deaver, Hiatt, Kawachika & Lezak, Honolulu, 1986—; mem. Hawaii Bd. of Bar Examiners, Honolulu; arbitrator Cir. Ct. Arbitration Program State of Hawaii, Honolulu, 1986—. Chmn. Disciplinary Bd. Hawaii Supreme Ct., 1991—; mem. U.S. dist. Ct. Adv. Com. on the Civil Justice Reform Act of 1990, 1991—. Mem. ABA, Hawaii Bar Assn. (bd. dirs. Honolulu chpt. 1975-76, young lawyers sect. 1983-84, 92-93, treas. 1987-88), 9th Crct. Jud. Conf. (lawyer rep., Honolulu chpt. 1988-90), Assn. Trial Lawyers Am. Office: Bays Deaver Hiatt Kawachika & Lezak Alii Pl 16th Fl 1099 Alakea St Honolulu HI 96813-4500

KAWAMOTO, HENRY K., plastic surgeon; b. Long Beach, Calif., 1937. Intern U. Calif. Hosp., L.A., 1965; resident Columbia Presbyn. Med. Ctr., N.Y., 1969-71; resident plastic surgery NYU, 1971-73; fellow craniofacial surgery Dr. Paul Tessier, Paris, 1973-74; clin. prof. plastic surgery U. Calif., L.A. Mem. Am. Assn. Plastic Surgery, Am. Soc. Plastic and Reconstructive Surgery, ASMS, AOA. Office: 1301 20th St # 460 Santa Monica CA 90404-2050

KAWASAKI, LILLIAN YURIKO, city general manager environmental affairs; b. Denver, Sept. 17, 1950. BS in Zoology, Calif. State L.A., 1974, MS in Biology, 1980. Dir. environ. mgmt. L.A. City Harbor, 1988-90; instr. part-time UCLA, 1990—; gen. mgr. City of L.A. Environ. Affairs, 1990—. Recipient Disting. Alumni award Calif. State L.A., 1992, Pres.'s award Asian-Am. Architects/Engrs., 1992. Mem. Nat. Adv. Coun. Environ. Policy & Tech., So. Calif. Acad. Scis. (bd. dirs. 1992—), Calif. State U. Found. (bd. dirs. 1993—), Am. Lung Assn. (bd. dirs. L.A. chpt. 1993—). Office: City of LA Environ Affairs Dept 200 N Spring St Ste 1500 Los Angeles CA 90012-4817

KAWESKI, SUSAN, plastic surgeon; b. Oil City, Pa., Jan. 27, 1955; d. Richard Francis and Lottie Ann (Malek) K.; m. Henry Nicholas Ernecoff, Aug. 7, 1983. BA, Washington and Jefferson Coll., 1976; MA, SUNY, Buffalo, 1979; MD, Pa. State U., 1983. Diplomate Am. Bd. Surgery, Am. Bd. Plastic Surgery. Commd. USN, 1983, advanced through grades to comdr.; head divsn. plastic surgery Naval Med. Ctr., San Diego, 1991—; chmn. Cleft Palate/Craniofacial Bd., San Diego, 1991—; plastic surgery advisor to surgeon gen. USN, 1994-95. Author chpt. to book. Recipient Ernest Witebsky Meml. award for proficiency in microbiology SUNY at Buffalo, 1978. Fellow ACS (assoc., 1st Place Rsch. award 1991); mem. Am. Assn. Plastic and Reconstructive Surgeons, Am. Cleft Palate Assn., Am. Assn. Women Surgeons, Am. Med. Women's Assn., Assn. Mil. Surgeons U.S., Univ. Club. Republican. Roman Catholic. Home: 1158 Barcelona Dr San Diego CA 92107 Office: Divsn Plastic Surgery Naval Med Ctr Bob Wilson Dr San Diego CA 92134

KAY, ALAN COOKE, federal judge; s. Harold Thomas and Ann (Cooke) K. BA, Princeton U., 1957; LLB, U. Calif., Berkeley, 1960. Assoc. Case, Kay & Lynch, Honolulu, 1960-64, ptnr., 1965-86; judge, now chief judge U.S. Dist. Ct. Hawaii, Honolulu, 1986—; bd. regents Internat. Coll. and Grad. Sch., 1994—. Mem. steering com. Fuller Theol. Sem. Hawaii, 1985-86; pres., trustee Hawaii Mission Children's Soc., Honolulu, 1980-86; bd. dirs. Good News Mission, 1980-86, Econ. Devel. Corp. Honolulu, 1985-86, Legal Aid Soc., Honolulu, 1968-71. Mem. ABA, Hawaii Bar Assn. (exec. com. 1972-73, bd. dirs. real estate sect. 1983-86), Fed. Judges Assn. 94—, 9th cir. Pacific Islands com. 1994—), Am. Inns of Ct. (counselor Aloha Inn 1987—). Republican. Office: US Dist Ct PO Box 50128 Honolulu HI 96850-0001

KAY, HERMA HILL, law educator; b. Orangeburg, S.C., Aug. 18, 1934; d. Charles Esdorn and Herma Lee (Crawford) Hill. BA, So. Meth. U., 1956; JD, U. Chgo., 1959. Bar: Calif. 1960, U.S. Supreme Ct. 1978. Law clk. to Justice Roger Traynor, Calif. Supreme Ct., 1959-60; asst. prof. law U. Calif., Berkeley, 1960-62; assoc. prof. U. Calif., 1962, prof., 1963, dir. family law project, 1964-67, Jennings prof., 1987—, dean, 1992—; co-reporter uniform marriage and div. act Nat. Conf. Commrs. on Uniform State Laws, 1968-70; vis. prof. U. Manchester, Eng., 1972, Harvard U., 1976; mem. Gov.'s Commn. on Family, 1966. Author: Text Cases and Materials on Sex-based Discrimination, 3rd edit., 1988, Supplement, 1994; (with R. Cramton, D. Currie and L. Kramer) Conflict of Laws: Cases, Comments, Questions, 5th edit., 1993; contbr. articles to profl. jours. Trustee Russell Sage Found., N.Y., 1972-87, chmn. bd., 1980-84; trustee, bd. dirs. Equal Rights Advs. Calif., 1976—, chmn., 1976-83; pres. bd. dirs. Rosenberg Found., Calif., 1987-88, bd. dirs. 1978—. Recipient rsch. award Am. Bar Found., 1990, award ABA Commn. Women in Profession, 1992, Marshall-Wythe medal, 1995; fellow Ctr. Advanced Study in Behavioral Sci., Palo Alto, Calif., 1963. Mem. Calif. Bar Assn., Bar U.S. Supreme Ct., Calif. Women Lawyers (bd. govs. 1975-77), Am. Law Inst. (mem. coun. 1985-), Assn. Am. Law Schs. (exec. com. 1986-87, pres.-elect 1988, pres. 1989, past pres. 1990), Am. Acad. Arts and Scis., Order of Coif (nat. pres. 1983-85). Democrat. Office: U Calif Law Sch Boalt Hall Berkeley CA 94720

KAY, MARGUERITE M., immunologist, geriatrician, medical educator; b. Washington, May 13, 1947; d. Ann Margot. BA in Zoology summa cum laude, U. Calif., Berkeley, 1970; D of Medicine, U. Calif., San Francisco, 1974. Staff fellow Gerontology Rsch. Ctr., Nat. Inst. Child Health and Devel., NIH, Balt. City Hosps., Balt. and Bethesda, Md., 1974, USPHS officer, chief high resolution lab, coord. human immunoepidemilolgy program, 1975-77; chief longitudinal immunology program Nat. Inst. on Aging, NIH, Balt. and Bethesda, 1975-77; chief lab. molecular and clin. immunology, dir. electron microscopy facilty chief lab Geriatric Rsch. Edn. and Clin. Ctr., VA Wadsworth Med. Ctr., L.A., 1977-81; staff geriatrician, rsch. assoc. dept. medicine UCLA, 1977-81; intern UCLA and VA Wadsworth Med. Ctr., 1978, resident in medicine, 1979-80, geriatric fellow, 1981; immunologist, internist, assoc. chief of staff rsch. Olin E. Teague Vets. Ctr., Temple, Tex., 1981-90; dir. div. geriatric medicine Tex. A&M U., College Station, 1981-90, prof. medicine, med. biochemistry, genetics, microbiology and immunology, 1981-90; regent's prof. microbiology, immunology and medicine U. Ariz. Coll. of Medicine, Tucson, 1990—; guest lectr. in basic microbiology Goucher Coll., Towson, Md., 1974-75, guest lab. instr. advanced microbiology, 1975-77; presenter, instr., participant numerous profl. symposia and seminars, 1974—. Author: (with J. Gaplin and T. Makinodan) Aging, Immunity and Arthritic Disease, 1980; (with T. Makinodan) CRC Handbook of Immunology in Aging, 1981; contbr. chpt. to Liver and Aging, 1977, Clinical Immunochemistry, 1978, Geriatric Dentistry, 1986, numerous others; contbr. numerous articles to profl. publs. and jours.; mem. editorial bd., Comprehensive Gerontology sect. editor Mechanisms of Aging and Development, 1985—; spl. issue editor Gerontology, 1985, 90, N.Am. editor, Gerontology, 1987—; author poems. NIH Med. Scientist Tng. fellow U. Calif., San Francisco, Pres.'s Undergrad. fellow, 1971-72, 72-73, 73-74, Edwin Letts Oliver scholar, Finkelstein scholar, Al Holman scholar, 1972-73; recipient Internat. Congress Gerontology Travel award, 1978, Arthur S. Fleming award, 1983; named Register Honoree in Sci. and Tech. Esquire mag., 1985; many other hons. and awards. Mem. Am. Soc. Clin. Investigation, Am. Soc. Biochemistry and Molecular Biology, Am. Assn. Immunologists, Am. Geriatrics Soc., Am. Soc. Cell Biology, Am. Soc. Hematology, Am. Fedn. Clin. Rsch., Gerontol. Soc., Sigma Xi. Home: PO Box 36018 Tucson AZ 85740-6018 Office: U Ariz Health Sci Ctr Dept Microbiology 1501 N Campbell Ave Rm 650 Lsn Tucson AZ 85724-0001

KAYALAR, SELAHATTIN, electrical engineer; b. Dinar, Turkey, Feb. 11, 1954; came to U.S., 1979; s. Salih and Ülfet (Taskoparan) K.; m. Lena Fazelian, Aug. 11, 1987; 1 child, Yasemin. BSEE, Boğaziçi U., Istanbul, Turkey, 1977; MSEE, Purdue U., 1981; MS in Engring., Johns Hopkins U., 1983, PhD in EE, 1987. Rsch. asst. Philips Rsch. Lab., Eindhoven, The Netherlands, 1978-79, Johns Hopkins U., Balt., 1981-87; vis. lectr. Ind. U. Purdue U., Indpls., 1979-81, asst. prof., 1987-91; mem. tech. staff Jet Propulsion Lab., Pasadena, Calif., 1991—. Recipient Tech. Achievement award NASA, 1993. Mem. IEEE, IEEE Comms. Soc., IEEE Control Engring. Soc. Muslim. Home: 45 Southwind Aliso Viejo CA 92656-1385 Office: Jet Propulsion Lab 4800 Oak Grove Dr Pasadena CA 91109-8001

KAYE, BRIAN RANDALL, rheumatologist, educator; b. Detroit, Dec. 13, 1957; s. Ronald Lee and Tobye Faye (Davidson) K.; m. Fran Alice Tannenbaum, Apr. 30, 1983; children: Naomi Shoshana, Joshua Hillel. AB summa cum laude, Princeton U., 1979; MD, Baylor Coll. Medicine, 1983. Diplomate Am. Bd. Internal Medicine, Am. Bd. Rheumatology. Resident in internal medicine Santa Clara Valley Med. Ctr., San Jose, Calif., 1983-86; fellow in rheumatology Stanford U., Palo Alto, Calif., 1986-88, clin. asst. prof. medicine, 1992—; pvt. practice, Oakland, San Leandro, Calif., 1988-91, Berkeley, Calif., 1992—; attending physician Highland Gen. Hosp., Oakland, Calif., 1988—; clin. asst. prof. medicine U. Calif., San Francisco, 1989—; manuscript reviewer Arthritis and Rheumatism, Atlanta, 1990—, Jour. Rheumatology, Toronto, Ont., Can., 1990—. Contbr. articles to med. jours. Mem. alumni schs. com. Princeton U., Castro Valley, Calif., 1983—; chmn. adult edn. Beth Jacob Congregation, Oakland, 1993—. Sr. thesis rsch. grantee Princeton U., 1978; Wexner Found. fellow, 1995—. Fellow ACP, Am. Coll. Rheumatology; mem. AMA, Calif. Med. Assn., Alameda-Contra Costa Med. Assn., No. Calif. Rheumatism Soc. (sec.-treas. 1988—). Office: The Arthritis Ctr 3010 Colby St Ste 118 Berkeley CA 94705-2059

KAYE, CAROLE, museum director and curator; b. Somerville, N.J., Apr. 24, 1933; d. Harry and Grace (Schwartz) Golison; m. Paul Littman, June 29, 1952 (dec. Apr. 1960); children: Fern, Alan; m. Barry Kaye; children: Howard. Student, Syracuse U. With Barry Kaye Assocs., L.A.; owner, curator Carole and Barry Kaye Mus. Miniatures, L.A. Past pres. Hadassah, Beverly Hills, Calif.; founder Music Ctr., Cedars-Sinai Hosp., L.A.; mem. Jewish Fedn. Mem. Friends of Ben Gurion U., Golden Key. Office: Carole & Barry Kaye Mus Miniatures 5900 Wilshire Blvd Los Angeles CA 90036

KAYE, IVAN NATHANIEL, writer; b. L.A., Aug. 24, 1932; s. Harry and Babette Dorothy (Richman) K. BA in History, U. Mich., 1954; MS in Journalism, Columbia U., 1958; postgrad., U. Calif., Berkeley, 1960, Harvard U., 1964-65. Reporter/writer UPI, Madison, Wis., 1958-60; Washington corres. Madison Capital Times, 1962-64; writer Newsweek Mag., N.Y.C., 1970-72; sci. writer People Mag., N.Y.C., 1974-82. Author: Good Clean Violence, A History of College Football 1973; articles pub. in Sports Illustrated, Harvard Mag., N.Y. Times, Michigan Alumnus, many others. With U.S. Army, 1954-56. Congl. fellow Am. Polit. Sci. Assn., 1960-61. Address: 950 6th St Boulder CO 80302-7125

KAYE, JEFFREY KENNETH, television reporter; b. London, Jan. 14, 1950; came to U.S., 1963; s. Harry and Rebecca (Richtiger) K.; m. Deborah Rose Klein, June 21, 1970; children: Sara Rachel, Sophie Emma. Student, UCLA, 1967-71. Reporter KPFK Radio (Pacifica), L.A., 1974-75; freelance reporter Radio New Zealand, NPR, AP, L.A., 1975-78; reporter KIIS Radio, L.A., 1976-77; reporter, producer KABC-TV, ABC, L.A., 1976-77; investigative reproter KNXT-TV, CBS, L.A., 1978; contbg. editor New West Mag., L.A., 1978-80; spl. corr. Washington Post, L.A., 1978-80; sr. prodr. KCET-TV, PBS, L.A., 1980—; corr. MacNeil/Lehrer NewsHour, L.A., 1984—. Recipient 3 Golden Mikes, Radio and TV News Assn., L.A., 1980, 82, 83, 5 Emmy awards Acad. TV Arts and Scis., L.A., 1977, 83, 84, 89, 91, Best Documentary award Valley Press Club, L.A., 1985. Mem. Investigative Reporters and Editors, Soc. Profl. Journalists. Jewish. Office: KCET 4401 W Sunset Blvd Los Angeles CA 90027-6017

KAYE, LORI, travel academy executive, consultant; b. N.Y.C.; d. Eldin Bert and Katherine Angeline Onsgard; student Detroit Inst. Art, 1951, 56, U. N.Mex., 1960. Actress, radio and TV commls., 1951-82; actress Warner Brothers, 1960-64; dir., v.p. John Robert Powers Schs., Los Angeles, 1961-71; v.p. Electron Industries, Torrance, Calif., 1963-65; owner, v.p., Lawrence Leon Photography Studio, Los Angeles, 1964-68; pres. Lori Kaye Cosmetics, Hollywood, Calif., 1964-70; co-owner, v.p. K and S Employment, Calif. Fashion Mart, 1965-67; dir., internat. cons. Airline Schs. Pacific, Van Nuys, Calif., 1972-74; dir. Caroline Leonetti Ltd. Sch., Hollywood, 1976-79; pres., Lori Kaye's Internat. Travel Acad., North Hollywood, Calif., 1980—; internat. cons. Internat. Career Acad., Van Nuys, 1978—, Glendale Coll. Bus. and Paramed. (Calif.), 1980—, Acad. Pacific, Hollywood, 1981—; pres. Molori Publs., Studio City, Calif., 1981—; cons. A&T Inst. Travel and Tourism, 1982; lectr., 1969—. Dir. project Camarillo State Hosp., 1963-69; cons. Job Corps. Recipient Mental Health Achievement award, 1967. Mem. Nat. Assn. Female Execs., Assn. for Promotion of Tourism Africa, AAU, Screen Actors Guild, AFTRA, Smithsonian Assocs., Am. Soc. Travel Agents, Internat. Airlines Travel Agents Network, Internat. Air Transport Assn., Soc. Travel Agents in Govt., Calif. Assn. Pvt. Postsecondary Schs., U.S. Masters-Internat. Swim Club, Nat. Geog. Soc., Internat. Platform Assn., Better Bus. Bur. (also arbitrator), L.A. World Affairs Coun., Universal City- No. Hollywood C. of C. Paintings included in UNICEF collection, 1967; hostess TV talk show The New You, KTTV, Hollywood, 1964-65. Office: Internat Travel Ctr 12123 Magnolia Blvd North Hollywood CA 91607-2609 also: Lori Kayes Internat Travel Acad 12123 Magnolia Blvd North Hollywood CA 91607-2609

KAYE, MICHAEL DUNCAN, physician, gastroenterologist, consultant; b. Coventry, Eng., July 26, 1939; came to U.S., 1969; s. Duncan Kaye and Rotha Valerie (Jones) Tyndall; m. Marina Sakellarides, July 26, 1962 (div. Sept. 8, 1987); children: Lydia Sophia, Delia Rosalind Julia, Duncan Edmund Alexander. BA, U. Oxford, Eng., 1960, MA, BM, BCh, 1963, MD, 1970. House physician, surgeon Radcliffe Infirmary, Oxford, 1964-65; sr. house officer, registrar Sully Hosp. Penarth, South Wales, 1965-67; professorial unit registrar Cardiff Royal Infirmary, South Wales, 1967-69; fellow in gastroenterology Med. Sch. U. Colo., Denver, 1969-72, asst. prof. medicine, 1972-74; assoc. prof. medicine U. Vt., Burlington, 1974-80, prof. medicine, 1980-87; cons. in gastroenterology Fronk Clinic, Honolulu, 1987-90, Straub Clinic and Hospital, Honolulu, 1990—. Contbr. more than 50 articles to profl. jours. Grantee NIH, 1972—. Fellow Royal Coll. Physicians (London); mem. Hawaii Gastroenterol. Assn. (pres.), Am. Gastroenterol. Soc., Am. Assn. for the Study of Liver Diseases, Brit. Soc. Gastroenterology, Honolulu Club, Oahu Country Club. Office: Straub Clinic 888 S King St Honolulu HI 96813-3009

KAYE, PETER FREDERIC, newspaper editor; b. Chgo., Mar. 8, 1928; s. Ralph A. and Sara Corson (Philipson) K.; m. Martha Louise Wood, Mar. 20, 1955; children: Loren, Terry, Adam. BA in Govt., Pomona Coll., 1949. Reporter Alhambra (Calif.) Post-Advocate, 1950-53; reporter, editorial writer, polit. writer The San Diego Union, 1953-68; news and pub. affairs dir. KPBS-TV, San Diego State Coll., 1968-72; corr., producer Nat. Pub. Affairs Ctr. for TV, Washington, 1972-74; comm. dir. So. Calif. First Nat. Bank, San Diego, 1974-75; press sec. The Pres. Ford Com., Washington, 1975-76; mgr. Copley Videotex, San Diego, 1982-84; assoc. editor The San Diego Union, 1976-94; freelance TV producer programs KPBS, PBS, BBC; San Diego corr. Newsweek, 1968-71, McGraw-Hill, 1959-67; lectr. comm. U. Calif., San Diego, 1971; copywriter Washburn-Justice Advt., San Diego, 1959-70. Producer 10 TV programs including including Jacob Bronowski: Life and Legacy, Twenty-Five Years of Presidency, The Presidency, The Press and the People. Press asst. Eisenhower-Nixon Campaign, L.A., 1952; asst. press sec. Richard Nixon Presdl. Campaign, Washington, 1960; dir. Pete Wilson for Mayor Campaign, San Diego, 1971; comm. dir. Flournoy for Gov. Campaign, Beverly Hills, Calif., 1974. With U.S. Mcht. Marines, 1945, U.S. Army, 1950-52. Jefferson fellow East-West Ctr., Honolulu, 1987; recipient Golden Mike awards So. Calif. TV News Dirs. Assn., 1969, 70, 71, Best Pub. Affairs Program award Nat. Ednl. TV, 1970, Best Local TV Series award Radio-TV Mirror, 1971, Nat. Emmy award Spl. Events Reporter, Watergate Coverage, 1973-74, Best Editorial awards Copley Newspapers Ring of Truth, 1979, Sigma Delta Chi, 1985, Calif. Newspaper Pubs. Assn., 1985; San Diego Emmy awards, 1985, 87, 91. Mem. NATAS, State Bar Calif. (bd. govs. 1991—, v.p. 1993-94), Sigma Delta Chi. Republican. Home: 240 Ocean View Ave Del Mar CA 92014-3322

KAYE, STUART MARTIN, lawyer; b. Bronx, N.Y., Dec. 2, 1946; s. Jules Krupnikoff and Gussie (Lipchinsky) Kaye; m. Christine Marie Heitkam, Sept. 25, 1970 (div. 1983); m. Eve C. Farkas, Apr. 2, 1988 (div. 1991); children: Joshua Brandon, Jeremy Jason, Kimberly I. Morlan. AA, Glendale Community Coll., 1971; BS in Polit. Sci., Ariz. State U., 1974; JD, Western State U., 1978. Bar: Calif. 1980, U.S. Dist. Ct. (no. dist.) Calif. 1980, (so. dist.) Calif. 1985, (cen. dist.) Calif. 1987. Assoc. mgmt. analyst State of Calif., Sacramento, 1978-84, legal counsel, 1984-85; indsl. relations counsel State of Calif., San Diego, 1985-92; legal asst. Ariz. Atty. Gen., Phoenix, 1992-93; indsl. rels. coun. State of Calif., Santa Ana, 1993—; pvt. practice, Shigle Springs, 1981-84. With U.S. Army, 1964-68. Democrat. Jewish. Office: State Calif Div Labor Standards 28 Civic Center Plz Ste 641 Santa Ana CA 92701-4035

KAYFETZ, VICTOR JOEL, writer, editor, translator; b. N.Y.C., July 20, 1945; s. Daniel Osler and Selma Harriet (Walowitz) K.; BA, Columbia U., 1966; postgrad. U. Stockholm (Sweden), 1966-67; MA in History, U. Calif.-Berkeley, 1969. Teaching asst. in Swedish, U. Calif., Berkeley, 1969-70; tchr., adminstr. Swedish adult edn. programs, 1970-75; corr. Reuters, Stockholm, 1975-78; sub-editor Reuters World Ser., London, 1978; corr. London Fin. Times, Stockholm, 1979-80; free lance translator Swedish, Danish, Norwegian, 1967—; free lance editor Swedish and Am. mags., 1980—. Henry Evans traveling fellow, 1966-67; Nat. Def. Fgn. Lang. fellow, 1967-69; Thord Gray fellow Am.-Scandinavian Found., 1970. Mem. Swedish Am. C. of C., Soc. Advancement Scandinavian Study, Am. Scandinavian Found., Swedish Assn. Profl. Translators, World Affairs Council No. Calif., Sierra Club, Phi Beta Kappa. Author: Sweden in Brief, 1974, 80; Invest in Sweden, 1984, Skanska, the First Century, 1987; editor, translator numerous books, ann. reports, mags. for Swedish govt. agys. interest orgns., univs., indsl. corps., banks. Office: Scan Edit 760 Market St Ste 1067 San Francisco CA 94102-2305

KAYLAN, HOWARD LAWRENCE, musical entertainer, composer; b. N.Y.C., June 22, 1947; s. Sidney and Sally Joyce (Berlin) K.; m. Mary Melita Pepper, June 10, 1967 (div. Sept. 1971); 1 child, Emily Anne; m. Susan Karen Olsen, Apr. 18, 1982; 1 child, Alexandra Leigh. Student, UCLA. Lead singer rock group The Turtles, Los Angeles, 1965-70, Mothers of Invention, Los Angeles, 1970-72, Flo and Eddie, 1972—; radio, TV, recording entertainer various broadcast organizations, Los Angeles, 1972—; screenwriter Larry Gelbart, Carl Gotleib prodns., Los Angeles, 1979-85; producer children's records Kidstuff Records, Hollywood, Fla., 1980—; singer, producer rock band Flo and Eddie, Los Angeles, 1976—; singer, producer The Turtles (reunion of original band), Los Angeles, 1980—; actor, TV and film Screen Actors Guild, Los Angeles, 1983—; background vocalist various albums for numerous performers; syndicated talk show host Unistar Radio Network, 1989—; radio personality Sta. WXRK-FM, N.Y.C., 1990-91, KLOU, St. Louis, 1993. Author: Hi Bob, 1995, The Energy Pals, 1995; contbr. articles to Creem mag., L.A. Free Press, Rockit mag., Phonograph Record; screenwriter: (film) Death Masque, 1985; actor: (film) Get Crazy, 1985, General Hospital; performed at the White House, 1970. Recipient 10 Gold and Platinum LP album awards while lead singer, 1965—, Fine Arts award, Bank of Am., L.A., 1965, Spl. Billboard Mag. award, 1992; recorded numerous top ten hit songs with Turtles, Bruce Springsteen, The Ramones, Duran Duran, T. Rex, John Lennon and others. Mem. AFTRA, Screen Actors Guild, Am. Fedn. Musicians, AGVA.

KAYMAN, SUSAN GOLDBERG, nutritionist, consultant; b. Houston, Aug. 5, 1944; d. Charles Goodman and Selma Beth (Selder) Goldberg; m. Harvey Kayman, June 27, 1965; children: Charles, Jessica Alexandra, Joshua. BS, Cornell U., 1965; MS, Columbia U., 1969; PhD, U. Calif., Berkeley, 1986; postgrad., Stanford U., 1986-88. Registered dietitian. Pub. health nutritionist Bur. of Nutrition N.Y.C. (N.Y.) Health Dept., 1969-71; pub. health nutritionist Contra Costa County Health Dept., Martinez, Calif., 1973-74; field program supr. Sch. Pub. Health, U. Calif., Berkeley, 1974-78, lectr., 1975-82; rsch. dir. weight maintenance study Kaiser Permanente Med. Offices, Fremont, Calif., 1984-86; NIH postdoctoral rsch. fellow Stanford Ctr. Rsch. in Disease Prevention, Stanford U., 1986-88, postdoctoral rsch. affiliate, cons., 1988-90; sr. cons. No. Calif. Regional Health Edn. The Permanente Med. Group, Kaiser Permanente, Oakland, 1988—; presenter in field. Contbr. articles to profl. jours. Grantee U. Calif., Berkeley, 1984-85, Biomed. Rsch. Support, 1984-86, NSF, 1986, ; Dowdle Endowment fellow U. Calif., Sch. Pub. Health, Berkeley, 1984-86. Office: Kaiser Permanente Med Care Program 17th Fl 1950 Franklin St Oakland CA 94612-5103

KAYTON, MYRON, engineering company executive; b. N.Y.C., Apr. 26, 1934; s. Albert Louis and Rae (Danoff) K.; m. Paula Erde, Sept. 5, 1954; children: Elizabeth Kayton Kerns, Susan Kayton Barclay. BS, The Cooper Union, 1955; MS, Harvard U., 1956; PhD, MIT, 1960. Registered engr., Calif. Sect. head Litton Industries, Woodland Hills, Calif., 1960-65; dep. mgr. NASA, Houston, 1965-69; mem. sr. staff TRW, Inc., Redondo Beach, Calif., 1969-81; pres. Kayton Engring. Co., Inc., Santa Monica, Calif., 1981—; chmn. bd. dirs. WINCON Conf., L.A., 1985-92; founding dir. Caltech-MIT Enterprise Forum, Pasadena, Calif., 1984—; tchr. tech. courses UCLA Extension, 1969-88. Author: Avionic Navigation Systems, 1966, Navigation: Land, Sea, Air and Space, 1990; contbr. numerous articles on engring., econs. and other profl. subjects. Founding dir. UCLA Friends of Humanities, 1971-75; West coast chmn. Cooper Union Fund Campaign,

1989-93. Fellow NSF, Washington, 1956-57, 58-60; recipient Gano Dunn medal The Cooper Union, N.Y.C., 1975. Fellow IEEE (pres. aerospace 1993-94, exec. v.p. aerospace 1991-92, v.p. tech. ops. 1988-90, nat. bd. govs. 1983—, vice chmn. L.A. coun. 1983-84, M.B. Carlton award 1988, disting. lectr.); mem. ASME, Harvard Grad. Soc. (coun. mem. chmn. nominating com. 1988-91), Inst. Navigation, Soc. Automotive Engr., Harvard Club So. Calif. (pres. 1979-80), MIT Club (L.A.). Office: Kayton Engring Co PO Box 802 Santa Monica CA 90406-0802

KAZENELSON DEANE, DEBORAH, public relations executive; b. Buffalo, Oct. 23, 1962; d. Gregorio Kazenelson and Mirtha (Cohen) Walsh; m. Jeffrey William Deane, Apr. 23, 1988; 1 child, Joshua Deane. BS in Psychobiology, UCLA, 1984, MS in Pub. Health, 1987. Cons. Herman Smith Assocs., Redwood City, Calif., 1986-88; exec. cons. Blue Shield Calif., San Francisco, 1988-89; sr. account supr. Hilland Knowlton Pub. Rels., L.A., 1989-92; v.p., gen. mgr. Paine & Assocs. Pub. Rels., L.A., 1992—; expert Hispanic mktg. Mem. Pub. Rels. Soc. Am. Democrat. Jewish. Office: Paine & Assocs Pub Rels 16633 Ventura Blvd Ste 1050 Encino CA 91436-1838

KAZLE, ELYNMARIE, producer; b. St. Paul, June 22, 1958; d. Victor Anton and Marylu (Gardner) K. BFA, U. Minn., Duluth, 1982; MFA, Ohio U., 1984. Prodn. mgr. Great Lakes Shakespeare, Cleve., 1983; prodn. stage mgr. San Diego (Calif.) Opera, 1984, PCPA Theaterfest, Santa Maria, Calif., 1986-87; stage mgr. Bklyn. Acad. Music, 1987; assoc. producer Assn. Am. Theater Actors, N.Y.C., 1988-89; prodn. stage mgr. Time Flies When You're Alive, West Hollywood, Calif., 1988—; asst. advt. display Wall St. Jour., L.A., 1988-89; West Coast adminstr. Soc. Stage Dirs. and Choreographers, 1991-93. Editor, pub. (newsletter) The Ohio Network, 1984-90; prodr. Santa Monica Playhouse, 1989-94; assoc. mng. dir. Actors Alley Repertory Theater, North Hollywood, Calif., 1994. Trustee Theatre/L.A., 1992-94. Mem. Stage Mgrs. Assn., Stage Mgrs. Assn. L.A., U.S. Inst. for Theatre Tech. (bd. dirs. 1990—), Actors Equity Assn., North Hollywood/Universal City C. of C. (bd. dirs. 1994—), Phi Kappa Phi, Delta Chi Omega (past pres. 1978). Office: Actors Alley PO Box 8500 Van Nuys CA 91409-8500

KEABLES, MICHAEL JOHN, geography educator; b. Denver, May 19, 1955; s. John Mayoll and Barbara Jean (Boettcher) K.; m. Dawn Alexandria Errickson, July 15, 1978; children: Paul Michael, Kevin Andrew. BA, U. Colo., 1978; MS, U. Wis., 1982, PhD, 1986. Lectr. dept. geography U. Wis., Madison, 1983-85, U. Md., Catonsville, 1985-86; asst. prof. dept. geography U. Denver, Colo., 1986-92; assoc. prof. dept. geography U. Denver, 1992—; prin. investigator rsch. grant U.S. Geol. Survey, 1990. Contbr. articles to profl. jours. Panelist State Auditors Office-Air Pollution Programs, Denver, 1991; mem. Coop. Decision Making-Denver (Colo.) Pub. Schs., 1992. Mem. Assn. Am. Geographers, Am. Meteorol. Soc., Am. Geophysical Union, Nat. Geographic Soc., Nat. Coun. for Geographic Edn. (Teaching Achievement award 1990), Sigma Xi. Democrat. Episcopalian. Office: Univ Denver Dept Geography 2130 S Race St Denver CO 80210-4639

KEALA, FRANCIS AHLOY, security executive; b. Honolulu, June 1, 1930; s. Samuel Louis and Rose (Ahloy) K.; m. Betty Ann Lyman, Nov. 28, 1952; children—Frances Ann, John Richard, Robert Mark. BA in Sociology, U. Hawaii, 1953. Patrolman Honolulu Police Dept., 1956-62, detective, 1962-65, lt., 1965-68, capt., 1968-69, chief of police, 1969-83; dir. security Hawaiian Telephone Co., 1983-93; trustee S. Keala Trust, 1989—; bd. dirs. Liliuokalani Trust. Bd. dirs. Aloha coun. Boy Scouts Am., 200 Club, Sex Abuse Treatment Center, Am. Automobile Assn. of Hawaii, Hawaii Meml. Park Assn., St. Louis Found., ARC-Hawaii chpt., St. Francis Med. Ctr.-West; bd. govs. Boys and Girls Clubs of Honolulu; mem. Civilian Adv. Group U.S. Army; mem. Commn. on Jud. Discipline. Served with U.S. Army, 1953-55. Mem. Internat. Assn. Chiefs of Police, Hawaii State Law Enforcement Ofcls. Assn., FBI Nat. Acad. Assocs. Clubs: Oahu Country, Pacific.

KEANE, EDMUND J., JR., banker; b. Syracuse, N.Y., June 29, 1933; s. Edmund J. and Elizabeth (Byrne) K.; m. Suzanne M. Lamica; children—Edmund J. III, Sean T., Catharine A., Timothy C., Michael P. B.S. in Bus. Adminstrn., Holy Cross Coll., 1955. Asst. bank examiner Fed. Res. Bank N.Y., 1958-61; asst. to pres. Gramatan Nat. Bank, Bronxville, N.Y., 1961-62; asst. v.p. Scarsdale Nat. Bank, N.Y., 1962-67; v.p. Key Bank of No. N.Y., N.A., Watertown, 1967-69, sr. v.p., sr. loan officer, 1969-75, exec. v.p., sr. loan officer, 1975-80, pres., 1980, pres., chief exec. officer, 1981-88; pres., chief exec. officer Key Bank of Idaho, Boise, 1988—. Bd. dirs. Samaritan Keep Home, United Way of Ada County, Bishop Kelly Found., Bronco Athletic Assn., BSU Found.; chmn. scholarship com. BSU; mem. Robert Morris Assocs. Served to capt. USAF, 1955-58. Office: Key Bank Idaho 702 W Idaho St Boise ID 83702-8901

KEANE, KEVIN PATRICK, philosopher, consultant; b. N.Y.C., June 7, 1944; s. William Arthur and Geraldine Ann (Maher) K.; m. Joan Wilhelmina Kelly, Aug. 30, 1970; children: Brigid Anne, Padraic Kevin. AB in Philosophy magna cum laude, Rockhurst Coll., 1967; MA in Theology & Religion, Fordham U., 1969, PhD in Philosophy & Religion, 1978. Lectr. in philosophy Nassau C.C., Garden City, N.Y., 1968-70; lectr. religion Good Counsel Coll., Pace U., White Plains, N.Y., 1968-70; lectr. philosophy Dowling Coll., Oakdale, N.Y., 1972-73; instr. depts. philosophy and fgn. langs. Colo. State U., 1973-77, dir. inter-disciplinary program in religion, 1975-76; cons. Robert Panero Assocs., N.Y.C., 1977-79; founder, dir. Presidents' Seminar No. Colo. Exec. Forum/Denver Exec. Forum, 1979—; mem. affiliate faculty dept. philosophy Colo. State U., 1986—; invited participant Liberty Fund Conf., Big Sky, Mont., 1991, South Woodstock, Vt., 1992, Jackson, Wyo., 1993. Mem. Bd. Editorial Contributors, Rocky Mountain News, 1991—; contbr. articles and essays to profl. publs. Recipient Elliott prize Mediaeval Acad. Am., 1977; fellow/specialist in philosophy Aspen Exec. Seminar, 1979. Mem. Alpha Sigma Nu. Roman Catholic. Home and Office: 4106 Attleboro Ct Fort Collins CO 80525-3445

KEARNEY, JOSEPH LAURENCE, athletic conference administrator; b. Pitts., Apr. 28, 1927; s. Joseph L. and Iva M. (Nikirk) K.; m. Dorothea Hurst, May 13, 1950; children: Jan Marie, Kevin Robert, Erin Lynn, Shawn Alane, Robin James. B.A., Seattle Pacific U., 1952, LL.D., 1979; M.A., San Jose State U., 1964; Ed.D., U. Wash., 1970. Tchr., coach Paradise (Calif.) High Sch., 1952-53; asst. basketball coach U. Wash., 1953-54; coach, tchr. Sunnyside (Wash.) High Sch., 1954-57; prin. high sch., coach Onalaska (Wash.) High Sch., 1957-61; prin. Tumwater (Wash.) High Sch., 1961-63; asst. dir. Wash. High Sch. Activities Assn., 1963-64; athletic dir., assoc. dir. U. Wash., 1964-76; athletic dir. intercollegiate athletics Mich. State U., East Lansing, 1976-80, Ariz. State U., Tempe, 1980; commr. Western Athletic Conf., Denver, 1980—; hon. chmn. Holiday Bowl, 1994, commr. emeritus, 1994. Pres. Community Devel. Assn., 1957-61; bd. dirs. U.S. Olympic Com., 1985—, mem. games preparation com., 1985—. Recipient Disting. Service award Mich. Assn. Professions, 1979, Citation for Disting. Svc., Colo. Sports Hall of Fame. Mem. Nat. Football Found. (ct. of honors com.), Nat. Collegiate Athletic Assn., Nat. Assn. Collegiate Dirs. Athletics (Corbett award 1991, Adminstr. Excellence award), Collegiate Commrs. Assn. (pres.). Home: 2810 W Magee Rd Tucson AZ 85741-1500 Office: Western Athletic Conf 14 W Dry Creek Cir Littleton CO 80120-4478

KEARNS, HOMER H., school system administrator. AA in Spanish, West Hills Coll., Coalinga, Calif., 1962; BA in Spanish and Life Sci., Calif. State U., Fresno, 1964, MA in Adminstrn., 1970; PhD in Adminstrn. Higher Edn. and Sociology, Mich. State U., 1971. Tchr., head tchr., prin. Clovis (Calif.) Unified Sch. Dist, 1964-70; asst. prof. edn. dept. curriculum and instrn. coll. edn., assoc. dir. Northwest Cmty. Edn. Devel. Ctr. U. Oreg., Eugene, 1971-72; supt. schs. Sisters (Oreg.) Sch. Dist., 1972-75, Redmond (Oreg.) Sch. Dist., 1975-81; county supt. schs. Deschutes County Edn. Svc. Dist., Bend, Oreg., 1978-81; assoc., dep. supt. Salem-Keizer Pub. Schs., Salem, Oreg., 1981-86, supt. schs., 1986—; mem. exec. com. Coalition for Equitable Sch. Funding, 1988-91; bd. dirs. Marion & Polk Schs. Credit Union, 1992-94, Salem Econ. Devel. corp., Northwest Regional Ednl. Lab., chair bd. equity com. Bd. dirs. Salem Family YMCA, 3rd Century Edn. Found.; past bd. dirs. Oreg. Congl. Awards Coun., Cascade Child Treatment Ctr.; bd. dirs. Salem Sch. Found.; active Oreg. 2000 Com., United Way, County Planning Commn., Econ. Devel. Strategic Planning Group; mem. panel Gannet Found. Named Supt of Yr., Oreg. Counseling Assn., 1988, Outstanding Adminstr. Oreg. Multicultural Edn. Assn., 1994. Mem. Am. Assn. Sch. Adminstrs. (chair suburban supts. adv. com. 1990, exec. com. 1992-94, pres. elect 1994-95, pres. 1995—), Oreg. Assn. Sch. Execs. (bd. dirs., pres. 1990, chair sch. funding coalition 1992, Supt. of Yr. award with Am. Assn. Sch. Adminstrs. 1990), Rotary Internat. Office: Salem/Keizer SD 24J PO Box 12024 Salem OR 97309-0024

KEARSE, DAVID GRIER, stage and screen writer, journalist; b. Annapolis, Md., June 24, 1937; s. Francis Grier and Esther Carlisle (McCusker) K. BA, U. Miami, 1959; postgrad., Columbia U., 1959-60, NYU, 1988-89. Reporter, editor Capital Gazette Press, Annapolis, 1961-67; critic, copy editor The Balt. Sun, 1967-78; creative dept. Young and Rubicam Advtg., N.Y.C., 1978-83; with pub. rels. dept. Stephen W. Brener Assoc., N.Y.C., 1985-89; ind. screenwriter Hollywood, Calif., 1989—. Author: (musical) Miranda, 1991; author, dir. (play) Once Bitten, 1978; author: (screenplay) Alfredo's Sunset, 1991; dir.: The Winter's Tale, 1978, Playformers, 1989. Co-founder Annapolis Fine Arts Festival, 1963; AIDS vol. Roosevelt Hosp., N.Y.C., 1988-89; mem. Spiritual Adv. Com. AIDS Project L.A.; assoc. Episcopal Order Holy Cross. Mem. The Dramatists Guild, Writers Guild Am. (assoc.), Westwood Village Rotary Club. Democrat.

KEATING, LARRY GRANT, electrical engineer, educator; b. Omaha, Jan. 15, 1944; s. Grant Morris and Dorothy Ann (Kauffold) K.; m. Barbara Jean Merley, Dec. 21, 1968. LLB, Blackstone Sch. Law, 1968; BS, U. Nebr., 1969; BS cum laude, Met. State Coll., 1971; MS, U. Colo., Denver, 1978. Chief engr. broadcast electronics 3 radio stas., 1965-69; coord. engring. reliability Cobe Labs., Lakewood, Colo., 1972-74; quality engr. Statitrol Corp., Lakewood, Colo., 1974-76; instr. electrical engring. U. Colo., Denver, 1976-78; from asst. prof. to prof. Met. State Coll., Denver, 1978—, chmn. dept., 1984-95; cons. Transplan Assocs., Boulder, Colo., 1983-84. 1st lt. U.S. Army, 1962-70. Recipient Outstanding Faculty award U. Colo., Denver, 1980, Outstanding Alumnus award Met. State Coll., 1985. Fellow Order of the Engr.; mem. IEEE (sr.), Instrument Soc. Am. (sr.), Am. Soc. Engring. Edn., Nat. Assn. Radio and Telecomm. Engrs. (cert. engr.), Eta Kappa Nu, Tau Alpha Pi, Chi Epsilon. Home: 6455 E Bates Ave # 4108 Denver CO 80222-7135 Office: Met State Coll PO Box 173362 Campus Box 29 Denver CO 80217-3362

KEATING, ROBERT CLARK, lawyer; b. Wallace, Idaho, Apr. 13, 1915; s. Charles August and Frances F. (McDiarmid) K.; m. Neysa B. Dalby, Nov. 13, 1944 (div. 1973); children: Robert D., Michael C., James M., Susan N.; m. Wanita Ekholm, Feb. 2, 1974. BA, U. Wash., 1937, JD, 1939. Bar: Wash. 1939, U.S. Dist. Ct. (we. dist.) Wash. 1941, U.S. Ct. Appeals (9th cir.) 1959. Claims atty. Ohio Casualty Ins. Co., Seattle, 1946-52; exec. v.p., gen. counsel Western Pacific Ins. Co., Seattle, 1952-66; ptnr. Merrick, Burgess, Hofstedt & Keating, Seattle, 1966-70; sr. ptnr. Keating, Bucklin & McCormack, Seattle, 1970—. Bd. dirs. Boy Scouts Am., Seattle, 1959-65, March of Dimes, Seattle, 1962-67, Nat. Football Found. and Hall of Fame, Seattle, 1965—. Served to capt. U.S. Army, 1942-46, PTO. Mem. ABA, Seattle-King County Bar Assn., Fedn. Ins. Counsel (sect. chmn.), Def. Rsch. Inst., Wash. Def. Trial Lawyers (pres. 1984-85), Pacific Claim Execs. Assn. (pres. 1965-66), Coll. Club, Harbor Club, Broadmoor Golf Club (pres. 1980-81), Wash. Athletic Club (Seattle), Delta Theta Phi, Sigma Nu. Republican. Lutheran. Home: 3414 81st Pl SE Mercer Island WA 98040-3038 Office: Keating Bucklin & McCormack 4141 Seafirst 5th Ave Seattle WA 98104

KEATINGE, CORNELIA WYMA, architectural preservationist consultant, lawyer; b. Poughkeepsie, N.Y., July 22, 1952; d. Edwin R. and Josephine B. (Brazis) Wyma; m. Robert Reed Keatinge, Aug. 21, 1982; 1 child, Courtney Elizabeth. BArch, U. Ky., 1974; MA in History and Theory of Architecture, U. Essex, Colchester, Eng., 1976; JD, U. Denver, 1982. Bar: Colo. 1982. Archtl. historian Kans. State Hist. Soc., Topeka, 1975-77; hist. architect Nat. Park Service, Denver, 1977-79; assoc. Richard E. Young, Denver, 1982-84; hist. architect Colo. Hist.Soc., Denver, 1984-86; sole practice, cons. architecture Denver, 1986; hist. preservation specialist Adv. Council Hist. Preservation, Golden, Colo., 1986—. Vol. Denver Art Mus., 1980—, Jr. League Denver, 1983—. Rotary fellow, 1974-75; recipient Spl. Achievement award, Nat. Park Service, 1980. Mem. ABA. Home: 460 S Marion Pky # 1904 Denver CO 80209-2544 Office: 730 Simms St Ste 401 Golden CO 80401-4798

KEATOR, CAROL LYNNE, library director; b. Annapolis, Md., Aug. 9, 1945; d. Lyle H. and Juanita F (Waits) K. BA, Syracuse U., 1967; MS, Simmons Coll., 1968. Librarian Bristol (Conn.) Pub. Sch.s, 1968-69, MIT, Cambridge, 1969-72; librarian Santa Barbara (Calif.) Pub. Library, 1972-77, br. supr., 1977-81, prin. librarian, 1981-88, library dir., 1988—. Mem. ALA, Calif. Libr. Assn., Pub. Libr. Assn. Unitarian. Office: Santa Barbara Pub Libr 40 E Anapamu St Santa Barbara CA 93101-2722

KECECIOGLU, DIMITRI BASIL, reliability engineering educator; b. Istanbul, Turkey, Dec. 26, 1922; came to U.S., 1946, naturalized, 1956; s. Basil C. and Mary (Melayios) K.; m. Lorene June Legan, Dec. 22, 1951; children: Zoe Diana Kececioglu Draelos, John Dimitri. BS, Robert Coll., Istanbul, 1942; MS, Purdue U., 1948, PhD, 1953. Asst. instr. Purdue U., Lafayette, Ind., 1943-47; instr. Purdue U., 1947-52; engring. scientist in charge mech. research labs. Allis-Chalmers Mfg. Co., Milw., 1952-57; asst. to dir. mech. engring. industries group Allis-Chalmers Mfg. Co., 1957-60, cons. engr. industries group, 1960-63, dir. corp. reliability program, 1960-63; prof. aerospace and mech. engring. U. Ariz., Tucson, 1963—; dir. reliability and maintainability engring. cons., Tucson, 1963—; dir. Reliability Engring. and Mgmt. Inst., 1963—, Reliability Testing Inst., 1975—; reliability cons. Northrop Space Labs., Gen. Elec. Co., Center for Mgmt. and Indsl. Devel., Rotterdam, Netherlands, Delco Radio div. Gen. Motors Corp., Aerojet-Gen. Corp., Westinghouse Elec. Co., U.S. Army Mgmt. Engring. Tng. Agy., Allied Signal, Data General, Polaroid, Storage Tek, Motorola, Digital Equipment, ITT, B.F. Goodrich, Gen. Dynamics, Xerox, Ford, JPL, Bendix, Cummins Engine, MOOG, Copeland, Eastman Kodak, Allied Chem.; Fulbright lectr. Nat. Tech. U., Athens, 1971-72; sr. extension tchr. UCLA, 1983; hon. prof. Shanghai U. Tech., 1984. Author: Bibliography on Plasticity, 1950, Introduction to Probabilistic Design for Reliability, 1975, Manual of Product Assurance Films and Videotapes, 1980, Reliability Engineering Handbook, Vols. 1-2, 1991, 4th printing, 1994 and 1995, The 1992-94 Reliability Maintainability and Availability Software Handbook, 1992, Reliability and Life Testing Handbook, Vols. 1-2, 1993, Environmental Stress Screening, 1995, Burn-in Testing, 1995, Maintainability, Availability and Operational Readiness Engineering Handbook Vol. 1; also more than 127 papers. Founder, fund raiser Dr. Dimitri Basil Kececioglu Reliability Engring. Rsch. Fellowships Endowment Fund, 1987. Recipient Presidency award Milw. Tech. Coun., 1962, Automotive Industries Author award, 1963, Ralph E. Teetor Outstanding Engring. Educator award Soc. Automotive Engrs., 1977, Anderson prize U. Ariz., 1983, U. Ariz. Scholarship Devel. Office award, 1991, Acad. of Achievement award in edn. Am. Hellenic Ednl. Progressive Assn., 1991-92. Mem. ASME (chmn. Milw. sect. 1960), IEEE, Soc. Exptl. Stress Analysis (chmn. Milw. sect. 1957), Am. Hellenic Ednl. Progressive Assn. (Adac. Achievement award in edn. 1992), Am. Soc. Engring. Edn., Am. Soc. Quality Control (Reliability Edn. Advancement award 1980, Allen Chop award for outstanding contbns. to reliability 1981), Soc. Reliability Engrs. (founder, pres. Tucson chpt. 1974-77), Hellenic Ops. Rsch. Soc. Greece, Phi Beta Kappa (hon.), Sigma Xi (pres. Univ. chpt. 1990-91), Tau Beta Pi, Phi Kappa Phi (pres. U. Ariz. chpt. 1988-89), Nat. Golden Key Soc. (hon.). Home: 7340 N La Oesta Ave Tucson AZ 85704-3119

KECHICHIAN, JOSEPH ALBERT, political scientist, educator; b. Bourj-Hammoud, Lebanon, Mar. 15, 1954; came to U.S., 1974; s. Albert and Josephine (Seraydarian) K.; m. Ritta Bardakjian, Oct. 1, 1994. BA, Immaculate Heart Coll., 1977; MA, Monterey Inst, 1980; PhD, U. Va., 1985. Lectr. Coll. William & Mary, Williamsburg, Va., 1985-86, U. Va., Charlottesville, 1986-89; assoc. polit. scientist Rand Corp., Santa Monica, Calif., 1989—; lectr. history UCLA, 1990—; cons. FBI Acad., Quantico, Va., 1986—; mem. adv. bd. Middle East Policy, Washington, 1994—. Author: Political Dynamics and Security in The Persian Gulf Through the 1990s, 1993; contbr. articles to profl. jours. Gulbenkian fellow U. Va., 1982-83, Kaprielian fellow, 1983-84, Hoover fellow U.S. State Dept., 1989. Mem. Middle East Inst., Middle East Studies Assn. (life), Soc. Armenian Studies (bd. dirs. 1989-92), Soc. Arab Gulf Studies. Armenian Catholic. Office: Rand Corp 1700 Main St PO Box 2138 Santa Monica CA 90407-2138

KEDDY, DIANE, nutrition consultant; b. Grand Forks, N.D., July 14, 1962; d. James Richard and Margaret Rose (Hagerott) Keddy; m. Gary Steven James, Jan. 6, 1990. BS in Dietetics summa cum laude, Calif. Poly. State U., 1984; MS in Nutrition Sci., Calif. State U., Long Beach, 1990. Registered dietician. Clin. dietician Capistrano by the Sea Hosp., Dana Point, Calif., 1985-88; pvt. practice Dana Point, 1986-93; assoc. faculty Saddleback Coll., Mission Viejo, Calif., 1989-93; asst. dir. clin. nutrition dept. Saddleback Meml. Med. Ctr., Laguna Hills, Calif., 1990-92; dir. nutrition svcs. Alternative Solutions, Newport Beach, Calif., 1991—; lectr. dept of nutrition Calif. State U., 1992—; pvt. practice Irvine, Calif., 1993—; adv. bd. Easting Disorders program Saddleback Coll., 1989-93. Author: Nutrition Knowledge of Eating Disorder Patients, 1990. Mem. Am. Dietetic Assn., Calif. Coun. Against Health Fraud, Calif. Dietetic Assn., Phi Kappa Phi, Phi Upsilon Omicron. Office: Diane Keddy MS RD 30 Corporate Park Ste 103 Irvine CA 92714-5132

KEEFER, DAVID KNIGHT, geologist; b. Laramie, Wyo., June 24, 1949; s. William Richard and Eleanor Audrey (Knight) K.; m. Karen Sue Harrison, Sept. 18, 1970; children: Bryan Richard, Alan Harrison. BS and MS in Geology, Stanford U., 1971; MSCE, U. Ill., 1973; PhD in Applied Earth Scis., Stanford U., 1977. Geotech. engr. Harza Engring. Co., Chgo., 1973; geologist U.S. Geol. Survey, Menlo Park, Calif., 1974—, group leader landslide research, 1986—; cons. geology Govt. Argentina, 1978-79, Govt. Japan, 1978, 84, Govt. Costa Rica, 1991, U. Ind. archeol. excavation Great Bedwyn, Eng., 1983-85. Contbr. articles to profl. jours. Recipient Spl. Achievement award U.S. Geol. Survey, 1985, 88, 90. Mem. AAAS, ASCE, Am. Geophys. Union, Geol. Soc. Am. Office: US Geol Survey 345 Middlefield Rd # 998 Menlo Park CA 94025-3561

KEEGAN, JANE ANN, insurance executive, consultant; b. Watertown, N.Y., Sept. 1, 1950; d. Richard Isidor and Kathleen (McKinley) K. BA cum laude, SUNY-Potsdam, 1972; MBA in Risk Mgmt., Golden Gate U., 1986. CPCU. Comml. lines mgr. Lithgow & Rayhill, San Francisco, 1977-80; risk mgmt. account coordinator Dinner Levison Co., San Francisco, 1980-83; ins. cons., San Francisco, 1983-84; account mgr. Rollins Burdick Hunter, San Francisco, 1984-85; account exec. Jardine Ins. Brokers, San Francisco, 1985-86; ins. cons., San Francisco, 1986-87, ins. adminstr. Port of Oakland, 1987—, risk mgr., 1989—. Vol. San Francisco Ballet vol. orgn., 1981—, Bay Area Bus., Govt. ARC disaster conf. steering com., 1987-88, 89, 90, 91-92; mem. Nob Hill Neighbors Assn., 1982—. Mem. Nat. Safety Mgmt. Soc., CPCU Soc. (spl. events chairperson 1982-84, continuing profl. devel. program award 1985, 88, chair loss prevention), Calif. Assn. of Port Authorities (ins. chair 1995), Risk and Ins. Mgr. Soc. (dep., sec. 1990—, dir. legis. 1993, dir. conf.). Democrat. Roman Catholic. Home: 1065 Las Gallinas Ave San Rafael CA 94903-2464

KEEGAN, JOHN CHARLES, state legislator, engineer, consultant; b. Tempe, Ariz., Feb. 21, 1952; s. William Edward and Lucille (Reay) K.; m. Mary Catherine Toschik, Oct. 22, 1971; children: Katherine, Mark, John II. BS in Engring., Ariz. State U., 1975; MS in Geography and Urban Planning, Western Pacific U., 1990. Registered profl. engr., Az., Tex., Utah, Nev.; registered land surveyor, Ariz. Pres. Accels/Keegan Consulting Engrs., Peoria, Ariz., 1987—; mem. Ariz. Ho. Reps., Phoenix, 1991—; commr. Planning and Zoning Commn., Peoria, 1989-91; mem. criminal justice task force Am. Legis. Exch. Coun., 1991—. Mem. selection com. Valley Leadership, Phoenix, 1988; chmn. Vision 2020 Com., Peoria, 1990-91. 1st lt. U.S. Army, 1975-79, comdr. USNR. Mem. Ariz. Soc. Profl. Engrs. (pres. 1990-91, Young Engr. of Yr. award 1980, Disting. Svc. award 1991). Republican. Episcopalian. Office: Ariz Ho Reps 1700 W Washington St Phoenix AZ 85007-2812

KEELER, THEODORE EDWIN, economics educator; b. Enid, Okla., Mar. 25, 1945; s. Clinton Clarence and Lorene Adda Keeler; m. Marjorie Ann Nathanson, Aug. 29, 1982; 1 child, Daniel C. B.A., Reed Coll., 1967; S.M., MIT, 1969, Ph.D., 1971. Asst. prof. econs. U. Calif.-Berkeley, 1971-77, assoc. prof., 1977-83, prof., 1983—; key faculty mem. Robert Wood Johnson Postdoctoral Fellows Program, 1993—. Author: Railroads, Freight, and Public Policy, 1983; co-author: Regulating The Automobile, 1986; also articles; editor: Research in Transportation Economics, vol. I, 1983, vol. II, 1985. Grantee NSF, 1973-75, 80-82, Dept. Transp. program, 1988-90, 93-94, NIH, 1990-91; prin. investigator project on transp. econs. Sloan Found., 1975-80; sr. fellow, vis. scholar Brookings Instn., Washington, 1980-82; co-prin. investigator Tobacco Tax Project Calif. Tobacco-Related Disease Fund, 1990—. Mem. Am. Econs. Assn. Democrat. Home: 617 Bonnie Dr El Cerrito CA 94530-3324 Office: U Calif Dept Econs Berkeley CA 94720-3880

KEELEY, JOSEPH, military officer, marketing professional; b. Boston, Sept. 20, 1937; s. Valentine J. and Margaret Theresa (Molloy) K.; m. Jane Watterson: children: John Christopher, Charles Andrew, Kathryn Jane. BS, U.S. Naval Acad., 1959; MBA, Nat. Univ., 1980. Commd. ensign USN, 1959, advanced through grades to cmmdr., 1975, retired, 1982; various staff positions Norden Systems, 1983-90, western region mktg. mgr., 1990-92; mkt. analyst Paramax Corp., 1992-93; ops. mgr. west coast Vail Rsch. and Tech., Pasadena, Calif., 1993-94; fed. programs mgr. Systems Integrated, Orange, Calif., 1994—. Mem. U.S. Navy League, So. Calif. Aerospace Representatives (chmn. activities com. 1993), Nat. Security Industry Assn. (bd. dirs. 1990-92), Armed Forces Comms. and Electronics Assn. Home and Office: 2080 Via Entrada Newport Beach CA 92660-3934

KEELY, GEORGE CLAYTON, lawyer; b. Denver, Feb. 28, 1926; s. Thomas and Margaret (Clayton) K.; m. Jane Elisabeth Coffey, Nov. 18, 1950; children: Margaret Clayton, George C. (dec.), Mary Anne, Jane Elisabeth, Edward Francis, Kendall Anne. BS in Bus, U. Colo., 1948; LLB, Columbia U., 1951. Bar: Colo. 1951. Assoc. Fairfield & Woods, Denver, 1951-58, ptnr., 1958-86, sr. dir., 1986-90, of counsel, 1990-91, ret., 1991; v.p. Silver Corp., 1966-86; mem. exec. com. Timpte Industries, Inc., 1970-78, dir., 1980-89. Mem. Colo. Commn. Promotion Uniform State Laws, 1967—; regional planning adv. com. Denver Regional Coun. Govts., 1972-74; bd. dirs. Bow Mar Water and Sanitation Dist., 1970-74; trustee Town of Bow Mar, 1972-74; trustee, v.p. Silver Found., 1970-90, mem. bd., 1983-90; trustee, v.p. Denver Area coun. Boy Scouts Am., 1985-90; bd. dirs. Pub. Broadcasting of Colo., Inc., 1986-90, Sta. KCFR. With USAF, 1944-47. Fellow Am. Bar Found., Colo. Bar Found.; mem. ABA (ho. of dels. 1977-79), Denver Bar Assn. (award of merit 1980), Colo. Bar Assn., Nat. Conf. Commrs. Uniform State Laws (sec. 1971-75, exec. com. 1971-79 , chmn. exec. com. 1975-77, pres. 1977-79), Am. Law Inst., Cath. Lawyers Guild of Denver (dir. 1965-67), Denver Estate Planning Coun., U. Club of Denver, (dir. 1966-75, pres. 1973-74), Law Club of Denver (pres. 1966-67, Lifetime Achievement award, 1994), Pinehurst Country Club, Hundred Club, Cactus Club, Rotary, Phi Delta Phi, Beta Theta Pi, Beta Gamma Sigma. Home: 5220 W Longhorn St Littleton CO 80123-1408 Office: Fairfield & Woods PC 1700 Lincoln St Denver CO 80203-4501

KEEN, RONALD LEE, career officer; b. Abilene, Tex., Jan. 28, 1959; s. Larry Lee and Betty Louise (Lesser) K.; Cindy Kaye Smedley, June 17, 1978; children: Cristina, Jordon, Brian. AA in Communication Mgmt., Community Coll. of USAF, 1983; BA in Applied Arts and Sci., Southwest Tex. S. U., 1986; MS in Aero. Sci., Embry Riddle A.U., 1991. Commd. 2d lt. USAF, 1979, advanced through grades to capt., 1990; sr. group comm. analyst 6920 ESG USAF, Misawa AB, Japan, 1980-83; Intel rsch. analyst HQ electronic securiry CMD USAF, Kelly AFB, Tex., 1983-86; instr. crew ICBM 44 strategic missle wing USAF, Ellsworth AFB, S.D., 1986-88, commdr. crew ICBM 68 strategic missle squad, 1988-89, commdr. post CMD ICBM 68 strategic missle squad, 1989-90, evaluator ICBM crew 44 strategic missile wing, 1990-91; officer squad activationHQ Air Force space command USAF, Peterson AFB, Colo., 1991-92; officer space ops. evaluator 4 space ops. USAF, Falcon AFB, Colo., 1992-94, officer space surveillance/orbit analysis 73 space ops., 1994—; ops. officer project SELM 90-1 44 strategic missile wing, Ellsworth AFB, 1990. Commr. T Ball league Ellsworth Youth Sports Assn., 1988-91; coach youth soccer Rapid City (S.D.) Youth Soccer Assn., 1989-91; cubmaster Boy Scouts Am., Ellsworth AFB, 1990-91, asst. cubmaster, Colorado Springs, 1991-93, chmn. pack com., 1992-93. Decorated Commendation medal with 1 and 4 oak leaf clusters.

Mem. Air Force Assn., Nat. Eagle Scout Assn. Republican. Home: Psc Box 7185 APO AP 96319-5000

KEENAN, EDWARD JOSEPH, management consultant; b. N.Y.C., Oct. 3, 1932; s. Edward Joseph and Leona (Tansey) K.; married; 2 children. BA, U. Minn., 1967; MA in Edn., Chapman Coll., 1977; MBA, Pepperdine U., 1984; PhD in Bus. Adminstrn., Kensington U., 1989. Served with U.S. Air Force, 1951-71; ptnr. Edman-Keenan & Assocs., San Bernardino, Calif., 1971-73; adminstr. for pvt. law firms, Los Angeles and Beverly Hills, Calif., 1973-78; cons. to law firms, small bus., and hosps., 1978—; instr. law office mgmt. U. So. Calif., U. West Los Angeles, Calif. State U., Long Beach; cons. in field. Mem. Am. Inst. Indsl. Engrs., Assn. Legal Adminstrs. (charter; pres. Beverly Hills chpt. 1977-78), Cons. Roundtable So. Calif. (chair profl. devel. com.). Republican. Lodges: Elks, Moose, K.C.

KEENAN, GERALD KEAN, writer, retired publishing company executive; b. Waukon, Iowa, Apr. 29, 1932; s. John Cyril and Mary Madeline (Entwisle) K.; m. Irma Ruth Scharninghausen, Sept. 28, 1968 (div. Aug. 1990); children: Kelly Marie, Andrew John; m. Carol Hammer Krismann, Aug. 29, 1992. Supr. cost/inventory control dept. Bruce Pub. Co., Milw., 1966-69; mng. editor, sr. editor Pruett Pub. Co., Boulder, Colo., 1969-90. Contbr. articles to Civil War Times Illustrated, America's Civil War, Jour. of the West, Montana: Mag. of Western History. Served to sgt. USMC, 1950-53, Korea. Mem. Western History Assn., Boulder Corral Westerners (founder, 1st sheriff 1990-91), Civil War Round Table of Colo. (founder, 1st pres. 1977-87). Democrat. Roman Catholic.

KEENAN, RETHA ELLEN VORNHOLT, nurse, educator; b. Solon, Iowa, Aug. 15, 1934; d. Charles Elias and Helen Maurine (Konicek) Vornholt; BSN, State U. Iowa, 1955; MSN, Calif. State U., Long Beach, 1978; m. David James Iverson, June 17, 1956; children: Scott, Craig ; m. Roy Vincent Keenan, Jan. 5, 1980. Publ. health nurse City of Long Beach, 1970-73, 94—, Hosp. Home Care, Torrance, Calif., 1973-75; patient care coord. Hillhaven, L.A., 1975-76; mental health cons. InterCity Home Health, L.A., 1978-79; instr. Community Coll. Dist., L.A., 1979-87; instr. nursing El Camino Coll., Torrance, 1981-86; instr. nursing Chapman Coll., Orange, Calif., 1982, Mt. Saint Mary's Coll., 1986-87; cons., pvt. practice, Rancho Palos Verdes, Calif., 1987-89. Contbg. author: American Journal of Nursing Question and Answer Book for Nursing Boards Review, 1984, Nursing Care Planning Guides for Psychiatric and Mental Health Care, 1987-88, Nursing Care Planning Guides for Children, 1987, Nursing Care Planning Guides for Adults, 1988, Nursing Care Planning Guides for Critically Ill Adults, 1988. Cert. nurse practitioner adult and mental health, 1979; mem. Assistance League of San Pedro, Palos Verdes, Calif. NIMH grantee, 1977-78. Mem. Sigma Theta Tau, Phi Kappa Phi, Delta Zeta. Republican. Lutheran. Avocations: travel, writing, reading. Home: 27849 Longhill Dr Rancho Palos Verdes CA 90275 Office: 2525 Grand Ave Long Beach CA 90815

KEENAN, ROBERT, architect; b. Rochester, N.Y., Jan. 8, 1950; s. John Lawrence and Frances (Hartigan) K.; m. Marianne Julia Janko, Sept. 9, 1989; 1 child, Robert John. BA, Fordham U., 1971; MArch, Harvard U., 1976. Registered architect, Mass., Calif.; cert. nat. coun. archtl. registration bds. Architect Archtl. Resources Cambridge Inc., Cambridge, Mass., 1977-79, Hoskins, Scott, Taylor & Ptnrs., Boston, 1979-81; architect Harry Weese & Assocs., Chgo., 1981-89, v.p., 1983-89; sr. resident architect Singapore Mass Rapid Transit Project, 1982-84; chief architect Metro Rail Transit Cons., 1986-89; architect, engrng. mgr., urban designer, Bechtel Corp., San Francisco, 1989—; chief architect Bay Area Transit Cons., 1989-91; chief architect for expansion/renovation Athens Metro System, 1991-94; dir. facility engrng. Light Rail Transit Sys. Two for Kuala Lumpur, Malaysia, 1994-95; mem. Western Corridor Feasibility Study team Kowloon Canton Railway Corp., Hong Kong, 1995—; speaker, session chmn. Internat. Conf. on Tall Bldgs, Singapore, 1984. Prin. works include Regis Coll. Athletic Facility, Weston, Mass., Singapore Mass Rapid Transit Sys., So. Calif. Metro Rail Project, L.A., Bay Area Rapid Transit Sys., San Francisco, Athens (Greece) Metro Projects, Kuala Lumpur Transis Sys. Mem. AIA, KCRC/WCR Project, Hong Kong. Republican. Roman Catholic. Office: Bechtel Corp Job # 22596 PO Box 19965 50 Beale St San Francisco CA 94119-3965

KEENE, CLIFFORD HENRY, medical administrator; b. Buffalo, Jan. 28, 1910; s. George Samuel and Henrietta Hedwig (Yeager) K.; m. Mildred Jean Kramer, Mar. 3, 1934; children: Patricia Ann (Mrs. William S. Kneedler), Martha Jane (Mrs. William R. Sproule), Diane Eve (Mrs. Gordon D. Simonds). AB, U. Mich., 1931, MD, 1934, MS in Surgery, 1938; DSc, Hahnemann Med. Coll., 1973; LLD, Golden Gate U., 1974. Diplomate Am. Bd. Surgery, Am. Bd. Preventive Medicine (occupational medicine). Resident surgeon, instr. surgery U. Mich., 1934-39; cons. surgery of cancer Mich. Med. Soc. and Mich. Dept. Health, 1939-40; pvt. practice surgery Wyandotte, Mich., 1940-41; med. dir. Kaiser-Frazer Corp., 1946-53; instr. surgery U. Mich., 1946-54; med. adminstrv. positions with Kaiser Industries and Kaiser Found., 1954-75, v.p., 1960-75; v.p., gen. mgr. Kaiser Found. Hosps. and Kaiser Found. Health Plan, 1960-67; med. dir. Kaiser Found. Sch. Nursing, 1954-67; dir. Kaiser Found. Research Inst., 1958-75; pres. Kaiser Found. Hosps. Health Plan, Sch. Nursing, 1968-75, dir., 1960-80; chmn. editorial bd. Kaiser Found. Med. Bull., 1954-65; lectr. med. econs. U. Calif.-Berkeley, 1956-75; mem. vis. com. Med. Sch., Stanford U., 1966-72, Harvard U., 1967-71, 79-85, U. Mich., 1973-78; Mem. Presdl. Panel Fgn. Med. Grads. (Nat. Manpower Commn.), 1966-69. Contbr. papers to profl. lit. Bd. visitors Harvard Bus. Adv. Council, 1972, Charles R. Drew Postgrad. Med. Sch., 1972-79; trustee Amman Civil Hosp., Jordan, 1973, Community Hosp. of Monterey Peninsula, 1983-92. Lt. col. M.C. AUS, 1942-46. Recipient Disting. Service award Group Health Assn. Am., 1974; Disting. Alumnus award U. Mich. Med. Center, 1976; Disting. Alumnus Service award U. Mich., 1985. Fellow ACS; mem. Am. Assn. Indsl. Physicians and Surgeons, Nat. Acad. Scis., Inst. Medicine, Calif. Acad. Medicine, Frederick A. Coller Surg. Soc., Calif., Am. med. assns., Alpha Omega Alpha (editorial bd., contbr. to Pharos mag. 1977—). Home: 3978 Ronda Rd PO Box 961 Pebble Beach CA 93953

KEENER, JOHN WESLEY, management consultant; b. Macedonia, Iowa, Apr. 10, 1927; s. Elza Lee and Florence Evelyn (Rhoades) K.; m. Loucille Clementine Wiedower, Nov. 19, 1949; children: Tonya Florence, Jonellyn Christine. BSEE, La. Tech., 1945; postgrad., St. Mary's Coll., 1971, Air War Coll., 1971. Owner 4K Motors, Medford, Oreg., 1948-51; purchasing agt. White City Lumber, Medford, 1951-52; asst. mgr. Woodbury & Co., Medford, 1952-57, Am. Steel & Supply, Medford, 1957-68; gen. mgr. Am. Steel & Supply, Medford and Redding, Calif., 1968-73, Medford, 1973-85; owner Rogue Pacific, Medford, 1985-91; mgmt. cons. Medford, 1991—; pres., bd. dirs. Jackson C.C. Found., Medford; cons. Oreg. div. Aeronautics, Salem, Oreg. Mem. Medford Planning Commn., 1972-75; chmn. Jackson County Econ. Devel., Medford, 1991; mem. County Airport Adv. Com., Medford, 1983—; chief instr. Oreg. Air Search and Rescue. With USN, 1944-46, col. USAF Aux. CAP, 1972—. Recipient Commendation for Community Svc. Gov. Oreg., 1992, Community Leader Spirit award Broadcasters, 1987. Mem. Loyal Order of Moose, Oreg. Wing Civil Air Patrol (comdr. 1981-82), Pacific Regional Civil Air Patrol (commendation 1981, nat. life saving awards (2)), Jackson County Airport Com. (past chmn., mem.), Rogue Valley Country Club. Republican. Methodist. Office: PO Box 22 Medford OR 97501-0002

KEENER, ROBERT W., retired gas company executive; b. 1931; married. Grad., U. Kans., 1958. Reservoir engr., then mgr. product and drilling Atlantic Richfield Co., Midland, Tex., 1958-69; v.p. ops. Tipperary Corp., Midland, 1969-73; with Apco Group (now Northwest Pipeline Corp.), from 1973; pres. Northwest Pipeline Corp., Salt Lake City, from 1983, pres., chief oper. officer, also bd. dirs. Served with USAF, 1950-53. Office: NW Pipeline Corp PO Box 8900 295 Chipeta Way Salt Lake City UT 84108-1220

KEENEY, EDMUND LUDLOW, physician; b. Shelbyville, Ind., Aug. 11, 1908; s. Bayard G. and Ethel (Adams) K.; m. Esther Cox Loney Wight, Mar. 14, 1950; children: Edmund Ludlow, Eleanor Seymour (Mrs. Cameron Leroy Smith). A.B., Ind. U., 1930; M.D., Johns Hopkins U., 1934. Diplomate Am. Bd. Internal Medicine. Intern Johns Hopkins Hosp., 1934-37, vis. physician, instr. internal medicine, 1940-48; practice medicine, specializing internal medicine San Diego, 1948- 55; dir. Scripps Clinic and Research Found., La Jolla, 1955-67; pres. Scripps Clinic and Research Found., 1967-77, pres. emeritus, 1977—; dir. rsch. on fungus infections OSRD, 1942-46. Author: Practical Medical Mycology, 1955, Medical Advice for International Travel; contbr. articles on allergy, immunology and mycology to med. jours. Bd. dirs. U. San Diego, Allergy Found. Am. Fellow A.C.P.; mem. A.M.A., Am. Soc. Clin. Investigation, Am. Acad. Allergy (pres. 1964), Western Assn. Physicians, Calif. Med. Assn., Western Soc. Clin. Research, Phi Beta Kappa, Alpha Omega Alpha, Beta Theta Pi. Republican. Presbyn. Clubs: El Dorado Country, La Jolla Country, Fox Acres Country. Lodge: Rotary. Home: 338 Via Del Norte La Jolla CA 92037-6539 Office: 10666 N Torrey Pines Rd La Jolla CA 92037-1027*

KEEP, JUDITH N., federal judge; b. Omaha, Mar. 24, 1944. B.A., Scripps Coll., 1966; J.D., U. San Diego, 1970. Bar: Calif. 1971. Atty. Defenders Inc., San Diego, 1971-73; pvt. practice law, 1973-76; asst. U.S. atty. U.S. Dept. Justice, 1976; judge Mcpl. Ct., San Diego, 1976-80; judge U.S. Dist. Ct. (so. dist.) Calif., San Diego, 1980—, chief judge, 1991—. Office: US Dist Ct 940 Front St Rm 6 San Diego CA 92101-8994*

KEES, BEVERLY, newspaper editor; b. Mpls., June 4, 1941; d. Burton Joseph and Dorothy Ann (White) K. BA, U. Minn., 1963. Reporter Mpls. Star, 1963-69, sect. editor, 1969-72; rsch. planning analyst Mpls. Star and Tribune Co., 1972-73; asst. mng. editor Mpls. Tribune, 1973-81; exec. editor Grand Forks (N.D.) Herald, 1981-84; editor Post-Tribune, Gary, Ind., 1984-88; exec. editor Fresno (Calif.) Bee, 1988-93; vis. profl. scholar Freedom Forum First Amendment Ctr. Vanderbilt U., 1993-94; editor-in-resident The Freedom Forum Pacific Coast Ctr., Oakland, Calif., 1994—; part-time journalism instr. Coll. St. Thomas, St. Paul, 1974. Author: Wonderful Ways With Chicken, 1970, Cook with Honey, 1973, Basic Breads Around the World, 1977; co-author Fondue on the Menu, 1970. Bd. dirs. greater Grand Forks Symphony Assn., 1982-84, Grand Forks chpt. Am. Red Cross, 1981-84, FKJN Pub. Radio Sta., 1981-84; mentor Career Beginnings Gary Ind. high schs., 1986-88; pres. Minn. Arts Forum, 1980-81; sec. The Acad., 1990-91, v.p., 1991-92, pres., 1992-93. Mem. Am. Soc. Newspaper Editors (chair bulletin com. 1989-90), Internat. Press Inst. (Am. com. bd. 1988—), Associated Press Mng. Editors Assn. (bd. dirs. 1985-91, sec. 1994), Minn. Alumnae Club (pres. 1977), U. Minn. Alumni Assn. (bd. dirs. 1975-79, exec. com. 1976-79). Episcopalian. Home: 201 Harrison St Apt 1127 San Francisco CA 94105-2000 Office: Freedom Forum Pacific Coast Ctr 70 Washington St Ste 210 Oakland CA 94607-3737

KEGLEY, JACQUELYN ANN, philosophy educator; b. Conneaut, Ohio, July 18, 1938; d. Steven Paul and Gertrude Evelyn (Frank) Kovacevic; m. Charles William Kegley, June 12, 1964; children: Jacquelyn Ann, Stephen Lincoln Luther. BA cum laude, Allegheny Coll., 1960; MA summa cum laude, Rice U., 1964; PhD, Columbia U., 1971. Asst. prof. philosophy Calif. State U., Bakersfield, 1973-77, assoc. prof., 1977-81, prof., 1981—; vis. prof. U. Philippines, Quezon City, 1966-68; grant project dir. Calif. Council Humanities, 1977, project dir. 1980, 82; mem. work group on ethics Am. Colls. of Nursing, Washington, 1984-86. Author: Introduction to Logic, 1978; editor: Humanistic Delivery of Services to Families, 1982, Education for the Handicapped, 1982; mem. editorial bd. Jour. Philosophy in Lit., 1979-84; contbr. articles to profl. jours. Bd. dirs. Bakersfield Mental Health Assn., 1982-84, Citizens for Betterment of Community. Recipinet Outstanding Prof. award Calif. State U., 1989-90, Golden Roadrunner award Bakersfield Community, 1991. Mem. N.Y. Acad. Scis., Philosophy of Sci. Assn., Soc. Advancement Am. Phil. soc. (chmn. Pacific div. 1979-83, nat. exec. com. 1974-79), Philosophy Soc., Soc. Interdisciplinary Study of Mind, Am. Philosophical Assn., Dorian Soc., Phi Beta Kappa. Democrat. Lutheran. Home: 7312 Kroll Way Bakersfield CA 93309-2320 Office: Calif State U Dept Philosophy & Religious Studies Bakersfield CA 93311

KEHL, RANDALL HERMAN, corporate executive, lawyer; b. Furstenfeldbruck, Fed. Republic of Germany, May 18, 1954; came to U.S., 1955; s. Raymond Herman and Annabelle (Fair) K.; m. Sharon Kay Barnes; children: Lindsey Elizabeth, Jessica Anne, Austin Randall. BS, USAF Acad., 1976; MBA, U. N.D., 1980; JD, Pepperdine U., 1983. Bar: N.D. 1983, D.C. 1988, U.S. Supreme Ct. 1990. Commd. 2d lt. USAF, 1976, advanced through grades to maj., 1986, chief civil law, 1983-84, chief criminal law, 1984-85; squadron commdr. Alaska Air Command, Anchorage, 1985, chief def. counsel, 1985-86; dep. base atty. Kirtland AFB, Albuquerque, 1986-89; spl. asst. U.S. atty. U.S. Dept. Justice, Albuquerque, 1986-89; chief energy litigation Office of USAF JAG, Washington, 1989-90; White House fellow, 1990-91; chmn., CEO POD Assocs., Inc., 1991—; cons., counsel to DESA-office of sec. of def. U.S. Dept. Def., Albuquerque, 1993; prin. Randall H. Kehl Consulting, Albuquerque, 1993—; mem. staff Pres.'s Coun. on Competiveness, 1990-91; vice-chmn. White House Working group on Commercialization of Fed. Lab. Tech.; chmn. Candeli, Ltd., Kerorioni, Ltd., Rep. of Georgia; adj. instr. law U. Alaska, 1985-86; bd. dirs., counsel Kirtland Fed. Credit Union, Albuquerque; bd. dirs., sec. Triad Communicaitons, Inc., Albuquerque; chmn. bd. POD Assocs., Inc., 1988-90. Asst. scoutmaster Boy Scouts Am., Minot, N.D., 1977-80; tchr. Officers Christian Fellowship, Minot, 1977-80; civic arbitrator Mediation and Conciliation Svc., 1983-86; mem. pvt. sch. bd. Anchorage, 1984-85, gov.'s Task Force for Utility Corp. Restructuring, 1987; vice-chmn. N.Mex. gov-elect transition team, 1994; vice-chmn. Gov.'s Bus. Adv. Coun., 1995—; mem. steering com. Rep. Campaign, 1995—. Mem. ABA, Albuquerque Acad. Capital Devel. Coun. and Assoc. Trustees, Phi Delta Phi. Republican. Presbyterian. Office: Pod Assocs 2309 Renard Pl SE Ste 201 Albuquerque NM 87106-4259

KEHLER, DOROTHEA FAITH, English educator; b. N.Y.C., Apr. 21, 1936; d. Nathan and Minnie (Coopersmith) Gutwill; (widowed 1981); children: Paul Dolid, Eve Boyd, Jessica, Ted. BA, CCNY, 1956; MA, Ohio U., 1967, PhD, 1969. Instr. MacMurray Coll., Ill., 1964-65; instr. Ohio U., Athens, 1965-66, teaching fellow, 1966-68; lectr. San Diego State U., 1969-70, asst. prof., 1970-85, assoc. prof., 1985-88, prof., 1988—. Author: Problems in Literary Research, 1975, 2d edit., 1981, 3d edit., 1987; editor: In Another Country: Feminist Perspectives on Renaissance Drama, 1991. Nat. Endowment for the Humanities fellow Harvard U., 1983; Folger Libr. Inst. grantee, 1988; San Diego State U. scholar, 1990—. Mem. ACLU, MLA, NOW, Internat. Shakespeare Assn., Rocky Mountain Modern Lang. Assn., Southeastern Renaissance Conf., Renaissance Conf. So. Calif., Philol. Assn. of Pacific Coast, Shakespeare Assn. Am., Amnesty Internat. Democrat. Office: San Diego State U English Dept San Diego CA 92182

KEHLER, RUTH, newspaper editor; b. Reedley, Calif., Jan. 1, 1956; d. Frank and Ruby Emma (Warkentin) Kehler; children: Jason Wedehase, Sarah Wedehase. AA, Kings River Coll., Reedley, 1983; BA, Calif. State U., Fresno, 1993. Editor Parlier (Calif.) Post, 1984-92, Orange Cove (Calif.) and Mountain Times, 1984-94; community editor Reedley Exponent, 1993-94; mng. editor Fowler (Calif.) Ensign, 1993-94; copy editor The Fresno (Calif.) Bee, 1994—. Hosted World Exch., Reedley, 1992. Calif. Press Women scholar, 1993, Paul Sheehan scholar, 1992; recipient Community Svc. awards. Mem. Calif. Press Women (sec. Ctrl. Dist. 1989), Orange Cove Women's Club (publicity chair 1987-94, Golden Key, Kappa Tau Alpha. Home: 1278 W Henley Creek Rd Reedley CA 93654-3628 Office: Reedley Exponent 1130 G St Reedley CA 93654-3004

KEHLMANN, ROBERT, artist, critic; b. Bklyn., Mar. 9, 1942. BA, Antioch Coll., 1963; MA, U. Calif., Berkeley, 1966. One-man shows include: Richmond Art Ctr., Calif., 1976, William Sawyer Gallery, San Francisco, 1978, 82, 86, Galerie M, Kassel, Fed. Republic Germany, 1985, Anne O'Brien Gallery, Washington, 1988, 90, Dorothy Weiss Gallery, San Francisco, 1993; group shows include: Am. Craft Mus., N.Y.C., 1978, 86, Corning (N.Y.) Mus. Glass, 1979, Tucson Mus. of Art, 1983, Kulturhuset, Stockholm, Sweden, 1985; represented in permanent collections at Corning Mus. Glass, Leigh Yawkey Woodson Art Mus., Hessisches Landes Mus., W.Ger., Bank of Am. World Hdqrs., San Francisco, Toledo Mus. Art, Hokkaido Mus. Modern Art, Sapporo, Japan, Huntington Mus. of Art, W.Va., Am. Craft Mus., N.Y.C., Musée des Arts Décoratifs, Lausanne, Switzerland; instr. glass design Calif. Coll. Arts and Crafts, Oakland, 1978-80, 91, Pilchuck Glass Ctr., Stanwood, Wash., 1978-80. Author: Twentieth Century Stained Glass: A New Definition, 1992; contbg. editor: New Glass Work mag.; editor: Glass Art Soc. Jour.,1981-84. Nat. Endowment Arts grantee, 1977-78. Mem. Glass Art Soc. (bd. dirs. 1980-84, 89-92, hon. life mem.). Office: Dorothy Weiss Gallery 256 Sutter St San Francisco CA 94108-4409

KEHOE, JAMES WILLIAM, JR., marketing manager; b. Sacramento, June 27, 1949; s. James William and Margaret Louise (Kennedy) K.; m. Brenda Lynn Magee, July 28, 1978; children: Michael Herrin Troyer, Aaron Max Troyer. BA in Geography, U. Colo., 1972; postgrad., No. Ariz. U., 1978-79. Mfg. rep. James Kehoe Co., San Francisco, 1976-78; divsn. head Hillsdale Sash & Door Co., Inc., Portland, Oreg., 1979-81, sales rep., 1981-86, sales mgr., 1986-94; dir. Am. Inst. Bldg. Design, Portland, 1985-86. Lt. USN, 1972-76, PTO. Office: Hillsdale Sash & Door Co PO Box 629 Wilsonville OR 97070-0629

KEHOE, VINCENT JEFFRÉ-ROUX, photographer, author, cosmetic company executive; b. Bklyn., N.Y., Sept. 12, 1921; s. John James and Bertha Florence (Roux) K.; m. Gena Irene Marino, Nov. 2, 1966. Student, MIT, 1940-41, Lowell Technol. Inst., 1941-42, Boston U., 1942; BFA in Motion Picture and TV Prodn., Columbia U., 1957. Dir. make-up dept. CBS-TV, N.Y.C., 1948-49, NBC Hallmark Hall of Fame series, 1951-53; make-up artist in charge of make-up for numerous film, TV and stage prodns., 1942—; dir. make-up Turner Hall Corp., 1959-61, Internat. Beauty Show, 1962-66; pres., dir. research Research Council of Make-up Artists, Inc., 1963—; chief press officer at Spanish Pavilion, N.Y. World's Fair, 1965; free-lance photographer, 1956—. Contbr. photographs to numerous mags. including Time, Life, Sports Illustrated, Argosy, Popular Photography; author: The Technique of Film and Television Make-up for Color, 1970, The Make-up Artist in the Beauty Salon, 1969, We Were There: April 19, 1775, 1974, A Military Guide, 1974, 2d rev. edit., 1993, The Technique of the Professional Makeup Artist, 1985, 2nd edit., 1995, Special Make-up Effects, 1991; author-photographer bullfighting books: Aficionado! (N.Y. Art Dirs. Club award 1960), Wine, Women and Toros (N.Y. Art Dirs. award 1962); producer: (documentary color film) Matador de Toros, 1959. Served with inf. U.S. Army, World War II, ETO. Decorated Purple Heart, Bronze Star, CIB; recipient Torch award Council of 13 Original States, 1979. Fellow Co. Mil. Historians; mem. Tenth Foot Royal Lincolnshire Regimental Assn. (life; Hon. Col. 1968), Soc. Motion Picture and TV Engrs. (life), Acad. TV Arts and Scis., Soc. for Army Hist. Research (Eng.) (life), Brit. Officers Club New England (life), 10th Mountain Div. Assn. (life), 70th Inf. Div. (life), DAV (life), Nat. Rifle Assn. (life). Home and Office: PO Box 850 Somis CA 93066-0850

KEIM, ELIZABETH M., computer company executive; b. El Paso, Tex., Apr. 8, 1958; d. Carl D. and Jeannette B. (Baker) K. BS in computer sci., Colo. State U., 1980; MBA in acctg. & fin., Regis U., 1988. Programmer IBM, Boulder, Colo., 1980-83, staff asst., 1983-86, project office mgr., 1986-91; mgr. of quality IBM/ISSC, Boulder, Colo., 1991—. Contbr. articles to profl. jours. Treas. Fountain Greens Home Owners Assn., Boulder, 1993. Mem. Am. Soc. Qualtiy Contorl, Denver Sect. Am. Soc. Quality Control (svc. industry com. chair 1991-93, chair 1993-94), Svc. Industry Divsn. Am. Soc. Quality Control (reg. counselor coord. 1992-94, group dir. 1992-94, vice chair 1994-95). Office: 5600 63rd St # 024K Boulder CO 80301-9269

KEIM, MICHAEL RAY, dentist; b. Sabetha, Kans., June 8, 1951; s. Milton Leroy and Dorothy Juanita (Stover) K.; m. Christine Anne Lorenzen, Nov. 20, 1971; children: Michael Scott, Dawn Marie, Erik Alan. Student, U. Utah, 1969-72; DDS, Creighton U., 1976. Pvt. practice Casper, Wyo., 1976—. Mem. organizing bd. dirs. Ctrl. Wyo. Soccer Assn., 1976-77; mem. Casper Mountain Ski Patrol, Nat. Ski Patrol System, 1980—, avalanche ski mountaineering advisor No. Div. Region III, 1992—; bd. dirs., dep. commr. for fast pitch Wyo. Amateur Softball Assn., 1980-84; bd. dirs. Ctrl. Wyo. Softball Assn., 1980-84. Recipient Purple Merit Star for Saving a Life, 1992. Mem. ADA, Fedn. Dentaire Internat., Pierre Fauchard Acad., Wyo. Acad. Gen. Dentistry (sec.-treas. 1980-82, pres. 1982-87), Wyo. Dental Assn. (bd. dirs. 1992—, chmn. conv. 1993, v.p. 1993-94, pres.-elect 1994-95, pres. 1995-96), Wyo. Dental Polit. Action Com. (sec.-treas. 1985—), Ctrl. Wyo. Dental Assn. (sec.-treas. 1981-82, pres. 1982-83), Wyo. Dental Hist. Assn. (bd. dirs. 1989-95), Kiwanis (v.p. Casper Club 1988-89, bd. dirs. 1986—, pres.-elect 1989-90, pres. 1990-91, internat. del. 1989-91), Creighton Club (pres. 1982-84). Methodist. Home: 58 Jonquil St Casper WY 82604-3863 Office: 1749 S Boxelder St Casper WY 82604-3538

KEIM, PAUL STEPHEN, molecular geneticist educator; b. Twin Falls, Idaho, Apr. 5, 1955; s. Robert Edgecomb and Sybil Odette (Miller) K.; m. Jenny Merete Bate, Dec. 28, 1985; children: Erika Karen, Stephen Paul. BS magna cum laude, No. Ariz. U., 1977; PhD, U. Kans., 1981. Asst. rsch. prof. biology U. Utah, Salt Lake City, 1981-87; rsch. assoc. Iowa State U., Ames, 1987-88; prof. biology No. Ariz. U., Flagstaff, 1988—; dir. Lowden Microbiology Endowment. Contbr. articles to profl. jours. Grantee rsch. Pioneer HiBred Inst., 1988, USDA Plant Genome, 1992, Nat. Sci. Fedn., Dept. of Energy, Program for Ecological Rsch. Fellow Assn. Western Univs.; mem. Am. Soc. Agronomy, Genetics Soc. Am., Sigma Xi. Office: No Ariz U Dept Biology PO Box 5640 Flagstaff AZ 86011

KEIMIG, ALAN CHARLES, architect; b. Torrington, Wyo., Oct. 9, 1942; s. Edwin Jack and Eunice Adaline (Goddard) K.; m. Judith Ann Hodgson, Mary Jane Polack (div.); children: Randall James, Angela Jane, John Joseph, Christina Carol, Jené Marie; m. Carol R. Nedderman. BS, U. Wyo., 1968. Engrng. technician U.S. Soil Conservation, Casper, Wyo., 1961-63; surveying asst. U.S. Forest Svc., Laramie, Wyo., 1964; designer J. T. Banner & Assocs., Laramie, 1964-66; undergrad. asst. U. Wyo., Laramie, 1966-68; planner The Boeing Co., Auburn, Wash., 1968; project mgr. Thompson/Hansen Architects, Federal Way, Wash., 1968-71, Ronald E. Thompson, Federal Way, 1971-73; owner, arch., planner The Keimig Assocs., Auburn, Wash., 1973—; bd. mem. Gov.'s Adv. Bd. on Indian Affairs, State of Wash., 1974-75; mem. exec. com., steering com., chairperson econ. restructuring Auburn Downtown Assn., 1993—; disting. spkr. Indian Affairs U.S. Govt., 1972. Coord. Am. Civil Liberties, South King County, 1970. Recipient Disting. Alumni Scholarship, 1966, James Kramlich award for outstanding committment and svc., 1994. Mem. Airlines of Am. (bd. dirs. 1995), City of Auburn Landmarks and Heritage Commn., Auburn C. of C. (EDC com.). Democrat. Office: The Keimig Assocs 216 A St NW Auburn WA 98001-4927

KEIPER, MARILYN MORRISON, elementary education educator; b. South Gate, Calif., June 12, 1930; d. David Cline and Matilda Ruth (Pearce) M.; m. Edward E. Keiper, June 18, 1962; children: Becky S. Swickard, Edward M. BA, Calif. State U., L.A., 1954; postgrad., UCLA, 1968. Elem. tchr. Rosemead (Calif.) Sch. Dist., 1954—; recreation leader L.A. County, 1951-62. 2d leader 1st Ch. Christ Scientist, Arcadia, Calif., 1991-94; mem. cons. Janson Adv. Group, Rosemead, 1985—; bd. dirs. Janson PTA, Rosemead, 1985—; participant Sta. KNBC Spirit of Edn., 1990-92. Named Tchr. of the Yr., L.A. County, 1983-84. Fellow Rosemead Tchrs. Assn., Delta Kappa Gamma.

KEIR, GERALD JANES, newspaper editor; b. Ludlow, Mass., Aug. 22, 1943; s. Alexander J. and Evelyn M. (Buckley) K.; m. Karen Mary Devine, July 22, 1972; children: Matthew J., Katherine B., Megan E. BA, Mich. State U., 1964, MA, 1966. Reporter Honolulu Advertiser, 1968-74, city editor, 1974-86, mng. editor, 1986-89, editor, 1989—. Co-author text: Advanced Reporting: Beyond News Events, 1985. Bd. dirs. Aloha United Way. Recipient Nat. Reporting award Am. Polit. Sci. Assn., 1971, Benjamin Fine Nat. award Am. Assn. Secondary Sch. Prins., 1981; John Ben Snow fellow, 1983, NEH fellow, 1973. Mem. Am. Soc. Newspaper Editors, Assoc. Press Mng. Editors, Am. Assn. Pub. Opinion Rsch. Soc. Profl. Journalists, Asian-Am. Journalists Assn., Social Sci. Assn., Pacific Club. Office: Honolulu Advertiser PO Box 3110 605 Kapiolani Blvd Honolulu HI 96813-5129

KEISER, MEGAN MARIE, neuroscience nurse specialist; b. Ann Arbor, Mich., Aug. 22, 1964; d. Franklin Delano McDonald and Mary Patricia (Ranere) Currier; m. Edward Vincent Keiser, Aug. 3, 1991; children: Johnathan Joseph, Kristi Marie, Patricia Ruthanne. BSN, U. Mich., 1986, MS in Med.-Surg. Nursing, 1990. RN, Mich., Calif.; cert. BCLS, ACLS, clin. specialist in med.-surg. nursing; cert. neurosci. RN. Nursing asst. in neuroscis. U. Mich. Hosp., Ann Arbor, 1984-86, staff nurse neuroscis., 1986-90; clin. nurse specialist in neurosurgery Detroit Receiving Hosp., 1990-92; clin. nurse specialist Comprehensive Epilepsy Program, L.A., 1993-94; BLS instr. Am. Heart Assn., 1990. Mem. AACN, ANA, Am. Assn. Neurosci. Nurses, Epi Found. of Am., Case Mgmt. Soc. Am. Roman Catholic.

KEISLING, PHILLIP ANDREW, state official; b. Portland, Oreg., June 23, 1955; s. Les and Ione Keisling; m. Pam Wiley, Sept. 4, 1988. BA, Yale U., 1977. Speech writer Gov. Tom McCall, Salem, Oreg., 1978; reporter Willamette Week, Portland, 1978-81; editor Washington Monthly mag., 1982-84; sr. legis asst. Oreg. Speakers of the Ho., Salem, 1985-88; mem. Oreg. Ho. of Reps., Salem, 1989-91; sec. of state State of Oreg., Salem, 1991—; mem. State Land Bd., Salem, 1991—, Hanford Waste Bd., Portland, 1991—. Chmn. Brooklyn Neighborhood Assn., Portland, 1986-88. Office: Office Sec of State State Capitol Rm 136 Salem OR 97310

KEISTER, JEAN CLARE, lawyer; b. Warren, Ohio, Aug. 28, 1931; d. John R. Keister and Anna Helen Brennan. JD, Southwesten, 1966. Bar: Calif. 1967, U.S. Supreme Ct. 1972, U.S. Dist. Ct. (so. dist.) Calif. 1988. Legal writer Gilbert Law Summaries, L.A., 1967; instr. Glendale (Calif.) Coll. Law, 1968; pvt. practice Glendale, 1967-70. Mem. Themis Soc., 1989-93. Recipient Golden Poet award World of Poetry. Mem. Burbank Bar Assn. (sec. 1993), Antelope Valley Bar Assn., Lancaster C. of C., Palmdale C. of C. Office: 1321 W Burbank Blvd Burbank CA 91506-1417

KEISTER, MARIE SILVER, public relations professional; b. Wooster, Ohio, Sept. 25, 1963; d. Thomas Edward and Donna Jean (Shellenberger) Silver; m. Mark Steven Keister, Aug. 1, 1987; 1 child, Tyler Daniel. BA in Comm., Ohio State U., 1981-85. Accredited Pub. Rels. Profl. Mktg. asst. YMCA of Columbus (Ohio), 1985; acct. exec. Sta. WBBY-FM, Columbus, 1986; acct. supr. Russell, Luke, Mercier Avt., Columbus, 1986-87; sr. acct. exec. Brooks Young Comms., Columbus, 1987-90; pub. info. officer Pierce Transit, Tacoma, Wash., 1990—; developer media rels seminars Pierce County Pub. Info. Officers Tacoma, 1992-93; speaker U. Wash., Pierce Coll., Tacoma, Seattle, 1991—; pub. rels. panelist Am. Gas Assn., Nat. Conf., Seattle, 1992; mem. Worldwide Leadership Panel, N.Y.C., 1989-93. Speaker in field; contbr. articles to profl. jours. Chair Pierce county bus. adv. coun. Resource Ctr. for the Handicapped, Seattle, 1993-94; pres. women's bd. Easter Seal Rehab. Ctr. of Cen. Ohio, Columbus, 1988-90; pub. rels. com. Childhood League, Children's Hosp., Columbus, 1988-90; publicity com. Jane Latane for State House of Reps., Columbus, 1986; pub. com. Bobbie Hall for County Treas., Columbus, 1984, 88. Recipient Comm. Achievement Merit award Am. Gas Assn., 1992, Employee Newsletter Adwheel award Am. Pub. Transit Assn., 1992, Wall of Fame award Wash. State Dept. Transp., 1995. Mem. Pub. Rels. Soc. Am. (chair southend group 1993-94, co-chair accreditation 1993, pub. rels. accreditation instr. 1993-94, Silver Totem Pub. Rels. Event award Tacoma, 1992, Silver Anvil Cert. of Commendation, N.Y.C., 1992), Pub. Info. Roundtable, Mcpl. League of Tacoma/ Pierce County. Home: 9206 81st St SW Tacoma WA 98498-3962 Office: Pierce Transit 3701 96th St SW Tacoma WA 98499-4431

KEITH, BRUCE EDGAR, political analyst, genealogist; b. Curtis, Nebr., Feb. 17, 1918; s. Edgar L. and Corinne E. (Marsteller) K.; m. Evelyn E. Johnston, Oct. 29, 1944; children: Mona Louise, Kent Marsteller, Melanie Ann. AB with high distinction, Nebr. Wesleyan U., 1940; MA, Stanford U., 1952; grad. Command and Staff, Marine Corps Schs., 1958, Sr. Resident Sch., Naval War Coll., 1962; PhD, U. Calif.-Berkeley, 1982. Commd. 2d lt. U.S. Marine Corps, 1942, advanced through grades to col., 1962, ret., 1971, OinC Marine Corps Nat. Media, N.Y.C., 1946-49, support arms coord. 1st Marines, Seoul, Chosin, Korea, 1950, comdg. officer 3d Bn., 11th Marines, 1958-59, ops. officer, Pres. Dwight D. Eisenhower visit to Okinawa, 1960, G-3 ops. officer Fleet Marine Force, Pacific, Cuban Missile Crisis, 1962, mem. U.S. del. SEATO, Planning Conf., Bangkok, Thailand, 1964, G-3, Fleet Marine Force, Pacific, 1964-65, head Strategic Planning Study Dept., Naval War Coll., 1966-68, genealogist, 1967—, exec. officer Hdqrs. Marine Corps programs, Washington, 1968-71; election analyst Inst. Govtl. Studies, U. Calif.-Berkeley, 1974-86, polit. analyst, 1986—; teaching asst. U. Calif.-Berkeley, 1973-74. Bd. dirs., Bay Area Funeral Soc., 1980-83, v.p., 1981-83. Decorated Bronze Star, Navy Commendation medal, Presdl. Unit citation with 3 bronze stars. Recipient Phi Kappa Phi Silver medal Nebr. Wesleyan U., 1940, Alumni award, 1964. Mem. Am. Polit. Sci. Assn., Acad. Polit. Sci., Am. Acad. Polit. and Social Sci., World Affairs Coun. No. Calif., Marine Corps Assn., Ret. Officers Assn. Phi Kappa Phi, Pi Gamma Mu. Republican. Unitarian. Clubs: Commonwealth of Calif. (San Francisco), Marines' Meml. (San Francisco). Lodge: Masons. Contbg. author: The Descendants of Daniel and Elizabeth (Disbrow) Keith, 1979-81; History of Curtis, Nebraska-The First Hundred Years, 1984; author: A Comparison of the House Armed Services Coms. in the 91st and 94th Congresses: How They Differed and Why, 1982; The Johnstons of Morning Sun, 1979; The Marstellers of Arrellton, 1978; The Morris Family of Brookville, 1977; Japan-the Key to America's Future in the Far East, 1962; A United States General Staff: A Must or a Monster?, 1950; co-author: California Votes, 1960-72, 1974; The Myth of the Independent Voter, 1992; Further Evidence on the Partisan Affinities of Independent " Leaners," 1983. Address: PO Box 156 El Cerrito CA 94530-0156

KEITH, DONALD MALCOLM, physician; b. Cordova, Alaska, May 18, 1932; s. Russell Monroe and Alverra Corinne (Anderson) K.; m. Betty Mae Riggers, Aug. 14, 1955; children: Heather Adair Moe, Allison Marie Ramsey. BS, Pacific Luth. Coll., 1954; MD, U. Wash., 1958. Diplomate Am. Bd. Family Practice. Family physician Ballenger Rd. Med. Ctr., Seattle, 1960-64; pvt. practice Seattle, 1965-86; family physician Highland Clinic, Seattle, 1986-89; pvt. practive Seattle, 1990—; clin. assoc. U. Wash. Sch. Medicine, Seattle, 1969-72, clin. instr., 1973-74, clin. asst. prof., 1975-87, clin. assoc. prof., 1987—; bd. dirs. Am. Bd. Family Practice, Wash. Physicians Health Program. Recipient Mead Johnson Grad. Tng. award Am. Acad. Gen. Practice, 1959, Disting. Alumnus award Pacific Luth. U., 1983, U. Wash. Sch. Medicine, 1986. Fellow Am. Acad. Family Physicians (bd. dirs. 1987-90); mem. AMA, Wash. Acad. Family Physicians (pres. 1974-75, Family Physician of Yr. 1980), King County Acad. Family Physicians (pres. 1969-70, Clin. Tchr. award 1986), Wash. State Med. Assn. (pres. 1982-83), King County Med. Soc. (pres. 1976). Republican. Lutheran. Office: 17191 Bothell Way NE Seattle WA 98155-5551

KEITH, KENT MARSTELLER, academic administrator, corporate executive, government official, lawyer; b. N.Y.C., May 22, 1948; s. Bruce Edgar and Evelyn E. (Johnston) K.; m. Elizabeth Misao Carlson, Aug. 22, 1976. BA in Govt., Harvard U., 1970; BA in Politics and Philosophy, Oxford U., Eng., 1972, MA, 1977; JD, U. Hawaii, 1977. Bar: Hawaii 1977, D.C. 1979. Assoc. Cades, Schutte, Fleming & Wright, Honolulu, 1977-79; coord. Hawaii Dept. Planning and Econ. Devel., Honolulu, 1979-81, dep. dir., 1981-83, dir., 1983-86; energy resources coord. State of Hawaii, Honolulu, 1983-86, chmn. State Policy Coun., 1983-86; chmn. Aloha Tower Devel. Corp., 1983-86; project mgr. Mililani Tech. Park Castle and Cooke Properties Inc., 1986-88, v.p. pub. rels. and bus. devel., 1988-89, pres. Chaminade U. Honolulu, 1989-95; bd. dirs. Grove Farm Co., Inc., 1990-93. Author: Jobs for Hawaii's People: Fundamental Issues in Economic Development, 1985, Hawaii: Looking Back from the Year 2050, 1987, For the Love of Students, 1992; contbr. articles on ocean law to law jours. Pres. Manoa Valley Ch., Honolulu, 1976-78; mem. platform com., Hawaii Dem. Conv., 1982, 84, 86; trustee Hawaii Loa Coll., 1986-89, vice chmn. 1987-89; mem. Diocesan Bd. Edn., 1990-95, chmn. 1990-93; bd. dirs. St. Louis Sch., 1990-95, Hanahauoli Sch., 1990—; chmn. Manoa Neighborhood Bd., 1989-91. Rhodes scholar, 1970; named one of 10 Outstanding Young Men of Am., U.S. Jaycees, 1984. Mem. Am. Assn. Rhodes Scholars, Internat. House of Japan, Nature Conservancy, Pla. Club, Pacific Club, Harvard Club of Hawaii (Honolulu, bd. dirs. 1974-78, sec. 1974-76), Rotary (Honolulu). Home: 2626 Hillside Ave Honolulu HI 96822-1716

KEITH, NORMAN THOMAS, aerospace company administrator; b. Antioch, Calif., Jan. 12, 1936; s. Dean Theodore and Edna Margaret (Doty) K.; m. Marla Mildred Osten, Sept. 9, 1962. B of Tech., Tex. State Tech. Inst. Cert. profl. mgr. Field service engr. Gen. Dynamics Corp., San Diego, 1955-66, supr. Data Ctr., 1966-76, chief data systems, 1976-81, chief property adminstrn., 1981-83, motivational mgr., 1983-86, sr. program adminstr., 1986-90, mgr. total quality mgmt.Convair divsn., 1990—. Contbr. articles to profl. jours. Mem. mil. adv. bd. congressman Ron Packard, 1983-86; sgt. Res. Dep. Sheriff's Office, San Diego County; bd. dirs. San Dieguito Boys/ Girls Clubs, Encinitas, 1966-69; loaned exec. United Way, San Diego, 1980-81. Mem. Nat. Mgmt. Assn. (bd. dirs., pres.), Nat. U. Alumni Assn. (life), Woodbury Coll. Alumni Assn., San Diego State U. Alumni Assn., Hon. Dep. Sheriff's Assn. (bd. dirs.). Republican. Lutheran. Lodges: Lions (sec. 1962-63), Elks. Home: 620 Cole Ranch Rd Encinitas CA 92024-6522 Office: Gen Dynamics Convair Div 5001 Kearny Villa Rd San Diego CA 92123-1407

KEITH, PAULINE MARY, artist, illustrator, writer; b. Fairfield, Nebr., July 21, 1924; d. Siebelt Ralph and Pauline Alethia (Garrison) Goldenstein; m. Everett B. Keith, Feb. 14, 1957; 1 child, Nathan Ralph. Student, George Fox Coll., 1947-48, Oreg. State U., 1955. Illustrator Merlin Press, San Jose, Calif., 1980-81; artist, illustrator, watercolorist Corvallis, Oreg., 1980—. Author 5 chapbooks, 1980-85; editor: Four Generations of Verse, 1979; contbr. poems to anthologies and mags. and articles to mags.; one-woman shows include Roger's Meml. Libr., Forest Grove, Oreg., 1959, Corvallis Art Ctr., 1960, Human Resources Bldg., Corvallis, 1959-61, Chintimini Sr. Ctr., 1994—, Corvallis Pastoral Counciling Ctr., 1992-94, Parteral Counseling Ctr., 1993, 94, Hall Gallery, Sr. Ctr., 1993, 94, Consumer Power, Philomath, Oreg., 1994; exhibited in group shows at Hewlett-Packard Co., 1984-85, Corvallis Art Ctr., 1992, Chintimini Sr. Ctr., 1992, Hall Gallery, Corvallis, 1994. Co-elder First Christian Ch. (Disciples of Christ), Corvallis, 1988-89, co-deacon, 1980-83, elder, 1991-93; sec. Hostess Club of Chintimini Sr. Ctr., Corvallis, 1987, pres., 1988-89, v.p., 1992-94. Recipient Watercolor 1st price Benton County Fair, 1982, 83, 88, 89, 91, 2d prize, 1987, 91, 3d prize, 1984, 90, 92. Mem. Oreg. Assn. Christian Writers, Internat. Assn. Women Mins., Am. Legion Aux. (elected poet post II Covallis chpt. 1989-90, elected sec. 1991-92, chaplain 1992-93, 94-95, v.p. 1994-95). Republican. Office: 304 S College Newberg OR 97132

KEITH, ROBERT ALLEN, Native American Indian tribal executive; b. Kotzebue, Alaska, May 15, 1957; s. Hugh A. and Lillian Nora (Daniels) K.; m. Evelyn Anna Saccheus, May 13, 1984; children: Robert, MaryAnn, Ernest, Raelane, Laurie. Resource mgr., board mem. Elim Native Corp., Elim, Alaska, 1990—; pres. Elim IRA Coun., Native Village Elim, Elim, Alaska, 1993—; bd. mem. Bering Straits Reg. Housing, Nome, Alaska, 1993—; RASC mem. Alaska Native Health Bd., Anchorage, Alaska, 1995—; chmn. Elim Shaktoolik Koyuk Marine Mammal Commn., Alaska, 1995—. Mem. Alcohol and Drug Prevention Cmty. Partnership, Elim., 1992—; mem. Adult Basic Edn. Aniiguin Sch., Elim, 1990—; bd. mem. Kawerak Non-Profit, Nome, Alaska, 1993—, exec. com. mem., 1994—. Office: Native Village of Elim PO Box 70 Elim AK 99739

KELBAUGH, DOUGLAS STEWART, architect, urban designer, architecture educator; b. Bklyn., Jan. 25, 1945; s. John Calvin and Marguerite Pretat (Travis) K.; m. Katherine Nolan, 1991; children from previous marriage: Casey Anderson, Tess McCook. BA magna cum laude, Princeton U., 1968, MArch, 1972. Registered architect N.J., Wash. Sr. planner, architect dept. planning & devel. City of Trenton, N.J., 1972-78; ptnr. Kelbaugh & Lee, Princeton, N.J., 1978-85; prof. architecture and urban design, chmn. dept. architecture U. Wash., Seattle, 1985-93; ptnr. Kelbaugh Calthorpe & Assocs., Seattle, 1989—; lectr. U. Pa., Phila., 1983-85; chmn. design arts panel, NEA, Washington, 1984-85; mem. nat. steering com. AIA Edn. Initiative. Editor: The Pedestrian Pocketbook, 1989; prin. investigator, editor: Housing Affordability and Density, 1993. Mem. Princeton Regional Planning Bd., 1977-78; bd. dirs. Mid Atlantic Solar Energy Soc., Phila., 1978-83. Recipient 2d pl. award Newtown Design Competition, Ile de Abeau, France, 1972, 1st pl. award Civic Ctr. Design Competition, Monroeville, Pa., 1982, 3d pl. award Cultural Arts Ctr. Design Competition, Newport News, Va., 1984, 1st prize Jacques Cartier Design Competition, Montreal, Can. Fellow AIA (v.p. Seatle chpt. 1987-88, Nat. Honor award 1985, mem. architects in edn. com. 1988, design com. 1989, honors awards com. 1991). Home: 2809 10th Ave E Seattle WA 98102-3925 Office: U Wash Dept Architecture JO-20 Seattle WA 98195

KELCH, VINCENT CHARLES, clinical pharmacist; b. Fort Lauderdale, Fla., Dec. 7, 1956; s. Carl John Koelsch and Beatrice Alberta (Obermeyer) Kelch. AA, Ventura (Calif.) Coll., 1977; D of Pharmacy, U. of the Pacific, 1979; M of Health Adminstrn., U. LaVerne, 1994. Registered pharmacist. Asst. pharmacy mgr. Salinas (Calif.) Care Pharmacy, 1980-82; asst. dept. head USN, Camp Lejeune, N.C., 1982-84; clin. pharmacist VA, Reno, Nev., 1984-87; asst. pharmacy mgr. VA, San Diego, 1987-88; asst. dept. mgr. U.S. Air Force, Riverside, Calif., 1988-90; clin. pharmacist St. John's Regional Med. Ctr., Oxnard, Calif., 1991—. Scoutmaster Boy Scouts of Am., Oxnard, 1964—; mem. Dem. Socialists of Am., Washington, 1991—. Mem. K.C., Am. Soc. Hosp. Pharmacists, Am. Pharm. Assn., Nat. Assn. of Retail Druggists. Roman Catholic. Home: 1120 Jamaica Ln Oxnard CA 93030-6773 Office: St Johns Regional Med Ctr 1600 N Rose Ave Oxnard CA 93030-3722

KELEN, JOYCE ARLENE, social worker; b. N.Y.C., Dec. 5, 1949; d. Samuel and Rebecca (Rochman) Green; m. Leslie George Kelen, Jan. 31, 1971; children: David, Jonathan. BA, Lehman Coll., 1970; MSW, Univ. Utah, 1974, DSW, 1980. Recreation dir. N.Y.C. Housing Authority, Bronx, 1970-72; cottage supr. Kennedy Home, Bronx, 1974; sch. social worker Davis County Sch. Dist., Farmington, Utah, 1976-86; clin. asst. prof. U. Utah., Salt Lake City, 1976—; sch. social worker Salt Lake City Sch. Dist., 1986—; cons. in field, Salt Lake City, 1981—. Editor: To Whom Are We Beautiful As We Go?, 1979; contbr. articles to profl. jours. Utah Coll. of Nursing grantee, 1985. Mem. Nat. Assn. Social Workers (chairperson Gerontology Council, 1983-84, Utah Sch. Social Worker of Yr., 1977), NEA, Utah Edn. Assn., Davis Edn. Assn. Democrat. Jewish. Home: 128 M St Salt Lake City UT 84103-3854 Office: Franklin Elem Sch 1100 W 400 S Salt Lake City UT 84104-2334

KELIN, DANIEL ALLEN, II, theatre director; b. Walnut Creek, Calif., Apr. 2, 1961; s. Daniel Allen and Ruth Noreen (Johnson) K. BA, U. Vt., 1983; postgrad., U. Miss., 1984; MFA, U. Hawaii, 1987. Assoc. dir. Honolulu Theatre for Youth, 1986—; assoc. artist Very Spl. Arts Hawaii, Honolulu, 1987-92; dir. theatre Jodrikdrik Nan Jodrikdrik, Majuro, Marshall Islands, 1991—; storyteller Hawaii State Libr., Honolulu, 1992—; scholar cons. Conf. on Lit. & Hawaii, Honolulu, 1994. 0ontbg. author: American Theatrical Company, 1986; contbr. articles and stories to jours.; playwright: He'e Nalu, 1994. Grantee Theatre Comms. Group, 1994, Rockefeller Found., 1993. Mem. Am. Alliance for Theatre and Edn. (com. chair 1993—, network coun. 1993—), Hawaii Alliance for Arts Edn., Soc. for Children's Book Writers, Archaeol. Assn., Hawaii Lit. Arts Coun., Storytelling Assn. Hawaii (adv. com. 1992-93). Home: 226 Kaimuohema Pl # A Honolulu HI 96817-1145

KELLAM, NORMA DAWN, medical, surgical nurse; b. Benton Harbor, Mich., June 13, 1938; d. Edgar Arnold and Bernice (Cronk) K. AA, San Bernardino Valley Coll., 1958; student, Calif. State Coll., Long Beach, 1961-1964, 1965, 1966, 1967; BS, San Diego State Coll., 1961; MS, Calif. State U., Fresno, 1972. Nursing instr. Porterville (Calif.) State Hosp., 1968-69; staff nurse Northside Psychiat. Hosp., Fresno, 1969-72; nursing instr. Pasadena (Calif.) City Coll., 1972-73; night shift lead Fairview Devel. Ctr., Costa Mesa, Calif., 1973—; Mem. Calif. Nurses Assn., Soc. Urologic Nurses and Assocs., Phi Kappa Phi. Contbr. articles to newspapers. Vol. Spanish translator for Interstitial Cystitis Assn. Recipient Cert. of Appreciation for vol. work Interstitial Cystitis Assn. Mem. Calif. Nurses Assn., Soc. Urologic Nurses and Assocs., Inc., Phi Kappa Phi.

KELLAR, MARTHA ROBBINS, artist; b. Alamogordo, N.Mex., Nov. 23, 1949; d. Raymond Hazen and Grace Beatrice (Crumbliss) Robbins; m. Robert William Kellar, Nov. 30, 1968; children: Jennifer, Robert, Molly, David. Student, Murray State U., 1967-69, N.Mex. State U., 1979-81. Co-founder Studio 5, Alamogordo, 1979-82; founder, owner Kellar Fine Art, La Luz, N.Mex., 1982—; represented by Thomas McMahon Fine Art Ruidoso, N.Mex.; instr. figure drawing Ea. N.Mex. U., Ruidoso, 1991—; instr. painting and drawing Carrizo Art Sch., Ruidoso, 1990—; mem. selection com. N.Mex. Arts Commn., Alamogordo, 1991; award judge various galleries including Gallery de la Luz 16th Ann. Minature Show, 1989, Mus. of the Horse Youth Exhibit, Ruidoso, 1993; vol. art tchr. La Luc Elem. Sch., 1977-83; guest lectr. art careers Alamogordo H.S., 1993-94, N.Mex. State U., 1985—; portrait artist various juried arts and crafts fairs in N.Mex., 1979-84. Exhibited in group shows at Nat. Arts Club, N.Y.C., 1985, 87, 88, Sacramento (Calif.) Fine Arts Ctr., 1987, 88, 89, N.Mex. State Profl. Fine Arts Exhbn., 1988, 89, 91, Salmagundi Club, N.Y.C., 1986, 87, 88, 93; commd. to paint portraits of deans N.Mex. State U. Coll. Bus. Adminstrn. and Econs., 1991. Recipient Cert. of Merit Salmagundi Club, N.Y.C., 1986, Jesse B. McReynolds award, 1987, Profl. Fine Arts awards N.Mex. State Fair, Albuquerque, 1986, 87, 88, 89, Collector's ribbon Gallery de La Luz, 1988, Scholarship award Scottsdale (Ariz.) Art Sch., 1990. Mem. Pastel Soc. Am. (Andrews/Nelson/Whitehead award 1985), Pastel Soc. West Coast (awards 1988, 89). Home and Office: Kellar Fine Art 4125 Lead Ave SE Apt 107 Albuquerque NM 87108-2691

KELLEHER, RICHARD CORNELIUS, marketing and communications executive; b. Buffalo, Nov. 21, 1949; s. Cornelius and Lucile Norma (White) K.; m. Sherri Fae Anderson, Mar. 17, 1981 (div. 1991); children: Erin Marie, Shawn Michael. BA, U. New Mex., 1975; MBA, U. Phoenix, 1984. Reporter, photographer Daily Lobo, Albuquerque, 1973-75; mgn. editor News Bulletin, Belen, New Mex., 1975-77; various corp. mktg. titles AT&T Mountain Bell, Denver, 1978-84; exec. editor Dairy Mag., Denver, 1984-86; communications dir. Am. Heart Assn., Phoenix, 1987-90; cons. Kelleher Communications & Mktg., Phoenix, 1990—; spl. writer Denver Post, 1977-82, Denver Corr. Billboard Mag., 1977-82. Mem. Gov.'s Roundtable on Employee Productivity, Gov. of Ariz., 1990-91; vol. communications Am. Cancer Soc., 1990-92. Recipient Harvey Communications Study award, 1986. Mem. Pub. Rels. Soc. Am., Toastmasters.

KELLEHER, ROBERT JOSEPH, federal judge; b. N.Y.C., Mar. 5, 1913; s. Frank and Mary (Donovan) K.; m. Gracyn W. Wheeler, Aug. 14, 1940; children: R. Jeffrey, Karen Kathleen. A.B., Williams Coll., 1935; LL.B., Harvard U., 1938. Bar: N.Y. 1939, Calif. 1942, U.S. Supreme Ct 1954. Atty. War Dept., 1941-42; asst. U.S. atty. So. Dist. Calif., 1948-50; pvt. practice Beverly Hills, 1951-71; U.S. dist. judge, 1971—. Mem. So. Calif. Com. Olympic Games, 1964; capt. U.S. Davis Cup Team, 1962-63; treas. Youth Tennis Found. So. Calif., 1961-64. Served to lt. USNR, 1942-45. Mem. So. Calif. Tennis Assn. (v.p. 1958-64, pres. 1983-85), U.S. Lawn Tennis Assn. (pres. 1967-68), Internat. Lawn Tennis USA, Internat. Lawn Tennis of Gt. Britain, Internat. Lawn Tennis of France, Internat. Lawn Tennis of Can., Internat. Lawn Tennis of Mex., Internat. Lawn Tennis of Australia, Internat. Lawn Tennis of India, Internat. Lawn Tennis of Israel, All Eng. Lawn Tennis and Croquet (Wimbledon), Harvard Club (N.Y./So. Calif.), Williams Club (N.Y.), L.A. Country Club, Delta Kappa Epsilon. Home: 15 St Malo Bch Oceanside CA 92054-5854 Office: US Dist Ct 255 E Temple St Ste 830 Los Angeles CA 90012-3334

KELLER, ARTHUR MICHAEL, computer science researcher; b. N.Y.C., Jan. 14, 1957; s. David and Luba K. BS summa cum laude, Bklyn. Coll., 1977; MS, Stanford U., 1979, PhD, 1985. Instr. computer sci. Stanford (Calif.) U., 1979-81, rsch. asst., 1977-85, acting asst. chmn. dept. computer sci., 1982, rsch. assoc., 1985, 89-91, vis. asst. prof., 1987-89, rsch. scientist, 1991-92, sr. rsch. scientist, 1992—; sr. rsch. scientist Advanced Decision Systems, Mountain View, Calif., 1989-92; chief tech. advisor Persistence Software, San Mateo, Calif., 1992—; bd. dirs. Persistence Software; sys. analyst Bklyn. Coll. Computer Ctr., 1974-77; summer rsch. asst. IBM, Thomas J. Watson Rsch. Ctr., Yorktown Heights, N.Y., 1980; acad. assoc. San Jose Rsch. Lab., 1981; asst. prof. U. Tex., Austin, 1985-88, adj. asst. prof., 1988-89; mem. program com. Internat. Conf. on Data Engring., L.A., 1986, 87, 89, Internat. Conf. on Very Large Data Bases, Amsterdam, The Netherlands, 1989. Author: A First Course in Computer Programming Using Pascal, 1982. Mem. IEEE (vice chmn. com. database engring. Computer Soc. 1986-87), Assn. Computing Machinery, TeX Users Group (fin. com. 1983-85, internat. coord. 1985-87), Chai Soc. (communications officer 1987-89, v.p. publicity 1989-90). Home: 3881 Corina Way Palo Alto CA 94303-4507 Office: Stanford U Dept Computer Sci Stanford CA 94305-2140

KELLER, BARBARA LYNN, special education educator; b. Great Falls, Mont., July 18, 1941; d. Edward Jerome and Alvina Elizabeth (Kampsnider) Daly; m. Ray B. Keller, Dec. 28, 1961; 1 child, Forest Ry. Student, Ea. Mont. Coll., 1967-69; BA, U. Mont., 1976; postgra., Mont. State U., 1976-79, No. Mont. Coll., 1989-91. Tchr. grades 1-4 Pub. Schs. Birch Creek Hutterite Colony, Dupuyer, Mont., 1962-63; tchr. grade 2 Pub. Sch. Blackfeet Indian Reservation, Heart Butte, Mont., 1963-64; tchr. reading remediation Pub. Sch., Fort Benton, Mont., 1967-68; tchr. emotionally disturbed Manzanita Ranch Residential Sch., Hyompom, Calif., 1968-69; tchr. reading remediation Pub. Schs., Bigfork, Mont., 1975-78; tchr. ESL Flathead C.C., Kalispell, Mont., 1978-82; pvt. practice tchr. reading, ESL, emotionally disturbed Bigfork, 1982-85; tchr. spl. edn. Pub. Schs. Blackfeet Indian Reservation, Browning, Mont., 1985-94; tchr. study skills and reading Browning (Mont.) H.S., 1994—; pres. Eagle's View Publs., Bigfork, 1989—; author-in-residence Am. Edn. Inst., 1994—. Author: Reading Pals--A Handbook for Volunteers, 1990, Reading Pals--A Teacher's Manual, 1990, The Parents' Guide--Studyng Made Easy, 1991, Gifts of Love and Literacy--A Parent's Guide to Raising Children Who Love to Read, 1993, Read with Your Child--Make a Difference, 1994; (ednl. program) Studying Made Easy--The Complete Program, 1992. Reading cons. Personal Vol. Svc., Bigfork, 1970—, Browning, Mont., 1985—. Recipient Author of Yr. award Am. Edn. Inst., 1993. Mem. ASCD, Internat. Reading Assn., Am. Fedn. Tchrs., Literacy Vols. Am., Glacier Reading Coun., Learning Disabilities Assn., COSMEP Internat. Assn. Ind. Publishers. Home: PO Box 1814 Browning MT 59417-1814 Office: Eagles View Publs 750 Cascade Ave Bigfork MT 59911-3625

KELLER, EDWARD LOWELL, electrical engineer, educator; b. Rapid City, S.D., Mar. 6, 1939; s. Earl Lowell and E. Blanche (Oldfield) K.; m. Carole Lynne Craig, Sept. 1, 1963; children: Edward Lowell, Craig, Morgan. BS, U.S. Naval Acad., 1961; PhD, Johns Hopkins U., 1971. Mem. faculty U. Calif., Berkeley, 1971—; asso. prof. elec. engring. U. Calif., 1977-79, prof., 1979-94, prof. emeritus, 1994—; sr. scientist Smith Kettlewell Eye Rsch. Inst., San Francisco, 1980—; chmn. bioengring. program U. Calif., Berkeley and San Francisco, 1989; chmn. engring. sci. program Coll. of Engring. U. C., Berkeley, 1991-94. Contbr. articles to sci. jours. Served with USN, 1961-65. Sr. Von Humboldt fellow, 1977-78. Mem. AAAS, IEEE, Assn. for Rsch. in Vision and Ophthalmology, Soc. for Neurosci., Internat. Neural Network Soc. Office: Smith-Kettlewell Eye Rsch Inst 2232 Webster St San Francisco CA 94115

KELLER, J(AMES) WESLEY, credit union executive; b. Jonesboro, Ark., Jan. 6, 1958; s. Norman Grady and Norma Lee (Ridgeway) Patrick; m. Patricia Maria Delavan, July 7, 1979. Student, U. Miss., 1976-78; BS in Bus. and Mgmt., Redlands U., 1991, MBA, 1994. Sr. collector Rodkwell Fed. Credit Union, Downey, Calif., 1978-79; acct. Lucky Fed. Credit Union, Buena Park, Calif., 1979-84; pres., chief exec. officer Long Beach (Calif.) State Employees Credit Union, 1984—. Mem. Credit Union Exec. Soc., Calif. Credit Union League (bd. govs. Long Beach chpt., treas. 1985-86), So. Calif. Credit Union Mgrs. Assn., U. Redlands Whitehead Leadership Soc., Nat. Assn. State Charted Credit Unions (vice chmn. 1993—), Kiwanis. Republican. Baptist. Office: Long Beach State Employees Credit Union 3840 N Long Beach Blvd Long Beach CA 90807-3312

KELLER, KENT EUGENE, advertising and public relations executive; b. Oil City, Pa., Oct. 5, 1941; s. George W. and Lois (Wallace) K.; divorced; children: Eric Trent, Todd Jason. BA, Kent State U., 1963; cert., Chrysler Inst., Detroit, 1968, UCLA, 1973. Editor Oil City (Pa.) Derrick, 1959-60; various mgmt. positions Chrysler Corp., Twinsburg, Ohio, 1960-64, prodn. cont. mgr., 1964-67; group mgr. Chrysler Corp. AMG, Detroit, 1967-69; dir. advt. and pub. rels. Zero Corp., Burbank, Calif., 1969-75; exec. v.p. Basso & Assocs. Inc., Newport Beach, Calif., 1975-80; pres. Jason Trent & Co., Inc., Fountain Valley, Calif., 1980—; pub. rels. counsel Electronic Convs. Inc., L.A., 1980-85; bd. dirs. Neurosci. Tech. Inc., Tarzana, Calif.; cons. Global Engring., Irvine, Calif., 1989—; co-founder Strategic Concepts, Fountain Valley, Calif., 1990. Editor (industry report) TOLD Report, 1985—, (mag.) Zero Dimensions, 1969-75. Mem. Town Hall of Calif., L.A., 1980—. Mem. Bus. & Profl. Advt. Assn., Pub. Rels. Soc. Am., Back Bay Club. Republican. Presbyterian. Home: 18072 Darmel Pl Santa Ana CA 92705-1916

KELLER, MICHAEL ALAN, librarian, educator, musicologist; b. Sterling, Colo., Apr. 5, 1945; s. Ephraim Richard and Mary Patricia (Warren) K.; m. Constance A. Kyle, Sept. 3, 1967 (div. Aug. 1979); children: Kristen J., Paul B.; m. Carol Lawrence, Oct. 6, 1979; children: Laura W., Martha M. BA, Hamilton Coll., 1967; MA, SUNY, Buffalo, 1970, postgrad., 1970-91; MLS, SUNY, Geneseo, 1972. Asst. libr. for reference and cataloging SUNY Music

Libr., Buffalo, 1970-73; acting undergrad. libr. Cornell U., Ithaca, N.Y., 1976; music libr., sr. lectr. Cornell U., Ithaca, 1973-81; head music libr. U. Calif.-Berkeley, 1981-86; assoc. univ. libr. for collection devel. Yale U., 1986-93; director Stanford U. Libraries, Stanford, Calif., 1993-94, univ. libr., dir. acad. info. resources, 1994—; cons. Colgate U., Hamilton, N.Y., 1976, Rutgers U., New Brunswick, N.J., 1982, Brown U., Providence, 1983, U. Alta., Edmonton, Can., 1983, NYU, 1984, L.A. Music Ctr. Operating Co., 1985-89, City of Ferrara, Italy, U. Pitts., Villa I Tatti-Biblioteca Berenson, Florence, Italy, Am. Physical Soc., Princeton U., Newsweek Mag.; mem. Bibliog. Commn., Repertoire Internat. de la Presse Mus. de XIXve Siecle, 1981-84; chmn. music program com. Rsch. Librs. Group, 1982-86; reviewer NEH, 1982-88, panelist, 1979—; chmn. Assoc. Music Librs. Group, Joint Com. Retrospective Conversion in Music, 1989—; collection mgmt. devel. com. Rsch. Librs. Group, 1986-91, chmn. 1989-91, program adv. com., 1991—; dir. Berkeley Italian Renaissance Project, 1985—, Renaissance Archive Database, 1989—. Author: MSS on Microfilm in Music Libr. at SUNYAB, 1971, (with Duckles) Music Reference and Rsch. Materials: an annotated bibliography, 1988, 94; contbr. articles to profl. jours. Firefighter, rescue squad mem. Cuyuga Heights Vol. Fire Co., N.Y., 1980-81. Recipient spl. commendation Nat. Music Clubs, 1978, Berkeley Bronze medal U. Calif.-Berkeley, 1983; NDEA Title IV fellow SUNY-Buffalo, 1967-70; Cornell Coll. Arts and Scis. rsch. grantee, 1973-81, U. Calif.-Berkeley humanities rsch. grantee, 1983-84, Coun. on Libr. Resources grantee, 1984, Libr. Assoc. U. Calif. grantee, 1985-86, NEH grantee, 1986, Deems Taylor award ASCAP, 1988. Mem. ALA, AAUP, Music Libr. Assn. (bd. dirs. 1975-77, fin. com. 1982-83, editl. com. index and bibliography series 1981-85), Internat. Assn. Music Librs., Am. Musicol. Soc. (com. on automated bibliography 1982-83, coun. 1986-88), Conn. Acad. Arts and Scis. (bd. dirs.), Ctr. Rsch. Librs. (mem. adv. com. 1988—), Conn. Ctr. for Books (bd. dirs.), Book Club of Calif., Roxburghe Club of San Francisco. Home: 4280 Los Palos Cir Palo Alto CA 94306-4310 Office: Cecil H Green Library Stanford CA 94305-6004

KELLER, MICHAEL CROSLEY, correctional facilities official; b. Salem, Oreg., Aug. 3, 1949; s. John L. and E. Ruth (Simmons) K.; m. Renée L. Romanko, June 30, 1975 (dec.Apr. 1984); m. Edie Ann Cannon, Mar. 25, 1989; children: Aaron Crosley, Alexis Catherine. BS, Western Oreg. State Coll., 1978; postgrad., Somona State U., 1978-84. Substitute tchr. Apache County Schs., Ganado, Ariz., 1972; correctional officer San Quentin (Calif.) State Prison, 1978-80, correctional sgt., 1980-82, correctional counselor, 1982-84, employee rels. officer, 1984-85; watch comdr., lt. Correctional Tng. Facility, Soledad, Calif., 1988-93; capt. North Kern State Prison, Delano, Calif., 1993-95; acad. adminstr. Correctional Training Acad., Galt, Calif., 1995—; asst. negotiator Dept. of Pers. Adminstrn., Sacramento, 1985. With U.S. Army, 1973-76, Korea. Republican. Office: Correctional Training Facility 9850 Twin CIties Rd Galt CA 95632

KELLER, PETER CHARLES, museum director, mineralogist; b. Allentown, Pa., Aug. 16, 1947; s. Charles Donald and Barbara Jean (Miller) K.; children: Bret Charles, Elizabeth Austin. BA, George Washington U., 1972; MA, U. Tex., 1974, PhD, 1977. Grad. gemologist, 1980. Curator mineralogy L.A. County Mus., Los Angeles, 1976-80; dir. edn. Gemological Inst. Am., Santa Monica, Calif., 1980-84; lectr. geology U. So. Calif., L.A., 1980-87; assoc. dirs. L.A. County Mus. Natural History, 1987-91; exec. dir. Bowers Mus. of Cultural Art, Santa Ana, Calif., 1991—. Assoc. editor: Gems and Gemology, 1980-91; contbr. articles in field to profl. jours. Trustee, Natural History Mus. Found., 1980-84; treas. Mineral Mus. Adv. Council, 1984. Fellow Leakey Found., Explorers Club; mem. Internat. Commn. Mus., Am. Assn. Mus., Mineral. Soc. Am., Gemol. Assn. Gt. Britain, Internat. Mineral. Assn. (U.S. rep. for mus.), Geol. Soc. Am., Mineral. Soc. Gt. Britain, Sigma Xi, Phi Kappa Phi. Home: 401 Seaward Rd Corona Del Mar CA 92625-2670 Office: Bowers Mus Cultural Art 2002 N Main St Santa Ana CA 92706-2731

KELLER, ROBERT M., bishop. Bishop Evang. Luth. Ch. in Am., Spokane, Wash. Office: Synod of E Washigton-Idaho 314 S A Spruce Spokane WA 99204

KELLER, SUSAN AGNES, insurance officer; b. Moline, Ill., July 12, 1952; d. Kenneth Francis and Ethel Louise (Odendahl) Hulsbrink. Grad. in Pub. Relations, Patricia Stevens Career Coll., 1971; grad. in Gen. Ins., Ins. Inst. Am., 1986. CPCU; lic. ins. and real estate agt.; notary public. Comml. lines rater Bitiminous Casualty Corp., Rock Island, Ill., 1973-78; with Roadway Express, Inc., Rock Island, 1978-81; front line supr. Yellow Freight System, Inc., Denver, 1982-83; supr. plumbing and sheet metal prodn. Bell Plumbing and Heating, Denver, 1983-84; v.p. underwriting farm/ranch dept. Golden Eagle Ins. Co., San Diego, 1985—; cons. real estate foreclosure County Records Svc., San Diego, 1986-89; tchr. Ins. Inst. of Am., 1991. Vol. DAV, San Diego, 1985—; tchr. IEA and CPCU courses. Mem. Soc. CPCU (pres., bd. dirs.), Profl. Women in Ins., NAFE. Roman Catholic. Home: 790 Camino De La Reina Apt 163 San Diego CA 92108-3227 Office: Golden Eagle Ins Co 7175 Navajo Rd PO Box 85826 San Diego CA 92116-5826

KELLER, WILLIAM D., federal judge; b. 1934. BS, U. Calif., Berkeley, 1956; LLB, UCLA, 1960. Asst. U.S. atty. U.S. Dist. Ct. (so. dist.) Calif., 1961-64; assoc. Dryden, Harrington, Horgan & Swartz, Calif., 1964-72; U.S. atty. U.S. Dist. Ct. (cen. dist.) Calif., Los Angeles, 1972-77; ptnr. Rosenfeld, Meyer & Susman, 1977-78; solo practice, 1978-81; ptnr. Mahm & Cazier, 1981-84; judge U.S. Dist. Ct. (cen. dist.) Calif., Los Angeles, 1984—; ptnr. Rosenfeld, Meyer & Susman, Calif., 1977-78; pvt. practice law Calif., 1978-81; ptnr. Hahn & Cazier, Calif., 1981-84. Office: US Dist Ct 312 N Spring St Los Angeles CA 90012-4701*

KELLERMAN, FAYE MARDER, novelist, dentist; b. St. Louis, July 31, 1952; d. Oscar and Anne (Steinberg) Marder; m. Jonathan Seth Kellerman, July 23, 1972; children: Jesse Oren, Rachel Diana, Ilana Judith, Aliza Celeste. AB in Math, UCLA, 1974, DDS, 1978. Author: The Ritual Bath, 1986 (Macavity award best 1st novel 1986), Sacred and Profane, 1987, The Quality of Mercy, 1989, Milk and Honey, 1990, Day of Atonement, 1991, False Prophet, 1992, Grievous Sin, 1993, Sanctuary, 1994, Justice, 1995; contbr. short stories to Sisters in Crime vols. 1 & 3, Ellery Queen Mag., A Woman's Eye, Women of Mystery, the year's 2d finest crime: mystery stories, The Year's 25 Finest Mystery and Crime Stories, A Modern Treasury of Great Detective and Murder Mysteries. UCLA rsch. fellow, 1978. Mem. Mystery Writers of Am. (So. Calif. bd. dirs.), Womens' Israeli Polit. Action Com., Sisters in Crime. Jewish.

KELLEY, BRUCE DUTTON, pharmacist; b. Hartford, Conn., Jan. 4, 1957; s. Roger Weston and Elizabeth Morrill (Atwood) K.: m. DawnReneé Cinocco, Jan. 19, 1990. Student, U. Hartford, 1975-77; BS in Pharmacy, U. Colo., 1985; diplomas in Russian, Pushkin Inst., Moscow, 1995; BA in Russian, U. Colo., 1995. RPh, Colo. Various part time jobs while attending school, 1975-85; pharmacist King Soopers, Inc., Boulder, Colo., 1990—; asst. tour leader in Russia U. Tex., El Paso, 1991; Russia asst. guide, U. Ariz., Tucson, 1992 (summer). Vol. Warderburg Student Health Ctr., U. Colo., Boulder, 1981-83, Am. Diabetes Assn. Mem. NRA, Am. Fedn. Police, Am. Pharm. Assn., Elks, Nat. Eagle Scout Assn., Am. Legion. Republican. Home: 6152 Willow Ln Boulder CO 80301-5356 Office: King Soopers Inc 6550 Lookout Rd Boulder CO 80301-3303

KELLEY, HAROLD EDWARD, metallurgical engineer; b. Butte, Mont., Sept. 8, 1960; s. Harold Arthur and Dorothy Gene (Barnes) K.; m. Kristine Marie Ganzer, Jan. 9, 1988; children: Tiffany Michelle, Harold Andrew. BS in Material Sci. and Engring., U. Utah, 1982; MS in Metall. Engring., Mont. Tech. U., 1984. Rsch. asst. Mont. Tech., Butte, 1982-84; mem. tech. staff Rockwell Internat., Anaheim, Calif., 1985-88; metall. engr. Kennametal, Inc., Fallon, Nev., 1988-93, sr. metall. engr., 1993—. Patentee arc hardfacing rod. Youth advisor Anaheim Meth. Ch., 1985-88; mem. Ptnrs. in Edn., Fallon, 1992—; CPR and first aid instr. ARC, Fallon, 1992—. Mem. ASM Internat. (exec. com. Orange county chpt. 1985-88), The Metall. Soc. Methodist. Home: 521 Michael Dr Fallon NV 89406-5725 Office: Kennametal Inc 347 N Taylor St Fallon NV 89406-5730

KELLEY, JAMES CHARLES, III, dean; b. L.A., Oct. 5, 1940; s. James Charles Jr. and Margaret (Fitzgerrell) K.; m. Susan Cotner, June 7, 1963; children: Jason Fitzgerrell, Megan Amber. BA, Pomona Coll., 1963; PhD, U. Wyo., 1966. Asst. prof. U. Washington, Seattle, 1966-71, assoc. prof., 1971-75; dean San Francisco State U., 1975—; chmn. East Pacific Oceanic Conf., 1986-89. Fulbright prof., Fulbright Commn., Athens, Greece, 1970. Fellow Calif. Acad. Scis. (v.p. 1983-86, pres. 1986—); mem. Am. Geophysical Union, Oceanography Soc., AAAS, Bohemian Club (San Francisco). Roman Catholic. Home: 380 4th St Montara CA 94037 Office: San Francisco State U Sch Sci San Francisco CA 94132

KELLEY, KEVIN PATRICK, security, safety, risk management administrator; b. Indpls., Apr. 21, 1954; s. Everett Lee and Emily Louise (Bottoms) K.; m. Kathie Jo Fluegeman, Oct. 13, 1984. BS, Calif. State U., Long Beach, 1984; cert. mgmt. supervision, UCLA, 1984. Mgmt. asst. FBI, Los Angeles, 1973-79; security/safety supr. U. Calif., 1979-82; security/safety adminstr. Micom Systems, Inc., Chatsworth, Calif., 1982-83; loss prevention, safety auditor Joseph Magnin, Inc., San Francisco, 1983-84; loss prevention, safety adminstr. Wherehouse Entertainment, Inc., Gardena, Calif., 1984-86; risk control cons. Indsl. Indemnity Co., Los Angeles, 1986-87, Kemper Group, City of Industry, Calif., 1987-90; account mgr. loss control engring. Tokio Marine Mgmt. Inc., Pasadena, Calif., 1990—; commr. pub. safety City of Norwalk, Calif., 1984-86. Mem. security com. Los Angeles Olympic Organizing Com., 1984. Mem. Am. Soc. Indsl. Security (cert., Peter Updike Meml. scholar 1985), Am. Soc. Safety Engrs., Chief Spl. Agts. Assn., Risk Ins. Mgmt. Soc., Nat. Safety Mgmt. Soc. (sec. 1985-86), Am. Heart Assn. (governing bd. chmn. 1986-88), Ins. Inst. Am. (cert.). Republican. Roman Catholic. Lodges: Rotary, Kiwanis.

KELLEY, LISA STONE, public guardian, conservator; b. Sacramento, Calif., Mar. 10, 1947; d. John William and Coral Frances (Roberts) Stone; m. Charles B. Kelley, Oct. 7, 1967 (div. Feb. 1987); children: Brian Christopher, Darren Matthew. Student, Sacramento City Coll., 1965-67, AA in Social Sci., 1978; BA in Social Work with honors, Calif. State U., Sacramento, 1982, MSW with honors, 1985; postgrad. in Psychology, Calif. Coast U., 1994—. Lic. clin. social worker, Calif. Pharmacy clerk S. Sacramento Pharmacy, 1966-68; temp. med. asst. Sacramento, 1978-80; adv., counselor El Dorado Women's Info. Ctr., Placerville, Calif., 1982; dep. patients rights adv. Sacramento County Office Patients Rights, 1983-84; sch. social worker Elk Grove (Calif.) Unified Sch. Dist., 1984-85; mental health counselor Sacramento Mental Health Ctr., 1986; dep. pub. guardian/conservator Sacramento County, 1986—. Mem. NASW, Sacramento County Employees Orgn., Am. Orthopsychiat. Assn., Menninger Found., Calif. State U. Alumni Assn., Calif. Coast U. Alumni Assn., Phi Kappa Phi. Democrat. Office: Sacramento County Pub Guardian/Conservator 4875 Broadway Ste I Sacramento CA 95820-1500

KELLEY, MARGARET SUE, sociology lecturer; b. Hutchinson, Kans., Nov. 26, 1967; d. Ronald D. and Lovella J. (Schamber) K. BA in Sociology, Wichita State U., 1990; postgrad. in sociology, NYU. Family tchr. Booth Family Svcs., Wichita, 1988-89; crisis counselor Parents Anonymous, Wichita, 1988-89, Women's Crisis Ctr., Wichita, 1989-90; rsch. lab. asst. Wichita State U., 1989-90; teaching asst. NYU, N.Y.C., 1991-93; lectr. sociology dept. San Jose (Calif.) State U., 1993-94; participant cultural workshops Wichita State U., 1987-89; internist Bedford Hills (N.Y.) Correctional Facility, 1988. Big Sister, Big Sisters/Big Bros., Wichita, 1988-90; student rep. sociology faculty meetings, NYU, 1991—. Rhodes Scholar nominee Wichita State U., 1989; recipient Continuing Svc. award Parents Anonymous, Wichita, 1989. Mem. Sociology Grad. Students (chairperson 1991-93), Delta Delta Delta Alumni Assn.

KELLEY, ROBERT PAUL, JR., management consultation executive; b. Mansfield, Ohio, Mar. 27, 1942; s. Robert Paul and Rachel Marie Kelley; m. Mimi Grant, June 15, 1975; children: Robert, Laura, Elizabeth. BBA, Notre Dame U., 1964; MBA, Harvard U., 1969. Corporate develp. exec., Holly Sugar Corp., 1969-70; mktg. cons., supr. Laventhol & Horwath, L.A., 1972-73; dir. mktg., entertainment and mdsg. Knott's Berry Farm, Buena Park, Calif., 1974-76; sr. v.p. mktg. Am. Warranty Corp., L.A., 1978-80; co-founder Gen. Group of Cos., 1981; CEO Strategy Network Corp., 1976—; dir. Orange County sect. So. Calif. Tech. Exec.'s Network, 1984-85, pres., CEO, 1985—; co-founder, CEO ABL Health Care Execs. Network, 1989-91; chmn. bd. Micro Frame Techs., Inc., 1990—, ABL Orgn., 1991—, Quick Start Tech., 1994, V-Sys., Inc., 1994—; vice chmn. bd. NTBG Venture Ptnrs., 1994—; chmn., CEO Quickstart Tech., 1993-94; chmn. bd. Ambience Redesign, Inc., 1995—. Author: The Board of Directors and its Role in Growing Companies, 1984; co-author: Better Than Money Resource Capitalism, 1993. Served with USNR, 1964-67. Home: 6004 E West View Dr Orange CA 92669-4314 Office: 17772 17th St Ste 200 Tustin CA 92680-1944

KELLEY, ROBERT SUMA, systems analyst; b. Chgo., July 2, 1961; s. Jerry Dean and Jean (Laine) K. BA in Philosophy, Western Md. Coll., 1985; MBA in MIS, Ind. U., 1989. Human resource specialist Marriott Corp., Gaithersburg, Md., 1985-86; mgr. in tng. Courtyard by Marriott, Fairfax, Va., 1986-87; sys. analyst Hewlett-Packard, Palo Alto, Calif., 1989—; mem. adv. com. for implementation of Calif. Assembly bill for improving edn. opportunities for learning disabled children, 1991-94. counselor Camp Allen for the Physically Handicapped, Manchester, N.H., 1977; track coach for disadvantaged youth Rockville (Md.) Recreation, 1980. Home: 408 Grant Ave Apt 309 Palo Alto CA 94306 Office: Hewlett-Packard 3000 Hanover St # 20bj Palo Alto CA 94304-1112

KELLEY, TERRY WAYNE, mechanical engineer; b. Eugene, Oreg., May 30, 1952; s. Edgar Harold and Esther Gwendolyn (Hansen) K.; m. Norma Kay Eberli, June 8, 1974; children: Stephanie Lynn, Sarah Elizabeth. BS in Mech. Engring., Oreg. State U., 1974, MS in Mech. Engring., 1975. Registered profl. engr., Calif. Engr. geothermal div. Unocal, Santa Rosa, Calif., 1975-78, prodn. engr., 1980-83, mech. engring. supr., 1983-93, advising prodn. engr., 1993—; project engr. Philippine Geothermal Inc., Manila, 1978-80; problem writer Nat. Coun. of Examiners for Engring. and Surveying Profl. Engrs. licensing exam, 1983-94. Mem. Geothermal Resource Coun., ASME, Pi Tau Sigma, Tau Beta Pi, Phi Kappa Phi. Democrat. Lutheran. Office: Unocal Geothermal 3576 Unocal Pl Santa Rosa CA 95403-1774

KELLOGG, DONALD RAY, surgeon, plastic surgeon; b. Hot Lake, Oreg., 1938. MD, Loma Linda U., 1965. Diplomate Am. Bd. Surgery; Am. Bd. Plastic Surgery. Intern Henry Ford Hosp., Detroit, 1965-66; residentgen. surgery Loma Linda Hosps., 1966-70; resident plastic surgery Washington U., St. Louis, 1970-72; resident Salinas Valley (Calif.) Meml. Hosp. Mem. AMA. Office: 242 E Romie Ln Salinas CA 93901-3128*

KELLOGG, FREDERICK, historian; b. Boston, Dec. 9, 1929; s. Frederick Floyd and Stella Harriet (Plummer) K.; m. Patricia Kay Hanbery, Aug. 21, 1954 (dec. 1975); 1 child, Kristine Marie Calvert. AB, Stanford U., 1952; MA, U. So. Calif., 1958; PhD, Ind. U., 1969. Instr., Boise State U., 1962-64, asst. prof., 1964-65; vis. asst. prof. U. Idaho, 1965; asso. prof. Boise State U., 1966-67; instr. history U. Ariz., 1967-68, asst. prof., 1968-71, asso. prof., 1971—. Founder, chmn. Idaho Hist. Conf., 1964. U.S.-Romania Cultural Exchange Research scholar, 1960-61; Sr. Fulbright-Hays Research scholar, Romania, 1969-70. Recipient Am. Council Learned Socs. Research grant, 1970-71; Internat. Research and Exchanges Bd. Sr. Research grant, 1973-74. Mem. Am. Hist. Assn., Am. Assn. Advancement Slavic Studies, Am. Assn. Southeast European Studies. Author: A History of Romanian Historical Writing, 1990, The Road to Romanian Independence, 1995; mng. editor Southeastern Europe, 1974—; contbr. articles to academic publs. Office: U Ariz Dept History Tucson AZ 85721

KELLOGG, GEORGE WILLIAM, psychiatrist; m. Betty L. BS in Chemistry, La. State U., 1963, MD, 1967; postgrad., U. Chgo.; MBA, Golden Gate U., 1982. Intern Letterman Hosp., San Francisco, 1967-68; resident Walter Redd Hosp., Washington, 1968-71; psychiatrist pvt. practice, Salinas, Calif., 1974—. Maj. U.S. Army, 1966-74, Vietnam. Office: 11 Maple St Ste A Salinas CA 93901-3249

KELLSHAW, TERENCE, bishop; b. Manchester, Eng., Oct. 4, 1936; m. Hazel Frederica Johnson, Nov. 3, 1963; 4 children. Student in theology, London Univ., attended Oakhill Theol. Coll.; D. Ministry, Pitts. Theol. Coll., 1985. Ordained deacon, The Ch. of Eng., 1967, priest, 1968. Med. technologist; sr. med. technologist Makerere Univ., Uganda; asst., Christ Ch., Clifton, Bristol, 1967-71, St. John's, Woking, Surrey, 1971-73, rector, inner-city parish group, from 1973; prof. pastoral theology Trinity Episc. Sch. for Ministry, Ambridge, Pa., from 1980; interim pastor Ch. of the Ascension, Pitts., 1984-85; bishop Diocese of the Rio Grande Episcopal Ch., Albuquerque, 1989—. Office: Rio Grande Episc Diocese 4304 Carlisle Blvd NE Albuquerque NM 87107-4811*

KELL-SMITH, CARLA SUE, federal agency administrator; b. Highland Park, Mich., Sept. 15, 1952; d. Carl William and Margie May (Cannon) Bodner; m. Joseph Mark Kell, Oct. 10, 1971 (div. Dec. 1980); m. Richard Charles Smith, Jan. 28, 1989; Student, Anderson Coll., 1970-71, Glendale Coll., 1976-77, Ariz. State U., 1978-79, Mesa Coll., 1979-80. Private tutor English, Fed. Republic of Germany, 1971-74; office mgr. Bell & Schore, Rochester, Mich., 1974-75, COL Press, Phoenix, 1978-80; publicity mgr. O'Sullivan Woodside & Col, Phoenix, 1980-81, gen. mgr., 1982-84; pub. relations/promotion cons. GPI Publs., Cupertino, Calif., 1985; pub. cons., 1985-88; project adminstr. FAA, 1986—; account coord. Bernard Hodes Advt., Tempe, Ariz., 1981; cons. freelance mktg., Phoenix, 1983. Vol., Fiesta Bowl Parade Com., Phoenix, 1983, FAA Airport Improvement Project. Office: 1200 Bayhill Dr Ste 224 San Bruno CA 94066

KELLY, BRIAN MATTHEW, industrial hygienist; b. Ogdensburg, N.Y., June 16, 1956; s. Lauris F. and Catherine M. (McEvoy) K. BA, SUNY, Oswego, 1978; BS, Clarkson U., 1981; MS in Indsl. Safety, Cen. Mo. State U., 1990. Cert. indsl. hygienist Am. Bd. Indsl. Hygiene; cert. accident investigator U.S. Dept. Energy, NASA and Nuclear Regulatory Commn. Maintenance engr. Kelly Sales Corp., Madrid, N.Y., 1978-80, carpenter, 1981-82; hygienist indsl. hygiene and toxicology ES&H assessments program office 7314 Sandia Nat. Labs., Albuquerque, 1983—; mem. tech. adv. bd. Albuquerque (N.Mex.) Tech. Vocat. Inst., 1989—. Mem. Air and Waste Mgmt. Assn., Am. Inst. Chemists, Am. Indsl. Hygienists Assn., N.Y. Acad. Scis., Am. Soc. Safety Engrs., Am. Acad. Indsl. Hygiene, Gamma Sigma Epsilon, Phi Kappa Phi. Republican. Roman Catholic. Home: 1455 Beall St Bosque Farms NM 87068-9109 Office: Sandia Nat Labs ES&H Assess Prog Ofc 7314 1515 Eubank Blvd SE Albuquerque NM 87123-3430

KELLY, CAROLYN SUE, newspaper executive; b. Pasco, Wash., Oct. 25, 1952; d. Jerald Davin and Margaret Helen (Nibler) K. BBA, Gonzaga U., 1974; MBA, Seattle U., 1985. CPA, Wash. Acct. Brajcich & Loeffler, Spokane, Wash., 1972-74; auditor Peat, Marwick, Mitchell & Co., Seattle, 1974-77; fin. analyst Seattle Times, 1977-81, asst. circulation mgr., 1981-83, spl. project advt. mgr., 1983-86, dir. mktg. and new bus., 1986-89, v.p., chief fin. officer, 1989—. Bd. dirs. Econ. Devel. Coun., Seattle, 1992, Campfire, Artists Unltd. Mem. Fin. Execs. Office: Seattle Times PO Box 70 Seattle WA 98111-0070*

KELLY, CHRISTINE ELISE, city planner; b. Hollywood, Calif., Nov. 22, 1952; d. Lorenzo Iral Alcott and Louise Jean Paule Ressier; children: Ryan, Jacqueline, Michael. BA, Calif. State U., Long Beach, 1978, MPA, 1986. Dir. cmty. devel. City of Cypress, Calif. Mem. Am. Planning Assn., Urban Land Inst., Comty. Redevel. Assn., Orange County Planning Dirs. Assn. (v.p. 1986, pres. 1987). Office: City of Cypress 5275 Orange Ave Cypress CA 90630-2957

KELLY, DANIEL GRADY, JR., lawyer; b. Yonkers, N.Y., July 15, 1951; s. Daniel Grady and Helene (Coyne) K.; m. Annette Susan Wheeler, May 8, 1976; children—Elizabeth Anne, Brigid Claire, Cynthia Logan. Grad., Choate Sch., Wallingford, Conn., 1969; BA magna cum laude, Yale U., 1973; JD, Columbia U., 1976. Bar: N.Y. 1977, U.S. Dist. Ct. (so. and ea. dists.) N.Y. 1977, Calif. 1986, U.S. Dist. Ct. (cen. dist.) Calif. 1987. Law clk. to judge U.S. Ct. Appeals (2d cir.), N.Y.C., 1976-77; assoc. Davis Polk & Wardwell, N.Y.C., 1977-83; sr. v.p. Lehman Bros., N.Y.C., 1983-85; sr. v.p., gen. counsel Kaufman & Broad, Inc., L.A., 1985-87; ptnr. Manatt, Phelps, Rothenberg & Phillips, L.A., 1987-90, Sidley & Austin, L.A., 1990—. Notes and comments editor Columbia Law Rev., 1975-76. Mem. ABA (com. on law firms), L.A. County Bar Assn. (exec. com. bus. and corps. law sect.). Office: Sidley & Austin 555 W 5th St Ste 4000 Los Angeles CA 90013-3000

KELLY, DENNIS RAY, sales executive; b. Olympia, Wash., Aug. 20, 1948; s. William E. and Irene (Lewis) K.; m. Pamela Jo Kresevich, Mar. 16, 1974. BA, Cen. Wash. U., 1972; postgrad., U. Wash., 1977-78. Sales rep. Bumble Bee Sea Foods, Seattle, 1972-74; retail sales mgr. Pacific Pearl Sea Foods, Seattle, 1974-76; regional sales mgr. Castle & Cooke Foods, Seattle, Phila., and N.Y.C., 1976-80; v.p. sales mktg. Frances Andrew Ltd., Seattle, 1980-82; regional sales mgr. Tenneco West, Seattle, 1982-85; sales and mktg. mgr. for western U.S. David Oppenheimer, Seattle, 1985—. Alumni advisor Cen. Wash. U., Ellensburg, 1979-87, alumni bd. dirs., 1986—, fund drive chmn., 1988, mem. sch. community group bd.; mem. Statue of Liberty Ellis Island Found.; chmn. ann. fund drive Cen. Wash. U., bd. dirs., 1992. Mem. New Zealand-Am. Soc., Mfrs. Reps. Club Wash. (bd. dirs.). Republican. Home: 2821 2nd Ave Apt 1204 Seattle WA 98121-1249

KELLY, EMMA JANE, veterinarian; b. Liverpool, Eng., July 16, 1965. AS, Wayne C.C., Goldsboro, N.C., 1983; BS in Animal Sci. summa cum laude, N.C. State U., 1985, DVM, 1989; MS in Bioveterinary Sci., Utah State U., 1992. Extern Liverpool U. Vet. Sch., 1988; clin. vet. resident Utah State U., Provo, 1989-91, asst. vet. diagnostician, 1991-94, diagnostician, 1994—; lectr. in field. Contbr. articles to profl. jours. Recipient Radiology award N.C. State U.-CVM, 1989; Winslow Found. scholar, 1982-83. Mem. Phi Kappa Phi, Phi Zeta, Gamma Sigma Delta, Phi Theta Kappa. Office: Utah State Univ Veterinary Diagnostic Lab 2031 S State St Provo UT 84606-6552

KELLY, FLORENCE ANN, writer, poet; b. Columbia, S.C., May 24, 1948; d. George Lafayette Austin and Minna Florence (Bolding) K. BA with honors, Columbia U., 1970; postgrad., U. Houston, 1982. Sec. Mass. Mut. Life Ins., 1983-84, Statesman Nat. Life Ins., Houston, 1985, O'Keefe Real Estate, Surprise, Ariz., 1987; adminstrv. asst. Periodontics Ltd., Phoenix, 1987-90; with Executemps, Phoenix, 1991—; with PAMS Temp. Agy., 1993—. Author poetry. Organizer New Alliance Party/Dem. Party high conservative br., N.Y.C. Houston and Phoenix, 1980-90. Recipient Am. Legion award for Citizenship, 1966, William W. Fairclough award Pelham Manor Club, N.Y., 1966, others.

KELLY, GABRIELLE MARY, film production executive; b. Galway, Ireland, Apr. 16, 1953; d. Gabriel Francis and Nora (Geraghty) K.; m. Allan Avrum Goldstein, May 30, 1986; children: Fiona Ann, Eamon Saul. BA in Am. Lit. with honors, U. Sussex, Brighton, Eng., 1976. Rsch. asst. BBC London/WGBH Boston, 1973-75; copy editor N.Y. Rev. of Books, N.Y.C., 1975-78; head devel. Lumet-Allen Co., N.Y.C., 1978-83; prodr. Paramount & Columbia Pictures, N.Y.C. & L.A., 1983-85; prodr., writer CBS Films, N.Y.C., 1985-86; v.p. prodn. Bud Yorkin Prodns., 1988-89; v.p. creative affairs Robert Evans Co., Paramount Pictures, L.A., 1990-93; prodr. Eddie Murphy Prodns., Paramount Pictures, L.A., 1993—. Democrat. Roman Catholic. Home and Office: 2509 Greenvalley Rd Los Angeles CA 90046-1437

KELLY, JEROME BERNARD, insurance company executive; b. Kankakee, Ill., Oct. 4, 1954; s. Joseph B. and Mary J. (Demerly) K.; m. Barbara Fawcett, June 21, 1986; children: Anna, Sarah. BA, Regis Coll., 1980; MBA, U. Phoenix, 1989. V.p. Shearson Hayden Stone, Denver, 1977-83, E.F. Hutton, Denver, 1983-85; portfolio mgr. 17th St. Fin. Mgmt., Denver, 1985-87; stockbroker Dain Bosworth, Denver, 1987-88; owner J.B. Kelly Ins. Agy., Denver, 1988—. Bd. dirs. United Cerebral Palsy Assn. Denver, 1987-90; mem. selection com. Cultural Facilities Tax Dist., Denver, 1995—. Mem. Colo. Bus. Sch. Club (pres. 1988-89), Trout Unltd., Nat. Assn. of Securities Dealers (bd. arbitration 1987—), Am. Arbitration Assn. (panel arbitrators 1990—). Office: JB Kelly Ins Agy 1863 S Pearl St Denver CO 80210-3136

KELLY, KATHLEEN FLO, personal and professional development company executive, cleaning service executive, cosmetologist; b. Loma Linda, Calif., Nov. 5, 1947; d. Boyde Jefferson and Nell (Miller) Henderson; m. Floyd Jerome Smith, Oct. 25, 1969 (div. 1972); 1 child, Robert Allen Smith;

m. Edwin Allen Blankinship, Oct. 15, 1977 (div. 1986); m. Steven Joe Kelly, May 30, 1993. Cert. bookkeeping/acctg. Calif. Bus. Sch., San Bernardino, 1966; AA, San Bernardino Valley Coll., 1975; student Riverside (Calif.) City Coll., 1985. Lic. Cosmetologist. Bookkeeper Laurentide Fin. Co., San Bernardino, 1969-70; loan officer Avco Thrift, San Bernardino, 1972-74; waitress Agro Land & Cattle, Colton, Calif., 1974-76; mem. advt. staff Holcombe Pub., San Bernardino, 1976-80; stylist, mgr. Mane St. Hair Design, Loma Linda, Calif., 1980-84; owner, profl. speaker, cons. U.&I Enterprises, Riverside, 1983—; organizational analyst Pomona Valley Praise Temple, Calif., 1985; rep. Equitable Life Assurance Soc. U.S., 1986; mentor Positive Force, Highland, Calif., 1985; owner Higher Image Hair, Riverside, 1988-92, ind. stylist, 1992—; fin. cons. BancVest Fin. Services Inc., 1986; stylist Ann & Friends, 1986-88. Author: Seasons of My Times, 1980, Winning Isn't For Everyone, 1986; contbr. monthly make-over column to mag., 1980-84. Mem. Vols. in Child Abuse and Neglect, 1978; campaign worker McCartney for Judge, 1969-70; Trainer Choices Program Riverside County Sch. Dist., 1986. Mem. Nat. Assn. Female Execs., Equitable Life Assurance Soc. U.S. (registered rep.), Women in Networking, Greater Riverside C. of C. (bd. dirs. 1986-92, chmn. Bus. in Action, chmn. edn. com. 1987-89, pres. La Sierra div. 1991-92), Redlands C. of C. (ambassador). Republican. Club: S.B. Pro-Club (bd. dirs.). Lodge: Toastmasters. Avocations: skiing, reading, personal development. Home and Office: 7 Bella Aliza Lake Elsinore CA 92532-0116

KELLY, KATHLEEN SUZANNE, marketing professional; b. Inglewood, Calif., Dec. 20, 1966; d. Robert Duane and Anne Margaret (Halpin) K. BS, U. So. Calif., L.A., 1989. Asst. media buyer Kelly, Scott & Madison, Chgo., 1989-90, pub. rels. rep. In N Out Burger, Baldwin Park, Calif., 1990-91, interim mktg. dir., 1991-92, advt. and pub. rels. adminstr., 1992-93; project mgr. L.A. Unified Sch. Dist., 1993—; cons. in field. Pres. bd. dirs. Haven House, 1995. Mem. NAFE, AAUW, Pub. Rels. Soc. Am., Am. Mgmt. Assn., Trojan Jr. Aux., San Gabriel Valley Trojan Club (bd. dirs.), Pasadena Jaycees (edn. com. 1993-94). Republican. Roman Catholic. Home: 1111 Cresthaven Dr Los Angeles CA 90042-1431 Office: Sch Vol Program 450 N Grand Ave Bldg G-253 Los Angeles CA 90012-2100

KELLY, MAXINE ANN, property developer; b. Ft. Wayne, Ind., Aug. 14, 1931; d. Victor J. and Marguerite E. (Biebesheimer) Cramer; m. James Herbert Kelly, Oct. 4, 1968 (dec. Apr. 74). BA, Northwestern U., 1956. Sec., Parry & Barns Law Offices, Ft. Wayne, 1951-52; trust sec. Lincoln Nat. Bank & Trust Co., 1956-58; sr. clk. stenographer div. Mental Health, Alaska Dept. Health, Anchorage, 1958-60; office mgr. Langdon Psychiat. Clinic, 1960-70; propr. A-1 Bookkeeping Svc., 1974-75; ptnr. Gonder-Kelly Enterprises & A-is-A Constrn., Wasilla, Alaska, 1965-92; sales assoc. Yukon Realty/Gallery of Homes, Wasilla, 1989; sec. Rogers Realty, Inc., Wasilla, 1989, MMC Constrn., Inc., 1992—. Dir. Alaska Mental Health Assn., Anchorage, 1960-61; pres., treas. Libertarian Party Anchorage, 1968-69, Alaska Libertarian Party, 1969-70. Mem. AAUW (life), Anchorage C. of C., Whittier Boat Owners Assn. (treas. 1980-84). Home: 8651 Augusta Cir Anchorage AK 99504-4202

KELLY, NANCY ANNE, nurse; b. San Diego, May 16, 1946; d. Jere Basil and Margaret Marcia (Kelly) Crepps; children: Christen, William, Bryce. AA, Golden West Coll., 1981; student, U. Calif., San Diego, 1990; chem. dependence counseling cert., U. Irvine, 1991, Graceland U., 1994. Nurse Huntington Intercommunity Hosp., Huntington Beach, Calif., 1981-92, William L. Kelly M.D., Huntington Beach, 1990-92, Home Health Agy., Mission Viejo, Calif., 1991; nursing supr. Monte Vista Hosp., Las Vegas, 1992-94; nurse So. Nev. Mental Health, Las Vegas, 1994—. Mem. Nat. Nurses Orgn., Nev. Nurses Orgn., Alliance Mentally Ill. Home: 8858 Scenic Bay Dr Las Vegas NV 89117-1026 Office: 1820 E Sahara Ave Ste 109 Las Vegas NV 89104-3736

KELLY, PAUL JOSEPH, JR., lawyer; b. Freeport, N.Y., Dec. 6, 1940; s. Paul J. and Jacqueline M. (Nolan) K.; BBA, U. Notre Dame, 1963; JD, Fordham U., 1967; m. Ruth Ellen Dowling, June 27, 1964; children—Johanna, Paul Edwin, Thomas Martin, Christopher Mark, Heather Marie. Bar: N.Mex. 1967. Law clk. Cravath, Swaine & Moore, N.Y.C., 1964-67; assoc. firm Hinkle, Cox, Eaton, Coffied & Hensley, Roswell, N.Mex., 1967-71, ptnr., 1971-92; judge U.S. Ct. Appeals (10th cir.), Santa Fe, 1992—; mem. N.Mex. Bd. Bar Examiners, 1982-85; mem. N.Mex. Ho. of Reps., 1976-81, chmn. consumer and public affairs com., mem. judiciary com. Mem. N.Mex. Pub. Defender Bd.; bd. of visitors, Fordham U. Sch. of Law, 1992—; pres. No. N.M. Am. Inn of Ct., 1993 ; pres. Roswell Drug Abuse Com., 1970-71; mem. Appellate Judges Nominating Commn., 1989-92. Pres. Chaves County Young Reps., 1971-72; vice chmn. N.Mex. Young Reps., 1969-71, treas., 1968-69; pres. No. N.Mex. Am. Inn of Court. Bd. dirs. Zia council Girl Scouts Am., Roswell Girls Club, Chaves County Mental Health Assn., 1974-77; bd. dirs. Santa Fe Orch., 1992-93, Roswell Symphony Orch. Soc., 1969-82, treas., 1970-73, pres., 1973-75; mem. Eastern N.Mex. State Fair Bd., 1978-83. Mem. ABA, Fed. Bar Assn., State Bar N.Mex. (v.p. young lawyers sect. 1969, co-chmn. ins. sub-com. 1972-73, mem. continuing legal edn. com. 1970-73). Roman Catholic (pres. parish council 1971-76). K.C. Office: US Court Appeals 10th Circuit Federal Courthouse PO Box 10113 Santa Fe NM 87504-6113

KELLY, PETER BERNARD, chemistry educator, researcher; b. Seneca Falls, N.Y., Sept. 10, 1954; s. Glenn Bernard and Ruth Margret (Larsen) K. AB, Dartmouth Coll., 1976; PhD, Pa. State U., State College, 1981. Postdoctoral assoc. Princeton (N.J.) U., 1981-83, U. Oreg., Eugene, 1983-86; asst. prof. U. Calif., Davis, 1986-93, assoc. prof., 1993-94; vis. assoc. prof. Rice U., Houston, 1994-95. Contbr. articles to profl. jours. Mem. Am. Chem. Soc., Am. Optical Soc., Western Spectroscopy Assn. Methodist. Office: U Calif Chemistry Dept Davis CA 95616

KELLY, RICHARD JOHN, anesthesiologist, physician, lawyer; b. Tamuning, Guam, July 10, 1959; s. Benjamin Harrison and Lourdes (Hawkins) K. Internat. Baccalaureate diploma, Washington Internat. Sch., 1981; AB, Harvard U., 1985; MPH, U. Calif., Berkeley, 1986; MD, JD, Stanford U., 1993. Diplomate Nat. Bd. Med. Examiners. Lyndon Baines Johnson congl. fellow U.S. Ho. of Reps., Washington, 1983; com. undergrad. edn. Harvard U., Cambridge, Mass., 1983-85; assoc. litigation dept. Musick, Peeler & Garrett, L.A., 1989; summer assoc. litigation dept. Berliner, Cohen & Biagini, San Jose, Calif., 1991; cons. coun. internat. orgns. med. scis. WHO, Geneva, 1991-92; resident physician dept. internal medicine U. Calif., San Francisco, 1993-94, resident physician dept. anesthesiology, 1994—. Contbr. chpts. to books, articles to profl. jours. Fellow Am. Coll. Legal Medicine; mem. ACP, AMA, Am. Soc. Law, Medicine and Ethics, Am. Soc. Anesthesiologists, Calif. House Officer Med. Soc., Calif. Med. Assn. Home: 2601 Valparaiso Ave Menlo Park CA 94025

KELLY, ROBERT EDWARD, engineer, educator; b. Abington, Pa., Oct. 20, 1934; s. Bernard Joseph and Rose Monica (Lautenschlager) K.; m. Karin Elizabeth Lampert, Aug. 15, 1964; children: Nicholas, Jennifer. BA, Franklin & Marshall Coll., 1957; BS, Rensselaer Poly. Inst., 1957; MS in Aero. Engring., MIT, 1959, ScD, 1964. Asst. prof. UCLA, 1967-70, assoc. prof., 1970-75, prof. dept. mech. and aerospace engring., 1975—, vice chair grad. affairs, 1976-94; sr. vis. fellow Imperial Coll. Sci. and Tech., London, 1974; vis. prof. Northwestern U., Evanston, Ill., 1985, U. Manchester, Eng., 1994; vis. scientist Japan Atomic Energy Rsch. Inst., Tokai-mura, 1991; cons. Hughes Aircraft Co., El Segundo, Calif., 1976-83. Assoc. editor Physics of Fluids, 1981-83, 92—; mem. editorial bd. Phys. Rev. E, 1990—; contbr. over 50 articles to profl. jours. Fellow Am. Phys. Soc. (chmn. divsn. fluid dynamics 1980 81); mem. ASME, AIAA. Office: MANE Dept UCLA Los Angeles CA 90095

KELLY, ROBERTO CONRADO (BOBBY KELLY), professional baseball player; b. Panama City, Panama, Oct. 1, 1964. Student, Jose Dolores Moscote Coll., Panama. With N.Y. Yankees, 1982-92, Cin. Reds, 1992-94, Atlanta Braves, 1994, Montreal Expos, 1994-95, L.A. Dodgers, 1995—; mem. Am. League All-Star Team, 1992, Nat. League All-Star Team, 1993. Office: LA Dodgers 1000 Elysian Park Ave Los Angeles CA 90012

KELLY, THOMAS J., sports association executive; b. Madison, Wis.; m. Carole Kelly. BA in Journalism, U. Wis., 1974. Photographer Madison's daily newspapers; sports editor weekly newspaper; pub. rels. dir. midwestern ski resort, 1977; asst. nat. nordic dir. U.S. Ski Assn., 1988-95; dir. comms. U.S. Skiing, 1988—, dir. ops., 1995—; mem. bd. dirs. Ski Utah. Mem. Rotary. Office: US Ski Team PO Box 100 Park City UT 84060-0100*

KELLY, TIMOTHY DONAHUE, state senator; b. Sacramento, Aug. 15, 1944; m. Lisa B. Nelson, Jan. 1, 1994; children: Ingrid Brose, Theodore Ambrose. Former legis. aide to Calif. and Nev. Legislatures; mortgage banker; mem. Alaska Ho. of Reps., 1976-78, Alaska Senate, 1978—, senate pres., 1989-90. With USMCR, Alaska Air NG. Office: State Capitol Juneau AK 99801-1182

KELLY, WILLIAM BRET, insurance executive; b. Rocky Ford, Colo., Sept. 28, 1922; s. William Andrew and Florence Gail (Yant) K.; m. Patricia Ruth Ducy, Mar. 25, 1944; children: Eric Damian, Kathryn Gail Kelly Schweitzer. BA cum laude, U. Colo., 1947. CPCU. With Steel City Agys., Inc., and predecessor, Pueblo, Colo., 1946—, pres., 1961-76, chmn. bd., 1977—; dir. United Bank Pueblo, 1963—, chmn. bd., 1983-88; mem. Pub. Expenditure Coun., 1984—; v.p. Colo. Ins. Edn. Found., 1981, pres., 1982. Mem. Pueblo Area Coun. Govts., 1971-73, Colo. Forum 1985—, trustee Pueblo Bd. Water Works, 1966-80, pres., 1970-71; pres. Pueblo Single Fund Plan, 1960-61, Pueblo Heart Coun., 1962, Family Svc. Soc. Pueblo, 1963; mem. 10th Jud. Dist. Nominating Com., 1967-71; trustee U. So. Colo. Found., 1967—, v.p., 1991, 92, 93, 94; trustee Jackson Found., 1972—, Farley Found., 1979—, Roselawn Cemetery Assn., 1982—, Kelly-Ducy Found., 1983—; sch. bus. adv. coun. mem. U. So. Colo., 1989—; hon. parade marshall Colo. State Fair, 1991. With inf. AUS, 1943-45. Decorated Silver Star, Bronze Star with oak leaf cluster, Purple Heart with oak leaf cluster; recipient Disting. Svc. award U. Colo., 1992; honored for cmty. svc. Parkview Episcopal Med. Ctr., 1992; named to Pueblo Hall of Fame, 1995. Mem. Soc. CPCU's, Pueblo C. of C. (past pres.), Pueblo Kiwanis (past pres.), Pueblo Country Club (treas. 1964-66), So. Colo. Press Club (Outstanding Community Svc. award 1991), Phi Beta Kappa. Democrat. Home: 264 S Sifford Ct Pueblo West CO 81007-2843 Office: 1414 W 4th St Pueblo CO 81004-1205

KELLY, WILLIAM STATES, data network engineer; b. Frederick, Md., Oct. 15, 1956; s. William Tolson III and Jane Randall (States) K. BS, Union Coll., Schenectady, 1978; MS, U. Ariz., 1983. City planner Bur. Planning, Schenectady, 1978-79; grad. teaching asst. systems engring. dept. U. Ariz., Tucson, 1981-83; systems engr. Gen. Dynamics, San Diego, 1983-85; staff engr. Martin Marietta, Littleton, Colo., 1985-88; data network engr. Apollo Travel Svcs./United Airlines, Englewood, Colo., 1988—; mem. user adv. coun. Quintessential Solutions, Inc., San Diego, 1991—; mem. user group AT&T-Accunet, Bridgewater, N.J., 1991; presenter C.A.C.I. Simulation Conf., 1988. Contbr. articles to profl. publs. Mem. Orchard Creek Park Assn., Greenwood Village, Colo., 1990—. Home: 5875 S Long Ln Greenwood Vlg CO 80121-1741 Office: Apollo Travel Svcs/United Airlines 5350 S Valentia Way Englewood CO 80111-3100

KELSEY, EDITH JEANINE, psychotherapist, consultant; b. Freeport, Ill., Oct. 15, 1937; d. John Melvin and Florence Lucille (Ewald) Anderson; divorced; children: Steven Craig, Kevin John. Student, Pasadena Coll., 1955-58; BA in Psychology, Calif. State U., San Jose, 1980; MA in Counseling Psychology, Santa Clara U., 1984. Lic. marriage, family and child counselor. Counselor, cons., cert. trainer Values Tech., Santa Cruz, Calif., 1981—, dir. research, 1982-84; intern in counseling Sr. Residential Services, San Jose, 1983-84; psychotherapist Process Therapy Inst., Los Gatos, Calif., 1983-86, Sexual Abuse Treatment Ctr., San Jose, 1984-87; cons. in field, Santa Clara Valley, 1982—; trainer, cons. Omega Assoc., 1987-88; teaching asst. Santa Clara U., 1987-88; pvt. practice psychotherapy, cons., tng., 1987—. Contbr. articles to profl. jours. Vol. Parental Stress Hotline, Palo Alto, Calif., 1980-85. Mem. Am. Assn. Marriage and Family Therapists, Am. Soc. Aging, Calif. Assn. Marriage and Family Therapists (clin.), Sierra Club. Democrat. Presbyterian. Home: 431 Casita Ct Los Altos CA 94022-1736 Office: 153 Forest Ave Palo Alto CA 94301-1615

KELSEY, FLOYD LAMAR, JR., architect; b. Colorado Springs, Colo., Jan. 2, 1925; s. Floyd Lamar and Myrtice (Graves) K.; m. Ruth Ann Witty, June 22, 1946; children—Patricia Ann, Carol Susan. Student, Colo. Coll., 1942-44; B.S. in Architecture with honors, U. Ill., 1947. Partner Bunts & Kelsey (architects), Colorado Springs, 1952-66; pres. Lamar Kelsey Assos., 1966-85, The LKA Ptnrs. Inc., 1985-88; cons. in arch. and planning, 1989—; cons. design rev. bd. U. Colo., 1969-70, 86—; adv. panel, region 8 Gen. Services Adminstrn. Author: Schools for America, 1967, Open Space Schools, 1971; Contbr. to profl. jours. Recipient design awards AIA, design awards Am. Inst. Steel Constrn., design awards Am. Assn. Sch. Adminstrs., design awards Nation's Schs. mag. Fellow AIA (former mem. nat. coms. on ednl. facilities, edn., architecture for arts and recreation); mem. Garden of the Gods Club, Kissing Camels Golf Club, Pinnacle Peak Country Club, Gargoyle Archtl. Hon. Soc., Phi Delta Theta. Presbyterian. Home (summer): 8408 E La Senda Dr Scottsdale AZ 85255-4268 Home (winter): 8408 E La Senda Dr Scottsdale AZ 85255-4268

KELSEY, MICHAEL LOYAL, geography educator; b. Greeley, Colo., Dec. 15, 1953; s. Loyal Lee and Luwanda Marie (Steffens) K. BS, Salisbury State U., 1976; MA in Geography, U. Northern Colo., 1988; PhD in Geography, Kent State U., 1993. Founder, mgr. Salisbury (Md.) State U. Book Co-op., 1975-76; mgmt. trainee J.C. Penney Co., Inc., Salisbury, 1976-77; cost acctg. and time study mgr. W.D. Byron & Sons, Inc., Williamsport, Md., 1978-83; corp. inventory controller Stuart McGuire Co., Inc., Salem, Va., 1983-84; owner, mgr. New Century Ribbon Co., Greeley, Colo., 1984-88; instr., doctoral teaching fellow Kent (Ohio) State U., 1988-91; instr. Montgomery Coll., Rockville, Md., 1991-93; prof., chmn. geography and econs. dept. Aims Coll., Greeley, 1993—; officer, bd. dirs. Seagulf Concepts, Inc., Salisbury, Md., 1975-76; cons. Laserhead Graphics, Greeley, 1993—. Recipient top bus. student award Rotary Internat., Salisbury, 1975, grad. fellowship U. Northern Colo., Greeley, 1986-87, grant IBM Corp., Rockville, Md., 1992. Mem. Assn. Am. Geographers, Nat. Coun. for Geographic Edn., Gamma Theta Upsilon (pres. U. No. Colo. 1987-89), Phi Kappa Phi, Omicron Delta Kappa. Home: 4040 W 12th St Apt 6 Greeley CO 80634 Office: Aims CC 5401 W 20th St Greeley CO 80634

KELSHAW, TERENCE, bishop; b. Manchester, Eng., Oct. 4, 1936; m. Hazel Frederica Johnson, Oct. 4, 1963; 4 children. Degree in Med. Tech., Univ. Med. Sch.; postgrad., London Univ., Oakhill Theol. Seminary; D in Ministry, Pitts. Theol. Coll., 1985; postgrad., Ecumenical Inst., Geneva, 1988. Ordained to diaconate, 1967 Episc. Ch., to priesthood, 1968. Pathologist various labs., Scotland and Far East; sr. med. technologist Makerere Univ., Uganda, 1961-64; asst. Christ Ch., Bristol, Eng., 1967-71, St. John's Ch., Woking, 1971-73; rector various inner city chs., Bristol, 1973-80; prof. pastoral theology Trinity Episc. Sch. Ministry, Ambridge, Pa., 1980-88; interim pastor Ch. Ascension, Pitts., 1984-85; elected bishop Diocese of Rio Grande, Albuquerque, 1989—; rector Christian Family Ctr., Easton, Eng.; formerly with nat. and diocesan re-organization com.; seminary commn. mission Panama Project Episc. Ch. Author: Three Streams, One River, Send This Message to My Church, (children's books) The Fernhill Series. Formerly active Ch. Fellowships Assn. Allen fellow, 1988. Office: 4304 Carlisle Blvd NE Albuquerque NM 87107-4811

KELTON, ARTHUR MARVIN, JR., real estate developer; b. Bennington, Vt., Sept. 12, 1939; s. Arthur Marvin and Lorraine (Millington) K.; m. Elaine White, Nov. 1, 1986; 1 child, Ashley. BA, Dartmouth Coll., 1961. Ptnr. Kelton and Assocs., Vail, Colo., 1966-77; pres. Kelton, Garton and Assocs. Inc., Vail, 1977-84, Kelton, Garton, Kendall, Vail, 1984-93, Christopher, Denton, Kelton, Kendall, Vail, 1993—. Head agt. Dartmouth Alumni Fund, Hanover, N.H., 1985-90, class pres., 1990—; pres. Vail Valley Med. Ctr. Found., 1991—. Republican. Congregationalist. Home: 1034 Homestake Cir Vail CO 81657-5111 Office: Kelton Garton Kendall 288 Bridge St Vail CO 81657-4523

KEMERY, WILLIAM ELSWORTH, psychotherapist, hypnotherapist; b. Portland, Oreg., Apr. 16, 1929; s. William Elsworth Jr. and Charlotte Francis (Leydic) K.; m. Norma Mae Ishmael, Nov. 22, 1963 (div. May 1972); children: William M., Robert Z.; m. Marlene Agnes Kwiatkowski, Dec. 15, 1983; children: William E., William M., Robert Z., Bradley E. DD, Episcopal Sem., Balt., 1953; BA, Fresno State U., 1954; PhD (hon.), Hamilton State, 1973; Masters, Newport Internat. U., 1976, PhD, 1979. Cert. psychotherapist, hypnotherapist, sex therapist. Psychotherapist Chula Vista, Calif., 1967—; founding dir. Calif. Hypnotists Examining Coun., Chula Vista, Calif., 1974; pres., fellow Acad. Sci. Hypnotherapy, San Diego, 1974—; bishop Holy Episcopal Ch., Chula Vista, 1978—; dir. Assn. of Spiritual Psychology, San Diego, 1968—. Contbr. articles to profl. jours. Named Hon. Mayor, Chula Vist C. of C., 1967, Knight of Grace, Order of St. John of Jerusalem, 1981. Fellow Nutrition and Preventive Medicine Assn.; mem. Internat. Assn. Clin. Hypnotherapy (life), Acad. Orthomolecular Psychiatry, Assn. Huministic Psychology, Internat. New Thought Alliance, Am. Guild Hypnotherapists, Am. Mental Health Counselors Assn., Am. Assn. Sex Educators, Counselors and Therapists. Republican. Home and Office: 379 G St Chula Vista CA 91910

KEMMERLY, JACK DALE, retired state official, aviation consultant; b. El Dorado, Kans., Sept. 17, 1936; s. Arthur Allen and Eythel Louise (Throckmorton) K.; m. Frances Cecile Gregorio, June 22, 1958; children: Jack Dale Jr., Kathleen Frances, Grant Lee. BA, San Jose State U., 1962; cert. in real estate, UCLA, 1970; MPA, Golden Gate U., 1973; cert. labor-mgmt. rels., U. Calif., Davis, 1978. Right of way agt. Calif. Div. Hwys., Marysville, 1962-71; adminstrv. officer Calif. Dept. Transp., Sacramento, 1971-82; dist. dir. Calif. Dept. Transp., Redding, 1982-83; chief aeros. Calif. Dept. Transp., Sacramento, 1984-94; mgmt. cons. U.S. Dept. Transp., Riyadh, Saudi Arabia, 1983-84; mem. tech. adv. com. on aeronautics Calif. Transp. Commn. Bd. dirs. Yuba-Sutter Campfire Girls, 1972-73. With USN, 1954-57. Recipient superior accomplishment award Calif. Dept. Transp., 1981. Mem. Nat. Assn. State Aviation Ofcls. (nat. pres. 1989—), Am. Assn. State Hwy. and Transp. Ofcls. (aviation com. 1985-94), Calif. Assn. Aerospace Educators (adv. bd. 1984—), Calif. Assn. Airport Execs., Calif. Aviation Coun., Aircraft Owners and Pilots Assn. (Western regional rep.), Elks (exalted ruler Marysville, Calif. 1974-75). Republican. Roman Catholic. Office: 1285 Charlotte Ave Yuba City CA 95991-2803

KEMMIS, DANIEL ORRA, mayor, author; b. Fairview, Mont., Dec. 5, 1945; s. Orra Raymond and Lilly Samantha (Shidler) K.; m. Jeanne Marie Koester, June 9, 1978; children: Abraham, Samuel; children by previous marriage: Deva, John. BA, Harvard U., 1968; JD, U. Mont., 1978. Bar: Mont. 1978. State rep. Mont. Ho. of Reps., Helena, 1975-84, minority leader, 1981-82, Speaker of House, 1983-84; ptnr. Morrison, Jonkel, Kemmis & Rossbach, Missoula, 1978-80, Jonkel & Kemmis, 1981-84; mayor City of Missoula, Mont., 1990—; cons. No. Lights Inst., Missoula, Mont., 1985-89. Author: Community and the Politics of Place, 1990, The Good City and the Good life, 1995; contbr. articles to profl. jours. Candidate for chief justice Mont. Supreme Ct.; mem. adv. bd. Nat. Civic League, Pew Partnership for Civic Change; chmn. leadership tng. coun. Nat. League Cities, 1992-94; bd. dirs. Charles F. Kettering Found.; fellow Dallas Inst. for Humanities & Culture. Named Disting. Young Alumnus U. Mont., 1981. Democrat. Home: 524 Benton Ave Missoula MT 59801-8635 Office: City of Missoula City Hall 435 Ryman St Missoula MT 59802-4207

KEMP, EDDY NELSON, investment advisory firm executive; b. Pike County, Ohio, June 29, 1938; s. Edward Clifton and Eulah Jessie (Martin) K.; m. Therese Helene Cisowski, June 25, 1960; children: Gregory, Christine, Brian. BA, Ball State U., 1965. CPA, registered investment advisor, Hawaii. Mgr. tax dept. Peat, Marwick, Mitchell & Co., Honolulu, 1965-74; dir. fin. and adminstrn. Estate of James Campbell, Honolulu, 1974-82; pres., part owner R.K. Marine, Inc., Honolulu, 1982-84; pres., owner E.N. Kemp & Assocs., Inc., Kaneohe, Hawaii, 1982—; bus. valuation cons. Bowen Hunsaker & Co. CPAs, Honolulu, 1992—, Tax Strategies, Honolulu, 1988-93. Envisioned, researched, co-designed and supervised constrn. of world's largest passenger catamaran. Mem. Kahaluu (Hawaii) Neighborhood Bd., 1988; pres. 15th House Dist., Reps. of Hawaii, Honolulu, 1990, chmn. 8th Senatorial Dist., 1992, 23d Senatorial Dist., 1993—; dir. Alger Found., Honolulu, 1986-90. With USAF, 1956-61. Mem. AICPA, Fin. Execs. Inst. (treas., sec. 2d v.p., 1st v.p., pres., dir. 1981-88), Hawaii Soc. CPAs (various coms. 1969—), Investment Soc. Hawaii, Inst. Bus. Appraisers, Hawaii Estate Planning Coun. Home and Office: E N Kemp & Assocs Inc 47-449 Ahuimanu Pl Kaneohe HI 96744-4676

KEMP, JEANNE FRANCES, office manager; b. L.A., Dec. 8, 1942; d. Damian Thomas and Helen Catherine (Bohin) Hanifee; m. Don H. Kemp, Dec. 16, 1966 (div. 1972). AB, San Francisco State U., 1965. Food svc. technician United Air Lines, San Francisco, 1961-65; clk. N.Y. Life Ins., San Francisco, 1965-66; inventory clk. Ingersoll-Rand, San Francisco, 1966; advt./order clk. Patrick's Stationers, San Francisco, 1966-67; sec. Dartmouth Travel, Hanover, N.H., 1967-68, Olsten Temp. Svcs., N.Y.C., 1968-70; office mgr. Brown U. Devel., N.Y.C., 1970-73; asst. dir. Cen. Opera Svc., N.Y.C., 1974-85; office mgr., sec. Payne, Thompson & Walker, San Francisco, 1986—. Editor: Career Guide...Singers, 1985, Operas...for Children, 1985; asst. editor COS Bull., 1976-85; editorial asst.: Who's Who in Opera, 1975. Democrat. Roman Catholic. Office: Payne Thompson & Walker 235 Montgomery St Ste 760 San Francisco CA 94104-2910

KEMP, SHAWN T., professional basketball player; b. Elkhart, Ind., Nov. 26, 1969. Student, U. Ky., Trinity Valley C.C., 1988-89. Basketball player Seattle Supersonics, 1989—. Named to NBA All-Star team, 1993, Dream Team II, 1994, All-NBA Second Team, 1994. Office: Seattle Supersonics PO Box C900911 190 Queen Anne Ave N Seattle WA 98109-9711

KEMPF, MARTINE, voice control device manufacturing company executive; b. Strasbourg, France, Dec. 9, 1958; came to U.S., 1985; d. Jean-Pierre and Brigitte Marguerite (Klockenbring) K. Student in Astronomy, Friedrich Wilhelm U., Bonn, Fed. Republic of Germany, 1981-83. Owner, mgr. Kempf, Sunnyvale, Calif., 1985—. Inventor Comeldir Multiplex Handicapped Driving Systems (Goldenes Lenkrad Axel Springer Verlag 1981), Katalavox speech recognition control system (Oscar, World Almanac Inventions 1984, Prix Grand Siecle, Comite Couronne Francaise 1985). Recipient Medal for Service to Humanity Spinal Cord Soc., 1986; street named in honor in Dossenheim-Kochersberg, Alsace, France, 1987; named Citizen of Honor City of Dossenheim-Kochersberg, 1985, Outstanding Businessperson of Yr. City of Sunnyvale, 1990. Office: 1080 E Duane Ave Ste E Sunnyvale CA 94086-2628

KEMPIS, JANET T., hospital executive; b. Kawit, Cavite, The Philippines, Sept. 21, 1944; came to U.S., 1979; d. Isidro A. Toledo and Ursula Fajardo; m. Richard A. Kempis, Jan. 6, 1965 (div. 1970); children: Joyce, Jenny, Denise. BSc, Far Eastern U., Manila, 1964; MPA, U. San Francisco, 1987, EdD in Orgn. and Leadership, 1991. Lic. nursing home adminstr., Calif. Internal auditor Philippine Airlines, Manila, 1968-70; internal auditor Sarmiento Internat., Manila, 1970-73, exec. asst. to chief exec. officer, 1973-77; adminstrn., fin. mgr. Pacific Woodworks Internat. Inc., Manila, 1977-79; health care billing clk. Laguna Honda Hosp., San Francisco, 1980-84, patient accounts supr., 1984-87; dir. patient acctg. French Hosp. Med. Ctr., San Francisco, 1987-89; dir. fin. svcs. Palo Alto (Calif.) Med. Found., 1989—; adminstr. Hillhaven Corp., 1992-94; exec. dir. Greenery Rehab. Group, 1994—. Vol. Freewheelers, San Francisco; pastoral aide Laguna Honda Hosp. Fellow NAFE, Healthcare Fin. Mgmt. Assn.; mem. Med. Group Practice Mgmt., Calif. Assn. Healthcare Facilities, Am. Colls. Healthcare Adminstrs., U. San Francisco Alumni Assn., Notarial Assn. Calif., Phi Delta Kappa. Office: 385 Esplanade Pacifica CA 94044-1882

KEMPTHORNE, DIRK ARTHUR, senator; b. San Diego, Oct. 29, 1951; s. James Henry and Maxine Jesse (Gustason) K.; m. Patricia Jean Merrill, Sept. 18, 1977; children: Heather Patricia, Jeffrey Dirk. BS in Polit. Sci., U. Idaho, 1975. Exec. asst. to dir. Idaho Dept. Lands, Boise, 1975-78; exec. v.p. Idaho Home Builders Assn., Boise, 1978-81; campaign mgr. Batt for Gov., Boise, 1981-82; lic. securities rep. Swanson Investments, Boise, 1983; Idaho pub. affairs mgr. FMC Corp., Boise, 1983-86; mayor Boise, 1986-93; U.S. Senator from Idaho, 1993—; 1st v.p. Assn. of Idaho Cities, 1990-93; chmn. U.S. Conf. of Mayors Standing Com. on Energy and Environment, 1991-93, mem. adv. bd., 1991-93, Environ. & Pub. Works Subcom. on Drinking Water, Fisheries, & Wildlife; sec. Nat. Conf. of Rep. Mayors and Mcpl. Elected Officials, 1991-93; mem. Armed Svcs. Com., Small Bus. Com., Nat. Republican Senatorial Com.; chmn. Fisheries, Drinking Water and Wildlife Subcom.; mem. Adv. Com. Intergovernmental Rels., 1995—. Pres. Associated Students U. Idaho, Moscow, 1975; chmn. bd. dirs. Wesleyan Presch.,

Boise, 1982-85; mem. magistrate commn. 4th Jud. Dist., Boise, 1986-93; mem. task force Nat. League of Cities Election, 1988; bd. dirs. Parents and Youth Against Drug Abuse, 1987—; mem. bd. vis. USAF Acad., 1994—. Recipient Idaho Citizen of Yr. award The Idaho Statesman, 1988. Republican. Methodist. Office: US Senate 367 Dirksen Senate Office Bldg Washington DC 20510-1204

KENAGY, JOHN WARNER, surgeon; b. Lincoln, Nebr., May 28, 1945; s. Wyman Black and Sylvia (Adams) K.; m. Barbara Penterman, Feb. 1968 (div. 1975); 1 child, Jennifer; m. Jonell Day, Apr. 21, 1978; children: Susanne, Emma, John Wyman. BS, U. Nebr., 1967, MD, U. Nebr., Omaha, 1971. Diplomate Am. Bd. Surgery; splty. cert. in gen. vascular surgery. Intern, Hosps. of U. Wash., Seattle, 1971-72, resident in surgery, 1971-76; surgeon Longview Surgical Group, Longview, Wash., 1976—; clin. instr. surgery U. Wash., Seattle, 1979-82, clin. asst. prof. surgery, 1982-89, clin. assoc. prof., 1989—; dir. peripheral vascular svcs. St. Johns Hosp., Longview, 1979-88, chmn. credentials com., 1989-90; dir. trauma svcs. St. Johns Med. Ctr., 1990-92; regional v.p. med. divsn. Lower Columbia Regional Health System. Editor current concepts in vascular diagnosis St. Johns Vascular Lab., Longview, 1979-88; contbr. articles to profl. jours. Chmn. bd. dirs. Cowlitz Med. Service, Longview, 1985-86. Regents scholar U. Nebr., Lincoln, 1963-67. Fellow ACS, Henry Harkins Surg. Soc. (trustee 1983-84), Seattle Surg. Soc.; mem. Internat. Cardiovascular Soc., Pacific N.W. Vascular Soc. (pres.-elect 1986-87, pres. 1987-88, chmn. com. on standards 1989-91), North Pacific Surg. Soc., Med. Group Mgmt. Assn., Am. Coll. Physician Execs., Alpha Omega Alpha, Theta Nu, Phi Gamma Delta. Republican. Office: Longview Gen & Thoracic Surgery 900 Fir St Ste 1J Longview WA 98632-2544

KENAROV, MIROSLAV IVANOV (MIRO KENAROV), artist, printmaker; b. Sofia, Bulgaria, May 2, 1961; came to U.S., 1993; s. Ivan Mirchev and Marina Mincheva K.; m. Maria Bogdanova Mitova, May 17, 1986; 1 child, Ivan Miroslavov. Grad., Nat. Sch. Fine Arts, Sofia, 1980; MFA, Nat. Acad. Fine Arts, 1988; degree in printmaking, Tamarind Inst., 1994. Freelance artist Albuquerque, 1985—; owner, pres. M&M Art Studio, Albuquerque, 1995—. One-man shows include Gallery 3, Harstad, Norway, 1992, Melbu (Norway) Hovedgard/Vesteralmuseet, 1992, Internat. Images, Ltd., Sewickley, Pa., 1993, Agora Gallery N.Y.C., 1993, Klosterbakken Gallery, Odense, Denmark, 1993, Galleriet Gallery, Stavenger, Norway, 1993, Geckos Gallery, Albuquerque, 1994; N.Mex. Arts & Crafts Fair, 1995; represented in permanent collections Nat. Art Gallery, Sofia, The Print Club, Varna, Bulgaria, Internat. Mus. of Exlibris and Small Graphics, Vollenhove, The Netherlands, Mus. of Internat. Contemporary Graphic Art, Fredrikstad, Norway, Kanagawa Prefectural Gallery, Japan, Galleriet Gallery, Stavanger, Pictor Gallery, Heberg, Sweden, Internat. Images, Ltd., Sewickley. Mem. Malaspina Printmakers Soc. (Can.), Assn. Difusora Obra Grafica Internat (Spain), Union of the Bulgarian Artists (nat. bd. dirs. 1992-93), Graphic Artists Guild. Home: 419 Cornell Dr SE # A Albuquerque NM 87106-3514 Office: M&M Art Studio 419 Cornell Dr SE Ste A Albuquerque NM 87106-3514

KENDALL, HARRY OVID, internist; b. Eugene, Oreg., Nov. 29, 1929; s. Edward Lee and Jessie Avis (Giem) K.; m. Katherine Alexander, June 20, 1951 (div. 1957); 1 child, Jessica Gail Gress; m. Barbara Ann Matt, Jan. 21, 1961 (div. June 1, 1977); children: David Lee, Brian Padraic; m. Wanda Eve Helmer, July 2, 1993. AB, U. Redlands, 1952; MD, Yale U., 1955. Diplomate Am. Bd. Internal Medicine, Am. Bd. Pulmonary Disease. Intern in internal medicine UCLA Med. Ctr., 1955-57; resident in internal medicine West L.A. VA Med. Ctr., 1957-59; staff physician U.S. Naval Regional Med. Ctr., San Diego, 1959-62, Tulare-Kings Counties Hosp., Springville, Calif., 1962-63; staff physician, ptnr. So. Calif. Permanente Med. Group, Fontana, Calif., 1963-67, Kaiser Hosp. and So. Calif. Permanente Med. Group, San Diego, 1967—; dir. respiratory care Kaiser Hosp., San Diego, 1967—; attending physician San Bernardino County Hosp., 1964-67; asst. clin. prof. medicine U. Calif. San Diego Med. Ctr., 1976—; com. mem. numerous hosps. and med. clinics. Mem. NAACP, Amnesty Internat., ACLU. Lt. USNR, 1954-56, lt. comdr. 1961, comdr. 1973. Mem. Am. Thoracic Soc., cAlif. Thoracic Soc., San Diego Pulmonary Soc.

KENDALL, JOHN WALKER, JR., medical educator, researcher, university dean; b. Bellingham, Wash., Mar. 19, 1929; s. John Walker and Mathilda (Hansen) K.; m. Elizabeth Helen Meece, Mar. 19, 1954; children—John, Katherine, Victoria. B.A., Yale Coll., 1952; M.D., U. Wash., 1956. Intern and resident in internal medicine Vanderbilt U. Hosp., Nashville, 1956-59; fellow in endocrinology Vanderbilt U. Hosp., 1959-60, U. Oreg. Med. Sch., Portland, 1960-62; asst. prof. medicine Oreg. Health Scis. U., Portland, 1962-66, assoc. prof. medicine, 1966-71, prof. medicine, 1971—, head div. metabolism, 1971-80; dean Sch. Medicine, Oreg. Health Scis. U., Portland, 1983-92, dean emeritus, 1992—; assoc. chief staff-research VA Med. Ctr., Portland, Oreg., 1971-83, dep. chief of staff, 1993, VA disting. physician, 1993—; cons. Med. Research Found. Oreg., Portland, 1975-83; sec., bd. dirs. Oreg. Found. Med. Excellence, Portland, 1984-89, pres., 1989-91. Served to lt. comdr. M.C., USN, 1962-64. Mem. AMA (governing coun. med. sch. sect. 1989-93, chair 1991-92, alt. del. 1992-93, Oreg. del. 1994—, rep. Coun. Grad. Med. Edn. 1993-94), Assn. Am. Physicians, Am. Soc. Clin. Investigation, Am. Fedn. Clin. Rsch., We. Soc. Clin. Rsch. (councillor 1972-75), Endocrine Soc., Multnomah County Med. Soc. (treas. 1989, pres. 1991), Med. Rsch. Found. (Mentor award 1992). Presbyterian. Home: 3131 SW Evergreen Ln Portland OR 97201-1816 Office: Oreg Health Scis U Sch Medicine 3181 SW Sam Jackson Park Rd Portland OR 97201-3011

KENDALL, PHILLIP ALAN, lawyer; b. Lamar, Colo., July 20, 1942; s. Charles Stuart and Katherine (Wilson) K.; m. Margaret Roe Greenfield, May 2, 1970; children: Anne, Timothy. BS in Engring., Stanford U., 1964; JD, U. Colo., Boulder, 1969; postgrad., U. Freiburg (Germany), 1965-66. Engr. Siemens Halske, Munich, 1965; ptnr. Kraemer, Kendall & Benson, Colorado Springs, Colo., 1969—; counsel Peak Health Care, Inc., Colorado Springs, 1979-87; bd. dirs. Norwest Banks Colorado Springs. Pres. bd. Colorado Springs Symphony Orch. Assn., 1977-80; bd. dirs. Penrose Hosps., Colorado Springs, 1982-88; pres. bd. Citizen's Goals, Colorado, 1984-86; bd. dirs. Legal Aid Found., Denver, 1988-94, chmn., 1991-93. Recipient Medal of Distinction-Fine Arts, Colorado Springs C. of C., 1983. Mem. ABA, Colo. Bar Assn. (bd. govs. 1985-88, outstanding young lawyer 1977), El Paso County Bar Assn. (bd. trustees 1983-85), Nat. Health Lawyers Assn., Colorado Springs Estate Planning Coun., El Paso Club. Home: 1915 Wood Ave Colorado Springs CO 80907-6714 Office: Kraemer Kendall & Benson PC 430 N Tejon St Ste 300 Colorado Springs CO 80903-1167

KENDALL, RICKY ALLEN, chemist; b. Jefferson, N.C., Mar. 8, 1961; s. Charles Richard and Ola Jean (Shepherd) K.; m. Angela Lynn Mikkelsen, June 1, 1991. BS magna cum laude, Ind. State U., 1983; PhD, U. Utah, 1988. Postdoctoral fellow Argonne (Ill.) Nat. Lab., 1988-89; staff scientist Pacific N.W. Lab., Richland, Wash., 1989—. Contbr. articles to profl. jours. Mem. sci. response com. Richland Sch. Dist., 1993. Rsch. fellow U. Utah, 1987-88. Mem. Am. Chem. Soc., Am. Phys. Soc., Phi Kappa Phi. Home: 1731 Goldfinch Ct Richland WA 99353 Office: Pacific NW Lab PO Box 999 Richland WA 99352-0999

KENDALL, WILLIAM FORREST, physicist; b. Clarksburg, W.Va., Apr. 2, 1936; s. Forrest O. and Yvonne O. (Quinet) K.; m. Elaine Ellen Reinhardt, May 26, 1973. AB, W.Va. U., 1958; MS in Health Physics, U. N.C., 1966, PhD in Med. Physics, 1973. Cert. Am. Bd. Health Physics, cert. diagnostic and therapeutic physics Am. Bd. Radiology. Commd. 2d lt. U.S. Army, 1960, advanced through grades to lt. col., ret., 1981; med. physicist Meth. Hosps. Dallas, 1981-94, Ariz. Oncology Svcs., Phoenix, 1994—. Mem. Am. Assn. Physicists in Medicine, Health Physics Soc., Am. Coll. Radiology. Republican. Methodist. Home: 16031 S 1st St Phoenix AZ 85048-2004 Office: Ariz Oncology Svcs 300 W Clarendon Ave Ste 350 Phoenix AZ 85013-3423

KENDLER, HOWARD H(ARVARD), psychologist, educator; b. N.Y.C., June 9, 1919; s. Harry H. and Sylvia (Rosenberg) K.; m. Tracy Seedman, Sept. 20, 1941; children—Joel Harlan, Kenneth Seedman. A.B., Bklyn. Coll., 1940; M.A., U. Iowa, 1941, Ph.D., 1943. Instr. U. Iowa, 1943; research psychologist OSRD, 1944; asst. prof. U. Colo., 1946-48; assoc. prof. NYU, 1948-51, prof., 1951-63; chmn. dept. Univ. Coll., 1951-61; prof. U. Calif., Santa Barbara, 1963-89, prof. emeritus, 1989—, chmn. dept. psychology, 1965-66; project dir. Office Naval Rsch., 1950-68; prin. investigator NSF, 1953-65, USAAF, 1951-53; mem. adv. panel psychobiology NSF, 1960-62; tng. com. Nat. Inst. Child Health and Human Devel., 1963-66; cons. Dept. Def., Smithsonian Instn., 1959-60, Human Resources Rsch. Office, George Washington U., 1960; vis. prof. U. Calif., Berkeley, 1960-61, Hebrew U., Jerusalem, 1974-75, Tel Aviv U., 1990; chief clin. psychologist Walter Reed Gen. Hosp., 1945-46. Author: Basic Psychology, 1963, 2d edit., 1968, 3d edit., 1974, Basic Psychology: Brief Version, 1977, Psychology: A Science in Conflict, 1981, Historical Foundations of Modern Psychology, 1987; co-author: Basic Psychology: Brief Edition, 1970; co-editor: Essays in Neobehaviorism: A Memorial Volume to Kenneth W. Spence; assoc. editor: Jour. Exptl. Psychology, 1963-65; contbr. to profl. jours., books. Served as 1st lt. AUS. Fellow Center for Advanced Studies in Behaviorial Scis., Stanford, Calif., 1969-70; NSF grantee, 1954-76. Mem. Am. Psychol. Assn. (pres. div. exptl. psychology 1964-65, pres. div. gen. psychology 1967-68), Western Psychol. Assn. (pres. 1970-71), Soc. Exptl. Psychologists (exec. com. 1971-73), Psychonomic Soc. (governing bd. 1963-69, chmn. 1968-69), Sigma Xi. Home and Office: 4596 Camino Molinero Santa Barbara CA 93110-1040

KENISON, LYNN T., chemist; b. Provo, Utah, Feb. 20, 1943; s. John Silves and Grace (Thacker) K.; m. Daralyn Wold, June 10, 1969; children: Marlene, Mark, Evan, Guy, Amy, Suzanne. BS in Chemistry, Brigham Young U., 1968, MS in Chemistry, 1971. Tchr. Weber County Sch. Dist., Ogden, Utah, 1968-69; bench chemist (drugs) Salt Lake City/County Health Dept., 1971-74; chemist U.S. Dept. Labor, OSHA Salt Lake Tech. Ctr., 1974—, bench chemist, 1974-77, supr., br. chief, 1977-84, sr. chemist, 1984—; tech. writer OSHA. Editor: Review Methods and Analytical Papers Before Publication, 1984—; tech. writer, 1984—. Councilman West Bountiful City, Utah, 1980-83, 85-89; scouting coord. Boy Scouts Am., cubmaster local pack, 1990-94; full-time missionary LDS Ch., Ark., Mo., Ill., 1962-64; vol. spkr. in local pub. schs., 1988—. Mem. Am. Indsl. Hygiene Assn., Fed. Exec. Assn. (Disting. Svc. award, Jr. Award for Outstanding Fed. and Cmty. Svc. 1980), Toastmasters Internat. (treas. Sale Lake City chpt. 1987-88). Home: 1745 N 600 W West Bountiful UT 84087-1150 Office: US Dept of Labor OSHA Salt Lake Tech Ctr 1781 S 300 W Salt Lake City UT 84115-1802

KENNARD, JOYCE L., judge. Former judge L.A. Mcpl. Ct., Superior Ct., Ct. Appeal, Calif.; assoc. justice Calif. Supreme Ct., San Francisco, 1989—. Office: Calif Supreme Ct South Tower 303 2nd St San Francisco CA 94107-1366

KENNEDY, CHARLENE FARRINGTON, head reference librarian; b. Cin., Sept. 17, 1947; d. Charles Winifred and Margaret Irene (Hurd) Farrington; m. Timothy Louis Kennedy, May 12, 1977 (div. 1981). BS in Sociology, U. Wis., 1969, MLS, 1971. Libr. intern Milw. Cen. Libr., 1969-71; reference libr. Atkinson Br. Libr., Milw., 1972-73; reference libr. sci. and bus. dept. Milw. Cen. Libr., 1973-78; reference libr., coord. on-line svcs. City of Carlsbad, Calif., 1978-85, head reference svcs., 1985—. Contbr. articles to profl. jours. Mem. Soroptimist Internat., Carlsbad, 1987. Mem. Calif. Libr. Assn., San Diego On-Line Users Group, North San Diego County Genealogical Soc., Bus. and Profl. Women (pres. Carlsbad chpt. 1983). Office: Carlsbad City Libr 1250 Carlsbad Village Dr Carlsbad CA 92008-1949

KENNEDY, CHARLES JOHN, marketing company executive; b. Phoenix, Nov. 18, 1928; s. Charles Ambrose and Katherine Anne (Conley) K.; m. Millicent B. Russell; 6 children. BS in English, Loyola U., 1953. Tech. writer Hughes Aircraft, Culver City, Calif., 1951-53; sales advt. L.A. Times, 1953-55; sales dist. mgr. Chrysler Corp., L.A., 1955-62; sales, mgr., pres. Motor Parts Depot, L.A., 1962-89; pres. Kennedy Mktg., Whittier, Calif., 1991-94; pres. Calif. Automotive Wholesalers, Sacramento, 1987, So. Calif. Jobbers, L.A., 1976, 84, Pacific Automotive Show, Anaheim, Calif., 1986. Author (sales column) Booster Mag., 1991-94. With USNR. Republican. Roman Catholic.

KENNEDY, CORTEZ, professional football player; b. Osceola, Ark., Aug. 23, 1968. Student, Northwest Miss. Jr. Coll.; BA, criminal justice, U. Miami, Fla. Defensive tackle Seattle Seahawks, 1990—. Named All-America team defensive tackle, The Sporting News, 1989; AP Defensive Player of Yr., 1992; named to Pro Bowl, 1991-93, NFL All-Pro team defensive tackle, The Sporting News, 1992, 93. Office: Seattle Seahawks 11220 NE 53rd St Kirkland WA 98033-7505

KENNEDY, DAVID MICHAEL, historian, educator; b. Seattle, July 22, 1941; s. Albert John and Mary Ellen (Caufield) K.; m. Judith Ann Osborne, Mar. 14, 1970; children: Ben Caufield, Elizabeth Margaret, Thomas Osborne. B.A., Stanford U., 1963; M.A., Yale U., 1964, Ph.D., 1968. Asst. prof. history Stanford (Calif.) U., 1967-72, assoc. prof., 1972-80, prof., 1980—, chmn. program in internat. relations, 1977-80, assoc. dean Sch. Humanities and Scis., 1981-85, William Robertson Coe prof. history and Am. studies, 1987-93, Donald J. McLachlan prof. history, 1993—, chair, history dept., 1990-94; vis. prof. U. Florence, Italy, 1976-77; lectr. Internat. Communications Agy., Denmark, Finland, Turkey, Italy, 1976-77, Ireland, 1980; Harmsworth prof. Am. history Oxford U., 1995-96. Author: Birth Control in America: The Career of Margaret Sanger, 1970, Over Here: The First World War and American Society, 1980, (with Thomas A. Bailey) The American Pageant: A History of the Republic, 10th edit., 1994, Power and Responsibility: Case Studies in American Leadership, 1986; mem. adv. bd. (TV program) The American Experience, Sta. WGBH, 1986—. Mem. nat. planning group Am. Issues Forum, 1974-75; bd. dirs. CORO Found., 1981-87, Environ. Traveling Companions, 1986—, Stanford U. Bookstore, 1994—. Recipient Bancroft prize, 1971, John Gilmary Shea prize, 1970, Richard W. Lyman award Stanford U. Alumni Assn., 1989; fellow Am. Council Learned Socs., 1971-72, John Simon Guggenheim Meml. Found., 75-76, Ctr. for Advanced Study in Behavioral Scis., 1986-87, Stanford Humanities Ctr., 1989-90. Mem. Am. Hist. Assn., Orgn. Am. Historians, Soc. Am. Historians. Democrat. Roman Catholic. Office: Stanford U Dept History Stanford CA 94305

KENNEDY, DEBRA JOYCE, marketing professional; b. Covina, Calif., July 9, 1955; d. John Nathan and Drea Hannah (Lancaster) Ward; m. John William Kennedy, Sept. 3, 1977 (div.); children: Drea, Noelle. BS in Communications, Calif. State Poly. U., 1977. Pub. rels. coord. Whittier (Calif.) Hosp., 1978-79, pub. relations mgr., 1980; pub. rels. dir. San Clemente (Calif.) Hosp., 1979-80; dir. pub. rels. Garfield Med. Ctr., Monterey Park, Calif., 1980-82; dir. mktg. and community rels. Charter Oak Hosp., Covina, 1983-85; mktg. dir. CPC Horizon Hosp., Pomona, 1985-89; dir. mktg. Sierra Royale Hosp., Azusa, 1989-90; mktg. rep. PacifiCare, Cypress, 1990-92; regional medicare mgr. Health Net, Woodland Hills, Calif., 1992-95; dist. sales mgr. Kaiser Permante Health Plan, Pasadena, Calif., 1995—. Mem. Am. Soc. Hosp. Pub. Rels., Healthcare Mktg. Assn., Healthcare Pub. Rels. and Mktg. Assn., Covina and Covina West C. of C., West Covina Jaycees. Republican. Methodist. Club: Soroptimists. Contbr. articles to profl. jours.

KENNEDY, JACK LELAND, lawyer; b. Portland, Oreg., Jan. 30, 1924; s. Ernest E. and Lera M. (Talley) K.; m. Clara C. Hagans, June 5, 1948; children: James M., John C. Student, U.S. Maritime Commn. Acad., Southwestern U., L.A.; JD, Lewis and Clark Coll., 1951. Bar: Oreg. 1951. Pvt. practice Portland; ptnr. Kennedy & King, Portland, 1971-77, Kennedy, King & McClurg, Portland, 1977-82, Kennedy, King & Zimmer, Portland, 1982—; trustee Northwestern Coll. Law, Portland; dir. Profl. Liability Fund, 1979-82. Contbr. articles to legal jours. Bd. overseers Lewis and Clark Coll. With USNR, 1942-46. Recipient Disting. Grad. award Lewis and Clark Coll., 1983. Fellow Am. Coll. Trial Lawyers, Am. Bar Found., Oreg. Bar Found. (charter); mem. ABA (ho. of dels. 1984-88), Oreg. State Bar (bd. govs. 1976-79, pres. 1978-79), Multnomah Bar Assn., City Club (Portland), Columbia River Yacht Club. Republican. Office: Kennedy King & Zimmer 1211 SW 5th Ave Ste 2600 Portland OR 97204-3726

KENNEDY, JOHN EDWARD, art dealer, appraiser, curator; b. Glens Falls, N.Y., Apr. 21, 1930; s. John Edward and Veronica Irene (Young) K.; m. Katherine Joan Donovan, July 14, 1956 (div. June 1973); children: Amy Joan Rosato, Gavin John; m. Ann Swift Kimball, Apr. 2, 1975 (dec. Aug. 1993); m. Blake Hale Whitney, Dec. 31, 1993. AB with hons., Boston Coll., 1951; JD, Harvard U., 1956; grad., U.S. Army Command and Gen. Staff Coll., 1964. Bar: Mass. 1956. Asst. counsel New England Mut. Life Ins., Boston, 1956-64; counsel Pa. Life Ins. Co., Beverly Hills, Calif., 1964-68; investment banker Smith Barney and Co., L.A. and N.Y.C., 1968-70; real estate developer Calif. and Hawaii, 1970-80; v.p. Galerie De Tours, Carmel, Calif., 1980-88; curator Gallery Americana, Carmel, 1988-92; patron Monterey Peninsula Mus. of Art., 1988—, Carmel Art Assn., 1985—. Trustee Harrison Meml. Libr., Carmel, 1986-88; commr. Planning commn., Carmel, 1988-94, chmn., 1992-94. With U.S. Army, 1952-53, Korea, Lt. Col., U.S. Army Res., 1969. Decorated Bronze Star for Valor, Purple Heart with cluster; recipient Disting. Mil. Svc. medal Republic of Korea, 1953. Mem. Am. Soc. of Appraisers (cert.), New England Appraisers Assn. (cert.), Am. Planning Assn., Marines Meml. Club. Republican. Episcopalian. Home: PO Box 1844 Carmel CA 93921-1844 Office: New Masters Gallery Dolores 7th Carmel CA 93921

KENNEDY, JOHN HARVEY, chemistry educator; b. Oak Park, Ill., Apr. 24, 1933; s. John Harvey and Margaret Helen (Drenthe) K.; m. Joan Corinne Hipsky, June 9, 1956 (div. Mar. 1969); children: Bruce Laurence, Bryan Donald, Brent Peter, Jill Amy.; m. Victoria Jane Matthew, July 2, 1970; 1 child, Karen Anne. BS, UCLA, 1954; AM, Harvard U., 1956, PhD, 1957. Sr. research chemist E.I. du Pont de Nemours, Wilmington, Del., 1957-61; asst. prof. chemistry U. Calif., Santa Barbara, 1961-63, 67-69, assoc. prof., 1969-76, prof., 1976-93, prof. emeritus, 1993—, chmn. dept., 1982-85; assoc. prof. Boston Coll., Chestnut Hill, 1963-64; head inorganic chemistry Gen. Motors, Santa Barbara, 1964-67; cons. Eveready Battery Co., Cleve., 1983—; vis. prof. U. N.C., Chapel Hill, 1980-81, Japan Soc. Promotion of Sci., Nagoya, 1974-75, Leningrad State U., 1989, China Acad. Scis., 1990. Author: Analytical Chemistry, Principles, 1990, Analytical Chemistry, Practice, 1990; contbr. articles to profl. jours.; patentee in field. Mus. dir. Christ the King Episcopal Ch., Santa Barbara, 1982—. Mem. Am. Chem. Soc., Electrochem. Soc. Democrat. Home: 5357 Agana Dr Santa Barbara CA 93111-1601 Office: U Calif Dept Chemistry Santa Barbara CA 93106

KENNEDY, MARJORIE ELLEN, librarian; b. Dauphin, Man., Can., Sept. 14, 1946; d. Stanley Harrison and Ivy Marietta (Stevens) May; m. Michael P.J. Kennedy, Apr. 3, 1980. BA, U. Sask., Regina, 1972; BLS, U. Alta., Edmonton, 1974; BEd, U. Regina, 1981. Profl. A cert. edn., Sask. Elem. sch. tchr. Indian Head (Sask) Pub. Sch., 1965-66, Elgin Sch., Weyburn, Sask., 1967-68; tchr., libr. Ctrl. Sch., Prince Albert, Sask., 1970-71; elem. sch. tchr. Vincent Massey Sch., Prince Albert, 1969-70, 72-73; children's libr. J.S. Wood br. Saskatoon (Sask.) Pub. Libr., 1974-77, asst. coord. children's svcs., 1977-79; programme head, instr. libr. tech. Kelsey Inst., Saskatoon, 1979—; presenter workshops on reference materials for elem. sch. librs., 1980—; vol. dir. Children's Lit. Workshops, Sask. Libr. Assn., 1979-80; mem. organizing com. Sask. Libr. Week, Saskatoon, 1988. Mem. Vanscoy (Sask.) and Dist. Agr. Soc., 1983—. Named to Libr. Edn. Honor Roll ALA, 1987. Mem. Can. Libr. Assn. (instl. rep. 1984—), Sask. Libr. Assn. (insl. rep. 1984—, mem. children's sect. 1982-83), Sask. Assn. Libr. Techs. (instl. rep. 1984—), Canadian Club (bd. mem. 1981-84). Mem. United Ch. Can. Office: Kelsey Inst Libr Tech Programme, Box 1520, Saskatoon, SK Canada S7K 3R5

KENNEDY, MARK ALAN, middle school educator; b. Oklahoma City, Okla., July 20, 1951; s. Millford Gordon and Lyn (Cheaney) Kennedy; m. Kim Danelle Kramer, Jan. 30, 1972; 1 child, Brianna Lynn. BA with honors, Calif. State U., 1978; postgrad., Western Sem., 1978-79, Fuller Sem., 1980-83. Cert. tchr., Calif. Sales mgr. Kennedy Investments, Ontario, Calif., 1980-83; regional v.p. A.L. Williams, Rancho Cucamonga, Calif., 1983-89; loan officer Funder's Mortgage Corp., Covina, Calif., 1989-90; math., social sci. tchr., lang. devel. specialist Ontario-Montclair Sch. Dist., 1990—; tchg. asst. Western Sem., Portland, Oreg., 1978-79, instr. cmty. inst., 1979; soccer coach DeAnza Mid. Sch., Ontario, 1990-93, core team leader, coop. tchr., student coun. advisor, 1992-93, bilingual adv. coun., 1992—, dist. lang. arts/social sci. trainer, 1993-94; advisor U. Calif. Riverside Honors Students' Inner City Literacy Program, 1993—; mentor tchr. Ont.-Montclair Sch. Dist., 1994—; cons. Inst. in Local Self Govt., Sacramento, 1994—, Assn. Calif. Sch. Adminstrs., 1994—. Contbr. articles to profl. jours. With USN, 1971-75. Mem. ASCD, Nat. Coun. Tchrs. Math., Nat. Coun. for Social Studies, Nat. Middle Schs. Assn., Nat. Dropout Prevention Network, Phi Alpha Theta (membership chair 1976-78). Baptist. Office: De Anza Mid Sch 1450 S Sultana Ave Ontario CA 91761-4236

KENNEDY, MATTHEW LAWRY, dance educator, writer; b. Redding, Calif., Mar. 14, 1957; s. Laurence Joseph and Carolyn (Cook) K. BA in Theater Arts, UCLA, 1979; MA in Anthropology, U. Calif., Davis, 1993. Dancer Margaret Jenkins Dance Co., San Francisco, 1982-83, Jonathon Apples and Co., N.Y.C., 1983-85; adminstr. Trisha Brown Co., Inc., N.Y.C., 1984-85; exec. asst. to dir. Calif. Arts Council, Sacramento, 1986-91; dir. programs and devel. City Celebration, San Francisco, 1993; cons. Nat. Endowment for Arts, 1988, Calif. Arts Coun., 1994; actor Berkeley (Calif.) Stage Co., 1983, Modern Theatre Ensemble, Sacramento, 1986; mem. meeting planning com. Nat. Assembly of State Arts Agys., Washington, 1988; tchr. City Coll. San Francisco, San Francisco Conservatory of Music. Contbr. articles to mags. and newspapers. Tutor Pub. Libr. Adult Literacy Program, Sacramento, 1987—. Scholar U. Calif., 1975, Merce Cunningham Dance Found., 1983-84; Fulbright fellow, 1992. Democrat. Office: City Coll San Francisco Box L213 50 Phelan Ave San Francisco CA 94112

KENNEDY, ORIN, film company executive; b. N.Y.C., May 24, 1939; s. Solomon Fuchs and Gertrude Krex. BFA, N.Y. Sch. Interior Design, 1963. Prodn. assoc. Fries Entertainment, Los Angeles, 1976-84; exec. location mgr. Metro-Goldwyn-Mayer subs. United Artists Entertainment, Culver City, Calif., 1984-85; exec. location mgr. The Twilight Zone TV series CBS Entertainment, Los Angeles, 1985-86; exec. location mgr. LA Law TV series 20th Century Fox Film Corp., Los Angeles, 1986-94, exec. location mgr. Picket Fences TV series, 1991-94; Chicago Hope TV series, 1994—.

KENNEDY, RAYMOND MCCORMICK, JR., interior designer; b. Glendale, Calif., Sept. 19, 1930; s. Raymond McCormick and June (Sparks) K.; adopted son Myrtle Abrahamson Kennedy. BA in Architecture, U. Calif.-Berkeley, 1956. Draftsman, Bechtel Corp., San Francisco, 1956-58; draftsman/designer Maher & Martens, Architects, San Francisco, 1956; free lance designer, San Francisco, 1966-67; designer Bernard J. Block, Architect, San Francisco, 1967-69; v.p. Rodgers Assocs., San Francisco, 1969-77; pres. RMK Design, Inc., San Francisco, 1977-83; pres. Kennedy-Bowen Assocs., Inc., San Francisco, 1983—; mem. faculty Acad. of Art Coll., San Francisco, 1982-86, mem. adv. coun., 1991—. Bd. dirs. San Francisco Easter Seals Soc., 1974-79; bd. dirs., pres. Design Found., Inc., 1986-87. Served with U.S. Army, 1952-54. Fellow Am. Soc. Interior Designers (dir., v.p. No. Calif. chpt. 1983, sec. bd. 1984, pres. 1987-88, nat. bd. dirs. 1989—, nat. v.p. 1990, nat. pres. 1991-92); mem. Golden Gate U. Assn., Am. Inst. Architects (affiliate), Internat. Furnishings and Design Assn., Nat. Trust for Hist. Preservation, Assocs. for San Francisco's Archtl. Heritage, Commonwealth Club, Press Club (San Francisco). Office: Kennedy-Bowen Assocs Inc 930 Lombard St San Francisco CA 94133-2218

KENNEDY, RICHARD JEROME, writer; b. Jefferson City, Mo., Dec. 23, 1932; s. Donald and Mary Louise (O'Keefe) K.; m. Lillian Elsie Nance, Aug. 3, 1960; children: Joseph Troy, Matthew Cook. BS, Portland State U., 1958. Author: (novel) Amy's Eye, 1985 (Internat. Rattenfanger Lit. prize, Fed. Republic Germany 1988), also 18 children's books including Richard Kennedy: Collected Stories, 1988 and 3 musicals; inclusion of stories in: The Oxford Book of Modern Fairy Tales, 1993, The Oxford Book of Children's Stories, 1993. With USAF, 1951-54. Home and Office: 415 W Olive St Newport OR 97365-3716

KENNEDY, SHEILA GRACE, medical social worker; b. San Jose, Calif., May 17, 1949; d. Irwin Thomas and Martha Ruth (Markey) O'Connell; m. Timothy Anthony Kennedy, Apr. 4, 1975; children: Maureen, Timmy, Patrick. BA in Social Work, Coll. Notre Dame, 1971; MA in Counseling Psychology, U. Santa Clara, 1977. Elem. sch. tchr. St. Louise de Marrillac Sch., Covina, Calif., 1971-72; dir. social svcs. and hospice Sequoia Hosp., Redwood City, Calif., 1972-89; hospice dir. Kaiser Med. Ctr., Redwood City, Calif., 1990—. Mem. adv. bd. peer counseling for srs. San Carlos (Calif.) Sr. Ctr., 1986-88; bd. dirs. San Mateo (Calif.) County com. on child abuse, 1981-83, Parish bd. edn., Nativity Ch., 1984—, pres. 1988; v.p. bd. dirs. Am. Cancer Soc., San Mateo County, Burlingame, Calif., 1983-85, pres.

bd. dirs., 1985-87. Named Woman of Yr. Notre Dame High Sch., San Jose, 1989. Mem. Nat. Assn. Social Workers, Am. Hosp. Assn., Hosp. Social Work Dirs. Democrat. Roman Catholic. Home: 67 Lorelei Ln Menlo Park CA 94025-1715 Office: Kaiser Med Ctr 1150 Veterans Blvd Redwood City CA 94063-2037

KENNEDY-MINOTT, RODNEY, international relations educator, former ambassador; b. Portland, Oreg.; s. Joseph Albert and Gainor (Baird) Minott; children: Katharine Pardow, Rodney Glisan, Polly Berry. AB, Stanford U., 1953, MA, 1956, PhD, 1960. Instr. history Stanford U., 1960-61, asst. prof., asst. dir. history of western civilization program, 1961-62, asst. dir. summer session, 1962-63, dir. summer session, 1963-65; assoc. prof. Portland State U., 1965-66; assoc. prof., assoc. dean instrn. Calif. State U., Hayward, 1966-67, prof., 1967-77, head div. humanities, 1967-69; ambassador to Sweden and chmn. Swedish Fulbright Com., 1977-80; adj. prof. Monterey Inst. Internat. Studies, Calif., 1981; exec. v.p. Direction Internat., Washington, 1982-83; sr. research fellow Hoover Instn., 1981-82, 85—; chmn. Alpha Internat., Washington, 1983-85; congl. staff mem., 1965-66; sr. fellow Ctr. Internat. rels., UCLA, 1986-90; prof. nat. security affairs tng. U.S. Naval Postgrad. Sch., Monterey, Calif., 1990—. Author: Peerless Patriots: The Organized Veterans and the Spirit of Americanism, 1962, The Fortress That Never Was: The Myth of Hitler's Bavarian Stronghold, 1964, The Sinking of the Lollipop: Shirley Temple v. Pete McCloskey, 1968, Regional Force Application: The Maritime Strategy and Its Affect on Nordic Stability, 1988, Tension in the North: Sweden and Nordic Security, 1989, Lonely Path to Follow: Nonaligned Sweden, United States/NATO, and the U.S.S.R., 1990. Mem. adv. bd. Ctr. for the Pacific Rim U. San Francisco, 1988—. With U.S. Army, 1946-48, USAR, 1948-54. Mem. Am. Hist. Assn., Orgn. Am. Historians, World Affairs Coun. No. Calif., Internat. Studies Assn., Am. Fgn. Svc. Assn. (assoc.), Internat. Inst. for Strategic Studies, Marines Meml. Assn., Stanford U. Faculty Club. Office: Dept Nat Security Affairs US Naval Postgrad Sch Monterey CA 93943

KENNELLY, SISTER KAREN MARGARET, college administrator; b. Graceville, Minn., Aug. 4, 1933; d. Walter John Kennelly and Clara Stella Eastman. BA, Coll. St. Catherine, St. Paul, 1956; MA, Cath. U. Am., 1958; PhD, U. Calif., Berkeley, 1962. Joined Sisters of St. Joseph of Carondelet, Roman Cath. Ch., 1954. Prof. history Coll. St. Catherine, 1962-71, acad. dean, 1971-79; exec. dir. Nat. Fedn. Carondelet Colls., U.S., 1979-82; province dir. Sisters of St. Joseph of Carondelet, St. Paul, 1982-88; pres. Mt. St. Mary's Coll., L.A., 1989—; cons. N. Cen. Accreditation Assn., Chgo., 1974-84, Ohio Bd. Regents, Columbus, 1983-89; trustee colls., hosps., Minn., Wis., Calif., 1972—; chmn. Sisters St. Joseph Coll. Consortium, 1989-93. Editor, co author: American Catholic Women, 1989; author: (with others) Women of Minnesota, 1977. Fulbright fellow, 1964, Am. Coun. Learned Socs. fellow, 1964-65. Mem. Am. Hist. Soc., Am. Cath. Hist. Soc., Medieval Acad., Am. Assn. Rsch. Historians on Medieval Spain. Roman Catholic. Home and Office: Mt St Marys Coll 12001 Chalon Rd Los Angeles CA 90049-1526

KENNER, RONALD W., writer, editor; b. Chgo., Apr. 21, 1935; s. Jack Morris and Sandra Cohan Kenner; m. Mary Abbott, Feb. 29, 1964. BA in English Lit., Calif. State U., 1975, postgrad., 1975-76. World news editor, deskman, staff writer Daily Pilot, Costa Mesa, Calif., 1960-61; editor Humboldt Star, Winnemucca, Nev., 1961-62; corr. No. Nev. United Press, 1961-62; deskman, staff writer The Register, Santa Ana, Calif., 1962-64; corr. Orange County (Calif.) Assoc. Press, 1962-64; writing cons. book editing Mexico City, 1964-65; reporter, staff writer L.A. Times, Metro, L.A., 1965-66; editor ctrl. desk Call-Enterprise Newspapers, Bellflower, Calif., 1966-67; mng. editor Norwalk Call, 1966-67; co-editor press & pub. rels. bur. News Features, Internat. & Kenner Press Features, Copenhagen, 1967-69; metro reporter, staff writer L.A. Times, 1969-70; v.p. pub. rels., press dir. Compu-Transit Corp., L.A., 1970-73; supr. publs. Santa Fe Internat. Corp., Orange, Calif., 1977-78; author, book editor, freelance, publs. rels. publicity dir. Kenner Press Features, L.A., 1978-89, News Features Internat., Copenhagen, 1978-89; author, book editor, editorial cons. L.A., 1990-95; guest lectr. writing classes UCLA, Calif. State U., Northridge, Northbridge H.S. Author: (biography) Max the Butcher, 1982; co-author: The Garbage People, 1971, 1995; editor numerous biographies; contbr. articles to profl. jours. Recipient John Swett award Calif. State Tchrs. Assn., 1967, Spl. Recognition award Nat. Assn. Adult Educators; co-recipient Pulitzer prize with 35-man L.A. Times metro staff for Watts Riot coverage, 1965. Home: Murray Hill Apt 103 1900 Vine St Los Angeles CA 90068-3973

KENNERKNECHT, RICHARD EUGENE, marketing executive; b. Glendale, Calif., Apr. 29, 1961; s. Richard and Sharon Mavis (Zane) K. Profl. sporting clays shooter, exhbn. shooter; v.p. mktg. Defense Tech. Corp. Am., Casper, Wyoming; pres. FDC, Inc., Lost Hills, Calif., 1989-91. Mem. U.S. Sporting Assn. (mem. team U.S.A. 1988, 89, all-Am. team 1988, 89, 90, winner gold medal U.S.-French Profl. Invitational 1990, 91), U.S. Sporting Clays Assn. (mem. rules and ethics com., capt. team Perazzi), Verdugo Hills Ducks Unltd. (founding mem.), Nat. Sporting Clays Assn. (mem. nat. adv. coun. 1991-92), Olin Winchester (adv. coun. 1991-93), Calif. Waterfowl Assn. (shooting sports dir. 1992-93), Western Outdoor News (outdoor columnist 1992-93). Republican. Episcoplian. Home: PO Box 903 Casper WY 82602-0903 Office: Def Tech Corp Am PO Box 240 2136 Oil Dr Casper WY 82602

KENNERLY, LINDA ANNE, marketing executive; b. Upper Darby, Pa., Apr. 9, 1948; d. Ronald Adams and Virginia Mary (Kehoe) MacKenzie; m. Scott Randall Kennerly, Nov. 17, 1990. BA, Met. State Coll. of Denver, 1986; Cert. in Internat. Bus., U. Denver, 1989. Exec. dir. Hist. Lancaster Walking Tour, Inc., Lancaster, Pa., 1977-78; comms. specialist Colo. State U. Ext. Svc., Golden, 1978-79; pub. info. officer Dist. Atty.'s Office, Golden, 1983-89; asst. dir. comms. Colo. Bar Assn., Denver, 1989-91; practice devel./client svcs. adminstr. Rothgerber, Appel, Powers & Johnson, Denver, 1991-94; mktg. mgr. Holland & Hart, Denver, 1994-95; pres. Kennerly Consulting Group, Denver, 1995—. Adv. bd. Colo. State U. Ext. Svc. in Jefferson County, Golden, 1987-94; campaign treas. Com. to Re-elect Woody Davis, Littleton (Colo.) Sch. Bd., 1993; mem. Jefferson County Prevention Task Force, 1984-89; speaker U. Colo. Sch. Journalism, Boulder, 1990, others. Recipient 1st place 1991 Comms. Contest in category of Info. to the Media, Nat. Fedn. Press Women, 1990, Colo. Press Women, Denver; recipient spl. achievement award Jefferson County Prevention Task Force, Golden, 1989. Mem. Nat. Law Firm Mktg. Assn., Pub. Rels. Soc. Am., Nat. Fedn. Press Women, Colo. Press Women. Mem. Christian Ch. Home and Office: Kennerly Consulting Group PO Box 367 Evergreen CO 80439-0367

KENNERSON, PAUL, lawyer, author, educator; b. Rochester, N.Y., Apr. 26, 1941; s. John V. and Margaret A. (Neary) K.; m. Kathleen M. Doran Snyder, Feb. 16, 1967 (div. Dec. 1986); children: Paul Gregory, Elliott Doran. AB summa cum laude, Georgetown U., 1963; LLB, Yale U., 1966. Bar: N.Y. 1967, Calif. 1970, D.C. 1990, U.S. Ct. Mil. Appeals 1967. Assoc. Welsh & Gibson, San Diego, 1969-72; ptnr. Gibson & Kennerson, successor firm, San Diego, 1972-92; of counsel Hollander & Grant, San Diego, 1992-95, Post Kirby Noonan & Sweat, 1995—; instr. U.S. Internat. U., San Diego, 1968-69, San Diego Inns of Ct., 1975—, San Diego Psychology Assn., 1989; judge pro tem San Diego County Superior Ct.; mem. Am. Bd. Trial Advs., 1975—. Author: (novel) The Oxymoron, 1993; contbr. articles to various publs. Bd. dirs. Children's Mus., San Diego, 1972, Defenders, Inc., San Diego, 1973-76; pres. Leukemia Soc. Am., San Diego, 1973-78; trustee Mus. Photog. Arts, San Diego, 1984-85; del. Calif. Dem. Convs., Sacramento. Lt. USNR, 1966-69. Mem. N.Y. State Bar Assn., D.C. Bar Assn., Calif. State Bar, San Diego County Bar Assn., Assn. So. Calif. Def. Counsel, Assn. Yale Alumni (del. 1991-93). Roman Catholic. Home: 6745 Muirlands Dr La Jolla CA 92037-6316 Office: Post Kirby Noonan & Sweat America Plz Ste 1100 600 W Broadway San Diego CA 92101

KENNETT, E. ALAN, agricultural products executive; b. 1944. Pres. Olokele Sugar Co. With U.S. Coast Guard, 1965-70. Office: Olokele Sugar Co 1 Kaumakani Ave Kaumakani HI 96747*

KENNETTE, JENNIE LAURA FAKES, medical/surgical nurse; b. Hanston, Kans., Jan. 16, 1935; d. Jack Delmont and Bertha Mabel (Law) Fakes; m. Leslie Cleland Koontz, Dec. 4 1958 (dec.); children: Kim, Lynn, Gay, Jan, Jay, Lee; m. Robert Ray Hamill, Oct. 21, 1979 (div.); m. Russell T. Kennette Jr., Nov. 17, 1990. ADN, Barton County Community Coll., 1971; BSN, U. Wyo., 1988. RN; cert. med.-surg. nurse, gerontol. nurse. Staff nurse clin. level III Laramie County Hosp., Cheyenne, Wyo.; asst. head nurse DePaul Hosp., Cheyenne; charge nurse St. Catherine's Hosp., Garden City, Kans.; DON Spearville (Kans.) Dist. Hosp.; charge nurse Meml. Hosp. Laramie County, Laramie County Hosp., Cheyenne, Wyo.; supr. Wyo. Retirement Ctr. Mem. ANA. Home: PO Box 841 Basin WY 82410-0841

KENNEY, JAMES JOSEPH, nutrition research specialist; b. Brockton, Mass., Apr. 20, 1945; s. James Henry and Margaret Teresa (McSweeny) K. BS in Food and Nutrition, U. Mass., 1969; MS in Nutrition, Rutgers U., 1972, PhD in Nutrition, 1974. Diplomate Am. Bd. Nutrition; registered dietitian, Calif. Postdoctoral fellow U. Pa., Phila., 1974-75; sr. sci. analyst Franklin Inst., Phila., 1976; asst. prof. Lehigh U., Bethlehem, Pa., 1977; dir. Nutrition Assocs., Santa Monica, Calif., 1978-81; dir. nutrition svcs. ALTA Inst., L.A., 1982-85; nutrition rsch. specialist Pritikin Longevity Ctr., Santa Monica, Calif., 1985—; instr. Pasadena (Calif.) City Coll., 1986; lectr. dept. kinesiology U. Calif., L.A., 1989-91; cons. Quaker Oats, Inc., Chgo., 1989-91; expert witness Mcpl. Ct., Encino, Calif., 1992. Author: The L.A. Diet, 1988; contbr. chpt. to book. Pvt. U.S. Army, 1968-69. Fellow Am. Coll. Nutrition; mem. Nat. Coun. Against Health Fraud (bd. dirs.). Home: 1239 19th St Apt 8 Santa Monica CA 90404-1250 Office: Pritikin Longevity Ctr 1910 Ocean Front Walk Santa Monica CA 90405

KENNEY, WILLIAM FITZGERALD, lawyer; b. San Francisco, Nov. 4, 1935; s. Lionel Fitzgerald and Ethel Constance (Brennan) K.; m. Susan Elizabeth Langfitt, May 5, 1962; children: Anne, Carol, James. BA, U. Calif.-Berkeley, 1957, JD, 1960. Bar: Calif. 1961. Assoc. Miller, Osborne Miller & Bartlett, San Mateo, Calif., 1962-64; ptnr. Tormey, Kenney & Cotchett, San Mateo, 1965-67; pres. William F. Kenney, Inc., San Mateo, 1968—; gen. ptnr. All Am. Self Storage, 1985—, Second St. Self Storage, 1990—. Trustee San Mateo City Sch. Dist., 1971-79, pres., 1972-74; pres. March of Dimes, 1972-73; bd. dirs. Boys Club of San Mateo, 1972-90, Samaritan House, 1989—, Lesley Found., 1992—. With U.S. Army, 1960-62. Mem. State Bar of Calif. (taxation com. 1973-76), San Mateo County Bar Assn. (bd. dir. 1973-75), Calif. Assn. Realtors (legal affairs com. 1978—), San Mateo C. of C. (bd. dirs. 1987-93), Self Storage Assn. (we. region, pres. 1989-90, nat. bd. dirs. 1990—, nat. v.p. 1994—), Rotary (pres. 1978-79, Elks (exalted ruler 1974-75). Republican. Roman Catholic. Home: 221 Clark Dr San Mateo CA 94402-1004 Office: William F Kenney Inc 120 N El Camino Real San Mateo CA 94401-2705

KENNICOTT, JAMES W., lawyer; b. Latrobe, Pa., Feb. 14, 1945; s. W.L. and Alice (Hayes) K.; m. Margot Barnes, Aug. 19, 1975 (div. 1977); m. Lynne Dratler Finney, July 1, 1984 (div. 1989). AB, Syracuse (N.Y.) U., 1967; JD, U. Wyo., 1979. Bar: Utah 1979. Prin. Ski Cons., Park City, Utah, 1969—; pvt. practice Park City, 1979-87, 89—; ptnr. Kennicott & Finney, Park City, 1987-89; pvt. practice Park City, 1989—; cons. Destination Sports Specialists, Park City, 1984—; judge pro tem Utah 3d Cir. Ct., Park City, 1988—; arbitrator Am. Arbitration Assn., 1989—. Chmn. Park City Libr. Bd. 1987; bd. dirs. Park City Libr. 1985-91, Park City Handicapped Sports, 1988-94, The Counseling Inst., 1993—, chmn. 1994-95, treas. 1995—; mem. program com. Gov.'s Commn. on Librs. and Info. Svcs., 1990-91. Mem. Utah Bar Assn., Am. Arbitration Assn. Home and Office: PO Box 2339 Park City UT 84060-2339

KENNY, ALAN DENNIS, international sales executive, computer educator; b. Quebec City, Quebec, Can., Nov. 12, 1963; s. Thomas Geer and Charlene Mae (Hecker) K. Student, U.S. Naval Acad., 1982, U. Minn., 1983-89. Engring. technician Honeywell, Inc., Hopkins, Minn., 1984-89; sales acct. mgr. Gen Rad, Inc., Chgo., 1989-90, Milpitas, Calif., 1990-93; internat. sales mgr. Gen Rad, Inc., Santa Clara, Calif., 1994—. Joint contbr. disk drive mounting patent. With USN, 1982. Recipient Spl. Achievement award Honeywell, Inc., 1985, 87, 88, Creative Sci. award 3M, Inc., 1981, Honeywell Math and Sci. Excellence scholarship, 1982. Mem. Ins. Environ. Scis. Office: Gen Rad Inc 2855 Bowers Ave Santa Clara CA 95051

KENNY, MICHAEL H., bishop; b. Hollywood, Calif., June 26, 1937. Ed., St. Joseph Coll., Mountain View, Calif., St. Patrick's Sem., Menlo Park, Calif., Cath. U. Am. Ordained priest Roman Cath. Ch., 1963; ordained bishop of Juneau, Alaska, 1979—. Office: Diocese of Juneau 419 6th St # 200 Juneau AK 99801-1072 Home: 2960 Howell Ave Juneau AK 99801*

KENOFF, JAY STEWART, lawyer; b. L.A., Apr. 29, 1946; s. Charles Kapp and Martha (Minchenberg) K.; m. Pamela Fran Benyas, Sept. 1, 1979 (div. Dec. 1981); m. Luz Elena Chavira, June 9, 1991. AB, UCLA, 1967; MS, U. So. Calif., L.A., 1972; JD, Harvard U., 1970. Bar: Washington 1970, Calif. 1971, U.S. Ct. Appeals (9th cir.) 1974, U.S. Dist. Ct. (so., cen. dists. Calif.) 1974, U.S. Ct. Mil. Appeals 1974. Assoc. Wyman, Bautzer, Rothman & Kuchel, Beverly Hills, Calif., 1974-76, Epport & Delevie, Beverly Hills, 1977-78; ptnr. Bushkin, Gaims, Gaines & Jonas, L.A., 1978-86; prof. Sch. of Law Northrup U., Inglewood, Calif., 1981-85; ptnr. Kenoff & Machtinger, L.A., 1986—; judge pro tem L.A. Mcpl. Ct., 1985—; arbitrator, mediator Ctr. for Comml. Mediation, L.A., 1986—; mediator L.A. Superior Ct., 1987—, mem. settlement panel, 1987—. Author: Entertainment Industry Contracts, 1986; contbg. editor Entertainment Law & Finance. Commdr. USN Navy Judge Adv. Corps, USNR, 1968-91. Mem. Beverly Hills Bar Assn., Harvard-Radcliffe Club. Democrat. Jewish. Office: Kenoff & Machtinger Bldg 1250 1999 Avenue Of The Stars Los Angeles CA 90067-6022

KENT, CHRISTOPHER ANDREW, history educator; b. Winnipeg, Man., Can., Oct. 28, 1940; s. Cecil Charles and Elizabeth McTaggart (Frame) K.; m. Mary Carolyn Marino, Oct. 26, 1977; 1 child, Andrew Michael. BA, U. Toronto (Ont., Can.), 1963, MA, 1964; DPhil, U. Sussex, Brighton, Eng., 1969. Asst. prof. Prince of Wales Coll., Charlottetown, P.E.I., Can., 1968-69, U. P.E.I., Charlottetown, 1969-70; asst. prof. U. Sask., Saskatoon, Can., 1970-73, assoc. prof., 1973-78, prof., 1978—, dept. head, 1987-90. Author: Brains and Numbers, 1976; editor Can. Jour. History, 1977-83, 95—; mem. editorial bd. Canadian Jour. History, Victorian Studies, Victorian Rev., Victorian Periodicals Rev. Mem. Victorian Studies Assn. (pres. 1986-88), Rsch. Soc. for Victorial Periodicals (bd. dirs. 1977—), Jane Austen Soc. N.Am. Office: U Sask, Dept History, Saskatoon, SK Canada S7N 0W0

KENT, DARREL ARTHUR, systems engineer; b. Colby, Kans., June 14, 1954; s. Norman Kent and LaVaughn (Hudson) Durkin; m. Diana Lynn Goodholm, Feb. 12, 1976; children: Nicole Christine, Jonathon Arthur, JEssica Suzanne. Student, Regis Coll., Denver, 1980-82, Community Coll., Westminster, Colo., 1982-84. Computer operator Mountain Bell Telephone Co., Denver, 1972-76, computer specialist, 1976-79, asst. mgr., 1979-82; systems programmer Mountain Bell/U.S. West, Denver, 1982-86; systems engr. Nat. Advanced Systems, Englewood, Colo., 1986-89; sr. systems engr. Hitachi Data Systems, Englewood, 1989—, dist. systems specialist, 1992—, cons. capacity planning, 1992—. Coach Little League Baseball Assn., Thornton, Colo., 1990-91; cubmaster Boys Scouts Am., Cub Scout Pack 564, Thornton, 1990—. Mem. Rocky Mountain Computer Measurement Group (founding dir. 1988-91), Computer Measurement Group (nat. adv. bd. 1990-91, author 1989). Mem. Christian Reformed Ch. Home: 5214 E 114th Pl Denver CO 80233-2814 Office: Hitachi Data Systems 5251 Dtc Pky Ste 990 Englewood CO 80111-2738

KENT, KARRI ANN, dietitian; b. Everette, Wash., Feb. 22, 1957; d. Donna Carol (Carscadden) Bosze; m. Joseph M. Kent, Dec. 15, 1979; children: Richard J., Stephanie M., Jennifer E. BA, U. North Colo., 1980, MA, 1981. Consulting nutritionist Homestead Nutrition Project, Hays, Kans., 1981-82; clin. dietitian Truman Med. Ctr., Kansas City, Mo., 1982-83; community health nutritionist Jefferson County Dept. Health, Lakewood, Colo., 1984—; mem. adv. bd. Mothers' Milk Bank, Denver, 1990—. Mem. Am. Dietetic Assn., Colo. Dietetic Assn. (chair consumer issues 1992—), Denver Dietetic Assn. (pres.-elect 1991-92, pres. 1992-93). Home: 531 Columbine Ave Broomfield CO 80020-6019 Office: Jefferson County Dept Health 6303 Wadsworth Byp Arvada CO 80003-4840

KENT, SHEILA KELLY, community volunteer; b. Chehalis, Wash., Oct. 20, 1932; d. John Caesar Jr. and Gladys Marie (Meenach) Kelly; m. Harry Christison Kent, Aug. 18, 1956 (dec. Apr. 1991); children: Colleen Kent de Ruiz, Bruce Kelly. BA with great distinction, Stanford U., 1953; postgrad., Golden Gate Coll., 1953-54, Whittier Coll., 1955. Cert. tchr., Calif. Jr. acct. Perkins & Trousdale, CPAs, San Francisco, 1953-55; tchr. kindergarten Glendora (Calif.) Sch. Dist., 1955-56. Spl. mem. United Meth. Women, 1979, dist. pres., 1989-93; vol. Santa Shop (Jeffco Action Ctr.), 1984—; mem. fin. com. Ch. Women United in Colo., 1994—; pres. Jefferson County Ch. Women United, 1995—. Mem. AAUW (named gift edn. found. 1982), Phi Beta Kappa. Democrat. Home: 5131 Jellison Ct Arvada CO 80002-3257

KENT, SUSAN GOLDBERG, library director, consultant; b. N.Y.C., Mar. 18, 1944; d. Elias and Minnie (Barnett) Solomon; m. Eric Goldberg, Mar. 27, 1966 (div. Mar. 1991); children: Evan, Jessica, Joanna; m. Rolly Kent, Dec. 20, 1991. BA in English Lit. with honors, SUNY, 1965; MS, Columbia U., 1966. Libr., sr. libr. N.Y. Pub. Libr., 1965-67, br. mgr. Donnell Art Libr., 1967-68; reference libr. Paedergaat br. Bklyn. Pub. Libr., 1971-72; reference libr. Finkelstein Meml. Libr., Spring Valley, N.Y., 1974-76; coord. adult and young adult svcs. Tucson Pub. Libr., 1977-80, acting libr. dir., 1982, dep. libr. dir., 1980-87; mng. dir. Ariz. Theatre Co., Tucson and Phoenix, 1987-89; dir. Mpls. Pub. Libr. and Info. Ctr., 1990-95; city libr. L.A. Pub. Libr., 1995—; tchr. Pima C.C., Tucson, 1978, grad. libr. sch. U. Ariz., Tucson, 1978, 79; panelist Ariz. Commn. Arts, 1981-85; reviewer pub. programs NEH, 1985, 89, panelist challenge grants, 1986-89, panelist state programs, 1988; cons. to librs. and nonprofit instns., 1989-90, 92—; mem. bd. devel. and fundraising Child's Play, Phoenix, 1983; bd. dirs., mem. organizing devel. and fundraising com. Flagstaff (Ariz.) Symphony Orch., 1988; cons., presenter workshops Young Adult Svcs. divsn. ALA, 1986-88; presenter in field. Contbr. articles to profl. jours. Chair arts and culture com. Tucson Tomorrow, 1981-85; bd. dirs., v.p. Ariz. Dance Theatre, 1984-86; bd. dirs. women's studies adv. coun. U. Ariz., 1985-90, Arizonans for Cultural Devel., 1987-89, YWCA Mpls., 1991-92; commr. Ariz. Commn. on Arts, 1983-87; participant Leadership Mpls., 1990-91. Fellow Sch. Libr. Sci., Columbia U., 1965-66. Mem. ALA (membership com., S.W. regional chair 1983-86, com. on appointments 1986-87, planning and budget assembly del. 1991-93, gov. coun. 1990—), Pub. Libr. Assn. (nominating com. 1980-82, v.p. 1986-87, pres. 1987-88, chair publs. assembly 1988-89, past pres. 1988-89, chair nat. conf. 1994, chair legis. com. 1994—), Minn. Librs. Assn., Urban Librs. Coun. (exec. bd. 1994—) Libr. Adminstrn. and Mgmt. Assn. (John Cotton Dana Award Com. 1994—). Office: LA Pub Libr 630 W 5th St Los Angeles CA 90071-2002

KENT, THEODORE CHARLES, psychologist; m. Shirley, June 7, 1948; children: Donald, Susan, Steven. BA, Yale U., 1935, MA, Columbia U., 1940, MA, Mills Coll., 1953, PhD, U. So. Calif., 1951; Dr. Rerum Naturalium, Johannes Gutenberg U., Mainz, Germany, 1960. Diplomate in clin. psychology. Clin. psychologist, behavioral scientist USAF, 1951-65, chief psychologist, Europe, 1956-60; head dept. behavioral sci. U. So. Colo., Pueblo, 1965-78, emeritus, 1978—; staff psychologist Yuma Behavioral Health, Ariz., 1978-82, chief profl. svcs., 1982-83; dir. psychol. svcs. Rio Colo. Health Systems, Yuma, 1983-85; clin. psychologist, dir. mental health Ft. Yuma (Calif.) Indian Health Svc., USPHS, 1985-88; exec. dir. Human Sci. Ctr., San Diego, 1982—. Columnist Yuma Daily Sun, 1982-86. Author (tests) symbol arrangement test, 1952, internat. culture free non-verbal intelligence, 1957, self-other location chart, 1970, test of suffering, 1982; (books) Skills in Living Together, 1983, Conflict Resolution, 1986, A Psychologist Answers Your Questions, 1987, Behind The Therapist's Notes, 1993, Mapping the Human Genome—Reality, Morality and Diety, 1995; plays and video Three Warriors Against Substance Abuse. Named Outstanding prof. U. So. Colo., 1977. Fellow APA (disting. visitor undergrad. edn. program); mem. AAAS, Deutsche Gesellschaft fur Antropologie, Internat. Assn. Study of Symbols (founder, 1st pres. 1957-61), Japanese Soc. Study KTSA (hon. pres.), Home and Office: PO Box 270169 San Diego CA 92198-2169

KENY, SHARAD VASANT, mathematics educator and researcher; b. Panaji, Goa, India, Jan. 21, 1946; d. Vishnu Roulu and Mandabai Vishnu Rao; m. Vasant Yeshwant Keny, May 26, 1969; children: Hemant, Shilpa, Ameet, Shveta. BS, Bombay U., 1966, MS, 1968; MA, UCLA, 1973; PhD, 1976. Instr. Dhempe Coll., Bombay, 1968-69, UCLA, Los Angeles, 1976-77; asst. prof. Calif. State U., Long Beach, Calif., 1977-86; adj. prof. Calif. State U., Fullerton, 1980-81, Golden West Coll., Huntington Beach, Calif., 1981-83, Orange Coast Community Coll., Costa Mesa, Calif., 1983-85; asst. prof. Whittier (Calif.) Coll., 1986-88, assoc. prof., 1989-94, prof., 1995—; adj. prof. Cypress (Calif.) Coll., 1990-91, chmn. dept. math; curriculum cons. La Serna High Sch., Whittier, Calif., 1989-90. Contbr. articles to profl. jours. Mem. Brahan Maharashtra Mandal, 1990, Maharashtra Mandal, 1974-90. Mem. Math. Assn. of Am., Am. Math. Soc., Am. Assoc. of U. Women, AM. Math. Coun., Indian Math. Soc., Maharashrian Assn. of L.A., Shantivan L.A., The Calif. Math. Projects. (adv. bd.). Home: 7901 Lemonwood Cir Buena Park CA 90623-1834 Office: Whittier Coll 13406 Philadelphia St Whittier CA 90601-4446

KENYON, CARLETON WELLER, librarian; b. Lafayette, N.Y., Oct. 7, 1923; s. Herbert Abram and Esther Elizabeth (Weller) K.; m. Dora Marie Kallander, May 21, 1948; children: Garnet Eileen, Harmon Clark, Kay Adelle. A.B., Yankton Coll., 1947; M.A., U. S.D., 1950, J.D., 1950; A.M. in L.S, U. Mich., 1951. Bar: S.D. 1950. Asst. law librarian, head catalog librarian U. Nebr., 1951-52; asst. reference librarian Los Angeles County Law Library, 1952-54, head catalog librarian, 1954-60; law librarian State of Calif., Sacramento, 1960-69; became cons. Library of Congress, Washington, 1963; asso. law librarian Library of Congress, 1969-71, law librarian, 1971—; cons. county law libraries; lectr. legal bibliography and research. Author: California County Law Library Basic List Handbook and Information of New Materials, 1967; compiler: Calif. Library Laws; assisted in compiling checklists of basic: Am. publs. and subject headings; contbr. articles and book revs. to law revs., library jours. Served with USAAC, 1943-46. Mem. ABA, State Bar S.D., Am. Assn. Law Librarians (chmn. com. on cataloging and classification 1969-71, mem. staff Law Library Inst. 1969, 71), Law Librarians Soc. Washington. Home: 4239 44th Ct NE Salem OR 97305-2117

KENYON, DAVID LLOYD, architect, architectural firm executive; b. Lockport, N.Y., Sept. 9, 1952; s. F. Robert and Betty Jane (Reviere) K.; m. Susan Clair Doyle, Jan. 6, 1990; children: Sean Phillip Kenyon, Colin Doyle Kenyon. A in Civil Tech., SUNY, Utica, 1972; BArch, Syracuse U., 1975. Lic. architect, N.Y., Pa., Ariz., Calif. Oreg., Ill., Washington. Assoc. The Myrus Group, Syracuse, N.Y., 1973-79; assoc. dir. design Chase Archtl. Assocs., Syracuse, N.Y., 1978-80; prin. Kenyon Archtl. Group, Phoenix, Ariz., 1980—; cons. Nat. Trust for Historic Preservation, Washington, 1978; faculty assoc. Ariz. State U. Coll. Architecture, Tempe, Ariz., 1983-89; with nat. solar study USAID, Morocco, 1991; with mission to Malaga and Morocco, OPEC, Washington, 1991-92; lectr. Assn. Construction Inspectors, 1993. Author: (textbook) A Hands on Approach to Construction Inspection, 1992. Recipient Energy Innovation award U.S. Dept. Energy, 1988, Environmental Excellence award Crescordia Valley Forward, 1991, Western Regional Design award Am. Inst. Architects, 1991, CAC Honor award, 1992. Fellow Ariz. Acad.; mem. Nat. Trust for Historic Preservation, Soc. Archtl. Historians, Internat. Conference Bldg. Officials. Office: Kenyon Archtl Group 398 S Mill Ave Tempe AZ 85281

KENYON, DAVID V., federal judge; b. 1930; m. Mary Cramer; children: George Cramer, John Clark. B.A., U. Calif.-Berkeley, 1952; J.D., U. So. Calif., 1957. Law clk. presiding justice U.S. Dist. Ct. (cen. dist.) Calif., 1957-58; house counsel Metro-Goldwyn-Mayer, 1959-60, Nat. Theatres and TV Inc., 1960-61; pvt. practice law, 1961-71; judge Mcpl. Ct. L.A., 1971-72, L.A. Superior Ct., 1972-80, U.S. Dist. Ct. (cen. dist.) Calif., L.A., 1980—. Office: US Dist Ct 312 N Spring St Los Angeles CA 90012-4701*

KEOGH, HEIDI HELEN DAKE, publishing executive; b. Saratoga, N.Y., July 12, 1950; d. Charles Starks and Phyllis Sylvia (Edmunds) Dake; m. Randall Frank Keogh, Nov. 3, 1973; children: Tyler Cameron, Kelly Dake. Student, U. Colo., 1972. Reception, promotions Sta. KLAK, KJAE, Lakewood, Colo., 1972-73; account exec. Mixed Media Advt. Agy., Denver, 1973-75; writer, mktg. Jr. League Cookbook Devel., Denver, 1986-88; chmn., coordinator Colorado Cache & Creme de Colorado Cookbooks, 1988-90; speakers bur. Mile High Transplant Bank, Denver, 1983-84, Writer's Inst., U. Denver, 1988; bd. dirs. Stewart's Ice Cream Co., Inc., Jr. League, Denver.

Contbr. 6 articles to profl. jours. Fiscal officer, bd. dirs. Mile High Transplant Bank; blockworker Heart Fund and Am. Cancer Soc., Littleton, 1978—, Littleton (Colo.) Rep. Com., 1980-84; fundraising vol. Littleton (Colo.) Pub. Schs., 1980—; vol. Hearts for Life, 1991—, Gathering Place, 1991—, Oneday, 1992, Denver Ballet Guild, 1992—, Denver Ctr. Alliance, 1993—. Mem. Jr. League Denver (pub. rels. bd., v.p. ways and means 1989-90, planning coun./ad hoc 1990-92, sustainer spl. events 1993-94), Community Emergency Fund (chair 1991-92), Jon D. Williams Cotillion at Columbine (chmn. 1991-93), Columbine Country Club, Gamma Alpha Chi, Pi Beta Phi Alumnae Club (pres. Denver chpt. 1984-85, 93-94). Episcopalian. Home: 63 Fairway Ln Littleton CO 80123-6648

KEOGH, RICHARD JOHN, management consultant; b. Woonsocket, R.I., Sept. 23, 1932; s. Michael Joseph and Dora Marie (Rumgay) K. BBA, U. Mass., 1958; MA, Pepperdine U., 1974. Lic. explosive disposal technician, Mass.; expert witness explosives, Hawaii. Commd. 2d lt. U.S. Army, 1958, advanced through grades to maj., 1967; stationed at Korea, S.C., Ala., 1958-73; ret. USAR, 1979; disposal specialist USN, Lualualei, Hawaii, 1973-76; mgmt. analyst Marine Corps Air Sta., Kaneohe Bay, Hawaii, 1976-93. Contbr. articles to profl. jours. Pres. Assn. of Owners Palms Condominium, Honolulu, 1978-80. With USAR, 1973-79. Decorated 3 Bronze Stars, 2 Purple Hearts, 2 Air medals, Cross of Gallantry; recipient Founders award, Order of the Arrow Boy Scouts Am., 1989, FBI Cert. of Appreciation, 1991, Silver Beaver award Boy Scouts Am., 1994. Mem. VFW (life), DAV (life), Internat. Assn. Bomb Technicians and Investigators (life), Nat. Auto Pistol Collectors Assn., Ohio Gun Collectors Assn., Bay Colony Weapons Collectors, Hawaii Rifle Assn. (pres. 1994-95), Gun Owners Action League, Am. Legion (life), Mil. Order Purple Heart (life). Home: 431 Nahua St Apt 203 Honolulu HI 96815-2915

KEPHART, FLOYD W., entertainment company executive; b. Ft. Oglethorpe, Ga., May 16, 1942; s. Floyd William Kephart and Zada (Whaley) Lindsay; m. Dolly Carlisle, Apr. 6, 1980 (div. Dec. 1991). BA, Mid. Tenn. State U., 1965. Rsch. asst. Kennedy staff White House, Washington, 1961-63; budget dir. Dept. Transp. Gov.'s Office, Tenn., 1963-68; assoc. prof. polit. sci. Mid. Tenn. State U., Murfreesboro, 1968-70; polit. analyst NBC, Nashville, 1970-80; chmn., CEO So. States Corp., Nashville, 1980-83; CEO, pres. McDowell Corp., Nashville, 1983-87; pres. Artists & Entertainment, Inc., Nashville, 1988-92; chmn., CEO Ventura Entertainment Group, L.A., 1992—; cons. Head Start, Washington, 1963-73; exec. dir. Fiscal Rev. Com., Nashville, 1967. Cons. Dem. Nat. Com., Washington, 1968-84; community spokesperson Boy Scouts Am., Nashville, 1971-73. Home: 1130 N Wetherly Dr Los Angeles CA 90069-1814

KEPLER, RAYMOND GLEN, physicist; b. Long Beach, Calif., Sept. 10, 1928; s. Glen Raymond and Erma Martina (Larsen) K.; m. Carol Flint, Apr. 19, 1953; children: Julianne, Linda, Russell B., David L. B.S., Stanford U., 1950; M.S., U. Calif.-Berkeley, 1955, Ph.D., 1957. Mem. tech. staff central research dept. E.I. duPont de Nemours & Co., 1957-64; div. supr. Sandia Nat. Labs., Albuquerque, 1964-69, dept. mgr., 1969-89, rsch. scientist, 1989—; vice chmn. panel 2 of Materials Sci. and Engring. Study Commn., NRC, 1985-88; mem. solid State scis. panel Nat. Acad. Sci., 1977-82; mem. evaluation panel for materials sci. Nat. Bur. Standards, 1982-88. Fellow Am. Phys. Soc. (chmn. edn. com. 1979-80); mem. AAAS, Sierra Club.

KEPNER, JANE ELLEN, psychotherapist, educator, minister; b. Lancaster, Pa., July 13, 1948; d. Richard Darlington and Miriam (Harclerode) K.; m. Raymond Earl Sparks Jr., July 23, 1969 (div. Apr. 1978); 1 child, Heather Elizabeth. AB, CCNY, 1975; MDiv, Harvard Divinity Sch., 1985. Vol. Vista, Auburn, Ala., 1967-69; creative drama tchr. East Harlem Day Care, N.Y.C., 1972-76; editl. asst. Bantam Books, Inc., N.Y.C., 1976-78; rschr. Theseus Prodns., Greenwich, Conn., 1978-82; homeless advocate Harvard Sq. Chs., Cambridge, Mass., 1984-85; cmty. organizer So. Middlesex Opportunity Coun., Marlboro, Mass., 1985-88; emergency psychiat. clinician Advocates, Inc., Framingham, Mass., 1988-89; assoc. prof. Curry Coll., Milton, Mass., 1989-90; psychologist, mental health advocate Portland (Oreg.) Health Svc., 1991—, bd. advisors, 1992-94. Organizer emergency food pantry Marlboro City Coun., 1987; tenants rights and housing rights advocates Tenants Action Com., Marlboro, 1985-87. Pfeiffer fellow Harvard U. Div. Sch., 1983. Mem. Am. Counseling Assn., Oreg. Friends of C.G. Jung, Club 53 (bd. dirs. 1992-94), Amnesty Internat., Oreg. Coalition to Abolish the Death Penalty. Office: Portland Health Svcs 1971 NW Overton St Portland OR 97209-1618

KERMAN, BARRY MARTIN, ophthalmologist, educator; b. Chgo., Mar. 31, 1945; s. Harvey Nathan and Evelyn (Bialis) K.; B.S., U. Ill., 1967, M.D. with high honors, 1970. Diplomate Am. Bd. Ophthalmology; m. Pamela Renee Berliant, Aug. 18, 1968 (div. 1989); children: Gregory Jason, Jeremy Adam. Intern in medicine Harbor Gen. Hosp., Torrance, Calif., 1970-71; resident in ophthalmology Wadsworth VA Hosp., L.A., 1971-74; fellow in diseases of the retina, vitreous and choroid Jules Stein Eye Inst. UCLA, 1974-75; fellow in ophthalmic ultrasonography Edward S. Harkness Eye Inst., Columbia U., N.Y.C. and U. Iowa Hosps., Iowa City, 1975; asst. prof. ophthalmology UCLA, 1976-78, Harbor Gen. Hosp., 1976-78; asst. clin. prof. ophthalmology UCLA, 1978-83, assoc. clin. prof., 1983—, dir. ophthalmic ultrasonography lab., 1976—; cons. ophthalmologist, L.A., 1976—; mem. exec. bd. Am. Registry Diagnostic Med. Sonographers, 1981-87. With USAFR, 1971-77. Fellow Am. Acad. Ophthalmology; mem. Am. Soc. Cataract and Refractive Surgery, L.A. Soc. Ophthalmology, Am. Soc. Ophthalmic Ultrasound, Am. Assn. Ophthalmic Standardized Echography, Societas Internat. Pro Diagnostica Ultrasonica in Opthalmic, Western Retina Study Club. Contbr. articles to profl. jours. Office: 2080 Century Park E Ste 800 Los Angeles CA 90067-2011

KERN, DONALD MICHAEL, internist; b. Belleville, Ill., Nov. 21, 1951; s. Donald Milton Kern and Dolores Olivia (Rust) Cohoon. BS in Biology, Tulane U., 1973; MD magna cum laude, U. Brussels, 1983. ECFMG cert.; lic. Calif. Intern in surgery Berkshire Med. Ctr., Pittsfield, Mass., 1983-84; intern in psychiatry Tufts New England Med. Ctr., Boston, 1984-85; resident in internal medicine Kaiser Found. Hosp., San Francisco, 1985-87; with assoc. staff internal medicine Kaiser Permanente Med. Group, Inc., San Francisco, 1987-89; assoc. investigator AIDS Clin. Trial Unit Kaiser Permanente Med. Ctr., Stanford U., Nat. Inst. Allergy & Infectious Disease, San Francisco, 1988-90; mem. staff internal medicine Kaiser Permanente Med. Group, South San Francisco, 1989—. Mem. Am. Coll. Physicians. Democrat. Roman Catholic. Office: Kaiser Permanente Med Group Inc 1200 El Camino Real South San Francisco CA 94080-3208

KERN, EUGENE FRANCIS, corporation executive; b. San Francisco, July 23, 1919; s. Eugene F. and Dorothy (Danforth) K.; m. Paula Stevenson, Oct. 3, 1942; children: Eugene, Tay, Kathy S.; m. 2d. Vida Del Fiorentino, June 10, 1964. AB, Stanford U., 1942. Wholesaleman, price clk. Tay Holbrook, Inc., Fresno, Calif., 1946-47, salesman, 1947-49; indsl. sales Tay Holbrook, Inc., Fresno, 1949-51, dir., 1951-64; asst. purchasing agt. Tay Holbrook, Inc., San Francisco, 1951-57, corp. sec., 1952-64, mgr., 1957-60, gen. sales mgr., 1960-62, exec. v.p., 1961-62, dir. purchases, 1962-63, exec. v.p. sales, 1963-64; pres., dir. Par-Kern Supply, Inc., San Leandro, Calif., 1964—. Dir. San Francisco Employers Council, 1959-66. Served from 2d lt. to maj. AUS, 1942-45. Decorated Bronze Star, Army Commendation medal. Mem. We. Suppliers Assn., Am. Arbitration Assn. (nat. panel arbitrators), Internat. Platform Assn., Stanford U. Alumni Assn., Olympic Club, Commonwealth Club, Stanford Buck Club. Home: 743 Park Way South San Francisco CA 94080-2512 Office: 888 Carden St San Leandro CA 94577-1119

KERN, LAWRENCE A., food products executive; b. 1947. BS, Ind. U., 1969, MBA, 1972. With FMC Corp., Riverside, Calif., 1972-76, San Jose, Calif., 1978-81; with Barnes-Kern Oil Co., Visalia, Calif., 1976-78, Shasta Beverages, Hayward, Calif., 1981-86, All Am. Gourmet, Orange, Calif., 1986-93; pres. Bud Antle Inc., Salinas, Calif., 1993—. *

KERN, PAUL ALFRED, advertising company executive, research consultant, realtor; b. Hackensack, N.J., Mar. 17, 1958; s. Paul Julian and Edith Helen (Colten) K. BS in Commerce, U. Va., 1980; MBA, U. So. Calif., 1983. Sales rep. Procter & Gamble, Cin., 1980-81; rsch. svcs. mgr. Opinion Rsch., Long Beach, Calif., 1984; consumer planning supr. Dentsu, Young & Rubicam, L.A., 1984-85; rsch. exec. DJMC Advt., Inc., L.A., 1986; realtor assoc. Tarbell Realtors, Santa Ana, Calif., 1988-89; corp. pres. Jennskore, Inc., Torrance, Calif., 1989-93, also bd. dirs.; bd. dirs. Applicon, Inc., Hillsdale, N.J., Kernokopia, Hillsdale; cons. Venture Six Enterprises, Encino, Calif., 1985-87, DFS/Dorland, Torrance, 1986, IMI Machinery Inc., Charleston, S.C., 1987—. Coach, supr. Little League Football, Alexandria, Va., 1981; active Surf and Sun Softball League (1987 champions). Recipient Most Calls Per Day award Procter and Gamble, 1980. Mem. Profl. Research Assn., Am. Mktg. Assn., Am. Film Inst., Internat. Platform Assn., U.S. Tennis Assn. (Michelob Light 4.5 Team Championship 1982), U. Va. Alumni Assn, Nat. Assn. Realtors, Calif. Assn. of Realtors, S. Bay Rd. of Realtors (Torrance-Lomita), Carson Bd. of Realtors. Club: Alta Vista Racquet. Home and Office: 48-253 Silver Spur Trl Palm Desert CA 92260-6611

KERNODLE, UNA MAE, home economics coordinator, retired secondary education educator; b. Jackson, Tenn., Mar. 4, 1947; d. James G. and Mary E. (McLemore) Sikes. B.S. in Home Econs., U. Tenn., 1969; M.Edn., U. Alaska, 1974. Tchr., head dept. vocat. edn. and electives Chugiak High Sch., Anchorage, ret.; home econs. coord. office career tech. King Career Ctr., Anchorage; edn. cons. State of Alaska, Anchorage Talent Bank; presenter Gov.'s Conf. on Child Abuse, Alaska Vocat. Edn. Assn. Conf., Alaska Home Econs. Inst., 1989; state officer Alaska Home Econs. Recipient Gruening award, 1989. Mem. Am. Home Econs. Assn., Anchorage Assn. Edn. Young Children, NEA, Am. Vocat. Assn. Democrat. Baptist. Office: Office of Career Tech 2650 E Northern Lights Blvd Anchorage AK 99508-4119

KERNS, PEGGY SHOUP, state legislator; b. Columbus, Ohio, Mar. 17, 1941; d. Ronald Traxler and Marie (Strausbaugh) Shoup; m. Pat L.J. Kerns, Nov. 9, 1963; children: Jerry, Deborah. BA, Duquesne U., 1963. Editor co. newspaper Samsonite Corp., Denver, 1978-83; mgr. customer svc. dept. Mt. Med. Equipment, Littleton, Colo., 1983-88; mem. State Ho. of Reps., Colo., 1989—; mem. bd. trustees Aurora (Colo.) Regional Med. Ctr., 1984—. Mem. coun. City of Aurora, 1983-89, mayor pro tem., asst. minority leader, 1993-94, minority leader, 1994—. Named Bus. and Profl. Women's Woman of Yr., 1991, Legislator of Yr. Colo. Assn. Commerce and Industry, 1993, Colo. Sch. Nurses Assn., Colo. Children's Campaign, 5th Most Effective Legislator by Colo. Bus. Mag., 1994, Legislator of Yr. by AP, 1994. Mem. AAUW, LWV, Aurora C. of C. (Woman of Yr. 1989), BPW. Democrat. Roman Catholic. Home: 1124 S Oakland St Aurora CO 80012-4260 Office: State Ho Reps State Capitol Denver CO 80201

KERPER, MEIKE, family violence, sex abuse and addictions educator, consultant; b. Powell, Wyo., Aug. 13, 1929; d. Wesley George and Hazel (Bowman) K.; m. R.R. Milodragovich, Dec. 25, 1963 (div. 1973); children: Dan, John, Teren, Tina, Stana. BS, U. Mont., 1973; MS, U. Ariz., 1975; postgrad. Ariz. State U., 1976-78, Columbia Pacific U., 1990—. Lic. marriage & family therapist, Oreg.; cert. domestic violence counselor, alcoholism and drug abuse counselor, mental health profl. and investigator. Family therapist Cottonwood Hill, Arvada, Colo., 1981; family program developer Turquoise Lodge, Albuquerque, 1982; co-developer abusers program Albuquerque Shelter Domestic Violence, 1984; family therapist Citizens Coun. Alcoholism and Drug Abuse, Albuquerque, 1984-86; pvt. practice cons. and trainer family violence and treatment, Albuquerque, 1987—; developer sex offender program Union County, Oreg. Co-author: Court Diversion Program, 1985; author Family Treatment, 1982. Lobbyist CCOPE, Santa Fe, 1983-86; bd. dirs. Union County Task Force on Domestic Violence, 1989-91; developer Choices program treatment of sex offenders and victims Union, Wallowa and Baker Counties, Oreg.; mem. Child Abuse Prevention Team, Union County, Baker County and Wallowa County, Oreg. Recipient commendation Albuquerque Shelter Domestic Violence, 1984. Mem. Assn. for the Treatment Sexual Abusers, Nat. Assn. Marriage and Family Therapists, Nat. Assn. Alcoholism Counselors, Delta Delta Delta. Republican. Episcopalian. Club: PEO. Avocations: Art history; reading; Indian culture; swimming; public speaking. Home: 61002 Love Rd Cove OR 97824-8211

KERR, CATHERINE SPAULDING, environmental advocate; b. Los Angeles, Mar. 22, 1911; d. Charles Edgar and Gertrude Mary (Smith) Spaulding; m. Clark Kerr, Dec. 25, 1934; children: Clark E., Alexander W., Caroline M. AB, Stanford U., 1932. Co-founder, environ. leader Save San Francisco Bay Assn., 1961—, v.p., 1987—. Editor Kensington Outlook, 1947-49. Advisor Mortar Bd., Theta Sigma Phi, Univ. YWCA, 1950-67; founder Fgn. Student Hospitality Program; mem. adv. bd. East Bay Regional Park Dist., 1976-82, 1985-88. Recipient Robert C. Kirkwood award, 1985, Calif. Council Landscape Architects citation, 1982, Sol Feinstone Environ. award, 1981, Carnegie Found. Advancement of Teaching cert. disting. service, 1979, Berkeley Citation award, 1974. Mem. Stanford U. Alumni Assn. (hostess com.). Democrat. Mem. Soc. Friends. Clubs: Town and Gown, Berkeley Fellows. Home and Office: 8300 Buckingham Dr El Cerrito CA 94530-2530

KERR, JAMES ARTHUR, logistics engineer; b. Colorado Springs, Mar. 1, 1943; s. George Jacob and Reah Lavetta (Morgan) K.; m. Eiko Furakawa, May 21, 1974; children: Cynthia Mirei, Marshal James. AS in Elec. Engring., Denver Engring. Inst., 1963. Cert. profl. logistician; acquisition profl. devel. cert. level III for program mgmt. and acquisition logistics level II for comm. F4B & RF4B engring. technician McDonnell Aircraft Co., St. Louis, 1963-66; 44OL OHR site comdr. Raytheon Co., Chitose AFB, Japan, 1966-75; mgr. acquisition airborne command post HQSAC, Offutt AFB, Nebr., 1975-80; dir. logistics Space Def. Systems Program, L.A. AFB, 1980-88; dep. dir. logistics MILSATCOM Joint Program Office, L.A. AFB, 1988—; dir. acquisition logistics MILSATCOM, Space & Missile Ctr./ALK, L.A. AFB, 1988—; dir. acquisition logistics antisatellite Space Sys. Divsn./ALN, L.A. AFB, 1980-88. Named Air Force Reservist of the Yr., Space System Divsn., 1990; recipient Dr. Alfred Rockefeller Jr. award for Outstanding Civilian, Air Force Assn. Chpt. 147, 1994. Mem. Soc. Logistics Engrs. Home: 4930 E Gayann Dr Anaheim CA 92807-3043 Office: HQ SMC/MCSL 2420 Vela Way Ste 1467-a8 El Segundo CA 90245

KERR, NANCY KAROLYN, pastor, mental health consultant; b. Ottumwa, Iowa, July 10, 1934; d. Owen W. and Iris Irene (Israel) K. Student Boston U., 1953; AA, U. Bridgeport, 1966; BA, Hofstra U., 1967; postgrad. in clin. psychology Adelphi U. Inst. Advanced Psychol. Studies, 1968-73; MDiv Associated Mennonite Bibl. Sems., 1986; m. Richard Clayton Williams, June 28, 1953 (div.); children: Richard Charles, Donna Louise. Ordained pastor Mennonite Ch., 1987; inducted pastor Presbyn. Ch., Can., 1992. Pastoral counselor Nat. Council Chs., Jackson, Miss., 1964; dir. teen program Waterbury (Conn.) YWCA, 1966-67; intern in psychology N.Y. Med. Coll., 1971-72; rsch. cons., 1972-73; coord. home svcs., psychologist City and County of Denver, 1972-75; cons. Mennonite Mental Health Svcs., Denver, 1975-78; asst. prof. psychology Messiah Coll., 1978-79; mental health cons., 1979-81; called to ministry Mennonite Ch., 1981, pastor Cin. Mennonite Fellowship, 1981-83, coord. campus peace evangelism, 1981-83, mem. Gen. Conf. Peace and Justice Reference Council, 1983-85; instr. Associated Mennonite Bibl. Sems., 1985; teaching elder Assembly Mennonite Ch., 1985-86; pastor Pulaski Mennonite Ch., 1986-89; v.p. Davis County Mins.' Assn., 1988-89; exec. dir., pastoral counselor Bethesda Counseling Svcs., Prince George B.C., 1989—; bd. dirs. Tri-County Counselling Clinic, Memphis, Mo., 1980-81; spl. ch. curriculum Nat. Council Chs., 1981; mem. Cen. Dist. Conf. Peace and Justice Com., 1981-89; mem. exec. bd. People for Peace, 1981-83. Mem. Waterbury Planned Parenthood Bd., 1964-67; mem. MW Children's Home Bd., 1974-75; bd. dirs. Boulder (Colo.) ARC, 1977-78; mem. Mennonite Disabilities Respite Care Bd., 1981-86; active Kamloops Presbytery Presbyn. Ch. Can., 1992—; P.G. Children's Svcs. com., 1992-94; bd. dirs. Prince George Neighborlink, 1995—; adv. com. Prince George Planning, 1995—. Mem. APA (assoc.), Soc. Psychologists for Study of Social Issues, Christian Assn. Psychol. Studies, Davis County Mins. Assn. (v.p. 1988-89), Prince George Ministerial Assn. (chmn. edn. and Airport chapel coms. 1990-92). Office: 575 Quebec St, Prince George, BC Canada V2L 1W6

KERRICK, DAVID ELLSWORTH, state senator, lawyer; b. Caldwell, Idaho, Jan. 15, 1951; s. Charles Ellsworth and Patria (Olesen) K.; m. Juneal Casper, May 24, 1980; children: Peter Ellsworth, Beth Anne, George Ellis, Katherine Leigh. Student, Coll. of Idaho, 1969-71; BA, U. Wash., 1972; JD, U. Idaho, 1980. Bar: Idaho 1980, U.S. Dist. Ct. Idaho 1980, U.S. Ct. Appeals (9th cir.) 1981. Senator State of Idaho, 1990—, majority caucus chmn., 1992-94, majority leader, 1994—. Mem. S.W. Idaho Estate Planning Coun. Mem. ABA, Assn. Trial Lawyers Am., Idaho Bar Assn. (3d dist. pres. 1985-86), Idaho Trial Lawyers Assn., Canyon County Lawyers Assn. (pres. 1985). Republican. Presbyterian. Lodge: Elks. Office: PO Box 44 Caldwell ID 83606-0044

KERSCHNER, LEE R(ONALD), former university president, political science educator; b. May 31, 1931; m. Helga Koller, June 22, 1958; children: David, Gabriel, Riza. B.A. in Polit. Sci. (Univ. fellow), Rutgers U., 1953; M.A. in Internat. Relations (Univ. fellow), Johns Hopkins U., 1958; Ph.D. in Polit. Sci. (Univ. fellow), Georgetown U., 1964. From instr. to prof. polit. sci. Calif. State U., Fullerton, 1961-69, prof., 1988—; state univ. dean Calif. State Univs. and Colls. Hdqrs., Long Beach, 1969-71, asst. exec. vice chancellor, 1971-76, vice chancellor for adminstrv. affairs, 1976-77, vice chancellor acad. affairs, 1987-92; exec. dir. Colo. Commn. on Higher Edn., Denver, 1977-83, Nat. Assn. Trade and Tech. Schs., 1983-85, Calif. Commn. on Master Plan for Higher Edn., 1985-87; interim pres. Calif. State U., Stanislaus, 1992-94, spl. asst. to the chancellor, 1994—; mem. Calif. Student Aid Commn., 1993—; cons. in field. Mem. exec. com. Am. Jewish Com., Denver, 1978-83; internat. bd. dirs. Amigos de las Americas, 1982-88 (chmn. 1985-87). Served with USAF, 1954-58; col. Res., ret. Home: PO Box 748 Weimar CA 95736-0748 Office: Calif State Univ #1160 915 L St Sacramento CA 95814-3786

KERSEY, TERRY L(EE), astronautical engineer; b. San Francisco, June 9, 1947; s. Ida Helen (Schmeichel) K. Houseman, orderly Mills Meml. Hosp., San Mateo, Calif., 1965-68; security guard Lawrence Security, San Francisco, 1973-74; electronic engr. and technician engring. research and devel. dept. McCulloch Corp., Los Angeles, 1977; warehouseman C.C.H. Computax Co., Redondo Beach, Calif., 1977-78; with material ops. and planning customer support dept. Allied-Signal Aerospace Co., Torrance, Calif., 1978-91; security guard Guardsmark Inc., L.A., 1993; electronic technician J. W. Griffin, Venice, Calif., 1993—. Participant 9th Space Simulation conf., Los Angeles, 1977, 31st Internat. Astronautical Fedn. Congress., Tokyo, 1980, Unispace 1982 for the U.N., Vienna. Served to sgt. USAF, 1968-72, Vietnam. Decorated Vietnam Service medal with 2 bronze stars, Republic of Vietnam Campaign medal, Air Force commendation medal for Vietnam campaign Service. Mem. AAAS, Nat. Space Inst., Am. Astronautical Soc., The Planetary Soc., Internat. L5 Soc., Ind. Space Rsch. Group, IEEE Computer Soc., Space Studies Inst. (sr. assoc.), sr. mem. AIAA (mem. space systems tech. com. 1981—, mem. aerodynamics com. 1980—, Wright Flyer Project Aerodynamics com. 1980—, pub. policy com. 1989—). Zen Buddhist.

KERSTEN, TIMOTHY WAYNE, economics educator, consultant; b. Algona, Iowa, Nov. 18, 1944; s. Harold Arthur and Marcella (Heger) K.; m. Carol Ann Oliver, Dec. 22, 1967; one child, Jeffrey Alexander. BA, Calif. State U., Sacramento, 1967; MA, U. Oreg., 1971, PhD, 1973. Asst. prof. econs. Calif. Poly. State U., San Luis Obispo, 1971-75, assoc. prof., 1976-80, prof., 1981—, chmn. acad. senate, 1980-82; mem. state-wide acad. sen. Calif. State U., 1983—, chmn. faculty affairs com., 1984-86, mem. govtl. affairs com. 1986-89, 93—, chmn., 1990-91, vice chmn., 1992-9, mem. exec. com., 1991-92. Author: Instructors Guide to Accompany Contemporary Economics, 1975. Mem. citizens adv. com. San Luis Obispo City Council, 1976-77. Fellow U.S. Govt., 1969-71. Mem. Am. Econ. Assn., Western Econ. Assn., Omicron Delta Epsilon, Phi Mu Alpha Sinfonia. Office: Calif Poly State U Dept Econs San Luis Obispo CA 93407

KERTZ, MARSHA HELENE, accountant, educator; b. Palo Alto, Calif., May 29, 1946; d. Joe and Ruth (Lazear) K. BSBA in Acctg., San Jose State U., 1976, MBA, 1977. CPA, Calif., cert. tax profl. Staff acct. Steven Kroff & Co., CPA's, Palo Alto, 1968-71, 73-74; contr. Rand Teleprocessing Corp., San Francisco, 1972; auditor, sr. acct. Ben F. Priest Accountancy Corp., Mountain View, Calif., 1974-83; tchr. San Jose Unified Regional Occupation Program, San Jose, 1977; pvt. practice accounting San Jose, 1977—; lectr. San Jose State U., 1977—. Mem. AICPA, Nat. Soc. of Tax Profls., Am. Inst. Tax Studies, Am. Acctg. Assn., Calif. Soc. CPAs, Beta Alpha Psi, Beta Gamma Sigma. Democrat. Jewish. Home: 4544 Strawberry Park Dr San Jose CA 95129-2213 Office: San Jose State U Acctg & Fin Dept San Jose CA 95192

KERVER, THOMAS JOSEPH, editor, consultant; b. Cleve., Nov. 9, 1934; s. William F. and Hope M. (Roberts) K.; m. Elizabeth G. Galloway, Apr. 12, 1969 (div. Apr. 1990); children: Kenneth, Stephen, Suzanne, Sarah. BA, Xavier U., 1956; M of Mil. Arts and Scis., U.S. Army Gen. Staff Coll., 1968; MA in Polit. Sci., U. Wis., 1972, MA in Journalism, 1972. Commd. 2d lt. U.S. Army, 1956, advanced through grades to lt. col., 1976; pres. Kerver People, Ft. Collins, Colo., 1976-80; dir. communications, publicity Colo. Bankers Assn., Denver, 1980-82; sr. editor Cardiff Pub. Co., Englewood, Colo., 1982-90; bus. editor Cablevision Mag., Denver, 1990—; prof. journalism Colo. State U., Ft. Collins, 1978-80; vice chmn. Larimer County Budget Adv. Com., Ft. Collins, 1978-79; chmn. Larimer Conty Pvt. Industry Coun., Ft. Collins, 1979-80. Contbr. articles to profl. jours. Organizer Larimer County Dem. Party, Ft. Collins, 1976-80; cons. Nat. Urban Indian Coun., Denver, 1980-81; organizer, affiliate Clinton for Pres. Campaign, Denver, 1992. Decorated Bronze Star (4), Legion of Merit (2); recipient Presdl. Citation award Pres. Jimmy Carter, 1980, Cert. of Distinction award Nat. Alliance Bus., 1980, Morton Margolin award Disting. Nat. Bus. Reporting, 1993, 94. Mem. Cable/Satellite Broadcasters Assn. Asia (chartered), Soc. Satellite Profls. Roman Catholic. Home: 7652 E Nassau Ave Denver CO 80237-2135 Office: Capital Cities/ABC Inc Chilton Comm 600 S Cherry St Ste 400 Denver CO 80222-1706

KERWIN, MARY ANN COLLINS, lawyer; b. Oconomowoc, Wis., Oct. 16, 1931; d. Thomas Patrick and Florence Mary (Morris) Collins; m. Thomas Joseph Kerwin, Dec. 27, 1954; children: Thomas, Edward, Gregory, Mary, Anne, Katherine, John, Michael. BA, Barat Coll., 1953; JD, U. Denver, 1986. Bar: Colo. 1987. Tchr. Country Grade Sch., Wheaton, Ill., 1953-54; travel agt. Chgo. Athletic Club, 1954-55; legal intern City Atty.'s Office, Denver, 1985, Dist. Atty.'s Office, Denver, 1985; atty. Kerwin and Assocs., Denver, 1987-92, Decker, DeVoss & O'Malley, P.C., Denver, 1992-93, King Peterson Brown, LLC, Englewood, Colo., 1993-95; assoc. Daniel F. Lynch, P.C., Denver, 1995—; legal compliance dept. editor United Banks Colo., Inc., Denver, 1988-93. Author: (with others) The Womanly Art of Breastfeeding, 1958, revised edit. 1991; contbr. articles to profl. jours. Mem. Colo. Breatfeeding Task Force mem., 1990-93; adv. bd. St. Luke's Woman's Hosp., Denver, 1986—, Colo. Sudden Infant Death Syndrome Program, 1992-94; sch. bd. Christ the King Sch., Denver, 1970-73; great books leader Jr. and Collegiate Great Books, Denver, 1963-82; marriage spkr. Cath. Archdiocese, Denver, 1965-75; co-founder, bd. dirs. La Leche League Internat., Franklin Park, Ill., 1956—, founder state orgn., 1960—, chmn. bd. 1980-83, sec. 1988-91. Named One of Ten Outstanding Alumnus Barat Coll., 1988. Mem. Colo. Bar Assn., Colo. Women's Bar Assn., Denver Bar Assn., Colo. Alumnae Assn. (pres. 1968-70), Theresians (pres. 1974-76). Home: 200 Cherry St Denver CO 80220-5638 Office: Daniel F. Lynch PC 4704 Harlan St Ste 610 Denver CO 80212-7421

KERWIN, WILLIAM JAMES, electrical engineering educator, consultant; b. Portage, Wis., Sept. 27, 1922; s. James William and Nina Elizabeth (Haight) K.; m. Madolyn Lee Lyons, Aug. 31, 1947; children: Dorothy E., Deborah K., David W. B.S., U Redlands, 1948; M.S., Stanford U., 1954, Ph.D., 1967. Aero. research scientist NACA, Moffett Field, Calif., 1948-59; chief measurements research br. NASA, Moffett Field, Calif., 1959-62, chief space tech. br., 1962-64, chief electronics research br., 1964-70; head electronics dept. Stanford Linear Accelerator Ctr., 1962; prof. elec. engring. U. Ariz., Tucson, 1969-85, prof. emeritus, 1986—. Author: (with others) Active Filters, 1970, Handbook Measurement Science, 1982, Instrumentation and Control, 1990, Handbook of Electrical Engineering, 1993; contbr. articles to profl. jours.; patentee in field. Served to capt. USAAF, 1942-46. Recipient Invention NASA, 1969, 70; recipient fellow NASA, 1966-67. Fellow IEEE (Centennial medal 1984). Republican. Episcopalian. Home: 1981 W Shalimar Way Tucson AZ 85704-1250 Office: U Ariz Dept Elec and Computer Engring Tucson AZ 85721

KERZIE, TED L., JR., painter, fine arts educator; b. Tacoma, May 10, 1943; s. Ted L. Sr. and Frances (Chesky) K.; m. Diane Vines; children: Kristin, Jennifer, Michael. BA, Wash. State U., 1966; MFA with honors,

Claremont Grad. Sch., 1972. Asst. prof. fine arts Claremont (Calif.) Grad. Sch., 1973-76; assoc. prof. Calif. State U., Bakersfield, 1976—, prof., 1986—; artist Cirrus Gallery, Los Angeles, 1980—; pres. Info-Sell, Los Angeles, 1986—. Exhibited in gallery shows nat. and internat. Served to capt. USAF, 1966-70;. Home: 14500 Las Palmas # 40 Bakersfield CA 93306

KESEY, KEN, writer; b. La Hunta, Colo., Sept. 17, 1935; s. Fred and Geneva (Smith) K.; m. Norma Faye Haxby, May 20, 1956; children: Shannon, Zane, Jed (dec. 1984) Sunshine. B.S., U. Oreg., 1957; postgrad., Stanford U., 1958-60. Pres. Intrepid Trips, Inc., 1964; editor, pub. mag. Spit in the Ocean, 1974—. Author: One Flew Over the Cuckoo's Nest, 1962, Sometimes a Great Notion, 1964, Garage Sale, 1973, Demon Box, 1986, Little Trickler the Squirrel Meets Big Double The Bear, 1988, (co-author) Caverns, 1989, The Further Inquiry, 1990, The Sea Lion, 1991, Sailor Song, 1992, (with Ken Babbs) Last Go Round: A Real Western, 1994. Address: 85829 Ridgeway Rd Pleasant Hill OR 97455-9627

KESSEL, BRINA, ornithologist, educator; b. Ithaca, N.Y., Nov. 20, 1925; d. Marcel and Quinta (Cattell) K.; m. Raymond B. Roof, June 19, 1957 (dec. 1968). BS (Albert R. Brand Bird Song Found. scholar), Cornell U., 1947, PhD, 1951; MS (Wis. Alumni Research Found. fellow), U. Wis.-Madison, 1949. Student asst. Patuxent Research Refuge, 1946; student teaching asst. Cornell U., 1945-47, grad. asst., 1947-48, 49-51; instr. biol. sci. U. Alaska, summer 1951, asst. prof. biol. sci., 1951-54, assoc. prof. zoology, 1954-59, prof. zoology, 1959—, head dept. biol. scis., 1957-66; dean U. Alaska (Coll. Biol. Scis. and Renewable Resources), 1961-72, curator terrestrial vertebrate mus. collections, 1972-90, curator ornithology collection, 1990—, adminstrv. assoc. for acad. programs, grad. and undergrad., dir. acad. advising, office of chancellor, 1973-80; project dir. U. Alaska ecol. investigation for AEC Project Chariot, 1959-63; ornithol. investigations NW Alaska pipeline, 1976-81, Susitna Hydroelectric Project, 1980-83. Author books, monographs; contbr. articles to profl. jours. Fellow AAAS, Am. Ornithologists' Union (v.p. 1977, pres.-elect 1990-92, pres. 1992-94), Arctic Inst. N.Am.; mem. Wilson, Cooper ornith. socs., Soc. for Northwestern Vertebrate Biology, Pacific Seabird Group, Assn. Field Ornithologists, Sigma Xi (pres. U. Alaska 1957), Phi Kappa Phi, Sigma Delta Epsilon. Office: PO Box 80211 Fairbanks AK 99708-0211

KESSELHAUT, ARTHUR MELVYN, financial consultant; b. Newark, May 18, 1935; s. Harry and Rela (Wolk) K.; m. Nancy Slater, June 17, 1956; children—Stuart Lee, Amy Beth. B.S. in Bus. Adminstrn, Syracuse (N.Y.) U., 1958; postgrad., NYU. With Coopers & Lybrand, N.Y.C., 1958-64; treas., chief fin. officer and sr. v.p. Anchor Group, Elizabeth, N.J., 1964-79; treas., sr. v.p. also Anchor Capital Fund, Anchor Daily Income Fund, Inc., Anchor Growth Fund, Inc., Anchor Income Fund, Inc., Anchor Spectrum Fund, Inc., Fundamental Investors, Inc., Westminster Fund, Washington Nat. Fund, Inc., Anchor Pension Mgmt. Co.; sr. v.p. corp. devel. USLIFE Corp., N.Y.C., 1979-82, exec. v.p.; chief operating officer, 1982-86; pres., chief exec. officer, dir. USLIFE Equity Sales Corp, 1985-86; exec. v.p. Pacific Mut. Life Ins. Co., Newport Beach, Calif., 1986-92; chmn., CEO, bd. dirs. Pacific Equities Network, Newport Beach, Calif., 1992-93; chmn., CEO Resource Network, San Juan Capistrano, 1993—; bd. dirs. Mut. Svc. Corp., United Planners Group, So. Calif. Entrepreneurship Acad. Commr. econ. devel., City of Dana Point, Calif. With U.S. Army, 1958-60. Home: 34300 Lantern Bay Dr Villa 69 Dana Point CA 92629

KESSELHEIM, A. DONN, environmental education educator; b. Billings, Mont., June 2, 1927; s. Bernhard and Bernice (Allen) K.; m. Chelsea Robbins, June 22, 1949; children: Alan Stanton, Craig, Ann Noel. BA in Econs., Stanford U., 1948; MA in Social Studies and History, U. Northern Colo., Greeley, 1951; EdD in Ednl. Adminstrn., Harvard, 1964. Assoc. dir., head sci. dept. Tarsus Coll., Tarsus, Turkey, 1952-57; physics tchr. Newton High Sch., Newtonville, Mass., 1957-59, housemaster, 1959-61; tchr. Newton Pub. Schs., Newton, Mass., 1957-61; prin. New Trier Twp. High Sch., 1963-65; with New Trier Twp. Pub. Schs., Winnetka, Ill., 1963-68; prin. New Trier High Sch. West, 1965-68; corp. planner Gen. Learning Corp., N.Y.C., 1967-68; coord. tng. Nat. Alliance of Businessmen, Gen. Learning Corp, Chgo., 1968; prof. Sch. Edn. U. Mass., Amherst, Mass., 1970-74; dep. supr. El Paso County Sch. Dist. 11, Colorado Springs, Colo., 1974-76; staff dir. Colo. Mt. Trail Found., Englewood, Colo., 1976-77; acting prin. Tarsus Am. Sch., Tarsus, Turkey, 1978-79; headmaster Woodstock Sch., Mussoorie, India, 1979-81, Robert Coll., Turkey, 1982-84; sr. cons. Turkey Devel. Found., Ankara, Turkey, 1984-85; dir edn. Wyoming Outdoor Coun., Lander, Wyo., 1985-94, Wyo. Riparian Assn., 1995—; dir. Antelope Retreat Ctr., Savery, Wyo., 1993—. Contbr. to profl. jours. Apptd. mem. United Ch. Bd. World Ministries, N.Y.C., 1952-81. With U.S. Navy, 1945-46. Mem. Phi Beta Kappa (delegate pres. 1992-94). Democratc. Mem. Soc. of Friends. Home and Office: 22 Pheasant Run Dr Lander WY 82520-9783

KESSLER, LILLIAN BERMAN, health facility administrator, retired; b. Phila., Dec. 28, 1925; d. Benjamin and Eva (Weissman) Berman; children: David Alan, Karen Allane, Diane Carol, Cheryl Beth. Diploma, Jewish Hosp. Sch. Nursing, 1948; BS, U. Redlands, 1984. RN, Calif. Staff nurse pediatrics Children's Hosp., Phila.; med./surg. staff nurse relief supr., charge nurse Kaiser Hosp., Panorama City, Calif.; admitting nurse coord. Sherman Oaks (Calif.) Hosp.; evening supr. Cigna Hosp. L.A.; ret. Cadet U.S. Nurses Corp., 1945-48. Home: 11926 Chandler Blvd Apt 1 Valley Vlg CA 91607-2124

KESSLER, LYNN ELIZABETH, state legislator; b. Seattle, Feb. 26, 1941; d. John Mathew and Kathryn (Berry) Eisen; m. Keith L. Kessler, Dec. 24, 1980; children: William John Moore, Christopher Scott Moore, Bradley Jerome Moore, Jamie. Attended, Seattle U., 1958-59. Mem. Wash. Ho. of Reps., 1993—, mem. health care, energy and utilities, fin. instns. and ins. coms. Exec. dir. United Way Grays Harbor, 1984-92; mem. adv. coun. Head Start, 1986-89, Cervical Cancer Awareness Task Force, 1990-91, vocat. adv. coun. Hoquiam High Sch., 1991—, strategic planning com. Grays Harbor Community Hosp., 1991-92, Grays Harbor Food Bank Com., 1991-92, Grays Harbor Dem. Ctrl. Com.; vice-chair Grays Harbor County Shorelines Mgmt. Bd., 1988-90; chair Disability Awareness Com., 1988-90, Youth 2000 Com., 1990-91; pres. Teenage Pregnancy, Parenting and Prevention Adv. Coun., 1989-91; v.p. Grays Harbor Econ. Devel. Coun., 1990-92; trustee Grays Harbor Coll., 1991—, Aberdeen YMCA, 1991—. Mem. Aberdeen Rotary (pres. 1993-94). Home: 62 Kessler Ln Hoquiam WA 98550-9742 Office: Wash State Legislature John L O'Brien Bldg Rm 318 Olympia WA 98504

KESSLER, MELODY SHERYL, information systems professional; b. Flushing, N.Y., Aug. 17, 1968; d. Melvin Lewis and Susan Penny (Linke) K. BSBA, U. Ariz., 1990. Infosystems engring. analyst Motorola, Inc., Tempe, Ariz., 1990—. Mem. Tempe Sister City Orgn., 1985—; pres., CEO Gamma Psi Corp.; alumni advisor Sigma Delta Tau, 1992—. Home: 631 E Manhatton Dr Tempe AZ 85282-5358

KESSLER, PETER BERNARD, computer scientist, researcher; b. N.Y.C., Apr. 5, 1952; s. Richard Howard and Marian Judith (Singer) K.; m. Monica Elaine McHenney, Dec. 27, 1984; children: Jacob Mitchell, Samuel Morris, Ryan Michael. BS, Yale Coll., 1973; MS, U. Calif., Berkeley, 1980, PhD, 1984. Mem. rsch. staff Xerox Palo Alto (Calif.) Rsch. Ctr., 1985-90; staff engr. Sun Microsystems Labs., Inc., Mountain View, Calif., 1990-94; sr. staff engr. Sun Soft, Mountain View, 1994—. Reviewer various confs. and jours.; contbr. articles to profl. jours. Judge paper airplanes Palo Alto Jr. Mus., 1990-94. Mem. IEEE, Assn. for Computing Machinery, Computer Profls. for Social Responsibility. Office: Sun Soft Inc 2550 Garcia Ave Mountain View CA 94043-1109

KESSLER, ROBERT ALLEN, data processing executive; b. N.Y.C., Feb. 2, 1940; s. Henry and Caroline Catherine (Axinger) K.; m. Marie Therese Anton, Mar. 17, 1967; children: Susanne, Mark. BA in Math., CUNY, 1961; postgrad., UCLA, 1963-64. EDP analyst Boeing Aircraft, Seattle, 1961-62; computer specialist System Devel. Corp., Santa Monica, Calif., 1962-66; mem. tech. staff Computer Scis. Corp., El Segundo, Calif., 1966-67, sr. mem. tech. staff, 1971-72, computer scientist, 1974-81; systems mgr. Xerox Data Systems, L.A., 1967-71; prin. scientist Digital Resources, Algiers, Algeria, 1972-74; sr. systems cons. Atlantic Richfield, L.A., 1981-94; computer cons., 1994—. Mem. Big. Bros. L.A., 1962-66; precinct capt. Goldwater for Pres., Santa Monica, 1964; mem. L.A. Conservacy, 1987. Mem. Assn. Computing Machinery. Home: 6138 W 75th Pl Los Angeles CA 90045-1634 Office: ARCO 515 S Flower St Los Angeles CA 90071-2201

KESSLER-HODGSON, LEE GWENDOLYN, actress, corporate executive; b. Wellsville, N.Y., Jan. 16, 1947; d. James Hewitt and Reba Gwendolyn (Adsit) Kessler; m. Bruce Gridley, June 22, 1969 (div. Dec. 1979); m. Jeffrey Craig Hodgson, Oct. 31, 1987. BA, Grove City Coll., 1968; MA, U. Wis., 1969. Prof. Sangamon State U., Springfield, Ill., 1969-70; pers. exec. Bullock's, L.A., 1971-74; owner Brunnen Enterprises, L.A., 1982—. Author: A Child of Arthur, 1981; producer, writer play including Anais Nin: The Paris Years, 1986; actress appearing in TV movies, mini-series including Roots, 1978, Backstairs at The White House, 1979, Blind Ambition, 1980, Hill Street Blues, 1984-87, Murder By Reason of Insanity, 1985, Hoover, 1986, Creator, 1987, Our House, 1988, Favorite Son, 1988, Lou Grant 1983, 84, Barney Miller, 1979, L.A. Law, 1990, Hunter, 1991, (screenplay) Settlers Way, 1988; recurring role TV series Matlock, L.A. Law, numerous others. Knapp Prize fellow U. Wis., 1969. Mem. AFTRA, SAG, Actors Equity Assn. Republican. Mem. Ch. Scientology. Home: 5629 Terrace Dr La Crescenta CA 91214-1548

KESTEN, PHILIP REED, physicist; b. N.Y.C., June 24, 1956; s. Seymour Ronald and Rose Edith (Posner) K.; m. Kathleen O'Shea, June 22, 1986; 1 child, Samuel O'Shea. BS in Physics, MIT, 1978; MS in Physics, U. Mich., 1980, PhD in Physics, 1985. Postdoctoral fellow Brandeis U., Waltham, Mass., 1985-88, lectr. physics, 1989-90; asst. prof. physics Santa Clara (Calif.) U., 1990—; cons. Pyramid Tech. Cons., Inc., Waltham, 1985-86. Contbr. articles to profl. jours. Mem. Am. Phys. Soc., Nat. Coun. on Undergrad. Rsch., Sigma Xi, Sigma Pi Sigma. Office: Santa Clara U Physics Dept Santa Clara CA 95053

KETCHEL, STEVEN J., internist; b. Cleve., May 5, 1946; s. Bertram J. and Ruth Sydney (Kavanau) K.; m. Marta Lee Fingado, May 29, 1972; children: Aron, Alana. AB, Stanford U., 1967; MD, U. Ariz., 1972. Diplomate Am. Bd. Internal Medicine. Intern and resident in internal medicine U. Ariz. Affiliated Hosps., Tucson, 1972-75; fellow in med. oncology M.D. Anderson Hosp., Houston, 1975-77; pvt. practice, Tucson, 1977—; trustee El Dorado Hosp., Tucson, 1992—, chief staff, 1993—. Bd. dirs. Pima County unit Am. Cancer Soc., Tucson, 1990—, vice chmn. 1994—. Fellow ACP; mem. AMA, Am. Soc. Internal Medicine, Am. Soc. Clin. Oncology. Office: Hematology-Oncology Physicians PC 2625 N Craycroft Ste 200 Tucson AZ 85712

KETCHUM, MILO SMITH, civil engineer; b. Denver, Mar. 8, 1910; s. Milo Smith and Esther (Beatty) K.; m. Gretchen Allenbach, Feb. 28, 1944 (dec. Dec. 21, 1990); children: David Milo, Marcia Anne, Matthew Phillip. B.S., U. Ill., 1931, M.S., 1932; D.Sc. (hon.), U. Colo., 1976. Asst. prof. Case Sch. Applied Sci., Cleve., 1937-44; engr. F.G. Browne, Marion, Ohio, 1944-45; owner, operator Milo S. Ketchum, Cons. Engrs., Denver, 1945-52; partner, prin. Ketchum, Konkel, Barrett, Nickel & Austin, Cons. Engrs. and predecessor firm, Denver, 1952—; prof. civil engring. U. Conn., Storrs, 1967-78; emeritus U. Conn., 1978—; mem. Progressive Architecture Design Awards Jury, 1958, Am. Inst. Steel Constrn. Design Awards Jury, 1975, James F. Lincoln Arc Welding Found. Design Awards Jury, 1977; Stanton Walker lectr. U. Md., 1966. Author: Handbook of Standard Structural Details for Buildings, 1956; editor-in-chief Structural Engineering Practice, 1981-84; contbr. engring. articles to tech. mags. and jours. Recipient Disting. Alumnus award U. Ill., 1979. Mem. Am. Concrete Inst. (hon., bd. dirs., Turner medal 1966), ASCE (hon., pres. Colo. sect.), Am. Cons. Engrs. Coun., Nat. Acad. Engring., Am. Engring. Edn., Internat. Assn. Shell and Space Structures, Structural Engrs. Assn. Colo. (pres.), Cons. Engrs. Coun. Colo. (pres.), Sigma Xi, Tau Beta Pi, Chi Epsilon, Phi Kappa Phi, Alpha Delta Phi.

KETCHUM, RHONDA J., hospital administrator; b. Beaumont, Tex., Nov. 14, 1954; children: Scott Webb, Traci Webb, Travis Ketchum. BSN, U. Tex. Health Sci. Ctr., 1978; MSN, U. Nev., Reno, 1988. Staff nurse neonatal ICU Jeff Davis Hosp., Houston, 1978; staff, charge nurse NB nursery St. Elizabeth Hosp., Beaumont, Tex., 1979-80; staff, charge nurse med.-surg. Beaumont (Tex.) Hosp., 1980; head nurse substance abuse Bapt. Hosp., Beaumont, 1980-81; nurse mgr. urology, nephrology Washoe Med. Ctr., Reno, 1981-87; staff nurse labor and delivery Washoe Med. Ctr., 1987-88; DON Senatobia (Miss.) Community Hosp., 1988-89; DON maternal-child, med.-surg. Good Shepherd Med. Ctr., Longview, Tex., 1989-93; v.p. patient care svcs. Meml. Med. Ctr., Las Cruces, N.Mex., 1993—. Mem. Am. Coll. Healthcare Execs., N.Mex. Nurses Assn., Assn. Women's Health, Obstetric, and Neonatal Nurses, N.Mex. Orgn. Nurse Execs. (bd. dirs.), Rotary Club (Las Cruces chpt.). Office: Meml Med Ctr Las Cruces NM 88011

KETCHUM, ROBERT GEORGE, college administrator; b. Spokane, Wash., Feb. 21, 1951; s. Robert Harris and Mary Catherine (Bach) K.; m. Heather Dawn Matheson, Feb. 17, 1985; 1 child, Tiernan Robert. BA, Ea. Wash. U., 1973, MEd, 1976; PhD in Edn., Wash. State U., 1985; postgrad., Maharishi European Rsch. U., 1976-77. Indsl. arts tchr. Sandy (Oreg.) Elem. Schs., 1973-75; instr. indsl. tech. dept. Ea. Wash. U., Cheney, 1977-78; dir. Spokane office Am. Fedn. for Sci. of Creative Intelligence, 1978-80; instr. tech. tng. program Maharishi Internat. U., Fairfield, Iowa, 1980-81, dir. tech. tng. program, 1981-82, dir. tech. tng. programs, asst. prof. tech. tng., 1985-90; assoc. dean instrn., workforce tng. and cmty. edn. North Idaho Coll., Coeur d'Alene, 1990—. Mem. ASCD, ASTD, Am. Vocat. Assn., Epsilon Pi Tau, Phi Delta Kappa. Home: 1376 Circle Dr Hayden ID 83835-9503 Office: North Idaho Coll Workforce Tng Ctr 525 W Clear Water Loop Post Falls ID 83854-9400

KETTEMBOROUGH, CLIFFORD RUSSELL, computer scientist, consultant, manager; b. Pitesti, Arges, Romania, June 8, 1953; came to U.S., 1983; s. Petre and Constanta (Dascalu) I. MS in Math., U. Bucharest, Romania, 1976; MS in Computer Sci., West Coast U., L.A., 1985; MS in Mgmt. Info. System, West Coast U., Los Angeles, 1986; PhD in Computer and Info. Sci., Pacific Western U., 1988; MBA, U. LaVerne, 1992. Lic. mathematician. Mathematician, programmer Nat. Dept. Chemistry, Bucharest, 1976-80; sr. programmer, analyst Nat. Dept. Metallurgy, Bucharest, 1980-82; sr. software engr. Xerox Corp., El Segundo, Calif., 1983-88; computer and info. scientist Jet Propulsion Lab. NASA, Pasadena, Calif., 1988-89; task mgr. Rockwell Internat., Canoga Park, Calif., 1989-91, cons., 1991-93; mgr. micro devel. Transam. Corp., L.A., 1993-95; dir. dept. devel. Maxicare Health Plans, L.A., 1995—. Contbr. articles to profl. jours. Sec. Romanian Nat. Body Bldg. Com., Bucharest, 1980-82; pres., chmn. Bucharest Mcpl. Body Bldg. Com., 1978-82. Served to lt. Romanian Army, 1978. Mem. IEEE, Assn. for Computing Machinery. Republican. Home: 6004 N Walnut Grove Ave San Gabriel CA 91775-2530

KETTER, DAVID E., lawyer; b. Ft. Benning, Ga., Jan. 1, 1945; s. Victor Eugene and Ruth Maxine (Ratekin) K. BA, Augustana Coll., Rock Island, Ill., 1967; MA, U. Ill., 1968; JD, Georgetown U., 1975. Bar: Iowa 1975, Ill. 1975, U.S. Dist. Ct. (so. dist.) Ill. 1975, U.S. Ct. Appeals (7th cir.) 1975, Wash. 1977, U.S. Dist. Ct. (we. dist.) Wash. 1978, U.S. Tax Ct. 1978, U.S. Ct. Appeals (9th cir.) 1978. Assoc. Klockau, McCarthy, Lousberg, Ellison & Rinden, Rock Island, 1975-77, Law Offices of W.V. Clodfelter, Seattle, 1977-78; pvt. practice Seattle, 1979-83; ptnr. Simburg, Ketter, Sheppard & Purdy, Seattle, 1984—; pres. Harper Farms, Inc., Seattle, 1979—. Trustee Fulghum Found., Seattle, 1990—; trustee New City Theatre, Seattle, 1978-93; pres. Sidney Fund, Seattle, 1979—. Mem. ABA, Ill. Bar Assn., Wash. Bar Assn., Seattle/King County Bar Assn., Omicron Delta Kappa. Office: Simburg Ketter Sheppard & Purdy 999 3rd Ave Ste 2525 Seattle WA 98104-4001

KETTERING, JAMES DAVID, microbiologist; b. Pekin, Ill., Mar. 27, 1942; s. Floyd Ransum and Elizabeth (McLyea) K.; m. Betty Jane Stevens, June 9, 1963; children: Brian Dean, Pamela Sue, David Eric. BA, Andrews U., 1964; MS, Loma Linda U., 1968, PhD, 1974. Microbiologist Indsl. Bio-Test Corp., Northbrook, Ill., 1964-66; instr. Loma Linda (Calif.) U., 1968-74, asst. prof., 1974-80, assoc. prof., 1980-89, prof. microbiolgy, 1989—; postdoctoral fellow Calif. Dept. Health, Berkeley, 1975-77; cons. Loma Linda U. Med. Ctr., 1984—. Author textbooks; contbr. articles to med. jours. Mem. Am. Soc. Microbiology, Am. Soc. Virology, Infectious Diseases Soc., Am. Assn. Dental Schs., Am. Assn. Dental Rsch., Sigma Xi, Omicron Kappa Epsilon. Republican. Seventh-day Adventist. Home: 11980 Canary Ct Grand Terrace CA 92313-5317 Office: Loma Linda Univ Dept Microbiology Loma Linda CA 92350

KEUTZER, KURT WILLIAM, computer scientist, researcher; b. Indpls., Nov. 9, 1955; s. William Dale and Mary Helen (Allgood) K. BS, Maharishi Internat., 1978; MS, Ind. U., 1981, PhD, 1984. Assoc. programmer analyst Computer Scis. Corp., Houston, 1978-79; rsch. assoc. Ind. U., Bloomington, 1979-83; asst. prof. Purdue U., Indpls., 1983-84; mem. tech. staff UNIX langs. dept. AT&T Bell Labs., Summit, N.J., 1984-85; mem. tech. staff Computing Sys. Rsch. Lab. AT&T Bell Labs., Murray Hill, N.J., 1985-91; sr. rsch. staff Synopsys, Inc., Mountain View, Calif., 1991-92, mgr. Advanced Tech. Group, 1992-93, dir. rsch., 1993—; chief scientist Advanced Tech. Group, 1994—; instr. computer architecture Purdue U., Indpls., 1984, instr. software engring., 1984; instr. data structures Fairleigh Dickenson U., Madison, N.J., 1984, instr. programming langs., 1985, instr. algorithms and data structures, 1986; instr. logic synthesis and optimization for VLSI Columbia U., N.Y.C., 1988; mem. numerous panels, confs. and tutorials. Co-author: Algorithms and Techniques for VLSI Synthesis, 1989, Logic Synthesis, 1994; assoc. editor IEEE Transaction on Computer-Aided Design, 1989—; mem. editl. bd. Formal Methods in System Design, 1990—, Integration, 1992—; mem. adv. bd. Bowker's CAD/CAM Abstracts, 1990—; contbr. articles to profl. jours. Mem. IEEE (sr., Best Paper award Internat. Conf. on Computer Design 1992), Assn. Computer Machinery (Best Paper award 1990, 91), Tibet Soc. Office: Synopsys Inc 700 E Middlefield Rd Mountain View CA 94043-4024

KEVANE, RAYMOND A., career consultant, management consultant; b. Rembrandt, Iowa, Dec. 18, 1928; s. Michael and Sarah A. (Distel) K.; m. Lillian A. Schiltz, July 26, 1972; children: Karen, Mark, Mary. B.A., Loras Coll., Dubuque, Iowa, 1950; S.T.L., Gregorian U., Rome, 1954; Doctorate, Lateran U., Rome, 1957. Adminstr. social programs and assistance to disadvantaged projects, 1957-71; chief cons., assoc. dir. J. Frederick Marcy & Assocs., Portland, Oreg., 1972-78; pres., chief cons. R.A. Kevane & Assocs., Inc., Portland and Seattle, 1978-91; pres., CEO R.A. Kerane & Assoc., Seattle, 1990—; founder, creator The Self Directed Career. Served to capt. Army N.G., 1959-61. Mem. Am. Counselling Assn., Seattle C. of C., Nat. Career Devel. Assn.Club: City (Portland). Author: Career Development Manual, 1979, Business Procedure Manual, 1982, Employment Power: Take Control of Your Career, 1994, Career Consultants Manual, 1995. Office: 801 2d Ave Ste 211 Seattle WA 98104

KEVLES, DANIEL JEROME, history educator, writer; b. Phila., Mar. 2, 1939; s. David and Anne (Rothstein) K.; m. Bettyann Holtzmann, May 18, 1961; children: Beth Carolyn, Jonathan David. BA in Physics, Princeton U., 1960; postgrad., Oxford U., 1960-61; PhD in History, Princeton U., 1964. From asst. to full prof. of history Calif. Inst. Tech., Pasadena, 1964-86, Koepfli prof. humanities, 1986—, head program in sci., ethics, and pub. policy, 1987—; vis. rsch. fellow U. Sussex, Brighton, Eng., 1976; vis. prof. U. Pa., Phila., 1979; dir. studies Ecole des Hautes Etudes en Sciences Sociales, Paris, 1991; chmn. of faculty, Calif. Inst. Tech., Pasadena, 1995—. Author: The Physicists, 1978 (Nat. Hist. Soc. prize 1979), In the Name of Eugenics, 1985; (mag. series) Annals of Eugenics (Page One award 1985); co-editor: The Code of Codes, 1992; contbr. articles to The New Yorker, N.Y. Rev. Books, other mags. Charles Warren fellow Harvard U., 1981-82, Ctr. for Advanced Study Behavorial Scis. fellow, 1986-87, Nat. Endowment for Humanities sr. fellow, 1981-82, Guggenheim fellow, 1983. Fellow AAAS (chmn. sect. L 1983-85); mem. PEN, Author's Guild, Am. Acad. Arts and Scis., Orgn. Am. Historians, Am. Hist. Assn., History Sci. Soc. (coun 1980-82, com. publ. 1984-88, Srton lectr. 1985), Princeton Club (N.Y.C.), Century Assn., Phi Beta Kappa. Democrat. Office: Calif Inst Tech 1201 E California Blvd Pasadena CA 91125-0001

KEY, JACK DAYTON, librarian; b. Enid, Okla., Feb. 24, 1934; s. Ernest Dayton and Janie (Haldeman) K.; m. Virgie Ruth Richardson, Aug. 12, 1956; children—Toni, Scot, Todd. B.A., Phillips U., Enid, Okla., 1958; M.A., U. N.Mex., 1960; M.S., U. Ill., 1962. Staff supr. Grad. Library U. Ill., 1960-62; pharmacy librarian U. Iowa, 1962-64; med. librarian Lovelace Found. for Med. Edn. and Research, Albuquerque, 1965-70; dir. Mayo Med. Ctr. Librs., Rochester, Minn., 1970-94, dir. emeritus, 1994—; prof. emeritus biomed. comm. Mayo Med. Sch.; cons. in field; participant Naval War Coll. Conf., 1979; Alberta A. Brown lectr. Western Mich. U., 1979. Author: The Origin of the Vaccine Inoculation by Edward Jenner, 1977, William Alexander Hammond (1828-1900), 1979; editor: Library Automation: The Orient and South Pacific, 1975, Automated Activities in Health Sciences Libraries, 1975-78, Classics and Other Selected Readings in Medical Librarianship, 1980, Journal of a Quest for the Elusive Doctor Arthur Conan Doyle, 1982, Medical Vanities, 1982, William A. Hammond, M.D., 1828-1900: The Publications of an American Neurologist, 1983, Classics in Cardiology, Vol. 3, 1983, Vol. 4, 1989, Medical Casebook of Dr. Arthur Conan Doyle from Practitioner to Sherlock Holmes and Beyond, 1984, Medicine, Literature and Eponyms: An Encyclopedia of Medical Eponyms Derived from Literary Characters, 1989, Conan Doyle's Tales of Medical Humanism and Values, 1992; contbr. articles to profl. jours. Served with USN, 1952-55. U. N.Mex. fellow, 1958-59; N.Mex. Library Assn. Marion Dorroh Meml. scholar, 1960; Rotary Paul Harris fellow, 1979; recipient Outstanding Hist. Writing award Minn. Medicine, 1980; decorated knight Icelandic Order of Falcon. Mem. Med. Library Assn., Am. Inst. History Pharmacy, Am. Assn. History Medicine, Am. Med. Writers Assn., Am. Osler Soc., Mystery Writers of Am., Alcuin Soc., Ampersand Club, Sigma Xi (cert. of recognition 1982). Mem. Christian Ch. (Disciples of Christ). Home: PO Box 231 54 Skyline Dr Sandia Park NM 87047 Office: Mayo Clinic Rochester MN 55905

KEY, MARY RITCHIE (MRS. AUDLEY E. PATTON), linguist, author, educator; b. San Diego, Mar. 19, 1924; d. George Lawrence and Iris (Lyons) Ritchie; children: Mary Helen Key Ellis, Harold Hayden Key (dec.), Thomas George Key. Student, U. Chgo., summer 1954, U. Mich., 1959; M.A., U. Tex., 1960, Ph.D., 1963; postgrad., UCLA, 1966. Asst. prof. linguistics Chapman Coll., Orange, Calif., 1963-66; asst. prof. linguistics U. Calif., Irvine, 1966-71; assoc. prof. U. Calif., 1971-78, prof., 1978—, chmn. program linguistics, 1969-71, 75-77, 87—; cons. Am. Indian langs., Spanish, in Mexico, 1946-55, S.Am., 1955-62, English dialects, 1968-74, Easter Island, 1975, Calif. Dept. Edn., 1966, 70-75, Center Applied Linguistics, Washington, 1967, 69; lectr. in field. Author: Comparative Tacanan Phonology, 1968, Male/Female Language, 1975, Paralanguage and Kinesics, 1975, Nonverbal Communication, 1977, The Grouping of South American Indian Languages, 1979, The Relationship of Verbal and Nonverbal Communication, 1980, Catherine the Great's Linguistic Contribution, 1980, Polynesian and American Linguistic Connections, 1984, Comparative Linguistics of South American Indian Languages, 1987, General and Amerindian Ethnolinguistics, 1989, Language Change in South American Indian Languages, 1991; founder, editor: newsletter Nonverbal Components of Communication, 1972-76; mem. editoral bd. Forum Linguisticum, 1976—, Lang. Scis., 1978—, La Linguistique, 1979—, Multilingua, 1987—; contbr. articles to profl. jours. Recipient Friends of Libr. Book award, 1976, hon. mention, Rolex awards for Enterprise, project Computerizing the Languages of the World, 1990; U. Calif. Regent's grantee, 1974, Fulbright-Hays grantee, 1975; faculty rsch. fellow, 1984-85. Mem. Linguistic Soc. Am., Am. Dialect Soc. (exec. council; regional sec. 1974-83), Internat. Reading Assn. (dir. 1968-72), Delta Kappa Gamma (local pres. 1974-76). Office: U Calif-Irvine Dept Of Linguistics Irvine CA 92717

KEYSTON, STEPHANI ANN, small business owner; b. Baytown, Tex., Aug. 6, 1955; d. Herbert Howard and Janice Faye (Stowe) Cruickshank; m. George Keyston III, Oct. 8, 1983; children: Jeremy George, Kristopher Samuel. AA with honors, Merced Coll., Merced, Calif., 1975; BA in Journalism with distinction, San Jose State U., 1976. Reporter, Fresno (Calif.) Bee, 1974-75; reporter, photographer Merced (Calif.) Sun-Star, 1974-77; pub. info. officer Fresno City Coll. (Calif.), 1977-80; dir. communications Aerojet Tactical Systems Co., Sacramento, 1980-83; co-owner, v.p. Keyco Landscape Contractor Inc., Auburn, Calif., 1984—. Co.-coordinator Aerojet United Way Campaign, 1981; Aerojet Tactical Systems Co. coordinator West Coast Nat. Derby Rallies, 1981-83; co-founder, pres. Calif. Lion Awareness. Mem. Internat. Assn. Bus. Communicators (dir. Sacramento chpt. 1983), Citrus Heights C. of C. (v.p. 1983). Republican. Home: 13399

Lakeview Pl Auburn CA 95602-8920 Office: Keyco Landscape Contractor Inc 3350 Swetzer Rd Loomis CA 95650

KEYT, DAVID, philosophy and classics educator; b. Indpls., Feb. 22, 1930; s. Herbert Coe and Hazel Marguerite (Sissman) K.; m. Christine Harwood Mullikin, June 25, 1975; children by previous marriage: Sarah, Aaron. A.B., Kenyon Coll., 1951; M.A., Cornell U., 1953, Ph.D., 1955. Instr. dept. philosophy U. Wash., 1957-60, asst. prof., 1960-64, assoc. prof., 1964-69, prof., 1969—, adj. prof. classics, 1977-79, acting chmn. dept. philosophy, 1967-68, 70, 86, winter, spring, 94, chmn. dept. philosophy, 1971-78; vis. asst. prof. dept. philosophy UCLA, 1962-63; vis. assoc. prof. Cornell U., 1968-69; vis. prof. U. Hong Kong, autumn 1987, Princeton U., autumn 1988, U. Calif., Irvine, autumn 1990. Co-editor: (with Fred D. Miller Jr.) A Companion to Aristotle's Politics, 1991; contbr. articles in field to profl. jours. Served with U.S. Army, 1955-57. Inst. for Research in the Humanities fellow U. Wis., 1966-67; Ctr. for Hellenic Studies fellow, 1974-75; Inst. for Advanced Study mem., 1983-84. Mem. Am. Philos. Assn., Soc. Ancient Greek Philosophy. Home: 12032 36th Ave NE Seattle WA 98125-5637 Office: U Wash Dept Philosophy Seattle WA 98195

KHAN, AHMED MOHIUDDIN, finance, insurance executive; b. Hyderabad, Andhra Pradesh, India, Nov. 14, 1955; s. Mohammad Mominuddin and Mehar-Unnisa Begum Hyderabad; m. Marjorie L. Klein-Khan, Mar. 31, 1983; 1 child, Yosuf F. MBA, U. Palm Beach, 1975; doctoral studies, Calif. Coast U. Inventory auditor RGIS, Inc., Chgo., 1975-78; staff acct. Sommerset, Inc., Chgo., 1979-84; fin. cons. Provident Mutual Fin. Svc., Inc., Phoenix, 1985-91; regional mgr. fin. svcs. US Life/Old Line Life Ins. Co. of Am., Phoenix, 1992—; pres. Khan and Assocs., Fin./Ins. Svcs., Phoenix, 1993—. Named to Execs. Hall of Fame, 1991. Mem. India Assn., U.S.A., Assn. MBA Execs., Nat. Assn. Life Underwriters, Ariz. Assn. Life Underwriters, Millon Dollar Round Table. Democrat. Islam. Home and Office: 4643 E Grandview Rd Phoenix AZ 85032-3416

KHAN, SARBULAND BILL, inventor, entrepreneur, consultant; b. Zanzibar, E. Africa, Apr. 11, 1951; came to U.S., 1984; s. Gulkhan Yusufzai and Sarfiraz (Abdulhakim) Awan; m. Stella Conner, May 12, 1979 (div. Nov. 1989); 1 child, Zenobia. Cert. telecommunications, Garrettsgreen Tech. Coll., Birmingham, Eng., 1969; cert. advanced level physics, Handsworth Tech. Coll., Birmingham, 1973. Telecommunications technician G.P.O. (name now Brit. Telecom), W. Midlands, Eng., 1968-71; sr. instr., co-owner Aston Martial Arts Centre, Birmingham, 1972-75; exec. dir. Dianetics & Scientology Centre, Birmingham, 1976-82, Am. Sun Solar, Inc., Redondo Beach, Calif., 1984-86; Hubbard adminstrv. tech. instr., supr. Singer Consultants, Beverly Hills, Calif., 1985-86; bus. cons., supr. W.I.S.E. Corp., L.A., 1986-88; pvt. practice rsch., discovery and mktg. L.A., 1987—. Author: How to Invent and Get Rich; patentee disposable diaper, biodegradable plastic, soft drink, tools and accesssories. Dancer Ballroom and Latin Am. Gold Medalist, 1970-71. Mem. Internat. Platform Assn., Planetary Soc., Children Internat., Millionaires Club of Hollywood (founder, chmn.). Home and Office: 8544 Burton Way # 307 Los Angeles CA 90048

KHAN, SHAHEER HASAN, chemist, research scientist; b. Shahjahanpur, India, Oct. 15, 1960; came to U.S., 1986; s. Shabbir Hasan and Moina Khan; m. Humaria Bano, Dec. 5, 1988; children: Muneeb H., Umme-Hani. BSc with honors, AMU, Aligarh, India, 1979, MSc, 1981; MSc, Brock U., St. Catharines, Ont., Can., 1985; PhD, SUNY, Buffalo, 1990. Rsch. asst. Brock U., St. Catharines, 1983-85; predoctoral rsch. fellow Roswell Park Cancer Inst., Buffalo, 1986-90, postdoctoral rsch. fellow, 1990-91; postdoctoral rsch. fellow U. Alta., Edmonton, Alta., Can., 1991-92; assoc. scientist applied biosys. divsn. Perkin-Elmer, Foster City, Calif., 1992—; lectr. SUNY, Buffalo, 1988-90. Contbr. numerous articles to profl. jours. Recipient Genzyme award Soc. for Complex Carbohydrates, 1990; Alta. Heritage Found. fellow for med. rsch., 1991. Mem. Am. Soc. for Glycobiology, Am. Chem. Soc. Office: Perkin-Elmer Applied Biosys Divsn 850 Lincoln Centre Dr Foster City CA 94404-1128

KHANDEKAR, SHEKHAR DINKAR, electrical engineer; b. Indore, India, Aug. 28, 1956; came to U.S., 1982; s. Dinkar N. and Sulochana D. (Dhavale) K.; m. Sandhya C. Bhave, July 22, 1982; children: Kunal, Kavita. BSEE, U. Indore, India, 1979; MSEE, Northwestern U., 1984. Electronics engr. Naidunia, Indore, 1980-81, Indian Express, Bombay, 1981-82; failure analysis engr. Tex. Instruments, Houston and Dallas, 1984-88; sr. component engr. Allen Bradley Co., Milw., 1988; mgr. device analysis Compaq Computer Corp., Houston, 1988-93; mgr. reliability assurance Level One Comms., Sacramento, 1993—. Author: Failure Analysis Handbook, 1993; author conf. papers. Mem. organizing com. Houston Marathi Mandal, 1985-86. Mem. IEEE (mem. tech. com. IRPS 1992—, chair tech. subcom. 1995), ASM Internat. (organizing com. internat. symposium on test and failure analysis 1990—). Democrat. Hindu. Office: Level One Comm 9750 Goethe Rd Sacramento CA 95827-3500

KHANJIAN, ARA, economics educator; b. Beirut, Lebanon, Apr. 2, 1956; came to U.S., 1976; BA in Econs., U. British Columbia, 1981; MA in Econs., Queen's U., 1982; PhD in Econs., The New Sch. for Social Rsch., N.Y.C., 1989. Econ. instr. St. John's U., N.Y.C., 1984-85, N.Y.U., 1985-88; prof. econs. Ventura (Calif.) Coll., 1989—; econ. instr. Hofstra U., Hempstead, N.Y., 1986-87; prof. econs. L.A. Harbor Coll., 1989; cons., researcher The Econ. Inst. of Ministry of Economy, Yerevan, Armenia, 1991. Rsch. fellow Govt. Can., 1981. Mem. Am. Econ. Assn., Assn. for Comparative Econ. Studies. Office: Ventura Coll 4667 Telegraph Rd Ventura CA 93003

KHASIMUDDIN, SYED, entomologist; b. Hyderabad, India, May 22, 1943; came to U.S., 1983; s. Taher Mohammad and Sardar (Begum) S.; m. Azher Ayesha Omar, Aug. 22, 1968; children: Ahsan, Mohsin, Ameen. B in Agriculture, A.P. Agrl. U. India, 1965, M in Entomology, 1967; PhD in Entomology, U. Calif., Riverside, 1972. Lectr. A.P. Agrl. U. India, Hyderabad, 1967-68; rsch. asst. U. Calif., Riverside, 1968-72; entomologist U.S. A.I.D./Rockefeller Found., Hyderabad, 1972-73; rsch. scientist Internat. Ctr. Insect Physiology & Ecology, Nairobi, Kenya, 1973-80; entomologist Tobacco Rsch. Bd., Harare, Zimbabwe, 1982-83; project coord. Wash. State U., Pullman, 1985-88; environ. specialist State Water Resources Control Bd., Sacramento, Calif., 1988—. Dir. Riverside Mosque, 1986-88. Mem. Islamic Soc. Riverside (pres. 1986-88), Muslim Mosque Assn. (bd. dirs. 1993—, pres. 1991-92). Republican. Home: 2709 Albany Ave Davis CA 95616-6113

KHATAIN, KENNETH GEORGE, psychiatrist, air force officer; b. Seattle, Oct. 11, 1953; s. Edward and LaVerne Mae (Bender) K.; m. Marla Dee Morgan, Aug. 12, 1978; children: Alanna E., Larissa E. AAS, Edmonds Community Coll., Lynnwood, Wash., 1976; BS in Molecular and Cellular Biology, U. Wash., 1978; MD, Wayne State U., 1986. Diplomate Am. Bd. Psychiatry and Neurology with qualifications in geriatric psychiatry, Nat. Bd. Med. Examiners. Resident in psychiatry Wright State U., Dayton, Ohio, 1986-90; commd. capt. USAF, 1986; advanced through grades to maj., 1992; chief inpatient psychiatry mental health svcs. Wilford Hall Med. Ctr., Lackland AFB, Tex., 1990-94; chief inpatient psychiatry VA Med. Ctr., Boise, Idaho, 1994—; guest reviewer AIDS articles Hosp. and Community Psychiatry, 1988—; clin. cons. Nat. Tng. Lab. Inst., Bethel, Maine, 1989; workshop presenter, guest speaker in field. Mem. adult edn. com. Westminster Presbyn. Ch., Dayton, 1989. Recipient physician recognition award AMA, 1989, Arnold Allen outstanding resident award Wright State U., 1990. Mem. Am. Psychiat. Assn., Tex. Soc. Psychiat. Physicians, Bexar County Psychiat. Soc., Bexar County Med. Soc., Phi Beta Kappa, Phi Theta Kappa. Office: VA Med Ctr 500 W Fort St Boise ID 83702-4501

KHOO, ROBERT E.H., colon and rectal surgeon; b. Sydney, New South Wales, Australia, Nov. 21, 1956; came to the U.S., 1992; s. Anthony and Patricia (Lim) K.; m. Sheryl Ann Khoo, Oct. 9, 1982; children: Justin, Jonathan. BS, U. British Columbia, 1978; MD, U. Calgary, Can., 1981. Diplomate Am. Bd. Surgery, Am. Bd. Colon and Rectal Surgery. Staff surgeon Calgary Dist. Hosp. Group, 1987-92, Rose Med. Hosp., Denver, 1992—; asst. clin. prof. surgery U. Colo., Denver, 1994—. Contbr. articles to profl. jours. Fellow ACS, Royal Coll. Physicians and Surgeons Can., Am. Soc. Colon and Rectal Surgeons. Office: 4500 E 9th Ave Ste 530 Denver CO 80220

KHOSLA, VED MITTER, oral and maxillofacial surgeon, educator; b. Nairobi, Kenya, Jan. 13, 1926; s. Jagdish Rai and Tara V. K.; m. Santosh Ved Chabra, Oct. 11, 1952; children: Ashok M., Siddarth M. Student, U. Cambridge, 1945; L.D.S., Edinburgh Dental Hosp. and Sch., 1950, Coll. Dental Surgeons, Sask., Can., 1962. Prof. oral surgery, dir. postdoctoral studies in oral surgery Sch. Dentistry U. Calif., San Francisco, 1968—; chief oral surgery San Francisco Gen. Hosp.; lectr. oral surgery U. of Pacific, VA Hosp.; vis. cons. Fresno County Hosp. Dental Clinic.; Mem. planning com., exec. med. com. San Francisco Gen. Hosp. Contbr. articles to profl. jours. Examiner in photography and gardening Boy Scouts Am., 1971-73, Guatemala Clinic, 1972. Granted personal coat of arms by H.M. Queen Elizabeth II, 1959. Fellow Royal Coll. Surgeons (Edinburgh), Internat. Assn. Oral Surgeons, Internat. Coll. Applied Nutrition, Internat. Coll. Dentists, Royal Soc. Health, AAAS, Am. Coll. Dentists; mem. Brit. Assn. Oral Surgeons, Am. Soc. Oral Surgeons, Am. Dental Soc. Anesthesiology, Am. Acad. Dental Radiology, Omicron Kappa Upsilon. Club: Masons. Home: 1525 Lakeview Dr Burlingame CA 94010-7330 Office: U Calif Sch Dentistry Oral Surgery Div 3D Parnassus Ave San Francisco CA 94117-4342

KHOURY, KENNETH ALAN, psychiatrist; b. Oklahoma City, Okla., Oct. 23, 1944. BS maxima cum laude, Notre Dame U., 1966; MD, Yale U., 1970. Intern, resident U. Calif., San Diego, 1970-73; pvt. practice Escondido, Calif., 1973—; asst. clin. prof. psychiatry U. Calif., San Diego, 1973—; chmn. dept. psychiatry Palomar Hosp., Escondido, Calif., 1974, 78, 83, 92; med. dir. psychiat. svcs. Palomar Med. Ctr., Escondido, 1986-91; staff psychiatrist Mercy and Mesa Vista Hosps., San Diego, 1973-74, Scripps Clinic, La Jolla, Calif., 1983, Palomar Med. Ctr., Escondido, 1973—, Charter Hosp., San Diego, 1989—, Harbor View, San Diego, 1992-93, Alvarado Pky. Inst., San Diego, 1992-93, Scripps Meml. Hosp., La Jolla, 1993—; mem. steering bd. Premier Mental Health Network, 1990—; bd. dirs. IPHC; cons. Western Inst. Human Resources, San Diego, 1973-74, Palomar Med. Ctr., 1974—, Escondido Youth Encounter, 1977, Maple Manor, Arcadian Gardens, 1992—; presenter in field. Contbr. articles to profl. jours. Participant Elizabeth Hospice, Escondido, 1977-78; mem. organizing and gov. bd. Friendship Ctr., Escondido, 1977-80; mem. med. adv. bd. Alzheimer's Family Ctr., San Diego, 1988—; mem. cancer adv. com. Palomar Pomerado Health Sys., 1991-93. Recipient scholarship Yale U., 1970. Fellow Am. Psychiat. Assn. (mem. panel confs. and meetings); mem. Calif. Psychiat. Assn., San Diego Soc. Psychiat. Physicians (chmn. hosp. com. 1989-91), San Diego Med. Soc., Calif. Med. Soc., Am. Assn. Psychiat. Adminstrs. (pres. San Diego chpt. 1990-91), Alpha Epsilon Delta. Office: 125 S Grape St Escondido CA 92025-4406

KIANG, ASSUMPTA (AMY KIANG), brokerage house executive; b. Beijing, Aug. 15, 1939; came to U.S., 1962; d. Pei-yu and Yu-Jean (Liu) Chao; m. Wan-lin Kiang, Aug. 14, 1965; 1 child, Eliot Y. BA, Nat. Taiwan U., 1960; MS, Marywood Coll., Scranton, Pa., 1964; MBA, Calif. State U., Long Beach, 1977. Data programmer IBM World Trade, N.Y.C., 1963; libr. East Cleve. Pub. Libr., 1964-68; lectr. Nat. Taiwan U., Taipei, 1971-73; with reference dept. U.S. Info. Svc., Taipei, 1971-74; v.p. Merrill Lynch, Santa Ana, Calif., 1977—. Author numerous rsch. reports in field. Founder Pan Pacific Performing Arts Inc., Orange County, Calif., 1987; treas. women league Calif. State. U., Long Beach, 1980-82. Mem. Chineses Bus. Assn. Soc. Calif. (chmn. 1987—, v.p. 1986-87), U.C.I. Chancellor's Club, Old Ranch Country Club. Democrat. Roman Catholic. Office: Merrill Lynch 2670 N Main St Santa Ana CA 92701-1224

KIANG, MIN, manufacturing executive; b. Taipei, Taiwan, Sept. 25, 1964; came to U.S., 1986; s. Tao and Ho (Yang) K.; m. Pascale Delain, Sept. 4, 1987; 1 child, Chrystelle A. Kiang. B of Engring., Nat. Taipei Inst. of Tech., Taipei, 1985; MS, SUNY, Stony Brook, 1988. Rsch. scientist Vactronic Equipment, Bohemia, N.Y., 1987-89; process engr. Ratheon Semiconductor, Mountain View, Calif., 1989; program mgr. Solectron Corp., San Jose, Calif., 1989-93; sr. program mgr. Pragmatech Inc., San Jose, 1993-94; co-founder Flash Electronics, Fremont, Calif., 1994—. Office: Flash Electronics 48607 Warm Springs Blvd Fremont CA 94539

KIBBLE, EDWARD BRUCE, insurance-investment advisory company executive; b. Seattle, May 11, 1940; s. Francis Bruce and Doris Kibble; m. Carol Kibble, July 8, 1961; 3 children. BA, U. Wash., 1972. CLU. Agt. Equitable of Iowa, Seattle, 1962-72; co-founder, co-chmn. Kibble & Prentice, Inc., Seattle, 1972—; bd. dirs. Seattle Best Coffee, Kibble & Prentice/KPI-Western Ins., Seattle, Drug Emporium, Bellevue, Wash., Northwestern Trust. Contbr. articles to profl. jours. Bd. dirs. Jr. Achievement Greater Puget Sound, Seattle Pacific Found. Mem. Assn. for Advanced Life Underwriting, Nat. Assn. Life Underwriters (Seattle Life Underwriter of Yr. award), Million Dollar Round Table, Estate Planning Coun. Seattle (past pres.), Wash. Athletic Club, Columbia Tower Club, Rainier Club, Seattle Yacht Club, Rotary (bd. dirs. Seattle). Republican. Office: 600 Stewart St Ste 1000 Seattle WA 98101-1217

KIBBY, CHARLES LEONARD, chemist; b. Wenatchee, Wash., Jan. 2, 1938; s. Leonard L. and Evy K. (McAuley) K.; m. Diana Lynn Morrison, Nov. 27, 1970; 1 child, Kenneth Charles. BA, Reed Coll., 1959; PhD, Purdue U., 1964. Fellow Harvard U., Cambridge, Mass., 1963-65; research assoc. Brookhaven Nat. Lab., Upton, N.Y., 1965-67; fellow Mellon Inst., Pitts., 1967-69; research chemist Gulf Research and Devel. Co., Pitts., 1970-75, sr. research chemist, 1977-81, research assoc., 1981-85; research chemist Pitts. Energy Tech. Ctr., 1976-77; sr. research assoc. Chevron Research Co., Richmond, Calif., 1985-92, staff scientist, 1992—. Contbr. articles to profl. jours.; patentee in field. NSF fellow, 1961-62. Mem. AAAS, Pitts.-Cleve. Catalysis Soc. (pres.-elect 1984-85, sec. 1983-84), Am. Chem. Soc. (bd. dirs. Pitts. sect. 1977-80, area rep. petroleum divsn. 1991-94), Phi Lambda Upsilon. Home: 846 Clifton Ct Benicia CA 94510-3639 Office: Chevron Rsch Co 100 Chevron Way Richmond CA 94802

KIDD, MELVIN DON, banker; b. Crowell, Tex., Oct. 10, 1937; s. Ewing Wilson and Joan (Solomon) K.; m. Sarrah Dee Whitley, Feb. 1, 1957; children: Vickye L. Kidd Faulk, Joan Renai Shuller, Sarah Dion Johnson. Student, Angelo State Coll., San Angelo, Tex., 1961-63, SW Grad. Sch. Banking, Dallas, 1972. Br. mgr. Pioneer Fin. Co., San Angelo, 1957-60, Southwestern Investment Co., Amarillo, Tex., 1960-67; v.p. Bank Commerce, Abilene, Tex., 1967-70, Coronado State Bank, El Paso, Tex., 1970-72; pres., chief exec. officer Western Commerce Bank, Carlsbad, N.Mex., 1973—, chmn. bd. dirs.; sr. chmn. bd. Western Bank Las Cruces, N.Mex.; CEO Western Bank Alamogordo, N.Mex.; pres. Western Bancshares Alamogordo, Inc., Western Commerce Bancshares Carlsbad (N.Mex.) Inc., Western Bancshares Clovis (N.Mex.), Inc., Western Bancshares Las Cruces, Inc.; pres., CEO, bd. dirs. Western Bank Clovis; past chmn. Albuquerque dist. adv. coun. SBA. Past pres. Eddy County Sheriff's Posse, Eddy County United Way; past chmn. Pres.'s Assn. N.Mex. State U., Carlsbad, past pres. bd. regents; mem. N.Mex. State U. Found.; bd. dirs. Carlsbad Dept. Devel., Western States Sch. Banking; chmn. bd. trustees N.Mex. Sch. Banking; state senator dist. 34. With USMCR. Mem. N.Mex. Bankers Assn. (past pres.), Carlsbad C. of C. (past pres.). Methodist. Home: PO Box 1358 Carlsbad NM 88221-1358 Office: Western Commerce Bank 127 S Canyon St Carlsbad NM 88220-5732

KIDD, REUBEN PROCTOR, management engineer; b. Bedford, Va., Feb. 18, 1913; s. Oscar Kibbler and Estelle (Johnson) K.; B.S., Va. Poly. Inst., 1936; m. Margaret Jerome, June 23, 1952. Pres., Frito Corp. of Roanoke (Va.), 1947-49; indsl. engr. USAF, Sacramento, 1956-73; chmn. bd. USDR, Inc., Sacramento, 1961-69, MEN Internat., Inc., Mpls., 1977—; owner The Kidd Cos., operator Precision Tune-Up, Sacramento, 1974—. Served to capt. U.S. Army, 1942-46, to maj., 1949-51. Decorated Silver Star; registered profl. engr., Calif. Republican. Presbyterian. Home: 5809 Northgrove Way Citrus Heights CA 95610-6522 Office: Precision Tune-Up 6241 Spruce Ave Sacramento CA 95841-2052

KIDDE, ANDREW JUDSON, sales executive, consultant; b. N.Y.C., Nov. 6, 1948; s. Fred Judson and Ellice (Welch) K.; m. Monica Bertell (div. 1981); m. Linda Jean Olsen, Feb. 24, 1983; children: Judson F., Briana P. BA in History, Polic. Sci., Hawthorne Coll., 1971; AA in Hotel Adminstrn., LaSalle U., 1993. Banquet mgr. Sheraton Hotel, Manchester, N.H., 1967-71; asst. dir. sales Hilton Hotel Corp., N.Y.C., 1971-75; regional dir. sales Ramada Inns, Detroit, 1975-77; regional sales mgr. Westin Hotels, Inc., Detroit, 1977-79; pres. Kidde & Assocs., San Diego, 1979-82; nat. sales mgr. Las Vegas (Nev.) Hilton, 1982-85; dir. sales, mktg. Madison Hotels, Washington, 1986-89; sr. nat. sales mgr. Walt Disney Resorts, Anaheim, Calif., 1989-93; sr. sales mgr. Hilton Hotel Corp., Anaheim, Calif., 1993—. Recipient Nat. Hotel Sales award Guiness Book, 1985, 86. Mem. Greater Washington D.C. Soc. of Assn. Execs. (assoc.), Am. Soc. Assn. Execs. (assoc.), Profl. Conv. Mgmt. Assn. (assoc.). Republican. Home: 30 Charca Rcho Station Marg CA 92688-2703 Office: Hilton Hotel Corp 777 W Convention Way Anaheim CA 92802-3425

KIDDE, JOHN EDGAR, food company executive; b. Kansas City, Mo., May 4, 1946; s. Gustave E. and Mary Sloan (Orear) K.; m. Donna C. Peterson, Aug. 4, 1973; children: Kari Lauren, Laurie Catherine, Kellie Ann. BA, Stanford U., 1968; MBA, Northwestern U., 1971. Corp. banking officer First Interstate Bank, L.A., 1971-73; v.p. ops. Colony Foods, Inc., Newport Beach, Calif., 1973-78; pres. Western Host Food Svcs., Inc., Newport Beach, 1978-81, Giuliano's Delicatessen & Bakery,Inc., Carson, Calif., 1981-90; pres., chief exec. officer Sona & Hollen Foods, Inc., Los Alamitos, Calif., 1990—, bd. dirs. Mem. adv. bd. Restaurant Institutions mag., 1975-78. Bd. trustees Harbor Day Sch., 1990—; mem. alumni admissions com. Phillips Acad., 1981—. 1st lt. U.S. Army, 1969-70. Mem. Stanford Club Orange County, Stanford Buck Club. Republican. Episcopalian. Home: 3907 Inlet Isle Dr Corona Del Mar CA 92625-1605 Office: Sona & Hollen Foods Inc 3712 Cerritos Ave Los Alamitos CA 90720-2419

KIDWELL, MARGARET GALE, ecology and biology educator; b. Askham, Notts, U.K., Aug. 17, 1933; came to the U.S., 1960; d. Frederick Everleish and Ethel Mary (Lowish) Gale; m. James Frederick Kidwell, Aug. 5, 1961 (dec. Oct. 1988); children: Mary Rachel, Stela Margaret. BSc, U. Nottingham, U.K., 1953; MS, Iowa State U., 1962; PhD, Brown U., 1973. Officer Nat. Agr. Adv. Svc., London, 1955-60; Kellogg Found. fellow Iowa State U., 1960-61; assoc. in rsch. Brown U., Providence, 1966-70, rsch. fellow, 1973-74, rsch. assoc., 1974-77, asst. prof. rsch., 1977-80, assoc. prof. rsch. biology, 1980-84, prof. biology, 1984-85; prof. ecology and evolutionary biology U. Ariz., Tucson, 1985—, head dept. ecology and evolutionary biology, 1992—, Regent's prof., 1994—. Fellow AAAS, Am. Acad. Arts and Scis.; mem. Am. Genetics Assn. (coun. mem. 1986-89, pres. 1992), Am. Soc. Naturalists (v.p. 1984), Genetics Soc. Am. (bd. dirs. 1985-87), Soc. for the Study Evolution, Soc. for Molecular Biology and Evolution (pres. elect 1995), Sigma Xi.

KIEFER, ROBERT JOHN, mechanical engineer; b. Cleve., Dec. 7, 1936; s. Paul Everette and Beulah Elizabeth (Moore) K.; m. Barbara Gayle Niemiec, June 14, 1958 (div. Aug. 1981); children: Kelly Jane, Paul Joseph; m. Aura Ann Knosby, Sept. 4, 1983 (div. Dec. 1989); children: Kimberly Fenske, Kerri Fenske. BSME, MSME, Ohio State U., 1959. Registered profl. engr., mechanical, nuclear, Ohio, Calif. Project officer Air Force Weapons Lab, Albuquerque, N.Mex., 1959-62; mgr., fuel applications engring. Gen. Atomic Co., San Diego, Calif., 1962-76; mgr. tech. tng. Scientific Atlanta, San Diego, 1976-93; staff cons. Air Force Space Div., L.A., 1976-87. Contbr. articles to profl. jours. Lt. col. USAFR, 1959-87. Mem. Soc. Am. Mil. Engrs. (gold medal, 1959), Sigma Xi, Pi Tau Sigma, Tau Beta Pi, Am. Soc. Mechanical Engrs., Inst. Environ. Scis., NSPE. Republican. Baptist. Home: 10215 Saunders Dr San Diego CA 92131-1313

KIEFT, THOMAS LAMAR, biology educator; b. Feb. 6, 1951; married; 1 child. BA in Biology, Carleton Coll., 1973; MS in Biology, N.Mex. Highlands U., 1978; PhD in Biology, U. N.Mex., 1983. Lab. scientist serology dept. Scientific Lab. Div., Albuquerque, 1978-80; teaching asst. biology dept. U. N.Mex., Albuquerque, 1980-81; asst. curator microbiology collection Mus. Southwestern Biology, Dept. Biology, U. N.Mex., Albuquerque, 1981-82; asst. prof. Div. Sci. and Math., N.Mex. Highlands U., Las Vegas, 1982-83; vis. asst. rsch. microbiologist Dept. Plan and Soil Biology, U. Calif., Berkeley, 1983-85; asst. prof. dept. biology N.Mex. Inst. of Mining and Tech., Socorro, 1985-89, assoc. prof., 1989-93, prof., 1993—, chmn., 1991—. Reviewer Applied and Environ. Microbiology, Biology and Fertility of Soils, Idaho DOE EPSCOR Program, Jour. Environ. Quality, NSF, N.Mex. Water Resources Rsch. Inst., Rsch. Found., U.S. EPA, U.S. Dept. Energy, Wyo. Abandoned Coal Mine Lands Rsch. Program; contbr. articles to profl. jours. including Cryobiology, Microbiology Ecology, Soil Biology and Biochemistry, Jour. Bacteriology, The Lichenologist, Applied and Environmental Microbiology, Current Microbiology, Geomicrobiology Jour., others. Numerous rsch. grants. Mem. AAAS, Am. Soc. Microbiology (N.Mex. br. sec.-treas. 1988—, br. rep. to the bd. edn. and tng. 1985-88, nominating com. div. N 1988, host state meeting at N.Mex. Tech, 1989), Sigma Xi (local membership com. 1985-88, treas. 1989, v.p. 1990-91). Office: NMex Inst Mining/Tech Dept Biology Socorro NM 87801

KIEHL, KATHLEEN SUZANNE, English language educator; b. La Grange, Ill., June 4, 1958; d. James Ogden and Barbara JoAnn (Andersen) K.; m. Dennis John Moberg, July 4, 1985; children: Christiaan Anders, Annalise Alleen. BA, San Jose State U., 1981, MA, 1989. C.C. cert., Calif. Adminstrv. asst. Kaiser Electronics, San Jose, Calif., 1978-83; dir. adminstrv. svcs. Leavey Sch. Bus. Santa Clara (Calif.) U., 1983-89; English instr. Cabrillo Coll., Aptos, Calif., 1989—; mem. writing awards com. and composition com. Cabrillo Coll., Aptos, 1994—; reader, presenter Porter Gulch Rev., Aptos, 1994. Author poetry and short fiction. Newsletter editor Glen Arbor Sch., Ben Lomond, Calif., 1992—; parent class rep. Quail Hollow Sch., Ben Lomond, 1993—; team mother San Lorenzo Valley Little League, Ben Lomond, 1994. Mem. MLA, Nat. Coun. Tchrs. English. Office: Cabrillo Coll 6500 Soquel Dr Aptos CA 95003-3119

KIEHN, ARTHUR JOHN, chemist, educator; b. Chgo., Nov. 1, 1944; s. Edgar Henry and Emma (Ritter) K.; m. Joan S. Stoltenberg, Aug. 9, 1980; 1 child, Katherine M. BS in Chemistry, U. Wash., 1968, BA in Edn.istry, 1974, MS in Meteorlogy, 1974. Chemist Bardhal Mfg., Seattle, 1968-74, chief chemist, 1975-84, dir. tech. svcs., 1984—; sci. tchr. Seattle Sch. Dist., 1974-75. Contbr. articles to profl. jours.; patentee in field. Mem. Soc. Tribiologists and Lubrication Engrs. (co-chair edn. 1986-94), Am. Chem. Soc., Soc. of Automotive Engrs. Office: Bardahl Mfg PO Box 70607 Seattle WA 98107

KIEHN, RUBEN LEWIS, construction cost estimator; b. Woodland, Calif., Dec. 25, 1941; s. Ruben and Ruby Elaine (Condrey) K.; m. Barbara Elaine Hilton, Dec. 2, 1968; children: Kenneth, Shannon, Jeffrey. BA in Econs., Calif. State U., Sacramento, 1981; Bechtel bus. cert., Golden Gate U., 1985. Estimator, project mgr. Woodland Electric Co., Inc., Yuba City, Calif., 1965-81; sr. cost engr. Bechtel Nuclear Fuel Ops., San Francisco, 1981-83; project cost engr. Bechtel Advanced Tech. Divsn., San Francisco, 1983-85; cost engring. supr. Office of the State Arch., Sacramento, 1985-93; mgr. cost control Divsn. of the State Arch., Sacramento, 1993—. Author: The Walls Family of Delaware, 1988, (computer program) Alta Vista Constrn. Estimator, 1993. With U.S. Army, 1961-64. Mem. Am. Assn. Cost Engrs., Del. Hist. Soc., Calif. State U. Sacramento Alumni Assn. Republican. Office: Divsn of the State Arch 8th Fl 1300 I St Sacramento CA 95814

KIELAROWSKI, HENRY EDWARD, marketing executive; b. Pitts., Dec. 29, 1946; s. Henry Andrew Kielarowski and Evelyn Marie Kline Boileau; m. Lynda Blair Powell, Aug. 1971 (div. 1976); children: Amorette, Blair. BA, Duquesne U., Pitts., 1969; MA, Duquesne U., 1974, PhD, 1974. Pres. Communicators, Inc., Pitts., 1974-76; mktg. specialist McGraw-Hill, Inc., N.Y.C., 1976-81; mktg. dir. Fidelity S.A., Allison Park, Pa., 1981-86; exec. v.p. ARC Systems, Inc., Pitts., 1986-88; v.p. mktg. Providian Bancorp, San Francisco, 1988—. Author: Microcomputer Consulting in the CPA Environment, 1987; contbr. articles to profl. jours. Mem. Am. Mktg. Assn. (mktg. excellence award 1988), Direct Mktg. Assn. Democrat. Home: 107 Lyon St San Francisco CA 94117-2112

KIELHORN, RICHARD WERNER, chemist; b. Berlin, Germany, June 17, 1931; s. Richard H. and Auguste (Lammek) K.; m. Anneliese Heinrich, Aug. 9, 1952; children: Anita, Margit. BS, Chem. Tech. Sch., Berlin, 1953. Lab. tech. Zoellner Werke, Berlin, 1950-57, Montrose Chem. Corp., Henderson, Nev., 1957-78; chief chemist Stauffer Chem. Corp., Henderson, 1978-88, Pioneer Chlor Alkali Co., Henderson, 1988-92; tax. cons. H&R Block, Las Vegas, Nev., 1972—, Exec. Tax Svc., instr., 1978—. Mem. ASTM, Am. Chem. Soc., Am. Soc. Quality Control, Nat. Soc. Tax Profls. Home: 1047

Westminster Ave Las Vegas NV 89119-1825 Office: Exec Tax Svc 3170 W Sahara Ave Las Vegas NV 89102-6004

KIELSMEIER, CATHERINE JANE, school system administrator; b. San Jose, Calif; d. Frank Delos and Catherine Doris (Sellar) MacGowan; M.S., U. So. Calif., 1964, Ph.D., 1971; m. Milton Kielsmeier; children—Catherine Louise, Barry Delos. Tchr. pub. schs. Maricopa, Calif.; sch. psychologist Campbell (Calif.) Union Sch Dist., 1961-66; asst. prof. edn. and psychology Western Oreg. State Coll., Monmouth, 1966-67, 70; asst. research prof. Oreg. System Higher Edn., Monmouth, 1967-70; dir. spl. services Pub. Schs., Santa Rosa, Calif., 1971-91; cons., 1991—. Mem. Sonoma County Council Community Services, 1974-84, bd. dirs. 1976-82, Sonoma County Orgn. for Retarded/Becoming Independent, 1978-84, bd. dirs. 1978-82. Mem. Council for Exceptional Children, Laubach Literacy Internat. Office: 7495 Poplar Dr Forestville CA 95436-9671

KIENAST, CHARLOTTE D., interior designer; b. Chgo., Mar. 25, 1955; d. George Bennet and Mary Frances (Potts) Norton; m. Robert Curt Wagner, Dec. 8, 1979 (div. 1989); children: Mandy Wagner, Sean Wagner; m. Gary Hanes Kienast, Sept. 26, 1991. BA in Interior Design, Auburn U., 1979. Interior designer S.E. Rykoff, Seattle, 1979-82; archtl. draftsman BBT Architects, Tyler, Tex., 1982-84; interior designer assoc. Betsy Shaw Interiors, Tyler, Tex., 1984-89; interior designer Hall Kienast Architects, Bellingham, Wash., 1989-90; prin. designer CDK Interior Design, Bellingham, Wash., 1990—. Vol. Emergency Med. Tech., Suquamish, Wash., 1979-81; vol., docent Whatcom Mus., Bellingham, Wash., 1994—. Mem. Am. Soc. Interior Designers. Office: CDK Interior Design 119 N Commercial St Ste 820 Bellingham WA 98225-4437

KIENHOLZ, LYN SHEARER, international arts projects coordinator; b. Chgo.; d. Mitchell W. and Lucille M. (Hock) Shearer; student Sullins Coll., Md. Coll. Women. Assoc. producer Kurt Simon Prodns., Beverly Hills, Calif., 1963-65; owner, mgr. Vuokko Boutique, Beverly Hills, 1969-75; bd. dirs. L.A. Inst. Contemporary Art, 1976-79, Fellows of Contemporary Art, 1977-79, Internat. Network for Arts, 1979-89, L.A. Contemporary Exhbns., 1980-82; exec. sec., bd. dirs. Beaubourg Found. (now George Pompidou Art and Culture Found.), 1977-81; visual arts adv. Performing Arts Coun., L.A. Music Ctr., 1980-89; bd. govs. Calif. Inst. Tech. Baxter Art Gallery, 1980-85; adv. bd. dirs. Fine Arts Communications, pub. Images & Issues mag., 1981-85; founder, chmn. bd. Calif./Internat. Arts Found., 1981—; bd. dirs., western chmn. ArtTable 1983-89; bd. dirs. Galef Inst., 1992—; exec. bd. Sovereign Fund, 1981-93; exec. bd. dirs. Scandinavia Today, 1982-83, Art L.A., 1987, 88, 89; mem. adv. bd. dirs. Otis/Parsons Sch. Design, 1983-85, U. So. Calif. dept. fine arts, 1983-85; bd. dirs. UK/LA Festival of Britain, 1986-88, 92-94; hon. bd. dirs. L'Ensemble des Deux Mondes, Paris, 1986-91; mem. Comité Internat. pour les Museés d'Art Moderne, 1985—, bd. dirs., 1991—; Bd. dirs. Arts, Inc., 1987-89. Co-host nat. pub. radio program ARTS/L.A., 1987-91; contbg. editor Calif. mag., 1984-89. Address: 2737 Outpost Dr Los Angeles CA 90068-2061

KIER, RAYMOND EDWARD, motel and restaurant owner; b. Denver, Jan. 21, 1942; s. Edward L. Kier and Georgine E. (Traber) Bond. BA, Oberlin Coll., 1963; MBA, NYU, 1965; profl. acctg. program, Northwestern U., Chgo., 1970. CPA, Calif., Ariz., Utah. Vol. Peace Corps, Santiago, Chile, 1966-68; acct. Arthur Young & Co., San Francisco, 1969-73; contr. Kaiser Aetna, Oakland, Calif., 1973-76; gen. mgr. Tomahawk Trucking, Vernal, Utah, 1976-81; account exec. Waddell & Reed, Kansas City, Mo., 1981-84; exec. v.p. Vernal Area C. of C., 1984-92, sec. Found., 1990-92, bd. dirs., 1982-84; owner Sage Motel and Restaurant, Vernal. Sec.-treas. Dinosaur Roundup Rodeo Assn., Vernal, 1985-92; mem. Unitah County Econ. Devel. Bd., Vernal, 1986-89. Fellow NYU Grad. Sch. Bus., 1964-65; recipient Outstanding Pub. Svc. award Vernal Area, 1992. Mem. Rotary (pres. Vernal 1978-79), Dinaland Country Club (sec. 1984-86). Home: 393 S 400 W Vernal UT 84078-3011 Office: Sage Motel and Restaurant 54 W Main St Vernal UT 84078-2502

KIERNAN, JUDITH ANN, health facility administrator and educator; b. South Weymouth, Mass., Nov. 19, 1937; d. Vincent Owen and Eunice (Warner) Kiernan; m. Robert Stanley Graff, Dec. 29, 1973 (div. Oct. 1983). Diploma, Mass. Meml. Hosp. Sch. Nursing, 1958; BSN, Boston U., 1961; MS in Nursing, U. Colo., Denver, 1965; PhD in Health Svcs. Adminstrn., U. Utah, 1992. RN, Utah; cert. nurse adminstr. advanced; cert. alt. dispute resolution. Nurse edn. advisor U.S. Agy. for Internat. Devel., Vietnam, 1969-71; dir. nursing Univ. Hosp., Boston, 1972-74; asst. prof. U. Utah Coll. Nursing, Salt Lake City, 1974-78, asst. prof., coord., 1978-81, clin. asst. prof., 1981-83; nurse cons. Intermountain Health Care, Inc., Salt Lake City, 1982-85; asst. prof. U. Utah Coll. Nursing, Salt Lake City, 1983-85, asst. prof., asst. dean, 1985-86, clin assoc. prof., 1986—; dir. nursing, med./surg. Univ. Hosp., Salt Lake City, 1986—; cons. Intermountain Health Care, Salt Lake City, 1982-83; lectr., speaker various orgns., 1986—. Contbr. articles to profl. jours. Recipient Medal of Civilian Svc., Min. Health, Vietnam, 1971, Danforth Found. nomination. Mem. ANA, Utah Nurses Assn. (Ednl. Adminstrn. award 1981), Western Inst. Nursing (gov. representing nursing practice 1991—), Western Soc. Rsch. in Nursing, Am. Orgn. Nurse Execs. (commr., policy/legis. advocacy), Am. Arbitration Assn. (. Democrat. Episcopalian. Home: 525 2nd Ave Apt 8 Salt Lake City UT 84103-2930 Office: Univ Utah Hosp 50 N Medical Dr Rm 1540 Salt Lake City UT 84132

KIERSCH, GEORGE ALFRED, geological consultant, retired educator; b. Lodi, Calif., Apr. 15, 1918; s. Adolph Theodore and Viola Elizabeth (Bahmeier) K.; m. Jane J. Keith, Nov. 29, 1942; children—Dana Elizabeth Kiersch Haycock, Mary Annan, George Keith, Nancy McCandless Kiersch Bohnett. Student, Modesto Jr. Coll., 1936-37; B.S. in Geol. Engring., Colo. Sch. Mines, 1942; Ph.D. in Geology, U. Ariz., 1947. Geologist 79 Mining Co., Ariz., 1946-47; geologist underground explosion tests and Folsom Dam-Reservoir Project U.S. C.E., Calif., 1948-50; supervising geologist Internat. Boundary and Water Commn., U.S.-Mex., 1950-51; asst. prof. geology U. Ariz., Tucson, 1951-55, dir. Mineral Resources Survey Navajo-Hopi Indian Reservation, 1952-55; exploration mgr. resources survey So. Pacific Co., San Francisco, 1955-60; assoc. prof. geol. sci. Cornell U., Ithaca, N.Y., 1960-63, prof., 1963-78, prof. emeritus, 1978—, chmn. dept. geol. scis., 1965-71; geol. cons., Ithaca, 1960-78, Tucson, 1978—; chmn. coordinating com. on environment and natural hazards, Internat. Lithosphere Program, 1986-1991. Author: Engineering Geology, 1955, Mineral Resources of Navajo-Hopi Indian Reservations, 3 vols., 1955, Geothermal Steam-A World Wide Assessment, 1964; author: (with others) Advanced Dam Engineering, 1988; editor/author: Heritage of Engineering Geology--First Hundred Years 1888-1988 (vol. of Geol. Soc. Am.), 1991; editor: Case Histories in Engineering Geology, 4 vols., 1963-69; mem. editorial bd. Engring. Geology/Amsterdam, 1965—. Mem. adv. coun. to bd. trustees Colo. Sch. Mines, 1962-71, pres. coms., 1990—; mem. nine coms. NAE/NAS, 1966-90; reporter coordinating com. 1 CC1 Nat. Hazards U.S. GeoDynamics Com., 1985-90. Capt. C.E., U.S. Army, 1942-45. Recipient award for best articles Indsl. Mktg. Mag., 1964; NSF sr. postdoctoral fellow Tech. U. Vienna, 1963-64. Fellow ASCE, Geol. Soc. Am. (chmn. div. engring. geology 1960-61, mem. U.S. nat. com. on rock mechanics 1980-86, Disting. Practice award 1986, Burwell award 1992); mem. Soc. Econ. Geologists, U.S. Com. on Large Dams, Internat. Soc. Rock Mechanics, Internat. Assn. Engring. Geologists (U.S. com. 1980-86, chmn. com. 1983-87, v.p. N.Am. 1986-90), Assn. Engring. Geologists (1st receipient Claire P. Holdredge award 1965, 93, hon. mem. 1985), Cornell Club (N.Y.C.), Statler Club, Tower Club (Ithaca), Mining Club of Southwest (Tucson). Republican. Episcopalian. Home and Office: 4750 N Camino Luz Tucson AZ 85718-5819

KIERSCH, THEODORE ALEXANDER, psychiatrist; b. Chgo., Oct. 29, 1916; s. Alexander Mark and Marie (Torbick) K.; m. Mary Omel, June 22, 1941 (dec. May 1970); children: Theodore Allen, Christine D.; m. Margaret Marie Bevan, Apr. 29, 1972. BS, U. Ill., Chgo., 1938, MD, 1940. Diplomate Am. Bd. Psychiatry and Neurology. Intern William Beaumont Gen. Hosp., El Paso, Tex., 1940-41; commd. first lt. U.S. Army, 1941; advanced through grades to col., 1959; instr. mil. field medicine U.S. Army Med. Field Svc. Sch., Carlisle Barracks, Pa., 1941-42, U.S. Army Tank Destroyer Sch., Camp Hood, Tex., 1942-44; exec. officer, chief ward sect. 131st Evacuation Hosp., Ft. Jackson, S.C., 1944-45; staff officer Chief Surgeon's Office, U.S. Army, 1945-47; post surgeon U.S. Disciplinary Barracks, Milw., 1947-48; rotating resident Madigan Gen. Hosp., Tacoma, 1948-50; resident psychiatry Fitzsimons Army Hosp., Denver, 1950-53, asst. chief, chief psychiatry svc., 1953-54; chief dept. neuropsychiatry 97th Gen. Hosp., Frankfurt, Germany, 1954-57; neuropsychiatric cons. to chief surgeon U.S. Army Hdqs., Europe, 1954-57; chief dept. neuropsychiatry Letterman Gen. Hosp., San Francisco, 1957-61; chmn. mental health divsn. U. Ill. Health Svc., Urbana, 1961-79; prof. life sci. U. Ill., Urbana, 1961-79; chief psychiatric svcs. Atacadero (Calif.) State Hosp., 1979-81, staff psychiatrist, 1981-87, cons. psychiatrist, 1987—; cons. in psychiatry Surgeon Gen. Dept. of the Army, 1960. Contbr. articles to profl. jours. Fellow ACP., Am. Psychiat. Assn. (life). Office: Atascadero State Hosp Drawer A Atascadero CA 93422

KIEST, ALAN SCOTT, social services administrator; b. Portland, Oreg., May 14, 1949; s. Roger M. and Ellen K.; 1 child, Jennifer S. BA in Polit. Sci., U. Puget Sound, Tacoma, 1970; MPA, U. Wash., 1979. Welfare eligibility examiner Wash. Dept. Social and Health Services, Seattle, 1970-72, caseworker, 1972-76, service delivery coordinator, 1976-82; community svcs. office adminstr. Wash. Dept. Social and Health Svcs., Seattle, 1982—; planning commr. City of Lake Forest Park, 1989, mem. city coun., 1990—, chair city fin. com., 1992—; mem. King County Mangaged Health Care Oversight Com., 1993-95; mem. King County Human Svcs. Roundtable, 1995—. Mem. Suburban Cities Assn. (mem. Met. King County Coun., Reg. Policy Com. 1994—). Home: 18810 26th Ave NE Lk Forest Park WA 98155 Office: Wash Dept Social & Health Svcs PO Box 6429 Bellevue WA 98008-0429

KIESWETTER, JAMES KAY, history educator; b. Dodge City, Kans., Mar. 8, 1942; s. Orville James and Ruth Margaret (Bredahl) K. BM, U. Colo., 1963, MA, 1965, PhD, 1968. Asst. prof. history Eastern Wash. U., Cheney, 1968-71, assoc. prof., 1971-76, prof., 1976—. Author: Metternich's Intervention Policy, 1970, Political Career of Etienne-Denis Pasquier, 1977; contbr. articles to profl. publs. Bd. dirs. Spokane Humane Soc., 1986—, Spokane Rose Soc., 1983-86. Recipient Faculty Achievement award Burlington No. Found., 1986. Mem. Am. Hist. Assn., Soc. French Hist. Studies, Western Soc. French History. Office: Eastern Wash U Dept History MS #27 Cheney WA 99004

KIKUCHI, RYOICHI, physics educator; b. Osaka, Japan, Dec. 25, 1919; came to U.S., 1950; m. Toshiko Sono; children: John M., Ann K. Snyder. BS, Tokyo U., 1942, PhD, 1951. Research assoc. MIT, Cambridge, 1951-53; asst. prof. U. Chgo., 1953-55; research physicist Armour Research Found., Chgo., 1955-56; assoc. prof. Wayne State U., Detroit, 1956-58; sr. scientist Hughes Research Labs., Malibu, Calif., 1958-85; research prof. U. Wash., Seattle, 1985-89; adj. prof. UCLA, 1975-86, 89—; vis. prof. Purdue U., West Lafayette, Ind., 1977-93, Tohoku U., Sendai, Japan, 1982, Technische Hugeschool, Delft, The Netherlands, 1980, 81. Contbr. articles to profl. jours. Recipient A. Von Humboldt Sr. U.S. Scientist award, Bonn, Fed. Republic of Germany, 1985. Mem. Am. Phys. Soc., Minerals, Metals, & Materials Soc., Phys. Soc. Japan. Office: UCLA Dept Materials Sci & Engring 6531 Boelter Hall Los Angeles CA 90095-1595

KILBOURN, ALDEAN GAE, secondary educator; b. Olympia, Wash., Apr. 27, 1951; d. Alfred Richard and Alda Jane (Gabel) Lewis; m. David Charles Kilbourn, June 24, 1972; children: Benjamin Lee, Adam Richard, Peter David. BA in Polit. Sci., U. Wash., 1972; teaching cert., U. Alaska, 1974. Tchr. fgn. lang. and social studies West Valley H.S., North Star Borough Sch. Dist., Fairbanks, Alaska, 1981-86; tchr. fgn. lang., social studies, reading North Pole Mid. Sch., Fairbanks, 1987—; mem. social studies curriculum com. Fairbanks North Star Borough Sch. Dist., 1990—; presenter dist. and statewide confs./insvc. for sch. dist. on various social studies and computer related topics, 1985—. Bd. mem. Cmty. Rsch. Ctr., Fairbanks, 1984—. Mem. AAUW, Nat. Mid. Sch. Assn., Alaska Coun. Social Studies (bd. mem. 1989—), Fairbanks Coun. Social Studies (pres. 1992—). Republican. Home: 3217 Riverview Dr Fairbanks AK 99709-4741 Office: North Pole Mid Sch 300 E 8th Ave North Pole AK 99705-7664

KILBOURN, LEE FERRIS, architect, specifications writer; b. L.A., Mar. 9, 1936; s. Lewis Whitman and Kathryn Mae (Lee) K.; m. Joan Priscilla Payne, June 11, 1961; children: Laurie Jane, Ellen Mae. BS in Gen. Sci., Oreg. State U., 1963; BS in Architecture, U. Oreg., 1965. Registered architect, Oreg. Specifier Wolff Zimmer Assocs., Portland, Oreg., 1965-75; specifier, assoc. Wolff Zimmer Gunsul Frasca, Portland, 1975-77; specifier, assoc. Zimmer Gunsul Frasca Partnership, Portland, 1977-81, specifier, assoc. ptnr., 1981—. Jr. warden, then sr. warden St. Stephen's Episcopal Parish, Portland. With U.S. Army, 1959-60. Fellow AIA (mem. masterspec rev. com. 1976-78, mem. documents com. 1981-89), Constrn. Specifications Inst. (mem. participating tech. documents com. 1976-78, certification com. 1980-82, Al Hansen Meml. award Portland chpt. 1987, Frank Stanton Meml. award N.W. region 1987, chpt. pres. 1979-80), Internat. Conf. Bldg. Ofcls. Home: 3178 SW Fairmount Blvd Portland OR 97201-1468 Office: Zimmer Gunsul Frasca Partnership 320 SW Oak St Ste 500 Portland OR 97204-2735

KILBURN, KAYE HATCH, medical educator; b. Logan, Utah, Sept. 20, 1931; d. H. Parley and Winona (Hatch) K.; m. Gerrie Griffin, June 7, 1954; children: Ann Louise, Scott Kaye, Jean Marie. BS, U. Utah, 1951, MD, 1954. Diplomate Am. Bd. Internal Medicine, Am. Bd. Preventive Medicine. Asst. prof. Med. Sch. Washington U., St. Louis, 1960-62; assoc. prof., chief of medicine Durham (N.C.) VA Hosp., 1962-69; prof., dir. environ. medicine Duke Med. Ctr., Durham, 1969-73; prof. medicine and environ. medicine U. Mo., Columbia, 1973-77; prof. medicine and cmty. medicine CUNY Mt. Siai Med. Sch., 1977-80; Ralph Edgington prof. medicine U. So. Calif. Sch. Medicine, L.A., 1980—; pres. Neurotest Inc., 1988—; pres. Workers Disease Detection Svc. Inc., 1986-95. Editor-in-chief Archives of Environ. Health, 1986—; editor Jour. Applied Physicology, 1970-80, Environ. Rsch., 1975—, Am. Jour. Indsl. Medicine, 1980—; contbr. over 200 articles to profl. jours. Capt. M.C., U.S. Army, 1958-60. Home: 1350 Elysian Park Dr Los Angeles CA 90026-3408 Office: U So Calif Sch Medicine 2025 Zonal Ave Los Angeles CA 90033-4526

KILE, RAYMOND LAWRENCE, aerospace project manager, consultant; b. Tucson, Oct. 3, 1946; s. Roddy Lloyd and Polly Ann (Vardalakes) K.; m. Sharon Kate Durham, June 5, 1969; 1 child, Kasey Sheridan. BSEE, U.S. Air Force Acad., 1969; MSEE, U. Mo., 1972. Commd. 2d lt. USAF, 1969, advanced through grades to capt., 1986, engr., 1969-78; software developer Westinghouse Hanford, Richland, Wash., 1978-79; communications mgr. Wash. Pub. Power Supply System, Richland, 1980-82; dir. projects Contel Info. Systems, Denver, 1982-86; cost estimation tech. mgr. Hughes Aircraft Co., Aurora, Colo., 1986-94; software cons. USAFR Contract Mgmt. Divsn., 1978-90, USAF/SC, 1991—, pvt. practice, 1988—; guest lectr. USAF Software Devel. Courses, 1987—, Chapman Coll., Colorado Springs, Colo., 1988; FAA flight instr.; owner RKK Enterprises, Inc., 1992—; guest lectr. U. Colo., 1992—. Author: (software) REVIC (cost estimating program), 1986, 87, 88, 89, 90, 91. Lt. col. USAFR, 1981—. Mem. Res. Officers Assn. (life), Assn. Grads. USAF Acad., Air Force Assn., NRA (life). Republican. Home: 1539 E Nichols Cir Littleton CO 80122-2940 Office: Hughes Aircraft Co 16800 E Centretech Pky Aurora CO 80011-9046

KILEY, ROBERT RALPH, political consultant; b. Honolulu, Apr. 21, 1948; s. Kenneth John and Dorothy Irene (Ambrozich) K.; m. Barbara Lynn Weber, Mar. 1985; children: Tiryn Marie, Kristin Leigh. AA, Fullerton Coll., 1971; BA, U. So. Calif., 1975. Specifications coord. Hughes Aircraft, Fullerton, Calif., 1967-70; adminstrv. aide Hon. Robert H. Finch for U.S. Senate, Fullerton, 1975-76; field supr. Rep. Nat. Com., Washington, 1976; exec. dir. Rep. Party Orange County, Orange, Calif., 1976-80; pres., cons. Robert Kiley & Assocs., Yorba Linda, Calif., 1980—; lead advancement Pres. and Mrs. Ronald Reagan, Washington, 1984-88; v.p. Am. Campaign Schs., Yorba Linda, 1989-95. Bd. dirs. Bd. Psychology, Sacramento, 1984-92; chmn. legis. com. Sacramento, 1986-92; co-founder Save Our State-Proposition 1987. Named One of Outstanding Young Men Am., 1977-81; recipient Cert. Appreciation Anaheim Lions Club, 1987, Calif.-Nev. Lions Internat., 1988. Mem. U. So. Calif. Alumni Assn. (life). Office: 5028 Vista Montana Yorba Linda CA 92686-4594

KILEY, THOMAS, rehabilitation counselor; b. Mpls., Aug. 18, 1937; s. Gerald Sidney and Veronica (Kennedy) K.; m. Jane Virginia Butler, Aug. 25, 1989; children: Martin, Truman, Tami, Brian. BA in English, UCLA, 1959; MS in Rehab. Counseling, San Francisco State U., 1989. Cert. rehab counselor, nat. and Hawaii. Former rsch. profl., businessman various S.E. Asian cos.; sr. social worker Episcopal Sanctuary, San Francisco, 1986-88; dir. social svcs. Hamilton Family Ctr., San Francisco, 1988-89; rehab. specialist Intracorp, Honolulu, 1989-91; pres., prin. rehab. counselor Heritage Counselling Svc., Honolulu, 1991—; pres. Hunter Vocat. Tng. Ctrs., Honolulu, 1993, Hallmark Assessment Svc., Honolulu, 1993—, Horizon Info. Sys., Honolulu, 1994—, Mission Med. Mgmt. Svcs., 1994, Hunter Employment Svcs., Yuma. Mem. Am. Counseling Assn., Nat. Assn. Rehab. Profls. in Pvt. Sector, Am. Rehab. Counselors Assn. (profl.), Nat. Rehab. Assn., Rehab. Assn. Hawaii, Phi Delta Kappa. Office: Heritage Counselling Svcs PO Box 3098 Mililani HI 96789-0098

KILGORE, CATHERINE C., economic geologist, researcher; b. L.A., Dec. 25, 1956; d. Donald Evan and Elsie Ellen (Walden) Cook; m. Thomas Jefferson Kilgore, III, Aug. 5, 1978; children: Devin Walden, Kyler Evan. BS in Geology, Fort Lewis Coll., 1978; postgrad. in mineral econs. Colo. Sch. Mines, 1981-82; grad. Office Pers. Mgmt., 1991. Geologist U.S. Geol. Survey, Denver, 1979, Colo. Dept. Health, Denver, 1979-80, U.S. Bur. Mines, Denver, 1980-88, supervisory minerals specialist, 1988-93, dep. chief, 1993—. Contbr. info. circulars, articles. Recipient spl. achievement award U.S. Bur. Mines, 1983, 86, 90. Mem. Soc. Mining Engrs. (session chmn. 1986). Avocations: stained glass art, gourmet cooking. Office: US Bur Mines MAFO Bldg 20 Denver Fed Ctr Denver CO 80225

KILLEA, LUCY LYTLE, state legislator; b. San Antonio, July 31, 1922; d. Nelson and Zelime (Pettus) Lytle; B.A., Incarnate Word Coll., San Antonio, 1943; M.A. in History, U. San Diego, 1966, Ph.D. in History, U. Calif., San Diego, 1975; m. John F. Killea, May 11, 1946; children: Paul, Jay. Research analyst for Western Europe, Army Intelligence, Spl. Br., Washington, 1944-48; adminstrv. asst. Dept. State, London, 1946; econ. officer Econ. Coop. Adminstrn., The Hague, Netherlands, 1949; research analyst CIA, Washington, 1948-56; part time book reviewer USIS, 1956-60; teaching and research asst. U. Calif., San Diego, 1967-72; exec. dir., exec. v.p. Fronteras de las Californias, San Diego, 1974-78; mem. City Council, San Diego, 1978-82, dep. mayor, 1982, mem. planning commn., 1978; mem. Calif. State Assembly, 1982-89; mem. Calif. State Senate, 1989—; lectr. socioeconomics of Baja, Calif. and Mex., Southwestern Coll., Chula-Vista, 1976; lectr. dept. history San Diego State U., 1976-77; participant, organizer, panelist, moderator confs. in field, U.S., Mex.; mem. Palm City Sanitation Dist., 1978-82, Met. Transit Devel. Bd., 1978-82. Regional Employment and Tng. Consortium Bd., 1978-80, City-County Reinvestment Task Force, 1978-80. Bd. trustees San Diego Zool. Soc., 1976-78; mem. San Diego County Cultural Heritage Com., 1971-78, vice chmn., 1973-75; mem. Hist. Site Bd., City San Diego, 1968-75, vice chmn., 1971-75; bd. dirs. San Diego Hist. Soc., 1971-77; chmn. Internat. Com. Conv. and Visitors Bur., 1978, host com., 1976-77; adv. bd. Sharp Hosp.; bd. dirs., com. mem. Friends of Library, U. Calif., San Diego; founding mem. Caridad Internacional; mem. James S. Copley Library Adv. Council, U. San Diego, 1981—; active community orgns. including LWV, Fine Arts Soc. San Diego, YWCA, San Diego Mus. Art, San Diego Chpt. ARC, Dimensions, Aardvarks Ltd., Pacific Beach Hist. Soc., San Diego Symphonic Assn. Research grantee, Justice Found., 1965, U. Calif., San Diego, 1971; recipient awards, Conf. Calif. Hist. Socs., 1966, Inst. for Protection of Children, City of Tijuana and Tijuana Com., 1966, Alice Paul Award, Nat. Women's Polit. Caucus, 1982; named one of 12 Women of Valor, Beth Israel Sisterhood of Temple Beth Israel, San Diego, 1966, Woman of Accomplishment, Bus. and Profl. Clubs. San Diego, 1979, Woman of Yr., San Diego Irish Congress, 1981; honored Leukemia Soc., 1980; named alumna of distinction Incarnate Word Coll., San Antonio, 1981. Mem. Nat. Women's Polit. Caucus, Calif., Women in Bus., Mus. Photog. Arts, San Diego Arts Center, Nat. Trust Historic Preservation, San Diego Hist. Soc. (life), San Diego County Congress of History, Travelers Aid Soc., Navy League, Vietnam Vets. Assn. Mid City C. of C., San Diego C. of C., Nat. Assn. State Legislatures, NCCJ, World Affairs Council, Am. Fgn. Service Assn., Incarnate Word Alumnae Assn., U. San Diego Alumni Assn., U. Calif. San Diego Alumni and Friends, Calif. Elected Women's Assn. for Edn. and Research (bd. 1980-85, sec., treas., 1980-81, v.p. 1982-85). Roman Catholic. Clubs: Catfish, Army-Navy (Arlington, Va.). Contbr. writings to publs. in field. Office: State Capitol Rm 4062 Sacramento CA 95814-4906

KILLEBREW, ELLEN JANE (MRS. EDWARD S. GRAVES), cardiologist; b. Tiffin, Ohio, Oct. 8, 1937; d. Joseph Arthur and Stephanie (Beriont) K.; BS in Biology, Bucknell U., 1959; MD, N.J. Coll. Medicine, 1965; m. Edward S. Graves, Sept. 12, 1970. Intern, U. Colo., 1965-66, resident 1966-68; cardiology fellow Pacific Med. Center, San Francisco, 1968-70; dir. coronary care, Permanent Med. Group, Richmond, Calif., 1970-83; asst. prof. U. Calif. Med. Center, San Francisco, 1970-83, assoc. prof., 1983-93, clin. prof. medicine, Univ. Calif., San Francisco, 1992—. Contbr. chpt. to book. Robert C. Kirkwood Meml. scholar in cardiology, 1970; recipient Physician's Recognition award continuing med. edn., Lowell Beal award excellence in teaching, Permante Med. Group/House Staff Assn., 1992. Diplomate in cardiovascular disease Am. Bd. Internal Medicine. Fellow ACP, Am. Coll. Cardiology: mem. Fedn. Clin. Rsch., Am. Heart Assn. (rsch. chmn. Contra Costa chpt. 1975—, v.p. 1980, pres. chpt. 1981-82, chm. CPR com. Alameda chpt. 1984, pres. Oakland Piedmont br. 1995—). Home: 30 Redding Ct Belvedere Tiburon CA 94920-1318 Office: 280 W Macarthur Blvd Oakland CA 94611-5642

KILLIAN, C(HARLES) RODNEY, school administrator, researcher; b. Lancaster, Pa., Dec. 8, 1941; s. Charles M. and Grace E. (Cooper) K.; m. Patricia D. Hale, Aug. 24, 1974; children: Jaima, Grant. BA, U. No. Colo., 1963; MS, Ball State U., 1968; PhD in Ednl. Stats. and Measurement, U. Iowa, 1973. Cert. adminstr. with supt. endorsement, Colo. Tchr. math. Del Norte (Colo.) H.S., 1964-69; cons. math. Joint County Sch. System, Ft. Dodge, Iowa, 1969-70; teaching asst. U. Iowa, Iowa City, 1970-73; rsch. assoc. Drake U., Des Moines, 1973-75; project evaluator Midwest Area Learning Resource Ctr., 1975-77; rsch. assoc. Met. State Coll., 1977-80; sr. cons. budget and evaluation Colo. Dept. Edn., 1980-81; statistician Dept. Def., 1981-82; dir. rsch. and govtl. rels. Aurora (Colo.) Pub. Schs., 1982—. Author articles. Active Dem. Party, Jefferson, Colo., 1976—; sr. warden Calvary Episcopal Ch., Golden, Colo., 1990-92; mem. Planning Commn., Wheat Ridge, Colo., 1988-89, chair, 1989. Recipient various awards, scholarships, grants. Mem. Colo. Assn. Sch. Execs. (pres. 1993-94), Assn. Colo. Ednl. Evaluators (past pres.), Colo. Ednl. Planners Assn., Phi Delta Kappa (past pres.). Office: Aurora Pub Schs 1085 Peoria St Aurora CO 80011-6203

KILLIAN, GEORGE ERNEST, association executive; b. Valley Stream, N.Y., Apr. 6, 1924; s. George and Reina (Moeller) K.; m. Janice E. Bachert, May 26, 1951 (dec.); children: Susan E., Sandra J.; m. Marilyn R. Killian, Sept. 1, 1984. BS in Edn., Ohio No. U., 1949; EdM, U. Buffalo, 1954; PhD in Phys. Scis., Ohio Northern U., 1989. Tchr.-coach Wharton (Ohio) High Sch., 1949-51; insp. USN, Buffalo, 1951-54; dir. athletics Erie County (N.Y.) Tech. Inst., Buffalo, 1954-69; asst. prof. health, phys. edn., recreation Erie County (N.Y.) Tech. Inst., 1954-60, asso. prof., 1960-62, prof., 1962-69; exec. dir. Nat. Jr. Coll. Athletic Assn., Colorado Springs, Colo., 1969—. Editor: Juco Rev., 1960—. Served with AUS, 1943-45. Recipient Bd. Trustees award Hudson Valley C. of C., 1969, Erie County Tech. Inst., 1969, Service award Ohio No. U. Alumni, 1972, Service award Lysle Rishel Post, Am. Legion, 1982; named to Ohio No. U. Hall of Fame, 1979. Mem. U.S. Olympic Com. (dir.), Am. Legion, Internat. Basketball Fedn. (pres. 1990—), Phi Delta Kappa, Delta Sigma Phi. Clubs: Masons, Rotary. Home: 325 Rangely Dr Colorado Springs CO 80921-2655 Office: Nat Jr Coll Athletic Assn PO Box 7305 Colorado Springs CO 80933-7305

KILLIAN, RICHARD M., library director; b. Buffalo, Jan. 13, 1942; m. Nancy Killian; children from previous marriage: Tessa, Lee Ann. BA, SUNY, Buffalo, 1964; MA, Western Mich. U., 1965; grad. advanced mgmt. library adminstrn., Miami U., Oxford, Ohio, 1981; grad. library adminstrn. devel. program, U. Md., 1985. Various positions Buffalo and Erie County Pub. Libraries, 1963-74, asst. dep. dir., personnel officer, 1979-80; dir. Town of Tonawanda (N.Y.) Pub. Library, 1974-78; asst. city librarian, dir. pub. svcs. Denver Pub. Library, 1978-79; exec. dir. Nioga Library System, Buffalo, 1980-87; library dir. Sacramento (Calif.) Pub. Library, 1987—. Mem. ALA, Calif. Library Assn., Rotary. Home: 3501 H St Sacramento CA 95816-4501 Office: Sacramento Pub Libr Adminstrn Ctr 828 I St Sacramento CA 95814-2508*

KILLINGSWORTH, KATHLEEN NOLA, artist, photographer, company executive; b. Eglin AFB, Fla., Sept. 5, 1952; d. Marlin Donald Evans and Winnifred Irene (Pelton) Yow; m. Thomas Marion, Dec. 31, 1973 (div. Feb. 1976). Grad. high sch., Myrtle Point, Oreg. Food svc. Internat. Trade Club, Mobile, Ala., 1970-73; food and beverage Gussies Restaurant and Night Club, Coos Bay, Oreg., 1973-77, Libr. Buttery and Pub, Las Vegas, Nev., 1977-79; beverage dir. Laughlin's (Nev.) Riverside Resort, 1979-80; food and beverage Hyatt Regency Maui, Lahaina, Hawaii, 1980-92; realtor assoc. Wailea (Hawaii) Properties, 1990; sole propr. K N Killingsworth Enterprises, Lahaina, 1990—; assoc. Kona Coast Resort II, 1992—; vol. Lahaina Arts Soc., 1992—; mem. Hui No'eau Visual Arts Ctr., Makawao, Maui, Hawaii, 1992—. Artist numerous watercolor and acrylic paintings; photographer nature greeting cards. Vol. The Word For Today, Lahaina, 1983-87, Kumalani Chapel, Kapalua, Hawaii, 1983-87, Maui Special Olympics, 1993—; founding mem. & vol. Maui Community Arts & Cultural Ctr.; supporter Teen Challenge, Lahaina, 1987—. Mem. Lahina Arts Soc., 1992—. Republican. Office: K N Killingsworth Enterprises PO Box 5369 Lahaina HI 96761-5369

KILLION, JACK CHARLES, newspaper columnist; b. L.A., Aug. 21, 1921; s. Roger William and Anna Virginia (Moser) K.; m. Elisabeth Horn, June 29, 1947; children: Joanna Barbara, Heidi Killion Gaul, Frederick John. Student, L.A. City Coll., 1940-42. Chief of spl. branch U.S. Army Mil. Govt., Bruchsal, Baden, Germany, 1945-47; sports editor Van Nuys News, Van Nuys, Calif., 1947-48; repair supr. L.A. Dept. Water & Power, 1948-81; columnist Simi Valley Enterprise, Simi Valley, Calif., 1986—, L.A. Daily News, 1989-90. Sgt. U.S. Army, 1942-45, ETO. Decorated Hon. Membership German Severely Wounded War Vets., Pacific Battle Star, European Battle Star; Commendation for work as Chief of Spl. Branch and Denazification, Bruchsal, Baden, Germany. Mem. Mensa. Republican. Lutheran. Home: 2403 Lukens Ln Simi Valley CA 93065-4909

KILLUS, JAMES PETER, JR., atmospheric scientist, consultant, writer; b. Nashville, June 1, 1950; s. James Peter Sr. and Lanis Sue (Embry) K. BS in Engring., Rensselner Poly. Inst., 1972, M of Engring., 1974. Teaching asst. Rensselaer Poly. Inst., Troy, N.Y., 1971-74; instr. Jr. Coll. of Albany, N.Y., 1973-74; staff scientist to sr. scientist Systems Applications, San Rafeal, Calif., 1975-85; cons. Berkeley, Calif., 1985—; cons. EPA, 1989—. Author: (novel) Book of Shadows, 1983, Sunsmoke, 1985. Mem. IEEE, AAAS, Am. Chem. Soc., Sci. Fiction Writers of Am. Home: 2305 Helena Ct Pinole CA 94564-1814

KILMER, JOSEPH CHARLES, secondary school educator; b. Omaha, Nov. 21, 1942; s. Randall Delmore and Helen June (Barber) K.; m. Marietta Josée van Eek, Dec. 21, 1963; children: Jason Robert, Ryan Patrick, Derek Christian. BS, U. Wash., 1965, MA, 1970. Cert. secondary tchr., Wash. Tchr. Sch. Dist. #121, Port Angeles, Wash., 1965—; coach various sports Sch. Dist. #121, Port Angeles, 1966-78; bldg. rep. Port Angeles Edn. Assn., 1966-68, 88-90, treas., 1968-69; tchr. assistance program mentor Olympic Ednl. Svc. Dist., 1992-93. Active Port Angeles Children's Theatre, 1982-85, Port Angeles Community Players, 1987-91; mem. exec. bd. Port Angeles YMCA, 1968-71, v.p. bd., 1969, pres. bd., 1970; cubmaster Port Angeles coun. Boy Scouts Am., 1979-84, exec. coun. Mt. Olympus dist., 1979-84; coach YBA youth soccer and basketball, 1979-86; precinct com. person Dem. Com., 1988—, pres. Clallam County Dem. Club, 1993—; mem. Friends of the Fine Arts Ctr., Friends of the Libr. Recipient Cubmaster of Yr. award Boy Scouts Am., 1982, Mt. Olympus Dist. Extra Mile award, 1982, Profl. Excellence award Northwest Svcs./Pvt. Industry Coun., 1993. Mem. NEA, Port Angeles Edn. Assn., Wash. Edn. Assn. (500-Hour Service award 1969), Princeton Parents Assn. Nat. Com., Phi Delta Kappa. Office: Roosevelt Mid Sch 400 Monroe Rd Port Angeles WA 98362-9328

KILMER, MAURICE DOUGLAS, marketing executive; b. Flint, Mich., Sept. 14, 1928; s. John Jennings and Eleanor Minnie (Gerholz) K.; m. Vera May Passino, Mar. 30, 1950; children: Brad Douglas, Mark David, Brian John, David Scott, Karen Sue. B of Indsl. Engring., Gen. Motors Inst., 1951; MBA, U. Minn., 1969. Quality svcs. mgr. ordnance div. Honeywell, Hopkins, Minn., 1964-69; product assurance dir. peripheral ops. Honeywell, San Diego, 1969-71; pres. Convenience Systems, Inc., San Diego, 1972-75; salesman real estate Forest E. Olson Coldwell Banker, La Mesa, Calif., 1976-77; resident mgr. Forest E. Olson Coldwell Banker, Huntington Beach, Calif., 1977-78; mgmt. cons. Century 21 of the Pacific, Santa Ana, Calif., 1978-83; dir. broker svcs. Century 21 of the Pacific, Anaheim, Calif., 1983-85; exec. dir. Century 21 of S.W., Phoenix, 1985-86; sales assoc. Century 21 Rattan Realtors, San Diego, 1986-88; mgr. Rattan Realtors, San Diego, 1988-92, relocation dir., 1993—. With U.S. Army, 1951-52. Mem. Am. Soc. for Quality Control, San Diego Bd. Realtors. Republican. Home: 668 Corte Raquel San Marcos CA 92069-7320 Office: Rattan Realtors 2878 Camino Del Rio S Ste 300 San Diego CA 92108-3846

KILMER, NEAL HAROLD, physical scientist; b. Orange, Tex., Apr. 24, 1943; s. Harold Norval and Luella Alice (Sharp) K. BS in Chemistry and Math., Northwestern Okla. State U., 1964; MS in Chemistry, Okla. State U., 1971; PhD in Chemistry, Mich. State U., 1979. Rsch. assoc. N.Mex. Petroleum Recovery Rsch. Ctr. N.Mex. Inst. Mining & Tech., Socorro, 1979-81, rsch. chemist, 1981-85, lectr. I geol. engring., 1984, asst. prof. mining engring., 1985-86; phys. scientist Phys. Sci. Lab. N.Mex. State U., Las Cruces, 1986—. Contbr. articles to profl. jours. Mem. Am. Chem. Soc., Am. Inst. Physics, Soc. Photo-Optical Instrumentation Engrs., Optical Soc. Am., Sigma Xi, Pi Mu Epsilon, Phi Lambda Upsilon. Presbyterian. Home: 2200 Corley Dr Apt 14G Las Cruces NM 88001-5827 Office: Phys Sci Lab PO Box 30002 Las Cruces NM 88003-8002

KILPATRICK, ANITA See **STAUB, ANITA**

KIM, CHAN-HIE, educator, clergyman; b. Hoeryung, Korea, June 7, 1935; came to U.S., 1961; s. Chong-Jin and Kansung (Moon) K.; m. Sook-Chung Kim, Sept. 9, 1962; 1 child, Alexis Hangin. BA, Yonsei U., Seoul, 1958; BD, Vanderbilt U., 1964, PhD, 1970. Ordained deacon United Methodist Ch., 1965, ordained elder, 1967. Acad. instr. Air Command and Staff Coll., Korean Air Force, 1958-60; asst. prof. religion Yonsei U., 1971-72; staff Bd. of Discipleship, United Meth. Ch., Nashville, 1974-77; dir. Ctr. for Asian-Am. Ministries, Claremont, Calif., 1977-87; affiliate prof. N.T. Sch. of Theology at Claremont, 1977-87, prof. N.T., 1987—; prof. religion Claremont Grad. Sch., 1987—; bd. dirs. U. So. Calif. Korean Heritage Libr., L.A., 1990—, Ctr. for Pacific-Asian Am. Ministries, Claremont, 1987—. Author: Form and Structure of Familiar Greek Letter of Recommendation, 1970. Vice chair Korea Town YMCA, L.A., 1989—; bd. dirs. Korean-Am. Mus., L.A., 1994—; rschr. Korean-Am. Rsch. Inst., L.A., 1994—. Mem. Soc. Bibl. Lit., Am. Acad. Religion. Office: Sch Theology at Claremont 1325 N College Ave Claremont CA 91711-3154

KIM, EDWARD WILLIAM, ophthalmic surgeon; b. Seoul, Korea, Nov. 25, 1949; came to U.S., 1957; s. Shoon Kul and Pok Chu (Kim) K.; m. Carole Sachi Takemoto, July 24, 1976; children: Brian, Ashley. BA, Occidental Coll., Los Angeles, 1971; postgrad. Calif. Inst. Tech., 1971; MD, U. Calif.-San Francisco, 1975; MPH, U. Calif.-Berkley, 1975. Diplomate Nat. Bd. Med. Examiners, Am. Bd. Ophthalmology. Intern, San Francisco Gen. Hosp., 1975-76; resident in ophthalmology Harvard U.-Mass. Eye and Ear Infirmary, Boston, 1977-79; clin. fellow in ophthalmology Harvard U., 1977-79; clin. fellow in retina Harvard, 1980; practice medicine in ophthalmic surgery, South Laguna and San Clemente, Calif., 1980—; vol. ophthalmologist Eye Care Inc., Ecole St. Vincent's, Haiti, 1980, Liga, Mex., 1989; chief staff, South Coast Med. Ctr., 1988-89; assoc. clin. prof. dept. ophthalmology, U. Calif., Irvine. Founding mem. Orange County Ctr. for Performing Arts, Calif., 1982, dir. at large, 1991; pres. Laguna Beach Summer Music Festival, Calif., 1984. Reinhart scholar U. Calif.-San Francisco, 1972-73; R. Taussig scholar, 1974-75. Fellow ACS, Am. Acad. Ophthalmology, Royal Soc. Medicine, Internat. Coll. Surgeons; mem. Calif. Med. Assn., Keratorefractive Soc., Orange County Med. Assn., Mensa, Expts. in Art and Tech. Office: Harvard Eye Assocs 665 Camino De Los Mares Ste 102 San Clemente CA 92673-2840

KIM, JAY, congressman; b. Korea, 1939; m. June, 1961; children: Richard, Kathy, Eugene. BS, U. So. Calif., MCE; MPA, Calif. State U. Mem. City Coun. city of Diamond Bar, Calif., 1990, mayor, 1991; mem. 103rd Congress from 41st dist. Calif., 1993—; pres., founder Jaykim Engrs. Inc. Recipient Outstanding Achievement in Bus. and Community Devel. award, Engr. of Yr. award, Caballero de Distinction award, Engr. Bus. of the Yr. award, others. Republican. Methodist. Office: US Ho of Reps Office of House Members Washington DC 20515*

KIM, JOUNG-IM, communication educator, consultant; b. Taejon, Choongnam, Republic of Korea, May 8, 1947; came to U.S., 1975; d. Yong-Kap Kim and Im-Soon Nam; m. James Andrew Palmore, Jr., Jan. 21, 1989 (div. Nov. 1993). BA in Libr. Sci., Yonsei U., Seoul, Korea, 1970, postgrad., 1974-75; postgrad., U. Hawaii at Manoa, 1975, MA in Sociology, 1978; PhD in Comm., Stanford U., 1986. Rschr. Korean Inst. Family Planning, Seoul, 1974-75; spl. resource person UN/East-West Ctr., Honolulu, 1976; rsch. asst. East-West Ctr., Honolulu, 1977-78; rsch., teaching asst. Stanford (Calif.) U., 1979-83, instr., 1984; asst. prof. U. Hawaii at Manoa, Honolulu, 1984—, also mem. faculty Ctr. Korean Studies; cons. UN Econ. and Social Commn. for Asia and Pacific, Bangkok, 1979, 84-86, 89, 90-92; cons. UN Devel. Program, Devel. Tng. Comm. Planning, Bangkok, 1984, UN Population Funds, N.Y.C., 1991, 92. Contbr. articles to profl. jours., monographs, and chpts. to books. Grantee East-West Ctr., 1972, 75-78; Population Libr. fellow U. N.C., 1973; Stanford U. fellow, 1978-79, 83, 84. Mem. Internat. Comm. Assn., Internat. Network for Social Network Analysis. Office: U Hawaii at Manoa 2560 Campus Rd # 336 Honolulu HI 96822-2217

KIM, KARL EUJUNG, urban planning educator; b. Junction City, Kans., Sept. 5, 1957; s. Yee Sik and Young Soon (Lee) K.; m. Shilla K.H. Yoon, Mar. 25, 1989; children: Kelly Hosue, Kenneth Taysoo. AB, Brown U., 1979; PhD, MIT, 1987. Asst. prof. urban and regional planning U. Hawaii Manoa, Honolulu, 1987-91, assoc. prof., 1991—; pres. Progressive Analytics, Inc., Honolulu, 1993. Mem. editl. bd. Korean Studies, 1989-94; contbr. articles to profl. publs. Commr. Rental Housing Trust Fund, Honolulu, 1992-93; mem. exec. bd. dirs. Common Cause Hawaii, 1993-94; elected to Manoa Neighborhood Bd., 1993. Fulbright fellow, Korea, 1991; scholar-in-residence Western Govs. Assn., Denver, 1990; grantee Hawaii CODES project U.S. Dept. of Transp./Nat. Hwy. Traffic Safety Adminstrn., 1992. Mem. Am. Planning Assn. (pub. issues chairperson 1991), Nat. Rsch. Coun. (mem. transp. rsch. bd. 1990-94), Nat. Safety Coun. (mem. traffic records com. 1990-94). Office: Univ Hawaii Manoa Porteus Hall 107 2424 Maile Way Honolulu HI 96822-2223

KIM, KWANG SIK, pediatrician, researcher; b. Seoul, Korea, June 9, 1947; came to U.S., 1974; s. Taejong and Kyung Ja (Cho) K.; m. Aeran Yoon, July 30, 1983; children: Melissa Yongsun, Brian Yongjin. BS, Seoul Nat. U. Korea, 1967, MD, 1971. Intern Ellis Hosp., Schenectady, N.Y., 1974-75; resident La. State U. Med. Ctr., New Orleans, 1975-78; fellow Harbor UCLA Med. Ctr., Torrance, 1978-80; asst. prof. pediatrics UCLA Sch. Medicine, 1980-86; assoc. prof. Children's Hosp. Los Angeles, 1986-91, prof. pediatrics, 1991-92, head divsn. of infectious diseases, 1992—. Recipient Basil O'Connor award March of Dimes, 1982; NIH grantee, 1984—. Mem. Western Soc. Pediatric Rsch., Soc. Pediatric Rsch., Am. Soc. Microbiology, Infectious Diseases Soc. Am., Am. Fedn. Clin. Rsch., Am. Heart Assn. (sr. investigator 1983), Am. Pediatric Soc. Office: Children's Hosp Los Angeles 4650 W Sunset Blvd # 51 Los Angeles CA 90027-6016

KIM, YONGMIN, electrical engineering educator; b. Cheju, Korea, May 19, 1953, came to U.S., 1976; s. Ki-Whan and Yang-Whi (Kim) K.; m. Eunai Yoo, May 21, 1976; children: Janice, Christine, Daniel. BEE, Seoul Nat. U., Republic of Korea, 1975; MEE, U. Wis., Madison, 1979, PhD, 1982. Asst. prof. U. Wash., Seattle, 1982-86, assoc. prof., 1986-90, prof., 1990—; bd. dirs. Optimedx, Precision Digital Images, Redmond, Wash.; cons. MITRE Corp., McLean, Va., 1990, Lotte-Canon, Seoul, 1991, Seattle Silicon, Bellevue, Wash., 1990-93, U.S. Army, 1989—, Neopath, Inc., Bellevue, Wash., 1989-90, Trinius Ptnrs., Seattle, 1989-91, Samsung Advanced Inst. Tech., Suwon, Republic of Korea, 1989-92, Daewoo Telecom Co., Seoul, 1989-91, Intel Corp., Santa Clara, 1992, Aptec Systems, Portland, Oreg., 1992—, Optimedx, Seattle, 1992—, Precision Digital Images, Redmond, Wash., 1994—, Micro Vision, Seattle, 1994—, Hitachi, Tokyo, 1995—; bd. dirs. Image Computing Systems Lab., 1984—, Ctr. for Imaging Systems Optimization, 1991, Optimedx, 1993—, U. Wash. Image Computing Libr. Consortium, 1995—. Contbr. numerous articles to profl. jours., chpts. in books; editor Proceedings of the Annual International Conference of the IEEE EMBS, vol. 11, 1989, Proceedings of the SPIE Medical Imaging Conferences, vol. 1232, 1990, vol. 1444, 1991, vol. 1653, 1992, vol. 1897, 1993, vol. 2164, 1994, vol. 2431, 1995; inventor in field. Mem. various nat. coms., chmn. steering com. IEEE TMI; chmn. numerous confs. Recipient Career Devel. award Physio Control Corp., 1982; grantee NIH, 1984—, NSF, 1984—, U.S. Army, 1986—, USN, 1986—; Whitaker Found. biomed. engring. grantee, 1986. Fellow Am. Inst. Med. and Biological Engring.; mem. IEEE (sr., Early Career Achievement award 1988, Disting. Speaker 1991), Assn. Computing Machinery, Soc Photo-Optical Instrumentation Engrs., Tau Beta Pi, Eta Kappa Nu. Presbyterian. Subspecialties: computer engring., multimedia, high-performance image computing workstations, image processing, computer graphics, medical imaging, and virtual reality. Home: 4431 NE 189th Pl Seattle WA 98155-2814

KIMBALL, CURTIS ROLLIN, investment advisor, appraiser; b. Grand Rapids, Mich., Dec. 21, 1950; s. Rollin Hibbard and Jane Ann (Walterman) K.; m. Marilyn M. Quaderer; 1 child, Neil Curtis. B.A., Duke U., 1972; M.B.A., Emory U., 1984. Comml. lending and trust portfolio mgr. Wachovia Bank and Trust Co., N.A., Winston-Salem, N.C., 1972-81; v.p., trust mgr. bus. owner services group Citizens and So. Nat. Bank, Atlanta, 1981-88; prin. Willamette Mgmt. Assocs., Inc., Portland, Oreg., 1988—. Chair activities coun. Portland Art Mus., 1993-94. Fellow Inst. Chartered Fin. Analysts; mem. Am. Soc. Appraisers (sr., pres. Atlanta chpt. 1985-86, treas. Portland chpt. 1993-94); mem. Nat. Assn. Bus. Econs. (pres. Portland chpt. 1992-93). Republican. Episcopalian. Avocations: running; fencing; tennis. Office: Willamette Mgmt Assocs Inc 111 SW 5th Ave Ste 2150 Portland OR 97204-3624

KIMBALL, DONALD W., electric utility corporate executive; b. Deadwood, S.D., Apr. 27, 1947; s. Garrett J. and Marietta (Alexander) K.; m. Sue Eide, Sept. 19, 1964; children: Lisa Gray, Tammi Bymers. BSEE, Colo. State U., 1974. Lineman Butte Electric Corp., Newell, S.D., 1965-68; journeyman lineman Poudre Valley Rural Electric, Ft. Collins, Colo., 1968-69; engr. Pourdre Valley Rural Electric, F. Collins, Colo., 1969-74; systems engr. Grand Valley Rural Power, Grand Juction, Colo., 1974-76, Heartland Consumers Power Dist., Madison, S.D., 1976-77; spl. projects enrg. East River Electric Power Corp., Madison, S.D., 1977; mgr. Clay Union Electric, Vermillion, S.D., 1978-88, Union County Electric Corp., Elk Point, S.D., 1984-88; exec. v.p., gen. mgr. Ariz. Electric Power Corp., Benson, Ariz., 1988—; bd. dirs., officer Heartland Consumers Power, Madison, S.C., 1979-88; cons. City of Elk Point, S.D., 1984-88; bd. pres. Ariz. Power Pooling Assn., Phoenix, Grand Canyon State Electric Coop. Assn., Inc., Western Power Producers, 1991. Mem. Nat. G&T Mgrs. Assn. (sec./treas.). Democrat. Lutheran. Home: 6828 E Calle Luciente Tucson AZ 85715-3208 Office: Ariz Electric Power Corp PO Box 670 Benson AZ 85602-0670

KIMBALL, K. RANDALL, broadcasting executive; b. Salt Lake City, June 3, 1951; s. Ralph Taylor and Marie (Seegmiller) K.; m. Rebecca Joye Cummings, Nov. 17, 1973; children: Jenifer, Nicklaus, Stefanie. BS in Acctg., U. Utah, 1975. Staff acct. Bonneville Internat. Corp., Salt Lake City, 1975-78; bus. mgr. B.I.C. KAAM-KAFM-Radio, Dallas, 1978-80, KCPX Inc. AM/FM Radio, Salt Lake City, 1980-84; controller Thomas, Phillips, Clawson Advt., Salt Lake City, 1984-85; bus. mgr. United TV Inc.-KTVX, Salt Lake City, 1985—. Contbr. articles to profl. jours. Mem. Broadcast Cable Fin. Mgmt. Assn. Mem. LDS. Home: 1361 Ridgemark Dr Sandy UT 84092-2916 Office: United TV Inc KTVX 1760 Fremont Dr Salt Lake City UT 84104-4215

KIMBALL, RICHARD WILSON, reporter; b. Nashua, N.H., Aug. 14, 1938; s. Rowe Wilson and Helen Louise (Thompson) K.; m. Barbara Helen Adams, Apr. 8, 1961 (div. Sept. 1975); children: Richard Michael, Daniel Wilson; m. Veronica Lucille McGovern/Barnes, Nov. 21, 1992. BA, U. N.Mex., 1976; Cert. mag. pub., NYU, 1978. Concession mgr. Benson's Wild Animal Farm, Hudson, N.H., 1953-59; typesetter Ray's Typesetting, Inc., Nashua, N.H., 1960-66; photo compositor U. N.Mex., Albuquerque, 1966-76; sr. VDT writer Westinghouse Electric Corp., Albuquerque, 1980-83; tech. writer Tiguex Editorial Svcs., Albuquerque, 1985-88; editor, reporter Chino Valley (Ariz.) Rev., 1988-92; reporter Prescott (Ariz.) Daily Courier, 1992—; editorial advisor Corrales Village Press, Corrales, N.Mex., 1975-76. Newsletter editor Distant Drums, 1985-86; inventor bd. game Patolli, the game of the Aztecs, 1986; pub., writer more than 100 limited edit. hist. booklets, 1980—. With USCG, 1977-79. Democrat. Buddhist. Home: 39 Woodside Dr Prescott AZ 86301-5092 Office: Prescott Daily Courier 147 N Cortez St Prescott AZ 86301-3097

KIMBALL, RUSSELL DREW, management consultant; b. Erie, Pa., Sept. 28, 1960; s. Gloyd Dene and Anita Amelia Claire (Gaudino) K. BSME summa cum laude, U. Mass., 1982; MBA, U. Wash., 1992. Cert. mgmt. cons. Project engr. Air Products and Chems., Inc., Pasadena, Tex., 1982-85; mktg. rep. Big Three Industries, Inc., Houston, 1985-87; sales rep. Nalco Chem. Co., Tex. and Wash., 1988-90; owner Operational Alignment Specialties, Seattle, 1991—; cons., instr. Green River C.C., Kent, Wash., 1991—, Lake Wash. Vocat. Coll., Kirkland, 1993—, Edmonds (Wash.) C.C., 1993—, Wash. Employers, Seattle, 1994—. Author: Strategic Alignment, 1993. Mem. indsl. adb. bd. U. Mass., Amherst, 1982-83; asst. scout master Boy Scouts Am., Allentown, Pa., 1982-83; pres. Washingont Hugh O'Brien Youth Found., Seattle, 1990-92; bd. dirs. Youth Advs., Seattle, 1994. Ron Crockett scholar, 1991-92. Mem. ASTD, Am. Proidn. and Inventory Control Soc., Jaycees (v.p. Seattle club 1990-91, state v.p. 1993-94, scholar 1991-92), Pi Tau Sigma, Phi Kappa Phi, Tua Beta Pi. Republican. Episcopalian. Home and Office: 10545 Greenwood Ave N Apt 207 Seattle WA 98133-8778

KIMBALL, SPENCER LEVAN, lawyer, educator; b. Thatcher, Ariz., Aug. 26, 1918; s. Spencer Woolley and Camilla (Eyring) K.; m. Kathryn Ann Murphy, June 12, 1939; children: Barbara Jean (Mrs. Thomas Sherman), Judith Ann (Mrs. William Stillion), Kathleen Louise, Spencer David, Kent Douglas, Timothy Jay. BS, U. Ariz., 1940; postgrad., U. Utah, 1946-47; BCL, Oxford (Eng.) U., 1949; SJD, U. Wis., 1958. Bar: Utah 1950, Mich. 1965, Wis. 1968, U.S. Dist. Ct. (we. dist.) Wis. 1968, U.S. Supreme Ct. 1982, U.S. Ct. Appeals (9th cir.) 1986. Assoc. prof. U. Utah Coll. Law, Salt Lake City, 1949-50, dean, 1950-54, prof., 1954-57, rsch. prof., 1993—; prof. U. Mich., 1957-68, dir. legal research Law Sch., 1962-67; staff dir. Wis. Ins. Law Revision Project, 1966-79; prof. law, dean U. Wis. Law Sch., 1968-72; exec. dir. Am. Bar Found., Chgo., 1972-82; prof. law U. Chgo., 1972-88, Seymour Logan prof., 1978-88, Seymour Logan prof. emeritus, 1988—. Lt. USNR, 1943-46. Fellow Am. Bar Found.; mem. ABA, Mich. State Bar, Utah State Bar, Wis. State Bar, Internat. Assn. Ins. Law (past pres. U.S. chpt., mem. presdl. council, hon. v.p.), Phi Beta Kappa, Phi Kappa Phi. Author: Insurance and Public Policy (Elizur Wright award), 1960; Introduction to the Legal System, 1966; Essays in Insurance Regulation, 1966, Cases and Materials on Insurance Law, 1992; (with Werner Pfenningstorf) The Regulation of Insurance Companies in the United States and the European Communities: A Comparative Study, 1981; co-editor: Insurance, Government and Social Policy, 1969, Legal Service Plans, 1977; bd. editors: Jour. Ins. Regulation, Internat. Jour. Ins. Law; contbr. articles to profl. jours. Home: 48 W Broadway Apt 2202N Salt Lake City UT 84101-2021 Office: U Utah Coll Law Salt Lake City UT 84112

KIMBELL, MARION JOEL, retired engineer; b. McDonough, Ga., Sept. 7, 1923; s. Charles Marvin and Mary (McMillian) K.; BS in Civil Engring., U. Houston, 1949, MChem Engring., 1953; m. Judy Weidner, Dec. 18, 1946; children: Nancy, Susan, Candice. Civil engr. U.S. Dept. Interior, Lemmon, S.D., 1954; chief piping engr. M.W. Kellog Co., Paducah, Ky., 1955; nuclear engr. Westinghouse Atomic Power Div., Pitts., 1956-59; control systems prin. engr. Kaiser Engrs., Oakland, Calif., 1959-80; control systems supervising engr. Bechtel Inc., San Francisco, 1980-86; ret., 1986; control systems tchr. Laney Coll. cons. engr. NASA, Gen. Atomic Co.; advisory bd. Chabot Collage on radiation tech. Served as sgt. U.S. Army, 1943-46. Registered profl. nuclear engr., Calif.; control systems engr., Calif. Mem. Instrument Soc. of Am. (sr. mem. exec. com.). Clubs: Moose. Contbr. articles to profl. jours. Home: 22324 Ralston Ct Hayward CA 94541-3336

KIMBERLEY, A. G., JR., industrial products, factory representative, management executive; b. Portland, Oreg., Oct. 29, 1939; s. A. Gurney and Meta (Horgan) K.; m. M. Susan Solie, Sept. 15, 1949 (div.); children: John Langton, Thea Ness; m. Roxanne Johannesen, Mar. 26, 1952. BS, Lewis & Clark Coll., 1959-62; postgrad., U. Oreg., 1963. Mgr. meat and dairy div. Hudson House Co., Portland, 1963-64; pres. Wall-Western Inc., Portland, 1964-92, Kimberley Indsl., Portland, 1982-92; owner Kimberley Boxwood Farm, Wilsonville, Oreg., 1987—, A. G. Kimberley & Co., 1992—. Republican. Episcopalian. Home: 16720 SW Wilsonville Rd Wilsonville OR 97070-9511

KIMBERLEY, BARRY PAUL, ear surgeon; b. Ont., Can.; s. Arthur and Maureen (Gibney) K.; m. Grace Khouri, May 13, 1989; children: Caleigh, Cameron. MD, Queen's U., Kingston, Ont., 1983; PhD, U. Minn., 1990. Registered profl. engr., Can.; diplomate Am. Bd. Otolaryngology. Mem. sci. staff Bell No. Rsch., Ottawa, Ont., 1979-81; intern, then resident U. Minn., 1983-88; asst. prof. U. Calgary, Alta., Can., 1990-92, assoc. prof., Campbell McLaurin chair in hearing deficiencies, 1990—. Contbr. articles to profl. publs., including Jour. Speech and Hearing Rsch., 1992 (Editor's award for best manuscript), Jour. Acoustical Soc. Am., 1989, Laryngoscope, 1992, Ear and Hearing. Recipient Clin. Investigator award Alta. Heritage Found. for Med. Rsch., 1991. Fellow Am. Acad. Otolaryngology, Royal Coll. of Physicians and Surgeons; mem. Acoustical Soc. Am., Assn. for Rsch. in Otolaryngology. Office: U Calgary, 3300 Hospital Dr NW, Calgary, AB Canada T2N 4N1

KIMBRELL, GRADY NED, author, educator; b. Tallant, Okla., Apr. 6, 1933; s. Virgil Leroy Kimbrell and La Veria Dee Underwood; m. Marilyn Louise King, May 30, 1953 (div.); m. Mary Ellen Cunningham, Apr. 11, 1973; children: Mark Leroy, Lisa Christine, Joni Lynne. BA, Southwestern Coll., Winfield, Kans., 1956; MA, Colo. State Coll., 1958. Cert. tchr. (life), Calif., Colo.; cert. adminstr., Calif. Bus. tchr. Peabody (Kans.) High Sch., 1956-58; bus. tchr. Santa Barbara (Calif.) High Sch., 1958-65, coordinator work edn., 1965-75, dir. research and evaluation, 1975-88; cons., textbook researcher and author. Author: Introduction of Business and Office Careers, 1974, The World of Work Career Interest Survey, 1986; co-author: Succeeding in the World of Work, 1970, 5th rev. edit., 1992, Entering the World of Work, 1974, 3rd rev. edit., 1988, The Savvy Consumer, 1984, Marketing Essentials, 1991, Office Skills for the 1990's, 1992, Advancing in the World of Work, 1992, Exploring Business and Computer Careers, 1992, Employment Skills for Office Careers, 1995. With U.S. Army, 1953-55. Mem. NEA, Calif. Assn. Work Experience Educators (life, v.p. 1968-70), Nat. Work Experience Edn. Assn., Calif. Tchrs. Assn., Coop. Work Experience Assn. Republican.

KIMBRELL, LESLIE CAITLIN, health science consultant; b. Kansas City, Mo., Apr. 19, 1944; d. William R. and Katherine L. (Maguire) K.; children: Chad M. Steele, Cristopher M. Steele. BS, Avila Coll., 1973; MS, U. Ariz., 1979; MA, U. Phoenix, 1986; PhD, Am. Inst. Holistic Theology. RN, Ariz.; cert. addictions counselor, Ariz.; cert. advanced group psychotherapist. Faculty instr. Ctrl. Mo. State U., Warrensburg, 1973-74; masters affiliate, RN U. Ariz. Med. Ctr., Tucson, 1974-75; supr. Tucson (Ariz.) Med. Ctr., 1976-77; counselor/cons. S.W. Counseling, Tucson, 1978-79; behavioral health psychotherapist So. Ariz. Mental Health Ctr., Tucson, 1979-84; program coord., psychotherapist CIGNA Healthplan of Ariz., Tucson, 1984-86; mgmt. cons. Kimbrooke-Stephens Assocs., Tucson, 1986-87; clin. health psychotherapist Carondelet/St. Joseph's Hosp., Tucson, 1989-94; complimentary health care clinician-cons. Desert Harmonies Health, Tucson, 1987—; lifestyle/stress mgmt. cons. Carondelet/St. Joseph's Hosp., Tucson, 1989-94; rschr., presenter Am. Heart Assn., Tucson, 1991; presenter Am. Spinal Cord Injury Assn., Tucson, 1992; faculty Pima C.C., 1995—, Prescott Coll., 1994—. Author: Emotional Needs of Parents of Premature Infants, 1979, Impact of Substance Abuse Treatment, 1986, Oriental Health Care as a Personal and Planetary Healing Modality, 1994; author, producer (tng. video) Interactive Group Psychotherapy, 1983. Mem. Am. Holistic Nurses Assn.

KIM-HAN, JEANNIE HYUN, educational administrator; b. Seoul, Korea; d. Hank Gil and Katherine (Lee) K.; m. Stefan Han, Sept. 3, 1994. BA in

Anthropology, UCLA, 1990. Asst. dir. student activities Vol. Programs Ctr. Occidental Coll., Eagle Rock, Calif., 1990-92, acting dir. student activities Vol. Programs Ctr., 1992; exec. dir. Calif. Campus Compact UCLA, 1992—; mem. Youth Svc. Calif. Steering Com., 1992—, CALSERVE Working Group, 1992-94, Nat. Svc. Seminar, 1993-94, Gov.'s Interim Com., 1993-94. Dir. Prison Coalition, 1988; chair Campus Outreach Opportunity League Nat. Conf. Bd. and Exec. Bd., 1989-90, mem. nat. bd. dirs., 1993—; commr. UCLA Cmty. Svc., 1989-90; founder So. Calif. Cmty. Svc. Consortium, 1992; bd. mgrs. N.E. YMCA, 1991-92, mem. adv. bd., 1992—; bd. dirs. L.A. Team Mentoring, Inc., 1993—; commr. Commn. on Improving Life through Svc., 1994—. Office: Calif Campus Compact 10920 Wilshire Blvd Los Angeles CA 90024-6502

KIMME, ERNEST GODFREY, communications engineer; b. Long Beach, Calif., June 7, 1929; s. Ernest Godfrey and Lura Elizabeth (Dake) K.; BA cum laude, Pomona Coll., 1952; MA, U. Minn., 1954, PhD, 1955; m. Margaret Jeanne Bolen, Dec. 10, 1978; children by previous marriage: Ernest G., Elizabeth E., Karl Frederick. Mem. grad. faculty Oreg. State U., Corvallis, 1955-57; mem. tech. staff Bell Telephone Labs., Murray Hill, N.J., 1957-65, supr. mobile radio rsch. lab., 1962-65; head applied sci. dept. Collins Radio Co., Newport Beach, Calif., 1965-72; rsch. engr. Northrop Electronics, Hawthorne, Calif., 1972-74; sr. staff engr. Interstate Electronics Corp., Anaheim, Calif., 1974-79; dir. advanced systems, dir. advanced comm. systems, tech. dir. spl. comm. programs Gould Navcomm Systems, El Monte, Calif., 1979-82; pres. Cobit, Inc, 1982-84; tech. staff Gen. Rsch. Corp., Santa Barbara, 1984-87; v.p. engring. Starfind, Inc., Laguna Niguel, Calif., 1987-88; dir. engring. R&D Unit Instruments, Orange, Calif., 1988-89; staff scientist Brunswick Def. Systems, Costa Mesa, Calif., 1989-90; v.p. engring. Redband Techs., Inc., 1990—; prin. assoc. Ameta Cons. Technologists; v.p. A.S. Johnston Drilling Corp., Woodland Hills, Calif.; adj. prof. U. Redlands, Golden Gate Univ., 1989—; mem. adj. faculty math. U. Redlands Whitehead Ctr., 1990—. Mem. AAAS, Aircraft Owners and Pilots Assn., Exptl. Aircraft Assn., Phi Beta Kappa, Sigma Xi. Contbr. articles to profl. jours. Home: 301 N Starfire St Anaheim CA 92807-2928

KIMMEL, MARK, venture capital company executive; b. Denver, Feb. 15, 1940; s. Earl Henry and Gerry Claire Kimmel; m. Gloria J. Danielewicz, Jan. 29, 1966 (div.); children: Kenton, Kristopher. BS in Elec. Engring., U. Colo., 1963, BS in Mktg., 1963; MBA in Fin., U. So. Calif., 1966. Sales engr., market research analyst 3M Co., Calif. and Minn., 1963-70; mktg. mgr. Am. Computer and Communications, Calif., 1970-71; mgr. new bus. devel. Motorola, Inc., Schaumburg, Ill., 1971-76; v.p. corp. devel. Nat. City Lines, Denver, 1976-77; pres. Enervest, Inc., Denver, 1977-84; gen. ptnr. Columbine Venture Fund Ltd., 1983-91, Columbine Venture Fund II, 1983-91, Columbine Venture Mgmt. I, 1983-91, Columbine Venture Mgmt. II, 1983-91; pres. Columbine Venture Mgmt. Inc., 1983-91, Paradigm Ptnrs., Inc., 1992—; exec. bd. dirs. Boulder Tech. Incubator; bd. dirs. Colo. Biomed. Venture Ctr., Colo. Incubator Fund. Mem. Nat. Assn. Small Bus. Investment Cos. (past bd. govs.), Venture Capital Assn. Colo. (past chmn.). Home: 4204 Tamarack Ct Boulder CO 80304-0991 Office: 1911 11th St Boulder CO 80302

KIMMICH, ROBERT ANDRÉ, psychiatrist; b. Indpls., Nov. 2, 1920; s. John Martin and Renée Marie (Baron) K.; m. Nancy Earle Smith, 1944 (div. 1952); children: Robert, John, Nancy. BS, Ind. U., 1940, MD, 1943. Diplomate Am. Bd. Psychiatry and Neurology; lic. physician, Calif. Intern St. Vincent's Hosp., Indpls., 1943-44; resident in psychiatry Inst. Pa. Hosp., Phila., 1944-45, U.S. Army Hosp., Phoenixville, Pa., 1945-47; chief male psychiat. div. Worcester (Mass.) State Hosp., 1947-48; resident in psychiatry Harvard Advanced Study Mental Health Ctr., Boston, 1948; asst. prof., asst. chief outpatient dept. Yale U. Sch. Medicine, 1949-51; chief psychosomatic svc. VA Hosp., Newington, Conn., 1949-51; med. dir. Territorial Psychiat. Hosp., Kaneohe, Hawaii, 1951-58; clin. dir. Ill. State Psychiat. Inst., Chgo., 1958-59; chief profl. edn. Stockton (Calif.) State Hosp., 1959-60; chief mental health program and svcs. City of San Francisco, 1960-64; dir. dept. mental health State of Mich., 1964-68; chmn. dept. psychiatry Children's Hosp., San Francisco, 1968-76; pvt. practice San Francisco, 1970—; asst. prof. psychiatry Yale U. Med. Sch., 1948-51; assoc. prof. Northwestern U. Med. Sch., 1958-59; asst. clin. prof. U. Calif., San Francisco, 1960-64; assoc. clin. prof. U. Mich. Med. Sch., Ann Arbor, 1964-68, Stanford U. Med. Sch., 1967-80; lectr. U. Hawaii, 1952-58; pres., founder San Francisco Coordinating Coun. on Mental Retardation, 1961-64; com. on psychiat. tng. State of Calif., 1963-64; chair adv. bd. Mich. Mental Health and Mental Retardation, 1964-67; cons. on mental retardation White House, 1965; exec. com. Children's Hosp., San Francisco, 1967-76; pres. Western Inst. for Rsch. in Mental Health, 1962-64, v.p., 1964-67; ind. med. examiner Calif. Bd. Indsl. Accidents, 1984—; bd. dirs. Children's Physicians Assocs. Editor Northern California Psychiatric Physician, 1985-94. Bd. dirs., chmn., fin. com. mem. Nat. Assn. State Mental Health, 1965-66; chmn., managed care com. No. Calif. Psychiat. Soc., 1991-93; bd. dirs. Westside Mental Health Ctr., San Francisco, 1967-77. Capt. M.C., U.S. Army, 1945-47. Fellow Am. Psychiat. Assn. (life, pres. Hawaii dist. branch 1954-55, rep. to nat. assembly 1986—, task force on ethics 1989-90, com. on procedures 1990—, com. on stds., 1966, spl. com. on prepayment health ins. 1965, com. on mental hosps., 1965, Am. Hosp. Assn. liaison 1964, nominating com. 1993—); mem. AMA, Mich. State Med. Soc., Calif. Med. Assn., San Francisco Med. Soc., Northern Calif. Psychiat. Soc. (pres. elect 1991-93, pres. 1993—, coun. mem. 1984—, editor 1984-94), San Francisco Psychiat. Soc. (pres. 1984-85). Office: 341 Spruce St San Francisco CA 94118-1830

KIMPORT, DAVID LLOYD, lawyer; b. Hot Springs, S.D., Nov. 28, 1945; s. Ralph E. and Ruth N. (Hutchinson) K.; m. Barbara H. Buggert, Apr. 2, 1976; children: Katrina Elizabeth, Rebecca Helen, Susanna Ruth. AB summa cum laude, Bowdoin Coll., 1968; postgrad. Imperial Coll., U. London, 1970-71; JD, Stanford U., 1975. Bar: Calif. 1975, U.S. Supreme Ct. 1978. Assoc. Baker & McKenzie, San Francisco, 1975-82, ptnr., 1982-90; ptnr. Nossaman, Guthner, Knox & Elliot, 1990—. Active San Francisco Planning and Urban Rsch., 1978—, Commonwealth Club of Calif., 1984—, The Family, 1987—. Served with U.S. Army, 1968-70. Decorated Bronze Star; Fulbright grantee, 1970. Mem. ABA, San Francisco Bar Assn., Phi Beta Kappa. Democrat. Episcopalian. Office: Nossaman Guthner Knox & Elliott 50 California St Fl 34 San Francisco CA 94111-4624

KIMPTON, DAVID RAYMOND, natural resource consultant, writer; b. Twin Falls, Idaho, Feb. 19, 1942; s. Lloyd and Retura (Robins) K.; m. Joanna Peak, June 2, 1984; foster children: Donnie, Derrick, Dustin. BS in Forestry, U. Idaho, 1964. Forester U.S. Forest Svc., Panguitch, Utah, 1966-68; with dept. interdisciplinary natural resources U.S. Forest Svc., Ely, Nev., 1968-71; with dept. interdisciplinary natural resources U.S. Forest Svc., Stanley, Idaho, 1971-72, dist. forest ranger, 1972-78; dist. forest ranger U.S. Forest Svc., Mountain City, Nev., 1978-84; natural resource cons. Idaho, 1984-92; range conservationist U.S. Forest Svc., Stanley, Idaho, 1992-93; program mgr. natural resources Sawtooth Nat. Recreation Area, Stanley, Idaho, 1993—; incident comdr. U.S. Forest Svc., Western States. 1978-86; botanist pvt. and govtl., Idaho, Nev., 11985-92; naturalist schs., pvt., govt., Idaho, Nev., 1988-95; bd. dirs. Salmon River Emergency Med. Clinic, Stanley, Idaho, 1984-86, v.p., 1987-92; bd. dirs., v.p. Idaho Mountain Health Clinics, Boise, 1985-92. Author Mining Law jour., 1990; author Life Saving Rescue mag., 1989. Pres. Meth. Youth Found., Twin Falls, 1960—; treas., v.p. Chrisman Bd. Dirs., Moscow, Idaho, 1960-63; bd. dirs. Vol. Fire Dept., Ely, 1968-71, Sawtooth Valley Meditation Chapel, 1974-76, Stanley Cmty. Bldg., 1977-78; mem. Sawtooth Valley Assn., Stanley, 1971-72, Vol. Fire Dept. Stanley, 1975-78, Mountain Search and Rescue, Stanley, 1972-78, Coalition of Taxpayers, Stanley, 1990-95. With U.S. Army, 1965-66, Vietnam. Recipient Presdl. Unit Citation award Pres. Johnson, 1965; named Outstanding Young Man Am., Bd. Nat. Advs., 1971, Outstanding Mem., White Pine Jaycees, 1969. Mem. Idaho Wildlife, Sawtooth Wildlife Coun. Mem. Christian Ch. Home: PO Box 32 Stanley ID 83278-0032

KIMSEY, RUSTIN RAY, bishop. s. Lauren Chamness K.; m. Gretchen Beck Rinehart, 1961; 2 children. BS U. Oreg., 1957, BD Episcopal Theol. Sem., 1960. Ordained priest, Episcopal Ch., 1960; vicar, St. John Ch., Hermiston, 1960-61; priest in charge, St. Paul NYSSA, 1961; vicar, St. Albany, 1961-67; rector, St. Stephen, Baker, 1967-71, St. Paul, the Dalles, 1971-80; consecrated bishop of Eastern Oreg., 1980; bishop, Episcopal Diocese Eastern Oreg., The Dalles, 1980—. Office: Episcopal Diocese Ea Oreg PO Box 620 The Dalles OR 97058-0620*

KIMURA, JOAN ALEXANDRA, artist, educator; b. L.A., July 10, 1934; children: Carey Tadao, Devin Isamu. Cert., Art Ctr. Coll. Design, 1955; BFA, U. Alaska, 1979; MFA, Syracuse U., 1984. Illustrator James Eng Assocs. and Sudler and Hennesey, N.Y.C., 1955-57; freelance illustrator N.Y.C., 1955-71; tchr. Anchorage C.C., 1976-87; prof. art U. Alaska, Anchorage, 1987-93; adj. instr. art Anchorage C.C., 1973-76; workshop leader Anchorage Mus. History and Art, 1988, Fairbanks Art Festival, 1989-91. One-woman shows include Chas. Z. Mann Gallery, N.Y.C., 1969, Anchorage Mus. History and Art, 1975, 83, 88, Westbroadway Gallery, Alternate Space, N.Y.C., 1981, 83, others; exhibited in group shows Nat. Soc. Painters in Casein and Acrylic, N.Y.C., 1968, Nat. Acad. Design, N.Y.C., 1969, Conn. Acad. Fine Arts, 1968, 71, 72, 74, 77, Audubon Artists, N.Y.C., 1968, 81, Art Ctr. Coll. Design Alumni Show, 1973, 74, 75, 76, 78, 80, 81, Visual Arts Ctr. Alaska, 1984, 8, Anchorage (Alaska) Mus. History, 1988-89, 90-91, numerous others; represented in permanent collections Alaska State Mus., Fairbanks, Juneau, Anchorage Mus. History and Art, Alaska State Coun. on Arts, Rainier Bank of Alaska, Atlantic Richfield Co.; reviewer Arts Mag., 1969, Artspeak, 1983; reviewer (book) Painting in the North, 1993. Grants panelist Alaska State Coun. Arts, 1984-87; bd. dirs. Anchorage Mus. History and Art, 1981-88, acquisition com., 1988-94; active Conn. Acad. Fine Art, 1971-94. Recipient Sage Allen award Conn. Acad. Fine Art, 1971, Mel Kohler award All Alaska Juried Show, 1972, Fine Art award Art Ctr. Coll. Design, 1973, Juror's Choice Anch Mus. of History & Art, 1974, Best of Show award All Alaska Juried Show, 1976, 1st prize Pacific N.W. Figure Drawing Competition, 1986, Painting award All Alaska Juried Show, 1988; travel grantee Alaska State Coun. Art, 1983, 90, fellowship grantee, 1984. Home: 15000 Stevens Rd SE Olalla WA 98359-9428

KINAKA, WILLIAM TATSUO, lawyer; b. Lahaina, Hawaii, Apr. 4, 1940; s. Toshio and Natsumi (Hirouji) K.; m. Jeanette Louisa Ramos, Nov. 23, 1968; children: Kimberly H., Kristine N.Y. BA in Polit. Sci., Whittier Coll., 1962; MA in Internat. Rels., Am. U., 1964, JD, 1973. Bar: D.C. 1975, U.S. Ct. Appeals (D.C. cir.) 1975, U.S. Dist. Ct. D.C. 1975, U.S. Tax Ct. 1975, U.S. Ct. Mil. Appeals 1975, Hawaii 1976, U.S. Dist. Ct. Hawaii 1976, U.S. Ct. Appeals (9th cir.) 1976. Career trainee CIA, Langley, Va., 1966; legis. asst. Sen. Hiram L. Fong, Washington, 1966-76; assoc. Ueoka & Luna, Wailuku, Hawaii, 1977-85; pvt. practice law Wailuku, Hawaii, 1985—; arbitrator circuit ct., 1989—; ct. arbitrator, 1989—; legal cons. Hale Mahaolu Elderly Housing, Kahului, 1976—. Active Dem. Party of Hawaii, Wailuku, 1988-89; pres. Nat. Eagle Scout Assn. of Boy Scouts Am., Wailuku, 1983-91; bd. dirs. Wailuku Main St. Assn., 1988-94, Maui Adult Day Care Ctr., Puunene, 1978; Maui coun. Boy Scouts of Am., 1983—; pres., bd. dirs. Maui Youth Intervention Program, Inc., 1993—. Mem. Hawaii Bar Assn., Maui Bar Assn., Maui Japanese C. of C., Maui C. of C., Nat. Eagle Scout Assn. (pres. Wailuku 1983-91). United Ch. of Christ. Home: 639 Pio Dr Wailuku HI 96793-2622 Office: 24 N Church St Ste 207 Wailuku HI 96793-1606

KINARD, J. SPENCER, television news executive; b. Long Beach, Calif., Aug. 29, 1940. BS in Speech and Journalism, U. Utah, 1966. Writer, producer CBS News, N.Y.C., 1970; corr. Salt Lake (City) Tribune; staff photographer Ogden (Utah) Standard Examiner; radio announcer Centerville, Utah; news dir., anchorman KSL-TV, Salt Lake City; account exec. Sta. KSL-TV, Salt Lake City, 1979-80, news dir., 1980-81; v.p., TV news dir. KSL-TV, Salt Lake City, 1981—. Announcer Mormon Tabernacle Choir, LDS Ch., Salt Lake City, Spoken Word program host, 1972—; past moderator Humana Hosp. Davis No.; past founding bd. mem. Children's Mus. of Utah. CBS fellow Columbia U., 1968. Mem. Nat. Radio-TV News Dirs. Assn. (past pres.). Office: Sta KSL TV Broadcast House 55 E 3rd Ave # D Salt Lake City UT 84107-4722

KINARD, R. CHRIS, real estate and agricultural company executive; b. West Point, N.Y., June 23, 1942; s. William Henry Kinard, Jr. and Jane Porter (Whitesides) Kinard Dellinger; m. Carol Ann Neitzke, Jan. 21, 1972 (sep.); children: Amy Louise, Nora Jane, Jonathan Garrett. BS in Engring., U.S. Military Acad., 1965; MS in internat. rels., Ohio State U., 1966. From staff employee rels. to coord. employee rels. Amoco, Chgo., N.Y.C., London, 1966-75; dir. employee rels. Levi Strauss Corp., San Francisco, 1975-78; mgmt. cons. Hay Assocs., San Francisco, 1978-79; dir. human resources Natomas Co., San Francisco, 1979-82; v.p., mgmt. advisor Natomas Co. IIAPCO, Jakarta, Indonesia, 1982-85; pres. Leeshore Prodns., Mill Valley, Calif., 1985-87; dir. human resources AMFAC/JMB Hawaii, Inc., Lihue (Kauai), Hawaii, 1987-89; v.p. human resources and adminstrn. AMFAC/JMB Hawaii, Inc., Honolulu, Hawaii, 1989—. Editor in chief The Pointer U.S. Military Acad., West Point, 1964-65. Treas. Kauai Mayor's Coun. on Adult Literacy, 1987-89; mem. County Salary Commn., Kauai County Govt., Lihue, Kauai, Hawaii, 1989, chmn. Bus. Coun. on Dependent Care, Honolulu, 1989-93, exec. com. Gov.'s Coun. on Family Ctrs., 1989—; steering com. Hawaii Bus. Health Coun., 1989—; cubmaster Boy Scouts of Am., Kauai, Hawaii, 1987-89. Named Cubmaster of Yr., 1987, Boy Scouts Am., Hawaii. Mem. Soc. Human Resource Mgmt., C. of C., Assn. Grads. U.S. Mil. Acad., Rotary internat., Phi Kappa Phi, Pi Sigma Alpha. Home: 1520 Ward Ave Apt 901 Honolulu HI 96822-3556 Office: AMFAC/JMB Hawaii PO Box 3230 700 Bishop St Honolulu HI 96801

KINASHI, DOREEN ANN, systems analyst, writer, editor; b. Plainfield, N.J., Jan. 2, 1957; d. Chester Paul and Helen Carol (Barsh) Cichurski; m. Yasuhiro Kinashi, Apr. 25, 1987; 1 child, Jason Philip. BSW, U. Evansville, Ind., 1979. Applications engr., support rep. NBI Inc. Govt. Systems, Washington, 1983-85; def. systems analyst Ultrasystems Inc., Irvine, Calif., 1985—; course instr. Def. Intelligence Agy., Washington, 1983-85. Author: Trends in Computer Ergonomic, 1984, Military Software Applications, 1987. Intelligence officer USAFR, Fayetteville, N.C., 1979-83, San Bernardino, Calif., 1985-87; jr. v.p. Res. Officers Assn., Arlington, Va., 1984; pres. Air Force Jr. Officers Com., Fayetteville, N.C., 1979-80. Capt. USAF, 1979-83. Mem. Nat. Historic Preservation Soc., AAUW. Home: 10426 Mount Sunapee Rd Vienna VA 22182-1523

KINBERG, JUD, producer; b. N.Y.C., July 4, 1925; s. Benjamin and Lillian (Pearlman) K.; m. Suzanne Dalbert, June 26, 1953 (dec. Dec. 1970); 1 child, Steven; m. Monica Menell, July 6, 1971; children: Simon, Robert. BA, U. N.C., 1948. V.p. TV Campbell-Ewald, N.Y.C., 1948-50; assoc. prodr. MGM Films, Culver City, Calif., 1951-57; prodr., writer CBS TV, N.Y.C., 1957-58; prodr. CBS TV, L.A., 1958-59, Weinstein Prodns., London, 1959-60; pres., writer, prodr. Blazer Films-Columbia Pictures, Hollywood, Calif., 1961-65; v.p., prodr. Horizon Films, London, 1965-68; pres., prodr., writer Valley Vista Prodns., London, 1969-74; freelance writer, prodr. London, Paris & L.A., 1975-76; exec. prodr. Universal Studios TV/NBC, Universal City, Calif., 1977-78; prodr. ABC TV, L.A., 1979-82; assoc. prof. dept. film and TV Calif. State U., Northridge, 1979-82; sr. v.p. Embassy TV, L.A., 1982-83; exec. prodr., writer Michael Grade Prodns., L.A., 1984-85; pres./prodr., writer Jud Kinberg Prodns., L.A., 1986—; vis. prof. film sch. Tel Aviv U., 1974-75. Assoc. producer (films) Bad & Beautiful, Julius Ceasar, Executive Suite, Moonfleet, Cobweb, Lust for Life, 1951-57, Blast in Centralia No. 5, 1959, The Collector, Reach ofr Glory, The Magus,. 1961-65; exec. producer Kane & Able, 1984-85; screenplays: Impossible Object, 1971, East of Sudan, 1963, The Saxons, 1962, Circus, 1972, The Sellout, 1974, When Hell Was in Session, 1978, Kiss of Gold, 1979, Stoning in Fulham County, 1988, To Catch a Killer, 1991, In the Best Interest of the Children, 1992. Sgt. U.S. Army, 1944-45. Mem. Writers Guild Am., Phi Beta Kappa. Jewish.

KINCHELOE, LAWRENCE RAY, state official; b. Twin Falls, Idaho, Jan. 1, 1941; s. Kenneth Kincheloe and Wilma Gladys (Barnett) Routt; children—Gerry, Corey, Michelle, Lawrence, Jeffrey; m. Elaine Lee Kempsky, April 2, 1995. BA, Mont. State U., 1963; MA, Pacific Luth. U., 1978. Assoc. supt. Dept. Corrections, Wash. State Penitentiary, Walla Walla, 1978-82, warden, 1982-89; dir. Div. of Prisons, Olympia, Wash., 1989-91; supt. Spring Creek Correctional Ctr., Seward, Ak, 1992—. Served to maj. U.S. Army, 1963-78. Decorated Silver Star, Bronze Star with oak leaf cluster, Legion of Merit, Air medal with oak leaf cluster, Army Commendation medal (2); Vietnamese Cross of Gallantry (3). Mem. Am. Corrections Assn., N.Am. Assn. Wardens, West Cen. Wardens and Supts. Assn. Home: PO Box 2109 Seward AK 99664-2109 Office: Alaska Dept Corrections PO Box 2109 Seward AK 99664-2109

KINCHELOE, WILLIAM ROBERTSON, JR., electrical engineering educator; b. Little Rock, June 17, 1926; s. William Robertson and Genevieve (Skinner) K.; m. Helen Joan Wehrly, Nov. 2, 1956 (div. 1993); children: Karen Lee, Robert Wallace, Wylliam Carl, John Stuart. BSEE, U. Okla., 1946, MIT, 1947; MSEE, Stanford U., 1951, PhD, 1962. Radio engr. Sta. WNAD, Norman, 1943-44; rsch. engr., prof. Stanford (Calif.) U., 1951-91; cons. Kincheloe Engring., Los Altos Hills, Calif., 1981-91. Lt. USN, 1947-50. Mem. IEEE (sr.), Tau Beta Pi, Sigma Xi.

KIND, KENNETH WAYNE, lawyer, real estate broker; b. Missoula, Mont., Apr. 1, 1948; s. Joseph Bruce and Elinor Joy (Smith) K.; m. Diane Lucille Jozaitis, Aug. 28, 1971; children: Kirstin Amber, Kenneth Warner. BA, Calif. State U.-Northridge, 1973; JD, Calif. Western U., 1976. Bar: Calif. 1976, U.S. Dist. Ct. (ea., so., no. dists.) Calif., 1976, U.S. Cir. Ct. Appeals (9th cir.); lic. NASCAR driver, 1987. Mem. celebrity security staff Brownstone Am., Beverly Hills, Calif., 1970-76; tchr. Army and Navy Acad., Carlsbad, Calif., 1975-76; real estate broker, Bakersfield, Calif., 1978—; sole practice, Bakersfield, 1976—; lectr. mechanic's lien laws, Calif., 1983—. Staff writer Calif. Western Law Jour., 1975. Sgt. U.S. Army, 1967-70. Mem. ABA, VFW, Nat. Order Barristers. Libertarian. Office: 4540 California Ave Ste 210 Bakersfield CA 93309-7019

KINDRICK, ROBERT LEROY, academic administrator, dean, English educator; b. Kansas City, Mo., Aug. 17, 1942; s. Robert William and Waneta LeVeta (Lobdell) K.; B.A., Park Coll., 1964; M.A., U. Mo., Kansas City, 1967; Ph.D., U. Tex., 1971; m. Carolyn Jean Reed, Aug. 20, 1965. Instr., Central Mo. State U., Warrenburg, 1967-69, asst. prof., 1969-73, assoc. prof., 1973-78, prof. English, 1978-80, head dept. English, 1975-80; dean Coll. Arts and Scis., also prof. English, Western Ill. U., Macomb, 1980-84; v.p. acad. affairs, prof. English, Emporia State U., Kans., 1984-87; provost, v.p. acad. affairs, prof. English, Eastern Ill. U., Charleston, 1987-91; provost, v.p. acad. affairs, dean grad. studies, prof. English U. Mont., 1991—. Chmn. bd. dirs. Mo. Com. for Humanities, 1979-80, Ill. Humanities Coun., 1991. Pres. Park Coll. Young Dems., 1963; v.p. Mo. Young Dems., Jefferson City, 1964; campus coordinator United Way, Macomb, Ill., 1983; mem. study com. Emporia Arts Council, 1985-86. U. Tex. fellow, 1965-66; Am. Council Learned Socs. travel grantee, 1975; Nat. Endowment for Humanities summer fellow, 1977; Mediaeval Acad. Am. grantee, 1976; Mo. Com. Humanities grantee, 1975-84; Assn. Scottish Lit. Studies grantee, 1979. Mem. Mo. Assn. Depts. English (pres. 1978-80), Mo. Philological Assn. (founding pres. 1975-77), Medieval Assn. Midwest (councillor 1977—, ex officio bd. 1980—, v.p. 1987-88, exec. sec. 1988—), Ill. Medieval Assn. (founding exec. sec. 1983-93), Mid-Am. Medieval Assn., Rocky Mountain MLA, Assn. Scottish Lt. Studies, Early English Text Soc., Société Rencesvals, Medieval Acad. N.Am. (exec. sec. com. on ctrs. and regional assns.), Internat. Arthurian Soc., Sigma Tau Delta, Phi Kappa Phi. Club: Rotary (editor Warrensburg club). Author: Robert Henryson, 1980; A New Classical Rhetoric, 1980, Henryson and the Medieval Arts of Rhetoric, 1993; editor: Teaching the Middle Ages, 1981—; editor Studies in Medieval and Renaissance Teaching, 1975-80; contbr. articles to profl. jours. Home: PO Box 9398 Missoula MT 59807-9398 Office: U Mont Main Hall Missoula MT 59812

KING, ALEXANDER LOUIS, pediatrician; b. Trenton, N.J., June 9, 1914; s. Edgar Emmanuel and Mildred Gertrude (Alexander) Klinkowstein; m. Carol Jean Leona Siegert, Jan. 23, 1958; 1 child, Susan Alexis. BA, Johns Hopkins U., 1933, MD, 1937. Diplomate Am. Bd. Pediatrics. Asst. prof. pediatrics Med. Sch. Wayne U., Detroit, 1946-47; dir. pediatrics Kaiser Found. Hosp., Oakland, Calif., 1950-65; sr. cons. pediatrics Kaiser Hosps., Oakland and Walnut Creek, Calif., 1965-79; blood bank physician Alameda-Contra Costa Med. Assn. Blood Bank, Oakland, 1980-93. Capt. USMC, 1942-46. Fellow Am. Acad. Pediatrics; mem. Calif. Med. Assn., No. Calif. Am. Acad. Pediatrics. Home and Office: 33 La Cresta Rd Orinda CA 94563-4143

KING, ARTHUR E., chemist, consultant; b. Fla., Mar. 22, 1947; m. Mary J. Britt, Dec. 6, 1975; 1 child, Eric Dane King. BS in Chemistry, U. West Fla., 1969; MS in Chemistry, Physics and Edn., Iowa State U., 1973, postgrad. Chief chemist Tecator Udy Analyzer Co., Boulder, Colo., 1974-76; dir. sales and mktg. Coulometrics, Inc., Wheat Ridge, Colo., 1977-83; pres. Custom Chem. Lab. Inc., Denver, 1983-85; tech. dir. UDY Corp., Fort Collins, Colo., 1985-94; sr. cons. Intelligo, Inc., Denver, 1994—, Teledyne Water Pik, Fort Collins, Colo., 1994—. Contbr. to profl. jours. Mem. Am. Soc. Testing and Materials (co-task group chmn.), Am. Chem. Soc., Soc. for Technical Communication, Phi Theta Kappa.

KING, BERNARD DAVID, cardiologist, pharmaceutical company executive; b. Lima, Ohio, Feb. 4, 1949; s. David Bernard and Edith Hedwig (Schimmens) K.; m. Kathleen Marek, Nov. 11, 1984; children: Matthew, Meaghan, Hillary, Michael. BS cum laude, U. Notre Dame, Ind., 1970; MD cum laude, Ohio State U., Columbus, 1973; MBA, U. Pa., 1992. Intern in medicine Riverside Meth. Hosp., Columbus, Ohio, 1973-74, sr. resident in medicine, 1978-79; resident in pathology The Ohio State Univ. Hosps., Columbus, 1977-78; fellow in cardiology Mt. Sinai Med. Ctr., N.Y.C., 1979-81; asst. prof. medicine N.Y. Med. Coll., Valhalla, 1981-86, asst. prof. physiology, 1984-89; dir. cardiology tng. program Westchester County Med. Ctr., Valhalla, 1983-86; dir. clin. cardiovascular investigation Smith Kline & French Labs., Phila., 1986-89; med. dir. ConvaTec div. Squibb Co., Princeton, N.J., 1989-90; v.p. med. and regulatory affairs Worldwide Convatec div. Bristol-Myers Squibb, Princeton, N.J., 1990-92; sr. v.p. rsch. and clin. devel. Advanced Tissue Scis., LaJolla, Calif., 1992-93; pres. Segenix, Inc., La Jolla, Calif., 1993-94; exec. v.p. med. & reg. affairs & strategic technical devel. Houghten Pharms., Inc., San Diego, Calif., 1995—; mem. com. for protection of human subjects, N.Y. Med. Coll., Valhalla, 1982-86, faculty senate, 1984-86. Contbr. articles to sci. jours. Served as capt. USAF, 1974-77. Grantee Am. Heart Assn., 1985-87. Fellow ACP, Am. Coll. Cardiology, N.Y. Cardiol. Soc., Soc. For Cardiac Angiography; mem. Am. Fedn. Clin. Research. Roman Catholic. Home: 4574 Mercurio St San Diego CA 92130-2731 Office: Houghten Pharms Inc 3550 Gen Atomics Ct San Diego CA 92121

KING, CHARLES LYNN, librarian; b. Olney, Ill., Oct. 31, 1949; s. Bernard DeWitt and Mary Catherine (Potts) K.; m. Esther Fukiko Fukui, May 16, 1987. AS Health Care Adminstrn., George Washington U., 1976; BS Health Care Adminstrn., So. Ill. U., 1977; MA in Mgmt., Webster Coll., 1978; M in Libr. and Info. Studies, U. Hawaii Manoa, 1992. Cert. health care exec. Pub. health adminstr. Ctrl. Oahu Mental Health, Pearl City, Hawaii, 1993; libr. Hawaii State Libr., Honolulu, 1993—. Lt. USN, 1970-91. Mem. ALA, Ret. Officers Assn., Hawaii Libr. Assn. Home: 98-1369 Koaheahe Pl Apt 89 Pearl City HI 96782-3091 Office: Hawaii State Libr 478 S King St Honolulu HI 96813-2901

KING, CHAROLETTE ELAINE, administrative officer; b. Baker, Oreg., Apr. 10, 1945; d. Melvin Howard and Rella Maxine (Gwilliam) Wright; m. Craig Seldon King, April 14, 1965; children: Andrea Karen, Diana Susan. Clerical positions various firms, Idaho, Va., Conn., 1964-71; nursing sec. VA, San Diego, 1974-77; sec. USN, Agana, Guam, 1972-73; procurement clk. USN, Bremerton, Wash., 1977-80; procurement clk. USN, San Diego, 1980, support svcs. supr., 1980-83, div. dir., 1983-87, program analyst, 1987-93, adminstrv. officer, 1993—. Recipient Model Agy. cup USN, San Diego, 1986. Republican. Office: USN Pub Works Ctr Code 139 2730 Mckean St Ste 1 San Diego CA 92136-5201

KING, CLAUDIA LOUAN, film producer, lecturer; b. Merced, Calif., May 1, 1940; d. Alvin Cecil and Thelma May (Matthew) K.; m. Douglas McLean, July 10, 1965 (div. 1975); children: Kia Gabrielle, Kendra Sue. BA, U. Calif., 1963; MA, Ind. U., 1969. Lectr. U. Fla., Gainesville, 1969-70; asst. prof. U. Nev., Las Vegas, 1973-79; producer Source 17 Prodns., Santa Monica, Calif., 1979-85; freelance producer Chico, Calif., 1985—. Author: Life Mastery: A Self-Esteem Handbook for Adults and Children, 1994, (screenplays) The Garden of Eden, 1983, My Sister's Keeper, 1986, (documentary) The Evolution of Women, 1988, 92 (short stories) In the Realm of the Invisible, 1991; prodr.: Rape is Everybody's Concern, 1978, Los Angeles Personally Yours, 1986; pub. Light Paths Communications, 1994—. Carnegie grantee, 1969; Nev. Endowment for Humanities grantee, 1978.

Mem. Women in Film, Coll. Art Assn. Democrat. Home: PO Box 3576 Chico CA 95927-3576

KING, DAVID BURNETT, history educator; b. Phila., Jan. 31, 1930; s. Karl Burnett and Edith (Loveless) K.; m. Mary Brownson, Mar., 1952 (div. 1962); children: Laura, Bonnie, Thomas; m. Paula Richter, Mar., 1963 (div. 1967); 1 child, Stephen; m. Juanita Parot, Sept. 3, 1974; 1 child, Hannah. BA, Hamilton Coll., 1951; MA, Rutgers U., 1955; postgrad., U. Heidelberg, 1957-58; PhD, Cornell U., 1962. Vis. instr. Culver (Ind.) Mil. Acad., 1964-65; from instr. to asst. prof. history Oreg. State U., Corvallis, 1962-64, from assoc. to prof. history, 1965—; head honors program Oreg. State U., 1967-68. Author: The Crisis of Our Time: Reflections on the Course of Western Civilization, 1988. 1st lt. U.S. Army, 1951-54. Schurman fellow Heidelberg U., 1957-58, Andrew White fellow Cornell U., 1958-59; Fulbright grantee Bonn, 1981. Mem. German Studies Assn., AAUP (v.p. Corvallis chpt. 1966-67). Home: 7950 NW Oxbow Dr Corvallis OR 97330-2830 Office: Oreg State U History Dept Corvallis OR 97331

KING, DAVID W., state treasurer; b. Albuquerque, June 28, 1946; m. Martha Lynn King; children: Shannon, David II, Kevin Sam. BS, N.Mex. State U., 1969, MS in Agrl. Dcons., 1970; computer short course, Rochester, N.Y., 1074. Ptnr. King Bros. and Sons Ranch, Stanley, N.Mex., 1964—, Pine Canyon Ranches, Inc. and King Land and Cattle Co., Stanley, 1969—; dir. state planning office State of Mex., Santa Fe, 1971-74; state dir. farmers home adminstrn. USDA, Albuquerque, 1977-78; gov.'s cabinet sec. Dept. Fin. and Adminstrn., chmn. state investment coun. State of Mex., 1979-80, gov.'s cabinet sec. Gen. Svcs. Dept., 1983-85; dept. state treas. State of N.Mex., Stanley, 1986-90, state treas., 1991—; exec. sec., gov.'s liaison Gov.'s N.Mex. Border Commission., 1071-75, 79-80. Mem. goodwill ambs. N.Mex. Amigos, 1973-86, Community Coun. of Albuquerque, 1974-79, N.Mex. Rural Devel. Coun., 1980-85; mem. resource conservation and devel. dist. exec. com. HUB, 1974-75; commn. mem. Internat. Space Hall of Fame., Alamogordo, N.Mex., 1975-81; supr. legal polit. subdiv. Edgewood Soil and Water Conservation Dist., 1976—; chmn. State Resource Conservation and Devel. Coun., 1971-77, N.Mex. Mortgage Fin. Authority, 1991—, Ednl. Assistance Found. Bd., 1991—; pres. N.Mex. Assn. Conservation Dists., 1977-79, nat. bd. dirs., 1980-81, N.Mex. State U. Bd. Regents, 1982-89; coord. 1st internat. border govs. conf. Mex. and U.S. El Paso, Tex. and Juarez Mex., 1980; mem., officer exec. bd. State Bapt. Ch., 1972-75; Sun. sch. dir. Calvary Bapt. Ch., 1983-85, Rodeo Road Bapt., 1985-88; elected to So. Bapt. conv. Nat. Christian Life Commn., Nashville, 1976-84; vice chmn. Border Devel. Authority, 1991—. Recipient State Minority and Human Devel. award N.Mex. State Conf. NAACP, 1972, Nat. Disting. Svc. award Nat. Assn. Conservation Dists., 1980-81, Supreme Ct. Excellence award State of Mex., 1985; named an Outstanding State Employee Soil Conservation Soc. Am., 1975. Mem. N.Mex. Technet (founding mem.), Rotary (past moriarty pres.), Omicron Delta Epsilon. Home: PO Box 85 Stanley NM 87056-0085 Office: Office of NMex State Treas PO Box 608 Santa Fe NM 87504-0608

KING, DONALD LATHAM, JR., computer software engineer; b. Washington, Feb. 4, 1961; s. Donald Latham and Nancy (Mowlds) K.; m. Janet Marie Novotny, Mar. 31, 1990; 1 child, Kyle Michael. BA in Philosophy, Emory U., 1983; MS in Computer Sci., Columbia U., 1986. Programmer, analyst WallSoft Sys., N.Y.C., 1984-89; sys. developer DynaMedix Corp., N.Y.C., 1989-90; software engr. Coord. Tech., Inc., Trumbull, Conn., 1990-91; arch., developer Columbia-Presbyn. Hosp., N.Y.C., 1988—; assoc. dir. Info. Resources, Inc., Darien, Conn., 1991-92; devel. mgr. Oracle Corp., Redwood Shores, Calif., 1992—; presenter in field. Contbr. articles to profl. jours.

KING, DOUGLAS JAMES CHRISTOPHER, mechanical engineering manager; b. Boston, Feb. 14, 1956; s. Walter Bradley Jr. and Mildred Lois (Antunez) K.; m. Sharon Lee Pastoriza, Apr. 7, 1979; children: Alden Pastoriza, Jonathan Lee, David Christopher. BS, MIT, 1978. Registered mech. engr.; cert. mfg. engr. Design engr. Chevron, USA, Richmond, Calif., 1978-80; assoc. engr. ESDM Corp., San Jose, Calif., 1980-82, engr., 1982-83, sr. engr., 1983-85, staff mech. engr., 1985-87; sr. engr. Bechtel Nat., Inc., San Francisco, 1987-89; sr. engr. RPC Industries, Hayward, Calif., 1989-91, staff mech. engr., 1991-93, mech. engring. mgr., 1993—. Mem. ASME, Soc. Mfg. Engrs. (sr.). Republican. Office: RPC Industries 21325 Cabot Blvd Hayward CA 94545-1650

KING, ELIZABETH ANN, writer; b. Malden, Mass., May 9, 1938; d. Richard H. Sheldon and Jane I. (Cotton) Killoran; m. Richard William King, Aug. 20, 1965 (div.); children: Kathy Ann, Richard Eric. AA, Moorpark Coll., 1977; BA, Calif. State U., Northridge, 1978. Adminstrv. sec. Northrop Corp., Newbury Park, Calif., 1981-86; freelance writer, 1987—. Author: Corridors, Winter Solstice, (with Sam Kane (Giancana)) Tales of the Vanguard: The Announcer; author of short stories; contbr. poetry to anthologies; lyricist: I Believe in Heroes, 1987, Journey's End, 1988. Home: 1021 Scandia Ave #4 Ventura CA 93004

KING, FRANK, investment company executive; b. Redcliff, Alta., Can.; married; 4 children. BSChemE, U. Alta., 1958; LLD (hon.), U. Calgary, 1988, U. Calgary, 1988. Chem. engr. various cos., 1958-72; pres. Met. Investment Corp., 1972—; pres., CEO The Inmark Group, Avanti Petroleums Ltd., Cambridge Environ. Sys. Inc.; also bd. dirs. other cos., Can. Chmn., chief exec. officer XV Olympic Winter Games Organizing Com.; active many community/sports programs. Decorated Officer Order of Can., Olympic Order in gold; recipient Air Can. Amateur Sports award, Premier's Award of Excellence, 1981, Champion d'Afrique Gold medal; inducted into Olympic Hall of Fame, Calgary. Mem. Assn. Profl. Engrs., Geologists and Geophysicists of Alta., World Pres. Orgn., Calgary Booster Club (hon., life), Men's Can. Club (hon., life), Can. 125 Corp. (co-pres.), Lions (hon., life). Office: 4600 400 3rd Ave SW, Calgary, AB Canada T2P 4H2

KING, FRANK WILLIAM, writer; b. Port Huron, Mich., Oct. 1, 1922; s. William Ernest and Catherine Theresa (Smith) K.; student U. Utah, 1963-65, Santa Monica City Coll., 1941, 48-49; BA, Marylhurst Coll., 1979; MA, U. Portland, 1982; m. Carma Morrison Sellers, Sept. 16, 1961; children: Rosanne, Jeanine Nell, Melanie, Lisa June; one stepson, Michael Sellers. Air traffic contr. FAA, Salt Lake City, Albuquerque and Boise, Idaho; 1949-65, info. officer Western Region, L.A., 1965-68; pub. affairs officer L.A. Dist. C.E., U.S. Army, 1968-69, Walla Walla (Wash.), 1969-77, N. Pacific div., Portland, Oreg., 1977-79; dir. pub. rels. U. Portland, 1979-80; adj. asst. prof. comm. U. Portland, 1982-83; instr. Portland (Oreg.) C.C., 1980-87; freelance writer, 1960—. Exec. asst. L.A. Fed. Exec. Bd., 1965-67; chmn. Walla Walla County Alcoholism Adminstrv. Bd., 1974-75; vice-chmn. Walla Walla County Human Services Adminstrv. Bd., 1976-78, chmn., 1977-78. Served with USMCR, 1942-45. Decorated Air medal; William Randolph Hearst scholar, 1965. Mem. Soc. Profl. Journalists, Pub. Relations Soc. Am. (accredited), Kappa Tau Alpha. Democrat. Roman Catholic. Home and Office: 310 N Fawn Dr Otis OR 97368-9323

KING, FRANKLIN WEAVER, lawyer; b. Alexandria, La., Aug. 8, 1942; s. William F. and Helen Kathleen (Weaver) K. BA, U. Ala., 1965; JD, Duke U., 1972. Bar: Calif. 1974. Pvt. practice law, San Francisco, 1974-88, Sacramento, 1988—. Served to lt. col. JAGC, USAFR, 1975-91. Mem. Am. Trial Lawyers Assn., Calif. Trial Lawyers Assn., ABA, Sacramento County Bar Assn., Calif. Bar Assn., Rancho Cordova C. of C. (bd. dirs.), Pi Kappa Phi, Phi Delta Phi. Office: Ste 211 2893 Sunrise Blvd Rancho Cordova CA 95742-6527

KING, FREDERIC, health services management executive, educator; b. N.Y.C., N.Y., May 9, 1937; s. Benjamin and Jeanne (Fritz) K.; m. Linda Ann Udell, Mar. 17, 1976; children by previous marriage—Coby Allen, Allison Beth, Lisa Robyn, Daniel Seth. B.B.A. cum laude, Bernard M. Baruch Sch. Bus. and Public Adminstrn., CUNY, 1958. Dir. adminstrn. Albert Einstein Coll. Medicine, Bronx, N.Y., 1970-72; assoc. v.p. health affairs Tulane Med. Ctr., New Orleans, 1972-77; dir. fin. Mt. Sinai Med. Ctr., N.Y.C., 1977-78; v.p. fin. Cedars-Sinai Med. Ctr., Los Angeles, 1978-82; pres. Vascular Diagnostic Services, Inc., Woodland Hills, Calif., 1982-84; exec. dir. South Bay Ind. Physicians Med. Group Inc., Torrance, Calif., 1984—; assoc. adj. prof. Tulane U. Sch. Pub. Health; asst. prof. Mt. Sinai Med. Ctr.; instr. Pierce Coll., Los Angeles; Bd. dirs Ohr Eliyahu Acad., AAPPO Pacific Region. Served with U.S. Army, 1959-62. Mem. Healthcare Forum, Am. Hosp. Assn., Pres.'s Assn., Calif. Assn. Hosps. and Health Systems. Republican. Jewish. Home: 1116 Rose Ave Venice CA 90291-2835

KING, GARR MICHAEL, lawyer; b. Pocatello, Idaho, Jan. 28, 1936; s. Warren I. King and Geraldine E. (Hanlon) Appleby; m. Mary Jo Rieber, Feb. 2, 1957; children: Mary, Michael, Matthew, James, Margaret, John, David. Student, U. Utah, 1957-59; LLB, Lewis and Clark Coll., 1963. Bar: Oreg. 1963, U.S. Dist. Ct. Oreg. 1965, U.S. Ct. Appeals (9th cir.) 1975, U.S. Supreme Ct. 1971. Dep. dist. atty. Multnomah County Dist. Atty.'s Office, Portland, Oreg., 1963-66; assoc. Morrison, Bailey, Dunn, Carney & Miller, Portland, 1966-71; ptnr. Kennedy & King, Portland, 1971-77, Kennedy, King & McClurg, Portland, 1977-82, Kennedy, King & Zimmer, Portland, 1982—. Active various pvt. sch. and ch. bds. Served as sgt. USMC, 1954-57. Fellow Am. Coll. Trial Lawyers (state chmn. Oreg. 1991-92); mem. ABA, Oreg. Bar Assn., Multnomah County Bar Assn. (pres. 1975), Jud. Conf. 9th cir. (del.), Northwestern Coll. Law Alumni Assn. (pres.). Democrat. Roman Catholic. Club: Multnomah Athletic (Portland). Office: Kennedy King & Zimmer 1211 SW 5th Ave Ste 2600 Portland OR 97204-3726

KING, GARY CURTIS, author, lecturer; b. Bonne Terre, Mo., Jan. 26, 1954; s. Curtis H. and Eunice C. (Veith) K.; m. Teresita Uson Engles, Mar. 5, 1983; children: Kirsten Nicole, Sarah Tiffany. Grad. high sch., Portland, Oreg. Freelance author Beaverton, Oreg., 1980—; lectr. Friends of Mystery, Portland, Oreg., 1993—. Author: Blood Lust: Portrait of a Serial Sex Killer, 1992 (featured selection True Crime Book Club 1993), Driven to Kill, 1993 (featured selection True Crime Book Club 1993), Web of Deceit, 1994 (featured selection True Crime Book Club 1994), Blind Rage, 1995; contbr. over 400 stories to crime mags. With USAF, 1972-76. Mem. Authors Guild, Authors League Am., Internat. Assn. Crime Writers, Mystery Writers Am., Nat. Press Club, Pacific N.W. Writers Conf. (lectr. 1993—), Willamette Writers (lectr. 1995—). Republican. Roman Catholic.

KING, GUNDAR JULIAN, retired university dean; b. Riga, Latvia, Apr. 19, 1926; came to U.S., 1950, naturalized, 1954; s. Attis K. and Austra (Dale) Kenins: m. Valda K. Andersons, Sept. 18, 1954; children: John T., Marita A. Student, J.W. Goethe U., Frankfurt, Germany, 1946-48; BBA, U. Oreg., 1956; MBA, Stanford U., 1958, PhD, 1964; DSc (hon.), Riga Tech. U., 1991; D Habil. Oecon., Latvian Sci. Coun., 1992. Asst. field supr. Internat. Refugee Orgn., Frankfurt, 1948-50; br. office mfr. Williams Form Engrng. Corp., Portland, Oreg., 1952-54; project mgr. Market Rsch. Assocs., Palo Alto, Calif., 1958-60; asst. prof., assoc. prof. Pacific Luth. U., 1960-66, prof., 1966—, dean Sch. Bus. Adminstrn., 1970-90; vis. prof. mgmt. U.S. Naval Postgrad. Sch., 1971-72, San Francisco State U., 1980, 1987-88; internat. econ. mem. Latvian Acad. Scis., 1990—; regent Estonian Bus. Sch., 1991—; vis. prof. Riga Tech. U., 1993—. Author: Economic Policies in Occupied Latvia, 1965; contbr. articles to profl. publs. Mem. Gov.'s Com. on Reorgn. Wash. State Govt., 1965-88; mem. study group on pricing U.S. Commn. Govt. Procurement, 1971-72; pres. N.W. Univs. Bus. Adminstrn. Conf., 1965-66. With AUS, 1950-52. Fulbright-Hayes scholar, Thailand, 1988, Fulbright scholar, Latvia, 1993-94. Mem. AAUP (past chpt. pres.), Am. Mktg. Assn. (past chpt. pres.), Assn. Advancement Baltic Studies (pres. 1970), Western Assn. Collegiate Schs. Bus. (pres. 1971), Latvian Acad. Scis., Alpha Kappa Psi, Beta Gamma Sigma. Home: PO Box 44401 Tacoma WA 98444-0401 Office: Pacific Luth U Tacoma WA 98447

KING, HARRY ALDEN, author; b. Juneau, Alaska, Apr. 3, 1928; s. Walter Bradley and Lillian Lucile K.; m. Anga Burt, Oct. 4, 1952. BSChemE, U. Colo., 1949; postgrad., MIT, 1950, U. Calif., 1951, U. Md., 1953. Tech. svc. dir. Nat. Starch Products, San Francisco, 1949-55; head rsch., composites divsn. Aerojet-Gen. Corp., Azusa, Calif., 1955-60, program mgr., 1962-68; tech. dir. Western Backing Corp., Culver City, Calif., 1960-62; mgr. rsch. & engring. Narmco/Whittaker Corp., Costa Mesa, Calif., 1968-70; pres. King Rsch., Yorba Linda, Calif., 1970-78; dir. rsch. Amicon/W.R. Grace, Lexington, Mass., 1978-90; pres. Spirit House Press, Tucson, 1993—; cons. King Rsch., 1960-90; featured spkr. and lectr. at many univs. and confs.; chmn. many tech. symposiums. Featured spkr. PBS TV program Innovations, 1967; author 25 tech. papers on variety of subjects, 1966-90; patentee in field; author: (Pure, Golden Light of Love, 1993; extensive article on tech. work L.A. Times, 1966. Aviation cadet USN, 1945-46; corp. U.S. Army, 1952-53. Office: Spirit House Press PO Box 37163 Tucson AZ 85740-7163

KING, HWA-KOU, anesthesiologist; b. Shanghai, Aug. 20, 1928; came to U.S., 1963, naturalized, 1982; m. Alice Lu-ping, Oct. 18, 1958; 5 children. M.D., Nat. Def. Med. Ctr. Sch. Medicine, Taipei, Taiwan, 1953. Diplomate Am. Bd. Anesthesiology. Resident in surgery Army First Gen. Hosp., Taipei, 1953-55, resident in anesthesiology, 1955-60; resident in anesthesiology Meml. Cancer Ctr., N.Y.C., 1963-65; fellow in anesthesiology, Mt. Sinai Med. Ctr., N.Y.C., 1965-67; attending staff anesthesiology Army First Gen. Hosp. and VA Gen. Hosp., Taipei, 1960-63; chief intensive care unit Triservice Gen. Hosp., Taipei, 1967-78, attending staff anesthesiology, 1967-78, chief accupuncture, 1973-78, chief out-patient dept., 1976-78; chief anesthesiology VA Gen Hosp., Taipei, 1978-81, Taiwan Adventist Hosp., Taipei, 1981-82; attending staff anesthesiology Harbor-UCLA Med. Ctr., Los Angeles, 1982-83, VA Med. Ctr., West Los Angeles, 1984-85; chmn. anesthesia rsch. Charles R. Drew U. of Medicine and Sci., Los Angeles, 1985—, assoc. prof., 1987—; clin. prof. Nat. Def. Med. Ctr. and Taipei Med. Coll., 1968-70; prof. China Med. Coll., Taichung, 1971-72; prof. Nat. Def. Med. Ctr., 1970-81; prof., chmn. anesthesiology Nat. Yang Ming Med. Coll., Taipei, 1978-81. Author: Clinical Anesthesiology (in Chinese), 1971, 4th edit., 1981; Introduction to Anesthesiology (in Chinese), 1982. Contbr. sci. papers to topical publs. Editor-in-chief Anesthesiologica Sinica; editor: Med. Research, Chinese Med. Jour., Clin. Medicine. Fellow Am. Coll. Anesthesiologists, Internat. Coll. Surgeons; mem. AAAS, Soc. Anesthesiology Republic of China (pres. 1976-80), Chinese Bd. Anesthesiology (examiner 1981—), Chinese Med. Assn., Formosa Med. Assn., Surg. Assn. Republic of China, Assn. Surgeons S.E. Asia, West Pacific Intensive Care Medicine, Am. Soc. Anesthesiology. Home: 30452 Via Rivera Palos Verdes Peninsula CA 90275-4472 Office: King/Drew Med Ctr Dept Anesthesiology 12021 Wilmington Ave Los Angeles CA 90059-3019

KING, INDLE GIFFORD, industrial designer, educator; b. Seattle, Oct. 23, 1934; s. Indle Frank and Phyllis (Kenney) K.; m. Rosalie Rosso, Sept. 10, 1960; children: Indle Gifford Jr., Paige Phyllis. BA, U. Wash., 1960, MA, 1968. Indsl. designer Hewlett-Packard, Palo Alto, Calif., 1961-63; mgr. indsl. design Sanborn Co., Boston, 1963-65; mgr. corp. design Fluke Corp., Everett, Wash., 1965—; prof. indsl. design Western Wash. U., Bellingham, 1985—; judge nat. competitions; cons. in field. Contbr. articles to profl. jours.; designer patents in field. Coach Mercer Island (Wash.) Boys' Soccer Assn., 1972-77; pres. Mercer Island PTA, 1973; advisor Jr. Achievement, Seattle, 1975-78. Mem. Idsl. Design Soc. Am. (Alcoa award 1965, v.p. Seattle chpt. 1986-88), Mercer Island Country Club. Office: Fluke Corp 6920 Seaway Blvd Everett WA 98203-5829

KING, JACK A., lawyer; b. Lafayette, Ind., July 29, 1936; s. Noah C. and Mabel E. (Pierce) K.; m. Mary S. King, Dec. 10, 1960; children: Jeffrey A., Janice D., Julie D. BS in Fin., Ind. U., 1958, JD, 1961. Bar: Ind. 1961. Ptnr. Ball, Eggleston, King & Bumbleburg, Lafayette, 1961-70; judge Superior Ct. 2 of Tippecanoe County (Ind.), 1970-78; assoc. gen. counsel Dairyland Ins. Co., 1978, v.p. and assoc. gen. counsel, 1979, v.p., gen. counsel and asst. sec., 1980-85; v.p. and counsel Sentry Ctr. West, 1981-85; asst. gen. counsel Sentry Corp., 1979-85; v.p., gen. counsel, and asst. sec. Gt. S.W. Fire Ins. Co., 1980-85, Gt. S.W. Surplus Lines Ins. Co., 1981-85; v.p. and gen. counsel Dairyland County Mut. Ins. Co. Tex., 1980-85; v.p. legal and asst. sec. Scottsdale Ins. Co., 1985—; asst. sec. Nat. Casualty Co. 1985—; v.p.-legal and asst. sec. Scottsdale Indemnity Co., 1992—; v.p., bd. dirs. Ariz. Ins. Info. Assn., 1988—; bd. dirs. Ariz. Joint Underwriting Plan, 1978-81, mem. exec. com., 1980-81; mem. Ariz. Property & Casualty Ins. Commn., 1985-86, vice chmn., 1986; mem. Ariz. Study Commn. on Ins., 1986-87; mem. Ariz. task force on Ct. Orgn. and Adminstrn., 1988-89; mem. adv. com. Ariz. Ho. Rep. Majority Leaders, 1989. Bd. dirs. Scottsdale (Ariz.) Art Ctr. Assn., 1981-84. Mem. ABA, Ind. Bar Assn., Maricopa County Bar Assn. Contbr. The Law of Competitive Business Practices, 2d edit. Office: 8877 N Gainey Center Dr Scottsdale AZ 85258-2108

KING, JANE CUDLIP COBLENTZ, volunteer, educator; b. Iron Mountain, Mich., May 4, 1922; d. William Stacey and Mary Elva (Martin) Cudlip; m. George Samuel Coblentz, June 8, 1942 (dec. June 1989); children: Bruce Harper, Keith George, Nancy Allison Coblentz Patch; m. James E. King, August 23, 1991 (dec. Jan. 1994). BA, Mills Coll., 1942. Mem. Sch. Resource and Career Guidance Vols., Inc., Atherton, Calif., 1965-69, pres., CEO, 1969—; part-time exec. asst. to dean of admissions Mills Coll., 1994—. Proofreader, contbr. Mills Coll. Quarterly mag. Life gov. Royal Children's Hosp., Melbourne, Australia, 1963—; pres. United Menlo Park (Calif.) Homeowner's Assn., 1994—; nat. pres. Mills Coll. Alumnae Assn., 1969-73, bd. trustees, 1975-83. Named Vol. of Yr., Sequoia Union High Sch. Dist., 1988, Golden Acorn award for outstanding svc. Menlo Park C. of C., 1991. Mem. AAUW (Menlo-Atherton branch pres. 1994—), Atherlons, Palo Alto (Calif.) Area Mills Coll. Club (pres. 1986), Phi Beta Kappa. Republican. Episcopalian. Home: 1109 Valparaiso Ave Menlo Park CA 94025-4412 Office: Menlo-Atherton HS Resource-Career Guid Vols 555 Middlefield Rd Atherton CA 94027

KING, JANE LOUISE, artist; b. South Bend, Ind., Aug. 9, 1951; d. Bill and Anne Luciel (Hopkins) Berta; m. Gerald William King Jr., July 7, 1973; children: Kelly Anne, Dinah Jolene. Student, Ind. U., South Bend, 1969-70, Ind. U., 1970-71; BFA, Ohio State U., 1973. Ind. artist Colo., 1974—; instr. Sangre de Cristo Art Ctr., Pueblo, Colo., 1982, Art Studio, Longmont, Colo., 1989. Exhibited oil and pastel paintings in numerous group shows including 5th Ann. Internat. Exhibit Kans. Pastel Soc., 10th and 22nd Ann. Pastel Soc. Am., N.Y., Colo. State Fairs, Poudre Valley Art League; prin. works represented in numerous pvt. collections; contbr. poems to At Days End, 1994. Leader 4-H Club, Longmont, 1986—; sec. Longmont Artists Guild Gallery, 1988-89, bd. dirs., 1989; supt. 1st Bapt. Ch., Longmont, 1990-91. Mem. Colo. Artists Assn. (area 1 rep. 1994), Longmont Artists Guild (Grumbacher award 1992), Longmont Arts Coun., Knickerbocker Artists N.Y, Audubon Artists N.Y. Republican. Home: 1508 Kempton Ct Longmont CO 80501-6716

KING, LEA ANN, community volunteer and leader; b. Elkhart, Ind., July 26, 1941; d. Lloyd Emerson and Mildred Salome (Hostetler) Hartzler; children: Thomas Ellsworth III, Alden Elizabeth. BA in History, DePauw U., 1963. participant in Intensive Workshop in Intercultural Comm. U. Calif., Irvine, 1993, Study Tour of Ethnic Minorites of China, UCLA Extension, 1990; audited The Ethics of War and Peace, Ethikon Inst., Jerusalem, 1993; attended Three Intercultural Colloquia of Family Life, Cultural Diversity and Human Values, Ethikon Inst., 1989. Producer, hostess Pub. Access cable TV programs; travel writer, photographer. Bd. dirs., chair The Ethikon Inst. for Study of Ethical Diversity and Intercultural Rels.; pres. Vol. Ctr. S. Bay-Harbor-Long Beach, 1993-95; v.p. Comty. Assn. of the Peninsula, chair multicultural com., chair PV 2000; sec. Planned Parenthood L.A., 1991—; past pres. Jr. League L.A.; past chair San Pedro Peninsula Hosp. Found.; founding chair Forward-Looking Strategies for Women Coalition, 1985; co-chair United Way System Wide Admissions Com.; mem. Nordstrom's Com. for Salute to Cultural Diversity, L.A., 1993-95. Named Woman of Yr. Nat. Women's Polit. Caucus, San Fernando Valley, 1986, South Bay YWCA; recipient John Anson Ford award L.A. County Commn. on Human Rels., 1992, Spirit of Volunteerism award Jr. League L.A., 1991, commendations from: L.A. Mayor Tom Bradley, L.A. County Bd. Suprs., Calif. State Sen. Robert Beverly, Congressmen Dana Rohrabcher and Howard Berman; appointed to L.A. County Commn. on Human Rels. by Supr. Deane Dana, 1993. Home and Office: 49 Strawberry Ln Rolling Hills Estates CA 90274

KING, LELAND W., architect; b. Battle Creek, Mich., Dec. 17, 1907; s. Leland Wiggins and Elizabeth Gale (Arnold) K.; m. Hametia Fielder, Nov. 29, 1934; children: Sheryl Letia, Louisa Sands. Student, Ga. Sch. Tech., 1927, Armour Inst. Tech. (Chgo. Art Inst., Beaux Arts Design), 1928-29. Registered architect, Colo., Ariz., N.Y., Calif., Nat. Council Archtl. Registration Bds. Archtl. draftsman, designer indsl., sch., hosp. and residential projects Ga., Ill., Mich., Wis., 1925-32; supr. architect's office U.S. Treasury, 1935-37; field insp. diplomatic and consular bldgs. Dept. State, 1937-40, in Scandinavia, Balkans, Europe, Middle East, C. and S. Am.; assoc. chief Fgn. Bldg. Ops. Dept. State, 1941-51; dir. and supervising architect, 1952-54; in charge U.S. diplomatic and consular bldg. design and constrn., worldwide; cons. Bd. Edn. White Fish Bay, Milw., 1931-32; tech. adviser to U.S. del. UNESCO Hdqrs. Bldg., Paris, 1952-53; exec. sec. Fgn. Service Bldgs. Com., U.S. Congress, 1952-54; gen. archtl. and indsl. design as asso. Norman Bel Geddes, 1954-55; asso. with James Gordon Carr (Architect), 1956; v.p., dir. architecture Pereira and Luckman, 1956-59; supervising archt. Ampex Corp., 1959-62; pvt. archtl. practice as Leland King, FAIA, 1961—; sr. partner King/Reif & Assos. (architecture and planning), Menlo Park, Calif.; Chmn. archtl. and constrn. engring. panel research, adv. council to postmaster gen., 1967, 68; dir., supervising architect U.S. Embassy projects, 1937-54, honor awards Stockholm, Paris, 1953, Memorex project, Santa Clara, Calif., 1972, Mission Control Air Force, 1982; chmn. Bodega Harbour Design Rev. Com. Works exhibited U.S. State Dept., Mus. Modern Art, N.Y.C., 1953, Octagon, 1954, San Jose Mus., 1980. Recipient McGraw-Hill Top Ten Plants award, 1971. Fellow AIA (honor award 1955, chpt. award 1974), Cosmos Club (Washington). Home: 21218 Heron Dr Bodega Harbour Bodega Bay CA 94923

KING, OSCAR LLOYD, astrodynamicist; b. Galveston, Tex., July 5, 1922; s. Oscar Lloyd and Lillie Dale (Johnson) K.; m. Ruth Norma, Feb. 1958. BA in Physics, Dartmouth Coll., 1948; postgrad., UCLA, 1950-66; MS in Engring., Cath. U. of Am., 1976. With USN, 1940-46; physicist GS-7 USN, China Lake, Calif., 1948-50; assoc. engr. North Am. Aviation, Downey, Calif., 1954-55, 61-66; rsch. analyst Douglas Aircraft, Santa Monica, Calif., 1956-59; sr. engr. McDonnell Douglas, St. Louis, 1966-68; satellite engr. Telesat-Canada, Ottawa, 1970-71; tech. staff Computer Sci. Corp., Silver Spring, Md., 1973-75; rsch. specialist Boeing, Kent, Wash., 1978-80, Wichita, Kans., 1983-88; staff engr. Martin Marietta, Denver, 1981-82; astrodynamicist Par Govt. Systems, Colorado Springs, 1989-90; cons. astrodynamics Correa Enterprises, Albuquerque, N.Mex., 1992—; pres. Wichita Astron., 1987; instr. Ferguson-Florisant Sch., St. Louis, 1967. Creator: Interplanetary Rendezvous Trajectory Software, 1992; author: Charts on Interrelationships of Math to Human Endeavor and Space Exploration Disciplines, 1991, 92. Tchr. Calif. Mus. of Sci. and Industry, L.A., 1965; mathematician Denver Pub. Librs., 1991. Mem. AIAA. Democrat. Home: 4264 S Nucla Way Aurora CO 80013-2927

KING, RAY JOHN, electrical engineer; b. Montrose, Colo., Jan. 1, 1933; s. John Frank and Grace (Rankin) K.; m. Diane M. Henney, June 20, 1964; children: Karl V., Kristin J. BS in Electronic Engring., Ind. Inst. Tech., 1956, BS in Elec. Engring., 1957; MS, U. Colo., 1960, PhD, 1965. Instr. Ind. Inst. Tech., 1956-58, asst. prof., 1960-62, acting chmn. dept. electronics, 1960-62; research asso. U. Colo., 1962-65; research assoc. U. Ill., 1965; assoc. prof. elec. engring. U. Wis., Madison, 1965-69; prof. U. Wis., 1969-82, assoc. dept. chmn. for research and grad. affairs, 1977-79; staff rsch. engr. Lawrence Livermore Nat. Lab. (Calif.), 1982-90, sr. scientist high power microwaves program, 1989-90; co-founder KDC Tech. Corp., 1983, v.p., 1990—, cons.; vis. Erskine fellow U. Canterbury, N.Z., 1977; guest prof., Fulbright scholar Tech. U. Denmark, 1973-74. Author: Microwave Homodyne Systems, 1978; contbr. articles to profl. jours.; patentee in field. NSF Faculty fellow, 1962-65. Fellow IEEE; mem. IEEE Soc. on Antennas and Propagation (adminstrv. com. 1989-91, chmn. wave propagation stds. com. 1986-89, gen. chmn. symposium 1989), IEEE Soc. Microwave Theory and Techniques, IEEE Soc. Instrumentation and Measurements, Forest Products Soc., Soc. Advancement Materials and Processing, Electromagnetics Acad., Internat. Sci. Radio Union (commns. A, B, F), Sigma Xi, Iota Tau Kappa, Sigma Phi Delta. Home: 2595 Raven Rd Pleasanton CA 94566-4605 Office: KDC Tech Corp 2011 Research Dr Livermore CA 94550-3803

KING, RHETA BARON, rehabilitation consultant; b. L.A., Dec. 15, 1935; d. Albert James and Marietta (Malcomson) Baron; m. Stuart Alan Walling, June, 11, 1956 (div. July 1968); children: S. Alan, Lynne Heather; m. Kenneth Bruce King, Oct. 11, 1968 (div. Apr. 1983). AB cum laude, Occidental Coll., 1957; postgrad., Calif. State U., Los Angeles, 1960-68, Calif. State U., Long Beach, 1963-64. Cert. rehab. counselor, ins. rehab. specialist, social security vocat. expert. Counselor Calif. Dept. Rehab., Burbank, 1972-74;

coordinator staff devel. Los Angeles, 1974, program supr., 1975-78; nat. dir. staff devel. Comprehensive Rehab. Services, Inc., Arcadia, Calif., 1978-80; dir. comprehensive rehab. ctr. Daniel Freeman Meml. Hosp., Inglewood, Calif., 1981-83, dir. vocat. programs, 1984-86; pvt. practice rehab. cons. Pasadena, Calif., 1981—; tech. advisor Devel. Disabilities Area Bd., L.A., 1978; cons. Social Security Office Hearings and Appeals, Pasadena and L.A., 1981—, Am. Coll. Neurology, 1986, Nat. Multiple Sclerosis Soc., 1986—, Calif. Applicants' Attys. Assn., Internat. Pers. Mgmt. Assn. Assessment Coun., Calif. State U., L.A.; rsch. scientist Human Interaction Rsch. Inst., L.A., 1986—; commr. Cert. Ins. Rehab. Specialist Commn., 1992—. Author graphic model, 1980. Mem. exec. bd. Calif. Gov.'s Com. for People With Disabilities, 1983-94, Calif. Health Care Plan Adv. Com., 1990-91; mem. L.A. Long-Term Care Task Force, 1987, Friends of Huntington Libr., San Marino, Calif., 1986-87; advisor, counselor edn. program Calif. State U., L.A., 1989—; mem. vestry Episc. Ch. of the Ascension, Sierra Madre, 1994—. Elizabeth Woods fellow, 1964; recipient Outstanding Svc. award Pasadena Mayor's Com., 1993. Mem. AAUW, ACA, Gov.'s Women Appointees Coun., Nat. Assn. Rehab. Profls. in Pvt. Sector, Am. Rehab. Counseling Assn., Occidental Coll. Alumni Assn. (bd. govs.), Pasadena Heritage Club. Republican. Episcopalian. Home and Office: 515 S Oakland Ave Apt 5 Pasadena CA 91101-3358

KING, ROBERT EUGENE, economic development consultant; b. Abilene, Kans., Jan. 8, 1935; s. Clarence Leroy and Margaret (Swift) K.; B.A., Kans. Wesleyan U., 1961; postgrad. U. Fla., 1963-64; m. Marilyn Jean Watts, May 17, 1977; children—Robert Eugene, Brian Stewart. Dir. indsl. devel. Kans. Dept. Econ. Devel., Topeka, 1973-77; dir. econ. devel. N.W. Kans. Econ. Devel. Dist., Hill City, 1977-80; dir. Econ. Devel. Council, Springfield, Ill., 1980-83; exec. dir. Econ. Devel. Commn., Midwest City, Okla., 1983—; with Clark County Cmty Resources, Las Vegas, Nev.; cons. King & Assocs., Henderson, Nev., 1995—. Sec.-treas. Great Lakes Area Devel. Council, 1980-81. Served with USN, 1954-58. Mem. Am. Econ. Devel. Council (dir.), Ill. Devel. Council, So. Indsl. Devel. Council, Nat. Assn. Rev. Appraisers, Indsl. Devel. Research Council, Methodist. Club: Elks. Office: King & Assocs 2352 Pickwick Dr Henderson NV 89014

KING, ROBERT LUCIEN, lawyer; b. Petaluma, Calif., Aug. 9, 1936; s. John Joseph and Ramona Margaret (Thorson) K.; m. Suzanne Nanette Parre, May 18, 1956 (div. 1973); children: Renee Michelle, Candyce Lynn, Danielle Louise, Benjamin Robert; m. Linda Diane Carey, Mar. 15, 1974 (div. 1981); 1 child, Debra; m. J'an See, Oct. 27, 1984 (div. 1989); 1 child, Jonathan F.; m. Marilyn Collins, June 15, 1991. AB in Philosophy, Stanford U., 1958, JD, 1960. Bar: Calif., N.Y. 1961. Asst. U.S. atty. U.S. Atty's. Office (so. dist.), N.Y.C., 1964-67; assoc. Debevoise & Plimpton, N.Y.C., 1960-64, 67-70, ptnr., 1970-89; mng. ptnr. Debevoise & Plimpton, L.A., 1989—; lectr. Practicing Law Inst., N.Y.C., ABA, Asia/Pacific Ctr. for Resolution of Internat. Bus. Disputes; bd. dirs. L.A. Ctr. Internat. Comml. Arbitration. Fellow Am. Coll. Trial Lawyers; mem. ABA, Assn. Bar City N.Y., Calif. Bar Assn., L.A. County Bar Assn., Assn. Bus. Trial Lawyers. Democrat. Home: 10000 Tikita Pl Toluca Lake CA 91602-2920 Office: Debevoise & Plimpton 601 S Figueroa St Fl 3700 Los Angeles CA 90017-5742

KING, SHELDON SELIG, medical center administrator, educator; b. N.Y.C., Aug. 28, 1931; s. Benjamin and Jeanne (Fritz) K.; m. Ruth Arden Zeller, June 26, 1955 (div. 1987); children: Tracy Elizabeth, Meredith Ellen, Adam Bradley; m. Xenia Tonesk, 1988. A.B., NYU, 1952; M.S., Yale U., 1957. Adminstrv. intern Montefiore Hosp., N.Y.C., 1952, 55; adminstrv. asst. Mt. Sinai Hosp., N.Y.C., 1957-60; asst. dir. Mt. Sinai Hosp., 1960-66, dir. planning, 1966-68; exec. dir. Albert Einstein Coll. Medicine-Bronx Mcpl. Hosp. Ctr., Bronx, N.Y., 1968-72; asst. prof. Albert Einstein Coll. Medicine, N.Y.C., 1968-72; dir. hosps. and clinics Univ. Hosp., assoc. clin. prof. U. Calif., San Diego, 1972-81; acting head div. health care scis., dept. community medicine U. Calif. (Sch. Medicine), 1978-81; assoc. v.p. Stanford U., 1981-85, clin. assoc. prof. dept. community, family and preventive medicine; exec. v.p. Stanford U. Hosp., 1981-85, pres., 1986-89; pres. Cedars-Sinai Med. Ctr., L.A., 1989-94; exec. v.p. Salick Health Care, Inc., L.A., 1994—; mem. adminstrv. bd. coun. teaching hosps., 1981-86, chmn. adminstrv. bd., 1985; preceptor George Washington U., Ithaca Coll., Yale U., U. Mo., CUNY; chmn. health care com. San Diego County Immigration Coun., 1974-77; adv. coun. Calif. Health Facilities Commn., 1977-82; chmn. ad hoc bd. advs. Am. Bd. Internal Medicine, 1985-91; bd. dirs. Am. Med. Internat., 1993-95, Nat. Com. Quality Health Care, chmn., 1993-94; bd. dirs. St. Joseph Health Sys., 1988-94, mem. exec. com., 1990-94; bd. dirs. Am. Health Properties, 1988—. Mem. editorial adv. bd.: Who's Who in Health Care, 1977; mem. editorial bd. Jour. Med. Edn, 1979-84. Bd. dirs. hosp. coun. San Diego and Imperial Counties, 1974-77, treas., 1976, pres., 1977; bd. dirs. United Way San Diego, 1975-80, B'rith Milah Bd., Vol. Hosps. Am., 1990-94, mem. exec. com., 1991-93; mem. Accreditation Coun. for grad. med. edn., 1987-90, Prospective Payment Assessment Commn., 1987-90, Inst. of Medicine, 1988—. With AUS, 1952-55. Fellow Am. Coll. Health Care execs., Am. Pub. Health Assn., Royal Soc. Health; mem. Am. Hosp. Assn. (governing coun. Met. sect. 1983-86, coun. on fin. 1987, ho. of dels. 1987-89), Calif. Hosp. Assn. (trustee 1978-81), Am. Podiatric Med. Assn. (project coun. 2000 1985-86), Hosp. Rsch. and Devel. Inst. (bd. dirs. 1993—, chmn. 1993-94). Home: 330 S Reeves Dr Apt 103 Beverly Hills CA 90212-4548

KING, SIDSEL ELIZABETH TAYLOR (BETH KING), hotel catering-hospitality professional; b. Edmonton, Alta., Can., July 27, 1932; d. Claude L. and Sadie (Hommy) Taylor; m. Otis A. King, Mar. 21, 1953; children: Ronald R., Lori Beth. AAS in Hotel Mgmt. and Food Svc Industry, U. Alaska, 1989. Sec. Sheriff's Office Courthouse, Edmonton, 1950-51; new accounts clk. First Nat. Bank Anchorage, 1952-53; sec., receptionist rate clk. Alaska Freight Lines, Anchorage, 1954-59; co-owner King's Rentals, Anchorage, 1953—; sec. State of Alaska Dept. Fish and Game, Anchorage, 1959-64, Anchorage Sch. Dist., West High, Wendler and East High, Anchorage, 1964—; exec. sec. Anchorage Daily News, 1969-70; with freight svc. Anchorage Slnd., 1970-71; caterer Clarion Hotel, Anchorage, 1989—; ambassador Clarion Hotel, Anchorage, 1991, Red Cross person, 1990-91. Preservation charter mem. Nat. Soc. Hist. Preservation, 1980's, Nat. Women in the Arts, Washington, 1980's, Nat. Secs. Assn. Anchorage, 1959—. Mem. Alaska Watercolor Soc., U. Alaska-Anchorage Alumni. Home: PO Box 244304 Anchorage AK 99524-4304 Office: Regal Alaskan Hotel 4800 Spenard Rd Anchorage AK 99517-3236

KING, TODD ALLEN, programmer, analyst; b. Downey, Calif., Feb. 15, 1959; s. John Flago and Audrey (Beaumont) K.; m. Patricia Irene Wallace, June 25, 1983; children: Garreth Merlin, Brendon Galen. BS in applied geophysics, UCLA, 1985. Programmer, analyst Inst. Geophysics and Planetary Physics, L.A., 1982—; cons. Space Environment Corp., Provo, Utah, 1992-94. Author: Dynamic Data Structures: Theory and Applications, 1983. Recipient Group Achievement award NASA, 1991, Adminstrn. and Profl. Devel. award UCLA, 1989, 91. Mem. IEEE, Assn. Computing Machines. Office: IGPP UCLA 5881 Slichter Hall Los Angeles CA 90024

KING, W. DAVID, professional hockey coach; b. North Battleford, Sask., Can., Dec. 22, 1947. Head coach Team Can. Internat. League, 1984-92; head coach Calgary (Can.) Flames, 1992—. Office: Calgary Flames, PO Box 1540 Sta M, Calgary, AB Canada T2P 3B9*

KING-ETTEMA, ELIZABETH DOROTHY, video and film editor, writer, photographer; b. Morristown, N.J., Sept. 29, 1953; d. James Claude and Marthe Helene (Dawson) King; m. Dale Frederic Ettema, Feb. 13, 1982; children: Taylor Braam, Claire Elizabeth. BA in Art History, UCLA, 1975; postgrad. U. N.Mex., 1977-78. Writer, Bettis & Parks Advt., Albuquerque, 1975-76; bus. mgr. N.Mex. Ballet Co., Albuquerque, 1976-78; asst. editor Dury Assocs., Los Angeles, 1978, Another Editing Pl., Los Angeles, 1978-79, Bullywood Prodn., Los Angeles, 1979, Alan Landsburg Prodn., Los Angeles, 1980-81, Columbia TV, Los Angeles, 1982-83; video editor Am. Film Inst., Los Angeles, 1983-85. Video editor Scenario, 1984, U.S. 49/Calif. 1, 1985; writer, photographer The Pumpkin Patch, 1990, Backyard Sunflower, 1993 (one of Outstanding Sci. Trade Books of Yr. for Children Nat. Sci. Tchrs. Assn. and Children's Book Coun.), Chile Fever, A Celebration of Peppers, 1995. Mem. Motion Picture and Videotape Editors Guild, Soc. Children's Book Writers. Democrat. Episcopalian. Club: Embroiderer's Guild of Am. (historian chpt. 1984-85, v.p., program chmn. 1987-88). Home and Office: 7235 Forbes Ave Van Nuys CA 91406-2736

KINGMAN, DONG, artist, educator; b. Oakland, Calif., Apr. 1, 1911; s. Dong Chuan-Fee and Lew Shee K.; m. Wong Shee, Sept. 1929 (dec. June 1954); children—Eddie, Dong Kingman Jr.; m. Helena Kuo, Sept. 1956. Student, Lingnan, Hong Kong, 1924-26; LHD (hon.), Acad. Art Coll., San Franciso, 1987. Tchr. art San Diego Art Gallery, 1941-43; tchr. Famous Artists Schs., Westport, Conn., Columbia U., Hunter Coll.; Lectr. tour around world sponsored by internat. cultural exchange program Dept. State, 1954. Represented in permanent collections, Whitney Mus. Am. Art, Am. Acad. Arts and Letters, Bklyn. Mus., Toledo Mus. Art, Joslyn Art Mus., Omaha, Mus. Fine Arts, Boston, Met. Mus. Art, Mus. Modern Art, N.Y.C., U. Nebr., Wadsworth Atheneum, Bloomington (Ill.) Art Assn., San Francisco Mus., Mills Coll., De Young Mus., Albert Bender Collection, Eleanor Roosevelt Collection, Chgo. Art Inst., N.Y. State Tchrs. Coll., Springfield (Ill.) Art Assn., Cranbrook Acad. Art, Butler Art Inst., Ft. Wayne Mus., Addison Gallery, U.S. Dept. State, many others; executed murals, Bank of Calif., San Francisco, N.Y. Hilton Hotel, R.H. Macy & Co., Franklin Sq., N.Y., Boca Raton Hotel, Fla., Hyatt Regency Hotel, Hong Kong, Ambassador Hotel, Kowloon, Hong Kong, Lincoln Savs. Bank, N.Y.C.; illustrator: The Bamboo Gate (Vanya Oakes), 1946, China's Story (Enid LaMonte Meadowcroft), 1946, Nightingale (Andersen), 1948, Johnny Hong in Chinatown (Clyde Robert Bulla), 1952, Caen's and Kingman's San Francisco (Herb Caen), 1964, City on the Golden Hill (Herb Caen), 1967; author: (with Helena Kuo Kingman) Dong Kingman's Watercolors, 1980, Paint the Yellow Tiger, 1991; Painted: (with Helena Kuo Kingman) title paintings for 55 Days at Peking, movie title paints for Flower Drum Song, 1964, movie poster Universal Studio Tour. Served in U.S. Army. Recipient award Chgo. Internat. Watercolor Exhbn., 1944, Gold medal of honor Audubon Artists Exhbn. 1946, award, 1956; Joseph Pennel Meml. medal Phila. Watercolor Club, 1950, award, 1968; Watercolor prize Pa. Acad., 1953, Am. Watercolor Soc. award, 1956, 60, 62-65, 67, 72, High Wings Medal award, 1973, V.K. McCracken Young award, 1976, Ford-Times award, 1978, Barse Miller Meml. award, 1979, Dolphin Medal award, 1987; 150th Anniversary Gold Medal award Nat. Acad. Design, 1975, Walter Bigg Meml. award, 1977; Key to City of Omaha, 1980, Key to City of Cin., 1980; San Diego Watercolor Soc. prize, 1984, 1st prize for Ch. No. 1, San Francisco Art Assn., 1936; named Hon. Admiral of Navy, Omaha, 1979, Hon. Citizen of Louisville, 1980, Hon. Capt. of Belle of Louisville, 1980, Man of Yr. Chinatown Planning Coun., N.Y.C., 1981, Man of Yr. Oakland (Calif.) Chinese Community Coun., 1985, Man of Yr. Rotary Club 1991, Man of Yr. Chinese Affirmative Action, San Francisco, 1991, Guest of Honor for Opening Internat. Book Fair, Hong Kong, 1991, judge Miss Universe and Miss U.S.A., 1963-85; Guggenheim fellow, 1942-43. Home: 21 W 58th St New York NY 10019-1604 Office: care Stary Sheet Gallery 14988 Sand Canyon Ave Irvine CA 92718-2107

KINGMAN, ELIZABETH YELM, anthropologist; b. Lafayette, Ind., Oct. 15, 1911; d. Charles Walter and Mary Irene (Weakley) Yelm; m. Eugene Kingman, June 10, 1939; children—Mixie Kingman Eddy, Elizabeth Anne Kingman. BA U. Denver, 1933, MA, 1935. Asst. in anthropology U. Denver, 1932-34; mus. asst. Ranger Naturalist Force, Mesa Verde Nat. Park, Colo., 1934-38; asst. to husband in curatorial work, Indian art exhibits Philbrook Art Ctr., Tulsa, 1939-42, Joslyn Art Mus., Omaha, 1947-69; tutor humanities dept. U. Omaha, 1947-50; chmn. bd. govs. Pi Beta Phi Settlement Sch., Gatlinburg, Tenn., 1969-72; asst. to husband in exhibit design mus. of Tex. Tech. U., 1970-75, bibliographer Internat. Ctr. Arid and Semi-Arid Land Studies, 1974-75; librarian Sch. Am. Research, Santa Fe, 1978-86; research assoc., 1986—; v.p. Santa Fe Corral of the Westerners, 1985-86. Mem. AAUW, LWV, Archeol. Inst. Am. (v.p. Santa Fe chpt. 1981-83), Santa Fe Hist. Soc. (sec. 1981-83). Home: 604 Sunset St Santa Fe NM 87501-1118 Office: Sch Am Rsch 660 Garcia St Santa Fe NM 87501-2858

KINGSBURY, CAROLYN ANN, software systems engineer; b. Newark, Ohio, Aug. 4, 1938; d. Cecil C. Layman and Orpha Edith (Hisey) Layman Dick; m. L.C. James Kingsbury, Apr. 25, 1959; children: Donald Lynn, Kenneth James. BS in Math., BS in Info. and Computer Scis., U. Calif., Irvine, 1979; postgrad. West Coast U., 1982-84. Systems engr., analyst Rockwell Internat., Downey, Calif., 1979-84, system and software engr. Northrop Corp., Pico Rivera, Calif., 1984-89; systems engr. Hughes Aircraft Co., Long Beach, Calif., 1989-90, Fullerton, Calif., 1990-91. Pres. PTA, Manhattan Beach, Calif., 1971-73; Cub Scout den mother Boy Scouts Am., Manhattan Beach, 1972-73; mem. Fountain Valley Regional Hosp. Guild, 1993—. Recipient Service award Calif. Congress Parents and Tchrs., 1973, Leadership Achievement award YWCA, Los Angeles, 1980, 84, NASA Achievement awards, 1983. Mem. NAFE, AAUW, Nat. Mgmt. Assn., Newtowners Club (pres. 1962). Republican. Home: 11392 Stonecress Ave Fountain Valley CA 92708

KINGSHILL, KONRAD, social sciences educator; b. Burgstädt, Saxony, Germany, June 22, 1923; naturalized U.S. citizen, 1944; s. William and Gertrude (Sachs) K.; m. Carolyn Ryberg; children: Christina, Kim Andrew, Kenneth Paul. BA magna cum laude, Hastings Coll., 1944; MS in Physics, U. Chgo., 1944; PhD in Anthropology, Cornell U., 1957; LHD (hon.), Hastings Coll., 1971. Instr. physics Morgan Pk. Jr. Coll., Chgo., 1946-47; instr. math., physics and English Prince Royal's Coll., Chiang Mai, Thailand, 1947-50; head univ. prep. divsn. Prince Royal's Coll., Chiang Main, Thailand, 1953-63; head secondary divsn. Bangkok Christian Coll., 1963-68; cons., instr. Nan (Thailand) Christian Sch., 1968-70; supt. of schs. Ch. of Christ in Thailand, various locations, 1966-74; v.p. Payap U., Chiang Mai, 1974-83, acting pres., then sr. v.p., 1984-88, hon. prof. sociology and anthropology, 1987, prof. emeritus, pres.'s rep. overseas, 1988—; vis. lectr. anthropology Hastings (Nebr.) Coll., 1970-71; advisor, mem. planning and devel. com. Christian Coll., Bangkok, 1993—. Author: Ku-Daeng -- The Red Tomb, A Village Study in Northern Thailand, A.D. 1954-64, 2nd edit., 1965, Ku Daeng - Thirty Years Later, NIU Ctr. for S.E. Asian Studies, 1991; contbr. or co-contbr. articles to profl. publs. Bd. dirs., chmn. acad. adv. bd. Chiang Mai Internat. Sch., 1984-88; mem. bd. edn. Ch. of Christ in Thailand, 1966-84, chmn. bd. edn., 1983-84, advisor to bd. edn., 1984-86, cons. welfare program, 1976-78, dir. bd. welfare, 1981-88, mem. commn. on structural orgn., 1977-88; chmn. bd. dirs. Chiang Mai Co-Ednl. Ctr., 1974-81; mem. founding bd. Payap Coll., 1971-74; mem. Foothill Master Chorale, 1989-91, Claremont (Calif.) Chorale, 1992—; treas. CROP Walk, Pomona Inland Valley Coun. of Chs., 1993-94; various positions Presbytery of San Gabriel, Synod of So. Calif. & Hawaii, Shepherd of the Valley Presbyn. Ch., Hacienda Heights, Calif., Claremont Presbyn. Ch. With USN, 1944-46. Named to Most Exalted Order of White Elephant, 3rd Class, King Bhumibol Adulyadej, Thailand, 1990. Mem. Siam Soc. (life). Home: 680 Avery Rd Claremont CA 91711-4222

KINKADE, KATE, publishing executive, magazine editor, insurance executive; b. N.Y.C., Jan. 22, 1951; d. Joel M. and Peeta S. (Sherman) Sandleman; m. Patrick Ramsey, June 27, 1981; children: Jamaa Ramsey, Kikanza Ramsey. BS in Speech, Emerson Coll., Boston, 1972; postgrad., Am. Coll., Bryn Mawr, Pa. CLU. Mgr. sales Equitable Life Ins., L.A., 1973-76; agy. v.p. Lincoln Nat. Life Ins. Co., Encino, Calif., 1976-80; chief exec. officer TIME Fin. Svcs., Reseda, Calif., 1980—; editor-in-chief Calif. Broker, Burbank, Calif., 1981—; exec. v.p. Life Underwriters Assn., Encino, 1978-81. Contbr. articles to profl. jours. Treas., trustee Labor Community Strategy Ctr., Van Nuys, Calif.. Recipient Asst. Prodn. awards Equitable Life, 1973, 77, Lincoln Nat. Life, 1978, 80, Pacific Mut. Life, 1983. Mem. Assn. CLU's. Democrat. Office: TIME Fin 7101 Baird Ave # 206 Reseda CA 91335-4150

KINLEN, JAMES GILBERT, publishing executive; b. Breckenridge, Pa., Aug. 25, 1933; s. George Sylvanius Kinlen and Bernice Carson; m. Rozonna Kinlen, Mar. 28, 1959; children: Christopher James, Leslie Loree. Student, Wayne State U. Mgr. State Securities, Dallas, 1956-66, Gen. Tire Co., Denver, Albuquerque, 1966-71; owner, pres. FLYING Review Publs., Albuquerque, 1972—; pres. Aviation Factors, Albuquerque, 1976—. Mem. Albuquerque C. of C., 1985-90. Staff sgt. U.S. Army, 1952-55, Korea. Recipient Cert. of Merit, Nat. Aeronautic Assn., 1990, Journalism award Ziff Daivs Pub., 1976; named Man of Yr., Mo. Pilots Assn., 1985. Mem. U.S. Pilots Assn. (bd. dirs., Mem. of Yr. 1986), N.Mex. Pilots Assn. (bd. dirs.), Irish Am. Soc., Air Force Assn., Aircraft Owners and Pilots Assn., VFW, Am. Legion. Republican. Methodist. Home: 4801 Charlotte Ct NE Albuquerque NM 87109-3009 Office: FLYING Review PO Box 9191 Albuquerque Airport Albuquerque NM 87119

KINNEY, BRIAN MALTBIE, plastic surgeon; b. Baton Rouge, Apr. 28, 1954; s. Kenneth Lee and Louise Estelle (Walker) K.; m. Laureen Alida McGillis, Aug. 29, 1980 (div. Jan. 1984). SB in Mechanical Engring., Mass. Inst. Tech., 1976, SM, 1980; MD, Tulane U., 1982. Intern, residency gen. surgery UCLA Med. Ctr., L.A., 1982-86, chief residency gen. surgery, 1987, resident divsn. plastic surgery, 1988, chief resident plastic surgery, 1989; pvt. practice L.A., 1989—; cons. An. Hosp. Supply Corp., 1978-80, Ingene Corp., Santa Monica, Calif., 1984—. Author: Lymphatic Drainage in Early and Chronic Lymphedema, 1984, Revascularization and the Pattern of Regeneration and Fibrosis in Free Muscle Grafts, 1984, Studies in Free Muscle Grafting, 1984-88. Treas. Tulane Med. Sch., 1986; vol. plastic reconstructive surgeon Mexican Red Cross, Los Mochis, Mexico, 1987-89; chief plastic surgeon Operation 2nd Chance, Croatia-Bosnia, 1992—. Walter C. Teagle Found. scholar, 1972-76, 76-78, 80-82, Grad. Rsch. Assistanship scholar, 1978-80; recipient Postdoctoral Scholar Rsch. award, 1983-84. Mem. AMA, IEEE, Am. Soc. Plastic & Reconstructive Surgeons. Am. Inst. Physics, Am. Soc. Mech. Engring., Calif. Med. Assn. Office: Ste 1110 2080 Century Park East Los Angeles CA 90067

KINNEY, JAY MACNEAL, editor, author, illustrator; b. Cleve., July 18, 1950; s. Del Jay and Analee (Lathrop) K.; m. Dixie Leone Tracy, July 8, 1978. Student, Baldwin Wallace Coll., Berea, Ohio, 1968-69, Pratt Inst., Bklyn., 1969-72. Prodn. asst. Whole Earth, Sausalito, Calif., 1980-83; editor Coevolution Quar., Sausalito, Calif., 1983-85; editor-in-chief Gnosis Mag., San Francisco, 1983—, pres. The Lumen Found., San Francisco, 1984—. Contbg. editor Whole Earth Rev., 1985—; editor/author comic art pubs.; contbr. articles to profl. jours.; freelance illustrator. Office: Gnosis Mag PO Box 14217 San Francisco CA 94114-0217

KINNEY, LISA FRANCES, lawyer; b. Laramie, Wyo., Mar. 13, 1951; d. Irvin Wayne and Phyllis (Poe) K.; m. Rodney Philip Lang, Feb. 5, 1971; children: Cambria Helen, Shelby Robert, Eli Wayne. BA, U. Wyo., 1973, JD, 1986; MLS, U. Oreg., 1975. Reference libr. U. Wyo. Sci. Libr., Laramie, 1975-76; outreach dir. Albany County Libr., Laramie, 1975-76, dir., 1977-83; mem. Wyo. State Senate, Laramie, 1984-94, minority leader, 1992-94, with documentation office Am. Heritage Ctr. U. Wyo., 1991-94; assoc. Corthell & King, Laramie, 1994—; owner Summit Bar Rev., 1987—. Author: (with Rodney Lang) Civil Rights of the Developmentally Disabled, 1986; (with Rodney Lang and Phyllis Kinney) Manual For Families with Emotionally Disturbed and Mentally Ill Relatives, 1988, rev. 1991; Lobby For Your Library; Know What Works, 1992; contbr. articles to profl. jours; editor, compiler pub. relations directory for ALA, 1982. Bd. dirs. Big Bros./Big Sisters, Laramie, 1980-83, Am. Heritage Ctr., Friends of Cmty. Health, Children's Mus. Recipient Beginning Young Profl. award Mt. Plains Libr. Assn., 1980; named Outstanding Wyo. Libr. Wyo. Libr. Assn., 1977, Outstanding Young Woman State of Wyo., 1980. Mem. ABA, Nat. Confs. of State Legislatures (various coms. 1985-90). Democrat. Avocations: photography, dance, reading, traveling, languages. Home: 2358 Jefferson St Laramie WY 82070-6420 Office: Corthell & King 221 S 2nd St Laramie WY 82070-3610

KINNEY, MARJORIE SHARON, marketing executive, artist; b. Gary, Ind., Jan. 11, 1940; d. David H. and Florence C. Dunning; student El Camino Coll., 1957, 58; LHD (hon.), West Coast U., 1982, Coll. San Mateo, 1987-88; MBA, Pepperdine U., 1989; m. Daniel D. Kinney, Dec. 31, 1958 (div. 1973); children: Steven Daniel, Michael Alan, Gregory Lincoln, Bradford David; m. Bradley Thomas Jr., Nov. 9, 1985 (div. Apr. 1987). Ptnr., Kinney Advt. Inc., Inglewood, Calif., 1958-68; pres. Greeters of Am., 1967-69; chmn. Person to Person Inc., Cleve., 1969-72; pres. Kinney Mktg. Corp., Encino, Calif., 1972-80; sr. v.p. Beverly Hills (Calif.) Savs. & Loan Assn., 1980-84; chmn., pres. Kinney & Assocs., Dana Point, Calif., 1985—; dir. Safeway Stores, Inc., Chubb/Pacific Indemnity Co.; freelance artist; lectr. Bd. dirs. ARC, 1976-81, United Way, 1979-81; trustee West Coast U.; v.p., trustee Capestrano Valley Symphony, 1989—; adv. bd. U.S. Human Resources, Womens Legal Edn. Fund; briefing del. to Pentagon Fed. Res. Dept. and White House, 1986; pres. Santa Fe Rep. Women, 1987; co-chair Childcare Action Day, 1986; participant Women of Faith and Courage, program for homeless girls, 1987—; chair Caps for Calypso, clothing project for homeless, 1988; v.p. Laguna Beach Art-A-Fair, 1992—. Presbyterian. Office: 81 Palm Beach Ct Dana Point CA 92629-4526

KINNEY, RALEIGH EARL, artist; b. Brainerd, Minn., Mar. 11, 1938; s. Earl Martin and Nancy Ann (Wolleat) K.; m. Darlene Joyce Fox, Sept. 12, 1964; children: Rodney Eric, Aaron Weston. BS, St. Cloud (Minn.) State U., 1965, MA, 1968. Cert. tchr. Art tchr. St. Cloud Jr. High Sch., 1965-70; art tchr., dept. chmn. St. Cloud Sr. High Sch., 1970-80; ind. instr. watercolor workshop, 1980—. Contbg. artist North Light Pub., 1993, 94. Served with USN, 1957-61. Named Artist of Yr. Phoenix C. of C., 1987. Mem. Ariz. Watercolor Soc. (signature), Midwest Watercolor Soc. (v.p. 1976-77, signature). Republican. Home: 1947 E Manhatton Dr Tempe AZ 85282-5815

KINNISON, HARRY AUSTIN, transportation engineer; b. Springfield, Ohio, Oct. 2, 1935; s. Errett Lowell and Audrey Muriel (Smith) K. BSEE, U. Wyo., 1964; M. in Transp. Engring., Seattle U., 1983; PhD in Civil Engring., U. Tenn., 1987. Enlisted USAF, 1958, commd. 2d lt., 1964, advanced through grades to capt., 1968, released from active duty, 1968; electronics engr. 1839th Electronics Installation Group, Keesler AFB, Biloxi, Miss., 1972-77; staff engr. Casper (Wyo.) Air Facilities Sector FAA, 1977; test engr. Boeing Aerospace Co., Seattle, 1977-81; grad. rsch. engr. U. Tenn. Transp. Ctr., Knoxville, 1983-87; avionics engr. Boeing Comml. Airplane Co., Seattle, 1981-83, 87-90, maintenance programs engr. customer svcs. div., 1990—. Mem. Inst. Transp. Engrs. (assoc.), Transp. Rsch. Bd. (assoc.). Republican. Mem. Christian Ch. Home: 11630 SE 219th Pl Kent WA 98031-3922 Office: Boeing Comml Airplane Group M/S 2-J-21 PO Box 3707 Seattle WA 98124

KINNISON, ROBERT WHEELOCK, accountant; b. Des Moines, Sept. 17, 1914; s. Virgil R. and Sopha J. (Jackson) K.; m. Randi Hjelle, Oct. 28, 1971; children—Paul F., Hazel Jo Huff. B.S. in Acctg., U. Wyo., 1940. C.P.A., Wyo., Colo. Ptnr. 24 hour auto service, Laramie, Wyo., 1945-59; pvt. practice acctg., Laramie, Wyo., 1963-71, Las Vegas, Nev., 1972-74, Westminster, Colo., 1974-76, Ft. Collins, Colo., 1976—. Served with U.S. Army, 1941-45; PTO. Mem. Wyo. Soc. C.P.A.s, Am. Legion (past comdr.), Laramie Soc. C.P.A.s (pres. 1966), VFW. Clubs: Laramie Optimist (pres. 1950), Sertoma. Home: PO Box 168 Fort Collins CO 80522-0168 Office: 401 N Summit View Dr Lot 288 Fort Collins CO 80524-1431

KINNUNE, WILLIAM P., forest products executive; b. 1939. Grad., U. Wash., 1961. With Willamette Industries, Inc., Portland, Oreg., 1961—, various sales and mgmt. positions, 1961-75, v.p., 1975-77, sr. v.p., from 1977, now exec. v.p. Office: Willamette Industries Inc 3800 1st Interstate Tower Portland OR 97201

KINSLER, BRUCE WHITNEY, air traffic controller, consultant, air traffic control engineer, air defense engineer; b. Ukiah, Calif., Jan. 11, 1947; s. John Arthur and Mary Helen (Hudson) K.; m. Mickey Kinsler, Apr. 1, 1969 (div. Nov. 1976); 1 child, Arthur Todd; m. Segundina L. Pangilinan, May 27, 1978; 1 stepchild, Stephanie Camalig. AA, El Camino Coll., 1979; BA, Calif. State U., Long Beach, 1984. Air traffic controller FAA, various locations, 1971-81; cen. sta. mgr. Times Mirror Security Communications, Irvine, Calif., 1982-84; supr. office services Law Offices Paul, Hastings, Janofsky & Walker, L.A., 1984-85; air traffic control cons. Hughes Aircraft Co., Fullerton, Calif., 1985-88; engr., scientist space sta. div. McDonnell Douglas, Huntington Beach, Calif., 1989-90; ATC/ADGE sr. sys. engr. Hughes Aircraft Co., Fullerton, Calif., 1990—; mem. citizens adv. com. Calif. Dept. Transp., Sacramento, 1982—. Author air traffic control tng. manuals. Res. dep. sheriff Orange County. With USNR, 1986—. Mem. Nat. Air Traffic Com. (nat. com.), Air Traffic Control Assn., Human Factors Soc. (pres. Orange County chpt.). Republican. Home: 283 Longbranch Cir Brea CA 92621-4420

KINSMAN, ROBERT PRESTON, biomedical plastics engineer; b. Cambridge, Mass., July 25, 1949; s. Fred Nelson and Myra Roxanne (Preston) K. BS in Plastics Engring., U. Mass., Lowell, 1971; MBA, Pepperdine U., Malibu, Calif., 1982. Cert. biomed. engr., Calif.; lic. real estate sales person, Calif. Product devel. engr., plastics divsn. Gen. Tire Corp., Lawrence, Mass., 1976-77; mfg. engr. Am. Edwards Labs. divsn. Am. Hosp. Supply Corp., Irvine, Calif., 1978-80, sr. engr., 1981-82; mfg. engring. mgr. Edwards Labs., Inc. subs. Am. Hosp. Supply Corp., Añasco, P.R., 1983; project mgr. Baxter Edwards Critical Care divsn. Baxter Healthcare Corp., Irvine, 1984-87, engring. and prodn. mgr., 1987-93; pres. Kinsman & Assocs., Irvine, Calif., 1993—; mem. mgmt. adv. panel Modern Plastics mag., N.Y.C., 1979-80. Instr. first aid ARC, N.D., Mass., Calif., 1971-82; vol. worker VA, Bedford, Mass., 1967-71; pres., bd. dirs. Lakes Homeowners Assn., Irvine, 1985-91; bd. dirs., newsletter editor Paradise Park Owners Assn., Las Vegas, Nev., 1988—; bd. dirs. Orange County, Calif., divsn. Am. Heart Assn., 1991—, chmn.-elect bd. dirs. 1994-95, chmn. bd. dirs. 1995—, v.p. bd. dirs., 1993-94, chmn. devel. com., 1993-95, mem. steering com. Heart and Sole Classic fundraiser, 1988—, subcom. chmn., 1989, event vice-chmn., 1990, event chmn., 1991-92, mem. devel. com. Calif. affiliate, 1993—. Capt. USAF, 1971-75, USAFR, 1975-81. Recipient Cert. of Appreciation, VA, 1971, Am. Heart Assn., 1991, 92, 93; Baxter Found. grantee, Deerfield, Ill., 1992, 93. Mem. Soc. Plastics Engrs. (sr., Mem. of Month So. Calif. sect. 1989), Am. Mgmt. Assn., Arnold Air Soc. (comptr. 1969, pledge tng. officer 1970), Plastics Acad., Demolay, Profl. Ski Instrs. Am., Mensa, Am. Legion, Elks, Phi Gamma Psi. Office: Kinsman & Assocs 4790 Irvine Blvd Ste 105-289 Irvine CA 92720-1973

KINSMAN, ROBERT WARREN, emergency management consultant; b. Palo Alto, Calif., Mar. 18, 1943; s. Karl Kenneth and Vera Evelyn (Romwall) K.; m. Susan Mary Hurtig, Oct. 26, 1968; 1 child, Erik Karl. BA, Calif. State U., San Francisco, 1965. Cert. secondary tchr., Calif., community coll.; registered environ. assessor, Calif. Probation officer San Mateo County Probation Dept., Redwood City, Calif., 1963-82; pub. edn. coord. San Mateo County Office of Emergency Svc., Redwood City, 1982-83, asst. area coord., 1983-90; emergency mgmt. cons. Emergency Mgmt. Assocs., Half Moon Bay, Calif., 1988—; project mgr. Indsl. Emergency Coun., San Carlos, Calif., 1992—. Author: Radiological Incident Management, 1990; contbr. articles to profl. jours. Bd. dirs. ARC Bay Area, San Mateo, 1988—, Coastside Emergency Coun., Half Moon Bay, 1975—, Bay Area March of Dimes, 1975-88, walk chmn.; coun. pres., treas. Coastside Luth. Ch., 1988-92. Recipient People Who Care award San Mateo County Bd. of Supr., 1981, Vol. of Yr. City of Half Moon Bay, 1979. Mem. Radiol. Emergency Mgmt. Soc. (state pres. 1983-88, Citation 1986), Nat. Coordinating Coun. on Emergency Mgmt., Internat. Soc. to Emergency/Diaster Medicine, Calif. Emergency Svcs. Assn. (industry rels. bd. 1983—, Citation 1990), Assn. of Profl. Emergency Planners. Republican. Lutheran. Home: 413 Casa Del Mar Dr Half Moon Bay CA 94019-1413 Office: Emergency Mgmt Assocs PO Box 3181 Half Moon Bay CA 94019-3181

KINTNER, WILLIAM LEROY, II, clergyman, psychotherapist; b. Princeton, Ind., July 23, 1945; s. William Leroy and Gladys Lucille (Woodburn) K.; m. Marilyn Louise King, Aug. 27, 1966 (div. Aug. 1981); 1 child, Kristina Marie; m. Colleen Mary Acord, Sept. 5, 1981; 1 child, Kristopher Jacob. BA, Calif. Western U., San Diego, 1967; ThM, Claremont Sch. Tehology, 1975, DMin, 1994. Ordained elder United Meth. Ch.; lic. marriage, family and child counselor, Calif.; lic. psychotherapist, Calif. Staff chaplain Meml. Hosp. Med. Ctr., Long Beach, Calif., 1968-72; psychotherapist in pvt. practice numerous locations, Calif., 1970—; staff min. First United Meth. Ch., North Hollywood, Calif., 1968-71; sr. pastor Wesley United Meth. Ch., Woodland Hills, Calif., 1971-73, La Canada United Meth. ch., La Canada-Flintridge, Calif., 1974-78, Sierra Madre (Calif.) United Meth. Ch., 1978-80, Artesia-Cerritos United Meth. Ch., Artesia, Calif., 1980-87, La Mirada (Calif.) United Meth.Ch., 1987-90, Valencia United Meth. Ch., Placentia, Calif., 1990—; v.p. United Leukodystrophy Found., Sycamore, Ill., 1986—; mem. Nat. Adv. Bd. in Pastoral Care and Human Genetics Issues, Washington, 1992—; mem. consumer com. and fiscal policy coms. Pacific S.W. Regional Genetics Network, Berkeley, Calif., 1991—; vis. lectr. Wasada U., Tokyo, 1987. Contbr. numerous articles to med. jours. Mem. alumni bd. dirs. U.S. Internat. U., San Diego, 1986-93; mem. alumni coun. Sch. Theology, Claremont, 1986-91; mem. bd. govs. Los Angeles County Mental Health Assn., L.A., 1972-75; mem. community adv. bd. Med. Ctr. of La Mirada, 1987-90; mem. bd. of ordained ministry Calif.-Pacific Conf. of United Meth. Ch., 1979-88, chair com. on counseling and guidance. Mem. Calif. Assn. Marriage and Family Therapists (life), Assn. for Clin. Pastoral Edn. Office: Valencia United Meth Ch 2050 Valencia Ave Placentia CA 92670-2040

KIPP, JUNE CAROL, health science laboratory administrator; b. Johnstown, Penn., Apr. 11, 1932; d. John Claude and Margaretta Olive (Firth) Saylor; m. David Franklin Kipp Sr., Aug. 18, 1951; children: Peggy Carol, David Franklin Jr., Matthew. AA, Lamar (Colo.) Coll., 1974; postgrad., U. Colo., Denver, 1978. Rsch. tech. Eli Lilly Co., Indpls., 1950-51; blood bank tech. Charleroi-Monessen Hosp., Penn., 1957-60; chief tech. Windber Hosp, Penn., 1960-70; technologist Nuclear Test Site, Mercury, Nev., 1970-71; blood bank tech ARC, Johnstown, Penn., 1971-72; chief tech. S.E. Colo. Hosp., Springfield, 1972-76; lab. supr. Smith Kline Clin. Labs., Denver, 1976-81, Indian Pub. Health Svc., Chinle, Ariz., 1982—. Mem. Am. Med. Tech. Assn., Colo. Med. Tech. Assn. (sec. 1977-81), Ariz. Med. Tech. Assn. Republican. Mem. Ch. of the Brethren. Office: Indian Pub Health Svc PO Drawer PH Chinle AZ 86503

KIPPUR, MERRIE MARGOLIN, lawyer; b. Denver, July 24, 1962; d. Morton Leonard and Bonnie (Seldin) Margolin; m. Bruce R. Kippur, Sept. 7, 1986. BA, Colo. Coll., 1983; JD, U. Colo., 1986. Bar: Colo. 1986, U.S. Dist. Ct. Colo. 1986, U.S. Ct. Appeals (10th cir.) 1987. Assoc. Sterling & Miller, Denver, 1985-88, McKenna & Cuneo, Denver, 1989-94; sr. v.p., gen. counsel 1st United Bank, Denver, 1994—; lectr. trial practice, bankruptcy article 4, uniform comml. code U. Colo., chpt. 9 bankruptcy and Real Estate Settlement Procedures Act. Author: Student Improvement in the 1980's, 1984, (with others) Ethical Considerations in Bankruptcy, 1985, Partnership Bankruptcy, 1986, Colorado Methods of Practise, 1988. Contract liaison Jr. League Denver, 1992-94; bd. dirs. Bylaws Parliamentarian, 1994-95, planning com., 1995-96. Mem. ABA, Colo. Bar Assn., Colo. Women's Bar Assn., Denver Bar Assn., Am. Judicature Soc., Am. Bankruptcy Inst., Gamma Phi Beta, Phi Delta Phi, Pi Gamma Mu. Democrat. Office: First United Bank 8095 E Belleview Ave Englewood CO 80111-6006

KIRBY, GEORGE WILLIAM, quality assurance professional, consultant; b. Springfield, Ill., May 7, 1939; s. George B. and Phillipa (Orel) Kardinsky; m. Linda Perkins Kirby, June 11, 1962 (div. June 1971); children: Jennifer, Brent, Michael; m. Judie Joy Hall Kirby, Oct. 15, 1975; 1 child, Gillian. Engring., St. Augustine, San Diego, 1957; polymer chemistry, San Diego State U., 1960; engring., Long Beach State U., 1970. Cert. quality engr., Calif. Sr. quality and rehab. engr. N. Am. Aviation, Downey, Calif., 1961-67; quality assurance staff Douglas Aircraft, Long Beach, Calif., 1967-69; quality assurance v.p. Hitco Corp., Gardena, Calif., 1969-79; quality assurance mgr. Armtec, Palm Springs, Calif., 1979-82; pres. Quality Assurance Consulting, Palm Springs, Calif., 1982-86; quality assurance mgr. Tracor Aviation, Goleta, Calif., 1986-89, Joslyn Elec. Sys., Goleta, Calif., 1989—. Patentee Acoustic Aircraft Interior, 1969; author: Quality Improvement, 1993, Tom Thru The Year 2000, 1993. Recipient 1st Place Mustang Restor, Vintage Collections, Palm Springs, Calif., 1983, Psychology of Achievement award Phoenix Corp., Santa Barbara, Calif., 1992. Mem. Soc. Aerospace Materials and Process Engrs.; fellow Santa Barbara Round Table. Republican. Roman Catholic. Office: Joslyn Electronic Systems 6868 Cortona Dr Goleta CA 93117-3021

KIRBY, ORVILLE EDWARD, potter; b. Wichita, Kans., Jan. 31, 1912; s. Charlie and Elizabeth J. (Sage) K. Student, U. Utah, 1935-36, U. So. Calif., L.A., 1934-35, St. Paul Sch. Fine Art, 1933-34. Owner Orville Kirby Pottery, L.A., 1941-47; owner Sleepy Hollow Pottery, Laguna Beach, Calif., 1948-54, Monroe, Utah, 1955—. Republican. Mormon. Home and Office: 95 W Center St Monroe UT 84754-4159

KIRBY, THOMAS PAUL, artist; b. San Francisco, June 10, 1926; s. Edward Thomas and Alice Madeline (Flood) K.; m. Virginia Gay Christianson, May 17, 1963 (div. Jan. 1984); children: Dawn, Paul, Alice, Steven, Thomas; m. Joan D. Truman, 1985. Student, Calif. Coll. Arts and Crafts, 1946-47, San Francisco Art Inst., 1948. Curator exhbns. dept. Mus. N.Mex., Santa Fe, 1970-74; concert hall and tour mgr. Santa Fe Chamber Music Festival, 1973. One man shows at East-West Gallery, San Francisco, 1954, 55, Lucien Labaudt Gallery, San Francisco, 1957, San Francisco Mus. Modern Art, 1964, Anchorage (Alaska) Fine Arts Mus., 1969, West Gallery, Santa Fe, 1970, Hill's Gallery, Santa Fe, 1972, 74, Hartnell Coll. Gallery, Salinas, Calif., 1980, Monterey (Calif.) Peninsula Mus. Art, 1981, Bay Window Gallery, Mendocino, Calif., 1987; group exhbns. include Bratta Gallery, N.Y.C., San Francisco Art Inst. Annual Exhbns. and Traveling Exhbns., 1959-62, Zellerbach Bldg., San Francisco, 1963, The deYoung Mus., San Francisco, 1963, Highlands U., Las Vegas, 1973, Roswell Mus. Fall Invitational, 1973, Francis McGray Gallery, Silver City, N.Mex; represented in permanent collections The Monterey (Calif.) Peninsula Mus. Art, The Mus. Fine Arts, Anchorage, The Fine Arts Mus., Santa Fe, The Roswell Mus. and Art Ctr., IBM Corp., ITEL, Torrance, Calif., SSI Corp., San Francisco, Mobil Oil Co., Denver, Kona Surf Hotel, Hawaii, Rosewood Hotel, Tex., The Fairmount, Tex., The Peabody Hotel, Orlando, Fla., Touche Ross & Co., San Jose, Calif. With USN, 1944-46. Mem. San Francisco Art Inst. Alumni. Home and Studio: 118 Willow St Salinas CA 93901

KIRCHMEIER, ROBERT LYNN, chemistry educator; b. Portland, Oreg., Apr. 25, 1942; s. A. H. and Ellen Mary (Dettmann) K.; m. Nancy Sue Bannon, June 20, 1970; children: Benjamin Robert, Samuel Bannon, Katherine Marie. BS in Chemistry, U. Mont., 1968; PhD in Chemistry, U. Idaho, 1975. Analytical environ. chemist U.S. AEC, Idaho Falls, Idaho, 1968-71; analytical rsch. chemist Pfizer, Inc., Groton, Conn., 1975-79; analytical prodn. chemist Parke-Davis (Warner Lambert), Holland, Mich., 1979-81; pres., founder West Analytical Lab., Bozeman, Mont., 1981-87; asst. rsch. prof. U. Idaho, Moscow, 1987-92, assoc. rsch. prof. chemistry, 1992—; cons. Dept. Def., Md., 1992, Catalytica, Mountain View, Calif., 1989-90. Contbr. numerous articles to profl. jours. With USAF, 1960-64. Grantee USAF Office Sci. Rsch., NSF, Dept. Energy, 1987—. Mem. Am. Chem. Soc. (exec. com. fluorine divsn. 1993—). Presbyterian. Office: U Idaho Dept Chemistry Moscow ID 83844

KIRCHNER, ERNST KARL, company executive; b. San Francisco, June 18, 1937; s. Karl Ewald and Theresa (Muller) K.; m. Ursula Martha Karmann, Sept. 3, 1960; children: Mark Ernst, Christl Elaine, Steven Thomas. BSEE, Stanford U., 1959, MSEE, 1960, PhD in EE, 1963. Tech. staff Teledyne MEC, Palo Alto, Calif., 1965-72; project engr. Teledyne MEC, Palo Alto, 1972-79, staff engr., 1979-81, mgr., 1981-82, ops. mgr., 1982-83, sr. mgr., 1983-84; mgr. engring. Teledyne Microwave, Mountain View, Calif., 1984-87; dir. engring. Teledyne Microwave, Mountain View, 1987-88, v.p. bus. devel., 1988-93; v.p. delay device product line Teledyne Microwave, 1990-93; dir. microwave components and microsys. Teledyne Electronics Techs., Mountain View, 1993—; tchr. U. Ariz., Tucson, 1963-65. Contbr. articles to profl. jours.; patentee in field. Com. mem. Town of Atherton, Calif., 1986-87; deacon, elder Menlo Park Presbyn. Ch.; bd. mem., vice chmn. Christian Found. for Mindanao; bd. dirs., vice chmn. Hope Unltd. Internat. Lt. U.S. Army, 1963-65. Recipient Army commendation medal and citation, U.S. Army, 1965. Mem. IEEE, Am. Phys. Soc., Am. Mktg. Assn., Assn. of Old Crows, Kappa Kappa Psi, Tau Beta Pi, Sigma Xi. Republican. Home: 41 Ashfield Rd Menlo Park CA 94027-3805 Office: Teledyne Electronic Techs 1274 Bella Ave Mountain View CA 94043-1885

KIRK, CARMEN ZETLER, data processing executive; b. Altoona, Pa., May 22, 1941; d. Paul Alan and Mary Evelyn (Pearce) Zetler. BA, Pa. State U., 1959-63; MBA, St. Mary's Coll. Calif., 1977. Cert. in data processing. Pub. sch. tchr. State Ga., 1965-66; systems analyst U.S. Govt. Dept. Army, Oakland, Calif., 1967-70; programmer analyst Contra Costa County, Martinez, Calif., 1970-76; applications mgr. Stanford (Calif.) U., 1976-79; pres. Zetler Assocs., Inc., Palo Alto, Calif., 1979—; cons. State Calif., Sacramento, 1985-88. Office: Zetler Assocs Inc PO Box 50395 Palo Alto CA 94303-0395

KIRK, CASSIUS LAMB, JR., lawyer, investor; b. Bozeman, Mont., June 8, 1929; s. Cassius Lamb and Gertrude Violet (McCarthy) K.; AB, Stanford U., 1951; JD, U. Calif., Berkeley, 1954. Bar: Calif. 1955. Assoc. firm Cooley, Godward, Castro, Huddleson & Tatum, San Francisco, 1956-60; staff counsel for bus. affairs Stanford U., 1960-78; chief bus. officer, staff counsel Menlo Sch. and Coll., Atherton, Calif., 1978-81; chmn. Eberli-Kirk Properties, Inc. (doing bus. as Just Closets), Menlo Park, 1981-94; mem. summer faculty Coll. Bus. Adminstrn. U. Calif., Santa Barbara, 1967-73; mem. adv. bd. Allied Arts Guild, Menlo Park. With U.S. Army, 1954-56. Mem. Stanford Assocs., Order of Coif, Phi Alpha Delta. Republican. Club: Stanford Faculty. Home and Office: 1330 University Dr Apt 52 Menlo Park CA 94025-4241

KIRK, GARY VINCENT, investment advisor; b. Wausau, Wis., Jan. 15, 1943; s. Kenneth Robinson and Mary (Fisher) K.; m. Cynthia Kimberly Monroe, Dec. 21, 1966; children: Alisa Kimberly, Randolph Monroe. BS in Chem. Engring., U. Wis., 1965; MBA, Stanford U., 1967. Analyst Nat. Air Pollution Control Adminstrn., Pub. Health Svc., Washington, 1967-69; fin. analyst Memorex Corp., Santa Clara, Calif., 1969-71; ptnr. Robertson, Colman, Siebel & Weisel, San Francisco, 1971-78; pres. Siebel Capital Mgmt., Inc., Larkspur, Calif., 1978-84; exec. v.p. Siebel Capital Mgmt., Inc., Larkspur, 1984-90; ptnr. Wood Island Assocs., Inc., Larkspur, 1992—, pres., 1993—. Deacon Menlo Park (Calif.) Presbyn. Ch., 1976-78; trustee St. Marks Sch. Bd., San Rafael, Calif., 1985-88. Lt. (j.g.) USPHS, 1967-69. Mem. Marin Country Club. Home: 40 Carnoustie Dr Novato CA 94949-5850 Office: Wood Island Assocs Inc 80 E Sir Francis Drake Blvd Larkspur CA 94939

KIRK, HENRY PORT, academic administrator; b. Clearfield, Pa., Dec. 20, 1935; s. Henry P. and Ann (H.) K.; m. Mattie F., Feb. 11, 1956; children: Timothy, Mary Ann, Rebecca. BA, Geneva Coll., 1958; MA, U. Denver, 1963; EdD, U. Southern Calif., 1973. Counselor, ednl. Columbia Coll., Columbia, Mo., 1963-65; dean Huron (S.D.) Coll., 1965-66; assoc. dean Calif. State U., L.A., 1966-70; dean El Camino Coll., Torrance, Calif., 1970-81; v.p. Pasadena (Calif.) City Coll., 1981-86; pres. Centralia (Wash.) Coll., 1986—. Contbr. articles to profl. jours. Mem. hist. commn., City Chehalis, 1990, pres. econ. devel. coun., 1992; campaign chmn., United Way, Centralia, 1989-90. Recipient PTK Bennett Disting. Pres. award, 1990; Exemplary Contbn. to Resource Devel. award Nat. Coun. of Resource Devel., 1993. Mem. Wash. Assn. Community Colls., Torrance Rotary Club (pres. 1987-88), Centralia Rotary Club (pres. 1990-91), Phi Theta Kappa, Phi Delta Kappa. Presbyterian. Office: Centralia Coll 600 W Locust St Centralia WA 98531-4035

KIRK, PAUL, architect; b. Salt Lake City, Nov. 18, 1914; s. Spencer B. and Malvina Zoe (Blair) K.; m. Helen Catherine Richardson, Feb. 16, 1939; children: Christopher Paul, Hannah Jo. BArch, U. Wash., 1932-37. Registered architect, Wash. Prin. Paul Kirk Architect, Seattle, 1939-45; ptnr. Chiarelli & Kirk, Seattle, 1945-50; prin. Paul Hayden Kirk AIA, Seattle, 1950-56, Paul Hayden Kirk, FAIA & Assocs., Seattle, 1956-60; ptnr. Kirk, Wallace, McKinley, AIA & Assocs., Seattle, 1968-78; prin. Paul Hayden Kirk FAIA, PSC; vis. critic Cornell U. Sch. Architecture, Ithaca, N.Y., jury for Nat. Conf. Ch. Architecture, jury for City Hall competition FHA, Wash. Former bd. dirs. Community Psychiat. Clinic, Pinel Mental Hosp. Found.; bd. dirs. Community Devel. Council, Seattle chpt. AIA; chmn. Gov. Com. Factory-Built Housing; mem. Hist. Seattle Preservation and Devel. Authority, Gov. Com. on Employment for Handicapped, Seattle, Mayor's Com. on Opportunities for Handicapped, Seattle. Named to U. Wash. Hall of Fame, 1986, U. Wash. Alumni Legends, 1987. Fellow AIA (past treas., former bd. dirs. Wash. state chpt., chmn. nat. com. aesthetics, chmn. Architect/Engr. Selection Com.); mem. Portland Devel. Commn. (mem. design adv. council), FHA (adv. com. honor awards for residential design), Jury for Nat. Conf. Ch. Architecture, Jury for City Hall Competition, AIA (past treas., former bd. dirs Wash. state chpt, chmn. nat. com. aesthetics), Forward Thrust Com. on Quality in Urban Design (chmn.), Gen. Services Adminstrn. (mem. design adv. commn.), Tau Sigma Delta, Alpha Rho Chi.

KIRK, REA HELENE (REA HELENE GLAZER), school administrator, educator; b. N.Y.C., Nov. 17, 1944; d. Benjamin and Lillian (Kellis) Glazer; 3 stepdaughters. B.A., UCLA, 1966; M.A., Eastern Mont. Coll., 1981; EdD U. So. Calif., 1995. Life cert. spl. edn. tchr., Calif., Mont. Spl. edn. tchr., Los Angeles, 1966-73; clin. sec. speech and lang. clinic, Missoula, Mont., 1973-75; spl. edn. tchr., Missoula and Gt. Falls, Mont., 1975-82; br. mgr. YWCA of L.A., Beverly Hills, Calif., 1989-91; sch. adminstrn., ednl. coord. Adv. Schs. of Calif., 1991-94; dir. Woman's Resource Ctr., Gt. Falls, Mont., 1981-82; dir. Battered Woman's Shelter, Rock Springs, Wyo., 1982-84; dir. Battered Victims Program Sweetwater County, Wyo., 1984-88, Battered Woman's Program, San Gabriel Valley, Calif., 1988, Spl. Edn., Pasadena, 1994—, prin., 1995; mem. Wyo. Commn. on Aging, Rock Springs; mem. Community Action Bd. City of L.A. Pres., bd. dirs. battered woman's shelter, Gt. Falls, Woman's Resource Ctr., Gt. Falls; founder, advisor Rape Action Line, Gt. Falls; founder Jewish religious svcs., Missoula; 4-H leader; hostess Friendship Force; Friendship Force ambassador, Wyo., Fed. Republic Germany, Italy; mem. YWCA Mont. and Wyo. Recipient Gladys Byron scholar U. So. Calif., 1993, Dept. Edn. scholar U. So. Calif., 1994, honors Missoula 4-H; recognized as significant Wyo. woman as social justice reformer and peace activist Sweetwater County, Wyo.; nominated Wyo. Woman of the Yr., 1981, 82. Mem. Council for Exceptional Children (v.p. Gt. Falls 1981-82), Assn. for Children with Learning Disabilities (Named Oustanding Mem. 1982), Phi Delta Kappa, Delta Kappa Gamma, Psi Chi, Pi Lamda Theta. Democrat. Jewish.

KIRK, SAMUEL ALEXANDER, psychologist, educator; b. Rugby, N.D., Sept. 1, 1904; s. Richard B. and Nellie (Boussard) K.; m. Winifred Eloise Day, June 25, 1933; children: Jerome Richard, Nancy Lorraine. Ph.B., U. Chgo., 1929, M.S., 1931; Ph.D., U. Mich., 1935; L.H.D., Lesley Coll., 1969; D.L., U. Ill., 1983. Research psychologist Wayne Country Tng. Sch., Northville, Mich., 1931-34, mental hygienist, 1934-35; dir. div. edn. for exceptional children State Tchrs. Coll., Milw., 1935-42, 46; chmn. grad. sch. vis. lectr. U. Mich, 1942; prof. edn. and psychology U. Ill., 1947-68, prof. emeritus, 1968—; dir. Inst. Research Exceptional Children, 1952-68; prof. spl. edn. U. Ariz., Tucson, 1968-86. Author: (with Hegge and W.D. Kirk) Remedial Reading Drills, 1936, Teaching Reading to Slow-Learning Children, 1940, (with Johnson) Educating the Retarded Child, 1951, (with Karnes and Kirk) You and Your Retarded Child, 1955, Early Education of the Mentally Retarded, 1958, Educating Exceptional Children, 1962, 2d edit, 1972, (with Gallagher) Educating Exceptional Children, 1979, 83, 86, 89, (with Gallagher and Anastasiow) Educating Exceptional Children, 1993, (with Wiener) Behavioral Research on Exceptional Children, 1964, (with J.J. McCarthy and Kirk) The Illinois Test of Psycholinguistic Abilities, rev. edit., 1968, (with Kirk) Psycholinguistic Learning Disabilities, 1971, (with Lord) Exceptional Children: Resources and Perspectives, 1974, (with J.M. McCarthy) Learning Disabilities, 1975, (with Kleibahn and Lerner) Teaching Reading to Slow and Disabled Readers, 1978, (with Chalfant) Academic and Developmental Learning Disabilities, 1984, (with Kirk and Minskoff) Phonic Remedial Reading Lessons, 1985, The Foundations of Special Education: Selected Papers and Speeches of Samuel A. Kirk, 1993; contbr. articles to profl. publs. Served as maj. AUS, 1942-46. Recipient 1st internat. award for profl. service in mental retardation Joseph P. Kennedy Jr. Found., 1962, J.E. Wallace Wallin ann. award Council for Exceptional Children, 1966, recognition award for early childhood edn., 1981, ann. award Assn. Children with Learning Disabilities, 1966, ann. award Caritas Soc., 1966, Internat. Milestone award Internat. Fedn. Learning Disabilities, 1975, Disting. Service award Am. Assn. Speech and Hearing, 1976, Disting. Citizen award U. Ariz. Alumni Assn., 1977, award for outstanding leadership Ill. Council Exceptional Children, 1980, recognition award Pa. Assn. Children with Learning Disabilities, 1980, Ariz. Div. Devel. Disability, 1980, Helen T. Devereaux Meml. award, 1981. Fellow Am. Psychol. Assn. (Edgar Bell award 1980); Am. Assn. for Mental Deficiency (award 1969); mem. Internat. Council Exceptional Children (pres. 1941-43), Nat. Soc. Study Edn. (chmn. 1950 yearbook com), Brit. Assn. Spl. Edn. (hon. v.p. 1962), Sigma Xi. Home: 7500 N Calle Sin Envidia Tucson AZ 85718-7300

KIRKBRIDE, RAYMOND WILLIAM, security officer; b. Wadsworth, Ohio, Oct. 5, 1962; s. Wilfred Edison and Marjorie May (Yoakem) K.; m. Hae Song Yi, July 18, 1983 (div. May 1994); children: Shawn O'Ryan, Sabin Allen. A in Indsl. Security, C.C. of the USAF, 1992. Enlisted USAF, 1981, advanced through grades to E-5, 1986, ret., 1992; security agt. Am Pro Protective Agy., Las Vegas, Nev., 1993-94; security officer MGM Grand Hotel, Las Vegas, 1994—. Active Amerasian Children Assn., Kunsan/Osan AFB, Korea, 1986-91; den father Cub Scouts Am., Las Vegas, 1993—. Decorated Commendation medals USAF, 1985, 91, Achievement medals USAF, 1988. Home: PO Box 356 Bainbridge OH 45612-0356 Office: MGM Grand Hotel Casino and Theme Park 3799 Las Vegas Blvd S Las Vegas NV 89109-4319

KIRKORIAN, DONALD GEORGE, college official, management consultant; b. San Mateo, Calif., Nov. 30, 1938; s. George and Alice (Sergius) K. BA, San Jose State U., 1961, MA, 1966, postgrad., 1968; postgrad., Stanford U., 1961, U. So. Calif., 1966; PhD, Northwestern U., 1972. Producer Sta. KNTV, San Jose, Calif., 1961; tchr. L.A. City Schs., 1963; instrnl. TV coord. Fremont Union High Sch. Dist., Sunnyvale, Calif., 1963-73; assoc. dean instrn. learning resources Solano C.C., Suisun City, Calif., 1973-85, dean instrnl. services, 1985-89, dean learning resources and staff devel., 1989—; owner, pres. Kirkorian and Assocs., Suisun City; field cons. Nat. Assn. Edn. Broadcasters, 1966-68; adj. faculty San Jose State U., 1968-69, U. Calif., Santa Cruz, 1970-73, U. Calif., Davis, 1973-76; chmn. Bay Area TV Consortium, 1976-77, 86-87; mem. adv. panel Speech Comm. Assn./Am. Theater Assn. tchr. preparation in speech., comm., theater and media, N.Y.C., 1973-77. Author: Staffing Information Handbook, 1990, National Learning Resources Directory, 1991, 93; editor: Media Memo, 1973-80, Intercom: The Newsletter for Calif. Community Coll. Librs., 1974-75, Update, 1980-90, Exploring the Benicia State Recreation Area, 1977, California History Resource Materials, 1977, Time Management, 1980; contbr. articles to profl. jours. Chmn. Solano County Media Adv. Com., 1974-76; bd. dirs. Napa-Solano United Way, 1980-82; mem. adv. bd. Calif. Youth Authority, 1986-93. Mem. Nat. Assn. Ednl. Broadcasters, Assn. for Edn. Comm. and Tech., Broadcast Edn. Assn., Calif. Assn. Ednl. Media and Tech. (treas.), Western Ednl. Soc. for Telecomm. (bd. dirs. 1973-75, pres. 1976-77, State Chancellor's com. on Telecomm. 1982-86), Learning Resources Assn. Calif. Comm. Colls. (exec. dir. 1976—, sec.-treas., pres.), Assn. Calif. C.C. Adminstrs. (bd. dirs. 1985-91), Phi Delta Kappa. Home: 1655 Rockville Rd Suisun City CA 94585-1373 Office: Solano CC 4000 Suisun Valley Rd Suisun City CA 94585-4017

KIRKPATRICK, DENNIS OERTING, management consultant, benefits and health care; b. Detroit, July 6, 1946; s. Henry O. and Mildred (Kalosek) K.; m. Jane Sanders (div. 1977); m. Carol E. Lagerquist, Mar. 7, 1982; 1 child, Mike. BS, U. Ala., 1970, MA, 1972. Dir. student union U. Ala., Tuscaloosa, 1968-70; v.p. ops. Morris Paper Co., Brunswick, Ga., 1970-77; branch mgr. Hosp. Svc. and Supply, Santa Clara, Calif., 1978-81; ops. mgr. Livingston Med., San Jose, Calif., 1982-83; mgmt. cons. Stockton, Calif., 1984—; benefit mgr. San Joaquin County, Stockton, 1991-93; adminstr. Lodi IPA, 1993—; pres. Unisys Computer Users Group, Redwood City, Calif., 1988-90. Mem. Med. Group Mgmt. Assn. Home: 2439 De Ovan Ave Stockton CA 95204-1513 Office: Med Mgmt Contractors 133 Arch St Redwood City CA 94062-1326

KIRKPATRICK, JOEY J., artist; b. Nov. 19, 1952. BFA, U. Iowa, 1975; postgrad. studies in Glass, Iowa State U., 1978-79, Pilchuck Glass Sch., Stanwood, Wash., 1979. Artist in residence Pilchuck Glass Sch., Stanwood, Wash., 1980, 87, Rhode Island Sch. of Design, Providence, 1980; guest instr. UCLA, 1981; faculty mem. U. Ill., Champaign, 1981-82; visiting faculty mem. U. Hawaii, Honolulu, 1993; artist in residence asst. Pilchuck Glass Sch., Stanwood, 1984; faculty mem. Haystack Mt. Sch. of Crafts, Deer Isle, Maine, 1985; visiting faculty mem. Lobmyer Factory, Sch., Vienna, 1985; guest lectr. Norisk Glas 1985, Rykjavik, Iceland, San Francisco State U., 1987, Harbourfront Studios, Toronto, Can., 1987, Nat. Coll. of Art, Craft and Design, Konstfack, Stockholm, 1987, Palm Springs (Calif.) Desert Mus., 1994; summer faculty mem. Pilchuck Glass Sch., Stanwood, 1986-90. Glass sculptress in collaboration with Flora C. Mace: solo exhbns. include: Heller Gallery, N.Y.C., 1982, 86, Seattle Art Mus., 1989, New Art Gallery, Paris, 1991, Riley Hawk Gallery, Cleve., 1992, 94, Foster/White Gallery, Seattle, 1994, Brunnier Mus., Ames, Iowa, 1992, Anne Reed Gallery, Sun Valley, Idaho, 1995, Metropolitan Mus. of Art, N.Y., others; numerous group exhbns. include: World Glass Now, Hokkaido Mus. Modern Art, Sapporo, Japan, 1985, 91, 94, Galsskunst, 1981, West Germany; included in pub.

collections in London, Switzerland, Japan, U.S., others. Mem. Bd. Trustees Pilchuck Glass Sch., Stanwood, Wash., 1991—.

KIRKPATRICK, RICHARD ALAN, internist; b. Rochester, Minn., Jan. 17, 1947; s. Neal R. and Ethel C. (Hull) K.; m. Susan Baxter; children: James N., Ronald S., David B., Mary J., Scott B., Christina Marie. BA in Chemistry with honors, U. Wash., 1968, BS in Psychology, 1968, MD, 1972. Diplomate Am. Bd. Internal Medicine. Intern, resident in internal medicine Mayo Grad. Sch., Rochester, 1972-76, spl. resident in biomed. communications, 1974-75; pvt. practice specializing in internal medicine Longview, Wash., 1976—; sr. ptnr. Internal Medicine Clinic of Longview; mem. clin. faculty U. Wash.; dir. cardiac rehab. program St. John's Hosp. . Editor: Drug Therapy Abstracts, Wash. Internists; mem. editorial adv. bd. Your Patient and Cancer, Primary Care and Cancer; weekly med. TV talk show host, 1978—; contbr. articles to med. jours. Bd. dirs., v.p. Columbia Theatre for Performing Arts; mem. City Coun., Longview; mem. S.W. Wash. Symphony; bd. dirs. S.W. Wash. Youth Symphony; pres., bd. dirs. Sta. KLTV. Fellow ACP (gov.'s coun.); mem. Wash. State Soc. Internal Medicine (trustee, past pres.), Am. Geriatrics Soc., Am. Soc. Echocardiography, Am. Soc. Internal Medicine, Wash. Med. Assn. (coun. med. svc.), Am. Cancer Soc. (local bd. dirs.), Am. Soc. Clin. Oncology, AMA, Am. Med. Writers Assn. Office: 748 14th Ave Longview WA 98632

KIRKPATRICK, SUSAN ELIZABETH D., political scientist; b. Niagara Falls, N.Y., Oct. 6, 1950; d. George Leo Jr. and Bette (Wadsworth) Dischinger; m. Allan Thomson Kirkpatrick, July 1, 1972; children: Anne Thomson, Robert Wadsworth. BA, U. Mich., 1971; MEd, Harvard U., 1975; PhD, Colo. State U., 1995. Social studies tchr. Walsingham Acad., Williamsburg, Va., 1972-74; adminstr. Wentworth Inst. Tech., Boston, 1977-80; polit. scientist Colo. State U., Fort Collins, 1987-91; asst. prof. polit. sci. U. No. Colo., Greeley, 1992—. City coun. mem. City of Fort Collins, 1986-93, mayor, 1990-93; exec. bd. Colo. Mcpl. League, 1990-93; chair state bd. Outdoors Colo. Trust, 1993—. Mem. Jr. League Fort Collins (newsletter editor 1984), Am. Polit. Sci. Assn., Women in Mcpl. Govt. (sec. 1989), Great Outdoors Colo. Trust (bd. dirs. 1993—, chair 1994—). Home: 2312 Tanglewood Dr Fort Collins CO 80525-1953

KIRKS, JAMES HARVEY, JR., librarian, administrator; b. L.A., Sept. 16, 1937; s. James Harvey Sr. and Grace Edna (Whitney) K.; m. Barbara Aileen Barry, June 1962 (div. July 1982); children: Cara Lynn, Laura Lee. AA, Compton Coll., 1957, UCLA, 1958; BA, UCLA, 1959; MS in LS, U. So. Calif., 1962. Head of reference, circulation and audiovisual City of Inglewood (Calif.) Pub. Libr., 1962, head of extension svcs., 1964-66; dir. pub. svcs. Arcadia (Calif.) Pub. Libr., 1966-70; city librarian Port Angeles (Wash.) Pub. Libr., 1970-73; dir. North Olympic Libr. System, Port Angeles, 1973-75; coord. North State Coop. Libr. System, Willows, Calif., 1975—. Contbr. articles to profl. jours. Pres. United Way, Clallum County, Wash., 1973, Port Angeles Symphony Orch., 1975, Faith Luth. Ch., Chico, Calif., 1981-82. With Signal Corps, U.S. Army, 1962-64, France. Mem. ALA (various coms.), Calif. Libr. Assn. (various coms.), Congress of Calif. Pub. Libr. System (pres. 1980s), Aid Assn. for Luths. (pres. br. 1990—), Rotary Internat. (bd. dirs. 1974). Home: 11 Hemming Ln Chico CA 95926-1076 Office: North State Coop Libr Sys 259 N Villa Ave Willows CA 95988-2607

KIRSCHNER, BRUCE HERBERT, federal official, political science educator; b. N.Y.C., Aug. 13, 1953; s. Arthur S. and Miriam (Edelman) K.; m. Janet P. Lowe, Aug. 16, 1978; children: Aron, Paul, Sam. BA English, Polit. Sci. magna cum laude, SUNY, Buffalo, 1975; MPA, U. New Mex., 1977; PhD in Pub. Adminstrn., U. Colo., Denver, 1990. Rsch. asst. Cmty. Planning Assitance Ctr. Western N.Y., Buffalo, 1974-75, N.Y. State Senate Com. on Consumer Protection, Albany, 1975-76, Divsn. Pub. Adminstrn. U. New Mex., Albuquerque, 1976-77; program specialist Inst. for Applied Rsch. Svcs. U. New Mex., Albuquerque, 1978; mgmt. analyst Office Nuclear Reactor Regulation U.S. Nuclear Reg. Commn., Bethesda, Md., 1978-79; program analyst Asst. Sec. for Conservation, Solar Energy U.S. Dept Energy, Washington, 1979-81, Western Area Power Adminstrn. U.S. Dept. Energy, Golden, Colo., 1981—; speaker various govt. sponsored panels and tech. orgn. confs.; adj. prof. polit. sci. & pub. adminstrn. U. Colo., Denver. Contbr. articles to profl. jours. Chmn. Denver Free-Net Policy/Procedures Com. Named one of Outstanding Young Men of Am., U.S. Jaycees, 1977. Mem. Alliance for Pub. Tech., The Electronic Frontier Found., The World Future Soc., Am. Soc. for Pub. Adminstrn.; Phi Beta Kappa, Pi Alpha Alpha. Office: Western Area Power Adminstrn 1627 Code Blvd Golden CO 80401

KIRSCHNER, MELVIN HENRY, physician; b. N.Y.C., Aug. 13, 1926; s. Philip S. and Belle (Lobel) K.; m. Geraldine Lee Williams, Dec. 30, 1961; children: Darin Markley, Corey Alan, Todd Andrew. BA, UCLA, 1948, BS, 1949; MPH, U. Calif., Berkeley, 1955; MD, U. So. Calif., 1960. Sanitarian Tulare (Calif.) County Health Dept., 1949-51, Oakland (Calif.) City Helath Dept., 1951-52, 55; cons. pub. health sanitarian City Health Dept., Berkeley, 1952-54; sanitary engr. Calif. State Health Dept., 1956-59; intern L.A. County Hosp., 1960-61; pvt. family practice Van Nuys, Calif., 1961—; mem., past chmn. Unihealth Bioethics Inst.; med. dir. San Fernando Valley Home Health Agy., Encino, Calif., 1968-71, Sheraton Convalescent Hosp., Sepulveda, Calif., 1968—, Beverly Manor Convalscent Hosp., Panorama City, Calif., 1967-92; dir. biomed. ethics Valley Hosp. Med. Ctr., Van Nuys, 1986—, Panorama Hosp. Med. Ctr., 1982-91; chmn. family practice com. Valley Presbyn. Hosp., 1992, Bioethics Mission Cmty. Hosp., Panorama City, 1993—. With USN, 1944-46. Mem. Am. Acad. Family Physicians (diplomate), AMA, Am. Pub. Health Assn., Nat. Coun. Against Health Fraud, Calif. Med. Assn., Calif. Acad. Family Practice, L.A. Co-med. Assn. (chmn. biomed. ethics com.). Office: 14411 Gilmore St Van Nuys CA 91401-1430

KIRSCHNER, RICHARD MICHAEL, naturopathic physician, speaker, author; b. Cin., Sept. 27, 1949; s. Alan George and Lois (Dickey) K.; 1 child, Aden Netanya; m. Lindea Bowe. BS in Human Biology, Kans. Newman Coll., 1979; D in Naturopathic Medicine, Nat. Coll. Naturopathic Medicine, 1981. Vice pres. D. Kirschner & Son, Inc., Newport, Ky., 1974-77; co-owner, mgr. Sunshine Ranch Arabian Horses, Melbourne, Ky., 1975-77; pvt. practice Portland, Oreg., 1981-83, Ashland, Oreg., 1983—; seminar leader, trainer Inst. for Meta-Linguistics, Portland, 1981-84; cons. Nat. Elec. Contractors Assn., So. Oreg., 1985-86, United Telephone N.W., 1986; spkr. Ford Motor Co., Blue Cross-Blue Shield, Balfour Corp., NEA, AT&T, Triad Sys., Supercuts, 1986-89, Hewlett-Packard, Pepsi Co., George Bush Co., 1990-91, Goodwill Industries Am., Motorola, 1992, The Homestead T.V.A., Federated Ambulatory Surg. Assn., V.H.A. Satellite Broadcast, 1993, Oreg. Dept. Edn., Anaheim Meml. Hosp., 1994, Inc. 500 Conf., U.S. C. of C., Inst. Indsl. Engrs., 1995; spkr., trainer Careertrack Seminars, Boulder, Colo., 1986-93; owner, spkr., trainer R & R Prodns., Ashland, Oreg., 1984—. Co-author: audio tape seminar How to Deal with Difficult People, 1987, video tape seminar, 1988; author (audio tape seminar) How to Find and Keep a Mate, 1988, (videotape seminar) How to Find a Mate, 1990, The Happiness of Pursuit, 1994, (videotape seminar) How to Deal with Difficult People, Vol. III, 1992, (book) Dealing With People You Can't Stand, 1994. Spokesman Rogue Valley PBS, 1986, 87. Mem. Am. Assn. Naturopathic Physicians (bd. dirs., chmn. pub. affairs 1989-93), Wilderness Soc., Internat. Platform Assn. Republican. Office: R&R Prodns PO Box 896 Ashland OR 97520-0030

KIRSHBAUM, HOWARD M., judge; b. Oberlin, Ohio, Sept. 19, 1938; s. Joseph and Gertrude (Morris) K.; m. Priscilla Joy Parmakian, Aug. 15, 1964; children—Audra Lee, Andrew William. B.A., Yale U., 1960; A.B., Cambridge U., 1962, M.A., 1966; LL.B., Harvard U., 1965. Ptnr. Zarlengo and Kirshbaum, Denver, 1969-75; judge Denver Dist. Ct., Denver, 1975-80, Colo. Ct. Appeals, Denver, 1980-83; justice Colo. Supreme Ct., Denver, 1983—; adj. prof. law U. Denver, 1970—; dir. Am. Law Inst. Phila., Am. Judicature Soc., Chgo., 1983-85, Colo. Jud. Inst. Denver, 1979-89; pres. Colo. Legal Care Soc., Denver, 1974-75. Bd. dirs. Young Artists Orch., Denver, 1976-85; pres. Community Arts Symphony, Englewood, Colo., 1972-74; dir. Denver Opportunity, Inc., Denver, 1972-74; vice-chmn. Denver Council on Arts and Humanities, 1969. Mem. ABA (commn. on coll. and legal studies), Denver Bar Assn. (trustee 1981-83), Colo. Bar Assn., Am. Judicature Soc. Office: Supreme Ct Colo 2 E 14th Ave Denver CO 80203-2115

KIRSHBAUM, JACK D., pathologist; b. Chgo., Dec. 31, 1902; s. David and Regina (Uno) K.; m. Florence R. Kirshbaum, Dec. 27, 1931; children: Gerald, Robert, Richard. MD, U. Ill., 1929, MS, 1934. Inter Cook County Hosp., Chgo., 1929-30, intern in pathology, 1932-41; instr. medicine U. Ill., 1932-34; prof. pathology, head dept. Chog. Med. Sch., 1946-47; sr. pathologist Nagasaki, Japan, 1968-70, Atomic Bomb Casualty Commn.; asst. prof. pathology Loma Linda, 1949-59; sr. pathologist Hadassah Hosp., Israel, 1978-79; mem. staff Emeritus Desert Hosp. Comdr. Jewish War Vets., Calif., 1947-48. Col. U.S. Army, 1942-47. Fellow ACP, Coll. Am. Pathologists; mem. U.S. Acad. Pathology, Can. Acad. Pathology, L.A. County Med. Assn., L.A. Pathology Soc., Calif. Pathology Soc., Am. Bd. Pathologists, Colo. Assn. Sch. Execs., Soc. Clin. Pathologists, Israel Red Cross Magen David (life), Hadassah (life fellow, assoc.), B'Nai Brith, Sigma Xi. Home: 24441 Calle Sonora Apt 250 Laguna Hills CA 92653-7705

KIRSLIS, PETER ANDRE CHRISTOPHER, computer science research and development specialist; b. Cambridge, Mass., Feb. 9, 1954; s. Peter Gabriel and Stephanie Leona (Szymczak) K. BA in Applied Math. cum laude, Harvard U., 1975; MS in Computer Sci., U. Ill., 1977, PhD in Computer Sci., 1986. Mem. tech. staff AT&T Bell Labs., Murray Hill, N.J., 1978-81, Denver, 1986—; rsch. analyst U. Ill., Urbana, 1981-86; tech. staff mem. Digital Tech., Inc., Champaign, 1982, Interactive Systems Corp., Estes Park, Colo., 1983. Co-author (chpt. in book) A Distributed Unix System, 1987; contbr. articles to profl. jours. Mem. IEEE Computer Soc., U.S. Amateur Ballroom Dance Assn. (winner various competitions 1980—), Assn. Computing Machinery, Rocky Mountain Harvard U. Alumni Assn. (chmn. scholarship 1987-89). Office: AT&T Bell Labs 11900 Pecos St Denver CO 80234-2703

KIRWAN, KATHARYN GRACE (MRS. GERALD BOURKE KIRWAN, JR.), retail executive; b. Monroe, Wash., Dec. 1, 1913; d. Walter Samuel and Bertha Ella (Shrum) Camp; m. Gerald Bourke Kirwan Jr., Jan. 13, 1945. Student, U. Puget Sound, 1933-34; BA, BS, Tex. Woman's U., 1937; postgrad., U. Wash., 1941. Libr. Brady (Tex.) Sr. High Sch., 1937-38, McCamey (Tex.) Sr. High Sch., 1938-43; mgr. Milady's Frock Shop, Monroe, 1946-62, owner, mgr., 1962-93. Meml. chmn. Monroe chpt. Am. Cancer Soc., 1961—; mem. Snohomish County Police Svcs. Action Coun., 1971; mem. Monroe Pub. Libr. Bd., 1950-65, pres. bd., 1964-65; mem. Monroe City Coun., 1969-73; mayor City of Monroe, 1974-81; commr. Snohomish County Hosp. dist. 1, 1970-90, chmn. bd. commrs., 1980-90; mem. East Snohomish County Health Planning Com., 1979—; mem. Snohomish County Law and Justice Planning Com., 1974-78, Snohomish County Econ. Devel. Coun., 1975-81, Snohomish County Pub. Utility Dist. Citizens Adv. Task Force, 1983; sr. warden Ch. of Our Saviour, Monroe, 1976-77, 89, sr. warden, 1976-77, 89-90; mem. Monroe Breast Cancer Screening Project community planning group Fred Hutchinson Cancer Rsch. Ctrs., 1991-93. With USNR, 1943-46. Mem. AAUW, U.S. Naval Inst., Ret. Officers Assn., Naval Res. Assn., Bus. and Profl. Women's Club (2d v.p. 1980-82, pres. 1983-84), Washington Gens., Snohomish County Pharm. Aux., C. of C. (pres. 1972), Valley Gen. Hosp. Guild (pres. 1994), VAlley Gen. Hosp. Found. (sec. 1993—). Episcopalian. Home: 538 S Blakely St Monroe WA 98272-2402 Office: 108 W Main St Monroe WA 98272-1810

KISCHER, CLAYTON WARD, embryologist, educator; b. Des Moines, Mar. 2, 1930; s. Frank August and Bessie Erma (Sawtell) K.; m.Linda Sese Espejo, Nov. 7. 1964; children: Eric Armine, Frank Henry. BS in Edn., U. Omaha, 1953; MS, Iowa State U., 1960, PhD, 1962. Asst. prof. biology Ill. State U., 1962-63; rsch. assoc. Argonne (Ill.) Nat. Lab., 1963; asst. prof. zoology Iowa State U., 1963-64; NIH postdoctoral fellow in biochemistry M.D. Anderson Hosp, Houston, 1964-66; chief sect. electron microscopy S.W. Found. Rsch. and Edn., San Antonio, 1966-67; assoc. prof. anatomy U. Tex. Med. Br., Galveston, 1967-77; assoc. prof. anatomy U. Ariz. Coll. Medicine, Tucson, 1977-92, prof. emeritus, 1993—; cons., dir. Scanning electron microscopy lab. Shrine Burns Inst., Galveston, 1969-73. Contbr. articles to profl. jours. Cubmaster pack 107 Island Dist., Galveston, 1974-76; bd. dirs. YMCA. With USN, 1947-49. NIH Rsch. grantee, 1968-89; Morrison Trust grantee, 1975-76. Mem. SAR, AAAS, Galveston Rsch. Soc. (pres. 1971-72), Am. Soc. Cell Biology, Electron Microscopy Soc. Am., Soc. Developmental Biology, Am. Assn. Anatomists, Tex. Soc. Electron Microscopy (hon.) (editor newsletter 1969-73, pres. 1975-76), Ariz. Soc. Electron Microscopy (pres. 1980-81), Gamma Pi Sigma. Home: 6249 N Camino Miraval Tucson AZ 85718-3024 Office: U Ariz Coll Medicine Dept Anatomy Tucson AZ 85724

KISER, NAGIKO SATO, retired librarian; b. Taipei, Republic of China, Aug. 7, 1923; came to U.S., 1950; d. Takeichi and Kinue (Sōma) Sato; m. Virgil Kiser, Dec. 4, 1979 (dec. Mar. 1981). Secondary teaching credential, Tsuda Coll., Tokyo, 1945; BA in Journalism, Trinity U., 1953; BFA, Ohio State U., 1956, MA in Art History, 1959; MLS, cert. in library media, SUNY, Albany, 1974. Cert. community coll. librarian, Calif., cert. jr. coll. tchr., Calif., cert. secondary edn. tchr., Calif., cert. tchr. library media specialist and art, N.Y. Pub. rels. reporter The Mainichi Newspapers, Osaka, Japan, 1945-50; contract interpreter U.S. Dept. State, Washington, 1956-58, 66-67; resource specialist Richmond (Calif.) Unified Sch. Dist., 1968-69; editing supr. CTB/McGraw-Hill, Monterey, Calif., 1969-71; multimedia specialist Monterey Peninsula Unified Sch. Dist., 1975-77; librarian Nishimachi Internat. Sch., Tokyo, 1979-80, Sacramento City Unified Sch. Dist., 1977-79, 81-85; sr. librarian Camarillo (Calif.) State Hosp. and Devel. Ctr., 1985-93. Editor: Short Form Test of Academic Aptitude, 1970, Prescriptive Mathematics Inventory, 1970, Tests of Basic Experience, 1970. Mem. Calif. State Supt.'s Regional Coun. on Asian Pacific Affairs, Sacramento, 1984-91. Library Media Specialist Tng. Program scholar U.S. Office Edn., 1974. Fellow Internat. Biog. Assn. (life); mem. ALA, Am. Biog. Inst. (life, dep. gov. 1988—), Calif. Libr. Assn., Med. Libr. Assn., Asunaro Shogai Kyoiku Kondankai (Lifetime Edn. Promoting Assn., Japan), The Mus. Soc., Internat. House of Japan, Matsuyama Sacramento Sister City Corp., Japanese Am. Citizens League, UN Assn. U.S., Ikenobo Ikebana Soc. Am., L.A. Hototogisu Haiku Assn., Ventura County Archeol. Soc., Internat. Platform Assn., Internat. Soc. Poets. Mem. Christian Science Ch. Office: Camarillo State Hosp & Devel Ctr Profl Libr PO Box 6022 Camarillo CA 93011-6022

KISER, ROBERTA KATHERINE, medical administrator, education educator; b. Alton, Ill., Aug. 13, 1938; d. Stephen Robert and Virginia Elizabeth (Lasher) Golden; m. James Robert Crisman, sept. 6, 1958 (div. May 1971); 1 child, Robert Glenn; m. James Earl Kiser, Dec. 19, 1971; 1 child, James Jacob. BEd, So. Ill. U., 1960. Cert. tchr., Ill., Calif. Librarian Oaklawn (Ill.) Elem. Sch., 1960-62, Alsip (Ill.) Elem. Sch., 1966-69; tchr. Desert Sands Unified Sch. Dist., Indio, Calif., 1969-79; prin. Mothercare Infant Sch., Rancho Mirage, Calif., 1980-89; substitute tchr. Greater Coachella Valley Sch., Calif., 1989-91; med. acct. Desert Health Care, Bermuda Dunes, Calif., 1990-92; mentor tchr., computing, typing skils Wilde Woode Children's Ctr., Palm Springs, Calif., 1990-92; chiropractic asst. Rapp Chiropractic Health Ctr, Palm Desert, Calif., 1992-93; sr. med. records clk. Eisenhower Med. Ctr., Rancho Mirage, 1993—. V.p. Palm Desert (Calif.) Community Ch. Montessori Sch. Bd., 1982-85. Republican. Presbyterian. Home: 39-575 Keenan Dr Rancho Mirage CA 92270-3610 Office: Eisenhower Med Ctr 39000 Bob Hope Dr Rancho Mirage CA 92270-3221

KISER, TERI DENISE, bank analyst; b. Oklahoma City, Aug. 22, 1968; d. Charles Ray Copple and Susan Camille (Adams) Furman; m. Darrell Keith Kiser, Aug. 20, 1988. BA in Polit. Sci. magna cum laude, U. N.Mex., 1992. Annuity/ins. sales rep. The Prin. Fin. Group, Albuquerque, 1990; fin. svcs. officer, br. mgr. tng. program Bank of Am., Albuquerque, 1992-93; S.W. region cmty. reinvestment act analyst First Interstate Bank Ariz., Phoenix, 1993—; fin. studies rschr. Bank of Am. N.Mex., Albuquerque, 1992-93; statewide instr. Toastmasters Internat., Phoenix, 1993—; bus. cons. Ergo-EESE, Ltd., Phoenix, 1993; criminal justice rschr. Maricopa County Sheriff's Office, Phoenix, 1994. Contbg. editor (tng. manual) Bank of Am. N.Mex. Br. Mgr. Tng. Program, 1992; editor T-Birds Talks Toastmaster Newsletter, 1994. Athletic asst. Spl. Olympics, College Station, Tex., 1988; active neighborhood beautification Tex. A&M U., College Station, 1988; civic events participant U. N.Mex., Albuquerque, 1991; posse mem., instr. Sheriff's Office, Maricopa County, Ariz., 1993—, editor (newsletter) The Call Out, 1994—. Mem. Am. Bus. Women's Assn. (chair scholarship com. 1993), Coun. on Internat. Rels., (founding mem., v.p. 1991), Internat. Bus. Students Assn., Toastmasters Internat. (club pres. 1994—, Outstanding Toastmaster 1993-94), Phi Beta Kappa, Golden Key Nat. Honor Soc. Home: 7429 W Paradise Dr Peoria AZ 85345

KISHIMOTO, YORIKO, business consultant; b. Shizuoka, Japan, Sept. 8, 1955; m. Leland D. Collins; 2 children. BA, Wesleyan U., 1977; MBA, Stanford U., 1981. Bus. fellow Nomura Rsch. Inst., Kamakura, Japan, 1979-81; prin. Japan Pacific Assocs., Palo Alto, Calif., 1982-93; Coalition for the Presidio Pacific Ctr., 1993—; speaker numerous internat confs. Pacific Rim. Pub. Biotech. in Japan News Svc., 1982-92; co-author: The Third Century, 1988; editor, co-pub. Biotech. in Japan Yearbook, 1990. Mem. Alliance Forum (co-founder), Coalition for The Presidio Pacific Ctr. Office: Coalition for the Presidio Pacific Ctr 467 Hamilton Ave Ste 2 Palo Alto CA 94301-1810

KISHIMOTO, YOSHIE KONDO, dietitian; b. Corinne, Utah, Aug. 21, 1935; d. Yuki and Michiko (Ogura) Kondo; divorced; 1 child, Carri. BS in Dietetics, U. Utah, 1957. Registered dietitian, lic. dietitian. Dietetic intern Harbor View Med. Ctr., Seattle, 1958; therapeutic dietitian Thomas Dee Meml. Hosp., Ogden, Utah, 1958-64; dietitian McKay Dee Hosp., Ogden, 1972-74, dir. dietary, 1974-75; clin. dietitian St. Benedict's Hosp., Ogden, 1976-79; adminstrv. dietitian, 1979-80, dir. dietary, 1980-89; asst. dir. food and nutrition St. Benedict's Hosp., Ogden, 1989-94, Ogden Regional Med. Ctr., 1994—. Mem. Am. Dietetic Assn., Utah Dietetic Assn. Home: 5424 S 300 W Ogden UT 84405-6817 Office: Ogden Regional Med Ctr 5475 South 500 East Ogden UT 84405

KISTNER, DAVID HAROLD, biology educator; b. Cin., July 30, 1931; s. Harold Adolf and Hilda (Gick) K.; m. Alzada A. Carlisle, Aug. 8, 1957; children—Alzada H., Kymry Marie Carlisle. A.B., U. Chgo., 1952, B.S., 1956, Ph.D., 1957. Instr. U. Rochester, 1957-59; instr., asst. prof. biology Calif. State U., Chico, 1959-64, assoc. prof., 1964-67, prof., 1967-92, prof. emeritus, 1992—; rsch. assoc. Field Mus. Natural History, 1967—, Atlantica Ecol. Rsch. Sta., Salisbury, Zimbabwe, 1970—; CEO Kistner family Trust, 1982—; dir. Shinner Inst. Study Interrelated Insects, 1968-75. Author: (with others) Social Insects, Vols. 1-3; editor Sociobiology, 1975-82; contbr. articles to profl. jours. Patron Am. Mus. Natural History; life mem. Republican Nat. Com., 1980—. Recipient Outstanding Prof. award Calif. State Univs. and Colls., L.A., 1976; John Simon Guggenheim Meml. Found. fellow, 1965-66; grantee NSF, 1960—, Am. Philos. Soc., 1972, Nat. Geog. Soc., 1988. Fellow Explorers Club, Calif. Acad. Scis.; mem. AAUP, AAAS, Entomol. Soc. Am., Pacific Coast Entomol. Soc., Kans. Entomol. Soc., Am. Soc. Naturalists, Am. Soc. Zoologists, Soc. Study of Systematic Zoology, Internat. Soc. Study of Social Insects, Mus. Nat. Hist. (life), Chico State Coll. Assocs. (charter). Home: 3 Canterbury Cir Chico CA 95926-2411

KITADA, SHINICHI, biochemist; b. Osaka, Japan, Dec. 9, 1948; came to U.S., 1975; s. Koichi and Asako Kitada. MD, Kyoto U., 1973; MS in Biol. Chemistry, UCLA, 1973, PhD, 1979. Intern Kyoto U. Hosp., Japan, 1973-74; resident physician Chest Disease Research Inst., 1974-75; rsch. scholar lab. nuclear medicine and radiation biology UCLA, 1979-87, rsch. scholar Jules Stein Eye Inst., 1988-91; rsch. biochemist La Jolla (Calif.) Cancer Rsch. Found., 1992—. Author papers in field. Japan Soc. Promotion Sci. fellow 1975-76. Mem. Am. Oil Chemists Soc., N.Y. Acad. Scis., Sigma Xi. Home: 920 Kline St Ste 301 La Jolla CA 92037-4320 Office: La Jolla Cancer Rsch Found 10901 N Torrey Pines Rd La Jolla CA 92037-1005

KITAGAWA, JOE, food products executive; b. 1945; s. Kiyoko Kitagawa. Pres. Y.K. Packing Co. (Inc.), Thermal, Calif., 1962—, Kitagawa & Sons, Inc., Thermal, 1967—, Golden Acres Farms. Office: Golden Acres Farms 87770 Ave 62 Thermal CA 92274*

KITAGAWA, KIYOKO, food products executive; b. 1924; m. Yeji Kitagawa (dec.). Sec.-treas. Kitagawa & Sons, Inc., Thermal, Calif., 1949—, Y.K. Packing Co., Inc., Thermal, 1962—; with Golden Acres Farm, 1972—. Office: Golden Acres Farms 87770 Ave 62 Thermal CA 92274*

KITANO, MASAMI, neurologist; b. Tokyo, Nov. 3, 1930; came to U.S., 1969; s. Rokuro and Teruyo (Yamaguchi) K.; m. Hiroko Umeda, June 6, 1966; children: Soichiro, Mariko. Grad. pre-med. sch., Keio U., Tokyo, 1950, MD, 1954, DMS, 1959. Intern/resident in Surgery Keio U. Hosp., Tokyo, 1954-59; resident in Surgery and Anesthesiology Jewish Hosp., St. Louis, 1959-62; rsch. fellow in Neurology UCLA, 1962-66; staff physician Keio U., Tokyo, 1966-68; resident in Neurology VA Hosp. UCLA, 1969-71, rsch. assoc., adj. asst. prof. Neurology, 1972-73; pvt. practice in Neurology Torrance, Calif., 1974—. contbr. 27 articles to profl. jours.; lectr. in field. V.p., bd. dirs. Japanese Am. Cultural Cmty. Ctr., L.A., 1987—. Mem. AMA, Japanese Med. Assn. (L.A.), Calif. Med. Assn., L.A. County Med. Assn., L.A. Soc. Neurosci., Am. Acad. Neurology. Office: 23441 Madison St Ste 280 Torrance CA 90505-4734

KITCHEN, JOHN MARTIN, historian, educator; b. Nottingham, Eng., Dec. 21, 1936; s. John Sutherland and Margaret Helen (Pearson) K. B.A. with honors, U. London, 1963, Ph.D., 1966. Mem. Cambridge Group Population Studies, Eng., 1965-66; mem. faculty Simon Fraser U., Burnaby, B.C., Can., 1966—. Author: The German Officer Corps 1890-1914, 1968, A Military History of Germany, 1975, Fascism, 1976, The Silent Dictatorship, 1976, The Political Economy of Germany 1815-1914, 1979, The Coming of Austrian Fascism, 1980, Germany in the Age of Total War, 1981, British Policy Towards the Soviet Union During the Second World War, 1986, The Origins of the Cold War in Comparative Perspective, 1988, Europe Between the Wars, 1988, A World in Flames, 1990, Empire and After: A Short History of the British Empire and Commonwealth, 1994, Nazi Germany at War, 1994, From Empire To Commonwealth: A Short History, 1994. Fellow Inter-Univ. Seminar on Armed Forces and Soc. Fellow Royal Hist. Soc., Royal Soc. Can. Office: Simon Fraser U, Dept History, Burnaby, BC Canada V5A 1S6

KITCHEN, MARK SCOTT, college administrator, college dean; b. Cheyenne, Wyo., Aug. 20, 1953; s. Otis Mead and Doris Charlene (Scott) K.; m. Sandra Gail Siel, June 23, 1984; children: Katherine Anne, Scott Edward. BA, U. Wyo., 1975. News editor Lovell (Wyo.) Chronicle, 1975-77; dir. pub. info. N.W. Coll., Powell, Wyo., 1977-80; asst. to pres. for coll. rels. N.W. Community Coll., Powell, Wyo., 1980-85, asst. to pres. info., alumni and devel., 1985-90; dean of coll. rels. and devel. N.W. Coll., Powell, Wyo., 1990—, interim pres., summer 1991. Editor Northwest Alumni News, 1980—. Pres. Powell Valley C. of C., 1984; chmn. N.W. Civic Orch. and Chorus Bd. Dirs., Powell, 1986, mem. Park County (Wyo.) Arts Coun., 1987-88; v.p. Friends of Sta. KEMC Bd. Dirs., Billings, Mont., 1990. Recipient Pacemaker award Wyo. Press Assn., 1990, 1st prize Paragon award in newsletter category Nat. Coun. Community Rels., 1987. Mem. Coun. for Advancement and Support of Edn. (adv. contest judge 1985, Award of Merit newsletter 1986), Nat. Coun. Mktg. and Pub. Rels. (dist. IV exec. coun. 1989-92). Home: 275 Stockade Ct Powell WY 82435-3201 Office: NW Coll 231 W 6th St Powell WY 82435-1898

KITCHEN, YVONNE RAE, public relations practitioner; b. Chgo., Nov. 20, 1953; d. Melvin and Ernestine (Warner) Mitchell; m. Willie JOnes, Feb. 15, 1977 (div. Sept., 1980); 1 child, Kwesi; m. Maurice Kitchen, June 22, 1991; 1 child, Kai. BS in Journalism, So. Ill. U., 1974. Reporter Fla. Sentinel Bulletin, Tampa, 1974; cmty. editor/reporter Citizens Newspaper Chain, Chgo., 1975; mng. editor The Lawndale Drum, 1976-78; from staff writer to editor media rels. Allstate Ins. Co., Northbrook, Ill., 1979-86; dir. comms. Mayor Harold Washington, Chgo., 1986-88; asst. press sec. Mayor Eugene Sawyer, Chgo., 1988-89; pub. rels. dir. Malcolm X Coll., Chgo., 1990-91; pub. affairs dir. Children's Bur. So. Calif., L.A., 1992—; asst. rsch. dir. Pyramidwest Devel. Corp., Chgo., 1976-78; pres. Raediant Comms., 1989—. V.p. Westside Cultural Arts Coun., Chgo., 1990-91; mem. Gov. James E. Thompson's Arson Adv. Bd., Ill., 1982; bd. dirs. Ill. Adv. Com. on Arson Prevention, 1981-86, newsletter editor, 1981-86; mem. Mayor's Arson Prevention Planning Com., East St. Louis, 1981. Recipient Silver Merit award Publicity Club Chgo., 1982, Kizzy award Black Women's Hall of Fame Found., 1984, Urban Focus achievement award Seanna Mag., Chgo., 1985; named among 100 Top African-Am. Bus. and Profl. Women, 1991. Mem. Nat. Assn. Media Women (past pres. Chgo. chpt.), Black Pub. Rels.

Soc. L.A. (co-chair scholarship com. 1992-93), Nat. Assn. Black Journalists. Home: 3613 Clarington Ave Los Angeles CA 90034-5001

KITTEL, PETER, research scientist; b. Fairfax, Va., Mar. 23, 1945; s. Charles and Muriel (Lister) K.; m. Mary Ellen Murchio, Aug. 12, 1972; 1 child, Katherine. BS, U. Calif., Berkeley, 1967; MS, U. Calif., La Jolla, 1969; PhD, Oxford U., 1974. Rsch. asst. U. Calif., La Jolla, 1967-69, Oxford (Eng.) U., 1969-74; rsch. assoc., adj. assoc. prof. U. Oreg., Eugene, 1974-78; rsch. assoc. Stanford (Calif.) U., 1978; rsch. assoc. Nat. Rsch. Coun. Ames Rsch. Ctr. NASA, Moffett Field, Calif., 1978-80, rsch. scientist, 1980—; dir. Cryogenic Engring. Conf., 1983-89, 92—. Adv. editor: Cryogenics, 1987—; editor: Advances in Cryogenic Engineering, 1992—; contbr. articles to profl. jours. Fellow Oxford U., 1972-74, Nat. Rsch. Coun., 1978-80; recipient medal for Exceptional Engring. Achievement NASA, 1990, Space Act award NASA, 1989, 91. Mem. Am. Phys. Soc., AAAS. Home: 3132 Morris Dr Palo Alto CA 94303-4037 Office: NASA 244-10 Ames Research Ctr Moffett Field CA 94035-1000

KITTLITZ, LINDA GALE, small business owner; b. Waco, Tex., Jan. 22, 1949; d. Rudolf Gottlieb and Lena Hulda (Landgraf) K. BA in Art, Tex. Tech. U., 1971. Sales rep. Taylor Pub. Co., San Francisco and Dallas, 1972-73, Internat. Playtex Corp., San Francisco, 1974-76, Faberge Inc., San Francisco, 1976-78, Soflens div. Bausch and Lomb Co., San Francisco, 1978-81, Ben Rickert Inc., San Francisco, 1981-86; mfr.'s sales rep. Dearing Sales, San Francisco, 1986-87; sales rep. Golden West Envelope Co., San Francisco, 1987-89; sales assoc. R.G. Creations, Inc., San Francisco, 1989-90; owner, mgr. Kittlitz & Assocs. (Custom Packaging and Printing Solutions), San Francisco, 1990—. Mem. NAFE, Profl. Women's Network San Francisco (bay area chpt.). Democrat. Baptist.

KITTO, FRANKLIN CURTIS, computer systems specialist; b. Salt Lake City, Nov. 18, 1954; s. Curtis Eugene and Margaret (Ipson) K.; m. Collette Madsen, Sept. 16, 1982; children: Melissa Erin, Heather Elise, Stephen Curtis. BA, Brigham Young U., 1978, MA, 1980. Tv sta. operator Sta. KBYU-TV, Provo, Utah, 1973-78; grad. teaching asst. Brigham Young Univ., 1978-80; cable TV system operator Instructional Media U. Utah, Salt Lake City, 1980-82, data processing mgr., 1982-83, media supr., 1983-85, bus. mgr., 1985-87; dir. computer systems tng. MegaWest Systems, Inc., Salt Lake City, 1987-90, dir. new product devel., 1990-91, mgr. tng. and installation, 1991-93, mgr. rsch. and devel., 1993; tng. and installation mgr. Total Solutions, American Fork, Utah, 1993-95, tng., support and installation mgr., 1995—. Recipient Kiwanis Freedom Leadership award, Salt Lake City, 1970, Golden Microphone award Brigham Young U., 1978. Mem. Assn. Ednl. Communications and Tech., Utah Pick Users Group (sec. 1983-87, pres. 1987-89, treas. 1989-90), Am. Soc. Tng. and Devel., Assn. for Computer Tng. and Support, Phi Eta Sigma, Kappa Tau Alpha. Mormon. Home: 10931 S Avila Dr Sandy UT 84094-5965 Office: Total Solutions 117 S 700 E American Fork UT 84003-2156

KITTREDGE, JOHN RUSSELL, physician; b. Ellsworth, Maine, Apr. 17, 1950; s. Russell Millard and Florence Elizabeth (Davis) K.; divorced; children: Crichton, Russa, Olivia, Clare, Clive. AB in Biology cum laude, Boston U., 1972; MD, Albany Med. Coll. Union U., 1976. Resident Overlook Hosp., Summit, N.J., 1976-79; staff physician Indian Health Svc., Shawnee, Okla., 1979-80, clin. dir., 1980-89; clin. dir. Indian Health Svc., Tucson, Ariz., 1989-92, coord. med. contracts, 1992—, acting chief med. officer, 1993—. Capt. USPHS, 1979—. Mem. Ariz. Acad. Family Practice, Officers Assn. USPHS, Soc. Tchrs. Family Medicine. Independent. Office: Indian Health Svc 7900 S J Stock Rd Tucson AZ 85746

KITTREDGE, WILLIAM ALFRED, humanities educator; b. Portland, Oreg., Aug. 14, 1932; s. Franklin Oscar and Josephine (Miessner) K.; m. Janet O'Connor, Dec. 8, 1952 (div. 1968); children: Karen, Bradley. BS, Oreg. State U., 1953; MFA in Creative Writing, U. Iowa, 1969. Rancher Warner Valley Livestock, Adel, Oreg., 1957-67; prof. U. Mont., Missoula, 1969—. Author: We Are Not In This Together, 1984, Owning It All, 1987, Hole in the Sky, 1992. With USAF, 1954-57. Recipient award for lit. Gov. of Mont., 1988, Frankel award-Humanist of Yr., NEH, 1994. Home: 143 S 5th St E Missoula MT 59801-2719 Office: U Mont Missoula MT 59801

KITZHABER, JOHN ALBERT, governor, physician, former state senator; b. Colfax, Wash., Mar. 5, 1947; s. Albert Raymond and Annabel Reed (Wetzel) K. BA, Dartmouth Coll., 1969; MD, U. Oreg., 1973. Intern Gen. Rose Meml. Hosp., Denver, 1976-77; Emergency physician Mercy Hosp., Roseburg, Oreg., 1974-75; mem. Oreg. Ho. of Reps., 1979-81; mem. Oreg. Senate, 1981-95, pres., 1985, 87, 89, 91; gov. State of Oregon, 1995—; assoc. prof. Oreg. Health Sci. U., 1986—. Mem. Am. Coll. Emergency Physicians, Douglas County Med. Soc., Physicians for Social Responsibility, Am. Council Young Polit. Leaders, Oreg. Trout. Democrat. Office: Office of the Gov State Capitol Bldg Salem OR 97310*

KIVELSON, MARGARET GALLAND, physicist; b. N.Y.C., Oct. 21, 1928; d. Walter Isaac and Madeleine (Wiener) Galland; m. Daniel Kivelson, Aug. 15, 1949; children: Steven Allan, Valerie Ann. AB, Radcliffe Coll., 1950, AM, 1951, PhD, 1957. Cons. Rand Corp., Santa Monica, Calif., 1956-69; asst. to geophysicist UCLA, 1967-83, prof., 1983—, also chmn. dept. earth and space scis., 1984-87; prin. investigator of magnetometer, Galileo Mission, Jet Propulsion Lab., Pasadena, Calif., 1977—; overseer Harvard Coll., 1977-83; mem. adv. coun. NASA, 1987-93; chair atmospheric adv. com. NSF, 1986-89, Com. Solar and Space Physics, 1977-86, com. planetary exploration, 1986-87, com. solar terrestial phys., 1989-92; mem. adv. com. geoscis. NSF. Editor: The Solar System: Observations and Interpretations, 1986; co-editor: Introduction to Space Physics, 1995; contbr. articlels to profl. jours. Named Woman of Yr., L.A. Mus. Sci. and Industry, 1979, Woman of Sci., UCLA, 1984; recipient Grad. Soc. medal Radcliffe Coll., 1983, 350th Anniversary Alumni medal Harvard U. Fellow AAAS, Am. Geophysics Union; mem. Am. Phys. Soc., Am. Astron. Soc., Internat. Inst. Astronautics (corr. mem.). Office: UCLA Dept Earth & Space Scis 6843 Slichter Los Angeles CA 90095-1567

KIZZIAR, JANET WRIGHT, psychologist, author, lecturer; b. Independence, Kans.; d. John L. and Thelma (Rooks) Wright; m. Mark Kizziar. BA, U. Tulsa, 1961, MA, 1964, EdD, 1969. Sch. psychologist Tulsa Pub. Schs.; pvt. practice psychology Tulsa, 1969-78, Bartlesville, Okla., 1978-88. Co-host: Psychologists' Corner program, Sta. KOTV, Tulsa.; author: (with Judy W. Hagedorn) Gemini: The Psychology and Phenomena of Twins, 1975, Search for Acceptance: The Adolescent and Self Esteem, 1979. Sponsor Youth Crisis Intervention Telephone Center, 1972-74; Bd. dirs. March of Dimes, Child Protection Team, Women and Children in Crisis, United Fund, YMCA Fund, Mental Health of Washington County., Alternative H.S.; edn. dir. Project Fresh Start, 1995. Named Disting. Alumni U. Tulsa, Outstanding Young Woman of Okla. Mem. APA, NOW, Internat. Twins Assn. (pres. 1976-77). Home: 9427 N 87th Way Scottsdale AZ 85258-1913 Office: PO Box 5227 Scottsdale AZ 85261-5227

KJOS, VICTORIA ANN, lawyer; b. Fargo, N.D., Sept. 17, 1953; d. Orville I. and Annie J. (Tanberg) K. BA, Minot State U., 1974; JD, U. N.D., 1977. Bar: Ariz. 1978. Assoc. Jack E. Evans, Ltd., Phoenix, 1977-78, pension and ins. cons., 1978-79; dep. state treas. State of N.D., Bismarck, 1979-80; freelance cons. Phoenix, 1980-81, Anchorage, 1981-82; asst. v.p., v.p., mgr. trust dept. Great Western Bank, Phoenix, 1982-84; assoc. Robert A. Jensen P.C., Phoenix, 1984-86; ptnr. Jensen & Kjos, P.C., Phoenix, 1986-89; assoc. Allen, Kimerer & LaVelle, Phoenix, 1989-90, ptnr., 1990-91; dir. The Yoga and Fitness Inst., Phoenix, 1994—; lectr. in domestic relations. Contbr. articles to profl. jours. Bd. dirs. Arthritis Found., Phoenix, 1986-89, v.p. for chpt. devel., 1988-89; bd. dirs. Ariz. Yoga Assn., 1993-95, v.p., 1993-95. Mem. ABA, ATLA, Ariz. Bar Assn. (exec. coun. family law sect. 1988-91), Maricopa Bar Assn. (sec. family law com. 1988-89, pres. family law com. 1989-90, judge pro tem 1989-91), Ariz. Trial Lawyers Assn.

KLADNEY, DAVID, lawyer; b. N.Y.C., Oct. 25, 1948; s. Rubin and Gloria Anita (Serotick) K.; m. Deborah Bayliss, Aug. 20, 1978; children: Mathew Blair, Blythe Nicole. BA in Journalism, U. Nev., 1972; JD, Calif. Western Sch. of Law, 1977. Bar: Nev. 1977, U.S. Dist. Ct. (no. dist.) Nev. 1977. Pvt. practice law Reno, Nev., 1977—; gen. counsel State of Nev. Employees Assn., Carson City, 1977-81; chairperson Truckee Meadows C.C. on Para-Legals. Writer, producer documentary Nevada Connection, 1973. Legal counsel B.U.R.N.S., Inc., 1992—, Make-A-Wish Found. of Nev., Reno, 1984—; chmn. of bd. dirs. Nev. Festival Ballet, Reno, 1984; bd. dirs. Washoe Legal Svcs., Reno, 1978-79. With USAR, 1966-72. Mem. ABA, Nev. Bar Assn., Washoe County Bar Assn., Assn. Trial Lawyers Am. (sustaining), Nev. Trial Lawyers Assn. (bd. dirs. 1979-85, Outstanding Svc. award 1985), Phi Delta Phi. Office: 1575 Delucchi Ln Ste 204 Reno NV 89502-6580

KLAGER, KARL, chemist; b. Vienna, Austria, May 15, 1908; came to U.S., 1949; s. Leopold and Barbara (Strasser) K.; m. Elisabeth Ramona Graven, Dec. 26, 1938; 1 child, Peter. PhD, U. Vienna, 1934. Instr., U. Vienna, 1931-34; asst. mgr. Neuman Bros., Arad, Rumania, 1934-36, Budapest, 1936-38; rsch./devel. chemist IG Farben Ind., Ludwigshafen, Ger., 1938-48; rsch. chemist Office Naval Research, Pasadena, Calif., 1949-50; v.p. Aerojet Gen., Sacramento, 1950-73; cons. in chemistry, Sacramento, 1973—. Contbr. articles to profl. jours.; patentee in field; author: Propellant Manufacturing, Hazards and Testing, 1966; contbr. book: Mechanics of Propellants, 1967. Recipient Disting. Pub. Service award U.S. Navy, 1958, Austrian Honor Cross award, 1989; named Inventor of Year, No. Calif., San Francisco Lawyers, 1975; Chem. Pioneer, Am. Inst. Chemists, 1978; J.H. Wyld Propulsion award AIAA, 1972. Fellow AIAA, Am. Inst. Chemists; mem. Am. Chem. Soc., Sigma Xi. Club: Mgmt. (pres. 1960-62).

KLAKEG, CLAYTON HAROLD, cardiologist; b. Big Woods, Minn., Mar. 31, 1920; s. Knute O. and Agnes (Folvik) K.; student Concordia Coll., Moorhead, Minn., 1938-40; BS, N.D. State U., 1942; BS in Medicine, N.D. U., 1943; M.D., Temple U., 1945; MS in Medicine and Physiology, U. Minn.-Mayo Found., 1954; children: Julie Ann, Robert Clayton, Richard Scott. Intern, Med. Ctr., Jersey City, 1945-46; mem. staff VA Hosp., Fargo, N.D., 1948-51; fellow in medicine and cardiology Mayo Found., Rochester, Minn., 1951-55; internist, cardiologist Sansum Med. Clinic Inc., Santa Barbara, Calif., 1955—; mem. staff Cottage Hosp., St. Francis Hosp. Bd. dirs. Sansum Med. Rsch. Found., pres., 1990. Served to capt. M.C., USAF, 1946-48. Diplomate Am. Bd. Internal Medicine. Fellow ACP, Am. Coll. Cardiology, Am. Coll. Chest Physicians, Am. Heart Assn. (mem. council on clin. cardiology); mem. Calif. Heart Assn. (pres. 1971-72, Meritorious Service award 1968, Disting. Service award 1972, Disting. Achievement award 1975), Santa Barbara County Heart Assn. (pres. 1959-60, Disting. Service award 1958, Disting. Achievement award 1971), Calif. Med. Assn., Los Angeles Acad. Medicine, Santa Barbara County Med. Assn., Mayo Clinic Alumni Assn., Santa Barbara Soc. Internal Medicine (pres. 1963), Sigma Xi, Phi Beta Pi. Republican. Lutheran. Club: Channel City. Contbr. articles to profl. jours. Home: 5956 Trudi Dr Santa Barbara CA 93117-2175 Office: Sansum Med Clinic Inc PO Box 1239 Santa Barbara CA 93102-1239

KLAMMER, JOSEPH FRANCIS, management consultant; b. Omaha, Mar. 25, 1925; s. Aloys Arcadius and Sophie (Nadolny) K.; BS, Creighton U., 1948; MBA, Stanford, 1950; cert. in polit. econs. Grad. Inst. Internat. Studies, U. Geneva, 1951. cert. mgmt. cons. Adminstrv. analyst Chevron Corp., San Francisco, 1952-53; staff asst. Enron Corp., Omaha, 1953-57; mgmt. cons., bd. dirs. Cresap, McCormick and Paget, Inc., San Francisco, 1957-75, v.p., mgr. San Francisco region, 1968-75; mgmt. cons., prin. J.F. Klammer Assocs., San Francisco, 1975—; CEO Isabelle Towers Homeowners Assn., pres. bd. dirs., 1993-94, mem. fin. com., 1994—. Past mem. bd. dirs. Conard House. Apptd. and attended U.S. Mil. Acad., West Point, N.Y.; served to 1st lt. USAAF, 1943-46; lt. col. USAF (ret.). Rotary Found. fellow, 1950-51. Republican. Roman Catholic. Mem. Isabelle Towers Home Owners Assn. (CEO, pres. 1993-94, bd. dirs. 1993-94, mem. fin. com.). Clubs: Univ., Omaha, Alpha Sigma Nu. Office: 1850 Union St Ste 1226 San Francisco CA 94123-4309

KLASING, SUSAN ALLEN, environmental toxicologist, consultant; b. San Antonio, Sept. 10, 1957; d. Jesse Milton and Thelma Ida (Tucker) Allen; m. Kirk Charles Klasing, Mar. 3, 1984; children: Samantha Nicole, Jillian Paige. BS, U. Ill., 1979, MS, 1981, PhD, 1984. Staff scientist Life Scis. Rsch. Office, Fedn. Am. Socs. Exptl. Biology, Bethesda, Md., 1984-85; assoc. dir. Alliance for Food and Fiber, Sacramento, 1986; postgrad. rschr. U. Calif., Davis, 1986-87; project dir. Health Officers Assn. Calif., Sacramento, 1987-89; cons. Klasing and Assocs., Davis, Calif., 1989—; mem. expert com. for substances-of-concern San Joaquin Valley Drainage Program, Sacramento, 1987, follow-up task force, 1990-91, drainage oversight com., 1992-94. Author: (chpt.) Consideration of the Public Health Impacts of Agricultural Drainage Water Contamination, 1991. Mem. AAAS. Office: Klasing and Assocs 515 Flicker Ave Davis CA 95616-0178

KLATSKY, ARTHUR LOUIS, cardiologist, epidemiologist; b. N.Y.C., Oct. 24, 1929; s. Martin Max and Rose M. (Hurwitz) K.; m. Eileen Selma Rohrberg, June 21, 1953; children: Jennifer Ann Klatsky Ferrer, Benjamin Paul. BA, Yale U., 1950; MD, Harvard U., 1954. Diplomate Am. Bd. Internal Medicine, Am. Bd. Cardiovascular Disease. Intern in medicine Boston City Hosp., 1954-56; resident in internal medicine and cardiology Boston VA Hosp., 1958-60; trainee in cardiology U. Calif., San Francisco, 1960-61; clin. instr. in medicine U. Calif. Med. Ctr., San Francisco, 1961-68, asst. clin. prof. medicine, 1968-80; staff physician internal medicine and cardiology Kaiser Found. Hosp., Oakland, Calif., 1961-80, sub-chief dpet. medicine, 1973, chief divsn. cardiology, 1978-94; assoc. divsn. rsch. Kaiser Permanente Med. Care Program, Oakland, 1975—; sr. cons. in Cardiology, 1995—; mem. med. adv. coun. Wine Inst., San Francisco, 1978—. Contbr. articles to profl. jours., chpts. to books. Mem. profl. edn. com. Alameda County Heart Assn., 1969—. With Med. Corps, 1956-58. Fellow Am. Heart Assn. Coun. on Epidemiology, 1975—; recipient rsch. award Med. Friends of Wine, 1984, 1st Thomas Turner award for Excellence in Alcohol Rsch., Alcoholic Beverage Med. Rsch. Found., 1992. Fellow ACP, Am. Coll. Cardiology; mem. Am. Wine Alliance for Rsch. and Edn. (bd. dirs. 1989—, Disting. Practioner in Medicine, Nat. Acad. of Practice. Office: Kaiser Found Hosp 280 W Macarthur Blvd Oakland CA 94611-5642

KLATT, JANET MARIE, sales and marketing executive; b. Great Falls, Mont., Feb. 19, 1959; d. Charles Auther and Betty Iola (Robuck) Loberg; m. Paul Howard Klatt, Jan. 27, 1990; 1 child, Courtney Marie. BA in Speech, Mont. State U., 1980; M in Interdisciplinary Studies, Oreg. State U., 1981; MBA, Alaska Pacific U., 1986. Mgr. advt. & pub. rels. Wien Air Alaska, Anchorage, 1982-84, MarkAir, Anchorage, 1984-88; asst. v.p. mktg. Alliance Bank, Anchorage, 1988; sales mgr. Clarion Hotel, Anchorage, 1989-91; dir. sales & mktg. McCaw/Cellular One, Anchorage, 1991—. Mem. Am. Mktg. Assn. (membership dir. 1992-93), Resource Devel. Coun. (dir. pub. rels. 1988-91), Anchorage C. of C. Office: Cellular One 4711 Business Park Blvd Ste 10 Anchorage AK 99503-7166

KLAUS, STEPHEN JOHN, immunologist; b. Bklyn., Jan. 25, 1960; s. Stephan and Rosa (Wendler) K. BS, Syracuse U., 1982; PhD, U. Mass., 1991. Sr. technician Sloan-Kettering Cancer Ctr., N.Y.C., 1984-85; grad. student U. Mass. Med. Ctr., Worcester, 1985-91; sr. post doctoral fellow U. Wash., Seattle, 1991—. Recipient post doctoral fellowship Am. Cancer Soc., 1993-96. Mem. Am. Assn. Immunologists. Office: Regional Primate Rsch Ctr SJ 50 U Wash Seattle WA 98195 Home: 617 5th Ave W Apt 4C Seattle WA 98119-4473

KLAUSNER, JACK DANIEL, lawyer; b. N.Y.C., July 31, 1945; s. Burt and Marjory (Brown) K.; m. Dale Arlene Kreis, July 1, 1968; children: Andrew Russell, Mark Raymond. BS in Bus., Miami U., Oxford, Ohio, 1967; JD, U. Fla., 1969. Bar: N.Y. 1971, Ariz. 1975, U.S. Dist. Ct. Ariz. 1975, U.S. Ct. Appeals (9th cir.) 1975, U.S. Supreme Ct. 1975. Assoc. counsel John P. McGuire & Co., Inc., N.Y.C., 1970-71; assoc. atty. Hahn & Hessen, N.Y.C., 1971-72; gen. counsel Equilease Corp., N.Y.C., 1972-74; assoc. Burch & Cracchiolo, Phoenix, 1974-78; ptnr. Burch & Cracchiolo, 1978—; judge pro tem Maricopa County Superior Ct., 1990—, Ariz. Ct. Appeals, 1992—. Bd. dirs. Santos Soccer Club, Phoenix, 1989-90; bd. dirs., pres. south Bank Soccer Club, Tempe, 1987-88. Home: 1390 W Island Cir Chandler AZ 85248-3700 Office: Burch & Cracchiolo 702 E Osborn Rd Phoenix AZ 85014-5241

KLEBANOFF, SEYMOUR JOSEPH, medical educator; b. Toronto, Feb. 3, 1927; s. Eli Samuel and Ann Klebanoff; m. Evelyn Norma Silver, June 3, 1951; children: Carolyn, Mark. MD, U. Toronto, 1951; PhD in Biochemistry, U. London, 1954. Intern Toronto Gen. Hosp., 1951-52; postdoctoral fellow Dept. Path. Chemistry, U. Toronto, 1954-57, Rockefeller U., N.Y.C., 1957-62; assoc. prof. medicine U. Washington, Seattle, 1962-68, prof., 1968—; mem. adv. coun. Nat. Inst. Allergy and Infectious Diseases, NIH, 1987-90. Author: The Neutrophil, 1978; contbr. over 200 articles to profl. jours. Recipient Merit award NIH, 1988, Mayo Soley award Western Soc. for Clin. Investigation, 1991. Fellow AAAS; mem. NAS, Am. Soc. Clin. Investigation, Am. Soc. Biol. Chemists, Assn. Am. Physicians, Infectious Diseases Soc. Am. (Bristol award 1993), Endocrine Soc., Reticuloendothelial Soc. (Marie T. Bonazinga rsch. award 1985), Inst. of Medicine. Home: 509 Mcgilvra Blvd E Seattle WA 98112-5047 Office: U Wash Dept Medicine SJ-10 Div of Allergy & Infectious Dis Seattle WA 98195

KLEE, VICTOR LA RUE, mathematician, educator; b. San Francisco, Sept. 18, 1925; s. Victor La Rue and Mildred (Muller) K.; m. Elizabeth Bliss; children—Wendy Pamela, Barbara Christine, Susan Lisette, Heidi Elizabeth; m. Joann Polack, Mar. 17, 1985. B.A., Pomona Coll., 1945, D.Sc. (hon.), 1965; Ph.D., U. Va., 1949; Dr. honoris causa, U. Liège, Belgium, 1984. Asst. prof. U. Va., 1949-53; NRC fellow Inst. for Advanced Study, 1951-52; asst. prof. U. Wash., Seattle, 1953-54, asso. prof., 1954-57, prof. math., 1957—, adj. prof. computer sci., 1974—, prof. applied math., 1976-84; vis. asso. prof. UCLA, 1955-56; vis. prof. U. Colo., 1971, U. Victoria, 1975, U. Western Australia, 1979; cons. IBM Watson Research Center, 1972; cons. to industry; mem. Math. Scis. Research Inst., 1985-86; sr. fellow Inst. for Math. and its Applications, 1987. Co-author: Combinatorial Geometry in the Plane, 1963, Old and New Unsolved Problems in Plane Geometry and Number Theory, 1991; contbr. more than 200 articles to profl. jours. Recipient Rsch. prize U. Va., 1952, Vollum award for disting. accomplishment in sci. and tech. Reed Coll., 1982, David Prescott Burrows Outstading Disting. Achievement award Pomona Coll., 1988, Max Planck rsch. prize, 1992; NSF sr. postdoctoral fellow, Sloan Found. fellow U. Copenhagen, 1958-60, fellow Ctr. Advanced Study in Behavioral Scis., 1975-76, Guggenheim fellow, Humboldt award U. Erlangen-Nürnberg, 1980-81, Fulbright fellow U. Trier, 1992. Fellow AAAS (chmn. sect. A 1975); mem. Am. Math. Soc. (assoc. sec. 1955-58, mem. exec. com. 1969-70), Math. Assn. Am. (pres. 1971-73, L.R. Ford award 1972, Disting. Svc. award 1977, C.B. Allendoerfer award 1980), Soc. Indsl. and Applied Math. (mem. coun. 1966-68), Assn. Computing Machinery, Math. Programming Soc., Internat. Linear Algebra Soc., Ops. Rsch. Soc., Phi Beta Kappa, Sigma Xi (nat. lectr. 1969). Home: 13706 39th Ave NE Seattle WA 98125-3810 Office: U Wash Box 354350 Dept Math Seattle WA 98195-4350

KLEEMAN, NANCY GRAY ERVIN, special education educator; b. Boston, Feb. 19, 1946; d. John Wesley and Harriet Elizabeth (Teuchert) Ervin; m. Brian Carlton Kleeman, June 27, 1969. BA, Calif. State U., Northridge, 1969; MS, Calif. State U., Long Beach, 1976, Calif. State U., Long Beach, 1976; cert. resource specialist, Calif. State U., Long Beach, 1982. Cert. spl. edn., learning disabilities and resource specialist tchr., Calif. Tchr. spl. edn., resource specialist Downey (Calif.) Unified Sch. Dist., 1972-86; tchr. spl. day class Irvine (Calif.) Sch. Dist., 1986—; tutor in field; speaker Commn. for Handicapped, L.A., 1975; advisor Com. to Downey Unified Sch. Dist., 1976-82; co-owner ISIS Design Pubs. Author: Rhyme Your Times, 1990; author numerous greeting cards. Vol. sec. UN, L.A., 1980-83; vol. coord., art dir., educator Sierra Vista Mid. Sch., Irvine, 1986-88; liaison Tustin (Calif.) Manor Convalscent Home and Regents Point Retirement Home, Irvine, 1988—; fundraiser Ronald McDonald House, Orange, Calif.; mem. Nat. Yough Svc., Washington; vol. Sr. Cheer Project, 1994—. Recipient award Concerned Students Orgn., Downey, 1984; named Tchr. Yr. Sierra Vista Middle Sch., 1988. Mem. NEA, Irvine Tchrs. Assn., Calif. Tchrs. Assn., Am. Carousel Assn., Dogs for the Blind. Office: Irvine Unified Sch Dist 2 Liberty Irvine CA 92720-2536

KLEESE, WILLIAM CARL, genealogy research consultant; b. Williamsport, Pa., Jan. 20, 1940; s. Donald Raymond and Helen Alice (Mulberger) K.; m. Vivian Ann Yeager, June 12, 1958; children: Scott, Jolene, Mark, Troy, Brett, Kecia, Lance. BS in Wildlife Biology, U. Ariz., 1975, MS in Animal Physiology, 1979, PhD in Animal Physiology, 1981. Sales rep. Terminix Co., Tucson, 1971-72; pest control operator, 1973-75; fire fighter Douglas Ranger Dist. Coronado Nat. Forest U.S. Forest Svc., 1975, biol. technician Santa Catalina ranger dist., 1975-76; lab. technician dept. animal scis. U. Ariz., 1977-78, rsch. technician dept. pharmacology and toxicology, 1978, rsch. asst. dept. biochemistry, 1979-81, rsch. specialist muscle biology group, 1981—; genealogy rsch. cons. Tucson, 1988—. Author: Introduction to Genealogy, 1988, Introduction to Genealogical Research, 1989, The Genealogical Researcher, Neophyte to Graduate, 1992, Genealogical Research in the British Isles, 1991; contbr. numerous articles to profl. jours. Chaplain Ariz. State Prisons, Tucson, 1988—. Mem. Ariz. Geneaolgy Adv. Bd. (com. chmn. 1990-92), Herpetologists League, Lycoming County Geneal. Soc., Nat. Geneal. Soc., Nat. Wildlife Fedn., Pa. Geneal. Soc., Soc. for the Study of Amphibians and Reptiles, Soc. of Vertebrate Paleontology, Ariz. State Geneal. Soc. (pres. 1990-93). Republican. Mormon. Home: 6521 E Fayette St Tucson AZ 85730-2220 Office: 6061 E Broadway Blvd Ste 128 Tucson AZ 85711-4020

KLEHN, HENRY, JR., engineering company executive; b. 1936. BS in Geol. Engring., U. Calif., MS in Engring. Sci. With Dames & Moore, L.A., 1960—. Office: Dames & Moore 911 Wilshire Blvd Ste 700 Los Angeles CA 90017-3436*

KLEHS, HENRY JOHN WILHELM, civil engineer; b. Dornbusch bez Stade, Germany, Dec. 7, 1910; s. Frederick and Anna (Mahler) K.; B.S., U. Calif., 1935; m. Clodell Peters, July 17, 1948; came to U.S., 1920, naturalized through father, 1922. Engr. So. Pacific Transp. Co., 1936-75, supr. hazardous materials control, until 1975; ret., 1975. Mem. Calif. Fire Chiefs Assn., Internat. Assn. Fire Chiefs, Steuben Soc. Am., Am. Ry. Engring Assn., ASCE. Home: 604 Glenwood Isle Alameda CA 94501-5605

KLEIMAN, VIVIAN ABBE, filmmaker; b. Phila., Oct. 11, 1950; d. Philip and Hilda (Kramer) K. BA, U. Calif., 1974. Filmmaker; bd. dirs. Cultural Rsch. & Comm., N.Y.C., Berkeley, Calif., The Living Room Festival, San Francisco, Catticus Corp., Berkeley; founding dir. Jewish Film Festival, Berkeley, 1981-85; adv. bd. Frameline, San Francisco, 1985—; pres., exec. dir. Signifyin' Works, Berkeley, 1991—; v.p. Film Arts Found., San Francisco, 1983-93; lectr. Stanford (Calif.) U., 92, 1995, U. Calif., Berkeley, 1990, 91, 92, 93; cinematographer Tongues Untied, 1989. Prodr., dir. films including Judy Chicago: The Birth Project, 1985, Ein Stehaufmannchen, 1991, My Body's My Business, 1992; prodr., rsch. dir. films including Routes of Exile: A Moroccan Jewish Odyssey, 1982, California Gold, 1984, Color Adjustment, 1992; assoc. prodr. films including We All Count In Family Math, 1984 ; assoc. prodr. The Disney Channel, 1982-83; rschr. for various films including A Woman Named Golda, 1982. Recipient George Foster Peabody award Sundance Film Festival, Outstanding Achievement award Internat. Documentary Assn., Nat. Emmy award nominee, The Eric Barnouw awards Orgn. Am. Historians, Red ribbon Am. Film and Video Festival, Best of Festival award Black Maria Festival, Black Internat. Cinema Berlin, Gold Plaque, Social/Polit. Documentary Chgo. Internat. Film Festival, N.C. Silver Juror's prize. Mem. Bay Area Video Coalition, Film Arts Found., Internat. Documentary Assn. Office: 2600 10th St Berkeley CA 94710-2522

KLEIN, ARNOLD WILLIAM, dermatologist; b. Mt. Clemens, Mich., Feb. 27, 1945; s. David Klein; m. Malvina Kraemer. BA, U. Pa., 1967, MD, 1971. Intern Cedars-Sinai Med. Ctr., Los Angeles, 1971-72; resident in dermatology Hosp. U. Pa., Phila., 1972-73, U. Calif., Los Angeles, 1973-75; pvt. practice dermatology Berverly Hills, Calif., 1975—; assoc. clin. prof. dermatology/medicine U. Calif. Ctr. for Health Scis; mem. med. staff Cedars-Sinai Med. Ctr.; asst. clin. prof. dermatology Stanford U., 1982-89; asst. clin. prof. to assoc. clin. prof. dermatology/medicine, UCLA; Calif. state commr., 1983-89; med. adv. bd. Skin Cancer Found., Lupus Found. Am., Collagen Corp.; presenter seminars in field. Reviewer Jour. Dermatologic Surgery and Oncology, Jour. Sexually Transmitted Diseases, Jour. Am. Acad. Dermatology; mem. editorial bd. Men's Fitness mag., Shape mag., Jour. Dermatologic Surgery and Oncology; contbr. numerous articles to med. jours. Mem. AMA, Calif. Med. Assn., Am. Soc. Dermatologic Surgery, Internat. Soc. Dermatologic Surgery, Calif. Soc. Specialty Plastic Surgery,

Am. Assn. Cosmetic Surgeons, Assn. Sci. Advosors, Los Angeles Med. Assn., Am. Coll. Chemosurgery, Met. Dermatology Soc., Am. Acad. Dermatology, Dermatology Found., Scleroderma Found., Internat. Psoriasis Found., Lupus Found., Am. Venereal Disease Assn., Soc. Cosmetic Chemists, AFTRA, Los Angeles Mus. Contemporary Art (founder), Dance Gallery Los Angeles (founder), Am. Found. AIDS Research (founder, dir.), Friars Club, Phi Beta Kappa, Sigma Tau Sigma, Delphos. Office: 435 N Roxbury Dr Ste 204 Beverly Hills CA 90210-5004

KLEIN, CORNELIS, geology educator; b. Haarlem, The Netherlands, Sept. 4, 1937; came to U.S., 1960; s. Cornelis and Wilhelmina (van'tHoen) K.; m. Angela M. Nobbs, Sept. 14, 1960; children: Marc Alexander, Stephanie Wilhelmina. BS in Geology with honors, McGill U., Montreal, Que., Can., 1958, MS in Geology, 1960; PhD in Geology, Harvard U., 1965. Lectr. in mineralogy Harvard U., Cambridge, Mass., 1965-69, assoc. prof., 1969-72, asst. dean, 1966-70; prof. mineralogy Ind. U., Bloomington, 1972-84; prof. geology U. N.Mex., Albuquerque, 1984—. Author: (with C.S. Hurlbut) Manual of Mineralogy, 21st edit., 1993, Minerals and Rocks: Exercises in Crystallography, Mineralogy, and Hand Specimen Pathology, 2d rev. edit., 1994; author (with S.M. Stoller Co.) minerology tutorials, interactive instrn. on CD-ROM, 1995; contbr. articles to profl. jours. Parker fellow Harvard U. fellow, 1962-63, Guggenheim fellow, 1978, Presdl. Tchg. fellow U. N.Mex., 1995—; recipient Faculty Achievement award Burlington Resources, U. N.Mex., 1991. Fellow Mineral. Soc. Am., Geol. Soc. Am., AAAS; mem. Soc. Econ. Goelogists, Mineral. Assn. Can. Home: 736 Val Verde Dr SE Albuquerque NM 87108-3468 Office: U NMex Dept Earth Planetary Sci 200 Yale Blvd SE Albuquerque NM 87106-4014

KLEIN, EDITH MILLER, lawyer, former state senator; b. Wallace, Idaho, Aug. 4, 1915; d. Fred L.B. and Edith (Gallup) Miller; m. Sandor S. Klein (dec. 1970). BS in Bus., U. Idaho, 1935; teaching fellowship, Wash. State U., 1936; JD, George Washington U., 1946, LLM, 1954. Bar: D.C. 1946, Idaho 1947, N.Y. 1955, U.S. Supreme Ct. 1954. Pers. spec. Labor and War Depts., Wash., 1942-46; practice law Boise, Idaho, 1947—; judge Mcpl. Ct., Boise, 1947-49; mem. Idaho Ho. Reps., 1948-50, 64-68, Idaho Senate, 1968-82; atty. FCC Wash., 1953-54; FHA N.Y.C., 1955-56. Chmn. Idaho Gov.'s Commn. Status Women, 1964-72, mem. 1965-79, 82-92; mem. Idaho Gov.'s Coun. Comprehensive Health Planning, 1969-76, Idaho Law Enforcement Planning Commn., 1972-82, Nat. Adv. Commn. Regional Med. Programs, 1974-76, Idaho Endowment Investment Bd., 1979-82; trustee Boise State U. Found. Inc., 1973—; pres. Boise Music Week, 1991-94; bd. dirs. Harry W. Morison Found. Inc., 1978—, St. Alphonsus Regional Med. Ctr. Found., 1982—; past pres. bd. dirs. Boise Philharm. Assn., Boise Opera. Named Woman of Yr. Boise Altrusa Club, 1966, Boise C. of C., 1970, Disting. Citizen, Idaho Statesman 1970, Woman of Progress, Idaho Bus. Prof. Women, 1978; recipient Women Helping Women award Soroptimist Club, 1980, Stein Meml. award Y.M.C.A., 1983, Silver and Gold award for Outstanding Svc., U. Idaho, 1985, March of Dimes award to Honor Outstanding Women, 1987, Cert. of Appreciation by Boise Br., AAUW, 1990, Morrison Ctr. Hall of Fame award, 1990, Disting. Cmty. Svc. award Boise Area C. of C., 1995. Mem. DAR (regent Pioneer chpt. 1991-93). Republican. Congregationalist. Home: 1588 Lenz Lane PO Box 475 Boise ID 83701 Office: 1400 West One Plaza PO Box 2527 Boise ID 83701

KLEIN, (MARY) ELEANOR, retired clinical social worker; b. Luzon, Philippines, Dec. 13, 1919; came to U.S., 1921; (parents Am. citizens); d. Roy Edgar and Edith Lillian Hay; m. Edward George Klein, June 24, 1955. BA, Pacific Union Coll., 1946; MSW, U. So. Calif., 1953. Lic. clin. social worker. Social worker White Meml. Hosp., Los Angeles, 1948-56; clin. social worker UCLA Hosp. Clinics, 1956-65, supr. social worker, 1965-67, assoc. dir., 1967-73, dir., 1973-82. Bd. dirs., treas. Los Amigos de la Humanidad, U. So. Calif. Sch. Social Work; hon. life mem. bd. dirs. Calif. div. Am. Cancer Soc., mem. vol. bd. Calif. div., 1964—, del. nat. dir., 1980-84, chmn. residential crusade for Orange County (Calif.) unit, 1985-86; bd. dirs. Vol. Exchange, 1988—, sec., 1991—. Recipient Disting. Alumni award Los Amigos de la Humanidad, 1984, Outstanding Performance award UCLA Hosp., 1968, various service awards Am. Cancer Soc., 1972-88. Fellow Soc. Clin. Social Work; mem. Nat. Assn. Social Workers (charter), Am. Hosp. Assn., Soc. Social Work Administrs. in Health Care (formerly Soc. Hosp. Social Work Dirs.) (nat. pres. 1981, bd. dirs. 1978-82, life mem. local chpt.), Am. Pub. Health Assn. Democrat. Adventist. Home: 1661 Texas Cir Costa Mesa CA 92626-2238

KLEIN, FAY MAGID, health administrator; b. Chgo., Jan. 12, 1929; d. Victor and Rose (Begun) Magid; m. Jerome G. Klein, June 27, 1948 (div. 1970); children: Leslie Susan Janik, Debra Lynne Maslov; m. Manuel Chait, Aug. 28, 1994. BA in English, UCLA, 1961; MA in Pub. Adminstrn., U. So. Calif., 1971. Cert. health adminstrn. Supr. social workers L.A. County, 1961-65; program specialist Econ. and Youth Opportunity Agy., L.A., 1965-69; sr. health planner Model Cities, L.A., 1971-72; dir. prepaid health plan Westland Health Svcs., L.A., 1972-74; exec. dir. Coastal Region Health Consortium, L.A., 1974-76; grants and legis. cons. Jewish Fed. Council of L.A., 1976-79; planning council Jewish Fed. Councils of So. Fla., Palm Beach to Miami, 1979-82; adminstrv. dir. program in kidney diseases Dept. Medicine UCLA, 1982-84; exec. dir. west coast Israel Cancer Rsch. Fund, L.A., 1984-94; cons. to non-profit orgns. Santa Monica, 1994—; cons. Arthritis Found., Los Angeles, 1984, Bus. Action Ctr., Los Angeles, 1982, Vis. Nurses Assn., Los Angeles, 1982. Charter mem. Los Angeles County Mus. of Art, Mus. of Contemporary Art, Los Angeles; cons. Los Angeles Mcpl. Art Gallery, 1979; mem. Art Council Wight Gallery, UCLA. Fellow U.S. Pub. Health, U. So. Calif., 1970-71. Mem. Am. Pub. Health, UCLA Alumni Assn. (life), U. So. Calif. Alumni Assn. (life).

KLEIN, FREDA, state agency administrator; b. Seattle, May 17, 1920; d. Joseph and Julia (Caplan) Vinikow; m. Jerry Jerome Klein, Oct. 20, 1946; children: Jan Susan Klein Waples, Kerry Joseph, Robin Jo Klein MacLeod. BA, U. Wash., 1942; MS, U. Nev., Las Vega, 1969, EdD, 1978. Owner, mgr. Smart Shop, Provo, Utah, 1958-60, Small Fry Shop, Las Vegas, 1961-66; vocat. counselor, test adminstr. Nev. Employment Security Dept., Las Vegas, 1966-77, local office mgr., 1978—. Contbr. articles to profl. jours. Exec. bd. Pvt. Industry Coun., Las Vegas, 1988—, Interstate Conf. on Employment Security Agys., Nev., 1988-90, Area Coordinating Com. for Econ. Devel., Las Vegas, 1988—. Recipient Achievement award Nev. Bus. Svc., 1990, Cert. of Spl. Congl. Recognition, 1992; named Outstanding Woman, Goodwill Industries sci. and rsch. divsn., 1977. Mem. AAUW, Internat. Assn. Pers. in Employment Security, U. Nev. Las Vegas Alumni Assn., Henderson C. of C. (exec. bd. 1986—), Soroptimist Internat. (pres. 1987-88), Phi Kappa Phi (scholastic hon.). Home: 2830 Phoenix St Las Vegas NV 89121-1312 Office: Nev Employment Security 119 S Water St Henderson NV 89015-7221

KLEIN, HENRY, architect; b. Cham, Germany, Sept. 6, 1920; came to U.S., 1939; s. Fred and Hedwig (Weiskopf) K.; m. Phyllis Harvey, Dec. 27, 1952; children: Vincent, Paul, David. Student, Inst. Rauch, Lausanne, Switzerland, 1936-38; BArch, Cornell U., 1943. Registered architect, Oreg., Wash. Designer Office of Pietro Belluschi, Architect, Portland, Oreg., 1948-51; architect Henry Klein Partnership, Architects, Mt. Vernon, Wash., 1952—. Bd. dirs. Wash. Pks. Found., Seattle, 1977—, Mus. N.W. Art, 1988—. With U.S. Army, 1943-46. Recipient Louis Sullivan award Internat. Union Bricklayers and Allied Craftsmen, 1981; Presdl. Design award Nat. Endowment Arts, 1988; George A. and Eliza Howard Found. fellow. Fellow AIA (Seattle charter medal 1995). Jewish. Home: 1957 Little Mountain Rd Mount Vernon WA 98273-8311 Office: Henry Klein Partnership 205 Matheson Mount Vernon WA 98273

KLEIN, JAMES MIKEL, music educator; b. Greenville, S.C., Aug. 27, 1953; s. Rubin Harry Klein and Billie (Mikel) Newton. BM, U. Tex., 1975, MM, 1977; MusD, U. Cincinnati, 1981. Prin. trombone player Austin (Tex.) Symphony Orch., 1973-77; conducting asst. U. Tex., Austin, 1975-77, U. Cin., 1977-78; dir. instrumental music Valparaiso (Ind.) U., 1978-84; prof. music Calif. State U. Stanislaus, Turlock, 1984—; mem. faculty Nat. Luth. Music Camp, Lincoln, Nebr., 1985-86, 95; guest conductor, clinician, adjudicator various states, internationally, 1978—; trombone player Modesto (Calif.) Symphony Orch., 1984—; conductor Stanislaus Youth Symphony, Modesto, 1985; music dir. Modesto Symphony Youth Orch., 1986—; site adminstr. Nat. Honors Orch., Anaheim, Calif., 1986, Indpls., 1988, Cin., 1992; faculty, coord. instrumental music Calif. State Summer Sch. of Arts, 1987-88. Pres. Turlock Arts Fund for Youth, 1986-88; mem. internat. Friendship Com., subcom., City of Modesto, 1990-92; vol. Big Bros. Am. Recipient Meritorious Prof. award Calif. State U., Stanislaus, 1988, Outstanding Young Man Am. award, 1990. Mem. Music Educators Nat. Assn., Nat. Sch. Orch. Assn. (pub. rels. chair 1992-94), Am. Fedn. Musicians (local 1), Condrs. Guild, Am. Symphony Orch. League, Calif. Orch. Dir.'s Assn. (pres.-elect 1988-90, pres. 1990-92, Orch. Dir. of the Year, 1994). Home: 840 Georgetown Ave Turlock CA 95382-0804 Office: Calif State U Dept Music 801 W Monte Vista Ave Turlock CA 95382-0256

KLEIN, JEREMY STEPHEN, editor; b. Newark, Apr. 17, 1945; s. Joe and Sylvia Klein; m. Janet Norma Raithel, Nov. 7, 1967; 1 child, Rachel Tamara. BA, U. Chgo., 1967. Pub. mgr. Internat. Soc. for Gen. Semantics, San Francisco, 1984-88; assoc. editor Western Real Estate News, South San Francisco, 1989—; grad. faculty advisor San Francisco Acad. of Art Coll., 1994-95. Editor-in-chief: (semantics jour.) ETC: A Review of General Semantics, 1990—; contbr.: (anthology) Creatical Thinking, 1991; contbr., co-editor: (anthology) To Be Or Not II, 1994; asst. editor: (newsletter) Glimpse, 1984-88. Mem. Internat. Soc. for Gen. Semantics (pres. San Francisco chpt. 1989—), Soc. for Gen. Sys. Rsch. (San Francisco chpt.). Home: PO Box 426336 San Francisco CA 94142-6336

KLEIN, MARC S., newspaper editor and publisher; b. Feb. 16, 1949; married; 2 children. BA in Journalism, Pa. State U., 1970. Bur. chief Courier-Post, Camden, N.J., 1970-75; asst. mng. editor Phila. Bull., 1975-81; editor Jewish Exponent, Phila., 1981-83; editor, pub. Jewish Bull. of No. Calif., San Francisco, 1984—. Past pres. Temple Israel, Alameda; former bd. dirs. Oakland-Piedmont Jewish Community Ctr. Recipient 1st place awards Phila. Press Assn., 1973, 1st place award N.J. Press Assn., 1973; Wall St. Jour. Newspaper Fund intern, fellow, 1969. Mem. Am. Jewish Press Assn. (past pres.), Soc. Profl. Journalists (past bd. dirs.). Office: 88 1st St Ste 300 San Francisco CA 94105-2522

KLEIN, M(ARY) A(LICE), fiber artist; b. Berwyn, Ill., Oct. 21, 1930; d. Ralph Logie and Dorothy (Tuttle) Low; m. Fred Arthur Hanson, Aug. 21, 1954 (div. 1974); children: Carol-Lynn, Kathryn, Susan, Linda; m. Charles Keith Klein, July 7, 1974; adopted children: Ellen, Elizabeth, Mary, Charles Jr. BA in Recreational Therapy, U. Calif., Berkeley, 1952; postgrad., Stanford U., 1954; degree Fine Arts, Famous Artists Sch., Westport, Conn., 1958-62. Recreational therapist Langley Porter Clinic, U. Calif. Hosp., San Francisco, 1952-53; exec. dir. Children's HomeSoc., San Francisco, 1954-55; designer, owner Hanson Handcrafts, Burlingame, Calif., 1968-74, Sunbow, Albuquerque, N. Mex., 1974-76, Monterey Bay Needleworks, Monterey, Calif., 1976-79; creator, owner M.A. Klein Design, Calif., 1980—; owner, mgr. M.A. Klein Co., Placerville, Portola Valley, Calif., 1991—; bd. dir. Calif. Needlework Assn., San Francisco, 1973-75; craftsmen's advisory bd. Goodfellow Craft Enterprises and Western Exhibitors, San Francisco, 1984; site nat. planner Nat. Standards Coun. of Am. Embroiders, Northbrook, Ill., 1989-91. Author: Stitchery Booklets with Slide Presentations, 1987-90; group shows include: Great Am. Needlework Show, Saratoga, Calif., 1982 (judges award 3 first prizes), Nat. Standards Coun. of Am. Embroiderers, Pitts. (best of show) 1985, Carmel Merchants Assn., Carmel, Calif. (best of show, purchase award), 1982, Art Quilt Internat. and Fiber Expression I, Mt. View, Calif. (selected as poster piece), 1994; prin. works include: (Wallhangings) Horizon Corp. Toronto, Can., St. Timothy's Ch., Danville, Calif., Libr. of Congress, Washington. Mem. Am. Crafts Assn., Coun. Am. Embroiderers (tchr. lectr. 1980—), Sacramento Ctr. Textile Arts (tchr. lectr. 1989—), Contemporary Quilters Fiber Artists (resource dir. 1994—), Pacific Art League. Episcopalian.

KLEIN, PERRY ANDREW, counselor; b. L.I., N.Y., May 4, 1964; s., Phillip Donald and Estelle (Truman) K.; m. Patricia Louise Hanson, Dec. 23, 1994. AA, Seminole Cmty. Coll., Sanford, Fla., 1985; BA in Psychology, U. Ctrl. Fla., 1987; postgrad., U. Phoenix, 1994—. Sr. case mgr. Mental Health Svcs. of Orange County, Orlando, Fla., 1987-90; case mgr. Temporary Living Ctr., Apopka, Fla., 1990-91; behavioral sci. specialist U.S. Army, Ft. Huachuca, Ariz., 1991-94; case mgr. Ariz. Ctr. for Clin. Mgmt., Tucson, 1994-95; cons. regarding clin. assessment and diagnosis, counseling Specialist U.S. Army, 1991-94; mem. Ariz. N.G., 1994-95. Decorated Expert Badge/M-16 Rifle, Army Achievemetn medal. Mem. Am. Counseling Assn., Am. Mental Health Counselors Assn., Golden Key Nat. Honor Soc. Home: 1620 E Blacklidge Dr # P-11 Tucson AZ 85719-2733

KLEIN, RALPH, provincial legislator, former city mayor; b. Calgary, Alta., Can.; ; m. 2nd, Colleen, 1972; 5 children. Dir. pub. rels. Alta. div. Red Cross; dir. pub. rels. Calgary United Way Fund, 1966-69; with CFCN, 1969-80; newsreader radio div., later television reporter, 1969-80; mayor City of Calgary, 1980-89; legislator Calgary-Elbow constituency Alta. Legislature, Edmonton, 1989—; minister of environment Alta. Legislature, 1989—. Office: Office of the Premier, 10800 97 Ave #307, Edmonton, AB Canada T5K 2B6

KLEIN, RAYMOND MAURICE, lawyer; b. Phila., Jan. 31, 1938; s. Maurice J. and Fay (Clearfield) K.; m. Roberta Steinberg, Apr. 8, 1984; children: Seth Grossman, Micah Grossman. AB, Williams Coll., 1959; JD, Harvard U., 1962. Bar: Pa. 1962, Calif. 1968, U.S. Supreme Ct. 1966. Lawyer Fed. Home Loan Bank Bd., Washington, 1963-67; ptnr. Hahn Cazier, L.A., 1967-78; lawyer Klein Law Corp., L.A., 1978-89, 93—; of counsel Davis Wright Tremaine, L.A., 1989-93; lectr. C. of C., Calif., 1988—, Young Pres.' Orgn., Ohio, 1990, Law Sch. for Entrepreneurs, L.A., 1990—; mem. exec. com. Cal Tech/MIT Enterprise Forum. Author: Putting a Lid on Legal Fees: How to Deal Effectively with Lawyers, 1987. Mem. ABA, Calif. State Bar Assn., L.A. Bar Assn. Home: 908 Kenfield Ave Los Angeles CA 90049-1405 Office: Cassady & Klein 908 Kenfield Ave Los Angeles CA 90049-1405

KLEIN, ROBERT GORDON, judge; b. Honolulu, Nov. 11, 1947; s. Gordon Ernest Klein and Clara (Cutter) Elliot; m. Aleta Elizabeth Webb, July 27, 1986; children: Kurt William, Erik Robert. BA, Stanford U., 1969; JD, U. Oreg., 1972. Dep. atty. gen. State of Hawaii, 1973, with state campaign spening commn., 1974, with state dept regulatory agys., 1975-78; judge State Dist. Ct. Hawaii, 1978-84; judge cir. ct. State of Hawaii, 1984-92, supreme ct. justice, 1992—. Office: Supreme Ct PO Box 2560 Honolulu HI 96804-2560

KLEIN, RUSS VINCENT, real estate developer; b. Vallejo, Calif., Mar. 24, 1951; s. Robert and Doris K. BS, Calif. Maritime Acad., 1972. Mgr. Shamrock Engring. Corp., Burlingame, Calif., 1972-84; mgr. of facilities Montgomery Wards Corp., Oakland, Calif., 1984-88, Indsl. Real Estate Corp., Hayward, Calif., 1988—. Mem. NSPE, Calif. Environmental Assessors. Office: Indsl Real Estate Corp 24468 Machado Ct Hayward CA 94541

KLEIN, SNIRA L(UBOVSKY), Hebrew language and literature educator; came to U.S., 1959, naturalized, 1974; d. Avraham and Devora (Unger) Lubovsky; m. Earl H. Klein, Dec. 25, 1975. Tchr. cert., Tchrs. Seminar, Netanya, Israel, 1956; B. Rel. Edn., U. Judaism, 1961, M in Hebrew Lit., 1963; BA, Calif. State U., Northridge, 1966; MA, UCLA, 1971, PhD, 1983. Tchg. asst. UCLA, 1969-71; instr., continuing edn. U. Judaism, L.A., 1971-76, 94—, instr., 1975-84; instr. continuing edn. U. Judaism, Los Angeles, 1994—; vis. lectr. UCLA, 1985-91; adj. asst. prof. U. Judaism, 1984-94. Mem. Assn. for Jewish Studies, Nat. Assn. of Profs. of Hebrew, World Union of Jewish Studies. Jewish. Office: U Judaism 15600 Mulholland Dr Los Angeles CA 90077-1519

KLEIN, STEPHEN PAUL, engineering and mathematics educator; b. L.A., Jan. 16, 1947; s. Paul Eugene and Frances (Lewis) K.; m. Cheryl Anne Harvey, June 14, 1968 (div. Aug. 1981); 1 child, Paul William; m. Lauren Ellin Syda, Aug. 11, 1984. BSME, U. Calif., Davis, 1968, postgrad., 1987; MSE, U. Mich., 1969; MS in Oceanography, U. Calif., San Diego, 1974. Rsch. asst. Scripps Instn. of Oceanography, La Jolla, Calif., 1969-73; test engr. Offshore Tech. Corp., Escondido, Calif., 1971-73; tech. engr. Oreg. State U., Corvallis, 1974-76; instr. engring. U. Calif., Davis, 1980-81; tenured instr. engring. and math., head engring. dept. Yuba Coll., Marysville, Calif., 1976—; participant NASA Space Tech. Summer Inst., U. So. Calif., 1967, Energy Summer Inst., U. Calif., Davis, 1978, NASA KC135 Zero G Rsch. Flight, Ellington AFB, Tex., 1987. Contbr. articles to profl. jours. Pres. Corvallis Velo Club, 1974-76. Mem. AAUP, Am. Soc. Engring. Edn., Yuba Sutter Bicycle Club (pres. 1977-80). Office: Yuba Coll 2088 N Beale Rd Marysville CA 95901-7605

KLEINBERG, JUDITH G., lawyer, children's advocate; b. Hartford, Conn., Jan. 28, 1946; d. Burleigh B. and Ruth (Leven) Greenberg; m. James Paul Kleinberg, Aug. 30, 1970; children: Alexander, Lauren. BA cum laude, U. Mich., 1968; JD, U. Calif., Berkeley, 1971. Atty. pvt. practice, San Francisco, 1971-74; legal affairs reporter comml. and pub. TV, San Francisco, 1974-76; prof. law Mills Coll., Oakland, Calif., 1977-84; chief of staff The Global Fund for Women, Los Altos, Calif., 1987-88; pub. interest atty., non-profit corp. law/orgn. specialist alternative dispute resolution Palo Alto, Calif., 1988-94; exec. dir. Kids in Common: A Children & Families Collaborative, Mountain View and San Jose, Calif., 1994—; arbitrator/mediator, legal adv. for abortion rights, women and children's rights and environ. groups, Santa Clara County and Calif., 1980—; speaker in field. Mem. Calif. Law Rev. Bd. Editors, 1969-71; moderator, host cmty. TV news program for San Francisco midpeninsula region, 1995—. Mem. steering com. lawyers coun. No. Calif. sect. ACLU, bd. dirs., 1990-92; founder, chairperson No. Calif. Friends of Pediat. AIDS Found.; past pres. Com. for Green Foothills; bd. dirs. Palo Alto SAFE, Support Network for Battered Women, 1990-92, Palo Alto Coun. PTAs, Leadership Midpeninsula; pres. Palo Alto Stanford divsn. Am. Heart Assn.; v.p. Assn. for Sr. Day Health; founder Safer Summer Project; pres., legal counsel Calif. Abortion Rights Action League, 1980-86. Mem. Am. Arbitration Assn. (mem. atty. panel), Calif. Women Lawyers (v.p. 1986-88).

KLEINFELD, ANDREW JAY, federal judge; b. 1945. BA magna cum laude, Wesleyan U., 1966; JD cum laude, Harvard U., 1969. Law clk. Alaska Supreme Ct., 1969-71; U.S. magistrate U.S. Dist. Ct. Alaska, Fairbanks, 1971-74; pvt. practice law Fairbanks, 1971-86; judge U.S. Dist. Ct. Alaska, Anchorage, 1986-91, U.S. Ct. Appeals (9th cir.), San Francisco, 1991—. Contbr. articles to profl. jours. Mem. Alaska Bar Assn. (pres. 1982-83, bd. govs. 1981-84), Tanana Valley Bar Assn. (pres. 1974-75), Phi Beta Kappa. Republican. Office: US Ct Appeals 9th Cir Courthouse Sq 250 Cushman St Ste 3-A Fairbanks AK 99701

KLEINSCHNITZ, BARBARA JOY, oil company executive, consultant; b. Granite Falls, Minn., Aug. 25, 1944; d. Arthur William and Joy Ardys (Roe) Green; m. Charles Lewis Kleinschnitz, Dec. 28, 1963; 1 child, Katheryn JoAnn Kleinschnitz Hartsock. BBA, U. Denver, 1983; student, Colo. Women's Coll. Leadman Schlumberger Well Services, Denver, 1968-76; supr., log processing Scientific Software-Intercomp, Denver, 1976-82; tech. cons. Tech. Log Analysis, Inc., Lakewood, Colo., 1982-83; customer support mgr. Energy Systems Tech., Inc., Englewood, Colo., 1983-86; cons. technical Littleton, Colo., 1986—; documentation specialist Q.C. Data, Inc., 1987-91; tng. specialist Advanced Data Concepts, Ft. Collins, Colo., 1991-93; tech. writer Computer Data Sys., Inc., Ft. Collins, 1993—; cons. Tech. Log Analysis, Inc., Denver, 1982-83, Energy Systems Tech., 1986—. Vol. Denver Police Reserve, 1973-75. Mem. NOW, NAFE, Assn. Women Geoscientists, Soc. Profl. Well Log Analysts (bd. dirs. 1989-90, v.p. 1990-91), Denver Well Log Soc. (bd. dirs. 1986-87, v.p. 1987-88, pres. 1988-89). Democrat. Roman Catholic. Home: 3024 Appaloosa Ct Fort Collins CO 80526-2646 Office: 2625 Redwing Rd Ste 120 Fort Collins CO 80526-2878

KLEINSMITH, BRUCE JOHN See **NUTZLE, FUTZIE**

KLEPINGER, JOHN WILLIAM, trailer manufacturing company executive; b. Lafayette, Ind., Feb. 7, 1945; s. John Franklin and R. Wanda (North) K.; m. Mary Patricia Duffy, May 1, 1976; 1 child, Nicholas Patrick. BS, Ball State U., 1967, MA, 1968. Sales engr. CTS Corp., Elkhart, Ind., 1969-70; exec. v.p. Woodlawn Products Corp., Elkhart, 1970-78; v.p. Period Ind., Henderson, Ky., 1976-78, Sotebeer Constrn. Co., Inc., Elkhart, 1978-81; gen. mgr. Wells Industries Inc., Ogden, Utah, 1981—; regional dir. Zion's First Nat. Bank, Ogden, 1986—. Bd. dirs. St. Benedict's Hosp., Ogden, 1986-94, chmn., 1987-94; bd. dirs. Weber County Indsl. Devel. Corp., Nat. Job Tng. Partnership Inc., 1986-89; mem. Weber-Morgan Pvt. Industry Coun., 1983—, Utah Job Tng. Coordinating Coun., 1988—, chmn. 1993-94. Named Ogden Bus. Man of Yr., Weber County Sch. Dist., 1984. Mem. Nat. Assn. Trailer Mfrs. (bd. dirs., vice chmn. 1994-95, chmn. 1995—), Weber County Prodn. Mgrs. Assn. (pres. 1984-85, 92-93), Nat. Assn. Pvt. Industry Couns. (pres., bd. dirs.), Nat. Alliance Bus. (bd. dirs. 1987-90), Ogden Area C. of C. (bd. dirs., treas. 1986—), Exch. Club (bd. dirs. 1984-86). Roman Catholic. Home: 5181 Aztec Dr Ogden UT 84403-4606 Office: Wells Industries Inc PO Box 1619 Ogden UT 84402-1619

KLEPPINGER, MOSELLE LEE, public relations professional; b. Worland, Wyo., Mar. 2, 1956; d. Kenneth Myron and Moselle Loretta (Shelton) K.; m. Tim Lee Romanek, May 28, 1983 (div. 1987); m. Mark David Cheesbrough, Dec. 30, 1994. BS, U. Wyo., 1978, MA, 1980, postgrad., 1980—. Pub. rels. officer Natrona County Sch. Dist., Casper, Wyo., 1976; corr., intern Casper Star-Tribune, 1976-78; corr., intern KTWO-TV, Casper, 1978-79, reporter, 1979-87; asst. dir. pub. rels. Casper Coll., 1987-95; bd. dirs. Conv. and Visitors Bur., Casper C. of C., mem. mktg. com., 1992-94. Participant Leaderhsip Casper, 1990-91, co-chair, 1991-92; bd. dirs. Cultural Affairs Com. Chamber, Casper, 1988-94, Troopers Drum and Bugle Corps, Casper, 1989-93, Big Bros.-Big Sisters, Casper, 1991-94; mem. Stage III Cmty. Theatre, Casper, 1980-94, bd. dirs., 1980-87, pres. 1984-87. Recipient Hist. award Wyo. State Hist. Soc., 1987; named Outstanding Young Women of Am., 1987. Mem. Casper Area Mktg. Profls., Soroptimist Internat. (exec. bd. ctrl. Wyo. chpt. 1990-94). Methodist. Home: 717 Independence Dr Longmont CO 80501-3924

KLEVIT, ALAN BARRE, business executive, motivational speaker; b. Balt., June 25, 1935; s. Robert and Minnie (Goodman) K.; m. Marilyn Rosenthal, Nov. 26, 1955; children: Mindy Faith, Lawrence Michael, Richard Steven. BS in Econs., Georgetown U., 1956, MA in Econs., 1960; MA in Pub. Adminstrn. and Urban Affairs, Am. U., 1970. Asst. mgr. AS Beck Shoe Co., Washington, 1956-57; stat., economist Commerce Dept., Washington, 1957-60; securities analyst, rsch. dir. T.J. McDonald & Co., Washington, 1960-62; mgmt. analyst, div. chief Fed. Aviation Adminstrn., Washington, 1962-73; chief exec. officer Art Fair, Inc., Silver Spring, Md., 1974—; founder, dir. Klevit Fine Art, Internat., Silver Spring and Malibu, Calif., 1987—; founder, exec. officer Robert Klevit Found. for Humanitarianism, Silver Spring and Malibu, Calif., 1987—; dir. Stardust Pub., Malibu, 1990—; co-founder, dir. Charity Editions, Silver Spring and Malibu, 1987; mem. faculty Mgmt. by Objectives Fed. Exec. Sch., Charlottesville, Va., 1969-71; motivational speaker, Malibu, 1988—. Author: Three Days in Sedona, 1990, How To Make Your Dreams Come True, 1991, Follow The Rainbow, 1991, (video) Journey Within, 1993; host: (radio show Today's Art World with Alan Klevit, 1983-84, (TV show) Off the Beaten Path with Alan Klevit, 1992; contbr. articles to profl. jours., mags. and newspapers. Bd. dirs. Summer Opera, Washington, 1987—, Marine & Mountain Wildlife Rescue, Malibu, 1991—; mem. Hammer Mus. Mem. Inst. for Econometric Rsch., World Wildlife Fedn., Inst. for Noetic Scis., Planetary Soc., Malibu C. of C., Masons. Office: Stardust Pub PO Box 6356 Malibu CA 90265-6356

KLEWENO, GILBERT H., lawyer; b. Endicott, Wash., Mar. 21, 1933; s. Melvin Lawrence and Anna (Lust) K.; m. Virginia Symms, Dec. 28, 1958; children: Stanley, Douglas, Phillip. BA, U. Wash., 1955; LLR, U. Idaho, 1959. Bar: Wash. 1960. Assoc. Read & Church, Vancouver, Wash., 1960-68, Boettcher & LaLonde, Vancouver, Wash., 1968—; part-time U.S. Magistrate Judge, 1979. Chmn. Bd. Adjustors, Vancouver, Civil Svc. Commn., Vancouver. Mem. Wash. State Bar Assn., Elks, Gyro Club. Office: Boettcher LaLonde Kleweno 610 Esther St Vancouver WA 98660-3022

KLIEGER, PAUL CHRISTIAAN, anthropologist, researcher; b. Great Falls, Mont., July 27, 1951; s. Samuel and Charlotte E. (Odegard) K. BA, U. Mont., 1973; MA in Asian Religions, U. Hawaii, 1980, MA in Anthropology, 1985, PhD, 1989. Lectr. Chaminade U., Honolulu, 1985-88, U. Hawaii, Honolulu, 1988; vis. lectr. U. Pitts., 1989; acting dir. Tibetan Cultural Ctr., Missoula, Mont., 1990; assoc. anthropologist Bishop Mus., Honolulu, 1991—; dir. Tibetan-U.S. resettlement Com., 1990-91, advisor, 1991-93; bd. dirs. Friends of Moku'ula, Lahaina, Hawaii, 1994. Author:

Tibetan Nationalism, 1992; entries in Asian Am. Encyclopedia, 1994; contbr. articles to anthrop. publs. Cons. U.S.-Tibet Com., Missoula, Mont., 1990-91. Pacific-Asian scholar U. Hawaii, Honolulu, 1985-86; grantee Lahaina (Maui, Hawaii) Restoration Found., 1993, Native Hawaiian Culture and Arts Program, Honolulu, 1994. Mem. Am. Anthrop. Assn. (com. on refugee issues 1989—, coun. on human rights 1989—), Soc. for Hawaiian Archaeology, Hawaiian Anthrop. Assn. (v.p. 1983, editor 1989). Buddhist. Office: Bishop Mus Dept Anthropology 1525 Bernice St Honolulu HI 96817

KLIEN, WOLFGANG JOSEF, architect; b. Hollabrunn, Austria, Sept. 29, 1942; s. Josef and Maria (Kainz) K.; Dipl. Ing., Vienna Tech. U., 1967; children: Christina Olga, Angelika Maria. Designer, E. Donau, Architect, Vienna, 1968; with C. Nitschke & Assos., Architects, Columbus, Ohio, 1968-71; project architect GSAS Architects, Phoenix, 1971-75, 77-78; prodn. architect Harry Glueck, Vienna, 1976-77; v.p. architecture Am. Indian Engrng. Inc., Phoenix, 1978-81; pres. S.W. Estate Group, Inc., real estate devel., San Diego, 1980-82; pres., tech. dir., branch mgr. Ariz. br. office SEG-S.W. Estate Group, Inc., Phoenix, 1982-86; prin. Klien & Assoc., Architecture, Planning, Devel. Cons., Phoenix, 1986—, Atlantic-Pacific Trading Corp., Internat. Trade, Phoenix, 1986-88; pres., gen. mgr. Polybau, Inc., Hayward, Calif., 1988-90; pres. Libra Cons., INc., Phoenix, 1989—; ptnr. Heart Devel. Co., LLC, dBa Heart Homes, 1993—. Recipient Great Silver Medal of Merit, Republic of Austria, 1993. Mem. AIA, Austro-Am. Council West, Austrian Soc. Ariz. (founder 1985, v.p. 1985-86, pres. 1987—). Roman Catholic. Home: 4524 S Willow Dr Tempe AZ 85282-7365 Office: Heart Devel 6220 W Thomas Rd # 205 Phoenix AZ 85033-5857

KLIMA, ROGER R., physiatrist; b. Prague, Czechoslovakia; came to U.S., 1982, naturalized, 1988; s. Josef and Radka Klima. BA, Zatlanka Coll., Prague, 1971; MD, Charles U., Prague, 1978. Diplomate Am. Bd. Phys. Medicine and Rehab., Am. Bd. Electrodiagnostic Medicine. Resident in surgery Charles U., 1978-79, resident in orthopedic surgery, 1979-81; fellow, clin. clk. Beverly Hills Med. Ctr. and Cedars-Sinai Med. Ctr., L.A., 1984-86; resident in surgery U. Medicine and Dentistry-N.J. Med. Sch., Newark, 1986-87; resident in phys. medicine and rehab. U. Medicine and Dentistry-N.J. Med. Sch./Kessler Inst., Newark and West Orange, 1987-90; mem. phys. medicine and rehab. faculty Stanford (Calif.) U. and affiliated hosps., 1990—; dir. phys. medicine and rehab. outpatient svcs. Palo Alto (Calif.) VA Med. Ctr., 1992—, also co-dir. comprehensive pain mgmt.; clin. instr. in phys. medicine and rehab. U. Medicine and Dentistry-N.J.Med. Sch., 1989-90, Stanford U. Sch. Medicine, 1990—. Contbr. articles to profl. jours. Recipient Thompson Humanitarian award Stanford U. Phys. Medicine and Rehab., 1994. Mem. Am. Acad. Phys. Medicine and Rehab. (liaison resident physician coun. 1989-90), Assn. Acad. Physiatrists, Am. Assn. Electrodiagnostic Medicine. Office: Stanford U Med Ctr Divsn Phys Medicine and Rehab Rm NC 104 Stanford CA 94305

KLIMKO, RONALD JAMES, music educator; b. Lena, Wis., Dec. 13, 1936; s. Robert Lewis and Evelyn Mary (Rosera) K.; m. Kathleen Screnson, Oct. 15, 1963 (div. July 1983); children: Karl Nicholas, Christopher Anthony, Julie Marie, Benjamin Andrew; m. Kathryn Paxton George, July 27, 1985; children: Kimberly George, Elizabeth Francene George. B in Mus. Edn., Milton Coll., 1959; postgrad., George Washington U., 1961; MusM, U. Wis., 1963, PhD, 1968. Asst. prof. music Moorhead (Minn.) State Coll., 1966-67, Ind. State U., Terre Haute, 1967-68; prof. music U. Idaho, Moscow, 1968—; vis. prof. Ind. U., Bloomington, 1980, Colo. U., Boulder, 1990-91; bassonist Madison (Wis.), 1961-66, Spokane (Wash.) Symphony, 1968-90. Author: Bassoon Performance Practices in U.S. and Canada, 1974, (with Marc Apfelstadt) Bassoon Performance and Teaching Mateirals, Methods, and Techniques, 1993. Mem. Am. Fedn. Musicians, Internat. Double Reed Soc. (Bassoon editor 1981—). Democrat. Home: 1020 W Cayuse Dr Moscow ID 83843-2461 Office: U Idaho Lionel Hampton Sch Music Moscow ID 83843

KLINE, ARTHUR JONATHAN, electronics engineer; b. Prescott, Ariz., Feb. 29, 1928; s. Sarah Ann (Odell) Kline; m. Marilyn Sue Lane, Nov. 14, 1959; children: Lee Ann, Jonathan Lane. BS in Engrng. Physics, U. Calif., Berkeley, 1953; MS in Applied Physics, UCLA, 1956. Electronics engr. Radio Corp. Am., Moorestown, N.J., 1953-55; electronics engr. Motorola Inc., Scottsdale, Ariz., 1956-93, retired, 1993; assoc. mem. Motorola Sci. Adv. Bd., 1972. With USN, 1946-52. Dan Noble fellow, 1975. Fellow AIAA (assoc., chmn. Phoenix chpt. 1968-69). Home: 6453 E Monterosa St Scottsdale AZ 85251-3136

KLINE, FRED WALTER, communications company executive; b. Oakland, Calif., May 17, 1918; s. Walter E. and Jean M. Kline; m. Verna Marie Taylor, Dec. 27, 1952; children—Kathleen, Nora, Fred Walter. B.A. in Calif. History, U. Calif.-Berkeley, 1940. With Walter E. Kline & Assocs. and successor Fred Kline Agy., Inc., from 1937; chmn. bd., pres. Kline Communications Corp., Los Angeles, 1956—; pres. Capitol News Service. Commr. Los Angeles County Fire Services Commn., Calif. Motion Picture Devel. Council; cons., advisor Calif. Film Commn.; former fed. civil def. liaison; developer state-wide paramedic rescue program; Calif. chmn. Office of Asst. Sec. Def.; mem. Calif. Com. for Employer Support of Guard and Res.; mem. Los Angeles Film Com. Served with USAAF, World War II; brig. gen. Calif. Mil. Dept. Recipient Inter-Racial award City of Los Angeles, 1963, named Man of Yr., 1964. Mem. Acad. Motion Picture Arts and Scis., Radio and TV News Assn. So. Calif., Pub. Relations Soc. Am., Calif. Newspaper Pubs. Assn., Cath. Press Council (founding mem.), Pacific Pioneer Broadcasters, Footprinters Internat., Am. Mil. Govt. Assn. (past pres.), Navy League, Calif. State Police Officers Assn., Internat. Assn. Profl. Firefighters (hon. life), Peace Officers Assn. Los Angeles County (life), Internat. Assn. Chiefs of Police, Internat. Assn. Fire Chiefs, Calif. Fire Chiefs Assn., Fire Marshals Assn. N.Am., Nat. Fire Protection Assn., Nat. Fin. Writers Assn., Hollywood C. of C., Nat. Fire Sci. Acad., Calif. State Mil. Forces, Calif. Pubs. Assn., So. Calif. Cable Club. Sigma Delta Chi. Clubs: Greater Los Angeles Press, Media (Los Angeles), Sacramento Press. Columnist Calif. newspapers. Office: 1180 Weber Way Sacramento CA 95822-1840

KLINE, HOWARD JAY, cardiologist; b. White Plains, N.Y., Nov. 5, 1932; s. Raymond Kline and Rose Plane; divorced; children: Michael, Ethan; m. Ellen Sawamura, June 13, 1987; 1 child, Christopher. BA, Dickinson Coll., 1954; MD, N.Y. Med. Coll., 1958. Intern San Francisco Gen. Hosp., 1958-59; resident Mt. Sinai Hosp., N.Y.C., 1959-61; sr. resident U. Calif. Med. Ctr., San Francisco, 1961-62; cardiology fellow Mt. Sinai Hosp., N.Y.C., 1962-64; dir. cardiology training program St. Mary's Hosp., San Francisco, 1970-90, Calif. Pacific Med. Ctr., San Francisco, 1992—; clin. prof. medicine U. Calif. Med. Ctr., San Francisco, 1984—; vis. prof. Nihon U., Tokyo, 1986. Editor (jours.) Hosp. Practice, Cardiology, 1992—; contbr. articles to Hosp. Practice. Lt. col. U.S. Med. Corps, 1967-69. Fellow ACP, Am. Heart Assn., Am. Coll. Cardiology, Am. Coll. Chest Physicians; mem. Burkes Tennis Club. Office: 2100 Webster St Ste 518 San Francisco CA 94115-2382

KLINE, LEE B., architect; b. Renton, Wash., Feb. 2, 1914; s. Abraham McCubbin and Pearl (Davidson) K.; m. Martha Myers, Aug. 29, 1936; children—Patricia, Joanne Louise Kline Kresse. B.Arch., U. So. Calif., 1937. Draftsman, designer, 1937-43; pvt. archtl. practice Los Angeles, 1943—; instr. engrng. extension U. Calif., 1947-53; mem. panel arbitrators Am. Arbitration Assn., 1964—. Pres. LaCanada Irrigation Dist., 1966—, dir., 1963—; Bd. dirs. Foothill Mcpl. Water Dist., 1980—, LaCanada br. ARC, 1959-81. Recipient Disting. Service citation Calif. council AIA, 1960, honor awards AIA, 1957, 59, Sch. of Month awards Nation's Schools, 1964, 71. Fellow AIA (pres. Pasadena chpt. 1957, pres. Calif. council 1959). Home: 5160 Oakwood Ave La Canada Flintridge CA 91011-2452 Office: Lee B Kline Inc 969 Colorado Blvd Los Angeles CA 90041-1715

KLINE, NATASHA CALE, biologist; b. Montclaire, N.J., Sept. 20, 1959; d. Arland Theodore and Gail (Hulslander) K.; m. Victor William Brown, Jun 13, 1986. BS in Zoology, U. Calif., Davis, 1982; MS in Biology, U. Miami, 1987. Biol. technician U.S. Fish and Wildlife Svc., Adak, Alaska, 1982-84; biol. technician U.S. Nat. Park Svc., Everglades Nat. Park, Fla., 1986-88, Grand Canyon Nat. Park, Ariz., 1990-91; nat. resource program mgr. USAF, Phoenix, 1991-93; wildlife biologist U.S. Nat. Park Svc., Tucson, Ariz., 1993—; regl. rep. Ptnrs. in Flight, USAF, Phoenix, 1992-93; cons. biologist U.S. Nat. Park Svc., Page, Ariz., 1990. Contbr. articles to profl. jours. Recipient Nat. Resource Response award U.S. Dept. Interior, Washington, 1989, Teagle Found. scholarship Exxon Corp., 1985, Maytag fellowship U. Miami, Coral Gables, Fla., 1984-86; rsch. grantee Tropical Audubon Soc., Miami, 1985. Office: Saguaro Nat Park Nat Park Svc 3693 S Old Spanish Trail Tucson AZ 85730

KLINE, PAMELA IRIS, consulting company executive; b. Pitts., Aug. 23, 1958; d. Robert Edward and Rae R. Kline. Cert., U. Paris, Sorbonne, 1979; AB magna cum laude, Harvard U., 1980, MBA, 1984. Asst. staff mgr. Bell of Pa., Phila., 1980-82; product mgr. Visa Internat., San Francisco, 1983; v.p. Prognostics, Palo Alto, Calif., 1984-91; dir. Diefenbach/Elkins, San Francisco, 1991-92; ptnr. Regis McKenna, Inc., 1992—. Vol. San Jose Civic Lights, 1987; dir. Harvard/Radcliffe Fundraising, Boston, 1980—; chmn. Harvard/Radcliffe Schs. com., San Mateo County, 1985—. Mem. Young Profl. Woman Assn., Radcliffe Club (dir. 1987—), Harvard Club. Republican. Home: 570 Beale St Apt 416 San Francisco CA 94105-2025 Office: Regis McKenna Inc 1755 Embarcadero Rd Palo Alto CA 94303-3304

KLINGENSMITH, ARTHUR PAUL, relocation and redevelopment consultant; b. L.A., May 23, 1949; s. Paul Arthur and Hermine Elinore K.; m. Donna J. Bellucci, Apr. 26, 1976 (div. Jan. 1981). AA in Social Sci., Indian Valley Jr. Coll., 1976; BA in Indsl. Psychology, San Francisco State U., 1979; MA in Indsl. Psychology, Columbia Pacific U., 1980. Enlisted USAF, Biloxi, Miss.; advanced through grades to staff sgt. USAF; instr. radio ops. USAF, Biloxi, 1968-72; air traffic control operator USAF, Hamilton AFB Novato, Calif., 1972-74; resigned USAF, 1974; elec. technician Calif. Dept. Transp., Oakland, 1975-78; right of way agt. Calif. Dept. Transp., San Francisco, 1978-85; sr. right of way agt. Calif. Dept. Transp., Sacramento, 1985-87, computer researcher, 1985-87; v.p., cons. Associated Right of Way Svcs., Inc., 1989-92; pvt. practice relocation and redevel. cons., 1987—. Mem. Internat. Right of Way Assn. (instr. 1982—), Am. Arbitration Assn., Marin County Bd. Realtors, Assn. Humanistic Psychology, Nat. Assn. Housing and Redevel. Ofcls., Inst. Noetic Scis., Am. Planning Assn. Republican. Office: Arthur P Klingensmith & Assocs PO Box 574 Sausalito CA 94966-0574

KLINGENSMITH, WILLIAM CLAUDE, III, radiologist; b. Pitts., Feb. 17, 1942; s. William Claude and Marian T. (Dale) K.; m. Georgeanna Seegar Jones, Apr. 22, 1972; children: William Claude IV, Theodore Emory. AB, Cornell U., 1964, MD, 1968. Med. intern U. Oreg. Med. Sch., Portland, 1968-69; radiology resident U. Colo. Med. Sch., Denver, 1969-72, asst. prof. radiology, 1976-80, assoc. prof. radiology, 1980-83; nuclear medicine fellow Johns Hopkins Med. Sch., Balt., 1974-75, instr., 1975-76; radiologist St. Joseph Hosp., Denver, 1983-90, Radiology Imaging Assoc., Denver, 1990—. Maj. USAF, 1972-74. Home: 4720 E Oxford Ave Englewood CO 80110-5118

KLINK, PAUL LEO, computer company executive; b. Auburn, N.Y., July 28, 1965; s. Charles Lawrence and Regina Joyce (Maniscalco) K. Student, SUNY, Cayuga, 1979-84. Pres., CEO Info. Tech., Honolulu, 1979—; v.p. Direct Mktg. Mgrs. divsn. Milici Valenti Ng Pack Assoc. Agy. DDB Needham, Honolulu, 1979—. Contbr. and edited articles for profl. jours. Co-chmn. direct mktg. com. Aloha United Way, Honolulu, 1989—; active computer affairs Friends of Rep. Paul O'Shiro, Ewa Beach, Hawaii, 1988—, Friends of Gov. Ben Cayetano, Honolulu, 1988—, Friends of Mayor Jer Harris, Honolulu, 1988—; bd. dirs. Postal Customer Coun., 1992-93; founder Rock 'n Vote; co-founder Live Aloha; inaugural attendee Pres. Williams Jefferson Clinton and V.P. Albert Gore. Mem. Info. Industry Assn. (dir. membership 1989—), Direct Mktg. and Advt. Assn. Hawaii (bd. dirs.), Database Mgmt. Assn. Hawaii (direct mktg. com.), Japanese C. of C. (strategic planning officer, steering com.), Puualoa Rifle and Pistol Club, Mensa, Honolulu Club, La Marianas Sailing Club, Nat. Press Club, Plaza Club, Georgetown Club, Honolulu Zool. Soc. (dir. Adolpt an Animal Fund). Office: Info Tech USA Inc Box 8578 330 Saratoga Rd Honolulu HI 96830-0578

KLIPPING, ROBERT SAMUEL, geophysicist; b. Glaston, N.D., Dec. 5, 1928; s. Roy Samuel and Marie (Peterson) K.; m. Gayle Cleone Swanson, Sept. 29, 1951; children: Barbara, Sharon, Joan. BS in Geology, Colo. Coll., Colorado Springs, 1953. Geophys. computer scientist Gen. Geophys. Co., Denver, 1953-57; geophys. supr. Mandrel Indsl. Inc., Denver, 1957-65, area mgr., 1965-69; geophys. Pennzoil Co., Denver, 1969-72, exploration mgr., 1972-78; geophys. cons., owner Klipping & Assocs., Denver, 1978—. Author: American Association of Petroleum Geologists, 1976, Montana Geological Society, 1978. Staff sgt. U.S. Army, 1946-48. Mem. Am. Assn. Petroleum Geologists, Soc. Exploration Geophysicists, Denver Geophys. Soc. (treas. 1972-73, sec. 1973-74). Republican. Methodist. Home: 14645 Sterling Rd Colorado Springs CO 80921-2618 Office: Klipping & Assocs 518 17th St Denver CO 80202-4102

KLOBE, TOM, art gallery director; b. Mpls., Nov. 26, 1940; s. Charles S. and Lorna (Effertz) K.; m. Delmarie Pauline Motta, June 21, 1975. BFA, U. Hawaii, 1964, MFA, 1968; postgrad., UCLA, 1972-73. Vol. peace corps Alang, Iran, 1964-66; tchr. Calif. State U., Fullerton, 1969-72, Santa Ana (Calif.) Coll., 1972-77, Orange Coast Coll., Costa Mesa, Calif., 1974-77, Golden West Coll., Huntington Beach, Calif., 1976-77; art gallery dir. U. Hawaii, Honolulu, 1977—; acting dir. Downey (Calif.) Mus. Art, 1976; cons. Judiciary Mus., Honolulu, 1982—, Maui (Hawaii) Arts and Cultural Ctr., 1984-94, curator Käia Wai Ola: This Living Water, 1994; exhibit designer Inst. for Astronomy, Honolulu, 1983-86; exhibit design cons. Japanese Cultural Ctr. Hawaii, 1993—; juror Print Casebooks. Recipient Best in Exhbn. Design award Print Casebooks, 1984, 86, 88, Vol. Svc. award City of Downey, 1977; Exhbn. grantee NEA, 1979—, State Found. Culture and the Arts, 1977—. Mem. Hawaii Mus. Assn., Nat. Assn. Mus. Exhbn. Roman Catholic. Office: U Hawaii Art Gallery 2535 The Mall Honolulu HI 96822-2233

KLOBUCHER, JOHN MARCELLUS, judge; b. Spokane, Wash., July 12, 1932; m. Virginia Rose Nilles; children—Marcella Marie, John Marcellus II, Christopher. Student Wash. State U., 1952; student Gonzaga U., 1954-57, J.D., 1960. Bar: Wash. 1960, U.S. Dist. Ct. (ea. dist.) Wash. 1961, U.S. Ct. Appeals (9th cir.) 1972. Law clk. to judge U.S. Dist. Ct. (ea. dist.) Wash., 1960-61; dep. pros. atty. criminal div. Spokane County Pros. Atty.'s Office, 1961-63; ptnr. Ennis & Klobucher, Spokane, 1963-78, Murphy, Bantz, Jansen, Klobucher, Clemons & Bury, Spokane, 1981; U.S. bankruptcy judge Eastern Dist. Wash., Spokane, 1981—. Served with U.S. Army, 1953-54. Mem. Wash. State Bar Assn., Spokane County Bar Assn. (pres. 1981), Inland Empire Fly Fishing (pres. 1977). Office: US Bankruptcy Ct PO Box 2164 Spokane WA 99210-2164

KLODZINSKI, BEATRICE DAVIS, management consultant; b. Berkeley, Calif., Dec. 28, 1950; d. H. Virgil and Margie (Snowden) D. BSBA, U. Denver, 1973, MBA, 1974. Asst. adminstr. Davis Nursing Home, Inc., Denver, 1972-76; prof. Universidad De Santo Tomas, Bogota, Colombia, 1977-78; writer, translater Sintesis Economica, Bogota, 1978-79; prof. Universidad Los Andes, Bogota, 1979-80; mgr. Serviminas Ltd., Medellin and Bogota, 1978-81; prof. Eafit U., Medellin, 1982-84; pres. Performance Plus, Sacramento and Trinidad, Colo., 1986-91; mayor Trinidad, Colo., 1991—; prof. Regis U., 1990—; pres. Negodianostics Ltd., Medellin, 1981-85. Adv. Colo. State Legisl. Register Health/Planning Bd., Denver, 1974-75; alt. del. Denver County Rep. Conv., 1971; del. Colo. Rep. Conv., 1990, Leadership Denver, 1975. Mem. Sacramento Women's Network (chair com. 1986), AAUW (pres. Trinidad chpt. 1989-90), Delta Sigma Pi (pres. 1975).

KLOEPFER, P(AUL) M(ICHAEL), economist, consultant, business psychologist; b. Guelph, Ont., Can., Mar. 4, 1949; came to U.S., 1985; s. Karl Joseph and Florence Mary (Kreller) K. PhD, Commonwealth U., New Hadley, Mass., 1971. Asst., aide to Senator W. M. Benidickson of Can. Kenora, Ont., Can., 1971-76; owner, chmn. The Premierre Co., St. Clair, Pa., 1985—, Premierre Clinics and Clubs, 1987—; chmn. Premierre Mgmt. Konsultants, Toronto, 1976—, Premierre Talent Reps, St. Clair, 1979—, Premierre Advt., L.A., 1985—, Premierre Fin. Consultants, St. Clair,1985—; commd. Ark. Amb. of Goodwill, 1991. Recipient Cert. of Award, Pres.'s Council Phys. Fitness and Sports, 1981; Spl. Recognition, Pres. Reagan, 1985; named to Ky. Col. Commonwealth of Ky, 1991. Home: 101-516 Ash St, New Westminster, BC Canada V3M 3N3

KLOHS, MURLE WILLIAM, chemist, consultant; b. Aberdeen, S.D., Dec. 24, 1920; s. William Henry and Lowell (Lewis) K.; m. Dolores Catherine Borm, June 16, 1946; children: Wendy C., Linda L. Student Westmar Coll., 1938-40; BSc, U. Notre Dame, 1947. Jr. chemist Harrower Lab., Glendale, Calif., 1947, Rexall Drug Co., L.A., 1947-49; sr. chemist Riker Labs., Inc., L.A., 1949-57, dir. medicinal chemistry, Northridge, Calif., 1957-69, mgr. chem. rsch. dept., 1969-72, mgr. pharm. devel. dept., 1972-73, mgr. tech. liaison and comml. devel., 1973-82; cons. chemist, 1982—. Contbr. articles to profl. jours. Served to lt. USNR, 1943-46. Riker fellow Harvard U., 1950. Mem. Am. Chem. Soc., Am. Pharm. Assn., Adventures Club (L.A.). Home and Office: 19831 Echo Blue Dr Lake Wildwood Penn Valley CA 95946

KLONTZ, JAMES MATHIAS, architect; b. Kent, Wash., May 3, 1920; s. George John and Mary Ellen (Lavin) K.; m. Angie Mary Gomes, Jan. 15, 1949; children: Melinda, Marsha, Nancy, Karen, Joyce. BArch, U. Wash., 1943. Registered arch., Wash., Alaska. Assoc. arch. Bliss Moore Jr. & Assoc., Seattle, 1946-51; prin. arch. Klontz & Assocs., Seattle, 1951—. Capt. U.S. Army, 1943-46, ETO. Mem. AIA. Office: Klontz & Assocs 4000 Aurora Ave N Seattle WA 98103-7853

KLOPFLEISCH, STEPHANIE SQUANCE, social services agency administrator; b. Rupert, Idaho, Dec. 21, 1940; d. William Jaynes and Elizabeth (Cunningham) Squance; B.A., Pomona Coll., 1962; M.S.W., UCLA, 1966; m. Randall Klopfleisch, June 27, 1970; children—Elizabeth, Jennifer, Matthew. Social worker, Los Angeles County, 1963-67; program dir. day care, vol. services Los Angeles County, 1968-71; div. chief children's services Dept. Public Social Services, Los Angeles County, 1971-73, dir. bur. of social services, 1973-79; chief dep. dir. Dept. Community Services, Los Angeles County, 1979—;with Area 10 Devel. Disabilities, 1981-82; bd. dirs. Los Angeles Fed. Emergency Mgmt. Act, 1985-91, pres., 1987; bd. dirs. Los Angeles Shelter Partnership, Pomona Coll. Assocs., 1988—. Mem. Calif. Commn. on Family Planning, 1976-79; mem. Los Angeles Commn. Children's Instns., 1977-78; bd. dirs. United Way Info., 1978-79; chmn. Los Angeles County Internat. Yr. of Child Commn., 1978-79; bd. govs. Sch. Social Welfare, UCLA, 1981-84. Mem. Nat. Assn. Social Workers, Am. Soc. Pub. Adminstrn., L.A. Philhamonic Affiliates, 1995, Soroptimist Internat. (bd. dirs. 1989—, pres. L.A. chpt. 1993).

KLOSINSKI, LEONARD FRANK, mathematics educator; b. Michigan City, Ind., July 16, 1938; s. Frank and Helen (Podgorna) K.; BS, U. Santa Clara, 1961; MA, Oreg. State U., 1963. Programmer NASA Ames Rsch. Ctr., Mountain View, Calif., 1963; instr. math. Santa Clara (Calif.) U., 1964-68, asst. prof., 1968-76, assoc. prof., 1976—; dir. Nat. Sci. Found. Insts., 1969-74; mng. editor, treas. Fibonacci Assn., 1975-80; dir. William Lowell Putnam Math. Competition, 1978—. Author: Santa Clara Silver Anniversary Contest Book/ Problems and Solutions of the University of Santa Clara High School Mathematics Contests, 1985, Students' Solutions Manual to Accompany Lynn E. Garner's Calculus and Analytical Geometry, 1988; editor: William Lowell Putnam Mathematical Competition Problems and Solutions , 1965-84, 1985; contbr. articles to profl. jours. Mem. Math. Assn. Am. (coun. on competitions 1992—, Putnam prize com. 1975—, adv. bd. Math. Horizons 1993—, sec.-treas. No. Calif. sect. 1979—). Democrat. Roman Catholic. Office: Santa Clara U Math Dept Santa Clara CA 95053

KLOTT, DAVID LEE, lawyer; b. Vicksburg, Miss., Dec. 10, 1941; s. Isadore and Dorothy (Lipson) K.; m. Maren J. Randrup, May 25, 1975. BBA summa cum laude, Northwestern U., 1963; JD cum laude, Harvard U., 1966. Bar: Calif. 1966, U.S. Ct. Claims. 1968, U.S. Supreme Ct. 1971, U.S. Tax Ct. 1973, U.S. Ct. Appeals (Fed. cir.) 1982. Ptnr. Pillsbury, Madison & Sutro, San Francisco, 1966—; mem. tax adv. group to sub-chpt. C J and K, Am. Law Inst.; tchr. Calif. Continuing Edn. of Bar, Practising Law Inst., Hastings Law Sch., San Francisco; bd. dirs. and counsel Marin Wine and Food Soc. Commentator Calif. Nonprofit Corp. Law; bd. dirs. Joan Shorenstein Barone Found. for Harvard, The Phyllis J. Shorenstein Fund for the Asian Art Mus. San Francisco; counsel Drum Found. Mem. ABA (tax exempt financing com.), Calif. State Bar Assn. (tax sect.), San Francisco Bar Assn., Am.-Korean Taekwondo Friendship Assn. (1st dan-black belt), Harvard Club, Northwestern Club, Olympic Club, City Club of San Francisco (founding mem.), Bay Club (charter mem.), Harbor Point Racquet and Beach Club, Internat. Wine and Food Soc. (bd. dirs., bd. govs. Ams.), Beta Gamma Sigma, Beta Alpha Psi (pres. local chpt.). Office: Pillsbury Madison & Sutro 235 Montgomery St Ste 1616 San Francisco CA 94104-2902

KLOTZ, SUZANNE RUTH, artist; b. Shawno, Wis., Oct. 15, 1944; d. Arthur Paul and Margaret Ruth (Pollard) K. BFA, Kansas City Art Inst., 1966; secondary art teaching cert., U. Mo., Kansas City, 1967; MFA, Tex. Tech U., 1972. tchr. art pub. secondary schs. and univs. in Ariz., Tex. and Calif.; vis. artist, Israel, 1990-91; art cons., South Australia, 1991; guest artist Mishkenot Sha'ananim, Jerusalem, 1992; vis. assoc. prof. U. Utah, Salt Lake City, 1992-93. Prin. works exhibited in numerous one-woman and group shows including Phoenix Art Mus., Mus. South Tex., Corpus Christi, Spencer Art Mus., Lawrence, Kans., Y. Tex., San Antonio, Schneider Mus. Art, Ashland, Oreg., Mesa Centennial Conf. Ctr.; childrens art unity workshops Senegal and Burkino Faso, 1995, Taipei, Taiwan, 1995; works represented in numerous collections including Nat. Mus. Am. Art, Smithsonian Instn., Baha'i World Ctr., Haifa, Israel, Minn. Mus. Art, St. Paul, many others. Craftsman fellow Nat. Endowment for Arts, 1975, 78, NEA fellow for performance and dance, 1983. Baha'i.

KLOWDEN, MARC JEFFERY, entomology educator; b. Chgo., June 6, 1948; s. Sam and Ruth (Ziskind) K.; m. Anne Janet Weitzman, Aug. 30, 1970; children: Daniel, Amanda. BS, U. Ill., Chgo., 1970, MS, 1973, PhD, 1976. Asst. entomologist U. Ga., Athens, 1976-81; asst. prof. U. Idaho, Moscow, 1981-83, assoc. prof., 1983-88, prof., 1988—. Editor Jour. of Vector Ecology; contbr. articles to profl. jours. Mem. AAAS, Entomolog. Soc. Am., Soc. Vector Ecology, Am. Soc. Zoologists, Am. Mosquito Control Assn., Sigma Xi. Office: U Idaho Div Entomology Moscow ID 83843

KLUCK, CLARENCE JOSEPH, physician; b. Stevens Point, Wis., June 20, 1929; s. Joseph Bernard and Mildred Lorraine (Helminiak) K.; divorced; children: Paul Bernard, Annette Louise Kluck Winston, David John, Maureen Ellen. BS in Med. Sci., U. Wis., 1951, MD, 1954. Resident San Joaquin Hosp., French Camp, Calif., 1955-56; asst. instr. medicine Ohio State U., Columbus, 1958-60; physician, chief of medicine Redford Med. Ctr., Detroit, 1960-69; practice medicine specializing in internal medicine Denver, 1969-83; med. dir. Atlantic Richfield Co., Denver, 1983-85; corp. med. dir. Cyprus Minerals Co., Englewood, Colo., 1985-92; pres. Kluck Med. Assocs., Englewood, 1992—; bd. dirs. Climbo Catering, Detroit, 1967-69, Met. Labs., Denver, 1970-81, Provost, Inc., Denver, 1985-92; pres., CEO, chmn. bd. Corpcare, Inc., Englewood, 1992; CEO, pres. Corpcare Med. Assocs., P.C., 1992, Denver Occupl. & Aviation Medicine Clinic, P.C., 1995—. Contbr. articles to profl. jours. Served to capt. U.S. Army, 1956-58. Recipient Century Club award Boy Scouts Am., 1972. Fellow Am. Occupational Med. Assn., Am. Coll. Occupational and Environ. Medicine, Am. Coll. Occupational Medicine; mem. Am. Acad. Occupational Medicine, Rocky Mountain Acad. Occupational Medicine (bd. dirs. 1985-88), Arapahoe County Med. Soc., Denver Med. Soc. (bd. dirs. 1973-74, council mem. 1981-87), Colo. Med. Soc. (del. 1973-74, 81-87), Am. Mining Congress Health Commn., Am. Soc. Internal Medicine, Colo. Soc. Internal Medicine. Roman Catholic. Clubs: Flatirons (Boulder, Colo.); Metropolitan. Home: 1900 E Girard Pl Englewood CO 80110-3151 Office: Ste 200 3700 Havana Denver CO 80239

KLUG, JOHN JOSEPH, secondary education educator, director of dramatics; b. Denver, Apr. 27, 1948; s. John Joseph Sr. and Dorthea Virginia (Feely) Carlyle. BA in English, U. N.C., 1974; MA in Theatre, U. Colo., 1984. Tchr. Carmody Jr. High Sch., Lakewood, Colo., 1976-78; tchr. Golden (Colo.) High Sch., 1978—, dir. of dramatics, 1978—; producer, dir. Children's Theatre Tours, 1978—; theatrical cons., 1983—; improvisational workshop leader, 1983—. Playwright, editor: Children's Theatre scripts, 1982—; producer, dir. Denver Theatre Sports, 1993—. Recipient Bravo/TCI Theatre award, 1995. Home: 4565 King St Denver CO 80211-1357 Office: Golden High Sch 701 24th St Golden CO 80401-2379

KLUGE, ARTHUR I., engineering company executive; b. 1938. BS in physics and math, Manhatten Coll., 1959; post grad., U. Calif., 1960-64. With N. Am. Rockwell Corp., Downey, Calif., 1964-68; sr. rsch. engr. Gen. Rsch. Corp., Santa Barbara, Calif., 1968-74; exec. v.p. Tecolote Rsch. Inc., Santa Barbara, Calif., 1974—. Office: Tecolote Research Inc 5290 Overpass Rd Ste D Santa Barbara CA 93111-2081*

KLUGER, MATTHEW JAY, physiologist, educator; b. Bklyn., Dec. 14, 1946; s. Morris and Gladys (Feit) K.; m. Susan Lepold, Sept. 3, 1967; children: Sharon, Hilary. BS, Cornell U., 1967; MS, U. Ill., 1969, PhD, 1970. Postdoctoral fellow Yale U., New Haven, 1970-72; asst. prof. U. Mich. Med. Sch., Ann Arbor, 1972-76, assoc. prof., 1976-81, prof. physiology, 1981-93; dir. inst. basic & applied med. rsch. The Lovelace Insts., Albuquerque, N.Mex., 1993—; vis. prof. St. Thomas' Hosp., London, 1979, U. Witwatersrand, South Africa, 1992; vis. scientist Cetus Corp., Palo Alto, Calif., 1986-87. Author: Fever: Its Biology, Evolution and Function, 1979; editl. bd. Jour. Thermal Biology, 1991—, Cytokine, 1991—, Am. Jour. Physiology, 1992—, Med. Sci. Sports Exercises, 1994—, NeuroImmuno Modulation, 1995—; author workbooks; co-editor text books. Grantee NIH, other agys. Mem. Am. Physiol. Soc., Am. Assn. Immunologists. Home: 6103 Blue Bird Ln NE Albuquerque NM 87122-1817 Office: Inst of Basic & Applied Med Rsch-The Lovelace Insts 2425 Ridgecrest Rd SE Albuquerque NM 87108

KLUGER, STEVE, writer, scriptwriter; b. Balt., June 24, 1952; s. Alan Charles and Florence Pearl (Shapiro) K. Student, U. So. Calif., 1970-71. Novelist, freelance scriptwriter and journalist, 1983—. Author: (novels) Changing Pitches, 1984, Bullpen, 1990; (nonfiction) Lawyers Say the Darndest Things, 1990, Yank: World War II From the Guys Who Brought You Victory, 1991; scriptwriter films including: Once Upon a Crime, 1992, Bye Bye Brooklyn, 1995; (plays) Bullpen, 1984, Cafe 50's, 1988, James Dean Slept Here, 1989, Jukebox Saturday Night, 1990, Plots of the Purple Twilights, 1991; (TV prodns.) Baseball, 1994, Yankee Doodle Boys, 1995. Democrat. Jewish. Office: care Sydelle Kramer Frances Goldin Agy 305 E 11th St # 3-F New York NY 10003

KLUMPH, MARK JON, electrical engineer; b. Memphis, Mar. 31, 1958; s. John F. and Berniece Faye (Huff) K.; m. Cheryl Ann Don, Feb. 22, 1986; children: Richard Anthony, Michael Jon. Student, Grossmont Coll., 1980-82, San Diego State U., 1984-86. From elec. tech. to sys. specialist Megatek Corp., San Diego, 1977-87; engr., owner True Images, San Diego, 1987—; engr., site mgr. Logicon, Inc., San Diego, Oklahoma City, 1988-92; engr., field engr. Oncor Instrument Sys. (formerly Am. Innovision), San Diego, 1992—. Mem. Soc. Mfg. Engrs. (Electronics Mfg. com., Computer and Automated Sys. com.), Machine Vision Assn. Office: Oncor Instument Sys 9581 Ridgehaven Ct San Diego CA 92123-1624

KLUSMIRE, JON DALTON, editor, writer; b. Aspen, Colo., June 4, 1956; s. Newton Eldo and Jeanette (Munroe) K.; children: Devin Wilkinson, Ansel, Mariah. BA, Western State Coll., 1980. Mem. advt. staff Central Phoenix Sun, 1980-81; reporter, bur. mgr. The Weekly Newspaper, Glenwood Springs, Colo., 1982-83, editor, 1983-86; media dir., staff writer/editor Rocky Mountain Inst., Snowmass, Colo., 1986-89; editor Trilogy Mag., Glenwood Springs, Colo., 1989-93; We. Colo. corr. Colo. Bus. mag., Lakewood, 1993—; columnist, editor Aspen (Colo.) Times, 1993—. Author: Colorado, A Compass American Guidebook, 1991; co-author: The Sacred Circle: A Healing Way for the Sickness of Alcoholism, 1992, Resource Efficient Housing Guide, 1987; editor: Financing Economic Renewal, 1988, Business Opportunities Casebook, 1988; contbr. articles and poetry to various publs. Bd. dirs. Sta. KDNK Pub. Radio, Carbondale, Colo., 1987-88, Garfield County United Way, 1989-91. Recipient 1st pl. Best News Story, Colo. Press Assn., 1982, 1st pl. Spot News, 1993, 3d pl. Best Coverage of Energy, Nat. Newspaper Assn., 1986. Home: 405 22nd Ln # 3B Glenwood Springs CO 81601-4355 Office: Aspen Times Box E Aspen CO 81612

KLYCINSKI, FREDERICK ALLEN See ALLEN, RICK

KMET, REBECCA EUGENIA PATTERSON, pharmacist; b. Ellisville, Miss., June 17, 1948; d. Eugene Roberts and Ruth Winn (Pettis) Patterson; m. Joseph Paul Kmet, Mar. 29, 1969. BS in Pharmacy, U. Ariz., 1971; MBA, Nat. U., 1981. Pharmacist Santa Monica (Calif.) Bldg. Profl. Pharmacy, 1972-73, Vets. Hosp., West Los Angeles, Calif., 1973-74, Kaiser Med. Ctr., San Diego, Calif., 1979-82, Farmersville Drug Store, Farmersville, Calif., 1991—. Community svc. vol. Lt. USN, 1975-78. Recipient Presdl. Achievement award Rep. Party Nat. Congl. com. Mem. Wilson Assoc., Navy League, Naval Hist. Found., Marine Corps Hist. Found., U.S. English, Am. Immigration Control Fedn., Rho Chi, Kappa Epsilon, NSDAR. Independent. Episcopalian. Home: 985 Murphy Dr Lemoore CA 93245-2181

KMETOVICZ, RONALD EUGENE, new product development educator, writer; b. May 31, 1947; m. Suzanne Marie Daley (div.); children: Kristyn, Cherisa; m. Gayle Anselmo. BSEE, Pa. State U., 1969; MSEE, Santa Clara U., 1978. Radio frequency/microwave engr. Goodyear Aerospace, Phoenix, 1969-72; hardware and software engr. Hewlett-Packard, Palo Alto, Calif., 1972-78, engring. mgr., 1978-88; founder, pres. Time to Market Assocs., Verdi, Nev., 1988—; cons. Sematech, Austin, 1988—; bus. advisor high tech. cos., 1988—. Author: New Product Development, 1992, It's About Time, 1994; author (column) Kmet's Korner in Elec. Design mag., 1990—; contbr. articles to mags. Mem. IEEE. Office: Time to Market Assocs PO Box 1070 Verdi NV 89439-1070

KNAPP, CLEON TALBOYS, business executive; b. Los Angeles, Apr. 28, 1937; s. Cleon T. and Sally (Brasfield) K.; m. Elizabeth Ann Wood, Mar. 17, 1979; children: Jeffrey James, Brian Patrick, Aaron Bradley, Laura Ann. Student, UCLA, 1955-58. With John C. Brasfield Pub. Corp. (purchased co. in 1965, changed name to Knapp Comm Corp. 1977, sold to Condé Nast Publs. in 1993); pres. Talwood Corp., Knapp Found., L.A.; Bd. dirs., bd. trustees Santa Fe Opera, Fulfillment Fund, Mus. Contemporary Art, L.A. County Mus., Craft and Folk Art Mus., chmn. bd. trustees; bd. visitors John E. Anderson Grad. Sch. of Mgmt., UCLA; chmn. bd. trustees Art Ctr. Coll. Design. Mem. Bel Air Country Club, Regency Club, Country Club of the Rockies, Eagle Springs Golf Club. Office: Talwood Corp 10100 Santa Monica Blvd Ste 20 Los Angeles CA 90067-4003

KNAPP, DONALD EUGENE, gastroenterologist; b. Burlington, Iowa, Aug. 17, 1931. Grad., Western Ill. U., 1955-58; MD, U. So. Calif., 1962. Diplomate Am. Bd. Internal Medicine, Am. Bd. Gastroenterology. Intern Valley Med. Ctr., Fresno, Calif., 1962-63, resident in internal medicine, 1963-65, chief med. resident, 1965-66; fellow in gastroenterology Valley Med. Ctr. and Mt. Sinai Hosp., Fresno and L.A., 1966-67; chmn. dept. medicine Valley Med. Ctr., Fresno, 1972-88, pres. attending staff, 1976-78, mem. active tchg. staff, 1967—; instr. of medicine UCLA, 1970-74; from asst. to assoc. clin. prof. medicine U. Calif., San Francisco, 1976-82; gastroenterologist Digestive Disease Cons. Corp., Fresno; mem. active staff St. Agnes Hosp. and Med. Ctr., 1967—, Fresno Cmty. Hosp. and Med. Ctr., 1967—. Trustee Cmty. Hosps. of Ctrl. Calif., 1988—; bd. med. quality assurance, chmn. Ninth Dist. Med. Quality Rev. Com., 1976-85; bd. dirs. Valley Med. Ctr. Found., 1971-80, Fresno Found. for Med. Care, 1975-80, Fresno-Madera PSRO, 1977-80, Fresno Cmty. Hosp. and Med. Ctr., 1987; v.p. Ctrl. Calif. Blood Bank, 1976—, pres. 1995. With USN, 1951-55. Mem. AMA, ACP, Am. Gastroent. Assn., Am. Soc. for Gastroent. Endoscopy, Calif. Med Assn. (del. 1975-87, jud. commn. 1982-87), Fresno-Madera Med. Soc. (pres. 1974, chmn. prof. rels. com. 1982-87), Am. Soc. Internal Medicine, Calif. Soc. Internal Medicine, Fresno Soc. Internal Medicine (pres. 1981-83). Office: Digestive Disease Cons 110 N Valeria St Ste 505 Fresno CA 93701-2168

KNAPP, EBER GUY, accountant; b. Seattle, Sept. 18, 1916; s. Eber G. and Ernestine C. (Venter) K.; m. M. Lorraine Knapp, July 2, 1947; children: Candyce Lorraine, Ardyce Christine, Carol Lynn. Student, Wilson's Bus. Coll., 1938-39, U. So. Calif., 1946-47. Accredited in acctg. Owner, Knapp's Tax & Bus. Svc., Westminster, Calif., 1959—; overall coordinator Orange County (Calif.) Am. Assn. Ret. Persons Tax-Aide Program, 1979-88. Mem. Vice chmn. Mobile Home Commn., Westminster, Calif. Served with U.S. Army, 1941-45. Mem. Am. Legion, Calif. Assn. Ind. Accts. (charter), Nat. Assn. Pub. Accts., Westminster C. of C. (life, hon.), VFW. Republican. Mem. Christian Ch. Home: 7152 Santee Ave PO Box 1 Westminster CA 92684

KNAPP, THOMAS EDWIN, sculptor, painter; b. Gillette, Wyo., Sept. 28, 1925; s. Chester M. and Georgia Mabel (Blankenship) K.; m. Dorothy Wellborn; children: Gordon, Kathy, Dan, Kent, Keith. Student, Santa Rosa Jr. Coll., 1952-53; A.A., Calif. Coll. Arts and Crafts, 1953-54; student, Art Ctr. Sch., Los Angeles, 1954-55. Animation artist Walt Disney Studios, Burbank, Calif., 1954-56, Portrait & Hobby Camera Shops, WyoFoto Studies, Cody, Wyo., 1956-64; owner Rocky Mountain Land Devel. Corp., Cody, Wyo., 1965-66; comml. artist Mountain States Telephone Co., Albuquerque, 1966-69; lectr. at art seminars. Exhibited one-man shows, Cody County Art League, 1968, Jamison Gallery, Santa Fe, 1969, Mesilla Gallery, 1971, Inn of Mountain Gods, Mescalero Apache Reservation, N.Mex., Mountain Oyster Club, Tucson, joint shows, Rosquist Gallery, Tucson, (with Michael Coleman), Zantman Gallery, Palm Desert Calif.; one and two person shows nationally with Dorothy Bell Knapp through 1988; group shows, Saddleback Inn, Santa Ana, Calif., Zantman Gallery, Carmel, Calif., Borglum Meml. Sculpture Exhbn. Nat. Cowboy Hall of Fame, Oklahoma City, 1975-76, Maxwell Gallery, San Francisco, 1975; represented permanent collections, Whitney Gallery Western Art, Cody, Senator Quinn Meml. Auditorium, Spencer, Mass., Heritage Mus., Anchorage, Indpls. Mus. Art, Mescalero Tribe, N.Mex.; works include Dance of the Mountain Spirits (Blue Ribbon award 1976), Laguna Eagle dancer (spl. award 1974, Blue Ribbon Los Angeles Indian Art Show, 1975-76), Santa Clara Buffalo dancer (Spl. award San Antonio Indian Nat. show 1974, Spl. award Los Angeles Indian show 1976), Mandan chieftan (Spl. award San Diego Indian show 1974, Spl. award Los Angeles Indian show 1976); commd. to sculpt bronze statue of Tex. ranger Capt. Bill McMurrey, now in Tex. Ranger Mus., San Antonio, bronze Giant Galapagos Tortoise in collection of Gladys Porter Zoo, Brownsville, Tex., Meijer Found., Grand Rapids, Mich., El Paso Mus. of Art, Mus. of Native Am. Cultures, Spokane, Wash., Cherokee Nat. Hist. Mus., Talequah, Okla., Diamond M. Found. Mus., Snyder, Tex., Buffalo Bill Hist. Ctr., Cody, Wyoming; Tex. Ranger (horseback) in bronze installed El Paso Mus. Art, 1989; commissioned giant Galapagos Tortoise in bronze for installation Sculpture Pk., Loveland, Colo., 1990, 13-foot bronze endangered salt water crocodile for Gladys Porter Zoo, Brownsville, Tex., 1990, heroic size bronze commd. for Rose Bowl, Tournament of Roses, 1992, heroic size Cahuilla Indian woman The Reed Gatherer, Waring Plaza, Palm Desert, Calif. Active Boy Scouts Am., 1947-68, World Wildlife Fund. Served with USN, World War II, Korea. Decorated Air medal; recipient Order Arrow award Boy Scout Am., 1968. Mem. Mensa, N.Y. Zool. Soc. Home and Office: PO Box 510 Ruidoso Downs NM 88346-0510

KNAUFF, HANS GEORG, physician, educator; b. Bad Hersfeld, Germany, July 8, 1927; s. Friedrich and Sophie (Sauer) K.; student U. Erlangen, 1947-49, U. Freiburg, 1949, U. Basel, 1949-51, U. Heidelberg, 1951-52; Dr. Med., U. Heidelberg, 1953; m. Sigrid W. Keppner, Aug. 28, 1956; children—Ursula v. Wrangel, Barbara K. Asst., pharmacology dept. Heidelberg (W. Ger.) U., 1953; with pharmacology dept. Univ. Coll., London, 1953, Royal Coll. Surgeons, London, 1954; with Pathol. Inst., Heidelberg U., 1955, Med. Clinic, U. Munchen, 1955-63; privat dozent for internal medizin Mü nchen and Marburg, 1961-67; prof. internal medizin, 1967; prof. Med. Clinic, U. Marburg (W. Ger.), 1967-83. Served with German Air Force, 1943-45. Mem. Deutsche Gesellschaft fü r Innere Medizin, Gesellschaft fur Verdauungs und Stoffwechselkrankheiten. Mem. Evangelical Luth. Ch. Contbr. articles to sci. jours. Home: 2155 Westhill Wynd, West Vancouver, BC Canada V7S 2Z3

KNEBEL, JACK GILLEN, lawyer; b. Washington, Jan. 28, 1939; s. Fletcher and Amalia Eleanor (Rauppius) K.; m. Linda Karin Ropertz, Feb. 22, 1963; children: Hollis Anne (dec.), Lauren Beth. BA, Yale Coll., 1960; LLB, Harvard U., 1966. Bar: Calif. 1966, U.S. Dist. Ct. (no. dist.) Calif. 1966, U.S. Ct. Appeals (9th cir.) 1966. Assoc. McCutchen, Doyle, Brown & Enersen, San Francisco, 1966-74, ptnr., 1974-94, of counsel, 1994—; bd. dirs. San Francisco Lawyers Com. for Urban Affairs, 1980-81, mem. exec. com., 1991-93; mem. adv. coun. Hastings Coll. Trial Advocacy, San Francisco, 1981-91, chair, 1990-91. Bd. dirs., pres. Orinda (Calif.) Assn., 1972-74, Sea Ranch (Calif.) Assn., 1978-79; co-chmn. Citizens to Preserve Orinda, 1983-85. Lt. (j.g.) USN, 1960-66. Fellow Am. Coll. Trial Lawyers (mem. com. on fed. rules civ. pro 1990-93); mem. ABA, Maritime Law Assn. of U.S. Democrat. Mem. United Ch. of Christ. Home: 5 Tarabrook Dr Orinda CA 94563-3120 Office: McCutchen Doyle Brown & Enersen Three Embarcadero Ctr San Francisco CA 94111

KNECHT, BEN HARROLD, surgeon; b. Rapid City, S.D., May 3, 1938; s. Ben and Ona K.; m. Jane Bowles, Aug. 27, 1961; children: John, Janelle. BA, U. S.D., 1960; MD, U. Iowa, 1964. Diplomate Am. Bd. Surgery. Intern Los Angeles County Gen. Hosp., 1964-65; resident in surgery U. Iowa Sch. Medicine, Iowa City, 1968-72; surgeon Wenatchee (Wash.) Valley Clinic, 1972—; dir. emergency rm. Ctrl. Wash. Hosp., Wenatchee, 1972-79, chief surgery, 1983-86; chmn. claims rev. panel Wash. State Med. Assn., Seattle, 1979—, profl. liability com. risk mgmt., 1985-90; clin. assoc. prof surgery U. Wash.; mem. adv. risk mgmt. com. Wash. State Physicians Ins. Subscribers, 1990—, regional adv. com. Nat. Libr. Medicine, 1991-93. Fundraiser Cen. Wash. Hosp. Found., 1987; del. Gov.'s Conf. on Librs., 1991. Lt. comdr. USN, 1965-68, Vietnam. Mem. AMA (alt. del. 1985-87, del. 1988—, surg. caucus exec. com. 1991-94), ACS (bd. dirs. Wash. chpt. 1981-84), North Pacific Surg. Assn., Wash. State Med. Assn. (trustee 1980—), Chelan-Douglas County Med. Soc., Rotary (chmn. youth com. 1976-78). Office: Wenatchee Valley Clinic 820 N Chelan Ave Wenatchee WA 98801-2028

KNEE, RICHARD ALAN, journalist; b. Chgo., Apr. 8, 1946; s. Aaron David Knee and Eva (Wolff) Sachs; m. Carolyn Becker, Sept. 17, 1988. BA in Journalism, Calif. State U., Northridge, 1972. Cert. C.C. tchr., Calif. Reporter Valley News, Van Nuys, Calif., 1969-73; pub. info. officer L.A. Harbor Coll., Wilmington, Calif., 1973-75; pub. rels. instr. East L.A. Coll., Monterey Park, Calif., 1975-78; copy editor Valley News, Van Nuys, 1978-80, Daily Rev., Hayward, Calif., 1980-81; mng. editor Daily Comml. News, San Francisco, 1981-84; assoc. editor Am. Shipper, San Francisco, 1984—. Bd. dirs. San Francisco Press Club, 1986-88. With U.S. Army, 1964. Mem. Soc. Profl. Journalists (bd. dirs. No. Calif. chpt., v.p. 1990-91, pres. 1991-93). Office: Am Shipper 5 3rd St Ste 1114 San Francisco CA 94103-3210

KNEEBONE, ALICE JEANNETTE, child care coordinator; b. Boulder, Colo., July 28, 1956; d. John William and Miriam Alice (Alcorn) K. AS in Med. Assistance, Parks Coll., 1981. Proof operator, asst. supr. Nat. State Bank, Boulder, 1975-80; child care coord. Mothers of Presch. Children, Boulder, 1982—, Moments with Mothers, Boulder, 1992—; child care coord. Doorways Internat., Inc., Boulder, 1982—, bd. dirs. officer; sec., shipping and receiving mgr. Video Accessory Corp., Boulder, 1984-91; office mgr. Arapahoe Chiropractic Clinic, Boulder, Colo., 1991-92; Home Day Care, 1992—; child care lead tchr. Joy of Living, 1st Presbyn. Ch., 1993—. Author ednl. materials for working mothers; dancer, co-leader Polynesian Dance Troop, 1974—, Hawaiian-Tahitian Dance Troop, 1989—. Tchr. Sunday sch. 1st Presbyn. Ch., Boulder, 1980—; med. asst. blood bank Health Fair, Boulder, 1983; election judge Boulder County Clk. and Recorder Office, 1992—; vol. asst. Home Health Care, 1992—; vol. preparation com. Vacation Bible Sch. Mem. Nat. Assn. Med. Assts., Boulder Assn. Med. Assts., 1st Priority Christian Singles, 20/30 Something Christian Singles Social Club, 20/30 Something Christian Singles (Bible Study), Neighborhood Eco-Cycle Block (asst. to coord.), Ivy Rebekah Lodge (jr. past noble grand of ivy 1993, elevator fund raising 1991—, rep. to dist. 8 odd fellows orgn., chmn. hosp./shut-in visitation, program com. 1991-92, bereavement com. 1992-93, mem. program com., 1994, del. to Colo. assembly, 1994, mem. auditing com. 1995), Odd Fellows (UN pilgrimage for youth fund raising 1992—, elevator fund raising 1991—, delgate to internat. order, 1993—). Republican. Office: Internat 1st Presbyn Ch Boulder Moments with Mothers/Doorways 1820 15th St Boulder CO 80302-5412 also: Calvary Bible Evang Free Ch Mothers of Presch Children 3245 Kalmia Ave Boulder CO 80301-1804 also: Arapahoe Chiropractic Clinic 2500 Broadway St Boulder CO 80304-4111

KNEESE, GEORGE VERNON, city manager; b. Fallon, Nev., June 9, 1944; s. George August and Lavern Mervel (Walton) K.; m. Susan Jane Kneese, Dec. 28, 1968; children: Alyce Lowenstein, Shepheard B. Glass. Student, Portland C.C., 1988, 89. Storm and sanitary sewer sys. foreman Granite Constrn. Co., Gardnerville, Nev., 1968-70; pipe crew supr. Boise Cascade Constrn. Co., Hayward, Calif., 1970-7; sewer-storm pipe crew laborer-foreman McSween Constrn. Co., Lake Tahoe, Nev., 1977-83; sewer maintenance supr. Dept. Pub. Works City of Hillsboro, 1983—; presenter Hillsboro City Hall, 1989, , City of Hillsboro, 1992-93, Am. Pub. Works Assn., Wilsonville, 1990-93, Oreg. Waste Water Collection Pers. Sect., North Bend, 1991, Roseburg, 1990, Clackamas C.C., 1993, 94; mem. regional steering com., command sys., ops. ICS, 1995; instr. basic skills course II & III, FEMA, 1994-95, exercise design course Earthquake Mgmt. Course, 1994. Mem. Oreg. Coun. on Alcoholism and Drug Addiction, 1984—; pres. Wash. County Boosters Club, 1992; v.p. Wash. County Rodeo Bd., 1990-91. Mem. Am. Pub. Works Assn., Am. Water Works Assn., Water Environment Fedn., Pacific N.W. Pollution Control Assn., Profl. Rodeo Cowboys Assn. Republican. Office: City of Hillsboro 123 W Main St Hillsboro OR 97123

KNEPP, GERALD EVERETT, hospital director; b. La Harpe, Kans., Jan. 21, 1934; s. Alvin Lester, Wilma Manetta (Johnson) K.; m. Tona Louise Shanks, Sept. 1, 1961 (div. May 1982); children—Kristopher Karsten, Karla Kristin (dec.); 1 stepchild, Steven Lynn York. B.S.B.A., U. Kans., 1956; M.P.A., U. Mo., 1971. Asst. controller St. Lukes Hosp., Kansas City, Mo., 1961-62; assoc. adminstr. North Kansas City Mem. Hosp., 1962-74; sr. cons. Peat-Marwick-Mitchell, 1974-75; adminstr. Panorama Community Hosp., Calif., 1975-80, Western Park Hosp., Los Angeles, 1980, Redding Med. Ctr., Calif., 1980—; preceptor masters program U. So. Calif., Los Angeles, 1970-80; bd. dirs. Downtown Hosp., Kansas City, 1974-76. Contbr. articles to profl. jours. Exec. sec. County Indigent Med. Fund, Clay County, Mo., 1965-75; mem. Gov.'s Adv. Council on Drug and Alcoholism, Planning Council Adv. Com., Shasta County Mental Health Adv. Com.; bd. dirs. Greater Redding C. of C. Served to capt. USAF, 1956-59. Recipient Disting. Service award Mo. Jaycees, 1968, Outstanding Young Man award 1968, Outstanding Young Man Am. award, 1970, Circle of Excellence award Nat. Med. Enterprises, Inc., 1985, 88. Mem. Hosp. Council No. Calif. (Blue Cross adv. com. 1982—, fin. and econ. com. 1982—), Healthcare Fin. Mgmt. Assn. (pres. 1968-69) (Follmer award 1968, Reeves award 1972, Muncie award 1978), Hosp. Council So. Calif. (bd. 1979-80), Am. Hosp. Assn., SAR. Republican. Methodist. Lodges: Rotary, Elks, Masons, Shriners. Home: 1620 E Willow Dr Apt 203 Olathe KS 66062-1854 Office: Mountain Home Health 393 Ridgecrest Circle Clayton GA 30525

KNIERIM, ROBERT VALENTINE, electrical engineer, consultant; b. Oakland, Calif., Sept. 27, 1916; s. Otto Valentine and Edith May (Bell) K.; m. Esther Perry Bateman, July 10, 1954; children: Kathleen Dianne, David Lyell, Daniel Goddard. BS, U. Calif., Berkeley, 1941; postgrad., U. Pitts., 1942, U. Colo., 1944-45, Raytheon Field Engring Sch, 1945. Registered profl. elec. engr., Calif. Student engr. Westinghouse Corp., East Pittsburgh, Pa., 1942; marine elec. engr. U.S. Maritime Commn., Oakland, 1943-44; elec. engr. U.S. Bur. Reclamation, Denver, 1944-45, Sacramento, 1945-48; field engr. Raytheon Corp., Waltham, Mass., 1945; electronics engr. Sacramento Signal Depot, 1948-49; assoc. elec. engr. Calif. Office Architecture and Constrn., 1949-57, sr. elec. engr., 1957-76; cons. engring., 1976. Mem. Century Club of Golden Empire Coun. Boy Scouts Am., 1969-87, instnl. rep. 1948-54, dist. chmn., camping and activities com. 1951-54; mem. Cascade Pacific Coun. Boy Scouts of Am. 1987—. Recipient James E. West Fellowship award Boy Scouts of Am., 1994. Mem. Sacramento Engrs. Club (charter), IEEE (sr., life), Nat. Rifle Assn. (life), Sierra Club (life, chpt. treas. 1962-65), Nat. Assn. Corrosion Engrs. (life), Calif. Alumni Assn. (life), Eta Kappa Nu, Alpha Phi Omega (life). Republican. Congregationalist. Lodge: Masons. Home and Office: Cons Elec Engring 10325 SW Ashton Circle Wilsonville OR 97070-9532

KNIGHT, CAROL BELL, author, lecturer, clergyperson; b. Girard, Kans., June 14, 1924; d. August William and Ethel Marie (Knight) Vilmure; m. William Porter Kinney, June 12, 1953 (div. 1971); children: David, Paul, Sheina. BA, Kans. State Tchrs. Coll., Pittsburg, 1947; DD, Kans. Meth. Sem., Topeka, 1950. Ordained to ministry United Ch. of Religious Sci., 1983. Founding dir. The Forum Found., Santa Fe, 1979—; minister The Forum Celebration, Santa Fe, 1990-93; world seminars with the Forum Found., Eng., Sweden, Denmark, Norway, Switzerland, Ireland, Can., U.S., 1990—; planner New Alexandrian Libr. Author: Passing the Torch, 1985, Thought Has Wings, 1990, Saturation: A Prosperity Manual, 1993, The Holy Place, 1994, Vortex of Fire, 1994, Soul Search, 1995. Mem. Inst. of Noetic Scis., Internat. New Thought Assn. Office: The Forum Found PO Box 5915 Santa Fe NM 87502

KNIGHT, CONSTANCE BRACKEN, writer, realtor, interior decorator, corporate executive; b. Detroit, Oct. 30, 1937; d. Thomas Francis and Margaret (Kearney) Bracken; m. James Edwards Knight, June 14, 1958 (div. Feb. 1968); children: Constance Lynne Knight Campbell, James Seaton, Keith Bracken. Student, Barry Coll., 1955-56, Fla. State U., 1958-60; AA, Marymount Coll., 1957. Columnist, feature writer Miami Herald, Ft. Lauderdale, Fla., 1954-55, 79-80; pub. rels. dir. Lauderdale Beach Hotel, 1965-67; columnist, feature writer Ft. Lauderdale News/Sun-Sentinel, 1980-81; owner Connie Knight and Assoc. Pub. Rels., Ft. Lauderdale, 1981-85; editor, pub. Vail (Colo.) Mag., 1986-89, contbg. freelance writer, 1989—; editorial cons. Vail Valley Mag., 1993; pres. Knight Enterprises, Vail, 1994—; instr. Colo. Mountain Coll., Vail, 1979; copywriter Colo. Ski Mus., Vail, 1986—. Mem. Planning and Environ. Commn., Vail, 1990-92. Mem. Soc. Profl. Journalists, N.Am. Ski Journalists (treas. 1990-93). Office: 5197 Black Gore Dr Vail CO 81657-5425

KNIGHT, EDWARD HOWDEN, retired hospital administrator; b. Vancouver, B.C., Can., Apr. 13, 1933; s. Edward Allen and Helen Blackley (Howden) K.; m. Glenda Carol Wiggins, Mar. 6, 1964; children: Carolyn, Patricia, Brett. B of Commerce, diploma in hosp. adminstrn., U. B.C., 1956. Adminstrv. asst. Vancouver Gen. Hosp., 1956-57; adminstr. Prince Rupert Gen. Hosp., 1957-61, Red Deer Gen. Hosp., 1961-72, Dr. Richard Parsons Aux. Hosp., 1963-72, Valley Park Manor Nursing Home, 1969-72; dep. exec. dir. Calgary (Alta.) Gen. Hosp., 1972-74, exec. dir., 1974-83, pres., 1983-88; pres. E.H. Knight & Assocs. Inc., Calgary, 1988-92; lectr. Red Deer Coll., 1968-72; adj. asst. prof. faculty medicine U. Calgary, 1978-91; trustee Alta. Blue Cross Plan, 1963-68; mem. Fed. Task Force on Cost of Health Services in Can., 1969. Recipient Queen's Silver Jubilee medal, 1977. Fellow Can. Coll. of Health Service Execs. (dir. 1972-74, founding charter mem.), Am. Coll. Healthcare Execs. (regent for Alta. 1973-76, 79-82); mem. Can. Hosp. Assn. (dir. 1981-83), Alta. Hosp. Assn. (dir. 1977-84, pres. 1983), Assn. Can. Teaching Hosps. (pres. 1986-87), Phi Delta Theta. Clubs: Red Deer, Kinsmen (pres. 1971-72), Glencoe. Lodge: Rotary. Home: 820 Windridge Cir San Marcos CA 92069-7917

KNIGHT, FRANK JAMES, medical sciences liaison; b. L.A., July 17, 1947; s. George Orlando Jr. and Virginia Clarabelle (Seig) K.; m. Mary Jane Vargo, Aug. 7, 1977 (div. July 1989); children: Cheryl Lynne, Michael Scott; m. Barbara Lorrene Garlick, June 19, 1993. BS, Okla. State U., 1970. Mktg. rep. Mobil Oil Corp., N.Y.C., 1971-73; sales rep. Monarch Crown Corp., N.Y.C., 1974-78; territory mgr. V.H. Monette, Inc., Smithfield, Va., 1978-81; profl. rep. Dermik Labs., Blue Bell, Pa., 1981-83; assoc. med. scis. liaison Sandoz Pharms., East Hanover, N.J., 1983—. Capt. U.S. Army, 1970. Mem. Harley Owners Group. Home: 14807 Velvet St Chino Hills CA 91709-2070 Office: Sandoz Pharms Corp 59 State Route 10 East Hanover NJ 07936-1011

KNIGHT, JANE MILLER, nurse-midwife, air force officer; b. Hampton, Va., Oct. 8, 1950; d. Donald Alexander and Elizabeth Harriet (Wilgus) Miller; m. David Ray Knight, Nov. 12, 1988. BSN, Med. Coll. Va., 1972; MA in Guidance and Counseling, Hampton (Va.) Inst., 1984. RN, Va.; cert. nurse-midwife. Staff nurse Mary Immaculate Hosp., Newport News, Va., 1972, Potomac Hosp., Woodbridge, Va., 1973, N.E. Bapt. Hosp., San Antonio, 1973-74, Hampton Gen. Hosp., 1974-76; commd. 1st lt. USAF, 1976, advanced through grades to lt. col., 1993; staff nurse USAF Hosp., Barksdale AFB, La., 1976-78; staff nurse, midwife USAF Hosp., Langley AFB, Va., 1979-84; instr. USAF Nurse-Midwifery program Malcolm Grow USAF Med. Ctr., 1984-91; staff nurse-midwife 416th Med. Group, Griffiss AFB, N.Y., 1991-94; speaker on women's health issues; workshop leader. Decorated Air Force Commendation medal, Meritorious Svc. medal. Mem.

Assn. Women's Health, Obstetric and Neonatal Nurses, Am. Coll. Nurse-Midwives, Air Force Assn., Am. Soc. Psychoprophylaxis in Obstetrics. Episcopalian. Home: 10210 Raygor Rd Colorado Springs CO 80908-4806

KNIGHT, JANET ANN, elementary education educator; b. Covina, Calif., July 22, 1937; d. Arnold M. and Thelma (Lyle) Ostrum; m. Ronald L. Knight, Sept. 14, 1957; children: Barbara Lynne, Susan Kaye. BA in Edn., Cen. Wash. U., 1979; MA in Edn., Heritage Coll., 1992. Cert. elem. secondary tchr., Wash. 2nd grade tchr. Kennewick (Wash.) Pub. Schs., 1980-81, 1st grade tchr., 1981-85, 3rd grade tchr., 1985-93, 4th grade tchr., 1993—; lang. arts dist. com. Kennewick Sch. Dist., 1985-89, curriculum, instrn. com., 1989-92, dist. curriculum and instruction renewal cycle for learning excellence, 1992-94, dist. assessment com., 1992—. Mem. Richland (Wash.) Light Opera Co., 1963-75. Mem. NEA, ASCD, Wash. Edn. Assn., Kennewick Edn. Assn., Wash. Orgn. Reading Devel., Benton County Coun. of Internat. Reading Assn., Order of Rainbow for Girls, Sigma Tau Alpha. Episcopalian. Home: 120 Heather Ln Richland WA 99352-9155 Office: Westgate Elem Sch 2514 W 4th Ave Kennewick WA 99336-3115

KNIGHT, JEFFREY RICHARD, systems requirements analyst; b. Salt Lake City, Apr. 22, 1962; s. Richard M. and Donna H. (Hallman) K.; m. Carrie Lyn Jackson. BBA, Calif. State Poly. Inst. U., 1984, MBA, 1986. With Unisys, Camarillo, Calif., 1985—; pres. Co. Activities Coordinating Com., Camarillo, 1991-93. Treas. Hillcrest Park Home Owners Assn., 1990-92, pres., 1992-93; chmn. Calif. State Poly. Inst. U. Rose Float Com., 1984-85. Mem. Co. Mgmt. Assn., Thailand Darts Assn., Rose Float Alumni Assn. (treas. 1985-86, bd. dirs. 1987-88, pres. 1991-93, historian/archivist 1994—), Gold Coast Chpt. of the Nat. Employee Svcs. and Recreation Assn. (pres. 1994—). Republican. Home: 2143 Saxe Ct Thousand Oaks CA 91360-3148 Office: Unisys 5151 Camino Ruiz Camarillo CA 93012-8601

KNIGHT, JEFFREY WILLIAM, publishing and marketing executive; b. Rome, Dec. 20, 1949; s. William Edwards and Ruth Leila (Lee) K.; m. Susan M. Dail, May 23, 1987; 1 child, Charlotte. BA, Yale U., 1971; JD, Catholic U., 1978. Bar: DC 1978. Nat. campaign staff McGovern for Pres., Washington, 1972; asst. legis. dir. Friends of the Earth, Washington, 1973-75, legis. dir., 1976-78; adminstrv. dir. Friends of the Earth, San Francisco, 1978-80, conservation dir., 1980-81, exec. dir., 1981-85; pub. ComputerLand Mag., Pleasanton, Calif., 1985-93; dir. direct mktg. Vanstar Corp. (formerly ComputerLand Corp.), Pleasanton, 1991-95, dir. product mktg., 1995—; dir. mktg. Computers 800 Catalog, 1995—; bd. dirs. Small Press Distbn., Inc., Berkely, Calif. Contbr.: Progress as if Survival Mattered, 1979, Ten Years of Not Man Apart, 1979. Dir. Child and Family Therapy Ctr., Concord, Calif. Mem. DC Bar Assn. Home: 4128 Gilbert St Oakland CA 94611-5114

KNIGHT, JOSEPH ADAMS, pathologist; b. Provo, Utah, Dec. 22, 1930; s. John Clarence and Martha Maude (Adams) K.; m. Pauline Brown, Oct. 18, 1949; children: David Paul, Leigh Knight Smith. BS in Chemistry, Brigham Young U., 1955, MS in Organic Chemistry, 1957; MD, U. Utah, 1963. Diplomate Am. Bd. pathology; lic. Utah, Calif., Nev., Wyo. Intern U. Utah Hosp., Salt Lake City, 1963-64, residency in pathology, 1964-67; instr. pathology Sch. Medicine U. Utah, Salt Lake City, 1966-67, clin. instr. pathology, 1967-70; assoc. pathologist Holy Cross Hosp., Salt Lake City, 1967-70; asst. clin. prof. pathology Sch. Medicine U. Utah., Salt Lake City, 1970-75; assoc. Health Svcs. Corp., Salt Lake City, 1969-75; assoc. pathologist Santa Rosa Med. Ctr., San Antonio, 1975-76; assoc. clin. prof. pathology Sch. Medicine U. Tex., San Antonio, 1975-76; dir. clin. labs. Primary Children's Med. Ctr., Salt Lake City, 1976-79; assoc. clin. prof. Sch. Medicine U. Utah, Salt Lake City, 1977-79, assoc. prof. pathology, 1979-88, prof. pathology, 1988—; assoc. chmn. pathology, head div. edn. VA Med. Ctr., Salt Lake City, 1986—, chief lab. svc., 1990—; vis. prof. pathology Sch. Medicine U. Conn., Farmington, 1985-86; mem. admissions com. Sch. Medicine U. Utah, 1981-82, chmn. pathology residency com., 1980-85, co-chmn. pathology residency com., 1987-90, mem. grad. sch. com. Sch. Med. Technologists U. Utah, 1981-85. Author: (with others) Laboratory Examination of Cerebrospinal, Synovial and Serous Fluids: A Textbook Atlas, 1982, Body Fluids: A Textbook Atlas, 2nd ed., 1986 , 3d edit., 1993; reviewer Clin. Chemistry, 1971, 77, 84, 86—; contrbr. articles to profl. jours. Served with U.S. Navy, 1948-52, Korea. Fellow Am. Soc. Clin. Pathologists, Coll. Am. Pathologists, Nat. Acad. Clin. Biochem.; mem. AMA, Am. Assn. Clin. Chemists, Utah Soc. Pathologists (pres. 1968-70, 79-80), Am. Bd. Pathology (test com. 1987-92), Am. Soc. Clin. Pathology (editorial rev. bd. 1987—, numerous others com.), Assn. Clin. Scientists (mem. com. 1985—, v.p. 1995), Coll. Am. Pathologists (inspector 1978—), Alpha Omega Alpha. Republican. Mormon. Office: U Utah Sch Medicine Dept Pathology 50 N Medical Dr Salt Lake City UT 84132-0001

KNIGHT, PATRICIA MARIE, optics researcher; b. Schnectady, N.Y., Jan. 25, 1952; d. Donald Orlin and Mary Ann (Rooney) K. BS in Engring. Sci., Ariz. State U., 1974, MS in Chem. Engring., 1976; PhD in Biomed. Engring., U. Utah, 1983. Teaching and rsch. asst. Ariz. State U., Tempe, 1974-76; product devel. engr. Am. Med. Optics, Irvine, Calif., 1976-79, mgr. materials rsch., 1983-87; rsch. asst. U. Utah, Salt Lake City, 1979-83; dir. materials rsch. Allergan Med. Optics, Irvine, 1987-88, dir. rsch., 1988-91, v.p. rsch., devel. and engring., 1991—; Contbr. articles to profl. jours. Mem. Soc. Biomaterials, Am. Chem. Soc., Soc. Women Engrs., Assn. Rsch. in Vision and Opthalmology, Biomed. Engring. Soc. Office: Allergan Med Optics 9701 Jeronimo Rd Irvine CA 92718-2020

KNIGHT, PHILIP H(AMPSON), shoe manufacturing company executive; b. Portland, Oreg., Feb. 24, 1938; s. William W. and Lota (Hatfield) K.; m. Penelope Parks, Sept. 13, 1968; children: Matthew, Travis. B.B.A., U. Oreg.; M.B.A., Stanford U. C.P.A., Oreg. Chmn., chief exec. officer, past pres. Nike, Inc., Beaverton, Oreg., 1967—. Bd. dirs. U.S.-Asian Bus. Coun., Washington, 1st lt. AUS, 1959-60. Named Oreg. Businessman of Yr., 1982, One of 1988's Best Mgrs., Bus. Week Magazine. Mem. AICPA. Republican. Episcopalian. Office: Nike Inc 1 SW Bowerman Dr Beaverton OR 97005-0979*

KNIGHT, ROBERT EDWARD, banker; b. Alliance, Nebr., Nov. 27, 1941; s. Edward McKean and Ruth (McDuffee) K.; m. Eva Sophia Youngstom, Aug. 12, 1966. BA, Yale U., 1963; MA, Harvard U., 1965, PhD, 1968. Asst. prof. U.S. Naval Acad., Annapolis, Md., 1966-68; lectr. U. Md., 1967-68; fin. economist Fed. Res. Bank of Kansas City (Mo.), 1968-70, research officer, economist, 1971-76, asst. v.p., sec., 1977, v.p., sec., 1978-79; pres. Alliance (Nebr.) Nat. Bank, 1979-94, also chmn., 1983-94; pres. Robert Knight Assocs., banking and econ. cons., Cheyenne, 1979—; vis. prof., chair banking and fin. E. Tenn. State U., Johnson City, 1988; mem. faculty Stonier Grad. Sch. Banking, 1972—, Colo. Grad. Sch. Banking, 1975-82, Am. Inst. Banking, U. Mo., Kansas City, 1971-79, Prochnow Grad. Sch. Banking, U. Wis.; mem. Coun. for Excellence for Bur. Bus. Rsch. U. Nebr., Lincoln, 1991-94, mem. Grad. Sch. Arts & Scis Coun., Harvard, 1994—; chmn. Taxable Mcpl. Bondholders Protective Com., 1991-94. Trustee, 1984-85, Knox Presbyn. Ch., Overland Park, Kans., 1965-69; bd. regents Nat. Comml. Lending Sch., 1980-83; mem. Downtown Improvement Com., Alliance, 1981-94; trustee U. Nebr. Found.; bd. dirs. Stonier Grad. Sch. Banking, Box Butte County Devel. Commn., Nebr. Com. for Humanities, 1986-90; mem. coun. for excellence for the Bur. of Bus. Rsch. U. Nebr., 1991; mem. fin. com. United Meth. Ch., Alliance, 1982-85, trustee, 1990-93; Box Butte County Indsl. Devel. Bd., 1987-94; mem. Nebr. Com. for the Humanities, 1986-90; amb. Nebr. Diplomats. Woodrow Wilson fellow, 1963-64. Mem. Am. Econ. Assn., Am. Fin. Assn., So. Econ. Assn., Nebr. Bankers Assn. (com. state legis. 1980-81, com. comml. loans and investments 1986-87), Am. Inst. Banking (state com. for Nebr. 1980-83), Am. Bankers Assn. (econ. adv. com. 1980-83, community bank leadership coun.), Western Econ. Assn., Econometric Soc., Harvard Grad. Sch. of Arts & Scis. Coun., Rotary, Masons. Contbr. articles to profl. jours. Home: 429 W 5th Ave Cheyenne WY 82001-1249 Office: 429 W 5th Ave Cheyenne WY 82001-1249

KNIGHT, THOMAS JOSEPH, history educator; b. Denton, Tex., Aug. 5, 1937; s. Thomas Daniel Knight and Laura Jo (Savage) Knight Myrick; m. Barbara Lorraine Jones, Dec. 29, 1955; children: Russell Alan, Karen Jeanne. BA, North Tex. State U., Denton, 1959; postgrad., U. Minn., 1959-61; PhD, U. Tex., 1967. Instr. history U. Nebr., Lincoln, 1964-65; asst. prof. humanities Mich. State U., East Lansing, 1966-68; asst. prof., then assoc. prof. Pa. State U., Harrisburg, 1968-76; assoc. dean, prof. social scis. Pa. State U., University Park, 1976-82; dean, prof. history U. W.Va., Morgantown, 1982-86, Colo. State U., Ft. Collins, 1986—; cons. Orgn. Econ. Coop. and Devel., Paris, 1982. Author: Latin America Comes of Age, 1979, Technology's Future, 1982. Trustee Univ. Press Colo., Niwot, 1989—. Mem. World History Assn., Nat. Assn. Sci., Tech. and Society, Am. Acad. Polit. and Social Sci., Phi Alpha Theta. Democrat. Unitarian. Home: 2006 Brookwood Dr Fort Collins CO 80525-1212 Office: Colo State U Dept History Fort Collins CO 80523

KNIGHT, VICK, JR. (RALPH KNIGHT), dean, education educator, counselor; b. Lakewood, Ohio, Apr. 6, 1928; s. Vick Ralph and Janice (Higgins) K. BS, U. So. Calif., 1952; MA, L.S. State Coll., 1956; postgrad. Whittier Coll., 1959-61, Long Beach State Coll., 1960-61, Calif. State Coll.-Fullerton, 1961-64, Claremont U., 1963-65; EdD, Calif. Coast U., 1991; m. Beverly Joyce McKeighan, Apr. 14, 1949 (div. 1973); children: Stephen Foster, Mary Ann; m. Carolyn Schlee, June 6, 1981; children: Kathy, Meri. Producer-dir. Here Comes Tom Harmon radio series ABC, Hollywood, Calif., 1947-50; tchr., vice-prin. Ranchito Sch. Dist., Pico Rivera, Calif., 1952-59; prin. Kraemer Intermediate Sch., Placentia, Calif., 1959-64; dir. instructional svcs. Placentia Unified Sch. Dist., 1964-65, asst. supt., 1965-71; program dir. World Vista Travel Svcs., 1970-72; bd. dir. grad. extension La Verne Coll., 1971-73; v.p. Nat. Gen. West Investments, 1971-74; bd. dir. community rels. and devel. Childrens Hosp. of Orange County (Calif.), 1974-84; sr. dir. curriculum and edn. svcs. Elsinore Union High Sch. Dist., Lake Elsinore, Calif., 1985-88; exec. dir. Elsinore Valley Community Devel. Corp., 1989-92; dean Sch. Edn. Newport U., Newport Beach, Calif., 1992—; pres. Aristan Assocs.; bd. dirs. Key Records, Hollywood. Dist. chmn. Valencia Coun. Boy Scouts Am.; chmn. Cancer Soc. Ptnrs. of Ams., also chmn. Sister City Com.; chmn. Community Chest Drives; chmn. adv. com. Esperenza Hosp.; mem. Educare; hon. life mem. Calif. PTA. Bd. dirs. U. Calif.-Irvine Friends of Library, pres., 1975-77; bd. trustees Lake Elsinore Unified Sch. Dist., 1991, pres. 1993; bd. dirs. Muckenthaler Cultural Groups Found.; chmn. bd. William Claude Fields Found. Club With USN, 1946-48. Recipient Disting. Citizen award Whittier Coll., 1960; Educator of Yr. award Orange County Press Club, 1971, Author and Book award U. Calif., 1973, Children's Lit. award Calif. State U.-Fullerton, 1979, Bronze Pelican award Boy Scouts Am.; named Canyon Lake Man of the Yr., 1994. Mem. Nat. Sch. Pub. Rels. Assn. (regional v.p.), U.S. Jr. C. of C. (bd. dir., Young Man of Calif. 1959), Calif. Jr. C. of C. (state v.p.), Pico Rivera Jr. C. of C. (pres.), Audubon Soc., Western Soc. Naturalists, Calif. Tchrs. Assn., NEA, Internat. Platform Assn., ASCAP, Soc. Children's Book Writers, Authors Guild, Authors League Am., Anti-Slubberdegullion Soc., Bank Dicks, Assn. Hosp. Devel., Art Experience, Good Bears of World, Los Compadres con Libros, Blue Key, Skull and Dagger, Les Amis du Vin, Phi Sigma Kappa, Alpha Delta Sigma, E Clampus Vitus, Theta Nu Epsilon, Kiwanian (pres.), Mason, Canyon Lake Home Owners Club (pres. 1989-91), West Atwood Yacht (commodore) Club. Writer weekly Nature Notebook newspaper columns, 1957—, wine columnist Riverside Press-Enterprise, 1991—; fine arts editor Placentia Courier; editor curriculum guides: New Math., Lang. Arts, Social Scis., Pub. Rels., Biol. Sci. Substitute Tchrs; author: (ecology textbooks) It's Our World; It's Our Future; It's Our Choice, Snakes of Hawaii, Earle the Squirrel, Night the Crayons Talked; My Word!; Send for Haym Salomon!. Joby and the Wishing Well; Twilight of the Animal Kingdom; A Tale of Twos, Who's Zoo, A Navel Salute, Friend or Enema?, John Sevier: Citizen Soldier, also math. instrn. units; contbr. articles to various jours. Home: 22597 Canyon Lake Dr S Canyon Lake CA 92587-7595

KNIGHT, WILLIAM J. (PETE KNIGHT), state legislator, retired military officer; b. Noblesville, Ind., Nov. 18, 1929; s. William T. and Mary Emma (Illyes) K.; m. Helena A Stone, June 7, 1958; children: William Peter, David, Stephen; m. Gail A. Johnson, Sept. 3, 1983. BS, Air Force Inst. Tech., 1958; student, Indsl. Coll. Armed Forces, 1973-74. Commd. 2d lt. USAF, 1953, advanced through grades to col., 1971; fighter pilot Kinross AFB, Mich., 1953-56; exptl. test pilot Edwards AFB, Calif., 1958-69; exptl. test pilot, Viet Nam, 1969-70; dir. test and deployment F-15 program, 1976; dir. Flight Attack System Program Office, 1977-79; vice comdr. Air Force Flight Test Ctr. Edwards AFB, 1979-82; ret. USAF, 1982; mayor City of Palmdale, Calif., 1988-92; elected rep. Calif. State Assembly, 1992—; v.p. Eidetics Internat., Torrance, Calif., 1988-92. Decorated D.F.C. with 2 oak leaf clusters, Legion of Merit with 2 oak leaf clusters, Air medal with 11 oak leaf clusters, Astronauts Wings; recipient Octave Chanute award, 1968, Harmony trophy, 1968, citation of honor Air Force Assn., 1969; winner Allison Jet Trophy Race, 1954;p named to Nat. Aviation Hall of Fame, 1988, Lancaster Aerospace Walk of Honor, 1990. Fellow AIAA (assoc.), Soc. Exptl. Test Pilots (past pres.); mem. Air Force Assn., Internat. Order of Characters, Aerospace Primus Club, Daedalians, Elks. Holder world's speed record for winged aircraft, 4520 m.p.h., 1967. Home: 220 Eagle Ln Palmdale CA 93551-3613 Office: 2196 State Capital Sacramento CA 95814

KNITTLE, WILLIAM JOSEPH, JR., media executive, psychologist, religious leader, management and marketing consultant; b. Santa Monica, Calif., June 11, 1945; s. William Joseph Knittle and Lahlee (Duggins) Morrell; m. Linda Catherine Black, Apr. 19, 1969 (div. Aug. 1977); 1 child, Kristen Elizabeth; m. Alexis Carrell Upton, Sept. 30, 1977; 1 child, Jonathan Kynan. BA in English, Loyola U., Los Angeles, 1966, MA in Communication Arts, 1970, MA in Counseling Psychology, 1973; PhD in Communication Theory and Social Psychology, Lawrence U., Santa Barbara, Calif., 1976; D of Dharma in Asian Religion and Philosophy, U. Oriental Studies, 1980; MBA, U. La Verne, 1983. Ordained Sramanera, Buddhist monk, 1976, ordained Bikkhu, 1977. Assoc. editor Black Belt mag., 1960-65; asst. news dir. Sta. KHJ-TV, Los Angeles, 1966-67; news editor Sta. KFWB Radio, Los Angeles, 1967-69; dir. news and pub. info. Loyola Marymount U., Los Angeles, 1969-75; gen. mgr. Media Five, Los Angeles, 1976-79, v.p., 1981-83; assoc. dir. div. of continuing edn. U. La Verne, Calif., 1979-81; pres. Western News Assocs., Los Angeles, 1983—; asst. to dean UCLA Sch. Medicine, 1985-86; advt./mktg. dir. summer sessions UCLA, 1986—; founder Realization Therapy, 1977. Author: Survival Strategies for the Classroom Teacher, 1982; columnist various newspapers, mags., 1970—; Hollywood corr. Columbia mag., 1974-87; contbr. articles to profl. jours. Asst. abbot Internat. Buddhist Med. Ctr., L.A., 1976-81; bd. mem. Dharma Vijaya Buddhist Vihara, L.A., 1985—; mem. So. Calif. Buddhist Sangha Coun., L.A. Buddhist Union. Recipient Martial Arts Pioneer award Am. Tae Kwon Do-Kung Fu Assn., 1976, Nat. Headliners award Wash. Press Club, 1968, Internat. Journalism award Sigma Delta Chi, 1968. Mem. AAAS, Assn. for Transpersonal Psychology, Inst. for Holistic Edn., Soc. Interdisciplinary Study of Mind, Internat. Brotherhood of Magicians, Internat. Imagery Assn., Am. Soc. Tng. and Devel., Nat. Book Critics Circle, Investigative Reporters and Editors, Am. Fedn. Police (chaplain 1985—), Nat. Police Acad. Home and Office: Western News Assocs PO Box 24130 Los Angeles CA 90024-0130

KNOBELOCH, JAMES JOSEPH, actor; b. Belleville, Ill., Mar. 18, 1950; s. Lester Irvin and Ruth Marsella (Fields) K.; m. Beth Sullivan, Oct. 17, 1992. BA in Art, Theatre, So. Ill. U., 1972; MFA, Ohio State U., 1975. Series regular Duncan Watts "Trials of Rosie O'Neill" CBS, L.A., 1990-92, series regular as Jake Slicker "Dr. Quinn, Medicine Woman", 1992—; founding mem. Mirror Repertory Theatre, N.Y.C., 1982-84, Powerhouse Repertory Theatre, L.A., 1992; mem. Actor's Alley Repertory Theatre, L.A., 1990-93, Theatre West, L.A., 1989-93. Mem. Farm Sanctuary, Ohio, 1992-94. Mem. SAG, Acotr's Equity Assn.

KNOEPFLER, GAYLE STEWART, sex therapist; b. Bottineou, N.D., Mar. 8, 1934; d. Alfred Earnest and Lois (Stewart) Kurth; m. Peter Tamas Knoepfler, July 3, 1960; children: David, Daniel, Paul. MS, Yeshiva U., 1960; PhB, U. N.D., 1957. Cert. sex therapist, mental health counselor, Wash. Caseworker ARC, St. Louis, Wichita Falls, Tex., Colorado Springs, Colo., 1957-59; copy writer KTRN, Wichita Falls; high sch. history tchr. A.B. Davis High Sch., Mt. Vernon, N.Y., 1959-61; sex educator Planned Parenthood, Seattle and Bellevue, Wash., 1972-82; sex educator, pvt. practice Bellevue, 1975—, sex therapist, 1975—, group therapist, 1975—; co-founder sex info. telephone line, Planned Parenthood, Seattle/King Co., 1979-81. Contbr. articles to profl. jours. State bd. dirs. LWV, Utah, 1968, eastside bd. dirs., Washington, 1971-72; chmn. bd. dirs., dean Unitarian/Eliot Inst., Pacific N.W. Dist., 1973, 89, 92; east shore ch. bd. mem. Unitarian Ch., Bellevue, 1993-95; chmn. Puget Sound Unitarian Coun., Seattle, 1980-82; precinct chmn. 41st Dist. Dem. Party. Vol. of Yr. Planned Parenthood Seattle, 1980. Mem. Am. Assn. Sex Education Therapists (chmn. dist. conv. 1983), Soc. for Scientific Study of Sex (conv. co-chair 1993). Unitarian. Office: 1621 114th Ave SE Ste 221 Bellevue WA 98004-6905

KNOEPFLER, PETER TAMAS, psychiatrist, organizational consultant; b. Vienna, Austria, Mar. 14, 1929; came to U.S., 1947, naturalized, 1962; s. Joseph and Claire (Farkas) K.; m. Gayle Kurth, July 3, 1960; children: David, Daniel, Paul. B.S., Calif. Inst. Tech., 1950; M.A., Columbia U., 1951; M.D., Cornell U., 1955. Diplomate Am. Bd. Psychiatry and Neurology. Intern Meth. Hosp. of Bklyn., 1955-56; resident Albert Einstein Coll. Medicine, N.Y.C., 1956-57, 59-61; practice medicine specializing in psychiatry Bellevue, Wash., 1970—; assoc. med. dir. U. Utah Student Health Service, Salt Lake City, 1962-69; staff psychiatrist Menninger Found., Topeka, 1969-70; mem. faculty Menninger Sch. Psychiatry, 1969-70; med. dir. Eastside Community Health Center, Bellevue, 1970-73; mem. staff Fairfax Hosp., Kirkland, Wash., Overlake Hosp., Bellevue, Snoqualmic Valley Hosp.; clin. assoc. prof. psychiatry and behavioral scis. U. Wash., Seattle, 1970-79; clin. prof. psychiatry U. Wash., 1979—; adj. faculty Union Grad. Sch., Yellow Springs, Ohio, 1974—, Antioch West, 1979—; lectr., cons. in field; instr. Am. Group Psychotherapy Ann. Inst., 1976-79; cons. AEC, 1966-68, Planned Parenthood of Bellevue, 1971—, Youth Eastside Services, Bellevue, 1970—, Rosehill Inst., Toronto, Ont., Can., 1973—, Peace Corps, 1964-66, Little Sch. Bellevue, 1972-74, Juvenile Ct. Kings County, Wash., 1972—, Skid Road Community Council, Seattle, 1973-76, Rice Inst., 1975—; mem. exec. med. com. Planned Parenthood Seattle, King County, 1974—. Editorial bd.: Adolescent Psychiatry, 1974—, Jour. Sex Edn. and Therapy. Mem. adv. bd. Solo Ctr., Seattle, 1974-77; mem. Radio Emergency Associated Citizens Team, 1977-79; bd. dirs. Eliot Inst., Friends of King County Libr., Seabeck Christian Conf. Group, Unitarian Universalist Assn., vice chmn., 1975-77; group leader Dean Ornish Retreat, 1995. Served to capt. M.C. USAF, 1957-59. Recipient Vol. of Yr. award Planned Parenthood of King County, 1980; named Physician of Yr., 1974, Citizen of Day. Fellow Am. Psychiat. Assn. (life), Am. Soc. Adolescent Psychiatry (life, exec. com. 1973-75); mem. Soc. Sci. Study Sex (pres. western region 1989), Am. Assn. Sex Educators, Counsellors and Therapists (dir. 1979-84, treas. N.W. region 1976-79), Am. Soc. Clin. Hypnotists, Internat. Soc. Adolescent Psychiatry (sci. adv. com.), Am. Group Psychotherapy Assn. (dir. 1979-81), N.W. Group Psychotherapy Assn. (pres. 1978-81), N.W. Soc. Adolescent Psychiatry (pres. 1973-75), Internat. Assn. Yoga Therapists, Preventive Medicine Rsch. Inst. (Dean Ormish Group 1995). Office: 1201 116th Ave NE #9 Bellevue WA 98004

KNOLLER, GUY DAVID, lawyer; b. N.Y.C., July 23, 1946; s. Charles and Odette Knoller; children: Jennifer Judy, Geoffrey David. BA cum laude, Bloomfield (N.J.) Coll., 1968; JD cum laude, Ariz. State U., 1971. Bar: Ariz. 1971, U.S. Dist. Ct. Ariz. 1971, U.S. Sup. Ct. 1976. Trial atty. atty. gen.'s honor program Dept. Justice, 1971-72; atty., adv., NLRB, 1972-73, field atty. region 28, Phoenix, 1972-74; assoc. Powers, Ehrenreich, Boutell & Kurn, Phoenix, 1974-79; ptnr. Froimson & Knoller, Phoenix, 1979-81; sole practice, Phoenix, 1981-84; ptnr. Fannin, Terry & Hay, P.A., 1984-85; sole practice, Phoenix, 1985—; of counsel Burns & Burns. Mem. bd. visitors Ariz. State U. Coll. Law, 1975-76; pres. Ariz. Theatre Guild, 1990, 91. Fellow Ariz. Bar Found.; mem. ABA, State Bar Ariz. (chmn. labor relations sect. 1977-78), Ariz. State U. Coll. Law Alumni Assn. (pres. 1977). Office: 3550 N Central Ave Ste 1401 Phoenix AZ 85012-2112

KNOOP, VERN THOMAS, civil engineer, consultant; b. Paola, Kans., Nov. 19, 1932; s. Vernon Thomas and Nancy Alice (Christian) K. Student, Kans. U., 1953-54; BSCE, Kans. State U., 1959. Registered profl. engr., Calif. Surveyor James L. Bell, Surveyors and Engrs., Overland Park, Kans., 1954; engr. asst. to county engr. Miami County Hwy. Dept., Paola, 1955; engr. State of Calif. Dept. Water Resources, L.A., 1959-85, sr. engr., 1986-88; chief, water supply evaluations sect. State of Calif. Dept. Water Resources, L.A., Glendale, 1989—; hydrology tchr. State of Calif. Dept. Water Resources, L.A., 1984; mem. Interagency Drought Task Force, Sacramento, 1988-91. Mem. Jefferson Ednl. Found., Washington, 1988-91, Heritage Found., Washington. 1988—, Nat. Rep. Senatorial Com., Washington, 1990—, Rep. Presdl. Task Force, Washington, 1990-91. With U.S. Army, 1956-57. Decorated Good Conduct medal U.S. Army, Germany, 1957. Mem. ASCE (dir. L.A. sect. hydraulics/water resources mgmt. tech. group 1985-86, chmn. 1984-85), Profl. Engrs. in Calif. Govt. (dist. suprs. rep. 1986—), Am. Assn. Individual Investors (life), Singles Internat. Baptist. Home: 116 N Berendo St Los Angeles CA 90004-4711 Office: State of Calif Dept Water Resources 770 Fairmont Ave Glendale CA 91203-1035

KNOPF, KENYON ALFRED, economist, educator; b. Cleve., Nov. 24, 1921; s. Harold C. and Emma A. (Underwood) K.; m. Madelyn Lee Trebilcock, Mar. 28, 1953; children—Kristin Lee, Mary George. A.B. magna cum laude with high honors in Econs., Kenyon Coll., 1942; M.A. in Econs.; Ph.D., Harvard U., 1949; LLD (hon.), Kenyon Coll., 1993. Mem. faculty Grinnell Coll., 1949-67, prof. econs., 1960-67, Jentzen prof., 1961-67, chmn. dept., 1958-60, chmn. div. social studies, 1962-64, chmn. faculty, 1964-67; dean coll. Whitman Coll., Walla Walla, Wash., 1967-70; prof. econs. Whitman Coll., 1967-89, Hollon Parker prof. econs., 1985-89, prof. emeritus, 1989—, provost, 1970-81, dean faculty, 1970-78, acting pres., 1974-75; pub. interest dir. Fed. Home Loan Bank, Seattle, 1976-83; mem. council undergrad. assessment program Ednl. Testing Service, 1977-80. Author: (with Robert H. Haveman) The Market System, 4th edit, 1981; A Lexicon of Economics, 1991; editor: Introduction to Economics Series (9 vols.), 1966, 2d edit., 1970-71; co-editor: (with James H. Strauss) The Teaching of Elementary Economics, 1960. Mem. youth coun. City of Grinnell, 1957-59; bd. dirs. Walla Walla United Fund, 1968-76, pres., 1973; mem. Walla Walla County Mental Health Bd., 1968-75; mem. Walla Walla CSC, 1978-84, chmn., 1981-84; councilman City of Grennell, 1964-67; pres. Walla Walla County Human Svcs. Adminstrv. Bd., 1975-77; mem. Iowa adv. coun. SBA; tax aide AARP/IRS Tax Counseling for Elderly, 1987—, local coord., 1990-91, assoc. dist. coord. S.E. Wash., 1991-94, assoc. dist. coord. tng., 1994—; bd. dirs. Shelter Bay Cmty., Inc., 1995—. With USAAF, 1943-46. Social Sci. Rsch. Coun. grantee, 1951-52. Mem. Am. Conf. Acad. Deans (exec. com. 1970-77, chmn. 1975), Am. Econ. Assn., Indsl. Rels. Rsch. Assn., Am. Assn. Ret. Persons, Kiwanis, Phi Beta Kappa, Delta Tau Delta. Office: 223 Skagit Way La Conner WA 98257-9602

KNOPOFF, LEON, geophysics educator; b. L.A., July 1, 1925; s. Max and Ray (Singer) K.; m. Joanne Van Cleef, Apr. 9, 1961; children—Katherine Alexandra, Rachel Anne, Michael Van Cleef. Student, Los Angeles City Coll., 1941-42; B.S. in Elec Engring, Calif. Inst. Tech., 1944, M.S. in Physics, 1946, Ph.D. in Physics, 1949. Asst., then assoc. prof. physics Miami U., Oxford, Ohio, 1948-50; mem. faculty UCLA, 1950—, prof. physics, 1961—, prof. geophysics, 1959—, rsch. musicologist, 1963—; assoc. dir. Inst. Geophysics and Planetary Physics, 1972-86; prof. geophysics Calif. Inst. Tech., 1962-63, research assoc. seismology, 1963-64; vis. prof. Technische Hochschule, Karlsruhe, Germany, 1966, Harvard U., 1972, U. Chile, Santiago, 1973; Chmn. U.S. Nat. Upper Mantle Com., 1963-71; sec. Internat. Upper Mantle Com., 1963-71; chmn. com. math. geophysics Internat. Union Geodesy and Geophysics, 1971-75; mem. Internat. Union Geodesy and Geophysics (U.S. nat. com.), 1973-75; vis. prof. U. Trieste, 1984. Recipient Wiechert medal German Geophys. Soc., 1978; Gold medal Royal Astron. Soc., 1979; NSF sr. postdoctoral fellow Cambridge (Eng.) U., 1960-61; Guggenheim Found. fellow, 1976-77; Selwyn Coll. Cambridge U. fellow. Fellow AAAS, Am. Acad. Arts and Scis., Royal Astron. Soc. (Jeffreys lectr.), Am. Geophys. Union (Gutenberg lectr. 1992), Nat. Acad. Scis., Seismol. Soc. Am. (hon., medal 1990); mem. Am. Phys. Soc., Am. Philosophical Soc. Office: U Calif Dept Physics Los Angeles CA 90024

KNORR, TOM JOHNSON, cultural organization administrator; b. Wichita, Kans., June 24, 1935; s. William Hayes and Margaret Ruth (Johnson) K. BS in Bus., Kans. U., 1958; MDiv, Seabury-Western Sem., 1966. Ordained to ministry Episcopal Ch. as priest, 1966. Priest Diocese Kans., Wichita, 1966-71; pvt. practice in psychotherapy Denver, 1980-93; exec. dir. Capitol Hill United Neighborhoods, Inc., Denver, 1993—; also bd. dirs. Capitol Hill United Neighborhoods, Inc.; Bd. dirs. Our House, Denver, 1991-92. Maj. USAF, 1971-80. Republican. Episcopalian. Home: 950 Pearl St Denver CO 80203-3214 Office: Capitol Hill United Neighborhoods Inc 1490 Lafayette St Ste 201 Denver CO 80218-2392

KNOTT, DONALD JOSEPH, golf course architect; b. Alameda, Calif., Apr. 11, 1946; s. Lester Joseph and Erna (Bell) K.; m. Victoria Susan Graves, Sept. 55, 1979 (div. 1994); children: Austin A., Alexander C. B Landscape Architecture, U. Calif., Berkeley, 1969, MArch, 1973. Registered, lic. landscape arch., Calif. Sr. v.p. Robert Trent Jones II Inc., Palo Alto, Calif., 1973—, R.T. Jones II Internat., Palo Alto, 1973—. Designer over 60 golf courses worldwide. 1st lt. U.S. Army, 1969-71, Vietnam. Mem. Am. Soc. Golf Course Archs. (bd. dirs. 1984—, exec. com. 1990-94, treas. 1991, sec. 1992, v.p. 1993, pres. 1994). Office: Robert Trent Jones II Inc 705 Forest Ave Palo Alto CA 94301-2102

KNOTT, RUSSELL H., food products executive; b. 1917. With Knott's Berry Farm, Buena Park, Calif., 1935—. Office: Knott's Berry Farm 8039 Beach Blvd Buena Park CA 90620-3225*

KNOTT, SYDNEY SULLIVAN, public relations executive; b. Santa Barbara, Calif., Oct. 16, 1956; d. Warren Arthur and Thelma Nadine (Adkins) Sullivan; m. Martin R. Wilson, Aug. 18, 1979 (div. July 1986); m. John J. Knott II, Sept. 4, 1988. AB in Pub. Relations, U. So. Calif., 1978. Mgr. dept. May Co., San Diego, 1979-80; acct. exec. Stoorza, Ziegaus & Metzger, San Diego, 1980-82; specialist pub. relations U.S. Dept. Treasury, Washington, 1983-84; acct. exec. Braun & Co., Los Angeles, 1984-85; dir. fin. Calif. Repub. Com., Burbank, Calif., 1985-86; dir. pub. relations Katersky Fin., Woodland Hills, Calif., 1987; v.p. Casey & Sayre, Inc., Malibu, Calif., 1987-94; mng. dir. Katz & Assocs., Inc., Las Vegas, 1994-95; prin. The PR Group, Las Vegas, 1995—; cons. Knott Communications, Los Angeles, 1987. Coord. campaign Gibson for Assembly, Huntington Beach, Calif., 1978; press asst. Pete Wilson for U.S. Senate, San Diego, 1982; network liaison Reagan for Pres. GOP Conv., Dallas, 1984. Mem. Pub. Rels. Soc. Am. (La. chpt. PRISM award for outstanding cmty. rels. program 1988, Silver Anvil award 1992), Nat. Assn. Real Estate Editors (assoc.), Jr. League (bd. dirs. 1986-87), Downtown Las Vegas Partnership, Comml. Mktg. Group. Office: The PR Group Ste 131 333 No Rancho Dr Las Vegas NV 89106

KNOTT, WILEY EUGENE, electronic engineer; b. Muncie, Ind., Mar. 18, 1938; s. Joseph Wiley and Mildred Viola (Haxton) K.; 1 child, Brian Evan. BSEE, Tri-State U., 1963; postgrad. Union Coll., 1970-73, Ga. Coll., 1987. Assoc. aircraft engr. Lockheed-Ga. Co., Marietta, 1963-65; tech. publs. engr. GE, Pittsfield Mass., 1965-77, sr. publs. engr., 1977-79, group leader, 1967-79; specialist engr. Boeing Mil. Airplane Co., Wichita, Kans., 1979-81, sr. specialist engr., 1981-84, 89-90, logistics mgr., 1984-85, customer support mgr., 1985-89; base mgr. Castle AFB, 1990-91; facilities plant ops. and maintenance engr. Everett (Wash.) div. Boeing Comml. Airplane Group, 1991-92, lead engr. 1992-93, prin. engr., 1993-95; part-time bus. cons., 1972—. Active Jr. Achievement, 1978-79, Am. Security Coun., 1975-90, Nat. Rep. Senatorial Com., 1979-86 , Nat. Rep. Congl. Com., 1979-87, Rep. Nat. Com., 1979-87 , Rep. Presdl. Task Force, 1981-86, Joint Presdl./Congl. Steering Com., 1982-86, Rep. Polit. Action Com., 1979-86, Mus. of Aviation, 1987-95; state advisor U.S. Congl. Adv. Bd., 1981-86; adviser Jr. Achievement, 1978-79. With AUS, 1956-59. Mem. Am. Def. Preparedness Assn. (life), Am. Mgmt. Assn., Soc. Logistics Engrs., U.S. Golf Assn. (assoc.), Fraternal Order Police (assoc.), Am. Fedn. Police (assoc.), Am. Assn. Retired Persons, Air Force Assn. (life), Assn. Old Crows, Boeing Mgmt. Club, Nat. Audubon Soc. Methodist.

KNOTT, WILLIAM ALAN, library director, library management and building consultant; b. Muscatine, Iowa, Oct. 4, 1942; s. Edward Marlan and Dorothy Mae (Holzhauer) K.; m. Mary Farrell, Aug. 23, 1969; children: Andrew Jerome, Sarah Louise. BA in English, U. Iowa, 1967, MA in L.S., 1968. Asst. dir. Ottumwa (Iowa) Pub. Libr., 1968-69; libr. cons. Iowa State Libr., Des Moines, 1968-69; dir. Hutchinson (Kans.) Pub. Libr. and S. Cen. Kans. Libr. System, Hutchinson, 1969-71; dir. Jefferson County Pub. Libr., Lakewood, Colo., 1971—. Served with U.S. Army, 1965-67. Mem. ALA, Colo. Libr. Assn. Author: Books by Mail: A Guide, 1973; co-author: A Phased Approach to Library Automation, 1969; editor: Conservation Catalog, 1982. Office: Jefferson County Pub Libr 10200 W 20th Ave Lakewood CO 80215-1402

KNOWLES, JAMES KENYON, applied mechanics educator; b. Cleve., Apr. 14, 1931; s. Newton Talbot and Allyan (Gray) K.; m. Jacqueline De Bolt, Nov. 26, 1952; children: John Kenyon, Jeffrey Gray, James Talbot. SB in Math., MIT, 1952, PhD, 1957; DSc (hon.), Nat. U. Ireland, 1985. Instr. math. MIT, Cambridge, 1957-58; asst. prof. applied mechanics Calif. Inst. Tech., Pasadena, 1958-61, assoc. prof., 1961-65, prof. applied mechanics, 1965—, William R. Kenan, Jr. prof., 1991—; vis. prof. MIT, 1993-94; cons. in field. Contbr. articles to profl. jours. Recipient Eringen medal Soc. Engring. Sci., 1991. Fellow ASME, Am. Acad. Mechanics. Home: 522 Michillinda Way Sierra Madre CA 91024-1066 Office: Calif Inst Tech Div Engring & Applied Sci 104-44 1201 E California Pasadena CA 91125-0001

KNOWLES, RICHARD THOMAS, state legislator, retired army officer; b. Chgo., Dec. 20, 1916; s. John T. and Signe (Almcrantz) K.; m. Elizabeth Wood Chaney, 1974; children: Diane T. Knowles Buchwald, Katherine T. Knowles Buck, Rebecca T. Knowles Crosby, Richard J., Stanley W. Crosby III, Steven W. Chaney. Student, U. Ill., 1938-42; student Command and Gen. Staff Coll., Armed Forces Staff Coll., 1956, U.S. Army War Coll., 1959. Commd. 2d lt. U.S. Army, 1942, advanced through grades to lt. gen., 1970; exec., bn. comdr. 96th F.S. Bn., Far East Command, 1950-51; student, then instr. Command and Gen. Staff Coll., Ft. Leavenworth, Kan., 1951-55; chief budget and plans br. Office Dep. Chief of Staff, Personnel, U.S. Army, Washington, 1956-58; chief Establishments Bur., Hdqrs. U.S. Army Element, SHAPE, 1959-60, mil. asst. Chief of Staff, 1960-62; comdg. officer 3d U.S. Army Missile Command, Ft. Bragg, N.C., 1962-63; div. arty. comdr., asst. div. comdr. 11th Air Assault Div., Ft. Benning, Ga., 1963-65; asst. div. comdr. 1st Cav. Div., (airmobile), Ft. Benning, Vietnam, 1965-66; chief of staff II Field Force, Vietnam, 1966; comdg. gen. 196th Light Inf. Brigade, Vietnam, 1966-67, Task Force Oregon, Vietnam, 1967; asst. dep. chief of staff for mil. operations U.S. Army, Washington, 1967-70; asst. to chmn. Joint Chiefs of Staff, Washington, 1970-72; comdg. gen. I Corps ROK/US Group, Korea, 1972-73; dep. comdr. 8th Army, Korea, 1973-74; ret., 1974; mgr. support services Northrop, Saudi Arabia, 1978-79; owner, operator The General's Store, 1980—; mem. N.Mex. Ho. of Reps. Mem. commn. Conquistador council Boy Scouts Am. Decorated D.S.M. with 3 oak leaf clusters, Silver Star, Legion of Merit with two bronze oak leaf clusters, D.F.C. with bronze oak leaf cluster, Bronze Star with V device and oak leaf cluster, Air medal with 25 oak leaf clusters, Purple Heart, Vietnam Nat. Order 5th Class, Vietnam Gallantry Cross,with 2 bronze palms, Vietnam Armed Forces Honor medal 1st Class, Order of Nat. Security Merit Guk-Seon medal Republic of Korea); recipient Silver Beaver award Boy Scouts Am., Disting. Citizens award Congrl. Medal Honor Soc.; Paul Harris Fellow. Mem. Roswell C. of C. (pres.' club). Club: Rotary. Home: PO Box 285 Roswell NM 88202-0285

KNOWLES, TONY, governor; b. Tulsa, Jan. 1, 1943; m. Susan Knowles; children: Devon, Lucas. BA in Econs., Yale U., 1968. Owner, mgr. The Works, Anchorage, 1968—, Downtown Deli, Anchorage, 1978—; mayor Municipality of Anchorage, 1981-87; now gov. State of Alaska. Mem. citizen's com. to develop comprehensive plan for growth and devel., Anchorage, 1972; mem. Borough Assembly, Anchorage, 1975-79; bd. dirs. Fairview Community Ctr., March of Dimes, Pub. TV Sta. KAKM, numerous sports facilities coms. Served with U.S. Army, Vietnam. Mem. Anchorage C. of C. (bd. dirs.). Office: Office of the Governor PO Box 110001 Juneau AK 99811-0001*

KNOWLES, WILLIAM LEROY (BILL KNOWLES), television news producer, journalism educator; b. L.A., June 23, 1935; s. Leroy Edwin and Thelma Mabel (Armstrong) K.; children from previous marriage: Frank, Irene, Daniel, Joseph, Ted; m. Sharon Weaver, Dec. 28, 1990. B.A. in Journalism, San Jose State Coll., 1959; postgrad., U. So. Calif., 1962-63. Reporter, photographer, producer KSL-TV, Salt Lake City, 1963-65; producer, editor, writer WLS-TV, Chgo., 1965-70; news writer ABC News, Washington, 1970-71; asso. producer ABC News, 1971-75, ops. producer, 1975-77; So. bur. chief ABC News, Atlanta, 1977-81; Washington bur. chief ABC News, 1981-82, West Coast bur. chief, 1982-85; prof. U. Mont., Missoula, 1986—; jazz writer and historian; v.p., co-owner Present Past Productions, Inc.; adv. U. Mont. Student Documentary Unit. Served with U.S. Army, 1959-62. Decorated Commendation medal; Gannett fellow Ind. U., 1987, Media Mgmt. fellow Poynter Inst. of Media Studies, 1988. Mem. Assn. for Edn. in Journalism, Mont. Traditional Jazz Soc. Office: U Mont Sch Journalism Missoula MT 59812

KNOX, ROBERT LESLIE, personnel professional; b. L.A., May 15, 1940. BS, U. So. Calif., L.A., 1962, postgrad., 1966-71; postgrad., UCLA, 1965-71. Pers. adminstr. City of L.A., 1965—; cons. pers. adminstr., L.A. Dir. Hollywood Knolls Community Club, Hollywood, Calif., 1986—, treas., 1990—. With USAF, 1966-72. Mem. So. Calif. Pers. Mgmt. Assn. (treas. 1980-83, bd. dirs. 1983-86). Office: City of LA 700 E Temple St #320 Los Angeles CA 90012

KNOX, YOLANDA YVETTE BRECKENRIDGE, legal/enforcement processor; b. Oakland, Calif., July 23, 1962; d. Orlandis Whitley and Ray Jean (Smith) Breckenridge; m. David Anthony Knox, June 24, 1989; 1 child, Alaina Nicole. BS in Criminal Justice Adminstrn., Calif. State U., Hayward, 1984; MS in Justice and Pub. Safety, Auburn U., 1992. Salesperson Montgomery Ward, Richmond, Calif., 1979-85; dep. sheriff I Alameda County Sheriff's Dept., Oakland, Calif., 1985; salesperson Macy's Calif., Richmond, 1985-89; police clk., criminal records officer El Cerrito (Calif.) Police Dept., 1986-87; fed. investigator U.S. Office Pers. Mgmt., San Francisco, 1987-88; sr. clk. undergrad. office asst. dept. English U. Calif., Berkeley, 1988-89; intern Lee County Sheriff's Dept., Opelika, Ala., 1991; sec., office mgr. ext. horticulture dept. Auburn (Ala.) U., 1989-92; legal/enforcement processor Stanislaus County Dist. Atty. Family Support Divsn., Modesto, Calif., 1992—. Link Program vol. Friends Outside, 1993-94. Recipient Spirit of Excellence award Auburn U., 1991. Mem. Lambda Alpha Epsilon, Alpha Phi Sigma.

KNUDSON, MELVIN ROBERT, management consultant, business executive; b. Libby, Mont., Oct. 27, 1917; s. John and Serina (Bakken) K.; BS in Wood Chemistry, Oreg. State U., 1942; m. Melba Irene Joice, Mar. 5, 1946; children—Mark Bradley, Kevin Marie, Kari Lynne. Mgr. quality control J. Neils Lumber Co., Libby, Mont., 1946-55; mgr. research and devel. St. Regis Paper Co., Libby, 1955-65, div. dir. tech. devel., Tacoma, Wash., 1965-69, div. dir. short and long-range planning, 1969-70; exec. v.p. Property Holding and Devel. Co., Tacoma, 1970-75; exec. v.p. and gen. mgr. U.S. Computers, Inc., Tacoma, 1975-79; corp. mgmt., orgn., univ. governance and adminstrn. cons., 1979—; owner Knudson Travel, Tacoma, 1981—; bd. dirs., special cons., incorporator Larex Internat. Corp. Mem. adv. bd. Coll. Engring., Wash. State U., 1967—, chmn., 1971-73; trustee 1st Luth. Ch., Libby, 1948-56, chmn., 1954-56; trustee Sch. Dist. # 4, Libby, 1964-65; trustee Christ Luth. Ch., Tacoma, 1966-71, com. chmn.; trustee Greater Lakes Mental Health Clinic, 1969-73, com. chmn., 1970-73; bd. regents Pacific Luth. U., Tacoma, 1969—, chmn., 1976-81; mem. Steilacoom Improvement Com., 1971-73; chmn. Pacific Luth. U. Pres. Search Com., 1974-75; dir. Wauna Dance Club, 1976-79; dir. Pacific Luth. Univ. "Q" Club, 1976-86; bd. dirs. Tenzler Library, Tacoma, 1980-83, Crime Stoppers, 1981-84, Operation Night Watch, 1989. Served to lt. col. F.A., Paratroops, U.S. Army, 1941-46. Recipient Disting. Service award Pacific Luth. U., 1986. Mem. Wash. Realtors Assn., Wash. Securities Sales, Am. Governing Bds., Center for Study of Democratic Institutions. Republican. Clubs: Tacoma Country and Golf, Normana Male Chorus (Norwegian Singers Assn. Am.). Patentee high-temperature wood-drying process, patentee Ultrarefined Arabinogalactan product; developer domestic natural gum. Home: 6928 100th St SW Tacoma WA 98499-1819 Office: 1103 A St Ste 200 Tacoma WA 98438-1301

KNUDSON, THOMAS JEFFERY, journalist; b. Manning, Iowa, July 6, 1953; s. Melvin Jake and Coreen Rose (Nickum) K. B.A. in Journalism, Iowa State U., 1980. Reporter/intern Wall Street Jour., Chgo., summer 1979; staff writer Des Moines Register, 1980—. Author: (series) A Harvest of Harm: The Farm Health Crisis, 1984 (Pulitzer Prize 1985); (series) Majesty and Tragedy; The Sierra in Peril, 1991 (Pulitzer Prize 1992). Recipient James W. Schwartz award Iowa State U., 1985, Nat. Press Club Robert Kozik award, 1992. Office: Sacramento Bee PO Box 15779 21st and Q Sts Sacramento CA 95852

KNUPP, LARRY SHELDON, judge; b. Whittier, Calif., Apr. 7, 1940; s. Wilber Sheldon and Mary Elmyra (Montgomery) K.; m. Jacque Lu Aldridge, Aug. 11, 1963; children: David, Linda. BA, Pomona Coll., 1961; JD, U. Calif., Berkeley, 1964. Bar: Calif. 1965. Ptnr. Knupp Knupp & Smith, Whittier, 1965-75; commr. Whittier Mcpl. Ct., Whittier, 1975-88, judge, 1989—. Mem. Sertoma Club (treas. 1988—). Republican. Office: Whittier Mcpl Ct 7339 Painter Ave Whittier CA 90601

KNUTH, DONALD ERVIN, computer sciences educator; b. Milw., Jan. 10, 1938; s. Ervin Henry and Louise Marie (Bohning) K.; m. Jill Carter, June 24, 1961; children: John Martin, Jennifer Sierra. BS, MS, Case Inst. Tech., 1960; PhD, Calif. Inst. Tech., 1963; DSc (hon.), Case Western Res. U., 1980, Luther Coll., Decorah, Iowa, 1985, Lawrence U., 1985, Muhlenberg Coll., 1986, U. Pa., 1986, U. Rochester, 1986, SUNY, Stony Brook, 1987, Valparaiso U., 1988, Oxford (Eng.) U., 1988, Brown U., 1988, Grinnell Coll., 1989, Dartmouth Coll., 1990, Concordia U., Montréal, 1991, Adelphi U., 1993; Docteur, U. Paris-Sud, Orsay, 1986; Marne-la-Vallée, 1993; D Tech., Royal Inst. Tech., Stockholm, 1991; Pochetnogo Doktora, St. Petersburg U., Russia, 1992. Asst. prof. Calif. Inst. Tech., Pasadena, 1963-66, assoc. prof., 1966-68; prof. Stanford (Calif.) U., 1968-92, prof. emeritus, 1993—; cons. Burroughs Corp., Pasadena, 1960-68. Author: The Art of Computer Programming, 1968 (Steele prize 1987), Computers and Typesetting, 1986. Guggenheim Found. fellow, 1972-73; recipient Nat. Medal of Sci., Pres. James Carter, 1979, Disting. Alumni award Calif. Inst. Tech., 1978, Priestly award Dickinson Coll., 1981, Franklin medal, 1988, J.D. Warnier prize, 1989, Adelsköld medal Swedish Acad. Scis., 1994. Fellow Am. Acad. Arts and Scis.; mem. IEEE (hon., McDowell award 1980, Computer Pioneer award 1982, von Neumann medal 1995), NAS, Nat. Acad. Engring., Assn. for Computing Machinery (Grace Murray Hopper award 1971, Alan M. Turing award 1974, Computer Sci. Edn. award 1986, Software Sys. award 1986), Acad. Sci. (fgn. assoc. Paris and Oslo). Lutheran. Office: Stanford Univ Computer Scis Dept Stanford CA 94305

KNUTH, ELDON LUVERNE, engineering educator; b. Luana, Iowa, May 10, 1925; s. Alvin W. and Amanda M. (Becker) K.; m. Marie O. Parrat, Sept. 10, 1954 (div. 1973); children: Stephen B., Dale L., Margot O., Lynette M.; m. Margaret I. Nicholson, Dec. 30, 1973. B.S., Purdue U., 1949, M.S., 1950; Ph.D. (Guggenheim fellow), Calif. Inst. Tech., 1953. Aerothermodynamics group leader Aerophysics Devel. Corp., 1953-56; asso. research engr. dept. engring. UCLA, 1956-59, asso. prof. engring., 1960-65, prof. engring. and applied sci., 1965-91, prof. emeritus, 1991—, head chem., nuclear thermal div. dept. engring., 1963-65, chmn. energy kinetics dept., 1969-75, head molecular-beam lab., 1961-88; Gen. chmn. Heat Transfer and Fluid Mechanics Inst., 1959; vis. scientist, von Humboldt fellow Max-Planck Inst. für Strömungsforschung, Göttingen, Fed. Republic Germany, 1975-76. Author: Introduction to Statistical Thermodynamics, 1966; also numerous articles. Served with AUS, 1943-45. Mem. AIAA, Am. Soc. Engring. Edn., Am. Inst. Chem. Engrs., Combustion Inst., Soc. Engring. Sci., AAAS, Am. Phys. Soc., Am. Vacuum Soc., Sigma Xi, Tau Beta Pi, Gamma Alpha Rho, Pi Tau Sigma, Sigma Delta Chi, Pi Kappa Phi. Club: Gimlet (Lafayette, Ind.). Home: 18085 Boris Dr Encino CA 91316-4350

KNUTZEN, RAYMOND EDWARD, federal official; b. Burlington, Wash., July 9, 1941; s. Erwin Edward Knutzen and Lillian Irene (Davis) Mowat; m. Cynthia Louise Neufeldt, Feb. 1, 1969; children: Traci Ann, Michael Edward. AAS with high honors, Everett Community Coll., 1970; BA magna cum laude, Pacific Luth. U., 1971; MA, Wash. State U., 1972. Ret. N.E. La. U., Monroe, 1992; cons. Everett, 1992—; freelance legal cons. Wash., 1992—; spl. dep. U.S. Marshal U.S. Marshal, Seattle, 1994—; dir. pub. safety Talolah, Wash., 1994—. Coord. Ouachita Valley coun. Boy Scouts Am., Monroe, 1979. With USAF, 1962-66, lt. col. USAR. Law Enforcement Edn. Program grantee Pacific Luth. U., 1970-71. Mem. Internat. Assn. Chiefs of Police, Mensa, acad. Criminal Justice Sci., La. Justice Educators Assn., Blue Key Soc., La. Soc. Criminal Justice and Criminology (state pres. 1990-91), Lambda Alpha Epsilon, Alpha Phi Sigma (nat. treas. 1971-72), Omicron Delta Kappa, Alpha Kappa Delta. Republican. Lutheran. Home: 5220 176th St SW SP 71 Lynnwood WA 98037-3045 Office: Police Dept PO Box 277 Taholah WA 98587-0277

KNYCHA, JOSEF, journalist; b. Summerside, P.E.I., Can., Apr. 19, 1953; s. Michael Stanley and Marjorie Mary (Gallant) K. Student pub. schs., Auburn, N.S., Can. Reporter Halifax Herald Ltd., N.S., 1971-81; editor The Mirror, Cameron Publs., Kentville, N.S., 1981-82, editor The Register, 1982-84; bus./markets/automotive editor Star-Phoenix, Saskatoon, Sask., Can., 1984-89, asst. news editor, 1990—; editor Cross Country Publs., Brandon Man., 1989-90. Southam fellow U. Toronto. Mem. Automobile Journalists Assn. Can. (bd. dirs.). Home: Box 239, Osler, SK Canada SOk 3AO Office: The Star Phoenix, 204 5th Ave N, Saskatoon, SK Canada S7K 2P1

KO, DENNY R. S., research & development executive; b. 1939. PhD, Calif. Inst. Tech., 1968. With TRW Sys., Redondo Beach, Calif., 1969-72, Dynatech Devel. Corp., Torrance, Calif., 1972—; v.p., gen. mgr. Flow Industries, Seattle, 1972-75; r & d Physical Dynamics, Inc., La Jolla, Calif., 1975-76; with Dynamics Tech., Inc., 1976—, now pres. Office: Dynamics Tech Inc 21311 Hawthorne Blvd Ste 300 Torrance CA 90503-5610*

KO, KATHLEEN LIM, health administrator; b. Shaker Heights, Ohio, Apr. 26, 1958; d. Wen Hsiung Ko and Christina Chen; m. Maurice Lim Miller, Mar. 29, 1986; children: Alicia Berta Lim, Nicholas Hilario Lim. BA, Stanford U., 1980; MS, Harvard U., 1984. Youth program coord. YWCA, San Francisco, 1979; instr. English Fudan U., Shanghai, China, 1980; asst. clinic mgr. Planned Parenthood, San Francisco, 1981; rsch. intern Inst. Health Policy Studies, U. Calif., San Francisco, 1981-82; analyst dept obgyn. San Francisco Gen. Hosp., 1983; ops. dir. Asian Health Svcs., Oakland, Calif., 1984-89, program planning and devel. officer, 1989-92, assoc. dir., 1993—; mem., pres. Bay Area Asian Health Alliance, Oakland, 1982—. Producer film/video Impossible Choices, 1995. Bd. dirs. Asian Women's Shelter, San Francisco, 1987-94, pres., 1989-93; v.p. Arts Sch. PTA, Oakland, 1994-95; bd. dirs. Californians United, San Francisco, 1986. Recipient Cmty. Svc. award Stanford Asian Pacifc Alumni Assn., 1993. Mem. Am. Pub. Health Assn., Asian Pacific Island Am. Health Forum. Democrat. Office: Asian Health Svcs 310 8th St Ste 200 Oakland CA 94607-4253

KO, SEUNG KYUN, educator, consultant; b. Seoul, Korea, July 13, 1936; came to U.S., 1957; s. Byong Ryon and Hung Sun (Song) K.; m. Sook Jin Bae, Aug. 29, 1972; children: Young Min, Young Eun. BA, Coll. of Wooster, Ohio, 1962; MA, U. Pa., 1963, PhD, 1969. Instr. Lake Superior State Coll., Sault Ste Marie, Mich., 1967-68; asst. prof. Maryville (Tenn.) Coll., 1968-69; rsch. commr. Ministry of Fgn. Affairs, Seoul, 1972; lectr. Seoul Nat. U., 1972; assoc. prof. Hawaii Loa Coll., Kaneohe, 1972-78, prof., 1978—. Contbr. articles to profl. jours. Pres. Korean Sr. Citizens Coll., Honolulu, 1985. Mem. United Korean Soc. Hawaii (v.p., pres. Honolulu chpt. 1984). Home: 45-209 Lilipuna Rd # A Kaneohe HI 96744-3106 Office: Hawaii Pacific U Hawaii Loa Campus 45-045 Kam Hwy Kaneohe HI 96744

KO, WEN-HSIUNG, plant pathology educator; b. Chao Chow, Taiwan, May 14, 1939; came to U.S., 1963; s. Ming-chu and Wang (Huang) K.; m. Sachi Su, Jan. 12, 1968; children: Subo, Supin. BS, Nat. Taiwan U., Taipei, 1962; PhD, Mich. State U., 1966. Postdoctoral rsch. assoc. Mich. State U., East Lansing, 1966-69; asst. prof. U. Hawaii, Honolulu, 1969-72, assoc. prof., 1972-74, prof. plant pathology, 1976—. Assoc. editor Plant Disease, 1988-90, Phytopathology, 1980-82; mem. editorial bd. Bot. Bull. Academia Sinica, 1988—; contbr. articles to profl. jours. Mem. Am. Phytopath. Soc. (Ruth Allen award 1984, Fellow award 1990), Mycological Soc. Am., Phytopath. Soc. Japan. Buddhist. Office: U Hawaii 461 W Lanikaula St Hilo HI 96720-4037

KOBAYASHI, ANN H., state legislator; b. Honolulu, Apr. 10, 1937; m.; 3 children. Student Pembroke Coll., Northwestern U. Officer family corp.; former legis. aide, adminstrv. asst. Hawaii Senate, now mem. Senate from 14th Dist. Republican. Home: 3657 Waaloa Way Honolulu HI 96822-1150 Office: Senate House State Capitol Honolulu HI 96813

KOBE, LAN, medical physicist; b. Semarang, Indonesia; naturalized; d. O.G. and L.N. (The) Kobe. BS in Physics, IKIP U., Bandung, Indonesia, 1964, MS in Physics, 1967; MS in Med. Physics and Biophysics, U. Calif.-Berkeley, 1975. Physics instr. Sch. Engring., Tarumanegara U., Jakarta, Indonesia, 1968-72; research fellow dept. radiation oncology U. Calif.-San Francisco, 1975-77; clin. physicist in residence dept. radiation oncology UCLA, 1977-78, asst. hosp. radiation physicist, 1978-80, hosp. radiation physicist, 1980—; instr. radiation oncology physics to resident physicians and med. physics graduate students. Contbr. sci. papers to profl. publs. Newhouse grantee U. Calif.-Berkeley, 1974-75, grantee dean grad. div. U. Calif.-Berkeley, 1975; recipient Pres. Work Study award U. Calif., Berkeley, 1974-75, Employee of Month award UCLA, 1983, Outstanding Service award UCLA, 1986; devel. Achievement award, UCLA, 1988. Mem. Am. Soc. for Therapeutic Radiology and Oncology, Am. Assn. Physicists in Medicine (nat. and So. Calif. chpts.), Am. Bd. Radiology (cert.), Am. Assn. Individual Investors (life). Office: UCLA Dept Radiation Oncology 200 UCLA Medical Plz Ste B265 Los Angeles CA 90024-6977

KOBLIN, DONALD DARYL, anesthesiologist, researcher; b. Chgo., Sept. 1, 1949; s. Alvin and Vera Koblin. BS, UCLA, 1971; PhD, U. Calif., Santa Cruz, 1975; MD, U. Miami, Fla., 1983. Diplomate Am. Bd. of Anesthesiology. Fellow Caltech, Pasadena, Calif., 1975-76; chemist U. Calif., San Francisco, 1976-81; resident in anesthesia Pa. State U., Hershey, 1983-86; assoc. prof. U. Calif., San Francisco, 1986-94; prof., 1994—. Contbr. numerous articles to profl. jours. Mem. Am. Soc. Anesthesiologist, Internat. Anesthesia Rsch. Soc. Office: VA Hosp Dept Anesthesia 4150 Clement St San Francisco CA 94121-1545

KOBZA, DENNIS JEROME, architect; b. Ullysses, Nebr., Sept. 30, 1933; s. Jerry Frank and Agnes Elizabeth (Lavicky) K.; B.S., Healds Archtl. Engring., 1959; m. Doris Mae Riemann, Dec. 26, 1953; children—Dennis Jerome, Diana Jill, David John. Draftsman, designer B.L. Schroder, Palo Alto, Calif., 1959-60; sr. draftsman, designer Ned Abrams, Architect, Sunnyvale, Calif., 1960-61, Kenneth Elvin, Architect, Los Altos, Calif., 1961-62; partner B.L. Schroder, Architect, Palo Alto, 1962-66; pvt. practice architecture, Mountain View, Calif., 1966—. Served with USAF, 1952-56. Recipient Solar PAL award, Palo Alto, 1983, Mountain View Mayoral award, 1979. Mem. C. of C. (dir. 1977-79, Archtl. Excellence award Hayward chpt. 1985, Outstanding Indsl. Devel. award Sacramento chpt., 1980) , AIA (chpt. dir. 1973), Constrn. Specifications Inst. (dir. 1967-68), Am. Inst. Plant Engrs., Nat. Fedn. Ind. Bus. Orgn. Club: Rotary (dir. 1978-79, pres. 1986-87). Home: 3840 May Ct Palo Alto CA 94303-4545 Office: 2083 Old Middlefield Way Mountain View CA 94043

KOCAOGLU, DUNDAR F., engineering management educator, industrial and civil engineer; b. Turkey, June 1, 1939; came to U.S., 1960; s. Irfan and Meliha (Uzay) K.; m. Alev Baysak, Oct. 17, 1968; 1 child, Timur. BSCE, Robert Coll., Istanbul, Turkey, 1960; MSCE, Lehigh U., 1962; MS in Indsl. Engring., U. Pitts., 1972, PhD in Ops. Rsch., 1976. Registered profl. engr., Pa., Oreg. Design engr. Modjeski & Masters, Harrisburg, Pa., 1962-64; ptnr. TEKSER Engring. Co., Istanbul, 1966-69; project engr. United Engrs., Phila., 1964-71; rsch. asst. U. Pitts., 1972-74, vis. asst. prof., 1974-76, assoc. prof. indsl. engring., dir. engring. mgmt., 1976-87; prof., dir. engring. mgmt. program, Portland State U., 1987—; pres. TMA-Tech. Mgmt. Assocs., Portland, Oreg., 1973—, pres. Portland Internat. Conf. Mgmt. Engring. and Tech., 1990—. Author: Engineering Management, 1981; editor: Management of R&D and Engineering, 1992; co-editor: Technology Management—The New International Language, 1991; series editor Wiley Series in Engring. and Tech. Mgmt.; contbr. articles on tech. mgmt. to profl. jours. Lt. C.E., Turkish Army, 1966-68. Fellow IEEE (Centennial medal 1984, editor-in-chief trans. on engring. mgmt. 1986—); mem. Informs (chmn. Coll. Engring. Mgmt. 1979-81), Am. Soc. Engring. Edn. (chmn. engring. mgmt. div. 1982-83), IEEE Engring. Mgmt. Soc. (fellow, publs. dir. 1982-85), ASCE (mem. engring. mgmt. bd. govs. 1988—), Muhendis, Ilim Adamlari ve Mimarlar Dernegi Soc. Turkish Engrs. and Scientists (hon.), Am. Soc. Engring. Mgmt. (dir. 1981-86), Omega Rho (pres. 1984-86).

KOCEN, LORRAINE AYRAL, accountant; b. Levittown, N.Y., July 20, 1956; d. Edward Joseph and Joan Dorothy (Destefanis) Ayral; m. Ross Kocen, Oct. 4, 1981; 1 child, Daniel. BS, Hofstra U., 1978; MBA, U. Minn., 1985. Engr. Sperry Systems Mgmt., Great Neck, N.Y., 1978-81; fin. analyst ITT Consumer Fin. Corp., Mpls., 1981-84; cost acct. Mercy Med. Ctr., Mpls., 1984-85, contr., 1985-86; bus. segments acct. GTE, Thousand Oaks, Calif., 1986-88, Cerritos project acct., 1988-90, Cerritos project adminstr., 1990-92, fin. adminstr., 1992-93, sr. sales adminstr., 1993-94, adminstr. mobile comms., 1994—. Asst. editor newsletter Healthcare Fin. Mgmt. Assn., Mpls., 1985-86. Mem. archtl. com. Foxmoor Hills Homeowners Assn., Westlake, Calif., 1989. Office: GTE 3500 Willow Ln Thousand Oaks CA 91361-4921

KOCH, GERALD DOUGLAS, social services administrator; b. Detroit, June 17, 1943; s. Albert Edward and Marjory M. (Mirovsky) K.; m. April Lee Wittrock, Aug. 14, 1965 (div. Jan. 1981); children: Bethany Lynne, Nathan Douglas; m. Janice Eva Faulk, Oct. 2, 1981; stepchildren: Ted Wilson, James Miller, DeAnna Miller Smith. BA, Asbury Coll., Wilmore, Ky., 1965; MSW, Ind. U., 1970. Cert. social worker. Social worker I Ky. State Hosp., Danville, 1965-67; casework supr. The Salvation Army, Indpls., 1967-68, 70-72; settlement dir. The Salvation Army, Chgo., 1973-78; dir. social svcs. The Salvation Army, Kansas City, Mo., 1978-80, Denver, 1980—; field instr. social work edn. U. Wyo, 1984, 85, U. Colo., Denver, 1987-89, U. No. Colo., 1988; tchr. tng. sessions for human svcs. cert., 1985, 89. Bd. dirs. Denver Santa Claus Shop, 1980—, Denver Emergency Housing Coalition, 1980—, LOVE Inc Met. Denver, 1987-89, Met. Denver Emergency Food and Shelter Bd., 1989—; mem. housing task force Denver Dept. Social Svcs., 1989—. Recipient Albert Schweitzer award Emergency Assistance Coalition, Kansas City, 1980, citation Dept. Health and Hosps., Denver, 1984. Mem. Nat. Assn. Social Workers, 50 for Housing, Piton Found., Colo. Coalition for Homeless. Republican. Home: 7296 S Lincoln Way Littleton CO 80122-1146 Office: The Salvation Army 1370 Pennsylvania Denver CO 80203

KOCH, PETER, wood scientist; b. Missoula, Mont., Oct. 15, 1920; s. Elers and Gerda (Heiberg-Jurgensen) K.; m. Doris Ann Hagen, Oct. 8, 1950. B.S., Mont. State Coll., 1942; Ph.D., U. Wash., 1954; D.Sc. (hon.), U. Maine, 1980. Asst. to pres., sales mgr. Stetson-Ross Machine Co., Seattle, 1946-52; owner Peter Koch Cons. Engr., Seattle, 1952-55; asso. prof. wood tech. Mich. State U., East Lansing, 1955-57; v.p., dir. Champlin Co., Rochester, N.H., 1957-62; project leader, chief wood scientist So. Forest Expt. Sta. Forest Service, U.S. Dept. Agr., Pineville, La., 1963-82; chief wood scientist, forest and range expt. sta. Forest Service, U.S. Dept. Agr., Missoula, Mont., 1982-84; pres. Wood Sci. Lab., Inc., Corvallis, Mont., 1984—; adj. prof. wood sci. N.C. State U. at Raleigh, 1973-82, U. Mont., Missoula, 1982—, Nanjing U. Forestry, China, 1985—; disting. affiliate prof. forest products U. Idaho, Moscow, 1982—. Author: Wood Machining Processes, 1964, Utilization of the Southern Pines, 2 vols, 1972; Utilization of Hardwoods Growing on Southern Pine Sites, 3 vols., 1986; contbr. articles to profl. jours. Served to capt., pilot USAAF, 1942-46. Decorated D.F.C. with oak leaf cluster, Air medal with 4 oak leaf clusters; named to Breast Order of Yun Hui Taiwan; recipient Woodworking Digest award for invention of chipping headrig, 1968, John Scott award for invention of chipping headrig, 1973, Superior Service award for invention of chipping headrig Dept. Agr., Forest Industries award for excellence, 1987. Fellow Internat. Acad. Wood Sci., Soc. Am. Foresters; mem. Forest Products Research Soc. (pres. 1972-73, exec. bd. 1967-74, Gottschalk award 1994), ASME, Soc. Wood Sci. and Tech. (Disting. Service award 1987), TAPPI, Sigma Xi, Tau Beta Pi, Phi Kappa Phi, Sigma Chi. Republican. Lutheran. Club: Rotarian. Home: 960 Little Willow Creek Rd Corvallis MT 59828-9326 Office: 942 Little Willow Creek Rd Corvallis MT 59828-9326

KOCH, RICHARD, pediatrician, educator; b. N.D., Nov. 24, 1921; s. Valentine and Barbara (Fischer) K.; m. Kathryn Jean Holt, Oct. 2, 1943; children: Jill, Thomas, Christine, Martin, Leslie. B.A., U. Calif. at Berkeley, 1958; M.D., U. Rochester, 1951. Mem. staff Children's Hosp., Los Angeles, 1952-75, 77—, dir. child devel. div., 1955-75; dep. dir. Calif. Dept. Health, 1975-76; prof. pediatrics U. So. Calif., 1955-75, 77—; co-dir. PKU Collaborative Study, 1966-82; med. dir. Spastic Children's Found., Los Angeles, 1980-85; mem. Project Hope, Trujillo, Peru, 1970; dir. Regional Center for Developmentally Disabled at Children's Hosp., Los Angeles, 1966-75; mem. research adv. bd. Nat. Assn. Retarded Citizens, 1974-76; mem. Gov.'s Council on Devel. Disabilities, 1981-83; bd. dirs. Down's Syndrome Congress, 1974-76; prin. investigator Maternal PKU Project Nat. Inst. Child Health and Human Devel., Washington, 1985—. Author: (with James Dobson) The Mentally Retarded Child and his Family, 1971, (with Kathryn J. Koch) Understanding the Mentally Retarded Child, 1974, (with Felix de la Cruz) Downs Syndrome, 1975; contbr. articles to profl. jours. Bd. dirs. Fair Housing Opportunities Coun., 1985—. Mem. Am. Assn. on Mental Deficiency (pres. 1968-69), Am. Acad. Pediatrics, Western Soc. Pediatric Research, Soc. for Study Inborn Errors Metabolism, Soc. Inborn Metabolic Disorders, Sierra Club (treas. Mineral King task force 1972). Home: 2125 Ames St Los Angeles CA 90027-2902 Office: MPKU # 73 4650 W Sunset Blvd Los Angeles CA 90027-6016

KOCH, WILLIAM FREDERICK, paleontologist; b. Paterson, N.J., Sept. 24, 1949; s. William F. and Lucille May (Gamberton) K.; m. Sheila Kavanagh Smith. BA in Geology, Rutgers Coll., 1971; MS in Geology, U. Mich., 1973; PhD in Geology, Oreg. State U., 1979. Vis. asst. prof. geology Portland (Oreg.) State U., 1980, St. Lawrence U., Canton, N.Y., 1980-81; asst. prof. geology Waynesburg (Pa.) Coll., 1981-83; rsch. assoc. zoology Oreg. State U., Corvallis, 1983—; cons. in field. Contbr. articles to profl. jours. Chmn. Waynesburg Food Coop., 1981-83. Mem. AAAS, Paleontol. Soc., Cactus and Succulent Soc., Odd Fellows, Sigma Xi. Democrat. Unitarian. Home and Office: 925 NW Merrie Dr Corvallis OR 97330-2335

KOCHER, CHARLES RODNEY, journalist; b. Portland, Oreg., Apr. 9, 1952; s. Kenneth Wilson and Kathlyn Elizabeth (Adams) K.; m. Gerry Kay Livingston, Apr. 18, 1981; children: KayLee Jean, Morgan Harris. BS in Journalism, Northwestern U., Evanston, Ill., 1974. Staff writer, copy editor The Idaho Statesman, Boise, 1973-75; city editor, staff writer The World Newspaper, Coos Bay, Oreg., 1975-82, mng. editor, 1992-95; econ. devel. specialsit, grant writer Coquille Econ. Devel. Corp., North Bend, Oreg., 1995—. Bd. dirs., vol. Helpline of the S. Coast, Coos Bay, 1976—; bd. dirs. Oreg. Geographic Names Bd., Portland, 1980—, Pacific Child Ctr., North Bend, Oreg., 1988—, Oreg. Coast Music Assn., Coos Bay, 1980-90, Friends of Shore Acres, 1992—. Recipient several state, regional and nat. writing and editing awards. Mem. Rotary (Coos Bay North Bend club, com. chmn.). Home: 3031 Sheridan Ave North Bend OR 97459-3038 Office: Coquille Econ Devel Corp The World Newspaper 3201 Tremont North Bend OR 97459

KOCKERBECK, CONRAD CAMPBELL, investment company executive; b. Calgary, Alberta, Can., July 31, 1952; came to U.S., 1993; s. Gunther E. and Anna M. K.; m. Joy Kockerbeck. Diploma in bus., So. Alberta Inst. Tech., 1971; B of Commerce, U. Calgary, 1974. Pres., CEO Global OA Systems Inc., Calgary, 1979-84; v.p. adminstrn., gen. mgr. Gunther's Bldg. Ctr. Ltd., Calgary, 1984-93; dir. Gunther's Bldg. Supplies Ltd., Calgary, 1985—; pvt. practice Scottsdale, Ariz., 1993—; dir. GBS Ltd., Calgary, 1985-94; cons. in field. Inventor lap top computer system, hemodynamic tracking system, insite MIS. Pres. Calgary Elbow Progressive Conservative Assn., 1983. Mem. Calgary C. of C., The Glencoe Club.

KODIS, MARY CAROLINE, marketing consultant; b. Chgo., Dec. 17, 1927; d. Anthony John and Callis Ferebee (Old) K.; student San Diego State Coll., 1945-47, Latin Am. Inst., 1948. Controller, div. adminstrv. mgr. Fed. Mart Stores, 1957-65; controller, adminstrv. mgr. Gulf Mart Stores, 1965-67; budget dir., adminstrv. mgr. Diana Stores, 1967-68; founder, treas., controller Handy Dan Stores, 1968-72; founder, v.p., treas. Handy City Stores, 1972-76; sr. v.p., treas. Handy City div. W.R. Grace & Co., Atlanta, 1976-79; founder, pres. Hal's Hardware and Lumber Stores, 1982-84; retail and restaurant cons., 1979—. Treas., bd. dirs. YWCA Watsonville,1981-84, 85-87; mem. Santa Cruz County Grand Jury, 1984-85. Recipient 1st Tribute to Women in Internat. Industry, 1978; named Woman of the Yr., 1986. Mem. Ducks Unltd. (treas. Watsonville chpt. 1981-89). Republican. Home and Office: 302 Wheelock Rd Watsonville CA 95076-9714

KODITUWAKKU, PIYADASA WIMALAGUNA, clinical neuropsychologist, educator; b. Tangalle, Sri Lanka, Sept. 12, 1949; came to U.S., 1981; s. Don Dionis and Heenhamy (Hewagama) K.; m. Elizabeth Louise Jackson, Sept. 1, 1984; children: Michael, Paul Armstrong. BA, U. Ceylon, 1971; MS, U. N.Mex., 1984, PhD, 1990. Asst. lectr. philosophy U. Ceylon (Sri Lanka), 1971-74; trainee clin. psychologist U. Ceylon, Colombo, Sri Lanka, 1975-79; probationer clin. psychologist Nat. Health Svc., Scotland, 1979-81; teaching and grad. asst. U. N.Mex., Albuquerque, 1981-90, clin. neuropsychologist, 1990—, asst. prof. psychiatry, 1992—. Developer progressive planning test, 1993. Vol. Albuquerque Rescue Mission, 1993—. Scholar Govt. of Sri Lanka, 1971; fellow WHO, 1979-81. Mem. AAAS, Internat. Neuropsychol. Soc., N.Mex. Psychol. Assn. (Miriani award 1991). Office: Dept Psychiatry U NMex Sch Medicine Albuquerque NM 87131

KOEHLER, AGNES THERESA, real estate sales executive, business executive; b. Hixton, Wis., June 8, 1921; d. August Carl and Hildegard (Capaul) K.; m. Bernard Van Eperen, Oct. 4, 1941 (div. 1978); children: David, Shari, Gary. Student, Tchrs. Coll., Oshkosh, Wis., 1940. Lic. real estate broker and sales, assessor. Real estate agt. Moder Realty, Appleton, Wis., 1965-66, Schwartzbauer Realty, Appleton, 1967-68, Kennedy Realty, Appleton, 1969-71; v.p., co-owner Van Eperen Painting, Inc., Appleton, 1960-77; assessor Town of Menasha, Wis., 1975-76; real estate agt. Farrow Realty, Carlsbad, Calif., 1979; pres. Aux. Wis. Painting & Decorating Contractor, Appleton, 1966. Artist various oils. Co-founder Fox Cities NOW, Appleton, 1973; mem. Menasha Planning Commn., 1975. Mem. LWV, Am. Assn. Retired Persons, United We Stand Am., San Diego Now, North Coast Dem. Club, San Diego Welcome Wagon, San Diego Floral Assn.. Home: 2147 Bulrush Ln Cardiff By The Sea CA 92007-1407

KOEHLER, JEREMY, tapestry artist; b. Detroit, Apr. 14, 1952; s. James Gerald and Maybelle Ralph (Thomas) K. BA, U. Mich., 1974. Benedictine monk Monastery of Christ in the Desert, Abiquiu, N.Mex., 1977-87; tapestry artist, 1987—; weaving tchr. Taos (N.Mex.) Inst. Arts, 1991-93. Exhibited in one/two person shows at Weaving S.W., Taos, 1992, Kent Galleries, Sante Fe, 1993, 95, Bentley Gallery, Scottsdale, Ariz., 1995; group shows include Wayrich Gallery, Albuquerque, 1986, Wichita Nat. All Media Crafts Exhibit, 1988, Santa Fe Festival of Arts, 1988, Taos Fall Arts Celebration, 1988, N.Mex. Arts and Crafts Fair, Albuquerque, 1986, 87, 88, 89, 90, 91, Stables Art Ctr., Taos, 1991, Am. Crafts Mus., N.Y., 1991, S.W. Arts and Crafts Festival, Albuquerque, 1987, 89, 90, 91, Mus. Fine Arts, Santa Fe, 1993, Nat. Tapestry Invitational Exhibit, Ohio State U., 1994, Contemporary Concepts IV, Los Carlos Mus., Corrales, N.Mex., 1994, Fiber Celebrated, Tucson Mus. Art, 1995. Home: PO Box 549 Ranchos De Taos NM 87557-0549 Studio: PO Box 279 Santa Fe NM 87504-0279

KOEL, BRUCE EDWARD, chemistry educator; b. Norton, Kans., June 30, 1955. BS in Chemistry with highest honors, Emporia State U., 1976, MS in Chemistry, 1978; PhD in Chemistry, U. Tex., 1981. Miller Inst. postdoctoral fellow U. Calif., Berkeley, 1981-83; asst. prof. chemistry and biochemistry U. Colo., Boulder, 1983-89, assoc. prof. chemistry and biochemistry, 1989, fellow Coop. Inst. for Rsch. in Environ. Scis., 1983-89; assoc. prof. chemistry U. So. Calif., L.A., 1990-93, prof. chemistry, 1993—; cons. Chemistry and Laser Scis.-2 Los Alamos Nat. Lab., 1984-92, Hewlett-Packard, 1985-89, J&A Assocs., 1986, Chemistry and Laser Scis.-1 Los Alamos Nat. Lab., 1992-94, Burge and Assocs., 1992-95, Chem Alert Corp., 1993-95; reviewer for proposals to Am. Chem. Soc.-Petroleum Rsch. Fund, Army Rsch. Office, Dept. Energy, ISF, NSF; lectr., spkr. in field. Mem. editorial adv. bd.: Langmuir; referee Applied Surface Sci., Catalysis Letters, Chemistry of Materials, Internat. Conf. on Metall. Coatings and Thin Films, Jour. Catalysis, Jour. Chem. Physics, Jour. Electron Spectroscopy and Related Phenomena, Jour. Phys. Chemistry, Jour. Am. Chem. Soc., Jour. Vacuum Sci. and Tech., Langmuir, Sci., Surface Sci.; contbr. articles to profl. jours. Recipient Dreyfus Found. grant for New Faculty, 1983, Exxon Edn. Found. award, 1987, Union Carbide Innovation Rsch. awards, 1990, 91; U. fellow U. Tex., Austin, 1978, NSF Energy Related trainee, 1978, Alfred P. Sloan Rsch. fellow, 1990. Mem. Am. Chem. Soc. (divsn. colloid and surface chemistry Proctor and Gamble fellowship 1980, various com. positions), Am. Phys. Soc., Am. Vacuum Soc., Materials Rsch. Soc. Office: Dept Chemistry Univ So Calif Los Angeles CA 90089-0482

KOELMEL, LORNA LEE, data processing executive; b. Denver, May 15, 1936; d. George Bannister and Gladys Lee (Henshall) Steuart; m. Herbert Howard Nelson, Sept. 9, 1956 (div. Mar. 1967); children: Karen Dianne, Phillip Dean, Lois Lynn; m. Robert Darrel Koelmel, May 12, 1981; stepchildren: Kim, Cheryl, Dawn, Debbie. BA in English, U. Colo., 1967. Cert. secondary English tchr. Substitute English tchr. Jefferson County Schs., Lakewood, Colo., 1967-68; sec. specialist IBM Corp., Denver, 1968-75, pers. adminstr., 1975-82, asst. ctr. coord., 1982-85, office systems specialist, 1985-87, backup computer operator, 1987—; computer instr. Barnes Bus. Coll., Denver, 1987-92; owner, mgr. Lorna's Precision Word Processing and Desktop Pub., Denver, 1987-89; computer cons. Denver, 1990—. Editor newsletter Colo. Nat. Campers and Hikers Assn., 1992—. Organist Christian Sci. Soc., Buena Vista, Colo., 1963-66, chmn. bd. dirs., Thornton, Colo., 1979-80; ch. organist, 1994—. Mem. NAFE, Nat. Secs. Assn. (retirement ctr. chair 1977-78, newsletter chair 1979-80, v.p. 1980-81), Am. Guild Organists, U. Colo. Alumni Assn., Alpha Chi Omega (publicity com. 1986-88). Republican. Club: Nat. Writers. Lodge: Job's Daus. (recorder 1953-54).

KOENIG, MARIE HARRIET KING, public relations director, fund raising executive; b. New Orleans, Feb. 19, 1919; d. Harold Paul and Sadie Louise (Bole) King; m. Walter William Koenig, June 24, 1956; children: Margaret Marie, Susan Patricia. Major in Voice, La. State U., 1937-39; Pre-law, Loyola U., 1942-43; BS in History, U. LaVerne, 1986. Adminstrv. asst. to atty. gen. State of La., New Orleans, 1940-44; contract writer MGM Studios, Culver City, Calif., 1944-46; asst. sec., treas. Found. for Ind., L.A., 1950-56, Found. for Social Rsch., L.A., 1950-56; dir. communications Incentive Rsch. Corp., L.A., 1969-78; rsch. supr., devel. dept. Calif. Inst. Technology, Pasadena, Calif., 1969; dir. funding devel. Rep. Party of L.A. County, South Pasadena, 1989-92. Author: Does the National Council of Churches Speak for You?, 1978; delivered lecture series on U.S. fgn. policy. Named Hon. Citizen Colonial Williamsburg Found., 1987; active Nat. Trust for Historic Preservation, 1986, Autry Western Heritage Mus., 1986, Friends of the Huntington Libr., 1986, Town Hall of L.A., 1986—, Pasadena City Women's Club, 1982-84, The Masquers Club; bd. mem. Coun. Women's Clubs; charter mem. Nat. Mus. of Women in Arts; bd. mem. Pasadena Opera Guild; contbg. mem. L.A. World Affairs Coun., 1990, L.A. County Mus. Art, 1990; pres., pub. chmn., Pasadene Rep. Women Federated; charter mem. Freedom Found. at Valley Forge L.A. County Chpt. Recipient Cert. Recognition Calif. State Assembly, 1989, 95, Recognition of Excellence, Achievement and Commitment U.S. Ho. Reps., 1989, Cert. Merit Rep. Presdl. Task Force, 1986, Cert. Appreciation U.S. Def. Com., 1984, Hon. Freedom Fighter award U.S. Def. Com., 1985, Cert. Appreciation Am. Conservative Union, 1983, Cert. Commendation Rep. Cen. Com. L.A. County, 1972, Cert. Appreciation Eisenhower-Nixon So. Calif. Com., 1952. Mem. Greater L.A. Press Club, Freedoms Found. at Valley Forge (charter L.A. chpt.). Republican. Home: 205 Madeline Dr Pasadena CA 91105-3311

KOEP, LAWRENCE JAMES, surgeon; b. Pasadena, Calif., May 6, 1944; s. Ambrose Urban and Loma Mary (Riordan) K.; m. Jennifer Leigh James, FEb. 4, 1982 (div. Jan. 1992); children: Alexander, Erik, Lauren. BS, Johns Hopkins U., 1966, MD, 1970. Diplomate Am. Bd. Surgery. Intern Johns Hopkins Hosp., Balt., 1970-71, resident, 1971-76; assoc. prof. U. Colo., Denver, 1976-81; pvt. practice Phoenix, 1981—; bd. dirs. Donor Network Ariz. Mem. ACS, Am. Soc. Transplant Surgeons, Western Surg. Assn. Home: 3729 E Rancho Dr Paradise Vly AZ 85253-5022 Office: 1410 N 3rd St Phoenix AZ 85004-1608

KOEPPEL, GARY MERLE, writer, publisher, art gallery owner; b. Albany, Oreg., Jan 20, 1938; s. Carl Melvin and Barbara Emma (Adams) K.; m. Emma Katerina Koeppel, May 20, 1984. BA, Portland State U., 1961; MFA, State U. Iowa, 1963. Writing instr. State U. Iowa, Iowa City, 1963-64; guest prof. English, U. P.R. San Juan, 1964-65; assoc. prof. creative writing Portland (Oreg.) State U., 1965-68; owner, operator Coast Gallery, Big Sur, 1971—, Pebble Beach, Calif., 1986—, Maui, Hawaii, 1985—, Hana, Hawaii, 1991—, Lahaina, Hawaii, 1992; owner Coast Pub. Co., Coast Seri Graphics, 1991—; editor, pub. Big Sur Gazette, 1978-81; producer, sponsor Maui Marine Art Expo., Calif. Marine Art Expo., Paris Marine Art Expo., Hawaiian Cultural Arts Expo., 1993; founder The Blue Movement, 1994; founder, pres. Global Art Expos, 1995. Founder Global Arts Expos, 1994. Author: Sculptured Sandcast Candles, 1974. Founder Big Sur Vol. Fire Brigade, 1975; chmn. coordinating com. Big Sur Area Planning, 1972-75; chmn. Big Sur Citizens Adv. Com., 1975-78. Mem. Internat. Soc. Appraisers, Big Sur C. of C. (pres. 1974-75, 82-84), Big Sur Grange, Audubon Soc., Cousteau Soc., Phi Gamma Delta, Alpha Delta Sigma. Address: Coast Gallery PO Box 223519 Carmel CA 93922-3519

KOERBER, JOHN ROBERT, computer programmer; b. L.A., Aug. 17, 1955; s. Thomas Joseph and Betty (Turner) Koerber; m. Kimberly Sue Rider, Mar. 15, 1986. BS, Yale U., 1977. Computer technician Tech Mart, Tarzana, Calif., 1977-79; programmer, ptnr. J&J Computer Svc., Northridge, Calif., 1979-80; sr. programmer Mitec Computer Bus. Systems, Chartsworth, Calif., 1980-87; sr. software engr. Dracon div. Harris Corp., Camarillo, Calif., 1987-88; programmer, cons. Sailing Computer Systems, Chatsworth, 1988—. Mem. IEEE (affiliate, Commns. Soc.), Assn. for Computing Machinery. Democrat. Home: 6657 Franrivers Ave West Hills CA 91307 Office: Sailing Computer Systems 10258 Glade Ave Chatsworth CA 91311-2812

KOESTEL, MARK ALFRED, geologist, photographer; b. Cleve., Jan. 1, 1951; s. Alfred and Lucille (Kemeny) K.; m. Deborah Leigh Caswell, Sept. 5, 1988; children: Jennifer Rose, Bonnie Leigh. BS, U. Ariz., 1978. Registered profl. geologist Wyo., Alaska, Ind.; registered environ. assessor, Calif. Sr. geologist Union Oil Co. of Calif., Tucson and Denver, 1978-86; mgr. geology Harmsworth Assocs., Laguna Hills, Calif., 1986-88; sr. project mgr. Applied GeoSystems, Irvine, Calif., 1988-90; geologist, photographer Adventures in Geology, Laguna Hills, Calif., 1986-88. Contbr. articles to profl. jours. N.Mex. state rep. Minerals Exploration Coalition, Tucson and Denver, 1982. Sci. Found. scholarship No. Ariz. U., 1969, Acad. Achievement scholarship, 1970, Disting. Scholastic Achievement scholarship, 1971. Mem. Am. Inst. of Profl. Geologists (cert.), Soc. of Mining Engrs., Aircraft Owners and Pilots Assn., Geol. Soc. of Am., Nat. Geographic Soc. Home and Office: 22891 Caminito Azul Laguna Hills CA 92653-1104

KOESTER, BERTHOLD KARL, lawyer, retired honorary consul; b. Aachen, Germany, June 30, 1931; s. Wilhelm P. and Margarethe A. (Witteler) K.; m. Hildegard Maria Buettner, June 30, 1961; children: Georg W., Wolfgang J., Reinhard B. JD, U. Muenster, Fed. Republic Germany, 1957. Cert. Real Estate Broker, Ariz. Asst. prof. civil and internat. law U. Muenster, 1957-60; atty. Cts. of Duesseldorf, Fed. Republic Germany, 1960-82; v.p. Bank J. H. Vogeler & Co., Duesseldorf, 1960-64; pres. Bremer Tank-u., Kuehlschiffahrtsges.m.b.H., 1964-72; atty., trustee internat. corps., Duesseldorf and Phoenix, 1973-82, Phoenix, 1983—; of counsel Tancer Law Offices, Phoenix, 1978-86; prof. internat. bus. law Am. Grad. Sch. Internat. Mgmt., Glendale, Ariz., 1978-81; with Applewhite, Laflin & Lewis, Real Estate Investments, Phoenix, 1981-86, ptnr., 1982-86, Beucler Real Estate Investments, 1986-88, Scottsdale, Ariz.; chief exec. officer, chmn. bd. German Consultants in Real Estate Investments, Phoenix, 1989—; hon. consul Fed. Republic of Germany for Ariz., 1982-92; chmn., chief exec. officer Arimpex Hi-Tec, Inc., Phoenix, 1981—; bd. dirs. Ariz. Ptnrship for Air Transp., 1988-92; chmn. Finvest Corp., Phoenix, 1990—. Contbr. articles to profl. jours. Pres. Parents Assn. Humboldt Gymnasium, Duesseldorf, 1971-78; active German Red Cross, from 1977. Mem. Duesseldorf Chamber of Lawyers, Bochum (Fed. Republic Germany) Assn. Tax Lawyers, Bonn German-Saudi Arabian Assn. (pres. 1976-79), Bonn German-Korean Assn., Assn. for German-Korean Econ. Devel. (pres. 1974-78), Ariz. Consular Corps (sec., treas. 1988-89), German-Am. C. of C., Phoenix Met. C. of C., Rotary (Scottsdale, Ariz.). Home: 6201 E Cactus Rd Scottsdale AZ 85254-4409 Office: PO Box 15674 Phoenix AZ 85060-5674

KOESTER, RUDOLF, educator; b. Mar. 16, 1936; s. Eric A. and Irmgard (Petzel) K.; m. Elizabeth Margriet Dane, Jan. 12, 1973. BA, UCLA, 1958, MA, 1959; PhD, Harvard U., 1964. Asst. prof. UCLA, 1964-69; assoc. prof. U. Nev., Las Vegas, 1969-76, prof., 1976—. Author: Hermann Hesse, 1975, Joseph Roth, 1982, Hermann Broch, 1987; contbr. articles to profl. jours. Baldwin Prize fellow in Germanics, Harvard U., 1959-60. Mem. Phi Beta Kappa. Home: 2349 Palora Ave Las Vegas NV 89109-1819

KOETHKE, CHARLES RICHARD, advertising specialist, consultant; b. Lewiston, Idaho, Feb. 13, 1945; s. George Richard and Bonna Jean (Lister) K.; m. Diana Kaye White, Mar. 8, 1966 (div. Apr. 1978); children: Timothy Richard, Richard Darin, Karie Jean, Michele Pamela; m. Sara Ann Savisky, Sept. 27, 1980. Grad. high sch., Ravenswood, W.Va. and Lewiston, Idaho. With Nu-Lawn Chem. Co., Redwood City, Calif., 1964, Potlatch Corp., Lewiston, 1964-67, Pacific Gamble Robinson, Lewiston, 1967-68; restaurant mgr. W. T. Grant & Co., Santa Rosa, Calif., 1968-70; owner Koethke's Grocery & Fountain, Lewiston, 1970-71; retail advt. sales dept. Lewiston Morning Tribune, Lewiston, 1971-72; classified advt. mgr. Lewiston Morning Tribune, 1972-77; classified/graphics/advt. svc. mgr. The Daily News, Longview, Wash., 1978-94, asst. computer technician, 1978-94; pvt. newspaper cons. Focus Media Svcs., Kelso, Wash., 1995—. Bd. dirs. Daily News Fed. Credit Union, Longview, 1983—, McClelland Arts Ctr., Longview, 1984—. Mem. Pacific N.W. Assn. Newspaper Classified Advt. Mgrs. (bd. dirs. 1980-82, 89—, v.p. 1983-84, 92-93, 93—, pres. 1984-85), Newspaper Pubs. Assn. (Wash., Oreg., Idaho, Mont., classified cons. 1987-90). Democrat. Home: 705 S 6th Ave Kelso WA 98626-2532 Office: Focus Media Svcs 705 S 6th Ave Kelso WA 98626-2532

KOETSER, DAVID, export company executive; b. Amsterdam, The Netherlands, July 22, 1906; came to U.S., 1939; s. Joseph and Mathilda Pauline (Hollander) K. Grad., Lyceum, Amsterdam, 1926. Owner Music Pub. Co., Amsterdam, 1935-39; exec. sec. The Netherlands C. of C., 1947-56; owner D.K. Co., Inc., San Francisco, 1957-84. Contbr. articles to profl. jours. Moderator U.S. Small Bus. Adminstrn., Score workshops, San Francisco, 1987—. Staff sgt. CIC, 1942-45, ETO. Mem. Holland Am. Soc. (treas. 1950—), World Trade Club (entertainment com. 1960—), Internat. Exporters Assn. (pres. 1965, recipient Pres. E award). Home and Office: 100 Thorndale Dr Apt 341 San Rafael CA 94903-4574

KOFAHL, ROBERT EUGENE, science and education consultant; b. Taft, Calif., Oct. 5, 1924; s. Lynn Hosey and Beatrice (Cotteral) K. BS in Chemistry, Calif. Inst. Tech., 1949, PhD in Chemistry, 1954. From instr. to profl. Highland Coll., Pasadena, Calif., 1950-71, pres., 1957-71; rsch. scientist Carter Rsch. Lab., Pasadena, 1955-57; sci. coord. Creation-Sci. Rsch. Ctr., San Diego, 1972—. Sr. author: The Creation Explanation, 1975; author: Handy Dandy Evolution Refuter, 1977, 92. Bd. dirs. Westminster Acad. Christian Day Sch., L.A., 1953—. With U.S. Army, 1943-46. Mem. AAAS, Creation Rsch. Soc. Republican. Presbyterian. Home: 1322 E Wilson Ave Glendale CA 91206-4632 Office: Creation-Sci Rsch Ctr 10625 Scripps Ranch Blvd San Diego CA 92131

KOFFLER, STEPHEN ALEXANDER, investment banker; b. Providence, R.I., Sept. 22, 1942; s. Irving I. and Jessie Lillian (Seltzer) K.; m. Enid Freya Mellion, June 15, 1963; children: Samara Rachel, Debra Lyn. BMetE, Rensselaer Poly. Inst., 1964, MS, 1967, PhD, 1968. Security analyst Auerbach Pollak & Richardson, N.Y.C., 1968-70; asst. v.p. investment banking A.G. Becker, Inc., N.Y.C., 1970-72; v.p., treas. Mattel, Inc., Hawthorne, Calif., 1972-74; sr. v.p., chief fin. officer Audio Magnetics, Inc., Gardena, Calif., 1974-75; cons. Koffler & Co., L.A., 1975-81; mng. dir. Becker Paribas, Inc., L.A., 1981-84, Merrill Lynch, L.A., 1984-91; exec. v.p., dir. investment banking dvsn. Sutro and Co., Inc., L.A., 1991-94; mng. dir. Smith Barney Inc., L.A., 1994—. Bd. dirs. L.A. Gear, 1991—, L.A. Music Ctr. Opera, 1989—. Mem. Am. Soc. for Metals, Nat. Assn. Securities Dealers Inc. (mem. corp. fin. com. 1994—), Riviera Tennis Club, Regency Club, Teton Pines Country Club. Office: Smith Barney Inc 333 S Grand Ave Los Angeles CA 90071-1504

KOFRANEK, ANTON MILES, floriculturist, educator; b. Chgo., Feb. 5, 1921; s. Antonin J. and Emma (Rehorek) K.; children—Nancy, John A. B.S., U. Minn., 1947; M.S., Cornell U., 1949, Ph.D., 1950. Asst. prof. to prof. U. Calif., Los Angeles, 1950-68; prof. hort. dept. U. Calif., Davis, 1968-87, ret. prof. emeritus, 1987; vis. prof. U. Wageningen, Netherlands, 1958,

Cornell U., 1966, Hebrew U., Rehovot, Israel, 1972-73, Lady Davis fellow, 1980; vis. prof. Glasshouse Crops Research Inst., Littlehampton, U.K., 1980, AID, Egypt, 1978-82, FAO-UN, India, 1985. Co-author: (with Hartmann, Rubatzky and Flocker) Plant Science Growth, Development and Utilization of Cultivated Plants, 2d edit., 1981; co-editor: (with R. A. Larson) U. Calif. Azalea Manual, 1975; contbr. articles to profl. jours. Served with AUS, 1942-45, ETO; Served with AUS, PTO. Recipient rsch. awards of merit Calif. State Florist Assn., 1966, Garland award 1974; named Young Man of Yr. Westwood Jr. C. of C., 1956; recipient rsch. and tchng. award Soc. Am. Florists, 1993. Fellow Am. Soc. Hort. Sci (dir., sectional chmn. 1973-74); mem. Sigma Xi, Pi Alpha Xi. Office: U Calif-Davis Dept Environ Hort Davis CA 95616

KOGA, ELAINE, controller; b. San Francisco, Feb. 8, 1942; d. Harry Takeo and Mitsuko Kaneko K.; m. Tad T. Murano, July 19, 1964 (div. 1981); children: Michael M., Kevin G. BS, U. San Francisco, 1980. Tax acct. Robert H. Mann, CPA, San Francisco, 1971-72; chief acct. H. Shenson, Inc., San Francisco, 1972-78; asst. controller, acctg. mgr. Esprit De Corp, San Francisco, 1978-80; controller Peat, Marwick, Mitchell, CPA, San Francisco, 1981; CFO Sofabed Conspiracy, Inc., Berkeley, Calif., 1982-83; asst. v.p., controller Montgomery Capital Corp., San Francisco, 1984-92; v.p., CFO Indsl. Environ. Mgmt., Inc., 1993—. Mem. Nat. Assn. Accts. (bd. dirs. 1981-84). Home: 1007 Arlington Ln Daly City CA 94014-3443

KOGA, ROKUTARO, astrophysicist; b. Nagoya, Japan, Aug. 18, 1942; came to U.S., 1961, naturalized, 1966; s. Toyoki and Emiko (Shinra) K.; m. Cordula Rosow, May 5, 1981; children: Evan A., Nicole A. B.A., U. Calif.-Berkeley, 1966; Ph.D., U. Calif.-Riverside, 1974. Research fellow U. Calif.-Riverside, 1974-75; research physicist Case Western Res U., Cleve., 1975-79, asst. prof., 1979-81; physicist Aerospace Corp., Los Angeles, 1981—. Mem. Am. Phys. Soc., Am. Geophys. Union, IEEE, N.Y. Acad. Scis., Sigma Xi. Contbr. articles to profl. confs.; research on gamma-ray astronomy, solar neutron observation, space scis., charged particles in space and the effect of cosmic rays on microcircuits in space. Home: 7325 Ogelsby Ave Los Angeles CA 90045-1356 Office: Aerospace Corp Space Scis Labs Los Angeles CA 90009

KOH, EUSEBIO LEGARDA, mathematics educator; b. Manila, Oct. 4, 1931; s. Enrique Legarda and Felisa Un (Makabuhay) K.; m. Donelita Mesina Viardo, Feb. 21, 1958; children—Eudonette, Elizabeth, Ethel, Denise. B.S. in Mech. Engring. cum laude, U. Philippines, Quezon City, 1954; M.S. in Mech. Engring., Purdue U., 1956; M.S., Birmingham, 1961; Ph.D., SUNY-Stony Brook, 1967. Research engr. Internat. Harvester Co., Chgo., 1956-57; asst. prof. mech. engring. U. Philippines, 1959-64, head dept., 1963-64; assoc. prof. math. U. Regina, Sask., Can., 1970-75, prof., 1975—, head dept. math., 1977-79; guest prof. math. Techn. Hochschule, Darmstadt, Fed. Republic Germany, 1975-76; prof. math. U. Petroleum/Minerals, Dhahran, Saudi Arabia, 1979-81. Contbr. research papers to profl. jours. Pres., Philippine Assn. Sask., 1971, bd. dirs., 1984; editor: Philippine Newsletter, 1985. Colombo Plan scholar Brit. Council, 1960; Travel fellow Nat. Research Council, Fed. Republic Germany, 1975; research grantee Nat. Sci. and Engring. Research Council, 1971—; named Outstanding Prof., U. Philippines Student Union, 1962, Outstanding Filipino-Can. in Edn., The Pinoy Digest, 1990. Mem. Soc. Indsl. and Applied Math., Am. Math. Soc., Math. Assn. Am., Can. Applied Math. Soc., Philippine Am. Acad. Sci. and Engring. (founding). Avocations: chess, bridge, tennis, golf. Office: U of Regina, Dept of Math and Stats, Regina, SK Canada S4S 0A2

KOHAN, DENNIS LYNN, international trade educator, consultant; b. Kankakee, Ill., Nov. 22, 1945; s. Leon Stanley and Nellie (Foster) K.; m. Julianne Johnson, Feb. 14, 1976 (dec. Sept. 1985); children: Toni, Bart, Elyse; m. Betsy Burns, Mar. 8, 1986; 1 child, David. BA, Ill. Wesleyan U., 1967; MPA, Gov.'s State U., 1975; postgrad., John. Marshall Law Sch., 1971-74. Police officer Kankakee County, 1967-75; loan counselor, security officer Kankakee Fed. Savs. & Loan, Kankakee, 1975-76; mgr. Bank Western, Denver, 1976-85; mgr. real estate lending dept. Cen. Savs., San Diego, 1985-87; maj. loan work-out officer Imperial Savs., San Diego, 1987-88; cons. Equity Assurance Holding Corp., Newport Beach, Calif., 1987-88; compliance officer Am. Real Estate Group and New West Fed. Savs. and Loan, Irvine, Calif., 1988-90; co-founder Consortium-Real Estate Asset Cons., Costa Mesa, Calif., 1990-91; investigator, criminal coord. Resolution Trust Corp., Newport Beach, Calif., 1991-94; instr. Inst. for Internat. Trade Anhui Inst. Fin. and Trade, Bengbu, People's Republic of China, 1994-95; instr. Gunghou Inst. Fgn. Trade, People's Republic of China, 1995—; instr. U. No. Colo. Coll. Bus., Greeley, 1981-85; chmn. bd. North Colo. Med. Ctr., Greeley, 1983-85; pres. bd. Normedco, Greeley, 1984-85. Vol. cons., chmn. ARC, Colo., 1979-85; campaign mgr. Donley Senatorial campaign, Colo., 1982, Kinkade City Coun. campaign, Colo., 1983; chmn. Weld County Housing Authority, 1981. Staff sgt. U.S. Army, 1969-71, Vietnam. Mem. Nat. Assn. Realtors, Shriners, Kiwanis.

KOHAN, DONALD ELLIOTT, molecular physiologist, medical educator; b. Wilmington, Del., July 1, 1953; s. Melvin I. and Beatrice (Nesson) K.; m. Sherrie L. Perkins; two children. BA, U. Del., 1975; PhD, Mayo Grad. Sch. Medicine, 1980; MD, U. Miami, 1982. Resident Barnes Hosp., St. Louis, 1982-85; fellow in nephrology Washington U., St. Louis, 1985-87, instr. medicine, 1987-89, asst. prof. medicine, 1989-90; asst. prof. medicine U. Utah, Salt Lake City, 1990-93, assoc. prof. medicine, 1993—. Contbr. articles to profl. jours. Mem. Am. Soc. for Clin. Investigation, Am. Physiol. Soc., Am. Soc. Nephrology, Nat. Kidney Found., Am. Heart Assn. Office: Divsn Nephrology Univ Utah Med Ctr Salt Lake City UT 84132

KOHL, HERBERT RALPH, education educator; b. Bronx, N.Y., Aug. 22, 1937; m. Judith Murdoch; children: Antonia, Erica, Joshua. AB in Philosophy magna cum laude, Harvard U., 1958; MA in Spl. Edn., Columbia U., 1962, postgrad., 1965-66. Tchr. Reece Sch. for Severely Disturbed, N.Y.C., 1961, N.Y.C. Pub. Schs., 1962-64; rsch. assoc., journalist Ctr. for Urban Edn., N.Y.C., 1965-67; dir. Tchrs. and Writers Collaborative, N.Y.C., 1966-67; rsch. assoc. Horace Mann-Lincoln Inst., N.Y.C., 1966-67; prin., tchr. Other Ways High Sch., Berkeley, Calif., 1968-71; co-dir. tchr. tng. Ctr. for Open Learning and Teaching, Berkeley, 1972-77; dir. ednl. devel. Coastal Ridge Rsch. and Ednl. Ctr., Point Arena, Calif., 1978—; tchr. Point Arean Pub. Schs., 1986-88; Gordon Sanders prof. edn. Hamline U., St. Paul, 1988-89; disting. prof. edn. Carlton Coll., Northfield, Min., 1989—; vis. assoc. prof. dept. English U. Calif.-Berkeley, 1967-68; vis. prof. edn. U. Alaska, Fairbanks, 1983; dir. software devel. Sci. Am. Books, N.Y.C., 1983-84; bd. dirs. Atari Inst., Calif. Poets in Schs., Childrens' Choice Book Club, Coastal Ridge Rsch. and Edn. Ctr., Computer Equity Project Nat. Women's Coalition, others; editorial bd. Learning Mag., The Lion and The Unicorn, Hungry Mind Rev., Interaction Mag., People's Yellow Pages, others; cons., lectr. pub., ednl. and profl. orgns. Author: The Age of Complexity, 1965, The Language and Education of the Deaf, 1967, Teaching the Unteachable, 1967, 36 Children, 1967, The Open Classroom, 1969, Fables: A Curriculum Unit, 1969, Golden Boy as Anthony Cool: A Photo Essay on Names and Graffiti, 1972, Reading: How To - A People's Guide to Alternative Ways of Teaching and Testing Reading, 1973, Games, Math and Writing in the Open Classroom, 1973, Half the House, 1974, On Teaching, 1976, A Book of Puzzlements, 1981, Basic Skills, 1982, Atari Games and Recreations, 1982, Insight: Reflections on Teaching, 1982, Conscience and Human Rights, 1983, Atari PILOT Games and Recreation for Learning, 1983, Atari Puzzlements, 1984, Commodore Puzzlements, 1984, 41 1/2 Things to do with your Atari, 41 1/2 Things to do with your Commodore, 1984, Growing Minds: On Becoming A Teacher, 1985, Mathematical Puzzlements, 1987, Making Theater: Developing Plays With Young People, 1988, The Question is College, 1989, I Won't Learn From You, 1991, From Archetype to Zeitgeist: An Essential Guide To Powerful Ideas, 1992, Powerful Mathematical Ideas, 1992, I Won't Learn From You and Other Thoughts on Maladjustment, 1994, Should We Burn Babar?, 1995; co-author: (with Judith Kohl) View From the Oak, 1977, Pack Band and Colony, 1983, (with Erica Kohl), Whatever Became of Emmett Gold, 1983, (with Myles Horton and Judith Kohl) The Long Haul, 1990; also numerous pamphlets, essays; columnist Teacher mag., 1968-82; editor: An Anthology of Fables (2 vols.), 1973, Stories of Sports and Society, 1973, Gamesmag, 1972-75, And Gladly Teach: A Dolores Kohl Education Foundation Anthology of Teaching and Learning Ideas, 1989, (with Victor Hernandez Cruz) Stuff, 1970; contbr. articles to profl. jours. Henry fellow in philosophy and logic Univ. Coll., Oxford, Eng., 1958-59; Woodrow Wilson Found. fellow Columbia U., 1959-60; recipient award for non-fiction article Nat. Endowment Arts, 1968, Nat. Book Award in CHildren's Lit., 1977, Robert Kennedy Book award, 1990; grantee Boehm Found., 1988, New World Found., 1988, Ford Found., 1970-71, Carnegie Corp. N.Y., 1968-70. Mem. PEN Am. Ctr., Nat. Assn. Devel. Educators, Authors Guild, Edn. Writers Assn. (Disting. Achievement award 1983, 84), Signet Soc., Phi Beta Kappa. Office: Coastal Ridge Rsch Edn Ctr 1 N College St Northfield MN 55057-4001

KOHL, JEANNE ELIZABETH, state senator, sociologist, educator; b. Madison, Wis., Oct. 19, 1942; d. Lloyd Jr. and Elizabeth Anne (Sinness) K.; m. Kenneth D. Jenkins, Apr. 15, 1973; children: Randall Hill, Brennan Hill, Terra Jenkins, Kyle Jenkins, Devon Jenkins; m. Alexander Sumner Welles, Nov. 10, 1985. BA, Calif. State U., Northridge, 1965, MA, 1970; MA, UCLA, 1973, PhD, 1974. Tchr. L.A. Sch. Dist., 1965-68; lectr. Calif. State U., Long Beach, 1973-85; vis. asst. prof. U. Calif., Irvine, 1974-77; So. Calif. mgr. Project Equity/U.S. Dept. Edn., 1978-84; asst. dean, coord. women's programs U. Calif., Irvine, 1979-82; lectr. Calif. State U., Fullerton, 1982-85, U. Wash., Seattle, 1985—; asst. prof. Pacific Luth. U., Tacoma, Wash., 1986-88; state legislator from 36th dist. Wash. Ho. of Reps., Olympia, 1992-94, majority whip, 1993-94; mem. Wash. Senate, Olympia, 1994—. Author: Explorations in Social Research, 1993, Student Study Guide-Marriage and the Family, 1993; contbr. articles to profl. jours. Bd. dirs. Com. for Children, Seattle, 1986-91, Queen Anne Cmty. Coun., Seattle, 1988-93, Stop Youth Violence, Wash., 1993—, Queen Anne Helpline, Seattle, 1992-94. Grantee U.S. Dept. Edn., 1988-89, 90-91. Home: 301 W Kinnear Pl Seattle WA 98119-3732 Office: Wash State Senate PO Box 40436 Bldg Olympia WA 98504-0436

KOHLER, DOLORES MARIE, gallery owner; b. Rochester, N.Y., June 26, 1928; d. Thomas Beranda and Kathryn (Held) White; m. Reuel S. Kohler, June 27, 1946; children: Richard, Kathryn Kohler Farnsworth, Linda Kohler Barnes, Pamela Kohler Conners. BMus, U. Utah, 1976. Lic. real estate broker, lic. cert. gen. real estate appraiser. Broker Kohler Investment Realty, Bountiful, Utah, 1962—; registered rep. Frank D. Richards, Salt Lake City, 1986-93; appraiser FHA/HUD, 1962—; owner Marble House Gallery, Salt Lake City, 1987—; owner Sandcastle Theaters, Bountiful, 1976—. Composer songs, 1973—. Music chmn. N. Canyon Stake LDS Ch., Bountiful, 1989-93; sec. North Canyon 3d Ward Sunday Sch., 1993—. Mem. Salt Lake Bd. Realtors, Salt Lake Art Dealers Assn. (v.p. 1988-90, pres. 1990-91), Nat. Assn. Real Estate Appraisers, Inst. Real Estate Mgmt. (pres. 1984), Mu Phi Epsilon. Home: 2891 S 650 E Bountiful UT 84010-4455 Office: Marble House Gallery 44 Exchange Pl Salt Lake City UT 84111-2713

KOHLER, ERIC DAVE, history educator; b. Cin., Oct. 24, 1943; s. Walter Joseph and Irmgard (Marx) K.; m. Kathryn D. K. Kohler, June 22, 1968. AB, Brown U., 1965; MA, Stanford U., 1967, PhD, 1971. Vis. asst. prof. history Calif. State U., Humboldt, 1970-71; asst. prof. U. Wyo., Laramie, 1971-78, assoc. prof., 1978—, acting head history dept., 1989-90. Chair Ivinson Hosp. La Grande Fleur Charity Ball, 1993. Recipient Deutcher Akademischer Austauchdienst award, 1968, U. Wyo. Faculty Devel. award, 1972. Mem. Am. Cath. Hist. Assn., Am. Hist. Assn., Am. Assn. for History of Medicine, German Studies Assn. (program dir. 1989). Club: Laramie Country. Office: U Wyo Dept History PO Box 3198 Laramie WY 82071-3198

KOHLER, FRED CHRISTOPHER, tax specialist; b. Cleve., Oct. 21, 1946; s. Fred Russell and Ruth Mary (Harris) K.; BS (Austin scholar), Northwestern U., 1968; MBA (Faville fellow), Stanford, 1970. Sr. analyst adminstrv. svcs. div. Arthur Andersen & Co., San Francisco, 1970-75, fin. systems analyst, sr. cost accountant Hewlett Packard Co., Palo Alto, Calif., 1975-77, internat. mktg. systems adminstr., 1977-80, sr. planning and reporting analyst corp. hdqrs., 1980-86, fin. planning and reporting mgr., 1986-90, tax mgr., 1990-92, sr. tax mgr., Hewlett Packard Co., 1992—. Mem. World Affairs Coun. No. Calif., Commonwealth Club, Churchill Club, Northwestern U. Alumni Club No. Calif., Stanford Alumni Assn., Beta Gamma Sigma. Home: 1736 Oak Creek Dr Palo Alto CA 94304-2112 Office: 3000 Hanover St Palo Alto CA 94304-1112

KOHLER, GARY JOSEPH, hotel and resort sales and marketing executive; b. N.Y.C., May 8, 1954; s. Raymond W. and Katherine Veronica (Christensen) K.; m. Carrie Lynn Catling, Sept. 1, 1958; children: Kristopher, Gabriel. Cert. hotel adminstr. Dir. food and beverage Atlas Hotels, 1978-82; gen. mgr. Red Lion Hotel, 1982-89; corp. sales mgr. Hyatt Regency Monterey (Calif.) and Conf. Ctr., 1992—. Mem. Monterey Conv. Bur., 1990. Mem. Meeting Planners Internat. (cert., bd. liaison 1992-93, bd. dirs. No. Calif. chpt. 1992-94, Outstanding Mem. of Yr. award), Bakersfield Innkeepers Assn. (pres. 1988-88), Bakersfield C. of C. (chmn. adminstrn., bd. dirs. 1988-89). Republican. Roman Catholic. Office: Hyatt Regency Resort One Old Golf Course Rd Monterey CA 93940

KOHLER, PETER OGDEN, physician, educator, university president; b. Bklyn., July 18, 1938; s. Dayton McCue and Jean Stewart (Ogden) K.; m. Judy Lynn Baker, Dec. 26, 1959; children: Brooke Culp, Stephen Edwin, Todd Randolph, Adam Stewart. BA, U. Va., 1959; MD, Duke U., 1963. Diplomate Am. Bd. Internal Medicine and Endocrinology. Intern Duke U. Hosp., Durham, N.C., 1963-64, fellow, 1964-65; clin. assoc. Nat Cancer Inst., Nat Inst. Child Health and Human Devel., NIH, Bethesda, Md., 1965-67, sr. investigator, 1968-73, head endocrinology service, 1972-73; resident in medicine Georgetown U. Hosp., Washington, 1969-70; prof. medicine and cell biology, chief endocrinology divsn. Baylor Coll. Medicine, Houston, 1973-77; prof., chmn. dept. medicine U. Ark., 1977-86, interim dean, 1985-86; chmn. Hosp. Med. Bd., 1980-82, chmn. council dept. chmn., 1979-80; prof., dean Sch. Medicine, U. Tex., San Antonio, 1986-88; pres. Oreg. Health Scis. U., Portland, 1988—; cons. endocrinology merit rev. bd. VA, 1985-86; mem. endocrinology study sect. NIH, 1981-85, chmn., 1984-85; mem. bd. sci counselors NICHD, 1987-92, chair, 1990-92; chair task force on health care delivery AAHC, 1991-92; bd. dirs. HealthChoice, Assn. Acad. Health Ctrs.; mem. adv. bd. Loaves and Fishes, 1989; Gov.'s Adv. Com. Commn. on Tech. Edn., 1989—; chair Oreg. Health Coun., 1993—; mem. bd. govs. Am. Bd. Internal Medicine, 1987-93, mem. endocrinology bd., 1983-91, chmn., 1987-91. Editor: Current Opinion in Endocrinology and Diabetes, 1994—, Diagnosis and Treatment of Pituitary Tumors, (with G. T. Ross), 1973, Clinical Endocrinology, 1986; assoc. editor: Internal Medicine, 1983, 87, 90, 94; contbr. articles to profl. jours. With USPHS, 1965-68. NIH grantee, 1973—; Howard Hughes Med. Investigator, 1976-77; recipient NIH Quality awrds, 1969, 71, Disting. Alumnus awrad Duke Med. Sch., 1992, MRF Mentor award, Med. Rsch. Found., 1994. Fellow ACP; mem. AMA (William Beaumont award 1988), Inst. Medicine, Am. Soc. Clin. Investigation, Am. Fedn. Clin. Rsch. (nat. coun. 1977-78, pres. so. sect. 1976), So. Soc. Clin. Investigation (coun. 1979-82, pres. 1983, Founder's medal 1987), Am. Soc. Cell Biology, Assn. Am. Physicians, Am. Diabetes Assn., Endocrine Soc. (coun. 1990-93), Raven Soc., Phi Beta Kappa, Sigma Xi, Alpha Omega Alpha, Omicron Delta Kappa, Phi Eta Sigma. Methodist. Office: Oreg Health Scis U Office of Pres 3181 SW Sam Jackson Park Rd Portland OR 97201-3011

KOHLS, DONALD WILLIAM, mineral exploration geologist, consultant; b. Mpls., Oct. 21, 1934; s. Alfred Julius and Grace Sarah (Cummings) K.; m. Marilyn Marshman, July 28, 1962; 1 child, Robert Alfred. BA, Carleton Coll., 1956; MS, U. Minn., 1958, PhD, 1961. Geologist Bur. Econ. Geology, Austin, Tex., 1961-64; supr. mineral rsch. N.J. Zinc Co., Palmerton, Pa., 1964-69; gen. mgr., asst. to pres. N.J. Zinc Co., Bethlehem, Pa., 1970-76; v.p. Gold Fields Mining Corp., Lakewood, colo., 1976-91; pres. Kohls Exploration Ltd., Lakewood, 1991—. Office: Kohls Exploration Ltd 12567 W Cedar Dr Lakewood CO 80228-2009

KOHN, ART, education educator; b. Detroit, Oct. 28, 1957; s. Art and Margaret K.; m. Wendy Lynn Koppel. BA, Oakland U., 1980; postgrad. in Japanese Studies, Nagoya U., Japan; PhD, Duke U. Prof. N.C. State U., Raleigh, 1987-88, Duke U., Durham, N.C., 1986-91, Meredith Coll., Raleigh, 1989-91, N.C. Cen. U., Durham, 1990-91, Janis Pannigs U., Pecs, Hungary, 1992-93, Pacific U., Forest Grove, Oreg., 1993—. Author: Communicating Psychology, 2 edits., 1989, 92; contbr. articles to profl. jours. Recipient Fulbright award Pecs, 1992, Internat. Study award Rotary, France, 1990. Mem. Am. Psychol. Soc., Am. Psychol. Assn. (Nat. Tchng. award 1989). Home: 7140 SW Lee Rd Gaston OR 97119-9175

KOHN, DAVID ZALMAN, human resources director; b. Washington, Apr. 4, 1949; s. Emanuel L. and Florence (Mandel) K.; m. Susan Alvarez, June 19, 1991. Student, Shimer Coll., 1968-70; BS, U. Wis., Green Bay, 1971; MS, W. Va. U., 1977; MBA, U. Ariz., 1984. Case mgr. Ill. Dept. Pub. Aid, Chgo., 1972-75; manpower analyst San Mateo County, Redwood City, Calif., 1977-79; pers. dir. N.E. Med. Svcs., San Francisco, 1979-80, Guadalupe Health Ctr., Daly City, Calif., 1980-81; program mgr. Berkeley (Calif.) Pvt. Industry Coun., 1981-82; human resources dir. El Rio Health Ctr., Tucson, 1985—; chief cons. The Musical Fruit Co., Tucson, 1988—; bd. dirs. The Profit Group, Tucson, 1993—. Editor: (book) How to Waste Time with Your PC, 1989; author: Creative Boredom, 1990. Office: El Rio Health Ctr 839 W Congress St Tucson AZ 85745-2819

KOHN, GERHARD, psychologist, educator; b. Neisse, Germany, Nov. 18, 1921; s. Erich and Marie (Prager) K.; m. Irene M. Billinger, Feb. 9, 1947; children: Mary, Eric. B.S., Northwestern U., 1948, M.A., 1949, Ph.D., 1952; postgrad. U. So. Calif., 1960. Instr., Northwestern U., 1947-49; instr., counselor, dir. pub. relations Kendall Coll., Evanston, Ill., 1947-51; psychologist, counselor Jewish Vocat. Services, Los Angeles, 1951-53, Long Beach Unified Sch. Dist., Calif., 1953-61; instr. Long Beach City Coll., 1955-61; asst. prof. psychology Long Beach State U., 1955-56; counselor, instr. Santa Ana Coll., Calif., 1961-65; prof. Calif. State U., Fullerton, 1971-72; lectr. Orange Coast Coll., 1972-75; asst. clin. prof. psychiatry U. Calif.-Irvine; dir. Reading Devel. Ctr., Long Beach, 1958-88, Gerhard Kohn Sch. Ednl. Therapy, 1967-85; exec. dir. Young Horizons; pvt. practice psychology, 1958—; for juvenile diversion program Long Beach Area, 1982—; cons. HEW, Bur. Hearing and Appeals, Social Security Adminstrn., Long Beach/Orange County B'nai B'rith Career and Counseling Svcs. (cons. to Long Beach Coun.), Long Beach Coun. of Parent Coop. Nursery Sch., Orange County Headstart, Orange County Coop. Pre-Schs. With AUS, 1942-47. Mem. NEA, Am. Pers. and Guidance Assn., Nat. Vocat. Guidance Assn., Am. Psychol. Assn., Calif. Psychol. Assn. (dir. 1976-79, 91-94, sec. 1980-81), Orange County Psychol. Assn. (dir., pres. 1974), Long Beach Psychol. Assn. (pres. 1985, 86, 93, 94, 95, sec. 1989, treas. 1991, chmn. govtl. affairs com.), L.A. County Psychol. Assn. (treas., sec.), Calif. Assn. Sch. Psychologists, Elks, Phi Delta Kappa, Psi Chi. Office: 320 Pine Ave Ste 308 Long Beach CA 90802-2307

KOHN, ROBERT SAMUEL, JR., real estate investment consultant; b. Denver, Jan. 7, 1949; s. Robert Samuel and Miriam Lackner (Neusteter) K.; m. Eleanor B. Kohn; children: Joseph Robert, Randall Stanton, Andrea Rene. BS, U. Ariz., 1971. Asst. buyer Robinson's Dept. Store, L.A., 1971; agt. Neusteter Realty Co., Denver, 1972-73, exec. v.p., 1973-76; pres. Project Devel. Svcs., Denver, 1976-78, pres., CEO, 1978-83; pres. Kohn and Assocs., Inc., 1979-83; pres. The Burke Co., Inc., Irvine, Calif., 1983-84, ptnr., 1984-91; sr. mktg. assoc. Iliff, Phoenix, 1992-94; owner RSKJ, Inc., 1992—; 1992-94. Mem. Bldg. Owners and Mgrs. Assn. (pres. 1977-78, dir. 1972-78, dir. S.W. Conf. Bd. 1977-78), Denver Art Mus., Denver U. Libr. Assn., Central City Opera House Assn., Inst. Real Estate Mgmt., Newport Beach Tennis Club. Republican. Jewish. Home: 5621 E Cambridge Ave Scottsdale AZ 85257-1013

KOHN, ROGER ALAN, surgeon; b. Chgo., May 1, 1946; s. Arthur Jerome and Sylvia Lee (Karlen) K.; m. Barbara Helene, Mar. 30, 1974; children: Bradley, Allison. BA, U. Ill., 1967; MD, Northwestern U., 1971. Diplomate Am. Bd. Opthalmology. Internship UCLA, 1971-72; residency Northwestern U., Chgo., 1972-75; fellowship U. Ala., Birmingham, 1975, Harvard Med. Sch., Boston, 1975-76; chmn. dept. ophthalmology Kern Med. Ctr., Bakersfield, Calif., 1978-87; asst. prof. UCLA Med. Sch., 1978-82, assoc. prof., 1982-86, prof., 1986—. Author: Textbook of Ophthalmic Plastic and Reconstructive Surgery, 1988; contbr. numerous articles to profl. jours.; author chpts. in 15 additional textbooks; patentee in field. Bd. dirs. Santa Barbara (Calif.) Symphony, 1990—. Capt. USAR, 1971-77. Named applied to med. syndrome Kohn-Romano Syndrome. Mem. Am. Soc. Ophthalmic Plastic and Reconstuctive Surgery (cert.), Pacific Coast Ophthal. Soc. (bd. dirs. 1986—, 1st v.p. 1990). Jewish. Office: 525 E Micheltorena St Ste 201 Santa Barbara CA 93103-2254

KOHNE, RAYMOND ERNEST, physician, educator; b. Orangeville, Ontario, Canada, Oct. 7, 1962; came to the U.S., 1981; s. Ernest Herman and Milda Lena (Thonigs) K.; m. Cathy Lynette Proctor, Aug. 11, 1985. BS, Andrews U., 1985, MS, 1988; MD, Loma Linda U., 1992. Researcher Andrews U., Berrien Springs, Mich., 1985-88, flight instr., 1985-90; resident Loma Linda (Calif.) Med. Ctr., 1992-93; intern in radiology Loma Linda U. Med. Ctr., 1993—; instr. anatomy Loma Linda U. Med. Ctr., 1992—. Contbr. articles to profl. jours. Mem. Radiologic Soc. North Am., AMA, San Bernadino Med. Assn., Housestaff Assn., Sigma Xi, Alpha Omega Alpha. Office: Loma Linda Med Ctr 11234 Anderson St Loma Linda CA 92354-2804

KOHNE, RICHARD EDWARD, retired engineering executive; b. Tientsin, China, May 16, 1924; s. Ernest E. and Elizabeth I. (Antonenko) K.; m. Gabrielle H. Vernaudon; children: Robert, Phillip, Daniel, Paul, Renee. B.S., U. Calif., Berkeley, 1948. Structural engr. hydro projects Pacific Gas & Electric Co., San Francisco, 1948-55; cons. engr. Morrison-Knudsen Engrs., Inc., San Francisco, 1955—, regional mgr. for Latin Am., then v.p., 1965-71, exec. v.p. world-wide ops. in engring. and project mgmt., 1971-79, pres., chmn., chief exec. officer, 1979-88; chmn., chief exec. officer Morrison-Knudsen Internat. Co., Inc., San Francisco, 1988-90, chmn. emeritus, 1990—. Decorated Chevalier Nat. Order of Leopold (Zaire). Mem. ASCE, U.S. Com. Large Dams, Cons. Engrs. Assn. Calif., World Trade Club (San Francisco). Democrat. Roman Catholic. Home and Office: 1827 Doris Dr Menlo Park CA 94025-6101

KOKALJ, JAMES EDWARD, retired aerospace administrator; b. Chgo., Oct. 29, 1933; s. John and Antoinette (Zabukovec) K. AA in Engring., El Camino Coll., Torrance, Calif., 1953. Dynomometer lab. technician U.S. Electric Motors, L.A., 1953-54; devel. lab. technician AiResearch divsn. Garrett, L.A., 1956-59; tech. rep. McCulloch, L.A., 1959-65; dist. mgr. Yamaha Internat., Montebello, Calif., 1965-67; salesman Vasek Polak BMW, Manhattan Beach, Calif., 1967-68; sr. svc. rep. Stratos-We. div. Fairchild, Manhattan Beach, 1968-70; asst. regional mgr. we. states J.B.E. Olson div. Grumman, L.A., 1970-71; gen. mgr. Internat. Kart Fedn., Glendora, Calif., 1971-73; logistics support data specialist mil. aircraft divsn. Northrop Grumman, Hawthorne, Calif., 1974-95; ret., 1995. Author: Technical Inspection Handbook, 1972; contbr. articles to profl. jours. With USN, 1954-56. Mem. U.S. Naval Inst., Internat. Naval Rsch. Orgn., Nat. Maritime Hist. Soc., So. Calif. Hist. Aircraft Found. Republican. Roman Catholic. Home: 805 Bayview Dr Hermosa Beach CA 90254-4147

KOKANOVICH, JON DOUGLAS, crime laboratory director, forensic chemist; b. Phoenix, Sept. 11, 1951; s. Dan and Doris (Schupbach) K.; m. Nancy Anne Freed, Apr. 14, 1974; children: Mark, Heidi, Holly, Tim. Student, Mesa (Ariz.) C.C., 1969-71; BA in Edn., Ariz. State U., 1973, MA in Edn., 1976. Sci. tchr. Paradise Valley High Sch., Phoenix, 1973-76; criminalist Ariz. Dept. Pub. Safety Crime Lab. System, 1977-80; criminalist, crime lab dir. Mesa Police Dept. Crime Lab., 1980—. Contbr. articles to profl. jours. Lay min. Apostolic Christian Ch., Phoenix, 1981. Mem. Am. Acad. Forensic Scis., Am. Soc. Crime Lab. Dirs., Assn. Firearms and Toolmark Examiners, Southwestern Assn. Forensic Scientists, Calif. Assn. Criminalists. Office: Mesa Police Crime Lab 130 N Robson Mesa AZ 85201-6609

KOLANOSKI, THOMAS EDWIN, financial company executive; b. San Francisco, Mar. 1, 1937; s. Theodore Thaddeus and Mary J. (Luczynski) K.; m. Sheila O'Brien, Dec. 26, 1960; children: Kenneth John, Thomas Patrick, Michael Sean. BS, U. San Francisco, 1959, MA, 1965. Cert. fin. planner; registered rep. Educator, counselor, adminstr. San Francisco Unified Sch. Dist.; adminstr. Huntington Beach (Calif.) Union, 1969-79; v.p. fin. svcs. Waddell & Reed, Inc., Ariz., Nev., Utah, So. Calif., 1979-94; retired Waddell & Reed, Inc., 1994; ind. contractor in field. Fellow NDEA, 1965. Mem. Nat. Assn. Secondary Sch. Prins., Internat. Assn. of Fin. Planners, Nat. Assn. Securities Dealers. Republican. Roman Catholic. Home: 1783 Panay

Cir Costa Mesa CA 92626-2348 also: 10218 N Central Ave Phoenix AZ 85020-1047

KOLAROV, KRASIMIR DOBROMIROV, computer scientist, researcher; b. Sofia, Bulgaria, Oct. 16, 1961; came to the U.S., 1987; s. Dobromir Krastev and Margarita Georgieva (Kurukafova) K.; m. Janet Louise Barba, July 4, 1990; children: April, Kathryn, Sonia, Elena. BS in Math. with honors, U. Sofia, Bulgaria, 1981, MS in Ops. Rsch. with honors, 1982, MA in English, 1982; MS in Mech. Engring., Stanford U., 1990, PhD in Mech. Engring., 1993. Rschr. Bulgarian Acad. Scis., Sofia, 1982-83; rsch. assoc., vis. prof. Inst. Mechanics and Biomechanics, Bulgarian Acad. Scis., Sofia, 1983-87; tchg. asst. Stanford (Calif.) U., 1988-92; mem. rsch. staff Interval Rsch. Corp., Palo Alto, Calif., 1992—; vis. prof. Inst. for Civil Engring., Sofia, 1983-86; lectr. H.S. U., Sofia, 1985; reviewer Jour. Robotic Sys., Palo Alto, 1991—, others. Contbr. articles to profl. jours. Mem. IEEE, Assn. for Computing Machinery, Soc. for Indsl. and Applied Math. Office: Interval Rsch Corp 1801 Page Mill Rd # C Palo Alto CA 94304-1216

KOLB, DOROTHY GONG, elementary education educator; b. San Jose, Calif.; d. Jack and Lucille (Chinn) Gong; m. William Harris Kolb, Mar. 22, 1970. BA (with highest honors), San Jose State U., 1964; postgrad., U. Hawaii, Calif. State U., L.A.; MA in Ednl. Tech., Pepperdine U., 1992. Cert. life elem. educator, mentally retarded educator K-12, learning handicapped pre-sch., K-12, adult classes. Tchr. Cambrian Sch. Dist., San Jose, Calif., 1964-66, Cen. Oahu (Hawaii) Sch. Dist., Wahiawa, 1966-68, Montebello (Calif.) Unified Sch. Dist., 1968—. Named to Pi Lambda Theta, Kappa Delta Pi, Pi Tau Sigma, Tau Beta Pi; recipient Walter Bachrodt Meml. scholar.

KOLB, KEITH ROBERT, architect, educator; b. Billings, Mont., Feb. 9, 1922; s. Percy Fletcher and Josephine (Randolph) K.; m. Jacqueline Cecile Jump, June 18, 1947; children: Brooks Robin, Bliss Richards. Grad. basic engring., US Army Specialized Training Rutgers U., 1944; BArch cum laude, U. Wash., 1947; MArch, Harvard U., 1950. Registered architect, Wash., Mont., Idaho, Calif., Oreg., Nat. Council Archtl. Registration Bds. Draftsman, designer various archtl. firms Seattle, 1946-54; draftsman, designer Walter Gropius and Architects Collaborative, Cambridge, Mass., 1950-52; prin. Keith R. Kolb, Architect, Seattle, 1954-64, Keith R. Kolb Architect & Assocs., Seattle, 1964-66; ptnr. Decker, Kolb & Stansfield, Seattle, 1966-71, Kolb & Stansfield AIA Architects, Seattle, 1971-89; pvt. practice Keith R. Kolb FAIA Architects, Seattle, 1989—; instr. Mont. State Coll., Bozeman, 1947-49; asst. prof. arch. U. Wash., Seattle, 1952-60, assoc. prof., 1960-82, prof., 1982-90, prof. emeritus, 1990—. Design architect Dist. II Hdqrs. and Comm. Ctr., Wash. State Patrol, Bellevue, 1970 (Exhbn. award Seattle chpt. AIA), Hampson residence, 1970 (nat. AIA 1st honor 1973, citation Seattle chpt. AIA 1980), Acute Gen. Stevens Meml. Hosp., 1973, Redmond Pub. Libr., 1975 (jury selection Wash. coun. AIA 1980), Tolstedt residence, Helena, Mont., 1976, Herbert L. Eastlick Biol. Scis. Lab. bldg. Wash. State U., 1977, Redmond Svc. Ctr., Puget Sound Power and Light Co., 1979, Computer and Mgmt. Svcs. Ctr., Paccar Inc., 1981 (curatorial team selection Mus. History and Industry exhbn. 100th anniversary of AIA 1994), Seattle Town House, 1960 (curatorial team selection Mus. History and Industry exhbn. 100th anniversary of AIA 1994), Comm. Tower, Pacific N.W. Bell, 1981 (nat. J.F. Lincoln bronze), Forks br. Seattle 1st Nat. Bank, 1981 (commendation award Seattle chpt. AIA 1981, nat. jury selection Am. Architecture, The State of the Art in the '80's 1985, regional citation Am. Wood Coun. 1981), Reg. ops. Control Ctr. Sacramento Dist. Corps Engrs. McChord AFB, Wash., 1982, Puget Sound Blood Ctr., 1983-88, expansion vis./dining/recreation facilities Wash. State Reformatory, Monroe, 1983, Univ. Sta. P.O., U.S. Postal Svc., Seattle, 1983, Guard Towers, McNeil Island Corrections Ctr. Wash., 1983, Magnolia Queen Anne Carrier Annex, U.S. Postal Svc., Seattle, 1986, Tolstedt residence, Seattle, 1987, Maxim residence, Camano Island, Wash., 1991, Carmean residence alterations/additions, Seattle, 1995. Pres. Laurelhurst Community Club, Seattle, 1966. Served with U.S. Army, 1943-45, ETO. Decorated Bronze Star medal ETO; recipient Alpha Rho Chi medal; selected Am. Architects, Facts on File, inc., 1989. Fellow AIA (dir. Seattle chpt. 1970-71, sec. Seattle chpt. 1972, Wash. state coun. 1973, pres. sr. coun. Seattle chpt. 1994-95, trustee Seattle Archtl. Found. 1994-95, Citation award Seattle chpt. for a Seattle 1960 Town House, 1990); mem. U. Wash. Archtl. Alumni Assn. (pres. 1958-59), Phi Beta Kappa, Tau Sigma Delta. Home and Office: 3379 47th Ave NE Seattle WA 98105-5326

KOLB, KEN LLOYD, writer; b. Portland, Oreg., July 14, 1926; s. Frederick Von and Ella May (Bay) K.; m. Emma LaVada Sanford, June 7, 1952; children: Kevin, Lauren, Kimrie. BA in English with honors, U. Calif., Berkeley, 1950; MA with honors, San Francisco State U., 1953. Cert. jr. coll. English tchr. Freelance fiction writer various nat. mags., N.Y.C., 1951-56; freelance screenwriter various film and TV studios, Los Angeles, 1956-81; freelance novelist Chilton, Random House, Playboy Press, N.Y.C., 1967—; instr. creative writing Feather River Coll., Quincy Calif., 1969; minister Universal Life Ch. Author: (teleplay) She Walks in Beauty, 1956 (Writers Guild award 1956), (feature films) Seventh Voyage of Sinbad, 1957, Snow Job, 1972, (novels) Getting Straight, 1967 (made into feature film), The Couch Trip, 1970 (made into feature film), Night Crossing, 1974; contbr. fiction and humor to nat. mags. and anthologies. Foreman Plumas County Grand Jury, Quincy, 1970; chmn. Region C Criminal Justice Planning commn., Oroville, Calif., 1975-77; film commr. Plumas County, 1986-87. Served with USNR, 1944-46. Establishment Ken Kolb Collection (Boston U. Library 1969). Mem. Writers Guild Am. West, Authors Guild, Mensa, Phi Beta Kappa, Theta Chi. Democrat. Club: Plumas Ski (pres. 1977-78). Home and Office: PO Box 30022 Cromberg CA 96103-2022*

KOLBE, JAMES THOMAS, congressman; b. Evanston, Ill., June 28, 1942; s. Walter William and Helen (Reed) K. BA in Polit. Sci., Northwestern U., 1965; MBA in Econs., Stanford U., 1967. Asst. to coordinating architect Ill. Bldg. Authority, Chgo., 1970-72; spl. asst. to Gov. Richard Ogilvie Chgo., 1972-73; v.p. Wood Canyon Corp., Tucson, 1973-80; mem. Ariz. Senate, 1977-83, majority whip, 1979-81; cons. Tucson, 1983-85; mem. 99th-104th Congresses from 5th dist. Ariz., 1985—; mem. appropriations com., 1987—, mem. budget com. Trustee Embry-Riddle Aero. U., Daytona Beach, Fla.; bd. dirs. Community Food Bank, Tucson; Republican precinct committeeman, Tucson, 1974—. Served as lt. USNR, 1977-79, Vietnam. Mem. Am. Legion, VFW. Republican. Methodist. Office: US Ho of Reps 205 Cannon HOB Washington DC 20515-0305

KOLBE, JOHN WILLIAM, newspaper columnist; b. Evanston, Ill., Sept. 21, 1940; s. Walter William and Helen (Reed) K.; m. Mary Bauman, Feb. 24, 1990; stepchildren: Erin Simmons, James Simmons; children by previous marriage: Karen, David. BS in Journalism, Northwestern U., 1961; MA in Polit. Sci., U. Notre Dame, 1962. Feature writer, polit. reporter Rockford (Ill.) Register-Republic, 1964-68; press aide Ogilvie for Gov. campaign, Chgo., 1968; asst. press sec. Office Gov., Springfield, Ill., 1969-73; polit. reporter, columnist Phoenix Gazette, 1973—. Elder Valley Presbyn. Ch., Scottsdale, Ariz., 1978-81; bd. dirs. Morrison Inst., Ariz. State U., Tempe, 1982—. Lt. (j.g.) USNR, 1962-64. Recipient Best Column of Yr. award Ariz. Press Club, 1976, 80, 84. Office: Phoenix Newspapers 120 E Van Buren St Phoenix AZ 85004-2227

KOLBESON, MARILYN HOPF, retired advertising executive, organization and management consultant, educator; b. Cin., June 9, 1930; d. Henry Dilg and Carolyn Josephine (Brown) Hopf; children: Michael Llen, Kenneth Ray, Patrick James, Pamela Sue Kolbeson Lang, James Allan. Student U. Cin., 1947, 48, 50. Sales and mktg. mgr. Cox Patrick United Van Lines, 1977-80; sales mktg. mgr. Creative Incentives, Houston, 1980-81; pres. Ad Sense, Inc., Houston, 1981-87, M.H. Kolbeson & Assocs., Houston, 1987, Seattle, 1987—, The Phoenix Books, Seattle, 1987-90; cons. N.L.P. Communications; lectr., cons. in field. Mem. adv. bd. Alief Ind. Sch. Dist., 1981-87, pres., 1983-84; bd. dirs. Santa Maria Hostel, 1983-86, v.p., 1983-84; founder, pres. Mind Force, Houston, 1978-87 and Seattle, 1987-95; ret., 1995; founder META Group, Seattle, 1991—. Mem. citizen's adv. bd. Arcola (Ill.) Sch. Bd., 1966-67; mem. Greater Houston Conv. and Visitors Coun., loaned exec., 1986-87; mem. adv. bd. Am. Inst. Achievement, 1986-87; vol. Seattle Pub. Schs., 1992—; charter mem. Rep. Task Force. Mem. Internat. Platform Assn., Houston Advt. Splty. Assn. (bd. dirs. 1984-87, treas. 1985, v.p. 1986-87), Inst. Noetic Scis. (charter), Galleria Area C. of C. (bd. dirs. 1986-87), Toastmasters (area gov. 1978), Grand Club (v.p. 1986), Lakewood Seward Park Community Club (bd. dirs. 1992—). Republican. Christian Scientist. Office: 5247 S Brandon St Seattle WA 98118-2522

KOLDE, BERT, professional basketball team executive. Vice chmn. Portland Trail Blazers. Office: Portland Trail Blazers Port of Portland Bldg 700 NE Multnomah St Ste 600 Portland OR 97232-4106*

KOLDE, RICHARD ARTHUR, insurance company executive, consultant; b. Pomona, Calif., Jan. 25, 1944; s. Arthur and Rosemary (Decker) K.; children: Nicole Rochelle, Eric Christian, Katarina R. Lic. CPCU. AA, Mt. San Antonio Coll., 1963; BS, U. So. Calif., 1965; AS, Mira Costa Coll., 1979. Asst. mgr., mgr. Lord Rebel Ind., Montclair, Costa Mesa and Carlsbad, Calif., 1971-74; agt. Conn. Mut. Life Ins. Co., San Diego and Carlsbad, 1974-77; pres., owner Investment Assocs., Carlsbad, 1977-82, 93—; mng. gen. agt. E.F. Hutton Life Ins. Co., San Diego, 1982—; cons. Hansch Fin. Group, Laguna Hills, Calif., 1984; cons., recruiter Ky. Gen. Life Ins. co., 1990-92; mng. gen agt. N.W. Life of Can. Ins. Co, 1991—. Bd. dirs. Boys Club Am., Carlsbad, 1980-84, adv. bd., 1984—; bd. dirs. YMCA, Pomona, 1960-64. Served with USAF, 1966-71. Decorated Outstanding Unit award, Small Arms Expert award, Security 1 & 2 Protection of Pres. U.S. award; named Largest Producing Mng. Gen. Agt. in Nation, E.F. Hutton Life Co., 1982, 83. Mem. Nat. Assn. Life Underwriters (legis. officer 1974—), Calif. Assn. Life Underwriters, Internat. Assn. Fin. Planners (Mem. of Yr. award 1977), U.S. Gymnastics Fedn. (coaching credentials, ofcl. judge collegiate level), VFW, Phi Sigma Beta. Republican. Lodge: Rotary.

KOLDEN, KENNETH DALE, semiconductor company executive; b. San Luis Obispo, Calif., Oct. 10, 1956; s. John Richard and Mary Louise K.; m. Rosymary Constance, Apr. 23, 1988; 1 child, Kristiana. BSChemE, Calif. Poly., 1981; MBA, U. So. Calif., 1993. Rsch. ops. mgr. J. C. Schumacher Co., Oceanside, Calif., 1981-86; yield mgr. Internat. Rectifier-Hexfet Am., Temecula, Calif., 1986-89; mgr. advanced products Alcoa Electronic Packaging, Rancho Bernardo, Calif., 1989-93; mgr. bus. devel. Athens Corp., Oceanside, Calif., 1993—. Patentee high frequency microwave package; contbr. papers to profl. publs. Pres. Royal Carlsbad (Calif.) Assn., 1991. Recipient George Putnum Engring. award Pasadena City Coll., 1979, Price fellowship U. So. Calif., 1992. Republican. Home: 3835 Nautical Dr Carlsbad CA 92008-3377 Office: Athens Corp 1922 Avenida Del Oro Oceanside CA 92056-5803

KOLDOVSKY, OTAKAR, pediatrics and physiology educator; b. Olomouc, Czechoslovakia, Mar. 31, 1930; came to U.S., 1968; s. Kvetoslav and Marie (Loukotska) K.; m. Eva Libicka, May 6, 1971. MD, Charles U., Prague, Czechoslovakia, 1955; PhD, Inst. Physiology, Prague, Czechoslovakia, 1962. Rsch. assoc. dept. Pediatrics Stanford (Calif.) U., 1965; vis. scientist dept. Clin. Biochemistry Lund (Sweden) U., 1967-68; from asst. prof. to prof. Pediatrics Rsch. U. Pa., Phila., 1969-79; prof. Pediatrics and Physiology U. Ariz., Tucson, 1980—. Author (books) Utiliz of Nutrients During Postnatal Development, 1967, Functional Development of the Gastrointestinal Tract in Mammals, 1968, Development of the Small Intestinal Function in Mammals and Man, 1969. Recipient Nutrition award Am. Acad. Pediatrics, 1986, Harry Shwachman award, 1991. Office: U Ariz 1501 N Campbell Ave Tucson AZ 85724-0001

KOLETTY, STEPHEN RONALD, geographer, educator; b. Jan. 17, 1949; s. John William and Margaret C. (Ford) K.; m. Yuhaniz Anang, Aug. 15, 1981; children: Manoah Koa'e, Gio Helaku. AA in Geology, L.A. Harbor Coll., 1969; BA in Geography/Earth & Space Sci., Calif. State U., Dominguez Hills, 1974; MA in Geography/Resource Mgmt., cert. Pacific Urban Studies and Planning, U. Hawaii at Manoa, 1983; postgrad., U. So. Calif., 1992—. Cert. c.c. instr., Calif. Evening coord. Office Student Affairs Calif. State U., Dominguez Hills, 1974-76, counselor, coord. internat. programs Office Student Devel., 1978—; rsch. asst., teaching asst. geography dept. U. So. Calif., L.A., 1993—; lectr. Calif. State U., Dominguez Hills, 1980, 81, 82, 85, 87, 89, 90, 91, 92, 93, asst. prof., summer 1982, 83, 86, instr., fall 1986, 87, 88, 89, 90, faculty pers. com. reappointment, tenure, promotion subcom. acad. senate, 1984-86, faculty advisor Polynesian Club, 1982-92, nat. student exch. del., 1988-92; instr. Cypress Coll., spring 1990, Fullerton Coll., spring 1989, El Camino Coll., 1990—; presenter in field. Mem. Assn. Am. Geographers, Assn. Pacific Coast Geographers, Calif. Geographic Soc., Calif. Coll. Pers. Assn., The Mongolia Soc. Home: 241 S Walker Ave San Pedro CA 90732-3245 Office: U So Calif Dept Geography Los Angeles CA 90089-0255

KOLFF, WILLEM JOHAN, internist, educator; b. Leiden, Holland, Feb. 14, 1911; came to U.S., 1950, naturalized, 1956; s. Jacob and Adriana (de Jonge) K.; m. Janke C. Huidekoper, Sept 4, 1937; children: Jacob, Adriana P., Albert C., Cornelis A., Gualtherus C.M. Student, U. Leiden Med. Sch., 1930-38; M.D. summa cum laude, U. Groningen, 1946; M.D. (hon.), U. Turin, Italy, 1969, Rostock (Germany) U., 1975, U. Bologna, Italy, 1983; D.Sc. (hon.), Allegheny Coll., Meadville, Pa., 1960, Tulane U., 1975, CUNY, 1982, Temple U., 1983, U. Utah, 1983; D. of Tech. Scis. (hon.), Tech. U. Twente, Enschede, The Netherlands, 1986; D.Sc. (hon.), U. Athens, 1988, Aix-Marseille II, 1993. Internist, head med. dept. Mcpl. Hosp., Kampen, Holland; dir. div. artificial organs Cleve. Clinic Found., 1950-67; privaat docent, dept. medicine U. Leiden, 1950-67; prof. surgery U. Utah Coll. Medicine, Salt Lake City, 1967—, Disting. prof. medicine and surgery, 1979—; prof. internal medicine U. Utah Coll. Medicine, 1981—, dir. Inst. for Biomed. Engring., dir. div. artificial organs, 1967-86. Patents include electrohydraulic heart with septum mounted pump, 1994, ventricular assist device with volume displacement chamber, 1994, muscle and air powered LVAD, 1995. Decorated commandeur Orde Van Oranje Netherlands, 1970; Orden de Mayo al Merito en el Grade de Gran Official Argentina, 1974; recipient Landsteiner medal for establishing blood banks during German occupation in Holland, Netherlands Red Cross, 1942, Cameron prize U. Edinburgh (Scotland), 1964, Gairdner prize Gairdner Found., 1966, Valentine award N.Y. Acad. Medicine, 1969, 1st Gold medal Netherlands Surg. Soc., 1970, Leo Harvey prize Technion, Israel, 1972, Sr. U.S. Scientist award Alexander Von Humboldt Found., 1978, Austrian Gewerbeverein's Wilhelm-Exner award, 1980, John Scott medal City of Phila., 1984, Japan prize Japan Found. Sci. and Tech., 1986, Rsch. prize Netherlands Royal Inst. Engrs., 1986, 1st Jean Hamburger award Internat. Soc. Nephrology, 1987, 1st Edwin Cohn-De Laval award World Apheresis Assn, 1990, Fed. prize Fedn. Sci. Med. Assn., 1990, Father of Artificial Organs award and medal Internat. Soc. Artificial Organs, 1992, Christopher Columbus Discovery award in biomed. rsch. NIH, 1992, Legacy of Life award LDS Deseret Found., 1995; named to Nat. Inventors Hall of Fame, 1985, named to On the Shoulders of Giants Hall of Fame, Cleve., 1989. Mem. AMA (Sci. Achievement award 1982), AAUP, Am. Physiol. Soc., Soc. Exptl. Biology and Medicine, AAAS, Nat. Acad. Engring. (City of Medicine award 1989), N.Y. Acad. Scis., Am. Soc. Artificial Internal Organs, Nat. Kidney Found., European Dialysis and Transplant Assn., ACP, Austrian Soc. Nephrology (hon.), Academia Nacional de Medicine (Colombia, hon.), NAE. Lodge: Rotary. Office: U Utah Coll of Engring Dept Biomed Engring 2460-A Merrill Engring Bldg Salt Lake City UT 84112

KOLIN, ALEXANDER, retired biophysics researcher; b. Odessa, Russia, Mar. 12, 1910; came to U.S., 1934; s. Rudolph and Luba (Gershberg) K.; m. Renée Bourcier, 1951. Student, Inst. Tech. and U. Berlin, Berlin, 1929-33; PhD in Physics, German U. Prague, Czechoslovakia, 1934. Rsch. fellow in biophysics Michael Reese Hosp., Chgo., 1935-37; physicist to hosp. Mt. Sinai Hosp., N.Y.C., 1938-41; rsch. fellow NYU Med. Sch., N.Y.C., 1941-42, asst. prof. physics, 1945; instr. CCNY, 1941-44; instr. Columbia U., N.Y.C., 1944-45, rsch. assoc., 1941-46; assoc. prof. U. Chgo., 1947-56; prof. UCLA, 1956-77, prof. emeritus, 1977—. Author: Physics, Its Laws, Ideas, Methods, 1951; inventor electromagnetic flow meter, method of analysis isoelectric focusing, also others; discoverer electromagnetophoresis phenomenon. Recipient John Scott medal City of Phila., 1965, Albert F. Sperry medal Instrument Soc. Am., 1967, Alexander von Humboldt award Fed. Republic Germany, 1977; rsch. grantee Office Naval Rsch., NIH, also others, 1954—. Mem. AAAS, Am. Phys. Soc., Am. Physiol. Soc., Biophys. Soc., Electrophoresis Soc. (hon. life, Founders' award 1980), Sigma Xi (pres. UCLA chpt. 1966-67). Office: UCLA Sch Med 100 Stein Plz Los Angeles CA 90024

KOLINSKI, ANDRZEJ, molecular biology researcher, educator; b. Wysokie Mazowieckie, Poland, June 25, 1951; came to U.S., 1985; s. Tadeusz and Halina (Biala) K.; m. Ewa Litwiniuk, June 30, 1973; children: Pawel, Michal, Dorota. MSc in Chemistry, U. Warsaw, Poland, 1974, PhD in Chemistry, 1979. Rsch. asst. chemistry U. Warsaw, 1974-79, asst. prof. chemistry, 1979-87, prof. chemistry, 1987—, dir. computational chemistry lab., 1989-91; vis. assoc. prof. chemsitry Washington U., St. Louis, 1985-89; vis. rsch. assoc. Scripps Rsch. Inst., La Jolla, Calif., 1990-91, adj. mem. molecular biology dept., 1991-93, assoc. mem. molecular biology dept., 1993—. Contbr. articles to profl. jours. Recipient Outstanding Work in Chemistry prize Polish Ministry of Higher Edn., 1992, Howard Huges Med. Inst. award, 1995; grantee Polish Acad. Scis., 1979-84, Polish Ministry Higher Edn., 1987-88, Com. Sci. Investigation (Poland), 1989-91. Office: Scripps Rsch Inst 10666 N Torrey Pines Rd La Jolla CA 92037

KOLKEY, DANIEL MILES, lawyer; b. Chgo., Apr. 21, 1952; s. Eugene Louis and Gilda Penelope (Cowan) K.; m. Donna Lynn Christie, May 15, 1982; children: Eugene, William, Christopher, Jonathan. BA, Stanford U., 1974; JD, Harvard U., 1977. Bar: Calif. 1977, U.S. Dist. Ct. (cen. dist.) Calif. 1979, U.S. Dist. Ct. (no. dist.) Calif. 1980, U.S. Dist. Ct. (ea. dist.) Calif. 1978, U.S. Dist. Ct. (so. dist.) Calif. 1994, U.S. Dist. Ct. Ariz. 1992, U.S. Ct. Appeals (9th cir.) 1979, U.S. Supreme Ct., 1983. Law clk. U.S. Dist. Ct. judge, N.Y.C., 1977-78; assoc. Gibson Dunn & Crutcher, L.A., 1978-84, ptnr., 1985-94; counsel to Gov. and legal affairs sec. to Calif. Gov. Pete Wilson, 1995—; arbitrator bi-nat. panel for U.S.-Can. Free Trade Agreement, 1990-94; commr. Calif. Law Revision Commn., 1992-94, vice chair, 1993-94, chair, 1994. Contbr. articles to profl. publs. Co-chmn. internat. rels. sect. Town Hall of Calif., L.A., 1981-90; chmn. internat. trade legis. subcom., internat. commerce steering com. L.A. Area C. of C., 1983-91 (mem. law & justice com., 1993-94); mem. adv. coun. and exec. com. Asia Pacific Ctr. for Resolution of Internat. Bus. Disputes, 1991-94; bd. dirs., L.A. Ctr. for Internat. Comml. Arbitration, 1986-94, treas., 1986-88, v.p. 1988-90, pres., 1990-94; assoc. mem. ctrl. com. Calif. Rep. Party, 1983-94, mem. ctrl. com., 1995—, dep. gen. coun. credentials com., Republican Nat. Convention, 1992, alt. Calif. Delegation, 1992; mem. L.A. Com. on Fgn. Rels., 1983—; mem. L.A. World Affairs Council; gen. counsel Citizens Rsch. Found., 1990-94. Mem. ABA, Internat. Bar Assn., L.A. County Bar Assn. (exec. com. internat. law sect. 1987—, vice chmn. 1989-91, chmn. 1991-92), Am. Arbitration Assn. (panel of arbitrators, arbitrator large complex case dispute resolution program, 1993—), Chartered Inst. Arbitrators, London (assoc.), Friends of Wilton Park So. Calif. (chmn. exec. com. 1986-94, exec. com. 1986—). Jewish. Office: Gov's Office State Capitol Sacramento CA 95814-4906

KOLLER, DUNCAN G., military officer; b. Felixstowe, Suffolk, Eng., Dec. 20, 1946; came to U.S., 1956; s. Carl Anthony and Grace Florence (Bunkell) K.; m. Cheryl Victoria Baccash, June 14, 1969; children: David Andrew, Elisha Anne. BS, Oreg. State U., 1969; MA in Edn., Chapman Coll., 1978; EdD, U. So. Calif., 1992. Commd. 2d lt. USAF, 1969, advanced through grades to col., 1991; squadron exec. officer 315th Security Police Squadron, Phan Rang, Vietnam, 1971-72; squadron comdr. Keesler Tech. Tng. Ctr., Biloxi, Miss., 1978-82; staff officer Hdqr. UN Command, Seoul, Korea, 1982-84; course dir. Armed Forces Staff Coll., Norfolk, Va., 1984-87; dep. base comdr. 8th Tactical Fighter Wing, Kunsan AB, Korea, 1987-88; joint sec. Hdqr. U.S. Pacific Command, Honolulu, 1989-92; prof. aerospace sci. Oreg. State U., Corvallis, 1992—. Pres. Radford High Sch. PTO, Honolulu, 1991-92. Decorated Bronze star. Mem. Phi Delta Kappa, Rotary. Episcopalian. Office: DET 685 AFROTC Oreg State U Corvallis OR 97331

KOLLER, THOMAS JOHN, engineering executive; b. Buffalo, N.Y., Feb. 16, 1942; s. Edward Jacob and Anna Dorthea (Christle) K.; m. Barbara Ann Mallozzi, Aug. 12, 1967; children: John J., Kevin E., Colleen M. BS in Physics, Canisius Coll., 1963; MS in Physics, U. Bridgeport, 1971. Devel. engr. Machlett Labs., Stamford, Conn., 1968-75, engring. mgr., 1975-89; sr. engr. Varian Assocs., Salt Lake City, 1989-93, R&D mgr., 1993—. Author: (with others) Radiology of Skull & Brain, 1981; contbr. articles to profl. jours.; co-author several patents. 1st lt. U.S. Army, 1964-66. Decorated Commendation medal. Home: 8363 S 3375 E Salt Lake City UT 84121-5874 Office: Varian Assocs 1678 Pioneer Rd Salt Lake City UT 84104-4205

KOLLITZ, JANICE ARLENE, English literature educator, freelance writer; b. Stockton, Calif., Sept. 8, 1937; d. Charles Millard and Anna Henrietta (Neidhardt) Morris; m. Richard LeRoy Hollenbeck (div. 1971); children: Richard Gordon Hollenbeck, John Morgan Hollenbeck, Margaret Joy Hollenbeck Stepe; m. Gerhard Kollitz. AA, Riverside (Calif.) C.C., 1986; BA, Calif. State U., San Bernardino, 1987, MA, 1989. Cert. cmty. coll. tchr., Calif. V.p. Concept Now, Inc., City of Commerce, Calif., 1971-72; owner wholesale giftwares co. GJK Enterprises, Riverside, Calif., 1972-85; art editor Elan Mag., Colton, Calif., 1987-90; prof. English Riverside C.C., 1988—; adj. instr. Chaffee Coll., Rancho Cucamonga, Calif., 1988-90, Valley Coll., San Bernardino, 1988-90, Crafton Hills Coll., Yucaipa, Calif., 1988-90; adj. lectr. Calif. State U., San Bernardino, 1989—; advisor Muse Lit. Mag., Riverside, 1992—; mem. editorial staff Pacific Rev., San Bernardino, 1987-88. Ghost writer: (biography) Machine Gun Kelly: To Right a Wrong, 1992; co-author: (hist. novel) Madagh, 1993; contbr. articles to Elan mag. Active in Republican politics, 1956, 64. Named Tchr. of Distinction, Latter Day Saints Student Orgn., 1994, 95, Most Influential Instr., Riverside C.C. Disabled Students, 1991, 93, 94, Tchr. of Yr. Assoc. Students Riverside C.C., 1991, 93, 95. Mem. MLA. Mem. Reformed Ch. in Am. Office: Riverside CC 4800 Magnolia Ave Riverside CA 92506-1242

KOLMAN, MARC RAND, public health administrator; b. Phila., May 14, 1960. BA, Brandeis U., 1982; MS in Pub. Health Policy Analysis, U. N.C., 1986. Rsch. tech. III dept. pathology U. N.Mex. Sch. Medicine, Albuquerque, 1989-90; health educator, tng. mgr. family planning program N.Mex. Dept. Health Pub. Health Div., Santa Fe, 1990-91; planner 3-C devel. disabilities divsn. N.Mex. Dept. Health, Santa Fe, 1992-94, mgmt. analyst, devel. disabilities div., 1994—; vol. N.Mex. AIDS Svcs., Albuquerque, 1988-89; vol. sponsor Parents Anonymous Program, All Faiths Family Svcs., Albuquerque, 1989-90; cons. Health Ctrs. of No. N.Mex., 1992. Contbr. articles to profl. jours. Mem. Am. Pub. Health Assn., N.Mex. Pub. Health Assn. Office: N Mex Dept Health 1190 S Saint Francis Dr Santa Fe NM 87505-4182

KOLODNY, STEPHEN ARTHUR, lawyer; b. Monticello, N.Y., June 25, 1940; s. H. Lewis and Ida K.; children: Jeffery, Lee. BA in Bus. Adminstrn., Boston U., 1963, JD, 1965. Bar: Calif. 1966, U.S. Dist. Ct. (cen. dist.) Calif. 1966; cert. family law specialist. Sole practice L.A., 1966-95; with Kolodny & Anteau, L.A., 1995—; lectr. on family law subjects. Co-author: Divorce Practice Handbook. Mem. ABA (family law sect., author ABA Advocate), Internat. Acad. Matrimonial Lawyers (bd. govs., pres. elect USA chpt.), Am. Acad. Matrimonial Lawyers (So. Calif. chpt. pres., bd. govs.), Calif. State Bar Assn. (cert. family law specialist, lectr. State Bar panel, CEB programs, mem. family law sect.), Los Angeles County Bar Assn. (lectr., mem. & past chmn. family law sect.), Beverly Hills Bar Assn. (lectr., mem. family law sect.).

KOLPAS, SIDNEY J., mathematician, educator; b. Chgo., Oct. 19, 1947; s. Irving and Molly Lou (Lubin) K.; m. Laurie Ann Puhn, June 27, 1971; children: Allison, Jamie. BA magna cum laude, Calif. State U., Northridge, 1969, MS, 1971; EdD, U. So. Calif., L.A., 1979. Tchr. Luther Burbank (Calif.) Jr. High Sch., 1971-79; tchr., author Tandy Corp., L.A., 1979-85; tchr. John Burroughs High Sch., Burbank, 1979-90; adj. instr. Coll. of the Canyons, Valencia, Calif., 1985-90; ind. cons. L.A., 1979—; instr. Glendale (Calif.) Coll., 1990—; statis. cons. U. So. Calif., L.A.; math. and computer sci. mentor Burbank Unified Sch. Dist., 1985-89; tchr. math. Korean Coll. Prep. Sch., 1989; instr. Moorpark (Calif.) Coll., 1990; tchr. computer programming L.A. Valley Jr. Coll., 1976-77. Author: Topics in Mathematics, 1971, A Theory of Motivation in Mathematics, 1972, Model 3 TRSDOS and Disk Basic, 1979, Computer Applications in Patient Care, 1986, Quest for James Coffin, 1990, The Pythagorean Theorem: 8 Classic Proofs, 1991; contbr. articles to profl. jours. Recipient Teaching award McLuhen Found., L.A., 1984, Honors Teaching award NASA/Nat. Coun. Tchrs. Math., 1987, teaching commendation L.A. County, 1992, Disting. Prof. award Glendale Coll. chpt. Alpha Gamma Sigma, 1993; named Outstanding Tchr., Kiwanis, 1985, Woodrow Wilson Master Tchr., Woodrow

Wilson Nat. Fellowship Found., Princeton, 1988, Ministerial and Burbank Tchr. of Yr., 1992. Mem. Nat. Coun. Tchrs. Math., Calif. Math. Coun. (com. chmn. 1985—), Foothill Math. Coun. (pres. 1989-90, 92-93), L.A. County Math. Tchrs. Assn. (bd. dirs. 1985-87), Phi Delta Kappa, Phi Eta Sigma, Alpha Mu Gamma. Democrat. Jewish. Office: Glendale Coll 1500 N Verdugo Rd Glendale CA 91208-2809

KOLSRUD, HENRY GERALD, dentist; b. Minnewaukan, N.D., Aug. 12, 1923; s. Henry G. and Anna Naomi (Moen) K.; m. Loretta Dorothy Cooper, Sept. 3, 1945; children—Gerald Roger, Charles Cooper. Student Concordia Coll., 1941-44; DDS, U. Minn., 1947. Gen. practice dentistry, Spokane, Wash., 1953—. Bd. dirs. Spokane County Rep. Com., United Crusade, Spokane; at-large-del. Republican Planning Com.; mem. Republican Presdl. Task Force. Capt. USAF, 1950-52. Recipient Employer of the Yr. award Lilac City Bus. and Profl. Women, 1994. Mem. ADA, Wash. State Dental Assn., Spokane Dist. Dental Soc. Lutheran. Clubs: Spokane Country, Spokane, Empire. Lodges: Masons, Shriners. Home: 2107 W Waikiki Rd Spokane WA 99218-2780 Office: 3718 N Monroe St Spokane WA 99205-2850

KOLSTAD, CHARLES DURGIN, economics and environmental studies educator; b. Warehan, Mass., Apr. 30, 1948; s. George Andrew and Christine Joyce (Stillman) K.; m. Dorothy Valerie Thompson, July 8, 1972; children: Jonathan, Kate. BS, Bates Coll., 1969; MA, U. Rochester, N.Y., 1973; PhD, Stanford U., 1982. Staff mem. Los Alamos (N. Mex.) Nat. Lab., 1974-83; asst. prof. econs. and environ. studies U. Ill., Urbana, 1983-88, assoc. prof., 1988-92, prof., 1992-94; vis. prof. econs. U. Calif., Santa Barbara, 1992, prof. econs. and environ. studies, 1993—; vis. scholar Norwegian Sch. Econs., Bergen, 1985; vis. asst. prof. MIT, Cambridge, 1986-87; vis. prof. Cath. U. Louvain, Belgium, 1993; pres. Resource Econs. Corp., Urbana, 1984—; mem. sci. adv. bd. U.S. EPA, 1992—; mem. bd. energy and environ. systems NRC/NAS. Editor: Resource and Energy Economics; assoc. editor Jour. Environ. Econs. and Mgmt., 1992-93; contbr. articles to profl. jours. Named Univ. Scholar, U. Ill., 1988. Mem. Assn. for Environ. and Resource Econs. (bd. dirs.), Am. Econ. Assn., Econometric Soc. Office: Dept Econs Univ Calif Santa Barbara CA 93106

KOLSTAD, ROBERT BRUCE, computer scientist; b. Montevideo, Minn., Aug. 21, 1953; s. Clayton Robert and Joanne Marie (Peterson) K. B in Applied Sci., So. Meth. U., 1974; MSEE, U. Notre Dame, 1976; PhD, U. Ill., 1982. Sr. engr., mgr. Convex Computer Corp., Dallas, 1982-88; sr. software engr. Prisma, Inc., Colorado Springs, 1988-89, v.p. software, 1989; sr. staff engr. Sun Micro Systems, Colorado Springs, 1989-91; pres. Berkeley Software Design, Inc., Colorado Springs, 1991—; sec., bd. officer USENIX, Berkeley, 1986-92. Patentee in field. Recipient Orange County Community Svc. award, 1989, UNIX Personality of the Yr. award, 1988; named to Guiness Book of World Records. Home: 7759 Delmonico Dr Colorado Springs CO 80919-1050 Office: 5575 Tech Center Dr Ste 110 Colorado Springs CO 80918

KOLTAI, STEPHEN MIKLOS, mechanical engineer, consultant, economist, writer, educator; b. Ujpest, Hungary, Nov. 5, 1922; came to U.S., 1963; s. Maximilian and Elisabeth (Rado) K.; m. Franciska Gabor, Sept. 14, 1948; children: Eva, Susy. MS in Mech. Engring., U. Budapest, Hungary, 1948, MS in Econs., MS, BA, 1955. Engr. Hungarian Govt., 1943-49; cons. engr. and diplomatic service various European countries, 1950-62; cons. engr. Pan Bus. Cons. Corp., Switzerland and U.S., 1963-77, Palm Springs, Calif., 1977—. Patentee in field. Charter mem. Rep. Presdl. task force, Washington, 1984—.

KOMAR, KATHLEEN LENORE, literature educator; b. Joliet, Ill., Oct. 11, 1949; d. Joseph Andrew and Sophie (Boldego) K. BA in English, U. Chgo., 1971; MA in Comparative Lit., Princeton U., 1975, PhD in Comparative Lit., German, 1977. Asst. prof. UCLA, 1977-84, assoc. prof. Germanic lang., comparative lit., 1984-90, prof. Germanic lang., comparative lit., 1990—, chair comparative lit., 1986-89, assoc. dean grad. div., 1992—. Author: Pattern & Chaos: Multilinear Novels by Dos Passos, Faulkner, Döblin, and Koeppen, 1983, Transcending Angels: Rainer Maria Rilke's Duino Elegies, 1987; contbr. articles to profl. jours. Grantee Am. Coun. Learned Socs., 1978, 86, UCLA, 1979, 81; Deutsche Akademische Austauschdienst fellow, 1971-72, Kent fellow Danforth Found., 1974-77; recipient Disting. Teaching award UCLA, 1989. Mem. MLA, Am. Comparative Lit. Assn., Internat. Comparative Lit. Assn., Soc. Values in Higher Edn., Am. Assn. Tchrs. German, Philol. Assn. Pacific Coast. Office: UCLA Grad Divsn 1237 Murphy Hall 405 Hilgard Ave Los Angeles CA 90024-1301

KOMDAT, JOHN RAYMOND, data processing consultant; b. Brownsville, Tex., Apr. 29, 1943; s. John William and Sara Grace (Williams) K.; m. Linda Jean Garrette, Aug. 26, 1965 (div.); m. Barbara Milroy O'Cain, Sept. 27, 1986; children: Philip August, John William. Student U. Tex., 1961-65. Sr. systems analyst Mass. Blue Cross, Boston, 1970-74; pvt. practice data processing cons., San Francisco, 1974-80, Denver, 1981—; prin. systems analyst mgmt. info. svcs. div. Dept. of Revenue, State of Colo., 1986-89; prin. systems analyst Info. Mgmt. Commn. Staff Dept. Adminstrn. State Colo., 1989—; mem. Mus. Modern Art, CODASYL End User Facilities Com., 1974-76, allocation com. Mile High United Way. Served with U.S. Army, 1966-70. Mem. IEEE, AAAS, ACLU, Colo. Info. Mgrs. Assn., Assn. Computing Machinery, Denver Art Mus., Friend of Pub. Radio, Friend of Denver Pub. Libr., Colo. State Mgrs. Assn, Nature Conservancy, Sierra Club, Common Cause, Trout Unlimited. Democrat. Office: PO Box 9757 Denver CO 80209-0757

KOMENICH, KIM, photographer; b. Laramie, Wyo., Oct. 15, 1956; s. Milo and Juanita Mary (Beggs) K. BA in Journalism, San Jose State U., 1979. Reporter/photographer Manteca (Calif.) Bull., 1976-77; staff photographer Contra Costa Times, Walnut Creek, Calif., 1979-82, San Francisco Examiner, 1982—; lectr. San Francisco Acad. Art. John S. Knight fellow Stanford U., 1993—; recipient 1st Pl. award UPI, 1982, 85, Nat. Headliner award, 1983, 88, 87 1st Pl. award World Press Photo Awards, 1983, 1st Pl. award AP, 1985, 87, Pulitzer prize, 1987, others. Mem. Sigma Delta Chi (Disting. Svc. award 1986). Office: San Francisco Examiner 110 5th St San Francisco CA 94103-2918

KOMISAR, JEROME BERTRAM, university administrator; b. Bklyn., Jan. 31, 1937; s. Harry and Fanny (Neumann) K.; m. Natalie Rosenberg, Sept. 8, 1957; children: Harriet, Wade, Frances, Aurenna. BS, NYU, 1957; MA, Columbia U., 1959, PhD, 1968. Asst. prof. econs. Hamilton Coll., Clinton, N.Y., 1961-66; asst. prof., then assoc. prof. mgmt. SUNY, Binghamton, 1966-74, asst. to pres., 1971-74; vice chancellor faculty and staff rels. SUNY System, 1974-81, provost, 1982-85, pres. Rsch. Found., 1982-90, exec. vice chancellor, 1985-90, acting chancellor, 1987-88; acting pres. SUNY, New Paltz, 1979-80, prof. econs. and adminstrn., 1988-90; pres. U. Alaska System, Fairbanks, 1990—; regents prof. U. Alaska, 1990—; Alaska commr. We. Interstate Commn. for Higher Edn., 1990—; chmn. Alaska Aerospace Devel. Corp., 1991—. Author: Work Scheduling in the Wholesale Trades in Manhattan's Central Business District, 1962, Social Legislation and Labor Force Behavior, 1968; co-author: (with John S. Gambs) Economics and Man, 1964. Bd. dirs. Sta. WAMC-FM, Albany, 1982-90; chair bd. overseers Rockefeller Inst., 1987-88. Office: U Alaska System 202 Butrovich Bldg 910 Yukon Dr Fairbanks AK 99775

KOMISSARCHIK, EDWARD A., computer scientist; b. Moscow, Russia, July 5, 1949; came to U.S., 1990; s. Alexander and Riva (Zilberstein) K.; m. Stella Mnatsakanian, Sept. 5, 1969; 1 child, Julia. M in Math., Lomonosov U., Moscow, 1971; PhD of Computer Sci., Inst. Cybernetics, Russia, 1978. Rsch. scientist Inst. Control Scis., Acad. Scis., Moscow, 1971-77, Inst. Sys. Studies, Acad. Scis., Moscow, 1977-90; assoc. prof. computer sci. Inst. Radio Electronics and Automation, Moscow, 1978-90; pres., chief tech. officer Accent, Inc., Mill Valley, Calif., 1993—. Contbr. articles to profl. jours. Mem. IEEE, N.Y. Acad. Scis., Russian Math. Soc., Scientists Club. Home: 137A Seminary Dr Mill Valley CA 94941-3111 Office: Accent Inc 591 Redwood Hwy Ste 5280 Mill Valley CA 94941-3064

KOMPALA, DHINAKAR SATHYANATHAN, chemical engineering educator, biochemical engineering researcher; b. Madras, India, Nov. 20, 1958; came to U.S., 1979; s. Sathyanathan and Sulochana Kompala; m. Sushila Viswamurthy Rudramuniappa, Nov. 18, 1983; children: Tejaswi Dina, Chytanya Robby. BTech., Indian Inst. Tech., Madras, 1979; MS, Purdue U., 1982, PhD, 1984. Asst. prof. chem. engring. U. Colo., Boulder, 1985-91, assoc. prof., 1991—; vis. assoc. chem. enging. Calif. Inst. Tech., 1991-92. Editor Cell Separation Sci. and Tech., 1991; contbr. articles to profl. jours. Recipient NSF Presdl. Young Investigators award, 1988-93; NSF Biotech. Rsch. grantee, 1986-89, 89-92, 95—; Dept. Commerce rsch. grantee, 1988; The Whitaker Found. grantee, 1990-93. Mem. Am. Inst. Chem. Engrs., Am. Chem. Soc. (program chair biochem. tech. divsn. 1993). Office: U Colo PO Box 424 Boulder CO 80309-0424

KOMPKOFF, GARY PHILLIP, chief of native village, fisherman; b. Tatitlek, AK, July 21, 1954; s. Carroll Mike and Mabel Seena (Allen) K.; m. Carolyn Marie Selanoff Kompkoff, Sept. 1, 1973; children: Katherine, Kristi, Kelly, Nanci, Kerry, Caroline. Grad. high sch., Cordova, AK, 1972. Chief, pres. Tatitlek (AK) Village IRA Coun., 1978-79, 80—; chmn. bd. dirs. The Tatitlek Corp., Cordova, AK, 1978-80, 86-92 (shareholder of the yr. 1992); bd. dirs. Chugachmiut, Anchorage, AK; vice chmn. Chugach Regional Resources Commn., Anchorage, AK, 1986—; mem. The North Pacific Rim Housing Authority Bd. Commr., Anchorage, AK, 1980—; adminstr. Fishing Vessels Alyeska/SERVS Oil Spill Response, Valdez, AK, 1990—. Bd. dirs. Prince William Sound Sci. Ctr., Cordova, AK; chmn. Tatitlek Ednl. Adv. Com., 1986-88, 90-92; mem. Prince William Sound Econ. Devel. Coun., Valdez, AK, 1991— (innovative econ. devel. award 1994), Prince William Sound Regional Citizen's Adv. Coun., Anchorage, AK, 1993—, Citizen's Oversight Coun. on Oil & Other Hazardous Substances, 1991—, South Ctrl. AK Subsistence Regional Adv. Coun., 1992-94; pres. The Copper Mountain Fdn., Anchorage, AK, 1991—, Chugach Environ. Protection Consortium, 1992—; dir. Tatitlek Emergency Med. Svcs., 1984-93; starosta St. Nicholas Orthodox Church, Tatitlek, 1988—. Russian Orthodox. Home: PO Box 170 103 Hillside Dr Tatitlek AK 99677 Office: Native Village of Tatitlek 585 Copper Mountain St Tatitlek AK 99677

KONDA, VENKATA REDDY, computer scientist, lecturer; b. Kollipara, India, Aug. 5, 1965; came to U.S., 1988; s. Siva Reddy and Raja Kumari (Jonnala) K.; m. V. L. Santha Devi Sompalli, Dec. 14, 1987. BTech in Elec. Engring., Nagarjuna U., Vijaywada, India, 1986; MTech in Elec. Engring., Indian Inst. Tech., Kharagpur, 1987; PhD in Computer Sci., U. Louisville, 1992. Staff scientist NCUBE Corp., Foster City, Calif., 1992-95; adj. lectr. computer engring. dept. Santa Clara (Calif.) U., 1994—; sr. engr., sci. Mitsubishi Electric Rsch. Lab. Inc., Sunnyvale, Calif., 1995—; referee tech. confs. and jours. Mem. IEEE, Assn. Computing Machinery. Home: 3996 Ellmar Oaks Dr San Jose CA 95136 Office: Mitsubishi Electric Rsch Labs 1050 East Arques Ave Sunnyvale CA 94536

KONDRASUK, JACK N. (JOHN KONDRASUK), business educator; b. Eau Claire, Wis., Jan. 23, 1942; s. Frank Mathew and Ruth (Norton) K. Student, Coll. St. Thomas, 1960-61; BS, U. Wis., Eau Claire, 1964; MA, U. Minn., 1966, PhD, 1972. Pers. adminstr. Honeywell, Inc., Mpls., 1967-68; instr. U. Minn., Mpls., 1969; mgmt. edn. specialist Control Data Corp., Mpls., 1969-71; mgmt. cons. J.N. Kondrasuk Co., Mpls., 1971-73; psychologist Persona Corp., Portland, Oreg., 1973; cons. Rohrer, Hibler & Repogle, Inc. (now called RHR Internat.), Portland, Oreg., 1973-74; asst. to pres. U. Portland, 1980-81, asst./assoc. prof., 1975—; vis. prof. Novgorod (Russia) Poly. Inst., 1993. Contbr. articles to profl. jours. Mem. adv. group City of Portland, 1978, State of Oreg., Salem, 1987-88; mem. Clackamas County Econ. Devel. Commn., 1992-94. Mem. ASTD (pres. 1987, nat. coms. 1987—, dir. HRD Cons. Network, regional conf. chair 1984-86), Soc. Human Resource Mgmt. (sr. profl. in human resources, tng. com. 1988—), N.W. Human Resource Mgmt. Assn. (chair 1979), Acad. of Mgmt. (div. newsletter editor 1982), Am. Psychol. Soc., Soc. Indsl. Orgn. Psychology. Office: U Portland Sch Bus 5000 N Willamette Blvd Portland OR 97203-5743

KONG, LAURA S. L., seismologist; b. Honolulu, July 23, 1961; d. Albert T.S. and Cordelia (Seu) K.; m. Kevin T.M. Johnson, Mar. 3, 1990. ScB, Brown U., 1983; PhD, MIT/Woods Hole Oceanog. Inst., 1990. Grad. rschr. Woods Hole (Mass.) Oceanog. Instn., 1984-90; postdoctoral fellow U. Tokyo, 1990-91; geophysicist Pacific Tsunami Warning Ctr., Ewa Beach, Hawaii, 1991-93; seismologist U.S. Geol. Survey Hawaiian Volcano Obs., 1993—; mem. grad. faculty dept. geology & geophysics U. Hawaii; mem. Hawaii State Earthquake Avd. Bd., 1993—; mem. equal opportunity adv. bd. Nat. Weather Svc. Pacific Region, Honolulu, 1992-93, Asian-Am./Pacific Islander spl. emphasis program mgr., 1992-93. Contbr. articles to profl. jours.; spkr., editl. reviewer in field. Rsch. fellow Japan Govt.-Japan Soc. for Promotion of Sci., 1990; recipient Young Investigator grant Japan Soc. for Promotion of Sci., 1990. Mem. Am. Geophys. Union, Seismol. Soc. Am., Hawaii Ctr. for Volcanology, Assn. Women in Sci., Sigma Xi. Office: US Geol Survey Hawaiian Volcano Obs PO Box 51 Hawaii National Park HI 96718-0051

KONG, XIANGLI (CHARLIE KONG), technical service company executive, educator; b. Chifeng, China, Mar. 11, 1953; came to U.S., 1988; s. Fanxin and Yuzhen Kong; m. Xiuxian Han, Jan. 17, 1978; children: Ling Xin, Brian Lingyu. BE, Shenyang Poly. U., 1978; MSc, Xian Jiaotong U., Xian, Shaanxi, China, 1981, PhD, 1985. Univ. lectr. Xian Jiotong U., 1981-86, assoc. prof., 1986-88; vis. assoc. prof. UCLA, 1988-89; engring. dir. Hill Equipment Corp., Whittier, Calif., 1989-92; pres., CEO MS-Tech. Corp., Cerritos, Calif., 1992—. Contbr. numerous articles to profl. jours. Named Outstanding Young Scientist, Chinese Sci. and Tech. Assn., Beijing, 1987, Outstanding Young Educator award Fok Yingtong Found., Beijing and Hong Kong, 1988, and many other awards. Address: MS-Tech Corp 13337 E South St # 349 Cerritos CA 90703

KONING, HENDRIK, architect; came to the U.S., 1979; BArch, U. Melbourne, Australia, 1978; MArch II, UCLA, 1981. Lic. architect Calif., 1982, contractor, 1984; registered architect, Australia; cert. Nat. Coun. Archtl. Registration Bds. Prin. in charge of tech., code, and prodn. issues Koning Eizenberg Architecture, 1981—; instr. UCLA, U. B.C., Harvard U.; lectr. in field. Exhbns. include "House Rules" Wexner Ctr., 1994, "The Architects Dream: Houses for the Next Millennium" The Contemporary Arts Ctr., 1993, "Angels and Franciscans" Gagosian Gallery, 1992, "Conceptual Drawings by Architects" Bannatyne Gallery, 1991, Exhbn. Koning and Eizenberg Projects Grad. Sch. Architecture & Urban Planning UCLA, 1990, and many others; prin. works include Digital Domain renovation and screening rm., Santa Monica, Lightstorm Entertainment offices and THX theater, Santa Monica, Gilmore Bank addition and remodel, L.A., 1548-1550 Studios, Santa Monica, (with RTA) Materials Rsch. Lab at U. Calif., Santa Barbara, Ken Edwards Ctr. Community Svcs., Santa Monica, Sepulveda Recreation Ctr., L.A., PS # 1 Elem. Sch., Santa Monica, A.L.A. Sr. Svc. Ctr., West Hollywood, Vitalize Fairfax Project, L.A., Famers Market additions and master plan, L.A. (Westside Urban Forum prize 1991), Stage Deli, L.A., Simone Hotel, L.A. (Nat. Honor award AIA 1994), Boyd Hotel, L.A., Community Corp. Santa Monica Housing Projects, St. John's Hosp. Replacement Housing Program, Santa Monica, Liffman Ho., Santa Monica, (with Glenn Erikson) Electric Artblock, Venice (Beautification award L.A. Bus. Coun. 1993), 6th St. Condominiums, Santa Monica, Hollywood Duplex, Hollywood Hills (Record Houses Archtl. Record 1988), California Avenue Duplex, Santa Monica, Millen Apts., Santa Monica, Tarzana Ho. (Award of Merit L.A. chpt. AIA 1991, Sunset Western Home Awards citation 1993-94), 909 Ho., Santa Monica (Award of Merit L.A. chpt. AIA 1991), 31st St. Ho., Santa Monica (Honor award AIACC 1994), others. Recipient 1st award Progressive Architecture, 1987; named one of Domino's Top 30 Architects, 1989. Fellow Royal Australian Inst. Archs., Am. Inst. Archs. (juror San Diego design awards 1992, panelist honor awards 1994); mem. Nat. Trust for Hist. Preservation, So. Calif. Assn. Non-Profit Housing, L.A. Conservancy. Office: Koning Eizenberg Architecture 1548 18th St Santa Monica CA 90404-3404

KONKEL, R(ICHARD) STEVEN, environmental and social science consultant; b. Denver, June 27, 1950; s. E. Vernon and Rojean (Templeman) K.; m. Jane Frances Ohlert, July 14, 1984; children: Kaitlin Brooke and Britt Edward (twins). BS in Archtl. Engring., U. Colo., 1972; M in City Planning, Harvard U., 1975; PhD in Urban and Environ. Planning, MIT, 1991. Economist, planner Edward C. Jordan Co., Portland, Maine, 1975-77; cost-benefit analyst Oak Ridge (Tenn.) Nat. Lab., 1977-79; prin. economist Konkel Environ. Cons., San Francisco, 1980-82; policy analyst State of Alaska Office of Gov. and Dept. Commerce and Econ. Devel., Juneau, 1982-84; pres. Konkel & Co., Cambridge, Mass., 1984-91; sr. rsch. sci. energy environ. policy and dispute resolution Battelle Pacific Northwest Lab., 1992-95; coord. MIT faculty seminar on risk mgmt., 1988-89. Author: Environmental Impact Assessment Rev., 1987; co-editor: MIT Faculty Seminar on Risk Management, 1989; rev. editor Soc. Risk Analysis. Co-chair Juneau Energy Adv. Com., 1984. Research grantee Nat. Inst. Dispute Resolution, Washington, 1986-87. Mem. Am. Inst. Cert. Planners (charter), Am. Planning Assn., Am. Econ. Assn., Internat. Assn. Energy Econs., Assn. Environ. and Resource Economists. Home: 112 S Van Buren St Kennewick WA 99336-1791 Office: Battelle Pacific NW Lab Energy and Environ Sci Bldg PO Box 999 Stop K8-03 Richland WA 99352-0999

KONKOL, PETER ADAM, engineer; b. Yonkers, N.Y., May 25, 1933; divorced; children: Deborah, Joliene. B of Engring., N.Y. Maritime Coll., 1955. Cert. mech. engr. Ariz., Ky., N.Y. Engr. trainee GE, 1955-56, mfg. engr., 1958-70; mfg. engr. Honeywell Computer, Phoenix, 1970-81, mgr. mfg. engring., 1981-84; pres. Engineered Adaptation Inc., Phoenix, 1984-89; mfg. engr. Honeywell Air Transport, Phoenix, 1989-92; pres. Engineered Adaptation Inc., 1992—. With U.S. Army, 1956-58. Mem. Am. Soc. Mech. Engr., (assoc.), Ariz. Printed Circuits Assn. (sec./treas. 1986—), Soc. Mfg. Engrs. Office: Engineered Adaptation Inc PO Box 82580 Phoenix AZ 85071-2580

KONNYU, ERNEST LESLIE, former congressman; b. Tamasi, Hungary, May 17, 1937; came to U.S., 1949; s. Leslie and Elizabeth Konnyu; m. Lillian Muenks, Nov. 25, 1959; children: Carol, Renata, Lisa, Victoria. Student, U. Md., 1960-62; BS in Acctg., Ohio State U., 1965. Mem. Calif. Assembly, Sacramento, 1980-86, 100th Congress from 12th Calif. dist., 1987-89; owner Premier Printing, San Jose, Calif., 1990—; chmn. Assembly Rep. Policy Com. of State Assembly, Sacramento, 1985-86; vice chmn. Assembly Human Services, Sacramento, 1980-86; vice chmn. Policy Research Com., Sacramento, 1985-86. Mem. Rep. State Cen. Com., Calif., 1977-88, Rep. Cen. Com., Santa Clara County, Calif., 1980-88; mem. adv. bd. El Camino Hosp., Mountain View, Calif., 1987-89. Served to maj. USAF, 1959-69. Recipient Nat. Def. Medal, 1968, Disting. Service award U.S. Jaycees, 1969, Nat. Security award Am. Security Council Found., 1987; named lifetime senator U.S. Jaycees, 1977. Mem. Am.- Hungarian C. of C. (v.p. 1995—). Republican. Roman Catholic.

KONRAD, PETER ALLEN, foundation administrator. BS in Biol. and Chemistry, U. Redlands, 1968; MS in Ecol., U. N.H., 1973; EdD in Ednl. Adminstrn., U. Northern Colo., 1979; BA in Accounting, Metro. State Coll., 1982. CPA, Colo.; prins. lic securities broker/dealer, Colo. secondary sch. administr. Founder, pres. Colo. Outdoor Educators, Denver, 1973-82; prin. Partner's Middle Sch., Denver, 1976-79; pres. Historic Shelter Investments, Inc., Denver, 1979-85; v.p., chief fin. officer The Colo. Trust, Denver, 1985—; faculty Grad. Sch. Pub. Affairs, U. Colo., Grad Sch. Profl. Studies, Regis U. Robert Kennedy Meml. fellow; recipient Disting. Svc. award U. Redlands. Home: 4650 E 18th Ave Denver CO 80220-1130 Office: The Colorado Trust 511 16th St Ste 700 Denver CO 80202-4232

KONTNY, VINCENT L., engineering and construction company executive; b. Chappell, Nebr., July 19, 1937; s. Edward James and Ruth Regina (Schumann) K.; m. Joan Dashwood FitzGibbon, Feb. 20, 1970; children: Natascha Marie, Michael Christian, Amber Brooke. BSCE, U. Colo., 1958, DSc honoris causa, 1991. Operator heavy equipment, grade foreman Peter Kiewit Son's Co., Denver, 1958-59; project mgr. Utah Constrn. and Mining Co., Western Australia, 1965-69, Fluor Australia, Queensland, Australia, 1969-72; sr. project mgr. Fluor Utah, San Mateo, Calif., 1972-73; sr. v.p. Holmes & Narver, Inc., Orange, Calif., 1973-79; mng. dir. Fluor Australia, Melbourne, 1979-82; group v.p. Fluor Engrs., Inc., Irvine, Calif., 1982-85, pres., chief exec. officer, 1985-87; group pres. Fluor Daniel, Irvine, Calif., 1987-88, pres., 1988—; pres. Fluor Corp., Irvine, 1990-94, vice chmn., 1994; ret., 1994; rancher Last Dollar Ranch, Ridgeway Co., Centennial Ranch, Ouray County, Co. Contbr. articles to profl. jours. Mem. engring. devel. coun., U. Colo.; mem. engring. adv. coun., Stanford U. Lt. USN, 1959-65. Mem. Am. Assn. Cost Engrs., Australian Assn. Engrs., Am. Petroleum Inst. Republican. Roman Catholic. Club: Cet. (Costa Mesa, Calif.).

KOO, GRACE, artist; b. Riverside, Calif., Jan. 5, 1921; d. Chung Sup and Ai Joo (Park) Koo; m. William F. Donoghue Jr., Jan. 26, 1974. BFA, U. Calif., Irvine, 1977. Mgr., owner Koo's Cafe, Santa Ana, Calif., 1942-61; clk. typist Civil Svc. U.S. Dept. Army, Korea, 1961-62; sec. Ford Aeronutronic, Newport Beach, Calif., 1962-65; adminstrv. asst., dept. math. U. Calif., Irvine, 1965-73; artist freelance, 1974—. Mem. U. Calif. Faculty Assocs., 1974—. Home: 22 Perkins Ct Irvine CA 92715-4043

KOOB, ROBERT DUANE, chemistry educator, educational administrator; b. Graetinger, Iowa, Oct. 14, 1941; s. Emil John and Rose Mary (Slinger) K.; m. E. Yvonne Ervin, June 9, 1960; children—Monique, Gregory, Michael, Angela, Julie, Eric, David. B.A. in Edn., U. No. Iowa, 1962; Ph.D. in Chemistry, U. Kans., 1967. From asst. prof. to prof. chemistry N.D. State U., Fargo, 1967-90, chmn. dept. chemistry, 1974-78, 79-81, dir. Water Inst., 1975-85, dean Coll. Sci. and Math., 1981-84, v.p., 1985-90, interim pres., 1987-88; v.p. for acad. affairs, sr. v.p. Calif. Poly. State U., San Luis Obispo, 1990-95; pres. U. No. Iowa, Cedar Falls, 1995—; cons. TrnasAlta, Edmonton, Alta., Can., Alta. Rsch. Coun., Mitre Corp., Washington; bd. dirs. State Bank Fargo, Fagro Cass County Econ. Devel. Corp.; chair bd. dirs. Cal Poly Found. Contbr. articles to profl. jours. Vice pres. Crookston Diocesan Sch. Bd., Minn., 1982; pres. elem. sch. bd. St. Joseph's Ch., Moorhead, Minn., 1982, parish council, 1983; pres. bd. Shanley High Sch., Fargo, 1985. Grantee in field. Roman Catholic. Office: U No Iowa Cedar Falls IA 50614

KOOMEY, JONATHAN GARO, energy and environmental analyst; b. N.Y.C., Feb. 15, 1962; s. Richard Alan Koomey and Cynthia Carol Chaffee. AB in History of Sci., Harvard U., 1984; MS in Energy and Resources, U. Calif., Berkeley, 1986, PhD in Energy and Resources, 1990. Rschr. Lawrence Berkeley Lab., 1984-90, postdoctoral rsch. fellow, 1990-91, staff scientist, 1991—. Co-author: Energy Policy in the Greenhouse, 1989; also articles. Office: Lawrence Berkeley Lab Bldg 90-4000 1 Cyclotron Rd Berkeley CA 94720

KOON, RAY HAROLD, management and security consultant; b. Little Mountain, S.C., Nov. 19, 1934; s. Harold Clay and Jessie Rae (Epting) K.; m. Bertha Mae Gardner, Aug. 19, 1958; children: Shari Madilyn Koon Goode, Schyler Michele, Kamela Suzanne. BSBA, Old Dominion U., 1957; postgrad., Columbia (S.C.) Coll., 1957-58. Lic. pvt. pilot. Supr. office svcs. FBI, Norfolk, Va., 1953-61, Las Vegas, Nev., 1961-62; agt. State Gaming Control Bd., Carson City, Nev., 1962-64, coord., 1967-80, chief of investigations, 1980-83; prodn. control mgr. Colite Industries, Inc., West Columbia, S.C., 1964-67; pres. Global Advisors, Ltd., Carson City, 1983; dir. gaming surveillance Hilton Hotels Corp., Beverly Hills, Calif., 1983-86; pres. JRJ Enterprises, Las Vegas, 1986-88, Assoc. Cons. Enterprises, Las Vegas, 1983—; pres. Assoc. Gaming Cons., Las Vegas, 1983—, CEO, 1990—; past sec. Sta. KNIS-FM; bd. dirs. Casino Mgmt. Internat., Carson City. Editor, pub. Ray Koon's Gaming Gram, 1986—; columnist Casino Gaming Internat., 1990-92. Chief vols. Warren Engine Co. 1, Carson City Fire Dept., 1962-83; mem. Carson City Sheriff's Aero Squadron, 1983—, past comdr.; past mem. exec. bd. Nev. Bapt. Conv. With U.S. Army, 1957-59. Mem. Nev. Arbitration Assn. (bd. dirs. 1986-90), Las Vegas C. of C. (mem. commerce crime prevention and legis. action coms. 1989-90), Zelzah Shrine Aviation Club (past comdr.), Toastmasters, Masons. Republican. Office: Assoc Cons Enterprises 3271 S Highland Dr Ste 705A Las Vegas NV 89109-1051

KOON, ROBIN CHARLES, retail pharmacy executive; b. Pasadena, Calif., Apr. 22, 1953; s. Charles John and Helene (Wickham) K.; m. Laura Lynn Robertson, Aug. 27, 1983; children: Casey Charles, Perry William. BSM, Pepperdine U., 1993. Lic. pharmacy technician. Store mgr. Imperial Drugs, L.A., 1977-81; mem. store mgmt. Thrifty Drugs, L.A., 1987-88; pharmacy technician Horton & Converse Pharmacies, Newport Beach, Calif., 1981-87, mgr. chain ops., 1988—. Unit commr. Boy Scouts Am., Hollywood, Calif.,

1984—. Mem. Calif. Pharmacy Assn., Orgn. Pharmacy Technicians, Optimists (v.p. Hollywood club 1986—). Home: 2730 N Kenneth Rd Burbank CA 91504-2305 Office: Horton Converse Pharmacies 1617 Westcliff Dr Newport Beach CA 92660-5524

KOONS, TODD L., agricultural products executive; b. 1959. Student, U. Oreg., 1980-82. Chef Chez Panisse, Berkeley, Calif., 1982-84; ind. rsch. Europe, 1984-85; rep. Calif. Dept. Agrl. World Wine Exposition, Bourdeaux, France, 1984-85; agrl. cons. Dalgety Ltd., Salinas, Calif., 1985-86; with Two Farms, Inc., 1986—, now pres. Office: Tko Farms Inc 85 Liberty Ship Way # 104 Sausalito CA 94965-1768*

KOONS, WILLIAM ALBRIGHT, quality engineer; b. Phila., Aug. 10, 1944; s. Albright Everett and Anna Christina (Fredlund) K.; m. Sandra F. Bailey, Dec. 31, 1967 (div. June 1978); children: Michael A., Paul G.; m. Fe Lusterio Panaligan, Feb. 16, 1985; 1 child, Hazel Mary. BS in Math., So. Nazarene U., 1970; MS in Quality Assurance, Calif. State U., Dominguez Hills, 1994. Cert. quality engr., cert. reliability engr., cert. quality auditor, cert. mech. inspector. Vocat. instr. Okla. Tech. Inst., Oklahoma City, 1967-68; test technician GE/Honeywell Corp., Oklahoma City, 1969-70; reliability engr., test engr., test supr., test technician Ampex Corp., El Segundo, Calif., 1971-86; sr. reliability engr. Kennedy Corp., Monrovia, Calif., 1986-87, Teradata Corp., El Segundo, 1987-91; quality engr. Cummins Recon Co., Santa Fe Springs, Calif., 1992—. Sec. Philippine Network, L.A., 1990; treas. Philippine Action Group for Environment, Carson, Calif., 1992. Mem. Am. Soc. for Quality Control (mem. L.A. sect. 1985-90, mem. Orange/Empire sect., edn. com. 1994—), Phi Kappa Phi. Democrat. Lutheran. Home: 1631 E Balard St Carson CA 90745-1821 Office: Cummins Recon Co 14014 Alondra Blvd Santa Fe Springs CA 90670-5803

KOP, TIM M., psychologist; b. Aug. 3, 1946; s. Michael and Antoinette Wanda (Stahurski) K.; m. Yoshino Fujita, Aug. 9, 1975; children: Maile K., Geoffrey M. BA in Psychology, U. Hawaii, 1972; MA in Edn., Mich. State U., 1976; MS in Psychology, Columbia Pacific U., 1989, PhD in Psychology, 1991. Air traffic controller FAA, Honolulu, 1968-74; with U.S. Dept. Def., 1974—; pres. PAOA, Inc., Honolulu, 1986—; cons. Tripler Army Med. Ctr., Honolulu, 1990-92, State of Hawaii, 1992—; adj. prof. Hawaii Pacific U., 1993—. Author: Neural Programming, 1991, Normal Language Learning, 1989, Normal Language Learning and Aphasia, 1988; editor: North Korean Military Forces, 1979; author manuscript: Counterinsurgency along the Thai-Malaysian Border, 1982. Vice pres. Waiau Gardens Community Assn., Pearl City, Hawaii, 1986-88. Capt. U.S. Army, 1965-68, 78. Recipient Sec. of the Navy Award for group achievement U.S. Sec. of Navy, 1982. Fellow Am. Orthopsychiat. Assn.; mem. APA, Am. Psychological Soc., Am. Assn. Artificial Intelligence, U. Hawaii Alumni Assn. (life), Assn. of Mil. Surgeons of U.S. (life). Democrat. Office: 1750 Kalakaua Ave Honolulu HI 96826-3766

KOPEL, GERALD HENRY, retired state legislator; b. Balt., June 16, 1928; m. Dolores Blanke, June 16, 1952; children: David, Stephen (dec.). BA, U. Colo., 1952; LLB cum laude, U. Denver, 1958. Bar: Colo. 1958. Asst. atty. gen. State of Colo., 1959-61; mem. Colo. Ho. of Reps., 1965-67, 71-77, 1979-93; chmn. ho. jud. com., 1975-77, legal svc. com., 1976-77, statutory revision com., 1981-85, Gov.'s adv. com. on consumer credit, 1976-93, asst. minority leader, 1983-89; advisor, 1993-95; mem. Ho.-Senate Sunrise-Sunset Com., 1983-93; commr. uniform state laws, 1975-77; mem. health facilities rev. com., 1977-80; Legis. Columnist Colo. Statesman Newspaper, 1993—; commr. Denver election, 1995. With AUS, 1946-48. Recipient Civil Rights award Am. Def. League, 1991, Disting. Legislator award ACLU, 1992, Nat. Legislator award CLEAR, 1992. Democrat. Home: 1755 Glencoe St Denver CO 80220-1342 Office: 1535 Grant St #280 Denver CO 80203

KOPETSKI, MIKE, former congressman; b. Oreg., Oct. 27, 1949; 1 child, Matthew. BA, Am. U.; JD, Lewis & Clark Coll. Congl. aide Senate Watergate Com., Washington, 1973-74; del. Dem. Nat. Conv., 1976; adminstr. coms. Oreg. State Legis., 1977-79, 81, state rep., 1985-89; cons. labor, mgmt. and edn.; community organizer Oreg. Law Related Edn. Project, 1986; v.p. Currier-McCormick Communications, 1989-90; mem. 102nd-103rd Congresses from 5th Oreg. dist., Washington, D.C., 1991-94, Ways and Means Com., Washington, D.C.; pres. House of Reps. 1st term Dem. class, 1992; v.p. Ho. Reps. 1st term Dem. Class, 1991. Address: 601 13th St NW Ste 410S Washington DC 20005-3807

KOPLIN, DONALD LEROY, health products executive, consumer advocate; b. Greenleaf, Kans., Dec. 31, 1932; s. Henry G. Koplin and Edith Mary Stevens; m. Patricia Joynes, June 2, 1962 (div. Aug. 1974); children: Marie Claire, Marie Joelle (adopted). Student, U. San Diego, 1956-59, 67-68. Electronics test insp. Gen. Dynamics, San Diego, 1956-59; cryptographer Dept. of State, Washington, 1959-67; communications program officer Dept. of State, France, Angola, Madagascar, Qatar, India, Oman, Benin and the Bahamas, 1977-86; tech. writer Ryan Aero. Corp., San Diego, 1967-68; comml. dir., tech. advisor, pub. rels. officer Societe AGM, San Francisco, Athens, Greece, Antananarivo and Morondava, Dem. Republic of Madagascar, 1968-72; founder, dir. Soc. Bells, Cyclone & Akai, Antananarivo, 1972-74; founder, ptnr., assoc. editor Angola Report, Luanda, 1974-75; polit. reporter Angola Report, Reuters, AP, UPI Corr., BBC, Luanda; supr. Tex. Instruments, Lubbock, 1976-77; exec. Dial A Contact Lens, Inc., La Jolla, Calif., 1986-90, Assn. for Retarded Citizens, San Diego, 1992-94, Club Med, Copper Mountain, Colo., 1992-94; CEO Vient Inc., 1994—. Active San Diego Zool. Soc. With USN, 1951-55, Korea. Mem. Am. Fgn. Svc. Assn. Republican. Roman Catholic. Home: 436 Rosemont St La Jolla CA 92037-6058

KOPP, CLAIRE JOAN BERNSTEIN, psychologist, educator; b. N.Y.C., July 8, 1931; d. Gerson Jerome and Martha Jane (Stavisky) Bernstein; m. Eugene Howard Kopp, Aug. 31, 1950; children: Carolyn, Michael, Paul. BS, NYU, 1951; MS, U. So. Calif., 1961; PhD, Claremont Grad. Sch., 1970. Cert. psychologist, Calif. Teaching staff UCLA, 1970-77, faculty, 1977—. Fellow APA (sec., treas. div. 7 1985-88, pres. 1993-94), Am. Occupational Therapy Assn.; mem. AAAS, Soc. Rsch. in Child Devel. (editor newsletter 1991—), Internat. Orgn. 99s (chmn. San Gabriel Valley chpt. 1985-86), Internat. Soc. for the Study of Behavioral Devel. (treas., membership sec. 1994—). Office: UCLA Psychology Dept Los Angeles CA 90024

KOPP, DAVID EUGENE, manufacturing company executive; b. St. Louis, Apr. 21, 1951; s. Doyle Eugene and Irene Audrey (Gloyeske) K. BA in English, U. South Fla., 1975. Supr. Titleist Golf Co., Escondido, Calif., 1979-80; supr. Imed Corp., San Diego, 1980-82, process engr., 1982-83, sr. process engr., 1983-85; area mgr. Husky Injection Molding Systems Inc., Newport Beach, Calif., 1985-91; dir. sales Tech C.B.I. Inc., Scottsdale, Ariz., 1991-93; exec. v.p. Top-Seal Corp., Phoenix, 1993—. Mem. Soc. Plastic Engrs. (affiliate, bd. dirs., student liaison person Canoga Park, 1985-87). Republican. Roman Catholic. Home: 9980 N 106th St Scottsdale AZ 85258-9203 Office: Top-Seal Corp 2236 E University Dr Phoenix AZ 85034

KOPP, HARRIET GREEN, communication specialist; b. N.Y.C., June 18, 1917; m. George A. Kopp, 1948 (dec. 1968); m. Kurt Friedrich, 1972. MA, Bklyn. Coll., 1939; diploma in edn. of deaf, Columbia U., 1939, PhD, 1962. Scientist Bell Telephone Labs., 1943-46; mem. faculty Eastern Mich. U., 1946-48; adj. prof. Wayne State U., Detroit, 1948-70; dir. communication clinics Rehab. Inst. Met. Detroit, 1955-59; dir. programs deaf and aphasic Detroit Bd. Edn., 1959-70; prof., chmn. communication disorders San Diego State U., 1970-80; acting dean Coll. Human Svcs., 1980-83; prof. emerita San Diego State U., 1983—; mem. Nat. Adv. Com. on Deaf, 1965-72, chmn., 1970-72; mem. Nat. Adv. Com. on Handicapped, 1972-73; adv., rev. panels Bur. Educationally Handicapped, HEW, 1963-83. Author: (with R. Potter, G.A. Kopp) Visible Speech, 1948, 68, Some Applications of Phonetic Principles, 1948, 65, 62, 68, 70, 78, 85, 86; editor: Curriculum, Cognition and Content, 1968, 75, Reading: Cognitive Input and Output, 49th Claremont Reading Conf. Yearbook, 1982, Bilingual Problems of the Hispanic Deaf, 1984. Chair quality of life bd. City of San Diego, 1978-92. Recipient Outstanding Faculty award San Diego State U., 1983. Fellow Am. Speech and Hearing Assn.; mem. AAAS, A.G. Bell Assn. (dir. 1964-68, chmn. edit. bd. 1966-75), Calif. Speech and Hearing Assn., Phi Kappa Phi. Address: 6711 Golfcrest Dr San Diego CA 92119-2427

KOPPA-WHITNEY, DIANE LYNN, interior designer; b. Wausau, Wis., Aug. 29, 1962; d. Lyle John and Shirley Jean (Kohnhorst) Koppa; m. Scott Cameron Whitney, June 16, 1990; children: Krystle, Erika, Benjamin. B Environ. and Textile Design, U. Wis., 1985. Designer F.A.C. Architects, Las Vegas, Nev., 1985; project designer Architronics, Las Vegas, 1985-86, SLC Design, Las Vegas, 1986-88; interior designer Morris & Brown Architects, Las Vegas, 1988-91; designer, dept. head Paul Steelman Ltd., Las Vegas, 1991—. Mem. Nat. Exec. Women in Hospitality. Office: 3330 W Desert Inn Rd Las Vegas NV 89102-8421

KOPPES, STEVEN NELSON, public information officer, science writer; b. Manhattan, Kans., Aug. 28, 1957; s. Ralph James and Mary Louise (Nelson) K.; m. Susan Camille Keaton, May 18, 1984. BS in Anthropology cum laude, Kans. State U., 1978; MS in Journalism, Kans. U., 1982. Rsch. asst. dept. anthropology Kans. State U., Manhattan, 1979; reporter The Morning Sun, Pittsburg, Kans., 1981-83; co-mgr. Doc's B.R. Others Restaurant, Tempe, Ariz., 1983-85; info. specialist Ariz. State U. New Bur., Tempe, 1985-87, asst. dir., 1987—. Contbr. to Ariz. State U. Rsch. Mag., 1984—; contbr. articles to various publs. Bd. dirs. Children's Mus. of Metro Phoenix, 1988. Recipient award of excellence Internat. Assn. Bus. Communicators, 1991-92, award of merit, 1989-93, Disting. Tech. Comm. award Soc. Tech. Comm. Phoenix Chpt., 1994-95. Mem. Nat. Assn. Sci. Writers, Ariz. Archaeol. Soc. (bd. dirs. Phoenix chpt. 1987-88), Rio Salado Rowing Club (charter mem. 1995—). Office: New Bur Ariz State U Tempe AZ 85287

KOPPETT, LEONARD, columnist, journalist, author; b. Moscow, Russia, Sept. 15, 1923; s. David and Marie (Dvoretskya) Kopeliovitch; m. Suzanne Silberstein, Apr. 24, 1964; children: Katherine, David. B.A., Columbia U., 1946. Sportswriter, columnist N.Y. Herald Tribune, 1948-54, N.Y. Post, 1954-63, N.Y. Times, 1963-78, 88-91, Sporting News, 1967-82; exec. sports editor Peninsula Times Tribune, 1980-81, editor, 1982-84, editor emeritus, 1984-93; free-lance columnist, 1978—; tchr. journalism Stanford (Calif.) U., 1977-81, San Jose State U., 1988-89. Books include A Thinking Man's Guide to Baseball, 1967, 24 Seconds to Shoot, 1969, The N.Y. Times Guide to Spectator Sports, 1970, The New York Mets, 1970, The Essence of the Game is Deception, 1974, Sports Illusion, Sports Reality, 1981, The New Thinking Fan's Guide to Baseball, 1991, The Man in the Dugout, 1993. Served with U.S. Army, 1943-45. Named to writer's wing Baseball Hall of Fame, 1992, Basketball Hall of Fame, 1994. Mem. Baseball Writers Assn. Am., Profl. Football Writers, Authors Guild. Democrat. Jewish.

KOPTA, JEAN MARILYN, voice educator, vocal performer; b. Wakonda, S.D., Nov. 13, 1928; d. Elmer and Alma (Gilbertson) Hesla; m. Robert Wenzel Kopta, Feb. 14, 1953 (div. Oct. 1978); children: Kathy, William, Joseph. BA in edn., Pacific Luth. U., 1950; MA, Cen. Washington U., 1978. Tchr. McDermoth Elem. Sch., Aberdeen, Wash., 1950-51, Catlin Elem. Sch., Kelso, Wash., 1951-52, Pinehurst Elem. Sch., Seattle, 1952-54; profl. opera chorus Seattle Opera Co., 1964-68; vocal music tchr. Shoreline Elem. Sch., Seattle, 1967-71; pvt. voice tchr. Seattle, 1975—; voice instr. Pacific Luth U., Parkland, Wash., 1979-83; choir dir. Gloria Dei Luth. Ch., Lynnwood, Wash., 1980-83, Christ Luth. Ch., Edmonds, Wash., 1985-88, Calvary Luth Ch., Seattle, 1991—. Contbr. articles to profl. jours. Mem. Ladies Musical Club, Nat. Assn. Tchrs. of Singing. Home: 738 N 161st Pl Seattle WA 98133-5671

KORAN, DENNIS HOWARD, publisher; b. L.A., May 21, 1947; s. Aaron Baer and Shirley Mildred (Kassan) K.; m. Roslynn Ruth Cohen, Apr. 6, 1979; 1 child, Michael; stepchildren: Jeff, Beth, Judy. Student, U. Leeds, Eng., 1966-67, UCLA, 1979-80; BA, U. Calif., Berkeley, 1980; postgrad., Loyola U., L.A., 1982-84, 86-89. Co-founder, co-editor Cloud Marauder Press, Berkeley, 1969-72, Panjandrum/Aris Books, San Francisco, 1973-81; founder, editor Panjandrum Books, San Francisco, 1971—, Panjandrum Press, Inc., San Francisco, 1971—; co-dir. poetry reading series Panjandrum Books, 1972-76. Author: (book of poetry) Vacancies, 1975, After All, 1993; editor Panjandrum Poetry Jour., 1971—; co-editor Cloud Marauder, 1969-72; author poetry pub. various jours. Liaison between U.S. Govt. and Saminole Indians VISTA, Sasakwa, Okla., 1969-70. Nat. Endowment for Arts Lit. Pub. grantee, 1974, 76, 79, 81, 82, 84, Coord. Coun. for Lit. Mags., 1971-80. Mem. Lovers of the Stinking Rose, Poets and Writers. Office: Panjandrum Books 6156 Wilkinson Ave North Hollywood CA 91606-4518

KORB, LAWRENCE JOHN, metallurgist; b. Warren, Pa., Apr. 28, 1930; s. Stanley Curtis and Dagna (Pedersen) K.; B.Chem.Engring., Rensselaer Poly. Inst., Troy, N.Y., 1952; m. Janet Davis, Mar. 30, 1957; children: James, William, Jeanine. Sales engr. Alcoa, Buffalo, 1955-59; metall. engr. N. Am. Rockwell Co., Downey, Calif., 1959-62; engring. supr. metallurgy Apollo program Rockwell Internat. Co., Downey, 1962-66, engring. supr. advanced materials, 1966-72, engring. supr. metals and ceramics space shuttle program, 1972-88; cons., 1988—; mem. tech. adv. com. metallurgy Cerritos Coll., 1969-74. Served with USNR, 1952-55. Registered profl. engr., Calif. Fellow Am. Soc. Metals (chmn. aerospace activity com. 1971-76, judge materials application competition 1969, handbook com. 1978-83, chmn. handbook com. 1983, chmn. publs. coun. 1984). Republican. Author articles, chpts. in books. Home: 251 S Violet Ln Orange CA 92669-3740

KORB, ROBERT WILLIAM, former materials and processes engineer; b. Warren, Pa., Mar. 12, 1929; s. Dallas Weigand and Evelyn Eleanor (Peterson) K.; m. Diane Marie Anderson, Oct. 14, 1964 (div. 1972); 1 child, Karen; m. Setsu Campbell, Aug. 9, 1980; children: Theresa Campbell, Mark Campbell, Laura Campbell. BS in Chemistry, U. Nev., 1951. Chemist Rezolin, Inc., Santa Monica, Calif., 1956-57; mem. tech. staff Hughes Aircraft Co., Culver City, Calif., 1957-64; mem. tech. staff Hughes Aircraft Co., Fullerton, Calif., 1971-74, group head materials engring., 1974-79, sect. head materials and processes engring., 1979-93; mem. tech. staff TRW Systems, Redondo Beach, Calif., 1964-71; ret., 1993. Contbr. articles to profl. jours.; patentee flexible cable process. 1st lt. USAF, 1951-56. Mem. Inst. for Interconnecting and Packaging Electronic Circuits (co. rep.), Soc. for Advancement Materials and Process Engring. Republican. Home: 12 Palmatum Irvine CA 92720-1862

KORELOV, NIKOLAI, artist; b. Kursk, USSR, Feb. 7, 1963; came to U.S., 1993; Red Diploma (with high honors), S. Samokish Coll., 1981; student, Kiev Acad. Art, Ukraine. Exhibited in group shows at St. Petersburg, Moscow, Kiev, Prague, Warsaw and Belgrade, internat. exhibit, Poland; pvt. collections include bus. and art galleries in Italy, Germany, Holland, France, U.S., and former Soviet Union. Studio: 1069 S Hayworth Ave Los Angeles CA 90035-2601

KORENIC, LYNETTE MARIE, librarian; b. Berwyn, Ill., Mar. 29, 1950; d. Emil Walter and Donna Marie (Harbutt) K. m. Jerome Dennis Reif, Dec. 31, 1988. BS in Art, U. Wis., 1977, MFA, 1979, MA in LS, 1981, MA in Art History, 1984. Asst. art libr. Ind. U., Bloomington, 1982-84; art libr. U. Calif., Santa Barbara, 1984-88, head Arts Libr., 1988—. Author articles. Mem. Art Librs. Soc. N.Am. (sec. 1983-84, v.p. 1989, pres. 1990), Beta Phi Mu. Office: U Calif Arts Libr Santa Barbara CA 93106

KORGE, PAAVO, cell physiologist; b. Tartu, Estonia, Sept. 6, 1943; came to U.S., 1989; s. Kuno and Elsa (Ruus) K.; m. Sirje Kipper, Dec. 26, 1964; children: Indrek, Kristjan. PhD in Physiology, Tartu U., 1969, DSc in Physiology, 1974. From jr. scientist to assoc. prof. Tartu U., 1967-76, prof., 1978-89; asst. prof. Washington State U., Pullman, 1989-92, prof., 1992—; vis. scientist Copenhagen U., 1976-78; sci. bd. dirs. Tartu U., 1976-89; chmn. all union conf. on hormonal regulation phys. activity, 1973, 77, 82, 87. Author: Molecular Mechanism of Glucocorticoid Action, 1981, Hormons and Physical Fitness, 1983, Glucocorticoids in the Regulation of Heart Function and Metabolism, 1984; contbr. articles to profl. jours. Grantee USSR Sports Com., 1978-82, Inst. Aviation, Leningrad, USSR, 1983-88; USSR Ministry Higher Edn. scholar, 1976; recipient Young Scientist award Estonian Govt., 1978. Mem. N.Y. Acad. Scis. Home: SE 1935 Valley Rd Pullman WA 99163 Office: Washington State U Pullman WA 99164-6520

KORIAT, RAPHAEL, manufacturing company executive; b. Meknes, Morocco, Mar. 18, 1947; came to U.S., 1979; s. Shlomo and Rivka (Adery) K.; m. Shimria Sobel, Aug. 11, 1971; children: Ravit, Dori, Sharon. BSME, Technion Inst. of Tech., Haifa, Israel, 1972; MSME, Drexel U., 1975; grad. exec. MBA program, Stanford U., Palo Alto, Calif., 1991. Chief engr. Kulso Ltd., Haifa, 1975-80; dir. bus. divsn. Kulicke & Soffa Ind., Willow Grove, Pa., 1985-88, dir. engring. and tech., 1989-90; corp. v.p. engring. tech. Kulicke & Soffa Ind., Willow Grove, 1990-92; gen. mgr. AG Assocs., Sunnyvale, Calif., 1992—. Contbr. articles to profl. jours. Mem. Mech. Engring. Soc., AEA Orgn., Entrepreneur Com. Home: 74 Ester Rabin St, Haifa 34789, Israel Office: AG Assocs 1325 Borregas Ave Sunnyvale CA 94089-1003

KORINS, LEOPOLD, stock exchange executive. Pres. Pacific Stock Exch., San Francisco, now chmn., chief exec. officer. Office: Pacific Stock Exch 301 Pine St San Francisco CA 94104-3301*

KORKUNIS, TONY WILLIAM, consumer products executive; b. L.A., Nov. 3, 1954; s. William Anthony and Christine (Raptis) K.; m. Deborah Maria Frederic, Oct. 24, 1984 (div. June 1990); 1 child, Amanda Christine; m. Kristin Kellogg Dutton, July 13, 1991; 1 child, Grace Kellogg. BS in Math., Harvey Mudd Coll., 1977; MA in Ops. Rsch., Claremont (Calif.) Grad. Sch., 1977; MBA, UCLA, 1989. Ops. rsch. analyst to retail mktg. specialist Products Co., Atlantic Richfield Co., L.A., 1977-80; economist Coun. on Wage and Price Stability, Office of the Pres., Washington, 1980; analyst Congl. Budget Office, U.S. Congress, Washington, 1981-82; supr. sales forecasting to supr. ops. planning Mars, Inc., Kal Kan Foods, Inc., Vernon, Calif., 1982-85, mgr. bus. sys., 1985-87, mgr. customer svc., 1987-89, mgr. svc. and fin., 1989-91; cons. bus. strategy Toranago Technologies, Calsbad, Calif., 1991-92; mgr. sales planning Buena Vista Home Video, Burbank, Calif., 1992-93, dir. forecasting, space planning, 1993—; bd. dirs. Lodestone Pacific, Anaheim; cons. Young Pres. Orgn. of Orange County, Newport Beach, Calif., 1994. Office: Walt Disney Co Buena Vista Home Video 350 S Buena Vista St Burbank CA 91521-7895

KORMONDY, EDWARD JOHN, university official, biology educator; b. Beacon, N.Y., June 10, 1926; s. Anthony and Frances (Glover) K.; m. Peggy Virginia Hedrick, June 5, 1950 (div. 1989); children: Lynn Ellen, Eric Paul, Mark Hedrick. BA in Biology summa cum laude, Tusculum Coll., 1950; MS in Zoology, U. Mich., 1951, PhD in Zoology, 1955. Teaching fellow U. Mich., 1952-55; instr. zoology, curator insects Mus. Zoology, 1955-57; asst. prof. Oberlin (Ohio) Coll., 1957-63, assoc. prof., 1963-67, prof., 1967-69, acting assoc. dean, 1966-67; dir. Commn. Undergrad. Edn. in Biol. Scis., Washington, 1968-72; dir. Office Biol. Edn., Am. Inst. Biol. Scis., Washington, 1968-71; mem. faculty Evergreen State Coll., Olympia, Wash., 1971-79, interim acting dean, 1972-73, v.p., provost, 1973-78; sr. profl. assoc., directorate sci. edn. NSF, 1979; provost, prof. biology U. So. Maine, Portland, 1979-82; v.p. acad. affairs, prof. biology Calif. State U., Los Angeles, 1982-86; sr. v.p., chancellor, prof. biology U. Hawaii, Hilo/West Oahu, 1986-93. Author: Concepts of Ecology, 1969, 76, 83, 95, General Biology: The Integrity and Natural History of Organisms, 1977, Handbook of Contemporary World Developments in Ecology, 1981; high school textbook Biology, 1984, 88; International Handbook of Pollution Control, 1989; contbr. articles to profl. jours. Served with USN, 1944-46. U. Ga. postdoctoral fellow radiation ecology, 1963-64; vis. research fellow Center for Bioethics, Georgetown U., 1978-79; research grantee Nat. Acad. Scis., Am. Philos. Soc., NSF, Sigma Xi. Fellow AAAS; mem. Ecol. Soc. Am. (sec. 1976-78), Nat. Assn. Biology Tchrs. (pres. 1981), Soc. Calif. Acad. Scis. (bd. dirs. 1985-86, 93—, v.p. 1995—), Sigma Xi, Phi Kappa Phi.

KORN, DAVID, educator, pathologist; b. Providence, RI, Mar. 5, 1933; s. Solomon and Cliare (Liebman) K.; m. Phoebe Richter, June 9, 1955 (div. Dec. 1993); children: Michael Philip, Stephen James, Daniel Clair. B.A., Harvard U., 1954, M.D., 1959. Intern Mass. Gen. Hosp., Boston, 1959-60; resident in Pathology Mass. Gen. Hosp., 1960-61; research asso. NIH, 1961-63; mem. staff Lab. Biochem. Pharmacology; also asst. pathologist NIH, 1963-68; prof. pathology Sch. Medicine Stanford (Calif.) U., 1968—, chmn. dept. pathology Sch. Medicine, 1968-84; physician-in-chief pathology Stanford Hosp., 1968-84, dean Sch. Medicine, 1984-95, v.p., dean, 1986-95; cons. pathology Palo Alto VA Hosp., 1968-84; sr. surgeon USPHS, 1961-66; mem. cell biology study sect. NIH, 1973-77, chmn., 1976-77; mem. bd. sci. counselors, div. cancer biology and diagnosis Nat. Cancer Inst., 1977-82, chmn., 1980-82; chmn. Nat. Cancer Adv. Bd., 1984-91. Mem. editorial bd. Human Pathology, 1969-74; assoc. editor, 1974-88; mem. editorial bd. Jour. Biol. Chemistry, 1973-79. Recipient Young Scientist award Md. Acad. Sci., 1967. Mem. Am. Soc. Biol. Chemists, Am. Assn. Pathologists, Am. Soc. Cell Biology, Am. Soc. Microbiology, Fedn. Am. Soc. Exptl. Biology (bd. dirs., mem. exec. com.), Inst. of Medicine. Office: Stanford U Sch Medicine MSOB X226 Stanford CA 94305

KORN, LESTER BERNARD, business executive, diplomat; b. N.Y.C., Jan. 11, 1936. BS with honors, UCLA, 1959, MBA, 1960; postgrad., Harvard Bus. Sch., 1961. Mgmt. cons. Peat, Marwick, Mitchell & Co., L.A., 1961-66, ptnr., 1966-69; chmn. emeritus, co-founder Korn/Ferry Internat., L.A., 1969; U.S. amb. and U.S. rep. Econ. and Social Coun. UN, 1987-88; chmn., founder Korn Tuttle Capital Group, Inc., 1991; alt. rep. 42nd and 43d UN Gen. Assembly; chmn., CEO Korn Tuttle Capital Group, Inc., 1991; bd. dirs. Continental Am. Properties, Music Ctr. Operating Co. L.A., Tenet Healthcare Corp. Author: The Success Profile, 1989. Trustee UCLA Found.; bd. overseers and bd. visitors Anderson Grad. Sch. Mgmt., UCLA; trustee, founding mem. Dean's Coun. UCLA; mem. adv. coun. Am. Heart Assn.; spl. advisor, del. UNESCO Inter-gov. Conf. on Edn. for Internat. Understanding, Coop., Peace, 1983; adv. bd. Women in Film Found., 1983-84; chmn. Commn. on Citizen Participation in Govt., State of Calif., 1979-82; bd. dirs. John Douglas French Found. for Alzheimer's Disease; mem. Republican Nat. Exec. Fin. Com., 1985, Pres.'s Commn. White House Fellowships, Republican Eagles; hon. chairperson 50th Am. Presdl. Inaugural, 1985; co-chmn. So. Calif. region NCCJ. Recipient Alumni Profl. Achievement award UCLA, 1984, Neil H. Jacoby Internat. award, 1990, Internat. Citizen of Yr. award Internat. Visitors Coun., 1991. Mem. AICPA, Calif. Soc. CPAs, Am. Bus. Conf. (founding mem.), Coun. Am. Ambs., Hillcrest Country Club, Regency Club (Calif.). Office: Korn/Ferry Internat 1800 Century Park E Ste 1100 Los Angeles CA 90067-1514

KORN, WALTER, writer; b. Prague, Czechoslovakia, May 22, 1908; came to U.S., 1950, naturalized, 1956; s. Bernard and Clara (Deutsch) K.; m. Herta Klemperer, Dec. 24, 1933. Dr.Comm., Charles U., Prague, 1938; postgrad. London Sch. Econs., 1949-50; cert. systems and procedures Wayne State U., 1957; cert. polit. sci. New Sch., N.Y.C., 1972-73. Dir. mktg. Kosmos Works, Prague, 1934-39; contract mgr. Cantie Switches, Chester, Eng., 1941-44; dir. UN Relief and Rehab. Adminstrn., U.S. Zone Occupation, Germany, 1945-47; country dir. Orgn. for Rehab. and Tng., Geneva, 1948-49; contract mgr. Royal Metal Mfg. Co., N.Y.C., 1951-55; bus. mgr. J. Cmty. Ctr., Detroit, 1956-59; dir. adminstrn. Am. Joint Distbn. Com., Tel Aviv, 1960-64; exec. asst. Self Help/United Help, N.Y.C., 1965-69; housing mgmt. cons. Exec. Dept. Divsn. Housing and Cmty. Renewal, State N.Y., N.Y.C., 1970-76; lectr. housing for aged and housing fin., 1958-74; lectr. Brit. Allied Council, Liverpool, Eng., 1942-44. Nat. field rep. United Jewish Appeal, 1968—; mem. Vols. for Internat. Tech. Assistance, 1968-71. Capt. Czechoslovakian Army, 1938. Mem. Acad. Polit. Sci., Acad. Polit and Social Sci., Am. Judicature Soc., Amnesty Internat., World Affairs Coun., Princeton Club of N.Y., Commonwealth Club of Calif., Press Club (San Francisco), Masons. Author: On Hobbies, 1936, Earn as You Learn, 1948, Learn As You Earn, 1949, The Brilliant Touch, 1950, Modern Chess Openings, 13th edit., 1990, America's Chess Heritage, 1978, American Chess Art, 1975, Moderne Schach Eroeffnungen I and II, 1968, 91, The Art of Chess Composition, 1995; contbr. essay on chess to Ency. Britannica, 1974. Home: 816 N Delaware St Apt 207 San Mateo CA 94401-1543

KORNBERG, ARTHUR, biochemist; b. N.Y.C., N.Y., Mar. 3, 1918; s. Joseph and Lena (Katz) K.; m. Sylvy R. Levy, Nov. 21, 1943 (dec. 1986); children: Roger, Thomas Bill, Kenneth Andrew; m. Charlene Walsh Levering, 1988. BS, CCNY, 1937, LLD (hon.), 1960; MD, U. Rochester, 1941, DSc (hon.), 1962; DSc (hon.), U. Pa., U. Notre Dame, 1965, Washington U., 1968, Princeton U., 1970, Colby Coll., 1970; LHD (hon.), Yeshiva U., 1963; MD honoris causa, U. Barcelona, Spain, 1970. Intern in medicine Strong Meml. Hosp., Rochester, N.Y., 1941-42; commd. officer USPHS, 1942, advanced through grades to med. dir., 1951; mem. staff NIH, Bethesda, Md., 1942-52, nutrition sect., div. physiology, 1942-45; chief sect. enzymes and metabolism Nat. Inst. Arthritis and Metabolic Diseases, 1947-

52; guest research worker depts. chemistry and pharmacology coll. medicine NYU, 1946; dept. biol. chemistry med. sch. Washington U., 1947; dept. plant biochemistry U. Calif., 1951; prof., head dept. microbiology, med. sch. Washington U., St. Louis, 1953-59; prof. biochemistry Stanford U. Sch. Medicine, 1959—, chmn. dept., 1959-69, prof. emeritus dept. biochemistry, 1988—; Mem. sci. adv. bd. Mass. Gen. Hosp., 1964-67; bd. govs. Weizmann Inst., Israel. Author: For the Love of Enzymes, 1989; contbr. sci. articles to profl. jours. Served lt. (j.g.), med. officer USCGR, 1942. Recipient Paul-Lewis award in enzyme chemistry, 1951; co-recipient of Nobel prize in medicine, 1959; recipient Max Berg award prolonging human life, 1968, Sci. Achievement award AMA, 1968, Lucy Wortham James award James Ewing Soc., 1968, Borden award Am. Assn. Med. Colls., 1968, Nat. medal of sci., 1979. Mem. Am. Soc. Biol. Chemists (pres. 1965), Am. Chem. Soc., Harvey Soc., Am. Acad. Arts and Scis., Royal Soc., Nat. Acad. Scis. (mem. council 1963-66), Am. Philos. Soc., Phi Beta Kappa, Sigma Xi, Alpha Omega Alpha. Office: Stanford U Med Ctr Dept Biochemistry Stanford CA 94305*

KORNELL, JIM, artificial intelligence researcher; b. Burbank, Calif., July 25, 1951; s. Hal Kornell and Mary (Serruys) Kornell Alfonte; m. Jane Hankey, Apt. 1972 (div. 1976); m. Ellen Kindl, Dec. 10, 1979; children: Nate, Max, Sam, Amy, Will. BS in Computer Sci., U. Calif., Santa Barbara, 1978. Software engr. Raytheon Electronic systems, Goleta, Calif., 1978-81; project engr. Delco Electronics, Goleta, Calif., 1981-83; dir. machine intelligence lab. Gen. Rsch. Corp., Santa Barbara, Calif., 1983-92; prin. Syukhtun Rsch., Santa Barbara, Calif., 1992—. Author: Knowledge Acquisition Guidebook, 1992; (with others) Knowledge Acquisition for Knowledge Based Systems, 1989; editor Santa Barbara Athletic Assn., 1988-91; author systems Eucalyptus, 1990, Katalyst, 1992. Convener Open Alternative Sch., Santa Barbara, 1983, 85, 89; v.p., bd. dirs. Forest Project, Santa Barbara, 1990—. Mem. AAAS, Am. Assn. Artificial Intelligence, Cognitive Sci. Soc. Office: Syukhtun Rsch 2740 Williams Way Santa Barbara CA 93105-2149

KORNELLY, IRENE LOUISE, state government affairs consultant; b. Chgo., Nov. 16, 1945; d. Raymond Mauritz and Hazel Marie (Whalen) Ring; m. Donald Elmer Kornelly, July 6, 1968 (div. Nov. 1987); 1 child, Sharon Irene. BA in Music History and Lit. cum laude, St. Olaf Coll., 1968; MM in Vocal Performance, Am. Conservatory of Music, Chgo., 1970; AB in Paralegal Sci., Southland U., Pasadena, Calif., 1983. Music assoc. First Presbyn. Ch., Colorado Springs, Colo., 1973-75; pvt. music instr. Colorado Springs, 1975-79; instr. music Geelong (Victoria, Australia) Coll., 1979-80; staff asst. U.S. Senator Gary Hart, 1981-85; coord. victim/witness program Office of Dist. Atty., 4th Jud. Dist., 1985-89; staff asst. U.S. Senator Timothy E. Wirth, 1989-93; cons. The Jefferson Group, Denver, 1993-94; dir. Office of Statewide Def. Initiatives, State of Colo., 1994—. Mem. State of Colo. Electoral Coll., 1992; mem. exec. com. Colo. Dem. Party, 1985-93, mem. rules com., 1995—; chair 5th Congl. Dem. Com., 1982-93; sec. El Paso County Dem. Com., 1977-79; mem. Colo. Capitol Adv. Com., 1993; pres. bd. Pikes Peak Community Action Agy.; mem. Exec. Clemency Adv. Bd. for State of Colo., 1987; mem. Citizens Goals Leadership 2000 Class, 1982; mem. Colo. Office of Space Advocacy. Mem. AAUW, LWV, Common Cause, Nat. Women's Polit. Caucus, Colorado Springs World Affairs Coun.

KORNER, HILDA, personnel executive; b. N.Y.C., June 2, 1931; d. Manuel and Sadie (Brookman) Troob; m. Herbert Korner, Aug. 1, 1953 (div. Feb. 1971); children—David, Peter. B.S. in Personnel Adminstrn, SUNY-Rochester, 1974. Owner, operator Gallery III, Marin County, Calif., 1964-69; supr. personnel services SUNY-Buffalo, 1970-72, dir. recruitment and promotion of women, 1972-75, coordinator human research devel., 1975-77; mgr. employment Stanford Linear Accelerator Ctr., Calif., 1977-83, asst. personnel dir., 1983-88, mgr. tng. and staff devel., 1988-93, owner Korner Training Svcs., 1993—; instr. D'Youville Coll., Buffalo, 1973-74, Ohlone Coll., Fremont, Calif., 1982-83; co-owner, ptnr. Korn Kompany, Palo Alto, Calif., 1985—. Workshop leader Resource Ctr. for Women, Palo Alto, 1981-83. Avocations: theater; symphony; chamber music; travel; reading. Home: 255 S Rengstorff Ave Apt 18 Mountain View CA 94040-1729

KORNEY, ELLEN LEMER, interior designer; b. N.Y.C., Dec. 27, 1943; d. Gerald J. and Gladys (Rosenberg) Halbreich; m. Albert Lemer, Apr. 16, 1969 (div. Jan. 1982); 1 child, Alison Hope; m. Michael Stanley Korney, Dec. 25, 1988. BA, Hofstra U., 1965; cert., N.Y. Sch. Interior Design, 1970-71. Asst. Virginia F. Frankel Interiors, N.Y.C., 1971; pres. Ellen Terry Lemer Ltd., N.Y.C., 1971-89; owner Ellen Lemer Korney Assocs., L.A., 1989—; instr. UCLA Extension, 1989, Parsons Sch. of Design, N.Y.C., 1987; guest lectr. Marymount Manhattan, N.Y.C., 1986. Contbr. articles to: Showcase of Interior Design, 1992, Very Small Spaces, 1988; contbr. articles to profl. jours. Mem. Allied Bd. of Trade, Met. Mus., L.A. County Mus. Art, Armand Hammer Mus., Am. Soc. Interior Designers (profl. mem., treas. 1993-94, bd. dirs. L.A. 1990-93, N.Y.C. 1986-89, 1st place award design competition residential L.A., 1991, Presdl. Citation 1991). Republican. Office: Ellen Lemer Korney Assocs 10170 Culver Blvd Culver City CA 90232-3152

KORNFELD, JUDITH R., product marketing consultant; b. Oklahoma City, July 31, 1948; d. Samuel and Ida (Charetsky) K. BA in Linguistics, U. Chgo., 1969; PhD in Linguistics/Psychology, MIT, 1974. Sr. systems engr. SofTech, Inc., Waltham, Mass., 1978-81, Higher Order Software, Cambridge, Mass., 1978-81; mem. tech. staff AT&T Bell Labs., Short Hills, N.J., 1981-84; project mgr. ALPHATECH, Burlington, Mass., 1984-85; product mgr. Fed. Systems Group Mktg. Symbolics, Inc., Cambridge, 1985-87; product mgr. fed. sys. mktg. Sun Microsystems, Mountain View, Calif., 1987; ind. cons. in product mktg. Menlo Park, Calif., 1987—. Mem. ACM, Sigchi, Bay Area Human Factors Soc. Home and Office: 967 Menlo Ave Menlo Park CA 94025-4606

KORNFELD, PETER, internist; b. Vienna, Austria, Mar. 16, 1925; came to U.S., 1939; s. Otto and Rosa (Weitzmann) K. BA summa cum laude, U. Buffalo, 1948; MD, Columbia U., 1952. Diplomate Am. Bd. Internal Medicine. Intern Mt. Sinai Hosp., N.Y.C., 1952-53; asst. resident, then chief resident in internal medicine Mt. Sinai Hosp., 1955-56; postdoctoral fellow cardiovascular physiology, physician Nat. Heart Inst. at Columbia U./Presbyn. Hosp., N.Y.C., 1953-54; pvt. practice, N.Y., N.J., 1956-88; clin. prof. medicine, attending physician Stanford U. Hosp., 1991—; cons. physician N.Y. State Bur. Disability Determination, 1960-87; attending physician Hackensack (N.J.) Hosp. Med. Ctr., 1988-91, Mt. Sinai Hosp., Englewood Hosp.; dir. Myasthenia Gravis Clinic, Englewood (N.J.) Hosp., 1965-91; mem. nat. med. adv. bd. Myasthenia Gravis Found., 1970-91; Clin. prof. Mt. Sinai Sch. Medicine, CUNY, 1968-92. Contbr. numerous articles to med. jours. Grantee, NIH, 1966-70, Hoffman-LaRoche, Inc., 1966-73, Muscular Dystrophy Assn., 1978-81, 81-82, Rosenstiel Found., 1979-82; recipient Globus award, Mt. Sinai Jour. Medicine, 1976-77. Fellow ACP, Am. Coll. Cardiology (assoc.), N.Y. Acad. Sci., N.Y. Acad. Medicine, Calif. Acad. Medicine; mem. AMA, Am. Fedn. Exptl. Biology, Am. Fedn. Clin. Rsch., Harvey Soc., Am. Diabetes Assn., Am. Heart Assn., Phi Beta Kappa, Alpha Omega Alpha, Sigma Xi.

KORNMAN, HENRY, marketing executive; b. Munich, Dec. 13, 1949; came to U.S., 1950; s. Julius and Helen (Lubocicz) K.; m. Shelley Jean Freed, Nov. 18, 1979. AB in History, Rutgers U., 1977. Sr. clk. B. Dalton Bookseller, Eatontown, N.J., 1975-76; sales rep. Avon Books/Hearst Corp., N.Y.C., 1977-78, regional sales mgr., 1979-80; product mgr. Follett Pub. Co., Chgo., 1980-84; exec. dir. U. Chgo. Med. Ctr., 1984-87; dir. mktg. and sales Books Nippan, Carson, Calif., 1988-94; owner HK Mktg. Svcs., L.A., 1994—; cons. Longman Trade, Chgo., 1984, Slawson Communications, San Diego, 1987. Contbg. editor sales manual, 1978. Vol. Jewish Community Ctr. Chgo., 1985. Office: HK Mktg Svcs 12621 Washington Pl Apt 203 Los Angeles CA 90066-4874

KORODY, ANTHONY VINCENT, corporate event producer, photographer; b. L.A., Mar. 4, 1951; s. Paul Alexander and Erica K.; m. Jaimie C. Korody, Mar. 13, 1982; 2 children. Student, U. So. Calif., 1970-72. Freelance photographer Black Star, Life, Newsweek, 1970; picture editor Daily Trojan, 1971; founder, chief exec. officer Fourth Estate Press, 1971—; photographer, co-founder SYGMA Agence de Press, Paris, 1973—; freelance photographer People, Time, Fortune, Newsweek, 1978-88; co-founder, v.p., dir. Image Stream, Inc., Los Angeles, 1978-86; contbg. photographer People Weekly Mag., 1979-87; lectr. Art Center; producer events for Apple Computer, Michelin, Toro, Taco Bell, Computerland, numerous others. Named Inc. 500 chief exec. officer, 1983, 84, 85. Mem. Nat. Press Photographers Assn., Sigma Delta Chi. Republican. Roman Catholic.

KOROLOFF, JOHN MICHAEL, environmental science educator, consultant; b. San Francisco, Dec. 26, 1942; s. Michael Nicolas and Frances Helen (Stout) K.; m. Beverly Virginia Dean, June 6, 1966 (dec. Nov. 1967); m. Nancy Margaret Koroloff, Mar. 5, 1946; children: Mary, Albert, Rachel. BA in biology, San Francisco State U., 1965, MA in biology, 1969; MPA, Portland State U., 1978; PhD, U. Oreg., 1985. Wildlife biologist U.S. Fish & Wildlife Svc., Sacramento, Calif., 1965-69; detective Mult County Sheriff, Portland, Oreg., 1969-71; dep. chair. Portland Cmty Coll., Portland, Oreg., 1971-89, instr., 1989—; cons. Emergy Curriculum project, Portland, 1993—. Active Healers Healty Planet, Portland, 1993—; Young Environ. Awareness Bd. Yea!, Portland, 1993—. Recipient U.S. Nat. Bank Excellence award U.S. Nat. Bank, 1992, Noram Paulus Excellence award, Oreg. Dept. Edn., 1991. Mem. Am. Assn. Advancement Sci., Oregon Sci. Tchrs., Nat. Sci. Tchrs. Assn. Democrat. Home: 2207 SW Iowa St Portland OR 97201-1908 Office: PCC Cascade Sci 705 N Killingswch Portland OR 97217

KORSON, GERALD MICHAEL, newspaper editor; b. Riverside, Calif., Oct. 19, 1960; s. Paul Joseph and Maryann (Eisenbart) K.; m. Christina Cecilia Bohner, June 23, 1984; children: Michael Allan, Monica Mary, Catherine Ruth, Raymond Paul, Sophia Rose, Adrienne Marie. BA, U. San Diego, 1981; MA, St. Mary's Coll., Moraga, Calif., 1987. Prodn. mgr. So. Cross newspaper Cath. Diocese of San Diego, 1979-82; owner, operator Korson Pub. Co., Oakland, Calif., 1984-88; editor The Mont. Cath. newspaper, dir. comm. Cath. Diocese of Helena, Mont., 1988—. Mem. Fellowship of Cath. Scholars, Cath. Press Assn., Unda-U.S.A., Religious Pub. Rels Coun. Republican. Roman Catholic. Office: Diocese of Helena 515 N Ewing St Helena MT 59601-4002

KOSECOFF, JACQUELINE BARBARA, health services researcher; b. Los Angeles, June 15, 1949; d. Herman Plaut and Betty (Bass) Hamburger; m. Robert Henry Brook, Jan. 17, 1982; children: Rachel Brook, Davida Brook. BA, UCLA, 1970; MS, Brown U., 1971; PhD, UCLA, 1973. Prof. medicine and pub. health UCLA, 1976—; pres. Value Health Scis., Santa Monica, Calif., 1988—; v.p. Value Health, Inc., Avon, Conn. Author: An Evaluation Primer, 1978, How to Evaluate Education Programs, 1980, Evaluation Basics, 1982, How to Conduct Surveys, 1985; contbr. numerous articles to profl. publs. Regents scholar UCLA, 1967-71; NSF fellow, 1971-72. Mem. Am. Pub. Health Assn., Assn. for Health Services Research. Democrat. Jewish. Home: 1474 Bienveneda Ave Pacific Palisades CA 90272-2346

KOSHALEK, RICHARD, museum director, consultant; b. Wausau, Wis., Sept. 20, 1941; s. H. Martin and Ethel A. (Hochtritt) K.; m. Elizabeth J. Briar, July 1, 1967; 1 child, Anne Elizabeth. Student, U. Wis., 1960-61, MA, 1965-67; BA, U. Minn., 1965. Curator Walker Art Ctr., Mpls., 1967-72; asst. dir. NEA, Washington, 1972-74; dir. Ft. Worth Art Mus., 1974-76, Hudson River Mus., Westchester, N.Y., 1976-80, Mus. Contemporary Art, L.A., 1980—; mem. Pres.' Coun. on Arts, Yale U., New Haven, Conn., 1989-94; mem. internat. bd. Biennale di Venezia, Italy, 1992-93; mem. internat. adv. bd. Wexner Ctr., Ohio State U., Columbus, 1990—; mem. com. of assesors The Tate Gallery of Art, London; cons. in field. Co-curator (exhibitions and books) Panza Collection, 1986, Ad Reinhardt, 1991, Arata Isozaki, 1991, Louis I. Kahn, 1992, Robert Irwin, 1993. Mem. Chase Manhattan Bank Art Com., N.Y.C., 1986—; chmn. architect selection Walt Disney Concert Hall, L.A., 1988-90; mem. adv. Neighborhood Revitalization Bd. for Pres. Clinton, Little Rock, Ark., 1993; bd. dirs. Am. Ctr. in Paris, 1993—. NEA fellow, 1972, Durfee Found. fellow, 1992, Design fellow IBM, 1984. Mem. Am. Inst. Graphic Arts (bd. dirs. 1992—), Am. Assn. Mus. Dirs. Office: Mus Contemporary Art 250 S Grand Ave California Plaza Los Angeles CA 90012

KOSSE, KRISZTINA MARIA, museum curator, archaeologist; b. Budapest, Hungary, Dec. 8, 1943; d. Elemer S. and Aranka (Gallai) Krudy; m. Alan D. Kosse, Nov. 25, 1971; 1 child, Jennifer. Student, U. Budapest, 1963-64; MA with honors, U. Edinburgh, Scotland, 1969; PhD, U. London, 1977. Intern Brit. Mus., Eng., 1968; program planner Iowa Dept. of Transp., 1977-80; curator of collections Maxwell Mus. of Anthropology U. N.Mex., Albuquerque, 1980—. Author: Settlement Ecology of Körös and Linear Pottery Cultures in Hungary, 1979; contbr.: A Zuni Artist Looks at Frank Hamilton Cushing: Cartoons by Phil Hughte, 1994. Abercrombie grantee U. Edinburgh, 1968. Mem. Soc. Am. Archaeology, N.Mex. Assn. of Mus. (treas. 1991-93). Office: U NMex Maxwell Mus of Anthropology Albuquerque NM 87131

KOST, GERALD JOSEPH, physician, scientist; b. Sacramento, July 12, 1945; s. Edward William and Ora Imogene K.; m. Angela Louise Baldo, Sept. 9, 1972; children: Christopher Murray, Laurie Elizabeth. BS in Engring., Stanford U., 1967, MS in Engring., 1968; PhD in Bioengring., U. Calif., San Diego, 1977; MD, U. Calif., San Francisco, 1978. Diplomate Nat. Bd. Med. Examiners, Am. Bd. Pathology. Resident dept. medicine UCLA, 1978-79, resident dept. neurology, 1979-80; resident dept. lab. medicine U. Wash., Seattle, 1980-81, chief resident dept. lab. medicine, 1981-82, cardiopulmonary-bioengring. and clin. chemistry researcher, 1982-83; asst. prof. pathology U. Calif., Davis, 1983-87, assoc. prof., 1987-93, prof., dir. clin. chemistry, faculty biomed. engring., 1993—; vis. prof. and Lilly scholar, 1990; numerous sci. cons., nat. and internat. speaker, invited lectr. Contbr. numerous articles to profl. and sci. jours.; various monographs, video and audio prodns. Recipient over 40 awards, honors and rsch. grants including Bank Am. Fine Arts award 1963, Millberry Art award, 1970, Nat. Rsch. Svc. award Nat. Heart, Lung and Blood Inst., 1972-77, Young Investigator award Acad. Clin. Lab. Physicians and Scientist, 1982, 83, Nuclear Magnetic Resonance award U. Calif., Davis, 1984-88; S.A. Pepper Collegiate scholar, 1963; fellowship Stanford U., 1967-68, Internat. scholar MOP, Venezuela, 1967, rsch. fellowship NIH, 1970, Highest Honor Calif. Scholarship Fedn.; grantee Am. Heart Assn., U. Calif., Davis, Lawrence Livermore Nat. Lab., others. Mem. Sigma Chi, Phi Kappa Phi, Mu Alpha Theta.

KOSTA, IVAN, sculptor; b. Košice, Czechoslovakia, Sept. 25, 1935; came to U.S., 1966; s. Jozef and Margita (Sobota) Koštòvà; m. Margerit Kosta, Apr. 26, 1958; 1 child, Yvette Kosta. Law degree, Charles U., Prague, Czechoslovakia, 1959; MFA in Sculpting, 1962. Executed numerous sculptures and commd. monumental pieces. Recipient several prestigious nat. and internat. sculpture awards. Mem. Internat. Sculpture Soc. Home and Office: 2569 Diamondback Dr Colorado Springs CO 80921-2310

KOSTKA, WILLIAM JAMES, JR., public relations executive; b. Mpls., Oct. 17, 1934; s. Dorothy Parmenter K.; m. Jerry Lee Swank, June 10, 1956 (div. 1973); children: Cheryl Elizabeth, Wendy Dorelle; m. Cynthia Sue Gleason, Apr. 6, 1974; children: Jennifer Anna, William James III. BA, U. Colo., 1956. Advt. mgr. Aurora (Colo.) Sentinel, 1958-59; reporter Rocky Mountain News, Denver, 1958-61; nat. new bur. chief Martin Marietta Corp., Balt., 1961-64; gen. mgr. William Kostka & Assocs., Denver, 1964-68; pres. William Kostra & Assocs., Denver, 1968-74; chmn. William Kostka & Assocs., Denver, 1974—; lectr. U. Colo., Boulder, 1974-87. Named Outstanding Grad. in Journalism, U. Colo., Boulder, 1977. Mem. Pub. Rels. Soc. Am. (chpt. pres. 1976, dist. chmn. 1977, nat. bd. dirs. 1978), Denver Press Club (pres. 1979, bd. dirs. 1968-79, 88-89), U. Colo. Alumni Assn. (bd. dirs. 1987-88), Greater Denver C. of C. Republican. Home: 13955 E Hamilton Dr Aurora CO 80014-3942 Office: William Kostka & Assocs 1407 Larimer St Denver CO 80202-1723

KOSTOULAS, IOANNIS GEORGIOU, physicist; b. Petra, Pierias, Greece, Sept. 12, 1936; came to U.S., 1965, naturalized, 1984; s. Georgios Ioannou and Panagiota (Zarogiannis) K.; m. Katina Sioras Kay, June 23, 1979; 1 child, Alexandra. Diploma in Physics U. Thessoloniki, Greece, 1963; MA, U. Rochester, 1969, PhD, 1972; MS, U. Ala., 1977, Instr. U. Thessaloniki, 1963-65; teaching asst. U. Ala., 1966-67, U. Rochester, 1967-68; guest jr. research assoc. Brookhaven Nat. Lab., Upton, N.Y., 1968-72; research physicist, lectr. UCLA, U. Calif.-San Diego, 1972-76; sr. research assoc. Mich. State U., East Lansing, 1976-78, Fermi Nat. Accelerator Lab., Betavia, Ill., 1976-78; research staff mem. MIT, Cambridge, 1978-80; sr. system engr., physicist Hughes Aircraft Co., El Segundo, Calif., 1980-86; sr. physicist electro-optics and space sensors Rockwell Internat. Corp., Downey, Calif., 1986—. Contbr. articles to profl. jours. Served with Greek Army, 1961-63. Research grantee U. Rochester, 1968-72. Mem. Am. Phys. Soc., Los Alamos Sci. Lab. Exptl. Users Group, Fermi Nat. Accelerator Lab. Users Group, High Energy Discussion Group of Brookhaven Nat. Lab., Pan Macedonian Assn., Save Cyprus Council Los Angeles, Sigma Pi Sigma. Club: Hellenic U. Lodge: Ahepa. Home: 2404 Marshallfield Ln # B Redondo Beach CA 90278-4406 Office: Rockwell Internat Co MC FD27 Space System Div 12214 Lakewood Blvd Downey CA 90242-2655

KOSTRIKIN, MARYBETH ELAINE, excavating company executive; b. Clarkston, Wash., Nov. 22, 1954; d. William Bruce and Rachel Ann (Osborn) Hodgson; m. David Kostrikin, Jan. 6, 1983; children: Troy James Pierson, Rachel Anne. Student, U. Idaho, 1972-75, Clackamas C.C., Oregon City, Oreg., 1976, 77. Meter reader, energy specialist Canby (Oreg.) Utility Bd., 1978-84; sec. Kostco Landscape Mgmt., Canby, 1983-91; v.p. KLM Excavating, Inc., Canby, 1991—. Mem. Nat. Fedn. Ind. Bus. Republican. Baptist.

KOTANSKY, ROY D., ancient languages, religion and culture educator; b. Montreal, Que., Can., Feb. 3, 1953; s. Daniel Joseph Kotansky and Jo-Anne (Dexter) Kells; m. Jeanne Marie Miller, Feb. 8, 1992. BA with honors, Westmont Coll., 1975; MA, Fuller Theol. Sem., 1977; PhD, U. Chgo., 1988. Samuel Sandmel Rsch. fellow in Hellenistic Judaism U. Chgo., 1980-81, rsch. specialist Corpus Hellenisticum Project, 1981-83; rsch. fellowship Alexander von Humboldt-Stiftung U. Cologne, Germany, 1990-91, 92-93. Author, editor: A Lex Sacra from Selinous, 1993, Greek Magical Amulets, 1994; consulting editor Greek Magical Papyri in Translation, 1981-83; contbr. articles to profl. jours. Recipient Noyes-Cutter Greek prize U. Chgo., 1980; fellow in antiquities, J. Paul Getty Mus., 1983-84. Mem. Am. Soc. Papyrologists, Nat. Assn. Profs. of Hebrew, Inst. Biblical Rsch., Soc. Biblical Lit. Home: 902 Idaho Ave Santa Monica CA 90403

KOTLER, RICHARD LEE, lawyer; b. L.A., Apr. 13, 1952; s. Allen S. Kotler and Marcella (Fromberg) Swarttz; m. Cindy Jasik, Dec. 9, 1990; children: Kelsey Elizabeth, Charles Max. BA, Sonoma State Coll., 1976; JD, Southwestern U., 1979. Bar: Calif. 1980, U.S. Dist. Ct. (cen. dist.) Cal. 1980. Sole practice Newhall, Calif., 1980-83, 88—; sr. ptnr. Kotler & Hann, Newhall, 1983-88; pvt. practice Law Offices of Richard L. Kotler, Newhall, 1984-86; judge pro temp Municipal Ct., 1981-84, Superior Ct., 1985—. Chmn. Santa Clarita Valley Battered Women's Assn., Newhall, 1983-87; bd. dirs. Santa Clarita Valley Hotline, Newhall, 1981-83. Recipient Commendation award L.A. County, 1983; named SCV Paintball champion. Mem. Santa Clarita Valley Bar Assn. (v.p. 1985—), Los Angeles Astronomy Soc., Newhall Astronomy Club. Office: 23942 Lyons Ave Ste 202 Santa Clarita CA 91321-2444

KOTNOUR, MARY MARGARET, elementary physical education educator; b. Winona, Minn., Jan. 28, 1956; d. Thomas and Maxine (Herber) K. BS in Phys. Edn., Winona State U., 1978; MEd in Counseling, U. Idaho, 1983. Cert. tchr. Minn., Idaho, Wash. Elem. phys. edn. specialist Sch. Dist. #211, Coeur d'Alene, Idaho, 1979-85; elem. phys. edn. coord. Sch. Dist. #271, Coeur d'Alene, 1985-86, elem. phys. edn. specialist, 1986—; Reviewer of Phys. Edn. Books, Prentice Hall, Inc., Englewood, N.J. Author: Physical Fitness Games and Activities Kit, 1990. Bd. dirs. Big Brothers and Big Sisters, Coeur d' Alene; coach, clinician, tng. chmn. Spl. Olympics, Coeur d' Alene; vol. chaplain County Jail. Recipient Disting. Young Alumni award Winona State U., 1987; named to Outstanding Young Women of Am., 1984. Mem. AAHPERD, NEA, Idaho Assn. Health Phys. Edn., Recreation and Dance (nominated for Outstanding Phys. Edn. Tchr. of Yr., 1986, '92), Idaho Edn. Assn., Coeur d' Alene Edn. Assn. (negotiating team 1988—), Delta Kappa Gamma. Office: Ramsay Elem Sch 1351 W Kathleen Ave Coeur D Alene ID 83814-8339

KOTTKAMP, JOHN HARLAN, lawyer; b. Portland, Oreg., Oct. 19, 1930; s. John Henry and Anna Margaret (Schnell) K.; m. Elizabeth Ann Lawrence, July 10, 1954; children: Elizabeth, Andrew, Molly, Jennifer, Carrie. B.S., U. Oreg., 1952, LL.B., 1957. Bar: Oreg. 1957, U.S. Dist. Ct. Oreg. 1957, U.S. Supreme Ct. 1971. Assoc. Kilkenny & Fabre, Pendleton, Oreg., 1957-59, Fabre, Collins & Kottkamp, Pendleton, 1959-61; pvt. practice, Pendleton, 1961-64; ptnr. Kottkamp & O'Rourke, Pendleton, Oreg., 1964—. Served with U.S. Army, 1952-54. Fellow Am. Bar Found., Am. Coll. Trial Lawyers. Republican. Club: Pendleton Country. Lodge: Elks. Office: Kottkamp & O'Rourke 331 SE 2nd St Pendleton OR 97801-2224

KOTTKE, FREDERICK EDWARD, economics educator; b. Menominee, Mich., Sept. 6, 1926; s. Edward Frederick and M. Marie (Braun) K.; BS, Pepperdine U., 1950; postgrad, U. Wis., 1950-52; MA, U. So. Calif., 1957, PhD, 1960; m. Lillian Dorathy Larson, Aug. 27, 1950; children: Karin Lee, Kurt Edward. Lectr., Pepperdine U., 1952-53; asst. prof. U. So. Calif., 1956-63; assoc. prof. econs., chmn. dept., speaker of gen. faculty Stanislaus State Coll., Calif. State U., Turlock, Calif., 1963-68, prof., also chmn. div. arts and scis., 1968—, prof. emeritus econs., 1992—; pres. KK Economic Consultants, Inc.; independent tax adviser, managerial adviser, 1960—; speaker in field. Chmn., Stanislaus County United Crusade, 1964-65; pres., Stanislaus State Coll. Found., 1972; trustee Emanuel Med. Ctr., 1974—; v.p. Good Shepherd Lutheran Ch., 1985-89. Served with USNR. 1943-46. Recipient Pologrammatic award Pepperdine Coll., 1952, Outstanding Prof. award Calif. State U., Stanislaus, 1987-88. Haynes Found. Postgrad. Research award U. So. Calif., 1959. Mem. Am., Western econ. assns., Nat. Tax Assn. (com. for fed. taxation 1989-90), Am. Finance Assn., C. of C., Omicron Delta Epsilon. Lodge: Kiwanis. Author: An Economic Analysis of Toll-Highway Finance, 1956, An Economic Analysis of Financing an Interstate Highway System, 1959; contbr. to econ. newsletter. Home: 1890 N Denair Ave Turlock CA 95382-1816 Office: Calif State U Stanislaus 801 W Monte Vista Ave Turlock CA 95382-0256

KOTTLER, DENNIS BRUCE, physician; b. Newark, N.J., May 19, 1949; married; 2 children. BA cum laude, Yale U., 1971; MD, Cornell U., 1975. Diplomate Am. Bd. Psychiatry and Neurology. Intern Med. Coll. Pa., Phila., 1976-77; resident N.Y. Hosp., N.Y.C., 1976-79; pvt. practice Westlake Village, Calif., 1979—; instr. Yale U., 1969; asst. dir. Payne Whitney Clinic, N.Y.C., 1979; assoc. med. dir. Pacific Shores Hosp., Oxnard, Calif., 1989-90; clin. dir. adult inpatient svcs. Woodview Calabasas (Calif.) Hosp., 1990—, med. dir., 1992—. Editor jour. Yale Daily News, 1970; contbr. articles to profl. jours. Mem. Am. Psychiatric Assn., So. Calif. Psychiatric Assn., L.A. County Med. Assn. Home: 31822 Village Center Rd # 203 Westlake Village CA 91361-4316

KOTTLOWSKI, FRANK EDWARD, geologist; b. Indpls., Apr. 11, 1921; s. Frank Charles and Adella (Markworth) K.; m. Florence Jean Chriscoe, Sept. 15, 1945; children: Karen, Janet, Diane. Student, Butler U., 1939-42; A.B., Ind. U., 1947, M.A., 1949, Ph.D., 1951. Party chief Ind. Geology Survey, Bloomington, summers 1948-50; fellow Ind. U., 1947-51, instr. geology, 1950; adj. prof. N.Mex. Inst. Mining and Tech., Socorro, 1970—; econ. geologist N.Mex. Bur. Mines and Mineral Resources, 1951-66, asst. dir., 1966-68, 70-74, acting dir., 1968-70, dir., 1974-91, state geologist, 1989-91, emeritust dir., state geologist, 1991—; geologic cons. Sandia Corp., 1966-72. Contbr. articles on mineral resources, stratigraphy and areal geology to tech. jours. Mem. Planning Commn. Socorro, 1960-68, 71-78, chmn., 86-90; mem. N.Mex. Energy Resources Bd.; chmn. N.Mex. Coal Surface Mining Commn.; sec. Socorro County Democratic Party, 1964-68. Served to 1st lt. USAAF, 1942-45. Decorated D.F.C.; decorated Air medal; recipient Richard Owen Disting. Alumni award in Govt. and Industry U. Ind., 1987. Fellow AAAS, Geol. Soc. Am. (councilor 1979-82, exec. com. 1981-82, Disting. Svc. award of Coal Geology divsn.); mem. AIME, Am. Assn. Petroleum Geologists (hon. mem., dist. rep. 1965-68, Disting. Svc. award, editor 1971-75, pres. energy minerals divsn. 1987-88), Assn. Am. State Geologists (pres. 1985-86), Soc. Econ. Geologists, Am. Inst. Profl. Geologists (Pub. Svc. award 1986), Am. Commn. Statigraphic Nomenclature (past sec., chmn.), Cosmos Club, Sigma Xi. Home: 703 Sunset St Socorro NM 87801-4657 Office: NMex Bur Mines NMex Tech Campus Sta Socorro NM 87801

KOUNALAKIS, MARKOS, foreign correspondent; b. San Francisco, Dec. 1, 1956; s. Antonios Markos and Vasiliki (Rozakis) K. BA in Polit. Sci. with honors, U. Calif., Berkeley, 1978; MS in Journalism, Columbia U.,

1988. Reporter, anchor Radio Sweden Internat., Stockholm, 1980-82; producer Spotlight on World Affairs, San Francisco, 1982-84; founder, ptnr. Earwax Prodns., San Francisco, 1984—; journalism fellow Robert Bosch Found., Germany, 1988-89; East European reporter Newsweek Mag., 1989-91; Moscow corr. NBC-Mut. News Network, Russia, 1991-92. Author: (book) Defying Gravity: The Making of Newton, 1993 (Gold award 1994).

KOURY, ALEAH GEORGE, retired church executive, minister; b. Toronto, Ont., Can., Sept. 26, 1925; came to U.S. 1952, naturalized, 1960; s. Aleah George and Alice Maude (Jackson) K.; m. Patricia Lee Reynolds, July 11, 1950; children: Patricia Koury Garrison, Aleah George Wayne, Gregory Scott, Rebecca Koury, Cynthia Koury Canaday. BA, U. Toronto, 1948; postgrad., Fresno Coll., 1956, U. Mo., Kansas City, 1971; M Divinity, Midwestern Bapt. Theol. Sem., Kansas City, 1983. Ordained to ministry Reorganized Ch. of Jesus Christ of Latter-day Saints, 1946; ordained Apostle, 1966. Editor Consol. Press, Toronto, 1948-49; minister Independence, Mo., 1949, B.C., Alta., Can., 1950-52, B.C. and Seattle, 1952-56, Cen. Calif. dist., 1956-60; pastor, dist. pres. Utah and S.E. Idaho, 1960-62; asst. to Council of Twelve, 1962; field dir. Europe and Africa, 1966-68, Europe, N. Atlantic States Region and Latin Am., 1973-80; field dir. Europe and Atlantic States Region, 1968-70, Europe, Ont. and Mich. Regions, 1970-73, Latin Am., 1973-80; chaplain dir. Independence Regional Health Ctr., 1985-89; ret., 1989. Author: Truth and Evidence, 1965, Appointee Handbook, 1966. Facilitator Bi-County Spl. Kids Project, Yuba and Sutter Counties, Calif., 1989. With Can. Army, 1944-46. Fellow Coll. of Chaplains (cert. chaplain); mem. Order of Evangelists (sec. 1980). Home: 2309 Pepperwood Dr Yuba City CA 95993-9690

KOUSSER, J(OSEPH) MORGAN, history educator; b. Lewisburg, Tenn., Oct. 7, 1943; s. Joseph Maximillian and Alice Holt (Morgan) K.; m. Sally Ann Ward, June 1, 1968; children: Rachel Meredith, Thaddeus Benjamin. AB, Princeton U., 1965; M.Phil., Yale U., 1968, PhD, 1971; MA, Oxford U., Eng., 1984. Instr. Calif. Inst. Tech., Pasadena, 1969-71; assoc. prof. Calif. Inst. Tech., Padadena, 1975-79, prof., 1979—; vis. prof. U. Mich., Ann Arbor, 1980, Harvard U., Cambridge, Mass., 1981-82, Oxford U., 1984-85, Claremont Grad. Sch., 1993; expert witness Minority Voting Rights Cases; researcher. Author: Shaping of Southern Politics, 1974; editor: Region, Race and Reconstruction, 1982. Guggenheim Found. fellow, 1984-85, Woodrow Wilson Ctr. fellow, 1984-85; grantee NEH, 1974, 82. Mem. Orgn. Am. Historians, Am. Hist. Assn., Social Scis. History Assn., So. Hist. Assn. Democrat. Office: Calif Inst of Tech 228-77 Caltech Pasadena CA 91125

KOUYMJIAN, DICKRAN, art historian, Orientalist, educator; b. Tulcea, Romania, June 6, 1934; came to U.S. (parents Am. citizens), 1939; s. Toros S. and Zabelle I. (Calusdian) K.; m. Angèle Kapoïan, Sept. 16, 1967. BS in European Cultural History, U. Wis., 1957; MA in Arab Studies, Am. U., Beirut, 1961; PhD in Near East Lang. and Culture, Columbia U., 1969. Instr. English Columbia U., N.Y.C., 1961-64; dir. Am. Authors, Inc., N.Y.C., 1965-67; asst. prof. and asst. dir. Ctr. for Arabic Studies Am. U., Cairo, 1967-71; assoc. prof. history Am. U. Beirut, 1971-75; prof. art history Am. U., Paris, 1976-77; prof. history and art, dir. Armenian Studies program Calif. State U., Fresno, 1977—; dir. Sarkis and Meline Kalfayan Ctr. for Armenian Studies, Calif. State U., Fresno, 1990—; Fulbright disting. lectr., prof. Armenian and Am. Lit., Yerevan (Armenia, USSR), 1987; cons. archaeology UNESCO, Paris, 1976; prof., chairholder Armenian Sect., Inst. Nat. des Langs. et Civilisations Orientales, U. Paris, 1988-91; 1st incumbent Haig & Isabel Berberian endowed chair Armenian Studies Calif. State U., Fresno, 1989—. Author: Index of Armenian Art, part I, 1977, part II, 1979, The Armenian History of Ghazar P'arpetzi, 1986, Arts of Armenia, 1992; co-author: (with A. Kapoïan) The Splendor of Egypt, 1975; author and editor: William Saroyan: An Armenian Trilogy, 1986, William Saroyan: Warsaw Visitor and Tales of the Vienna Streets, 1990; editor: (books) Near Eastern Numismatics, Iconography, Epigraphy and History, 1974, Essays in Armenian Numismatics in Honor of C. Sibilian, 1981, Armenian Studies: In Memoriam Haïg Berbérian, 1986; editorial bd. Armenian Rev., 1974—, Ararat Lit. mag., 1975—, Revue des Etudes Arméniennes, 1978—, NAASR Jour. Armenian Studies; contbr. articles to profl. jours. Served with U.S. Army, 1957. Recipient Outstanding Prof. award Am. U., Cairo, 1968-69, 69-70, Outstanding Prof. of Yr. award Calif. State U., 1985-86, Hagop Kevorkian Disting. Lectureship in Near Eastern Art and Civilization, NYU, 1979; Fulbright fellow, USSR, 1986-87; grantee NEH, Paris, 1980-81, 95. Mem. Am. Oriental Soc., Am. Numismatic Soc., Mid. East Studies Assn. (charter), Coll. Arts Assn., Soc. Armenian Studies (charter, pres. 1985-86, 92-94), Société Asiatique, Medieval Acad., Assn. Internat. des Etudes Armeniennes, others. Home: 30 rue Chevert, 75007 Paris France Office: Calif State U Armenian Studies Program Fresno CA 93740-0004

KOVACH, RONALD, footwear manufacturing executive; b. N.Y.C., Dec. 22, 1946; s. Edward Joseph and Louise Christine (Ragno) K.; m. Linda Cathrine Clark, May 5, 1969; children: Meredith Alexa, Matthew Alexander. BA with honors, U. Calif., Riverside, 1968, MA, 1970; postgrad., UCLA, 1970-74. Asst. v.p. Big 5 Sporting Goods, El Segundo, Calif., 1972-91; dir., founder Eagle Claw Saltwater Fishing Schs., Huntington Beach, Calif., 1989—; ind. cons. to sporting goods industry Huntington Beach, 1992—; bd. dirs. Penn Fishing U.; lectr., condr. seminars, Huntington Beach, 1985—; frellance photojournalis, Huntington Beach, 1985—; co-owner FX (fishing expeditions outdoor apparel); bd. dirs. Advt. Maj. Footwear Co.; cons. in field. Author: Bass Fishing in California: Secrets of the Western Pros, 1985, Trout Fishing in California: Secrets of the Top Western Anglers, 1987, Saltwater Fishing in California: Secrets of the Pacific Experts, 1989, Serious Bass Fishing: Winning Secrets of Advanced Bass Anglers, 1994, The Serious Pacific Angler: Advanced Secrets of The Eagle Claw Fishing School, 1994; host: Fishing Expeditions KABC-Radio; co-host: World of Big Game Fishing Show ESPN-TV; contbr. numerous articles to various publs. Organizer Proposition 132, Calif. anti-gill net initiative, 1990. Calif. State scholar U. Calif., 1970; rsch. NIMH fellow UCLA, 1972. Mem. Internat. Game Fish Assn., Nat. Resource Def. Coun., Calif. Trout, Bass Anglers Sportsman Soc., Outdoor Writers Assn. Am., Outdoor Writers Calif., United Anglers. Home and Office: 17911 Portside Cir Huntington Beach CA 92649-4931

KOVACH, THOMAS ALLEN, educator; b. Providence, Oct. 22, 1949; s. George Paul and Madeline Elizabeth (Besnyö) K.; divorced; children: Leah Beth; 1 step-child, Sarah Shanti Stein. BA in German magna cum laude, Columbia U., 1971; PhD in Comparative Lit., Princeton (N.J.) U., 1978. Asst. prof. Dept. Langs. U. Utah, Salt Lake City, 1978-85; assoc. prof. Dept. Langs. and Lit., U. Utah, Salt Lake City, 1985-90; assoc. prof., dept. chair Dept. German and Russian, U. Ala., Tuscaloosa, 1990-94; assoc. prof., dept. head German studies U. Ariz., Tucson, 1994—. Author: Hofmannsthal and Symbolism, 1985; contbr. articles to profl. jours. Recipient Deutscher Verein Prize Columbia U., 1971; Fulbright-Hays Grad. fellowship, 1974-75; Fulbright-Hays faculty grant, 1983. Mem. MLA, South Atlantic Modern Lang. Assn., Am. Comparative Lit. Assn., Phi Beta Kappa. Jewish. Home: 701 N Palo Verde Blvd Tucson AZ 85716-4615 Office: U Ariz Dept German Studies 571 Modern Langs Bldg Tucson AZ 85721

KOVACHY, EDWARD MIKLOS, JR., psychiatrist; b. Cleve., Dec. 3, 1946; s. Edward Miklos and Evelyn Amelia (Palenscar) K.; m. Susan Eileen Light, June 21, 1981; children: Timothy Light, Benjamin Light. BA, Harvard U., 1968, JD, 1972, MBA, 1972; MD, Case Western Reserve U., 1977. Diplomate Nat. Bd. Med. Examiners. Resident in psychiatry Stanford U. Med. Ctr., Stanford, Calif., 1977-81; pvt. practice psychiatry mediator mgmt. cons. Menlo Park, Calif., 1981—; mediator, mgmt. cons. Columnist The Peninsula Times Tribune, 1983-85. Bd. trustees Mid Peninsula H.S., Palo Alto, Calif., 1990—; mem. gift com. Harvard Coll. Class of 1968, 25th reunion chmn. participation, San Francisco, 1993. Mem. Am. Psychiat. Assn., Physicians for Social Responsibility, Assn. Family and Conciliation Cts., No. Calif. Psychiat. Soc., San Francisco Acad. Hypnosis. Presbyterian. Office: 1187 University Dr Menlo Park CA 94025-4423

KOVARIK, JOSEPH LEWIS, surgeon; b. Omaha, Sept. 16, 1927; m. Delores Marie Casey, June 20, 1953; children: Jane Ann, Joseph Edward, Patricia Marie, James John, Karen Rose, Kenneth Michael. Student, Creighton U., 1944, Ctrl. Mo. State U., Warrensburg, 1945, Brown U., 1945-46; MD, U. Nebr., 1950. Diplomate Am. Bd. Surgery, Am. Bd. Thoracic Surgery; lic. physician Nebr., Ill., Colo. Intern U. Ill. Rsch. and Ednl. Hosps., Chgo., 1950-51; resident in gen. surgery St. Francis Hosp., Peoria, Ill., 1951-53, Presbyn. Hosp., Chgo., 1953-55; resident in thoracic surgery Chgo. State Tuberculosis Sanitarium, 1955, VA Hosp., Hines, Ill., 1956; fellow in thoracic and cardiovascular surgery Rush-Presbyn.-St. Luke's Med. Ctr., Chgo., 1957; pvt. practice surgery Englewood, Colo.; active staff Presbyn.-St. Luke's Med. Ctr., Denver; staff St. Anthony Hosp., Denver, St. Joseph Hosp., Denver, Mercy Med. Ctr., Denver; cons. in thoracic surgery VA Hosp., Albuquerque, 1961-66; cons. in surgery Colo. State Hosp., Pueblo, Colo., 1960-80; attending in thoracic surgery VA Hosp., Denver, 1959-85; asst. clin. prof. surgery U. Colo. Health Scis. Ctr., Denver, 1965-76, assoc. clin. prof., 1976-87, clin. prof. surgery, 1987—; staff surgeon Gate Med. Clinic, Denver, 1973-93. Contbr. numerous articles to profl. jours.; mem. physician's adv. panel Med. World News, 1980. Pres. Colo. divsn. Am. Cancer Soc., 1981-83, adv. com., 1986—, exec. com., 1965-86); bd. dirs., chmn. profl. adv. com. Cmty. Homemaker Svc., Denver, 1964-68; v.p., chmn. med. adv. com. Colo. Cystic Fibrosis Assn., 1964-69; surg. rev. com. Blue Cross/Blue Shield of Colo., 1981-88, cons., 1988—; bd. govs. QuaLife Wellness Cmty., Denver, 1988-91; bd. dirs. Denver Boys, Inc., 1992-93; health care adminstrv. adv. bd. Denver Tech. Coll., 1993—; physician advisor Colo. Found. Med. Care, 1988—. With U.S. Naval Air Corps, 1945-46. Mem. ACS (bd. govs. 1979-85, Colo. chpt. pres. 1976-77), AMA, Southwestern Surg. Congress (pres. 1986-87), Denver Med. Soc. (pres. 1969-70, chmn. bd. trustees 1970-71), Colo. Med. Soc. (del. 1982-85), Rush Surg. Soc. (pres. 1989-90), Western Thoracic Surg. Assn., Am. Assn. for Thoracic Surgery, Western Surg. Assn., Am. Coll. Chest Physicians, Colo. Trudeau Soc., Am. Thoracic Soc., Denver Acad. Surgery (bd. dirs. 1985-86), Rotary.

KOVTYNOVICH, DAN, civil engineer; b. Eugene, Oreg., May 17, 1952; s. John and Elva Lano (Robie) K. BCE, Oreg. State U., 1975, BBA, 1976. Registered profl. engr., Calif., Oreg. V.p. Kovtynovich, Inc., Contractors and Engrs., Eugene, 1976-80, pres., chief exec. officer, 1980—. Fellow ASCE; mem. Am. Arbitration Assn. (arbitrator 1979—), N.W. China Coun., Navy League of U.S., Eugene Asian Coun. Republican. Office: Kovtynovich Inc 1595 Skyline Park Loop Eugene OR 97405-4466

KOWALCZEWSKI, DOREEN MARY THURLOW, communications company executive; b. London, May 5, 1926; came to U.S., 1957, naturalized, 1974; d. George Henry and Jessie Alice (Gray) Thurlow; BA, Clarke Coll., 1947; postgrad. Wayne State U., 1959-62, Roosevelt U., 1968; m. Witold Dionizy Kowalczewski, July 26, 1946; children: Christina Julianna, Janet Alice, Stephen Robin. Agy. supr. MONY, N.Y.C., 1963-67; office mgr. J.B. Carroll Co., Chgo., 1967-68; mng. editor Sawyer Coll. Bus., Evanston, Ill., 1968-71; mgr. policyholder svc. CNA, Chgo., 1971-73; EDP coord. Canteen Corp., Chgo., 1973-75; mgr. documentation and standards LRSP, Chgo., 1975-77; data network mgr. Computerized Agy. Mgmt. Info. Svcs., Chgo., 1977-86; founder, chmn. Tekman Assocs., 1982—; chpt. sec. Soc. Tech. Communications, 1988-90. Bd. dirs. Wash. E. chpt. LWV, 1993—. Pres., Univ. Park Assn., 1980-84. Mem. Bus. Profl. Women, Women's Bus. Exch., Assn. Profl. Writing Cons., Soc. Tech. Communications, Mensa. Bd. dirs. Lake View Estates, 1993—.

KOWALSKI, KAZIMIERZ, computer science educator, researcher; b. Turek, Poland, Nov. 7, 1946; came to U.S., 1986; naturalized, 1994; s. Waclaw and Helena (Wisniewska) K.; m. Eugenia Zajaczkowska, Aug. 5, 1972. MSc, Wroclaw (Poland) U. Tech., 1970, PhD, 1974. Asst. prof. Wroclaw U. Tech., 1970-76, assoc. prof., 1976-86; assoc. prof. Pan Am. U., Edinburg, Tex., 1987-88; prof. computer sci. Calif. State U.-Dominguez Hills, Carson, 1988—; lectr. U. Basrah, Iraq, 1981-85; cons. XXCal, Inc., L.A., 1987-91; conf. presenter in field; rsch. fellow Power Inst. Moscow, USSR, 1978; info. sys. tng. UNESCO, Paris, 1978. Co-author: Principles of Computer Science, 1975, Organization and Programming of Computers, 1976; also articles. Recipient Bronze Merit Cross, Govt. of Poland, 1980. Mem. IEEE Computer Soc., The N.Y. Acad. Scis., Assn. for Computing Machinery, Am. Assn. for Artificial Intelligence, Mensa, Sigma Xi. Home: 5042 N Raton Cir Long Beach CA 90807-1140 Office: Calif State U 1000 E Victoria St Carson CA 90747-0001

KOWDLEY, KRIS V., gastroenterologist/hepatologist, educator; s. V. S. and Geetha (Iyer) K.; m. Bonnie Dixit. AB, Columbia U., 1981; MD, Mount Sinai, N.Y.C., 1985. Diplomate Am. Bd. Gastroenterology. Intern Oreg. Health Sci. U., Portland, 1985-86, resdient in internal medicine, 1986-88; gastrointestinal fellow New Eng. Med. Ctr., Boston, 1989-91; asst. prof. Case Western U., Cleve., 1991-93, U. Wash., Seattle, 1993—. Author: Collagen Diseases of Liver, 1993, Difficult Decisions in Digestive Disease, 1994; contbr. articles to Gastroenterology and Hepatology. Mem. Am. Gastroenterology Assn., Am. Assn. Study Liver Diseases, Am. Soc. Gastroenterology Endoscopy, Am. Coll. Gastroenterologists. Office: U Wash RG-24 Seattle WA 98195

KOZAR, MARTHA CECILE, corporate executive; b. Davenport, Iowa, May 4, 1963; d. Albert Eugene and Carol Margaret (Sejrup) Lorenz; m. Paul J. Kozar, June 30, 1990. BA in Computer Sci., Lewis U., Romeoville, Ill., 1985; MBA, U. Notre Dame (Ind.), 1989. Systems analyst GE, Morris, Ill., 1984-86; MIS supr. Blistex Inc., Oak Brook, Ill., 1986-87; mktg. intern Whirlpool Corp., LaPorte, Ind., 1988; mktg. asst. Miles Inc., Elkhart, Ind., 1989-90, asst. product mgr., 1990-91; asst. brand mgr. The Dial Corp., Phoenix, 1991-93, brand mgr., 1993-95, sr. brand mgr., 1995—.

KOZAREK, RICHARD ANTHONY, gastroenterologist, educator; b. Duluth, Minn., Apr. 22, 1947; s. Clarence Edward and Patricia Ann (Koors) K.; m. Linda Jane Kozarek, June 9, 1973; children: Katherine, Ellen. BA in Philosophy, U. Wis., 1969, MD, 1973. Diplomate Am. Bd. Internal Medicine; bd. cert. internal medicine and gastroenterology. Intern Dalhousie U., Halifax, N.S., Can., 1973-74; resident Good Samaritan Hosp., Phoenix, Ariz., 1974-76; fellow U. Ariz.-Phoenix VA Med. Ctr., Tucson, 1976-78; asst. chief gastroenterology Phoenix VA Med. Ctr., Tucson, 1978-83; asst. clin. prof. medicine U. Wash., Seattle, 1978-83; chief sect. gastroenterology Virginia Mason Med. Ctr., Seattle, 1983—; chief gastroenterology Va. Mason Med. Ctr., Seattle, 1989—; clin. prof. medicine U. Wash., Seattle, 1990—. Author 4 books, 40 book chpts., numerous sci. articles. Recipient Eddy D. Palmer award William Beaumont Soc., 1982. Fellow ACP, Am. Coll. Gastroenterology; mem. Am. Gastroenterology Assn., Soc. for Gastrointestinal Endoscopy (gov. bd. 1990-95), Pacific N.W. Gastroenterology Soc. (sec. 1990, pres. 1991). Office: Virgina Mason Med Ctr 1100 9th Ave Seattle WA 98101-2756

KOZINSKI, ALEX, federal judge; b. Bucharest, Romania, July 23, 1950; came to U.S., 1962; s. Moses and Sabine (Zapler) K.; m. Marcy J. Tiffany, July 9, 1977; children: Yale Tiffany, Wyatt Tiffany, Clayton Tiffany. AB in Econs. cum laude, UCLA, 1972, JD, 1975. Bar: Calif. 1975, D.C., 1978. Law clk. to Hon. Anthony M. Kennedy U.S. Ct. Appeals (9th cir.), 1975-76; law clk. to Chief Justice Warren E. Burger U.S. Supreme Ct., 1976-77; assoc. Covington & Burling, Washington, 1979-81; asst. counsel Office of Counsel to Pres., White House, Washington, 1981; spl. counsel Merit Systems Protection Bd., Washington, 1981-82; chief judge U.S. Claims Ct., Washington, 1982-85; judge U.S. Ct. Appeals (9th cir.), 1985—; lectr. law U. So. Calif., 1992. Office: US Ct Appeals 125 S Grand Ave Ste 200 Pasadena CA 91105-1621*

KOZOJET, CHRISTINE HOFFMAN, university official; b. Pasadena, Calif., Apr. 23, 1962; d. Eugene Francis and Kathleen Joanne (Schumacher) Hoffman; m. Robert B. Kozojet, Sept. 5, 1987; 1 child, Makenzie Madeline. BA in Polit. Sci., Tulane U., 1984. Staff asst. U.S. Congressman William Dannemeyer, Washington, 1984-85; asst. to v.p. fin. and adminstrn. Wilderness Soc., Washington, 1985-86; asst. dir. devel. Hood Coll., Frederick, Md., 1986-88; assoc. dir. ann. giving Calif. Inst. Tech., Pasadena, 1988-92; dir. devel. Coll. Arts and Scis. U. N.Mex., Albuquerque, 1992—. Co-author: Annual Giving Strategies: A Conprehensive Guide to Better Results, 1990. Mem. exec. com. Orgn. for Women at Caltech, 1990-92; mem. Jr. League Albuquerque, 1992-94. Mem. Coun. for Advancement and Support Edn. Office: U NMex Ortega Hall # 201 Albuquerque NM 87131

KRACHT, THEODORE ANDREW, career officer; b. Wooster, Ohio, Mar. 15, 1967; s. William and Edna Lucille (Radcliffe) K. BS in History, USAF Acad., 1989. Commd. 2d lt. USAF, 1985, advanced through grades to capt., 1993, comdr. for missle crews, 1990-93, instr., 1993—. Recipient 20th Air Force Crewmember Excellence award 20th Air Force and USAF Space Command, 1993; named one of Outstanding Young Men of Am., 1992. Mem. Am. Hist. Assn., Air Force Assn,. Assn. Grad.-USAF Acad. Roman Catholic. Home: 3345 11th Ave S Apt 116 Great Falls MT 59405-5445

KRAEMER, KENNETH LEO, architect, urban planner, educator; b. Plain, Wis., Oct. 29, 1936; s. Leo Adam and Lucy Rose (Bauer) K.; m. Norine Florence, June 13, 1959; children: Kurt Randall, Kim Rene. BArch, U. Notre Dame, 1959; MS in City and Regional Planning, U. So. Calif., 1964, M of Pub. Adminstrn., 1965, PhD, 1967. From instr. to asst. prof. U. So. Calif., Los Angeles, 1965-67; asst. prof. U. Calif., Irvine, 1967-71, assoc. prof., 1971-78, prof., 1978—, dir. Pub. Policy Research Orgn., 1974-92, dir. Ctr. for Rsch. on Info. Tech. and Orgns., 1992—; cons. Office of Tech. Assessment, Washington, 1980, 84-85; pres. Irvine Research Corp., 1978—. Author: Management of Information Systems, 1980, Computers and Politics, 1982, Dynamics of Computing, 1983, People and Computers, 1985, Modeling as Negotiating, 1986, Data Wars, 1987, Wired Cities, 1987, Managing Information Systems, 1989. Mem. Blue Ribbon Data Processing Com., Orange County, Calif., 1973, 79-80, Telecomm. Adv. Bd., Sacramento, 1987-92. Mem. Am. Soc. for Pub. Adminstrn. (Disting. Research award 1985), Internat. Conf. on Info. Systems, Am. Planning Assn., Assn. for Computing Machinery. Democrat. Roman Catholic. Club: Notre Dame. Office: U Calif Ste 320 Berkeley Pl N Ctr Rsch Info Tech & Orgns Irvine CA 92717

KRAFT, ELAINE JOY, community relations and communications official; b. Seattle, Sept. 1, 1951; d. Harry J. and Leatrice M. (Hanan) K.; m. Lee Somerstein, Aug. 2, 1980; children: Paul Kraft, Leslie Jo. BA, U. Wash., 1973; MPA, U. Puget Sound, 1979. Reporter Jour. Am. Newspaper, Bellevue, Wash., 1972-76; editor Jour./Enterprise Newspapers, Wash. State, 1976; mem. staff Wash. State Senate, 1976-78, Wash. Ho. of Reps., 1978-82, pub. info. officer, 1976-78, mem. leadership staff, asst. to caucus chmn., 1980—; ptnr., pres. Media Kraft Communications; mgr. corp. info., advt. and mktg. communications Weyerhaeuser Co., 1982-85; dir. communications Weyerhaeuser Paper Co., 1985-87; dir. community rels. N.W. region Coors Brewing Co. 1987—. Recipient state and nat. journalism design and advt. awards. Mem. Nat. Fedn. Press Women, Women in Communications, Wash. Press Assn. Home: 14329 SE 63rd St Bellevue WA 98006-4802 Office: PO Box 5921 Bellevue WA 98006-0421

KRAFT, GEORGE HOWARD, physician, educator; b. Columbus, Ohio, Sept. 27, 1936; s. Glen Homer and Helen Winner (Howard) K.; m. Mary Louise Wells, Oct. 2, 1965; children: Jonathan Ashbrook, Susannah Mary. AB, Harvard U., 1958; MD, Ohio State U., 1963, MS, 1967. Cert. Am. Bd. Phys. Medicine and Rehab., Am. Bd. Electrodiagnostic Medicine. Intern U. Calif. Hosp., San Francisco, 1963-64, resident, 1964-65; resident Ohio State U., Columbus, 1965-67; assoc. U. Pa. Med. Sch., Phila., 1968-69; asst. prof. U. Wash., Seattle, 1969-72, assoc. prof., 1972-76, prof., 1976—, chief of staff Med. Ctr., 1993-95; dir. electrodiagnostic medicine U. Wash. Hosp., 1987—, dir. Multiple Sclerosis Clin. Ctr., 1982—, co-dir. Muscular Dystrophy Clinic, 1974—; assoc. dir. rehab. medicine Overlake Hosp., Bellevue, Wash., 1989—; bd. dirs. Am. Bd. Electrodiagnostic Medicine, 1993—. Cons. editor Phys. Med. and Rehab. Clinics, 1990—, EEG and Clin. Neurophysiology, 1992—; assoc. editor Jour. Neurologic Rehab., 1988—; mem. editorial bd. Am. Jour. Phys. Medicine and Rehab., 1987-93; contbr. aritcles to profl. jours. Adv. com. World Rehab. Fund., N.Y.C., 1988—; sci. peer rev. com. C Nat. Multiple Sclerosis Soc., N.Y.C., 1990—, chmn., 1993—, med. adv. bd., exec. com. med. adv. bd., 1991—, clinic com. mem., 1993—; bd. sponsors Wash. Physicians for Social Responsibility, Seattle, 1986—. Rsch. grantee Rehab. Svcs. Adminstrn., 1978-81, HEW, 1976-79, Nat. Inst. Handicapped Rsch., 1984-88, Nat. Multiple Sclerosis Soc., 1990-92, 94—. Fellow Am. Acad. Phys. Medicine and Rehab. (pres. 1984-85, Zeiter award 1991); mem. Am. Assn. Electrodiagnostic Medicine (cert., pres. 1982-83), Assn. Acad. Physiatrists (pres. 1980-81), Am. Acad. Clin. Neurophysiology (treas. 1989-93, pres.-elect 1993-95, pres. 1995—), Am. Congress Rehab. Medicine, Am. Acad. Neurology, Internat. Rehab. Medicine Assn. Episcopalian. Office: U Wash Dept Rehab Dept Rehab PO Box 356490 Seattle WA 98195-0004

KRAFT, HENRY R., lawyer; b. Los Angeles, Apr. 27, 1946; s. Sylvester and Freda (Schochat) K.; m. Terry Kraft, July 21, 1968; children: Diana, Kevin. BA in History, San Fernando Valley State Coll., 1968; JD, U. So. Calif., 1971. Bar: Calif. 1972, U.S. Dist. Ct. (cen. dist.) Calif. 1972, U.S. Ct. Appeals (9th cir.) 1985. Dep. pub. defender San Bernardino (Calif.) County, 1972-78; sole practice Victorville, Calif., 1979—; city atty. Victorville, 1987—; atty. City of Barstow, Calif., 1980—; instr. Victor Valley Coll., Victorville, 1986—. Atty. Barstow Community Hosp., 1980-88. Mem. San Bernardino Bar Assn. (fee dispute com., jud. evaluation com.), High Desert Bar Assn. (pres., v.p., sec. 1979-81), Calif. Soc. Health Care Attys. Democrat. Jewish. Office: 14350 Civic Dr Ste 270 Victorville CA 92392-2343

KRAFT, RICHARD JOE, sales executive; b. Toppenish, Wash., Apr. 20, 1944; s. Joseph Nian and Rose Goldie (Merrick) K.; m. Karolyn Idell Keyes, Oct. 9, 1963 (div. 1982); children: Craig J., Jeffrey Eugene; m. Margaret Celeste Porter, Apr. 9, 1983. Student, Yakima Valley Coll., 1962-63; student, U. Wash., 1964-70. Project engr. Gray & Osborne Consulting Engrs., Seattle, 1965-76; project engr., constrn. cons. Pool Engring., Ketchikan, Alaska, 1976-81; project mgr. Cape Fox Corp., Ketchikan, 1982; project engr. Buno Constrn., Woodinville, Wash., 1983, Straiger Engring. Svcs., Ketchikan, Sitka, Alaska, 1984; owner Kraft Constrn. Svcs., Kirkland, Wash., 1984-85; dir. mcpl. projects ESM, Inc., Renton, Wash., 1985-86; estimator Active Constrn., Inc., Gig Harbor, Wash., 1987; sr. sales engr. Advanced Drainage Systems, Inc., Woodinville, 1987-93; project mgr. TY-Matt, Inc., Ketchikan, 1993-94; storm sewer/sanitary specification subcom. Am. Pub. Works Assn., Wash. state chpt., 1985-93. Pres. Snohomish (Wash.) Camp, Gideons Internat., 1990-91; pres. exec. com. Maltby (Wash.) Congl. Ch. Mem. Utility Contractors Assn. Wash. (bd. dirs. 1990-92). Mem. Christian Ch. Home and Office: PO Box 6384 Ketchikan AK 99901-1384

KRAFT, SCOTT WALLACE, writer, actor; b. Cambridge, Mass., July 30, 1960; s. Robert Alan and Carol Louise (Wallace) K.; m. Nadine Marie van der Velde, Oct. 28, 1990. Student, Am. Coll. in Paris, 1980; BA in English Lit., U. Pa., 1983; student, Padua Hills Playwrights Conf., L.A., 1988. Writer CBS, HBO, Viacom, others, L.A., 1988—; actor BCS, ABC, NBC, NFB, others, L.A., 1982—; producer CBS, L.A., 1990—; playwright Essential State, Wilton Project, L.A., 1986—; lit. advisor Audrey Skirall-Kenis Theater, L.A., 1990-92; founding mem. Wilton Project Theater Co., L.A., 1991—; book reviewer L.A. Times, 1992—. Author: (play) The Big One Shot, 1992; co-author: (film) A Little Death, 1993; actor in film For the Moment, 1993, in play Hurleyburley, 1989, Genie, 1994 (nominated Best Supporting Actor 1994). Mem. PEN, SAG, Writers Guild Am., Alliance of Can. Cinema, TV and Radio Artists. Office: care 3 Arts Mgmt 7920 W Sunset Blvd Ste 350 Los Angeles CA 90046-3300

KRAFT, WILLIAM ARMSTRONG, retired priest; b. Rochester, N.Y., Apr. 13, 1926; s. William Andrew and Elizabeth Ruth (Armstrong) K. BA, St. Bernard Coll., 1947; ThM, Immaculate Heart Theol. Coll., 1951; D of Ministry, Claremont Sch. of Theology, 1981. Ordained priest Roman Cath. Ch., 1951. Dir. and founder of Newman Apostolate Diocese of San Diego, Calif., 1951-63; dir. of pub. rels. Diocese of San Diego, 1956-63, dir. of cemeteries, 1964-70, exec. dir. of devel., 1979-91; founding pastor St. Therese of Child Jesus Parish, San Diego, 1956-70, Good Shepherd Parish, San Diego, 1970-77; pastor St. Charles Borromeo Parish, San Diego, 1977-79; bd. dirs. Cath. Charities, San Diego; bd. of consultors Diocese of San Diego, 1985-91, mem. Presbyteral Coun., 1985-91, mem. bldg. commn., 1977-91. Bd. dirs. Am. Nat. Red Cross, San Diego, 1956-63, Legal Aid Soc., San Diego, 1956-65, Travelers' Aid Soc., San Diego, 1956-65; mem. Presdl. Task Force, Washington, 1984—. Named Prelate of Honor to Pope, Pope John Paul II, Vatican City, 1985, Knight Comdr. of Equestrian, Order of The Holy Sepulchre, Latin Patriarcii, Jerusalem, 1984, Knights of Columbus 4th degree. Mem. Benevolent and Protective Order of Elks, Univ. Club Atop Symphony Towers, Nat. Cath. Conf. for Total Stewardship (bd. dirs.), Nat. Cath. Devel. Conf., Nat. Soc. Fund Raising Execs. (cert.). Republican. Home: 6910 Cibola Rd San Diego CA 92120-1709

KRAG, OLGA, interior designer; b. St. Louis, Nov. 27, 1937; d. Jovica Todor and Milka (Slijepcevic) Golubovic. AA, U. Mo., 1958; cert. interior design UCLA, 1979. Interior designer William L. Pereira Assocs., L.A., 1977-80; assoc. Reel/Grobman Assocs., L.A., 1980-81; project mgr. Kaneko/Laff Assocs., L.A., 1982; project mgr. Stuart Laff Assocs., L.A., 1983-85; restaurateur The Edge, St. Louis, 1983-84; pvt. practice comml. interior design, L.A., 1981—, pres., R.I., 1989—. Mem. invitation and ticket com. Calif. Chamber Symphony Soc., 1980-81; vol. Westside Rep. Coun., Proposition 1, 1971; asst. inaugural presentation Mus. of Childhood, L.A., 1985. Recipient Carole Eichen design award U. Calif., 1979. Mem. Am. Soc. Interior Designers, Inst. Bus. Designers, Phi Chi Theta, Beta Sigma Phi. Republican. Serbian Orthodox. Home and Office: 700 Levering Ave Apt 10 Los Angeles CA 90024-2797

KRAHMER, DONALD L., JR., financial services company executive; b. Hillsboro, Oreg., Nov. 11, 1957; s. Donald L. and Joan Elizabeth (Karns) K.; m. Suzanne M. Blanchard, Aug. 16, 1986; children: Hillary, Zachary. BS, Willamette U., 1981, MM, 1987, JD, 1987. Bar: Oreg. 1988. Fin. analyst U.S. Bancorp, Portland, 1977-87; intern U.S. Senator Mark Hatfield, 1978; legis. aide State Sen. Jeannette Hamby, Hillsboro, Oreg., 1981-83, State Rep. Delna Jones, Beaverton, Oreg., 1983; bus. analyst Pacificorp, Portland, 1987; mgr. mergers/acquisitions Pacificorp Fin. Svcs., Portland, 1988-89; dir. Pacificorp Fin. Svcs., 1990; CEO, pres. Atkinson Group, Portland, 1991—; atty. Black Helterline, Portland, 1991—; bd. dirs., sec. Marathon Fin. Assocs., Portland, 1989; bd. dirs. Self-Enhancement, Inc., Willamette Forum, chmn. adv. bd.; adv. bd., editor Oreg. Enterprise Forum, 1991—; bd. dirs. Concordia Univ. Found. Treas. Com. to Re-Elect Jeannette Hamby, 1986; bd. dirs. fin. com./devel. com. Am. Diabetes Assn., Portland, 1990—; founder Needle Bros., 1994; chmn. Atkinson Grad. Sch. Devel. Com., Salem, 1989-92; founder Conf. of Entrepreneurship, Salem, 1984, chmn. Entrepreneurship Breakfast Forum, Portland, 1993; chmn., founder Oreg. Conf. on Entrepreneurship and Awards Dinner, 1994. Recipient Pub.'s award Oreg. Bus. Mag., 1987, Founders award Willamette U., 1987, award Scripps Found., 1980, others. Mem. ABA, Oreg. Bar Assn. (chmn. exec. com., fin. instns. com., exec. com., bus. law sect.), Multnomah County Bar Assn., Washington County Bar Assn., Portland Soc. Fin. Analysts, Japan-Am. Soc. Oreg., Assn. Investment Mgmt. and Rsch., City Club. Republican. Lutheran. Home: 16230 SW Copper Creek Dr Portland OR 97224-6500 Office: Black Helterline 1200 Bank of Calif Tower 707 SW Washington St Portland OR 97205-3536

KRAKOWER, BERNARD HYMAN, management consultant; b. N.Y.C., May 11, 1935; s. David and Bertha (Glassman) K.; m. Sondra Joan Fishbein, Apr. 14, 1968; children: Lorna, Victoria, Ariela Shauna. BA in Advt., UCLA, 1959, cert. in real estate, 1966, cert. in indsl. relations, 1972; MBA, Pepperdine U., 1979. Loan officer Lytton Fin. Corp., Los Angeles, 1961-65; mgmt. cons. James R. Colvin & Assocs., Los Angeles, 1965-67; sr. indsl. relations rep. Sci. Data Systems (Xerox), 1967-68; dir. ops. Tratec, Inc., Los Angeles, 1968-70; chmn. Krakower/Brucker Internat., Inc., Los Angeles, 1970-88; sr. ptnr. Krakower Finnegan Assocs., Los Angeles, 1988-90; pres. Krakower Group, Inc., 1990—; bd. dirs. Columbia Nat. Bank, Santa Monica, Calif. Mem. citizens liaison com. Los Angeles Dept. Recreation and Parks, 1973; apptd. commr., v.p. L.A. Countywide Citizens Planning Coun. by L.A. County Bd. Suprs., 1988—, v.p., 1991—, pres. 1993—; pres., bd. dirs. L.A. Bus. Coun. past chmn. bd. Recipient cert. of Appreciation City Angeles, 1974, 77-79, commendation Pres. George Bush, 1989, commendation for establishment of Westwood Regional Pk. City of L.A. Dept. Recreation and Pks., 1992, numerous city, county and state awards. Mem. Los Angeles West C. of C. (treas. 1983, v.p. 1984, v.p. corp. fin. 1986, vice chmn. 1987-88, chmn. bd. bus. council 1988-89), UCLA Alumni Assn., Pepperdine U. Alumni Assocs., Calif. Exec. Recruiters Assn., Sierra Club (exec. com. West Los Angeles 1971-72). Office: 1821 Wilshire Blvd Ste 400 Santa Monica CA 90403-5678

KRAMARSIC, ROMAN JOSEPH, engineering consultant; b. Mokronog, Slovenia, Feb. 15, 1926; came to U.S., 1957; s. Roman and Josipina (Bucar) K; m. Joanna B. Ruffo, Oct. 29, 1964; children: Joannine M., Roman III. Student, U. Bologna, Italy, 1947-48; BS, U. Toronto, Can., 1954, MS, 1956; PhD, U. So. Calif., 1973. Registered profl. engr., Ont., Can. Rsch. engr. Chrysler Rsch., Detroit, 1957-58; chief design engr. Annin Corp., Montebello, Calif., 1959-60; mgr. Plasmadyne Corp., Santa Ana, Calif., 1960-62; sr. rsch. engr. NESCO, Pasadena, Calif., 1962-64; asst. prof. U. So. Calif., L.A., 1971-77; mgr. engring. div. MERDI, Butte, Mont., 1977-78; sr. rsch. engr. RDA, Albuquerque, 1978-85; sr. staff mem. BDM, Albuquerque, 1985-90; owner Dr. R.J. Kramarsic's Engring. Svcs., Albuquerque, 1985—; cons. various tech. cos., So. Calif., 1964—; mem. various govt. coms. evaluating high power lasers. Author tech. presentations; contbr. articles to profl. jours. Violinist Albuquerque Civic Light Opera, 1980-85. Mem. ASME (sr.), AIAA (sr.), ASM Internat., Nat. Ski Patrol (aux. leader 1990-94). Roman Catholic. Office: Kramarsic's Engring Svcs PO Box 608 Laguna Beach CA 92605-0608

KRAMER, ALEXANDER GOTTLIEB, financial director; b. DesPlaines, Ill., Sept. 21, 1964; s. Gottlieb G. and Norma L. Kramer. BA in Econ. Devel. and Internat. Rels., Lake Forest Coll., 1987; M in Internat. Fin., Am. Grad. Sch. Internat. Mgmt., Glendale, Ariz., 1990. Asst. to dir. parliamentary affairs Spanish Parliament, Madrid, 1985-87; intern to chief polit. consular U.S. Dept. State, Rabat, Morocco, 1987-88; project mgr. H. Shapiro & Assocs., Inc., Chgo., 1988-90; dir. fin. and logistics Pacific Inter-Trade Corp., Westlake Village, Calif., 1990-93; fin. dir. Export SBOC Sr. Counsel Internat., L.A., 1993—; prof. internat. fin,. West Coast U., L.A., 1991—; corp. advisor World Trade Ctr., Ventura Calif.; mem. adv. bd. Bestone Group, Hong Kong and Shanghai; mem. Calif. USSR Trade Assn. Mem. Peruvian Arts Soc., Phi Sigma Iota. Home: 7266 Franklin Ave Apt 306 Los Angeles CA 90046-3080

KRAMER, BARRY ALAN, psychiatrist; b. Phila., Sept. 9, 1948; s. Morris and Harriet (Greenberg) K.; m. Paulie Hoffman, June 9, 1974; children—Daniel Mark, Steven Philip. B.A. in Chemistry, NYU, 1970; M.D., Hahnemann Med. Coll., 1974. Resident in psychiatry Montefiore Hosp. and Med. Ctr., Bronx, N.Y., 1974-77; practice medicine specializing in psychiatry, N.Y.C., 1977-82; staff psychiatrist L.I. Jewish-Hillside Med. Ctr., Glen Oaks, N.Y., 1977-82; asst. prof. SUNY, Stony Brook, 1978-82; practice medicine specializing in psychiatry, L.A., 1982—; asst. prof. psychiatry U. So. Calif., 1982-89, assoc. prof. clin. psychiatry, 1989-94, prof. clin. psychiatry U. So. Calif. U. Hosp., 1994—; ward chief Los Angeles County/U. So. Calif. Med. Ctr., 1982—; mem. med. staff USC U. Hosp., Cedars Sinai Hosp.; cons. Little Neck Nursing Home (N.Y.), 1979-82, L.I. Nursing Home, 1980-82; dir. ECT U. So. Calif. Sch. Medicine, 1990. Reviewer: Am. Jour. Psychiatry, Hospital and Community Psychiatry; mem. editorial bd. Convulsive Therapy; contbr. articles to profl. jours., papers to sci. meetings. NIMH grantee, 1979-80; fellow UCLA/U. So. Calif. Long-Term Gerontology Ctr., 1985-86. Fellow Am. Psychiat. Assn., Mem. AMA, AAAS, Internat. Soc. Chronobiology, Assn. Convulsive Therapy (editorial bd.), Soc. Biol. Psychiatry, Calif. Med. Assn., Los Angeles Med. Assn., Am. Assn. Geriatric Psychiatry, West Coast Coll. Biol. Psychiatry, Gerontol. Soc. Am., So. Calif. Psychiat. Soc. (chair ETC com.). Jewish. Office: U So Calif U Hosp 1500 San Pablo St Fl 3 Los Angeles CA 90033-4508 also: PO Box 5792 Beverly Hills CA 90209-5792

KRAMER, DONOVAN MERSHON, SR., newspaper publisher; b. Galesburg, Ill., Oct. 24, 1925; s. Verle V. and Sybil (Mershon) K.; m. Ruth A. Heins, Apr. 3, 1949; children: Donovan M. Jr., Diana Sue, Kara J. Kramer Bugbee, Eric H. BS in Journalism, Pub. Mgmt., U. Ill., 1948. Editor, publisher, ptnr. Fairbury (Ill.) Blade, 1948-63, Forrest (Ill.) News, 1953-63; ptnr. Gibson City (Ill.) Courier, 1952-63; pres., publisher, editor Casa Grande (Ariz.) Valley Newspapers, Inc., 1963—; mng. ptnr. White Mt. Pub. Co., Show Low, Ariz., 1978—. Wrote, edited numerous articles and newspaper stories. Many award-winners including Sweepstakes award in Ill. and Ariz. Mem., chmn. Econ. Planning and Devel. Bd. State of Ariz., Phoenix, 1976-81; pres. Indsl. Devel. Authority of Casa Grande, 1977—; founding pres. Greater Casa Grande Econ. Devel. Found., bd. dirs., 1982-94, 91 (Lifetime Achievement award 1994); gov. apptd. bd. mem. Ariz. Dept. Transp., 1992—. Sgt. U.S. Army Air Corps, 1943-46, PTO. Recipient Econ. Devel. plaque City of Casa Grande, 1982, Lifetime Achievement award Greater Casa Grande Econ. Devel. Found., 1994. Mem. Ariz. Newspapers Assn. (pres. 1980, Master Editor-Pub. 1977), Cmty. Newspapers Ariz. (pres. 1970-71), Inland Newspapers Assn., Newspapers Assn. Am., Ctrl. Ariz. Project Assn., Nat. Newspapers Assn., Greater Casa Grande C. of C. (pres. 1981-82, Hall of Fame 1991), Soc. Profl. Journalists. Republican. Lutheran. Home: PO Box 15002 1125 E Cottonwood Ln Casa Grande AZ 85230-5002

KRAMER, GEORGE H., historic preservation consultant; b. Mayfield Heights, Ohio, Sept. 21, 1958; s. Allen Kramer and Jean Shirley (Hirsch) Mains; m. Joyce Van Anne, May 28, 1981; 1 child, Benjamin Allen. BA in History, Sonoma State U., 1980; MS in Hist. Preservation, U. Oreg., 1989. Hist. preservation cons. Ashland, Oreg., 1989—; hist. cons. City of Talent, Oreg., 1993—, City of Grants Pass, Oreg., 1992, City of Medford, Oreg., 1994—, Anchorage Hist. Property, 1988. Author: Camp White: City in the Agate Desert, 1992. Chmn. Ashland Hist. Commn., 1984-87, Jackson City Hist. Adv. Com., Medford, 1993—; bd. dirs. Hist. Preservation League Org., Ashland, 1989—, Nat. Alliance of Preservation Commns., 1994—; mem. bd. advisors Nat. Trust for Hist. Preservation, Washington, 1993—. Named Preservationist of Yr., City of Ashland, 1992. Mem. Soc. for Comml. Archeology, N.W. Pacific Coast chpt. Soc. Archtl. Historians, Siskiyou Pioneer Sites Found. (sec. 1989—, v.p. 1994—). Democrat. Home and Office: 386 N Laurel St Ashland OR 97520-1154

KRAMER, GORDON, mechanical engineer; b. Bklyn., Aug. 1937; s. Joseph and Etta (Grossberg) K.; m. Ruth Ellen Harter, Mar. 5, 1967 (div. June 1986); children: Samuel Maurice, Leah Marie; m. Eve Burstein, Dec. 17, 1988. BS Cooper Union, 1959; MS, Calif. Inst. Tech., 1960. With Hughes Aircraft Co., Malibu, Calif., 1959-63; sr. scientist Avco Corp., Norman, Okla., 1963-64; asst. div. head Batelle Meml. Inst., Columbus, Ohio, 1964-67; sr. scientist Aerojet Electrosystems, Azusa, Calif., 1967-75; chief engr. Beckman Instrument Co., Fullerton, Calif., 1975-82; prin. scientist McDonnell Douglas Microelectronics Co., 1982-83, Kramer and Assocs., 1983-85; program mgr. Hughes Aircraft Co., 1985—; cons. Korea Inst. Tech. NSF fellow, 1959-60. Mem. IEEE. Democrat. Jewish. Home: 153 Lake Shore Dr Rancho Mirage CA 92270-4055 Office: 2000 E El Segundo Blvd El Segundo CA 90245-4501

KRAMER, GORDON EDWARD, manufacturing executive; b. San Mateo, Calif., June 22, 1946; s. Roy Charles and Bernice Jeanne (Rones) K.; BS in Aero. Engring., San Jose State Coll., 1970; m. Christina Hodges, Feb. 14, 1970; children: Roy Charles, Charlena. Purchasing agent Am. Racing Equipment, Brisbane, Calif., 1970-71, asst. to v.p. mktg., 1971-72; founder, pres. Safety Direct Inc., hearing protection equipment, Sparks, Nev., 1972—; dir. Hodges Transp., Condor Inc.; mem. adv. bd. to pres. Truckee Meadows Community Coll., 1991—. Named Nev. Small Businessperson of Yr., Nev. Small Bus. Adminstrn., 1987, Bus. Person of Yr. Sparks Community C. of C., 1987. Mem. Am. Soc. Safety Engrs., Safety Equipment Distributors Assn., Indsl. Safety Equipment Assn., Nat. Assn. Sporting Goods Wholesalers, Nat. Sporting Goods Assn., Nev. State Amature Trapshooting Assn. (dir. 1978-79), Pacific Internat. Trapshooting Assn. (Nev. pres. 1979-80, 80-81), Nev. Mfrs. Assn. (dir. 1992—), Advanced Soccer Club (pres.1985-86). Republican. Methodist. Rotary Club (pres. Spark Club 1988-89). Office: Safety Direct Inc 56 Coney Island Dr Sparks NV 89431-6335

KRAMER, JAMES JOSEPH, artist, painter; b. Columbus, OH, Oct. 24, 1927; s. James Joseph and Louise Julia (Eireman) K.; m. Barbara Peters, Apr. 11, 1959; children: Susan Kramer Erickson, Joan Kramer Busick. Student, OH State U., 1950, Cleve. Sch. of Art, Cleve., 1949. Archtl. Lic. Exhibited w/ Ohio Watercolor Soc., Columbus, OH, 1948-50; pvt. archtl. practice Columbus, OH, 1950-57; architect Hertzka and Knowles, Arch., San Francisco, CA, 1957-59; assoc. Burde, Shaw and Assoc., Arch., Carmel, CA, 1959-70; retired from arch. Carmel, CA, 1970-76; artist, painter Santa Fe, N.Mex., 1976—; instr. Valdes Art Workshop, Santa Fe, N.Mex., 1985—, Scottsdale Artists Sch., Scottsdale Ariz., 1986-88, Ghost Ranch Workshop, Abiquiu, N.Mex., 1980, Mont. Art Edn., Assn., Great Falls, Mont., 1974. Exhibited in group shows at Royal Watercolor Soc., London, Taiwan Mus., N.Mex. Mus. Fine art, Santa Fe, Mus. Western Art, Denver, Gilcrease Mus., Tulsa, Millicent Rogers Mus., Taos, N.Mex., Albuquerque Mus., Colo. Heritage Ctr. Mus., Denver, others; represented in permanent collections at Monterey Peninsula Mus. Art, Calif., Georgetown Hist. Soc., Colo., U. Nev., Reno, Colo. Heritage Ctr. Mus., Mus. Western Art. Recipient Silver Medal, Nat. Acad. of West Art, Okla. City, 1989, Frederic Remington award for artistic merit, 1991, Calif. Art Club, L.A., 1974, Gold Medal, 1973, Best of Show, Mother Lode Art Assn., Sonora, Calif., 1971.

KRAMER, JOANN MARY, insurance agency executive; b. Bristol, Pa., Jan. 18, 1956; d. Vincent Louis and Alberta (Hoynoski) gardener; m. Robert E. Kramer, June 16, 1973; children: Jody, Vincent. BS, Mission Viejo (Calif.) C.C., 1978. Mgr. Bob's Custom Cycle Works, Morrisville, Pa., 1973-75; office mgr. Futuristic Custom Paint Studios, Orange, Calif., 1975-78; sales rep. Tandy Corp., Cherry Hill, N.J., 1983-84; appraiser Kramer Real Estate Appraisers, Fountain Hills, Ariz., 1985-86; sales, mgmt. Kramer & Kramer Agy., Mesa, Fountain Hills, and Scottsdale, Ariz., 1986—, pres., 1987—; sales rep. Western Fidelity, Scottsdale, 1986-87; sales mgmt. Am. Svc. Life, Mesa, Ariz., 1987-91, United Benefit Life, Fountain Hills, 1991—; pres. Lifestyle Consumer Benefits, Fountain Hills, 1990-91, Health Ins. Rating program, Phoenix, Ariz., 1991. Pres. Sr. Info. Update, 1993—. Democrat. Roman Catholic. Home: 15414 E Thistle Dr Fountain Hills AZ 85268-4339

KRAMER, LAWRENCE STEPHEN, journalist; b. Hackensack, N.J., Apr. 24, 1950; s. Abraham and Ann Eve (Glasser) K.; m. Myla F. Lerner, Sept. 3, 1978; children: Matthew Lerner, Erika. B.S. in Journalism, Syracuse U., 1972; M.B.A., Harvard U., 1974. Reporter San Francisco Examiner, 1974-77; reporter Washington Post, 1977-80; exec. editor Trenton Times, N.J., 1980-82; asst. to exec. editor Washington Post, 1982, asst. mng. editor, 1982-86; exec. editor San Francisco Examiner, 1986-91; pres. Datasport Inc., San Mateo, Calif., 1991-94; v.p. Data Broadcasting Corp., San Mateo, 1994—. Recipient W.R. Hearst Found. award 1971-72, Gerald Loeb award 1977. Mem. Soc. Profl. Journalists. Home: 8 Auburn Ct Belvedere Tiburon CA 94920-1349

KRAMER, LORNE C., protective services official. BA in Pub. Mgmt., U. Redlands, 1977; MPA with honors, U. So. Calif., 1979; Advanced Exec. Cert., Calif. Law Enforcement Coll., 1987; grad., Nat. Exec. Inst., 1993. Comdr. L.A. Police Dept., 1963-91; chief police Colorado Springs (Colo.) Police Dept., 1991—; Cons., instr. drugs and gangs Nat. Inst. Justice, Office Juvenile Justice U.S. Dept. Justice. Active Colo. State DARE Adv. Bd.; bd. dirs. Ctr. Prevention Domestic Violence, Pikes Peak Mental Health. Mem. Colo. Assn. Chiefs Police (bd. dirs., major cities rep.), Internat. Assn. Chiefs Police (juvenile justice com.), Police Exec. Rsch. Forum. Office: Police Dept 224 E Kiowa St Colorado Springs CO 80903-1748*

KRANAK, PETER VAL, geologist; b. Pasadena, Calif., Oct. 7, 1951; s. Andrew Anthony and Virginia (Wherritt) K.; m. Margaret Fitting, Dec. 29, 1973; children: Virginia Meghan, Joseph Anthony. BS, U. Wash., 1974; MS, Okla. State U., 1978; MBA, U. Denver, 1991. Computer programmer Call Computer, Palo Alto, Calif., 1967-71; mineral explorationist Conoco, Reno, Nev., 1975-76; rsch. asst. Okla. State U., Stillwater, 1977-78; mineral explorationist Texaco, Corpus Christi, Tex., 1979-82; petroleum geologist Texaco, Midland, Tex., 1982-84; petroleum geologist Texaco, Denver, 1984-90, exploration risk specialist, 1990-92, planning mgr.-exploration, 1992—. Mem. Am. Assn. Petroleum Geologists (jr.). Office: Texaco USA PO Box 2100 Denver CO 80201-2100

KRANTZ, BARRY E., restaurant executive; b. Cleve., June 17, 1944; s. Milton S. and Helen (Abrams) K.; m. Janet L. Dishlip, Aug. 24, 1969; children: Brandi, Cory. AB, U. Pa., 1966; MBA, Stanford U., 1968. Product mgr. Gen. Foods Corp., White Plains, N.Y., 1968-72; account supr. Foote, Cone & Belding-Honig, San Francisco, 1972-75; mng. ptnr. Ted Thompson & Ptnrs., Inc., San Francisco, 1975-77; dir. mktg. Victoria Sta., Inc., Lakespur, Calif., 1977-78; sr. v.p. mktg. and concept devel. Denny's, Inc., La Mirada, Calif., 1979-88; pres. family restaurant div. Restaurant Enterprises Group, Inc., Irvine, Calif., 1989—; cons. Sea Galley Stores, Inc., Mountlake Terrace, Wash., 1988. Office: CoCos Restaurants Inc 2701 Alton Pky Irvine CA 92714-5811

KRANTZ, WILLIAM BERNARD, chemical engineering educator; b. Freeport, Ill., Jan. 27, 1939; s. Peter Thomas and Caroline (Dorer) K.; m. June Clair Gaspar, Sept. 7, 1968; 1 child, Brigette. BA, St. Joseph Coll., Rensselaer, Ind., 1961; BS, U. Ill., 1962; PhD, U. Calif., Berkeley, 1968. Registered profl. engr., Colo. Fulbright lectr. chem. engring. Istanbul (Turkey) Tech. U., 1974-75; NSF-NATO sr. fellow U. Essex, Colchester, Eng., summer 1975; Fulbright rsch. fellow Aachen (Fed. Republic of Germany) Tech. U., 1981-82; Keating-Crawford prof. Notre Dame U., South Bend, Ind., fall 1985; Fulbright Rsch. fellow and Guggenheim fellow U. Oxford, Eng., 1988-89; asst. prof. U. Colo., Boulder, 1968-73, assoc. prof., 1974-79, prof., 1980—, pres.'s teaching scholar, 1990—; co-dir. NSF Industry/U. Coop. Rsch. Ctr. Separations Using Thin Films, 1990—; rsch. fellow Inst. Arctic and Alpine Rsch., 1991—; program dir. NSF, Washington, 1977-78; cons./advisor various orgns. including U.S. Coun. for Internat. Exch. of Scholars, Dow Chem. Co., Midland, Mich., 1969-71, U.S. Dept. Energy, Laramie, Wyo., 1979-81, U.S. Nat. Bur. Standards, Boulder, 1979-80, Martin Marietta Corp., Denver, 1982, Bend (Oreg.) Rsch. Inc., 1990—. Contbr. numerous articles to profl. publs. Recipient Innovation in Coal Conversion award Pitts. Internat. Coal Conf., 1987, Spl. Achievement award, Outstanding Performance award NSF, Cert. of Appreciation U.S. Dept. Energy; Pres. teaching scholar U. Colo., 1990—. Fellow AAAS (pres. southwestern and Rocky Mountain divsn. 1993-94, John Wesley Pwell Meml. Lectr., 1995); mem. AIChE (chmn. tech. program com.), Am. Soc. Engring. Edn. (George Westinghouse award 1980), Am. Chem. Soc., Fulbright-Hays Alumni Assn., Union Concerned Scientists, Sigma Xi (nat. rsch. lectr. 1984-87), Alpha Chi Sigma. Roman Catholic. Home: 35412 Boulder Canyon Dr Boulder CO 80302-9658 Office: Univ Colo Dept Chem Engring Campus Box 424 Boulder CO 80309-0424

KRANZLER, JAY D., pharmaceutical executive; b. Nyack, N.Y., Feb. 17, 1958; s. Moses Nathan Kranzler and Eveline Leah Shuchatowitz; m. Bryna Wincelberg, June 22, 1980; children: Michael Jared, Jesse Ryan. BA, Yeshiva U.; MD, Yale U., D of Philosophy-Pharmacology. Mgmt. cons. McKinsey & Co., 1985-89; pres., ceo Cytel Corp., San Diego, 1989—; psychiatry prof. Yale U.; pres., ceo, chmn. bd. dirs. Sequel Therapeutics, San Diego, 1992—. Adj. mem. Rsch. Inst. of Scripps Clinic, 1989—. Office: Cytel Corp 3525 John Hopkins Ct San Diego CA 92121

KRASNER, OSCAR JAY, business educator; b. St. Louis, Dec. 3, 1922; s. Benjamin and Rose (Persov) K.; BS in Pub. Adminstrn., Washington U., St. Louis, 1943; MA in Mgmt. with honors, U. Chgo., 1950; MS in Quantitative Bus. Analysis, U. So. Calif., 1965, DBA in Mgmt., 1969; m. Bonnie Kidder, June 4, 1944; children: Bruce Howard, Glenn Evan, Scott Allan, Steve Leland, Michael Shawn, Bettina Jeanine. Mem. staff Exec. Office of Sec., U.S. Dept. Navy, 1944-56; supervising cons. Bus. Research Corp., Chgo., 1956-57; mem. staff flight propulsion div. Gen. Electric Co., Cin., 1957-61, mgr. VTOL project planning, 1959-61; exec. adviser long range planning space div. N.Am. Rockwell Corp., Downey, Calif., 1962-64, dir. tech. resources analysis exec. offices, 1964-70; pres. Solid State Tech. Corp. Calif., 1968-71; prof. mgmt. Pepperdine U., Los Angeles, 1970-92; pres. Rensark Assocs., 1976-92; founder Rsch. Inst. Spl. Entrepreneurs, 1992—. Active community orgns.; mem. nat. adv. bd. Nat. Congress Inventor Orgns., 1983-84; bd. dirs. Long Beach (Calif.) JCC, 1969-70; People-to-People del. to Peoples' Republic China, 1987, Russia, 1991. Served with Anti-Aircraft, AUS, 1942-44. Recipient Edwin M. Appel prize Price-Babson Inst. for Entrepreunurial Edn., 1990. Mem. Am. Acad. Mgmt., MBA Internat. (chmn. 1976-77), AIAA, AAAS, World Future Soc., Beta Gamma Sigma. Home and Office: 7656 N Sonoma Way Tucson AZ 85743-9489

KRASNEY, MARTIN, organization executive, educator; b. Phila., Apr. 2, 1945; s. Leonard and Sarah (Allen) K.; m. Pamela Parker Sanderson, Aug. 10, 1984; children: Samantha Sanderson, Parker Leonard Krasney. AB, Princeton U., 1967; MA, U. Mich., 1968; postgrad., Stanford U., 1968-69; MBA, Harvard U., 1975. Asst. to dir. Nat. Humanities Series/Woodrow Wilson Nat. Fellowship Found., Princeton, N.J., 1969-70, program dir., 1970-73; asst. to pres. Aspen Inst., N.Y.C., 1975-76, dir. exec. seminars, 1976-81; mgr. exed. devel. Atlantic Richfield Co., L.A., 1981-82; pres. Am. Leadership Forum, Houston, 1982-83; dir. pub. affairs Levi Strauss & Co., San Francisco, 1983-85; pres. Ctr. for the Twenty-First Century, San Francisco, 1986—; exec. dir. Coalition fo the Presidio Pacific Ctr., San Francisco, 1991—; con. to found., ednl. orgns. and corps. Editor Aspen Institute Readings, 1976-81. Bd. dirs. Calif. Tomorrow, 1988—, Inform, 1980—, San Francisco Film Soc., 1992—; trustee Marin Country Day Sch., 1992—; mem. adv. bd. Commonweal, Global Fund for Women. Mem. Citizens Network for Sustaining Devel. Home: 122 Santa Rosa Ave Sausalito CA 94965-2035 Office: Coalition for Presidio Pacific Ctr 220 Sansome St Ste 1300 San Francisco CA 94104-2728

KRASTMAN, HANK, psychology educator; b. The Haque, The Netherlands, Mar. 15, 1935; came to U.S., 1960; s. Gert Hendrik and Hendrika (Bataille) K.; m. Cherry Zorbag, Mar. 26, 1954; children: Christ, Sharon, Cheryl. MA in Sociology, Royal Dutch Govt. U., 1959; MA, U. Ariz., 1963; DD, S.O.M.S. Bible Coll., 1971; PhD in Psychology, Kansas City U., 1972; postgrad., Northwestern Calif. U., 1994—. Cert. contractor, Calif., bldg. insp. 1st lt. Royal Dutch Navy, 1953-60; constrn. mgr. Farm & Home Co., Tucson, 1963-66; mng. dir. Powermatic Co., Nymegen, The Netherlands, 1966-67; engr. Efficiency Engring. Co., Rotterdam, The Netherlands, 1967-69; constrn. cons. Shell Oil Co., The Netherlands, 1969-70; contractor, mgr. Nat. Constrn. Co., Van Nuys, Calif., 1973-86; insp. Dept. Bldg. and Safety, L.A., 1986-90, comml. bldg. insp., 1990-94; mem. faculty LTU Univ., Chatsworth, Calif., 1991—; lectr. in field. Author: Mysteries of Life Explained, Kopavi, The Men in Black, Cave Tunnels of Garvanza, George Van Tassel and Integratron, Secrets of the Crystal Skulls (videos) Secrets of the Lines, Palatkwapi: A Hopi City in the Inner Earth, The Men in Black, Earth Chackra Alaska, The Unexplained Magazine. Missionary to Navajo Am. Indians, So. Bapt. Conv., 1961-63; mem. faculty, adv. bd. regents Fla. State Christian Coll., 1971-72. Office: 5941 Texhoma Ave PO Box 16790 Encino CA 91416-6790

KRATKA, ILENE, artist, sculptor; b. Bridgeton, N.J., May 31, 1941; d. William Herbert Kratka and Zelda Verna (Fox) Osdin; companion Lawrence A. Healey, Oct. 15, 1983. BA, American U., 1965; postgrad., Corcoran Sch. Art, 1968-71. Presch. tchr. Headstart Program, Washington, 1963-65; pottery tchr. Centering, Cambridge, Mass., 1971-77, Hui Noeau, Maui, Hawaii, 1977-78. Exhibited in group shows including Hawaii Craftsman, 1979, Art Maui, 1989, Lahaina Arts Soc., 1985, Hui Noeau, 1987, Viewpoints Gallery, 1990, 93, 94; in collections of H.M.S. Assocs., San Francisco, The Willkinsburg Drop-In Ctr., Pitts. Mem. Centering Pottery Coop., Cambridge, Mass., 1970-77. Mem. Centering Pottery (co-founder), Maui Crafts Guild (bd. dirs., display chairperson), Viewpoints Artists Collective (mem. bd. dirs. and installations). Studio: Viewpoints Artists Collective 3620 Baldwin Ave Makawao HI 96768-9547

KRAUS, JOE, editor and publisher, writer; b. Portland, Oreg., Sept. 8, 1939; s. Joseph Kraus and Ethel Riggs; m. Karren Kraus, Apr. 10, 1968; children: Heidi, Peter, Becky. Student, Citrus Coll., Azusa, Calif., 1966-68. Mng. editor Prescott (Ariz.) Evening Courier, 1970-72, Banning (Calif.) Daily Record, 1973-75, Daily Ledger-Gazette, Lancaster, Calif., 1976-85; editor, pub. Autograph Collector Mag., 1986-92, Child Stars Mag., 1992—. Author: Alive in the Desert, 1978; author more than 300 nat. mag. articles in more than 60 publs. Scoutmaster, Boy Scouts Am., 12 yrs. Served with USN, 1961-63. Democrat. Mormon. H and Office: PO Box 55328 Stockton CA 95205-8828

KRAUS, JOHN WALTER, former aerospace engineering company executive; b. N.Y.C., Feb. 5, 1918; s. Walter Max Kraus and Marian Florance (Nathan) Sandor; m. Janice Edna Utter, June 21, 1947 (dec. Feb. 1981); children: Melinda Jean Kraus Peters, Kim Kohl Kraus; m. Jean Curtis, Aug. 27, 1983. BS, MIT, 1941; MBA, U. So. Calif., 1972. Registered indsl. engr., Calif. From indsl. engr. to indsl. engring. mgr. TRW, Inc., Cleve., 1941-61; spl. asst. Atomics Internat., Chatsworth, Calif., 1961-65; br. chief McDonnell Douglas Astronautics Co., Huntington Beach, Calif., 1966-74; sr. mgr. McDonnell Douglas Space Systems Co., Huntington Beach, Calif., 1983-93; pres. Kraus and DuVall, Inc., Santa Ana, Calif., 1975-83; retired, 1993; cons. Tech. Assocs. So. Calif., Santa Ana, 1974-75. Author: (handbook) Handbook of Reliability Engineering and Management, 1988. Mem. Am.

Def. Preparedness Assn. (life, chmn. tech. div. 1954-57), Nat. Soc. Profl. Engrs. (life). Republican. Home: 2001 Commodore Rd Newport Beach CA 92660-4307

KRAUS, PANSY DAEGLING, gemology consultant, editor, writer; b. Santa Paula, Calif., Sept. 21, 1916; d. Arthur David and Elsie (Pardee) Daegling; m. Charles Frederick Kraus, Mar. 1, 1941 (div. Nov. 1961). AA, San Bernardino Valley Jr. Coll., 1938; student Longmeyer's Bus. Coll., 1940; grad. gemologist diploma Gemological Assn. Gt. Britain, 1960, Gemological Inst. Am., 1966. Clk. Convair, San Diego, 1943-48; clk. San Diego County Schs. Publs., 1948-57; mgr. Rogers and Boblet Art-Craft, San Diego, 1958-64; part-time editorial asst. Lapidary Jour., San Diego, 1963-64, assoc. editor, 1964-69, editor, 1970-94, sr. editor, 1984-85; pvt. practice cons., San Diego, 1985—; lectr. gems, gemology local gem, mineral groups; gem & mineral club bull. editor groups. Mem. San Diego Mineral & Gem Soc., Gemol. Soc. San Diego, Gemol. Assn. Great Britain, Mineral. Soc. Am., Epsilon Sigma Alpha. Author: Introduction to Lapidary, 1987; editor, layout dir.: Gem Cutting Shop Helps, 1964, The Fundamentals of Gemstone Carving, 1967, Appalachian Mineral and Gem Trails, 1968, Practical Gem Knowledge for the Amateur, 1969, Southwest Mineral and Gem Trails, 1972, Introduction to Lapidary, 1987; revision editor Gemcraft (Quick and Leiper), 1977; contbr. articles to Lapidary jour., Keystone Mktg. catalog. Home and Office: PO Box 600908 San Diego CA 92160-0908

KRAUSE, THOMAS EVANS, record promotion consultant; b. Mpls., Dec. 17, 1951; s. Donald Bernhard and Betty Ann (Nokleby) K.; m. Barbara Ann Kaufman, Aug. 17, 1974 (div. Apr. 1978); m. Nicole Michelle Purkerson, Aug. 13, 1988; 1 child, Andrew Todd Evans. Student, Augsburg Coll., 1969-73; BA, Hastings Coll., 1975. Lic. 3d class with broadcast endorsement FCC. Air personality Sta. KHAS Radio, Hastings, Nebr., 1974-75; air personality, news dir. Sta. KWSL Radio, Sioux City, Iowa, 1975-76; asst. program dir. Sta. KISD Radio, Sioux Falls, S.D., 1976-78; music dir. Sta. KVOX Radio, Fargo, N.D., 1978; program dir. Sta. KPRQ Radio, Salt Lake City, 1978-79; air personality Sta. KIOA Radio, Des Moines, 1980; program dir., ops. mgr. Sta. KKSS Radio, Sioux Falls, 1981-83; program dir. Stas. KIYS/KBBK Radio, Boise, Idaho, 1983-87; program dir., ops. mgr. Sta. WSRZ AM/FM Radio, Sarasota, Fla., 1988-90; owner, cons. Tom Evans Mktg., Seattle, 1990—; editor., pub. Northwest Log, Seattle, 1991—; co-founder Sta. KCMR Radio, Augsburg Coll., Mpls., 1973; TV show coord./host Z-106 Hottraxx, Sarasota, 1988-90; air personality/guest disc jockey various radio stas., Pacific N.W., 1990—; host Am. Music Report. Sta. KIX-106 Radio, Canberra, Australia, 1992; instr. Sta. KGRG, Green River Coll., Auburn, Wash., 1994—. Contbr. articles to various trade publs., mags. Bd. judges Loyola U. Marconi Awards, Chgo., 1992-93; bd. dirs. Habitat for Humanity, Snohomish County, Wash., 1992—, Martin Luther King Day Celebration, Sarasota County, Fla., 1989-90, Shoreline/So. County YMCA, 1992—; dist. coord. Carter for Pres., Nebr. 1st Dist., 1975-76; hon. chairperson March of Dimes Walk Am., Sioux Falls, 1977; media vol., MC or spokesperson M.S. Soc., MDA, Am. Diabetes Assn., Human Soc., others. Mem. Free Methodist Ch. Office: Tom Evans Mktg 16426 65th Pl W Lynnwood WA 98037-2710

KRAUSS, MICHAEL EDWARD, linguist; b. Cleve., Aug. 15, 1934; s. Lester William and Ethel (Sklarsky) K.; m. Jane Lowell, Feb. 16, 1962; children: Marcus Feder, Stephen Feder, Ethan, Alexandra, Isaac. Bacc. Phil. Islandicae, U. Iceland; BA, U. Chgo., 1953, Western Res. U., 1954; MA, Columbia U., 1955; Cert. d'études supérieures, U. Paris, 1956; PhD, Harvard U., 1959. Postdoctoral fellow U. Iceland, Reykjavik, 1958-60; rsch. fellow Dublin Inst. Advanced Studies, Ireland, 1956-57; vis. prof. MIT, Cambridge, 1969-70; prof. linguistics Alaska Native Lang. Ctr., U. Alaska, Fairbanks, 1960—, dir., 1972—, head Alaska native lang. program, 1972—; panel mem. linguistics NSF. Author: Eyak Dictionary, 1970, Eyak Texts, 1970, Alaska Native Languages: Past, Present and Future, 1980; editor: In Honor of Eyak: The Art of Anna Nelson Harry, 1982, Yupik Eskimo Prosodic Systems, 1985; mem. editorial bd.: Internat. Jour. Am. Linguistics, Arctic Anthropology; edited dictionaries and books in Alaska Eskimo and Indian langs. Halldor Kiljan Laxness fellow Scandinavian-Am. Found., Iceland, 1958-60, Fulbright fellow Leningrad, USSR, 1990; Fulbright study grantee Iceland, 1958-60; grantee NSF, 1961—, NEH, 1967; named Humanities Forum, 1981; recipient Athabaskan and Eyak rsch. award NSF, 1961—. Mem. Linguistics Soc. Am. (chair com. endangered langs. and preservation 1991-95), Am. Anthropol. Assn., Soc. Study Indigenous Langs. of the Ams. (pres. 1991). Jewish. Office: U Alaska Alaska Native Lang Ctr Fairbanks AK 99775

KRAVITZ, ELLEN KING, musicologist, educator; b. Fords, N.J., May 25, 1929; d. Walter J. and Frances M. (Prybylowski) Kokowicz; m. Hilard L. Kravitz, Jan. 9, 1972; 1 child, Julie Frances; stepchildren: Kent, Kerry, Jay. BA, Georgian Ct. Coll., 1964; MM, U. So. Calif., 1966, PhD, 1970. Tchr. 7th and 8th grade music Mt. St. Mary Acad., North Plainfield, N.J., 1949-50; cloistered nun Carmelite Monastery, Lafayette, La., 1950-61; instr. Loyola U., L.A., 1967; asst. prof. music Calif. State U., L.A., 1967-71, assoc. prof., 1971-74, prof., 1974—; founder Friends of Music at Calif. State U., L.A., 1976. Author: Finding Your Way Through Music in World Culture, 1995; editorial bd. Jour. Arnold Schoenberg Inst., L.A.; jour. editor Vol. I, No. 3, 1977, Vol II, No. 3, 1978; author (with others) Catalog of Schoenberg's Paintings, Drawings and Sketches. Mem. Schoenberg Centennial Com., 1974, guest lectr., 1969—. Recipient award for masters thesis U. So. Calif., 1966. Mem. Am. Musicol. Soc. (treas. Pacific S.W. chpt. 1994—), L.A. County Mus. Art, L.A. Music Ctr., Mu Phi Epsilon, Phi Kappa Lambda. Home: PO Box 5360 Beverly Hills CA 90209-5360

KRAVITZ, HILARD L(EONARD), physician; b. Dayton, Ohio, June 26, 1917; s. Philip and Elizabeth (Charek) K.; divorced; children: Kent C., Kerry, Jay; m. Ellen King, Jan. 9, 1972; 1 child, Julie Frances. BA, U. Cin., 1939, MD, 1943. Lic. physician, Calif., Ohio. Resident in internal medicine Miami Valley Hosp., VA Hosp., Dayton, 1946-49; practice medicine specializing in internal medicine Dayton, 1950-54, Beverly Hills and Los Angeles, Calif., 1955—; practice medicine specializing in internal medicine and cardiology Los Angeles, 1955—; attending physician Cedars-Sinai Med. Ctr., 1955—; cons., med. dir. Adolph's Ltd., Los Angeles, 1955-74; mem. exec. com. Reiss-Davis Clinic, Los Angeles, 1966-70; chmn. pharmacy and therapeutic com. Cent City Hosp., Los Angeles, 1974-79; mem. pain commn. service Dept. Health and Human Services, Washington, 1985-86. Patentee sugar substitute, 1959, mineral-based salt, 1978. V.p. Friends of Music Calif. State U., Los Angeles, 1979-81. Served to capt. U.S. Army, 1944-46, ETO. Decorated Bronze Star with oak leaf cluster; Fourragere (France). Mem. AMA, Calif. Med. Assn., Los Angeles County Med. Assn., Am. Soc. Internal Medicine, Calif. Soc. Internal Medicine (del. 1974). Jewish. Office: 436 N Bedford Dr Ste 211 Beverly Hills CA 90210-4312

KRAVJANSKY, MIKULAS, artist; b. Rudnany, Slovakia, May 3, 1928; came to U.S., 1978; s. Imrich and Anna (Kubicekova) K.; m. Ruzena Horvath, Jan. 4, 1958; 1 child, Vladimir. Magister, Acad. Muzas Arts, Czechoslovakia, 1957. Scenographer State Theatre of J.Z., Czechoslovakia, 1957-62, Nat. Theatre Czechoslovakia, Bratislava, 1958-68; head of art and design Czechoslovakian Tel., Bratislava, 1962-68; asst. master Humber Coll., Toronto, Ont., Can., 1969-75; creator, dir. Black Box Theatre Can., Toronto, 1969-78; pres. Kravjansky Arts Inc., Pampano Beach, Fla., 1978-88, Napa, Calif., 1988—; asst. prof. Acad. of Muzas Art, Bratislava, 1962-68. Bd. dirs. Assn. Slovak Artists, Bratislava, 1965-68. Recipient Golden medal Bienale of Art, Sao Paulo, 1958. Mem. Kiwanis Internat. (bd. dirs. 1989-90). Home: 23 Newport Dr Napa CA 94559-4819

KRAW, GEORGE MARTIN, lawyer, essayist; b. Oakland, Calif., June 17, 1949; s. George and Pauline Dorothy (Herceg) K.; m. Sarah Lee Kenyon, Sept. 3, 1983. BA, U. Calif.-Santa Cruz, 1971; student, Lenin Inst., Moscow, 1971; MA, U. Calif.-Berkeley, 1974, JD, 1976. Bar: Calif. 1976, U.S. Dist. Ct. (no. dist.) Calif. 1976, U.S. Supreme Ct. 1980, D.C., 1992. Pvt. practice, 1976—; ptnr. Kraw & Kraw, San Jose, 1988—; Mem. ABA, Am. Soc. Law, Medicine and Ethics, Nat. Assn. Health Lawyers, Inter-Am. Bar Assn., Union Internationale des Avocats, Internat. Bar Assn. Office: Kraw & Kraw 333 W San Carlos St Ste 1050 San Jose CA 95110-2711

KREBS, EDWIN GERHARD, biochemistry educator; b. Lansing, Iowa, June 6, 1918; s. William Carl and Louise Helena (Stegeman) K.; m. Virginia Frech, Mar. 10, 1945; children: Sally, Robert, Martha. AB in Chemistry, U. Ill., 1940; MD, Wash. U., St. Louis, 1943; DSc honoris causa, U. Geneva, 1979; hon. degree, Med. Coll. Ohio, 1993; DSc (hon.), U. Ind., 1993; D honoris causa, Universidad Nacional De Cuyo, 1993. Intern, asst. resident Barnes Hosp., St. Louis, 1944-45; rsch. fellow biol. chemistry Wash. U., St. Louis, 1946-48; asst. prof. biochemistry U. Wash., Seattle, 1948-52, assoc. prof. biochemistry, 1952-57, prof. biochemistry, 1957-66; prof., chmn. dept. biol. chemistry, Sch. Medicine U. Calif., Davis, 1968-76; prof., chmn. dept. pharmacology U. Wash., Seattle, 1977-83; investigator, sr. investigator Howard Hughes Med. Inst., Seattle, 1983-90, sr. investigator emeritus, 1991—; prof. biochemistry and pharmacology U. Wash., Seattle, 1984—; mem. Phys. Chemistry Study Sect. NIH, 1963-68, Biochemistry Test Com. Nat. Bd. Med. Examiners, 1968-71, rsch. com. Am. Heart Assn., 1970-74, bd. sci. counselors Nat. Inst. Arthritis, Metabolism and Digestive Diseases, NIH, 1979-84, Internat. Bd. Rev., Alberta Heritage Found. for Med. Rsch., 1986, External Adv. Com. Weis Ctr. for Rsch., 1987-91; mem. subgroup interconvertible enzymes IUB Spl. Interest Group Metabolic Regulation; mem. internat. adv. bd. Advances in Second Messenger Phosphoprotein Rsch.; adv. com., Rowe chair U. Calif., Davis; adv. bd. Sam and Rose Stein Inst. Rsch. on Aging U. Calif., San Diego; external adv. com. Cell Therapeutics Inc., Seattle; adv. bd. Vollum Inst., Portland, Oreg. Mem. editorial bd. Jour. Biol. Chemistry, 1965-70; mem. editorial adv. bd. Biochemistry, 1971-76; mem. editorial and adv. bd. Molecular Pharmacology, 1972-77; assoc. editor Jour. Biol. Chemistry, 1971-93; mem. internat. adv. bd. Advances in Cyclic Nucleotide Rsch., 1972—; editorial advisor Molecular and Cellular Biochemistry, 1987—. Recipient Nobel Prize in Medicine or Physiology, 1992, Disting. lectureship award Internat. Soc. Endocrinology, 1972, Gairdner Found. award, Toronto, Ont., Can., 1978, J.J. Berzelius lectureship, Karolinska Institutet, 1982, George W. Thorn award for sci. excellence, 1983, Sir Frederick Hopkins Meml. lectureship, London, 1984, Rsch. Achievement award Am. Heart Assn., Anaheim, Calif., 1987, 3M Life Scis. award FASEB, New Orleans, 1989, Albert Lasker Basic Med. Rsch. award, 1989, CIBA-GEIGY-Drew award Drew U., 1991, Steven C. Beering award, Ind. U., 1991, Welch award in chemistry Welch Found., 1991, Louisa Gross Horwitz award Columbia U., 1989, Alumni Achievement award Coll. Liberal Arts & Scis. U. Ill., 1992; John Simon Guggenheim fellow, 1959, 66. Mem. NAS, Am. Soc. Biol. Chemists (pres. 1986, ednl. affairs com. 1965-68, councillor 1975-78), Am. Acad. Arts and Scis., Am. Soc. Pharmacology and Exptl. Therapeutics. Office: U Wash Dept Pharmacology Box 357370 Seattle WA 98195

KREBS, NINA BOYD, psychologist; b. Phoenix, Sept. 9, 1938; d. Hugh Lewis and Elizabeth Bevette (Burleson) Boyd; m. Richard Lee Schafer, Aug. 13, 1960 (div. 1969); children: Erica Schafer, Karen Fleming; m. David O. Krebs, Aug. 27, 1973. BA in Edn., Ariz. State U., 1960, MA in Edn., 1964; EdD in Counseling and Guidance, Ball State U., Muncie, Ind., 1971. Lic. psychologist, Calif. Counseling psychologist Calif. State U., Sacramento, 1971-76; ptnr. Ctr. for Family, Individual and Orgnl. Devel., Sacramento, 1976-83; pvt. practice psychology Sacramento, 1976—; psychology examiner Calif. State Bd. of Med. Quality Assurance, 1978-93; ind. contractor U.S. Bur. Reclamation, Mid-Pacific Region, 1979; cons. in field; presenter workshops in field; lectr. in field, creator, presenter 7-session workshop series, Feminine Power at Work, 1990—. Author: Changing Woman Changing Work, 1993; co-author: (with Robert Allen) Psychotheatrics, the New Art of Self-Transformation, 1979; contbr. articles to profl. jours. Mem. Sacramento Valley Psychol. Assn. (divsn. 1 pres. 1991-92), Orgn. of Calif. Counseling Ctr. Dirs. in Higher Edn., Calif. Pers. Assn. (statewide chair counseling ctr., 1974-75). Office: 2200 L St Sacramento CA 95816-4927

KREGER, MELVIN JOSEPH, lawyer; b. Buffalo, Feb. 21, 1937; s. Philip and Bernice (Gerstman) K.; m. Patricia Anderson, July 1, 1955 (div. 1963); children: Beth Barbour, Arlene Roux; m. Renate Hochleitner, Aug. 15, 1975. JD, Mid-valley Coll. Law, 1978; LLM in Taxation, U. San Diego, 1988. Bar: Calif. 1978, U.S. Dist. Ct. (cen. dist.) Calif. 1979, U.S. Tax Ct. 1979; cert. specialist in probate law, trust law and estate planning law, Calif., cert. specialist in taxation law, Calif. Life underwriter Met. Life Ins. Co., Buffalo, 1958-63; bus. mgr. M. Kreger Bus. Mgmt., Sherman Oaks, Calif., 1963-78, enrolled agt., 1971-78; sole practice North Hollywood, Calif., 1978—. Mem. Nat. Assn. Enrolled Agts., Calif. Soc. Enrolled Agts., State Bar of Calif., L.A. Bar Assn., San Fernando Valley Bar Assn. (probate sect.). Jewish. Office: 11424 Burbank Blvd North Hollywood CA 91601-2301

KREIL, CURTIS LEE, research chemist; b. Milw., Aug. 22, 1955; s. Hugo Harvey and Sofia (Patelski) K. AA, U. Wis. Ctr., West Bend, 1975; BS in Chemistry, U. Wis., Madison, 1977; PhD in Chemistry, U. Calif., Los Angeles, 1983. Tech. prodn. asst. DIMAT Inc., Cedarburg, Wis., 1973-75; rsch. asst. U. Wis., Madison, 1975-77; rsch. fellow Columbia U., N.Y.C., 1976; rsch. asst. U. Calif., L.A., 1977-82; sr. rsch. chemist 3M, St. Paul, 1983-86; quality assurance supr. 3M, Camarillo, Calif., 1986-90, tech. mgr., 1990-92; tech. specialist, 1993—; chmn. photochemistry chpt. 3M Tech. Forum, St. Paul, 1984-85; chmn. 3M Tech. Forum, Camarillo, 1989-90. Contbr. articles to profl. jours.; inventor electron beam adhesion-promoting treatment of polyester film base for silicone release liners, electron beam adhesion promoting treatment of polyester film base. 1st lt. CAP. Recipient Merck Index award Merck & Co., 1977; grad. fellow NSF, 1977-80. Mem. Am. Chem. Soc., Aircraft Owners and Pilots Assn., Exptl. Aircraft Assn. (v.p. 1991), 3M Aviation Club (pres. 1985-86), Phi Beta Kappa. Office: 3M 350 Lewis Rd Camarillo CA 93012-6617

KREINBERG, PENELOPE PETTIT, counselor; b. N.Y.C., Aug. 3, 1946; d. William Dutton and Carole (Earle) P.; m. Robert Lee Kreinberg, July 4, 1968; children: Joshua Adam, Patricia Dawn, Sarah Lynn. BA in Psychology/Sociology/Anthropology, Cornell U., 1968; MA in Counseling Psychology, Lewis & Clark Coll., 1993. Portland (Oreg.) chair Candlelighters for Children, 1982, 87, Oreg. pres., 1988-90; instr., counselor Clackama C.C., Portland, 1993—; pvt. practice counselor Portland, 1994—; bd. dirs. Candlelighters for Children, Oreg., 1984—; bd. dirs. Candlelighters Childhood Cancer Found., Washington, 1990-94. Bd. dirs. Camp Ukandu, Am. Cancer Found., Portland, 1985-89, mem. adv. bd. svc. and rehab. com., 1987-89; mem. local sch. adv. com. Grant H.S. PTA, Portland, 1984-88, 92—; vol. U.S. Peace Corps, Colombia, 1968-70; vol. facilitator Dougy Ctr. for Grieving Children, Portland, 1994—; vol. Ronald McDonald House, Portland, 1988-89. Recipient Cmty. Svc. award J. C. Penney, 1990, Met. Family Svc. award City of Portland, 1988. Mem. Nat. Counseling Assn., Oreg. Counseling Assn., Am. Assn. Mental Health Counselors, Oreg. Assn. Aging and Devel., Phi Beta Kappa, Delta Gamma. Democrat. Episcopalian. Home: 3145 NE 20th Ave Portland OR 97212-2410

KREISSMAN, STARRETT, librarian; b. N.Y.C., Jan. 4, 1946; d. Bernard and Shirley (Relis) K.; m. David Dolan, Apr. 13, 1985; 1 child, Sonya. BA, Grinnell Coll., 1967; MLS, Columbia U., 1968. Asst. circulation libr. Columbia U., N.Y.C., 1968-70; sci. libr. N.Y. Pub. Libr., N.Y.C., 1970-71; outreach libr. Stanislaus County Free Libr., Modesto, Calif., 1971-73, Oakdale libr., 1974-79, acquisitions libr., 1979-85, br. supr., 1985-92, county libr., 1992—. Writer book revs. Stanislaus County Commn. on Women. Mem. ALA, Pub. Libr. Assn., Calif. Libr. Assn. (legis. com. 1993-95), Rotary. Office: Stanislaus County Free Libr 1500 I St Modesto CA 95354-1120

KREITLER, RICHARD ROGERS, company executive; b. Summit, N.J., Nov. 15, 1942; s. Carl John and Juliette (Rogers) K.; children: Kent, Kim; m. Robin Morris, June 9, 1994. BA, Washington and Lee U., 1965; MA, George Washington U., 1966. Tchr. Pembroke Country Day Sch., Kansas City, Mo., 1966-67; salesman B. C. Christopher & Co., Kansas City, 1967-70; v.p. Faulkner, Dawking & Sullivan, N.Y.C., 1970-72, Donaldson, Lufkin Jenrett, N.Y.C., 1972-75; sr. v.p. White Weld, N.Y.C., 1975-76; v.p. Goldman Sachs, N.Y.C., 1976-80; gen. ptnr. Dakota Ptnrs., Ketchum, Idaho, 1980-91. Trustee Sun Valley (Idaho) Sky Edn. Found., 1984-87, 89-91, Ketchum Sun Valley Cmty. Sch., 1984-88; mem. Monticello Cabinet, Charlottesville, Va. Republican. Episcopalian. Home: 449 Wood River Dr Ketchum ID 83340 Office: Box 2360 Ketchum ID 83340

KREITZBERG, FRED CHARLES, construction management company executive; b. Paterson, N.J., June 1, 1934; s. William and Ella (Bohen) K.; m. Barbara Braun, June 9, 1957; children: Kim, Caroline, Allison, Bruce, Catherine. BSCE, Norwich U., 1957, DS in Bus. Adminstrn. (hon.), 1994. Registered profl. engr., Ala., Alaska, Ariz., Ark., Calif., Colo., Del., D.C., Fla., Ga., Idaho, Ill., Ind., Iowa, Kans., Ky., Md., Mass., Minn., Miss., Mo., Nebr., Nev., N.H., N.J., N.Mex., N.Y., Ohio, Okla., Oreg., S.C., S.D., Tenn., Va., Vt., Wash., W.Va., Wis., Wyo. Asst. supt. Turner Constrn. Co., N.Y.C., 1957; project mgr. Project Mercury RCA, N.J., 1958-63; schedule cost mgr. Catalytic Constrn. Co., Pa., 1963-65, 65—; cons. Meridien Engring., 1965-68; prin. MDC Systems Corp., 1968-72; chmn., CEO O'Brien-Krietzberg Inc., San Francisco, 1972—; lectr. Stanford (Calif.) U., U. Calif., Berkeley. Author: Crit. Path Method Scheduling for Contractor's Mgmt. Handbook, 1971; tech. editor Constrn. Inspection Handbook, 1972; contbr. articles to profl. jours. bd. dirs. Partridge Soc.; trustee Norwich U. 2d lt. C.E., U.S. Army, 1957-58. Recipient Disting. Alumnus award Norwich U., 1987; named Boss of Yr., Nat. Assn. Women in Constrn., 1987; named in his honor Kreitzberg Amphitheatre, 1987, Kreitzberg Libr. at Norwich U., 1992; Bay Area Discovery Mus.-Birthday rm. and snack bar named in honor of Kreitzberg family, 1989. Fellow ASCE (Constrn. Mgr. of Yr. 1982); mem. Am. Arbitration Assn., Constrn. Mgmt. Assn. Am. (founding, bd. dirs.), Soc. Am. Value Engrs., Community Field Assn., Ross Hist. Soc., N.J. Soc. Civil Engrs., N.J. Soc. Profl. Planners, Project Mgmt. Inst., Constrn. Industry Pres. Forum. Home: 19 Spring Rd PO Box 1200 Ross CA 94957-1200 Office: OBrien-Kreitzberg Inc 188 The Embarcadero San Francisco CA 94105

KREJCI, ROBERT HENRY, aerospace engineer; b. Shenandoah, Iowa, Nov. 15, 1943; s. Henry and Marie Josephine (Kubicek) K.; m. Carolyn R. Meyer, Aug. 21, 1967; children—Christopher S., Ryan D. B.S. with honors in Aerospace Engring., Iowa State U., Ames, 1967, M.Aerospace Engring., 1971. Commd. 2d lt. U.S. Air Force, 1968, advanced through grades to capt., 1978; lt. col. Res.; served with systems command Space Launch Vehicles Systems Program Office, Advanced ICBM program officer; research assoc. U.S. Dept. Energy Lawrence Livermore lab.; dept. mgr. advanced tech. programs Strategic div. Thiokol Corp., 1978-84, mgr. space programs, 1984-85, mgr. Navy spl. projects, 1986—. Decorated A.F. commendation medal, Nat. Def. Service medal, Meritorious Svc. medal. Fellow AIAA. Home: 885 N 300 E Brigham City UT 84302-1310 Office: Thiokol Corp PO Box 689 Brigham City UT 84302-0689

KREMPEL, RALF HUGO BERNHARD, artist, art gallery owner; b. Groitzsch, Saxony, Germany, June 5, 1935; came to U.S., 1964; s. Curt Bernhard and Liesbeth Anna Margarete (Franz) K.; m. Barbara von Eberhardt, Dec. 21, 1967 (div. 1985); 1 child, Karma. Student, Wood and Steel Constrn. Coll., Leipzig, German Democratic Republic, 1955. Steel constructor worldwide, 1955-73; co-owner San Francisco Pvt. Mint, 1973-81; prin. artist San Francisco Painter Magnate, 1982—; dir. Stadtgalerie Wiprechtsburg Groitzsch, Germany, 1991—, Museumsgalerie am Markt, Groitzsch, 1994—. Exhbns. Centre Internat. d'Art Contemporain, 1985, Art Contemporain Cabinet des Dessins, 1986, Galerie Salammbo-Atlante, 1987—, Mus.-gallery Borna, 1993, and others; inventor, designer Visual Communication System; registration Libr. of Congress, Washington, 1991. Home: 2400 Pacific Ave San Francisco CA 94115-1280 Office: San Francisco Painter Magnate Rincon Ctr San Francisco CA 94119-3368 also: Brühl 2, 04539 Groitzsch Germany

KREMPEL, ROGER ERNEST, public works management consultant; b. Waukesha, Wis., Oct. 8, 1926; s. Henry and Clara K.; m. Shirley Ann Gray, June 16, 1948; children: John, Sara, Peter. Student Ripon College, 1944, Stanford U., 1945; BCE, U. Wis.-Madison, 1950. Registered profl. engr., Wis., Colo.; registered land surveyor, Wis. Asst. city engr., Manitowoc, Wis., 1950-51; city engr. dir. pub. works, Janesville, Wis., 1951-75; dir. water utilities, pub. works Ft. Collins, Colo., 1975-84, dir. natural resources, streets and stormwater utilities, Ft. Collins, 1984-88; pub. works mgmt. cons., 1988—; lectr. various univ., coll., nat. confs. and seminars. Contbr. articles to profl. pubs. Past pres. bd. Janesville YMCA. Served with U.S. Army, 1944-46. Recipient numerous tech. and profl. awards, Distin. Svc. citation U. Wis. Coll. Engring., 1989. Fellow ASCE (life); mem. NSPE, Am. Pub. Works Assn. (life mem., past pres. Colo. and Wis. chpts., past mem. rsch. found., Man of Yr. 1971), Pub. Works Hist. Soc. (pres. 1993-95), Wis. Soc. Profl. Engrs. (past pres.), Am. Acad. Environ. Engrs. (diplomate, 1982-91), Colo. Engrs. Coun. (pres. 1990-91, honor award 1989), Am. Soc. Civil Engrs. (mgmt. award 1990)

KREMS, SUSAN ALEXANDER, telecommunications specialist; b. Chgo., May 25, 1940; d. Joseph B. and Florence Jean (Cassel) Alexander; children: Steven M., Stacy Krems Polinsky. Student, U. Ill. Pres. Tel-Us Ltd., Beverly Hills, Calif., 1979, 1 800 Telemktg. Inc., Beverly Hills, 1988; ptnr. Pvt. Lines, Inc., Beverly Hills, Calif.; co-founder Uni Call, Beverly Hills; developer, tchr. seminars on inbound telemktg., order entry and direct response mktg. for numerous telemessaging and telemktg. trade assns.; advisor Startel/Comverse USA and Doyle-Logan Sys. Co-author order entry/inbound telemktg. manual. Mem. NAFE, Assn. Calif. Enchanced Telemessaging Svcs., LA. Ad Club, Calif. Assn. Employers, Telephone Answering Svcs. Calif. (bd. dirs., sec.), Assn. Telemessing Svcs. Internat. (bd. dirs.), Beverly Hills C. of C., Startel Nat. Users Group (pres. 1990-91). Office: 400 S Beverly Dr Ste 214 Beverly Hills CA 90212-4482

KREND, WILLIAM JOHN, secondary education educator; b. Chgo., Oct. 25, 1947; s. Patrick H. and Irene (Dmytryk) K.; m. Marjorie J. Tow, Aug. 15, 1970; children: Andrew William, Kira Loren. BA, U. Calif., Santa Barbara, 1969; MA, Calif. State U., Fresno, 1978. Cert. secondary, community coll. tchr., Calif. Tchr. Avenal (Calif.) High Sch., 1970-73; tchr. history Lemoore (Calif.) High Sch., 1973—; faculty history West Hills Coll., Lemoore, 1978-86, Chapman U., Nas Lemoore, Calif., 1979—; curriculum cons. Kings County Office of Edn., Hanford, Calif., 1990-91. Contbr. articles to profl. jours.; contbr: World History supplement, 1990. Coord. History Day, Kings County, 1987—, Am. Youth Competition, 1992, We the People for Calif. 20th Congl. Dist., 1992—; bd. dirs. Avenal Recreation Com., 1973-74. CLIO Project/U. Calif.-Berkeley fellow, 1986, Calif. History Project/Calif. State U.-Fresno fellow, 1990, Ctr. for Energy Edn. fellow. Mem. Nat. Coun. for Social Studies (presenter), Calif. Coun. for Social Studies (bd. dirs. 1992—, no. co-chmn. govt. rels. com., co-chair publs. com. 1995—), Calif. Hist. Soc., Nat. Geog. Soc., Calif. Fedn. Tchrs., San Joaquin Coun. for Social Studies (bd. dirs. 1991, pres. 1995—). Home: 14230 16th Ave Lemoore CA 93245-9517 Office: Lemoore High Sch 101 E Bush St Lemoore CA 93245-3601

KREPKY, CYNTHIA D., technical publishing administrator; b. Columbus, Ohio, Apr. 1, 1956; d. Donald Rex, Jr., and Nancy May (Dawson) Barnes; m. David Morris Krepky, June 1, 1991. BS in Botany and Marine Sci., U. Wash., 1981, MPA, 1985; cert. exec. mgmt. U. Wash., 1990. Water quality technician Ohio EPA, Columbus, 1978; exec. sec. Dan A. Carmichael, AIA, Columbus, 1978-79; supr. publs. Vitro Corp., Silverdale, Wash., 1982-85; sr. tech. writer water pollution control dept. Municipality Met. Seattle (Metro), 1985-87, supr. 1987—; founder, pres., CEO Dolphin Tech. Comms., Inc., 1995—; bd. dirs. Hood Canal Environ. Council, Seabeck, Wash., 1985-88; chmn. conservation com. Kitsap Audubon, Poulsbo, Wash., 1982-84; mem. adv. bd. dirs. U. Washington Extension Tech. Writing Cert. Program, Green River C.C. Multimedia Design Program. Author: Citizen's Guide to Municipal Incorporation in the State of Washington, 1985. Tech. advisor and publicity co-chmn. Silverdale Inc. Com., 1983-85. Mem. Am. Soc. Pub. Adminstrn. (student rep. Evergreen chpt. Council 1984-85, coun. mem. Evergreen chpt. 1986-90), Water Environ. Fedn., Am. Mgmt. Assn., Cityclub (Seattle). Avocations: backpacking, canoeing, scuba diving, gardening, stained glass. Home: 2245 E Crescent Dr Seattle WA 98112-3415 Office: Metro 821 2nd Ave Seattle WA 98104-1519

KREPS, DAVID MARC, economist, educator; b. N.Y.C., Oct. 18, 1950; s. Saul Ian and Sarah (Kaskin) Kreps; m. Anat Ruth Admati, Jan. 4, 1984; children: Tamar, Oren. AB, Dartmouth Coll., 1972; MA, PhD, Stanford U., 1975. Asst. prof. Stanford U., 1975-78, assoc. prof., 1978-80, prof., 1980-84, Holden prof., 1984—; rsch. officer U. Cambridge, Eng., 1978-79, fellow commoner Churchill Coll., Cambridge, 1978-79; vis. prof. Yale U., New Haven, 1982, Harvard U., Cambridge, Mass., 1983, U. Paris, 1985; vis. prof. U. Tel Aviv, 1989-90, sr. prof. by spl. appointment, 1991—. Author: Notes on the Theory of Choice, 1988, A Course in Microeconomic Theory, 1990, Game Theory and Economic Modelling, 1990; co-editor Econometrica, 1984-88. Alfred P. Sloan Found. fellow, 1983, John S. Guggenheim fellow, 1988. Fellow Econometric Soc.; mem. Am. Econ. Assn. (J.B. Clark medal 1989),

Am. Acad. Arts and Scis. Office: Stanford U Grad Sch of Bus Stanford CA 94305-5015

KRESA, KENT, aerospace executive; b. N.Y.C., Mar. 24, 1938; s. Helmy and Marjorie (Boutelle) K.; m. Joyce Anne McBride, Nov. 4, 1961; 1 child, Kiren. BSAA, MIT, 1959, MSAA, 1961, EAA, 1966. Sr. scientist research and advanced devel. div. AVCO, Wilmington, Mass., 1959-61; staff mem. MIT Lincoln Lab., Lexington, Mass., 1961-68; dep. dir. strategic tech. office Def. Advanced Research Projects Agy., Washington, 1968-73; dir. tactical tech. office Def. Advanced Research Project Agy., Washington, 1973-75; v.p., mgr. Research & Tech. Ctr. Northrop Corp., Hawthorne, Calif., 1975-76; v.p., gen. mgr. Ventura div. Northrop Corp., Newbury Park, Calif., 1976-82; group v.p. Aircraft Group Northrop Corp., L.A., 1982-86, sr. v.p. tech. devel. and planning, 1986-87, pres., COO, 1987-90; chmn. bd., pres., CEO Northrop Grumman Corp., L.A., 1990—; bd. dirs. John Tracy Clinic.; mem. Chief of Naval Ops. exec. panel Washington, Def. Sci. Bd., Washington, DNA New Alternatives Working Group, L.A., Dept. Aeronautics and Astronautics Corp. Vis. Com. MIT. Recipient Henry Webb Salsbury award MIT, 1959, Arthur D. Flemming award, 1975; Sec. of Def. Meritorious Civilian Service medal, 1975, USN Meritorious Pub. Service citation, 1975, Exceptional Civilian Service award USAF, 1987. Fellow AIAA; mem. Naval Aviation Mus. Found., Navy League U.S., Soc. Flight Test Engrs., Assn. U.S. Army, Nat. Space Club, Am. Def. Preparedness Assn., L.A. Country Club. Office: Northrop Grumman Corp 1840 Century Park E Los Angeles CA 90067-2101*

KREUTEL, RANDALL WILLIAM, JR., electrical engineer; b. Norwood, Mass., May 3, 1934; s. Randall William Sr. and Dorothy Elizabeth (Reynolds) K.; m. Kay Irene Dadmun, Oct. 10, 1950 (div. Nov. 1973); children: John William, James Thomas, Karen Irene, Robert Steven; m. Alice Jean Guillory, June 26, 1975. BSEE, Northea. U., 1961, MSEE, 1964; DSc, George Washington U., 1978. Rsch. engr. Sylvania Electronic System, Waltham, Mass., 1957-66; tech. staff Comsat Corp., Washington, 1966-68; dept. mgr. antenna dept. Comsat Corp., Clarksburg, Md., 1968-77, dir. optics lab., 1977-81, div. dir. devel. engr., 1981-84; div. dir. System Planning Corp., Arlington, Va., 1984-87; mgr. Sci.-Atlanta Corp., 1987-89; prin. engr. Electromagnetic Scis., Inc., Norcross, Ga., 1989-92; tech. staff mem. Motorola Satcom Div., Chandler, Ariz., 1992—. Contbr. McGraw-Hill Encyclopedia of Science and Technology, 6th, 7th editions; patentee in field; contbr. articles to profl. jours. Bd. dirs. System Planning Antenna Corp., 1986-88. Fellow AIAA (assoc.); mem. IEEE (sr.), Internat. Union Radio Sci., Antenna and Propagation Soc. (vice chmn. Washington and no. Va. chpt. 1986-87, chmn. 1987-880, Sigma Xi, Eta Kappa Nu. Home: 2005 E Granite View Dr Phoenix AZ 85048-4503 Office: Motorola Satcom 2501 S Price Rd Chandler AZ 85248-2802

KREVANS, JULIUS RICHARD, university administrator, physician; b. N.Y.C., May 1, 1924; s. Sol and Anita (Makovetsky) K.; m. Patricia N. Abrams, May 28, 1950; children: Nita, Julius R., Rachel, Sarah, Nora Kate. B.S. Arts and Scis, N.Y. U., 1943, M.D., 1946. Diplomate: Am. Bd. Internal Med. Intern, then resident Johns Hopkins Med. Sch. Hosp., mem. faculty, until 1970, dean acad. affairs, 1969-70; physician in chief Balt. City Hosp., 1963-69; prof. medicine U. Calif., San Francisco, 1970—, dean Sch. Medicine, 1971-82, chancellor, 1982-93, chancellor emeritus, 1993—. Contbr. articles on hematology, internal med. profl. jours. Served with M.C. AUS, 1948-50. Mem. A.C.P., Assn. Am. Physicians. Office: U Calif Chancellor Emeritus 500 Parnassus Ave San Francisco CA 94122-2723

KRICH, KENNETH L., computer dealer executive; b. L.A., May 19, 1946; s. Percy and Rita (Shane) K.; m. Nancy Leahong, Dec. 12, 1982. BA, U. Chgo., 1967; MBA, U. Calif., Berkeley, 1983. V.p., gen. mgr. Westbrae Nat. Foods, Berkeley, Calif., 1974-79; ptnr. Bear Valley Foods, Berkeley, 1979-81; fin. analyst Harris Farinan, San Carlos, Calif., 1983-84; mgr. fin. planning internat. divsn. Computerland, Oakland, Calif., 1984-85; dir. ops. GTL divsn. Computerland, Hayward, Calif., 1985-87; exec. v.p., gen. mgr. Jasmine Techs., San Francisco, 1987-88; v.p. ops. Computerware, Palo Alto, Calif., 1988-91, pres., CEO, 1991—. Office: ComputerWare 2800 W Bayshore Rd Palo Alto CA 94303

KRICHMAR, LEE, information systems executive; b. Santa Ana, Calif., May 26, 1965; d. Sidney and Jeanette (York) K. BS, DeVry Inst. Tech., Calif., 1986. Ops. mgr. GTECH Corp., Whittier, Calif., 1986-90; ops. supr. Pacific States Casualty Co., Chino, Calif., 1990-93; info. sys. mgr. VNA Home Health Systems, Orange, Calif., 1993—. Republican. Jewish. Home: 5995 Sunstone Ave Alta Loma CA 91701-2731 Office: VNA Home Health Systems 1337 W Braden Ct Orange CA 92668-1123

KRICK, IRVING PARKHURST, meteorologist; b. San Francisco, Dec. 20, 1906; s. H. I. and Mabel (Royal) K.; m. Jane Clark, May 23, 1930; 1 dau., Marilynn; m. Marie Spiro, Nov. 18, 1946; 1 son, Irving Parkhurst II. BA, U. Calif., 1928; MS, Cal. Inst. Tech., 1933; PhD, Calif. Inst. Tech., 1934. Asst. mgr. radio sta. KTAB, 1928-29; meteorologist, 1930—; became mem. staff Calif. Inst. Tech., 1933, asst. prof. meteorology, 1935-38, assoc. prof., prof. and head dept., 1938-48; organizer, pres. Am. Inst. Aerological Rsch. and Water Resources Devel. Corp., 1950; pres. Irving P. Krick Assocs., Inc., Irving P. Krick, Inc., Tex., Irving P. Krick Assocs. Can. Ltd.; now, chmn. emeritus, sr. cons. strategic Weather Svc. Krick Ctr. Weather R & D, Palm Springs, Calif.; established meteorology dept. Am. Air Lines, Inc., 1935, established Internat. Meteorol. Cons. Svcs., 1946, mng. dir.; cons. in field, 1935-36; mem. sci. adv. group Von Kármán Army Air Force, 1945-46. Pianist in concert and radio work, 1929-30; Co-author: Sun, Sea and Sky, 1954; Writer numerous articles on weather analysis, weather modification and forecasting and its application to agrl. and bus. industries. Served as lt. Coast Arty. Corps U.S. Army, 1928-36; commd. ensign USNR, 1938; maj., then lt. col. USAAF, 1943; Weather Directorate, Weather Central Div. unit comdr. of Long Range Forecast Unit A 1942-43; dep. dir. weather sect. U.S. Strategic Air Forces Europe, 1944; chief weather information sect. SHAEF 1945. Decorated Legion of Merit, Bronze Star with Oak leaf cluster U.S.; Croix de Guerre France; recipient Distinguished Service award Jr. C. of C.; chosen one of 10 outstanding men under age 35 by U.S. Jr. C. of C. Fellow AIAA (assoc.), Royal Soc. Arts; mem. AAAS (patron), Royal Meteorol. Soc., Am. Meteorol. Soc., Am. Geophys. Union (supporting mem.), Sigma Xi (supporting mem.). Republican. Home: 1200 S Orange Grove Blvd Apt 13 Pasadena CA 91105-3353 Office: Krick Ctr Weather R & D 610 S Belardo Rd Palm Springs CA 92264-7466

KRIEGEL, ARLYN ALVIN, accounting company executive; b. Clovis, N.Mex., Mar. 26, 1931; s. Alvin E. and Eleonora H. (Schwede) K.; m. Elizabeth A. Kallsen, Jan. 26, 1958; children: Joan L., Beth A. BBA in Acctg., Tex. Tech U., 1954. CPA, Tex., N.Mex. Mem. staff Neff & Co., Albuquerque, 1958-62; ptnr. Neff & Co., Las Cruces, N.Mex., 1963-78; pres. Kriegel & Co. Ltd., Las Cruces, 1978—; bd. dirs. First Nat. Bank of Dona Ana County. Bd. dirs. N.Mex. State Found., 1970-90, pres., 1989-90; bd. dirs. Mem. Med. Ctr. Found., 1989-91. Served to 1st lt. USAF, 1954-58. Mem. AICPAs, N.Mex. Soc. CPAs (pres. Dona Ana chpt. 1974), Las Cruces C. of C. Las Cruces Rotary. Presbyterian. Home: 2955 Sundance Cir Las Cruces NM 88011-4609

KRIEGER, JOHN NEWTON, urology educator; b. Phila., May 3, 1948; s. Rivan and Leah (Moses) K.; m. Monica Schoelch, July 22, 1972. AB, Princeton U., 1970; MD, Cornell U., 1974. Diplomate Am. Bd. Urology. Resident in surgery N.Y. Hosp., N.Y.C., 1974-76, resident in urology, 1976-80; fellow in urology U. Va., Charlottesville, 1980-82; asst. prof. urology U. Wash., Seattle, 1982-86, assoc. prof., 1986-90, prof., 1990—. Author 2 books; contbr. more than 200 articles to profl. jours. Mem. Am. Urol. Assn. (F.C. Valentine prize, N.Y.C. sect. 1977, Scholar award, Balt. 1980), ACS, Am. Soc. Microbiology, Am. Venereal Disease Assn., Infectious Disease Soc. Am. Office: U Wash Dept Urology RL-10 Pacific St NE Seattle WA 98195

KRIEGER, MARTIN H., planning and design educator; b. Bklyn., Mar. 10, 1944; s. Louis and Shirley Krieger. BA, Columbia U., 1964, MA, 1965, PhD in Physics, 1969. Lectr., researcher U. Calif., Berkeley, 1968-73; asst. prof. U. Minn., Mpls., 1974-80; lectr., researcher MIT, Cambridge, 1980-84; assoc. prof. planning U. So. Calif., Los Angeles, 1985-92; prof. planning, 1992—; vis. prof. entrepreneurship U. Mich., 1990-91. Author: Advice and Planning, 1981, Marginalism and Discontinuity, 1989, Doing Physics, 1992. Fellow: Am. Council Learned Societies, Ctr. for Advanced Study in Behavioral Scis., Nat. Humanities Ctr.; mem. Am. Phys. Soc. Office: U So Calif Sch Urban and Regional Planning Los Angeles CA 90089-0042

KRIEGER, MICHAEL RAYMOND, computer manufacturing executive, writer; b. Bklyn., Feb. 4, 1954; s. Joseph Ezra and Sally (Gelberg) K.; m. Barbara Gale Rothman, Sept. 27, 1981; children: Rachael, Zachary. Student, Polytech. Inst. N.Y., 1970-72, New Sch. Social Rsch., N.Y.C., 1972-73, Actor's Studio, N.Y.C., 1974-75. Programmer, analyst Inflight Motion Pictures, Queens, N.Y., 1975-77; pres., CEO Solution Bus. Systems, Port Washington, N.Y., 1978-84; v.p. devel. Techland Systems, N.Y.C., 1984-86; dir. advanced systems AST Computer, Irvine, Calif., 1986-93; dir. Ziff-Davis Mag. Network, Foster City, Calif., 1993—; mem. mktg. com. Common-Users Group, Chgo., 1977-93; founding mem. Extended Industry Standard Architecture Consortium Bd., Houston, 1988-93. Author: Smartsizing, 1993; editorial advisor System 3X World, 1989. Recipient Product of Yr. award Lan Mag., 1993. Democrat. Office: Ziff Davis Pub Co 950 Tower Ln Foster City CA 94404-2121

KRIEGER, MURRAY, English language educator, author; b. Newark, Nov. 27, 1923; s. Isidore and Jennie (Glinn) K.; m. Joan Alice Stone, June 15, 1947; children: Catherine Leona, Eliot Franklin. Student, Rutgers U., 1940-42; M.A., U. Chgo., 1948; Ph.D. (Univ. fellow), Ohio State U., 1952. Instr. English Kenyon Coll., 1948-49, Ohio State U., 1951-52; asst. prof., then asso. prof. U. Minn., 1952-58; prof. English U. Ill., 1958-63; M.F. Carpenter prof. lit. criticism U. Iowa, 1963-66; prof. English, dir. program in criticism U. Calif. at Irvine, 1966-85; prof. English UCLA, 1973-82; univ. prof. U. Calif., 1974-94, univ. rsch. prof., 1994—; co-dir. Sch. Criticism and Theory U. Calif., 1975-77, dir., 1977-81, hon. sr. fellow, 1981—; assoc. mem. Ctr. Advanced Study, U. Ill., 1961-62; dir. U. Calif. Humanities Rsch. Inst., 1987-89. Author: The New Apologists for Poetry, 1956, The Tragic Vision, 1960, A Window to Criticism: Shakespeare's Sonnets and Modern Poetics, 1964, The Play and Place of Criticism, 1967, The Classic Vision, 1971, Theory of Criticism: A Tradition and Its System, 1976, Poetic Presence and Illusion, 1979, Arts on the Level, 1981, Words About Words About Words: Theory, Criticism and the Literary Text, 1988, A Reopening of Closure: Organicism Against Itself, 1989, Ekphrasis: The Illusion of the Natural Sign, 1992, The Ideological Imperative: Repression and Resistance in Recent American Theory, 1993, The Institution of Theory, 1994; editor: (with Eliseo Vivas) The Problems of Aesthetics, 1953, Northrop Frye in Modern Criticism, 1966, (with L.S. Dembo) Directions for Criticism: Structuralism and its Alternatives, 1977, The Aims of Representation: Subject/Text/History, 1987. Served with AUS, 1942-46. Recipient rsch prize Humboldt Found., Fed Republic Germany, 1986-87, medal U. Calif. at Irvine, 1990, 91; Guggenheim fellow, 1956-57, 61-62; Am. Coun. Learned Socs. postdoctoral fellow, 1966-67; grantee NEH, 1971-72; Rockefeller Found. humanities fellow, 1978; resident scholar Rockefeller Study Ctr., Bellagio, 1990. Fellow Am. Acad. Arts and Scis. (council and exec. com. 1987-88); mem. MLA, Internat. Assn. Univ. Profs. English, Acad. Lit. Studies. Home: 407 Pinecrest Dr Laguna Beach CA 92651-1471 Office: U Calif Dept English Comparati Irvine CA 92717

KRIEGER, WILLIAM CARL, English language educator; b. Seattle, Mar. 21, 1946; s. Robert Irving Krieger and Mary (McKibben) Durfee; m. Patricia Kathleen Callow, Aug. 20, 1966; children: Richard William, Robert Irving III, Kathleen Elizabeth. BA in English, Pacific Luth. U., 1968, MA in Humanities, 1973; PhD in Am. Studies, Wash. State U., 1986. Instr. Pierce Coll., Tacoma, 1969—, chmn. English dept., 1973-79, 81-84, 95—, chmn. humanities divsn., 1979-81, prof. English, 1969—; adj. prof. hist. and English Cen. Wash. State U., 1980; vis. prof. hist. and English So. Ill. U., Carbondale, 1981-84, Pacific Luth. U., Tacoma, 1981-84; head coach Gig Harbor High Sch. Wrestling, 1990—; bd. dirs. Thoreau Cabin Project, Tacoma, 1979—; project dir. Campus Wash. Centennial Project, Tacoma, 1984-89; spl. cons. Clover Park Sch. Dist., Tacoma, 1985; lang. arts cons. Inst. for Citizen Edn. in Law, U. Puget Sound Law Sch., 1990. Apptd. Wash. State Centennial Commn., Constitutions Com., Pierce County Centennial Com.; mem. bd. dirs. Tacoma Symphony; choir dir. Rosedale Ch.; mem. Peninsula Cmty. Chorus, 1993—; dir. Peninsula Madrigal Singers, 1995. Recipient Disting. Achievement award Wash. State Centennial Commn., 1989, Outstanding Achievement award Pierce County Centennial Commn., 1989, Centennial Alumni recognition Pacific Luth. U., 1990; named Outstanding Tchr. Nat. Inst. Staff and Orgnl. Devel., 1992; NEH rsch. fellow Johns Hopkins U. and Peabody Conservatory of Music, 1994. Mem. Thoreau Soc. (life), Community Coll. Humanities Assn. (standing com. 1982-83), Am. Studies Assn., Wash. Community Coll. Humanities Assn. (bd. dirs. 1982-84, grantee, 1984), Western Wash. Ofcls. Assn. Home: 4415 68th Street Ct NW Gig Harbor WA 98335-8312 Office: Pierce Coll 9401 Farwest Dr SW Tacoma WA 98498-1919

KRIENKE, CAROL BELLE MANIKOWSKE (MRS. OLIVER KENNETH KRIENKE), realtor; b. Oakland, Calif., June 19, 1917; d. George and Ethel (Purdon) Manikowske; student U. Mo., 1937; BS, U. Minn., 1940; postgrad. UCLA, 1949; m. Oliver Kenneth Krienke, June 4, 1941 (dec. Dec. 1988); children: Diane (Mrs. Robert Denny), Judith (Mrs. Kenneth A. Giss), Debra Louise (Mrs. Ed Paul Davalos). Demonstrator, Gen. Foods Corp., Mpls., 1940; youth leadership State of Minn. Congl. Conf., U. Minn., Mpls. 1940-41; war prodn. worker Airesearch Mfg. Co., Los Angeles, 1944; tchr. L.A. City Schs., 1945-49; realtor DBA Ethel Purdon, Manhattan Beach, Calif., 1949; buyer Purdon Furniture & Appliances, Manhattan Beach, 1950-58; realtor O.K. Krienke Realty, Manhattan Beach, 1958—. Manhattan Beach bd. rep. Community Chest for Girl Scouts U.S., 1957; bd. dirs. South Bay council Girl Scouts U.S.A., 1957-62, mem. Manhattan Beach Coordinating Coun., 1956-68, South Coast Botanic Garden Found., 1989—; v.p. Long Beach Area Childrens Home Soc., 1967-68, pres. 1979; charter mem. Beach Pixies, 1957-93, pres. 1967; chmn. United Way, 1967; sponsor Beach Cities Symphony, 1953—, Little League Umpires, 1981-91. Recipient Long-standing Local Bus. award City of Manhattan Beach, 1993. Mem. DAR (life, citizenship chmn. 1972-73, v.p. 1979, 83—), Calif. Retired Tchrs. Assn. (life), Colonial Dames XVII Century (charter mem. Jared Eliot chpt. 1977, v.p., pres. 1979-81, 83-84), Friends of Library, South Bay Bd. Realtors, Nat. Soc. New England Women (life, Calif. Poppy Colony), Internat. Platform Assn., Soc. Descs. of Founders of Hartford (life), Friends of Banning Mus., Hist. Soc. of Centinela Valley, Manhattan Beach Hist. Soc., Manhattan Beach C. of C. (Rose and Scroll award 1985), U. Minn. Alumni (life). Republican. Mem. Community Ch. (pres. Women's Fellowship 1970-71). Home: 924 Highview Ave Manhattan Beach CA 90266-5813 Office: OK Krienke Realty 1716 Manhattan Beach Blvd Manhattan Beach CA 90266-6220

KRIEPS, MARA J., marketing professional. BA in Advt., U. Wis., 1986; MS in Direct Mktg., Northwestern U., 1987. Mktg. analyst Eddie Bauer, Inc., Seattle, 1988-91; mktg. supr. Egghead Software, Seattle, 1991-92; ind. sales rep. Collette Unique Edits., Portsmouth, N.H., 1992-94; regional mktg. mgr. ADVO, Inc., Seattle, 1994—. United Way campaign mgr., 1994. Recipient scholarship U. Wis., 1985, 86. Mem. NAFE, Am. Mktg. Assn., Wash. Software Assn. (mktg. com. 1994—), Phi Kappa Phi. Office: ADVO Inc 6020 S 226th St Kent WA 98032-4814

KRIEGER, PETER WILSON, healthcare administrator; b. San Francisco, Jan. 22, 1936; s. Peter Clark and Dorothy Margaret (Noethig) Wilson; children: Peter W., Marilyn, Nicole. Student, Humboldt State Coll., Arcata, Calif., Antioch U., San Francisco; postgrad., U. Calif., Berkeley, Cornell U. Adminstr. Klamath-Trinity Hosp., Hoopa, Calif., 1961-66; asst. adminstr. St. Joseph Hosp., Eureka, Calif., 1966-75, adminstr., exec. v.p., 1975-83, pres., CEO, 1983-91; adminstr. Eureka Internal Medicine, 1992—; mem. hosp. rels. com. Blue Cross Calif., 1986-91, bd. dirs., 1988-91, mem. audit com., 1989-91; pres. No. Redwood Empire Hosp. Conf., 1966-68, 88; mem. health occupations adv. com. Coll. of Redwoods, 1972-76. Mem. Humbold County Hist. Soc.; treas., chmn. budget and fin. com. Humboldt-Del Norte unite Am. Cancer Soc., 1978; bd. dirs. Calif. affiliate Am. Heart Assn., 1976; mem. Rhododentron Festival Com., 1984-88, chmn. awards and judging, 1986-88; bd. regents St. Bernard H.S., 1987-89, chmn., 1988-89; mem. AIDS Task Force, County of Humboldt, 1989-91. Served with Med. Svc. Corps, U.S. Army. George H. Walker fellow, 1989. Fellow Am. Coll. Healthcare Execs.; mem. Am. Hosp. Assn. (ho. of dels. 1982-86), Calif. Hosp. Assn. (bd. dirs. 1983-86), Hosp. Coun. No. Calif. (bd. dirs. 980-86, exec. com. 1981-82, chmn. fin. and econs. com. 1982-83), Cath. Health Assn. (rural hosp. study group 1988-90), Rotary Club of Eureka (bd. dirs. 1987-89, chmn. blood bank com. 1983-84, 91-92). Home: 1928 Greenbriar Ln Eureka CA 95503 Office: Eureka Internal Medicine 2280 Harrison Ave Ste B Eureka CA 95501

KRIKEN, JOHN LUND, architect; b. Calif., July 5, 1938; s. John Erik Nord and Ragnhild (Lund) K.; m. Anne Girard (div.); m. Katherine Koelsch. BArch, U. Calif., Berkeley, 1961; MArch, Harvard U., 1968. Ptnr. Skidmore, Owings and Merrill, San Francisco, 1970—; tchr. Washington U., St. Louis, 1968, U. Calif., Berkeley, 1972, Rice U., Houston, 1979. Commr. Bay Conservation and Devel. Commn., Calif., 1984—, Arts Commn. City and County San Francisco, 1989-95; mem. design rev. bd. Berkeley campus, U. Calif., 1986—; mem. Harvard U. Alumni Coun., 1989-92. With U.S. Army, 1961-63. Fellow AIA; mem. Am. Inst. Cert. Planners, Sunday Afternoon Watercolor Soc. (founding mem.). Office: Skimore Owings & Merrill 333 Bush St San Francisco CA 94104-2806

KRINSKY, IRA WALTER, executive search consultant; b. Long Beach, N.Y., Jan. 15, 1949; s. Rubin and Lillian Evelyn (Tucker) K.; m. Susan Lois Paul, June 6, 1971 (div. July 15, 1989); 1 child, Brian Paul. BA, Hofstra U., 1971; MA, N.Y. U., 1974; EdD, Harvard U., 1979. Tchr. Monticello (N.Y.) Pub. Schs., 1971-72; tchr., admisntr. Huntington (N.Y.) Pub. Schs., 1972-75; asst. supt. Levittown (N.Y.) Pub. Schs., 1978-79; dep. supt. Pomona (Calif.) Unified Sch. Dist., 1979-82; mng. v.p. Korn/Ferry Internat., L.A., 1982-88, 92—; pres. Ira W. Krinsky and Assoc., L.A., 1988-92; adv. bd. mem. Supt.'s Prepared, Washington, 1992—. Mem. editorial adv. bd. Interant. Jour. of Edn. Reform, Lancaster, Pa., 1992—; author: The Careers Makers, 1990, 92, 94, contbr. articles to profl. jours. Trustee Southwestern U. Sch. of Law, 1985—. With U.S. Army, 1966-69, Vietnam. Mem. Am. Philatellic Soc., Am. Air Mail Soc., Harvard Club of So. Calif. (bd. mem. 1986—), Phi Delta Kappa (Harvard Chpt.). Office: Korn/Ferry Internat 1800 Century Park E Ste 900 Los Angeles CA 90067-1512

KRIPPNER, STANLEY CURTIS, psychologist; b. Edgerton, Wis., Oct. 4, 1932; s. Carroll Porter and Ruth Genevieve (Volenberg) K.; m. Lelie Anne Harris, June 25, 1966; stepchildren: Caron, Robert. BS, U. Wis., 1954; MA, Northwestern U., 1957, PhD, 1961; PhD (hon.), U. Humanistic Studies, San Diego, 1982. Diplomate Am. Bd. Sexology. Speech therapist Warren Pub. Schs. (Ill.), 1954-55, Richmond Pub. Schs. (Va.), 1955-56; dir. Child Study Ctr. Kent State U. (Ohio), 1961-64; dir. dream lab. Maimonides Med. Ctr., Bklyn., 1964-73; prof. of psychology Saybrook Inst., San Francisco, 1973—; disting. prof. psychology Calif. Inst. Integral Studies, San Francisco, 1991—; vis. prof. U. P.R., 1972, Sonoma State U., 1972-73, U. Life Scis., Bogotá, Colombia, 1974, Inst. for Psychodrama and Humanistic Psychology, Caracas, Venezuela, 1975, West Ga. Coll., 1976, John F. Kennedy U., 1980-82, Inst. for Rsch. in Biopsychophysics, Guritiba, Brazil, 1990; lectr. Acad. Pedagogical Scis., Moscow, 1971, Acad. Scis., Beijing, 1981, Minan Gerais U., Belo Horizonte, Brazil, 1986-87. Author: (with Montague Ullman) Dream Telepathy, 1973, rev. edit., 1989, Song of the Siren: A Parapsychological Odyssey, 1975; (with Alberto Villoldo) The Realms of Healing, 1976, rev. edit., 1987, Human Possibilities, 1980, (with Alberto Villoldo) Healing States, 1987; (with Jerry Solfvin) La Science et les Pouvoirs Psychiques de l'Homme, 1986, (with Joseph Dillard) Dreamworking, 1988, (with David Feinstein) Personal Mythology, 1988, (with Patrick Welch) Spiritual Dimensions of Healing, 1992, (with Dennis Thong and Bruce Carpenter) A Psychiatrist in Paradise, 1993; editor: Advances in Parapsychological Research, Vol. 1, 1977, Vol. 2, 1978, Vol. 3, 1982, Vol. 4, 1984, Vol. 5, 1987, Vol. 6, 1990, Vol. 7, 1994, Psychoenergetic Systems, 1979; co-editor: Galaxies of Life, 1973, The Kirlian Aura, 1974, The Energies of Consciousness, 1975, Future Science, 1977, Dreamtime and Dreamwork, 1990; mem. editorial bd. Gifted Child Quar., Internat. Jour. Paraphysics, Jour. Humanistic Psychology, Jour. Transpersonal Psychology, Revision Jour., Jour. Indian Psychology, Metanoia, Dream Network, Humanistic Psychologist, Internat. Jour. Psychosomatics, Jour. Creative Children and Adults; contbr. 500 articles to profl. jours. Bd. dirs., adv. bd. Acad. Religion and Phys. Rsch., Survival Rsch. Found., Hartley Film Found., Inst. for Multilevel Learning, Humanistic Psychology Ctr. N.Y., Life Action Found. Recipient Svc. to Youth award YMCA, 1959, Citation of Merit Nat. Assn. Creative Children and Adults, 1975, Cert. Recognition Office Gifted and Talented, U.S. Office Edn., 1976, Volker medal South Africa Soc. Psychical Rsch., 1980, Bicentennial medal U. Ga., 1985, Charlotte and Karl Bühler award, 1992, Dan Overlade Meml. award, 1994. Fellow Am. Soc. Clin. Hypnosis, Am. Psychol. Assn., Am. Psychol. Soc., Soc. Sci. Study Religion, Soc. Sci. Study Sex; mem. AAAS, Am. Soc. Psychical Rsch., N.Y. Soc. Clin. Psychologists (assoc.), Am. Acad. Social and Polit. Sci., Am. Ednl. Rsch. Assn., Am. Assn. of Counseling and Devel., Internat. Council Psychologists, Assn. for Study of Dreams (pres. 1993-94), Soc. for the Anthropology Consciousness, Internat. Kirlian Rsch. Assn., Com. for Study Anomalistic Rsch., Inter-Am. Psychol. Assn., Assn. Humanistic Psychology (pres. 1974-75), Assn. Transpersonal Psychology, Internat. Psychomatics Inst., Internat. Soc. Hypnosis, Internat. Soc. for Study Multiple Personality and Dissociative States, Nat. Assn. for Gifted Children, Sleep Rsch. Soc., Soc. Sci. Exploration, Biofeedback Soc. Am., Coun. Exceptional Children, Soc. Accelerative Learning and Teaching, Soc. Gen. Systems Rsch., Swedish Soc. Clin. and Exptl. Hypnosis, Western Psychol. Assn., World Coun. for Gifted and Talented Children, Internat. Soc. Gen. Semantics, Menninger Found., Nat. Soc. Study of Edn., Parapsychol. Assn. (pres. 1983), Soc. Clin. and Exptl. Hypnosis, World Future Soc. Home: 79 Woodland Rd Fairfax CA 94930-2153 Office: Saybrook Inst 450 Pacific Ave # 300 San Francisco CA 94133-4640

KRISTIANSEN, MICHAEL SIGURD, botanical gardens director; b. Durban, Natal, Republic of South Africa, Apr. 27, 1942; came to U.S., 1978; s. Sigurd and Claire (Reed) K.; m. Terry Ellen O'Reilly; children: Matt, Erik Colin. BSc in Landscape Architecture, Calif. State Poly. U., 1970. Cert. park adminstr. and ornamental horticulturist Inst. Park Adminstrn. Durban, 1966, cert arborist. Landscape draftsman Keith French Assocs., L.A., 1970-72; landscape architecture planning Kristiansen Assoc., Johannesburg, 1972-78; horticultural cons. Kristiansen Assoc., 1979—; instr. horticulture Dept. Arts UCLA, 1979-89; instr. landscape architecture Dept. of Scis., UCLA, 1979-89; instr. horticulture West Valley Occupational Ctr., L.A., 1980-89; mentor tchr., 1985-89. Mem. Mayor's Com. on Graffitti Tech. Resource, L.A., 1988-89, Wahiawa (Hawaii) Task Force, 1994—, Am. the Beautiful, Honolulu, 1992—, Hawaii Job Corps Adv. Com., 1990—. William Poulton scholar City of Durban (2) 1966, (1) 1967. Home: 45-685 Luluku Rd Kaneohe HI 96744-1857 Office: Honolulu Botanical Gardens 50 N Vineyard Blvd Honolulu HI 96817-3759

KRISTOF, NICHOLAS DONABET, journalist; b. Chgo., Apr. 27, 1959; s. Ladis K.D. and Jane (McWilliams) K.; m. Sheryl WuDunn; children: Gregory, Geoffrey. BA, Harvard U., 1981; BA and MA in Law, U. Oxford, Eng., 1983; diploma in Arabic, Am. U. in Cairo, 1983-84; student, Taipei Lang Inst., 1987-88. Econs. reporter N.Y. Times, N.Y.C., 1984-85, fin. corr. L.A. bur., 1985-86, chief Hong Kong bur., 1986-87, chief Beijing bur., 1988-93, chief Tokyo bur., 1995—; vis. fellow East-West Ctr., 1993; vis. scholar Linfield Coll., 1994. Author: (with S. WuDunn) China Wakes: The Struggle for the Soul of the Rising Power, 1994. Recipient Pulitzer prize for fgn. reporting, 1990, George Polk award for fgn. reporting L.I. U., N.Y., 1990, Hal Boyle award Overseas Press Club, 1990; Rhodes scholar, 1981-83. Home: 23050 NW Roosevelt Dr Yamhill OR 97148-8336

KRIVE, IRWIN, new products development company executive; b. Bklyn., Nov. 12, 1929; m. Sylvia Stall; children: Taryn, Risa, Lance. BS, NYU, 1951, MA, 1957. Cert. chief sch. adminstr., secondary sch. prin., vocat. and indsl. arts tchr., N.Y. Tchr. Port Washington (N.Y.) Unified Free Dist. 4, asst. supt., coord. redesign; prin. H.S., Oceanside (N.Y.) Bd. Edn.; dir. tech. tng. Plainedge (N.Y.) Bd. Edn.; pres., founder Heartfelt Products Co., West Hills, Calif. Patentee muscle mimicry exerciser for ski industry. Former asst. scoutmaster troop 181 Boy Scouts Am., Bklyn. With U.S. Army, 1951-53. Home and Office: 6720 Capistrano Ave West Hills CA 91307-3733

KRIVOKAPICH, JANINE, physician, educator; b. Raton, N.Mex., Jan. 18, 1947; d. John and Mary Edith (Stewart) K; 1 child, Julie Kathleen Frazee. BA in Biology, Stanford U., 1969; MD, Harvard U., 1973. Diplomate Am. Bd. Internal Medicine, Am. Bd. Cardiovascular Disease. Intern, resident, fellow UCLA, 1973-78, prof. medicine, div. cardiology, 1978—; Contbr. articles to Circulation, Circulation Rsch., Am. Jour. Cardiology,

Jour. Am. Coll. Cardiology. NIH rsch. grantee, 1981-85, 86-91. Fellow Am. Coll. Cardiology; mem. Phi Beta Kappa, Alpha Omega Alpha. Office: UCLA Med Ctr Dept Medicine CHS47-123 Los Angeles CA 90095-1679

KRIZ, GEORGE STANLEY, chemistry educator; b. Santa Cruz, Calif., Oct. 20, 1939; s. George S. and Mary L. (Semelka) K.; m. Carolyn M. Anderson, Aug. 25, 1989; children: Sonja M. Dyer, Brian G., Erik W. Leininger, Kenneth M., Michelle L. BS, U. Calif., Berkeley, 1961; PhD, Ind. U., 1966. Fgn. asst. faculty of scis. U. Montpellier, France, 1965-66; vis. rsch. assoc. Ohio State U., Columbus, 1966-67; asst. prof. Western Wash. U., Bellingham, 1967-72, assoc. prof., 1972-79, prof. of chemistry, 1979—; vis. prof. of chemistry Ind. U., Bloomington, 1984-87. Co-author: Introduction to Organic Laboratory Techniques, 1976, 4th edit., 1989, Introduction to Spectroscopy, 1979, Introduction to Organic Laboratory Techniques: A Microscale Approach, 1990, 2d edit., 1995; contbr. articles to profl. jours. Fellow Royal Soc. Chemistry; mem. AAAS, Am. Chem. Soc. Democrat. Lutheran. Office: Western Wash U Dept Chemistry MS 9150 Bellingham WA 98225-9150

KROEGER, KARL, retired musicologist, librarian, composer, and editor; b. Louisville, Apr. 13, 1932; s. Carl Robert and Lillian (Gnadinger) K.; m. Marie Jasper, July 20, 1955; 1 child, Paul Edmond. BM, U. Louisville, 1954, MM, 1959; MS, U. Ill., 1961; PhD, Brown U., 1976. Curator Am. Music Coll. N.Y. Pub. Libr., N.Y.C., 1962-64; composer-in-residence Eugene (Oreg.) Pub. Schs., 1964-67; asst. prof. Ohio U., Athens, 1967-68, Moorhead (Minn.) State Coll., 1971-72; dir. Moravian Mus. Found., Winston-Salem, N.C., 1972-80; prof./music libr. U. Colo., Boulder, 1982-94; ret., 1994. Author: American Fuging Tunes, 1770-1820, 1994, Catalog of the Music of William Billings, 1991; editor: Complete Works of William Billings, 3 vols., 1981-90, Pelissier's Columbian Melodies, 1984. Ford Found. grantee, 1964-67; Leverhulme Trust fellow, U. Keele, Eng., 1980-81, Sr. Rsch. fellow NEH, 1981-82, 88. Mem. Am. Musicol. Soc., Music Libr. Assn., Internat. Assn. Music Librs., Sonneck Soc. for Am. Music. Home: 9260 Newton St Westminster CO 80030-3128

KROGH, PETER SUNDEHL, III, family physician; b. Chgo., Jan. 29, 1953; s. Peter Sundehl Krogh Jr. and Audrey Rose (Kalal) Morgan; m. Cynthia Marie Umano, Mar. 4, 1978. BS, USAF Acad., 1975; MD, Rush Med. Coll., 1979. Diplomate Am. Acad. Family Practice. Commd. 2nd lt. USAF, 1975, advanced through grades to lt. col., 1991; family physician resident David Grant USAF Med. Ctr., Travis AFB, Calif., 1979-82, family physician, 1986—; family physician Scott USAF Med. Ctr., Scott AFB, Ill., 1982-84, Iraklion USAF Hosp., Iraklion AB, Crete, 1984-86. Mem. Uniformed Svcs. Acad. Family Physicians, Am. Acad. Family Physicians, Soc. Tchrs. Family Medicine. Republican. Mem. Evangelical Free Ch. Office: USAF David Grant Med Ctr/SGHF Travis AFB CA 94535

KROGIUS, TRISTAN ERNST GUNNAR, international marketing consultant, lawyer; b. Tammerfors, Finland, Apr. 13, 1933; came to U.S., 1939; s. Helge Lorenz and Valborg Isolde (Antell) K.; m. Barbara Jane Brophy, Aug. 29, 1952; children—Ferril Anne, Lars Anthony, Karin Therese, Eric Lorenz, Marian Elaine, Rebecca Kristina. B.A., U. N.Mex., 1954; M.A., Calif. State U.-Los Angeles, 1962; student Advanced Mgmt. Program, Harvard U., 1980; JD, Western State U., 1990. Bar: Calif. 1991. With Scott Paper Co., Phila., 1960-65, Hunt-Wesson Foods, Fullerton, Calif., 1965-75; pres. Hunt-Wesson Foods Can., Ltd., Toronto, Ont., 1969-71, pres. frozen and refrigerated foods div., 1971-75; pres., chief exec. officer Dalgety Foods, Salinas, Calif., 1975-78; v.p., gen. mgr. food div. Tenneco West, Inc., Bakersfield, Calif., 1978-80, pres., chief exec. officer, 1981-87; pres. Landmark Mgmt., Inc., 1987-88; ptnr. The Cons. Co., South Laguna, 1988-90, Internat. Mktg. Consultancy, 1990—; adj. prof. Western State U. Coll. of Law, 1992—. Bd. dirs. South Coast Med. Ctr., Laguna Beach, Calif., 1969-74, pres., CEO, 1974; bd. dirs. South Sierra coun. Boy Scouts Am., 1981-87, Calif. State Coll. Found., Bakersfield, 1983-87, Found. for 21st Century, 1987-90; mgr. elder abuse program Pub. Law Ctr., 1992-93. Capt. USMC, 1954-60. Recipient World Food award Ariz. State U., Tempe, 1982. Mem. Orange County Bar Assn. Republican. Episcopalian. Office: 15 Monarch Bay Plz Ste 200 Dana Point CA 92629-3441

KROHN, KENNETH ALBERT, radiology educator; b. Stevens Point, Wis., June 19, 1945; s. Albert William and Erma Belle (Cornwell) K.; m. Marijane Alberta Wideman, July 14, 1968; 1 child, Galen. BA in Chemistry, Andrews U., 1966; PhD in Chemistry, U. Calif., 1971. Acting assoc. prof. U. Wash., Seattle, 1981-84, assoc. prof. radiology, 1984-86, prof. radiology and radiation oncology, 1986—, adj. prof. chemistry, 1986—; guest scientist Donner Lab. Lawrence Berkeley (Calif.) Lab., 1980-81; radiochemist, VA Med. Ctr., Seattle, 1982—. Contbr. numerous articles to profl. jours.; patentee in field. NDEA fellow. Fellow AAAS; mem. Am. Chem. Soc., Radiation Rsch. Soc., Soc. Nuclear Medicine, Acad. Coun., Sigma Xi. Home: NE 550 Lake Ridge Dr Belfair WA 98528 Office: U Washington Imaging Rsch Lab RC-05 Seattle WA 98195-6004

KROKENBERGER, LINDA ROSE, chemist, environmental analyst; b. Ridley Park, Pa., July 17, 1954; d. Roy Frank and Rose Marie (Kraffert) K. BS in Chemistry, Syracuse U., 1976. Radiopharm. chemist Upstate Med. Ctr., SUNY, Syracuse, 1976-78; chemist, asst. mgr. lab. IT Corp., Cerritos, Calif., 1978-86; mgr. data control Enseco-Cal Lab., West Sacramento, Calif., 1987; asst. mgr. lab. Sci. Applications Internat. Corp., San Diego, 1987-89; ind. cons. in environ. compliance and analytical chemistry Poway, Calif., 1989—. Recipient Citizenship award DAR, 1972. Republican. Methodist. Home and Office: 12974 Cree Dr Poway CA 92064-3830

KROLL, JAMES XAVIER, librarian; b. Michigan City, Ind., July 9, 1951; s. John Stephen and Clara Marie (Widelski) K.; m. Joan Marie Spadacene, Aug. 6, 1977; children: Michael James, John Xavier. BA, Gannon U., 1973; MS, U. Denver, 1979; MLS, Emporia State U., 1993. Libr. Denver Pub. Libr., 1980-86, sr. libr., 1986-88, mgr. humanities dept., 1989-94, mgr. gen. reference and nonfiction dept., 1995—. 1st lt. U.S. Army, 1973-79. Mem. Colo. Geneaol. Soc. (pres. 1984-88). Home: 2307 Ivy St Denver CO 80207-3410 Office: Denver Pub Libr 10 14th Ave Pkwy West Denver CO 80204

KRONENBERG, JACALYN (JACKI KRONENBERG), nurse administrator; b. N.Y.C., July 21, 1949; d. Martin Jerome and Joyce (Weinberg) Jacobs; m. Robert Kronenberg, Jan. 23, 1971 (div.); 1 child, Joshua Louis. BA, William Paterson Coll. of N.J., 1971; ADN, Phoenix Coll., 1977. RN, Calif.; cert. IV nurse, chemo, ACLS, PALS. Asst. charge nurse Phoenix Gen. Hosp.; nurse Ariz. State Crippled Children's Hosp., Tempe; maternal, child nurse Desert Samaritan Hosp., Mesa, Ariz.; nurse mgr. PPS Inc., Phoenix, Med-Pro 2000, Phoenix; clin. nurse II Phoenix Children's Hosp.; nurse mgr. adolescent unit Shriners Hosp., L.A.; nurse mgr. pediatrics, oncology, gynecology, med./surg. Santa Monica (Calif.) Hosp. Med. Ctr., 1993-94; dir. nurses, dir. patient care svcs. NMC Homecare, Anaheim, Calif., 1994; mgr. med.-surg. svcs., house supr.'s staffing office Midway Hosp. Med. Ctr., L.A., 1995—, mgr. nursing office, urgent care clinic, 1995—. Nursing Lab. Tech. scholar, 1976. Mem. Oncology Nursing Soc., Soc. Pediatric Nurses. Office: Midway Hosp Med Ctr 5925 San Vicente Blvd Los Angeles CA 90019-6630

KRONENBERG, JOHN ROBERT, retired magistrate judge; b. Spokane, Wash., Mar. 15, 1923; s. George C. and Agnes Isabel (Monaghan) K.; m. Marilyn Elizabeth Miller, Feb. 24, 1962; children: John, Karl, Kathryn. LL.B., Loyola U., Los Angeles, 1958. Bar: Calif. 1959, U.S. Dist. Ct. (cen. dist.) Calif. 1959. Dep. pub. defender Los Angeles County (Calif.) Pub. defender, 1959-73; magistrate judge U.S. Dist. Ct. (cen. dist.) Calif., 1973-92, recalled 1994-95, ret., 1995. Served with U.S. Army, 1943-45. Roman Catholic. Office: US Courthouse 312 N Spring St Los Angeles CA 90012-4701

KRONENFELD, DAVID BRIAN, anthropologist; b. Miami Beach, Fla., Dec. 21, 1941; s. John and Elsie Rodlyn (Weinkle) K.; m. Judy Zahler, June 21, 1964; children: Daniel Aaron, Mara Gianna. AB, Harvard U., 1963; MA, PhD, Stanford U., 1970; vis. student, Oxford U., 1968-69; student, Yale U., 1963-64. Asst. prof. dept. anthropology U Calif., Riverside, 1969-77, assoc. prof., 1977-81; prof. dept. anthropology U. Calif., Riverside, 1981—, dept. chmn., 1980-93, chair com. on linguistics, 1991—. Contbr. numerous articles to profl. jours. Pres. PTA, Longfellow Elementary Sch. PTA, Riverside, 1982-83, Univ. Heights Middle Sch. PTSA, Riverside, 1987-88; coach soccer teams, 1981-88. Fellow Am. Anthropol. Assn., Royal Anthropol. Inst.; mem. Linguistic Soc. of Am., Am. Ethnol. Soc., Southwestern Anthropol. Assn. (pres. 1988-89). Democrat. Home: 3314 Celeste Dr Riverside CA 92507-4051 Office: Univ of Calif-Riverside Dept Of Anthropology Riverside CA 92507

KROPOTOFF, GEORGE ALEX, civil engineer; b. Sofia, Bulgaria, Dec. 6, 1921; s. Alex S. and Anna A. (Kurat) K.; came to Brazil, 1948, to U.S., 1952, naturalized, 1958; BS in Engring., Inst. Tech., Sofia, 1941; postgrad. in computer sci. U. Calif., 1968; Registered profl. engr., Calif.; m. Helen P., July 23, 1972. With Standard Eletrica S.A., Rio de Janeiro, 1948-52, Pacific Car & Foundry Co., Seattle, 1952-64, T.G. Atkinson Assocs., Structural Engrs., San Diego, 1960-62, Tucker, Sadler & Bennett A-E, San Diego, 1964-74, Gen. Dynamics-Astronautics, San Diego, 1967-68, Engring. Sci., Inc., Arcadia, Calif., 1975-76, Incomtel, Rio de Janeiro, Brazil, 1976, Bennett Engrs., structural cons., San Diego, 1976-82; project structural engr. Hope Cons. Group, San Diego and Saudi Arabia, 1982-84; cons. structural engr. Pioneered engring. computer software. With U.S. Army, 1945-46. Fellow ASCE; mem. Structural Engrs. Assn. San Diego (assoc.), Soc. Am. Mil. Engrs., Soc. Profl. Engrs. Brazil. Republican. Russian Orthodox. Home: 9285 Edgewood Dr La Mesa CA 91941-5612

KROTKI, KAROL JOZEF, sociology educator, demographer; b. Cieszyn, Poland, May 15, 1922; emigrated to Can., 1964; s. Karol Stanislaw and Anna Elzbieta (Skrzywanek) K.; m. Joanna Patkowski, July 12, 1947; children—Karol Peter, Jan Jozef, Filip Karol. B.A. (hons.), Cambridge (Eng.) U., 1948, M.A., 1952; M.A., Princeton U., 1959, Ph.D., 1960. Civil ser. Eng., 1948-49; dep. dir. stats. Sudan, 1949-58; vis. fellow Princeton U., 1958-60; research adviser Pakistan Inst. Devel. Econs., 1960-64; asst. dir. census research Dominion Bur. Stats., Can., 1964-68; prof. sociology U. Alta., 1968-83, univ. prof., 1983-91, univ. prof. emeritus, 1991—; vis. prof. U. Calif., Berkeley, 1967, U. N.C., 1970-73, U. Mich., 1975, U. Costa Rica, 1993; coord. program socio-econ. rsch. Province Alta., 1969-71; dir. Can. Futures Rsch. Inst., Edmonton, 1993—; cons. in field. Author 12 books and monographs; contbr. numerous articles to profl. jours. Served with Polish, French and Brit. Armed Forces, 1939-46. Recipient Achievement award Province of Alta., 1970, Commemorative medal for 125th Anniversary of Can., 1992; grantee in field. Fellow Am. Statis. Assn., Royal Soc. Can. (v.p. 1986-88), Acad. Humanities and Social Scis. (v.p. 1984-86, pres. 1986-88); mem. Fedn. Can. Demographers (v.p. 1977-82, pres. 1982-84), Can. Population Soc., Association des Demographes du Quebec, Soc. Edmonton Demographers (founder, pres. 1990—), Cen. and E. European Studies Soc. (pres. 1986-88), Population Assn. Am., Internat. Union Sci. Study Population, Internat. Statis. Inst., Royal Statis. Soc. Roman Catholic. Home: 10137 Clifton Pl, Edmonton, AB Canada T5N 3H9 Office: U Alta, Dept Sociology, Edmonton, AB Canada T6G 2H4

KROUT, BOYD MERRILL, psychiatrist; b. Oakland, Calif., Jan. 31, 1931; s. Boyd Merrill and Phoebe Lenore (Colby) K.; m. Helena Luise Keel, Aug. 25, 1965. AB, Stanford U., 1951, MD, 1955. Diplomate Am. Bd. Psychiatry and Neurology. Intern San Francisco Hosp., 1954-55; resident Boston U. Hosps., 1958-60, Boston Va Hosp., 1960-61; asst. to clin. prof. UCLA Sch. Medicine, 1961—; chief physician Harbor/UCLA Med. Ctr., Torrance, 1961—. Capt. USAF, 1955-58. Fellow Am. Psychiat. Assn., So. Calif. Psychiat. Soc. (councillor 1988-91), Am. Psychiat. Soc.; mem. L.A. County Med. Soc. Republican. Office: Harbor/UCLA Med Ctr PO Box 2910 Torrance CA 90509-2910

KROZEL, JIMMY ALAN, research scientist, artist; b. Morton Grove, Ill., Dec. 13, 1963; s. Walter A. and Irene (Bogard) K. AS, Purdue U., W. Lafayette, Ind., 1984; BS, 1985, MA, 1988, PhD, 1992. Rsch. scientist Hughes Info. Scis. Lab., Malibu, Calif., 1987—. Contbr. articles to profl. jours. Recipient Am. Inst. Aeronautics and Astronautics scholarship Washington, 1984; Ames Rsch. Ctr. fellowship NASA, Moffett Field, Calif., 1985; Hughes Doctoral fellowship Hughes Aircraft Co., L.A., 1987. Home: 1148 9th St Apt 21 Santa Monica CA 90403-5242 Office: Hughes Info Scis Lab RL69 3011 Malibu Canyon Rd Malibu CA 90265-4737

KRUEGER, JAMES, lawyer; b. N.Y.C., Oct. 27, 1938; s. Carl and Ida (Levey) K.; m. Merry Michael Hill, July 5, 1967; children—Melissa Carlton, James Michael. BA, UCLA, 1960; LLB, Loyola U., L.A., 1965. Bar: Hawaii 1966, U.S. Dist. Ct. Hawaii 1966, U.S. Ct. Appeals (9th cir.) 1967, U.S. Tax Ct. 1974, U.S. Supreme Ct. 1982. Assoc. firm Padgett, Greeley, Marumoto & Akinaka, Honolulu, 1967-72; atty. Krueger & Cahill, Attys. at Law, Wailuku, Maui, Hawaii, 1973—; mem. Hawaii com. Pattern Jury Instrns., 1992-93. Contbr. articles to profl. jours. Co-founder Nat. Bd. of Trial Advocacy, Hawaii Acad. of Plaintiffs Attys.; Gold Trustee Thomas F. Lambert Chair; mem. Commn. Hawaii Ct. Annexed Arbitration, Hawaii State Commn. on Lawyer Professionalism, 1988-90, Hawaii State Commn. on Solicitation and Advt.; del. Hawaii Jud. Conf., 1986-88, Fed. Jud. Conf., 1989. Fellow Internat. Soc. Barristers, Internat. Acad. Trial Lawyers; mem. ABA (trial techniques com. 1974-76, com. medicine and law, nat. vice-chmn. sect. on tort and ins. practice 1977-81), Assn. Trial Lawyers Am. (gov. 1976-82, state committeeman 1975-76, constl. revisions com. 1977-78, nat. exec. com. 1981-82, amicus curiae com. 1979-80, fed. liaison com. 1980-81, nat. vice chmn. profl. rsch. and devel. com. 1980-81, nat. vice-chmn. publs. dept. 1982-83, nat. vice chmn. edn. policy bd. 1983-84, chmn. Nat. Midwinter Convs., 1988, 91, chmn. Nat. Pub. Rels. Com. 1986-88), Hawaii Bar Assn., Fed. Bar Assn., Maui County Bar Assn. (pres. 1975), Melvin M. Belli Soc. (trustee), Am. Coll. Legal Medicine, Am. Soc. Hosp. Attys., Am. Bd. Profl. Liability Attys., Western Trial Lawyers Assn. (pres. 1978-79, v.p. 1977-78, bd. govs. 1982—), Calif. Trial Lawyers Assn., N.Y. Trial Lawyers Assn., Pa. Trial Lawyers Assn., Tex. Trial Lawyers Assn., NITA Advocates Assn., Hawaii Inst. Cont. Legal End. (pres. 1994), Hawaii Trial Lawyers Assn. (pres. 1995—), Million Dollar Advocates Forum, Olympic Club, Phi Alpha Delta. Jewish. Clubs: Outrigger Canoe, Oahu (Honolulu); Olympic Club (San Francisco); Transpacific Yacht (Los Angeles); Maui Country; Maui Ocean Swim. Office: 2065 Main St PO Box 1460 Wailuku HI 96793

KRUEGER, JAMES A., lawyer; b. Detroit, Sept. 21, 1943; s. A.A. and Margaret E. (Hurley) K.; m. Therese Eileen Connors, Aug. 2, 1968; 1 child, Colleen. B.A. cum laude, Gonzaga U., 1965; J.D., Georgetown U., 1968; LL.M., NYU, 1972. Bar: Wash. 1969, U.S. Supreme Ct. 1972, U.S. Tax Ct. 1972, U.S. Dist. Ct. (we. dist.) Wash. 1980, U.S. Ct. Appeals (9th cir.) 1982. With staff U.S. senator from Wash., 1967-68; assoc. firm Kane, Vandeberg & Hartinger, Tacoma, 1972-76, ptnr. Kane, Vandeberg, Hartinger & Walker, 1976-90; shareholder Vandeberg & Johnson, P.S., 1990—; spl. dist. counsel Wash. State Bar Assn., 1984-94; adj. prof. law, U. of Puget Sound, 1974-76. Chmn. bd. dirs. Cath. Community Svcs. of Pierce and Kitsap Counties, 1983-84; bd. dirs. United Way of Pierce County, 1973-82. Capt. U.S. Army, 1968-72. Decorated Bronze star, Army Commendation medal. Mem. ABA, Wash. State Bar Assn. (spl. dist. counsel), Tacoma-Pierce County Bar Assn. Roman Catholic. Contbr. chpt. to Representing the Close Corporation, 1979, Partnership Agreements, 1981, Planning for the Small Business Enterprise, 1982, The Partnership Handbook, 1984. Office: First Interstate Pla 1201 Pacific Ave Ste 1900 Tacoma WA 98402-4301

KRUEGER, JOHN CHARLES, financial planner, investment advisor; b. St. Louis, Oct. 5, 1951; s. Edward Rice and Frances (Lingel) K.; m. Mary Jo Holtz, Apr. 20, 1979; children: Kimberly Ann, Eric John. BS in Bus., U. Miss., 1974; MBA, U. Phoenix, 1987. CLU; cert. fin. planner; chartered fin. cons.; registered investment advisor. With Aetna Life Ins., Phoenix, 1975-76; fin. planner, investments advisor Krueger Fin. Services Inc., Phoenix, 1976—; guest instr. Ariz State U., 1983-86; lectr. and coordinator cable TV programs on fin., Ariz., 1983, 84; adj. faculty mem. Coll Fin. Planning, Denver, 1984—. Guest instr. in fin. planning. City of Phoenix Retirement Ctr., 1984—, City of Mesa (Ariz.) Retirement Ctr., 1984, City of Tempe (Ariz.) Retirement Ctr., 1984-85. Mem. Inst. Cert. Fin. Planners (past pres. greater Phoenix chpt.), Am. Soc. CLU's. Republican. Presbyterian. Home: 2159 E La Vieve Ln Tempe AZ 85284-3543 Office: Krueger Fin Svcs 7776 S Pointe Pky W Ste 136 Phoenix AZ 85044-5424

KRUEGER, KURT ARNOLD, sports psychologist, institute administrator; b. L.A., Jan. 29, 1946; s. Charles H. and Adlaide M. Krueger; m. Teresa Anne Krueger, May 10, 1992; 1 child, Keith Charles. AA in History, L.A. Valley Coll., 1967; BA in History, Classics and Phys. Edn., U. Colo., 1969; MS in Edn., Mt. St. Mary's Coll., L.A., 1972. Cert. Calif. Std. secondary tchr.; cert. mediation and yoga instr. Tchr. social studies Belvedere Jr. High Sch. L.A. Unified Sch. Dist., 1969; tchr. social studies and phys. edn. Torrance (Calif.) Unified Sch. Dists., 1969-71; tchr. social studies Berendo Jr. High Sch. L.A. Unified Sch. Dist., 1971-76, tchr. social studies Crenshaw High Sch., 1977-81, tchr. phys. edn. Webster Jr. High Sch., 1984, tchr. social studies and phys. edn. Pastuer Jr. High Sch., 1984-87, tchr. social studies Palms Jr. High Sch., 1987-91, substitute secondary tchr., 1992-93; tchr. social studies Van Nuys (Calif.) Mid. Sch., 1993—; mem. faculty phys. edn. and psychology Calif. State U., L.A., 1978-81, 93, phys. edn. Glendale Coll., 1979-81; tchr. Calif. State U. at L.A., Long Beach and Dominguez Hills, 1978-81, 93, Stockholm U., 1983, Calif. State U., L.A., Nat. Inst. Sports, India, 1982; condr. workshops in stress mgmt., peak performance, yoga, meditation, winning ways, practical sports psychology, 1975—; dir., instr., co-founder Inst. Sports Psychology, Bombay and L.A., 1982—; tchr. stress mgmt. or succes systems. Author: Japan Hijack, 1978; (audio tapes) Winning Ways: The Neuropsychology of Sports Excellence, 1988; contbr. articles to profl. jours. and mags.; appearances on TV KNBC, Everywhere Show, 1981, Theta Cable You Are That, 1981, Century Cable, 1988, KCAL Weekend Gallery, 1988, KCBS Barbara De Angeles Show on Twins, 1992, radio KABC Tom Hall Program, 1981, KMDY, 1987, KGIL HealthChoice, 1988, others. Recipient Sr. Olypmic Swim Championship medals, 1979, 80, 81, 84, 85. Mem. Assn. for Advancement of Applied Sports Psychology, Internat. Soc. Sport Psychology,Calif. Assn. Health, Phys. Edn. and Recreation and Dance. Home: 5175 Mecca Ave Tarzana CA 91356-4133

KRUEGER, KURT DONN, lawyer; b. Worthington, Minn., May 8, 1952; s. Donn Kurt and Lola (Lueck) K.; m. Kim Short, Jan. 2, 1983; children: Krista Marie, Kurt Derrick. BA in Gov., Mont. State U., 1974; JD, George Mason U., 1978. Bar: Va. 1978, U.S. Dist. Ct. (ea. dist.) Va. 1979, U.S. Ct. Appeals (4th and D.C. cirs.) 1979, Mont. 1980, U.S. Dist. Ct. Mont. 1980, U.S. Ct. Appeals (9th cir.) 1985, U.S. Supreme Ct. 1990. Law clk. to superior ct. judge Washington, 1978-80; staff atty. Mont. Legal Svcs. Assn., Butte, 1980-83; pvt. practice Butte, 1984—; bd. dirs Mont. Legal Svcs. Assn., Helena, 1984—, pres., 1988-89. State rep. Mont. State Legis., Helena, 1985-87; bd. dirs. Big Bros. and Big Sisters, Butte, 1985-88, Butte Silver Bow Zoning Bd. Adjustment, 1989-92; adv. bd. vigilante dist. Boy Scouts Am., 1989—. Mem. Va. Bar Assn., Mont. Bar Assn., Butte Silver Bar Assn., Assn. Trial Lawyers Am., Mont. Trial Lawyers Assn., Trout Unlimited, Ducks Unlimited. Democrat. Methodist. Office: 66 W Park St Ste 211 Butte MT 59701-1714

KRUEGER, KURT EDWARD, environmental management company official; b. Santa Monica, Calif., June 24, 1952; s. Richard L. and Peggy J. (Cisler) K.; m. Maureen S. Catland, Aug. 4, 1973; children: Corey Edward, Brendan Kurt, Alyssa Marie. BA in Biology, Calif. State U., Northridge, 1978; MS in Environ. and Occupational Health & Safety, Calif. State U., 1980; MBA, Pepperdine U., 1988. Registered environ. health specialist. Regional health and safety coord. Internat. Tech. Corp., Wilmington, Calif., 1979-82, mgr. emergency response program, 1982-85, ops. mgr., 1985-88, gen. mgr., 1988-89; dir. health and safety Internat. Tech. Corp., Torrance, Calif., 1989—. Mem. Am. Soc. Safety Engrs., Am. Indsl. Hygiene Assn. (cert.), Nat. Fire Protection Assn., Nat. Safety Mgmt. Soc., Hazardous Waste Action Coalition (vice chmn. health and safety subcom.), Masons. Home: 24143 Archwood St West Hills CA 91307-2902 Office: Internat Tech Corp 23456 Hawthorne Blvd Ste 300 Torrance CA 90505-4719

KRUG, AL JOHN, social services administrator; b. Elizabeth, N.J., July 3, 1946; s. Albert John and Margaret (MacMillan) K.; m. Cheryl Jeanne Black, June 4, 1968; children: Tracy, Joseph. BA, Iowa Wesleyan U., 1968; MS, U. Oreg., 1972, PhD candidate, 1975. Juvenile counselor Linn County Juvenile Dept., Albany, Oreg., 1971-73; juvenile counselor Benton County Juvenile Dept., Corvallis, Oreg., 1973-75, asst. dir., 1975-79, 81-85, dir., 1985—; exec. asst. to adminstr. Children's Svcs. Div., Salem, Oreg., 1980; bd. dirs. Juvenile Svcs. Commn., Corvallis, 1981-89, YM-YWCA Round Table, Coorvallis, 1981-84; facilitator parent edn. groups, Corvallis, 19775-88; chmn. Student Retention Initiative, Coorvallis, 1987-88; bd. dirs. Linn Benton Community Coordinated Child Care Coun., Corvallis, 1971-81, Coun. Social Agys., Corvallis, 1977-78, Shelter Care Task Force, Corvallis, 1977-79. With U.S. Army, 1969-71, Vietnam. Mem. Nat. Coun. Juvenile and Family Ct. Judges, Oreg. Juvenile Dirs. Assn., Oreg. Together, Oreg. Children's Agenda. Office: Benton County Juvenile Dept 530 NW 27th St Corvallis OR 97330-5223

KRUG, DONNA REBECCA DONDES, history educator, small business owner; b. Decatur, Ga., Feb. 17, 1947; d. Aaron and Gladys (Lynch) Dondes; m. John A. Krug, Nov. 30, 1968. BA in History summa cum laude, Calif. State U., Northridge, 1980; MA in Am. History, U. Calif., Irvine, 1983, PhD in History, 1990. Student rsch. asst. Calif. State U., Northridge, 1979-80; teaching asst., teaching assoc. U. Calif., Irvine, 1982-88, rsch. asst., 1988-90; asst. prof. history Va. State U., Petersburg, 1990-93; owner Donna's Korner Kollectibles, Orange, Calif., 1984—; instr. summer sch. U. Calif., Irvine, 1989; adj. history instr. Rancho Santiago Cmty. Coll., Santa Ana, 1990. Active mem. Orange County Bd. Electors. Regents Dissertation fellow U. Calif., Irvine, 1987. Mem. AAUW, Am. Hist. Assn., Orgn. Am. Historians, So. Hist. Assn., So. Hist. Assn. Women Historians, Phi Kappa Phi, Phi Alpha Theta. Home and Office: 2689 N Galley St Orange CA 92665-2420

KRUGER, CHARLES HERMAN, JR., mechanical engineering educator; b. Oklahoma City, Oct. 4, 1934; s. Charles H. and Flora K.; m. Nora Nininger, Sept. 10, 1977; children—Sarah, Charles III, Elizabeth, Ellen. S.B., M.I.T., 1956, Ph.D., 1960; D.I.C., Imperial Coll., London, 1957. Asst. prof. MIT, Cambridge, 1960; research scientist Lockheed Research Labs., 1960-62; prof. mech. engring. Stanford (Calif.) U., 1962—, chmn. dept. mech. engring., 1982-88, sr. assoc. dean engring., 1988-93, vice provost, dean rsch. and grad. policy, 1993—; vis. prof. Harvard U., 1968-69, Princeton U., 1979-80; mem. Environ. Studies Bd. NAS, 1981-83; mem. hearing bd. Bay Area Air Quality Mgmt. Dist., 1969-83. Co-author: Physical Gas Dynamics, 1965, Partially Ionized Gases, 1973, On the Prevention of Significant Deteriorization of Air Quality, 1981; asso. editor: AIAA Jour, 1968-71; contbr. numerous articles to profl. jours. NSF sr. postodoctoral fellow, 1968-69. Mem. AIAA (medal, award 1979), Combustion Inst., ASME, Am. Phys. Soc., Materials Res. Soc. Office: Stanford U Bldg 10 Stanford CA 94305-2061

KRUGER, DENNIS GEORGE, nurse; b. Jackson, Minn., Feb. 22, 1946; s. Benjamin Henry and Lois Lila (Wolff) K. Diploma in nursing, Sioux Valley Hosp., 1967; BSN, U. Phoenix, 1995. RN. Commd. 2d lt. U.S. Army, 1966, advanced through grades to lt. col., 1987; staff nurse 312th Evacuation Hosp. U.S. Army, Chulai, Vietnam, 1968-70; head nurse Walter Reed Hosp., Washington, 1970-71, McAfee Health Clinic, White Sands, N.Mex., 1975-77, DDEAMC, Augusta, Ga., 1977-79; staff nurse USAH Augsburg, Fed. Republic Germany, 1972-75; asst. head nurse Univ. Hosp., Augusta, 1980-92, sexuality counselor, 1982-90; sr. staff nurse St. Joseph Hosp., Denver, 1991—. Decorated Bronze Star; recipient Army Achievement medal, 1984. Mem. Oncology Nursing Soc., Nat. League for Nursing, Chu Lai Med. Soc., Res. Officers Assn. Baptist. Home: PO Box 300536 Denver CO 80203-0536 Office: St Joseph Hosp 1835 Franklin St Denver CO 80218-1126

KRUGER, KENNETH CHARLES, retired architect; b. Santa Barbara, Calif., Aug. 19, 1930; s. Thomas Albin and Chleople (Gaines) K.; m. Patricia Kathryn Rasey, Aug. 21, 1955; children: David, Eric. B.Arch., U. So. Calif., 1953. Registered architect, cert. Calif. and Nat. Councils Archtl. Registration Bds. Pres. Kruger Bensen Ziemer, Santa Barbara, 1960-89; part-time instr. architecture dept. Calif. Poly., San Luis Obispo, 1993—; part-time architect, 1993—. Bd. dirs. Transition House, United Boys & Girls Club. Fellow AIA; mem. Archtl. Found. Santa Barbara (pres. 1987-89). Democrat. Unitarian. Home: 1255 Ferrelo Rd Santa Barbara CA 93103-2101

KRUGER, PAUL, nuclear civil engineering educator; b. Jersey City, June 7, 1925; s. Louis and Sarah (Jacobs) K.; m. Claudia Mathis, May 19, 1972; children: Sharon, Kenneth, Louis. BS, MIT, 1950; PhD, U. Chgo., 1954. Registered profl. engr., Pa. Rsch. physicist GM, Detroit, 1954-55; mgr. dept. chemistry Nuclear Sci. and Engring. Corp., Pitts., 1955-60; v.p.

Hazleton Nuclear Sci. Corp., Palo Alto, Calif., 1960-62; prof. civil engring. Stanford (Calif.) U., 1962-87, prof. emeritus, 1987—; cons. Elec. Power Rsch. Inst., Palo Alto, 1975—, Los Alamos (N.Mex.) Nat. Lab., 1985—. Author: Principles of Activation Analysis, 1973, Geothermal Energy, 1972. 1st lt. USAF, 1943-46, PTO. Recipient achievement cert. U.S. Energy R & D Adminstrn., 1975. Fellow Am. Nuclear Soc.; mem. ASCE (divsn. chmn. 1978-79). Home: 819 Allardice Way Stanford CA 94305-1050 Office: Stanford U Civil Engring Dept Stanford CA 94305

KRUGER, PAUL ROBERT, insurance broker; b. Ft. Dodge, Iowa, Nov. 16, 1957; s. Robert Wayne and Corinne Maxine (Wierson) K.; m. Lisa Diane Rouselle, June 9, 1990; children: Whitney Katherine, Austin Jacob and Garrett Jackson (twins). BSBA in Fin. and Mktg., Iowa State U., 1980. Claims rep. IMT Ins. Co., Des Moines, 1981-82; sales mgr. JCPenney Fin. Svcs., Plano, Tex., 1982-89, GranTree Furniture Rental, Aurora, Colo., 1989-90; sales rep. Sentry Ins., Denver, 1990—; with Preferred Risk Ins., Englewood, Colo., 1991—; ins. broker The Urman Co., Englewood, 1992—. Mem. Life Underwriting Tng. Coun., Boulder C. of C., Apt. Assn. Met. Denver (social com. 1989-90, amb. club 1989-90, trade show com. 1989-90), Boulder Jaycees (bd. dirs. 1983-84), Phi Kappa Tau (song leader 1979-80, pledge trainer 1977-78, asst. treas. 1978-79). Republican. Mem. Ch. of Nazarene. Home: 3350 Kassler Pl Westminster CO 80030-2747

KRUGER-HAMILTON, ERICA, interior designer, small business owner; b. Jersey City, Sept. 22, 1956; d. Lawrence and Alice Mae (Lee) Lai; m. Richard L. Hamilton, Mar. 31, 1995. Diploma, Interior Design Inst., Las Vegas. Design cons. J.C. Penney, Las Vegas, 1986-87; drapery cons. Design Ctr., Las Vegas, 1987-90; interior designer Fabrics West, Las Vegas, 1990, interior designer, owner Elite Designs by Erica, Las Vegas, 1991—. Home: 9404 Calico Garden Ave Las Vegas NV 89109 Office: Elite Designs by Erica 5410 S Cameron Ste 210 Las Vegas NV 89118

KRUGGEL, JOHN LOUIS, physician; b. Lake Mills, Iowa, Jan. 27, 1931; s. August and Elizabeth (Gleitz) K.; m. Kathleen Ann Lawson, June 1958 (div. 1972); children: Deborah, Natalie, Victoria, Pamela, Michae; m. Donna Marie Koerner, mar. 2, 1978; 1 child, Matthew. AS, Waldorf Coll., 1951; MD, U. Iowa, 1957. Diplomate Am. Bd. Plastic Surgery, Am. Bd. Surgery. Intern Mercy Hosp., San Diego; resident Orange Meml. Hosp., Orlando, Fla., Mercy Hosp., San Diego, U. Calif., San Francisco; pvt. practice in plastic surgery San Diego, 1966—. Capt. USAF, 1959-61. Mem. Am. Soc. Plastic and Reconstructive Surgery, Calif. Soc. Plastic and Reconstructive Surgery, Calif. Med. Soc., San Diego County Med. Soc. (del. to Calif. Med. Assn.). Office: 4060 4th Ave # 120 San Diego CA 92103-2116

KRUGMAN, PAUL ROBIN, economics educator; b. Albany, N.Y., Feb. 28, 1953; s. David Krugman and Anita Alman; m. Robin Leslie Bergman, Oct. 23, 1983. BA, Yale U., 1974; PhD, MIT, 1977. Asst. prof. Yale U., New Haven, Conn., 1977-80; assoc. prof. MIT, Cambridge, 1980-83, prof. econs., 1983—; research assoc. Nat. Bur. Econ. Research, Cambridge, 1979—; economist internat. policy U.S. Council Econ. Advisers, Washington, 1982-83; mem. bd. economists L.A. Times. Author: Exchange Rate Instability, 1988, Geography and Trade, 1991; co-author: Market Structure and Foreign Trade, 1985, Internat. Economics: Theory and Policy, 1988, Trade Policy and Market Structure, 1989, Rethinking International Trade, 1990, The Age of Diminished Expectations, 1990; co-author: Foreign Direst Investment in the United States, 1989; editor: Strategic Trade Policy and The New International Economics, 1986, Exchange Rate Targets and Currency Bonds, 1991. Fellow Econometric Soc.; mem. Group of Thirty. Home: 669 Mirada Ave Stanford CA 94305-8476 Office: MIT Dept Econs 77 Massachusetts Ave Cambridge MA 02139-4301

KRUGMAN, STANLEY LEE, international management consultant; b. N.Y.C., Mar. 2, 1925; s. Harry and Leah (Greenberg) K.; m. Helen Schorr, June 14, 1947; children: Vicky Lee, Thomas Paul; m. Carolyn Schambra, Sept. 17, 1966; children: David Andrew, Wendy Carol; m. Gail Jennings, Mar. 17, 1974. B Chem. Engring., Rensselaer Poly. Inst., 1947; postgrad., Poly. Inst. Bklyn., Columbia U., 1947-51. Process devel. engr. Merck & Co., Rahway, N.J., 1947-51; sr. process and project engr. C.F. Braun & Co., Alhambra, Calif., 1951-55; with Jacobs Engring. Co., Pasadena, Calif., 1955-76; from chief engr. to v.p. engring. and constrn. to v.p. gen. mgr. to exec. v.p. to pres., also dir.; exec. v.p., dir. Jacobs Engring. Group Inc., Pasadena, Calif., 1974-82; pres., dir. Jacobs Constructors of P.R., San Juan, 1970-82; pres. Jacobs Internat. Inc., 1971-82, Jacobs Internat. Ltd., Inc., Dublin, Ireland, 1974-82; dep. chmn. Jacobs LTA Engring., Ltd., Johannesburg, South Africa, 1981-82; pres. Krugman Assocs., Inc., 1982—; internat. mgmt. cons.; dir. Mediscan Tech., Inc. Served to lt. (j.g.) USNR, 1944-46, PTO. Mem. Am. Inst. Chem. Engrs., Am. Chem. Soc., Ireland-U.S. Council of Industry. Presbyterian. Home and Office: 24452 Portola Rd Carmel CA 93923-9327

KRULAK, VICTOR HAROLD, newspaper executive; b. Denver, Jan. 7, 1913; s. Morris and Besse M. (Ball) K.; m. Amy Chandler, June 1, 1936; children: Victor Harold Jr., William Morris, Charles Chandler. B.S., U.S. Naval Acad., 1934; LL.D., U. San Diego. Commd. 2d lt. USMC, 1934; advanced through grades to lt. gen.; service in China, at sea, with USMC (Fleet Marine Forces), 1935-39; staff officer, also bn. and regimental comdr., World War II; chief staff (1st Marine Div. Korea); formerly comdg. gen. (Marine Corps Recruit Depot), San Diego; formerly spl asst. to dir., joint staff counterinsurgency and spl. activities (Office Joint Chiefs Staff); comdg. gen. Fleet Marine Force Pacific, Pacific, 1964-68; ret., 1968; v.p. Copley Newspaper Corp., 1968-79; pres. Words Ltd. Corp., San Diego. Trustee Zool. Soc. San Diego. Decorated D.S.M., Navy Cross, Legion of Merit with 3 oak leaf clusters, Bronze Star, Air medal, Purple Heart (2) U.S.; Cross of Gallantry; Medal of Merit Vietnam; Distinguished Service medal (Korea), Order of Cloud and Banner, Republic of China. Mem. U.S. Naval Inst., U.S. Marine Corps Assn., Am. Soc. Newspaper Editors, InterAm. Press Assn., U.S. Strategic Inst. (vice chmn.). Home: 3665 Carleton St San Diego CA 92106-2163 Office: Words Ltd 3045 Rosecrans St San Diego CA 92110-4827

KRUMPE, PETER E., medical educator; b. Jamaica, N.Y., July 26, 1943; s. Edward George K.; m. Joane Krumpe, Nov. 24, 1990; children: Katherine, Kara, Stephanie, Stephen. BA, Vanderbilt U., 1965; MD, Emory U., 1969. Resident New Eng. Med. Ctr., Boston, 1969-71; fellow pulonoary medicine McGill U., Montreal, 1973-75; asst. assoc. prof. U. Calif., DEavis, 1975-91. Contbr. chpts. to books. Lt. comdr. USNR, 1973-75. Mem. Am. Heart Assn., Am. Lung Assn. Home: 3715 Brighton Way Reno NV 89509-6800 Office: Reno VA Med Ctr 1000 Locust St Reno NV 89520-0102

KRUPP, EDWIN CHARLES, astronomer; b. Chgo., Nov. 18, 1944; s. Edwin Frederick and Florence Ann (Olander) K.; m. Robin Suzanne Rector, Dec. 31, 1968; 1 son, Ethan Hembree. B.A., Pomona Coll., 1966; M.A., UCLA, 1968, Ph.D. (NDEA fellow, 1970-71), 1972. Astronomer Griffith Obs., Los Angeles Dept. Recreation and Parks, 1972—, dir., 1976—; mem. faculty El Camino Coll., U. So. Calif., extension divs. U. Calif.; cons. in ednl. TV Community Colls. Consortium; host teleseries Project: Universe. Author: Echoes of the Ancient Skies, 1983, The Comet and You, 1986 (Best Sci. Writing award Am. Inst. Physics 1986), The Big Dipper and You, 1989, Beyond the Blue Horizon, 1991, The Moon and You, 1993; editor, co-author: In Search of Ancient Astronomies, 1978 (Am. Inst. Physics-U.S. Steel Found. award for Best Sci. Writing 1978), Archaeoastronomy and the Roots of Science; editor-in-chief Griffith Obs., 1984—; contbg. editor Sky & Telescope, 1993—. Mem. Am. Astron. Soc. (past chmn. hist. astronomy div.), Astron. Soc. Pacific (past dir., recipient Klumpke-Roberts outstanding contbns. to the public understanding and appreciation of astronomy award 1989), Internat. Astron. Union, Explorers Club, Sigma Xi. Office: Griffith Observatory 2800 E Observatory Ave Los Angeles CA 90027-1255

KU, CECILIA CHOU YUAN, analytical chemist, researcher; b. Peking, China, Jan. 9, 1942; came to U.S., 1966; naturalized, 1974; d. Hsiao-Hsing and Chin-Chung (Shih) Yuan; m. James Chen Ku, June 3, 1967; children: Grace, Philip. BS, Nat. Taiwan Normal U., Taiwan, 1966; MS, Carnegie-Mellon U., 1968. Cert. tchr., Pa. Chemist U. Pitts., 1969-71, Research Triangle Inst., N.C., 1974-75; chemist, scientist Carnegie-Mellon U., Pitts., 1971-73; analytical chemist, quality control chemist, US Dept. Labor Occupational Safety and Health Adminstrn. Tech. Ctr., Salt Lake City, 1976—, cons., 1982—. Mem. Am. Indsl. Hygiene Assn. Mem. Evangelical Free Ch. Avocations: computers, statistical process control, cooking, piano. Office: US Dept Labor Occupational Safety & Health Adminstrn 1781 S 300 W PO Box 15200 Salt Lake City UT 84115

KU, TEH-LUNG, geological sciences educator; b. Shanghai, People's Republic of China, Aug. 30, 1937; came to U.S., 1961; s. Hou-Hsi and Hwei-Feng (Chang) Ku; m. Theresa S. Shen, June 13, 1970; children: Pamela T.M., Christina T.L., Joanna T.H. BSc, Nat. Taiwan U., Republic of China, 1959; PhD, Columbia U., 1966. Asst. scientist Woods Hole (Mass.) Oceanographic Inst., 1967-69; assoc. prof. geol. scis. U. So. Calif., L.A., 1969-75, prof. geol. scis., 1975—; Author (with others) books; contbr. articles to profl. jours. Fellow John Simon Guggenheim Meml. Found., 1983-84, Japan Soc. for the Promotion of Sci., 1991; Fulbright Sr. scholar, 1983-84. Office: U So Calif Dept Geol Scis Los Angeles CA 90089

KUBOTA, MIYOKO, artist; b. Kapaa, Hawaii, June 9, 1921; d. Kikuji and Suye (Tomosada) Shimizu; m. Toyoshi Kubota, July 20, 1942 (dec. 1988); children: Stephen T., Alan T., Louise T. Kubota Taniguchi. Cert., Wally Young Sch. Fine Arts, 1981; studied gyotaku with, Yoshihiko Takahashi, Japan, 1987; studied oils with, Ed Furuike, 1985. Presch. tchr., 1955-64; artist Honolulu Zoo Fence, 1981-84; resident artist Upstart Crow Book Store, Honolulu, 1986-87; coop. mem. South Shore Gallery, Honolulu, 1986-88, Ko'olau Gallery, Kaneohe, Hawaii, 1989—. Exhibited in solo shows Terr. Savs. and Loan, 1982, Ctrl. Pacific Bank, 1987; groups shows include Artists of Hawaii Exhbn., 1983, 85, Vox Populi Exhibit, 1984, Cherry Blossom Festival, 1984, Windward Artist Guild, 1984, ARC, 1985, Whale Expo, 1987, Hawaii Med. Assn., 1986, Koolau Gallery, Windward Mall Shows, 1990-94, Shirokiya Gyotaku Show, 1985, Hawaii Med. Assn., 1986; represented in various pvt. collections. Mem. Artist of Hawaii Assn., Hawaii Audubon Soc., Windward Artist Guild, Nature Printing Soc., Nat. Mus. Women in Arts (charter mem.). Baptist. Home: 44-281 Mikiola Dr Kaneohe HI 96744-2442

KUCERA, GREGORY MICHAEL, art dealer; b. Seattle, May 6, 1956; life ptnr. Larry W. Yocom, Feb. 14, 1985. BA in Art, U. Wash., 1980. Art dealer Greg Kucera Gallery, Seattle. Pres. Seattle (Wash.) Art Dealers Assn., 1990-92, 94-95. Democrat. Office: Greg Kucera Gallery 608 Second Ave Seattle WA 98104

KUCHEMAN, CLARK ARTHUR, religion educator; b. Akron, Ohio, Feb. 7, 1931; s. Merlin Carlyle and Lucile (Clark) K.; m. Melody Elaine Frazer, Nov. 15, 1986. BA, U. Akron, 1952; BD, Meadville Theol. Sch., 1955; MA in Econs., U. Chgo., 1959, PhD, 1965. Instr., then asst. prof. U. Chgo., 1961-67; prof. Claremont (Calif.) McKenna Coll., 1967—, Claremont Grad. Sch., 1967—. Co-author: Belief and Ethics, 1978, Creative Interchange, 1982, Economic Life, 1988; contbg. editor: The Life of Choice, 1978; contbr. articles to profl. jours. 1st lt. USAF, 1955-57. Mem. Am. Acad. Religion, Hegel Soc. Am., N.Am. Soc. for Social Philosophy. Democrat. Mem. United Ch. of Christ. Home: 10160 60th St Riverside CA 92509-4745 Office: Claremont McKenna Coll Dept Philosophy and Religion Pitzer Hall Claremont CA 91711

KUCIJ, TIMOTHY MICHAEL, engineer, composer, organist, pianist, conductor, minister, theologian; b. Whittier, Calif., Sept. 2, 1954; m. Paulina V. Jimenez, 1979. BA in Music, Calif. State Poly. U., Pomona, 1978; ThM cum laude, Christian Bible Coll., 1983; studies with Frank Sanucci, Dr. Edward D. Berryman, Thurla Wallis, Kathreen Prout, Eddy L. Manson, Henry Charles Smith, Dr. Joseph P. Free, Dr. Ronald Gearman, 1964-78; student, Sherwood Music Sch. of Chgo., 1965-68; postgrad., Cen. Bapt. Theol. Sem., Maranatha Bapt. Bible Coll. Lic. Bapt. minister, 1982. Tech. writer Honeywell Inc., West Covina (Calif.) and Mpls., 1977-84; hydromech. reliability engr. Advanced Systems div. Northrop Corp., Pico Rivera, Calif., 1984-86; sr. engr. quality and reliability Swedlow, Inc., Garden Grove, Calif., 1986-88, mgr., quality assurance, composites div., 1988-90, quality assurance staff specialist, 1990-92; div. quality assurance engr. Rexroth Corp. (Piston Pump Div.), Fountain Inn, S.C., 1992-94; pastor 1st Missionary Bapt. Ch., Gardena, Calif., 1994—; lectr. tech. and engring.; tchr. piano, organ and composition, 1971-81; active pulpit supply local Bapt. chs., So. Calif., S.C. Performer (pipe organ) Wiltern Theater, L.A., 1966-68, Busch-Reisinger Mus., Harvard U., Cambridge, Mass., 1972, 73, 74; composer over 40 piano compositions including Persistence and the Storm, Remembrance, Purity, Your Song, Yearning, Compassion, A Little Jingle, A Familiar Song, Images, Paulina, Afterthought, Blue Fragrance, Sunset, Then, Piano Lesson #1, Chase, Unrest, Nebulae, Distress, Retrograde, Frolic, The Happy Whistler, The Little Toy March, Hope, Teardrops, Reminisce, Wind Chimes, A Place Somewhere, Rainbows, The Bicentennial Rag, The Pulsar Rag, Dazzling Fingers, The Butterfly Rag, first 25 original pieces written in honor of Am. bicentennial; compositions (scores and recs.) housed in numerous libraries including L.A. Pub. Libr., Covina Pub. Libr., Calif. State Poly. U. Libr., Libr. of Congress, Smithsonian Instn. Collection of Recordings, Washington, Archive of Contemporary Music, N.Y.C., Whittier Pub. Libr, Greenville County Libr., Furman U. Libr., U. S.C. Libr., Calif. Baptist Coll. Libr., New York Pub. Libr., Cleve. Pub. Libr., Boston Pub. Libr., and numerous others; debut 1966, records for KRC Records 1993— including A Place Somewhere, 1995, LifeSongs, 1995; concertized nationally (piano, pipe organ); scored comprehensive piano arrangements Jesus Loves Me, Over the Rainbow; songwriter Jesus Is the Answer, O Jesus; contbr. numerous articles to newspapers and jours. Bd. dirs. Garden Grove Symphony Orch., 1989-90; asst. to pastors local Bapt. chs. in Tex., Ga., Wis., Minn. and Calif., 1978-82; pastor Victory Bapt. Ch., Pine City, Minn., 1982-83; music dir., Bible tchr. Calvary Bapt. Ch., LaVerne, Calif., 1988-92, mem. sch. bd., ch. coun., 1989-92; music dir., youth dir. Covina Bapt. Temple, 1985-87; pastor First Missionary Bapt. Ch., Gardena, Calif., 1994—. Named one of Outstanding Young Men in Am., U.S. Jaycees, 1980; recipient First prize So. Calif. Organ Competition, 1966, Performer's certificate, 1967, Disting. Alumnus award Calif. State Poly. U., 1989. Mem. Minn. Composer's Forum, Bible-Sci. Assn., Creation Rsch. Soc., Soc. Am. Quality Control, Majority Text Soc., Broadcast Music, Inc. Republican. Home: 1148 W 182nd St Gardena CA 90248-3320

KUCK, MARIE ELIZABETH BUKOVSKY, retired pharmacist; b. Milw., Aug. 3, 1910; d. Frank Joseph and Marie (Nozina) Bukovsky; Ph.C., U. Ill., 1933; m. John A. Kuck, Sept. 20, 1945 (div. Nov. 1954). Pharmacist, tchr. Am. Hosp., Chgo., 1936-38, St. Joseph Hosp., Chgo., 1938-40, Ill. Masonic Hosp., Chgo., 1940-45; chief pharmacist St. Vincent Hosp., Los Angeles, 1946-48, St. Joseph Hosp., Santa Fe, 1949-51; dir. pharm. services St. Luke's Hosp., San Francisco, 1951-76; pharmacist Mission Neighborhood Health Center, San Francisco, 1968-72; docent Calif. Acad. Sci., 1977—, DeYoung Mus., 1989—; mem. peer rev. com. Drug Utilization Com., Blue Shield Calif. and Pharm. Soc. San Francisco. Recipient Bowl of Hygeia award Calif. Pharm. Assn., 1966. Mem. No., Calif. (legis. chmn. aux. 1967-69, chmn. fund raising luncheon 1953-71, pres. San Francisco aux. 1974), Nat., Am., No. Calif. (pres. 1955-56, pres. San Francisco aux. 1965-66, editor ofcl. publ. 1967-70), San Francisco (sec. 1977-79, treas. 1979-80, pres. 1982-83; Pharmacist of Yr. award 1978) pharm. socs., Am. Pharm. Assn. (pres. No. Calif. br. 1956-57, nat. sec. women's aux. 1970-72, hon. pres. aux. 1975—), Calif. Council Hosp. Pharmacists (organizer 1962, sec.-treas. 1962-66), Am. Soc. Hosp. Pharmacists, Assn. Western Hosps. (gen. chmn. hosp. pharmacy sect. conv. San Francisco 1958), Internat. Pharmacy Congress (U.S. del. Brussels 1958, Copenhagen 1960), Fedn. Internationale Pharmaceutique, Lambda Kappa Sigma. Home: 2261 33rd Ave San Francisco CA 94116-1606

KUCZAJ, STAN ABRAHAM, II, comparative psychologist; b. Jersey Shore, Pa., Oct. 20, 1950; s. Stan A. and Rosalie Audrey (Frogge) K.; m. Maggie Kirkpatrick, July 16, 1991. BA in Psychology, U. Tex., 1972; PhD in Child Psychology, U. Minn., 1976. Asst. prof. Sch. Meth. U., Dallas, 1976-80, assoc. prof., chmn. psychology, 1982-86, prof., 1985-94; dir. Ctr. for Comparative Cognition, Santa Fe, N.Mex., 1994—; vis. prof. U. Minn., Mpls., 1980-81, U. Hawaii, Honolulu, 1989; vis. fellow Oxford (England) U., 1986; cons. NSF, 1976—, NIH, 1976—, Sea World, 1991—. Author: Crib Speech, 1983, Development of Word Meaning, 1985, Developmental Psychology, 1992, Ontogeny of Creativity, 1994; editorial bd. mem. Development Review, 1980—. Fellow Am. Psychol. Assn. (Boyd McCandless Young Scientist award 1980), Am. Psychol. Soc., Internat. Soc. for Study of Child Language (pres. exec. com.); mem. Psychonomic Soc., Soc. fo Marine Mammalogy, Animal Behavior Soc. Office: Ctr Comparative Cognition 211 Old Santa Fe Trl Santa Fe NM 87501-2160

KUDENOV, JERRY DAVID, zoology educator; b. Lynwood, Calif., Dec. 19, 1946; s. William and Marion Kudenov; m. Kathryn Anne Brown, May 30, 1969; children: Peter Alexander, Michael William. BA, U. Calif., San Diego, 1968; MS, U. Pacific, 1970; PhD, U. Ariz., 1974. Research scientist Ministry for Conservation, Melbourne, Australia, 1974-79; asst. prof. zoology U. Alaska, Anchorage, 1980-82, assoc. prof., 1982-86, prof., 1987—, chmn. dept. biol. sci., 1986-90; vis. asst. prof. U. So. Calif., Los Angeles, 1979-80. Mem. AAAS, Am. Soc. Zoologists, Sci. Research Soc. N. Am., Biol. Soc. Wash., So. Calif. Acad. Scis. (bd. dirs. 1980), Internat. Polychaete Assn. Home: 3930 Alitak Bay Cir Anchorage AK 99515-2366 Office: U Alaska Anchorage Dept Biol Scis 3211 Providence Dr Anchorage AK 99508-4614

KUDO, EMIKO IWASHITA, former state official; b. Kona, Hawaii, June 5, 1923; s. Tetsuzo and Kuma (Koga) Iwashita; BS, U. Hawaii, 1944; MS in Vocational Edn., Pa. State U., 1950; postgrad. U. Hawaii, U. Ore., others; m. Thomas Mitsugi Kudo, Aug. 21, 1951; children: Guy J.T., Scott K., Candace F. Tchr. jr. and sr. high sch., Hawaii, 1945-51; instr. home econs. edn. U. Hawaii Tchrs. Coll., Honolulu, 1948-51, Pa. State U., State College, 1949-50; with Hawaii Dept. Edn., Honolulu, 1951-82, supr. sch. lunch svc., 1951-64, home econ. edn., 1951-64, dir. home econ. edn., 1964-68, adminstr. vocat.-tech. edn., 1968-76, asst. supt. instructional svcs., 1976-78, dep. supt. State Dept. Edn., 1978-82; cons. Am. Samoa vocat. edn. state plan devel., 1970-71, vocat. edn. U. Hawaii, 1986, internat. secondary program devel. Ashiya Ednl. System, Japan, 1986-91, cons. to atty. gen. mental health svcs. for children and adolescents State of Hawaii, 1994, state coord. industry-labor-edn., 1972-76; mem. nat. task force edn. and tng. for minority bus. enterprise, 1972-73; steering com. Career Info. Ctr. Project, 1973-78; co-dir. Hawaii Career Devel. Continuum project, 1971-74; mem. Nat Accreditation and Instl. Eligibility Adv. Council, 1974-77, cons., 1977-78; mem. panel Internat. Conf. Vocat. Guidance, 1978, 80, 82, 86, 88; state commr. edn. commn. of the states, 1982-90; mem. Hawaii edn. coun., 1982-90; dir. Dept. Parks and Recreation, City and County of Honolulu, 1982-84; bd. dirs. Honolulu Neighborhood Housing Svcs., 1991—. Exec. bd. Aloha council Boy Scouts Am., 1978-88. Japan Found. Cultural grantee, 1977; Pa. State U. Alumni fellow, 1982; bd. trustees St. Louis High Sch., 1988—; mem. Gov.'s Commn. on Sesquicentennial Observance of Pub. Edn. In Hawaii, 1990-91; mem. Commn. State Rental Housing Trust Fund, 1992—; mem. steering com. Hawaii Long Term Care Coalition, 1992-94. Mem. Am. Assn. Retired Persons (mem. state legis. com. 1990-92), Pa. State U. Disting. Alumni, Western Assn. Schs. and Colls. (accreditation team mem. Ch. Coll. of Hawaii 1972-73), Am. Vocat. Assn., Hawaii Practical Arts and Vocat. Assn., NEA, Hawaii Edn. Assn. (trustee 1992—), Hawaii State Ednl. Officers Assn., Am., Hawaii home econ. assn., Nat., Hawaii assns. for supervision and curriculum devel., Am. Tech. Edn. Assn., Hawaii Recreation and Park Assn., Omicron Nu, Pi Lambda Theta, Phi Delta Kappa, Delta Kappa Gamma. Author handbooks and pamphlets in field. Home and Office: 217 Nenue St Honolulu HI 96821-1811

KUDRONOWICZ, JUANITA HELEN, occupational health nurse; b. Culdesac, Idaho, Feb. 19, 1935; d. Leonard Augustine and Christine Mae (Funnemark) Yochum; m. Ambrose Andrew Kudronowicz, June 11, 1955; children: Doloris, Kevin, Kathleen, Sharon, Ambrosine, Allen. AD, Lewis and Clark State Coll., 1969. Occupational health nurse Potlatch Corp., Lewiston, 1969, lead nurse, 1980—. Vol. ARC, Lewiston, 1989—. Mem. Emergency Dept. Nursing Assn. (publicity chmn. 1971-73), Nat. League Nursing, Idaho Nurses Assn. (sec. dist. 4, 1970-71), Occupational Health Nurses Assn., Women of Moose (Acad. of Friendship, Coll. of Regents, recorder). Roman Catholic. Home: 3129 7th St Lewiston ID 83501 Office: Potlatch Corp 805 Mill Rd Lewiston ID 83501-9710

KUEBLER, RICHARD ARTHUR, theatre educator, consultant; b. Lincoln, Nebr., July 31, 1947; s. Richard Arthur Sr. and Phyllis Darlene (Belka) K. BA, Wayne (Nebr.) State Coll., 1970; MFA, U. Nebr., 1980, postgrad., 1980-81. Dir., actor Nettlecreek Players, Inc., Hagerstown, Ind., summers 1975-76; dir. of theatre Kearney (Nebr.) Pub. Schs., 1971-78; dir., actor Kearney Pks. & Recreation, summers 1973-77; workshop and tour dir. U. Nebr., Lincoln, 1978-80, teaching asst., 1979-80; scenic supr. Doane Coll., Crete, Nebr., 1980-81; dir. theatre Northeastern Jr. Coll., Sterling, Colo., 1981—; state festival chmn., adjudicator Colo. Community Theatre Coalition, Sterling, 1989-90; regional adjudicator Am. Coll. Theatre Festival; state theatre chmn. Colo. Community Coll./Occupational Edn. System, Denver, 1988-89; drama chmn. Sterling Arts Coun., 1990—; mem. theatre grant rev. panel Colo. Coun. on the Arts and Humanities, 1990—, community theatre liaison to the organizational assistance program; U.S. rep. The Enniskillen (No. Ireland) Internat. Community Theatre Festival, 1990, The Dundalk (Republic Ireland) Internat. Amateur Theatre Festival, 1990; mem. community theatre liaison Alliance for Colo. Acts; mem. coll./univ. adv. panel to the Denver Ctr. Theatre Comp.; guest dir. U. Wyo., summer 1993. Dir. (play) Luann Hampton Laverty Oberlander, 1980 (Best Dir.), Vanities, 1989 (Best Dir. 1989), The Shadow Box, 1990 (Best Dir.). Pres. Prairie Players, Sterling, 1986-90; bd. dirs. Colo. Community Theatre Coalition, 1989-90, state ajudicator; bd. dirs. Sterling Arts Coun., 1988—; sponsor Northeastern Jr. Coll. Players, 1981-90. Recipient All State Co. Directing award Colo. Cmty. Theatre Coalition, 1995, Bd. Mem. of Yr. award, 1990, Higher Edn. Theatre Educator of Yr., Alliance of Colo. Theatre award, 1992; Formfit-Rogers scholar, 1965, Knights of Ak-Sar-Ben scholar. Mem. Am. Assn. Community Theatre (rep. region VII 1989-90). Home: 116 S 3rd Ave # 7 Sterling CO 80751-3616 Office: Northeastern Jr Coll ES French Hall Sterling CO 80751

KUECHLE, ROLAND KOERNER, architect; b. Columbus, Ohio, Aug. 4, 1916; s. Theodore Frederick and Josephine (Koerner) K.; m. Nayaulderson Webb, July 13, 1940; children: Richard Roland, Joel Frederick. BArch, Ohio State U., 1940. Registered architect, Ohio, Calif. Assoc. engr. Appalachian Electric Power Co., Huntington, W.Va., 1939-41; architectural draftsman Ohio State U. Architect, Columbus, 1941, Basic magnesium, Inc., Henderson, Nev., 1941-43, Corlet & Anderson, Ponsford & Price, Oakland, Calif., 1943-45; assoc. architect Confer & Willis, Oakland, 1945-55; architect Rosner Engring., Inc., San Francisco, 1955-58, Roland K. Kuechle, Architect, Oakland, 1950-61; engr./architect Lawrence Livermore (Calif.) Nat. Labs., 1961-85, engr./architect indeterminate, 1985—. Photographer (recipient Photo/Travel Slide of Yr. award No. Calif. Coun. of Camera Clubs 1982); architectural designer residence (Hon. mention Rich's Progressive Architecture Mag. competition 1946), naval supply depot (Meritorious Civilian Svc. medal 1945). Recipient sch. medal AIA, Ohio State U., 1940. Mem. East Bay Assn. Architects (treas. 1946-52), Rossmoor Camera Club (pres. 1987-88, numerous awards), No. Calif. Coun. of Camera Clubs (assoc., rep. 1991-93). Republican. Presbyterian. Home: 3100 Rossmoor Pky Apt 2 Walnut Creek CA 94595-3327

KUEHN, JODEE STAHLECKER, information technology consultant; b. Thornton, Colo., Aug. 25, 1966; d. Robert James Stahlecker; m. Carl Kuehn, Aug. 13, 1994. BS, U. Denver, 1988; MBA, U. Ariz., 1993. Tech. trainer Info. Found., Denver, 1988-90, programmer/analyst, 1990-91; bus. systems cons. Am. Mgmt. Systems, Inc., Lakewood, Colo., 1993—. Big sister Big Sisters Colo., Denver, 1989-91; nursing hostess vol. Humana Mountain View Hosp., Thornton, 1989-90. Hornbeck scholar U. Denver, 1984-85. Mem. Golden Key, Pi Mu Epsilon. Office: Am Mgmt Systems 66 S Van Gordon St Lakewood CO 80228-1705

KUEHN, KLAUS KARL ALBERT, ophthalmologist; b. Breslau, Germany, Apr. 1, 1938; came to U.S., 1956, naturalized, 1971; s. Max and Anneliese (Hecht) K.; m. Eileen L. Nordgaard, June 22, 1961 (div. 1972); children—Stephan Eric, Kristina Annette; m. Lynda O. Hubbs, Oct. 2, 1974. Student, St. Olaf Coll., 1956-57; B.A., B.S., U. Minn., 1961; M.D., 1963. Diplomate Am. Bd. Ophthalmology. Resident in ophthalmology UCLA Affiliated Hosps., 1968-71; practice medicine specializing in ophthalmology, San Bernardino, Calif., 1971—; chief ophthalmology dept. San Bernardino County Med. Ctr., 1979-80; assoc. clin. prof. ophthalmology Jules Stein Eye Inst. and UCLA Med. Ctr., 1978-81. Served to capt. U.S. Army, 1963-64. Fellow Am. Acad. Ophthalmology; mem. AMA, Calif. Med. Assn., Calif.

Assn. Ophthalmology (bd. dirs.). Office: 902 E Highland Ave San Bernardino CA 92404-4007

KUEST, MARILYN SIBYL, school nurse; b. Seattle, Feb. 24, 1938; d. Richard Austin and Bernadette (McMahon) Smith; m. Harold LeRoy Kuest, Oct. 1, 1960; children: Carole Kiele, Kristi Drake, Coleen Arndt, Karen, Cathie, Kelly. BSN, Seattle U., 1960; M Edn. Guidance and Counseling, City U., Bellevue, Wash., 1993. RN, Wash. Nurse delivery rm. Providence Hosp., Seattle, 1960; pub. health nurse Seattle-King County Health Dept., 1960-61; sch. nurse Sequim (Wash.) Sch. Dist., 1980—; mem. sch. nurse adv. bd. Wash. State Bd. Edn., 1995—. Active High Priority Infant Tracking, Child Devel. Screening, Adolescent Access to Health Care, AIDS task force Clallam County, Wash., Teenage Pregnancy Prevention Coalition, Clallam County Interagy. Coord. Coun. Bd., cmty. clubs and orgns.; instr. First Aid-CPR, 1976—; bd. dirs. Umbrella Svcs., United Way; com. chair United Way; eucharistic min., lector, parish coun., v.p. Altar Soc. v.p. and treas., Guild chair, stewardship com. chair St. Joseph's Ch. Mem. Nat. Assn. Sch. Nurses (cert.), Sch. Nurse Orgn. Wash. (v.p. 1988-89, chmn. scholarship com., adv. bd. profl. edn. Pacific Luth. U. 1989-94, mem. legis. com. 1989—, alt. area III rep. 1990, area III rep. 1993—, Sch. Nurse of Yr. award 1992), Am. Sch. Health Assn., Sch. Health Assn. Wash., Ft. Worden Alumni Assn., Delta Kappa Gamma (co-v.p., program chmn. Beta Nu chpt. 1994-96). Roman Catholic. Home: 1079 Finn Hall Rd Port Angeles WA 98362-8115 Office: Sequim Sch Dist 503 N Sequim Ave Sequim WA 98382-3161

KUGA, MARK WAYNE, economist; b. Renton, Wash., Oct. 5, 1959; s. Henry S. and O. Lavonne (Ninnemann) K.; m. Nanette K. Starr, Apr. 27, 1990. BA in Econs., U. Wash., 1982; MA, UCLA, 1984, PhD, 1989. Econ. Lexecon, Inc., Chgo., 1987-89; sr. econ. Econ. Analysis Corp., L.A., 1989-93; prin. Willamette Mgmt. Assocs., Portland, Oreg., 1993—; adj. instr. Portland State U., 1993—. Rsch. fellow Alfred P. Sloan Found., 1984-87. Mem. Am. Econ. Assn., Am. Acad. Econ. and Fin. Experts, Am. Arbitration Assn. (nat. panel of comml. arbitrators), Nat. Assn. Bus. Econs., Nat. Assn. Forensic Econs. Office: Willamette Mgmt Assocs 111 SW 5th Ave Ste 2150 Portland OR 97204-3624

KUH, ERNEST SHIU-JEN, electrical engineering educator; b. Peking, China, Oct. 2, 1928; came to U.S., 1948, naturalized, 1960; s. Zone Shung and Tsia (Chu) K.; m. Bettine Chow, Aug. 4, 1957; children: Anthony, Theodore. BS, U. Mich., 1949; MS, MIT, 1950; PhD, Stanford U., 1952. Mem. tech. staff Bell Tel. Labs., Murray Hill, N.J., 1952-56; assoc. prof. elec. engring. U. Calif., Berkeley, 1956-62, prof., 1962—, Miller rsch. prof., 1965-66, William S. Floyd Jr. prof. engring., 1990-92, William S. Floyd Jr. prof. engring. emeritus, 1993—, chmn. dept. elec. engring. and computer sci., 1968-72, dean Coll. Engring., 1973-80; cons. IBM Research Lab., San Jose, Calif., 1957-62, NSF, 1975-84; mem. panel Nat. Bur. Standards, 1975-80; vis. com. Gen. Motors Inst., 1975-79, dept. elec. engring. and computer scis. MIT, 1986-91; mem. adv. council elec. engring. dept. Princeton (N.J.) U., 1986—; mem. bd. councilors sch. engring. U. So. Calif., 1986-91; mem. sci. adv. bd. Mills Coll., 1976-80. Co-author: Principles of Circuit Synthesis, 1959, Basic Circuit Theory, 1967, Theory of Linear Active Network, 1967; Linear and Nonlinear Circuits, 1987. Recipient Alexander von Humboldt award, 1980, Lamme medal Am. Soc. Endring. Edn., 1981, U. Mich. Disting. Alumnus award, 1970, Berkeley citation, 1993; Brit. Soc. Engring. and Rsch. fellow, 1982. Fellow IEEE (Edn. medal 1981, Centenial medal 1984, Circuits and Systems Soc. award. 1988), AAAS; mem. Nat. Acad. Engring., Academia Sinica, Sigma Xi, Phi Kappa Phi. Office: U Calif Elec Engring and Computer Sci Depts Berkeley CA 94720

KUHL, RONALD WEBSTER, marketing executive; b. Chgo., Dec. 12, 1938; s. Robert Emerson and Kathleen (Webster) K.; m. Mary Walls, Sept. 28, 1968; children: David Douglas, Kevin Lathrop. BS in Econs., U. Pa., 1960; MBA, Harvard U., 1964. Account exec. Young & Rubicam Advt., N.Y.C., 1964-71; v.p. mgmt. supr. Young & Rubicam Advt., San Francisco, 1988-90; mgr. promotion and design The First Ch. of Christ Scientist, Boston, 1971-75; account exec. BBDO Advt., San Francisco, 1975-77; acct. supr. Ketchum Communications, San Francisco, 1977-80; dir. mktg. ComputerLand Corp., Hayward, Calif., 1985-88; v.p. mktg. communications Ventura Software Inc., San Diego, 1990-92; v.p. mktg. Castelle, Santa Clara, Calif., 1992-94; v.p. advt. and mktg. svcs. Interactive Video Enterprises, San Ramon, Calif., 1994—. 1st lt. U.S. Army, 1960-62. Office: Interactive Video Enterprises #210 3000 Executive Pkwy San Ramon CA 94583

KUHL, WAYNE ELLIOTT, physician; b. Des Moines, Mar. 8, 1947; s. Leonard Peter and Florence Agnes Kuhl; m. Judith A. Kuhl, Aug. 3, 1968; children; Jason, Aaron, Brian. BS, Loras Coll., 1969; MD, U. Iowa, 1972. Staff emergency physician St. Joseph Hosp. & Med. Ctr., Phoenix, 1972-73; fellow in internal medicine Mayo Clinic, Rochester, Minn., 1974-77; physician in internal medicine Phoenix Med. Assocs., Ltd., 1977—; pres. Mamakai Med. Asscs., Phoenix, 1989; team physician Phoenix Cardinal NFL Football Team, 1990—. Fellow ACP; mem. AMA, Am. Soc. Internal Medicine, Nat. Football League Physicians Soc., Paradise Valley C. of C. (bd. dirs. 1989—), Thunderbirds (bd. dirs. Phoenix chpt. 1982—). Republican. Roman Catholic. Office: Physicians Med Assocs Ltd 3600 N 3rd Ave Phoenix AZ 85013-3904 Home: 3501 E Rose Ln Paradise Vly AZ 85253-3735

KUHLMAN, ERIKA ANN, historian, educator; b. Billings, Mont., Jan. 4, 1961; d. Paul Theodore and Dolores (Geiss) K. BA, U. Mont., 1983, MA, 1987; postgrad., Washington State U., 1994—. Historical cons. State History Preservation Office, Helena, Mont., 1988-89; humanities instr. U. Mont., Missoula, 1989-91; Am. hist., culture prof. Washington State U., Pullman, Wash., 1991—; book discussing group leader Mont. Com. for the Humanities, 1990-91; conf. presenter; book reviewer Choice Mag., Hartford, Conn., 1990-94. Contbr. articles to profl. jours. Canvasser Mont. Dem. Party, Missoula, 1980s; cons. Mont. Pub. Interest Rsch. Group, Missoula, 1980s. Recipient Hist. grant Nat. Endowment for the Humanities, 1989-90, grant Washington State U., 1994. Mem. Phi Alpha Theta. Home: 1615 SE Bleasner Dr Apt 63 Pullman WA 99163-5426 Office: Washington State U History Dept Pullman WA 99164-4030

KUHLMAN, GLORIA JEAN, mental health and geriatric nurse, educator; b. Wichita, Nov. 9, 1949; d. Virgil D. and Gladys (Plett) Coleman; m. Thomas A. Kuhlman, Sept. 12, 1969; 1 child, Jeffrey Paul. Diploma, St. Francis Sch. Nursing, Wichita, 1974; BSN, Wichita State U., 1976, MN, 1979; D. in Nursing Sci., U. Calif., San Francisco, 1992. Cert. community coll. instr. Prof., clin. coord. Ohlone Coll., Fremont, Calif., 1979—. Mem. NLN, Alzheimers Disease Assn., Am. Soc. on Aging, Gerontol. Soc. Am., Calif. Coun. on Gerontology and Geriatrics, Nat. Coun. on Aging. Home: 674 Giraudo Dr San Jose CA 95111-2680 : Ohlone Coll 43600 Mission Blvd Fremont CA 94539

KUHLMAN, WALTER EGEL, artist, educator; b. St. Paul, Nov. 16, 1918; s. Peter and Marie (Jensen) K.; m. Nora McCants; 1 son, Christopher; m. Tulip Chestman, April 9, 1979. Student, St. Paul Sch. Art, 1936-40; BS, U. Minn., 1941; postgrad., Tulane U., Academiè de la Grand Chaumierè, Paris, Calif. Sch. Fine Arts. mem. faculty U. Calif. Sch. Fine Arts, Stanford, U. Mich., Santa Clara (Calif.) U., U. N.Mex., Sonoma State U., Rohnert Park, Calif., (prof. emeritus, 1988—). One person shows include U. N.Mex., Walker Art Center, Mpls., The Berkshire Museum, Mass., La Jolla Museum of Contemporary Art, Calif., Santa Barbara Mus. of Art, Calif., San Francisco Mus. of Modern Art, New Arts Gallery, Houston, 1959-61, Roswell Mus. Palace of Legion of Honor, 1956, 59, 61, 62, 64, San Francisco Mus. Art, "20-yr. Retrospective" De Saisset Mus., Jonson Gallery U. N.Mex., 1963, 64, 65, Charles Campbell Gallery, San Francisco, 1981, 83, 85, Djurovich Gallery, Sacramento, The Carlson Gallery, San Francisco, Kuhlman: Historic Survey Bay Area Abstract Expressionists, 1945-60, 1989, Gump's Gallery, San Francisco, 1976, 1992, University Gallery, Sonoma State U., "40 year Retrospective, Natsoulis Gallery Davis, Calif. "Kuhlman: Abstract Expressionist Works", Albuquerque, Mus.Fine Arts; group shows include N.Y. World's Fair, St. Paul Gallery "WPA Exhibition", (Walter Kuhlman/Cameron Booth), Lawson Galleries, San Francisco, "A 1948 Portfolio: 16 Lithographs (Diebenkorn, Lobdell, Hultberg), All Annual Invitational Exhibitions, San Francisco Mus. Modern Art, 1948-58, Petit Palais Mus., Paris, "Salon Des Realities Nouvelles", San Francisco Mus. Modern Art, "Art in the 20th Century", III Biennial of Sao Paulo, Museo de Arte Moderna, Brazil, L.A. County Mus., Mus. Modern Art, Rio de Janiero, San Francisco Mus. Modern Art, Graham Found., Chgo, "Pacific Coast Biennial", L.A. County Mus., Calif. Palace of the Legion of Honor, Santa Barbara Mus., The Contemporary Art Mus., Houston, Virginia Mus. Fine Arts, Richmond, "American Painting", Stanford U., Gallery, "Selective Survey of Recent Western Painting," Roswell Mus., 1961-62, Univ. Art Mus., Austin, Texas "Recent American Painting", Santa Fe Mus. Fine Arts, NM, Ca. Palace of Legion of Honor, "Painters Behind Painters", Richard L. Nelson Gallery, UC Davis, "A Survey of Three Decades", Natsoulis Gallery, "Northern Calif. Figuration" Expositions Art USA, 1992, 93, 94, George Krevsky Fine Art, San Francisco Art Mus. Santa Cruz, Calif. "Paper Tracings", 93, Pasquale Ianetti Art Galleries, San Francisco, "Four Centuries of Master Works", 1994, Robert Green Fine Art, "Kuhlman, Diebenkorn, Francis, McDonald", Ross, Calif. 1994, 95, Acad. Arts and Letters, N.Y. 1995, "Abstract Expressionism," The San Francisco Sch.; permanent Collections include: The Phillips Collection" D.C., Nat. Gallery Am. Art, D.C., San Francisco Mus. Modern Art, British Mus., Met. Mus. Art, Nat. Acad. Design, Papers in the Archives of Am. Art, Smithsonian. Recipient Maestro award Calif. Arts Coun., Outstanding Calif. Working Artist and Tchr. award; fellow Tiffany Found., Graham Found., Cummington Found. Mem. Nat. Acad. Design. Studio: Industrial Center Bldg Gate 5 Rd Sausalito CA 94965

KUHN, DONALD MARSHALL, marketing professional; b. Miami, Fla., Nov. 2, 1922; s. Paul Carlton Kuhn and Helen (Merrick) Bond; m. Jane Emma Williams, Dec. 24, 1948 (dec. 1988); children: Marshall Merrick, Richard Williams, Diane Joan, Paul Willard; m. Kay Bardsley, Feb. 25, 1990. BA in Journalism and Drama, U. Miami, 1949. Cert. fundraising executive. Advt. copywriter Sears Roebuck and Co., Chgo., 1949-50; dir. pub. relations Tb Inst. Chgo. and Cook County, 1950-54; dir. fundraising Dade County Tb Assn., Miami, 1955-59, Minn. Tb and Health Assn., St. Paul, 1959-60, Mich. Lung Assn., Lansing, 1960-68, Am. Lung Assn., N.Y.C., 1968-78; nat. founder, dir. regional fin. program Rep. Nat. Com., Washington, 1978-79; exec. v.p., dir. fundraising div. Walter Karl, Inc., Armonk, N.Y., 1979-90, cons., 1990-93; cons. May Devel. Svcs., Greenwich, Conn., 1993—; mem. direct mktg. task force Am. Red Cross, Washington, 1983-84; mem. direct mail task force Am. Heart Assn., Dallas, 1982. Editor: Non-profit Council Info. Exchange, 1987-90; contbr. articles to Fundraising Mgmt. Mag. Bd. dirs. Isadora Duncan Internat. Inst., N.Y.C., 1987—. Mem. Nat. Soc. Fundraising Execs. (bd. dirs. 1978-80), Direct Mktg. Assn. (mem. operating com., non-profit coun. 1987-90, recipient non-profit coun. fundraising achievement award 1991). Republican. Congregational. Home and Office: 6305 S Geneva Cir Englewood CO 80111-5437

KUHN, JANE ELIZABETH, nursing administrator; b. Pitts., Oct. 10, 1948; d. William James and Mary Louise (Mongell) K. Diploma in nursing, St. Joseph's Hosp., Pitts., 1969; BSN, Calif. State U., Dominguez Hills, 1992; MSN, U. San Francisco, 1994. Cert. oper. rm. nurse. Staff nurse Montefiore Hosp., Pitts., 1969-71, Mt. Sinai Med. Ctr., Miami Beach, Fla., 1971-72; pvt. duty nurse Catalano's Nurse Registry, Miami, Fla., 1972-74; staff nurse oper. rm. Mercy Hosp., Miami, 1974-76; adminstr. oper. rm. U. Calif., San Francisco, 1977-86; splty. supr. oper. rm. Children's Hosp. San Francisco, 1986-88; adminstrv. supr. French Hosp., San Francisco, 1988-90; nurse educator oper. rm. Kaiser Med. Ctr., Oakland, Calif., 1990-92; dept. mgr. perioperative svcs. Kaiser Med. Ctr., San Francisco, 1992-94; adminstrv. supr. St. Luke's Hosp., San Francisco, Fla., 1994—, San Francisco, 1995—; bd. dirs. Nat. Cert. Bd. Perioperative Nursing, Denver, 1990-93; cons. Higman Healthcare, 1994. Active local polit. campaigns. Mem. Assn. Oper. Rm. Nurses (nominating com. 1991-92, chmn. nominating com. 1992-93, chmn. spl. com. on HIV 1992-93), Oper. Rm. Nursing Coun. Calif. (sec. 1988-90, chmn. 1990-92), Golden Gate Nurses Assn. (chair govt. rels. com. 1990), Calif. Nurses Assn. (legis. liaison 1992-93). Democrat. Home: 1340 20th Ave Apt 4 San Francisco CA 94122-1752 Office: Saint Luke's Hosp 3555 Cesar Chavez St San Francisco CA 94110

KUHN, JOHN ALAN, gas products plant executive; b. Evanston, Ill., Sept. 9, 1963; s. Wayne Allen and Enid Grant (Robertson) K. BS in Engring., Colo. Sch. Mines, 1988; MBA, Pepperdine U., 1995. Field engr. Schlumberger Internat., Cairo, 1989; systems engr. EDS/GM, Fairfax, Kans., 1989-91; prodn. supr. Lever Bros. Co., Commerce, Calif., 1991-93; plant mgr. Matheson Gas Products, Cucamonga, Calif., 1993—. Mem. ASME. Home: 4317 E Vermont St Long Beach CA 90814-2949

KUHN, ROBERT LAWRENCE, investment banker, corporate financier, strategist, author, educator; b. N.Y.C., Nov. 6, 1944; s. Louis and Lee (Kahn) K.; m. Dora Elana Serviarian, June 23, 1967; children: Aaron, Adam, Daniella. AB in Human Biology, Johns Hopkins U., 1964; PhD in Brain Sci., UCLA, 1968; MS in Mgmt., MIT, 1980. Investment banker, fin adv. representing various firms, N.Y.C., L.A., Beijing, Tokyo, 1980—; cons. corp. strategy and fin., N.Y.C., L.A., Beijing, Tokyo, 1980—; pres. The Geneva Cos., Irvine, Calif, 1991—; adj. prof. Grad. Sch. Bus. Adminstrn., NYU, 1981-89; exec.-in-residence U. So. Calif., 1990; bd. advisors, U. So. Calif. Sch. Bus., 1992—; internat. adviser in fin. and high tech. to govts. U.S., Israel, Fed. Republic Germany, China, 1984—; vice chmn. bd. dirs. Data Software and Systems; bd. dirs. Tower Semiconductor, N.Y.C.; cons. and lectr. in field. Author: Mid-Sized Firms: Success Strategies and Methodology, 1982, Creativity and Strategy in Mid-Sized Firms, 1988, (with George Geis) The Firm Bond: Linking Meaning and Mission in Business and Religion, 1984, Micromanaging: Transforming Business Leaders with Personal Computers, 1987, To Flourish Among Giants: Creative Management for Mid-Sized Firms, 1985 (Japanese translation, 1986, Macmillan Book Club main selection), (with Arie Lavie) Industrial Research and Development in Israel, 1986, Dealmaker: All the Negotiating Skills and Secrets You Need, 1988, Investment Banking: The Art and Science of High-Stakes Dealmaking, 1989, Japanese translation, 1990, Chinese translation, 1995, (with Don Gamache) The Creativity Infusion, 1989; editor: Commercializing Defense-Related Technology, 1984; (with Raymond Smilor) Corporate Creativity: Robust Companies and the Entrepreneurial Spirit, 1984; (with Margaret Maxey) Regulatory Reform: Private Enterprise and Risk Assessment, 1985; (with Eugene Konecci) Technology Venturing: American Innovation and Risk Taking, 1985; (with Raymond Smilor) Managing Take-Off in Fast Growth Companies, 1985; Frontiers in Creative and Innovative Management, 1985; (with Yuji Ijiri) New Directions in Creative and Innovative Management, 1988; Medical Information Sciences, 1988; Commercializing Strategic Defense Technologies, 1986, Commercializing SDI Technologies (with Stewart Nozette, 1987). Editor-in-chief: Handbook for Creative and Innovative Managers, 1987, Libr. of Investment Banking, 7 vols., 1990; contbg. editor, columnist Jour. Bus. Strategy, 1984—. Sloan fellow MIT, Cambridge, 1979; sr. research fellow in creative and innovative mgmt. IC2 Inst., U. Tex., Austin, 1983—. Mem. Phi Beta Kappa. Avocations: weight-lifting, table tennis, chess, classical music. Office: The Geneva Coms 5 Park Plaza Irvine CA 92714

KUHNER, ARLENE ELIZABETH, English language educator, reviewer, academic administrator; b. Victoria, B.C., Can., May 1, 1939; d. Theodore Foort and Gladys Virginia (Evans) Huggins; m. Robert Henry Kuhner, Dec. 17, 1971; children: Mary Kathleen, Gwynne Elizabeth, Benjamin David. BA in English, Seattle U., 1960; postgrad., U. Calif., Berkeley, 1960-61; MA in English, U. Wash., 1966, PhD in English, 1978. Editor English dept. U. Wash., Seattle, 1964-66; instr. Seattle U., 1966-69, asst. prof., 1969-71; mem. adj. faculty Anchorage Community Coll., 1971-81, tchr., 1981-87; assoc. prof. U. Alaska, Anchorage, 1987-90, chair women's studies dept., 1989-93, prof., chair English dept., 1990-93, assoc. dean for acad. program & curriculum, prof. English, 1993—. Contbr. numerous papers to profl. confs. Contbg. mem. Oreg. Shakespeare Festival; nat. assoc. Folger Shakespeare Libr., Washington, 1987—; ptnr. in conscience Amnesty Internat., 1985—; bd. dirs. Tudor Community Sch., Anchorage, 1975-77. Woodrow Wilson Found. fellow, 1960; Western State Project grantee, 1986, 87, various others. Mem. MLA, Women's Caucus for Modern Langs., Nat. Coun. Tchrs. of English, Renaissance Soc. Am., Nat. Women's Studies Assn., N.W. Women's Studies Assn., Philos. Assn. of the Pacific Coast, Assn. for Can. Studies in U.S., Marlowe Soc. Am., Margaret Atwood Soc., Phi Kappa Phi. Democrat. Roman Catholic. Office: U Alaska Coll Arts and Scis 3211 Providence Dr Anchorage AK 99508-4614

KUHNS, CRAIG SHAFFER, business educator; b. Spokane, Wash., Apr. 14, 1928; s. Theodore Lewis and Audrey Grace (Shaffer) K. BS, U. Calif., Berkeley, 1950, BA, 1954, MBA, 1955. Analyst Standard Oil Co. of Calif., San Francisco, 1955-57; bus. educator U. Calif./San Jose State U., 1958-63, City Coll. of San Francisco, 1963—; exec. mng. dir. Blumentec Corp., USA, San Francisco, 1989—; adj. faculty U. San Francisco, 1977-90; bd. dirs. Blumentec Corp. USA. 1st lt. U.S. Army, 1951-52, col. Mil. Intelligence USAR, 1953-80, col. AUS, ret. Mem. Calif. Alumni Assn., U.S. Army War Coll. Alumni Assn., Res. Officers Assn,. Japan Soc. Republican. Home: 8 Locksley Ave Apt 8A San Francisco CA 94122-3850 Office: City Coll of San Francisco 50 Phelan Ave San Francisco CA 94112-1821

KUIVINEN, NED ALLAN, pathologist; b. Mt. Vernon, Ohio, May 19, 1936; s. Thomas Oscar and Pauline Ruthella (Pealer) K.; m. Deborah Berle Miller, Feb. 5, 1972; children: David Joseph, Matthew Thomas. BS, Ohio State U., 1958, MD, 1962. Diplomate Am. Bd. Pathology. Pathologist St. Joseph's Hosp., Phoenix, 1969—; dir. clin. lab. W. O. Boswell Meml. Hosp., Sun City, Ariz., 1970—; pathologist D. E. Webb Meml. Hosp., Sun City, Ariz., 1988—; dir. clin. lab. Vencor Hosp. Phoenix, Youngtown, Ariz., 1990-92. Lt. comdr. U.S. Navy, 1966-68. Fellow Am. Soc. Clin. Pathology, Coll. Am. Pathology; mem. Ariz. Med. Assn., Ariz. Soc. Pathologists (pres. 1993-95). Home: 5835 N 2nd Ave Phoenix AZ 85013-1535 Office: Pathology Assocs Ltd 555 W Catalina Dr Ste 12 Phoenix AZ 85013-4413

KUKLIN, JEFFREY PETER, lawyer, talent agency executive; b. N.Y.C., Dec. 13, 1935; s. Norman Bennett and Deane (Cable) K.; m. Jensina Olson, Nov. 18, 1960; 1 son, Andrew Bennett; m. 2d, Ronia Levene, June 22, 1969; children—Adam Blake, Jensena Lynne, Jeremy Brett. AB, Columbia U., 1957, JD, 1960. Bar: N.Y. 1962, U.S. Supreme Ct. 1965, Calif. 1973. Atty., TV sales adminstrn. NBC-TV, N.Y.C., 1966-67; asst. to dir. bus. affairs CBS News, N.Y.C., 1967-69; atty., assoc. dir. contracts ABC-TV, N.Y.C. and Los Angeles, 1969-73; v.p. bus. affairs and law Tomorrow Entertainment, Inc., Los Angeles, 1973-75; v.p. legal and bus. affairs Billy Jack Enterprises, Inc., Los Angeles, 1975-76; atty., bus. affairs exec. William Morris Agy., Inc., Beverly Hills, Calif., 1976-79, head TV bus. affairs, 1979-93, v.p., 1981—. Mem. ABA, Acad. TV Arts and Scis., Los Angeles Copyright Soc. Office: 5465 White Oak Ave Van Nuys CA 91316

KULATILAKE, PINNADUWA H.S.W., mining and geological engineering educator; b. Colombo, Sri Lanka, Sept. 21, 1953; came to U.S., 1978; s. Samee De Silva and Koruwage Theadora (Wijewardane) K.; m. Thili Nayana Chandradasa Kulatilake; 1 child, Roy Sheyhan Kulatilake. BS in Civil Engring. with honors, U. Sri Lanka, Peradeniya, Sri Lanka, 1976; MEng in Soil Engring., Asian Inst. of Techol., Bangkok, Thailand, 1978; PhD in Civil Engring., Ohio State U., 1981. Registered Civil Engr., Calif. Chief instr. in geotechnical lab. U. Sri Lanka, Peradeniya, Sri Lanka, 1976; grad. scholar, teaching assoc. Geotechnical Engring. Dept. of Civil Engring. U. Calgary, Calgary, Alberta, Can., 1978; grad. rsch. assoc. Geotechnical Engring. Dept. of Civil Engring. Ohio State U., Columbus, 1978-81, sr. rsch. assoc., 1981; grad. teaching assoc. mathematics Dept. of Mathematics Ohio State U., Columbus, 1980-81; asst. prof. Geotechnical Engring. Dept. of Mining and Geological Engring. U. Ariz., Tucson, 1981-88, assoc. prof., 1988—; vis. rsch. fellow Norwegian Geotechnical Inst., 1988; vis. rsch. prof. Lulea U. of Technol., 1988-89, 1990; civil engr. Dept. of Nat. Housing, Colombo, Sri Lanka, U.N. Gunasekara & Co., Sri Lanka, Water Supply & Drainage Bd., Sri Lanka. Reviewer 6 jours.; contbr. articles to profl. jours.; invited speaker in field. Exxon Ednl. Fdn. awards, 1982-85. Mem. ASCE (mem. geotechnical safety and reliability com., EMD divsn. properties of materials com.), Am. Soc. for Testing and Materials (head com. stability, erosion control & damage mitigation of mine slopes geotech. divsn.), Am. Soc. of Mining Engrs., Internat. Assn. for Civil Engring. Reliability and Risk Analysis, Internat. Assn. for Computer Methods and Advances in Geomechanics, Internat. Soc. for Soil Mechanics and Fdn. Engring., Internat. Soc. for Rock Mechanics, Internat. Assn. for Mathematical Geology, Phi Kappa Phi. Home: 5277 W Peridot St Tucson AZ 85742 Office: U Ariz Dept Mining & Geological Engring Tucson AZ 85721

KULBIN, VELLO, publisher, writer; b. Valga, Karula, Estonia, May 8, 1937; came to U.S., 1949, naturalized, 1956; s. Jaan and Emilie (Sona) K.; m. Juta Meius, 1967; children: Kalev Mark, Lembit Jaan. Student U. Ill., 1956-59, Ambassador Coll., 1969-70, Valley Coll., 1976—. Pres. Western Mktg. Assn., Pasadena, Calif., 1972-78, Penny Stocks Newsletter, Redlands, Calif., 1978—; pub. Vello Kulbin's Investments Newsletter, 1981—, Vello Kulbin's Commentary, 1984—. Author: Your Resume and Job Campaign, 1973. Mem. Alpha Delta Phi. Club: Spokesman (past pres.) (Yucaipa, Calif.). Office: Penny Stocks Newsletter 31731 Outer Highway 10 Redlands CA 92373-8610

KULHAVY, RAYMOND WILLIAM, psychology educator; b. San Diego, Dec. 20, 1940; s. Lumir Oldrich and Virginia Dawn (Walker) K.; m. Linda Claire Caterino, July 17, 1977; children: Nicole Dawn Marie, Kathryn Elisabeth Dawn. AB, Calif. State U., San Diego, 1967, MA, 1968; PhD, U. Ill., 1971. Lic. psychologist, Ariz. Rsch. scientist USN, San Diego, 1975; with Ariz. State U., Tempe, 1971-72, prof. psychology, 1979-88, regents prof., 1989—; scholar-in-residence U. Tubingen, Germany, 1993; vis. scholar U. Newcastle, NSW, Australia, 1986-87; sr. Fulbright fellow U. Rome, 1986. Editor: Contemporary Edn. Psychology Jour., 1989; contbr. numerous articles to profl. jours. Recipient Palmer O. Johnson award AERA, 1974. Fellow Am. Psychol. Soc., Nat. Consortium for Instruction and Cognition; mem. Psychonomic Soc., AAAS. Office: Ariz State U Psychology In Edn Dept Tempe AZ 85287-0611

KULIS, STEPHEN STANLEY, sociologist, educator; b. Balt., Sept. 13, 1953; s. Stephen S. and Dorothy E. (Sellner) K. BA, George Washington U., 1975; MA, Columbia U., 1977, PhD, 1984. Instr. St. Xavier H.S., Louisville, Ky., 1975-76; rsch. assoc. Columbia U., N.Y.C., 1982-84; asst. prof. Ariz. State U., Tempe, 1984-90, assoc. prof., 1990—. Author: Why Honor Thy Father and Mother, 1991; contbr. articles to profl. jours. Grantee NSF, 1990-92, Spencer Found., 1993—, Brookdale Inst. on Aging and Human Devel., 1981-82. Mem. Am. Sociol. Assn., Pacific Sociol. Assn., Phi Beta Kappa. Home: 1978 E Stephens Dr Tempe AZ 85283-4914 Office: Ariz State U Dept Sociology Tempe AZ 85287

KULKARNI, KISHORE GANESH, economics educator, consultant; b. Poona, Maharashtra, India Oct. 31, 1953; came to U.S., 1976; s. Ganesh Y. and Sindhu G. Dhekane; m. Jayu K., Aug. 17, 1980; children: Lina, Aditi. BA, U. Poona, India, 1974, MA, 1976; MA, U. Pitts., 1978, PhD, 1982. Teaching asst. U. Pitts., 1976-78, teaching fellow, 1978-80, asst. prof., Johnstown, Pa., 1981-82; asst. prof. U. Central Ark., Conway, 1982-86; assoc. prof. N.E. La. U., Monroe, 1986-89, Met. State Coll. Denver, 1989-93, prof., 1993—, prof. and chmn. dept. econs., 1994—; prof. semester at sea program U. Pitts., 1994. Author: First Principles of Monetary Theory; author (with others): Role of LIC in Economic Development of India; contbr. articles to profl. jours. Research fellow Winrock Internat., Morrilton, Ark., 1984-85; vis. research fellow Nat. Inst. Bank Mgmt., Pune, India, 1986, 87; recipient K. Shinde prize, Poona, India, 1974, First prize, essay competition, Forum of Free Enterprise, Bombay, India, 1975, Rama Watumull Fund award, Honolulu, 1977. Mem. Am. Econ. Assn., Southwestern Econ. Assn., So. Econ. Assn., Assn. Indian Econ. Studies. Avocation: tennis.

KULKOSKY, PAUL JOSEPH, psychology educator; b. Newark, N.J., Mar. 3, 1949; s. Peter Francis and Rose Mary (Leonetti) K.; m. Tanya Marie Weightman, Sept. 16, 1978. BA, Columbia U., N.Y.C., 1971, MA, 1972; PhD, U. Wash., 1975. Research assoc. Cornell U., White Plains, N.Y., 1980-81, instr. psychiatry, 1981-82; asst. prof. psychology U. So. Colo., Pueblo, 1982-86, assoc. prof., 1986-89, chmn. dept. psychology, 1988-91, prof., 1989—; bd. advisors Pueblo Zool. Soc., 1984-85, 1988-91, bd. dirs., 1985-88; editorial cons. to pubs. Contbr. chpts. to books, articles to profl. jours.; referee psychol. jours. Liaison Rocky Mountain region Coun. Undergrad. Psychology Programs, 1990-91. Named Hon. Affiliate Prof. Am. U., Washington, 1977; rsch. grantee NIH, 1984—; staff fellow Nat. Inst. Alcohol Abuse and Alcoholism, 1976-80. Mem. AAAS (vice chair psychol. scis. sect. Southwestern and Rocky Mountain divsn. 1990-91, chmn. 1991-92, exec. com. Colo. rep. 1991-94, pres.-elect 1994-95, pres. 1995—), Consortium of Aquariums, Univs. and Zoos, N.Y. Acad. Scis., Internat. Brain Rsch. Orgn., Soc. Neurosci., Internat. Soc. Biomed. Rsch. on Alcoholism (charter),

Psychonomic Soc., Soc. Study Ingestive Behavior (charter) U. So. Colo. Club, Sigma Xi (treas. 1986—), Colo.-Wyo. Acad. Sci., others. Home: 417 Tyler St Pueblo CO 81004-1405 Office: U So Colo 2200 Bonforte Blvd Pueblo CO 81001-4901

KULL, LORENZ A., scientific research company executive; b. 1937. PhD, Mich. State U., 1967. With Gen. Atomics Co., San Diego, 1967-70; mgr. applied sci. and tech. group Sci. Applications Internat. Corp., 1970-71, corp. v.p., mgr. applied sci. and tech. group, 1971-76, sr. v.p., 1976-79, exec. v.p., 1979-88, pres., 1988—, also bd. dirs. Office: Science Applications Inter Corp 10260 Campus Point Dr San Diego CA 92121-1522

KULL, WILLIAM FRANKLIN, civil engineer, land surveyor; b. Houston, Nov. 21, 1956; s. William Fredrick and Rita Francis (Natiello) K. BS in Civil Engring., U. Santa Clara, 1979. Registered civil engr., land surveyor, Calif. Jr. engr. Nowack & Assocs., San Jose, Calif., 1978-82; sr. engr. Sandis & Assocs., Mountain View, Calif., 1982-87; prin. engr. Civil Cons. Group, Cupertino, Calif., 1987-88; founder, prin. Giuliani & Kull Inc., Cupertino, 1988—. Mem. ASCE (assoc. 1978—). Republican. Episcopalian. Home: 8406 Oak Crest Ct Oakdale CA 95361-9248 Office: Giuliani & Kull Inc 20431 Stevens Creek Blvd Cupertino CA 95014-2252

KULONGOSKI, THEODORE R., state attorney general; b. St. Francois County, Mo., Nov. 5, 1940; married; 3 children. Grad., U. Mo., law degree, 1970. Ptnr. Kulongoski, Durham, Drummonds, and Colombo, Portland, Oreg., 1974-87; dir., Oreg. ins. commr., Oreg. corp. commr., dir. Oreg. fin. institutions, dir. Oreg. workers' compensation program Oreg. Dept. Ins. and Fin., 1987-91; exec. dir. Met. Family Svcs., 1991-93; atty. gen. Oreg., 1993—; gen. counsel Oreg. AFL-CIO; mem. Oreg. legis., 1975-83; chair Ho., Senate labor coms., senate banking and ins. com., mem. Ho. and Senate jud. coms., environ. and energy coms., agriculture and forestry coms. Dem. Party nominee Gov. Oreg., 1982. With USMC. Office: 100 Justice Bldg Salem OR 97310

KUMAGAI, STACEY, broadcast executive. Student, Acad. Radio Broadcasting, Orange Coast Coll.; cert., U. Calif., Irvine. Broadcast studio counselor Acad. Radio Broadcasting, Huntington Beach, Calif., 1987; quality control dir. sta. KDOC-TV, Anaheim, Calif., 1987-88; mktg. promotional graphics sales Blue White Ind., Westminster, Calif., 1989-92; mktg., promotions rep. sta. KIIS-FM, L.A., 1992-93; on-camera talent, voiceover artist Berzon Talent Agy., Costa Meda, Calif.; broadcast media coord. Jill Lloyd & Assocs., Costa Mesa, Calif.; v.p. Audio-dition, Inc., Fountain Valley, Calif., 1993-94; dir. broadcast affiliate rels. Who Did That Music?, L.A., 1994—; mktg./acct. exec. Bood Music Advertising, Irvine; sales mgr. MSC, Westminster ; assoc. prodr., writer Larger Than Life, Century Cable, Santa Monica, Calif.; mktg. cons. Infotrex Network Sys., Westminster; mktg. promotions asst. O'Brien & Shore Broadcast Enterprises, Downey, Calif.; reporter BNN-BournsNews Network Pilot, Orange, Calif.; co-host JCET Ednl. Network Spl., Huntington Beach, Calif.; host, writer Local Cable Update, Garden Grove, Calif.; radio personality Sta. KBCH-FM, Huntington Beach. Mem. Women in Communications, Unity Media Access Project. Office: 18030 Brookhurst St Ste 7 Fountain Valley CA 92708

KUMAR, ANIL, nuclear engineer; b. Agra, India, Aug. 3, 1952; came to U.S., 1988; s. Vedprakash and Satyawati (Sudhir) Parashar; m. Geeta Sharma, Nov. 29, 1979; 1 child, Amitabh. MSc in Physics, Agra U., 1973; PhD in Nuclear Engring., U. Bombay, India, 1981. Sci. officer Bhabha Atomic Rsch. Ctr., Bombay, 1974-81; sr. researcher Ecole Poly. Fed. Lausanne, Switzerland, 1982-88; devel. engr. UCLA, 1988-90, sr. devel. engr., 1990—. Contbr. articles to Jour. Fusion Energy, Nuclear Sci. and Engring., Fusion Tech., Fusion Engring. and Design, Atom Kern Energie, proc. internat. confs. and symposia. Mem. Am. Nuclear Soc., Am. Phys. Soc., Soc. Indsl. and Applied Math. Office: UCLA 43-133 Eng IV 405 Hilgard Ave Los Angeles CA 90025

KUMAR, RAJENDRA, electrical engineering educator; b. Amroha, India, Aug. 22, 1948; came to U.S., 1980; s. Satya Pal Agarwal and Kailash Vati Agarwal; m. Pushpa Agarwal, Feb. 16, 1971; children: Anshu, Shipra. BS in Math. and Sci., Meerut Coll., 1964; BEE, Indian Inst. Tech., Kanpur, 1969, MEE, 1977; PhD in Electrical Engring., U. New Castle, NSW, Australia, 1981. Mem. tech. staff Electronis and Radar Devel., Bangalore, India, 1969-72; rsch. engr. Indian Inst. Tech., Kanpur, 1972-77; asst. prof. Calif. State U., Fullerton, 1981-83, Brown U., Providence, 1980-81; prof. Calif. State U., Long Beach, 1983—; cons. Jet Propulsion Lab., Pasadena, Calif., 1984-91. Contbr. numerous articles to profl. jours.; patentee; efficient detection and signal parameter estimation with applications to high dynamic GPS receivers; multistage estimation of received carrier signal parameters under very high dynamic conditions of the receiver; fast frequency acquisition via adaptive least squares algorithms. Recipient Best Paper award Internat. Telemetering Conf., Las Vegas, 1986, 10 New Technology awards NASA, Washington, 1987-91. Mem. IEEE (sr.), NEA, AAUP, Calif. Faculty Assn., Auto Club So. Calif. (Cerritos), Sigma Xi, Eta Kappa Nu, Tau Beta Pi (eminent mem.). Home: 13910 Rose St Cerritos CA 90703-9043 Office: Calif State U 1250 N Bellflower Blvd Long Beach CA 90840-0006

KUMLER, ROSE MARIE, career counselor, educator; b. Detroit, Dec. 22, 1935; d. Charles and Aida (Oliveri) Fiorini; m. Frank Wozniak, May 17, 1958 (div. 1975); children: Corrine, Paul. BBA, Western Internat. U., 1982; MA, U. Phoenix, 1985. Lic. career counselor, Ariz. Sales rep. Vestal Labs., Phoenix, 1978-79; personnel cons. Ford Personnel Cons. Inc., Phoenix, 1979-81; owner, career counselor Specialized Employment Evaluation Devel., Phoenix, 1980—; dist. supr. Grand Canyon Color Lab., Phoenix, 1981-83; acad. dean Lamson Colls., Glendale, Ariz., 1983-86, instr. Phoenix Coll., Ottawa U., Phoenix, 1986—; speaker in field, 1987—. Chair subcom. of task force Ariz. Gov.'s Offices Women's Svcs.; active Ariz. Affirmative Action Assn., 1990—. Mem. Fellow Impact (strategic planning com. 1988, edn. com. 1988), The Network, Ariz. Career Devel. Assn. (pres. 1994-95), Am. Bus. Women's Assn. (sec. 1975), Soroptimists (judge 1988). Roman Catholic. Home and Office: 13630 N 34th Pl Phoenix AZ 85032-6108

KUMMER, EDWARD WOLFGANG, film company executive; b. Santa Monica, Calif., Dec. 30, 1962; s. Wolfgang Helmut and Mary (Mau) K.; m. Nancy Dufour, Mar. 27, 1993. BS in Computer Sci. & Engring., UCLA, 1985; MS in Computer Sci., U. So. Calif., 1988. Mem. tech. staff II Hughes Aircraft Co., El Segundo, Calif., 1983-88; mgr. computer graphics imergy Walt Disney Pictures, Burbank, Calif., 1988—. Tech. dir. Oliver & Company, The Little Mermaid, Rescuers Down Under, Aladdin, Beauty and the Beast; mgr. The Lion King.

KUMMER, GLENN F., construction and automotive executive; b. Park City, Utah, 1933. B.S., U. Utah, 1961. Sr. acct. Ernst & Ernst, 1961-65; trainee Fleetwood Enterprises Inc., Riverside, Calif., 1965-67, purchasing mgr., 1967-68, plant mgr., 1968-70, gen. mgr. recreational vehicle div., 1970-71, asst. v.p. ops. to v.p. ops., 1971-72, sr. v.p. ops., 1972-77, exec. v.p. ops., 1977-82, pres., 1982—, dir. Office: Fleetwood Enterprises Inc 3125 Myers St Riverside CA 92503-5527

KUNC, JOSEPH ANTHONY, physics and engineering educator, consultant; b. Baranowicze, Poland, Nov. 1, 1943; came to U.S., 1978; s. Stefan and Helena (Kozakiewicz) K.; m. Mary Eva Smolska, May 24, 1979; 1 child, Robert. PhD, Warsaw Tech. U., 1974. Assoc. prof. Warsaw Tech. U., 1974-79; rsch. assoc. prof. U. So. Calif., L.A., 1980-84, assoc. prof., 1985-89, prof. dept. aerospace engring., dept. physics, 1990—; rsch. affiliate Jet Propulsion Lab., Calif. Inst. Tech., 1982-83; vis. scholar Inst. Theoretical Atomic and Molecular Physics, Harvard U., Cambridge, Mass., 1991; vis. scholar dept. high-temperature plasma Nat. Inst. for Nuclear Studies, Warsaw, 1991; vis. scholar atomic and plasma radiation div. Nat. Bur. Standards, Washington, 1979; cons. Nat. Tech. Systems, L.A., 1984-86, Phys. Optics Corp., Torrance, Calif., 1988—, Wolfsdorf and Assocs., L.A., 1991—; mem. com. on arcs and flames Nat. Rsch. Coun., 1985-86; mem. internat. adv. bd. Internat. Symposia Rarefied Gas Dynamics, 1994—; chmn., adv. bd. numerous sci. workshops and symposia. Author: (with others) Advances in Pulsed Power Technology, 1991, Progress in Astronautics and Aeronautics, vol. 116, 1989: contbr. over 150 articles to profl. jours., confs., symposia. Recipient award of merit U.S. Congl. Adv. Bd., 1986, Nat. Bur. Stds., 1979; fellow Nat. Bur. Stds., 1978, Harvard/Smithsonian fellow Inst. Theoretical Atomic and Molecular Physics, Harvard U., 1991. Fellow AIAA (assoc., com. on thermo-physics 1994—), Am. Phys. Soc.; mem. IEEE (sr.), Phi Beta Delta (co-founder Beta Kappa chpt.). Office: U So Calif University Park MC-1191 Los Angeles CA 90275

KUNG, FRANK F. C., medical products executive; b. 1948. MBA, U. Calif., Berkeley, PhD in Molecular Biology. With Clin. Bio-Rsch., Emeryville, Calif., 1978-80, Cetus Immune Corp. (subs. of Cetus Corp.), Emeryville, Calif., 1980-83; with Genelabs Techs., Inc., 1983—, now pres., CEO, chmn. bd. Office: Genelabs Tech Inc 505 Penobscot Dr Redwood City CA 94063-4737*

KUNIYASU, KEITH KAZUMI, secondary education educator; b. Honolulu, Apr. 16, 1955; s. Hajime and Betty Mieko (Yamamoto) K. AA in Liberal Arts, U. Hawaii, Pearl City, 1978, AS in Graphic Arts, 1978; BS in Tech. Edn., Western Wash. U., 1982; MEd in Tech. Edn., Oreg. State U., 1987. Cert. vocat. adminstr. Instrumental music instr. Aiea (Hawaii) Intermediate Sch., 1978-88; spl. edn. instr. Highlands Intermediate Sch., Pearl City, 1983-84; visual comm. instr. Oak Harbor (Wash.) High Sch., 1982-83; photography instr. Olympic Coll., Bremerton, Wash., 1984-85; comm. techs. instr. North Kitsap High Sch., Poulsbo, Wash., 1984-93; instr. comm. techs. River Ridge High Sch., Lacey, Wash., 1993—; edn. rep. curriculum/competency validation com. Wash. State Supt. Pub. Instrn., Olympia, 1988-93; cons. Wash. State Assn. Vocat. Indsl. Clubs Am., 1990—; pvt. woodwind instr., 1974-94; counselor, woodwind specialist Maui (Hawaii) Intermediate Select Band Camps, 1975-80; advisor Leeward C.C. Graphic Arts Club, Pearl City, 1978-80; sch. accreditation teams for various high schs. throughout Wash., 1988—; writing com. leadership curriculum Washington State Supt. Instrn. Edn., Olympia, 1993—. Author: (pamphlet series) Care of Single Reeds, 1983, (brochures) Addressing Technology Education, 1988-92; VisCom Student Study Guide, 1987, 2nd edit., 1990, 3rd edit., 1993, From Goods to Services, 1988, Technology Education Facility, 1988, Communication Technologies at North Kitsap High School, 1989, Visual Communications, 1990. Organizer, pres. Pacific Islanders Club at Western Wash. U., Bellingham, 1981-82; organizer, bd. dirs. Leeward Fine Arts Coun., Pearl City, 1981-94. Named Advisor of Yr. Wash. State Assn. Vocat. Indsl. Clubs Am., 1993. Mem. NEA, Internat. Tech. Edn. Assn. (affiliate rep. 1990-94), Internat. Graphic Arts Educators Assn., Vocat. Indsl. Clubs Am. (advisor, regional coord. 1990-93, 94—), Graphic Arts Tech. Found., Am. Vocat. Assn., Wash. Vocat. Assn., Wash. Tech. Edn. ASsn. Office: River Ridge H S 8929 Martin Way E Lacey WA 98516-5932

KUNKEE, RALPH EDWARD, viticulture and enology educator; b. San Fernando, Calif., July 30, 1927; s. Azor Frederick and Edith Electa (Engle) K. AB, U. Calif., Berkeley, 1950, PhD, 1955. Research biochemist E.I. Du Pont De Nemours, Wilmington, Del., 1955-60; prof. enology U. Calif., Davis, 1963-92, prof. emeritus, 1992; cons. UNFAO, Bangalore, India, 1986. Co-author: Technology of Winemaking, 1971. Fulbright fellow, Mainz, Fed. Republic Germany, 1970-71, France fellow, Montpellier, France, 1977-78. Mem. Am. Chem. Soc., Am. Soc. Microbiology, Am. Soc. Enology and Viticulture (sec./treas. 1983-85). Home: 820 Radcliffe Dr Davis CA 95616-0941 Office: U Calif Dept Viticulture and Enology Davis CA 95616

KUNKEL, GEORGIE MYRTIA, writer, retired school counselor; b. Chehalis, Wash.; d. George Riley and Myrtia (McLaughlin) Bright; m. Norman C. Kunkel, Apr. 25, 1946; children: N. Joseph D.C., Stephen Gregory, Susan Ann, Kimberly Jane Waligorska. BA in Edn., Western Wash. U., 1944; MEd, U. Wash., 1968. Typist, clk. FHA, Seattle, 1940; tchr. pub. schs. Vader, Centralia, Wash., Seattle, 1941-67; pvt. cons., Seattle, 1970—; counselor Highline Pub. Schs., Seattle, 1967-82; sch. counselor rep. State of Art Conf., Balt., 1980. Editor Women and Girls in Edn., 1972-75. Author (under pseudonym Dorothy Bright): My Sex Secrets, 1989, How Do You Know You're Dying, 1991, Grandma's Holiday Greetings, 1992; contbr. articles to profl. jours. Organizer Women and Girls in Edn., Wash. state, 1971; pres. Wash. State NOW, 1973; mem. West Seattle Community Council, 1980. Grantee Women Adminstrs. Wash. State, 1971, Edn. Service Dist., Seattle, 1980. Mem. NEA (sec. pub. relations), Am. Assn. Counseling and Devel. (pres. state br. 1982-83), Am. Sch. Counseling Assn. (pres. state div. 1980-81), Seattle Counselors Assn. (organizer, past pres. office exec., Counselor of Yr. 1990), Holmes Harbor Homeowners Assn. (organizer and pres.), West Seattle C. of C., Past Pres. Club (Seattle), West Seattle Dem. Women's Club (pres.). Unitarian Universalist. Club: Past Presidents (Seattle). Avocation: singing. Home and Office: 3409 SW Trenton St Seattle WA 98126-3743

KUNKEL, GERALD ROBERT, marketing professional, interior designer; b. Red Bud, Ill., May 23, 1956; s. Robert Francis and Alberta Louise (Lang) K. BS in Bus. Adminstrn., U. Ark., 1985. Mgr. Porta-King Bldg. Sys., Earth City, Mo., 1984-89; rep/ ITW-Paslode, Lincolnshire, Ill., 1988-89; contract furniture and design rep. The Stationers, Inc., Tacoma, 1989-92, design dept. mgr., 1991-92; owner Kelly & Lang, Seattle, 1993—; contract position Emerald City Arts, Seattle, 1993—; mem. Greater Seattle Bus. Assn., 1991—, ACLU Seattle, 1993—, DIFFA/Greater Seattle, 1992—; founding mem., sec. Diffa/Greater Seattle, 1992-93. lead mgr. collectors NW AIDS Found.-AIDS Walk, Seattle, 1991—; com. person NW AIDS Found.-Salute to Cultural Diversity/Nordstrom Event, Seattle, 1992; Angel for Angel Itiman Theatre Angels in Am., Seattle, 1994, 95. Mem., fellow Greater Seattle Bus. Assn.; mem. Seattle Men's Chorus. Office: Kelly & Lang PO Box 20805 Seattle WA 98102-1805

KUNKEL, SCOTT WILLIAM, strategic management and entrepreneurship educator; b. St. Louis, May 26, 1945; s. Robert Scott and Mary (Muldowney) K.; divorced; children: Mary Charlotte, Deborah Ann. BBA in Accountancy, Memphis State U., 1974, MS in Finance, 1979; PhD in Bus. Adminstrn., U. Ga., 1991. Asst. v.p., controller First Fed. Savs. & Loan, Memphis, 1976-79; v.p. Maury County Fed. Savs. & Loan, Columbia, Tenn., 1979-81, Great Southern Fed. Savs. & Loan, Gainesville, Ga., 1981-82; assoc. prof. Brenau U., Gainesville, 1982-88; asst. prof. U. Nev., Reno, 1988-92; asst. prof., dir. Family Bus. Inst. U. San Diego, 1992—. Mem. U.S. Assn. Small Bus. and Entrepreneurship, Acad. Mgmt., Internat. Family Bus. Program Assn., Family Firm Inst., Acad. Entrepreneurship. Libertarian. Roman Catholic. Office: U San Diego Sch Bus San Diego CA 92110-2492

KUNTZ, CHARLES POWERS, lawyer; b. L.A., May 7, 1944; s. Walter Nichols and Katherine (Powers) K.; m. June Emerson Moroney, Dec. 23, 1969; children: Michael Nicholas, Robinson Moroney, Katie Moroney. AB with honors, Stanford U., 1966, JD, 1969; LLM, NYU, 1971. Bar: Calif. 1970, N.Y. 1970, U.S. Dist. Ct. (no. dist.) Calif. 1970, U.S. Ct. Appeals (9th cir.) 1970, U.S. Supreme Ct. 1979. Staff atty. project for urban affairs Office Econ. Opportunity, N.Y.C., 1969-71; dep. pub. defender Contra Costa County Pub. Defender's Office, Martinez, Calif., 1971-75; assoc. Treuhaft, Walker & Brown, Oakland, Calif., 1976-78; ptnr. Hirsch & Kuntz, San Rafael, Calif., 1979-85; pvt. practice San Rafael, 1985-89; ptnr. Coombs & Dunlap, Napa, Calif., 1989—. Mem. ABA, Assn. Trial Lawyers Am., Calif. Trial Lawyers Assn., Napa County Bar Assn. Home: 1271 Monticello Rd Napa CA 94558-2019 Office: Coombs & Dunlap 1211 Division St Napa CA 94559-3372

KUNZ, CHARLES ALAN, programs manager; b. St. Louis, May 16, 1945; s. Glennon Charles and Lillian Margaret (Nies) K.; m. Teresa Anne Klutenkamper, Oct. 8, 1966; children: Leanne Teresa, Karl Thomas, Alicia Marie, Andrew Conrad. Diploma in Nursing, St. Louis City Hosp., 1966; BS, Regis Coll., 1985; MA in Computer Resource Mgmt., Webster U., 1989; Cert. in Anesthesia, Wilford Hall USAF Med. Ctr., San Antonio, 1980. RN. Commd. 2d lt. USAF, 1966, advanced through ranks to lt. col., 1966; operating room nurse Bethesda Gen. Hosp., St. Louis, 1986; gen. duty nurse USAF, Amarillo, Tex., 1967-68; flight nurse USAF DaNang AB, Vietnam, 1968-69; oper. room nurse USAF Hosp., Wiesbaden, Fed. Republic Germany, 1970-73; oper. room supr. USAF Altus AFB, Okla., 1974-77; staff nurse anesthetist USAF Hosp., Lakenheath, Eng., 1980-83; chief nurse anesthetist USAF Acad., Colorado Springs, 1983-88; nursing systems coord. Keesler AFB, Biloxi, Miss., 1988-91; chief clin. systems Keesler AFB, Biloxi, 1991-92; program mgr. Loral Tng. & Tech. Svcs., Colorado Springs, Colo., 1992-94, Las Vegas, Nev., 1994—; cons. in nurse anesthesia to USAF Surgeon Gen., 1982-83, cons. med. systems, 1989-92. Asst. scoutmaster Boy Scouts Am., Ocean Springs, Miss., 1988-92; mem. CAP, 1990-92. Recipient Agatha Hodgins Meml. award to Outstanding Grad., Am. Assn. Nurse Anesthetists, 1980, Wall Street Jour. Student Achievement award, 1985. Mem. Nat. Model R.R. Assn. (life), Keesler Amateur Radio Club (pres. 1990-92), Pikes Peak Computer Applications Soc. (pres. 1988), Ret. Officers' Assn. (life), Am. Radio Relay League (life). Roman Catholic. Home: 7573 Lorinda Ave Las Vegas NV 89128-0213 Office: Loral Tng & Tech Svc 2400 N Tenaya Way Las Vegas NV 89128-0420

KUNZ, MICHAEL LENNEY, archaeologist; b. Galveston, Tex., Sept. 1, 1942; s. Thomas John and Catherine Rita (Lenney) K.; m. Patricia Ann Allan, Jan. 28, 1965; children: Kelly Heather, Joshua Allan. BS in Anthropology, Ea. N.Mex. U., 1967. Instr. anthropology Ea. N.Mex. U., Portales, 1969-70; rsch. assoc. U. Alaska, Fairbanks, 1971-77; archaeologist, chief environ. monitor Bur. Land Mgmt., Fairbanks, 1977-80; archaeologist, quality assurance N.W. Alaskan Pipeline Co., Fairbanks, 1981-82; archaeologist Nat. Park Svc., Fairbanks, 1983-88, Bur. Land Mgmt., Fairbanks, 1989—; cons. Kunz & Assocs., Fairbanks, 1980—. Contbr. articles to profl. jours. Rsch. grantee Wenner-Gren Found., 1967, Sigma Xi, 1969, Bur. Land Mgmt., 1991—. Mem. Soc. Profl. Archaeologists, Plains Anthropol. Soc., Soc. for Am. Archaeology, Alaska Anthropol. Assn. Home: Box 80087 College Station Fairbanks AK 99708 Office: Bureau of Land Mgmt 1150 University Ave Fairbanks AK 99709-3844

KUNZ, PHILLIP RAY, sociologist, educator; b. Bern, Idaho, July 19, 1936; s. Parley P. and Hilda Irene (Stoor) K.; m. Joyce Sheffield, Mar. 18, 1960; children: Jay, Jenifer, Jody, Johnathan, Jana. B.S., Brigham Young U., 1961, M.S. cum laude, 1962; Ph.D. (fellow), U. Mich., 1967. Instr. Eastern Mich. U., Ypsilanti, 1964, U. Mich., Ann Arbor, 1965-67; asst. prof. sociology U. Wyo., Laramie, 1967-68; prof. sociology Brigham Young U., Provo, Utah, 1968—; acting dept. chmn. Brigham Young U., 1973; dir. Inst. Geneal. Studies, 1972-74; cons. various ednl. and research instns., 1968—; missionary Ch. Jesus Christ LDS, Ga. and S.C., 1956-58, mem. high coun., 1969-70, bishop; mission pres. La. Baton Rouge Mission, 1990-93. Author: (book) 10 Critical Keys for Highly Effective Families and other books; contbr. articles on social orgn., family rels. and deviant behavior to profl. jours. Housing commr. City of Provo, 1984—. Served with AUS, 1954-56. Recipient Karl G. Maeser research award, 1977. Mem. Am. Sociol. Assn., Rocky Mountain Social Sci. Assn., Am. Council Family Relations, Rural Sociol. Soc., Am. Soc. Criminology, Soc. Sci. Study of Religion, Religious Research Assn., Sigma Xi, Phi Kappa Phi, Alpha Kappa Delta. Democrat. Home: 3040 Navajo Ln Provo UT 84604-4820 Office: Brigham Young Univ Dept Sociology Provo UT 84602

KUO, FRANKLIN F., computer scientist, electrical engineer; b. Hankow, People's Republic of China, Apr. 22, 1934; came to U.S., 1950, naturalized, 1961; s. Steven C. and Grace C. (Huang) K.; m. Dora Lee, Aug. 30, 1958; children: Jennifer, Douglas. BS, U. Ill., 1955, MS, 1956, PhD, 1958. Asst. prof. dept. elec. engring. Poly. Inst. Bklyn., 1958-60; mem. tech. staff Bell Telephone Labs., Murray Hill, N.J., 1960-66; prof. elec. engring. U. Hawaii, Honolulu, 1966-82; exec. dir. SRI Internat., Menlo Park, Calif., 1982-94; v.p. Gen. Wireless Comm. Corp., 1994—; dir. info. systems Office Sec. of Def., 1976-77; cons. Lawrence Radiation Labs., 1966-71; liason scientist U.S. Office Naval Research, London, 1971-72; cons. prof. elec. engring. Stanford U., Calif., 1982—; mem. exec. panel Chief of Naval Ops., 1980-85. Author: Network Analysis and Synthesis, 1962, (2d edit.), 1966, Linear Circuits and Computations, 1973; co-author: System Analysis by Digital Computer, 1966, Computer Oriented Circuit Design, 1969, Computer Communications Networks, 1973, Protocols and Techniques in Data Communication Networks, 1981; cons. editor, Prentice-Hall Inc., 1967—; mem. editorial bd. Future Generations Computer Systems; contbr. articles to profl. jours.; developer Alohanet packet broadcast radio network. Mem. Pres. coun. U. Ill.; adv. bd. Beckman Inst. Fellow IEEE (gen. chmn. 6th Data Communications Symposium 1979, mem. editorial bd.); mem. Assn. Computing Machinery (coun. mem. 1986-90), The Internet Soc., Tau Beta Pi, Eta Kappa Nu. Home: 824 La Mesa Dr Portola Valley CA 94028

KUO, PING-CHIA, historian, educator; b. Yangshe, Kiangsu, China, Nov. 27, 1908; s. Chu-sen and Hsiao-kuan (Hsu) K.; m. Anita H. Bradley, Aug. 8, 1946. A.M., Harvard U., 1930, Ph.D., 1933. Prof. modern history and Far Eastern internat. relations Nat. Wuhan U., Wuchang, China, 1933-38; editor China Forum, Hankow and Chungking, 1938-40; counsellor Nat. Mil. Council, Chungking, China, 1940-46, Ministry Fgn. Affairs, 1943-46; participated in Cairo Conf. as spl. polit. asst. to Generalissimo Chiang Kai-shek, 1943; during war yrs. in Chungking, also served Chinese Govt. concurrently in following capacities: mem. fgn. affairs com. Nat. Supreme Def. Council, 1939-46; chief, editorial and pubs. dept. Ministry Information, 1940-42, mem. central planning bd., 1941-45; tech. expert to Chinese delegation San Francisco Conf., 1945; chief trusteeship sect. secretariat UN, London; (exec. com. prep. commn. and gen. assembly), 1945-46; top-ranking dir. Dept. Security Council Affairs, UN, 1946-48; vis. prof. Chinese history San Francisco State Coll., summers 1954, 58; assoc. prof. history So. Ill. U., 1959-63, prof. history, 1963-72, chmn. dept. history, 1967-71, prof. emeritus, 1972—; sr. fellow Nat. Endowment for Humanities, 1973-74; Pres. Midwest Conf. Asian Studies, 1964. Author: A Critical Study of the First Anglo-Chinese War, with Documents, 1935, Modern Far Eastern Diplomatic History (in Chinese), 1937, China: New Age and New Outlook, 1960, China, in the Modern World Series, 1970; Contbr. to Am. hist. pubs. and various mags. in China and Ency. Brit. Decorated Kwang Hua medal A-1 grade Nat. Mil. Council, Chungking, 1941; Auspicious Star medal Nat. Govt., Chungking, 1944; Victory medal, 1945. Mem. Am. Hist. Assn., Assn. Asian Studies. Club: Commonwealth (San Francisco). Home: 8661 Don Carol Dr El Cerrito CA 94530-2752

KUPPERMAN, HENRY JOHN, lawyer; b. N.Y.C., May 18, 1957; s. Ben J. and Roma M. (Ash) K.; m. Rebecca Beauchamp, 1990; 1 child, Jonathan Andrew. BA, Johns Hopkins U., 1978; JD, St. John's U., 1982. Bar: N.Y. 1983, U.S. Ct. Appeals (3d cir.) 1983, Pa. 1984, Calif. 1987, U.S. Ct. Appeals (9th cir.) 1987, U.S. Supreme Ct. 1988. Student law clk. to judge U.S. Dist. Ct., N.Y.C., 1981-82; law clk. to chief judge U.S. Dist. Ct., Wilmington, Del., 1982-83; assoc. Drinker, Biddle & Reath, Phila., 1984-86; assoc. Brobeck, Phleger & Harrison, L.A., 1986-89, ptnr., 1990-93; gen. counsel The Investigative Group, Inc., L.A., 1994—. Mem. ABA (co-chmn. subcom. on fed. local procedure 1986-88), Calif. Bar Assn. L.A. Bar Assn., Beverly Hills Bar Assn. Jewish. Office: The Investigative Group Inc 333 S Grand Ave Ste 3650 Los Angeles CA 90071-1540

KURAISHI, AKARI LUKE, real estate company executive; b. Nagano, Japan, July 29, 1959; came to U.S. 1984; s. Atsushi and Kuniko (Tomita) K.; m. Hiromi Lydia Hatae, Oct. 10, 1987; children: Katrina Ayumi, Kristin Kasumi. BA, Nat. Def. Acad., Yokosuka, Japan, 1982; MBA, U. Dallas, 1986. Registered internat. mem. Internat. Real Estate Inst. Mgr. Gateway Travel & Tours, Dallas, 1985-87; with portfolio investments dept. Mitsui Real Estate Sales USA Co., Ltd., L.A., 1987-90; mgr., 1990-91; asst. v.p. Mitsui Real Estate Sales USA Co., Ltd., L.A., 1991-95; v.p. Mitsui Real Estate Sales U.S.A. Co., Ltd., L.A., 1995—; dir. ALKALY Inc., Orange, Calif., 1991—; v.p. Santa Ana (Calif.) Corp., 1992—, Santa Ana Mgmt. Corp., 1992—; sec. MI Ptnrs. (L.A.) Co., Ltd., 1993—. Mem. NRA, U. Dallas Alumni Assn., Orange County Japanese Am. Assn. (bd. dirs. 1994—), Japanese-Am. Network (charter mem.). Home: 2348 E Trenton Ave Orange CA 92667-4454 Office: Mitsui Real Estate Sales USA Co Ltd 601 S Figueroa St Fl 4600 Los Angeles CA 90017-5751

KURNICK, JOHN EDMUND, hematologist, educator; b. N.Y.C., Feb. 9, 1942; s. Nathaniel B. and Dorothy (Manheimer) K.; m. Luann Fogliani, July 9, 1969; children: David, Katherine. BA, Harvard U., 1962; MD, U. Chgo., 1966. Diplomate Am. Bd. Internal Medicine, Am. Bd. Oncology, Am. Bd. Hematology. Intern U. Wash., Seattle, 1966-67; resident Stanford U., Palo Alto, Calif., 1967-68; asst. prof. medicine U. Colo. Med. Ctr., Denver, 1973-78; chief hematology VA Hosp., Denver, 1973-78; pvt. pracice Downey, Calif., 1979—; assoc. clin. prof. medicine U. Calif., Irvine, 1979—; lectr., expert witness in field. Contbr. articles to med. jours. Maj. Med. Corps., USAR, 1970-73. Fellow U. Colo., 1968-70. Fellow ACP; mem. Am. Soc. Hematology, Am. Soc. Clin. Oncology, Western Soc. Clin. Rsch., Internat. Soc. Hematology, Am. Fedn. Clin. Rsch., Am. Assn. Cancer Edn. Democrat. Office: 11411 Brookshire Ave Downey CA 90241-5003

KURODA, YUTAKA, management consultant; b. Kobe, Hyogo, Japan, Dec. 16, 1950. BS, Waseda U., Tokyo, 1973; MS, Stanford U., 1982. Adv. systems engr. IBM Japan, Tokyo, 1973-85; product mgr. IBM Asia Pacific Group Hdqrs., Tokyo, 1985-88; sr. cons. SRI Internat., Menlo Park, Calif., 1988—. Home: 4769 Williams Rd San Jose CA 95129-3232 Office: SRI International 333 Ravenswood Ave Menlo Park CA 94025-3453

KURRI, JARI, professional hockey player; b. Helsinki, Finland, May 18, 1960; m. Tina Kurri; children: Joonas, Ville. Hockey player Jokerit, Finland, 1977-80, Edmonton Oilers, Alta., Can., 1980-90; with Milan Devils, Italian Hockey League, 1990-91, L.A. Kings, Inglewood, Calif., 1991—; mem. NHL All-Star team, 1984-85, 86-87; player NHL All-Star game, 1983, 85,86, 88-90, 93, Stanley Cup Championship teams, 1984, 85, 87, 88, 90. Recipient Lady Byng Meml. Trophy, 1984, 85; named Sporting News All Star first team, 1984-85. Office: care LA Kings Gt Western Forum PO Box 17013 Inglewood CA 90308-7013*

KURSEWICZ, LEE Z., marketing consultant; b. Chgo., Oct. 26, 1916; s. Antoni and Henryka (Sulkowska) K.; ed. Chgo. and Bata ind. schs.; m. Ruth Elizabeth Venzke, Jan. 31, 1940; 1 son, Dennis. With Bata Shoe Co., Inc., 1936-78, plant mgr., Salem, Ind., 1963-65, v.p., mng. dir., Batawa, Ont., Can., 1965-71; v.p., dir. Bata Industries, Batawa, 1965-71, plant mgr., Salem, 1971-76; pres. Bata Shoe Co., Inc., Belcamp, Md., 1976-77, sr. v.p., dir., 1977-79; gen. mgr. Harford Insulated Panel Systems div. Hazleton Industries, 1981-82. City mgr. City of Batawa, 1965-71; vice chmn. Trenton (Ont.) Meml. Hosp., 1970-71; pres. Priestford Hills Community Assn., 1979-80; chmn. adv. bd. Phoenix Festival Theatre, Hartford County Community Coll., 81; vice chmn. Harford County chpt. ARC, 1980-81, chmn., 1982-83; chmn. Harford County Econ. Devel. Adv. Bd., 1983-85; mem. Susquehanna Region Pvt. Industry Council, 1983-85. Mem. Am. Mgmt. Assn. Clubs: Rotary, Bush River Yacht (commodore 1956), Bush River Power Squadron (comdr. 1957), Western Hills Country of Salem (pres. 1975), Trenton Country (pres. 1968-69), Md. Country. Home and Office: 31382 Abanita Way Laguna Niguel CA 92677-2725

KURTIN, SANDRA ELAINE, nurse; b. Tucson, Oct. 28, 1958; m. Thomas Henry Kurtin, June 18, 1983; children: John Thomas, Katherine Isabelle. BS, U. Ariz., 1985, MS, 1990. Rsch. asst. U. Ariz., Tucson, 1985; staff nurse med. oncology U. Med. Ctr., Tucson, 1986-90, oncology nurse specialist, 1990—, program coord. case mgmt., 1994—; oncology rsch. nurse U. Ariz. Coll. Medicine, Tucson, 1988-89; program coord. differentiated group profl. practice nursing U. Ariz./U. Med. Ctr., Tucson, 1989-90; asst. clin. prof. U. Ariz., 1990—. Contbg. author: Patient Centered Care, 1994. Am. Cancer Soc. grad. scholar, 1988-90. Mem. Am. Cancer Soc., Oncology Nursing Soc. (mem. govt. rels. com. 1993—, cert. oncology nurse), Nightingale Soc., Sigma Theta Tau. Democrat. Office: U Med Ctr 1501 N Campbell Ave Tucson AZ 85724-0001

KURTZ, MAXINE, personnel executive, lawyer; b. Mpls., Oct. 17, 1921; d. Jack Isadore and Beatrice (Cohen) K. BA, U. Minn., 1942; MS in Govt. Mgmt., U. Denver, 1945, JD, 1962; postdoctoral student, U. Calif., San Diego, 1978. Bar: Colo. 1962; U.S. Dist. Ct., Colo., 1992. Analyst Tri-County Regional Planning, Denver, 1945-47; chief rsch. and spl. projects Planning Office, City and County of Denver, 1947-66, dir. tech. and evaluation Model Cities Program, 1966-71; pers. rsch. officer Denver Career Service Auth., 1972-86, dir. pers. svcs., 1986-88, sr. pers. specialist, 1988-90; pub. sector pers. cons., 1990—, atty., 1990—; expert witness nat. com. on urban problems U.S. Ho. of Reps., U.S. Senate. Author: Law of Planning and Land Use Regulations in Colorado, 1966; co-author: Care and Feeding of Witnesses, Expert and Otherwise, 1974; bd. editors: Pub. Adminstrn. Rev., Washington, 1980-83, 88-92; editorial adv. bd. Internat. Pers. Mgmt. Assn.; prin. investigator: Employment: An American Enigma, 1979. Active Women's Forum of Colo.; Denver Dem. Com.; chair Colo. adv. com. to U.S. Civil Rights Commn., 1985-89, mem. 1989—. Sloan fellow, U. Denver, 1944-45; recipient Outstanding Achievement award U. Minn., 1971, Alumni of Notable Achievement award, 1994. Mem. ABA, Am. Inst. Planners (sec. treas. 1968-70, bd. govs. 1972-75), Am. Soc. Pub. Adminstrn. (nat. council 1978-81, Donald Stone award), Colo. Bar Assn., Denver Bar Assn., Order St. Ives., Pi Alpha Alpha. Jewish. Home and Office: 2361 Monaco Pky Denver CO 80207-3453

KURTZMAN, ALAN, cosmetics company executive. Pres. U.S. div. Max Factor & Co. subs. Revlon Group Inc., L.A.; bd. dirs. Certron Corp. Office: Max Factor & Co 12100 Wilshire Blvd Los Angeles CA 90025-7120

KURTZMAN, RALPH HAROLD, biochemist, researcher; b. Mpls., Feb. 21, 1933; s. Ralph Harold, Sr. and Susie Marie (Elwell) K.; m. Nancy Virginia Leussler, Aug. 27, 1955; children: Steven Paul, Sue. BS, U. Minn., 1955; MS, U. Wis., 1958, PhD, 1959. Asst. prof. U. R.I., Kingston, 1959-62, U. Minn., Morris, 1962-65; biochemist U.S. Dept. Agriculture, Albany, Calif., 1965—; instr. U. Calif., Berkeley, 1981-82; cons. Bliss Valley Farms, Twin Falls, Idaho, 1983-84. Editor Internat. Jour. Mushroom Scis., 1995—; inventor mushroom substrate (compost) preparation, 1982, decaffeination of beverages, 1973; contbr. articles to profl. jours. Chmn. Berkeley YMCA Camp Program Com., 1971-72; official Amateur Athletic Union (swimming), San Francisco, 1973-80; treas. Calif. Native Plant Soc., 1970. Mem. Am. Mushroom Inst., Mushroom Growers of Great Britain, Mycological Soc. Am., Sigma Xi. Home: 445 Vassar Ave Berkeley CA 94708-1215 Office: US Dept Agriculture Western Regional Rsch Ctr 800 Buchanan St Berkeley CA 94710-1105

KURZ, EDWARD PHILIP, lawyer; b. Chgo., Mar. 8, 1921; s. William and Barbara (Duy) K.; m. Lavonne Shirley Kemmerer, Sept. 27, 1953; children: Sharon Marie, Kevin Edward, David Wayne. BSBA, U. Denver, 1948, JD, 1953. Bar: Colo. 1953, Ill. 1954, U.S. Dist. Ct. Colo. 1957, U.S. Ct. Appeals (10th cir.) 1957, U.S. Supreme Ct. 1959, U.S. Tax Ct. 1965; CPA, Colo., Ill. Acct. Cordle & Assocs., CPAs, Denver, 1948-53; ptnr. Davis & Kurz, Denver, 1954-60; pvt. practice Aurora, Colo., 1960—; tax analyst Commonwealth Edison Co., Chgo., 1953-54; exec. dir. Four County Met. Capital Improvement Dist., Denver, 1961-62; magistrate Denver County Ct., 1979-92, Arapahoe County Ct., 1989—; instr. in contracts U. Denver Law Sch., 1956-58. Chmn. fin. com. Billy Graham Colo. Crusade, 1965. Capt. U.S. Army, 1940-46, PTO. Mem. ABA, Colo. Bar Assn., Denver Bar Assn., Colo. Soc. CPAs, Am. Arbitration Assn., Denver C. of C. (hon. life; coordinator spl. state tax study 1959-61), Kiwanis (pres. 1968, lt. gov. 1980-81). Republican. Lutheran. Home: 3161 S Holly Pl Denver CO 80222-7623 Office: 3090 S Jamaica Ct # 110 Aurora CO 80014-2628

KURZ, MORDECAI, economics educator; b. Nathanya, Israel, Nov. 29, 1934; came to U.S., 1957, naturalized, 1973; s. Moshe and Sarah (Kraus) K.; m. Lillian Rivlin, Aug. 4, 1963 (div. Mar. 1967); m 2d Linda Alice Cahn, Dec. 2, 1979. BA in Econs. and Polit. Sci., Hebrew U., Jerusalem, 1957; MA in Econs., Yale U., 1958, PhD in Econs., 1961; MS in Stats., Stanford U., 1960. Asst. prof. econs. Stanford U., 1962-63, assoc. prof., 1966-68, prof., 1969—, dir. econs. sect. Inst. for Math. Studies, 1971-89; sr. lectr. in econs. Hebrew U., 1963-66; cons. econs. SRI Internat., Menlo Park, Calif., 1963-78; spl. econ. advisor Can. health and Welfare Ministry, Ottawa, Ont., 1976-78; spl. econ. advisor Pres.'s Commn. on Pension, Washington, 1979-81; rsch. assoc. Nat. Bur. Econ. Rsch., 1979-82; Lady Davis vis. prof. Hebrew U., Jerusalem, 1993. Author: (with Kenneth J. Arrow) Public Investment, the Rate of Return and Optimal Fiscal Policy, 1970. Ford Found. faculty fellow Stanford U., 1973; Guggenheim Found. fellow Stanford U., Harvard U., Jerusalem, 1977-78; Inst. Advanced Studies fellow Hebrew U., Mt. Scopus, Jerusalem, 1979-80; prin. investigator NSF, 1969-93. Fellow Econometric Soc. (assoc. editor Jour. Econ. Theory 1976-90); mem. Am. Econ. Assn. Democrat. Jewish. Office: Stanford U Econs Dept Serra St at Galvez Stanford CA 94305-6702

KUSHLA, JOHN DENNIS, forester, researcher; b. Norristown, Pa., Feb. 3, 1955; s. Walter and Helen K.; m. Michele Ankenmann, Apr. 1, 1989; 1 child, Melanya Eve. BS in Forest Sci. with honors, Pa. State U., 1977; MS in Forest Sci., minor in Soil Sci., U. Fla., 1979. Grad. rsch. asst. U. Fla., Gainesville, 1977-79; supr. soil and water Union Camp Corp., Savannah, Ga., 1980-90; grad. rsch. asst. Oreg. State U., Corvallis, 1990—, mgr. environ. remote sensing applications lab., 1992-93; pvt. practice soil cons., Savannah, 1987-90. Contbr. articles Soil Sci. Soc. Am. Jour., Environmental Management. Mem. Am. Soc. Agronomy, Am. Soc. Photogrammetry and Remote Sensing, Soc. Am. Foresters, Soil Sci. Soc. Am., Phi Kappa Phi, Xi Sigma Pi, Gamma Sigma Delta, Alpha Zeta. Office: Oreg State U Peavy Hall A 108 Corvallis OR 97331

KUSTER, ROBERT KENNETH, scientist; b. Los Angeles, July 11, 1932; s. Arthur Rollo Kuster and Ermine Rosebud (Prittchett) Woodward. AS, Gavilan Coll., 1974, AA in Humanities, 1981; student, San Jose State U., 1955, 1974-76, UCLA, 1977. Installer Western Electric Co., Inc., Corpus Christi, Tex., 1951-52, 1955, San Jose, Calif., 1957-58, 1960-83; ptnr., scientist, cons. WE-Woodward's Enterprises, Morgan Hill, Calif., 1975—; technician AT&T Tech., Inc., San Jose, 1983-85; scientist pvt. practice, Gilroy, 1978—. Served to sgt. U.S. Army Corps Engrs., 1952-54. Mem. AAAS, Astron. Soc. Pacific, Calif. Acad. Scis., N.Y. Acad. Scis., Am. Legion, VFW. Baptist. Lodge: Elks. Home: 17506 Hoot Owl Way Morgan Hill CA 95037-6524 Office: Woodward's Enterprises 179 Bender Cir Morgan Hill CA 95037-3533

KUTA, CHARLES STANLEY, computer engineer; b. Lafayette, Ind., Jan. 7, 1956; s. Edwin Joseph and Meryl (Goodman) K.; m. Eva Rosa Echemendia, Sept. 24, 1989. BA in Engring. Sci. with honors, Oxford (U.K.) U., 1977, MA, 1981; MSEE, Stanford U., 1985. Programmer Harold Beck & Sons, Inc., Newtown, Pa., 1977-81; mem. tech. staff Silicon Graphics, Inc., Mountain View, Calif., 1982-92; engring. fellow Media Vision Tech. Inc., Fremont, Calif., 1992-94, dir. software engring., 1995—. Mem. IEEE, Assn. for Computing Machinery. Home: 55 Chestnut Ave Los Gatos CA 95030-5803

KUTER, KAY E., writer, actor; b. L.A., Apr. 25, 1925; s. Leo E. and Evelyn Belle (Edler) K. Student, Pomona Coll., UCLA; BFA, Carnegie Inst. Tech., 1949. Radio actor NBC, 1944; actor, 1944—. Actor in 189 musicals Off Broadway, Stock, Repertory, Touring and Shakespearean Stage Prodns.; 43 feature films; more than 400 TV shows, including 7 yrs. as a series regular (Newt Kiley) in Green Acres and Petticoat Junction; voiceover actor for Disney cartoon series The Little Mermaid, Aladdin, Prince Valiant, Biker Mice From Mars; author: Carmen Incarnate, 1946, Ships that Never Sailed, 1994, Hollywood Houdini, Picture Perfect World, 1995; editor: The Jester, 1956-60, The Jester 25th Anniversary, 1960, The Jester 50th Anniversary, 1976. Bd. dirs. Family Svc. of L.A., 1950-70. Mem. SAG (bd. dirs. 1970-73), AEA, AFTRA, Book Publicists of So. Calif., Nat. Soc. Hist. Preservation, Smithsonian, Carnegie Mellon U. Westcoast Drama Alumni Clan (founding mem., officer, bd. mem. 1968-80), Ephebian Soc., Andrew Carnegie Soc., Pacific Pioneer Broadcasters, Carnegie Mellon U. Alumni Assn. (regional v.p. 1976-79, Svc. award 1979), Masquers Club (bd. dirs. 1953-75, rec. sec. 1956-70, corr. sec. 1957-69, v.p. 1971-75), Actors Fund of Am. (life mem.), Calif. Artists Radio Theatre. Democrat. Home: 6207 Satsuma Ave North Hollywood CA 91606-3819

KUTINAC, JOHN GEORGE, JR., psychologist; b. Chgo., Dec. 26, 1947; s. John G. Sr. and Ann (Michalec) K.; m. Linda S. Derrico, Aug. 3, 1968; children: John Eric, Jason Edward, Erin Elizabeth. BA, Avila Coll., 1978; MA, N.Mex. State U., 1980. Program dir. Open Door Ctr., Las Cruces, N.Mex., 1978-81; counselor Las Cruces Pub. Sch., 1981-90; psychologist pvt. practice, Las Cruces, 1990—. Bd. dirs., pres. Shalom Family Svcs., Las Cruces, 1990—; v.p. Trinity Luth. Ch. Coun., Las Cruces, 1987-90. With U.S. Army, 1968-70, Vietnam. Mem. Am. Counseling Assn., Am. Mental Health Counseling Assn. Office: 715 E Idaho 1-D Las Cruces NM 88001

KUTVIRT, DUDA CHYTILOVA (RUZENA), scientific translator; b. Pilsen, Czechoslovakia, Sept. 17, 1919; came to U.S., 1949; d. Frantisek and Ruzena (Vitousek) Chytil; m. Otakar Kutvirt, July 10, 1942 (dec.); children: Thomas (dec.), Daniel. BA, Smith Coll., 1940; MA, Mills Coll., 1942. Rsch. asst. U. Rochester Med. Sch., 1942-44; scientific translator Eastman Kodak Rsch. Labs., Rochester, 1944-45, 61-78. Voter registrar LWV, Albuquerque, 1980—, Rochester, 1955-70; vol. U. N.Mex. Hosp. Svc. League, Albuquerque, 1979—; mem. Albuquerque com. for fgn. affairs. Home: 5 Pool St NW Albuquerque NM 87120-1809

KUWABARA, DENNIS MATSUICHI, optometrist; b. Honolulu, July 20, 1945; s. Robert Tokuichi and Toshiko (Nakashima) K.; m. Judith Naomi Tokumaru, June 28, 1970; children: Jennifer Tomiko, Susan Kazuko. BS, So. Calif. Coll. Optometry, 1968, OD cum laude, 1970. Pvt. practice optometry Waipahu, Honolulu, Hawaii, 1972—; pres. 1st Study Club for Optometrists, Honolulu, 1982-83; chmn. Bd. Examiners in Optometry, Honolulu, 1982-90; state dir. Optometric Extension Found., Honolulu, 1980-88. Served to lt. Med. Service Corps, USN, 1970-72. Named Outstanding Young Person of Hawaii, Hawaii State Jaycees, 1979. Fellow Am. Acad. Optometry (diplomate cornea and contract lens sect. 1991); mem. Hawaii Optometric Assn. (pres. 1979-80, Man of Yr. award 1976, Optometrist of Yr. 1983), Am. Optometric Assn., Armed Forces Optometric Soc. Home: 94-447 Holaniku St Mililani HI 96789-1710 Office: 94-748 Hikimoe St Waipahu HI 96797-3350 also: 1441 Kapiolani Blvd Ste 710 Honolulu HI 96814-4404

KUWAHARA, STEVEN SADAO, biochemist; b. Lahaina, Hawaii, July 20, 1940; s. Toshio and Hideko (Sasaki) K.; m. Rene Mikie Miyajima, June 24, 1972; children: Daniel T., Sara S. BS, Cornell U., 1962; MS, U. Wis., 1965, PhD, 1967. Research assoc. U. Wash., Seattle, 1966-67; asst. prof. biochemistry Calif. State U., Long Beach, 1967-71; asst. research biologist U. Calif., Irvine, 1971-73; unit chief Mich. Dept. Pub. Health, Lansing, 1973-76, sect. chief, 1976-82; mgr. test tech. Hyland Therapeutics, Los Angeles, 1982-89; mgr. validations Baxter Immunotherapy, Irvine, Calif., 1989-95; tech. dir. Pyramid Labs., Costa Mesa, Calif., 1995—; adj. rsch. assoc. Mich. State U., East Lansing, 1980-82. Contbr. articles to profl. jours. Asst. cubmaster Boy Scouts Am., Claremont, Calif., 1984-85, com. mem., 1985-94, scoutmaster, 1988-94; bd. dirs. West Covina (Calif.) Buddhist Ch., 1985-93, treas., 1986-92. Recipient Award of Merit, Long Beach Heart Assn., 1969; NIH spl. rsch. fellow, 1971-73. Mem. AAAS, Am. Chem. Soc., Am. Soc. Quality Control, Soc. Exptl. Biology and Medicine, Am. Fedn. Clin. Rsch., Am. Soc. Microbiology, N.Y. Acad. Scis., Parenteral Drug Assn., Regulatory Affairs Profls. Soc. Club: Torch (Lansing) (v.p. 1981-81). Home: 975 W Amador St Claremont CA 91711-3621 Office: Pyramid Labs 3505 Cadillac Ave Bldg B-2 Costa Mesa CA 92626-1430

KUWAYAMA, GEORGE, curator; b. N.Y.C., Feb. 25, 1925; s. Senzo and Fumiko Kuwayama; m. Lillian Yetsuko Yamashita, Dec. 5, 1961; children: Holly, Mark, Jeremy. B.A., Williams Coll., 1948; postgrad., NYU, 1948-54; M.A., U. Mich., 1956. Curator Oriental art L.A. County Mus. Art, L.A., 1959-70, sr. curator Far Ea. art, 1970—; lectr. U. So. Calif., UCLA; organizer spl. exhbns. Author: Far Eastern Lacquer, 1980, Shippo: The Art of Enameling in Japan, 1980; author, editor: Japanese Ink Painting, 1983, The Quest for Eternity, 1987, Ancient Mortuary Traditions of China, 1991, New Perspective on the Art of Ceramics in China, 1992; author, co-editor: Imperial Taste, 1989. Served with parachute inf. U.S. Army, 1944-46. Charles Freer scholar U. Mich., 1955-56; Inter-Univ. fellow Ford Found., 1957-58; rsch. travel grantee Nat. Endowment for Arts, 1974, 88. Mem. Assn. for Asian Studies, Am. Oriental Soc. (Louise Hackney fellow 1956), Coll. Art Assn., Japan Soc., Internat. House Japan, China Colloquium, Far Ea. Art Coun. Democrat. Methodist. Home: 1417 Comstock Ave Los Angeles CA 90024-5316 Office: LA County Mus Art 5905 Wilshire Blvd Los Angeles CA 90036-4523

KUYPER, PETER WALK, motion picture company executive; b. L.A., Apr. 4, 1942; s. A.B. and Mina (Walk) K.; m. Christine Anne Thomas, Feb. 27, 1966; children: Jonathan, Peter Jr., T. Christopher, Katherine. BA, Pomona Coll., 1964; MBA, U. Chgo., 1966. Master's lic. U.S. Coast Guard. V.p. Paramount TV, L.A., 1968-72, Paramount Pictures Corp., N.Y., 1972-78; pres. Newport (R.I.) Comm., 1978-80; v.p. MGM Film Co., N.Y.C., 1980-82; pres. MGM/United Artists Home Entertainment, N.Y.C., 1982-87; chmn. Motion Picture Licensing Corp., L.A., 1987—. Mem. Royal Prince Alfred Yacht Club, St. Francis Yacht Club, Calif. Yacht Club, N.Y. Athletic Club. Office: Motion Picture Licensing Corp 5458 Centinela Ave Los Angeles CA 90066-6970

KUZELL, WILLIAM CHARLES, physician, instrument company executive; b. Great Falls, Mont., Dec. 13, 1914; s. Charles R. and Theresa (O'Leary) K.; m. Françoise Lavelaine de Maubeuge, Oct. 15, 1945; children: Anne Frances Kuzell Hackstock, Elizabeth Jacqueline, Charles Maubeuge. Exchange student, Lingnan U., Canton, China, 1934-35, U. de Grenoble, summer 1935; BA, Stanford U., 1936, MD, 1941. Diplomate: Am. Bd. Internal Medicine. Research assoc. therapeutics Stanford U., 1948-56, physician in charge arthritis clinic, 1956-59, clin. prof. medicine emeritus, 1986—; chief div. rheumatology Presbyn. Med. Center, San Francisco, 1959-85; dir. emeritus Kuzell Inst. for Arthritis and Infectious Disease Research, Calif. Pacific Med. Ctr., San Francisco, 1985—; chmn. bd., chief exec. officer Oxford Labs., Inc., Foster City, to 1974; guest lectr. Japan Rheumatism Assn., 1964. Editor: Stanford Med. Bull, 1950-53. Pres. Fund for Arthritis and Infectious Disease Rsch., San Francisco, 1989—, No. Calif. chpt. Arthritis Found., 1971-72, chmn. bd., 1972-80. Capt. M.C. AUS, 1942-46. Named Man of Yr. in Medicine Shoong Found. Hall of Fame, 1980; recipient Disting. Service award Arthritis Found., 1981. Fellow ACP, Am. Coll. Rheumatology; mem. AMA, Japan Rheumatism Assn. (hon.), Sigma Xi, Sigma Nu, Nu Sigma Nu. Clubs: Olympic, Presidio Golf. Home: 25 W Clay St San Francisco CA 94121-1230 Office: 450 Sutter St Rm 1035 San Francisco CA 94108-3912

KUZMA, GEORGE MARTIN, bishop; b. Windber, Pa., July 24, 1925; s. Ambrose and Anne (Marton) K. Student, Benedictine Coll., Lisle, Ill.; BA, Duquesne U., postgrad.; postgrad., U. Mich.; grad., SS Cyril and Methodius Byzantine Cath. Sem. Ordained priest Byzantine Cath. Ch., 1955. Asst. pastor SS Peter and Paul Ch., Braddock, Pa., 1955-57; pastor Holy Ghost Ch., Charleroi, Pa., 1957-65, St. Michael Ch., Flint, Mich., 1965-70, St. Eugene Ch., Bedford, Ohio, 1970-72, Annunciation Ch., Anaheim, Calif., 1970-86; rev. monsignor Byzantine Cath. Ch., 1984, titular bishop, 1986, consecrated bishop, 1987; aux. bishop Byzantine Cath. Diocese of Passaic, N.J., 1987-90; bishop Van Nuys, Calif., 1991—; judge matrimonial tribunal, mem. religious edn. commn., mem. commn. orthodox rels. Diocese of Pitts., 1955-69; judge matrimonial tribunal, vicar for religious Diocese of Parma, 1969-82; treas., bd. dirs., chmn. liturgical commn., mem. clergy & seminarian rev. bd., liaison to ea. Cath. dirs. religious edn., bd. dirs. diocesan credit union, chmn. diocesan heritage bd., chmn. diocesan ecumenical commn. Diocese of Van Nuys, 1982-86; vicar gen. Diocese of Passaic; episcopal vicar for Ea. Pa.; chmn. Diocesan Retirement Plan Bd.; pres. Father Walter Cizsek Prayer League; chaplain Byzantine Carmelite Monastery, Sugarloaf, Pa. Assoc. editor Byzantine Cath. World; editor The Apostle. With USN, 1943-46, PTO. Office: Pastoral Ctr 18024 Parthenia St Northridge CA 91325-3150*

KVAM, ROBERT LARS, geological engineer, educator; b. Reno, Mar. 27, 1953; s. Arthur Christian and Grace Marie (Thomas) K.; m. Jean Marie Dailey, Aug. 16, 1980; children: Jay Jensen, Eric Michael. BS in Geol. Engring., U. Nev., 1975. Registered profl. engr., Nev.; engr. in tng., Nev. Staff geol. engr. S.E.A. Engrs./Planners, Carson City, Nev., 1979-83, Lumos & Assocs., Carson City, 1983; civil engr. Nev. Dept. Transp., Carson City, 1983—; engr.-in-tng. instr., Nev. Dept. Transp., Carson City, 1990-95. Mem. ASCE (dir.-at-large, treas., 1993-95). Democrat. Presbyterian. Home: 805 Crain St Carson City NV 89703 Office: Nev Dept Transp 1263 S Stewart St Carson City NV 89712

KVENVOLDEN, KEITH ARTHUR, geochemist; b. Cheyenne, Wyo., July 16, 1930; s. Owen Arthur and Agnes B. Kvenvolden; m. Mary Ann Lawrence, Nov. 7, 1959; children: Joan Agnes, Jon William. Geophys. Engr., Colo. Sch. Mines, 1952; MS, Stanford U., 1958, PhD, 1961. Registered geologist, Calif. Jr. geologist Socony Mobil Oil Co., Caracas, Venezuela, 1952-54; sr. rsch. technologist Mobil Oil Corp., Dallas, 1961-65; rsch. sci. Ames Rsch. Ctr. NASA, Mountain View, Calif., 1965-75, br. chief Ames Rsch. Ctr., 1971-75, div. chief Ames Rsch. Ctr., 1974-75; geologist U.S. Geol. Survey, Menlo Park, Calif., 1975-92, sr. scientist, 1992—; cons. prof. geology Stanford (Calif.) U., 1967—; courtesy prof. oceanography Oreg. State U., Corvallis, 1988—. Editor: Geochemistry and the Origin of Life, 1974, Geochemistry of Organic Molecules, 1980; contbr. articles to profl. jours. With U.S. Army, 1952-54. Gilbert fellow U.S. Geol. Survey, 1989; recipient Meritorious Svc. award U.S. Dept. of Interior. Fellow AAAS, Geol. Soc. Am., Explorers Club, Am. Geophys. Union; mem. Internat. Assn. Geochemistry and Cosmochemistry, Am. Assn. Petroleum Geologists, Geochemical Soc. (chmn. Organic Geochemical div., Best Paper award 1971). Office: US Geol Survey M/S 999 345 Middlefield Rd Menlo Park CA 94025-3561

KWAN, EDDY MAN KIN, research mechanician, consultant; b. Hong Kong, Apr. 30, 1959; came to U.S., 1967; s. Kim Lun and Sue (Wong) K.; m. Mary Yuen, May 20, 1990. BA in Maths., U. Calif., Berkeley, 1983. Design engr. Petrogen Inc., Richmond, Calif., 1978-81; sr. lab. mechanician U. Calif., Berkeley, 1983—; design cons. Bio-Rad, Cambridge, Mass., 1990—. Inventor underwater steel cutting system with gasoline and oxygen. Mem. U. Calif. Alumni Assn. Baptist. Office: U Calif 54 Mulford Hall 1170 VLSB Berkeley CA 94720

KWOCK, ROYAL, architect; b. San Bernardino, Calif., Sept. 29, 1947; s. Eddie Sing and Jeanie K.; m. Irene L. Leau, June 26, 1983. BArch, Calif. Poly. U., 1972. Registered architect, Calif.; Cert. Nat. Coun. Archtl. Registration Bds. Draftsman Martinskis & Prodis, San Jose, Calif., 1973-74; intern architect, staff architect, assoc. Hawley, Stowers & Assoc., San Jose, 1974-83; project architect Winston & May, Santa Clara, Calif., 1983-86; prin. May & Kwock, Santa Clara, 1986—. Bd. dirs. Youth Sci. Inst. Santa Clara Valley, 1985; mem. Nat. Trust Hist. Preservation, San Jose, 1984. Corp. mem. AIA (corr. mem. Interiors Commn. 1982-83), Kiwanis Club of West San Jose (bd. dirs. 1993). Office: May & Kwock AIA Architects 2290 Walsh Ave Santa Clara CA 95050-2514

KWONG, DANIEL WAI-KIN, management and financial consultant, educator, writer; b. Hong Kong, Aug. 1, 1958; came to U.S., 1978; s. Moon Kwok and Fung Ha (Leung) K.; m. Oriana Bao-er Ou, Sept. 2, 1985 (div. Mar. 1993); 1 child, Cassandra Anthea. AA, East L.A. Coll., 1980; BA, Calif. State U., L.A., 1982; postgrad., Am. Grad. Sch. Internat. Mgmt., 1983; JD, Thomas Jefferson Coll. Law, 1993. Lic. fire and casualty insurance broker and agt., life ins. agt., notary pub., Calif.; cert. adult edn. educator, substitute tchr., Calif. Pvt. practice mgmt. cons., fin. cons. Monterey Park, Calif., 1984—; translator, Monterey Park, 1989—; high sch. guest tchr. Los Angeles County, 1989—; law book cons., critic Glansville Pubs., Dobbs Ferry, N.Y., 1986—; prof., faculty advisor LaSalle U., Slidell, La., 1994—. Author: A Hidden Tool, 1990; translator: (from Chinese to English) The Tales of Marsh-Land, 1990; critic, cons. various law and political books; contbr. book critic to New Asia Review, 1994—; columnist Favorites newsletter. Founding life mem., chmn.'s coun. Rep. Nat. Com., 1992—, mem. Free Enterprise Coun., 1993—; founding mem. U.S. Holocaust Mus., Washington, 1992; consul-gen. Holy See of Antioch, U.K., 1994; assoc. State Ctrl. Com., Calif. Rep. Party, 1992—, founding mem. Victory Fund, 1993; founding ptnr. Competitiveness Ctr. Hudson Inst., 1993—; founding mem. Rep. Presdl. Trust, 1992—, Rep. Nat. Candidate Trust, 1992—; presdl. election com. Bush-Quayle, 1992; at-large del. Rep. Platform Planning Com., 1992—; sponsor Nat. Rep. Congrl. com., 1992—, Population Comm. Internat., 1993—; mem. Rep. Senatorial Inner Circle, 1993—, Rep. Fund for the 90s, 1993—, Heritage Found., 1993—; mem. adv. bd. Oliver North for U.S. Senate Com.; mem. campaign team Matt Fong for State Treas. Com.-Calif.; mem. Bush for Tex. Gov. Com., Jeb Bush for Fla. Gov. Com., Sen. Orrin Hatch Com., Sen. Daniel Moynihan Com., Mike Huffington for U.S. Senate Com., Gov. Pete Wilson Com.-Calif.; mem. Pub. Concern Found., U.S. Justice Found., Ctr. Marine Conservation, Sino Charity Found., Inc., Am. Conservative Union; del., lobbyist, activist Calif. Coun. Internat. Trade; invited Rep. Presdl. Roundtable summer policy forum, Washington, 1994; founding nat. mem. U.S. Libr. Congress; chair blingual adv. coun., Repetto Sch., Alhambra Sch. Dist., Calif., 1994—, mem site coun., 1994—; founding mem. invited by House Speaker Gingrich The Speaker's Citizen Task Force, 1995—; mem. exploratory com. 250 Club of Dole, 1995—; co-sponsor Nat. Tax Limitation Com., 1994—; mem. Coll. Rep. Nat. Com., 1994—; commr. 1996 Congl. Platform Commn.; nat. campaign advisor Nat. Rep. Senatorial Com.;. Recipient Presdl. award Rep. Presdl. Legion Merit, 1994, presdl. honor roll, 1993, Cert. Commendation, U.S. Vice Pres. Dan Quayle, 1992, Presdl. Election Yr. recognition Rep. Nat. Com., 1992, Cert. Appreciation, Order of Liberty, Nat. Rep. Congl. Com., 1993, Congressional Order of Freedom, 1995; named VIP guest del. Rep. Nat. Conv., 1992; Knight Grand Cross, Order Golden Fleece, The Holy See of Antioch, 1994, Order Golden Seraphim, 1994. Mem. AAAS, N.Y. Acad. Scis., Rep. Presdl. Task Force (founding life mem., trustee 1991, honor roll 1991,ofcl. del. 1994), Chinese Assn. Internat. Trade, Ctr. Modern China (rschr. 1992—), Asia Soc., Hong Kong Assn. So. Calif., Pres.'s Club, Orgn. Chinese Ams., L.A.-Quangzhou Sister City Assn., Internat. Churchill Soc., Monterey Park Rep. Club, Songwriter's Club Am. (life), Acad. Polit. Sci., Poet's Guild, Ripon Soc., Acad. Polit. Sci., Am. Biographical Inst. N.C. (editl. adv. bd., rsch. bd.), Nat. Authors Registry. Home: 601 S Cecil St Monterey Park CA 91755

KWONG, JAMES KIN-PING, geological engineer; b. Kowloon, Hong Kong, Sept. 12, 1954; came to U.S., 1985; s. Joseph and Mary (Sung) K.; m. Annie May-Ching Loh, June 7, 1980; 1 child, John Richard. BSc with honors, U. London, Eng., 1977; MSc, U. Leeds, Eng., 1978, PhD, 1985. Registered profl. civil engr., Hawaii; chartered engr., Eng. Engrng. geologist Maunsell Cons., Hong Kong, 1978-80, Palmer & Turner Geotechnics, Hong Kong, 1980-82; cons., rsch. assoc. U. Guelph, Ont., Can., 1982-85; project mgr. Geolabs Hawaii, Honolulu, 1985-87, Dames & Moore, Honolulu, 1987-91; v.p. Pacific Geotech. Engrs., Inc., Honolulu, 1991—; guest lectr. dept. civil engrng. U. Hawaii, Honolulu, 1990—. Contbr. articles to profl. jours. Recipient J.F. Kirkaldy's prize U. London, 1977. Mem. ASCE (exec. bd. dirs., past pres. Hawaii sect., mem. nat. com. on microtunneling, mem. nat. com. stds. of practice), NSPE, Inst. Mining and Metallurgy, Cons. Engrs. Coun. Hawaii (pres.-elect, chmn. internat. bus. com.), Can. Geotech. Soc. Office: Pacific Geotech Engrs Inc 1030 Kohou St Ste 101 Honolulu HI 96817-4434

KYD, MARILYN GRATTON, writer, editor; b. Wichita, Kans., Jan. 26, 1948; d. Robert and Celia (Goldman) Gratton; m. Charles W. Kyd, Mar. 25, 1984. AA, Pasadena City Coll., 1967; BA in English, UCLA, 1969. Cert. secondary tchr., Calif. Tchr. English Glendora (Calif.) High Sch., 1970-72; tchr. English and creative writing Hueneme High Sch., Oxnard, Calif., 1972-76; employment counselor Snelling & Snelling, Oxnard, 1976-77; ptnr., mgr. MG Pers. Agy., Santa Monica, Calif., 1977-78; tech. writer, editor Stanwick Corp., Ventura, Calif., 1978-80; engrng. writer Northrop Corp., Newbury Park, Calif., 1980; logistics analyst Automation Industries, Vitro Labs., Oxnard, 1980-81; mgr. documentation Computer Data Corp., Westlake Village, Calif., 1981-82; dir. mktg. Kiely Profl. Svcs., Westlake Village, 1983-84; pres., owner CashMaster Bus. Systems, Inc., Seattle, 1984—; owner, operator profl. resume preparation bus.; free-lance tech. writer and editor. Author: It's A Good Thing I'm Not Married, 1975, The Leopard and his Brother, 1995; contbr. articles to profl. jours. Named Young Careerist Bus. Profl. Women, 1975; recipient 3rd pl. Nat. Writers Club articles contest, 1976, 2nd pl. for photography Port Hueneme Harbor Days, 1976, Honorable mention Writer's Digest Articles Contest, 1987. Mem. Nat. Writers Club, UCLA Alumni Assn., Mensa (columnist 1978).

KYL, JON, senator; b. Oakland, Nebr., Apr. 25, 1942; s. John and Arlene (Griffith) K.; m. Caryll Louise Collins, June 5, 1964; children: Kristine Kyl Gavin, John Jeffry. BA, U. Ariz., 1964, LLB, 1966. Atty. Jennings, Strouss & Salmon, Phoenix, 1966-86; mem. 100th-103rd Congresses from 4th Ariz. dist., 1987-94; senator Ariz., 1995—; mem. Energy & Natural Resources Com., Jud. Com., select com. on Intelligence. Past chmn. Phoenix C. of C.; founding dir. Crime Victim Found., Phoenix Econ. Growth Corp.; past bd. dirs. Ariz. Acad.; past chmn. Young Rep.; gen. coun. Ariz. Rep. Party. Mem. Ariz. State Bar Assn. Office: 702 Hart Senate Bldg Washington DC 20515-0302

KYLE, RICHARD DANIEL, state legislator, fundraising consultant; b. Flint, Mich., July 31, 1960; s. Roland W. and Mary Louise Kyle Tubbs; m. Cyndi Kingaan, Apr. 30, 1994. BS, Ea. Mich. U., 1984. Cons. RDK Comms., Phoenix, 1984-89; dir. adminstrn. U.S. Census Bur., Phoenix, 1989-90; exec. dir. Epilepsy Soc., Scottsdale, Ariz., 1990-93; mem. Ariz. Ho. of Reps., Phoenix, 1993—. Mem. Ariz. Young Reps., Scottsdale, 1988—; pres. Mich. Young Reps., Ann Arbor, 1987. Named to Outstanding Young Men in Am., 1985, 86. Mem. Chandler C. of C. Roman Catholic. Home: PO Box 51742 Phoenix AZ 85076-1742 Office: Ho of Reps 1700 W Washington St Phoenix AZ 85007-2812

KYTE, LYDIANE, botanist; b. L.A., Jan. 6, 1919; d. Aurele and Helen Scott (Douglas) Vermeulen; m. Robert McClung Kyte, June 2, 1939; children: Katherine Liu, Bobbin Cave, William Robert Kyte. BS, U. Wash., 1964. Supt. Weyerhaeuser Co., Rochester, Wash., 1972-77; lab mgr. Briggs Nursery, Olympia, Wash., 1977-80; owner Cedar Valley Nursery, Centralia, Wash., 1980—; cons. Internat. Exec. Service Corps, Brazil, 1987, Egypt, 1990. Author: Plants From Test Tubes: An Introduction to Micropropagation, 1983, 2d rev. edit., 1988. Mem. Internat. Plant Propagators' Soc., Tissue Culture Assn., Internat. Assn. Plant Tissue Culture, Am. Assn. for Hort. Sci., Am. Assn. Univ. Women. Home and Office: Cedar Valley Nursery 3833 Mcelfresh Rd SW Centralia WA 98531-9510

LAALY, HESHMAT OLLAH, research chemist, roofing consultant, author; b. Kermanshah, Iran, June 23, 1927; came to Germany, 1951, Can., 1967, U.S., 1984; s. Jacob and Saltanat (Afshani) L.; m. Parvaneh Modarai, Oct. 7, 1963; (div. 1971); children: Ramesh, Edmond S.; m. Parivash M. Farahmand, Feb. 7, 1982. BS in Chemistry, U. Stuttgart, Germany, 1955; MS in Chemistry, U. Stuttgart, Republic of Germany, 1958, PhD in Chemistry, 1962. Chief chemist Kress Sohne, Krefeld, Germany, 1963-67; analytical chemist Gulf Oil Research Ctr., Montreal, Que., Can., 1967-70; material scientist Bell-Northern Research, Ottawa, Ont., Can., 1970-71; research officer NRC of Can., Ottawa, 1972-84; pres. Roofing Materials Sci. and Tech., L.A., 1984—; Patentee in field. Author: The Science and Technology of Traditional and Modern Roofing Systems, 1992 (World Lifetime Achievement award Am. Biog. Inst. 1992); patentee bi-functional photovoltaic single ply roofing membrane. Mem. AAAS (Can. chpt.), ASTM, Inst. Roofing and Waterproofing Cons., Single-Ply Roofing Inst., Assn. Profl. Engrs. Ontario, Am. Chem. Soc., Internat. Union of Testing and Rsch. Labs. for Material and Structures (tech. com. 75), Constrn. Specifications Inst., Nat. Roofing Contractors Assn., UN Indsl. Devels. Orgn., Internat. Conf. Bldg. Ofcls., Roofing Cons. Inst., Inst. for Roofing and Waterproofing Cons., Can. Standard Assn., Can. Gen. Standards Bd. Office: Roofing Materials Sci & Tech 9037 Monte Mar Dr Los Angeles CA 90035-4235

LABA, MARVIN, management consultant; b. Newark, Mar. 17, 1928; s. Joseph Abraham and Jean Cecil (Saunders) L.; m. Sandra Seltzer, Apr. 16, 1961 (div. May 1974); children: Stuart Michael, Jonathan Todd; m. Elizabeth Luger, June 11, 1974 (div. 1979). BBA, Ind. U., 1951. Buyer Bamberger's (Macy's N.J.), Newark, 1951-67; v.p., mdse. adminstr. Macy's N.Y., 1967-73; v.p., gen. mdse. mgr. Howland/Steinback, White Plains, N.Y., 1973-75, Pomeroy's, Levittown, Pa., 1975-76; v.p., gen. mdse. mgr., sr. v.p., exec. v.p. May Co. Calif., North Hollywood, 1976-79; pres., chief exec. officer G. Fox & Co. (div. of the May dept. stores), Hartford, Conn., 1979-82; pres. Richard Theobald & Assocs., L.A., 1983; pres., chief exec. officer Marvin Laba & Assocs., L.A., 1983—. With U.S. Army, 1946-48. Office: Marvin Laba & Assoc 6255 W Sunset Blvd Ste 617 Los Angeles CA 90028-7407

LABBE, ARMAND JOSEPH, museum curator, anthropologist; b. Lawrence, Mass., June 13, 1944; s. Armand Henri and Gertrude Marie (Martineau) L.; m. Denise Marie Scott, Jan. 17, 1969 (div. 1972). BA in Anthropology, Univ. Mass., 1969; MA in Anthropology, Calif. State U., 1986; lifetime instr. credential in anthropology, State Calif. Curator collections Bowers Mus., Santa Ana, Calif., 1978-79, curator anthropology, 1979-86, chief curator, 1986-91, dir. rsch. and collections, 1991—; tchr. Santa Ana Coll., 1981-86, Calif. State U., Fullerton, 1982, 83, 88, U. Calif., Irvine, 1983, 87, 91, 93; trustee Balboa Arts Conservation Ctr., San Diego, 1989—, Ams. Found., Greenfield, Mass., 1985-94, Quintcentenary Festival Discovery, Orange County, Calif., 1990-91; mem. adv. bd. Elan Internat., Newport Beach, Calif., 1992—; trustee Mingei Internat. Mus., LaJolla, Calif., 1993—; inaugural guest lectr. Friends of Ethnic Art, San Francisco, 1988; hon. bd. dirs. Ethnic Arts Coun. of L.A. Author: Man and Cosmos, 1982, Ban Chiang, 1985, Colombia Before Columbus, 1986 (1st prize 1987), Leigh Wiener: Portraits, 1987, Colombia Antes de Colón, 1988 (honored at Gold Mus. Bogotá, Colombia, 1988), Images of Power: Master Works of the Bowers Museum of Cultural Art, 1992; co-author Tribute to The Gods: Treasures of the Museo del Oro, Bogotá, 1992, Guardians of the Life Stream: Shamans, Art and Power In Prehispanic Central Panama, 1995. Hon. bd. dirs. Ethnic Arts Coun. L.A.; cons. Orange County Coun. on History and Art, Santa Ana, 1981-85; mem. Task Force on County Cultural Resources, Orange County, 1979; cons., interviewer TV prodn. The Human Journey, Fullerton, 1986-89. With USAF, 1963-67. Recipient cert. of Recognition Orange County Bd. Suprs., 1982, award for outstanding scholarship Colombian Community, 1987; honored for authorship Friends of Libr., 1987, 88. Fellow Am. Anthrop. Assn.; mem. AAAS, Am. Assn. Mus., N.Y. Acad. Scis., S.W. Anthrop. Assn. Home: 2854 Royal Palm Dr # C Costa Mesa CA 92626-3828

LABBY, DANIEL HARVEY, medical educator, psychiatry educator; b. Portland, Oreg., Sept. 1, 1914; s. Harry A. and Sonia (Goldfarb) L.; m. Margaret Selling, Dec. 28, 1940; children: Joan, David, Louise. BA, Reed Coll., 1935; MD, U. Oreg., 1939. Intern Johns Hopkins Hosp., Balt., 1939-40; resident medicine N.Y. Hosp., N.Y.C., 1943-45; fellow psychiatry Tavistock Inst. for Human Rels., London, Eng., 1970-71, 77-78; prof. medicine Oreg. Health Sci. U., Portland, 1948—, prof. psychiatry, 1978—; asst. The Rockefeller Inst., N.Y.C., 1945-48; vis. prof. medicine Med. Coll. Va., 1958, U. Strasbourg, France, 1960-61, U. Colo. Med. Sch., 1964; sr. scholar Ctr. for Ethics in Health Care, Oreg. Health Sci. Ctr., 1989—. Contbr. articles to profl. jours. Capt. USMC, 1941-44. Noble Wiley Jones fellow in pathology U. Oreg. Med. Sch., 1937-38, A Blaine Brower fellow Ames Coll., 1953, Commonwealth fellow, 1960-61, Disting. Svc. award Reed Coll., 1995; named Alumnus of Yr. Oreg. Health Sci. Ctr., 1991. Mem. Sigma Xi, Alpha Omega Alpha. Home: 5931 SW Hamilton St Portland OR 97221-1231 Office: Univ Oreg Health Scis Ctr 3181 SW Sam Jackson Park Rd Portland OR 97201-3011

LABOVITZ, EARL A., allergist; b. Cleveland, Miss., July 12, 1949. MD, U Miss, 1975. Allergist Desert Samaritan Hosp., Mesa, Ariz. Office: Mesa-Tempe Allergy & Asthma Clinic 2945 S Dobson Rd Ste 1 Mesa AZ 85202-7980*

LABOWE, MARK LAWRENCE, plastic surgeon; b. L.A., Aug. 5, 1953. MD, UCLA. Plastic surgeon St. John's Hosp., Santa Monica, Calif.; asst. clin. prof. Sch. Med. UCLA. Office: 100 Ucla Medical Plz Ste 747 Los Angeles CA 90024-6970*

LA BRUE, TERRY J., advertising executive; b. Fresno, Calif., Feb. 25, 1949; s. John Lawrence and Zepha Ruth (Frankum) La B.; m. Linda Johnson; 1 child, Annique Noel. BA in Journalism and Fine Arts, Calif. State U., Fresno, 1972. Art dir. San Francisco Progress Newspaper, 1973-74, Carter Hawley Hale, Oakland, Calif., 1974-75, Nordstrom, Inc., Seattle, 1975-77; art dir., writer Meyers, Wolfe, Kilgore & Sutter, Seattle, 1977-79; pres. Fisher, Brady & La Brue, Seattle, 1979-89; mktg. cons., Wash., 1976—; dir. mktg. Bogle & Gates, Seattle, 1995—. Editor: Great British Breakfasts, 1982, British Recipes from Country Inns, 1983. Mem. vestry and comm. com. Emmanuel Parish, Mercer Island; active Rep. campaigns for elected Wash. offices, 1980—; bus. vol. for the arts. Recipient MAME Grand award Seattle Master Builders, 1985, 91, John Cotton Dana award ALA. Mem. Am. Inst. Graphic Arts, Pub. Relations Soc. Am. (citation of excellence 1985, Totem award 1985, 86, 87, 89), Am. Advt. Fedn. (awards com. 1984), Northwest Culinary Alliance (bd. dirs., dir. communications 1984-86), Seattle C. of C., Am. Inst. Graphic Arts, Wash. Athletic Club, Mercer Island Country Club, Seattle Art Dirs. and Copywriters Club, Delta Upsilon Fraternity Alumni Assn. Episcopalian. Clubs: Seattle Ad (Silver award 1982, 83, 84, 85), Portland Ad (Best of Show award 1982, Mature Media award 1993, 94). Home: 7236 78th Ave SE Mercer Island WA 98040-5511 Office: La Brue Communications 150 Circle Dr SE Lacey WA 98503-2526

LACEY, RONALD EDWARD, minority outreach advisor; b. Chgo., Apr. 6, 1958; s. Marion and Grace (Taylor) L.; m. Rochelle Rhone, Oct. 6, 1979 (div. Sept. 1983); children: Isaiah, Rhonda, Seraiah. Student, Yuba C.C., Marysville, Calif., 1985-87; BA, Chico State U., 1990. Outreach advisor Butte C.C., Oroville, Calif., 1991—; instr. Butte C.C., Oroville, 1991—. Activist Pan African Union, Chico, Calif., 1989; actor Martin Luther King Prodn. Co., Chico, 1989; big brother C.A.V.E., Chico, 1988; baseball mgr. Chico Little League, 1989—. With USN, 1976-80. Minority Equity fellow Chico State U., 1990, Lt. Rawlins award Chico State U., 1990.

LACHEMANN, MARCEL, professional baseball manager; b. L.A., June 13, 1941. BSBA, U. So. Calif., 1962. Former player Kansas City A's (moved to Oakland); pitching coach Calif. Angels, 1983-92, mgr., head coach, 1994—; pitching coach Fla. Marlins, 1992-94. Office: California Angels 2000 E Gene Autry Way Anaheim CA 92806-6100

LACITIS, ERIK, journalist; b. Buenos Aires, Argentina, Dec. 10, 1949; came to U.S., 1960, naturalized, 1965; s. Erik and Irene Z. L.; m. Malorie Nelson, Aug. 30, 1976. Student, Coll. Forest Resources, U. Wash., 1967-71. Editor U. Wash. Daily, 1970; pub. New Times Jour., 1970-71; reporter, pop-music cons. Seattle Post Intelligencer, 1972—; reporter, columnist Seattle Times, 1972; v.p., treas. Malorie Nelson, Inc., 1980—. Recipient numerous awards from Wash. State chpt. Sigma Delta Chi; Nat. Headliners Club award, 1978; winner gen. interest competition Nat. Soc. Newspaper Columnists, 1987. Lutheran. Office: The Seattle Times PO Box 70 Fairview Ave N & John St Seattle WA 98111-0070

LACK, LARRY HENRY, small business owner; b. Richland, Wash., Aug. 27, 1952; s. Eugene Herman and Myrtle (Wellman) L.; m. Patricia Ann Henry, Aug. 19, 1978; children: Vicki Marie, Rachel Ann. Enlisted USAF, 1970, disabled vet., 1978; aircraft mechanic Ill., S.C., Okla. AFBs., 1970-78; inventor, prin. Lack Industries, Inc., Shreveport, La., 1979-85, Phoenix, 1985—; CEO Stellar Internat., Phoenix, 1991-92; cons. U.S. Air Force, Altus AFB, 1978-80, Cates & Phillips Patent Attys., Phoenix, 1985—; pres. La. Innovators Tech., Shreveport, 1981-82; lectr. Glendale Community Coll. 1987-88; guest lectr. Ariz. State U., 1989-90; authored legislation to regulate invention promotion cos. in Ariz., 1989. Patentee in field. Mem. Internat. Platform Assn. Republican. Home: 3106 W Vogel Ave # 110 Phoenix AZ 85051-2636 Office: 2420 W 1st St Ste 65 Tempe AZ 85281-2335

LACKEY, LAWRENCE BAILIS, JR., retired architect, urban designer; b. Santa Fe, Nov. 7, 1914; s. Lawrence Bailis and Mary (McFie) L.; children: Merryl, Stephen Byrne. Student in liberal arts, U. N.Mex., 1936; BS in Architecture, U. Mich., 1938; postgrad. (Acad. fellow in town planning), Cranbrook Acad. Art, 1939-41; grad. seminar on computer aids in urban design, M.I.T., 1969. Registered architect, Calif., Alaska. Designer Eliel and Eero Saarinen, Bloomfield Hills, Mich., 1940-41, Wurster, Bernardi & Emmons, San Francisco, 1946-48; architect Skidmore, Owings & Merrill, San Francisco, 1948-54, John Lord King (Architect), San Francisco, 1954-56, John Carl Warnecke & Assos., San Francisco, 1956-59; prin. Lawrence Lackey (Urban Design Cons.), San Francisco, 1959-63, Sasaki, Walker, Lackey & Assos., San Francisco, 1963-65, Lawrence Lackey & Assos., San Francisco and San Rafael, Calif., 1965-75, Lawrence Lackey (Architect), San Rafael, Calif., 1978-91; cons. architect U. Alaska, 1959-71; mem. faculty U. Mont., 1964-71. Designer: preliminary concept Golden Gateway Redevel, San Francisco, 1956, U. N.Mex. Campus Devel. Plan, 1960, U. Mont. Campus Devel. Plan, 1964, Okla. Health Center Devel. Plan, Oklahoma City, 1968, U. Alaska Campus Devel. Plan, 1968, Sci. Teaching Complex Design Concept at, U. Kans. Med. Center, 1970, Creekside Center Complex, San Rafael, 1979. Mem. coordinating com. for redevel. San Francisco C. of C., 1955-58, chmn. com. urban design, 1971. Served as officer USN, 1942-45. Fellow AIA (dir. No. Calif. chpt. 1962); mem. San Francisco Planning and Urban Renewal Assn. (dir., mem. exec. com. 1959-63), San Francisco Planning and Housing Assn. (pres. 1956-59). Office: 623 Cherry Ave Sonoma CA 95476-4183

LACOM, WAYNE CARL, artist, writer; b. Glendale, Calif., Oct. 11, 1922; s. Frdinand and Blanche Charlotte (Heinmiller) LaC.; m. Diana Crystal Strode LaCom, Aug. 27, 1949; children: Lawrence Carl, Laura Diana, Eric Wayne. Student, Art Ctr. Sch., L.A., 1942-43, Chouinard Art Inst., L.A., 1943-45, Jepson Art Inst., L.A., 1945-47. Cert. Dept. Edn., Calif. Artist Conners-Joyce, L.A., N.Y.C., 1943-45; freelance artist pvt. practice, L.A., 1946-47; artist, tchr. L.A. Unified Sch. Dist., 1948-78; artist, graphic designer Emerson Gallery, Encino, Tarzana, Calif., 1964-84; owner, dir., pres. Internat. Art Svcs., Inc., Encino, Calif., 1975—; in-svc. tng. cons. L.A. Unified Sch. Dist., 1950-63; treas. Artists for Ednl. Action, L.A., 1972-75. 100 one man shows Watercolor Painting, 1943—; TV demos, 1960-65; designer: Sculputre and Stained Glass, 1964—; publisher: over 300 edits., 1975—; paintings reporduces in numerous art books including The California Style and The California Romantics. Recipient various Juried Shows awards, 1949—; named 1st Place Catalina Art Assn., 1989, Best of Show Lahainatown Poster Comp, Hawaii, 1993. Mem. Nat. Watercolor Soc. (past pres.). Home: 16703 Alginet Pl Encino CA 91436-4119 Office: International Art Services 16703 Alginet Pl Encino CA 91436-4119

LACOMBE, RITA JEANNE, bank consultant; b. Panama City, Fla., Sept. 28, 1947; d. Robert Rosario and Virginia May (Mauldin) L. AA, Los Angeles Pierce Coll., 1967; BSBA, Calif. State U., Northridge, 1969; postgrad., Stanford U., 1986. Br. mgr. Security Pacific Nat. Bank, San Fernando Valley, Calif., 1970-78; bankcard compliance officer, asst. v.p. Security Pacific Nat. Bank, Woodland Hills, Calif., 1978-82; sect. mgr., v.p. Security Pacific Nat. Bank, Los Angeles, 1982-87; sr. sales rep. corp. microcomputer sales ComputerLand, L.A., 1987-88; corp. sales rep. microcomputer sales ComputerLand, Northridge and Laguna Hills, Calif., 1988-89; sr. mgmt. cons. fin. industries group Deloitte & Touche, CPA, L.A., 1989—. Membership chair Sierra Club, Los Angeles, 1982. Mem. Nat. Assn. Female Execs. Democrat. Roman Catholic.

LACOUNTE, CHERYL DEWERFF, academic director, educator; b. Long Beach, Calif., Aug. 13, 1961; d. Duane Lee DeWerff and Margery Carol (Plumb) Singer; m. Christopher Thomas LaCounte, Aug. 27, 1983; 1 child: Brendan Alexander. BBA with honors, Ea. N.Mex. U., 1983; MS, Troy State U., 1993. Cert. hotel mgr., housekeeping supr. Bridal cons. Jordan Marsh, Framingham, Mass., 1983-84; exec. asst. Sheraton Tara Hotel, Framingham, 1984-85, pers. dir., 1985-87; coll. instr. Newbury Coll., Brookline, Mass., 1987-91; campus dir. Newbury Coll., Framingham, 1990-91; dir. student affairs, instr. Ea. N.Mex. U., Ruidoso, 1991—. Counselor Parental Stress Hotline, Mass., 1987-91; mem. steering com. Big Bros./Big Sisters of Lincoln County, 1994—, 1st and 2nd ann. Ctrl. Mountain Women's Conf., 1992, 93; facilitator N.Mex. Gov. Conf. on Sch. and Cmty., 1993. Mem. NAFE, Acad. Women Achievers, Delta Mu Delta. Republican. Office: Ea N Mex U 1400 Sudderth Dr Ruidoso NM 88345-6103

LACY, CAROL ANGELA, insurance executive; b. Watford, Eng., July 15, 1943; came to U.S., 1967, naturalized, 1976; d. Thomas and Winifred Joan (Stromberg) Carney; m. Floyd Raymond Lacy, May 25, 1968 (dec. July 1988); children: Susan, Timothy. Claims adjuster Central Mut. Ins. Co., Toronto, Can., 1964-68; exec. sec. TransFresh Corp., Salinas, Calif., 1968-70; claims examiner Monterey Bay Found., Salinas, 1972-78; pres., account mgr. ABC Med. Claims Services, Salinas, 1978—; chmn. bd. dirs. Monterey County Spl. Health Care Authority, Salinas, 1982-85. mem. adv. bd. Natividad Hosp., Salinas, 1979-82, North Monterey County Bd. Edn., Salinas, 1977-83; mem. 101 Bypass com., 1983—, chmn. exec. bd. 1986—; treas. Monterey County Bds. Assn., Salinas, 1981-83; mem. Monterey County Grand Jury, Salinas, 1984-85; pres. Prunedale PTA, Salinas, 1976; founding trustee Med. Ctr. Found. Monterey County, 1988; co-chmn. Yes on Measure B Com., 1989; chmn. Com. to elect Judy Pennycook, 1989, 92, also to elect Bill Kennedy, 1992; chmn. Com. to Elect Flip Baldwin, 1989; commr. Monterey County Planning Commn., 1995—; mem. tech. adv. com. 101 Bypass, 1989. Recipient Honorary Service award Prunedale PTA, 1982. Mem. Monterey Bay Life Underwriters Assn., League of Women Voters. Republican. Baptist. Avocations: stamp collecting, fishing. gardening.

LACY, CAROLYN JEAN, elementary education educator, secondary education educator; b. Marshall, Ark., Apr. 6, 1944; d. Charles Ira Bolch and Edna Rebecca Cherry; 1 child, Kelli Jean. AA with distinction, Riverside City Coll., 1980; BA, U. Calif., Riverside, 1982, postgrad., 1983; MEd, U.S. Internat. U., 1993. Cert. social sci. tchr., Calif. Educator Perris (Calif.) Elem. Sch. Dist., 1984-89, Rialto (Calif.) Unified Sch. Dist., 1989—; instr. Developing Capable People, Riverside, Calif., 1986-89; presenter, lectr. Jurupa Unified Sch. Dist., Riverside, 1990, Rialto Unified Sch. Dist., 1990; developer peer tutor proglram Perris Elem. Sch. Dist., 1989; dir. chess club Dollahan Elem. Sch., 1995, computer chmn., 1995—. Editor: (newsletter) Perris Lights, 1989. Active Students in Environ. Action, Riverside, 1978; mem. Riverside County Task Force for Self-Esteem. Named Mentor Tchr. State of Calif., 1988. Mem. AAUW, NEA, Calif. Tchrs. Assn., Internat. Reading Assn., U. Calif. Alumni Assn., Phi Delta Kappa, Alpha Gamma Sigma. Democrat. Mem. LDS Ch. Home: 4044 Wallace St Riverside CA 92509-6809

LACY, GEORGE M., plastic surgeon; b. Tulsa, 1933. MD, Johns Hopkins U., 1959. Plastic surgeon St. Luke's Hosp., Denver. Office: 360 S Garfield St Ste 690 Denver CO 80209-3136*

LACY, LEE MARVA LOU, mathematics educator; b. Longview, Tex., Dec. 28, 1942; d. Louis and Grace Tecumseh (Davis) Armstrong; BS in Math., Prairie View (Tex.) A&M U., 1965; MA in Secondary Math. Edn. (grantee Roosevelt Sch. Dist. 1977-78), Ariz. State U., 1978; m. Troy Lee Lacy, June 20, 1965; children: Corwyn Enrico, Aimee Siubhan, Gardenia Catriona. Tchr. math. schs. in Tex., Nebr., Md. and Ariz., 1965-68, 69-77; sr. gen. edn. instr., counselor Washington Jobs Corps, 1968; tchr. math., spl. tchr. for gifted C.O. Greenfield Jr. High Sch., Phoenix, 1978-82; math and gifted resource tchr. T.B. Barr Sch., Phoenix, 1982-85; instr. math. South Mountain C.C. at Ariz. State U., Tempe, 1985-87, Glendale C.C., 1987—; faculty assoc. Prairie View A&M U., 1981-83; vis. math. tchr. South Mountain C.C., Phoenix, 1982-85; workshop leader, cons. in field. Vol., Arthritis Found., Leukemia Soc.; v.p., trustee sanctuary choir First Instl. Bapt. Ch., Phoenix. Mem. Nat. Council Tchrs. Math., NEA, Assn. Supervision and Curriculum Devel., Ariz. Edn. Assn., Ariz. Assn. Tchrs. Math., Roosevelt Classroom Tchrs. Assn., Ariz. State U. Alumni Assn., Am. Math. Assn. 2-Yr. Colls., Math. Assn. Am., Maricopa County NAACP, Delta Sigma Theta Alumnae. Baptist. Home: 9404 S Kenneth Pl Tempe AZ 85284-4104 Office: Glendale CC Faculty Office Bldg 04-120 Glendale AZ 85302

LACY, STEVEN DOUGLAS, bio-electrical engineer; b. Champagne, Ill., June 10, 1970; s. Jeffrey Lynn and Mary Lee (Schoenbeck) L. ScB, Brown U., 1992; postgrad., Stanford U., 1992—. Rsch. asst. Brown U., Providence, R.I., 1989-92; elec. engr. Affymax Rsch. Inst., Palo Alto, Calif., 1993—; sound engr. Idle Hands, Palo Alto, 1994—. Educator Sexual Assault Peer Edn. Program, Brown U., 1991-92. Faculty scholar Brown U., 1991-92. Mem. Brown Biomed. Engrng. Soc. (pres. 1991-92), Calif. Athletic Club, Concordia Sports Club, Sigma Xi. Democrat. Office: Affymax Rsch Inst 3380 Central Expy Santa Clara CA 95051

LADAR, JERROLD MORTON, lawyer; b. San Francisco, Aug. 2, 1933. AB, U. Wash., 1956; LLB, U. Calif., Berkeley, 1960. Bar: Calif. 1961, U.S. Supreme Ct. 1967. Law clk. to judge U.S. Dist. Ct. (no. dist.) Calif., 1960-61; asst. U.S. atty. San Francisco, 1961-70; chief criminal div., 1968-70; mem. firm MacInnis & Donner, San Francisco, 1970-72; prof. criminal law and procedure U. San Francisco Law Sch., 1962-83; pvt. practice San Francisco, 1970-94; ptnr. Ladar & Knapp, San Francisco, 1994—; lectr. Hastings Law Coll. Trial Advocacy, 1984—; chair pvt. defender panel U.S. Dist. Ct. (no. dist.) Calif., 1980-90; chair stats. and tech. subcom. Fed. Civil Justic Reform Act Com. (no. dist.) Calif., 1990-95; ct. apptd. mem. Fed. Ct. Rules Revision Com. (no. dist.) Calif., 1994—; mem. continuing edn. of bar criminal law adv. com. U. Calif., Berkeley, 1978-83, 89—. Author: (with others) Selected Trial Motions, California Criminal Law Procedure and Practice, 1986, (supplements to) California Criminal Law and Procedure, 1987-92, (chpts.) Calif. Criminal Law and Procedure, 2d edit., 1993, Direct Examination-Tips and Techniques, 1982; co-author: Criminal Trial Tactics, 1985, 88, 89; co-author chpts. Grand Jury Practice, California Asset Forfeiture in California Criminal Law and Procedure 2d, U. Calif. Continuing Edn. of the Bar, 1994. Trustee Tamalpais Union High Sch. Dist., 1968-77, chmn. bd., 1973-74; mem. adv. com. Nat. PTA Assn., 1972-78; apptd. mem. criminal justice act com. U.S. Ct. Appeals (9th cir). Fellow Am. Bd. Criminal Lawyers; mem. ABA, San Francisco Bar Assn. (editor in Re 1974-76), State Bar Calif. (pro-tem disciplinary referee 1976-78, vice chmn. pub. interest and edn. com. criminal law sect., mem. exec. com. criminal law sect. 1980-87, editor Criminal Law Sect. News 1981-87, chmn. exec. com. 1983-

84), Am. Inns of Ct. (exec. com. 1994—). Office: 507 Polk St Ste 310 San Francisco CA 94102-3339

LADD, ALAN WALBRIDGE, JR., motion picture company executive; b. L.A., Oct. 22, 1937; s. Alan Walbridge and Marjorie Jane (Harrold) L.; m. Patricia Ann Beazley, Aug. 30, 1959 (div. 1983); children: Kelliann, Tracy Elizabeth, Amanda Sue; m. Cindra Kay, July 13, 1985. Motion picture agt. Creative Mgmt., L.A., 1963-69; v.p. prodn. 20th Century-Fox Film Corp., L.A., 1973-74; sr. v.p. 20th Century-Fox Film Corp. (Worldwide Prodns. div.), Beverly Hills, Calif., 1974-76; pres. 20th Century-Fox Pictures, 1976-79, Ladd Co., Burbank, Calif., 1979-83; pres., chief oper. officer MGM/UA Entertainment Co., 1983-86; chief exec. officer MGM/UA Entertainment Co, from 1986, also chmn. bd. dirs.; chmn., chief exec. officer Metro-Goldwyn-Mayer Pictures, Inc., Culver City, Calif., until 1988; pres., chmn. Pathe Entertainment, L.A., 1989-90; co-chmn. MGM-Pathe, L.A., 1990-93, MGM, L.A., 1990-93; chmn., CEO MGM-Pathe Communications, L.A., 1991-93; pres. The Ladd Co., L.A., 1993—. Producer: (films) Walking Stick, 1969, A Severed Head, 1969, TamLin, 1970, Villian Zee and Co, 1971, Fear is the Key, 1973, Braveheart, 1995; exec. producer: (films) Nightcomers, 1971, Vice Versa, 1988, The Brady Bunch, 1995. Served with USAF, 1961-63. Office: The Ladd Co c/o Paramount 5555 Melrose Ave Los Angeles CA 90038

LADEHOFF, ROBERT LOUIS, bishop; b. Feb. 19, 1932; m. Jean Arthur Burcham (dec. Feb. 1992); 1 child, Robert Louis Jr. Grad., Duke U., 1954, Gen. Theol. Sem., 1957, Va. Theol. Sem., 1980. Ordained deacon, priest The Episcopal Ch., 1957;. Priest in charge N.C. parishes, 1957-60; rector St. Christopher's Ch., Charlotte, N.C., 1960-74, St. John's Ch., Fayetteville, 1974-85; bishop, co-adjutor of Oreg., 1985, bishop, 1986—. Office: Diocese of Oreg PO Box 467 Lake Oswego OR 97034-0467

LA FLEUR, WALTER J., engineering executive; b. Carrizozo, N.Mex., July 22, 1933; s. Walter J. and Miriam Evelyn (Grumbles) La F.; m. Vera Jean Scott Shupe, Dec. 20, 1953 (div. Mar. 1970); children: Walter IV, Ian; m. Mary Lee Johenning, May 6, 1972 (dec. Dec. 1994). BS in Physics, N.Mex. State U., 1955, MS in Electronic Engring., 1960. Assoc. physicist Phys. Sci. Lab. N.Mex. State U., University Park, 1956-60; dir. Bermuda Sta. NASA, Goddard Space Flight Ctr., 1961-67; chief tracking and data systems br. NASA, Goddard Space Flight Ctr., Greenbelt, Md., 1967-70, assoc. chief support divsn., 1971, chief ops. divsn., 1972-78, dep. dir. networks, 1980-84; asst. assoc. adminstr., tech. NASA, Office Tracking and Data Acquisition, Washington, 1979; dep. dir. tech. ops. Voice of Am., Washington, 1984-88; dir. engring. Voice of Am. and Worldnet, Washington, 1989-93; chmn. bd. Marconi Comm., Inc., Reston, Va., 1994—. Recipient Rank of Meritorious Exec. Pres. Bush, Washington, 1989, Rank of Disting. Exec. Pres. Bush, Washington, 1991. Mem. IEEE, Nat. Assn. Radio and TV Engrs. (sr.), Radio Club Am., Am. Radio Relay League. Home and Office: PO Box 1029 Silver City NM 88062-1029

LA FORCE, JAMES CLAYBURN, JR., economist, educator; b. San Diego, Dec. 28, 1928; s. James Clayburn and Beatrice Maureen (Boyd) La F.; m. Barbara Lea Latham, Sept. 23, 1952; children: Jessica, Allison, Joseph. BA, San Diego State Coll., 1951; MA, UCLA, 1958, PhD, 1962. Asst. prof. econs. UCLA, 1962-66, assoc. prof., 1967-70, prof., 1971-93, prof. emeritus, 1993—, chmn. dept. econs., 1969-78, dean Anderson Sch. Mgmt., 1978-93; acting dean Hong Kong U. Sci. & Tech., 1991-93; bd. dirs. Rockwell Internat., Eli Lilly & Co., Jacobs Engring. Group Inc., The Timken Co., The Black Rock Funds, Imperial Credit Industries, Inc., Payden & Rygel Investment Trust, Providence Investment Coun. Mut. Funds; chmn. adv. com. Calif. Workmen's Compensation. Author: The Development of the Spanish Textile Industry 1750-1800, 1965, (with Warren C. Scoville) The Economic Development of Western Europe, vols. 1-5, 1969-70. Bd. dirs. Nat. Bur. Econ. Rsch., 1975-88, Found. Francisco Marroquin, Lynde and Harry Bradley Found., Pacific Legal Found., 1981-86; trustee Found. for Rsch. in Econs. and Edn., 1970—, chmn., 1977—; mem. bd. overseers Hoover Inst. on War, Revolution and Peace, 1979-85, 86-93; mem. nat. coun. on humanities NEH, 1981-88; chmn. Pres.'s Task Force on Food Assistance, 1983-84. Social Sci. Research Council research tng. fellow, 1958-60; Fulbright sr. research grantee, 1965-66; Am. Philos. Soc. grantee, 1965-66. Mem. Econ. History Assn., Mont Pelerin Soc., Phi Beta Kappa. Office: UCLA Anderson Grad Sch Mgmt 405 Hilgard Ave Los Angeles CA 90095-1481

LAFRANCHI, STEPHEN HENRY, pediatric endocrinologist, educator, researcher; b. St. Helena, Calif., Aug. 26, 1943; s. Edward Henry and Marion Blanche (Holcomb) LaF.; m. Pamela Ann Fisher; children: Christopher, Alexander. BA in Biology, U. So. Calif., 1965; MD, UCLA, 1969. Resident in pediat. UCLA, 1969-72, fellow in pediat. endocrinology, 1972-75; asst. prof. pediat. Oreg. Health Scis. U., Portland, 1975-80, assoc. prof. pediat., 1980-85, prof. pediat., 1985—; vis. prof. Chiba Children's Hosp., Okinawa, 1987, U. Ariz., Phoenix, 1987. Contbr. numerous articles and abstracts to med. jours. Mem. Physicians for Social Responsibility, 1975—. Fogarty Sr. Internat. fellow NIH, Zurich, Switzerland, 1982-83. Fellow Am. Acad. Pediat. (exec. com. endocrine sect. 1994—); mem. Am. Acad. Pediat., Lawson Wilkins Pediat. Endocrine Soc. (treas. 1988-93), The Endocrine Soc., Am. Thyroid Assn., Portland Acad. Pediat. (pres. 1991), European Soc. Pediat. Rsch. Office: Oregon Health Svcs Univ Dept of Pediatrics 3181 SW Sam Jackson Park Rd Portland OR 97201-3011

LAGASSE, BRUCE KENNETH, structural engineer; b. Bklyn., Feb. 1, 1940; s. Joseph F. Lagasse and Dora S. Gould. BSME, U. Calif., Berkeley, 1964. Structures engr. Rockwell Internat., Canoga Park, Calif., 1964-69; mem. tech. staff Hughes Aircraft Co., Los Angeles, 1969-70; scientist/engr. Hughes Aircraft Co., El Segundo, Calif., 1972—; sr. engr. Litton Ship Systems, Los Angeles, 1971-72; lectr. Hughes Aircraft Co., El Segundo, 1980—; cons. in field, Van Nuys, Calif., 1979—. Libertarian state chmn., L.A., 1977-79, nat. committeeman, Washington, 1979-81. Mem. ASME. Home: 7247-C Balboa Blvd Van Nuys CA 91406

LAGER, DOUGLAS ROY, property tax consultant; b. Eau Claire, Wis., Dec. 10, 1947; m. Barbara Joyce Johnston, Oct. 5, 1985; 1 child, Jeffrey D. BSBA in Acctg., Rockhurst Coll., Kansas City, Mo., 1971. Cert. gen. appraiser, Colo. Head dept. personal property Jackson County Assessor, Kansas City, Mo., 1971-74; property assessment specialist Wis. Dept. Revenue, Madison, 1974-80; property tax cons. Property Tax Svc., Mpls., 1980-84, Denver, 1984-87; property tax cons. Avtax, Inc., Denver, 1987—. Home: 9 White Alder Littleton CO 80127-3598 Office: Avtax Inc 5555 DTC Pkwy Ste C-3300 Englewood CO 80111

LAGERBERG, RANDALL ERLAND, mental health specialist; b. Seattle, June 1, 1959; s. Floyd R. and Rose M. (Nixon) L. AA, Shoreline C.C., Seattle, 1988; BA in Comms., U. Wash., 1991. Registered counselor. Customer svc. rep. Speakerlab, Inc., Seattle, 1978-82; svc. rep. Linde Homecare, Redmond, Wash., 1984-88; mng. editor The Ebbtide, Seattle, 1988; reporter The Daily, Seattle, 1989-91; staff reporter North Seattle Press, 1991; mental health specialist N.W. E&T, Seattle, 1991—. Photographer: Spindrift, 1988, 2d edit., 1989; author mag. Seafair, 1991. Vol. Audubon Soc.

LAGLE, JOHN FRANKLIN, lawyer; b. Kansas City, Mo., Jan. 22, 1938; s. Ernest J. and Hilda B. L.; m. Nina E. Weston, Aug. 1, 1959; m. Diana G. Fogle, July 14, 1962; children—Robert, Gregory. BBA, UCLA, 1961, JD, 1967. Bar: Calif. 1967, U.S. Dist. Ct. (no. dist.) Calif. 1967. Assoc. Hindin, McKittrick & Marsh, Beverly Hills, Calif., 1967-70, Macco Corp., Newport Beach, Calif., 1970, Rifkind & Sterling, Beverly Hills, 1971; mem. Fulop & Hardee, and predecessor Fulop, Rolston, Burns & McKittrick, Beverly Hills, 1971-82; ptnr. Leff & Stephenson, Beverly Hills, 1983; sole practice, Los Angeles, 1984; ptnr. Barash & Hill (formerly Wildman, Harrold, Allen, Dixon, Barash & Hill), Los Angeles, 1985-91; pvt. practice, L.A., 1992—. Served with U.S. Army, 1961-63. Mem. ABA, Calif. Bar Assn., Los Angeles County Bar Assn. Republican. Contbr. to Practice Under the California Corporate Securities Law of 1978. Office: 16750 Marquez Ave Pacific Palisades CA 90272-3240

LAGORIA, GEORGIANNA MARIE, curator, writer, editor, visual art consultant; b. Oakland, Calif., Nov. 3, 1953; d. Charles Wilson and Margaret Claire (Vella) L.; m. David Joseph de la Torre, May 15, 1982; 1 child, Mateo Joseph. BA in Philosophy, Santa Clara U., 1975; MA in Museology, U. San Francisco, 1978. Exhbn. coordinator Allrich Gallery, San Francisco, 1977-78; asst. registrar Fine Arts Mus., San Francisco, 1978-79; gallery coordinator de Saisset Mus., Santa Clara, Calif., 1979-80, asst. dir., 1980-83, dir., 1983-86; dir. Palo Alto (Calif.) Cultural Ctr., 1986-91; ind. writer, editor and cons. mus. and visual arts orgns., Hawaii, 1991-95; dir. The Contemporary Mus., Honolulu, 1995—; V.p. Non-Profit Gallery Assn., San Francisco, 1980-82; bd. dirs. Fiberworks, Berkeley, Calif., 1981-85; field reviewer Inst. Mus. Services, Washington, 1985-87; adv. bd. Hearst Art Gallery, Moraga, Calif., 1986-89, Womens Caucus for Art, San Francisco, 1987—; mem. adv. bd. Weigand Art Gallery, Notre Dame Coll., Belmont, Calif. Curator exhbns. The Candy Store Gallery, 1980, Fiber '81, 1981; curator, author exhbn. catalogue Contemporary Hand Colored Photographs, 1981, Northern Calif. Art of the Sixties, 1982, The Artist and the Machine: 1910-1940, 1986; author catalogue, guide Persis Collection of Contemporary Art at Honolulu Advertiser, 1993; co-author: The Little Hawaiian Cookbook, 1994; coord. exhbn. selections Laila and Thurston Twigg-Smith Collection and Toshiko Takaezu ceramics for Hui No'eau Visual Arts Ctr., Maui, 1993; editor Nuhou (newsletter Hawaii State Mus. Assn.), 1991—; spl. exhbn. coord. Honolulu Acad. Arts, 1995. Mem. Arts Adv. Alliance, Santa Clara County, 1985-86; grant panelist Santa Clara County Arts Council, 1987. Exhbn. grantee Ahmanson Found., 1981, NEA, 1984, Calif. Arts Coun., 1985-89. Mem. Am. Assn. Mus., ArtTable, 1983—, Calif. Assn. Mus. (bd. dirs. 1987-89), Hawaiian Craftsmen (bd. dirs. 1994—), Honolulu Jr. League, Key Project (bd. dirs. 1993-94). Democrat. Roman Catholic. Home and Office: 47-665 Mapele Rd Kaneohe HI 96744-4918

LAGREEN, ALAN LENNART, public relations executive, radio personality; b. Burbank, Calif., May 20, 1951; s. Lennart Franklin and Mary (Cassara) LaG.; m. Wendy Diane Gilmaker, June 28, 1975; 1 child, Cara Diane. BA, U. So. Calif., L.A., 1972. Pub. rels. asst. Dames & Moore, L.A., 1972-75; asst. pub. Orange County Illustrated, Newport Beach, Calif., 1975; asst. exec. dir. Toastmasters Internat., Santa Ana, Calif., 1975-86; meetings and conv. mgr. Fluor Corp., Irvine, Calif., 1986-87; v.p. CCRA, Inc., Santa Ana, 1987—; morning radio personality Sta. KSBR-FM Jazz Radio, Mission Viejo, Calif. Home: 120 W 20th St Santa Ana CA 92706-2722

LAGUARDIA, RONALD PAUL, career counselor, educator; b. Sidney, N.Y., May 16, 1950; s. Enrico Donato and Leta Mae (Milks) LaG.; m. Karen Lucille Freleigh Hill, Oct. 4, 1968 (div. Mar. 1980); 1 child, Mark; m. Yayoi Nagashima, Sept. 10, 1994. AAS, SUNY, Cobleskill, 1970; BS cum laude, SUNY, Albany, 1975; MS, Elmira Coll., 1981. Cert. tchr., Calif., N.Y. Instr., wrestling coach Corning (N.Y.) East H.S., 1975-87; instr. Calif. State U.-Dominguez Hills, Santa Barbara, 1988-90, Santa Barbara C.C., 1988-90; career devel. specialist, instr. Santa Barbara Bus. Coll., 1991-94; career counselor New Directions Career & Life Style Devel. Ctr., Thousand Oaks, Calif., 1994—; cons. LaGuardia Consulting, Santa Barbara, 1991; computer cons. Louis J. Nessle CPA, Corning, 1987; antique post card dealer Crystal City Cards, Corning and Santa Barbara, 1981-94. Author: On Purpose: Finding and Following Your Path of Fulfillment, 1994. Mem. curriculum devel. com. Leadership Santa Barbara County, 1992-93. Mem. Am. Counseling Assn., Nat. Career Devel. Assn., Conejo Valley C. of C. (edn. com. 1994), Santa Barbara C. of C. (small bus. com. 1991-94), Pi Omega Pi. Office: New Directions Career and Life Style Devel Ctr 101 Moody Ct Ste 206 Thousand Oaks CA 91360-6068

LAGUERRE, MICHEL SATURNIN, anthropology educator; b. Lascahobas, Haiti; came to U.S., 1971; s. Magloire Laguerre and Anilia Roseau. BA in Philosophy, U. Quebec, 1971; MA in Sociology, Roosevelt U., 1973; PhD in Social Anthropology, U. Ill., 1976. Asst. prof. sociology Fordham U., N.Y.C., 1977-78; asst. prof. anthropology and African-Am. studies U. Calif., Berkeley, 1978-82, assoc. prof., 1982-90, prof., 1990—; trustee Refugee Policy Group, Washington, 1982-90. Author: American Odyssey: Haitians in N.Y.C., 1984, Urban Poverty in the Caribbean, 1990, The Military and Society in Haiti, 1993, The Informal City, 1994; co-editor Am. Anthropologist, 1990-94. Fellow Am. Anthrop. Assn.; mem. Am. Sociol. Assn. Roman Catholic. Office: U Calif Berkeley CA 94720

LAHAY, DAVID GEORGE MICHAEL, ballet company director; b. Barrie, Ont., Can., July 15, 1949; s. George Anthony and Edna Alice (Silverberg) LaH. B.A., Trent U., Peterborough, Ont., 1971; B.F.A. with honors, York U., Toronto, 1973. Prin. dancer Les Grands Ballets Canadiens, Montreal, 1978-87, asst. ballet master, 1987-91; prin. dancer Atlanta Ballet, 1978; ballet master Ottawa Ballet, 1991. Choreographer Canadian Heritage Festival, 1989, 90, 91. Ont. scholar, 1968; Can Council grantee, 1973, 75, 78. Office: Alberta Ballet Nat Christie Ctr, 141 18th Ave, Calgary, AB Canada T2S 0B8

LAHRI, RAJEEVA, electronics executive; b. Kanpur, India, Sept. 12, 1955; came to U.S., 1980; s. Rajni Kant and Pushpa (Srivastava) Lehri; m. Sangeeta Srivastava, Dec. 1, 1983; children: Shephalie, Shilpika. MSc in Physics, Indian Inst. of Tech., Kanpur, 1974, MTech in Materials Sci., 1976; PhD in Elec. Engring., SUNY, Buffalo, 1982. Mem. tech. staff Hewlett Packard Co., Corvallis, Oreg., 1982-86; mgr. Bipolar/BiCMOS devel. Fairchild/Nat. Semiconductor, Puyallup, Wash., 1986-90; dir. tech. devel. Nat. Semiconductor Corp., Santa Clara, Calif., 1990—. Co-author: BiCMOS Technology and Its Applications, 1989; patentee BJT device formation related, 1992. Home: 643 Pilgrim Loop Fremont CA 94539-6285

LAI, HIM MARK, writer; b. San Francisco, Nov. 1, 1925; s. Mark Bing and Hing Mui (Dong) L.; m. Laura Jung, June 12, 1953. AA, San Francisco Jr. Coll., 1945; BS in Engring., U. Calif., Berkeley, 1947. Mech. engr. Utilities Engring. Bur., San Francisco, 1948-51, Bechtel Corp., San Francisco, 1953-84; lectr. Chinese Am. history San Francisco State U., 1969, 72-75, U. Calif., Berkeley, 1978-79, 84; researcher, writer on Chinese Am. history San Francisco, 1967—; dir. Chinese of America 1785-1980 Exhbn. Chinese Cultural Found. San Francisco, 1979-80; mem. adv. bd. Chinese Am. Women's Project, 1981-83; coord. Chinese Am. In Search of Roots Program, 1991—; cons. proposed El Pueblo de L.A. State Hist. Park Chinese Am. Mus., 1987, 89, 93, Asian Am. Studies Program Chinese Materials Rsch. Collection, U. Calif., Berkeley, 1986-88; adj. prof. Asian Am. studies dept. San Francisco State U., 1990—; coord. Chinese Cmty. Hour, Cantonese radio program, 1971-84. Co-author: Chinese of America, 1785-1980: Exhibition Catalog, 1980, Island: Poetry and History of Chinese Immigrants on Angel Island, 1910-1940, 1980; author: A History Reclaimed: An Annotated Bibliography and Guide of Chinese Language Materials on the Chinese of America, 1986, From Overseas Chinese to Chinese American: History of Development of Chinese American Society During the Twentieth Century, 1992; assoc. editor: A History of the Chinese in California, A Syllabus, 1969; co-editor: Collected Works of Gilbert Woo, 1991; mem. editl. bd. Amerasia Journal, 1979—, Chinese America: History and Perspectives, 1986—; contbr. articles to profl. jours. Mem. Chinese Hist. Soc. Am. (pres. 1971, 76, 77, bd. dirs. 1972-81, 84, 85-91, 93—), Chinese Culture Found. San Francisco (bd. dirs. 1975-85, 87-94, pres. 1982, bd. chairperson 1983, 84, 85, 89). Home: 357 Union St San Francisco CA 94133-3519

LAI, LIWEN, molecular geneticist, educator; b. Taipei, Taiwan, 1957; d. Kwan-Long Lai. BS, Nat. Taiwan U., 1980; MS, U. Calif., San Francisco, 1983; PhD, U. Tex., Dallas, 1987. Diplomate Am. Coll. Med. Genetics. Postdoctoral fellow NIH, Bethesda, Md., 1987-89; asst. rsch. sci. U. Ariz., Tucson, 1990-94, asst. dir. Molecular Diagnostic Lab., 1992—, rsch. asst. prof., 1995—. Rsch. grantee Elks, 1994-95, Dialysis Clinic Inc., 1994-95. Mem. Am. Soc. Human Genetics. Office: U Ariz Dept Pediats 1501 N Campbell Ave Tucson AZ 85724

LAI, WAIHANG, art educator; b. Hong Kong, Jan. 7, 1939; s. Sing and Yu-ching L.; came to U.S., 1964; BA, Chinese U. Hong Kong, 1964; MA, Claremont Grad. Sch., 1967; m. Celia Cheung, Aug. 13, 1966. Asst. prof. art Maunaolu Coll., Maui, Hawaii, 1968-70; prof. art Kauai (Hawaii) Community Coll., 1970—. Vis. prof. art Ariz. State U., Tempe, summer 1967. Recipient Excellence in Teaching award U. Hawaii, 1992, Nat. Inst. Staff and Orgnl. Devel. Excellence award U. Tex., 1993. Mem. Kauai (pres. 1974—) Watercolor Socs., Phila. Watercolor Club, Hawaii Computer Art Soc., Kauai Oriental Art Soc. (pres. 1981—). Author: The Chinese Landscape Paintings of Waihang Lai, 1966, The Watercolors of Waihang Lai, 1967; illustrator: The Tao of Practice Success, 1991, Advertisements for Acupuncturists, 1992. Home: PO Box 363 Lihue HI 96766-0363 Office: Kauai Community Coll Lihue HI 96766

LAIDIG, ELDON LINDLEY, financial planner; b. Oberlin, Kans., Jan. 20, 1932; s. Ira Lawless and Minnie Lorene (Williams) L.; m. Mary Jane Urban, Feb. 13, 1953 (dec. June 1981); 1 child, Larry Wayne; m. Lois Audrey Davey Cameron, Feb. 11, 1983. BS, Ft. Hay Kans. State U., 1954; MS, U. Tex., 1960, PhD, 1967. CFP. Jr. high prin. Jefferson County Pub. Schs., Arvada, Colo., 1963-88; pvt. practice fin. planner Personal Benefit Svcs., Arvada, 1988—. Author: The Influence of Situational Factors on Administrative Behavior, 1967, An Organizational Manual, 1979; editor various local and state newsletters. Bd. dirs. Highlander's Inc., Denver, 1978-83, Arvada Coun. for the Arts and Humanities, 1982, chmn., 1988-93; pres. Jefferson County Sch. Adminstrs., Lakewood, Colo., 1971-72; elder Arvada Presbyn., 1964—; v.p. Arvada Sister Cities Internat., 1992—. Named as Comdg. Officer of Outstanding Coast Guard Unit, 2nd Coast Guard Dist., 1968; recipient Disting. Svc. citation U.S. Dept. of Def., 1974, Unit citation Def. Civil Preparedness Agy., 1974, Don Kemp award for outstanding fundraising Arvada Ctr. for the Arts & Humanities, 1983. Mem. Arvada Hist. Soc. (v.p. 1983-85), Res. Officers Assn. (pres. Denver chpt. 1974, pres. Dept. of Colo., nat. councilman 1979), Arvada Sentinel and N.W. Metro C. of C. (Arvada Man of Yr. 1990), Rotary (bd. dirs. Arvada chpt. 1989-94). Home: 7038 Ammons St Arvada CO 80004-1849 Office: Personal Benefit Svcs 5400 Ward Rd Arvada CO 80002-1819

LAIDLAW, HARRY HYDE, JR., entomology educator; b. Houston, Apr. 12, 1907; s. Harry Hyde and Elizabeth Louisa (Quinn) L.; BS, La. State U., 1933, MS, 1934; PhD (Univ. fellow, Genetics fellow, Wis. Dormitory fellow, Wis. Alumni Rsch. Found. fellow), U. Wis., 1939; m. Ruth Grant Collins, Oct. 26, 1946; 1 child, Barbara Scott Laidlaw Murphy. Teaching asst. La. State U., 1933-34, rsch. asst., 1934-35; prof. biol. sci. Oakland City (Ind.) Coll., 1939-41; state apiarist Ala. Dept. Agr. and Industries, Montgomery, 1941-42; entomologist First Army, N.Y.C., 1946-47; asst. prof. entomology, asst. apiculturist U. Calif.-Davis, 1947-53, assoc. prof. entomology, assoc. apiculturist, 1953-59, prof. entomology, apiculturist, 1959-74, asso. dean Coll. Agr., 1960-64, chair agr. faculty, staff, 1965-66, prof. entomology emeritus, apiculturist emeritus, 1974—; coord. U. Calif.-Egypt Agrl. Devel. Program, AID, 1979-83. Rockefeller Found. grantee, Brazil, 1954-55, Sudan, 1967; honored guest Tamagawa U., Tokyo, 1980. Trustee, Yolo County (Calif.) Med. Soc. Scholarship Com., 1965-83. Served to capt. AUS, 1942-46. Recipient Cert. of Merit Am. Bee Jour., 1957, Spl. Merit award U. Calif.-Davis, 1959, Merit award Calif. Central Valley Bee Club, 1974, Merit award Western Apicultural Soc., 1980, Gold Merit award Internat. Fedn. Beekeepers' Assns., 1986; recipient Disting. Svc. award Ariz. Beekeepers Assn., 1988. Cert. of Appreciation Calif. State Beekeepers' Assn., 1987, award Alan Clemson Meml. Found., 1989: NIH grantee, 1963-66; NSF grantee, 1966-74. Fellow AAAS, Entomol. Soc. Am. (honoree spl. symposium 1990, C.W. Woodworth award Pacific br. 1981); mem. Am. Inst. Biol. Scis., Am. Soc. Naturalists, Am. Soc. Zoologists, Nat. Assn. Uniformed Svcs., Ret. Officers Assn. (2d v.p. Sacramento chpt. 1984-86), Scabbard and Blade, Sigma Xi (treas. Davis chpt. 1959-60, v.p. chpt. 1966-67), Alpha Gamma Rho (pres. La. chpt. 1933-34, counsellor Western Province 1960-66). Democrat. Presbyterian. Author books including Instrumental Insemination of Honey Bee Queens, 1977; Contemporary Queen Rearing, 1979; author slide set: Instrumental Insemination of Queen Honey Bees, 1976. Achievements include determination of cause of failure of attempts to artificially inseminate queen honey bees; invention of instruments and procedures to consistently accomplish same; elucidation of genetic relationships of individuals of polyandrous honey bee colonies; design of genetic procedures for behavioral study and breeding of honey bees for general and specific uses. Home: 761 Sycamore Ln Davis CA 95616-3432 Office: U Calif Dept Entomology Davis CA 95616

LAIDLAW, ROBERT, aircraft maintenance executive; b. 1927. V.p. N.Am. Aviation, Newport Beach, Calif., 1967-69; pres., founder Flight Sys., Inc., Newport Beach, 1969-81; CEO, chmn. bd. dirs. Aerotest, Inc., Santa Ana, Calif., 1986—. Office: Aerotest Inc 2062 N Bush St # 230 Santa Ana CA 92706-2884*

LAIDLAW, VICTOR D., construction executive; b. 1946. Officer Moran Cons., Alhambra, Calif., 1968-88; pres. Koll Cons., 1988—. Office: Koll Cons 3020 Old Ranch Pky Seal Beach CA 90740-2748*

LAING-MALCOLMSON, SALLY ANNE, enrolled tax agent, tax consultant; b. Seattle, Sept. 25, 1957; d. Ian Laing-Malcolmson and Frances Rutherford (Arold) Cook; children: Rhiannon Ethel Quandt, Peter Eugene Stone, Benjamin Elliott Stone. AS in Bus., SUNY, 1989. With accounts payable dept. King County Airport, Seattle, 1984-86; bookkeeper Driftmeir Architects, P.S., Kirkland, Wash., 1986; pvt. practice tax cons. Bellevue, Wash., 1987—; tax specialist Puget Sound Nat. Bank, Tacoma, 1990-92; bookkeeper Papillon, Inc.; sec. Washington State Tax Cons., Bellevue, 1991—, Am. Bus. Women's Assn., Bellevue, 1992—. Active Word of His Grace Fellowship, PTA, newsletter editor, 1991—. Mem. Pentecostal Ch. Home and Office: 16227 SE 8th St Bellevue WA 98008-4928

LAIRD, ANDREW KENNETH, radio broadcast engineer; b. Stockton, Calif., May 28, 1943; s. Andy George and Helene (Nielsen) L.; m. Diane Louise Bradley, Nov. 7, 1981; 1 stepchild, Jason McCoy. BS in Physics, Coll. of Principia, 1965; postgrad., U. Denver, 1965-66. Staff engr. Sta. KWGN-TV, Denver, 1966-67; chief engr. Sta. KLAK-AM-FM, Denver, 1967-72, Sta. KDAY, L.A., 1972-88; v.p. engring./radio group Heritage Media Corp., Bellevue, Wash., 1988—; cons. Laird Audio/Studio Design, L.A., 1976-88. Columnist Radio & Record Mag., 1974-76; contbr. articles to profl. jours. Staff sgt. Colo. Air N.G., 1966-72. Mem. Soc. Broadcast Engrs., Profl. Broadcast Engrs. (cert.).

LAIRD, HUGH EDWARD, II, pharmacologist, toxicologist; b. Phoenix, Mar. 30, 1939; s. Clyde Wesley and Juanita (Gregg) L.; m. Marilyn Jo Long, June 11, 1961; children: Michael Edward, Deborah Gayle. BS in Pharmacy, U. Ariz., 1962, PhD in Pharmacology/Toxicology, 1974. Registered pharmacist, Ariz., Calif. Pharmacist, mgr. Laird Pharmacies, Tempe, 1962-68; prof. pharmacology/toxicology U. Ariz., Tucson, 1974—; cons. Ariz. Poison Control Ctr., Tucson, 1974-80, Legal Profession, Tucson, 1989-94. Co-editor: Neurotransmitters and Epilepsy, 1987; contbr. numerous articles to profl. jours. Pres. Glenn Heights Neighborhood Assn., Tucson, 1991-94; chair Arcadia-Alamo Area Plan-City of Tucson, 1992. Grantee NIH, 1978-81, 92—, Ariz. Disease Control Commn., 1987-92. Mem. Am. Soc. Pharmacology and Experimental Therapeutics, Soc. for Neuroscis., Soc. for Experimental Biology and Medicine, Am. Assn. for Cancer Rsch., Tissue Culture Assn. Office: U Ariz Dept Pharm/Toxicology Bldg #207 Coll of Pharmacy Tucson AZ 85721

LAIRD, JERE DON, news reporter; b. Topeka, Aug. 8, 1933; s. Gerald Howard and Vivian Gertrude (Webb) L.; m. Alexandra Berezowsky, Aug. 4, 1957; children: Lee, Jennifer, Christopher. BA in Journalism, U. Nev., 1960. Disc jockey Sta. KHBC Radio, Hilo, Hawaii, 1949-50; announcer, chief engr. Sta. KOLO Radio, Reno, Nev., 1951-58; program dir. Sta. KOLO-TV, Reno, 1958-60; news reporter Sta. KCRA Radio and TV, Sacramento, Calif., 1960-61, Sta. KRLA Radio, L.A., 1962-63; news reporter, editor Sta. KNXT-TV, L.A., 1964-68; news reporter, fin. editor Sta. KNX-CBS Radio, L.A., 1968—; fin. reporter Sta. KCBS-TV, L.A., 1990—; lectr. U. So. Calif., L.A., 1984-85; instr. Calif. State U., Northridge, 1978-79. Cpl. U.S. Army, 1953-55. Recipient Emmy award, L.A., 1964, Peabody award, U. Ga., 1984, Best Bus. News award, L.A. Press Club, 1983, 84, 86, 87, 88, 89, Martin K. Gainsburgh award, Fiscal Policy Coun., Fla., 1978. Mem. Radio TV News Assn. (bd. dirs. 1966-68, Golden Mike award 1984), Sigma Delta Chi. Office: Sta KNX-CBS 6121 W Sunset Blvd Los Angeles CA 90028-6455

LAIRD, MARY See WOOD, LARRY

LAIRD, WILBUR DAVID, JR., librarian; b. Kansas City, Mo., Mar. 15, 1937; s. Wilbur David and Alma Blanche (Turner) L.; children: Wendy, Cynthia, Brian Andrew, David Alexander; m. Helen M. Ingram, July 12, 1984. Student, U. Wichita, 1959-60; BA, UCLA, 1965, MLS, 1966. Reference libr. U. Calif., Davis, 1966-67; acquisitions libr. U. Utah, 1967-70, asst. dir. for tech. svcs., 1970-71, assoc. dir., 1971-72; univ. libr. U. Ariz., Tucson, 1972-90; pres. Books West S.W., Tucson, 1990—. Author: Hopi Bibliography, 1977; editor: Books of the Southwest, 1977—. Bd. dirs. Westerners Internat., 1974-87, Tucson Civic Ballet, 1975-76, S.W. Pks. and Mon.

Assn., 1993—. With USN, 1955-59. Mem. ALA, Ariz. State Libr. Assn. (pres. 1978-79), Western History Assn., Western Lit. Assn., Guild Ariz. Antiquarian Booksellers. Home: 3329 E 2nd St Tucson AZ 85716-4213 Office: Books West Southwest Inc 2452 N Campbell Ave Tucson AZ 85719-3368

LAJOIE, DENISE HELENA, psychology educator; b. Woonsocket, R.I., Jan. 23, 1947; d. Edgar T. and Stasia S. (Kinash) L.; children: Joseph John Robbins, Kevin Patrick Robbins. BA, Roger Williams U., 1989; MA, U. Hawaii, Manoa, 1991, postgrad. Instr. Leeward C.C., Pearl City, Hawaii, 1992—, U. Hawaii West Oahu, Pearl City, 1993—; adj. faculty Chaminade U., Honolulu, 1992—, Hawaii Pacific U., Honolulu, 1994—. Assoc. editor: Internat. Jour. Transpersonal Studies, 1993—; contbr. articles to profl. jours. Vol. Unity Ch., Hawaii, 1992-93. Recipient award U. Hawaii Manoa, Honolulu, 1992; grantee Fetzner Inst., 1993. Mem. Assn. Transpersonal Psychology, Inst. Noetic Scis., Assn. Humanistic Psychology, Am. Counseling Assn., Transpersonal Psychology Interest Group (sec. 1992). Office: U H West Oahu 96-043 Ala Ike St Pearl City HI 96782-3366

LAKATOS, JOSEPH SANDOR, software company executive, engineer; b. Jaszladany, Hungary, Mar. 26, 1950; came to U.S., 1986; s. Gustav and Laura (Balogh) L.; div.; children: Emese Lakatos, Laura Lakatos. Bachelor, Polytechnic, Budapest, Hungary, 1971, Master, 1977. Registered profl. engr., Calif. Sr. power engr. Energy Tech. Lab., Modesto, Calif., 1986-87; project engr. Johnson Control, Inc., City of Industry, Calif., 1988-92; corp. project engr. Plaxicon, Inc., Rancho Cucamonga, Calif., 1992-94; owner, pres. Ohmsberry Tech., Rancho Cucamonga, Calif., 1994—. Inventor cavitative water treatment, ultrasonic heat exchanger, self-sealing blow core, cavity plasticizer. Mem. N.Y. Acad. Scis., Internat. Plastics Soc., Soc. Plastics Engrs. Office: Ohmsberry Technology 10022 5th St Unit O Rancho Cucamonga CA 91730

LAKE, DAVID S., publisher, lawyer; b. Youngstown, Ohio, July 17, 1938; s. Frank and Charlotte (Stahl) L.; m. Sandra J. Levin, Dec. 18, 1960 (div. Aug. 14, 1987); children: Joshua Seth, Jonathan Daniel. B.A. in Math, Youngstown State U., 1960; J.D. cum laude, Cleve. State U., 1965. Bar: Ohio 1965, D.C. 1970, U.S. Supreme Ct. 1969. Gen. counsel World Pub. Co., Cleve., 1965-68; dir. devel. Cath. U. Am., Washington, 1968-69; v.p., gen. counsel Microform Pub. Corp., Washington, 1969-70; dir. spl. projects Library Resources, Inc., Chgo., 1970-72; gen. mgr., partner Nat. Textbook Co., Skokie, Ill., 1972-76; pres. David S. Lake Pubs., Belmont, Calif., 1976-89, pres, owner, 1984-89; owner Lake Pub. Co., Belmont, 1989—. Contbr. to: Cleve. Marshall Law Rev, 1964. Served with USMC, 1960-62. Jewish. Office: Lake Pub Co 500 Harbor Blvd Belmont CA 94002-4021*

LAKE, KEVIN BRUCE, medical association administrator; b. Seattle, Jan. 25, 1937; s. Winston Richard and Vera Emma (Davis) L.; m. Suzanne Roto, Oct. 25, 1986; children from previous marriage: Laura, Kendrick, Wesley. BS, Portland State U., 1960; MD, U. Oreg., 1964. Intern, Marion County Gen. Hosp. and Ind. Med. Center, Indpls., 1964-65; resident U. Oreg. Hosps. and Clinics, 1968-70; fellow in infectious and pulmonary diseases, 1970-71; fellow in pulmonary diseases U. So. Calif., 1971-72, instr. medicine, 1972-75, asst. clin. prof., 1975-79, assoc. clin. prof., 1979-84, clin. prof., 1986—; dir. med. edn. and research La Vina Hosp., 1972-75; dir. respiratory therapy Methodist Hosp., Arcadia, Calif., 1975—; mem. staff Los Angeles County/U. So. Calif. Med. Center, Santa Teresita Hosp., Duarte, Calif., Huntington Meml. Hosp., Pasadena, Calif.; attending physician, mem. med. adv. bd. Foothill Free Clinic, Pasadena. Mem. exec. com. Profl. Staff Assn. U. So. Calif. Sch. Medicine; 2d v.p. bd. mgmt. Palm St. br. YMCA, Pasadena, 1974, 1st v.p., 1975, chmn., 1976-78, met. bd. dirs., 1976-84; bd. dirs. Mendenhall Ministries, La Vie Holistic Ministries, Hospice of Pasadena, Hastings Found. co-pres. PTA, Allendale Grade Sch., Pasadena, 1975-76; deacon Pasadena Covenant Ch., 1976-79. Served to lt. U.S. Navy, 1965-68. NIH grantee, 1971-72. Fellow ACP, Am. Coll. Chest Physicians; mem. Am. Thoracic Soc., Calif. Thoracic Soc., Oreg. Thoracic Soc., Trudeau Soc., Am. Soc. Microbiology, N.Y. Acad. Scis., Calif. Med. Assn., Los Angeles County Med. Assn. Democrat. Contbr. articles to profl. jours. Home: 875 S Madison Ave Pasadena CA 91106-4404 Office: 50 Alesandro Pl Ste 330 Pasadena CA 91105-3149

LAKE, STANLEY JAMES, security consulting company executive, motel chain executive, locksmith; b. Oklahoma City, June 3, 1926; s. Clyde Edward Lake and Helene Frances (Herndon) Hunnicut; m. Lila Marguarite Mosley, Mar 29, 1947 (div. Aug. 1952); children: Katherine, Marilyn, Stanley James II; m. Norma Jean Phelps, Jan. 21, 1960. Student, Mont. State U., 1946-48. Owner, mgr. Lake Oil Co., Glendive, Mont., 1949-53, Lake Mining Co., Salt Lake City, 1954-57, Lake Realty Co., Denver, 1958-63, Stanlake Corp., Denver, 1964—, Stanlake Luxury Budget Motels, Denver, 1979—, Lake's Security and Lock Svc., Englewood, Colo., 1979—; co-owner, instr. Colo. Karate Assn., Denver, 1965-73, 2d degree black belt. Originator modular budget motel concept, 1963. Chmn. bd. for karate Rocky Mountain region AAU, 1972-73. With USAAC, 1945-46. Recipient Presdl. award for teaching karate to disadvantaged and civic orgns., 1972, numerous others. Mem. Assn. Locksmiths Am. (cert. master locksmith), Rocky Mountain Locksmiths Assn., Japan Karate Assn. Rocky Mountain Area (chmn. bd. 1970-73), Masons, Shriners. Republican. Methodist. Home: 6026 S Elizabeth Way Littleton CO 80121-2816 Office: Lake's Security & Lock Svc 6200 S Syracuse Way Ste 125 Englewood CO 80111-4738

LAKIER, NANCY S., health facility administrator; b. Ft. Madison, Iowa, Nov. 17, 1952; d. Bernard A. and Ruth Mary (Dyer) Mehmert; m. Richard Stephen Lakier, Nov. 12, 1983; 1 child, Andrea. BSN, Creighton U., 1975; MBA, U. Nebr., 1985. Staff and mid. mgmt. positions various orgns., 1975-83; v.p. nursing Children's Hosp., Omaha, 1983-86, Ft. Hamilton (Ohio)-Hughes, 1986-88, San Bernardino (Calif.) Community Hosp., 1988-90; assoc. adminstr. Scripps Meml. Hosp., La Jolla, Calif., 1990—; mem. nurse adminstrs. coun. of San Diego and Imperial Counties. Case Mgmt. and Critical Path Documentation System, 1991, CareTracs, 1991. Pres. alumni adv. bd. dirs. Creighton U., Omaha, 1984-88. Recipient Alumni Merit award Creighton U., Omaha, 1986, 87. Mem. Am. Orgn. Nurse Execs., Calif. Nurses Assn., VHA Nat. Nursing Adv. Bd. Office: Scripps Meml Hosp 9888 Genesee Ave La Jolla CA 92037-1200

LAKOFF, EVELYN, music association executive; b. Bklyn., Apr. 8, 1932; d. Boris and Ray (Feldman) Schleifer; m. Sanford Allan Lakoff, June 4, 1961. BA, Queens Coll., 1953; MA in Music Edn., Columbia U., 1955; MA in Musicology, Harvard U., 1963. Pres. San Diego (Calif.) Early Music Soc.; music tchr. N.Y.C. 1955-60, Northport, N.Y., 1965-67. Office: San Diego Early Music Soc 3510 Dove Ct San Diego CA 92103-3904

LAL, DEEPAK KUMAR, economics educator; b. Lahore, Punjab, Pakistan, Jan. 3, 1940; s. Nand and Shanti (Devi) L.; m. Barbara Ballis, Dec. 11, 1971; children: Deepika, Akshay. BA with honors, St. Stephens Coll., 1959; MA, Jesus Coll., Oxford, Eng., 1962, B. Philosophy, 1965. 3d sec. Indian Fgn. Svc., New Delhi, Tokyo, 1963-66; lectr. Christchurch Coll., Oxford, 1966-68; rsch. fellow Nuffield Coll., Oxford, 1968-70; lectr. Univ. Coll. London, 1970-79, reader, 1979-84, prof. polit. economy, 1984-93, emeritus prof. polit. economy, 1993—; James S. Coleman prof. devel. studies UCLA, 1991—; co-dir. trade policy unit Ctr. Policy Studies, London, 1993—; cons. Indian Planning Commn., New Delhi, 1973-74, ILO, UNCTAD, OECD, UNIDO, World Bank, Ministry of Planning Republic of Korea, Sri Lanka; rsch. adminstr. World Bank, Washington, 1983-87. Author: Wells and Welfare, 1972, Methods of Project Analysis, 1974, Appraising Foreign Investment in Developing Countries, 1975, Unemployment and Wage Inflation in Industrial Economies, 1977, Men or Machines, 1978, Prices for Planning, 1980, The Poverty of Development Economics, 1983, 85, The Hindu Equilibrium, 2 vols., 1988, 89, The Repressed Economy, 1993, Against Dirigisme, 1994; co-author: (with P. Collier) Labour and Poverty in Kenya, 1986; editor: Development Economics, 4 vols., 1991. Home: 2 Erskine Hill, London NW11 6HB, England also: 213 Park Wilshire 10724 Wilshire Blvd Los Angeles CA 90024-4447 Office: UCLA Dept Econs 405 Hilgard Ave Los Angeles CA 90024-1301

LAL, PREETI GUPTA, microbiologist, researcher; b. Delhi, India, June 14, 1963; came to U.S., 1989; d. Prem Chand and Vimla (Aggarwal) Gupta; m. Anil Mohan Lal, Dec. 15, 1990. PhD, Med. U. S.C., 1993. Lectr. Bombay U., 1985-89; fellow tumor biology program Stanford U., Palo Alto, Calif., 1994—. Contbr. articles to profl. jours. Organizer ann. health fair Med. U. S.C., Charleston, 1990, 91. Recipient Svc. award Minority Affairs Office, 1990, 91; Merit scholar Bombay U., 1983-85. Mem. AAAS. Hindu. Home: 1270 Vicente Dr Apt A Sunnyvale CA 94086-7248

LALA, TAPAN KANTI, computer and communications engineering manager, consultant, researcher. BEE, Jadaupur U., Calcutta, India, 1972; MSEE, Queen's U., Kingston, Ont., Can., 1977; postgrad., U. Toledo, 1977-79. Instr., teaching asst. U. Toledo, 1975-79, Queen's U., 1975-79; design engr. AVCO Corp., Everett, Mass., 1979-81; mem. tech. staff Mitre Corp., Bedford, Mass., 1981, AT&T Bell Labs., Holmdel, N.J., 1981-84; prin. engr. Motorola, Cupertino, Calif., 1984-85; sr. engr. Fujitsu Am., San Jose, Calif., 1985-86; mgr., group leader Granger Assoc., San Jose, 1986; mgr. NEC Am., San Jose, 1986—; pres. Lala-D-Net, San Jose, 1990—. Merit-Cum-Means scholar Govt. India, Jadaupur U., 1967-72, grad. fellow, 1974-75. Mem. IEEE, IEEE Computer Soc., IEEE Comm. Soc. (assoc. editor, editor Comm. mag.), IEEE Engring. Mgmt. Soc. (sec., program com. Silicon Valley chpt.), Soc. Photo-optical Instrument Engrs., Internat. Soc. Optical Engring. Home: 15771 Simoni Dr San Jose CA 95127-2751 Office: NEC Am 110 Rio Robles San Jose CA 95134-1813

LA LANDE, JEFFREY MAX, historian; b. Troy, N.Y., Nov. 14, 1947; s. Albert Max and Georgia Louise (Vogel) LaL.; m. Judith Kay Vantil, Apr. 23, 1988; 1 child, Daniel Ethan. BS, Georgetown U., 1969; MA, Oreg. State U., 1981; PhD, U. Oreg., 1993. Historian and writer-editor Rogue River Nat. Forest, Medford, Oreg., 1976-79; archaeol. rsch. asst. Oreg. State U., Corvallis, 1979-80; tchg. fellow U. Oreg., Eugene, 1991-92; archaeologist U.S. Forest Svc., Medford, Oreg., 1980—; hist. rsch. cons. and writer Ashland, Oreg., 1978—; adj. prof. history So. Oreg. State Coll., Ashland, 1985—. Author: (books) First Over the Siskiyous: Peter Ogden, 1987, Medford Corporation: A History, 1979, (monograph) The Indians of Southwestern Oregon, 1991; contbr. articles to hist. jours. Trustee So. Oreg. Hist. Soc., Jacksonville, 1980-83; bd. dirs. City Hist. Commn., Ashland, 1977-79. Recipient certs. of merit USDA, 1980-92, Regional Forester's Archaeology award U.S. Forest Svc., 1994. Mem. Orgn. of Am. Historians, Pacific Coast Br./Am. Hist. Assn., Soc. for Am. Archaeology, Oreg. Hist. Soc., Wash. State Hist. Soc. (Charles Gates award 1993), Forest and Conservation History Soc. Democrat. Roman Catholic. Home: 1110 Hillview Dr Ashland OR 97520-3574 Office: US Forest Svc/Rogue River PO Box 520 Medford OR 97501

LALLY, NORMA ROSS, federal agency administrator, retired; b. Crawford, Nebr., Aug. 10, 1932; d. Roy Anderson and Alma Leona (Barber) Lively; m. Robert Edward Lally, Dec. 4, 1953 (div. Mar. 1986); children: Robyn Carol Murch, Jeffrey Alan, Gregory Roy. BA, Boise (Idaho) State U., 1974, MA, 1976; postgrad., Columbia Pacific U., 1988—. With grad. admissions Boise State U., 1971-74; with officer programs USN Recruiting, Boise, 1974; pub. affairs officer IRS, Boise and Las Vegas, 1975-94; ret., 1994; speaker in field, Boise and Las Vegas, 1977—. Contbr. articles to newspapers. Mem. task force Clark County Sch. Dist., Las Vegas. Staff sgt. USAF, 1950-54. Mem. NAFE, Internat. Assn. Bus. Communicators, Mensa, Toastmasters (Las Vegas), Marine's Meml. Club (life), Am. Legion. Home: 3013 Hawksdale Dr Las Vegas NV 89134-8967

LALONDE, ROBERT FREDERICK, state senator, retired; b. Bay City, Mich., Dec. 1, 1922; s. Joseph and Mildred Amanda (Brimmer) LaL.; m. Betty Ellen Schwartz, Aug. 2, 1941; 1 child, Rose Marie Tibbitts. BGE in Bus., U. Omaha, 1965. Airport mgr. Jackson Hole Airport, Jackson, Wyo., 1972-80; county commr. Teton County, Jackson, 1982-86, rental property owner, 1970-88; Wyo. state senator Jackson, 1989-95. Author: The Dangerous Trilogy, 1973. Chmn. Teton County Rep. Com., Jackson, 1975-77; del. Rep. Nat. Conv., Detroit, 1980; mem. Electoral Coll., Cheyenne, Wyo., 1980; sec. Wyo. Rep. party, 1980-82; chmn. Teton County Planning Commn., Jackson, 1973-78. Col. USAF, 1943-70. Mem. Am. Legion (comdr. 1989-94), Wyo. Airport Operators Assn. (founder, pres. 1973-75, Disting. Svc. award 1979), Jackson Hole C. of C. (pres. 1977-79, Citizen of Yr. 1975, Disting. Svc. award 1980), Rotary (pres. 1976-77). Christian Scientist. Home: PO Box 1707 Jackson WY 83001-1707

LA LUZERNE-OI, SALLY ANN, humanities educator; b. Green Bay, Wis., Nov. 21, 1953; d. Bernard Joseph and Bernice Lucille (Mommaerts) La L.; m. Sadaji Oi, July 25, 1987. BS in French and Spanish, U. Wis., Green Bay, 1976; MA in ESL, U. Ariz., 1983. Cert. tchr. French and Spanish, Wis. Tchr. English as Fgn. Lang./French Inst. de la Salle, Querétaro, Mexico, 1977; migrant tchr. Coop. Ednl. Svc. Agy., Hartford, Wis., 1977; instr. ESL Systran Corp., Oshkosh, Wis., 1978; tchr. French St. Joseph Acad., Green Bay, Wis., 1978-80, Colegio Internat. de Caracas, Venezuela, 1980-82; instr. English as Fgn. Lang. Interlingua Instituto de Linguas, Lagos, Portugal, 1983-84, Trident Coll., Nagoya, Japan, 1984-87; ESL instr., asst. coord. spl. English programs U. Hawaii, Manoa, 1988; instr. ESL, French Hawaii Pacific U., Honolulu, 1989—; tchr. trainer, Ukraine, summers 1994, 95; conf. presenter Kyoto, Japna, Nagoya, Japan, Honolulu, Hong Kong, Long Beach, Calif. Author: (with Cynthia McKeag Tsukamoto) (text) Tell Me About It!, (instrs. manual) Tell Me About It!, (Cassette) Tell Me About It!, 1993. Lectr. Sacred Heart Parish, Honolulu, 1992—; letter writer Amnesty Internat., N.Y.C., 1991—. Recipient Profl. Devel. Funding award Hawaii Pacific U., Honolulu, 1993, 95. Mem. TESOL, Hawaii Coun. Tchrs. English, Hawaii ESL Caucus, Hawaii Assn. Lang. Tchrs. Roman Catholic. Office: Hawaii Pacific U 1188 Fort Street Mall Honolulu HI 96813-2713

LAM, DAVID C., lieutenant governor; b. Hong Kong; arrived in Can., 1967; Businessman, philanthropist; lt. gov. Province of B.C., Can. Office: Govt House, 1401 Rockland Ave, Victoria, BC Canada V8S 1V9

LAM, KIT SANG, medical educator; b. Hong Kong, Jan. 10, 1954; came to U.S., 1972; s. Kang To Lam and Chuen Fong But; m. Bonita M.S. Soohoo; 1 child, Reina Y.H. BA in Microbiology, U. Tex., 1975; PhD in Oncology, U. Wis., 1980; MD, Stanford U., 1984. Intern in internal medicine U. Ariz., Tucson, 1984-85, resident in internal medicine, 1985-87, fellow in med. oncology, 1987-89, asst. prof. medicine, 1989-94; assoc. prof., 1994—; founding scientist Selectide Corp., Tucson, 1990, chief cons. scientist, 1990—. Leukemia spl. fellow Leukemia Soc. Am., 1989-92, leukemia scholar, 1992—. Mem. AAAS, Am. Assn. Cancer Rsch., Am. Chem. Soc., Am. Peptide Soc., Am. Soc. Clin. Oncology, Soc. Chinese Bioscientists in Am. Office: Ariz Cancer Ctr 1501 N Campbell Ave Tucson AZ 85724

LAM, LUI, physicist; b. Lianxian, China, Nov. 17, 1944; came to U.S., 1966; s. Lap-Chung and Lai-Jane (Wong) L.; m. Heung-Mee Lee, July 1, 1972; 1 child, Charlene. B.S., U. Hong Kong, 1965; M.S., U. of B.C., 1968; M.A., Columbia U., 1969, Ph.D., 1973. Research assoc. City Coll. CUNY, 1972-75; research scientist U. Instelling Antwerpen, Belgium, 1975-76, U. Saarlandes, Saarbrucken, Fed. Republic Germany, 1976-77; assoc. research prof. Inst. Physics, Academia Sinica, Beijing, China, 1978-83, adj. prof., 1984—, City Coll.; assoc. prof. Queensborough Community Coll., CUNY, 1984-87; prof., San Jose State U., 1987—; founder, co-editor Springer Series on Partially Ordered Systems, 1987—, Woodward Conf. Series, 1988—; elected mem. planning and steering com. Internat. Liquid Crystal Conf., 1984-90. Co-editor: Wave Phenomena, 1989, Nonlinear Structures in Physical Systems, 1990, Solitons in Liquid Crystals, 1992, Modeling Complex Phenomena, 1992, Liquid Crystalline and Mesomorphic Polymers, 1994, Novel Laser Sources and Applications, 1994, Introduction to Nonlinear Physics, 1995, Nonlinear Physics for Beginners, 1995; assoc. editor Jour. Molecular Crystal and Liquid Crystals, 1981-93; editorial mem. Liquid Crystals, 1986-90. Li Po Kwai scholar U. Hong Kong, 1963-65; Eugene Higgin fellow Columbia U., 1966-67, Nordita fellow, 1976. Mem. Am. Phys. Soc., Internat. Liquid Crystal Soc. (founder, bd. dir., chmn. conf. com. 1990-94). Office: San Jose State U Dept Physics San Jose CA 95192-0106

LAMAN, JERRY THOMAS, mining company executive; b. Muskogee, Okla., Mar. 1, 1947; s. Thomas J. and Juanita J. (Pittman) L.; m. Lenora J. Laman, July 1, 1972; children: Troy T., Brian D. Silver Diploma, Colo. Sch. Mines, 1969. Refinery engr. ARCO, Torrance, Calif., 1969-71; chem. engr. Cleveland-Cliffs Iron Co., Mountain City, Nev., 1971-73, asst. mine supt., 1973-77; chief uranium metallurgist Cleveland-Cliffs Iron Co., Casper, Wyo., 1977-83; project mgr. In-Situ, Inc., Laramie, Wyo., 1983-85, v.p., 1985—; also bd. dirs. In-Situ, Inc.; pres. Solution Mining Corp., Laramie, Wyo., 1990—, also bd. dirs., 1990—. Mem. Soc. for Mining, Metallurgy and Exploration, Optimist (pres. Laramie club 1989). Home: 1085 Colina Dr Laramie WY 82070-5014

LAMB, BERTON LEE, II, policy analyst, researcher; b. Torrance, Calif., July 4, 1945; s. Berton Lee and Phyllis Jean (Schultz) L.; m. Susan Elizabeth Snow, June 22, 1968; 1 child, Kara Lee. BA, Calif. Luth. U., 1967; MA in Internat. Polits., San Francisco State U., 1970; PhD in Polit. Sci., Wash. State U., 1976. Instr. polit. sci. George Fox Coll., Newberg, Oreg., 1969-72; rsch. asst. Water Rsch. Ctr. Wash. State U., Pullman, 1974-75; asst. prof. polit. sci. Ea. Ky. U., Richmond, 1975-76; water res. policy specialist U.S. Fish and Wildlife Svc., Ft. Collins, Colo., 1976-79, policy analyst Nat. Ecology Rsch. Ctr., 1979-86, leader water resources analysis sect., Nat. Ecology Rsch. Ctr., 1986-90; project leader Nat. Ecology Rsch. Ctr., Ft. Collins, Colo., 1990-93; sect. leader Midcontinent Ecol. Sci. Ctr. Nat. Biol. Svc., 1993—. Editor: Water Quality Administration, 1980; co-editor: Water Resources Administration. Symposium in Public Administration Review, 1976; bd. editors P.A. Times, 1988-91; author chpts. in Instream Flow Protection in the West, 2d edit., 1993, Inland Fisheries Management, 1993, At the Nexus: Science Policy, 1995; contbr. articles to Water Resources Bull., Water Resources Rsch., Jour. Water Resources Planning and Mgmt., Social Sci. Micro-Computer Rev., The Environ. Profl., Boston Coll. Environ. Affairs law Rev. and others. Pres. Trinity Luth. Ch. Coun., Ft. Collins, 1981-82. Future faculty fellow Am. Luth. Ch., 1973; faculty devel. grantee George Fox Coll., 1972; scholar, diplomat Internat. Studies Assn.-Dept. of State, 1973; rsch. fellow Nat. Resources Law Ctr., Sch. of Law, U. Colo., 1990. Mem. Am. Soc. Pub. Administrs. Western Social Sci. Assn. (exec. coun. 1989-92, pres.-elect 1995—). Lutheran. Office: Nat Biol Svc Midcontinent Ecol Sci Ctr 4512 Mcmurray Ave Fort Collins CO 80525-3400

LAMB, DARLIS CAROL, sculptor; b. Wausa, Nebr.; d. Lindor Soren and June Berniece (Skalberg) Nelson; m. James Robert Lamb; children: Sherry Lamb Sobh, Michael, Mitchell. BA in Fine Arts, Columbia Pacific U., San Rafael, Calif., 1988; MA in Fine Arts, Columbia Pacific U., 1989. Exhibited in group shows at Nat. Arts Club, N.Y.C., 1983, 85, 89, 90, 91, 92 (Catherine Lorillard Wolfe award sculpture 1983, C.L. Wolfe Horse's Head award 1994), N.Am. Sculpture Exhibit, Foothills Art Ctr., Golden, Colo., 1983, 84, 86, 87, 90, 91 (C. Percival Dietsch Sculpture Prize 1991), Loveland Mus. and Gallery, 1990, 91, Allied Artists Am., 1992, Pen and Brush, 1993, 95 (Roman Bronze award 1995), others; represented in permanent collections: Nebr. Hist. Soc., Am. Lung Assn. of Colo., Benson Park Sculpture Garden, Loveland, others. Mem. Catherine Lorillard Wolfe Art Club, N.Am. Sculpture Soc. Office: PO Box 9043 Englewood CO 80111-0301

LAMB, H. RICHARD, psychiatry educator; b. Phila., Sept. 18, 1929; s. Julius R. and Lillian (Beerman) L.; m. Doris Murial Koehn, Feb. 10, 1969; children: Jonathan Howard, Carolyn Elizabeth, Thomas Warren. BA, U. Pa., 1950; MD, Yale U., 1954. Diplomate Am. Bd. Psychiatry and Neurology. Chief rehab. svcs. San Mateo (Calif.) County Mental Health Svcs., 1960-76; prof. psychiatry U. So. Calif. Sch. Medicine, L.A., 1976—; vis. prof. U. Wales, Coll. Medicine, Cardiff, 1991; chmn. Hosp. & Comty. Psychiatry Inst. Program Planning Com., 1990—. Editor: New Directions for Mental Health Services, 1979—; mem. editl. bd.: Hosp. & Comty. Psychiatry, 1981-90, Psychosocial Rehab. Jour., 1982—, Internat. Jour. Social Psychiatry, 1988—; author 6 books; contbr. chpts. to books, articles to profl. jours. Capt. U.S. Army, 1958-60. Named Exemplary Psychiatrist, Nat. Alliance for Mentally Ill, 1992. Fellow Am. Psychiat. Assn. (chmn. task force on homeless mentally ill 1983-84, mem. com. on chronically mentally ill 1986—, Presdl. Commendation 1985), Am. Coll. Psychiatrists. Office: U So Calif Dept Psychiatry 1934 Hospital Pl Los Angeles CA 90033

LAMB, LOWELL DAVID, physicist; b. Abilene, Tex., Nov. 8, 1955; s. Donald Wayne Lamb and Gaylon (Jordan) Monteverde; m. Victoria Irene Russo, May 8, 1985. BS in Physics, BS in Math., Abilene Christian U., 1977; MA in Physics, Johns Hopkins U., 1983; PhD in Physics, U. Ariz., 1991. Systems programmer Fed. Res. Bank of N.Y., N.Y.C., 1981-85; asst. dir. Ariz. Fullerene Consortium, U. Ariz., Tucson, 1991—. Contbr. articles to profl. jours. Fellow ARCS Found., 1988, 89; faculty scholar U. Ariz., 1985. Mem. Am. Phys. Soc. Home: 5214 E Alberta Dr Tucson AZ 85711-3121 Office: Dept Physics U Ariz Tucson AZ 85721

LAMB, ROBERT CHARLES, plastic surgeon; b. Rockville Center, N.Y., Oct. 30, 1947. MD, U. Autonoma de Guadalajara, Mex., 1976. Plastic surgeon Chino (Calif.) Cmty. Hosp.; asst. clin. prof. Med. Coll. U. Calif., Irvine. Office: 5365 Walnut Ave Ste E-f Chino CA 91710-2622*

LAMB, RONALD ALFRED, computer book editor; b. Seattle, Mar. 17, 1948; s. Lowell Rendall and Esther Irene (Fischer) L.; m. Nancy Sandine, Apr. 20, 1973; children: Braden Daniel, Kirsten Marie. AA, Highline Coll., 1968; BA, U. Wash., 1970. Sports writer Federal Way/Des Moines (Wash.) News, 1972-74; sports writer Skagit Valley Herald, Mt. Vernon, Wash., 1975-77, reporter, 1977-79; reporter Bremerton (Wash.) Sun, 1979-84; editor Microsoft Press, Bellevue and Redmond, Wash., 1984—. Editor: Command Performance: Microsoft Excel, 1986 (Achievement award Puget Sound chpt. Soc. Tech. Comm. 1986), Computer Lib/Dream Machines, 1987 (Non-fiction Computer Book of Yr. award Computer Press Assn. 1988), Variations in C, 2d edit., 1989 (Merit award Puget Sound chpt. Soc. Tech. Comm. 1989), Inside OLE 2, 1994 (Merit award Puget Sound chpt. Soc. Tech. Comm. 1994), Word 6 for Windows Companion, 1994 (Excellence award Puget Sound chpt. Soc. Tech. Comm. 1994); contbg. author: Tukwila: Community at the Crossroads, 1991 (1st pl. non-fiction books--history Wash. Press Assn. 1992). Del. to state conv. Wash. State Dem. Party, Tacoma, 1984; sec. South Ctrl. Schs. Adv. Coun., Tukwila, 1987-88; mem. Foster Friends of Libr., Tukwila, 1988—; chmn. South Ctrl. 2000 Com., Tukwila, 1987-89, Foster Annexation Com., Tukwila, 1988-89; bd. dirs. South Ctrl. Sch. Dist., Tukwila, 1989-93, chmn. bd. dirs., 1991-93. Mem. Soc. Profl. Journalists, King County Dirs. Assn. (bd. dirs. 1992-93), Wash. State Sch. Dirs. Assn. (urban schs. com. 1993). Democrat. Home: 4251 S 139th St Tukwila WA 98168-3260 Office: Microsoft Press 1 Microsoft Way Redmond WA 98052-8300

LAMB, WILLIS EUGENE, JR., physicist, educator; b. L.A., July 12, 1913; s. Willis Eugene and Marie Helen (Metcalf) L.; m. Ursula Schaefer, June 5, 1939. BS, U. Calif., 1934, PhD, 1938; DSc (hon.), U. Pa., 1953, Gustavus Adolphus Coll., 1975, Columbia U., 1990; MA (hon.), Oxford (Eng.) U., 1956, Yale, 1961; LHD (hon.), Yeshiva U., 1965. Mem. faculty Columbia U., 1938-52, prof. physics, 1948-52; prof. physics Stanford U., 1951-56; Wykeham prof. physics and fellow New Coll., Oxford U., 1956-62; Henry Ford 2d prof. physics Yale U., 1962-72, J. Willard Gibbs prof. physics, 1972-74; prof. physics and optical scis. U. Ariz., Tucson, 1974—, Regents prof., 1990—; Morris Loeb lectr. Harvard U., 1953-54; Gordon Shrum lectr. Simon Fraser U., 1972; cons. Philips Labs., Bell Telephone Labs., Perkin-Elmer, NASA; vis. com. Brookhaven Nat. Lab. Recipient (with P. Kusch) Nobel prize in physics, 1955, Rumford premium Am. Acad. Arts and Scis., 1953; award Rsch. Corp., 1954, Yeshiva award, 1962; Guggenheim fellow, 1960-61, sr. Alexander von Humboldt fellow, 1992-94. Fellow Am. Phys. Soc., N.Y. Acad. Scis.; hon. fellow Inst. Physics and Phys. Soc. (Guthrie lectr. 1958), Royal Soc. Edinburgh (fgn. mem.); mem. Nat. Acad. Scis., Phi Beta Kappa, Sigma Xi. Office: U Ariz Optical Scis Ctr Tucson AZ 85721*

LAMB-BRASSINGTON, KATHRYN EVELYN, writer, genealogist; b. Yakima, Wash., Apr. 3, 1935; d. Victor Earl and Anna (Kauzlarich) Lamb; m. Donald Morley Brassington, Dec. 27, 1956 (div. 1968); children: Andrew Stuart, Perry Sanford, Van Victor, Keith Bennett. Student, Wash. State U., 1954-55, U. Wash., 1955-56. Author: A Leg of Lamb, 1985; assoc. editor quar. newsletter Lamb's Pastures. Mem. DAR, Towne Family Assn., Colonial Dames 17th Century, Nat. Soc. Women Descendants of Ancient and Honorable Artillery Co. Republican. Presbyterian. Home: PO Box 290 311 B St Roslyn WA 98941-0290

LAMBERT, DENNIS ALVIN, radio news director; b. Allegan, Mich., Sept. 14, 1947; s. Alvin Millard and Myrta Gertrude (Ellinger) L.; m. Pamela Sue Hoeksema, Dec. 20, 1969; children: Matthew Dennis, Nicole Leigh. BA, Mich. State U., 1971. Disc jockey Sta. WAOP, Osego, Mich., 1969; asst. news dir. Sta. WJIM, Lansing, Mich., 1969-75; news reporter Sta. WVIC,

East Lansing, 1975-76; news and sports anchor Sta. WCAR, Detroit, 1976; news reporter, editor Sta. WXYZ, Detroit, 1976-84; mng. editor Sta. KTAR, Phoenix, 1984-85, news dir., 1985—. Recipient various news related awards Ariz. AP, 1984, 86, 87. Mem. Ariz. Press Club, Radio, TV and News Dirs. Assn. Office: Sta KTAR Radio 301 W Osborn Rd Phoenix AZ 85013-3921

LAMBERT, MARK ALLEN, aero-mechanical engineer; b. Dallas, Oct. 13, 1964; s. William A. and Elizabeth A. (Rowland) L. BS in Mech. Engring., U. N.Mex., 1987; MS in Mech. Engring., Calif. State U., Northridge, 1990. Engr. in tng., N.Mex. Aero-mech. staff engr. Naval Air Warfare Ctr., China Lake, Calif., 1987—; acad. grad. sch. fellow Naval Postgrad. Sch., Monterey, Calif., 1993—. Patentee in field. Vol. tutor Seaside (Calif.) Homework Ctr., 1994. Recipient Navy award of merit for group achievement Naval Weapons Ctr., China Lake, 1991. Mem. AIAA, ASME, Tau Beta Pi, Pi Tau Sigma. Republican. Home: 184 Lillian Pl Marina CA 93933-2204

LAMBERT, RICHARD WILLIAM, mathematics educator; b. Gettysburg, Pa., May 1, 1928; s. Allen Clay and Orpha Rose (Hoppert) L.; m. Phyllis Jean Bain, Sept. 2, 1949 (div. May 1982); children: James Harold, Dean Richard; m. Kathleen Ann Waring, Aug. 30, 1982; stepchildren: Gregory Scott Gibbs, LeAnn Marie Gibbs. BS, Oreg. State U., 1952; MA in Teaching Math., Reed Coll., 1962. Instr. Siuslaw High Sch., Florence, Oreg., 1954-55, David Douglas High Sch., Portland, Oreg., 1955-67; instr. Mt. Hood Community Coll., Gresham, Oreg., 1967-87, ret., 1987. NSF grantee, 1959, 60, 62. Mem. Nat. Coun. Tchr. Math., Am. Math Soc., Math. Assn. Am., Am. Math. Assn. of Two Yr. Colls., Oreg. Coun. Tchrs. Math. Democrat. Methodist. Home: 11621 SE Lexington St Portland OR 97266-5933

LAMBERTI, JOHN JOSEPH, cardiovascular surgeon; b. Yonkers, N.Y., Jan. 4, 1942; s. John Joseph and Gertrude Margaret (Dean) L.; m. Maureen Estelle McCarthy, June 17, 1967 (div. Dec. 1989); children: Andrea, Amy. BS, Mass. Inst. Tech., 1963; MD, U. Pitts., 1967. Diplomate Am. Bd. Surgery, Am. Bd. Thoracic Surgery. Surgical intern Peter Bent Brigham Hosp., Boston, 1967-68, surgical resident, 1968-72, chief resident cardiac and thoracic surgery, 1972-73; chief resident cardiac surgery Children's Hosp. Medical Ctr., Boston, 1973; asst. in surgery Peter Bent Brigham Hosp., 1973-74, jr. assoc. in surgery, 1974; instr. in surgery Harvard Medical Sch., Boston, 1974; asst. prof. surgery The Univ. Chgo., 1974-77, assoc. prof. surgery, 1977-78; assoc. clinical prof. cardiothoracic surgery U. Calif., San Diego, 1980; dir. cardiovascular surgery Children's Hosp. and Health Ctr., San Diego, 1981-88, 90—, chmn. dept. surgery, 1989—, dir. cardiovascular inst., 1990—; attending surgeon Donald N. Sharp Meml. Hosp., Children's Hosp. and Health Ctr., Scripps Meml. Hosp., 1978—. Contbr. numerous articles to profl. jours. Actice Am. Heart Assn. Recipient Pa. Heart Assn. Rsch. award, 1967. Fellow Am. Coll. Surgeons, Am. Coll. Cardiology, Am. Coll. Chest Physicians; mem. Assn. Acad. Surgery, Am. Fedn. Clinical Rsch., Soc. Thoracic Surgeons, Am. Soc. Artificial Internal Organs, Am. Assn. Thoracic Surgery, Western Thoracic Surgical Soc., Pacific Coast Surgical Soc., Calif. Soc. Pediatric Cardiology. Office: 3030 Childrens Way Ste 310 San Diego CA 92123-4228

LAMBROS, VASILIOS S., II, plastic surgeon; b. Washington, 1948. MD, Rush Med. Coll., 1974. Plastic surgeon Western Med. Ctr., Santa Ana, Calif.; clin. instr. U. Calif., Irvine. Office: 2200 E Fruit St Santa Ana CA 92701-4479*

LAMDEN, EVELYN OLSON, advertising executive; b. Akron, Ohio, Nov. 10, 1950; d. Myrle Mylo Olson and Luz (Talaña) Swartz; m. William Edward Lamden, Aug. 31, 1986. BA in Mass Media Communications magna cum laude, U. Akron, 1980. Sec. Goodyear Tire Co., Akron, 1968-74, field merchandiser, 1975-76, display coordinator, 1976-79, regional advt. mgr., 1979-83; ptnr., dir. Budji Corp., Los Angeles, 1983-85; sr. account exec. Internat. Communications Group, Los Angeles, 1985-87, account dir., 1987-88; ptnr. Lamden Property Mgmt., San Diego, 1988-90, Century 21 Triad-Realtor, 1990-93; media mgr. Foodmaker, Inc., San Diego, 1993—. Pres., Goodyear Cmty. Theater, Akron, 1976-79; bd. dirs., Dallas Repertory Theater, 1980-83, La Jolla Stage Co., 1990—, pres. 1993-94. Recipient Best Speaker award Toastmasters Internat., Akron, 1972. Mem. Women in Communications, Nat. Assn. Female Execs. Democrat. Roman Catholic. Office: Foodmaker Inc 9330 Balboa Ave San Diego CA 92123

LAMEIRO, GERARD FRANCIS, research institute director; b. Paterson, N.J., Oct. 3, 1949; s. Frank Raymond and Beatrice Cecilia (Donley) L.; BS, Colo. State U., 1971, MS, 1973, PhD, 1977. Sr. scientist Solar Energy Rsch. Inst., Golden, Colo., 1977-78; asst. prof. mgmt. sci. and info. systems Colo. State U., Fort Collins, 1978-83, mem. editorial bd. energy engring., 1978-82, editorial bd. energy econs. policy and mgmt., 1981-82, lectr. dept. computer sci., 1983, lectr. dept. mgmt., 1983; pres. Successful Automated Office Systems, Inc., Fort Collins, 1982-84; product mgr. Hewlett Packard, 1984-88; computer networking cons., 1988-89, Ft. Collins.; mem. editorial bd. The HP Chronicle, 1986-88, columnist, 1988, mgmt. strategist, 1988-91; dir. Lameiro Rsch. Inst., 1991—. Author: Campaign Code of Ethics, 1988, Ten Laws for Winning Presidential Elections, 1992; mem. editorial bd. Hp Chronicle, 1986-88, Energy Engring., Policy and Mgmt., 1981-82, Energy Engring., 1978-82. Mem. Presdl. Electoral Coll., 1980. Recipient nat. Disting. Svc. award Assn. Energy Engrs., 1981, Honors Prof. award Colo. State U., 1982; Colo. Energy Rsch. Inst. fellow 1976; NSF fellow 1977. Mem. Assn. for Computing Machinery, Assn. Energy Engrs. (pres. 1980, Nat. Distinguish Service award 1981, internat. bd. dirs. 1980-81), Am. Mgmt. Assn., Am. Soc. for Tng. and Devel., Am. Mktg. Assn. (exec.), Am. Soc. For Quality Control, IEEE Computer Soc., Inst. Indsl. Engrs., U.S. C. of C., Crystal Cathedral Golden Eagles Club, The Heritage Found., Sigma Xi, Phi Kappa Phi, Beta Gamma Sigma, Kappa Mu Epsilon. Roman Catholic. Author: Ten Laws for Winning Presidential Elections, 1992, Campaign Code of Ethics, 1988; contbr. articles in mgmt. and tech. areas to profl. jours. Home: PO Box 9580 Fort Collins CO 80525-0500 Office: 3313 Downing Ct Fort Collins CO 80526-2315

LAMEIRO, PAUL AMBROSE, manufacturing executive; b. Bay Shore, N.Y., July 31, 1957; s. Frank R. and Beatrice C. Lameiro. BS in Physics, Colo. State U., 1982. Engr. Hewlett Packard, Loveland, Colo., 1977-91; pres. Wavefront Acoustics, Aurora, Colo., 1983—. Mem. Audio Engring. Soc., Am. Soc. Quality Control. Office: Wavefront Acoustics 1610 Magnolia St Denver CO 80220-1636

LAMENDOLA, WALTER FRANKLIN, human services, information technology consultant; b. Donora, Pa., Jan. 29, 1943. BA in English, St. Vincent Coll., 1964; MSWin Community Orgn., U. Pitts., 1966; diploma in Sociology and Social Welfare, U. Stockholm, 1970; PhD in Social Work, U. Minn., 1976. Community svcs. dir. Ariz. tng. programs State Dept. Mental Retardation, Tucson, 1970-73; assoc. prof. social welfare adminstrn. Fla. State U., 1976-77; pres., chief exec. officer Minn. Rsch. and Tech., Inc., 1977-81; assoc. prof., dir. Allied Health Computer Lab. E. Carolina U., 1981-84; prof., dir. info. tech. ctr. Grad. Sch. Social Work U. Denver, 1984-87; cons. info. tech., rsch. human svcs., 1987-90; v.p. rsch. The Colo. Trust, Denver, 1990-93, info. tech. and rsch. cons., 1993—; cons. European Network Info. Tech. & Human Svcs.; mem. adv. bd. ctr. human svcs. U. Southampton, Brit. Rsch. Coun. Univs., Human Svc. Info. Tech. Applications, CREON Found., Netherlands; lectr. conf., symposia, univs. U.S., Europe; mem. nat. adv. bd. Native Elder Health Resource Ctr., 1994—; co-founder Denver Free Net, 1993—; info. tech. cons. Healthy Nations Program Robert Wood Johnson Found., 1993—; evaluator Nat. Libr. Rsch. Program, Access Colo. grant, 1994, Nat. Info. Infrastrure grant Colo. State Libr.; cons. set up on the Internet for U.S. Cts.-Ct. Futures Network; rschr. telemedicine Ctr. for Mental Health Svcs., NIH, Frontier Mental Health Svcs. Network grant. Co-author: Choices for Colorado's Future, 1993, The Integrity of Intelligence: A Bill of Rights for the Information Age, 1992, Choices for Colorado's Future: Executive Summary, 1991, Choices for Colorado's Future: Regional Summaries, 1991; co-editor: A Casebook of Computer Applications in Health and Social Services, 1989; contbr. numerous articles to profl. jours. Capt. U.S. Army, 1966-69. Recipient Innovative Computer Application award Internat. Fedn. Info. Processing Socs., 1979; Nat. Lib. Rsch. Evaluator grantee, Colo., 1994—, Nat. Info. Infrastructure grantee Dept. Edn., State Libr. and Adult Literacy, 1994-95; Funds & Couns. Tng. scholar United Way Am., 1964-66, Donaldson Fund scholar, 1965-66, NIMH scholar, 1964-66, 73-76, St. Vincent Coll. Benedictine Soc. scholar, 1963-64; vis. fellow U. Southampton. Office: 4098 Field Dr Wheat Ridge CO 80033-4358

LAMFERS, ERIC BERNARD, forester; b. Grand Rapids, Mich., Aug. 11, 1961; s. Bernard Lamfers and Martha (DeVries) L. AA, Reformed Bible Coll., 1985; BS in Forestry, Mich. State U., 1989, MS in Forestry, 1991. Biol. chem. def. specialist staff sgt. U.S. Army Res., Mich. and Oreg., 1983-93; forestry technician Boise Cascade, Medford, Oreg., 1992—. With U.S. Army, 1980-83. Mem. Soc. Am. Foresters. Mem. Christian Reformed Ch. Home: PO Box 4384 3083 Springbrook Medford OR 97501

LAMIE, EDWARD LOUIS, computer science educator; b. Kingsley, Mich., Aug. 27, 1941; s. Louis Edward Lamie and Pauline Theresa (Harrand) La Bonte; children from previous marriage: William, David, Marla, Melissa; m. Frances Moore Jeffries, Jan. 2, 1988. AB, San Diego State U., 1969; MS, U. So. Calif., 1971; PhD, Mich. State U., 1974. Drafter Security Title Ins. Co., San Diego, 1962-64; engring. aide City of San Diego, 1964-69; mem. tech. staff Rockwell Internat., Downey, Calif., 1969-71; prof. computer sci. Cen. Mich. U., Mount Pleasant, Mich., 1971-82; chmn. dept. Cen. Mich. U., Mount Pleasant, 1972-82; prof., chmn. dept. Calif. State U. Stanislaus, Turlock, 1982-93, prof., dir. instl. rsch., 1993—. Author: PL/1 Programming, 1982, Pascal Programming, 1987; contbr. articles to profl. jours. Served with USN, 1959-62. Recipient Meritorious Service award Calif. State U. Stanislaus, 1984. Mem. Assn. Computing Machinery, IBM Computer Club. Republican. Roman Catholic. Home: 1713 Fairington Ln Modesto CA 95355-1543 Office: Calif State U Stanislaus Computer Sci Dept 801 W Monte Vista Ave Turlock CA 95382-0256

LAMKINS, ROBERT GERALD, fundraising executive; b. Medicine Lodge, Kans., Nov. 13, 1938; s. Charles Nelson and Thelma Fanelle (Peterie) L.; m. Marcia Lane Johnson, June 23, 1962; children: Carla Elaine, Martha Elizabeth. BA, Friends U., 1960; MS, Boston U., 1966. Dir. alumni rels. Friends U., Wichita, Kans., 1961-64; dir. devel. William Woods Coll., Fulton, Mo., 1965-70; dir. ann. giving Calif. Inst. Tech., Pasadena, 1970-78; pres. Little Co. of Mary Hosp. Found., Torrance, Calif., 1978-93; regional v.p. Western region J. Donovan Assocs., Inc., Salem, Mass., 1993—; pres., corr. sec. Nat. Cons. Group Inc., Marina Del Rey, Calif., 1984-92; bd. dirs., v.p. Vol. Ctr., Torrance. Fellow Assn. for Healthcare Philanthropy (regional dir. 1990-92); mem. So. Calif. Assn. for Hosp. Devel. (pres. 1983), Nat. Soc. Fund Raising Execs., Rotary (pres. Palos Verdes chpt. 1988-89, Chmn. of Yr. 1991, Rotarian of Yr. 1993), Kiwanis, Toastmasters (treas. local chpt. 1992, Competent Toastmaster 1992). Republican. Office: J Donovan Assocs Inc 655 Deep Valley Dr Ste 125 Rolling Hills Estates CA 90274

LAMMER, EDWARD JAMES, geneticist; b. Dubuque, Feb. 26, 1953. MD, U. Iowa, 1979. Dir. med. genetics Children's Hosp., Oakland, Calif.; asst. prof. Stanford U. Office: Stanford U Sept of Ped Stanford CA 94305*

LAMONICA, JOHN, food executive; b. Bklyn., Apr. 26, 1954; s. Lou and Alda (Merola) L.; m. Nancy Lamonica. BS in Acctg., Bklyn. Coll., 1977. With N.S.L. Enterprises, 1982—; with Aniellos Pizza, 1979—, Lamonicas N.Y. Pizza, 1980—; restaurant cons. Developer of new pizzas. Republican. Mem. Beverly Hills Gun Club, Shelby Am. Club. Office: 1066 Gayley Ave Los Angeles CA 90024-3402

LAMONT, SANDERS HICKEY, journalist; b. Atlanta, Nov. 9, 1940; s. Louis Earnest and Dorothy Rebecca (Strickland) LaM.; m. Patricia Jean Taylor, Aug. 5, 1966; children—Patricia Ruth, Zachary Taylor. A.A., Marion Mil. Inst., Ala., 1960; B.A. in Journalism, U. Ala., 1962; postgrad. U. Mich., 1977-78. Reporter, bur. chief Gannett News Service, various locations, 1961-74; mng. editor Ft. Myers News Press, Fla., 1974-77; exec. editor Marietta Times, Ohio, 1978-80, Modesto Bee, Calif., 1980—; chmn. AP News Execs. Council, Calif., 1984-85. NEH journalism fellow, U. Mich., 1977-78; Pulitzer prize juror, 1984-85. Served to 1st lt. U.S. Army, 1963-65. Mem. Am. Soc. Newspaper Editors, AP Mng. Editors, Soc. Profl. Journalists. Methodist. Office: The Modesto Bee PO Box 5256 Modesto CA 95352-5256

LA MONT, TAWANA FAYE, video director, public relations executive; b. Ft. Worth, May 12, 1948; d. Jerry James and Roberta Ann (Wilkinson) La M. AA, Antelope Coll., 1979; BA in Anthropology, UCLA, 1982. Forest technician, trail constrn. supr. Angeles Nat. Forest, Region 9 U.S. Forest Svc., Pear Blossom, Calif., 1974-79; trail constrn. supr., maintenance asst. Calif. State Parks, 1979-81; cable TV installer Sammons Comm., Glendale, Calif., 1981-83; camera operator Sammons Comm., San Fernando, Calif., 1984—; video studio and ENG remotes dir., mgr., program mgr. channels 6 and 21 Sammons Comm., Glendale, Calif., 1987—; video dir., prodr. LBW & Assocs. Internat., Ltd., 1988—; mem. edl. access channel satellite program evaluation com., Glendale and Burbank, 1990-92; mem. Foothill Cmty. TV Network, Glendale and Burbank, 1987—; pres./CEO Chamblee Found., Ltd., 1995—. Prodr., dir. (homeless video) Bittersweet Streets, 1988; cameraperson Rockin in A Hard Place, 1988-93; dir., editor over 1000 videos. Active Glendale Hist. Soc., 1992—; bd. dirs. Am. Heart Assn., 1992—, comms. chair; bd. dirs. ARC, 1993—, mem. disaster svcs. team, cultural diversity chair, 1994—; mem. mktg. com. Burbank YMCA, 1994—; bd. dirs. Glendale Rose Float Assn., 1995—. Recipient award of appreciation LBW and Assocs. Internat., 1988, Bur. Census, 1990, USMC, 1991, Verdigo Disaster Recovery Project, 1995, ARC, 1995, ARC Spl. citation for exceptional vol. svc., 1995, award of outstanding pub. svc. Social Security Adminstrn. HHS, 1989, dedicated svc. award Am. Heart Assn., 1992, cert. of appreciation, 1994, 95. Mem. NFA, NRA, Am. Women in Radio and TV, Am. Bus. Women Assn., UCLA Alumni ASsn. (lfie), Wildlife Waystation, Alpha Gamma. Democrat. Home and Office: The Chamblee Found Ltd PO Box 142 Lake Hughes CA 93532-0142

LAMONT-WELLS, TAWANA F., video director; b. Ft. Worth, May 12, 1948; d. Jerry James and Roberta Ann (Wilkinson) LaMont. AA, Antelope Valley Coll., 1979; BA in anthropology, UCLA, 1982. Forest technician, trail constrns. supr. Angeles Nat. Forest Region 9 U.S. Forest Svc., Pear Blossom, Calif., 1974-79; installer Sammons Comm., Glendale, Calif., 1981-83, cameraperson, 1983-87, video dir./program mgr., 1987—; video dir., prodr. L.B.W. & Assocs., Internat. Ltd., Glendale, 1988—. prodr./dir.: (video) Bittersweet Streets, 1988; cameraperson: Rockin' In A Hard Place, 1988; dir./editor over 1000 videos. Bd. dirs. ARC, Glendale, 1993—, mem. disaster svcs. team, 1994; com. chair bd. dirs. Am. Heart Assn., 1992—; active Glendale Hist. Soc., 1992—. Recipient Outstanding Pub. Svc. award, U.S. Social Security Dept., 1989; recipient award of appreciation Bur. of Census, 1990, U.S. Marine Corps, 1991, Dedicated Svc. award Am. Heart Assn., 1993, First Yr. pin ARC, 1994, ARC exceptional Vol. Svc. award, 1995. Mem. Am. Women in Radio and TV, Wildlife Waystation, Foothill Cmty. TV Network, Ednl. Access Channel Satellite Program (evaluation com.), Alpha Gamma, UCLA ALumni Assn. (life), Am. Bus. Women's Assn., 1995—. Democrat. Office: Sammons Comm 6246 San Fernando Rd Lake Hughes CA 93532

LAMORE, BETTE, rehabilitation counselor, motivational speaker; b. Chgo., Oct. 1, 1948. BA in Polit. Sci., U. Ariz., 1971, MS in Rehab. Counseling, 1974. Cert. rehab. counselor & ins. rehab. specialist. Social worker Pima County Welfare Dept., Tuscon, 1971-72; residential therapist So. Arix. Mental Health Clinic, Tuscon, 1972-73; drug counselor Awareness House Drug Clinics, Tuscon, 1973-74; dir. residential intervention ctr. YWCA, Tuscon, 1974-75; rehab. counselor Calif. State Dept. Rehab., Ventura and Thousand Oaks, 1975-77; job placement specialist, counselor Moorpark (Calif.) C.C., 1977-81; co-owner, rehab. counselor Experienced Rehab. Advisors, Atascadero, Calif., 1981—; breeder Arabian horses Whispering Oaks Arabians, Atascadero, 1987—; cons. for drug abuse programs Ventura (Calif.) County Health Svcs., 1975; expert witness in field. Author: My Friend Joe, 1984; co-author: Injured Workers Guide to California Workers Compensation System, 1988. Scholar NIMH, 1973. Mem. Calif. Assn. Rehab. Profls., Internat. Arabian Horse Assn. (v.p. Los Robles chpt. 1991), Am. Horseshow Assn., Phi Kappa Phi, Phi Beta Kappa, Pi Lambda Theta. Democrat. Home: PO Box 2863 Atascadero CA 93423-2863 Office: Experienced Rehab Advisors 5411 El Camino Real Atascadero CA 93422-3355

LA MOTHE, SUZANNE MARIE, career counselor; b. Long Beach, Calif., Apr. 15, 1966; d. Thomas Jay and Louise Mary (Jacobs) La M. Student, Inst. Am. Univs., Aix-en-Provence, France, 1988; BA in Behavioral Sci., U. San Diego, 1989, MEd of Counseling in Edn., 1994. Counselor kindergarten-12th grade St. Judes sch. Concern Counseling Svcs., San Diego, 1991-92; asst. program coord. continuing edn. U. San Diego, 1992-94; career counselor intern U. Calif., San Diego, 1993-94; career counselor Loyola Marymount U., L.A., 1994—. Fellow Am. Counseling Assn., Calif. Career Devel. Assn.; mem. Chi Sigma Iota. Roman Catholic. Office: Loyola Marymount U Loyola Blvd at W 80th St Los Angeles CA 90045

LAMOUREUX, CHARLES HARRINGTON, botanist, arboretum administrator; b. West Greenwich, R.I., Sept. 14, 1933; s. Emile and Cora May (Harrington) L.; m. Florence May Kettelle, Aug. 28, 1954; children: Mark Harrington, Anne Maile. BS in Botany, U. R.I., 1953; MS in Botany, U. Hawaii, 1955; PhD in Botany, U. Calif., Davis, 1961. From asst. to assoc. prof. botany U. Hawaii, Honolulu, 1959-71, prof., 1971—, chair dept. botany, 1962-65, 76-78, acting assoc. dean curriculum coll. arts and scis., 1976-77, 83, project coord. instrnl. assistance unit, 1977-79, assoc. dean acad. affairs coll. arts and scis., 1985-91, dir. Lyon arboretum, 1992—; rsch. assoc. botany Bernice P. Bishop Mus., Honolulu, 1963—; vis. asst. prof. botany U. B.C., Can., summer 1963; vis. colleague dept. botany Canterbury U., Christchurch, New Zealand, 1965-66; mem. sci. adv. com. Pacific Tropical Bot. Garden (name changed to Nat. Tropical Bot. Garden), 1967-94; dir. summer inst. sci. amd math. tchrs. U.S. children Far East NSF, Chofu, Japan, 1968-71, reviewer, mem. various rev. panels; faculty mem. ctr. Pacific islands studies U. Hawaii, 1971—; guest sci. Nat. Biol. Inst. Indonesia, Bogor, 1972-73, 79-80; mem. adv. com. plants and animals quarantine br. Hawaii State Dept. Agr., 1973-79, 89—; study lectr./leader Smithsonian Assocs. Study Tours S.E. Asia, 1985, 86, 88-95, Melanesia, 1987; report reviewer U.S. Congl. Office Tech. Assessment; rschr. in field; bot. and ecol. cons. to various businesses and agys. including State Hawaii Dept. Bus. and Econ. Devel., UNESCO, UN Devel. Programme. Author: Trailside Plants of Hawaii's National Parks, 1976, (U.S. Nat. Pk. Svc. Dir.'s award 1977, Nat. Pks. Coop. Assn. Award of Excellence 1977-78), rev. edit., 1982; bd. editors Pacific Sci., 1965—, editor-in-chief, 1985-86; mem. editorial com. Allertonia, 1977-90; manuscript reviewer for various jours. and presses; contbr. articles to profl. jours. Active Hawaii Audubon Soc., 1959—, past pres., 1st v.p., Hawaiian Bot. Gardens Found., 1959-67, 1st v.p.; life mem. Conservation Coun. Hawaii, 1959—, state bd. dirs., mem. com. flora conservation, Hawaiian Bot. Soc., 1959—, trustee endowment fund, past pres., v.p., sec., treas., newsletter editor; mem. adv. com. Hawai'i Earth Day, 1990; bd. dirs. Friends Honolulu Bot. Garden, 1992—. Mem. Bot. Soc. Am., Am. Assn. Bot. Gardens and Arboreta, Hawaiian Acad. Sci. (councillor 1991-93, pres.-elect 1993, pres. 1994-95), Pacific Sci. Assn. (life, standing com. botany 1971—), Internat. Assn. Plant Taxonomists, Internat. Assn. Wood Anatomists. Home: 3426 Oahu Ave Honolulu HI 96822-1254 Office: Harold L Lyon Arboretum 3860 Manoa Rd Honolulu HI 96822-1180

LAMPERT, ELEANOR VERNA, employment development specialist; b. Porterville, Calif., Mar. 23; d. Ernest Samuel and Violet Edna (Watkins) Wilson; student in bus., fin. Porterville Jr. Coll., 1977-78; grad. Anthony Real Estate Sch., 1971; student Laguna Sch. of Art, 1972, U. Calif.-Santa Cruz, 1981; m. Robert Mathew Lampert, Aug. 21, 1935; children—Sally Lu Winton, Lary Lampert, Carol R. John. Bookkeeper, Porterville (Calif.) Hosp., 1956-71; real estate sales staff Ray Realty, Porterville, 1973; sec. Employment Devel. Dept., State of Calif., Porterville, 1973-83, orientation and tng. specialist CETA employees, 1976-80. Author: Black Bloomers and Han-Ga-Ber, 1986. Sec., Employer Adv. Group, 1973-80, 81—; mem. U.S. Senatorial Bus. Adv. Bd., 1981-84; charter mem. Presdl. Republican Task Force, 1981—; mem. Rep. Nat. Congl. Com., 1982-88; pres. Sierra View Hosp. Vol. League, 1988-89 ; vol. Calif. Hosp. Assn., 1983-89, Calif. Spl. Olympics Spirit Team. Recipient Merit Cert., Gov. Pat Brown, State of Calif., 1968. Mem. Lindsay Olive Growers, Sunkist Orange Growers, Am. Kennel Club, Internat. Assn. Personnel in Employment Security, Calif. State Employees Assn. (emeritus Nat. Wildlife Fedn., NRA, Friends of Porterville Library, Heritage Found., DAR (Kaweah chpt. rec. sec. 1988—), Internat. Platform Assn., Dist. Fedn. Women's Clubs (recording sec. Calif. chpt. 1988—), Ky. Hist. Soc., Women's Club of Calif. (pres. Porterville chpt. 1988-89, dist. rec. sec. 1987-89), Mo. Rep. Women of Taney County, Internat. Sporting and Leisure Club, Ladies Aux. VFW (No. 5168 Forsyth, Mo.), Ozark Walkers League.

LAMPHERE, LOUISE, anthropology and women's studies educator; b. St. Louis, Oct. 4, 1940; d. Harold and Miriam (Bretschneider) L.; 1 child, Peter Bret. BA, Stanford U., 1962; MA, Harvard U., 1966, PhD, 1968. Asst. prof. Brown U., Providence, 1972-75, assoc. prof., 1979-85; assoc. prof. U. N.Mex., Albuquerque, 1976-79, adj. prof., 1979-85; fellow Wellesley (Mass.) Coll., 1981; prof. anthropology Brown U., Providence, 1985-88; prof. anthropology U. N.Mex., Albuquerque, 1986—, acting dir. women studies, 1993-95. Author: From Working Daughters to Working, 1987, (with others) Sunbelt Working Mothers, 1993; editor: Structuring Diversity, 1992, Newcomers in the Workplace, 1993, (with others) Woman, Culture and Society, 1974; editor Frontiers: A Jour. of Women Studies, Albuquerque, 1990-93. Recipient Conrad Arensberg award Soc. for Anthropology of Work, 1994; grantee NSF, 1981-83, Russell Sage Found., 1985-86, Ford Found., 1987-90. Mem. Am. Ethnological Soc. (counsellor 1981-84, pres.-elect 1987, pres. 1987-89), Am. Anthropol. Soc. (exec. com. 1987-89), Assn. for Feminist Anthropology (bd. dirs. 1989-91, pres.-elect 1993-95, pres. 1995—). Office: U NMex Dept Anthropology Albuquerque NM 87131

LAMPSON, FRANCIS KEITH, metallurgical engineer; b. Mpls., Aug. 7, 1924; s. Albert Dean and May (Miner) L.; m. Margaret Elaine Snyder, Sept. 30, 1945; children: Michael, Jan Colleen, Andrea, Kevin. BS in Metall. Engring., U. Ill., 1949. Jr. Met. N.E.P.A. N.E.P.A., Fairchild Engring. & Airplane Corp., Oak Ridge, Tenn., 1949-51; exptl. metallurgist Allison div. GMC, Indpls., 1951-54; metallurgist, group leader Marquardt Co., Van Nuys, Calif., 1954-57; tech. rep. Pacific Coast Allegheny Ludlum Steel Corp., L.A., 1957-65; dir. materials engring. Marquardt Co., Van Nuys, Calif., 1965-91; pres. F.K. Lampson Assocs., Northridge, Calif., 1975—. recipient Disting. Merit award U. Ill., 1983, Engr. '80 Merit award, San Fernando Valley Engring. Coun., 1980, Outstanding Achievement award San Fernanco Valley Engrs. Coun., 1982. Fellow ASM (trustee 1978-81), Masons, Shriner. Republican. Baptist. Home: 10000 Aldea Ave Northridge CA 91325-1661

LAMSON, ROBERT WOODROW, retired school system administrator; b. L.A., Dec. 28, 1917; s. Ernest K. and Mabel (Mahoney) L.; m. Jeannette Juett, July 22, 1949; children: Robert Woodrow Jr., Nancy Virginia, Kathleen Patricia. BA, Occidental Coll., 1940; MA, U. So. Calif., 1955. Cert. tchr., prin., supt., Calif. Tchr. El Monte (Calif.) Sch. Dist., 1940-43; tchr. L.A. City Sch. Dist., 1945-49, prin., 1949-55, supr., 1955-57, adminstrv. asst., 1957-59, area supt., 1959-78; ret., 1978; agt. Keilholtz Realtors, La Canada, Calif., 1979—; instr. various colls. and univs. so. Calif., 1948—; a founder, v.p., bd. dirs. U.S. Acad. Decathlon, Cerritos, Calif., 1981-86. Bd. dirs. 10th Dist. PTA, L.A., 1965-78; chmn. Scout-O-Rama, Gt. Western coun. Boy Scouts Am., 1980. Lt. comdr. USNR, 1943-46, mem. Res. ret. Mem. Am. Assn. Sch. Adminstrs., Assn. Adminstrs. L.A., Alumni Occidental Coll. in Edn. (a founder, past pres., bd. dirs.), Town Hall, Nat. PTA (hon. life), Calif. PTA (hon. life, bd. dirs. 1978-80), 31st Dist. PTA (hon. life, bd. dirs. 1965-78, auditorium named in his honor 1978), Phi Beta Kappa, Alpha Tau Omega. Republican. Home: 4911 Vineta Ave La Canada Flintridge CA 91011-2624 Office: Richard Keilholtz Realtors 727 Foothill Blvd La Canada Flintridge CA 91011-3405

LAN, ZHIYONG, public administration educator; b. Nanchang, Jiangxi, China, Dec. 3, 1955; came to U.S., 1984; s. Handing Liu and Wanying Lan; m. Xiangning Zhang, Jan. 1983; 1 child, Kenneth Tianyi. BA, Nanjing (China) U., 1982; MPA, N.C. State U., 1986; PhD in Pub. Adminstrn., Syracuse U., 1991. Adminstrv. asst. fgn. affairs office Nanjing U., 1982-84; rsch. assoc. Syracuse (N.Y.) U., 1987-90; instr. publ. affairs Ariz. State U., Tempe, 1990-91, asst. prof., chair com. pub. info. mgmt., 1991—; cons. in field. Author: Bureaucracy and Administration, 1994; co-editor: Taiwan in Transition: Observations & Reflections, 1994; contbr. articles to profl. jours. Faculty grantee Ariz. State U., 1990, 91, 93. Mem. Am. Pub. Adminstrn. Soc., Chinese Scholars Assn. Polit Sci. and Internat. Rels., Inc. (editor jour. 1992-93, bd. dirs. 1992-93, v.p. 1993—, program dir. conf. 1994), Washington Ctr. China Studies (bd. dirs. 1993—). Office: Ariz State U Sch Pub Affairs Tempe AZ 85287-0603

LANCASTER, JOHN HOWARD, civil engineer; b. Bklyn., July 3, 1917; s. George York and Alice Eliot (Littlejohn) L.; m. Phyllis Elaine Metcalf, June 1, 1938; children: Judith Ann, Barbara Jean, Marylin Sharon, Kathryn Joy, Debra Elizabeth. B.S., Worcester (Mass.) Poly. Inst., 1939. Registered profl. engr., N.Y., N.Mex.; lic. master mariner USCG. Engr. Austin Co., N.Y.C., 1939-40; engr. C.E., 1940-42; asst. to div. engr. C.E., N.Y.C., 1942-43; chief engring. and constrn. AEC, Upton, N.Y., 1946-54; chief project engr. Brookhaven Nat. Lab., Upton, 1954-72; asst. dir. Nat. Radio Astronomy Obs. and program mgr. very large array radiotelescope program, Socorro, N.Mex., 1972-81; propr. John H. Lancaster & Assos. (cons. engrs.), 1950-72; cons. NRAO/Associated Univs. Inc., 1981—; cons. in field, 1970—; bd. dirs., sec. corp. Seven Seas Cruising Assn.; cons. NSF, 1970, Cornell U., 1971, Fermi Nat. Accelerator Lab., 1980. Bd. dirs. Good Samaritan Nursing Home; treas. Socorro Pub. Libr. With USNR, 1942-46. Recipient Meritorious Service award NSF, 1976. Mem. NSPE, N.Y. Soc. Profl. Engrs., N.Mex. Soc. Profl. Engrs., Rotary, Masons, Ea. Star, Sigma Xi, Alpha Tau Omega.

LAND, CAROL JEANNE, marketing professional, writer; b. N.Y.C., Feb. 8, 1948; d. Alexander E. and Shirley (Wolfson) L.; m. John Campbell McTiernan, Oct. 12, 1974 (div. Feb. 1984); m. Barry Howard Slobin, May 20, 1984; 1 child, Noah Land Slobin. BA in Theater Arts and Comm., Brandeis U.; grad. study, Am. Film Inst., UCLA Sch. Mgmt. Asst. press agt. The Tony Awards, N.Y.C., 1969, HAIR Boston Nat. Co., 1970; asst. stage mgr. Joffrey Ballet Co. Chgo Tour, 1970, N.Y.C. Opera Lincoln Ctr., 1971; free lance producer, prodn. mgr. Various motion picture companies, 1975-80; writer, producer, prodn. mgr. Martin Brinkerhoff & Assocs., Inc., Irvine, Calif., 1980-82; producer, dir. of Devel. Land McTiernan, Inc., L.A., 1974-88; freelance writer Walt Disney Devel. Co., Orlando, Fla., 1990-92; owner, producer The Family Network, Studio City, Calif., 1988-91; v.p. Mktg., creative dir. Ovation Body Solutions, L.A., 1991-93. Co-producer (video) Open Adoption: The Experts Speak Out, 1989; writer, producer, dir. (audio, video) Winning At Adoption, 1991. Home: PO Box 1995 Studio City CA 91614-0995

LAND, DAVID BENJAMIN, obstetrician/gynecologist; b. Reading, Pa., May 18, 1950; s. Edward Herbert and Marjorie (Kline) L. BS in Chemistry, U. Miami, Fla., 1972; BS in Pharmacy summa cum laude, U. Tex., 1977; DO cum laude, Tex. Coll. Osteopathic Med., Ft. Worth, 1985. Registered pharmacist, Tex. Indsl. auctioneer David Weis Co., L.A., 1972-74; pharmacist Revco Drug/K-Mart, Ft. Worth, Tex., 1977-81; intern West Allegheny Hosp., Oakdale, Pa.; resident Mich. Health Ctr., Detroit, 1986-90; v.p., dir. residency clinic Physician's Svc. Corp., Detroit, 1991—; staff gynecologist Northeastern Regional Hosp., Las Vegas, N.Mex., 1992—. Recipient Merck Sharpe & Dohme Excellence in Rsch. award, 1990. Mem. Am. Osteo. Assn., Tex. Coll. Osteo. Medicine Alumni Assn., N.Mex. Osteo. Med. Assn., Am. Coll. Osteo. Obstetricians and Gynecologists, Am. Soc. Colposcopic Pathologists, Rho Chi. Democrat. Jewish. Home: 752 Diane Ave Las Vegas NM 87701-4910 Office: Rio Vista OB Gyn PA 1620 7th St Las Vegas NM 87701

LAND, KENNETH DEAN, test and balance agency executive, energy and environmental consultant; b. Central City, Nebr., Oct. 5, 1931; s. Adrew Kenneth Land and Marie Eveline (Weaver) Gehrke. Student, El Camino Coll., Gardena, Calif., 1954-56, Long Beach City Coll., 1958, Calif. State Coll., Long Beach, 1959. Gen. mgr. Air Heat Engrs., Inc., Santa Fe Springs, Calif., 1956-61; sales and estimating engr. Thermodyne Corp., Los Alamitos, Calif., 1962-64; pres., founder Air Check Co., Inc., Santa Ana, Calif., 1964-69; chief engring. technician Nat. Air Balance Co., Los Angeles, 1969-73; gen. mgr. B&M Air Balance Co., South El Monte, Calif., 1973-78; chief exec. officer, founder Land Air Balance Tech. (LABTECH), Las Vegas, Nev., 1978—; bd. dirs. Energy Resources and Mgmt., Inc., San-I-Pac, Internat., Inc., Energy Equities Group, Inc.; founder, pres. Utility Connection, 1990—. Active Las Vegas Founders Club-Las Vegas Invitational PGA Tournament, 1983—, player, 1992; former trustee Assoc. Air Balance Coun.-Sheet Metal Workers Internat. Apprenticeship Tng. Fund; mem. Citizens Against Govt. Waste, 1990—, YNOT Night for YMCA, 1987—; co-founder The Golf Com., operators charity golf tournament for Am. Cancer Soc., 1990, 91, Am. Diabetes Assn., 1992, Nev. Child Seekers, 1992—. With USN, 1951-54. Mem. ASHRAE (pres. so. Nev. chpt. 1983-84, editor chpt. bull. 1979-89, Citizen of Yr. 1989), CSI (co-founder Las Vegas chpt., pres. 1989-90, editor, founder chpt. bull. 1987-90, S.W. regional mem. chmn. 1990-91), Assn. Energy Engrs., Am. Soc. Profl. Cons., Associated Air Balance Coun. (cert. test and balance engr. 1966—, internat. pres. 1988-89, bd. dirs. 1982-90, mem. numerous coms.), Sheet Metal Workers Internat. Tng. Fund, Internat. Conf. Bldg. Officials, Internat. Assn. Plumbing and Mech. Officials, Nat. Fedn. Ind. Businessmen, Rotary (So. El Monte Calif. Club 1977-78, bull. editor, Las Vegas S.W. Nev. Club 1978-94, bd. dirs. 1983-85, 88-90, photographer 1987-90, chmn. internat. svc., 4 Paul Harris fellowships, charter mem. Las Vegas West Club, Nev., 1994—), Citizens for Pvt. Enterprise, Nev. Taxpayers Assn., UNLV Golf Found., UNLV Presdl. Assocs. Group, Nev. Devel. Assn., Nev. Nuclear Waste Study Com. adv. coun., Sheet Metal and Air Conditioning Contractors Assn. (nat. and so. Nev. chpt. bd. dirs.), Associated Gen. Contractors (nat. and Las Vegas chpt.), Nat. Energy Mgmt. Inst. (cert., co-chmn. Nev. adv. coun., instr. Energy Mgmt. Tng. 1991), Nev. Energy Resources Assn., Las Vegas C. of C., Nat. Inst. Bldg. Scis., Nev. Assn. Ind. Businessman, Nat. Fire Protection Assn., Am. Soc. Hosp. Engrs., Nev. Profl. Facility Mgrs. Assn., 1992—, Las Vegas Country Club. Office: Land Air Balance Tech Inc PO Box 26389 Las Vegas NV 89126-0389

LANDAR, HERBERT JAY, linguistics educator, author; b. N.Y.C., Dec. 7, 1927; s. Leo and Mildred (Mann) L.; m. Muriel Anne Epstein; children: Clifford, Nancy, Stephen. BA, Queens Coll., 1949; MA, Yale U., 1955, PhD, 1960. Instr. Reed Coll., Portland, Oreg., 1957-59; prof. linguistics Calif. State U., L.A., 1960-91, prof. emeritus, 1991—; vis. prof. Ind. U., Bloomington, 1976-77, Université Blaise Pascal, Clermont-Ferrand, France, 1987-88. Author: Language and Culture, 1966, (in Japanese) Kotoba-To Bunka, 1977; contbr. numerous articles to profl. jours. Cpl. U.S. Army, 1950-52. Guggenheim Found. fellow, 1967-68; Fulbright Commn. grantee, 1987-88. Home: 220 San Anselmo Ave San Francisco CA 94127-2030

LANDAU, ELLIS, gaming company executive; b. Phila., Feb. 24, 1944; s. Manfred and Ruth (Fischer) L.; m. Kathy Suzanne Thomas, May 19, 1968 (div.); children: Rachel, David; m. Yvette Ehr Cohen, Nov. 1, 1992. BA in Econs., Brandeis U., 1965; MBA, Columbia U., 1967. Fin. analyst SEC, Washington, 1968-69; asst. treas. U-Haul Internat., Phoenix, 1969-71; v.p., treas. Ramada, Inc., Phoenix, 1971-90; CFO Boyd Gaming Corp., Las Vegas, Nev., 1990—. Home: 7895 Harbour Towne Ave Las Vegas NV 89113-1387 Office: Boyd Gaming Corp 2950 S Industrial Rd Las Vegas NV 89109-1100

LANDAU, FELIX, lawyer; b. Hof/Salle, Germany, June 29, 1947; came to U.S., 1950; s. Fiszel and Ursula (Wahncau) L.; m. Kay Ellen Krutza, Aug. 10, 1979; children: Erik Lloyd, Kelly Anne, Kristine Marie. BS, U. Colo., 1969; MA, U. Northern Colo., 1972; JD cum laude, Gonzaga U., 1982. Bar: Wash. 1983, Wis. 1988. Atty. USAF, 1983-87; assoc. Liebman, Conway, Olejniczak and Jerry, S.C., Green Bay, Wis., 1987-90; pvt. practice Bellevue, Wash., 1990—. Assoc. editor Gonzaga U. Law Rev., 1981-82. Capt. USAF, 1983-87. Fellow ABA; mem. Wash. Bar Assn., Wash. State Trial Lawyers Assn., East King County Trial Lawyers Assn., Wis. Bar Assn., Phi Delta Phi. Office: 14670 NE 8th St Bellevue WA 98007-4127

LANDAU, HENRY GROH, geoenvironmental consulting engineer; b. N.Y.C., Mar. 1, 1943; s. Henry G. and Ann Marie (Skvarich) L.; m. Joyce Kathryn Van de Merlen, July 27, 1965; children: Greg, Amy, Michael. BS in Civil Engring., CCNY, 1965; MS in Geotech. Engring., Purdue U., 1966, PhD in Engring., 1973. Profl. engr., Wash., N.Y., Alaska. Civil engr. Geotechnica, Sao Paulo, Brazil, 1966-67; officer U.S. Army C.E., South Vietnam, 1967-70; sr. engr. Dames & Moore, Seattle, 1973-82; sr. prin. Landau Assocs., Inc., Edmonds, Wash., 1982—; vis. prof. Fed. U., Paraiba, Brazil, 1978-79; mem. Gov.'s Sci. Adv. Bd., Olympia, Wash., 1987-90, chmn., 1990—. Contbr. articles to profl. jours. Tutor math. & sci. Edmonds Sch. Dist.; scout leader Boy Scouts Am., Edmonds, 1986-90. 1st lt. U.S. Army, 1967-70, Vietnam. Mem. ASCE, Soc. Am. Mil. Engrs., Assn. Groundwater Scientists & Engrs. Office: Landau Assocs Inc 23107 100th Ave W Edmonds WA 98020-5017

LANDAU, JOSEPH WHITE, dermatologist; b. Buffalo, N.Y., May 23, 1930; s. Fred and Carolyn (White) L.; children: Brenda, Kenneth, Jason. BA, Cornell U., 1951, MD, 1955. Diplomate Am. Bd. Pediatrics, Am. Bd. Dermatology; spl. competence cert. in dermatopathology. Intern Gen. Hosp., Buffalo, 1955-56; pediatric resident Children's Hosp., Buffalo, 1956, Boston, 1959-60; pediatric resident UCLA, 1960-61; pediatric hematology trainee Children's Hosp., L.A., 1961-62; postdoctoral trainee in mycology UCLA, 1962-63, asst. rsch. dermatologist, 1964, asst. prof. medicine-dermatology, 1964-68, assoc. prof. medicine-dermatology, 1968-74, assoc. clin. prof. medicine-dermatology, 1974—. Contbr. articles to profl. jours. Comdr. USNR, 1957-59. Mem. AAAS, Am. Soc. Dermatopathology, San Fernando Valley Dermatologic Soc., L.A. Dermatologic Soc., Am. Acad. Dermatology, Soc. for Pediatric Dermatology, L.A. Pediatric Soc., Soc. for Investigative Dermatology, Alpha Omega Alpha, Phi Beta Kappa, Alpha Epsilon Delta. Office: 2428 Santa Monica Blvd #401 Santa Monica CA 90404

LANDAY, ANDREW HERBERT, lawyer; b. N.Y.C., Mar. 8, 1920; s. Max and Ida Rose (Fox) L.; m. Carolyn Anne Greco, Aug. 22, 1962; children: Vincent, Mark, James, Roseanne. BA, UCLA, 1946; BA, Mt. Angel Sem., Oreg., 1950; M.S., Columbia U., 1953; JD, Southwestern U., 1964. Bar: Calif. 1964, U.S. Dist. Ct. (cen. dist.) Calif. 1964, U.S. Tax Ct. 1965, U.S. Ct. Appeals (9th cir.) 1966, U.S. Supreme Ct. 1971. Sole practice, L.A., 1964-68, ptnr. Rozner, Yorty, Landay, Gibbs, Hodges, Bernstein & Wagner, Los Angeles, 1968-73, Bernstein, Wagner, Hodges & Landay, Beverly Hills, Calif., 1974-78; of counsel H. Bradley Jones, Inc., Beverly Hills, Calif., 1978-89; arbitrator Calif. Superior Ct., L.A., 1979—; judge pro-tem, arbitrator Santa Monica (Calif.) Mcpl. Ct., 1971—, L.A. Mcpl. Ct., 1971—, Culver Mcpl. Ct., 1988—, Malibu Mcpl. Ct., 1988—; mem. security com. Superior Ct., L.A., 1995—. Bd. dirs. Santa Monica Republican Club, 1983-91. Served with AUS, 1942-46. Mem. L.A. County Bar Assn. (mcpl. cts. com. 1977-78, state cts. com. 1992—), Am. Judicature Soc., L.A. County Lawyers Club (chmn. profl. ethics and unauthorized practice com. 1968-70, 77-78, bd. govs. 1988—), KC, Phi Alpha Delta. Republican. Roman Catholic. Office: 322 12th St Santa Monica CA 90402-2014

LANDBERG, ANN LAUREL, nurse, psychotherapist; b. Chgo., June 20, 1926; d. Carl Ryno and Ebba Sadie Elvira (Engstrom) Granlund; m. Harry Morton Landberg, Apr. 1, 1953 (dec. Feb. 1967); stepchildren: Rosabel, Marcene. RN, Swedish Hosp. Sch. Nursing, Seattle, 1948. Asst. head nurse Halcyon Hosp., Seattle, 1948; doctor's asst. Office of H.M. Landberg, M.D., Seattle, 1948-50, psychotherapist, 1950-67; pvt. practice psychotherapy, Seattle, 1967—; cons. Good Shepherd Sch. for Disturbed Girls, Seattle, 1954—, bd. dirs., 1954-60. Mem. Am. Psychotherapy Assn., King County Med. Aux., Stevens Hosp. Aux. (life), Swedish Hosp. Alumni (pres. 1952-53), Nat. Council Jewish Women, City of Hope, Edmonds Arts Assn. (life patron), Seattle Forensic Inst. (charter). Club: Swedish (Seattle). Home: 16900 Talbot Rd Edmonds WA 98026-5051 Office: 1007 Spring St Seattle WA 98104-1235

LANDEN, SANDRA JOYCE, psychologist, educator; b. L.A., May 8, 1960; m. Bernard B. Reifkind, Aug. 15, 1981. BA, UCLA, 1982, MA, 1984, PhD, 1988. Lic. clin. psychologist, Calif. Rsch. asst. UCLA Autism Clinic, 1980-82, UCLA Teaching Homes for Devel. Disabilities Project, 1981-82; rsch. assoc. UCLA Project for Devel. Disabilities, 1982-87; co-coord. parent tng. program UCI-UCLA Program for ADHD Children, 1984; teaching assoc. psychology dept. UCLA, 1984-87; psychology intern Hathaway Home for Children, Lakeview Terrace, Calif., 1985-86, clin. staff, 1986-87; clin. postdoctoral fellow Childrens Hosp. L.A., 1987-88; adj. faculty Grad. Sch. Edn. and Psychology Pepperdine U., L.A., 1988—; psychologist L.A., 1987—; dir. Westside Parenting Ctr., L.A., 1992—. Contbr. articles to profl. jours. Recipient scholarship UCLA, 1978-82, fellowship UCLA, 1982-85, dissertation rsch. grant UCLA, 1985-87. Mem. APA (div. psychoanalysis), Calif. Psychol. Assn., L.A. Psychol. Assn., Am. Assn. Mental Retardation, L.A. Child Devel. Ctr. Office: 11340 W Olympic Blvd Ste 245 Los Angeles CA 90064-1612

LANDERS, DANIEL MACARTHUR, psychology educator; b. Oakland, Calif., May 3, 1942; s. Jack Ignatius Landers and Alice Mary (Anderson) Elliott; m. Laverne Alice Witcosky Buckman, 1964; children: Lisa Sue Landers Olivas, Frederick Jack Landers Buckman; m. 2d Donna Marie Harney, Dec. 16, 1972; children: Tracey Ann, Daniel Joseph. BA, San Jose State U., 1964; MS, U. Ill., 1965, PhD, 1968. Asst. prof. U. Ill., Champaign, 1967-70, SUNY, Brockport, 1970-72; assoc. prof. U. Wash., Seattle, 1972-74; prof. Pa. State U., University Park, 1974-81; prof. Ariz. State U., Tempe, 1981-90, regent's prof., 1990—. Founding editor: Jour. Sport and Exercise Psychology, 1975-82. Fellow APA (pres. divsn. 47 1990-92), Am. Coll. Sports Medicine; mem. N.Am. Soc. for Psychology of Sport and Phys. Activity (pres. 1985-86). Office: Ariz State U Box 850404 Tempe AZ 85287-0404

LANDERS, TERESA PRICE, librarian; b. N.Y.C., Dec. 28, 1954; d. Stanley and June Ethel (Novick) Price; m. Gary David Landers, Sept. 2, 1979; children: Joshua Price, Alisha Rose. BA in History cum laude, Williams Coll., 1976; MA in LS, U. Denver, 1978; postgrad., Ctrl. Wash. U., 1980. Libr., asst. analyst Earl Combs, Inc., Mercer Island, Wash., 1979; reference libr. Yakima (Wash.) Valley Regional Libr., 1981-83, coord. youth svcs., 1983-84; libr. Tempe (Ariz.) Pub. Libr., 1984-85; supervisory libr. Mesa (Ariz.) Pub. Libr., 1985-90; head telephone reference Phoenix Pub. Libr., 1990-91, head bus. and scis., 1991—; cons. Fed. Dept. Corrections, Phoenix, 1993. Mem. Ariz. Right To Choose, Phoenix, 1992—. Mem. ALA, Ariz. Libr. Assn., Phoenix C. of C. (libr. rep. 1993—), Nat. Wildlife Fedn. (life), Beta Phi Mu. Democrat. Unitarian. Office: Phoenix Libr Bus & Scis Dept 12 E Mcdowell Rd Phoenix AZ 85004-1627

LANDERS, VERNETTE TROSPER, writer, educator, association executive; b. Lawton, Okla., May 3, 1912; d. Fred Gilbert and LaVerne Hamilton (Stevens) Trosper; m. Paul Albert Lum, Aug. 29, 1952 (dec. May 1955); 1 child, William Tappan; m. 2d, Newlin Landers, May 2, 1959 (dec. Apr. 1990); children: Lawrence, Marlin. AB with honors, UCLA, 1933, MA, 1935, EdD, 1953; Cultural doctorate (hon.) Lit. World U., Tucson, 1985. Tchr. secondary schs., Montebello, Calif., 1935-45, 48-50, 51-59; prof. Long Beach City Coll., 1946-47; asst. prof. Los Angeles State Coll., 1950; dean girls Twenty Nine Palms (Calif.) High Sch., 1960-65; dist. counselor Morongo (Calif.) Unified Sch. Dist., 1965-72, coordinator adult edn., 1965-67, guidance project dir., 1967; clk.-in-charge Landers (Calif.) Post Office, 1962-82, ret., 1982. V.p., sec. Landers Assn., 1965—; sec. Landers Vol. Fire Dept., 1972—; life mem. Hi-Desert Playhouse Guild, Hi-Desert Meml. Hosp. Guild; bd. friends Copper Mountain Coll., 1990-91; bd. dirs., sec. Desert Emergency Radio Service; mem. Rep. Senatorial Inner Circle, 1990-92, Regent Nat. Fedn. Rep. Women, 1990-92, Nat. Rep. Congl. Com., 1990-91, Presdl. Task Force, 1990-92; lifetime mem. Girl Scouts U.S., 1991. Recipient internat. diploma of honor for community service, 1973; Creativity award Internat. Personnel Research Assn., 1972, award Goat Mt. Grange No. 818, 1987; cert. of merit for disting. svc. to edn., 1973; Order of Rose, 1978, Order of Pearl, 1989, Alpha Xi Delta; poet laureate Center of Internat. Studies and Exchanges, 1981; diploma of merit in letters U. Arts, Parma, Italy, 1982; Golden Yr. Bruin UCLA, 1983; World Culture prize Nat. Ctr. for Studies and Research, Italian Acad., 1984; Golden Palm Diploma of Honor in poetry Leonardo Da Vinci Acad., 1984; Diploma of Merit and titular mem. internat. com. Internat. Ctr. Studies and Exchanges, Rome, 1984; Recognition award San Gorgonio council Girl Scouts U.S., 1984—; Cert. of appreciation Morongo Unified Sch. Dist., 1984, 89; plaque for contribution to postal service and community U.S. Postal Service, 1984; Biographee of Yr. award for outstanding achievement in the field of edn. and service to community Hist. Preservations of Am.; named Princess of Poetry of Internat. Ctr. Cultural Studies and Exchange, Italy, 1985; community dinner held in her honor for achievement and service to Community, 1984; Star of Contemporary Poetry Masters of Contemporary Poetry, Internat. Ctr. Cultural Studies and Exchanges, Italy, 1984; named to honor list of leaders of contemporary art and lit. and apptd. titular mem. of Internat. High Com. for World Culture & Arts Leonardo Da Vinci Acad., 1987; named to honor list Foremost Women 20th Century for Outstanding Contbn. to Rsch., IBC, 1987; Presdl. Order of Merit Pres. George Bush-Exec. Coun. of Nat. Rep. Senatorial Com., Congl. cert. of Appreciation U.S. Ho. of Reps.; other awards and certs. Life fellow Internat. Acad. Poets, World Lit. Acad.; mem. Am. Personnel and Guidance Assn., Internat. Platform Assn., Nat. Ret. Tchrs. Assn., Calif. and Nat. Assn. for Counseling and Devel., Am. Assn. for Counseling and Devel. (25 yr. membership pin 1991), Nat. Assn. Women Deans and Adminstrs., Montebello Bus. and Profl. Women's Club (pres.), Nat. League Am. Pen Women (sec. 1985-86), Leonardo Da Vinci Acad. Internat. Winged Glory diploma of honor in letters 1982), Landers Area C. of C. (sec. 1985-86, Presdl. award for outstanding service, Internat. Honors Cup 1992-93), Desert Nature Mus., Phi Beta Kappa, Pi Lambda Theta (Mortar Bd., Prytanean UCLA, UCLA Golden Yr. Bruin 1983), Sigma Delta Pi, Pi Delta Phi. Clubs: Whittier Toastmistress (Calif.) (pres. 1957); Homestead Valley Women's (Landers). Lodge: Soroptimists (sec. 29 Palms chpt. 1962, life mem., Soroptimist of Yr. local chpt. 19, Woman of Distinction local chpt. 1987-88). Author: Impy, 1974, Talkie, 1975, Impy's Children, 1975; Nineteen O Four, 1976, Little Brown Bat, 1976; Slo-Go, 1977; Owls Who and Who Who, 1978; Sandy, The Coy, 1979; The Kit Fox and the Walking Stick, 1980; contbr. articles to profl. jours., poems to anthologies. Guest of honor ground breaking ceremony Landers Elem. Sch., 1989, dedication ceremony, 1991. Home: 632 N Landers Ln PO Box 3839 Landers CA 92285

LANDING, BENJAMIN HARRISON, pathologist, educator; b. Buffalo, Sept. 11, 1920; s. Benjamin Harrison Sr. and Margaret Catherine (Crohen) L.; m. Dorothy Jean Hallas; children: Benjamin H., Susan L. Phillips, William M., David A. AB, Harvard U., 1942, MD, 1945. Diplomate Am. Bd. Pathology (anatomic pathology and pediatric pathology). Intern pathology Children's Hosp., Boston, 1945-46, asst. resident, then resident pathology, 1948-49; resident pathology Boston Lying-in Hosp., 1949, Free Hosp. for Women, Brookline, Mass., 1949; pathologist Children's Med. Ctr., Boston, 1950-53, Cin., 1953-61; pathologist-in-chief Children's Hosp., L.A., 1961-88, rsch. pathologist, 1988—; asst. pathologist Harvard U. Med. Sch., Boston, 1950-53; from asst. prof. to assoc. prof. U. Cin. Coll. Medicine, 1953-61; prof. pathology and pediatrics U. So. Calif. Sch. Medicine, L.A., 1961-91, prof. emeritus, 1991—. Author: Butterfly Color/Behavior Patterns, 1984; author chpts. in books; contbr. articles to profl. jours. Chmn. Pacific S.W. Dist. Unitarian-Universalist Assn., 1968-70; pres. Burbank (Calif.) Unitarian Fellowship, 1964-66. Capt. Med. Corps AUS, 1946-48. Mem. Soc. for Pediatric Pathology (pres. 1973-74), Internat. Pediatric Pathology Soc. (pres. 1980). Democrat. Unitarian-Universalist. Home: 4513 Deanwood Dr Woodland Hills CA 91364-5622 Office: Childrens Hosp LA Box 103 4650 W Sunset Blvd Los Angeles CA 90027-6016

LANDIS, RICHARD GORDON, retired food company executive; b. Davenport, Okla., Apr. 5, 1920; s. John William and Venna Marie (Perrin) L.; m. Beth L. Throne, Nov. 6, 1943; children: Gary Perrin, Dennis Michael, Kay Ellen. BA, U. LaVerne, 1942; postgrad., Claremont U., 1947; LLD (hon.), U. LaVerne, 1981. Mgmt. Delmonte Corp. San Francisco, 1942-83, pres., 1971-77, pres. & chief exec. officer, 1977-78, chmn. & chief exec. officer, 1978-81; pres. Pacific div. R.J. Reynolds, Inc., San Francisco, 1981-83; former chancellor U. LaVerne, Calif.; bd. dirs. Oregon Steel, Portland, Stanford Rsch. Internat., Menlo Park, Calif. Mem. Commn. of Calif., 1984—; chmn. Pacific Basin Econ. Coun., 1975-83; officer Boy Scouts Am., 1946—, Invest in Am.; Lt. USAF, 1942-46. Mem. Pacific Union Club, Bohemian Club, Claremont C. of C., Peachtree C. of C. Republican. Office: 120 Montgomery St Ste 1880 San Francisco CA 94104-4321

LANDIS, RICHARD PRESTON, corporate executive; b. Yakima, Wash., July 12, 1946; s. Richard Paul and Louise Beverly (Fletcher) L.; m. Diane Susan Hathaway, Apr. 8, 1972. AA in Law Enforcement, Ariz. Western Coll., 1978; BSBA, St. Mary's Coll. of Calif., 1979. Divsn. comdr./state police officer Ariz. Dept. Pub. Safety, Phoenix, 1971-91; assoc. adminstr. for motor carriers Fed. Hwy. Adminstrn./U.S. Dept. Transp., Washington, 1985-93; exec. dir., CEO Heavy Vehicle Electronic Lic. Plate, Inc., Phoenix, 1993—; transp. specialist Nat. Hwy. Traffice Safety Adminstr., U.S. Dept. Transp., 1979-80. With USNR, 1965-68, Vietnam. Mem. Am. Soc. Assn. Execs., It's America, Rotary (bd. dirs. Estrella club 1993-94), Intelligent Transp. Soc. Am. (chmn. commercial vehicle ops. com.). Republican. Home: 608 N La Loma Ave Litchfield Park AZ 85340-4324 Office: Help Inc 40 N Central Ave Ste 2250 Phoenix AZ 85004-4451

LANDMAN, HOWARD ANDREW, electronics engineer; b. San Francisco, Feb. 3, 1952; s. Louis and Helen Mary (Marchick) L.; m. Gail Louise Archibald, June 27, 1982; children: Maya, Arella, Robert. AB in Math with honors, U. Calif., Berkeley, 1973; postgrad., U. Calif., 1974-75, MS in Computer Sci., 1982; postgrad., Princeton U., 1973-74. Bus. planner, fin. sys. analyst Amdahl Corp., Sunnyvale, Calif., 1976-78; rsch. intern Xerox PARC, Palo Alto, Calif., 1979-81; dir. software engring. SynMos Corp., Palo Alto, 1981-82; VLSI/CAD designer Metheus Corp., Hillsboro, Oreg., 1982-84; software engr. Silicon Compilers, Inc., San Jose, Calif., 1984-85; sr. software engr. Intel Corp., Chandler, Ariz., 1986-88; sr. engr. Sun Microsystems, Mountain View, Calif., 1988-91, Crosspoint Solutions, Santa Clara, Calif., 1991-92, Hal Computer Sys., Campbell, Calif., 1992—; program com. mem. Internat. Design Engring. & ASIC Conf., 1990-92; tech. program com. mem. Synopsys User's Group, 1993—. Contbr. articles to profl. jours.; patentee in field. Precinct worker Humphrey-Muskie Campaign, Santa Clara, 1968. Shodan Seidokan Aikido Inst., 1988. Mem. IEEE, Am. Go Assn., Foresight Inst., Calif. Alumni Assn. (life). Office: Hal Computer Sys 1315 Dell Ave Campbell CA 95008-6609

LANDOVSKY, JOHN, artistic director; b. Riger, Latvia, Jan. 2, 1935; came to U.S., 1950; s. Jains and Olga (Kalnins) L. Dancer Weïrtterberg Stadiis Opera House, Stuttgart, Fed. Republic Germany, 1965, Internat. Ballet Co., Chgo., 1960-70, Lyric Opera of Chgo., 1960-70; asst. prof. U. Ill., Urbana, 1976-80; director Duluth (Minn.) Ballet Co., 1980-82, Ballet Hawaii, Honolulu, 1982, Hawaii State Ballet, Honolulu, 1982—. Office: Hawaii State Ballet 1418 Kapiolani Blvd Honolulu HI 96814-3603

LANDRE, DEBRA ANN, mathematics educator; b. Quantico, Va., Sept. 15, 1955; d. Thomas F. and Joy L. (Carstens) L. BA in French and Math., Bradley U., 1976, MS in Edn., 1977; MS in Math., Ill. State U., 1979. Math. instr. Bradley U., Peoria, Ill., 1977-79, Ill. Valley Community Coll., Peru, 1980, Ill. Wesleyan U., Bloomington, 1981; computer sci. instr. Lincoln Coll., Bloomington, 1981-85; math. instr. Ill. State U., Normal, 1979-85; pres. Quality Input Inc., Normal, 1983-85; dir. acad. computing San Joaquin Delta Coll., Stockton, Calif., 1985-88; math. instr. San Joaquin Delta Coll., Stockton, 1988—. Author: Explorations in Elementary Algebra, 1992, Explorations in Intermediate Algebra, 1992, Explorations in College Algebra, 1992, Explorations in Statistics and Probability, 1992; co-author: Mathematics: Theory into Practice, 1980, Microprocessor-Based Operations: Systems Software, 1985, Microprocessor-Based Operations, 1985, Data Acquisition, 1985, Explorations in Elem. Algebra, 1992, Explorations in Intermediate Algebra, 1992, Explorations in Coll. Algebra, 1992, Explorations in Statistics and Probability 1992.; contbr. articles to profl. jours. Mem. Am. Statis. Assn., Calif. Assn. Dirs. Acad. Computing (pres. 1988-90), Calif. Ednl. Computer Consortium (bd. dirs. 1987-90, editor 1988-90), No. Calif. Cmty. Coll. Computer Consortium (sec./editor 1986-91), Calif. Math. Coun. (editor exec. bd. 1990—, pres. elect 1991-93, pres. 1994-95, past pres. 1995—), Am. Math. Assn. of Two Yr. Colls. (del. 1993—, editor 1994—), Calif. Tchrs. Assn. (pres.-elect 1994—), Calif. Assn. Women in Edn. and Rsch. Office: San Joaquin Delta Coll 5151 Pacific Ave Stockton CA 95207-6304

LANDRUM, BRETT JOHN DAVID, automobile sales executive; b. Cin., June 12, 1958; s. James David and Maxine Elizabeth (Jordan) L.; m. Dannita Michelle Coleman, Aug. 29, 1987. BA in Physiology, U. Calif., Berkeley, 1980; MBA, U. So. Calif., L.A., 1984. Owner Discount Auto Ctr., Oakland, Calif., 1990—. Author: Chess Workbook, 1992; creator: (bd. game) Word Challenge, 1990. Grad. bus. scholar Consortium for Grad. Study in Mgmt., 1984. Home and Office: Word Challenge 181 Montecito Ave Oakland CA 94610-4530

LANDRUM, LARRY JAMES, computer engineer; b. Santa Rita, N.Mex., May 29, 1943; s. Floyd Joseph and Jewel Helen (Andreska) L.; m. Ann

Marie Hartman, Aug. 25, 1963 (div.); children: Larry James, David Wayne, Andrei Mikhail, Donal Wymore; m. 2d, Mary Kathleen Turner, July 27, 1980. Student N.Mex. Inst. Mining and Tech., 1961-62, N. Mex. State U., 1963-65; AA in Data Processing, Eastern Ariz. Coll., 1971; BA in Computer Sci., U. Tex., 1978. Tech. svc. rep. Nat. Cash Register, 1966-73; with ASC super-computer project Tex. Instruments, Austin, 1973-80, computer technician, 1973-75, tech. instr., 1975-76, product engr., 1976-78, operating system programmer, 1978-80; computer engr. Ariz. Pub. Svc., Phoenix, 1980-84, sr. computer engr., 1984-87, lead computer engr., 1987-88, sr. computer engr., 1988-90, sr. control systems engr., 1990-94; pres., chmn. bd. dirs. Glendale Community Housing Devel. Orgn., 1993; instr. computer fundamentals Eastern Ariz. Coll., 1972-73, Rio Salado C.C., Phoenix, 1985-86; mem. bd. trustees Epworth United Meth. Ch., 1987-89, chmn. 1988; mem. community devel. adv. com. City of Glendale (Ariz.), 1988-90, chmn., 1991-92; local arrangements chmn. Conf. on Software Maintenance, 1988. Mem. IEEE Computer Soc., Assn. Computing Machinery, Mensa, Phi Kappa Phi. Methodist. Home: 6025 W Medlock Dr Glendale AZ 85301-7321

LANDSBOROUGH, RON JAMES, health care executive; b. Jerome, Idaho, Oct. 9, 1955; s. James Ron and Lola Cora (Kinsey) L. BS in Engring., Ariz. State U., 1981, M in Health Service Adminstrn., 1985. Registered profl. engr., Calif. Indsl. mfg. engr. Gen. Instrument Corp., Chandler, Ariz., 1981; systems engr. Samaritan health Service, Phoenix, 1982-85; healthcare systems cons. Shared Med. Systems, Phoenix, 1985-90; healthcare industry specialist Gateway Data Scis., Tempe, Ariz., 1990-91; sr. sales rep. IBAX Healthcare Systems, Orange, Calif., 1991-92; v.p. program devel. Guynes Designs, Inc., Phoenix, 1992—; cons. Ariz. Dept. Transp., Phoenix, 1980. Author: Proceedings of the Summer Regional Conference of the Hospital Management Systems Society of the American Hospital Association, 1984, Hospital and Health Services Administration, 1985. Mem. Am. Coll. Healthcare Execs. (diplomate), Healthcare Fin. Mgmt. Assn., Health Adminstrs. Forum, Active 20/30 Internat., Soc. for Arts Phoenix, Toastmasters. Republican. Methodist. Home: 3442 E Hazelwood St Phoenix AZ 85018-3434 Office: Guynes Design Inc 1555 E Jackson St Phoenix AZ 85034-2310

LAND-WEBER, ELLEN, photography educator; b. Rochester, N.Y., Mar. 16, 1943; d. David and Florence (Miller) Epstein; 1 child, Julia. BA, U. Iowa, 1965, MFA, 1968. Faculty mem. UCLA Extension, 1970-74, Orange Coast Coll., Costa Mesa, Calif., 1973, U. Nebr., Lincoln, 1974; asst. prof. photography Humboldt State U., Arcata, Calif., 1974-79, assoc. prof., 1979-83, prof., 1983—; photographer Seagram's Bicentennial Courthouse Project, 1976-77, Nat. Trust for Hist. Preservation/Soc. Photographic Edn., 1987. Author: The Passionate Collector, 1980; contbr. sects. to books; photographs pub. in numerous books and jours. Nat. Endowment for Arts fellow, 1974, 79, 82; Artist's support grantee Unicolor Corp., 1982, Polaroid 20X24 Artist's support grantee, 1983, 90-93; Fulbright sr. fellow, 1993-94. Mem. Soc. for Photog. Edn. (exec. bd. 1979-82, treas. 1979-81, sec. 1981-83). Office: Humboldt State U Art Dept Arcata CA 95521

LANE, GLORIA JULIAN, foundation administrator; b. Chgo., Oct. 6, 1932; d. Coy Berry and Katherine (McDowell) Julian; m. William Gordon Lane (div. Oct. 1958); 1 child, Julie Kay Rosewood. BS in Edn., Cen. Mo. State U., 1958; MA, Bowling Green State U., 1959; PhD, No. Ill. U., 1972. Cert. tchr. Assoc. prof. William Jewell Coll., Liberty, Mo., 1959-60; chair forensic div. Coral Gables (Fla.) High Sch., 1960-64; assoc. prof. No. Ill. U., DeKalb, 1964-70; prof. Elgin (Ill.) Community Coll., 1970-72; owner, pub. Lane and Assocs, Inc., San Diego, 1972-78; prof. Nat. U., San Diego, 1978-90; pres., chief exec. officer Women's Internat. Ctr., San Diego, 1982—; founder, dir. Living Legacy Awards, San Diego, 1984—. Author: Project Text for Effective Communications, 1972, Project Text for Executive Communication, 1980, Positive Concepts for Success, 1983; editor Who's Who Among San Diego Women, 1984, 85, 86, 90—, Systems and Structure, 1984. Named Woman of Accomplishment, Soroptimist Internat., 1985, Pres.'s Coun. San Diego, 1986, Center City Assn., 1986, Bus. and Profl. Women, San Diego, 1991, Woman of Yr., Girls' Clubs San Diego, 1986, Woman of Vision, Women's Internat. Ctr., 1990, Wonderwoman 2000 Women's Times Newspaper, 1991; recipient Independence award Ctr. for Disabled, 1986. Home and Office: 6202 Friars Rd Apt 311 San Diego CA 92108-1008

LANE, HENRY WALLACE, physician, consultant; b. Chgo., Aug. 31, 1911; s. Henry Higgins and Mary June (Harper) L.; m. Mary Jane Whitaker, Aug. 26, 1938 (dec. Jan. 1984); children: Edwin Wallace, William Robert. AB, U. Kans., 1933, MA in Immunology, 1935, MD, 1939; MPH, Johns Hopkins U., 1951. Resident in pathology Kans. Med. Ctr., Kansas City, Kans., 1940-41; physician Student Health Svcs., Lawrence, Kans., 1946-48; dir. pub. health U.S. Civil Adminstrn., Naha Ryukyu Islands, 1954-55; assoc. prof. Dept. Preventive Medicine, Seattle, 1957-73; chief div. adult health State Dept. Health, Seattle, 1958-61; chief div. local health State Dept. Health, Olympia, Wash., 1961-68, dir., 1968-73; asst. sec. Dept. Social & Health Svc., Olympia, Wash., 1970-73; preventive medical cons. Olympia, Wash., 1973—. With M.C., U.S. Army, 1953-55. Recipient Oread medal U. Kans., 1929. Mem. AMA, N.Y. Acad. Sci., Phi Sigma, Phi Beta Kappa, Sigam Xi, Alpha Omega Alpha. Home and Office: 1817 Governor Stevens Ave SE Olympia WA 98501-3711

LANE, JAMES F., software engineer; b. Jersey City, Nov. 6, 1953; s. Francis Robert and Margaret Ellen Lane. BS in Computer Sci., Worcester Poly. Inst., 1971-75; postgrad., U. Colo., 1978. Software engr. LFE Corp., Waltham, Mass., 1975-76, Martin Maretta, Waterton, Colo., 1976-77; sr. software engr. Digital Group, Denver, 1977; systems analyst Johns-Manville, Littleton, Colo., 1977-78; systems software designer, project leader Microsoft, Redmond, Wash., 1978-85; pres. Elvyn Software, Inc., Redmond, Wash., 1985-87; mgr. PDL group, mgr. software engring. dept. Hanzon Data Inc., Bothell, Wash., 1985-90; owner Novelty Hill Software, Inc., Redmond, 1987—. Editor (newsletter) Madrone Leaf, 1983-84. Vol. Seattle Folklife Fest., 1988-95. Mem. Ind. Computer Cons. Assn., Seattle Lindyhoppers Performance Dance Co., Ballos Argentinos Tango Performance Troupe. Home: 22006 NE 114th St Redmond WA 98053-5701 Office: Novelty Hill Software Inc Redmond WA 98053

LANE, JOAN FLETCHER, educational administrator; b. San Francisco, May 7, 1928; d. Howard French and Kathryn Elizabeth (Kraft) Fletcher; m. Melvin Bell Lane, Feb. 15, 1953; children: Whitney Lane-Miller, Julie Lane-Gay. AB, Smith Coll., 1949. Staff World Affairs Coun. No. Calif., San Francisco, 1949-51, Inst. Internat. Edn., Stanford, Calif., 1952; spl. asst., dean Sch. H&S Stanford U., 1982-93, spl. asst. bd. trustees, 1993—; bd. dirs. The Brown Group, St. Louis, McClatchy Newspapers, Sacramento, The James Irvine Found., San Francisco. Trustee San Francisco Found., 1984-92; trustee Smith Coll., Northampton, Mass., 1978-85, chmn. bd. trustees, 1982-95, v.p. alumnae assn., 1975-78; bd. dirs. Internat. House, U. Calif., Berkeley, 1971-80; pres., assoc. coun. Mills Coll., Oakland, Calif., 1974-78. Recipient John M. Green award Smith Coll., 1988. Home: 99 Tallwood Ct Atherton CA 94027-6431

LANE, JOHN RODGER, art museum director; b. Evanston, Ill., Feb. 28, 1944; s. John Crandall Lane and Jeanne Marie (Rodger) L. Moritz; m. Inge-Lise Eckmann, 1992. B.A., Williams Coll., 1966; M.B.A., U. Chgo., 1971; A.M., Harvard U., 1973, Ph.D., 1976; DFA (hon.), San Francisco Art Inst., 1995. Asst. dir. Fogg Art Mus., Cambridge, Mass., 1974; exec. asst. to dir., adminstr. curatorial affairs, asst. dir. curatorial affairs Bklyn. Mus., N.Y.C., 1975-80; dir. Carnegie Mus. Art, Pitts., 1980-86, San Francisco Mus. Modern Art, 1987—. Author: Stuart Davis: Art and Art Theory, 1978; co-editor: Abstract Painting and Sculpture in America, 1927-1944, 1983, Carnegie International, 1985; exec. editor: The Making of a Modern Museum/SFMOMA, 1995. Served to lt. USNR, 1966-69. Nat. Endowment Arts Mus. fellow, 1974-75. Mem. Assn. Art Mus. Dirs., Am. Assn. Museums, Internat. Council Museums, Coll. Art Assn. Office: San Francisco Mus Modern Art 151 3rd St San Francisco CA 94103-3159

LANE, KATHLEEN MADDEN, emergency/trauma nurse, family nurse practitioner; b. Danville, Pa., July 24, 1955; d. Albert LeRoy and Margaret Regina (Cero) Madden; m. John Patrick Lane Jr., June 1, 1985; children: Jamie McKenzie, Colin Thomas. BSN, Ind. U. Pa., 1977; M in Nursing, UCLA, 1982, postgrad., 1995—; cert. in sch. nursing, Calif. State U., Northridge, 1992. RN, Calif.; CEN; CCRN; FNP; cert. mobile intensive care nurse, BCLS, ACLS and first aide instr. Staff nurse emergency Pottsville (Pa.) Hosp., 1978-79, White Meml. Med. Ctr., L.A., 1979-84, Santa Monica (Calif.) Hosp., 1980-82; trauma nurse coord. Hollywood Presbyn. Med. Ctr., L.A., 1983-85; coord. emergenyc svc. Glendale (Calif.) Adventist Med. Ctr., 1985-87, Simi Valley (Calif.) Hosp. and Health Care Svc., 1987—; health svcs. specialist Moorpark (Calif.) Unified Sch. Dist., 1989—; nurse Coneja Valley Family Care Ctr., 1995—; affiliate faculty Am. Heart Assn. BLS and ALS, 1993-95. Contbr. articles to profl. jours. Bd. dirs. Am. Heart Assn., L.A., 1984-85. Mem. Nat. Sch. Nurses Assn., Emergency Nurses Assn.

LANE, LARRY K., air industry service executive; b. 1948. BS in Social Scis., Oreg. Coll. Edn., 1974. With Evergreen Aviation Ground Logistics, 1967-78, 1984—, now pres.; regional sales rep. Skyline Mobile Home Mfr., McMinnville, Oreg., 1978-84. With USAR, 1969-75. Office: Evergeen Avation Ground Logistics 3850 Three Mile Ln Mcminnville OR 97128*

LANE, LINDA PATRICIA, scriptwriter; b. L.A.; m. Warder Ray Harrison, 1981 (div. 1983); 1 child, Lucy Lane; m. Gunnar Magg, 1983 (div. 1986). BA, U. So. Calif., 1976. Screenwriter Writer's Guild Am., L.A., 1974—; screenwriter Warner Bros., Burbank, Calif., 1979-80; interactive writer Hands of Time Animation and Design, L.A., 1994. Co-author: Malibu 90265, 1990, (with Hermien Lee) The Spot Reducing Diet: How to Lose Weight Where You Want, 1983; screenwriter (movie) Crosstalk, 1982, (TV) Full House, 1994.

LANE, PATRICIA BAUMGARTNER, medical office manager; b. Scottsbluff, Nebr., Mar. 15, 1927; d. Casper and Myrtice A. (Edwards) Baumgartner; m. James A. Lane, Sept. 4, 1949; children: Leann Keller, Rene Rickabaugh. BBA, U. Denver, 1949. Sec. Edwin Shields Hewitt & Assocs., Chgo., 1949-51, C. of C., Newcastle, Wyo., 1951, Newcastle Sch. Dist., 1952-53; office mgr. Dr. James A. Lane, Newcastle, 1970—, optometric technician, 1980—. Pres. Wyo. Assn. Retarded Citizens, 1976-77; nat. bd. mem. Assn. Retarded Citizens, 1978-80, regional nat. v.p., 1980-84; bd. mem. United Fund of Weston County, Wyo., 1976-78; bd. trustees United Meth. Ch., Newcastle. Named Vol. of Yr. Assn. Retarded Citizens, Wyo., 1977. Mem. PEO Sisterhood, Wyo. Optometric Aux. (pres. 1960), 20th Century Club (treas. 1976—), Order Eastern Star. Republican. Home: 204 E Warwick St Newcastle WY 82701-2235

LANE, SYLVIA, economist, educator; b. N.Y.C.; m. Benjamin Lane, Sept. 2, 1939; children: Leonard, Reese, Nancy. A.B., U. Calif., Berkeley, 1934, M.A., 1936; postgrad., Columbia U., 1937; Ph.D., U. So. Calif., 1957. Lectr., asst. prof. U. So. Calif., Los Angeles, 1947-60; asso. prof. econs. San Diego State U., 1961-65; assoc. prof. finance, assoc. dir. Ctr. for Econ. Edn. Calif. State U., Fullerton, 1965-69, chmn. dept. fin., 1967-69; prof. agrl. econs. U. Calif., Davis, 1969-82, prof. emerita, 1982—; prof. emerita and economist Giannini Found., U. Calif.-Berkeley, 1982—; vis. scholar Stanford U., 1975-76; econ. cons. Pres.'s Com. Consumer Interests, 1966-72; cons. Calif. Adv. Commn. Tax Reform, 1963, Office Consumer Affairs, Exec. Office of Pres., 1972-77, FAO, UN, 1983. Author: (with E. Bryant Phillips) Personal Finance, 1963, rev. edit., 1979, The Insurance Tax, 1965, California's Income Tax Conformity and Withholding, 1968; also articles. Project economist Los Angeles County Welfare Planning Council, 1956-59; del. White House Conf. on Food and Nutrition, 1969, Pres.'s Summit Conf. on Inflation, 1974; mem. adv. com. Center for Bldg. Tech., Nat. Bur. Standards, 1975-79; Bd. dirs. Am. Council Consumer Interests, 1973, Consumers Union, 1974-76. Ford Found. fellow UCLA, 1963; Ford Found. fellow U. Chgo., 1965; fellow U. Chgo., 1968. Fellow Am. Agrl. Econ. Assn. (life, Sylvia Lane Fellowship Fund 1993); mem. Am. Econ. Assn., Am. Coun. Consumer Info., Omicron Delta Epsilon (pres. 1973-75, trustee 1975-83, chmn. bd. trustees 1982-84). Home: 1241 Grizzly Peak Blvd Berkeley CA 94708-2127 Office: U Calif Dept Agrl & Resource Econs Berkeley CA 94720

LANE, THOMAS ALFRED, laboratory manager; b. Sidney, Mont., July 22, 1947; s. Alfred Ralph and Agnes Lillian (Johnson) L.; m. Shirley Ann Niemuth, June 14, 1970; children: Andrew, Stephanie. BA, Linfield Coll., McMinnville, Oreg., 1969; MS, Oreg. State U., 1976. Chemist Deschutes Valley Sanitation, Terre Bonne, Oreg., 1975-76, Atlantic Richfield Hanford Co., Richland, Wash., 1976-77; chemist Rockwell Hanford Co., Richland, 1977-79, program rep., 1979-82, mgr. plutonium process devel., 1982-86, mgr. applied tech., 1986-87; mgr. applied tech. Westinghouse Hanford Co., Richland, 1987-90, dep. mgr. analytical ops., 1990-92; site mgr. Oak Ridge Rsch. Inst., Richland, 1992-93. Loaned exec. United Way, 1990, key person, 1989, 92; leadership officer CAP, 1989—, adminstrv. officer, 1989—, pers. officer, 1989—. Sgt. U.S. Army, 1971-74. Mem. Nat. Mgmt. Assn. (treas. 1984-85, sr. v.p. 1985-86, v.p. 1986-87, pres. 1987-88, dir. 1988-89, Svc. awards 1986, 87, 88), Am. Chem. Soc. (sec. Richland sect. 1984, chair elect 1985, chmn. 1986), Inst. Cert. Profl. Mgrs. (cert. mgr.), Nat. Registry Environ. Profls. (registered).

LANE, WILLIAM KENNETH, physician; b. Butte, Mont., Nov. 5, 1922; s. John Patrick and Elizabeth Marie (Murphy) L.; m. Gilda Antoinette Parision, Aug. 21, 1954; children: William S., Francine Deirdre. Student, U. Mont., 1940-41, Mt. St. Charles Coll., 1941-43; MD, Marquette U., 1946. Intern Queen of Angels Hosp., L.A., 1946-47, resident physician, 1954-56; pvt. practice internal medicine San Francisco, 1947-51; resident in urology VA Hosp., Long Beach, Calif., 1956-58; physician VA Hosp., Long Beach, Oakland and Palo Alto, Calif., 1958—; lectr. on psychology of the elderly Foothill Coll., Los Altos, 1972-74; rschr. in field. Bd. dirs., mem. No. Cheyenne Indian Sch.; mem. Josef Meier's Black Hills Theatrical Group, S.D., 1940. With U.S. Army, 1943-46, ETO, lt. USN, 1951-54, Korea. Mem. AMA, Am. Geriatrics Soc., Nat. Assn. VA Physicians, San Francisco County Med. Soc., Woodrow Wilson Ctr. (assoc.), St. Vincent de Paul Soc., Cupertino Landscape Artists (past pres.), Audubon Soc., Stanford Hist. Soc., San Jose Movie/Video Club, San Jose Camera Club. Roman Catholic. Home: 18926 Sara Park Cir Saratoga CA 95070-4164 Office: Stanford VA Med Ctr 3801 Miranda Ave # 171 Palo Alto CA 94304-1207

LANE-OREIRO, LAVERNE TERESA, former tribal official; b. Bellingham, Wash., Aug. 29, 1951; d. Vernon Adrian and Nancy Ann (Solomon) Lane; m. David William Cagey Oreiro, Oct. 27, 1979; children: Tyson Hawk, Cody Lane. Student, Grenoble, France, 1972-73; BA in Humanities, Seattle U., 1974. Asst. dir. social svcs. Lummi Indian Tribe, Bellingham, 1974-77, dir. fed. contracts, 1977-78, exec. dir., 1978-81; real estate agt. Ron Bennett & Assocs., Bellingham, 1982-86; Indian edn. coord. Ferndale (Wash.) Pub. Schs., 1984—; vice-chairperson Lummi Indian Nation, 1991-93; pub. spkr. and presenter for local confs., media press confs., talk shows and cmty. functions; bd. chmn. Lummi Tribal Enterprises, Bellingham, 1978-80; bd. dirs. minority sci. and engring. adv. bd. U. Wash., Seattle, 1987-91; mem. minority cmty. adv. bd. Western Wash. U., Bellingham, 1989-93; Wash. state del.-at-large White House Conf. on Indian Edn., Washington, 1992, mem. U. Wash. Women's Ctr. Com. Advisory Bd., 1995. Writer eulogies for variety of tribal mems. including tribal leaders, elders, etc. Co-chairperson Nat. Indian Women's Fast Pitch, Lummi Indian Reservation, 1978, co-MC Nat. Indian Edn. Opening Rec., Spokane, Wash., 1985; mem. cmty. adv. bd. U. Wash. Women's Ctr., 1995—. Recipient Cmty. Svc. Diversity award Western Wash. U., 1994. Mem. Wash. State Indian Edn. Assn. (bd. sec. 1985-86, 1st v.p. 1986-87), Western Wash. Native Am. Edn. Consortium (vice-chairperson 1985-86, chairperson 1986-87). Democrat. Roman Catholic. Home: 2210 Lummi View Dr Bellingham WA 98226-9208 Office: Ferndale Sch Dist # 502 PO Box 428 Ferndale WA 98248-0428

LANEY, LEROY OLAN, economist, banker; b. Atlanta, Mar. 20, 1943; s. Lee Edwin and Paula Izlar (Bishop) L.; m. Sandra Elaine Prescott, Sept. 3, 1966; children: Prescott Edwin, Lee Olan III. B Indsl. Engring., Ga. Inst. Tech., 1965; MBA in Fin., Emory U., 1967; MA in Econs., U. Colo., 1974, PhD in Econs., 1976. Budget analyst Martin-Marietta Corp., Denver, 1971-72; economist Coun. Econ. Advisers, Washington, 1974-75; internat. economist U.S. Treasury Dept., Washington, 1975-78; sr. economist Fed. Res. Bank Dallas, 1978-88; prof. econs., chmn. dept. Butler U., Indpls., 1989-90; sr. v.p. 1st Hawaiian Bank, Honolulu, 1990—; chmn. Fed. Res. Com. on Internat. Rsch., Washington, 1981-83; vis. prof. U. Tex., Arlington and Dallas, 1978-85; adj. prof. So. Meth. U., Dallas, 1982-85. Editor bank periodicals, 1975-88; contbr. articles to profl. jours. Mem. Internat. Fin. Symposium, Dallas, 1982-85; Hawaii Coun. on Revenues. Lt. USN, 1967-71. Scholar Ga. Inst. Tech., 1961; rsch. fellow Emory U., 1965-67, teaching fellow U. Colo., 1972-73; rsch. grantee Butler U., 1989-90. Mem. Am. Econ. Assn., Western Econ. Assn., Indpls. Econ. Forum, Plaza Club, Honolulu Rotary, Omicron Delta Epsilon, Lambda Alpha, Kappa Sigma. Office: 1st Hawaiian Bank PO Box 3200 Honolulu HI 96847-0001

LANEY, STEPHEN FAYNE, art educator; b. Salt Lake City, Jan. 1, 1942; s. Fayne and Elzina (Maylett) L.; m. Iva Elizabeth Allen; children: Stephen Shon, Laura Kathleen, Michael Allen, David Brian, Patrick Henrie, Joseph Fayne. BA in Art, Brigham Young U., 1969; MA in Art Edn., Ariz. State U., 1972; postgrad., Brigham Young U., 1983-87. Art, photography tchr. Westwood High Sch., Mesa, Ariz., 1969-84; tchr. figure drawing, painting, basic design, illustration Mesa C.C., 1974-84; tchr. photography Rio Salado C.C., 1978-83; art tchr. Brigham Young U., 1983-84; art & photography tchr. Lakeridge Jr. High Sch., 1985-87, Mountain View High Sch., Orem, Utah, 1988—. Named Art Tchr. of Yr., 1992, Tchr. Artist of Yr., 1992. Mem. NEA, Utah Edn. Assn., Nat. Arts Edn. Assn. Home: 5256 W 10400 S Payson UT 84651-9608 Office: Alpine Sch Dist Mountain View High Sch 665 W Center St Orem UT 84057-5340

LANG, GEORGE FRANK, insurance executive, consultant, lawyer; b. Orange, N.J., Aug. 21, 1937; s. Frank W. and Hilda I. (Pierson) L.; m. Grace B. Preisler, Jan. 30, 1960; children: Christine, Gregg, Cynthia; m. Valerie J. Hanson, Nov. 24, 1978. BS, Ill. Wesleyan U., 1960; JD, Ill. Inst. Tech., 1968. Account exec. Scarborough & Co., Chgo., 1960-67; dir. fin. inst. George F. Brown & Sons, Chgo., 1967-69; v.p., dir. Fin. Ins. Svc., Schaumburg, Ill., 1969-79; pres. City Ins. Svc., Elizabeth, N.J., 1980-84; mng. dir. Res. Fin. Mgmt., Miami, Fla., 1984-85; v.p. Beneficial Ins. Group, Newport Beach, Calif., 1985-86; v.p. Ask Ins. Svc., Irvine, Calif., 1986-89, cons. product ctr. sales, 1989; cons. Nat. Dealer Ins. Systems, 1989, New Liberty Adminstrn., 1990—, Home Crest Ins., 1991—, Great Western Ins. Agy., 1992—; cons. in field. Bd. dirs. Woodview Civic Assn., Mt. Prospect, Ill., 1964-70, pres., bd. dirs., 1969; bd. dirs. Chippendale Assn., Barrington, Ill., 1972-76, v.p., bd. dirs., 1976. Home: 203 E Avenida San Juan San Clemente CA 92672-2325

LANG, KURT, sociologist, educator, writer; b. Berlin, Jan. 25, 1924; came to U.S., 1936; s. Ernst and Ilse (Kass) L; m. Gladys Engel, June 9, 1950; children: Glenna Engel, Kevin Engel. BA, U. Chgo., 1949, MA, 1852, PhD, 1953. Rsch. analyst Office of U.S. Milit. Govt., Berlin, 1945-47; asst. prof. U. Miami, Fla., 1953-54; rsch. sociologist Can. Broadcasting Corp., Ottawa, Ont., 1954-56; from asst. to assoc. prof. Queens Coll. CUNY, Flushing, N.Y., 1956-62, assoc. prof., chair, 1963-64; prof. SUNY, Stony Brook, 1964-84, chair, 1965-68; prof. U. Wash., Seattle, 1984—, dir. Sch. Comm., 1984-87; vis. assoc. prof. U. Calif., Berkeley, 1962-63; cons. CBS, N.Y.C., 1964-65, Nat. Adv. Commn. Civil Disorder, Washington, 1967. Author: Collective Dynamic, 1961, Television and Politics, 1968, 84, Battle for Public Opinion, 1983, Etched in Memory, 1990. U.S. Army Rsch. Inst. grantee, 1975-78, NEH fellow, 1971, Woodrow Wilson Ctr. fellow, 1978-79, Nat. Humanities Ctr. fellow, 1983-84, Sr. Fullbright fellow, 1994. Mem. Am. Polit. Sci. Assn. (Disting. Career award in polit. comm. 1994), Am. Assn. Pub. Opinion Rsch. (coun. 1975-77, Disting. Contbn. award 1989), Am. Sociol. Assn. (Edward L. Bernays award 1952), Internat. Inst. Comm. Democrat. Home: 1249 20th Ave E Seattle WA 98112-3530 Office: U Washington Dept Sociology Seattle WA 98195

LANG, MARGO TERZIAN, artist; b. Fresno, Calif.; d. Nishan and Araxie (Kazarosian) Terzian; m. Nov. 29, 1942; children: Sandra J. (Mrs. Ronald L. Carr), Roger Mark, Timothy Scott. Student, Fresno State U., 1939-42, Stanford U., 1948-50, Prado Mus., Madrid, 1957-59, Ariz. State U., 1960-61; workshops with, Dong Kingman, Ed Whitney, Rex Brandt, Millard Sheets, George Post. Maj. exhbns. include, Guadalajara, Mex., Brussels, N.Y.C., San Francisco, Chgo., Phoenix, Corcoran Gallery Art, Washington, internat. watercolor exhbn., Los Angeles, Bicentennial shows, Hammer Galleries, N.Y.C., spl. exhbn. aboard, S.S. France, others, over 50 paintings in various Am. embassies throughout world; represented in permanent collections, Nat. Collection Fine Arts Mus., Smithsonian Instn.; lectr., juror art shows; condr. workshops.; interviews and broadcasts on Radio Liberty, Voice of Am. Bd. dirs. Phoenix Symphony Assn., 1965-69, Phoenix Musical Theater, 1965-69. Recipient award for spl. achievements Symphony Assn., 1966, 67, 68, 72, spl. awards State of Ariz., silver medal of excellence Internat. Platform Assn., 1971; honoree U.S. Dept. State celebration of 25 yrs. of exhbn. of paintings in embassies worldwide, 1989. Mem. Internat. Platform Assn., Ariz. Watercolor Assn., Nat. Soc. Arts and Letters (nat. dir. 1971-72, nat. art chmn. 1974-76), Nat. Soc. Lit. and Arts, Phoenix Art Mus., Friends of Mexican Art, Am. Artists Profl. League, English-Speaking Union, Musical Theater Guild, Ariz. Costume Inst., Phoenix Art Mus., Scottsdale Art Ctr., Ariz. Arts Commn. (fine arts panel 1990-91). Home: 6127 E Calle Del Paisano Scottsdale AZ 85251-4212

LANG, NORMA ELLEN, art educator; b. Newton, Iowa, Mar. 11, 1931; d. Roger Hesser and Norma (Davis) Hostetler; m. Archibald Barrie Lang, Mar. 17, 1951; children: Stephanie, Christopher, Kimberly, Tracy. BA, Calif. State U., Northridge, 1973; BFA, Otis Art Inst., 1974, MFA, 1976. Cert. community coll. instr., Calif. Art instr. Coll. of the Redwoods, Crescent City, Calif., 1977-91, Southwestern Oreg. Community Coll., Coos Bay, 1979—; mem. Mayors Study Com. on the Arts, Glendale, Calif., 1972-76. Mem. budget com. Dist. 17C Sch. Dist., Brookings, Oreg., 1978-79, mem., chmn. sch. bd., 1979-84; mem. adv. coun. Libr. Bd., Brookings, 1990-93; vol. tax preparer AARP, Brookings Sr. Ctr., 1991-93; chmn. county safety campaign Curry County (Oreg.) Vol. Fire Assn., 1992. Mem. PEO, DAR (auditor), LWV (sec., treas. 1980—, cand. forum moderator 1984—). Home: PO Box 1859 Brookings OR 97415-0060

LANG, RICHARD ARTHUR, mayor, educator; b. Modesto, Calif., June 22, 1937; s. Frank Herbert and Joyce C. (Crowell) L.; m. Judith Karen Haertling, June 29, 1957; children: Susan Diane, Richard Arthur Jr., Julie Diane. BA in Polit. Sci., Calif. State U., Fresno, 1959; MA in Mgmt. Sys., Chapman Coll., 1973. Cert. tchr., Calif., cert. adminstr., Calif. Vice prin. Roosevelt Jr. H.S., 1974-77, La Loma Jr. H.S., 1977-79; asst. prin. in charge of student pers. svcs. Downey H.S., 1980; prin. Modesto (Calif.) H.S., 1980-90; govt. tchr. Downey H.S., Modesto, 1990—; mayor City of Modesto, 1991—. Elected to City Coun., City of Modesto, 1977, 81, 85, 89, vice mayor, 1981, chmn. citizen housing and comty. devel. com., 1983-92, chmn. solid waste com., 1984-92, chmn. downtown renaissance com., 1986—, chmn. econ. devel., comty. & intergovtl. rels. com., transp. policy com., utility svcs. & franchise com., pub. projects, budget and Stanislaus County solid waste adv. coms.; mem. Presdl. Mayors Task Force on Urban Affairs, 1992—; chmn. Modesto Bi-Centennial Com.; bd. dirs. Stanislaus chpt. ARC, 1992—, Assn. Retarded Citizens, Hanot Found., United Way, Family Tree. Named Man of Yr., VFW, 1992, Friend of the Chamber, Hispanic C. of C., 1991. Mem. Nat. Assn. Secondary Sch. Prins., Assn. Calif. Sch. Adminstrs., Modesto Rotary Club, Moose (lodge # 675), Phi Delta Kappa. Republican. Methodist. Office: 801 11th St Modesto CA 95354

LANG, WENDY FRANCES, artist, photographer; b. Cleve., Feb. 15, 1938; d. H. Jack and Frances (Wise) L. BA, Antioch Coll., 1961; MA, Stanford U., 1963; student, Colegio de Mex., Mexico City, 1962, Inst. des Hautes Etudes, Paris, 1964-65. Assoc. film producer Richard Kaplan Prodns., Inc., N.Y.C., 1966; human resource specialist Community Devel. Agy., Project Head Start, N.Y.C., 1966-68; adminstrv. assoc. Model Cities Com., Office of Mayor, N.Y.C., 1968; tech. asst. Volt Tech. Corp., N.Y.C., 1968-69; photographer self-employed, N.Y.C., 1969-79; tchr. photography L.A. City Coll. Community Svcs., 1979-82; coord. The Photography Mus., L.A., 1980-81; interpreter Pasadena City Coll. Hearing Impaired Program, 1981-83; freelance interpreter L.A., 1984—, freelance photographer, 1984—; bd. dirs., coord. Internat. Theatre Festivl XV World Games for the Deaf, L.A., 1983-85; bd. dirs., 2d v.p. So. Calif. Recreation Assn. of the Deaf, 1983-87; bd. dirs., sec.-treas. Self-Actualizatio Inst. for the Deaf, 1983—; bd. dirs., treas. Damien Project, L.A., 1990-91. Exhibited works in one-person show at Cleve. Playhouse Gallery; group exhbns. include Soho/Cameraworks, L.A., Friends of Photography, Carmel, Steps into Space, L.A., Butler Inst. Am. Art, Youngstown, Ohio, Status Gallery, L.A., Clarence Kennedy Gallery, Cambridge, Mss., others. Mem. Soc. for Photog. Edn., Friends of Photography, Ctr. for Creative Photography, Greater L.A. Council on Deafness, Nat. Assn. of the Deaf, So. Calif. Registry of Interpreters for the

Deaf, Calif. Assn. of the Deaf. Home: 1231 Kipling Ave Los Angeles CA 90041-1616

LANG, WILLIAM EDWARD, mathematics educator; b. Salisbury, Md., Oct. 22, 1952; s. Woodrow Wilson and Clara T. L. BA, Carleton Coll., 1974; MS, Yale U., 1975; PhD, Harvard U., 1978. Vis. mem. Inst. for Advanced Study, Princeton, N.J., 1978-79; exch. prof. Universite de Paris, Orsay, 1980; C.L.E. Moore instr. MIT, Cambridge, 1980-82; asst. prof. U. Minn., Mpls., 1982-83, assoc. prof., 1983-89; vis. assoc. prof. Brigham Young U., Provo, Utah, 1988-89, prof., 1989—. Contbr. articles to profl. jours. Fellow NSF 1974-77, 79-80. Mem. Am. Math. Soc., Math. Assn. Am., Math. Scis. Rsch. Inst., Sigma Xi. Republican. Office: Brigham Young Univ Dept Math Provo UT 84602

LANGAGER, CRAIG T., artist; b. Seattle, July 5, 1946; s. Clarence John and Maybelle (Sandve) L.; m. Sarah Clark, 1979. BS in Art, Minn. State U., Bemidji, 1971; MFA, U. Oreg., 1974. Guest artist U. Minn., Mpls., 1975, Dartington (Eng.) Coll. Arts, 1977; chmn., tchr. coord. spl. events gallery Cornish Inst., Seattle, 1976-78; coord. Earthworks: Land Reclamation as Sculpture King County Arts Commn., Seattle, 1978-79; vis. sculptor Syracuse (N.Y.) U., 1982, U. Colo., Boulder, 1985. One-man shows include Foster/White Gallery, Seattle, 1975, 77, 79, Susan Caldwell, Inc., N.Y.C., 1980, 81, 83, 84, Inst. Contemporary Art, Boston, 1982, Ruth Siegel Ltd., N.Y.C., 1986, Bemidji (Minn.) State U., 1986, William Traver Gallery, Seattle, 1991, Security Pacific Gallery, Seattle, 1991-92, Winnipeg (Man.) Art Gallery, 1984, Edith Baker Gallery, Dallas, 1987; exhibited in group shows at Foster/White Gallery, Seattle, 1973, 74, 76, Seattle Art Mus., 1975, 77, 87, Cornish Inst., Seattle, 1978, Goddard-Riverside Cmty. Ctr., N.Y.C., 1981, Wave Hill, Bronx, N.Y., 1981, Met. Mus. and Art Ctr., Coral Gables, Fla., 1982-83, Indpls. Mus. Art, 1982, 86, Contemporary Arts Ctr., Cin., 1985, Susan Caldwell Inc., N.Y.C., 1982, 83, 84, Siegel Contemporary Art, N.Y.C., 1983, Contemporary Arts Ctr., Cin., 1985-87, Ruth Siegel Ltd., N.Y.C., 1986, 87, 89, Edith Baker Gallery, Dallas, 1988, Colo. U. Art Galleries, 1992, U. Hawaii Art Gallery, Honolulu, 1994, many others; represented in permanent collections at Bklyn. Mus. Art, Denver Art Mus., Met. Mus. Art, N.Y.C., Mus. Art, U. Oreg., Eugene, Seattle Arts Commn., U. Colo. Galleries, Winnipeg Art Gallery, Can.; commd. by Niagara Frontier Transp. Authority Buffalo, Utica Station, 1982-83. Minn. State Arts grantee Minn. Coun. Arts, Mpls., 1975, Whitney Found. grantee, 1977.

LANGBERG, MIKE, newspaper reporter, columnist; b. Princeton, N.J., Sept. 6, 1954; s. Edwin and Meredith (Stern) L.; m. Debra Gordon, Nov. 14, 1993. BS in Journalism, Northwestern U., 1976; MA, Stanford U., 1980. Bus. reporter Sun-Sentinel, Ft. Lauderdale, Fla., 1981-84, Pioneer Press, St. Paul, 1985-88; bus. reporter, columnist San Jose (Calif.) Mercury News, 1989—. Author: CD-ROM Superguide, 1995; author weekly column "New on CD-ROM", 1993—. Office: San Jose Mercury News 750 Ridder Park Dr San Jose CA 95131-2432

LANGDON, PAUL RUSSELL, retired accountant; b. Columbus, Ohio, Feb. 17, 1914; s. Waren Elmore and Ethel Hulda (Cowgill) L.; m. Marjorie Clark, Nov. 28, 1935; children: Larry R., Robert C. BSc, Ohio State U., 1935; postgrad., Am. U., Northwestern U. CPA, Ohio. Pub. acct. W.E. Langdon & Sons, Columbus, 1935-39, 47-48; dir. fin. U.S. R.R. Retirement Bd., Chgo., 1939-46; procedures analyst Nationwide Ins. Co., Columbus, 1948-49; asst. treas. Battelle Meml. Inst., Columbus, 1949-79. Mem. Columbus Sch. Bd., 1953-83, pres., 1958, 63, 65, 78; pres. Ohio Sch. Bds. Assn., Westerville, 1971; chmn. exec. com. Billy Graham Ctrl. Ohio Crusade, Columbus, 1964; trustee, sec. Malone Coll., Canton, Ohio, 1955-75; trustee mem. Columbus Tech. Inst., 1966-69. Recipient Spl. award for vocat. gidance Columbus Kiwanis, 1983, Emmerling Mgmt. award Adminstrv. Mgmt. Soc., 1960, Bronze Leadership award Jr. Achievement, Columbus, 1983. Mem. Ohio Soc. CPAs (life), PTA (life), Fin. Execs. Inst. (life). Republican. Presbyterian. Home: 4952 Farnham Dr Newark CA 94560-1408

LANGDON, STEPHANIE DAVIS, orthotist, prosthetist, educational coordinator; b. White Plains, N.Y., May 27, 1955; d. Richard Huntington Langdon and Sarah Stevens (Davison) Aston. BA in Biology, Hartwick Coll., 1977; cert. in Orthotics, Rancho Los Amigos Med. Ctr., 1984; cert. in Prosthetics, UCLA, 1990. Cert. prosthetist, orthotist, Am. Bd. Certification. Orthotist Cert. Orthotics, Phoenix, 1986-89; orthotist, prosthetist Rehab Systems, Long Beach, Calif., 1990-91; orthotist Rancho Los Amigos Med. Ctr., Downey, Calif., 1982-86; ednl. coord. Rancho Los Amigos Med. Ctr., Downey, 1991—; presenter to health profls. on Orthotics, 1986—. Mem. Am. Acad. Orthotists and Prosthetists (bd. dirs. 1992—). Republican. Episcopalian. Office: Rancho Los Amigos Med Ctr Orthotics 7450 Leeds St Downey CA 90242

LANGE, CLIFFORD E., librarian; b. Fond du Lac, Wis., Dec. 29, 1935; s. Elmer H. and Dorothy Brick (Smithers) L.; m. Janet M. LeMieux, June 6, 1959; children: Paul, Laura, Ruth. Student, St. Norbert Coll., 1954-57; B.S., Wis. State U., 1959; M.S.L.S. (Library Services Act scholar), U. Wis., 1960, Ph.D. (Higher Edn. Act fellow), 1972. Head extension dept. Oshkosh (Wis.) Public Library, 1960-62, head reference dept., 1962-63; asst. dir. Jervis Library, Rome, N.Y., 1962; dir. Eau Claire (Wis.) Public Library, 1963-66; asst. dir. Lake County Public Library, Griffith, Ind., 1966-68; asst. prof. Sch. Library Sci., U. Iowa, 1971-73; dir. Wauwatosa (Wis.) Public Library, 1973-75; asst. prof. U. So. Calif., 1975-78; state librarian N.Mex. State Library, Santa Fe, 1978-82; dir. Carlsbad City Library, Calif., 1982—. Served with U.S. Army, 1958. Mem. ALA, Calif. Libr. Assn. Home: 3575 Ridge Rd Oceanside CA 92056-4952 Office: 1250 Carlsbad Village Dr Carlsbad CA 92008-1949

LANGE, GARY DAVID, periodontist; b. Mpls., Dec. 13, 1936; s. Emil and Esther Catherine (Schwartzkopf) L.; m. Donna Lynn Hall, Mar. 23, 1969; 1 child: Christian Elizabeth. BA, Augsburg Coll., Mpls., 1959; BS, U. Minn., 1961, DDS, 1963, MSD, 1971. Lic. periodontist. Dental intern U. S. Army Dental Corps, Tacoma, 1963-64; staff dentist and commdg. officer U. S. Army Dental Sect., Fulda, Fed. Republic of Germany, 1964-67; staff dentist U. S. Army Dental Corps, Ft. Bragg, N.C., 1967-69; periodontal resident U. Minn., Mpls., 1969-71; pvt. practice Rochester, Minn., 1971-74; staff periodontist VA, St. Petersburg, Fla., 1974-83, dir. gen. practice residency, 1983-86; chief dental svcs. VA, Columbia, Mo., 1986-92; chief dental svc. VA Med. Ctr., Prescott, Ariz., 1992—; asst. prof. Sch. Dentistry U. Minn., 1971-73, Kansas City Dental Sch., divsn. Grad Periodontics, U. Mo., 1987-92. Maj. U.S. Army, 1963-69. Mem. ADA, Am. Acad. Periodontology. Republican. Home: 2069 Meadowbrook Rd Prescott AZ 86303-5696

LANGENHEIM, JEAN HARMON, biology educator; b. Homer, La., Sept. 5, 1925; d. Vergil Wilson and Jeanette (Smith) H.; m. Ralph Louis Langenheim, Dec. 1946 (div. Mar. 1961). BS, U. Tulsa, 1946; MS, U. Minn., 1949, PhD, 1953. Rsch. assoc. botany U. Calif., Berkeley, 1954-59, U. Ill., Urbana, 1959-61; rsch. fellow biology Harvard U., Cambridge, Mass., 1962-66; asst. prof. biology U. Calif., Santa Cruz, 1966-68, assoc. prof. biology, 1968-73, prof. biology, 1973—; academic v.p. Orgn. Tropical Studies, San Jose, Costa Rica, 1975-78; mem. sci.adv. bd. EPA, Washington, 1977-81; chmn. com. on humid tropics U.S. Nat. Acad. Nat. Research Council, 1975-77; mem. com. floral inventory Amazon NSF, Washington, 1975-87. Author: Botany-Plant Biology in Relation to Human Affairs.; Contbr. articles to profl. jours. Grantee NSF, 1966-88; recipient Disting. Alumni award U. Tulsa, 1979. Fellow AAAS, AAUW, Calif. Acad. Scis., Bunting Inst.; mem. Bot. Soc. Am., Ecol. Soc. Am. (pres. 1986-87), Internat. Soc. Chem. Ecology (pres. 1986-87), Assn. for Tropical Biology (pres. 1985-86), Soc. for Econ. Botany (pres. 1993-94). Home: 191 Palo Verde Ter Santa Cruz CA 95060-3214 Office: U Calif Dept Biology Sinsheimer Labs Santa Cruz CA 95064

LANGER, GLENN ARTHUR, cellular physiologist, educator; b. Nyack, N.Y., May 5, 1928; s. Adolph Arthur and Marie Catherine (Doscher) L.; m. Beverly Joyce Brawley, June 5, 1954 (dec. Nov. 1976); 1 child, Andrea; m. Marianne Phister, Oct. 12, 1977. BA, Colgate U., 1950; MD, Columbia U., N.Y.C., 1954. Diplomate Am. Bd. Internal Medicine. Asst. prof. medicine Columbia U. Coll. Physicians and Surgeons, N.Y.C., 1963-66; assoc. prof. medicine and physiology UCLA Sch. Medicine, 1966-69, prof., 1969—, Castera prof. of cardiology, 1978—, assoc. dean rsch., 1986-91, dir. cardiovascular rsch. lab., 1987—; Griffith vis. prof. Am. Heart Assn., L.A., 1979; cons. Acad. Press, N.Y.C., 1989—. Editor: The Mammalian Myocardium, 1974, Calcium and the Heart, 1990; mem. editorial bd. Circulation Rsch., 1971-76, Am. Jour. Physiology, 1971-76, Jour. Molecular Cell Cardiology, 1974—; contbr. over 170 articles to profl. jours. Capt. U.S. Army, 1955-57. Recipient Disting. Achievement award Am. Heart Assn. Sci. Coun., 1982, Heart of Gold award, 1984, Cybulski medal Polish Physiol. Soc., Krakow, 1990, Pasarow Found. award for Cardiovascular Sci., 1993; Macy scholar Josiah Macy Found., 1979-80. Fellow AAAS, Am. Coll. Cardiology; mem. Am. Soc. Clin. Investigation, Am. Assn. Physicians. Office: UCLA Sch Medicine Los Angeles CA 90094-1760

LANGER, STEPHEN MARC, clinical psychologist; b. Richland, Wash., May 22, 1955; s. Otto Heinrich and Erdmute Johanna (Heidtman) L.; m. Donna Marie Mendenhall; 1 child, Anneliese Mendenhall. BS magna cum laude, U. Wash., 1977; MA, U. Mont., 1980, PhD, 1983. Lic. psychologist, Wash.; cert. biofeedback Biofeedback Cert. Inst. Am., cert. health svc. provider in psychology Nat. Register Health Svc. Providers in Psychology. Counselor Mercer Inn Psychiat. Half-way House for Women, Seattle, 1976-77; psychology trainee level I psychology svc. VA Hosp., Battle Creek, Mich., 1978; instr. divsn. continuing edn. U. Mont., 1979, teaching asst. psychology dept., 1980-81, practicum asst. Clin. Psychology Ctr., 1980-81; psychology trainee level II psychology svc. VA Med. Ctr., Richmond, Va., 1980; intern psychology svc. VA Med. Ctr., Pitts., 1981-82; staff psychologist Behavioral Medicine Clinic, Olympia, Wash., 1982-86; psychologist Olympia, 1983—; part-time student psychologist Mont. State Prison, Deer Lodge, 1977-78, 81; part-time extern Children's Hosp., Pitts., 1982; staff psychologist St. Peter Hosp., Olympia, 1985-88; expert Madigan Army Med. Ctr., Tacoma, 1986—; staff privileges St. Peter Hosp., Olympia, Madigan Army Med. Ctr., Tacoma; mem. Thurston-Mason County Mental Health Adv. Bd., 1985-88; dir. N.W. Brief Therapy Tng. Ctr., 1994—. Contbr. articles to profl. jours. Chmn. Henderson Inlet Watershed Coun., Thurston County, 1989—; vol. counselor phone crisis intervention Open Door Clinic, Seattle, 1975-77. Honors scholar U. Wash., 1975, 76, 77. Mem. APA (assoc.), Assn. for Advancement of Behavior Therapy, Assn. for Applied Psychophysiology and Biofeedback, Internat. Coun. Psychologists, Soc. for Clin. and Exptl. Hypnosis (assoc.), Wash. State Psychol. Assn., Biofeedback Soc. Wash. (past pres.), Deschutes Psychol. Assn. (past pres.), Phi Beta Kappa. Home: 3238 Lindell Rd NE Olympia WA 98506-3628 Office: 1021 Legion Way SE Olympia WA 98501

LANGEREIS-BACA, MARIA, speech-language pathologist; b. Hoorn, Netherlands, Dec. 16, 1930; came to U.S., 1956; d. Jan and Ditje (Schollée) Langereis; m. Stanley H. Skigen (dec.); 1 child, Michelle Arlene; m. Wilhelm Voebel (div.); children: George L., Helene Patimah; m. Gregorio Baca. BS, N.Mex. State U., 1982, MS in Speech, MS in Ednl. Mgmt. Devel., 1985, EdD in Ednl. Mgmt. Devel., 1989. Cert. elem. tchr., ednl. adminstr., speech-lang. pathologist. Asst. personnel mgr. D.M. Read Inc., Bridgeport, Conn., 1960-62; order librarian U. Bridgeport (Conn.), 1962-65; dir. community house Nichols Improvement Assn., Trumbull, Conn., 1960-65; speech-lang. pathologist Las Cruces (N.Mex.) Pub. Schs., 1984-88, Hatch (N.Mex.) Pub. Schs., 1985-89, Albuquerque Pub. Schs., 1989—; cons. Hospice Inc., Las Cruces, 1985-89, Associated Health Service, Las Cruces, 1986-89; ednl. cons., 1988—. Leader Girl Scouts Am., Las Cruces, 1976-77; leader 4H Club, Las Cruces, 1978-80; vol. Las Cruces Pub. Schs., 1978-79. Mem. Am. Speech Hearing and Lang. Assn., N.Mex. Speech Hearing and Lang. Assn., Assn. Supervision and Curriculum Devel., Phi Kappa Phi, Phi Delta Kappa. Republican. Roman Catholic. Club: Singles Scene (bd. dirs. 1985—). Home: 6309 Loftus Ave NE Albuquerque NM 87109-2717

LANGFORD, ROBERT BRUCE, chemistry educator; b. San Francisco, Mar. 7, 1919; s. Stephen George and Carrie Anna (Williams) L.; m. Wilma Ruth Ostrander, Feb. 1, 1957. BS in Chemistry, UCLA, 1948; MS in Chemistry, U. So. Calif., L.A., 1963, PhD in Pharm. Chemistry, 1972. Registered U.S. Patent Agt. Analytical chemist So. Pacific Co., L.A., 1949-54; rsch. chemist Stauffer Chem. Co., Torrance, Calif., 1954-58; prodn. mgr. Cyclo Chem. Corp., L.A., 1958-61; chemistry educator Marshall High Sch., L.A., 1961-64; prof. chemistry E. L.A. Coll., Monterey Park, Calif., 1964-86; prof. chemistry, emeritus E. L.A. Coll., Monterey Park, 1986—, head chemistry dept., 1968-74. Patentee in field; contbr. articles to profl. jours. Staff sgt. USAF, 1941-45. Mem. Am. Chem. Soc., Masonic Lodge, Elks Lodge, Sigma Xi. Home: 644 Haverkamp Dr Glendale CA 91206-3117

LANGFORD, THOMAS L., construction executive; b. 1941. BS, U. Calif., Berkeley, 1963, MBA, 1964. With Price Waterhouse, L.A., 1964-70, Parsons Corp. and subs., 1970—. Office: Parsons Corp 100 W Walnut St Pasadena CA 91124-0001*

LANGGUTH, EARL LEONARD, clergyman, writer, poet; b. San Diego, Apr. 7, 1927; s. Earl Chester and Kathleen Dakyne (Webster) L.; m. Mary Lu Langguth, Dec. 28, 1952; 1 child, Robert Leonard. AB, San Diego State U., 1951; postgrad., Columbia U., 1952-53; MDiv cum laude, Pacific Sch. Religion, Berkeley, Calif., 1956. Ordained minister Meth. Ch., 1956. Youth pastor Laurel Meth. Ch., Oakland, Calif., 1953-54; pastor Elverta (Calif.) Meth. Ch., 1954-56, Kings Beach (Calif.) Meth. Ch., 1956-60; pastor First Meth. Ch., Livingston, Calif., 1960-64, Dinuba, Calif., 1964-74; pastor Palm United Meth. Ch., Dinuba, 1970-74, Grass Valley (Calif.) United Meth. Ch., 1974-83, Faith United Meth. Ch., Sacramento, 1983-89, Montclair United Meth. Ch., Oakland, 1989-93, Laurel United Meth. Ch., Oakland, 1993—; assoc. statistician Cali.f-Nev. Conf., Dinuba, 1964-68, conf. statistician, 1968-88. Editor Bay View Rev., Oakland, 1991—. Mem. Montclair Lions Club (bull. editor). Home: 4254 Detroit Ave Oakland CA 94619-1602 Office: Laurel United Meth Ch 3525 Kansas St Oakland CA 94619-1415

LANGHOUT-NIX, NELLEKE, artist; b. Utrecht, The Netherlands, Mar. 27, 1939; came to U.S., 1968, naturalized, 1978; d. Louis Wilhelm Frederick and Geertruida Nix; m. Ernst Langhout, July 26, 1958; 1 child, Klaas-Jan Marnix. MFA, The Hague, 1958. Head art dept. Bush Sch., Seattle, 1969-71; dir. creative projects Project Reach, Seattle, 1971-72; artist-in-residence Fairhaven Coll., Bellingham, Wash., 1974, Jefferson Cmty. Ctr., Seattle, 1978-82, Lennox Sch., N.Y.C., 1982; dir. NN Gallery, Seattle, 1970—; guest curator Holland-U.S.A. Bicentennial show U. Wash., 1982; project dir. Women in Art Today, Wash., 1989, Wash. State Centennial Celebration; Washington to Washington traveling exhibition, 1989; mem. nat. adv. bd. Nat. Mus. Women in Arts. Executed wall hanging for King County Courthouse, Seattle, 1974; one-woman shows include: Nat. Art Center, N.Y.C., 1980, Gail Chase Gallery, Bellevue, Wash., 1979, 80, 83, 84, Original Graphics Gallery, Seattle, 1981, Bon Nat. Gallery, Seattle, 1981, Kathleen Ewing Gallery, Washington, 1986, Ina Broerse Laren, Holland, 1992, Charlotte Daneel Gallery, Holland, 1992, Christopher Gallery, Tucson, 1992, Mercer Island Cmty. Arts Ctr., 1992, Lisa Harris Gallery, Seattle, 1994; group shows include: Cheney Cowles Mus., Spokane, 1977, Bellevue Art Mus., 1978, 86, Renwick Gallery, Washington, 1978, Kleinert Gallery, Woodstock, N.Y., 1979, Artcore Meltdown, Sydney, Australia, 1979, Tacoma Art Mus., 1979, 83, 86, 87, Ill. State Mus., Springfield, 1979, Plener Sandomierz, Poland, 1980, Plener Kielce, Poland, 1980, Western Assn. Art Museums traveling show, 1979-80, Madison Square Garden, N.Y.C., 1981, Exhbn. Space, N.Y.C., 1982, Lisa Harris Gallery, 1985, 87, 88, Wash. State Centennial, Tacoma, 1989, Nordic Heritage Mus., Seattle, 1994; represented in permanent collections Plener Collection, Sandomierz, Poland, Bell Telephone Co. Collection, Seattle, Wash. U., Seattle, Children's Orthopedic Hosp., Seattle, Nat. Mus. Women in Arts, Washington; installations Tacoma Art Mus. Bd. dirs. Wing Luke Mus., Seattle, 1978-81, Wash. State Trust Hist. Preservation, 1990-93; v.p. Denny Regrade Cmty. Coun., 1978-79; mem. Seattle Planning Commn., 1978-84. Author (with others) Step Inside th Sacred Circle, 1989, an Artist's Book 1940-45 Remembered, 1991. Recipient Wallhanging award City of Edmonds (Wash.), 1974; Renton 83 merit award, 1984; Merit award Internat. Platform Assn. Art Exhibit, 1984, Silver medal 1st place, 1985, 87, Gold medal, Internat. Platform Assn., 1989. Mem. Denny Regrade Arts Coun. (co-founder), Internat. Platform Assn., Women in Arts N.Y.C., Nat. Mus. Women in Arts (founding mem., Libr. fellow, chairperson Wash. State com. 1988-89, mem. nat. adv. com. 1993—), Internat. Platform Assn., Seattle-King County Cmty. Arts Network (bd. dirs. 1983-85, chmn. 1984-85), Nat. Artist Equity Assn. Address: PO Box 375 Mercer Island WA 98040-0375

LANGLEY, MICHAEL DOUGLAS, secondary education educator; b. Martinez, Calif., Aug. 24, 1949; s. Harrold Lloyd and June Celeste (Lindstrom) Cline; m. Claudia Jane Neumann, July 20, 1974; children: Jennifer Jessen, Nicole Suzanne. BA in History cum laude, Calif. State U., Hayward, 1988. Tchg. credential in social studies. Sheet metal worker Prescolite, San Leandro, Calif., 1973-74; prodn. scheduler Prescolite, San Leandro, 1974-75; tchr. U.S. history El Dorado Middle Sch., Concord, Calif., 1989—; social studies dept. chair El Dorado Middle Sch., Concord, 1992—; interdisciplinary team leader El Dorado Middle Sch., Concord, 1992-93. Staff sgt. U.S. Army, 1976-84. Decorated Army Commendation medal with two oak leaf clusters, Joint Svc. Commendation medal Dept. Def., 1984; recipient Single Computer in Classroom grant Mt. Diablo Unified Sch. Dist., 1990; named Mid. Sch. History Tchr. of 1994, DAR, 1994. Mem. Nat. Assn. Mid. Schs., Calif. Tchrs. Assn. Democrat. Home: 3829 Chatworth St Pittsburg CA 94565-5709 Office: El Dorado Middle Sch 1750 West St Concord CA 94521-1008

LANGLEY, ROCKY D., consumer products company executive; b. Albuquerque, Oct. 14, 1953; s. Ralph L. and Selia D. (Francis) L.; m. Debra Houston, May 17, 1975; children: Kristy K., Steven P. BS, N.Mex. State U., 1975. Asst. country supr. FmHA, Taos, N.Mex., 1975-77; acctg. mgr. Price's Valley Gold Dairies, Inc., Bernalillo, N.Mex., 1977-79, gen. mgr., sr. v.p., 1979—. Leathercraft leader 4-H, Bernalillo, 1993-95, dairy team leader, 1994-95; mem. N.Mex. State Engr. Water Conservancy Group, Sante Fe, 1992-93, Water Adv. Bd.-Torrance County, Estancia, N.Mex., 1994-95. Mem. MRGDHIA (pres. 1987), Dairy Prodrs. N.Mex. (v.p. 1993-95). Republican. Home: 618 Hwy 528 Box 10862 Bernalillo NM 87004 Office: Price's Valley Gold Dairies PO Box 850 Bernalillo NM 87004

LANGMAN, ALAN WAYNE, physician; b. Phila., Feb. 28, 1956. BA, Temple U., 1978; MD, Hahnemann U., 1982. Diplomate Am. Bd. Otolaryngology. Resident in otolaryngology U. Calif., San Francisco, 1983-89; fellow U. Mich., Ann Arbor, 1989-90; staff physician Virginia Mason Med. Ctr., Seattle, 1990—. Contbr. articles to profl. jours. Fellow Am. Acad. Otolaryngology-Head and Neck Surgery, Am. Neurotology Soc. (assoc.); mem. Seattle Surg. Soc. Office: Virginia Mason Med Ctr 1100 Ninth Ave Seattle WA 98101-2756

LANGONI, RICHARD ALLEN, civil engineer; b. Trinidad, Colo., Aug. 7, 1945; s. Domenic and Josephine (Maria) L.; A of Applied Sci., Trinidad State Jr. Coll., 1966; BSCE Colo. State U., 1968; MA, U. No. Colo., 1978; m. Pamela Jill Stansberry, Aug. 19, 1972; children: Kristi, Kerri. Civil engr. Dow Chem. Co., Golden, Colo., 1968-71; city engr., dir. public works City of Trinidad, 1971-74; civil engr. Clement Bros. Constrn. Co., 1974-75; instr. Trinidad State Jr. Coll., 1975-78; city engr., dir. public works City of Durango (Colo.), 1978-82; region traffic engr. Colo. Dept. Transp., Durango, 1982—. Recipient Meritorious Svc. award City of Durango; registered profl. engr. Colo., N.Mex. Mem. Nat. Soc. Profl. Engrs., ASCE, Am. Public Works Assn., Water Pollution Control Fedn., Profl. Engrs. Colo., Durango C. of C., Nat. Ski Patrol (Purgatory and Wolf Creek), Phi Theta Kappa, Chi Epsilon. Home: 30 Moenkopi Dr Durango CO 81301-8599

LANG-PERALTA, LINDA ANN, English language educator; b. Coronado, Calif., July 13, 1953; d. William Harper and Catherine Margaret (Ray) Lang; m. Timothy Peralta, Apr. 2, 1982. BA in English, Calif. State U., Long Beach, 1980, MA in Comparative Lit., 1983; PhD in Comparative Lit., U. Calif., Irvine, 1991. Tchg. asst./assoc. U. Calif., Irvine, 1983-88, lectr. humanities, 1991-94; instr. humanities U. Redlands, Calif., 1991-94, Irvine (Calif.) Valley Coll., 1992-94; lectr. English U. Nev., Las Vegas, 1994—. Editor: Visions of Peace, 1982. Mem. MLA, Am. Lang. Assn., Am. Soc. for 18th Century Studies, Phi Delta Gamma, Phi Kappa Phi. Office: U Nev Las Vegas Dept English PO Box 455011 4505 S Maryland Pky Las Vegas NV 89154-9900

LANGS, TED CHARLES, aerospace company executive; b. Orlando, Fla., July 20, 1954; s. Theodore Charles and Katherine Elizabeth (Willette) L.; m. Lois Ann Grimaldi, July 22, 1978; children: Eric Christopher, Samantha Ann. Student, Bryant Coll., 1973-76, U. R.I., 1976-78, Mira Mesa Coll., 1981-82. Cert. telecomm. I. Br. supr., loan officer Columbus Nat. Bank, Providence, 1977-82; sr. analyst Travelodge-Trusthouse/Forte Hotels, 1982-86; chief fin. analyst/strategist Radelow/Gittins, San Diego, 1986-92; v.p. Arrow Aviation Spares, Oceanside, Calif., 1993—; Prin. Langs. and Assoc. Bus. Cons., Oceanside, 1992—. CPR instr., co-author new instrn. methods ARC, San Diego chpt.; vol. Oceanside Econ. Devel. Summit, 1994. Mem. Ind. Cons. Network, Internat. Cons. Network, Am. Mgmt. Assn., Am. Hotel Motel Assn., Am. Bankers Assn., Profl. Assn. Diving Instrs., Oceanside C. of C., San Diego C. of C.

LANGSTON, J. WILLIAM, neurologist; b. Mar. 22, 1943. BS, Drury Coll., 1962; MS, U. Mo., 1963, MD, 1967. Diplomate Am. Bd. Psychiatry and Neurology. Intern, resident Stanford (Calif.) U., 1967-74, physician specialist, clin. asst., 1974-76, asst. prof. neurology, 1976-85; sr. scientist, dir. Parkinson's Disease Rsch. program Inst. Med. Rsch., San Jose, Calif., 1985-93; pres. Parkinson's Inst. (formerly Calif. Parkinson Found.), Sunnyvale, Calif., 1988—; chief neurology divsn. Santa Clara Valley Med. Ctr., San Jose, 1974, 81, med. dir. electroencephalography lab., 1975-85. Contbr. numerous articles to profl. jours. lt. comdr. USPHS, 1968-70, med. cons. and dir. HEW, 1970-71. Recipient Sarah L. Poiley Meml. award N.Y.Acad. Scis., 1986, 30th Anniversary award Parkinson's Disease Found., 1987, Disting. Clin. Investigator award Hoffman-LaRoche, 1989, Disting. Achievement award Jour. Clin. Medicine - Modern Medicine, 1991. Mem. AMA, AAAS, Am. Neurol. Assn., Am. Acad. Neurology, Behavioral Neurology Soc., Movement Disorders Soc., Soc. Neurosci., Parkinson's Study Group, Calif. Med. Assn., Santa Clara County Med. Soc., Alpha Omega Alpha. Office: Parkinson's Inst 1170 Morse Ave Sunnyvale CA 94089-1605

LANGSTON, MARK EDWARD, professional baseball player; b. San Diego, Aug. 20, 1960; m. Michelle Langston; 1 child, Katie. Student, San Jose State U. Baseball player Seattle Mariners, 1981-89, Montreal Expos, 1989—, California Angels, 1989—. Named AL Rookie Pitcher of Yr. 1984 by the Sporting News, Am. League All-Star Team, 1987, 91-93; recipient AL Gold Glove, 1987-88, 1991-94. Office: care Calif Angels Anaheim Stadium 200 State College Blvd Anaheim CA 92806*

LANGUM, W. SUE, civic worker; b. Kennett, Mo., Jan. 10, 1934; d. Howard S. and Lucille (Hubble) Walker; m. Norman H. Nelson, June 22, 1957 (dec. Sept. 1969); 1 child, Kirby Walker Nelson; m. John K. Langum, Dec. 28, 1972. Student, Northwestern U., 1952-53, Crane Jr. Coll., 1953-54. Svc. rep. Ill. Bell Tel. Co., Chgo., 1956-57; receptionist Tri-City Animal Hosp., Elgin, Ill., 1967-69; rsch. asst. Bus. Econs. Inc., Chgo., 1969-73, dir., 1973—. V.p. Elgin Coun. PTA, 1969-73; bd. dirs. OEO, 1972-73, Meals on Wheels, Elgin, 1972-93, Coloquy Coffee House, 1968-70, Judson Coll. Friends, 1976-87, Elgin Area Hist. Soc., 1982—, Elgin Symphony Orch. Assn., 1984-93, Elgin Symphony League, 1982-93, pres. 1984-86; bd. dirs. United Meth. Women, 1978-93, pres., 1980-84; vol. Fish, 1974-76; bd. dirs., treas. Easter Seal Assn. for Crippled Children, 1977-90; mem. Elgin Beautification Commn., 1986-88, Tuesday Morning Bible Study Club. Mem. Sister Cities Assn. Elgin (bd. dirs. 1990), LWV (v.p. Elgin Club 1965), Tucson Women's Club, Current History Forum Club. Home: Diamond T Ranch 9820 E Old Spanish Trl Tucson AZ 85748-7547 also: Balsam Bay Is Manitowish Waters WI 54545

LANHAM, URLESS NORTON, curator; b. Grainfield, Kans., Oct. 17, 1918; s. Urless R. and Frankie V. (Norton) L.; m. Caroline Jane Combs, Sept. 1, 1945; children: Robert, Margaret, Carl. B.A. cum laude, U. Colo., 1940; Ph.D., U. Calif., Berkeley, 1948; postgrad., UCLA, La Jolla, 1940-42, U. Chgo., 1945-46. Asst. prof., research asso. U. Mich., Ann Arbor, 1948-62; asso. prof. Monteith Coll., Wayne State U., 1959-62; vis. curator, asso. curator entomology U. Colo. Mus., Boulder, 1962-73, curator, 1973-89, prof. natural history, 1973-89, prof. emeritus, 89—, mem. Tunisian expdn., 1976; asst. prof. biophysics U. Colo. Med. Center, Denver, 1968-71; vis. lectr. Arctic-Alpine Inst., Dept. Devel. Biology, 1966-67; vis. investigator Carnegie Mus. Pitts., 1982; editor biol. sci. curriculum studies Am. Inst. Biol. Scis., 1963-66; cons. Smithsonian Instn., Washington, 1967. Author: The Fishes, 1962, The Insects, 1964, Origins of Modern Biology, 1968, German transl., 1972; The Bone Hunters, 1973, 91, The Enchanted Mesa, 1974, The Sapphire

Planet, 1978, transl. into Arabic and Spanish; also tech. papers; adv. editor, Columbia U. Press, 1964-72. Served to capt. USAAF, 1942-46, PTO. Mem. Kans. Entomol. Soc., Phi Beta Kappa, Sigma Xi. Home: 2670 Stephens Rd Boulder CO 80303-5762 Office: U Colo Museum Campus Box 218 Boulder CO 80309

LANIER, WILLIAM JOSEPH, college program director; b. Great Falls, Mont., Dec. 20, 1963; s. Bolder Lanue and Nancy Jo (Kiszczak) L. AS, No. Mont. Coll., 1985, B Tech., 1987, MEd, 1989. Drafting intern Columbus Hosp., Great Falls, 1985-87; grad. asst. No. Mont. Coll., Havre, 1987-89; dir. student life Mont. State U. -No. (formerly No. Mont. Coll.), Havre, 1989-95, 1995—. Bd. dirs. Havre Encourages Long Range Prevention, 1992—, Hill County Crimestoppers, 1991-93; adv. bd. No. Ctrl. Mont. Upward Bound, Harlem, 1992—; mem. Nat. Eagle Scout Assn., Irving, Tex., 1991—. Recipient Golden N award student senate No. Mont. Coll., 1992. Mem. Am. Counseling Assn., Am. Coll. Pers. Assn., Nat. Assn. Student Pers. Adminstrs., No. Mont. Coll. Alumni Assn. (bd. dirs 1990—). Home: MacKenzie Hall Havre MT 59501 Office: Mont State U - No Box 7751 Havre MT 59501

LANIER-GRAHAM, SUSAN D., writer; b. Lynchburg, Va., June 8, 1963; d. Ralph Douglas and Shirley M. (Arthur) Lanier; m. William Patrick Graham, Dec. 23, 1979; 1 child, Patrick Douglas. AA in Liberal Arts, Colo. Mountain Coll., 1983; BS in Govt. and Politics magna cum laude, U. Md., 1986; MA in Liberal Studies and Social Sci. with honors, Regis U., 1993. Pres. THOT Info. Svcs., Scottsdale, Ariz., 1987—. Author: The Nature Directory, 1991 (one of Best Reference Books of N.Y. Pub. Libr. 1991), The Ecology of War, 1993. Sec. Craig-Moffat County Librs., 1991-93, pres., 1994; chairperson Moffat County Dem. Party, 1994. Mem. Soc. Environ. Journalists. Home: 11048 N 109th St Scottsdale AZ 85259-6911 Office: 7119 E Shea Blvd # 109-303 Scottsdale AZ 85254-6107

LANKFORD, DUANE GAIL, investment banker, mountaineer; b. Ft. Collins, Colo., July 18, 1932; s. William Oliver and Mary Martha (Lago) L.; m. Eleanor Polly, June 18, 1955 (div. 1983); children: Scott, Kurt Edwin, Rebecca Ann; m. Jariyaporn Ekkanasing, Nov. 8, 1991. Student, Colo. State Coll. of Edn., 1950-51, Denver U., 1952-55. Lic. stockbroker over 40 states security commns. Mgr. Dial Fin., Denver, 1953-59; mgr. investment banking Peters Writer & Christianson, Denver, 1959-60, E.I. DuPont De Nemours, Denver, 1960; mgr. mcpl. investment banking Bache & Co., Denver, L.A., N.Y.C., 1961-68; v.p. sales Fin. Programs, Inc., San Francisco, 1968-69; fin. advisor Lankford & Co., Denver, 1969; mgr. muni bonds W.E. Hutton & Co., Denver, 1969-71; owner/operator Lankford & Co., Denver, 1972—, The Wilderness Inst./Lankford Mountain Guides, Denver, 1978—; chmn. Denver Lenders Exch., 1957-58; cons. advisor numerous cities, towns, states and corps.; expert witness in investment banking and mountaineering; cons. numerous legal firms; cons./advisor numerous fed. agys. Contbr. articles to profl. jours. Worldwide mountaineer numerous maj. peaks. Mem. Am. Alpine Club, Pioneers. Republican.

LANNI, JOSEPH TERRENCE, hotel corporation executive; b. Los Angeles, Mar. 14, 1943; s. Anthony Warren and Mary Lucille (Leahy) L. B.S., U. So. Calif., 1965, M.B.A., 1967. Vice pres. Intervest, Inc., Los Angeles, 1967-69; treas. Republic Corp., L.A., 1969-76; treas., chief fin. officer Caesars World Inc., L.A., 1977-78, sr. v.p., 1978-79, exec. v.p., 1979-81, pres., chief oper. officer, dir., 1981—; pres., chief oper. officer, dir. Caesars N.J., Inc., 1981—. Author: Anthology of Poetry, 1965. Trustee St. John's Hosp. and Med. Ctr., Archdiocese of L.A. Edn. Found., Loyola Marymount U.; bd. councillors U. So. Calif. Sch. Bus. Adminstrn. Mem. Calif. C. of C. (bd. dirs.), Commerce Assocs., Regency Club, Rep. Senatorial Inner Circle, Clermont Club (London), Annabel's (London. Clubs: Bachelors; Crockfords (London), Beach (London). Office: Desert Palace Inc 3570 Las Vegas Blvd S Las Vegas NV 89109-8924 Office: Caesars Palace Corp 3570 Las Vegas Blvd S Las Vegas NV 89109-8924

LANS, CARL GUSTAV, architect, economist; b. Gothenburg, Sweden, Oct. 19, 1907; came to U.S., 1916; s. Carl and Ida Carolina (Schon) L.; m. Gwynne Iris Meyer, Dec. 21, 1935; children: Douglas C., C. Randolph. Student, CCNY, 1925-26, Sch. Architecture, Columbia U., 1926-30. Registered architect, Calif. Architect with Harry T. Lindeberg N.Y.C., 1930-32; architect Borgia Bros. Ecclesiastical Marble, N.Y.C., 1932-34; with architects Paist & Stewart, Miami, Fla., 1934-35; chief engr. insp. Dept. Agr., 1936-38; asst. tech. dir. FHA, 1938-48; tech. dir. Nat. Assn. Home Builders, Washington, 1948-52; with Earl W. Smith Orgn., Berkeley, Calif., 1952-56; architect, economist Huntington Beach, Calif., 1956—; ptnr. John Hans Graham & Assocs. Architects, Washington, 1947-55; spl. adviser Pres. Rhee, Republic of Korea, 1955-56; guest lectr. various univs., 1949-52. Author: Earthquake Construction, 1954. Chmn. bd. edn. adv. com., Arlington, Va., 1948. Recipient Outstanding and Meritorious Svcs. citation Republic of Korea, 1956. Mem. AIA (citation), Nat. Acad. Scis. (bldg. rsch. adv. bd. dirs.), S.W. Rsch. Inst., Seismol. Soc. Am., Prestressed Concrete Inst., Urban Land Inst., Nat. Press Club. Home and Office: 21821 Fairlane Cir Huntington Beach CA 92646-7902

LANSDOWNE, KAREN MYRTLE, retired English language and literature educator; b. Twin Falls, Idaho, Aug. 11, 1926; d. George and Effie Myrtle (Ayotte) Martin; B.A. in English with honors, U. Oreg., 1948, M.Ed., 1958, M.A. with honors, 1960; m. Paul L. Lansdowne, Sept. 12, 1948; children: Michele Lynn, Larry Alan. Tchr., Newfield (N.Y.) High Sch., 1948-50, S. Eugene (Oreg.) High Sch., 1952; mem. faculty U. Oreg., Eugene, 1958-65; asst. prof. English, Lane Community Coll., Eugene, 1965-82, ret., 1982; cons. Oreg. Curriculum Study Center. Rep., Cal Young Neighborhood Assn., 1978—; mem. scholarship com. First Congl. Ch., 1950-70. Mem. MLA, Pacific N.W. Regional Conf. Community Colls., Nat. Council Tchrs. English, U. Oreg. Women, AAUW (sec.), Jaycettes, Pi Lambda Theta (pres.), Phi Beta Patronesses (pres.), Delta Kappa Gamma. Co-author: The Oregon Curriculum: Language/Rhetoric, I, II, III and IV, 1970. Home: 15757 Rim Dr La Pine OR 97739-9412

LANSDOWNE, WILLIAM M., police chief; b. May 10, 1944; s. Leonard M. and Grace (Dabuque) L.; m. Sharon L. Young, June 12, 1994; children: Greg, Erik. BS in Law Enforcement, San Jose State U., 1971. Asst. chief San Jose (Calif.) Police Dept., 1966-94; chief Richmond (Calif.) Police Dept., 1994—; bd. dirs. Los Medanos Coll. Law Enforcement, Pittsburgh, Calif. bd. dirs. Christmas in April, Richmond, YMCA. Mem. Internat. Assn. Chiefs of Police, Calif. Police Chiefs Assn., Rotary. Office: Richmond Police Dept 401 27th St Richmond CA 94804

LANTER, SEAN KEITH, software engineer; b. Los Alamos, N.Mex., May 8, 1953; s. Robert Jackson and Norma Esther (Jonas) L.; m. Lauri Jane Willand, July 16, 1977; children: Tully Erik, Sarah Elizabeth, Rachel Erin. BA in Physics, U. Utah, 1974, MS in Mech. Engring., 1977. Registered profl. engr. Wash. Sr. engr. Boeing Comml. Airplane Co., Seattle, 1977-82; systems analyst Internat. Submarine Tech. Ltd., Redmond, Wash., 1982-83; engr. software Advanced Tech. Labs., Bellevue, Wash., 1983-84; engr. contract Rho Co., Redmond, 1984-85; sr. mem. tech. staff Cedar Software Inc., Redmond, 1985-87; pres. Connexions Engring. and Software, Woodinville, Wash., 1987-88; pres., chief engr. Connexions Engring., Inc., Woodinville, 1988—; cons. Unison Group, Bothell, Wash., 1990-92; cons., contract programmer, 1992-94; sr. software engr. AccessLine Techs., Inc., Bellevue, 1994—. Contbr. articles to profl. jours. Mem. Assn. Computing Machinery, NSPE. Lutheran. Office: Connexions Engring PO Box 3007 Woodinville WA 98072-3007

LANTING, FRANS MARTEN, photographer, writer; b. Rotterdam, The Netherlands, July 13, 1951; came to U.S., 1978; s. Frans and Geertruida (Stravers) L. MS in Econs., Erasmus U., 1977. Ind. photographer, writer Nat. Geographic Mag., 1987—; roving editor Nat. Wildlife Fedn., Washington, 1992—. Author: Madagascar, A World Out of Time, 1990, Okavango, Africa's Last Eden, 1993, Peace on Earth, 1993; co-author: Forgotten Edens, 1993; columnist: Outdoor Photographer Mag., 1994—. Recipient 1st prize World Press Photo, 1st prize Nat. Press Photographers Assn., 1994; named Wildlife Photographer of Yr., BBC Wildlife, 1991. Mem. Am. Soc. Media Photographers (mem. adv. bd. N.C. chpt. 1993—), N.Am. Nature Photography Assn. (bd. dirs. 1993—), World Wildlife Fund Holland (editl. cons. 1993—). Home and Office: Frans Lanting Photography 1985 Smith Grade Santa Cruz CA 95060-9758

LANTOS, THOMAS PETER, congressman; b. Budapest, Hungary, Feb. 1, 1928; m. Annette Tillemann; children: Annette, Katrina. B.A., U. Washington, 1949, M.A., 1950; Ph.D., U. Calif.-Berkeley, 1953. Mem. faculty U. Wash., San Francisco State U., 1950-83; TV news analyst, commentator, sr. econ. and fgn. policy adviser to several U.S. senators; mem. Presdl. Task Force on Def. and Fgn. Policy, 97th-104th Congresses from 11th (now 12th) Calif dist., 1981—; ranking minority mem., mem. internat. rels. subcom. on internat. ops. and human rels., chmn. internat. rels. subcom. on western hemisphere human rights, mem. gov. reform and oversight com.; founder study abroad program Calif. State U. and Coll. System. Mem. Millbrae Bd. Edn., 1950-66. Democrat. Office: US Ho of Reps 2217 Rayburn HOB Washington DC 20515-0512*

LANTZ, NORMAN FOSTER, electrical engineer; b. Pekin, Ill., June 8, 1937; s. Norman Gough and Lenore (Elsbury) L.; m. Donnis Maureen Ballinger, Sept. 7, 1958 (div. Aug. 1991); children: Katherine, Deborah, Norman Daniel; m. Judith Eliane Peach, Dec. 7, 1991. BSEE, Purdue U., 1959, MSEE, 1961. System engr. GE Co., Phila., 1961-72; mem. tech. staff The Aerospace Corp., El Segundo, Calif., 1972-75, mgr., 1975-79, dir., 1979-83, prin. dir., 1983-90, sr. project engr., 1991—; dir. Internat. Found. for Telemetering, Woodland Hills, Calif., 1985—. 2d lt. U.S. Army, 1960-61. Mem. AIAA (sr.), IEEE, Internat. Test and Evaluation Assn., Am. Mgmt. Assn. Office: The Aerospace Corp El Segundo CA 90245-4691

LANZ, ROBERT FRANCIS, corporate financial officer; b. Greenwich, Conn., Oct. 30, 1942; s. John Edwin and Katheryn Loretto (Jerman) L.; m. Elizabeth Kienlen, Nov. 11, 1967; children—Christopher, Jennifer. B.A., LaSalle Coll., Phila., 1964; postgrad., Law Sch., Fordham U., 1966-67; M.B.A., U. Conn., 1975. Corp. trust officer Chase Manhattan Bank, N.Y.C., 1966-71; cons. Stone & Webster, N.Y.C., 1971; sr. cons. EBASCO Services, N.Y.C., 1971-73; v.p., treas. Pacific/Corp., Inc., Portland, Oreg., 1973—; treas. Pacific/Corp., Inc., 1985—; sr. v.p. Pacific/Corp. Credit, Inc., Portland, Oreg., 1986—; pres. Willamette Devel. Corp. Mem. legal budget com. City of Lake Oswego, Oreg., 1975-80. Served with U.S. Army, 1964-66. Mem. Edison electric Inst. (fin. com. 1980-85), Northwest Electric Light and Power Assn. Democrat. Roman Catholic. Home: 17351 Canyon Dr Lake Oswego OR 97034-6711 Office: PacifiCorp 851 SW 6th Ave Portland OR 97204-1337

LAPENA, FRANK RAYMOND, art educator; b. San Francisco, Oct. 5, 1937; s. Henry and Evelyn Gladys (Towndolly) LaP.; m. Catherine Alice Sell Skinner, Aug. 19, 1966 (div. Apr. 1984); children: Kari Renee, Vincent Craig; stepchildren: Ivy, Peggy, Dan, Paul, Nancy. Student, Calif. State U., Chico, 1956-65; secondary cert., San Francisco State Coll., 1968; MA in Ethnography, Calif. State U., Sacramento, 1978. Cert. silversmith, 1977, secondary teacher. Instr. Shasta Jr. Coll., Redding, Calif., 1969-71; from instr. to asst. prof. art Calif. State U., Sacramento, 1971-73, dir. Nat. Am. Standards, 1974—; instr. Pena-Adobe, Vacaville, Calif., 1970, U. Alberta, Leithbridge, Can., 1974; dir. HEW Designegration Project D.Q. U., Davis, Calif., 1972; rsch. assoc. U.S. Dept. Interior, Fair Oaks, Calif., 1984; cons. Calif. Arts Coun., Sacramento, 1980—. Author, illustrator: (poems) Singing of Earth, 1993, The Sound of Rattles and Clappers, 1994; cover artist: Keeping Slug Woman Alive, 1993; co-author, artist: California Indian Shamanism, 1992; co-editor, artist: Smithsonian Nat. Mus. Am. Indian, 1991-94; numerous one-man shows and group exhibits. Grantee Smithsonian Inst., 1976; recipient People On the Move award YMCA, 1975, Order of the Hornet and Disting. Svc. award Calif. State U. Alumni Assn., 1995. Office: Calif State Univ 6000 J St Sacramento CA 95819-2605

LAPHAM, SANDRA C., research scientist, physician; b. Detroit, Sept. 2, 1948; d. Wendell E. and Eva E. (Youngblut) L.; m. Gary L. Simpson, Feb. 22, 1983; children: Cassandra A., Courtney M. BA in Psychology, U. Mich., 1970; MD, Wayne State U., 1975; MPH, Harvard U., 1978. Cert. in treatment of alcoholism and other drug dependencies. Internship Mount Auburn Hosp., Cambridge, Mass., 1975-76, residency dept. of medicine, 1976-78; emergency med. staff Amesbury (Mass.) Hosp., 1978; asst. clin. prof. Dept. Preventive Medicine U. Colo. Sch. of Medicine, 1979-80; E.I.S. officer Epidemic Intelligence Svc. Ctrs. for Disease Control, Atlanta, 1979-81; clin. assoc. Dept. Family, Cmty. and Emergency Medicine U. N.Mex. Sch. of Medicine, Albuquerque, 1981—; environ. epidemiologist Environ. Improvement divsn. Health and Environment Dept., 1981-84; co-ptnr. Placitas Consulting Group, 1984—; epidemiologist Clin. Studies Divsn. The Lovelace Insts., Albuquerque, 1986-88, dir. substance abuse rsch. program, 1989—; resource persons network Office of Minority Health Resource Ctr., 1989; editorial rev. bd. Jour. of Human Lactation, 1988-92; editorial reviewer Family of Medicine, 1993; peer rev. cons. NIH/ADAMHA, 1993; lectr. in field. Contbr. numerous articles to profl. publs., chpts. to books. Mem. N.Mex. Alcohol Issues Consortium, 1989—, N.Mex. Prenatal Care Network, 1989-92; mem. substance abuse adv. com. Health Care for the Homeless, 1991—; mem. task force on DWI, N.Mex. Atty. Gen., 1992—. Robert Wood Johnson fellow, 1976, AID grantee, 1977, Fogerty Sr. Internat. fellow, 1995. Mem. APHA, Am. Soc. Addiction Medicine, Am. Coll. Physicians, Rsch. Soc. on Alcoholism, Soc. Behavioral Medicine, N.Mex. Pub. Health Assn. Office: The Lovelace Insts 1650 University Blvd NE Ste 302 Albuquerque NM 87102-1732

LA PLANTE, PATRICIA ANN, counselor, radio broadcaster; b. Bklyn., Feb. 13, 1955; d. Kenneth Charles and Patricia Ann (Duffy) La P. BA in Comms., Va. Tech., 1982; postgrad., Dallas Theol. Sem., 1989; MA in Bib. Counseling, Colo. Christian U., 1990; postgrad., Denver Sem. Radio announcer Pillar of Fire Ch., Zarephath, N.J. & Denver, 1987-90, 91-94; radio coord. Hope for the Heart, Dallas, 1990-91; counselor Crossroads Bapt. Ch., Northglenn, Colo., 1992—; dir. cmty. rels. Sta. KPOF, Westminster, Colo., 1991—; owner, dir. Anchor Counseling and Comm., Northglenn, 1990-92; guest lectr. Denver Sem., 1992-94. Crisis intervention pers. dir. Drop-in Ctr./The RAFT, N.J. and Va., 1974-77, 80-82; coord. blood drs. Crossroads Bapt. Ch., Northglenn, 1992—; active Share Colo., 1991—. Mem. Am. Counseling Assn., Am. Assn. Christian Counselors, Nat. Religious Broadcasters. Home: 1057 C W 112th Ave Westminster CO 80234-3318 Office: KPOF Radio 3455 W 83rd Ave Westminster CO 80030-4005

LAPLANTE, PEGGY LYNN, financial executive; b. Glencoe, Minn., Feb. 23, 1960; d. Kenneth L. and Joann L. (Selchow) LaPlante; m. Joel Scott Johnson, Nov. 18, 1989. BS in Acctg., U. S.D., 1982; MBA, U. Wyo., 1986. Adminstrv. analyst Amoco Prodn. Co., Casper, Wyo., 1982-86; acctg. supr. Amoco Corp., Tulsa, 1986-88; gen. acctg. mgr. The Federated Group, Sunnyvale, Calif., 1988-89; account mgr. Domain Tech., Milpitas, Calif., 1989-90; controller Psi Star, Fremont, Calif., 1990; chief fin. officer Rancho Santa Fe Assn., Rancho Santa Fe, Calif., 1990—. Yankton Savs. & Loan Fin. scholar, U. S.D., 1981. Home: 1689 S Deframe St Lakewood CO 80228-4140 Office: PO Box A Rancho Santa Fe CA 92067-0359

LAPOTA, DAVID, oceanographer; b. L.A., June 1, 1949; s. M.H. and J.E. (Cassell) L.; m. Jeannette Harward, June 28, 1975. BS in Zoology, San Diego State U., 1973, MA in Geography, 1982; postgrad., U. Calif., Santa Barbara, 1992—. Data analyst San Diego State Found., 1974-79; biologist Naval Ocean Systems Ctr., San Diego, 1979-82, scientist, 1982—. Patentee in field; contbr. articles and abstracts to profl. jours. and chpts. to books. With USAR, 1969-75. Fellow Explorers Club; mem. Am. Geophys. Union, Biol. Soc. Washington, Oceanography Soc., AAAS. Home: 6678 Hemingway Dr San Diego CA 92120-1616 Office: Naval Command Control Ocean Surveillance Ctr Marine Environ Br Code 522 San Diego CA 92152-5000

LAPSLEY, JAMES NORVELL, JR., minister, pastoral theology educator; b. Clarksville, Tenn., Mar. 16, 1930; s. James Norvell and Evangeline (Winn) L.; m. Brenda Ann Weakley, June 4, 1953 (dec. May 1989); children: Joseph William, Jacqueline Evangeline; m. Helen Joan Winter, Feb. 24, 1990. BA, Rhodes Coll., 1952; BD, Union Theol. Sem., 1955; PhD (Div. Sch. fellow, Rockefeller fellow), U. Chgo., 1961. Ordained to ministry Presbyn. Ch., 1955; asst. min. Gentilly Presbyn. Ch., New Orleans, 1955-57; instr. Princeton (N.J.) Theol. Sem., 1961-63, asst. prof., 1963-67, assoc. prof., 1967-76, prof. pastoral theology, 1976-80, Carl and Helen Egner prof. pastoral theology, 1980-92, acad. dean, 1984-89, prof. emeritus, 1992—; mem. editl. bd. Jour. Pastoral Care, 1966-69, 91—; bd. dirs. N.W. Maricopa UN Assn., 1994—, v.p., 1995. Editor: The Concept of Willing, 1967, Salvation and Health, 1972, Renewal in Late Life Through Pastoral Counseling, 1992; editor: (with B.H. Childs, D.W. Waanders), Festschrift: The Treasure of Earthen Vessels, 1994; chmn. editl. bd. Pastoral Psychology Jour., 1975-84. Bd. dirs. Westminster Found., Princeton U., 1970-76. Danforth fellow Menninger Found., 1960-61. Mem. Am. Acad. Religion, Phi Beta Kappa. Presbyterian. Home: 16610 N Meadow Park Dr Sun City AZ 85351-1758

LARA, ADAIR, columnist, writer; b. San Francisco, Jan. 3, 1952; d. Eugene Thomas and Lee Louise (Hanley) Daly; m. James Lee Heig, June 18, 1976 (div. 1989); children: Morgan, Patrick; m. William Murdock LeBlond, Nov. 2, 1991. BA in English, San Francisco State U., 1976. Reader Coll. of Marin, Kentfield, Calif., 1976-83; freelance editor, 1983-86; mng. editor San Francisco Focus mag., 1986-89; exec. editor San Francisco mag., 1988-89; columnist San Francisco Chronicle, 1989—. Author: History of Petaluma: A California River Town, 1982, Welcome to Earth, Mom, 1992, Slowing Down in a Speeded-up World, 1994, At Adair's House, More Columns by America's Funniest Formerly Single Man, 1995; contbr. articles to profl. publs. Recipient Best Calif. Columnist award AP, 1990. Democrat. Office: San Francisco Chronicle 901 Mission St San Francisco CA 94103-2905

LARA, TONY RICHARD, industrial engineer, consultant; b. Prescott, Ariz., June 9, 1947; s. Brigido S. and Antonio (Abril) L.; m. Marilyn Larson, July 31, 1969; children: Jennifer, Kristen. AA in Tech. Edn., Yavapai C.C., Prescott, 1972; BA in Tech. Edn. cum laude, Ariz. State U., 1974; AA in Supervision, Maricopa Tech. C.C., Phoenix, 1978. Facility engr. Airesearch Mfg. Co., Phoenix, 1973-79; maintenance coord. Garrett Engine divsn. Allied-Signal Aerospace Co., Phoenix, 1979-80; capital/facility engr. Garrett Fluid Systems divsn. Allied-Signal Aerospace Co., Tempe, Ariz., 1980-89, supr. time std., 1989-91, supr. N/C programming, 1991-92, sr. indsl. engr., 1992—. Mem. adv. bd. Maricopa County Skill Ctr., Phoenix, 1981-92. Sgt. USMC, 1966-69, Vietnam. Mem. Soc. Mfg. Engrs., Kappa Delta Pi. Roman Catholic.

LARBALESTRIER, DEBORAH ELIZABETH, writer; b. Pitts., July 17, 1934; d. Theron Benjamin and Granetha Elizabeth (Crenshaw) Cowherd; m. Dec. 25, 1969 (div.). AB, Storer Coll., 1954; student, Robert H. Terrell Law Coll., 1954-58, Woodbury Coll., 1959-60; certs., Univ. W. Los Angeles, 1971-73. Cert. legal asst., paralegal specialist. Author Prentice-Hall Inc., Englewood Cliffs, N.J., 1975—; prof. Southland Career Inst., L.A., 1985—; paralegal mgr. Lynberg & Watkins, L.A., 1988-95; ret., 1995; bd. dirs. Am. Paralegal Assn., Los Angeles, 1975-80, exec. dir., 1980—; nat. chmn. Am. Inmate Paralegal Assn., 1984—; cons. Fed. Bur. Prisons, 1983—. Mem. Los Angeles Police Dept. (Wilshire div.) Community Police Council, 1985—, Harbor Human Relations Council, Wilmington, Calif., 1985—; vol., crime prevention specialist Los Angeles Police Dept. (Wilshire div.), 1985—. Recipient gold plaque Am. Paralegal Assn. Chpt. Pres., Los Angeles, 1975, Nat. Notary Assn., Hawaii, 1979, cert. of acknowledgment Los Angeles Police Dept., 1985, Humanitarian Award of Spl. Merit, So. Calif. Motion Picture Council, 1987. Mem. U. of W. Los Angeles (adv. bd. 1980, 88), Am. Paralegal Assn. (exec. dir. 1975), Am. Inmate Assn. (nat. chmn. 1983), U. W. Los Angeles Paralegal Alumni Assn. Republican. Jewish. Home: 1321-1/2s Sycamore Ave Los Angeles CA 90019

LARIZADEH, M(OHAMMED) R(EZA), business educator; b. Tehran, Iran, Apr. 14, 1947; came to U.S., 1966; s. Hassan and Nosrat (Saremi) L.; m. Dianne Ellen Pincus, Mar. 25, 1973; children: Dariush, Darya Anna. BA in Econs., Bus., UCLA, 1972, cert. in acctg., 1974. Cert. colls. teaching credential, Calif. (life); lic. real estate agent, Calif. Auditor Peat, Marwick & Mitchell, Los Angeles, 1972-74; controller Petromain Constrn. Co., Tehran, 1975-77; v.p. fin. Pilary Marine Shipping Co., Tehran, 1977-79; prof. Iranian Inst. Banking, Tehran, 1975-78; pres. Audicount Acctg. and Auditing Group, L.A., 1984—; prof. bus. and acctg. East L.A. Coll., 1980-87, vice-chmn. dept. bus. and acctg., 1987—, chmn. dept. bus. adminstrn., 1988—; prof. acctg. Santa Monica (Calif.) Coll., 1987—; mgmt. cons. L.P. Assocs. Mfg. Co., Los Angeles, 1981—; mng. dir. Barrington Enterprises, Los Angeles; prof. Santa Monica (Calif.) Coll., 1987. Author/translator: Accounting/Auditing, 1975. Mem. NEA, Internat. Fedn. Bus. Edn., Am. Mgmt. Assn., Am. Acctg. Assn., Faculty Assn. Calif. C.C.s, Am. Fedn. Tchrs., Calif. Tchrs. Assn., Am. Entrepreneur Assn., Nat. Assn. Realtors, Am. Assn. Pub. Accts., Calif. Assn. Bus. Educators, Calif. Assn. Realtors, Nat. Soc. Pub. Accts., Calif. Bus. Edn. Assn., Internat. Fedn. Bus. Edn., Inst. Mgmt. Accts., UCLA Alumni Assn. (life), Alpha Kappa Psi.

LARK, KARL GORDON, microbiology educator. PhB in Sci., U. Chgo., 1948; PhD in Microbiology, NYU, 1953. Instr. St. Louis U. Sch. Medicine, 1956-57, sr. instr., 1957-58, asst. prof., 1958-61, assoc. prof., 1961-63; prof. Kans. State U., 1963-70; chmn. dept. biology U. Utah, Salt Lake City, 1970-76, prof. dept biology, 1977—; cons. Eli Lilly and Co., 1968-73; mem. Genetics Study Sect., NSF, 1966-69, Ctrs. of Excellence Rev. Panel, 1987, Tng. Grant Rev. Panel, 1990, com. of visitors Rev. of Genetics Program, 1992; mem. Genetics Study Sect., Extramural Grant Program, NIH, 1971-75; mem. Cell Biology and Virology Study Sect., Am. Cancer Soc., 1972-76, chmn., 1975; ad hoc mem. Nat. Inst. Gen. Med. Scis. Adv. Coun., 1978, mem., 1979-84. Nat. Found. for Infantile Paralysis predoctoral fellow, NYU, 1951-53, Nat. Found. for Infantile Paralysis fellow, U. Geneva, 1955-56, NSF sr. postdoctoral fellow, U. Edinburgh, Scotland, 1961, Am. Cancer Soc. fellow, Statenserum Inst., Copenhagen, 1953-55; recipient Eli Lilly award in microbiology, 1965, Career Devel. award, 1963-70. Fellow Am. Acad. Microbiology. Office: Univ of Utah Dept Biology 201 Biology Building Bldg Salt Lake City UT 84112-1196

LARK, M. ANN, management consultant, strategic planner; b. Denver, Feb. 28, 1952; d. Carl Eugene and Arlena Elizabeth (Bashor) Epperson; m. Larry S. Lark, Apr. 1, 1972 (div. 1979). Cert. seminar leader. Asst. corp. sec., savs. dir. Imperial Corp. dba Silver State Savs. & Loan, Denver, 1972-75; client svcs. mgr. 1st Fin. Mgmt. Corp., Englewood, Colo., 1977-81; regional account mgr. Ericsson Info. Systems, Chatsworth, Calif., 1981-82; ind. cons. Denver, 1982-84; regional account mgr. InnerLine/Am. Banker, Chgo., 1984-85; chief info. officer Security Pacific Credit Corp., San Diego, 1985-88; prin. The Genessee Group, Thousand Oaks, Calif., 1988—. Home and Office: 1144 El Monte Dr Thousand Oaks CA 91362-2117

LARK, RAYMOND, artist, art scholar; b. Phila., June 16, 1939; s. Thomas and Bertha (Lark) Crawford. Student, Phila. Mus. Sch. Art, 1948-51, Los Angeles Trade Tech. Coll., 1961-62; B.S., Temple U., 1961; L.H.D., U. Colo., 1985. Ednl. dir. Victor Bus. Sch., Los Angeles, 1969-71; public relations exec. Western States Service Co., Los Angeles, 1968-70; owner, mgr. Raymond Lark's House of Fine Foods, Los Angeles, 1962-67; exec. sec. to v.p. Physicians Drug and Supply Co., Phila., 1957-61; lectr. L.A. Trade Tech. Coll., 1973, Compton (Calif.) Coll., 1972, Nat. Secs. Assn., Hollywood, Calif., UCLA, U. Utah, Salt Lake City, 1993, numerous others. One-man shows include, Dalzell Hatfield Galleries, Los Angeles, 1970-80, Arthur's Gallery Masterpieces and Jewels, Beverly Hills, Calif., 1971, Dorothy Chandler Pavillion Music Center, L.A., 1974, Honolulu Acad. Arts, 1975, UCLA, 1983, U. Colo. Mus., 1984, Albany State Coll. Art Gallery, Albany, Ga., 1988, Utah Mus. Fine Arts, Salt Lake City, 1989, Mind's Art Gallery, Dickinson U., Dickinson, N.D., 1989, Trinton Mus. Art, Santa Clara, Calif., Greenville (N.C.) Mus. of Art, 1993, others; group exhbns. include, Smithsonian Instn., 1971, N.J. State Mus., Trenton, 1971, Guggenheim Mus., N.Y.C., 1975, Met. Mus. Art, 1976, La Galerie Mauffe, Paris, 1977, Portsmouth (Va.) Mus., 1979, Ava Dorog Galleries, Munich, W. Ger., 1979, Accademia Italia, Parma, 1980, Ames Art Galleries and Auctioneers, Beverly Hills, 1980, Le Salon des Nations at Centre International d'Art Contemporain, Paris, 1983; represented in permanent collections, Library of Congress, Ont. Coll. Art, Toronto, Mus. African and African Am. Art and Antiquities, Buffalo, Carnegie Inst., numerous others; art commns. for TV and film studios include, All in the Family, Carol Burnett Show, Maude, The Young and the Restless, Universal City Studios, Palace of the Living Arts, Movie Land Wax Mus.; author works in field; author and contbr. more than 50 scholarly treatises on art, edn. and the hist. devel. of Black Ams., chpts. to encyclopedias and textbooks, articles to jours., introductions to mus. exhbn. catalogues. Recipient gold medal Acad. Italia, 1980, also numerous gold medals and best of show awards, 3 presdl. proclamations; award Internat. Platform Assn.; Dr. Raymond Lark Day proclaimed by State of Md., 1994; grantee Nat. Endowment Arts, ARCO Found., Colo. Humanities Program, Adolph Coors Beer Found. Mem. Art West Assn. (pres. 1968-70). Address: PO Box 76169 Los Angeles CA 90076-0169

LARKIN, NELLE JEAN, computer programmer, analyst; b. Ralston, Okla., July 4, 1925; d. Charles Eugene and Jennivea Pearl (Lane) Reed; m. Burr Oakley Larkin, Dec. 28, 1948 (div. Aug. 1969); children: John Timothy, Kenneth James, Donald Jerome, Valerie Jean Larkin Rouse. Student, UCLA, 1944, El Camino Jr. Coll., 1946-49, San Jose (Calif.) City Coll., 1961-62. Sr. programmer, analyst III Santa Clara County, San Jose, Calif., 1963-69; sr. analyst, programmer Blue Cross of No. Calif., Oakland, 1971-73; sr. programmer, analyst Optimum Systems, Inc., Santa Clara, Calif., 1973-75, Crocker Bank, San Francisco, 1975-77, Greyhound Fin. Service, San Francisco, 1977-78; analyst, programmer TRW, Mountain View, Calif., 1978-79; sr. programer analyst Memorex, Santa Clara, 1979-80; staff mgmt. cons. Am. Mgmt. System, Foster City, Calif., 1980-82; sr. programmer, analyst, project leader Tymeshare, Cupertino, Calif., 1982-83; sr. programmer, analyst Beckman Instruments, Palo Alto, Calif., 1983-89; analyst, programmer U.S. Postal Svc., San Mateo, Calif., 1989—. Mem. Calif. Scholarship Fedn. (life mem. 1943), Alpha Sigma Gamma. Home: 3193 Londonderry Dr Santa Clara CA 95050-6632 Office: US Postal Svc 2700 Campus Dr San Mateo CA 94497-0001

LAROCK, BRUCE EDWARD, civil engineering educator; b. Berkeley, Calif., Dec. 24, 1940; s. Ralph W. and Hazel M. (Lambert) L.; m. Susan E. Gardner, June 17, 1968; children: Lynne M., Jean E. BS in Civil Engring., Stanford U., 1962, MS in Civil Engring., 1963, PhD, 1966. Registered profl. engr., Calif. Asst. prof. U. Calif., Davis, 1966-72, assoc. prof., 1972-79, prof., 1979—; sr. vis. fellow U. Wales, Swansea, 1972-73; U.S. sr. scientist Tech. U., Aachen, Germany, 1986-87. Author: (with D. Newnan) Engineer-in-Training Examination Review, 3d edit., 1991; contbr. over 70 tech. articles to profl. jours. Mem. ASCE, Sigma Xi, Tau Beta Pi. Lutheran. Office: U Calif Davis Dept Civil & Eviron Engring Davis CA 95616-5294

LAROCQUE, MARILYN ROSS ONDERDONK, public relations executive; b. Weehawken, N.J., Oct. 14, 1934; d. Chester Douglas and Marion (Ross) Onderdonk; B.A. cum laude, Mt. Holyoke Coll., 1956; postgrad. N.Y. U., 1956-57; M. Journalism, U. Calif. at Berkeley, 1965; m. Bernard Dean Benz, Oct. 5, 1957 (div. Sept. 1971); children: Mark Douglas, Dean Griffith; m. 2d, Rodney C. LaRocque, Feb. 10, 1973. Jr. exec. Bonwit Teller, N.Y.C., 1956; personnel asst. Warner-Lambert Pharm. Co., Morris Plains, N.J., 1957; editorial asst. Silver Burdett Co., Morristown, 1958; self-employed as pub. rels. cons., Moraga, Calif., 1963-71, 73-77; pub. relations mgr. Shaklee Corp., Hayward, 1971-73; pub. rels. dir. Fidelity Savs., 1977-78; exec. dir. No. Calif. chpt. Nat. Multiple Sclerosis Soc., 1978-80; v.p. pub. rels. Cambridge Plan Internat., Monterey, Calif., 1980-81; sr. account exec. Hoefer-Amidei Assocs., San Francisco, 1981-82; dir. corp. communications, dir. spl. projects, asst. to chmn. Cambridge Plan Internat., Monterey, Calif., 1982-84; dir. communications Buena Vista Winery, Sonoma, Calif., 1984-86, asst. v.p. communications and market support, 1986-87; dir. communications Rutherford Hill Winery, St. Helena, Calif., 1987-88; pres. LaRocque Pub. Rels. and Pub. Affairs, Napa, Calif., 1988-91; pres. LaRocque Profl. Svcs., Inc., 1991—; instr. pub. rels. U. Calif. Extension, San Francisco, 1977-79. Mem. exec. bd., rep-at-large Oakland (Calif.) Symphony Guild, 1968-69, Napa County Landmarks, Inc.; co-chmn. pub. rels. com. Oakland Mus. Assn., 1974-75; cabinet mem. Lincoln Child Ctr., Oakland, 1967-71, pres. membership cabinet, 1970-71, 2d v.p. bd. dirs., 1970-71; bd. dirs. Calif. Spring Garden and Home Show, 1971-77, 1st Agrl. Dist., 1971-77, Dunsmuir House and Gardens, 1976-77; mem. Calif. State Rep. Cen. Com., 1964-66; v.p. Piedmont coun. Boy Scouts Am., 1977. Mem. U. Calif. Alumni Assn., Pub. Rels. Soc. Am. (chpt. dir. 1980-82; accredited), Sonoma Valley Vintners Assn. (dir. 1984-87), Internat. Wine and Food Soc. (Marin chpt.), San Francisco Mus. Soc., Smithsonian Assocs., Sonoma Valley C. of C. (bd. dirs. 1984-87), Napa County Landmarks Inc. (bd. dirs., 1993-94), Am. Assn. Univ. Women (Napa Valley chpt.), Napa Valley Republican Women, Knights of the Vine (master lady 1985-90), Mount Holyoke Coll. Alumnae Club, Silverado Country Club, DAR (vineyard trails chpt.). Office: LaRocque Profl Svcs Inc 1800-A Soscol Ave Napa CA 94559-1345

LA ROSA, FRANCISCO GUILLERMO, pathologist, researcher, educator; b. Lima, Peru, Jan. 17, 1949; came to U.S., 1981; s. Anibal and Carmen (de la Pascua) La R.; m. Clara Ann Dufficy, May 21, 1989; children: David, Anamaria. MD, U. Nacional Federico Villarreal, Lima, 1975. Instr. U. Nacional Federico Villarreal, Lima, 1973-79, asst. prof., 1979-81; resident in clin. pathology U. de San Marcos, Lima, 1977-79; postdoctoral fellow in immunology U. Colo., Denver, 1981-85, instr., 1985-87, asst. prof., 1987-94, resident in pathology, 1992-95, fellow in molecular pathology, 1995—; cons. Ortho Pharm., Lima, 1979-81, Reaads Med. Products, Inc., Denver, 1991. Contbr. chpts. to books, revs. and articles to profl. jours. Krock Found. fellow, 1985-86, Juvenile Diabetes Found. fellow, 1985-86; NIH grantee, 1988-91; recipient Enrique Leon Garcia Best MD Thesis award Peruvian Pediat. Soc., Lima, 1975, award Diabetes Rsch. and Edn. Found., 1987-88. Mem. AMA, The Transplantation Soc., Soc. Española Immunologia, Am. Assn. Immunologists, Coll. Am. Pathologists, Am. Soc. Clin. Pathologists, Peruvian Soc. Clin. Pathology, Peruvian Soc. Immunology and Allergy. Roman Catholic. Home: 1231 Hudson St Denver CO 80220-2607 Office: Univ of Colo HSC 4200 E 9th Ave # C321 Denver CO 80220-3706

LAROSA, GIANNI, aerospace industry executive; b. S. Biagio Platani, Italy, Jan. 22, 1937; came to U.S., 1954; s. Alfonso and Santa (Marino) LaR.; m. Maria Cappello, Jan. 6, 1958; children: Alfonso, Sandra, Claudio, Julio. Student, Cass Tech., 1962; diploma in art, Musée de Art Modern, Tonneins, France, 1993. Lic. contractor, Calif. Owner indsl./comml. kitchen equipment bus. Detroit, 1970-74; supr. aerospace industry, 1985—; supr. The Aerospace Corp., El Segundo, Calif. Exhbns. include San Bernardino County Mus., Calif., 1992, San Clemente (Calif.) Art Fest, 1992, Paris City Hall, 1993, Modern Art Mus., Bordeaux, France, 1993, Modern Art Mus. Unet, Tonneins, France, 1993, Soho Internat. Art Competition, N.Y.C., 1993, Wirtz Gallery, Miami, 1993. Recipient award Fine Arts Inst., 1992, award Soho Internat. Competition, 1993, award Mayor of Paris, Internat. Art Competition, 1993; named Disting. Vis., Mayor of Miami, Fla., 1994. Home: 26641 Domingo Dr Mission Viejo CA 92692-4114

LARSEN, DONNA KAY, public relations executive, writer, consultant; b. Anniston, Ala., Feb. 14; d. James Murray and Lucy B. Bible. BA, U. Ala.; cert. in pub. rels., UCLA. Feature writer L.A. Times; pres. Larsen Promotions, L.A.; pub. rels. cons., L.A., 1987—. Co-author: Superior Healing Power; contbr. feature articles to various newspapers and mags. Mem. Internat. Women's Media Found., L.A. World Affairs Coun., Book Publicists So. Calif. (sec.-treas. 1995), Ebell of L.A., L.A. City Hist. Soc. Office: Donna Larsen Comm. 720 S Plymouth Blvd Los Angeles CA 90005-3776

LARSEN, GWYNNE E., computer information systems educator; b. Omaha, Sept. 10, 1934; d. Melvin and Vernetta (Allen) Bannister; m. John M. Larsen, June 8, 1958; children: Bradley Allen, Blair Kevin, Randall Lawrence. A in Bus. Adminstrn., Denver U., 1956, MBA, 1975, PhD, 1979; BS, Met. State Coll., 1971. Instr. Met. State Coll. Denver, 1979-81, asst. prof., 1981-85, assoc. prof., 1985-88, prof., 1989—, acting chair computer dept., 1991-92; book reviewer McGraw Hill, 1991, Harcourt Brace Jovanovich, 1991, Macmillan Pub. Co., 1993, Southwestern Pub. Co., 1993; presenter Mountain Plains Mgmt. conf., Denver, 1982, Rocky Mountain Bus. Expo, Denver, 1982, Red Rocks C.C., 1984, Colo.-Wyo. Acad. Sci. conf., 1985, Boulder, 1986, Colorado Springs, 1987; local coord. John Wiley & Sons, Denver, 1982, 83; panel chmn. on office automation Assn. for Computing Machinery, Denver, 1985; spkr. ASTD, 1986, Am. Pub. Works Assn., 1986; participant numerous presentations and confs. Author: (with others) Computerized Business Information Systems Workbook, 1983, Collegiate Microcomputer, 1992, (with Verlene Leeberg) Word Processing: Using WordPerfect 5.0, 1989, Word Processing: Using WordPerfect 5.1, 1991, First Look at WordPerfect 5.1, 1991, First Look at DOS, 1991, First Look at NetWare, 1992, Using WordPerfect for Windows, 1993, (with Marold and Shaw) Using Microsoft Works: An Introduction to Computing, 1993, Using Microsoft Works, An Introduction to Computing, 1993, First Look at WordPerfect 6.0 for Windows, 1994, Using WordPerfect 6.0 for Windows, 1994, Using Microsoft Works for Windows, An Introduction to Computing, 1994; apptd. editl. bd. Jour. Mgmt. Systems, 1988, Jour. Microcomputer Systems Mgmt., 1989, Info. Resources Mgmt. Jour., 1991; mem. editl. review bd. Jour. Info. Resources Mgmt. Systems, 1985—, Jour. Mgmt. Info. Systems, 1986—, Jour. Database Mgmt. Systems, Jour. Database Mgmt. Systems, 1987—, Jour. End User Computing, 1990—; contbr. articles to profl. jours. Mem. Info. Resources Mgmt. Assn., Colo.-Wyo. Acad. Scis., Office Automation Soc. Internat. Home: 8083 S Adams Way Littleton CO 80122 Office: Met State Coll Denver Campus Box 45 PO Box 173362 Denver CO 80217-3362

LARSEN, PATRICIA JANE, nursing administrator; b. Traverse City, Mich., June 27, 1933; d. Elton Brentwood and Lola L. (Cook) Bigger; m. Walter Christian Larsen, Nov. 22, 1956; children: Elysia Kim Kary, Kip Anne Hopper, Janice Kirstin. Diploma, Butterworth Hosp. Sch. Nursing, Grand Rapids, Mich., 1957. RN, Nev.; Diplomate Am. Bd. Quality Assurance Utilization Rev. Emergency rm. head nurse Sinai Hosp., Detroit, 1960-65; pediatric/ICU head nurse U. N.Mex. Med. Ctr., Anna Kaseman Hosp., Albuquerque, 1969-71, 72-75; nurse mgr. chem. dependency unit U. N.Mex., Albuquerque, 1977-78; ICU, CCU nurse mgr. Columbia Meml. Hosp., Astoria, Oreg., 1979-81; nurse Washoe Med. Ctr., Reno, Nev., 1981-84; nurse coord. Nev. Peer Rev., Reno, 1984-85, Western Health Plan HMO, Reno, 1985-87; dir. Health Benefit Cons. Med. Benefit Cons. and Superior Health Care Preferred Provider Orgn., Reno, 1987—; mem. Nev. Hosp. Assn. Task Force on Utilization Rev. Providers, 1990. Mem. Citizens Pvt. Enterprise, Reno, 1990-92. Mem. Am. Bd. Quality Assurance and Utilization Rev., Nev. Nurses Assn., Reno C. of C., Mich. State Student Assn. (pres. elect 1956, pres. 1957). Republican. Home: 1440 Huntington Cir Reno NV 89509-5803 Office: Superior Health Care 3400 Kauai Ct Reno NV 89509-4832

LARSEN, PAULA ANNE, operating room nurse; b. Norfolk, Va., Oct. 2, 1962; d. Larry Gene and Sue Frances (Williams) P. ADN, Labette C.C., 1982. RN, Mo.; CNOR, TNCC. Lab. asst. Labette County Med. Ctr., Parsons, Kans., 1979-82; RN operating rm. St. John's Regional Med. Ctr., Joplin, Mo., 1982-85, RN oper. rm., shift coord., 1989-94; head nurse Mason Gen. Hosp., Shelton, Wash., 1994—; with Mo. Lions Eye Bank, 1989-94. Mem. adv. coun. Organ and Tissue Donation. Mem. Assn. Operating Rm. Nurses (del. 1991). Republican. Baptist. Office: Mason Gen Hosp 901 Mountain View Dr Bldg 1 Shelton WA 98584-4401

LARSEN, RICHARD LEE, former city manager, business, municipal and labor relations consultant, arbitrator; b. Jackson, Miss., Apr. 16, 1934; s. Homer Thorsten and Mae Cordelia (Amidon) L.; m. Virginia Fay Alley, June 25, 1955; children: Karla, Daniel, Thomas (dec.), Krista, Lisa. B.S. in Econs. and Bus. Adminstrn, Westminster Coll., Fulton, Mo., 1959; postgrad., U. Kans., 1959-61. Fin. dir. Village of Northbrook, Ill., 1961-63; city mgr. Munising, Mich., 1963-66, Sault Ste. Marie, Mich., 1966-72, Ogden, Utah, 1972-77, Billings, Mont., 1977-79; mcpl. cons., 1979—, pub./pvt. sector labor relations cons., arbitrator, 1979—; elected mayor City of Billings, 1989—; dep. gen. chmn. Greater Mich. Found., 1968. Bd. dirs. Central Weber Sewer Dist., 1972-77; chmn. labor com. Utah League Cities and Towns, 1973-77, Mont. League Cities and Towns, 1977-79; bd. dirs., coach Ogden Hockey Assn., 1972-77, Weber Sheltered Workshop, 1974-77, Billings YMCA, 1980-86, Rimrock Found., 1980-86; chmn. community relations council Weber Basin Job Corps Center, 1973-77. Served with USCG, 1953-57. Recipient Cmty. Devel. Disting. Achievement awards Munising, 1964, Cmty. Devel. Disting. Achievement awards Sault Ste. Marie, 1966-70, Citizen award Dept. of Interior, 1977, Alumni Achievement award Westminster Coll., 1990, Dist. award of merit Boy Scouts Am., 1993, Silver Beaver award Boy Scouts Am., 1994; named Utah Adminstr. of Yr., 1976. Mem. Internat. City Mgmt. ASsn. (L.P. Cookingham career devel. award 1974, Clarence Ridley in-service tng. award 1979), Utah City Mgrs. Assn. (pres. 1972-74), Greater Ogden C. of C. (dir.), Phi Gamma Delta. Mem. LDS Ch. Club: Rotary. Home and Office: 1733 Parkhill Dr Billings MT 59102-2358

LARSEN, SAMUEL HARRY, minister, educator; b. Sterling, Kans., Feb. 3, 1947; s. Harold Julius and Edna Marguerite (Wasson) L.; m. Natalie Louise Mahlow, June 21, 1969; children: Samuel Eric, Kristen Joy, Hans Joseph. BS, U.S. Naval Acad., 1969; MDiv, Covenant Theol. Sem., 1979; D of Ministry, Reformed Theol. Sem., 1989. Ordained to ministry Presbyn. Ch., 1981. Various assignments USN, Norfolk, Va., 1969-72; instr. U.S. Naval Acad., Annapolis, Md., 1972-75; pastoral intern Community Presbyn. Ch., Nairobi, Kenya, Africa, 1977-78; officer-in-charge Naval Res. Shipboard Simulator Lab. and Sch., New Orleans, 1979-81; church planter Mission to the World, Brisbane, Australia, 1982-84; team coord. Mission to the World, Queensland, Australia, 1984-86; regional dir. Mission to the World, Australia, 1986-89; squadron chaplain Destroyer Squadron Five, San Diego, 1989-92; chaplain Naval Air Sta. Whidbey Island, Oak Harbor, Wash., 1992—; dean Westminster Theol. Coll., Brisbane, 1986-88; del. La. Congress on World Evangelism, Manila, 1989. Pres. Covenant Sem. Student Assn., St. Louis, 1976-77; chaplain Chs. Soccer Assn., Sunshine Coast, Australia, 1984-86; tutor Logan Elem. Sch., San Diego, 1991-92; adv. bd. YMCA, Oak Harbor, 1992—. Recipient Meritorious Svc. medal Sec. of Navy, 1981. Mem. Res. Officers Assn. Home: 1208 Cascade Dr Oak Harbor WA 98277-4126 Office: Chapel NAS Whidbey Island Oak Harbor WA 98278

LARSON, BRENT T., broadcasting executive; b. Ogden, Utah, Sept. 23, 1942; s. George Theodore and Doris (Peterson) L.; m. Tracy Ann Taylor; children: Michelle, Brent Todd. Student, pub. schs., Los Angeles; diploma in radio operational engring., Burbank, Calif., 1962. Owner, mgr. Sta. KAIN, Boise, Idaho, 1969-77; owner, operator Sta. KXA Radio, Seattle, 1975-83, Sta. KYYX Radio, Seattle, 1980-83, Sta. KGA Radio, Spokane, Wash., 1978-84, Sta. KUUZ Radio, Boise, 1976-82, Sta. KOOS Radio, North Bend, Oreg., 1980-81, Sta. KODL Radio, The Dalles, Oreg., 1974-80, Sta. KKWZ Radio, Richfield, Utah, 1980—, Sta. KSVC Radio, Richfield, 1980—, Sta. KSOS-FM & AM, Salt Lake City, 1984—; v.p. Casey Larson Fast Food Co., Oreg. and Idaho, 1976-94, Imperial Broadcasting Corp., Idaho, 1970—, Sta. KSOS FM & AM, 1983—; pres. First Nat. Broadcasting Corp., 1970—; v.p. Larson-Wynn Corp., 1974—, Brentwood Properties, Ogden, 1977—; pres. Sta. KSIT Broadcasting, Rock Springs, Wyo., 1980—, Gold Coast Communications Corp., Oreg., 1980-81, Sevier Valley Broadcasting Co., Inc., Utah, 1980—, Brent Larson Group Stas., Western U.S., 1969—; v.p. mktg. Internat. Foods Corp., Boise, 1983-95; ptnr. Larson Tours and Travel, Burley, Idaho, 1977-87; founder 1st Nat. TV Div., 1990; bd. dirs. Casey-Larson Foods Co., La Grande, Oreg. Bd. dirs. Met. Sch., 1981—, Children's Aid Soc., 1991-94. Mem. Am. Advt. Fedn., Nat. Assn. Broadcasters, Nat. Radio Broadcasters Assn., Wash. Broadcasters Assn., Oreg. Broadcasters Assn., Idaho Broadcasters Assn., Utah Broadcasters Assn, Citizens for Responsible Broadcasting (bd. dirs.). Republican. Mormon. Home: 2613 Seashore Dr Las Vegas NV 89128 Office: First Nat Broadcasting Corp 385 24th St Ste 820 Ogden UT 84401-1446

LARSON, CHARLES LESTER, television writer, producer, author; b. Portland, Oreg., Oct. 23, 1922; s. Charles Oscar and Ina May (Couture) L.; m. Alice Mae Dovey, Aug. 25, 1966; 1 stepson, Wyn Donavan Malotte. Student, U. Oreg., 1940. Contract writer MGM Studios, Culver City, Calif., 1943-46; freelance mag. writer, 1941-51. Assoc. producer: TV program Twelve O'Clock High, 1964; producer: TV program The FBI, 1965-68, The Interns, 1970-71, Cades County, 1971-72; exec. producer: TV program Nakia, 1974; producer: TV movie Crime Club, 1973; co-creator: TV series Hagen, 1979-80; author: The Chinese Game, 1969, Someone's Death, 1973, Matthew's Hand, 1974, Muir's Blood, 1976, The Portland Murders, 1983. Mem. Writers Guild Am. West, Producers Guild, Mystery Writers Am. (spl. award 1974), Authors League Am. Democrat. Home: 14205 SE 38th St Vancouver WA 98684-3912

LARSON, DAYL ANDREW, architect; b. Denver, Aug. 13, 1930; s. Andrew and Esther (Freiberg) L.; m. Kay W. Larson; children: Linda, Lesli, Lucy. BS in Architecture, BSBA, U. Colo., 1953. Pres. Haller & Larson Architects, Denver, 1962-92. Served to capt. C.E., U.S. Army, 1953-55. Fellow AIA (pres. Denver chpt. 1978, pres-elect 1986-87); mem. Colo. AIA (pres.). Home: 2153 S Beeler Way Denver CO 80231-3409 Office: Haller & Larson 1621 18th St Denver CO 80202-1266

LARSON, DOROTHY ANN, business educator; b. Nekoosa, Wis., Feb. 27, 1934; d. Edwin E. and Ruby E. (Burch) L.; children: Jean Marie Fitz Harkey, Kenneth Lee Fitz, Cynthia Ann Fitz Whitney. BS with high distinction in Bus. and English, No. Ariz. U., 1969; MA in English, 1971; EdD in Bus., Ariz. State U., 1980. Tchr. English, Cottonwood (Ariz.) Oak Creek Elem. Sch., 1969-70; tchr. bus. and English, Mingus Union High Sch., Cottonwood, 1970-79, dir. vocat. edn., 1976-79; mem. faculty dept. bus. adminstrn. Yavapai Coll., 1979—, chairperson bus. divsn., 1981-86, prep. coord. Yavapai Tech., 1994—; cons. Ariz. Dept. Edn.; mem. adv. coun. Gov's. Coun. Practitioners. Mem. Ariz. Bus. Edn. Assn. (pres. 1980-81), Nat. Bus. Edn. Assn., Am. Vocat. Assn., Ariz. Edn. Assn., NEA, Nat. Tech. Prep. Network, Pi Omega Pi, Delta Pi Epsilon, Phi Kappa Phi, Alpha Delta Kappa, Phi Delta Kappa. Republican. Editor Ariz. Bus. Edn. Newsletter, 1972-74. Home: 2173 Elkhorn Dr Apt B Prescott AZ 86301-4323 Office: 1100 E Sheldon St Prescott AZ 86301-3220

LARSON, ERIC HUGH, public health scientist; b. Mpls., Mar. 19, 1957; s. Marvin Claire and Jean Elizabeth (Firmage) L.; m. Mary Alice Hausladen, Aug. 13, 1987; 1 child, Sarah Elizabeth. BA in Geography, U. Minn., 1980; MS, U. Calgary, 1985; postgrad., U. Wash., 1990—. Rsch. asst. imaging scis. lab. Xerox Palo Alto (Calif.) Rsch. Ctr., 1981-83, rsch. asst. exploratory devel. lab., 1985-87; grad. rsch. asst. dept. geography U. Calgary, Alberta, Canada, 1984; teaching asst. dept. geography U. Wash., Seattle, 1988, rsch. asst., scientific programmer rural health rsch. ctr., 1988-89, rsch. scientist, 1990-91, assoc. dir. rsch., 1991—; presenter in field. Contbr. articles to profl. jours. Mem. Am. Pub. Health Assn., Assn. Am. Geographers, Can. Assn. Geographers, Nat. Rural Health Assn., Wash. Rural Health Assn. Office: U Wash Dept Family Medicine # Hq-30 Seattle WA 98195

LARSON, GALE KJELSHUS, English language educator, consultant; b. Ekalaka, Mont., Aug. 31, 1937; s. Roland Walter and Hazel Annette (Kjelshus) L.; m. Cathy Frances Sechser, Aug. 11, 1962; 1 child, Michael Dale. BA, Carroll Coll., 1960; MA, Creighton U., 1963; PhD, U. Nebr., 1968. Prof. English Calif. State U., Northridge, 1967—, dir. freshman composition, 1969-71, asst. chmn. dept. English, 1971-72, acting assoc. dean Sch. Letters and Scis., 1972-73, assoc. dean Sch. Humanities, 1973-83, acting assoc. v.p. acad. program, 1983-84, chmn. dept. English, 1985-91, coord. writing proficiency exam., 1980-87, 91—; coord. London semester Calif. State U., Northridge, 1982—; pres. Calif. State U. English Coun., Calif. State U. Sys., 1986-90, v.p. English Coun., 1994—. Editor: Caesar and Cleopatra (Bernard Shaw), 1974; contbg. author: (bibliography) Annotated Bibliography of Bernard Shaw, vol. III, 1986. Mem. MLA, Nat. Coun. Tchrs. of English, Shaw Soc. of Am. (London), Sigma Tau Delta, Phi Beta Delta. Democrat. Roman Catholic. Home: 10965 Bluffside Dr # 39 Studio City CA 91604 Office: Calif State U 18111 Nordhoff Northridge CA 91330

LARSON, GERALD LEE, auditor; b. Billings, Mont., Apr. 18, 1937; s. Phillip Antone and Eunice (LaPoint) L. Student, U. Nev., 1955-59; AS, Western Nev. U., 1975. Mil. pers. mgr. Nev. Air NG, Reno, 1973-81; mgr. employee rels. Nev. Mil. Dept., Carson City, 1981-82, mil. pers. mgr., 1982-88; auditor Nev. State Indsl. Ins., Reno, 1989-92; sr. auditor Nev. State Indsl. Ins., Carson City, 1992—. State pres. Nev. Enlisted NG Assn., Carson City, 1983-87; nat. conf. chmn. Enlisted Assn. NG U.S., Reno, 1989; project chmn. 40th ann. book Nev. Air NG, 1988. CM Sgt. Nev. Air NG, USAF, 1955-88. Named Outstanding Sr. Non-Commissioned Officer of Yr., Nev. Air NG, 1979. Office: State Indsl Ins System 515 E Musser St Carson City NV 89701-4262

LARSON, JAMES LEE, Scandinavian languages educator; b. Newport, Wash., Sept. 17, 1931; s. Lars W. and Norma (Newburn) L. PhD, U. Calif., Berkeley, 1965; PhD honors cause, Uppsala U., Sweden, 1983. Asst. prof. U. Pa., Phila., 1965-67, U. Calif., Berkeley, 1967-72; assoc. prof. U. Calif., 1972-79, prof. Scandinavian lang., 1979—. Author: Reason and Experience, 1971, Songs of Something, 1982, Interpreting Nature, 1994; editor/translator: Linnaeus, 1983, Gothic Renaissance, 1991. With U.S. Army, 1953-55. Mem. Am. Soc. 18th Century Studies, Western Soc. 18th Century Studies, History of Sci. Soc. Home: 2451 Ashby Ave Berkeley CA 94705-2034 Office: U Calif Dept Scandinavian Berkeley CA 94720

LARSON, KENNETH GERARD, real estate professional; b. Bklyn., Apr. 6, 1949; s. Lawrence Joseph and Agnes Lucy (Hannon) L.; m. Diane Marie D'Amico, May 24, 1980. BSBA, Pfeiffer Coll., 1971. Lic. real estate broker, Colo. Real estate salesman Van Schaack & Co., Denver, 1979-80; real estate broker Perry & Butler Realty, Denver, 1980-87, Re/Max Internat., Denver, 1987-90; owner, broker Profl. Relocation Assocs. Realty, Broomfield, Colo., 1993—; relocation specialist Relocation Resources, Inc., Norwell, Mass., 1991—. Contbr. articles to profl. jours. Mem. ethics com. Jeffco Bd. Realtors, Lakewood, Colo., 1985-87; task force mem. Denver Ctr. for Performing Arts, Denver, 1993-94. Mem. Colo. Archaeol. Soc. (v.p. 1993-94, dir. 1995—). Republican. Office: Relocation Resources Inc 1099 18th St Ste 1900 Denver CO 80202

LARSON, KIRK DAVID, pomologist and extension specialist; b. Pasadena, Calif., July 1, 1953; s. David and Martha Louise (Munn) L.; m. Katherine Ann Whitson, June 29, 1985; children: Kyle Galen, Kaelyn Ann. BS, U. Calif., Davis, 1980, MS, 1984; PhD, U. Fla., 1991. Horticulturist Aponte Farms, Peñuelas, P.R., 1971-75, Guatemalan Agrl. Project, San Juan Comalapa, Guatemala, 1977-78; agronomist IRI Rsch. Inst., Tinaco, Venezuela, 1980; orchard prodn. mgr. Pike Mt. Apples, North San Juan, Calif., 1981; rsch., teaching asst. Dept. of Pomology U. Calif., Davis, 1982-84; fruit crops ext. agt. Dade County Coop. Ext. Svc., Homestead, Fla., 1985-86; orchard prodn. mgr. J. R. Brooks & Son, Inc., Homestead, Fla., 1986-88; rsch. and teaching asst., dept. fruit crops U. Fla., Gainesville, 1988-91; pomologist, ext. specialist U. Calif., Davis, 1991—; horticultural cons. U.S. Agrl. Svc., Miami, Fla., 1989-91, Agridec, Inc., Miami, 1990. Contbr. articles to profl. jours. and chpt. to book. Recipient citation for Outstanding Achievement in Internat. Agrl. Devel., U. Calif. Davis, 1979; grantee Calif. Strawberry Commn., 1992, 93, 94. Mem. Am. Soc. for Horticultural Sci., N.Am. Strawberry Growers Assn., Fla. State Horticultural Soc., Phi Kappa Phi, Gamma Sigma Delta. Office: U Calif South Coast Rsch Ctr 7601 Irvine Blvd Irvine CA 92718-1201

LARSON, KURT PAUL, fire chief; b. Arlington, Va., Jan. 6, 1958; s. Leonard Paul and June Audrey (Kruck) L.; m. Linda Kay Black, Sept. 21, 1991. BS, U. Colo., 1980; MEd, U. Ariz., 1988. Firefighter Wheat Ridge (Colo.) Fire Dept., 1986-89, fire marshal, 1989-90, lt., 1989-90, dep. fire chief, 1991—; performer Up With People, Broomfield, Colo., 1987—; fire investigator Castlewood Fire Dept., Englewood, Colo., 1990-91; fire svc. lectr., instr., Wheat Ridge, 1989—; bd. dirs. Wheat Ridge Fire Dept.; cons., Wheat Ridge, 1989—. Named Legion of Honor Am. Legion, Denver, 1968, Chevalier Internat. Order of DeMolay, Denver, 1990, Hon. Fire Chief SW Colo. Firefighters Assn., Durango, 1992. Mem. Internat. Assn. Arson Investigators, Scottish Rite of Freemasonry (officer 1982—), Wheat Ridge Masons (presiding officer 1982—, Past Master 1992), Fire Safety Educators (treas. 1988—), Fire Marshals Assn. Colo., Up With People. Republican. Office: Cherryvale Fire Dept 7700 Baseline Rd Boulder CO 80303

LARSON, MARY BEA, elementary education educator; b. Brookings, S.D., Apr. 19, 1946; d. Theodore Orville and Doris Rose (Conway) Larson; children: Christie DiRé, Corey DiRe. BA, Wash. State U., 1968, Portland State U., 1973; MA, U. Guam, 1975; postgrad., Seattle Pacific U. Cert. tchr., Wash. Tchr. early childhood and creativity Chemeketa C. C., Salem, Oreg.; tchr. kindergarten-1st grade Govt. Guam, Agana; tchr. kindergarten, 3rd grade Canal Zone Govt., Balboa; tchr. kindergarten, 2d and 3d grades, elem. art specialist Marysville (Wash.) Sch. Dist., 1994—; mem. profl. adv. bd. coll. edn. Western Wash. U., 1989—. Active Snohomish County Arts Coun. Mem. NEA (del. to Nat. Rep. Assembly, Washington 1992, San Francisco 1993), Wash. Edn. Assn., Marysville Edn. Assn. (pres. 1990-92), Nat. Mus. Women in Arts, Seattle Art Mus. (landmark), Alpha Delta Kappa (state sgt.-at-arms 1990-92, state chaplain 1992-94, state v.p. 1994—). Home: 15605 N Spring Tree Ct SE Mill Creek WA 98012-5825

LARSON, MAUREEN INEZ, rehabilitation consultant; b. Madison, Minn., Mar. 10, 1955; d. Alvin John and Leona B. (Bornhorst) L.; m. Michael Earl Klemetsrud, July 7, 1979 (div. Sept. 1988); m. Kenneth Bell, Dec., 1993. BA in Psychology cum laude, U. Minn., 1977; MA in Counseling, U. N.D., 1978. Cert. rehab. counselor, ins. specialist. Employment counselor II, coordinator spl. programs Employment Security div. State of Wyo.,

Rawlins, 1978-80; employment interviewer Employment Security div. State of Wash., Tacoma, 1980; lead counselor Comprehensive Rehab. Counseling, Tacoma, 1980-81; dir. counseling Cascade Rehab. Counseling, Tacoma, 1981-87, dist. mgr., 1987-90; regional mgr. Rainier Case Mgmt., Tacoma, 1991-92; owner Maureen Larson and Assocs., Tacoma, Wash., 1992—; state capt. legis. div. Provisions Project Am. Personnel and Guidance Assn., 1980. Advocate Grand Forks (N.D.) Rape Crisis Ctr., 1977-78; mem. Pierce County YMCA; bd. dirs. Boys and Girls Clubs of Tacoma, chairperson sustaining drive, 1991, sec.-treas., 1993, pres., 1994, auction com. and spl. events com. State of Minn. scholar, 1973-77; recipient Alice Tweed Tuohy award U. Minn., 1977, Nat. Disting. Svcs. Registry award Libr. of Congress, 1987; named bd. mem. vol. of Yr. Boys and Girls Clubs of Tacoma, 1992. Mem. Nat. Fedn. Bus. and Profl. Women (rec. sec. 1978-80, runner-up Young Careerists' Program 1980), Nat. Rehab. Assn. (bd. dirs. Olympic chpt. 1988—, pres. 1990-91, chairperson state conf. planning com. 1990, 93), Nat. Rehab. Counseling Assn. (bd. dirs. 1993, State of Wash. Counselor of Yr. 1991, Pacific Region Counselor of Yr. 1992), Nat. Rehab. Adminstrs. Assn. (bd. dirs. 1993), Women in Workers Compensation Orgn., Wash. Self-Insured Assn., Nat. Assn. Rehab. Profls. in Pvt. Sector, Pi Gamma Mu. Home: 13504 82nd Ave NW Gig Harbor WA 98329-8642 Office: M Larson & Assocs 4007 Bridgeport Way W Tacoma WA 98466-4330

LARSON, MEL, retired hotel facility executive, corporate executive, helicopter pilot; b. Detroit, Oct. 1, 1929; s. Algot E. and Oleta M. (Murphy) L.; m. Marilyn Gowens, Jan. 14, 1979. Grad. high sch., Plymouth, Mich., 1946. Track owner, auto racing driver, promoter, publicist, 1953-73; v.p. pub. rels., advt. C. W. Pine, Phoenix, 1964-68; various promotional positions Mint Hotel/Casino, 1968-73; mktg. dir. Circus Circus Hotel/Casino, Las Vegas, Nev., 1974-75, v.p. mktg., 1976-85; corp. v.p. mktg. Circus Circus Enterprises, Inc., Las Vegas, 1985-87, exec. v.p., 1987-92; ret., 1992; also bd. dirs. Circus Circus Enterprises, Inc., Las Vegas. Sgt. USAF, 1948-52. Mem. Nat. Assn. Stock Car Auto Racing, Helicopter Assn. Internat., Helicopter Club Am.

LARSON, NEIL EDWIN, accountant; b. Bellingham, Wash., May 10, 1954; s. Theodore Earl and Carolyn (Hawley) L.; m. Kirby Miltenberger, Sept. 6, 1975; children: Tyler Kenton, Quinn Louis. BA, Western Wash. U., 1976; MS in Tax, Golden Gate U., 1987. CPA, Wash. From payroll to fish clk. Alaska Packers Assn., Chignik, 1973-74; credit and sales clk. Sears Roebuck & Co., Bellingham, Wash., 1974-76; intern Larson, Gross & Assoc., Bellingham, 1976; acct. Benson & McLaughlin, Seattle, 1976-78; sr. acct. Bashey & Co., Bellevue, Wash., 1978-80; supr. Peterson Sullivan & Co., Seattle, 1980-84; mgr. Simonson, Moore & Olson, Bellevue, 1984-86; tax ptnr., sec.-treas. Rabern, Larson & North, PS, Seattle, 1986—. Pres. Prince Peath Luth. Ch., Seattle, 1988-89, treas. 1986-88; legis. com. PTA, Bothell, Wash., 1991-92; legis. v.p. Northshore Coun. PTA, 1992-93; outdoor leader Campfire Girls, Bothell, 1992—; bd. dirs. Arboretum Found., 1994—. Mem. AICPA, Wash. Soc. CPAs (chmn. programs 1978, not for profit com.), Associated Gen. Contractors, Constrn. Fin. Mgmt. Assn., Rotary (Seattle # 4). Office: Rabern Larson & North PS 1800 9th Ave Ste 1150 Seattle WA 98101-1322

LARSON, PAUL MARTIN, lawyer; b. Tacoma, June 8, 1949; s. Charles Philip and Margeret (Kobervig) L.; m. Kristina Simonson, June 19, 1971; children: Kristin Ilene, Paul Philip, Erika Louise. AB, Stanford U., 1971; JD, Gonzaga U., 1974. Bar: Wash. 1975, U.S. Dist. Ct. (we. dist.) Wash. 1975, U.S. Dist. Ct. (ea. dist.) Wash. 1978, U.S. Ct. Appeals (9th cir.) 1981. Assoc. Hoff & Cross, Tacoma, 1975-76; ptnr., prin. Brooks & Larson, P.S., Yakima, Wash., 1976-87; ptnr. Bogle & Gates, Yakima, 1987-93, Larson & Perkins, 1994—. Author: (with others) Commercial Law Deskbook, 1981. Pres. Cardio & Pulmonary Inst., Yakima, 1981; bd. dirs. Yakima YMCA, 1981—, Yakima Youth Commn., 1989-93, Yakima Valley chpt. ARC, 1990-93; bd. dirs. Sisters of Providence Med. Ctr.-Yakima Found., 1986—, pres., 1992-93. Mem. ABA (standing com. lawyer's responsibility for client protection 1984-89), Wash. State Bar Assn. (spl. dist. counsel, 1985—, pres. corp. bus. and banking sect. 1987-88), Yakima Estate Planning Coun. (pres. 1981), Rotary. Republican. Home: Larson & Perkins 2311 W Chestnut Ave Yakima WA 98902-3746 Office: Bogle & Gates 105 N 3rd St Yakima WA 98901-2704

LARSON, PEGGY LOUISE See TILLMAN, PEGGY LOUISE

LARSON, RONALD ALLEN, information specialist and programmer/analyst; b. Bakersfield, Calif., Aug. 22, 1950; s. Roger Keith and Frances Ann (Appel) L. BS in BA, Calif. Poly. State U., 1979, MS in Computer Sci., 1981. With Hewlett-Packard, Mountain View, Calif., 1980—. Home: 148 S Lake Merced Hls San Francisco CA 94132-2935

LASAROW, WILLIAM JULIUS, retired federal judge; b. Jacksonville, Fla., June 30, 1922; s. David Herman and Mary (Hollins) L.; m. Marilyn Doris Powell, Feb. 4, 1951; children: Richard M., Elisabeth H. BA, U. Fla., 1943; JD, Stanford U., 1950. Bar: Calif. 1951. Counsel judiciary com. Calif. Assembly, Sacramento, 1951-52; dep. dist. atty. Stanislaus County, Modesto, Calif., 1952-53; pvt. practice law L.A., 1953-73; bankruptcy judge U.S. Cts., L.A., 1973-94; chief judge U.S. Bankruptcy Ct., Central dist., Calif., 1978-90; judge Bankruptcy Appellate Panel 9th Fed. Cir., 1980-82; fed. judge U.S. Bankruptcy Ct., L.A., 1973; faculty Fed. Jud. Ctr. Bankruptcy Seminars, Washington, 1977-82. Contbg. author, editor legal publs.; staff: Stanford U. Law Review, 1949. Mem. ABA, Am. Coll. Bankruptcy, Am. Bankruptcy Inst., L.A. County Bar Assn., Wilshire Bar Assn., Blue Key, Phi Beta Kappa, Phi Kappa Phi. Home: 11623 Canton Pl Studio City CA 91604-4164

LASCH, ROBERT, former journalist; b. Lincoln, Neb., Mar. 26, 1907; s. Theodore Walter and Myrtle (Nelson) L.; m. Zora Schaupp, Aug. 22, 1931 (dec. 1982); children: Christopher (dec. 1994), Catherine; m. Iris C. Anderson, Sept. 14, 1986. A.B., U. Nebr., 1928; postgrad. (Rhodes scholar), Oxford, 1928-31; Nieman fellow, Harvard, 1941-42. Reporter, state editor, editorial writer Omaha World-Herald, 1931-41; editorial writer, then chief editorial writer Chgo. Sun and Sun-Times, 1942-50; editorial writer St. Louis Post-Dispatch, 1950-57, editor editorial page, 1957-71, ret. Contbr. to: Newsmen's Holiday, 1942; Author: For a Free Press, 1944 (Atlantic Monthly prize), Breaking The Building Blockade, 1946. Recipient; St. Louis Civil Liberties award, 1966; Pulitzer prize for distinguished editorial writing, 1966. Home: 685 S La Posada Cir # 703 Green Valley AZ 85614-5118

LASHLEY, ROBERT H., engineering manager; b. Lawrence, Kans., Nov. 4, 1955; s. Richard H. and Virginia L. (Stephenson) L.; m. Anne Regine Deveaux, Mar. 29, 1980; children: Randall H., Scott B. BSEE, U. Calif., Berkeley, 1978, MSEE, 1979. Jr. engr. Ampex Corp., Redwood City, Calif., 1978; mem. tech. staff Apple Computer, Inc., Cupertino, Calif., 1979-83; engr. Gavilan Computers, Campbell, Calif., 1983-84; ptnr., prin. engr. Tech. Assocs., Los Gatos, Calif., 1984-94; founder, sr. engr. The Engring. Dept., Inc., Los Gatos, 1985-89; c.a.e. mgr. Radius, Inc., San Jose, Calif., 1989-94, G.E.C. Plessey Semiconductors Inc., Scotts Valley, Calif., 1994—. Inventor/patentee Monitor Control Systems and Methods for Monitoring and Controlling Atmospheres in Containers for Respiring Perishables, 1991. Home: 15018 Charlotte Ave San Jose CA 95124-5037

LASHLEY, VIRGINIA STEPHENSON HUGHES, retired computer science educator; b. Wichita, Kans., Nov. 12, 1924; d. Herman H. and Edith M. (Wayland) Stephenson; m. Kenneth W. Hughes, June 4, 1946 (dec.); children: Kenneth W. Jr., Linda Hughes Tindall; m. Richard H. Lashley, Aug. 19, 1954; children: Robert H., Lisa Lashley Van Amberg, Diane Lashley Tan. BA, U. Kans., 1945; MA, Occidental Coll., 1966; PhD, U. So. Calif., 1983. Cert. info. processor, tchr. secondary and community coll., Calif. Tchr. math. La Canada (Calif.) High Sch., 1966-69; from instr. to prof. Glendale (Calif.) Coll., 1970—, chmn. bus. div., 1977-81, coord. instructional computing, 1974-84; 88—; sec., treas., dir. Victory Montessori Schs., Inc., Pasadena, Calif., 1980—; pres. The Computer Sch., Pasadena, 1983-92; ret., 1992; pres. San Gabriel Valley Data Processing Mgmt. Assn., 1977-79, San Gabriel Valley Assn. for Systems Mgmt., 1979-80; chmn. Western Ednl. Computing Conf., 1980, 84. Editor Jour. Calif. Ednl. Computing, 1980. Mem. DAR. NSF grantee, 1967-69, EDUCARE scholar U. So. Calif., 1980-82; John Randolph and Dora Haynes fellow, Occidental Coll., 1964-66; student computer ctr. renamed Dr. Virginia S. Lashley Ctr., 1992. Mem. AAUP, AAUW, DAR, Data Processing Consortium (bd. dirs. 1979—, v.p. 1983—, pres. 1985-87, ret. 1992), Orgn. Am. Historians, San Marino Women's Club, CDXVIIC Colonial Dames, XVII Century Club, Phi Beta Kappa, Pi Mu Epsilon, Phi Alpha Theta, Phi Delta Kappa, Delta Phi Upsilon, Gamma Phi Beta. Republican. Congregationalist. Home: 1240 S San Marino Ave San Marino CA 91108-1227

LASIC, DANILO DUSAN, physicist; b. Ljubljana, Slovenia, Aug. 7, 1952; came to U.S., 1988; s. Dusan H. and Vida (Tom) L.; m. Alenka Dvorzak, Jan. 7, 1988; 1 child, Eva. BS in Chemistry, U. Ljubljana, 1975, MS in Chemistry, 1977, PhD in Physics, 1979. Rsch. assoc. Inst. J. Stefan, Ljubljana, 1977-81; postdoctoral fellow Duke U., Durham, N.C., 1981-82; vis. scientist Eidgenossische Technische Hochschule, Zurich, Switzerland, 1982-84; prof. Biophysics U. Ljubljana, 1984-86; vis. prof. U. Waterloo (Ont., Can.), 1986-88; sr. scientist Liposome Tech. Inc., Menlo Park, Calif., 1988-94, Mega Bios Corp., San Carlos, Calif., 1994—; dir. Nuclear Magnetic Resonance Inst. U. Waterloo, Ont., 1986-88; cons. Immunotherapeutics, Fargo, N.D., 1987-88, Liposome Tech. Inc., Menlo Park, 1994—. Author: Liposomes: From Physics to Applications, 1993; co-editor: Nuclear Magnetic Resonance in Physics, Chemistry and Biology, 1989, Stealth Liposomes, 1994, Nonmedical Applications of Liposomes, Vols. I, II, and III; contbr. over 130 articles to profl. jours. Home: 7512 Birkdale Dr Newark CA 94560-1512 Office: MegaBios Corp 863A Mitten Rd Burlingame CA 94010

LASKIN, BARBARA VIRGINIA, legal association administrator; b. Chgo., July 2, 1939; d. Cyril Krieps and Gertrude Katherine (Kujawa) Szymanski; children: Dawn Katherine Doherty, Amy Lynn Anderson. BA, U. Ill., Chgo., 1967; MA, Am. U. Beirut, 1978, Georgetown U., 1985. Asst. buyer Carson, Pirie, Scott & Co., Chgo., 1967-69; fgn. svc. officer Dept. State, Washington, 1969-79; mgr. gift shops Marriott Hotels, Washington, 1979-81; office mgr. Robt Schwinn & Assoc., Bethesda, Md., 1983-85; exec. dir. Internat. Acad. Trial Lawyers, San Jose, Calif., 1985—. Fellow Rotary Club San Jose; mem. AAUW (v.p. 1987), Am. Soc. Assn. Execs., Meeting Planners Internat., Internat. Spl. Events Soc. (v.p. edn. 1995), Profl. Conservation Mgrs. Assn. Roman Catholic. Office: Internat Acad Trial Lawyers 4 N 2nd St Ste 175 San Jose CA 95113-1306

LASKO, ALLEN HOWARD, pharmacist; b. Chgo., Oct. 27, 1941; s. Sidney P. and Sara (Hoffman) L.; BS (James scholar), U. Ill., 1964; m. Janice Marilynn Chess, Dec. 24, 1968 (div. Aug. 1993); children: Stephanie Paige, Michael Benjamin. Staff pharmacist Michael Reese Hosp. and Med. Center, Chgo., 1964-68; clin. pharmacist City of Hope Med. Center, Duarte, Calif., 1968-73; chief pharmacist Monrovia (Calif.) Cmty. Hosp., 1973-74, Santa Fe Meml. Hosp., L.A., 1974-77; pvt. investor, 1977-93; clin. pharmacist Foothill Presbyn. Hosp., Glendora, Calif., 1993—. Recipient Roche Hosp. Pharmacy Rsch. award, 1972-73. Mem. Magic Castle, Flying Samaritans, Mensa, Rho Pi Phi. Jewish. Author: Diabetes Study Guide, 1972, A Clinical Approach to Lipid Abnormalities Study Guide, 1973, Jet Injection Tested As An Aid in Physiologic Delivery of Insulin, 1973. Home: 376 Hill St Monrovia CA 91016-2340

LASLETT, LAWRENCE J., physician, educator; b. Boston, Apr. 17, 1942. BS, Iowa State U., Ames, 1964; MD, U. Iowa, Iowa City, 1969. Diplomate Am. Bd. Internal Medicine, sub-bd. Cardiology. Asst. prof. clin. medicine U. Calif., Davis, 1978-85, assoc. prof. clin medicine, 1985—, dir. fellowship tng. in cardiology, 1994—; dir. cardiac catheterization lab. U. Calif. Davis Med. Ctr., Sacramento, 1984-94. Contbr. articles to med. jours. Mem. tech. adv. com. on free-standing catheterization labs. Calif. Dept. Health Svcs., Sacramento, 1990-94. Served to lt. comdr. USPHS, 1979-81. Fellow Am. Coll. Cardiology (chair Calif. chpt. health care issues com.); mem. ACP, Am. Heart Assn. Office: Div Cardiology 4150 V St Sacramento CA 95817

LASORDA, THOMAS CHARLES (TOMMY LASORDA), professional baseball team manager; b. Norristown, Pa., Sept. 22, 1927; s. Sam and Carmella (Covatto) L.; m. Joan Miller, Apr. 14, 1950; children: Laura, Tom Charles. Student pub. schs., Norristown. Pitcher Bklyn. Dodgers, 1954-55, Kansas City A's, 1956; with L.A. Dodgers, 1956—; mgr. minor league clubs L.A. Dodgers, Pocatello, Idaho, Ogden, Utah, Spokane, Albuquerque, 1965-73; coach L.A. Dodgers, 1973-76, mgr., 1976—. Author: (with David Fisher) autobiography The Artful Dodger, 1985. Served with U.S. Army, 1945-47. L.A. Dodgers winner Nat. League pennant, 1977, 78, 81, 88, winner World Championship, 1981, 88; 2d Nat. League mgr. to win pennant first two yrs. as mgr.; named Nat. League Mgr. Yr. UPI, 1977, AP, 1977, 81, Baseball Writers' Assn. Am., 1988, Sporting News, 1988; recipient Milton Richman Meml. award Assn. Profl. Baseball Players Am. Mem. Profl. Baseball Players Am. Roman Catholic. Club: Variety of Calif. (v.p.). Office: care Los Angeles Dodgers 1000 Elysian Park Ave Los Angeles CA 90012-1112*

LASPINO, ANDREW JOSEPH, business executive, consultant; b. New Haven, Mar. 19, 1940; s. Anthony C. and Dagmar (Allen) L.; m. R. Laspino, June 24, 1961 (div. Aug. 1976); children: Lisa, Laura; m. Jane Laspino, Oct. 18, 1987. BA, So. Conn. State Coll., New Haven, 1967, MA, 1969. Owner, operator nationwide ops. Self-Employment, 1962-89; field cons. The Southland Corp., L.A., 1989-90; dir. bus. devel. we. region The Great Frame-Up Systems, Inc., Franklin Park, Ill., 1990—; owner The Flower Cart, Milford, Conn., 1972-76, Nibbler Ice Cream Factory, Milford, 1973-83, Ice Cream Maker of Beverly Hills, Calif., 1984-85, Lickety Split Restaurants, Milford, 1980-83, Redondo Beach, Calif., 1986-88, Laspino's Cons. Svc., Redondo Beach, 1985-89. Mem. Nat. Franchise Assn., C. of C. Home: 1750 Beach St Apt 2 San Francisco CA 94123-1665

LASSA, RALPH E., plastic surgeon; b. Milw., 1944. DDS, Marquette U., 1968; MD, Med. Coll. Wis., 1972. Plastic surgeon Meml. Hosp., Santa Rosa, Calif.; assoc. clin. prof. U. Calif. San Francisco. Office: 1210 Sonoma Ave # A Santa Rosa CA 95405-6621*

LASSER, THOMAS EDWARD, career officer; b. Mt. Clemens, Mich., Apr. 29, 1946; s. Edward Harry and Lottie Barbara (Dwyer) L.; m. Laura Elena Hermosillo, Apr. 2, 1978; 1 child, Ami Colette. AA in Adminstrn. of Justice, San Joaquin Delta Coll., Stockton, Calif., 1974; BS in Orgnl. Behavior, U. San Francisco, 1984. Master army aviator. Commanding officer 49th Medium Helicopter Co., Stockton, 1972-80; ops. officer Stockton AASF # 2, 1972-91; commanding officer 3/140 (Cu-47), Stockton, 1991-94; ops. officer Los Alamitos (Calif.) AASF # 1, 1994—. Lt. col. U.S. Army, 1965-72, Vietnam. Decorated D.F.C., Bronze Star, Air medal (35 awards), Purple Heart, Vietnam. Mem. Army Aviation Assn., Nat. Guard Assn. of Calif., Nat. Guard Assn. of U.S., Vietnam Helicopter Pilots Assn., Order of Purple Heart, Am. Legion. Home: 232 S Guadalupe Ave # A Redondo Beach CA 90277-3411 Office: Los Alamitos AASF # 1 AFRC # 913 11600 Lexington Los Alamitos CA 90720-5002

LAST, DIANNA LINN SCHNEIDER, marketing company executive; b. Canton, Ohio, Dec. 29, 1944; d. Ld Mervyn and Veronica Lee Schneider; m. David D. Last, Nov. 29, 1969; 1 child, Jason Holden. BA in German, Ohio State U., 1966. Rsch. asst., programmer trainee high-energy physics dept. Ohio State U., Columbus, 1964-66; mfg. programmer RANCO, Inc., Columbus, 1966-68; sr. edn. rep. Honeywell Info. Systems, Cleve., 1968-72; dist. mgr. Honeywell Info. Systems, Orlando, Fla., 1972-78, telecommunications cons., 1978-79; mgr. networking edn. Honeywell Info. Systems, Phoenix, 1979-81, mgr. distributed systems, 1981-84; account and tech. mgr. Honeywell Info. Systems, Beijing, People's Republic of China, 1985; resident dir., chief rep. Honeywell Bull (formerly Honeywell Info. Systems), Beijing, People's Republic of China, 1985-87; dir. Integrated Info. Architecture Honeywell Bull, Phoenix, 1987-88; dir. info. mgmt. U.S. mktg. Bull (formerly Honeywell Bull), Phoenix, 1988-90; pres. Last Concepts Internat. Mktg. & Export Mgmt. Co., Phoenix, 1990—; bd. advisors Internat. Bus. Orgn., Am. Grad. Sch. Internat. Mgmt., 1981-84, 90—; cons., speaker in field; co-founder, vice chmn. Ariz. Internat. Trade Orgn., 1992—; co-founder, chmn. Am. High-Tech Forum, Beijing, 1985-87; mktg. com. Enterprise Network, 1990—; adj. faculty internat. bus. Maricopa Colls., 1994—. Chalice bearer, lay reader St. John Baptist Episcopal Ch., Phoenix, 1983—, mem. bishop's com., 1980-83, mem. vestry, 1991-92; adv. bd. Ariz. Assn. Children and Adults with Learning Disabilities, 1983-84; design task force Maricopa C.Cs., 1984; active World Trade Ctr. Ariz., 1992—; mem. internat. adv. coun. Paradise Valley Coll., 1994—; bd. dirs. Ctr. for New Dirs., Phoenix, 1987-90. Mem. IEEE (past vice chmn. programs), Coun. Fgn. Rels. (mem. Phoenix com. 1994—), Ariz. Software Assn. (internat. com. 1990-92). Home: 1274 E Marconi Ave Phoenix AZ 85022-3232

LAST, MARIAN HELEN, social services administrator; b. L.A., July 2, 1953; d. Henry and Renee (Kahan) Last. BA, Pitzer Coll., 1975; postgrad., U. So. Calif., 1975-84; MS, Long Beach State U., 1980. Lic. marriage therapist. Coordinator City of El Monte, Calif., 1975-76, project dir., 1976—; pvt. practice psychotherapist Long Beach, Calif., 1982—; div. mgr. City of El Monte, 1982—; cons. U. So. Calif. Andrus Ctr., L.A., 1977-78; bd. dirs. Coord. Coun., City of El Monte, 1975—, Sr. Pres.'s Coun., 1982—; Congl. del. White House Conf. on Aging, 1995; chair Nutrition Focus Group, L.A. Co. Area Agy. On Aging, 1993—. Co-author rape survival guide, 1971. Dir., co-founder Rape Response Program, Pomona, San Gabriel Valley, Calif., 1971-80; cons. on sexual assault Pitzer Coll., Claremont, Calif., 1975-78; past pres. El Monte-South El Monte Coord. Coun. Recipient Susan B. Anthony award NOW, Pomona, 1976. Mem. Am. Soc. on Aging, Calif. Assn. Sr. Ctr. Dirs. (dist. dir. XIII), Calif. Parks and Recreation Soc. (Profl. Citation award 1993), Calif. Assn. Marriage and Family Therapists, Emergency Resources Assn. (bd. dirs.), Women's Club, Civitan, Chi Kappa Rho Gamma. Democrat. Jewish. Office: City of El Monte 3120 N Tyler Ave El Monte CA 91731-3354

LASTOVICKA, JOHN LADDIE, marketing and advertising educator; b. Berwyn, Ill., Apr. 15, 1950; s. Laddie John and Ella Marie (Doubek) L.; m. Terry Jeanne Mau, June 23, 1973; children: Ian, Maura. BS, U. Ill., 1972, MS, 1973, PhD, 1978. Prof. U. Kans., Lawrence, 1979-92, Ariz. State U., Tempe, 1992—. Mem. editorial bd. Jour. Consumer Rsch., Jour. Advt., Psychology & Mktg., Jour. Pub. Policy and Mktg.; contbr. articles to profl. jours. Mem. Am. Mktg. Assn., Am. Acad. Advt., Assn. Consumer Rsch. Office: Ariz State U PO Box 874106 Tempe AZ 85287-4106

LATHAM, DEBRA LYNNE, radio station administrator; b. Neillsville, Wis., Aug. 24, 1960; d. Franklin Richard and Ruth Ann (Eddy) Schneider; m. James Leroy Latham, Dec. 28, 1982; children: Adrianne, Joanna. BS, Oreg. State U., 1983, MS, 1988. Exec. dir. Sunrise, Inc., Portland, 1983-85; gen. mgr. Radio Sta. KFIR, Sweet Home, Oreg., 1986-88, Radio for Peace Internat., Portland, 1988—; sec. Starfire Prodn., Sweet Home, 1986-88; mem. bd. dirs. Univ. Global Edn., Portland, 1983—, Earth Comms., Portland, 1992—. Editor: (periodical) Vista, 1988—. Reporter Radio For Peace Internat., Costa Rica, 1990—. Recipient Scholarship Oreg. Dairy Industries, Corvallis, 1981, Inst. Good Tech., 1982-83, Disting. Svc. award World Peace U., Portland, 1992, Earth Comms. award, 1994. Home: 911 NE 122 # 12 Portland OR 97220 Office: Radio for Peace Internat, APDO 88, Santa Ana Costa Rica

LATHAM, JAMES RICHARD, research scientist; b. Pomona, Calif., July 1, 1946; s. James Richard and Norma Elizabeth (Mills) L.; m. Pamela June Staley Latham, Aug. 31, 1968, 1 child, Joan Elizabeth Latham. Student, U. Calif., Berkeley, 1964-65, Chabot Coll., Hayward, Calif., 1965-72. Technician Coast Mfg./Hexel Co., Livermore, Calif., 1966-69, Crown Zellerbach Co., San Leandro, Calif., 1969-70; sr. rsch. technician Kaiser Aluminum & Chem. Corp., Pleasanton, Calif., 1970-82; sr. technician Clorox Tech. Ctr., Pleasanton, Calif., 1982—. Patentee in field. Named Merit Scholarship Finalist; recipient NROTC scholarship. Mem. AAAS, Am. Chemical Soc., Div. Chemical Technicians (treas.), N.Y. Acad. Sci. Mem. LDS Ch. Office: Clorox Technical Ctr 7200 Johnson Dr Pleasanton CA 94588-8005

LATHI, BHAGAWANDAS PANNALAL, electrical engineering educator; b. Bhokar, Maharashtr, India, Dec. 3, 1933; came to U.S., 1956; s. Pannalal Rupchand and Tapi Pannalal (Indani) L.; m. Rajani Damodardas Mundada, July 27, 1962; children: Anjali, Shishir. BEEE, Poona U., 1955; MSEE, U. Ill., 1957; PhD in Elec. Engring., Stanford U., 1961. Research asst. U. Ill., Urbana, 1956-57, Stanford (Calif.) U., 1957-60; research engr. Gen. Electric Co., Syracuse, N.Y., 1960-61; cons. to semicondr. industry India, 1961-62; assoc. prof. elec. engring. Bradley U., Peoria, Ill., 1962-69, U.S. Naval Acad., Annapolis, Md., 1969-72; prof. elec. engring. Campinas (Brazil) State U., 1972-78, Calif. State U., Sacramento, 1979—; vis. prof. U. Iowa, Owa City, 1979; founder, sope proprieter Berkeley-Cambridge Press. Author: Signals, Systems and Communication, 1965, Communication Systems, 1968 (transl. into Japanese 1977), Random Signals and Communication Theory, 1968, Teoria Signalow I Ukladow Telekomunikacyjnych, 1970, Sistemy Telekomunikacyjne, 1972, Signals, Systems and Controls, 1974, Sistemas de Comunicacion, 1974, 86, Sistemas de Comunicacao, 1978, Modern Digital and Analog Communication Systems, 1983, 89 (transl. into Japanese 1986, 90), Signals and Systems, 1987, Linear Systems and Signals, 1992; contbr. articles to profl. jours. Fellow IEEE. Office: Calif State U 6000 J St Sacramento CA 95819-2605

LATHROP, ANN, librarian, educator; b. L.A., Nov. 30, 1935; d. Paul Ray and Margaret (Redfield) W.; divorced; children: Richard Harold, John Randolph, Rodney Grant. BA in History summa cum laude, Ea. N.Mex. U., 1957; MLS, Rutgers U., 1964; PhD, U. Oreg., 1988. Cert. elem. tchr., Calif.; cert. libr., Calif; adminstrv. credential, Calif. Elem. sch. tchr. Chalfont (Pa.) Boro Sch., 1960-61, Livingston Elem. Sch., New Brunswick, N.J., 1961-63, Rosedale Elem. Sch., Chico, Calif., 1964-65; libr. Chico (Calif.) H.S., 1965-72, Princeton (Calif.) H.S., 1972-73, Santa Maria (Calif.) H.S., 1973-77; libr. coord. San Mateo County Office Edn., Redwood City, Calif., 1977-89; assoc. prof. Calif. State U., Long Beach, 1989-92, prof., 1993—; dir. Calif. Software Clearinghouse, Calif. State U. Long Beach. Author: Online Information Retrieval as a Research Tool in Secondary School Libraries, 1988; co-author: Courseware in the Classroom, 1983; editor: Online and CD-ROM Databases in School Libraries, 1989, the 1988-89 Educational Software Preview Guide, 1988, Technology in the Curriculum Recource Guides, 1988; editor, founder: (jours.) The Digest of Software Reviews: Education, 1983-86, Software Reviews on File, 1985-86; editor: (database) California Online Resources in Education, 1989—; contbr. chpts. to books, articles to prof. jours. Mem. ALA, NEA, Am. Assn. Sch. Librs., Assn. State Tech. Using Tchr. Educators, Calif. Faculty Assn., Calif. Media and Libr. Educators Assn., Calif. Reading Assn., Computer Using Educators, Internat. Soc. for Tech. in Edn., Phi Delta Kappa. Office: Calif State U 1250 N Bellflower Blvd Long Beach CA 90840-0006

LATHROP, MITCHELL LEE, lawyer; b. L.A., Dec. 15, 1937; s. Alfred Lee and Barbara (Mitchell) L.; m. Denice Annette Davis; children: Christin Lorraine Newlon, Alexander Mitchell, Timothy Trewin Mitchell. B.Sc., U.S. Naval Acad., 1959; J.D., U. So. Calif., 1966. Bar: D.C. 1966, Calif. 1966, U.S. Supreme Ct. 1969, N.Y. 1981; registered environ. assessor, Calif. Dep. counsel Los Angeles County, Calif., 1966-68; with firm Brill, Hunt, DeBuys and Burby, L.A., 1968-71; ptnr. Macdonald, Halsted & Laybourne, L.A. and San Diego, 1971-80; sr. ptnr. Rogers & Wells, N.Y.C., San Diego, 1980-86; sr. ptnr. Adams, Duque & Hazeltine, L.A., San Francisco, N.Y.C., San Diego, 1986-94, exec. com., 1986-94, firm chmn., 1992-94; sr. ptnr. Luce, Forward, Hamilton & Scripps, San Diego, N.Y.C., San Francisco, L.A., 1994—; presiding referee Calif. Bar Ct., 1984-86, mem. exec. com., 1981-88; lectr. law Calif. Judges Assn., Practicing Law Inst. N.Y., Continuing Edn. of Bar, State Bar Calif., ABA. Author: State Hazardous Waste Regulation, 1991, Environmental Insurance Coverage, 1991, Insurance Coverage for Environmental Claims, 1992. Western Regional chmn. Met. Opera Nat. Coun., 1971-81, v.p., mem. exec. com., 1971—, now chmn.; trustee Honnold Libr. at Claremont Colls., 1972-80; bd. dirs. Music Ctr. Opera Assn., L.A., sec., 1974-80; bd. dirs. San Diego Opera Assn., 1980—, v.p., 1985-89, pres.-elect, 1993, pres., 1994—; bd. dirs. Met. Opera Assn., N.Y.C.; mem. nat. steering coun. Nat. Actors Theatre, N.Y. Capt. JAGC, USNR, ret. Mem. ABA, N.Y. Bar Assn., Fed. Bar Assn., Fed. Bar Council, Calif. Bar Assn., D.C. Bar Assn., San Diego County Bar Assn. (chmn. ethics com. 1980-82, bd. dirs. 1982-85, v.p. 1985), Assn. Bus. Trial Lawyers, Assn. So. Calif. Def. Counsel, Los Angeles Opera Assos. (pres. 1970-72), Soc. Colonial Wars in Calif. (gov. 1970-72), Order St. Lazarus of Jerusalem, Friends of Claremont Coll. (dir. 1975-81, pres. 1978-79), Am. Bd. Trial Advocates, Judge Advocates Assn. (dir. Los Angeles chpt. 1974-80, pres. So. Calif. chpt. 1977-78), Internat. Assn. Def. Counsel, Brit. United Services Club (dir. Los Angeles 1973-75), Mensa Internat., Calif. Soc., S.R. (pres. 1977-79), Calif. Club (Los Angeles), Valley Hunt Club (Pasadena, Calif.), Met. Club (N.Y.C.), The

Naval Club (London), Phi Delta Phi. Republican. Home: 455 Silvergate Ave San Diego CA 92106-3327 Office: Luce Forward Hamilton and Scripps 600 W Broadway Fl 26 San Diego CA 92101-3311 also: Citicorp Ctr 153 E 53rd St Frnt 26 New York NY 10022-4611

LATINI, HENRY PETER, real estate management executive; b. Portland, Maine; s. Joseph and Mary Rose (Di Santo) L.; m. Betty Shevock, Oct. 20, 1951; children: Mary Celeste, Lisa Ann Kirkendall, Monica Louise King. AB, U. Miami, Coral Gables, Fla., 1951; postgrad., U. Maine, 1980-81, U. Hawaii, 1984. Spl. agt. FBI, Washington, 1951-79; owner, pres. Nat. Bur. Spl. Investigations, Portland, 1979-84; owner, v.p. Data Base Inc., Reston, Va., 1980-84; v.p. Cert. Mgmt. Inc., Honolulu, 1985-94, Latini-Kirkendall: Architecture, Seattle and Honolulu, 1992—; owner Residential Mgmt. Cons., Seattle, Wash., 1992—; managing ptnr. Latini-Kirkendall Architecture, Seattle and Honolulu, 1992—; owner Koapaka Ctr Inc., Honolulu, 1992—; chmn. bd. dir. A.R. Corp., Honolulu, 1987-92, CMI, 1992—; mem. Community Assns. Inst., Honolulu; pres. Common Area Maintenance Co., 1991—; co-owner Koapaka Ctr., Inc. Membership chair Portland Club, 1980-84; mem. Civil Svc. Commn., Cape Elizabeth, Maine, 1981-83; dir. security Mus. of Art, Portland, Maine, 1982-83; vol. Hawaiian Open and Ko'Olina Sr. Invitational Tournament. Mem. Soc. Former Spl. Agts. of the FBI Inc. (Hawaii chpt., sec. 1987-88, v.p. 1988-89, chmn. 1989-90), Inst. Real Estate Mgmt. Am. Soc. for Indsl. Security (Maine chpt., founder 1980, pres. 1980-82), Elks. Republican. Roman Catholic. Office: Cert Mgmt Inc 3179 Koapaka St Honolulu HI 96819-1927

LATNER, BARRY P., pathologist; b. L.A., Oct. 8, 1957; m. Claudia Pinilla, Sept. 3, 1988. BA, UCLA, 1979; MD, Chgo. Med. Sch., 1984. Diplomate Am. Bd. Pathology. Intern/resident Calif. Pacific Med. Ctr., San Francisco, 1984-89; pathologist Mt. Diablo Med. Ctr., Concord, Calif., 1989—; asst. clin. prof. U. Calif., Berkeley, Calif., 1989—. Contbr. articles to profl. jours. Fellow Coll. Am. Pathologists; mem. Am. Soc. Clin. Pathologists, Am. Assn. Clin. Chemists, Calif. Soc. Pathologists, South Bay Pathology Soc. Office: Mt Diablo Med Ctr 2540 East St Concord CA 94520-1906

LATTANZIO, STEPHEN PAUL, astronomy educator; b. Yonkers, N.Y., June 29, 1949; s. Anthony Raymond and Anella Lattanzio; m. Barbara Regina Knisely, Aug. 14, 1976; children: Gregory Paul, Timothy Paul. BA in Astronomy, U. Calif., Berkeley, 1971; MA in Astronomy, UCLA, 1973, postgrad., 1973-75. Planetarium lectr. Griffith Obs., Los Angeles, 1973-75; instr. astronomy El Camino Coll., Torrance, Calif., 1974-75; planetarium lectr. Valley Coll., Los Angeles, 1975; prof. astronomy Orange Coast Coll., Costa Mesa, Calif., 1975—, planetarium dir., 1975—; mem. adv. commn. Natural History Found. Orange County, Calif., 1988-91; scientific advisor instructional TV series Universe: The Infinite Frontier, 1992—. Co-author: Study Guide for Project: Universe, 1978, 2d rev. edition 1981; textbook reviewer, 1978—; co-screenwriter Project: Universe instructional TV series episode, 1979; contbr. articles to profl. jours. Mem. Astron. Soc. Pacific, Nat. Space Soc., The Planetary Soc., Space Studies Inst. Sigma Xi (assoc.), Phi Beta Kappa. Office: Orange Coast Coll 2701 Fairview Rd Costa Mesa CA 92626-5563

LATTMAN, LAURENCE HAROLD, retired academic administrator; b. N.Y.C., Nov. 30, 1923; s. Jacob and Yetta (Schwartz) L.; m. Hanna Renate Cohn, Apr. 12, 1946; children—Martin Jacob, Barbara Diane. BSChemE, Coll. City N.Y., 1948; MS in Geology, U. Cin., 1951, PhD, 1953. Instr. U. Mich., 1952-53; asst. head photogeology sect. Gulf Oil Corp., Pitts., 1953-57; asst. prof. to prof. geomorphology Pa. State U., 1957-70; prof., head dept. geology U. Cin., 1970-75; dean Coll. of Mines U. Utah, 1975-83, dean Coll. Engring., 1978-83; pres. N.Mex. Tech., Socorro, 1983-93, pres. emeritus, 1993—; bd. dirs. Pub. Svc. Co. of N.Mex.; cons. U.S. Army Engrs., Vicksburg, Miss., 1965-69, also major oil cos. Author: (with R.G. Ray) Aerial Photographs in Field Geology, 1965, (with D. Zillman) Energy Law; Contbr. articles to profl. jours. Served with AUS, 1943-46. Fenneman fellow U. Cin., 1953. Fellow Geol. Soc. Am.; mem. Am. Assn. Petroleum Geologists, Am. Soc. Photogrammetry (Ford Bartlett award 1968), Soc. Econ. Paleontologists and Mineralogists, AIME (Disting. mem. 1981, Mineral Industries Edn., award 1986—), Assn. Western Univs. (chmn. bd. dirs. 1986-87), Sigma Xi. Home: 11509 Penfield Ln NE Albuquerque NM 87111

LAU, BENNETT MUN KWAI, plastic surgeon, educator; b. Honolulu, May 28, 1930; s. Luck Yee and Juliette (Kaiuaola) L.; m. Yvonne Yip, Apr. 21, 1961; 1 child, DeeAnne Karyl. BA, La Sierra U., 1951; MD, Loma Linda U., 1955. Commd. capt. U.S. Army, 1956, advanced through grades to col., 1970, gen. surgeon, 1956-66, plastic surgeon, 1966-77, ret., 1977; pvt. practice plastic surgeon Honolulu, 1978—; clin. assoc. prof. U. Hawaii Med. Sch., Honolulu, 1978—; cons. plastic surgeon Micronesia, 1970-84, Tripler Army Med. Ctr., 1978—. Mem. ACS, Am. Soc. Plastic Surgery, Pan Pacific Surg. Soc. Office: 1380 Lusitana St Ste 702 Honolulu HI 96813-2449

LAU, BETH, English language educator; b. Milw., Dec. 16, 1951; d. Milford H. and Janet (Towse) L.; m. Martin J. Camargo, Dec. 27, 1974 (div. 1982). BA in English, U. Ill., 1974, MA, 1976, PhD, 1980. Teaching asst. U. Ill., Urbana, 1974-78; adj. prof. various colls. and univs., Ala., Mo., 1979-82; asst. prof. N.Mex. State U., 1982-85, Ripon Coll., 1985-90; assoc. prof. Calif. State U., Long Beach, 1990—. Author: Keats's Reading of the Romantic Poets, 1991; co-editor Approaches to Teaching Brontë's Jane Eyre, 1993; contbr. articles and revs. to profl. jours. Travel grantee Am. Coun. Learned Socs., 1986. Mem. MLA, Keats-Shelley Assn., Wordsworth-Coleridge Assn., Interdisciplinary 19th Century Studies, Philological Assn. Pacific Coast, N.Am. Soc. for Study of Romanticism. Home: 2621 E 20th St Unit 17 Signal Hill CA 90804-1004 Office: Calif State U Dept English 1250 N Bellflower Blvd Long Beach CA 90840-0006

LAU, CHARLES KWOK-CHIU, architect, architectural firm executive; b. Hong Kong, Oct. 19, 1954; came to U.S., 1973; s. Oi-Ting and Wai-Han L. BFA in Environ. Design, U. Hawaii Manoa, Honolulu, 1977. Registered architect, Hawaii. Designer CJS Group Architects, Honolulu, 1977-78, Fox Hawaii, Honolulu, 1978-80, Wimberly Allison Tong & Goo, Honolulu, 1980-82, Architects Hawaii, Honolulu, 1982-84; assoc., designer Stringer & Assocs., Honolulu, 1984-85; pres. AM Ptrns., Inc., Honolulu, 1985—; instr. U. Hawaii, Honolulu, 1987. Principal works include Crystal Fantasy, Hyatt Regency Hotel, Honolulu, 1988 (Merit award Hawaii chpt. AIA 1988), Dole Cannery Sq., Honolulu, 1989 (Merit award Hawaii Renaissance 1989), Danelle Christie's, Ala Moana Hotel, Honolulu, 1989 (Hawaii Region award Illuminating Engring. Soc. N.Am. 1989, Grand and Nat. Grand awards Hawaii Renaissance 1989, Tiger Restaurant, Lahaina, Hawaii, 1990 (Gold Key Excellence in Interior Design award Am. Hotel and Motel Assn. 1990, Nat. and Merit awards Hawaii Renaissance 1990), La Pierre du Roi, ANA Kalakaua Ctr., Honolulu, 1990 (Grand and Nat. Grand awards 1990), Crazy Shirts, Honolulu, 1991 (Grand and Overall awards Hawaii Renaissance 1991), Grand Hyatt Wailea, Maui, Hawaii, 1992 (Merit award Hawaii chpt. AIA 1992), Carrera y Carrera, Ala Moana Ctr., Honolulu, 1992 (Merit award Hawaii chpt. AIA 1992), Danelle Christie's, Outrigger Waikiki Hotel, Honolulu, 1992 (Merit award Hawaii Renaissance 1992), Exec. Ctr. Hotel, Honolulu, 1992 (Merit award Hawaii Renaissance 1992), Centre Ct. Restaurant, Honolulu, 1993 (Merit award Hawaii Renaissance 1993), Lani Huli, Kailua, 1993 (Spl. Recognition award Parade of Homes 1993), 218 Plantation Club Dr., Kapalua, Maui, 1993 (Interior Design award Am. Soc. Interior Design 1993), Royal Garden Restaurant, Alamoana Hotel, Honolulu, 1994 (Brand and Overall award Hawaii Renaissance, 1994, Lani Huli, Kailua, Hawaii (Project of Yr., City and County of Honolulu 1994). Mem. AIA (mem. design award jury selection com. Honolulu chpt. 1990), C. of C. Hawaii, Chinese C. of C. Hawaii, Pacific Club. Office: AM Partners Inc 1164 Bishop St Ste 1000 Honolulu HI 96813-2824

LAU, CHERYL A., former state official. BM, Ind. U.; JD, U. San Francisco. Bar: 1986. Formerly dep. atty. gen. Nev. Motor Vehicles and Pub. Safety Dept., Carson City, Nev.; sec. of state, State of Nev. State of Nev., Carson City, 1991-94; gen. coun. U.S. Ho. of Reps., Washington, 1995—. Office: House of Reps 219 Cannon House Office Bldg Washington DC 20515

LAU, EUGENE WING IU, lawyer; b. Canton, China, Sept. 23, 1931; came to U.S., 1939; s. Eugene K. F. and Ann (Leung) L.; m. Dierdre Florence, July 20, 1962; children: Elyse M., Jennifer M. AB, U. Mich., 1953; LLB, Yale U., 1960. Bar: Hawaii 1960, U.S. Supreme Ct. 1965. Dep. Pros. Attys. Office, Honolulu, 1960-63; pvt. practice Honolulu, 1963-67, 73—; v.p. Hawaii Corp., Honolulu, 1967-73; del. People to People Legal Del. to China, 1987; mem. Commn. on Manpower and Full Employment, Honolulu, 1965-67. With U.S. Army, 1954-55. Mem. ABA, Hawaii Bar Assn., Punahou Tennis Club (Honolulu). Home: 3079 La Pietra Cir Honolulu HI 96815-4736 Office: 1188 Bishop St Ste 1912 Honolulu HI 96813-3308

LAU, GLEN K., plastic surgeon; b. China, 1946. MD, Tufts U., 1972. Plastic surgeon Samuel Merritt Hosp., Oakland, Calif. Office: 3300 Webster St Ste 1005 Oakland CA 94609-3106*

LAU, KAM YUNG, physician, educator; b. Hong Kong, Oct. 7, 1951; came to U.S., 1974; s. Hong Wai and Wong Yee Lau; m. Sylvia Ho, June 30, 1979; 1 child, Jason. MB, Nat. Def. Med. Coll., Taipei, Taiwan, 1973. Diplomate Am. Bd. Internal Medicine, sub-splty. Bd. Critical Care Medicine, sub-splty. Bd. Pulmonary Disease, Am. Bd. Pediats.; lic. physician, Calif., Tex., Va., Wash.; cert. advanced cardiac life support instr. Intern in pediats. Misericordia Hosp., Bronx, N.Y., 1974-75, resident in pediats., 1975-76; resident in pediats. Meml. U. Nfld., St. John's, Can., 1976-77; hosp. privileges Bon Secours Hosp., Lawrence (Mass.) Gen. Hosp., Methuen, 1977-78; pvt. practice specializing in pediats. Kadlec Hosp., Richland, Wash., 1978-80; resident in internal medicine Tex. Tech. U. Health Scis. Ctr., El Paso, 1980-82; pvt. practice specializing in emergency medicine Sierra Med. Ctr., El Paso, 1982-83; fellow in pulmonary medicine of internal medicine UCLA, 1983-85; attending physician, chief pulmonary svcs. dept. medicine, med. dir. dept. of respiratory therapy R. E. Thomason Gen. Hosp., El Paso, 1985-88; attending physician dept. medicine Riverside (Calif.) Comty. Hosp., 1988—, 1988—; co-dir. critical care unit R. E. Thomason Gen. Hosp., El Paso, 1987-88; asst. prof. medicine, chief pulmonary divsn. Tex. Tech. U. Health Scis. Ctr., El Paso, 1985-88; asst. clin. prof. medicine Loma Linda (Calif.) U. Med. Ctr., 1989—; presenter in field. Contbr. articles to profl. jours. Recipient Outstanding Overseas Student award Overseas Affairs Commn., Govt. of Republic of China, 1973. Fellow ACP, Am. Acad. Pediats., Am. Coll. Chest Physicians; mem. Am. Thoracic Soc., Tex. Soc. for Respiratory Care (med. dir. S.W. region 1986-88). Office: Riverside Med Clinic 3660 Arlington Ave Riverside CA 92506-3912

LAU, LAWRENCE JUEN-YEE, economics educator, consultant; b. Guizhou, China, Dec. 12, 1944; came to U.S., 1961, naturalized, 1974; s. Shai-Tat and Chi-Hing (Yu) Liu; m. Tamara K. Jablonski, June 23, 1984. BA with great distinction, Stanford U., 1964; MA, U. Calif.-Berkeley, 1966, PhD, 1969. Acting asst. prof. econs. Stanford U., Palo Alto, Calif., 1966-67, asst. prof., 1967-73, assoc. prof., 1973-76, prof., 1976—, Kwoh-Ting Li prof. econ. devel., 1992—; co-dir. Asia/Pacific Rsch. Ctr., 1992—; cons. The World Bank, Washington, 1976—; vice chmn. Bank of Canton of Calif. Bldg. Corp., San Francisco, 1981-85; dir. Bank of Canton of Calif., San Francisco, 1979-85; dir. Property Resources Equity Trust, Los Gatos, 1987-88; vice-chmn. Complete Computer Co. Far Eat Ltd., Hong Kong, 1981-89. Co-author: (with D.T. Jamison) Farmer Education and Farm Efficiency, 1982, Models of Devlopment: A Comparative Study of Economic Growth in South Korea and Taiwan, 1986, rev. edit., 1990; contbr. articles to profl. jours. Adv. bd. Self-Help for Elderly, San Francisco, 1982—; bd. dirs. Chiang Ching-Kuo Found. for Internat. Scholarly Exch., 1989—; govs. coun. econ. policy advisors State of Calif., 1993—. John Simon Guggenheim Meml. fellow, 1973; fellow Ctr. for Advanced Study in Behavioral Scis., 1982; Overseas fellow Churchill Coll., Cambridge U., Eng., 1984. Fellow Econometric Soc.; mem. Academia Sinica, Conf. Research in Income and Wealth. Republican. Episcopalian. Office: Stanford U Dept Econs Stanford CA 94305

LAUB, DONALD R., plastic surgeon; b. Milw., 1935. MD, Marquette Sch. Medicine, 1960. Plastic surgeon U. Stanford Med. Ctr.; clin. assoc. prof. surgery Stanford U. Office: Ober Bldg 1515 El Camino Real Palo Alto CA 94306-1010*

LAUBE, ROGER GUSTAV, retired trust officer, financial consultant; b. Chgo., Aug. 11, 1921; s. William C. and Elsie (Drews) L.; m. Irene Mary Chadbourne, Mar. 30, 1946; children: David Roger, Philip Russell, Steven Richard. BA, Roosevelt U., 1942; postgrad., John Marshall Law Sch., 1942, 48-50; LLB, Northwestern U., 1960; postgrad., U. Wash., 1962-64. Cert. fin. cons. With Chgo. Title & Trust Co., Chgo., 1938-42, 48-50, Nat. Bank Alaska, Anchorage, 1950-72; mgr. mortgage dept. Nat. Bank Alaska, 1950-56, v.p., trust officer, mgr. trust dept., 1956-72; v.p., trust officer, mktg. dir., mgr. estate and fin. planning div. Bishop Trust Co., Ltd., Honolulu, 1972-82; instr. estate planning U. Hawaii, Honolulu, 1978-82; exec. v.p. Design Capital Planning Group, Inc., Tucson, 1982-83; pres., sr. trust officer, registered investment adviser Advanced Capital Advisory, Inc. of Ariz., Tucson, 1983-89; registered rep., pres. Advanced Capital Investments, Inc. of Ariz., Prescott, 1983-89; pres., chief exec. officer Advanced Capital Devel., Inc. of Ariz., Prescott, 1983-89; mng. exec. Integrated Resources Equity Corp., Prescott, 1983-89; pres. Anchorage Estate Planning Coun., 1960-62, Charter mem., 1960-72, Hawaii Estate Planning Coun., 1972-82, v.p., 1979, pres., 1980, bd. dirs., 1981-82; charter mem. Prescott Estate Planning Coun., 1986-90, pres. 1988. Charter mem. Anchorage Community Chorus, 1946, pres., 1950-53, bd. dirs., 1953-72, Alaska Festival of Music, 1960-72; mem. Anchorage camp Gideons Internat., 1946-72, Honolulu camp, 1972-82, mem. Cen. camp, Tucson, 1982-85, Prescott, 1985-90, Port Angeles-Sequim Camp, 1990—; mem. adv. bd. Faith Hosp., Glenallen, Alaska, 1960—, Cen. Alaska Mission of Far Ea. Gospel Crusade, 1960—; sec., treas. Alaska Bapt. Found., 1955-72; bd. dirs. Anchorage Symphony, 1965-72; bd. dirs. Bapt. Found. of Ariz., 1985-90; bd. dirs., mem. investment com. N.W. Bapt. Found., 1991—; mem. mainland adv. coun. Hawaii Bapt. Acad., Honolulu, 1982—; pres. Sabinovista Townhouse Assn., 1983-85; bd. advisers Salvation Army, Alaska, 1961-72, chmn., Anchorage, 1969-72, bd. advisers, Honolulu, 1972-82, chmn. bd. advisers, 1976-78; asst. staff judge adv. Alaskan Command, 1946-48; exec. com. Alaska Conv., 1959-61, dir. music Chgo., 1938-42, 48-50, Alaska, 1950-72, Hawaii, 1972-82, Tucson, 1982-85, 1st So. Bapt. Ch., Prescott Valley, Ariz., 1985-90; 1st Bapt. of Sequim, Wash., 1990—; chmn. bd. trustees Hawaii, 1972-81, Prescott Valley, 1986-89, Sequim, Wash., 1991—; worship leader Waikiki Ch., 1979-82. 1st lt., JAGD, U.S. Army, 1942-48. Recipient Others award Salvation Army, 1972. Mem. Am. Inst. Banking (instr. trust div. 1961-72), Am. Bankers Assn. (legis. com., trust div. 1960-72), Nat. Assn. Life Underwriters (nat. com. for Ariz.), Yavapai County-Prescott Life Underwriters Assn. (charter), Anchorage C. of C. (awards com. 1969-71), Internat. Assn. Fin. Planners (treas. Anchorage chpt. 1969-72, exec. com. Honolulu chpt. 1972-82, Ariz. chpt. 1982-90, del. to World Congress Australia and New Zealand 1987), Am. Assn. Handbell Ringers. Baptist. Home: Sunland Country Club 212 Sunset Pl Sequim WA 98382-8515

LAUBER, MIGNON DIANE, food processing company executive; b. Detroit, Dec. 21; d. Charles Edmond and Maud Lillian (Foster) Donaker. Student Kelsey Jenny U., 1958, Brigham Young U., 1959; m. Richard Brian Lauber, Sept. 13, 1963; 1 child, Leslie Viane (dec.). Owner, operator Alaska World Travel, Ketchikan, 1964-67; founder, owner, pres. Oosick Soup Co., Juneau, Alaska, 1969—. Treas., Pioneer Alaska Lobbyists Soc., Juneau, 1977—. Mem. Bus. and Profl. Women, Alaska C. of C. Libertarian, Washington Athletic Club. Author: Down at the Water Works with Jesus, 1982; Failure Through Prayer, 1983, We All Want to Go to Heaven But Nobody Wants to Die, 1988. Home: 321 Highland Dr Juneau AK 99801-1442 Office: PO Box 1625 Juneau AK 99802-0078

LAUBSCHER, RODERICK, engineering company executive; b. San Francisco; s. Fred and Myrtle Louise (Bazzini) L. BA in History, U. Calif., Santa Cruz, 1970; MS in Journalism, Columbia U., 1972. News reporter KSFO Radio, San Francisco, 1970-74, KGTV (NBC), San Diego, 1975-77, KRON-TV (NBC), San Francisco, 1977-80; pvt. practice polit. cons. San Francisco, 1980-81; mgr. corp. comm. Becntel Group, Inc., San Francisco, 1981—. Dir. San Francisco (Calif.) C. of C., 1986-87, San Francisco (Calif.) Beautiful, 1990-93; mem. Citizen's Adv. Com. on Transp., San Francisco, 1991—. Pulitzer fellow Columbia U., N.Y.C., 1972; recipient Emmy award Acad. TV Arts and Sci., San Francisco, 1978. Mem. City Club San Francisco (founding chmn., gov. 1988—). Office: Bechtel Group Inc 19/A33 50 Beale St San Francisco CA 94105-1813

LAUCHENGCO, JOSE YUJUICO, JR., lawyer; b. Manila, Philippines, Dec. 6, 1936; came to U.S., 1962; s. José Celis Sr. Lauchengco and Angeles (Yujuico) Sapota; m. Elisabeth Schindler, Feb. 22, 1968; children: Birthe, Martina, Duane, Lance. AB, U. Philippines, Quezon City, 1959; MBA, U. So. Calif., 1964; JD, Loyola U., L.A., 1971. Bar: Calif. 1972, U.S. Dist. Ct. (cen. dist.) Calif. 1972, U.S. Ct. Appeals (9th cir.) 1972, U.S. Supreme Ct. 1975. Banker First Western Bank/United Calif. Bank, L.A., 1964-71; assoc. Demler, Perona, Langer & Bergkvist, Long Beach, Calif., 1972-73; ptnr. Demler, Perona, Langer, Bergkvist, Lauchengco & Manzella, Long Beach, 1973-77; sole practice Long Beach and L.A., 1977-83; ptnr. Lauchengco & Mendoza, L.A., 1983-92; pvt. practice L.A., 1993—; mem. commn. on jud. procedures County of L.A., 1979; tchr. Confraternity of Christian Doctrine, 1972-79; counsel Philippine Presdl. Commn. on Good Govt., L.A., 1986. Chmn. Filipino-Am. Bi-Partisan Polit. Action Group, L.A., 1978. Recipient Degree of Distinction, Nat. Forensic League, 1955. Mem. Criminal Cts. Bar Assn., Calif. Attys. Criminal Justice, Calif. Pub. Defenders Assn., L.A. County Bar Assn., Assn. Trial Lawyers Am., Calif. Trial Lawyers Assn., L.A. Trial Lawyers Assn., Philippine-Am. Bar Assn. (bd. dirs.), U. Philippines Vanguard Assn. (life), Beta Sigma. Roman Catholic. Lodge: K.C. Office: 3545 Wilshire Blvd Ste 247 Los Angeles CA 90010-2305

LAUCHLAN, DOUGLAS MARTYN, performing arts administrator; b. Pine Falls, Man., Feb. 18, 1931; s. William Martyn and Laura Maud (Douglas) L.; m. Margaret Roberta Hanley, Sept. 11, 1953; children: John (dec.), Andrea, Michael, Scott. BA, U. Man., Winnipeg, 1952; Diploma in Theology, U. Winnipeg, 1955; BDiv, St. Andrews Coll., Saskatoon, Sask., 1967; grad. diploma in Ednl. Adminstrn., U. Calgary, 1971. Min. United Ch. Can., Winnipeg, Edmonton and Saskatoon, 1954-66; chaplain U. Calgary, 1966-69; v.p. Mt. Royal Coll., Calgary, Alta., 1969-75, pres., 1975-80; leader Liberal Party of Man., Winnipeg, 1980-83; exec. dir. United Way of Calgary, 1983-86; gen. mgr. Calgary Ctr. for Performing Arts, 1986—. Past chmn. Calgary Convention and Vis. Bur., Performing Arts Ctr. Consortium; dir. Can. Ctr. for Philanthropy, Can. Voice Care Found., Calgary Internat. Organ Festival, Child Friendly Calgary, United Way of Calgary, Can. Speech Communicators Assn., Can. Country Music Assn.; vice chmn. Esther Honens Internat. Piano Competition. Mem. Can. Music. Assn., Willow Park Golf and Country Club, Can. Speech Communicators Assn. (Calgary White Hatter of the Year 1994). Office: Calgary Ctr Performing Arts, 205 8th Ave SE, Calgary, AB Canada T2G 0K9

LAUER, GEORGE, environmental consultant; b. Vienna, Austria, Feb. 18, 1936; came to U.S., 1943; s. Otto and Alice (Denton) L.; m. Sandra Joy Comp, Oct. 1, 1983; children by previous marriage: Julie Anne, Robert L. BS, UCLA, 1961; PhD, Calif. Inst. Tech., 1967. Mem. tech. staff N.Am. Aviation, Canoga Park, Calif., 1966-69; mgr. Rockwell Internat., Thousand Oaks, Calif., 1969-75; div. mgr. ERT, Inc., Westlake Village, Calif., 1975-78; dir. Rockwell Internat., Newbury Park, Calif., 1978-85; dir. Tetra-Tech Inc., Pasadena, Calif., 1985-86; pres. Environ. Monitoring and Services, Inc., 1986-88; sr. cons. Atlantic Richfield, Inc., Los Angeles, 1988—. Contbr. articles to profl. jours.; patentee in field. Mem. adv. bd. Environment Rsch. and Tech. Served with U.S. Army, 1957-59. Fellow Assn. for Computing Machinery; mem. Am. Chem. Soc., Am. Statistical Soc., Air Pollution Control Assn. Republican. Jewish. Home: 6009 Maury Ave Woodland Hills CA 91367-1052 Office: Atlantic Richfield Inc 515 S Flower St Los Angeles CA 90071-2201

LAUER, ROBERT HAROLD, human behavior educator, minister; b. St. Louis, June 28, 1933; s. Earl Ervin and Frances Pauline (Bushen) L.; m. Jeanette Carol Pentecost, July 2, 1954; children: Jon Robert, Julie Anne, Jeffrey David. BS, Washington U., St. Louis, 1954; BD, So. Sem., Louisville, 1958; MA, So. Ill. U., Edwardsville, 1969; PhD, Washington U., St. Louis, 1970. Ordained to ministry Bapt. Ch., 1956. Min. Salem Bapt. Ch., Florissant, Mo., 1958-68; prof. So. Ill. U., 1968-82; prof. dept. human behavior U.S. Internat. U., San Diego, 1983—, dean, 1983-90; min. Christian edn. La Jolla (Calif.) Presbyn. Ch., 1991—. Author: Temporal Man, 1983, Spirit & The Flesh, 1983, 'Till Death Do Us Part, 1986, Watersheds, 1988, The Quest for Intimacy, 1991, No Secrets?, 1993. Mem. Am. Sociol. Assn., Nat. Coun. on Family Rels., Nat. Communal Socs. Assn., Pacific Sociol. Assn. Democrat. Presbyterian. Office: La Jolla Presbyn Ch 7715 Draper Ave La Jolla CA 92037-4301

LAUER, STEFANIE DOROTHEA, painter, writer; b. Berlin, Apr. 28, 1928; came to U.S., 1945; d. Max and Margaret Minna (Stöckel) Blank; m. James Lothar Lauer, Sept. 4, 1955; children: Michael Solon, Ruth Lauer Manenti. Diploma in Theatre, Dramatic Workshop of New Sch., N.Y.C., 1947; BA in English with honors, Smith Coll., 1950; MA in English with distinction, Harvard U., 1952; postgrad. in art, SUNY, Albany, 1981. Cert. tchr. English Pa., N.Y., art, N.Y. Instr. Mitchell Coll., New London, Conn., 1952-54; asst. prof. SUNY, Cortland, 1954-55; asst. editor Curtis Publishing Co., Phila., 1955-56; asst. prof. Brandywine Coll., Wilmington, Del., 1974-77; copy editor United Ch. of Christ, N.Y.C., 1978-80; artist pvt. practice, Burnt Hills,, N.Y., 1980-93, San Diego, 1994—. Author: Home is the Place, 1959; contbr. reviews art mags.; editor (newsletter) DASH, 1980-90; artist: solo exhibitions: (paintings and photography) Penn Wynne (Pa.) Libr., 1976, Schenectady, N.Y. C. of C., 1982, Smith Coll., Northampton, Mass., 1984, Galeria Grupo Arte, Albany, N.Y., 1993, KEX Copy Source Corp. Hdqs., Albany, 1993; group shows include: SUNY Fine Arts Bldg., Albany, 1981, U. Tex., Tyler, 1988, Ariel Gallery, N.Y.C., 1988, 89, Stuyvesant Plaza Invitational, 1989 (award), others. Program chmn., pres., chmn. nominating com. Penn Wynne Sch. Parents Assn., 1970-80; Braille Inst. reader Temple Beth Hillel, Wynwood, Pa., 1978; writer, editor, bd. mem., officer Congregation Ohav Shalom, Albany, N.Y., 1983-89; interviewer Harvard Club Ea. N.Y., Albany, 1980-92; interviewer Harvard Club of San Diego, 1994—. Named fellow Breadloaf Writers Conf., 1955, finalist Artists' Mag. Still-life Competition, 1988; recipient 1st prize Montgomery County Arts Coun., Amsterdam, N.Y., 1987, RCCA landscape competition 1st, 1990, gallery exhibit 2nd, 1990, photography exhibit 1 of 5 awards, 1993. Mem. Phi Beta Kappa. Democrat. Home: 7622 Palmilla Dr # 78 San Diego CA 92122

LAUGHLIN, CHARLES WILLIAM, agriculture educator, research administrator; b. Iowa City, Iowa, Dec. 9, 1939; s. Ralph Minard and Geraldine (O'Neill) L.; m. Barbara Waln, Dec. 17, 1966; children: Shannon Morris, Charles Tudor. BS, Iowa State U., 1963; MS, U. Md., 1966; PhD, Va. Tech., 1969. Asst. extension nematologist U. Fla., Gainesville, 1968-69; asst. prof., extension nematologist Mich. State U., East Lansing, 1969-73, assoc. prof., asst. dir. acad. and student affairs, 1973-78, prof., asst. dean, dir. acad. and student affairs, 1978-80; prof., dept. head plant pathology and weed sci. Miss. State U., Starkville, 1980-83; prof., assoc. dir. Ga. Agrl. Expt. Sta. U. Ga., Athens, 1983-92; dir. co., Agrl. Expt. Sta. Colo. State U., Ft. Collins, 1992—; cons. Brazilian Ministry of Edn. and Culture, Brasilin, Brazil, 1975-77, Brazilian Nat. Agrl. Rsch. Agy., 1978, W.K. Kellogg Found., Battle Creek, Mich., 1983—, Latin Am. Inst. of Creativity, São Paulo, Brazil, 1991. Recipient Colleague award Creative Edn. Found., 1988. Mem. Soc. Nematologists, Am. Phytopathological Soc., Brazilian Soc. Nematologists. Address: 16 Administration CSU Fort Collins CO 80523-0001

LAURANCE, DALE R., oil company executive; b. Ontario, Oreg., July 6, 1945; s. Rolland D. and Frances S. (Hopkins) L.; m. Lynda E. Dolmyer, Sept. 11, 1966; children—Catherine Megan, Brandy Nichole, Holly Elizabeth. B.S. in Chem. Engring., Oreg. State U., 1967; M.S. in Chem. Engring., U. Kans., 1971, Ph.D. in Chem. Engring., 1973. Mem. mgmt., research staff E.I. DuPont de NeMours, Lawrence, Kans., 1967-77; mgr. process technology Olin Corp., Lake Charles, La., 1977-80; bus. mgr. urethanes Olin Corp., Stamford, Conn., 1980-82, gen. mgr. urethane and organics, 1982-83; sr. v.p. Occidental Chem. Corp., Darien, Conn., 1983-84; exec. v.p. Occidental Petroleum Corp., Los Angeles, 1984-91, exec. v.p., sr. oper. officer, 1991—, also bd. dirs.; chmn. adv. bd., mem. dept. chem. and petroleum engring., U. Kans., Lawrence, 1985—. Contbr. articles to profl. jours. Patentee in field. Recipient Disting. Engring. Svc. award Sch. Engring., U. Kans., 1991. Mem. Am. Petroleum Inst., Chem. Mfrs. Assn., Soc. Chem. Industry, L.A. Area C. of C. (bd. dirs.). Republican. Club: Riveria Country (Los Angeles). Office: Occidental Petroleum Corp 10889 Wilshire Blvd Los Angeles CA 90024-4201

LAURANCE, MARK RODNEY, optics instrumentationist; b. Seattle, Nov. 27, 1959; s. Sidney Laurance and Patricia Louise Sadlier. BS in Astronomy, U. Wash., 1984, BS in Physics, 1984, MS in Astronomy, 1992. Computer ops. programmer Seattle Police Dept., Seattle, 1980-85; researcher U. Wash., Seattle, 1984-90; lighting engr. Korry Electronics Co., Seattle, 1990-92; optics instrumentationist Can.-France-Hawaii Telescope Corp., Kamuela, Hawaii, 1992—. Contbr. articles to profl. jours. Mem. chpt. mgmt. program mgr., exec. bd. dirs. Hawaii State Jaycees, 1995; exec. v.p. Kona Jaycees, 1994, cmty. fundraising dir., 1993; cert. prime trainer Jr. Chamber Internat., 1994. Recipient C. William Brownfield Meml. award for outstanding first yr. jaycee Kona Jaycees, 1994, Presdl. Excellence award Hawaii State Jaycees, 1995, First Place Speak-Up Competition award Hawaii State Jaycees, 1995; named Outstanding Young Men of Am. award Jaycees, 1989, Outstanding Exec. V.P. of Quar., Hawaii Jaycees, 1995, Ten Outstanding Young Persons of Hawaii Jaycees, 1995. Mem. S.P.I.E. Internat. Soc. Optical Engring.

LAURANT, VAN, III, entrepreneur; b. New Orleans, Sept. 3, 1948; s. Van Jr. and Mary Louise (Baldwin) L. BS in Acctg., Woodbury U., 1973; MA in Mgmt. and Adminstrn., Columbia Pacific U., 1993. Security examiner Sec-Los Angeles Reg., L.A., 1975-76; sr. auditor New Orleans br. Def. Contract Audit Agy., 1976-81; sr. auditor western region Def. Contract Audit Agy., L.A., 1982-94; sr. overhead monitor L.A. region Def. Contract Adminstrn. Svcs. Mgmt. Area, 1981-82;, 1993-95; founder Natchez Computerized Acctg. & Bookkeeping Svcs., 1995—, Laurant's Small Bus. Cons. Group, Natchez, 1995—; founder Fin. Info. Publs., L.A., 1993—. Author: Study of Relationships: Education: Employment; and Wealth, 1993 (award 1993), Study of Personal Financial Planning, 1993 (award 1993), Weight Loss Control, 1994. Vol. Shelter for Homeless, L.A. County, 1993, Gateways*Paths to Learn, L.A. County, 1993. Sgt. USAF, 1966-70. Recipient Letter of Appreciation for Vol. Svc., local ch., 1992, Gateways, 1993. Mem. Am. Black Book Writers Assn., Book Publicist of So. Calif., Nat. Trust for Hist. Preservation, Pubs. Mktg. Assn., Black Agenda. Home and Office: 809 N Rankin St Natchez MS 39120

LAURE, PHILLIP JOHN, industrial engineer; b. Ann Arbor, Mich., May 9, 1949; s. Daniel Pierre and Elizabeth Ann (Arigan) L.; m. Nelda Jane Griffing, June 8, 1973; children: Michael James Whitham, Steven Duane Whitham, Charles Allen Whitham, Deanna Jane Hainey. BA, Calif. State U., San Bernardino, 1978. Sr. engring. technician County of San Bernardino, San Bernardino, 1974-80; prodn. planning supr. Lily-Tulip, Inc., Riverside, Calif., 1980-85; mfg. cons. Laure & Assocs., Riverside, 1985-86; indsl. engr. Northrop Corp., Hawthorne, Calif., 1986-88; sr. indsl. engr. Rohr Industries, Riverside, 1988-92; owner Profit Technologies, an ISO 9000 cons. firm, 1993—. Sponsor Kids Against Drugs, Moreno Valley, Calif., 1988, '89, '90. Mem. Inst. Indsl. Engrs. (bull. editor 1988, 90, chpt. pres. 1991, 92, 93), Am. Soc. Quality Control (chair cmty. quality coun. sect. 1994—), Inland Empire Quality Improvement Network (co-founder), Riverside C. of C., Elks. Republican. Roman Catholic.

LAUREN, PAUL GORDON, history educator; b. Seattle, Feb. 17, 1946. BA with highest honors, Wash. State U., 1968; MA, Stanford U., 1969, PhD, 1973. Prof. history U. Mont., Missoula, 1974-86, dir. Mansfield Ctr., 1986-91, regents prof., 1992—; vis. prof. history Stanford U., Calif., 1973, 79, 82; bd. dirs. Mansfield Found. Author: Diplomats and Bureaucrats, 1976, Power and Prejudice, 1988, 95; editor: Diplomacy: New Approaches, 1979, The China Hands' Legacy, 1989, Destinies Shared, 1989; contbr. articles to profl. jours. and chpts. to books. Named Disting. Speaker UN, Geneva, 1990; Woodrow Wilson fellow, Nat. Peace fellow, Rockefeller Found. fellow, 1980, Paul Harris fellow, 1994; sr Fulbright scholar, 1994. Office: U Mont Dept History Missoula MT 59812

LAURI, JOHN PETER, hospital administrator; b. Marquette, Mich., Apr. 25, 1946; s. T.J. and Elsie Elizabeth (Storstrang) L.; m. Cynthia Judith Barr, June 22, 1968; children—Brian Barr, Christian Matthew. B.A., Morehead State U., 1968; M.A. in Health Care Adminstrn., George Washington U., 1972. Cert. secondary tchr., Mich. High sch. tchr. Roseville Pub. Schs., Roseville, Mich., 1968-70; adminstrv. resident Baptist Med. Ctrs., Birmingham, Ala., 1971-72; asst. adminstr. Foote Meml. Hosp., Jackson, Mich., 1972-73; assoc. adminstr. Foote Meml. Hosp., Jackson, 1973-78; adminstr. Miami Heart Inst., Fla., 1978—; mem. S. Fla. Hosp. Assn., Miami, 1979-84, chmn., 1982-83; adj. prof. U. Miami Grad. Program, 1982—. Mem. Miami Beach Health Adv. Bd., 1984—, Rediscover Miami Beach Task Force, 1984—, Becon Council, Miami, 1984—. Mem. Greater Miami C. of C., Miami Beach C. of C., Am. Coll. of Hosps. Adminstrs. Am. Hosp. Assn., Fla. Hosp. Assn. (dir.). Republican. Presbyterian. Club: LaGorce County (Miami Beach). Home: 4470 S Lemay Ave Apt 415 Fort Collins CO 80525-4823

LAUTER, JAMES DONALD, stockbroker; b. L.A., Sept. 3, 1931; s. Richard Leo and Helen M. (Stern) L.; BS, UCLA, 1956; m. Neima Zwieli, Feb. 24, 1973; children: Walter James (dec.), Gary. Market rsch. mgr. Germain's Inc., L.A., 61; sr. v.p. investments, former branch mgr. Dean Witter Reynolds, Inc., Pasadena, Calif., 1961—. With Armed Forces, 1954-56. Recipient Sammy award L.A. Sales Execs. Club, 1961. Mem. AARP, UCLA Alumni Assn.), Pasadena Bond Club (pres. 1995—), Bruin Athletic Club. Home: 17237 Sunburst St Northridge CA 91325-2922 Office: Dean Witter Reynolds Inc 55 S Lake Ave Ste 800 Pasadena CA 91101-2626

LAUTZENHEISER, MARVIN WENDELL, computer software engineer; b. Maximo, Ohio, Feb. 19, 1929; s. Milton Leander and Mary Lucetta (Keim) L.; m. Jean Bethene Baker, Oct. 26, 1946 (div. Nov. 1986); children: Constance Kay, Thomas Edward, Jan Stephen; m. Paula Ann Keane, Mar. 10, 1990. BS in Math., Mt. Union Coll., 1953. Spl. agt. FBI, Washington, 1953-59; computer analyst Tech. Ops., Washington, 1959-64; pres. Anagram Corp., Springfield, Va., 1964-83; computer analyst Onyx Corp., McLean, Va., 1983, Inmark, Springfield, 1983-84, Memory Scis., McLean, 1984-85; software scientist Zitel Corp., San Jose, Calif., 1985—. Inventor, designer in field. Mem. Mensa, Am. Iris Soc. Home: 7216 Neuman St Springfield VA 22150-4421 Office: Zitel Corp 47211 Bayside Pky Fremont CA 94538-6517

LAVALLEE, DEIRDRE JUSTINE, marketing professional; b. Woonsocket, R.I., June 14, 1962; d. Albert Paul and Margaret Justine (O'Brien) L. BS in Chem. Engring., U. R.I., 1984. Sales engr. NGS Assocs. Inc., Canton, Mass., 1985-87; mgr. dist. sales MKS Instruments Inc., Andover, Mass., 1987—. V.p., bd. dirs. Nat. Conf. Standards Labs.; mem. adv. bd. Tex. State Tech. Coll. Mem. AIChE (sec. chpt.), Am. Soc. Materials, Am. Inst. Physics, Am. Vacuum Soc. Home: 845 13th St Boulder CO 80302-7503 Office: MKS Instruments Inc 5330 Sterling Dr Boulder CO 80301-2351

LAVE, CHARLES ARTHUR, economics educator; b. Phila., May 18, 1938; s. Israel and Esther (Axlerod) L.; 1 child, Rebecca. BA, Reed Coll., 1960; PhD, Stanford U., 1968. Mem. faculty U. Calif., Irvine, 1966—, prof. econs., chmn. dept. econs., 1978-85, 89-92; vis. prof., vis. scholar Hampshire Coll., 1972, Stanford U., 1974, MIT, 1982, Harvard U., 1982, U. Calif., Berkeley, 1988, 94. Author: (with James March) An Introduction to Models in the Social Sciences, 1975, Energy and Auto Type Choice, 1981, Urban Transit, 1985, others. Trustee Reed Coll., Portland, Oreg., 1978-82; bd. dirs. Nat. Bur. Econ. Rsch., Cambridge, 1991—; chmn. bd. Irvine Campus Housing Authority, Inc., 1982—. Served with USAF, 1957. Recipient Pyke Johnson award Transp. Rsch. Bd., 1987, Extraordinarius award U. Calif., 1993. Fellow Soc. Applied Anthropology; mem. Am. Econ. Assn., AAAS, Transp. Research Bd. Office: U Calif Dept Econs Irvine CA 92717

LAVELLE, BETTY SULLIVAN DOUGHERTY, legal professional; b. Omaha, Nov. 12, 1941; d. Marvin D. and Marie C. (Sery) Sullivan; children from previous marriage: Clayton B. Dougherty, Lance A. Dougherty; m. James S. LaVelle, 1986; 1 child, Lindsay L. A of Pre-Law, U. Nebr., 1960; student, U. Colo., 1964-66; BA in Philosophy, Metro State Coll., 1979; cert. legal assistant, U. San Diego, 1979. Teaching asst. Metro State Coll., Denver, 1978; paralegal Holland and Hart, Denver, 1979-85; litigation paralegal Rothgerber, Appel, Powers and Johnson, Denver, 1985-88; pres. Vivant, Inc., Boulder, 1987—; owner, adminstr. Homestead Group Home for Elderly, Longmont, 1987-92; ptnr. LaVelle & McMillan, Boulder, 1989-90; water law and litigation paralegal Moses, Wittemyer, Harrison and Woodruff, P.C., Boulder, 1990—; mediator domestic relations 20th Jud. Dist., Boulder, 1984-85. Contbr. articles to profl. jours. Vol. legal aid Thursday Night Bar, Denver Bar Assn., 1979-86, paralegal coordinator, panelist, speaker, 1983-85; sr. paralegal Boulder County Legal Svcs., 1988-89; mediator landlord/tenant project City of Boulder, 1983-87; coach, trainer Ctr. for Dispute Resolution, Denver and Boulder, 1984-86; vol. Shelter for Homeless, Boulder, 1988. Recipient cert. U. Denver Coll. Law, 1981, Hoagland award Colo. Bar Assn., 1984. Mem. Colo. Bar Assn., Boulder Bar Assn. (assoc.), Soc. Profls. in Dispute Resolution, Rocky Mountain Legal Assts. (mem. adv. bd. 1980-81, bd. dirs. 1983-85, 94—, rep. to Colo. Bar Assn. 1994—, dir. pro bono svcs. 1984-85). Republican. Home: 1660 Bradley Ct Boulder CO 80303-7300

LAVELLE-NICHOLS, ROBIN ANN, accountant; b. Tacoma, Wash., Nov. 27, 1959; d. Gregory Henry and Shirley Ann (Heggen) L.; m. Gordon L. Nichols, Aug. 20, 1983; children: Melinda Ann, Angela Elizabeth, Lindsey Katherine. BBA cum laude, Pacific Luth. U., 1985. CPA, Wash. V.p. acctg. and fin. Sorrento Enterprises, Inc., Spanaway, Wash., 1980-85; accountant, audit mgr. Ernst & Young, Seattle, 1985-90; audit. mgr. Dwyer, Pemberton & Coulson, Tacoma, Wash., 1990-92; pvt. practice Tacoma, Wash., 1992—. Mem. AICPA, Wash. Soc. CPAs, Inst. Mgmt. Accts. (dir. acquisition 1985-87, dir. tech. programs 1989-90, v.p. profl. devel. 1990-91, Outstanding Achievement Mem. Acquisition award 1985-86, v.p. membership and mktg. 1991-92, v.p. fin. and adminstrn., 1993-94, chair corp. and acad. devel.), Pacific Luth. U. Bus. Alumni Assn. (founding bd. dirs.), Wash. State Horseman Assn., Beta Alpha Psi (pres. Delta Rho chpt.). Home and Office: 4104 145th St E Tacoma WA 98446-1674

LAVENTHOL, DAVID ABRAM, newspaper editor; b. Phila., July 15, 1933; s. Jesse and Clare (Horwald) L.; m. Esther Coons, Mar. 8, 1958; children: Peter, Sarah. BA, Yale U., 1957; MA, U. Minn., 1960; LittD (hon.), Dowling Coll., 1979; LLD (hon.), Hofstra U., 1986. Reporter, news editor St. Petersburg (Fla.) Times, 1957-62; asst. editor, city editor N.Y. Herald-Tribune, 1963-66; asst. mng. editor Washington Post, 1966-69; assoc. editor Newsday, L.I., N.Y., 1969, exec. editor, 1969, editor, 1970-78, pub., chief exec. officer, 1978-86; group v.p. newspapers Times Mirror Co., L.A., 1981-86, sr. v.p., 1987-93, pres., 1987-93; pub., chief exec. officer L.A. Times, 1989-93; editor-at-large Times Mirror Co., L.A., 1994—; mem. Pulitzer Prize Bd., 1982-91, chmn., 1988-89; chmn. Internat. Press Inst., 1992—, vice chmn., 1985-93; dir. Am. Press Inst., 1988—. Bd. dirs. United Negro Coll. Fund, 1988, Times Mirror Found., 1987, Mus. Contemporary Art, L.A., 1989—, chmn., 1993—; bd. dirs. Associated Press, 1993—, Columbia Journalism Sch., 1993—. With Signal Corps AUS, 1953-55. Recipient Columbia Journalism award for Disting. Svc., 1994. Mem. Am. Soc. Newspaper Editors (chmn. writing awards bd. 1980-83), Council Fgn. Relations. Clubs: Century (N.Y.C.), Regency (L.A.). Office: LA Times Times Mirror Sq Los Angeles CA 90053-3816*

LAVEY, ELLIOTT BRUCE, plastic surgeon; b. Chgo., Aug. 31, 1951. MD, Stanford U., 1977. Plastic surgeon San Ramon Regional Med. Ctr., Calif.; with Mt. Diablo Hosp., 1983—. Office: Contemp Plas Surg Med Ste 288 913 San Ramon Valley Blvd Danville CA 94526-4031*

LAVI, EFRAIM, allergist; b. Petah, Tiqua, Israel, 1946. MD, U Tel Aviv Sacleler Sch Medicine, 1975. Allergist Kaiser Found. Hosp., Sacramento. Office: Kaiser Hosp Al Clin 2025 Morse Ave Sacramento CA 95825-2115*

LAVIN, LAURENCE MICHAEL, lawyer; b. Upper Darby, Pa., Apr. 27, 1940; s. Michael Joseph and Helen Clair (McGonigle) L. BS, St. Joseph's U., Phila., 1962; JD, Villanova (Pa.) U., 1965. Bar: Pa., S.C. Vol. U.S. Peace Corps, Thika, Kenya, 1966-67; atty. Community Legal Svcs., Phila., 1968-70, exec. dir., 1971-79; exec. dir. Palmetto Legal Svcs., Columbia, S.C., 1981-85; dir. Law Coordination Ctr., Harrisburg, Pa., 1985-88, Nat. Health Law Program, L.A., 1988—; chmn. Orgn. Legal Svc. Backup Ctrs., 1991—; bd. dirs., chmn. civil com. Nat. Legal Aid and Defender, Washington, 1976-78; bd. dirs. Ctr. for Health Rights. Editor Health Advocate, 1988—. Founding mem. Pa. Coun. to Abolish Death Penalty, Harrisburg, 1986. Mem. ABA, Pa. Bar Assn. (chmn. legal svcs. to pub. com. 1985-88), Legal Assistance Assn. Calif. (bd. dirs.). Democrat. Home: 1133 22nd St Santa Monica CA 90403-5727 Office: Nat Health Law Program 2639 S La Cienega Blvd Los Angeles CA 90034-2603

LAVIN, MATTHEW T., horticultural educator. Prof. biology dept. Mont. State U., Bozeman. Recipient N.Y. Botanical Garden award Botanical Soc. Am., 1993. Office: care Dept Biology Montana State U Bozeman MT 59717-0002

LAVINE, STEVEN DAVID, college president; b. Sparta, Wis., June 7, 1947; s. Israel Harry and Harriet Hauda (Rosen) L.; m. Janet M. Sternburg, May 29, 1988. BA, Stanford U., 1969; MA, Harvard U., 1970, PhD, 1976. Asst. prof. U. Mich., Ann Arbor, 1974-81; asst. dir. arts and humanities Rockefeller Found., N.Y.C., 1983-86, assoc. dir. arts and humanities, 1986-88; pres. Calif. Inst. Arts, Valencia, 1988—; adj. assoc. prof. NYU Grad. Sch. Bus., 1984-85; cons. Wexner Found., Columbus, Ohio, 1986-87; selection panelist Input TV Screening Conf., Montreal, Can., and Granda, Spain, 1985-86; cons., panelist Nat. Endowment for Humanities, Washington, 1981-85; faculty chair Salzburg Seminar on Mus., 1989; co-dir. Arts and Govt. Program, The Am. Assembly, 1991. Editor: The Hopwood Anthology, 1981, Exhibiting Cultures, 1991, Museums and Communities, 1992; editor spl. issue Prooftexts jour., 1984. Bd. dirs. Sta. KCRW-FM (NPR), 1989—, J. Paul Getty Mus., 1990—, Inst. for African Humanities, Northwestern U., 1990—, Am. Coun. on the Arts, 1991—, L.A. Philharm. Assn., 1994—, Endowments, Inc., Bond Portfolio for Endowments, Inc., 1994—. Recipient Class of 1923 award, 1979, Faculty Recognition award, 1980 U. Mich.; Charles Dexter traveling fellow Harvard U., 1972, Ford fellow, 1969-74, vis. rsch. fellow Rockefeller Found., N.Y.C., 1981-83. Jewish. Office: Calif Inst Arts Office Pres 24700 Mcbean Pky Santa Clarita CA 91355-2340

LAVOIE, STEVEN PAUL, columnist, library director; b. Madison, Minn., Oct. 9, 1953; s. Clarence Donald and Lovetta (Gearhart) L.; m. Teresa Pei-Shiung Shen. BA, U. Calif., Berkeley, 1975, M of Libr. and Info. Studies, 1986. Head libr., writer Marin Ind. Jour., Novato, Calif., 1986-89; columnist, dir. of librs. Oakland (Calif.) Tribune, 1989—; reading coord. New Coll. Calif., San Francisco, 1978-82; founder Black Bart Poetry Soc., Oakland, 1982; local v.p. Communications Workers of Am., Cedar Rapids, Iowa, 1984-85; pres. Pacific Ctr. for Book Arts, San Francisco, 1990-92, treas., 1994—; rep. Newspaper Guild, San Francisco, 1992-93; bd. dirs. U. Calif. Sch. of Libr. & Info. Studies Alumni Assn. Author: On The Way, 1982, Erosion Surface, 1984, Nine Further Plastics, 1984. Recipient Doris Green award Doris Green Editions, 1982, Mark Twain prize Mid-Am. Writing, 1984. Mem. Spl. Librs. Assn., Soc. Am. Baseball Rsch., Ina Coolbrith Cir. Home: 4085B Lincoln Ave Oakland CA 94602

LAW, CHRISTOPHER K., plastic surgeon; b. Hong Kong, Nov. 18, 1955. MD, U Pa., 1982. Chief plastic reconstructive surgery Denver Gen. Hosp., 1990—; with U. Colo. Health Sci. Ctr., Denver, 1990—; asst. prof. plastic surgery U. Colo., 1990—. Office: Univ Colo Health Sci Ctr Box C 309 8th & Colorado Blvd Denver CO 80262*

LAW, FLORA ELIZABETH (LIBBY LAW), retired community health and pediatrics nurse; b. Biddeford, Maine, Sept. 11, 1935; d. Arthur Parker and Flora Alma (Knutti) Butt; m. Robert F. Law, 1961; children : Susan E., Sarah F., Christian A., Martha F.; m. John F. Brown, Jr., 1982. BA, Davis and Elkins (W.Va.) Coll., 1957; postgrad., Cornell U.-N.Y. Hosp., N.Y.C., 1960; BSN, U. Nev., Las Vegas, 1976, MS in Counseling Edn., 1981. RN, Nev.; cert. sch. nurse. Staff nurse So. Nev. Community Hosp. (now Univ. Med. Ctr.), Las Vegas, 1975-76; relief charge nurse Valley Psychiat. Inst., Las Vegas, 1976; pub. health nurse Clark County Dist. Health Dept., Las Vegas, 1977-78; sch. nurse Clark County Sch. Dist., Las Vegas, 1978-94; ret., 1994. Chair task force on sch. nursing Nev.'s Commn. for Profl. Standards in Edn.; mem. nurse practice act revision com. Nev. State Bd. Nursing. Mem. Nat. Assn. Sch. Nurses (past state dir., sch. nurse liaison Clark County Tchrs. Assn.), NEA, Clark County Assn. Sch. Nurses (past pres.), Sigma Theta Tau. Home: 3420 Clandara Ave Las Vegas NV 89121-3701

LAW, JOHN MANNING, retired lawyer; b. Chgo., Dec. 5, 1927; s. Fred Edward and Elisabeth (Emmons) L.; m. Carol Lufkin Ritter, May 14, 1955; children: John E., Lucy L., Frederick R., Beth K. Student, U. Chgo., 1944-45, St. Ambrose Coll., 1945; BA, Colo. Coll., 1948; JD, U. Colo., 1951. Bar: Colo. 1952, U.S. Ct. Appeals (10th cir.) 1954, U.S. Supreme Ct. Atty. trust dept. Harris Bank, Chgo., 1951-52; ptnr. Law, Nagel & Clark, Denver, 1958-84; assoc. Dickerson, Morrissey, Zarlengo & Dwyer, 1952-57; also bd. dirs. Law, Nagel & Clark, Denver; ptnr. Law & Knous, Denver, 1984-93, retired, 1993; mem. law com. Colo. Bd. Law Examiners, 1971-81, Colo. Ofcls. Compensation Commn., 1985-89. Mem. Moffatt Tunnel Commn., Denver, 1966-90. Capt. USNR, 1945-77, ret. Fellow Colo. Bar Found. (charter); mem. ABA (legal assistance to mil. person 1972-77, past chair), Colo. Bar Assn. (mem. bd. govs. 1968-71), Denver Bar Assn. (trustee 1971-74), Internat. Soc. Barristers, Law Club, Univ. Club Denver, Denver Country Club. Republican. Presbyterian. Home: 3333 E Florida Ave Apt 35 Denver CO 80210-2541

LAWES, PATRICIA JEAN, art educator; b. Mathis, Tex., June 28, 1940; d. Thomas Ethan and Alma Dena (Pape) Allen; m. Elmer Thomas Lawes, Apr. 9, 1960; children: Linda Lee, Tracy Dena. BA in Art Edn., U. Wyo., 1976; MA in Curriculum and Instruction, Leslie Coll., 1988. Cert. tchr., Wyo. Elem. art tchr. Laramie County Sch. Dist. # 1, Cheyenne, Wyo., 1977—, facilitator elem. art. and gifted edn., 1979-87; ret. Laramie County Sch. Dist. #1, 1994; owner, sec. Dundele Ltd. Liability Co., Mesa, Ariz., 1994—; artist in the sch. Mesa, Ariz., 1994-95; judge F.E. Warren AFB Artist Craftsman Show, Cheyenne, 1988-92, adjudicator for music festival for Assn. of Christian Sch Internat., Tempe, Ariz. Author, mem. visual arts task force various curricula; Author, dir: The Apron Caper, 1989 (recognition 1990), Oh Where Oh Were Have Those Little Dawgs Gone, 1989 (recognition 1990); exhibitions include Wyoming Artists Assn., Wyo., 1977, Washington Congressional Exhibit, 1977-78. Recipient Cert. of Appreciation Mayor Erickson, Cheyenne, 1986, MWR Vol. Recognition F.E. Warren Moral, Welfare, Recreation Dept., Cheyenne, 1988-93; grantee Coun. on Arts, Cheyenne, 1987-91. Mem. NEA, Am. Fedn. Tchrs., Nat. art Edn. Assn., Wyo. Assn. Gifted Edn. (bd. dirs., W.E. rep. 1986—, presenter, chmn. state ass. award 1992—), Wyo. Arts Alliance for Edn. (presenter, bd. dirs. 1987—, sec. 1988-91, visual arts task force, chmn. state arts award 1990-92), Wyo. Coun. Arts (slide bank 1986—), Wyo. Odessey of Mind (bd. dirs. 1991-92), Wyo. Women's Fedn. Club (chmn. state safety 1972-75), Order of Eastern Star (presiding officer, worthy matron 1984-85, grand officer 1990-91), Daughters of Nile, Assn. of Christian Schs. Internat. Music Festival (adjudicator 1995). Office: Laramie County Sch Dist # 1 2810 House Ave Cheyenne WY 82001-2860

LAWES, ROBERT BROCK, marketing educator, academic administrator; b. Lake Charles, La., Oct. 27, 1937; s. Robert Bonnabel and Clara Rose (Thompson) L.; m. JoAnna Pace, June 15, 1957 (div. Aug. 1972); children: Alita, Guion; m. Paige Nickson Elrod, Nov. 19, 1972; 1 child, Christiaan DeValle. BSBA, U. S.W. La., 1958; M in Internat. Mgmt., Am. Grad. Sch. Internat. Mgmt., 1976, U. Hawaii, 1985-91. Sales rep. JAX Beer Co., Lake Charles, La., 1959-62, advt. mgr., 1962-65, gen. mgr., 1965-68, pres., CEO, 1968-72; stores mgr. U.S. Mil. Sealift Command, Bklyn., 1973-74; dir., rsch. Ctr. Am. Grad. Sch., Glendale, Ariz., 1975-77; gen. mgr. Gen. Distbrs., Tamuning, Guam, 1977-80; instr. U.S. Navy Edn. and Tng. Command, Pearl Harbor, Hawaii, 1981-84; assoc. prof. Chaminade U., Honolulu, 1984—; acting dir. MBA program Chaminade U., 1995—; lectr. Small Bus. Adminstrn. SCORE Honolulu, 1984—, small bus. mgmt. U. Hawaii,, 1985, Windward Community Coll., Kaneohe, 1985, 91; cons. Bus. Consulting Resources, Honolulu, 1985. Editor: ISRC Jour., 1976; contbr. articles to profl. jours. Pres. Young Men's Bus. Club, Lake Charles, 1970, With USMCR, 1955-60. Grantee Weyerhauser Found. Am. Grad. Sch. Internat. Mgmt., Glendale, 1976. Mem. Am. Mktg. Assn., Direct Response Advt. and Mktg. Assn. Hawaii, Am. Advt. Fedn. Office: Chaminade U Bus Sch 3140 Waialae Ave Honolulu HI 96816-1510

LAWIT, JOHN WALTER, lawyer; b. Phila., Aug. 13, 1950; s. Alfred and Marilyn Jane (Balis) L.; m. Susan Scarborough, Nov. 24, 1974 (div. May 1980); m. Susan Stein, July 15, 1984; children: Andrew Alejandro, Samuel Martin and Ivan Luis (twins). Student, U. Bridgeport, 1968-70; B of Univ. Studies, U. N.Mex., 1972; JD, Franklin Pierce Law Ctr., Concord, N.H., 1977. Bar: Pa. 1978, N.Mex. 1980, Tex. 1992, U.S. Dist. Ct. (ea. dist.) Pa. 1978, U.S. Dist. Ct. N.Mex. 1980. Investigator Franklin Pierce Law Ctr., 1976-77; social researcher Commun. Svc. Coun., Concord, 1977-78; sole practitioner N.Y.C., 1978-79; atty., assoc. McCallister, Fairfield, Query, Strotz & Stribling, Albuquerque, 1979-80; sole practitioner Albuquerque, 1980—; adj. prof. immigration law U. N.Mex. Sch. Law, 1983, 84, 88; spl. immigration counsel U. N.Mex., Albuquerque, 1987—; U.S. immigration judge US. Dept. Justice, 1985; apptd. mem. N.Mex. Internat. Trade/Investment Coun., 1984-87, N.Mex. Border Commn., 1982-86; hon. cons. atty. Ministry Fgn. Affairs Republic of Mex., 1983; lobbyist, author, drafter N.Mex. Immigration & Nationality Law Practice Act. Presenter in field. Founder, profl. cons. Jewish Family Svcs. of Albuquerque, 1988—; bd. dirs., pres. Rainbow House Internat. Adoption, Belen, N.Mex., 1987—; v.p. N.Mex. Refugee Assn., Albuquerque, 1979-84; bd. dirs. N.Mex. Civil Liberties Union, 1988-90; mem. adv. bd. Healing the Children, Albuquerque, 1989—; bd. dirs. Inst. for Spanish Arts, 1994—. Recipient Disting. Svcs. award Cath. Social Svcs., 1988. Mem. N.Mex. State Bar (chair internat. and immigration lawyers sect. 1990-91, bd. dirs. 1988-90), Albuquerque Bar Assn., Am. Immigration Lawyers Assn. (nat. chair 1988-89), El Paso Assn. Immigration and Nationality Lawyers. Office: 900 Gold Ave SW Albuquerque NM 87102-3043 also: 121 E Palace Ave Santa Fe NM 87501-2010

LAWLER, ALICE BONZI (MRS. OSCAR T. LAWLER), retired college administrator, civic worker; b. Milan, Italy, Dec. 25, 1914; came to U.S. 1920, naturalized 1925; d. Ercole and Alice (Spalding) Bonzi; m. Morris Warner Mothershead, Sept. 15, 1935 (dec.); children: Warner Bonzi, Maria (Mrs. Andrei Rogers); m. Oscar Thom Lawler, May 1989 (dec.). Pvt. pupil music and art; student Pasadena City Coll., 1958-60. Ptnr. Floal Toy Co., Pasadena, Calif., 1942-44; community adv. Fgn. Student Program, Pasadena City Coll., from 1952, past dir. Community Liaison Ctr. Chmn. Am. Field Service Internat. Scholarships, Pasadena, 1953-55; mem. West Coast adv. bd. Inst. Internat. Edn., San Francisco, 1957-70; v.p. San Rafael Sch. PTA, Pasadena, 1945-46; active Community Chest, ARC, Pasadena; chmn. Greater Los Angeles Com. Internat. Student and Visitor Services, 1962; mem. Woman's Civic League Pasadena, chmn. city affairs com., 1985, pres., 1986-87; bd. dirs. Fine Arts Club of Pasadena, 1983-85, Pasadena City Coll. Found., 1983-85; commr. City of Pasadena Cultural Heritage Commn., 1984-89; active Caltech Y. Bd., 1993—, Caltech Assocs., 1993—. Decorated knight Govt. of Italy, 1975; recipient citation City of L.A., 1992; named Woman of Yr., Federated Italians City of L.A., County of L.A., State of Calif., 1992. Fellow Nat. History Mus., L.A.; mem. Assn. Internat. Educators (life, chmn. community sect. and v.p. 1964-65, chmn. U.S. study abroad com. 1969-70), Am. Assn. UN (chpt. 2d v.p. 1964), Soc. Women Geographers, Am. Friends Middle East, Zonta Internat. (hon. mem.), Am. Women for Internat. Understanding, Pasadena City Coll. Retirees Assn. (bd. dirs. 1991), Omicron Mu Delta. Club: International (Pasadena). Author: Social Customs and Manners in the United States, 1957; Dining Customs Around the World, 1982; co-author: 15 Years of the Foreign Student Program at Pasadena City College, 1965. Editor: Students to People to Future, 1971. Home: 480 S Orange Grove Blvd Apt 12 Pasadena CA 91105-1721

LAWLER, RICK M., publishing executive; b. Watsonville, Calif., June 13, 1949; s. Myrle W. and Mae A. (Summers) L.; m. Alice T. Tang, May 28, 1981; 1 child, Sara. Tech. instr., USAF Tech. Sch., Tex., 1970; career acctg., Heald Bus. Coll., Fresno, Calif., 1973; student, CSU, Fresno, 1974-76. News editor Shafter (Calif.) Press, 1977-82; editor Los Gatos (Calif.) Times-Observer, 1982-83; media rels. mgr. Systems Plus, Inc., Palo Alto, Calif., 1983-84; adminstrv. asst. U. Calif. Davis Dept. Internal Medicine, Sacramento, 1984-88; sr, word processing specialist U.Calif Davis Dept. Math., 1988-90; adminstrv. asst. U. Calif. Davis Office Continuing Med. Edn., Sacramento, 1990-93; programmer, analyst U. Calif.-Davis Med. Ctr. Info. Svcs., Davis, Calif., 1993—; owner, pub. MinRef Press, Sacramento, 1989—; co-owner, pub. Lawriel-Gabler Publ., Inc., San Jose, 1982-84. Author: Valley Fire, 1991, How to Write to World Leaders, 1992; editor: Abortion Stories, 1992, Myth: The Extinction Factor, 1994. Sgt. USAF, 1968-72. Mem. Authors Guild, Nat. Writers Club. Mem. Seventh-day Adventists. Home: 8379

Langtree Way Sacramento CA 95823-5645 Office: U Calif Davis Med Ctr IS User Support 2525 Stockton Blvd # 1025 Sacramento CA 95817-2207

LAWLESS, MICHAEL WILLIAM, strategic management educator; b. N.Y.C., June 20, 1948; s. Harvey Edward and Anne Elizabeth (Hindenlang) L.; m. Margaret Elizabeth Minton, May 24, 1986; 1 child, Blake Minton. BS, St. John's U., 1970; MBA, UCLA, 1974, PhD, 1980. Asst. prof. U. Colo., Boulder, 1982-90, assoc. prof. strategic mgmt., 1990—; dir. Tech. and Innovation Mgmt. Rsch. Ctr., Boulder, 1987—; vis. prof. UCLA, 1986, Dartmouth Coll., 1992; cons. IBM, Wickes, Phillips Petroleum Corp., US West Corp., U.S. Dept. Def., 1980—. Author: Technology and Strategy, 1994; editor High Tech. Mgmt. Rsch. Jour., 1990, Org. Sci. Jour., 1990; mem. editorial bd. Acad. of Mgmt. Jour.; contbr. articles to profl. jours. Lt. comdr. USNR. Mem. Acad. Mgmt. (program chmn. 1990, consortium chmn. 1990, div. chmn. 1991, editor Jour. 1993), Ascendant scholar 1990), Am. Econ. Assn., Strategic Mgmt. Soc., Inst. Mgmt. Sci., USN Inst., USNR Assn., Beta Gamma Sigma. Office: U Colo Grad Sch Bus PO Box 419 # U Boulder CO 80309-0419

LAWLOR, GLENN JOSEPH, allergist; b. Reno, 1940. MD, UCLA, 1966. With UCLA Student Health Allergy Clinic; assoc. prof. pediatrics UCLA. Office: 4835 Van Nuys Blvd Van Nuys CA 91403-2109*

LAWRENCE, DAVID M., health facility administrator; b. 1940. MD, U. Ky., 1966; MPH, U. Wash., 1973. Intern in internal medicine, pediat.; with Kaiser Found. Health Plan and Hosps., Oakland, Calif., 1981—, now chmn., CEO; various professorships, directorships and fellowships with U. Wash., Johns Hopkins U., U. Ky.; dir. Pacific Gas and Electric Co., 1994—, Hewlett Packard, Healthcare Forum, Bay Area Coun., Urban Strategies Coun., CCAC. Mem. APHA, Am. Hosp. Assn., Am. Coll. Preventive Medicine, Calif. Assn. Hosps. and Health Sys., Group Health Assn. of Am., Western Consortium for Pub. Health, Calif. Bus. Roundtable Collective Bargaining Forum. Office: Kaiser Found Health Plan & Hosp 1 Kaiser Plz Oakland CA 94612-3610

LAWRENCE, DEAN GRAYSON, retired lawyer; b. Oakland, Calif.; d. Henry C. and Myrtle (Grayson) Schmidt; A.B., U. Calif.-Berkeley, 1934, J.D., 1939. Admitted to Calif. bar, 1943, U.S. Dist. Ct., 1944, U.S. Ct. Appeals, 1944, Tax Ct. U.S., 1945, U.S. Treasury Dept., 1945, U.S. Supreme Ct., 1967; asso. Pillsbury, Madison & Sutro, San Francisco, 1944, 45; gen. practice Oakland, 1946-50, San Jose, 1952-60, Grass Valley, 1960-63, 66—; county counsel Nevada County, 1964-65. Nevada County Bd. Suprs., 1969-73, chmn., 1971. Vol. animal welfare movement; sec. Nev. County Humane Animal Shelter Bd., 1966-86; state humane officer, 1966-82; pres. Nev. County Humane Soc., 1974-86, mem. Humane Soc. U.S., Fund for Animals; pres. Humane Information Svc., 1992—; bd. dirs. Nevada County Health Planning Council, Golden Empire Areawide Health Planning Council, 1974, 75; trustee Grass Valley Pub. Libr., 1962-64. Mem. People for Ethical Treatment of Animals, Doris Day Animal League, Farm Animal Reform Movement, Performing Animal Welfare Soc., Pet Adoption League, Bus. and Profl. Women's Club, AAUW, Animal Protection Inst. Am. (Humanitarian of Yr. 1986), Animal Legal Defense Fund, Golden Empire Human Soc. (Lifetime Achievement award 1990), League Unbiased Women, Phi Beta Kappa, Sigma Xi, Kappa Beta Pi, Pi Mu Epsilon, Pi Lambda Theta. Episcopalian. Office: PO Box 66 Grass Valley CA 95945-0066

LAWRENCE, DEBORAH JEAN, statistician; b. San Jose, Calif., June 25, 1960. BA in Math., San Jose State U., 1982; MS in Stats., Stanford U., 1985. Math. aide Info. Mgmt. Internat., Moffet Field, Calif., 1980-82; group engr. Lockheed Missiles and Space Co., Sunnyvale, Calif., 1982-89; total quality mgmt. mgr. Analog Devices, Inc., Santa Clara, Calif., 1989—; reengring. spl. interest group leader Coun. for Continuous Improvement, 1994—. Author tech. papers. Mem. Am. Soc. for Quality Control (sr. mem., cert. engr.), Am. Statis. Assn. Office: Analog Devices Inc. M/S 431 1500 Space Park Dr Santa Clara CA 95054-3434

LAWRENCE, GARY SHELDON, academic administrator; b. Portland, Oreg., Aug. 31, 1946; s. Harry Sheldon and Nellie Maude (Mackey) L.; m. Maya Tsuji, Sept. 22, 1974; children: Katherine, Matthew. BA cum laude, Claremont Men's Coll., 1968; MLS, U. Calif., Berkeley, 1973, M in Pub. Policy, 1975, D in Libr. and Info. Studies, 1980. Lab. asst. Inst. Libr. Rsch. U. Calif., Berkeley, 1973, cons. to Office of Asst. Chancellor-Budget and Planning, 1974-75, rsch. asst. Inst. Libr. Rsch., 1976, tchg. assoc. Sch. Libr. and Info. Sci., 1976, project mgr. online catalog evaluation project, 1981-83, statis. cons. mgmt. affirmative action working group, 1981-83, sr. ad.ninstrv. analyst Libr. Studies and Rsch. Divsn., 1976-80, assoc. mgr. rsch. and analysis Office of Pres., 1980-82, dir. Libr. Studies and Rsch. Divsn. Office of Pres., 1982-87, coord. libr. affairs Office Assoc. V.P. Acad. Affairs, 1987-93, coord. librs. & academic computing Office Vice Provost Rsch.; cons. Manifest Sys., Inc., Coun. on Libr. Resources, Inc., J. Matthews and Associates, Inc., Grass Valley, Calif., Libr. and Info. Svcs. for the N.W., Fred Meyer Charitable Trust, Portland, Oreg., Assn. Coll. and Rsch. Librs., ALA, Chgo., Ohio Bd. Regents, Columbus, U. Ariz., Capital Facilities Planning Office; prin. investigator costs and features of online catalogs Coun. on Libr. Resources, Inc., 1982-83; U. Calif. del. Document Delivery Com. of Calif. Libr. Authority for Sys. and Svcs., 1983-84. Author: (with others) Advances in Library Organization and Administration, 1984; rsch. notes editor Coll. and Rsch. Librs., 1984-90; contbr. articles to profl. jours. 1st lt. U.S. Army, 1969-71. Mem. ALA (mem. editl. bd. Assn. Coll. and Rsch. Librs. 1984-90; chair rsch. com. Libr. and Info. Tech. Assn. 1993-94, Gaylord award com. 1993-94, chair libr. rsch. task force 1992-93, rep. to ALA rsch. and statistics assembly 1992-94, chair fuzzy match interest group 1986-89; co-chair machine-assisted ref. sect. ann. conf. program com. Ref. and Adult Svcs. Divsn. 1987, Libr. Rsch. Round Table 1977-89, Libr. Rsch. Roundtable 1977-78), Am. Soc. for Info. Sci. (treas. Bay Area chpt. 1979). Office: U Calif Office Libr Affairs 300 Lakeside Dr 18th Fl Oakland CA 94612-3550

LAWRENCE, GLENN SCOTT, state official; b. Salt Lake City, Apr. 7, 1950; s. Don Pershing and Helen (Heath) L.; m. Jana Kirby, Sept. 2, 1976; children: Kari, Rebecca, Jill, David. AS, Coll. Ea. Utah, 1971; BS, Weber State U., 1976; MPA, Brigham Young U., 1979. Dir. legis. printing Utah State Legis., Salt Lake City, 1976-85; dir. div. ctrl. svcs. Utah State Dept. Adminstrv. Svc., Salt Lake City, 1985-89, state PC lab. coord., 1989-90; support svcs. coord. Utah State Dept. Environ. Quality, Salt Lake City, 1990-91; quality coord. Utah State Tax Commn., Salt Lake City, 1991 ; v.p. Am. Western Press Assn., Layton, Utah, 1985—; sr. ptnr. Am. Western Cons., Layton, 1993—. Writer, editor, designer: (tech. booklet) Guidelines for Desktop Publishing, 1987-90, (tech. periodical) Support Notes, 1989-91; writer, designer: (info. booklet) Successful Resume Writing, 1994. Mem. Layton City Recycling Com., 1993—; team leader, facilitator State of Utah Mgr. of Yr. Award, Salt Lake City, 1993-94. Mem. ASTD, ASPA, In Plant Printing Mgmt. Assn. (Mem. of Yr. award 1988). Home: 1514 Tartan Way Layton UT 84040-8232

LAWRENCE, JEROME, playwright, director, educator; b. Cleve., July 14, 1915; s. Samuel and Sarah (Rogen) L. BA, Ohio State U., 1937, LHD (hon.), 1963; DLitt, Fairleigh Dickinson U., 1968; DFA (hon.), Villanova U., 1969; LittD, Coll. Wooster, 1983. Dir. various summer theaters Pa. and Mass., 1934-37; reporter, telegraph editor Wilmington (Ohio) News Jour., 1937; editor Lexington Daily News, Ohio, 1937; continuity editor radio Sta. KMPC, Beverly Hills, Calif., 1938-39; sr. staff writer CBS, Hollywood, Calif. and N.Y.C., 1939-42; pres., writer, dir. Lawrence & Lee, Hollywood, N.Y.C. and London, 1945—; vis. prof. Ohio State Univ., 1969, Salzburg Seminar in Am. Studies, 1972, Baylor Univ., 1978; prof. playwriting Univ. So. Calif. Grad. Sch., 1984—; co-founder, judge Margo Jones award, N.Y.C., 1958—; co-founder, pres. Am. Playwrights Theatre, Columbus, Ohio, 1970-85; bd. dirs. Am. Conservatory Theatre, San Francisco, 1970-80, Stella Adler Theatre, L.A., 1987—, Plumstead Playhouse, 1986—; keynote speaker Bicentennial of Bill of Rights, Congress Hall, Phila., 1991; hon. mem. Nat. Theatre Conf., 1993; adv. bd. Am. Theatre in Lit. Contemporary Arts Ednl. Project, 1993—. Scenario writer Paramount Studios, 1941; master playwright NYU Inst. Performing Arts, 1967-69; author-dir. for: radio and television UN Broadcasts; Army-Navy programs D-Day, VE-Day, VJ-Day; author: Railroad Hour, Hallmark Playhouse, Columbia Workshop; author: Off Mike, 1944, (biography, later made into PBS-TV spl.) Actor: Life and Times of Paul Muni, 1978 (libretto and lyrics by Lawrence and Lee, music by Billy Goldenberg); co-author, dir.: (album) One God; playwright: Live Spelled Backwards, 1969, Off Mike, (mus. with Robert E. Lee) Look, Ma, I'm Dancin', 1948 (music by Hugh Martin), Shangri-La, 1956 (music by Harry Warren, lyrics by James Hilton, Lawrence and Lee), Mame, 1966 (score by Jerry Herman), Dear World, 1969 (score by Jerry Herman), (nonmus.) Inherit the Wind (translated and performed in 34 langs., named best fgn. play of year London Critics Poll 1960), Auntie Mame, 1956, The Gang's All Here, 1959, Only in America, 1959, A Call on Kuprin, 1961, Diamond Orchid (revised as Sparks Fly Upward, 1966), 1965, The Incomparable Max, 1969, The Crocodile Smile, 1970, The Night Thoreau Spent in Jail, 1970, (play and screenplay) First Monday in October, 1978, (written for opening of Thurber Theatre, Columbus) Jabberwock: Improbablilities Lived and Imagined by James Thurber in the Fictional City of Columbus, Ohio, 1974, (with Robert E. Lee) Whisper in the Mind, 1994, The Angels Weep, 1992, (novel) A Golden Circle: A Tale of the Stage and the Screen and Music of Yesterday and Now and Tomorrow and Maybe the Day After Tomorrow, 1993; Decca Dramatic Albums, Musi-Plays.; contbg. editor Dramatics mag., mem. adv. bd., contbr. Writer's Digest; Lawrence and Lee collections at Libr. and Mus. of the Performing Arts, Lincoln Ctr., N.Y., Harvard's Widener Libr., Cambridge, Mass., Jerome Lawrence & Robert E. Lee Theatre Rsch. Inst. at Ohio State U., Columbus, est. 1986. A founder, overseas corr. Armed Forces Radio Service; mem. Am. Theatre Planning Bd.; bd. dirs. Nat. Repertory Theatre, Plumstead Playhouse; mem. adv. bd. USDAN Center for Creative and Performing Arts, East-West Players, Performing Arts Theatre of Handicapped, Inst. Outdoor Drama; mem. State Dept. Cultural Exchange Drama Panel, 1961-69; del. Chinese-Am. Writers Conf., 1982, 86, Soviet-Am. Writers Conf., 1984, 85; Am. Writers rep. to Hiroshima 40th Anniversary Commemorative, Japan, 1985; mem. U.S. Cultural Exchange visit to theatre communities of Beijing and Shanghai, 1985; adv. coun. Calif. Ednl. Theatre Assn., Calif. State U., Calif. Repertory Co., Long Beach, 1984—. Recipient N.Y. Press Club award, 1942, CCNY award, 1948, Radio-TV Life award, 1948, Mirror awards, 1952, 53, Peabody award, 1949, 52, Variety Showmanship award 1954, Variety Critics poll 1955, Outer-Circle Critics award 1955, Donaldson award, 1955, Ohioana award,Ohio Press Club award, 1959, Brit. Drama Critics award, 1960, Moss Hart Meml. award, 1967, State Dept. medal, 1968, Pegasus award, 1970, Lifetime Achievement award Am. Theatre Assn., 1979, Nat. Thespian Soc. award, 1980, Pioneer Broadcasters award, 1981, 95, Diamond Circle award, 1995, Ohioana Library career medal, Master of Arts award Rocky Mountain Writers Guild, 1982, Centennial Award medal Ohio State U., 1970, William Inge award and lectureship Independence Community Coll., 1983, 86—, Disting. Contbr. award Psychologists for Social Responsibility, 1985, ann. awards San Francisco State U., Pepperdine U., Career award Southeastern Theatre Conf., 1990; named Playwright of Yr. Baldwin-Wallace Coll., 1960; named to Honorable Order of Ky. Colonels, 1965, Tenn. Colonels, 1988; named to Theater Hall of Fame, 1990. Fellow Coll. Am. Theatre, Kennedy Ctr.; mem. Nat. Theatre Conf. (hon.), Acad. Motion Picture Arts and Scis., Acad. TV Arts and Scis. (2 Emmy award 1988), Authors League (coun.), ANTA (dir., v.p.), Ohio State U. Assn. (dir.), Radio Writers' Guild (founder, pres.), Writers Guild Am. (dir., founding mem. Valentine Davies award), Dramatists Guild (coun.), ASCAP, Calif. Ednl. Theatre Assn. (Profl. Artist award 1992), Century Club N.Y., Phi Beta Kappa, Sigma Delta Chi.

LAWRENCE, KELLY JOY, federal agency administrator; b. Amsterdam, N.Y., May 2, 1958; d. Carl Douglas and Patricia Louise (Brown) Pearson; m. Lawrence J. Lawrence, June 19, 1982. BA in Orgnl. Adminstrn., Alaska Pacific U., 1994. Clk. U.S. Postal Svc., Anchorage, 1980-87, account rep., 1987-90, mgr. comml. accounts, 1990-92, mgr. postal bus. ctr., 1992—; coord. Postal Customer Coun., Anchorage, 1990-92. Dir. hospitality Am. Mktg. Assn., Anchorage, 1992-93; v.p. Bus. Profl. Women's Assn., Anchorage, 1991. With U.S. Army, 1976-79. Named Profl. Bus. Woman of Yr., Bus. Profl. Women's Orgn., 1991. Office: US Postal Svc 3201 C St Ste 505 Anchorage AK 99503-3934

LAWRENCE, PAUL FREDERIC, educational consultant; b. Paterson, N.J., Mar. 20, 1912; s. Joshua Emanuel and Louise (Hill) L.; m. Vivian Ann Hall, Sept. 21, 1941; children: Katherine Louise, Robin Ann. BS in Edn., Kean Coll., 1935; MA in Edn., Stanford U., 1945, EdD, 1947; LHD, Kean Coll., 1965. Teaching and adminstrn. credentials, N.J., Calif. Tchr., art supr. Princeton (N.J.) Pub. Schs., 1935-41; assoc. prof., asst. dir. Howard U., Washington, 1948-56; supt. of schs. Willowbrook Sch. Dist., L.A., 1956-60; prof. edn., dean counseling State Coll. Alameda County, Hayward, Calif., 1960-63; assoc. state supt. pub. instrn., chief Divsn. Higher Edn. State Calif., 1963-67; regional commr. edn. Region IX Federal Govt., 1967-73; dep. assoc. commr. U.S. Office Edn., Washington, 1973-77; dir. postsecondary liaison U.S. Office of Edn., Washington, 1978-83; owner, dir. Cons. in Edn. Policy and Adminstrn., Sacramento, 1983—; bd. dirs. Scholastic Mag., N.Y.C.; com. mem. Nat. Acad. Sci., Washington, Nat. Conf. Christians and Jews, L.A.; desegregation monitor 9th Dist. Fed. Ct., San Francisco, spl. monitor desegregation case, 1984—. Co-author: Negro American Heritage, 1965, Opportunities in Interracial Colleges, 1947; contbr. articles to profl. jours. With USAF, 1942-46, Lt. col. USAFR, 1946-70. Recipient Disting. Svc. award NABSE, New Orleans, Outstanding Svc. awards City of San Bernardino, Calif., U.S. Dept. HEW, Washington, Calif. Senate and Assembly, Sacramento. Mem. Nat. Conf. Parents and Tchrs., USAF Acad. (liason advisor), Calif. State Commn. on Edn., Exploratory Commn. on Edn., Select Com. Study Higher Edn., Phi Delta Kappa. Home: 4837 Crestwood Way Sacramento CA 95822-1660 Office: Cons in Ednl Policy 615 J St Sacramento CA 95814-2405

LAWRENCE, PAULA DENISE, physical therapist; b. Ft. Worth, May 21, 1959; d. Roddy Paul and Kay Frances (Spivey) Gillis; m. Mark Jayson Lawrence, Apr. 20, 1985. BS, Tex. Women's U., 1982. Lic. phys. therapist, Tex., Calif. Sales mgr. R and K Camping Ctr., Garland, Tex., 1977-82; staff physical therapist Longview (Tex.) Regional Hosp., 1982-83, dir. phys. therapy, 1983-87, dir. rehab. svcs., 1987-88; staff phys. therapist MPH Home Health, Longview, Tex., 1983-84; owner, pres. Phys. Rehabil. Ctr., Hemet, Calif., 1988—; mem. adv. com. div. health occupations Kilgore (Tex.) Coll., 1985-88; mem. profl. adv. bd. Hospice Longview, 1985-88. Mem. NAFE, Am. Phys. Therapy Assn., Calif. Phys. Therapy Assn., Am. Bus. Women's Assn. (v.p. 1987, 89, pres. 1990, Woman of Yr. 1988, 91), Assistance League Aux., Soroptimist (corr. sec. 1992, dir. 1993-95, sec. 1995), Psi Chi, Alpha Rho Alpha. Home: 899 Kristin Ln Hemet CA 92545-1645 Office: 901 S State St Ste 500 Hemet CA 92543-7127

LAWRENCE, RICHARD A., plastic surgeon; b. Portsmouth, Ohio, 1937. MD, U Mich, 1963. Plastic surgeon St. Mary Corwin Hosp., Pueblo. Office: 202 W 21st St Pueblo CO 81003-2514*

LAWRENCE, ROBERT DON, pathologist, consultant; b. Oakland, Calif., Jan. 2, 1941; s. Ernest Orlando and Mary (Blumer) L.; m. Eleanor Long Ardery, Apr. 2, 1967; children: Amy, Beth. BS in Chemistry, U. Pacific, 1962; MD, UCLA, 1966. Diplomate Am. Bd. Pathology. Intern UCLA Hosp, 1966-67; resident Mayo Clinic, Rochester, Minn., 1969-72; Ptnr. Delta Pathology Assocs., Stockton, Calif., 1972—; forensic pathologist San Joaquin County Coroner's Office, Stockton, 1972—; lab. dir. SmithKline Beecham Clin. Lab., Stockton, 1972—; med. dir. Found. Health Plan, Sacramento/ Stockton, 1980-92. Author: Snap Diagnoses in Pathology, 1976, Forensic Pathology For The Primary Care Physician, 1982; contbr. aarticles to profl. jours. Bd. dirs. San Joaquin County Child Abuse Prevention Coun., Stockton, 1983-89; bd. dirs., v.p. Delta Blood Bank, Stockton, 1975—. Lt. USN, flight surgeon, 1967-69. Pathology fellow Mayo Clinic, Rochester, Minn., 1970-73. Mem. San Joaquin Young Man's Marching and Chowder Soc. Republican. Home: 1811 Monty Ct Stockton CA 95207-2402 Office: Delta Pathology Assocs 2291 W March Ln # 179E Stockton CA 95207-6652

LAWRENCE, SANFORD HULL, physician, immunochemist; b. Kokomo, Ind., July 10, 1919; s. Walter Scott and Florence Elizabeth (Hull) L. AB, Ind. U., 1941, MD, 1944. Intern Rochester (N.Y.) Gen. Hosp., 1944-45; resident Halloran Hosp., Staten Island, N.Y., 1946-49; chief med. svce. Ft. Ord Regl. Hosp., 1945-46; dir. biochemistry rsch. lab. San Fernando (Calif.) VA Hosp.; asst. prof. UCLA, 1950—; cons. internal medicine and cardiology U.S. Govt., Los Angeles County; lectr. Faculte de Medicine, Paris, various colls. Eng., France, Belgium, Sweden, USSR, India, Japan; chief med. svc. Ft. Ord Regional Hosp.; chmn. Titus, Inc., 1982—. Author: Zymogram in Clinical Medicine, 1965; contbr. articles to sci. jours.; author: Threshold of Valhalla, Another Way to Fly, My Last Satyr, and other short stories; traveling editor: Relax Mag. Mem. Whitley Heights Civic Assn., 1952—; pres. Halloran Hosp. Employees Assn., 1947-48. Served to maj. U.S. Army, 1945-46. Recipient Rsch. award TB and Health Assn., 1955-58, Los Angeles County Heart Assn., 1957-59, Pres. award, Queen's Blue Book award, Am. Men of Sci. award; named one of 2000 Men of Achievement, Leaders of Am. Sci., Ky. Col., named Hon. Mayor of West Point, Ky. Mem. AAAS, AMA, N.Y. Acad. Scis., Am. Fedn. Clin. Research, Am. Assn. Clin. Investigation, Am. Assn. Clin. Pathology, Am. Assn. Clin. Chemistry, Los Angeles County Med. Assn. Republican. Methodist. Home: 2014 Whitley Ave Los Angeles CA 90068-3235 also: 160 rue St Martin, 75003 Paris France

LAWRENCE, WILLIAM, JR., elementary education educator; b. L.A., Mar. 2, 1930; s. Willie and Nellie (January) L.; m. Elizabeth Johnson, Jan. 13, 1951; children: William III, Timothy Dwight, Walter Fitzgerald. BA in Psychology, Columbia Coll., Mo., 1981; LLB, LaSalle U., 1982; MA in Edn., Claremont Coll., 1992; postgrad., Calif. Coast U., 1992—. Enlisted U.S. Army, 1947, advanced through grades to lt., 1957, commd. sgt. maj., 1965; served U.S. Army, Vietnam, 1965-70; instr. U.S. Military Acad., West Point, N.Y., 1970-73; with Berlin Brigade, U.S. Army, Berlin, Germany, 1973-76; dep. sheriff L.A., 1958-65; probation officer San Berdnardino County, Calif., 1985-89; tchr. Pomona Unified Sch. Dist., Pomona, Calif., 1989—. Decorated U.S. Army Dist. Svc. Cross for Extraordinary Heroism in Combat, Silver Star, 7 Purple Hearts. Mem. Legion of Valor, 555Th Parachute Battalion (pres.). Democrat. Roman Catholic. Home: 1456 S Lilac Ave Bloomington CA 92316-2130 Office: Pomona Unified Sch Dist 800 N Garey Ave Pomona CA 91767-4616

LAWS, JULIE AUGUSTADT, computer consultant; b. Valley Stream, N.Y., Nov. 6, 1936; d. Herbert Walter and Ada Therese (Munroe) Augustadt; m. Richard E. Laws, June 21, 1958; children: Karen Laws Callaway, Kip. BA, Cornell U., 1957; MLS, U. Calif., 1970. Dir. libr. tech. svcs. Golden Gate Bapt. Theological Sem. Libr., Mill Valley, Calif., 1970-80; coll. libr. World Coll. West, Petaluma, Calif., 1980-86; pres. R & H Wholesale Hardware, San Francisco, 1987-91, computer cons., 1991-93; computer cons., 1994—. Home: 152 Hamerton Ave San Francisco CA 94131-3228

LAWSON, DANIEL DAVID, chemist, consultant; b. Tucson, Jan. 13, 1929; s. Morris and Virginia (Lawson) Duncan-Lawson; m. Margaret Charlotte Schaeffer, Aug. 18, 1957; children: David Dale, Monica Ann. BA, U. So. Calif., 1957, MS, 1960. Rsch. fellow Hastings Found., Altadena, Calif., 1960-61; chemist Jet Propulsion Lab. Calif. Inst. Tech., Pasadena, 1961-92, ret., 1992; dir. rsch. Spectra Rsch., Arcadia, Calif., 1958—. Contbr. articles to profl. jours.; patentee in field. With U.S. Army, 1948-61, Korea. Fellow Am. Inst. Chemists; mem. AAAS, Am. Chem. Soc., Electro Chem. Soc., So. Calif. Alumni Assn., Royal Chem. Soc. Home: 919 S Golden West Ave Arcadia CA 91007-6567

LAWSON, J(ENICE) EVELYN, quality assurance professional, pharmacist; b. Ozark, Mo., Jan. 20, 1952; d. Robert Evelyn and Jenice Gemima (Spiess) L. AA, East Cen. Coll., 1972; BS in Pharmacy, U. Mo., Kansas City, 1975; BS in Chemistry, Northwest Mo. State U., 1979; MS in Pharmaceutics and Pharm. Chemistry, Ohio State U., 1985. Registered pharmacist, Mo. Pharmacy intern Federmann Drug Store, Kansas City, 1974; staff pharmacist The Corner Drug, Maryville, Mo., 1975, St. Francis Hosp., Maryville, Mo., 1976-78, Easter's Ben Franklin Pharmacy, Maryville, Mo., 1979; grad. rsch., teaching assoc. Ohio State U., Columbus, 1980-84; pharmacist Boehringer Ingelheim, Ingelheim, Fed. Rep. Germany, 1985; computer programmer, cons., coll. pharmacy Ohio State U., Columbus, 1986-87; mgr. Lynn Drug Co., Columbus, 1987-88; regulatory compliance specialist Clorox Tech. Ctr., Pleasanton, Calif., 1989—; preposition 65 coord., 1989-94, monitor of upcoming legis. pertaining to co., rev. materials for compliance with regulations, submit documents to fed. EPA, Clorox Tech. Ctr., Pleasanton, 1989—. Tutor Laubach Literacy Action, Livermore, Calif., 1989; adult choir, handbell choir, children's choir, pianist, single adult min. worker Trinity Bapt. Ch., Livermore. Mem. Am. Pharm. Assn. Contra Costa German-Am. Club, Soc. Risk Analysis and Exposure Assessment, Diamond Toastmasters (sec. dist. 57 club 4582, 1991, treas. 1991—, pres. 1991, Competent Toastmaster award 1991, Able Toastmaster award 1993), Kappa Epsilon (Nellie Wakeman award 1983). Southern Baptist. Office: Clorox Tech Ctr PO Box 493 Pleasanton CA 94566-0803

LAWSON, KAY, political science educator; b. Salem, Oreg., Apr. 21, 1933; d. Arlo C. and Ethel L. (Jones) Davis; m. William Vincent Lawson, Apr. 30, 1952; children—Kevin Stuart, Marta Elizabeth. B.A. with honors in English Lit., U. Calif.-Berkeley, 1959, M.A. in Polit. Sci., 1962, Ph.D. in Polit. Sci., 1971. Postgrad. research polit. scientist Inst. Internat. Studies, U. Calif.-Berkeley, 1963-66, instr. extension div., 1963, 64; instr. dept. polit. sci. San Francisco State U., 1963, 1964-66, prof., 1968—; vis. prof. dept. polit. sci. Rutgers U., 1982, Columbia U., N.Y.C., 1982, U. London, 1987, London Sch. Polit. Sci. and Econs., 1987, U. Paris, Nanterre, France, 1987, U. Paris, Sorbonne, 1992, 94, 95, Fondation Nat. des Scis. Politiques, 1992, 94; participant, presenter papers profl. jours., meetings. Author: Political Parties and Democracy in the U.S.; The Comparative Study of Political Parties, The Human Polity. Editor: How Political Parties Work, Political Parties and Linkage, When Parties Fail. Mem. editorial bd. Western Polit. Quar. Jour., Polity, Comparative Political Studies, Party Politics, Modern and Contemporary France. Mem. Conf. Group on French Politics and Society, Bay Area Women in Polit. Sci., Calif. Com. on Fed. Constl. System, African Studies Assn. (nominating com. 1971-72, placement com. 1972-74, exec. bd. dirs. 1977-79), Am. Polit. Sci. Assn. (founder, sec. local sect. 1979-82, nominating com. women's caucus 1981-82, pres. 1989-90, mem. exec. coun. 1989-91, dissertation award com. 1983), Internat. Studies Assn., Com. for Party Renewal (exec. bd. dirs. 1979—), Western Polit. Sci. Assn. (exec. council 1979-81), Calif. Com. for Party Renewal (founder, chmn. 1982-84), Democrat. Home: 389 Gravatt Dr Berkeley CA 94705-1503 Office: San Francisco State U Dept Polit Sci San Francisco CA 94132 also: U Paris I Sorbonne, Dept Scis Politiques, 75005 Paris France

LAWSON, SCOTT LAWRENCE, dean, consultant; b. Greenwich, Conn., Mar. 20, 1964; s. James Archibald and Georgene Eva (Ricard) L.; m. Randi Lou Gammell, Sept. 27, 1986; children: Karli Anne Elizabeth, Makai Makana Caspian. BA in English, Calif. State U., 1990, MA in English, 1992. cert. microsoft cert. profl., microcomputer instr. Editor Community Presbyn., San Juan, Calif., 1992-93; textbook author/editor New Horizons Computer, Santa Ana, Calif., 1992-93; computer instr. Focus Automation, Costa Mesa, Calif., 1993-94; dean computer edn. The Focus Inst., Costa Mesa, Calif., 1994—; computer cons. San Juan Capistrano, Calif., 1991—. Author: (poems) Negative Capability, 1992, (book) Beginning QuarkXPress, 1992, The Music of Poetry, 1992, CorelDRAW Series, 1993. Recipient First Place award in Los Escribeantes poetry contest, 1985. Mem. MLA. Presbyn. Home: 32865 Calle Miguel San Juan Capistrano CA 92675-4430 Office: Automatic Data Processing 400 Covina Blvd San Dimas CA 91773

LAWSON, THOMAS, artist; b. Glasgow, Scotland, July 16, 1951; came to U.S., 1975; s. Edward and Margaret Lawson; m. Susan Morgan. MA (hons), U. St. Andrews, Scotland, 1973; MA, U. Edinburgh, Scotland, 1975; MPhil, CUNY, 1979. Artist various cities worldwide, 1975—; founding editor Real Life Mag., N.Y.C., 1979-94; instr. Sch. Visual Arts, N.Y.C., 1981-90; dean Calif. Inst. of the Arts, Valencia, 1990—; N.Y. advisor Alba Mag., Edinburgh, 1984-89; vis. instr. Rhode Island Sch. Design, Providence, N.Y., 1988-89; vis. faculty Calif. Inst. of the Arts, Valencia, 1986-89. Executed mural Manhattan Mcpl. Bldg., 1989-92; contbr. articles to profl. jours. Artist advisor Rotunda Gallery, Bklyn., 1985-90. Nat. Endowment for the Arts artists fellow, 1982-83, 85-86, 89-90; Real Life Mag. publ. grantee Nat. Endowment for the Arts, 1979-94, N.Y. State Coun. Arts, 1980-89. Mem. Coll. Art Assn. Office: Calif Inst of the Arts 24700 Mcbean Pky Valencia CA 91355-2340

LAWSON, THOMAS CHENEY, fraud examiner; b. Pasadena, Calif., Sept. 21, 1955; s. William McDonald and Joan Bell (Jaffee) L.; children: Christopher, Brittany. Student, Calif. State U., Sacramento, 1973-77. Cert. internat. investigator, fraud examiner. Pres. Tomatron Co., Pasadena, 1970-88, Tom's Tune Up & Detail, Pasadena, 1971-88, Tom's Pool Svc., Sacramento,

1975-78, Tom Supply Co., 1975—; mgmt. trainee Permoid Process Co., L.A., 1970-75; prof. automechanics Calif. State U., Sacramento, 1973-75; regional sales cons. Hoover Co., Burlingame, 1974-76; mktg. exec. River City Prodns., Sacramento, 1977-78; territorial rep. Globe div. Burlington House Furniture Co., 1978; So. Calif. territorial rep. Marge Carson Furniture, Inc., 1978-80; pres. Ted L. Gunderson & Assos., Inc., Westwood, Calif., 1980-81; pres., CEO Apscreen, Newport Beach, Calif., 1980—; founder Creditbase Co., Newport Beach, Worldata Corp., Newport Beach, Trademark Enforcement Corp., L.A.; pres. Carecheck, Inc., Newport Beach, Calif., 1990—; CEO Badchex, Inc., Newport Beach, Calif., 1992—. Calif. Rehab. scholar, 1974-77. Mem. Christian Businessmen's Com. Internat., Coun. Internat. Investigators, Am. Soc. Indsl. Security (cert., chmn. Orange County chpt. 1990), Nat. Pub. Records Rsch. Assn., Pers. and Indsl. Rels. Assn., World Assn. Detectives, Assn. Cert. Fraud Examiners, Soc. Human Resource Mgmt. Office: 2043 Westcliff Dr Ste 300 Newport Beach CA 92660-5511

LAWTON, LARRY DAVID, lawyer; b. Cheyenne, Wyo., June 12, 1942; s. David Dwight and June Creole (Estes) L.; m. Ida Beth Aullman, June 8, 1966; children: Lynn David, Lowell Dale, Lance Donald, Lorin Michael. BS in Polit. Sci., U. Wyo., 1969; JD, Duke U., 1970. Bar: Calif. 1971, Wyo. 1973, U.S. Dist. Ct. Wyo., U.S. Dist. Ct. (no. dist.) Calif., U.S. Supreme Ct., U.S. Cir. Ct. (10th cir.). Law clk. Arter & Hadden, Cleve., 1969; law clk. L.A. County Dist. Atty., 1970-71, dep. dist. atty., 1971-73; assoc. Guy, Williams & White, Cheyenne, 1973-78; trial atty., founder Lawton, Edwards & Johnson, Cheyenne, 1978-86; sole practice Oakland, Calif., 1986-90; Superfund atty., advisor Office of Regional Counsel, USAF, San Francisco, 1990—. Rep. nominee for dist. atty. Laramie County, Cheyenne, 1982; pres. Larmaie County Young Reps., 1980. Mem. LDS Ch. Home: 1271 New Hampshire Dr Concord CA 94521-3820 Office: HQ USAF Office Regional Counsel 630 Sansome St S 1336 San Francisco CA 94111

LAWTON, MICHAEL JAMES, entomologist, pest management specialist; b. Balt., Aug. 6, 1953; s. James William and Mary Eileen (O'Connor) L.; m. Barbara Ann Byron, Dec. 19, 1983. BS, U. Md., 1975. Cert. entomologist. Technician, tech. dir. Atlas Exterminating Co., Towson, Md., 1975-78; asst. tech. dir. Western Exterminator Co., Irvine, Calif., 1978-83, tng. and tech. dir., 1984—. Republican. Office: Western Exterminator Co 1732 Kaiser Ave Irvine CA 92714-5706

LAX, KATHLEEN THOMPSON, federal judge. BA, U. Kans., 1967; JD, U. Calif., L.A., 1980. Law clk. U.S. Bankruptcy Ct., L.A., 1980-82; assoc. Gibson, Dunn & Crutcher, L.A., 1982-88; judge U.S. Bankruptcy Ct., L.A., 1988—; bd. dirs. L.A. Bankruptcy Forum, 1988—; bd. govs. Fin. Lawyers Conf., L.A., 1991-92, 94—. Bd. editors: Calif. Bankruptcy Jour., 1988—. Office: US Bankruptcy Court 255 E Temple St Rm 1334 Los Angeles CA 90012-3334*

LAYCOCK, ANITA SIMON, psychotherapist; b. Cheyenne, Wyo., Dec. 17, 1940; d. James Robert and Dorothy (Dearmin) Simon; m. Maurice Percy Laycock, June 18, 1965(dec. 1976); 1 child, (dec.). BA, U. Wyo., 1962, MA, 1971. Lic. counselor, Wyo., nationally cert. addiction specialist. Grad. student counselor, psychometrist Wyo. State Prison, Rawlins, 1971-73; counselor, trainer Dept. of Insts. State of Colo., Denver, 1973-75; counselor, tchr. supr. Jefferson County Evaluation-Diagnostic Ctr., Rawlins, 1975-78; psychometrist Wyo. State Penitentiary, Rawlins, 1978-79; counselor, therapist Rocky Mountain Arts and Scis., Cheyenne, 1979-81; counselor, therapist supr., dir. SWARA, Rock Springs, Wyo., 1981-85; therapy dir. St. Joseph Residential Treatment, Torrington, Wyo., 1985-88; dir. psychiatric unit Nat. Med. Enterprises Hill-Haven-Pk. Manor, Rawlins, 1988-89; chief exec. officer Simon-Laycock & Assocs., Rawlins, 1989—; cons. Kids in Distressed Situations, Rawlins, 1990-91, Child Devel. Ctr., Rawlins, 1991—; dir. Pub. Offender and Forensic Mental Health Program, Rawlins, 1988-91. Author: (programs) related to sex offenders. Pres. Cheyenne City Panhellenic, 1965-68. Named Miss Wyo.-Miss Universe, 1960; named Miss Wool of Wyo., 1965. Mem. ACA, Nat. Sex Offenders Counselors, Nat. Assn. Drug and Alcohol Counselors, Pub. Offenders Counselors Assn., Western Corrections Assn., Wyo. Assn. Addiction Specialists (pres. 1988—). Home: PO Box 3027 Cheyenne WY 82003-3027 Office: Simon Laycock & Assocs 1716 Yellowstone hwy Cheyenne WY 82009

LAYDEN, FRANCIS PATRICK (FRANK LAYDEN), professional basketball team executive, former coach; b. Bklyn., Jan. 5, 1932; m. Barbara Layden; children: Scott, Michael, Katie. Student, Niagara U. High sch. basketball coach L.I., N.Y.; head coach, athletic dir. Adelphi-Suffolk Coll. (now Dowling Coll.); head basketball coach, athletic dir. Niagara U., Niagara Falls, N.Y., 1968-76; asst. coach Atlanta Hawks, 1976-79; gen. mgr. Utah Jazz, Salt Lake City, 1979-88, head coach, 1981-88, v.p. basketball ops., until 1988, pres., 1989—. Bd. dirs. Utah Soc. Prevention Blindness; bd. dirs. Utah chpt. Multiple Sclerosis Soc., Utah Spl. Olympics. Served to 1st lt. Signal Corps, AUS. Office: Utah Jazz Delta Ctr 301 W South Temple Salt Lake City UT 84101-1216*

LAYE, JOHN E(DWARD), contingency planning and disaster recovery consulting executive; b. Santa Monica, Calif., May 26, 1933; s. Theodore Martin and Evelyn Rosalie (Young) L.; m. Jeanne Tutt Curry, Dec. 23, 1955; children: John Russell, Linda Helen. A.A., Los Angeles Community Coll., 1952; B.A., Naval Postgrad. Sch., 1967; M.S., U. So. Calif., 1975. Enlisted U.S. Navy, 1951, advanced through grades to lt. comdr., 1965; naval aviator, project mgr., worldwide, 1955-75; ret., 1975; emergency services exec. Marin County, Calif., 1975-76, Solano County, Calif., 1976-82; cons., pres. Cartingency Mgmt. Cons. (formerly Applied Protection Systems), Moraga, Calif., 1982—; cons. disaster med. com. Calif. Gov.'s Earthquake Task Force, 1981-89 ; mem. faculty Emergency Mgmt. Inst., Nat. Emergency Tng. Ctr., Emmitsburg, Md., 1982—; mem. bus. mgmt. faculty U. Calif. Bus. and Mgmt. extenstion, 1993—; pres. Calif. Emergency Services Assn., 1988; lectr. internat. contingency planning and disaster recovery, 1976—. Decorated Air medal, Navy Commendation medal, Navy Achievement medal, Viet Nam cross of Gallantry; recipient commendation Gov.'s Office Emergency Svcs., State Fire Marshal, Calif. Emergency Svcs. Assn., City Orinda. Mem. Nat. Coordinating Council Emergency Mgmt. (chmn. bus. and industry com. 1992—), Orinda Assn. (bd. dirs. 1988-90, pres. 1989, Vol. Yr. award 1991), U. So. Calif. Alumni (bd. dirs. 1980-87, pres. east bay club 1984), U. So. Calif. Inst. Safety and Systems Mgmt. Triumvirate (founding bd. mem.). Presbyterian. Office: Contingency Mgnt Cons 346 Rheem Blvd Ste 202 Moraga CA 94556-1588

LAYMAN, CHARLES DONALD, plastic surgeon; b. Portland, Mar. 20, 1949. MD, U Oreg. Health Scis. U., 1975. Plastic surgeon St. Vincent Med. Ctr., Portland; clin. instr. plastic surgery U. Oreg. Health Sci. Ctr. *

LAYMON, STEPHEN ADAIR, research scientist; b. Albany, Calif., Mar. 16, 1948; s. Fredrick Sylvester Laymond and Winifred Edith (Risser) Rishel; m. Phyllis Sydney Bailey, July 20, 1968 (div. Sept. 1981); m. Pamela Lorraine Williams, Apr. 7, 1991. AA, Shasta C.C., 1968; BA, Sacramento State Coll., 1970; MA, Calif. State U., Chico, 1981; PhD, U. Calif., Berkeley, 1988. Archivist Tehama County Libr., Red Bluff, Calif., 1979; wildlife biologist USDA Forest Svc., Yreka, Calif., 1980-81; wildlife and ecol. cons., Chico and Berkeley, 1974-90; postdoctoral fellow dept. forestry U. Calif., Berkeley, 1991-92; co-exec. dir. and rsch. dir. Kern River Rsch. Ctr., Weldon, Calif., 1990—; mem. adv. bd. Nature Conservancy, Kern River Preserve, Weldon, 1994—. Mem. editorial bd. Western Birds-Western Field Ornithologists, 1978—; contbr. articles to profl. publs. Mem. Wildlife Soc. (chpt. pres. 1981, symposium organizer 1994, steering com. Wildlife 2000 symposium 1984), Soc. for Conservation Biology, Ecol. Soc. Am., Soc. for Ecol. Restoration, Am. Ornithologists Union, Cooper Ornithol. Soc. (chpt. pres. 1981, chmn. of implementation bd. of Calif. Riparian Habitat Joint Venture 1995). Office: Kern River Rsch Ctr PO Box 990 Weldon CA 93283-0990

LAYTON, DONALD MERRILL, aeronautics educator; b. Cuyahoga Falls, Ohio, Sept. 23, 1922; s. Clifton Merrill and Flossie Belle (Payne) L.; m. Kathleen Gingras, Sept. 3, 1948; children: Mary, Patricia, Jane, Susan (dec.), Carol, James, Robert (dec.). BS in Sci., U.S. Naval Acad., 1945; MS in Aeros., Princeton U., 1954; MS in Mgmt., Naval Postgrad. Sch., 1968. Registered profl. safety engr., Calif. Commd. ensign USN, 1945, advanced through grades to comdr., 1960, ret., 1968; from faculty to prof., del. chmn. dept. Naval Postgrad. Sch., Monterey, Calif., 1968-88; vis. prof. Stellenbosch U., South Africa, 1985-89; lectr., pilot Nat. Test Pilot Sch., 1985-95; pres. Per Safe, Salinas, Calif., 1985—. Author: System Safety, 1981, Helicopter Performance, 1984, Performance for Flight Test, 1985, Aircraft Performance, 1986, Handling Qualities for Flight Test, 1987. Fellow AIAA (assoc., chpt. pres. 1976-78, mem. tech. com. 1975—); mem. Am. Soc. Safety Engrs., System Safety Soc. (sr., bd. dirs. 1974-77, Safety Educator of Yr. 1985), Navy League of U.S. (bd. dirs. 1978—, past pres.), Sigma Xi (Rsch. award 1976), Masons. Republican. Episcopalian. Home and Office: 44 Seca Pl Salinas CA 93908-8817

LAYTON, MARILYN SMITH, English language educator; b. Des Moines, Nov. 29, 1941; d. Sam Solomon and Mollie (Leiserowitz) Hockenberg; m. Charles Kent Smith, July 1, 1962 (div. Nov. 1974); children: Laurence Joseph, Eleanor Gwen; m. Richard Howard Layton, Dec. 14, 1975. BA, Northwestern U., 1963; MA, U. Mich., 1964; postgrad., U. Wash., 1972-74. Instr. part time English and humanities North Seattle Community Coll., 1969-74, tenured instr., 1975—; lectr., cons. on pedagogy. Author: (with others) Let Me Hear Your Voice, 1983 (Gov.'s Writers' award 1984), (with H. Collins) Intercultural Journeys Through Reading and Writing, 1991, Choosing to Emerge As Readers and Writers, 1993; mem. editorial bd. Jour. Basic Writing, 1986-89, Teaching English in the Two-Yr. Coll., 1987-90; contbr. articles to profl. jours. Mem. Conf. on Coll. Composition and Communication (mem. exec. com. 1983-86, editorial bd. 1987-90), Nat. Coun. Tchrs. English (chmn. nat. two-yr. coll. coun. 1985-86), Pacific N.W. Conf. on English in the Two-Yr. Coll. (chmn., 1982-83), Wash. C.C. Humanities Assn. Office: North Seattle Community Coll Dept Humanities 9600 College Way N Seattle WA 98103-3514

LAYTON, WILLIAM FREDERICK, JR., school counselor; b. Coos Bay, Oreg., Apr. 21, 1947; s. William Frederick Sr. and Lois Catherine (Hansen) L.; m. M. Linda Lang, Aug. 3, 1973 (div. Nov. 1989); 1 child, Shannon Marie; m. Brenda Kay Weygandt, Aug. 10, 1990; children: Jenni Lynn, Evan John. BS in Elem. Edn., Mt. Angel Coll., 1969; MS in Edn., Portland State U., 1978; MS in Counseling, Oreg. State U., 1994. Cert. tchr., counselor, Oreg. 2d and 6th grade tchr. Washington Elem. Sch., Woodburn, Oreg., 1969-72; tchg. supt., prin. Cloverdale Elem. Sch., Turner, Oreg., 1972-82; 3d grade tchr. Aumsville (Oreg.) Elem. Sch., 1982-85, child devel. specialist, 1985-86; counselor Talmadge Mid. Sch., Independence, Oreg., 1986—; chmn. adv. bd. Polk County Pub. Health, Dallas, Oreg., 1990-94, chair, 1994-95. Mem. adv. bd. Salem (Oreg.) Bicycle Club, 1994. Mem. NEA, Oreg. Edn. Assn., Oreg. Sch. Counselor Assn. (profl. recognition chair 1992-94, pres.-elect 1994-95, pres. 1995—), Oreg. Counselor Assn., Am. Sch. Counselor Assn., Am. Counselor Assn. Office: Talmadge Mid Sch 510 16th St Independence OR 97351-1012

LAZARUK, KIRK MAURICE, real estate developer, land use planner, consultant; b. Santa Monica, Calif., Dec. 18, 1958; s. Robert Lazaruk and Michele L. BA in Environ. Studies, U. Calif., Santa Barbara, 1983; postgrad., Calif. State U., Northridge, 1984-87. Pres. The KML Group, L.A., 1983—; coastal analyst Calif. Coastal Commn., Long Beach, 1983-84; planning project mgr. Joel Silverman & Assocs., Calabasas, Calif., 1984-87; dir. acquisitions AR Devel., Beverly Hills, Calif., 1987-88; dir. ops. Concord Devel., Century City, Calif., 1988-90; pres. owner Due Diligence and Mktg. Analysis. Mem. numerous mayoral apptd. ad hoc coms., Los Angeles and Ventura counties; mem. U.S. water polo team Macabbiah Games. Recipient Silver Water Polo medal Maccabiah Olympian. Mem. Bldg. Industry Assn. (pres. No. L.A. Region, exec. bd. dirs. So. Calif.), Internat. U.S. Rep. Water Polo Teams. Office: The KML Group 11755 Wilshire Blvd Ste 1140 Los Angeles CA 90025

LAZARUS, RICHARD STANLEY, psychology educator; b. N.Y.C., Mar. 3, 1922; s. Abe and Matilda (Marks) L.; m. Bernice H. Newman, Sept. 2, 1945; children—David Alan, Nancy Eve. A.B., City Coll. N.Y., 1942; M.S., U. Pitts., 1947, Ph.D., 1948; Dr. honoris causa, Johannes Gutenberg U., Mainz, Fed. Republic Germany, 1988; D Honoris Causa, U. Haifa, Israel, 1995. Diplomate in clin. psychology Am. Bd. Examiners in Profl. Psychology. Asst. prof. Johns Hopkins, 1948-53; psychol. cons. VA, 1952—; assoc. prof. psychology, dir. clin. tng. program Clark U., Worcester, Mass., 1953-57; assoc. prof. psychology U. Calif. at Berkeley, 1957-59, prof. psychology, 1959-91, prof. emeritus, 1991—; prin. investigator Air Force contracts dealing with psychol. stress, 1951-53, USPHS grant on personality psychol. stress, 1953-70; NIA, NIDA, and NCI grantee on stress, coping and health, 1977-81, MacArthur Found. research grantee, 1981-84; USPHS spl. fellow Waseda U., Japan, 1963-64. Author 18 books, numerous publs. in profl. jours. Served to 1st lt. AUS, 1943-46. Recipient Disting. Sci. Achievement award Calif. State Psychol. Assn., 1984, Div. 38 Health Psychology, 1989; Guggenheim fellow, 1969-70; Army Rsch. Inst. rsch. grantee, 1973-75. Fellow AAAS, APA (Disting. Sci. Contbn. award 1989); mem. Western Psychol. Assn., Argentina Med. Assn. (hon.). Home: 1824 Stanley Dollar Dr Apt 3B Walnut Creek CA 94595-2833 Office: Univ Calif Dept Psychology Berkeley CA 94720

LAZEAR, EDWARD PAUL, economics and industrial relations educator, researcher; b. N.Y.C., Aug. 17, 1948; s. Abe and Rose (Karp) L.; m. Victoria Ann Allen, July 2, 1977; 1 child, Julia Ann. A.B., UCLA, 1971, A.M., 1971; Ph.D., Harvard U., 1974. Asst. prof. econs. U. Chgo., 1974-78, assoc. prof. indsl. relations, 1978-81, prof. indsl. relations, 1981-85, Isidore and Gladys Brown prof. urban and labor econs., 1985-92; sr. fellow Hoover Instn. Stanford (Calif.) U., 1985—, coord. domestic studies Hoover Instn., 1987-90, prof. econs. and human resource mgmt. Grad. Sch. Bus., 1992—; econ. advisor to Romania, Czechoslovakia, Russia, Ukraine, Georgia; rsch. assoc. Nat. Bur. Econ. Rsch., Econs. Rsch. Ctr. of Nat. Opinion Rsch. Ctr.; fellow Inst. Advanced Study, Hebrew U., Jerusalem, 1977-8; lectr. Inst. Advanced Study, Vienna, 1983-84, Nat. Productivity Bd., Singapore, 1982, 85; vis. prof. Inst. des Etudes Politiques, Paris, 1987; Wicksell lectr., Stockholm, 1993. Author: with R. Michael) Allocation of Inclome Within the Household, 1988; (with J.P. Gould) Microeconomic Theory, 1989, Personnel Economics, 1995; editor: Economic Transition in Eastern Europe and Russia, 1995; founding editor Jour. Labor Econs., 1982—; assoc. editor Jour. Econ. Perspectives, 1986-89; contbr. numerous articles to scholarly jours. NSF grad. fellow, 1971-74. Fellow Econometric Soc.; mem. Am. Econs. Assn. Home: 277 Old Spanish Trl Portola Valley CA 94028-8129 Office: Stanford U Grad Sch Bus Stanford CA 94305-5015 also: Hoover Inst Stanford CA 94305-6010

LAZECHKO, D. M. (MOLLY LAZECHKO), former state legislator; b. Innisfail, Alta., June 3, 1926; came to U.S., 1960; d. Archibald Donald and Violet Georgina (Adams) Manuel; m. Walter Vladmir Lazechko, Apr. 16, 1960; children: William Donald, Robert James. BA, Boise State U., 1976. Cert. elem. tchr. Tchr. Olds Sch. Dist., Stewart Sch., Alta., 1945-46, Innisfail (Alta.) Sch. Dist., 1946-50; tchr., vice prin. Calgary (Alta.) Sch. Dist., 1950-59; exchange tchr. Edinburgh, Scotland, 1954-55; math tutor mgr. Title I, Boise, Idaho, 1974-76; elem. tchr. Boise (Idaho) Sch. Dist., 1976-87; jr. high tchr. Chpt. I, Boise, 1987-88; ret., 1988-90; mem. Idaho Ho. of Reps., Boise, 1991, 92; pres. div. I Alta. Tchrs. Assn., Calgary, 1958-59, Whittier PTA, Boise, 1969-70, 73-74; pres., 3d v.p. Dist. 8 Idaho State PTA, 1973-75; sec., elem. dir. Boise (Idaho) Edn. Assn., 1978-81. Treas. LWV, Boise, 1988-90, House Dems. Campaign. Com., Boise, 1991-92; precinct capt. Ada County Dems. Dist. 16, Boise, 1988-90; sec. Boise Ret. Tchrs., 1989-90, pres., 1993-94; bd. mem. Boise Neighborhood Housing Svcs., 1990-92, Cmty. Contbn. Ctr., 1991-92, Idaho Housing Coalition, 1991-92; gov. appt. to bd. of Idaho Coun. on Domestic Violence, 1994—; bd. dirs. Epilepsy League of Idaho, 1993-94; candidate Idaho Legis. Ho. Reps., 1994. Mem. NEA, Idaho Edn. Assn., Idaho Conservation League, Idaho Women's Network, Grassroots Women's Lobby, Idaho Citzen's Network. Episcopalian.

LE, KHANH TUONG, utility executive; b. Saigon, Vietnam, Feb. 25, 1936; parents Huy Bich and Thi Hop; m. Thi Tri Nguyen, Apr. 22, 1961; children: Tuong-Khanh, Tuong-Vi, Khang, Tuong-Van. BS in Mech. Engring., U. Montreal, 1960, MS in Mech. Engring., 1961. Cert. profl. engr. Project mgr. Saigon Met. Water Project Ministry Pub. Works, Saigon, 1961-66; dep. dir. gen. Cen. Logistics Agy. Prime Min. Office, Saigon, 1966-70; asst. dir., chief auditor Nat. Water Supply Agy. Min. Pub. Works, Saigon, 1970-75; mgr. Willows Water Dist., Englewood, Colo., 1975—; dean sch. mgmt. scis., asst. chancellor acad. afairs Hoa-Hao U., Long-Xuyen, Vietnam, 1973-75; chmn. bd. dirs. Asian Pacific Devel. Ctr.,; adv. bd. Araphoe County Utility Douglas County Water Authority. Treas. Met. Denver Water Authority, 1989-92; mem. Araphoe County Adv. Bd., Doughas County Water Authority, 1993—; mem. Front Range Water Forum presided by Gov. Roy Romer, Colo., 1993—. Recipient Merit medal Pres. Republic Vietnam, 1966 Pub. Health Svc. medal, 1970, Svc. award Asian Edn. Adv. Coun., 1989; co-recipient Engring. Excellence award Am. Cons. Engrs. Coun. 1994; named to Top Ten Pub. Works Leaders in Colo., Am. Pub. Works Assn., 1990. Mem. Am. Water Works Assn., Vietnamese Profl. Engrs. Soc. (founder), Amnesty Internat. Buddhist. Office: Willows Water Dist 6970 S Holly Cir Ste 200 Englewood CO 80112-1066

LE, NGUYEN MINH, computer company executive; b. Kien Phong, Vietnam, Mar. 22, 1952; came to U.S., 1975; s. Vinh Phat Le and Banh Thi Nguyen; m. Nuong Thi Liet Huynh, 1973; children: Dan, Long. Bachelor, Saigon Law Sch., Vietnam, 1974. Painter Dallas Apartments, 1976-77; machinist N.W. Industries, Oklahoma City, 1978-79; auto mechanic Harbor Auto Sales, Long Beach, Calif., 1980-81; operator L.A. County Sanitation Dist., Carson, 1981-84; pres. Dan Long Landscape, Long Beach, 1982-85, Dolphin Microcomputer Corp., Long Beach, 1985—; pres. Tinvi USA, Long Beach, 1991—. Mem. Rep. Senatorial Trust, Washington, 1992—, Alliance for Democracy of Vietnam, Houston, 1982—, Nat. Progressive Movement, Saigon, 1969-75; pres. Nguyen Ngoc Huy Found., Long Beach, 1991—. Buddhist. Home: 6466 E Bixby Hill Rd Long Beach CA 90815-4709 Office: Dolphin Microcomputer Corp 1234 E South St Long Beach CA 90805-4321

LEABHART, THOMAS GLENN, art educator; b. Charleroi, Pa., Oct. 23, 1944; s. Thomas G. and Tresa Rose (Lacher) L.; m. Sally Diane Garfield, Apr. 29, 1972. BA, Rollins Coll., Winter Park, Fla., 1966; MA, U. Ark., 1968; postgrad., Ecole de Mime Decroux, Paris, France, 1968-72. Instr. U. Ark., Fayetteville, 1972-76; artistic dir. Wis. Sch. of Mime, Spring Green, 1976-78; resident artist Grand Valley State Coll., Allendale, Mich., 1978-81; asst. prof. Ohio State U., Columbus, 1981-82; assoc. prof., resident artist Pomona Coll., Claremont, Calif., 1982—; mem. artistic staff Internat. Sch. Theatrical Anthropology, Holstobro, Denmark. Author: Modern and Post Modern Mime, 1989; editor: Mime Jour., 1974—. Fulbright fellow, 1968-69, Ohio Arts Coun. Choreography fellow, 1982, NEA fellow, 1980, 84, 85; grantee Calif. Arts Coun. for Mime Jour., 1985, 87, 88, Internat. Rsch. Exchs. Bd, 1975. Mem. (founder, pres. 1986, 87) Nat. Movement Theatre Assn., Assn. Theatre in Higher Edn. Office: Pomona Coll Theatre Dept Claremont CA 91711

LEACH, ANTHONY RAYMOND, financial executive; b. Gerrards Cross, Eng., Nov. 11, 1939; came to U.S., 1969; s. John Raymond Geoffrey and Edith Eileen (Blackburn) L.; m. Shirley Ann Kidd, Apr. 17, 1965; children: Mark Irwin, Amanda Jane, Christopher John. Supr. Ernst & Whinney, London, 1957-63, San Francisco, 1967—; mgr. Ernst & Whinney, Paris, 1963-69; mgr. fin. acctg. Occidental Petroleum Corp., Los Angeles, 1965-74, asst. controller, 1974-81, v.p. acctg., 1981-91, v.p., contr., exec. v.p., CFO, 1991—. Fellow Inst. Chartered Accts.; mem. Fin. Execs. Inst. Club: Palos Verdes Breakfast. Office: Occidental Petroleum Corp 10889 Wilshire Blvd Los Angeles CA 90024-4201

LEACH, DEANNA DARLENE, publisher; b. Stephenville, Tex., Sept. 28, 1959; d. Eugene Frank and Barbara Ann (Layland) L. Cert., San Diego State U., 1988. Logistics analyst Gen. Dynamics, Electronics, San Diego, 1979-81; property adminstr. M/A-Com Linkabit, San Diego, 1981-89, contract adminstr., 1987-90; pub. Paradigm Pub., San Diego, 1989—; freelance cons. on govt. property adminstrn. and laser typesetting, San Diego, 1990—. Comm. dir. Ctr. for Social Svcs., 1985-89; bd. liaison San Diego AIDS Walk, 1989. Recipient Ms. Gay Pride award San Diego Pride awards, 1985, Female Personality award Hillcrest 92103 Awards, 1986. Democrat. Office: Paradigm Pub Co 2323 Broadway Studio # 202 San Diego CA 92102

LEACH, GARY EDWARD, urologist, educator; b. Detroit, Nov. 20, 1950; s. John and Antoinette (Isca) L.; m. Barbara Jean Williams; children: Andrew, Jody, Cory. BS in Biology, U. Mich., 1972; MD, Wayne State U., 1976. Diplomate Am. Bd. Urology. Intern and resident Kaiser Permanente, L.A., 1976-81; fellow in female urology UCLA, 1981-82; Chief, urology Kaiser Permanente, L.A., 1988-94; assoc. clin. prof. urology UCLA, 1990—. Author: chpts. in urology texts; contbr. articles to profl. jours. Patentee in field. Advisor Help Incontinent People, Union, S.C., 1990—. Mem. Am. Urol. Assn. (chmn. guidelines panel 1993—, mem. Western sect.), Calif. Urologic Assn., Soc. Internat. de Urology, L.A. Urologic Soc. (v.p. 1994—), Urodynamics Soc. (v.p. 1994—). Office: Kaiser Permanente 4900 W Sunset Blvd Los Angeles CA 90027-5814

LEACH, JOHN F., newspaper editor, journalism educator; b. Montrose, Colo., Aug. 6, 1952; s. Darrell Willis and Marian Ruth (Hester) L.; m. Deborah C. Ross, Jan. 2, 1982; children: Allison, Jason. BS in Journalism, U. Colo., 1974, MA in Journalism, 1979; MA in Am. Studies, U. Sussex, Falmer, Brighton, Eng., 1983. News reporter Boulder (Colo.) Daily Camera, 1974-79; news reporter Ariz. Republic, Phoenix, 1979-85, asst. city editor, 1985-93; news editor Phoenix Gazette, 1993-94, asst. mng. editor, 1994—; faculty assoc. Ariz. State U., Tempe, 1990—; pres., dir. First Amendment Funding Inc., Phoenix. Bd. Regents scholar U. Colo., 1970, Rotary Found. scholar, 1982. Mem. Ariz. Press Club (treas. 1984-86, pres. 1986-87), Investigative Reporters and Editors, Soc. Profl. Journalists, Reporter's Com. for Freedom of Press. Home: 4313 E Calle Redonda Phoenix AZ 85018-3733 Office: Phoenix Gazette 300 E Van Buren St Phoenix AZ 85004-2227

LEACH, RICHARD MAXWELL, JR. (MAX LEACH, JR.), corporate professional; b. Chillicothe, Tex., June 14, 1934; s. Richard Maxwell and Lelia Booth (Page) L.; m. Wanda Gail Groves, Feb. 4, 1956; children: Richard Clifton, John Christopher, Sandra Gail, Kathy Lynn. BS in Acctg. magna cum laude, Abilene Christian U., 1955. Registered Fin. Planner., CLU. Asst. dir. agys. Am. Founders Ins. Co., Austin, Tex., 1960-62; owner A.F. Ins. Planning Assocs., Temple, Tex., 1962-65; v.p. sales Christian Fidelity Life Ins. Co., Waxahachie, Tex., 1966-67; exec. v.p. Acad. Computer Tech., Inc., Dallas, 1968-69; pres., chief exec. officer Inta-Search Internat., Inc., Dallas, 1969-71; prin., chief exec. officer, fin. cons. Leach and Assocs., Albuquerque, 1971—; pres. The Wright Edge, Inc., 1988-90; pres., CEO Action Mktg. Programs, Inc., 1989-92; CEO Vacation Premiums Internat., Inc., 1990-92; pres. ITM Corp., Albuquerque, 1993—; chmn. bd. United Quest Inc., Albuquerque, Hosanna Inc., Albuquerque; real estate broker; commodity futures broker; exec. dir., bd. dirs. New Heart, Inc., Albuquerque, 1975-85; owner Insta-Copy, Albuquerque, 1973-76, Radio Sta. KYLE-FM, Temple, 1963-64. Editor, author Hosanna newspaper, 1973-74. Gen. dir. Here's Life, New Mexico, Albuquerque, 1976; exec. dir. Christians for Cambodia, Albuquerque, 1979-80. Served with U.S. Army, 1955-57. Home: 3308 June St NE Albuquerque NM 87111-5029 Office: 9920 Bell Ave SE # B Albuquerque NM 87123-3313

LEAF, NORMAN, plastic surgeon, educator. MD, U Chgo, 1966. Plastic surgeon Cedars-Sinai Med. Ctr., Calif.; clin. asst. prof. plastic surgery, UCLA. Office: 436 N Bedford Dr Beverly Hills CA 90210-4310*

LEAHY, GERALD PHILIP, hospital administrator; b. Vancouver, B.C., Canada, Feb. 16, 1936; married. B, U. Portland, 1959; MHA, St. Louis U., 1961. Adminstrv. asst. Sacred Heart Med. Ctr., Spokane, Wash., 1961-63, asst. adminstr., 1963-68, assoc. adminstr., 1968-81, exec. v.p., 1981-88, pres., chief exec. officer, 1988—. Mem. Am. Coll. Healthcare Execs., Am. Hosp. Assn. (del. 1979-81, reg. adv. bd. 1977-83) Wash. Hosp. Assn. (chmn. 1977-78, bd. dirs. 1970-82). Home: 4925 S Perry St Spokane WA 99223-6337 Office: Sacred Heart Med Ctr PO Box 2555 Spokane WA 99220-2555

LEAHY, JOHN HENRY, JR., telecommunications executive; b. Portland, Oreg., Sept. 17, 1951; s. John Henry and Maryanne (Shrauger) L.; m. Monique Catherine McCall, Aug. 30, 1980; children: Shea Nicolas, Sean Michael. BA in Econs., Whitman Coll., 1973; MBA in Fin., U. Wash., 1978. Fin. assoc. devel. program GTE, Stamford, Conn., 1978-80; program mgr. GTE-N.W., Everett, Wash., 1980-86; group mgr. bus. devel. US Sprint, Kansas City, Mo., 1986-91; dir. mktg. programs Metromedia Comm. Co., San Antonio, 1992; dir. mktg. Minitel Devel. Corp., Englewood, Colo., 1992-93; v.p. sales and mktg. Minitel Devel. Corp., Englewood, 1993—; instr. fin. U. Puget Sound, Seattle, 1981-83; sr. ptnr. Overbrook Consulting, Leawood,

Kans., 1991-92. Com. chair Boy Scouts Am., Kansas City, Mo., 1991-92. Mem. Silicon Prairie Tech. Assn. Home: 12014 Aintree Ln Reston VA 22091-2110 Office: Minitel Devel Corp 198 Inverness Dr E Ste 600 Englewood CO 80112-5113

LEAKE, PHILIP GREGORY, exercise physiologist, consultant; b. L.A., Mar. 1, 1958; s. Philip Matthew and Carroll Rita (Hithe) L.; m. Barbara June Ehrhardt, July 99, 1983; children: Galen Alexander, Benjamin Matthew. BA in Phys. Edn., Calif. State U., Northridge, 1983; MA in Phys. Edn., Calif. State U., 1988. Exercise physiologist JMP Ctr. for Sports Medicine, Van Nuys, Calif., 1983-87, Daniel Freeman Meml. Hosp. Ctr. for Heart and Health, Inglewood, Calif., 1988-90; program dir., exercise physiologist Heart Disease Prevention and Test Ctr., Sacramento, 1990-94; program dir., cons. Preventive Health and Fitness of Sacramento, 1994—. Contbr. articles to profl. jour. Mem. Am. Coll. Sports Medicine (S.W. newsletter editor), Am. Heart Assn. Democrat. Baptist.

LEAKE, ROSEMARY DOBSON, physician; b. Columbus, Ohio, July 14, 1937; d. Joseph Lawrence and Rosemary Elizabeth (Brockmeyer) Dobson; m. Donald Leake, Aug. 20, 1964; children: John, Elizabeth, Catherine. BA, Ohio State U., 1959, MD, 1962. Diplomate Am. Bd. Neonatal-Perinatal Medicine. Intern, pediatrics Mass. Gen. Hosp., Boston, 1962-63, resident, pediatrics, 1963-64; rsch. fellow Maternal Infant Health Collaborative Study The Boston Lying-In Hosp., Boston, 1965-67; neonatal fellow Stanford U. Hosp., Palo Alto, Calif., 1968-69; co-dir. NIH sponsored perinatal tng. program Harbor-UCLA Med. Ctr., Torrance, 1979, program dir. NIH sponsored perinatal rsch. ctr., 1980—; prof. pediatrics UCLA Sch. of Medicine, L.A., 1982—; dir. regionalized fellowship Harbor-UCLA/King-Drew Med. Ctr., Torrance, 1986—; chair pediatrics Harbor-UCLA Med. Ctr., Torrance, 1992—; dir. perinatal crisis care program Harbor-UCLA Med. Ctr., Torrance, 1972-76, dir. neonatal ICU, 1974-81, assoc. prof. pediatrics, 1976-82, assoc. chief div. neonatology, 1976-77. Named UCLA Woman of Sci., 1985, Outstanding Woman Acadmician of Yr. Nat. Bd. Award of the Med. Coll. of Pa., 1989; recipient Alumni Achievement award Ohio State U. Sch. Medicine, 1987. Mem. Am. Pediatric Soc., Soc. for Pediatric Rsch. Home: 2 Crest Rd W Rolling Hills CA 90274-5003 Office: Harbor-UCLA Med Ctr 1000 W Carson St Torrance CA 90502-2004

LEAL, GEORGE D., engineering company executive; b. 1934. B in Civil Engring., MA, Santa Clara U., 1959. With Dames & Moore, Inc., L.A., 1959—, CEO, 1981—, now CEO, pres.; bd. dirs. BW/IP Internat. Inc. Office: Dames & Moore Inc 911 Wilshire Blvd Ste 700 Los Angeles CA 90017-3436*

LEALE, OLIVIA MASON, import marketing company executive; b. Boston, May 5, 1944; d. William Mason and Jane Chapin (Prouty) Smith; m. Euan Harvie-Watt, Mar. ll, 1967 (div. Aug. 1979); children: Katrina, Jennifer; m. Douglas Marshall Leale, Aug. 29, 1980. BA, Vassar Coll., 1966. Sec. to dir. Met. Opera Guild, N.Y.C., 1966; sec. to pres. Friesons Printers, London, 1974-75; guide, trainer Autoguide, London, 1977-79; ptnr. Inmark Internat. Mktg. Inc., Seattle, 1980—. Social case worker Inner London Ednl. Authority, 1975-76. Democrat. Presbyterian. Home and Office: 5427 NE Penrith Rd Seattle WA 98105-2842

LEAMAN, JACK ERVIN, landscape architect, community/regional planner; b. Mason City, Iowa, Jan. 24, 1932; s. Theodore R. and Dorothy M. (Schrum) L.; m. Darlene A. McNary, June 15, 1952; children: Jeffrey A., Danna J., Jay M., Duree K. B.S. in Landscape Architecture and Urban Planning, Iowa State U., 1954, M. Community and Regional Planning, 1982. Registered landscape architect, Calif., Iowa, Minn., N.Mex. Landscape architect Sam L. Huddleston Office, Denver, 1954-55, Phillips Petroleum Co., Bartlesville, Okla., 1955-58; landscape architect for Price Tower and residence with architect Frank Lloyd Wright Bartlesville, Okla., 1957-58; planning technician Santa Barbara County, Calif., 1958-60; planning cons. Engring. Planners, Santa Barbara, 1960-63; planning dir. City of Santa Barbara, 1963-66, City of Mason City, 1966-72; landscape architect, planning cons. Midwest Research Inst., Kansas City, Mo., 1972-74, Hansen, Lind, Meyer, Iowa City, Iowa, 1974-76, Sheffler, Leaman, Rova, Mason City, 1976-78, RCM Assocs., Inc., Hopkins, Minn. and Ames, Iowa, 1978-82; planning dir. City-County Planning, Albuquerque, 1982-86, City of Colorado Springs, Colo., 1986-90; landscape architect, pvt. practice planning cons. Mason City, Iowa, 1990-92; assoc. ptnr., landscape architect, community/regional planner Yaggy Colby Assocs., Mason City, 1992—. Recipient Residential Landscape Design award Calif. Landscape Contractors Assn., 1962, Design Achievement award Coll. of Design Iowa State U., 1988. Fellow Am. Soc. Landscape Architects (chpt. pres. 1967-68, 90-91, trustee Iowa 1980-82, N.Mex. 1982-86, Award of Excellence 1954); mem. Am. Inst. Cert. Planners, Am. Planning Assn. (chpt. pres. Iowa 1969-70), Urban Land Inst., Tau Sigma Delta.

LEAMING, MARJ P(ATRICIA), management and marketing consultant, researcher; b. Denver; d. Taylor J. Sr. and Augie R. Leaming. BA, U. Colo., 1969, MBA, 1970; PhD, Colo. State U., 1979; JD, U. Denver, 1993. Bar: Colo., Tex. Asst. supr. State Approving Agy. Vets. Edn., Denver, 1973-82; asst. assoc. dir. State Bd. Community Colls. and Occupational Edn., Denver, 1982-85; mgmt. cons. divsn. mgmt. services Colo. Dept. Adminstrn., 1985-86; pres. Edventure Systems, Lakewood, Colo., 1986—; bd. dirs. Colo. Retail Coun., Denver, 1982-85; asst. grad. prof. MBA program Regis Coll., Denver, 1982; vis. asst. prof. Bus. Leadership Inst., U. Alaska, Fairbanks, 1986; pres. Nat. Entrepreneurship Consortium, 1984-85; commr. Colo Productivity-Study Team, 1988-89; sr. assoc., bd. dirs. Affiliated Cons. Colo., 1993. Author: (coll. textbook) Administrative Office Management, 1970, (coll. casebook) Administrative Management Cases, 1970, (handbook) Entrepreneurship, 1988; author, editor: Entrepreneurship Models, 1985, Economic Value of Entrepreneurship, 1985; contbr. articles to nat. jours. Active fin. devel. ARC, Jefferson County, 1988, Mile High, 1988; mem. Denver Art Mus., 1983-88; mem. adv. com. Jefferson County Pub. Schs., 1986-88, Jefferson County Small Bus. Ctr.; mem. Gov. apptd. Commn. on Privatization, 1988—. NSF grantee, Denver, 1972. Mem. SBA (bd. dirs. region VIII 1987-88), ABA, Women Bus. Owners Assn., Exec. Women Internat. (nat. del. 1986), U.S. Assn. for Small Bus., Am. Entrepreneurs Assn., Colo. Bar Assn., Tex. Bar Assn., Phi Kappa Phi. Office: Edventure Systems PO Box 15767 Lakewood CO 80215

LEARY, LORY DIANE MARY B., publishing executive; b. New Haven, June 20, 1936; d. James Vincent and Eileen Marie (Kennedy) Bica; m. Robert Arthur Leary (dec. Oct. 1991). Dir., owner Alaskan Art Gallery, Seward, 1976-86; owner, pub. Alaskan Viewpoint Pub., Seward, 1986—. Author: Dreamwish, 1991, An Alaskan Child's Garden of Verse, 1990, (reference) Who's Who in Alaskan Art, 1990; author, pub. (collection) Jour. of Alaskan Women, 1994. Bd. dirs., grant officer Moose Pass Sportsmen Club; chmn. Moose Pass Rep. Com., 1990—; adv. planning commn. mem. Kenai Borough, Alaska; mem. Moose Pass Vol. Fire Co. Mem. Nat. Fedn. Ind. Bus., Nat. Press Women, Alaska Press Women (past v.p.), United Alaska Artists, Moose Pass C. of C. (founder, pres. 1994), Rebekan Lodge 6A (vice grand 1994). Roman Catholic. Office: Alaskan Viewpoint Pub HC 64 Box 453 Seward AK 99664-9707

LEARY, TIM, software microbiologist, electrical engineer; b. Phoenix, May 5, 1951; s. Kelvin and Lisa Ninny (Sweatsmith) L.; m. Ginny Earl Diner, Aug. 19, 1975 (div.); children: Mike, Bob, James, Earl. Degree in software microbiology, Ariz. State U., 1973, BSEE, 1977. Engr. Xerox, Phoenix, 1972-78, Greyhound Bus Lines, Phoenix, 1978-80; software microbiologist Sperry Flight Systems, Phoenix, 1980-89; elec. engr. Motorola, Scottsdale, Ariz., 1989—. Author: Fone Phracking, 1989, Blue Boxing in the 90's, 1991. With USN, 1971. Mem. Tip & Ring Assn. (bd. dirs. 1985—), Colo. Diving Club. Office: Motorola PO Box 2743 Phoenix AZ 85002-2743

LEASE, JANE ETTA, librarian; b. Kansas City, Kans., Apr. 10, 1924; d. Joy Alva and Emma (Jaggard) Omer; B.S. in Home Econs., U. Ariz., 1957; M.S. in Edn., Ind. U., 1962; M.S. in L.S., U. Denver, 1967; m. Richard J. Lease, Jan. 16, 1960; children—Janet (Mrs. Jacky B. Radifera), Joyce (Mrs. Robert J. Carson), Julia (Mrs. Earle D. Marvin), Cathy (Mrs. Edward F. Warren); stepchildren—Richard Jay II, William Harley. Newspaper reporter Ariz. Daily Star, Tucson, 1937-39; asst. home agt. Dept. Agr., 1957; homemaking tchr., Ft. Huachuca, Ariz., 1957-60; head tchr. Stonebelt Council Retarded Children, Bloomington, Ind., 1960-61; reference clk. Ariz. State U. Library, 1964-66; edn. and psychology librarian N.Mex. State U., 1967-71; Amway distbr., 1973—; cons. solid wastes, distressed land problems reference remedies, 1967; ecology lit. research and cons., 1966—. Ind. observer 1st World Conf. Human Environment, 1972; mem. Las Cruces Community Devel. Priorities Adv. Bd. Mem. ALA, Regional Environ. Edn. Research Info. Orgn., NAFE, P.E.O., D.A.R., Internat. Platform Assn., Las Cruces Antique Car Club, Las Cruces Story League, N.Mex. Library Assn. Methodist (lay leader). Address: 2145 Boise Dr Las Cruces NM 88001-5149

LEASE, RICHARD JAY, police science educator, former police officer; b. Cherokee, Ohio, Dec. 10, 1914; s. Harold and Mabelle (Fullerton) L.; m. Marjorie Faye Stoughton, Sept. 2, 1939 (div. Apr. 1957); children: Richard Jay II, William Harley; m. Jane Etta Omer, Jan. 16, 1960; stepchildren: Janet Radifera, Joyce Carson, Julia Marvin, Catherine Warren; adopted children: Alan Fudge, Stephen V. Graham. Student, Wittenberg U., 1932-33; BA, U. Ariz., 1937, MA, 1961; postgrad., Ind. U., 1950, 60, Ariz. State U., 1956, 63-65, 67—; grad., U. Louisville So. Police Inst., 1955. Grad. asst . U. Ariz., Tucson, 1937-38; with Tucson Police Dept., from 1938; advanced from patrolman to sgt., also served as safety officer Pima County Sheriff's Dept., Tucson, 1953, patrol supr., 1953-55, investigator, 1955-56; tchr. sci. pub. schs. Tucson, 1957-59; lectr. dept. police adminstrn. Ind. U., Bloomington, 1960-65; asst. prof. dept. police sci. N.Mex. State U., Las Cruces, 1965—; cons. law enforcement problems HEW, 1960, Indpls. Police Dept., 1962, Harrisburg Community Coll. Police Sci. Dept., 1967, Phoenix Police Dept., 1968—; advisor police tng. programs several small city police depts., Ind., 1960-63, Indpls., 1962; mem. oral bd. for selection chief in Bateville, Ind., 1962, oral bd. for selection sgts. and lts., Las Cruces Police Dept., 1966—. Author: (with Robert F. Borkenstein) Alcohol and Road Traffic: Problems of Enforcement and Prosecution, 1963, The Dreams, Hopes, Recollections and Thoughts of a Professional Good Samaritan; cons. editor Police, various rsch. publs. on chem. intoxification tests, psychol. errors of witnesses, reading disabilities, delinquency. Participant numerous FBI seminars; active youth work, philanthropy, among Am. Indians in Southwest; founder awards outstanding ROTC cadets N.Mex. State U., 1967—; founder Wiltberger ann. awards Nat. Police Combat Pistol Matches; scoutmaster Yucca council Boy Scouts Am., 1966—. Served to 1st lt. USMCR, 1942-45, PTO. Fellow Am. Acad. Forensic Scis. (sec. gen. sect.); mem. Internat. Assn. Chiefs of Police, Internat. Assn. Police Profs., Brit. Acad. Forensic Scis., Can. Soc. Forensic Sci., Am. Soc. Criminology, Ret. Officers Assn., Assn. U.S. Army (2d v.p. 1969—), NEA, N.Mex. Edn. Assn., N.Mex. Police and Sheriffs Assn., Internat. Crossroads, NRA (benefactor mem.), Marine Corps League (life), Sigma Chi. Lodges: Masons, Elks. Home and Office: 2145 Boise Dr Las Cruces NM 88001-5149

LEASON, JODY JACOBS, newspaper columnist; b. Margarita, Venezuela, June 8, 1926; came to U.S., 1928; d. Jose Cruz Caceres and Graciela Rodriguez; m. Russell L. Jacobs (div.); 1 child, Jessica Jacobs Vitti; m. Barney Leason, Dec. 29, 1976. BA, Hunter Coll., 1940's. Assoc. fashion editor Women's Wear Daily, N.Y.C., 1969-70; West Coast fashion editor Women's Wear Daily, Los Angeles, 1957-69; London fashion editor Women's Wear Daily, N.Y.C., 1970-72; soc. editor L.A. Times, 1972-86. Author: (novel) The Right Circles, 1988.

LEASURE, ROBERT ELLIS, writer, photographer; b. Lamar, Colo., Oct. 20, 1921; s. Henry Naley and Pansy Margaret (Leatherman) L.; m. Betty Jean Stulck, July 4, 1945; twins: Mary Margaret and David Lee. Grad. high sch., Lamar, Colo. Cryptographer 15th Air Force Air Def. Command, Colorado Springs, Colo., 1946; staff Colorado Springs (Colo.) Post Office, 1946-76; freelancer photographer, writer, 1976—. Author: Black Mountain, 1975; exhibited at Tex. Fine Art Assn. Mem. Colorado Springs Fine Arts Guild.Sgt. U.S. Army, 1942-45. Mem. VFW. Presbyterian. Home: 1210 Milky Way Colorado Springs CO 80906-1715

LEATHERS, MARGARET WEIL, foundation administrator; b. Princeton, Ind., Dec. 22, 1949; d. Albert J. and Nora Jewel (Franklin) Weil; m. Charles L. Leathers, June 19, 1971 (div. Dec. 1987); children: Julianna L., Kevin Sean. AB, U. Ill., 1971; MS, Russell Sage Coll., 1979. Cert. tchr., N.Y., health edn. specialist. Employment counselor Snelling & Snelling, Schenectady, N.Y., 1972-76; substitute tchr. Monahasen High/Jr. High Sch., Schenectady, 1978-79; grant abstractor State of N.Y., Albany, 1979; program coordinator Am. Lung Assn. Santa Clara-San Benito Counties, San Jose, Calif., 1982-84, dir. programs, 1984-87, nat. clinic leader trainer, 1986—, acting exec. dir., 1987-88, exec. dir., 1988—. Author: Camp Superstuff Workbook and Teachers Manual, 1983; contbr. articles to profl. publs. and mags. Bd. dirs., officer Santa Clara Valley Coun. Parent-Participating Nursery Schs., 1980-81; resource vol. Lyceum Santa Clara Valley, 1983-87; leader Explorer post Boy Scouts Am., San Jose, 1988; mem. adminstrv. bd. coun. ministries United Meth. Ch.; mem. staff 1st asthma camp Young Tchrs. of Health, Soviet Union, 1989, Seattle, 1990; mem. citizen's oversight com. Local Transp. Commn. for Santa Clara County, 1993—; mem. steering com. for Measure A., 1992. Mem. APHA, Soc. Pub. Health Educators, Am. Sch. Health Assn., Assn. of United Way Agys. (exec. bd. 1993), ALA Calif. Coun. Execs. (v.p. 1994). Democrat. Home: 341 Springpark Cir San Jose CA 95136-2144 Office: Am Lung Assn 1469 Park Ave San Jose CA 95126-2530

LEAVENGOOD, WILLIAM SAMUEL, playwright; b. St. Petersburg, Fla., Mar. 11, 1960; s. Charles Richard and Pauline Clara (Moeller) L.; m. Diana Lucas Leavengood, Oct. 12, 1991. BA, Rollins Coll., Winter Park, Fla., 1982. Playwright in residence Theater-In-The-Schools, N.Y.C., 1984-90; playwright, 1990—. Author: Florida Bound: The Collected Plays of William S. Leavenwood, 1995; plays include What Is Art?, Dreams of the Afternoon, The Family Curse, The Preservation Society, 17 Black, Spacehunter, The Head, Laughter in the Rain, The Winter of Youth, Cold Fact and Concrete, Florida Crackers. Recipient Brodkin scholarship award, 1993, grant for playwriting Berilla Kerr Found, 1995, O'Neill Playwright, 1993, 95; play competitions The Winter of Youth, Ctrl. Fla. Civic Theatre, Cold Fact and Concrete (Fla. Internat. U.). Mem. Circle Repertory Playwright's Lab, Dramatist's Guild, Writer's Guild Am. Home: 12002 Laurel Ter North Hollywood CA 91604

LEAVITT, DANA GIBSON, management consultant; b. Framingham, Mass., Dec. 4, 1925; s. Luther C. and Margaret (Gibson) L.; m. Frances Smith, Apr. 12, 1952; children: Margaret Gibson, Jonathan. BA, Brown U., 1948; postgrad., Harvard U. Bus. Sch., 1954-55. Home office rep. Aetna Life Ins. Co., Boston, also Long Beach, Calif., 1949-54; v.p., sec.-treas., exec. v.p. N. Am. Title Ins. Co., Oakland, Calif., 1955-64; pres. Transam. Title Ins. Co., Oakland, 1964-72; v.p. Transam. Corp., 1969-71, group v.p., 1971-77, exec. v.p., 1977-81; bd. dirs. Chgo. Title and Trust Co., Chgo. Title Ins. Co., World Minerals, Inc., Am. Ctr. for Wine, Food and the Arts, Napa Valley, Calif., pres., 1994—. Bd. dirs. Children's Hosp. Med. Ctr. and Found., 1969-72; trustee Lewis and Clark Coll., Portland, Oreg., 1972-75, Queen of Valley Hosp., Napa, Calif., 1988-90, Nat. Wildflower Rsch. Ctr., Austin, Tex., 1988-90, pres., 1991-94, Brown U., Providence, 1973-78, trustee emeritus, 1978—. With USMCR, WWII. Mem. World Presidents Orgn. (bd. dirs. 1986), Delta Kappa Epsilon. Republican. Clubs: Brown U. of No. Calif, Harvard Bus. Sch. of No. Calif, Napa Valley Country; Bohemian (San Francisco). Office: 2201 3rd Ave N Napa CA 94558-3836

LEAVITT, MAIMON, psychiatrist; b. Bklyn., Jan. 26, 1921; s. William and Leah (Wolson) L.; m. Peggy Berne, May 19, 1943; children: Richard M., Andrew M., Susan J., Jane E. BS, Harvard Coll., 1940; MD, NYU Coll. Medicine, 1943. Intern Michael Reese Hosp., Chgo., 1944; resident in neurology Goldwater Meml. Hosp., N.Y., 1945; resident in psychology Menninger Fedn., Topeka, 1945-47, staff psychiatrist, 1945-50; psychiatrist pvt. practice, L.A., 1950—; dir. L.A. Psychoanalytic Inst., 1970-73; prof. UCLA, 1960—; pres. Stoller Found., L.A., 1992—. contbr. articles to profl. jours. Com. chmn. Boy Scouts Am., L.A., 1955-58. Maj. U.S. Army, 1950-53. Mem. L.A. Psychoanalytical Soc. & Inst. (dir. 1970-73, pres. 1965-68). Office: 1800 Fairburn Ave Los Angeles CA 90025-4968

LEAVITT, MICHAEL OKERLUND, governor, insurance executive; b. Cedar City, Utah, Feb. 11, 1951; s. Dixie and Anne (Okerlund) L.; m. Jacalyn Smith; children: Michael Smith, Taylor Smith, Anne Marie Smith, Chase Smith, Weston Smith. BA, So. Utah U., 1978. CPCU. Sales rep. Leavitt Group, Cedar City, 1972-74, account exec., 1974-76; mgr. underwriting Salt Lake City, 1976-82; chief operating officer, 1982-84, pres., chief exec. officer, 1984—, gov., state of Utah, 1993—; bd. dirs. Pacificorp, Portland, Oreg., Utah Power and Light Co., Salt Lake City, Great Western Thrift and Loan, Salt Lake City. Utah Bd. Regents, chmn. instl. coun. So. Utah State U., Cedar City, 1985-89; campaign chmn. U.S. Sen. Orrin Hatch, 1982, 88, U.S. Sen. Jake Garn, 1980, 86; cons. campaign Gov. Norman Angerter, 1984; mem. staff Reagan-Bush '84. 2d lt. USNG, 1969-77. Named Disting. Alumni So. Utah State Coll. Sch. Bus., 1986. Mem. Chartered Property Casualty Underwriters. Republican. Mormon. Office: Office of the Governor 210 State Capitol Building Salt Lake City UT 84114-1202*

LEAVY, EDWARD, judge; m. Eileen Leavy; children: Thomas, Patrick, Mary Kay, Paul. AB, U. Portland, 1950, LLB, U. Notre Dame, 1953. Dist. judge Lane County, Eugene, Oreg., 1957-61, cir. judge, 1961-76; magistrate U.S. Dist. Ct. Oreg., Portland, 1976-84, judge, 1984-87, cir. judge U.S. Ct. Appeals (9th cir.), 1987—. Office: US Ct Appeals Pioneer Courthouse 555 SW Yamhill St Ste 216 Portland OR 97204-1323

LE BARD, JEFFREY MITCHELL, English language educator; b. Lynwood, Calif., July 1, 1955; s. Tommy Joe and Mona L. (McKinzie) Barton. BA in English and Spanish, Pacific Union Coll., 1977; MA in English, Calif. State U., Long Beach, 1984; PhD in English, U. Calif., Riverside, 1991. Tech. editor SCS Engrs., Long Beach, 1978-90; adj. asst. prof. West Coast U., Orange, Calif., 1991-94; tchg. asst. U. Calif., 1986-91, lectr. English, 1994—. Mem. Phi Delta Gamma.

LEBEAU, CHARLES PAUL, lawyer; b. Detroit, Dec. 11, 1944; s. Charles Henry Jr. and Mary Barbara (Moran) L.; m. Victoria Joy (Huchin), May 15, 1970; children: Jeffrey Kevin, Timothy Paul. AA, Macomb County Community Coll., Warren, Mich., 1967; BA, Wayne State U., 1969; JD, U. Detroit, 1972; grad. tax program, NYU Sch. Law, 1972-73. Bar: Mich. 1973, U.S. Tax Ct. 1973, Calif. 1987, U.S. Ct. Internat. Trade. 1988, U.S. Supreme Ct. 1988, U.S. Dist. Ct. (so. dist.) Calif. 1988. Tax atty. Ford Motor Co., Dearborn, Mich., 1973-75; assoc. Hoops & Huff, Detroit, 1975-76, Miller, Canfield, Paddock & Stone, Detroit, 1976-78; tax mgr. Oceaneering Internat., Santa Barbara, Calif., 1978-79; tax counsel Signal Cos. Inc., Beverly Hills and La Jolla, Calif., 1979-83; assoc. Gray, Cary, Ames & Frye, San Diego, 1983-84; of counsel James Watts Esq., La Jolla, 1985, Murfey, Griggs & Frederick, La Jolla, 1986; pvt. practice La Jolla and San Diego, 1987—; lectr. grad. tax program Golden Gate U., San Diego, 1979-87; adj. prof. law U. San Diego, 1982-85, 88-89; mem. Law Rev., U. Detroit, 1971-72; lectr. in taxation. Contbr. articles on internat. tax to profl. jours.; monthly tax case commentator Taxes Internat., London, 1981-85. Campaign coord. United Way, Santa Barbara, 1979. Mem. ABA, Mich. Bar Assn., Calif. Bar Assn., San Diego County Bar Assn., Pi Sigma Alpha. Republican. Roman Catholic. Home: 1999 Via Segovia La Jolla CA 92037-6441 Office: Law Offices Charles LeBeau Ste 1070 4660 La Jolla Village Dr San Diego CA 92122-4606

LEBEAU, CHARLES RAY, futures trading advisor; b. Oklahoma City, Sept. 6, 1938; s. Robert Eugene and Louise Juanita (McCombs) LeB.; m. Patricia Jo Dillard, Jan. 20, 1963; children: Suzanne, Robert. BA in Fin., Calif. State U., Long Beach, 1963. V.p. E.F. Hutton & Co., L.A., 1967-88, Paine Webber Inc., Rolling Hills Estate, Calif., 1988—; pres. Island View Fin. Group, Inc., Torrance, Calif., 1989—. Co-author: Computer Analysis of the Futures Market, 1992; editor, pub. Tech. Traders Bull., 1989-93. Capt. U.S. Army, 1963-67. Mem. Nat. Futures Assn. (mem. bus. conduct com. 1983—, waiver rev. bd. 1986—), Managed Futures Assn., Bond Club L.A. Office: Island View Fin Group Inc 25550 Hawthorne Blvd Ste 100 Torrance CA 90505-6831

LEBEJOARA, OVIDIU, artist; b. Ciupa, Romania, Dec. 14, 1952; came to U.S., 1986; s. Petre and Ileana (Telegaru) L. BFA, N. Tonitza Sch., Bucharest, Romania, 1973; BA, Otis Parsons Sch., L.A., 1988. Graphic artist Recom, Bucharest, 1975-79, Siderma, Bucharest, 1979-86, L.A. Signs & Graphics, 1987-94; artist Arts & Signs, L.A., 1994—. Exhibited in group shows in Romania, 1975-86, Anca Colbert Gallery, L.A., 1987, 88, Julleux Gallery, Kansas City, Mo., 1989, Main Street Gallery, Visalia, Calif., 1990, 91, L.A. Modern Art Gallery, 1990, Calif. Expn. and State Fair, 1991, United Pastelists Am., N.Y., 1991, Cedar-Lily Gallery, Murfreesboro, Tenn., 1991-92, Barakat Gallery, Beverly Hills, Calif., 1992, Modern Art Mus. Unet, France, 1993, New Eng. Fine Art Inst., Boston, 1993, City Hall Paris, May Mus. Modern Art, 1994, Romfest, Downey, Calif., 1994, Napoleon Found., 1995, City Hall Paris, 1995, Agora Gallery, Soho, N.Y., 1995, numerous others. Founder Romanian Am. Ctr., L.A., 1989. Recipient award of merit Calif. Expn. and State Fair, 1991, Discovery award Art of Calif. mag., 1993, 94. Mem. Knickerbocker Artists, Am. Pastelists, Graphic Artists Guild. Orthodox. Home and Studio: 3115 Montrose Ave # 12 Glendale CA 91214

LE BERTHON, ADAM, lawyer; b. L.A., June 12, 1962; s. Edward Lynch and Veronica Rose (Franks) Le B. BA cum laude, U. San Diego, 1985; JD, U. So. Calif., L.A., 1989. Bar: Calif. 1989, U.S. Dist. Ct. (ctrl. dist.) Calif. 1989, U.S. Ct. Appeals (9th cir.) 1989, U.S. Dist. Ct. (so. dist.) Calif. 1990, (no. dist.) Calif. 1990, (ea. dist.) Calif. 1990. Assoc. White & Case, L.A., 1989-91, Straw & Gilmartin, Santa Monica, Calif., 1991—. Editor So. Calif. Law Rev., 1988-89; contbr. articles to profl. jours. Recipient Am. Jurisprudence award U. So. Calif., 1987. Mem. Calif. State Bar Assn., L.A. County Bar Assn., Order of the Coif, Phi Alpha Delta, Omicron Delta Epsilon, Kappa Gamma Pi. Home: 125 Montana Ave Apt 207 Santa Monica CA 90403-1054 Office: Straw & Gilmartin 100 Wilshire Blvd Ste 1325 Santa Monica CA 90401-1114

LEBL, MICHAL, peptide chemist; b. Prague, Czechoslovakia, Aug. 21, 1951; came to U.S., 1991; s. Bedrich and Olga (Krystofova) Leblova; m. Zuzana Bucinova, June 9, 1973; children: Martin, George. MS, Inst. Chem. Tech., Prague, 1974; PhD, Inst. Organic Chemistry and Biochemistry, Prague, 1978, DSc, 1992. Scientist Inst. Organic Chemistry and Biochemistry, Prague, 1978-87, group leader, 1987-89, dept. head, 1989-91; dir., owner CSPS, Prague, Tucson, 1990—; dir. chemistry Selectide Corp., Tucson, 1991—; pres. Spyder Instruments Inc., 1993—; vis. prof. McMaster U., Hamilton, Can., 1982, U. Ariz., Tucson, 1983, 86, cons., 1989; mem. bd. chemistry Czechoslovak Acad. Sci., Prague, 1988-91; mem. program com. European Peptide Symposium, Interlaken, Switzerland, 1992; mem. Debiopharm Award Com., Bonmot, Switzerland, 1992. Author, editor: Handbook of Neurohypophysial Hormone Analogs, 1987, numerous sci. publs.; author: (software) Peptide Companion, 1994; editor-in-chief. (jour.) Collection of Czechoslovak Chem. Commn., 1987-91; editor: Molecular Diversity, 1995—; edtl. bd. Internat. Jour. Peptide and Protein Rsch., 1989—, Peptide Rsch. jour., 1988—; contbr. articles to profl. jours. Sci. grantee NIH, 1992-95, Czechoslovak Acad. Scis., 1991-93; recipient prize Czech Republic. Govt., 1990, Czechoslovak Acad. Scis., 1980, 86, 89. Mem. Am. Chem. Soc., Am. Peptide Soc., European Peptide Soc. (Zervas prize 1990), Czechoslovak Chem. Soc. Office: Selectide Corp 1580 E Hanley Blvd Tucson AZ 85737-9525

LEBLON, JEAN MARCEL, retired French language educator, consultant; b. Chimay, Hainaut, Belgium, June 7, 1928; came to U.S., 1947; s. Alfred and Marcelle (Lefèvre) L.; m. Mary Lorraine Hovorka, June 3, 1952; children: Mitzi, Simone. BS in Edn., Emporia State U., 1951; PhD, Yale U., 1960. Instr. Conn. Coll., New London, 1953-59, CCNY, 1959-62; assoc. prof. Hollins (Va.) Coll., 1962-65; prof. French Vanderbilt U., Nashville, 1966-87; chmn., 1976-85; teaching assoc. U. Wash., Seattle, 1988-90; vis. prof. U. Maine, Orono, 1962, Emporia (Kans.) State U., 1965, Fairfield (Conn.) U., 1966; cons. Ednl. Testing Svc., Princeton, N.J., 1963-87, Oxford U. Press, London, 1985-86, Champs-Elysees, Inc., Nashville, 1985-90, Wash. Acad. Lang., Seattle, 1987—. Co-author: Précis de Civilisation Française, 1966; translator: Zola (Marc Bernard), 1960; editor Les Choses (Georges Perec), 1969; editor, terminologist Microsoft Corp., 1990—. Mem. MLA (regional del. 1974-76), Am. Assn. Tchrs. French, N.W. Translators & Interpreters Soc. (pres. 1991-93), Am. Translators Assn., Seattle-Nantes Sister City Assn. (bd. dirs. 1990—), Alliance Française (bd. dirs. 1990—). Home: 1130 5th Ave S Apt 104 Edmonds WA 98020-4666

LE BON, DOUGLAS KENT, investment manager; b. Rapid City, S.D., Oct. 27, 1953; s. Stanley and Elodis (Holm) LeB. BSBA, Calif. State U., Dominguez Hills, 1976, MBA, 1979. Valuation cons. Houlihan, Lokey, Howard & Zukin, L.A., 1979-83; v.p., prin. Wilshire Assocs., Inc., Santa Monica, Calif., 1983-90; founder, mng. dir. Pathway Capital Mgmt., L.A., 1990—. Vice chmn., chmn. fin. com. L.A. area coun. Boy Scouts Am., 1991-95. Office: Pathway Capital Mgmt 18101 Von Karman Ave Ste 1860 Irvine CA 92715

LEBOW, BENNETT S., communications executive; b. Phila., 1938; 1 child, Geri. BEE, Drexel U.; postgrad., Princeton U. Prin. DSI Systems Inc., Rockville, Md., from 1961, B.S. LeBow Inc.; chmn. Western Union Corp., Upper Saddle River, N.J., New Valley Corp. (formerly Western Union Corp.), Upper Saddle River, 1993—. Office: Mai Basic Four Inc 14101 Myford Rd Tustin CA 92680-7020 also: New Valley Corp 1 Mack Centre Dr Paramus NJ 07452

LEBRATO, MARY THERESA, lawyer, psychologist; b. Ft. Wayne, Ind., June 13, 1950; d. Joseph James and Veronica (Adamonis) L. BA, U. Dayton, 1971; MA, U. Ala., Tuscaloosa, 1973, PhD, 1975; JD, Lincoln Law Sch., 1986. Bar: Calif. 1986; lic. psychologist, Calif. Psychologist Ala. Dept. Mental Hygiene, Tuscaloosa, 1975, Calif. Dept. Health, Eldridge, Calif., 1975-77; chief statewide evaluation devel. svcs. Calif. Dept. Health, Eldridge, 1977-79; dir. evaluation Oakland Perinatal Health Project, Calif. Dept. Health, Sacramento, 1979-81; coord. Maternal, Child and Adolescent Health, Sacramento, 1981-82; dir. sexual harassment in employment project Calif. Commn. on Status of Women, Sacramento, 1982-85; chief long range planning Calif. Dept. Devel. Svcs., Sacramento, 1985-88; staff counsel Calif. State Lottery, Sacramento, 1988-91. Co-author (with Marilyn Pearman) Sexual Harassment Investigators Guidebook, 1984; author, editor: Help Yourself: A Manual for Dealing with Sexual Harassment, 1986. Adv. bd. mem. Calif. State Pers. Bd., Appeals Div. Adv. Com., 1987-91; bd. mem. Sacramento Rape Crisis Ctr., 1988. Recipient fellowships in psychology NIMH, U. Ala., Tuscaloosa, 1971, 72, 73, teaching asst. in psychology U. Ala., Tuscaloosa, 1974-75. Mem. APA, ABA, Am. Assn. on Mental Deficiency, Calif. State Bar Assn., Calif. State Psychol. Assn., Calif. Women Lawyers, Sacramento County Bar Assn., Women Laywers Sacramento (bd. mem., chair del. com. 1989, chair scholarship 1990). Home: 335 Del Wes Ln Rio Linda CA 95673-2031

LECKART, BRUCE, psychologist; b. N.Y.C., Mar. 8, 1940; s. Samuel and Adele (Chesler) L.; m. Karen Iris Leckart, Mar. 30, 1969; 1 child, Steven. BA, Mich. State U., 1962, MA, 1963, PhD, 1965. Lic. psychologist, Calif. Asst. prof. Ohio U., Athens, 1965-68; assoc. prof. psychology San Diego State U., 1968-72, prof. psychology, 1972-93, prof. emeritus, 1994—; psychologist Westwood Evaluation and Treatment Ctr, L.A., 1986-94; postdoctoral clin. intern L.A. Cmty. Mental Health Ctr., Long Beach, Calif., 1971-73, supr. clin. psychologist Family Svc., Cerritos, Calif., 1985-86; vis. prof. Calif. State U., L.A., 1974-75; qualified med. evaluator State of Calif., 1990-94; pvt. practice, L.A., San Diego, Oxnard, and Ventura, Calif., 1977-94. Author: Up From Boredom, Down From Fear, 1979; editl. cons. psychol. jours.; contbr. articles to profl. jours. USPHS fellow, 1963-65. Mem. APA, Psi Chi. Office: Westwood Evaluation Ctr and Treatment 11300 W Olympic Blvd Los Angeles CA 90064-1637

LE CLAIR, DOUGLAS MARVIN, lawyer; b. Montreal, Nov. 13, 1955; s. Lawrence M. and Joan B. Le Clair; m. Debra L. Garland, Oct. 12, 1985. BA, Loyola U., 1977; JD, Southwestern U., 1980; peace officer cert., Mesa Community Coll. Law Enforcement Acad., 1985. Bar: Ariz. 1982, U.S. Dist. Ct. Ariz. 1983, U.S. Ct. Appeals (9th cir.) 1983, U.S. Tax. Ct. 1987, U.S. Ct. Claims 1987, U.S. Supreme Ct. 1987. Corp. counsel Great Western Trading Co., Los Angeles, 1982-83; pvt. practice Mesa, Ariz., 1983—; mem. faculty law & acctg. Sterling Sch., Phoenix, Ariz., 1992—; chief exec. officer, gen. counsel DL Industries, Inc., Mesa, 1983—; corp. counsel various corps., Ariz. Author: Le Clair/Morgan Income Tax Organizer, 1982-83; prodn. editor Computer Law Jour., 1979-80; producer TV Advt., 1983. Res. officer Mesa Police Dept., 1984-92. Named One of Outstanding Young Men Of Am., 1979. Mem. ABA, Ariz. Bar Assn., Maricopa County Bar Assn., Internat. Platform Assn., Southwestern Student Bar Assn. (exec. bd. 1978-79), Southwestern U. Tax Law Soc., Mesa C. of C., Delta Theta Phi, Phi Alpha Theta. Home and Office: PO Box 223 Mesa AZ 85211-0223

LECRON, MARY FRAZER See FOSTER, MARY FRAZER

LEDBETTER, CARL SCOTIUS, counselor, educator; b. Pyatt, Ark., Aug. 19, 1910; s. James Oliver and Lillie Belle (Wall) L.; student Phillips U., Enid, Okla., 1930-32; A.B., Ky. Christian Coll., 1937; AB, Butler U., 1939, MA, 1940; MA, U. Redlands, 1967; postgrad. Claremont Grad. Sch., 1961-64, Mankato (Minn.) State Coll., 1970-73, Calif. State Coll., 1974-76; m. Ruth Slocum Weymouth, June 20, 1948; children: Carla Sue Ledbetter Holte, Carl Scotius, Charles Stephen, Craig Slocum, Candace Sybil Ledbetter Heidelberger, Christa Sharyn Nuxoll. Ordained to ministry Christian Ch., 1933; student pastor, Huntington, W.Va., 1935-36, Russell, Ky., 1936-39, Atlanta, Ind., 1939-40; mem. editorial staff Standard Pub. Co., Cin., 1940-41; commd. 1st lt. U.S. Army, 1941; advanced through grades to col., 1961; command chaplain Augsburg (W. Ger.) area, 1950-53; div. chaplain 3d Inf. Div., 1953-55; dep. army chaplain 6th U.S. Army, 1955-58; command chaplain 5th Region Army Air Def. Command, 1959-61; ret., 1961; dean men U. Redlands, 1961-69; dir. counseling, v.p. acad. affairs Lea (Minn.) Coll., 1969-74; rehab. counselor J.O.B. Work Activities Ctr., Hesperia, Calif., 1976-80, dir., 1980-85, dir. emeritus, 1985—; adj. prof. psychology and religion Chapman Coll., 1976-85. Recipient award of merit Boy Scouts Am., 1967, Silver Beaver award, 1969. Mem. Am. Personnel and Guidance Assn., Nat. Vocat. Guidance Assn., Am. Rehab. Counselors Assn., Alpha Phi Gamma, Phi Delta Kappa, Pi Ch, Pi Gamma Mu, Alpha Phi Omega. Democrat. Club: Masons. Home: 611 Juniper Ct Redlands CA 92374-6236

LEDBETTER, LOGAN SCOTT, management consultant; b. Phila., Oct. 2, 1958; s. Thomas Velt and Elizabeth Kinloch (Logan) L. BA in Polit. Sci., U. Ga., 1982; MS in Strategic Intelligence, Def. Intelligence Coll., 1991. Commd. ensign USN, 1983, advanced through grades to lt. comdr., 1993; naval intelligence officer USS Dwight D. Eisenhower, Norfolk, Va., 1984-86, Def. Intelligency Agy., Washington, 1986-89, USS Am., Norfolk, 1989-91; resigned USN, 1991; mgmt. cons. Booz, Allen and Hamilton, Inc., Mountain View, Calif., 1992-93, Colorado Springs, 1993—. With USNR. mem. U.S. Naval Inst., The Woodrow Wilson Ctr., The Naval Res. Assn. Episcopalian. Office: Booz Allen & Hamilton Inc 1050 S Academy Blvd Ste 148 Colorado Springs CO 80910

LEDBURY, DIANA GRETCHEN, adult education educator; b. Denver, Mar. 7, 1931; d. Francis Kenneth and Gretchen (Harry) Van Ausdall; m. Chander Parkash Lall, Dec. 26, 1953 (div. Aug. 1973); children: Anne, Neil, Kris; m. Eugene Augustus Ledbury, Sept. 13, 1976; stepchildren: Mark, Cindy, Rob. BA in Sociology, Colo. U., 1953. Instr. Home, and Family Life Seattle Pub. Schs. Adult Edn., 1957-62, Seattle C.C., Seattle, 1962-69, Green River C.C., 1969-71; asst. tchr. Renton Sch. Dist., Wash., 1974-83; adult edn. instr. Mental Health Network, Renton, 1984—; coord. Inter-Study, Renton, 1985—, program dir. Crossroads Child Care, 1985-86, family svcs. coord. , 1986-87, program supr. Candyland Too Child Care Ctr., 1987—, Candyland Also, 1987-90; coord. child care staff Washington Fitness Ctr., 1991-93. Mem. Renton Area Youth Svcs. Bd., Sch. and Community Drug Prevention Program, Renton dist. coun. PTA, Renton Citizen's Com. on Recreation; vol. Griffin Home for Boys; coord. Modern Dance Prodn., Carco Theater; adult leader Camp Fire Girls' Horizon Club; mem. bd. Allied Arts of Renton; mem. Bicentennial Com. for a Cultural Arts, Edn. and Recreation Ctr.; PTA rep. Dimmit Jr. High Sch.; mem. Sch. and Community Recreation Com.; founder Handicapped Helping Themselves, Mental Health Network; precinct committeeperson 11th dist. Republican party, Wash., 1976-85. Recipient Golden Acorn award Wash. State Congress PTA, Renton, 1972. Mem. AAUW (legis. chair 1983-87, mem. com. on strategic sch. policy safety in schs. 1993-94, com. on getting parents involved. 1994-95, pub. policy chair AAUW 1994—), Assn. Social and Health Services (mem. com. 1984-85). Episcopalian. Avocations: arts; culture; recreation; child and family advocate.

LEDERER, MARION IRVINE, cultural administrator; b. Brampton, Ont., Can., Feb. 10, 1920; d. Oliver Bateman and Eva Jane (MacMurdo) L.; m. Francis Lederer, July 10, 1941. Student, U. Toronto, 1938, UCLA, 1942-45. Owner Canoga Mission Gallery, Canoga Park, Calif., 1967—; cultural heritage monument Canoga Mission Gallery, 1974—; Vice pres. Screen Smart Set women's aux. Motion Picture and TV Fund, 1973—; founder sister city program Canoga Park-Taxco, Mexico, 1963; Mem. mayor's cultural task force San Fernando Valley, 1973—; mem. Los Angeles Cultural Affairs Commn., 1980-85. Mem. Los Angeles Cultural Affairs Commn., 1980-85. Recipient numerous pub. service awards from mayor, city council, C. of C. Mem. Canoga Park C. of C. (cultural chmn. 1973-75, dir. 1973-75). Presbyn. Home: PO Box 32 Canoga Park CA 91305-0032 Office: Canoga Mission Gallery 23130 Sherman Way Canoga Park CA 91307-1402

LEDERER, THOMAS FELIX, secondary education educator, consultant; b. San Francisco, Oct. 10, 1944; s. Wolfgang and Hanni (Hirschberg) L.; m. Gale Jennings, June 20, 1972 (div. June 1988); children: Katrina, Mark. Student, San Diego State U., 1962-64; BA, San Francisco State U., 1967. Cert. elem., secondary tchr., adminstr., Calif. Tchr. Peace Corps, Somalia, 1967-70; tchr., prin. Cienega Elem. Sch., Hollister, Calif., 1970-72; tchr. English, Fairfield (Calif.) H.S., 1972—; cons. Ednl. Testing Svc., Calif., N.J., 1974—. NEH grantee, U. Md., 1985, U. Del., 1990. Mem. NEA, Nat. Coun. Tchrs. English, Ctrl. Calif. Coun. Tchrs. English (speaker Asilomar 1993, 94). Home: 726 Pomona Ave El Cerrito CA 94530-3255 Office: Fairfield High Sch 205 Atlantic Ave Fairfield CA 94533-1538

LEDFORD, GARY ALAN, real estate developer; b. San Diego, Dec. 30, 1946; s. Loren Oscar and Madge Francis (Condon) L.; children: Kelly, Jeanne, Robert, Kevin. BSCE, U.S. Army Engring. Coll., 1967. Pres. Mastercraft Contractors/Mastercraft Diversified Svcs., Inc./Masterplan, Inc., Colo. Springs, 1969-73; v.p. K.L. Redfern, Inc., Orange, Calif., 1973-75; pres. Ledford Industries, Inc./G.A. Ledford & Assocs., 1975-82, Watt Jess Ranch, Inc., Apple Valley, Calif., 1985-94; chmn. Jess Ranch, Apple Valley, 1994—; pres. Jess Ranch Water Co., Apple Valley, 1986—; gen. ptnr. GLBT Assocs., 1978-79; chmn. Watt-Jess/Ledford, Apple Valley, 1992-94; pres. LJ&J Investments, Inc., Apple Valley, Ledford-Schaffer/Rogers, Apple Valley. Designer computer software, 1979. Past pres. Cultural Arts Found., 1991-92, Victorville, Calif; bd. trustees Apple Valley Christian Care Ctr., High Desert Questors, Victorville; past pres. Victor Valley Mus. Assn., Baldy View B.I.A. Capt. C.E., U.S. Army, 1967-69, Vietnam. Mem. Internat. Coun. Shopping Ctrs., Nat. Assn. Home Builders', Nat. Planning Assn., NRA (life), High Desert Constrn. Indsutry Assn. (past v.p.), Bldg. Industry Assn., VFW, Sr. Housing Coun. Republican. Home: 11401 Apple Valley Rd Apple Valley CA 92308-7503 Office: Jess Ranch 11401 Apple Valley Rd Apple Valley CA 92308-7503

LEE, ALDORA G., social psychologist; b. Schenectady, N.Y.; d. Alois W. and M. Dorothy (Swigert) Graf. AB, Ind. U.; MA, Stanford U.; PhD, U. Colo. Dir. women studies Wash. State U., Pullman, 1976-78, dir. unit on aging, 1976-81; cons. in market research Syva, Palo Alto, Calif., 1982; staff market rsch. analyst Allstate Rsch. and Planning Ctr., Menlo Park, Calif., 1983—; rep. Wash. Assn. Gerontol. Edn., N.W. region rep. Nat. Women's Studies Assn., 1978-81. Contbr. articles to profl. jours. Mem. Menlo Park Libr. Commn., 1984-92, chmn., 1985-87; instr. Career Action Ctr., Palo Alto, 1984-87; Menlo Park rep. system adv. bd. Peninsula Libr. System, 1992—. Recipient Allstate Good Hands award for Cmty. Svc., 1994. Mem. Am. Mktg. Assn., Am. Psychol. Soc., Am. Sociol. Assn., Western Psychol. Assn., SRI Organon Toastmasters (Toastmaster of Yr. 1989, Able Toastmaster, Competent Toastmaster, mentor GeoSpeakers 1994), Phi Beta Kappa, Sigma Xi.

LEE, BEVERLY ING, educational administrator; b. Honolulu, Oct. 10, 1932; d. Tim Sheu and Helen (Heu) Ing; m. Daniel David Lee, June 21, 1962; children: Helen Ann Esq, Terence Daniel, Scott David. BA, Coll. of the Pacific, Stockton, Calif., 1954; MA, Columbia U., 1957. Policewoman Honolulu Police Dept., 1957-61; counselor Ewa Elem., Highlands Intermediate and Waipahu High Schs., 1961-69; adminstr. Dept. Edn. State of Hawaii, Honolulu, 1969-89; contr., v.p., pres. Classic Travel, Honolulu, 1988—; bd. dirs. Hawaii State Employees Credit Union, Honolulu, vice chair, 1994, chair, 1995; bd. dirs. Mahalo Airport Travel Agy.; mem. adv. bd. Travel Univ. Internat. Adv. Bd., 1994—. Mem. Gov.'s Commn. on Child Abuse, Honolulu, 1985-89; bd. dirs. Hawaii Family Stress Ctr., Honolulu, 1983—, Child and Family Svc., 1975-85; mem. Casey Family Program Adv. Com., 1986—, Parents Anonymous, 1988-92, Prevent Child Abuse Hawaii, 1975—. Mem. AAUW (life), Hawaiian Airlines Travel Agy. (adv. bd. 1991-93), Mahalo Airlines Travel Agy. (adv. bd. 1994—), Travel U. Internat. (adv. bd. 1994—), Casey Family (adv. bd. 1986—), Prevent Child Abuse Hawaii (bd. dir. 1975—), Child & Family Svcs. (bd. dir. 1975-85), Delta Kappa Gamma, Tri Delta. Office: Classic Travel 1413 S King St Ste 201 Honolulu HI 96814-2505

LEE, BLAINE NELSON, educational executive, consultant, educator; b. Olympia, Wash., Apr. 3, 1946; s. Elwyn Earl and Thelma Marie (Woods) Reeder; m. Shawny Christian Lee; children: Blaine, Benjamin, Adam, Michal, Joseph, Joshua, Casey, Abraham, Eliza, Gabriel, Celeste. BS in Psychology, Brigham Young U., 1969, MS in Ednl. Psychology, 1972; PhD in Ednl. Psychology, U. Tex., 1982. Cert. ednl. specialist, secondary edn., ednl. adminstrn. Dir. instrnl. sys. USAF, San Antonio, 1972-75; assoc. prof. USAF Acad., Colorado Springs, Colo., 1975-78; edn. dir. Heritage Sch., Provo, Utah, 1978-81; asst. prof. Utah Valley C.C., Orem, Utah, 1981-84; pres. Skills for Living, Salem, Utah, 1984-86; v.p. Covey Leadership Ctr., Provo, 1986—; ednl. cons. in field. Author: Affective Objectives, 1972, Personal Change, 1982, Stress Strategists, 1986; contbr. articles to profl. jours. High councilman LDS Ch., mem. gen. bd., 1970-72; pres. Provo PTO. Named Outstanding Young Man in Am., U.S. C. of C., 1976, 84. Mem. APA, ASTD, Am. Mgmt. Assn., Nat. Spkrs. Assn., Phi Delta Kappa. Home: 10435 S 600 E Salem UT 84653-9389 Office: Covey Leadership Ctr 3507 N University Ave Provo UT 84604-4478

LEE, CANDIE CHING WAH, retail executive; b. Hong Kong, British Crown Colony, June 17, 1950; came to U.S., 1973:; d. Willard W. and Yuk Ching (Yau) L. Student, Hong Kong Tech. Coll., Kowloon, 1968-70. Office mgr. Crown Enterprises, Ltd., Hong Kong, 1970-73; buyer, mgr. Hawaii Resort Industries, Inc., Honolulu, 1973-76, v.p., 1976-82; pres. Hawaii Resort Shops, Inc., Honolulu, 1983—. Mem. Am. Mgmt. Assn. Republican. Office: Hawaii Resort Shops Inc 2270 Kalakaua Ave Ste 1000 Honolulu HI 96815-2558

LEE, CAROLINE DURED, art appaiser, consultant, curator; b. Ft. Worth, Nov. 27, 1934; d. Willis Frank and Virginia C. (McIntyre) L.; m. Tom T. Adams, Aug. 25, 1956 (div. 1971); children: Holly, Erin; m. Robert M. Ellis, Dec. 22, 1990. Student, Stephens Coll., 1952-53, U. Ariz., 1953-55, Tex. Christian U., 1955, U. Tex., Austin and San Antonio, 1955, 78-79, San Antonio Art Inst., 1968-70, Trinity U., San Antonio, 1970-71, U. Mex., San Antonio, 1979, No. C.C., Taos, N.Mex., 1992, Lindenwood Coll., 1992. Dir. Southwest Craft Ctr. Gallery, San Antonio, 1971-75; owner, dir. Objects Gallery, San Antonio, 1980-84, Exvoto Gallery, San Antonio and Houston, 1985-86; owner, dir. Caroline Lee Gallery, San Antonio, 1984-87, Houston, 1986-88; owner, dir. Caroline Lee Gallery and Consulting Office, Taos, N.Mex., 1990-92, Caroline Lee Fine Art Appraising, Taos, 1991—; hon. instr. art segment Integration of Abilities Trinity U., San Antonio, 1970-71; juror, curator numerous Tex. art exhbns., 1973—; pvt. cons. various collectors, architects, designers, 1988-95; cons., art curator Taos Inn, 1992—; lectr., panel participant various mus. and orgns. One-woman show: San Antonio Art Inst., 1969; group shows: The Hand and the Spirit Gallery, Scottsdale, Ariz., 1979, Hadler-Rodriguez Gallery, Houston, 1979, Houston Designer/Craftsmen Exhbn., 1979 (award of excellence), Tex. Women Artists, 1980 (2d prize mixed media); invitational exhbns.: Of Paper and Porcelain, The Hand and Spirit Gallery, Scottsdale, 1980, 80 Texans, Galveston Arts Ctr., 1980; permanent collections: Archives of Am. Art, Smithsonian Inst., Washington, Mountain Bell Telephone Co., U. Tex. Health Sci. Ctr., pvt. individuals; author essays for catalogue and newsletter. Bd. mem. Santa Rosa Children's Hosp. Vol. Orgn., San Antonio, McNay Mus. Art, San Antonio, San Antonio Art League, Witte Mus. Art, San Antonio, Tex. Sculpture Symposiums, San Antonio; mem. Com. for Benefit for N.Mex. AIDS Svcs., Santa Fe, Com. for Friends of Santa Fe Opera-Apprentice Program, Com. for Vis. Nurse Svcs. Benefit, Santa Fe; mem. adv. bd. Rio Grande Planned Parenthood of Taos; chairwoman Fundraiser Benefits for the Harwood Mus., Taos. Named Accredited Sr. Appraiser, Am. Soc. Appraisers, 1993. Democrat. Home and Office: PO Box 1449 Taos NM 87571-1449

LEE, CHARLTON ROBERT, psychology educator; b. Jan. 13, 1930. BA in Psychology, Calif. State U., Long Beach, 1952, postgrad, 1960; MA in Psychology, UCLA, 1958. Lic. marriage, family, child counselor, Calif.; lic. ednl. psychologist, Calif. Intern Olive View Hosp., Sylmar, Calif., 1956-57, Rancho Los Amigos Hosp., Downey, Calif., 1957-58; counseling psychologist Calif. Dept. Edn., Long Beach, 1958-60; pvt. practice Lakewood, Calif., 1959-65; psychologist Los Alamitos (Calif.) Sch. Dist., 1960-67; staff psychologist Psychiat. Clinic for Youth Meml. Med. Ctr., Long Beach, 1964—; prof. Psychology Cypress (Calif.) Coll., 1967—; staff therapist Crystal Cathedral Counseling Ctr., Garden Grove, Calif., 1989—; dir. Attention Deficit Hyperactivity Disorder program Minirth-Meier Clinic West, Newport Beach, Calif., 1991-92, Am. Psychol. Inst., Anaheim Hills, Calif., 1992-93; staff therapist New Hope Counseling, Tustin, Calif., 1983—; ind. constractor Orange County Children's Svcs., 1992—. Mem. ASCD, AAAS, Western Psychol. Assn., Calif. Assn. Marriage and Family Therapists, Calif. C.C. Faculty Assn., Christian Assn. for Psychol. Studies, N.Y. Acad. Scis., Calif. Assn. Sch. Psychometrists and Psychologists, Am. Assn. Sex Educators Counselors and Therapists, Am. Psychol. Assn., Nat. Assn. Sch. Psychologists. Home: 3946 Walnut Ave Long Beach CA 90807-3750

LEE, DAVID WOON, chemist, lawyer; b. Hong Kong, July 14, 1949; came to U.S., 1967; s. Kwoon and Sau Yuen Lee; m. Helen Lee, May 23, 1970; children: Victor, Malinda. BS, U. Winnipeg, Can., 1970; BS with honors, U. Waterloo, Can., 1979; JD, Glendale (Calif.) U., 1991. Bar: Calif. 1992, U.S. Dist. Ct. (cen. dist.) Calif. 1992, U.S. Ct. Appeals (9th cir.) 1993, U.S. Patent & Trademark Office 1993. Rsch. chemist Atomic Energy of Can., Pinawa, 1970-80; supr. maj. facilities Atomic Energy of Can., Chalk River, 1980-87; indsl. waste specialist County of L.A., 1987-88; chemist City of L.A., 1988—; del. citizen amb. program nuclear waste mgmt. U.S.S.R., 1989. Contbr. articles to Can. Jour. of Chemistry, Jour. of Colloid and Interface Sci., Jour. Electrochem. Soc., Electrochimica Acta 22; contbr. over 20 articles to profl. jours. Br. rep. Atomic Energy of Can. Profl. Employees Assn., Chalk River, 1984-87; judge Pembroke (Can.) Regional Sci. Fair, 1985-86. Mem. Am. Nuclear Soc., People-to-People Internat. Office: David & Raymond 108 N Ynez Ave Ste 118 Monterey Park CA 91754-1680

LEE, DONNA JEAN, retired hospice and respite nurse; b. Huntington Park, Nov. 12, 1931; d. Louis Frederick and Lena Adelaide (Hinson) Munyon; m. Frank Bernard Lee, July 16, 1949; children: Frank, Robert, John. AA in Nursing, Fullerton (Calif.) Jr. Coll., 1966; extension student, U. Calif., Irvine, 1966-74; student, U. N.Mex., 1982. RN, Calif. Staff nurse Orange (Calif.) County Med. Ctr., 1966-71, staff and charge nurse relief ICU, CCU, Burn Unit, ER, Communicable Disease, Neo-Natal Care Unit, 1969-71, charge nurse communicable disease unit, 1969-70; staff and charge nurse ICU, emergency rm., CCU, med./surg. units Anaheim (Calif.) Meml. Hosp., 1971-74; charge and staff nurse, relief Staff Builders, Orange, 1974-82; agy. nurse Nursing Svcs. Internat., 1978-89; asst. DON Chapman Convalescent SNF, Orange, 1982; geriatric and pedicatrics nurse VNASS, 1985-93; hospice/respite nurse VIA Upjohn Home Healthcare Svcs and VNA Support Svcs. of Orange, 1985-93; ret.; staff relief nurse ICU/CCU various hosps. and labs, including plasmapheresis nurse Med. Lab. of Orange, 1978. Life mem. Republican, pres. task force, 1982—; past mem. Republican adv. com., Rep. Presdl. Trust; mem. Rep. Presdl. Legion of Merit. Mem. AACN, RNCC, RNSC, ADA, ASA. Inst. Noetic Scis., The Heritage Found., Aria, Intravenous Therapy Assn. U.S.A. (cert. 1994), Am. Cancer Soc., Am. Lung Assn., Am. Heart Assn., Nat. Multiple Sclerosis Soc., Easter Seal Soc., Internat. Platform Assn. Baptist. Home: 924 S Hampstead St Anaheim CA 92802-1740

LEE, DOROTHY WONG, secondary art educator; b. L.A., Aug. 17, 1948; d. Leonard G.Y. and Ginger (Hom) Wong; m. Kenny Lee, Nov. 24, 1973; children: Brandon Joel, Brittany Jene. BA, UCLA, 1971; std. secondary tchg. credential, Calif. State U., L.A., 1973. Secondary art tchr. L.A. (Calif.) Unified Sch. Dist., 1973—; buyer, retailer Imperial Dragon Gifts, Inc., L.A., 1978-94. Recipient Tchg. award Otis Art Inst., L.A., 1992, Bravo award L.A. (Calif.) County Music Ctr., 1994. Mem. United Tchrs. L.A., Art Educators L.A., L.A. County Art Mus. Home: PO Box 29893 Los Angeles CA 90029-0893

LEE, EDMUND, photojournalist; b. San Francisco, Mar. 2, 1968; s. Jeffrey Kuenka and Maria Lai Ping (Chan) L. AS in Photography, City Coll. San Francisco, 1992; student, San Francisco State U., 1992—. Photo editor/staff photographer The Guardsman, San Francisco, 1989-90; stringer photographer San Mateo (Calif.) Times, 1992-93, Petaluma (Calif.) Argus-Courier, 1992-94, Marin Ind. Jour., Novato, Calif., 1992-94, AP, San Francisco, 1992-94; photography intern Metro Newspaper Group, San Jose, Calif., 1994, staff photographer, 1994-95. Recipient awards for photography. Mem. Asian Am. Journalists Assn., Soc. Profl. Journalists, Nat. Press Photographers Assn., Calif. Press Photographers Assn., San Francisco Bay Area Press Photographers Assn. Home: 7 Crestview Ave Daly City CA 94015-4502 Office: Metro Newspaper Group 245 Almendra Ave Los Gatos CA 95030-7210

LEE, ELIZABETH ANNE, marketing executive; b. Carbondale, Ill., Sept. 5, 1952; d. Kenneth O. and Velma Marquerite (Mizner) McGee; m. Steven Robin Lee, Mar. 27,1987; 1 child, Kelsey Erin. BS in Applied Sci., Miami U., 1974; MBA, St. Louis U., 1978. Staff supr. Southwestern Bell, St. Louis, 1978-80; mgr. market rsch. Angelica Uniform Group, St. Louis, 1980-83; sr. analyst consumer rsch. May Dept. Stores Co., St. Louis, 1983-84; v.p. Data Support Svcs., Inc., St. Louis, 1984-87; pres. Concours Rsch., Inc., St. Louis, 1987-89, also bd. dirs.; ptnr. Steve Lee & Assocs., 1994—; cons. Project Bus., St. Louis, 1983-84; mem. adj. faculty U. Mo., 1987—, Webster U., 1988—, Menlo Coll., 1995. Editor: Quantitative Models for Bus. Decisions (Kwak), 1978. Bd. dirs. The St. Louis Ballet, 1989-90. Fellow St. Louis U., 1977-78. Mem. BBB, Am. Mktg. Assn., San Francisco C. of C. Republican. Congregationalist. Office: The Fitzpatrick Bldg 2000 Broadway St Redwood City CA 94063-1802

LEE, ELIZABETH TAN, mathematics educator; b. Singapore, July 7, 1944; came to U.S., 1962; d. Keng Huat and Siok Eng (Chan) Tan; m. David Oi Lee, Aug. 7, 1966 (div. Dec. 1994); 1 child, Andrea K.E. Lee-Wolf. BA, North Ctrl. Coll., Naperville, Ill., 1966; MA, U. N.Mex., 1981. Cert. tchr., N.Mex. Computer programmer Continental Casualty Co., Chgo., 1966; computer programmer, substitute tchr., math. tchr. Albuquerque Pub. Schs., 1967-72; tchr. math. Los Lunas (N.Mex.) H.S., 1977-78; tchr. math. and computer sci. Albuquerque Pub. Schs., 1978—. Republican. Methodist. Office: Cibola HS 1510 Ellison Dr NW Albuquerque NM 87114-5101

LEE, GILBERT BROOKS, retired ophthalmology engineer; b. Cohasset, Mass., Sept. 10, 1913; s. John Alden and Charlotte Louise (Brooks) L.; m. Marion Corrine Rapp, Mar. 7, 1943 (div. Jan. 1969); children: Thomas Stearns, Jane Stanton, Frederick Cabot, Eliot Frazar. BA, Reed Coll., 1937; MA, New Sch. for Social Rsch., 1949. Asst. psychologist U.S. Naval Submarine Base Civil Svc., Psychophysics of Vision, New London, Conn., 1950-53; rsch. assoc. Project Mich., Vision Rsch. Labs., Willow Run, 1954-57; rsch. assoc. dept. ophthalmology U. Mich., Ann Arbor, 1958-72, sr. rsch. assoc., 1972-75, sr. engring. rsch. assoc. ophthalmology, 1975-82, part-time sr. engr. ophthalmology, 1982—; sec. internat. dept., 23d St. YMCA, N.Y.C.; cons. W.K. Kellogg Eye Ctr., Ann Arbor, 1968—. Local organizer, moderator (TV program) Union of Concerned Scientists' Internat. Satellite Symposium on Nuclear Arms Issues, 1986; producer (TV show) Steps for Peace, 1987; designer, builder portable tristimulus Colorimeter; (videotape) Pomerance Awards, UN.; broken lake ice rescue procedure rsch., by one person in a dry suit, all weather conditions, 1966, 89-93 (videotape). Precinct del. Dem. County Conv., Washtenaw County, 1970, 74; treas. Dem. Club, Ann Arbor, Mich., 1971-72, 74-79; vice chmn. nuclear arms control com., 1979; chmn. Precinct Election Inspectors, 1968-75; scoutmaster Portland (Oreg.) area coun. Boy Scouts Am., 1932-39. Capt. AUS, 1942-46, 61-62. Mem. AAAS, Nat. Resources Def. Coun., Fedn. Am. Scientists, N.Y.

Acad. Sci., Nation Assocs., ACLU, Sierra Club, Amnesty Internat. Home: 4131 E Pinchot Ave Phoenix AZ 85018-7115

LEE, GLENN RICHARD, medical administrator, educator; b. Ogden, Utah, May 18, 1932; s. Glenn Edwin and Thelma (Jensen) L.; m. Pamela Marjorie Ridd, July 18, 1969; children—Jennifer, Cynthia. B.S., U. Utah, 1953, M.D., 1956. Intern Boston City Hosp.-Harvard U., 1956-57, resident, 1957-58; clin. asso. Nat. Cancer Inst., NIH, 1958-60; postdoctoral fellow U. Utah, 1960-63; instr. U. Utah Coll. Medicine, 1963-64, asst. prof. internal medicine, 1964-68, assoc. prof., 1968-73, prof., 1973—, assoc. dean for acad. affairs, 1973-76, dean, 1978-83; chief of staff Salt Lake VA Med. Ctr., 1985-95. Author: (with others) Clinical Hematology, 9th edit, 1993; Contbr. (with others) numerous articles to profl. jours.; editorial bd.: (with others) Am. Jour. Hematology, 1976-79. Served with USPHS, 1958-60. Markle Found. scholar, 1965-70; Nat. Inst. Arthritis, Metabolic and Digestive Disease grantee, 1977-82. Mem. A.C.P., Am. Soc. Hematology, Am. Soc. Clin. Investigation, Western Assn. Physicians, Am. Inst. Nutrition. Mem. LDS Ch. Home and Office: 3781 Ruth Dr Salt Lake City UT 84124-2331

LEE, GRACE TZE, controller; b. Taipei, Republic of China, Aug. 11, 1953; came to U.S., 1974; d. Tang Chi and Ming (Shu) L. BA, Nat. Taipei U., 1974; BS, U. Nev., 1977; postgrad., UCLA, 1988. Fgn. currency specialist Deak-Perera Co., L.A., 1977-80; asst. mgr. Universal Supply Co., L.A., 1980; contr. AJR Electronics Inc., L.A., 1981-84; western zone asst. mgr. Samsung Electronics Co., L.A., 1984; contr. Gideon Nol Inc., L.A., 1985-87, James G. Wiley Co., L.A., 1987-91, Jetset Tours Inc. (N.Am.), L.A., 1991—; pres. G.L. Fin. Svc., 1988—, Real Estate Investment Svc., 1988—. Home: 23442 Batey Ave Harbor City CA 90710-1204

LEE, HAMILTON H., education educator; b. Zhouhsien, Shandong, China, Oct. 10, 1921; came to U.S., 1956, naturalized, 1972; s. Peiyuen and Huaiying L.; BA, Nat. Beijing Normal U., 1948; MA, U. Minn., 1958; EdD, Wayne State U., 1964; m. Jean Chang, Aug. 24, 1945; children-Wei, Clarence, Karen, Kate. Rsch. assoc. Wayne State U., Detroit, 1958-64; asst. prof. Moorhead (Minn.) State U., 1964-65; assoc. prof. U. Wis., LaCrosse, 1965-66; prof. edn. East Stroudsburg (Pa.) U., 1966—, now prof. emeritus; vis. prof. Seton Hall U., summer 1964; vis. scholar Harvard U., summer 1965, 66; vis. fellow Princeton U., 1976-78; hon. mem. adv. coun. Internat. Biographical Ctr., Cambridge, England, 1995. Recipient numerous poetry contest awards. Mem. Acad. Am. Poets, Poetry Soc. Am., Pa. Poetry Soc., Internat. Soc. Poets (life mem. adv. panel), Phi Delta Kappa. Author: Readings in Instructional Technology, 1970, (chapbook) Reflection, 1989, (chapbook II) Revelation, 1991; contbg. editor Edn. Tomorrow, 1972-74; contbr. articles and poetry to profl. jours., anthologies. Address: PO Box 980 Los Altos CA 94023-0980

LEE, HO JOHN, electrical engineer; b. Boston, Nov. 4, 1962; s. Kwan Young and Kum Hwa (Yoo) L.; m. Insook Amy Jeon, May 8, 1993. BSEE, MSEE, MIT, 1985. Mem. tech. staff HP Labs., Palo Alto, Calif., 1983—; project leader HP Labs., Palo Alto, 1988-89; founder, pres. Tetra Systems Inc., Palo Alto, 1989-93; project mgr. HP Labs., Palo Alto, 1994—; mem. faculty dept. elec. engring. Northwestern Poly. U., 1985-88. Me, IEEE, Assn. Computing Machinery, Korean Am. Profl. Soc. (bd. dirs. 1992-95).

LEE, HOSIN, civil engineer, educator; b. Seoul, Feb. 24, 1958; came to U.S., 1980; s. Youngjae and Jungsup (Chung) L.; m. Jounghee Veronica Lee, Dec. 22, 1984; 1 child, Charles Sangjune. BS, Seoul Nat. U., 1980; MS, Stanford U., 1981; PhD, U. Tex., 1985. Registered profl. engr., Utah. Rsch. engr. Austin (Tex.) Rsch. Engrs., 1986; project engr. Vanasse/Hangen Inc., Boston, 1986; asst. prof. Youngstown (Ohio) State U., 1986-88, Wash. State U., Pullman, 1988-91, U. Utah, Salt Lake City, 1992—; dir. Ctr. for Advanced Constrn. Materials, Salt Lake City, 1994—. Mem. ASCE, ASTM, Transp. Rsch. Bd. (univ. rep.), Am. Concrete Inst., Am. Soc. Engring. Edn. Office: U Utah 3220 MEB Civil Engring Salt Lake City UT 84112

LEE, IVY, JR., public relations consultant; b. N.Y.C., July 31, 1909; s. Ivy and Cornelia (Bigelow) L.; m. Marie F. Devin, Oct. 14, 1988; children: Peter Ivy III (dec.), Jean Downey. BA, Princeton U., 1931; MBA, Harvard U., 1933. Ptnr. Ivy Lee & T.J. Ross, N.Y.C., 1933-45; with Pan Am. World Airways, Miami, Fla. and San Francisco, 1942-45; adminstrv. asst. S.D. Bechtel, Bechtel Cos., San Francisco, 1950-54; pres. Ivy Lee Jr. & Assocs., San Francisco, 1945-85; pres., cons. Ivy Lee Jr. & Assocs., Inc., San Francisco, 1985—. Trustee Princeton (N.J.) U., 1965-69; bd. dirs. San Francisco TB Assn., Bay Area Red Cross, San Francisco, Edgewood Childrens Ctr. Mem. Pub. Relations Soc. Am., Internat. Pub. Relations Assn. (pres. 1976-77). Republican. Presbyterian. Clubs: Bohemian, Pacific Union. Home: 1940 Broadway San Francisco CA 94109-2216 Office: 210 Post St Ste 609 San Francisco CA 94108-5108

LEE, JAI JUNG, accountant; b. Seoul, Republic of Korea, Feb. 22, 1949; came to U.S., 1977; s. Sung B. and Young A. (Koo) L.; m. In S. Choi, Aug. 20, 1980; children: Marcus, Michael. LLB, Kyung Hee U., Seoul, 1972; postgrad., USAMMCS, 1973; MBA, Calif. State U., L.A., 1984. Cert. tax preparer, Calif. Staff acct. Pyramid Optical Co., Irvine, Calif., 1978-80; sr. acct. Kim, Kang Yun & Co., CPA's, L.A., 1981-84, Simon, Steemke & Co., CPA's, Rolling Hills Estates, Calif., 1984-91; pvt. practice Lee & Co., Artesia, Calif., 1991—. Referee Am. Youth Soccer Orgn., Torrance, Calif., 1990—. Roman Catholic. Office: Lee & Co 18021 Norwalk Blvd Ste 201 Artesia CA 90701-4254

LEE, JAMES GORDON, air force officer; b. Willimantic, Conn., Nov. 7, 1956; s. Jesse Richard and Mary Francis (Kelley) L.; m. Debevon Deneice Duncan, Aug. 15, 1980; 1 child, Shaun Duncan. BS in Computer Sci., N.Mex. State U., 1978; MA in Computer Resources, Webster U., 1985; MA in Airpower Studies, Air U., Maxwell AFB, Ala., 1993. Commd. 2d lt. USAF, advanced through grades to lt. col., 1994; space computer plans officer Hdqs. USAF Space Command, Colorado Springs, Colo., 1982-85; space weapons officer Hdqs. USAF, Washington, 1985-86; exch. officer Hdqs. U.S. Army, Washington, 1986-87; space and strategic def. analyst Hdqs. USAF, Washington, 1987-89; dir. systems and logistics 5 Def. Space Comm. Squadron, Woomera, South Australia, 1989-91; dep. chief space policy, doctrine and strategy Hdqs. Air Force Space Command, Colorado Springs, 1993-94, comdr. 4th space surveillance squadron, 1994—. City councilman Woomera (South Australia) Bd., 1989-91; mem. com. Boy Scouts Am., Montgomery, Ala., 1992-93, Colorado Springs, San Antonio, 1992-94. Mem. Air Force Assn.

LEE, JAMES KING, technology corporation executive; b. Nashville, July 31, 1940; s. James Fitzhugh Lee and Lucille (Charlton) McGivney; m. Victoria Marie Marani, Sept. 4, 1971; children: Gina Victoria, Patrick Fitzhugh. BS, Calif. State U., Pomona, 1964; MBA, U. So. Calif., 1966. Prodn. and methods engring. foreman Gen. Motors Corp., 1963-65; engring. adminstr. Douglas MSSD, Santa Monica, Calif., 1965-67; mgr. mgmt. systems TRW Systems, Redondo Beach, Calif., 1967-68; v.p. corp. devel. DataStation Corp., L.A., 1968-69; v.p., gen. mgr. Aved Systems Group, L.A., 1969-70; mng. ptnr. Corp. Growth Cons., L.A., 1970-81; chmn., pres., CEO Fail-Safe Tech. Corp., L.A., 1981-93; pres., COO The Flood Group Inc., Torrance, Calif., 1994—. Author industry studies, 1973-79. Mem. L.A. Mayor's Community Adv. Com., 1962-72, aerospace task force L.A. County Econ. Devel. Commn., 1990-92; bd. dirs. USO of Greater L.A., 1990-92, v.p. personnel 1990-92, exec. v.p., 1992-93, pres. 1993—; asst. adminstr. SBA, Washington, 1974; vice chmn. Traffic Commn., Rancho Palos Verdes, Calif., 1975-78; chmn. Citizens for Property Tax Relief, Palos Verdes, 1976-80; mem. Town Hall Calif. Recipient Golden Scissors award Calif. Taxpayers' Congress, 1978. Mem. So. Calif. Tech. Execs. Network, Am. Electronics Assn. (chmn. L.A. coun. 1987-88, vice chmn. 1986-87, nat. bd. dirs. 1986-89), Nat. Security Industries Assn. Republican. Baptist. Home: 28874 Crestridge Rd Palos Verdes CA 90275-5063 Office: The Flood Group 3521 Lomita Blvd Ste 201 Torrance CA 90505-5016

LEE, JAMES NORMAN, bioengineering researcher, educator; b. Santa Monica, Calif., Dec. 20, 1956; s. Robert Martin and Nila (Stubbs) L.; m. Carolyn Kim Bailey, Aug. 23, 1957; children: Bethany, Jessica, Christina. BA in Applied Physics, U. Utah, 1980, MS in Physics Instrumentation, 1982; PhD in Biomed. Engring., Duke U., 1986. Postdoc. fellow Duke U., Durham, N.C., 1986-88; rsch. asst. prof. Dept. Radiology U. Utah, Salt Lake City, 1988-93; adj. asst. prof. Dept. Bioengring. U. Utah, Salt Lake City, 1993—; reviewer small bus. innovation rsch. grants Dept. HHS, Washington, 1993—; prin. investigator The Whitaker Found., 1990-93, GE Med. Systems, 1993, NIH, 1993-94. Patentee in field of biomed. engring. instrumentation; contbr. articles to profl. jours. Mem. Soc. Magnetic Resonance Imaging, Soc. Magnetic Resonance in Medicine. Republican. Mem. Ch. Latter Day Sts. Office: U Utah Med Imaging Rsch Labs AC 213 Sch Medicine Salt Lake City UT 84108

LEE, JOHN JIN, lawyer; b. Chgo., Oct. 20, 1948; s. Jim Soon and Fay Yown (Young) L.; m. Jamie Pearl Eng, Apr. 30, 1983. BA magna cum laude, Rice U., 1971; JD, Stanford U., 1975; MBA, 1975. Bar: Calif. 1976. Assoc. atty. Manatt Phelps & Rothenberg, L.A., 1976-77; asst. counsel Wells Fargo Bank N.A., San Francisco, 1977-79, counsel, 1979-80, v.p., sr. counsel, 1980, v.p., mng. sr. counsel, 1981—; mem. governing com. Conf. on Consumer Fin. Law, 1989-93. Bd. dirs. Asian Bus. League of San Francisco, 1981—, gen. counsel, 1981. Fellow Am. Coll. Consumer Fin. Svcs. Attys., Inc., (bd. regents 1995—), mem. ABA (chmn. subcom. on housing fin., com. on consumer fin. svcs., bus. law sect. 1983-90, vice chmn. subcom. securities products, com. consumer fin. svcs. bus. law sect. 1993—), Consumer Bankers Assn. (lawyers com.), Soc. Physics Students, Stanford Asian-Pacific Am. Alumni/ae Club (bd. dirs. 1989-93, v.p. 1989-91). Democrat. Baptist. Office: Wells Fargo Bank NA Legal Dept 111 Sutter St San Francisco CA 94104-4504

LEE, JOHN PATRICK, hospital administrator; b. Portland, Oreg., Apr. 29, 1942; s. Patrick and Margaret Ann (Molahan) L.; m. Feb. 27, 1965; children—Kevin, Kelly, Jason. B.B.A., U. Portland, 1964, M.B.A., 1973; M.P.A. in Hosp. Adminstrn., UCLA, 1970. Asst. adminstr. fin. and gen. adminstrn. Good Samaritan Hosp. and Med. Center, Portland, 1970-75; dep. adminstr., St. Vincent's Hosp. and Med. Center, Portland, 1975-79; adminstr. Providence Med. Center, Portland, 1979-89; regional v.p. Sisters of Providence Health System, 1989—. Served to capt. Med. Service Corps, USAF, 1964-68. Fellow Am. Coll. Hosp. Adminstrs., Hosp. Adminstrv. Mgmt. Assn. Office: Sisters of Providence 1235 NE 47th Ave Ste 299 Portland OR 97213-2100

LEE, JONG HYUK, accountant; b. Seoul, Korea, May 6, 1941; came to U.S., 1969, naturalized, 1975; s. Jung Bo and Wol Sun L. B.A., Sonoma State U., Rohnert Park, Calif., 1971; M.B.A. in Taxation, Golden Gate U., San Francisco, 1976. CPA, Calif.; m. Esther Kim, Jan. 24, 1970. Cost acct., internal auditor Foremost-McKesson Co., San Francisco, 1971-74; sr. acct. Clark, Wong, Foulkes & Barbieri, CPAs, Oakland, Calif., 1974-77; pres. J.H. Lee Accountancy Corp., Oakland, 1977-89, Bay Cities Restaurants, Inc. Wendy's Franchise, 1989—; instr. Armstrong Coll., Berkeley, Calif., 1977-78; lectr. acctg., dir. sch. of bus. The U.S.-Korea Bus. Inst., San Francisco State U.; adv. bd. mem. Ctr. for Korean Studies, Inst. of East Asian Studies U. Calif, Berkeley. Bd. dirs. Korean Residents Assn., 1974, Multi-svc. Ctr. for Koreans, 1979, Better Bus. Bur., 1984-87; chmn. caucus Calif.-Nev. ann. conf. United Meth. Ch., 1977; commr. Calif. State Office Econ. Opportunity, 1982-86; pres. Korean-Am. Dem. Network; mem. Dem. Nat. Fin. Coun.; regional chmn. Adv. Coun. on Peaceful Unification Policy, Republic of Korea; commr. Asian Art Mus. San Francisco, 1988-91. With Korean Marine Corps, 1961-64; 1st lt. Calif. State Mil. Res. Mem. Am. Inst. CPAs, Nat. Assn. Asian Am. CPAs (bd. dir.), Am. Acctg. Assn., Nat. Assn. Accts., Internat. Found. Employee Benefit Plans, Calif. Soc. CPAs, Oakland C. of C., Korean Am. C. of C. (pres. Pacific North Coast, Rotary. Democrat. Author tax and bus. column Korea Times, 1980. Home: 180 Firestone Dr Walnut Creek CA 94598-3645 Office: 369 13th St Oakland CA 94612-2636

LEE, KAI-FU, computer company executive; b. Taipei, Taiwan, Dec. 3, 1961; came to the U.S., 1973; s. Tien-Min and Yah-Ching (Wong) L.; m. Shen-Ling Hsieh, Aug. 6, 1983; 1 child, Jennifer Lee. BA in Computer Sci. summa cum laude, Columbia U., 1983; PhD in Computer Sci., Carnegie Mellon U., Pitts., 1988. Rsch. scientist, asst. prof. Sch. Computer Sci. Carnegie Mellon U., Pitts., 1988-90; prin. speech scientist spl. projects Apple Computer, Inc., Cupertino, Calif., 1990-91, mgr. speech and lang. lab., advanced tech. group, 1991-93, dir. interactive media lab., advanced tech. group, 1993—; adj. prof. Carnegie Mellon U. Sch. Computer Sci., 1990—; keynote spkr. Eurospeech Conf., Paris, 1989, Berlin, 1993, AVIOS Mtg., San Jose, Calif., 1993; lectr. in field; cons. to major corps. Reviewer, numerous profl. jours., book proposals and grant proposals in field; author: Automatic Speech Recognition: The Development of the SPHINX System, 1989, (with A.H. Waibel) Readings in Speech Recognition, 1990; contbr. chpt. to Recent Progress in Speech Signal Processing, 1990, Recent Advances in Speech Understanding and Dialog Systems, 1987; contbr. numerous articles, conf. papers and tech. reports to profl. publs. NSF grad. fellow, 1983-86; recipient paper award IEEE Signal Processing Soc., 1991, Most Innovative Sci. Innovation award Bus. Week, 1988; named Othello champion N.Am. Computer, 1989. Mem. IEEE (reviewer procs. and transactions, mem. speech tech. com. 1991-95, IEEE ICASSP Conf. organizing com. 1992, organizing com. workshop on speech recognition 1991), Acoustical Soc. Am. (reviewer jour.), DARPA (coord. com. spoken lang. 1989=90, lang. and speech workshop com. 1991, chair speech session workshop on speech and lang. 1989), Chinese Software Profl. Assn. (adv. com. 1993—); Sigma Xi, Phi Beta Kappa. Office: Apple Computer, Inc. 1 Infinite Loop Cupertino CA 95014-2083

LEE, KENNETH, computer aided design educator; b. Seoul, Korea, Feb. 26, 1958; came to U.S., 1981; s. M.H. and N.Y. Lee; m. Kristie E. Lee, Oct. 18, 1991. B of Landscape Architecture cum laude, Seoul Nat. U., Seoul, 1980; M of Landscape Architecture, Cornell U., 1984. Project landscape architect Space Goup of Korea, Seoul, 1980-81; project planner Sullivan Assocs., Phila., 1984-86; project mgr. The SWA Group, Laguna Beach, Calif., 1986-88; sr. assoc. Florian Martinez Assocs., Tustin, Calif., 1988-91; sr. prin. LDI, Irvine, Calif., 1991—; pres. PowerPlay Prodn., Irvine, 1992—; instr. U. Calif., Irvine, 1993—; computer cons. Lynn Capouya, Inc., Newport Beach, Calif., 1991—, Landvista, Irvine, 1991—, Sebastian & Assocs., Laguna Beach, 1991—. Republican. Methodist. Office: LDI 396 Deerfield Ave Irvine CA 92714-7650

LEE, LILA JUNE, historical society officer, library director; b. Ukiah, Calif., July 12, 1923; d. Arthur L. and Leila Edna (Rose) Romer; m. Dale R. Laney, May 1, 1944 (div. Sept. 1952); m. Robert James Lee, Apr. 16, 1955; children: Arthur John, Margarett June. Officer Mendocino County Hist. Soc., Ukiah, 1960—; libr. dir. Held Poage Libr., Ukiah, 1970—. Mem. conf. of Calif. Hist. Soc. (regional v.p 1980—), Mendocino County Hist. Soc. (v.p., treas., fin. sec.). Republican. Presbyterian. Office: Mendocino County Hist Soc 603 W Perkins St Ukiah CA 95482-4726

LEE, LILY KIANG, scientific research company executive; b. Shanghai, China, Nov. 23, 1946; came to U.S., 1967, naturalized, 1974; d. Chi-Wu and An-Teh (Shih) Kiang; m. Robert Edward Lee; children: Jeffrey Anthony, Michelle Adrienne, Stephanie Amanda, Christina Alison. BS, Nat. Cheng-Chi U., 1967; MBA, Golden Gate U., San Francisco, 1969. Acct., then acctg. supr. Am. Data Systems, Inc., Canoga Park, Calif., 1969-73; sr. acct. Pertec Peripheral Equipment div. Pertec Corp., Chatsworth, Calif., 1973-76; mgr. fin. planning and acctg., then mgr. fin. planning, program and internal control Sci. Ctr. div. Rockwell Internat. Corp., Thousand Oaks, Calif., 1976—. Mem. NAFE, Am. Mgmt. Assn., Nat. Mgmt. Assn., Nat. Property Mgrs. Assn. Republican. Baptist. Office: Rockwell Internat Corp PO Box 1085 1049 Camino Dos Rios Thousand Oaks CA 91358

LEE, LONG CHI, electrical engineering and chemistry educator; b. Kaohsiung, Taiwan, Oct. 19, 1940; came to U.S., 1965; s. Chin Lai Lee and Wen Wang; m. Laura Meichau Cheng, Dec. 1, 1967 (dec. Dec. 1988); children: Gloria, Thomas; m. Masako Suto, Jan. 6, 1990. BS in Physics, Taiwan Normal U., Taiwan, 1964; MA in Physics, U. So. Calif., L.A., 1967, PhD in Physics, 1971. Rsch. staff U. So. Calif., L.A., 1971-77; physicist SRI Internat., Menlo Park, Calif., 1977-79, sr. physicist, 1979-81; prof. elec. engring. San Diego State U., 1982—, adj. prof. chemistry, 1986—; adj. asst. prof. U. So. Calif., L.A., 1977; chmn. bd. Fiber Does, Inc., 1994—, Superior Evaporants, Inc., 1994—. Contbr. papers to profl. jours. Pres. Taiwanese Cultural Assn. in San Diego, 1983, 93. Rsch. grantee NSF, 1990-94, NASA, 1979-94, Air Force Office Sci. Rsch., 1980-89, Naval Rsch. Office, 1986-89. Mem. IEEE, Am. Phys. Soc., Am. Geophys. Union, Inter-Am. Photochem. Soc., Formesan Assn. for Pub. Affairs (pres. San Diego chpt. 1990-91), Taiwanese-Am. Investment Club (pres. 1995—). Office: San Diego State U Dept Elec & Computer Engring San Diego CA 92182

LEE, LORRIN L., marketing executive, architect, designer, author, speaker; b. Honolulu, July 22, 1941; s. Bernard Chong and Betty (Lum) L.; m. Nina Christine Fedoroscko, June 10, 1981. BArch, U. Mich., 1970; MBA, Columbia Pacific U., 1981, PhD in Psychology, 1981. Registered arch., Hawaii. Arch. Clifford Young AIA, Honolulu, 1971-72, Aotani & Oka AIA, Honolulu, 1972-74, Geoffrey Fairfax FAIA, Honolulu, 1974-76; seminar leader Lorrin Lee Program, Honolulu, 1976-81; star grand master coord. Enhance Corp., 1981-83; 5-diamond supr. Herbalife Internat., L.A., 1984-85, mem. global expansion team, 1993—; presdl. dir. Uni-Vite Internat., San Diego, 1989-92. Author: Here is Genius, 1980. Editor Honolulu Chinese Jaycees, Honolulu, 1972, v.p., 1983; active Makiki Cmty. Ctr., Honolulu, 1974. 1st lt. U.S. Army, 1967-70, Okinawa. Recipient Braun-Knect-Heimann award, 1959, 1st prize in design Kidjel Cali-Pro Internat., 1975, Kitchen Design award Sub-zero Contest, 1994; named Honolulu Chinese Jaycee of Yr., Honolulu Chinese Jaycees, 1973. Mem. Nature Conservancy, Sierra Club. Office: 1750 Kalakaua Ave # 3140 Honolulu HI 96826-3795

LEE, LOU S., printing company executive, developer; b. Liuzhou, Guangsi, Peoples Republic of China, Nov. 5, 1943; came to U.S., 1959; s. So Sat and Yuen Ching (Leung) L.; m. Irene Woo Lee, Apr. 21. 1971; children: Derrick Chin-Chang, Aaron Cin-Hung. AA, Los Angeles City Coll., 1965; BA, San Jose (Calif.) State U., 1968; MBA, Golden Gate U., 1971. Cert. coll. instr., Calif. Mktg. rep. IBM, San Francisco, 1973-75; chief exec. officer VIP Litho, San Francisco, 1976—; assoc. producer Gold Mountain Prodns., San Francisco, 1986. Active Cathedral Sch. for Boys Christmas Boutique, San Francisco, 1981-82, Merola Opera program, San Francisco, 1983-84, Katherine Delmar Burke Sch. Festival, San Francisco, 1985; v.p. and bd. dirs. Marin Chinese Cultural Group, Calif., 1985; mem. fin. com. Kentfield Sch. Found., Calif., 1986-88; dir. Kentfield Sch. Found., 1987-88; hon. com. mem. San Francisco Boys Chorus Bracebridge Feast, 1986, San Francisco Opera Ctr. Shanghai Fund, 1987—; adv. bd. Asian Performing Arts, San Francisco, 1988; mem. Calif. Spl. Olympic spirt Team, San Francisco, 1988. Named Man of the Yr., Univ. High Sch., San Francisco, 1987. Mem. Asian Bus. Assn., Sierra Club Found., Sierra Club. Club: City (San Francisco). Office: VIP Litho 1 Newhall St San Francisco CA 94124-1420

LEE, MARGARET ANNE, social worker, psychotherapist; b. Scribner, Nebr., Nov. 23, 1930; d. William Christian and Caroline Bertha (Benner) Joens; m. Robert Kelly Lee, May 21, 1950 (div. 1972); children: Lawrence Robert, James Kelly, Daniel Richard. AA, Napa Coll., 1949; student, U. Calif., Berkeley, 1949-50; BA, Calif. State Coll., Sonoma, 1975; MSW, Calif. State U., Sacramento, 1977. Diplomate clin. social worker; lic. clin. social worker, Calif.; lic. marriage and family counselor, Calif.; tchr. Columnist, stringer Napa (Calif.) Register, 1946-50; eligibility worker, supr. Napa County Dept. Social Services, 1968-75; instr. Napa Valley Community Coll., 1978-83; practice psychotherapy Napa, 1977—; oral commr. Calif. Dept. Consumer Affairs, Bd. Behavioral Sci., 1984—; bd. dirs. Project Access, 1978-79. Trustee Napa Valley C.C., 1983—, v.p. bd., 1984-85, pres. bd., 1986, 90, 95, clk., 1988-89; bd. dirs. Napa County Coun. Econ. Opportunity, 1984-85, Napa chpt. March of Dimes, 1957-71, Mental Health Assn. Napa County, 1983-87; vice chmn. edn. com. Calif. C.C. Trustees, 1987-88, chmn. edn. com., 1988-89, legis. com., 1985-87, bd. dirs., 1989—, 2d v.p., 1991, 1st v.p., 1992, pres., 1993; mem. student equity rev. group Calif. C.C. Chancellors, 1992; bd. dirs. C.C. League Calif., 1992—, 1st v.p. 1992. Recipient Fresh Start award Self mag., award Congl. Caucus on Women's Issues, 1984. Mem. NASW, Mental Health Assn. Napa County, Calif. Assn. Physically and Handicapped, Women's Polit. Caucus, Calif. Elected Women's Assn. Edn. and Rsch., Am. Assn. Women in Community and Jr. Colls. Democrat. Lutheran. Office: 1100 Trancas St Napa CA 94558-2908

LEE, MARIANNA, editor; b. N.Y.C., Aug. 23, 1930; d. Isaac and Charlotte (Steiner) Lubow; m. Edward Lee, June 17, 1968 (div. 1978); 1 child, Susanna. BA, Smith Coll., 1952; postgrad, Columbia U., 1952-53; postgrad., Oxford (Eng.) U., 1957-58. Asst. editor Watson-Guptill Publs., N.Y.C., 1958-59; chief copy editor Grolier, Inc., N.Y.C., 1960-61; mng. editor Portfolio & Art News Ann., N.Y.C., 1961-62; assoc. editor Parade Publs., N.Y.C., 1962-66; mng. editor The Johns Hopkins Press, Balt., 1966-68, U. Tex. Press, Austin, 1968-69; sr. publs. mgr. Scripps Inst. of Oceanography, La Jolla, Calif., 1979-82; mng. editor Harcourt Brace and Co., San Diego, 1982—. Contbr. articles to profl. jours. Democrat. Jewish. Office: Harcourt Brace and Co 525 B St San Diego CA 92101-4403

LEE, MARTHA, artist, writer; b. Chehalis, Wash., Aug. 23, 1946; d. William Robert and Phyllis Ann (Herzog) L.; m. Peter Reynolds Lockwood, Jan. 25, 1974 (div. 1982). BA in English Lit., U. Wash., 1968; student, Factory of Visual Art, 1980-82. Reporter Seattle Post-Intelligencer, 1970; personnel counselor Theresa Snow Employment, 1971-72; receptionist Northwest Kidney Ctr., 1972-73; proprietress The Reliquary, 1974-77; travel agt. Cathay Express, 1977-79; artist, 1980—; represented by Pulliam Deffenbaugh Gallery, Portland, Oreg., Uppertown Antiques, Astoria, Oreg., Lucia Douglas Gallery, Bellingham, Wash., Whitebird Gallery, Cannon Beach, Oreg. Painter various oil paintings; exhibitor group and one-person shows. Home and Studio: 24409 Pacific Hwy Ocean Park WA 98640-3823

LEE, MARVIN JUN HUNG, architectural firm executive; b. Honolulu, Dec. 8, 1961; s. Christopher and Judith L.; m. Mika Tanaka Lee, Apr. 28, 1990. B in interior environ. design, UCLA, 1991. Interior architect Architect & Assoc. Will Gentile, L.A., 1988-92; project mgr. Yamada Design Mgmt., Irvine, Calif., 1992-93; pres. IONICA Interior Architecture, Honolulu, 1993—. Chmn. Kaimuki Main St. Assn., Honolulu, 1994—. Mem. Retail Mchts. Hawaii, Kaimuki Bus. Profl. Assn. (bd. dirs. 1994—), Honolulu Japanese C. of C. (program chair econ. divsn. 1993—), Hawaii C. of C. Office: IONICA Interior Archt 1154 Fort Street Mall # 315 Honolulu HI 96813-2709 Home: 4337 Lanihale Pl Apt F Honolulu HI 96816-3359

LEE, MEREDITH, German language educator; b. St. Louis, July 11, 1945; m. Anthony Battaglia, Nov. 18, 1977. BA summa cum laude, St. Olaf Coll., Northfield, Minn., 1968; MPhil with distinction, Yale U., 1971, PhD, 1976. Asst. prof. U. Calif., Irvine, 1974-81; assoc. prof. U. Calif., 1981-93; prof. U. Calif., Irvine, 1993—, dean undergrad. studies, 1984-88, assoc. dean humanities, 1982-84, chair dept. German, 1991—; sec., treas., dir. Goethe Soc. N.Am., 1979-94, exec. sec., 1994—; chair area adv. com. Coun. for Internat. Exch. Scholars, Washington, 1986-88. Author: Studies in Goethe's Lyric Cycles, 1978; co-editor: Interpreting Goethe's Faust Today, 1994; contbr. articles to profl. jours. Danforth fellow, 1968-74; Fulbright scholar, Göttingen, Fed. Republic Germany, 1972-73. Mem. Am. Assn. Tchrs. German, Am. Soc. for 18th Century Studies, Soc. For Values in High Edn., Modern Lang. Assn., German Studies Assn. (exec. com. 1983-86), Phi Beta Kappa. Lutheran. Office: U Calif Dept German Irvine CA 92717

LEE, MICHAEL ANTHONY, cardiologist; b. Tucson, Jan. 6, 1954; s. Tony S.B. and Bella (Wong) L.; m. Mei-Gee Chang, June 1, 1980; children: Michael Jr., Andrew. BS in Biology, MIT, 1976; MD, U. Calif., San Francisco, 1980. Diplomate Am. Bd. Internal Medicine, Nat. Bd. Med. Examiners; lic. MD, Calif. Intern V.A. Wadsworth Med. Ctr., L.A., 1980-81; resident U. Calif., San Francisco, 1981-83; clin. instr. Georgetown U., Washington, 1984-86; cardiology fellow U. Ariz. Med. Ctr., Tucson, 1986-88; cardiac electrophysiology fellow U. Calif., San Francisco, 1988-90, asst. clin. prof. medicine, 1990—. Contbr. articles to profl. jours. Fellow Lincoln Found., 1975, NIH, 1983-86; grantee Am. Heart Assn., 1987-88. Mem. AMA, Cardiac Electrophysiology Soc., N.Am. Soc. Pacing and Electrophysiology. Republican. Office: E Bay Arrhythmia & Electrophys Ctr 365 Hawthorne Ave Ste 201 Oakland CA 94609

LEE, MICHAEL ERIC, magazine editor; b. Eugene, Ore., Apr. 28, 1959; s. M. James and Aileen May (Kronquist) L. BA in Journalism, U. Ore., 1981, MA in Philosophy, 1991. News editor News Register, McMinnville, Ore., 1981-83; from morning music host to devel. dir. KWAX-FM, Eugene, 1985-90; from assoc. editor to editor Ore. Quarterly, Eugene, 1990—; pub. Intangible Pubs., Eugene, 1993—. Office: Ore Quarterly Mag 5228 U Ore Eugene OR 97403

LEE, MURLIN E., program manager; b. Crescent City, Calif., Jan. 4, 1957; s. George Lee and Ida Burl (Wilson) M.; m. Jeanine Marie Metcalfe, Apr. 13, 1985; children: Kimberly, Kristen, Gina. BS in Bus. Adminstrn., Calif. Poly. U., Pomona, 1981; MS in Software Engring., Nat. U., San Jose, Calif., 1988. Mgr. George M. Lee Enterprises Inc., Crescent City, Calif., 1979-80, Wells Aviation, Ontario, Calif., 1980-81, Bard Software, San Jose, Calif., 1982-84; software engr. Litton Applied Techology, San Jose, 1984-89; program mgr. Condor Systems, Inc., San Jose, 1989—. Republican. Home: 4081 Will Rogers Dr San Jose CA 95117-2730 Office: Condor Systems Inc 2133 Samaritan Dr San Jose CA 95124-4406

LEE, MYUNG-SHIK, medical researcher; b. Seoul, Korea, Nov. 14, 1956; came to U.S., 1992; s. Sung-Su and Sung-Sook (Hong) L.; m. Shin-Heh Kang, Sept. 23, 1984; children: Ji-Yeon Lee, Chang-Sup Lee. MD, Seoul Nat. U., 1981, PhD, 1990. Lic. physician Calif. Bd. Medicine. Resident Seoul Nat. U. Hosp., 1981-84; chief in internal medicine Seoul Dist. Armed Force Gen. Hosp., 1985-88; staff physician in internal medicine Korea Cancer Ctr. Hosp., Seoul, 1989-91; rsch. assoc. Scripps Rsch. Inst., La Jolla, Calif., 1992—. Author: Lessons from Animal Diabetes, 1992, Transgenesis and Targeted Mutagenesis for Immune System Analysis, 1994. Editl. bd. Korean Jour. of Endocrinology, 1989-91. Capt. Korean Med. Hosp., 1985-88. Fellow Nat. Multiple Sclerosis Soc. (advanced post-doctoral fellowship N.Y.C. 1992). Home: 7861 Avenida Navidad Apt 234 San Diego CA 92122-4433

LEE, NANCY JANE MCCLEARY, American studies educator; b. Indpls., Jan. 21, 1951; d. John Albert and Sue Jane (Lapping) McCleary; m. Thomas Eugene Lee, Dec. 30, 1971; children: Bryan Thomas Stephen, Dustin David Adam, Travis Scott James. Student, U. Calif., Santa Barbara, 1969-70, L.A. Pierce Coll., 1970, 71; BA in History, English and Edn., Adams State Coll., 1974; MA in History, Calif. State U., Northridge, 1979; postgrad., Calif. Luth. U., U. Calif., Santa Barbara, LaVerne Coll. Cert. secondary edn. tchr. Substitute tchr. Conejo Unified Sch., 1975-78; home tchr., 1977; tchr. Simi Valley H.S., 1978-90, Apollo H.S., 1990—; tchr./trainer curriculum program Simi Valley Unified Sch. Dist., 1990—, facilitator student support groups, 1984—, faculty senate, acad. standards com., sch. site coun.; sch. site coun. Apollo H.S., rep. dist. curriculum coun., 1990—. Mem. adv. bd. Scholastic Search mag., 1993-95. Active polit. elections and campaigns. Mem. NEA, CTA, Calif. Edn. Assn., Calif. Assn. Dirs. Activities, Nat. Coun. for Social Studies, Nat. Coun. for Tchrs. English, Calif. Continuing Edn. Assn., Simi Educators Assn. (rep. coun., exec. bd. dirs.). Democrat. Home: 3093 Cobb Cir Simi Valley CA 93065-5261 Office: Apollo H S 3150 School St Simi Valley CA 93065-3967

LEE, OLIVER MINSEEM, political science educator; b. Shanghai, Dec. 7, 1927; came to U.S., 1946; s. Ginffa and Gerta (Scheuermann) L.; m. May Yee Lee, July 9, 1950; children: Vivien, Steven, Anthony. AB, Harvard Coll., 1951; MA, U. Chgo., 1955, PhD, 1962. Intelligence analyst U.S. Army Res., Chgo., 1957-58; instr. govt. and politics U. Md., College Park, 1958-62; Far Eastern analyst Legis. Reference Svc., Libr. Congress, Washington, 1962-63; asst. prof. U. Hawaii, Honolulu, 1963-73, assoc. prof. polit. sci., 1973—. Candidate for U.S. Senate, Peace and Freedom party, Hawaii, 1968. Mem. Harvard Club Hawaii, U. Chgo. Club Honolulu. Home: 690 Hao St Honolulu HI 96821 Office: U Hawaii at Manoa Dept Polit Sci 2424 Maile Way Honolulu HI 96822-2223

LEE, PALI JAE (POLLY JAE STEAD LEE), retired librarian, writer; b. Nov. 26, 1929; d. Jonathan Everett Wheeler and Ona Katherine (Grunder) Stead; m. Richard H.W. Lee, Apr. 7, 1945 (div. 1978); children: Lani Catherine, Karin Lee Robinson, Ona G., Laurie Brett, Robin Louise Lee Halbert; m. John K. Willis, 1979 (dec. 1994). Student, U. Hawaii, 1944-46, Mich. State, 1961-64. Cataloguer and processor U.S. Army Air Force, 1945-46; with U.S. Weather Bur. Film Library, New Orleans, 1948-50, FBI, Wright-Patterson AFB, Dayton, Ohio, 1952, Ohio Wholesale Winedealers, Columbus, Ohio, 1956-58, Coll. Engring., Ohio State U., Columbus, 1959; writer tech. manual Annie Whittenmeyer Home, Davenport, Iowa, 1960; with Grand Rapids (Mich.) Pub. Library, 1961-62; dir. Waterford (Mich.) Twp. Libraries, 1962-64; acquisition librarian Pontiac (Mich.) Pub. Libraries, 1965-71, dir. East Side br., 1971-73; librarian Bishop Mus., Honolulu, 1975-83; pub. Night Rainbow Pub., Honolulu, 1984—. Author: Mary Dyer, Child of Light, 1973, Giant: Pictorial History of the Human Colossus, 1973, History of Change: Kaneohe Bay Area, 1976, English edit., 1983, Na Po Makole-Tales of the Night Rainbow, 1981, rev. edit., 1988, Mo'olelo O Na Pohukaina, 1983, Ka Ipu Kukui, 1994; contbr. articles to profl. jours. Chmn. Oakland County br. Multiple Sclerosis Soc., 1972-73, co-chmn. Pontiac com. of Mich. area bd., 1972-73; sec. Ohana o Kokua, 1979-83, Paia-Willis Ohana, 1982-91, Ohana Kame'ekua, 1988-91; bd. dirs. Detroit Multiple Sclerosis Soc., 1971; mem. Mich. area bd. Am. Friends Svc. com., 1961-69; mem. consumer adv. bd. Libr. for Blind and Physically Handicapped, Honolulu, 1991—; pres. consumer 55 plus bd. Honolulu Ctr. for Ind. Living, 1990-94; pres. Honolulu chpt. Nat. Fedn. of Blind, 1991-94, 1st v.p. #93 state affiliate, 1991-94, editor Na Na Maka Aloha newsletter, 1990-94; 1st v.p. Hawaii chpt. Talking Book Readers Club, 1994—. Recipient Mother of the Yr. award Quad City Bus. Men, 1960, Bowl of Light award Hawaiian Community of Hawaii, 1989. Mem. Internat. Platform Assn., Soc. Friends. Office: PO Box 10706 Honolulu HI 96816

LEE, PAMELA ANNE, accountant, financial analyst; b. San Francisco, May 30, 1960; d. Larry D. and Alice Mary (Reece) L. BBA, San Francisco State U., 1981. CPA, Calif. Typist, bookkeeper, tax acct. James G. Woo, CPA, San Francisco, 1979-85; tutor bus. math. and statistics San Francisco State U., 1979-80; teller to ops. officer Gibraltar Savs. and Loan, San Francisco, 1978-81; sr. acct. Price Waterhouse, San Francisco, 1981-86; corp. acctg. mgr. First Nationwide Bank, Daly City, Calif., 1986-89, v.p., 1989-91, v.p., project mgr., 1991-92, sr. conversion and bus. analyst, 1992-93; sr. bus. analyst, asst. v.p. Bank of Am., 1993—; acctg. cons. New Performance Gallery, San Francisco, 1985, San Francisco Chamber Orch., 1986. Founding mem., chair bd. trustees Asian Acctg. Students Career Day, 1988-89. Mem. NAFE, Am. Inst. CPA's, Calif. Soc. CPA's, Nat. Assn. Asian-Am. CPA's (bd. dirs. 1986, news editor 1987, pres. 1988). Republican. Avocations: reading, music, travel, personal computing, needlework. Office: 50 California St Fl 11 San Francisco CA 94111-4624

LEE, PAUL PAK-HING, artist, educator; b. Hong Kong, July 2, 1962; came to U.S., 1982; BA, Hamilton Coll., 1985; MFA, Cranbrook Acad. Art, Bloomfield Hills, Mich., 1987. Vis. instr. Cleve. Inst. Art, 1987-88; asst. prof. San Antonio Art Inst., 1988-89, Wash. State U., Pullman, 1989—. Solo exhbns. include San Antonio Art Inst., 1988, Hartung Theatre, U. Idaho, Moscow, 1990, Columbia Arts Ctr., Vancouver, Wash., 1991, Greg Kucera Gallery, Seattle, 1994; two-person exhbns. include Johnson Bldg., Clinton, N.Y., 1984, Pontiac (Mich.) Art Ctr., 1987, S p a c e s Gallery, Cleve., 1989; group exhbns. include Munson Williams Proctor Inst., Utica, N.Y., 1985, Muhlenberg Coll., Pa., 1986, Emerson Gallery, Clinton, 1986, Detroit Inst. Art, 1986, Kingswood Gallery, Bloomfield Hills, 1986, Cleve. Inst. Art, 1987, Indpls. Art League, 1987, 88, N.A.M.E. Gallery, Chgo., 1988, Cleve. Mus. Art, 1988, U. Tex. San Antonio, 1989, Blue Star, San Antonio, 1989, Mus. Art, Washington State U., 1989, 90, Ridenbaugh Art Gallery, U. Idaho, 1989, Evanston (Ill.) Art Ctr., 1991, Prichard Gallery, Moscow, Idaho, 1992, Cheney Cowles Mus., Spokane, Wash., 1992, Cranbrook Acad. Art Mus., Bloomfield Hills, 1992, Bumbershoot 93, Seattle, 1993, Bellevue (Wash.) Art Mus., 1993, Cyberspace Gallery, L.A., 1993, N.Mex. State U. Art Mus., Las Cruces, Evergreen State Coll., Olympia, Wash., 1993, Artetage Gallery, Vladivostok, Russia, 1994. NEH fellow 1994; grantee Rockefeller Found., 1993, 94, Wash. State China Rels. coun. Project, 1994, others. Home and Studio: SW 220 Blaine St Pullman WA 99163

LEE, PETER Y., electrical engineer, consultant; b. Taipei, Taiwan, May 20, 1959; s. Jack T. and Joanna C. (Chen) L. BSEE, U. So. Calif., MSEE. MTS TTI/Citicorp, Santa Monica, Calif., 1981-82; project mgr. Tomy Corp., Carson, Calif., 1982-83; program devel. officer City Net Rsch. and Devel., L.A., 1983-86; system mgr. Hughes Aircraft Co./EDSG, El Segundo, Calif., 1986-87; founder, pres. Hyper Systems, Walnut, Calif., 1985—. Mem. IEEE. Republican. Roman Catholic. Home: 254 Viewpointe Ln Walnut CA 91789-2078 Office: Hyper Systems 20199 Valley Blvd # C Walnut CA 91789-2632

LEE, QWIHEE PARK, plant physiologist; b. Republic of Korea, Mar. 1, 1941; came to U.S., 1965; d. Yong-sik and Soon-duk (Paik) Park; m. Ick-whan Lee, May 20, 1965; children: Tina, Amy, Benjamin. MS, Seoul Nat. U., Republic of Korea, 1965; PhD, U. Minn., 1973. Head dept. plant physiology Korea Ginseng and Tobacco Inst., Seoul, 1980-82; instr. Sogang U., Seoul, 1981, Seoul Women's U., 1981; research assoc. U. Wash., Seattle, 1975-79. Exec. dir. Korean Community Counseling Ctr., Seattle, 1983-86. Named one of 20 Prominent Asian Women in Wash. State, Chinese Post Seattle, 1986. Mem. AAAS. Buddhist. Home: 13025 42nd Ave NE Seattle WA 98125-4624 Office: U Wash Dept Pharm SJ-30 1959 NE Pacific St Seattle WA 98195-0004

LEE, RALPH KELLY, real estate developer; b. Salt Lake City, Oct. 9, 1951; s. Ralph Hugh and Hattie (Hadlock) L.; m. Jacquelyn Dowdle, Jan. 15, 1974 (div. Sept. 1985); children: Ralph Adam Lee, Daniel Spencer Lee, Linzl Lee, Jayme Lee, Jordan Duke Lee; m. Carol Elaine Redelings, Oct. 24, 1987; 1 child, Annie Rebecca Anderson. Urban Planning Cert., U. Utah, 1979, BS in Polit. Sci., 1979, BS in Geography, 1979; MBA, U. Phoenix, 1987. Assoc. planner CKK Engrs. & Planners, Holiday, Utah, 1978-79; planner I Salt Lake County Planning Dept., 1979-80; planner II West Valley City (Utah) Community Devel., 1980-81; exec. dir. Redevel. Agy. of Murray City (Utah), 1981-83; forward planning dir. PF West, Inc., Dallas, 1983-88, Systems Constrn. Co., Anaheim Hills, Calif., 1989-90; project mgr. The Orange Coast Group, Inc., Seal Beach, Calif., 1990-91; seminary tchr. Ch. Ednl. Svcs., Cypress, Calif., 1990-93; dir. spl. projects Hill Williams Devel. Corp., Anaheim Hills, 1991-93; mem. faculty U. Phoenix, Fountain Valley, Calif., 1991—; computer programmer, nat. title coord. Stewart Title, L.A., Calif., 1990-93; EDI team mem. Landata Sys. Inc., Glendale, Calif., 1993-95; project mgr. Glenwood Devel. Co., 1995—; minister LDS Ch., Perth, Australia, 1971-72, Adelaide, Australia, 1972-73. Composer/performer: (albums) City Moods, 1987, Lucky Dreams, 1987. Recipient Duty to God award LDS Ch., Salt Lake City, 1971, Seminary Ch. Ednl. System award, Anaheim Hills, 1991, 92, 93. Mem. Nat. Assn. Home Builders, Bldg. Industry Assn. So. Calif., Bldg. Industry Assn. So. Calif., Bldg. Industry Assn. So. Calif., Inc., Am. Land Title Assn., Calif. Land Title Assn. Republican. Home: 530 South Ranchview Circle # 43 Anaheim Hills CA 92807-4318 Office: Glenwood Devel Co 100 W Broadway # 990 Glendale CA 91210

LEE, REX E., university president, lawyer; b. Los Angeles, Feb. 27, 1935; s. Rex E. and Mabel (Whiting) L.; m. Janet Griffin, July 7, 1959; children: Diana, Thomas Rex, Wendy, Michael, Stephanie, Melissa, Christie. B.A., Brigham Young U., 1960; J.D., U. Chgo., 1963. Bar: Ariz., D.C., Utah. Law clk. Justice Byron R. White, U.S. Supreme Ct., 1963-64; atty. Jennings, Strouss & Salmon, 1964-72, ptnr., 1967-72; founding dean J. Reuben Clark Law Sch., Brigham Young U., Provo, Utah, 1972-81; solicitor gen. U.S.A., Washington, 1981-85; ptnr. Sidley & Austin, Washington, 1985-89; pres. Brigham Young U., Provo, Utah, 1989—; asst. U.S. atty-gen. in charge civil div. Justice Dept., Washington.; lectr. Am. Inst. Fgn. Trade, 1966-68, U. Ariz. Sch. Law, 1968-72; George Sutherland prof. law Brigham Young U., 1985—. Mem. gen. bd. Young Men's Mut. Improvement Assn., Ch. of Jesus Christ of Latter-day Saints, 1958-60; bd. dirs. Theodore Roosevelt council Boy Scouts Am., 1967-72. Mem. Am. Law Inst. Home: 2840 Iroquois Dr Provo UT 84604-4318 Office: Brigham Young U D346 ASB Provo UT 84602

LEE, RICHARD CARL, government official; b. Chgo., July 19, 1950; s. Carl Lee and Helen Louise (Webster) L. BSME, Calif. State Poly. U., Pomona, 1973; BFA in Printmaking, U. Oreg., 1980; postgrad., U. Mo., 1982-83, Calif. State U., L.A., 1984-85. Pipeline engr. pipeline div. Bechtel Corp., San Francisco, 1973-74; test engr. power sys. div. United Techs., South Windsor, Conn., 1974-76; salesman Ea. Mountain Sports, hartford, Conn., 1976-77; grad. teaching asst. visual arts resources U. Oreg. Art Mus., 1977-80; iron worker Eugen, Oreg., 1980-81; energy auditor Student Conservation Assn., Vashon Island, Wash., 1981-82; house painter Fontana, Calif., 1982-83; printing procurement specialist U.S. Govt. Printing Office, San Francisco, 1986—. Mem. Sierra Club, Tau Beta Pi, Pi Tau Sigma. Office: US Govt Printing Office Treasure Is # 99 San Francisco CA 94130

LEE, RICHARD FRANCIS JAMES, evangelical clergyman, apologist, researcher; b. Yakima, Wash., Sept. 13, 1967; s. Richard Francis and Dorothy Aldean (Blackwell). Diploma, Berean Coll., Springfield, Mo., 1989; BA, U. Wash., Seattle, 1990; postgrad., Gonzaga Sch. Law, 1994—. Lic. clergyman Gen. Coun. of the Assemblies of God, Seattle, 1989—. Author: Tell Me the Story, 1982. Named Most Likely to be President, Franklin High Sch., Seattle, 1986. Pentecostal. Home: 2604 E Boone Ave Spokane WA 99202-3718 Office: Evangel Outreach Ministries 2604 E Boone Ave Spokane WA 99202-3718

LEE, ROBERT, telecommunications executive; b. Los Angeles, Sept. 19, 1948; s. Ben Yow and Ngun Hung (Chin) L.; m. Carolyn Louise Coffman, Sept. 11, 1971; children: Robyn Jennifer, Tracy Christine. BS, U. So. Calif., Los Angeles, 1970; MBA, U. Calif., Berkeley, 1972. With Pacific Telephone, 1972—; asst. mgr. Los Angeles, 1972-74; mgr. Los Angeles, Huntington Pk., El Segundo, Calif., 1975-78; dist. mgr. Inglewood, Buena Pk., El Segundo, Torrance, Calif., 1978-80; div. mgr. Torrance, San Francisco, Calif., 1983-84; gen. mgr. San Francisco, San Ramon, Calif., 1984-85; v.p.-ops. San Francisco, 1986; v.p.-consumer market San Ramon, 1986-87, exec. v.p.-mktg., 1987—. Recipient Asian Am. Achievement award Orgn. Chinese Ams., Los Angeles, 1985, Corp. Leadership award Asian Bus. League, San Francisco. Democrat. Office: Pacific Bell 2600 Camino Ramon Rm 3100cn San Ramon CA 94583-5041

LEE, ROBERT, association executive, former theological educator, consultant, author; b. San Francisco, Apr. 28, 1929; s. Frank and Shee (Fong) L.; m. May Gong, Feb. 4, 1951; children: Mellanie Lynn, Marcus Arthur, Matthew John, Wendy Gale, Michele Miko. A.B., U. Calif.-Berkeley, 1951; M.A., Pacific Sch. Religion, 1953; B.D. magna cum laude, Union Theol. Sem., 1954; Ph.D., Columbia U., 1958. Ordained to ministry United Ch. Christ, 1954; transferred to U.P. Ch., 1961; Western regional exec. sec. Chinese Student Christian Assn., 1949-50; assoc. sec. Stiles Hall, Univ. YMCA, Berkeley, Calif., 1950-52; dir. rsch. Protestant Council N.Y., 1954; from instr. to asst. prof. ch. and community Union Theol. Sem., 1955-61; lectr. philosophy Mills Coll. Edn., 1956-57; Margaret Dollar prof. social ethics, dir. Inst. Ethics and Soc., San Francisco Theol. Sem., 1961-83; v.p. acad. affairs Alaska Pacific U., 1983-85; pres., dir. Enfield Resources, 1985-87; dean Internat. Student Studies Heald Coll. Inst. of Tech., San Francisco, 1987-88; rsch. cons. Ctr. for Pacific Rim, U. San Francisco, 1989—; asst. v.p., dir. Asian Am. Philanthropy, United Way of Bay Area, 1990—; coord. community rels. Peace Corps, 1991—; prof., area chmn. Grad. Theol. Union, 1962-70; vis. prof. Union Theol. Sem., summer 1964, Internat. Christian U., Tokyo, Japan, 1964-65, Assn. S.E. Asian Sems., Hong Kong, 1966; vis. scholar Stanford Grad. Sch. Bus., 1971-72; co-optd staff World Council Chs. Conf. Ch. and Soc., Geneva, 1966; lectr., TV appearances, 1956—; cons. ISI Corp., 1971-72, World Coll. West, 1977-83, Coun. on Founds., 1989—; theologian-in-residence Windward Coalition, Kilua, Hawaii, 1980; moderator Inst. Religion and Social Studies, Jewish Theol. Sem., 1960; assoc. Columbia Seminar, 1961; sr. fellow East-West Center, Honolulu, 1972-73; bd. advisors Walden U.; nursing home care specialist Found. Health Corp., 1987; mem. exec. com. Calif. State Bar Ct., 1989—. Author: Social Sources of Church Unity (selected for Kennedy White House Library), 1960, Religion and Leisure in America, 1964, Directory of Centers for the Study of Society, 1965, Stranger in the Land, 1967, The Schizophrenic Church, 1969, The Promise of John C. Bennett, 1969, (with Marjorie Casebier) The Spouse Gap, 1971, Marriage Enrichment Sharing Sessions, 1979, China Journal, 1980, Faith and the Prospects of Economic Collapse, 1981, Guide to Chinese American Philanthropy and Charitable Giving Patterns, 1990; editor: Cities and Churches, 1962, (with Martin E. Marty) Religion and Social Conflict, 1964, The Church and The Exploding Metropolis, 1965, Action/Reaction; Pacific Theol. Rev., (book revs. edit.) East/West; contbr. to profl. jours., books. Mem. adv. com. problems met. soc. U.P. Ch., 1961—, Center Study Democratic Instns., Coll. Marin, 1965—; bd. sponsers Christianity and Crisis; bd. dirs. Chinese for Affirmative Action, Am. Soc. Christian Ethics, Ctr. for Family in Transition, Family Svc. Agy. of Marin, Festival Theatre Found., Pacific S.W. Student YMCA, ISI Trust Fund, ISI Growth Fund, ISI Income Fund, Found. for Theol. Edn. S.E. Asia; asst. v.p., bd. dirs. Asian Am. and Internat. Philanthropy, United Way Bay Area: bd. dirs. Marin Chinese Culture Ctr.; commn. Marin County Human Rights Comm., 1995—; hon. chairperson U.N 50 Marin Com., 1995—. Recipient Martin Luther King, Jr. Humanitarian award Marin County, 1994. Mem. Religious Rsch. Assn. (book rev. editor jour. 1959-65), Am. Sociol. Assn., Soc. Religion Higher Edn., Soc. for Sci. Study Religion, Center for Ethics and Social Policy, United Presbyn. Found. (trustee), Asians and Pacific Islanders in Philanthropy, Nan Hai Art Ctr. (trustee). Home: 717 Montecillo Rd San Rafael CA 94903-3135

LEE, ROBERT ANDREW, librarian; b. Washington, Dec. 7, 1923; s. Frederic Edward and Edna (Stewart) L. BA in English, Oberlin Coll., 1947; MLS, U. So. Calif., 1966. Jr. cataloger Columbia U. Law Library, 1950-51; reference librarian N.Y. Daily Mirror, 1952-54; researcher for Dore Schary MGM, Culver City, Calif., 1955; with Universal City Studios, Calif., 1955—, research librarian, 1960-69, head research dept., 1969-89. Contbr. articles to profl. jours. Served with AUS, 1943-46. Decorated Bronze Star with oak leaf cluster. Mem. Acad. Motion Picture Arts and Scis. (gov. 1973-75), Acad. TV Arts and Scis., Am. Film Inst., Am. Cinematheque. Home: 400 Hauser Blvd Apt 11A Los Angeles CA 90036-5522

LEE, ROBERT EDWARD, medical educator, researcher; b. Worcester, Mass., Sept. 15, 1942; s. Robert Edward and Helen Carol (Thomas) L.; m. Patricia Ann Grasso, July 6, 1968; children: Nicole Regina, Alana May, Christian Robert. BSc, Cornell U., 1964; PhD, U. Mass., 1971. Lectr. U. Witwatersrand, Johannesburg, South Africa, 1971-76; assoc. prof. Shiraz (Iran) U., 1977-79; staff fellow Schepens Eye Rsch. Inst., Boston, 1979-81; mem. affiliate faculty Med. Sch. Harvard U., Cambridge, Mass., 1979-81; prof. anatomy, mgr. Colo. State U., Ft. Collins, 1981—. Author: Phycology, 1st edit., 1981, 2d edit., 1989, Scanning Electron Microscopy, 1992. 1st lt. U.S. Army, 1964-66, Vietnam. Mem. Phi Kappa Phi. Office: Colo State U Dept Anatomy and Neurobiol Fort Collins CO 80523

LEE, ROBERT ERICH, information technology consultant; b. Spokane, Wash., Dec. 26, 1955; s. Robert Edward Lee and Edith Freida (Klasen) Moore; m. Vicky Ann Rowland, Jan. 31, 1981; children: Erich Rowland, Christopher Michael. Student, Vanderbilt U., 1973-77, Corpus Christi (Tex.) State U., 1977, U. Tex., El Paso, 1980. Mgr., instr. Neptune Equipment Co., Nashville, 1976-77; customer engr. Hewlett-Packard Co., Los Angeles, 1977-82, dist. service mgr., 1982-85; region service adminstrn. mgr. Hewlett-Packard Co., North Hollywood, Calif., 1985-86; dir. mgmt. info. Tova Corp., Beverly Hills, Calif., 1986-87; dir. info. tech. PrimeSource/Sequoia Supply, Inc., Irvine, Calif., 1987-92; pres. Results From Tech.!, 1992—; spkr. in field. Columnist Interex Press, 1995—; writer Interact, 1995—. Mem. Town Hall Calif., Eagle Scout, Cub Scout Woodbadge. Mem. IEEE, Assn. for Computing Machinery, Interex. Republican. Home and Office: Results From Tech! 1 Shenandoah Irvine CA 92720-2554

LEE, ROBERT W(ILLIAM), journalist, researcher; b. Salt Lake City, June 19, 1937; s. William Orme Jr. and Golda Alice (Anderson) L.; m. Karen Brinkerhoff, Nov. 24, 1958; children: Michael Don, Gary Dean, William Reed, Robert Bruce, Lawrence Alan. BS, U. Utah, 1960. Pres. Thermotech, Inc., Salt Lake City, 1960-65; adminstrv. asst. John Birch Soc., Washington, 1965-72, Washington rep., 1972-77; adminstrv. asst. Salt Lake County Commn., 1979-81; contbg. editor Am. Opinion Mag., Belmont, Mass., 1981-85, Rev. of the News Mag., Belmont, 1969-85, Conservative Digest Mg., Ft. Collins, Colo., 1985-89; talk-show host Radio Sta. KTKK, Salt Lake City, 1989-94; contbr. The New Am. Mag., Appleton, Wis., 1985—. Author: The United Nations Conspiracy, 1981; co-author: A Taxpayer Survey of the Grace Commission Report, 1984, Flight 007: Were There Survivors?, 1986; editor/pub. newsletter Comments and Corrections, 1981—. Mormon.

LEE, RONALD DEMOS, demographer, economist, educator; b. Poughkeepsie N.Y., Sept. 5, 1941; s. Otis Hamilton and Dorothy (Demetracopoulou) L.; m. Melissa Lee Nelken, July 6, 1968; children: Sophia, Isabel, Rebecca. BA, Reed Coll., 1963; MA, U. Calif.-Berkeley, 1967; PhD, Harvard U., 1971. Postdoctoral fellow Nat. Demographic Inst., Paris, 1970-71; asst. prof. to prof. U. Mich., Ann Arbor, 1971-79; prof. demography and econs. U. Calif., Berkeley, 1979—, chair dept. demography, dir. Berkeley Ctr. on Econs. and Demography of Aging; cons. in field; dir. Ctr. Demography and Econs. of Aging. Peace Corps. vol., Ethiopia, 1963-65. NIH fellow, 1965-67; NSF fellow, 1968-69; Social Sci. Research Council fellow, 1970-71; NIH grantee, 1973—; Guggenheim fellow, 1984-85. Mem. NAS (mem. com. on population), Population Assn. Am. (pres. 1987), Am. Econ. Assn., Internat. Union Sci. Study of Population. Democrat. Author: Econometric Studies of Topics in Demographic History, 1978; Population Patterns in the Past, 1977, others; contbr. articles to profl. jours. Home: 2933 Russell St Berkeley CA 94705-2333 Office: U Calif Dept Demography 2232 Piedmont Ave Berkeley CA 94720

LEE, RUBY BEI-LOH, computer systems and multimedia architect; b. Singapore; came to the U.S., 1970; m. Howard F. Lee, July 27, 1974; children: Patrick, Josephine. AB in Computer Sci. and Comparative Lit. with distinction, Cornell U., 1973; MS in Computer Sci., Stanford U., 1975, PhD in Elec. Engring., 1980. Asst. prof. elec. engring. Stanford (Calif.) U., 1980-81; lead arch. Hewlett Packard Co., Palo Alto, Calif., 1982-84; lead designer microprocessors Hewlett Packard Co., Palo Alto, 1984-86; project mgr. Hewlett Packard Co., Cupertino, Calif., 1987-90; chief arch. computer sys. arch., multimedia Hewlett Packard Co., Cupertino, 1991—; cons. assoc. prof. elec. engring. Stanford (Calif.) U., 1990—. Designer PA-RISC architecture; contbr. articles to profl. jours.; inventor and patentee in field. Mem. IEEE (exec. com., tech. com. on microprocessors, program com. Compcon conf. San Francisco 1991—, program chair Hot-Chips Symposium Stanford 1992-93), Assn. Computing Machinery, Phi Beta Kappa, Alpha Lambda Delta. Methodist. Home: 12933 Atherton Ct Los Altos Hls CA 94022-3405 Office: Hewlett-Packard Co 19410 Homestead Rd Cupertino CA 95014-0606

LEE, SAMMY, retired physician, surgeon; b. Fresno, Calif., Aug. 1, 1920; s. Soonkee Rhee and Eunkee Chun; m. Rosalind M.K. Wong, Oct. 1, 1950; children: Pamela Alicia, Sammy Lee II. BA, Occidental Coll., 1943; MD, U. So. Calif., 1947, DSc (hon.), 1984. Diplomate Am. Bd. Otorhinolaryngology. Pvt. practice limited to otology Orange, Calif., 1955-90; intern Orange County Hosp., Calif., 1946-47; resident in otolaryngology Letterman Army Hosp., 1949-53; presdl. rep. Melbourne Olympics, 1956, Munich Games, 1972, Seoul Olympics, 1988; coach diving U.S. Olympics, Rome, 1960, Bob Webster, Rome Olympics, 1960, Tokyo Olympics, 1964, Greg Louganis, Montreal Olympics, 1976; cons. Mission Viejo Nadadores Diving Team, Mission Viejo, Calif.; mem. President's Coun. on Phys. Fitness and Sports, 1971-80; adv. U.S. Internat. Olympic Diving Com. Author: (with other) DIVING, 1983, Not Without Honor, 1987; editor: The New Book of Knowledge, Diving, 1986. Commr. Pres. Commn. on White House Fellows, 1981-88; pres. Coun. on Phys. Fitness and Sports, 1991; hon. chmn. Korean Am. Coalition, L.A., 1986-88, Korean Am. Rep., Orange County, Calif., 1986-88; Olympic flag bearer/torch runner, 1984. Maj. U.S. Army, 1943-55, Korea. Recipient Gold high diving and Bronze medal 3 meter springboard diving London Olympics, 1948, Gold high diving medal Helsinki Olympics, 1952, James E. Sullivan award for outstanding amateur athlete in U.S.A., 1953, Excellence 2000 awards, 1990; named Outstanding Am. Korean Ancestry, Am. Korean Soc., 1967, Outstanding Am. Korean Ancestry, League of Korean Ams., 1986, named to U.S. Olympic Hall of Fame, 1990. Republican. Home: 16537 Harbour Ln Huntington Beach CA 92649-2105

LEE, SHI-CHIEH (SUCHI LEE), international tax specialist; b. Taipai, Taiwan, Sept. 6, 1960; came to U.S., 1971; s. Shien-Ming and Piyao (Chien) L. BSBA, creSo. Calif., 1983; M in Bus. Taxation, U. So. Calif., 1990. CPA, Calif. Mem. staff, sr. acct. Price Waterhouse, Century City, Calif., 1983-86; tax mgr., spl. tech. advisor Tax Tech. Group Price Waterhouse, Chgo., 1988; sr. tax cons. Price Waterhouse, L.A., 1986-88, tax mgr. internat. tax, 1989-91, sr. mgr. internat. tax, 1992—; lead instr. Becker CPA Rev., Encino, Calif., 1985—; guest lectr. Masters of Taxation program U. So. Calif., 1991—, mem. part-time faculty, 1993—; lectr. in field. Bd. dirs. Zeta Collectivwe Performance Arts, L.A., 1991-93. Mem. AICPA, Calif. Soc. CPAs, L.A. World Affairs Coun., Town Hall. Home: 19860 Archwood St

Winnetka CA 91306-4318 Office: Price Waterhouse 400 S Hope St Fl 23 Los Angeles CA 90071-2801

LEE, STUART MILTON, materials scientist, consultant; b. N.Y.C., Apr. 14, 1920; s. Herman and Bertha (Horowitz) L.; m. Miriam Drucker, Apr. 28, 1948; children: Gary, Scott, Randy. BS, L.I. U., 1941; MS, U. Nev., 1947; PhD, Fla. State U., 1953. Research chemist Aerojet-Gen., Azusa, Calif., 1959-61; mgr., chem. research and devel. Electro-optical systems, Pasadena, Calif., 1961-64; sr. tech. specialist Rockwell Internat., Anaheim, Calif., 1964-71; sr. staff scientist Ford Aerospace and Communications, Palo Alto, Calif., 1971-85; cons. materials, processes Palo Alto, 1985—. Editor-in-chief Technomic Pub. Co., Lancaster, Pa., 1985—, VCH Publishers, 1987; editor: Internat. Encyclopedia of Composites; contbr. author or editor 23 books; contbr. articles to profl. jours.; patentee in field. Research corp. fellow Fla. State U., 1950-52. Fellow Soc. Adv. Material and Process Engring. (editor jour. 1979-95, editor emeritus 1995—, bronze award 1982, space award 1995, internat. tech. dir.); mem. Am. Chem. Soc. (emeritus). Office: 3718 Cass Way Palo Alto CA 94306-3111

LEE, VIN JANG THOMAS, financial company executive, physicist; b. Honan Province, China, Feb. 14, 1937; came to U.S., 1958; s. Tsin-Yin and Hwa-Neu (Mar) L.; m. Doris Y. Feng, Apr. 21, 1957; 1 child, Maxwell. Diploma in ChemE Ordnance Engring. Coll., Taipei, Taiwan, 1958; MSChemE, U. Notre Dame, 1959; PhD, U. Mich., 1963. Assoc. prof. chem. engring. U. Mo., Columbia, 1965-74; pres. Econo Trading Co., Santa Monica, Calif., 1975-80, Cyberdyne Inc., Santa Monica, 1980—; vis. prof. catalysis and physical chemistry UCLA, 1972-73. Contbr. numerous articles to sci. jours. Mem. Sigma Xi. Lodge: Masons. Office: Cyberdyne Inc 1045 Ocean Ave Apt 2 Santa Monica CA 90403-3539

LEE, YUAN T(SEH), chemistry educator; b. Hsinchu, Taiwan, China, Nov. 29, 1936; came to U.S., 1962, naturalized, 1974; s. Tsefan and Pei (Tasi) L.; m. Bernice Wu, June 28, 1963; children: Ted, Sidney, Charlotte. BS, Nat. Taiwan U., 1959; MS, Nat. Tsinghua U., Taiwan, 1961; PhD, U. Calif., Berkeley, 1965. From asst. prof. to prof. chemistry U. Chgo., 1968-74; prof. U. Calif., Berkeley, 1974—, also former prin. investigator Lawrence Berkeley Lab. Contbr. numerous articles on chem. physics to profl. jours. Recipient Nobel Prize in Chemistry, 1986, Ernest O. Lawrence award Dept. Energy, 1981, Nat. Medal of Sci., 1986, 90, Peter Debye award for Phys. Chemistry, 1986; fellow Alfred P. Sloan, 1969-71, John Simon Guggenheim, 1976-77; Camille and Henry Dreyfus Found. Tchr. scholar, 1971-74, Harrison Howe award, 1983. Fellow Am. Phys. Soc.; mem. NAS, AAAS, Am. Acad. Arts and Scis., Am. Chem. Soc. Office: U Calif Dept Chemistry Berkeley CA 94720*

LEEB, CHARLES SAMUEL, clinical psychologist; b. San Francisco, July 18, 1945; s. Sidney Herbert and Dorothy Barbara (Fishstrom) L.; m. Storme Lynn Gilkey, Apr. 28, 1984; children: Morgan Evan, Spencer Douglas. BA in Psychology, U. Calif.-Davis, 1967; MS in Counseling and Guidance, San Diego State U., 1970; PhD in Edn. and Psychology, Claremont Grad. Sch., 1973. Assoc. So. Regional Dir. Mental Retardation Ctr., Las Vegas, Nev., 1976-79; pvt. practice, Las Vegas, 1978-79; dir. biofeedback and athletics Menninger Found., Topeka, 1979-82, dir. children's div. biofeedback and psychophysiology ctr. The Menninger Found., 1979-82; pvt. practice, Claremont, Calif., 1982—; dir. of psychol. svcs. Horizon Hosp., 1986-88; dir. adolescent chem. dependency and children's program Charter Oak Hosp., Covina, Calif., 1989-91; founder, chief exec. officer Rsch. and Treatment Inst., Claremont, 1991; lectr. in field. Contbr. articles to profl. jours. Mem. Am. Psychol. Assn., Calif. State Psychol. Assn. Office: 937 W Foothill Blvd Ste D Claremont CA 91711-3358

LEED, JEAN ANN, religious organization administrator; b. Akron, Ohio, Feb. 8, 1942; d. Clifford John and Laura Rosetta (Drescher) Burg; m. Roger Melvin Leed, Apr. 1, 1967; children: Craig, Maren, Jennifer. BA magna cum laude, Radcliffe Coll., 1964; MA, U. Mich., 1965, candidate in philosophy, 1967. Dir. devel. A Contemporary Theatre, Seattle, 1979-82; dir. devel. Arts and Scis. U. Wash., Seattle, 1982-90; dir. major gifts Sta. KCTS, Seattle, 1991-92; v.p. for devel. Sta. KTCA, St. Paul, 1992-93; dir. stewardship and devel. Episcopal Diocese of Olympia, Seattle, 1993—; instr. cert. program in fundraising, U. Wash., Seattle, 1986-89. Editor: Part-Time Careers in Seattle, 1976. Bd. dirs. YWCA, Seattle, 1978-81. Woodrow Wilson fellow, 1964. Mem. Nat. Soc. Fund Raising Execs. (pres. Wash. chpt. 1988-89, bd. dirs. 1986-90, 93—), City Club (bd. dirs. 1986-90), Phi Beta Kappa. Democrat. Episcopalian. Office: Episcopal Diocese Olympia PO Box 12126 Seattle WA 98102-0126

LEED, ROGER MELVIN, lawyer; b. Green Bay, Wis., July 15, 1939; s. Melvin John and Veronica Sarah (Flaherty) L.; m. Jean Ann Burg, Mar. 1967; children: Craig, Maren, Jennifer. AB, Harvard U., 1961; JD cum laude, U. Mich., 1967. Bar: Wash. 1967, U.S. Dist. Ct. (we. dist.) Wash. 1968, U.S. Ct. Appeals (9th cir.) 1969, U.S. Supreme Ct. 1973. Law clk. Wash. Supreme Ct., Olympia, 1967-68; assoc. Perkins, Coie et al, Seattle, 1968-70; ptnr. Schroeter, Goldmark et al, Seattle, 1970-77; sole practice Seattle, 1977—; adj. prof. law U. Puget Sound, Tacoma, 1974-77. Editor Shorelines Mgmt., the Wash. Experience, 1972. Pres. Cen. Seattle Community Council Fedn., 1972, Wash. Environ. Council, 1980-82; bd. dirs. Allied Arts, Seattle, 1971-72, Downtown Human Services Council, Seattle, 1985-92. Mem. Wash. State Bar Assn., Seattle-King County Bar Assn., Assn. Trial Lawyers Am. Clubs: Met. Dem., Washington Athletic. Office: 4705 16th Ave NE Seattle WA 98105-4208

LEEDS, ELIZABETH LOUISE, miniature collectibles executive; b. L.A., July 24, 1925; d. Charles Furnival and Etta Louise (Jackson) Mayes; m. Walter Albert Leeds, Jan. 20, 1973 (dec.); children: Pam Ravey Lewis, Linda Ravey McCallam, Diane Ravey Lathrop, Tom Ravey. Student pub. sch., Prescott, Ariz. Lic. real estate agt., Ariz., cert. motel mgr. Real estate agt., Prescott, Ariz., 1962-64; sec. to mgr. Kon Tiki Hotel, Phoenix, 1964-65; draftsman Goleta Water Dist., Calif., 1965-68; asst. to v.p. rsch. and design House of Mosaics, Santa Barbara, Calif., 1968-69; exec. chmn. poster design, dept. music U. Calif.-Santa Barbara, 1969-74; v.p. Colorform West, Inc., Santa Barbara, 1974-75; pres. Leeds Miniatures, Inc., Lincoln City, Oreg., 1975-86, Leed's Co., Inc., 1989—; cert. instr. Technologies for Creating, DMA, Inc., 1986—; lamp and silk screen designer Colorform West, Inc.; ind. assoc. The Environ. Network. Illustrator: Just A Story by Gustav Coenod, 1964. Active Global Vols., 1993, Oceanic Soc. Expeditions, 1993. Mem. Hobby Industry Am., Miniatures Industry Assn. Am., Nat. Assn. Female Execs., Eugene C. of C., Eugene Bus. and Profl. Women (cert. practitioner neuro-linguistic programming, trainer values realization). Republican. Clubs: Assn. Humanistic Psychology, Internat. New Thought Alliance, Assn. Transpersonal Psychology. Home: 2290 Arthur Ct Eugene OR 97405-1525

LEEDS-HORWITZ, SUSAN BETH, school system administrator, speech-language pathology educator; b. L.A., Mar. 14, 1950; d. Henry Herbert and Lee (Weiss) Leeds; m. Stanley Martin Horwitz, Nov. 28, 1975; 1 child, Brian David. BA, Calif. State U., Northridge, 1971; MEd, U. S.C., 1973; adminstrv. credential, U. LaVerne, 1984. Itinerant speech pathologist L.A. City Schs., 1973-74; severe lang. disorders tchr. L.A. County Bd. Edn., Downey, Calif., 1974-88; tchr. on spl. assignment Santa Clarita Valley Spl. Edn. Local Plan Area, Newhall, Calif., 1986-88; coord. spl. programs, testing, evaluation and migrant edn. Castaic (Calif.) Union Sch. Dist., 1988-94, adminstr., 1988-1994; ednl. cons. Richmond, Calif., 1994-95; coord. grands & project devel. Glendale (Calif.) Unified Sch. Dist., 1995—. Author: Project Próspero: A Traditional Bilingual Education Program for Grades 2-8, 1991. Active Santa Clarita Valley Spl. Edn. PTA, Newhall, 1984—; grantee Project VISTA ValVerde-Castaic involvement sports, team activities, 1992—. Grantee student enhancement program Kaiser-Permanente Community Svcs., 1992. Mem. ASCD, Am. Speech Lang and Hearing Assn. (cert.), So. Calif. Assn. Alumnae Panhellenic (pres. 1993-94), Down Syndrome Congress, Assn. Calif. Sch. Adminstrs., San Fernando Valley Panhellenic Assn. (rep. 1976—, pres. 1993-95), Santa Clarita Valley C. of C. (edn. com., anti-gang com., tchr. tribute com.), Delta Kappa Gamma, Alpha Xi Delta (Edna Epperson Brinkman award 1985), Phi Delta Kappa. Office: 223 N Jackson St Glendale CA 91206-4380

LEEFE, JAMES MORRISON, architect; b. N.Y.C., Aug. 28, 1921; s. Charles Clement and Suzanne (Bernhardt) L.; m. Miriam Danziger, Oct. 31, 1949; 1 dau., Molly Elizabeth. Cert., U.S. Mcht. Marine Acad., 1943; B.Arch., Columbia U., 1950. Practice architecture San Francisco, 1955-60; chief architect power and indsl. div. Bechtel Inc., San Francisco, 1960-64; prin. urban designer Bechtel Inc., 1974-80; chief architect San Francisco Power div. Bechtel Power Corp., 1980-89; v.p., asst. sec. Bechtel Assos. (P.C.), N.Y., 1978-89; v.p. Bechtel Assos. (P.C.), D.C. and Va., 1978-89; pvt. cons. architect Sausalito, Calif., 1989—; ptnr. Leefe & Ehrankrantz Architects, San Francisco, 1964-68; v.p. Bldg. Systems Devel. Inc., San Francisco and Washington, 1965-70; also dir.; dir. architecture Giffels Assos. Inc., Detroit, 1971-74; lectr. in architecture Columbia U., 1951-52, U. Calif., Berkeley, 1954-60; mem. faculty U. for Pres's., Young Pres's. Orgn., 1967; adj. prof. U. Detroit, 1971-72; mem. adv. bd. Nat. Clearing House for Criminal Justice Planning and Architecture, 1974-76. Works include Mus. West of Am. Craftsmen's Council, San Francisco, 1964 (Archtl. Record award for interior design 1971), Wells Hydrocombine Dam and Power Generating Facility, Columbia River, Wash., 1965, Boundary Dam, Pend Orielle River, Wash., 1965 (Am. Public Power Assn. honor award 1975), Detroit Automobile Inter-Ins. Exchange Corp. Hdqrs, Dearborn, Mich., 1972 (Detroit chpt. AIA honor award 1975), PPG Industries Research Center, Allison Park, Pa., 1973 (Detroit chpt. AIA honor award 1975, Am. Inst. Steel Constrn. Archtl. award of excellence 1975, Mich. Soc. Architects honor award 1976), Gen. Electric Research Center, Twinsburg, Ohio, 1973 (Detroit chpt. AIA honor award 1977), Appliance Buyers Credit Corp. Hdqrs. Office, Benton Harbor, Mich., 1974 (Engring. Soc. Detroit Design award 1976), Standard Tng. Bldg. Commonwealth Edison, 1989-90, Strybing Arboretum, San Francisco, 1990; contbr. articles to profl. jours.; originator various techniques for analysis of human factors in the working environment. Chmn. bd. Mus. West of Am. Crafts Coun., San Francisco, 1966-68; vice chmn. Franklin (Mich.) Hist. Dist. Commn., 1973-74; trustee So. Marin Land Trust. With U.S. Mcht. Marine, 1942-46. Recipient Hirsh Meml. prize Columbia U., 1950, 1st prize (with Miriam Leefe) Dow Chem. Co. Competition for Interior Design, 1960. Fellow AIA; hon. mem. Internat. Union Architects Working Group Habitat, trustee, So. Marin Land Trust. Home and Office: James Leefe FAIA Architect 131 Spencer Ave Sausalito CA 94965-2022

LEELAND, STEVEN BRIAN, electronics engineer; b. Tampa, Fla., Dec. 27, 1951; s. N. Stanford and Shirley Mae (Bahner) L.; m. Karen Frances Hayes, Dec. 20, 1980; children: Crystal Mary, April Marie. BSEE, MSEE magna cum laude, U. South Fla., 1976. Registered profl. engr., Ariz. Engr. Bendix Avionics, Ft. Lauderdale, Fla., 1976-77; prin. engr., instr. Sperry Avionics, Phoenix, 1977-84; prin. staff engr. Motorola Govt. Electronics Group, Scottsdale, Ariz., 1984-88; sr. staff engr., mgr. dept. software engring. Fairchild Data Corp., Scottsdale, 1988—; cons. Motorola Govt. Electronics Group, 1991. Patentee systolic array, 1990; contbr. articles to profl. jours. Mem. IEEE (Phoenix chpt. Computer Soc. treas. 1978-79, sec. 1979-80, chmn. 1980-81, 81-82), Tau Beta Pi, Pi Mu Epsilon, Phi Kappa Phi, Omicron Delta Kappa, Themis. Republican. Adventist. Home: 10351 E Sharon Dr Scottsdale AZ 85260-9000 Office: Fairchild Data Corp 350 N Hayden Rd Scottsdale AZ 85257-4601

LEEMING, FRANK, JR., newspaper editor, publisher; b. Oklahoma City, Aug. 10, 1938; s. Frank and Louise (Linder) L.; m. Sally Schuske, 1960 (div. 1968); children: Patricia, Frank III; m. Joyce Barnett, Oct. 28, 1973; children: Dusty, Scott, Lewis. B in Bus. and Pub. Adminstrn., U. Mo., 1960. Reporter St. Louis Dispatch, 1960-69; corr. Life Mag., St. Louis, 1967-69; editorial editor Lindsay-Schaub Newspapers, Decatur, Ill., 1969-70; bus. editor The Phila. Inquirer, 1970-71, city editor, 1972, asst. to exec. editor, 1973-75, circulation sales and mktg. mgr., 1976-78; circulation sales and mktg. mgr. Daily News, Phila., 1976-78; pub. Kinsport (Tenn.) Times-News, 1978-83; editor, pub. Jour. of San Juan Islands, Friday Harbor, Wash., 1983—. Contbr. editorials, news series and columns. Bd. dirs. Econ. Devel. Coun. San Juan County, Wash., 1986-89. Mem. Lions. Presbyterian. Home: 37 Mesero Way Hot Springs National Park AR 71909-6007 Office: Leeming Communications Co PO Box 519 301 Tucker Ave Friday Harbor WA 98250-8021

LEEN, TODD KEVIN, physicist; b. Glen Ridge, N.J., Dec. 24, 1955; S. Albert and Miriam (Proskauer) L. BS in Physics, Worcester Poly. Inst., 1977; MS in Physics, U. Wis., 1979; PhD in Physics, U. Wis., Milw., 1982. Research and teaching asst. U. Wis., Madison, 1979-82; scientist, engr. IBM, Burlington, Vt., 1982-87; rsch. assoc. Neurol. Scis. Inst. Good Samaritan Hosp., Portland, Oreg., 1987-89; sr. scientist Oreg. Grad. Inst., Beaverton, Oreg., 1989-90; assoc. prof. Oreg. Grad. Inst., Beaverton, 1990—. Contbr. articles to profl. jours. Mem. Am. Phys. Soc., Internat. Neural Network Soc., Tau Beta Pi, Sigma Pi Sigma, Phi Kappa Phi. Jewish. Office: Oreg Grad Inst Dept Computer Sci & Engring 19600 NW Von Neumann Dr Beaverton OR 97006-6904

LEESON, THOMAS AUBERT, painter; b. Chgo., Mar. 16, 1945; s. Cecil Burton and Louise Larose (Gamble) L.; m. Lee Ann Carroll, June 3, 1967 (div. Mar. 1992). BS, Ball State U., 1968; MA, UCLA, 1971. instr. UCLA, 1977-79, 83-94, U. Calif., Santa Barbara, 1982. One-man shows include Kenmore Galleries, Phila., 1973, Dobrick Gallery, Chgo., 1976, OK Harris, N.Y.C., 1979, Peperdine U., Malibu, Calif., 1980, L.A. County Mus. Art, 1985-86, Ovsey Gallery, L.A., 1986, 89, 95; exhibited in group shows at James Yu Gallery, N.Y.C., 1974, John Gunn Gallery, L.A., 1976, L.A. Inst. Contemporary Art, 1977, L.A. Mcpl. Art Gallery, 1978, 82, Western Assn. Art Mus., 1983, Loyalo Law Sch., L.A., 1984, Riverside (Calif.) Art Mus., 1989, and others. Home and Office: 4748 W Washington Blvd Los Angeles CA 90016-1526

LEETS, PETER JOHN, outplacement consulting firm executive; b. London, Mar. 12, 1946; came to U.S., 1948; s. Earl Edward and Doris Eileen L.; m. Anne E. Shahinian, May 15, 1982. BS in Mktg., Ind. U., 1969. Salesman Ortho Pharm. Corp., Raritan, N.J., 1969-74; account mgr. Revlon Inc., Indpls., 1974-76; regional dir. Revlon Inc., Cleve., 1976-79; field sales mgr. Revlon Inc., Bay Village, Ohio, 1979-83; nat. field sales mgr. Binney & Smith, Bethlehem, Pa., 1983-85; v.p., dir. sales Dell Pub. Co., Inc., N.Y.C., 1985-87; exec. v.p. Geneva Corp., Irvine, Calif., 1987-88; pres. Geneva Cos., Costa Mesa, Calif., 1988-90; exec. v.p. Exec. Assets Corp., Irvine, Calif., 1990-91; pres. Exec. Assets Corp., 1992-94; sr. v.p. Right Assocs., Irvine, Calif., 1994—; guest instr. U. Calif., Irvine, Exec. Spkr. Series; bd. dirs. Career Beginnings; bd. dirs. Career Transition Ptnrs. Chairperson Orange County Econ. Outlook Conf., Orange Coast Venture Group; mem. Internat. Forum for Corp. Dirs. Mem. Assn. for Corp. Growth, Internat. Assn. Career Mgmt. Profls. (bd. dirs.), Ind. U. Alumni Assn. (life), U. Calif. Irvine Chancellor's Club (bd. dirs.), Delta Chi. Office: Exec Assets Corp 3333 Michelson Dr Ste 400 Irvine CA 92715-1684

LEFEVRE, GREG, bureau chief; b. Los Angeles, Jan. 28, 1947; s. Robert Bazille and Anna Marie (Violé) L.; m. Mary Deborah Bottoms, July 10, 1971. AA, Valley Coll., 1970; BS, San Diego State U., 1972, postgrad. Asst. news dir. Sta. KDEO, San Diego, 1971-73; reporter Sta. KFMB-TV, San Diego, 1973-75; sr. reporter Sta. KDFW-TV, Dallas, 1976-81; news dir. Sta. KSEE-TV, Fresno, Calif., 1981-83; corr. Cable News Network, San Francisco, 1983-89, bur. chief, 1989—. Mem. AP Broadcasters (bd. dirs. 1981-90), Soc. Profl. Journalists (pres. 1979-81), Radio and TV News Dirs. Assn. (bd. dirs. 1988-90). Club: Dallas Press (v.p. 1978-81). Office: CNN Am Inc 50 California St Ste 950 San Francisco CA 94111-4606

LEFF, ROBERT S., computer company executive; b. 1947. BA, MS, SUNY at Albany. With RCA Labs., 1971, Neisner Bros., Inc., 1971-72, BASF Wyandotte Corp., 1972-78, Transaction Tech., 1978-80; pres. Merisel Internat. (formerly Softsel Computer Products), from 1980, co-chmn. bd., 1985—. Office: Merisel Internat 200 Continental Blvd El Segundo CA 90245-4526*

LEFFLER, ADRIENNE KAREL, political science educator; b. Chgo., Sept. 24, 1934; d. Bernard and Lenore (Siegal) Karel; m. Robert Leffler, Aug. 28, 1960 (dec. 1990); 1 child, Lawrence Steven. BA in Social Sci. with distinction, San Diego State U., 1969, MA in Polit. Sci., 1975. Instr. ESL Converse Sch. Langs., San Diego, 1976-80; adj. faculty, instr. polit. sci. San Diego C.C. Dist., 1976-85, Grossmont Coll., El Cajon, Calif., 1978—. Author: Wine Country (California), 1992; freelance writer for newspapers and jours. Mem. United Faculty Grossmont Coll. Office: 5156 Judson Way San Diego CA 92115-1625

LEFFLER, STACY BRENT, government employee; b. Quincy, Ill., May 22, 1944; s. Burl William and Eva Elaine (Wood) L.; m. Shirley Mazer, Oct. 6, 1970; children: Sean Alisha, Bar-El Haim. BS in Math., N.Mex. Inst. Mining & Tech., 1974; MA in Internat. Rels., N.Mex. State U., 1982. Ops. rsch. analyst Dept. of the Navy, China Lake, Calif., 1974-76; ops. rsch. analyst Dept. of the Army, White Sands Missile Range, N.Mex., 1976-89, Ft. Bliss, Tex., 1989-94; chmn. Joint Svcs. Command and Control Decision Aids Working Group, 1991-92. With U.S. Army, 1963-67. Mem. NRA (life), Mil. Ops. Rsch. Soc., Assn. of the U.S. Army, Jewish War Vets., Mensa, Intertel, Pi Sigma Alpha. Jewish. Home: PO Box 742 Santa Teresa NM 88008-0742

LEFORCE, JACQUETTA K., interior designer; b. Prescott, Ariz., Nov. 22, 1955; d. Jack Douglas and W. Janice LeF; m. W. Lynn Bartol, Jan. 21, 1995. BS, U. Ariz., 1977. Cert. Nat. Coun. Interior Design Qualification, 1980; ASID. Interior designer J.W. Goebel Interiors, Tucson, 1976-77; asst. mgr. decorative accessories Bullocks, Phoenix, 1977-78; interior designer Barrows, Phoenix, 1978-81; owner, interior designer Jacquetta Porta Interior Design, Oklahoma City, 1981-90; market mgr. Haworth, Inc., L.A., 1990-92; acct. exec. Vater's Office Interior Syss., Tulsa and Oklahoma City, 1992; ter. market mgr. Haworth, Inc., Phoenix, 1992-94; interior designer Interior Studio Group, Scottsdale, Ariz., 1995—; vis. prof. of interior design U. Okla. Coll. Arch., 1987-90; pub. mem., bd. govs. lic. archs., Oklahoma City, 1987-91, pres. ASID Oklahoma chpt., 1989-90; nat. task force licensing for ASID with AIA, IBD, 1989. Docent, com. chmn. Okla. Mus. Art, 1981-90; mem. Okla. Hist. Soc., Okla. City, 1986-90, Junior League, Okla. City, L.A., Phoenix, 1989—;. Recipient Colcord award Okla. Hist. Soc., 1988, 1st Place Nat. Pub. Svc. award ASID, 1988. Profl. mem. ASID, Mortar Bd. (sr. hon.), Alpha Zeta Agrl. (hon.). Office: Interior Studio Group 7633 E Acoma Dr Ste 104 Scottsdale AZ 85260

LEFRANC, MARGARET (MARGARET SCHOONOVER), artist, illustrator, editor, writer; b. N.Y.C., Mar. 15, 1907; d. Abraham and Sophie (Teplitz) Frankel; m. Raymond Schoonover, 1942 (div. 1945). Student, Art Students League, N.Y.C., Kunstschule des Westerns, Berlin, NYU Grad. Sch., Acad. Grande Chaumiere, Paris. Tchr. art Adult Edn., Los Alamos, 1946, Miami (Fla.) Mus. Modern Art, 1975-76. Exhibited in one-person shows at Mus. N.Mex., Santa Fe, 1948, 51, 53, Okla. Art Ctr., 1950, Recorder Workshop, Miami, 1958, St. John's Coll., Santa Fe, 1993; group shows include Salon de Tuileries, Paris, 1928, 29, 30, Art Inst. Chgo., 1936, El Paso Mus. Art, 1964, Mus. Modern Art, 1974, North Miami Mus. Contemporary Art, 1984, Miami Collects, 1989, Women's Caucus Invitational, 1990, Gov.'s Gallery, Santa Fe, 1992; in collections at Belles Artes, Mexico City, Mus. Fine Arts, Santa Fe, others. Bd. dirs., pres. Artist Equity of Fla., 1964-68; v.p. Miami Art Assn., 1958-60; founder, bd. dirs. Guild Art Gallery, N.Y.C., 1935-37. Recipient Illustration award Fifty Best Books of Yr., Libr. of Congress; Honorable Mention award Rodeo of Santa Fe, Mus. N.Mex., others.

LEFTWICH, JAMES STEPHEN, management consultant; b. Stevenage, Eng., Nov. 30, 1956; came to U.S., 1957; s. James Wright and Del Maureen (Thomson) L.; m. Carol Petersen, Nov. 7, 1980 (div. Jan. 1982). AA in Criminal Justice, Butte Coll., Oroville, Calif., 1981; BA, S.W. U., 1993. Lic. internat. accredited safety auditor; cert. hazardous material specialist. Prodn. mgr. Artistic Dyers Inc., El Monte, Calif., 1976-80; mgr. loss control and risk mgmt. Mervyn's Dept. Stores, Hayward, Calif., 1982-91; dir. risk mgmt. Save Mart Corp., Modesto, Calif., 1991-93; v.p. ops. I.C.S. Corp., San Ramon, Calif., 1993-94; pres. I.C.S. Corp., Irvine, Calif., 1994—; cons. R.I.M. Assocs., Walnut Creek, Calif., 1989—; instructor Claims Mgmt., 1993; speaker in field. Scriptwriter, tech. advisor 12 safety videos; contbr. articles on safety and risk mgmt. to profl. publs. Res. police officer Cotati (Calif.) Police Dept., 1983-85; fundraiser United Way, Hayward, 1986, Am. Found. for AIDS Rsch., L.A., 1990; bd. dirs. Bay Area Safety Coun., Oakland, Calif., 1987-88; trustee Calif. Safety Ctr., Sacramento, 1990-91, dir., 1991—. Mem. Am. Soc. for Safety Engrs., Nat. Safety Mgmt. Soc., Nat. Fire Protection Assn., Risk and Ins. Mgmt. Soc., Nat. Assn. Chiefs Police, Nat. Environ. Tng. Assn. Office: ICS Corp San Ramon CA 94583

LÉGARÉ, HENRI FRANCIS, archbishop; b. Willow-Bunch, Sask., Can., Feb. 20, 1918; s. Phillippe and Amanda (Douville) L. B.A., U. Ottawa, 1940; theol. student, Lebret, Sask., 1940-44; M.A., Laval U., 1946; Dr. Social Sci., Cath. U. Lille, France, 1950; LL.D. (hon.), Carleton U., Ottawa, 1959, Windsor (Ont.) U., 1960, Queens U., Kingston, Ont., 1961, U. Sask., 1963, Waterloo (Ont.) Luth. U., 1965, U. Ottawa, Can., 1984; Doctor of Univ., U. of Ottawa. Ordained priest Roman Cath. Ch., 1943; prof. sociology Laval U., 1947, U. Ottawa, 1951; exec. dir. Cath. Hosp. Assn. Can., 1952-57; dean faculty social scis. U. Ottawa, 1954-58, pres., 1958-64; provincial Oblate Fathers, Winnipeg, Man., 1966-67; bishop of Labrador, 1967-72; archbishop Grouard-McLennan, Alta., 1972—. Contbr. articles to profl. jours. Chmn. Canadian Univs. Found., 1960- 62. Decorated grand cross merit Order Malta, 1964; order merit French Lang. Assn. Ont., 1965. Mem. Assn. Canadian Univs. (pres. 1960-62), Can. Conf. Cath. Bishops (pres. 1981-83), Internat. Assn. Polit. Sci. Address: Archbishop's House, CP 388, McLennan, AB Canada T0H 2L0

LEGER, RICHARD ROUBINE, public relations executive, writer; b. Schenectady, N.Y., Oct. 27, 1935; s. Roubine Joseph and Catherine Bernice (Waikas) L.; m. Lawrence Lowell Putnam, Sept. 14, 1957 (div. 1971); children: Philip Augustus, William Richard, Catherine Lowell; m. Dianne Lee Williams, May 14, 1978. BA, U. Rochester, 1957. Reporter Wall St. Jour., N.Y.C., 1960-63, 69-70, Atlanta, 1963-69, San Francisco, 1972-76; fgn. corr. Wall St. Jour., London, 1976-78; bur. chief Wall St. Jour., Nairobi, Kenya, 1978-80; econ. editor San Francisco Chronicle, San Francisco, 1982-84; owner/pub. Sebastopol Times, Sebastopol, Calif., 1985-86; pres. Leger Networks, Inc., San Francisco, 1988—.

LEGG, DAVID E., entomologist, educator; b. Kansas City, Mo., Sept. 25, 1955; s. William J. and Ruth Ann (Thompson) L.; m. Cynthia Sue Volden, July 20, 1985; children: Sarah Kirsten, Taylor Marie. BS in Agr., U. Mo., 1978, MS in Entomology, 1980; PhD in Entomology, U. Minn., 1983. Postdoctoral fellow U. Ky., Lexington, 1983-84; prin. investigator Ky. State U., Frankfort, 1984-88; assoc. prof. integrated pest mgmt. U. Wyo., Laramie, 1988—; cons. FAO, Bangkok, 1986, 87. Contbr. articles to refereed sci. jours. Grantee USDA, 1985, 86, 87. Mem. Colo.-Wyo. Acad. Sci., Ky. Acad. Sci. (governing bd. 1987-88), Entomol. Soc. Am., S.C. Entomol. Soc., Sigma Xi., Gamma Sigma Delta. Office: Univ Wyo PO Box 3354 Laramie WY 82071-3354

LEGGAT, JANET COCHRANE, nutritionist; b. Lowell, Mass., Nov. 18, 1954; d. William Douglas and Doris (Russell) L. BS in Human Nutrition, U. Mass., 1976; MBA in Human Resources, Rivier Coll., Nashua, N.H., 1986. Asst. dir. Chelmsford (Mass.) Sch. Food Svcs., 1977-79; sales rep. Princess House Products, Nashua, N.H., 1981-82; program mgr. St. Joseph Community Svcs., Inc., Merrimack, N.H., 1979-87, enterprise mgr., 1987-94; child and adult care food program coord. Assn. for Supportive Child Care, Inc., Tempe, Ariz., 1994—; state rep. Nat. Assn. Meals Programs, Washington, 1985-94. Vol. Hands Across Am. Mass., Boston, 1986, gen. Greater Lowell (Mass.) Regatta Festival Com., 1975-94, Nat. Park Svc., Lowell, 1986-94, Headstart Nutrition Edn., 1989. Mem. NAFE, Am. Dietetic Assn., N.H. Dietetic Assn. (sec. bd. dirs. 1990-93), Kiwanis (pres. Lowell chpt.). Republican. Episcopalian. Office: Assn Supportive Child Care 4701 S Lakeshore Dr Ste 101 Tempe AZ 85282-7158

LEGGE, CHARLES ALEXANDER, federal judge; b. San Francisco, Aug. 24, 1930; s. Roy Alexander and Wilda (Rampton) L.; m. Janice Meredith Sleeper, June 27, 1952; children: Jeffrey, Nancy, Laura. AB with distinction, Stanford U., 1952, JD, 1954. Bar: Calif. 1955. Assoc. Bronson, Bronson & McKinnin, San Francisco, 1956-64, ptnr., 1964-84, chmn., 1978-84; judge U.S. Dist. Ct. (no. dist.) Calif., San Francisco, 1984—. Served with U.S. Army, 1954-56. Fellow Am. Coll. Trial Lawyers; mem. Calif. Bar Assn. (past chmn. adminstrn. justice com.). Republican. Clubs: Bohemian, World Trade (San Francisco); Orinda (Calif.) Country. Office: US Dist Ct PO Box 36060 16700 Valley View Ave Ste 300 La Mirada CA 90638-5841*

LEGINGTON, GLORIA R., middle school educator. BS, Tex. So. U, Houston, 1967; MS, U. So. Calif., L.A., 1973. Cert. adminstr. (life). Tchr., mentor L.A. Unified Sch. Dist., 1991-93; grade level chair L.A. Unified Schs., 1975-78, faculty chairperson, 1978, 80, 84, Black history/Martin Luther King program chair, 1978, 80, 83, 86, 88, 90-92, social chair, bus. coord., svc. club sponsor, 1978-80, Indian edn. chair, 198084, opportunity chair, 1976-78, grade level chair, 1984; Black edn. commn. liaison, 1989-90, impact tchr., 1991-92, human rels. sponsor, 1991-92, coun. Black adminstrs.-student conf. facilitator, 1992, tchr. inservice classes for area colloqium, parents, tchrs., faculty shared decision making coun., 1993-94, mem. faculty senate, 1992-93, mem. sch. improvement, 1993-94, mem. discipline com., 1993-94. Chair United Way, 1988, 90; sponsor, 8th Grade, 1994-95. Mem. NEA, Internat. Reading Assn., United Tchrs. L.A., Calif. League of Mid. Schs.

LEGRAND, SHAWN PIERRE, computer systems programmer; b. San Diego, Nov. 27, 1960; s. Roger and Violet Louise (Howe) L. Grad. high sch., El Cajon, Calif.; student, U. Calif., San Diego, 1992—. Cert. computer programmer; cert. in neural networks. Computer operator Grossmont CCD, El Cajon, 1978-79; computer systems programmer ICW, San Diego, 1979—. Recipient Math. Achievement award Bank of Am., 1978. Mem. Astron. Soc. Pacific. Republican. Office: ICW 10140 Campus Point Dr San Diego CA 92121-1520

LEHAN, JONATHAN MICHAEL, judge; b. Los Angeles, Apr. 25, 1947; s. Bert Leon and Frances (Shapiro) L.; m. Annett Jean Garrett, Aug. 1, 1970; children: Joshua Michael, Melanie Janine. BA, Calif. State U., Fullerton, 1968; JD, Calif. Western Sch. Law, 1971. Bar: Calif. 1972, U.S. Dist. Ct. (no. dist.) Calif. 1973, U.S. Supreme Ct. 1975. Law clk. to presiding and assoc. justice Calif. Dist. Ct. Appeals, San Bernardino, 1971-73; dep. dist. atty. Mendocino County, Ukiah, Calif., 1973-76; coast asst. dist. atty. Mendocino County, Fort Bragg, Calif., 1976-83; sole practice Fort Bragg, 1983-84; ptnr. Lehan & Kronfeld, Fort Bragg, 1984-90; judge Ten Mile Justice Ctr., Ft. Bragg, 1990—; instr. Barstow C.C., Calif., 1972, Mendocino C.C., Ukiah, 1974-75, Coll. Redwoods, Ft. Bragg, 1981-82; seminar faculty Calif. Jud. Coll., U. Calif., Berkeley, 1993. Bd. dirs. Salmon Restoration Assn., Fort Bragg, Gloriana Opera Co., Mendocino, Mendocino Art Ctr. Editor Calif. Western Sch. Law Law Rev., 1971. Mem. ABA, Mendocino County Bar Assn. (pres. 1989), Phi Delta Phi, Mendocino C. of C. (bd. dirs.). Democrat. Office: Ten Mile Justice Ctr 700 S Franklin St Fort Bragg CA 95437-5464

LEHANE, ANDREW DESMOND, civil engineer; b. San Francisco, June 23, 1964; s. Thomas Jeremiah and Evelyn Marie (Desmond) L.; m. Nena Duran, May 27, 1989; 1 child, Christopher Joseph. BS, U. Santa Clara, 1986. Cert. engr.-in-tng., Calif., cert. profl. engr./Calif. Project mgr. Interstate Constrn., Inc., South San Francisco, Calif., 1986-87, T.I. Systems, Inc., Los Altos, Calif., 1987-89; project engr. Pacific Environ. Group, Inc., San Jose, Calif., 1989—. Mem. Am. Soc. Civil Engrs., NSPE, U. Santa Clara Alumni Assn. Democrat. Roman Catholic. Office: Pacific Environ Group Inc 2025 Gateway Pl Ste 440 San Jose CA 95110-1006

LEHMAN, GARY DOUGLAS, real estate broker; b. Abington, Pa., Feb. 7, 1951; s. Robert Ralston Sr. and Jane Anna (Springer) L. BA in Social Sci., Mich. State U., 1971; postgrad., Calif. Culinary Acad., San Francisco, 1976-77. Exec. chef Holiday Inn, Honolulu, 1979-80; domestic chef Allan Carr, Honolulu, Beverly Hills, Calif., 1980-81, Clare Boothe Luce, Honolulu, 1981-83, Mr. and Mrs. Bernard Cantor, Beverly Hills, 1984-85, Mr. Joseph Ridder, Honolulu, 1985-86, Mr. and Mrs. Sid Bass, Ft. Worth, 1986-87, Mr. and Mrs. John Devine, Tuxedo Park, N.Y., 1987, Mr. and Mrs. Frank Pearl, Washington, 1989; realtor Wiser Realty, Lompoc, Calif., 1990—; state dir. Calif. Assn. Realtors, 1993—; pres. Lompoc Valley Bd. Realtors, 1994. Named Realtor of Yr., Lompoc Valley Bd. Realtors, 1994. Democrat. Home: 517 Venus Ave Lompoc CA 93436-1935 Office: Wiser Realty 119 E Walnut Ave Lompoc CA 93436-6832

LEHMAN, I. ROBERT, biochemist; b. Tauroggen, Lithuania, Oct. 5, 1924; s. Herman B. and Anne (Kahn) L.; m. Sandra Teper, Aug. 5, 1959; children: Ellen R., Deborah, Samuel M. AB, Johns Hopkins U., 1950, PhD, 1954; MD (hon.), U. Gothenberg, Sweden, 1989; DSc. (hon.), U. Paris, 1992. Instr. microbiology Washington U., St. Louis, Mo., 1957-59; from asst. to assoc. prof. biochemistry Stanford (Calif.) U., 1959-66, prof., 1966—, chmn., 1984-86; sci. advisor U.S. Biochem. Corp., Cleve., 1984—, Amersham Life Scis., Eng., 1993—, Ribozyme Pharms., Boulder, Colo., 1992—. Author: Principles of Biochemistry, 7th edit., 1979. Sgt. U.S. Army, 1943-46, ETO. Recipient Merck award Am. Soc. Biol. Chemistry, 1995. Fellow Am. Acad. Arts and Scis.; mem. NAS, Am. Soc. Biol. Chemists, Soc. Scholars. Democrat. Jewish.

LEHMAN, ROBERT GEORGE, electrical engineer; b. Geneva, N.Y., Oct. 17, 1953; s. Robert Frederick and Genevieve Victoria (Grodzicki) L.; m. Melanie Lynn Hendershot, Sept. 13, 1981; children: Paul Andrew, Miranda Elizabeth, Bethany Ellen. BSEE, Wilkes U., Wilkes-Barre, Pa., 1975. Sr. engr. Aerospace Svcs. divsn. Pan Am. World Airways, Patrick AB/Cape Canaveral, Fla., 1975-84; prin. engr. Sperry Corp., Glendale, Ariz., 1984-87; prin. engr. Honeywell, Inc., Glendale, 1987-94, staff engr., 1994—; Contbr. articles to profl. jours.; patentee in field. Dean's scholar Wilkes U., 1975. Office: Honeywell Inc MS AZ77 2AA81A3 5353 W Bell Rd Glendale AZ 85308-3912

LEHMAN, RUTH GILLESPIE, newspaper executive; b. Denver, Feb. 28, 1924; d. Dean Milton and Lillie Mae (Baldwin) Gillespie; m. Edward Lehman, Apr. 22, 1949; children: Lauren Lehman Kivimaki, Dean G. Student, U. Colo., 1941-44; LLB, Columbia U., 1947. Bar: Colo., 1947. Lawyer Denious & Denious, Denver, 1947-51, Burnett, Lehman & Lehman, Denver, 1951-57; pres. Colo. Century Corp., Denver, 1953-80; editl. page editor Longmont (Colo.) Daily Times Call, Loveland (Colo.) Daily Reporter-Herald, Canon City (Colo.) Daily Record, 1965—; v.p., treas. Lehman Comm. Corp., Longmont, 1987—; bd. mem., pres. Colo. Press Assn., Denver, 1976-82; bd. mem., treas. Inland Press Assn., Chgo., 1982-86; bd. mem. Mountain States Employers Coun., Denver, 1989—. Bd. mem. Colo. Legal Aid Found., Denver, 1984-91, Colo. Coun. Econ. Edn., Denver, 1988—, Longmont Art in Pub. Pls., 1989-92. Named Woman of Achievement, Colo. Press Women, 1982. Mem. Internat. Newspaper Fin. Exec., Am. Soc. Newspaper Editors, Nat. Conf. Editl. Writers, Colo. Bar Assn. Office: Lehman Comm Corp 350 Terry St Longmont CO 80501-5440

LEHMANN, ERICH LEO, statistics educator; b. Strasbourg, France, Nov. 20, 1917; came to U.S., 1940, naturalized, 1945; s. Julius and Alma Rosa (Schuster) L.; m. Juliet Popper Shaffer; children: Stephen, Barbara, Fia. M.A., U. Calif. at Berkeley, 1943, Ph.D., 1946; D.Sc. (hon.), U. Leiden, 1985, U. Chgo., 1991. Asst. dept. math. U. Calif. at Berkeley, 1942-43, asso., 1943-46, instr., 1946-47, asst. prof., 1947-51, asso. prof., 1951-54, prof., 1954-55, prof. dept. statistics, 1955-88, emeritus, 1988—, chmn. dept. statistics, 1973-76; vis. assoc. prof. Columbia, 1950-51, Stanford, 1951-52; vis. lectr. Princeton, 1951. Author: Testing Statistical Hypotheses, 1959, 2d edit., 1986, (with J.L. Hodges, Jr.) Basic Concepts of Probability and Statistics, 1964, 2d edit, 1970, Nonparametrics: Statistical Methods Based on Ranks, 1975, Theory of Point Estimation, 1983. Recipient Fisher award Coms. of Pres. Stats. Socs. in N.Am., 1988; Guggenheim fellow, 1955, 66, 79; Miller research prof., 1962-63, 72-73. Fellow Inst. Math. Statistics, Am. Statis. Assn., Royal Statis. Soc. (hon.); mem. Internat. Statis. Inst., Am. Acad. Arts and Scis., Nat. Acad. Scis. Office: U Calif Dept Statistics Berkeley CA 94720

LEHMANN, WERNER HANS, mail order company executive; b. Bronx, N.Y., July 4, 1946; s. William Charles and Grete (Mueller) L.; m. Noreen V. Warren, Aug. 17, 1985. Student, Collegiate Bus. Inst., 1969. Systems adviser IBM, Germany, 1970-75; sales rep. Zeitelhack Steel, Germany, 1976-77; store mgr. Warren Co., Germany, 1977-82; proprietor Euro Posters, N.Y.C., 1982-92, Denver, 1992—. With U.S. Army, 1964-67. Home and Office: 531 Clayton St Denver CO 80206-4232

LEHNER, GREGORY MICHAEL, federal agency administrator; b. Buffalo, Sept. 29, 1948; s. Albert M. and Dorothy J. (Nawrocki) L.; m. Karen A. Boeheim, July 25, 1970; children: Beth M., Kelly M., Michael G. BA in Psychology, St. Bonaventure U., 1970, postgrad., 1972-74; postgrad., U. Ariz., 1976-78. Therapist N.Y. State Dept. Mental Hygiene, Buffalo, 1970, 72-74; intelligence officer U.S. Army Intelligence Ctr., Fort Huachuca, Ariz., 1971-72; mktg. mgr. Master Distbrs., Tucson, Ariz., 1974-75; mgr. Circle K Corp., Tucson, 1975-76; gen. mgr. McDonald's Corp., Tucson, 1976-80; letter carrier U.S. Postal Svc., Tucson, 1980, EEO counselor, 1981-82, supr., 1982-85, mgr., 1985-94, postmaster, 1995—; co-owner, operator K&G Enterprises, Tucson, 1992—; treas. M.D.U. Cable, Phoenix, 1995—. Cubmaster Cub Scouts Am., Tucson, 1985-87; mem. planning com. Cmty. Food Bank, Tucson, 1992-95; active PTO, 1975—. Major USAR, 1970-89. Recipient Leadership award Niagara Mohawk Power Corp., 1970. Mem. DAV, Res. Officers Assn., Am. Legion, Nat. Assn. Postal Suprs. Home: 3035 N Tomas Rd Tucson AZ 85745-9370 Office: US Postal Svc 1501 S Cherrybell Stra Tucson AZ 85726-9998

LEHR, JEFFREY MARVIN, immunologist, allergist; b. N.Y.C., Apr. 29, 1942; s. Arthur and Stella (Smellow) L.; m. Suzanne Kozak, June 10, 1946; children: Elisa, Alexandra, Vanessa. BS, City Coll., Bklyn., 1963; MD, NYU, 1967. Resident, fellow Beth Israel Hosp., N.Y.C., 1968-72; resident in allergy/immunology, internal medicine Roosevelt Hosp., N.Y.C., 1968-72; allergist, immunologist Monterey, Calif., 1974—. Chmn. Monterey Bay Ari Pollution Hearing Bd., 1982-95; v.p. Lyceum of Monterey, 1977-83. Fellow Am. Acad. Allergy/Immunology, Am. Coll. Allergy/Immunology, Am. Assn. Cert. Allergists; mem. Am. Lung Assn. (v.p. 1989-91), Monterey County Med. Soc. (pres. 1988-89). Office: 798 Cass St Monterey CA 93940-2918 also: 262 San Jose St Salinas CA 93901-3901

LEHRER, WILLIAM PETER, JR., animal scientist; b. Bklyn., Feb. 6, 1916; s. William Peter and Frances Reif (Muser) L.; m. Lois Lee Meister, Sept. 13, 1945; 1 child, Sharon Elizabeth. BS, Pa. State U., 1941; MS in Agr., MS in Range Mgmt., U. Idaho, 1946, 55; PhD in Nutrition and Biochemistry, Wash. State U., 1951; LLB, Blackstone Sch. Law, 1972; JD, U. Chgo., 1974; MBA, Pepperdine U., 1975. Mgmt. trainee Swift & Co., Charleston, W.Va., 1941-42; farm mgr. Maple Springs Farm, Middletown, N.Y., 1944-45; rsch. fellow U. Idaho, Moscow, 1945; asst. prof. to prof. U. Idaho, 1945-60; dir. nutrition Albers Milling Co., L.A., 1960-62; dir. nutrition and rsch. Albers Milling Co., 1962-74, Albers Milling Co. & John W. Eshelman & Sons, L.A., 1974-76, Carnation Co., L.A., 1976-81; ret.; cons. in field; speaker, lectr. more than 40 univs. in U.S. and abroad. Contbr. 115 articles to profl. jours.; co-author: The Livestock Industry, 1950, Dog Nutrition, 1972; author weekly column Dessert News, Salt Lake City. Mem. rsch. adv. co. U.S. Brewers Assn., 1969-81; mem. com. on dog nutrition, com. animal nutrition Nat. Rsch. Coun. NAS, 1970-76. With U.S. Army Air Corps, 1942-43. Named Disting. Alumnus, Pa. State U., 1963, 83, Key Alumnus, 1985; named to U. Idaho Alumni Hall of Fame, 1985; recipient Alumni Achievement award Wash. State U., 1993. Fellow AAAS, Am. Soc. Animal Sci.; mem. Am. Inst. Nutrition, Coun. for Agrl. Sci. & Tech., Am. Registry of Profl. Animal Scientists, Am. Inst. Food Technologists, Animal Nutrition Rsch. Coun., Am. Dairy Sci. Assn., Am. Soc. Agrl. Engrs., Am. Feed Mfrs. Assn. (life, nutrition coun. 1962-81, chmn. 1969-70), Calif. State Poly. U. (adv. coun. 1965-81, Meritorious Svc. award), The Nutrition Today Soc., Am. Soc. Animal Sci., Poultry Sci. Assn., Nat. Block & Bridle Club, Hayden Lake Country Club, Alpha Zeta, Sigma Xi, Gamma Sigma Delta (Alumni Award of Merit), Xi Sigma Pi. Republican. Home: Rocking L Ranch 12180 Rimrock Rd Hayden Lake ID 83835

LEHRMAN, LEWIS BARRETT, artist, writer; b. N.Y.C., May 18, 1933; s. Joseph D. and Minna (Agranoff) L.; m. Lola Glanzberg, Aug. 26, 1961; children: Matthew Robert, Jo Ann Lehrman Tierney. BS in Printing Mgmt., Carnegie Inst. Tech., 1954. Prodn. asst. United Catalog Pubs., Hempstead, N.Y., 1957-58; pres. Design Unltd./Culinary Concepts, Hempstead, N.Y., 1958-84; profl. artist Mill River, Mass., 1985-92, Scottsdale, Ariz., 1992—; watercolor instr. Scottsdale Artists' Sch., 1992—; producer, moderator panel discussion series Insight: Art, 1993-95. Author: Being An Artist, 1992, Energize Your Paintings with Color, 1993, Freshen Your Paintings with New Ideas, 1994, Oil Painting Fresh and Bright with Ted Goerschner, 1995. With U.S. Army, 1954-56. Home: 9123 N 115th Pl Scottsdale AZ 85259-5922 Office: Lewis B Lehrman Studio Studio 6 5734 E First St Scottsdale AZ 85251

LEHTIHALME, LARRY (LAURI) K., financial planner; b. Montreal, Que., Can., Feb. 26, 1937; came to U.S., 1964; s. Lauri Johann and Selma Maire (Piispanen) L.; m. Elizabeth Speed Smith, Sept. 9, 1961; children: Tina Beth, Shauna Lyn. Student, Sir George Williams U., Montreal, 1960-64, Mission Coll., San Fernando, Calif., 1978-80, Pierce Coll., Woodland Hills, Calif., 1990-92. Lic. in variable annuity, life and disability ins., Calif.; lic. securities series 7 SEC, series 63. Acct., customer svc. cons. No. Electric, Montreal, 1957-64; salesman Remington Rand Systems, Wilmington, Del., 1964-67; account exec., comm. cons. Pacific Tel. & Telegraph Co., L.A., 1968-84; tech. customer support specialist AT&T, L.A., 1984-85; fin. planner, registered rep. IDS Fin. Svcs., L.A., 1987—. Mem. ctrl. com. Calif. 39th Assembly Dist. Rep. Com., 1976-81, City of L.A., 12th dist.; pres. North Hills Jaycees, 1969-70; sec.-treas. Com. Ind. Valley City and County Govt., 1978-82; subchmn. allocations United Way, Van Nuys, Calif., 1990; fundraiser North Valley YMCA, 1986—; formerly active numerous comty. and polit. orgns. in San Fernando Valley. Named Jaycee of Yr., Newark (Del.) Jaycees, 1966, Granada Hills Jaycees, 1971; recipient cert. of merit U.S. Ho. of Reps., 1973, cert. appreciation City of L.A., 1980, 84, State of Calif., 20th senate dist., 1983, Comty. Spirit award, 1990. Mem. L.A. Olympic Organizing Com. Alumni Assn., Jr. Chamber Internat. (life, senator 1973), U.S. Jaycees (life, Jaycee of Yr. 1965, Outstanding Local Jaycee 1965-66, Presdl. award Honor 1967, Jaycee of Month 1966-67, asst. gen. chmn. 1970-71, state dir. N. Hollywood chpt. 1970-71, Cert. Merit 1971, state gen. chmn., 1971-72, 72-73, Outstanding State Chmn. Calif. dist. 22 1973-74), Granada Hills C. of C. (bd. dirs. 1976-83, Man of Yr. award 1973), Granada Hills Jr. C. of C. Episcopalian. Home: 11408 Haskell Ave Granada Hills CA 91344-3959 Office: Am Express Fin Advisors 11145 Tampa Ave Ste 20A Northridge CA 91326-2255

LEIBACHER, LISE HELENE, French language and literature educator; b. Flers, Orne, France, Jan. 29, 1952; came to U.S., 1976; d. Georges and Jane (Guillaume) Ouvrard; m. John W. Leibacher, Dec. 21, 1976. Degree in English, U. Lille III, 1975; MA in French, San Jose State U., 1977; PhD in French, Stanford U., 1982. Asst. prof. French U. Ariz., Tucson, 1985-91, assoc. prof. French, 1991—, interim dept. head, 1991-92; mem. adv. bd. Syracuse (N.Y.) U. Press, 1988—; reviewer, panelist NEH, Washington, 1992-94. Author: Libertinage et Utopies, 1989; editor: (collected essays) Pascal Corneille Desert, 1984, Utopian Studies IV, 1991, Esprit Créateur, Winte,r 1994; mem. editl. bd. Utopian Studies, 1988—. Mem. MLA, Am. Assn. Tchrs. French, Am. Soc. for Eighteenth Century Studies, N.Am. Soc. for 17th Century French Lit., N.Am. Soc. for Utopian Studies, Popular Culture Assn. Office: U Ariz Dept French Modern Langs 549 Tucson AZ 85721

LEIBERT, RICHARD WILLIAM, special events producer; b. N.Y.C., Nov. 11, 1948; s. Richard William and Rosemarie Martha (Bruns) L. BS, Boston U., 1966-70; student, Northwestern U., 1971. Producer Sta. WBZ AM/FM, Boston, 1968-70; prodn. dir. Sta. WMMR-FM, Phila., 1970; exec. producer Sta. WIND-AM, Chgo., 1970-72; program dir. Sta. KGB AM-FM, San Diego, 1972-80; pres. Events Mktg., Inc., L.A., 1980—; dir. Nat. Fireworks Ensemble, Los Angeles, Calif., 1985—. Creator (mascot, publicity stunts) Sta. KGB Chicken, 1974; creator, producer (radio fireworks show) Sta. KGB Sky Show, 1976; writer, producer (network radio show) New Music News, 1983; creator, dir. (touring co.) Nat. Fireworks Ensemble, 1985. Recipient Emmy award, 1978; named Program Dir. of Yr. Billboard Mag., 1976, Radio Program of Yr. Billboard Mag., 1976. Office: Events Mktg Inc PO Box 65694 Los Angeles CA 90065-0694

LEIBOWITZ, ARLEEN A., economist; b. Binghamton, N.Y., June 11, 1942; d. Albert E. and Mae (Forman) Smigel; m. Robert D. Leibowitz, Aug. 22, 1965; children: Nora, Karen. BA, Smith Coll., 1964; PhD, Columbia U., 1972. Economic analyst Arthur D. Little, Cambridge, Mass., 1965-67; rsch. assoc. Nat. Bureau of Econ. Rsch., N.Y.C., 1971-74; vis. asst. prof. econs. Brown U., Providence, R.I., 1972-75; adj. asst. prof. U. Miami, 1975-76; rsch. prof. law U. Miami (Fla.), 1976-77; economist Rand Corp., Santa Monica, Calif., 1977—; adj. prof. UCLA Sch. Pub. Health. Mem. L.A. Task Force on Access to Health Care, 1992-94. Office: The Rand Corp 1700 Main St Santa Monica CA 90401-3208

LEIDL, PETER JANOS, internist; b. Budapest, Hungary, Mar. 4, 1942; came to U.S., 1959; s. Erno T. and Klara (Mellinger) L.; m. Rose Dumlao, July 26, 1991. BA in Chemistry, Lehigh U., 1965; MS in Chemistry, Fairleigh Dickinson U., 1975; MD, Autonomous U., Guadalajara, Mex., 1981. Diplomate Am. Bd. Internal Medicine. Rsch. chemist Schering Plough Corp., Bloomfield, N.J., 1965-77; intern St. Barnabas Med. Ctr., Livingston, N.J., 1981-82; resident Chgo. Med. Sch., North Chicago, Ill., 1982-85; staff physician FHP Inc., Long Beach, Calif., 1986—. Mem. AMA, ACP, Long Beach Soc. Internal Medicine. Home: 424 N Bellflower Blvd Unit 307 Long Beach CA 90814-2006 Office: 628 Alamitos Ave Long Beach CA 90802-1513

LEIGH, SHARI GREER, software consulting firm executive; b. Reading, Pa., Mar. 1, 1959; d. Martin and Francine Rita (Gross) Rothenstein; m. Martin Brad Greer, Dec. 31, 1979; children: Shannon Leigh, Krista Heather. BA in Biochemistry, Wellesley Coll.-MIT, 1980; postgrad. in bus. adminstrn., Colo. State U., 1982-83. Lead thermal engr. Rockwell Internat. Space div., Downey, Calif., 1980-81; systems engr. Martin Marietta Aerospace, Denver, 1981-82, aerospace new bus. analyst, 1982-84; v.p. Miaco Corp. (Micro Automation Cons.), Englewood, Colo., 1984-87, pres., CEO, 1987—. Co-designer life systems monitor for Sudden Infant Death Syndrome, 1980. Exec. bd. dirs. Mile High chpt. ARC, 1991—. Recipient Recognition award for 500 fastest growing cos. Inc. Mag., 1990, 91, Blue Chip Enterprise award Am.'s Best Small Bus., U.S. C. of C., 1991; named Bus. Leader to Watch in the 90's Corp. Connection; finalist Colo. Small Bus. of the Yr. award C. of C., 1992-93, Person of Yr., U.S. Small Bus. Bus. Adminstrn., South Metro Small Bus. Person of Yr., 1992-93. Mem. Greater Denver Chamber (coun. mem. small bus. bd. 1991-93), So. Met. C. of C. (bd. dirs. 1994—). Office: Miaco Corp 6300 S Syracuse Way Ste 415 Englewood CO 80111-6724

LEIGHNINGER, DAVID SCOTT, cardiovascular surgeon; b. Youngstown, Ohio, Jan. 16, 1920; s. Jesse Harrison and Marjorie (Lightner) L.; m. Margaret Jane Malony, May 24, 1942; children: David Allan, Jenny. BA, Oberlin Coll., 1942; MD, Case Western Res. U., 1945. Intern Univ. Hosps. of Cleve., 1945-46, resident, 1949-51, asst. surgeon, 1951-68; rsch. fellow in cardiovascular surgery rsch. lab. Case Western Res. U. Sch. Medicine, Cleve., 1948-49, 51-55, 57-67, instr. surgery, 1951-55, sr. instr., 1957-64, asst. prof., 1964-68, asst. clin. prof., 1968-70; resident Cin. Gen. Hosp., 1955-57; practice medicine specializing in cardiovascular surgery, Cleve., 1957-70; pvt. practice medicine specializing in cardiovascular and gen. surgery Edgewater Hosp., Chgo., 1970-82, staff surgeon, also dir. emergency surg. services, 1970-82; staff surgeon, also dir. emergency surg. svcs. Mazel Med. Ctr., Chgo., 1970-82; emergency physician Miner's Hosp., Raton, N.Mex., 1982-83, 84-85, No. Colfax County Hosp., Raton, 1983-84, Mt. San Rafael Hosp., Trinidad, Colo., 1984-85; assoc., courtesy, or cons. staff Marymount Hosp., Cleve., Mt. Sinai Hosp., Cleve., Geauga Community Hosp., Chardon, Ohio, Bedford Community Hosp (Ohio), 1957-70. Tchr. tng. courses in CPR for med. personnel, police, fire and vol. rescue workers, numerous cities, 1950-70. Served to capt., M.C., AUS, 1946-48. Recipient Chris award Columbus Internat. Film Festival, 1964, numerous other award for sci. exhibits from various nat. and state med. socs., 1953-70; USPHS grantee, 1949-68. Fellow Am. Coll. Cardiology, Am. Coll. Chest Physicians; mem. AMA, N.Mex. Med. Assn., Colfax County Med. Assn., Ill. Med. Assn., Chgo. Med. Assn., U. Cin. Grad. Sch. Surg. Soc. Contbr. numerous articles to med. jours., chpts. to med. texts; spl. pioneer research (with Claude S. Beck) in physiopathology of coronary artery disease and CPR; developed surg. treatment of coronary artery disease; achieved 1st successful defibrillation of human heart, 1st successful reversal of fatal heart attack; provided 1st intensive care of coronary patients. Home: HC 68 Box 77 Fort Garland CO 81133-9708

LEIGHTON, HENRY ALEXANDER, physician, consultant; b. Manila, Nov. 12, 1929; (parents U.S. citizens).; s. Raymond Harry and Theola Marie (Alexander) L.; m. Helga Maria Hell, Jan. 17, 1970; children: Alan Raymond, Henry Alexander, Michael Ballinger, John, Marni, Tammy Ballinger. BA in History, U. Calif., Berkeley, 1952, MPH, 1971; MD, U. Calif., San Francisco, 1956. Diplomate Am. Bd. Preventive Medicine. Intern So. Pacific Gen. Hosp., San Francisco, 1956-57; resident in surgery Brooke Gen. Hosp., Ft. Sam Houston, Tex., 1960-62; commd. 2d. lt. U.S. Army, 1957, advanced through grades to col., 1971; div. surgeon 8th Inf. div. U.S. Army, Germany, 1964-66; comdr. 15th Med. Bn. U.S. Army, Vietnam, 1966-67; instr. Med. Field Service Sch. U.S. Army, San Antonio, 1968-70; resident preventive medicine U.S. Army, Ft. Ord, Calif., 1971-72, chief preventive medicine, 1973-76; chief preventive medicine U.S. Army-Europe, 1976-79, ret., 1979; chief occupational health MEDDAC U.S. Army, Ft. Ord, 1981-89; pvt. practice Salinas, Calif., 1990—. Neighborhood commr. Boy Scouts Am., 1964-66; bd. dirs. Am. Lung Assn. of Calif., 1982-84, and of affiliate, 1980-86, The Calif. Acad. Preventive Medicine, 1994—; pres. The Bluffs Homeowners Assn., 1986. Decorated Air medal with oak leaf cluster, Bronze Star, Legion of Merit, Meritorious Service medal. Fellow Am. Coll. Preventive Medicine; mem. Am. Pub. Health Assn., Am. Coll. Occupational Medicine, Assn. Mil. Surgeons, Ret. Officers Assn., Assn. U.S. Army, Theta Xi. Lodges: Masons, Shriners. Office: 14096 Reservation Rd Salinas CA 93908-9208

LEIGHTON, LARRY J., nonprofit organization administrator; b. Wenatchee, Wash., June 28, 1941; s. Lyle L. and Gwen E. (Jones) L.; m. Uvieja Good , Aug. 6, 1977. AB, Guilford Coll., 1964. Scout exec. Boy Scouts Am., Tucson, 1977-81, Sacramento, Calif., 1981-88; exec. dir. Cen. Ohio Coun. of Camp Fire, Inc., Columbus, 1990-94, Big Brothers/Big Sisters of Greater Sacramento Area, 1994—. Chmn. Guilford Coll. Loyalty Fund, Class 1964; bd. dirs. United Way. Named to Honorable Order of Ky. Cols., 1971; recipient Disting. Svc. award Kiwanis Club, Louisville, Ky., 1972. Mem. Nat. Soc. Fund Raising Execs., Boy Scouts Am., Sacramento C. of C., Rotary Club of Sacramento, Agys. Exec. Assn. (v.p.). Republican. United Methodist. Home: 2044 Granite Bar Way Gold River CA 95670-8333 Office: Big Brothers/Big Sisters 2856 Arden Way Ste 150 Sacramento CA 95825-1374

LEIGHTON, PETER ELLIOTT, advertising executive; b. Millbrae, Calif., Jan. 31, 1962; s. Elliott Leighton and Barbara (Reines) Lazear; m. Joy Robin Brown, Mar. 22, 1987; children: Sarah R., Allison J. Student, U. Fla., 1980-84, New Sch. for Social Rsch., 1984. Account exec. G/D Advt., Miami, Fla., 1984; sr. account exec. Goldcoast Advt., Miami, 1985; exec. v.p. Advisors, Ft. Lauderdale, Fla., 1985-89; pres. Leighton/Brydger/Gottron, Ft. Lauderdale, 1989-91; account dir. Gauger & Silva Assocs., San Francisco, 1991—; pres., contbg. editor Bus. Builders, San Francisco, 1992-93. Recipient Price Waterhouse's Up & Comer Achievement awards, 1988, 91. Democrat. Jewish. Office: Gauger Silva Inc 129 Hyde St San Francisco CA 94102-3605

LEINBERGER, CHRISTOPHER BROWN, urban development consultant, writer; b. Charleston, W.Va., Jan. 2, 1951; s. Frederick Arthur and Helen (Brown) L.; children: Christopher Brown, Rebecca. BA in Urban Sociology, Swarthmore Coll., 1972; MBA, Harvard U., 1976. Asst. to pres. ARA Food Svcs., Inc., Phila., 1973-74, 76-77; dir. concept devel. Saga Corp., Menlo Park, Calif., 1977-79; exec. v.p. Robert Charles Lesser & Co., Beverly Hills, Calif., 1979-82, mng. dir., co-owner, 1982—; bd. dirs. Avalon Properties. Author: Strategic Planning for Real Estate companies: contbr. articles to profl. jours. and nat. print media including The Wall Street Jour., L.A. Times, The Atlantic Monthly, The Nation, Chgo. Tribune. Bd. dirs. Swarthmore (Pa.) Coll., Coll.of Santa Fe, Realen Homes, Phila., Avalon Properties. Fellow NSF, 1971, NCAA, 1972, Coro Found., 1972-73. Mem. Urban Land Inst. (coun. mem. 1984—). Democrat. Home: Las Urracas Rte 4 Box 48 Santa Fe NM 87501 Office: Robert Charles Lesser & Co RR 4 Santa Fe NM 87501-9804

LEININGER, CHRIS J., physician; b. Chgo., Oct. 27, 1947; s. Philip W. and Lorie (Dodge) L.; m. Jyl P. Jacobowitz, Sept. 8, 1979; 1 child, Alex Carl. BA, Amherst Coll., 1969; MS, U. Pa., 1971; MD, NYU, 1975. Diplomate Am. Bd. Family Practice. Resident, chief resident in family practice Doctors Hosp., Seattle, 1975-78; physician Greenlake Med. Ctr.,

Seattle, 1979-85; physician Greenwood Family Medicine, Seattle, 1985-94, med. mgmt. cons., 1992—; dir. profl. svcs. Swedish Med. Svcs., Seattle, 1994—; asst. clin. prof. Sch. Medicine, U. Wash., Seattle, 1978—; attending faculty Swedish Family Practice Program, Seattle, 1980—. Fellow Am. Acad. Family Practice; mem. AMA. Home: 7606 E Green Lake Dr N Seattle WA 98103-4911 Office: Swedish Medical Services 1101 Madison St Ste 1000 Seattle WA 98104-1320

LEININGER, ROBERT FARNES, author, screenwriter; b. Berkeley, Calif., Sept. 13, 1946; s. Robert Farnes Leininger and Patricia (MacNeil) Geary; m. Patricia Mary Bradbrook. BS in Mech. Engring., U. Nev., 1980. Mech. engr. Northrop Corp., Newbury Park, Calif., 1981-85; author, writer pvt. practice Reno, Nev., 1985—. Author: Killing Suki Flood, 1991, Black Sun, 1991; screenwriter: The Lemonmobile, 1991. With USN, 1964-71. Mem. Pi Mu Epsilon.

LEINO, DEANNA ROSE, business educator; b. Leadville, Colo., Dec. 15, 1937; d. Arvo Ensio Leino and Edith Mary (Bonan) Leino Malenck; adopted child, Michael Charles Bonan. BSBA, U. Denver, 1959, MS in Bus. Adminstrn., 1967; postgrad. Community Coll. Denver, U. No. Colo., Colo. State U., U. Colo., Met. State Coll. Cert. tchr., vocat. tchr., Colo. Tchr. Jefferson County Adult Edn., Lakewood, Colo., 1963-67; retired tchr. bus., coordinator coop. office edn., Jefferson High Sch., Edgewater, Colo., 1959-93, ret., 1993; sales assoc. Joslins Dept. Store, Denver, 1978—; mem. ea. team, clk. office automation Denver Svc. Ctr. Nat. Park Svc, 1993-94, U.S. Dept. Labor, 1994—, wage hour asst.; instr. Community Coll. Denver, Red Rocks, 1967-81, U. Colo. Denver, 1976-79, Parks Coll. Bus. (name now Parks Jr. Coll.), 1983—; dist. adviser Future Bus. Leaders Am. Active City of Edgewater Sister City Project Student Exchange Com.; pres. Career Women's Symphony Guild; treas. Phantoms of Opera, 1982—; active Opera Colo. Assocs. & Guild, I Pagliacci; ex-officio trustee Denver Symphony Assn., 1980-82. Recipient Disting. Svc. award Jefferson County Sch. Bd. 1980, Tchr. Who Makes A Difference award Sta. KCNC/Rocky Mountain News, 1990, Youth Leader award Lakewood Optimist Club, 1993; inducted into Jefferson High Sch. Wall of Fame 1981 Mem. NEA (life), Colo. Edn. Assn., Jefferson County Edn. Assn., Colo. Vocat. Assn., Am. Vocat. Assn., Colo. Educators for and about Bus., Profl. Secs. Internat., Career Women's Symphony Guild, Profl. Panhellenic Assn., Colo. Congress Fgn. Lang. Tchrs., Wheat Ridge C. of C. (edn. and scholarship com.), Federally Employed Women, Delta Pi Epsilon, Phi Chi Theta, Beta Gamma Sigma, Alpha Lambda Delta. Republican. Roman Catholic. Club: Tyrolean Soc. Denver. Avocations: decorating wedding cakes, crocheting, sewing, music, world travel. Home: 3712 Allison St Wheat Ridge CO 80033-6124

LEIS, MARIETTA PATRICIA, artist; b. Newark; d. George Francis and Marietta Roma (Napoliello) L. BA, Antioch Coll. West, 1975; MA in Painting/Drawing, U. N.Mex., 1985, MFA in Painting/Drawing, 1988. Art instr. dept. art and art history Coll. Fine Arts, Albuquerque, 1985-88; art instr. cmty. coll. divsn. continuing edn. U. N.Mex., Albuquerque, 1988—; artist-tchr. MFA program Vt. Coll. of Norwich U., Montpelier, 1991—. One-person shows include St. John's Coll., Santa Fe, N.Mex., 1990, Pacific Internat. Art Gallery, Palo Alto, Calif., 1991, U. N.Mex. Continuing Edn. Conf. Ctr., Albuquerque, 1993; exhibited in group shows at Oakland C.C., Farmington Hills, Mich., 1993, Gallery Per Tutti, Boston, 1993, Merrill Chase Galleries, Buffalo Grove, Ill., 1993, Cooperstown (N.Y.) Art Assn., 1993, Allentown (Pa.) Art Mus., 1993, also pub. collections; contbr. articles to profl. jours. Artist grantee Artist Space, N.Y.C.; recipient Hon. Distinction award Internat. Art Biennial, Mus. Hisico, Capranica, Italy, 4th Ann. Faber Birren Color award Stanford (Conn.) Art Assn., Art-in-Opera Merit award Met. Opera Guild, Inc. Mem. Nat. Assn. Women Artists. Home and Office: PO Drawer D Corrales NM 87048-0159

LEISSRING, JOHN COTHER, pathologist; b. Milw., Mar. 29, 1935; s. William Frederick and Alice Jane (Webb) Leissring; m. Judith Lee Lentz, June 1959 (div. 1981); children: Matthew William, Malcolm Arthur. BS, U. Wis., 1957, MS in Anatomy, 1961, MD, 1961. Diplomate Bd. Med. Examiners, Wis., Calif., Am. Bd. Pathology, Am. Bd. Dermatology. Instr. pathology Stanford (Calif.) Med. Sch., 1968-69; asst. clin. prof. U. Calif. Med. Sch., San Francisco, 1969-74; pathologist Santa Rosa (Calif.) Meml. Hosp., 1969—. Author: Life and Work of Michael Brenner, 1991; contbr. articles to profl. jours. Lt. comdr. USN, 1959-65. Recipient Border award in rsch. Borden Inst., Madison, Wis., 1961. Fellow Coll. Am. Pathologists, Am. Soc. Clin. Pathologists; mem. Pacific Derm. Soc., Calif. Soc. Pathologists, Press Club of San Francisco, Musicians Union, AFL/CIO. Home: 1015 Mcdonald Ave Santa Rosa CA 95404-3524 Office: Drs Leissring and DeMeo 1144 Montgomery Dr Santa Rosa CA 95405-4802

LEISURE, ROBERT GLENN, physics educator; b. Cromwell, Ky., Jan. 29, 1938; s. Roscoe B. and Lova Leisure; m. Jeanine Smith, Aug. 18, 1962. BS, Western Ky. U., 1960; PhD, Wash. U., St. Louis, 1967. Staff scientist Boeing Sci. Rsch. Labs., Seattle, 1967-70; asst. prof. physics Colo. State U., Ft. Collins, 1970-73, assoc. prof. physics, 1973-78, prof. physics, 1978—, chmn. physics dept., 1984-90; vis. scientist U. Paris, 1978-79; collaborator Los Alamos Nat. Lab., 1990—; mem. operating bd. Colo. Advanced Materials Inst., 1991—. Contbr. numerous articles to profl. jours. NSF grantee, 1973-85; SERC fellow U.K., 1983, 87. Mem. Internat. EPR Soc., Am. Ceramic Soc., Am. Phys. Soc., Phi Kappa Phi, Sigma Xi. Home: 926 Cottonwood Dr Fort Collins CO 80524-1521 Office: Colo State U Dept Physics Fort Collins CO 80523

LEIWEKE, TIMOTHY, sales executive, marketing professional; b. St. Louis, Apr. 21, 1957; s. John Robert and Helen (Caicuey) L.; m. Pamela Leiweke, Nov. 1, 1984. Grad. high sch., St. Louis. Salesperson New Eng. Mut. Life Ins. Co., St. Louis, 1976-79; asst. gen. mgr. St. Louis Steamers/MISL, 1979-80; gen. mgr. Balt. Blast/MISL, 1980-81; v.p., gen. mgr. Kansas City (Mo.) Comets/MISL, 1981-84; v.p. Leiweke and Co., Kansas City, 1984-85; pres. Kansas City Comets/MISL, 1986-88; v.p. sales and mktg. div. Minn. Timberwolves, Mpls., 1988-91; sr. v.p. of bus. ops. Denver Nuggets, Denver, 1991-92; pres. Denver Nuggets, Denver, CO, 1992—. Bd. dirs. Kidney Found., Minn., 1989—, Spl. Olympics, Minn., 1989—, Timberwolves Community Found., Minn., 1989—. Named Rookie of the Yr., Mo. Life Underwriters, 1976, Kansas Citian of the Yr., Kansas City Press Club, 1983; recipient William Brownfield award U.S. Jaycees, 1978, William Brownfield award Mo. Jaycees, 1978, Excalibur award Am. Cancer Soc., 1987. Mem. Kansas City Mktg. and Sales Execs., Mpls. Club. Home: 1635 Clay St Denver CO 80204-1799 Office: Denver Nuggets McNichols Sports Arena 1635 Clay St Denver CO 80204-1799*

LEKA, FANTU WOLDE, quality assurance engineer; b. Addis Ababa, Ethiopa, May 7, 1958; came to U.S., 1986; s. Wolde and Birke (Gebre) L. BS in Mech. Engring., Anna U., 1985; MS in Mech. Engring., San Diego State U., 1989. Quality assurance dept. Contract Sys. Assocs., San Diego, 1986-87; mfg. engr. Cipher Data, San Diego, 1987-89; mech. engr. Taylor Made Golf, Carlsbad, Calif., 1989-91; quality assurance engr., gen. supr. 3M/Unitek, Monrovia, Calif., 1991—; spkr. Minority Engring. & Sci. Students, 1992-93. Exec. bd., employment assistance com. Ethiopian Ednl. Assistance at L.A., 1993-94. Mem. ASME, Am. Soc. Quality Control. Home: 2276 Stratford Way La Verne CA 91750-5142 Office: 3M/Unitek 2824 Peck Rd Monrovia CA 91016-5005

LEKASHMAN, JOHN RAYMOND, company executive; b. N.Y.C., Jan. 9, 1961; s. John Quentin and Barbara Ann (Bianco) L.; m. Karen Jeanne Karasinski, Feb. 26, 1989; children: Andrew, Kenneth. BS, MIT, 1983. Engr. Megatest Corp., Santa Clara, Calif., 1983-85; sys. engr. GE, San Jose, Calif., 1985-89; network mgr. NASA, Moffett Field, Calif., 1989-93; CEO Alleged Assocs. Inc., Los Gatos, Calif., 1989—. Mem. Assn. for Computing Machinery, Internet Engring. Task Force. Home: PO Box 390045 Mountain View CA 94039-0045

LEKSON, STEPHEN HENRY, archaeologist; b. West Point, N.Y., May 18, 1950; s. John S. and Gladys M. (Pecsok) K.; m. Catherine M. Cameron, Jan. 12, 1979. BA, Case Western Res. U., 1972; MA, Ea. N.Mex. U., 1978; PhD, U. N.Mex., 1988. Archaeologist, project dir. U. Tenn., Knoxville, 1973; archaeologist Ea. N.Mex. U., Portales, 1974-75, Nat. Park Svc., Albuquerque, 1976-86; rsch. assoc. Ariz. State Mus., Tucson, 1987-90; curator archaeology Mus. of N.Mex., Santa Fe, 1991-92; pres., CEO Crow Canyon Archaeol. Ctr., Cortez, Colo., 1992—. Author: Great Pueblo Architecture of Chaco Canyon, N.Mex., 1986, Nana's Raid, 1987, Mimbres Archaeology, 1990, Ancient Land, Ancestral Places, 1993. Mem. Am. Anthropol. Assn., Soc. Am. Archaeology, Am. Assn. Mus., World Archaeol. Congress. Home: 7279 W Kentucky Dr Apt B Lakewood CO 80226-4914 Office: Crow Canyon Archaeol Ctr 23390 County Road K Cortez CO 81321-9408

LEM, RICHARD DOUGLAS, painter; b. L.A., Nov. 24, 1933; s. Walter Wing and Betty (Wong) L.; B.A., UCLA, 1958; M.A., Calif. State U.-Los Angeles, 1963; m. Patricia Ann Soohoo, May 10, 1958; 1 son, Stephen Vincent. Exhibited in one-man shows at Gallery 818, Los Angeles, 1965; group shows at Lynn Kottler Galleries, N.Y.C., 1973, Palos Verdes Art Gallery, 1968, Galerie Mouffe, Paris, France, 1976, Le Salon des Nations, Paris, 1984, numerous others; represented in permanent collections; writer, illustrator: Mile's Journey, 1983; cover illustrator: The Hermit, 1990, The Hermit's Journey, 1993. Served with AUS, 1958-60. Mem. UCLA Alumni Assn. Address: 1861 Webster Ave Los Angeles CA 90026-1229

LEMAN, LOREN DWIGHT, civil engineer; b. Pomona, Calif., Dec. 2, 1950; s. Nick and Marian (Broady) L.; m. Carolyn Rae Bratvold, June 17, 1978; children: Joseph, Rachel, Nicole. BSCE, Oreg. State U., 1972; MS in Civil, Environ. Engring., Stanford U., 1973. Registered profl. engr., Alaska. Project mgr. CH2M Hill, San Francisco, 1973, Reston, Va., 1973-74, Ketchikan, Alaska, 1974-75, Anchorage, 1975-87; state rep. State of Alaska, 1989-93, state senator, 1993—; owner Loren Leman, P.E., Anchorage, 1987—; mem. Anchorage Hazardous Materials Commn., Local Emergency Planning Com., 1989-93. Contbr. articles to profl. jours. Mem. Breakthrough Com., Anchorage, 1978; del. to conv. Rep. Party of Alaska, 1976-90; basketball coach Grace Christian Sch., Anchorage, 1985-88; commr. Pacific States Marine Fisheries Commn.; del. Pacific Fisheries Legis. Task Force. Mem. ASCE, Alaska Water Mgmt. Assn., The Nature Conservancy, Am. Legis. Exch. Coun., Water Environment Fedn., Toastmasters (pres.). Republican. Home: 2699 Nathaniel Ct Anchorage AK 99517-1016 Office: Alaska State Legis 716 W 4th Ave # 540 Anchorage AK 99501-2107

LEMASTER, SUSAN M., marketing consultant, writer; b. Cody, Wyo., May 9, 1953; d. Floyd Morris and Virginia Kristena (Renner) LeM.; B.A., U. Wyo., Casper, 1979; A.A., Casper Coll., 1977. Reporter, night editor Casper Star Tribune, 1972-76; copy editor, editor In Wyo. mag., Casper, 1979; info. dir. Wyo. Rural Electric Assn., Casper, 1980-81; story editor Wyo. Horizons mag., Casper, 1981-82; asst., instr. English lab. Casper Coll., 1982-84; mktg. mgr. Chen & Assocs., Inc., 1984-87; mktg. cons., 1987-90; dir. mktg. KaWES and Assocs., Inc., 1990-91, pub. rels./mktg. cons., 1992—; freelance writer and editor, 1982—; night sch. instr. Casper Coll., 1983-84, summer sch. instr., 1984. Editor Casper Jour., 1983-84. Recipient First Place News Story, Wyo. Press Assn., 1973; first pl. Editing award Wyo. Press Women, 1980. Mem. Soc. Mktg. Profl. Svcs. (bd. dirs. L.A. chpt. 1990-94), L.A. Press Club, Phi Theta Kappa, Phi Kappa Phi, Alpha Mu Gamma. Democrat.

LEMASURIER, WESLEY ERNEST, geology educator, researcher; b. Washington, May 3, 1934; s. E. Howard and V. May (Van Arnum) LeM.; m. C. Heather Nelson, Sept. 21, 1963; children: Michelle, Susanne, John. Student, St. Andrews U., Fifeshire, Scotland, 1954-55; BS, Union Coll., Schenectady, N.Y., 1956; MS, U. Colo., 1962; PhD, Stanford U., 1965. Geologist U.S. Geol. Survey, Denver, also Menlo Park, Calif., 1956-63; asst. prof. geology Cornell U., Ithaca, N.Y., 1964-68; from assoc. prof. to prof. geology U. Colo., Denver, 1968—; dir. Guilin Coll. (China)-U. Colo. Denver Scholarly Exch. Program, 1986—. Editor, author: Volcanoes of the Antarctic Plate and Southern Oceans, 1990. Pvt. U.S. Army, 1960. Recipient Antarctic Svc. medal, 1971; NSF grantee, 1968-85; Mt. LeMasurier named in his honor, 1971; exch. scholar St. Andrews U., 1954-55. Fellow Geol. Soc. Am.; mem. Am. Geophys. Union, Internat. Assn. Volcanology. Presbyterian. Home: 1333 Mariposa Ave Boulder CO 80302-7841 Office: U Colo at Denver 1200 Larimer St Denver CO 80204-5300

LEMERT, JAMES BOLTON, journalist, educator; b. Sangerfield, N.Y., Nov. 5, 1935; s. Jesse Raymond and Caroline Elizabeth (Brown) L.; m. Rosalie Martha Bassett, Mar. 23, 1972. A.B., U. Calif.-Berkeley, 1957, M.J., 1959; Ph.D., Mich. State U., 1964. Newspaper reporter Oakland Tribune, Calif., 1955-56; Newspaper reporter Chico Enterprise-Record, Calif., 1957, 58-60; asst. prof. journalism So. Ill. U., Carbondale, 1964-67, U. Oreg., Eugene, 1967-69; assoc. prof. U. Oreg., 1969-76, prof., 1976—, dir. div. communication rsch., 1967—, dir. grad. program Sch. Journalism, 1983-86, 88-93; chair U. Oreg. Task Force to Revise Faculty Governance, 1983-84; mem. senate U. Oreg., 1981-83, 86-88, 93-94, chmn. senate rules com., 1987-88, chmn. intercollegiate athletics com., 1986-89, pres.'s adv. coun., 1990-91, chair, 1991-92, mem. grad. coun., 1984-86, 89-90, 94—, chair, 1993-94, chair task force on rsch. and grad. edn., 1990-91, mem. rsch. com., 1994-95. Prodr., on-air host Old Grooves show, KWAX-FM, 1977-80, 82-84; author: Does Mass Communication Change Public Opinion After All? A New Approach to Effects Analysis, 1981, Criticizing the Media: Empirical Approaches, 1989, News Verdicts, The Debates and Presidential Campaigns, 1991, Politics of Disenchantment: Bush, Clinton, Perot and the Press, 1995; editor Daily Californian, 1957; contbr. articles to profl. jours. Mem. Oreg. Alcohol and Drug Edn. Adv. Com., 1968-69; pres. South Hills Neighborhood Assn., 1976-77, bd. dirs., 1982-84, 86-88; bd. dirs. Traditional Jazz Soc. Oreg., 1981-83, 87; v.p. Met. Cable Access Corp., 1983-84; mem. exec. bd. AAUP, 1975-76, 91-94; mem. state exec. com., head chpt. Assn. Oreg. Faculties, 1981-83, 85-87, state v.p., 1987-89, del. to Oreg. Faculties Polit. Action Com., 1986-89. Recipient Outstanding Journalist award Sigma Delta Chi, 1957, Donald M. McGammon Communication Rsch. Ctr. critical rsch. grantee, 1988-89, Allen Family Found. grantee; NSF fellow, 1963, 64; Calif. Newspaper Pubs. fellow, 1957; Butte County Alumni scholar, 1953-54. Mem. Assn. Edn. Journalism, Am. Assn. Pub. Opinion Rsch., Am. Polit. Sci. Assn., Speech Comm. Assn., Phi Beta Kappa (membership chmn. 1985-86, v.p., pres. 1989-91). Home: 10 E 40th Ave Eugene OR 97405-3487

LEMIEUX, LINDA DAILEY, museum director; b. Cleve., Sept. 6, 1953; d. Leslie Leo LeMieux Jr. and Mildred Edna (Dailey) Tutt. BA, Beloit Coll., 1975; MA, U. Mich., 1979; assoc. cert., Mus. Mgmt. Program, Boulder, Colo., 1987. Asst. curator Old Salem, Inc., Winston-Salem, N.C., 1979-82; curator Clarke House, Chgo., 1982-84; curator Western Mus. Mining and Industry, Colorado Springs, Colo., 1985-86, dir., 1987—. Author: Prairie Avenue Guidebook, 1985; editor: The Golden Years--Mines in the Cripple Creek District, 1987; contbr. articles to mags. and newspapers. Fellow Hist. Deerfield, Mass., 1974—. Research grantee Early Am. Industries Assn., 1978. Mem. Am. Assn. Mus., Am. Assn. State and Local History, Colo.-Wyo. Mus. Assn., Colo. Mining Assn., Nev. Mining Assn., Mountain Plains Assn. Mus., Women in Mining. Republican. Presbyterian. Home: 1337 Hermosa Way Colorado Springs CO 80906-3050 Office: Western Mus of Mining & Industry 1025 N Gate Rd Colorado Springs CO 80921-3018

LEMIRE, DAVID STEPHEN, school psychologist, educator; b. Roswell, N.Mex., May 23, 1949; s. Joseph Armon and Jeanne (Longwill) L.; BA, Linfield Coll., 1972, MEd, 1974; EdS, Idaho State U., 1978; postgrad. U. Wyo.; EdS in Ednl. Adminstrn. and Instructional Leadership, U. Wyo., 1988; postgrad. U. Wyo. Cert. sch. counselor, student pers. worker, psychology instr., Calif. Sch. counselor, psychol. technician and tchr. Goshen County Sch. Dist. 1, Torrington, Wyo., counselor Aspen High Sch., Aspen, Colo.; sch. counselor Unita County Sch. Dist., Evanston, Wyo., coord. R&D Lifelong Learning Ctr. 1986-87, dir. spl. svcs. and sch. psychologist Bighorn County Sch. Dist. #4, Basin, Wyo., 1989-90; sch. psychologist Sweetwater County Sch. Dist. #2, Green River, Wyo., 1990-91; dir. housing, residence supr. Pratt (Kans.) Community Coll., 1991-92; pres. David Lemire Software Enterprises, Evanston; dir. Inst. for Advanced Study of Thinkology. Mem. ASCD, Nat. Assn. Sch. Psychologists (cert.), Am. Psychol. Assn. Former editor WACD Jour.; former mng. editor Jour. Humanistic Edn.; contbr. articles to profl. jours. Address: PO Box 21097 Topeka KS 66621 also: Creative Therapeutics Adminstrv Offices 2390 Riviera St Reno NV 89509-1144

LEMKHIN, MIKHAIL, photographer; b. Leningrad, USSR, Feb. 11, 1949; came to U.S., 1983, naturalized, 1990; s. Abram and Anna (Denkevich) L.; m. Irina Margolin, July 18, 1969; children: Nathan, Marina. MA in Journalism and Photo-journalism, Leningrad State U., 1973. Freelance and staff journalist, photographer various newspapers and publs., Leningrad; freelance photographer San Francisco, 1983—. Numerous photographic portraits, including Joan Baez, Joseph Mankeiwicz, Allen Ginsberg, Dizzy Gillespie, Richard Avedon, Peter Gabriel, Julian Lennon, Randy Newman, Joyce Carol Oats, Sting, Pete Seeger, Paul Simon, Joseph Brodsky, Andrey Sakharov, Michalangelo Antonioni, Czeslaw Milosh, and many others; one-man shows include Viborgsky Cultural Ctr., Leningrad, Russia, 1965, 66, Leningrad State U., 1968, Koret Gallery, Palo Alto, Calif., 1987, Stanford (Calif.) U., 1989, St. John's Coll., Santa Fe, 1989, Montgomery Gallery, San Francisco, 1990, Lenin Cultural and Hist. Ctr. Ukraine, Kiev, 1991, Concourse Pavilion, San Francisco, 1991, 3287 Folsom, San Francisco, 1992, Park Lane's Parc Fifty Five Hotel, San Francisco, 1993, San Francisco Internat. Airport, 1993, Eighth St. Gallery, Berkeley, Calif., 1993, Cafe Les Croissants, San Francisco, 1993, Owl and Monkey Cafe, San Francisco, 1994, St. John's Coll., Santa Fe, 1989, Montgomery Gallery, San Francisco, 1990, Peter and Paul Fortress, Leningrad, 1991, Lenin Cultural and Hist. Ctr., Kiev, Ukraine, 1991; group exhibits include 3287 Folsom, 1992, Eighth St. Gallery, Berkeley, 1993, Jewish Mus., San Francisco, 1993, Belcher Gallery, San Francisco, 1995; represented in pub. and pvt. collections such as U. Calif. Pacific Film Archive, Stenford U. Green Libr. Contbd. photographs to The Christian Science Monitor, San Francisco Chronicle, Nikon News, Moscow News, Ogonyok Mag.; author: Missing Frames, 1995. Mem. P.E.N. Club, Nat. Press Photographers Assn. Home: 1811 38th Ave San Francisco CA 94122-4147

LEMMON, PHILIP DOUGLAS, publishing company executive; b. Pocatello, Idaho, Sept 4, 1943; s. Eugene and Shirley (Walton) L.; m. M. Kathleen Jensen; Dec. 13, 1943; children: Kari, Steven. Student, Idaho State U., 1961-63, 67. Regular performances Egyptian Theatre; Boise on Robert Morton Theatre Pipe Organ; conductor Church Organist Seminars; recital series for Dunkley Music Boise; Instn. sales dir. Dunkley Music, Boise; tchr., arranger, composer; owner Douglas Pub. Co., Spiral Studios and Prodns., Odyssey Records. Author: By Special Invitation, 1983, Essentials for Organists, 1986, Beginning Organist Workshop, 1985, Sweet Is The Work, 1991. Mem. Egyptian Theatre Organ Found. (chmn.), Am. Guild Organists. Republican. Mem. LDS Ch. Home: 8465 Westchester Ave Boise ID 83704-4375

LEMON, LESLIE GENE, consumer products and services company executive, lawyer; b. Davenport, Iowa, June 14, 1940. BS, U. Ill., 1962, LLB, 1964. Bar: Ill. 1964, Ariz. 1972. Asst. gen. counsel Am. Farm Bur. Fedn., Chgo., 1964-69; sr. atty. Armour and Co., Chgo., 1969-71; with The Dial Corp (formerly Greyhound Corp.), Phoenix, 1971—, sr. asst. gen. counsel, 1975-77, gen. counsel, 1977—, v.p., 1979—; bd. dirs. FINOVA Group. Vestryman All Saints Episcopal Ch., Phoenix, 1975-81; trustee Phoenix Art Mus., 1985—; bd. dirs. Phoenix Children's Hosp., 1985—; bd. visitors U. Calif. Med. Sch., Davis, 1983—. Mem. ABA, Assn. Gen. Counsel, Maricopa County Bar Assn., State Bar Ariz., Phoenix C. of C. (bd. dirs. 1989-95). Home: 1136 W Butler Dr Phoenix AZ 85021-4428 Office: The Dial Corp Dial Tower 1850 N Central Ave Phoenix AZ 85077-0001

LENARD, MICHAEL BARRY, merchant banker, lawyer; b. Chgo., May 20, 1955; s. Henry Madart and Jacqueline Jo Anne (Silver) L.; m. Amy Jeanne Rifenbergh, Oct. 10, 1987; children: Madeline M., Nicholas X. BBA, U. Wis., 1977; postgrad., NYU, 1981-82; JD, U. So. Calif., 1982. Assoc. Whitman & Ransom, N.Y.C., 1982-83; assoc. Latham & Watkins, L.A., 1984-91, ptnr., 1992-93; mng. dir., counsellor William E. Simon & Sons, L.A., 1993—; bd. dirs. William E. Simon & Sons (Asia), Hong Kong. With So. Calif. Law Rev. mag., 1980-81. V.p. U.S. Olympic Com., 1989—, mem. exec. com., bd. dirs., 1985—, mem. athletes' adv. coun., 1981-89, vice chmn. athletes' adv. coun., 1985-89; named to Internat. Coun. for Arbitration of Sport, Internat. Olympic Com., 1994—; bd. dirs. L.A. Sports Coun., 1988—, Atlanta Com. for Olympic Games, 1990—. Named semi-finalist Outstanding Undergrad. Achievement award, 1977; recipient Harry A. Bullis scholarship, 1977; named USA Team Handball Athlete of the Yr., 1985, USOC Olympian Mag. Team Handball SportsMan of the Yr., 1985; mem. 1984 Olympic Team, U.S. Nat. Team, 1977-85 (capt. 1985). Mem. Order of the Coif, Phi Kappa Phi, Beta Gamma Sigma, Beta Alpha Psi, Phi Eta Sigma. Home: 1433 El Bosque Ct Pacific Palisades CA 90272-1915 Office: William E Simon & Sons 10990 Wilshire Blvd Ste 1750 Los Angeles CA 90024-3913

LENDRUM, JAMES THOBURN, architect; b. Oxford, N.Y., Jan. 21, 1907; s. Frederick Alexander and Mary Emma (Crist) L.; m. Dorothea Lombard, Sept. 8, 1931; children—Peter Alexander, Nancy Caroline. Student, Ohio Wesleyan U., 1925-26; B. Arch., U. Mich., 1930; M.Arch., U. Ill., 1946. Registered architect, Ill., Fla., Pa., Ariz., Calif. Partner George E. Ramey & Co., Champaign, Ill., 1934-43; mem. firm Lendrum & Pusey (archtl. cons.), 1955-58; mem. faculty gen. engring. drawing U. Ill.; also dir. small homes council, prof. architecture; chief mission Archtl. Edn. Cons., Ford Found., Pakistan, 1957; prof. architecture U. Fla., 1957-69, head dept. architecture, 1957-67; housing cons. HHFA, 1950; v.p., dir. Environs, Inc., Phoenix; mem. firm Peter Lendrum & Assos., Phoenix, 1969-87, ret., 1987; Mem. archtl. standards adv. com. FHA, 1954-66; mem. bldg. research adv. bd. Nat. Acad. Scis., 1954-66; asst. dir. Bur. Archtl. and Community Research, 1955-67; mem.-at-large Internat. Council for Bldg. Research Studies and Documentation, Rotterdam; dir. Fla. Found. for Advancement Bldg., Inc. Author: (with F.M. Porter) Architectural Projections; also articles. Cons. House and Home. Fellow A.I.A.; mem. Archtl. Assn. London, Fla. Assn. Architects (dir.), Alpha Rho Chi, Tau Sigma Delta. Methodist. Club: Kiwanian (Gainesville). Home: 1233 E Escondido Dr Phoenix AZ 85014-2342 Office: Peter Lendrum & Assocs 3033 S 44th St Phoenix AZ 85040-1706

LENEAU, THOMAS ERVIN, gas company executive; b. Mpls., Aug. 3, 1950; s. Thomas J. and Evelyn F. (Schwantees) LeN. BS in Math., St. Cloud State U., 1972; MEd, U. Minn., 1977; B in Acctg., U. Minn., Duluth, 1979; MBA, Ariz. State U., 1985. CPA, Ariz., Minn. Math. instr. Duluth Pub. Schs., 1972-78; acctg. instr. U. Minn., Duluth, 1978-79; auditor Deloitte, Haskins & Sells, Mpls., 1979-81; v.p. fin. Rio Verde Devel., Scottsdale, Ariz., 1981-86; pres., CEO Black Mountain Gas Co., Cave Creek, Ariz., 1986—, also bd. dirs. Treas. Foothills Community Found., Carefree, Ariz., 1989-94. Mem. AICPA. Office: Black Mountain Gas Co PO Box 427 Cave Creek AZ 85331-0427

LENGYEL, CORNEL ADAM (CORNEL ADAM), author; b. Fairfield, Conn., Jan. 1, 1915; s. Elmer Alexander and Mary Elizabeth (Bismarck) L.; m. Teresa Delaney Murphy, July 10, 1933; children: Jerome Benedict, Paul Joel, Michael Sebastian, Cornelia (Mrs. Charles Burke). LittD (hon.), World Acad. of Arts and Culture, Taiwan, 1991. Editor, supr. Fed. Research Project, San Francisco, 1938-41; music critic The Coast, San Francisco, 1937-41; shipwright, personnel officer Kaiser Shipyard, Richmond, Calif., 1942-44; mgr. Forty-Nine Theatre, Georgetown, Calif., 1946-50; editor W.H. Freeman Co., San Francisco, 1952-54; founder, exec. editor Dragon's Teeth Press, Georgetown, 1969—; vis. prof., lectr. English lit. Sacramento State Coll., 1962-63; writer-in-residence Hamline U., St. Paul, 1968-69; guest lectr. MIT, 1969; transl. from Hungarian; editorial cons. HEW; ednl. dir. ILGWU. Author: (history) American Testament: The Story of the Promised Land, 1956, Four Days in July, 1958, I, Benedict Arnold: The Anatomy of Treason, 1960, Presidents of the U.S.A., 1961, Ethan Allen and the Green Mountain Boys, 1961, Jesus the Galilean, 1966, The Declaration of Independence, 1969; (poetry) Thirty Pieces, 1933, First Psalms, 1950, Fifty Poems, 1965, Four Dozen Songs, 1970, The Lookout's Letter, 1971, Late News from Adam's Acres, 1983, El Dorado Forest: Selected Poems, 1986; (plays) The World's My Village, 1935, Jonah Fugitive, 1936; The Giant's Trap, 1938, The Atom Clock, 1951, Eden, Inc., 1954, rev. edit. Omega, 1963, Will of Stratford, 1964, Three Plays, 1964, The Case of Benedict Arnold, 1975, Doctor Franklin, 1976, The Shadow Trap, 1977, The Second Coming, 1985, Mengele's Passover, 1987, A Clockmaker's Boy: Part One, 1987; (essays) The Creative Self, 1971; contbr. to anthologies The Golden Year, 1960, Interpretation in Our Time, 1966, The Britannica Library of Great American Writing, 1961, The Menorah Treasury, 1964, Interpretation for Our Time, 1966, The Courage to Grow Old, 1988, From These Hills, 1990, Blood to Remember, 1991, Anthology of Contemporary Poets, 1992, World Poetry, 1993, We Speak for Peace, 1993, also Poet Lore, The Coast, The Argonaut, Saturday Rev., Menorah Jour., others. Served with U.S. Merchant Marine,

1944-45. Recipient Albert M. Bender award in lit., 1945; recipient 1st prize Maritime Poetry Awards, 1945, 1st prize Poetry Soc. Va., 1951, Maxwell Anderson award drama, 1950, Di Castagnola award Poetry Soc. Am., 1971, Internat. Who's Who in Poetry award, 1972; Huntington Hartford Found. resident fellow, 1951, 64; MacDowell Colony resident fellow, 1967; Ossabaw Island Found. fellow, 1968; Nat. Endowment for Arts fellow, 1976-77. Mem. MLA, AAUP, PEN, Poetry Soc. Am., Poetry Soc. Eng., Authors Guild. Address: Adam's Acres Georgetown CA 95634

LENHART, JAMES ROBERT, sales manager, foodservice administrator; b. Detroit, Apr. 29, 1952; s. Robert Bernard and Harriett Frances (Ebert) L.; m. Lauren Michi Fujimoto, Oct. 1, 1983; children: Amanda Mariko, Samuel James Kai. Student, Naval Schs. of Photography, Pensacola, Fla., 1973, U. Hawaii, 1977-79. Beverage mgr. Bobby McGee's, Honolulu, 1978-79, Marriott Hotels, Maui, Hawaii, 1979-81; bartender various restaurants, Maui, 1981-82; owner Plantation Prime Rib Restaurant, Kauai, Hawaii, 1982-85; account exec. Inter Island Distributors, Kauai, 1985-86; sales mgr. Superior Coffee and Foods, Honolulu, 1986—. With USN, 1973-77, PTO. Mem. VFW, Am. Culinary Assn., Internat. Food Svc. Execs., Hawaii Mfrs. Assn., Chefs de Cuisine/Hawaii. Republican. Methodist. Home: 7007 Hawaii Kai Dr Honolulu HI 96825 Office: Superior Coffee and Foods 99-910 Iwaena St Aiea HI 96701

LENING, JANICE ALLEN, physical education educator; b. Topeka, Mar. 10, 1946; d. John Otis and Bertha May (Simon) Allen; m. Jay Ridley Lening, Dec. 26, 1976; children: Brooke Michelle, Chad Allen. BA in Phys. Edn., U. Denver, 1968; MA in Elem. Edn., U. No. Colo., 1980. Lic. tchr. phys. edn., elem. edn., Colo. Tchr. Denver Pub. Schs., 1968-69; phys. edn. tchr. Jefferson County Schs., Lakewood, Colo., 1969—, gymnastics coach, 1969, 76-79, gymnastics judge, 1970-75; mem. budget com. Shaffer Elem. Sch., Littleton, 1985-86, accountability com., 1985-86; wellnes rep. Shaffer, Colorow, Gov. Racn Elem., Littleton, 1985-94; mem. social com. Lasley, Green Gables, Shaffer, Gov. Ranch Elem. Lakewood and Littleton, 1970-93; student coun. supr. Green Gables Elem., Lakewood, 1978-85, credit union rep., 1980-85. Leader Girl Scouts, Littleton, 1986-87; coach Columbine Soccer Assn., Littleton, 1986-91; judge Odyssey of the Mind, Littleton, 1986-94. Recipient Gold medal Am. Heart Assn., Denver, 1991, Bronze award, 1994-95 State Champion award sch. Pres. Coun. on Phys. Fitness, 1990-94. Mem. AAPHERD, NEA, PAC, Colo. Edn. Assn., JCEA. Republican. Home: 6546 W Hoover Pl Littleton CO 80123-3632 Office: Govs Ranch Elem Sch 5354 S Field St Littleton CO 80123-7800

LENNOX, GLORIA (GLORIA DEMEREE), real estate executive; b. Baden, Pa., Feb. 14, 1931; d. Gilbert and Marion (Slosson) Whetson; m; William Lennox, June 19, 1954 (div. 1985); children: Cheryl Lennox Watson, Lynda Lennox Huerta, Jim; m. Philip Demeree, July 4, 1985. BS in Edn., Kent State U., 1954; MA in Spl. Edn., Ariz. State U., 1968; grad., Realtor's Inst. Grad. Realtor Inst.; cert. residential specialist, cert. residential broker state and nat. Tchr. Maple Leaf Sch., Garfield Heights, Ohio, 1954-55, Madison (Ind.) Dist. Elem. Sch., 1958, Scottsdale (Ariz.) Schs., 1961-68, Devereux Sch., 1968-70, Tri-City Mental Health Sch., Mesa, Ariz., 1970-71; br. mgr. M. Leslie Hansen, Scottsdale, 1972-74; v.p., gen. mgr. John D. Noble and Assocs., Scottsdale, 1974-83; pres., broker Gloria Lennox & Assocs., Inc., Scottsdale, 1983—. Chmn. bd. Interfaith Counseling Svc., 1988, 89; trustee Scottsdale Congl. United Ch. of Christ, 1986-88, 92. Kent State U. scholar, 1950-54. Mem. Nat. Assn. Realtors, Ariz. Assn. Realtors (Realtor Assoc. of Yr. 1975), Scottsdale Assn. Realtors (life, Hall of Fame award 1992, Disting. Career award 1994), Women's Coun. Realtors, Realtor Nat. Mktg. Inst., Scottsdale Bd. Realtors (pres. 1981-82, Realtor of Yr. 1982), Ariz. Town Halls, Ariz. Country Club. Republican. Home: 7561 N Via Camello Del Sur Scottsdale AZ 85258-3005 Office: Gloria Lennox and Assocs 4533 N Scottsdale Rd Ste 200 Scottsdale AZ 85251-7618

LENNOX BUCHTHAL, MARGARET AGNES, neurophysiologist; b. Denver, Dec. 28, 1913; d. William Gordon and Emma Stevenson (Buchtel) L.; m. Gerald Klatskin, 1941 (div. 1947); 1 child, Jane Herner; m. Fritz Buchthal, Aug. 19, 1957. BA, Vassar Coll., 1934; MD, Yale Sch. Medicine, 1939; D of Medicine, Copenhagen U., 1972. Intern pediatrics Strong Meml. Hosp., Rochester, N.Y., 1939-40; asst. resident pediatrics N.Y. Hosp., N.Y.C., 1941-42; instr. Yale Sch. Medicine, New Haven, Conn., 1942-44, asst. prof. dept. psychiatry, 1945-51; asst. prof. U. Copenhagen, Inst. Neurophysiology, Denmark, 1957-72, assoc. prof., 1972-81; ret., 1981; head clin. electroencephalography Yale U. Sch. of Medicine, 1942-51, head clinic epileptology, 1942-51; chief editor Epilesia Pub. by Elsevire, 1967-73. Contbr. articles to profl. jours. Republican. Methodist. Home: 289 El Cielito Rd Santa Barbara CA 93105-2306

LE NOIR, MICHAEL A., allergist; b. Tex., Feb. 22, 1942. MD, U Tex, 1967. Allergist Childrens Hosp., Oakland, Calif., Summit Med. Ctr., Oakland, Calif. Office: 401 29th St Ste 201 Oakland CA 94609-3581*

LENTES, DAVID EUGENE, corporate executive; b. Spokane, Wash., Dec. 14, 1951; s. William Eugene and Ellen Elsie L.; m. Debra Kay White, May 19, 1973 (div. 1984); children: Janette Adele, Damon Arthur; m. Marlene J. Livingston, Sept. 15, 1990. AA, Spokane Falls C.C., 1972; BBA, Gonzaga U., 1975. V.p. Dellen Wood Products, Inc., Spokane, 1972—, also bd. dirs.; v.p. Custom Computer Services, Inc., Spokane, 1980-87, also bd. dirs.; mng. ptnr. Com-Lease, 1980-87, Len-Lease, 1980—; v.p., bd. dirs. DWP Trucking, Inc., 1982-85, Sentel Corp., 1983-88, BDR Investment Corp., 1983—; pres., bd. dirs. ASA Mgmt. Corp., 1984—, also Lenmark Corp., Inc., 1985—. Treas. Dishman Hills Natural Area Assn., 1970—; elder Bethany Presbyn. Ch., 1980-83; active Spokane Econ. Devel. Council. Mem. Assn. Wash. Bus., Nat. Fedn. Ind. Businessmen, Am. Fedn. Bus., Better Bus. Bur. (Spokane chpt.), U.S. C. of C., Spokane C. of C., Coeur D'Alene C. of C., Post Falls C. of C., Timber Products Mfrs. (mem. bd. dirs.), Hoo-Hoo Internat. Republican. Office: 3014 N Flora Rd Spokane WA 99216-1802

LENZ, PHILIP JOSEPH, municipal administrator; b. Monterey Park, Calif., Sept. 15, 1940; s. Philip George and Irene Mary (Bowers) L.; m. Mary Lou Antista, July 16, 1966; children: Brian Joseph, Jonathan Thomas. BA, Calif. State U., L.A., 1966; MS, Pepperdine U., 1974. Dir. West Valley div. San Bernardino County (Calif.) Probation Dept., 1977-79, dir. juvenile div., 1979-82, dir. adminstrv. services, 1982-88, dir. dist. services, 1988-90; dep. chief probation officer, 1990—; instr. dept. bus. Calif. State U., San Bernardino; instr. dept. social rels. Loma Linda U., 1988. Sec. bd. trustees Upland (Calif.) Sch. Dist., 1986—, pres. sch. bd., 1989-90, 94-96; mgr., coach Upland Am. Little League, 1981-90, bd. dirs., 1982-90; pres. Fontana (Calif.) Family Svc. Agy., 1972-74; mem. adv. com. corrections Chaffey Coll., Alta Loma, Calif., 1977—; mem. Upland Parks and Recreation Com., 1986—, chmn., 1989-91; bd. dirs. Highlander Ednl. Found., v.p., 1991—; mem. Calif. Youth Authority CADRE of Cons. Recipient Tim Fitzharris award Chief Probation Officers of Calif., 1987. Mem. Calif. Probation, Parole and Correctional Assn. (liaison, regional v.p. 1981-83, 2d v.p. 1985-86, 1st v.p. 1986—, pres. 1987—), Probation Bus. Mgr.'s Assn. (regional chmn. 1984-86, v.p. 1987), Western Correctional Assn., Assn. for Criminal Justice Rsch. (bd. dirs.), Probation Adminstrs. Assn. (regional chair 1992-93). Democrat. Roman Catholic. Home: 1375 Stanford Ave Upland CA 91786-3147 Office: San Bernardino County Dept Probation 175 W 5th St San Bernardino CA 92401-1401

LENZEN, CONNIE LOU, genealogist; b. Portland, Oreg., Feb. 1, 1939; d. Grayland Dudley and Agnes Cecilia (Stariha) Miller; m. Gerald Sylvester Lenzen, Sept. 19, 1959; children: Daniel Mark, Jennifer Anne. BS in Edn., Portland State Coll., 1960; MS in Edn., Portland State U., 1981. Cert. geneal. record specialist, 1983. Elem. tchr. Pleasant Valley Sch., Portland, Oreg., 1960-63, Portland Pub. Schs., 1969-94; profl. genealogist Portland, 1983—. Author: Huiras Family in America (8 vols.), 1986-89, Oregon Guide to Genealogical Resources, 1991, St. Mary's Cemetery, Portland, Oregon, 1987, How to Find Naturalization Records in Oregon, 1989; contbr. articles to geneal. mags. Mem. Assn. Profl. Genealogists (trustee 1992-94), Nat. Geneal. Soc. (conf. author 1991, Excellence award, 1995), Geneal. Coun. Oreg. (membership chair), Geneal. Forum Oreg. (1st. v.p., 1994—), Oreg. Hist. Soc., Oreg. Hist. Cemeteries Assn. Democrat. Roman Catholic. Home and Office: 10411 SW 41st Ave Portland OR 97219-6984

LENZI, JERRY C., state official; b. Pocahantas, Ark., Oct. 21, 1944. BSCE, St. Martin's Coll., 1970; MPA, Evergreen State Coll., 1982; postgrad., U. Ind., 1992. Registered profl. engr., Wash.; profl. land surveyor, Wash.; cert. value engring. facilitator. Journeyman retail clk. Seamart Grocery, 1967-69; engring. technician I, 2 and 3, dist. 3 Wash. State Dept. Transp., Tumwater, 1966-67, 69-70; hwy. engr. I Wash. State Dept. Transp., Trimwater, 1970-72, project inspector, hwy. engr. 2, 1972-76, field/design engr., hwy. engr. 3, 1976-78, asst. project engr., 1978-80, project engr., 1980-85, mgr. multimodal br. planning, rsch. and pub. transp. divsn., 1985-87, mgr. transp. planning office, 1987-90; dist. adminstr. Wash. State Dept. Transp., Spokane, 1990—; mem. subcom. on rail issues, subcom. on multimodal investment optimization, subcom. on characteristics and changes in freight transp. demand Transp. Rsch. Bd.; mem. Wash. State Rail Devel. Commn.; mem. acad. adv. com. St. Martin's Coll.; mem. engring. adv. coun. Gonzaga U.; mem. Rd. Jurisdiction Com.; mem. exec. com. Wash. State Transp. Rsch. Coun.; mem. Disappearing Task Force for Curriculum Devel., South Puget Sound C.C., Upper Gt. Plains Transp. Inst., S.E. Wash. Transp. Needs. Contbr. articles to profl. jours. Mem. Spokane Regional Transp. Coun. Mem. ASCE (student chpt. advisor), Order of Engr., Nat. Conf. State Rwy. Ofcls. (vice chair), Am. Assn. State Hwy. Transp. Ofcls. (standing subcom., mem. policy rev. com., domestic freight policy devel. and intermodal issues com., Pres. Intermodal award), Rotary of Spokane. Office: Wash State Dept Transp Eastern Region 2714 N Mayfair St Spokane WA 99207

LENZIE, CHARLES ALBERT, utility company executive; b. South Wilmington, Ill., Sept. 5, 1937; s. Charles and Dorothy Rosita (Fritz) L.; children: Ann Marie, Michael Charles, Jody Ann. Student Ill. State Normal U., 1955-58; BS in Acctg., U. Ill., 1960. CPA, Ill. Audit Mgr. Arthur Andersen & Co., Chgo., 1960-70, L.A., 1970-74; v.p. fin. Nev. Power Co., Las Vegas, 1974-78, sr. v.p., 1978-83, pres., 1983-89, chmn. bd., chief exec. officer, 1989—, also bd. dirs. Bd. dirs. Las Vegas YMCA, Nev. Taxpayers' Assn., Nev. Devel. Authority. Mem. Rotary. Cpl. U.S. Army, 1961-63. Office: Nevada Power Co 6226 W Sahara Ave Las Vegas NV 89151-0001

LENZO, THOMAS JOHN, training and development consultant; b. Waterbury, Conn., Nov. 19, 1949; s. John Anthony and Mary Louise (Perezella) L. BA, Fairfield U., 1971; MEd, Calif. State U., L.A., 1980. Media coord. Valley Vocat. Ctr., Industry, Calif., 1977-78; libr. Washington Sch., Pasadena, Calif., 1978-79; tng. specialist Data Electronics Inc., Pasadena, 1979-82; engring. instr. Litton Data Systems, Van Nuys, Calif., 1982-83; cons. B.P.W. Inc., Costa Mesa, Calif., 1983-86; pvt. practice Pasadena, 1986—. Contbr. articles to profl. jours. Instr. ARC, Pasadena, 1983-85; mem. Towards 2000 mayoral com., Pasadena, 1984-85; speaker advisor All Sts. Ch., Pasadena, 1989—; with USAF, 1972-76. Mem. Am. Soc. Tng. & Devel., Nat. Soc. Performance & Instrn., Soc. Tech. Communications, Pasadena IBM PC User Group (bd. dirs.). Roman Catholic. Home: 2473 Oswego St Apt 10 Pasadena CA 91107-4239

LEO, LOUIS J., university administrator; b. Chgo.; m. Karen Ann Leo. BA, U. Mich., 1966, JD, 1969. Dean for adminstrn., dean of students Calif. State U., Stanislaus, 1969-77; vice chancellor student svcs. U. Calif., Riverside, 1977—. Office: U Calif 3108 Hinderker Hall Riverside CA 92521

LEO, MARY GAYE, school administrator; b. Colorado Springs, Colo., Oct. 19, 1951; d. Bernard Johnston and Mary Ellen (Hardy) Lamar; m. Dominick Louis Leo; children: Dominick Christopher, Rachel Gabreilla. BA, U. Colo., 1973, MA, 1978; PhD in Ednl. Adminstrn. Denver U., 1985. Cert. bicultural/bilingual instr. Communications & group dynamics instr., Denver area, 1972-73; with Denver Pub. Sch. Sys., 1973-94, arts mgmt./theater dir., 1973-87; asst. prin. Lake Mid. Sch., 1987-89, Martin Luther King Mid. Sch., Denver Pub. Schs., 1989-91; asst. prin. West H.S., Denver, 1991-94; prin. Skyview H.S., Denver, 1994—; with Mapleton Pub. Sch. Sys., 1994—. adj. faculty U. Colo., Boulder, Colo.; adj. edn. faculty Met. State Coll., Denver; prof. edn. adminstrn. U. Phoenix. Author: (musical) Celebration, 1979, (children's fantasy) Bob, The Magical Unicorn, 1981, (book) The Raven and I-E Locus of Control as Measures of High Ability; dir., designer, producer profl. & ednl. theatrical prodns. including Godspell, 1974, Guys and Dolls, 1975, My Fair Lady, 1976, Carousel, 1977, Music Man, 1978, Celebration!, 1979, Annie Get Your Gun, 1980, Jesus Christ Superstar, 1982, Grease, 1982, Camelot, 1983, Guys and Dolls, 1987; developer Authentic School Project for Drop Out Prevention, Academy Model for Middle Level Education. Lectr., workshop coord. Colo. Arts and Humanities Coun., 1974-75. Gov.'s Creativity grantee, 1990-91. Mem. ASCD, NAFE, Am. Theatre Assn., Women in Theatre, Nat. Council Tchrs. English, Colo. Assn. Sch. Execs., Colo. Partnership. Home: 4554 S Alton St Englewood CO 80111-1207

LEOFSKY, JOAN CAROLE, business owner; b. Tonawanda, N.Y., Mar. 11, 1938; d. Frances Joseph Leofsky and Rose Marie (Karkoski) Horst; m. Arlen Dale Goodwine, June 27, 1959 (div. June 1971); children: Stirling Lance Goodwine, Andrew Raleigh Goodwine. BS, Ea. Wash. State Coll., 1973; MA, U. Wash., 1979. Rschr. Hunger Action Ctr., Seattle, 1975; nutritionist Rainier Vista Health Clinic & Neighborhood House, Inc., Seattle, 1975-79; project mgr. Rainier Vista Health Clinic, Seattle, 1979-81; owner Leofsky Art Glass, Seattle, 1981-84; bus. broker agt. VR Bus. Brokers, Bellevue, Wash., 1984-87; owner Cheers & Chocolates, Bellevue, 1987—. Weekly columnist Womanspeak, 1978-80. Founder, coord. South Seattle Women's Network, 1979-81, Seattle Women's Craft Fair, 1979-81. Office: PO Box 1087 Bellevue WA 98009-1087

LEON, BRUNO, architect, educator; b. Van Houten, N.Mex., Feb. 18, 1924; s. Giovanni and Rose (Cunico) L.; m. Louise Dal-Bo, Sept. 4, 1948 (dec. 1974); m. Bonnie Bertram, Sept. 12, 1976; children: Mark Jon, John Anthony, Lisa Rose. Student, Wayne State U., 1942, U. Detroit, 1945-48; LHD (hon.), U. Detroit, 1984; BArch, N.C. State Coll., 1953. Registered architect, Mich., N.C., Mass., N.Y., N.Mex., Fla. Head design staff Fuller Research Found., Raleigh, N.C., 1954-55; archtl. designer I.M. Pei & Assos., N.Y.C., 1955-56; instr. Mass. Inst. Tech., 1956-59; designer Catalano & Belluschi (architects), Cambridge, Mass., 1958-59; asst. prof. U. Ill. at Urbana, 1959-61; dean Sch. Architecture, U. Detroit, 1961-93, dean emeritus, 1993; pvt. practice architecture, 1956—. Served with USAAF, 1942-45. Fellow AIA (dir. Detroit 1963-64); mem. Alpha Sigma Nu (hon.), Phi Kappa Phi. Home: 9 Redonda Ct Santa Fe NM 87505-8308

LEONARD, ANGELINE JANE, psychotherapist; b. McKeesport, Pa., Dec. 9, 1940; d. Paul James Franklin and Jane Angeline (McKee) L.; m. Tom L. Kregel, Aug. 25, 1962 (div. 1970). BFA, U. Okla., 1962; MA in Art History, UCLA, 1965; MA in Clin. Art Therapy, Immaculate Heart Coll., 1980; PhD in Clin. Psychology, Cambridge Grad. Sch., 1991. Lic. marriage, family, child counselor, Calif., marriage and family counselor, N.C.; registered art therapist/bd. cert.; cert. hypnotherapist, guided imagery, domestic violence. Tchr. San Gabriel (Calif.) Mission High Sch., 1964-66, L.A. Valley Coll., Van Nuys, 1966-90, L.A. Unified Sch. Dist., 1980-90; pvt. practice psychotherapy, Reseda, Calif., 1982—; spkr. in field. Author: California Art Therapy Trends, 1993; author of poems. Bd. dirs., v.p. Ch. of Religious Sci., North Hollywood, Calif., 1989-93. Mem. Am. Art Therapy Assn., Am. Assn. Marriage and Family Therapists, Artist Equity Assn. (sec.), Calif. Assn. Marriage and Family Therapists, So. Calif. Art Therapy Assn. (bd. dirs.), No. Calif. Art Therapy Assn. Democrat. Home and Office: 19520 Vose St Reseda CA 91335-3637

LEONARD, DEBI LYNN (DELYN KYNTA LEONARD), advertising and marketing executive; b. Dodge City, Kans., May 6, 1955; d. Harold Duane and Kynta Lov (Kennedy) L. Student, Marymount Coll., 1972-76, Vo-Tech. U., Salina, Kans. 1976-78. Comml. art sales rep. Shoppers Guide, Salina, 1977-81; sales rep. Sta. KYEZ-AM, Salina, 1981-82, Freedom News, Denver, 1982-83; designer Delyns Fashions, Denver, 1983-86; mktg. mgr. Lenko Enterprises, Cripple Creek, Colo., 1981-88, Cellular One Mobile Communications, 1988—; product devel., fashion designer, sr. sales mgr., Silver-Mine, Cripple Creek, Colo., 1988-92; advt. and mktg. mgr. Silver Mine Casino, 1992—. Vol. Annual Bridal Show, Salina, 1985; active Am. Cancer Soc., membership drive YMCA. Mem. Life Underwriters Assn., Am. Bus. Womens Assn. Midwest Corvette Assn., Nat. Assn. Female Execs.; Denver Advt. Assn. Avocations: windsurfing; skiing; swimming; hot air ballooning. Office: Silver Mine Casion Advt and Mktg Dept PO 9032 Woodland Park CO 80866-9032

LEONARD, GEORGE EDMUND, real estate, bank, and consulting executive; b. Phoenix, Nov. 20, 1940; s. George Edmund and Marion Elizabeth (Fink) L.; m. Gloria Jean Henry, Mar. 26, 1965 (div. Feb. 1981); children: Tracy Lynn, Amy Theresa, Kristin Jean; m. Mary C. Short, Sept. 22, 1990. Student, Ariz. State U., 1958-60; BS, U.S. Naval Acad., 1964; postgrad., Pa. State U., 1969-70; MBA, U. Chgo., 1973. Commd. ensign, USN, 1964, advanced through grades to lt. comdr., 1975; v.p. 1st Nat. Bank Chgo., 1970-75; exec. v.p., chief banking, chief fin. and chief lending officer Mera Bank, Phoenix, 1975-90, also bd. dirs., 1982-90; pres., chief exec. officer Cen. Savs., San Diego, 1985-87; chmn., CEO AmBank Holding Co. of Colo., Scottsdale, Ariz., 1990-91; pres., CEO Diversified Mgmt. Svcs., Inc., Phoenix, 1991—, GEL Mgmt. Inc., Phoenix, 1991—; bd. dirs. Beverly Hills (Calif.) Savs., Am. Nat. Bank of Scottsdale, Bank of Santa Fe, 1990-91, 1st Am. Bank of Colo. Springs. Active Phoenix Thunderbirds, 1979—; bd. dirs. Maricopa Community Colls. Found., treas., 2d v.p., 1991-93, 1st v.p., 1993-94, pres. 1994-95, Camelback Charitable Trust, 1991-92, Samaritan Charitable Trust, 1993—, chmn. fin. com., 1994—. Mem. Phoenix Met. C. of C. (bd. dirs. 1975-82), Inst. Fin. Edn. (bd. dirs. 1980-87, nat. chmn. 1985-86), Ariz. State U. Coll. of Bus. Deans Coun. of 100, Paradise Valley Country Club (bd. dirs. 1991—, treas. 1992-95, pres. 1995—), Univ. Club (San Diego), Kiwanis. Republican. Roman Catholic. Home: 3064 E Stella Ln Phoenix AZ 85016-2244 Office: Diversified Mgmt Svcs Inc 3001 E Camelback Rd Ste 140 Phoenix AZ 85016-4427

LEONARD, GLEN M., museum administrator; b. Salt Lake City, Nov. 12, 1938; s. Burnham J. and Allene (Green) L.; m. Karen Wright, Mar. 15, 1968; children: Cory, Kyle, Keith. BA, U. Utah, 1964, MA, 1966, PhD, 1970. Mng. editor Utah State Hist. Soc., Salt Lake City, 1970-73; sr. rsch. assoc. history div. Ch. of Jesus Christ of Latter-day Saints, Salt Lake City, 1973-78; dir. Mus. Ch. History and Art, Salt Lake City, 1979—; mem. adv. bd. editors Utah Hist. Quarterly, Salt Lake City, 1973-88; assoc. editor Jour. Mormon History, Provo, Utah, 1974-80; bd. dirs. Western Studies Ctr., Brigham Young U., Provo. Co-author: The Story of the Latter-day Saints, 1976; contbr. articles to profl. publs. Mem. Hist. Preservation Commn., Farmington, Utah, 1986-92; mem. adv. coun. Mormon Pioneer Nat. Hist. Trail, Nat. Park Svc., 1980-86. Recipient Dale Morgan Article award Utah State Hist. Soc., 1973. Mem. Orgn. Am. Historians, Western History Assn., Am. Assn. Mus. (museum assessment program cons.), Assn. Utah Historians (bd. dirs. 1981-83), Utah Mus. Assn. (bd. dirs. 1980-83), Am. Assn. State and Local History. Office: Mus Ch History and Art 45 N West Temple Salt Lake City UT 84150

LEONE, STEPHEN ROBERT, chemical physicist, educator; b. N.Y.C., May 19, 1948; s. Dominic and Annie Frances (Sappa) L. BA, Northwestern U., 1970; PhD, U. Calif., Berkeley, 1974. Asst. prof. U. So. Calif., L.A., 1974-76; physicist/fellow Nat. Inst. Standards and Tech., Boulder, Colo., 1976-94, acting chief Quantum Physics divsn., 1994—; adj. prof. U. Colo., Boulder, 1976—. Contbr. over 200 articles to profl. publs.; mem. editorial bd. Optics Letters, Jour. Chem. Physics, Chem. Revs., Jour. Phys. Chemistry, Molecular Physics, Chem. Physics Letters, Progress in Reaction Kinetics; patentee in field. Recipient silver and gold medals Dept. Commerce, 1980, 85, Coblentz award Coblentz Soc., 1984, Arthur S. Flemming award U.S. Govt., 1986, Samuel Wesley Stratton award Nat. Inst. Standards and Tech., 1992; Alfred P. Sloan fellow Sloan Found., 1977-81, Guggenheim fellow, 1988. Fellow AAAS, Optical Soc. Am., Am. Phys. Soc. (chair div. chem. physics 1987-88, Herbert P. Broida prize 1989); mem. Am. Chem. Soc. (Pure Chemistry award 1982, Nobel Laureate Signature award 1983). Office: Joint Inst for Lab Astrophysics Univ of Colo Campus Box 440 Boulder CO 80309

LEONE, WILLIAM CHARLES, retired manufacturing executive; b. Pitts., May 3, 1924; s. Joseph and Fortuna (Sammarco) L.; m. Sara Jane Hollenback, Aug. 26, 1950; children: William Charles, David M., Patricia Ann, Mary Jane. BS, Carnegie Inst. Tech., 1944, MS, 1948, DSc, 1952. Asst. prof. engring. Carnegie Inst. Tech., Pitts., 1946-53; mgr. Indsl. Sys. divsn. Hughes Aircraft, L.A., 1953-59; v.p., gen. mgr., dir. Rheem Califone, L.A., 1960, Rheem Electronics, L.A., 1960-68; group v.p. Rheem Mfg. Co., 1968-71; exec. v.p. Rheem Mfg. Co., N.Y.C., 1971-72, pres., 1972-76; also dir. Rheem Mfg. Co.; pres. City Investing Co. Internat., Inc., 1972-76; pres., dir. Farah Mfg. Co., El Paso, Tex., 1976-77; bus. cons., 1977-79; acting vice chmn. McCulloch Oil Corp. (MCO), L.A., 1979-80, also bd. dirs.; pres., dir. MAXXAM Inc. (formerly MCO Holdings, Inc.), 1980-90; vice chmn. MAXXAM Inc., 1990-92; chmn., CEO, dir. Pacific Lumber Co., 1986-90, Horizon Corp., 1984-89. Trustee Carnegie Mellon U., 1986-92. Mem. ASME, IEEE, Am. Inst. Aerospace and Aeronautics, Sigma Xi, Tau Beta Pi, Pi Tau Sigma, Theta Tau, Pi Mu Epsilon. Home: 2209 Chelsea Rd Palos Verdes Peninsula CA 90274-2603

LEONG, ALBIN B., allergist, educator; b. Astoria, Oreg., 1950. MD, U. Calif., San Diego, 1977. Clin. asst. prof. U. Calif. Med. Sch., Davis; mem. med. staff Sacramento Kaiser Fedn. Hosp. Office: Sacramento Kaiser Fedn Hosp Pediats Pulmonary & Allergy 6600 Bruceville Rd Sacramento CA 95823*

LEONG, CAROL JEAN, electrologist; b. Sacramento, Jan. 9, 1942; d. Walter Richard and Edith (Bond) Bloss; m. Oliver Arthur Fisk III, Apr. 12, 1964 (div. 1973); 1 child, Victoria Kay. BA in Sociology, San Jose (Calif.) State Coll., 1963; degree, Western Bus. Coll., 1964; cert. in electrolysis, Bay Area Coll. Electrolysis, 1978. Registered and cert. clin. profl. electrologist, Calif. Model various orgns., Calif., 1951-64; employment counselor Businessmen's Clearinghouse, Cin., 1966-67; dir. personnel Kroger Food Corp., Cin., 1967-68; prin. Carol Leong Electrolysis, San Mateo, Calif., 1978—; prin. Designs by Carol, San Mateo, 1987—; mem. Profl. Women's Forum, 1988—. Contbr. articles to profl. publs. Recipient Cert. of Appreciation San Francisco Lighthouse for the Blind, 1981-82, 83. Mem. Internat. Guild Profl. Electrologists (mem. continuing edn. com.), NAFE, Profl. Women's Forum, Peninsula Humane Soc., San Francisco Zool. Soc., Friends of Filoli, Am. Electrologists Assn., Electrologists Assn. Calif., Internat. Platform Assn, Chi Omega. Republican. Presbyterian. Home: 1447 Woodberry Ave San Mateo CA 94403-3712 Office: Carol Leong Electrolysis 359 M San Mateo Dr Ste 4 San Mateo CA 94401-2513

LEONG, LAM-PO (LANBO LIANG), artist, educator; b. Canton, Guangdong, China, July 3, 1961; came to U.S., 1983; BFA in Chinese Brush Painting, Canton Fine Arts Inst., 1983; MFA in Painting with high distinction, Calif. Coll. Arts & Crafts, 1988. Instr. art U. Calif. Extension, Oakland, 1986-87, U. Calif. Ext. & ASUC, Berkeley, 1989, 90—, San Jose (Calif.) State U. Ext., 1989-91; lectr. San Francisco State U., 1988—; instr. art Chabot Coll., Hayward, Calif., 1989—; artistic dir. Oakland Asian Cultural Ctr., Calif., 1990—; lectr./speaker in field. One-man shows include Markings Gallery, Berkeley, 1984, Sumitomo Bank, Albany, Calif., 1985, Calif. Coll. Arts & Crafts, 1985, Rosicrucian Egyptian Mus., San Jose, 1986, U. Utah, Salt Lake City, 1986, Patrick Gallery, Regina, Sask., Can., 1986, Mus. Macao Luis De Camoes, Macao, 1986, Kai Ping County Mus., Guangdong, 1987, Chinatown Gallery, San Francisco, 1987, Guangzhou Fine Arts Mus., Canton, 1988, The Arlington Gallery, Oakland, 1989, Moy Ying Ming Gallery, Chgo., 1990, Chinese Culture Ctr., San Francisco, 1991, Stanwood Gallery, San Francisco, 1992, Sanuk Fine Asian Collectables, San Francisco, 1992, The Univ. Gallery, San Francisco, 1994, Michael Thompson Gallery, San Francisco, 1995; exhibited in group shows at Hong Kong Arts Ctr., 1980, Chinese Painting Exhibit Guangdong Province, 1981 (3d Prize award 1981), Macao Artists Assn. Exhbn., 1982, Mus. Canton Fine Arts Inst., 1983, Nat. Mus. Art, Beijing, 1985, Macao Young Artist Exhbn. (Excellence award, 1st prize 1985), Pacific Art Ctr., Seattle, 1985, Chinese Culture Ctr., 1986, Faculty & MFA Show Calif. Coll. Arts & Crafts, San Francisco Campus, 1986, Chinese-Am. Artist Exhbn., Taipei, Taizhong, Taiwan, 1986, Sullivan Galleries, Salt Lake City, 1987, Oriental Gallery, N.Y., 1987, Santa Cruz Art League (Spl. award 1988, 1st prize 1990), Asian Resource Gallery, Oakland, 1988, Nat. Mus. Fine Arts, Beijing, 1988, 90, Chinese Art Gallery, San Leandro, Calif., 1989, Stanwood Gallery, 1989, Gallery Imago, San Francisco, 1990, Sun Gallery, Hayward, 1990, N.Y. Art Expo, N.Y.C., 1991, Gallery 5, Santa Monica, Calif., 1991, Butterfield & Butterfield Auction, San Francisco, 1992, 95, Asian Art Mus., San

Francisco, 1992, Ke Shan Art Gallery, Taipei, 1993, Wan Fung Art Gallery, Hong Kong, 1993, Gallery On The Rim, San Francisco, 1994, Resource for Art, 1995, Ginsberg Collection, 1995; work represented in various mus., corp. and pvt. collections including Guangzhou Arts Mus., Macao Camoes Mus., Mus. Canton Fine Arts Inst., Asian Art Mus. San Francisco, United Savs. Bank, Calif., Hotel East 21, Tokyo, The Westin Hotel, Tokyo, Comml. Bank, San Francisco; author: Brush Paintings of Lam-Po Leong, 1986, Journey of the Heart, 1994; illustrator: Brushstrokes-Styles and Techniques of Chinese Painting, 1993, The Tao of Power, 1986; designer (granite courtyard) New Chinatown Pk., San Francisco, 1993. Recipient Outstanding Merit award Young Art Now Competition, 1980, Decade of Achievement award Asian/Pacific Heritage Week, 1988, 2d prize Zunyi Internat. Brush Painting Competition, 1989; inductee Pan-Pacific Asian Hall of Fame at San Francisco Internat. Expo., 1987; grantee City of Oakland, 1994. Mem. Asian Artists Assn. Am., Oriental Art Assn., U.S.A. (v.p.), Macao Soc. Social Scis., Hai-Ri Artists Assn. (China), Nat. Modern Delicate Painting Soc. (China), Chinese Am. Culture Exch. Assn. (co-founder, dir. 1992—). Office: Brushwork Gallery 166 Palisades Dr Daly City CA 94015-4517

LEONG, YVONNE C., literacy consultant; b. Honolulu; d. Henry Y. K. and Betty (C.) Ching; m. Douglas H. Leong, Aug. 1964; children: Deborah, Darryl. BA in Speech/English, Humboldt State U., 1963; MA in Speech Edn., Northwestern U., 1965. Cert. adminstr. of non-profit vol. programs, Master Laubach Way to English/Reading tutor, supr. tutor trainer, secondary edn. educator; lic. realtor. Tchr. Roosevelt High Sch., Honolulu, 1960; coll. instr. Northeastern Ill. State Coll., Chgo., 1965-66; speech instr., forensics dir. Chgo. City Coll., 1966-68; grad. sch. office coord. Ill. Inst. Tech., Chgo., 1969-70; prin. Lang. & Cultural Sch. of Orange County, 1978-80, coord. cultural program, 1979-87; exec. dir. Ctrl. Orange County Literacy Coun., Santa Ana, Calif., 1989-90; CASAS testing coord. Orange County Literacy Coun., Santa Ana, Calif., 1989-91; literacy/ESL cons., instr. various orgns., Santa Ana, Calif., 1988—; literacy cons. Head Start Orange County, Santa Ana, Calif., 1991—; literacy trainer Hacienda (Calif.) La Puente Unified Sch. Dist., 1992, Rancho Santiago Coll., Santa Ana, 1992—; bd. dirs. Orange County Literacy Network, Santa Ana, 1986—; dir., trainer FV Literacy Ctrs., Fountain Valley, Calif., 1986—; master tutor Laubach Literacy Action, Syracuse, N.Y., 1982, supr., tutor trainer, 1994—; conf. workshop speaker in field. leader, svc. team, cmty. events chair WIGS-Girl Scouts, Fountain Valley; bd. dirs. Chineses Assn. Recipient Gold award Roosevelt High Sch., 1960, Girls Scouts Orange Owl County award, 1986, Bruce William award Vol. Ctr.-West, 1988, Carnation Silver Bowl award Vol. Ctr. Orange County, 1991, 10 Yr. Svc. award Ctrl. Orange County Literacy Coun., 1992. Mem. Calif. Literacy, Inc. (field devel. chmn. bd. dirs. 1990—, Orange County field rep. vol. 1991—, Outstanding leader 1989), Ctrl. Oragne County Literacy Coun. (bd. dirs., adv. coun., pres., dir. tng. 1982—), Orange County Advancing Literacy (dir., founder 1992—, Disneyland award 1994). Office: PO Box 548 Midway City CA 92655-0548

LEONIS, JOHN MICHAEL, aerospace executive; b. Whittier, Calif., Oct. 21, 1933; s. Michael Arthur and Minnie Augusta (Peterson) L.; m. Edith Ann Pattison, Aug. 30, 1958; children: Susan Elizabeth, Carolyn Ann, Linda Maria. BEE, U. Ariz., 1959. Past pres. Litton Guidance and Control Systems, Woodland Hills, Calif.; pres., CEO Litton Industries, Inc., Beverly Hills, Calif., 1994—. Mem. AIAA, Inst. Navigation, Air Force Assn., Assn. U.S. Army, Assn. Naval Aviation, Naval Helicopter Assn., Am. Electronics Assn. Office: Litton Industries Inc 360 N Crescent Dr Beverly Hills CA 90210-4802

LEONTE, DINU IOAN, software engineer; b. Ploiesti, Romania, July 16, 1941; came to U.S., 1990; s. Dumitru and Filotea (Dinescu) L.; m. Oana Mariana Vetrici, July 11, 1964; 1 child, Laura Daria Leonte Lawson. MS in Math., U. Bucharest, Romania, 1965; MSEE, Poly. Inst., Bucharest, 1972, PhD, 1983. Programmer analyst Nat. Electric Power Dispatch, Bucharest, 1969-82, sr. software engr., 1984-90; software engr. EMS and SCADA systems/Siemens, Erlangen, Germany, 1982-84; CAD software engr. Popa Kihlthau S.e.C., Campbell, Calif., 1990-92; software engr. A.D. Costas Projects, Pleasanton, Calif., 1992; sr. software engr. First Pacific Networks, Inc., San Jose, Calif., 1992-95, Automatic Data Processing, San Ramon, Calif., 1995—. Democrat. Roman Catholic. Home: 1137 Walpert St Apt 69 Hayward CA 94541-6724 Office: Automatic Data Processing 2010 Crow Canyon Pl San Ramon CA 94583

LEOPOLD, MICHELLE RAEANNA SAEVKE, public relations executive; b. Alameda, Calif., June 14, 1965; d. Peter Frido and Barbara Louise (Gremminger) Saevke; m. Jeff Leopold, July 15, 1995. BA in Sociology, Bus., UCLA, 1987. Account asst., account coord. Grey Avt., San Francisco, 1987-89, asst. account exec., 1989-90; mktg. asst. The St. Francis Hotel, San Francisco, 1990-91, pub. rels. mgr., 1991-93, dir. pub. rels., 1993-94, dir. mktg. comm., 1994—; speaker in field. Pres. Bay Area UCLA Bruin Alumni, mem. alumni scholarship com., 1988-93; head counselor Job's Daughters Leadership Camp, No. Calif., 1988-90. Mem. Pub. Rels. Soc. Am., San Francisco Bay Area Publicity Club, San Francisco Acad. Travel and Tourism (bd. dirs.), Women in Comms., Inc., Calif. Hist. Soc., San Francisco Hist. Soc. Office: Westin St Francis 335 Powell St San Francisco CA 94102-1804

LEPAGE, KERRY LEIGH, marketing executive; b. Manhatten, Kans., Mar. 6, 1965; d. William Ludwig and Montague Kay (Epps) Tillman; m. John David LePage, May 15, 1993. BA in Comms., Ariz. State U., 1987; MBA, U. Phoenix, 1991. Account coord. The Quale Group, Phoenix, 1987-88, prodn. mgr., 1988-89; employee comms. coord. Phoenix Transit Sys., 1989-90, bus. devel./pub. rels. supr., 1990-92; mgr. mktg. comms. Aquapore Moisture Sys., Inc., Phoenix, 1992-95; owner Momentum Mktg., Tempe, Ariz., 1995—; project mgr. mktg. program Bus. Card PLUS, 1991. Editor/project mgr.: Grow and Tell Children's Gardening, 1993 (Copper Quill award 1993). Vol. Aid to Ind. Living, Tempe, 1992—. Recipient Clarion award, 1992. Mem. Women in Comms. Inc. (newsletter editor 1989-91, sec. 1991-92, pres. 1992-94, polit. com. organizer 1993-94), Internat. Assn. Bus. Communicators (v.p. membership 1992-93, Excellent Mem. award 1992), Ariz. Recycling Coalition, Nat. Recycling Coalition. Office: Momentum Mktg 1112 E Laguna Dr Tempe AZ 85282-5516

LEPIE, ALBERT HELMUT, chemist, reseacher; b. Malapane, Silesia, Germany, Aug. 6, 1923; came to U.S., 1963; s. Albert and Emilia (Zachlod) L.; m. Claire Kortz, 1956 (div. 1964); 1 child, Karin. Degree in chem. engring., Staatliche Ing. Schule, Essen, Germany, 1953; diploma in chemistry, Tech. Hochschule, Aachen, Germany, 1959; D in Natural Scis., Tech. Hochschule, Munich, Germany, 1961. Chem. engr. Pahl'sche Gummi & Asbest, Düsseldorf, 1953-59; chemist Deutsche Versuchanstalt für Luftfahrt, Munich, 1961-63; rsch. chemist U.S. Naval Propellant Plant, Indian Head, Md., 1963-64, Naval Weapons Ctr., China Lake, Calif., 1964—; chmn. mech. properties panel Joint Army, Navy, NASA, and Air Force Interagy. Rocket Propulsion, 1977-84. Inventor air curtain incinerator for energetic materials and fiber peal force measurement device, flywheel high rate tensile tester for viscoelastic materials. Recipient Joint Army, Navy, NASA, and Air Force award, 1984, William B. McLean award Naval Weapons Ctr. Mem. AAAS, Am. Chem. Soc. (sec. China Lake chpt. 1968, 69), China Lake Astron. Soc., Sigma Xi. Roman Catholic. Home: 121 S Desert Candles St Ridgecrest CA 93555-4218

LEPOME, PENELOPE MARIE, rehabilitation counselor, educator; b. Buffalo, Dec. 17, 1945; d. Raymond Arthur and Mildred Evelyn (Johnson) Kramer; m. Robert Charles LePome, May 26, 1966 (div. Jan. 1982); children: Lisa Anne, Kathryn Jane, Robert Charles II. BA in Biology, SUNY, Buffalo, 1967; MS in Vocat. Rehab., U. Nev., Las Vegas, 1984, postgrad., 1993—. Cert. rehab. counselor, substance abuse counselor, ins. rehab. specialist; lic. substitute tchr. and sch. counselor, Nev. Co-owner, salesman Flamingo Realty, Las Vegas, Nev., 1974-76; substitute tchr. Clark County Sch. Dist., Las Vegas, 1969-74, 1982-84; adj. faculty Clark County Community Coll., Las Vegas, 1984-86, Truckee Meadows Community Coll., Reno, 1987; bus. and industry field specialist, Tng. Inst. Clark County Community Coll., 1985-86; probation officer on call Clark County Juvenile Services, Las Vegas, 1984; counselor Nike House, Las Vegas, 1984; mental health techician III, State of Nev., 1984-86; rehab. coord. I, Nev. Bur. Vocat. Rehab., Reno, 1986-92; pvt. practice rehab. counseling, 1984-86; rehab. counselor GENEX Svcs. Inc. (formerly Gen. Rehab. Svcs., Inc.), Reno, 1992—. Active Nev. Womens Polit. Caucus, Las Vegas, 1983-85; carnival chmn. Rex Bell PTA, Las Vegas, 1974-75, treas., 1975-76; leader Frontier Area Girl Scouts U.S., Las Vegas, 1975-76, cookie sale chmn., 1980; treas., bd. dirs. Young Audiences, Las Vegas, 1979-80; mem. Reno City Coun. Adv. Com. Persons With Disabilities, 1991-93. N.Y. State Regents scholar, 1963. Mem. Am. Counseling Assn., AAUW (div. officer Nev. 1983-85, pres. 1982-83, v.p. programming 1981-82, v.p. membership 1980-81, life mem.), Assn. Part-time Profls. (bd. dirs.). Republican. Office: 1325 Airmotive Way # 175X Reno NV 89502-3201

LEPORE, KEN, financial services executive; b. 1957. BS, Cal Poly U., 1981. V.p. Tital Capital Corp., Tustin, Calif., 1985-87; dir. compliance Transamerica Fin. Resources, Carlsbad, Calif., 1987-89; v.p., CFO ASB Fin. Svcs., Inc., Irvine, Calif., 1989—. Office: ASB Fin Svcs Inc 17875 Von Karman Ave Fl 2 Irvine CA 92714*

LEPORE, VINCENT DONALD, JR., plastic surgeon; b. Rome, Mar. 30, 1955; came to U.S., 1957; s. Vincent Donald and Mary Louise Lepore; m. Margaret Mary Scura; 1 child, Nicholas. AB, Dartmouth Coll., 1977; MD, U. Cin., 1981. Diplomate Am. Bd. Plastic Surgery. Resident in plastic surgery Stanford (Calif.) U., 1981-87; founder, owner Plastic & Reconstructive Surgery Assocs., Inc., Palo Alto, Calif., 1987—. Rufus Choate scholar Dartmouth Coll., 1977. Mem. Am. Soc. Plastic and Reconstructive Surgeons, Calif. Med. Assn., Calif. Soc. Plastic Surgeons, Alpha Omega Alpha. Office: Plastic & Reconstructive Surgery Assocs Inc 900 Welch Rd Ste 110 Palo Alto CA 94304

LEPORIERE, RALPH DENNIS, quality engineer; b. Elizabeth, N.J., Nov. 8, 1932; s. Maximo and Christian (Lello) L.; m. Judith Louise Crowhurst, Nov. 19, 1960; children: Bonnie Ann, David Anthony. BS in Chemistry, Rutgers U., 1954. Registered profl. engr., Calif. Chemist N.Y. Quinine & Chemical Works, Newark, 1954-55; asst. to chief quality control C.D. Smith Pharmacal Co., New Brunswick, N.J., 1955-56; asst. supr. quality control White Labs., Kenilworth, N.J., 1958-60; statistician Calif. and Hawaiian Sugar Co., Crockett, Calif., 1960—; instr., chmn. quality control dept. Laney C.C., Oakland, Calif., 1967-87; asst. prof., chmn. quality control dept. John F. Kennedy U., Martinez, Calif., 1967-72; instr., mem. adv. com. ann. statis. short course U. Calif., Davis, 1969-94. Pres. PTA Napa Junction Elem. Sch., Napa County, Calif., 1971-73; mem. early childhood com., program adv. com. Napa Valley Unified Sch. Dist., Napa County, 1972-76; v.p. Am. Canyon County Water Dist., American Canyon, Calif., 1971-73, pres., 1973-83, gen. mgr., 1981. Recipient Hon. Service award Calif. State PTA, 1973. Fellow Am. Soc. Quality Control (cert. quality engr., chmn. San Francisco sect., founder East Bay Subsect. 1970-71); mem. Soc. Mfg. Engrs. (sr.), Am. Statis. Soc., Am. Chem. Soc. Republican. Roman Catholic. Home: 618 Kilpatrick St Vallejo CA 94589-1305 Office: Calif & Hawaiian Sugar Co 830 Loring Ave Crockett CA 94525-1104

LEPP, STEPHEN HENRY, physicist, educator; b. Duluth, Minn., June 7, 1956; s. Henry and Maxine (Foster) L. BS in Physics, U. Minn., Duluth, 1978; PhD in Physics, U Colo., 1984. Postdoctoral fellow Harvard U., Cambridge, Mass., 1984-87, rsch. assoc., 1987-91; asst. prof. physics U. Nev., Las Vegas, 1991-95, assoc. prof., 1995—. Contbr. articles to profl. jours. Mem. Am. Astron. Soc., Internat. Astron. Union (Young Astronomer grant 1991). Office: U Nev Physics Dept 4505 S Maryland Pky Las Vegas NV 89154-9900

LERAAEN, ALLEN KEITH, financial executive; b. Mason City, Iowa, Dec. 4, 1951; s. Myron O. and Clarice A. (Handeland) L.; m. Mary Elena Partheymuller, Apr. 14, 1978. BBA in Data Processing and Acctg., No. Ariz. U., 1975. CFA. Data processing supr. Stephenson & Co., Denver, 1978-81, contr., 1981-85, arbitrageur, trader, 1985-88, v.p., 1985-90, exec. v.p., 1990—; v.p., sec. bd. dirs. Circle Corp., Denver, 1985—. Mem. Assn. Investment Mgmt. and Rsch., Denver Soc. Security Analysts. Home: 5692 S Robb St Littleton CO 80127-1942 Office: 100 Garfield St Fl 4 Denver CO 80206-5550

LERMAN, EILEEN R., lawyer; b. N.Y.C., May 6, 1947; d. Alex and Beatrice (Kline) L. BA, Syracuse U., 1969; JD, Rutgers U., 1972; MBA, U. Denver, 1983. Bar: N.Y. 1973, Colo. 1976. atty. FTC, N.Y.C., 1972-74; corp. atty. RCA, N.Y.C., 1974-76; corp. atty. Samsonite Corp. and consumer products div. Beatrice Foods Co., Denver, 1976-78, assoc. gen. counsel, 1978-85, asst. sec., 1979-85; ptnr. Davis, Lerman, & Weinstein, Denver, 1985-92, Eileen R. Lerman & Assocs., 1993—; bd. dir. Legal Aid Soc. of Met. Denver, 1979-80. Bd. dirs., vice chmn. Colo. Postsecondary Ednl. Facilities Authority, 1981-89; bd. dirs., pres. Am. Jewish Com., 1989-92; mem. Leadership Denver, 1983. Mem. ABA, Colo. Women's Bar Assn. (bd. dir. 1980-81), Colo. Bar Assn. (bd. govs.), Denver Bar Assn. (trustee), N.Y. State Bar Assn., Rhone Brackett Inn (sec. 1994), Denver Law Club, Rutgers U. Alumni Assn., University Club. Home: 1018 Fillmore St Denver CO 80206-3332 Office: Eileen R Lerman & Assocs 50 S Steele St Ste 420 Denver CO 80209-2809

LERNER, ALAN BURTON, financial service executive, lawyer; b. N.Y.C., Nov. 17, 1930; s. Samuel A. and Helen (Zisfein) L.; m. Elisabeth Waltraud Bruttel, July 5, 1959; children: Raissa, Anthony, Jessica, James. BBA, CCNY, 1951; LLB, Yale U., 1954. Bar: N.Y. 1954, D.C. 1973. Assoc. Chadbourne, Parke, Whiteside & Wolff, N.Y.C., 1956-60; with legal dept. C.I.T. Fin. Corp., N.Y.C., 1960-81; gen. counsel, sec. C.I.T. Fin. Corp., 1976-81, v.p., 1977-81; sr. exec. v.p. Assocs. Corp. of N.Am., Dallas, 1981-93; sr. exec. v.p. corp. staff Assocs. Corp. of N.Am.; also sr. exec. v.p. Assocs First Capital Corp.; cons. Fed. Res. Bd., 1973, Nat. Conf. Commrs. on Uniform State Laws, 1966-68. mem. adv. coun. Sch. Mgmt. and Adminstrn., U. Tex., Dallas, 1981-87; mem. Fin. Commn. of State of Tex., 1983-89; mem. adv. bd. Salvation Army Dallas County, 1991—. Mem. ABA, D.C. Bar Assn., Assn. Bar City N.Y., Am. Fin. Svcs. Assn. (bd. dirs. 1983-88, 90—, vice chmn. 1991-92, chmn. 1992-93, chmn. exec. com. 1993-94). Office: Assocs Corp NAm PO Box 660237 Dallas TX 75266-0237 also: Assocs Corp NAm 250 Carpenter Fwy Irving TX 75062

LERNER, ALEXANDRIA SANDRA, artist; b. Phila., Jan. 1, 1946. Student, Pa. Acad. Fine Arts, 1970-75; BFA, Phila. Coll. Art, 1978. founding mem., trustee Found. for Toaday's Art, 1975—; co-dir. Synapse: A Visual Art Press, 1980-85. Exhibited works in shows at Nexus Gallery, Phila., 1976, 77, 78, 80, 94, Marion Locks Gallery, Phila., 1976, 82, Phila. Coll. Art, 1977, 1977, A.C.T. Gallery, Toronto, 1978, N.A.M.E. Gallery, Chgo., 1979, Phila. Art Alliance, 1979, 80, 89, So. Alleghenies, Mus., Loretteo, Pa., 1979, 80, 82, Phila. Acad. Fine Arts, 1980, A.I.R. Gallery, N.Y.C., 1980, A.B.F. Gallery, Hamburg, Germany, 1980, Art Inst. Chgo., 1980, Washington Sq. Gallery, N.Y.C., 1980, Tweed Mus., Duluth, Minn., 1981, Mus. Found. for Visual Arts, Phila., 1981, For Art's Sake Gallery, Martha's Vineyard, Mass., 1981, Kathryn Markel Gallery, N.Y.C., 1983, Port of History Mus., Phila., 1989, Phila. Mus. Art, 1990, Mangel Gallery, Phila., 1991, Harwood Found. Mus., Taos, N.Mex., 1991, Spirit Gallery, Santa Fe, 1993; permanent collections include Phila. Mus. Art, So. Alleghenies Mus., Art Inst. Chgo., Jean Brown Archives, Shaker Seed House, Maine, Franklin Furnace Archive, N.Y.C., Tweed Mus., Nat. Inst. Design, Ahmedabad, New Delhi, India, Phila. Sci. Ctr., others. Home: Box 5304 Taos NM 87571

LERNER, SHELDON, plastic surgeon; b. N.Y.C., Mar. 3, 1939; s. Louis and Lillian L.; AB with honors, Drew U., 1961; MD, U. Louisville, 1965. Intern, resident Albert Einstein Coll. Medicine, Bronx-Mcpl. Hosp. Center, 1965-73; practice medicine, specializing in plastic surgery Plastic Cosmetic and Reconstructive Surgery Center, San Diego, 1973—. Served with USPHS, 1968-70. Mem. AMA, Am. Soc. Plastic and Reconstructive Surgeons, Calif. Med. Soc., San Diego County Med. Soc., San Diego Internat. Plastic Surgery Assn. Clubs: Masons, Shriners. Office: 3399 1st Ave San Diego CA 92103-5601

LEROY, NORBERT GHISLAIN, management and financial consultant; b. Boitsfort, Belgium; came to U.S., 1940; s. Julian J. and Marie (Huygens) L.; m. Janet E. Dishington, Feb. 11, 1967 (div. Mar. 1974). BA, Iona Coll., 1947; BS, Columbia U., 1949; BA, MA, Cambridge U., Eng., 1951. Various to v.p. J.P. Morgan & Co., N.Y.C., 1951-66; dir., pres., treas. Polyroy, Inc., Montroy Properties, Ltd., N.Y./Mont., 1968-79; dir., v.p. The Pilot Corp. (merged with Polyroy, Inc.), Billing, Mont., 1988—. With Royal Air Force, 1941-45. Mem. The Brook Club (N.Y.), Racquet and Tennis Club (N.Y.), Coun. on Fgn. Rels., The Travellers (Paris), Billings Area C. of C., others. Roman Catholic. Office: Polyroy Inc Ste 321 769 Fallow Ln Apt 321 Billings MT 59102-7051

LERUD, JOANNE VAN ORNUM, library administrator; b. Jamestown, N.D., Nov. 21, 1949; d. Elbert Hiel and Dorothy Arlene (Littrick) Van Ornum; m. Gerald Henry Groenewold, Jan. 15, 1971 (div. Nov. 1978); 1 child, Gerd Heil Groenewold; m. Jeffrey Craig Lerud, Aug. 30, 1980; 1 child, Jesse Currier. BS in Geology, U. N.D., 1971, MS in Geology, 1979; MA in Librarianship and Info. Mgmt., U. Denver, 1979. Assoc. tech. info. specialist Marathon Oil Co., Littleton, Colo., 1980-86; libr. dir. Mont. Coll. Mineral Sci. and Tech., Butte, 1986-89, Colo. Sch. Mines, Golden, 1989—; report investigator in field. NSF grantee, 1970. Mem. Geosci. Info. Soc. (v.p. 1988, pres. 1989). Office: Colo Sch Mines Arthur Lakes Libr Golden CO 80401

LERUDE, WARREN LESLIE, journalism educator; b. Reno, Oct. 29, 1937; s. Leslie Raymond and Ione (Lundy) L.; m. Janet Lagomarsino, Aug. 24, 1961; children: Eric Warren, Christopher Mario Leslie, Leslie Ann. BA in Journalism, U. Nev., 1961. Reporter, editor, correspondent The AP, Las Vegas, Reno, Nev., 1960-63; reporter, editor, pub., pres. Reno Evening Gazette, Nev. State Jour., 1963-81; prof. journalism U. Nev., Reno, 1981—; bd. dirs. Oakland (Calif.) Tribune; lectr. Am. Press Inst.; cons. ABA, Nat. Broadcasting Co., Nat. Jud. Coll. Co-author: American Commander in Spain, Robert Hale Merriman and the Abraham Lincoln Brigade, 1986; mem. editorial bd. USA Today, 1982—. Trustee U. Nev.-Reno Found.; trustee, mem. cmty. adv. bd. Sta. KNPB-TV, Reno; mem. legis. com. Greater Reno C. of C.; mem. bd. dirs. Squaw Valley Ski Corp. Served with USNR, 1957-59. Co-recipient Pulitzer prize, 1977. Mem. Nev. State Press Assn. (past pres.), Calif.-Nev. News Execs. Council of the AP, Calif. Newspaper Pub. Assn. (editors conf.), Sigma Delta Chi. Club: Rotary. Home: 3825 N Folsom Dr Reno NV 89509-3015 Office: U Nev Reynolds Sch Journalism Reno NV 89557

LESAVOY, MALCOLM A., plastic surgeon, educator. MD, U. Health Scis., 1969. Prof. plastic surgery UCLA, 1976—; mem. med. staff UCLA Med. Ctr. Office: UCLA Med Ctr 10833 Le Conte Ave Los Angeles CA 90024*

LESHER, MARGARET LISCO, newspaper publisher, songwriter; b. San Antonio, Tex., May 4, 1932; d. Lloyd Elmo Lisco and Dovie Deona (Maynard) Lisco Welch; m. William Jarvis Ryan (dec.); children: Patricia Ryan Simmonds, Wendi Ryan Alves, Jill Ryan Heidt, Roxanne Ryan Gibson; m. Dean Stanley Lesher, Sr., Apr. 2, 1973 (dec.). Student Coalinga (Calif.) Jr. Coll. Dir. sales Chatmar, Inc., Concord, Calif., 1970-73; dir. cmty. svcs. Contra Costa Times Newspaper, Walnut Creek, Calif., 1973-94; chmn. bd. Lesher Comm., Inc., Walnut Creek, 1974—, Calif. Delta Newspapers, Inc., Antioch, 1975—, No. Calif. Publs., Inc., Telegraph.-News Publs., Inc.; pres., ceo, dean Margaret Lesher Found. Composer, lyricist gospel song Margaret Lesher Album, 1976 (So. Calif. Motion Picture Coun. Bronze Halo award 1982); author 14 published poems. Pres., exec. dir. Dean and Margaret Lesher Found.; regent Holy Names Coll., Oakland, Calif., 1979-86; chief of protocol Contra Costa County, 1980—; dir. Bay Area Sports Hall of Fame, San Francisco, 1982—; bd. overseers U. Calif., San Francisco, 1983-90; bd. dirs. Yosemite Fund; mem. San Francisco Host Com., 1983—, Internat. Host Com. of Calif., 1983-86, Nat. Reading Initiative Coordinating Coun., 1988—; dir. emeritus Alameda-Contra Costa Regional Parks Found.; developed Contra Costa County Citizen Recognition Awards Program with County Police Chiefs Assn.; founded Contra Costa Literacy Alliance; commr. Port of Richmond, Calif., 1983-86; chmn. adv. bd. Crisis Nursery of Bay Area, Concord, 1983-86; adv. bd. Oakland A's Baseball Team, 1984-85, Battered Women, 1983—; pres. bd. dirs. Mt. Diablo Hosp. Found., 1980-81; bd. dirs. Contra Costa Council, 1984-90; mem. adv. bd. Las Trampas Sch. Mentally Retarded, chmn., 1984-90; trustee Oakland Symphony Orch., 1985-86; host Informed Viewer pub. svc. program Sta. KFCB-TV. Recipient Spl. Merit award State of Calif., 1982, Charles E. Scripps award Outstanding Contbn. in the Promotion of Literacy, 1988, 2 Internat. Silver Angel awards, 1st pl. for lit. program Calif. Newspaper Pub.'s Assn., 1988; named Calif. Assembly Woman of Yr. Mem. Am. Newspaper Pub. Assn. (ednl. svcs. com. 1988—), Gospel Music Assn., ASCAP, Nat. TV Acad. Arts & Scis., Calif. Cattlemen's Assn., Cancer of the Prostate Cure, Walnut Creek Rotary, Blackhawk Country Club. Republican. Christian. Avocation: horses. Office: Contra Costa Times Lesher Comm Inc 2640 Shadelands Dr Walnut Creek CA 94598-2513

LESKO, RONALD MICHAEL, osteopathic physician; b. Homestead, Pa., Mar. 25, 1948; s. Andrew Paul and elizabeth Ann (Tarasovic) L.; m. Elena Alexandra Shalayeva, July 29, 1990. BS, U. Pitts., 1970; DO, Coll. Osteo. Medicine & Surgery, Des Moines, 1973; MPH, Loma Linda U., 1985. Diplomate Am. Osteo. Bd. Family Physicians, Am. Osteo. Bd. Preventive Medicine (bd. dirs., chmn. pub. health rep., chmn. bd. exam. com. 1991-97). Famiy physician pvt. practice Port Richey, Fla., 1974-80; flight surgeon USN, NAS Chase Field Beeville, Tex., 1981-83; resident gen. preventive medicine Loma Linda (Calif.) U. Med. Ctr., 1983-85; pvt. practice family and preventive medicine, pvt. practice, Del Mar, Calif., 1988—; flight surgeon, capt. USNR, NAS Miramar, San Diego, 1988—; attending physician ambulatory care svc. J.L. Pettis Meml. VA Hosp., Loma Linda, Calif., 1986-88; staff physician Scripps Meml. Hosp., La Jolla, Calif., 1990—; lectr., 1985—; cons. Jour. Am. Osteo. Assn., Chgo., 1987, phys. rediness div. USN, Washington, 1988; med. advisor blue ribbon adv. com. Nutrition Screening Initiative, Washington, 1991. Contbr. articles to med. jours. Med. adviser March of Dimes Suncoast chpt., New Port Richey, 1977-79; bd. dirs. Fla. Gulf Health Systems Agy., Region IV, 1977-79, Price-Pottenger Nutrition Found., San Diego, 1988—. Fellow Am. Osteo. Coll. Preventive Medicine (trustee 1989-91, chmn. pub. health divisional com. 1989-91); mem. APHA, Am. Osteo. Assn., San Diego Osteo. Med. Assn., San Diego County Med. Soc., Osteo. Physicians and Surgeons Calif., Calif. Med. Assn., Am. Coll. Family Physicians-Osteo., U.S. Naval Flight Surgeons. Office: 13983 Mango Dr Ste 102 Del Mar CA 92014-3146

LESLIE, JACQUES ROBERT, JR., journalist; b. L.A., Mar. 12, 1947; s. Jacques Robert and Aleen (Wetstein) L.; m. Leslie Wernick, June 21, 1980; 1 child, Sarah Alexandra. BA, Yale U., 1968. Tchr. New Asia Coll., Chinese U., Hong Kong, 1968-70; free-lance journalist Washington, 1970-71; fgn. corr. L.A. Times, Saigon, 1972-73, Phnom Penh, 1973, Washington, 1974; chief New Delhi (India) bur. L.A. Times, 1974-75, Madrid, 1975-76; chief Hong Kong bur. L.A. Times, 1976-77; freelance journalist, 1977—. Author: The Mark: A War Correspondent's Memoir of Vietnam and Cambodia. Recipient Best Fgn. Corr. award Sigma Delta Chi, 1973, citation reporting Overseas Press Club, 1973. Home: 124 Reed St Mill Valley CA 94941-3448

LESLIE, ROBERT LORNE, lawyer; b. Adak, Alaska, Feb. 24, 1947; s. J. Lornie and L. Jean (Conelly) L.; children—Lorna Jean, Elizabeth Allen. B.S., U.S. Mil. Acad., 1969; J.D., Hastings Coll. Law, U. Calif.-San Francisco, 1974. Bar: Calif. 1974, D.C. 1979, U.S. Dist. Ct. (no. dist.) Calif. 1974, U.S. Ct. Claims 1975, U.S. Tax Ct. 1975, U.S. Ct. Appeals (9th and D.C. cirs.), U.S. Ct. Mil. Appeals 1980, U.S. Supreme Ct. 1980. Commd. 2d lt. U.S. Army, 1969, advanced through grades to maj., 1980; govt. trial atty. West Coast Field Office, Contract Appeals, Litigation Div. and Regulatory Law Div., Office JAG, Dept. Army, San Francisco, 1974-77; sr. trial atty. and team chief Office of Chief Trial Atty., Dept. Army, Washington, 1977-80; ptnr. McInerney & Dillon, Oakland, Calif., 1980—; lectr. on govt. contracts CSC, Continuing Legal Edn. Program; lectr. in govt. procurement U.S. Army Materiel Command. Col. USAR. Decorated Silver Star, Purple Heart. Mem. ABA, Fed. Bar Assn., Associated Gen. Contractors, The Beavers. Office: Ordway Building Fl 18 Oakland CA 94612-3610

LESLIE, SHEILA LOUISE, human services consultant; b. Carmel, Calif., Nov. 6, 1955; d. John T. and Julia (Gonser) L.; m. Robert Fulkerson, Jan. 19, 1985 (div.); 1 child, Emma. BA in Spanish Lang. and Lit., Sonoma State U., 1977; MA in Spanish Lang. and Lit., U. Nev., 1979. Food bank adminstr. Cmty. Svcs. Agy., Reno, Nev., 1981-84; planning adminstr. Cmty. Svcs. Agy., Reno, 1986; acting exec. dir. El Centro - Latin Am. Info. Ctr.,

Reno, 1985-86; exec. dir. Tahoe Human Svcs., South Lake Tahoe, Calif., 1984-86, Children's Cabinet, Reno, 1987-93; pvt. practice human svcs. cons. Reno, 1994—; Founding mem. bd. dirs. Gang Alternatives Partnership, Reno, 1991-93; bd. dirs. Nat. Network of Runaway/Homeless Youth Svcs., Washington, 1992-93; chair Western States Youth Svcs. Network, Calif., Nev., Ariz., Hawaii, 1992-93; mem. Nev. Family Acad., Reno, 1993—. Editor: Nevada's Children: Our Most Precious Resource?, 1989. Bd. dir. Truckee Meadows Human Svcs. Assn., Reno; chair Coalition for Future of Juvenile Justice and Youth Svcs., Reno; mem. Guatemalan Judges Exch., Reno; adv. mem. Family Cabinet Inc., Las Vegas, 1992, Children's Cabinet at Incline Village, Lake Tahoe, 1992—. Named Woman of Distinction Soroptimist of Reno South, 1992, Woman of Achievement Nev. Women's Fund, Reno, 1993, Citizen of Yr. Nev. Assn. Social Workers, 1994; Am. Field Svc. scholar, 1973-74. Mem. Sierra Nev. Cmty. Access TV, Soroptimist of Truckee Meadows. Democrat. Methodist. Home and Office: Cmty Partnerships 725 Mcdonald Dr Reno NV 89503-3415

LESLY, CRAIG EDWARDS, marketing professional; b. Evanston, Ill., Sept. 14, 1942; s. Philip and Ruth (Edwards) L.; m. Carole McLaughlin, July 31, 1964 (div.); children: Elizabeth Lesly Stevens, Melissa Lesly Cooper; m. Penni McRoberts, Aug. 16, 1986; 1 child, Alexander McRoberts. BA, DePauw U., 1964; MBA, Stanford U., 1966. Group mgr. new products Libby, McNeill and Libby, Chgo., 1966-70; sr. acct. exec. N. W. Ayer, Chgo., 1970-73; v.p. McCann-Erickson, San Francisco and L.A., 1973-81; v.p. mktg. and sales Chef America, Sylmar, Calif., 1981-84; v.p., dir. acct. mgmt. Hakuhodo Advt., L.A., 1984-86; gen. mgr. Four 'N Twenty, Tustin, Calif., 1986-91; mktg. cons. Santa Ana, Calif., 1991-95. Named Outstanding Young Men, Jr. C. of C., 1976. Republican. Home: 2007 Fruit St Santa Ana CA 92701

LESNICK, STEPHEN WILLIAM, artist. BA, Silvermine Coll. of Art, Art Career Sch., N.Y.; studied with Revington Arthur, Jon McClelland, Gail Symon, Herb Olson. Tchr. comml. and fine arts various locations; owner Lesnick Art Studio, Inc., Las Vegas, Nev., 1965—; art dir. Kelly-Reber Advt. Agy.; comml. artist, illustrator E.G. & G.; art editor, columnist Las Vegas Sun, 1971-90; art instr. Clark County C.C.; advisor on art tax fraud to FBI and IRS. Contbr. illustrations to numerous mags., including Readers Digest, Bus. Week, Newseek; exhibited in 31 one man shows; represented in pvt. and pub. permanent collections, including Burndy Libr. Arts and Scis., Norwalk, Conn.; designer Helldorado Medallions to commemorate Boulder Dam, 1971-80 series, Commerative Medallions Nev. State Mus., 50th Anniversary Gambling Medallion for State of Nev.; author (books) How to Draw, Figure Drawing; inventer Funny Brush, The Leaning Bridge, The Pen-Save, the Artist's Palette, The Artist Brush Holder. Recipient 1st and 2d ann. prize Conn. Religious Show, 1st Place award All New Eng. Show, purchase prize Barnum Festival, 1st place award Internat. Art Competition, Tokyo, 1st place and purchase prize Helldorado Western Art Show, 1st place prize designer Nev. Medallion for Franklin Mint Bicentennial Yr., 1987, The Lincoln Meml. Region I Painting award Nat. Arts for Parks. Office: Lesnick Art Studio Inc PO Box 71945 Las Vegas NV 89170-1945

LESONSKY, RIEVA, editor-in-chief; b. N.Y.C., June 20, 1952; d. Gerald and Muriel (Cash) L. BJ, U. Mo., 1974. Researcher Doubleday & Co., N.Y.C., 1975-78; researcher Entrepreneur Mag., L.A., 1978-80, rsch. dir., 1983-84, mng. editor, 1985-86, exec. editor, 1986-87; editor Entrepreneur Mag., Irvine, Calif., 1987-90; editor-in-chief Entrepreneur Mag. Bus. Start-Ups Entrepreneur Group, Irvine, Calif., 1990—; rsch. dir. LFP Inc., L.A., 1980-82; speaker, lect. in field. Editor: 184 Businesses Anyone Can Start, 1990, Complete Guide to Owning a Home-based Business, 1990, 168 More Businesses Anyone Can Start, 1991, 111 Businesses You Can Start for Under $10,000, 1991; contbr. articles to mags. Apptd. SBA Nat. Adv. Coun., 1994-96. Named Dist. Media Advocate of Yr., Small Bus. Adminstrn., 1993, Dist. Women in Bus. Advocate, Small Bus. Adminstrn., 1995. Mem. Women's Network for Entrepreneurial Tng. (bd. dirs., advisor, nat. steeri. Office: Entrepreneur Mag Group 2392 Morse Ave Irvine CA 92714-6234

LESSER, GERSHON MELVIN, physician, lawyer, medical and legal commentator; b. N.Y.C., Apr. 3, 1933; s. Herman and Dora (Kronfeld) L.; m. Michelle Elyse Lesser; children: Hadrian, Aaron, Jason. BA, UCLA, 1954; MD, U. So. Calif., 1958; JD, UWLA, 1977. Atty. in pvt. practice L.A., 1977-82; med. dir. Westside Hosp., Am. Med. Internat., L.A., 1964-71; pvt. prctice cardiology L.A., 1963-92; mem. pres.'s coun. Salk Inst., La Jolla, Calif.; broadcaster KGIL Radio, San Fernando Valley, 1984-92, KCRW-Nat. Pub. Radio, Santa Monica, Calif., 1980-94; med. broadcaster KTTV, Hollywood, Calif., 1984-86; med. dir. CD, L.A., 1978-89; adj. prof. law West L.A. Sch. Law, 1980; instr. regional medicine U. So. Calif. Sch. Medicine, 1978-80. Author: Growing Younger, 1987, When You Have Chest Pain, 1989; TV commentator Alive and Well, USA Cable, L.A., 1984-95. Fellow Am. Coll. Legal Medicine, Royal Soc. Health, Am. Coll. Angiology, Am. Geristrics Soc.; mem. Am. Acad. Preventive Medicine, Am. Coll. Thoracic Medicine, Soc. Internal Medicine, Phi Delta Epsilon. Office: 8230 Beverly Blvd Los Angeles CA 90048

LESSER, JOAN L., lawyer; b. L.A.. BA, Brandeis U., 1969; JD, U. So. Calif., 1973. Bar: Calif. 1973, U.S. Dist. Ct. (cen. dist.) Calif. 1974. Assoc. Irell and Manella, L.A., 1973-80, ptnr., 1980—; mem. planning com. Ann. Real Property Inst., Continuing Edn. of Bar, Berkeley, 1990—; speaker at profl. confs. Trustee Windward Sch.; grad. Leadership L.A., 1992. Mem. Orgn. Women Execs., Order of Coif. Office: Irell and Manella 1800 Avenue of the Stars Ste 900 Los Angeles CA 90067-4211

LESSER, WENDY, literary magazine editor, writer, consultant; b. Santa Monica, Calif., Mar. 20, 1952; d. Murray Leon Lesser and Millicent (Gerson) Dillon; m. Richard Rizzo, Jan. 18, 1985; 1 stepchild, Dov Antonio; 1 child, Nicholas. BA, Harvard U., 1973; MA, Cambridge (Eng.) U., 1975; PhD, U. Calif., Berkeley, 1982. Founding ptnr. Lesser & Ogden Assocs., Berkeley, 1977-81; founding editor The Threepenny Rev., Berkeley, 1980—; vis. lectr. U. Calif., Santa Cruz, 1983, 86, 90; Bellagio resident Rockefeller Found., Italy, 1984. Author: The Life Below the Ground, 1987, His Other Half, 1991, Pictures at an Execution, 1994; editor: Hiding in Plain Sight, 1993. Fellow NEH, 1983, 92, Guggenheim fellow, 1988. Democrat. Office: The Threepenny Rev PO Box 9131 Berkeley CA 94709-0131

LESTER, JOHN JAMES NATHANIEL, II (SEAN LESTER), engineer, environmental analyst, human rights activist; b. Houston, May 7, 1952; s. John James Nathaniel Lester and Margaret Louise (Tisdale) Sharp. Student, U. Tex., 1970, Lee Coll., 1971; AS, Grossmont Coll., 1979; BA in Behavioral Sci., Nat. U., 1987; y. Registered profl. stationary engr., Tex. Nuclear power specialist USN, various, 1971-77; microbiology lab. technician VA, San Diego, 1978; prin. engring. asst. San Diego Gas & Electric, 1979-85, engring. environ. analyst, 1985-88; owner Calif. Triad Gem & Mineral Co.; founder Ctr. for Creative Healing. Dir. logistics, mem. regional bd. Gary Hart Presdl. Campaign, San Diego, 1984; founding mem. Inlet Drug Crisis Ctr., Houston, 1970; vol. dir. Aid for Guatemalan Refugees and Orphans, 1988; vol. for Dali Lama, Tibetan Refugee Rights and Ceremonies, 1989; mem. bldg. com. Tibetan Sch. Medicine, Crestone, Colo.; mem. San Luis Valley Tibetan Project, Crestone; active Clinton Presdl. Campaign, 1992; founder Padma Tashi Ling Found. for Tibetan Studies, 1992—. Mem. ASME, IEEE (interim pres., founding mem. San Diego region Ocean Engring. Soc. 1984-85), Mensa, Assn. Humanistic Psychology, Amnesty Internat., Hunger Project, Earth Stewards, Human Rights Watch, Tibet Watch, Sierra Club. Buddhist. Home and Office: PO Box 710 Makawao HI 96768-0710

LETTS, J. SPENCER, federal judge; b. 1934. BA, Yale U., 1956; LLB, Harvard U., 1960. Commd. U.S. Army, 1956, advanced through grades to capt., resigned, 1965; pvt. practice law Fulbright & Jaworski, Houston, 1960-66, Troy, Malin, Loveland & Letts, L.A., 1973-74, Hedlund, Hunter & Lynch, L.A., 1978-82, Latham & Watkins, L.A., 1982-85; gen. counsel Teledyne, Inc., 1966-73, 75-78, legal cons., 1978-82; judge U.S. Dist. Ct. (cen. dist.) Calif., L.A., 1986—. Contbr. articles to profl. jours. Mem. ABA, Calif. State Bar, Tex. State Bar, L.A. Bar Assn., Houston Bar Assn. Office: US Dist Ct 312 N Spring St Los Angeles CA 90012-4701*

LETZ, EILEEN KORBER, community health nurse; b. Custer, Mont., Dec. 31, 1916; d. Louis Charles and Gertrude Helen (Jackman) Korber; m. Arthur P. Letz, May 17, 1941 (dec.); children: Philip, Richard, Nancy. RN, Bozeman Deaconess Hosp., 1939; BSN, Mont. State U., 1964; MPH, U. Hawaii, 1968. RN, Mont. Supr. surg. fl. Billings (Mont.) Deaconess Hosp., 1952-56; community health nurse Yellowstone County, Billings, 1964-67, 68-70; community health nurse Ft. Peck reservation Indian Health Svc., Poplar, Mont., 1970-72; community health nurse Crow reservation Indian Health Svc., Crow Agency, Mont., 1972-75; nursing cons., program mgr. commun. helath nursing Indian Health Svc., Billings, 1975-82, ret., 1982. Mem. Mont. league for Nursing (bd. dirs. 1980-84, 91-92, v.p. 1984-91), Am. Assn. Ret. Persons. Democrat. Seventh Day Adventist. Home: 2316 Miles Ave Billings MT 59102-4705

LEUBE, KURT RUDOLPH, economics educator; b. Salzburg, Austria, June 27, 1943; came to U.S., 1983; s. G. Werner and Elfriede (Haselhof) L.; m. Elisabeth A. Payer, Dec. 30, 1968; children: Philipp, Michael, Christian, Jakob. BA, Gymnasium, Salzburg, 1963; AJD, U. Salzburg, 1971. Sr. researcher, univ. assoc. to F.A. von Hayek IFN at U. of Salzburg, 1968-77; sr. economist, resident scholar Austrian Enterprize Inst., Vienna, 1977-83; prof. econs. Calif. State U., Hayward, 1984—; rsch. fellow Hoover Instn. Stanford Univ., 1983—; dir. Internat. Inst. for Austrian Econs., Stanford, 1988—; vis. prof. Université d'Aix en Provence, Institut Für Liberalismus, Vienna, 1992; editor-in-chief Internat. Carl Menger Libr., Munich, 1978; leading authority in Austrian economics. Editor: Essence of Hayek, 1985, Essays in Honor of F.A. von Hayek, 1985, The Political Economy of Freedom, Essays in Honor of F.A. von Hayek, 1985, Essence of Friedman, 1987, Essence of Stigler, 1988, Marktwirtschaft Aufsätze F.A. von Hayek zum Gedenken, 1992; contbr. articles and essays to profl. jours. Recipient numerous awards including F. Leroy Hill award Inst. for Humane Studies, George Mason U., 1984. Mem. Libertas Internat. (founding mem. 1983), Inst. Europeum, Ludwig Erhard Stiftung, Wirtschaftsforum der Führungskräfte, Mont Pelerin Soc. (awards). Office: Stanford U Hoover Instn Stanford CA 94305

LEUNG, DAVID WAI-HUNG, molecular biologist; b. Hong Kong, Aug. 2, 1951; came to U.S., 1969; BA, Whittier Coll., 1973; PhD, U. Ill., 1978. Post-doctoral fellow U. B.C., Vancouver, Can., 1978-80; sr. scientist Genentech, Inc., South San Francisco, Calif., 1980-92; dir. molecular biology Cell Therapeutics, Inc., Seattle, 1992—. Office: Cell Therapeutics Inc 201 Elliott Ave W Seattle WA 98119-4230

LEUNG, KASON KAI CHING, computer specialist; b. Hong Kong, July 2, 1962; came to U.S., 1963; s. Patrick Kin Man and Esther Mo Chee (Shum) L. BA in Computer Sci., U. Calif., 1984. Microcomputer specialist Coopers & Lybrand, San Francisco, 1985-87; freelance computer specialist San Francisco, 1988-90; computer applications specialist T.Y. Lin Internat., San Francisco, 1990-92; tech. specialist ZD Labs., Foster City, Calif., 1993-94; tech. analyst PC Mag., Foster City, Calif., 1995—. Mem. Assn. for Computing Machinery. Home: 90 Stanford Heights Ave San Francisco CA 94127-2318

LEUNG, PUI-TAK (PETER LEUNG), physicist, educator, researcher; b. Macau, China, Aug. 23, 1953; s. Chin-Pang and Hon-Yin (Luk) L.; m. Pei-Yi Feng, Apr. 19, 1985; children: Jonathan Li-Chung, Rosalyn Roh-Shi. BSc, Chinese U. Hong Kong, 1976; MEd, MA, SUNY, Buffalo, 1979, PhD, 1982. Assoc. prof. physics Tamkang U., Tamsui, Taiwan, 1982-85; rsch. assoc. SUNY, Buffalo, 1985-88; asst. prof. physics Portland (Oreg.) State U., 1988-91, assoc. prof. physics, 1991—; affiliate staff scientist Pacific Northwest Labs., Richland, Wash., 1994—; cons. in biosensor rsch. Amersham Internat. plc, Buckinghamshire, Eng., 1989-92; vis. scientist in laser rsch. IBM Almaden Rsch. Ctr., San Jose, Calif., 1991-92; invited speaker Soc. Photo-Optical Instrumentation Engrs. conf., 1989; invited visitor Pollards Wood Labs., Eng., 1989. Contbr. 51 articles to profl. jours.; presenter in field. Equipment grantee Amersham Internat. plc, 1989, IBM, 1992; recipient Outstanding Jr. Faculty award Portland State U., 1992; Faculty fellow U.S. Dept. of Energy, 1995. Mem. Am. Phys. Soc. Home: 3342 NW Brandt Pl Portland OR 97229-8508 Office: Portland State University Dept of Physics PO Box 751 Portland OR 97207-0751

LEUS MCFARLEN, PATRICIA CHERYL, water chemist; b. San Antonio, Mar. 12, 1954; d. Norman W. and Jacqueline S. (Deason) Leus; m. Randy N. McFarlen (div.); 1 child, Kevin Bryant. AA, Highline Community Coll., 1974; BS in Chemistry, Eastern Wash. U., 1980. Cert. operator grade II water treatment and distbn., grade I wastewater and collection operator Ariz. Dept. Environ. Quality; cert. in asbestos identification through microscopy. Lab. technician, oil analyst D.A. Lubricant, Vancouver, Wash., 1982-83; plant chemist Navajo Generating Sta., Page, Ariz., 1983-92, chemist, 1992—. Sci. judge Page Schs. Sci. Project Fair, 1985, 91; chemist Navajo Generating Sta./Page Sch. Career Day, 1986, 89, 90; life mem. Girl Scouts Am. Mem. Sigma Kappa (life mem., treas. 1976-78). Methodist. Office: Navajo Generating Sta Lab Svcs Dept PO Box W Page AZ 86040-1949

LEUTHE, ANDREW PETER, manufacturing company executive; b. Naha, Japan, Nov. 29, 1961; s. Alvin William and Kinuyo (Yamauchi) L.; m. Dedra Lee Lewis, Mar. 31, 1985; children: Robert Frank Wong, Aaron Mathew, Alan Peter. AAS, Erie C.C., Williamsville, N.Y., 1981. Dir. market mgmt. Mitchell Internat., San Diego, 1985—. contbr. articles to profl. jours. Div. dir. Continental Little League, Escondido, Calif., 1988. Mem. Am. Nat. Standards Inst., Colision Industry Elec. Commerce Assn. (co-chmn. 1993-94), Ivans (adv. bd. 1994—). Republican. Roman Catholic. Office: Mitchell Internat 9889 Willow Creek Rd San Diego CA 92131-1119

LEUTY, GERALD JOHNSTON, osteopathic physician and surgeon; b. Knoxville, Iowa, July 23, 1919; s. John William and Mable Reichard (Johnston) L.; m. Martha L. Weymouth, Jan. 24, 1940 (div. 1957); children: Maxine Joanne, Robert James, Gerald Johnston Jr., Karl Joseph; m. Norma Jean Hindman, Dec. 30, 1969; children: Barbara Jayne, Patrick Jack. AB, Kemper Mil. Sch., Boonville, Mo., 1939; postgrad., Drake U., Des Moines, 1944-45; DO, Des Moines Coll. Osteopathy, 1949; embalmer, Coll. Mortuary Sci., St. Louis, 1941. Mortician/embalmer Cauldwell-McJihon Funeral Home, Des Moines, 1939-40; aero. engr. Boeing Aircraft Co., Wichita, Kans., 1941-42; osteopathic physician and surgeon Knoxville (Iowa) Osteopathic Clinic, 1949-56; dir. Leuty Osteopathic Clinic, Earlham, Iowa, 1957-77; osteopathic physician and surgeon in pvt. practice Santa Rosa, Calif., 1977—; prof. clin. med. Coll. Osteopathic Medicine of the Pacific, Pomona, Calif., 1985—. With U.S. Army, 1942-46. Named Physician of the Yr., 6th Dist. Iowa Osteopathic Soc., 1975, Disting. Leadership award, Am. Biog. Inst., 1988, others. Fellow Internat. Co.. Angiologists; mem. Am. Osteopathic Assn. (ho. of dels., life mem. 1989), Iowa Osteopathic Soc. (pres. 6th dist. 1974), Soc. Osteopathic Physicians, No. Calif. Osteopathic Med. Soc. (pres. 1981), Osteopathic Physicians and Surgeons of Calif. (pres. 1982), Am. Acad. Osteopathy (chmn. component socs. com. 1988, Calif. div. pres. 1987), North Coast Osteopathic Med. Assn. (pres. 1992), Am. Med. Soc. Vienna (life mem.), Am. Legion (6th dist. comdr. 1974-75), Lions (pres. 1946). Republican. Presbyterian. Home: 5835 La Cuesta Dr Santa Rosa CA 95409-3914

LEVADA, WILLIAM JOSEPH, archbishop; b. Long Beach, Calif., June 15, 1936; s. Joseph and Lorraine (Nunez) L. B.A., St. John's Coll., Camarillo, Calif., 1958; S.T.L., Gregorian U., Rome, 1962, S.T.D., 1971. Ordained priest Roman Cath. Ch., 1961, consecrated bishop, 1983. Assoc. pastor Archdiocese of L.A., 1962-67; prof. theology St. John's Sem., Camarillo, Calif., 1970-76; ofcl. Doctrinal Congregation, Vatican City, Italy, 1976-82; exec. dir. Calif. Cath. Conf., Sacramento, 1982-84; aux. bishop, vicar for Santa Barbara County, 1983-86; archbishop Archdiocese of Portland in Oreg., 1986—. Trustee Cath. U. Am.; chmn. bd. dirs. Pope John XXIII Med.-Moral Rsch. and Edn. Ctr. Mem. Nat. Conf. Cath. Bishops (com. on doctrine), U.S. Cath. Conf., Cath. Theol. Soc. Am., Canon Law Soc. Am. Office: Archdiocese of Portland 2838 E Burnside St Portland OR 97214-1830

LEVENSON, COREY HOWARD, chemist; b. N.Y.C., Aug. 26, 1954; s. Edgar Alan and Joanne Leah (Schriver) L.; m. Katherine Mary Ovitt, Feb. 14, 1982; children: Lauren Elyse, Maia Katherine. BS, Hampshire Coll., 1976; PhD, U. Calif., San Francisco, 1981. Regents fellow U. Calif., 1976-80; assoc. scientist Cetus Corp., Emeryville, Calif., 1981-84, scientist, mgr. DNA synthesis lab., 1984-88, sr. scientist, assoc. dir. chemistry dir., 1988-90, dir. nucleic acid chemistry, 1990-91; sr. rsch. investigator Roche Molecular Systems, Alameda, Calif., 1991—; adj. prof. dept. pharm. chemistry U. Calif. San Francisco, 1994—. Contbr. numerous articles to profl. jours.; patentee in oligonucleotide functionalizing reagents, precursor to nucleic acid probe, others. Mem. AAAS, Am. Chem. Soc., Am. Assn. Clin. Chemistry, N.Y. Acad. Scis.

LEVENSTEIN, ROSLYN M., advertising consultant, writer; b. N.Y.C., Mar. 26, 1920; d. Leo Rapoport and Stella Schimmel Rosenberg; m. Justin Seides, June 7, 1943 (div. 1948); 1 child, Leland Seides.; m. Lawrence Levenstein, June 25, 1961. BA in Advt., NYU, 1940. Sr. v.p., assoc. creative dir. Young and Rubicam, Inc., N.Y.C., 1962-79; cons. Young and Rubicam, Inc., Los Angeles and San Diego, 1979-83; advt. cons., writer mag. articles La Jolla, Calif., 1979—. Creator: Excedrin Headache commls. (Andy awards 1967, 68, 69), I'm Only Here for the Beer (Cannes award 1970, Clio Jury award 1970). Recipient: Silver Lion award Cannes Film Festival, 1968, multiple advt. awards U.S. and Eng.; named one of YWCA Women of Yr., 1978. Mem. Charter 100, Women's Com. Brandies U., Nat. Pen Women, San Dieto Writers & Editors Guild. Home: 5802 Corral Way La Jolla CA 92037-7423

LE VEQUE, MATTHEW KURT, public affairs and marketing consultant; b. Los Angeles, May 24, 1958; s. Edward Albert and Vera Eleanora (Behne) LeV. BA in Polit. Sci., UCLA, 1981. Reapportionment cons. Calif. State Legislature, Sacramento, 1981; cons. Berman and D'Agostino Campaigns, Inc., L.A., 1982-91; coord. L.A. Olympic com., 1984; spl. asst. Congressmen H. Waxman and H. Berman, Calif., 1982-85; cons. The Helin Orgn., Newport Beach, Calif., 1984-86; sr. cons. Calif. State Senate, L.A. and Sacramento, 1985-92; campaign fin. coord Levine for U.S. Senate, L.A., 1991; sr. assoc. Pacific West Comms. Group, L.A., 1992-93; chief staff L.A. State Assemblyman Terry Friedman, 1993-94; pub. affairs and mktg. exec. Rogers & Assocs., L.A., 1995—. Active numerous local and nat. Dem. polit. campaigns. Office: 531 24th St Hermosa Beach CA 90254-2618

LEVER, JANET RAE, sociology educator, television talk show host, columnist; b. St. Louis, Dec. 5, 1946; d. Harry H. and Sophia (Goldberg) L. BA summa cum laude, Wash. U., St. Louis, 1968; MPhil, Yale U., 1971, PhD in Sociology, 1974. Instr. Yale U., New Haven, 1974; asst. prof. sociology Northwestern U., Evanston, Ill., 1974-82; vis. asst. prof. U. Calif. San Diego, La Jolla, 1983-85; vis. lectr. UCLA, 1985-87; cons. The RAND Corp., Santa Monica, Calif., 1987—; vis. lectr. U. So. Calif., 1989; assoc. prof. Calif. State U., L.A., 1990—; sr. analyst readers' sex survey Playboy Mag., Chgo., 1981-83; cons. Playboy Cable Channel, L.A., talk show host, 1983-87; numerous TV appearances as expert on health aspects of sexuality; author and analyst readers' sex surveys The Advocate, L.A., 1994, 95. Author: Soccer Madness, 1983, 95; co-author: Women at Yale, 1971; columnist "Sex & Health", Glamour mag., 1991—; contbr. articles to mags. and profl. jours. Pew Health Policy Career fellow, 1987-88; grantee Am. Found. AIDS Rsch., 1988-89. Mem. Am. Sociol. Assn., Soc. Sci. Study of Sexuality, Phi Beta Kappa. Office: RAND Corp SP/7 1700 Main St Santa Monica CA 90401-3208

LEVETON, IAN SINCLAIR, civil engineer; b. Birmingham, Eng., Nov. 27, 1942; came to U.S., 1953; s. Eric Karl and Zena (Altman) L. BA in Physics and Econs., NYU, 1965; cert. of achievement, Orange Coast Coll., Costa Mesa, Calif., 1990. Computer programmer trainee Bklyn. Union Gas Co., 1969; computer programmer Elizabeth Arden Sales Corp., N.Y.C., 1970; electronics expeditor Bendix Navigation & Controls, Teterboro, N.J., 1971; inventory control supr. Roman Products Inc., South Hackensack, N.J., 1972; nuclear mech. engr. Pub. Svc. N.J., Newark, 1973; mech. engr. Chemplant Designs divsn. DuPont, N.Y.C., 1974-78, Holmes and Narver, Inc., Orange, Calif., 1978-82; tech. writer nuclear safety So. Calif. Edison, Rosemead, Calif., 1983-85; civil engr. tech. City of Santa Ana, Calif., 1985—; cons. Islian Assocs., Teaneck, N.J., 1970-71. Mem. Teaneck Bicentennial Com., 1976; coord. United Way, City Pub. Works Agy., Santa Ana, 1992. Mem. KP (sec. 1974-76). Home: 19302 Steven Ln Huntington Beach CA 92646-2711

LEVI, DAVID F., federal judge; b. 1951. BA, Harvard U., MA, 1973; JD, Stanford U. Bar: Calif. 1983. U.S. atty. ea. dist. State of Calif., Sacramento, 1986-90; judge U.S. Dist. Ct. (ea. dist.) Calif., 1990—; chmn. 9th Cir. Task Force on Race, Religious and Ethnic Fairness, 1994—. Adv. com. on Civil Rules, 1994-95; chair 9th cir. task force on Race, Religious and Ethnic Fairness, 1994-95. Office: 2504 Fed Bldg 650 Capitol Mall Sacramento CA 95814-4708

LEVI, HERBERT A., deputy city manager, consultant; b. Dunkirk, Ind., May 31, 1931; s. Lawrence Warren and Virginia Roselyn (Avery) L.; m. Virginia Elizabeth Webster, Dec. 7, 1950; children: Victor Herbert, Michael David, Demetrius Titus. BA, Ball State U., Muncie, Ind., 1952; MPA, Calif. State U., Long Beach, 1978. Cert. tchr., Calif. Debit mgr. Mammoth Life Ins. Co., Muncie, 1951-53; chemist City of L.A. Pub. Works, 1954-55, sr. indsl. waste inspector, 1959-66, safety engring. asst., 1967-69, sr. personnel analyst, 1969-71, contract compliance officer, 1971-75; adminstrv. analyst III City of Long Beach (Calif.) City Mgr., 1975-78; personnel analyst III City of Long Beach Personnel, 1978-82; adminstrv. officer Long Beach Pub. Libr., 1982-90; dep. city mgr., exec. dir. police complaint commn. City of Long Beach, 1990-91; ret., 1991—, cons. to bus. and govt., 1993—; mem. policy bd. Ctr. for Pub. Policy and Adminstrn., Calif. State U., 1986-90. Author: Equal Opportunity Compliance for Cities, 1978; co-author: Contract Compliance Manual, 1976. Founder Vet. Stadium Citizen's Com., Long Beach, Calif., 1983; mem. Lakewood (Calif.) High Sch. Community Adv. Coun., 1974; chair Hamilton High Sch. Community Adv. Coun., L.A., 1969; mem. KLON-FM 88 Community Adv. Bd., Long Beach, 1985. Recipient Excellence in Performance award City of L.A. Bd. Pub. Works, 1977, Employee of Yr. award City of Long Beach, Personnel, 1981. Mem. Am. Soc. Pub. Adminstrn., Internat. Personnel Mgmt. Assn., Equal Opportunity Compliance Officers Assn. (pres., co-founder 1971-77), So. Calif. Personnel Mgmt. Assn. (v.p. programs 1983-84), Long Beach Mgmt. Club, Pi Alpha Alpha (v.p. 1989-91). Home and Office: 5153 E Hanbury St Long Beach CA 90808-1845

LEVI, STEVEN C(HANNING), freelance writer, historian; b. Chgo., Dec. 9, 1948; s. Mario and Janice (Houghton) L. BA in History, U. Calif.-Davis, 1970; MA in History, San Jose State U., 1973; Teaching Credential, U. Calif., Riverside, 1972. Hist. researcher Mus. Comparative Zoology, Harvard U., 1972-73; part-time instr. Chapman Coll., 1974—, various mil. bases, Alaska, 1976-77, instr. Elmendorf AFB, Alaska, 1974—; staff cons. Ernst & Ernst, 1978; research analyst State of Alaska, Alaska Pub. Utilities Commn., 1977-78, Div. Energy and Power Devel., 1978-79; dir. pub. affairs Resource Devel. Council, Anchorage, 1979-80; coordinator Alaska Trade Shows, Inc. and Am. Diabetes Assn., Anchorage, 1980; editor Parsnackle Press, Anchorage, 1981—; legis. aide Alaska Senate and Ho. of Reps., 1981-84; free-lance writer, Anchorage, 1984—; part time instr. Victor Valley Coll., Calif., Riverside Unified Sch. Dist.; reading and math. cons. Appleton-Century-Crofts, 1971-73. Author poetry: Alaskan Phantasmagoria, 1978; The Last Raven, 1979; The Phantom Bowhead, 1979; Fish-Fed Maize, 1980; We Alaskans, 1980; author: Sourdough Journalist, 1981, The Committee of Vigilance of 1916: A Case Study in Official Hysteria, 1983, Our National Tapestry, 1986, The Pacific Rim, The Emerging Giants, 1988, Deadwood Dick, 1988, The Alaska Traveler, 1989, Making It, Personal Survival in the Corporate World, 1990, Bush Flying, 1992, A Treasury of Alaskan Humor, 1993; also articles, short stories. Home: PO Box 241467 Anchorage AK 99524-1467

LEVIN, ALAN SCOTT, pathologist, allergist, immunologist; b. Chgo., Jan. 12, 1938; s. John Bernhard and Betty Ruth (Margulis) L.; m. Vera S. Byers, June 15, 1971. BS in Chemistry, U. Ill., Champaign-Urbana, 1960; MS in Biochemistry, U. Ill., Chgo., 1963, MD, 1964; JD, Golden Gate U., 1995. Diplomate Am. Bd. Allergy and Immunology, Am. Bd. Pathology. Intern Children's Hosp. Med. Ctr., Boston, 1964-65; adj. instr. pediatrics U. Calif., San Francisco, 1971-72, asst. prof. immunology dept. dermatology, 1972-78, adj. assoc. prof., 1978-88; dir. lab. immunology U. Calif. & Kaiser Found. Rsch. Inst. Joint Program Project, San Francisco, 1971-74; attending physician dept. medicine Mt. Zion/U. Calif. San Francisco Hosps., 1971—; dir. div. immunology Western Labs., Oakland, Calif., 1974-77; med. dir. MML/Solano Labs. Div. Chemed-W.R. Grace, Inc., Berkeley, Calif., 1977-

79; med. dir. Levin Clin. Labs., Inc., San Francisco, 1979-81; pvt. practice San Francisco, 1981—. Contbr. articles to profl. jours., chpts. to books. Lt. USN, 1966-69, Vietnam. Decorated Bronze Star, Silver Star, 4 Air medals; Harvard Med. Sch. traineeship grantee, 1964, USPHS hematology tng. grantee U. Calif., San Francisco Med. Ctr., 1969-71; recipient Faculty Rsch. award Am. Cancer Soc., 1970-74. Fellow Coll. Am. Pathologists, Am. Coll. Emergency Physicians, Am. Soc. Clin. Pathologists; mem. AMA, Am. Acad. Allergy and Immunology, Am. Coll. Allergy and Immunology, Am. Assn. Clin. Chemists, Am. Acad. Environ. Medicine, Calif. Med. Assn., San Francisco Med. Soc. Jewish.

LEVIN, ALVIN IRVING, composer, educator; b. N.Y.C., Dec. 22, 1921; s. David and Frances (Schloss) L.; m. Beatrice Van Loon, June 5, 1976 (div. 1981). BMus in Edn., U. Miami (Fla.), 1941; MA, Calif. State U., L.A., 1955; EdD with honors, UCLA, 1968. Composer, arranger for movies, TV, theater Allied Artists, Eagle-Lion Studios, Los Angeles, 1945-65; tng. and supervising tchr. Los Angeles City Schs., 1957-65, adult edn. instr., 1962-63; research specialist Los Angeles Office Supt. Edn., 1965-67; asst. prof. edn. research Calif. State U., Los Angeles, 1968; asst. prof. elem. edn. Calif. State U., Northridge, 1969-73; self-employed, Northridge, 1973—; founder, pres. Alvin Irving Levin Philanthropic Found., 1973—; ordained to ministry Ch. of Mind Sci., 1975; founder, pres. Divine Love Ch.-An Internat. Metaphys. Ch., 1977—. Meet Your New Personality, A Mind Expansion Program, 1975-77. Bd. overseers Calif. Sch. Profl. Psychology, 1974—; gen. chmn., producer Fiftieth Anniversary Pageant of North Hollywood Park, 1977. Author: My Ivory Tower, 1950, Symposium: Values in Kaleidoscope, 1973, (TV series) America, America!, 1978-79, (docudrama) One World, 1980; composer: Symphony for Strings, 1984, Tone Poem for Male Chorus and Brass, 1984, Hymn to the United Nations for chorus and symphony orch., 1991, Hiawatha Suite for Chorus and Symphony Orch., 1994, (music-drama) Happy Land, 1971, (musical plays) A Tale of Two Planets, 1988, Blueprint for a New World Model, 1991; producer UN Festival Calif. State U., Northridge, 1991; compiler, contbr. U.S. Dept. Edn. reports Adult Counseling and Guidance, 1967, Parent Child Preschool Program, 1967, English Classes for Foreign Speaking Adult Professionals, 1967, Blueprint for New World Order, 1991. Recipient plaque State of Calif., 1977, Golden Merit medal Rep. Presdl. Task Force, 1985. Named to Rep. Task Force Presdl. Commn., 1986. Mem. Nat. Soc. for Study Edn., AAUP, Am. Statis. Assn., Internat. Council Edn. for Teaching, Los Angeles World Affairs Council, Internat. Platform Assn., World Federalist Assn. (pres. San Fernando Valley chpt. 1991—), North Hollywood C. of C. (dir. 1976—), Phi Delta Kappa. Home and Office: 5407 Colfax Ave Apt 223 North Hollywood CA 91601-5209

LEVIN, BARRY RAYMOND, rare book dealer; b. Phila., June 11, 1946; s. Sidney and Bertha (Zwerman) L.; m. Sally Ann Fudge, Aug. 19, 1983. Student, Santa Monica City Coll., 1964-65. Various aerospace positions McDonnell Douglas, AstroPeen, 1967-72; owner Barry R. Levin Sci. Fiction & Fantasy Lit., 1973—; cons. sci. fiction, fantasy and horror films, 1976—. Author: (rare book catalogs) Titles from the Back Room, 1981, Great Works and Rarities of Science Fiction and Fantasy, 1982, One Small Step, 1983, Newsletters, 1980—, others; contbr. articles to profl. jours. With U.S. Army, 1965-67. Mem. Antiquarian Booksellers Assn. Am., Am. Booksellers Assn., Bibliog. Soc. Am., Bibliog. Soc. Great Britain, New Eng. Sci. Fiction Assn., So. Calif. Booksellers Assn., Internat. League Antiquarian Booksellers, Internat. Assn. of the Fantastic in the Arts, Internat. Platform Assn., Sci. Fiction Writers Am., Horror Writers Am., Manuscript Soc., Sci. Fiction Rsch. Assn., Assn. Sci. Fiction and Fantasy Artists, Lewis Carroll Soc., others. Jewish. Office: Barry R Levin Sci Fiction & Fantasy Lit 720 Santa Monica Blvd Santa Monica CA 90401-2602

LEVIN, BARRY SHERWIN, physician; b. Dec. 17, 1940. BS in Hisotry, U. Wis., 1962; MD, U. Ill., 1966. Diplomate Am. Bd. Internal Medicine, Am. Bd. Nephrology. Intern then resident U. Ill. Rsch. and Edn. Hosp., Chgo., 1966-68; resident U. Calif., San Francisco, 1967-68, asst. clin. prof. medicine, 1975-82; fellow Peter Brent Brigham Hosp., Boston, 1969-71; asst. prof. medicine U. Chgo., 1974-75; med. dir. transplantation program Calif. Pacific Med. Ctr., San Francisco, 1979—; med. dir. Calif. Transplant Donor Network, 1987-88; staff physician Andrews AFB, Md., 1971-73, Washingotn Hosp., Calif. Pacific Med. Ctr., San Francisco, 1975—; assoc. attending physician, dir. Michael Reese Hosp., Chgo., 1974-75. Contbr. articles to profl. jours. NIH fellow, 1969-71. Mem. Am. Soc. Nephrology, Am. Soc. Transplant Physicians (pres. 1988-89), Internat. Soc. Nephrology, Transplantation Soc., Alpha Omega Alpha. f. Office: Calif Pacific Med Ctr 2340 Clay St San Francisco CA 94115-1932

LEVIN, HAL ALAN, psychiatrist; b. Bklyn., Feb. 13, 1935; s. David and Rose M. (Rosen) L.; children of former marriage: Julie Levin Keith, Susan Levin Davis, Mark D. Levin; m. Sharon Greenleaf, Feb. 9, 1973; children: Anne Levin Warrick, Julie Elizabeth, Alisa M., Kimberly L. Grimes, Christopher Lenk. BS, Roosevelt U., 1958; MD, Tulane Med. Sch., New Orleans, 1967. Diplomate Am. Bd. Psychiatry & Neurology, 1982, Am. Bd. Forensic Examiners, 1995. Intern Norfolk (Va.) Gen. Hosp., 1967-68; resident in psychiatry Sheppard & Enoch Pratt Hosp., Towson, Md., 1968-70, Crownsville (Md.) Hosp., 1970-71; fellow in forensic psychiatry U. So. Calif., L.A., 1983-84; staff psychiatrist Atascadero (Calif.) State Hosp., 1971-72; pvt. practice psychiatry San Bernardino, Calif., 1972-85; asst. prof. clin. psychiatry Mich. State U., East Lansing, 1985-86; asst. dir. mental health State of Mich., Lansing, 1985-86; dir. mental health State of Ariz., Phoenix, 1986-87; pvt. practice psychiatry Tempe, Ariz., 1987—; cons. psychiatrist San Bernardino County Hosp., 1972-85, San Bernardino Superior Ct., 1972-85; dir. Desert Valley Clinic, Apple Valley, Calif., 1973-80; med. dir. Big Bear (Calif.) Psychiat. Clinic, 1980-84; med. dir. Ctr. for Behavioral Health, Tempe, 1989—. cons. Jewish Family Svcs., Tempe, 1990—, Interfaith Counseling, Mesa, Ariz., 1991—. Mem. AMA, Am. Psychiat. Assn., Ariz. Med. Assn., Am. Acad. Psychiatry & the Law, Am. Bd. Forensic Examiners, Friends of Phoenix Symphony. Democrat. Office: 5410 S Lakeshore Dr # 103 Tempe AZ 85283-2171

LEVIN, JACK, physician, educator, biomedical investigator; b. Newark, Oct. 11, 1932; s. Joseph and Anna (Greengold) L.; m. Francine Corthesy, Apr. 13, 1975. B.A. magna cum laude, Yale U., 1953, M.D. cum laude, 1957. Diplomate: Am. Bd. Internal Medicine. Intern in medicine Grace-New Haven Hosp., 1957-58, asst. resident in medicine, 1960-62; chief resident in medicine Yale-New Haven Med. Ctr., 1964-65; clin. assoc. Nat. Cancer Inst., Bethesda, Md., 1958-60; fellow in hematology Johns Hopkins U. Sch. Medicine and Hosp., Balt., 1962-64, mem. faculty, 1965-82, prof. medicine, 1978-82; prof. lab. medicine, prof. medicine U. Calif. Sch. Medicine, San Francisco, 1982—; dir. hematology lab. and blood bank San Francisco VA Med. Ctr., 1982-93, dir. flow cytometry facility, 1987-90; cons. in field. Author: (with P.D. Zieve) Disorders of Hemostasis, 1976; editor: (with E. Cohen and F.B. Bang) Biomedical Applications of the Horseshoe Crab (Limulidae), 1979, (with S.W. Watson and T.J. Novitsky) Endotoxins and Their Detection with the Limulus Amebocyte Lysate Test, 1982, Detection of Bacterial Endotoxins with The Limulus Amebocyte Lysate Test, 1987, (with others) Bacterial Endotoxins. Structure, Biomedical Significance, and Detection with the Limulus Amebocyte Lysate Test, 1985, Megakaryocyte Development and Function, 1986, Bacterial Endotoxins. Pathophysiological Effects, Clinical Significance, and Pharmacological Control, 1988, Molecular Biology and Differentiation of Megakaryocytes, 1990, Bacterial Endotoxins: Cytokine Mediators and New Therapies for Sepsis, 1991, Bacterial Endotoxin: Recognition and Effector Mechanisms, 1993, Bacterial Endotoxins: Basic Science to Anti-Sepsis Strategies, 1994; mem. editorial bd. Blood Cells, Jour. Endotoxin Rsch.; contbr. numerous articles to profl. jours; developer (with F.B. Bang) Limulus test for bacterial endotoxins. Mem. Yale Alumni Schs. Com. for Md., 1967-82, for San Francisco, 1986—; mem. sci. adv. bd. Nat. Aquarium, Balt., 1978-82; mem. corp. Marine Biol. Lab., 1965—; trustee Marine Biol. Lab., 1988-93. Served with USPHS, 1958-60. Markle scholar, 1968-73; recipient USPHS Rsch. Career Devel. award, 1970-75; Royal Soc. Medicine fellow Oxford (Eng.) U., 1972; Josiah Macy Jr. Found. faculty scholar, 1978-79; Frederik B. Bang award for rsch. in bacterial endotoxins, 1986. Fellow ACP; mem. Am. Soc. Hematology, Am. Soc. Clin. Investigation, Internat. Soc. Hematology, Internat. Soc. Explt. Hematology, Am. Soc. Investigative Pathology, Am. Fedn. Clin. Rsch., Soc. Exptl. Biology and Medicine, Internat. Endotoxin Soc., So. Soc. Clin. Investigation, Western Assn. Physicians, Soc. Invertebrate Pathology, Soc. Analytical Cytology, Cell Kinetics Soc., Calif. Acad. Medicine, Phi Beta Kappa, Sigma Xi. Clubs: 14 W Hamilton St, Tudor and Stuart; Yale (San Francisco).

LEVIN, WILLIAM EDWARD, lawyer; b. Miami, Fla., June 13, 1954; s. Harold A. and Phyllis (Wolfson) L.; m. Mary Catherine Egan, June 25, 1994. Student, Conn. Coll., 1972-74; BA, Emory U., Atlanta, 1976; JD, U. Miami, 1979. Bar: Fla. 1979, Calif. 1982; lic. real estate broker, Calif. Distbr. N.Y. Times, Atlanta, 1975-76; legis. intern Congressman William Lehman, Washington, 1974; law clk. Superior Ct. Hillsborough County, Tampa, Fla., 1974; legal asst./law clk. U. Miami Sch. Law, 1977-78; law clk. Shevin, Shapo & Shevin, Miami, 1977-79; assoc. Law Offices of John Cyril Malloy, Miami, 1979-82; assoc./ptnr. Flehr, Hohbach, Test, Albritton & Herbert, San Francisco, 1982-87; ptnr. Cooper, White & Cooper, San Francisco, 1987-88; trademark atty., pvt. practice San Francisco, 1988-92; broker/sole proprietor Levin Realty, San Francisco, 1987-92; of counsel Goldstein & Phillips, San Francisco, 1988-91, Hawes & Fischer, Newport Beach, Calif., 1992-93, Hilborne, Hawkin & Co., 1993-94; fo counsel Gauntlett & Assocs., Irvine, Calif., 1995—; co-chmn. trademark com. San Francisco Patent & Trademark Assn., 1985-86; moot ct. judge Giles Rich Moot Ct. Competition, San Francisco, 1986; ofcl. arbitrator Am. Arbitration Assn., 1987—; mem. exec. com. L.A. Complex Inns of Ct., 1994—; lectr. in field. Editorial bd. Trademark World, London, 1987-90, Trademark Reporter, 1987-89, 93—, Trademark Reporter Task Force, 1994—, San Francisco Atty., 1986-89; contbr. articles to profl. jours. Adm. bd. Californians for Missing Children, San Francisco, 1989-92, Hebrew Inst. Law, San Francisco, 1986-88; atty's. steering com. Jewish Community Fedn., San Francisco, 1987-88; fin. com. Temple Emanu-El, San Francisco, 1985-86. Mem. ABA, Internat. Trademark Assn., Orange County Bar Assn. (fed. ct. com.), Orange County Patent Law Assn. (trademark com.). Democrat. Jewish. Home and Office: 5405 Alton Pkwy Ste 554 Irvine CA 92714

LEVINE, ARNOLD MILTON, retired electrical engineer, documentary filmmaker; b. Preston, Conn., Aug. 15, 1916; s. Samuel and Florence May (Clark) L.; m. Bernice Eleanor Levich, Aug. 31, 1941; children: Mark Jeffrey, Michael Norman, Kevin Lawrence. BS in Radio Engring., Tri-State U., Angola, Ind., 1939, DSc (hon.), 1960; MS, U. Iowa, 1940. Head sound lab. CBS, N.Y.C., 1940-42; asst. engr., div. head ITT, N.Y.C. and Nutley, N.J., 1942-65; lab. head, lab. dir. ITT, San Fernando, Calif., 1965-71; v.p. aerospace, gen. mgr., sr. scientist ITT, Van Nuys, Calif., 1971-86; ret., 1986. Patentee fiber optics, radar, communications and TV fields. Past mem. bd. dirs., v.p., pres. Am. Jewish Congress, L.A. Recipient San Fernando Valley Engr. of Yr. award, 1968; Profl. designation Motion Picture Art & Scis., UCLA, 1983. Fellow IEEE (life), Soc. Motion Picture and TV Engrs., USCG Aux. (vice comdr. 1990-91, flotilla cmdr. 1992-94). Home: 10828 Fullbright Ave Chatsworth CA 91311-1737

LEVINE, BENJAMIN JACOB, secondary education educator; b. L.A., Jan. 14, 1940; s. Leo Harry and Rebecca (Haim) L. BA, U. Calif., L.A., 1962; MS, Calif. State U., Northridge, 1971. Calif. standard tchg. credential; Calif. C.C. instr. credential. Tchr. Hillel Acad., Beverly Hills, Calif., 1965-67, Mary Star of the Sea H.S., San Pedro, Calif., 1967-68, Alemany H.S., Mission Hills, Calif., 1968-70; part-time instr. Los Angeles Harbor Coll., Wilmington, Calif., 1971-79, Santa Monica (Calif.) Coll., 1974-79; programmer Gen. Motors-Hughes Electronics, El Segundo, Calif., 1979-88; tutor Colin McEwen H.S., Malibu, Calif., 1992-93; tchr. grades 8-12 Noonnoppi, La Crescenta, Calif., 1994—; grievance com. chair Santa Monica (Calif.) Coll. United Faculty Assn., 1976-78. Mem. Chamber Pot Soc. Home: 6261 Condon Ave Los Angeles CA 90056-1905 Office: Noonnoppi 1521 W Glenoaks Blvd Glendale CA 91201

LEVINE, DAVID KNUDSEN, economics educator; b. New Haven, Sept. 11, 1955; s. Robert Arthur and Carol (Knudsen) L.; m. Joyce Nira Davidson, Jan. 6, 1985; 1 child, Milena Davidson-Levine. BA in Math., UCLA, 1977, MA in Econs., 1977; PhD in Econs., MIT, 1981. Asst. prof. UCLA, 1981-86, assoc. prof., 1986-87, prof., 1987—; assoc. prof. U. Minn., Mpls., 1987-88; vis. prof. Calif. Inst. Tech., Pasadena, 1990-91; vis. scholar Cambridge (Eng.) U., 1985, Math. Scis. Rsch. Inst., Berkeley, Calif., 1985; visitor Fed. Res. Bank Mpls., 1987-88, U. Automa de Barcelona (Spain), 1990. Co-editor: Economic Theory, 1992—; assoc. editor Jour. Econ. Theory, 1987—. NSF grantee. Fellow Econometric Soc.; mem. Am. Econ. Assn., Ecometric Soc. Office: UCLA Dept Econs Los Angeles CA 90024

LEVINE, GENE NORMAN, sociology educator; b. Medford, Mass., May 15, 1930; s. Joseph Michael and Jennie (Herman) L.; children: John Albert, Edgar. AB summa cum laude, Boston U., 1952; PhD, Columbia U., 1959. Rsch. assoc. Bur. Applied Social Rsch., Columbia U., N.Y.C., 1954-64; project dir. UN Rsch. Inst. for Social Devel., Geneva, 1964-65, 66-68; prof. sociology UCLA, 1965-91, prof. emeritus, 1991—; adj. prof. U. N.Mex., Albuquerque, 1992—; mem. core faculty Walden U., Mpls., 1986—. Author: Workers Vote, 1962, Inducing Social Change in Developing Communities, 1967, Japanese American Community, 1981. Mem. bd. scholars Japanese Am. Nat. Mus., L.A., 1989—. Grantee Russell Sage Found., 1959-60, NIMH, 1965-75; rsch. scholar U. Judaism, L.A., 1976-80. Fellow Am. Sociol. Assn. (emeritus); mem. Am. Soc. for Sociol. Study Jewry (v.p. 1976-77), N.Mex. Psychoanalytic Soc., UCLA Emeriti Assn. Democrat. Home: (B37) 7303 Montgomery Blvd NE Albuquerque NM 87109-1512 Office: Dept Sociology U NM Albuquerque NM 87131

LEVINE, HOWARD HARRIS, health facility executive; b. Bklyn., Sept. 30, 1949; s. Roy and Lucille Levine. MPH in Hosp. Administrn., UCLA, 1974; BBA in Mktg., Baruch Coll., 1972. Adminstrv. resident Inter-Community Hosp., Covina, Calif., 1973-74; adminstrv. asst. to exec. dir. John F. Kennedy Med. Ctr., Edison, N.J., 1974-75; assoc. exec. dir. John F. Kennedy Med. Ctr., Edison, 1975-78; adminstr. Robert Wood Johnson Jr. Rehab. Inst., Edison, 1975-78; asst. dir. Beth Israel Med. Ctr., N.Y.C., 1978-81, assoc. dir., 1981-84, sr. assoc. dir. for ops., 1984-87; v.p. Staten Island Univ. Hosp., 1988, sr. v.p., chief oper. officer, 1988-91; exec. dir. Chapman Gen. Hosp., Orange, Calif., 1992—; v.p. OrNda Health Corp., 1994—; adj. lectr. dept. health care adminstrn. Bernard M. Baruch Coll./Mt. Sinai Sch. Medicine, N.Y.C., 1982—; Health Profl. adv. com. March of Dimes, 1992—; joint com. patient svcs. Calif. Hosp. Assn., 1992—; guest lectr. NYU Grad. Sch. Pub. Adminstrn., 1984-86; mem. mental health and substance abuse com. Greater N.Y. Health Adminstrn., 1988-91, profl. affairs and hosp. ops. com., 1989-91, chmn. com. on utilization rev., 1988-91; exec. and planning com. Hosp. Coun. So. Calif., 1992—, coun. on profl. practices N.J. Hosp. Assn., Princeton, 1977-78, dist. bd. Health Svcs. Adminstrn., N.Y.C., 1979-80. Mem. editorial adv. bd. The Malpractice Reporter, N.Y.C., 1980-88. Mem. ins. profl. adv. com. Fedn. Jewish Philanthropies Ins., 1981-87; mem. tech. adv. panel N.J. State Health Coordinating Coun., Princeton, 1976-78; bd. dirs. Meals-on-Wheels Program, Metuchen, Edison and Woodbridge, N.J., 1974-76; mem. budget com. United Crusade L.A., 1973-74. Fellow Am. Coll. Healthcare Execs.; mem. Coun. Hosp. Adminstrs. (pres. 1986-87), Met. Health Adminstrs. Assn. (pres. 1980-82), Am. Coll. Healthcare Mktg., Hosp. Adminstrs. Discussion Group. Home: 309 Bay Hill Dr Newport Beach CA 92660-5235 Office: OrNda Health Corp 2601 E Chapman Ave Orange CA 92669-3206

LEVINE, JOEL SETH, medical school and hospital administrator; b. Key West, Fla., Feb. 22, 1947; s. Carl Michael and Sophie Barbara (Halpern) L.; m. Frieda Zylberberg, Aug. 1, 1970; children: Daniel Ian, Steven Neal, Karyn Ann. BS, Bklyn. Coll., 1967; MD, SUNY, Bklyn., 1971. Asst. prof. medicine U. Colo., Denver, 1978-84; vice chmn. dept. medicine U. Colo., 1984-92, assoc. prof. medicine, 1984—, assoc. dean clin. affairs, 1989—; dir. gastroenterology unit Univ. Hosp., Denver, 1989—; pres. med. staff Univ. Hosp., 1989-92. Editor: Decision Making in Gastroenterology, 1985, 92; contbr. articles to profl. jours. Trustee Kern Rsch. Found., Denver, 1982—. Lt. comdr. USN, 1973-75. NIH grantee, 1977-78, Clin. Investigator awardee, 1978-81; Robert Wood Johnson Found. fellow, 1988-89. Fellow ACP; mem. Am. Gastroenterological Assn., Am. Fedn. Clin. Rsch., Western Soc. Clin. Rsch., N.Y. Acad. Scis. Jewish. Office: Univ of Colo Health Sci Ctr B-158 4200 E 9th # 9th Ave Denver CO 80262

LEVINE, MICHAEL JOSEPH, insurance company executive; b. Boston, Mar. 23, 1945; s. Sam and Helen Alice (Michelman) L.; m. Margaret Mary Gutierrez, Aug. 6, 1983; children: Samuel Jacob, Rebecca Lynn. BA, Boston U., 1967; MBA, N.Mex. State U., 1991. Supr. underwriting Comml. Union. Ins., Boston, 1969-73; mgr. Harris-Murtagh Ins., Boston, 1973-75, Cohen-Goldenberg Ins. Agy., Boston, 1975-77; v.p. Southwest Underwriters Ins., Deming, N.Mex., 1977-83, pres., 1983-86; pres. Consol. Ins. Cons., Deming, N.Mex., 1985—; instr. fin. and ins., N.Mex. State U., Las Cruces. V.p. Border Area Mental Health Svcs., So. N.Mex., 1978—; pres. Deming Arts Council, 1979-81; treas. Luna County (N.Mex.) Crimestoppers, Inc., 1979—. Mem. Mensa, Soc. CPCU's (cert.), Soc. Cert. Ins. Counselors (cert.), Ins. Mktg. Assocs., Luna County C. of C. (v.p. 1981-84), Ind. Ins. Agts. N.Mex. (state dir. 1985—), Southwest N.Mex. Ind. Ins. Agts. (treas. 1981-83, pres. 1983-85). Home: PO Box 6028 Alpine TX 79832-0001 Office: Consol Ins Cons Inc 318 S Columbus Rd Deming NM 88030-3867

LEVINE, NORMAN GENE, insurance company executive; b. N.Y.C., Sept. 14, 1926; s. Harris J. and Dorothy S. (Podolsky) L.; m. Sandra Leibow, Dec. 11, 1969; children—Linda, Daniel, Donald. Student, U. Wis.-Madison, 1943-48. Agt. Aetna Life Ins. Co., N.Y.C., 1948-56; supr. Aetna Life Ins. Co., 1956-59, gen. agt., 1959-75; mng. gen. agt. Mut. Benefit Life Ins. Co. in No. Calif., San Francisco, 1975-91; br. mgr. Sun Life of Can., 1991—; pres. Levine Fin. Group, 1975—; internat. speaker in field; past div. v.p. Million Dollar Round Table; nat. chmn. Life Underwriters Tng. Council, 1983-84; nat. pres. Gen. Agts. and Mgrs. Conf., 1986-87. Author: How To Build a $100,000,000 Agency in Five Years or Less, Yes You Can, Life Insurance to Diversification; editor: bi-weekly news report Probe; contbr. numerous articles to profl. jours.; author tapes on ins., mgmt., photography, Americanism. Past mem. bd. dirs. Calif. Law Enforcement Needs Com. Served with AUS, 1944-46, ETO. Recipient Julian Myrick award, 1969, John Newton Russell Meml. award, 1986; named to Hall of Fame Gen. Agts. and Mgrs. Conf., 1982. Mem. N.Y.C. Assn. Life Underwriters (pres. 1967-68), N.Y. State Assn. Life Underwriters (pres. 1968-69), Nat. Assn. Life Underwriters (pres. 1974-75, dir. polit. action com. 1967-69), N.Y.C. Life Mgrs. Assn. (pres. 1974-75), Assn. Advanced Life Underwriters, Am. Soc. C.L.U.s, San Francisco Gen. Agts. and Mgrs. Assn. (pres. 1983), Golden Key Soc., Linnaean Soc., San Francisco C. of C., Audubon Soc., Am. Israel Friendship League (trustee). Mem. Order B'nai Zion (pres. 1964-67). Home: 251 Crest Rd Woodside CA 94062-2310 Office: 1 California St San Francisco CA 94111-5401

LEVINE, PHILIP, poet, educator; b. Detroit, Jan. 10, 1928; s. A. Harry and Esther Gertrude (Priscol) L.; m. Frances Artley, July 12, 1954; children: Mark, John, Teddy. B.A., Wayne State U., 1950, A.M., 1955; M.F.A., U. Iowa, 1957, studied with John Berryman, 1954. Instr. U. Iowa, 1955-57; instr. Calif. State U., Fresno, 1958—; prof. English Calif. State U., 1969-92, Tufts U.; tchr. Princeton U., Columbia U., U. Calif., Berkeley.; Elliston lectr. poetry U. Cin.; poet-in-residence Vassar Coll., Nat. U. Australia; chmn. lit. panel Nat. Endowment Arts, 1985; adj. prof. NYU, Spring, 1984; Univ. prof. Brown U., spring 1985; tchr. NYU, U. Iowa, Vanderbilt U. Author: On the Edge, 1961, Silent in America: Vivas for Those Who Failed, 1965, Not This Pig, 1968, 5 Detroits, 1970, Thistles, 1970, Pili's Wall, 1971, Red Dust, 1971, They Feed They Lion, 1972, 1933, 1974, On The Edge & Over, 1976, The Names of the Lost, 1976 (Lenore Marshall award Best Am. Book Poems 1976), 7 Years from Somewhere, 1979 (Nat. Book Critics Circle prize 1979, Notable Book award Am. Libr. Assn. 1979), Ashes, 1979 (Nat. Book Critics Circle prize 1979, Nat. Book award 1979), Don't Ask, 1979, One for the Rose, 1981, Selected Poems, 1984, Sweet Will, 1985, A Walk with Tom Jefferson, 1988 (Bay Area Book Reviewers award), What Work Is, 1991 (L.A. Times Book Prize 1991, Nat. Book award for poetry, 1991), New Selected Poems, 1991, Earth, Stars, and Writers, 1992, The Bread of Time: Toward an Autobiography, 1994, Simple Truth, 1994 (Pulitzer Prize for poetry 1995); editor: (with Henri Coulette) Character and Crisis, 1966, (with E. Trejo) The Selected Poems of Jaime Sabines, (with Ada Long) Off the Map, The Selected Poems of Gloria Fuertes, 1984, (with D. Wojahn and B. Henderson) The Pushcart Prize XI, 1986, The Essential Keats, 1987. Active anti-Vietnam war movement. Recipient Joseph Henry Jackson award San Francisco Found., 1961, The Chaplebrook Found. award, 1968, Frank O'Hara Meml. prize, 1973; Amer. Academy of Arts and Letters Award of Merit, 1974; Levinson Prize, 1974; Harriet Monroe Meml. prize for poetry, 1976; Golden Rose award New Eng. Poetry Soc., 1985, Ruth Lilly Poetry Prize, Modern Poetry Assn. and Am. Council Arts, 1987, Elmer Bobst award NYU, 1990, Lit. Lion New York Public Library 1993; named outstanding lectr. Calif. State U., Fresno, 1971, outstanding prof. Calif. State U. System, 1972; Stanford U. poetry fellow, 1957, Nat. Inst. Arts and Letters grantee, 1973, Guggenheim fellow, 1973-74, 80; Nat. Endowment for Arts grantee, 1969, 70 (refused), 76, 81, 87. Home: 4549 N Van Ness Blvd Fresno CA 93704-3727

LEVINE, THOMAS JEFFREY PELLO, lawyer; b. Santa Monica, Calif., Mar. 6, 1952; s. Allan Lester and Shirley Elaine (Pello) L.; m. Margaret Louise Adlon, Aug. 27, 1977; children: Marissa, Matthew, Molly. Student, U. Denver, 1970-71, Calif. State U., Northridge, 1971-73; BA, Calif. State U., Sacramento, 1974; JD, Southwestern U., 1977. Bar: Calif. 1977, U.S. Dist. Ct. (cen. dist.) Calif. 1978. Partner Levine & Levine, L.A., 1977-83; staff atty. Fed. Deposit Ins. Corp., Newport Beach, Calif., 1983-85; v.p., assoc. counsel Imperial Bank, Inglewood, Calif., 1985-88; v.p., counsel Community Bank, Pasadena, Calif., 1988; gen. counsel, sr. v.p., sec. Calif. Commerce Bank, Banamex USA Bancorp, L.A., 1988—; legal affairs com. mem. Calif. Bankers Assn., San Francisco, 1990—; Am. Bankers Assn. Bank Counsel Com. 1993—. Author: (course materials) Bank Counsel Symposium, 1991. Dir. Angelino Heights Historic Preservation Assn., L.A., 1985; sec., dir. Carroll Ave. Restoration Found., L.A., 1979-87; dir. Wilshire C. of C., L.A., 1982. Mem. L.A. County Bar Assn. Jewish. Office: Banamex USA Bancorp 811 Wilshire Blvd Los Angeles CA 90017-2606

LEVINGSTON, JOHN COLVILLE BOWRING, telecommunications executive; b. Rawalpindi, Punjab, Pakistan, Apr. 10, 1929; came to U.S. 1961; s. Thomas Clarke and Kathleen Patricia (Farley) L.; m. Elizabeth Ann Baumer, June 6, 1958 (div. Apr. 1968); m. Paula Angela Eriksen, Feb. 29, 1980; children: Thomas Arthur, Alexandra Jane. Grad., Harrow Sch., Eng.; student, Sandhurst, Eng. Sales mgr. British-Am. Tobacco Co., East Africa, 1952-55, W.L. Mackenzie Co., Vancouver, B.C., Can., 1957-61; v.p. Precipitator Inc., Santa Fe Springs, Calif., 1973-78; cons. Calif. Inst. Tech., Pasadena, 1979; v.p. Kingmont Oil, Pine Knot, Ky., 1980; cons. Sta. KCET-TV, Hollywood, Calif., 1981; founder, chmn. Straightley Films, Hollywood, 1982-86; founder, chmn., chief exec. officer Interactive Telemedia, Sherman Oaks, Calif., 1986-89; chmn. Levingston & Assocs., Beverly Hills, Calif., 1989—. Inventor Straightley automobile, 1969. Lt. Parachute Regt., 1950-52. Mem. Internat. Platform Assn., Acad. Television Arts Scis., SAG, Masons. Office: Levingston & Assocs PO Box 1951 Beverly Hills CA 90213-1951

LEVINSON, ARTHUR DAVID, molecular biologist; b. Seattle, Mar. 31, 1950; s. Sol and Malvina (Lindsay) L.; m. Rita May Liff, Dec. 17, 1978; children: Jesse, Anya. BS, U. Wash., 1972; PhD, Princeton U., 1977. Postdoctoral fellow U. Calif., San Francisco, 1977-80; sr. scientist Genentech, South San Francisco, 1980-84, staff scientist, 1984—, dir. cell genetics dept., 1988-89, v.p. rsch., 1990-93, sr. v.p. rsch. and devel., 1993-95; pres., CEO Genentech, Co., 1995—. Mem. editorial bd. Virology, 1984-87, Molecular Biology and Medicine, 1986-90, Molecular and Cellular Biology, 1987—, Jour. of Virology, 1988-91. Mem. Am. Soc. Microbiology, Am. Soc. Biochemistry and Molecular Biology. Office: Genentech Inc 460 Point San Bruno Blvd South San Francisco CA 94080-4918

LEVINSON, DAVID W., engineering educator, consultant; b. Chgo., Feb. 24, 1925; s. Louis E. and Ethel (Paul) L.; m. Betty L. Sachnoff Levinson, Aug. 28, 1949; children: Louis E., Joseph P., Jeanne L. BSChemE, Ill. Inst. Tech., Chgo., 1948; MS in Metall. Engring., 1949, PhD, 1953. Instr. Ill. Inst. Tech., Chgo., 1949-53; rsch. metallurgist Armour Rsch. Found., Chgo., 1953-56, supr. non-ferrous met., 1956-60; asst. dir. met. rsch. IIT Rsch. Inst., Chgo., 1960-62, scientific advisor met. & ceramics, 1962-64; prof. Dept. Engring. U. Ill., Chgo., 1964-87, dean of engring., 1968-70; dir. forensic sci. Triodyne Taussig Inc., Niles, Ill., 1987-89; adjunct prof. metallurgy U. Ariz., Tucson, 1990—; pres. David W. Levinson Cons., Inc., Northbrook, Ill., 1966-87; panel mem. U.S. Natl. Adv. Bd., Washington, 1963-64; v.p, engring. Fotofabrication Corp., Chgo., 1970-87. Contbr. over 40 articles to profl. jours. Dir. Northbrook Civil Def., 1960-64. Mem. Am. Soc. for Materials, Am. Inst. Mining, Metallurgical and Petroleum Engrs. Home: 990 W

Placita De La Cotonia Green Valley AZ 85614-1305 Office: Dept MSE Univ Arizona Tucson AZ 85721

LEVINSON, KENNETH LEE, lawyer; b. Denver, Jan. 18, 1953; s. Julian Charles and Dorothy (Milzer) L.; m. Shauna Titus, Dec. 21, 1986. BA cum laude, U. Colo.-Boulder, 1974; JD, U. Denver, 1978. Bar: Colo. 1978, U.S. Ct. Appeals (10th cir.) 1978. Assoc. atty. Balaban & Lutz, Denver, 1979-83; shareholder Balaban & Levinson, P.C., 1984—, pres., 94—. Contbr. articles to profl. jours. Pres. Dahlia House Condominium Assn., 1983-85, bd. dirs., 1991-94; intern Reporters Com. For Freedom of the Press, Washington, 1977; atty. grievance hearing bd., 1988—. J.V. volleyball coach Good Shephard Catholic Sch., 1992-95. Recipient Am. Jurisprudence award Lawyers Co-op., 1977; 3rd Place award Rocky Mt. Fiction Writers Mystery Novel Contest, 1994. Mem. Denver Bar Assn., Colo. Bar Assn. (profl. liability com. 1991-94), Am. Arbitration Assn. (arbitrator). Club: Denver Law.

LEVINSON, MARK, retired engineering educator; b. Bklyn., June 12, 1929; s. Samuel Eleazer and Rose (Tartakow) L.; m. Suzanne Josephson, Dec. 27, 1953; children: Robert Matthias, Madeline Jane. B Aero. Engring. summa cum laude, Poly. Inst. Bklyn., 1951, MS, 1960; PhD, Calif. Inst. Tech., 1964. Registered profl. engr., Ont., Can. Stress and vibration analyst Foster Wheeler Corp., N.Y.C., 1957-59; asst. prof. mech. engring. Oreg. State U., Corvallis, 1960-61; assoc. prof. mech. engring. Clarkson Coll. Tech., Potsdam, N.Y., 1964-66; assoc. prof. theo. and applied mech. W.Va. U., Morgantown, 1966-67; prof. engring. mech. McMaster U., Hamilton, Ont., Can., 1967-80; A.O. Willey prof. mech. engring., dir. tech./soc. project U. Maine, Orono, 1980-90; engring. educator, rschr. U. Wash., Seattle, 1989—; cons. in field, 1963-94. Contbr. over 50 articles to profl. jours. V.p. Heritage Hamilton Ltd., 1973-78. With U.S. Army, 1952-54. Fellow Ford Found., 1961-62, Woodrow Wilson Found., 1964, A. W. Mellon Found., 1984-85, NSF, 1988-89. Fellow AAAS, AIAA (assoc.); mem. ASME, Soc. for History of Tech., Soc. for Indsl. and Applied Math., Am. Aviation Hist. Soc. Home: 630 Giltner Ln Edmonds WA 98020-3001 Office: U Wash Dept Aero and Astronautics FS-10 Seattle WA 98195

LEVISTER, ERNEST CLAYTON, JR., physician; b. N.Y.C., Feb. 4, 1936; s. Ernest Clayton and Ruth D. Levister; m. Sandra P. Levister (div.); children: Michelle N., E. Clay; m. Christine M. Miller, May 18, 1991. AB in Chemistry, Lincoln U., Pa., 1958; BS in Chem. Engring., Lafayette Coll., 1958; MD, Howard U., 1964. Diplomate Am. Bd. Internal Medicine. Maj., physician internal medicine & cardiology U.S. Army European Command, Fed. Republic Germany, 1969-72; pvt. practice internal medicine & cardiology Houston, 1972-73, Group Health Assn., Washington, 1973-74, Norfolk, Va., 1974-78; med. attaché Embassy of the U.S., 1978-79; internal med. & cardiology Occupational Med. & Toxicology, San Bernardino, Calif., 1979—; ind. med. examiner Dept. Indsl. Rels., Divsn. Ind. Accidents, San Bernardino, 1979—, qualified med. examiner, 1991—. Columnist (newspaper) Voice News. Mem. environ. protection commn. City of Riverside, Calif., 1989-92. Recipient Alumni award Lincoln U., 1988, Award Nat. Assn. for Equal Opportunity in High Edn., 1995, NAFTA award, 1995, Media award, 1995. Fellow ACP, Royal Coll. Physicians, Am. Coll. Preventive Medicine. Office: 1738 N Waterman Ave Ste 1 San Bernardino CA 92404-5131

LEVIT, VICTOR BERT, lawyer, foreign representative, civic worker; b. Singapore, Apr. 21, 1930; s. Bert W. and Thelma (Clumeck) L.; m. Sherry Lynn Chamove, Feb. 25, 1962; children: Carson, Victoria. A.B. in Polit. Sci. with great distinction, Stanford, 1950; LL.B., Stanford U., 1952. Bar: Calif. 1953. Assoc. Long & Levit, San Francisco and Los Angeles, 1953-55, ptnr., 1955-83; mng. ptnr. Long & Levit, San Francisco and L.A., 1971-83; ptnr. Barger & Wolen, San Francisco, L.A. and Newport Beach, 1983—; assoc. and gen. legal counsel U.S. Jaycees, 1959-61; legal counsel for consul gen. Ethiopia for San Francisco, 1964-71; hon. consul for Ethiopia for San Francisco, Ethiopia, 1971-76; guest lectr. Stanford U. Law Sch., 1958—, Haile Selassie I Univ. Law Sch., 1972-76; mem. com. group ins. programs State Bar Calif., 1980—; Mem. Los Angeles Consular Corps, 1971-77; mem. San Francisco Consular Corps, 1971-77, vice dean, 1975-76; Grader Calif. Bar Exam., 1956-61; del. San Francisco Mcpl. Conf., 1955-63, vice chmn., 1960, chmn., 1961-63. Author: Legal Malpractice in California, 1974, Legal Malpractice, 1977, 2d edit., 1983; Note editor: Stanford Law Rev, 1952-53; legal editor: Underwriters' Report, 1963—; Contbr. articles to legal jours. Campaign chmn. San Francisco Aid Retarded Children, 1960; mem. nat. com. Stanford Law Sch. Fund, 1959—; mem. Mayor's Osaka-San Francisco Affiliation Com., 1959-65, Mayor's Com. for Mcpl. Mgmt., 1961-64; mem. San Francisco Rep. Country Cen. Com., 1956-63; assoc. mem. Calif. Rep. Cen. Com., 1956-63, 70-72; campaign chmn. San Francisco Assemblyman John Busterud, 1960; bd. dirs. San Francisco Comml. Club, 1967-70, San Francisco Planning and Urban Renewal Assn., 1959-60, San Francisco Planning and Urban Renewal Assn. Nat. Found. Infantile Paralysis, 1958, Red Shield Youth Assn., Salvation Army, San Francisco, 1960-70, bd. dirs. NCCJ, San Francisco, 1959—, chmn., No. Calif., 1962-64, 68-70; mem. nat. bd. dirs., 1964-75; bd. dirs. San Francisco Tb and Health Assn., 1962-70, treas., 1964, pres., 1965-67; bd. dirs. San Francisco Assn. Mental Health, 1964-73, pres., 1968-71; mem. com. Nat. Assn. Mental Health, 1969-71; trustee United Bay Area Crusade, 1966-74, Ins. Forum San Francisco; bd. visitors Stanford Law Sch., 1969-75; mem. adv. bd. Jr. League San Francisco, 1971-75. Named Outstanding Young Man San Francisco mng. editors San Francisco newspapers, 1960, One of Five Outstanding Young Men Calif., 1961. Fellow ABA (chmn. profl. liability com. for gen. practice sect. 1979-81, council gen. practice sect. 1982-86, sec.-treas. gen. practice sect. 1986-87); mem. San Francisco Bar Assn. (chmn. ins. com. 1962, 73, chmn. charter flight com. 1962-66), State Bar Calif. (com. on group ins. programs 1980—, chmn. gen. practice sect. 1988—), Consular Law Soc., Am. Arbitration Assn. (arbitrator), World Assn. Lawyers (chmn. parliamentary law com. 1976—), Am. Law Inst. (adviser restatement of law governing lawyers 1985—), Internat. Bar Assn., San Francisco Jr. C. of C. (dir. 1959, pres. 1958), U.S. Jaycees (exec. com. 1959-61), Jaycees Internat. (life, senator), Calif. Scholarship Fedn., U.S. C. of C. (labor com. 1974-76), San Francisco C. of C. (dir.), Phi Beta Kappa, Order of Coif, Pi Sigma Alpha. Clubs: Commercial (San Francisco) (dir.); Commonwealth (quar. chmn.), California Tennis; World Trade; Bankers. Home: 59 Lupine # 303 San Francisco CA 94418 Office: Barger & Wolen 101 California St Ste 4725 San Francisco CA 94111-5802

LEVITAN, ROGER STANLEY, lawyer; b. Washington, Jan. 31, 1933; s. Simon Wolfe and Bessie (Abramson) L.; m. Maria Anneli Stennius, May 27, 1975 (div. 1980); 1 child, Mark Howard; m. Laurel Lynn Allen, July 9, 1982; 1 child, Brandon Wolfe. BS in Econs., U. Pa., 1954; JD, Columbia U., 1957. Bar: D.C. 1957, U.S. Ct. Appeals (D.C. cir.) 1957, Ariz. 1976. Tax specialist, reorgn. br. IRS, Washington, 1957-62; atty. McClure & Trotter, Washington, 1962-65; assoc. ptnr. Main Lafrentz, Washington and N.Y.C., 1970-72; dir. taxes U.S. Industries, Inc., N.Y.C., 1972-73; asst. tax counsel Am. Home Products Co., N.Y.C., 1973-75; ptnr., Bilby & Shoenhair, P.C., Tucson, 1976-89; ptnr. Snell & Wilmer, Tucson, 1989-90; ptnr. Molloy, Jones & Donohue P.C., Tucson, 1991-92; counsel Hecker, Phillips & Zeeb, 1992—; lectr. Am. Law Inst., State Bar Ariz. Trustee, Tucson Community Found., 1981—. Contbr. articles to profl. jours. Mem. ABA (chmn. ann. report com. 1965-67, continuing legal edn. com. 1969-70), Ariz. Bar Found., State Bar Ariz. (chmn. sect. taxation 1987-88, mem. tax specialization adv. bd., 1991-93), D.C. Bar Assn. Home: 727 E Chula Vista Rd Tucson AZ 85718-1028 Office: 405 W Franklin St Tucson AZ 85701-8209

LEVITON, ALAN EDWARD, museum curator; b. N.Y.C., Jan. 11, 1930; s. David and Charlotte (Weber) L.; m. Gladys Ann Robertson, June 30, 1952; children: David A., Charlotte A. AB, Stanford U., 1949, MA, 1953, PhD, 1960; student, Columbia U., summers 1947, 48, 53, NYU, 1948, U. Nebr., 1954. Asst. curator herpetology Calif. Acad. Scis., San Francisco, 1957-60, assoc. curator, 1960-61, chmn., curator, 1962-82, 89-92, curator, 1983-88, 93—; chmn. computer svcs. Calif. Acad. Scis., 1983-92; editor Sci. Publs., 1994—; assoc. curator zool. collections Stanford, 1962-63; lectr. biol. sci., 1963-70; professorial lectr. Golden Gate U., 1953-63; adj. prof. biol. sci. San Francisco State U., 1967—. Author: North American Amphibians and Reptiles, 1972; Amphibians and Reptiles of the Middle East, 1992; contbr. numerous articles to sci. and profl. jours. Am. Philos. Soc. grantee, 1960, NSF grantee, 1960-61, 77-79, 80, 83-86, 86-89, 91-93, Belvedere Sci. Fund grantee, 1958-59, 62. Fellow AAAS (coun. 1976—, com. coun. affairs 1983-85, sec.-treas. PAcific divsn. 1975-79, exec. dir. 1980—), Calif. Acad. Scis., Geol. Soc. Am. (vice chmn. history geology divsn. 1989-90, chmn. 1990-91); mem. Am. Soc. Ichthyologists and Herpetologists (bd. govs. 1960-84), Soc. Systematic Zoology (sec.-treas. Pacific sect. 1970-72), Forum Historians of Sci. Am. (coord. com. 1986-88, sec.-treas. 1988-90), Herpetologists League (pres. 1961-62), Hist. of Sci. Soc. Home: 571 Kingsley Ave Palo Alto CA 94301-3225 Office: Calif Acad Scis Golden Gate Park San Francisco CA 94118

LEVITT, IRENE HANSEN, secretarial staff, writer; b. Berkeley, Calif., Aug. 18, 1953; d. Alvin Kenneth and Bertha (Schiff) Hansen; m. Kim De Wayne, Oct. 22, 1983. BA in Art, Calif. Luth. U., 1976. Bookkeeper, data processor, sec. pvt. contractor, 1984—. Photographer with exhibits of greeting card prints in numerous art galleries in the Seattle area; exhibited in art show, Seattle, 1994; author: (plays) A Cancer of Proximity, 1987, The Price of the Retreat, 1987, Sacrifices to the Compromise, 1987, In Order to Bury Our Dead, 1987, Foxtrot, 1993, The Loom, 1993, (novel) The Renaiisance of the Poppy, 1991, (anthology) Diaries of the Affluent, 1993. Vol., alumni rep. Calif. Luth. U., Thousand Oaks, Calif., 1987; vol. Am. Cancer Soc., Modesto, Calif., 1991-92. Recipient award in art Alameda County Art Com., 1972, Mark Van Doren Meml. Poetry prize Calif. Luth. U., 1976; Undergrad. scholar VA, 1972-76, U.S. Civil Svc. Commn., 1972-75.

LEVITT, LAWRENCE DAVID, insurance agent; b. Los Angeles, Apr. 18, 1944; s. Albert Herbert and Reva (Narvey) L.; m. Cinda Sue Coffee, Apr. 8, 1967; 1 child, Rachel Diane. AA, Solano Community Coll., 1970; B, U. San Francisco, 1976. Officer, detective Fairfield (Calif.) Police Dept., 1968-78; officer, supr. Douglas (Wyo.) Police Dept., 1978-79; comdr. Rock Springs (Wyo.) Police Dept., 1979-83, chief of police, 1983-86; owner CoServe, Rock Springs, 1986—; instr. Solano Community Coll., Fairfield, 1972-78, Western Wyo. Coll., Rock Springs, 1979—; mem. curriculum com. Wyo. Law Enforcement Acad., Douglas, 1985—. V.p. admissions and allocations, bd. dirs. United Way Sweetwater County, 1989—; v.p., bd. dirs. Rock Springs C. of C., 1990-93, pres., 1993; elected to city coun. Councilman Ward III, City of Rock Springs, 1991-95; apptd. Wyo. Pari-Mutuel Commn., 1993, chmn., 1995; mem. adv. bd. Youth Home, Inc., ROck Springs, 1980, S.W. Wyo. Alcohol Rehab. Assn., Rock Springs, 1984-86; mem. Upper Solano County Assn. for Retarded Children, Fairfield, 1974-78. Recipient Red Cross Life Saving award ARC, 1970; named Police Officer of Yr., Fairfield-Suisun Exchange Club, 1973. Mem. Internat. Assn. Chiefs of Police, Wyo. Assn. Chief's Police (v.p. 1985-86, chmn. edn. com. 1985—), Wyo. Peace Officers Assn., Rock Springs C. of C., Am. Assn. Life Underwriters, Wyo. Assn. Life Underwriters. Democrat. Jewish. Club: Wyo. Paint Horse (Douglas). Lodges: Lions, Shriners, Masons, Elks. Home: 9 Spotted Tail Cir Rock Springs WY 82901-9614 Office: Allstate Ins 175 Riverview Dr Ste F Green River WY 82935-4811

LEVY, AARON, marketing executive; b. 1934. BA in Comms., San Jose State U., 1956. With Field Rsch. Corp., 1956—, v.p., 1961, pres., 1976, chmn., 1993. Office: Field Research Corp 550 Kearny St Ste 900 San Francisco CA 94108-2527*

LEVY, ALAN DAVID, real estate executive; b. St. Louis, July 19, 1938; s. I. Jack and Natalie (Yawitz) L.; grad. Sch. Real Estate, Washington U., 1960; m. Abby Jane Markowitz, May 12, 1968; children: Jennifer Lynn, Jacqueline Claire. Property mgr. Solon Gershman Inc., Realtors, Clayton, Mo., 1958-61; gen. mgr. Kodner Constrn. Co., St. Louis, 1961-63; regional mgr. Tishman Realty & Constrn. Co., Inc., N.Y.C., 1963-69, v.p., Los Angeles, 1969-77; exec. v.p., dir. Tishman West Mgmt. Corp., 1977-88; pres. Tishman West Cos., 1988-92, chmn. Tishman Internat. Cos., 1993—; guest lectr. on real estate mgmt. to various forums. Mem. L.A. County Mus. Art; chmn. Am. Art Coun.; trustee Archives Am. Art, Harvard-Westlake Sch.; bd. govs. W.L.A. coun. Boy Scouts Am. Mem. Bldg. Owners and Mgrs. Assn. L.A. (dir.), N.J. (co-founder, hon. dir.), Inst. Real Estate Mgmt. (cert. property mgr.), Urban Land Inst., Internat. Council Shopping Centers. Contbr. articles on property mgmt. to trade jours. Office: 10900 Wilshire Blvd Ste 510 Los Angeles CA 90024-6525

LEVY, DAVID, lawyer, insurance company executive; b. Bridgeport, Conn., Aug. 3, 1932; s. Aaron and Rachel (Goldman) L. BS in Econs., U. Pa., 1954; JD, Yale U., 1957. Bar: Conn. 1958, U.S. Supreme Ct. 1963, D.C. 1964, Mass. 1965, N.Y. 1971, Pa. 1972; CPA, Conn. Acct. Arthur Andersen & Co., N.Y.C., 1957-59; sole practice Bridgeport, 1959-60; specialist tax law IRS, Washington, 1960-64; counsel State Mut. Life Ins. Co., Worcester, Mass., 1964-70; assoc. gen. counsel taxation Penn Mut. Life Ins. Co., Phila., 1971-81; sole practice Washington, 1982-87; v.p., tax counsel Pacific Mut. Life Ins. Co., Newport Beach, Calif., 1987—. Author: (with others) Life Insurance Company Tax Series, Bureau National Affairs Tax Management Income Tax, 1970-71. Mem. adv. bd. Tax Mgmt., Washington, 1975-90, Hartford Inst. on Ins. Taxation, 1990—; bd. dirs. Citizens Plan E Orgn., Worcester, 1966-70. With AUS, 1957. Mem. ABA (vice-chmn. employee benefits com. 1980-86, ins. cos. com. 1984-86, torts and ins. practice sect., subcom. chair ins. cos. com. tax sect. 1994—), Assn. Life Ins. Counsel, AICPA, Beta Alpha Psi. Jewish.

LEVY, DAVID, broadcasting executive; b. Phila.; s. Benjamin and Lillian (Potash) L.; m. Lucile Alva Wilds, July 25, 1941 (div. 1970); children: Lance, Linda; m. Victoria Robertson, Apr. 23, 1987; 1 stepchild, Kate Jolson. BS in Econs., U. Pa., 1934, MBA, 1935. With Young & Rubicam, Inc., N.Y.C., 1938-59, v.p., assoc. dir. radio-TV dept.; v.p. charge network programs and talent NBC, N.Y.C., 1959-61; exec. producer Filmways, L.A., 1964-68, Goodson-Todman Prodns., West Coast, 1968-69; exec. v.p., dir. Golden Orange Broadcasting Co., Anaheim, Calif., 1969-88, bd. dirs.; exec. v.p. charge TV activities Four Star Internat., Inc., Beverly Hills, Calif., 1970-72; pres. Wilshire Prodns. Inc., Beverly Hills, 1972—; mem. faculty Calif. State U., Northridge, 1973-77; TV adviser Citizens for Eisenhower, 1952, 56, Haig for Pres., 1988; dir. radio and TV for Citizens for Eisenhower-Nixon, 1956; prodr., writer 3-network program for closing Rep. campaign broadcast Four More Years, 1956; writer, co-prodr. closing program election eve Behalf of Wendell Willkie, 1940; cons. Sec. Treasury, 1944-46; chief radio sect. war fin. divsn. Treasury Dept. Exec. producer Double Life of Henry Phyffe, 1965; exec. producer, creator TV series Addams Family, 1964-66, The Pruitts of Southampton ABC-TV, 1966-67; producer world premier Sarge, also exec. producer, creator TV series Universal Studios NBC, 1971-72; creator Hollywood Screen Test, Bat Masterson, Appointment with Adventure, Outlaws, The Americans, Real West, The Kate Smith Daytime Hour, others; launched Maverick, Shirley Temple, National Velvet, Father Knows Best, Godfrey's Talent Scouts, People's Choice, I Married Joan, Life of Riley, Dr. Kildare, Bonanza, Hitchcock Presents, Thriller, Saturday Night at the Movies, Walt Disney's Wonderful World of Color, Robert Taylor and The Detectives, The Deputy (starring Henry Fonda), Car 54, 1st Bob Newhart Show, 1st Phil Silver's Show, Goodyear TV Playhouse, Peter Pan (starring Mary Martin), What's My Line, Make the Connection, Say When, others; producer Paramount TV, 1972-73, Hanna Barbera Prodns. NBC, 1973-74; creative cons. The Addams Family, Name That Tune, Ralph Edwards Prodns., 1974-81, new series You Asked for It; TV cons. Mark Goodson Prodns., 1989—; co-creator, exec. producer Face the Music TV series, 1980-81; author: (novels) The Chameleons, 1964, The Network Jungle, 1976, The Gods of Foxcroft, 1970, Potomac Jungle, 1990; contbr. short stories to popular mags. Lt. USN, 1944-46. Recipient Treasury medal and disting. svc. citation U.S. Treasury Dept., 1946. Mem. ASCAP, TV Acad., Writers Guild Am., Prodrs. Guild Am. (sec., bd. dirs.), Hollywood Radio-TV Soc. (pres. 1969-70, award 1970), Caucus for Prodrs., Writers and Dirs. (sec., steering com., exec. dir. 1974—, Disting. Svc. award 1985, Spl. award of merit for 20 yrs. svc. 1994). Republican. Jewish. Office: 210 S Spalding Dr Beverly Hills CA 90212-3608

LEVY, DAVID STEVEN, college administrator; b. L.A., Mar. 9, 1955; s. Henry and Gloria Grace (Barouh) L. BA, Occidental Coll., 1977; MA, 1979. Asst. dir. fin. aid Calif. State Coll., San Bernardino, 1978-79; fin. aid counselor Calif. State U.-Northridge, 1979-80; assoc. dir. student fin. aid Calif. State U.-Dominguez Hills, 1980-82; dir. fin. aid Occidental Coll., L.A., 1982-88; dir. fin. aid Calif. Inst. Tech., Pasadena, Calif., 1988—, assoc. dean of students, 1991—; mem. Title IA Adv. Com. Calif., 1977—; negotiator U.S. Dept Edn. Mem. life-long learning com. Calif. Postsecondary Edn. Commn., 1980—, mem. student fin. aid issues com., 1984—. Richter fellow Princeton U., 1976; Calif. State U. adminstrv. fellow, 1981—. Mem. Nat. Assn. Student Fin. Aid. Adminstrs. (Meritorious Achievement award 1988, bd. dirs. 1991—, commn. dir. 1994-95), Mortar Board Alumni Assn. (pres. 1977—), Calif. Assn. Student Fin. Aid Adminstrs. (ind. segmental rep. 1984, sec. 1985, treas. 1986-88, Pres.'s award 1986, 93, Meritorious Svc. award 1994, Segmental Leadership award 1992, Creative Leadership award 1990), Western Assn. Student Fin. Aid Adminstrs. (Disting. Svc. award 1990, Pres. Disting. Svc. award 1992), Nat. Assn. Student Fin. Aid Adminstrs., Phi Beta Kappa, Delta Phi Epsilon, Psi Chi, Phi Alpha Theta, Sigma Alpha Epsilon. Jewish. Co-editor Calif. Student Aid Commn. Student Aid Workbook, 1977—; co-author, contbr. Playing the Selective College Admissions Game, 1994. Home: 368 Mount Carmel Dr Glendale CA 91206 Office: CalTech 515 S Wilson Ave Pasadena CA 91106-3212

LEVY, EZRA CESAR, aerospace scientist, real estate broker; b. Habana, Cuba, Sept. 22, 1924; s. Mayer D. and Rachel Levy; m. Gaynor D. Popejoy, 1980; children from previous marriage: Daniel M., Diana M. Levy Friedman, Linda R. Levy Brenden. MS, UCLA, 1951. Sect. head Douglas Aircraft Co., Santa Monica, Calif., 1951-54; dept. head Lockheed Aircraft Co., Van Nuys, Calif., 1954-56, Librascope, Glendale, Calif., 1956-57, Radioplane, Van Nuys, 1957-58; asst. dept. mgr. Space Tech. Labs., Redondo Beach, Calif., 1958-60; asst. divsn. dir. TRW, Redondo Beach, Calif., 1960-74; now real estate broker Regency Realty Corp., Temple City, Calif. Author: Laplace Tranfer Tables, 1958; contbr. articles to profl. jours. Cpl. U.S. Army, 1944-46. Mem. Temple City C. of C. (bd. dirs. 1992—), Masons (past master and sec.). Democrat. Jewish.

LEVY, JEROME, dermatologist; retired naval officer; b. Bklyn., Aug. 17, 1926; s. Alexander and Pauline (Wollkof) L.; m. Leona Elsie Eligator, June 6, 1948; children—Andrew B., Eric J., Peter C., David J. Student, Wesleyan U., 1944-45; postgrad., 1952-54; A.B., Yale U., 1947; M.D., Albany Med. Coll., 1958. Diplomate Am. Bd. Dermatology. Commd. ensign M.C., U.S. Navy, 1957, advanced through grades to capt., 1972; intern U.S. Naval Hosp., Newport, R.I., 1958-59; resident U.S. Naval Hosp., Phila., 1960-62, U. Pa. Grad. Sch. Medicine, Phila., 1962-63; chief dept. dermatology U.S. Naval Hosp., Memphis, 1963-67, Yokosuka, Japan, 1967-70, Long Beach, Calif., 1974-75; head outpatient dermatology clinic San Diego Naval Hosp., 1970-72; sr. med. officer Keflavik, Iceland, 1972-74; ret., 1975; med. dir. dermatology Westwood Pharm Co., Buffalo, 1975-82; acting chief dermatology dept. Buffalo Gen. Hosp., 1981-82; cons. Erie County Health Dept., 1979-82; clin. assoc. prof. SUNY, Buffalo Med. Sch., 1980-82; practice medicine specializing in dermatology, Coronado, Calif., 1982-90. Contbr. articles to med. jours. Decorated Navy Commendation medal, Joint Service Commendation medal; Knight's Cross of the Order of Falcon (Iceland). Fellow Am. Acad. Dermatology, ACP; mem. AMA, So. Med. Assn., Assn. Mil. Surgeons, U.S., Navy League, Alpha Omega Alpha. Republican. Jewish. Home: 3352 Lucinda St San Diego CA 92106-2932

LEVY, JERROLD EDGAR, anthropology educator; b. N.Y.C., Mar. 9, 1930; s. Julien Samson Levy and Joella Synara (Haweis) Bayer; m. Patricia Blake (div. Dec. 1963); 1 child, Kimrey; m. Marie Dolores Charley, Mar. 1964; children: Modesta, Jonathan. Student, Black Mountain Coll., 1947-50; MA, U. Chgo., 1956, PhD, 1959. Lectr. in pub. health U. Calif., Berkeley, 1959-62; rsch. ethnologist USPHS Indian Health Svc., Navajo Reservation, 1962-64; prof. anthropology Portland (Oreg.) State U., 1964-72, U. Ariz., Tucson, 1972—; prof. emeritys, 1995—; mem. profl. adv. bd. Epilepsy Found. Am., Landover, Md., 1979-87; mem. suicide task force USPHS Indian Health Svc., Washington, 1986—; mem. bd. advisors Nat. Ctr. for Am. Indian and Alaska Native Mental Health Rsch., Denver, 1981. Author: (with others) Indian Drinking, 1974, Hand Trembling, Frenzy Witchcraft and North Mdness, 1987, Navajo Aging, 1991, Orayvi Revisited, 1992. Recipient Career Devel. award NIMH, 1966-71; Resident scholar NEH, Sch. Am. Rsch., Santa Fe, 1988-89. Fellow AAAS, Am. Anthropol. Assn.; mem. Soc. for Med. Anthropology, Soc. Psychol. Anthropology, Am. Ethnol. Soc., Soc. for Cross-Cultural Rsch. Office: Dept Anthropology Univ Ariz Tucson AZ 85721

LEVY, LOUIS, chess master; b. N.Y.C., Feb. 10, 1921; s. Victor and Sarah (Caffina) L.; m. Gloria Alice Cressy, Jan. 21, 1972. B.S., N.Y. U., 1941. Engaged in car washing business, 1947-66, chess and bridge player, 1939—; Bd. dirs. N.J. Bridge League, 1969-73. Served with USAAF, 1942-46. Named U.S. Internat. Master Am. Contract Bridge League, 1972. Mem. Marshall, Manhattan chess clubs, Am. Contract Bridge League. Address: 12317 Ridge Cir Los Angeles CA 90049-1183

LEVY, MARIAN MULLER, transportation executive; b. N.Y.C., Mar. 10, 1942; d. Arthur Russ and Diana Elise (Ornstein) Muller; m. Richard Dennis Levy, Nov. 16, 1962; children: Dawn, Nicole, Jason, Adam. Student, Bklyn. Coll., 1959-61, 68-70. Sec. ASCAP, N.Y.C., 1959-61; tchr. spl. edn Garden Park Sch., Phoenix, 1974-76; v.p. Pac Expediters, Ltd., Scottsdale, Ariz., 1976—. Bd. dirs. Outreach, Phoenix, 1982-92; co-chmn. Council Jews Spl. Needs, Phoenix, 1987-88; chairperson Hospice of the Valley Art Com. Recipient Paul D. Mahoney Outstanding Svc. award Hospice of the Valley, 1991. Mem. Scottsdale Ctr. for Arts, Fine Art for Fine Causes, Phoenix Art Mus., The Heard Mus. Home: 7850 E Camelback Rd Unit 602 Scottsdale AZ 85251-2291 Office: Pac Expediters Ltd 3020B N Scottsdale Rd Scottsdale AZ 85251-7210

LEVY, RICARDO BENJAMIN, chemical company executive; b. Quito, Ecuador, Jan. 11, 1945; came to U.S., 1962; s. Leopoldo and Kate (Bamberg) L.; m. Noella Luke, June 15, 1967; children: Tamara, Brian. BS, Stanford U., 1966, PhDChemE, 1972; MS, Princeton U., 1967. Gen. mgr. Sudamericana, Quito, 1967-70; research engr. Exxon Research & Engring. Corp. subs. Exxon Corp., Florham Park, N.J., 1972-74; v.p., co-founder Catalytica Inc., Mountain View, Calif., 1974—, exec. v.p., chief operating officer, 1982—, pres., CEO, 1991—. Co-Author: Catalysis in Coal Conversion; patentee in field. Mem. Am. Inst. Chem. Engrs., Comml. Devel. Assn., Phi Beta Kappa. Office: Catalytica Inc 430 Ferguson Dr Bldg 3 Mountain View CA 94043

LEW, ALAN AUGUST, geography and urban planning educator, consultant; b. Sacramento, Calif., Apr. 13, 1955; s. Gimpock P. and Inger Ida (Berg) L.; m. Mable Wong, Dec. 26, 1987; children: Lauren Asia, Skylan Sunjong, Chynna Kymberlee. BA in Geography, U. Hawaii, Hilo, 1981; MA in Geography, U. Oreg., 1983, M in Urban Planning, 1983, PhD in Geography, 1986. Rsch. asst. pub. works and planning divsn. U. Oreg., Eugene, 1981-82, grad. tchg. fellow in geography, 1981-86; asst. prof. geography and pub. planning No. Ariz. U., Flagstaff, 1986-92, assoc. prof. geography and urban planning, 1992—; prin. ptnr. Lew Assocs., Flagstaff, 1991—; vis. asst. prof. geography U. Oreg., summer 1986; vis. prof. geography U. Tubingen, Germany, spring 1989; cons. Willamette Pass Ski Corp., 1982, Grand Canton Mgmt. Inc., 1986, Uavpai=Apache Nation, 1986-87, Tohonto O'odham Nation, 1987-89, Hope Tribe, 1990-91, 94-95, Coconino County Recorders Office, 1991, Bur. Land Mgmt., 1992, City of Williams, 1993, Ariz. State Parks Dept., 1993, U. Ariz., 1994, Ea. Ariz. Counties Orgn., 1994-95, Yavapai County, 1995; organizer and chair numerous confs. and workshops in field. Author: (with others) Politics and Public Policy in Arizona, 1993, Travel, Tourism and Hospitality Research: A Handbook for Managers and Researchers, 1994; editor, author: (with others) Tourism in China: Geographical, Political and Economic Perspectives, 1995; contbr. articles to profl. jours. Grantee Environ. Sys. Rsch. Inst., 1992; Fulbright award Nat. U. Singapore, 1983-84. Mem. Assn. Am. Geographers (bd. dirs. recreation, tourism and sport specialty group 1987-89, 93-95, chmn. 1995—), Assn. Pacific Coast Geographers (sec.-treas. 1993—), Am. Planning Assn. (info. sys. divsn., univ. liaison Ariz. chpt. 1989-90), Am. Inst. Cert. Planners, Nat. Coun. Geog. Edn., Assn. Collegiate Schs. Planning, Assn. for Asian Studies, Nat. Recreation and Parks Assn. (soc. park and recreation edn., comml. recreation and tourism sect.), Travel and Tourism Assn., Internat. Geog. Union (U.S. rep., Sustainable Tourism Study Group 1995—). Democrat. Home: 716 W Aspen Ave Flagstaff AZ 86001-5312 Office: No Ariz U Dept Geog/Urban Planning Flagstaff AZ 86011-5016

LEW, DONALD EVAN, accountant; b. Sacramento, Calif., Jan. 13, 1948; s. Sam Gene and Mamie (Quon) L.; m. Linda Elkins, July 8, 1972; children: Brian Danforth, Karissa Lynae. BS, Oreg. State U., 1975. CPA, Oreg. Prodn. planner, shipper GE Co., Portland, Oreg., 1969-72; acctg. clk. Oreg

Dept. of Commerce, Salem, 1972-73; acct. Oreg. System of Higher Edn., Corvallis, 1974; audit mgr., sr. auditor Audits divsn. Oreg. Sec. of State, Salem, 1974-94; acctg. analyst Oreg. State Contr.'s Divsn., Salem, 1994—; staff acct. Morgan, Holland & Connelly, CPA's, Salem, 1975; prin. Donald E Lew, CPA, Salem, 1978—. Bd. chair, trustee 1st Congl. Ch., Salem, 1986-88, moderator, pres., 1985-90; mgr., coach Battlecreek Little League, Salem, 1989-93; equipment chair Sprague High sch. Band Boosters, Salem, 1993-95, v.p. Mem. AICPA. Home: 155 Kevin Way SE Salem OR 97306-1928 Office: Oregon State Contrs Divsn Dept Adminstrv Svcs 155 Cottage St NE Salem OR 97310

LEW, RONALD S. W., federal judge; b. L.A., 1941; m. Mamie Wong; 4 children. BA in Polit. Sci., Loyola U., L.A., 1964; JD, Southwestern U., 1971. Bar: Calif. 1972. Dep. city atty. L.A. City Atty's. Office, 1972-74; ptnr. Avans & Lew, L.A., 1974-82; commr. fire and police pension City of L.A., 1976-82; mcpl. ct. judge County of L.A., 1982-84, superior ct. judge, 1984-87; judge U.S. Dist. Ct. (cen. dist.) Calif., L.A., 1987—; Bar: Calif. 1971. Mem. World Affairs Council of L.A., 1976—, Christian Businessmen's Com. of L.A., 1982—. 1st lt. U.S. Army, 1967-69. Recipient Vol. award United Way of L.A., 1979, cert. of merit L.A. Human Relations Commn., 1977, 82. Mem. Am. Judicature Soc., Calif. Assn. of Judges, So. Calif. Chinese Lawyer's Assn. (charter mem. 1976, pres. 1979), Chinese Am. Citizens Alliance, San Fernando Valley Chinese Cultural Assn., Delta Theta Phi. Office: US Dist Ct 312 N Spring St Los Angeles CA 90012-4701

LEW, WEYMAN, artist; b. San Francisco, Feb. 17, 1935; s. Jee and Him Jeung (Ng) L. BS, U. Calif., Berkeley, 1957. Guest instr. M.H. De Young Meml. Mus., San Francisco, 1970-72. One-man shows include Kelley Galleries, San Francisco, 1967, 68, John Bolles Gallery, San Francisco, 1969, 73, M.H. de Young Meml. Mus., San Francisco, 1970, Instituto de Arte Contemporaneo, Lima, Peru, 1970, Shaw Rimmington Gallery, Toronto, 1970, 72, 75, Santa Barbara (Calif.) Mus. Art, 1971, Galeria Lirolay, Buenos Aires, 1971, Jodi Scully Gallery, L.A., Galerie Smith Andersen, Palo Alto, Calif., Ames Gallery, Berkeley, Calif., 1972, 75, Husstege Gallery, Amsterdam, Wallnuts Gallery, Phila., 1972, 74, 77, 80, Bonython Art Gallery, Sydney, Australia, 1972, 75, Galerie Unicorn, Copenhagen, 1972, Art Gallery Greater Victoria, Can., 1972, Linda Farris Gallery, Seattle, 1973, Rubicon Gallery, Los Altos, Calif., 1974, 76, Muirhead Galleries, Costa Mesa, Calif., 1977, 78, Gryphon Galleries, Denver, 1980, Marshall-Myers Gallery, San Francisco, 1983, Sande Webster Gallery, Phila., 1984, Hank Baum Gallery, San Francisco, 1987, Internat. Art Exhbn. Ctr., Beijing, 1991, Chinese Culture Ctr., San Francisco, 1991, Acad. Art Gallery, San Francisco, 1994; selected pub. collections include M.H. de Young Meml. Mus., San Francisco Mus. Modern Art, Oakland (Calif.) Mus., Bklyn. Mus., Instituto de Arte Contemporaneo, Lima, Chinese Artists Assn., Beijing; author, artist: Weyman Lew Sketches Away, 1981; illustrator: Echoes of Oxford, 1991. Mem. art adv. bd. Chinese Cultural Found., San Francisco. Recipient Disting. award for culture and svc. Chinese Cultural Found., 1991. Mem. Calif. Soc. Printmakers, Phi Beta Kappa, Beta Gamma Sigma. Home: 2810 Pacific Ave San Francisco CA 94115-1107

LEWIN, RALPH ARNOLD, biologist; b. London, Apr. 30, 1921; came to U.S., 1947; s. Maurice and Ethel Lewin; m. Joyce Mary Chismore, June, 1950 (div. 1965); m. Cheng Lanna, June 3, 1969. BA, Cambridge U., Eng., 1942, MA, 1946; PhD, Yale U., 1950; ScD, Cambridge U., Eng., 1973. Instr. Yale U., New Haven, Conn., 1951-52; sci. officer Nat. Research Council, Halifax, N.S., Can., 1952-55; ind. investigator NIH, Woods Hole, Mass., 1956-59; assoc. prof., now prof. U. Calif., La Jolla, 1960—. Editor: Physiology and Biochemistry of Algae, 1962, Genetics of Algae, 1976, Biology of Algae, 1979, Biology of Women, 1981, Origins of Plastids, 1993; co-editor: Prochloron, a microbial enigma, 1989; transl. Winnie-La-Pu (Esperanto), 1972, La Dektri Horlogoj, 1993. Served with British Army, 1943-46. Mem. Phycological Soc. Am. (pres. 1970-71, Darbaker prize 1963). Home: 8481 Paseo Del Ocaso La Jolla CA 92037-3024 Office: U Calif San Diego Scripps Inst Oceanogra # 0202 La Jolla CA 92093

LEWIN, SUSAN O., medical geneticist; b. Johannesburg, South Africa, Feb. 27, 1953. MD, U. Witwatersrand, Johannesburg, 1976. Med. geneticist Shodair Childrens Hosp., Helena, Mont. Office: Shodair Childrens Hosp Dept Med Genetics 840 Helena Ave # 5539 Helena MT 59601-3423*

LEWIN, WERNER SIEGFRIED, JR., lawyer; b. San Francisco, Apr. 13, 1954; s. Werner Siegfried and Libby (Lewis) L.; married. BS, Cornell U., 1975; JD, U. Calif., Hastings, 1980. Bar: Calif. 1980. Assoc. Lynch, Loofbornraow et al, San Francisco, 1980-82, Rudy Rapoport & Holden, San Francisco, 1982-86, Hanson, Bridgett, Marcus, Vlahos & Rudy, San Francisco, 1986-87; prin. Werner S Lewin Jr., Esq., Novato, Calif., 1987—; founder, pres. Atty. Assistance, San Francisco Bay Area, 1987—. Office: Atty Assistance Co Hdqs 55 Cavalla Cay Novato CA 94949-5341

LE WINN, LAURENCE RYNES, plastic & reconstructive surgeon; b. Phila., Nov. 12, 1940; s. Claire Le Winn; married; children: Kaja Z., Laurence Jr. BS, Trinity Coll., 1962; MD, Jefferson Med. Coll., 1966. Diplomate Am. Bd. Plastic & Reconstructive Surgery. Gen. surgery N.Y. Hosp./Cornell U., 1966-72, plastic surgery, 1972-74; dir. dept. plastic surgery Geisinger Med. Ctr., Danville, Pa., 1980-86; dir. The Plastic Surgery Inst., Palm Springs, Calif.; dir. divsn. plastic surgery Eisenhower Med. Ctr., Rancho Mirage, Calif.; com. mem. ASPRS Edn. Found., 1976-77; co-chmn. awards program Robert Ivy Soc., 1983-84; spokesman Am. Soc. Aesthetic Surgery (mem. pub. edn. com.). Inventor of Le Winn Needleholder, Aesculap Instrument Co. and Le Winn Tissue Expander, McGhan Med. Corp. Chmn. Palm Valley High Campaign Com., Palm Springs, Calif.; vol. surgeon Barbara Sinatra Ctr., Rancho Mirage, Calif. Lt. Commdr. U.S. Navy Res. Mem. Am. Bd. Plastic and Reconstructive Surgeons. Office: Plastic Surgery Inst 73 122 Fred Waring Dr # 102 Palm Desert CA 92260

LEWIS, B(ENJAMIN) EARL, criminal justice system consultant; b. L.A., June 16, 1926. AB, San Jose State Coll., 1952, MS in Law Enforcement Adminstrn., 1969; postgrad. in pub. adminstrn., polit. and social sci., and criminology, U. Calif. and U. So. Calif., 1954-70. Sgt., dep. sheriff Santa Clara County Sheriff's Dept., lt. and sgt., capt., detention divsn. commdr.; policeman traffic bureau L.A. Police Dept.; adminstrv. asst. Dept. of Justice Office of Atty. Gen., Calif.; cons. CJ Systems Cons., Bend, Oreg.; coord. adminstrn. justice program Foothill and De Anza Colls., 1967-74; field dir. Pres.' commn. on law enforcement and adminstrn justice Sch. Criminology U. Calif., Berkeley, 1966; cons. U. Calif., Santa Cruz, 1973, Police Orgn. and Police Contract Svc., Saratoga and Los Altos Hills, Calif.; chmn. task force on edn. and tng. Assn. Bay Area Govt., region V Calif. Coun. Criminal Justice; coord. courses Calif. Commn. Peace Officer's Standards and Tng., 1969-73; coord. criminology program U. Calif. Extension, Santa Cruz, 1969-73; project dir. evaluation Calif. Specialized Tng. Inst., Camp San Luis Obispo, 1974-75. Contbr. articles to profl. jours. Pres. Acad. Criminal Justice Scis., 1969-70; mem. Calif. Commn. on Criminal Justice, 1974; mem. com. on manpower devel. Calif. Criminal Justice Planning Bd., 1974; com. mem. Calif. Commn. Criminal Justice-Standards and Goals, 1974. With USMC, 1943-45, PTO; col. USAR, 1952-80. Mem. Internat. Assn. Police Profs. (pres. 1969-70). Office: CJ Systems Cons 515 S Brancirorte Santa Cruz CA 95062

LEWIS, CARSON MCLAUGHL, plastic surgeon; b. Dallas, 1931. MD, U. Tex., Galveston, 1956. Plastic surgeon Scripps Meml. Hosp., Calif.; mem. tchg. staff U. Hosp., San Diego. Office: 9900 Genesee Ave Ste B La Jolla CA 92037-1210*

LEWIS, DAVID HOWARD, nuclear medicine physician; b. Alexandria, Va., June 3, 1959; s. Frederick Roland and Frances Patricia (Urchak) L.; m. Mary Helen Mayer, Dec. 17, 1983; 1 child, Piper Elizabeth. BA, U. Va., 1981; MD, Med. Coll. Va., 1985. Diplomate Nat. Bd. Med. Examiners, Am. Bd. Internal Medicine, Am. Bd. Nuclear Medicine. Resident internal medicine U. Wash., Seattle, 1985-88, resident nuclear medicine, 1988-90; dir. nuclear medicine Harborview Med. Ctr., Seattle, 1990—; asst. prof. radiology U. Wash., Seattle, 1990—. Author: (with others) Nuclear Medicine in Oraland Maxillofacial Surgery, 1990; contbr. articles and abstracts to profl. jours. Named one of Outstanding Young Men of Am., Jaycees, Richmond, Va., 1984. Mem. Soc. Nuclear Medicine, Alpha Omega Alpha, Phi Beta Kappa, Phi Kappa Phi, Sigma Delta Pi.

LEWIS, EDWARD A., investment manager; b. Detroit, July 12, 1929; s. Harry A. and Clara K. (Klein) L.; children: Eden Salenger, Meredith D. Salenger; m. Dorathy M., Nov. 12, 1977; children: James R. Lewis, Karen S. Lewis. BA in Polit. Sci., U. Mich., 1951; LLB, Yale U., 1955. Bar: N.Y., R.I. Lawyer Delson Levin & Gordon, N.Y.C., 1955-58, Adler Pollock & Shehan, Providence, 1958-62, Merrill Lynch PF & S, N.Y.C., 1962-69, Internat. Industries, Beverly Hills, Calif., 1969-72; owner Brit. Oversees Investment, Santa Monica, Calif., 1972-76, Bell-Lewis Assn., L.A., 1976-82, Lewis Energy Partnerships, L.A., 1982—. Office: Lewis Enterprises 11845 W Olympa Blvd #995 Los Angeles CA 90064

LEWIS, EDWARD B., biology educator; b. Wilkes-Barre, Pa., May 20, 1918; s. Edward B. and Laura (Histed) L.; m. Pamela Harrah, Sept. 26, 1946; children: Hugh, Glenn (dec.), Keith. B.A., U. Minn., 1939; Ph.D., Calif. Inst. Tech., 1942; Phil.D., U. Umea, Sweden, 1982; DSc, U. Minn., 1993. Instr. biology Calif. Inst. Tech., Pasadena, 1946-48, asst. prof., 1949-56, prof., 1956-66, Thomas Hunt Morgan prof., 1966-88, prof. emeritus, 1988—; Rockefeller Found. fellow Sch. Botany, Cambridge U., Eng., 1948-49; mem. Nat. Adv. Com. Radiation, 1958-61; vis. prof. U. Copenhagen, 1975-76, 82; researcher in developmental genetics, somatic effects of radiation. Editor: Genetics and Evolution, 1961. Served to capt. USAAF, 1942-46. Recipient Gairdner Found. Internat. award, 1987, Wolf Found. prize in medicine, 1989, Rosenstiel award, 1990, Nat. Medal of Sci. NSF, 1990, Albert Lasker Basic Med. Rsch. award, 1991, Louisa Gross Horowitz prize Columbia U., 1992. Fellow AAAS; mem. NAS, Genetics Soc. Am. (sec. 1962-64, pres. 1967-69, Thomas Hunt Morgan medal), Am. Acad. Arts and Scis., Royal Soc. (London) (fgn. mem.), Am. Philos. Soc., Genetical Soc. Great Britian (hon.). Home: 805 Winthrop Rd San Marino CA 91108-1709 Office: Calif Inst Tech Div Biology 1201 E California Blvd Pasadena CA 91125-0001

LEWIS, EDWARD C., plastic surgeon; b. L.A., May 7, 1925. MD, U. Pitts., 1949. Plastic surgeon VA Med. Ctr., St. Mark's Hosp., Salt Lake City; clin. assoc. prof. surgery U. Utah Sch. Medicine, Salt Lake City. Office: St Marks Med Office Bldg 1220 E 3900 S Ste 2-h Salt Lake City UT 84124-1327*

LEWIS, EDWARD NORMAN, marketing executive; b. Canandaigua, N.Y., Aug. 8, 1951; s. Raymond Eugene and Marion Francis (Norman) L.; m. Valerie Lynn Tomlin, Sept. 5, 1970 (div. 1979); 1 child, Christopher Edward; m. Nancy Doyle, June 8, 1980. AA, Pasadena City Coll., 1971; BA, Calif. State U., L.A., 1973, MS in Pub. Adminstrn., 1988. Athletic dir., program specialist Pasadena (Calif.) Boys Club, 1968-73; mktg. rep. Mchts. & Mfrs. Assn., L.A., 1973-77; mgr. sales and promotions Marineland, Palos Verdes, Calif., 1977-80; exec. dir. L.A. County Rep. Party, 1979-80; area mgr. L.A. C. of C., 1980-84; v.p. mktg. and sales Hollywood (Calif.) C. of C., 1984-87, exec. v.p., COO, 1987-90; dir. devel. Riverside (Calif.) Cmty. Hosp. Found., 1991-93, exec. dir., 1993-95; dir. devel. San Antonio Hosp. Found., Upland, Calif., 1995—; originator, new cause-related mktg. programs Hollywood Walk of Fame, Hollywood Sign, Hollywood cmty. name; instr. mktg. and comm. U. Calif., Riverside, La Sierra U. Mem. Nat. Soc. Fund Raising Execs. (found. devel. chair Calif. Inland chpt. 1993-94). Republican. Presbyterian. Office: San Antonio Hosp Found 999 San Bernardino Rd Upland CA 91786

LEWIS, EDWIN REYNOLDS, biomedical engineering educator; b. Los Angeles, July 14, 1934; s. Edwin McMurtry and Sally Newman (Reynolds) L.; m. Elizabeth Louise McLean, June 11, 1960; children: Edwin McLean, Sarah Elizabeth. AB in Biol. Sci., Stanford U., 1956, MSEE, 1957, Engr., 1959, PhD in Elec. Engring., 1962. With research staff Libraoscope div. Gen. Precision Inc., Glendale, Calif., 1961-67; mem. faculty dept. elec. engring. and computer sci. U. Calif., Berkeley, 1967—, dir. bioengring. tng. program, 1969-77, prof. elec. engring. and computer sci., 1971-94, prof. grad. sch., 1994—, assoc. dean grad. div., 1977-82, assoc. dean interdisciplinary studies coll. engring., 1988—; chair joint program bioengring. U. Calif., Berkeley and San Francisco, 1988-91. Author: Network Models in Population Biology, 1977, (with others) Neural Modeling, 1977, The Vertebrate Inner Ear, 1985, also numerous articles. Grantee NSF, NASA, 1984, 87, Office Naval Rsch., 1990-93, NIH, 1975—; Neurosci. Rsch. Program fellow, 1966, 69; recipient Disting. Teaching Citation U. Calif., 1972; Jacob Javits neurosci. investigator NIH, 1984-91. Fellow IEEE, Acoustical Soc. Am.; mem. AAAS, Assn. Rsch. in Otolaryngology, Soc. Neurosci., Toastmasters (area lt. gov. 1966-67), Sigma Xi. Office: Dept Elec Engring & Computer Scis U Calif Berkeley CA 94720

LEWIS, FREDERICK THOMAS, insurance company executive; b. Tacoma, Apr. 1, 1941; s. Arthur Thomas and June Louise (Levenhagen) L.; m. Sarah Carolyn Boyette, Apr. 18, 1971; adopted children: Johanna, Elizabeth, Sarah, Jonathan, Matthew. Student, Concordia Coll., Portland, Oreg., 1959-61, Dominican Coll., San Rafael, Calif., 1967-71. Registered health underwriter. Enroute coord. Trans World Airlines, N.Y.C., 1961-62, 64-66; customer svc. rep. Trans World Airlines, Oakland, Calif., 1966-75; dist. rep. Aid Assn. for Luths., Twin Falls, Idaho, 1975-84, dist. mgr., 1984—. Vocalist Oakland Symphony Chorus, 1972-75; soloist Magic Valley Chorale, Twin Falls, 1979-83. Cantor Immanuel Luth. Ch., Twin Falls, 1984—; organizer Theos of Magic Valley, Filer, Idaho, 1984. Served with U.S. Army, 1962-64. Mem. Nat. Assn. Life Underwriters (tng. coun. fellow 1984, nat. quality award, nat. sales achievement award, health ins. quality award 1978—), So. Idaho Life Underwriters (pres. 1980-81, edn. chmn. 1984-86, nat. local com. mem. 1986-89), So. Idaho Health Underwriters (bd. dirs. 1986-88), Idaho State Assn. Life Underwriters (area v.p. 1988-89, sec. 1989-90, pres.-elect 1990-91, pres. 1991-92, state conv. exhibitor chmn. 1992-94, Bill Rankin Life Underwriter of Yr. award 1993), Idaho Fraternal Congress (ins. counselor 1976, bd. dirs. 1976-85, pres. 1981-82), Lions (local v.p. 1979-81, pres. 1982-83, organizer women's aux. 1983, sec. 1986-87, 92-93, treas. 1993-94, sec./treas. multiple dist. 31 1994-95, vice dist. gen. 39W 1995—). Republican. Home and Office: 1612 Targhee Dr Twin Falls ID 83301-3546

LEWIS, GERALD ANTHONY, film company executive. Student, Swansea Art Coll., 1968-71. Asst. film cameraman BBC, Wales, 1971-73; owner, pres. Tybach Prodns., Inc. Producer Goodyear, 1975, Survival of the Fittest (Second Pl. award The Cannes Film Festival), 1981, Little People (Best Documentary at the Independent TV awards), 1983, Lebanon, A World Apart, 1983, Internat. Storybook, 1987, Sacred Encounters, 1993. Mem. Internat. Alliance Theatrical & Stage Employees, Assn. Cinemagraphic & TV Technicians (London). Home: 7557 N Hurst Portland OR 97203 Office: 733 NW Everett St Ste 5B Portland OR 97209-3517

LEWIS, GERALD JORGENSEN, judge; b. Perth Amboy, N.J., Sept. 9, 1933; s. Norman Francis and Blanche M. (Jorgensen) L.; m. Laura Susan McDonald, Dec. 15, 1973; children by previous marriage: Michael, Marc. AB magna cum laude, Tufts Coll., 1954; JD, Harvard U., 1957. Bar: D.C. 1957, N.J. 1961, Calif. 1962, U.S. Supreme Ct. 1968. Atty. Gen. Atomic, LaJolla, Calif., 1961-63; ptnr. Haskins, Lewis, Nugent & Newnham, San Diego, 1963-77; judge Mcpl. Ct., El Cajon, Calif., 1977-79; judge Superior Ct., San Diego, 1979-84; assoc. justice, Calif. Ct. of Appeal, San Diego, 1984-87; dir. Fisher Scientific Group, Inc., 1987—; Bolsa Chica Corp., 1991-93; of counsel Latham & Watkins, 1987—; dir. Wheelabrator Techs., Inc., 1987—, Henley Mfg., Inc., 1987-89; adj. prof. evidence Western State U. Sch. Law, San Diego, 1977-85, exec. bd., 1977-89; faculty San Diego Inn of Ct., 1979—, Am. Inn of Ct., 1984—. Cons. editor: California Civil Jury Instructions, 1984. City atty. Del Mar, Calif., 1963-74, Coronado, Calif., 1972-77; counsel Comprehensive Planning Orgn., San Diego, 1972-73; trustee San Diego Mus. Art., 1986-89; bd. dirs. Air Pollution Control Dist., San Diego County, 1972-76. Served to lt. comdr. USNR, 1957-61. Named Trial Judge of Yr., San Diego Trial Lawyers Assn., 1984. Mem. Am. Judicature Soc., Soc. Inns of Ct. in Calif., La Jolla Wine and Food Soc., Confrerie des Chevaliers du Tastevin, Order of St. Hubert, Friendly Sons of St. Patrick. Republican. Episcopalian. Clubs: Bohemian; LaJolla Country (dir. 1980-83); Venice Island Hunt Club; Prophets. Home: 6505 Caminito Blythefield La Jolla CA 92037-5806 Office: Latham & Watkins 701 B St Ste 2100 San Diego CA 92101-8116

LEWIS, GORDON CARTER, auditor; b. Billings, Mont., June 14, 1960; s. Gene Eskil and Vanda (Carter) L. Student, U. Utah, 1978-79, 81-82; AA, LDS Bus. Coll., 1984; BBA, Nat. Coll., Denver, 1986. Market rsch. interviewer Colo. Market Rsch. Svcs. Inc., Denver, 1984-87, 93-94; mgmt. trainee Yellow Front Stores, Aurora, Colo., 1987; auditor, 1987-93; computer office coord. US EPA, Denver, 1989-81; store mgr. Trans Pacific Stores, Denver, 1994—. Ch. leadership, 1979—, bowling league officer. Mem. Assn. Govt. Accts., Am. Bowling Congress, Am. Philatelic Soc. Republican. Mem. LDS Ch.

LEWIS, GREGORY ALLEN, computer programmer and analyst, consultant; b. Ft. Morgan, Colo., Nov. 24, 1961; s. John Marion and Mary Loretta (Dorsey) L.; m. Tina Helena Hofer, Aug. 13, 1983; children: Daniel Gregory, Cynthia Grace, Sarah Ashley, Maria Bethany, Amanda Naomi. BS, Regis Coll., Colorado Springs, Colo., 1989. Operator, jr. programmer Cen. Electric Co., Denver, 1983; tech. leader Logical Systems, Colorado Springs, 1983-86; sr. programmer, analyst Fed. Express Corp., Colorado Springs, 1986-94; lead software engr. Optika Imaging Sys., Inc., Colorado Springs, 1994—; cons. Colorado Springs. Neurol. Assocs., 1986-88, Rose Rehab., Colorado Springs, 1987. Tchr. World Bible Sch., 1989—. Home: 6712 Fredrick Dr Colorado Springs CO 80918-1345

LEWIS, GREGORY WILLIAMS, scientist; b. Seattle, Mar. 3, 1940; s. Delbert Srofe and Eileen Juliann (Williams) L.; m. Stephanie Marie Schwab, Sept. 18, 1966; children: Jeffrey Williams, Garrick Peterson. BS, Wash. State U., 1962, MA, 1965, PhD, 1970. Tchr., rsch. asst. Wash. State U., Pullman, 1965-69; prin. investigator U.S. Army Med. Rsch. Lab., Ft. Knox, Ky., 1970-74; prin. investigator USN Pers. R & D Ctr., San Diego, 1974—, head neurosci. lab., 1980—, leader security systems, 1981-83, head neurosci. projects office, 1987-89, div. head neurosci., 1989-95, sr. prin. scientist, 1995—; cons. in field. Contbr. articles to profl. jours. Bd. dirs., pres. Mesa View Homeowners Assn., Calif., 1980-82; bd. dirs. Santa Fe Hills Homeowners Assn., Calif., 1994—. Capt. U.S. Army, 1967-74. Fellow Internat. Orgn. Psychophysiology; mem. AAAS, Soc. Neurosci., Internat. Brain Rsch. Orgn., N.Y. Acad. Scis., Soc. Psychophysiol. Rsch., Sigma Xi, Alpha Kappa Delta, Delta Chi, Psi Chi. Home: 410 Santa Cecelia Solana Beach CA 92075-1505 Office: US Navy Pers R&D Ctr 53335 Ryne Rd San Diego CA 92152-7207

LEWIS, IAN DAVID, special education educator; b. London, Dec. 10, 1955; s. Louis Sol and Rebecca Katherine (Moses) L.; m. Terrie Reiss Spritzer, July 8, 1984 (div. 1987); 1 child, Charles Laurence. BA honors, U. York, Eng., 1978; MA, Calif. State U., Northridge, 1986; postgrad. cert. in edn., U. Cambridge, Eng. Tchr. music and spl. edn. Cambridgeshire County Coun., Eng., 1979-81, L.A. Unified Sch. Dist., 1982-87; asst. prof. spl. edn. L.A. Mission Coll., 1992—, learning disability specialist, 1993—; asst. prof. spl. edn., learning disability specialist L.A. Valley Coll., 1992—; ednl. cons. entertainment industry, Hollywood, Calif., 1989-94. Mem. Calif. Assn. Post-Secondary Educators (jour. editor 1994), Assn. Ednl. Therapists (profl. mem.). Home: 939 Palm Ave West Hollywood CA 90069-6403

LEWIS, JANIE CAROL, tax preparer, accounting consultant; b. Hollandale, Miss., Mar. 20, 1957; d. Elijah Elbert and Josephine (Clay) Lewis. BBA, Delta State U., 1978. Data entry supr. II Hughes Aircraft Co., El Segundo, Calif., 1980-89; pvt. practice tax preparer Inglewood, Calif., 1989—; beauty cons. Aloette Cosmetics of Long Beach, Calif. Mem. Alpha Kappa Alpha (charter). Democrat. Mem. Pentecostal Ch. Home: 536 Evergreen St Apt 4 Inglewood CA 90302-1959

LEWIS, JASON ALVERT, JR., communications executive; b. Clarksville, Tex., Aug. 17, 1941; s. Jason Allen and Mary (Dinwiddie) L. Student, Stockton Coll., 1959-60, San Jose Jr. Coll., 1962-63. Field engr. telephone tech. Pacific Bell, San Francisco, 1983-84; systems technician AT&T, San Francisco, 1984—. Patentee in field. With U.S. Army, 1964-66. Mem. Internat. Platform Assn., Cousteau Soc., Astron. Soc. Pacific, San Francisco Zool. Soc., Planetary Soc., U.S. Naval Inst. Democrat. Home: 139 Pecks Ln South San Francisco CA 94080-1744

LEWIS, JERRY, congressman; b. Oct. 21, 1934. BA, UCLA, 1956. Former underwriter life ins. underwriter; field rep. for former U.S. Rep. Jerry Pettis; mem. Calif. State Assembly, 1968-78; vice chmn. rules com., chmn. subcom. on air quality; mem. 96th-103rd Congresses from 35th (now 40th) Calif. dist., 1979—; chmn. appropriation com. Va.-HUD subscom., mem. defense subcom., select com. on intelligence, chmn. subcom. on human intelligence. Presbyterian. Office: 2112 Rayburn Bldg Washington DC 20515*

LEWIS, JOHN CHRISTOPHER, allergist; b. Boston, Oct. 15, 1950. MD, Loyola U., Maywood, 1982. Instr. medicine Mayo Med. Sch., Scottsdale, Ariz., Scottsdale Meml. Hosp. North. Office: Mayo Clinic Scottsdale 13400 E Shea Blvd Scottsdale AZ 85259-5404*

LEWIS, JOHN CLARK, JR., manufacturing company executive; b. Livingston, Mont., Oct. 15, 1935; s. John Clark and Louise A. (Anderson) L.; m. Carolyn Jean Keesling, Sept. 4, 1960; children: Robert, Anne, James. BS, Fresno (Calif.) State U., 1957. With Service Bur. Corp., El Segundo, Calif., 1960-70, Computer Scis. Corp., 1970; with Xerox Corp., El Segundo, 1970-77, pres. bus. systems div., 1977; pres. Amdahl Corp., Sunnyvale, Calif., 1983-87, chief exec. officer, 1983—, chmn., 1987—. Served with USNR, 1957-60. Roman Catholic. Office: Amdahl Corp PO Box 3470 1250 E Arques Ave Sunnyvale CA 94086-4730*

LEWIS, JOHN THOMSON CONDELL, aerospace company executive; b. Castro Valley, Calif., Nov. 18, 1955; s. Ernest Edward John and Catherine Evangeline (Thomson) L. BA, U. Calif., Santa Barbara, 1977; MBA, Santa Clara U., 1980, MBA (Extended Edition), 1990. Systems analyst Gen. Electric Co., Sunnyvale, Calif., 1978-82; mem. tech. staff Applied Research, Inc., Santa Clara, Calif., 1982-83; co-founder, mng. ptnr. The Delphi Group, Fremont, Calif., 1982-83; aerospace planner Loral Space and Range Systems (formerly Ford Aerospace Corp), Sunnyvale, Calif., 1983—. Mem. Commonwealth Club of Calif. (program com. Contra Costa chpt.). Republican. Presbyterian. Home: 7835 Cross Ridge Rd Dublin CA 94568-3710 Office: Loral Space and Range Systems 1260 Crossman Ave Sunnyvale CA 94089-1116

LEWIS, JOHN WILSON, political science educator; b. King County, Wash., Nov. 16, 1930; s. Albert Lloyd and Clara (Lewis) Seeman; m. Jacquelyn Clark, June 19, 1954; children: Cynthia, Stephen, Amy. Student, Deep Springs Coll., 1947-49; AB with honors, UCLA, 1953, MA, 1958, PhD, 1962; hon. degree, Morningside Coll., 1969, Lawrence U., 1986. Asst. prof. govt. Cornell U., 1961-64, assoc. prof., 1964-68; prof. polit. sci. Stanford U., 1968—, William Haas prof. Chinese politics, 1972—, co-dir. arms control and disarmament program, 1971-83, co-dir. NE Asia U.S. Forum on Internat. Policy, 1980-90, co-dir. Ctr. for Internat. Security and Arms Control, 1983-91, sr. fellow, 1991—, dir. Project on Peace and Cooperation in the Asian-Pacific Region; chmn. Internat. Strategic Inst., 1983-89; chmn. joint com. on contemporary China Social Sci. Rsch. Coun.-Am. Coun. Learned Socs., 1976-79; former vice chmn. and bd. dirs. Nat. Com. on U.S.-China Relations; cons. Senate Select Com. on Intelligence, 1977-81, Lawrence Livermore Nat. Lab., Dept. of Defense; mem. Def. Policy Bd.; chmn. com. advanced study in China Com. Scholarly Communication with People's Republic of China, 1979-82; mem. com. on internat. security and arms control Nat. Acad. Scis., 1980-83; organizer first univ. discussion arms control and internat. security matters Chinese People's Inst. Fgn. Affairs, 1978, first academic exchange agreement Dem. People's Rep. of Korea, 1988; negotiator first univ. tng. and exchange agreement People's Rep. of China, 1978. Author: Leadership in Communist China, 1963, Major Doctrines of Communist China, 1964, Policy Networks and the Chinese Policy Process, 1986; co-author: The United States in Vietnam, 1967, Modernization by Design, 1969, China Builds the Bomb, 1988, Uncertain Partners: Stalin, Mao, and the Korean War, 1993, China's Strategic Seapower: The Politics of Force Modernization in the Nuclear Era, 1994; editor: The City in Communist China, 1971, Party Leadership and Revolutionary Power in China, 1970, Peasant Rebellion and Communist Revolution in Asia, 1974, Uncertain Partners: Stalin, Mao and the Korean War, 1993, China's Strategic Seapower: The Politics of Force Modernization in the Nuclear Era, 1994; contbr.: Congress and Arms Control, 1978, China's Quest for Independence, 1979, others.; mem. editorial bd.: Chinese Law and Govt, China Quar.,

Survey, The Pacific Rev. Served with USN, 1954-57. Mem. Assn. Asian Studies, Am. Polit. Sci. Assn., Coun. Fgn. Rels. Home: 541 San Juan St Palo Alto CA 94305-8432 Office: Stanford U 320 Galvez St Palo Alto CA 94305-6105

LEWIS, KAREN MAXINE, nurse, pharmaceutical sales executive; b. Salem, Oreg., Jan. 18, 1942; d. Karl Julius and Margaret Emma (Kimbrough) Pluemke; m. Daniel John Braxmeyer III, June 15, 1963 (div. June 1980); children: Debbra Marie Braxmeyer, Daniel John Braxmeyer IV; m. Ted Lewis, Sept. 27, 1981; children: Vance Leland, Danielle Leann. Diploma, Good Samaritan Hosp. RN, Oreg.; cert. adult nurse practitioner; lic. diagnostic radiology technician; cert. diabetes educator. Staff nurse, charge nurse, head nurse Good Samaritan Hosp. and Med. Ctr., Portland, Oreg., 1963-80; nurse practitioner, rsch. coord., diabetes educator Portland Diabetes Ctr., Good Samaritan Hosp., 1973-84, with pvt. physician, 1984-86; terr. sales rep., area trainer Novo Nordisk, 1986-90; regional sales mgr. Novo Nordisk, Portland, 1986—. Mem. ANA, Oreg. Nurses Assn., Am. Diabetes Assn., Oreg. Diabetes Educators. Home: 1106 NE 131st Cir Vancouver WA 98685-2641

LEWIS, KENNETH, shipping executive; b. N.Y.C., Aug. 23, 1934; b. Nathaniel and Hana Evelyn (Kotler) L.; m. Carol Ann Schnitzer, Aug. 3, 1958 (div. 1982); children: Scott, Laurence, Kathleen; m. Colleen Anne Wesche, Nov. 27, 1983. AB, Princeton U., 1955; JD, Harvard U., 1958. Bar: N.Y. 1959, Oreg., 1959. Law clk. to judge U.S. Dist. Ct., N.Y.C., 1958-59; assoc. King, Miller, Anderson, Nash & Yerke, Portland, Oreg., 1959-61; gen. counsel Indsl. Air Products Co., Portland, 1961-63; v.p. to exec. v.p. Lasco Shipping Co., Portland, 1963-79, pres., 1979-94; ret. 1994; bd. dirs. Britannia Steam Ship Ins. Assn., Ltd., London, 1986-94, The Swedish Club, Gothenburg, 1987-89, dep. chmn., 1988-89. Mem. Port of Portland Commn., 1974-81, treas., 1977, v.p., 1978, pres., 1979; trustee Lewis and Clark Coll., 1974-83; bd. dirs. I Have Dream Found., N.Y.C., 1992—, exec. com. 1994—; bd. dirs. Columbia River Maritime Mus., 1987-93, I Have a Dream Found., Oreg., 1990—, chmn., 1990—, The Appleseed Found., 1994—, Pacific Ballet Theater, 1986-89, Oreg. Ballet Theater, 1989—, chmn., 1991-92; pres., 1989-93, Oreg. Community Found., 1982-89, treas., 1986-89; mem. Portland Met. Area Boundary Commn., 1974-74, Portland Met. Mass Transit Dist. Bd., 1973-74; pres. Portland Zool. Soc., 1970, World Affairs Council of Oreg., 1969. Mem. Am., Oreg. Bar Assns., Soc. Maritime Arbitrators, Inc. Democrat. Jewish. Clubs: Multnomah Athletic, Arlington, University, Masons, City (Portland). Office: 1 SW Columbia St Ste 1990 Portland OR 97258-2041

LEWIS, LAURA HESTER SHEPHERD, clinical psychologist, consultant; b. Rulo, Nebr., Nov. 18, 1921; d. Ernest Charles and Marian Eloise (Cook) Shepherd; divorced, 1978; 1 child, Ellen Lewis Anderson. RN, NE Methodist Hosp., Omaha, 1942; BS, Nebr. Wesleyan U., 1959; PhD, U. Nebr., 1967. Lic. psychologist, Nebr., N.Mex.; diplomate Am. Bd. Profl. Psychology. Asst. staff psychologist U. Nebr. Psychol. Clinic, Lincoln, 1961-64; from asst. clin. psychologist to staff psychologist Lincoln State Hosp., 1964-65; intern Nebr. Psychiatric Inst., Omaha, 1964-65; practicum supr. field placement child psychiatry fellows and residents Lincoln Regional Ctr. Nebr. Psychiat. Inst., Omaha, 1966-67; dir. training for paraprofessionals children's and adolescent psychiat. unit Lincoln Regional Ctr., Nebr., 1966-70; psychology practicum supr. dept. psychology U. Nebr., Spring 1967; coord. clin. svcs. children's/adolescent psychiat. unit Lincoln Regional Ctr., 1966-69, acting dir., 1969-70; dir. inpatient psychiatric svcs. Children's Meml. Hosp., Chgo., 1972-74, dir. tng. psychology divsn. of child psychiatry, 1970-74; asst. prof. clin. psychiatry & pediatrics Northwestern U. Med. Sch., Chgo., 1973-74; dir. Harbor City (Calif.) Outpatient Clinic, 1974-78; clin. adminstr., clin. child psychologist So. Calif. Permanente Med. Group-Kaiser Divsn., Lomita, 1974-78; pvt. practice, cons. Calif., 1978-92, Las Vegas, N.Mex., 1992-94; contract instr. Calif. Sch. Profl. Psychology, L.A., 1978-79; instr. clin. psychology Calif. State U., Dominguez Hills, Spring 1978; asst. clinical prof. dept. psychiatry L.A. Harbor Gen. Hosp. L.A. Harbor-UCLA Sch. Medicine, Torrance, Calif., 1980-89; clinical prof. psychology Fuller Theol. Sem., Pasedena, Calif., 1981; pvt. practice N.Mex., 1993-94; mem. med. staff Northeastern Regional Hosp., 1994—; vis. lectr. psychology Nebr. Wesleyan U., Lincoln, 1969-70; cons. telephone hot line, Village of Oak Park, Ill., 1974, UCLA Sch. Medicine, 1976, Rivera Hall, Redondo Beach, Calif., 1978, Rehab. Svcs., Bay Harbor Hosp., Harbor City, Calif., 1993, Project for Prevention of Sexual Abuse of Presch. Children, Children's Svcs. Dept. Psychiatry, Harbor-UCLA Sch. Medicine, Torrance, 1993; bd. dirs. Harbor View House, San Pedro, Calif.; delegate People-to-People Program, People's Rep. of China, 1989, USSR, 1991; speaker presentations and seminars at hospitals, religious centers, corps., 1973-91; cons. adminstrn. Northeastern Regional Hosp., 1994—. Author: (with others) Group Therapy with Children and Adolescents: A Treatment Manual, 1985; contbr. articles to profl. jours. Mem. Nebr. Little White House Conf. on Children and Youth, 1968; mem. health svcs. task force Village of Oak Park, Ill., 1974. 1st lt. U.S. Army Nurse Corps, 1942-45, PTO. Fellow Acad. Clin. Psychologists; mem. APA (divsn. 12, sect. 1), Soc. Personality Assessment, N.Mex. Psychol. Assn., Nebr. Psychol. Assn. (com. legis. affairs and profl. relationships 1969), Sigma Xi. Democrat. Methodist. Home: PO Box 2956 1214 6th St Las Vegas NM 87701

LEWIS, MARION ELIZABETH, social worker; b. Los Alamos, Calif., Dec. 7, 1920; d. James Henry and Carolina Sophia (Niemann) Eddy; m. William Ernest Lewis, May 30, 1943 (dec. Oct. 1954); children: Doris Lenita Lewis Terrill, Paul William. Student, Jr. Coll., Santa Maria, Calif., 1939-40, Bus. Coll., Santa Barbara, Calif., 1940-41, Alan Hancock Coll., 1958-61; BA in Sociology cum laude, Westminster Coll., Salt Lake City, 1964. Office clk. Met. Life Ins. Co., Santa Barbara, 1942-43; sales clk. Sprouse Reitz Co., Laguna Beach, Calif., 1943-44; office clk. U.S. Army, Santa Maria AFB, 1944-45; sch. crossing guard Calif. Hwy. Patrol, Los Alamos, 1956-58; office clk. Holaday Children's Ctr., Salt Lake City, 1964; social worker Sonoma County Social Svc., Santa Rosa, Calif., 1964-78, ret., 1978; sales rep. Avon Products, Los Alamos, 1957-61; sales clk. Gen. Store, Los Alamos, 1957-59; office clk. Sonoma County Pub. Health Dept., 1979-80. Deacon Presbyn. Ch., 1956—, moderator Presbyn. Women, 1990-91, vice moderator, 1989-90, sem. rep., 1978-80, 92—. Mem. AAUW, R.I. Geneal. Soc., Sonoma County Geneal. Soc. (hospitality com.), Calif. Automobile Assn., Nat Geographic Soc., Sonoma County Assn. Ret. Employees, Commonwealth Club Calif., Sequoia Club, Alpha Chi. Republican. Home: 61 Sequoia Cir Santa Rosa CA 95401-4992

LEWIS, MARK EARLDON, city manager; b. Boston, June 27, 1951; s Frederick Cole Lewis and Barbara (Forsyth) Corrigan; m. Kristine Mietzner, May 1, 1983; children: Anna Kristine, Benjamin Mark. BA, Washington State U., 1975; BS, We. State U., 1993, JD, 1995. Adminstrv. asst. City and Borough of Juneau, Alaska, 1975-77; city mgr. City of Valdez, Alaska, 1978-82; commr. State of Alaska Dept. of Community and REgional Affairs, Juneau, 1982-83; dep. city mgr. City of South San Francisco, Calif., 1984-87, city mgr., 1987-88; city mgr. City of Monterey Park, Calif., 1988-91, City of Colton, Calif., 1991-93, Union City, 1995—. Dir. Monterey Park Boys' and Girls' Club, 1990; vice chmn. allocation team United Way, 1990, area group chmn. 1989-90; exec. com. mem. Calif., colo., Ariz. and Nev. Innovation Group, 1987. Home: 453 Charleston Dr Claremont CA 91711-1916 Office: City of Colton 650 N La Cadena Dr Colton CA 92324-2823

LEWIS, NANCY PATRICIA, speech and language pathologist; b. Miami, Fla., Sept. 23, 1956; d. James and Sara (Gilman) L. BS, U. Fla., 1978; MS, U. Ariz., 1980. Postgrad. fellow U. Tex. Med. Br., Galveston, 1979-80, speech lang. pathologist, 1980-81; speech lang. pathologist Albuquerque Pub. Schs., 1982-84; child devel. specialist Albuquerque Spl. Presch., 1984—; pvt. practice speech-lang. pathology Albuquerque, 1985—; coord. Project Ta-kos, 1987—; artist Trash Warrior wearable art; instr. Express Ability in movement, 1992—; speaker in field. Author (dianostic procedure) Khan-Lewis Phonological Analysis, 1986; (therapeutic materials) Familiar Objects and Actions, 1985. Labor coord. Lama Found., San Cristobal, 1988, fundraiser, 1988-91, speech pathology cons., 1990—, bd. dirs., 1990—; bd. dirs. Vol. for Outdoors, Albuquerque, 1984—; cmty. vol. mediator N.Mex. Ctr. for Dispute Resolution, 1993—; cons. Robert Wood Johnson Found. City of Santa Fe Carino Children's Project, 1993—; developer, instr. Conflict Resolution Curriculum, 1993—. Fellow U. Tex. Med. Br., Galveston, 1981. Mem. Am. Speech Lang. and Hearing Assn., N.Mex. Speech Lang. and Hearing Assn. Democrat.

LEWIS, NATHAN SAUL, chemistry educator; b. L.A., Oct. 20, 1955. BS in Chemistry with highest honors, MS in Chemistry, Calif. Inst. Tech., 1977; PhD in Chemistry, MIT, 1981. Asst. prof. chemistry Stanford (Calif.) U., 1981-86, assoc. prof., 1986-88; assoc. prof. Calif. Inst. Tech., 1988-90, prof., 1990—; cons. Lawrence Livermore (Calif.) Nat. Lab., 1977-81, 84-88, Solar Energy Rsch. Assocs., Santa Clara, Calif., 1981-85, Am. Hosp. Supply, Irvine, Calif., 1983-85, Molecular Devices, Palo Alto, Calif., 1983-88; mem. U.S. Japan Joint Conf. Photochemistry and Photoconversion, 1983, Chem. Revs. Adv. Bd., 1989-92, long range planning com. Electrochem. Soc., 1991-94, Adv. Bd. Progress Inorganic Chemistry, 1992-94, vis. com. dept. applied sci. Brookhaven Nat. Lab., 1993—. Divisional editor Jour. Electrochemical Soc., 1984-90; mem. editorial adv. bd. Accounts Chem. Rsch., 1993—. Recipient Presdl. Young Investigator award, 1984-88, Fresenius award Phi Lambda Upsilon, 1990, Pure Chemistry award Am. Chem. Soc., 1991; Achievement Rewards Coll. Scientists Found. scholar Calif. Inst. Tech., 1975-77, Calif. State scholar, 1976-77, Carnation Co. Acad. Merit scholar, 1976-77, Camille and Henry Dreyfus Tchr. scholar, 1985-90; Fannie and John Hertz Found. fellow MIT, 1977-81, Alfred P. Sloan Rsch. fellow, 1985-87. Office: Calif Inst Tech Dept Chem 127-72 Pasadena CA 91125

LEWIS, NORMAN, English language educator, writer; b. N.Y.C., Dec. 30, 1912; s. Herman and Deborah (Nevins) L.; m. Mary Goldstein, July 28, 1934; children—Margery, Debra. B.A., CUNY, 1939; M.A., Columbia U., 1941. Instr., lectr CUNY, N.Y.C., 1943-52; assoc. prof. English NYU, N.Y.C., 1955-64; instr. Compton Coll., Calif., summers 1962-64, UCLA, 1962-69; prof. English Rio Hondo Coll., Whittier, Calif., 1964-91, chmn. communications dept., 1964-75. Author: (with others) Journeys Through Wordland, 1941, Lessons in Vocabulary and Spelling, 1941, (with Wilfred Funk) Thirty Days to a More Powerful Vocabulary, 1942, rev. edit., 1970, Power with Words, 1943, How to Read Better and Faster, 1944, rev. edit., 1978, The Lewis English Refresher and Vocabulary Builder, 1945, How to Speak Better English, 1948, Word Power Made Easy, 1949, rev. edit., 1978, The Rapid Vocabulary Builder, 1951, rev. edit., 1980, 3d edit., 1988, How to Get More Out of Your Reading, 1951, Twenty Days to Better Spelling, 1953, The Comprehensive Word Guide, 1958, Dictionary of Correct Spelling, 1962, Correct Spelling Made Easy, 1963, rev. edit. 1987, Dictionary of Modern Pronunciation, 1963, New Guide to Word Power, 1963, The New Power with Words, 1964, Thirty Days to Better English, 1964, The Modern Thesaurus of Synonyms, 1965, RSVP-Reading, Spelling, Vocabulary, Pronunciation (books I-III), 1966, 77, See, Say, and Write! (books I and II), 1973, Instant Spelling Power, 1976, R.S.V.P. for College English Power (books I-III), 1977-79, R.S.V.P. with Etymology (books I and II), 1980-81, Instant Word Power, 1980, New American Dictionary of Good English, 1987; editor: New Roget's Thesaurus of the English Language in Dictionary Form, 1961; also numerous articles in nat. mags.

LEWIS, NORMAN G., academic administrator, researcher, consultant; b. Irvine, Ayrshire, Scotland, Sept. 16, 1949; Came to U.S., 1985; s. William F. and Agnes H. O. L.; m. Christine I. (div. Oct. 1994); children: Fiona, Kathryn. BSc in Chemistry with honors, U. Strathclyde, Scotland, 1973; PhD in Chemistry 1st class, U. B.C., 1977. NRC postdoctoral fellow U. Cambridge, Eng., 1978-80; rsch. assoc. chemistry dept. Nat. Rsch. Coun., Can., 1980; asst. scientist fundamental rsch. divsn. Pulp and Paper Rsch. Inst. Can., Montreal, 1980-82, group leader chemistry and biochemistry of woody plants, grad. rsch. chemistry divsn., 1982-85; assoc. prof. wood sci. and biochemistry Va. Poly. Inst. and State U., Blacksburg, 1985-90; dir. Inst. Biol. Chemistry, Wash. State U., Pullman, 1990—; Eisig-Tode disting. prof.; cons. NASA, DOE, USDA, NIH, NSF, AIBS, other industries, 1985—. Mem. editl. bd. Holzforschung, 1986, TAPPI, 1986, 89, Jour. Wood Chemistry and Tech., 1987, Cellulose Chemistry and Tech., 1987—, Phytochemistry, 1992—, Polyphenols Actualities, 1992—; author, co-author over 90 articles to books, profl. jours. Hon. mem. Russian Assn. Space and Mankind. Recipient ICI Merit awards Imperial Chem. Industries, 1968-69, 69-70, 70-71, 71-72, ICI scholar, 1971-73, Chemistry awards Kilmarnock Coll., 1969-70, 70-71; NATO/SRC scholar U. B.C., 1974-77; named Arthur M. and Kate E. Tode Disting. Prof. Mem. Am. Chem. Soc. (at-large cellulose divsn., organizer symposia, programme subcom. cellulose, paper and textile divsn. 1987-90, editorial bd.), Am. Soc. Plant Physiologists, Am. Soc. Gravitational and Space Biology, Phytochemical Soc. N.A. (phytochemical bank com. 1989—), Chem. Inst. Can. (treas. Montreal divsn. 1982-84, Am. Inst. Chemists and Chem. Inst. Can. Montreal conf. 1982-84), Can. Pulp and Paper Assn., Tech. Assn. of Pulp and Paper Industry, Societe de Groupe Polyphenole, Gordon Rsch. Conf. (vice-chmn. raenewable resources com. 1993—). Presbyterian. Home: 1710 NE Upper Dr Pullman WA 99163-4624 Office: Washington State U Inst Biol Chemistry Clark Hall Pullman WA 99164

LEWIS, PHILIP CHRISTIE, psychiatrist; b. Lincoln, Nebr., July 19, 1942; s. Norman R. and Annabeth (Kurtzweil) L.; m. Rosa E. Dragone, Sept. 17, 1965; children: Diana Patricia, Miriam Elizabeth, Susana Graciela. MD, U. Nat. Cordoba, Argentina, 1969; MA, Western Sem., Portland, Oreg., 1993. Diplomate Am. Bd. Psychiatry and Neurology. Commd. capt. U.S. Army, 1971, advanced through grades to col., 1984; intern Madigan Gen. Hosp., Tacoma, Wash., 1971-72; resident Letterman Army Med. Ctr., San Francisco, 1972-75; chief cmty. mental health svc. U.S. Army Meddac, Ft. Clayton, Canal Zone, 1975-79; pvt. practice Cordoba, 1979-88; chief dept. psychiatry SB Hays Army Cmty. Hosp., Fort Ord, Calif., 1988-93, dep. comdr. clin. svcs., 1993-94; chief dept. psychiatry Tripler Army Med. Ctr., Honolulu, 1994—. Decorated Meritorious Svc. medal. Mem. Am. Psychiatric Assn., Christian Med. and Dental Soc. Evangelical. Office: US Army Dept Psychiatry Tripler Army Med Ctr Honolulu HI 96859

LEWIS, RALPH JAY, III, management and human resources educator; b. Balt., Sept. 25, 1942; s. Ralph Jay and Ruth Elizabeth (Schmeltz) L. BS in Engring., Northwestern U., 1966; MS in Adminstrn., U. Calif., Irvine, 1968; PhD in Mgmt., UCLA, 1974. Rsch. analyst Chgo. Area Expressway Surveillance Project, 1963-64, Gen. Am. Transp. Co., Chgo., 1965-66; assoc. prof. mgmt. and human resources mgmt. Calif. State U., Long Beach, 1972—; cons. Rand Corp., Santa Monica, Calif., 1966-74, Air Can., Montreal, Que., 1972-73, Los Angeles Times, 1973;. Co-author: Studies in the Quality of LIfe, 1972; author instructional programs, monographs; co-designer freeway traffic control system. Bd. dirs. Project Quest, Los Angeles, 1969-71. Mem. AAAS, Am. Psychol. Assn., Assn. for Humanistic Psychology, The World Future Soc., Soc. of Mayflower Desc., SAR (Ill. soc.), Beta Gamma Sigma. Democrat. Office: Calif State U Dept Human Resources Mgmt Long Beach CA 90840

LEWIS, ROBERT TURNER, psychologist; b. Taft, Calif., June 17, 1923; s. D. Arthur and Amy Belle (Turner) L.; m. Jane Badham, Mar. 23, 1946; children: Jane, William, Richard. BA, U. So. Calif., 1947, MA, 1950; PhD, U. Denver, 1952. Diplomate Am. Bd. Profl. Disability Cons.; lic. psychologist, Calif. Chief psychologist Hollywood Presbyn. Hosp., Los Angeles, 1953-58; dir. psychol. svcs. Salvation Army, Pasadena, Calif., 1958-68; dir. Pasadena Psychol. Ctr., 1964-74; successively asst. prof., assoc. prof. and prof., Calif. State U.-L.A., 1952-83, prof. emeritus, 1984—; assoc. dir Cortical Function Lab., L.A., 1972-84; clin. dir. Diagnostic Clinic, West Covina, Calif., 1983-85; dir. Job Stress Clinic, Santa Ana, Calif., 1985—. Author: Taking Chances, 1979, A New Look at Growing Older, 1995, Money Hangups, 1995; co-author: Money Madness, 1978; Human Behavior, 1974; The Psychology of Abnormal Behavior, 1961. Served to lt. (j.g.) USNR, 1943-46, PTO. Mem. APA, Calif. State Psychol. Assn., Nat. Acad. Neuropsychology. Republican. Office: Job Stress Clinic 2670 N Main St # 280 Santa Ana CA 92701-1224

LEWIS, ROGER ALLEN, biochemistry educator; b. Wellington, Kans., June 1, 1941; s. B. Kenneth and Marjorie (Crockett) L.; m. Kathy Joanne Milldrum, Aug. 26, 1962; children: Carrie Joanne, Christine Joy, Jennifer Dianne. BA, Phillips U., 1963; PhD, Oreg. State U., 1968. Rsch. assoc. Stanford (Calif.) U., 1968-69; asst. prof. biochemistry U. Nev., Reno, 1969-75, assoc. prof. biochemistry, 1975-82, prof. biochemistry, 1982—, assoc. dean coll. agr., 1992—; mem. edn. com. No. Calif. Cancer Program, 1977-80. Contbr. articles to profl. jours. Mem. Gov.'s Cancer Adv. Coun., 1975-77; trustee No. Nev. Cancer Program, 1977-83. Mem. Am. Soc. of Biochemistry and Molecular Biology, Am. Soc. Pharmacology and Exptl. Therapeutics, Am. Chem. Soc. (biol. chemistry sect.), AAAS. Office: U Nev Dept Biochemistry Reno NV 89557

LEWIS, ROSE, plastic surgeon; b. New Orleans, 1942. MD, U. Calif., San Francisco, 1974. Plastic surgeon Mt. Zion Hosp., San Francisco. Office: 203 Willow St Ste 303 San Francisco CA 94109-7731*

LEWIS, SHEILA MURIEL, retired communications management specialist; b. Glendive, Mont., Sept. 23, 1937; d. John Edward and Muriel Christine (Johnson) O'Neil; m. Lyndell W. Lewis, Dec. 14, 1957 (div. 1973); children: Sheri Lynne, Debra Lynne, Linda Marie, Valerie Jean. AA, Colo. Women's Coll., 1957; BS, U. No. Colo., 1976; postgrad., Stanford U. Adminstrv. asst. DAFC/Dept. Defense DOT/FAA, Denver, 1956-64; substitute tchr. Portland (Oreg.) Public Schs., 1964-72; communications operator Denver Air Rt. Traffic Control Ctr., 1972-78, communications specialist, 1978-80, computer programmer, 1980-82, air traffic controller, 1982-86; communications specialist Air Force Space Command, Falcon AFB, Colo., 1986-95, retired, 1995. Troop leader Campfire Girls, Las Vagas, 1964-72, pres. PTA, Las Vegas, 1964-72. .. Mem. AAUW, Armed Forces Communications and Electronics Assn., Aviation Space Edn. Assn., Civil Air Patrol, Univ. Aviation Assn., Order of Eastern Star, Order of White Shrine Jerusalem, Chi Omega. Democrat. Lutheran. Home: 4934 Daybreak Cir Colorado Springs CO 80917-2657

LEWIS, SHIRLEY JEANE, psychology educator; b. Phoenix, Aug. 23, 1937; d. Herman and Leavy (Hutchinson) Smith; AA, Phoenix C.C., 1957; BA, Ariz. State U., 1960; MS, San Diego State U., 1975, MA, 1986; MA, Azusa Pacific U., 1982; PhD, U. So. Calif., 1983. Cert. Tchr., Calif.; m. Edgar Anthony Lewis, June 25, 1966 (div. May 1980); children: Edgar Anthony, Roshaun, Lucy Ann Jonathan. Recreation leader Phoenix Parks and Recreation Dept., 1957-62; columnist Ariz. Tribune, Phoenix, 1958-59; tchr. phys. edn. San Diego Unified Schs., 1962—; adult educator San Diego C.Cs., 1973—, instr. psychology, health, Black studies, 1977—, counselor, 1981—; community counselor S.E. Counseling and Cons. Svcs. and Narcotics Prevention and Edn. Systems, Inc., San Diego, 1973-77; counselor educator, counselor edn. dept. San Diego State U., 1974-77; marriage, family, child counselor Counseling and Cons. Ctr., San Diego, 1977—; inservice educator San Diego Unified and San Diego County Sch. Dists., 1973-77; Fulbright Exch. counselor, London, 1994—; lectr. in field. Girl Scout phys. fitness cons., Phoenix, 1960-62; vol. community tutor for high sch. students, San Diego, 1963; sponsor Tennis Club for Youth, San Diego, 1964-65; troop leader Girl Scouts U.S., Lemon Grove, Calif., 1972-74; vol. counselor USN Alcohol Rehab. Center, San Diego, 1978; mem. sch. coun.'s adv. bd. San Diego State U. Named Woman of Year, Phoenix, 1957, One of Outstanding Women of San Diego, 1980; recipient Phys. Fitness Sch. award and Demonstration Sch. award Pres.'s Coun. on Phys. Fitness, Taft Jr. High Sch., 1975, Excel award Corp. Excellence Edn., 1989; Delta Sigma Theta scholar, 1957-60; Alan Korrick scholar, 1956. Mem. NEA, Calif. Tchrs. Assn., San Diego Tchrs. Assn., Assn. Marriage and Family Counselors, Am. Personnel and Guidance Assn., Calif. Assn. Health, Phys. Edn. and Recreation (v.p. health), Am. Alliance of Health, Phys. Edn. and Recreation, Assn. Black Psychologists (corr. sec. 1993), Assn. African-Am. Educators, Delta Sigma Theta (Delta of Yr. 1987). Democrat. Baptist. Contbr. articles to profl. jours. Home: 1226 Armacost Rd San Diego CA 92114-3307 Office: 2630 B St San Diego CA 92102-1022

LEWIS, TONY LLOYD, pastor; b. Lake Charles, La., Sept. 4, 1951; s. Gloria Mae Lewis-Smith; m. Esther Ann Craven, Oct. 1, 1988; 1 child, Kimberly Josephine. Bachelors, Bishop Coll., 1979; Masters, Pitts. Theol. Sem., 1981; DD (hon.), Bethany Theol. Sem., 1987; D of Ministry, Triune Bible Coll. and Sem., 1990. Ordained to ministry, Bapt. Ch., 1980. Youth minister Prosperity Bapt. Ch., L.A., 1975-76; minister of evangelism Concord Bapt. Ch., Dallas, 1977-79; assoc. minister Ctrl. Bapt. Ch., Pitts., 1979-81; sr. pastor Morning Star Bapt. Ch., Portland, Oreg., 1982-91, Macedonia Bapt. Ch., Pomona, Calif., 1991—. Author: (tract) Whatever Happened to that Family Who Joined Our Church Last Month, 1993. Exec. bd. dirs. NAACP, Pomona, 1994; invitee White House Inauguration, 1988. Recipient Outstanding Leadership award Bapt. Ministers Fellowship of Portland, 1991, Cert. of Appreciation, Census Complete County Com., 1990. Mem. Nat. Bapt. Conv. Am. (bd. dirs. 1982—), Calif. United Bapt. State Conv. (statistician 1991—), San Gabriel Valley Bapt. Assn. of Pomona Calif. and Vicinity, Inc. (founder, exec. dir. 1991—). Office: 710 S Hamilton Blvd Pomona CA 91766-2823

LEWITT, MILES MARTIN, computer engineering company executive; b. N.Y.C., July 14, 1952; s. George Herman and Barbara (Lin) L.; m. Susan Beth Orenstein, June 24, 1973; children: Melissa, Hannah. BS summa cum laude, CCNY Engring., 1973; MS, Ariz. State U., 1976. Software engr. Honeywell, Phoenix, 1973-78; architect iRMX line ops. systems, x86 line microprocessors Intel Corp., Santa Clara, Calif., 1978; engring. mgr. Intel, Hillsboro, Oreg., 1978-80, 1981-89, corp. strategic staff, 1981-82; engring. mgr. Intel, Israel, 1980-81; v.p. engring. Cadre Techs., Inc., Beaverton, Oreg., 1989-91; v.p. rsch. and devel. ADP, Portland, Oreg., 1991—; instr. Maricopa Tech. Coll., Phoenix, 1974-75. Contbr. articles to profl. jours. Recipient Engring. Alumni award CCNY, 1973, Eliza Ford Prize CCNY, 1973, Advanced Engring. Program award, Honeywell, 1976, Product of Yr. award Electronic Products Mag., 1980. Mem. IEEE (sr.), IEEE Computer Soc. (voting mem.), Assn. Computing Machinery (voting mem.), Am. Electronics Assn. (exec. com. Oreg. Coun.). Democrat. Office: Automatic Data Processing 2525 SW 1st Ave Portland OR 97201-4753

LEWITZKY, BELLA, choreographer; b. Los Angeles, Jan. 13, 1916; d. Joseph and Nina (Ossman) L.; m. Newell Taylor Reynolds, June 22, 1940; 1 child, Nora Elizabeth. Student, San Bernardino Valley (Calif.) Jr. Coll., 1933-34; hon. doctorate, Calif. Inst. Arts, 1981; PhD (hon.), Occidental Coll., 1984, Otis Parsons Coll., 1989, Juilliard Sch., 1993; DFA, Santa Clara U., 1995. Chmn. dance dept., chmn. adv. panel U. So. Calif., Idyllwild, 1956-74; founder Sch. Dance, Calif. Inst. Arts, 1969, dean, 1969-74; vice chmn. dance adv. panel Nat. Endowment Arts, 1974-77, mem. artists-in-schs. adv. panel, 1974-75; mem. Nat. Adv. Bd. Young Audiences, 1974—, Joint Commn. Dance and Theater Accreditation, 1979; com. mem. Am. chpt. Internat. Dance Coun. of UNESCO, 1974—; bd. dirs. Am. Arts Alliance, 1974-88; trustee Nat. Found. Advancement Arts, 1982-90, 92-95, Calif. Arts Coun., 1983-86; trustee Calif. Assn. Dance Cos., 1976—, Idyllwild Sch. music and Arts, 1986—, Dance/USA, 1988—, Calif. State Summer Sch. of Arts, 1988—; cons. the dance project WNET, 1987—. Co-founder, co-dir., Dance Theatre, Los Angeles, 1946-50; founder, dir., Dance Assocs., Los Angeles, 1951-55; founder 1966, since artistic dir., Lewitzky Dance Co., Los Angeles; choreographer, 1948—; founder, former artistic dir. The Dance Gallery, Los Angeles; contbr. articles in field.Works choreographed include Trio for Saki, 1967, Orrenda, 1969, Kinaesonata, 1971, Pietas, 1971, Ceremony For Three, 1972, Game Plan, 1973, Five, 1974, Spaces Between, 1975, Jigsaw, 1975, Inscape, 1976, Pas de Bach, 1977, Suite Satie, 1980, Changes and Choices, 1981, Confines, 1982, Continuum, 1982, Walking/Falling, 1982, 1990, The Song of the Woman, 1983, Nos Duraturi, 1984, 8 Dancers/8 Lights, 1985, Facets, 1986, Impressions #1, 1987, Impresssions #2, 1988, Agitime, 1989, Impressions #3, 1989, Episode #1, 1990, Glass Canyons, 1991, Episode #2, 1992, Episode #3, 1992, Episode #4, 1993. Mem. adv. com. Actors' Fund of Am., 1986—, Women's Bldg. Adv. Council, 1985-91, Calif. Arts Council, 1983-86, City of Los Angeles Task Force on the Arts, 1986—; mem. artistic adv. bd. Interlochen Ctr. for Arts, 1988—. Recipient Mayoral Proclamation, City of L.A., 1976, 1982, ann. award Dance mag., 1978, Dir.'s award Calif. Dance Educators Assn., 1978, Plaudit Award, Nat. Dance Assn., 1979, Labor's Award of Honor for Community Svc., L.A. County AFL-CIO, 1979, L.A. Area Dance Alliance and L.A. Junior C. of C. Honoree, 1980, City of L.A. Resolution, 1980, Distguished Artist Award, City of L.A. and Music Ctr., 1982, Silver Achievement award YWCA, 1982, California State Senate Resolution, 1982, 1984, Award of Recognition, Olympic Black Dance Festival, 1984, Distinguished Women's Award, Northwood Inst., 1984, California State U. Distinguished Artist, 1984, Vesta Award, Women's Bldg, L.A., 1985, L.A. City Council Honors for Outstanding Contributions, 1985, Woman of the Year, Palm Springs Desert Museum, Women's Committee, 1986, Disting. Svc. award Western Alliance Arts Adminstrs., 1987, Woman of Achievement award, 1988, Am. Dance Guild Ann. award, 1989, So. Calif. Libr. for Social

Studies & Rsch. award, 1990, Am. Soc. Journalists & Authors Open Book award, 1990, Internat. Soc. Performing Arts Adminstrs. Tiffany award, 1990, Burning Bush award U. of Judaism, 1991, 1st recipient Calif. Gov.'s award in arts for individual lifetime achievement, 1989; honoree L.A. Arts Coun., 1989, Heritage honoree, Nat. Dance Assn., 1991, Vaslav Nijinsky award, 1991, Hugh M. Hefner First Amendment award, 1991, Artistic Excellence award Ctr. Performing Arts U. Calif., 1992, Lester Horton Lifetime Achievement award Dance Resource Ctr. of L.A., 1992, Occidental Coll. Founders' award, 1992, Dance/USA honor, 1992, Visual Arts Freedom of Expression award Andy Warhol Found., 1993, Artist of Yr. award L.A. County High Sch. Arts, 1993, Freedom of Expression honor Andy Warhol Found. Visual Arts, 1993, Calif. Alliance Edn. award, 1994; grantee Mellon Found., 1975, 81,ggenheim Found., 1977-78, NEA, 1969-94. Mem. Am. Arts Alliance (bd. dirs. 1977), Internat. Dance Alliance (adv. council 1984—), Dance/USA (bd. dirs. 1988). Office: Lewitzky Dance Co 1055 Wilshire Blvd Ste 1140 Los Angeles CA 90017-2498

LEWTHWAITE, GORDON ROWLAND, geography educator; b. Oamaru, Otago, N.Z., Aug. 12, 1925; came to U.S., 1959; s. Harry Stanley and Mary Elizabeth (Savage) L.; m. Lydia Luft, Dec. 21, 1953; children: Rebecca, Karen. BA, U. Canterbury, Christchurch, N.Z., 1946, MA, 1948; diploma of honors, U. Auckland, N.Z., 1950; PhD, U. Wis., 1956. Cert. secondary edn. tchr., N.Z. Tchr. Gisborne (N.Z.) High Sch., 1950; instr. U. Okla., Norman, 1953-54; lectr. geography dept. U. Auckland, 1955-59; prof. geography Calif. State U., Northridge, 1959-92, prof. emeritus, 1992—; vis. prof. U. Hawaii, Honolulu, summer 1964, U. B.C., Vancouver, Can., 1966-67, U. Newcastle, N.S.W., Australia, 1973, U. Auckland, 1980, U. Calif., Santa Barbara, winter 1987, L.A., winter 1993. Contbr. numerous articles to profl. jours. Lectr, tchr. in ch. and community groups. Fulbright fellow U. Wis., 1950, Knapp fellow, 1952; Wenner-Gren Found. grantee, 1964, Calif. State U. Rsch. grantee. Fellow Am. Sci. Affiliation; mem. Assn. Am. Geographers, Assn. Pacific Coast Geographers, N.Z. Geographical Soc. (asst. editor 1955-59), Calif. Geographical Soc., Polynesian Soc. (life). Home: 18908 Liggett St Northridge CA 91324-2844

LEWY, ALFRED JONES, psychiatrist, educator; b. Chgo., Oct. 12, 1945; s. Robnert Barnard and Evelyn (Bluestone) L. BS in Biochemistry, U. Chgo., 1967, MD, 1973, PhD in Pharmacology, 1973. Diplomate Am. Bd. Neurology and Psychiatry. Clin. assoc. NIMH, Bethesda, Md., 1975-77; staff fellow NIMH, Bethesda, 1977-80; asst. prof. to prof. psychiatry, ophthalmology, pharmacology Oregon Health Sci. U., Portland, 1981—. Contbr. almost 100 articles to profl. jours. Lt. commdr. USPHS, 1972-75. Recipient several rsch. awards and NIH grants. Home: 14047 SE Fairoaks Way Portland OR 97267 Office: Oregon Health Scis U 3181 SW Sam Jackson Park Rd Portland OR 97201-3011

LEX, STEPHEN FRANCIS, plastic surgeon; b. Oceanside, Calif., Sept. 22, 1955. MD, La. State U., Shreveport, 1982. Plastic surgeon Flagstaff (Ariz.) Med. Ctr. *

LEY, ROBERT DUNCAN, plastic surgeon; b. Santa Cruz, Calif., Sept. 12, 1948. MD, Stanford U. Plastic surgeon Watsonville (Calif.) Cmty. Hosp., 1981, Dom SC Hosp., 1981—. Office: 150 Carnation Dr Ste 4 Freedom CA 95019-3132*

LEYDEN, NORMAN, conductor; m. Alice Leyden; children: Robert, Constance. Grad., Yale U., 1938; MA, Columbia U., PhD, 1970. Bass clarinetist New Haven Symphony; arranger Glenn Miller Air Force Band, Eng., France; chief arranger Glenn Miller Orch., 1946-49; freelance arranger N.Y.C.; mus. dir. RCA Victor Records, Arthur Godfrey, 1956-59; with Oreg. Symphony, 1970—, assoc. conductor, 1974—; music dir. Seattle Symphony Pops, 1975-93; tchr. Columbia U.; guest condr. over 30 Am. symphony orchs. including Boston Pops, Minn. Orch., Pitts. Symphony, St. Louis Symphony, San Diego Symphony, San Francisco Symphony, Nat. Symphony, Utah Symphony; condr. Army Air Force. Author: The Big Band Style: A Guide for Performers. Office: Oreg Symphony Orch 711 SW Alder St Ste 200 Portland OR 97205*

LEYDET, FRANÇOIS GUILLAUME, writer; b. Neuilly-sur-Seine, France, Aug. 26, 1927; came to U.S., 1940, naturalized, 1956; s. Bruno and Dorothy (Lindsey) L. AB, Harvard, 1947, postgrad. Bus. Sch., 1952; postgrad. Johns Hopkins Sch. Advanced Internat. Studies, 1952-53; Bachelier-es-lettres-philosophie, U. Paris (France), 1945; m. Patience Abbe, June 17, 1955 (div.); step-children: Catherine Abbe Geissler, Lisa Amanda O'Mahony; m. Roslyn Carney, June 14, 1970; step-children: Walter E. Robb IV, Rachel R. Avery, Holly H. Prunty, Mary-Peck Peters. Bd. advisers Am. Wilderness Alliance; past dir. Marin County Planned Parenthood Assn., Planned Parenthood Center Tucson; docent Ariz.-Sonora Desert Mus. 1st lt. French Army, 1947-48. Mem. Nat. Parks Assn., Wilderness Soc., Sierra Club, Nat. Audubon Soc., World Wildlife Fund, Am. Mus. Natural History, Environ. Def. Fund, Friends of the Earth, Ariz.-Sonora Desert Mus., Ariz. Hist. Soc., LWV, Ariz. Opera League, Western Writers Assn., Commonwealth Club. Author: The Last Redwoods, 1963, Time and the River Flowing: Grand Canyon, 1964, The Coyote: Defiant Songdog of the West, 1977; editor: Tomorrow's Wilderness, 1963; editor Noticias; contbr. to Nat. Geog. mag. Home: 5165 N Camino Real Tucson AZ 85718-5026

LI, CINDY, scientist; b. Shanghai, People Republic China, Mar. 30, 1962; came to U.S., 1990; s. Mao-Shen Li and Wang-Ying (Mo) Mo; m. Xiang Y. Yao, Dec. 18, 1986; 1 child, Jamie L. Yao. MD, Shanghai Medical U., 1985. Rsch. assoc. Osaka (Japan) Univ. Sch. Medicine, 1987-90; rsch. fellow Hosp. of the Good Samaritan, L.A., 1990-94; staff scientist Allymax Rsch. Inst., Santa Clara, Calif., 1994—. Contbr. articles to profl. jours. Recipient rsch. scholarship Osaka U., 1988-89. Home: 1043 Ridgemont Dr Milpitas CA 95035-7838 Office: Affymax Rsch Inst Santa Clara CA 95051

LI, FU, electrical engineering educator, editor; b. Chengdu, Sichuan, China, Sept. 12, 1958; came to U.S., 1985; s. Zhi and Xu-Juan (Ding) L.; m. Grace Hui Fang, Mar. 18, 1984; children: Susan J., Karen M. BS in Physics, Sichuan U., 1982, MS in Physics, 1985; PhD in Elec. Engring., U. R.I., 1990. Rsch./teaching asst. U. R.I., Kingston, 1986-89; rsch. staff Philips Labs., Briarcliff Manor, N.Y., summer 1987; tech. staff Prime Computer, Inc., Bedford, Mass., 1989-90; asst. prof. elec. engring. Portland (Oreg.) State U., 1990-94, assoc. prof. elec. engring., 1994—; session chair Internat. Conf. on Acoustics, Speech and Signal Processing, 1993, 94. Author chpts. to 4 books, 1991-94; contbr. articles to profl. jours. Recipient Faculty Devel. award Portland State U., 1991, Pew Teaching Leadership award 2d Nat. Conf. on Teaching Assts., 1989, Excellent Paper award Chinese Assn. Sci. and Tech., 1986. Mem. IEEE (sr., assoc. editor IEEE Transactions on Signal Processing 1993—, organizer Oreg. chpt. 1993, chair 1993-95, exec. com. 1993—, session chair statis. signals and array processing workshop 1992, 94, tech. com. on statis. signals and array processing 1992—, chair tech. subcom. power spectrum estimation 1992—, chair 1994—, Recognition award 1993), Eta Kappa Nu. Office: Portland State Univ Dept Elec Engring 1800 SW 6th Ave Portland OR 97201-5204

LI, GERALD, architect, film producer; b. Washington, Mar. 4, 1942; s. Chen Sheng and Gloria (Mark) L.; m. Annemarie van Kersen, Oct. 31, 1972 (div. 1990); children: Alexis, Madison. BS, Rensselaer Poly. Inst., 1963, BArch, 1965. Architect Edward Larabee Barnes, N.Y.C., 1965-67; with Romaldo Guirgola, N.Y.C., 1967-68, Brown-Daltas, Rome, 1969-70, Conklin-Rossant, N.Y.C., 1970-72; chief designer Odell Assocs., Charlotte, N.C., 1972-73; prin. Clark Tribble Harris and Li, Charlotte, N.C., 1973-86; chmn., CEO Tribble Harris Li, Inc., Charlotte, N.C., 1986-90; dir. Young Pres'. Orgn., N.Y.C., L.A., 1988-90, Covell Matthews Wheatley, PLC, London, 1987-90, THL, Inc., Delaware, 1986-90. Principal works include Saatchi-Saatchi World Hdqs., Georgetown Park shopping mall, Northwest Mutual Office Bldg., Milw., Ritz Carlton Hotel, Aspen, Bank of Spain, N.Y.C. Recipient Young Profls. Design award Building Design Construction Mag., 1980. Fellow AIA (award Hist. Preservation for Market House 1981, Honor award for Discovery Place Mus. 1984); mem. Nat. Coun. Archtl. Registration Bds. Home: 929 E 2nd St Ste 202 Los Angeles CA 90012-4337

LI, JOSEPH KWOK-KWONG, molecular biologist; b. Hong Kong, UK, Jan. 13, 1940; came to U.S. 1963; s. Kan and Wai Ching (Chan) L.; m. Livia Say, June 28, 1970; children: Karen, Brenda. BS, U. Redlands, 1967; MS, State U. Calif., 1970; PhD, UCLA, 1975. Rsch. asst. UCLA, 1970-74; from postdoctoral fellow to med. rsch. assoc. Duke U. Med. Ctr., Durham, N.C., 1975-80; mgr. Becton Dickinson Rsch. Ctr., Rsch. Triangle Pk., N.C., 1980-82; rsch. assoc. prof. U. N.C., Chapel Hill, 1982-83; from assoc. prof. to prof. Utah State U., Logan, 1984-93, dir. program in molecular biology, 1992—; scientist -at-resident N.C. Mus. Arts & Scis., Durham, 1983. Contbr. articles to profl. jours. Named Capt., all-star, conf. NCAA, S. Calif. Soccer Conf., 1964, 1965; recipient grad. rsch. awd. State U. Calif., L.A., 1970. Mem. Am. Soc. Microbiology, Am. Soc. Virologist, Soc. Chinese Bioscientists Am. (regional coord., exec. sec.), N.Y. Acad. Sci., Sigma Xi. Office: Biology Dept UMC 5500 Utah State U Logan UT 84322

LI, PETER WAI-KWONG, mathematics educator; b. Hong Kong, Apr. 18, 1952; came to U.S., 1971; s. Chun Tat and Lai Mui (Sum) L.; m. Glenna Marie Seaver, Oct. 30, 1982; children: Tiana, Natasha, Talia. BA, Calif. State U., 1974; MA, U. Calif., Berkeley, 1977, PhD, 1979. Rsch. mem. Inst. for Advanced Study, Princeton, N.J., 1979-80; asst. prof. Stanford (Calif.) U., 1980-83; assoc. prof. Purdue U., West Lafayette, Ind., 1983-85; prof. U. Utah, Salt Lake City, 1985-89, U. Ariz., Tucson, 1989-91, U. Calif., Irvine, 1991—; chair math. dept. U. Calif., 1993—. Editor Rocky Mountain Jour. Math., 1989-91, Procs. of Am. Math. Soc., 1991—; Editor-in-Chief Comm. in Analysis and Geometry, 1992—. Grantee NSF, 1980—; fellowship Sloan, 1982-83, Guggenheim, 1989-90. Mem. Am. Math. Soc., Phi Beta Kappa. Office: U Calif Irvine Dept Math Irvine CA 92717

LI, SHENGQIANG, virologist; b. Ziyang, Sichuan, China, Feb. 28, 1964; came to U.S., 1990; s. Guojun and Suzhen (Zhu) L.; m. Ou He, Dec. 27, 1989; 1 child, Helen. MS, BS, Justus-Liebig U., Giessen, Germany, 1987, DVM, 1990. Grad. rsch. asst. Sch. Vet. Medicine, Giessen, 1987-89; postdoctoral fellow Mt. Sinai Sch. Medicine, N.Y.C., 1990-93; staff scientist Aviron, Burlingame, Calif., 1993—. Contbr. articles to profl. jours.; patentee in field. Recipient Karl-Pfizer prize, 1990; SBIR grantee NIH, 1995; Alexander von Humbolt Found. fellow, 1987-89, Fritz-Thyssen Found. fellow, 1989-90. Office: Aviron 1450 Rollins Rd Burlingame CA 94010

LI, SHUGUANG, research scientist; b. Taiyuan, China, June 22, 1953; came to U.S., 1991; s. Yu Li and Yu Wu; m. Suyu Liu, July 25, 1979; 1 child, Lei Li. MD, Nanjing Railway Med. U., China, 1978; MS, Hunan Med. U., China, 1981; PhD, Leiden U., The Netherlands, 1989. Lectr. Dept. Immunology Hunan Med. U., China, 1981-85; vis. scholar, PhD Rsch. Dept. Immunohematology and Rsch. Blood Bank Leiden U., The Netherlands, 1986-89; post doctoral rsch. fellow Inst. Immunology and Rheumatology Oslo U., Norway, 1990-91; sr. rsch. scientist Specialty Labs., Inc., Santa Monica, Calif., 1991—; referee Scandanavian Jour. Immunology, Oslo, Norway, 1990-92. Mem. AAAS, Assn. Immunologists, Clin. Immunology Soc., Internat. Union Immunological Soc., Norwegian Soc. for Immunology, Chinese Soc. for Immunology, Chinese Soc. for Microbiology. Home: 1909 Warwick Ave Santa Monica CA 90404-5038 Office: Specialty Labs Inc 2211 Michigan Ave Santa Monica CA 90404

LI, VICTOR ON-KWOK, electrical engineering educator; b. Hong Kong, Oct. 11, 1954; came to the U.S., 1973; s. Chia-Nan and Wai-Ying (Chan) L.; m. Regina Yui-Kwan Wai, Aug. 14, 1977; children: Ronald, Nathan. SB in Elec. Engring. and Computer Sci., MIT, 1977, SM in Elec. Engring. and Computer Sci., 1979, ScD in Elec. Engring. and Computer Sci., 1981. Asst. prof. dept. elec. engring. U. So. Calif., L.A., 1981-87, assoc. prof. dept. elec. engring., 1987-92, prof. dept. elec. engring., 1992—, comm. group leader dept. elec. engring., 1988-91, co-dir. dept. elec. engring. Comm. Scis. Inst., 1991-93, dir., 1993-94; Disting. lectr. Nat. Sci. coun., Taiwan, 1993; hon. speaker IEE, 1995; lectr. in field. Editor: IEEE Networks, 1986-92, ACM/BaltzerWireless Networks, 1993—, Telecom.Sys., 1991-95; guest editor spl. issue IEEE Jour. on Selected Areas in Comm., 1987; contbr. articles to profl. jours. Named Disting. lectr. Calif. Poly. Inst., Pomona, 1990. Fellow IEEE (Svc. award 1984, 85, gen. chmn., tech. program chmn. 4th Annual Computer Comm. Workshop, Dana Point, Calif., Oct. 1989, Comm. Soc. tech. com. on computer comm. 1987-89, chmn. L.A. chpt. IEEE Info. Theory Soc. 1983-85, steering com. chair Internat. Conf. on Computer Comm. and Networking, 1992—, tech. program chair symposium on personal comm. svcs., 1995), Inst. for Advancement Engring. Office: Dept Elec Engring Univ So Calif Los Angeles CA 90089-2565

LI, ZHI, process engineer; b. Bazhong, Sichuan, People's Republic of China, Apr. 2, 1961; s. Qingxiang Li and Kamin Zhou; m. Fan Yang, Dec. 20, 1987; 1 child, Rosa Jane. BSEE, Sichuan U., Chengdu, People's Republic of China, 1982; MSEE, U. Wash., 1987, PhD in Elec. Engring., 1993. Electronics engr. Sichuan U., 1982-85; process engr. Lattice Semiconductor Co., Hillsboro, Oreg., 1991—. Mem. Tau Beta Pi, Eta Kappa Mu. Office: Lattice Semiconductor Corp 5555 NE Moore Ct Hillsboro OR 97124-6421

LIANG, JEFFREY DER-SHING, retired electrical engineer, civil worker, diplomat; b. Chungking, China, Oct. 25, 1915; came to U.S., 1944, naturalized, 1971; s. Tze-hsiang and Sou-yi (Wang) L.; m. Eva Yin Hwa Tang, Jan. 2, 1940; 1 child, Shouyu. BA, Nat. Chengchih U., Chungking, 1940; BAS, U. B.C., Vancouver, 1960. Office asst. Ministry of Fgn. Affairs, Chungking, 1940-43; vice consul, Chinese consulate Ministry of Fgn. Affairs, Seattle, 1944-50; consulate-gen. Ministry of Fgn. Affairs, San Francisco, 1950-53; consul, Chinese consulate-gen. Ministry of Fgn. Affairs, Vancouver, 1953-56; engr.-in-tng. Can. Broadcasting Corp., Vancouver, 1960-65; assoc. engr. Boeing Co., Seattle, 1965-67, rsch. engr., 1967-70, engr., 1970-73, sr. engr., 1973-75, specialist engr., 1975-78; cons. Seattle, 1979-81. Mem. chancelor's cir. Wesbrook Soc. U. B.C., Vancouver, 1986—, Seattle-King County Adv. Coun. on Aging, 1984-88, Gov.'s State Coun. on Aging, Olympia, 1986-88, Pres. Coun., Rep. Nat. Com.; permanent mem. Rep. Nat. Senatorial Com., Washington State Rep. Party, Seattle Art Mus.; life mem. Am. Assn. Individual Investors, Rep. Presdl. Task Force; sustaining mem. Rep. Nat. Congl. Com., Rep. Presdl. Adv. Com.,. Mem. IEEE (life), Heritage Found., Nat. Trust for Hist. Preservation, Hwa Sheng Chinese Music Club (v.p. 1978-79, chmn. nomination com. 1981-88, 90-94). Republican. Mem. Christian Ch. Home: 1750 152d Ave NE Apt 302 Bellevue WA 98007-4270

LIANG, LOUISE LINDA, health facility administrator. MD, Georgetown U., 1972. Diplomate Am. Bd. Med. Mgmt., Am. Acad. Pediatrics. Intern, resident in pediatrics Tufts U., Boston, 1972-75; divsn. head pediatrics and adolescent medicine Henry Ford Hosp., Dearborn, Mich., 1975-77; White House fellow, spl. asst. to sec. Dept. Health, Edn. and Welfare, Washington, 1977-78; program mgr. Nat. Childhood Immunization Initiative Dept. Health and Human Svcs., 1978-79; dir. divsn. of health svc. del. USPHS, Boston, 1979-81; asst. to assoc. med. dir. Harvard Cmty. Health Plan, Boston, 1981-83; health ctr. dir. Harvard Cmty. Health Plan, Peabody, Mass., 1983-85; assoc. med. dir., corp. officer Harvard Cmty. Health Plan, Boston, 1985-92; v.p. clin.ops. and chief operating officer Straub Clinic and Hosp., Inc., Honolulu, 1992—; instr. pediatrics Harvard Med. Sch., Boston, 1983-92; clin. instr. pediatrics U. Mich., Ann Arbor, 1976-77; assoc. clin. prof. pediatrics Mercy Coll. Detroit, 1976-77; asst. pediatrician Mass. Gen. Hosp., Boston, 1983-92; courtesy staff Children's Hosp. Med. Ctr., Boston, 1982-92; program co-chair Nat. Forum on Quality Improvement in Healthcare, 1990-91; bd. dirs. Inst. for Healthcare Improvement, 1995—. coord. benchmarking and innovation track Nat. Forum on Quality Improvement in Health Care, 1992; sec. bd. registration Commonwealth Mass., 1987-88, bd. dirs., bd. registration medicine, 1985-89, maternal and child health grant rev. com. Dept. of Pub. Health, 1982; mem. com. health care delivery Med. Found., Boston, 1986-89. Mem. Quality Mgmt. Network (exec. com. 1994—), Group Practice Improvement Netowk (steering com. 1993—), Alpha Omega Alpha. Office: Straub Clinc and Hosp 888 S King St Honolulu HI 96813-3009

LIBBY, LAUREN DEAN, foundation executive; b. Smith Center, Kans., Jan. 9, 1951; s. Dean L. and Elizabeth V. (Hansen) L.; m. June Ellen Hofer, Apr. 29, 1979; 1 child, Grant Lauren. BS in Agrl. Econs., Kans. State U., 1973; MBA, Regis U., 1988. Radio sta. employee, 1968-72; asst. program dir. info. br. Kans. State Extension Svc., Manhattan, 1969-73; economist Howard Houk Assocs., Chgo., 1973-75; asst. to pres. The Navigators, Colorado Springs, Colo., 1975-78, ministry devel. coord., 1979-86, dir. min. advancement, 1986-90, v.p., 1990—; pres. New Horizons Found., Colorado Springs, 1990—; bd. dirs. Navigators, Colorado Springs, 1993—; founding bd. dirs. Sta. KTLF-FM/Ednl. Comms. of Colorado Springs, 1987—; cons. 12 listener-supported radio stas., 1989—. Contbr. articles to mags. Mem. Nat. Soc. Fundraising Execs., Ctrl. States VHF Soc. (pres.). Home: 6166 Del Paz Dr Colorado Springs CO 80918-3004 Office: The Navigators 3820 N 30th St Colorado Springs CO 80904-5001

LICENS, LILA LOUISE, administrative assistant; b. Puyallup, Wash., Feb. 18, 1949; d. C.L. and Joan L. (Rubert) Vormestrand. Cert., Knapp Bus. Coll., 1968. Cert. profl. sec. Adminstrv. asst. Weyerhaeuser Co., Tacoma, 1968-93, adminstrv. asst. bleached paperboard, 1993—. Mem. adv. bd. Bates Tech. Coll., 1994—. Mem. Profl. Sec. Internat. (pres. Mt. Rainier chpt. 1994—, pres. Wash.-Alaska divsn. 1990-91, sec. 1987-89, pres. Sea-Tac chpt. 1985-87), Fed. Way Women's Network (treas. 1988, sec. 1989, pres. 1995). Home: 771 108th St S Tacoma WA 98444-5666

LICHTENBERG, LARRY RAY, chemist, consultant, researcher; b. Marceline, Mo., July 25, 1938; s. Kenneth Ray and Evelyn (Lauck) L.; m. Clarice Elaine Dameron, Dec. 23, 1961; children: Julia-Isabel Dameron. BS in Chemistry, Northeast Mo. State U., 1962. Chemist Bell & Howell, Chgo., 1962-62; jr. chem. engr. Magnavox Corp., Urbana, Ill., 1963-64; process engr. Gen. Electric Co., Bloomington, Ill., 1964-70; mfg. engr. Burr-Brown, Tucson, 1970-72; sr. staff engr. Motorola, Scottsdale, Ariz., 1972—; mem. corp. tech. council Motorola, Scottsdale, 1982—. Contbr. articles to profl. jours. Mem. Am. Chem. Soc., Internat. Soc. Hybrid Microelectronics (pres. Phoenix chpt. 1981-82). Republican. Baptist. Home: 13018 N 32nd Ave Phoenix AZ 85029-1206 Office: Motorola SPS 5005 E McDowell Rd Phoenix AZ 85008

LICHTENSTEIN, CHASE WALTER, management consultant; b. Meriden, Conn., Sept. 22, 1936; s. Harry Charles and Josefa Rose (Weil) L.; m. Marie Agnes Sullivan, June 11, 1959; children: Helen, Paul, Jeremy, Caroline. B Chem. Engring., Cornell U., 1959. Registered profl. engr., N.J. Project mgr., plant engr. M&T Chems., div. Am. Can, Rahway, N.J., 1961-68; project mgr. E.R. Squibb, New Brunswick, N.J., 1968-72, prodn. mgr., 1972-74; plant mgr. Medi-Physics Inc., South Plainfield, N.J., 1974-75; mgr. corp. plant engring. and good mfg. practices Baxter Healthcare, Deerfield, Ill., 1975-78; dir. engring. Hyland div. Baxter Healthcare, Glendale, Calif., 1978-85; pres., owner Planning Masters, Newbury Park, Calif., 1985—. Contbr. articles to profl. jours. Chmn. Housing Authority, Edison, N.J., 1972-75. 1st lt. U.S. Army, 1959-61. Mem. Am. Soc. Tng. and Devel. (chpt. pres. 1989), Am. Inst Chem. Engrs., Nat. Soc. Profl. Engrs., Project Mgmt. Inst. Home and Office: 3343 William Dr Newbury Park CA 91320-2931

LICHTENSTEIN, ROBERT MOOHR, allergist; b. Milw., 1920. MD, Northwestern U., 1950. Allergist Kaiser Found. Hosp., Richmond, Calif. Office: 901 Nevin Ave Richmond CA 94801-3143*

LICHTENWALTER, KAY GILLES, molecular biologist; b. St. Louis, Mar. 30, 1941; d. Jacob Sell and Mary Ellen (Kaylor) Welty; m. Scott Edwin Gilles, Feb. 4, 1961 (div. Feb. 1979); children: Heather Lynn, Richard Scott, Karin Leigh; m. Guy Evan Lichtenwalter, Dec. 24, 1987. BFA, U. Colo., Denver, 1976, MA, 1979; PhD, U. Calif., Santa Cruz, 1984. Teaching asst. U. Colo., 1976-79; teaching asst. U. Calif., Santa Cruz, 1981-83, head teaching asst., 1983-84, vis. lectr., 1985; NIH postgrad. rsch. fellow U. Calif., San Francisco, 1985-87; sr. postgrad. rsch. assoc. U. Calif., Berkeley, 1987-89; instr. Cabrillo Coll., Aptos, Calif., 1984, Palmer Coll., Santa Clara, Calif., 1985; tech. project leader Hewlett Packard Labs., Palo Alto, Calif., 1989—; cons. Cetus, Emeryville, Calif., 1979-80. Author: Lab Guide for Vertebrate Microanatomy, 1980; contbr. articles to profl. jours.; patentee 20 in field. Parent aide, role model Adult and Child Guidance Ctr., San Jose, Calif., 1993-94. Grantee Calif. Sea, 1979-82, NIH, 1985-87. Mem. AAAS, Am. Soc. Human Genetics, Am. Assn. Clin. Chemistry, Am. Soc. Microbiology, No. Calif. Soc. Microbiology, Phi Sigma. Home: 1286 City View Pl San Jose CA 95127-4333 Office: Hewlett Packard Labs 3500 Deer Creek Rd PO Box 10350 Bldg 26 U Palo Alto CA 94303

LIDDELL, BARBARA ANNE, school administrator; b. Chgo., Jan. 4, 1938; d. Harold and Margaret (Schutte) Fly; m. Wingham John Hunter Liddell, Jr., Apr. 6, 1961 (div. Dec. 1982); 1 child, Letitia. BA, Stanford U., 1959; MA, San Francisco State U., 1970; MEd, St. Mary's Coll., Moraga, Calif., 1980. Tchr. Orinda (Calif.) Schs., 1964-78; prin. Hillsborough (Calif.) City Schs., 1978-81, dir. adminstrv. svcs., 1981-84; asst. supt. Piedmont (Calif.) City Schs., 1984-87; assoc. supt. Palo Alto (Calif.) Schs., 1987—. Bd. dirs. Consortium of Calif. Edn. Founds., San Francisco, 1984-88, Bay Area Global Edn. Project, San Francisco, 1985-88. Fulbright-Hays fellow, 1993, Japan Found. fellow, 1990. Mem. ASCD, Am. Assn. Sch. Adminstrs., Calif. Sch. Adminstrs. Assn. Office: Palo Alto Sch Dist 25 Churchill Ave Palo Alto CA 94306-1005

LIDDICOAT, RICHARD THOMAS, JR., association executive; b. Kearsarge, Mich., Mar. 2, 1918; s. Richard Thomas and Carmen (Williams) L.; m. Mary Imogene Hibbard, Sept. 21, 1939. BS in Geology, U. Mich., 1939, MS in Mineralogy, 1940; grad. gemologist, Gemological Inst. Am., 1941; MS in Meteorology, Calif. Inst. Tech., 1944. Cert. gemologist (hon.). With Gemological Inst. Am., L.A., 1940-42, 46—; dir. edn. Gemological Inst. Am., 1942, 46-49, asst. dir., 1950-52, exec. dir., 1952-83, pres., 1970-83, chmn. bd., 1983—, also author courses; editor Gem and Gemology, 1952—; hon. mem. rsch. staff L.A. Mus. Natural History, 1968—; U.S. dep. to Internat. Gem Conf., 1960, 64, 66, 68, 70, 72, 75, 77, 79, 81, 83, 85, 89; del. Pres.'d Conf. on Small Bus., 1957. Author: Handbook of Gem Identification, 12th edit, 1987, (with others) The Diamond Dictionary, 1960, 2d edit., 1977, (with Copeland) Jewelers Manual, 2d edit, 1967; numerous articles.; contbr. to Ency. Britannica Jr., Ency. Americana, McGraw-Hill Ency. of Sci. and Tech. Trustee Nat. Home Study Coun., 1988-88. Recipient Lifetime Achievement award Modern Jeweler's mag., 1985, award Internat. Soc. Appraisers, 1985, Spl. award Internat. Colored Stone Assn., 1984, Lifetime Achievement award Morris B. Zale, 1987; named Man of Yr., Consol. Jewelers Assn. Greater N.Y., 1984; named to Nat. Home Study Coun. Hall of Fame, 1991; Liddicoatite species of tourmaline group named for him. Fellow Mineral. Soc. Am., Geol. Soc. Am., Gem Assn. Gt. Britain (hon.); mem. AAAS, Am. Gem Soc. (supr. ednl. sessions ann. conclaves 1948-83, Shipley award 1976), Am. Gem Trade Assn. (hon.), Gem Assn. Australia (hon. v.p.), Gem Testing Lab. Gt. Britain (1st hon. life mem.), Bel Air Country Club (bd. dirs. 1980-83, Twenty-Four Karat Club (N.Y.C. and So. Calif.), Sigma Xi, Sigma Gamma Epsilon. Home: 1484 Allenford Ave Los Angeles CA 90049-3614 Office: Gemological Inst Am 1660 Stewart St Santa Monica CA 90404-4020

LIDDLE, ALAN CURTIS, architect; b. Tacoma, Mar. 10, 1922; s. Abram Dix and Myrtle (Maytum) L. B.Arch., U. Wash., 1948; postgrad., Eidgenoissche Technische Hochschule, Zurich, Switzerland, 1950-51. Asst. prof. architecture U. Wash., 1954-55; prin. Liddle & Jones, Tacoma, 1957-67, Alan Liddle (architects), Tacoma, 1967-90, Liddle & Jacklin, Tacoma, 1990—. Architect oceanography bldgs, U. Wash., 1967, Tacoma Art Mus., 1971, Charles Wright Acad., Tacoma, 1962, Pacific Nat. Bank Wash., Auburn, 1965. Pres. bd. Allied Arts Tacoma, 1963-64, Civic Arts Commn. Tacoma-Pierce County, 1969; commr. Wash. Arts Commn., 1971; Bd. dirs. Tacoma Art Mus., Tacoma Zool. Soc., Tacoma Philharmonic, Inc. Served with AUS, 1943-46. Fellow A.I.A. (pres. S.W. Wash. chpt. 1967-68); mem. Wash. Hist. Soc., U. Wash. Alumni Assn. (all life). Home: 12735 Gravelly Lake Dr SW Tacoma WA 98499-1459 Office: 703 Pacific Ave Tacoma WA 98402-5207

LI DESSAU, KATHRYN DAIROH, product manager; b. Red Bank, N.J., Oct. 4, 1965; d. Tingye and Edith (Wu) Li; m. Daniel Stephen Dessau, Sept. 9, 1990. AB, Princeton U., 1987; MA, Stanford U., 1989, PhD, 1992. Product mgr. New Focus, Inc., Sunnyvale, Calif., 1992—. Contbr. articles to profl. jours. Recipient Fannie and John Hertz fellow Hertz Found., 1987-92, Grad. Rsch. Program for Women grant AT&T, 1987-92, Achievement award Coll. Scientists Found. scholarship, 1992. Mem. IEEE, Optical Soc. Am. Office: New Focus Inc 2630 Walsh Ave Santa Clara CA 95051

LIDGATE, DOREEN WANDA, retired librarian; b. Seattle, Jan. 27, 1925; d. Robert Jesse and Doris Ivy (Giffin) L. BA, U. Wash., 1946, M in Librarianship, 1966. Tchr. music St. Nicholas Sch., Seattle, 1948-70, libr., 1950-70, dean of students, 1968-70; reference libr. depts. edn., sociology, psychology Seattle Pub. Libr., 1971-74; libr. in charge Ratti Perbix Clark, Seattle, 1974-90; ret., 1990; cons. libr. rsch., 1990—. Mem. The Mountaineers, Wash. Athletic Club (v.p. 1955, associate women's bd. 1954), Beta Phi Mu, Alpha Chi Omega. Home: 2214 Viewmont Way W Seattle WA 98199-3824

LIDICKER, WILLIAM ZANDER, JR., zoologist, educator; b. Evanston, Ill., Aug. 19, 1932; s. William Zander and Frida (Schroeter) L.; m. Naomi Ishino, Aug. 18, 1956 (div. Oct., 1982); children: Jeffrey Roger, Kenneth Paul; m. Louise N. DeLonzor, June 5, 1989. B.S., Cornell U., 1953; M.S., U. Ill., 1954, Ph.D., 1957. Instr. zoology, asst. curator mammals U. Calif., Berkeley, 1957-59; asst. prof., asst. curator U. Calif., 1959-65, assoc. prof., assoc. curator, 1965-69; assoc. dir. Mus. Vertebrate Zoology, 1968-81, acting dir., 1974-75, prof. zoology, curator mammals, 1969-89, prof. integrative biology, curator of mammals, 1989—. Contbr. articles to profl. jours. Bd. dirs. No. Calif. Com. for Environ. Info., 1971-77; bd. trustees BIOSIS, 1987-92, chmn., 1992; N.Am. rep. steering com., sect. Mammalogy IUBS, UNESCO, 1978-89; chmn. rodent specialist group Species Survival Commn., IUCN, 1980-89; mem. sci. adv. bd. Marine World Found. at Marine World Africa USA, 1987—; pres. Dehnel-Petrusewicz Meml. Fund, 1985—. Fellow AAAS, Calif. Acad. Scis.; mem. Am. Soc. Mammalogists (hon. mem., dir., 2d v.p. 1974-76, pres. 1976-78, C.H. Merriam award 1986), Am. Soc. Naturalists, Berkeley Folk Dancers Club (pres. 1969, tchr. 1984—), others. Office: U Calif Mus Vertebrate Zoology Berkeley CA 94720

LIDMAN, ROGER WAYNE, museum director; b. June 8, 1956; s. Arthur Arvid and Elna G. (Bernson) L.; m. Cynthia Louise Platt, May 26, 1988. BA in Anthropology, Ariz. State U., 1987, postgrad. studies, 1987-91. Mus. aide Pueblo Grande Mus., Phoenix, 1976-84, exhibit preparator, 1984-86, ops. coord., 1986-89, acting dir., 1989-90, dir., 1990—. Mem. Am. Assn. Mus. (officer small mus. adminstr. com. 1993-94, treas. 1994-95), Mus. Assn. Ariz. (v.p. 1994-95), Ctrl. Ariz. Mus. Assn. (v.p. 1992, pres. 1993-94). Office: Pueblo Grande MUs 4619 E Washington St Phoenix AZ 85034-1909

LIDOFSKY, STEVEN DAVID, medical educator; b. Bklyn., Jan. 19, 1954; s. Leon Julian and Eleanor Helen (Liebman) L.; m. Elisabeth Tang Barfod, May 3, 1982; children: Benjamin Barfod, Anna Barfod. BA, Columbia U., 1975, PhD, 1980, MD, 1982. Bd. cert. in gastroenterology and internal medicine Am. Bd. Internal Medicine. Intern U. Colo., Denver, 1982-83, resident, 1983-85, chief med. resident, 1985-86; fellow in gastroenterology U. Calif., San Francisco, 1986-90, asst. prof. medicine, 1990—. Contbr. articles to profl. jours. Recipient Liver Scholar award Am. Liver Found., 1990-93. Mem. Am. Assn. for Study of Liver Diseases, Am. Fedn. for Clin. Rsch., Am. Gastroenterol. Assn. (Fiterman Found. Rsch. award 1994), Calif. Acad. Medicine. Office: Univ Calif San Francisco GI Unit S357 San Francisco CA 94143-0538

LIDSTONE, HERRICK KENLEY, JR., lawyer; b. New Rochelle, N.Y., Sept. 10, 1949; s. Herrick Kenley and Marcia Edith (Drake) L.; m. Mary Lynne O'Toole, Aug. 5, 1978; children: Herrick Kevin, James Patrick, John Francis. AB, Cornell U., 1971; JD, U. Colo., 1978. Bar: Colo. 1978, U.S. Dist. Ct. Colo. 1978. Assoc. Roath & Brega, P.C., Denver, 1978-85, Brenman, Epstein, Raskin & Friedlob, P.C., Denver, 1985-86; shareholder Brenman, Raskin & Friedlob, P.C., Denver, 1986-94, Friedlob Sanderson Raskin Paulson & Tourtilott, LLC, Denver, 1995—; adj. prof. U. Denver Coll. Law, 1985—; speaker in field various orgns.; fluent in Spanish. Editor U. Colo. Law Rev., 1977-78; co-author: Federal Income Taxation of Corporations, 6th edit.; contbr. articles to profl. jours. Served with USN, 1971-75, with USNR, 1975-81. Mem. ABA (Am. Law Inst.), Colo. Bar Assn., Denver Bar Assn., Denver Assn. Oil and Gas Title Lawyers. Office: Friedlob Sanderson Raskin Paulson & Tourtillott LLC 1400 Glenarm Pl Denver CO 80202-5030

LIEBAU, FREDERIC JACK, JR., investment manager; b. Palo Alto, Calif., Sept. 30, 1963; s. Frederic Jack and Charlene (Conrad) L. BA, Stanford U., 1985. Press aide Office of V.P., Washington, 1982; intern L.A. Times, 1983; analyst Capital Rsch. Co., L.A., 1984-86; v.p. Primecap Mgmt. Co., Pasadena, Calif., 1986—; owner Liebau Farms, Arcadia, Calif. Home: 1014 Fairview Ave Apt 5 Arcadia CA 91007-7163 Office: Primecap Mgmt Co 225 S Lake Ave Pasadena CA 91101

LIEBERMAN, BRANDON STUART, broadcast executive; b. L.A., July 30, 1961; s. Barry Sherwin L. and Joan Yvonne (Fischer) Drabkin. Music dir. Sta. KBVR-FM Radio, Corvallis, Oreg., 1982-85, sta. mgr., 1983-85; import and ind. buyer Tower Records, Beaverton, Oreg., 1985-87; ind. buyer Music Millennium, Portland, Oreg., 1987—; music dir. Sta. KBOO-FM Radio, Portland, 1990—; pvt. practice as concert promoter, Corvallis, Portland, 1983—. Contbr. articles to profl. jours. Office: Sta KBOO-FM Radio 20 SE 8th Ave Portland OR 97214-1203

LIEBERMAN, CAROLE ILENE, media psychiatrist, consultant. BA in Psychology with honors, SUNY, Stony Brook; MD, U. de Louvain, Belgium. Diplomate Am. Bd. Psychiatry and Neurology. Intern Mt. Sinai Hosp., Hartford, Conn., N.Y. Infirmary, N.Y.C.; resident in psychiatry NYU/Bellevue Psychiatry Hosp., N.Y.C.; ednl. cons. Met. State Hosp., L.A.; mem. attending staff Motion Picture and TV Hosp., L.A.; mem. assoc. staff Cedars Sinai Hosp./Thalians Mental Health Ctr., L.A.; pvt. practice Beverly Hills; asst. clin. prof. psychiatry UCLA/Neuropsychiat. Inst.; med. advisor/med. editor (cable TV programs) Your Mental Health-Informathon, 1984, Depression Informathon, 1985, The Nephronauts, 1986; lectr. in field. Author: Love Transplant: A High Risk Affairs of the Heart, 1990; columnist Show Biz Shrink Nat. Examiner, 1994—; columnist, contbr. The Malibu Times, 1986—, Malibu Surfside News, 1984-89, Working World mag., 1990, Ency. Britannica, 1990, Michael Jackson, The Magic and the Madness, Your View, 1991, Health Net News, 1992, Doctors Book of Home Remedies for Children, Glam Scam, Abuse of Discretion: The Rodney King Story; (TV scripts) Stranger Dangers, My House to Yours, Seeds of Success, What If It Were Real?, Feeling Female and Fine, Feelings Behind the Masks, (with Ginny Weissman) America's Un-Wanted and Mouseketeers Become Imagineers...And You Can Too!; contbr. articles to profl. jours., mags., and newspapers; host/prodr. (cable TV series) Real Talk about Reel Life, 1992, What You Always Wanted to Know about Psychiatry...But Were Afraid to Ask, The Seven Warning Signals of Mental Illness, (dramatic therapy) Psycho-Theatre; host Understanding Asthma, Lifetime TV, 1987-88, (weekly radio series) Life Perspectives with Dr. Carole Lieberman, 1990, Dr. Carole Lieberman with Real Talk about Reel Life, 1990-91, Real Talk about Reel Life with Dr. Carole Lieberman, Sta. KWNK, 1991-92, Sta. KGIL, 1992; host (radio shows) Psychiatry and the Media, 1990-92, Hollywood Correspondent, 1993—; numerous TV, radio appearances and psychology call-in shows. Mem. Pub. Access Producer's Acad., 1985-87, Calif. Theater Coun., 1985-87. Recipient Film Adv. Bd. Excellence award, 1990, Mayor Bradley commendation for scipt consulting, City of L.A., Emmy award, 1992, 93, O'Henry prize for lit. N.Y. Mem. Am. Psychiat. Assn., So. Calif. Psychiat. Soc. (pub. info. com. 1980—, co-chair 1982-85), Malibu Med. Soc. (chair pub. info. com. 1986-89), Nat. Insts. for Profl. Edn. (bd. govs. 1983-86, NYU/Bellevue Psychiat. Soc., Los Angeles County Med. Women's Assn., Am. Assn. Dirs. Psychiat. Residency Tng., Soc. for Liaison Psychiatry, Nat. Coalition on TV Violence (chair 1992-93, bd. dirs. 1990-93, spokesperson 1987-93), Writers Guild Am. (Outstanding Achievement TV Children's Script award 1992), AFTRA, Motion Picture Assn. Am. (press credentials), Acad. TV Arts and Scis.

LIEBERMAN, FREDRIC, ethnomusicologist, educator; b. N.Y.C., Mar. 1, 1940; s. Stanley and Bryna (Mason L.). MusB, U. Rochester, 1962; MA in Ethnomusicology, U. Hawaii, 1965; PhD in Music, UCLA, 1977; diploma in Electronics, Cleve. Inst. Electronics, 1973; cert. Inst. for Ednl. Mgmt., Harvard U., 1984. Asst. prof. music Brown U., Providence, 1968-75; assoc. prof. U. Wash., Seattle, 1975-83, chmn. dir. ethnomusicology, 1977-80, dir. sch. music, 1981-83; prof. U. Calif., Santa Cruz, 1983—, dir. dept. arts, 1983-85, provost Porter Coll., 1983-85; chmn. Bd. of Studies in Music, 1988-92; fieldworker, Taiwan and Japan, 1963-64, Sikkim, winter 1970, Madras, India, winters 1977, 78, 82, 83; mem. folk arts panel Nat. Endowment for Arts, 1977-80, internat. panel, 1979-80; panelist basic rsch. divsn. NEH, 1982-84, Calif. Arts Coun., 1993, Mass. Cultural Coun., 1995; fieldworker, presenter Smithsonian Instn. Festival Am. Folklife, 1978-82; reviewer Ctr. for Scholarly Comm. with People's Republic China, 1979—; exch. lectr. U. Warsaw, Poland, spring 1980; co-dir. summer seminar for coll. tchrs. NEH, 1977; dir. Am. Mus. Heritage Found., 1991—. Author: Chinese Music: An Annotated Bibliography, 1970, 2d edit., 1979, A Chinese Zither Tutor: The Mei-An Ch'in-P'u, 1983, (with Mickey Hart) Drumming at the Edge of Magic, 1990, Planet Drum: A Celebration of Percussion and Rhythm, 1991; editor (with Fritz A Kuttner) Perspectives on Asian Music: Essays in Honor of Lawrence Picken, 1975; gen. editor Garland Bibliographies in Ethnomusicology, 1980-86; mem. editorial bd. Musica Asiatica, 1984—; contbr. numerous articles and revs. to profl. publs.; composer: Suite for Piano, 1964, Sonatina for Piano, 1964, Two Short String Quartets, 1966, Leaves of Brass (for brass quartet), 1967, Psalm 137; By the Rivers of Babylon (for chorus), 1971; records include China I: String Instruments, 1969, China II: Amoy Music, 1971, Music of Sikkim, 1975; ethnomusicology cons. 360 Degrees Prodns., 1988—; filmer, editor (with Michael Moore) Traditional Music and Dance of Sikkim, Parts I and II, 1976; producer, dir., editor videotape Documenting Traditional Performance, 1978. Mem. exec. bd. Pub. Radio Sta. KRAB-FM, Seattle, 1977-78; mem. King County Arts Commn., Seattle, 1977-80. Grantee Nat. Endowment for the Arts, 1978, NEH, 1978, 80.; N.Y. State Regents fellow, 1958-62, East-West Ctr. fellow and travel grantee, 1962-65, UCLA Chancellor's teaching fellow, 1965-69, John D. Rockefeller 3d Fund research fellow, 1970-71. Mem. NARAS, Soc. for Ethnomusicology (editor Ethnomusicology 1977-81, nat. coun. 1970-72, 74-76, 78-81, 83-86), Soc. for Asian Music (editorial bd. Asian Music 1968-77, editor publs. series 1968—), Coll. Music Soc. (nat. coun. 1973-75, exec. bd. 1974-75, 76-77), Conf. on Chinese Oral and Performing Lit. (exec. bd. 1971-74, 78-80), ASCAP, Internat. Coun. Traditional Music, Am. Musical Heritage Found. (treas. 1991—), Phi Mu Alpha Sinfonia. Office: U Calif Porter Coll Santa Cruz CA 95064

LIEBERMAN, GERALD J., statistics educator; b. N.Y.C., Dec. 31, 1925; s. Joseph and Ida (Margolis) L.; m. Helen Herbert, Oct. 27, 1950; children—Janet, Joanne, Michael, Diana. B.S. in Mech. Engring., Cooper Union, 1948; A.M. in Math. Stats., Columbia U., 1949; Ph.D., Stanford U., 1953. Math. statistician Nat. Bur. Standards, 1949-50; mem. faculty Stanford U., 1953—, prof. statistics and indsl. engring., 1959-67, prof. statistics and operations research, 1967—, chmn. dept. operations research, 1967-75, assoc. dean Sch. Humanities and Scis., 1975-77, acting v.p. and provost, 1979, vice provost, 1977-85, dean research, 1977-80, dean grad. studies and research, 1980-85, provost, 1992-93; cons. to govt. and industry, 1953—. Author: (with A.H. Bowker) Engineering Statistics, 1959, 2d edit., 1972, (with F.S. Hillier) Introduction to Operations Research, 1967, 6th edit., 1995. Ctr. Advanced Studies in Behavioral Scis. fellow, 1985-86. Fellow Am. Statis. Assn., Inst. Math. Statistics, Am. Soc. Quality Control (Shewhart medal 1972), AAAS; mem. Nat. Acad. Engring., Inst. Mgmt. Sci. (pres. 1980-81), Ops. Research Soc. Am., Sigma Xi, Pi Tau Sigma. Home: 811 San Francisco Ter Stanford CA 94305-1021

LIEBERT, MARTHA ANN, public librarian; b. Grand Forks, N.D., Mar. 25, 1933; d. Paul E. and Margaret Eva (Libby) Barr; m. Joseph H. Liebert; children: Paul A., Thor M., Mark J. BS in Edn., U. N.D., 1955; MA in Art, U. N.Mex., 1957. Librarian Town of Bernalillo, N.Mex., 1965-89; archivist Sandoval County Hist. Soc., Bernalillo, 1969—. County chmn. Easter Seals, Sandoval County, 1960s; mem. Housing Authority Town of Bernalillo, 1969-70; co-chair LWV, Sandoval County, 1974; bd. dirs. N.Mex. State Libr. Assn., Santa Fe, 1987. Recipient Jefferson award N.Mex. Award Com., 1985, Cmty. Achievement award N.Mex. Libr. Assn., 1986; named Gov.'s Outstanding Women of N.Mex., N.Mex. Gov.'s Commn. on Status of Women, 1989; Pub. Libr. Named in Honor of Martha Ann Liebert, Town of Bernalillo, 1985; grantee and dir. N.Mex. Endowment for the Humanities, Photographic History of Sandoval County. Mem. N.Mex. State Hist. Soc., Sandoval County Hist. Soc. (pres. 1980-85), AAUW, Westerners Corral, Alumni of U. Of N.D. (Alumni award 1987), P.E.O. Sisterhood. Home: PO Box 223 Bernalillo NM 87004-0223

LIEBHABER, MYRON I., allergist; b. Dec. 28, 1943. MD, U. Ariz., 1972. Allergist College Hosp., Santa Barbara, Calif.; asst. vis. clin. prof. UCLA. Office: Santa Barbara Med Found Clinic 215 Pesetas Ln Santa Barbara CA 93110*

LIECHTY, CLINTON, lawyer; b. Logan, Utah, Feb. 28, 1949; s. Mada (Hulse) L.; m. Carol Ann Mathews, July 1, 1972; children: Brian, Heidi, Matthew, Heather, Jennifer, Tyler. BS, Utah State U., 1975; JD, Gonzaga Law Sch., 1978. Bar: Ariz. 1979, U.S. Ct. Appeals (9th cir.) 1980, U.S. Supreme Ct. 1982. Pvt. practice Tucson, 1979—; talk show host, You and The Law Radio, Tucson, 1979-92. Century mem. Boy Scouts Am., Tucson, 1988, com. chmn. 1984—, dist. adv. chmn., 1993—; With USAR, 1967-73. Named Most Valuable Com. Chmn., Boy Scouts Am., Tucson, 1989; Rockefeller Found. research grantee, Utah State U., 1973; J. Reuben Clark fellowship Provo, Utah, 1989—. Mem. Pima County Bar Assn. (ed. com. mem. 1979—), Tucson Rod & Gun Club. Mem. LDS Ch. Office: 360 N Court Ave Tucson AZ 85701-1035

LIEHR, ROBERT JOSEPH, private school educator; b. N.Y.C., Oct. 5, 1947; s. Arthur and Gloria Margaret (Sadlier) Carcanis. AA, Alpena (Mich.) C.C., 1967; BA, San Jose State U., 1969; postgrad., U. Calif., Santa Cruz, 1973, U. Santa Clara, 1974. Standard scondary edn. credential, Calif. Tchr. history Woodrow Wilson Jr. H.S., San Jose, Calif., 1970, Bret Harte Jr. H.S., San Jose, 1971-75, John Steinbeck Jr. H.S., San Jose, 1975-82; tchr. history, head dept. Gunderson H.S., San Jose, 1982-92; tchr., internat. baccalaureate instr. San Jose High Acad., 1992—; mem. Ctr. for Rsch. on Context Secondary Sch. Teaching, Stanford U., Palo Alto, Calif., 1988-92. With U.S. Army, 1970-76. Mem. NEA, Calif. Tchrs. Assn., San Jose Tchrs. Assn., San Jose State U. Alumni Assn. Office: San Jose High Acad 275 N 24th St San Jose CA 95116-1109

LIEN, ERIC JUNG-CHI, pharmacist, educator; b. Kaohsiung, Taiwan, Nov. 30, 1937; came to U.S., 1963, naturalized, 1973; m. Linda L. Chen, Oct. 2, 1965; children: Raymond, Andrew. B.S. in Pharmacy (Frank Shu China Sci. scholar), Nat. Taiwan U., 1960; Ph.D. in Pharm. Chemistry, U. Calif., San Francisco, 1966; postdoctoral fellow in bio-organic chemistry, Pomona Coll., Claremont, Calif., 1967-68. Hosp. pharmacist 862 Hosp. of Republic of China, 1960-61; asst. prof. pharmaceutics and biomedicinal chemistry U. So. Calif., L.A., 1968-72; assoc. prof. U. So. Calif., 1972-76, prof., 1976—, coord. sects. biomedicinal chemistry and pharms., 1975-78, coord. sect. biomedicinal chemistry, 1975-84; cons. Internat. Medication Sys., Ltd., 1978, NIH, 1971, 82-87, 92, 94, Inst. Drug Design, Inc., Calif., 1971-73, Allergan Pharms, Inc., 1971-72, EPA, 1985, 89, Ariz. Disease Control Rsch. Commn., 1986—; sci. adv. nat. labs. Dept. Health, Foods and Drugs, Exec., Yuan, China, Dept. Health Taipei, Taiwan, 1992-94; referee Jour. Pharmacokinetics and Biopharmaceutics, Jour. Medicinal Chemistry, Jour. Food Agr. Chemistry, Jour. Pharm Sci., Pesticide Biochemistry and Physiology, Chem. Resv., Jour. Organic Chemistry, Pharm. Rsch., Internat. Jour. Oriental Medicine, Am. Jour. Pharm. Edn. Author 3 books; mem. editorial bd. Jour. Clin. Pharmacy and Therapeutics, 1979—, Internat. Jour. Oriental Medicine, Med. Chem. Rsch., 1991—, Chinese Pharm. Jour., 1991-93, Acta Pharmaceutica, 1992—; contbr. numerous articles to profl. jours. Grantee Merck, 1970, Abbott, 1971-72, NSF, 1972-74, 76-77, IMS, 1979, H & L Found., 1989-95. Fellow AAPS, AAAS, Louis Pasteur Found.; mem. Am. Assn. Cancer Rsch., Acad. Pharm. Scis., Am. Chem. Soc., Am. Assn. Pharm. Scientist, Internat. Union Pure and Applied Chemistry, Sigma Xi, Rho Chi, Phi Kappa Phi. Office: U So Calif Sch Pharmacy 1985 Zonal Ave Los Angeles CA 90033-1058

LIESMAN, WILLIAM RUSSELL, oil company executive; b. Reading, Pa., Apr. 12, 1950; s. William Elbert and Helen Elizabeth (Russell) L.; m. Peggy Darlene Jacoby, June 24, 1977; children: Lauren Elizabeth, Alexis Christina, Aniela Catherine. BA, Coll. Holy Cross, Worcester, Mass., 1972; MA, Columbia U., N.Y.C., 1974. Commodities trader Philipp Brothers Div., N.Y.C., 1974-76; dir. mineral exports Philipp Brothers Australia Ltd., Sydney, 1976-78; mng. dir. Philipp Brothers Thai Ltd., Bangkok, 1978-81, Philipp Brothers Singapore Ltd., 1981-85; dir. regional mgr. Phibro Energy Singapore Ltd., 1985-88; pres., br. mgr. Phibro Energy Taiwan, Inc., Taipei, 1988-93; Asia-Pacific mgr. Phibro Energy, Winchester, Calif., 1993-94; pvt. practice bus. cons., 1994—. Bus. editor Jour. Internat. Affairs, 1972-74. Bd. dirs. Singapore Trade Devel. Bd., 1986-88. Office: 34155 Winchester Rd Winchester CA 92596-9771

LIGGETT, THOMAS MILTON, mathematics educator; b. Danville, Ky., Mar. 29, 1944; s. Thomas Jackson and Virginia Corinne (Moore) L.; m. Christina Marie Goodale, Aug. 19, 1972; children: Timothy, Amy. AB, Oberlin Coll., 1965; MS, Stanford U., 1966, PhD, 1969. Asst. prof. UCLA, 1969-73, assoc. prof., 1973-76, prof., 1976—. Author: Interacting Particle Systems, 1985; editor Jour. Annals of Probability, 1985-87; contbr. articles to profl. jours. Fellow Sloan Found., 1973. Fellow Inst. Math. Stats.; mem. Am. Math. Soc., Math. Assn. Am., Bernoulli Soc. Office: UCLA Math Dept 405 Hilgard Ave Los Angeles CA 90024-1301

LIGGINS, GEORGE LAWSON, microbiologist, diagnostic company executive; b. Roanoke, Va., June 19, 1937; m. Joyce Preston Liggins, Sept. 3, 1966; 1 child, George Lawson Jr. BA, Hampton U., 1962; cert. med. technician, Meharry Med. Sch., 1963; MPH, U. N.C., 1969; PhD, U. Va., Charlottesville, 1975. Med. technician Vets. Hosp., Hampton, Va., 1963-66; rsch. technician U. N.C. Med. Sch., Chapel Hill, 1966-69; postdoctoral fellow Scripps Clinic, La Jolla, Calif., 1975-76, Salk Inst., La Jolla, 1976-77; rsch. mgr. Hyland div. Baxter, Costa Mesa, Calif., 1977-78; R & D dir. diagnostics div. Baxter, Roundlake, Ill., 1978-83; pres., COO Internat. Immunology, Murrieta, Calif., 1983-86; chmn., CEO Bacton Assay Systems, Inc., San Marcos, Calif., 1986—; cons. Beckman Instruments, Inc., Brea, Calif., 1987-90, Paramax divsn. Baxter, Irvine, Calif., 1988-90, Scantibodies Lab., Santee, Calif., 1990-92; presenter in field; mem. virology study Cold Spring Harbor Lab., L.I., N.Y., 1974. Contbr. articles to profl. jours. Fellow NIH, 1975, Am. Cancer Soc., 1976. Mem. Am. Soc. Microbiology, Am. Assn. Clin. Chemistry, Van Slyke Soc. of Am. Assn. Clin. Chemistry, Am. Heart Assn., Nat. Hampton Alumni, Inc. (pres. 1991—), Omega Psi Phi. Republican. Methodist. Office: Bacton Assay Systems Inc 772-A N Twin Oaks Valley Rd San Marcos CA 92069

LIGHT, IVAN HUBERT, sociology educator; b. Chgo., Nov. 3, 1941; s. Ivan Huber and Lily Ann (Schulz) L.; m. Leah Lazarovitz, June 15, 1966; children: Matthew, Nathaniel. BA, Havard, 1963; MA, PhD, U. Calif., 1969. Prof. U. Calif., L.A., 1969—. Author: Ethnic Enterprise in America, 1972, Immigrant Entrepreneurs, 1988, Cities in World Perspective, 1983, Immigration & Entrepreneurship, 1993, Race, Ethnicity and Entrepreneurship in Urban America, 1995. Pres. Claremont Dem. Club, 1993-94. Rsch. fellowship Nat. Sci. Found., Washington, 1976-79, 85-86, 88-89. Mem. Am. Assn. Univ. Profs. (pres. UCLA chpt. 1994-95), Am. Sociological Assn. (pres. 1969), Sierra Club (pres. 1971). Democrat. Episcopalian. Office: UCLA Dept Sociology 405 Hilgard Ave Los Angeles CA 90024-1301

LIGHTON, JOHN REGINALD BRANDE, biologist, educator; b. Johannesburg, Traansvaal, South Africa, Aug. 25, 1952; came to the U.S., 1984; s. Reginald Eliot and Lorna Catherine (Brande) L.; m. Monika Ritter, Aug. 25, 1985. BA, U. Cape Town, South Africa, 1975; BSc, U. Cape Town, 1981, MSc, 1984; PhD, UCLA, 1987. Postdoctoral fellow UCLA, 1987-88, adj. asst. prof., 1989; guest prof. U. Zurich, Switzerland, 1990; asst. prof. U. Utah, Salt Lake City, 1991—; pres. Sable Sys., Salt Lake City, 1987—. Contbr. articles to profl. jours. Packard fellow D & L Packard Found., Montery, Calif., 1993. Fellow Packard Found.; mem. AAAS, Am. Soc. Zoologists. Office: Biology Dept Univ Utah Salt Lake City UT 84112

LIGHTSTONE, RONALD, lawyer; b. N.Y.C., Oct. 4, 1938; s. Charles and Pearl (Weisberg) L.; m. Nancy Lehrer, May 17, 1973; 1 child, Dana. AB, Columbia U., 1959; JD, NYU, 1962. Atty. CBS, N.Y.C., 1967-69; assoc. dir. bus. affairs CBS News, N.Y.C., 1969-70; atty. NBC, N.Y.C., 1970; assoc. gen. counsel Viacom Internat. Inc., N.Y.C., 1970-75; v.p., gen. counsel, sec. Viacom Internat. Inc., 1976-80; v.p. bus. affairs Viacom Entertainment Group Viacom Internat., Inc., 1980-82, v.p. corp. affairs, 1982-84, sr. v.p. corp. and legal affairs, 1984-87; exec. v.p. Spelling Entertainment Inc., L.A., 1988-91, COO, 1991-93; chmn. Multimedia Labs. Inc., 1994—, Producers Entertainment Group, 1995—; bd. dirs. Starsight Telecast, Inc.; chmn. Prodrs. Entertainment Group, Ltd., 1995—. Served to lt. USN, 1962-66. Mem. ABA (chmn. TV, cable and radio com.), Assn. Bar City N.Y., Fed. Communications Bar Assn.

LIGHTWOOD, CAROL WILSON, writer; b. Tacoma, Wash., Oct. 2, 1941; d. Harry Edward and Cora H. Wilson; m. Keith G. Lightwood (div. Dec. 1968); children: Miles Francis, Clive Harry. BA, Smith Coll., 1963. Writer various advt. agencies, 1968-82; v.p. Wakeman & DeForrest, Newport Beach, Calif., 1985-86; owner Lightwood & Ptnrs., Santa Barbara, Calif., 1986—. Author: Malibu, 1984; contbr. articles to profl. jours. Chair mus. coun. Long Beach Mus. Art, 1989; docent William O. Douglas Outdoor Classroom. Mem. Sierra Club, Sisters in Crime. Episcopalian.

LIGON, PATTI-LOU E., real estate investor, educator; b. Riverside, Calif., Feb. 28, 1953; d. Munford Ernest and Patsy Hazel (Bynum) L. BS, San Diego State U., 1976; BBA, Nat. U., San Diego, 1983, MA in Bus. Adminstrn., 1984; Clear Profl. Credential, Nat. U., 1986. Cert. profl. counselor. Escrow asst. Cajon Valley Escrow, El Cajon, Calif., 1978-79; escrow asst. Summit Escrow, San Diego, 1979-81; escrow officer Fidelity Nat. Title, San Diego, 1982-84, Dawson Escrow, San Diego, 1984; owner, property mgr., investment adviser Ligon Enterprises, San Diego, 1980—, cons., 1982—. Chmn. com., alumnae and assocs. San Diego State U., 1983, 84, 85; com. chmn. San Diego Zool. soc., 1985; pres. Friends of Symphony, Riverside, Calif., 1978. Recipient commendation City and County of Honolulu, 1981. Mem. Nat. Notary Assn., Calif. Escrow Assn., Am. Home Ecns. Assn., Nat. Assn. Female Execs, Internat. Platform Assn., Calif. Bus. Edn. Assn., Jr. League of San Diego, Sigma Kappa (pres. 1974, v.p. sorority corp. 1976—). Republican. Methodist. Club: Spinster (pres. 1981), Univ. (San Diego). Avocations: racquetball; clothing design; photography; travel. Home and Office: Ligon Enterprises 7937 Wetherley St La Mesa CA 91941-6335

LIGRANI, PHILLIP MEREDITH, mechanical engineering educator, consultant; b. Cheyenne, Wyoming, Feb. 2, 1952; s. Alfred Joseph Ligrani and Marilyn Virginia (Waugh) Whittaker. BS, U. Tex., 1974; MS, Stanford U., 1975, PhD, 1980. Asst. prof. Von Karman Isnt. for Fluid Dynamics, Rhode St. Genese, Belgium, 1979-82; sr. rsch. fellow Imperial Coll. U. London, 1982-84; assoc. prof. mech. engring. Naval Postgrad. Sch., Monterey, Calif., 1984-92, U. Utah, Salt Lake City, 1992—. Author 4 book chpts.; contbr. over 40 articles to profl. jours. Recipient Menneken award for excellence sci. rsch. Menneken Found., 1990. Mem. ASME (K-14 heat transfer com. 1986—). Office: U Utah Mech Engring MEB 3209 Salt Lake City UT 84112

LIKENS, JAMES DEAN, economics educator; b. Bakersfield, Calif., Sept. 12, 1937; s. Ernest LeRoy and Monnie Jewel (Thomas) L.; m. Janet Sue Pelton, Dec. 18, 1965 (div.); m. Karel Carnohan, June 4, 1988 (div.); children: John David, Janet Elizabeth. BA in Econs., U. Calif., Berkeley, 1960, MBA, 1961; PhD in Econs., U. Minn., 1970. Analyst Del Monte Corp., San Francisco, 1963; economist 3M Co., Mpls., 1968-71; asst. prof. econs. Pomona Coll., 1969-75, assoc. prof. econs., 1975-83, prof. econs., 1983-85, Morris B. Pendleton prof. econs., 1989—; vis. asst. prof. econs. U. Minn., 1970, 71, vis. assoc. prof., 1976-77; pres., dean Western CUNA Mgmt. Sch., Pomona Coll., 1975—; chmn. bd. 1st City Savs. Fed. Credit Union, 1978—; coord. So. Calif. Rsch. Coun., L.A., 1980-81, 84-85; mem. adv. coun. Western Corp. Fed. Credit Union, 1993—; cons. in field. Author: (with Joseph LaDou) Medicine and Money, 1976, Mexico and Southern California: Toward A New Partnership, 1981, Financing Quality Education in Southern California, 1985; contbr. articles to profl. jours. Served with USCG, 1961-67. Rsch. grantee HUD-DOT, Haynes Found., Filene Rsch. Inst. Mem. ABA, Am. Econ. Assn., Western Econ. Assn. Home: 725 W 10th St Claremont CA 91711-3719 Office: Pomona Coll Dept Econs Claremont CA 91711

LIKENS, SUZANNE ALICIA, physiologist, researcher; b. Chgo., Nov. 12, 1945; d. Harry Ross and Sibyle Lovelett (Butler) L. BS in Biology, U. N.Mex., 1969, MS in Physiology, 1982. Research asst. biology dept. U. N.Mex, Albuquerque, 1969; sr. research technologist Inhalation Toxicology Research Inst., Albuquerque, 1974-93; lab. scientist II state lab. divsn.

N.Mex. Dept. Pub. Health, Albuquerque, 1994—; mgr. dressage horse shows Am. Horse Show Assn./U.S. Dressage Fedn. Contbr. sci. papers and articles to profl. jours. Mem. N.Mex. Mus. Natural History & Sci. Found. Mem. AAAS, N.Mex. Natural History and Sci. Mus. Found. (docent, operator planetarium, lectr. on astronomy), N.Mex. Zool. Soc., N.Mex. Herpetol. Soc. (charter), Cousteau Soc., Women in Sci. and Engring., Am. Horse Show Assn., U.S. Dressage Fedn., N.Mex. Dressage and Combined Tng. Assn., S.W. Dressage Assn. (bd. dirs. 1989-94), N.Y. Acad. Scis., Sigma Xi. Republican. Presbyterian. Home: 1311 Dartmouth Dr NE Albuquerque NM 87106-1803

LILLA, JAMES A., plastic surgeon; b. Comfrey, Mont., June 12, 1943. MD, Stanford U., 1969. Plastic surgeon Sutter Cmty. Hosp., Calif.; asst. clin. prof. plastic surgery U. Calif. Davis. Office: Hand Surg Assocs 1201 Alhambra Blvd Ste 410 Sacramento CA 95816-5243*

LILLEGRAVEN, JASON ARTHUR, paleontologist, educator; b. Mankato, Minn., Oct. 11, 1938; s. Arthur Oscar and Agnes Mae (Eaton) L.; m. Bernice Ann Hines, Sept. 5, 1964 (div. Feb. 1983); children: Brita Anna, Ture Andrew; m. Linda Elizabeth Thompson, June 5, 1983. BA, Long Beach State Coll., 1962; MS, S.D. Sch. Mines and Tech., 1964; PhD, U. Kans., 1968. Professional geologist, Wyo. Postdoctoral fellow Dept. Paleontology U. Calif., Berkeley, 1968-69; from asst. prof. to prof. zoology San Diego State U., 1969-75; from assoc. prof. to prof. geology and zoology U. Wyo., Laramie, 1975—; program dir. NSF Systematic Biology, Washington, 1977-78; assoc. dean U. Wyo. Coll. Arts and Scis., 1984-85, temporary joint appointment Dept. Geography, 1986-87; U.S. sr. scientist Inst. for Paleontology Free U., Berlin, 1988-89. Author, editor: Mesozoic Mammals the First Two Thirds of Mammalian History, 1979, Vertebrates, Phylogeny and Philosophy, 1986; editorial bds. of Research and Exploration (Nat. Geographic Soc.), Jour. of Mammalian Evolution, Jour. of Vertebrate Paleontology; contbr. articles to profl. jours. Recipient numerous rsch. grants NSF, 1970-95, George Duke Humphrey Disting. Faculty award, Humboldt prize. Mem. Am. Soc. Mammalogists, Am. Assn. Petroleum Geologists, Paleontol. Soc., Soc. Vertebrate Paleontology (pres. 1985-86), Linnean Soc. London, Soc. Mammalian Evolution, Sigma Xi. Office: U Wyo Dept Geology and Geophysics Laramie WY 80271-3006

LILLEY, WESLEY WAYNE, oil and gas industry consultant, geologist; b. Edmond, Okla., Dec. 5, 1948; s. William Wesley and Twyla Joan (Fuller) L.; m. Patricia Sue Reed, June 20, 1970; children: Nathan James, Travis Reed. BS, Ft. Hays Kans. State Coll., 1970; MS, Idaho State U., 1972; PhD, U. Kans., 1976. Cert. prof. geologist, Wyo.; registered appraiser, Colo. Geologist Sun Oil Co., Midland and Dallas, 1974-78; chief geologist Bow Valley Exploration (U.S.) Inc., Denver, 1978-79; ind. geologist Denver, 1979-80; v.p., dir., founder Dakota Resources, Inc., Denver, 1980-84; geologist, pres., owenr Quivira Energy Corp., Littleton, Colo., 1984—; ind. real estate cons. and appraiser, Littleton, 1994—. Contbr. numerous articles to profl. jours. Asst. scoutmaster, den leader Boy Scouts Am., Littleton, 1982—; coach, referee Littleton Soccer Assn., 1982—. Am. Assn. Petroleum Geologists grantee, 1973; Sigma Xi grantee, 1973. Mem. Am. Assn. Petroleum Geologists, Rocky Mountain Assn. Geologists, Mid-Continent Exploration Assn.

LILLIE, JOHN MITCHELL, transportation company executive; b. Chgo., Feb. 2, 1937; s. Walter Theodore and Mary Ann (Hatch) L.; m. Daryl Lee Harvey, Aug. 23, 1987; children: Alissa Ann, Theodore Perry. BS, Stanford U., 1959, MS, MBA, 1962-64. Various positions including dir. systems devel., also asst. to pres. Boise Cascade Corp., 1964-68; v.p., chief financial officer Arcata Nat. Corp., Menlo Park, Calif., 1968-70; exec. v.p., chief operating officer Arcata Nat. Corp., 1970-72; pres., chief exec. officer Leslie Salt Co., Newark, Calif., 1972-79; exec. v.p. Lucky Stores Inc., Dublin, Calif., 1979-81, pres., 1981-86, chmn., chief exec. officer, 1986-89; gen. ptnr. Sequoia Assocs., Menlo Park, Calif., 1989-90; pres., COO, Am. Pres. Cos., Ltd., Oakland, Calif., 1990-91, chmn., pres., CEO, 1991—; bd. dirs. Am. Pres. Co., Gap Inc. Trustee Stanford (Calif.) U., 1988—; bd. dirs. Am. Pres. Co. Mem. Beta Theta Pi, Tau Beta Pi. Office: Am Pres Cos 1111 Broadway Oakland CA 94607-4036*

LILLY, LUELLA JEAN, university administrator; b. Newberg, Oreg., Aug. 23, 1937; d. David Hardy and Edith (Coleman) L. BS, Lewis and Clark Coll., 1959; postgrad., Portland State U., 1959-61; MS, U. Oreg., 1961; PhD, Tex. Woman's U., 1971; postgrad., various univs., 1959-72. Tchr. phys. edn. and health, dean girls Cen. Linn Jr.-Sr. High Sch., Halsey, Oreg., 1959-60; tchr. phys. edn. and health, swimming, tennis, golf coach Lake Oswego (Oreg.) High Sch., 1960-63; instr., intramural dir., coach Oreg. State U., Corvallis, 1963-64; instr., intercollegiate coach Am. River Coll., Sacramento, 1964-69; dir. women's phys. edn., athletics U. Nev., Reno, 1969-73, dir. women's athletics, 1973-75, assoc. dir. athletics, 1975-76, assoc. prof. phys. edn., 1971-76; dir. women's intercollegiate athletics U. Calif., Berkeley, 1976—; organizer, coach Lue's Aquatic Club, 1962-64; v.p. PAC -10 Conf., 1990-91. Author: An Overview of Body Mechanics, 1966, 3d rev. edit., 1969. Vol. instr. ARC, 1951; vol. Heart Fund and Easter Seal, 1974-76, Am. Heart Assn., 1991-95, ofcl. Spl. Olympics, 1975; mem. L.A. Citizens Olympic Com., 1984. Recipient Mayor Anne Rudin award Nat. Girls' and Women's Sports, 1993; inducted Lewis and Clark Coll. Athletic Hall of Fame, 1988. Mem. AAHPER (life), AAUW, Nat. Soc. Profs., Nat. Assn. Coll. Women Athletic Adminstrs. (divsn. I-A women's steering com. 1991-92), Women's Athletic Caucus, Council Collegiate Women Athletics Adminstrs. (membership com. 1989-92), Western Soc. Phys. Edn. Coll. Women (membership com. 1971-74, program adv. com. 1972, exec. bd. 1972-75), Western Assn. Intercollegiate Athletics for Women (exec. bd. dirs. 1973-75, 79-82), Oreg. Girls' Swimming Coaches Assn. (pres. 1960, 63), Cen. Calif. Bd. Women Ofcls. (basketball chmn. 1968-69), Calif. Assn. Health, Phys. Edn. and Recreation (chmn.-elect jur. coll. sect. 1970), Nev. Bd. Women Ofcls. (chmn. bd., chmn. volleyball sect., chmn. basketball sect. 1969), No. Calif. Women's Intercollegiate Conf. (sec. 1970-71, basketball coordinator 1970-71), No. Calif. Intercollegiate Athletic Conf. (volleyball coordinator 1971-72), Nev. Assn. Health, Phys. Edn. and Recreation (state chmn. 1974—), No. Calif. Athletic Conf. (pres. 1979-82, sec. 1994—), Phi Kappa Phi, Theta Kappa. Lodge: Soroptimists (bd. dirs. 1988-93, v.p. 1989, 92-93). Home: 60 Margrave Ct Walnut Creek CA 94596-2511 Office: U Calif 177 Hearst Gym Berkeley CA 94720

LILLY, MICHAEL ALEXANDER, lawyer; b. Honolulu, May 21, 1946; s. Percy Anthony Jr. and Virginia (Craig) L.; m. Kathryn I. Collins, Aug. 10, 1991; children: Michael Jr., Cary J., Laura B., Claire F., Winston W. AA, Menlo Coll., Menlo Park, Calif., 1966; BA, U. Calif., Santa Cruz, 1968; JD with honors, U. of Pacific, 1974. Bar: Calif. 1974, U.S. Dist. Ct. (no., so. and ea. dists.) Calif. 1974, U.S. Ct. Appeals (9th cir.) 1974, Hawaii 1975, U.S. Dist. Ct. Hawaii 1975, U.S. Ct. Appeals (D.C. cir.) 1975, U.S. Supreme Ct. 1978, U.S. Ct. Appeals (7th cir.) 1979. Atty. Pacific Legal Found., Sacramento, 1974-75; dep. atty. gen. State of Hawaii, Honolulu, 1975-79, 1st dep. atty. gen., 1981-84, atty. gen., 1984-85; ptnr. Feeley & Lilly, San Jose, Calif., 1979-81, Ning, Lilly & Jones, Honolulu, 1985—. Author: If You Die Tomorrow-A Layman's Guide to Estate Planning. Bd. dirs. Diamond Head Theatre; Lt. USN, 1968-71, Vietnam; capt. USNR. Named hon. Ky. col. Mem. Nat. Assn. Attys. Gen., Hawaii Law Enforcement Ofcls. Assn., Navy Res. Assn. (pres. 14th dist. 1986-89), Navy League (nat. dir., contbg. editor Fore 'N Aft mag., pres., dept. judge adv. to bd. Honolulu coun.), Outrigger Canoe Club. Home: 2769 Laniloa Rd Honolulu HI 96813-1041

LILLY-HERSLEY, JANE ANNE FEELEY, nursing researcher; b. Palo Alto, Calif., May 31, 1947; d. Daniel Morris Sr. and Suzanne (Agnew) Feeley; children: Cary Jane, Laura Blachree, Claire Foale; m. Dennis C. Hersley, Jan. 16, 1993. BS, U. Oreg., 1968; student, U. Hawaii, 1970; BSN, Sacramento City Coll., 1975. Cert. ACLS, BCLS. Staff and charge nurse, acute rehab. Santa Clara Valley Med. Ctr., San Jose, Calif., staff nurse, surg. ICU and trauma unit; clin. project leader mycophenolate mofetil program team Syntex Rsch., Palo Alto. Co-founder, CFO and dir. non profit scientific rsch. CURE (Citizens United Responsible Environmentalism), Inc. Mem. AACN.

LIM, ALAN YOUNG, plastic surgeon; b. St. Louis, Apr. 11, 1953. MD, U. Calif., San Diego, 1979. Plastic surgeon Kaiser-Permanente, Sacramento, Calif.; asst. clin. prof. U. Calif. Davis. Office: Plastic Surg 2025 Morse Ave Sacramento CA 95825-2115*

LIM, JOHN K., state senator, business executive; b. Yeoju, South Korea, Dec. 23, 1935; came to U.S., 1966, naturalized, 1976; s. Eun Kyu and Seu Nyu (Chung) L.; m. Grace Young-Hee Park, Dec. 9, 1963; children: Peter, Billy, Gloria. BA in Religion, Seoul Theol. Coll., 1964; MDiv, Western Evang. Sem., Portland, Oreg., 1970. Founder, chmn. Am. Royal Jelly Co., 1972—; founder, pres. ARJ Co., 1973—; pres. Realty Resources, 1981-91; mem. Oreg. State Senate, 1993—; chair Senate Trade and Econ. Devel. Com., 1995; vice chair Senate Bus. and Consumer Affairs Com., 1995; mem. Govs. Adv. Com. on DUII, 1993—; mem. sheriffs forum Multnomah County, Oreg., 1994; asst. majority leader Oreg. State Senate, 1995. Pub.: World Korean Conference Journal, 1989; editor, pub.: (directory) World Korean C. of C., 1990, The World Korean Soc. Directory, 1989. Oreg. Gubernatorial Candidate, 1990; nat. chair Asian Am. Voters Coalition, 1990-91; bd. dirs. Rep. Nat. Com. Asian Adv., 1992; mem. exec. com. Billy Graham Crusade, Portland, Oreg., 1992; mem. Oreg.-Korea Econ. Coop., 1986-88; mem. Cmty. Bd. Mt. Hood Med. Ctr., 1993—; bd. mem. Western Evang. Sem., 1995—. Mem. Korean Am. Soc. U.S.A., Korean Soc. Oreg. (pres. 1986), Oreg. Royal Rosarian Soc., Portland Rose Soc. Republican. Office: 3630 SE Division St Portland OR 97202-1546

LIM, KENNETH TING, interactive multimedia analyst; b. Tucson, Mar. 29, 1958; m. Nancy Ann Wong, Aug. 10, 1985; children: Brian Christopher, Jordan Kendall. BS in Bus. Mgmt. and Mktg., San Jose State U., 1980, MS in cybernetic systems, 1980. Rsch. assoc. Search for Extra-Terrestrial Intelligence NASA Ames Rsch. Ctr., Mountain View, Calif., 1975-77; industry analyst personal computers Dataquest, Inc., San Jose, Calif., 1981-86; mgr. market intelligence Apple Computer, Inc., Cupertino, Calif., 1986-90, mgr. corp. tech. devel., chief futurist, 1991-93; chmn., chief futurist The CyberMedia Group, Cupertino, 1994—; chmn. U.S. Microcomputer Statistics Consortium, Washington, 1992-93, mem. exec. com., 1990-93; mem. Computer Market Analysis Group, 1991-93. Author: (with others) Demistifying Multimedia, 1993, New Media Industry: Report from Hakone Forum, 1993. Mem. Internat. Interactive Comm. Soc., Computer Game Devels.' Assn., Multimedia Devels.' Group. Home and Office: The CyberMedia Group 10410 San Fernando Ave Cupertino CA 95014-2833

LIM, LARRY KAY, university official; b. Santa Maria, Calif., July 4, 1948; s. Koonwah and Nancy (Yao) L.; m. Louise A. Simon, Aug. 15, 1988. BA, UCLA, 1970, teaching cert., 1971. Asst. engr. Force Ltd., L.A., 1969; teaching asst. UCLA, 1970-71; tchr. L.A. Sch. Dist., 1971-82; dir. minority programs Sch. Engring., U. So. Calif., L.A., 1979—; presenter minority math.-based intervention symposium U. D.C., Washington, 1988. Newsletter editor, 1981-92. Bd. dirs. Developing Ednl. Studies for Hispanics, L.A., 1983-88. Named Dir. of Yr., Math., Engring., Sci. Achievement Ctr. Adv. Bd., 1986, 91, 92. Mem. Nat. Assn. Pre-Coll. Dirs., Nat. Assn. Minority Engring. Program Adminstr., Lotus/West Club (pres. 1977-83). Office: U So Calif Sch Engring OHE 104 Los Angeles CA 90089-1455

LIM, SALLY-JANE, insurance consultant; b. Manila; came to U.S., 1990; d. Teddy and Sonia (Yii) L.; children: Robin Michael, Rodney Jovin, Romelle Gavin Lim Velasco. BA, BS in Commerce magna cum laude, Coll. of Holy Spirit, Manila. CPA, Manila. Treas, contr. Ky. Fried Chicken, Makati, Philippines, 1968-73; ins. rep. Insular Life Assurance Co., Makati, 1972-82; project analyst Pvt. Devel. Corp. of Philippines, Makati, 1972-78; account exec. Genbancor Devel. Corp., Makati, 1978-80; risk mgr. Filcapital Devel. Corp., Makati, 1978-82; pres., gen. mgr., ins. broker Sally-Jane Multiline Insce., Inc., Makati, 1978-90; real estate broker Sally-Jane Realty, Inc., Manila, 1980-90; ins. rep. Sun Life of Can./AIU (Philippines) AFIA, Makati, 1982-91; rep. Prudential Ins. & Fin. Svcs., 1990-91; registered rep. L.A. dist. Pruco Securities Corp., South Pasadena, Calif., 1990-91; registered rep. Asian Pacific dist. Pruco Securities Corp., 1992—. Recipient Young Achiever award Young Achiever Found., Quezon City, Philippines, 1988, Golden Scroll award Philippine Ednl. Youth Devel., Inc., Quezon City, 1988, Young Famous Celebrity Mother's award Golden Mother/Father Found., Quezon City, 1990, Recognition of Excellence cert. San Gabriel Valley YWCA, 1992, Most Outstanding Ins. Exec. of The Philippines bronze trophy Consumers' Union of Philippines, Manila, 1983, 88, Ten Outstanding Profl. Svc. award Achievement Rsch. Soc., Manila, 1988, numerous others. Fellow Life Underwriters Tng. Coun.; mem. Nat. Assn. Life Underwriters, Arcadia C. of C., Asian Bus. Assn., Filipino C. of C., Monrovia C. of C., Duarte C. of C., Million Dollar Round Table (life), Foothills Assn. Life Underwriters, Chinese C. of C. (bd. dirs. L.A. 1992—). Home: 1006 A Royal Oaks Dr Monrovia CA 91016-3737 Office: Prudential of Am Penthouse 1255 Corporate Center Dr Monterey Park CA 91754

LIM, SHIRLEY GEOK LIN, English language educator; b. Malacca, Malaysia, Dec. 27, 1944; came to U.S., 1969; d. Chin Som and Chye Neo; m. Charles Bazerman, Nov. 1972; 1 child, Gershom Kean. BA with 1st class honors, U. Malaya, 1967, postgrad., 1967-69; MA, Brandeis U., 1971, PhD, 1973. Tchg. fellow Queens Coll. CUNY, Flushing, 1972-73; asst. prof. Hostos C.C. CUNY, Bronx, 1973-76; assoc. prof. Westchester C.C. SUNY, Valhalla, 1976-90; prof. Asian Am. studies U. Calif., Santa Barbara, 1990-93, prof. women's studies and English, 1990—; part-time lectr. U. Malaya, Kuala Lumpur, 1967-69, U. Sains, 1974; vis. fellow Nat. U. of Singapore, 1982, writer in residence, 1985; Asia Found. fellow Ctr. for Advanced Studies, 1989; Mellon fellow Grad. Ctr. CUNY, 1983, 87; minority discourses fellow Interdisciplinary Rsch. Ctr. U. Calif., Irvine, 1993; writer in residence East-West Ctr., Honolulu, 1988; presenter workshops in field. Author: Crossing the Peninsula and Other Poems, 1980 (Commonwealth Poetry prize 1980), Another Country and Other Stories, 1982, No Man's Grove, 1985, Modern Secrets: New and Selected Poems, 1989, Nationalism and Literature: English-Language Writers from the Philippines and Singapore, 1993, Monsoon History, 1994, Writing South/East Asia in English, 1994, Life's Mysteries, 1995; editor: Approaches to Teaching Kingston's "The Woman Warrior", 1991; co-editor: Reading Asian-American Literatures, 1992, One World of Literature, 1992; co-editor, author: Introduction: The Forbidden Stitch: An Asian American Women's Anthology, 1989 (Am. Book award 1989). Mem. N.Y. Gov.'s Commn. on Librs., 1990. Wein internat. fellow, 1969-72; Fulbright scholar, 1969-72; grantee NEH, 1978, 87, Westchester Found., 1987. Mem. MLA (exec. com. divsn. Lit. in English Other Than Brit. and Am. 1986-90, founder discussion group on Asian Am. lit. 1985, chair exec. com. 1989, exec. com. divsn. ethnic lit. 1993—, chair com. langs. and lit. of the U.S. 1995), Internat. PEN, Am. Studies Assn. (programs com. 1994, chair minority scholars com. 1995—), Assn. Asian Am. Studies, Nat. Women's Studies Assn., Multi-Ethnic Lit. of U.S., Coord. Coun. Lit. Mags. (bd. dirs. 1983-88, chair 1986-87, exec. com. 1987-88), Assn. Commonwealth Langs. and Lits. Office: U Calif Dept of English Santa Barbara CA 93106

LIM, TIMOTHY ALTON, plastic surgeon; b. Tucson, 1949. MD, UCLA, 1974. Plastic surgeon Anaheim Meml. Hosp., Calif. Office: 1801 W Romneya Dr Ste 302 Anaheim CA 92801-1825*

LIMA, DONALD ALLAN, oil company executive; b. Pasadena, Calif., Nov. 21, 1953; s. John Kenneth and Fay Gwynneth (Strangman) L.; m. Tina Marie Clark, Nov. 23, 1979 (div. May 9, 1984); m. Joyce Close Cirre, Jan. 17, 1985 (div. Oct. 15, 1987). BS, Calif. State U., Long Beach, Calif., 1982. Research technician Union Oil Co. Calif., Brea, Calif., 1979-84; chief chemist Pennzoil Products Co., Vernon, Calif., 1984-86; tech. service engring. Asia Pacific Region Tribol, Woodland Hills, Calif., 1986-88; engring. mgr. internat. ops. ICI Tribol, Woodland Hills, 1988-94. Mem. Am. Soc. Lubrication Engrs. (publicity chmn. 1986-87), Soc. Automotive Engrs. Home: 1137 Mooring Walk Oxnard CA 93030-6759

LIMBERIS, LUCY JANE, English studies educator; b. Glens Falls, N.Y., Oct. 31, 1967; d. William Nicholas and Jane Catherine (Kelley) L.; m. Paul Joseph Bardis, July 13, 1992. BS in Edn., SUNY, Plattsburgh, 1989, MALS, 1990; MEd, U. Mont., 1992. Cert. tchr., N.Y., Mass., Mont. English educator Upward Bound Program, Plattsburgh, N.Y., 1990, Missoula, Mont., 1994; English educator Chazy (N.Y.) Ctrl. Rural Sch., 1990-92, Equal Opportunity Program, Plattsburgh, 1995. Contbg. poet American Poetry Anthology, 1990. Mem. Grad. Student Assn. (faculty rep. 1994), Kappa Delta Pi. Home: 611 Pioneer Ct N Missoula MT 59801-7000

LIMBURG, VAL EVERT, media educator; b. Ogden, Utah, Feb. 14, 1938; s. Evert J. and Madge (Garner) L.; m. Janet Nims, May 26, 1961; children: Blake V., Lonna, Alisa, Krista, Eric. BA, Brigham Young U., 1962, MA, 1964; postgrad., U. Ill., 1964-67. Assoc. prof. communications dept. Wash. State U., Pullman, 1967—; TV producer, dir. Office of Instructional Resources, Urbana, Ill., 1965-68. Author, narrator (radio program) Radio Looks at TV, 1979-83; author: Electronic Media Ethics. Grantee Nat. Assn. Broadcasters, Wash. State Assn. Broadcasters (sec.). Mem. Broadcast Edn. Assn. (bd. dirs.), Assn. for Edn. in Journalism and Mass Communication, Internat. Visual Literacy Assn., Alpha Epsilon Rho (nat. exec. sec. 1968-72). Mormon. Office: Wash State U Murrow Sch Communication Murrow Communications Ctr Pullman WA 99164

LIN, CHING-FANG, engineering executive; b. Taiwan, Mar. 23, 1954. BEE, Nat. Chiao-Tung U.; MS, PhD in Computer, Info. Control Engr., U. Mich. Rsch. engr. U. Va., Charlottesville, 1977-78; lectr. U. Mich., Ann Arbor, 1978-80, adj. prof. elec. and computer engring., 1980-82; sr. rsch. scientist Applied Dynamics Internat., 1980-82; mem. faculty elec. and computer engring., dir. control engr. U. Wis., Madison, 1982-83; lead engr., project supr. flight controls tech. Boeing Mil. Aircraft Co., Seattle, 1983-86; pres. Am. GNC Corp., Chatsworth, Calif., 1986—. Contbr. 150 articles to profl. publications; author: Modern Navigation, Guidance and Control Processing, 1991, Advanced Control Systems Design, 1993. Recipient numerous grants. Fellow (assoc.) AIAA; mem. IEEE (sr.), SCS, IMACS, IFIP, Sigma Xi, Tau Beta Pi. Office: Am GNC Corp PO Box 10987 Canoga Park CA 91309-1987

LIN, HENRY C., gastroenterologist, researcher; b. Taiwan, China, Mar. 10, 1958; came to U.S., 1969; s. Titus S.M. and Helen J.Y. (Jin) L.; m. Susan Kao, Nov. 18, 1989; 1 child, Jessica Yoon-en. BS magna cum laude, CCNY, 1980; MD cum laude, SUNY, Syracuse, 1982. Diplomate Am. Bd. Internal Medicine, Am. Bd. Gastroenterology. Intern Harbor-UCLA Med. Ctr., Torrance, 1982-83, resident, 1983-85; fellow integrated tng. program UCLA, 1985-87; assoc. investigator Sepulveda (Calif.) VA Med. Ctr., 1987-90; dir. sect. nutrition Cedars-Sinai Med. Ctr., L.A., 1990—, dir. GI motility program, 1991—. Fellow ACP, Am. Coll. Nutrition; mem. ACP, Am. Gastroenterology Assn., Am. Soc. Parenteral & Enteral Nutrition, Am. Fedn. Clin. Rsch., Am. Motility Soc. Office: Cedars Sinai Med Ctr 7511/GI Unit 8700 Beverly Blvd Los Angeles CA 90048

LIN, HUN-CHI, molecular biologist; b. Yun-Lin, Taiwan, Republic of China, Nov. 8, 1953; came to U.S., 1980; s. Shun-Tsu and Yu-Hwa (Tsai) L.; m. Shau-Ping Lei, July 6, 1980; 1 child, Victoria Lei. BS, Nat. Taiwan U., Taipei, 1976, MS, 1978; PhD, UCLA, 1984. Teaching asst. UCLA, 1983; rsch. scientist Ingene, Santa Monica, Calif., 1984-85, project dir., 1985-87, prin. investigator, 1985-87; rsch. dir. Sinogen, L.A., 1987; pres., dir. rsch. Trigen Inc., Santa Monica, 1987—. Contbr. articles to profl. jours. Lt. Chinese Army, 1978-80. Mem. AAAS, Am. Soc. Microbiology. Office: Trigen Inc 2211 Michigan Ave Santa Monica CA 90404-3905

LIN, JAMES PEICHENG, mathematics educator; b. N.Y.C., Sept. 30, 1949; s. Tung Hua and Susan (Zsiang) L.; m. Julie Sano, June 24, 1990. BS, U. Calif., Berkeley, 1970; PhD, Princeton U., 1974. Asst. prof. U. Calif., LaJolla, 1974-76, assoc. prof., 1977-81; prof. U. Calif., San Diego, 1982-83, 1985-90, 90—; vis. prof. Princeton (N.J.) U., 1976, Inst. at Hewbrew U., Jersulem, 1981-82, MIT, Cambridge, 1983-84, Neuchatel (Switzerland) U., 1984; prof. Math Sci. Rsch. Inst., Berkeley, 1989; bd. dirs. Asians in Higher Edn. Author: Steenrod Connections, 1988. Sloan fellow; grantee NSF, 1974—; recipient Excellence in Edn., U. Pan Asian Communities, 1986. Mem. Asian Educators, Pan Asian Staff (bd. dirs., chair panel on equity and diversity, math. scis. edn. bd.), Sierra Club, Am. Math. Soc., Phi Beta Kappa. Office: Dept Math C-012 U Calif San Diego La Jolla CA 92093

LIN, JIAN-ZHONG, English language educator; b. Putian, Fujian, China, June 18, 1955; came to U.S., 1985; s. Jinzhu Lin and Xiumei You. Diploma, Xiamen (China) U., 1980; MA in English, U. Calif., Riverside, 1983, PhD in English, 1991. Lectr. English Xiamen U., 1983-85, dir. English lit. program, 1984-85; assoc. Chinese and English U. Calif., Riverside, 1988-89; lectr. English Calif. State U., Fullerton, 1990-91; asst. prof. English Teikyo Loretto Heights U., Denver, 1991—, dir. intercultural studies program, 1994—; chair college entrance exam com., Putian, 1985; mem. curriculum com. Teikyo Loretto Heights U., Denver, 1992—, mem. faculty issues and acad. programs com., 1994—. Contbr. articles to profl. jours. Pres. Assn. Chinese Students and Scholars, Riverside, 1986-88. New China Edn. Found. fellow, 1980-83. Mem. MLA, Soc. Study of the Multi-Ethnic Lit. of the U.S., Mid-Atlantic Region Assn. for Asian Studies, Phi Beta Kappa. Office: Teikyo Loretto Heights Univ 3001 S Federal Blvd Denver CO 80236-2711

LIN, LAWRENCE SHUH LIANG, accountant; b. China, July 5, 1938; s. Wan Chow and Inn Chi Lin; came to U.S., 1967, naturalized, 1979; LLB, Soochow U., 1963; MBA, Pepperdine U., 1970; m. Grace Yu, July 31, 1966; children: Ray, Lester. Spl. project acctg. supr. Motown Records, Hollywood, Calif., 1975; chief acct. Elektra/Asylum/Nonesuch Records, Beverly Hills, Calif., 1976-77, United Artists Music Pub. Group, Hollywood, 1977-80; contr.-adminstr. Pasadena (Calif.) Guidance Clinics (name now Pacific Clinics, 1980-86; v.p. Stew Kettle Corp., L.A., 1986-87; pres. LKL Corp., L.A., 1987-89; internat. fin. cons. Pacific Capital Mgmt., Alhambra, Calif., 1989—. Mem. Inst. Mgmt. Accts., Nat. Assn. Security Dealers. Baptist. Office: Pacific Capital Mgmt 29 N Garfield Ave Alhambra CA 91801-3545

LIN, SHENG HSIEN, chemist and educator; b. Changhwa, Taiwan, China, Sept. 17, 1937; children: Huei C., Bing C. BSc, Nat. Taiwan U., 1958, MSc, 1960; PhD, U. Utah, 1964. Rsch. asst. Nat. Taiwan U., Taipei, 1961-62; postdoctoral fellow Columbia U., N.Y.C., 1964-65; asst. prof. Ariz. State U., Tempe, 1965-68, assoc. prof., 1968-72, prof. chemistry, 1972—; dir. Inst. Atomic and Moledular Sci., Academia Sinica, Taiwan, 1994—; vis. prof. dept. theoretical chemistry U. Cambridge, Royal Inst., London, 1972-73; lectr. Nat. Chung-Shang Inst. of Sci. and Tech., Taiwan; disting. vis. prof. Tech. U. Munich, 1979, 80, 87, U. Louis Pasteur, France, 1987, 93; adj. prof. Shandong U., 1990—; lectr. in field; organizer Symposium Honoring Henry Eyring in His 80th Year, Am. Chem. Soc., 1980; sci. advisor Inst. Atomic and Molecular Scis. of Academica Sinica, 1983—; Cherry Emerson lecture Dept. Chemistry, Emory U., 1990, others. Editor: Advances in Multi-photo Processes, 1982—; editor Jour. Molecular Scis., 1981—; contbr. articles to profl. jours.; editor Lecture and Course Note Series, World Sci. Pub. Co., 1990—; editl. adv. com. Newton Sci. Mag. (Taiwan), 1987—. Recipient Alexander von Humboldt Found. U.S. Sr. Scientist award, 1979-80, 86, Disting. Rsch. award Ariz. State U., 1983-84; named Hon. Prof. Nanking U., 1988 , Regent's Prof. Ariz. State U., 1988—, Kai-Ying Tsing Disting. Lectr., 1993; Alfred P. Sloan fellow, 1967-71, Guggenheim fellow, 1971-73, Disting. Rsch. fellow Academic Sinica, 1993. Mem. AAAS, Am. Phys. Soc., Am. Chem. Soc., Soc. of Columbia Chemists, Chinese Chem. Soc., Inter-Am. Photochem. Soc., Sigma Xi, Phi Kappa Phi, Phi Lambda Upsilon. Office: Academia Sinica, Inst Atomic/Molecular Sci, PO Box 23-166, Taipei Taiwan, China

LIN, TAO, software engineer; b. Shanghai, Aug. 6, 1958; came to U.S., 1986; s. Zheng-hui Lin and Wei-jing Wu; m. Ping Kuo, Aug. 18, 1989; children: Jason, Jessie. BS, East China Normal U., Shanghai, 1982; MS, Tohoku U., Sendai, Japan, 1985; PhD, Tohoku U., 1990. Technician Dongtong Electronics Inc., Shanghai, 1977-78; rsch. asst. Electronics Rsch. Lab U. Calif., Berkeley, 1986-87, postgrad. researcher, 1987-88; applications engr. Integrated Device Technology Inc., Santa Clara, Calif., 1988-90; sr. applications engr. Sierra Semiconductor Corp., San Jose, Calif., 1990-91; applications mgr. Sierra Semicondr. Corp., San Jose, Calif., 1991-92, software engring. mgr., 1992-94; strategic planning and applications engring. mgr. IC Works Inc., San Jose, 1994—. Contbr. articles to profl. jours. Mem. IEEE. Home: 3552 Rockett Dr Fremont CA 94538-3425 Office: IC WORKS Inc 3725 N 1st St San Jose CA 95134-1708

LIN, THOMAS WEN-SHYOUNG, accounting educator, researcher, consultant; b. Taichung, Republic of China, June 3, 1944; came to U.S., 1970; s. Ju-chin and Shao-chin (Tseng) L.; m. Angela Kuei-fong Hou, May 19, 1969; children: William Margaret. BA in Bus. Adminstrn., Nat. Taiwan U., Taipei, 1966; MBA, Nat. Chengchi U., Taipei, 1970; MS in Acctg. and Info. Systems, UCLA, 1971; PhD in Acctg., Ohio State U., 1975. Cert. mgmt.

acct., Calif. Internal auditor Formosa Plastics Group, Taipei, 1967-69, spl. asst. to the pres., 1969-70; asst. prof. U. So. Calif., L.A., 1975-80, assoc. prof., 1980-86, prof. acctg., 1986-90, acctg. cir. prof., 1990—, dir. doctoral studies acctg., 1982-86; cons. Intex Plastics, Inc., Long Beach, Calif., 1979-81, Peat, Marwick, Mitchell, L.A., 1982, City of Chino, Calif., 1982. Author: Planning and Control for Data Processing, 1984, Use of Mathematical Models, 1986, Advanced Auditing, 1988; mem. editl. bd. Acctg. Horizons, Jour. Mgmt. Acctg. Rsch., Quarterly Jour. Bus. and Econs., Am. Jour. Math. and Mgmt. Scis., Chinese Acctg. Rev., Hong Kong Jour. Bus. Mgmt., 1988—; contbr. articles to profl. jours. Bd. dirs. U. So. Calif. Acctg. Circle, L.A., Taiwan Benevolent Assn. Am., Washington, 1986; pres. Taiwan Benevolent Assn. Calif., L.A., 1986-88. 2d lt. China Army, 1966-67. Recipient cert. appreciation L.A. City Mayor Tom Bradley, 1988, Congressman Martinez award for outstanding community svc., 1988; Faculty Rsch. scholar U. So. Calif. Bus. Sch., L.A., 1984-87. Mem. Am. Acctg. Assn. (bd. dirs. 1986-88), Chinese Acctg. Profs. N.Am. (founding pres. 1976-80), Inst. Cert. Mgmt. Accts. (cert. of disting. performance 1978), Inst. Mgmt. Accts. (coord. 1984—, Author's trophy 1978, 79, 81, 87), EDP Auditor Assn., Inst. Mgmt. Scis. Republican. Baptist. Home: PO Box 8023 Rowland Hghts CA 91748-0023 Office: U So Calif Sch Acctg Univ Park ACC 109 Los Angeles CA 90089-1421

LIN, YU-CHONG, physiology educator, consultant; b. Republic of China, Apr. 24, 1935; came to U.S., 1962; s. Shing-Chern and Shern Lin; m. Dora D.R. Liaw, Apr. 27, 1960; children: Mimi C.W., Betty L.W. PhD, Rutgers U., 1968. Rsch. assoc. U. Calif., Santa Barbara, 1968-69; asst. prof. physiology U. Hawaii, Honolulu, 1969-74, assoc. prof., 1974-76, prof., 1976—; cons. on environ. physiology Tripler Army Med. Ctr., Honolulu, 1979—, Nat. Def. Med. Ctr., Taipei, Republic of China, 1989—; advisor panel on diving physiology NOAA, Washington, 1986—. Editor: Hyperbaric Medicine and Physiology, 1988, Man in the Sea, Vol. I and 2, 1990; contbr. over 100 articles to profl. jours. Mem. Am. Physiol. Soc., Undersea and Hyperbaric Med. Soc., Honolulu Country Club. Office: U Hawaii Sch Medicine 1960 E West Rd Honolulu HI 96822-2319

LINAHON, JAMES JOSEPH, music educator, musician; b. Mason City, Iowa, Sept. 6, 1951; s. Robert Eugene and Teresa Darlene (Mulaney) L.; m. Kathryn Anne Tull, Apr. 12, 1987; children: Michael, Katie, Joseph. BA in Music, U. No. Iowa, 1973; M in Music Edn., North Tex. State U., 1975. Assoc. dir. jazz studies Chaffey Coll., Rancho Cucamonga, Calif., 1975-80; prof. music, dir. jazz studies Fullerton (Calif.) Coll., 1980—; cons. U. No. Colo., U. Alaska, U. Calif., U. Ariz., U. Hawaii, DePaul U., Chgo., U. So. Calif., Wash. State U., S.D. State U., 1978—; cons., artist Playboy Jazz Festival, Reno Internat. Jazz Festival, Queen Mary Jazz Festival, Disneyland, All That Jazz; record producer MCA, Warner Bros, ABC, Columbia; performer for Frank Sinatra, Henry Mancini, Beverly Sills, Ella Fitzgerald, Sarah Vaughan, Tony Bennett, Merv Griffin. Artist, producer: (jazz compact disc) Time Tripping, 1984 (Album of Yr. Downbeat Mag., 1987), (classical compact disc) Gradus Ad Parnassum, 1990, (compact disk) Season of Our Lives, 1994; composer: (musical composition) Snow Wisp, 1986 (finalist Columbia Artists search). Performer, producer Theatre Palisades, Pacific Palisades, Calif., 1986, Claremont (Calif.) Community Found., 1992; guest soloist Claremont (Calif.) Symphony Orch., 1991. Recipient Major Landers scholarship Iowa Band Master's Assn., Iowa, 1969; named Dee Bee Album of Yr. (5 awards) Downbeat Mag., 1978-87. Mem. NARAS (Oustanding Recordings 1989), Internat. Assn. Jazz Educators (higher edn. rep. 1992-93), Internat. Trumpet Guild, Internat. Assn. Jazz Edn., Am. Soc. Composers, Authors and Publishers, Nat. Assn. Coll. Wind and Percussion Instrs., Am. Fedn. Musicians. Roman Catholic. Home: 560 W 10th St Claremont CA 91711-3714 Office: Fullerton College 321 E Chapman Ave Fullerton CA 92632-2011

LINAWEAVER, WALTER ELLSWORTH, JR., physician; b. San Pedro, Calif., Oct. 16, 1928; s. Walter Ellsworth and Catherine Breathed (Bridges) L.; m. Lydia Anne Whitlock, Oct. 6, 1957; children: Catherine Ann, Nancy Alyn, Walter E. III. BA cum laude, Pomona Coll., 1952; MD, U. Rochester, 1956. Diplomate Am. Bd. Allergy and Immunology, Am. Bd. Pediatrics, Am. Bd. Pediatric Allergy. Intern pediatrics Med. Ctr. U. Rochester, N.Y., 1956-57, resident pediatrics Med. Ctr., 1958-59; asst. resident pediatrics Med. Ctr. UCLA, 1957-58; fellow allergy and immunology Med. Ctr. U. Colo., Denver, 1959-61, instr. pediatrics Sch. Medicine, 1961; pvt. practice Riverside (Calif.) Med. Clinic, 1962—; bd. dirs. Riverside Med. Clinic. Elder Presbyn. Ch. Staff sgt. U.S. Army, 1946-48. Inducted into Athletic Hall of Fame Pomona Coll., Claremont, Calif., 1979. Fellow Am. Acad. Allergy and Immunology, Am. Acad. Pediat., Southwestern Pediat. Soc. (emeritus, v.p. 1978), L.A. Acad. Medicine; mem. Riverside County Med. Soc. (councillor), Riverside County Heart Assn. Republican. Home: 1296 Tiger Tail Dr Riverside CA 92506-5475 Office: Riverside Med Clinic 3660 Arlington Ave Riverside CA 92506-3912

LINCOLN, ALEXANDER, III, financier, lawyer, private investor; b. Boston, Dec. 1, 1943; s. Alexander Jr. and Elizabeth (Kitchel) L.; m. Isabel Fawcett Ross, Dec. 27, 1969. BA, Denver U., 1967; JD, Boston U., 1971. Bar: Colo. 1972, U.S. Ct. Appeals (10th cir.) 1972, U.S. Supreme Ct. 1979. Atty. Dist. Ct. Denver, 1973-78, Colo. Ct. Appeals, Denver, 1978-80; mng. ptnr. Alexander Lincoln & Co., Denver, 1980—. Mem. Colo. Bar Assn. (fin. com. 1975-76), Colo. Soc. Mayflower Descendants (life, bd. dirs. 1975—), Order of Founders and Patriots (life). Republican. Home and Office: 121 S Dexter St Denver CO 80222-1052

LINCOLN, SANDRA ELEANOR, chemistry educator; b. Holyoke, Mass., Mar. 11, 1939; d. Edwin Stanley and Evelyn Ida (Mackie) L. BA magna cum laude, Smith Coll., 1960; MSChem, Marquette U., 1970; PhD in Inorganic Chemistry, SUNY, Stony Brook, 1982. Tchr., prin. Oak Knoll Sch., Summit, N.J., 1964-74; tchr. Holy Child High Sch., Waukegan, Ill., 1974-76; lectr. chemistry, dir. fin. aid Rosemont (Pa.) Coll., 1976-78; teaching asst. SUNY, Stony Brook, 1978-82; assoc. prof. chemistry U. Portland, Oreg., 1982—; researcher Oreg. Grad. Ctr., Beaverton, 1982—. Contbr. articles to profl. jours. Cath. sister Soc. Holy Child Jesus, 1963—. Recipient Pres.'s award for Teaching, SUNY, Stony Brook, 1981; Burlington No. Outstanding scholar, 1987. Mem. Am. Chem. Soc., Phi Beta Kappa, Sigma Xi. Democrat. Home: 5431 N Strong St Portland OR 97203-5711 Office: U Portland 5000 N Willamette Blvd Portland OR 97203-5743

LIND, CARL BRADLEY, retired museum director; b. Bethel, Vt., Apr. 22, 1929; s. Carl Olaf and Signe Alfield (Anderson) L.; m. Barbara Ann Eskridge, Oct. 22, 1951; children: Carl Garrett, Susan Ann, Craig Ira. BA, Norwich U., 1951; cert., Command and Gen. Staff Coll., Fort Leavenworth, Kans., 1960; MA, Columbia U., 1963; cert., NATO Def. Coll., Rome, 1976. Commd. 2d lt. U.S. Army, advanced through grades to col., 1968; asst. prof. U.S. Mil. Acad., West Point, N.Y., 1961-64; comdr. 1st Squadron 3d Armored Cavalry Rgt. U.S. Army, Fed. Republic Germany, 1965-67; sr. advisor Vietnamese Nat. Mil. Acad. U.S. Army, Dalat, Vietnam, 1967-68; chief Congl. Inquiry Div., Office Sec. of the Army U.S. Army, Washington, 1968-71; area comdr. 2d ROTC Region U.S. Army, Fort Knox, Ky., 1973-75; exec. for interoperability to SACEUR, SHAPE NATO, Mons, Belgium, 1977-79; exec. v.p. Evans Llewellyn Securities, Bellevue, Wash., 1979-81; dep. dir. Mus. of History and Industry, Seattle, 1984-88, exec. dir., 1988-91; bd. dirs. Museum of History and Industry, Seattle, Coast Guard Mus. of Northwest, Seattle. Contbr. articles to jours. in field. Neighborhood commr. Boys Scouts Am., Baumholder, Fed. Rep. Germany, 1965-66; pres. PTA, Baumholder, 1965-66; commr. King County (Wash.) Landmarks & Heritage Commn., 1992—, Wash. State Heritage Caucus, 1990—; bd. dirs. Hydroplane and Antique Race Boat Mus., Seattle, 1993—; exec. bd. Bigelow House Preservation Assn., Olympia, Wash., 1993—. Decorated Bronze star, Dept. Def. Superior Svc. medal. Legion of Merit, Meritorious Svc. medal. Mem. VFW (comdr. Mercer Island, Wash. post 5760 1984-85), Assn. of U.S. Army, U.S. Armor Assn., Ret. Officer Assn., Am. Assn. State and Local History, Lions, Rotary. Home: 3023 Country Club Rd NW Olympia WA 98502-3738

LIND, TERRIE LEE, social services administrator; b. Spokane, Wash., June 5, 1948; d. Clifford and Edna Mae (Allenbach) Presnell; m. Stephen George Lind, Aug. 29, 1970 (div. Mar. 1981); children: Erica Rachel, Reid Christopher. BA cum laude, Wash. State U., 1970, MA, 1971. Cert. tchr., Wash., Ariz.; cert. in Porch Index Communicative Ability. Specialist communication disorders U. Tex., Houston, 1971-73; clin. supr. The Battin Clinic, Houston, 1973-76; specialist communication disorders Spokane Guilds Sch., 1980-82; program coord. Fresno (Calif.) Community Hosp., 1982-87; program adminstr. Advantage 65* sr. access program Health Dimensions, Inc., San Jose, Calif., 1987-90; dir. patient svcs. San Jose Med. Ctr., 1990-92; dir. cmty. svcs. Planned Parenthood Mar Monte, San Jose, 1992—; cons. Adolescent Chem. Dependency Unit, Fresno, 1984-87. Mem. AAUW (officer 1976-82), Am. Speech and Hearing Assn. (cert., Continuing Edn. award 1985-86), Wash. Speech and Hearing Assn. (co-chmn. state conv. program com. 1981-82), Soc. Consumer Affairs Profls. in Bus., Wash. State U. Alumni Assn. Office: Planned Parenthood 1691 The Alameda San Jose CA 95126-2203

LINDAMOOD, GEORGE EDWARD, computer consultant; b. Marietta, Ohio, Sept. 15, 1938; s. Lee Marcus and Mildred Katherine (Young) L.; m. Diane Kay Haugen, Feb. 2, 1962 (div. July 1980); children: Brian Avery, Elden Kirk; m. Annette Irene Powell, July 18, 1980; 1 stepchild, Nina Powell. BS, Wittenberg U., 1960; MA, U. Md., 1964, postgrad., 1964-69; postgrad., Johns Hopkins U., 1972-73. Assoc. engr. Westinghouse Electric Corp., Balt., 1962-63; instr. in computer sci. U. Md., College Park, 1963-70; sr. computer scientist Nat. Bur. Standards, Gaithersburg, Md., 1970-81; visiting fellow MIT, Cambridge, 1981-82; sr. scientist U.S. Office Naval Rsch., Tokyo, 1982-84; dir. industry analysis Burroughs Corp., Tokyo, 1984-85; assoc. prof. computer sci. Hood Coll., Frederick, Md., 1986-87; prog. dir. industry svc. Gartner Group, Inc., Stamford, Conn., 1987-90, dir. high performance computing, 1991, v.p., high performance computing, 1991-93; dir. Wash. State dept. of info. svcs. Cybertiger, Sequim, 1993-95, chmn., CEO, 1995—; cons. to numerous pvt. cos. and fed. agencies, 1963-87; mem. numerous adv. coms. and study teams of U.S. govt., 1971-87; U.S. rep. at internat. meetings, Manila, Paris, Bangkok, India, Jamaica, 1976-84. Author pub. poems, humorous articles; contbr. articles to profl. jours. Mem., sec. Planning & Zoning Commn., Woodsboro, Md., 1975-78; pres. Woodsboro Elem. PTA, 1976-77, v.p. 1975-76; pres. Frederick (Md.) County Coun. PTAs, 1978, v.p., 1977. Recipient Silver medal U.S. Dept. Commerce, 1973, fellowship Woodrow Wilson Found., 1960-61, scholarship Nat. Merit Scholarship Found., 1956-60. Mem. IEEE. Lutheran. Home: 91 Brittany Ln Sequim WA 98382 Office: CyberTiger 155 W Cedar St #142 Sequim WA 98382

LINDAUER, JOHN HOWARD, II, newspaper publisher; b. Montclair, N.J., Nov. 20, 1937; s. John Howard and Louise (Platts) L.; m. Jacqueline Shelly, Sept. 2, 1960 (dec. 1992); children: Susan, John Howard. BS, Ariz. State U., 1960; PhD in Econs., Okla. State U., 1964. Asst. prof. econs. Occidental Coll., L.A., 1964-66; assoc. prof. Claremont (Calif.) Men's Coll. and Grad Sch., 1966-70, prof., chmn. econs., 1970-74; dean Coll. Bus. Murray (Ky.) State U., 1974-76; chancellor U. Alaska, Anchorage, 1976-78; commr. Alaska Pipeline, Anchorage, 1978; pres., chief exec. officer Alaska Industry and Energy Corp., Anchorage, 1978—; mem. Alaska Ho. of Reps., 1983-84; Rep. candidate for gov., 1990; bd. dirs. various cos.; owner various newspapers and radio sta.; cons. econ. policy and devel. U.S. Congress; cons. econs. U.S. corps; mem. AF Adv. Bd. Author: Macroeconomics, 1968, 71, 76, Economics: The Modern View, 1977, Land Taxation and the Indian Economic Development, 1979; editor Macroeconomic Readings; contbr. articles to profl. jours. Co-founder, vice chmn. Group against Smog Pollution, 1968; pres. So. Calif. Econ. Assn., 1974. With Army U.S., 1955-57. Fulbright prof., India, 1972; vis. prof. U. Sussex, Eng., 1972-73. Home: 3933 Geneva Pl Anchorage AK 99508-5055*

LINDBECK, STEPHEN EMANUEL, state agency administrator; b. Tacoma, Wash., Jan. 14, 1955; s. Edwin Emanuel and Mary Ann (Persson) L.; m. Martha Jane Ginsburg, July 18, 1992. BA in Polit. Sci., Stanford U., 1980. News editor Anchorage Daily News, 1979-81, editorial page editor, 1981-85, contbg. editor, 1987-88; John S. Knight profl. journalism fellow Stanford (Calif.) U., 1985-86; copy editor Boston Globe, 1986-87; editorial page editor Everett (Wash.) Herald, 1988-89; freelance reporter, 1989; chief writer and editor Alaska Oil Spill Commn., 1989-90; issues dir., ofcl. spokesman Knowles for Alaska Campaign, 1990; exec. dir. Alaska Humanities Forum, Anchorage, 1991—. Home: 2600 Redwood St Anchorage AK 99508-3973 Office: Alaska Humanities Forum 421 W 1st Ave Ste 210 Anchorage AK 99501-1635

LINDBURG, DONALD GILSON, researcher in animal behavior; b. Wagner, S.D., Nov. 6, 1932; s. Kenzie Ray and Lela Almeta (Wilhelm) L.; m. Linda L. Gildea, Aug. 27, 1982. BA, Houghton (N.Y.) Coll., 1956; MA, U. Chgo., 1962; PhD, U. Calif., Berkeley, 1967. With Nat. Ctr. for Primate Biology, U. Calif., Davis, 1964-69; asst. prof. dept. anthropology U. Calif., Davis, 1969-72; assoc. prof., chair dept. anthropology Ga. State U., Atlanta, 1973-75; assoc. prof. anthropology UCLA, 1975-79; head behavior div. Zool. Soc. San Diego, 1979—; mem. comparative medicine rev. com. NIH, 1992—. Editor: The Macaques, 1980; editor Zoo Biology, 1989—; author sci. articles. County coord. McGovern for Pres., Yolo County, Davis, 1972. Recipient Centennial award for excellence in zoo rsch. Nat. Zool. Park, 1990; grantee Inst. for Mus. Svcs., Washington, 1984, 89, 93, NIH, 1989. Mem. Am. Soc. Primatologists (founding mem. 1976, pres. 1984-86), Am. Zoo Assn. (coord.-behavior Rhino Rsch. Coun. 1993—). Office: Zool Soc San Diego PO Box 551 San Diego CA 92112-0551

LINDE, GARY J., goldsmith; b. Rolla, Mo., Sept. 9, 1950; s. Kenneth P. and Willowe J. (Palmer) L.; m. Karen M. Anderson, May 22, 1979. Grad Goldsmith and Gemologist, U. Kans., 1972; degree in diamond & diamond grinding, Gemological Inst. Am., 1989, 90; student, Carlyle Smith at U. Kans. Owner, master goldsmith Del Oro-Goldsmith, Alamogordo, N.Mex., 1972—. Bd. dirs., treas. City Zoo; bd. dirs., founding pres., treas., v.p. Alamogordo Friends of Zoo. Recipient numerous trophies for antique cars. Home: PO Box 1242 Alamogordo NM 88311-1242 Office: Del Oro-Goldsmith 800 New York Ave Alamogordo NM 88310-7108

LINDE, LUCILLE MAE (JACOBSON), motor-perceptual specialist; b. Greeley, Colo., May 5, 1919; d. John Alfred and Anna Julia (Anderson) Jacobson; m. Ernest Emil Linde, July 5, 1946 (dec. Jan. 1959). BA, U. No. Colo., 1941, MA, 1947, EdD, 1974. Cert. tchr. Calif., Colo., Iowa, N.Y.; cert. ednl. psychologist; guidance counselor. Dean of women, dir. residence C.W. Post Coll. of L.I. Univ., 1965-66; asst. dean of students SUNY, Farmingdale, 1966-67; counselor, tchr. West High Sch., Davenport, Iowa, 1967-68; instr. grad. tchrs. and counselors, univ. counselor, researcher No. Ariz. U., Flagstaff, 1968-69; vocat. edn. and counseling coord. Fed. Exemplary Project, Council Bluffs, Iowa, 1970-71; sch. psychologist, counselor Oakdale Sch. Dist., Calif., 1971-73; sch. psychologist, intern Learning and Counseling Ctr., Stockton, Calif., 1972-74; pvt. practice rsch. in motor-perceptual tng. Greeley, 1975—; researcher ocumeter survey, Lincoln Unified Sch. Dist., Stockton, 1980, 81, 82, Manteca (Calif.) High Sch., 1981; motor perceptual tng. LUSD, 1981, 82, YMCA, Stockton, 1983, 84, others; spkr. Social Sci. Edn. Consortium, Colo. U., 1993; presenter seminars in field. Author: Psychological Services and Motor Perceptual Training, 1974, Guidebook for Psychological Services and Motor Perceptual Training (How One May Improve in Ten Easy Lessons!), 1992, Manual for the Lucille Linde Ocumeter: Ocular Pursuit Measuring Instrument, 1989, Target, 1991, Motor-Perceptual Training and Visual Perceptual Research (How Students Improved in Seven Lessons!), 1992, Effects of Motor Perceptual Training on Academic Achievement and Ocular Pursuit Ability, 1992; inventor ocumeter, instrument for measuring ocular tracking ability, 1989, target for use, 1991; patentee in field. Mem. Rep. Presdl. Task Force, 1989-90, trustee, 1991, life, charter mem., 1994—; mem. Rep. Nat. Com., 1990, 93-94, Rep. Nat. Com. on Am. Agenda, 1993, Nat. Rep. Congrl. Com., 1990, 92, 93, 95; adv. Sen. Bob Dole for Pres.; charter mem. Congressman Newt Gingrich's Speaker's Task Force; at-large del. Rep. Platform Planning Com.; active The Heritage Found., Attention Deficit Disorder Adv. Group, Christian Bus. Men's Assn., Friends of U. N.C. Librs. Recipient Presdl. medal of merit and lapel insignia, 1988, 90, Nat. Rep. Senatorial Com., 1991-95, cert. appreciation Nat. Rep. Congl. Com., 1992, lapel pin Rep. Senatorial Inner Cir., 1990-95, rep. Presdl. commemorative honor roll, 1993, rep. senatorial freedom medal, 1994, rep. legion of merit award, 1994, rep. congl. order of freedom award, 1995; named to Rep. Nat. Hall of Honor, 1992. Mem. AAUP, NAFE, Nat. Assn. Sch. Psychologists and Psychometrists (speaker at conf. 1976), Nat. Fedn. Rep. Women, The Smithsonian Assocs., Nat. Trust for Hist. Preservation, Am. Pers. and Guidance Assn., Nat. Assn. Student Pers. Adminstrs., Nat. Assn. Women Deans and Counselors, Calif. Tchrs. Assn., Internat. Platform Assn., Independence Inst., Learning Disabilities Assn. (speaker internat. conv. 1976), Rep. Senatorial Inner Circle (senatorial commn. & cert. 1991, 93), Greeley Rep. Women's Club, Pi Omega Pi, Pi Lambda Theta. Home: 1954 18th Ave Greeley CO 80631-5208

LINDEGREN, JACK KENNETH, elementary and secondary education educator; b. Fresno, Calif., Feb. 9, 1931; s. Henry Jack and Katherine (Metzler) L.; m. Betty Jo Rowland, Dec. 1960 (div. Apr. 1963); m. Elaine Finnegan, Apr. 27, 1963; children: Susan Carol, Karen Ann. BA, Fresno State Coll., 1954; MA, Calif. State U., Fresno, 1976. Educator, adminstr. Fresno County, Firebaugh, Calif., 1954-5; educator Calaveras County Schs., San Andreas, Calif., 1964-66, Kings County Schs., Corcoran, Calif., 1966-80, Kern County Schs., Bakersfield, Calif., 1985-87, L.A. Unified Schs., 1985—; educator L.A. Unified Schs., 1977-92; instr. ARC, Hanford, Calif., 1974-79.; instr. County Sci. Insvc., 1985. Inventor electroanalysis device Chrysler award., 1965. Participant Desert Opera, Palmdale, Calif., 1986-88; bd. mem., chmn. ARC, Hanford, 1973-78. Sgt. U.S. Army, 1955-57. Mem. NAS, AAAS, NEA, Nat. Assn. Legions of Honor, Nat. Space Soc., Tehran Shrine, Fresno East/West Game Corcoran Band Club, Santa Clara U. Alumni Assn., N.Y. Acad. Scis., Internat. DeMolay Alumni Assn. (life), Assn. Calif. Sch. Adminstrs., Calif. State U. of Fresno Alumni Assn. (life), Scottish Rite (life), Corcoran/Tulare Masons (life, Bethel guardian 1978-80, Pin 1980), Odd Fellows (30 Yr. Mem. award 1991), Mensa (elder, deacon bushop, 10 v.p. Membership award). Presbyterian.

LINDEMAN, ROBERT DEAN, medical educator, researcher, consultant; b. Ft. Dodge, Iowa, July 19, 1930; s. Verlus F. and Dorothy L. (Cawelti) L.; m. Janet Ruth Lyman, Apr. 12, 1954 (div. June 1982); children: William Douglas, Ann Denise Hendrix, James Lawrence, Peter Verlus, David Matthew; m. Edith Lynn Lind, Aug. 14, 1982; stepchildren: Laurel Lind Lisinski, Lisa Lind Ringhoff, Kristine Lind Cannaday. BS, SUNY, Syracuse, 1952, MD, 1956. Diplomate Am. Bd. Internal Medicine. Intern in internal medicine Blodgett Meml. Hosp., Grand Rapids, Mich., 1956-57; resident in internal medicine Upstate Med. Ctr., Syracuse, 1957-60; chief renal sect. Dept. Medicine U. Okla., Oklahoma City, 1966-77; assoc. chief of staff in rsch. Oklahoma City VA Med. Ctr., 1966-76; chief of staff Louisville VA Med. Ctr., 1977-83; assoc. dean VA affairs Sch. Medicine U. Louisville, 1977-83; chief of staff VA Med. Ctr., Washington, 1983-88; assoc. dean VA affairs, prof. medicine Sch. Medicine George Washington U., Washington, 1983-88; prof. medicine, chief divsn. gerontology U. N.Mex., Albuquerque, 1988—; mem. panel chair nutrition U. S. Pharmacopeia, Rockville, Md., 1975—; mem. adv. bd. Am. Assn. Ret. Persons, Washington, 1990—. Contbr. more than 140 articles to profl. jours. Pres. Nat. Kidney Found. (Okla. chpt.), Oklahoma City, 1970-71, pres.-elect and pres., Ky. chpt., Louisville, 1978-81. Recipient Ralph C. Williams Rsch. award U. N.Mex., 1992, Gerontology Assoc. award, 1992. Fellow ACP, Am. Geriat. Soc., Am. Coll. Nutrition (pres., pres.-elect, v.p. 1981-87); mem. Nat. Assn. VA Chiefs of Staff (pres., pres.-elect 1984-86), Gerontol. Soc. Am., Am. Soc. Nephrology, Internat. Soc. Nephrology, So. Soc. for Clin. Investigation, Ctrl. Soc. for Clin. Rsch., Western Assn. Physicians. Democrat. Home: 2513 Myra Pl NE Albuquerque NM 87112 Office: U NMex Sch Medicine 2121 Lomas Ave NE Albuquerque NM 87131

LINDEMANN, GEORGE, agricultural products executive; b. 1942. Pres. Lindemann Produce Co., 1963—. Office: Lindemann Produce Co 300 E 2nd St Reno NV 89501*

LINDEN, CHRISTOPHER, financial analyst. BA, U. So. Calif., 1971. Various positions First Pacific Advisors, Inc., L.A., 1972—, now sr. v.p.; investment analyst Rotan Mosle, Houston, 1974-75; securities broker/dealer, sr. assoc. Carl H. Phorzheimer & Co., N.Y.C., 1975-77; sr. v.p. Source Capital, L.A., 1977—; dir., chmn., COO FPA Paramount Fund, Inc., L.A.; dir. pres., chief investment officer FPA Perennial Fund, Inc., L.A.; sr. v.p. FPA New Income Inc., L.A., FPA Capital Fund, Inc., L.A. Office: First Pacific Advisors Inc 11400 W Olympic Blvd Los Angeles CA 90064-1550*

LINDENMEYER, MARY KATHRYN, secondary education educator; b. Denver, Dec. 9, 1952; d. Edward L. and Margaret Mary (Hogan) L. BA in English and History, St. Mary Coll., Leavenworth, Kans., 1975; MA in History, U. No. Colo., 1990. Cert. tchr., Mo., Colo., N.Mex. Tchr. Bishop Hogan High Sch., Kansas City, Mo., 1976-82, St. Pius X High Sch., Kansas City, Mo., 1982-84, Machebeuf Cath. High Sch., Denver, 1984-89; prin. Trinidad (Colo.) Cath. High Sch., 1989-90; tchr. Navajo Pine High Sch., Navajo, N.Mex., 1990—, chair dept. lang. arts, 1992—; adj. faculty Navajo C.C., Window Rock, Ariz., 1991—. Recipient Dickerson award U. No. Colo. History Fellowship, 1989; named Disting. Tchr., Gallup-McKinley County, 1993; NEH scholar, 1985, 89. Mem. ASCD, Nat. Coun. Tchrs. English. Roman Catholic. Office: Navajo Pine High Sch PO Box 1286 Gallup NM 87305-1286

LINDER, GLORIA ANN, medical librarian, educator; b. La Salle, Ill., Jan. 1, 1943; d. Cletus Frank and Mary Louise (Mahnich) L.; m. Robert Drake Boyington, Aug. 26, 1983 (dec. Nov. 1984). BA in History, U. Ill., 1964, MS in LS, 1965; MS in Biol. Sci., Stanford U., 1981. Teaching asst. U. Ill. Libr. Sch., Urbana, 1964-65; reference libr. Mich. State U., East Lansing, 1965-67, Hoover Instn., Stanford U., 1967-69; med. reference librarian, instr. Medline Lane Med. Libr. Stanford U., 1969—. Contbr. articles to profl. jours. Docent/elephant seals Ano Nuevo State Res., San Mateo County, Calif., 1990—; docent Pescadero State Preserve, San Mateo County, 1990—. Mem. AAAS, Med. Libr. Assn., Am. Soc. for Info. Sci., No. Calif. Med. Libr. Group, Nev. Med. Libr. Group. Office: Lane Med Libr Stanford U Med Ctr Stanford CA 94305

LINDER, RONALD JAY, accountant, lawyer; b. Dayton, Ohio, Aug. 7, 1934; s. Sam C. and Amelia (Diamond) L.; m. Sandra Loving, June 12, 1966; children: Jeffrey Arthur, Carey Anne. BS in Econ., U. Pa., 1958; LLB, U. Mich., 1959; LLM, NYU, 1960. Bar: Calif. 1961, Ohio 1960. Mgr. Arthur Young & Co., San Francisco, 1964-67, prin., 1967-69, ptnr., 1969-85; ptnr. Delagnes, Mitchell & Linder, CPA, San Francisco, 1985—, Delagnes, Linder & Zippel, Attys. at Law, San Francisco, 1985—. Author: Tax Strategies in Financial Planning, 1992. Mem. AICPA (exec. com. div. pers. fin. plan 1991—), Calif. CPA Soc. (chmn. pers. fin. plan com. 1991-93), State Bar of Calif., Ohio State Bar Assn. Office: Delagnes Mitchell & Linder 300 Montgomery St Ste 1050 San Francisco CA 94104-1912

LINDHOLM, DWIGHT HENRY, lawyer; b. Blackduck, Minn., May 27, 1930; s. Henry Nathanial and Viola Eudora (Gummert) L.; m. Loretta Catherine Brown, Aug. 29, 1958; children: Douglas Dwight, Dionne Louise, Jeanne Marie, Philip Clayton, Kathleen Anne. Student, Macalester Coll., 1948-49; BBA, U. Minn., 1951, LLB, 1954; postgrad., Mexico City Coll. (now U. of Ams.), 1956-57. Bar: Minn. 1954, Calif. 1958. Sole practice Los Angeles, 1958-65, 72-81, 84—; ptnr. Lindholm & Johnson, Los Angeles, 1965-69, Cotter, Lindholm & Johnson, Los Angeles, 1969-72; sole practice Los Angeles, 1972-81; of counsel Bolton, Dunn & Moore, Los Angeles, 1981-84. Mem. Calif. Republican Central Com., 1962-63, Los Angeles Republican County Central Com., 1962-66; bd. dirs. Family Service Los Angeles, 1964-70, v.p., 1968-70; bd. dirs. Wilshire YMCA, 1976-77; trustee Westlake Girls Sch., 1978-81; hon. presenter Nat. Charity League Coronet Debutante Ball, 1984; bd. dirs. Calif. State U.-Northridge Trust Fund, 1989-93; bd. dirs. Queen of Angeles/Hollywood Presbyn. Med. Ctr., 1990—. Served as capt. JAG Corps USAF, 1954-56. Recipient Presdl. award Los Angeles Jr. C. of C., 1959. Mem. ABA, Calif. Bar Assn., L.A. County Bar Assn., Wilshire Bar Assn. (bd. govs. 1989-91), Internat. Genealogy Fellowship of Rotarians (founding pres. 1979-86), Calif. Club, Ocean Cruising Club Eng. (Newport Harbor port officer), Rotary (dir. 1975-78), Delta Sigma Pi, Delta Sigma Rho, Delta Theta Phi (state chancellor 1972-73). Presbyterian. Home: 3580 Wilshire Blvd Los Angeles CA 90010-2501 Office: 3580 Wilshire Blvd Fl 17 Los Angeles CA 90010-2501

LINDHOLM, RICHARD THEODORE, educator; b. Eugene, Oreg., Oct. 5, 1960; s. Richard Wadsworth and Mary Marjorie (Trunko) L. m. Valaya Nivasananda, May 8, 1987. BA, U. Chgo., 1982, MA, 1983, PhD, 1993. Ptnr. Lindholm and Osanka, Eugene, 1986-89, Lindholm Rsch., Eugene, 1989—; guest lectr. Nat. Inst. Devel. Adminstrn., Bangkok, Thailand, 1989; pres. Rubicon Inst., Eugene, 1988—; adj. asst. prof. U. Oreg., Eugene,

1988—. Campaign co-chmn. Lane C.C. Advocates, Eugene, 1988; coord., planner numerous state Rep. Campaigns, Oreg., 1988—; campaign mgr. Jack Roberts for Oreg. State Labor Commn., 1994; mem. staff Oreg. Senate Rep. Office, 1989-90; precinct committeeperson Oreg. Rep. Party, 1987-92, 94—; bd. dirs. Rubicon Soc., Eugene, 1987—, pres., 1993—. Republican. Lutheran. Home: 3335 Bardell Ave Eugene OR 97401-8021

LINDLEY, F(RANCIS) HAYNES, JR., foundation president, lawyer; b. L.A., Oct. 15, 1945; s. Francis Haynes and Grace Nelson (McCanne) L.; m. Hollinger McCloud Lindley, Apr. 1, 1977; 1 child, Anne Hollinger Lindley. BA, Claremont (Calif.) Men's Coll., 1967; MFA, Claremont (Calif.) Grad. Sch., 1972; JD, Southwestern U. Sch. Law, L.A., 1976. Bar: Calif. 1976, U.S. Supreme Ct. 1980. Deputy pub. defender Office of Pub. Defender, L.A., 1977-79; staff atty., Dept. Trial Counsel The State Bar of Calif., L.A., 1979-81; pvt. practice, 1981-90; pres. John Randolph Haynes and Dora Haynes Found., L.A., 1987—; trustee John Randolph Haynes and Dora Haynes Found., L.A., 1978—. Mem. bd. dirs. TreePeople, L.A., 1985-87, Southern Calif. Assn. Philanthropy, L.A., 1985-89; mem. bd. fellows Claremont (Calif.) U. Ctr. and Grad. Sch., 1987—. Recipient Disting. Svc. award The Claremont (Calif.) Grad. Sch., 1994. Mem. The Calif. Club. Home: PO Box 1404 Ross CA 94957-1404 Office: John Randolph Haynes and Dora Haynes Found 888 W Sixth St Ste 1150 Los Angeles CA 90017

LINDLEY, NORMAN DALE, physician; b. Henrietta, Tex., July 18, 1937; s. Hardie Lindley and Hope (Clement) Mourant; m. Luise Ann Moser, May 29, 1964; children: Norman Dale Jr., Roger Paul. BS, N.Mex. Highlands U., 1960; MD, U. Colo., 1964. Diplomate Am. Bd. Ob-Gyn. Rotating intern Kans. City (Mo.) Gen. Hosp., 1964-65; resident in ob-gyn. St. Joseph Hosp., Denver, 1965-68; med. officer USAF, Cheyenne, Wyo., 1968-70; pvt. practice physician Alamogordo, N.M., 1970—; dir. N.Mex. Found. for Med. Care, Albuquerque, 1985-88, N.Mex. Med. Rev. Assn., Albuquerque, 1985-88; physician liaison Am. Assn. Med. Assts., Chgo., 1987-93; physician advisor N.Mex. Soc. Med. Assts., 1984—. Bd. dirs. Otero County Boys and Girls Club, Alamogordo, 1977—, pres., 1979-81; bd. dirs. Otero County Assn. for Retarded Citizens, 1985-91, pres., 1989-90; bd. dirs. Otero County chpt. Am. Cancer Soc., 1970-72. Capt. USAF, 1968-70. Rsch. grantee NSF, 1959, 60. Fellow Am. Coll. Ob-Gyn.; mem. AMA, Am. Fertility Soc., Am. Inst. Ultrasound in Medicine, Am. Soc. Colposcopists and Cervical Pathologists, M.Mex. Med. Soc. (councilor 1985-88), Otero County Med. Soc. (pres. 1972-73, 83-84), Rotary (pres. White Sands chpt. 1981-82, bd. dirs. 1988-89, Svc. Above Self award 1979, Paul Harris fellow 1987). Home: 2323 Union Ave Alamogordo NM 88310-3849 Office: Thunderbird Ob-Gyn 1212 9th St Alamogordo NM 88310-5842

LINDLY, DOUGLAS DEAN, elementary school educator, administrator; b. San Diego, Aug. 22, 1941; s. George A. and Jessie V. L.; m. Brenda J., Oct. 22, 1971; children: Elizabeth, David. MA in Curriculum, Pepperdine U., 1967, student, 1975; credential edn., USC, 1971; student, U. Oreg., 1981-85, Oreg. State U., 1981-85; credential adminstrn., Calif. State U., Fullerton, 1991; cert. in spl. edn., Calif. State U., L.A., 1994. Cert. in profl. adminstrv. svcs., Calif., gen. teaching, Calif., standard designated adult edn., Calif., standard elem. teaching, Oreg., standard adminstrv., Oreg.; cert. lang. devel. specialist, Calif., Learning Handicapped and Resource Specialist credential. Supervising tchr. Imperial Schs., Pasadena, Calif., 1965-70; tchr. Charter Oak Unified Sch. Dist., Covina, Calif., 1970-78, Sweet Home (Oreg.) Unified Sch. Dist., 1978-81, Rialto (Calif.) Unified Sch. Dist., 1989-90; prin. Lewis and Clark Sch. Dist., Astoria, Oreg., 1981-86, Barstow (Calif.) Unified Sch. Dist., 1986-88; spl. edn. dir. River Delta Unified Sch. Dist., Walnut Grove, Calif., 1988-89; tchr. of learning handicapped Los Angeles Unified Sch. Dist., South Gate, 1990—; tchr. motivational program Great Kids Club, 1982—. Author: A Handbook for Parents, 1967, Summer Education Handbook, 1970; contbr. numerous articles on ednl. programs to newspapers and mags., 1970-89. Vol. ARC, Pasadena/Covina, 1970-78; cubmaster Boy Scouts Am., Astoria and Barstow, 1982-88 (Outstanding Svc. award 1988); coach Little League, Astoria, 1985; leader youth group Ch. of God, 1975-81. Grantee Adventures in Success, 1976-78; scholar Future Tchrs. Am. and Eugene Tchrs. Assn., 1959; named San Gabriel Valley Outstanding Educator, San Gabriel Valley Endl. Consortium, 1977; recipient Outstanding Speaker award Toastmasters Internat., 1986, Outstanding Svc. award PTA, 1988. Mem. NEA, ASCD, Calif. Assn. Gifted, Calif. Tchrs. Assn., Assn. Calif. Sch. Adminstrs. (assoc.), Kappa Delta Pi. Home: PO Box 1058 962 E Mountain View Ave Glendora CA 91741-2871

LINDOW, LOUISA ROSE, lawyer; b. San Antonio, Jan. 25, 1922; d. George Edward and Louisa Augusta (Schweizerhof) L.; m. Richard J. Nugent, May 5, 1950 (div. 1953). BA, U. Colo., 1944; JD, Hastings Coll., 1956. Bar: Calif. 1956, Hawaii 1981. Asst. atty to exec. sec. Calif. Law Revision Commn., Stanford, Calif., 1957-61; sr. staff atty. Calif. Dist. Ct. Appeal, Sacramento, 1961-78; pvt. practice Honolulu, 1981—. Home: 1707 Alencastre St Honolulu HI 96816-1907

LINDQUIST, LOUIS WILLIAM, artist, writer; b. Boise, Idaho, June 26, 1944; s. Louis William and Bessie (Newman) L.; divorced; children: Jessica Ann Alexandra, Jason Ryan Louis. BS in Anthropology, U. Oreg., 1968; postgrad., Portland State U., 1974-78. Researcher, co-writer with Asher Lee, Portland, Oreg., 1977-80; freelance artist, painter, sculptor Oreg., 1980-91. Sgt. U.S. Army, 1968-71, Vietnam. Mem. AAAS, Internat. Platform Assn., N.Y. Acad. Scis. Democrat. Home and Office: PO Box 991 Bandon OR 97411-0991

LINDSAY, DONALD GENE, retired dermatologist, educator, writer; b. Kokomo, Ind., Mar. 27, 1922; s. Clifford George and Velma L.; m. Mary Katharine Smith, June 20, 1945 (div. 1972); children: Jan Corwin, Diane Kay, James Christopher; m. Donann Sisler, July 10, 1986. BS, U. Ill., 1943, MD, 1947; postgrad., UCLA, 1955-58, U. So. Calif., 1972-74. Diplomate Am. Bd. Dermatology, Am. Bd. Dermal Pathology, Am. Bd. Endocrinology. Intern Calif. Hosp., Los Angeles, 1947-48; resident in gen. practice San Luis Obispo County Hosp., San Luis Obispo, Calif., 1948-49; pvt. practice specializing in gen. practice Dinuba, Calif., 1949-52; resident in internal medicine Good Samaritan Hosp., L.A., 1954-55; resident in dermatology U. So. Calif., Long Beach Vets. Hosp., L.A. and Long Beach, 1955-58; dermatologist, clin. prof. U. So. Calif., Ventura and L.A., 1958-90; postdoctoral fellow in endocrinology Harbor Hosp., Torrance and L.A., 1972-74; tng. in psychiatry U.S. Army Hosp., Fort Sam Houston, Tex., 1951-52; pres. Found. for Research in Aging, Ventura, Calif., 1965—; rsch. cons. Pickard, Lowe & Garrick Inc., Newport Beach, Calif., Washington, 1987-88; genetic engring. rsch. tng. Univ. Colorado, Boulder, 1989. Author: Medical Cost Crisis! A Solution, 1993 (Best Seller 1994). Active various govt. orgns., 1992—. Capt. U.S. Army M.C., Korea, 1952-54. Mem. AMA, Am. Acad. Dermatology, Pacific Dermatol. Soc., Am. Geronotol. Soc., Calif. Med. Assn., Ventura County Med. Soc., Alpha Omega Alpha. Republican. Home: 5300 Cliffside Cir Ventura CA 93003-1125

LINDSAY, ELENA MARGARET, nurse; b. Evansville, Ind., Oct. 6, 1941; d. Gordon Graham and Irma Louise (Berkemeier) Kuhn; m. Robert Dean Lindsay Jr., Dec. 29, 1988; children: Maria, Robert. BS in Nursing, U. Evansville, 1963. RN. Evening coord., head nurse Welborn Meml. Bapt. Hosp., Evansville, 1969-74; dir. nurses Warrick Hosp., Boonville, Ind., 1975-76; head nurse St. Mary's Med. Ctr., Evansville, 1976-87; staff nurse, HIV counselor BCLS and ACLS instr. VA Med. Ctr., Salt Lake City, 1987-95. Mem. Epilepsy Found. 2d lt. U.S. Army, 1961-64. Mem. DAV (life aux. mem.), AACN, Soc. Orthopedic Nurses (past pres.). Republican. Mem. United Ch. of Christ. Home: 5064 South Heath Ave Kearns UT 84118-6972 Office: 500 Foothill Dr Salt Lake City UT 84148-0001

LINDSAY, GEORGE EDMUND, museum director; b. Pomona, Calif., Aug. 17, 1916; s. Charles Wesley and Alice (Foster) L.; m. Geraldine Kendrick Morris, 1972. Student, San Diego State Coll., 1936-39; B.A., Stanford U., 1951, Ph.D., 1956. Dir. Desert Bot. Gardes, Phoenix, 1939-40, San Diego Natural History Mus., 1956-63; Dir. Calif. Acad. Scis., San Francisco, 1963-82, dir. emeritus, 1982—. Served to capt. USAAF, 1943-46. Decorated Air medal with 3 clusters, Bronze Star. Fellow San Diego Soc. Natural History, Zool. Soc. San Diego, Calif. Acad. Scis., A.A.A.S., Cactus and Succulent Soc. Home: 87 Barbaree Way Tiburon CA 94920-2223 Office: Calif Acad Scis San Francisco CA 94118

LINDSAY, NORMAN ROY, systems consultant; b. Pitts., May 17, 1936; s. Norman Ward and Beverly Mae (Norris) L.; m. Camille Kaye Biddinger, Nov. 29, 1969. BA, Oberlin Coll., 1958; tech. degree, Control Data Inst., San Francisco, 1977. Budget analyst First Ch. Christ Scientist, Boston, 1965-68; office mgr. Christian Sci. Benevolent Assn., San Francisco, 1968-70; instr. Turner Enterprises, Orlando, Fla., 1970-73; various, 1973-77; computer specialist Lawrence Livermore Nat. Lab., Livermore, Calif., 1977-84; assoc. systems analyst Pacific Bell, San Ramon, Calif., 1984-90; cons. Solution Software, Inc., Livermore, Calif., 1990-92; owner RCL Enterprises, Livermore, 1993—. Contbr. articles to profl. jours. Capt. USAF, 1958-65. Mem. USE (com. chair 1987-90, treas. 1991-93, plaque 1990, 91), UNITE (v.p. 1993—, Star award 1994). Republican. Christian Scientist. Home: 130 El Caminito Livermore CA 94550-4004 also: 977 E Stanley Blvd Ste 262 Livermore CA 94550-4009

LINDSAY, RICHARD PAUL, artist, jewelry designer; b. Aurora, Colo., Nov. 21, 1945; s. Paul Francis and Geraldine Evelyn (Goulet) L.; 1 child, Jared Nicholas. BA in Polit. Sci., Colo. State U., 1967. Profl. ski patrol Santa Fe (N.M.) Ski Basin, 1974-80; prin. Richard Lindsay Designs, Santa Fe, 1973—. Copyrighted designs include Walking Trout (R), Happy Critters (R), Roadkill Rabbit (R), Kachina Klan (R); exhibited in numerous galleries, N.Y.C., Colo., N.M., Tex., France, also others. Served to lt. U.S. Army, 1968-71, Vietnam. Recipient Design award Silversmith Santa Fe Film Festival, 1983, Best Ad Yr., Colo. Press Assn., 1972; decorated Bronze Star, Army Commendation medal. Mem. Jewelers Bd. of Trade. Office: Richard Lindsay Designs 1404 Luisa St Ste 4 Santa Fe NM 87505-1012

LINDSELL, HAROLD, clergyman, educator, editor; b. N.Y.C., Dec. 22, 1913; s. Leonard Anthony and Ella Briggs (Harris) L.; B.S., Wheaton Coll., 1938; M.A., U. Calif., 1939, Ph.D., N.Y. U., 1942; D.D., Fuller Theol. Sem., 1964; m. Marion Joanne Bolinder, June 12, 1943; children: Judith Ann (Mrs. William C. Wood), Joanne (Mrs. Robert Webber), Nancy J. (Mrs. Daniel Sharp), John H. Prof. history, missions, registrar Columbia Bible Coll., 1942-44; ordained to ministry Baptist Ch., 1944; prof. missions, assoc. prof. ch. history No. Bapt. Theol. Sem., 1944-47, prof., 1947-51, registrar, 1947-50, dean, 1950-51; dean faculty, prof. missions Fuller Theol. Sem., 1951-61, v.p., prof. missions, 1961-64; assoc. editor Christianity Today, 1964-67, editor, pub., 1968-78; prof. Bible, Wheaton (Ill.) Coll., 1967-68; prof. apologetics Simon Greenleaf Sch. Law, 1983-89, dir. M.A. program, 1984-89. Mem. exec. com. Internat. Congress on World Evangelization. Trustee emeritus Westmont Coll., Wheaton Coll.; chmn. emeritus Gordon Conwell Theol. Sem., Outreach, Christianity Today. Mem. Tournament Roses, Nat. Assn. Bible Instrs., Am. Hist. Assn., Am. Soc. Ch. History, Nat., Greater Washington (pres. 1966-67) assns. evangelicals, NEA, Am. Acad. Polit. and Social Scis., Evang. Theol. Soc. (pres. 1970-71), Pi Gamma Mu, Pi Kappa Delta, Alpha Gamma Omega. Republican. Clubs: Nat. Press, Cosmos (Washington). Author: Abundantly Above, 1944; The Thing Appointed, 1949; A Christian Philosophy of Missions, 1949; Park Street Prophet, 1951; (with C.J. Woodbridge) Handbook of Christian Truth, 1953; Missionary Principles and Practice, 1955; The Morning Altar, 1956; Daily Bible Readings from the Revised Standard Version, 1957; Christianity and the Cults, 1963; Harper Study Bible (rev. standard version), 1964, 91; When You Pray, 1969; The World, The Flesh and The Devil, 1974; The Battle for the Bible, 1976; God's Incomparable Word, 1978; The Bible in the Balance, 1979; The Lindsell Study Bible in the Living Bible, 1980; The Gathering Storm, 1980; Free Enterprise: a Judeo-Christian Defense, 1982; The Holy Spirit in the Latter Days, 1983; Armageddon Spectre, 1984, The People's Study Bible in King James and Living Bible, 1986, The New Paganism, 1987; also articles; editor: The Church's Worldwide Mission, 1966, Harper Study Bible (New Am. Standard Version), 1985, The Everyday Pocket Bible, 1988, Tyndale Words of God for Every Day, 1989, New Harper Study Bible (New Rev. Standard Version), 1991. Home: 23442 El Toro Rd Apt E344 Lake Forest CA 92630-6927

LINDSEY, D. RUTH, physical education educator; b. Kingfisher, Okla., Oct. 26, 1926; d. Lewis Howard and Kenyon (King) L. BS, Okla. State U., 1948; MS, U. Wis., 1954; PEd, Ind. U., 1965. Cert. kinesiotherapist, 1970. Instr. Okla. State U., Stillwater, 1948-50, Monticello Coll., Alton, Ill., 1951-54, DePauw U., Greencastle, Ind., 1954-56; prof. Okla. State U., Stillwater, 1956-75; vis. prof. U. Utah, Salt Lake City, 1975-76; prof. phys. edn. Calif. State U., Long Beach, 1976-88; prof. emeritus phys. edn. Calif. State U., 1988—; freelance author, cons. Westminster, Calif. Co-author: Fitness for the Health of It, 6th edit., 1989, Concepts of Physical Fitness, 8th edit., 1994, Fitness for Life, 4th edit., 1992, Concepts of Physical Fitness and Wellness, 1994, The Ultimate Fitness Book, 1984, Survival Kit for Those Who Sit, 1989; editor: Perspectives: Jour. of Western Soc. for Phys. Edn. Coll. Women, 1988—. Amy Morris Homans scholar, 1964; recipient Disting. and Meritorious Svc. Honor award Okla. Assn. Health, Phys. Edn. and Recreation, 1970, Meritorious Performance award Calif. State U., 1987, Julian Vogel Meml. award Am. Kinesiotherapy Assn., 1988. Fellow AAHPERD, Am. Kinesiotherapy Assn., Calif. Assn. Health, Phys. Edn., Recreation and Dance, Nat. Coun. Against Health Fraud, Orange County Nutrition Coun., Tex and Acad. Authors Assn., Phi Kappa Phi. Republican. Baptist.

LINDSEY, HENRY JACKSON, III, psychologist, educator; b. Anderson, S.C., Aug. 27, 1949; s. Henry Jackson Jr. and Susan Blanche (Bouchillon) L.; m. Jean Catherine Gutshall, Oct. 11, 1986. AA in Biology, MiraCosta Coll., 1970; BA in Psychology, Loretto Hts. Coll., 1983; MA, U. No. Colo., 1986, PhD, 1992. Cert. sch. psychologist. Owner Undersea Sys. Co., 1973-80; supr. res. dept. U. Denver, 1981-85; counselor, therapist Bethesda Cmty. Mental Health Ctr., Denver, 1983-89; instr. psychology dept. U. No. Colo., Greeley, 1989-90; pvt. practice Colo., 1990-92; psychologist Adams County Sch. Dist., Westminster, Colo., 1990-91, Denver Pub. Schs., 1992—; adj. faculty Met. State Coll., denver, 1992—; curriculum-based measurement adv. com. Colo. State Dept. Edn., 1990-92; child custody evaluation tng. State Colo. Interdisciplinary Com. on Child Custody, 1989; teaching asst. psychology dept. U. Denver, 1983; panelist Metro Speech/Lang. Symposium, Denver, 1991. Health edn. dir., bd. dirs. ARC, Denver, 1987-89. Colo. Grad. scholar, 1989, Johnson Found. scholar, 1982, Agnes Kraugh Hearn scholar. Mem. AACD, Assn. Multicultural Counseling and Devel., Colo. Soc. for Behavior Analysis and Therapy (past pres.), Kappa Delta Pi.

LINDSEY, JOHN CUNNINGHAM, sales executive; b. Aliceville, Ala., July 23, 1953; s. Joe Alvin and Anne (Cunningham) L.; m. Karen Lynn Skaczkowski, May 3, 1980; children: Christina, Alissa, Jenna. BS, U. So. Calif., 1975, MBA, 1976. Sales rep. Jantzen, Inc., Portland, Oreg., 1977-87, western regional sales mgr., 1987-90; western regional mgr. OshKosh B'Gosh, L.A., 1990-92; v.p., gen. mgr. men's divsn. Basic Elements, Inc., L.A., 1992-93; dir. product mgmt. BWS Brands, Salinas, Calif., 1993-94; pres., COO Organik Technologies, Tacoma, Wash., 1994—; cons. D&K Enterprises, Moorpark, Calif., 1990—. Co-author, editor manual: Principles of Retail Math Related to Apparel Sales, 1991. Mem. Mayor's Adv. Coun., Moorpark, 1991, Tacoma-Pierce County Leadership Coun. Mem. Am. Mgmt. Assn., Jonathan Club (jr. com. 1984, 86), Sigma Alpha Epsilon (v.p. 1975). Presbyterian. Office: Organik Technologies 4020 S 56th St Tacoma WA 98409

LINDSEY, JOHN HALL, JR., software company executive; b. Malvern, Ark., July 29, 1938; s. John Hall and Jeannette Francis (Stuart) L.; m. Renetta Louise Harms, July 14, 1962; children: Sabra, Lemecia, Lance. Student, Ark. Poly. U., 1956-58, Okla. State U., 1958-60; BS in Bus., U. Utah, 1964; MBA, U. So. Calif., 1968. Data base mgr. NCR corp., Rancho Bernardo, Calif., 1966-75; data base adminstr. Kal Kan Foods, Vernon, Calif., 1975-77; data base supr. Kaiser Steel, Fontana, Calif., 1977-79; mgr. data base and tech. support Western Gear, Lynwood, Calif., 1979-84; mgr., sr. cons. data base Citicorp/TTI, Santa Monica, Calif., 1984-86; prin. Lindsey & Assocs., Eureka, Calif., 1986—; ptnr. Lazio Family Products, 1990-94; ptnr. Lindsey/Milligan Cos., Houston; mem. computer adv. com. Ontario/Montclare Schs., Calif. 1980-82; mem. industry advisor Cullinet Corp., Westwood, Mass., 1986-91; bd. dirs. IDMS User Assn., Westminster, chmn. large users adv. com., 1985-88; bd. dirs. S.W. User Assn., L.A.; guest lectr. U. So. Calif., 1975-76. Author: IDMS DB Design Review, 1982. Elder local Presbyn. Ch., 1980-82; vol. Culver City (Calif.) YMCA, 1986, Santa Monica (Calif.) Real Soccer Club, 1985-86; pres. Mt. Baldy Swim Team, Upland, Calif., 1975-80; bd. dirs. Ontario Community Credit Union, 1979-80; pres. Redwood Heritage Found, Inc., 1990—. Served with USNG, 1956-64. Mem. IDMS User Assn., SW Area IDMS User Assn. (chmn. 1982-84), Assn. System Mgmt. (v.p. 1966-68), Soc. for Mgmt. Info. (co-founder), Eureka C. of C., North Coast Fly Fishers, Trout Unltd., Rotary. Home and Office: 327 2nd St Ste 201 Eureka CA 95501-0486

LINDZEY, GARDNER, psychologist, educator; b. Wilmington, Del., Nov. 27, 1920; s. James and Marguerite (Shotwell) L.; m. Andrea Lewis, Nov. 28, 1944; children: Jeffrey, Leslie, Gardner, David, Jonathan. AB, Pa. State U., 1943, MS, 1945; PhD, Harvard U., 1949; LHD (hon.), U. Colo., 1990; DSc (hon.), Rutgers U., 1992. Research analyst OSRD, 1944-45; instr. psychology Pa. State U., 1945-46; teaching fellow Harvard U., Cambridge, Mass., 1946-47, research fellow, 1947-49, research assoc., asst. prof., 1949-53, lectr., chmn. psychol. clinic staff, 1953-56, prof., chmn. dept., 1972-73; prof. psychology Syracuse (N.Y.) U., 1956-57, U. Minn., 1957-64; prof. psychology U. Tex., 1964-72, chmn., 1964-68, v.p. acad. affairs, 1968-70, v.p. ad interim, 1971, v.p., dean Grad. Studies, prof. psychology, 1973-75; dir. Ctr. for Advanced Study in Behavioral Scis., Stanford (Calif.) U., 1975-89, dir. emeritus, 1989—; mem. psychopharmacology study sect. NIMH, 1958-62, mem. program-project com., 1963-67, mem. adv. com. on extramural research, 1968-71; mem. com. faculty research fellowships Social Sci. Research Council, 1960-63, bd. dirs., 1962-76, mem. com. problems and policy, 1963-70, 72-76, chmn., 1965-70, mem. exec. com., 1970-75, chmn., 1971-75, mem. com. genetics and behavior, 1961-67, chmn., 1961-65; mem. com. biol. bases social behavior, 1967—; mem. com. work and personality in middle years, 1972-77; mem. sociology and social psychology panel NSF, 1965-68, mem. spl. commn. social scis., 1968-69, mem. adv. com. research, 1974—, mem. Waterman award com., 1976-79; mem. exec. com., assembly behavioral and social sci. NAS-NRC, 1970—, mem. com. life sci. and pub. policy, 1968-74, mem. panel nat. needs for biomed. and behavioral research personnel, 1974—, mem. com. social sci. in NSF, 1975—, mem. Inst. Medicine, 1975—; mem. com. on drug abuse Office Sci. and Tech., 1962-63; mem. Presdl. Com. Nat. Medal Sci., 1966-69; bd. dirs. Found.'s Fund Research in Psychiatry, 1967-70; bd. dirs. Am. Psychol. Found., 1968-76, v.p., 1971-73, pres., 1974-76. Author: (with Hall) Theories of Personality, 1957, 70, 78; (with Allport and Vernon) Study of Values, 1951, 60; Projective Techniques and Cross-Cultural Research, 1961; (with J.C. Loehlin and J.N. Spuhler) Race Differences in Intelligence, 1975; (with C.S. Hall and R.F. Thompson) Psychology, 1975; also articles; editor: Handbook of Social Psychology, Vols. 1 and 2, 1954, Vols. 1-5, 1969, Assessment of Human Motives, 1958, Contemporary Psychology, 1967-73, History of Psychology in Autobiography, Vol. 6, 1974, vol. 7, 1980, vol. 8, 1989; assoc. editor Psychol. Abstracts, 1960-62, Ency. Social Scis., 1962-67; co-editor Century Psychology Series, 1960-74, Theories of Personality: Primary Sources and Research, 1965, History of Psychology in Autobiography, Vol. V, 1968, Behavioral Genetics: Methods and Research, 1969, Contributions to Behavior-Genetic Analysis, 1970. Fellow Ctr. Advanced Study Behavioral Scis., Stanford, 1955-56, 63-64, 71-72, Inst. Medicine, 1975—. Fellow Am. Psychol. Assn. (bd. dirs. 1962-68, 70-74, mem. publs. bd., 1956-59, 70-73, chmn. 1958-59, mem. council of reps. 1959-67, 68-74, pres. divsn. social and personality psychology 1963-64, mem. policy and planning 1975, 78, pres. assn. 1966-67, mem. council of editors 1968-73, chmn. com. sci. award 1968-69, pres. divsn. gen. psychology 1970-71), Am. Acad. Arts and Scis., Am. Philos. Soc., Inst. Medicine, NAS, AAAS; mem. Am. Eugenics Soc. (bd. dirs. 1962-70), Soc. Social Biology (bd. dirs. 1972—, pres. 1978—), Am. Psychol. Assn. (dir. ins. trust 1973—), Univs. Research Assn. (bd. dirs. 1973-75). Home: 109 Peter Coutts Cir Palo Alto CA 94305-2517

LINFORD, LAURANCE DEE, cultural organization administrator; b. Cheyenne, Wyo., Mar. 2, 1951; s. Dee Verl and Helen Grace L.; m. Karen Page Stephens, Nov. 23, 1971; children: Justin, Micah. BA, U. N.Mex., 1973; MA, U. Ariz., 1978. Archaeologist Sch. Am. Research, Santa Fe, 1967-75, Ariz. State Mus., Tucson, 1975-77, Nat. Park Service, Tucson, 1977-78, Navajo Nation, Window Rock, Ariz., 1978-82; exec. dir. Inter-Tribal Indian Ceremonial Assn., Gallup, N.Mex., 1982—; bd. dirs. St. Michaels (Ariz.) Hist. Mus., 1979-86. Author: A Measure of Excellence, 1992; author, editor: The Pinon Project, 1982; editor: The Caremonial Mag., 1986-89, Inter-tribal Am. Mag, 1990-92. Pres. Indian Country Tourism Coun., 1982-86; mem. tourism com. Gallup McKinnley County Chamber, 1985-86; bd. dirs. Gallup Conv. and Visitors Bur., 1987-89, 91—. Mem. N.Mex. Assn. Execs. Democrat. Office: Inter-Tribal Indian Ceremonial Assn PO Box 1 Church Rock NM 87311-0001

LING, DANIEL, audiology consultant, educator emeritus, former university dean; b. Wetherden, Suffolk, Eng., Mar. 16, 1926; came to Can., 1963; s. Arthur George and Edith (Rowe) L.; m. Agnes Ling, Sept. 2, 1958 (div. 1979); m. Jane Elizabeth Hansel, Dec. 18, 1982; children: Philip John Ashman, Alister Rowland. Diploma Ed., St. John's Coll., York, Eng., 1950; Diploma Audiology, Manchester (Eng.) U., 1951; MSc, McGill U., Montreal, Que., Can., 1966, PhD, 1968. Tchr. Sch. for Deaf, Sheffield, Eng., 1951-55; organizer deaf edn. Reading Edn. Com., Berkshire, Eng., 1955-63; prin. Montreal Oral Sch. for Deaf, 1963-66; prof. McGill U., 1966-84; dean applied health scis. U. Western Ont., London, Can., 1984-91; cons. audiology, 1991—; dir. McGill Project Deaf Children, Montreal, 1966-84. Author: Speech and the Hearing Impaired, 1976, Aural Habilitation, 1978, Foundations of Spoken Language for Hearing-Impaired Children, 1989; editor: Early Intervention for the Hearing Impaired, 1984. Recipient various grants. Fellow Am. Speech, Lang. and Hearing Assn.; mem. A.G. Bell Assn. for Deaf (pres. 1984-86). Home and Office: 956 Cherry Point Rd RR3, Cobble Hill, BC Canada V0R 1L0

LING, DAVID CHANG, international book dealer; b. Shanghai, Feb. 17, 1939; s. H.C. and Katherine (Chang) L.; m. Janine Peters, June 20, 1970 (div. Feb. 1975). BA, U. Ore., 1962; MA, U. Wis., 1964, PhD, 1971. Vis. instr. U. of the South, Sewanee, Tenn., 1964-65; asst. prof. U. Wis., Kenosha, 1969-73; owner Ling's Internat. Books, San Diego, 1974—. Mem. Phi Beta Kappa. Democrat. Home: 5012 Westminster Ter San Diego CA 92116-2103 Office: Ling's Internat Books 7531 Convoy Ct San Diego CA 92111-1113

LINHARDT, ANTHONY LAKATOS, electrical engineer; b. Kispest, Hungary, Aug. 24, 1929; came to U.S., 1956; s. Antal and Elizabeth (Simon) L.; m. Agi Sarlo, Feb. 1, 1951 (div. Feb. 1971); children: Peter, Paul. BSME, Tech. Inst. Budapest, 1951, MS in Aeronautical Engring., 1951. Registered profl. engr., Calif., Nev., Tex., Ariz., Wyo., Colo., Oreg., Hawaii, N.Y. Prin. Anthony L. Linhardt & Assocs., L.A., 1964—. Recipient Leadership award YMCA, 1983. Mem. IEEE, Internat. Assn. Elec. Insps., Illuminating Engring. Soc., Assn. Cons.Elec. Engrs. (pres. 1993-95). Democrat.

LINK, GEORGE HAMILTON, lawyer; b. Sacramento, Calif., Mar. 26, 1939; s. Hoyle and Corrie Elizabeth (Evans) L.; m. Betsy Leland; children—Thomas Hamilton, Christopher Leland. AB, U. Calif., Berkeley, 1961; LLB, Harvard U., 1964. Bar: Calif. 1965, U.S. Dist. Ct. (no., ea., ctrl. and so dists.) Calif. 1965, U.S. Ct. Appeals (9th cir.) 1965. Assoc. Brobeck, Phleger & Harrison, San Francisco, 1964-69, ptnr., 1970—; mng. ptnr. Brobeck, Phleger & Harrison, L.A., 1973-93; mng. ptnr. firmwide Brobeck Phleger & Harrison, 1993—; chmn. Pacific Rim Adv. Coun., 1992—. Bd. regents U. Calif., 1971-74; trustee Berkeley Found., Jr. Statesmen Am.; bd. govs. United Way, 1979-81; trustee, v.p. Calif. Hist. Soc., 1987—. Fellow Am. Bar Found.; mem. ABA, Calif. Bar Assn., L.A. Bar Assn., U. Calif. Alumni Assn. (pres. 1972-75), Calif. Club, Bohemian Club, Jonathan Club. Republican. Methodist. Home: 315 N Carmelina Ave Los Angeles CA 90049-2701 Office: Brobeck Phleger & Harrison 550 S Hope St Los Angeles CA 90071-2627

LINK, MICHAEL PAUL, pediatrics educator; b. Cleve., Jan. 3, 1949; s. J. Alexander and Betty Irene (Lewis) L.; m. Vicki L. Rumpf, May 30, 1985; 1 child, Alexis Arielle. AB, Columbia Coll., 1970; MD, Stanford U., 1974. Diplomate Am. Bd. Pediatrics, subbd. Pediatric Hematology/Oncology. Prof. pediatrics Stanford (Calif.) U., 1991—. Mem. Phi Beta Kappa, Alpha Omega Alpha. Office: Stanford U Children's Hosp 725 Welch Rd Palo Alto CA 94304-1601

LINKER, DAVID T., cardiologist; b. Reykjavik, Iceland, July 27, 1951. BS in Biology, Stanford (Calif.) U., 1972, MD, 1976. Diplomate Am. Bd. Internal Medicine, Am. Bd. Pediatrics, Am. Bd. Pediatric Cardiology, Am. Bd. Cardiology. Intern in internal medicine U. Calif. Davis/Sacramento Med. Ctr., 1976-77; resident in internal medicine U. Wash. Hosp., 1977-79, resident in pediatrics, 1979-81, fellowship adult cardiology, 1981-83; fellowship pediatric cardiology Stanford U. Med. Ctr., 1983-84; asst. prof. biomed. engrng. U. Trondheim, 1985-91, chmn. dept. of biomed. engrng., 1990-91; assoc. prof. divsn. of cardiology Dept. of Medicine, U. Wash., 1993—; acting attending physician, divsn. of cardiology Regional Hosp., Tondheim, 1985-86; attending physician divsn. of cardiology, 1987-91; head divsn. of echocardiography, dept. of cardiology, Thorax Ctr. Academic Hosp. of Rotterdam, 1991-93; attending physician, dvisn. cardiology, dept. medicine, U. Wash., 1993—. Contbr. articles to profl. jours. Grantee Fulbright-Hays, 1985-86; recipient Nedron award for Rsch., 1988. Fellow Am. Coll. Cardiology (echocardiography com.), European Soc. Cardiology (organizer subgroup on intravascular ultrasound 1991-93); mem. Am. Soc. Echocardiography (physics and instrumentation com.), Soc. Pediat. Echocardiography, IEEE, IEEE Computer Soc., Seattle Seafair Clowns (Charlie Choate award 1983), Norwegian Soc. for Diagnostic Ultrasound, Norwegian Soc. for Pattern Analysis and Image Processing (exec. com. 1987-88), Norwegian Med. Assn., Internat. Cardiac Doppler Soc. (sec. Euro-African sect. 1993), Am. Heart Assn. Office: U Wash Divsn Cardiology PO Box 356422 Seattle WA 98195

LINKLETTER, ARTHUR GORDON, radio and television broadcaster; b. Moose Jaw, Sask., Can., July 17, 1912; s. Fulton John and Mary (Metzler) L.; m. Lois Foerster, Nov. 25, 1935; children: Jack, Dawn, Robert (dec.), Sharon, Diane (dec.). A.B., San Diego State Coll., 1934. Program dir. Sta. KGB, San Diego, 1934; program dir. Calif. Internat. Expn., San Diego, 1935; radio dir. Tex. Centennial Expn., Dallas, 1936; San Francisco World's Fair, 1937-39; pres. Linkletter Prodns.; ptnr., co-owner John Guedel Radio Prodns.; chmn. bd. Linkletter Enterprises; owner Art Linkletter Oil Enterprises. Author: theme spectacle Cavalcade of Golden West, 1940; author and co-producer: theme spectacle Cavalcade of Am, 1941; writer, producer, star in West Coast radio shows, 1940-55; former star, writer: People Are Funny, NBC-TV and radio, Art Linkletter's House Party, CBS-TV and radio; Author: People Are Funny, 1953, Kids Say The Darndest Things, 1957, The Secret World of Kids, 1959, Confessions of a Happy Man, 1961, Kids Still Say The Darndest Things, 1961, A Child's Garden of Misinformation, 1965, I Wish I'd Said That, 1968, Linkletter Down Under, 1969, Oops, 1969, Drugs at My Door Step, 1973, Women Are My Favorite People, 1974, How to be a Super Salesman, 1974, Yes, You Can!, 1979, I Didn't Do It Alone, 1979, Public Speaking for Private People, 1980, Linkletter on Dynamic Selling, 1982, Old Age is not for Sissies, 1988; lectr. convs. and univs. Nat. bd. dirs. Goodwill Industries; commr. gen. to U.S. Exhibit at Brisbane Expo 88, Australia, 1987; amb. to The 200th Anniversary Celebration, Australia, 1987—; bd. regents Pepperdine U.; bd. advisors Ctr. On Aging UCLA; ch. bd. French Fn for Alzheimers Rsch. Recipient numerous awards. Address: 8484 Wilshire Blvd Ste 205 Beverly Hills CA 90211-3220

LINN, BRIAN JAMES, lawyer; b. Seattle, July 8, 1947; s. Bruce Hugh and Jeanne De V. (Weidman) L.; m. Renee Diane Mousley; children: Kelly, Kareem, Kari. BA in Econs., U. Wash., 1972; JD, Gonzaga Sch. Law, 1975. Bar: Wash. 1975, U.S. Supreme Ct. 1979. Mng. atty. Legal Svcs. for Northwestern Pa., Franklin, 1975-76; staff atty. The Nat. Ctr. for Law and the Handicapped, 1976-78, U. Notre Dame Law Sch., South Bend, Ind., 1976-78; pvt. practice, Seattle, 1978—; lectr. Seattle U., 1980-85. Chmn. civil and legal rights subcom. Gov.'s Com. on Employment of the Handicapped, 1981-87; arbitrator King County Superior Ct., 1981—, judge pro tem, 1989—. Editor Gonzaga Law Rev., 1974-75. Mem. Wash. State Devel. Disabilities Planning Council, 1980-83; trustee Community Service Ctr. for the Deaf and Hard of Hearing, Seattle, 1982-84; chmn. legal rights task force Epilepsy Found. Am., 1979-81; mem. Witness for Peace Delegation, Nicaragua, 1993. Served with U.S. Army, 1967-69; Vietnam. Mem. Wash. State Bar Assn. (chair world peace through law sect. 1990-91, spl. dist. counsel 1991-95), Omicron Delta Epsilon. Democrat. Methodist. Hon. editor DePaul Law Rev., 1978; contbr. articles to profl. jours. Home: 9716 S 204th Ct Kent WA 98031-1400 Office: 245 SW 152nd St Seattle WA 98166-2307

LINN, CAROLE ANNE, dietitian; b. Portland, Oreg., Mar. 3, 1945; d. James Leslie and Alice Mae (Thorburn) L. Intern, U. Minn., 1967-68; BS, Oreg. State U., 1963-67. Nutrition cons. licensing and cert. sect. Oreg. State Bd. Health, Portland, 1968-70; chief clin. dietitian Rogue Valley Med. Ctr., Medford, Oreg., 1970—; cons. Hillhaven Health Care Ctr., Medford, 1971-83; lectr. Local Speakers Bur., Medford. Mem. ASPEN, Am. Dietetic Assn., Am. Diabetic Assn., Oreg. Dietetic Assn. (sec. 1973-75, nominating com. 1974-75, Young Dietitian of Yr. 1976), So. Oreg. Dietetic Assn., Alpha Lambda Delta, Omicron Nu. Democrat. Mem. Christ Unity Ch. Office: Rogue Valley Med Ctr 2825 E Barnett Rd Medford OR 97504-8332

LINN, DAVID EDWARD, artist; b. Palo Alto, Calif., Sept. 2, 1959; s. Charles William and Dixie Joyce (Rawlins) L. BFA, Brigham Young U., 1986, postgrad., 1994—. Selected exhbns. include Am. Inst. Graphic Artists Invitational Exhbn., San Francisco 1987 (Purchase award 1987), Soc. of Illustrators, N.Y.C., 1988 (award of merit 1988), Commn. Arts, Palo Alto, Calif., LDS Internat. Art Exhbn, Salt Lake City, 1992 (award of Merit, Peoples Choice award 1992), 1994 (award of Merit, Purchase award 1994, Visitors Choice award 1994), Springville Mus. Art, 1994 (Dirs. Choice award 1994). Missionary LDS Ch., Buenos Aires, 1980-82. Named Outstanding Young Men of Am., 1988. Home: 12305 Stonebrook Ct Los Altos CA 94022

LINN, GARY DEAN, golf course architect; b. Wichita, Kans., May 11, 1955; s. Richard W. and Marilyn (Hanson) L.; m. Vicki Duncan, Aug. 6, 1977; children: Rachel, Jason, Nathan. B of Landscape Architecture, Kans. State U., 1978. Registered landscape architect Kans., 1979. Mem. Am. Soc. Landscape Architects, Am. Soc. Golf Course Architects. Office: 705 Forest Ave Palo Alto CA 94301-2102

LINSCHEID, DAN EDWIN, land surveyor; b. Amity, Oreg., Aug. 23, 1947; s. Walter Edwin and Cora Elizabeth (Cross) L.; m. Annita Louise Sims, Sept. 10, 1969; children: James, Jonathan, Dawn. Assoc., Chemeketa C.C., 1971. Registered profl. land surveyor, Oreg. Engrng. technician Yamhill County Rd. Dept., McMinnville, Oreg., 1971-79; county rd. surveyor Yamhill County Pub. Works, McMinnville, Oreg., 1979-84, asst. dir., 1984-94. Elected Dem. County Surveyor, McMinnville, 1994—. Served to Cpl., USMC, 1966-69. Recipient Award of Merit, Oreg. Assn. County Engrs., Surveyors, 1991-92. Mem. Profl. Land Surveyors Oreg. (Willamette chpt. pres. 1984). Home: 9273 Gopher Valley Rd Sheridan OR 97378-9758 Office: Yamhill County Surveyor Ofc 2060 Lafayette Ave Mcminnville OR 97128

LINSTONE, HAROLD ADRIAN, management and systems science educator; b. Hamburg, Fed. Republic Germany, June 15, 1924; came to U.S., 1936; s. Frederic and Ellen (Seligmann) L.; m. Hedy Schubach, June 16, 1946; children: Fred A., Clark R. BS, CCNY, 1944; MA, Columbia U., 1947; PhD, U. So. Calif., 1954. Sr. scientist Hughes Aircraft Co., Culver City, Calif., 1949-61, The Rand Corp., Santa Monica, Calif., 1961-63; assoc. dir. planning Lockheed Corp., Burbank, Calif., 1963-71; prof. Portland (Oreg.) State U., 1970—; pres. Systems Forecasting, Inc., Santa Monica, 1971—; cons. 1973—. Author: Multiple Perspectives for Decision Making, 1984; co-author: The Unbounded Mind, 1993, The Challenge of the 21st Century, 1994; co-editor The Delphi Method, 1975, Technological Substitution, 1976, Futures Research, 1977; editor-in-chief Technol. Forecasting Social Change, 1969—. NSF grantee, Washington, 1976, 79, 85. Mem. Inst. Mgmt. Scis., Ops. Rsch. Soc., Internat. Soc. Systems Scis. (pres. 1993-94). Office: Portland State U PO Box 751 Portland OR 97207-0751

LINTHICUM, GARY REX, construction company executive; b. Tulsa, Mar. 3, 1940; s. Rex R. and Theo Murtle (Mace) L.; m. Dianne Davis, May 28, 1960; children: David, Dana, Eric. BS in Engring. and Constrn., Ariz. State U., 1964; postgrad., U. Ariz., 1974, Stanford U., 1980. Field engr. Craig & Keithline Emgrs., Tulsa, 1960-61; project engr. Kitchell Contractors, Phoenix, 1964, estimator, project mgr., ops. mgr., exec. v.p., pres., 1980-84; pres. Linthicum Constructors Inc., Scottsdale, Ariz., 1984—. Named Mgr. of Yr. City of Scottsdale, 1986. Mem. Associated Gen. Contractors (special contracting methods com. 1980-82, bd. dirs. 1982-83, collective bargaining com. 1983, contract documents coordinating com. 1983, spl. contracting methods com. 1983, chmn. edn. com. Ariz. chpt. 1980-82, bd. dirs. 1982-83, chmn. collective bargaining com. 1982-83, 2d v.p. 1987, 1st v.p. 1988, pres. Ariz. chpt. 1989), Ariz. State Alumni Assn. (bd. dirs. 1983-85). Republican. Methodist. Office: Linthicum Constructors Inc 9322 N 94th Way Ste 102 Scottsdale AZ 85258-5522

LINTON, MARGARET ANN, curator; b. Pontiac, Mich., Mar. 17, 1967; d. Frederick Melvin and Peggy Ruth (Jensen) L. BA in English, U. Calif., Irvine, 1989; postgrad. in exhbn. design, Calif. State U., Fullerton, 1992-95. Trademark paralegal Knobbe, Martens, Olson, Bear, Newport Beach, Calif., 1991-94; asst. dir. devel. Sch. Arts Calif. State U., Fullerton, 1994-95; curator Griffin Fine Art, Costa Mesa, Calif., 1994—. Office: Griffin Fine Art PO Box 11240 Costa Mesa CA 92627-1240

LINTON, MARIGOLD L., psychology educator; b. Morongo Reservation, Banning, Calif.; d. Walter Alexander and Wistaria (Hartmann) L.; m. Robert Ellis Barnhill, Feb. 12, 1983; children: John, Margaret. BA, U. Calif.-Riverside, 1958; postgrad., U. Iowa, 1960; PhD, UCLA, 1964. Lectr., prof. San Diego State U., 1964-74; prof. U. Utah, Salt Lake City, 1974-86; dir. edn. svcs. Coll. Edn. Ariz. State U., Tempe, 1986-94; dir. Am. Indl. Program SUMMS Inst. Ariz. State U., Tempe, 1994—; vis. prof. U. Calif.-San Diego, 1971-72; vis. scholar Learning Research and Devel. Ctr. U. Pitts., 1980-81; mem. nat. adv. research resources council NIH, 1982-86. Co-author: (with Gallo) The Practical Statistician, 1975. Contbr. articles to profl. jours., chpts. to books. Bd. dirs. Malki Mus., 1971-78; bd. dirs. Soc. Adv. Chicanos Native Am. Sci., 1989-95, treas., 1994-95; trustee Carnegie Found. Advancement Teaching, 1977-85. NIH research grant, 1980, Edn. grant NASA, 1994-95, Edn. grant NSF, 1994-95; recipient Founders medal Soc. Adv. Chicanos Native Am. Sci., 1993; Svc. award Soc. Adv. Chicanos Native Am. Sci., 1994. Fellow APA (bd. advancement psychol. pub. interest 1993—), Am. Psychol. Soc.; mem. Am. Ednl. Rsch. Assn., Nat. Indian Edn. Assn. (founder, Cert. Honor award 1976), Phi Beta Kappa, Phi Kappa Phi. Office: Ariz State U Dept Math Tempe AZ 85287-1804

LINTON, WILLIAM HENRY, power industry consultant, engineer; b. Jersey Shore, Pa., Feb. 20, 1925; s. John Henry Linton and Emily Helena (Scouten) Linton Sims; m. Mary Bishop Clarke, Aug. 12, 1949; 1 child, Susan Bishop. BSME, Bucknell U., 1949. Registered profl. engr., Calif. Constrn. engr. Penna Power and Light Co., Allentown, Pa., 1949-53, Grinnell Corp., Portsmouth, Ohio, 1953-54; engring. mgr. Bettis Atomic Power Lab., Pitts., 1954-64, 66-69; resident mgr. Bettis Atomic Power Lab., Newport News, Va., 1964-66; resident mgr. west coast Bettis Atomic Power Lab., L.A., 1970-72; mgr. constrn. Westinghouse Hanford, Richmond, Wash., 1972-74; project mgr. Bechtel Corp., San Francisco, 1974-90; ind. cons. to power industry Sausalito, Calif., 1990—; Patentee naval nuclear field. Grand Juror Marin County Grand Jury, San Rafael, 1991. 2nd lt. U.S. Army, 1943-45, ETO. Mem. ASME (life), Masons, Marin County Dog Tng. Club. Republican. Home: 14 Cypress Pl Sausalito CA 94965-1536

LINXWILER, JAMES DAVID, lawyer; b. Fresno, Calif., Apr. 9, 1949; s. George Edwin and Stella Ruth (Schmidt) L.; m. Robyn Kenning, July 12, 1986; children: Elizabeth Ann, John Edwin, Jeffrey David. BA, U. Calif.-Berkeley, 1971; JD, UCLA, 1974. Bar: D.C. 1976, Alaska 1977, U.S. Ct. Appeals (9th and D.C. cirs.), U.S. Dist. Ct. Alaska, U.S. Supreme Ct. Lawyer, Dept. Interior, Washington, 1974-76; lawyer, Cook Inlet Region Inc., Anchorage, 1976-78; lawyer Sohio Petroleum Co., Anchorage, 1978-81; ptnr. Guess & Rudd, Anchorage, 1981—; speaker seminars on environ. and natural resources law. Contbr. chpts. to book, articles to profl. jours. Chmn. Alaska Coalition Am. Energy Security, 1986-87, Alliance Arctic Nat. Wildlife Refuge Com., 1986-87; bd. dirs., Commonwealth N., 1993-95. Mem. ABA, Alaska Bar Assn. (chmn., exec. com. nat. resources sect. 1988-93), Fed. Bar Assn., D.C. Bar Assn.Democrat. Home: 2407 Loussac Dr Anchorage AK 99517-1272 Office: Guess & Rudd 510 L St Ste 700 Anchorage AK 99501-1959

LINXWILER, LOUIS MAJOR, JR., retired finance company executive; b. Blackwell, Okla., Mar. 7, 1931; s. Louis Major and Flora Mae (Horton) L.; m. Susan Buchanan, July 27, 1963; children: Louis Major III, Robert William. BS, Okla. State U., 1954. Mgr. credit dept. Valley Nat. Bank, Tucson, 1957-60; sales rep. Vega Industries, Syracuse, N.Y., 1960-62; program dir. Am. Cancer Soc., Phoenix, 1962-67; v.p., mgr. credit dept. United Bank Ariz., Phoenix, 1967-76; dean edn. Am. Inst. Banking, Phoenix, 1976-80; cons. Phoenix, 1980-81, United Student Aid Funds Inc., Phoenix, 1981-82; founder, pres., chief exec. officer Ariz. Student Loan Fin. Corp., Phoenix, 1982-88, also bd. dirs.; founder, chmn., chief exec. officer Western Loan Mktg. Assn., Phoenix, 1984-90, also bd. dirs.; pres. Precision Design and Engring., Inc., Escondido, Calif., 1993—. Editor: Money and Banking, 1978. Pres. City Commn. Sister Cities, Phoenix, 1986-87, Am. Inst. Banking, Phoenix, 1973-74, Phoenix YMCA Bd. Dirs., 1974-75; v.p. North Mountain Behavioral Inst., Phoenix, 1975-77. Served to 1st lt. U.S. Army, 1954-56. Mem. Shriners, Hiram Club, Rotary (bd. dirs. 1982-83, 93-94), Beta Theta Pi. Republican. Presbyterian. Home: 3311 E Georgia Ave Phoenix AZ 85018-1424

LIONAKIS, GEORGE, architect; b. West Hiawatha, Utah, Sept. 5, 1924; s. Pete and Andriani (Protopapadakis) L.; student Carbon Jr. Coll., 1942-43, 46-47; BArch., U. Oreg., 1951; m. Iva Oree Braddock, Dec. 30, 1951; 1 dau., Deborah Jo. With Corps Engrs., Walla Walla, Wash., 1951-54; architect Liske, Lionakis, Beaumont & Engberg, Sacramento, 1954-86, Lionakis-Beaumont Design Group, 1986—. Mem. Sacramento County Bd. Appeals, 1967—, chmn., 1969, 75, 76; pres. Sacramento Builders Exchange, 1976. Served with USAAF, 1943-46. Mem. AIA (pres. Central Valley chpt., 1972—), Constrn. Specifications Inst. (pres. Sacramento chpt., 1962; nat. awards, 1962, 63, 65), Sacramento C. of C. (code com., 1970—). Club: North Ridge Country (pres. 1987). Lodge: Rotarian (pres. East Sacramento 1978-79). Prin. works include Stockton (Calif.) Telephone Bldg., 1968, Chico (Calif.) Main Telephone Bldg., 1970, Mather AFB Exchange Complex Sacramento, 1970, Base Chapel Mather AFB, Sacramento, 1970, Woodridge Elementary Sch., Sacramento, 1970, Pacific Telephone Co. Operating Center Modesto, Calif., 1968, Sacramento, 1969, Marysville, Calif., 1970, Red Bluff, Calif., 1971, Wells Fargo Banks, Sacramento, 1968, Corning, Calif., 1969, Anderson, 1970, Beale AFB Exchange Complex, Marysville, 1971, Cosumnes River Coll., Sacramento, 1971, base exchanges at Bergstrom AFB, Austin, Tex., Sheppard AFB, Wichita Falls, Tex., Chanute AFB, Rantoul, Ill., McChord AFB, Tacoma, Wash., health center Chico State U., Sacramento County Adminstrn. Center, Sacramento Bee Newspaper Plant. Home: 160 Breckenwood Way Sacramento CA 95864-6968 Office: Lionakis Beaumont Design Group 1919 19th St Sacramento CA 95814-6714

LIPCHIK, HAROLD, company executive; b. N.Y.C., Apr. 17, 1928; s. Samuel and Ida (Gutterman) L.; m. Elaine Greenberg, Mar. 23, 1952; children: Alan Scott, Debra Anne. BS in Mech. Engring., Carnegie Mellon U., 1948; postgrad., NYU, 1948-49, 49-50. Project engr. Pub. Svc. Commn. N.Y. State, N.Y.C., 1950-51, Bendix Aviation, South Bend, Ind., 1951-52, Hamilton Standard div. United Aircraft, Windsor Locks, Conn., 1952-66; v.p. AMF Inc., N.Y.C., 1966-71, Chromalloy Am. Corp., Clayton, Mo., 1968-71; pres. Water Treatment Corp., City of Industry, Calif., 1971-82, Halco Industries, Glendale, Calif., 1982—, Halco Assocs., Tarzana, Calif., 1984—; v.p. Nat. Tech. Systems, Calabasas, Calif., 1982—; dir. Halco Assocs., Tarzana. Pres. United Synagogue Am., L.A., 1976-78, L.A. Hebrew High Sch., L.A., 1978-84. Jewish. Home: 4429 Trancas Pl Tarzana CA 91356-5302 Office: Nat Tech Systems 24007 Ventura Blvd Calabasas CA 91302-1458

LIPKE, JAMES SCOTT, municipal official; b. Lakewood, Ohio, Sept. 17, 1947. BA in Biology, U. Calif. San Diego, La Jolla, 1975. Cert. tchr. cmty. coll., Calif. Tchr. computer info. scis. San Diego Mesa Coll., 1984-95; coord. data sys. City of San Diego, 1979-95; spkr. Computer Fair, San Diego, 1991-95. With USN, 1966-70. Mem. AFIO, Internat. Spl. Interest Group, Assn. Former Intelligence Officers (pres. 1990), San Diego Computer Soc. Office: City of San Diego 202 C St MS 2A San Diego CA 92101

LIPKIN, MARY CASTLEMAN DAVIS (MRS. ARTHUR BENNETT LIPKIN), retired psychiatric social worker; b. Germantown, Pa., Mar. 4, 1907; d. Henry L. and Willie (Webb) Davis; m. William F. Cavenaugh, Nov. 8, 1930 (div.); children: Molly C. (Mrs. Gary Oberbillig), William A.; m. Arthur Bennett Lipkin, Sept. 15, 1961 (dec. June 1974). Student, Pa. Acad. Fine Arts, 1924-28; attended, U. Wash., 1946-48. Nursery sch. tchr. Miquon (Pa.) Sch., 1940-45; caseworker Family Soc. Seattle, 1948-49, Jewish Family and Child Service, Seattle, 1951-56; psychiat. social worker Stockton (Calif.) State Hosp., 1957-58; supr. social service Mental Health Research Inst., Fort Steilacoom, Wash., 1958-59; engaged in pvt. practice, Bellevue, Wash., 1959-61. Former mem. Phila. Com. on City Policy. Former diplomate and bd. mem. Conf. Advancement of Pvt. Practice in Social Work; former mem. Chestnut Hill women's com. Phila. Orch; mem. Bellevue Art Mus., Assoc. Am. Assn. of U. Women, Wing Luke Mus. Mem. ACLU, LWV, Linus Pauling Inst. Sci. and Medicine, Inst. Noetic Scis., Menninger Found., Smithsonian Instn., Union Concerned Scientists, Physicians for Social Responsibility, Center for Sci. in Pub. Interest, Asian Art Council, Seattle Art Mus., Nature Conservancy, Wilderness Soc., Sierra Club, Nassau Club (Princeton, N.J.). Home: 10022 Meydenbauer Way SE Bellevue WA 98004-6041

LIPMAN, CAROL KOCH, designer; b. Lincoln, Nebr., Mar. 23, 1960; d. Robert Carl and Gertrude Evelyn (Kornmuller) Koch; m. Ken Lipman, Dec. 16, 1989. B.S., Drexel U., 1982. Design asst. Sydney Carvin Milliken, N.Y.C., 1981, 82-83, Jones New York, N.Y.C., 1983-84; sales rep., designer Asymmetry, N.Y.C., 1984-85; designer Rayman/Ridless, N.Y.C., 1985-87; designer Echo Design Group, Albert Nipon Belts, 1987-88; designer Philip Sand Belts, 1988; designer, mgr. product devel. Karl Lagerfeld Bijoux div. Victoria Internat., 1988-89; designer The 1928 Jewelry Co., 1989-91; brand mgr. Hair Jewelry divsn. Crystals, 1991-92; brand mgr. Aurora R.S.V.P. Collection, 1993, vice pres. design, 1994; mgr. design dept. Leegin Creative Leather Products, Inc., 1994—. Mem. NAFE, Phi Eta Sigma, Phi Kappa Phi, Omicron Nu. Avocations: art, art history, jewelry making.

LIPOMI, MICHAEL JOSEPH, health facility administrator; b. Buffalo, Mar. 9, 1953; s. Dominic Joseph and Betty (Angelo) L.; m. Brenda H. Lipomi, Dec. 23, 1977; children: Jennifer, Barrett. BA, U. Ottawa, 1976; MS in Health Adminstrn., U. Colo., 1994. Mktg. dir. Am. Med. Internat. El Cajon Valley Hosp., Calif., 1980-83; dir. corp. devel. Med. Surg. Ctrs. Am., Calif., 1983-85; exec. dir. Stanislaus Surgery Ctr., Modesto, Calif., 1985—. Author: Complete Anatomy of Health Care Marketing, 1988; co-host med. TV talk show Health Talk Modesto. Bd. dirs. Am. Heart Assn., Modesto, 1988-89; pres. Modesto Community Hospice, 1987-88; active local govt.; sec.-treas. Modesto Industry and Edn. Council, 1989. Mem. Calif. Ambulatory Surgery Assn. (pres. 1988-89, mem. legis. com. 1994, mem. rsch. and edn. found. bd. 1994—), No. Calif. Assn. Surgery Ctrs. (pres. 1986-88), Federated Ambulatory Surgery Assn. (mem. govt. rels. com. 1988, bd. dirs. 1989—, chmn. govt. rels. com. 1990), Modesto C. of C. (bd. dirs. 1989-92), Rotary. Office: Stanislaus Surgery Ctr 1421 Oakdale Rd Modesto CA 95355-3359

LIPPA, ERIK ALEXANDER, ophthalmologist; b. Mpls., Nov. 7, 1945; s. Walter and Cecilie (Buchman) L.; m. Linda Susan Mottow, Mar. 6, 1980; children: David Abram, Andrew Moss. BS, Calif. Inst. Tech., 1967; MS, U. Mich., 1968, PhD in Math., 1971; MD, Albert Einstein Coll. Medicine, 1980. NATO postdoctoral fellow Oxford (Eng.) U., 1971-72; asst. prof. Purdue U., West Lafayette, Ind., 1972-78; med. intern NYU Med. Ctr./Manhattan (N.Y.) VA Hosp., 1980-81; resident ophthalmology Ill. Eye and Ear Infirmary, Chgo., 1981-84; ophthalmologist St. Paul, 1984-85; asst. dir. clin. rsch. Merck & Co. Inc., West Point, Pa., 1985-89, dir. clin. rsch., 1989-93; dir. med. affairs Allergan, Inc., Irvine, Calif., 1993—; adj. clin. asst. prof. Jefferson Med. Coll., Phila., 1986-91, adj. clin. assoc. prof., 1991—; clin. assoc. U. Pa., Phila., 1987-93; asst. surgeon Wills Eye Hosp., Phila., 1991-93, instr., 1986-91. Author: Mathematics for Freshmen in the Life Sciences, 1976; contbr. articles to profl. jours. Treas. Cub Scout Pack #665, Ft. Washington, Pa., 1988-93. Fellow Am. Acad. Ophthalmology; mem. AMA, Assn. Rsch. in Vision and Ophthalmology, Internat. Soc. Eye Rsch., Am. Glaucoma Soc., European Glaucoma Soc., Sigma Xi, Tau Beta Pi. Home: PO Box 16517 Irvine CA 92713-6517 Office: Allergan Inc 2525 Dupont Dr Irvine CA 92715-1531

LIPPE, PHILIPP MARIA, neurosurgeon, educator; b. Vienna, Austria, May 17, 1929; s. Philipp and Maria (Goth) L.; came to U.S., 1938, naturalized, 1945; m. Virginia M. Wiltgen, 1953 (div. 1977); children: Patricia Ann Marie, Philip Eric Andrew, Laura Lynne Elizabeth, Kenneth Anthony Ernst; m. Gail B. Busch, Nov. 26, 1977. Student Loyola U., Chgo., 1947-50; BS in Medicine, U. Ill. Coll. Medicine, 1952, MD with high honors, 1954. Rotating intern St. Francis Hosp., Evanston, Ill., 1954-55; asst. resident gen. surgery VA Hosp., Hines, Ill., 1955, 58-59; asst. resident neurology and neurol. surgery Neuropsychiat. Inst., U. Ill. Rsch. and Ednl. Hosps., Chgo., 1959-60, chief resident, 1962-63, resident neuropathology, 1962, postgrad. trainee in electroencephalography, 1963; resident neurology and neurol. surgery Presbyn.-St. Luke's Hosp., Chgo., 1960-61; practice medicine, specializing in neurol. surgery, San Jose, Calif., 1963—; instr. neurology and neurol. surgery U. Ill., 1962-63; clin. instr. surgery and neurosurgery Stanford U., 1965-69, clin. asst. prof., 1969-74, clin. assoc. prof., 1974—; staff cons. in neurosurgery O'Connor Hosp., Santa Clara Valley Med. Ctr., San Jose Hosp., Los Gatos Cmty. Hosp., El Camino Hosp. (all San Jose area); chmn. divsn. neurosugery Good Samaritan Hosp. 1989—; founder, exec. dir. Bay Area Pain Rehab. Center, San Jose, 1979—; clin. adviser to Joint Commn. on Accreditation of Hosps.; mem. dist. med. quality rev. com. Calif. Bd. Med. Quality Assurance, 1976-87, chmn., 1976-77. Served to capt. USAF, 1956-58. Diplomate Am. Bd. Neurol. Surgery, Nat. Bd. Med. Examiners. Fellow ACS, Am. Coll. Pain Medicine (pres. 1992-93, bd. dirs. 1991-94, v.p. 1991-92, pres. 1992-93, exec. v.p. 1994—); mem. AMA (Ho. of Dels. 1981—), Am. Coll. Physician Execs., Calif. Med. Assn. (Ho. of Dels. 1976-80, sci. bd., council 1979-87, sec. 1981-87, Outstanding Svc. award 1987), Santa Clara County Med. Soc. (coun. 1974-81, pres. 1978-79, Outstanding Contbn. award 1984, Benjamin J. Cory award 1987), Chgo. Med. Soc., Congress Neurol. Surgeons, Calif. Assn. Neurol. Surgeons (dir. 1974-82, v.p. 1975-76, pres. 1977-79), San Jose Surg. Soc., Am. Assn. Neurol. Surgeons (chm. sect. on pain 1987-90, dir. 1983-86, 87-90, Disting. Svc. award 1986, 90), Western Neurol. Soc., San Francisco Neurol. Soc., Santa Clara Valley Profl. Standards Rev. Orgn. (dir., v.p., dir. quality assurance 1975-83), Fedn. Western Socs. Neurol. Sci., Internat. Assn. for Study Pain, Am. Pain Soc. (founding mem.), Am. Acad. Pain Medicine (sec. 1983-86, pres. 1987-88, Philipp M. Lippe Disting. Svc. award, 1995), Am. Coll. Pain Medicine (bd. dir. 1991-94, v.p., 1991-92, pres. 1992-93), Am. Bd. Pain Medicine (exec. v.p., 1994—), Alpha Omega Alpha, Phi Kappa Phi. Assoc. editor Clin. Jour. of Pain; contbr. articles to profl. jours. Pioneered med. application centrifugal force using flight simulator. Office: 2100 Forest Ave Ste 106 San Jose CA 95128-1422

LIPPINCOTT, JANET, artist, art educator; b. N.Y.C., May 16, 1918. Student Emil Bisttram, Taos., N.Mex., Colorado Springs Fine Art Ctr., Art Students League N.Y.C., San Francisco Art Inst. Artist in residence, Durango, Colo., 1968; guest artist Tamarind Inst., Albuquerque, 1973; participant TV ednl. programs, Denver, Albuquerque; art instr. Santa Fe Community Coll., N.Mex., 1984—. Participant juried exhbns. including: Denver Mus., 1968, N.Mex. Arts Commn. traveling shows, 1967, Chautauqua Exhbn. Am. Art, N.Y., 1967, High Mus., Atlanta, Butler Inst. Am. Art, Springfield, Ohio, Dallas Mus. Fine Art, Mid Am. Exhbn., Nelson Atkins Mus., Kansas City, Kans., Mus. Fine Arts, Houston, Denver Art Mus., U. N.Mex. Art Gallery, Albuquerque, Ball State Tchrs. Coll., Muncie, Ind., N.Mex. Painting Invitational, 1968, Colorado Springs Fine Art Ctr., 1968, N.Mex. Biennial, Santa Fe, 1969, 72, 73 (award 1962), Tyler Mus. Art, Tex, 1977, Santa Fe Arts Festival, 1978, 79, 80, Enthios Gallery, Santa Fe, 1987; participant invitation exhbns. including: Albuquerque Mus. Art, 1977, Bethune & Moore, Denver, 1969, Yellowstone Art Ctr., Billings, Mont., 1967, Tucson Fine Art Ctr., 1965, Hockaday Sch., Dallas, 1965, Hayden Calhoun Galleries, Dallas, 1966, Leone Kahl Gallery, Dallas, 1965, U. Utah, Salt Lake City, 1966, Roswell Mus. and Art Ctr., N.Mex., 1963, Lucien Labaudt Gallery, San Francisco, 1963, Denver U.S. Nat. Ctr., 1963, Muse d'Art Moderne, Paris, 1962, Instituto Cultural, Mexico City, 1957, Colo. State Coll., Greeley, 1961, Highland U., Las Vegas, N.Mex., 1960-70, St. John's Coll., Santa Fe, 1965, 75, 80, Coll. Santa Fe, 1968, 81, 4748 Galleries, Oklahoma City, 1965, Owen Gallery, Denver, 1970, New West Gallery,

Albuquerque, 1970, 71, 72, 73, 74, Columbia Fine Arts Mus., S.C., 1972, Arts and Crafts Mus., Columbus, Ga., 1972, Dubose Gallery, Houston, 1972, Jamison Gallery, Santa Fe, 1972, Tex. Tech U., Lubbock, 1973 (award), Triangle Gallery, Tulsa, 1973, Gallery 26, Tulsa, 1974, West Tex. Mus., Lubbock, 1976, Britton Gallery, Denver, 1975, 77, 78, 79, 80, Osborne Gallery, Winnipeg, Ont., Can., 1979, Blair Gallery, Santa Fe, 1979, 80; works represented in pvt. and mus. collections; represented by Fletcher Gallery, Santa Fe, 1989-90; Day Star Internat. Galleries, Albuquerque, 1990; New Directions Gallery, Taos, N.Mex., 1995—; Laurel Seth Gallery, Santa Fe, N.Mex., 1995—; Tartan Pony Gallery, 1995—; New Directions Gallery, Taos N. Mex., 1995. With WAC, 1943-45, ETO. Purchase awards and prizes include: Southwestern Biennial, Santa Fe, 1966, N.Mex. Mus. Fine Arts, 1957, Roswell Mus., 1958, Okla. Art Ctr., Oklahoma City, 1962, Atwater Kent award, Palm Beach, Fla., 1963, Chautauqua Art Award Assn. prize, 1963, El Paso Mus. prize, 1962, 76. Home and Office: 1270 Upper Canyon Rd Santa Fe NM 87501-6189

LIPPITT, ELIZABETH CHARLOTTE, writer; b. San Francisco; d. Sidney Grant and Stella L. Student Mills Coll., U. Calif.-Berkeley. Writer, performer own satirical monologues, nat. and polit. affairs for 85 newspapers including Muncie Star, St. Louis Globe-Dem., Washington Times, Utah Ind., Jackson News, State Dept. Watch. Singer debut album Songs From the Heart; contbr. articles to 85 newspapers including N.Y. Post, L.A. Examiner, Orlando Sentinel, Phoenix Rep., The Blue Book; author: 40 Years of American History in Published Letters 1952-1992. Mem. Commn. for Free China, Conservative Caucus, Jefferson Ednl. Assn., Presdl. Adv. Commn. Recipient Congress of Freedom award, 1959, 71-73. Mem. Amvets, Nat. Trust for Hist. Preservation, Am. Security Coun., Internat. Platform Assn., Am. Conservative Union, Nat. Antivivisection Soc., High Frontier, For Our Children, Childhelp U.S.A., Free Afghanistan Com., Humane Soc. U.S., Young Ams. for Freedom, Coun. for Inter.-Am. Security, Internat. Med. Corps, Assn. Vets for Animal Rights, Met. Club, Olympic Club. Home: 2414 Pacific Ave San Francisco CA 94115-1238

LIPPITT, LOUIS, physical science educator, aerospace engineer; b. N.Y.C., Mar. 19, 1924; s. Louis Sr. and Susan Davie (Anderson) L.; m. Adele Dorothy Wissmann, June 27, 1948; children: Laurie, Craig, Bonnie, Nancie. BS, CUNY, 1947; MA, Columbia U., 1953, PhD, 1959. Registered geologist, geophysicist, Calif. Physicist Columbia U., N.Y.C., 1947-51, NYU, N.Y.C., 1951-53; geophysicist Chevron, Calif., 1954-58; staff engr. Lockheed Missiles and Space Co., Vandenberg AFB, Calif., 1958-87; tchr. part time Hancock Coll., Santa Maria, Calif., 1967—, Chapman Coll., Vandenberg AFB, 1985-86. Project leader, 4H, Calif., 1960-77. Recipient Honorarium, State of N.Y., 1952. Fellow Geol. Soc. Am. (sr.); mem. Am. Geophys. Union. Lutheran. Home: 696 Raymond Ave Santa Maria CA 93455-2760

LIPPOLD, ROLAND WILL, surgeon; b. Staunton, Ill., May 1, 1916; s. Frank Carl and Ella (Immenroth) L.; m. Margaret Cookson, June 1, 1947; children: Mary Ellen Lippold Elvick, Catherine Anne Lippold Rolf, Carol Sue Lippold Webber. BS, U. Ill., 1940, MD, 1941. Diplomate Am. Bd. Surgery. Intern Grant Hosp., Chgo., 1941-42, resident in surgery, 1942-43, 47-48; resident in surgery St. Francis Hosp., Evanston, Ill., 1946-47; fellow in pathology Cook County Hosp., Chgo., 1947-48, resident in surgery, 1949-50; practice medicine specializing in surgery Chgo., 1950-53; also asst. in anatomy U. Ill., Chgo., 1950-53; practice medicine specializing in surgery Sacramento, 1953-68; chief med. officer No. Reception Ctr.-Clinic, Calif. Youth Authority, Sacramento, 1954-68, chief med. services, 1968-79; cons. in med. care in correctional instns.; cons. Calif. State Personnel Bd. Contbr. articles to med. publs. Chmn. Calif. Expn. Hall of Health, 1971-72. Comdr. M.C., USNR, 1943-73, PTO. Mem. Sacramento Surg. Soc., Sacramento County Med. Soc., Calif. Med. Assn., AMA, Assn. Mil. Surgeons U.S., Sacramento Hist. Soc. (life). Republican. Lutheran. Home: 1811 Eastern Ave Sacramento CA 95864-1724

LIPPS, DOUGLAS JAY, mechanical engineer; b. Lincoln, Nebr., June 13, 1954; s. Robert E. and Ruth L. (Stryson) L.; m. Jan A. Henry, Aug. 12, 1978; children: Erik A., Emily K. BSME, U. Nebr., 1978; MBA, Golden Gate U., 1984. Registered profl. mech. engr. Sr. engr. Bechtel Corp., San Francisco, 1979—. Office: Bechtel Corp 50 Beale St San Francisco CA 94105-1813

LIPPS, JERE HENRY, paleontology educator; b. L.A., Aug. 28, 1939; s. Henry John and Margaret (Rosaltha) L.; m. Karen Elizabeth Loeblich, June 25, 1964 (div. 1971); m. Susannah McClintock, Sept. 28, 1973; children: Jeremy Christian, Jamison William. BA, UCLA, 1962, PhD, 1966. Asst. prof. U. Calif., Davis, 1967-70, assoc. prof., 1970-75, prof., 1975-88; prof. U. Calif., Berkeley, 1988—, prof. paleontology, 1988-89, prof. integrative biology, 1989—; dir. Mus. Paleontology, Berkeley, 1989—; dir. Inst. Ecology, U. Calif., Davis, 1972-73, chmn. dept. geology, 1971-72, 78-84, chmn. dept. integrative biology, Berkeley, 1991-94. Contbr. articles to sci. publs. Fellow, dir. Cushman Found. Recipient U.S. Antarctic medal NSF, 1975; Lipps Island, Antarctica named in his honor, 1979. Fellow AAAS, Calif. Acad. Scis., Geol. Soc. Am., Cushman Found. Office: Mus Paleontology U Calif 1101 Valley Life Scis Bldg Berkeley CA 94720

LIPSCOMB, ANNA ROSE FEENY, small business owner, arts organizer, fundraiser b. Greensboro, N.C., Oct. 29, 1945; d. Nathan and Matilda (Carotenuto) L. Student langs., Alliance Francaise, Paris, 1967-68; BA in English and French summa cum laude, Queens Coll., 1977; diploma advanced Spanish, Forester Instituto Internacional, San Jose, Costa Rica, 1990; postgrad. Inst. Allende San Miguel de Allende, Mex., 1991. Reservations agt. Am. Airlines, St. Louis, 1968-69, ticket agt., 1969-71; coll. rep. CBS, Holt Rinehart Winston, Providence, 1977-79, sr. acquisitions editor Dryden Press, Chgo., 1979-81; owner, mgr. Historic Taos (N.Mex.) Inn, 1981-89, Southwest Moccasin and Drum, Taos; pres., co-owner Southwest Products, Ltd., 1991—; fundraiser Taos Arts Celebrations, 1989—; bd. dirs. N.Mex. Hotel and Motel Assn., 1986—; sem. leader Taos Women Together, 1989; founder All One Tribe Found., 1994, All One Tribe Fall Drumming Workshop Series, 1992—. Editor: Intermediate Accounting, 1980; Business Law, 1981. Contbr. articles to profl. jours.; patentee in field. Bd. dirs., 1st v.p. Taos Arts Assn., 1982-85; founder, bd. dirs. Taos Spring Arts Celebration, 1983—; founder, dir. Meet-the-Artist Series, 1983—; bd. dirs. and co-founder Spring Arts N.Mex., 1986; founder Yuletide in Taos, 1988, A Taste of Taos, 1988; bd. dirs. Music from Angel Fire, 1988—; founding mem. Assn. Hist. Hotels, Boulder, 1983—; organizer Internat. Symposium on Arts, 1985; bd. dirs. Arts in Taos, 1983, Taoschool, Inc., 1985—; mem. adv. bd. Chamisa Mesa Ednl. Ctr., Taos, 1990—; founder All One Tribe Found., 1994. Recipient Outstanding English Student of Yr. award Queens Coll., 1977; named Single Outstanding Contbr. to the Arts in Taos, 1986. Mem. Millicent Rogers Mus. Assn., Taos Lodgers Assn. (mktg. task force 1989), Taos County C. of C. (1st v.p. 1988-89, bd. dirs. 1987-89, advt. com. 1986-89, chmn. nominating com. 1989), Internat. Platform Assn., Phi Beta Kappa. Democrat. Home: Talpa Rte Taos NM 87571 Office: PO Drawer N Taos NM 87571

LIPSICK, JOSEPH STEVEN, research scientist, medical educator; b. Sharon, Pa., Jan. 6, 1955; m. Laurel Most, June 30, 1978; children: Samuel, Leslie. BA, Oberlin Coll., 1974; PhD, U. Calif., San Diego, 1981; MD, U. Calif., 1982. Resident pathology, postdoctoral UCLA, 1983-85; asst. prof. U. Calif., San Diego, 1986-89; assoc. prof. SUNY, Stony Brook, 1989-93, Stanford (Calif.) U., 1993—. Recipient Career Devel. award VA, 1986-89, Rsch. Career Devel. award Nat. Cancer Inst., 1989-94, Scholar award Leukemia Soc. Am., 1989-94. Office: Stanford U Dept Pathology 300 Pasteur Dr Palo Alto CA 94304-2203

LIPSKY, IAN DAVID, contracting executive; b. Bklyn., May 26, 1957; s. Eugene Herman and Janet Dorothy (Heller) L. BS in Marine Engring., Maine Maritime Acad., 1979. Third asst. engr. Interlake Steamship Co., Cleve., 1979-81; port engr. Exxon Internat. Co., Florham Park, N.J., 1981-84; prodn. supr. Alfred Conhagen Inc. Calif., Hercules, 1984-87, gen. mgr., 1987-89, v.p., 1989—. Mem. Soc. Naval Architects & Marine Engrs., Marine Port Engrs. N.Y., Inst. Marine Engrs., Port Engrs. San Francisco, Nat. Soc. Profl. Engrs. Democrat. Jewish. Home: 153 Koch Rd Corte Madera CA 94925-1263 Office: Alfred Conhagen Inc Calif 3900 Oregon St [illegible] CA 94510-1102

LIPSON, PHILIP BRUCE, librarian; b. Darby, Pa., Oct. 30, 1948; s. Herbert Leon and Alice Louise (Mandell) L. BS in Edn., Wayne State U., 1970, MS in Libr. Sci., 1972. Libr. Detroit Pub. Libr., 1973-76; researcher Detroit, 1977-83; head libr. As-You-Like-It Metaphys. Libr., Seattle, 1983—. Mem. Ind. Order of Odd Fellows. Jewish. Office: As-You-Like-It Libr 915 E Pine St # 401 Seattle WA 98122-3849

LIPSTONE, HOWARD HAROLD, television production executive; b. Chgo., Apr. 28, 1928; s. Lewis R. and Ruth B. (Fischer) L.; m. Jane A. Nudelman, Apr. 7, 1957; children—Lewis, Gregory. BA in Cinema, U. So. Calif., 1950. Asst. to gen. mgr. Sta. KTLA, Los Angeles, 1950-54; program dir. Sta. KABC-TV, Los Angeles, 1955-61, film and program dir., 1961-63; exec. asst. to pres., exec. producer Selmur Prodns., Inc. subs. ABC-TV, Los Angeles, 1963-69; exec. v.p. Ivan Tors Films and Studios, Inc., 1969-70; pres. Alan Landsburg Prodns., Inc., Los Angeles, 1970-85; pres., chief oper. officer The Landsburg Co., Los Angeles, 1985—. Mem. NATAS, Soc. Motion Picture and TV Engrs., Motion Picture Acad. Arts and Scis., Radio Club Am. Office: The Landsburg Co 11811 W Olympic Blvd Los Angeles CA 90064-1113

LISA, ISABELLE O'NEILL, law firm administrator, mergers and acquisitions executive; b. Phila., Mar. 12, 1934; d. Thomas Daniel and Margaret Marie (Hayes) O'Neill; m. Donald Julius Lisa, June 15, 1957; children: Richard Allan, Steven Gregory. Student, Harper Community Coll., Rolling Meadows, Ill., 1976, Scottsdale Community Coll., 1980, Ariz. State U., 1981-82. Cost control clk. Curtis Pub. Co., Phila., 1952-56; sec. United Ins. Co., Annapolis, Md., 1956-57; firm adminstr., legal sec. Law Offices Donald J. Lisa, Bloomingdale, Ill., 1987; legal sec. Lisa & Kubida, P.C., Phoenix, 1987-88, firm adminstr., 1987-89; firm adminstr. Lisa & Assocs., Phoenix, 1989-90, Lisa & Lisa, Phoenix, 1990-91, Lisa & Assocs., 1991—; v.p. adminstrn. Lisa & Co., Phoenix, 1987—. Den mother Cub Scouts Am., Millburn, N.J., 1965; founder, pres. Pro-Tem Rutgers U. Law Wives Assn., 1962-63; bd. advisors Am. Inst., Phoenix, 1991—. Mem. NAFE, Maricopa County Bar Assn. (legal adminstrs. sect. 1992—), Internat. Platform Assn., Rotary. Republican. Roman Catholic. Home: 8989 E Via Linda Ste 215 Scottsdale AZ 85258-5409

LISALDA, SYLVIA ANN, primary educator; b. San Diego, Oct. 14, 1949; d. Joseph and Irene (Valdez) Lisalda; m. Robert Holguin Marquez, Sept. 1, 1979 (div. 1986). AA, Valley Coll., Van Nuys, Calif., 1964; BA in English, Calif. State U., Northridge, 1971. Tchr. kindergarten L.A. Unified Schs., 1965—. Democrat. Roman Catholic. Office: Sylmar Elem Sch 13291 Phillippi Ave Sylmar CA 91342-2810

LISCHER, LOWELL KARL, geologist, administrator; b. Elmwood, Ill., Sept. 28, 1946; s. Armin Arthur and Norma Christine (Fanke) L.; m. Janice Lynn Driskill, Aug. 13, 1971; 1 child, Jennifer Anne. B.S. in Agr., U. Mo.-Columbia, 1972, M.A. in Geology, 1974. Cert. petroleum geologist; profl. geologist, Wyo. Devel. geologist Chevron, Lafayette, La., 1974-75; devel. geologist Marathon Oil Co., Lafayette, 1975-79, exploration geologist, Casper, Wyo., 1979-81; mgr. geol. services Moxa Energy Corp., Casper, 1981-82; chief geologist True Oil Co., Casper, 1982—. Bd. dirs. Casper Youth for Christ, Inc., 1982-91. Served with U.S. Army, 1964-67. Mem. Am. Assn. Petroleum Geologists, Rocky Mountain Assn. Geologists, Wyo. Geol. Assn., Dallas Geol. Soc., Houston Geol. Soc. Office: True Oil Co PO Box 2360 Casper WY 82602

LISONI, GAIL MARIE LANDTBOM, lawyer; b. San Francisco, Mar. 11, 1949; d. William A. and Patricia Ann (Cruden) Landtbom; m. Joseph Louis Lisoni, Mar. 24, 1984. B.A., Dominican Coll., Calif., 1971; J.D., U. West Los Angeles, 1978, cert. paralegal, 1974. Bar: Calif. 1979. Campaign treas. Calif. for Lisoni, Arcadia, 1979-81; assoc. Joseph Lisoni, Esq., Los Angeles, 1981, Arnold S. Malter, Esq., Los Angeles, 1982; ptnr. Lisoni & Lisoni, Los Angeles, 1983—. Mem. Assn. Trial Lawyers Am., Calif. Trial Lawyers Assn., Los Angles Trial Lawyers Assn., ABA, Italian Am. Lawyers Assn. Democrat. Roman Catholic. Lodge: Sons of Italy. Office: Lisoni & Lisoni 225 S Lake Ave Fl 9 Pasadena CA 91101

LISS, NORMAN RICHARD, insurance executive; b. Bronx, N.Y., May 29, 1947; s. Jacob Melvin and Terry Ruth (Stoppler) L.; student Athens (Ala.) Coll., 1965-67, U. Albuquerque, 1967; m. Orlinda P. Olivas, Apr. 11, 1970; children—Maria, Jacqueline Melissa. With First Nat. Life Ins. Co., Albuquerque, 1969-70; founder, pres. Ins. Planners of N.Mex., Albuquerque, 1970—. Active Heart Fund, United Way, Arthritis Found., Boy Scouts Am.; pres. N.Mex. Track Athletic Congress; bd. dirs. N.Mex. chpt. March of Dimes, N.Mex. Kidney Found. Served with USAF, 1967-69. Recipient various ins. sales awards, Dublin award for public service. Mem. Assn. Life Underwriters (local sec.-treas., bd. dirs., state chmn. pub. service, instr. and moderator Tng. Council), Million Dollar Round Table (life), Ct. of Table (charter mem.), Albuquerque Rotary Club Del Norte (charter, chmn. Ryla and Youth Exch. program, Rotarian of Yr. 1990-91). Republican. Jewish. Home: 11433 Nassau Dr NE Albuquerque NM 87111-2741 Office: 3644 Thaxton Ave SE Albuquerque NM 87108-4385

LISTER, KEITH FENIMORE, publishing executive; b. Clio, Iowa, Aug. 29, 1917; s. W. Frank and Maude (Fenimore) L.; m. Margaret Boman, Sept. 1, 1941; children: Janet, Priscilla. Student, Drake U., 1936-41. Pres. Lister Investment Co., San Diego, 1955-61, Southcoast Capital Co., San Diego, 1961-65, City Bank San Diego, 1965-69; pub. San Diego Daily Transcript, 1972-94. Mem. San Diego Yacht Club, Univ. Club. Presbyterian.

LISTERUD, MARK BOYD, retired surgeon; b. Wolf Point, Mont., Nov. 19, 1924; s. Morris B. and Grace (Montgomery) L.; m. Sarah C. Mooney, May 26, 1954; children: John, Mathew, Ann, Mark, Sarah, Richard. BA magna cum laude, U. Minn., 1949, BS, 1950, MB, 1952, MD, 1953. Diplomate Am. Bd. Surgery. Intern King County Hosp., Seattle, 1952-53; resident in surgery U. Wash., Seattle, 1953-57; practice medicine specializing in surgery Wolf Point, 1958-93; mem. admission com. U. Wash. Med. Sch., Seattle, 1983-88; instr. Dept. Rural and Community Health, U. N.D. Med. Sch., 1991. Contbr. articles to med. jours. Mem. Mont. State Health Coordinating Council, 1983, chmn. 1986—; bd. dirs. Blue Shield, Mont., 1985-87. Served with USN, 1943-46. Fellow Am. Coll. Surgeons, Royal Soc. Medicine; mem. N.E. Mont. Med. Soc. (pres.), Mont. Med. Assn. (pres. 1968-69), AMA (alt. del., del. 1970-84). Clubs: Montana, Elks. Home: Rodeo Rd Wolf Point MT 59201 Office: 100 Main St Wolf Point MT 59201-1530

LISTON, AARON IRVING, botanist; b. Cleve., Dec. 2, 1959; s. Herbert Liston and Seema Beatrice Feinstein; m. Sara Noelle Meury, Nov. 11, 1990. BSc in Biology, The Hebrew Univ., Jerusalem, 1982, MSc cum laude in Botony, 1984; PhD in Botany, Claremont Grad. Sch., 1990. Herbarium asst. The Hebrew Univ., Jerusalem, 1982-86; rsch. asst. Rancho Santa Ana Botanic Garden, Claremont, Calif., 1987-89; postdoctoral rschr. dept. Genetics U. Calif., Davis, 1990; asst. prof., dir. herbarium, dept. botany & plant pathology Oreg. State U., Corvallis, 1991—. Contbr articles to profl. jours. Grantee Claremont Grad. Sch., 1986, 87, 89, Sigma Xi, 1988, NSF, 1988, 93, 94, Oreg. Dept. Agr., 1991, M.J. Murdock Charitable Trust, 1991-92, Hardman Found., 1993, 94, Hardman Found. and Hoover Trust, 1993, 94, NAS/Nat. Rsch. Coun., 1993; recipient G. Ledyard Stebbins award Calif. Native Plants Soc., 1987, The Nature Conservancy, 1994. Mem. AAAS, Am. Soc. Plant Taxonomists, Assn. Systematics Collections, Bot. Soc. Am., Soc. for Molecular Biology and Evolution, Soc. Systematic Biologists, Calif. Bot. Soc. Office: Oregon State University Cordley Hall # 2082 Corvallis OR 97331-2902

LISTON, ALBERT MORRIS, administrator, educator, investor; b. Carlinville, Ill., Aug. 6, 1940; s. Joseph Bostick and Hazel Marie (Smalley) L.; AB in Econs., U. Calif., Davis, 1963; MA in Govt., Calif. State U., Sacramento, 1970; postgrad., U. Calif., Santa Barbara, 1980—; m. Phyllis Clayton, Feb. 27, 1967 (div. July 1970). Rsch. analyst Ombudsman Activities Project polit. sci. dept. U. Calif., Santa Barbara, 1970-72; asst. prof. polit. sci. dept. Calif. State U., Fullerton, 1973-79; investor, 1980—. Lt. Supply Corps, USNR, 1963-66. Mem. Am. Polit. Sci. Assn., Commonwealth Club Calif., Kappa Sigma, Phi Kappa Phi. Democrat. Office: PO Box 8027 Missoula MT 59807-8027

LITINSKY, VADIM ARPADOVICH, geophysicist, geologist; b. Petrozavodsk, Russia, Oct. 9, 1929; came to U.S., 1980; s. Arpad Szabados and Nina Nikolaevna Litinsky; m. Mina E. Ratner, Oct. 29, 1964 (div. Sept. 1990); children: E. Eugene, Alla V.; m. Elena Davidovna Sirochinsky, Oct. 29, 1991; 1 child, Tanya N. MS, Sch. Mines, Leningrad, USSR, 1953; PhD, State U., Moscow, 1972. Sr. engr., sr. geophysicist, chief engr. Polar expdn. NIIGA-Sci. Rsch. Inst. for the Geology of the Arctic, Leningrad, 1953-79; sr. geophysicist EDCON-Exploration Data Cons., Inc., Denver, 1980-86; cons. geophysicist Denver, 1986-88, Vadim Litinsky, Geocons. on Russia and Former Soviet Union, Denver, 1989—; Contbr. numerous articles to profl. jours. Mem. Am. Geophys. Union, Soc. Exploration Geophysicist, Am. Assn. Petroleum Geologists. Republican. Home and Office: 1075 Dawson St Aurora CO 80011-6914

LITMAN, ROBERT BARRY, physician, author, television and radio commentator; b. Phila., Nov. 17, 1947; s. Benjamin Norman and Bette Etta (Saunders) L.; m. Niki Thomas, Apr. 21, 1985; children: Riva Belle, Nadya Beth, Caila Tess, Benjamin David. BS, Yale U., 1967, MD, 1970, MS in Chemistry, 1972, MPhil in Anatomy, 1972, postgrad. (Life Ins. Med. Rsch. Fund fellow) Yale U., Univ. Coll. Hosp., U. London, 1969-70; Am. Cancer Soc. postdoctoral rsch. fellow Yale U., 1970-73. Diplomate Am. Bd. Family Practice. Resident in gen. surgery Bryn Mawr (Pa.) Hosp., 1973-74; USPHS fellow Yale U. Sch. Medicine, 1974-75; pvt. practice medicine and surgery, Ogdensburg, N.Y., 1977-93, San Ramon, Calif., 1993—; mem. med. staff A. Barton Hepburn Hosp., 1977-93, John Muir Med. Ctr., 1993—, San Ramon (Calif.) Regional Med. Ctr., 1993—, also chmn. med. edn.; commentator Family Medicine Stas. WWNY-TV and WTNY-Radio, TCI Cablevision; clin. preceptor dept. family medicine State Univ. Health Sci. Ctr., Syracuse, 1978—. Author: Wynnefield and Limer, 1983, The Treblinka Virus, 1991, Allergy Shots, 1993; contbr. articles to numerous sci. publs. Pres. Am. Heart Assn. No. N.Y. chpt., 1980-84. Fellow Am. Coll. Allergy, Asthma, and Immunology, Am. Acad. Family Physicians; mem. AMA (Physicians Recognition award 1970—), Calif. State Med. Assn., Alameda-Contra Costa County Med. Assn., Joint Coun. Allergy and Immunology, Nat. Assn. Physician Broadcasters (charter), Acad. Radio and TV Health Communicators, Book and Snake Soc., Gibbs Soc. of Yale U. (founder), Sigma Xi, Nu Sigma Nu, Alpha Chi Sigma. Home: PO Box 1857 San Ramon CA 94583-6857 Office: 3160 Crow Canyon Rd Ste 150 San Ramon CA 94583-1331

LITROWNIK, ALAN JAY, psychologist, educator; b. Los Angeles, June 25, 1945; s. Irving and Mildred Mae (Rosin) L.; m. Hollis Merle, Aug. 20, 1967; children: Allison Brook, Jordan Michael. BA, UCLA, 1967; MA, U. Ill., Champaign-Urbana, 1969, PhD, 1971. Psychologist Ill. Dept. Mental Health, Decatur, 1970-71; asst. prof. psychology San Diego State U., 1971-75, assoc. prof., 1975-78, prof., 1978—, chmn. dept. psychology, 1981-87, assoc. dean for curriculum and acad. planning, North County Campus, 1987-88; co-dir. Ctr. for Behavioral and Community Health Studies, San Diego, 1989—; cons. San Diego County Dept. Edn. Program Evaluation, 1975-81; project dir. Self-Concept and Self-Regulatory Processes in Developmentally Disabled Children and Adolescents, 1975-78; co-dir. Child Abuse Interdisciplinary Tng. Program, 1987—; project dir. tobacco use prevention in youth orgns., 1989-92. Research, publs. in field. Contbr. chpts. to books. Mem. San Diego County Juvenile Justice Commn., 1989-92; mem. juvenile systems adv. group San Diego County Bd. Suprs., 1989-91. Grantee U.S. Office Edn., 1975-78, 80-81, Nat. Ctr. Child Abuse, 1987—, Calif. Dept. Health, 1989-92, U. Calif. Tobacco-Related Disease Rsch. Program, 1992-94. Office: Ctr Behavioral/Comm Health Studies 9245 Sky Park Ct San Diego CA 92123-4311

LITTLE, ALEX GRAHAM, thoracic surgeon, educator; b. Atlanta, Aug. 24, 1943; s. Alex G. and Roline (Adair) L.; m. Louise Rogers, June 7, 1975; children: Ashley Suzanne, Jody Louise. AB, U. N.C., 1965; MD, Johns Hopkins U., 1974. Diplomate Am. Bd. Surgery and Am. Bd. Thoracic Surgery. Intern surgery Johns Hopkins Hosp., Balt., 1974-75, resident, 1975-76; resident in gen. and thoracic surgery U. Chgo., 1977-81, asst. prof. dept. surgery, 1981-84, assoc. prof., 1984-87; prof., chmn. dept. U. Nev., Las Vegas, 1988—. Editor: Lung Cancer and Diseases of Esophagus, Vol. 1, 1987, Vol. 2, 1990; contbr. over 100 articles to sci. jours., 50 chpts. to books. Lt. M.C., USNR, 1965-69. Fellow ACS, Am. Coll. Chest Physicians (pres. 1991-92), Soc. Thoracic Surgeons, Am. Assn. for Thoracic Surgery, Soc. for Surgery Alimentary Tract, Am. Surg. Assn.; mem. Phi Beta Kappa, Alpha Omega Alpha. Home: 2501 Rancho Bel Air Dr Las Vegas NV 89107-2310 Office: U Nev Sch Medicine Dept Surgery 2040 W Charleston Blvd Las Vegas NV 89102-2227

LITTLE, BILL, food products executive; b. 1928. With Stadelman Fruit INc., 1965—. Office: Stadelman Fruit Ind 314 S 2nd Ave Yakima WA 98902-3535*

LITTLE, CARL MAURICE, performing arts administrator; b. Campbellton, N.B., Can., Mar. 17, 1924; s. George Everett and Ada (Boucher) L.; m. Frances R. Corner, Aug. 27, 1949; children—Christine, Jennifer, Geoffrey, Stephen; m. Barbara Wolfond, Dec. 8, 1978. B.Sc., Dalhousie U., Halifax, N.S., Can., 1945, Licentiate of Music, 1945, Diploma Engring., 1944; Asso., Royal Coll. Music, London, 1952; Licentiate, Royal Acad. Music, London, 1952. Tchr. music public schs. Outremont, Que., Can., 1949-50; pvt. tchr. music Montreal, Que., 1946-59, Toronto, Ont., 1959-70; producer music CBC Radio, Montreal, 1952-59; producer music CBC Radio, Toronto, 1959-65, nat. network supr. serious music, 1965-75; mgr. Nat. Arts Centre Orch., Ottawa, 1975-78; co-founder, pres. Little Gallery of the Arts, Ottawa, 1979-80; pres. Arts Connection, Victoria, B.C., 1980—; exec. dir., festival adminstr. Courtenay Youth Music Centre (B.C.), 1983; organist Holy Trinity Anglican Ch., Saanichton, B.C., 1984—. Pianist, 1945-52; juror for internat. music competitions including Scriabin Piano Competition, Oslo, Norway, Internat. String Quartet, Stockholm, Sweden, Let The Peoples Sing, Choir, London; jury chmn. Kathaumixw Internat. Choral Festival Powell River, B.C., Can. Mem. Royal Can. Coll. Organists (program chmn. 1985), Can. Conf. of Arts, Can. Music Council, Can. Amateur Musicians Assn. (dir.; co-founder), Ont. Choral Fedn., Nat. Arts Centre Orch. Assn. Address: 2171-2600 Ferguson Rd, Saanichton, BC Canada V8M 2C1

LITTLE, LOREN EVERTON, musician, ophthalmologist; b. Sioux Falls, S.D., Oct. 28, 1941; s. Everton A. and Maxine V. (Alcorn) L.; m. Christy Gyles; 1 child, Nicole Moses; children from previous marriage: Laurie, Richard. BA, Macalester Coll., 1963; BS, U. S.D., 1965; D. Medicine, U. Wash., 1967. Prin. trumpeter Sioux Falls Mcpl. Band, 1956-65; trumpeter St. Paul Civic Orch., 1960-62; leader, owner Swinging Scots Band, St. Paul, 1960-63; trumpeter Edgewater Inn Show Room, Seattle, 1966-67, Jazztet-Arts Council, Sioux Falls, 1970-71, Lee Maxwell Shows, Washington, 1971-74; residency in ophthalmology Walter Reed Med. Ctr., Washington, 1974; co-leader, trumpeter El Paso (Tex.) All Stars, 1975; freelance trumpeter, soloist various casinos and hotels, Las Vegas, Nev., 1977—. Trumpeter (album) Journey by R. Romero Band, 1983; soloist for numerous entertainers including Tony Bennet, Burt Bacharach, Jack Jones, Sammy Davis Jr., Jerry Lewis Telethon, for video Star Salute to Live Music, 1989; with Stan Mark Band Nat. Pub. Radio Broadcast, 1994, 95. Trustee Nev. Sch. of the Arts, Las Vegas, 1983—. Served to lt. col. U.S. Army, 1968-76, Vietnam. Decorated Silver Star, Purple Heart, Bronze Star, Air medal; fellow Internat. Eye Found., 1974; Dewitt Wallace scholar Readers Digest, 1963-65. Fellow ACS, Am. Acad. Ophthalmology; mem. Am. Fedn. Musicians, Nat. Bd. Med. Examiners. Presbyterian.

LITTLETON, GAYE DARLENE, nonprofit executive director; b. Parma, Idaho, Nov. 1, 1938; d. Donald Lyle and June E. (Shelton) Graham; m. Jerry M. Littleton, June 11, 1960; children: Leslie, Clark, Laura, Stacey. BS in Edn., U. Idaho, 1960; MS in Ednl. Adminstrn., Utah State U., 1980. Tchr. Seattle, 1960-62; tchr. jr. high sch. Ogden (Utah) Sch. Dist., 1975-76; tchr. Utah State Sch. for the Blind, Ogden, 1976-80; ednl. equity program coord. Weber State Coll., Ogden, 1979-81; councilwoman Ogden City Coun., 1983—; exec. dir. Your Cmty. Connection, 1981—; bd. dirs. Zion's State Bank, First Security Bank Housing Com.; rschr. in field. Contbr. articles to profl. jours. Commr. Ogden Redevel. Agy., Ogden Housing Agy., 1993; mem. human devel. com. Nat. League of Cities; bd. dirs. Weber County Dept. Aging, City Parks and Recreation, Nature Ctr., Arts Commn., Equal Employment Opportunity; mem. Weber County Social Svcs. Coordinating

Coun.; past chair Weber County Title XX Coun.; mem. Weber County Resource Coalition, Weber County Human Rights Coalition, Weber County Homeless Coordinating Com.; mem. ethics com. McKay Dee Hosp., 1990—. Recipient Acad. scholarship for Cmty. Svc., 1956, Thesian award U. Idaho, 1959, LWV Cmty. Svc. award Weber County Mental Health, 1974, Cmty. Svc. award, VIP award Hill AFB, Utah, 1977, Liberty Bell award Utah Bar Assn., 1977, Leadership award Nat. YWCA, 1979, Susa Young Gates award Utah Women's Polit. Caucus for Outstanding Contbn. to Women and Minorities, 1980, Jane Addams award, 1982, Women Helpin Women award, 1983, Utah Woman of Achievement award, 1984, Golden Deeds award, 1988, Athena award. Mem. LWV, AAUW (Woman of Yr. 1988), Nat. Family Resource Coun., Utah Citizens Coun., Ogden Rotary Club (First Woman Rotarian 1992), Ogden C. of C. (Athenia award 1992). Home: 1708 Hislop Dr Ogden UT 84404-5320 Office: Your Cmty Connection 2261 Adams Ave Ogden UT 84401-1510

LITTMAN, RICHARD ANTON, psychologist, educator; b. N.Y.C., May 8, 1919; s. Joseph and Sarah (Feinberg) L.; m. Isabelle Cohen, Mar. 17, 1941; children—David, Barbara, Daniel, Rebecca. AB, George Washington U., 1943; postgrad., Ind. U., 1943- 44; PhD, Ohio State U., 1948. Faculty U. Oreg., 1948—, prof. psychology, 1959—, chmn. dept., 1963-68, vice provost acad. planning and resources, 1971-73; Vis. scientist Nat. Inst. Mental Health, 1958-59. Contbr. articles to profl. jours. Sr. postdoctoral fellow NSF, U. Paris, 1966-67; sr. fellow Nat. Endowment for Humanities, U. London, 1973-74; Ford Found. fellow, 1952-53; recipient U. Oreg. Charles H. Johnson Meml. award, 1980. Mem. Am., Western, psychol. assns., Soc. Research and Child Devel., Psychonomics Soc., Animal Behavior Soc., Soc. Psychol. Study of Social Issues, Internat. Soc. Developmental Psychobiology, History of Sci. Soc., Am. Philos. Assn., AAUP, Sigma Xi. Home: 3625 Glen Oak Dr Eugene OR 97405-4736 Office: U Oreg Dept Psychology Eugene OR 97403

LITTON, MARTIN, conservationist. Recipient John Muir award Sierra Club, 1993. Address: 180 Bear Gulch Dr Portola Valley CA 94028

LITVAK, JOHN, neurosurgeon; b. Denver, Oct. 5, 1927; s. Isadore and Celia (Luper) L.; m. Adrienne Kirshenbaum, Dec. 7, 1947; children: Stacy Michael, David Lee, Jacqueline Beth, Jeffrey Scott. BA, U. Denver, 1952; MD, U. Colo., 1954; MS, McGill U., 1959. Diplomate Am. Bd. Neurol. Surgery. Resident in surgery Montreal Children's Hosp./Gen. Hosp., 1955-56; fellow in exptl. surgery McGill U., Montreal, 1956; resident in neurology Montreal Neurol. Inst., 1956-57, fellow in neuropathology, 1957; resident in neurol. surgery The Neurol. Inst., N.Y.C., 1957-60; asst. prof. neurosurgery U. Colo. Med. Ctr., Denver, 1974—; pvt. practice neurosurgery, 1960—; chief of surgery St. Anthony Hosp., 1978-79, chair neurosurgical divsn., 1970-72, 76-77, 94—. Served in U.S. Navy, 1956-46. Fellow Am. Coll. Surgeons; mem. AMA, Colo. State Med. Soc., Am. Assn. Neurol. Surgeons, Rocky Mountain Neurol. Soc., Congress Neurol. Surgeons, Colo. Neurol. Soc. Office: 1471 Stuart St Denver CO 80204-1244

LIU, ALAN FONG-CHING, mechanical engineer; b. Canton, China, Mar. 25, 1933; came to U.S., 1958; s. Gee Call and Shuk Hing (Chen) L.; m. Iris P. Chan, Sept. 2, 1962; children: Kent, Willy, Henry. BSME, U. Chiba, Japan, 1958; MSME, U. Bridgeport, 1965. Sr. structures engr. Lockheed Calif. Co., Burbank, Calif., 1968-73; sr. tech. specialist/project mgr. Rockwell Internat. Space div., Downey, Calif., 1973-76; sr. tech. specialist Northrop Corp. Aircraft div., Hawthorne, Calif., 1976-88; sr. engring. specialist/projectmgr. Rockwell Internat./N.Am. Aircraft, El Segundo, Calif., 1988—. Developer structural life analysis methodologies in support of various aircraft projects; contbr. articles to Jour. of Aircraft, AIAA Jour., Res Mechanica, Jour. Engring. Materials and Tech., Engring. Fracture Mechanics, procs. nat. and internat. confs. and symposia. Fellow AIAA (assoc.); mem. ASTM, Am. Soc. Metals Internat.

LIU, CHAOQUN, staff scientist; b. Yizheng, Jiangsu, China, Apr. 8, 1945; came to U.S., 1986; s. Jixiang and Guiying (Han) L.; m. Weilan Jin, Dec. 25, 1972; children; Haiyan, Haifeng. MS, Tsinghua U., Beijing, China, 1981; PhD, U. Colo., 1989. Asst. prof. Nanjing Aero. Inst., Nanjing, China, 1981-86; vis. scholar Miss. State U., 1986; rsch. asst. U. Colo., Denver, 1986-89; staff scientist Ecodynamics Rsch. Assocs., Inc., Denver, 1990—; asst. prof. adj. U. Colo., Denver, 1990-93, assoc. prof. adj., 1993—. Contbr. articles to profl. jours. Grantee USN, 1992-93, 95-97, NASA, 1990-93, 92-95, 93-94, 94-95, USAF, 1991, 95-97. Mem. AIAA, Soc. for Indsl. and Applied Math. Office: Univ of Colorado Denver Computational Math Group Campus Box 170 Denver CO 80217

LIU, DON, ophthalmologist, medical researcher; b. Nanjing, China, July 17, 1947; came to the U.S., 1964; s. Robert Ching Ming and I. Tu Liu; m. Helen Cheng, June 21, 1975; children: David, Grace, Glory, Daniel. BS in Physics, Purdue U., 1969; MS in Physics, U. Mass., 1971; MD, SUNY, Buffalo, 1977. Dir. oculoplastics/orbit. Ford Hosp., Detroit, 1982-90; dir. oculoplastics/orbit. svc. U. So. Calif.-L.A. County Hosp., L.A., 1990—; organizer Internat. Conf., China and Hong Kong, Taiwan, 1985, 87, 89, 92, 93, 95; cons. to med. industries. Sci. referee Am. Jour. Ophthalmology, 1991—, Ophthalmic Plastic & Reconstructive Surgery, 1990—, Opthalmology; mem. editl. bd. Ophthalmic Plastic & Reconstructive Surgery, 1991—; mem. adv. bd. Med. Books for China, Internat., 1985—; contbr. numerous book chpts. and articles to textbooks and profl. jours.; designer five surg. instruments. Campaign fundraiser Mike Woo for Maj., L.A., 1993; South Calif. coord. Bush/Quayle '92, L.A., 1992; sponsor San Marino (Calif.) Sch. Dist., 1990—; active Boy Scouts Am., Amnesty Internat., church activities. Recipient numerous tchg. awards. Fellow ACS, Am. Acad. Facial Plastic and Reconstructive Surgery (com. mem. 1992-96), Am. Soc. Ophthalmic Plastic and Reconstructive Surgery (fellowship dir. 1994—, Outstanding fellow 1981), Am. Acad. Ophthalmology (Honor award 1994), Am. Bd. Ophthalmology (assoc. examiner 1991—); mem. AMA, Chinese Am. Ophthalmologic Soc. (treas.-sec. 1988-92). Home: 1066 Kewen Dr San Marino CA 91108-1013

LIU, EDWIN CHIAP HENN, biochemical ecologist; b. Honolulu, Apr. 11, 1942; s. Edward F. and Margaret (Yuen) L. AB, Johns Hopkins U., 1964; PhD, Mich. State U., 1971. Asst. prof. U. S.C., Columbia, 1973-81; rsch. prof. Savannah River Ecology Lab., Aiken, S.C., 1981-86; coord. Newport Bay Santa Ana Regional Water Quality Control Bd., Riverside, Calif., 1986-88; monitoring coord. EPA, San Francisco, 1988—; newsletter editor Am. Bot. Soc., Columbia, 1981. Contbr. numerous rsch. papers to profl. publs. Recipient Young Scientist award Am. Soc. Plant Physiologists, 1977, Faculty Recognition award U. S.C., 1977. Mem. Ecol. Soc. of Am., Sigma Xi, Phi Kappa Psi. Home: 1510 Ashby Ave Berkeley CA 94703-2302

LIU, FU-TONG, biomedical researcher, dermatologist; b. Taipei, Taiwan, July 16, 1948; came to the U.S., 1971; s. Yung-Piao and Chu-Yeh (Muira) L.; m. Sheimei Rose Chen, July 29, 1972; children: Jane May, Ray Chung. BS in Chemistry, Nat. Taiwan U., 1970; PhD, U. Chgo., 1976; MD, U. Miami, 1987. Asst. mem. Scripps Rsch. Inst., La Jolla, Calif., 1979-82, assoc. mem., head allergy rsch. sect., 1990—; assoc. mem. Med. Biology Inst., La Jolla, 1982-87, mem., 1987-90; mem. divsn. dermatology Scripps Clinic Med. Group, La Jolla, 1993—; mem. adv. com. allergy & immunology NIH, Bethesda, Md., 1985-89, allergy, immunology and transplantation, 1993—. Assoc. editor: Jour. Clin. Investigation, 1993—. Scholar Leukemia Soc. Am., 1982. Mem. Am. Chem. Soc., Am. Assn. Immunologists, Am. Soc. for Investigative Pathology, Am. Soc. for Clin. Investigation, Soc. Investigative Dermatology, Am. Acad. Dermatology. Home: 4351 Mensha Pl San Diego CA 92130-2448 Office: Scripps Rsch Inst 10666 N Torrey Pines Rd La Jolla CA 92037-1027

LIU, JIA-MING, electrical engineering educator, physicist, researcher; b. Taichung, Taiwan, Republic of China, July 13, 1953; came to U.S., 1978; s. Min-chih and Hsin (Lin) L.; m. Vida H. Chang, July 8, 1990; 1 child, Janelle Jen-Wu. BS in Electrophysics, Nat. Chiao Tung U., 1975; SM in Applied Physics, Harvard U., 1979, PhD in Applied Physics, 1982. Registered profl. engr., Taiwan. Asst. prof. SUNY, Buffalo, 1982-84; sr. mem. tech. staff GTE Lab., Inc., Waltham, Mass., 1983-86; assoc. prof. elec. engr. UCLA, 1986-93, prof., 1993—; cons. JAYCOR, San Diego, 1987—, Battelle, Rsch. Triangle Park, N.C., 1989-90. Contbr. articles to profl. jours. Patent award GTE Labs., Inc., Waltham, 1986, 87, 88, 89. Fellow Optical Soc. Am.; mem. IEEE Laser and Electro-Optics Soc. (sr.), Am. Physical Soc., Photonics Soc. Chinese Americans (founding), Sigma Xi, Phi Tau Phi. Office: UCLA 56-147 Engring Iv # C Los Angeles CA 90024

LIU, JUANITA CHING, travel industry educator; b. Honolulu, Aug. 9, 1947; d. Albert Y.A. Ching and Winifred Liu; children: Anthony, Deborah. BA in Math. magna cum laude, U. So. Calif., 1969; MA in Regional Sci., U. Pa., 1971; PhD in Econ. Geography, Simon Fraser U., 1979. Rsch. asst. Comex Air Pollution Project, L.A., 1967-68; computer programmer Statewide Info. System State of Hawaii, 1968; rsch. asst. Regional Sci. Rsch. Inst., Phila., 1969-70; doctoral fellow Energy Mgmt. and Policy U. Pa., Phila., 1971-72; teaching asst. Simon Fraser U., Vancouver, 1973-80; asst. prof. Sch. Travel Industry Mgmt. U. Hawaii, Manoa, 1980-85, assoc. prof. Sch. Travel Industry Mgmt., 1985-89, prof. Sch. Travel Industry Mgmt., 1989—, asst. to exec. vice chancellor, 1994; rschr., presenter in field. Author: Pacific Islands Ecotourism: A Public Policy and Planning Guide, 1994; assoc. editor Jour. Leisure Scis., 1986-89; reports editor, coordinating referee Annals of Tourism Rsch., 1982-91; contbr. articles to profl. jours. Bd. dirs. Hawaii Visitors Bur., 1989-93; sec. bd. dirs. Family Peace Ctr. Recipient Grad. Rsch. Engring. and Tech. award B.C. Dept. Edn., 1978-79, Regents'medal for Excellence in Teaching, 1993. Mem. Am. Assn. Geographers, Am. Statis. Assn., Ecotourism Soc., Western Regional Sci. Assn. (bd. dirs. 1994—), Phi Beta Kappa, Phi Kappa Phi, Alpha Mu Gamma, Alpha Lambda Delta. Office: U Hawaii Sch Travel Industry Mgmt 2560 Campus Rd Honolulu HI 96822-2217

LIU, KATHERINE CHANG, artist, art educator; b. Kiang-si, China; came to U.S., 1963; d. Ming-fan and Ying (Yuan) Chang; m. Yet-zen Liu; children: Alan S., Laura Y. MS, U. Calif., Berkeley, 1965. tchr. U. Va. Ext., Longwood Coll.; mem. teaching staff master class Hill Country Arts Found., Tex., 1995; mem. invited L.A. Artcore Reviewing and Curatorial Bd., 1993; invited juror, lectr. more than 75 exhibits and orgns., 1980—. One-woman shows include Harrison Mus., Utah State U., Riverside (Calif.) Art Mus., Ventura (Calif.) Coll., Fla. A&M U., Louis Newman Galleries, L.A., L.A. Artcore, Lung-Men Gallery, Taipei, Republic of China, State of the Arts Invitational Biennial, Parkland Coll. Ill., 1989, 91, Watercolor U.S.A. Hon. Soc. Invitational, 1989, 91, 93, 95, Hunter Mus. Art, Tenn., 1993, Bakersfield Art Mus., 1994, Chgo. Navy Pier Internat. Art Expo, 1994, Sandra Walters Gallery, Hong Kong, 1994; Invitational, U. Brit. Columbia Art Gallery, 1992, U. Sydney Art Mus., 1992, Ruhr-West Art Mus., Wise, 1992, Macau Art Mus., 1992, Rosenfeld Gallery, Phila., 1994, Mandarin Oriental Fine Arts, Hong Kong, 1994, Horwitch-Newman Gallery, Scottsdale, Ariz., 1995, Watercolor USA Honor Soc. Biennial, 1995; contbr. works to 20 books and 31 periodicals. Co-curator Taiwan-USA-Australia Watermedia Survey Exhbn., Nat. Taiwan Art Inst., 1994; sole juror San Diego Watermedia Internat., 1993, Triton Mus. Open Competition, 1994, Northern Nat. Art Competition, 1994, Watercolor West Nat., 1993, Tenn., Utah, Hawaii, N.C. Watercolor Socs.; co-juror Rocky Mountain Nat., San Diego Internat. and West Fedn. Exhibts; sole juror N.Am. Open, Midwest, Southwest and over 30 state-wide competitions in watermedia or all-media. Recipient Rex Brandt award San Diego Watercolor Internat., 1985, Purchase Selection award Watercolor USA and Springfield (Mo.) Art Mus., 1981, Gold medal, 1986, Mary Lou Fitzgerald meml. award Allied Arts Am. Nat. Arts Club, N.Y.C., 1987, Achievement award of Artists Painting in Acrylic Am. Artists Mag., 1993; NEA grantee, 1979-80. Mem. Nat. Watercolor Soc. (life, chmn. jury 1985, pres. 1983, Top award 1984, cash awards 1979, 87), Watercolor U.S.A. Honor Soc., Nat. Soc. Painters in Casein and Acrylic (2nd award 1985), Rocky Mountain Nat. Watermedia Soc. (juror 1984, awards 1978, 80, 86).

LIU, ROBERT SHING-HEI, chemistry educator, researcher; b. Shanghai, China, Aug. 1, 1938; came to U.S., 1958; s. George C.C. and Aline (Tang) L.; m. Regina S.L. Ro, Nov. 22, 1967; children: Corey Wei, Conan Chung. BA, Howard Payne Coll., 1961; PhD, Calif. Inst. Tech., 1965. Research chemist E.I. DuPont de Nemours & Co., Wilmington, Del., 1964-68; assoc. prof. U. Hawaii, Honolulu, 1968-72, prof. chemistry, 1972—; vis. research assoc. biol. lab. Harvard U., Cambridge, Mass., 1974-75: vis. researcher Royal Instn., London, 1975. Contbr. articles to profl. jours. Sloan fellow, 1970-72, Guggenheim fellow, 1974-75; Fujio Matsuda scholar U. Hawaii Found., 1985-86; recipient Medal for Excellence in Rsch. U. Hawaii Bd. Regents, 1986, Medal for Excellence in Teaching U. Hawaii Bd. Regents, 1988, Creativity award NSF, 1986, Merit award NIH, 1988. Mem. Golden Key Nat. Hon. Soc. Office: U Hawaii Chemistry Dept 2545 The Mall Honolulu HI 96822-2233

LIU, SHU QIAN, biomedical engineer, researcher; b. Lian-cheng, China, Dec. 22, 1956; came to U.S., 1985; s. Din-An and Jin-Zhen L.; m. Wu Yu-Hua, Feb. 3, 1983; children: Diana Liu, Charley Liu. BS in Medicine, Med. Sch. of NeiMongu, China, 1980; MS, Med. Sch. of NeiMongu, 1983; PhD, U. Calif., San Diego, 1990. Post doctoral fellow U. Calif., San Diego, 1990-92, asst. rsch. bioengineer, 1992—. Contbr. articles to profl. jours. Recipient Melville medal ASME, 1994, best paper award, 1995, Tobacco Rsch. award State of Calif., 1990-92, Whitaker Rsch. award Whitaker Found., 1993-96. Mem. AAAS, Biomed. Engring. Soc. Home: 4620 Porte De Palmas #62 San Diego CA 92122 Office: Inst Biomed Engring UCSD 0412 9500 Gilman Dr La Jolla CA 92093-5003

LIVERMORE, DONALD RAYMOND, elementary education educator, library media specialist, educational consultant; b. Stockton, Calif., May 14, 1947; s. Harry Guy and Cora Edith (Ambrose) L. AA, Delta Jr. Coll., Stockton, Calif., 1967; BS, BA, Chico State U., 1971; MLS, San Jose State U., 1995. Cert. elem., sec. tchr., Calif. Salesman/mgr. Magor's Mens Wear, Tracy, Calif., 1961-75; tchr., K-6 Monterey (Calif.) Peninsula Unified Sch. Dist., 1971—, mentor tchr., cons., trainer and presenter multimedia presentations, 1984—, trainer and presenter multimedia presentations, 1995; instr. Chapman Coll., Monterey, 1982—; aquarium guide Monterey Bay Aquarium, 1985-93, mentor guide, trainer, 1986-92, VVIP tour guide, 1988—; program quality reviewer State of Calif., Monterey County Office Edn., Salinas, 1982-92; mem. IMEP history and social sci. textbook adoption com. Calif. Bd. Edn., 1990, 93; libr. media specialist Manzanita Elem. Model Tech. Sch. Author: (resource workbook) Hands on History; collaborator (with Randy Reinstedt): More Than Memories, 1985; coord. history project curriculum Memories Shared, 1984—. Pres. bd. dirs. PTA, Olson, 1976-78, Hayes, 1986-88. Apple Computers Ptnrs. in Edn. grantee, 1994-95; recipient Kern County Hist. award, Social Sci. Consortium award, Fresno, Calif., 1985; named Tchr. in Marine Rsch., Monterey County Office Edn., Salinas, 1988, Vol. of Yr., Monterey Peninsula Hospitality Industry, 1993. Mem. Monterey Bay Tchrs. Assn. (faculty rep. 1975-77). Democrat. Lutheran. Office: Manzanita Elem Sch Model Technology Sch Calif 1720 Yosemite St Seaside CA 93955-3914

LIVESAY, THOMAS ANDREW, museum administrator, lecturer; b. Dallas, Feb. 1, 1945; s. Melvin Ewing Clay and Madge Almeda (Hall) L.; m. Amanda Haralson, 1985; children: Heather Marie, Russell Lee. BFA, U. Tex., Austin, 1968, MFA, 1972; postgrad., Harvard U. Inst. Arts Adminstrn., 1978. Curator Elisabet Ney Mus., Austin, 1971-73; dir. Longview (Tex.) Mus. and Arts Center, 1973-75; curator of art Amarillo (Tex.) Art Center, 1975-77, dir. center, 1977-80; asst. dir. for adminstrn. Dallas Mus. Fine Arts, 1980-85; dir. Mus. of N.Mex., Santa Fe, 1985—; mem. touring panel Tex. Commn. Arts; mem. panel Nat. Endowment Arts, Inst. Mus. Services; adj. tchr. U. Okla., Coll. Liberal Studies, 1992—, U. N.Mex., 1992—. Author: Young Texas Artists Series, 1978, Made in Texas, 1979; editor: video tape American Images, 1979, Ruth Abrams, Paintings, 1940-85, NYU Press. Served with U.S. Army, 1969-71. Mem. Am. Assn. Mus. (coun. 1986-89, commn. on ethics 1992—, accreditation commn. 1994—), Tex. Assn. Mus. (v.p. 1981, pres. 1983), N.Mex. State Records and Archives Commn. (chmn. 1986—), Rotary. Methodist. Office: Mus of New Mexico PO Box 2087 Santa Fe NM 87504-2087

LIVINGSTON, ALAN WENDELL, communications executive; b. McDonald, Pa.; s. Maurice H. and Rose L. (Wachtel) L.; m. Nancy Olson, Sept. 1, 1962; children: Peter, Laura, Christopher. BS, U. Pa., 1940. Exec. v.p. Capitol Records, Inc., Hollywood, Calif., 1946-55, pres., chmn., 1960-68; v.p. programming NBC, Burbank, Calif., 1955-60; pres. Mediarts, Inc., Los Angeles, 1968-76; exec. v.p., pres. entertainment group 20th Century Fox Film Corp., Beverly Hills, Calif., 1976-80; pres. Pacific Rim Entertainment, Los Angeles, 1980—. Creator various children's books, records and Bozo the Clown, 1946—; author: Ronnie Finklehof, Superstar, 1988; writer, producer (animated film) Sparky's Magic Piano, 1988. Bd. dirs. Ctr. Theater Group, Los Angeles. Served to 2d lt. inf. U.S. Army, 1943-46. Mem. ASCAP, Nat. Acad. Rec. Arts and Scis., Acad. TV Arts and Scis., Acad. Motion Picture Arts and Scis. Office: Pacific Rim Entertainment Inc 9229 W Sunset Blvd Los Angeles CA 90069-3402

LIVINGSTON, ALVIN JACOB, state official; b. New Orleans, June 12, 1929; s. Bernard and Annette H. (Steckler) L.; m. Rita Cornelia Powers, Oct. 29, 1961. BS with honors, UCLA, 1953. Spl. asst. to pres. So. Calif. Freight Lines, L.A., 1954-57; v.p., gen. mgr. Torre Safety Devices, L.A., 1957-59; v.p. fin. and adminstrn., sec.-treas., conglomerate of Twentieth Century Engring. Corp., Radiant Industries Inc., Mammoth Mountain Inn Corp. and affiliates; pres. subs. Qualimetrics, L.A., 1959-78; cons. fin., mgmt., pub. rels., career guidance, polit. campaign mgmt., L.A., 1958-83; dep. dir. Calif. Dept. Motor Vehicles, Sacramento, 1983—. Past pres. L.A. Libr. Assn., Cedars-Sinai Med. Ctr. Young Men's Group, Fernando Awards Inc., various polit. orgns.; past officer, dir. United Chambers of San Fernando Valley, Pacific Lodge Boy's Home, Gt. Western Coun. Boy Scouts Am.; mem. 1972 Electoral Coll.; past pres. Sacramento Vol. Ctr.; sec. Safety Ctr., Inc., Sacramento. Mem. UCLA Alumni Assn. (life, former bd. dirs., pres. Class of 1953, mem. govt. affairs steering com., pres. No. Calif. 1985-90), Masons. Republican. Jewish. Editl. bd. L.A. County Guide to Govt. Almanac, 1964-83, chmn., 1971-75, editor, 1983; editor various polit. newspapers and bus. publs. Office: Dept Motor Vehicles 2415 1st Ave Sacramento CA 95818

LIVINGSTON, MYRA COHN, poet, writer, educator; b. Omaha, Aug. 17, 1926; d. Mayer L. and Gertrude (Marks) Cohn; m. Richard Roland Livingston, Apr. 14, 1952 (dec. 1990); children: Joshua, Jonas Cohn, Jennie Marks. BA, Sarah Lawrence Coll., 1948. Profl. horn player, 1941-48; book reviewer Los Angeles Daily News, 1948-49, Los Angeles Mirror, 1949-50; asst. editor Campus Mag., 1949-50; various public relations positions and pvt. sec. to Hollywood (Calif.) personalities, 1950-52; tchr. creative writing Dallas (Tex.) public library and schs., 1958-63; poet-in-residence Beverly Hills (Calif.) Unified Sch. Dist., 1966-84; sr. instr. UCLA Extension, 1973—; cons. to various sch. dists., 1966-84, cons. poetry to publishers children's lit., 1975—. Author: Whispers and Other Poems, 1958, Wide Awake and Other Poems, 1959, I'm Hiding, 1961, See What I Found, 1962, I Talk to Elephants, 1962, I'm Not Me, 1963, Happy Birthday, 1964, The Moon and a Star and Other Poems, 1965, I'm Waiting, 1966, Old Mrs. Twindlytart and Other Rhymes, 1967, A Crazy Flight and Other Poems, 1968, The Malibu and Other Poems, 1972, When You Are Alone/It Keeps You Capone: An Approach to Creative Writing with Children, 1973, Come Away, 1974, The Way Things Are and Other Poems, 1974, 4-Way Stop and Other Poems, 1976, A Lollygag of Limericks, 1978, O Sliver of Liver and Other Poems, 1979, No Way of Knowing: Dallas Poems, 1980, A Circle of Seasons, 1982, How Pleasant to Know Mr. Lear!, 1982, Sky Songs, 1984, A Song I Sang to You, 1984, Monkey Puzzle, 1984, The Child as Poet: Myth or Reality?, 1984, Celebrations, 1985, Worlds I Know and Other Poems, 1985, Sea Songs, 1986, Earth Songs, 1986, 1987, Higgledy-Piggledy, 1986, Space Songs, 1988, There Was a Place and Other Poems, 1988, Up in the Air, 1989, Birthday Poems, 1989, Remembering and Other Poems, 1989, My Head Is Red and Other Riddle Rhymes, 1990, Climb Into the Bell Tower: Essays on Poetry, 1990, Poem-making: Ways to Begin Writing Poetry, 1991, Light and Shadow, 1992, I Never Told and Other Poems, 1992, Let Freedom Ring: A Ballad of Martin Luther King, Jr., 1992, Abraham Lincoln, A Man for All the People, 1993, Platero Y Yo/Platero and I (trans. 1994, Flights of Fancy and other poems, 1994, Keep on Singing: A Ballad of Marian Anderson, 1994; The Writing of Poetry, film strips; co-editor: The Scott-Foresman Anthology, 1984; editor 36 anthologies of poetry; contbr. articles on children's lit. to ednl. publs., essays on lit. and reading in edn. to various books; mem. editorial adv. bd. The New Advocate, The Reading Teacher. Officer Beverly Hills PTA Council, 1966-75; pres. Friends of Beverly Hills Public Library, 1979-81; bd. dirs. Poetry Therapy Inst., 1975—, Reading is Fundamental of So. Calif., 1981—. Recipient honor award N.Y. Herald Tribune Spring Book Festival, 1958, excellence in poetry award Nat. Coun. Tchrs. of English, 1980, Commonwealth Club award, 1984, Nat. Jewish Book award, 1987, Kerlan award U. Minn., 1994, Transl. award Internat. Bd. on Books for Young People, 1994. Mem. Authors Guild, Internat. Reading Assn., Soc. Children's Book Writers (honor award 1975), Tex. Inst. Letters (awards 1961, 80), So. Calif. Council on Lit. for Children and Young People (Comprehensive Contribution award 1968, Notable Book award 1972, Poetry Quartet award 89), PEN. Address: 9308 Readcrest Dr Beverly Hills CA 90210-2533

LIVINGSTON, PATRICIA ANN, marine biologist, researcher; b. Detroit, Dec. 10, 1954. BS, Mich. State U., 1976; MS, U. Wash., 1980, M in Pub. Adminstrn., 1987. Ecosystem modeller Nat. Marine Fish Svc., Seattle, 1977-82, trophic interactions program leader, 1983—; mem. sci. and tech. bd. The Sea Use Council, Seattle, 1986—. Contbr. articles on ecosystem modelling and marine fish trophic interactions to profl. jours. Bd. dirs. Little Anchor Child Care Ctr., 1992-93, treas., 1992, pres. bd., 1993. Mem. Am. Fisheries Soc. (officer and regional fish corr. Marine Fish sect. 1982-84, membership chair internat. sect. 1992, soc. membership com. 1991-92). Office: NW and Alaska Fisheries Ctr Bldg 15700 7600 Sand Point Way NE Seattle WA 98115-6349

LIVINGSTON, STANLEY C., architect. BArch, U. So. Calif., 1961; student, U. Calif., San Diego. Lic. architect Calif., N.Mex., Nev.; cert. Nat. Coun. Archtl. Registration. Prin. Salerno/Livingston Architects, San Diego; lectr. numerous instns. Archtl. projects include Residence Hall Tower & Multi Purpose Bldg. San Diego State U., Pacific Southwest Airlines Adminstrv. Offices & Hangar Facility, Fujitsu Microelectronics, Inc., Belden Village Low Income Sr. Housing Project, Atkinson Marine Corp. Hdqs. & Ship Repair Facility, Campbell Industries, Islandia Hotel Tower, Marlin Club, Sportfishing Facility and 500 Boat Marina, Branch Libr., Belmont Park Master Plan, Expert Witness Projects; other comml. projects include U.S. Fin. Office Bldg., Lake Murray Office Bldg., San Diego Fed. Branch Bank (5 locations), Nat. U. Office Bldg., Harbor Boat & Yacht Shipyard Renovation, Pacific Southwest Airlines Passenger Lounges & Gates (2 locations), and others. Symposia chmn. "Frank Lloyd Wright-Living in the Wright Century...An Evaluation" San Diego Archtl. Found./San Diego Mus. Art, 1990; mem. design competition adv. panel Balboa Park Organ Pavilion Parking Garage, 1990; mem. urban design com. San Diego Centre City, 1982-86; founder Orchids and Onions Program, 1976, com. chmn. 1984, jury chmn. 1985; chmn. design adv. com. San Diego Center City Devel. Corp., 1980. Fellow AIA (San Diego chpt., past pres. 1978-79, chmn. urban design com. 1978-86, chmn. task force Balboa Pk. master plan); mem. Am. Planning Assn. (mem. bd. dirs. San Diego 1981-82), Soc. Mktg. Profl. Svcs., Am. Arbitration Assn. (mem. panel arbitrators 1988—), Urban Land Inst. (assoc.), Urban Design & Planning Com., Bldg. Industry Assn. (mem. construction quality com.), Community Assn. Inst., San Diego Archtl. Found. (bd. dirs.), SCARAB. Office: Salerno/Livingston Architects 363 5th Ave 3rd Fl San Diego CA 92101-6909

LIVZIEY, JAMES GERALD, secondary school educator; b. Buffalo, July 30, 1927; s. James Ephlyn and Helena Charlote (Kiener) L.; m. June Ellen Andersen, July 25, 1955; children: Naomi Lynn, Patricia Ellen. AA, Southwestern Jr. Coll., 1970; BA, San Diego State U., 1972. Enlisted U.S. Navy, 1945, advanced through grades to lt. comdr., 1967, ret., 1969; high sch. instr. SWHS Dist., Chula Vista, Calif., 1972—. Recipient award Freedoms Found., 1991; fellow Taft Inst., 1977, Pacific Acad. Advanced Studies, 1978. Fellow Alpha Gamma Sigma; mem. Naval Inst. USN, Masons, Knight Comdr. Ct. Honor (32d degree). Home: 675 Mariposa Cir Chula Vista CA 91911-2510

LJUBICIC DROZDOWSKI, MILADIN PETER, consulting engineer; b. Zajecar, Yugoslavia, Sept. 28, 1921; came to U.S., 1959; s. Peter Miladin and Martha Jovan (Viktorovic) Ljubicic; m. Dusica Cile Pavic, Sept. 9, 1948. Diploma in engring., U. Belgrade, Yugoslavia, 1951, 52; ancien élève, Ecole Nationale Superieure de l'Armement, Paris, 1956; MSME, UCLA, 1964, PhD in Mec. Engring., 1971. Design and test engr. Fed. Mogul Bower, El Monte, Calif., 1959-62; chief advanced armament analytical support Hughes Helicopters, Culver City, Calif., 1962-78; engring. supr. Bechtel Power Corp., Norwalk, Calif., 1978-80; engring. [illegible]

Madrid, 1980-87; v.p. Koach Engring., Sun Valley, Calif., 1987; engring. cons. Mission Viejo, Calif., 1987—; asst. to chmn. continuum mechanics, Belgrade, 1955-56; guest lectr. Sch. Engring. and Applied Sci., UCLA, 1971; prof., Loyola Marymount U., L.A., 1978-80. Contbr. to profl. publs. Mem. Am. Soc. Mech. Engrs., Am. Def. Preparedness Assn., Spanish Nuclear Soc. Home and Office: 26426 Lope De Vega Dr Mission Viejo CA 92691-3316

LLAURADO, JOSEP G., nuclear medicine physician, scientist; b. Barcelona, Catalonia, Spain, Feb. 6, 1927; s. José and Rosa (Llaurado) García; m. Deirdre Mooney, Nov. 9, 1966; children—Raymund, Wilfred, Mireya; m. Catherine D. Entwistle, June 28, 1958 (dec.); children—Thadd, Oleg, Montserrat. B.S., B.A., Balmes Inst., Barcelona, 1944; M.D., Barcelona U., 1950; Ph.D. in Pharmacology, 1960; M.Sc. Biomed. Engring., Drexel U., 1963. Diplomate: Am. Bd. Nuclear Medicine. Resident Royal Postgrad. Sch. Medicine, Hammersmith Hosp., London, 1952-54; fellow M.D. Anderson Hosp. and Tumor Inst., Houston, 1957-58, U. Utah Med. Coll., Salt Lake City, 1958-59; asst. prof. U. Otago Dunedin, N.Z., 1954-57; sr. endocrinologist Pfizer Med. Research Lab., Groton, Conn., 1959-60; assoc. prof. U. Pa., 1963-67; prof. Med. Coll. Wis., Milw., 1970-82, Marquette U., 1967-82; clin. dir. nuclear medicine service VA Med. Ctr., Milw., 1977-82; chief nuclear medicine service VA Hosp., Loma Linda, Calif., 1983—; prof. dept. radiation scis. Loma Linda U. Sch. Medicine, 1983—; U.S. rep. symposium on dynamic studies with radioisotopes in clin. medicine and research IAEA, Rotterdam, 1970, Knoxville, 1974. Editor: Internat. Jour. Biomed. Computing; dep. editor Environ. Mgmt. and Health; contbr. numerous articles to profl. jours. Merit badge counselor Boy Scouts Am., 1972—; pres. Hales Corners (Wis.) Hist. Soc., 1981-83. Recipient Commendation cert. Boy Scouts Am., 1980. Fellow Am. Coll. Nutrition; mem. Soc. Nuclear Medicine (computer and acad. councils), IEEE (sr.), IEEE in Medicine and Biology Soc. (nat. adminstrv. Com. 1986-89), Biomed. Engring. Soc. (charter), Am. Physiol. Soc., Am. Soc. Pharmacology and Exptl. Therapeutics, Soc. Math. Biology (founding), Endocrine Soc., Royal Soc. Health, Societat Catalana de Biologia, Casal dels Catalans de Calif. (pres. 1989-91), Calif. Med. Assn. (sci. adv. panel nuclear medicine 1983—). Office: Nuclear Med Svc #115 11201 Benton St Loma Linda CA 92357-1000

LLEWELLYN, FREDERICK EATON, real estate executive; b. Mexico, Mo., Mar. 28, 1917; s. Frederick William and Mabel (Eaton) L.; BS, Calif. Inst. Tech., 1938; MBA (Baker scholar), Harvard, 1942; LLD, Pepperdine U., 1976; m. Yvonne Maples, July 18, 1990; children: Richard, John, Ann Marie. Asst. gen. mgr., dir. Forest Lawn Life Ins. Co., Glendale, Calif., 1940-41, pres., 1959-61; asst. to gen. mgr. Forest Lawn Meml. Park, Glendale, 1941-42, exec. v.p., 1946-66, gen. mgr., 1966-89; pres. Forest Lawn Found., 1961—, Forest Lawn Co., 1967-88; chmn. bd. Am. Security & Fidelity Corp., Forest Lawn Co., 1988—, Upstairs Galleries Inc., 1974-91, Met. Computer Center, 1973-81, Calif. Citrus Corp., 1971-80, Forest Lawn Mortgage Corp., 1976-92; dir. IT Corp., Trust Svcs. Am., Inc.(chmn. 1983-91). Mem. Found. for the 21st Century, 1986-91, Orthopaedic Hosp., 1976-82, chmn., 1980; chmn. Glendale Meml. Hosp., 1980, trustee, 1982-85; pres. So. Calif. Visitors Coun., 1976-77; chmn. Coun. of Regents, Meml. Ct. of Honor, 1966-93. Mem. Mayor's Ad Hoc Energy Com., L.A., 1973-74, L.A. County Reorgn. Commn., 1978; bd. dirs. L.A. County Heart Assn., 1957; trustee U. Redlands, 1966-77, chmn. bd., 1969-72; mem. Univ. Bd., Pepperdine Coll. (life), chmn. bd. regents, mem. exec. bd., 1977-86; bd. dirs. Pasadena Found. Med. Rsch., 1967-72, So. Calif. Bldg. Funds, 1975-85, Met. YMCA L.A., 1975—; trustee San Gabriel Valley coun. Boy Scouts Am., 1968-74; trustee Calif. Mus. Sci. and Industry, 1977-89, pres., 1983-85, chmn., 1985-86; bd. govs. Dept. Mus. Natural History, L.A. County, 1968-72; mem. L.A. County Energy Commn., 1974-80; chmn. Mayor's Ad Hoc Water Crisis Commn., 1977. Served with USNR, 1942-45. Decorated knight Order of Merit (Italy). Mem. Nat. Assn. Cemeteries (pres. 1956-57), L.A. Area C. of C. (dir. 1969-78, bd. chmn. 1974, pres. 1973), Calif. C. of C. (dir. 1977-89), Newcomen Soc., Tau Beta Pi. Clubs: California, Lincoln, One Hundred, Twilight. Contbr. articles to profl. jours. Home: 1521 Virginia Rd San Marino CA 91108-1933 Office: 1712 S Glendale Ave Glendale CA 91205-3320

LLOYD, DOUGLAS GEORGE, watercolor artist, educator; b. Portsmouth, Hampshire, Eng., Jan. 8, 1918; came to U.S., 1946; s. John Albert and Jessie (Lavender) L.; m. Dorothy May Van Alphen, June 10, 1944 (dec. Apr. 1984); children: Ian Douglas (dec.), Lawrence Merrill, Robert Rodney, Jess Andrew, Robin Lee, Barbara Jeanne; m. Martha Clydesdale Amoia, June 21, 1986. Student, Portsmouth Jr. Tech., 1933-36; cert., Royal Naval Extension Coll., Dartmouth, Eng., 1944. Photography tchr. Boston Coll. Photography, 1946-47; photography editor Harvard Film Svc., Boston, 1947-48; microfilm specialist Hall & McChesney, Syracuse, N.Y., 1948-50; exec. v.p. Dakota So. Microfilm, Miami, Fla., 1950-54; microfilm cons. Miami, 1954-60, Oakland, Calif., 1961-67; microfilm specialist, special courses instr. Datagraphix Inc., San Diego, 1968-78; watercolor artist Las Vegas, Nev., 1978—; cons., Indio, Calif.; microfilm cons. Clk. of Cir. Ct., Deland, Fla., 1950-52, Bahamian Govt., Nassau, Bahamas, 1954. Author: (series of articles) Gremlins in the Computer Output Microfilm System, 1975 (monetary award 1975); artist: (series of ink drawings) The California Scene, 1981 (monetary award 1986). Alderman Hayling Island (Eng.) Coun., 1945; fire commr. City Fire Commn., Lake Helen, Fla., 1950-52; spl. dep. to Clk. of Cir. Ct., DeLand, 1950-52; pilot and cadet commandant CAP, Miami, 1952-54; mem. Vols. in Police Program, City of Indio, Calif., 1993-95; apptd. to City of Indio Cultural Arts Commn., 1994—, chmn. spl. art show projects, 1994; treas. San Diego Watercolor Soc., 1980. With Royal Navy, 1936-45. Mem. Nev. Watercolor Soc. (Signature award 1988), San Diego Watercolor Soc. (treas. 1982), Western Fedn. Watercolor Socs., Cochella Valley Watercolor Soc., Riverside Art Mus., 1993—. Republican. Episcopalian. Home and Office: Douglas Lloyd Arts 81297 Avenida Gaviota Indio CA 92201-7812

LLOYD, ELISABETH ANNE, philosophy educator; b. Morristown, N.J., Sept. 3, 1956; d. Stuart Phinney and Ruth Elisabeth (Sorensen) L. BA in Gen. Studies summa cum laude, U. Colo., 1980; PhD in Philosophy, Princeton U., 1984. Asst. in instrn. philosophy dept. Princeton (N.J.) U., 1983; vis. scholar dept. genetics Harvard U., Cambridge, Mass., 1983-84; vis. lectr. dept. philosophy U. Calif.-San Diego, La Jolla, 1984-85, asst. prof. dept. philosophy, 1985-88; asst. prof. dept. philosophy U. Calif., Berkeley, 1988-90; rsch. assoc. Mus. Comparative Zoology Harvard U., Cambridge, 1989; vis. sr. lectr. philosophy dept. U. Auckland, New Zealand, 1990; affiliated faculty history & philosphy of sci. program U. Calif., Davis, 1990—; assoc. prof. dept. philosophy U. Calif., Berkeley, 1990—; mem. panel oversight rev. com. NSF, Washington, 1988, 89, 92. Author: The Structure and Confirmation of Evolutionary Theory, 1988, 94; editor: Keywords in Evolutionary Biology, 1992 (Newbridge Book Club 1993); contbr. articles to profl. jours.; cons. referee NSF jours., 1985-94; mem. editl. bd. Biology and Philosophy jour., Dordrecht, The Netherlands, 1989—; assoc. Behavioral and Brain Scis. jour., 1994—; contbr. photographic portraits to The Economist, MIT Press, Oxford U. Press, Blacknell, Penguin Press, Routledge, 1984—. Campaign writer, contbr. Calif. and Nat. Dem. Party, Sacramento, 1984—; mem., contbr. Nature Conservancy, Washington, 1985—, Fairness & Accuracy in Reporting, N.Y.C., 1993—; mem., activist NOW, Washington, 1980-92. Grad. fellow NSF, 1980-83, fellow U. Calif. Humanities Rsch. Inst., 1989, 91; scholarly rsch. grantee NSF, 1986, 87, 88. Mem. Internat. Soc. for History, Philosophy, and Social Studies of Biology (bd. dirs. 1991-95), Soc. for Social Studies of Sci. (program com. 1989), Philosophy of Sci. Assn. (nominating com. 1990-91, program com. 1991-92), Am. Philos. Assn. (program com. 1988-91, award referee for Matchette prize 1992-94), Bay Area Philosophy of Sci. Reading Group (founder 1988—), Phi Beta Kappa. Unitarian. Office: U Calif Philosophy Dept 314 Moses Hall Berkeley CA 94720

LLOYD, JOSEPH WESLEY, physicist, researcher; b. N.Mex., Jan. 31, 1914; s. William Washington and Mattie May (Barber) L.; m. Lenora Lucille Hopkins, Jan. 24, 1944 (dec. June 1969); 3 children (dec.); m. Ruth Kathryn Newberry, Nov. 19, 1988; children: Kathryn Ruth Jordan, Mary Evelyn Jordan. Student, Pan Am. Coll., 1942. Plumber Pomona, Calif., 1951-57; plumber, pipefitter Marysville, Calif., 1957-79; ret., 1979; ind. researcher in physics and magnetism, Calif., 1944—. With CAP, 1944-45. Mem. AAAS, N.Y. Acad. Scis. Mem. Ch. of Christ.

LLOYD, LLYN ALLAN, association executive; b. Evergreen Park, Ill., Jan. 14, 1938; s. Russell Donald and Gladys Marie (Bladholm) L.; m. Helen Elizabeth Main, Mar. 22, 1959; children: Leanne, Douglas, Bradley. BS in Pharmacy, Ohio No. U., 1960; MA in Pub. Adminstrn., Boise State U., 1980. Lic. pharmacist, Ohio, Idaho, Ariz. With various pharmacies, Ohio and Idaho, 1960-63; pharmacist, owner Arco (Idaho) Drug, 1963-76; pharmacist City of Boise, Idaho, 1976-82; exec. dir. Idaho Bd. Pharmacy, Boise, 1982-86, Ariz. State Bd. Pharmacy, Phoenix, 1986—. Chmn. Butte County unit ARC, Arco, Idaho, 1968-74; mem. forest adv. com. Challis (Idaho) Nat. Forest, 1969-72. Recipient A.H. Robbins Bowl of Hygiene award Challis Nat. Forest, 1973. Mem. Nat. Assn. Bds. Pharmacy (exec. com. 1986—), Ariz. Pharmacy Assn., Ariz. Soc. Hosp. Pharmacists (Svc. to Pharmacy award 1988), Rotary, Lions, Masons. Home: 3044 W Myrtle Ave Phoenix AZ 85051-7541 Office: Ariz State Bd Pharmacy 5060 N 19th Ave Phoenix AZ 85015-3210

LLOYD, WILLIAM JUDD, JR., obstetrician/gynecologist; b. Sacramento, Calif., Feb. 22, 1948; s. William Judd Lloyd Sr. and Dorothea Theresa (Munz) Jones; m. Cheri Beatrice Jacobsen, May 3, 1969; children: William III, Alaina, Tricia, Natalie. BS, U. Nev., 1971, postgrad., 1973; MD, U. Iowa, 1975. Diplomate Am. Bd. Ob-Gyn. Rotating intern Akron Gen. Med. Ctr., 1975-76; ob-gyn. resident Kaiser Found. Hosp., Sacramento, Calif., 1976-79; ob-gyn. staff physician Darnall Army Hosp., Ft. Hood, Tex., 1979-81; pvt. practice Carson City, Nev., 1981-87, Reno, Nev., 1987—. Maj. U.S. Army, 1979-81. Fellow Am. Coll. Ob-Gyn.; mem. AMA, Nev. State Med. Assn., Am. Assn. Gyn. Laparoscopists, No. Nev. Ob-Gyn. Soc., Am. Fertility Soc., Washoe County Med. Soc. Republican. Office: 601 Ralston St # 200 Reno NV 89503-4436

LO, SUZANNE JAY, librarian; b. Berkeley, Calif., Apr. 23, 1950; d. Bock Seow and Hong Ting (Chin) Gee; m. John Wing-Sum Lo, Jan. 19, 1970 (div. 1986); 1 child, Roxanne April. B in Sociology, U. Calif., Berkeley, 1972, MLS, 1973. Adult ref. libr. San Francisco Pub. Libr., 1974-75, children's libr., 1976-83; br. sr. libr. Oakland (Calif.) Pub. Libr., 1983—; reader Libr. Svcs. and Constrn. Act Title V Fgn. Lang. program U.S. Dept. Edn., Washington, 1991, 92, 93. Contbr.: (chpt.) Our Family, Our Friends, Our World, 1992, Global Voices, Global Visions, 1994. V.p. Asian Pacific Employees Assn., Oakland, 1992—; task force mem. Oakland Sharing the Vision, 1992; mem. Chinese Am. Citizens Alliance, Oakland, 1995. Recipient Svc. award City of Oakland Vol. Program, 1992, scholarship Calif. State Libr., 1992, Transition into Mgmt. Ind. Honoree award East Bay Asian Local Devel. Corp., 1993. Mem. ALA (mem. com. 1990—), Oakland Asian Cultural Ctr. (bd. dirs. 1985-87, 93—), Chinese Am. Librs. Assn. (life, v.p., pres., treas. 1990—), U. Calif. Libr. Sch. Alumni Assn. (life, bd. dirs. 1992-94), Calif. Libr. Assn. (gen. assembly 1994—). Office: Oakland Pub Libr Asian Br 388 9th St Ste 190 Oakland CA 94607-4292

LO, WAITUCK, artist; b. Honolulu, June 9, 1919; s. Wai Tong and Kam T. Lo; m. Agnes Ching, Jan. 4, 1958; children: Edwina, Felix, Lisa Ann. BS, Utopia U., Shanghai, China, 1942; postgrad., Yen Yu Inst. Fine Art, Shanghai, Ind. U. Exhibited in group shows at Assn. Honolulu Artist Jury Art Show, 1956, 57 (Most Decorative award 1956, 57), Assn. Honolulu Artists non-jury show, 1957 (Popular award 1957), Narcissus Festival Art Exhbn., 1960 (Kaiser award 1960, Most Popular award 1960), Maui County Fair Art Exhbn., 1963 (2d prize 1963); commd. silk painting Pepsi-Cola U.S.A., 1987; paintings reproduced by Regency Card Co. Recipient 1st Place Water Color award Assn. Honolulu Artists, 1965, 68, Hayward award Assn. Honolulu Artists, 1968, 1st Place Water Color award Home Builders Assn. Art Show, 1966; Honorable Mention in Oil and Water Color, Assn. Honolulu Artists, 1966, Internat. Assn. Artists, 1979. Club: Toastmasters (Honolulu) (pres. 1986). Home: 6080 Keoki Pl Honolulu HI 96821-2224

LOARIE, JOHN ADAMS, engineer; b. Evanston, Ill., Jan. 15, 1942; s. Willard John and Lucille V. (Finnegan) L.; divorced; children: Michael, Julie, Christopher, Jennifer, Amy, Carrie; m. Barbara Fitzpatrick, Apr. 24, 1993. BSME, U. Notre Dame, 1964; MBA, Long Beach State U., 1977. Engr. Am. Can Co., Vernon, Calif., 1970-73; engring. mgr. Pharmaseal divsn. Am. Hosp. Supply, Duarte, Calif., 1973-78; prodn. mgr. Dupaco divsn. Pharmaseal, San Marcos, Calif., 1977-78; v.p. tech. and regulatory affairs GST Labs., La Jolla, Calif., 1978-79; v.p. ops. KIMCO, San Marcos, Calif., 1979-85; prodn. mgr. Astromec, Carson City, Nev., 1986-88; v.p. engring. Shurflo, Santa Ana, Calif., 1988-92, v.p. recreation vehicle marine, 1992—. Lt. USN, 1964-70; Vietnam. Recipient Achievement award Sec. of Navy, 1968. Home: 13 Princeton Irvine CA 92720-2644 Office: Shurflo 12650 Westminster Ave Santa Ana CA 92706-2139

LOARIE, THOMAS MERRITT, healthcare executive; b. Deerfield, Ill., June 12, 1946; s. Willard John and Lucile Veronica (Finnegan) L.; m. Stephanie Lane Fitts, Aug. 11, 1968 (div. Nov. 1987); children: Thomas M., Kristin Leigh. BSME, U. Notre Dame, 1968; Student, U. Minn., 1969-70, U. Chgo., 1970-71, Columbia U., 1978. Registered profl. engr., Calif. Prodn. engr. Honeywell, Inc., Evanston, Ill., 1968-70; various positions Am. Hosp. Supply Co., Evanston, Ill., 1970-83, pres. Heyer-Schulte divsn., 1979-83; pres. COO Novacor Med. Corp., Oakland, Calif., 1984-85, also bd. dirs.; pres. ABA Bio Mgmt., Danville, Calif., 1985-87; chmn., CEO Keravision, Inc., Santa Clara, Calif., 1987—; founder, chmn., med. device CEO Roundtable, 1993—; asst. prof. surgery Creighton U. Med. Sch., Omaha, 1986-94; spkr. in field. Contbr. articles on med. tech. and pub. policy to Wall St. Jour., others. Bd. dirs. Marymount Sch. Bd., 1981-84; bd. dirs. United Way Santa Barbara, 1981-84, assoc. chairperson, 1982-83, treas., 1983. Named One of 50 Rising Stars: Exec. Leaders for the 80's Industry Week mag., 1983. Mem. Assn. for Rsch. in Vision and Ophthalmology, Contact Lens Assn. Ophthalmology, Med. Mktg. Assn., Am. Entrepreneurs for Econ. Growth, Health Industry Mfrs. Assn. (spl. rep. bd. dirs. 1993—). Roman Catholic. Office: KeraVision Inc 48630 Milmont Dr Fremont CA 94538-7353

LOBACH, MELISSA RENEE, English language educator; b. San Diego, Nov. 28, 1965; d. James Edward Lobach and Dyahna Rose (Brittain) Riall; children: Corinthea Procopis, Beau Williams. BA, Met. State Coll., Denver, 1994. Cert. secondary tchr., Colo. Security officer Laird Internat. Studios, Culver City, Calif., 1984; sr. staff asst. Met. State Coll., Denver, 1989-94; asst. dir. Hollywood for Kids, Denver, 1992; tchr.-participant Westridge Young Writers Workshop, Lakewood, Colo., 1993, 95. Contbr. articles to profl. jours. Tchg. asst. Cherry Creek (Colo.) Schs. Spl. Needs Summer Program, 1992. Recipient Colo. Scholars scholarship Met. State Coll., Denver, 1991-94. Mem. NEA, Internat. Reading Assn. (Colo. coun.), Writers Anonymous (co-founder, bd. dirs. 1991—), Golden Key Honor Soc.

LOBANOV-ROSTOVSKY, OLEG, arts association executive; b. San Francisco, July 12, 1934; s. Andrei and Grace S. (Pope) L-R.; m. Susan Waters, Sept. 8, 1979; 1 child, Alexandra; children by previous marriage: Christopher, Nicholas. BA, U. Mich., 1956. Community concert rep. Columbia Artists Mgmt. Inc., 1958-59; mgr. Columbus (Ohio) Symphony Orch., 1959-62, Hartford (Conn.) Symphony Orch., 1962-65, Balt. Symphony, 1965-69; program officer div. humanities and arts Ford Found., 1969-75; exec. dir. Denver Symphony Orch., 1975-76; mng. dir. Nat. Symphony Orch., Washington, 1977-80; cons. Fed. Coun. on Arts, 1980-81; exec. dir. Del. Ctr. for Performing Arts, 1981-82; exec. v.p., mng. dir. Detroit Symphony Orch., 1982-83, pres., 1983-89; ind. cons., 1989-90; mng. ptnr. Middle Am. div. Jerold Panas, Young & Ptnrs. Inc., Chgo., 1990-91; pres. Calif. Ctr. for the Arts, Escondido, Calif., 1991—.

LOBAUGH, LESLIE E., JR., holding company executive, corporate lawyer. AB, Santa Clara U., 1967; JD, Georgetown U., 1970. Bar: Calif. Assoc. Holdberg, Finger, Brown & Abramson, 1971-75; staff atty. Pacific Lighting, 1975-77, sr. counsel, 1977-82, asst. gen. counsel, 1982-85, assoc. gen. counsel, 1985-86; v.p., gen. counsel Pacific Enterprises, 1986—, So. Calif. Gas Co., 1986—. Office: Pacific Enterprises 633 W 5th St Ste 5200 Los Angeles CA 90071-2015

LOBDELL, FRANK, artist; b. Kansas City, Mo., 1921; m. Ann Morency, 1952; children: Frank Saxton, Judson Earle. Studied, St. Paul Sch. Art, 1938-39, Calif. Sch. Fine Arts, 1947-50, Academie de la Grande Chaumiere, Paris, France, 1950-51. Tchr. Calif. Sch. Fine Arts, 1957-65; prof. art, Stanford, 1965—. One man shows, Lucien Labaudt Gallery, 1949, Martha Jackson Gallery, 1958, 60, 63, 72, 74, de Young Meml. Mus., San Francisco, 1959, Ferus Gallery, 1962, Pasadena Art Mus., 1961, San Francisco Mus. Art, 1969, Benador Gallerie, Geneva, Switzerland, 1964, Gallerie Anderson-Mayer, Paris, 1965, Smith-Anderson Gallery, San Francisco, 1982, Oscarsson Hood Gallery, N.Y.C., 1983, 84, 85, John Berggruen Gallery, San Francisco, 1987, Charles Campbell Gallery, San Francisco, 1988, 90, 92, Stanford Mus. Art, 1988, retrospective show, Pasadena Art Mus. and Stanford Mus., 1966, San Francisco Mus. Modern Art, 1983, Stanford Mus., 1993; exhibited group Shows, Salon du Mai, Paris, 1950, III Sao Paulo Biennial, 1955, Whitney Mus. Am. Art, 1962-63, 72, Guggenheim Mus., N.Y.C., 1964, Van Abbemuseum, Eindhoven, Holland, 1970, Corcoran Gallery Art, Washington, 1971, U. Ill., 1974; represented in permanent collections, San Francisco Mus. Art, Oakland Mus. Art, L.A. County Mus., Nat. Gallery Washington, others. Served with AUS, 1942-46. Recipient Nealie Sullivan award San Francisco Art Inst., 1960, award of merit AAAL, 1988. Home: 2754 Octavia St San Francisco CA 94123-4304

LOBEL, CHARLES IRVING, physician; b. Phila., Nov. 9, 1921; s. Maurice and Dora (Barnett) L.; m. Julia Valentine Skellchock, June 12, 1955; children: Meredith Anne Lobel-Angel. AA, San Jose State U., 1948; student, Stanford U., 1948-49; MD, U. So. Calif., 1953. Physician Permanente Med. Group, Inc., South San Francisco, 1954-65; physician, courtesy staff Chope Community Hosp., San Mateo, Calif., 1965-89, Sequoia Hosp., Redwood City, Calif., 1965—; physician Permanente Med. Group, Inc., Redwood City, Calif., 1965-95; clin. prof. medicine div. rheumatology Stanford U. Sch. Medicine, 1965—; chief profl. edn. Kaiser Found. Hosp., Redwood City, 1968-80, rehab. coord, 1968-80, pres med. staff, 1968-70; mem. Calif. Med. Assn. Staff Survey Com., San Francisco, 1970-90; mem. 4th dist. Bd. Med. Quality Assurance State Calif., 1979-84. 1st Lt. U.S. Army, 1942-46. Decorated Combat Infantry Badge, Bronze Star, Presdl. Unit citation, 3 Battle Stars. Fellow Am. Acad. Family Physicians, Am. Coll. Rheumatology; mem. AMA, AAAS, San Mateo County Med. Soc. (bd. dirs. 1975-78), Calif. Med. Soc. (alt. del. 1979-83), N.Y. Acad. of Sci., Am. Heart Assn., Royal Soc. of Med., Med. Friends of Wine, Arthritis Found. No. Calif., Phi Delta Epsilon. Office: Stanford U Clinic Dept Rheumatology 900 Blake Wilbur Dr Palo Alto CA 94304-2205

LOBIG, JANIE HOWELL, special education educator; b. Peoria, Ill., June 10, 1945; d. Thomas Edwin and Elizabeth Jane (Higdon) Howell; m. James Frederick Lobig, Aug. 16, 1970; 1 child, Jill Christina. BS in Elem. Edn., So. Ill. U., 1969; MA in Spl. Edn. Severely Handicapped, San Jose State U., 1989. Cert. elem. tchr., Calif., Mo., Ill., handicapped edn., Calif., Mo.; ordained to ministry Presbyn. Ch. as deacon, 1984. Tchr. trainable mentally retarded children Spl. Luth. Sch., St. Louis, 1967-68; tchr. trainable mentally retarded and severly handicapped children Spl. Sch. Dist. St. Louis, 1969-80, head tchr., 1980-83; tchr. severly handicapped children San Jose (calif.) Unifed Sch. Dist., 1983-86; tchr. autistic students Santa Clara County Office Edn., San Jose, 1986—; tchr. Suzanne Dancers, 1991-92. Vol. Am. Cancer Soc., San Jose, 1986-89, 92, St. Louis Reps., 1976-82, Am. Heart Assn., 1985—, Multiple Sclerosis Soc., 1990—; troop leader Camp Fire Girls, San Jose, 1984-85; moderator bd. deacons Evergreen Presbyn. Ch., 1986-89; mem. exec. bd. Norwood Creek Elem. Sch. PTA, 1983-86. Mem. Council for Exceptional Children, Assn. for Severly Handicapped, Nat. Edn. Assn., Calif. Tchrs. Assn. Independent. Home: 3131 Creekmore Way San Jose CA 95148-2805 Office: Weller Elem Sch 345 Boulder Dr Milpitas CA 95035

LOBSINGER, THOMAS, bishop; b. Ayton, Ont., Can., Nov. 17, 1927. Ordained priest Roman Cath. Ch., 1954, bishop, 1987. Bishop Whitehorse, Y.T., Can., 1987—. Home: 5119 5th Ave, Whitehorse, YK Canada Y1A 1L5*

LOBUE, ANGE JOSEPH, psychiatrist, writer; b. Hammond, La., Aug. 12, 1937; s. Joseph Vincent and Augustine (Palmintier) L. BS in Pharmacy, U. Miss., 1960; MD, La. State U., 1964; MPH, UCLA, 1968. Diplomate Am. Bd. Psychiatry and Neurology. Med.-surg. intern So. Pacific Meml. Hosp., San Francisco, 1964-65; resident in psychiatry Dept. Preventive and Social Medicine UCLA Sch. Medicine, 1968-71, resident in psychiatry Dept. Psychiatry, 1969-72, asst. clin. prof., 1972—; instr. Sch. Cinema-TV U. So. Calif., L.A., 1987—; pvt. practice Santa Rosa, Calif., 1988—, Mill Valley, 1995—; vis. fellow U. Belgrade (Yugoslavia) and the Fed. Inst. Pub. Health, U. Edinburgh (Scotland) and the Ministry of Health, 1969, St. Thomas' Hosp. and the Ministry of Health, London, 1969; vis. scholar, spl. asst. to adminstr. Health Svcs. and Mental Health Adminstrn., HEW, Washington, 1970; vis. scholar, asst. to pres. N.Y.C. Health and Hosps. Corp., 1970-71; registered pharmacist, mgr. Briargrove Pharmacy, Houston, Tex., 1960; spkr., lectr., program presenter numerous workshops, hosps., colls., univs., TV, assns.; apptd. staff Meml. Hosp. Med. Ctr., Long Beach, Calif., Santa Rosa Meml. Hosp., UCLA Ctr. Health Scis., Warrack Hosp., Santa Rosa. Editor: Psychiatry and the Media, 1983; contbr. articles to profl. jours. Sr. pub. health physician Venice Youth Clinic, L.A., 1969. Capt. U.S. Army Med. Corps, 1965-67. Fellow Acad. Psychosomatic Medicine, Am. Coll. Preventive Medicine (assoc.), Am. Geriatrics Soc. (founding), Royal Soc. Health; mem. NATAS, Am. Film Inst. Alumni Assn., Am. Med. Writers Assn., Biofeedback Cert. Iinst. Am., Mendocino-Lake County Med. Soc., Nat. Thespian Soc., Physician's Coun. on Drug Dependence, Sonoma County Med. Assn., UCLA Alumni Assn., Delta Omega. Office: Waterfall Towers 2455 Bennett Valley Rd Santa Rosa CA 95404-5663 also: 45121 Ukiah St Mendocino CA 95460-2390

LOCATELLI, PAUL LEO, university president; b. Santa Cruz, Calif., Sept. 16, 1938; s. Vincent Dino and Marie Josephine (Piccone) L. B.S. in Acctg., Santa Clara U., 1961; MDiv, Jesuit Sch. Theology, 1974; DBA, U. So. Calif., 1971. CPA, Calif. Ordained priest Roman Cath. Ch., 1974. Acct., Lautze & Lautze, San Jose, Calif., 1960-61, 1973-74; prof. acctg. Santa Clara (Calif.) U., 1974-86, assoc. dean Bus. Sch. and acad. v.p., 1978-86, pres., 1988—. bd dirs. Silicon Valley, Tech. Mus.; bd. govn., Inst. of Eur & Asian Studies; mem. Nat. Cath. Bishops and Pres.' Com., Acctg. Edn. Change Commn.; mem. adv. couns. Parents Helping Parents and Community Found.; past rector Jesuit Community at Loyola Marymount U. Trustee Regis U.; past trustee U. San Francisco, Seattle U., St. Louis U. and Loyola Marymount U.; past mem. Sr. Commn. of Western Assn. Schs. and Colls. Mem. AICPA, Calif. Soc. CPAs (Disting. Prof. of the Yr award, 1994), Am. Acctg. Assn., NCCJ (bd. dirs.), Assn. Jesuit Colls. and Univs. (chair), Ind. Colls. Calif., Am. Leadership Forum (bd. dirs.). Democrat. Office: Santa Clara U Office of Pres Santa Clara CA 95053

LOCH, PATRICIA ANN, software company executive, consultant; b. Omaha, May 2, 1944; d. Frank and Elizabeth (Duffield) Barrick; m. Charles Joseph Loch, Nov. 25, 1967; children: Michelle Kathleen, Justin Randall. BS in Math., Wake Forest U., 1966. Programmer IBM, Raleigh, N.C., 1966-68, Almay Cosmetics, Raleigh, N.C., 1968; contract programmer Kelly Assocs., Mpls., 1969-70, Bre-Mar Systems, N.Y.C., 1971; systems analyst Met. Life Ins. Co., N.Y.C., 1970-71; cons. Bd. Coop. Edn. Svcs., Yorktown, N.Y., 1972-75; pres., cons. P. Loch Assocs., Danville, Calif., 1975—; cons. Target Pub., Pleasanton, Calif., 1976-88. Mem. Assn. Small System Users (dir. membership 1981-82, dir. facilities 1985-87), NAFE, AAUW, Round Hill Country (Alamo, Calif.), Amador Athletic Club (Pleasanton). Home: 8071 E Del Trigo Scottsdale AZ 85258-1751

LOCHANKO, ELIZABETH ALEXANDRA, communications executive; b. Toronto, Ontario, Can., Apr. 30, 1957; came to U.S., 1960; d. Adam and Alexandra (Zabuga) L. BA, Rutgers U., 1979; M of Music, Johns Hopkins U., 1982. Office mgr. Simos C. Dimas Esquire, N.Y.C., 1982-84; pub. rels. mgr. 'K' Lines/Cloud Tours, N.Y.C., 1984-86; sr. acct. exec. Peter Martin Assocs., N.Y.C., 1986-88; sr. v.p. corp. communications Sony Pictures Entertainment, L.A., 1988—. Mem. NAFE, Johns Hopkins Alumni Assn., Douglass Rutgers Alumni Assn., Phi Beta Kappa.

LOCHER, MARIANNE, marketing professional; b. Washington, Oct. 27, 1959; d. Paul R. and Anne (Farrelly) L. BA cum laude, Rosemont Coll., 1981; Cert., N.Y. Sch. Interior Design, 1986; MFA, Columbia U., 1989. Asst. to dir. of mktg. Sotheby's, N.Y.C., 1983-85; spl. asst. to pres. Asprey, N.Y.C., 1985-88; asst. to exec. dir. Assoc. Art Mus. Dirs., N.Y.C., 1988-89; dir. communications Paul Segal Assocs., Architects, N.Y.C., 1989; bus. devel. profl. Archtl. Interiors, Washington, 1991-92; mktg. mgr. Hornberger & Worstell, Inc., Kentfield, Calif., 1992-94, Hellmuth, Obata & Kassabaum, 1994—. Mem. Delta Epsilon Sigma.

LOCHER, WALTER, agricultural products company; b. 1943. With Volcom (formerly Volkart Holding AG), Winterhur, Switzerland, 1966—; pres. Volkart Am. Inc., Phoenix, 1988—; CEO Anderson Clayton Corp., Phoenix, 1990—. Office: Anderson Clayton Corp 615 S 51st Ave Phoenix AZ 85043-4706*

LOCHHEAD, ROBERT BRUCE, lawyer; b. St. Louis, June 20, 1952; s. Angus Tulloch and Matilda Evangeline (Thurman) L.; m. Klynn Walker, June 21, 1974; children: Robert, Richard, Cynthia, Melinda, Rebekah, Elizabeth. BA, Brigham Young U., 1975; JD, Columbia U., 1978. Bar: D.C. 1979, Utah 1980, U.S. Dist. Ct. Utah 1980, U.S. Ct. Appeals (10th cir.) 1980, U.S. Supreme Ct. 1986. Law clk. to judge U.S. Ct. Appeals (10th cir.), Salt Lake City, 1978-79; assoc. Hogan & Hartson, Washington, 1979-80, Larsen, Kimball, Parr & Crockett, Salt Lake City, 1980-82; shareholder Kimball, Parr, Waddoups Brown & Gee and predecessor firm, Salt Lake City, 1982—; judge pro tem Small Claims Ct., Salt Lake City, 1985-88. Harlan Fiske Stone scholar, 1976-78. Mem. ABA, Am. Bankruptcy Inst. Mormon. Home: 492 N Flint St Kaysville UT 84037-9777 Office: Kimball Parr Waddoups Brown & Gee 185 S State St Ste 1300 Salt Lake City UT 84111-1537

LOCK, ROBERT GRAHAM, utilities executive; b. Innisfail, Alta., Can., 1943; m. Margaret Ellen; children: Heather Katherine, Robert Duncan. B-SChemE, U. Alberta, 1965; MSChemE, U. Calgary, 1975. Devel. engr., program analyst Chemcell ltd., 1965-67; ops. rsch. analyst Federated Coop. Ltd., 1967-69; inst. in chem. engring. So. Alberta Unst. of Tech., 1969-77; devel. engr. Can. Western Natural Gas Co. Ltd., 1977, sr. gas supply engr., 1978, mgr. of prodn., transmission, 1978; v.p., gen. mgr. Northwestern Utilities, Ltd., Edmonton, AB, Can., 1982, pres., 1982—. Mem. Baniff Sch, of Advanced Mgmt., Assn. Profl. Engrs, Geologists and Geophysicists of Alberta, Am. Gas Assn., Can. Gas Assn., Can. Mfrs. Assn., Can. Std. Assn., Edmonton C of C, Can. Gas Processors' Assn., Cmty. Planning Assn. of Alberta, Edmonton Club, Edmonton Petroleum Club, Royal Glenora Club. Office: Can Utilities Ltd, 10035 105 St NW, Edmonton, AB Canada T5J 3T2

LOCK, WILLIAM JOSEPH, lawyer; b. Chgo., June 4, 1946; s. Howard Bryant and Dorothy Helen (Felts) L.; m. Judith Marie Swan Hooper, June 14, 1969; children: Jennifer, Elizabeth, Robert, John. AB, Coll. William and Mary, 1968; JD, Ind. U., 1973. Bar: N.Mex. 1973. Assoc. atty. Oldaker & Oldaker, Albuquerque, 1973-74, Robinson, Stevens & Wainwright, Albuquerque, 1974-78; pvt. practice Albuquerque, 1978-80, 87—; ptnr., atty. Mercer, Lock & Keating, Albuquerque, 1980-87; pres. Albuquerque Lawyer's Club, 1986-87. Note editor: Indiana University Law Review, 1971-73. Vestryman, jr. warden St. John's Episcopal Cathedral, 1982-85; dir. N.Mex. Hist. Soc., Santa Fe, 1982-92; pres., founder, chmn. bd. dirs. Friends of the C&TSRR, Inc., N.Mex., 1988—; mem. Bishop's Long Range Planning Task Force, 1994-95. With U.S. Army, 1968-70. Mem. N.Mex. Bar Assn., Albuquerque Bar Assn., Railroad Club N.Mex. (sec./treas. 1983—), Kiwanis (pres. Albuquerque club 1979-80). Office: 5732 Osuna Rd NE Albuquerque NM 87109-2527

LOCKART, BARBETTA, counselor, jeweler, artwear designer, artist; b. Sacramento, Calif., Feb. 28, 1947; d. Bernard Elwood and Naomi Joyce (Wilson) L.; m. Michael Stanley Ray, Dec. 29, 1982 (div). AA in English, Southwestern Coll., Chula Vista, Calif., 1974; BA, San Diego State U., 1975; MA in Edn. Adminstrn., N.Mex. State U., Las Cruces, 1979, MA in Counseling and Guidance, 1981. Sec., interim coord., tchr. Indian Edn. Project, Palm Springs (Calif.) Unified Sch. Dist., 1976-79; outreach counselor Tecumseh House/Boston Indian Coun., 1980-81, asst. dir., 1981; acad. counselor, coord. native Am. affairs Ea. N.Mex. U., Portales, 1981-82; ind. researcher in field of counseling, Albuquerque, 1982-89, Sacramento, Calif., 1989—; pres., Sacramento, 1989—; owner Dearwater Designs, Albuquerque, 1985-88, Sacramento, 1988-90, Barbetta's Beads & Art, Sacramento, 1990—; speaker in field of community edn., alcoholism, urban native Am. women. Rockefeller Found. fellow, 1978-79; Nat. Inst. Edn. fellow, 1979-80. Author: Resolving Discipline Problems for Indian Students: A Preventative Approach, 1981, Auctions and Auction-Going: Make Them Pay Off for You; contbr. articles to profl. jours.

LOCKE, FRANCIS PHILBRICK, retired editorial writer; b. Lincoln, Nebr., May 1, 1912; s. Walter Leonard and Annette Elizabeth (Philbrick) L.; m. Carroll Day, Dec. 31, 1936; children: Margaret Locke Newhouse, Alice Locke Carey, Walter Day. BA, Harvard Coll., 1933; posgrad., Harvard U., 1946-47. Reporter Miami (Fla.) Daily News, 1934-36, editorial writer, 1936-41; editorial writer St. Louis Post-Dispatch, 1941; editor of editorial page Miami Daily News, 1941-46; Nieman fellow Harvard U., Cambridge, Mass., 1946-47; assoc. editor Dayton (Ohio) Daily News, 1947-63; editorial writer Riverside (Calif.) Press-Enterprise, 1963-72. Author: (chpt.) Public Men In & Out of Office, 1943; contbr. articles to profl. jours. Bd. dirs. Mission Inn Found., Riverside, 1987—; mem. adv. bd. YWCA, Riverside; trustee Miami U., Oxford, Ohio, 1954-63; div. chmn. United Way, Dayton, 1957-63. Recipient aviation writing award TWA, 1956. Mem. Nat. Conf. Editl. Writers, Soc. Profl. Journalists (nat. editl. writing prize 1946), Harvard U. Alumni Assn. (S.W. and Pacific regional bd. dirs. 1980-86, Harvard medal 1983), Harvard-Radcliffe Club So. Calif. (bd. dirs. 1975-92), Harvard Club Dayton (pres. 1961-63). Democrat. Congregationalist. Home: 7368 W Westwood Dr Riverside CA 92504-2729

LOCKE, JOHN GARDNER, chemical company executive; b. Chgo., Sept. 2, 1926; s. John Gardner and Hildur Marie (Ericsson) L.; m. Janyce B. Hill, June 25, 1960; children: James Walter, John Gardner III. BS, U. So. Calif., L.A., 1950, MBA, 1960. Account rep. Kerr & Bell Investments, L.A., 1950-51; salesman, v.p. mktg. Am. Mineral Spirits Co., Western, L.A., 1951-69; regional mgr. Union Oil Co., Amsco div., L.A., 1969-71; pres. Angeles Chem., Santa Fe Springs, Calif., 1971—; bd. dirs. Angeles Chem., Santa Fe Springs. Mem. Nat. Assn. Chem. Distbrs., Nat. Assn. Paint Mfrs., Balboa Yacht Club. Republican. Home: 20449 E Rancho Los Cerritos Rd Covina CA 91724-3528 Office: Angeles Chem Co Inc 8915 Sorensen Ave Santa Fe Springs CA 90670-2638

LOCKE, TIMOTHY ATWATER, marketing communications executive; b. Rochester, N.Y., Feb. 4, 1962; s. Laurance George and Linda Daly (Feldman) L.; m. Catherine Jean Marineau, Sept. 12, 1987; children: Natalie Suzanne, Charles Atwater. BA, U. Buffalo, 1984. Editorial asst. Nat. Asphalt Pavement Assn., Riverdale, Md., 1985-87; pub. rels. coord. Am. Diabetes Assn., Portland, Oreg., 1987-89; pub. rels. mgr. Wilson, Donaldson & Assocs., Portland, Oreg., 1989-92; product publicity mgr. Western Wood Products Assn., Portland, Oreg., 1992—. Mem. Pub. Rels. Soc. Am. (com. chair., bd. dirs.). Republican. Office: Western Wood Products Assn 522 SW 5th Ave Portland OR 97204

LOCKETT, BARBARA ANN, librarian; b. Northampton, Mass., Feb. 21, 1936; d. William M. and Anna A. (Vachula) Prabulos; m. Richard W. Rice, June 2, 1957 (div. Feb. 1966); 1 child, Annamarie Louise; m. Benjamin B. Lockett, June 7, 1985. BS, U. Mass., 1957; MLS, U. Calif., Berkeley, 1967. Documents librarian Knolls Atomic Power Lab., Schenectady, N.Y., 1968-74; coordinator bibliog. devel. SUNY, Albany, 1974-81; prin. librarian reference services N.Y. State Library, Albany, 1981-85; dir. libraries Rensselaer Poly. Inst., Troy, N.Y., 1985-94; cons. Office Mgmt. Svcs., Assn. Rsch. Librs., Washington, 1981-86. Contbr. articles on collection devel., mgmt. and info. systems to profl. jours. Mem. ALA (cons. collection mgmt. and devel. com., Resources and Tech. Svcs. div. 1983-87), Assn. Coll. and Rsch. Librs. (chmn. standards and accreditation com. 1988-90), N.Y. State Edn. and Rsch. Network (chmn. info. resources com. 1988-89), N.Y. State Libr./NYSERNet (joint planning team 1991-94, del. N.Y. State Gov.'s Conf. on Librs., 1990), Sigma Xi, Phi Kappa Phi, Beta Phi Mu. Mem. Unitarian Ch. Home: 1772 Calle Poniente Santa Barbara CA 93101-4916

LOCKLIN, WILLIAM RAY, financial planner; b. Joplin, Mo., Dec. 16, 1942; s. Jack and Audrey R. (Miller) L.; B.S. in Mech. Engring., U. Ariz., 1966, M.B.A., 1968; m. Karen E. Bjorklund, Dec. 29, 1979; children—Kevin Russell, Matthew William. Securities and ins. sales rep. Bell Funding Corp., Los Angeles, 1970-72; gen. agt., mgr., 1972-76; fin. planner Bill Locklin and Co., Santa Monica, Calif.; prin., mgr. Fin. Planners Equity Corp., Santa Monica; now stockholder, registered prin. Associated Securities Corp. Cert. fin. planner; pres. Econ. Profiles, 1988—; bd. dirs. Associated Fin. Group, Inc., 1992—; C.L.U. Mem. Internat. Assn. Fin. Planning (L.A. chpt. dir. 1983-89 , v.p. 1984-87, pres. 1987-88, chmn. bd. 1988-89), Inst. Cert. Fin. Planners, Registry Fin. Planning Practitoners. Office: Econ Profiles Associated Securities Corp 27431 Enterprise Cir W # 101 Temecula CA 92590

LOCKWOOD, ROBERT WILSON, paper and pulp executive; b. Chgo., July 12, 1960; s. Glynn H. and Lorri (Wilson) L.; m. Ann E. Longwell, May 21, 1983. BA in Econs., Whitman Coll., Walla Walla, Wash., 1982; MA in Fin. and Econs., Webster U., 1984. Purchasing mgr. LTI-Auto. Products, Farmington Hills, Mich., 1983; planning and control coord. Simpson Timber Co., Shelton, Wash., 1985-86; contr. Commencement Bay Mill Co., Tacoma, Wash., 1986-88; asst. contr. Simpson Tacoma Kraft Co., 1988-91; contr. Simpson Pasadena Paper Co., Houston, 1991-93; mgr. planning and control Simpson Paper Co., Seattle, 1993-94, strategic planning mgr., 1995—.

LODGE, EDWARD JAMES, federal judge; b. 1933. BS cum laude, Coll. Idaho, 1957; LLB, U. Idaho, 1961. Mem. firm Smith & Miller, 1962-63; probate judge Canyon County, Idaho, 1963-65; judge Idaho State Dist. Ct., 1965-88; U.S. bankruptcy judge State of Idaho, 1988; dist. judge, now chief judge U.S. Dist. Ct. Idaho, 1989—. Recipient Kramer award for excellence in jud. adminstrn.; named three time All-Am., disting. alumnus Coll. Idaho, Boise State U.; named to Hall of Fame Boise State U., Coll. Idaho. Mem. ABA, Idaho Trial Lawyer Assn., Idaho State Bar Assn., Idaho Dist. Judges Assn., U.S. Federal Judges Assn., Boise State Athletic Assn., Elks Club. Office: US Dist Ct PO Box 040 550 W Fort St Boise ID 83724-0101

LOEB, JOYCE LICHTGARN, interior designer, civic worker; b. Portland, Oreg., May 20, 1936; d. Elias Lichtgarn and Sylvia Amy (Margulies) Freedman; m. Stanley Robinson Loeb, Aug. 14, 1960; children: Carl Eli, Eric Adam. Student U. Calif.-Berkeley, 1954-56; BS, Lewis and Clark Coll., 1958; postgrad. art and architecture, Portland State U., 1976. Tchr. art David Douglas Sch. Dist., Portland, 1958-59, 61-64; tchr., chmn. art dept. Grant Union High Sch. Dist., Sacramento, 1959-60; designer, pres. Joyce Loeb Interior Design, Inc., Portland, 1976—; cons. designer to various developers of health care facilities. Chairperson fundraisers for civic orgns. and Jewish orgns.; mem. women's com. Reed Coll.; bd. dirs., mem. exec. com. Inst. Judaic Studies, 1989-92; bd. dirs. Young Audiences, Inc., Portland, 1970-76, chmn. long range planning, 78-80; bd. dirs. Met. Family Svc., Portland, 1968-71, Portland Opera Assn., 1978-84, Arts Celebration, Inc., Portland, 1984—, Friends of Chamber Music; chmn. Artquake Festival, 1985, Operaball, 1987, Children's Charity Ball Com., 1989, Women's Bd. Jewish Fedn. Portland, 1993—; sec. exec. com., bd. dir. Oreg. Children's Theatre, 1992—; v.p. Beth Israel Sisterhood, 1981-83; bd. dirs., trustee Congregation Beth Israel, 1986-92, chmn. art interior design com.; trustee Robison Home, 1990—; bd. dirs. Friends of Chamber Music, 1994—. Recipient Women of Distinction award in architecture and design Girl Scouts Columbia River Coun., 1994. Mem. Am. Soc. Interior Design (allied, bd. dirs. 1993-95), Multnomah Athletic Club. Democrat. Home: 1546 SW Upland Dr Portland OR 97221-2651

LOEB, PAUL ROGAT, writer, lecturer; b. Berkeley, Calif., July 4, 1952; s. Yosal Rogat and Magd (Kosches) Rogat Loeb Waingrow; m. Bette Jean Bullert. Student, Stanford U., 1970-72; BA in Social Scis., New Sch. for Social Rsch., 1972. Writer, critic, 1977—, lectr., 1982—; vis. lectr. numerous colls. and univs. including Harvard U., MIT, Cath. U., Brandeis U., Emory U., Trinity U., U. Calif., U. Wis.; scholar-in-residence Dartmouth U., Mercer U., Hobart and William Smith Coll., La. State U., U. Wash., SUNY, Plattsburgh, others. Author: Nuclear Culture: Living and Working at The World's Largest Atomic Complex, 1982, 86, Hope in Hard Times: America's Peace Movement and the Reagan Era, 1987, Generation at The Crossroads: From Apathy to Action in American College Students, 1994; editor: Liberation mag., 1974-76; cons. editor: Nuclear X-Change, 1983-86; assoc. editor: Clinton St. Quar., 1985-91; contbr. revs. to numerous publs. including the Washington Post, L.A. Times, Psychology Today, Mother Jones, Utne Reader, Village Voice, Internat. Herald Tribune. Mem. Inst. for Global Security Studies. Home: 3232 41st Ave SW Seattle WA 98116-3445

LOEBIG, LARRY E., realtor, consultant; b. Bklyn., Nov. 28, 1951; s. Lawrence and Margaret (Hurtle) L.; m. C.L. Tree, Nov. 6, 1983. Student, Emerson Coll., 1969-71; AA, Framingham (Mass.) State U., 1972; PhD (hon.), Sankhaver Inst., Houston, 1987. Grad. Realtors Inst. Mgr. Charles Playhouse, Boston, 1972; dir. Hatch Shell Concert Series, Boston, 1975, Wayland (Mass.) Recreation Dept., 1977-79; v.p. Interel, San Francisco, 1984; officer, coord. New Games Found., San Francisco, 1979-82; gen. mgr. Black World Found., Oakland, Calif., 1985-89, Ctrl. Realty Svc., Oakland, 1989-91; v.p. ERA Network Real Estate, Oakland, 1991-93; owner, broker Home Buyers Network, Oakland, 1993—; cons. Interel, 1985-87; cons.-investigator Office Paranormal Investigation, Orinda, Calif., 1988-94; basic trainer coach Coaches Tng. Inst., San Francisco, 1994; conf. coord. Coun. Sci. Investigation Claims of Paranormal, Buffalo, 1991; host Creative Real Estate forum Delphi Internet. Author: New Games Book II, 1989; author mag., newspaper and jour. articles. Actor, owner Seance Fiction Theater, Oakland, 1992; mem./performer Acad. Magical Arts, Hollywood, 1987; cons. Gov.'s Coun. Phys. Fitness, Boston, 1978. Mem. Soc. Am. Magicians (occult com.), Nat. Assn. Realtors (edn. com.), Oakland Assn. Realstors (edn. com.), Real Estate Buyers Agt. Coun. (co-chair membership), Magic Castle Hollywood (occult com.). Home: 4163 Shafter Ave Oakland CA 94609-2619 Office: Home Buyers Network 330 41st St Oakland CA 94609-2653

LOEHMAN, RONALD ERNEST, materials scientist; b. San Antonio, Feb. 22, 1943; s. Roland Albert and Charlotte (Herweck) L.; m. Edna Tusak, June 26, 1965 (div. Oct. 1981), 1 child, Rachel Andrea; m. Ellen Louise Griffith, July 10, 1982; 1 child, Matthew Charles. BA, Rice U., 1964; PhD, Purdue U., 1969. Asst. prof. U. Fla., Gainesville, 1970-75, assoc. prof., 1975-78; sr. materials scientist SRI Internat., Menlo Park, Calif., 1978-82; mem. tech. staff Sandia Nat. Labs., Albuquerque, 1982-86, div. supr., 1986-87, mgr. chemistry and ceramics dept., 1987-92; mgr., co-dir. Advanced Materials Lab., Albuquerque, 1992—; nat. labs. disting. prof. U. N.Mex., 1992—. Contbr. articles to profl. jours.; patentee in field. Mem. AAAS, Am. Ceramic Soc. (assoc. editor jour. 1988—, Roland Snow award 1984, Fulrath award 1988), Nat. Inst. Ceramic Engrs., Sigma Xi. Office: Advanced Materials Lab 1001 University Blvd SE Albuquerque NM 87106-4342

LOEHR, THOMAS MICHAEL, chemist, educator; b. Munchen, Germany, Oct. 2, 1939; came to the U.S., 1951; s. Max and Irmgard (Kistenfeger) L.; m. Joann Sanders, June 20, 1965. BS in Chemistry, U. Mich., 1963; PhD, Cornell U., 1967. Asst. prof. Cornell U., Ithaca, N.Y., 1967-68, Oreg. Grad. Ctr., Portland, 1968-74; assoc. prof. Oreg. Grad. Ctr., Beaverton, 1974-78, prof., 1978—, acting head dept. chem. and bio. scis., 1981-82; acting head dept. chem. and bio. scis. Oreg. Grad. Inst. Sci. and Tech., Beaverton, 1992-93; vis. prof. Portland State U., 1974-75, adj. prof., 1979—; vis. assoc. Calif. Inst. Tech., Pasadena, 1978-79; chmn. Metals in Biology/Gordon Rsch. Conf., 1987; mem. Metallobiochemistry study sect. NIH, 1978-82. Editor: Iron Carriers and Iron Proteins, 1989; contbr. more than 125 articles to profl. jours. Mem. Am. Chem. Soc. Office: Oreg Grad Inst Sci Tech PO Box 91000 20000 NW Walker Rd Portland OR 97291-1000

LOEHWING, RUDI CHARLES, JR., publicist, radio broadcasting executive; b. Newark, July 26, 1957; s. Rudy Charles Sr. and Joan Marie (Bell) L.; m. Claire Popham, Sept. 4, 1987; children: Aspasia Joyce, Tesia Victoria, Rudi Douglas, Anna Marie, Samantha Diane, Ian Ryan. Student, Biscayne U., 1975, Seton Hall U., 1977, Hubbard Acad., 1980. Announcer radio sta. WHBI FM, N.Y.C., 1970-72; producer Am. Culture Entertainment, Belleville, N.J., 1973-74; exec. producer Am. Culture Entertainment, Hollywood, Calif., 1988-94; CEO Broadcaster's Network Internat., Hollywood, U.K., 1989—; sr. v.p. bus. devel., pub. rels. The Dohring Co., Hollywood; pub. rels. dir. The Dohring Co.; acct. exec. Michael Baybak & Co., Inc., Beverly Hills Calif., 1989—; bd. dirs. 1st Break, Hollywood and Eng., 1988—. Author: Growing Pains, 1970; exec. producer TV documentaries and comml. advertisements, 1983; patentee in field. Devel. dir. Tricentennial Found., Washington, 1989-90; bd. dirs. Just Say No to Drugs, L.A., 1983, Hand Across the Atlantic, First Bank, Internat. Country Top 10, The Rock of Russia, Job Search, Hollywook, U.K. and Russia. Named Youngest Comml. Radio Producer and Announcer for State of N.Y., Broadcaster's Network Internat., 1972. Mem. Broadcaster's Network Assn. (bd. dirs. 1977—). Office: Broadcasters' Network Internat Ltd 2624 Medlow Ave Ste B Los Angeles CA 90065-4617

LOEPPKY, JACK ALBERT, physiologist, researcher; b. Saskatoon, Sask., Can., Jan. 14, 1944; came to U.S., 1967; s. George and Sarah (Martens) L.; m. Janet Sue By, Nov. 22, 1974; children: Kristopher, Ninya. BA with distinction, U. Sask., 1966; MS, U. N.Mex., 1969, PhD, 1973; postgrad. Colo. State U., 1969-70. Instr., U. Sask., Saskatoon, 1966-67; technician Lovelace Med. Found., Albuquerque, 1968-69, rsch. assoc., 1970-75, assoc. scientist, 1975-90, scientist, 1990—, head dept. cardiopulmonary physiology, 1981-83; head respiratory technologist Wellington (N.Z.) Hosp., 1975; adj. asst. prof. U. N.Mex., Albuquerque, 1982—. Editor: Oxygen Transport to Human Tissues, 1982; contbr. articles to profl. jours. Max Planck fellow physiology, 1983-84; grantee Am. Heart Assn., 1982, 88, NSF, 1984, NASA, 1989. Mem. Am. Physiol. Soc., N.Mex. Mountain Club. Office: The Lovelace Insts 2425 Ridgecrest Dr SE Albuquerque NM 87108-5129

LOETE, STEVEN DONALD, pilot; b. Tacoma, Aug. 21, 1959; s. Donald Kenneth and Ida Lorraine (Buck) L.; 1 child, Samantha. BA, Pacific Luth. U., 1984. Pilot contracting office USAF, Williams AFB, Ariz., 1985; flight instr. Clover Park Tech. Coll., Tacoma, 1986; charter pilot Stellar Exec., Chandler, Ariz., 1986-87; pilot, airline capt. Maui Airlines, Guam, 1987; airline capt., checkairman Westair Airlines, Fresno, Calif., 1987—. Contbr. Save the Children, 1988-90; mem. Angel Flight, U. Puget Sound, 1981-83; bd. dirs. aviation adv. com. Clover Park Tech. Coll., 1991—. 1st lt. USAF, 1983-93. Mem. Airline Pilots Assn. (chmn. organizing com. 1989, chmn. coun. 1989-91). Republican. Methodist. Home and Office: 6102 84th Avenue Ct W Tacoma WA 98467-4042

LOEUP, KONG, counselor; b. Battambang, Cambodia, May 26, 1944; s. Kong Niem and Chhit Roeun; m. Ly Keo Thim, Aug. 1968; children: Kong Bandaul, Kong Panlauk. Diploma in edn., U. Phnom Penh, 1965; BA, Antioch U., 1983; MA, U. Colo., Denver, 1987; PhD, Columbia Pacific U., 1987. Tchr. Ministry Edn., Phnom Penh, 1964; counselor, community case worker Internat. Refugee Ctr., Denver, 1983; refugee program coord./counselor Refugee Camps, Thailand; cons. Cambodian Buddhist Soc. of Colo., Denver; counselor Cambodian Community Colo., Denver; pres. Cambodian Cultural Ctr., Denver, 1992—. Pres. Cambodian Fine Arts Preservation Group Colo.; mem. Asian Edn. Adv. Coun., Rep. Presdl. Task Force, 1986. Mem. ASCD. Home and Office: 1804 S Eliot St Denver CO 80219-4904

LOEWENSTEIN, WALTER BERNARD, nuclear power technologist; b. Gensungen, Hesse, Germany, Dec. 23, 1926; came to U.S., 1938; s. Louis and Johanna ((Katz) L.; m. Lenore C. Pearlman, June 21, 1959; children: Mark Victor, Marcia Beth. BS, U. Puget Sound, 1949; postgrad., U. Wash., 1949-50; PhD, Ohio State U., 1954. Registered profl. engr., Calif. Rsch. asst., fellow Ohio State U., Columbus, 1951-54; rsch. asst. Los Alamos Nat. Lab., 1952-54; sr. physicist, divsn. dir. Argonne (Ill.) Nat. Lab., 1954-73; dept. dir., dep. divsn. dir. Electric Power Rsch. Inst., Palo Alto, Calif., 1973-89, profl. cons., 1989—, mem. large aerosol containment experiment project bd., 1983-87; mem. Marviksen project bd. Studsvik Rsch. Ctr., Stockholm, 1978-85; mem. LOFT project bd. Nuclear Energy Agy., Paris, 1982-89; mem. tech. adv. nuclear safety Ontario Hydro Corp., 1990—; mem. nuclear engring. dept. adv. com. Brookhaven Nat. Lab., 1992—. With USNR, 1945-46. Recipient Alumnus Cum Laude award U. Puget Sound, 1976. Fellow Am. Phys. Soc., Am. Nuclear Soc. (v.p., pres. 1988-90); mem. Am. Assn. Engring. Socs. (sec., treas. 1990), Nat. Acad. Engring. Jewish. Home and Office: 515 Jefferson Dr Palo Alto CA 94303

LOEWENTHAL, NESSA PARKER, communications educator; b. Chgo., Oct. 13, 1930; d. Abner and Frances (Ness) Parker; m. Martin Moshe Loewenthal, July 7, 1951 (dec. Aug. 1973); children: Dann Marcus, Ronn Carl, Deena Miriam; m. Gerson B. Selk, Apr. 17, 1982 (dec. June 1987). BA in Edn. and Psychology, Stanford U., 1952. Faculty Stanford Inst. for Intercultural Communication, Palo Alto, Calif., 1973-87; dir. Trans Cultural Svcs., San Francisco, 1981-86, Portland, Oreg., 1986—; dir. dependent svcs. and internat. edn. Bechtel Group, San Francisco, 1973-81, internat. edn. cons., 1981-84; mem. adv. com. dept. internat. studies Lesley Coll., Cambridge, Mass., 1986—; mem. Oreg. Ethics Commons, 1990—; mem. Bay Area Ethics Consortium, Berkeley, 1985-90; chmn. ethics com. Sietar Internat., Washington, 1987—, mem. governing bd., 1992-95; mem. faculty Summer Inst. for Internat. Comms., Portland, Oreg., 1987—. Author: Professional Integration, 1987, Update: Federal Republic of Germany, 1990, Update: Great Britain, 1987; author, editor book series Your International Assignment, 1973-81; contbr. articles to profl. jours. Mem. equal opportunity and social justice task force Nat. Jewish Rels. Adv. Coun.; bd. dirs. Kids on the Block, Portland; mem. Lafayette (Calif.) Traffic Commn., 1974-80; bd. dirs. Ctr. for Ethics and Social Policy, 1988-91; mem. exec. bd. and planning com. Temple Isaiah, Lafayette, 1978-82; bd. dirs. Calif. Symphony, Orinda, 1988-90; mem. exec. com. overseas schs. adv. com. U.S. Dept. State, 1976-78. Named Sr. Interculturalist, Sietar Internat., 1986. Mem. ASTD, Soc. for Intercultural Edn., Tng. and Rsch. (chmn. 1986-87, nomination com. 1985-86, co-chmn. 1989-90, chmn. ethics com. 1989—, governing bd. 1992-95), World Affairs Coun. (exec. bd. internat. profl. performance area 1993—), Am. Women for Internat. Understanding, Portland City Club. Democrat. Home: 712 NW Westover Ter Portland OR 97210-3136

LOEWUS, FRANK ABEL, biochemistry and plant physiology educator; b. Duluth, Minn., Oct. 22, 1919; s. David G. and Alyce (Abel) L.; m. Mary Esther Walz, Dec. 26, 1947; children: Rebecca, David I., Daniel. BSc, U. Minn., 1942, MSc, 1950, PhD, 1952. Rsch. assoc. dept. biochemistry U. Chgo., 1952-55; chemist Western Regional Rsch. Lab., USDA, Berkeley, Calif., 1955-64; prof. dept. biology SUNY, Buffalo, 1964-75; prof., fellow inst. of biol. chemistry Wash. State U., Pullman, 1975-90, prof. emeritus, fellow emeritus Inst. Biol. Chem., 1990—; instr.-in-charge Exptl. Marine Botany, Marine Biol. Lab., Woods Hole, Mass., summers, 1970-74. Author/editor: Biogenesis of Plant Cell Wall Polysaccharides, 1973; co-editor: Encyclopedia of Plant Physiology, New Series, Vol. 13 A&B, 1982, Inositol Metabolism in Plants, 1990. 1st lt. USAAF, 1942-46. Mem. AAAS, Phytochem. Soc. N.Am. (life; pres. 1975-76, editor-in-chief Recent Advances in Phytochemistry 1977, 80-84), Am. Soc. Plant Physiologists (Charles Reid Barnes Life Mem. award 1993), Am. Chem. Soc., Am. Soc. Biochem. and Molecular Biology, N.Y. Acad. Sci. Home: 1700 NE Upper Dr Pullman WA 99163-4624 Office: Wash State U Inst of Biol Chemistry Pullman WA 99164-6340

LOEWUS, MARY WALZ, retired biochemist; b. Duluth, Minn., Feb. 15, 1923; d. Ivan George and Mary Ellen (McLennan) Walz; m. Frank Abel Loewus, Dec. 26, 1947; children: Rebecca Ruth, David Ivan, Daniel. BA, U. Minn., 1945, MSA, 1950, PhD, 1953. Teaching asst. biochemistry U. Minn., St. Paul, 1946-51; jr. rsch. biochemist U. Calif., Berkeley, 1956-58, jr. rsch. biochemist Kearney Found. soils, 1958-63, postgrad. rsch. asst. genetics, 1963-64; rsch. assoc. biology SUNY, Buffalo, 1965-75; rsch. assoc. dept. agrl. chemistry Wash. State U., Pullman, 1975-80; rsch. assoc. Inst. Biol. Chemistry, Wash. State U., Pullman, 1980-85, assoc. scientist, 1985-86; vis. prof. botany U. Nijmegen, the Netherlands, 1976. Contbr. articles to profl. jours. Pres. Pullman-Moscow Jewish Community, 1978-80, treas., 1986-90. NSF grantee, 1965-67. Mem. Am. Soc. Biol. Chemists, Assn. Faculty Women. Home: 1700 NE Upper Dr Pullman WA 99163-4624

LOFFER, LINDA V., small business owner; b. Portland, Oreg., Aug. 15, 1952; d. Verl O. and Mary R. (Parmenter) Wells; m. James E. Loffer, Oct. 7, 1978; children: Robert, Jennifer. Degree in legal adminstrv. skills, Western Bus. U., 1971. Legal sec., internat. sec. Georgia-Pacific, Portland, 1973-77; adminstrv. sec. Dwyer Overseas Timber, Portland, 1977-79, Cambrian Forest Products, Portland, 1979-80; legal technician Law Office of Richard Van Hoomissen, Portland, 1983-85; sr. legal sec. Stoel Rives Boley Jones & Grey, Portland, 1986-94; adminstrv. asst. Northwest Occuptl. Medicine Ctr., Portland, 1994—; owner, pres. Shoppers Shuttle Inc., Tualatin, Oreg., 1992—. Team leader March of Dimes Walk, Portland, 1993-94; sec., bd. dirs. Byrom Elem. PSO, Tualatin, 1987-92; treas. Hazelbrook Mid. Sch. PSO, Tualatin, 1991-94, pres., 1993—; mem. tax bond and planning coms. Tigard-Tualatin Sch. Dist., 1990—; mem. care ministry Our Lady of the Lake Ch., Lake Oswego, 1991—. Mem. Portland Rose Festival Assn., Portland-Oreg.

Visitors Assn. Republican. Roman Catholic. Home and Office: Shoppers Shuttle Inc PO Box 1550 9721 SW Alsea Dr Tualatin OR 97062

LOFGREN, CHARLES AUGUSTIN, legal and constitutional historian; b. Missoula, Mont., Sept. 8, 1939; s. Cornelius Willard and Helen Mary (Augustin) L.; m. Jennifer Jenkins Wood, Aug. 6, 1986. AB with great distinction, Stanford U., 1961, AM, 1962, PhD, 1966. Instr. history San Jose State Coll., 1965-66; asst. prof. Claremont McKenna Coll., 1966-71, assoc. prof., 1971-76, prof., 1976—, Roy P. Crocker prof. Am. history and politics, 1976—. Served with USAR, 1957-63. Mem. Am. Soc. Legal History, Orgn. Am. Historians, Am. Hist. Assn. Republican. Roman Catholic. Author: Government from Reflection and Choice, 1986, The Plessy Case, 1988; contbr. articles to profl. jours. Office: Claremont McKenna Coll Dept History 850 Columbia Ave Claremont CA 91711-3901

LOFGREN, ZOE, county government official; b. San Mateo, Calif., Dec. 21, 1947; d. Milton R. and Mary Violet L.; m. John Marshall Collins, Oct. 22, 1978; children: Sheila Zoe Lofgren Collins, John Charles Lofgren Collins. BA in Polit. Sci., Stanford U., 1970; JD cum laude, U. Santa Clara, 1975. Bar: Calif., 1975. D.C. Adminstrv. asst. to Congressman Don Edwards, San Jose, Calif., 1970-79; ptnr. Webber and Lofgren, San Jose, 1979-81; mem. Santa Clara County Bd. Suprs., 1981-94; congresswoman 104th U.S. Congress, Calif. 16th Dist., 1995—; part-time prof. Law, U. Santa Clara, 1978-80; jud. com. on crime; house com. on sci., subcommittee on tech., basic rsch. Exec. dir. Community Housing Developers, Inc., 1979-80; trustee San Jose Community Coll. Dist., 1979-81; bd. dirs. Community Legal Svcs., 1978-81, San Jose Housing Svc. Ctr., 1978-79; mem. steering com. sr. citizens housing referendum, 1978; del. Calif. State Bar Conv., 1979-82, Dem. Nat. Conv., 1976; active Assn. Immigration and Nationality Lawyers, 1976-82, Calif. State Dem. Cen. Com., 1975-78, Santa Clara County Dem. Cen. Com., 1974-78, Notre Dame High Sch. Blue Ribbon Com., 1981-84, Victim-Witness Adv. Bd., 1981-94. Recipient Bancroft-Whitney award for Excellence in Criminal Procedure, 1973. Mem. Santa Clara County Bar Assn. (trustee 1979—), Santa Clara County Women Lawyers Com. (exec. bd. 1979-80), Sanata Clara Law Sch. Alumni Assn. (v.p. 1977, pres. 1978), Nat. Women's Polit. Caucus, Assn. of Bay Area Govts. (exec. bd. 1981-86). Office: US House Reps 118 Cannon House Office Bldg Washington DC 20515-0516 also: 635 N First St Ste B San Jose CA 95112*

LOFTHOUSE, RUSS WILBERT, school administrator; b. Chgo., Jan. 21, 1945; s. Russell Wilber and Anne Marie (Daker) L.; m. Pamlin I. Axelson, Aug. 7, 1976; one child, James. BA in Elem. Edn., U. Denver, 1971; MA in Elem. Edn., U. Colo., Denver, 1978, PhD in Edn., 1991. Cert. elem tchr., Colo., elem. prin., Colo. Tchr. Cherry Creek Schs., Englewood, Colo., 1971-86, prin., 1986—; mem. adv. bd. Teaching and Computers, N.Y.C., 1986—. Recipient Disting. Tchr. award Cherry Creek Schs., 1985; named Colo. Tchr. of Yr., Colo. Dept. Edn., 1986; runner-up Nat. Tchr. of Yr., 1986. Mem. Assn. Supervision and Curriculum Devel., Am. Acad. and Inst. Human Reason (dir. community leaders and succesful schs.), Fulbrite Tchrs. Alumni Assn., NEA, Nat. State Tchs. of Yr., Phi Delta Kappa. Home and Office: 8505 E Temple Dr Apt 502 Denver CO 80237-2545

LOFTIN, ORRIN KEITH, career officer; b. Fayetteville, N.C., Mar. 16, 1960; s. Leonza and Willie Elizabeth (Adams) L.; m. Sandra Denise Chisholm, Apr. 3, 1985; 1 child, Jauté Desireé, Procasius Darnell. BS in Math., Fayetteville State U., 1984; MA in Space Sys. and Computer Sys., Webster U., 1992. Enlisted USAF, 1985, advanced through grades to capt., 1985—; pres., founder Loftin, Algorithms, Inc., 1993-94. Author: (poetry) Infinity of Blue, The Rent, Am. Poetry Assn. award, 1990. Republican. Presbyterian. Home: 3805 7th St NE Trlr 114 Great Falls MT 59404-1155

LOFTUS, THOMAS DANIEL, lawyer; b. Seattle, Nov. 8, 1930; s. Glendon Francis and Martha Helen (Wall) L. BA, U. Wash., 1952, JD, 1957. Bar: Wash. 1958, U.S. Ct. Appeals (9th cir.) 1958, U.S. Dist. Ct. Wash. 1958, U.S. Ct. Mil. Appeals 1964, U.S. Supreme Ct. 1964. Trial atty. Northwestern Mut. Ins. Co., Seattle, 1958-62; sr. trial atty. Unigard Security Ins. Co., Seattle, 1962-68, asst. gen. counsel, 1969-83, govt. rels. counsel, 1983-89; of counsel Groshong, LeHet & Thornton, 1990—; mem. Wash. Commn. on Jud. Conduct (formerly Jud. Qualifications Commn.), 1982-88, vice-chmn., 1987-88; judge pro tem Seattle Mcpl. Ct., 1973-81; mem. nat. panel of mediators Arbitration Forums, Inc., 1990—. Sec., treas. Seattle Opera Assn., 1980-91; pres., bd. dirs. Vis. Nurse Svcs., 1979-88; pres., v.p. Salvation Army Adult Rehab. Ctr., 1979-86; nat. committeeman Wash. Young Rep. Fedn., 1961-63, vice chmn., 1963-65; pres. Young Reps. King County, 1962-63; bd. dirs. Seattle Seafair, Inc., 1975; bd. dirs., gen. counsel Wash. Ins. Coun., 1984-86, sec., 1986-88, v.p., 1988-90, Am. Mediation Panel of Mediators; bd. dirs. Arson Alarm Found., 1987-90; bd. visitors law sch. U. Wash., 1993—. 1st lt. U.S. Army, 1952-54, col. Res., 1954-85. Fellow Am. Bar Found.; mem. Am. Arbitration Assn. (nat. panel arbitrators 1965—), Am. Arbitration Forums, Inc. (nat. panel arbitrators 1992), Am. Mediation Panel, Wash. Bar Assn. (gov. 1981-84), Seattle King County Bar Assn. (sec., trustee 1977-82), ABA (ho. of dels. 1984-90), Internat. Assn. Ins. Counsel, U.S. People to People (del. Moscow internat. law-econ. conf. 1990), Def. Rsch. Inst., Wash. Def. Trial Lawyers Assn., Wash. State Trial Lawyers Assn., Am. Judicature Soc., Res. Officers Assn., Judge Advocate General's Assn., U. Wash. Alumni Assn., Coll. Club Seattle, Wash. Athletic Club, Masons, Shriners, Ranier Club, Pi Sigma Alpha, Delta Sigma Rho, Phi Delta Phi, Theta Delta Chi. Republican. Presbyterian. Home: 3515 Magnolia Blvd W Seattle WA 98199-1841 Office: 2133 3rd Ave Seattle WA 98121-2321

LOGAN, APRIL CHARISE, lawyer; b. Wauconda, Ill., Oct. 6, 1952; d. G. Edwin and Virginia June (Walker) L. BS in Biology and Genetics, Aurora (Ill.) U., 1974; MS in Human Med. Genetics, Ind. U., 1977; JD, U. Tulsa Coll. Law, 1985. Bar: Calif. 1985, U.S. Patent Office 1989, U.S. Ct. Appeals (fed. cir.) 1990. Rsch. asst. dept. med. genetics Ind. U., Indpls., 1974-77; geneticist, med. educator Indpls. Sickle Cell Ctr., 1977-78; lectr. histology Marian Coll., Indpls., 1978; vol. technologist genetics dept. Children's Med. Ctr., Tulsa, 1979-82; instr. biology Oral Roberts U., Tulsa, 1978-1984; assoc. Rogers & Wells, San Diego, 1985-86, Adams, Duque & Hazeltine, San Diego, 1986-87, Spensley Horn Jubas & Lubitz, San Diego, 1987-88, Knobbe, Martens, Olson & Bear, San Diego, 1988-91; with Office of Patent Counsel The Scripps Rsch. Inst., La Jolla, Calif., 1991—. Contbr. poetry to lit. mags. Recipient Gold Ivy Leaf award Aurora U., 1974; doctoral tng. grantee Ind. U., 1976. Mem. ABA, Am. Intellectual Property Law Assn., San Diego County Bar Assn., San Diego Intellectual Property Law Assn. (sec.-treas. 1990-91, v.p. 1991-92, pres. 1992-93), Biotech. in Cyte, Fed. Cir. Bar Assn., Licensing Execs. Soc., Calif. Women Lawyers, Mensa, Beta Beta Beta, Phi Delta Phi. Republican. Office: Office of Patent Counsel The Scripps Rsch Inst TPC-8 10666 N Torrey Pines Rd La Jolla CA 92037-1027

LOGAN, GLENN RAYMOND, mental health professional, counselor; b. Indio, Calif., Mar. 23, 1937; s. Raymond Nelson Logan and Ardis Lenore (McComb) Mangold; m. Rosalie Theresa Gallegos, Oct. 5, 1956; children: Glenn M., Benjamin N., Leonard F., James R., Patricia L., Karen M. BS in Mil. Sci., U. Md., 1969; MA in Counseling, U. Colo., 1989. Lic. profl. counselor, Colo.; cert. sr. chem. addictions counselor, Colo. Enlisted U.S. Army, 1953, advanced through grades to 1st lt., 1960, intelligence analyst, 1961-72, sr. intelligence ops. supr., 1972-74, ret., 1974; CEO Techtran Corp., Glen Burnie, Md., 1974-77, GlenRo Inc., Colorado Springs, Colo., 1977-87; counselor The Ark, Green Mountain Falls, Colo., 1991-92, Vet. Ctr., Colorado Springs, 1993—. Contbr. articles to profl. jours. Mgr. Little League, Odenton, Md., 1966-76; comdg. officer U.S. Naval Sea Cadets, Colorado Springs, 1986. Maj. USAR. Decorated twelve air medals. Mem. Assn. Former Intelligence Officers (life), Disabled Am. Vets. (life), Ret. Officers Assn. (life), Vietnam Vets. Am. (life, chpt. sec. 1989-90), Vets. of Underage Mil. Svc. (charter), Clin. Mental Health Counselors Assn. Republican. Roman Catholic.

LOGAN, JAMES SCOTT, SR., emergency management program specialist; b. Stanford, Ky., June 18, 1948; s. James M.H. and Lillian Elizabeth (Givens) L.; m. Rose Marie Helm, Aug. 31, 1968; children: James Matthew, Tasha Marie. AA, Columbia (Mo.) Coll., 1990, BS/BA cum laude, 1992; postgrad., U. Colo., 1992—. Unit adminstr. USAR, Lakewood, Colo., 1972-82; continuity of govt. planner Fed. Emergency Mgmt. Agy. Region VIII, Lakewood, 1983-90, tech. hazards program specialist, 1991-92, sr. tech. hazards program specialist, 1992-95; team leader state and local programs Fed. Emergency Mgmt. Agy. Region VIII, Lakewood, Colo., 1995—; exercise planning co-dir. Fed. Emergency Mgmt. Agy., Region VIII, Denver, 1992-95; bd. dirs. Rocky Mountain Human Svcs. Coalition, 1995—. Mem. NAACP, Denver, 1992; mem. NCOA NCO Assn., Devner, 1979—; mem. citizen's adv. com. polit. sci. dept. U. Colo., Denver. With U.S. Army, 1968-71, Vietnam, USAR, 1973—. Decorated Meritorious Svc. medal. Mem. VFW, Am. Legion, Pi Sigma Alpha. Democrat. Baptist. Home: 16952 E Bates Ave Aurora CO 80013-2243 Office: FEMA Region VIII PO Box 25267 Bldg 710A Denver CO 80225-0267

LOGAN, LEE ROBERT, orthodontist; b. L.A., June 24, 1923; s. Melvin Duncan and Margaret (Seltzer) L.; m. Maxine Nadler, June 20, 1975; children: Fritz, Dean, Scott, Gigi, Chad, Casey. BS, UCLA, 1952; DDS, Northwestern U., 1956, MS, 1961. Diplomate Am. Bd. Orthodontics. Gen. practice dentistry, Reseda, Calif., 1958-59; practice dentistry specializing in orthodontics, Northridge, Calif., 1961—; pres. Lee R. Logan DDS Profl. Corp.; mem. med. staff Northridge Hosp., Tarzana Hosp., dir. dentist edn.; owner Maxine's Prodn. Co.; owner Maxine's Talent Agy.; guest lectr. UCLA, U. So. Calif., dir dental edn. Northridge Med. Ctr. Contbr. articles to profl. jours. Served to lt. USNR, 1956-58. Named (with wife) Couple of Yr. Autistic Children Assn., 1986; recipient Nat. Philanthropy award, 1987, 1st Pl. winner Austistic Jogathon, 1981-95, 1st Pl. winner Best Treated Orthodontic Cases So. Calif., 1990. Mem. Am., San Fernando Valley Dental Assn (v.p.), Am. Assn. Orthodontists, Pacific Coast Soc. Orthodontists (dir., pres. so. sect. 1974-75, chmn. membership 1981-83), Found. Orthodontic Research (charter mem.), Calif. Soc. Orthodontists (chmn. peer rev. 1982-93), G.V. Black Soc. (charter mem.), Angle Soc. Orthodontists (pres. 1981-82, bd. dirs. 1982-95, nat. pres. 1985-87, dir. 1985—), U. S.C. Century Fraternity, Xi Psi Phi. Home: 4830 Encino Ave Encino CA 91316-3813 Office: 18250 Roscoe Blvd Northridge CA 91325-4226

LOGAN, STEVE DEAN, pharmacy administrator; b. Portland, Oreg., July 22, 1953; s. Norman Dean and Kathleen Ruth (Anderson) L.; m. Sally Gail Garrison, Aug. 7, 1982; children: Sarah Abigail, Rachel Elizabeth. BS in Pharmacy, Oreg. State U., 1980. Asst. dir. pharmacy Gresham (Oreg.) Comty. Hosp., 1981-82; dir. pharmacy Physicians and Surgeons Hosp., Portland, 1982-84; dir. pharmacy location Kaiser Permanente, Portland, 1984—. Mem. Oreg. Soc. Hosp. Pharmacists (ann. seminar com. mem.). Office: Kaiser Permanente 19500 SE Stark St Portland OR 97233-5757

LOGE, GARY WAYNE, scientist; b. Evansville, Ind., June 23, 1951; s. Howard Ellis and Doris Elizabeth (Elmendorf) L. BS in Chemistry, Purdue U., 1973; MS in Chemistry, U. Cin., 1976; PhD in Chem. Physics, Ind. U., 1979. Postdoctoral rsch. assoc. Cornell U., Ithaca, N.Y., 1980-81; postdoctoral staff photochemistry and photophysics group Los Alamos (N.Mex.) Nat. Lab., 1981-84, staff mem. photochemistry and photophysics group, 1984-90, guest scientist isotope geochemistry group, 1991-93, subcontractor to Ewing Tech. Design, Inc., 1993-94; pres. Laser Diagnostics, Los Alamos, 1992—. Contbr. articles to tech. jours. Mem. Am. Chem. Soc., Optical Soc. Am., Toastmasters Internat. Office: Laser Diagnostics PO Box 4627 35 Bonnieview Dr Ste B Los Alamos NM 87544

LOGES, WILLIAM EARL, communications educator; b. Chgo., May 17, 1961; s. James and Beverly Jane (McGuire) L.; m. Cathleen Lynn Armstead, Feb. 14, 1986 (div. July 1, 1992); 1 child, Jessica Rachel Armstead-Loges. BA in Comm., U. Calif., San Diego, 1983; MA in Comm. Theory, U. So. Calif., L.A., 1989, PhD in Comm. Theory, 1992. Unit supr. Travelers Ins. Co., Brea, Calif., 1983-86; rsch. asst. Annenberg Sch. for Comm., L.A., 1986-92; lectr. comm. Loyola Marymount U., L.A., 1990-92, U. Denver, 1992-95; asst. prof. Baylor U., Waco, Tex., 1995—; vis. assoc. prof. comms. U. So. Calif., L.A., 1994. Contbr. articles to profl. jours. Mem. Am. Sociol. Assn., Internat. Comm. Assn. Democrat.

LOGGANS, SUSAN VON BROCKHOEFT, nurse; b. New Orleans, June 29, 1955; d. George Emmett and Dorothy Claire (Castellano) Von Brockhoeft; m. Joseph Stewart Loggans, May 12, 1977. BS in Nursing La. State U., New Orleans, 1977. Cert. rehab. nurse. Staff nurse Oktibbeha County Gen. Hosp., Starkville, Miss., 1977-78, Lowdnes County Gen. Hosp., Columbus, Miss., 1978-79, F.E. Hebert Hosp., New Orleans, 1979-81; asst. unit dir. East Jefferson Hosp., Metairie, La., 1981-87; charge nurse Health South Rehabilitation Ctr., 1987-88, Touro Infirmary Rehabilitation Unit, 1989-93; staff nurse SW Wash. Med. Ctr., 1993-94; clin. mgr. Covington Med. and Rehab. Ctr., Vancover, Wash., 1995—. Mem. Ctr. for Costal Studies, Rehab. Nurses Assn. Republican. Home and Office: 14706 SE 5th Cir Vancouver WA 98684-7417

LOGGINS, WILLIAM CONLEY, industrial engineer; b. Springfield, Ohio, July 15, 1953; s. Harvey Quinn and Madelyn Mary (Conley) Licklider. BS in Psychology, Wright State U., 1977; MEd in Counseling and Guidance, U. Ariz., 1981, MS in Indsl. Engring., 1989. Social worker Head Start, Dayton, Ohio, 1976-78; collective mem. Small Planet Bakery, Tucson, 1978-81; human rels. trainer Prescott, Ariz., 1982-83; domestic violence counselor Tucson Ctr. for Women and Children, Tucson, 1983-84; info. engr. Tucson Med. Ctr., 1987; indsl. engr. Allied Signal Aerospace Co., 1987; ops. analyst Tucson Pub. Libr., 1987-88; tech. analyst Pima (Ariz.) Assn. of Govts., 1988-89; info. analyst Evans and Sutherland Computer Corp., 1989-91; data analyst and info. engr. Execusoft, Inc., 1992-94; indsl. engr. Merit Decision Tech., Inc., Salt Lake City, 1993—. Youth leader and career night organizer St. Francis in the Foothills Meth. Ch., Tucson, 1986-89; tennis instr. and youth leader Parks and Recreation Dept./YMCA, Springfield, 1970-73. Mem. ACM Spl. Interest Groups on Human Computer Interaction and Simulation, No. Utah Computer-Human Interaction Spl. Interest Group of ACM, Toastmasters (Award for best table topic and humor speeches 1993), Wasatch Mountain Club (bd. dirs. 1991-92, Outstanding Leader 1991, 93). Office: Merit Decision Techs Inc 1422 E 7380 S Salt Lake City UT 84121

LOGIE, DENNIS WAYNE, minister; b. Longmont, Colo., Mar. 18, 1940; s. Wayne Edward and Fern Maxine (Jacobson) L.; m. Burgl Dagmar Kaiser, Jan. 15, 1961; children: Hans Dennis, Heidi Elisabeth. Student, Stanford U., 1958-60, Fuller Sem., 1978. Ordained to ministry Christian Ch., 1977. Systems officer Crocker Nat. Bank, San Francisco, 1964-76, dir. data processing edn., 1976-78; minister 1st Christian Ch., Redwood City, Calif., 1978-81, sr. minister, 1981—; del. Heavenly Hills Christian Camp, Twain-Harte, Calif., 1978—; founder, bd. dirs. No. Calif. Ministers Retreat, San Rafael, Calif., 1983—. Contbr. articles and essays to various publs. Mem. parents adv. group Selby Ln. Sch., Atherton, Calif., 1974-76; treas. Band-Aids, Woodside (Calif.) H.S., 1976-79; co-founder, bd. dirs. Lay Inst. for Tng., Redwood City, 1976-81; bd. dirs. San Jose (Calif.) Christian Coll., 1976-82, 88-94; founding mem. South County Coalition for Prevention of Substance Abuse, 1991—; chaplain Redwood City Police Dept., 1994—. Mem. No. Calif. Evangelistic Assn. (bd. dirs. 1987--), Redwood City Clergy Assn. (pres. 1979-85, 88--), Calif. PTA (life). Republican. Home: 164 Oakfield Ave Redwood City CA 94061-3622 Office: 1st Christian Ch 233 Topaz St Redwood City CA 94062-2817

LOH, EDITH KWOK-YUEN, oncology nurse; b. Hong Kong, May 1, 1948; came to U.S., 1972; d. Chun Wing and Pui King (Chan) Lee; m. Kevin Kai-Tsu Loh, Mar. 30, 1972; children: Elizabeth, Jennifer, Jeffrey. RN, Hong Kong Govt. Nursing Sch., 1971, Tex. Woman's U., 1976; BSN magna cum laude, Hawaii Loa Coll., 1989; MPH, U. Hawaii, 1990, postgrad., 1994—. RN, Hawaii, Tex., Hong Kong, Eng. Student gen. nurse Hong Kong Govt. Hosps., 1968-70; pediatric nurse Queen Elizabeth Hosp., Hong Kong, 1971-72; head nurse oncology Ctr. Pavillion Hosp., Houston, 1972-75; oncology nurse Dr. Kevin Loh, Inc., Honolulu, 1978-90; nurse coord., health instr. Hawaii Hematology, Oncology, Inc., Honolulu, 1991-92; vol. rschr. immunol. studies U. Hawaii, 1990; health instr. baby S.A.F.E. Dept. Health, Honolulu, 1993-94; presenter Am. Indian and Alaska Native Caucus 123d ann meeting, APHA, San Diego, 1995. Vol. recruitor Hawaii Bone Marrow Donor Registry, Honolulu, 1992; chmn. cmty. svc. com., Honolulu, 1992—; dir. Health Svcs. for Sr. Citizens, 1993; bd. dirs. Hawaii Cancer Children Found., 1992-94. Mem. AMA, Am. Cancer Soc., Soc. for Pub. Health Edn.-Hawaii (bd. dirs., sec. life), Orgn. Chinese Am. Women, Associated Chinese Univ. Women, Inc. (chmn. welfare com. 1992, chmn. cmty. svc. com. 1991—, mem. in parliamentary procedure legis. com. 1992), Soc. Pub. Health Edn. (bd. dirs., sec. 1992, 93, bd. dirs. 1994), Sigma Theta Tau. Home: 1815 Kumakani Pl Honolulu HI 96821-1327

LOHMAN, LORETTA CECELIA, social scientist, consultant; b. Joliet, Ill., Sept. 25, 1944; d. John Thomas and Marjorie Mary (Brennan) L. BA in Polit. Sci., U. Denver, 1966, postgrad., 1985—; MA in Social Sci., U. No. Colo., 1975. Lectr. Ariz. State U., Tempe, 1966-67; survey researcher Merrill-Werthlin Co., Tempe, 1967-68; edn. asst. Am. Humane Assn., Denver, 1969-70; econ. cons. Lohman & Assocs., Littleton, Colo., 1971-75; rsch. assoc. Denver Rsch. Inst., 1976-86; rsch. scientist Milliken Chapman Rsch. Group, Littleton, 1986-89; owner Lohman & Assocs., Littleton, 1989—; affiliate Colo. Water Resources Rsch. Inst., Ft. Collins, Colo., 1989-91; tech. adv. com. Denver Potable Wastewater Demo Plant, 1986-90; cons. Constrn. Engring. Rsch. Lab., 1984—; peer reviewer NSF, 1985-86, Univs. Coun. Water Resources, 1989—; WERC consortium reviewer N.Mex. Univs.-U.S. Dept. Energy, 1989—; course cons. Regis Coll., Denver, 1992—. Contbr. articles to profl. jours. Vol. Metro Water Conservation Projects, Denver, 1986-90; vol. handicapped fitness So. Suburban Parks and Recreation. Recipient Huffsmith award Denver Rsch. Inst., 1983; Nat. Ctr. for Edn. in Politics grantee, 1964-65. Mem. ASCE (social and environ. objectives com.), Am. Water Works Assn., Am. Water Resources Assn., Orgn. Am. Historians, Colo. Water Congress, Water Environ. Fedn., Sigma Xi, Pi Gamma Mu, Phi Alpha Theta. Democrat. Home and Office: 3375 W Aqueduct Ave Littleton CO 80123-2903

LOHN, ROGER LOWELL, management consultant; b. Wessington Springs, S.D., Feb. 6, 1934; s. Kenneth Fairbairn and Irma Gladys Lohn; m. Eleanor Terlinden, Nov. 7, 1958; children: Cinty Lou, Mark David, Matthew Eric. Student, Phoenix Jr. Coll., 1958-60, Ariz. State U., 1960-63. Quality assurance technician Sperry Phoenix, 1950-60; engr. Motorola Mil., 1961-65; reliability product mgr. Siemens, Scottsdale, Ariz., 1965-67; dir. quality assurance Motorola Mobile Comm. Products, Fort Worth, 1967-83; dir. quality and productivity Codex-Phoenix Ops., 1983-86; mgr. reliability and quality assurance Motorola, Inc., Schaumburg, Ill., 1986—, mem. semiconductor group, 1987-91, cons., 1991—. Editor: The Quality System, 1981, revised, 1990.contbr. articles to profl. jours. lst lt. USAF, 1952-57. Mem. Am. Soc. Quality Control (various com. positions). Home: 145 N Centennial Way Mesa AZ 85201-6750

LOHR, GEORGE E., state supreme court justice; b. 1931. BS, S.D. State U.; JD, U. Mich. Bar: Colo. 1958, Calif. 1969. Former judge Colo. 9th Dist. Ct., Aspen; assoc. justice Colo. Supreme Ct., Denver, 1979—. Office: Supreme Ct Colo State Judicial Bldg 2 E 14th Ave Denver CO 80203-2115

LOHRE, JOHN OWEN, retired leasing company executive; b. Vermillion, S.D., Apr. 21, 1932; s. George Herman and Sanna (Nelson) L.; m. Mary Belle Biggert, Aug. 6, 1960; children: Kathryn, Philip. BS, U. S.D., 1954; MBA, Harvard U., 1959. With Chgo. Bridge and Iron Co., 1959-65; v.p. First Nat. Bank of Chgo., 1965-74; with First Mcpl. div. BancOne Leasing Corp., Denver, 1974-93, pres., 1980-93. Treas. Cmty. Renewal Soc., Chgo., 1973-74; bd. dirs. Crow Canyon Ctr. for Southwestern Archaeology, 1985-93, Cascade Village Met. Dist., 1985. 1st lt. U.S. Army, 1955-57. Mem. University Club Chgo., Harvard Club, Harvard Bus. Sch. of Colo. (v.p. 1979-80, dir. 1980—, pres. 1986-87), Cherry Hills Country, Denver Athletic, Eagle Springs Golf Club. Presbyterian. Home: 3333 E Florida Ave Apt 122 Denver CO 80210-2539 Office: 333 Logan St Ste 203 Denver CO 80203-4089

LOKA, RAGHAVENDRA RAO, software engineer; b. Angara, India, Apr. 4, 1954; came to U.S., 1976; s. Vyasa Rao and Seshuparavati (Angara) L. B of Tech., Indian Inst. of Tech., Madras, India, 1976; MS, Case Western Res. U., 1979, Ind. U., 1980; PhD, Ind. U., 1986. Software engr. Digital Equipment Corp., Nashua, N.H., 1981-83; lectr. U. N.C., Charlotte, 1985-86; mem. tech. staff AT&T Bell Labs., Naperville, Ill., 1986-90; staff software engring. Microtec Rsch. Inc., Santa Clara, Calif., 1990—. Contbr. articles to profl. jours. Mem. ASME, Assn. of Computing Machinery, IEEE Computer Soc. Home: 1145 Amarillo Ave Apt 10 Palo Alto CA 94303-3711 Office: Microtec Rsch Inc 2350 Mission College Blvd Santa Clara CA 95054-1532

LOKEY, FRANK MARION, JR., broadcast executive, consultant; b. Ft. Worth, Oct. 15, 1924; s. Frank Marion Sr. and Corinne (Whaley) L. Student, Smith-Hughes Evening Coll., 1955-59. Asst. gen. mgr., mgr. sales, news anchor Sta. WLW-A TV (now named WXIA-TV), Atlanta, 1955-66; co-owner, gen. mgr. Sta. WAIA, Atlanta, 1960-62; S.E. news corr., talk show host CBS News N.Y., N.Y.C., 1960-66; asst. to owner, gen. mgr. Sta. WBIE-AM-FM, Atlanta, 1962-64; asst. to pres., gen. mgr. Stas. KXAB-TV, KXJB-TV, KXMB-TV, Aberdeen, Fargo, Bismarck, S.D., N.D., 1966-67; exec. v.p., gen. mgr. St. WEMT-TV, Bangor, Maine, 1967-70; pres., gen. mgr. Stas. KMOM-TV, KWAB-TV, Odessa-Midland, Big Spring, Tex., 1970-75; exec. v.p., gen. mgr. Sta. KMUV-TV (now named KRBK-TV), Sacramento, Calif., 1975-77; CEO Lokey Enterprises, Inc., Sacramento, L.A., El Centro, Calif., 1977—, also chmn. bd. dirs.; cons., Troubleshooter 16 TV stas. nationwide, 1977—; cons., actor 5 movie prodn. cos., Hollywood, Calif., 1980—; cons., outside dir. Anderson Cons., Manhattan, L.I., N.Y., 1981—; network talk show host/news corr. for 7 news orgns. worldwide, 1984—; bd. dirs. Broadcast Audience Behavior Rsch., Manhattan, 1986—, mem. inner circle, 1986—; owner franchise The Party Place. Creator, originator approach to real estate mktg. Hon. mem. Imperial County Bd. Suprs., El Centro, 1986—, El Centro City Coun., 1987—. Mem. Am. Legion. Baptist. Home: 592 Wensley Ave El Centro CA 92243-3955 Office: Lokey Enterprises Inc 626 W Main St El Centro CA 92243-2920

LOKEY, R. EUGENE, legislative consultant; b. Washington, Ga., Sept. 3, 1944; s. Walter Eugene and Zelma (May) L. BA, San Jose State U., 1966, BA, 1968, MA, 1974. Pres., Calif. Planners & Cons., Sacramento, 1970—; ptnr. Patrick Andrews Advt. Co., San Jose, 1974-75; pres. Save-A-Bee, San Jose, 1975-83; dir. Physicians and Surgeons Ins. Exchange, Los Angeles, 1976—. Contbr. articles to profl. jours. Pres., San Jose Dem. Club, 1972, San Jose Community Theatre, 1973; bd. dirs. Frances Gulland Child Care Ctr., San Jose, 1974; mem. Data Confidentiality Commn., Santa Clara County, 1980; bd. dirs. Nat. Council Alternative Health Care Policy, 1984. Recipient La Torre award San Jose State U., 1968; Community Service award Nat. Assn. Social Workers, 1970. Mem. Am. Polit. Sci. Assn., Am. Assn. Polit. Cons., San Jose Airport Assn. (bd. dirs.), Tau Delta Phi, Psi Sigma Alpha. Home: 5875 Gloria Dr Apt 5 Sacramento CA 95822-3294 Office: Calif Planners and Cons Inc 1029 K St Ste 48 Sacramento CA 95814-3816

LOKKEN, FRED BRUCE, political scientist, educator; b. La Crosse, Wis., Nov. 4, 1955; s. Lawrence A. and Theresa E. (Kloss) L.; m. Sandra K. Mc Millen, May 16, 1987; children: Theresa M., Sean A. BS, U. Wis.-La Crosse, 1977; MA, Wash. State U., 1979; doctoral candidate, U. B.C., Vancouver, 1985—. Project coord. Cmty. Housing Resource Bd., La Crosse, Wis., 1982-85; instr., asst. prof. U. Wis.-La Crosse, 1982-85, 87-91; mem. faculty Truckee Meadows C.C., Reno, 1991—, chair dept social scis./humanities, 1994; social sci. divsn. senator Truckee Meadows C.C., Reno, 1992—, commr. strategic planning commn., 1993—, chair acad. stds. com. faculty senate, 1993—, chair internat. edn. com., 1991-92, chair election com., 1993—, mem. curriculum com. faculty senate, 1992, mem. strategic planning commn. taskforce, 1992. Chair City of Sparks Mayor's Com./Citizen's Adv. Com., 1992-95; mem. tech. com. Sparks Redevel. Authority, 1992—; mem. Washoe At Risk Taskforce/Washoe County Sch. Dist., 1993—, Quality of Life Taskforce/Truckee Meadows Regional Planning Commn. Govt. and Edn. Coms., 1993—; commr. Sparks Planning Commn., 1995—. Recipient U.S. Housing and Urban Devel. Recognition award, 1985, Outstanding Young American award, 1988, Outstanding Tchr. of Yr. award, 1992-93, Outstanding Educator award UCCSN, 1995. Mem. Western Polit. Sci. Assn., Midwest Polit. Sci. Assn., Wis. Inst.: A Consortium for the Study of War, Peace and Global Cooperation, Internat. Conflict Mgmt. Assn. Home: 1256 Pullman Dr Sparks NV 89434-4046 Office: Truckee Meadows C C 7000 Dandini Blvd Reno NV 89512-3901

LOLMAUGH, SCOTT DEVERE, engineering executive; b. Ann Arbor, Mich., Nov. 17, 1955; s. Starr Devere and Marjorie Adella (Anderson) L.; m. Constance Elisa Alamat, Aug. 23, 1975; children: Jacob Scott, Katrina Charity. BS in Indsl. Engring., Ea. Mich. U., 1978. Ordained to ministry, Chrisitan Ch., 1991. Assoc. indsl. engring. Burroughs Corp., Plymouth, Mich., 1979-81; indsl. engr. Universal Elec. Co., Owosso, Mich., 1981-82; staff indsl. engr. Wavetek Ind., Inc., Beech Grove, 1982-87; sr. mfg. engr. United Med. Mfg., Indpls., 1987-90; prin. prodn. engr. Honeywell, Inc. IAC, Phoenix, 1990—; owner, CEO Soft Answers, Indpls., 1982—; tech. cons. IPC

Video, Ranchos De Taos, N.Mex., 1982—. Mem. ASTM, Suface Mount Tech. Assn. (chmn. 1988-89), Internat. Soc. for Hybrid Microelectronics, Inst. of Indsl. Engrs., Am. Soc. for Quality Control, Instrument Soc. Am., Soc. of Packaging and Handling Engrs., Wavetek PC Users Group (founder, pres. 1984-87). Republican. Home: 1017 W Muriel Dr Phoenix AZ 85023-2655 Office: Honeywell Inc MS A15 IAC 2500 W Union Hills Dr Phoenix AZ 85027

LOMBARD, LAWRENCE JOHN, chemical dependency counselor; b. Seattle, June 5, 1952; s. John Cutler and Dorothy Marie (Brandt) L.; m. Helen Angela Crannell-Godeloson, Mar. 13, 1973 (div. Feb. 1987); children: Christopher, Lisa, Michael. BS in Pharmacy,BA in History of Medicine, U. Wash., 1979; AAS in Chem. Dependency Counseling, Shoreline C.C., Seattle, 1988. Cert. chem. dependency counselor level II. Rsch. scientist U. Wash., 1972-77; staff pharmacist Group Health Hosp., 1974-79; hosp. pharmacist Swedish Hosp., 1980-83; cmty. pharmacist Eatonville (Wash.) Drugs, 1984-86; group leader north rehab. facility King County Jail, 1986; case mgr. Meridian Recovery Ctr., 1986-88, Eastside Alcohol Ctr., 1988-89; asst. dir. pharmacy svcs. Pharmacy Corp. Am., 1989-91; program adminstr. Coming 2, 1991-92; intake counselor CareUnit Hosp., Kirkland, Wash., 1992-93; case mgr. Lakeside Recovery Ctr., Everett, Wash., 1993—; v.p. Wash. State Coun. on Alcoholism and Drug Dependency, Bellevue, 1989—; pvt. practice cons., 1991—. Pres. Eatonville C. of C., 1984-86; lt. Vol. Fire Dept., 1984-86. Home: PO Box 771 Everett WA 98206-0771

LOMBARDI, EUGENE PATSY, orchestra conductor, violinist, educator, recording artist; b. North Braddock, Pa., July 7, 1923; s. Nunzio C. and Mary (Roberto) L.; m. Jacqueline Sue Davis, Mar. 1955; children: Robert, Genanne. BA, Westminster Coll., 1948; MA, Columbia U., 1948; Edn. Specialist, George Peabody Coll., 1972; MusD, Westminster Coll., 1981. Band dir. Lincoln High Sch., Midland, Pa., 1948-49; orch. dir. Male High Sch., Louisville, 1949-50, Phoenix Union High Sch., 1950-57; orch. dir., prof. Ariz. State U., Tempe, 1957-89. Condr. Phoenix Symphonette, 1954-61, 70-73, Phoenix Symphony Youth Orch., 1956-66, Phoenix Pops Orch., 1971-83, Fine Arts String Orch., 1995—; asst. concertmaster Phoenix Symphony Orch., 1950-62, concermaster, 1962-69, asst. condr., 1968-69; mem. Newart String Quartet, 1965-89; concertmaster Flagstaff Festival Symphony, 1967-81, Flagstaff Festival Chamber Orch., 1967-81, Phoenix Chamber Orch., 1970-83; condr., music dir. Sun City (Ariz.) Symphony Orch., 1983-87. Served with USAAF, 1943-46. Decorated Bronze Star; named Outstanding Grad. Westminster Coll., 1948; recipient Alumni Achievement award, 1976, gold medal Nat. Soc. Arts and Letters, 1973, Disting. Tchr. award Ariz. State U. Alumni, 1974, Phoenix Appreciation award, 1983. Mem. Music Educators Nat. Conf., Am. String Tchrs. Assn. (pres. Ariz. unit 1965-67), Am. Fedn. Musicians, Ariz. Music Educators Assn. (pres. higher edn. sect. 1973-75, Excellence in Teaching Music award 1989), Ind. Order Foresters, Phi Delta Kappa, Phi Mu Alpha. Republican. Presbyterian. Home: 920 E Manhatton Dr Tempe AZ 85282-5520

LOMELI, MARTA, elementary education educator; b. Tijuana, Baja Calif, Mex., Oct. 28, 1952; came to U.S. 1954; d. Jesus and Guadalupe (Ascencio) Lomeli; m. Rudolph Benitez, 1978 (div. 1982); children: Pascual Lomeli Benitez; m. David E. Miller, Aug. 16, 1991. BA, San Diego State U., 1977. With M & N Tree Nursery, Vista, Calif., 1957-70; libr. Vista Boys Club, 1969-70; vol. tutor MECHA U. Calif. San Diego, La Jolla, 1971-73; tchr. aide San Diego City Schs., 1976-77; bilingual educator National City (Calif.) Schs., 1978—; mem. restructuring com. Lincoln Acres Sch., 1991. Author numerous poems. Mem. Lincoln Acres Com. to Advise the Prin., National City, 1986-88, Com. to Advise the Supt., National City, 1986-88; art editor Lincoln Jr. H.S., Vista, Calif., 1964-65, Third World U. Calif., San Diego, 1970-73; mem. Lincoln Acres Sch. Site Coun., 1988-89; mem. high tech. com. Nat. Sch. Dist., 1993-94; vol. tchr. St. Vincent de Paul's Ctr. for Homeless, San Diego, 1991-93, Shaolin Kempo; mem. Paradise Hills Citizens Patrol, 1994—. Karate Black belt, 1st degree. Mem. Calif. Tchrs. Assn. (site rep. Nat. City 1985), Calif. Assn. Bilingual Edn. (sec. 1986), Nat. Assn. Bilingual Edn., La Raza Club (pres., co-founder 1970). Democrat. Home: 6920 Alsacia St San Diego CA 92139-2101

LOMELÍ, REFUGIO (JESSE LOMELÍ), athletics educator; b. Aguascalientes, Mex., July 23, 1941; came to U.S., 1954, naturalized, 1965; s. J. Jesus and Maria Guadalupe (Ascencio) L.; m. Barbara L. McMinn, Aug. 24, 1968; children: Lorena, Maya, Marc. Assoc., Palomar Coll., 1962; Bachelors degree, U. of the Americas, Mexico City, 1965; Masters degree, San Diego State U., 1972; postgrad., U. Pitts., 1972-74. Firefighter U.S. Forest Service, So. Calif. region, 1962-66; tchr. Santana H.S., Santee, Calif., 1967-73; counselor, tchr., soccer coach Mira Costa Coll., Oceanside, Calif., 1973—. Named Community Coll. Soccer Coach of Yr., Pacific Coast Conf., 1985. Mem. Nat. Assn. Fgn. Student Advisors, Am. G.I. Forum. Lodge: KC. Home: 1250 Vista Colina Dr San Marcos CA 92069-4956 Office: Mira Costa Coll PO Box 586312 Oceanside CA 92058-6312

LOND, HARLEY WELDON, editor, publisher; b. Chgo., Feb. 5, 1946; s. Henry Sidney and Dorothy (Shaps) L.; m. Marilyn Moss, Aug. 20, 1981. BA in Journalism, Calif. State U., L.A., 1972. Adminstrv. dir. Century City Ednl. Arts Project, L.A., 1972-76, hon. dir., 1982—; founder, editor Intermedia mag., L.A., 1974-80; prodn. mgr. FilmRow Publs., L.A., 1981; assoc. editor Box Office mag., Hollywood, Calif., 1981-84, editor, assoc. pub., 1984-94; dir. publs. Entertainment Data, Inc., 1994-95; pres. CyberPod Prodns., 1995—; syndicated columnist Continental Features, Washington, Tel-Aire Publs., Dallas, 1986—; hon dir. Monterey (Calif.) Film Festival, 1987; mem. media adv. bd. Cinetex Internat. Film Festival, 1988; cons. Take 3 Info. Svc. Editor: Entertainment Media Electronic Info. Svc.; contbr. articles to profl. publs. Calif. Arts Council grantee, 1975, Nat. Endowment for Arts grantee, 1976-77. Mem. MLA, Soc. Profl. Journalists, Assn. for Edn. in Journalism and Mass Communication, Speech Communication Assn., Soc. for Cinema Studies. Office: CyberPod Prodns 1109 Longwood Ave Los Angeles CA 90019

LONDON, ADELE, poet; b. Brussels, Aug. 25, 1930; came to U.S., 1952; d. Charles and Helen (Hecht) Lubin; m. Ed F. London, Sept. 17, 1960; 1 child, Alan Lewis. Student, U. Belgium. Underwriter Ins. Co., L.A., 1952-60; writer of short stories in English and French, 1960—, French poet, 1950—; provider readings for French groups in Calif. and Can., 1952. Author: Maintenant et Jadis, 1992, Sentiments, 1994; poems written in French publs., translated into English, 1993-94. Pres. L.A. PTA, 1972-74; other sch. offices. Mem. Alliance Francaise, 1939 Club.

LONDON, ANDREW BARRY, film editor; b. Bronx, N.Y., Jan. 1, 1949; s. Max Edward and Nellie (Steiner) L. BA in Cinema magna cum laude, U. So. Calif., 1970. Represented by Mont. Artists, Santa Monica, Calif. Prin. works include (features) The Meteor Man, 1993, F/X 2, 1991, Rambo III, 1988, Planes, Trains and Automobiles, 1987, Link, 1986, Cloak & Dagger, 1984, Psycho II, 1983, The True Story of Eskimo Nell, 1975, (TV shows) Don't Talk to Strangers, 1994, Day of Reckoning, 1993, Mortal Sins, 1992, Running Delilah, 1992, True Tales, 1992, Sweet Poison, 1991, Tales from the Crypt, 1989-90, (pilot) Beauty and the Beast, 1987, The Christmas Star, 1986; sound editor: Wolfen (MPSE Golden Reel award 1982), Hammett, Roadgames, Psycho II, I'm Dancing As Fast As I Can, Perfect, Protocol, Coal Miner's Daughter, The Long Riders, others. Mem. Acad. Motion Picture Arts and Scis., Motion Picture Sound Editors (Golden Reel award 1982), Phi Beta Kappa. Office: Montana Artists 2d Fl 625 Montana Ave Fl 2 Santa Monica CA 90403-1409

LONEGAN, THOMAS LEE, restaurant corporation executive; b. Kansas City, Mo., July 4, 1932; s. Thomas F. and Edna L. (Payton) L.; m. Donna F. Ednie, Apr. 11, 1958; children: Timothy L., John M. BSME, Gen. Motors Inst., 1955; MS in Mgmt., USN Post Grad Sch., 1963; grad., Indsl. Coll. Armed Forces, Washington, 1970; postgrad., Calif. State U., Long Beach, 1979-83; grad., Coll. for Fin. Planning, Denver, 1984. Registered profl. engr.; CFP. Commd. ensign USN, 1956, advanced through grades to comdr., 1978; dir. pub. works Naval Weapons Sta., Seal Beach, Calif., 1974-78; ret., 1978; dir. cen. staff McAthco Enterprises, Inc., Camarillo, Calif., 1985, exec. v.p., CFO, 1986-90, pres., CEO,, 1991-93, exec. v.p., CFO, 1994—; gen. ptnr. 4 restaurants, 1985—. Author: Analysis and Attenuation of Air Borne Noise in Industrial Plants, 1955, Formalized Training of Maintenance Personnel, 1963. Vol. various couns. Boy Scouts Am., 1968-74. Decorated Bronze Star with combat device, Meritorious Svc. medal, Jt. Svcs. Commendation medal, Navy Achievement medal; recipient Order of Chamoro Govt.of Guam; named Sr. Engr./Arch. Yr. Naval Facilities Engr. Command, 1972. Fellow Soc. Am. Mil. Engrs., Inst. CFP's, Ret. Officers Assn., GM Inst. Robots Honor Soc.; mem. Beta Gamma Sigma. Home: 8578 Amazon River Cir Fountain Valley CA 92708-5510 Office: McAthco Enterprises Inc 3687 Las Posas Rd Ste 188 Camarillo CA 93010-1431

LONERGAN, MICHAEL HENRY, development administrator, journalist; b. Richland, Wash., Sept. 19, 1949; s. Joseph Thornberg and Gertrude (Foxen) L.; m. Cyndi Lou Kniffin, Jan. 8, 1971 (div. 1981); m. Paula Elizabeth Wallace, Jan. 8, 1983; children: Joseph, Ricardo. Student, U. Chgo., 1967-69; BA in History, U. Wash., 1979. News reporter Sta. WTRC Radio, Sta. WSJV-TV, Elkhart, Ind., 1968-71; gen. mgr. Sta. KURB, Mountlake Terrace, Wash., 1972-73; advt. rep. Enterprise Newspaper, Lynnwood, Wash., 1974-77; news dir. Sta. KBRO-AM-FM, Bremerton, Wash., 1977-78; communications rep. Motorola, Inc., Bellevue, Wash., 1980-81; radio announcer Sta. KTNT/KPMA, Tacoma, 1981-84; dir. mktg. TAC-COMM, Tacoma, 1984-85; dir. community rels. The Salvation Army, Tacoma, 1985-92; exec. dir. Tacoma Rescue Mission, 1993—. Host Cityline TV program, 1992—. Rep. candidate 6th dist. U.S. Congress, Wash., 1984. Mem. NAACP, Tacoma N.W. Gideons (pres. 1990-94), Tacoma Downtown Kiwanis, Phi Beta Kappa. Mem. Christian Ch. Home: 3715 N 27th St Tacoma WA 98407-5810 Office: Tacoma Rescue Mission PO Box 1912 702 Pacific Ave Tacoma WA 98402-5208

LONERGAN, THOMAS FRANCIS, III, criminal justice consultant; b. Bklyn., July 28, 1941; s. Thomas Francis and Katherine Josephine (Roth) L.; m. Irene L. Kaucher, Dec. 14, 1963; 1 son, Thomas F. BA, Calif. State U., Long Beach, 1966, MA, 1973; MPA, Pepperdine U., L.A., 1976; postgrad., U. So. Calif., L.A., 1976. Dep. sheriff Los Angeles County Sheriff's Dept., 1963-70; U.S. Govt. program analyst, 1968—; fgn. service officer USIA, Lima, Peru, 1970-71; dep. sheriff to lt. Los Angeles Sheriff's Office, 1971-76, aide lt. to div. chief, 1976-80; dir. Criminal Justice Cons., Downey, Calif., 1977—; cons. Public Adminstrv. Service, Chgo., 1972-75, Nat. Sheriff's Assn., 1978, 79; cons. Nat. Inst. Corrections, Washington, 1977—, coordinator jail ctr., 1981-82 ; tchr. N. Calif. Regional Criminal Justice Acad., 1977-79; lectr. Nat. Corrections Acad., 1980-83; spl. master Chancery Ct. Davidson County, Tenn., 1980-82, U.S. Dist. Ct. (no. dist.) Ohio, 1984-85, Santa Clara Superior Ct. (Calif.), 1983-89, U.S. Dist. Ct. Ga., Atlanta, 1986-87, U.S. Dist. Ct. (no. dist.) Calif., 1982—, U.S. Dist. Ct. (no. dist.) Idaho, 1986, U.S. Dist. Ct. Oreg. 1986, U.S. Dist. Ct. Portland 1987, U.S. Dist. (no. dist.) Calif. 1984-89. Author: California-Past, Present & Future, 1968; Training-A Corrections Perspective, 1979; AIMS-Correctional Officer; Liability-A Correctional Perspective; Liability Law for Probation Administrators; Liability Reporter; Probation Liability Reporter; Study Guides by Aims Media. Mem. Am. Correctional Assn., Nat. Sheriff's Assn. Roman Catholic.

LONERGAN, WALLACE GUNN, economics educator, management consultant; b. Potlatch, Idaho, Mar. 18, 1928; s. Willis Gerald and Lois (Gunn) L.; m. Joan Laurie Penoyer, June 1, 1952; children: Steven Mark, Kevin James. BA, Coll. Idaho, 1950; MBA, U. Chgo., 1955, PhD, 1960. Asst. dir., asst. prof. bus. Indsl. Relations Ctr. U. Chgo., 1960-70, assoc. dir., assoc. prof., 1970-74, dir., prof., 1974-84; vis. prof. Rikkyo U., Tokyo, 1985; vis. fellow Merton Coll. Oxford (Eng.) U., 1986; chair, prof. bus., econs. divsn. Albertson Coll. Idaho, Caldwell, 1987—; v.p. Human Resources Research Cons., Chgo., 1980-87. Author: Leadership and Morale, 1960, Group Leadership, 1974, Performance Appriasal, 1978, Leadership and Management, 1979. Chmn. Episcopal Commn. on Higher Edn., Chgo., 1970-80, mgmt. com. United Way Chgo., 1982-85. 1st lt. U.S. Army, 1950-53, Korea. Named Disting. Alumni Coll. Idaho, 1962; vis. scholar Internat. Anglican Exchange, N.Y.C., 1976, Tokyo, 1986. Mem. Internat. House Japan, Internat. Indsl. Relations Research Assn., Acad. Mgmt., Rotary. Home: 812 E Linden St Caldwell ID 83605-5335 Office: Albertson Coll Idaho Bus Econs Divsn 2112 Cleveland Blvd Caldwell ID 83605-4432

LONG, ALEXIS BORIS, weather modification scientist, educator; b. N.Y.C., Sept. 9, 1944; s. Robert Long and Mary Elizabeth (Rogers) Fisk; m. Loretto Margaret Crowe, Sept. 7, 1974; children: Leonora Elizabeth, Andrew Alexis, Louisa Margaret. BA, Reed Coll., 1965; MS, Syracuse U., 1966; PhD, U. Ariz., 1972. Grad. assoc., NASA trainee, rsch. asst. U. Ariz., Tucson, 1966-72; NSF postdoctoral fellow divsn. cloud physics Commonwealth Sci. and Indsl. Rsch. Orgn., Sydney, NSW, Australia, 1972-73; rsch. assoc. U. Colo., Boulder, 1973-75; design and evaluation group head Nat. Ctr. for Atmospheric Rsch., Boulder, 1975-79; assoc. rsch. scientist, lectr. dept. meteorology Tex. A&M U., College Station, 1979-81; prin. rsch. scientist divsn. atmospheric rsch. Commonwealth Sci. and Indsl. Rsch. Orgn., Melbourne, Victoria, Australia, 1987-93; assoc. rsch. prof. Atmospheric Scis. Ctr., Reno, 1981—. Contbr. articles to sci. jours. and ency. Fellow Royal Meteorol. Soc.; mem. Am. Meteorol. Soc. (cert. cons. meteorologist 1984—, com. on cloud physics 1976-82), Am. Geophys. Union, Australian Meteorol. and Oceanographic Soc., Sigma Xi. Office: Desert Rsch Inst PO Box 60220 Reno NV 89506-0220

LONG, BETTY JEAN, library director; b. Olton, Tex., Aug. 30, 1951; d. Fred D. and Thelma Bennie (Cowart) L. BA, Tex. Woman's U., 1972, MLS, 1973. Br. libr. east br. Amarillo (Tex.) Pub. Libr., 1976-80; youth libr. southwest branch Amarilla (Tex.) Pub. Libr., 1973-74, youth libr. east branch, 1974-76; asst. coord. Tex. Panhandlw Libr. System, Amarillo, 1980-85; dir. Roswell (N.Mex.) Pub. Libr., 1985—; del. second N.Mex. Conf. on Librs. and Info. Svcs., 1991, White House Conf. on Librs. and Info. Svcs., 1993; chair adult basic edn. adv. coun. Eastern N.Mex. U., 1991-92, 92-93. Bd. dirs. N.Mex. Coalition for Literacy, 1989-91, co-chair pub. rels. com. 1990-91; sec. Roswell Literacy Coun., 1986, v.p. 1987, pres. 1988-89; sec. Altrusa Club of Roswell, 1987, dir. 1988-89, v.p. 1989-90, pres. 1990-91; v.p. Altrusa Found., 1992-93, pres. 1993-94; com. mem. Chaves County Courthouse Restoration and Preservation; K-6 com. mem. Reach 2000, 1990-91; steering com. Roswell Indep. Sch. Dist. Master Plan; active Friends of Roswell Pub. Libr., Chaves County Literacy Action Coalition. Mem. ALA, N.Mex. Libr. Assn. (chair conf. arrangements com. 1987, membership com. 1987-88, chair libr. devel. com. 1988-89, 93-94, co-chair conf. arrangements com. 1991, 2d v.p. 1995—), Mcpl. Librs. Assn. N.Mex. (mclp. leagud vice-chair 1987-88, chaor 1988-89), Los Pocos Locos (pres. 1990-91, 93-94), Roswell Rotary. Office: Roswell Pub Libr 301 N Pennsylvania Ave Roswell NM 88201-4663

LONG, DAVID R., cardiologist, internist, medical consultant. BA, Ohio Wesleyan U., 1944; MD, Western Res. U. Med. Sch., 1946. Diplomate Am. Bd. Internal Medicine; licensure: Ohio, 1946, Ariz., 1953, Calif., 1968, Nev., 1968. Rotating internship Cleve. City Hosp., 1946-47, internal medicine residency, 1948-50; pathology Crile Vets. Adminstrn. Hosp., Cleve., 1947-48; examining physician Armed Forces Induction Sta., 1950-51; chief of medicine Luke AFB, 1951, Williams AFB, 1951-53; pvt. practice, 1953-72; dir. med. care delivery sys. Ariz. Health Plan, 1973-76, dept. head cardiology, 1972-83; med. dir., v.p. med. affairs Sunworld Internat. Airways, Las Vegas, 1981-86; dir. cardiac rehabilitation St. Luke's Hosp., Phoenix, 1983-94; clinic dir. Ariz. Diagnostic Cardiology, P.C., Phoenix, 1983-87; dir. Occupl. Health Network, Phoenix, 1987-88; dir. exec. health program, 1987-94; contract cardiologist Cigna Health Plan, Phoenix, 1988-92; med. dir. VIP/PHN PPO, 1989—, contract cardiologist, internist, 1989—; med. cons. Health Advancement Svcs., 1991; adj. prof. dept. psychology Ariz. State U., 1984-89; part-time med. dir. Bonanza, Air West, Hughes Airwest, Republic Airline, 1967-78; prin. investigator Tenabe's Diltiazem Harris Lab, 1990—, clin. trials in use of Acebutolol Wyeth, 1969-70; co-investigator Metoprolol in treatment of hypertension, 1986; regional adv. group of regional med. program, 1968; mem., officer Comprehensive Health Planning Ariz., 1969; original mem. cardiac catherization team St. Luke's Hosp.; original mem. First Open Heart Surgical Team, St. Luke's Hosp.; introduced CPR Tng. in Ariz., 1962. Capt. USAF, 1951-53; 2d lt. USAR, 1942-43. Fellow Am. Coll. Cardiology; mem. ACP, Am. Soc. Internal Medicine, Am. Heart Assn. (bd. dirs., past bd. mem.), Ariz. Med. Assn., Aerospace Med. Assn., Airline Med. Dir. Assn. (past officer), Maricopa County Med. Soc. (sec. 1965). Home: 4128 Lakeside Ln Paradise Valley AZ 85253 Office: 3315 W Indian Sch Rd Phoenix AZ 85017

LONG, EMMETT THADDEUS, communication educator; b. Kaufman, Tex., Dec. 31, 1923; s. Emmett Thaddeus Sr. and Ruth Eliza (Jones) L.; m. Marjorie Ruth Harris, Feb. 22, 1946; children: David Alan, Steven Harrison. BA, Pepperdine U., 1945, U. Calif., Berkeley, 1946; MA, U. Calif., Berkeley, 1948; EdD, U. So. Calif., L.A., 1965. Asst. prof. Pepperdine U., L.A., 1948-54, dir. admissions, 1954-57; admissions officer Calif. State Poly. U., Pomona, 1957-59; assoc. dean Calif. State U., Fullerton, Calif., 1959-72; assoc. dean office of chancellor Calif. State U., L.A., 1972-75; prof. Calif. State U., Fullerton, 1975-86, prof. emeritus, 1986—. Author: (legis. report) School Relations in California, 1969; editor: Liberal Studies in Communication. Parliamentarian United Ch. of Christ Conf., 1975-94. Named for Disting. Svc., Pi Kappa Delta, 1958, Articulation Conf., Calif., 1975. Mem. Calif. Faculty Assn., U. Club Claremont (pres. 1993-94), Calif. State Emeritus Assn. (pres. 1993-95), Phi Delta Kappa. Democrat. Home: 653 N California Dr Claremont CA 91711-4141 Office: California State U Fullerton CA 92634

LONG, HENRY (HANK LONG), librarian; b. Macon, Miss., Aug. 4, 1946; s. Robert Gray and Eula Mae (Hendrix) L.; m. Marilyn Eiland, Mar. 23, 1973 (div. Oct. 1982); 1 child, Michelle Robin; m. Diane Houser, Aug. 30, 1986. BS in History, Livingston (Ala.) U., 1965-67, 72-73; MLS, U. So. Miss., 1974-75; Cert. in Pub. Mgmt., U. Denver, 1990. Ref. libr. Aurora (Colo.) Pub. Libr., 1975-77, tech. svcs. libr., 1977-78, staff svcs. mgr., 1978-80, TV svcs. mgr., 1980-82, regional supr., 1982-84; libr. svcs. mgr. Englewood (Colo.) Pub. Libr., 1984-90, libr. dir., 1990—; bd. dirs. Cen. Colo. Libr. System, Interfaith Task Force; adv. bd. mem. Englewood Family Literacy Project; numerous successful grant proposals in field. Contbr. articles to profl. jours. With U.S. Army Nat. Guard, 1981-82, USN, 1967-71. Mem. ALA, Colo. Libr. Assn., Greater Englewood C. of C. (outreach com.), Englewood Libr. Coun., Colo. Dynix Users Group, Colo. Front Range Libr. Dirs. Democrat. Unitarian. Home: 12355 E Arizona Dr Aurora CO 80012-4321 Office: Englewood Pub Libr 3400 S Elati St Englewood CO 80110-2304

LONG, HOWARD, agricultural products executive; b. 1934. With Coronet Foods, Inc., Wheeling, W.Va., 1956—; pres. Weimer Packing Co., Inc., Wheeling, W.Va., 1974-81; with KGM Harvesting Co., Inc., 1982—, now pres. Office: KGM Harvesting Co Inc 20800 Spence Rd Salinas CA 93908*

LONG, JEANINE HUNDLEY, state legislator; b. Provo, Utah, Sept. 21, 1928; d. Ralph Conrad and Hazel Laurine (Snow) Hundley; m. McKay W. Christensen, Oct. 28, 1949 (div. 1967); children: Cathy Schuyler, Julie Schulleri, Kelly M. Christensen, C. Brett Christensen, Harold A. Christensen; m. Kenneth D. Long, Sept. 6, 1968. AA, Shoreline C.C., Seattle, 1975; BA in Psychology, U. Wash., 1977. Mem. Wash. Ho. of Reps., 1983-87, 93-94, mem. bd. joint com. pension policy, Inst. Pub. Policy; mem. Wash. Senate, 1995—. Mayor protem, mem. city coun. City of Brier, Wash., 1977-80. Republican. Office: PO Box 40482 Olympia WA 98504-0482

LONG, MARIE KATHERINE, public relations consultant, researcher; b. Cleve., Dec. 8, 1925; d. Mike Kurilich and Katherine (Grasso) Kurilich; m. Elgen Marion Long, May 12, 1946; children: Donna Marie Long Weiner, Harry Elgen. Student, Cleve. Coll., 1943-44, Harbor Jr. Coll., L.A., 1954-55. Lic. real estate agt., Calif. Exec. sec. Fawick Airflex Co., Cleve., 1943-44, Pillsbury and Globe Mills, L.A., 1944-48; ptnr. Elgen Long, gen. contractor, San Mateo, Calif., 1958-77, Woodside (Calif.) Investment Co., 1964-71; logistics mgr. pub. rels. Crossroads Endeavor, Woodside, 1971—; pub. rels. cons. Elgen Long Enterprises, San Mateo, 1971—; research on Amelia Earhart disappearance, San Mateo, 1972—; adminstrv. coord., project mgr. pub. rels. Internat. Human Potential Orgns., San Francisco, 1977-82; cons. to books and mags., 1971—. Troop leader Girl Scouts U.S.A., San Mateo, 1954-61; fundraiser Woodside High Sch. Band, 1966-68; Am. Heart Assn., also other orgns., San Mateo, 1973—; v.p. Western Aerospace Mus., Oakland, Calif., 1982—, also life mem.; mem. People to People, Hunger Project; adv. com. USN Meml. Found. Mem. Internat. Platform Soc., Peninsula Press Club. Democrat. Home and Office: 11975 Danvers Cir San Diego CA 92128-4343

LONG, OPHELIA, hospital administrator; b. Birmingham, Ala., Dec. 5, 1940; m. Henry Long; children: Donald, Celeste, Camile. AA, Los Angeles City Coll., 1962; BS, Calif. State U., Los Angeles, 1971; postgrad., U. So. Calif., 1985—. Jr. staff nurse Kaiser Found. Hosp., Los Angeles, 1962-63, gen. duty staff nurse, 1963-65, specialty unit staff nurse, 1965, nursing care coordinator ICU, 1966, supr. ICU, 1966-70, instr., 1970-72, asst. dir. critical care nursing, 1972-81; dir. nursing Kaiser Permanente Med. Ctr., West Los Angeles, 1981-84, hosp. adminstr., 1984—; Instr. leadership skills, Kaiser Permanente Med. Ctr., Los Angeles, 1975; apptd. Dist. XI Med. Quality Assurance com. Bd. Med. Examiners, 1976-81; mem. staff West Los Angeles Community Coll., 1981—. Dir. Operation Learn, 1970-72; active Youth Motivational Task Force, 1974—, Calif. State U. at Los Angeles Adv. Com., 1979—, Los Angeles SW Coll., 1979—, Los Angeles Trade-Tech. Coll., 1979—; Joint Nat. Com. High Blood Pressure of NIH Heart, Blood and Lung Inst., 1982—, Joint Nat. Com. Heart Blood and Lung Inst., 1983—; bd. dirs. U. So. Calif. Community Freedom Sch., 1970-73. Named Outstanding Alumni, Los Angeles Community Coll., 1984, Distng. Alumni, Calif. State U. at Los Angeles, 1985; recipient Outstanding Nurse of Yr. award, 1983. Mem. Nat. Black Nurses' Assn., Inc. (1st v.p. 1978-82, bd. dirs. 1982-83, pres. 1983—), Council Black Nurses (chairperson Ways and Means com. 1972-74, pres. 1974-75, award 1973), Critical Care Nurses Assn., Nephrology Nurses Assn., Calif. Nurses Assn., Black Congress on Health and Law, Congl. Black Caucus-Health Brain Trust, Nursing Alumni Assn. Los Angeles City Coll. (pres. 1970-72), Chi Eta Phi. Home: 2431 W 116th St Inglewood CA 90303

LONG, RANDALL CRAIG, financial advisor; b. Salem, Oreg., Mar. 28, 1958; s. Gerald R. and Dorothy (Larson) L.; m. Mary Fels Long, Sept. 3, 1983; children: Kristina M. Long, Kellie N. Long, Kyle C. Long. BSBA, San Diego State U., 1980. Cons. Scribner, Sciarra & Taylor, Inc., L.A., 1980-81; sr. mktg. advisor Integrated Fin., Irvine, Calif., 1981-89; prin. First Fin. Resources, Newport Beach, Calif., 1990—; regional dir Fin. Network Investment Corp., Newport Beach, 1992—. Bd. dirs. ABSC, San Diego, 1979-80. Mem. Orange County Life Underwriters Assn., Internat. Assn. Fin. Planners, Million Dollar Round Table, Delta Sigma Pi (bd. dirs. 1979-80). Republican. Office: First Fin Resources 20281 SW Birch St Ste 100 Newport Beach CA 92660-1753

LONG, ROBERT MERRILL, retail drug company executive; b. Oakland, Calif., May 19, 1938; s. Joseph Milton and Vera Mai (Skaggs) L.; m. Eliane Quilloux, Dec. 13, 1969. Student, Brown U., 1956-58; BA, Claremont Men's Coll., 1960. With Longs Drug Stores Inc., Walnut Creek, Calif., 1960—, dist. mgr., 1970-72, exec. v.p., 1972-75, pres., 1975-77, pres., chief exec. officer, 1977-91; chmn., chief exec. officer Longs Drug Stores, Walnut Creek, Calif., 1991—. Mem. Nat. Assn. Chain Drug Stores (dir.). Office: Longs Drug Stores Corp PO Box 5222 141 N Civic Dr Walnut Creek CA 94596-3858

LONG, TOM, manufacturing company executive; b. Charleston, W.Va., Apr. 19, 1932; s. Mary (Saunders) Nielsen; m. Delores Faye Holt, Aug. 6, 1954; children: Gary, Tom Jr., Debra, Rex. BSEE, U. Dayton, 1965, MBA, 1967; grad. advanced mgmt. program, Harvard U., 1985. Field engr. Tektronix Inc., Chgo., 1960-61, Dayton, Ohio, 1961-67; mktg. mgr. Beaverton, Oreg., 1967-71, engring. mgr.-gen. instruments, 1971-74, div. gen. mgr., 1973-74, v.p., gen. mgr. communications group, 1981-83, v.p., gen. mgr. design automation group, 1984-87, v.p., gen. mgr. tech. group, 1988—; pres. Grass Valley (Calif.) Group, 1974-81; exec. v.p. Analogic, Peabody, Mass., 1983-84; trustee Tektronix Found., Beaverton, 1985—; pres. Tektronix Devel. Co., Beaverton, 1984—; chmn., chief exec. officer TriQuint Semicondr. Inc., Beaverton, 1985-91. Served to staff sgt. USAF, 1950-54. Mem. Soc. Motion Picture and TV Engrs. Republican. Office: Tektronix Inc M/S 50-408 PO Box 500 Beaverton OR 97077-0001

LONG, WILLIAM JOSEPH, software engineer; b. Kokomo, Ind., Feb. 1, 1956; s. George Alexander and Rebecca Bethina (Burgan) L. BA, Harvard U., 1979; cert. in project mgmt., U. Calif., Berkeley, 1994. Cons. Bechtel Corp., San Francisco, 1982-85; assoc. prof. Dalian (Liaoning, China) Inst. Tech., 1985-86; software engr. Bechtel Corp., San Francisco, 1986-92; EDI project mgr. Pacific Gas & Electric Co., San Francisco, 1992-94; software engr. Am. Pres. Lines, Oakland, Calif., 1994—; mem. adv. bd. Synetics, Inc., San Francisco, 1987—; owner SerenSoft Cons., Oakland, Calif., 1990—. Vol. English tutor, Oakland, Calif., 1983—. Rsch. grantee Smithsonian Astrophys. Obs., Cambridge, Mass., 1976. Mem. IEEE, Assn. Computing Machinery, Am. Assn. Artificial Intelligence, Math. Assn. Am. Home: 2225 7th Ave # 33 Oakland CA 94606-1969 Office: Am Pres Lines 1111 Broadway Oakland CA 94607-4036

LONG, WILLIAM ROBERT, automotive engineer; b. Glendale, June 10, 1948; s. George Willis and Jean (Olmstead) L.; m. Cindy Jade Dobbins, Mar. 1, 1980; children: W. Robert Long, Kellie A. Long. BSME, U. Calif., Santa Barbara, 1970; postgrad., Stanford U., 1971. Various positions PACCAR Inc., 1976-84; dir. engring. Crown Coach Corp., L.A., 1984-85; ops. mgr., chief engr. Servicair Co. divsn. G&H Tech./Penn Ctrl. Corp., Glendale, Calif., 1985-88; chief engr., mgr. suspensions Rancho Suspension divsn. Monroe Auto Equipment/Tenneco Co., Long Beach, Calif., 1988—. Inventor damping sys. for secondary harmonics in a leaf spring. Mem. Soc. Automotive Engrs., Soc. of Plastics Engrs., Packards Internat., Soc. of Mech. Engrs. Home: 5301 Via Ramon Yorba Linda CA 92687-2562 Office: Tenneco Automotive Rancho Suspension 6925 Atlantic Ave Long Beach CA 90805-1415

LONG, ZELMA REED, winery administrator; b. The Dalles, Oreg., Dec. 1, 1943; d. Leo Casper and Lulu Jean (Lovell) Reed; m. Phillip Freese, Dec. 1, 1990. BS, Oreg. State U., 1965. Lic. dietician. Dietetic intern U. Calif. Med. Ctr., San Francisco, 1965; dietitian Highland Alameda Hosp., Oakland, Calif., 1967-68; asst. enologist Robert Mondavi Winery, Napa, Calif., 1970-71, chief enologist, 1972-79; sr. v.p., winemaker Simi Winery, Healdsburg, Calif., 1979-88, pres., 1988-90, pres., CEO, 1990—; cons. Ruffino Chianti, 1983-84, Bodegas Chandon, 1992—; mem. Vitis Corp. adv. com. Adv. Group to Nat. Plant Germplasm Sys. U.S. Dept. Agr., 1987-89; mem. indsl. adv. com. Found. Plant Material Sci., U. Calif., Davis, 1987-89, policy adv. com. Sch. Agr., 1987-89, mem. dept. viticulture and enology, industry adv. com., 1989—; co-owner, Long Vineyards, Napa Valley, Calif., 1977—; lectr. panel discussions. Contbr. articles to profl. jours. Mem. Calif. Regional Water Quality Control Bd., North Coast Region, 1985-90; mem. Internat. Womens Forum, Bay Area chpt., Calif., 1990-93, dir., 1994—; bd. trustees UC Davis Found., Calif. Agrl. Found., U. Calif., Davis, 1991-93, exec. bd., 1994—. Recipient Wine and Food Achievement award No. Calif. chpt. Am. Soc. Wine and Food, 1989, MASI award , Verona, Italy, 1991; named Calif. Wine Pioneer, 1993, Woman of Yr. Roundtable for Women in Food Svc., 1994, Woman of the Yr. Women for WineSense, 1995. Mem. Napa Valley Wine Tech. Group (past pres.), Sonoma County Wine Tech. Group (past dir.), Am. Soc. Enology and Viticulture (dir. 1982-83), Am. Vineyard Found. (bd. mem.), Women for Wine Sense (dir. 1990-93, adv. bd. 1990-94), North Coast Viticultural Rsch. Group (founder), United Winegrowers (dir. 1990—), Alexander Valley Winegrowers (founder, pres. 1992—), Am. Vinters Assn. (bd. dir. 1994—). Office: Simi Winery 16275 Healdsburg Ave Healdsburg CA 95448-9618

LONGO, PATRIZIA, political science educator; b. Vicenza, Italy, May 29, 1957; d. Domenico and Maria Grazia (Tramma) L.; 1 child, David. BA in Langs., Scuola Superiore per Interpret, Traduttori, Florence, Italy, 1980; BA in Polit. Sci., U. Pa., 1983; MA in Polit. Sci., U. Calif., Berkeley, 1984, PhD in Polit. Sci., 1989. Part-time instr. Italian, translator and interpreter The Berlitz Sch. of Langs., Jenkintown, Pa., 1981-83; rsch. asst. Dept. English U. Pa., 1982-83; translator/interpreter Am. Translators Internat., Stanford, Calif., 1984—; tchng. asst. in polit. theory U. Calif., Berkeley, 1984-87, instr. of Italian, 1987-89; instr. dept. polit. sci. Calif. State U., Hayward, 1991; instr. St. Mary's Coll., Moraga, Calif., 1991—. Contbr. articles to profl. pubis. Grantee NEH, 1993, Irvine Grant Workshop, 1992, 93. Mem. Soc. Utopian Studies, Am. Polit. Sci. Assn., Western Polit. Sci. Assn., So. Soc. Philosophy and Psychology, Bay Area Women in Polit. Sci. Office: Dept of Govt St Marys Coll Moraga CA 94575

LONGSTREET, STEPHEN (CHAUNCEY LONGSTREET), author, painter; b. N.Y.C., Apr. 18, 1907; m. Ethel Joan Godoff, Apr. 22, 1932; children: Joan, Harry. Student, Rutgers Coll., Harvard U.; grad., N.Y. Sch. Fine and Applied Art, 1929; student in Rome, Paris. Ind. artist, writer, 1930—; staff lectr. Los Angeles Art Assn., 1954, UCLA, 1955, 58-59, lectr. Los Angeles County Mus., 1958-59; staff mem. arts and humanities dept. UCLA, 1965—; prof. art, dir. dept. Viewpoints Inst. of Gen. Semantics, Los Angeles, 1965; prof. modern writing U. So. Calif., Los Angeles, 1975-80. Began as painter; contbr. to French, Am. and English mags.; also cartoonist; radio writer for NBC, CBS, and other networks, writer shows for Rudy Vallee, Deems Taylor, John Barrymore, Bob Hope, Ellery Queen; writer popular series detective stories for Lippincott and Morrow under pen name Paul Haggrad, 1936; film critic Saturday Rev., 1941; mem. editorial staff Time mag., 1942, Screenwriters mag., 1947-48; critic L.A. Daily News, Book Pages, 1948; assoc. producer Civil War series The Blue and Gray, NBC, 1959—; author: All or Nothing, 1983, Delilah's Fortune, 1984, Our Father's House, 1985; painting exhibited: L.A., 1946, 48, N.Y., 1946, London, 1947; one-man shows include Padlia Galleries, L.A., 1970, Memphis Mus., 1979, Erie Mus., 1981, Coll. of Libr. of Congress, 1980, Jazz Age Revisited, 1983, Smithsonian Nat. Portrait Gallery, 1983, Sr. Eye Gallery, Long Beach, Calif., 1990, Columbus (Ohio) Mus. Art, 1992, tour of Japan, 1994; retrospective show Longstreet the Mature Years, L.A., 1983, Jazz-The Chgo. Scene, Regenstein Libr. U. Chgo., 1989, Columbus (Ohio) Mus. Fine Arts; author: The Pedlocks, 1951, The Beach House, 1952, The World Revisited, 1953, A Century of Studebaker on Wheels, 1953, The Lion at Morning, 1954, The Boy in the Model-T, 1956, Real Jazz, 1956, The Promoters, 1957, The Bill Pearson Story, 1957, (in French), Complete Dictionary of Jazz, 1957, Man of Montmatre, 1958, The Burning Man, 1958, The Politician, 1959, The Crime, 1959, Geisha, 1960, Gettysburg, 1960, A Treasury of the World's Great Prints, 1961, Eagles Where I Walk, 1961, The Flesh Peddler, 1962, A Few Painted Feathers, 1963, War In Golden Weather, 1965, Pedlock & Sons, 1965, The Wilder Shore: San Francisco '49 to '06, 1968, A Salute to American Cooking, (with Ethel Longstreet), 1968, War Cries on Horseback, An Indian History, 1970, The Canvas Falcons, 1970, Chicago: 1860-1920; a history, 1973, The General, 1974, (with Ethel Longstreet) World Cookbook, 1973, Win or Lose, 1977, The Queen Bees, 1979, Storm Watch, 1979, Pembroke Colors, 1981, From Storyville to Harlem - 50 years of the Jazz Scene, 1987, Magic Trumpets--The Young Peoples Story of Jazz, 1989, (poems) Jazz Solos, 1990, My Three Nobel Prizes; Life with Faulkner, Hemingway and Sinclair Lewis, 1994; editor, illustrator: The Memoirs of W.W. Windstaff Lower Than Angels, 1993; writer screen plays including Uncle Harry, 1943, Rider on a Dead Horse, The Imposter, First Travelling Saleslady, Stallion Road, 1946, The Jolson Story, 1947, Helen Morgan Story, 1956, plays including High Button Shoes, 1947, Gauguin, 1948, All Star Cast, Los Angeles, A History, 1977, (TV series) Playhouse 90, TV writer for Readers Digest Theatre, 1955; contbr. dialogue for films Greatest Show on Earth, Duel In the Sun. Pres. Los Angeles Art Assn., 1973-90. Recipient Stafford medal London, 1946, Bowman prize, 1948, Photo-Play mag. Gold medal for The Jolson Story, 1948, Billboard-Donaldson Gold medal for High Button Shoes, 1948. Mem. Motion Picture Acad. Arts and Letters, Writers Guild Am. (bd. dirs. 1948), Phi Sigma (charter mem.). Clubs: Sketch, Daguerreotype Society, Winadu Players.

LONGSWORTH, EILEEN CATHERINE, library director; b. N.Y.C., Feb. 7, 1950; d. Francis L. and Maurine E. (Romkey) Brannigan; m. Laurence S. Woodworth, June 16, 1970 (div. 1982); 1 child, David; m. Bruce Todd Longsworth, May 28, 1983. Student, Dunbarton Coll., 1966-68; BA, U. Md., 1970; MS in Libr. Sci., Cath. U., Washington, 1973. Dept. head Anne Arundel County Pub. Libr., Annapolis, Md., 1974-75, br. librarian, 1975-79; adult services specialist Enoch Pratt Free Libr., Balt., 1979-84; asst. dir. Salt Lake City Pub. Libr., 1984-87; dir. Salt Lake County Libr. System, 1987—. Mem. ALA, Utah Libr. Assn. Democrat. Home: 860 Terrace Hills Dr Salt Lake City UT 84103-4021 Office: Salt Lake County Libr System 2197 E 7000 S Salt Lake City UT 84121-3139

LONNER, THOMAS DUNSTAN, museum director; b. San Francisco, May 27, 1942; s. Ernest B. and Lisa K. Lonner; m. Elizabeth Ward. BA, San Francisco State U., 1966, MA, 1970; PhD, U. Calif., San Francisco, 1976. Projects coordinator Peat, Marwick, Mitchell & Co, Anchorage, 1976-79; [illegible]sistence div. Alaska Fish and Game, Juneau, 1979-81; dir. Ctr. for Alcohol Studies, Anchorage, 1981-85, Alaska State Museums, Juneau, 1986—. Contbr. articles to profl. jours. Home: 2318 Columbia St SW Olympia WA 98501-2844 Office: Alaska State Mus 395 Whittier St Juneau AK 99801-1718

LONSDALE, HAROLD KENNETH, retired high technology company executive; b. Westfield, N.J., Jan. 19, 1932; s. Harold K. and Julia (Papandrea) L.; children: Karen Anne Trachsel, Harold Kenneth Jr. BS in Chemistry, Rutgers U., 1953; PhD in Phys. Chemistry, Pa. State U., 1957. Staff mem. Gen. Atomic Co., San Diego, 1959-70; prin. scientist Alza Corp., Palo Alto, Calif., 1970-72; vis. scientist Max Planck Inst. for Biophysics, Frankfurt, W.Ger., 1973-74, Weizmann Inst. Sci., Rehovot, Israel, 1974; pres. Bend Research, Inc., Oreg., 1975-89; bd. dirs. Oreg. Bus. Coun. 1985-89; chair Gov's. Sci. Coun., 1987-88. Editor: Reverse Osmosis Membrane Research, 1972; founder, editor Jour. Membrane Sci.; contbr. articles to profl. jours. Candidate U.S. Senate, 1990-92. Served to 1st lt. USAF, 1957-59. Named Small Bus. Entrepreneur of Yr., Oreg. Bus. Mag., 1982.

LOO, KATHERINE HAUGHEY, nonprofit organization consultant; b. Concordia, Kans., June 24, 1939; d. James M. and Katherine (Hurd) Haughey; m. Lester B. Loo, June 14, 1961; children: Susan Loo Pattee, James O. BA in Polit. Sci., U. Kans., 1961. Pres. Jr. League, Colorado Springs, Colo., 1974-75, Brockhurst Boy's Ranch, Colorado Springs, Colo., 1973-77; dir. Assn. Jr. Leagues, N.Y.C., 1976-78; pres. founder docent aux., chair capital campaign Cheyenne Mt. Zoo, Colorado Springs, 1969-94; dir. UMB Bank Colo., Colorado Springs, 1994-95; mem. Colorado Springs Urban Renewal Bd., 1979-85; pres. Colo. Women's Forum, Denver, 1990-91; founder, bd. dirs. Colo. Women's Found.; advisor Cheyenne Mt. Zoo. Composer, performer piano music. Councilwoman City of Colorado Springs, 1979-85; vice chair Colo. Commn. on Higher Edn., Denver, 1985-87; bd. trustees, chair music dir. search com. Colorado Springs Symphony, 1994-95. Recipient Silver Bell award Assistance League, Colorado Springs, 1975. Mem. Broadmoor Garden Club (civic chair 1992-94), Phi Beta Kappa. Home: 19 Northgate Rd Colorado Springs CO 80906-4331

LOOMIS, CHRISTOPHER KNAPP, metallurgical engineer; b. San Francisco, May 6, 1947; s. Richard and Evaline Elsie (Crandal) L.; m. Merril Ellen Purdy, Dec. 8, 1968; 1 child, Nicole Lee; m. Sandra Lee Marsh, Feb. 14, 1993. Profl. Engring. degree, Colo. Sch. Mines, 1969. Cert. quality engr. Process engr. Alcan Aluminum Corp., Riverside, Calif., 1969-73, prodn. supt., 1973-76; process engr. Alcan Aluminum Corp., Oswego, N.Y., 1976-78, maintenance engr., 1978-80; metall. engr. Hazelett Strip-Casting Corp., Colchester, Vt., 1980-81; chief engr. ARCO Metals Co., Chgo., 1981-84; maintenance supt. Cerro Metal Products, Paramount, Calif., 1984-85, mgr. engring. and maintenance, 1985-86; supt. tech. svcs. Golden Aluminum Co., Ft. Lupton, Colo., 1987-88; process devel. engr. Golden Aluminum Co., Lakewood, Colo., 1988-91, corp. environ. and process engr., 1991; engr. IV Coors Brewing Co., Golden, Colo., 1991-93, material engr. V, 1993—. Mem. Am. Soc. for Metals, Metall. Soc., Colo. Sch. Mines Alumni Assn., Am. Soc. for Quality Control, Fedn. Fly Fishers (life), Trout Unltd. (life). Episcopalian. Home: 6572 Owens Ct Arvada CO 80004-2765 Office: Coors Brewing Co Mail Stop RR820 Golden CO 80401

LOOMIS, RICHARD FRANK, entertainment company executive; b. Eugene, Oreg., Aug. 24, 1947; s. Frank Clark and Elsie Jane (Allgood) L. BA in Acctg., Ariz. State U., 1975. Owner, founder, pres. Flying Buffalo Computer Conflict Simulation, Inc., Scottsdale, Ariz., 1970—. Author game book: Buffalo Castle, 1976; designer play by mail game: Starweb, 1976 (Best Game 1984, 87), Heroic Fantasy, 1982 (Best Game 1989); developer card game: Nuclear Escalation, 1983 (Best Game 1983). Pres. YMCA Ch. Softball League, Scottsdale, 1981-84. With U.S. Army, 1969-71. Recipient Meritorious Svc. to Gaming award Hobby/Metro Detroit Gamers, 1979. Mem. Play by Mail Assn. (exec. dir. 1985-88, 90—), Game Mfrs. Assn. (bd. dirs. 1986—, 1st pres. 1978-79, treas. 1980-86, Hall of Fame 1989, Honor of Svc. award 1991). Republican. Methodist. Office: Flying Buffalo Inc PO Box 1467 Scottsdale AZ 85252-1467

LOONEY, CLAUDIA ARLENE, academic administrator; b. Fullerton, Calif., June 13, 1946; d. Donald F. and Mildred B. (Gage) Schneider; m. James K. Looney, Oct. 8, 1967; 1 child, Christopher K. BA, Calif. State U., 1969. Dir. youth YWCA No. Orange County, Fullerton, Calif., 1967-70; dir. dist. Camp Fire Girls, San Francisco, 1971-73; asst. exec. dir. Camp Fire Girls, Los Angeles, 1973-77; asst. dir. community resources Childrens Hosp., Los Angeles, 1977-80; dir. community devel. Orthopaedic Hosp., Los Angeles, 1980-82; sr. v.p. Saddleback Meml. Found./Saddleback Meml. Med. Ctr., Laguna Hills, Calif., 1982-92; v.p. planning and advancement Calif. Inst. Arts, Santa Clarita, Calif., 1992—; instr. U. Calif., Irvine, Univ. Irvine; mem. steering com. U. Irvine. Mem. steering com. United Way, Los Angeles, 1984-86. Fellow Assn. Healthcare Philanthropy (nat. chair-elect, chmn. program Nat. Edn. Conf. 1986, regional dir. 1985-89, fin. com. 1988—, pres., com. chn. 1987—, Give To Life com. chmn. 1987-91, Orange County Fund Raiser of Yr. 1992); mem. Nat. Soc. Fund Raising Execs. Found. (cert., vice chmn. 1985-90, chair 1993—), So. Calif. Assn. Hosp. Devel. (past pres., bd. dirs.), Profl. Ptnrs. (chmn. 1986, instr. 1988—), Philanthropic Ednl. Orgn. (past pres.). Office: Calif Inst of the Arts 24700 Mcbean Pky Valencia CA 91355-2340

LOONEY, GERALD LEE, medical educator, administrator; b. Bradshaw, W.Va., Nov. 22, 1937; s. Noah Webster and Anna Belle (Burris) L.; m. Linda Louise Pluebell, Oct. 19, 1962 (div. Apr. 1975); children: Deborah Lynn, Catherine Ann, Karen Marie, Kelli Rachelle; m. Patricia Marie Terrazas, Dec. 22, 1987. AB, Johns Hopkins U., 1959, MD, 1963; MPH, Harvard U., 1968. Diplomate Am. Bd. Preventive Medicine, Am. Bd. Pediatrics. Resident pediatrics Tufts-New Eng. Med. Ctr., Boston, 1965-67; physician-in-chief Kennedy Meml. Hosp., Boston, 1969-71; asst. prof. family and cmty. medicine U. Ariz. Coll. Medicine, Tucson, 1971-72; asst. prof. emergency medicine U. So. Calif. Sch. Medicine, L.A., 1972-77; assoc. clin. prof. medicine U. Calif., Irvine, 1991—; emergency dept. dir. Glendale (Calif.) Adventist Med. Ctr., 1978-84; edn. dir. Orthopaedic Hosp., L.A., 1985-88; urgent care dir. Bay Shore Med. Group, Torrance, Calif., 1988-93; med. dir. Surecare and LAX Clinics Centinela Hosp., Inglewood, Calif., 1993—; bd. dirs. Beach Cities Health Dist., Redondo Beach, Calif., 1992-93. Home: 230 S Catalina Ave Apt 413 Redondo Beach CA 90277-3367 Office: Centinela Airport Clinic 9601 S Sepulveda Blvd Los Angeles CA 90045

LOONEY, J. ANNA, corporate affairs executive; b. Winnemucca, Nev., Oct. 22, 1951; d. Robert Holland and Gladys Frances Raring; m. James E. Looney, May 13, 1978; 1 child, Emily Claire. BA, Ursinus Coll., 1973; MA, SUNY, Stony Brook, 1986. Pub.. policy research Va. Power, Richmond, 1983-87; asst. corp. sec., mgr. corp. affairs Black & Decker Corp., Towson, Md., 1987-90; mgr. corp. communications, exec. speechwriter Gen. Pub. Utilities, Parsippany, N.J., 1991-93; adj. tchr. Coll. St. Elizabeth, Convent Station, N.J., 1991-93; dir. corp. affairs, asst. corp. sec. Freedom Communications, Inc., Irvine, Calif., 1993—; chmn. steering com. GPU Leadership in Edn. Co-author: Middle Scots Poets Reference Guide, 1985. Mem. Am. Soc. Corp. Secs., Internat. Assn. Bus. Communicators. Republican. Presbyterian. Office: Freedom Communications Inc 17666 Fitch Irvine CA 92714-6022

LOONEY, RALPH EDWIN, newspaper editor, author, photographer; b. Lexington, Ky., June 22, 1924; s. Arville Zone and Connie Elizabeth (Boyd) L.; m. Clarabel Richards, Dec. 7, 1944. B.A., U. Ky., 1948. Various positions including proof reader, photographer, chief photographer, sports writer, reporter Lexington Leader, 1943-52; reporter Albuquerque Tribune, 1953-54; reporter, copy editor, chief copy editor St. Louis Globe-Democrat, 1955-56; city editor Albuquerque Tribune, 1956-68, asst. mng. editor, 1968-73, editor, 1973-80; editor Rocky Mountain News, Denver, 1980-89; columnist Scripps Howard News Svc., 1989-93, Tribune, Albuquerque, 1989-93. Author: Haunted Highways, the Ghost Towns of New Mexico, 1969, O'Keeffe and Me, 1995; contbr. articles to mags. including Nat. Observer, others; photographs to mags. Founder, mem. N.Mex. Motion Picture Commn., 1967-76; v.p., bd. dirs. Albuquerque C. of C., 1971-75; bd. dirs. Albuquerque Indsl. Devel. Svc., 1971-80; bd. advisors Lovelace Med. Ctr., Albuquerque, 1976-80; bd. advs. UPI, 1983-86; bd. dirs. Newspaper Features Coun., 1984-89; mem. exec. coun. St. Joseph Hosp., 1986—. Recipient N.Mex. medal of Merit, 1968, Robert F. Kennedy Journalism award, 1970, George Washington Honor medal Freedoms Found., 1969, 19 E.H. Shaffer awards N.Mex. Press Assn., 1965-80; named Colo. Newspaper Person of the Yr., 1988, Newspaper Features Coun. Jester award, 1989. Mem. N.Mex. Press Assn. (state pres. 1976), Colo. Press Assn. (bd. dirs. 1982-85), Sigma Delta Chi (N. Mex. pres. 1960). Methodist. Home: 6101 Casa De Vida Dr NE Albuquerque NM 87111-1140

LOOS, WILLIAM CHRISTENSEN, lawyer, academic administrator; b. Ogden, Utah, Feb. 16, 1944; s. Walter Howard and Mary Alice (Loos) Christensen; m. Frances Ann Coltharp, July 17, 1973; children: William, David, Katherine, Robert, Stephen. BS, U. Utah, 1966, JD, 1969. Bar: Utah 1969, U.S. Dist. Ct. Utah, U.S. Ct. Appeals (10th cir.) 1970. Clk. to justice Utah Supreme Ct., 1968-69; assoc. Romney, Nelson & Cassity, Salt Lake City, 1969-73; chief asst. atty. gen. Atty. Gen.'s Office State of Utah, Salt Lake City, 1973-74; gen. counsel Utah State U., Logan, 1974-80; dir. Utah offices U.S. Senator Orrin Hatch, Salt Lake City, 1980-84; asst. to pres., dir. govt. rels. U. Utah, Salt Lake City, 1984-89; v.p. univ. advancement Weber State U., Ogden, 1989-95; v.p. Smith Mktg. Group, Salt Lake City, Atlanta, 1995—. Founder, chair Western State Govtl. Rels. Con., 1986-92; dir. Utah Boys Ranch, Salt Lake City, 1987-88; bd. dirs., mem. exec. com. No. Utah United Way, 1991—. Mem. Salt Lake Area C. of C., Ogden-Weber C. of C., Ogden Golf and Country Club, Rotary, Sigma Gamma Chi (nat. v.p. 1989-93). LDS. Office: Smith Mktg Group 3761 S 700 E Ste 202 Salt Lake City UT 84106

LOPATA, MARTIN BARRY, executive; b. Bronx, N.Y., Apr. 6, 1939; s. Julius A. and Rose (Silverman) L.; m. Sarah G. Lopata, July 4, 1965 (div. 1978; children: Warren A., Lawrence M.; m. Lynette Wyrick, May 6, 1989 (div. 1991). Grad., High Sch. of Art and Design, N.Y.C.; attended N.Y.C. Community Coll., Bklyn. Sales mgr. H. Natoway Co., Los Angeles, 1961-62; contract mgr. A.S. Aloe Co., Los Angeles, 1962-64; merchandise mgr. S.E. Rykoff Co., Los Angeles, 1964-70; v.p. Kirby Sales, Los Angeles, 1970-71; pres. MBL Industries Inc., Santa Ana, Calif., 1971-87, Unicorn Seminars Inc., Huntington Beach, Calif., 1987-88, Unicorn Investments Internat., Huntington Beach, 1988-91; chair Yes Educational Systems, Reno, Nev., 1995—; chmn. Soviet Am. Internat. Co., 1988-92; joint venture Sovaminco Soviet Am. Internat. Co. #104, Moscow; pres. Coastal-West Industries, 1991-92. Patron Am. Mus. Nat. History, N.Y.C., 1984-91; bus. chmn. Ctr. for Soviet-Am. Dialogue, Washington, 1987-91; chmn. Com. on Bus.-A New Way of Thinking in a New Age, Moscow, 1987; bd. dirs. Three Mountain Found., Lone Pine, Calif., 1987-88, Inside Edge, Irvine, Calif., 1987-94, found. pres., 1993-94; vice chmn. United Ch. Religious Science, Los Angeles, 1986-87, pres. Huntington Beach Ch. Religious Sci., 1985. Mem. Masons (32d degree), Shriners. Home: 16391 Wimbledon Ln Huntington Beach CA 92649-2188 Office: Yes Educational Systems 1135 Terminal Way Ste 209 Reno NV 89502

LOPER, JAMES LEADERS, broadcasting executive; b. Phoenix, Sept. 4, 1931; s. John D. and Ellen Helen (Leaders) L.; m. Mary Louise Brion, Sept. 1, 1955; children: Elizabeth Margaret Sehran (Mrs. Michael K. Sehran), James Leaders Jr. BA, Ariz. State U., 1953; MA, U. Denver, 1957; PhD, U. So. Calif., 1967; DHL (hon.), Columbia Coll., 1973; LLD (hon.), Pepperdine U., 1978. Asst. dir. bur. broadcasting Ariz. State U., Tempe, 1953-59; news editor, announcer Sta. KTAR, Phoenix, 1955-56; dir. ednl. TV, Calif. State U., Los Angeles, 1960-64; v.p. Community TV So. Calif., Los Angeles, 1962-63; asst. to pres. Sta. KCET-Pub. TV, Los Angeles, 1963-65, sec., 1965-66, dir. ednl. services, 1964-65, asst. gen. mgr., 1965-66, v.p., gen. mgr., 1966-69, exec. v.p., gen. mgr., 1969-71, pres., gen. mgr., 1971-76, pres., CEO, 1976-82; exec. dir. Acad. TV Arts and Scis., 1983—; bd. dirs., chmn. audit com. Western Fed. Savs. and Loan Assn., L.A., 1979-93; bd. dirs. Global View, Washington; chmn. bd. dirs. Tennessee Ernie Ford Enterprises, 1994—; chmn. bd. Pub. Broadcasting Service, Washington, 1969-72; dir. Calif. Arts Coun., 1991—; adj. prof. Sch. Cinema and TV U. So. Calif., 1984—; sr. lectr. U. So. Calif., Los Angeles, 1969-70; pres. Western Ednl. Network, 1968-70; mem. Gov.'s Ednl. TV and Radio Adv. Com., Calif., 1968-74; U.S. rep. CENTO Conf. Radio and TV, Turkey, 1978, trustee Internat. Council Nat. Acad. TV Arts and Scis., 1988—. Contbr. articles to profl. jours; contbr. to ETV: The Farther Vision, 1967, Broadcasting and Bargaining: Labor Relations in Radio and Television, 1970. Mem. adv. bd. Jr. League of Los Angeles, 1970-76, Jr. League of Pasadena, 1972-75, Los Angeles Jr. Arts Ctr., 1968-72; exec. v.p. Assocs. of Otis Art Inst., 1971-77, pres., 1975-77; chmn., dir. The Performing Tree, Los Angeles; bd. dirs. Los Angeles Civic Light Opera Co., 1974—, v.p., 1975—; bd. dirs. Sears-Roebuck Found., 1976-79; chmn. bd. visitors Annenburg Sch. Communications, U. So. Calif., 1975-80; trustee Poly. Sch., Pasadena; mem. Calif. State Arts Commn., 1991. Recipient Disting. Alumnus award Ariz. State U., 1972; Alumni award of Merit, U. So. Calif., 1975; Gov's. award Hollywood chpt. Nat. Acad. TV Arts and Scis., 1975; Alumni Achievement award Phi Sigma Kappa, 1975; named Centennial Alumnus Nat. Assn. of State Univs. and Land Grant Colls., 1988. Named to Hall of Fame Walter Cronkite Sch. Comms., Ariz. State U., 1994 Mem. Acad. TV Arts and Scis. (past gov., v.p. Hollywood chpt., trustee nat. acad.), TV Acad. Found., Hollywood Radio and TV Soc. (treas., dir.), Western Ednl. Soc. Telecommunications (past pres.), Assn. Calif. Pub. TV Stas. (past pres.), Young Pres.'s Orgn., Phi Sigma Kappa, Pi Delta Epsilon, Alpha Delta Sigma, Sigma Delta Chi. Presbyterian (chmn. Mass Media Task Force So. Calif. synod 1969-75). Clubs: Valley Hunt (Pasadena), Bel-Air Bay, California, Los Angeles, 100 of Los Angeles, Calif. (Los Angeles). Office: Acad TV Arts and Scis PO Box 7344 North Hollywood CA 91603-7344

LOPER, WARREN EDWARD, computer scientist; b. Dallas, Aug. 2, 1929; s. Leon Edward and Belva (Fannin) L.; BS in Physics, U. Tex. at Austin, 1953, BA in Math. with honors, 1953; m. Ruth M. Wetzler, June 17, 1967; 1 child, Mary Katherine. Commd. ensign U.S. Navy, 1953, advanced through grades to lt., 1957; physicist U.S. Naval Ordnance Test Sta., China Lake, Calif., 1956-61; operational programmer U.S. Navy Electronics Lab., San Diego, 1962-64; project leader, systems programming br., digital computer staff U.S. Fleet Missile Systems Analysis and Evaluation Group, Corona, 1964-65, sr. systems analyst digital computer staff U.S. Naval Ordnance Lab., Corona, 1965-69; head systems programming br. Naval Weapons Center, Corona Labs, 1969; computer specialist compiler and operating systems devel., Naval Electronics Lab. Ctr., San Diego, 1969-76; project leader langs., operating systems and graphics Naval Ocean Systems Ctr., San Diego, 1977-90, employee emeritus, 1990-93, retired 1993. Navy rep. on tech. subgroup Dept. Def. High Order Lang. Working Group, 1975-80. Recipient Disting. Svc. award Dept. Def., 1983. Democrat. Roman Catholic. Home: 6542 Alcala Knolls Dr San Diego CA 92111-6947

LOPEZ, ANA MARIA, physician; b. Bolivia, Apr. 23, 1960. AB, Bryn Mawr (Pa.) Coll., 1982; MD, Jefferson Med. Coll., 1988; MPH, U. Ariz., 1994. Diplomate Am. Bd. Internal Medicine, Nat. Bd. Med. Examiners. Resident in internal medicine U. Ariz. Health Ctr., Tucson, 1988-91, fellow in gen. internal medicine, 1991-92, chief med. resident, 1991-92, fellow hematology/oncology, 1992-95, postdoctoral NIH rsch. fellow, 1993-95, instr. Coll. of Pharmacy, 1992—, instr. Coll. of Medicine, 1991—; asst. prof. medicine, 1995—; presenter in field. Contbr. numerous articles to profl. jours. Mem. ACP (assoc., health and pub. policy com. Ariz. chpt. 1991—, chair coun. of assocs. Ariz. chpt. 1992—, coun. of assoc. 1991-93, house staff rep. to the Assn. of Program Dirs. in Internal Medicine, 1992-94, health and pub. policy com. 1993-94, membership enhancement com. 1994—), Soc. Gen. Internal Medicine (membership devel. com. 1994—), Ariz. Women's Cancer Network (legis. policy and advocacy com. 1993—), Am. Med. Women's Assn. (faculty advisor to student chpt. 1992—, Scholarship award 1986, 87, 88), Am. Cancer Soc. (profl. edn. com. 1990—, Vol. award So. Ariz. chpt. 1990), Ariz. Pub. Health Soc. (mem. legis. com. 1990-92), Physicians Social Responsibility, (mem. spkrs. bur. 1983). Office: Sect of Hematology/Oncology Ariz Cancer Ctr 1501 N Campbell Ave Tucson AZ 85724-0001

LOPEZ, ANDY, university athletic coach. Head coach Pepperdine U. Waves, 1989-94, U. Florida, 1994—. NCAA Divsn. 1A Champions, 1992. Office: U Florida Athletic Dept Gainesville FL 32611*

LOPEZ, ANGELO CAYAS, freelance illustrator; b. Norfolk, Va., Mar. 29, 1967; s. Felizardo Pardo and Teresita (Cayas) L. BS in Graphic Design, San Jose State U., 1992. Cashier Marriott's Great Am., Santa Clara, Calif., 1985; page tech. svc. dept. Sunnyvale (Calif.) Pub. Libr., 1985-90, tech. svc. clk.,

1993—; intern Palo Alto (Calif.) Fast Stats, 1990-91; framer Aaron Bros., Sunnyvale, 1991-92; cashier Linden Tree Children's Bookstore, Los Altos, Calif., 1992-94; libr. page Santa Clara (Calif.) Pub. Libr., 1992—. Contbr. illustrations to books including Two Moms A Zark and Me, 1993, Night Travelers, 1994; contbr. illustrations and cartoons to mags. Vol. Arts Project, Santa Clara, 1990; tutor San Jose (Calif.) Chinese Alliance Ch., 1993—; active Santa Clara U. Mission Ch., 1992—. Mem. Philia. Democrat. Home: 1302 Socorro Ave Sunnyvale CA 94089-2621

LOPEZ, DANIEL HERALDO, academic administrator; b. Puerto de Luna, N.Mex., Feb. 14, 1946; s. Julian and Tiofila (Ocaña) L.; m. Linda Vigil, July 12, 1975. BA in Polit. Sci., U. N.Mex., 1970, MA in Polit. Sci., 1972, PhD in Polit. Sci., 1982. Cabinet sec. N.Mex. Dept. Fin. and Adminstrn., Santa Fe, 1984-86; chief of staff for senate fin. and sr. staff analyst House Appropriations and Fin. Com., Santa Fe, 1987-89; assoc. and dep. dir. terminal effects rsch. and analysis N.Mex. Inst. Mining and Tech., Socorro, 1987-89, adj. prof., 1994—; v.p. institutional devel. N.Mex. Inst. Mining and Technology, Socorro, 1989-93, pres., 1993—; exec. dir. N.Mex. Adv. Coun. on Vocat.-Tech. Edn., 1973-82; adj. prof. U. N.Mex., Albuquerque, 1975-82, N.Mex. Inst. Mining and Tech., Socorro, 1994—; cabinet sec. N.Mex. Employment Security Dept., Santa Fe, 1983-84. Mem. League of United Latin Am. Citizens, Albuquerque; mem., past pres. Albuquerque Hispano C. of C. Staff Sgt. USAF, 1968-69, Korea. Mem. N.Mex. Tech. Rsch. Found. (v.p. 1994), N.Mex. First Exec. Com. (v.p. 1994), N.Mex. Children's Found., N.Mex. Industry Network Corp. (exec. com. 1994), N.Mex. Amigos, Rio Grande Tech. Found. Home: One Olive Ln Socorro NM 87801 Office: NMex Inst Mining and Tech Office of the Pres Socorro NM 87801

LOPEZ, DAVID ALFRED, geologist; b. Embudo, N.Mex., Dec. 19, 1949; s. Alfredo Abel and Anna Maria (Silva) L.; m. Carolyn Rene Pease, Sept. 10, 1973; children—Amy, Paul, Matthew, Martin and Mia (twins). B.A., U. Colo., 1973; M.S., U. N.Mex., 1975; Ph.D., Colo. Sch. Mines, 1981. Research geologist geologic div. U.S. Geol. Survey, Denver, 1975-82; sr. geologist N.Am. Resources Co., Billings, Mont., 1982-92; sr. rsch. geologist Mont. Bur. Mines and Geology, Billings, 1992—. Author numerous research papers. Grantee Gulf Oil Co., Albuquerque, 1974, Colo. Sch. Mines, Golden, 1979. Mem. Am. Assn. Petroleum Geologists, Geol. Soc. Am., Mont. Geol. Soc. Mem. Pentecostal-Full Gospel Ch. Home: 5723 Us Highway 87 E Billings MT 59101-9034 Office: Mont Bur Mines and Geology MSU-B Campus Box 112 1500 N 30th St Billings MT 59101-0245

LOPEZ, RAMON ROSSI, lawyer; b. Vallejo, Calif., Aug. 14, 1950; s. Louis and Katherine Rita (Rossi) L.; m. Jamie Gray, May 26, 1973; children: James Louis, Matthew Ramon, Scott Nicholas, Katherine Joan. BS, Loyola U., L.A., 1972, JD, 1978. Bar: Calif. 1979, U.S. Dist. Ct. (so. dist.) Calif. 1979. Sales rep. Eaton Labs., L.A., 1972-75; claims rep. Chubb/Pacific Indeminity, L.A., 1975-78; assoc. Cummins, White, Robinson & Robinson, L.A., 1979-80, Robinson & Robinson, Newport Beach, Calif., 1981-82; ptnr. Barth & Lopez, Newport Beach, 1982-87, Barth, Lopez & Hodes, Newport Beach, 1987-90, Lopez & Hodes, Newport Beach, Calif., 1991—. Bd. dirs. Newport Nat. Little League, 1988, Our Lady Queen of Angels Sch., 1989-90, Am. Youth Soccer Assn., 1988—. Mem. Assn. Trial Lawyers Am., Calif. Trial Lawyers Assn., L.A. Trial Lawyers Assn., Orange County Bar Assn., Balboa Bay Club. Democrat. Roman Catholic. Home: 5 Canyon Ct Newport Beach CA 92660-5918 Office: Lopez & Hodes 2424 SE Bristol St Ste 250 Newport Beach CA 92660-0757

LOPEZ, STEVEN RICHARD, small business owner, consultant; b. Flagstaff, Ariz., Dec. 14, 1944; s. John and Trinidad (Rodriquez) L.; (div. 1983); children: David Allen, Laura Marie, Jonel Christina, Steven Christopher. BFA, U. Ariz., 1968; MBA, U. Phoenix, 1992. Art dir. Curran-Morton Advt., Phoenix, 1968-70; owner Steve Lopez Graphic Design, Phoenix, 1970-73; asst. art dir. Ulrich Studios, Phoenix, 1973-78; artist, illustrator Goodyear (Ariz.) Aerospace/Loral Def. Systems, 1978-90; pres. Z-Boz, Inc., Glendale, Ariz., 1990-92; owner L&A Janitorial/Clean Room Specialists, 1994—; pres. Exigency Alert, Inc., Glendale, 1988-90; owner Lopez & Assocs., Glendale, 1989—, pres., 1991; v.p. South Paw, Inc., Peoria, Ariz., 1990-91; cons. Teddy Bear Factory, Inc., Peoria, 1990-91, Beanies Soft Toy Factory, Phoenix, 1990, Maquiladoras, Mex.; exec. advisor Jr. Achievement, Phoenix, 1979-80; amb. to Mex., U.S. JCI Senate, Tulsa, 1987-88. Patentee eyeglass floatation apparatus. Mem. adv. com. City of Glendale, 1985, City of Glendale Cable TV Task Force, 1987; bd. dirs. All Am. Cities Com., Glendale; bd. trustees Valley of the Sun United Way, Phoenix. Mem. Glendale C. of C., U.S. Jaycees (Excellence award 1977, Upson award 1982), Ariz. Jaycees (life, pres. 1985-86, Excellence award 1986), Glendale Jaycees (pres. 1978-81, Chmn. of the Yr. 1977). Democrat. Roman Catholic. Home: 4927 W Mclellan Rd Glendale AZ 85301-4010

LOPEZ-NAVARRO, EDUARDO LUIS, family therapist; b. Santiago de Cuba, Oriente, Cuba, June 29, 1959; came to U.S, 1970; s. Eduardo Regino and Alicia Del Pilar (Navarro) Lopez. BA, UCLA, 1982; MS in Psychology with honors, Calif. State U., L.A., 1991. Counselor L.A. Unified Sch. Dist., 1982-90; family therapist Family Counseling Svcs., San Gabriel, Calif., 1990-93; program coord. El Centro del Pueblo, L.A., 1993—; family therapist Hillsides Home for Children, Pasadena, Calif., 1992—, El Centro Del Pueblo, L.A., 1993—; dir. North Ctrl. L.A. Family Preservation Project; cons. (counselor) UCLA/Valley Alternative Magnet Sch., Van Nuys, 1990; rsch. asst. UCLA/Fernald Sch., 1981; lectr. in field; expert presenter and cons. various TV programs including KMEX-Channel 34, L.A., 1993—. Contbr. articles to profl. jours.; author video: The World of Perpetual Night: Insights into the Psychology of Street Prostitution, 1990. Counselor Hollywood Sunset Cmty. Clinic, L.A., 1986-89; family counselor St. Matthias Ch.; mem. san Gabriel Valley Child Abuse Coun.; educator/trainer Latino Family Preservation, L.A., 1994. Recipient Counseling Dept. Spl. Recognition award Hollywood Sunset Cmty. Clinic, 1988, Am. Assn. for Marriage and Family Therapy Minority fellowship, 1991. Mem. Calif. Assn. Marriage and Family Therapists, Am. Assn. Marriage and Family Therapists. Roman Catholic. Office: El Centro Del Pueblo 1157 Lemoyne St Los Angeles CA 90026-3206

LOPINA, LOUISE CAROL, artist; b. Chgo., Nov. 24, 1936; d. Don and Eva Bernice (Rice) Petersen; m. Robert Ferguson Lopina, June 21, 1958; children: Kimberly, Sandra, Amy. BS, Purdue U., 1958. One-woman shows include Norwood Galleries Ltd., Denver, 1970, Garden of the Gods Gallery, Colorado Springs, Colo., 1972, Air Univ. Libr., Montgomery, Ala., 1977, Christ Ch. Little Gallery, Kettering, Ohio, 1980, 81, Cin. Club, 1981, Nissequoque Golf Club, L.I., N.Y., 1986, Nat. Mgmt. Assn., Newport Beach, Calif., 1991; exhibited in group shows at Ill. Woman's Fedn., Internat. Red Cross Round the World Tour, Colorado Springs (Colo.) Fine Arts Ctr., 1974, Nat. Scholastic Art Awards, Nat. Nature Art Exhn. (Best Painting in Show 1978, 79, 82, Salmagundi Club, N.Y.C., 1979, Clayton Bruckner Meml. award), Cin. Mus. Natural History, 1980, Adler Gallery, N.Y.C., 1981, Game Coin Internat., San Antonio, Tex., Wondrous Wildlife, Cin., 1983, G&R Gallery, 1983, Nora Gallery, Great Neck, N.Y., 1985, Country Gallery, Locust Valley, N.Y., Outdoor Expo, Albany, N.Y., 1985, So. Alleghenies Mus. Art, 1986, Calif. Acad. Scis., San Francisco, 1986, Cumming Nature Ctr.-Rochester Mus. and Sci. Ctr., 1988, St. Hubert's Giralda, Madison, N.J., Prestige Gallery Ltd., 1989, 90, Mus. Sci., Boston, 1989-90, Wichita (Kans.) Kennel Club, Dog Mus., St. Louis, 1992, 94, San Bernardino County Mus., Redlands, Calif., 1992, 93, 94, East African Wild Life Soc., Nairobi, 1991-92, So. Vt. Fine Arts Ctr., Columbus Ohio Fine Arts Ctr., Grand Ctrl. Galleries, N.Y.C., Owen Gallery, Oklahoma City, Denver Mus. Natural History, Cleve. Mus. Natural History, Exhbn. Hall Crown Ctr., Kansas City, and numerous other gallery exhbns.; represented in permanent collections Cin. Club, Miami Bank Ohio, G and R Tackle Co., Nissequoque Golf Club, Hartwood Club, San Bernardino County Mus., The Dog Mus., Cin. Natural History Mus., Bronx Zoo, Cin. Zoo, Bank Smithtown; commissioned poster for 8th Annual Snow Leopard Symposium, Islamabad, Pakistan. Chmn. landscape com. Sea Pointe Estates, 1993—. Mem. Soc. Animal Artists (chmn. exhbns. 1985-88). Home and Office: Wild Brook Studio 7 Calle Agua San Clemente CA 92673-2749

LOPINA, ROBERT FERGUSON, aerospace company executive; b. Jamestown, N.Y., May 13, 1936; s. Konrad Stephen and Elizabeth (Ferguson) L.; m. Louise Carol Peterson, June 21, 1958; children: Kimberly, Sandra, Amy. BSME, Purdue U., 1957; SMME, MIT, 1965, Mech. Engr., 1966, PhD, 1967. Commd. 2d lt. USAF, 1957, advanced through grades to col., ret., 1983; comdr., dir. avionics lab. USAF, Aero. Systems Div., Wright Patterson AFB, Ohio, 1978-80, dep. enring., 1980-82, dep. reconnaissance, strike and electronic warfare, 1982-83; v.p. Fairchild Republic Co., Farmingdale, N.Y., 1983-87; dir. advanced devel. Ford Aerospace Corp., Detroit, 1987-89, v.p. advanced programs aeronutronic div., Newport Beach, Calif., 1988-90, v.p. Loral Aernoutronic div., 1990—; cons. W.Va. U. Aerospace/Mech., Morgantown, 1981-83; advisor N.Y. Inst. Tech., Woodbury, 1983-85. Co-author: Introduction to Aeronautics, 1971. Decorated Legion of Merit, Meritorious Service medal. Mem. AIAA (treas., vice-chmn. 1970-72), ASME, Air Force Assn., Assn. Old Crows, Tau Kappa Epsilon. Republican. Presbyterian. Avocations: fishing, boating, running, scubadiving. Home: 7 Calle Agua San Clemente CA 92673-2749

LOPP, SUSAN JANE, insurance underwriter; b. Billings, Mont., Feb. 16, 1944; d. Russell and Edith (Trapp) Wallace; m. Robert J. Lopp, June 2, 1963; children: Robert J. Jr., Cheryl J. BA, U. Mont., 1972. CLU, ChFC; registered rep. Reporter Park County News, Livingston, Mont., 1965-66; tchr. Sch. Dist. #5, Kalispell, Mont., 1968-73; planner Areawide Planning Orgn., Kalispell, 1974-77; econ. devel. dir. NW MT HRDC, Inc., Kalispell, 1978-79; ins. underwriter The Equitable, Kalispell, 1979-88, The Prudential, Kalispell, 1989—; mem. Mont. Supreme Ct. Gender Bias Task Force, Helena, 1990—, Mont. Pvt. Industry Coun., Helena, 1988—; commr. Mont. Human Rights Commn., 1993—, chair, 1995—; dir., sec.-treas. Mont. Life and Health Ins. Guaranty Assn. Bd., 1994—; Govs. Coun. for Monts. Future, Helena, 1992; chair Govs. Coun.-Women & Employment, Helena, 1981-83, Mont. Bd. Printing, Helena, 1991-92. Active Flathead City-County Health Bd., Kalispell, 1987—, chair, 1989—; mem. Flathead Coop. Planning Coalition Campaign Bd., 1993-94, Mont. Sch. for Deaf and Blind Found., Great Falls, 1988—, Mont. Rep. Women Bd., 1980-85; exec. com. United Way Flathead County, Kalispell, 1986-92; chair Mont. Womens Prison Site Selection Com., Helena, 1991. Recipient Mont. Centennial Equity award Mont. Depts. Labor and Pub. Instrn. and Higher Edn., 1989, 4-H Silver Clover award Mont. State U./Mont. Ext. Svc., 1980. Mem. AAUW (Mont. pres. 1980-82, Named Gift 1982, 93), N.W. Mont. Life Underwriters (pres. 1988-89), Flathead County Rep. Women (pres. 1985), Am. Soc. CLU and ChFC, Glacier County Pachyderm Club. Republican. Mem. Seventh Day Adventist. Office: The Prudential 295-3d Ave EN Box 7547 Kalispell MT 59904

LORANC, WAYNE SCOTT, geophysicist; b. Houston, Aug. 17, 1951; s. Arthur Rufo Jr. and Margaret (Wood) L.; children from previous marriage: Wayne Scott (dec. 1992), Marshall; m. Karen Tobler, 1992; children: Michelle, Mari. A, Del Mar Jr. Coll., Corpus Christi, Tex., 1974; BS in Wildlife Biology, Tex. A&I U., 1976; BS in Geology and Geophysics, Metro State Coll., 1981. Geophys. analyst Geophys. Svc., Inc., Denver, 1977-79; geophys. technician Amoco Prodn. Co., Denver, 1979-81; CEO, pres. LoCo Exploration Corp., Inc., Arvada, Colo., 1981—; geophysicist Cantenna/Al Aquitaine, Denver, 1981-84; salesman U.S. Sprint, Denver, 1990-94; pres. Big Horn Geophys., Denver, 1981—; mgr. Arrowstar Geophys., Denver, 1981—; owner Ecology Action of Corpus, Corpus Christi, 1974. Rep. Colo. Sch. Mines, Golden, 1985; scout master Gateway coun. Boy Scouts Am., Denver, 1987—; coach Arvada Soccer Assn., 1991-93; asst. coach Arvada Baseball Assn., 1991-94. Mem. Am. Assn. Petroleum Geophys., Denver Geophys. Soc. (picnic chmn. 1985), Soc. Exptl. Geophysicist, Wildlife Soc., Forestry Soc. Republican. Home and Office: 13613 W 66th Way Arvada CO 80004-2004

LORANCE, ELMER DONALD, organic chemistry educator; b. Tupelo, Okla., Jan. 18, 1940; s. Elmer Dewey and Imogene (Triplett) L.; m. Phyllis Ilene Miller, Aug. 31, 1969; children: Edward Donald, Jonathan Andrew. BA, Okla. State U., 1962; MS, Kansas State U., 1967; PhD, U. Okla., 1977. NIH research trainee Okla. U., Norman, 1966-70; asst. prof. organic chemistry So. Calif. Coll., Costa Mesa, 1970-73, assoc. prof., 1973-80, prof., 1980—, chmn. div. natural scis. and math., 1985-89, chmn. chemistry dept., 1990-93, chmn. divsn. natural scis. and math., 1993—. Contbr. articles to profl. jours. Mem. AAAS, Am. Chem. Soc., Internat. Union Pure and Applied Chemistry (assoc.), Am. Inst. Chemists, Am. Sci. Affiliation, Phi Lambda Upsilon. Republican. Mem. Ch. Assembly of God. Office: So Calif Coll 55 Fair Dr Costa Mesa CA 92626-6520

LORANCE, JANE, librarian; b. Sept. 16, 1946; d. Robert Clark and Evagene (Davis) Richardson; m. Frank Velasques Martinez Jr., May 28, 1966 (div. July 1970); 1 child, Robert Louis Martinez; m. William John Lorance, Feb. 14, 1983. BA in History, U. Wyo., 1971; MLibr, U. Wash., 1972. Reference and fine arts libr. Clark County Libr., 1973; dept. head Clark County Libr. Dist., 1974-77; br. supr./adminstr. Newport Beach (Calif.) Pub. Libr., 1978-82; on-call libr. Santa Ana and Newport Beach Pub. Librs., Calif. State U., Fullerton, 1984; br. adminstr. Las Vegas-Clark County Libr. Dist., 1985—. Mem. Freedom to Read Found. Mem. ALA, Popular Culture Assn., Nev. Libr. Assn., Mountain Plains Libr. Assn., So. Calif. On-Line Users Group, Newport Beach Profl. and Tech. Employees Assn. Office: Las Vegas-Clark County Libr 833 Las Vegas Blvd N Las Vegas NV 89101-2030

LORBEER, GEORGE COE, retired science educator; b. Cedarville, Calif., May 4, 1920; s. George Coe Sr. and Jeannette (Reeves) L.; m. Dorothea Margaret Weber, July 17, 1943; children: Kathleen, Mary, George, Rebecca. BA, San Francisco State U., 1942; MA, Stanford U., 1946; EdM, U. Ill., 1950, EdD, 1953. Cert. tchr., Calif. Tchr. Jordan Jr. H.S., Palo Alto, Calif., 1946-50; rsch. asst. U. Ill., Urbana, 1950-53; asst. prof. edn. L.A. State Coll., 1953-56; assoc. prof. edn. San Fernando Valley State Coll., Northridge, Calif., 1956-58; prof. edn. Calif. State U., Northridge, Calif., 1958-89; retired Calif. State U., Northridge, 1989; secondary dept. chmn. Calif. State U., Northridge, 1956-62, 68-72, 78-82; coord. program instrn. L.A. Unified Sch. Dist., 1968-79, rep. edn. forum, 1958-75; cmty. adv. bd. Chatsworth (Calif.) H.S., 1962-66; adj. prof. Lawrence U., Santa Barbara, Calif., 1972-74. Author: Science Activities for Elementary Children, 1952—, Science Activities for Children, vol. II, 1992—; editor: Circle of the World, 1971, Readings in Educational Leadership, 1969. pres. Chatsworth Cmty. Coord. Coun., 1968-72; chmn. fund drive ARC, Chatsworth, 1969, water safety instr., 1958; active PTA, 1962—. Lt. comdr. USN, 1942-47. Mem. AAAS, NEA, Nat. Sci. Tchrs. Assn., Calif. Coll. and U. Assn., B Sharp Square Dancers, Rotary (pres. 1962, 68, 72). Democrat. Roman Catholic. Home: 16439 Knollwood Dr Granada Hills CA 91344-1805

LORD, CAROLYN MARIE, artist; b. L.A., Oct. 6, 1956; m. Robert Bryce Anglin, Nov. 1, 1980; 1 child, Devin Lord Anglin. BA, Principia Coll., 1978. Artist, 1978—; juror of award Ariz. Aqueous Tubac Ctr. of Arts, 1992; juror of slide Adirondack Nat. Exhbn. Am. Watercolor, Arts Ctr. Old Forge, N.Y., 1993; workshop instr. La Romita Sch. Art, Terni, Italy, 1991, Santa Cruz (Calif.) Art League, 1990-95. One-woman shows include Maybeck Gallery, Elsah, Ill., 1978-83, Fireside Gallery, Carmel, Calif., 1978-92, Northeastern Nev. Mus., Elko, 1985, 90, Art e Espaco, Aracatuba, Brazil, 1988, Ojai (Calif.) Gallery and Design Studio, 1990, Stary-Sheets Fine Art Galleries, Irvine, Calif., 1983—, Banaker Gallery, San Francisco, 1993—; exhibited in group shows at Valley Art Ctr., Walnut Creek, Calif., 1987-94, Winfield Gallery, Carmel, Calif., 1995—; artist art reproduction notecards. Recipient Rouse medallion Adirondack Nat. Exhbn. Am. Watercolor, 1987, Exhbn. award Watercolor U.S.A., 1988, Exhbn. award San Diego Art Inst., 1992, Hon. Mention award Triton Mus. Watercolor Biennial, 1994. Mem. Nat. Watercolor Soc., Watercolor U.S.A. Honor Soc., Calif. Lawyers for Arts. Christian Scientist.

LORD, HAROLD WILBUR, electrical engineer, electronics consultant; b. Eureka, Calif., Aug. 20, 1905; s. Charles Wilbur and Rossina Camilla (Hansen) L.; B.S., Calif. Inst. Tech., 1926; m. Doris Shirley Huff, July 25, 1928; children—Joann Shirley (Mrs. Carl Cook Disbrow), Alan Wilbur, Nancy Louise (Mrs. Leslie Crandall), Harold Wayne. With Gen. Electric Co., Schenectady, 1926-66, electronics engr., 1960-66; pvt. cons. engr., Mill Valley, Calif., 1966—. Coffin Found. award Gen. Electric Co., 1933, GE Inventors award, 1966. Fellow IEEE (life, tech. v.p. 1962, Centennial medal 1984, IEEE Magnetics Soc. 1984 Achievement award). Contbr. articles to profl. jours. Patentee in field. Home and Office: 1565 Golf Course Dr Rohnert Park CA 94928-5638

LORD, JACKLYNN JEAN, student services representative; b. Sacramento, Feb. 2, 1940; d. Jasper Jackson and Celia (Moreno) Opdyke; m. Brent Andrew Nielsen, Aug. 6, 1966 (dec. Sept. 1974); 1 child, Taumie Celia; m. Mark William Lord, Mar. 5, 1983; 1 child, Jacklynn Michelle. Student, Sacramento State U., 1958-60, Cabrillo Coll., 1962-66, Sacred Coll. of Jamilian Theology and Div. Sch., Reno, 1976—. Ordained Ch. Internat. Community Christ. Communications cons. Pacific Telephone Co., San Jose, Calif., 1966-74, Nev. Bell Co., Reno, 1974-76; student services rep. for extension program Jamilian U. of Ordained, Reno, 1976—; asst. music dir. Internat. Community Christ, Reno, 1980—; choral instr. Jamilian Parochial Sch., Reno, 1976—; sexton Jamilian Handbell Choir, Reno, 1981—; organist Symphonietta, Reno, 1983—. Mem. Nat. League Concerned Clergywomen. Republican. Home: 1990 Humboldt St Reno NV 89509-3645 Office: Internat Community Christ 643 Ralston St Reno NV 89503-4436

LORD, MIA W., peace activist; b. N.Y.C., Dec. 2, 1920; m. Robert P. Lord (dec. Nov. 1977); children: Marcia Louise, Alison Jane. BA in Liberal Arts cum laude, Bklyn. Coll., 1940; postgrad., San Francisco State U., 1984—. Hon. sec. Commonwealth of World Citizens, London; membership sec. Brit. Assn. for World Govt., London; sec. Ams. in Brit. for U.S. Withdrawal from S.E. Asia, Eng.; organizer Vietnam Vigil to End the War, London; pres. Let's Abolish War chpt. World Federalist Assn., San Francisco State U.; appointed hon. sec. Commonwealth of World Citizens, London; officially invited to Vietnam, 1973; organizer Vietnam Vigil to End the War, London. Author: The Practical Way to End Wars and Other World Crises: the case for World Federal Government: listed in World Peace through World Law, 1984, and in Strengthening the United Nations, 1987, War: The Biggest Con Game in the World, 1980. Hon. sec., nat. exec. mem. Assn. of World Federalists-U.K.; founder, bd. dirs. Crusade to Abolish War and Armaments by World Law. Nominated for the Nobel Peace Prize, 1975, 92, 93; recipient four Merit awards Pres. San Francisco State U. Mem. Secretariat of World Citizens USA (life), Assn. of World Federalists USA, Brit. Assn. for World Govt. (membership sec.), Crusade to Abolish War and Armaments by World Law (founder, dir.), World Govt. Orgn. Coord. Com., World Fed. Authority Com., Campaign for UN Reform, Citizens Global Action, World Constitution and Parliament Assn., World Pub. Forum, Internat. Registry of World Citizens. Home: 174 Majestic Ave San Francisco CA 94112-3022

LORENZ, BRIAN, finance company executive; b. Bombay, India, 1939. Grad., Williams Coll., 1960; JD, Harvard U., 1963. Ptnr. Bleakley Platt & Schmidt; sec. Franklin Custodian Funds, San Mateo, Calif. Home: One Pine Ter Bronxville NY 10708 Office: Franklin Calif Tax Free Inc 777 Mariners Island Blvd San Mateo CA 94404*

LORENZ, CONNIE ELIZABETH, nutritionist; b. Cottonwood, Idaho, July 11, 1955; d. Robert G. and Anna E. (Schmidt) Gehring; m. Robert M. Lorenz, Oct. 29, 1979; children: Sara E., Jennifer A., Christopher R. BS in Food and Nutrition, U. Idaho, 1978, MS in Food and Nutrition, 1991. Clin. dietitian Saga Corp., Lewiston, Idaho, 1978-88; clin. dietitian St. Joseph Regional Med. Ctr., Lewiston, Idaho, 1988-93, clin. nutrition mgr., 1993—; mem. dietetic licensure bd. Idaho Bd. Medicine, Boise, 1994—; nutrition rep. North Ctrl. Dist. Health Dept. Adv. Bd., Lewiston, 1993—; alumni rep. Margaret Ritchie Disting. Spkr. Com., Moscow, Idaho, 1990—. Mem. Am. Assn. Diabetes Educators, Am. Dietetic Assn., Am. Soc. Parenteral Nutrition. Roman Catholic. Office: St Joseph Regional Med Ctr 415 6th St Lewiston ID 83501-2434

LORENZ, TIMOTHY CARL, real estate agent; b. Glendale, Calif., June 9, 1947; s. Raymond Jerome and Majorie Nadine (Bevis) L.; m. Jeanann Carrington, Apr. 16, 1966 (div. 1982); children: Julianne, Todd; m. Nadyne Claire Buck, Sept. 11, 1982; stepchildren: Ron, Eve, SeAnn, Dray. BA in Psychology, Calif. State U., Los Angeles, 1969, MA in Psychology, 1972. Lic. real estate agt., Calif. Chief investigator L.A. County Dept. Consumer Affairs, 1976-81; co-owner Newport Holistic Health Clinic, Newport Beach, Calif., 1981-83; chief investigator Orange County Office Consumer Affairs, Santa Ana, Calif., 1983-86; agt. Century 21 Niguel, Laguna Niguel, Calif., 1986—, mgr.; owner The Carousel, San Juan Capistrano, Calif., 1987-93, Depot...Pourri Gift Shop, San Juan Capistrano, 1991-93; instr. psychology Mt. San Antonio, Walnut, Calif., 1976-83; chmn. bd. dirs. Real Reasons, Laguna Niguel; distbr. Amway, Dana Point, Calif., 1983—; instr. Saddleback Coll., 1992-93; dir., treas.-sec. Landingham Composites, 1994. Co-author Renter Rights and Responsibilities, 1978; producer T.V. talk show Coping in Today's World, 1982 (Best of Pub. Access award 1982). Pres. Bur. Electronic and Appliance Repair Bd., Sacramento, Calif., 1980, 86, legis. com., 1979; founding mem. Nat. Automobile Dealers Consumer Action Panel, L.A., 1978-81. Recipient Letter Commendation Atty. Gen., L.A., 1980. Mem. Nat. Assn. Realtors, Assn. Foster Parents North Cen. South Orange County (pres. 1986-88), State Calif. Foster Parent Assn., Nat. Assn. Foster Parents, Dana Point C. of C., Newport Beach C. of C. Republican. Home: 33391 Ocean Hill Dr Dana Point CA 92629-1122 Office: Century 21 Niguel Realty 30232 Crown Valley Pky Laguna Beach CA 92677-2366

LORENZEN, ROBERT FREDERICK, ophthalmologist; b. Toledo, Ohio, Mar. 20, 1924; s. Martin Robert and Pearl Adeline (Bush) L.; m. Lucy Logsdon, Feb. 14, 1970; children: Roberta Jo, Richard Martin, Elizabeth Anne. BS, Duke, 1948, MD, 1948; MS, Tulane U., 1953. Intern, Presbyn. Hosp., Chgo., 1948-49; resident Duke Med. Center, 1949-51, Tulane U. Grad. Sch., 1951-53; practice medicine specializing in ophthalmology, Phoenix, 1953—; mem. staff St. Joseph's Hosp., St. Luke's Hosp., Good Samaritan Hosp., Surg. Eye Ctr. of Ariz. Pres. Ophthalmic Scis. Found., 1970-73; chmn. bd. trustees Rockefeller and Abbe Prentice Eye Inst. of St. Luke's Hosp., 1975—. Recipient Gold Headed Cane award, 1974; named to Honorable Order of Ky. Cols. Fellow ACS, Internat. Coll. Surgeons, Am. Acad. Ophthalmology and Otolaryngology, Pan Am. Assn. Ophthalmology, Soc. Eye Surgeons; mem. Am. Assn. Ophthalmology (sec. of ho. of dels. 1972-73, trustee 1973-76), Ariz. Ophthal. Soc. (pres. 1966-67), Ariz. Med. Assn. (bd. dirs. 1963-66, 69-70), Royal Soc. Medicine, Rotary (pres. Phoenix 1984-85). Republican. Editor in chief Ariz. Medicine, 1963-66, 69-70. Office: 367 E Virginia Ave Phoenix AZ 85004-1202

LORIAUX, D. LYNN, internist, endocrinologist; b. Bartlesville, Okla., Apr. 29, 1940; s. Maurice Lucien and Susan Elizabeth (Bowman) L.; m. Judith Ann Draggon, Nov. 4, 1961 (div. July 1986); children: Marc, Aubyn; m. Teresa Marie Choate, Sept. 14, 1986; children: Dylan, Daniel, Grant. BS, Colo. State U., 1962; MD, Baylor Med. Coll., 1967, PhD, 1968. Intern and resident in internal medicine Peter Bent Brigham Hosp., Boston, 1967-70; fellow in endocrinology and metabolism NIH, Bethesda, Md., 1970-772, clin. dir. Nat. Inst. Child Health and Devel., 1980-90, br. chief, 1980-90; head endocrinology Oreg. Health Sci. U., Portland, 1990—, chmn. dept. medicine, 1994—. Served with USPHS, 1970-90. Mem. Endocrine Soc. (pres. 1995-96). Office: Oreg Health Sci U 3181 SW Sam Jackson Park Rd Portland OR 97201-3011

LORING, THOMAS JOSEPH, forest ecologist; b. Haileybury, Ont., Can., May 27, 1921; s. Ernest Moore and Margaret Evangeline (Bacheller) L.; m. Beth Rogers McLaughlin, Oct. 29, 1966; children: John Francis, Christopher Thomas. BSc in Forestry, Mich. Tech. U., 1946; M Forestry, N.Y. State Coll. Forestry, 1951. Forester McCormick Estates, Champion, Mich., 1947; cons. Porteous and Co., Seattle, 1948-49; forester Penokee Veneer Co., Mellon, Wis., 1951-53; cons. E.M. Loring Consulting, Noranda, Que., Can., 1954-55; forester USDA Forest Svc., Albuquerque, 1956-81; cons. Tom Loring, Cons., Victoria, B.C., Can., 1986—; mem. Parks and Recreation Commn., Victoria, 1988-92, mem. environment adv. com., 1993—. Editor: Directory of the Timber Industry in Arizona and New Mexico,1 972; coeditor: Ecology, Uses and Management of Pinyon-Juniper Woodlands, 1977. Pres. Shawnigan Lake Residents and Rate Payers Assn., B.C., 1985-86. Mem. Soc. Am. Foresters (sect. chair 1960-62), Ecol. Soc. Am., Forest Products Rsch. Soc. (regional rep. 1980-81), Can. Inst. Forestry, Soc. Ecol. Restoration. Home: 59 Moss St, Victoria, BC Canada V8V 4M1

LOS, STANLEY CORNELIUS, JR., security consultant, private investigator; b. N.Y.C., Mar. 23, 1942; s. Stanley Cornelius and Terri S. (Latopolski) L.; m. Lenore Marie Stoffel, Mar. 19, 1966 (div. May 1988); Constance Lynette O'Shaughnessy; children: Stephanie Lynn, Jennifer Marie. BS in Physics, Ill. Benedictine Coll., 1963; MS in Physics, Ill. Inst. Tech., 1966. Rsch. physicist Argonne (Ill.) Nat. Lab., 1963-67; spl. agt. FBI, Washington,

New Orleans, L.A., 1967-92; sr. resident agt. FBI, Santa Barbara, Calif., 1992; mng. dir., founder Summit Rsch. Group, Santa Barbara, Calif., 1992—. Contbr. articles to profl. jours. Bd. dirs. Santa Barbara Youth Found., 1987-88. Mem. Former FBI Agts. Soc., Calif. Assn. Licensed Investigators, Santa Barbara Yacht Club (commodore 1988), Rancheros Visitadores, Lincoln Club of Santa Barbara. Home: 4626 Sierra Madre Rd Santa Barbara CA 93110-1321 Office: Summit Rsch Group PO Box 6905 Santa Barbara CA 93160-6905

LOSH, SAMUEL JOHNSTON, engineering administrator; b. Hershey, Pa., Nov. 11, 1932; s. Charles Seibert and Esther Dora (Johnston) L.; m. Llewellyn Mathews Hall, Sept. 26, 1964 (div. Oct., 1994); children: Elizabeth Mathews, Stephen Johnston. BSME, MIT, 1954; postgrad., Syracuse U., Utica, 1956-57, UCLA, 1968-74, U. So. Calif., 1975-81. Cert. profl. mgr. Inst. Cert. Profl. Mgrs. Engr. RCA, Camden, N.J., 1954-55; instr. Syracuse U., Utica, 1956; mem. tech. staff TRW, L.A., 1957-59; systems engr. Hoffman Electronics, L.A, 1959-62; spacecraft systems engr. Lockheed Calif. Co., Burbank, 1962-64; sr. systems specialist Xerox Spl. Info. Systems, Pasadena, Calif., 1964-87; sr. systems engr. Datametrics Corp., Chatsworth, Calif., 1987-89; pres. Milner Street, Inc., Pasadena, 1980—; sec. Regina Properties, Inc., Pasadena, 1981-92. Chmn. L.A. chpt. MIT Ednl. Coun., 1978—; facilitator Math. Standards Program, L.A. Unified Sch. Dist., 1994. Recipient George Morgan award MIT Ednl.Coun., 1987; named Silver Knight of Mgmt., Nat. Mgmt. Assn., 1980. Mem. IEEE, AIAA, MIT Alumni Assn. (bd. dirs. 1981-83). Republican. Unitarian. Home and Office: PO Box 50368 Pasadena CA 91115-0368

LOTHROP, GLORIA RICCI, historian, educator; b. L.A., Dec. 30, 1934; d. Leo N. and Maria (Angeli) R. AB in English (with honors), Immaculate Heart Coll., 1956, MA in Edn., 1963; student, U. of Pisa, Italy, 1960, U. Mysore, India, 1963; postgrad., U. Calif., L.A., 1964-65; PhD in History, U. So. Calif., 1970. Tchr. English, History Sacred Heart High School, 1956-60; tng. tchr., teaching internship program UCLA, 1964; tchr. History Beverly Hills High School, 1962-64; part time supr. of teaching interns Las Virgenes Unified Sch. Dist., 1964-65, Univ. Calif., Riverside, 1965; coord. of tchr. tng., summer internship program Univ. Calif., L.A., 1965; part time instr., U.S. History L.A. Valley C.C., 1966-67; archivist Southwest Regional Lab. for Ednl. Rsch. and Devel., 1967; lecture series coord., Current Affairs Loyola Marymount Univ, 1969-72; vis. lectr., Western Am. History Univ. Calif., 1969-70; supr. student tchrs., asst. prof., History Calif. State Polytechnic Univ., Pomona, 1970-74, supr. student tchrs., assoc. prof., History, 1974-79; vis. prof. Art Ctr. Coll. of Design, 1978-80; acting chair, Dept. of Liberal Studies Calif. State Polytechnic Univ., 1974, 77; adj. prof., Master in Liberal Arts Program Univ. So. Calif., 1980-86; CSU adminstrv. fellow, Office of the Dean of Sch. of Letters and Sci. Calif. State Univ., L.A., 1981-82; prof. history State Polytechnic U., 1979-94; Whitsett chair Calif. history Calif. State U., Northridge, 1994—; cons. Ontario Mus. of History and Art, 1992, Rancho Los Cerritos, 1991, Constitutional Rights Found., 1988, USC Sch. of Cinema, 1988-89, CSU Inst. for Teaching and Learning, 1989—, Calif. Heritage Quilt Project, 1987-88, L.A. History Project, Public T.V. Sta. KCET, 1986-88, Calif. Project, 1987-89, Afro-Am. Mus., 1985-88, El Pueblo State Historic Park, 1986—, Cattlekate Productions, 1987, So. Calif. Gas Co. and Radio Sta., 1980-88, Ontario Centennial Celebration, 1980, CBS T.V. "Bicentennial Minutes", 1979-80, and participation in numerous other profl. activities. Author: Recollections of the Flathead Mission: The Memorie of Fr. Gregory Mengarini, S.J., 1977, Chi Siamo: The Italians of L.A., 1981, California Woman, A Historic Profile, 1986, Guide to the Historic Resources of the State of Calif., 1989, Rancho San Jose, A Sesquacentennial Tribute, 1987, Pomona Valley: A Centennial History, 1988, A Guide to Historic Outings in Southern Calif., 1991, Quality of Life at California State Polytechnic University, Pomona, 1991, Los Angeles Ethnic Profile, 1994; contbr. articles to numerous profl. jours. bd. govs. Calif. Maritime Acad., 1980-82, 82-85, bd. dirs. Photo Friends, L.A. Public Libr., 1990—, hist. adv. Com. to Save Italian Hall Com., 1990—, mem. State and Local Hist. Day Coms., 1987-89, pres. bd. dirs. El Pueblo Park Assn., 1984-85, bd. dirs., 1986-87, pres. emeritus 1988, mem. L.A. 200 Exec. Com. and acting chair edn. com., 1979-91, mem. citizens Adv. Com. for the 1984 Olympics, 1981-84, bd. dirs. L.A. Internat. Visitors Coun., 1981-87, sec. to the exec. com. L.A. Archdiocesan Archival Ctr., 1982-89, chair publications com. and bd. mem. Calif. Hist. Soc., 1987-88. Recipient Community Enrichment award Hist. Soc. of Southern Calif., 1993, Carl Wheat award, 1990, Woman of Distinction award Today's Women's Forum Citrus Coll., 1987, Outstanding Achievement award Southern Calif. Social Sci. Assn., 1987, Calif. Polytechnic Authors Golden Leaves award, 1986, 87, 89, 90, tchr award Daughters of Colonial Wars award, 1983, Outstanding Italian Am. award Targhe d'Oro, Regione Puglia, Italia, 1982, Dist. Alumnae award, Immaculate Heart Coll. Alumnae Assn., 1981, George Danielson Historical Writing Excellence award Westerners Internat., 1978, Outstanding Feminist of the Pomona Valley award NOW, 1974; Haynes Huntington Rsch. fellow Huntington Library, 1986, 91, Fulbright fellow, 1963, Daniel Murphy Found. grantee, 1987. Fellow Calif. Hist. Soc.; mem. Am. Hist. Assn., Am. Italian Hist. Assn., Orgn. of Am. Historians, Women's Studies Assn., Nat. Coun. for the Social Studies, Western Hist. Assn., Southwest Labor Studies Assn., West Coast Assn. for Women Historians, Hist. Soc. of So. Calif., Friends of the Huntingt. Democrat. Roman Catholic. Home: 880 Paige Dr Pomona CA 91768-1644 Office: Calif State Univ Northridge CA 91330

LOTT, DAVIS NEWTON, advertising agency executive, publisher; b. San Antonio, May 8, 1913; s. James and Sissilla (Davis) L.; m. Arlene Marion Peterson, Nov. 1, 1942; children: Vicki Arlene, Christy Sue, Laurie Ann. B.S., Northwestern U., 1935; post-grad. UCLA. With Better Homes and Gardens and Successful Farming, Des Moines, Iowa, 1935-36; with Abbott, Labs., North Chicago, Ill., 1936-37; copywriter J. Walter Thompson, Chgo., 1938-39; owner and pres. Lott Advt. Agy., L.A., 1939-41, 46—; pres. USA Corp., Marina Del Rey, Calif.; pres. Lott Publs., Santa Monica, Calif.; pub. Am. Carwash Rev., Am. Personal Protection Rev., Candy WORLD, Tobacco and Sundries WORLD, Specialty/Fancifoods WORLD, Chocolate and Nut WORLD, SugarFree WORLD, New Inventions WORLD, Organic WORLD, Teen Scene, Bubble 'n' ChewinGum WORLD, Cracker/Snack WORLD, Surfing Illustrated, Smoker's Digest, Books and Authors WORLD, New Products and Mail Order WORLD, The Cosa News; dir. spl. projects Microlert Systems Internat. Past bd. dirs. Los Angeles Library Assn. Comdr. USNR, 1941-46, 1951-52, World War II, Korea. Named Assoc. Dean of Candy Industry, Nat. Candy Wholesalers Assn., 1974. Author: Rules of the Road, 1942, Handbook of the Nautical Road; Emergency Shiphandling Manual, 1943, Collision Prevention, 1947, Treasure Trail, 1944, Star Spangled Broadcast, 1950, Mystery of Midnight Springs, 1954, Dodge City Justice, 1957, The Inaugural Addresses of the American Presidents, 1964, The Presidents Speak, 1965, See How They Ran 1972, The Presidents Illustrated, 1976, Jimmy Carter-And How He Won, 1976; co-author: (with Bruce Greenland) musical comedy The Music Room, 1982, The Presidents Speak-The Inaugural Addresses from Washington to Clinton, 1994. Home: 13222 Admiral Ave Unit B Marina Del Rey CA 90292 Office: PO Box 9669 Marina Del Rey CA 90295

LOTT, IRA TOTZ, pediatric neurologist; b. Cin., Apr. 15, 1941; s. Maxwell and Jeneda (Totz) L.; m. Ruth J. Weiss, June 21, 1964; children: Lisa, David I. BA cum laude, Brandeis U., 1963; MD cum laude, Ohio State U., 1967. Intern Mass. Gen. Hosp., Boston, 1967, resident in pediatrics, 1967-69, resident in child neurology, 1971-74; clin. assoc. NIH, Bethesda, Md., 1969-71; from clin. rsch. fellow to asst. prof. Harvard Med. Sch., Boston, 1971-82; clin. dir. Eunice Kennedy Shriver Ctr. for Mental Retardation, Waltham, Mass., 1974-82; assoc. prof. U. Calif., Irvine, 1983-91, prof., 1992—; chmn. dept. pediatrics U. Calif., Irvine, 1992—, dir. pediatric neurology, 1983—; pres. Prof. Child Neurology, Mpls., 1992—. Editor: Down Syndrome-Medical Advances, 1991; contbr. articles to profl. jours. Sec., treas. Child Neurology Soc., Mpls., 1987-90. Lt. comdr. USPHS, 1969-71. NIH grantee, 1974—; recipient Career Devel. award Kennedy Found., 1976. Fellow Am. Acad. Neurology; mem. Am. Pediatric Soc., Am. Neurol. Assn., Nat. Down Syndrome Soc. (sci. acad. bd. 1985—), Western Soc. for Pediatric Rsch. (councillor 1989-91). Office: U Calif Irvine Med Ctr Dept Pediatrics 101 The City Dr S # 27 Orange CA 92668-3201

LOTZ, TREY, scientology auditor; b. Buffalo, N.Y., Apr. 13, 1945; s. Albert Frank and Carolyn Kathleen (Rouse) L.; m. Delores Ismay Simons Pierson, Oct. 25, 1968 (div. June 1978); m. Barbara Sager, Aug. 26, 1989. BA, Hamilton Coll., 1967. Cert. class 8 scientology auditor. Minister Trey Lotz Field Ministry, L.A., 1970, pastoral counselor, 1970-94. Named Field Auditor of Yr., Ch. of Scientology, L.A., 1976.

LOUCKS, GORDON CRAIG, business educator, consultant; b. Erie, Pa., Aug. 8, 1947; s. Warren M. and Betty Jean (Anderson) L.; m. June Masters, Dec. 21, 1969 (div. 1977); children: David Eric, Michelle Elaine; m. Judith Allen, Dec. 1, 1979; 1 child, Jessica Allene Law. BS in Bus. Adminstrn., Ariz. State U., 1974, M of Quantitative Systems, 1992. Cert. fellow in prodn. and inventory mgmt.; cert. acad. assoc. Goldratt Inst. Asst. dir. admissions DeVry Inst. Tech., Phoenix, 1974-77; dir. admissions Mo. Inst. Tech., Kansas City, Mo., 1977-79; from asst. prof. to prof. DeVry Inst. Tech., Phoenix, 1981-92, sr. prof. bus. ops., 1992—; cons. in field. Contbr. articles to profl. jours. With U.S. Army, 1970-72. Mem. Am. Prodn. and Inventory Control Soc. (region staff 1991—, chpt. acad. liaison 1988—, pres. Phoenix chpt. 1994—), Prodn. and Ops. Mgmt. Soc. Democrat. Office: DeVry Inst Tech 2149 W Dunlap Ave Phoenix AZ 85021-2982

LOUDEN, WILLARD CHARLES, artist, environmental consultant; b. Trinidad, Colo., Jan. 16, 1925; s. Roy D. and Zita P. (Bradley) L.; m. Virginia M. Hudson, Juen 1964 (div. 1969); 1 child, Tamara; m. Mary Ann Thiel, Jan. 1, 1973. AA, Trinidad (Colo.) State Coll., 1947; BA, U. Mo., 1949; postgrad., Colo. State U., 1973. Rancher Branson, Colo., 1946-86; tchr. Branson High Sch., 1952-57; wildlife cinematographer Branson, 1955-62; vol. Peace Corps, Iran, 1962-64; geology, anthropology, mus. tech. instr. Trinidad State Coll., 1973-76, bldg. renovator Trinidad, 1977—; environ. cons. Branson, 1977—; mus. dir., curator A.R. Mitchell Mus. & Gallery, Trinidad, 1980—; Bd. dirs. Louden-Henritze Archeol. Mus., 1990—. One man shows include Columbian Hotel, Trinidad, Colo., 1960, Colo. Bank and Trust, Delta, Colo., La Rennaisance, Pueblo, Colo., 1993; three person show A.R. Mitchell Mus. and Gallery, Trinidad, 1985; exhibited in group shows at Folsom Art Group, Raton, N.Mex., Trinidad, 1960-67, Trinidad Roundup Shows, 1975-87, Nat. Art Shows, LaJunta, Colo., 1979-90, Wildlife Art Exhbn., Denver, 1983, Artists of the West Show, Colorado Springs, 1988, Santa Fe Trail Days Show, Trinidad, 1989-90; included in permanent collections: Trinidad Nat. Bank, Otero Jr. Coll., LaJunta, Nuzum Nurseries, Boulder, Bob Doak Oil Explorations, Albuquerque. Pres. So. Colo. Heritage Conservancy, Pueblo, 1987—, S.E. Colo. Area Health Edn. Ctr., 1990—, Friends of Purgatory, 1993—; adv. com. Pinon Canyon Manuever Area Land Utilization Tech. Adv. Com., 1984—; chmn. bd. Mid-Town Investment Corp., Trinidad, 1975-87. With U.S. Army, 1943-46. Recipient Outstanding Svc. award, Colo. Nature Conservancy, 1986, Internat. Peace Prize, Beyond War, 1987, Stephen Hart award, Colo. State Hist. Soc., 1988, Outstanding Svc. award, A.R. Mitchell Mus. and Gallery, 1990. Mem. Colo. Archaeol. Soc. (chpt. pres.), Trinidad Art League (pres. 1975-77), Trinidad Hist. Soc. (hon. life mem.). Home: 83500 County Rd 10 Branson CO 81027-9501 Office: AR Mitchell Mus & Gallery PO Box 95 Trinidad CO 81082-0095

LOUDERBACK, TRUMAN EUGENE, environmental project manager; b. Sterling, Colo., Jan. 17, 1946; s. George DeWayne and Lillian Louise (Harrach) L.; m. Dena Marie Chambers, June 1, 1985; children: Nicole Marie, Kyle Eugene, Matthew Joseph. BS, Colo. State U., 1968; postgrad., U. Colo., 1974-75. Project investigator and biologist, research inst. Colo. Sch. Mines, Golden, 1972-78; adminstr. quality assurance Cleveland-Cliffs Iron Co., Casper, Wyo., 1979, dir. environ. affairs, 1980-83; dir. environ. affairs Cleveland-Cliffs Iron Co., Rifle, Colo., 1984-88, Cliffs Engring., Inc., Rifle, Colo., 1984-88; pvt. practice cons. Lakewood, Colo., 1978-79, Rifle, 1988-89; sr. project mgr., quality asurance mgr. Roy F. Weston, Inc., Lakewood, Colo., 1989—; chmn. environ. com. Pacific Shale Project, Rifle, 1983-87, also mgr. environ. impact statement, 1983-84. Contbr. articles to profl. jours. Industry rep. Colo. Joint Rev. Process Team, Colo. Dept. Nat. Resources, 1983. Republican. Methodist. Lodge: Rotary (bd. dirs. Rifle chpt. 1984), Masons. Home: 13736 W Auburn Ave Lakewood CO 80228-4700 Office: Roy F Weston Inc 215 Union Blvd Ste 600 Lakewood CO 80228-1842

LOUGANIS, GREG E., former Olympic athlete, actor; b. San Diego, Jan. 29, 1960; s. Peter E. and Frances I. (Scott) L. Student, U. Miami, Fla., 1978-80; B.A. in Drama, U. Calif., Irvine, 1983. Mem. U.S. Nat. Diving Team, 1976—. Author: Breaking The Surface, 1995. Recipient Silver medal Olympic Games, 1976, 2 Olympic Gold medals, 1984, 2 Olympic Gold medals, 1988; James E. Sullivan award, Olympic Games, 1984; inducted into Olympic Hall of Fame, 1985; winner 48 U.S. nat. diving titles, World Diving Champion (platform and springboard) 1986, Jesse Owens award, 1987, Pan Am Gold medal, 1979, 83, 87; Gold medalist (platform and springboard) Seoul Olympics, 1988. Home: PO Box 4130 Malibu CA 90264-4130*

LOUGHMAN, WILLIAM DOSTER, cytogenetics/pre-natal diagnosis lab director; b. Oklahoma City, July 10, 1932; s. William Noland and Mary Vyola (Bubb) Loughman; m. Linnet Neale Goodrich, 1956 (div. 1966); children: Paul Owen, Elizabeth Leigh, Donald Ewan; m. Katharine Jean Hershey, Feb. 11, 1967. BS, U. Calif., Berkeley, 1960, MS, 1964, PhD, 1973. Diplomate Am. Bd. Med. Genetics. Biophysicist U. Calif., Berkeley, 1965-74; dir. cytogenetics lab. U. Calif., San Francisco, 1975-82; spl. cytogeneticist Children's Hosp., Oakland, Calif., 1982-89, dir. cytogenetics lab., 1989—; adj. assoc. prof. pediatrics U. Calif., San Francisco, 1980-82; cons. CDC, Atlanta, 1980, Pacific States Regional Genetics Network, Berkeley, 1987-93, Sutter Meml. Hosp., Sacramento, 1993-94, Stanford (Calif.) U. Med. Ctr., 1994—. Contbr. over 60 articles to profl. jours. Active, office holder various mountain rescue groups, Calif., 1960-90. Fellow Am. Coll. Med. Genetics (founding); mem. AAAS, Am. Soc. Human Genetics, Sigma Xi. Office: Childrens Hosp Med Genetics 747 52nd St Oakland CA 94609

LOUIE, DAVID MARK, lawyer; b. Oakland, Calif., Oct. 8, 1951; s. Paul and Emma (Woo) L.; m. Johanna C. Chuan, Sept. 6, 1986; children: Ryan David, Jenna Rachel. AB cum laude, Occidental Coll., 1973; JD, U. Calif., Berkeley, 1977. Bar: Calif. 1977, U.S. Dist. Ct. (no. Dist.) Calif. 1977, U.S. Ct. Appeals (9th cir.) 1977, Hawaii 1978, U.S. Dist. Ct. Hawaii 1978. Ptnr. Case & Lynch, Honolulu, 1977-88; sr. ptnr. Roeca, Louie & Hiraoka, Honolulu, 1988—. Contbg. author: Going Back, 1972, Hawaii Tort Liability Issues in Work Site Accident Cases, 1989, Trying the Automobile Accident Case, 1991, Hawaii Tort Law Update, 1992, 94. Bd. dirs. Jr. Achievement Hawaii, Honoulu. Mem. ABA, Hawaii Bar Assn. (bd. dirs. 1994—), Calif. Bar Assn., Hawaii Def. Lawyers Assn. (bd. dirs. 1990—, sec.-treas. 1994-95), Nat. Asian Pacific ABA (Hawaii chpt. pres. 1992-95), Mensa, Oahu Country Club, Pacific Club. Home: 4122 Pakolu Pl Honolulu HI 96816-3930 Office: Roeca Louie & Hiraoka 841 Bishop St Ste 900 Honolulu HI 96813-3910

LOUIS, NIKKI NOJIMA, playwright, actress; b. Seattle, Dec. 7, 1937; d. Shoichi and Michiyo (Nakatsu) Nojima; m. Daniel K. Louis, Nov. 22, 1968; 1 child, Kimberly Kay. BA in Lit., Calif. State U., 1962. Co-author, performer Word of Mouth Physicians/Educators for Social Responsibility, Seattle, 1984-90; author, rschr., performer Japanese Am. Citizens League, Seattle, 1985; playwright Pioneer Sq. Theatre, Seattle, 1985, N.W. Asian Am. Theatre, Seattle, 1987; playwright, educator, dramaturg Seattle Group Theatre, 1987—; writer, educator, prodr. Local Access, Seattle, 1990—; vis. artist Oberlin (Ohio) Coll., 1988; commd. playwright Mus. of History and Industry, Seattle, 1990, 91-92, Women's Internat. League for Peace & Freedom, Seattle, Bryn Mawr, Pa., Swarthmore, Pa., Concord W.Va., San Jose, 1990-94, Bainbridge Performing Arts, Bainbridge Island, Wash., 1993; multicultural educator Seattle Repertory Theatre, 1992-94; playwriting tchr. Seattle Children's Theatre, 1994; drama specialist Wash. Alliance for Arts Edn., Seattle, 1994—. Author: (plays) Changing Faces, 1988, Our Mothers' Stories, 1989 (Wash. State Centennial award 1989), Issei, 1993, I Am Furious Yellow, 1994, Shirley Temple at the Alamo, 1995; author documentary theatre: Breaking the Silence, 1985, Most Dangerous Women, 1990, Winds of Change, 1990, I Dream A World, 1991. Benefit organizer Physicians for Social Responsibility, Seattle, 1984, Japanese Am. Citizens League, Seattle and Tacoma, 1985, Rainbow Coalition, Seattle, 1992; vol. Mayoral race of Norm Rice, Seattle, 1990; bd. dirs. Winfred Ward Meml. Fund, 1992—; v.p. Local Access for Arts and Edn., 1989—; founder Playwrights in Progress, 1987-89; founder Women Who Write Too Much, 1992—. Artist Trust fellow in playwriting, 1988; grantee Jane Addams Peace Assn., N.Y.C., 1990, 93, Bill of Rights Edn. Collaborative, Washington, 1991, Ptnrs. in Pub. Edn., Seattle, 1992, 93, Washington Commn. for the Humanities, 1994, Washington Arts Commn., 1995. Mem. N.W. Playwrights Guild (mem. steering com. 1986-88), Wash. Alliance for Arts and Edn. (bd. dirs.), Seattle Playwrights Alliance, Assn. for Asian Am. Performers, Alliance of Asian Am. Artists, Matrix Table. Office: Local Access 4203 Brooklyn Ave NE Seattle WA 98105

LOUNSBURY, JOHN FREDERICK, geographer, educator; b. Perham, Minn., Oct. 26, 1918; s. Charles Edwin and Maude (Knight) L.; m. Dorothea Frances Eggers, Oct. 3, 1943; children—John Frederick, Craig Lawrence, James Gordon. B.S., U. Ill., 1942, M.S., 1946; Ph.D., Northwestern U., 1951. Asst. dir. rural land classification program Insular Govt., P.R., 1949-52; cons., research analyst Dayton Met. Studies, Inc., Ohio, 1957-60; chmn. dept. earth scis., prof. geography Antioch Coll., 1951-61; prof. geography, head dept. geography and geology Eastern Mich. U., 1961-69; chmn. dept. geography Ariz. State U., 1969-77; dir. Ctr. for Environ. Studies, 1977-80; prof. emeritus Ariz. State U., 1987—; project dir. Geography in Liberal Edn. Project, Assn. Am. Geographers, NSF, 1963-65, project dir. commn. on coll. geography, 1965-74; dir. environment based edn. project US. Office Edn., 1974-75; dir. spatial analysis of land use project NSF, 1975-85. Author articles, workbooks, textbooks. Mem. Yellow Springs Planning Commn., Ohio, dir. research, 1957-60; mem. Ypsilanti Planning Commn., 1961-66; research com. Washtenaw County Planning Commn., 1961-69; mem. cons. Ypsilanti Indsl. Devel. Corp., 1961-63. Served with AUS, 1942-46, ETO. Named Man of Yr., Yellow Springs C. of C., 1956-57. Fellow Ariz.-Nev. Acad. Sci.; mem. Assn. Am. Geographers (chmn. East Lakes div. 1959-61, mem. nat. exec. council 1961-64, chmn. liberal edn. com. 1961-65), Nat. Council Geog. Edn. (chmn. earth sci. com. 1961-68, regional coord. 1961-63, mem. exec. bd. 1968-71, 77-83, v.p. 1977-78, pres. 1979-80, Disting. Svc. award 1988, Disting. Mentor award 1990), Mich. Acad. Sci. Arts and Letters (chmn. pub. relations com. 1964-69, past chmn. geography sect.), Ohio Acad. Sci. (past exec. v.p.), Mich. Acad. Sci., Ariz. Acad. Sci., Am. Geog. Soc., AAAS, Sigma Xi, Delta Kappa Epsilon, Gamma Theta Upsilon. Home: 7850 E Vista Dr Scottsdale AZ 85250-7641 Office: Ariz State U Dept Geography Tempe AZ 85281

LOUSBERG, SISTER MARY CLARICE, hospital executive; b. Fleming, Colo., Aug. 21, 1929; d. Edward P. and M. Irene (Berg) L. R.N., St. Joseph Hosp., Denver, 1952; B.S. in Nursing Edn., St. Mary Coll., Leavenworth, Kans., 1969; M.P.A. in Health Care Adminstrn., U. So. Calif., 1971. Nursing supr. St. John's Hosp., Helena, Mont., 1954-59, supr. obstetrics, Santa Monica, Calif., 1959-63; operating room supr. Providence Hosp., Kansas City, Kans., 1963-66; dir. nursing service DePaul Hosp., Cheyenne, Wyo., 1966-68, pres., 1979-88; adminstr. St. James Community Hosp., Butte, Mont., 1972-79; patient representative St. Mary's Hosp. & Med. Ctr., 1991—; bd. dirs. St. Joseph Hosp., Denver, 1980-87, 92—, Laramie County Health Planning Com., Cheyenne, 1980-84. Mem. Wyo. State Cert. of Need Rev. Bd., Cheyenne, 1982-83, Cheyenne MX Impact Com., 1982-87. Named Boss of Yr., Am. Bus. Women's Assn., Cheyenne, 1980. Fellow Am. Coll. Hosp. Adminstrs. (Regent Wyo. 1982-88); mem. Wyo. Hosp. Assn. (chmn. bd. dirs. 1986), Catholic Hosp. Assn., Mont. Hosp. Assn. (pres. 1976-77).

LOUVAU, GORDON ERNEST, management consultant, educator; b. Oakland, Calif., May 29, 1928; s. Ernest and Ella Meta (Meins) L.; m. Lois Louvau Peterson, June 9, 1984; children: John Pierre, Tanya Lissette, Charles Frederic. Student U. Calif., 1946-49; postgrad. Calif. State U., Hayward, 1975-77; MBA, John F. Kennedy U., 1980. Cert. mgmt. acct., 1975. Accountant, Oakland, 1950-59; asst. controller U.S. Leasing, Inc., San Francisco, 1960-61; pres. Louvau Systems Co., Oakland, 1962-66; v.p., gen. mgr. Prescolite div. U.S. Industries Co., San Leandro, Calif., 1966-68; cons. acctg. systems, 1969—; vis. prof. acctg. U. S.Africa, 1970-71; dir. Inst. Research and Bus. Devel., asst. prof. acctg. Calif. State U. at Hayward, 1972-80; asst. dean., asso. prof. mgmt., dir. acctg. programs J.F. Kennedy U., 1969-85; adj. prof. Golden Gate U., San Francisco, 1985—; instr. U. Calif. Ctr. Media and Independent Learning, 1973—; lectr. Naval Postgrad. Sch., Monterey, 1990—. Mem. Inst. Mgmt. Accts. (dir. 1972-74), Am. Acctg. Assn. Author: Financial Management of the Clinical Laboratory, 1974; Management and Cost Control Techniques for the Clinical Laboratory, 1977; Computers in Accountant's Offices, 1981. Office: PO Box 5808 Carmel CA 93921-5808

LOUX, GORDON DALE, organization executive; b. Souderton, Pa., June 21, 1938; s. Curtis L. and Ruth (Derstine) L.; m. Elizabeth Ann Nordland, June 18, 1960; children: Mark, Alan, Jonathan. Diploma, Moody Bible Inst., Chgo., 1960; BA, Gordon Coll., Wenham, Mass., 1962; BD, No. Bapt. Sem., Oak Brook, Ill., 1965, MDiv, 1971; MS, Nat. Coll. Edn., Evanston,Ill., 1984; LHD (hon.), Sioux Falls Coll., 1985. Ordained to ministry, Bapt. Ch., 1965. Assoc. pastor Forest Park (Ill.) Bapt. Ch., 1962-65; alumni field dir. Moody Bible Inst., Chgo., 1965-66, dir. pub. rels., 1972-76; dir. devel. Phila. Coll. Bible, 1966-69; pres. Stewardship Svcs., Wheaton, Ill., 1969-72; exec. v.p. Prison Fellowship Ministries, Washington, 1976-84, pres., CEO, 1984-88; pres., CEO Prison Fellowship Internat., Washington, 1979-87, Internat. Students, Inc., Colorado Springs, Colo., 1988-93; pres. Stewardship Svcs. Group, Colorado Springs, 1994—. Author: Uncommon Courage, 1987, You Can Be a Point of Light, 1991; contbg. author: Money for Ministries, 1989, Dictionary of Christianity in America, 1989. Bd. dirs. Evang. Coun. for Fin. Accountability, Washington, 1979-92, vice chmn., 1981-84, 86-87, chmn., 1987-89; vice chmn. Billy Graham Greater Washington Crusade, 1985-85; bd. dirs. Evang. Fellowship of Mission Agys., 1991—. Named Alumnus of Yr., Gordon Coll., 1986. Mem. Broadmoor Golf Club (Colo. Springs). Republican. Home: 740 Bear Paw Ln Colorado Springs CO 80906-3215 Office: PO Box 60037 Colorado Springs CO 80960-0037

LOVATO, ROBERTO, association executive; b. San Francisco, Nov. 14, 1963; s. Ramon Alfredo and Maria Elena (Alvarenga) L. BA in Rhetoric with honors, U. Calif., Berkeley. Fundraiser various orgns., San Francisco; exec. dir. Ctrl. Am. Resource Ctr., L.A.; v.p. SEED, Inc., L.A. Active Calif. Latino Civil Rights Network, 1993-94. Fellow Eureka Found., Washington and L.A., 1994—. Office: CARECEN 1636 W 8th St Ste 215 Los Angeles CA 90017

LOVATT, ARTHUR KINGSBURY, JR., manufacturing company executive; b. Ventura, Calif., Mar. 12, 1920; s. Arthur Kingsbury and Flora (Mercedes) L.; B.S., U. So. Calif., 1941; M.B.A., Queens U., 1943; m. Juanita Gray, Feb. 1, 1946; children—Sherry Lynn, Tim Arthur. Leaseman, Shell Oil Co., Los Angeles, 1946-51; dir. indsl. relations Willys-Overland Motors, Inc., Los Angeles, 1952-55; asst. to pres. and gen. mgr. Pastushin Aviation Corp., Los Angeles, 1955-57; pres. Lovatt Assos., Los Angeles, 1957-66; chemn. bd., pres., gen. mgr. Lovatt Tech. Corp., Santa Fe Springs, Calif., 1966—, also dir.; chmn. bd. Lovatt Sci. Corp., Santa Fe Springs, Metal Ore Processes, Inc., Santa Fe Springs; dir. Lovatt Industries, Inc., others. Mem. Calif. Rep. State Central Com., 1964—; chartered mem. Rep. Pres. Task Force, citizens adv. commn.; state adviser U.S. Congl. Adv. Bd. With U.S. Army, 1943-45. Mem. Am. Legion (post comdr. 1946), AAAS, Nat. Space Inst., Am. Soc. Metals, Los Angeles C. of C., U. So. Calif. Alumni Assn. (life), Nat. Hist. Soc. (founding assoc.), N.Y. Acad. Scis., Internat. Oceanographic Found., Smithsonian Assos., Am. Ordnance Assn., Disabled Am. Vets., U.S. Senatorial Club, Nat. Rifle Assn. Club: Masons (past master, Shriner). Inventor, developer tech. processes. Office: Lovatt Tech Corp 10106 Romandel Ave Santa Fe Springs CA 90670-3434

LOVE, GORDON LEE, pathologist, researcher; b. Concord, Calif., Dec. 11, 1951; s. Curtis and Violet (Cota) L.; m. Margaret Fuller, Jan. 12, 1985. B.S., La. Tech. U., 1973; M.D., Tulane Med. Sch., 1978. Diplomate Am. Bd. Pathology, Anatomic and Clin. Pathology, Am. Bd. Med. Microbiology, Mycology; spl. qualification in med. microbiology, cytopathology. Resident in pathology Charity Hosp., New Orleans, 1978-83, vis. pathologist, 1984-93; staff pathologist VA Hosp., New Orleans, 1983-93; instr. pathology La. State U. Med. Sch., New Orleans, 1984-86; asst. prof., 1986-92, assoc. prof., 1992-93; dir. labs. VA Northern Calif. System Clinics, Martinez, 1993—; clin. assoc. prof. U. Calif., Davis, 1994—. Contbr. articles to profl. jours. Fellow Coll. Am. Pathologists; mem. Internat. Acad. Pathologists, Am. Soc. for Microbiologist. Democrat. Presbyterian. Avocation: computing. Home: 1300 Bonita Bahia Benicia CA 94510-2406 Office: VA Clin 150 Muir Rd Martinez CA 94553-4612

LOVE, JACK WAYNE, surgeon; b. Belleville, Ill., Sept. 20, 1930; s. Charles H. and Helen M. (Golden) L.; student Harvard, 1948-49, U.S. Mil. Acad., 1950-51, U. Ill., Chgo., 1951-52; MD cum laude, Yale U., 1958; D Phiosophy

(Rhodes scholar), Oxford U., Eng., 1956; m. Elizabeth J. Vogt, Nov. 19, 1960; children: Charles S., John W., Elizabeth P., Richard M., George F., Sarah L. Intern Barnes Hosp., St. Louis, 1959-60, resident in gen. surgery, 1960-61, fellow in thoracic surgery, 1961-63; resident in gen. surgery Walter Reed Gen. Hosp., Washington, 1963-65; practice medicine specializing in cardiovascular surgery; chief of thoracic surgery William Beaumont Gen. Hosp., El Paso, Tex., 1965-67, dir. intern tng., 1966-67; chief div. thoracic and cardiovascular surgery Balt. City Hosps., 1967-69; asso. prof. surgery Johns Hopkins U. Sch. Medicine, Balt., 1967-70; staff surgeon Johns Hopkins Hosp., 1967-70, Greater Balt. Med. Center, 1969-70; Union Meml. Hosp., 1969-70, Md. Gen. Hosp., 1969-70; cons. thoracic surgeon Good Samaritan Hosp., 1969-70, Mt. Wilson State Hosp., 1969-70, Santa Barbara (Calif.) Cottage Hosp., 1970—, Goleta (Calif.) Valley Community Hosp., 1970—, attending thoracic surgeon Harbor Gen. Hosp., Los Angeles, 1974—; assoc. clin. prof. surgery U. Calif., Los Angeles, 1974-89; pres. Love Med. Rsch., 1985—; pres., CEO Autogenics, 1990-95. Served from capt. to maj. U.S. Army, 1963-67. Diplomate Am. Bd. Surgery, Am. Bd. Thoracic Surgery. Fellow ACS, Am. Coll. Cardiology, Am. Coll. Chest Physicians; mem. Soc. for Vascular Surgery, Internat. Cardiovascular Soc., Am. Assn. Thoracic Surgery, Soc. of Thoracic Surgeons, Western Thoracic Surg. Assn., Pacific Coast Surg. Assn., N.Y. Acad. Scis., Am. Trauma Soc., Pan-Pacific Surg. Assn., Soc. Internat. Chirurgie, Internat. Soc. for Artificial Organs, Internat. Soc. for Cardiac Biol. Implants, Sigma Xi, Alpha Omega Alpha. Republican. Roman Catholic. Contbr. numerous articles to med. jours.; editorial bd. Jour. AMA, 1973-77; patentee blood oxygenator, prosthetic heart valve. Home: 785 Carosam Rd Santa Barbara CA 93110-2201

LOVE, LAURIE MILLER, science editor; b. Fed. Republic Germany, May 7, 1960; came to U.S., 1961; d. Thomas Walter and Jacquelyn (Jolley) Miller; m. Raymond Lee Love. Student, U. Minn., 1979-80; BA in Psychology, Scripps Coll., 1983; postgrad., UCLA. Programmer specialist Control Data Corp., San Diego, 1982, asst. mgr. software retail store, 1983-84; support technician Ashton-Tate, Torrance, Calif., 1984, editor-in-chief, 1985-87; mgr. tech. pub. Ashton-Tate, Torrance, 1986-87; product mgr. Apple Products Nantucket Corp., Los Angeles, 1987-88; sr. mktg. cons. Macintosh Market Launch Systems, Rancho Palos Verdes, Calif., 1988; pres. Miller Tech. Pub., Santa Cruz, 1987—; contractor, writer, editor Claris Corp., Santa Clara, Calif., Apple Computer, Cupertino, Calif., Live Picture, Inc., Soquel, Calif., Aladdin Sys., Watsonville, Calif. Tech. and devel. editor Addison-Wesley, Osborne/McGraw Hill, TAB books; author Using ClarisWorks, 1992, Using ClarisWorks for Windows, 1993; contbr. feature articles to monthly mag., 1985—, computer product manuals, 1987—. Mem. Soc. Tech. Comm. (sr., Silicon Valley chpt.), Women in Tech. (internat.), Phi Beta Phi (asst. treas. 1980). Democrat. Methodist.

LOVE, SANDRA RAE, information specialist; b. San Francisco, Feb. 20, 1947; d. Benjamin Raymond and Charlotte C. Martin; B.A. in English, Calif. State U., Hayward, 1968; M.S. in L.S., U. So. Calif., 1969; m. Michael D. Love, Feb. 14, 1971. Tech. info. specialist Lawrence Livermore (Calif.) Nat. Lab., 1969—. Mem. Spl. Libraries Assn. (sec. nuclear sci. div. 1980-82, chmn. 1983-84, bull. editor 1987-89), Beta Sigma Phi. Democrat. Episcopalian. Office: Lawrence Livermore Nat Lab PO Box 808 # L387 Livermore CA 94551-0808

LOVE, SUSAN DENISE, accountant, consultant, small business owner; b. Portland, Oreg., Aug. 5, 1954; d. Charles Richard and Betty Lou (Reynolds) Beck; m. Daniel G. Oliveros, Dec. 21, 1979 (div. Nov. 1983); m. Michael Dean Love, Aug. 24, 1984 (div. Mar. 1989); m. Michael Eugene Watson, July 28, 1990 (div. Dec. 1994). BA in Graphic Design, Portland State U., 1976. Office mgr. Rogers Machinery Co., Portland, 1972-77; exec. sec. Creighton Shirtmakers, N.Y.C., 1977-80; dir. adminstrn. Henry Grethel div. Manhattan Industries, N.Y.C., 1980-81; exec. asst. S.B. Tanger and Assocs., N.Y.C., 1981-83; exec. asst., bookkeeper M Life Ins. Co., Portland, 1983-84; acct. cons., owner Office Assistance, Portland, 1984—; owner WE LOVE KIDS Clothing Store, Portland, 1985—; owner, pres. Oreg. Music and Entertainment, 1989—; sec./treas. Designers' Roundtable, Portland, 1985-88; co-owner, The Tuxedo Club, 1992—. Mem. Oreg. State Pub. Interest Rsch. Group, Portland, 1985-90, Oreg. Fair Share,Salem, 1987, mem. adv. bd. career and life options program Clackamas Community Coll., 1989-91. Mem. Women Entrepreneurs Oreg. (bd. dirs. 1988-92, pres. 1992-93, 94-95, Mem. of Yr. award 1991), Brentwood-Darlington Neighborhood Assn. (treas. 1993—), North Clackamas County C. of C., Nat. Fedn. Ind. Bus., Outer Southeast Coalition. Democrat. Office: Oreg Music & Entertainment PO Box 1784 Clackamas OR 97015-1784

LOVE, SUSAN MARGARET, surgeon, educator, medical administrator; b. N.J., Feb. 9, 1948; d. James Arthur and Margaret Connick (Schwab) L.; life ptnr. Helen Sperry Cooksey, Sept. 8, 1982; 1 child, Katherine Mary Love-Cooksey. BS, Fordham U., 1970; MD, SUNY, N.Y.C., 1974; DSc (hon.), Northeastern U., 1991; D of Humane Sci. (hon.), Simmons Coll., 1992. Clin. fellow in surgery Harvard Med. Sch., Boston, 1977-78, clin. instr. in surgery, 1980-87; dir. breast clinic Beth Israel Hosp., Boston, 1980-88; clin. assoc. in surg. oncology Dana Farber Cancer Inst., Boston, 1981-92; dir. Faulkner Breast Ctr. Faulkner Hosp., Boston, 1988-92; asst. clin. prof. surgery Harvard Med. Sch., Cambridge, 1987-92; assoc. prof. clin. surgery UCLA Sch. Medicine, L.A., 1992—; dir. UCLA Breast Ctr., L.A., 1992—; mem. adv. coun. Breast & Cervical Cancer Coun., State of Calif. Dept. Human Svcs., 1994—; mem. NSABP Oversight Com., Pitts., 1994—; mem. adv. com. Women's Health Initiative Program, Washington, 1993—; prin. investigator Nat. Surg. Adjuvant Breast and Bowel Project, 1985—. Author: Dr. Susan Love's Breast Book, 1990, (book chpts.) Breast Disease, 1987, Clinics in Oncology: Breast Cancer, 1989, The Woman's Guide to Good Health, 1991; contbr. articles to profl. jours. Founder, bd. dirs. Nat. Breast Cancer Coalition, 1991—; mem. breast cancer subcom. divsn. cancer treatment Bd. Sci. Counselors, Nat. Cancer Inst., 1992—; conf. com. co-chair Sec.'s Conf. to Establish Nat. Action Plan on Breast Cancer, 1993—. Recipient Rose Kushner award Am. Med. Writers Assn., 1991, Achievement award Am. Assn. Physicians for Human Rights, 1992, Women Making History award U.S. Senator Barbara Boxer, 1993, Woman of Yr. award YWCA, 1994; prin. investigator grantee Dept. of Def., 1994. Mem. Am. Med. Women's Assn. (pres. br. 39 1987), Soc. for Study of Breast Disease, Am. Soc. Preventive Oncology, Southwestern Oncology Group (women's health an breast com. 1992—, surg. rep. 1992—), L.A. Med. Soc., Boston Surg. Soc. Office: Revlon/UCLA Breast Ctr Ste 150 200 UCLA Med Plaza Los Angeles CA 90095-7028

LOVELAND, WALTER DAVID, chemist, chemistry educator; b. Chgo., Dec. 23, 1939; s. Walter Hubert and Anna Emelia (Reese) L.; m. Patricia Marie Rice, Sept. 7, 1962. SB, MIT, 1961; PhD, U. Wash., Seattle, 1965. Postdoctoral fellow Argonne (Ill.) Nat. Lab., 1966-67; rsch. asst. prof. Oreg. State U., Corvallis, 1967-68, from asst. to prof., 1968—; vis. scientist Argonne (Ill.) Nat. Lab., 1968, 76, Lawrence Berkeley (Calif.) Lab., 1976-77, 83-84. Author: Radiotracer Methods, 1975, Nuclear Chemistry, 1982, Elements Beyond Uranium, 1990; contbr. numerous articles to profl. jours. NSF fellow, 1962, Tartar fellow Oreg. State U., 1977. Mem. Am. Chem. Soc., Am. Phys. Soc., AAAS, MIT Alumni Assn., Sigma Xi. Democrat. Office: Oreg State U Radiation Ctr Corvallis OR 97331

LOVELESS, EDNA MAYE, English language educator; b. Keene, Tex., Jan. 15, 1929; d. Luther Ray and May (Willhelm) Alexander; m. William Alfred Loveless, Aug. 17, 1952; children: Marti Sue Loveless Olson, Marilynn Kaye Loveless Stepniak. BA, Walla Walla Coll., 1950; PhD, U. Md., 1969. Instr. English Walla Walla Coll., College Place, Wash., 1950-52, Columbia Union Coll., Takoma Park, Md., 1952-53; prof. English Columbia Union Coll., Takoma Park, 1980-90; textbook writer, editor Review Publishers, Hagerstown, Md., 1970-80; prof. English La Sierra U., Riverside, Calif., 1990—; advisor student newspaper Columbia Union Coll., Takoma Park, 1980-90, dir. writers' conf., 1988, 89; lectr. Profl. Writers' Conf., Review Publs. Hagerstown, 1989; dir. freshman English program La Sierra U., Riverside, 1991—; participant and presenter Internat. Conf. on Critical Thinking, 1991, 94, 95; presenter Nat. Conf. on Critical Thinking, 1992, Pa. State Conf. in Rhetoric, 1994. Author: (book and tchr.'s manual) What Shall I Live For?, 1976, What Is of Most Worth?, 1978; author: (with others) Penn's Example to the Nations, 1987, Masterplots II, Juvenile and Adult Fiction, 1991, Critical Thinking, 1994. Recipient NDEA fellowship U. Md., 1964-68, 2nd prize Scholastic Mag. Writing Contest for High Sch. Tchrs., 1967. Office: La Sierra U 4700 Pierce St Riverside CA 92505-3331

LOVELL, CHARLES C., federal judge; b. 1929; m. Ariliah Carter. BS, U. Mont., 1952, JD, 1959. Assoc. Church, Harris, Johnson & Williams, Great Falls, Mont., 1959-85; judge U.S. Dist. Ct. Mont., Helena, 1985—; chief counsel Mont. Atty Gen.'s Office, Helena, 1969-72. Served to capt. USAF, 1952-54. Mem. ABA, Am. Judicature Soc., Assn. Trial Lawyers Am. Office: US Dist Ct PO Drawer 10112 301 S Park Ave Helena MT 59626*

LOVELL, MARGARETTA M., art history educator, museum curator; b. Pitts., Oct. 30, 1944; m. Jonathan H. Lovell, June 17, 1967; children: Stephanie, Helen. B.A., Smith Coll., 1966; M.A., U. Del., 1975; Ph.D., Yale U., 1980. Curatorial asst. Yale Art Gallery, New Haven, 1972-75; acting instr. dept. art history Yale U., 1978-80, asst. prof. dept. art history, 1980-81; asst. prof. dept. art history U. Calif., Berkeley, 1981-90; Duane and Virginia S. Dittman prof. Am. studies Coll. William & Mary, 1990-92; assoc. prof. art history U. Calif., Berkeley, 1992—; curator Am. paintings collection Fine Arts Mus., San Francisco, 1981-85; adv. com. Archives Am. Art Western div., Smithsonian Instn., Washington; exec. com. Yale Ctr. for Study Am. Art and Material Culture, New Haven, 1978-81; R. Stanton Avery vis. chair Huntington Libr., 1994-95. Author book: A Visitable Past: Views of Venice by American Artists, 1860-1925, 1989; author catalogues: American Paintings 1730-1960: A Selection from the Collection of Mr. and Mrs. John D. Rockefeller 3rd., 1982; William Morris: The Sanford and Helen Berger Collection, 1984; Venice: The American View, 1860-1920, 1984-85. Nat. Endowment for Arts Mus. Profl. fellow, 1973, Danforth Found. Women's fellow, 1975-78, Rsch. fellow Henry E. Huntington Library and Art Gallery, 1987, 89, 93, DAAD fellow, 1988, fellow For Univ. Profs. Nat. Endowment for Humanities Rsch., 1989-90; Gladys Krieble Delmas Found. grantee, 1978, ACLS grantee, 1988; recipient Ralph Henry Gabriel prize Am. Studies Assn., 1981, Clifford prize Hon. Mention Am. Soc. for 18th Century Studies, 1992. Office: U Calif Dept History of Art 405 Doe Library Berkeley CA 94720

LOVEN, CHARLES JOHN, human resource executive; b. N.Y.C., Feb. 17, 1937; s. John and June Emma (Custer) Azzaro. BA, Occidental Coll., 1962; MA, Calif. State U., L.A., 1967. Group scheduler Douglas Space Systems, Huntington Beach, Calif., 1963-65; personnel rep. Shell Oil Co., L.A., 1965-71; dir. indsl. rels. Calif. Computer Products, Anaheim, 1971-80; sr. v.p., dir. personnel dept. Thompson Recruitment Advt., L.A., 1980-92; dir. pers. dept. UAW/Labor Employment and Tng. Corp., Bell, Calif., 1994—. With USCG, 1954-58. Mem. Employment Mgrs. Assn., Personnel and Indsl. Rels. Assn., Am. Soc. Personnel Adminstrs., Exec. Human Resources Round Table. Office: UAW-LETC 5150 Gage Ave Bell CA 90201-1529

LOVENTHAL, MILTON, writer, playwright, lyricist; b. Atlantic City, Jan. 19, 1923; s. Harry and Clara (Feldman) L.; m. Jennifer McDowell, July 2, 1973. BA, U. Calif., Berkeley, 1950, MLS, 1958; MA in Sociology, San Jose State U., 1969. Researcher Hoover Instn., Stanford, Calif., 1952-53; librarian San Diego Pub. Library, 1957-59; librarian, bibliographer San Jose (Calif.) State U., 1959-92; tchr. writing workshops, poetry readings, 1969-73; co-producer lit. and culture radio show Sta. KALX, Berkeley, 1971-72; editor, pub. Merlin Press, San Jose, 1973—. Author: Books on the USSR, 1951-57, 57, Black Politics, 1971 (featured at Smithsonian Inst. Special Event, 1992), A Bibliography of Material Relating to the Chicano, 1971, Autobiographies of Women, 1946-70, 72, Blacks in America, 1972, The Survivors, 1972, Contemporary Women Poets an Anthology, 1977, Ronnie Goose Rhymes for Grown-Ups, 1984; co-author: (Off-Off-Broadway plays) The Estrogen Party to End War, 1986, Mack the Knife, Your Friendly Dentist, 1986, Betsy & Phyllis, 1986, The Oatmeal Party Comes to Order, 1986, (plays) Betsy Meets the Wacky Iraqi, 1991, Bella and Phyllis, 1994; co-writer (mus. comedy) Russia's Secret Plot to Take Back Alaska, 1988. Recipient Bill Casey Award in Letters, 1980; grantee San Jose State U., 1962-63, 84. Mem. Assn. Calif. State Profs., Calif. Alumni Assn., Calif. Theatre Coun. Office: PO Box 5602 San Jose CA 95150-5602

LOVERING, LORELI, nurse practitioner, secretary; b. Renton, Pa., Dec. 28, 1934; d. Harry and Mary (Romanco) Federoff; m. Francis J. Piekarski, May 4, 1957 (dec. Mar. 1973); children: Jill C., Beth S. Hammack, Karen, James; m. Larry J. Lovering. Diploma in nursing, West Pa. Hosp. Sch. Nursing, 1955; nurse practitioner, U. Pitts., 1969; cert. nurse practitioner, Russellton Med. Group, 1973. Cert. Nurse Practitioner, 1978; ordained to ministry Eckankar, 1990. Staff and rehab. nurse Angelus Rehab. Ctr., Pitts., 1955-56; psychiat. nurse Vets. Hosp., Pitts., 1956-58; nurse part-time Citizen Gen. Hosp./Columbia Hosp., New Kensington, Pa., 1958-63; from nurse to nurse practitioner Penn Plum Med. Bldg. (merged with Miners Clinic, Inc., New Kensington, 1963-78; nurse practitioner VA Nursing Home Care Unit, Phoenix, 1978—; coord. Profl. Hearing Healthcare Ctrs., Sun City, Ariz., 1987—; chmn. nursing com. VA, 1992-94; pres. Nat. Assurance Svcs., Inc., Phoenix, 1986—; owner, pres. Interiors by Loreli, 1987-93. Co-editor Ariz. Geriatrics Jour. Mem. Mem. Ariz. Geriatrics Soc. (bd. dirs. 1992—), Women's Bus. Clubs (scholar 1952), Advanced Practice Nurse, Geriatric Jour. Club, Toastmasters. Republican. Home: 2745 E Winchcomb Dr Phoenix AZ 85032-5037 Office: Carl T Hayden Vets Med Ctr 650 E Indian School Rd Phoenix AZ 85012

LOVIN, HUGH TAYLOR, history educator; b. Pocatello, Idaho, Dec. 10, 1928; s. Robert Scott and Hazel Viora (Gleim) L.; m. Ida Carolyn Edwards, June 3, 1956; 1 child, Jeffrey Douglas. BA, Idaho State Coll., 1950; MA, Wash. State U., 1956; PhD, U. Wash., 1963. Instr. history U. Alaska Mil. Br., Elmendorf AFB, 1957-61; asst. prof. history Southwestern Oreg. Coll., North Bend, 1963-64, Kearney (Nebr.) State Coll., 1964-65; assoc. prof. history Boise (Idaho) State U., 1965-68, prof. history, 1968-93, emeritus prof. history, 1993—; abstracter pub. hist. materials Am. Bibiog. Ctr., CLIO Press, Santa Barbara, Calif., 1970—; book reviewer in profl. history jours., 1969—. Editor: Labor in the West, 1986; contbr. numerous articles to profl. jours. including Pacific N.W. Quarterly, Jour. of the West, The Old Northwest. Fellow Nat. Endowment for Humanities, 1982. Home: 1310 Gourley St Boise ID 83705-6042 Office: Boise State U Dept History Boise ID 83725

LOVINS, L. HUNTER, public policy institute executive; b. Middlebury, Vt., Feb. 26, 1950; d. Paul Millard and Farley (Hunter) Sheldon; m. Amory Bloch Lovins, Dept. 6, 1979; 1 child, Nanuq. BA in Sociology, Pitzer Coll., 1972, BA in Polit. Sci., 1972; JD, Loyola U., L.A., 1975; LHD, U. Maine, 1982. Bar: Calif. 1975. Asst. dir. Calif. Conservation Project, L.A., 1973-79; exec. dir., co-founder Rocky Mountain Inst., Snowmass, Colo., 1982—; vis. prof. U. Colo., Boulder, 1982; Henry R. Luce vis. prof. Dartmouth Coll., Hanover, N.H., 1982; pres. Nighthawk Horse Co., 1993, Lovins Group, 1994. Co-author: Brittle Power, 1982, Energy Unbound, 1986, Least-Cost Energy Solving the CO2 Problem, 2d edit., 1989. Bd. dirs. Renew Am., Basalt and Rural Fire Protection Dist., Telluride Inst., E Source, Roaring Park Polocrosse Assn.; vol. firefighter. Recipient Mitchell prize Woodlands Inst., 1982, Right Livelihood Found. award, 1983, Best of the New Generation award Esquire Mag., 1984. Mem. Am. Quarter Horse Assn. Office: Rocky Mountain Inst 1739 Snowmass Creek Rd Snowmass CO 81654-9115

LOVITT, JOHN R., software company executive; b. Vermillion, Kans., Feb. 6, 1945; s. Charles H. and Frances J. (Campfield) L.; m. Diane L. Rasmussen, June 4, 1966; children: Jennifer R., Angela J., Christofer J. BS in Aeronautical Engring., Wichita State U., 1968; MS in Computer Sci., U. Mo., 1970. Programmer Beech Aircraft, Wichita, Kans., 1965-68; engr. McDonnell Dougas, St. Louis, 1968-73; sales mgr. Hewlett Packard, St. Louis, 1973-86; sr. v.p. field ops. Rational Software, Santa Clara, Calif., 1986—. Office: Rational Software Corp 2800 San Tomas Expwy Santa Clara CA 95051-0951

LOVVIK, DARYL VAUGHN, consulting geologist; b. Eau Claire, Wis., July 26, 1941; s. Oscar W. and Pearl B. (Johnson) L.; m. Sherly Berog; children: Liezel Bayo, Lenie, Panging, Alexander Wilhelm, Sheila Najivi. B.S. in Geology, W. Tex. State U., 1975; MBA, U. of Phoenix. Cert. profl. geologist; registered profl. geologist, Alaska, Ariz., Ark. Cons. geologist, Golden, Colo., 1975-77; exploration geologist Cotter Corp., Moab, Utah, 1977-79; pres. Southwestern Geol. Survey, Mesa, Ariz., 1979-86; water resource dir. Tohono O'Odham Nation, Sells, Ariz., 1986-89, Ariz. Dept. Water Resources, 1990—; pres. Southwestern Geol., Tempe, Ariz., 1971—, Pac-Isle Enterprises, Tacloban, Philippines, 1994—, Philippine Connection, Tempe, 1993—. Contbr. articles to profl. jours. With USAF, 1960-64. Mem. Am. Inst. Profl. Geologists, Geol. Soc. Am., Am. Assn. Petroleum Geologists, Soc. Mining Engrs. Republican. Episcopalian. Home: 410 E Beatrice St Tempe AZ 85281-1004

LOW, MARISSA E., health care administrator; b. San Francisco; d. Fred and Winifred L. AA, Fashion Inst. of Design and Mdse., 1979; Cert. Corp. Communications, Calif. State U.-Long Beach, 1987; BSBA, U. Redlands, 1992. Assoc. area mgr. Buffums, Glendale, Calif., 1979-80; asst. buyer Buffums, Long Beach, Calif., 1981-83; mdse. control mgr. Buffums, Long Beach, 1983-86, advt. mgr., 1987-89; account rep. CompuMed, Culver City, Calif., 1989-91; physician recruiter Pioneer Ind. Physician Network, Artesia, Calif., 1991-92; provider rels. mgr. Mullikin Ind. Physician Assn., Long Beach, Calif., 1992-93; dir. provider rels. Mullikin Ind. Physician Assn., Daly City, 1993-94; regional network mgr. AHI Healthcare Systems, Inc., San Mateo, Calif., 1994—. Judge Miss Lakewood Pageant of Beauty, 1987; vol. Long Beach Conv. and Visitors Coun., 1987; pub. rels. chmn. March of Dimes, Calif., 1986; v.p. programs, spl. projects, chmn. bd. dirs., nomination com. chmn. Women's Coun., 1985-91; sec. Women's Bus. Conf., 1985; com. mem. Interval House Le Bal des Papillons. Recipient Cert. Appreciation Orange County Commn. on Status of Women, 1991, Interval House, 1991. Mem. NAFE, Am. Mktg. Assn., Group Health Assn. of Am., Acad. Health Svcs. Mktg. (chmn. managed care com. Health Futures Forum 1992), Healthcare Fin. Mgmt. Assn. Office: 951 Mariners Island Blvd San Mateo CA 94404-1560

LOW, MERRY COOK, civic worker; b. Uniontown, Pa., Sept. 3, 1925; d. Howard Vance and Eleanora (Lynch) Mullan; m. William R. Cook, 1947 (div. 1979); m. John Wayland Low, July 8, 1979; children: Karen, Cindy, Bob, Jan. Diploma in nursing, Allegheny Gen. Hosp., Pitts., 1946; BS summa cum laude, Colo. Women's Coll., 1976. RN, Colo. Dir. patient edn. Med. Care and Rsch. Found., Denver, 1976-78. Contbr. chpt. to Pattern for Distribution of Patient Education, 1981. Bd. dirs. women's libr. assn. U. Denver, 1982—, vice chmn., 1985-86, chmn., 1986-87, co-chmn. spl. event, 1992, bd. dirs. Humanities Inst., 1993—, co-chair Founders' Day, 1994, chair Culture Fest, 1994; docent Denver Art Mus., 1979—, mem. vol. exec. bd., 1988—, mem. nat. docent symposium com., 1991, chmn. collectors' choice benefits, 1988, pres. vols., trustee, 1988-90; mem. alumni assn. bd. U. Denver, 1994—; bd. dirs. Lamont Sch. Music Assocs., 1990—; mem. search com. for dir. Penrose Libr., 1991-92; trustee ch. coun., chmn. invitational art show 1st Plymouth Congl. Ch., Engelwood, Colo., 1981-84; co-chmn. art auction Colo. Alliance Bus., 1992, 93, com., 1994—. Recipient Disting. Svc. award U. Denver Coll. Law, 1988, King Soopers Vol. of Week award, 1989, Citizen of Arts award Fine Arts Found., 1993, Outstanding Vol. Colo. Alliance of Bus., 1994. Mem. Am. Assn. Museums (vol. meeting coord. 1990-91), P.E.O. (pres. Colo. chpt. DX 1982-84), U. Denver Alumni Assn. (bd. dirs.), Rocky Mountain Women's Inst. (bd. dirs. 1995—). Republican. Congregationalist. Home: 2552 E Alameda Ave Apt 11 Denver CO 80209-3324

LOWDEN, SUZANNE, state legislator; b. Camden, N.J., Feb. 8, 1952; m. Paul W. Lowden; children: Christopher, Jennifer, Paul, William. BA magna cum laude, Am. U.; MA cum laude, Fairleigh Dickinson U. Resort industry exec.; mem. Nev. State Senate, 1993—, majority whip, 1993—. Active Juvenile Diabetes Found., United Way of So. Nev. With USO, 1971, Vietnam. Recipient Woman of Achievement award Women's Coun. of Las Vegas C. of C. Republican. Home: 992 Pinehurst Dr Las Vegas NV 89109-1569 Office: Nev State Senate State Capitol Carson City NV 89710

LOWE, CLAUDIA MARIE, childbirth assistant; b. Cleve., Mar. 7, 1955; m. Michael Lowe, Feb. 23, 1980; children: Alexander, Adam, Aaron. Cert. perinatal educator. Childbirth educator Am. Acad. Husband-Coached Childbirth, San Jose, Calif., 1983—, Cert. Perinatal Educators Assn., 1983-89; dir. Nat. Assn. Childbirth Assts., 1985—, Women's Resources (formerly Health Awareness Ctr.), 1991—, Birth Support Providers Internat., 1992—; guided self-hypnosis practitioner, 1990—; clin. hypnotherapist Nat. Guild of Hypnotists, 1991—; breast feeding counselor Breastfeeding Support Cons., 1992—; birth ball trainer and cons., 1995—. Editor, pub. The Childbirth Asst. Jour., 1987—, Birth Support Providers Internat., (newsletters) You and Me, 1989, Inside NACA, 1992; author: (manual) Becoming a Childbirth Assistant, 1990, (guidebook) Planning for a Positive Pregnancy, 1990; Guided Self-Hypnosis for Childbirth and Beyond, 1994, Critical Concepts of Obstetric and Maternity Care for the 21st Century, Marketing Tips for Birth Support Providers, 1994, Perinatal Fitness with the Birth Ball, 1995. Com. mem. Calif. State Assembly Cesarean Info. Bill, Sacramento, 1990-91. Mem. Nat. Assn. Childbirth Assts. (founder 1985—), Internat. Childbirth Edn. Assn., Hypnosis Info. Network, La Leche League Internat. (leader), Internat. Cesarean Awareness Network, ASPO Lamaze. Office: 4 David Ct Novato CA 94947

LOWE, OARIONA, dentist; b. San Francisco, June 17, 1948; d. Van Lowe and Jenny Lowe-Silva; m. Evangelos Rossopoulos, Dec. 18, 1985; 1 child, Thanos G. BS, U. Nev., Las Vegas, 1971; MA, George Washington U., 1977; DDS, Howard U., 1981; pediatric dental cert., UCLA, 1984. Instr. Coll. Allied Health Scis. Howard U., Washington, 1974-76, asst. prof., 1976-77; research asst. Howard U. Dental Sch., Washington, 1977-81; resident gen. practice Eastman Dental Ctr., Rochester, N.Y., 1981-82; dir. dental services City of Hope Med. Ctr., Duarte, Calif., 1984-86; chief dental staff Whittier (Calif.) Presbyn. Hosp., 1992-94; asst. prof. Loma Linda (Calif.) U., 1991—; vis. lectr. pediatric dentistry UCLA; mem. oral cancer task force Am. Cancer Soc., Pasadena, Calif., 1985—. Contbr. articles to profl. jours. Del. People to People Internat. Mem. ADA, Am. Soc. Dentistry for Children (v.p.), Nat. Soc. Autistic Children, Calif. Dental Assn., Am. Acad. Pediatric Dentistry, San Gabriel Valley Dental Soc. (chmn. 1991—), Sigma Xi, Alpha Omega. Republican. Presbyterian. Office: 8135 Painter Ave Ste 202 Whittier CA 90602-3154

LOWE, RICHARD GERALD, JR., computer programming manager; b. Travis AFB, Calif., Nov. 8, 1960; s. Richard Gerald and Valerie Jean (Hoefer) L.; m. Claudia Maria Arevalo, 1993; 1 child, Alvaro Arevalo. Student, San Bernardino Valley Coll., 1978-80. Tech. specialist Software Techniques Inc., Los Alamitos, Calif., 1980-82, sr. tech. specialist, 1982-84, mgr. tech. services, 1984-85; mgr. cons. services Software Techniques Inc., Cypress, Calif., 1985-86; sr. programmer BIF Accutel, Camarillo, Calif., 1986-87; systems analyst BIF Accutel, Camarillo, 1987-88; mgr. project Beck Computer Systems, Long Beach, Calif., 1986-91, v.p. devel., 1991-93; dir. tech. svcs. Trader Joe's Co., S. Pasadena, Calif., 1994—. Author: The Autobiography of Richard G. Lowe, Jr., 1991, The Lowe Family and Their Relatives, 1992; contbr. articles to profl. jours. Vol. min., field staff mem. L.A. Found. Ch. of Scientology, 1993—; active Concerned Citizens for Human Rights. Mem. Assn. Computing Machinery, Digital Equipment Corp. Users Group, UniData Users Group, Internat. Assn. Scientologists. Office: Trader Joe's Co 538 Mission St South Pasadena CA 91030-3036

LOWE, ROBERT STANLEY, lawyer; b. Herman, Nebr., Apr. 23, 1923; s. Stanley Robert and Ann Marguerite (Feese) L.; m. Anne Kirtland Selden, Dec. 19, 1959; children: Robert James, Margaret Anne. AB, U. Nebr., 1947, JD, 1949. Bar: Wyo. 1949. Ptnr. McAvoy & Lowe, Newcastle, 1949-51, Hickey & Lowe, Rawlins, 1951-55; county and pros. atty. Rawlins, 1955-59, pvt. practice, 1959-67; assoc. dir. Am. Judicature Soc., Chgo., 1967-74, 1968-74; counsel True Oil and affiliated cos., Casper, Wyo., 1974—; bd. dirs., sec. Hilltop Nat. Bank, Casper; mem. legal adv. div. Nat. Ski Patrol Sys., 1975-88; pres. Snowy Range Ski Corp., 1963-66; city atty. City of Rawlins, 1963-65; atty., asst. sec. Casper Mountain Ski Patrol, 1988—. Co-editor: Selected Readings on the Administration of Justice and its Improvement, 1969, 71, 73, Current Issues on the Judiciary, 1971, Judicial Disability and Removal Commissions, Courts and Procedures, 1969, 70, 72, 73, others; contbr. articles to legal jours. Mem. Wyo. Ho. of Reps., 1952-54; del. Dem. Nat. Conv., 1952, alt. del., 1956; mem. exec. com. Wyo. Dem. Ctrl. Com., 1953-55; bd. dirs. Vols. in Probation, 1969-82; leader legal del. to China, People to People, 1986; mem. Wyo. Vets. Affairs Coun., 1994—; mem. legis. com. United Vets. Coun. Wyo., 1993—; trustee, pres. Troopers Found., Inc., 1994—; pres. WW II Commemorative Cmty. Program. Lt. (j.g.) U.S. Maritime Svc., U.S. Mcht. Marine, 1943-46. Recipient Dedicated Community

Worker award Rawlins Jr. C. of C., 1967, Yellow merit award Nat. Ski Patrol System, 1982, 85, 87, 88. Fellow Am. Bar Found. (life); mem. VFW (post adv. 1991—, nat. aide-de-camp 1993-94, judge advocate dist. 3 Dept. Wyo., 1994—), Am. Judicature Soc. (dir. 1961-67, 85-89, bd. editors 1975-77, Herbert Harley award 1974), ABA (sec. jud. adminstrn. divsn. lawyers conf., exec. com. 1975-76, chmn. 1977-78, chmn. judicial qualification and selection com. 1986-93, coun. jud. adminstrn. div. 1977-78, mem. com. to implement jud. adminstrn. standards 1978-82, Ho. of Dels. state bar del. 1978-80, 86-87, state del. 1987-93, Assembly del. 1980-83), Wyo. State Bar (chmn. com. on cts. 1961-67, 77-87), Nebr. State Bar Assn., Ill. State Bar Assn., D.C. Bar Assn., Inter-Am. Bar Assn., Selden Soc., Inst. Jud. Adminstrn., Rocky Mountain Oil and Gas Assn. (legal com. 1976—, chmn. 1979-82, 90-91), Rocky Mountain Mineral Law Found. (trustee 1980-94), Am. Law Inst., Newcomen Soc., Order of Coif, Mil. Order of Cootie (grand judge advocate 1994—), Delta Theta Phi (dist. chancellor 1982-83, chief justice 1983-93, assoc. justice 1993—; Percy J. Power Meml. award 1983, Gold Medallion award 1990), Casper Rotary Club (pres. 1985-86). Mem. Ch. of Christ, Scientist. Home: 97 Primrose St Casper WY 82604-4018 Office: 895 River Cross Rd Casper WY 82601-1758

LOWE, ROLLAND CHOY, surgeon; b. San Francisco, Sept. 29, 1932; s. Laurence and Eva (Chan) L.; m. Kathryn Lew, Jan. 7, 1957; children: Larry, Randall, Yvonne. AB, U. Calif., Berkeley, 1952; MD, U. Calif., San Francisco, 1955. Diplomate Am. Bd. Surgeons. Intern San Francisco Gen. Hosp., 1956; resident in surgery U. Calif., San Francisco, 1958-63, assoc. clin. prof., 1964-92; pvt. practice San Francisco, 1992—; commr. bd. med. examiners State of Calif., 1979-80; chmn. bd. Chinese Hosp., 1984-85, 91, vice chmn., 1979-81, 83, 90, 92, chief of staff, 1971, 73-74, chief of surgery, 1977-78, bd. dirs., 1979-93. Trustee San Francisco Found., Asian Am. Health Forum, mem. exec. com.; trustee U.S.-China Edn. Inst.; mem. exec. com. San Francisco Comprehensive Health Planning Coun., 1974-76, bd. dirs., 1972-76; mem. bd. overseers U. Calif., San Francisco, 1990-91; chair Lawrence Choy Lowe Meml. Fund, Found. for Chinese Democracy; vice chair San Francisco 2000, 1990-92; chair Mayor's Citizen Adv. Com. on I-Hotel Block Devel., 1980-92; civil svc. commr. City and County of San Francisco, 1979-80. Capt. USAR, 1956-58. Mem. ACS, Howard Naffziger Surg. Soc., San Francisco Surg. Soc., San Francisco Med. Soc. (treas. 1979-80, pres.-elect 1981, pres. 1982), Calif. Med. Assn. (trustee 1987-94, chair bd. trustees 1994). Office: 929 Clay St # 401 San Francisco CA 94108-1556

LOWE, SUE ESTHER, optometrist; b. Scottsburg, Ind., July 22, 1954; d. Donald and Etta (Helton) L.; m. Eric Stephen Lundell, May 24, 1953; 1 child, Sven Olaf Lundell. BA, U. Wyoming, 1976; OD, Pacific U., Forest Grove, Oreg., 1980. Rsch. asst. Pacific U. Coll. of Optometry, Forest Grove, Oreg., 1976-77; pvt. practice optometrist, 1980—; assoc. Snowy Range Vision Ctr., Laramie, Wyo., 1980-82, ptnr. Trustee Albany County Hosp. Dist., 1985-88, mem. Episcopal Ch., 1983—, bd. dirs. LWV, 1981—, Wyoming Infant Stimulation, 1982—, Precinct Com. Woman, 1983-84; interviewer Albany County Oral History Project, 1983-86. Named One of the Outstanding Young Women of Am, 1976, 1978, Outstanding Greek Woman, 1976. Fellow Acad. of Optometry, Coll. Optometrists in Vision Devel.; mem. Am. Optometric Assn., Wyoming Optometric Assn., Calif. Optometric Assn., Colo. Optometric Assn., Am. Pub. Health Assn., Infant Stimulation Edn. Assn., Am. Optometric Found., Zontas Internat. Lioness, Omega Epsilon Phi, Alpha Epsilon Delta, Alpha Chi Omega Alumna Club. Democrat. Home: 1704 Skyline Rd Laramie WY 82070-8932 Office: Snowy Range Vision Ctr 301 S 8th St Laramie WY 82070-3914

LOWELL, GERALD RAY, librarian, academic information technology administrator; b. Sioux Falls, S.D., Feb. 11, 1949; s. G. James and Alice Kristine (Nelson) L.; m. Mitchell S. Block, Aug. 16, 1981. BA in Russian Area Studies, Gustavus Adolphus Coll., 1971; MA in Librarianship, U. Wash., 1977. Head title II-C serials project, asst. serials libr. U. Wash. Librs., Seattle, 1977-79; v.p., mgr. dir. N.Am. Faxon Co., Westwood, Mass., 1979-82; cons. Libr. of Congress, Washington, 1983-84, chief cataloging distbn. svc., 1984-86; assoc. univ. libr., dir. for tech. svcs. Yale Univ. Libr., New Haven, Conn., 1986-93; univ. libr., assoc. vice chancellor acad. info. tech. U. Calif., San Diego, 1993—. Contbr. articles to profl. jours. Mem. ALA, Libr. and Info. Tech. Assn., Assn. Coll. and Rsch. Librs., Assn. Libr. Collections and Tech. Svcs. Office: Univ Calif 9500 Gilman Dr La Jolla CA 92093-5003

LOWELL, JAMES DILLER, geologist; b. Lincoln, Nebr., Aug. 17, 1933; s. James Russell and Pearl Evelyn (Diller) L.; m. Suzanne Hewitt, Nov. 1, 1957; children: Jennifer, Carey, Elizabeth, Alexandra. BS, U. Nebr., 1955; MA, Columbia U., 1957, PhD, 1958. Sr. geologist Am. Overseas Petroleum Ltd., Tripoli, Libya and The Hague, The Netherlands, 1958-65; asst. prof. geology Washington and Lee U., Lexington, Va., 1965-66; sr. rsch. specialist Esso Prodn. Rsch., Houston, 1966-73; exploration geologist Exxon Co., USA, Englewood, Colo., 1973-74; mgr. geology N.W. Exploration Co., Denver, 1974-76; pres. Colexcon Inc., Littleton, Colo., 1976—; mem. adv. bd. U. Nebr., Lincoln, 1984-87, 89—, Schramm prof., 1987; Crosby vis. prof. MIT, Cambridge, 1987. Author: Structural Styles in Petroleum Exploration, 1985; editor: Foreland Basins and Uplifts, 1983; contbr. articles to profl. jours. Recipient Disting. Alumni award U. Nebr., 1994, Esso Disting. Lectr., Esso Australia/U. Sydney, 1989. Fellow Geol. Soc. Am.; mem. Am. Assn. Petroleum Geologists (adv. bd. 1985-94, Disitng. lectr. 1994-95), Rocky Mountain Assn. Geologists (pres., 1st v.p., Scientist of Yr. 1979), Wyo. Geol. Assn., Explorers Club. Home: 5836 Colorow Dr Morrison CO 80465-2210 Office: Colexcon Inc 2200 W Berry Ave Littleton CO 80120-1100

LOWELL, RICHARD WILLIAM, naval officer; b. San Francisco, Aug. 7, 1952; s. Richard Leslie and Shirley May (VanOrnum) L.; m. Barbara Ann Conmy, May 29, 1976; children: Jacqueline, Richard William Jr., Christopher. BS in English, U.S. Naval Acad., 1975; MS in Mgmt., Naval Postgrad. Sch., Monterey, Calif., 1987. Commd. ensign USN, 1975, advanced through grades to comdr., 1990; asst. engr. USS Badger (FF1072), Honolulu, 1976-80; exec. asst. to comdr. in chief Pacific Fleet, Honolulu, 1980-83; engr. USS A.W. Radford (DD968), Norfolk, Va., 1983-84; officer-in-charge Engrng. Mobile Tng. Team, Norfolk, 1985-86; exec. officer USS Bowen (FF1078), Norfolk, 1987-89; engrng. tng. officer Comdr. Naval Surface Force Atlantic, Norfolk, 1989-91, force tng. officer, 1990-91; bd. dirs. info. Fed. Women's Program, Norfolk, 1989-91; chmn. Inport Tng. Bd., Norfolk, 1990-91, Patrol Coastal Quality Mgmt. Bd., 1992—; active Navy Tng. Appraisal, 1991, Conventional Marine Propulsion Steering Com., 1989, Surface Warfare Tng. Rev. Bd., 1991, Spl. Warfare Worldwide Exec. Steering Com., 1992—. Editor PCJR Newsletter, 1987, Synergy newsletter, 1990. Mem. Hampton Roads Quality Mgmt. Coun., 1992; coach Virginia Beach (Va.) Youth Soccer, 1985, Virginia Beach Youth Football, 1986, Norfolk Youth Soccer, 1989-91. Roman Catholic.

LOWELL, WAVERLY B., archivist; b. N.Y.C., Mar. 2, 1951; d. Allan and Evelyn S. Lowell. BA in History, U. R.I., 1972; MA, Rutgers U., 1976; MLS, U. Calif., Berkeley, 1979. Grad. student instr. women's studies Rutgers U., New Brunswick, N.J., 1975-76; asst. photography curator San Francisco Maritime Mus., 1977-78; libr. San Francisco Mus. Art, 1978-79; curator of manuscripts, archivist Calif. Hist. Soc., 1980-84; acting curator historic documents Nat. Maritime Mus., 1985; archives ad rsch. cons., 1984—; dir. Calif. Coop. Preservation of Archtl. Records, 1985-87, Nat. Archives-Pacific Sierra Region, 1987—; cons. to Carey & Co. Architects, Calif. Acad. Scis., Sequoia Kings Canyon Nat. Parks, Chevron Corp., numerous others; instr. Calif. State U., San Jose, John F. Kennedy Univ. Ctr. for Mus. Studies; mem. faculty Soc. Calif. Archivists, Western Archives Inst.; presenter in field. Author: Architectural Records in the San Francisco Bay Area: A Guide to Research, 1988; editor Friends of Terra Cotta newsletter, 1980-86; contbr. articles to profl. jours. Recipient Archivist award of excellence Calif. Heritage Preservation Commn., 1993. Mem. Soc. Am. Archivists (coun. 1991-94), Nat. Assn. Govt. Archives and Records Adminstrs. (bd. dirs. 1989-91), AIA, Soc. Calif. Archivists (pres. 1989-90), Friends of Terra Cotta (bd. dirs. 1980-88).

LOWELL, WAYNE BRIAN, financial officer; b. Lakeland, Fla., Apr. 20, 1955; s. Robert Earle and Joan (Weber) L.; m. Nan Jean Bjornstad, May 31, 1980; children: Christopher Earle, Jonathan Paul. BS summa cum laude, U. Md., 1977; MBA with honors, U. Calif., Irvine, 1985. Sr. acct. Deloitte, Haskins and Sells, Costa Mesa, Calif., 1977-81; asst. controller Burlington Air Express Irvine, Calif., 1981-86; corp. controller Pacificare Health Systems, Cypress, Calif., 1986, chief fin. officer, 1986-92, exec. v.p., 1992—; bd. dirs. Columbia Gen. Life Ins. Co., Laguna Hills, Calif., Pacific Care Oreg., Portland. Mem. Am. Ins.t CPA's, Fin. Execs. Inst. (cert.) Nat. Assn. Accts., Beta Alpha Psi (pres., sec. 1975-77). Republican. Office: PacifiCare Health Systems 5995 Plaza Dr Cypress CA 90630-5028

LOWEN, ROBERT MARSHALL, plastic surgeon; b. Detroit. MD, U. Mich. Med. Sch., 1971. Diplomate Am. Bd. Plastic Surgery, cert. surgery of the hand. Internship Pacific Presbyn., San Francisco, 1971-72; resident general surgery Stanford U. Med. Ctr., 1983-85; resident plastic surgery U. Okla. HSC, Okla. City, 1985-86; fellow hand surgery U. Colo. HSC, Denver, 1986-87, resident plastic surgery, 1987-88; pvt. practice Mountain View, Calif.; staff El Camino Hosp., Mountain View, Calif., 1988. Mem. Am. Soc. Plastic and Reconstructive Surgeons, Am. Soc. Lasers in Medicine aSurgery, Calif. Med. Soc., Lipoplasty Soc. North Am., Santa Clara County Med. Assn. Office: 305 South Dr Ste 2 Mountain View CA 94040-4207

LOWENTHAL, TINA MARIE, contract negotiator; b. Wyandotte, Mich., Dec. 8, 1961; d. Donald Allen and Namiko (Endo) Pocock; m. Marc Allan Lowenthal, Oct. 27, 1985. BA, Mich. State U., 1984; cert. in govt. contract adminstrn., UCLA, 1989; MBA, U. La Verne, 1991. Asst. mgr. Bakers Square Restaurant, La Verne, Calif., 1985-86; contract negotiator Jet Propulsion Lab., Pasadena, Calif., 1986—. Mem. Nat. Contract Mgmt. Assn., Mich. State U. Alumni Assn. Democrat. Home: 1124 W Juanita Ave San Dimas CA 91773-1647 Office: Jet Propulsion Lab 4800 Oak Grove Dr Pasadena CA 91109-8001

LOWENTROUT, PETER MURRAY, religious studies educator; b. Salinas, Calif., Mar. 14, 1948; m. Christine Ione, Sept. 30, 1980; children: Mary, Brandon. AB, U. Calif., Riverside, 1973; PhD, U. So. Calif., L.A., 1983. Prof. religious studies Calif. State U., Long Beach, 1981—. Contbr. articles to profl. jours. Capt. Orange County Fire Dept., Orange, Calif., 1977—. Mem. Am. Acad. Religion (regional pres. 1989-90), Ctr. for Theology and Lit. U. Durham (Eng.). Office: Calif State U Dept Religious Studies 1250 N Bellflower Blvd Long Beach CA 90840-0006

LOWERY, DOUGLAS LANE, retired environmental engineer; b. Ft. Madison, Iowa, Jan. 24, 1939; s. Frank Onel and Buelah Muree (Pechstein) Lowery; m. Sally Ann Giggey, Dec. 23, 1962; children: Lynda Denise, Lori Diane. BCE, Colo. State U., 1962; MS in Sanitary Engring., U. Mo., 1963; postgrad., Calif. Inst. Tech., Pasadena, 1965-66. Registered profl. engr., Calif., Alaska. Sanitary engring. asst. L.A. Dept. Water and Power, 1963-68; sanitary engring. assoc. L.A. Bur. of Sanitation, 1968-72; environ. conservation mgr. Alaska Dept. Environ. Conservation, Fairbanks, 1972-86, environ. specialist, 1986-94. Various offices Fairbanks Arctic Swim Team, Fairbanks, San Gabriel Valley Orchid Hobbyists, Arcadia, Calif., No. Area Aquatics, del. to U.S. Swimming Assn. Mem. ASCE (pres. Fairbanks br. 1974-75), Am. Water Works Assn., Am. Pub. Works Assn. (v.p. Alaska 1974-75), Rotary (Paul Harris fellow, past pres., dist. officer, youth exch. chmn.), Sigma Tau, Chi Epsilon, Omicron Delta Kappa, Phi Kappa Tau, Kappa Mu Epsilon.

LOWERY, LAWRENCE FRANK, mathematic science and computer educator; b. Oakland, Calif., June 26, 1932. AA, U. Calif., Berkeley, 1952, BA, 1954, MA, 1962, EdD, 1965. Assoc. dean Sch. Edn. U. Calif., Berkeley, 1980-84, prof., 1965—. Contbr. articles to profl. jours.; also, books, videos and films; prolific writer. Numerous leadership roles in field. With U.S. Army, 1954-56. Mem. AAAS, ASCD, Am. Edn. Rsch. Assn. (res. rev. bd.), Assn. for the Edn. Tchrs. Sci., Phi Delta Kappa. Home: 650 Diablo Rd Danville CA 94526-2802

LOWEY-BALL, ALBERT EDWARD, health plan management consultant, educator; b. Delft, The Netherlands, July 8, 1942; came to U.S., 1951; s. Jacobus Johannes and Agatha Wilhelmina (Van Uye) Lowey; m. Hanna Chen Sadan, Nov. 4, 1971 (div. Oct. 1980); 1 child, Adam; m. Joyce Corinne Johnston, Feb. 11, 1982; children: Jeremy, Marisa. BA, Rice U., 1964; MS, Georgetown U., 1966; MA, U. Md., 1969, postgrad., 1970. Economist Pub. Interest Econs. Ctr., Washington, 1971-75; dir. econ. analysis Health Policy Ctr., Georgetown U., Washington, 1974-76; cons. Orkand Corp., Silver Spring, Md., 1975-77; economist U.S. Health Care Financing Adminstrn., Washington, 1977-78; exec. dir. Calif. Health Facilities Commn., Sacramento, 1978-80; CEO Santa Barbara (Calif.) Health Initiative, 1980-84; dir. IIMO svcs. Computer Scis. Corp., El Segundo, Calif., 1985-87; pres. Albert Lowey-Ball Assocs. Inc., Sacramento, 1983—; adj. prof. U. San Francisco, 1984—. Author: Hospital Cost Containment in the U.S., 1980, HMOs, Managed Competition and CalPERS in the Early 1990s, 1993; editor: Health Economics Reader, 1987. Mem. Harry Truman Dem. Club, Sacramento, 1987-91; health advisor Gary Hart Campaign, Washington, 1984. Grantee Johnson Found., 1975, Hartford Found., 1980, Am. Enterprise Inst., 1982, Kaiser Family Found., 1993. Mem. Am. Managed Care Rev. Assn., Group Health Assn. Am., Friends of the River. Office: Albert Lowey-Ball Assocs Inc 1421 16th St Sacramento CA 95814

LOWI, ALVIN, JR., mechanical engineer, consultant; b. Gadsden, Ala., July 21, 1929; s. Alvin R. and Janice (Haas) L.; m. Guillermina Gerardo Alverez, May 9, 1953; children: David Arthur, Rosamina, Edna Vivian, Alvin III. BME, Ga. Inst. Tech., 1951, MSME, 1955; PhD in Engring., UCLA, 1956-61. Registered prof. engr., Calif. Design engr. Garrett Corp., Los Angeles, 1956-58; mem. tech. staff TRW, El Segundo, Calif., 1958-60, Aerospace Corp., El Segundo, 1960-66; prin. Alvin Lowi and Assocs., San Pedro, 1966—; pres. Terraqua Inc., San Pedro, Calif., 1968-76; v.p. Daeco Fuels and Engring. Co., Wilmington, Calif., 1978—; also bd. dirs. Daeco Fuels and Engring. Co.; pres. Lion Engring., Inc.; vis. research prof. U. Pa., Phila., 1972-74; sr. lectr. Free Enterprise Inst., Monterey Park, Calif., 1961-71; bd. dirs. So. Calif. Tissue Bank; research fellow Heather Found., San Pedro, 1966--. Contbr. articles to profl. jours.; patentee in field. Served to lt. USN, 1951-54, Korea. Fellow Inst. Humane Studies; mem. ASME, NSPE, Soc. Automotive Engrs., Soc. Am. Inventors, So. Bay Chamber Music Soc., Scabbard and Blade, Pi Tau Sigma. Jewish. Home and Office: 2146 W Toscanini Dr Palos Verdes Peninsula CA 90275

LOWMAN, MARY BETHENA HEMPHILL (MRS. ZELVIN D. LOWMAN), civic worker, realtor; b. Lewis, Kans., Feb. 10, 1922; d. Frederick William and Gladys (Follin) Hemphill. A.B., Western State Coll., Colo., 1945; m. Zelvin D. Lowman, Oct. 24, 1943; children: Freda Ruth, James Fredrick, William Martin, Elizabeth June (Mrs. Joseph Herbst) (dec.). Tchr. Stout Creek Sch., Colo., 1942-43, San Diego City Sch. Dist., 1944-45, L.A. City Sch. Dist., 1948-50; pvt. sch. tchr. So. Inst. Music, 1956-57. Troop leader Frontier coun. Girl Scouts U.S., 1957-70, mem. exec. bd., 1961-73, 2d v.p., 1962-63, pres., 1968-71, chmn. established camp com., 1963-67, dir. Camp Foxtail, 1965, 67, chmn. Gold award com., 1986-87; mem. Calico Task Group, 1986-89, chmn., 1988-89; mem. Girl Scouts U.S. Region VI Com., 1973-75, chmn. Region VI Com., mem. nat. bd., mem. exec. com. and couns. com., 1975-78; mem. Am. Field Svc. Exchange Student Bd. So. Nev., 1961. Parliamentarian, West Charleston PTA, 1957-59, Nev. Congress, 1960-61; elder, trustee Presbyn. Ch., 1964-67, 89—; chmn. Christian Edn. Commn., 1964-65; chmn. Commn. on Mission of Ch., 1966; chmn. exec. com. Clark County Bicentennial Commn., 1974-76; chmn. bd. First Presbyn Pre-Sch. Day Care Ctr., 1982-85; chmn. stewardship fin. com. 1st Presbyn. Ch., 1990-92; chmn. bd. dirs. 1st Presbyn. Acad. and Preschool, 1990—. Family chosen as Nev. All-Am. Family, 1960. Recipient Thanks Badge U.S. Girl Scouts U.S., 1963, Thanks Badge II, 1989; Mary and Zel Lowman Sch. named in honor, 1992. Mem. Gen. Fedn. Women's Clubs (dir. 1958-60, 62-64, 72-78, chmn. scholarships and student aid 1974-76, chmn. family living div., 1976-78; treas. Western States Conf. 1968-70, sec. 1970-72, pres. 1972-74), Nev. Fedn. Women's Clubs, (past pres.), Md. fedn. women's Clubs (past jr. dir.), Clark County Pan-Hellenic Assn., So. Nev. Alumni Club (pres. 1961-62), Internat. Platform Assn. Presbyn. (elder, dir. capital stewarship canvas program, 1987-88), Las Vegas Bd. Realtors (chmn. membership com. 1988-90, chmn. bylaws com. 1990-91), Las Vegas Mesquite Club (past pres.), Jr. Women's Club (past pres., College Park, Md.), Newcomers Club (past pres.), Nat. Presbyn. Mariners Club (past pres.), Nevada-Sierra District Mariners Club, Las Vegas Nautilus Mariners Club. Home: 1713 Rambla Ct Las Vegas NV 89102-6103

LOWNDES, DAVID ALAN, programmer analyst; b. Schenectady, N.Y., Oct. 28, 1947; s. John and Iris Anne (Hepburn) L.; m. Peggy Welco, May 3, 1970; children: Diana Justine, Julie Suzanne. AB, U. Calif., Berkeley, 1969, postgrad., 1972-73. Acct., credit mgr. The Daily Californian, Berkeley, 1973-75; bus. mgr. The Daily Californian, 1975-76; acct. Pacific Union Assurance Co., San Francisco, 1976-77, acctg. mgr., 1977-78; sr. acct. U. Calif., San Francisco, 1978-88, programmer analyst, 1988—. Home: 1829 Gaspar Dr Oakland CA 94611-2350 Office: U Calif Ste 2000 250 Executive Park Blvd San Francisco CA 94143-0976

LOWNEY, BRUCE STARK, artist; b. Los Angeles, Oct. 16, 1937; s. Franklin and Thelma (Poirier) L. B.A., North Tex. State U., 1959; M.A., San Francisco State U., 1966. printer-fellow Tamarind Lithography Workshop Inc., Los Angeles, 1967; printmaking supr. Mpls. Coll. Art and Design, 1971; vis. artist Chgo. Art Inst., 1972, 77, Western Ill. State U., 1973. One man shows, Elaine Horwitch Galleries, Santa Fe, 1975, 80, Louise Allrich Gallery, San Francisco, 1975, Martha Jackson Gallery, N.Y.C., 1975, Hill's Gallery, Santa Fe, 1978, Elaine Horwitz, Santa Fe, 1982, Rettie y Martinez, Santa Fe, 1986; group shows include, Library of Congress, 1975, U. N.D., 1978, Allrich Gallery, 1977, Mus. of Albuquerque, 1980; represented in permanent collections, Chgo. Art Inst., Yale U., Mus. Fine Arts, Santa Fe, Mpls. Mus. Art, No. Ill. U. Vol. Peace Corps, Papua New Guinea, 1992-94. Served with U.S. Army, 1962-64. Nat. Endowment for Arts grantee, 1974; Western States Art Found grantee, 1979; recipient Louis Comport Tiffany award, 1974. Home and Studio: 800 Oso Ridge Rt El Morro Grants NM 87020

LOWRANCE, MURIEL EDWARDS, program specialist; b. Ada, Okla., Dec. 28, 1922; d. Warren E. and Mayme E. (Barrick) Edwards; B.S. in Edn., East Central State U., Ada, 1954; 1 dau., Kathy Lynn Lowrance Gutierrez. Accountant, adminstrv. asst. to bus. mgr. East Central State U., 1950-68; grants and contracts specialist U. N.Mex. Sch. Medicine, Albuquerque, 1968-72, program specialist IV, dept. orthopaedics, 1975-86; asst. adminstrv. officer N.Mex. Regional Med. Program, 1972-75. Bd. dirs. Vocat. Rehab. Center, 1980-84. Cert. profl. contract mgr. Nat. Contract Assn. Mem. Am. Bus. Women's Assn. (past pres. El Segundo chpt., Woman of Yr. 1974), AAUW, Amigos de las Americas (dir.). Democrat. Methodist. Club: Pilot (Albuquerque) (pres. 1979-80, dir. 1983-84, dist. treas. 1984-86, treas. S.W. dist., 1984-86, gov.-elect S.W. dist. 1986-87, gov. S.W. dist. 1987-88). Home: 3028 Mackland Ave NE Albuquerque NM 87106-2018

LOWRY, CANDACE ELIZABETH, human resource administrator, consultant; b. Miles City, Mont., Sept. 27, 1950; d. James A. and Nathlee (Azar) Zadick; m. Michael Roy Lowry, June 7, 1980; 1 child, Natalie. BSW with high honors, U. Mont., 1971; MSW with high honors, U. Iowa, 1975; DSW, U. Utah, 1984. Clin. social worker, Utah; cert. marriage and family therapist and supr.; diplomate clin. social work, 1987—. Inpatient social worker II U. Iowa Psychiat. Hosps., Iowa City, 1975-76, inpatient social worker III, 1976-79, coordinator, Iowa Autism Program, 1979-80; coordinator, social work specialist U. Utah Counseling Ctr., Salt Lake City, 1980-86, assoc. dir., 1986; prog. dir. adult unit Wasatch Canyons Hosp., Salt Lake City, 1986—; dir. all adult svcs. Wasatch Canyons Hosp., 1990—; clin. instr. U. Utah, Salt Lake City, 1981—. Co-author: Meeting the Needs of Autistic Children, 1980; contbr. articles to profl. jours. Grantee NIMH, 1986—. Mem. Nat. Assn. Social Workers, Acad. Cert. Social Workers (cert.), Nat. Register Clin. Social Workers, Am. Group Psychotherapy Assn., Salt Lake City C. of C. Home: 2705 Eagle Way Salt Lake City UT 84108-2804 Office: Wasatch Canyons Hosp 5770 S 1500 W Salt Lake City UT 84123-5216

LOWRY, LARRY LORN, management consulting company executive; b. Lima, Ohio, Apr. 12, 1947; s. Frank William and Viola Marie L.; m. Jean Carroll Greenbaum, June 23, 1973; 1 child, Alexandra Kristin. BSEE, MIT, 1969, MSEE, 1970; MBA, Harvard U., 1972. Mgr. Boston Consulting Group, Menlo Park, Calif., 1972-80; sr. v.p., mng. ptnr. Booz, Allen & Hamilton Inc, San Francisco, 1980—. Western Electric fellow, 1969, NASA fellow, 1970. Mem. Sigma Xi, Tau Beta Pi, Eta Kappa Nu. Presbyterian. Home: 137 Stockbridge Ave Atherton CA 94027-3942

LOWRY, MIKE, governor, former congressman; b. St. John, Wash., Mar. 8, 1939; s. Robert M. and Helen (White) L.; m. Mary Carlson, Apr. 6, 1968; 1 child, Diane. B.A., Wash. State U., Pullman, 1962. Chief fiscal analyst, staff dir. ways and means com. Wash. State Senate, 1969-73; govtl. affairs dir. Group Health Coop. Puget Sound, 1974-75; mem. council King County Govt., 1975-78, chmn., 1977; mem. 96th-100th congresses from 7th dist. Wash., 1979-1989; governor State of Wash., 1993—. Chmn. King County Housing and Community Devel. Block Grant Program, 1977, pres. Wash. Assn. Counties, 1978. Democrat. Address: Legislative Bldg PO Box 40002 Olympia WA 98504*

LU, GUIYANG, electrical engineer; b. Guiyang, China, May 10, 1946; came to U.S., 1982; s. Wen and Yunqiu Deng; m. Jing Du; 1 child, Jia. Degree in elec. engring., Tsing Hua U., Beijing, 1970; postgrad., South China U. Tech., Guangzhou, 1980-81; MA in Math., Calif. State U., Fresno, 1984; MSEE, Poly. U., N.Y.C., 1986. Instr. in elec. engring. South China U. Tech., Guangzhou, 1973-80; v.p. engring. Kawahara Corp., N.Y.C., 1986-88; H.S. math. tchr. N.Y.C. Bd. Edn., 1988-90; sr. R&D engr. Avid Inc., Norco, Calif., 1991—. Mem. IEEE. Office: Avid Inc 3179 Hamner Ave Norco CA 91760-1983

LU, PAUL HAIHSING, mining engineer, geotechnical consultant; b. Hsinchu, Taiwan, Apr. 6, 1921; came to U.S., 1962; m. Sylvia Chin-Pi Liu, May 5, 1951; children: Emily, Flora. BS in Mining Engring., Hokkaido U., Sapporo, Japan, 1945; PhD in Mining Engring., U. Ill., 1967. Sr. mining engr., br. chief Mining Dept. Taiwan Provincial Govt., Taipei, 1946-56; sr. indsl. specialist mining and geology U.S. State Dept./Agy. for Internat. Devel., Taipei, 1956-62; rsch. mining engr. Denver Rsch. Ctr. Bur. of Mines, U.S. Dept. Interior, 1967-90; geotech. cons. Lakewood, Colo., 1991—. Contbr. over 60 articles to profl. jours. Rsch. fellow Hokkaido U., 1945-46, Ill. Mining Inst., 1966-67. Mem. Internat. Soc. for Rock Mechanics, Soc. for Mining, Metallurgy, and Exploration (AIME), Mining and Materials Processing Inst. Japan, Chinese Inst. of Mining and Metall. Engrs. (dir., mining com. chair 1960-62, Tech. Achievement award 1962). Home and Office: 1001 S Foothill Dr Lakewood CO 80228-3404

LU, WUAN-TSUN, microbiologist, immunologist; b. Taichung, Taiwan, July 8, 1939; came to U.S., 1964; s. Yueh and Jinmien Lu; m. Rita Man Rom, July 25, 1970; children: Dorcia, Loretta. BS in Agrl. Econs., Nat. Taiwan U., 1960; MS in Microbiology, Brigham Young U., 1968; PhD, U. Okla., 1978. Microbiologist, chemist Murray Biol. Co., L.A., 1969-71; microbiologist Reference Lab., North Hollywood, Calif., 1971-73; rsch. assoc. U. Okla., Okla. City, 1973-78; lab. supr. Reference Med. Lab., San Jose, Calif., 1980; mng. dir. Anakem Labs., Los Gatos, Calif., 1981-85; toxicologist SmithKline Labs., San Jose, 1981; founder, pres. United Biotech, Inc., Mountain View, Calif., 1983—, dir., chmn., mng. dir., 1987—; bd. dirs. Sino-U.S. Hunan Bioengring. Co., Ltd., Bios Instrment Lab., Inc., Mountain View, Calif.. Mem. Am. Soc. Clin. Pathologists, Am. Soc. Clin. Chemists, Delta Group. Office: United Biotech Inc 110 Pioneer Way # C Mountain View CA 94041-1517

LUBECK, MARVIN JAY, ophthalmologist; b. Cleve., Mar. 20, 1929; s. Charles D. and Lillian (Jay) L. A.B., U. Mich., 1951, M.D., 1955, M.S., 1959. Diplomate Am. Bd. Opthamology; m. Arlene Sue Bitman, Dec. 28, 1955; children: David Mark, Daniel Jay, Robert Charles. Intern, U. Mich. Med. Ctr., 1955-56, resident ophthalmology, 1956-58, jr. clin. instr. ophthalmology, 1958-59; pvt. practice medicine, specializing in ophthalmology, Denver, 1961—; mem. staff Rose Hosp., Porter Hosp., Presbyn. Hosp., St. Luke's Hosp.; assoc. clin. prof. U. Colo. Med. Ctr.; cons. ophthalmologist State of Colo. With U.S. Army, 1959-61. Fellow ACS; mem. Am. Acad. Ophthalmology, Denver Med. Soc., Colo. Ophthalmol. Soc., Am. Soc. Cataract & Refractive Surgery. Home: 590 S Harrison Ln Denver CO 80209-3517 Office: 3865 Cherry Crk North Dr Denver CO 80209-3803

LUBY, CHARLES STRONG, company executive; b. Pitts., Dec. 8, 1937; s. Charles Leopold and Helen Marie (Adams) L.; m. Robin Dorothy Briscoe, Aug. 10, 1963. BA in Chemistry, San Diego State U., 1959, MS in

Chemistry, 1964. Materials engr. Gen. Atomics, San Diego, 1960-68, mgr. nuclear fuel testing, 1968-71, mgr. fuel planning, 1971-73, exec. asst., 1973-76, mgr. internat. programs, 1977-82, mgr. proposals, 1982—. Patentee in field. Mem. Am. Nuclear Soc. (sect. chmn. 1978), Univ.Club. Office: Gen Atomics 3550 General Atomics Ct San Diego CA 92121-1122

LUCARELLI, PETER RAYMOND, fire chief; b. Walla Walla, Wash., Mar. 30, 1938; s. Anthony E. and Rhea (Cavalli) L.; m. Millie Bennett Lucarelli, Feb. 17, 1974; children: Kathleen, Marjorie, Tami, Peter. AS, Harbor Coll., 1984; BA, U. Redlonds, 1986; exec. fire officer, Nat. Fire Acad., 1988. From firefighter to asst. chief City of L.A., 1963-90; fire chief City of Bellevue(Wash.), 1990—; adj. faculty Nat. Emergency Tng. Ctr. and Fire Acad., Emmitsburg, Md., 1989—. Office: Bellevue Fire Dept 766 Bellevue Way SE Bellevue WA 98006

LUCAS, BETH ANNE, television producer; b. Grand Rapids, Mich., Sept. 15, 1960; d. Gordon Patrick and Phyllis (Sablack) Galka; m. Mark Fordham, Mar. 19, 1982 (div. 1985); m. Gus Lucas, June 3, 1991. BA in Psychology, Antioch U., 1995. Segment producer Breakaway, Metromedia TV, Hollywood, Calif., 1983; asst. dir. Anything for Money, Paramount TV, Hollywood, 1984; post prodn. supr. Heathcliff DIC, Hollywood, 1984; post prodn. supr. Beauty and the Beast, Witt-Thomas Prodns., Hollywood, 1986-88; assoc. producer Anything But Love, 20th Century Fox, Hollywood, 1989; assoc. producer Easy Street Viacom Prodns., Hollywood, 1984-85; mgr. post prodn. Matlock, Perry Mason, Father Dowling, Jack and the Fatman, Hollywood, 1990-91. Vol. Children Are Our Future, Haven Hills Battered Woman's Shelter; mem. AIDS Project L.A., L.A. Mission. Mem. NOW, Amnesty Internat., The Nature Conservancy, Nat. Parks and Conservation Assn., Am. Film Inst., Women in Arts, Feminist Majority, Nat. Abortion Rights Action League, Greenpeace, Smithsonian Assocs., Mus. Contemporary Art, L.A. County Mus., Sta. KCET, UCLA Alumni Assn., Child Help USA, Childreach, Mus. of Tolerance.

LUCAS, DONALD LEO, private investor; b. Upland, Calif., Mar. 18, 1930; s. Leo J. and Mary G. (Schwamm) L.; BA, Stanford U., 1951, MBA, 1953; m. Lygia de Soto Harrison, July 15, 1961; children: Nancy Maria Lucas Thibodeau, Alexandra Maria Lucas Ertola, Donald Alexander Lucas. Assoc. corp. fin. dept. Smith, Barney & Co., N.Y.C., 1956-59; gen., ltd. ptnr. Draper, Gaither & Anderson, Palo Alto, Calif., 1959-66; pvt. investor, Menlo Park, Calif., 1966—; bd. dirs. Cadence Design Systems, San Jose, Calif., Delphi Info. Systems, Inc., ICOT Corp., San Jose, Kahler Realty Corp., Rochester, Minn., Oracle Corp., Redwood Shores, Calif., Quantum Health Resources Inc., Racotek, Inc., Mpls., Macromedia, San Francisco, TriCord Systems, Inc., Plymouth, Minn., Trascend, Inc., Atlanta; Mem. bd. regents Bellarmine Coll. Prep., 1977—; regent emeritus U. Santa Clara, 1980—. 1st lt. AUS, 1953-55. Mem. Am. Coun. for Capital Formation, Stanford U. Alumni Assn., Stanford Grad. Sch. Bus. Alumni Assn., Order of Malta, Stanford Buck Club, Vintage Club (Indian Wells, Calif.), Menlo Country Club (Woodside, Calif.), Menlo Circus Club (Atherton, Calif.), Jackson Hole Golf and Tennis Club, Teton Pines Club, Zeta Psi. Home: 224 Park Ln Atherton CA 94027-5411 Office: 3000 Sand Hill Rd # 3-210 Menlo Park CA 94025-7116

LUCAS, ELIZABETH COUGHLIN, educator; b. Youngstown, Ohio, May 5, 1918; d. Joseph Anthony and Gertrude Elizabeth (Handel) Coughlin; m. Charles Edward Lucas, Apr. 7, 1945. BS magna cum laude, Notre Dame Coll. of Ohio, 1940; Diploma, Harvard U., 1944; MA in Edn., Calif. State Poly U., 1980. Cert. tchr., Calif. (life), secondary tchr., Pa., Ohio. Tech. sec. for v.p. engring and purchasing Patterson Foundry and Machine Co., East Liverpool, Ohio, 1941-42; tchr. chemistry Point Marion (Pa.) High Sch., 1942, Lincoln High Sch., Midland, Pa., 1942-44; radar specialist Thunderstorm Project U.S. Weather Bur., St. Cloud, Fla., 1946, Wilmington, Ohio, 1947; substitute tchr. math, sci. Chaffey (Calif.) Union High Schs., 1971-75; tchr. math Claremont (Calif.) High Sch., 1975-80; tchr., counselor, head sci. dept. San Antonio High Sch., Claremont, 1980-88; substitute tchr. Claremont Unified Sch. Dist., Claremont, 1988—; mem. dist. adv. com. for math. and sci., Claremont, 1983-85; substitute tchr. San Antonio (Calif.) High Sch., 1988—, Upland (Calif.) High Sch., 1988-89, Hillside High Sch., 1988-89. Author, editor: A Descriptive Study of the Effects of the New Math Syndrome on the Average High School Student, 1980. Lt. (j.g.) USNR, 1944-48. Mem. NAFE, Nat. Coun. of Tchrs. of Math., Nat. Sci. Tchrs. Assn., Assn. for Supervision and Curriculum Devel., Cath. Daus. of the Ams. (regent 1975-77, diocesan chmn. 1979-81). Republican. Roman Catholic. Home and Office: 9185 Regency Way Alta Loma CA 91701-3439

LUCAS, ELIZABETH HELENE, artist, calligrapher, educator; b. Pasadena, Calif., Aug. 21, 1936; d. Edward A. and Anona Marie (Snyder) Buse; m. Justice Campbell M. Lucas, Dec. 17, 1960; children: Scott, Stephen, Lisanne. AA, Long Beach City Coll., 1956, BA, Whittier Coll., 1958, MA, 1984. Cert. gen. secondary tchr., Calif. Chmn. dept. sci. Bolsa Grande High Sch., Garden Grove, Calif., 1960-65; ind. tchr. calligraphy Long Beach, Calif., 1976-90; instr. Sch. for Adults, Long Beach, 1978-80; assoc. prof. calligraphy Calif. State U.-Long Beach, 1979-90, coord. cert. in calligraphy program, 1982-90; instr. calligraphy and bookbinding U. Calif.-Riverside, 1982-85; instr. calligraphy Whittier Coll., Calif., 1984-85; designer books Great Quotations, Inc.; free-lance calligrapher and graphic designer, 1976—; designer, pub. line of calligraphy greeting cards, 1978—, owner Elizabeth Lucas Designs. Author: Calligraphy, The Art of Beautiful Writing, 1984; one-Woman calligraphy shows Long Beach Mus. Art Bookshop/Gallery, 1981, 84, Sr. Eye Gallery, Long Beach, 1982, 85, Gt. Western Savs. and Loan, Long Beach, 1983, David Scott Meier Gallery, Mendocino, Calif., 1983, Whittier Coll. Mendenhall Gallery, 1983; also group shows. Active, past mem. bd. dirs. Long Beach Law Aux., 1960—, Jr. League, Long Beach, 1968—; pres. Lowell Sch. PTA, Long Beach, 1972; pres., bd. dirs. Am. Heart Assn., 1991—. Named Sci. Tchr. of Yr., So. Calif. Edison Co., 1963; recipient art awards, including First Place award Calif. State Lawyers' Wives, 1984. Mem. Soc. for Calligraphy (past presL.A. chpt. 1982-83), Soc. Scribes and Illuminators, Friends of Calligraphy, Soc. Scribes, Profl. Writers League, Calif. State PTA (hon. life 1973—), Long Beach Mus. Art Found. (co-chairperson dir.'s circle 1985), Long Beach Art Assn., Pub. Corp. for Arts, Fine Art Affiliates of Calif. State U. at Long Beach. Republican. Lodge: Soroptimists (com. chairperson local club 1981-86), Cameo, Profl. Auxiliary, Assistance League of Long Beach, Rotary (Long Beach). Home: 518 Monrovia Ave Long Beach CA 90814-1843 Office: Elizabeth Lucas Designs 10542 Calle Lee Ste 118 Los Alamitos CA 90720-2550

LUCAS, GLENN EUGENE, materials engineering educator, consultant; b. Los Angeles, Mar. 8, 1951; s. Glenn Edwin and Mary Lorraine (Shaw) L.; m. Susan R. Ricketts, Sept. 2, 1972; children: Kelly Christopher, Ryan Geoffrey, Shannon Michael. BS, U. Calif., Santa Barbara, 1973; MS, MIT, 1975, ScD, 1977. Cons. on nuclear materials, mech. metallurgy, composite materials, Santa Barbara, 1975—; engr. Exxon Nuclear Co., Inc., Richland, Wash., 1978; asst. prof. nuclear engring. U. Calif., Santa Barbara, 1978-83, assoc. prof., 1983-87, prof. chem. engring. and materials, 1987—; vis. prof. U. Tokyo and Hokkaido U., 1985. Author: Effects of Anisotropy and Irradiation on the Creep Behavior of Zircaloy, 1979; co-author: Creep of Zirconium Alloys in Nuclear Reactors, 1983; co-editor: The Use of Small Scale Specimens for Testing Irradiated Materials, 1986; contbr. over 100 articles to profl. jours. and conf. procs. Recipient Outstanding Nuclear Engring. Faculty award U. Calif., Santa Barbara, 1980, 81, 83, 84, 89, 94; Joseph Warren Barker fellow, 1975, Babcock and Wilcox fellow, 1977. Mem. Am. Soc. for Metals, AAAS, Am Nuclear Soc. (significant contbn. awards 1982, 91, 92, exec. com. 1984-92, chair 1992-93, Young Mem. Engring. Achievement award 1991). Home: 529 Dorset Ct Goleta CA 93117-1643 Office: U Calif Dept Chem & Mech Engring Santa Barbara CA 93106

LUCAS, JAMES BRUNO, public relations consultant; b. Berkeley, Calif., Nov. 15, 1950; s. James M. and Elizabeth A. (Pilorz) L.; m. Liesel C. Friedrich, Dec. 21, 1985; children: Charles M., Benjamin A. BA, Kenyon Coll., 1973; MA, Duke U., 1980. Accredited Pub. Rels. Soc. Am. Staff writer The Raleigh (N.C.) Times, 1978-80; sr. pub. info. rep. Met. Water Dist. So. Calif., L.A., 1981-84; copywriter Corp. Comm. Group, Marina del Rey, Calif., 1984-87; sr. account exec. Burson-Marsteller, L.A., 1987-89; cons. J. Lucas Corp. Pub. Rels. and Investor Rels., Santa Monica, Calif., 1989-90, 94—; dir. Pub. Rels. Health Net, Woodland Hills, Calif., 1990-94. Recipient 1st place investigative reporting N.C. Press Assn., 1979, Annual Report awards Fin. World Mag., N.Y., 1992, 93. Home and Office: PO Box 1305 Santa Monica CA 90406-1305

LUCAS, JAMES GREGORY, marketing executive; b. Nampa, Idaho, Oct. 24, 1957; s. Joseph Lorimer Berry and Donna Jeuell (Warner) Janicek; m. Josephine Ann Palajac, June 6, 1981; children: William Bradley, Jessica Lauren. BSBA in Mgmt. cum laude, San Diego State U., 1981. POEM channel mgr., 1984-87; LaserJet III product mgr. Hewlett Packard, 1987-90; U.S. sales devel. mgr. Hewlett Packard, Boise, Idaho, 1990-93; worldwide market devel. mgr. Hewlett Packard, San Diego, 1993, worldwide current product mktg. mgr., 1993-94; mgr. worldwide mktg. Hewlett-Packard, Bergamo, Italy, 1994—. Republican. Roman Catholic. Office: Hewlett Packard, Vialo Europa 2, 24040 Stezzano Italy

LUCAS, JOE NATHAN, research scientist; b. Lake Providence, La., Dec. 18, 1945; s. Bennie and Mary (Wright) L.; 1 child, Aziza K. BS in Physics, UCLA, 1970, MS in Med. Radiation Physics, 1972; PhD in Biophysics, U. Calif., Berkeley, 1977. Cert. tchr., Calif. Instr. sci. and math. Mills Coll., Oakland, Calif., 1972-75; tchg. fellow physics and phys. chemistry U. Calif., Berkeley, 1972-75, biophysicist Lawrence Berkeley Lab., 1977-78; sr. scientist biophysics Lawrence Livermore Lab. U. Calif., Livermore, 1978—; adj. prof. biology Calif. State U., Hayward, 1993—. Contbg. author chpts. to books; contbr. articles, abstracts to profl. jours. and conf. procs.; co-developer Chromosome Painting; inventor/developer 3-Color Chromosome Painting. Founder, chmn. bd. dirs. The Lucas Ednl. Found., Inc., San Ramon, Calif., 1978—. Fulbright scholar, U. Calif., 1977; grantee USPH Biophysics Tng. Fellowship, U. Calif., Berkeley, 1972-76, U. Calif. Univ. Scholar, Berkeley, 1975, U. Calif. Biophysics Rsch., Berkeley, 1974-75; recipient U. Calif. Regents scholarship, 1967-70, USPH fellowship, 1970-72, Bay Area Image Builders award, 1983. Mem. Radiation Rsch. Soc., Cell Biology Soc., Internat. Soc. Analytical Cytometry. Office: Univ of Calif PO Box 808 Livermore CA 94551-0808

LUCAS, LINDA LUCILLE, dean; b. Stockton, Calif., Apr. 22, 1940; d. Leslie Harold Lucas and Amy Elizabeth (Callow) Farnsworth. BA, San Jose State Coll., 1961, MA, 1969; EdD, U. San Francisco, 1982. Dist. libr. Livermore (Calif.) Elem. Schs., 1962-64; libr. Mission San Jose High Sch., Fremont, Calif., 1964-69; media reference libr. Chabot Coll., Hayward, Calif., 1969-75; asst. dean instrn. Chabot-Las Positas Coll., Livermore, 1975-91; assoc. dean instrn. Las Positas Coll., Livermore, 1991-94, dean acad. svcs., 1994—; participant Nat. Inst. for Leadership Devel., 1991. Bd. dirs. Tri-Valley Community TV, Livermore, 1991—, Valley Choral Soc., 1993—, Chabot-Las Positas Colls. Found., Pleasanton, Calif., 1991-94; mem. needs assessment com Performing Arts Coun., Pleasanton. Mem. ALA, Coun. Chief Librs., Assn. Calif. Community Coll. Adminstrs., Calif. Libr. Assn. Office: Las Positas Coll 3033 Collier Canyon Rd Livermore CA 94550-9797

LUCAS, MALCOLM MILLAR, state supreme court chief justice; b. Berkeley, Calif., Apr. 19, 1927; s. Robert and Georgina (Campbell) L.; m. Joan Fisher, June 23, 1956; children: Gregory, Lisa Georgina. B.A., U. So. Calif., 1950, LL.B., 1953. Bar: Calif. 1954. Ptnr. firm Lucas, Deukmejian and Lucas, Long Beach, Calif., 1955-67; judge Superior Ct., L.A., 1967-71, U.S. Dist. Ct. (cen. dist.) Calif., 1971-84; assoc. justice Calif. Supreme Ct., 1984-87, chief justice, 1987—. Republican. Office: Calif Supreme Ct South Tower 303 2nd St San Francisco CA 94107-1366*

LUCAS, SUZANNE, statistician, entrepreneur; b. Baxter Springs, Kans., Jan. 16, 1939; d. Ralph Beaver and Marguerite (Sansocie) L.; children: Patricia Sue Jennings, Neil Patric Jennings. BA in Math., Calif. State U., Fresno, 1967, MA in Ednl. Theory, 1969; MS in Stats., U. So. Calif., 1979. Asst. to dir. NSF Inst., Calif. State U., Fresno, 1968; Tchr. secondary math. Fresno city schs., 1968-78; statistician corp. indsl. relations Hughes Aircraft Co., Los Angeles, 1979-80; personnel adminstr. Hughes Aircraft Co. Space and Communications Group, Los Angeles, 1981-82, mem. tech. staff in math., 1982-85, staff engr., 1986-87; mem. tech. staff cost analysis The Aerospace Corp., 1987-90; sr. staff engr. Hughes Aircraft Co. Electro Optical Systems, 1990-93, scientist, engr., 1993—; owner, math. cons. Lucas Ednl. Consultants, Manhattan Beach, Calif., 1989—; owner Lucas Enterprises, Manhattan Beach, 1993—; lectr. in biostats. U. So. Calif., 1979. Kiwanis scholar, 1958. Mem. Internat. Soc. Parametric Analysts (pres. So. Calif. chpt. 1991-92), Soc. Cost Estimating and Analysis (cert.), Am. Psychol. Assn., Am. Statis. Assn., U. So. Calif. Alumni Assn. (life), Internat. Platform Assn., Kappa Mu Epsilon. Office: Hughes Aircraft Co EOS PO Box 902 EO/E1/A118 El Segundo CA 90245-0902 also: Lucas Ednl Cons PO Box 3868 Manhattan Beach CA 90266-1868

LUCCHETTI, LYNN L., advertising executive, military officer; b. San Francisco, Calif., Aug. 21, 1939; d. Dante and Lillian (Bergeron) L. AB, San Jose State U., 1961; MS, San Francisco State U., 1967; grad. U.S. Army Basic Officer's Course, 1971, U.S. Army Advanced Officer Course, 1976, grad. U.S. Air Force Command and Staff Coll., 1982, U.S. Air Force War Coll., 1983, Sr. Pub. Affairs Officer Course, 1984. Media buyer Batten, Barton, Durstine & Osborn, Inc., San Francisco, 1961-67; producer-dir. Sta. KTVA-TV, Anchorage, 1967-68; media supr. Bennett, Luke and Teawell Advt., Phoenix, 1968-71; commd. 1st lt. U.S. Army, 1971; advanced through ranks to lt. col., 1985, col., 1989, brig. gen. 1993; officer U.S. Army, 1971-74, D.C. N.G., , 1974-78, U.S. Air Force Res., 1978—, program advt. mgr. U.S. Navy Recruiting Command, 1974-76; exec. coordinator for the Joint Advt. Dirs. of Recruiting (JADOR), 1976-79; dir. U.S. Armed Forces Joint Recruiting Advt. Program (JRAP), Dept. Def., Washington, 1979-91; resources mgr. Exec. Leadership Devel. Program Dept. Def., Washington, 1991-94. Author: Broadcasting in Alaska, 1924-1966. Decorated U.S. Army Meritorious Svc. medal, Nat. Def. medal, U.S. Air Force Longevity Ribbon, U.S. Navy Meritorious Unit Commendation, Dept. Def. Joint Achievement medal, 1984. Sigma Delta Chi journalism scholar, 1960. Mem. Women in Def., Sr. Profl. Wommens Assn. Home: 11401 Malaguena Ln NE Albuquerque NM 87111-6899

LUCE, R(OBERT) DUNCAN, psychology educator; b. Scranton, Pa., May 16, 1925; s. Robert Rennselaer and Ruth Lillian (Downer) L.; m. Gay Gaer, June 6, 1950 (div.); m. Cynthia Newby, Oct. 5, 1968 (div.); m. Carolyn A. Scheer, Feb. 27, 1988; 1 child, Aurora Newby. BS, MIT, 1945, PhD, 1950; MA (hon.), Harvard U., 1976. Mem. staff research lab electronics MIT, 1950-53; asst. prof. Columbia U., 1953-57; lectr. social relations Harvard U., 1957-59; prof. psychology U. Pa., Phila., 1959-69; vis. prof. Inst. Advanced Study, Princeton, 1969-72; prof. Sch. Social Scis., U. Calif., Irvine, 1972-75; Alfred North Whitehead prof. psychology Harvard U., Cambridge, Mass., 1976-81, prof., 1981-83, Victor S. Thomas prof. psychology, 1983-88, Victor S. Thomas prof. emeritus, 1988; chmn. Harvard U., 1988-94; disting. prof. cognitive sci. U. Calif., Irvine, 1988-94, dir. Irvine Rsch. Unit in math. behavioral sci., 1988-92, disting. rsch. prof. cognitive sci. and rsch. prof. econs., 1994—; dir. Inst. for Math. Behavioral Sci., 1992—; chmn. assembly behavioral and social scis. NRC, 1976-79. Author: (with H. Raiffa) Games and Decisions, 1957, Individual Choice Behavior, 1959, (with others) Foundations of Measurement, I, 1971, II, 1989, III, 1990, Response Times, 1986, (with others) Stevens Handbook of Experimental Psychology, I and II, 1988, Sound & Hearing, 1993. Served with USNR, 1943-46. Ctr. Advanced Study in Behavioral Scis. fellow, 1954-55, 66-67, 87-88, NSF Sr. Postdoctoral fellow, 1966-67, Guggenheim fellow, 1980-81; recipient Disting. award for Rsch. U. Calif., Irvine, 1994. Fellow AAAS, APA (disting. sci. contbn. award 1970, bd. sci. affairs 1993—), Am. Psychol. Soc. (bd. dirs. 1989-91); mem. Am. Acad. Arts and Scis., Am. Philos. Soc., Nat. Acad. Scis. (chmn. sect. psychology 1980-83, class behavioral and social scis. 1983-86), Am. Math. Soc., Math. Assn. Am., Fedn. Behavioral Psychol. and Cognitive Scis. (pres. 1988-90), Psychometric Soc. (pres. 1976-77), Psychonomic Soc., Soc. Math. Psychology (pres. 1979), Sigma Xi, Phi Beta Kappa, Tau Beta Pi. Home: 20 Whitman Ct Irvine CA 92715-4057 Office: U Calif Social Sci Tower Irvine CA 92717

LUCE, SUSAN MARIE, library director; b. Ypsilanti, Mich., Mar. 4, 1948; d. Walter Stanley and Irene Elizabeth (Gallaway) Rybka; m. Paul Trescott Jackson, July 10, 1971 (div. Apr. 1986); m. John Archer Luce, Jr., Nov. 19, 1988. BA in History, U. Mich., 1968, AMLS, 1969. Acquisitions libr. Oakland U., Rochester, Mich., 1969-71; head circulation dept. Lincoln Libr., Springfield, Ill., 1972-73; dir. Alpha Park Pub. Libr. Dist., Bartonville, Ill., 1973-87, Ontario (Calif.) City Libr., 1988—. Mem. ALA, Calif. Libr. Assn. Office: Ontario City Library 215 E C St Ontario CA 91764-4111

LUCENTE, ROSEMARY DOLORES, educational administrator; b. Renton, Wash., Jan. 11, 1935; d. Joseph Anthony and Erminia Antoinette (Argano) Lucente; BA, Mt. St. Mary's Coll., 1956, MS, 1963. Tchr. pub. schs., Los Angeles, 1956-65, supr. tchr., 1958-65, asst. prin., 1965-69, prin. elem. sch., 1969-85, 86—, dir. instrn., 1985-86, 1986—; nat. cons., lectr. Dr. William Glasser's Educator Tng. Ctr., 1968—; nat. workshop leader Nat. Acad. for Sch. Execs.-Am. Assn. Sch. Adminstrs., 1980; L.A. Unified Sch. Dist. rep. for nat. pilot of Getty Inst. for Visual Arts, 1983-85, 92—, site coord., 1983-86, team leader, mem. supt.'s adv. cabinet, 1987—. Recipient Golden Apple award Stanford Ave. Sch. PTA, Faculty and Community Adv. Council, 1976, resolution for outstanding service South Gate City Council, 1976. Mem. Nat. Assn. Elem. Sch. Prins., L.A. Elem. Prins. Orgn. (v.p. 1979-80), Assn. Calif. Sch. Adminstrs. (charter mem.), Assn. Elem. Sch. Adminstrs. (vice-chmn. chpt. 1972-75, city-wide exec. bd., steering com. 1972-75, 79-80), Asso. Adminstrs. Los Angeles (charter), Pi Theta Mu, Kappa Delta Pi (v.p. 1982-84), Delta Kappa Gamma. Democrat. Roman Catholic. Home: 6501 Lindenhurst Ave Los Angeles CA 90048-4733 Office: Figueroa St Sch 510 W 111th St Los Angeles CA 90044-4231

LUCHTERHAND, RALPH EDWARD, financial advisor; b. Portland, Oreg., Feb. 9, 1952; s. Otto Charles II and Evelyn Alice (Isaac) L.; m. JoAnn Denise Adams, Aug. 13, 1983; children: Anne Michelle, Eric Alexander, Nicholas Andrew. BS, Portland State U., 1974, MBA, 1986. Registered profl. engr., Oreg.; gen. securities broker NYSE/NASD, CFP. Mech. engr. Hyster Co., Portland, 1971-75, svc. engr., 1975-76; project engr. Lumber Systems Inc., Portland, 1976-79; prin. engr. Moore Internat., Portland, 1979-81, chief product engr., 1981-83; project engr. Irvington-Moore, Portland, 1983, chief engr., 1983-86; ind. cons. engr., 1986; engring. program mgr. Precision Castparts Corp., Portland, 1986-87; personal fin. adv., Am. Express Fin. Advs., Clackamas, Oreg., 1987-94, sr. fin. adv., 1994—; apptd. to Silver Team, 1991, Gold Team, 1994. Treas. Village Bapt. Ch., Beaverton, Oreg., 1988-91; bd. dirs. Carus Community Planning Orgn., Clackamas, Oreg., 1993—. Republican. Home: 24440 S Eldorado Rd Mulino OR 97042-9629 Office: American Express Fin Advisors Inc 8800 SE Sunnyside Rd Ste 300 Clackamas OR 97015-9786

LUCKETT, BYRON EDWARD, JR., air force chaplain; b. Mineral Wells, Tex., Feb. 2, 1951; s. Byron Edward and Helen Alma (Hart) L.; m. Kathryn Louise Lambertson, Dec. 30, 1979; children: Florence Louise, Byron Edward III, Barbara Elizabeth, Stephanie Hart. BS, U.S. Mil. Acad., 1973; MDiv, Princeton Theol. Sem., 1982; MA, Claremont Grad. Sch., 1987. Commd. 2d lt. U.S. Army, 1973, advanced through grades to maj.; stationed at Camp Edwards, Korea, 1974-75; bn. supply officer 563rd Engr. Bn., Kornwestheim, Germany, 1975-76; platoon leader, exec. officer 275th Engr. Co., Ludwigsburg, Germany, 1976-77; boy scout project officer Hdqrs., VII Corps, Stuttgart, Germany, 1977-78; student intern Moshannon Valley Larger Parish, Winburne, Penn., 1980-81; Protestant chaplain Philmont Scout Ranch, Cimarron, N.Mex., 1982; asst. pastor Immanuel Presbyn. Ch., Albuquerque, 1982-83, assoc. pastor, 1983-84; tchr. Claremont High Sch., 1985-86; Protestant chaplain 92nd Combat Support Group, Fairchild AFB, Wash., 1986-90; installation staff chaplain Pirinclik Air Station, Turkey, 1990-91; protestant chaplain Davis-Monthan AFB, Ariz., 1991-95, OFFUTT AFB, Nebr., 1995; mem. intern program coun. Claremont (Calif.) Grad. Sch. Contbr. articles to profl. jours. Bd. dirs. Parentcraft, Inc., Albuquerque, 1984, United Campus Ministries, Albuquerque, 1984, Proclaim Liberty, Inc., Spokane, 1987-90; bd. dirs. western region Nat. Assn. Presbyn. Scouters, Irving, Tex., 1986-89, chaplain, 1991-93; mem. N.Mex. Employer Co, in Support of the Guard and Reserve, Albuquerque, 1984, Old Baldy coun. Boy Scouts Am., 1986; chmn. Fairchild Parent Coop., Fairchild AFB, 1986-87; pres. Co. Grade Officers Coun., Fairchild AFB, 1987-88. Capt. U.S. Army Reserve; chaplain USAF Reserve 1983-86, maj. 1990—. Recipient Dist. Award of Merit for Disting. Svc. Boy Scouts Am., 1977. Mem. Soc. Cin. Md., Mil. Order Fgn. Wars U.S. Presbyterian. Home: 12909 S 29th Ave Bellevue NE 68123 Office: 55 WG/HC 301 Lincoln Hwy Bellevue NE 68123-5000

LUCKMAN, CHARLES, architect; b. Kansas City, Mo., May 16, 1909; m. Harriet McElroy, 1931; children: Charles, James M., Stephen A. Grad. magna cum laude, U. Ill., 1931; LLD, U. Miami, Fla., 1950; AFD (hon.), Calif. Coll. Arts and Crafts, 1958; DFA (hon.), Adelphi U., 1986; LLD (hon.), Pepperdine U., 1989. Lic. architect, 1931 Registered architect, 48 states and D.C. sr. registration Nat. Archtl. Registration Bds. Employed in architect's office for license qualifications, 2 years; joined Colgate- Palmolive-Peet Co. as retail salesman, 1931, Chgo. sales supr., 1933; mgr. Colgate-Palmolive-Peet Co. as retail salesman (Wis. dist.), 1934; divisional mgr. Colgate- Palmolive-Peet Co. as retail salesman (Cin. hdqrs.), 1935; with Pepsodent Co. (later Pepsodent Div. of Lever Bros. Co.), 1935-50, sales promotion mgr., sales mgr., 1935-36, v.p. in charge sales, 1936, in charge sales and advt., 1937, v.p., gen. mgr., 1938, exec. v.p., 1942-43, pres., 1943-46; exec. v.p. Lever Bros., Jan.-July 1946, pres., 1946-50; pres., partner Pereira & Luckman, Los Angeles, 1950-58; founder, ptnr. The Luckman Partnership, Inc., 1958—; chmn. bd., chief exec. officer Ogden Devel. Corp., 1968-74, Luckman Mgmt. Co., 1973—; dir. Hollywood Bowl. Maj. projects include Madison Sq. Garden, N.Y.C., Conv. and Exhbn. Center, Los Angeles, U.S. World's Fair Pavilion, N.Y.C., Los Angeles World Zoo, U. Calif. at Santa Barbara, Civic Plaza, Phoenix, Prudential Center, Boston, State Office Bldg, Madison, Wis., Phoenix Civic Plaza, Los Angeles Internat. Airport, First Nat. Bank of Ariz, Phoenix, Broadway Plaza, Los Angeles, United Calif. Bank, Los Angeles, U. Del. Student Living Center, La Jolla VA Hosp, Aloha Stadium, Honolulu, 9200 Sunset Tower, Los Angeles, Manned Space Craft Center, Houston, VA Hosp, West Los Angeles, Calif., Hoover Library and Linear Accelerator Center, Stanford U., 1st Natl Bank of Oreg, Portland, Forum, Inglewood, Calif., Ralph M. Parsons Co. hdqrs, Pasadena, Calif., Nat. Security and Resources Study Center, Los Alamos, Hyatt Regency Hotels, Dearborn, Mich., Phoenix, City Hall and Police Bldg., Inglewood, Xerox Corp. hdqrs., Stamford, Conn., Warner Bros. Office Bldg., Burbank, Calif., Orange County Conv./Civic Ctr., Orlando, Fla.; also numerous other pub. bldgs; author: (autobiography) Twice in a Lifetime, 1988. Pres., chmn. bd. Los Angeles Orchestral Soc., 1962; v.p., dir. So. Calif. Symphony Assn.; mem. bd. assocs., pres. council George Pepperdine Found., Los Angeles; trustee Calif. State Colls.; chmn. bd. trustees, 1963-65; bd. govs. Library Presdl. Papers; trustee Nat. Art Mus. Sport; mem. U. Ill. Found.; Calif. mem. Ednl. Commn. of States; mem. bd. Am. Nat. Red Cross, YMCA; bd. dirs., past pres. AID-United Givers.; Mem. Pres.'s Commn. on Equality of Treatment and Opportunity in Armed Services and Civil Rights, Gov.'s Commn. Met. Area Problems; dir. Advt. Council; trustee Adelphi U.; chmn. Citizens Food Com., 1947; mem. Commerce and Industry Assn. N.Y.C., Los Angeles World Affairs Council, Com. Econ. Devel., Council U.S. Assocs. of Internat. C. of C.; bd. dirs. Nat. Advt. Council Community Chest, Am. Heritage Found.; bd. assocs. Northwestern U., Calif. Inst. Tech.; chmn. Nat. Council Trustees of Freedoms Found. at Valley Forge, 1986. Decorated Star of Solidarity Republic of Italy; chevalier Nat. Order Legion of Honor France; Order of St. John; recipient Horatio Alger award Am. Schs. and Colls. Assn., George Washington Honor medal Freedom's Found., 1964, 67, 68, Make Am. Beautiful award Nat. Assn. Realty Bds.; named Outstanding Mgmt. Exec. N.Y. Mgmt. Club, Man of Year Constrn. Industries, 1974; Disting. Achievement award U. Ill., 1970; Henry Laurence Gantt medal Am. Mgmt. Assn. and ASMF, 1981. Mem. AIA (Fellowship award 1963), Ill. Soc. Architects, U.S. Jr. C. of C. (One of Outstanding Young Men 1945, dir.), Tau Beta Pi, Theta Tau, Gargoyle. Home and Office: The Luckman Management Co 9220 W Sunset Blvd West Hollywood CA 90069-3501

LUCKOW, ELIZABETH ELLEN, retired nurse; b. Stromsburg, Nebr., Jan. 31, 1934; d. Paul William and Lillian Marcella (Anderson) James; children: Michael, Erin Elizabeth. Diploma in nursing, Lincoln Gen. Hosp., 1954; BS, U. Colo., 1966, cert. pediatric nurse practitioner, 1967, MS, 1970. RN, Colo. Charge nurse sick baby nursery Children's Hosp., Fresno, Calif., 1955-56; pediatric nurse Pediatric Group, Fresno, 1956-62; emer. rm. nurse Gen. Rose Hosp., Denver, 1962; pediatric nurse emer. rm. Children's Hosp., Denver, 1963; pediatric nurse pvt. practice med. office, Denver, 1964; migrant nurse, child care nurse dept. pediatrics U. Colo., Boulder, 1967; clinic coord. Boulder County Devel. Evaluation Clinic, Boulder, 1969-82; child devel. cons. Boulder County Social Svcs., Boulder, 1983-84; staff nurse

Boulder Psychiat. Inst., 1985-88; ret., 1988. Mem. Boulder County Child Abuse Team, 1978-79; bd. dirs. Boulder County Bd. Devel. Disabilities, 1980-82; mem., adviser Colo. Subcom. on Mental Retardation, Denver, 1969-78; pres. Colo. Nurses Assn., Boulder, 1973; treas. Boulder Valley Bd. Edn., 1973-76; mem. adv. bd. Boulder Valley Sch. Adv. Bd., 1970-82; mem. Boulder County Mental Health-Child Team, 1978-80. Mem. Non Practicing and Part Time Colo. Nurses Assn. (program com. 1991—), Sigma Theta Tau (life). Methodist. Home: 3111 14th St Boulder CO 80304-2611

LUDIN, ROGER LOUIS, physics educator; b. Jersey City, June 13, 1944; s. Fredric E. and Gwendolyn C. (Rogers) L.; m. Diane E. Wilson, Aug. 26, 1966; children: Stephen L., Joyce E. BS in Physics, Brown U., 1966; MS in Physics, Worcester Polytech. Inst., 1968, PhD in Physics, 1969. Postdoctoral fellow Worcester (Mass.) Polytech. Inst., 1969-70; prof. Burlington County Coll., Pemberton, N.J., 1970-85; lectr. Calif. Poly. State U., San Luis Obispo, 1984—. Author lab. manuals for introductory physics; author computer assisted instrn. for gen. physics. Active Medford Lakes (N.J.) Bd. Edn., 1976-84, pres. 1978-84; bd. dirs. Medford Lakes Athletic Assn., 1974-84; soccer coach Morro Bay (Calif.) High Sch., 1985—. Named Tchr. of Yr. Burlington County Coll., 1982, 83. Mem. Am. Assn. Physics Tchrs. (sec., treas. N.J. sect. 1976-84, named Outstanding Contbr. to Physics Edn. 1984, editor So. Calif. sect. 1985-87, v.p. 1987-89, pres. 1989-92), Am. Phys. Soc., AAAS, Lions, Sigma Xi. Home: 2691 Koa St Morro Bay CA 93442-1709 Office: Calif Poly State U Physics Dept San Luis Obispo CA 93407

LUDWIG, MYLES ERIC, writer, editor, publishing executive, art director; b. Bklyn., Apr. 12, 1942; s. Solomon and Muriel (Levine) L.; m. Hendrieka Van Riper (div.); 1 child, Lindsay Anne; m. Marsha Daniel (div.). BA, U. N.C., 1967, MA in Mass. Comms., 1969. Editl. dir. Art Direction Mag., N.Y.C., 1970-73; creative asst. to pub. Penthouse/Viva Internat., N.Y.C., 1973-75; editor, pub. Olympic mag., N.Y.C., 1978-80; editl. dir. SMC/Carnegie Corp., N.Y.C., 1978-82; founding editor, pub. North Shore/The Sandwich Islands Quar., Kauai Style, Visions, BayNotes, Kauai, Hawaii, 1985—; mng. dir. Inter-Pacific Media, Inc., Kauai, 1988—; cons. Ludwig/Christensen, N.Y.C., 1982-85, Leber/Katz Ptnrs., N.Y.C., 1983-84; instr. creative writing NYU, N.Y.C., Kauai Acad. Creative Arts, 1971-72; instr. concept design N.Y. Inst. Advt., N.Y.C.; exhbn. judge Art Dirs. Club Denver, Art Dirs. Club N.C., N.Y. Art Dirs. Club; mem. Garden Island Arts Coun., founding editor and pub. ARTS, Mirage Princeville Resort Mktg. Bd. Author: (novel) Golem, 1969, (non-fiction) Creativity, 1972, The Detectives, 1980, Kauai in the Eye of Iniki, 1992, The Handbook of Magazine Design; contbr. numerous articles to profl. and consumer publs. Active Hawaii Internat. Film Festival, 1000 Friends of Kauai; advisor to mayor County of Kauai, 1993; advisor to Rep. Carl Stepath, 1993-94. Recipient Pele award Am. Assn. Advt. Agys., 1993, Pa'l award (2) Hawaii Pub. Assn., 1993; MCA fellow in creative writing Thomas Wolfe Award for Fiction, N.Y. Art Dirs. Mem. Soc. Pub. Designers (pres. 1983-84), N.Y. Type Dirs. Club (Ozzie award), Kauai Hist. Soc. Jewish. Home: 3667 Anini Beach Rd Hanalei HI 96714 Office: Inter-Pacific Media Inc PO Box 1545 Hanalei HI 96714-1545

LUDWIG, ROLF MARTIN, internist; b. Bautzen, Germany, June 3, 1924; came to U.S., 1953; s. Martin Max and Doris (Metz) L.; m. Shirley Jean Ray, Oct. 26, 1956 (div. June 1983); 1 child, Mark Stephen. M.D., Eberhard Karls U. Tuebingen, Germany, 1953. Intern, Mary's Help Hosp., San Francisco, 1953-54, then resident in internal medicine; resident in internal medicine Franklin Hosp., San Francisco, Huntington Meml. Hosp., Pasadena, Calif., Wadsworth VA Gen. Hosp., Los Angeles, 1959-60. Internist, Kaiser/Permanente, Fontana, Calif., 1960-63, 73-87; practice medicine specializing in internal medicine, Yucaipa, Calif., 1963-72; retired, 1987. Served to capt. M.C., U.S. Army, 1956-59. Mem. Am. Soc. Internal Medicine, Calif. Soc. Internal Medicine, Inland Soc. Internal Medicine. Republican. Lutheran. Home: 11711 Holmes St Yucaipa CA 92399-4014

LUEBTOW, JOHN GILBERT, artist; b. Milw., Apr. 2, 1944; s. Gilbert and Evelyn Luebtow; 1 child, Matthew John. BA, Calif. Luth. Coll., 1967; MA, UCLA, 1969, MFA, 1976. Dir. archtl. and exptl. ceramics depts. De Porcelyne Fles Co., Delft, The Netherlands, 1969-71; instr. Harvard Sch., North Hollywood, Calif., 1971—, chairperson arts dept., 1980; part time instr. painting Calif. Luth. Coll., Thousand Oaks, 1972-73. Exhibited in numerous group and one-man shows including Patricia Correia Gallery, Venice, Calif., 1994, Glass Now '94, Tokyo, 1994, Mus. Collectors Coun. Santa Barbara Mus. Art, 1993, Finegood Art Gallery, West Hills, Calif., 1993, many others; works commd. by numerous orgns. including Kawamura Haneda Hotel, Japan, Shaeraton Hotel, Bal Harbor, Fla., Supreme Ct. Nev., Am. Airlines, N.Y.C., Atlantic Richfield Corp., L.A., MCI, Atlanta, and numerous pvt. collections. Active art com. L.A. Bicentennial, 1980-81, Mus. Contemporary Art, L.A., L.A. County Mus. Art, Craft and Folk Art Mus., L.A. Mem. Nat. Coun. on Edn. Ceramics, Glass Arts Soc., Am. Crafts Coun., Calif. Art Edn. Assn., Nat. Art Edn. Assn., L.A. Inst. Contemporary Art, Calif. Assn. Ind. Schs. Home and Studio: 10954 Independence Ave Chatsworth CA 91311-1560

LUEGGE, WILLARD ARTHUR, chemist, consultant; b. Oak Park, Ill., Mar. 19, 1931; s. Theodore Wilhelm and Irma Minnie (Schoepfer) L.; m. Joanna Carleen Wechter, Sept. 1, 1951; children: Sherylene, Lynette. BA, Ind. U., 1953; postgrad., Ind. U., U. Louisville, UCLA, 1954-64. Rsch. chemist Louisville Cement Co., Speed, Ind., 1956-60; quality control chemist Cal Portland Cement Co., Mojave, Calif., 1960-61; chemistry tchr. Palmdale (Calif.) High Sch., 1961-90; owner-dir. PM Labs, Lancaster, Calif., 1968-89; cons. extractive metallurgical chemistry Lancaster, 1989—; sci. dept. chmn. Palmdale High Sch., 1964-79; mem. Calif. Assn. Chemistry Tchrs., 1963-89; rsch. chemist USAF Rocket Propulsion Lab., Edwards AFB, summers, 1966, '67, '68; bd. dirs. Bryman Refining Co., Inc. Inventor assay kit, 1970. Recipient Tchr. of the Yr. award Am. Chem. Soc., 1967; NSF grantee, 1963, 64. Mem. Western Mining Coun., Western States Pub. Lands Coalition. Presbyterian. Home and Office: 560 E Avenue J1 Lancaster CA 93535-3828

LUEHRS, PAUL RICHARD, hospital administrator; b. Sheboygan, Wis., Dec. 29, 1948; s. Richard and Rosemary (Kelm) L.; m. Linnae Marie Aalgaard, Mar. 3, 1972. BS, N.D. State U., 1972; cert., Concordia Coll., 1972; MS, Washington U., St. Louis, 1977. Diplomate Am. Coll. Healthcare Execs. Field cons. Am. Hosp. Assn., Des Moines, Iowa, 1972-75; staff specialist Am. Hosp. Assn., Chgo., 1977-81; asst. v.p. Meth. Hosps. Dallas, 1981, 1982-84; adminstr. Meth. Ctrl. Hosp., Dallas, 1981-82; asst. adminstr. Trinity Med. Ctr., Carrollton, Tex., 1984-86; assoc. adminstr. Irving (Tex.) Healthcare System, 1986-89; chief operating officer San Ramon (Calif.) Regional Med. Ctr., 1989—. Mem. San Ramon C. of C. (bd. dirs. 1993—), Rotary (program chmn. Danville/Sycamore Valley chpt. 1989). Home: 6520 Platt Ave # 621 West Hills CA 91307-3218 Office: San Ramon Regional Med Ctr 6001 Norris Canyon Rd San Ramon CA 94583-5400

LUEPKE, GRETCHEN, geologist; b. Tucson, Nov. 10, 1943; d. Gordon Maas and Janice (Campbell) Luepke; B.S., U. Ariz., 1965, M.S., 1967; U. Colo., summer, 1962. Geol. field asst. U.S. Geol. Survey, Flagstaff, Ariz., 1964; with U.S. Geol. Survey, Menlo Park, Calif., 1967—, geologist, Pacific Br. of Marine Geology, 1976—. Registered geologist, Ore. Mem. U.S. Congress Office Tech. Assessment Workshop, Mining and Processing Placers of EEZ, 1986. Mem. Soc. Econ. Paleontologists and Mineralogists (chmn. com. libraries in developing countries 1988-91), Geol. Soc. Am.(Interdisciplinary Perspectives on the Hist. Earth Scis., Penrose Conf. 1994), Ariz. Geol. Soc., Peninsula Geol. Soc., Bay Area Mineralogists (chmn. 1979-80), History of the Earth Scis. Soc., Internat. Assn. Sedimentologists, Internat. Marine Minerals Soc. (charter), Geospeakers Toastmasters Club (charter), Sigma Xi. Editor: Stability of Heavy Minerals in Sediments; Econ. Analysis of Heavy Minerals in Sediments; editor book rev. Earth Scis. History, 1989—. Contbr. articles on heavy-mineral analysis to profl. jours. Office: 345 Middlefield Rd Menlo Park CA 94025-3561

LUEVANO, FRED, JR., computer systems executive; b. Alamogordo, N.Mex., June 21, 1943; s. Fred Macias and Margaret (Baca) L.; m. Lupe Olmos, July 11, 1964; children: Michael, James Paul. AA in bus., Fullerton Coll., 1975; BA in Mgmt., U. Redlands, 1979, MA in Mgmt., 1985. Cert. data processing mgr., disaster recovery planner. Mgr. computer ops. Hoffman Electronics, El Monte, Calif., 1971-76; mgr. computer ops. and tech. services City of Anaheim, Calif., 1976-79; mgr. data processing Wyle Data Services, Huntington Beach, Calif., 1979-83; mgr. corp. computer ops. Northrop Grumman Corp., Pico Rivera, Calif., 1983, mgr. corp. computing, 1985—, dir. disaster revovery program, 1983—, dir. disaster recovery and security, 1988-90; Northrop Grumman Corp. Pico Rivera, Calif., 1990-92; mgr. data processing Northrop Grumman Corp., Pico Rivera, Calif., 1992—; cons. on info. sys., La Habra, Calif., 1971—; chmn. cert. bd. dirs. Disaster Recovery Inst., spkr., 1991-95. Cub master Boy Scouts Am., La Habra, 1979-84, chmn. com. 1975-79; councilman candidate City of La Habra Heights, Calif., 1982; pres. Red Coach Club, 1979-80, 86-88; pres. La Habra Parents for Swimming Inc., 1986-88. Served with USN, 1961-65. Mem. Am. Mgmt. Assn., Telecom. Assn., Assn. Computer Ops. Mgrs. (speaker 1983-94), Northrop Mgmt. Club. Republican. Roman Catholic. Office: Northrop Grumman Corp MS 770/XC 8900 Washington Blvd Pico Rivera CA 90660-3765

LUFKIN, LIZ, newspaper editor. Entertainment editor The San Francisco Chronicle, Calif. Office: The San Francisco Chronicle 901 Mission St San Francisco CA 94103-2905

LUFT, HERBERT, former dean; b. Frankfurt, Germany, Aug. 17, 1942; came to U.S., 1961; s. Theodor and Hedwig (Theismann) L.; married, Mar. 25, 1965; children: Sebastian, Rebecca. BA, Pepperdine U., 1965, MA, 1966; PhD, U. So. Calif., 1976. Prof. Pepperdine U., Malibu, Calif., 1967—; prof. history Pepperdine U., L.A., 1982—; exec. v.p. Pepperdine U., Malibu, Calif., 1981-83; dean European Programs Pepperdine U., Malibu, London, Heidelberg (Germany) and Florence (Italy), 1983-93. Mem. Kiwanis Club, Phi Alpha Theta. Mem. Ch. of Christ. Home: 24 155 PCH Malibu CA 90263

LUFT, RENE WILFRED, civil engineer; b. Santiago, Chile, Sept. 21, 1943; came to U.S., 1968; s. David and Malwina (Kelmy) L.; m. Monica Acevedo, Aug. 24, 1970; children: Deborah Elaine, Daniel Eduardo. CE, U. Chile, 1967; MS, MIT, 1969, DSc, 1971. Registered profl. engr., Alaska, Calif., Wash., Mass., N.H., R.I., Republic of Chile; registered structural engr., Vt. Asst. prof. civil engring. U. Chile, 1967-68; research asst. MIT, Cambridge, Mass., 1969-71, vis. lectr., 1983-84; staff engr. Simpson, Gumpertz & Heger Inc., Arlington, Mass., 1971-74, sr. staff engr., 1975-78, assoc., 1978-83, sr. assoc., 1984-90; prin. Simpson, Gumpertz & Heger Inc., San Francisco, 1990-91; head design div. Simpson, Gumpertz & Heger Inc., 1991—; sec. seismic adv. com. Mass. Bldg. Code Commn., 1978-80, chmn., 1981-82; mem. Boston seismic instrumentation com. U.S. Geol. Survey; mem. slabs on ground com. Post-Tensioning Inst., 1994—. Contbr. articles to profl. jours. Mem. design overview com., bldg. seismic safety coun. Earthquake Hazards Reduction Program, 1983-91, chmn. rsch. com. 1987-88. Mem. ASCE, Boston Soc. Civil Engrs. (chmn. seismic design adv. com. 1981-86, Clemens Herschel award for tech. paper 1980, pres.'s award for leadership in earthquake engring. 1984), Am. Concrete Inst., Earthquake Engring. Research Inst., Structural Engrs. Assn. Calif., NSPE (Young Engr. of Yr., 1979), Sigma Xi, Chi Epsilon. Home: 109 Ardith Dr Orinda CA 94563-4201 Office: 221 Main St Ste 1500 San Francisco CA 94105-1934

LUGG, JAMES R., agricultural products executive; b. 1934. Agrl. agent U. Calif., Salinas, 1956-63; rsch. Bruce Church, Inc., Salinas, Calif., 1963-66; with Transfresh Corp., 1996—. Office: Transfresh Corp 607 Brunken Ave Salinas CA 93901-4362*

LUHN, ROBERT KENT, writer, magazine editor; b. Oakland, Calif., Nov. 23, 1953; s. Joel Adrian and Norma Jeanne (Arnold) L.; m. Marla Mieko Miyashiro, Sept. 14, 1992; 1 child, Pudge. Student, U. Calif., Davis, 1972-76. Freelance writer, 1968—; broadcaster, 1979-80; sr. editor PC World mag., San Francisco, 1983-90, contbg. editor, 1990-94; contbg. editor Calif. Republic mag., San Francisco, 1990-94, editor in chief Computer Currents Mag., 1994—. Author: The Swedish Catfish & Other Tales, 1979, Collected Works, Vol. 3, 1985, Going West, 1988, The Wit is Out, 1993; contbr. fiction, features and poetry to numerous publs., including Harper's, Mother Jones, Omni, Am. Film, Hudson Rev., Nantucket Rev., Christian Sci. Monitor, San Francisco Chronicle, Chgo. Tribune, Phila. Inquirer, PC mag., Computerworld, The Oregonian, Exec. Update, Grapevine Weekly; columnist Computer Currents, 1993—. Adv. bd. mem. Baykeeper, San Francisco, 1994—. Mem. ACLU, Amnesty Internat., Greenpeace, Environ. Defense Fund. Home: 955 B Stannage Ave Albany CA 94706

LUIZZI, RONALD, wholesale distribution executive; b. Neptune, N.J., Apr. 7, 1953; s. Alfredo Luizzi and Mary Kay (Mumford) Figart; m. Kim T. Richardson, May 14, 1994. BA in Psychology, Trenton State Coll., 1975. Pres., chief exec. officer Profl. Divers, Inc., Neptune, 1975-78; nat. dir. projects Nat. Assn. Scuba Diving Schs., Long Beach, Calif., 1978-81; sales mgr. TW Systems, Inc., Honolulu, 1981-85; gen. mgr. TW Systems, Ltd.-Kona, Kailua-Kona, Hawaii, 1985—; East coast regional dir. Nat. Assn. Scuba Diving Schs., Neptune, 1977-78. Contbg. author: (tng. manual) Gold Book, 1977, Safe Scuba, 1977. Scuba advisor YMCA-Kona, Kailua-Kona, 1985—. Mem. Nat. Assn. Instnl. Laundry Mgrs. (cert.), Hawaii Assn. Instnl. Laundry Mgrs. (allied), Nat. Exec. House Keepers Assn. (allied), Hawaii Hotel Assn. (allied), Rotary (sec. 1988-89, v.p. 1989-90, pres. 1990-91), Kona-Kohala C. of C. Home: 76-6303 Kaheiau St Kailua Kona HI 96740-2275 Office: TW Systems Ltd-Kona 74-5622 Alapa St Kailua Kona HI 96740-3108

LUJAN, HERMAN D., university president; m. Carla Lujan; 3 children. B in Polit. Sci., St. Mary's Coll. Calif.; M in Polit. Sci., U. Calif., Berkeley; PhD in Polit. Sci., U. Idaho. Faculty mem., adminstr. U. Kans., dir. inst. social and environ. studies, 1972-78; dir. divsn. state planning and rsch. Gov. of Kans., 1974-75; prof. polit. sci. dept. U. Wash., lectr. Japanese exec. mgmt. program, sch. bus., v.p. minority affairs, 1978-88, vice provost, 1988-91; pres. U. No. Colo., 1991—; bd. dirs. Bank One, Greeley, Colo. Author several books; contbr. articles to profl. jours. Bd. dirs. Boy Scouts Am., Latin Am. Ednl. Found. Mem. Rotary (Greeley). Office: U No Colo Office of Pres Greeley CO 80639*

LUKATHER, CHRISTIAN ERIC, graphic designer and author; b. Burbank, Calif., Dec. 12, 1959; s. Wesley Stanley and Teddie Joy (Brooks) Remhild. BFA, Calif. Inst. of the Arts, Valencia, 1984. Art dir. S.W. Advt., Santa Monica, Calif., 1985-87, LFP, Inc., Beverly Hills, Calif., 1987-90, PROMAX Internat., Hollywood, Calif., 1990—. Author: Advanced Modeling Techniques, 1986, Abandon Dyke, 1987; illustrator: Image mag., 1991, 92. Mem. Motor Press Guild, Pro Passport Network. Democrat. Home: PO Box 93613 Los Angeles CA 90093-0613

LUKE, DAVID KEVIN, investment company executive; b. Las Vegas, Nev., Dec. 14, 1960; s. Freddie Allen and Janet Anne (Shelton) L.; m. Lee-Ann Marie Petryshyn, Apr. 22, 1983; children: Krista Lee-Ann, David Nathan, Spencer Matthew, Ruth Alyssa. BA, Brigham Young U., 1984; M of Internat. Mgmt., Am. Grad. Sch. of Internat. Mgmt., 1986. cert. investment broker. Cons. Internat. Small Bus. Inst., Denver, 1985; mgmt. trainee Gen. Motors of Can., Oshawa, Can., 1986-87; supr. Gen. Motors Acceptance Corp. of Can., Toronto, Can., 1987-89; investment broker A.G. Edwards & Sons, Scottsdale, Ariz., 1989—; incorporator Protip, Inc., 1991-93. instr. Ariz. Coun. on Econ. Edn., Tucson, Ariz., 1990-93; treas. Kyrene Schs. Cmty. Found., Tempe, Ariz., 1993-94, appointee Supt. Fin. Com., den leader Troop 375, Phoenix, 1992-94. Mem. Ch. Jesus Christ Latter Day Saints. Home: 1706 E Brookwood Ct Phoenix AZ 85048 Office: AG Edwards & Sons 6045 N Scottsdale Rd Ste 103 Scottsdale AZ 85250-5405

LUKE, DENNIS ROBERT, state legislator, home building company executive; b. Salem, Oreg., Dec. 13, 1946; s. LeRoy Willard and Alice Lucille (Magnason) L.; m. Joanne Elaine Copley, Jan. 13, 1968; children: Matthew Mark, Brian Lee. Student, Oreg. State U., 1965-68. Owner, mgr. Luke Builders Inc., Bend, Oreg., 1974—; mem. Oreg. Ho. of Reps., Salem, 1993—. Contbr. articles to various publs. Bd. dirs., sec. Ctrl. Oreg. People's Utility Dist., Bend, Redmond, 1980-84; scoutmaster troop 25, com. mem., bd. dirs. Boy Scouts Am., 1977—. Recipient 10-yr. award Boy Scouts Am., 1987. Mem. Nat. Assn. Home Builders (nat. bd. dirs., com.), Oreg. Builders Assn. (past pres., bd. dirs., com., State Builder of Yr. 1991, dir. builders ins. agy. 1991—), Ctrl. Oreg. Builders Assn. (past pres., bd. dirs.), Deschutes County Far Bur., Ea. Star Grange, Elks, Eagles. Republican. Lutheran. Home: PO Box 9069 Bend OR 97708-9069

LUKE, LANCE LAWTON, real estate and construction consultant; b. Wahiawa, Hawaii, Dec. 27, 1955; s. Samuel C. and Florence (Ng) L.; m. Leilani M. Reelitz, Aug. 12, 1979; children: Samuel E., Solomon L., Spencer L. AA, Windward Community Coll., Hawaii, 1975; student, U. Hawaii; grad. in bldg. constrn., NRI, 1989. Investor, contractor pvt. practice, Honolulu, 1975-79; pres. Lance L. Luke & Assocs., Honolulu, 1979—; constrn. cons. Contbr. articles to profl. jours. Com. chmn. Boy Scouts Am., Kailu Cub Scout Pack 311, 1989—; reviewer Fed. Emergency Mgmt. Agy., 1989—, Nat. Inst. of Bldg. Scis., 1990—; sch. inspector State Sch. Inspection Team, Kailua, Kaneohe, Hawaii, 1990—. Mem. Numerous profl. and related orgns. including: Am. Concrete Inst., Internat. Coun. Bldg. Ofcls., Bldg. Ofcls. and Code Adminstrs., Concrete Reinforcing Steel Inst., Constrn. Specifications Inst., Hawaii Assn. Realtors, Honolulu Bd. of Realtors, Nat. Assn. Home Inspectors, Inc., Project Mgmt. Inst., Real Estate Educators Assn. Republican. Roman Catholic. Office: Lance L Luke & Assocs Inc 470 N Nimitz Hwy Ste 216 Honolulu HI 96817-5089

LUKER, KRISTIN, sociology educator; b. San Francisco, Aug. 5, 1946; d. James Wester and Bess (Littlefield) L. BA, U. Calif., Berkeley, 1968; PhD, Yale U., 1975. Postdoctoral fellow U. Calif., Berkeley, 1974-75, asst. prof. sociology, San Diego, 1975-81, assoc. prof., 1981-85, prof., 1985-86, co-dir. women's studies program, 1984-85, prof. jurisprudence and social policy, sociology, Berkeley, 1986—; Doris Stevens prof. women's studies, prof. sociology Princeton (N.J.) U., 1993-95. Author: Taking Chances: Abortion and the Decision Not to Contracept, 1976 (hon. mention Jessie Bernard award), Abortion and the Politics of Motherhood, 1984 (Charles Horton Cooley award 1985), Dubious Conceptions: The Myths of Teenage Pregnancy, 1995. Bd. dirs. Ctr. for Women's Studies and Services, San Diego, Ctr. for Population Options, Washington. Recipient Disting. Teaching award U. Calif., San Diego, 1984; Guggenheim Found. grantee, 1985. Mem. Am. Sociol. Assn., Sociologists for Women in Soc. Office: U Calif Berkeley Jurisprudence & Social Policy 2240 Piedmont Ave Berkeley CA 94704

LUKOS, GLENN CHARLES, environmental biologist; b. Ypsilanti, Mich., Nov. 9, 1946; s. Alex Charles and Esther Exilda (Smith) L.; m. Judith Merrylin Hon, June 2, 1985; 1 child, Cameron Hon. Student, Wayne State U., 1964-67; BS, SUNY, Brockport, 1968, MS, 1974; postgrad., U. South Fla., 1974-77. Vol. Peace Corps, Dominican Republic, 1967-69; tchr. Vershire (Vt.) Sch., 1969-71, Rochester (N.Y.) City Sch. Dist., 1971-72; instr. SUNY, 1973-74; environ. specialist Fla. Dept. Environ. Regulation, Tallahassee, 1977-79, U.S. Army C.E., New Orleans, 1979-83; chief South Coast sect. U.S. Army C.E., L.A., 1983-87; dir. regulatory svcs. Michael Brandman Assocs., Santa Ana, Calif., 1987-89; pres. Glenn Lukos Assocs., Inc., Laguna Hills, Calif., 1989—. Vol. pub. TV, Tallahassee, 1977-79, New Orleans, 1979-83. Mem. Soc. Wetland Scientists, Assn. State Wetland Mgrs., Calif. Native Plant Soc. Office: 23441 S Pointe Dr Ste 150 Laguna Hills CA 92653-1522

LUM, HERMAN TSUI FAI, retired state supreme court chief justice; b. Honolulu, Nov. 5, 1926; s. K.P. and Helen (Tom) L.; m. Almira Ahn, June 17, 1949; children: Forrest K.K., Jonathan K.K. Student, U. Hawaii, 1945-46; LL.B., U. Mo., 1950. Bar: Hawaii 1950. Asst. public prosecutor City and County Honolulu, 1950-52; chief atty. Hawaii Ho. of Reps., 1955, chief clk., 1956-61; partner Suyenaga, Sakamoto & Lum, Honolulu, from 1956; atty. U.S Dist. Ct. Hawaii, 1961-67; judge Cir. Ct. Honolulu, 1967-76, sr. judge Family Ct., 1977-80; assoc. justice Supreme Ct. Hawaii, 1980-83, chief justice, 1983-93; Pres. Jr. Bar Assn. Hawaii, 1957. Mem. ABA, Bar Assn. Hawaii, Fed. Bar Assn. Hawaii (pres. 1963), Phi Delta Phi, Lambda Chi Alpha. Home: 2508 Makiki Heights Dr Honolulu HI 96822-2548 Office: Hawaii Supreme Ct PO Box 2560 Honolulu HI 96804-2560

LUM, JEAN LOUI JIN, nurse educator; b. Honolulu, Sept. 5, 1938; d. Yee Nung and Pui Ki (Young) L. BS, U. Hawaii, Manoa, 1960; MS in Nursing, U. Calif., San Francisco, 1961; MA, U. Wash., 1969, PhD in Sociology, 1972. Registered nurse, Hawaii. From instr. to prof. Sch. Nursing U. Hawaii Manoa, Honolulu, 1961—, acting dean, 1982, dean, 1982-89; project coordinator Analysis and Planning Personnel Svcs., Western Interstate Commn. Higher Edn., 1977; extramural assoc. div. Rsch. Grants NIH, 1978-79; mem. mgmt. adv. com. Honolulu County Hosp., 1982—; mem. exec. bd. Pacific Health Rsch. Inst., 1980-88; mem. health planning com. East Honolulu, 1978-81; mem. rsch. grants adv. coun. Hawaii Med. Svcs. Assn. Found., Nat. Adv. Coun. for Nursing Rsch., 1990-93. Contbr. articles to profl. jours. Trustee Straub Pacific Health Found., Honolulu; bd. dirs. Friends of the Nat. Inst. of Nursing Rsch., 1994—. Recipient Nurse of Yr. award Hawaii Nurses Assn., 1982; named Disting. Practitioner in Nursing, Nat. Acads. of Practice, 1986; USPHS grantee, 1967-72. Fellow Am. Acad. Nursing; mem. Am. Nurses Assn., Am. Pacific Nursing Leaders Conf. (pres. 1983-87), Council Nurse Researchers, Nat. League for Nursing (bd. rev. 1981-87), Western Council Higher Edn. for Nurses (chmn. 1984-85), Western Soc. for Research in Nursing, Am. Sociol. Assn., Pacific Sociol. Assn., Assn. for Women in Sci., Hawaii Pub. Health Assn., Hawaii Med. Services Assn. (bd. dirs. 1985-92), Western Inst. Nursing, Mortar Bd., Phi Kappa Phi, Sigma Theta Tau, Alpha Kappa Delta, Delta Kappa Gamma. Episcopalian. Office: U Hawaii-Manoa Sch Nursing Webster 409 2528 The Mall Honolulu HI 96822

LUM, JODY MAE KAM QUON, real property appraiser; b. Honolulu, Sept. 15, 1961; d. Joseph Tai and Alice Moi (Lau) L. BA, U. Hawaii, 1983. Cert. residential appraiser. Asst. appraiser Hanamura Appraisal Co., Honolulu, 1986-87; real estate staff appraiser Am. Savs. Bank, Honolulu, 1987-89; real property appraiser III City and County of Honolulu, Hawaii, 1989-90; real property appraiser IV City and County of Honolulu, 1990—. Named Outstanding Woman of Yr., 1991. Mem. Nat. Assn. Rev. Appraisers, Honolulu Chinese Jaycees (rec. sec. 1989-90, mem. devel. v.p. 1990-91, community devel. v.p. 1991-92, Woman of Yr. 1989-90, Outstanding mem. 1990-91, Outstanding Community Devel. v.p. 1991-92). Office: City and County Honolulu 842 Bethel St Honolulu HI 96813-4320

LUM, PAUL, writer; b. Canton, Republic of China, Jan. 10, 1923; came to U.S., 1927; s. Hing and Lae Jun (Ng) L. BA in Sociology, U. Oreg., 1945. Sales rep., ptnr. Worchung, Portland, 1946-67; advt. mgr. Walnut Restaurant, 1972-73. Vol. reception Ambassador from Taiwan, Portland, 1973. Mem. AAAS, Am. Statis. Assn., Sci. and Engring. Group, Navy League U.S. Republican. Home: 16485 SW Pacific Hwy Portland OR 97224-3446

LUMMIS, CYNTHIA MARIE, lawyer, rancher; b. Cheyenne, Wyo., Sept. 10, 1954; d. Doran Arp and Enid (Bennett) L.; m. Alvin L. Wiederspahn, May 28, 1983; children: Annaliese Alex. BS, U. Wyo., 1976, U. Wyo., 1978; JD, U. Wyo., 1985. Bar: Wyo. 1985, U.S. Dist Ct. of Wyo. 1985, U.S. Ct. of Appeals (10th cir.) 1986. Rancher Lummis Livestock Co., Cheyenne, 1972—; law clk. Wyo. Supreme Ct., Cheyenne, 1985-86; assoc. Wiederspahn, Lummis & Liepas, Cheyenne, 1986—; mem. Wyo. Ho. Judiciary Com., 1979-86, Ho. Agriculture, Pub. Lands & Water Resources Com., 1985-86, Wyo. State Senate, 1993-94, Senate Judiciary Com., 1993-94, Senate Mines, Minerals, Econ. Devel. Com., 1993-94, U. Wyo. Inst. for Environment and Natural Resource Policy and Rsch.; chmn. County Ct. Planning Com., Wyo., 1986-88, Ho. Rev. Com., 1987-92, Joint Revenue Interim Com., 1988-89, 91-92. Sec. Meals on Wheels, Cheyenne, 1985-87; mem. Agrl. Crisis Support Group, Laramie County, Wyo., 1985-87; mem. adv. com. U. Wyo. Sch. Nursing, 1988-90; mem. steering com. Wyo. Heritage Soc., 1986-89. Republican. Lutheran. Club: Rep. Women's (Cheyenne) (legis. chmn. 1982). Office: Wiederspahn Lummis & Liepas 2020 Carey Ave Ste 704 Cheyenne WY 82001-3639*

LUMSDEN, IAN GORDON, art gallery director; b. Montreal, Que., Can., June 8, 1945; s. Andrew Mark and Isobel Dallas (Wilson) L.; m. Katherine Elizabeth Carson, July 28, 1979; 1 child, Craig Ian. B.A., McGill U., 1968; postgrad., Mus. Mgmt. Inst., U. Calif., Berkeley, 1991. Curator art dept. N.B. Mus., Saint John, 1969; curator Beaverbrook Art Gallery, Fredericton, N.B., 1969-83, dir., 1983—; bd. dirs. ArtsAtlantic; mem. Cultural Property Export Rev. Bd., 1982-85; mem. program com. 49th Parallel Ctr. for Contemporary Can. Art., 1990-92. Author exhbn. catalogues; contbr. numerous articles to Can. art periodicals. Mem. Can. Museums Assn. (sec.-treas. 1973-75), Can. Art Mus. Dirs. Orgn. (1st v.p. 1977-83, pres. 1983-85), Atlantic Provinces Art Gallery Assn. (chmn. 1970-72), Am. Assn. Museums, Union Club (St. John, N.B.). Mem. Anglican Ch. of Can. Home: Fernholme, 725 George St, Fredericton, NB Canada E3B 1K6

LUNA, CASEY, retired state official; b. Canon de Jemez, N. Mex., May 26, 1931; m. Beverly Fulton; 6 children. Pres. Casey Luna Ford & Mercury Co., Belen, N. Mex.; lt. gov. State of N.Mex., 1993, retired, 1994; mem. Albuquerque Hispano C. of C. With U.S. Army, 1948-51. Office: Top 100 Hispanic Bus in US CLFM Belen NM 87002

LUND, VICTOR L., retail food company executive; b. Salt Lake City, 1947; married. BA, U. Utah, 1969, MBA, 1972. Audit mgr. Ernst and Whinney, Salt Lake City, 1972-77; sr. v.p. Skaggs Cos. Inc., from 1977; v.p., contr. Am. Stores Co., 1980-83, sr. v.p., contr., from 1983, exec. v.p., co-chief exec. officer, vice-chmn., chief fin. and adminstrv. officer, now pres., CEO, dir., 1992—. Office: Am Stores Co PO Box 27447 Salt Lake City UT 84127-0447 also: Am Stores Co 709 E South Temple Salt Lake City UT 84102-1205

LUNDBERG, DOUGLAS TAYLOR, biology educator; b. Atlanta, Nov. 7, 1947; widowed Dec. 1988; 1 child, Claire Jeanette; m. Christa Reichert, Dec. 21, 1991. BS, Wayne State U., Detroit, 1970; MA, Adams (Colo) State Coll., 1985. Instr. Northwestern Jr. High Sch., Battle Creek, Mich., 1970-72, Upwey (Victoria, Australia) High Sch., 1972-75, Air Acad. High Sch., U.S. Air Force Acad., Colo., 1975—; rschr. Agrigenetics Corp., Boulder, Colo., 1986-87, Lawrence Livermore (Calif.) Nat. Lab., 1990; cons. Coll. Bd., Princeton, N.J., 1986—. Contbr. articles to profl. jours. Mem. Pikes Peak Edn. Assn. (pres. Colorado Springs, Colo. chpt. 1986-88), Acad. Edn. Assn. (pres. Colorado Springs chpt. 1982-85). Home: 15270 Pleasant View Dr Colorado Springs CO 80921-2226 Office: Air Acad High Sch U S A F Academy CO 80840

LUNDBERG, LARRY THOMAS, general manager; b. Pleasanton, Kans., Mar. 19, 1938; s. William Rex and Lucille Maxine (Rosebrook) L.; m. Sharon Colleen Kirksey, Jan. 26, 1957; children: Julie, John, William. BA, U. Wash., 1965; postgrad., Wash. State U., 1974-80. Cert. secondary tchr. Clerk G.N.Ry., Wenatchee/Seattle, 1957-65; tchr. Grandview (Wash.) Sch. Dist., 1965-66, South Kitsap Sch. Dist., Port Orchard, Wash., 1966-67; acctg. supr. Weyerheauser Co., Tacoma, 1967-69; pres., chief exec. officer Commander Bd. Wash., Seattle, 1969-70; asst. exec. dir. Wash. State Sch. Dirs., Olympia, 1970-80; gen. mgr., chief exec. officer Trout, Inc., Chelan, Wash., 1980—. Author: Negotiations, 1978. Bd. dirs. Traffic Assn., Wenatchee, Wash., 1987—. With U.S. Army, 1957-60. Mem. Internat. Apple Inst. (bd. dirs. 1988—), Chelan, Wash. C. of C. (bd. dirs. 1989—). Office: Trout Inc PO Box 669 Chelan WA 98816-0669*

LUNDBLAD, ROGER LAUREN, research director; b. San Francisco, Oct. 31, 1939; s. Lauren Alfred and Doris Ruth (Peterson) L.; m. Susan Hawly Taylor, Oct. 15, 1966 (div. 1985); children: Christina Susan, Cynthia Karin. BSc, Pacific Luth. U., 1961; PhD, U. Wash., 1965. Rsch. assoc. U. Wash., Seattle, 1965-66, Rockefeller U., N.Y.C., 1966-68; asst. prof. U. N.C., Chapel Hill, 1968-71, assoc. prof., 1971-77, prof. pathology and biochemistry, 1977-91; adj. prof., 1991—; dir. sci. tech. devel. Baxter-Biotech, Duarte, Calif., 1991—; vis. scientist Hyland div. Baxter Healthcare, Glendale, Calif., 1988-89. Author: Chemical Reagents for Protein Modification, 1984, 2d edit., 1990; editor: Chemistry and Biology of Thrombin, 1977, Chemistry and Biology of Heparin, 1980, Techniques in Protein Modification, 1994; contbr. articles to profl. jours. Recipient Career Achievement award U. N.C., 1986. Mem. Am. Soc. Biochem. Molecular Biology, Am. Soc. Microbiology, Am. Heart Assn., Sigma Xi. Office: Baxter Biotech Hyland Divsn 1720 Flower Ave Duarte CA 91010-2923

LUNDE, DOLORES BENITEZ, retired secondary education educator; b. Honolulu, Apr. 12, 1929; d. Frank Molero and Matilda (Francisco) Benitez; m. Nuell Carlton Lunde, July 6, 1957; 1 child, Laurelle. BA, U. Oreg., 1951, postgrad., 1951-52; postgrad., U. So. Calif., L.A., 1953-54, Colo. State U., 1957-58, Calif. State U., Fullerton, 1967-68. Cert. gen. secondary tchr., Calif.; cert. lang. devel. specialist. Tchr. Brawley (Calif.) Union High Sch., 1952-55; tchr. Fullerton (Calif.) Union High Sch. Dist., 1955-73; tchrs. aide Placentia (Calif.) Unified Sch. Dist., 1983-85; tchr. continuing edn. Fullerton Union High Sch. Dist., 1985-91; tchr. Fullerton Sch. Dist., 1988, Fullerton Union H.S. Dist., 1989-94; presenter regional and state convs., so. Calif., 1986-88. Innovator tests, teaching tools, audio-visual aids. Vol. Luth. Social Svcs., Fullerton, 1981-82, Messiah Luth., Yorba Linda, Calif., 1981-88, 91-94. Recipient Tchr. of Yr. award Fullerton Union High Sch. Dist., 1989. Mem. NEA, AAUW (life, bull. editor 1979-80, corr. sec. 1981-83, program v.p. 1983-84, gift honoree Fullerton br. 1985), Calif. State Tchrs. Assn., Fullerton Secondary Tchrs. Assn., Internat. Club/Spanish Club (advisor La Habra, Calif. 1965-72), Tchrs. English to Speakers Other Langs., Calif. Assn. Tchrs. English to Speakers Other Langs. Home: 4872 Ohio St Yorba Linda CA 92686-2713

LUNDE, DONALD THEODORE, physician; b. Milw., Mar. 2, 1937; m. Marilynn Krick; children: Montgomery, Christopher, Glenn, Evan, Bret. BA with distinction, Stanford U., 1958, MA in Psychology, 1964, MD, 1966. Diplomate Nat. Bd. Med. Examiners. Ward psychologist Palo Alto (Calif.) VA Hosp., 1965-66, chief resident in psychiatry, 1969-70, assoc. chief tng. and research sect., 1970-72, acting chief tng. and research sect., 1971-72; intern in internal medicine Palo Alto/Stanford Hosp., 1966-67; resident in psychiatry Stanford (Calif.) U. Sch. Medicine, 1967-69, instr. psychiatry, 1969-70, asst. prof. psychiatry, 1970-75, dir. med. sch. edn. in psychiatry, 1971-74, clin. assoc. prof. psychiatry, 1978-89, clin. prof. psychiatry, 1989—; staff physician Atascadero (Calif.) State Hosp., 1968. Author books and articles in field. Served with USN, 1958-61. Fellow Am. Psychiat. Assn., Am. Coll. Forensic Psychiatry; mem. Am. Psychiat. Assn., No. Calif. Psychiat. Soc., Phi Beta Kappa, Alpha Omega Alpha. Office: Stanford U 900 Welch Rd Ste 400 Palo Alto CA 94304-1804

LUNDEEN, SAMUEL EDWARD, elementary education educator; b. Crookston, Minn., Feb. 16, 1944; s. Arthur Gehard and Agatha Margit (Hamre) L.; m. Angela F. Fitzhugh, Jan. 11, 1968; children: Gairdt, Bjorn. BA, Humboldt State U., 1968, postgrad., 1971, 80. Cert. elem. tchr., Calif. Tchr. mid. sch. Escambia County Pub. Schs., Pensacola, Fla., 1969-70; tchr. elem. sch. Arcata (Calif.) Elem. Sch. Dist., 1971—; house painter, Arcata, 1970-71; mem. sch. site coun., Arcata, 1989-93. With USN, 1967-69. Mem. Sierra Club, Greenpeace, Nature Conservancy. Democrat. Lutheran/Unity. Home: PO Box 2055 Trinidad CA 95570-2055

LUNDEN, SAMUEL EUGENE, architect; b. Chgo., July 14, 1897; s. Albert Axel and Christina Eugenia (Erickson) L.; m. Leila Burton Allen, Mar. 13, 1925; children: Alice Marie, Robert Allen, Ardelle Leila. Student, Calif. Inst. Tech., Pasadena, 1918; SB in Architecture, MIT, 1921. Mem. Am. Students Reconstrn. Unit, Verdun, France, 1921; traveled and studied architecture in Europe, 1921, 51, 61, 68; asso. with office Cram & Ferguson, Boston, 1921-27; began practice architecture, L.A., 1928; partner Lunden, Hayward & O'Connor, 1949-57; prin. Samuel E. Lunden, FAIA,, 1958-60; ptnr. Samuel E. Lunden-Joseph L. Johnson, architects,, L.A., 1960-78; cons. architect Lyon Assocs., Inc., Los Angeles, 1978-83; prin. Samuel E. Lunden FAIA Cons. Architect, 1983-94, ret., 1994. Author: The Interiors of the Church of St. Vincent de Paul, 1931, Community Development Through an Exposition for Los Angeles, 1944, Personal Service to the Client, 1989; assoc. architect: interiors of St. Vincent de Paul Ch., 1928 (declared Heritage Cultural Monument 1978); architect: Pacific Coast Stock Exchange, 1929 (declared Heritage Cultural Monument 1979), (residence halls) U. So. Calif., Hosp. Good Samaritan Med. Ctr., Los Angeles, 1943-73; City Hall South, Civic Ctr., Los Angeles, 1954; (master plans) Temple Urban Renewal Project, Los Angeles, 1958; Las Palmas Sch. Girls, Probation Dept. County Los Angeles, 1959; Los Angeles Unified Sch. Dist.; Vets. Meml. Regional County Park, Sylmar, Calif., 1976, Temple Israel, Hollywood, Calif.; designer: Carveyor People Mover Systems, Los Angeles area, 1956-65; cons. architect: Allan Hancock Biol. Research Found. Bldg; co-architect: Edward L. Doheny Meml. Library, U. So. Calif., 1932; Harbor Police Sta., City Los Angeles, 1961; Western Fed. Bldg., (co-architect) Univ. Ctr., Calif. State U., Fullerton, 1975; mem. planning commn.: (master plans and design) sch. bldgs. City Manhattan Beach. Mem. Town Hall Calif., 1943—, bd. of govs., 1955-60, 62-68, pres., 1965, hon. life gov, 1984—; sec. South Bay Beach and Hwy. Assn., 1944-45; vice chmn. Citizens Traffic Transp. Com., Los Angeles Area, 1954-55; mem. Am. Arbitration Assn., 1953—; mem. alumni fund bd. MIT, 1967-70, mem. corp. devel. com., 1965—. Recipient 1st prize Am. Hosp. Assn. competition for design small community hosp. and med. ctr., 1945; certificate merit So. Calif. chpt. AIA, Kemper award AIA, 1963; Town Hall award, 1960; Beaver award MIT, 1962; Marshall B. Dalton award MIT, 1980. Mem. AIA (v.p. 1945-47, pres. So. Calif. chpt. 1942-43, mem. Coll. Fellows 1945, bd. dirs. Calif. coun. 1965), L.A. Area C. of C. Clubs: MIT of So. Calif. (pres. 1955), Life Assocs. of U. So. Calif., Calif. (Los Angeles). Home and Office: 6205 Via Colinita Rancho Palos Verdes CA 90275

LUNDERVILLE, GERALD PAUL, bilingual education educator; b. Springfield, Mass., Feb. 22, 1941; s. Leon Albert and Florence Marion (Jolivette) L.; m. Martha Ann Sumner, Mar. 26, 1966 (div. Aug. 1971); m. Bony Lek, June 30, 1984. BA cum laude, U. N.H., 1963; MA, Middlebury Coll., 1969, U. Rochester, 1973, Calif. State U., Long Beach, 1994. Instr. Spanish Berwick Acad., South Berwick, Maine, 1963-64; tchr. French, Spanish Barnstable High Sch., Hyannis, Mass., 1967-68; instr. Spanish Cape Cod Community Coll., West Barnstable, Mass., 1968-71; tchr. French, Spanish Stevens High Sch. Annex, Claremont, N.H., 1973-74; tchr. English Centro de Estudios Norteamericanos, Valencia, Spain, 1974-75; dept. head fgn. langs. Merrimack (N.H.) High Sch., 1975-80; tchr. Spanish El Camino Coll., Torrance, Calif., 1980-85; tchr. ESL Wilson High Sch., Long Beach, Calif., 1980—, dept. head ESL, 1987-88, tchr. bilingual edn./Spanish, 1992—. Author: 20th Century Baseball Trivia, 1992; contbr. articles to Am. Atheist Mag. Active Long Beach Area Citizens Peace, 1982—, Animal Protection Inst. Am., Sacramento., 1983—. Served with U.S. Army, 1964-67, Vietnam. Mem. NEA, ACLU, NOW, Modern and Classical Lang. Assn. So. Calif., Tchrs. of English as a 2d Lang., Soc. for Preservation of English Lang. and Lit., VERBATIM, Nat. Humane Edn. Soc., Merrimack Tchrs. Assn. (sec. 1977-80), Lambda Pi. Home: 1740 E Washington St Long Beach CA 90805-5535

LUNDGREN, LEONARD, III, retired secondary education educator; b. San Francisco, June 22, 1933; s. Leonard II and Betty (Bosold) L.; m. Jane Gates, June 12, 1976. AA, City Coll. San Francisco, 1952; AB, San Francisco State U., 1954, MA, 1958, postgrad., 1958-71. Cert. tchr., Calif. Phys. edn. tchr., athletic coach Pelton Jr. High Sch., San Francisco, 1958-59; social studies tchr., dept. chair, phys. edn. tchr., athletic coach Luther Burbank Jr. High Sch., San Francisco, 1959-78; history, govt. econs., geography tchr. George Washington High Sch., San Francisco, 1978-93; water safety instr. ARC, San Francisco, 1946-61; mem. Calif. Quality Teaching Ctr. Conf. Bd., 1965-67. Author: Guide for Films and Filmstrips, 1966, Teacher's Handbook for Social Studies, 1966, Guide for Minority Studies, 1968. V.p. Lakeside Property Owners Assn., San Francisco, 1986-88, legis. advocate, 1988-95; v.p. West of Twin Peaks Coun., San Francisco, 1986-87; pub. affairs polit. econ. cons., Calif., 1993—. With USN, 1954-56. Fulbright scholar, Greece, 1963; recipient Svc. Pin, ARC, 1961. Mem. NEA (life, del. 1970, 72-76), Calif. Tchrs. Assn. (state coun. rep. 1963-74), Nat. Coun. Social Studies, Calif. Coun. Social Studies (v.p. San Francisco chpt. 1969-70), San Francisco Classroom Tchrs. Assn. (pres. 1972-73, Gavel award 1973), PTA (sch. v.p.1980-81), Calif. Ret. Tchrs. Assn. (life., legislation chmn. San Francisco div. 1995-96), San Francisco State U. Alumni Assn. (life, treas.1959), Calif. Asn. Health, Phys. Edn., Recreation and Dance (life, treas. San Francisco chpt. 1959-60), Nat. Geog. Soc. (life), Phi Delta Kappa (life, pres. chpt. 1965-66).

LUNDGREN, SUSAN ELAINE, counselor, educator; b. Martinez, Calif., May 31, 1949; d. Elmer Alfred and Shirley (Bright) L.; 1 child, Alicia Hadiya. AA, Diablo Valley Coll., 1969; BA in English, San Francisco State U., 1971, MA in Counseling, 1975; EdD, U. San Francisco, 1983; cert. in gen. mgmt., John F. Kennedy U., 1988. Instr., counselor Diablo Valley Coll., Pleasant Hill, Calif., 1976—, coordinator, 1986-90, women's ctr. faculty dir., 1983-85; adj. prof. grad. career devel. John F. Kennedy U., Orinda, Calif., 1982—. Sec., bd. dirs. Rape Crisis Ctr., Concord, Calif., 1985. Named participant in leadership devel. inst. AAUW and Nat. Assn. Community Colls., 1985. Mem. Eureka Consortium (conf. speaker 1984, 86). Home: 3738 Victor Ave Oakland CA 94619-1533 Office: Diablo Valley Coll 321 Golf Club Rd Pleasant Hill CA 94523-1529

LUNDGREN, SUSAN ELIZABETH, information technology consultant, musician; b. Tacoma, June 21, 1964; d. Lawrence L. and Diane E. Lundgren. BS in Math., U. Wash., 1988; postgrad., U. Alaska, 1995—. Software tester Logicon/RDA, Tacoma, 1988, software engr., 1989, project mgr., 1990-92; software engr. ctg-Alaska, Anchorage, 1992-93, sr. software engr., 1993—, project leader, 1993—, instr., 1994. Mem. Assn. for Computing Machinery.

LUNDSTROM, MARJIE, newspaper editor. Grad., U. Nebr. Columnist, editor, nat. corr. The Denver Post, 1981-89; with The Sacramento Bee, 1989-90, 91—; nat. corr. Gannett News Svc., Washington, 1990-91. Recipient Pulitzer Prize for nat. reporting, 1991. Office: The Sacramento Bee 2100 Q St PO Box 15779 Sacramento CA 95852

LUNDSTROM, MARY MEYER, museum curator, museum store manager, educator; b. Hollywood, Calif., June 23, 1948; d. Archibald deNorville and Ivy Kate (Whitworth) Meyer; 1 child, Tara Carina. BA in Art, San Diego State U., 1971. Lic. real estate salesperson, Calif. Draftsman Genge Industries, Ridgecrest, Calif., 1967-68; draftsman Naval Weapons Ctr., China Lake, Calif., 1969, illustrator, 1970; substitute tchr. Albuquerque Pub. Schs., 1971-72, Kern County High Sch. Dist., China Lake, 1972-74; real estate salesperson Coldwell Banker Best Realty, Ridgecrest, 1974-86; art instr. Cerro Coso C.C., Ridgecrest, 1986-91; art curator Maturango Mus., Ridgecrest, 1987—; mus. store mgr. Matruango Mus., Ridgecrest, 1993—; freelance artist, 1970—. Juror Lancaster Art Mus. Mixed Media Show, 1990, Millie Funk Western ARt Show, 1991. Mem. AAUW (past pres., name grant award 1987), High Desert Coun. of Arts, Kern Arts Coun., Am. Assn. Mus., Enamel Guild West, Enamelist Soc., Calig. Assn. Mus., Inst. Mus. Svcs. (grant reviewer), Rotary. Home: 731 W Howell Ave Ridgecrest CA 93555-3445 Office: Maturango Mus 100 E Las Flores Ridgecrest CA 93555-3654

LUNDY, GILBERT MOULTON, JR., computer science educator; b. New Orleans, Sept. 29, 1954; s. Gilbert Moulton and Loretta Maureen (Taylor) L.; m. Yong Ae Yi, Feb. 18, 1978 (div. 1988); children: Benjamin Lee, Miriam Yong. BA in Math., Tex. A&M U., 1976; MS in Computer Sci., U. Tex., Dallas, 1983; PhD in Computer Sci., Ga. Inst. Tech., 1988. Software engr. E-Systems, Inc., Dallas, 1981-84; rsch. asst. Ga. Inst. Tech., Atlanta, 1984-88; assoc. prof. computer sci. U.S. Naval Postgrad. Sch., Monterey, Calif., 1988—. Contbr. articles on computer and telecom. networks to sci. jours. 1st lt. U.S. Army, 1977-81. Mem. IEEE, Assn. for Computing Machinery. Office: US Naval Postgrad Sch Dept Computer Sci Code CS Monterey CA 93943

LUNGREN, DANIEL EDWARD, state attorney general; b. Long Beach, Calif., Sept. 22, 1946; s. John Charles and Lorain Kathleen (Youngberg) L.; m. Barbara Kolls, Aug. 2, 1969; children: Jeffrey Edward, Kelly Christine, Kathleen Marie. A.B. cum laude, Notre Dame U., 1968; postgrad., U. So. Calif. Law Sch., 1968-69; J.D., Georgetown U., 1971. Bar: Calif. 1972. Staff asst. Sen. George Murphy, Sen. William Brock, 1969-71; spl. asst. to co-chmn. Rep. Nat. Com., dir. spl. programs, 1971-72; assoc., selected as ptnr. Ball, Hunt, Hart, Brown & Baerwitz, Long Beach, 1973-78; mem. 96th-97th Congresses from 34th, 98th-100th Congresses from 42d Calif. Dist., 1979-1989, Rep. State Cen. Com. Calif., 1974-89; ptnr. Diepenbrock, Wulff, Plant & Hannegan, Sacramento, 1989-90; atty. gen. State of Calif., Sacramento, 1991—. Bd. dirs. Long Beach chpt. ARC, Boy's Club, 1976-88; committeeman Rep. Nat. Com., Calif., 1988—. Recipient Good Samaritan award Los Angeles Council Mormon Chs., 1976. Republican. Roman Catholic. Office: Office of the Atty Gen 1300 I St Sacramento CA 95814

LUNIEWSKI, ALLEN WILLIAM, computer scientist; b. Pitts., Aug. 5, 1952; s. Alphonse and Helen (Ruszkowski) L.; m. Patsy Ann Fenerin, Nov. 19, 1983; 1 child, Catherine Ann. BS in Math., Carnegie-Mellon U., 1974; SM in Computer Sci., Elect. Engring., MIT, 1977, PhD in Computer Sci., 1979. Devel. mgr. Xerox Corp., Palo Alto, Calif., 1979-86; research staff mem. IBM, San Jose, Calif., 1986-91, mgr. object oriented systems, 1991—. Mem. IEEE, Assn. Computing Machinery. Roman Catholic. Home: 7624 De Foe Dr Cupertino CA 95014-4307 Office: IBM 650 Harry Rd San Jose CA 95120-6001

LUNINE, JONATHAN IRVING, planetary scientist, educator; b. N.Y.C., June 26, 1959. BS magna cum laude, U. Rochester, 1980; MS, Calif. Inst. Tech., 1983, PhD, 1985. Rsch. assoc. U. Ariz., Tucson, 1984-86, asst. prof. planetary scis., 1986-90; vis. asst. prof. UCLA, 1986, assoc. prof., 1990-95, prof., 1995—, faculty mem. program in applied math., 1992—; interdisciplinary scientist on joint U.S.-European Cassini mission to Saturn; mem. com. planterary and lunar exploration space sci. bd. Nat. Acad. Scis., 1986-90; chmn. NASA Solar System Exploration subcom., 1990-95. Contbr. articles to profl. jours.; co-editor: Protostars and Planets III, 1993. Mem. Internat. Mars Exploration Adv. Panel NASA, 1993-94, space sci. adv. com., 1993-94. Recipient Cospar Zeldovich prize Soviet Intercosmos and Inst. for Space Rsch., 1990. 1 of the 50 emerging leaders Time Mag., 1994. Mem. Am. Astron. Soc. (Harold C. Urey prize 1988), Am. Geophys. Union, (Macelwane medal, 1995), Internat. Coun. Sci. Unions, Sigma Xi. Office: U Ariz Lunar and Planetary Lab Tucson AZ 85721

LUO, HORNG J., electrical engineer; b. China, 1962; came to U.S., 1985; s. Chu H. and Yueh O. (Liu) L.; m. Teresa C. Liu, June 2, 1990; 1 child, Rachel S. BS, Nat. Taiwan U., 1985; PhD, U. Fla., 1993. Rsch. asst. U. Fla., Gainesville, 1987-93, postdoctoral assoc., 1993; sr. device engr. Nat. Semicondr., Santa Clara, Calif., 1993—. Contbr. articles to profl. jours. Vol. worker First Bapt. Ch., Gainesville, 1992-93; team leader Chinese Student Assn., Gainesville, 1987. Semicondr. Rsch. Conf grantee, 1987-88, Fla. High Tech. Indsl. Coun. grantee, 1990-93. Mem. IEEE (reviewer 1989—), Optical Soc. Am., Internat. Soc. for Optical Engring., Lasers and Optoelectronics Soc. (organizer 1990). Office: Nat Semicondr D3-677 2900 Semiconductor Dr Santa Clara CA 95051-0606

LUPASH, LAWRENCE OVIDIU, computer analyst, researcher; b. Bucharest, Romania, May 29, 1942; came to U.S., 1980; s. Ovidiu Dumitru and Stefania Maria (Lebu) L. BS, Polytechnic Inst. of Bucharest, 1964; MS, Polytechnic Inst. Bucharest, Romania, 1965, PhD, 1972. Sr. engr., researcher Inst. Automation, Bucharest, 1971-72; sr. analyst, researcher, computing ctr. U. Bucharest, 1972-79; sr. analyst Intermetrics, Inc., Huntington Beach, Calif., 1980-94, LL Consulting, Fullerton, Calif., 1994—; asst. prof. Polytechnic Inst. Bucharest, 1966-67, 67-68, 71-72; lectr. U. Bucharest, 1973-78; vis. prof. U. Tirana, Albania, 1973. Co-author: Numerical Methods in Systems Theory, 1974; contbr. numerous articles to profile pubs. Recipient Rep. award Polytechnic Inst. Bucharest, 1962; grantee Case Western Reserve U., 1968, Romanian Acad. Scis., 1968. Mem. IEEE, Soc. Indsl. and Applied Math., Assn. Computing Machinery, Am. Philatelic Soc., Orange County Philatelic Soc. Mem. Greek Orthodox Ch. Office: Intermetrics Inc 5312 Bolsa Ave Huntington Beach CA 92649-1020

LUPPER, EDWARD, artist; b. Trenton, N.J., Jan. 4, 1936; s. Julius Lupper and Irene Rich. Studied with, Wesley Lea, Frenchtown, N.J., 1952-54; student, Trenton Jr. Coll., 1953, Parsons Sch. Design, 1958, San Francisco Art Inst., 1959-60, San Francisco State Coll., 1960-61. One man shows include Naples (Fla.) Art Gallery, 1986-95; exhibited in group shows at Balt. Mus. Art, 1955, Tucson Art Ctr., San Francisco Mus. of Art, Am. Embassy, Belgium, 1977-78, Ft. Worth Art Ctr.; artist Sunrise Pub. Co., 1988—, Gt. Am. Puzzle co., 1994—; represented in collections Teddy Bear Mus., Naples, L.A. Maritime Mus.; represented in pvt. and corp. collections in U.S., Europe, Asia, Australia, U.K. and Can. With USN, 1954-57. Huntington Hartford fellow, 1964. Mem. San Francisco Pub. Health Found., San Francisco Nat. Wildlife Fedn. (donor 1993-94). Democrat. Studio: 1255 Pacific Ave San Francisco CA 94109-2715

LURIE, RON, mayor. Former city councilman Las Vegas, Nev.; mayor, 1987—. Office: City Hall Office of Mayor 400 Stewart Ave Las Vegas NV 89101-2942

LURVEY, IRA HAROLD, lawyer; b. Chgo., Apr. 6, 1935; s. Louis and Faye (Grey) L.; m. Barbara Ann Sirvint, June 24, 1962; children: Nathana, Lawrence, Jennifer, Jonathan, David, Robert. BS, U. Ill., 1956; MS, Northwestern U., 1961; JD, U. Calif., Berkeley, 1965. Bar: Calif. 1965, Nev. 1966, U.S. Dist. Ct. (cen. dist.) Calif. 1966, U.S. Tax Ct. 1966, U.S. Ct. Appeals (9th cir.) 1966, U.S. Supreme Ct. 1975. Law clk. to hon. justices Nev. Supreme Ct., Carson City, 1965-66; from assoc. to ptnr. Pacht, Ross, Warne, Bernhard & Sears, Inc., 1966-84; predecessor firm Shea & Gould, Los Angeles; founding ptnr. Lurvey & Shapiro, Los Angeles, 1984—; lectr. legal edn. programs; mem. Chief Justice's Commns. on Ct. Reform, Weighted Caseloads; mediator family law L.A. Supreior Ct. Editor Community Property Jour., 1979-80, Primary Consultant CFL 2d, 1994; columnist Calif. Family Law Monthly; contbr. articles to profl. jours. Former chmn. L.A. Jr. Arts Ctr.; past pres. Cheviot Hills Homeowners Assn.; exec. v.p., counsel Hillel Acad. Sch., Beverly Hills, Calif., 1977—. With U.S. Army, 1957-58. Fellow Am. Acad. Matrimonial Lawyers (pres. So. Calif. chpt. 1991-92, mem. nat. bd. govs. 1992-94), Internat. Acad. Matrimonial Lawyers; mem. ABA (vice chair 1994-95, chair elect. family law sect. 1995—, governing coun. 1986—, fin. officer 1991-92, chmn. support com., chmn. continuing legal edn., chmn. policy and issues com., vice chmn. com. arbitration and mediation, bd. of editors Family Adv. mag.), Calif. Bar Assn. (editor jour. 1982-85, chmn. family law sect. 1986-87, exec. com. family law sect. 1982-88, specialization adv. bd. family law 1979-82), L.A. County Bar Assn. (chmn. family law sect. 1981-82, exec. com. family law 1989-92), Beverly Hills Bar Assn. (chmn. family law sect. 1976-77). Home: 2729 Motor Ave Los Angeles CA 90064-3441 Office: Lurvey & Shapiro Ste 1550 2121 Avenue Of The Stars Los Angeles CA 90067-5010

LUSH, PAMELA GRACE MEINE, international publishing company executive; b. Wellsboro, Pa., Apr. 1, 1961; d. Stanley Gale and Karen (Kohler) L. BA, Colo. State U., 1983. Traffic coord. Leo Burnett Advt., Chgo., 1983-85; sr. account exec. Cardiff Pub., Englewood, Colo., 1985-88; pres. PGL Assocs., Denver, 1988-90; v.p. Interfax-US, Denver, 1991-92; pres. DGL Internat. Pub., Denver, 1990—, DGL Publs., Denver, 1990—. Editor, pub.: The Child Care Directory, 1991; pub.: The Family Resource Guide, 1992, The Petroleum Tech. Resource Guide, 1992, The Agricultural Technical Resource Guide, 1992, The Mining/Environmental Technical Resource Guide, 1992. Mem. Soviet Task Force Under Gov. Roy Romer, Denver, 1990—, Internat. Gateway Com., Denver, 1990—. Named nominee for Pulitzer Prize for Internat. Reporting, 1991, Pulitzer Prize for Meritorious Pub. Svc., 1991. Presbyterian.

LUSK, HARLAN GILBERT, national park superintendent; b. Jersey City, June 22, 1943; s. Harlan H. and Mary M. (Kuhl) L.; m. Catherine L. Rutherford, Oct. 11, 1986. BA in History, Gettysburg Coll., 1965. Supervisory historian Cape Hatteras Nat. Seashore, Manteo, N.C., 1968; historian Nat. Pk. Svc., Washington, 1968-69; programs specialist So. Utah Group, Cedar City, 1968-70; pk. supt. Wolf Trap Farm Pk., Vienna, Va., 1970-72; supervisory pk. ranger Blue Ridge Pkwy., Roanoke, Va., 1972-74; pk. supt. Appomattox (Va.) Courthouse, Nat. Hist. Pk., 1974-76, Valley Forge (Pa.), Nat. Hist. Pk., 1976-81, Big Bend (Tex.) Nat. Pk., 1981-86, Glacier Nat. Pk., West Glacier, Mont., 1986-94; pk. supt. Albright Tng. Ctr. Grand Canyon Nat. Pk., Ariz., 1994—; chief, Divsn. Tng. and Employee Nat. Park Svc., Washington, 1995—; organizer 1st regional conf. Rio Grande Border, States on Pks. and Wildlife, Laredo, Tex., 1985. Bd. dirs. Tech. Com. on Pks. & Recreation Cen. Va. Planning Dist., 1972-74, Fed. Exec. Assn. Roanoke Valley, 1972-74, Flathead Basin Commn., 1986—, Flathead Conv. & Visitor Assn., 1986—; prin. founder, 1st pres., Appomattox County Hist. Soc., 1974-76; trustee Sci. Mus. Assn. Roanoke Valley, 1972-74, Nature Conservancy Mont., 1994—; ex-officio Friends of Valley Forge, 1977-81; founder, ex-officio, bd. dirs. Valley Forge Pk. Interpretive Assn., 1977-81; founder Big Bend Area Travel Assn., chmn., 1984-86. Recipient Meritorious Svc. award. Dept. Interior, 1986. Mem. Glacier Natural History Assn. (ex officio 1986-94), Glacier Nat. Pk. Assocs. (founder, ex-officio 1989-94), George Wright Soc., Lions, Rotary. Office: Grand Canyon Nat Pk Albright Tng Ctr West Glacier MT 86023

LUST, PETER, JR., microwave engineer, consultant; b. Montreal, Que., Can., Apr. 21, 1960; came to U.S., 1975, naturalized, 1987; s. Peter Clark and Evelyn (Heymanson) L.; Gloria Ruth Bingle, Apr. 5, 1985; children: Peter Alexander III, Elizabeth Ann, Matthew Eric. Student, Lowry Tech. Tng. Ctr., Community Coll. A.F., Albuquerque, USAF Acad.; BSEE, Pacific Western U., 1990. Computer meterologist Electro Rent, Burbank, Calif., 1982-84; microwave engr., program mgr. satellite and space shuttle communications systems Transco Products, Camarillo, Calif., 1984-90, internat. tech. mktg. mgr., 1990-93; prin. Electronic Note Co., Port Hueneme, Calif., 1984—; spacecraft cons. in field, Port Hueneme, 1984—; rep. ANT, Teldix, Germany, Spar Space Systems, Can. With USAF, 1979-82. With USAF, 1979-82. Recipient Technol. award USAF, 1980, Discovery award NASA, 1987, Internat. Leaders in Achievement award, Cambridge. Mem. Assn. Old Crows, Channel Islands Health Club. Office: Electronic Note Co 300 Esplanade Dr Ste 900 Oxnard CA 93030

LUSTICA, KATHERINE GRACE, publisher, artist, marketing consultant; b. Bristol, Pa., Nov. 20, 1958; d. Thomas Lustica and Elizabeth Delores (Moyer) De Groat. Student, Hussian Sch. Art, Phila., 1976-78, Rider Coll., 1980-82, U. Utah, 1993—. Comml. artist, illustrator Bucks County Courier Times Newspapers, Levittown, Pa., 1978-82; account exec. Trenton (N.J.) Times Newspapers, 1982-84; promotions and account exec. Diversified Suburban Newspapers, Murray (Utah) Printing, 1984-88; pub. Barclays Ltd. Salt Lake City, 1988—; cover artists, illustrator Accent mag., Bristol, 1978-82; freelance artist, 1978—; advt. and creative cons. Everett & Winthrop Products Group, Salt Lake City, 1988-90, Multi Techs. Internat., Salt Lake City, 1990-91. Newcombe scholar, 1981-82. Mem. Art Dirs. Salt Lake City. Presbyterian. Office: 4640 Stratton Dr Salt Lake City UT 84117-5558

LUTALI, A. P., governor of American Samoa; b. Aunu'u, American Samoa, Dec. 24, 1919; married. Gov. Am. Samoa, 1985-89, 93—; spkr. of the House Senate, Am. Samoa, 1956-57, pres., 1965-67, v.p., 1988—; chair Constnl. Conv., 1966. Mem. Am. Samoa Bar Assn. (founder 1972). Office: Governor's Office Pago Pago AS 96799

LUTES, DONALD HENRY, architect; b. San Diego, Mar. 7, 1926; s. Charles McKinley and Helen (Bjoraker) L.; m. Donnie Wageman, Aug. 14, 1949; children: Laura Jo, Gail Eileen, Dana Charles. B.Arch., U. Oreg., 1950. Pvt. archtl. practice Springfield, Oreg., 1956-58; ptnr. John Amundson, Springfield, 1958-70; pres. Lutes & Amundson, Springfield, 1970-72; ptnr. Lutes/Sanetel, 1973-86; adj. assoc. prof. architecture U. Oreg., 1964-66, 89—; chmn. Springfield Planning Commn., 1956-64, Urban Design and Devel. Corp., 1968-70, Eugene Non-Profit Housing, Inc., 1970. Architect: Springfield Pub. Library, 1957, Mt. Hood Community Coll, 1965-79, Shoppers Paradise Expt. in Downtown Revitalization, 1957. Chmn. Springfield United Appeal, 1959. Served to 1st lt. AUS, 1943-46, 51-52. Decorate Bronze Star; named Jr. 1st Citizen, Springfield C. of C., 1957, 1st Citizen, 1968, Disting. Citizen, 1994. Fellow AIA (bd. dirs. 1987-90, v.p. 1991); mem. Rotary, Theta Chi. Home and Office: 778 Crest Ln Springfield OR 97477-3601

LUTHER, LUANA MAE, editor; b. L.A., Mar. 7, 1939; d. Chester Harry and Mildred P. (Knight) L.; m. O. Solorzano, Sept. 6, 1958 (div. 1974); children: Suzanne, Troy, Stephanie, Paul; m. Edwin J. Salzman, Apr. 4, 1981. BA, Calif. State U., Sacramento, 1974. Law indexer, legis. counsel State Calif., Sacramento, 1975-80, analyst, adminstrv. law, 1981-84; communications dir. Townsend & Co., Sacramento, 1985-87; adminstrv. asst., dept. justice State of Calif., Sacramento, 1987-88; editorial asst. Golden State Report Mag., Sacramento, 1986-88; mktg. cons. Lake Oswego, Oreg., 1989—; editor-in-chief Doral Pub., Wilsonville, Oreg., 1990—. Author: Red Mack Truck Massacre, 1981; contbr. articles to numerous publs.; columnist: Sacramento Bee, 1982-84; editor: (newsletter) Sacramento Youth Band, 1985. Dir. pub. rels., pres. LWV, West Clackamas County, Oreg., 1993—; vol. numerous polit. campaigns, Sacramento; fundraiser Dem. Women's Com., Sacramento, 1986. Mem. Mex.-Am. Ednl. Assn. (treas. 1964, Cert. Appreciation 1971). Democrat. Home: 17701 Blue Heron Way Lake Oswego OR 97034-6619

LUTHER, ROBERT CHESTER, former psychiatrist, consultant; b. Palo Alto, Calif., July 9, 1934, s. Chester Francis and Helen Eva (Yeomans) L.; m. Norma Gene Juenemann, June 18, 1960; children: Douglas Robert, Andrew Donald, David Allen. BS, Whitman Coll., 1955; MD, U. Oreg. Med. Sch., 1959. Psychiat. resident, fellow Menninger Sch. Psychiatry, Topeka, Kans., 1960-62, 64-65; pvt. practice psychiatry Psychiat. Assocs., Medford, Oreg., 1965-94; mem. psychiat. dept. staff Rogue Valley Med. Ctr., Medford, 1965—, bd. dirs., 1986-93; bd. dirs. So. Oreg. Leadership Coun., Medford, 1992—, Prime Care IPA, Medford, 1993—; lectr. in psychiatry Kans. U. Med. Ctr., 1961-65; clin. instr. psychiatry U. Oreg. Med. Sch., 1967-77, clin. asst. prof. psychiatry, 1977—; psychiat. cons. Ft. Vannoy Job Corps Ctr., 1965-68, Josephine County Mental Health Clinic, 1965-74; med. dir. methadone program Jackson County Mental Health Svcs., 1970-82, med. svcs. cons., 1995—. Mem. adv. com. Medford Sch. Dist., 1970-79; mem. So. Oreg. steering com. Re-Elect Mark Hatfield Com., 1990; bd. dirs. Medford Babe Ruth Baseball, 1976-78; pres. So. Oreg. Tennis Club, Medford, 1981-82; v.p. U. Oreg. Med. Sch. Alumni Assn., 1973-74; mem. citizen adv. bd. So. Oreg. State Coll., 1990—; chmn. Jackson County Bd. Health, 1974-76, 80-82; treas. Jackson County Rep. Ctrl. Com., 1994—. Capt. U.S. Army, 1962-64. Mem. Am. Psychiat. Assn., Oreg. Med. Assn. (bd. med. examiners liaison com. 1991—), ho. dels. 1970-72, Oreg. Psychiat. Assn. (mem. liaison com. 1991—, exec. coun. 1990-93), Jackson County Med. Soc. (pres. 1974), Medford Rotary Club (pres. 1976-77), Rogue Valley Country Club. Congregationalist. Home: 2241 Dellwood Ave Medford OR 97504-8012

LUTIN, DAVID LOUIS, real estate development and finance consultant; b. East Hartford, Conn., Apr. 18, 1919; s. Solomon and Esther (Newman) L.; A.B., Ohio No. U., 1946; M.B.A., Syracuse U., 1949; m. Dorothy Marmor, Dec. 3, 1944; children—Gary, Marnie (Mrs. George Wittig). Housing economist and field rep. HHFA, Washington, 1950-57; dir. urban renewal City of Brookline, Mass., 1957-58; cons. on urban renewal and housing Com. for Econ. Devel., N.Y.C., 1958-59; propr. David L. Lutin Assocs., real estate devel. and fin. cons., Rye, N.Y., 1959-73, Phoenix, 75—; v.p. real estate and mortgages Am. Bank and Trust Co., N.Y.C., 1973-75. Research assoc. Albert Farwell Bemis Found., M.I.T., 1951-52. Served to capt. AUS, 1942-46. Decorated Purple Heart. Mem. Am. Econ. Assn., Nat. Planning Assn., Mortgage Bankers Assn., Urban Land Inst., Am. Planning Assn., Am. Statis. Assn., Nat. Assn. Home Builders. Contbr. articles and reports on econs., housing and urban devel. to profl. jours. Home and Office: 11419 N Century Ln Scottsdale AZ 85254-4827

LUTRIN, CARL EDWARD, political science educator; b. Far Rockaway, N.Y., June 11, 1940; s. Louis and Mildred S. (Fertel) L.; m. Patricia Lutrin, Aug. 24, 1982; 1 child, Lawren. BA, Adelphi U., 1962; MS, U. Wis., 1965; PhD, U. Mo., 1971. Prof. polit. sci. Calif. Poly. Inst., San Luis Obispo, Calif., 1970—. Author: American Public Administration, 5th edit., 1995. Mem. Am. Polit. Sci. Assn., Am. Soc. Pub. Adminstrn., Western Polit. Sci. Assn. Democrat. Jewish. Home: 74 Rafael Way San Luis Obispo CA 93405-1524 Office: Calif Poly Inst Dept Polit Sci San Luis Obispo CA 93407

LUTTRELL, DAN CURTIS, savings and loan company executive; b. Tucson, Dec. 20, 1952; s. Lonnie Calvin and Lois Ann (Jaesche) L.; m. Kathy Lou Sword, Aug. 30, 1975; children: Jason Matthew, Ryan David. Student, Boise State U., 1970-75. Packer, loader Compton Mayflower, Boise, Idaho, 1970-72; billing clk. St. Alphonsus Hosp., Boise, 1972-75; br. mgr. Assocs. Fin. Svcs., Boise, 1975-80; v.p. Farmers & Mchts. State Bank, Meridian, Idaho, 1980-87; asst. v.p. Wash. Fed. Svgs., Nampa, Idaho, 1987—. Chmn. United Way of Ada County, Meridian, 1984-85; judge Am. Cancer Soc. Jail & Bail, Nampa, 1987-88; treas. Soap Box Derby Boise, 1991—; exec. bd. United Way Canyon area, 1991-95; bd. dirs. Nampa Downtown Econ. Devel. Com., 1992—. Mem. Consumer Credit Counseling Svc. (pres. 1986—), Inst. Fin. Edn. (sec.-treas. 1988—), Snake River Valley Bldg. Contractors (sec.-treas. 1988-90), Better Bus. Bur. (bd. dirs. 1984-87), Optimist Club (pres. 1979), Sunrise Exch. Club (v.p. 1976), Kiwanis Club Nampa. Republican. Episcopalian. Home: 11491 W Arlen St Boise ID 83713-1512 Office: Washington Fed Svgs & Loan 223 11th Ave S Nampa ID 83651-3920

LUTTRELL, ERIC MARTIN, oil company executive; b. Wheeling, W.Va., May 12, 1941; s. Lauren Robert and Gertrude Dorothy (Olson) L.; m. Janet Marie Quigg, June 8, 1963; children: Dawn Alexandra, Brooke Catherine. BS in Geology, U. Wis., 1963, MS in Geology, 1965; PhD in Geology, Princeton U., 1968. Geologist Texaco Inc., New Orleans, 1968-70; rsch. geologist Texaco Inc., Bellaire, Tex., 1970-75, rsch. supr., 1975-79; exploration mgr. Texaco Inc., New Orleans, 1979-80; divsn. geologist Sohio Petroleum Co., Dallas, 1980-82, exploration mgr., 1986-86; exploration mgr. onshore U.S. BP Exploration, Houston, 1986-89; exploration mgr. L.Am. BP Exploration, London, 1989-91; v.p. exploration BP Exploration, Anchorage, 1991—. Bd. dirs., v.p. United Way of Anchorage, 1992-94; bd. dirs. Performing Arts Ctr., Anchorage, 1994. Mem. Am. Assn. Petroleum Geologists, Geol. Soc. Am. Office: BP Exploration Alaska 900 E Benson Blvd Anchorage AK 99508-4254

LUTVAK, MARK ALLEN, computer company executive; b. Chgo., Feb. 9, 1939; s. Joseph Issac and Jeanette Nettie (Pollock) L.; B.S. in Elec. Engring., U. Mich., 1962; M.B.A., Wayne State U., Detroit, 1969; m. Gayle Helene Rotofsky, May 24, 1964; children—Jeffrey, Eric. Sales rep. IBM Corp., 1962-64; successively sales rep., product mktg. mgr., corp. product mgr. Burroughs Corp., Detroit, 1964-76; mgr. product mktg. Memorex Corp., Santa Clara, Calif., 1976-80, product program gen. mgr., 1980-81; dir. product mktg. Personal Computer div. Atari, Inc., Sunnyvale, Calif., 1981-83; dir. mktg., v.p. Durango Systems, San Jose, Calif., 1983-85; dir. mktg. ITTQUME Corp., San Jose, 1985-87; v.p. mktg. Optimem, Mountain View, Calif., 1987-88; dir. mktg. Priam Corp., San Jose, 1988-91; dir. Memorex, Santa Clara, Calif. 1991—; prof. Applied Mgmt. Center, Wayne State U., 1967-72, Walsh U., Troy, Mich., 1974-76, West Valley Coll., Saratoga, Calif., 1977-78. Trustee, pres. brotherhood Temple Emanuel, San Jose, Calif., 1979-80. Mem. IEEE, Soc. Applied Math., Alpha Epsilon Pi. Home: 1364 Box Canyon Rd San Jose CA 95120-5627

LUTZ, JOHN SHAFROTH, lawyer; b. San Francisco, Sept. 10, 1943; s. Frederick Henry and Helena Morrison (Shafroth) L.; m. Elizabeth Boschen, Dec. 14, 1968; children: John Shafroth, Victoria. BA, Brown U., 1965; JD, U. Denver, 1971. Bar: Colo. 1971, U.S. Dist. Ct. Colo. 1971, U.S. Ct. Appeals (2d cir.) 1975, D.C. 1976, U.S. Supreme Ct. 1976, U.S. Dist. Ct. (so. dist.) N.Y. 1977, U.S. Tax Ct. 1977, U.S. Ct. Appeals (10th cir.) 1979, N.Y. 1984, U.S. Ct. Appeals (9th cir.) 1990, U.S. Dist. Ct. (no. dist.) Calif. 1993. Trial atty. Denver regional office U.S. SEC, 1971-74; spl. atty. organized crime, racketeering sect. U.S. Dept. Justice, So. Dist. N.Y., 1974-77; atty. Kelly, Stansfield and O'Donnell, Denver, 1977-78; gen. counsel Boettcher & Co., Denver, 1978-87, Kelly, Stansfield and O'Donnel, Denver, 1987; spl. counsel, 1987-88, ptnr., 1988-93; of counsel LeBoeuf, Lamb, Greene and Mac Rae, L.L.P., 1993-94, ptnr. 1995—; allied mem. N.Y. Stock Exch., 1978-87; speaker on broker, dealer, securities law and arbitration issues to various profl. orgns. Contbr. articles to profl. jours. Bd. dirs. Cherry Creek Improvement Assn., 1980-84, Spalding Rehab. Hosp., 1986-89; chmn., vice-chmn. securities sub sect. Bus. Law Sect. of Colo. Bar, 1990, chmn., 1990-91. Lt. (j.g.), USNR, 1965-67. Mem. ABA, Colo. Bar Assn., Denver Bar Assn., Am. Law Inst., Securities Industry Assn. (state regulations com. 1982-86), Nat. Assn. Securities Dealers, Inc. (nat. arbitration com. 1987-91), St. Nicholas Soc. N.Y.C., Denver Law Club, Denver Country Club, Denver Athletic Club (dir. 1990-93), Rocky Mountain Brown Club (founder, past pres.), Racquet and Tennis Club. Republican. Episcopalian. Office: LeBoeuf Lamb Greene & MacRae LLP 633 17th St Ste 2800 Denver CO 80202-3628

LUTZE, ROBERT STEPHEN, engineering manager; b. Sheboygan, Wis., Apr. 3, 1954; s. Ernest A. and Elva E. (Lund) L.; m. Mary E. Hoel, Oct. 1, 1983; children: Kyle S., Alexandra E. BS in Applied Math. and Physics, U. Wis., 1976, BSEE, 1977, MSEE, 1978. Engr. Hewlett Packard, Ft. Collins, Colo., 1979-82; engring. mgr. Honeywell Solid State, Mpls., 1982-88, Brooktree Corp., San Diego, 1988—. Contbr. numerous papers to tech. jours. and confs. Mem. IEEE.

LUTZKY, FRANK JOSEPH, JR., science educator; b. Flagtown, N.J., Feb. 4, 1934; s. Frank J. and Esther (Buckshaw) L.; m. Donna Wyglendowski, June 17, 1943; children: Angela, Robert, Albert, David, Kristen, Scott. BS in Engring., Rutgers U., 1955. Lic. real estate broker. Instr. sci. Ctrl. Oreg. C.C., N.Y.C., 1955-61; supr. svc. ops. Bell Labs., Murray Hill, N.J., 1961-69; dept. head ops. svc. ops. Bell Labs., Holmdel, N.J., 1969-72; dept. head engring. svc. ops. Bell Labs., Murray Hill, N.J., 1972-75, dept. head space planning plant engring., 1975-79; dir. svc. ops. Bell Labs., Holmdel, 1979-84, dir. facilities mgmt. adminstrn. systems, 1984-86; v.p. Weichert Comml. Realtors, Princeton, N.J., 1986-89; pres. Weichert Comml. Realtors, Morris Plains, N.J., 1989-90; sci. instr. Cen. Oreg. Community Coll., Bend, 1991—; cons., 1988—. Mgr. Little League, Hillsborough, 1980-83; sponsor dir. Jr. Achievement, Holmdel, 1976-86. 2d lt. U.S. Army, 1957-58. Mem. Nat. Assn. Corp. Real Estate Execs., Morris County Bd. Realtors, Princeton Area C. of C. Roman Catholic. Home: 60612 Brasada Way Bend OR 97702-9655 Office: Ctrl Oreg CC Bend OR 97701

LUX, JOHN H., corporate executive; b. Logansport, Ind., Feb. 3, 1918; s. Carl Harrison and Mary Emma (Dunn) L.; m. Betty F. Passow, Aug. 27, 1940; children: John Ernst, Courtney Rae; m. Bernice Weitzel Brown, 1965; m. Linda Merrill Brown, Mar. 2, 1978; children: Julia Elizabeth, Jenifyr Claire. B.S., Purdue U., 1939; Ph.D., 1942. Asst. dir. research and devel. The Neville Co., 1943-46; v.p., cons. Atomic Basic Chems., 1946-47; dir. research Witco Chem. Co., 1947-50; mgr. new product devel. Gen. Electric Co., 1950-52; v.p. Shea Chem. Co., 1952-55; pres., dir. Haveg Industries, Inc., Wilmington, Del., 1955-66, Haveg Corp., Tourlux Mgmt. Corp. (P.R.); chmn. bd. Hemisphere Products Corp. (P.R.), Reinhold Engring. & Plastics Co., Norwalk, Calif., Am. Super-Temperatures Wires Co.; pres. Ametek, Inc., 1966-69, chmn. bd., chief exec. officer, 1969-90, chmn. bd., 1990-93; ret., 1993. Mem. Am. Inst. Chem. Engrs., Am. Chem. Soc., Phi Lambda Upsilon. Club: Met.

LUZOVICH, STEVEN ALBERT, computer engineer; b. San Jose, Calif., Mar. 2, 1960; s. Albert and Betty (Compton) L. BSECE, U. Calif., Santa Barbara, 1982. Test engr. Tandem Computers, Watsonville, Calif., 1983-84; electronics engr. MCT/Synerception, Santa Cruz, Calif., 1984-89; systems engr. Meridian Data, Scotts Valley, Calif., 1989-90; sr. electronics engr. Worthington Data Solutions, Santa Cruz, 1990—. Home: 750 Edwardo Ave Ben Lomond CA 95005-9408 Office: Worthington Data Solutions 3004 Mission St Ste 220 Santa Cruz CA 95060-5700

LYASHENKO, NIKOLAI NIKOLAEVICH, mathematician, educator; b. Leningrad, Russia, Jan. 19, 1946; came to U.S., 1990; s. Nikolai Makarovich and Rufina Stepanovna (Poshekhonova) L.; m. Tatiana Vasilievna Giga, June 21, 1969; 1 child, Anna Nikolaevna. BS, Leningrad U., 1966, MS, 1969, PhD in Physics and Math. Scis., 1974, D in Phys. Math. Scis., 1986. Assoc. prof. Leningrad Elec. Engring. Inst., 1975-85; prof. Leningrad Poly. Inst., 1986-88; dir. info. processing lab. Leningrad Inst. Informatics and Automation, 1988-90; vis. prof. George Mason U., Fairfax, Va., 1991—; v.p. Empirical Inference Corp., Schenectady, N.Y. Contbr. numerous articles to profl. jours.; patentee in field. Home and Office: 4614 W 131st St Hawthorne CA 90250-5107

LYBARGER, MARJORIE KATHRYN, nurse; b. Holland, Mich., Apr. 23, 1956; d. Richard Simon and Mary Kathryn (Homan) Denuyl; m. John Steven Lybarger, Aug. 22, 1981; children: Ashley Ann, Ryan Christopher. BA in Psychology, Biola U., Calif., 1979, BS in Nursing, 1984. RN, Calif. Staff nurse Presbyn. Intercommunity Hosp., Whittier, Calif, 1985-86, Healthcare Med. Ctr., Tustin, Calif., 1986-88; staff nurse med.-telemetry unit Friendly Hills Regional Med. Ctr., La Habra, Calif., 1988-90; staff nurse telemetry unit Riverside (Calif.) Community Hosp., 1990-93; staff nurse med. telemetry unit St. Anthony's Ctrl. Hosp., Denver, 1993-94; staff nurse cardiovascular intermediate care unit St. Anthony's Ctr., Denver, 1994—. Mem. Med.-Surg. Nurses Assn., Gamma Phi Beta. Republican. Home: 8489 W 95th Dr Broomfield CO 80021-5330

LYDICK, LAWRENCE TUPPER, federal judge; b. San Diego, June 22, 1916; s. Roy Telling and Geneva (Lydick) L.; m. Gretta Grant, Aug. 7, 1938; children: Gretta Grant, Lawrence Tupper; m. Martha Martinez, Oct. 1969; 1 child, Chip. A.B., Stanford U., 1938, LL.B. (Crothers law scholar), 1942; Sigma Nu exchange scholar, U. Freiburg, Germany, 1938-39; postgrad., Harvard U., 1943, Mass. Inst. Tech., 1943-44. Bar: Calif. 1946. Since practiced in L.A.; dir. disputes div. 10th region Nat. War Labor Bd., San Francisco, 1942-43; asst. to pres., gen. counsel U.S. Grant Export-Import, Ltd., L.A., 1946-48; assoc. Adams, Duque & Hazeltine, L.A., 1948-53, ptnr., 1953-71; U.S. dist. ct. judge Central Dist. Calif., 1971—. Bd. vis. Stanford Law Sch. Lt. USNR, 1943-46. Mem. Am. Law Inst. Republican. Office: US Dist Ct 34 Civic Center Plz Santa Ana CA 92701-4025

LYE, WILLIAM FRANK, history educator; b. Kimberley, B.C., Can., Feb. 19, 1930; came to U.S., 1955, naturalized, 1981; s. Arthur Percy and Jessie Loretta (Prince) L.; m. Velda Campbell, Oct. 16, 1953; children: William Mark, Matthew Campbell, David Arthur, Victoria, Regina. Student Ricks Coll., 1953-55, Duke U., 1963; BS, Utah State U., 1959; MA, U. Calif.-Berkeley, 1959; PhD, UCLA, 1969. Instr. polit. sci. Ricks Coll., Rexburg, Idaho, 1959-63, 67-68, head dept. polit. sci., 1959-63; teaching asst. dept. history UCLA, 1964-65; asst. prof. Utah State U., Logan, 1968-69, acting head dept. history and geography, 1969-70, assoc. prof., head dept. history and geography, 1970-73, prof., head dept. history and geography, 1973-76, dean Coll. Humanities, Arts and Social Scis., 1976-83, v.p. for univ. relations, prof. dept. history and geography, 1983-91, prof. history, 1991—; vis. lectr. dept. history Brigham Young U., Provo, Utah, 1970; temporary lectr. dept. history U. Cape Town, Republic of South Africa, 1974; social cons. for project design teams in land conservation, U.S. Agy. for Internat. Devel. Khartoum, Sudan, 1978, Maseru, Lesotho, 1979; mem. higher edn. taskforce on telecommunications, Utah, 1977-82; chmn. State of Utah Telecommunications Coop., 1987, Regents' Com. on Credit by Exam., Utah, 1976; mem. adv. com. Sta. KULC-TV, State Ednl. Telecommunications Operating Ctr., 1986-90; bd. dirs., exec. com. Children's Aid Soc. Utah, 1985-88, pres., 1990-91; mem. Utah Statehood Centennial Commn., 1990—, Utah Christopher Columbus Quincentenary Commn., 1990-91. Author: (with Colin Murray) Transformations on the Highveld: The Tswana and Southern Sotho, 1980, paperback edit., 1985; editor: Andrew Smith's Journal of His Expedition into the Interior of South Africa, 1834-36, 1975. Producer (TV series) Out of Africa, 1977, The God Seekers, 1978; contbr. articles and book revs. to profl. publs. Chmn. State Day celebration, Logan, Utah, 1973, univ. drive for new Logan Regional Hosp; bishop LDS Ch., 1993—. Recipient Leadership award Standard of Calif., 1957, Idea of Yr. award Utah State U., 1971, Faculty Service award Associated Students, Utah State U., 1977-78, Nicholas and Mary Kay Leone Leadership award, 1991; Woodrow Wilson Nat. fellow 1958, Foreign Area fellow Social Sci. Research Council, Republic of South Africa, England, 1966-67, 67-68; faculty devel. grantee Utah State U., 1972, Human Sci. Research Council of South Africa publ. grantee, 1975, Mauerberger Trust grantee, 1976. Mem. African Studies Assn., Royal African Soc., Western Assn. Africanists (program chmn. 1972-74, pres. 1974-76), Am. Soc. Landscape Architects (accreditation bd. 1967-93), Phi Kappa Phi, Phi Alpha Theta. Home: 696 E 400 N Logan UT 84321-4218 Office: Utah State U Dept History 650 N 1100 E Logan UT 84322-0710

LYKINS, JAY ARNOLD, economic development director; b. Shattuck, Okla., Feb. 13, 1947; s. George Eldridge and Lucy Lee (Croom) L.; m. (Mary) Lynn Turner, Jan. 3, 1970; children: Mary Lee and Amy Lynn (twins), Jason. BA, Covenant Coll., 1973; MBA in 3rd World Econ. Devel., Kennedy-Western U., 1987, PhD in Internat. Bus., 1988. Credit specialist Gen. Electric Supply Co., Nashville, 1974-75; owner, mgr. Environment Control Co., Nashville, 1975-78; bus. adminstr. Youth for Christ, Atlanta, 1978-81; controller Young Life, Colorado Springs, Colo., 1981-82, internat. adminstr., 1982-86; exec. dir. Global Reach, Pleasanton, Calif., 1982—; cons. Royal Donuts, Lima, Peru, Barnabas Group, Vancouver, B.C., Manna Corp., Bulawayo, Zimbabwe, Denver Bridge Corp.; started more than 110 businesses in 30 countries, serving over 50 chs., missions. Author: Values in the Marketplace, 1985, Development and Technology: Economics for the Third World, 1987, Islamic Business: Philosophy and Methods, 1988. Served with USN, 1966-68. Mem. Internat. Council for Small Bus., Am. Cons. League, Assn. MBA Execs., Ctr. Entrepreneurial Mgmt. Club: Nob Hill Country (Snellville, Ga.) (pres. 1980). Office: Global Reach 39 California Ave Ste 203 Pleasanton CA 94566-6281

LYLE, GLENDA SWANSON, state legislator; b. Knoxville, Tenn.; d. Richard and Olivia Swanson; children: Kipp, Elsie, Jennifer, Anthony. BA, U. Denver, 1964; MA, U. Colo., 1973. Former dir. cmty. and personal svcs., instr. early childhood edn., dir. preschool lab C.C. of Denver/Auraria; owner Planners, Inc.; mem. Colo. Ho. of Reps., 1992—, mem. various coms., 1993—. Del. White Ho. Conf. Small Bus., 1980-86; mem. Regional Transp. Dist. Bd., 1986-92, Regulatory Agy. Adv. Bd., Mayor's Planning Bd., Nat. Pub. Lands Adv. Coun., Gov.'s Small Bus. Coun., Colo. Mkt. and Distributive Edn. Adv. Coun., Va Neal Blue Ctr. Mem. Am. Planning Assn., Conf. Minority Transp. Ofcls. (nat. bd. dirs.), Black Women Polit. Action (founding mem.), Black C. of C. (bd. dirs.). Democrat. Office: Colo House of Reps State Capitol Denver CO 80203

LYLE, JOHN TILLMAN, landscape architecture educator; b. Houston, Aug. 10, 1934; s. Leo Tillman and Martha Ellen (Rawlins) L.; m. Harriett Laverna Fancher, Dec. 28, 1967; children: Alexander Tillman, Cybele Katsura. BArch, Tulane U., 1957; postgrad., Royal Acad. of Fine Arts, Copenhagen, 1965-67; M of Landscape Architecture, U. Calif., Berkeley, 1966. Registered architect, Calif. Architect Stanford (Calif.) U., 1959-62; urban designer John Carl Warnecke & Assocs., San Francisco, 1963-65; prof. Calif. State Poly. U., Pomona, 1968—; vis. prof. Liubliana (Yugoslavia) U., 1982, Instituto Universitario Di Architectura, Venice, Italy, 1988, U. Sao Paulo, Brazil, 1989, Kyushu Inst. Design, Fukuoka, Japan, 1990; dir. design bldg. and landscape Inst. for Regenerative Studies, 1984—. Author: Design For Human Ecosystems, 1985 (award Assn. Am. Pubs. 1985, Am. Soc. Landscape Architects 1986); contbr. articles to profl. jours. Mem. bd. govs. Desert Studies Consortium, Mojave Desert, 1984-88. Recipient Honor award Calif. Coun. Landscape Architects, 1988; named Fulbright Disting. prof., U.S. Dept. State, 1982, Disting. Educator, Coun. Educators in Landscape Architecture, 1989; Fulbright scholar U.S. Dept. State, 1966-68. Fellow Am. Soc. Landscape Architects (Design for Sustainable Devel. award 1994). Democrat. Home: 580 N Hermosa Ave Sierra Madre CA 91024-1117 Office: Calif State Poly U 3801 W Temple Ave Pomona CA 91768-2557

LYLES, DARA LYNN, sales executive; b. Jacksonville, Fla., Mar. 4, 1964; d. Royce and Ruth Anna (Lipscomb) L. BSBA, U. Fla., 1986. From sales mgr. lingerie to buyer lingerie Macy's/Bullock's, Atlanta, Houston, 1986-91; nat. sales mgr. Lingerie Live, Inc., L.A., 1991-94; western sales mgr. lingerie Guess Innerwear, N.Y.C., 1994—.

LYMAN, RICHARD WALL, foundation and university executive, historian; b. Phila., Oct. 18, 1923; s. Charles M. and Aglae (Wall) L.; m. Elizabeth D. Schauffler, Aug. 20, 1947; children: Jennifer P., Holly Lyman Antolini, Christopher M., Timothy R. BA, Swarthmore Coll., 1947, LLD (hon.), 1974; MA, Harvard U., 1948, PhD, 1954, LLD (hon.), 1980; LLD (hon.), Washington U., St. Louis, 1971, Mills Coll, 1972, Yale U., 1975; LHD (hon.), U. Rochester, 1975, Coll. of Idaho, 1989. Teaching fellow, tutor Harvard U., 1949-51; instr. Swarthmore Coll., 1952-53; instr., then asst. prof. Washington U., St. Louis, 1953-58; mem. faculty Stanford U., 1958-80, 88-91, prof. history, 1962-80, 88-91, Sterling prof., 1980-91, assoc. dean Sch Humanities and Scis., 1964-66, v.p., provost, 1967-70, pres., 1970-80, pres. emeritus, 1980—, dir. Inst. Internat. Studies, 1988-91, prof. dept. history, 1991—; pres. Rockefeller Found., 1980-88; spl. corr. The Economist, London, 1953-66; bd. dirs. Council on Founds., 1982-88, Independent Sector, 1980-88, chair, 1983-86, Nat. Com. on U.S.-China Relations, 1986—; dir. IBM, 1978—, Chase Manhattan Corp., 1981-82. Author: The First Labour Government, 1957; editor: (with Lewis W. Spitz) Major Crises in Western Civilization, 1965, (with Virginia A. Hodgkinson) The Future of the Nonprofit Sector, 1989; editorial bd. Jour. Modern History, 1958-61. Mem. Nat. Council on Humanities, 1976-82, vice chmn., 1980-82; chmn. Commn. on Humanities, 1978-80; trustee Rockefeller Found., 1976-88 , Carnegie Found. Advancement of Teaching, 1976-82; bd. dirs. Nat. Assn. Ind. Colls. and Univs., 1976-77; chmn. Assn. Am. Univs., 1978-79. Served with USAAF, 1943-46. Decorated officier Legion of Honor; Fulbright fellow London Sch. Econs., 1951-52, hon. fellow, 1978—; Guggenheim fellow, 1959-60. Fellow Royal Hist. Soc.; mem. Am. Acad. Arts and Scis., Am. Hist. Assn., Council on Fgn. Relations, Conf. Brit. Studies, Phi Beta Kappa. Office: Stanford U Sch Edn Stanford CA 94305

LYNCH, EUGENE F., federal judge; b. 1931. B.S., U. Santa Clara, 1953; LL.B., U. Calif., 1958. Assoc. O'Connor, Moran, Cohn & Lynch, San Francisco, 1959-64, ptnr., 1964-71; judge Mcpl. Ct., San Francisco, 1971-74; justice Superior Ct. City and County San Francisco, 1974-82; judge U.S. Dist. Ct. (no. dist.) Calif., San Francisco, 1982—. Office: US Dist Ct PO Box 36060 450 Golden Gate Ave San Francisco CA 94102*

LYNCH, LINDA LOU, reading and language arts specialist/educator; b. L.A., Feb. 9, 1941; d. Alexander Alfred and Gizella Mary (Bajus) Laszloffy; m. John Joseph Lynch, June 13, 1964; children: Valerie Ann, Colinda Lee, Lee Anne Ellen. BS, Calif. State U., Northridge, 1964; MEd, Loyola Marymount U., L.A., 1990; EdD, Pepperdine U., 1995. Cert. tchr., Calif. Computer programmer Union Bank, L.A., 1962-64; substitute tchr. various sch. dists. Calif., 1964-68, 79-80; tchr. Richard H. Dana Mid. Sch., Hawthorne, Calif., 1980-88; reading specialist Wiseburn Sch. Dist., Hawthorne, 1988-91, 94—; elem. sch. tchr. Juan de Anza Elem. Sch., Hawthorne, 1991-93; reading specialist Wiseburn Sch. Dist., 1994—; adj. faculty mem. Loyola Marymount U., L.A., 1991—, dir. reading program Grad. Sch., 1992; rsch. asst. Pepperdine U., L.A., 1992-94, teaching asst., 1993, asst. dir. student tchrs., 1993, adj. prof., 1994—; adj. prof. Chapman U., L.A., 1995—. Mem. NEA, AAUW, ASCD, Am. Edn. Rsch. Assn., Internat. Reading Assn., Calif. Reading Assn., Ventura County Reading Assn., Calif. Tchrs. Assn., Wiseburn Faculty Assn., Phi Delta Kappa. Democrat. Roman Catholic.

LYNCH, MARTIN ANDREW, retail company executive; b. Chgo., Oct. 5, 1937; s. George Irwin and Cecilia Veronica (Corley) L.; m. Shirley Ann McKee, Oct. 20, 1962; children: Kathleen Marie, Kevin Michael, Karen Ann, Daniel Patrick, Michelle Eileen. BSc, DePaul U., 1962. CPA, Ill., Calif. Audit mgr. Price Waterhouse & Co., Chgo., 1962-69; asst. to pres. Scot Lad Foods, Chgo., 1969-70; v.p. fin. N.Am. Car Corp., Chgo., 1970-76; sr. v.p. fin. Tiger Internat. Inc., L.A., 1976-83; exec. v.p., chief fin. officer Duty Free Shoppers Group Ltd., San Francisco, 1983-89, Casino USA Inc., Santa Barbara, Calif., 1989—, Smart & Final Inc., Santa Barbara, 1989—. Mem. AICPA, Calif. CPA Soc., Fin. Execs. Inst., Nat. Assn. Whole Grogery, Inst. Food Distbn. Assn., Bel Air Country Club (L.A.). Roman Catholic. Office: Casino USA 524 Chapala St Santa Barbara CA 93101-3412

LYNCH, PATRICK MICHAEL, insurance agent, risk management consultant; b. Lebanon, Oreg., Aug. 26, 1951; s. Luther Bryan and Genevieve Colleen (Clarno) L.; m. Katherine Anne Sofranko, Sept. 6, 1972; children: Daniel Patrick, Sara Maria. BA in Philosophy, Psychology cum laude, Calif. State U., Chico, 1973; MA, Grad. Theol. Union, Berkeley, 1976. Exec. asst. Com. on Children's TV, San Francisco, 1974-76; instr. Grad. Theolog. Union, Berkeley, 1975-76; cons. Standard Oil Co., San Francisco, 1975; agt., broker CalFarm Ins., Chico, CAlif., 1976—; cons. PSI, Inc., Vacaville, Calif., 1989—. Chmn. Sch. Site Coun., Chico, 1987—, Music Scholarship Com., Chico, 1993—; mem. Chico Unified Sch. Dist. Planning Com., 1993. Mem. Ins. Inst. Am. (accredited ins. advisor, assoc. in risk mgmt.), Soc. for the Preservation and Encouragement, Barbershop Quartet Singing in Am., Inc., A Capella Singing Orgn. (v.p. N. Valley chpt., Internat. Choral Conducting Scholar, nat. and Kenosha chpt., 1991, 92, Man of Yr., Chico chpt. 1991), N. Valley Chorus (dir.), Greater Chico Kiwanis Club (pub. rels., bd. dirs.). Republican. Presbyterian. Office: CalFarm Ins Agy 1215C Mangrove Ave Chico CA 95926-3527

LYNCH, ROBERT BERGER, lawyer; b. LaCrosse, Wis., June 10, 1931; s. Jan P. and Eve (Berger) L.; B.S., U.S. Merchant Marine Acad., 1955; J.D., U. of the Pacific, 1967; m. Ann Godfrey, May 30, 1980; children: Jan Fredrick Lynch, Jerry Wayne Coggins. Engr. Aerojet Gen. Corp., Sacramento, Calif., 1955-61, proposal mgr., 1961-63, asst. contract adminstrn. mgr., 1963-66, contract adminstrn. mgr., 1967-70; admitted to Calif. bar, 1969, U.S. Supreme Ct. bar, 1972; individual practice law. Rancho Cordova, Calif., 1969—; instr. bus. law Solano Community Coll., 1977-79, San Joaquin Delta Coll., 1978-79. Active various charity fund-raising campaigns in Sacramento Calif., 1966-68; mem. mission com. St. Clements Episcopal Ch., Rancho Cordova, Calif., 1967-68; trustee Los Rios Community Coll. Dist., Calif., 1971-79. With USCG, 1949-51, USNR 1951-80, Nat. Guard 1988-91, Maj. AUS, ret. Mem. IEEE, Calif. Wildlife Fedn., Internat. Turtle Club, Marines Meml. Assn., Am. Legion, Mensa. Office: 10615 Coloma Rd Rancho Cordova CA 95670-3939

LYNCH, ROBERT MONTGOMERY, newspaper publisher; b. San Francisco, Aug. 9, 1920; s. Ernest Glenn and Alice Romona (Granice) L.; m. Jean Helen Allen, Nov. 9, 1941; children: William, James, John, AA, Santa Rosa Jr. Coll., 1940; postgrad., Cornell U., 1945. Petty officer 1st class U. S. Naval Intelligence, San Francisco, 1942-45; ensign instr. U.S. Naval Reserve, Port Deposit, Md., 1945-46; reporter and ad salesman The Sonoma (Calif.) Index-Tribune, 1946-49, editor and publ., 1949-90, publ., owner, 1990—. Recipient Svc. to Media award Sonoma Co. Sch. Bd. Assn., 1989. Mem. Calif. Newspaper Publ. Assn. (pres. 1980), San Francisco Press Club, Calif. Press Assn. (pres. 1981, 92, bd. dirs. 1978—, Calif. Newspaper Exec. of Yr. 1989), Sonoma Men's Golf Assn., Sonoma Kiwanis Club (pres. 1965). Home: P O Box C Sonoma CA 95476 Office: The Sonoma Index-Tribune 117 W Napa St Sonoma CA 95476-6639

LYNCH, TIMOTHY BRUCE, city adminstrator; b. Lewistown, Pa., Dec. 30, 1949; s. James F. and Elsie (Holloman) L.; m. Cecilia P. Resendez; children: Dennis, Kelly, Johnny, Michael. BS in Biology, U. Calif., Riverside, 1971; MPA, Harvard U., 1984. Rsch. asst. U. Calif., Riverside, 1971-72, spl. asst., 1985; campaign mgr. Brown for Congress, Riverside, 1972; legis. asst. Congressman George Brown, Washington, 1973-80, adminstrv. asst., 1980-84; exec. asst. Memel, Jacobs, Pierno, Gersh & Ellsworth, L.A., 1985-87; membership and devel. dir. The Planetary Soc., Pasadena, Calif., 1987-91; dep. contr. City of L.A., 1991—. Active Riverside Press Coun., 1973-74, Environ. Protection Com., Riverside, 1973-74; bd. dir. Return Brown to Cong. campaign, San Bernardino, 1984. Recipient Internat. Achievement award Am. Soc. Assn. Execs. for internat. mktg. for the planetary soc., 1989. Mem. AAAS, U. Calif.-Riverside Alumni Assn., U. Calif. Advocates, Common Cause. Democrat. Home: 12753 Emelita St North Hollywood CA 91607-1018 Office: City Hall Rm 220 Los Angeles CA 90012

LYNCH, TIMOTHY JEREMIAH-MAHONEY, lawyer, theologian, realtor, educator; b. June 10, 1952; s. Joseph David and Margaret Mary (Mahoney) L. MS, JD in Taxation, Golden Gate U., 1981; MA, PhD in Modern European History, U. San Francisco, 1983; Licentiate, Inter-Am. Acad., Rio de Janeiro, 1988; PhD in Classics and Divinity/Theology, Harvard U., 1988; JSD in Constl. Law, Hastings Law Ctr., 1990. Bar: D.C. 1989, Calif., U.S. Ct. Appeals (2d cir.) 1989, U.S. Ct. Appeals (4th cir.) 1990; mem. Bar/Outer Temple/Comml. Bar of U.K.; European Econ. Ct. of 1st Instance. Legal bus., tax, counsel Lynch Real Estate, San Francisco, 1981-85; researcher, writer Kolb, Roche & Sullivan, San Francisco, 1986-88; chmn. internat. law dept. Timothy J.M. Lynch & Assocs., San Francisco, 1987-88, chmn., mng. dir. law dept., 1988—; chmn., pres., CEO Lynch Real Estate Investment Corp., San Francisco, 1989—; ptnr. Lynch Investment Corp.; bd. lawyer/arbitrators Pacific Coast Stock Exch., NASD, 1994—; chmn. bd. Lynch Holding Corp. Group; corp. counsel, sr. ptnr. L.A. Ctr. Internat. Comml. Arbitration, 1991—; vis. fellow classics, Inst. of Classical Studies, U. London; rsch. prof. Canon law and ecumenical ch. history grad. Theological Union U. Calif. Berkeley, 1992—; vis. scholar Patristic theology and classical philosophy of ecumenical doctrines, U. Laval, Quebec, Can., 1993—; vis. scholar Medieval ch. history U. Leeds, Eng., 1993-95; arbitrator Iran-U.S. Claims Tribunal, The Hague, 1993; mem. internat. corp. adv. bd. J.P. Morgan and Co., N.Y.C.; bd. dirs. Morgan-Stanley Corp., N.Y.C.; chmn. Latin Am., African and Middle East Corp. Groups J.P. Morgan Internat., Corp.; adv. bd. Morgan Stanley Corp., N.Y.C.; mem. Orgn. Econ. Cooperation and Devel., mem. adv. com. Internat. Labor Orgn.; participant Forum/A Group of Internat. Leaders, Calif., 1995, mem. adv. bd. U.S.-Saudi Arabia Bus. Coun., others. Author: (10 vol. manuscript) History of Ecumenical Doctrines and Canon Law of Church; editorial bd. Internat. Tax Jour., 1993; author: Publishers National Endowment for Arts and Humanities Classical Translations: Latin, Greek, and Byzantine Literary Texts for Modern Theological-Philosophical Analysis of Social Issues; Essays on Issues of Religious Ethics and Social, Public Policy Issues, others; editorial bd. Internat. Tax Jour., 1993; contbr. articles to profl. jours. Dir., vice chmn. Downtown Assn. San Francisco; councillor, dir. Atlantic Coun. U.S., 1984—; corp. counsel, chmn. spl. arbitrator's tribunal on U.S.-Brazil trade, fin. and banking rels. Inter-Am. Comml. Arbitration Commn., Washington; chmn. nat. adv. com. U.S.-Mid. East rels. U.S. Mid. East Policy Coun., U.S. State Dept., Washington, 1989—; mem. Pres. Bush's Adv. Commn. on Econ. and Public Policy Priorities, Washington, 1989; mem. conf. bd. Mid. East Policy Coun., U.S. State Dept., Washington, 1994—. Recipient Cmty. Svc. honors Mayor Dianne Feinstein, San Francisco, 1987, Leadership awards St. Ignatius Coll. Prep., 1984, Calif.'s Gold State award, 1990, AU-ABA Achievement award, 1990; named Civic Leader of Yr., Nat. Trust for Hist. Preservation, 1988, 89; named to Presdl. Order of Merit, 1991; recipient Internat. Leader of Achievement award Internat. Biographical Ctr., Cambridge, Eng., 1994-95, named Internat. Man of Yr., IBC and Brit. Fgn. Ministry. Mem. ATLA, Internat. Bar Assn. (various coms., internat. litigation, taxation, labor issue), Am. Arbitration Assn. (panelist), Am. Fgn. Law Assn. (various coms.), Am. Soc. Ch. History, Am. Inst. Archaeology (Boston), Pontifical Inst. Medieval Studies (Toronto, Can.), Am. Hist. Assn., Am. Philol. Assn., Inst. European Law, Medieval Acad. Am., U.S. Supreme Ct. Hist. Soc., J Canon Law Soc. U.S., Nat. Planning Assn., Nat. Assn. Scholars (Eminent Scholar of Yr. 1993), Netherlands Arbitration Inst. (mem. Gen. Panels of Arbitrators, mem. Permanent Ct. Arbitration), Calif. Coun. Internat. Trade (GATT com., tax com., legis. com.), Practicing Law Inst., Am. Fgn. Law Assn. (mem. editl. bd Groups on Rsch. Jour. for Legal systems of Africa, Mid. East, Latin Am., EEC and Soviet Union), U.S.-China Bus. Coun. (export com., GATT com., banking and fin. com., import com.), Bay Area Coun. (corp. mem.), Nat. Acad. Conciliators (Spl. award), Internat. Bar (mem. U.S. Group on Model on Insolvency Corp. Acts), Ctr. Internat. Comml. Arbitration, Comml. Club (various positions), Am. Soc. Internat. Law, Washington Fgn. Law Soc., Asia-Pacific Lawyers Assn., Soc. Profls. in Dispute Resolution, British Inst. Internat. and Comparative Law, Internat. Law Assn. (U.S. br.), Commercial Bar Assn. of United Kingdom (London), Inter-Pacific Bar Assn. (Tokyo; mem. arbitration intellectual property, consitutional taxation, labor, legal groups), Inst. European Law Faculty of Laws (United Kingdom), Urban Land Inst. Internat., Mid. East Inst. (Am.-Arab Affairs Coun.), Inter-Am. Bar Assn., 1987—, Calif. Trial Lawyers Assn., Ctr. Reformation Rsch. (co-chmn. Calif. State Com. on U.S.-Mid. East Econ. and Polit. Rels.), Am. Com. on U.S.-Japan Rels., Japan Soc. No. Calif., Pan-Am. Assn. San Francisco, Soc. Indsl./Office Realtors, Assn. Entertainment Lawyers London, Royal Chartered Inst. Arbitrators (London), Soc. Indsl. and Office Realtors, Urban Land Inst., San Francisco Realtors Assn., Calif. Realtors Assn., Coun. Fgn. Rels., Chgo. Coun. Fgn. Rels., Conf. Bd., San Francisco Urban and Planning Assn., U.S. Trade Facilitation Coun., Asia Soc., Am. Petroleum Inst., Internat. Platform Assn., San Francisco C. of C. (bus. policy com., pub. policy com., co-chmn. congl. issues study group), Am. Inst. Diplomacy, Overseas Devel. Coun. (Mid. East, Russian Republics, Latin Am. studies group), Internat. Vis. Ctr. (adv. bd.), Fin. Execs. Inst., Nat. Assn. Corp. Dirs., Heritage Found. (bd. dirs.), Archaeological Inst. Am. (fellow coun. near east studies, Egyptology), Nat. Assn. Indsl. and Office Properties, Pres. Club, Nat. Assn. Bus. Economists, Villa Taverna Club, Palm Beach Yacht Club, Pebble Beach Tennis Club, Calif. Yacht Club, Commonwealth Club, City Club San Francisco, British Bankers Club, London, San Diego Track Club (registered athlete). Republican. Roman Catholic. Home: 501 Forest Ave Palo Alto CA 94301-2631 Office: 540 Jones St Ste 201 San Francisco CA 94102-2022

LYNDE, GARY GRAY, human resource manager; b. Jamestown, N.D., May 7, 1950; s. William Edward and Nancy Ellen (Gray) L.; m. Carol Jean O'Connor, June 10, 1972; children: Jennifer, Rebecca, Scott. BS, N.D. State U., 1972; MA, U. No. Colo., 1976. Instr. U.S. Army, Ft. Polk, La., 1972-74; co. commdr. U.S. Army, White Sands Missle Range, N.Mex., 1974-79; hdqtrs. commdr. U.S. Army, Germany, 1979-82; asst. prof. mil. sci. N.D. State U. and U.S. Army, Fargo, 1982-85; dir. tng. devel. N.D. State U. and U.S. Army, Ft. Rucker, Ala., 1986-88, v.p., human resources svcs., 1988-90; prof., dept. chmn. Cen. Wash. U. and U.S. Army, Ellensburg, 1990-94; prof., program coord. Ctrl. Wash. U., 1994-95, acting dean continuing edn., 1995—. Home: 208 S Lookout Mountain Dr Ellensburg WA 98926-9032

LYNDON, DONLYN, architect, educator; b. Detroit, Jan. 7, 1936; s. Maynard and Dorothea Katherine (Zentgrebe) L.; m. Alice Wingwall, Dec. 28, 1963; children: Andrew, Audrey, Laura. BA, Princeton U., 1957, MFA, 1959. Registered architect Calif., Oreg., Mass. Asst. prof. architecture U. Calif., Berkeley, 1960-64; assoc. Maynard Lyndon FAIA, L.A., 1960-62; ptnr. Moore, Lyndon, Turnbull, Whitaker (MLTW), Berkeley, 1962-65; pvt. practice Eugene, Oreg., 1965-78; head dept. architecture U. Oreg., Eugene, 1964-67; ptnr. Moore, Lyndon, Turnbull, Boston, 1967-71; prof. architecture MIT, Cambridge, 1967-78, head dept. architecture, 1967-75; prin. Lyndon Assocs., Cambridge, 1971-78; ptnr. Lyndon/Buchanan Assocs., Berkeley, Calif., 1978—; prof. architecture U. Calif., Berkeley, 1978—; chmn. panel design guidelines GSA fed. devel. projects NAS, 1990; coord. Mayor's Inst. City Design West, Berkeley, 1990—; resource person Mayor's Inst. City design, Charlottesville, Va., 1991, Midwest, Minn., 1989; chmn. panel design arts policy NEA, 1988-91, rev. panel state of arts, 1988-91; chmn. design com. The Sea Ranch, 1984-88; mem. design rev. com., Newton, Mass., 1972-75; bd. dirs. Internat. Lab. Architecture and Urban Design, Italy, 1977—, Kronos Performing Arts Assn., 1987—. Author: The City Observed: Boston, 1982, The Place of Houses, 1974, (with Charles W. Moore) Chambers for a Memory Palace, 1994; editor: Places, MIT Press, 1982-89, Places, Design Hist. Found., 1989—; contbr. articles to profl. jours.; editor Jour. Archtl. Edn., 1967-69. Recipient Gov.'s Design award, Calif., 1967, First Design award Progressive Architecture, 1970, Honor awards, Boston Soc. Architects, 1977, First Design award Pacific Coast Builders Conf., 1983-84, citation Sunset Mag., 1983, honorable mention U. Calif. Santa Barbara Mus. competition, 1984, First place Harbor Bay Isle Neighborhood Four competition, 1985, Sunset Mag. Western Homes awards, 1985-86, Honor award Am. Wood Coun., 1991, First Place Miles/Cutter Pilot Plant competition, 1991; Fulbright scholar India, 1959-60; study grantee Graham Found., 1978. Fellow AIA (Honor award 1967, 80, 84, Excellence in Edn. award Calif. coun. 1991, urban design award of excellence 1992, Twenty-Five Yr. award 1992), Inst. for Urban Design; mem. St. Botolph Club (Boston). Democrat. Office: 2604 9th St Berkeley CA 94710-2518

LYNN, FREDRIC MICHAEL, sportscaster, former professional baseball player; b. Chgo., Feb. 3, 1952; s. Fredric Elwood and Marie Elizabeth (Marshall) L.; m. Natalie Brenda Cole, Oct. 7, 1986; children from previous marriage: Jason Andrew, Jennifer Andrea. Student, U. So. Calif., 1971-73. Center fielder Boston Red Sox, 1973-81, Calif. Angels, 1981-84, Balt. Orioles, 1985-88, Detroit Tigers, 1988-89, San Diego Padres, 1990; sportscaster ESPN, 1992—. Am. League batting champion, 1979; mem. Am. League All-Star Team, 1975-79, All-Star Team, 1975-83; named Most Valuable Player and Rookie of Yr., Am. League, 1975, Most Valuable Player in Play-Offs, Am. League, 1982, Most Valuable Player All Star Game, 1983, Center Fielder of 70's; recipient Rawlings Gold Glove award, 1975, 78, 79, 80, Seagrams Seven Crowns of Sports award, 1979. Mem. Major League Baseball Players Assn. Republican. Lutheran. Home: 7336 El Fuerte St Carlsbad CA 92009-6409*

LYNN, JONATHAN ADAM, director, writer, actor; b. Bath, England, Apr. 3, 1943; s. Robin and Ruth (Eban) L.; m. Rita Merkelis, Aug. 1, 1967; 1 child. MA, Pembroke Coll., 1964; MA (hon.), Sheffield U. Actor Cambridge Circus, N.Y.C., 1964, The Ed Sullivan Show, 1964; repertory actor Leicester, Edinburgh, Bristol Old Vic, London; artistic dir. Cambridge Theatre Co., 1977-81. Author: (novel) A Proper Man, 1976; co-author: (with Anthony Jay) The Complete Yes Minister, 1984, Yes, Prime Minister, the Diaries of the Rt. Hon. James Hacker, vol. I, 1986, vol. II, 1987; performed in: (plays) Green Julia, 1965, Fiddler on the Roof, 1967-68, Blue Comedy, 1968, The Comedy of the Changing Years, 1969, When We are Married, 1970, (TV movies) Barmitzvah Boy, 1975, The Knowledge, 1979, Outside Edge, 1982, Diana, 1984; dir.: (London) The Plotters of Cabbage Patch Corner, 1970, The Glass Managerie, 1977, The Gingerbread Man, 1977, 78, The Unvarnished Truth, 1978, The Matchmaker, 1978, Songbook, 1979 (SWET award 1979), Tonight at 8:30, 1981, Arms and the Man, 1981, Pass the Butler, 1982, Loot, 1984, A Little Hotel on the Side, 1984, Jacobowski and the Colonel, 1986, Three Men on a Horse, 1987 (Olivier award), RSC: Anna Christie, 1980, (Broadway) The Moony Shapiro Songbook, 1981, (short film) Mick's People, 1982; TV scriptwriter situation comedies, including: My Brother's Keeper, 1974, 75 (also co-starred), Yes, Minister (also radio scripts), 1980, 81, 82, (Pye TV Writers award 1981), Yes, Prime Minister, 1986, 87 (Pye TV Writers award 1986, ACE award 1988); film scriptwriter: The Internecine Project, 1974; film scriptwriter and dir.: Clue, 1986, Nuns on the Run, 1990, My Cousin Vinny, 1991. Recipient award Broadcasting Press Guild, 1980, 86, Writer's award BAFTA, 1987,. Home: 29 Etheldene Ave, London N 10, England Office: ICM 8942 Wilshire Blvd Beverly Hills CA 90211-1934 also: Peters Fraser & Dunlop, The Chambers Lots Rd 5th fl, London SW10 0XF, England also: c/o Barry Burnett Orgn, Princess House 190 Piccadilly Ste 409, London W1 EN, England

LYNN, KATHERINE LYN, engineer, chemist; b. Nagoya, Japan, June 25, 1954; (parents Am. citizens); d. Jimmie Frank and Barbara Sue (Whiteside) Sutton; m. Richard Shelly Lynn, Feb. 28, 1981. BS in Chemistry cum laude, Calif. State U., Fullerton, 1979. Technician U.S. Borax Corp., Anaheim, Calif., 1974-79; chemist Armstrong World Industries, Southgate, Calif., 1979-82; project engr. Hydril Co., Whittier, Calif., 1982-84; project mgr. So. Calif. Gas Co., L.A., 1984—. Patentee fluorspar flotation. Bd. dirs. East Side Christian Ch., 1987-89. Mem. So. Calif. Thermal Analysis Group (chair 1988, sec. 1985-87), Soc. Plastic Engrs., Am. Soc. for Quality Control, Am. Chem. Soc., Sierra Club. Mem. Christian Ch. Home: 5120 Faust Ave Lakewood CA 90713-1924 Office: So Calif Gas Co Box 3249 Terminal Annex ML 24EØ Los Angeles CA 90051

LYNN, RICHARD JOHN, Chinese language and literature educator; b. Binghamton, N.Y., June 28, 1940; s. Joseph Richard Lynn and Margaret Krutulis; m. Rosie Lucia Chu, Apr. 25, 1964 (div. Sept. 1979); children: Anne Margaret, Joseph Paul; m. Anne Mihelich Knight, Jun. 12, 1994; stepchildren: Benjamin, Daniel. BA in Art and Archaeology magna cum laude, Princeton U., 1962, postgrad., 1962-63; MA in Chinese Lit. and History, U. Wash., 1966; postgrad., U. Chgo., 1966-67; PhD in Asian Langs., Stanford U., 1971. Lectr. dept. Asian langs. and lits. U. Auckland, New Zealand, 1970-72; asst. prof. Chinese and comparative lit. U. Mass., Amherst, 1972-75, Ind. U., Bloomington, 1975-77; sr. lectr., head dept. Chinese Macquarie U., Sydney, Australia, 1977-80; dir. Corp. Asian Lang. Tng., Palo Alto, Calif., 1983—; prof., chair Dept. East Asian Studies U. Alberta, Edmonton, Can., 1993—; vis. scholar dept. Asian langs. Stanford (Calif.) U., 1980-81, 86-92; vis. asst. prof. U. B.C., Vancouver, 1981-82; vis. lectr. Chinese lang. and lit. U. Calif., Santa Barbara, 1983; cons., data base editor Rsch. Librs. Group, Stanford, 1983, 84, 87, 88; vis. prof. Chinese lang. and lit. U. Calif., Berkeley, 1987-88, 1988-89; program officer, humanities adminstr. NEH, Washington, 1992-93. Author: Chinese Literature: A Draft Bibliography in Western European Languages, 1980, Kuan Yun-shih, 1980, Guide to Chinese Poetry and Drama, 1984, The Classic of Changes: A New Translation of the I Ching as Interpreted by Wang Bi, 1994; editor: Language-Paradox-Poetics: A Chinese Perspective, 1988; contbr. articles and revs. to profl. jours., chpts. to books. Nat. Def. Fgn. Langs. fellow, 1962-63, 63-64, 66-67, 71; Rsch. Tng. fellow Kyoto U., Humanistic Scis. Rsch. Ctr., 1969; Fgn. Area fellow Ford Found., 1969; Am. Coun. Learned Socs. fellow, 1980-81; NEH fellow, 1986; Princeton Alumni scholar, 1958-62. Mem. Assn. Asian Studies. Democrat. Home: 9239-118 St, Edmonton, AB Canada T6G 1T8 Office: U Alberta Dept East Asian Studies, 400 Arts Bldg, Edmonton, AB Canada T6G 2E6

LYON, CAROLYN BARTEL, civic worker; b. Richmond, Ind., Mar. 28, 1908; d. Frederick John and Cora Caroline (Eggemeyer) Bartel; m. E. Wilson Lyon, Aug. 26, 1933 (dec.); children: Elizabeth Lyon Webb, John Wilson. BA, Wellesley Coll., 1928; MA, U. Chgo., 1930; LHD (hon.), Pomona Coll., 1974. Editorial asst. U. Chgo. Press, 1930-33. Alumna trustee Wellesley Coll., 1958-65; bd. trustees United Bd. for Christian Higher Edn. in Asia, N.Y.C., 1966-83; mem. women's coun. KCET Pub. TV, L.A., 1965—; active LWV, Claremont, Calif., 1941—, bd. dirs., 1945-50; pres. Foothill Philharmonic Com., L.A. Philharmonic, 1970-72. Mem. UN Assn. U.S. Congregationalist. Home: 900 E Harrison Ave Pomona CA 91767

LYON, IRVING, biochemist, researcher, consultant; b. L.A., May 10, 1921; s. Charles and Belle (Kvitky) L.; m. Harriette Goodman, Oct. 16, 1948; children: David, Charles, Lawrence. AB in Zoology, UCLA, 1942, MA in Physiology, 1949; postgrad., U. So. Calif., 1946-47; PhD in Physiology, U. Calif., Berkeley, 1952. Rsch. gen. lab. asst. U. Calif., Berkeley, 1949-52; rsch. biochemist med. dept. The Toni Co., Chgo., 1954-58; asst. prof. biol. chemistry U. Ill. Coll. Medicine, Chgo., 1958-62; assoc. prof. biochemistry The Chgo. Med. Sch., 1962-67; prof. biology Bennington (Vt.) Coll., 1967-72; spl. cons. State Energy Resources Conservation & Devel. Commn., L.A., 1975; cons. environ. health and nutrition L.A., 1975—; asst. rsch. physiologist UCLA Med. Sch., 1979-89; rsch. biochemist U.S. V.A. Wadsworth Hosp. Ctr., L.A., 1979-89; cons. New England Coalition vs. Nuclear Pollution, Bennington and Brattleboro, Vt., 1968-72, Another Mother for Peace, Beverly Hills, Calif., 1974-79, Psychemedics Corp., Santa Monica, Calif., 1988-89; invited lectr. various univs. and rsch. insts. Contbr. articles to profl. jours.; patentee in field. Capt. U.S. Army, 1942-46. Fellow Rockefeller Found., 1952-54. Fellow AAAS; mem. Am. Physiol. Soc., N.Y. Acad. Scis., Sigma Xi (pres. 1967-68). Home and Office: Unit A 708 Grant St Santa Monica CA 90405-1221

LYON, JAMES KARL, German language educator; b. Rotterdam, Holland, Feb. 17, 1934; came to U.S., 1937; s. T. Edgar and Hermana (Forsberg) L.; m. Dorothy Ann Burton, Dec. 22, 1959; children: James, John, Elizabeth, Sarah, Christina, Rebecca, Matthew, Melissa. BA, U. Utah, 1958, MA, 1959; PhD, Harvard U., 1963. Instr. German Harvard U., Cambridge, Mass., 1962-63, asst. prof., 1966-71; assoc. prof. U. Fla., Gainesville, 1971-74; prof. U. Calif. San Diego, La Jolla, 1974-94, provost Fifth Coll., 1987-94; prof. dept. Germanic and Slavic langs. Brigham Young U., Provo, Utah, 1994—; vis. prof. U. Augsburg, Germany, 1993. Author: Konkordanz zur Lyrik Gottfried Benns, 1971, Bertolt Brecht and Rudyard Kipling, 1975, Brecht's American Cicerone, 1978, Bertolt Brecht in America, 1980, Brecht in den USA, 1994. Capt. M.I., U.S. Army, 1963-66. NEH fellow, 1970, Guggenheim Found. fellow, 1974; Ford Found. grantee, 1988, 91. Mem. MLA, Am. Assn. Tchrs. German, Internat. Brecht. Soc., Phi Beta Kappa. Democrat. Mormon. Office: BYU Dept Germanic & Slavic Langs 4094 Jesse Knight Human Bld Provo UT 84602-6120

LYON, JEAN COZAD, family nurse practitioner, educator; b. San Francisco, Mar. 6, 1952; d. Charles Earle and Phoebe (LaMunyan) Cozad; m. Robert L. Lyon, Oct. 23, 1976. RN, Sacred Heart Sch. Nursing, 1973; BA in Health Edn., U. Wash., 1975; MS in Health Edn., San Francisco State U., 1980; BSN, Calif. State U., Long Beach, 1984; MSN, San Jose State U., 1986; PhD in Nursing, U. Calif., San Francisco, 1991; family nurse practitioner cert., Sonoma State U., 1994. RN, Calif.; cert. pub. health nurse; cert. clin. nurse specialist, family nurse practitioner, cmty. health nurse ANA. Staff nurse intensive care nursery Washoe Med. Ctr., Reno, 1976; staff nurse, charge nurse cardiopulmonary unit Presbyn. Hosp. Pacific Med. Ctr., San Francisco, 1976-78; staff nurse coronary care unit and emergency dept. Mt. Diablo Hosp. and Med. Ctr., Concord, Calif., 1978-79; clin. instr. nursing edn. dept. Herrick Hosp. and Health Ctr., Berkeley, Calif., 1979-80; asst. DON Peralta Hosp., Oakland, Calif., 1980-84; dir. edn. Hosp. Consortium of San Mateo County, 1984-86; dir. nursing systems and staff devel. Valley Meml. Hosp., Livermore, Calif., 1986-87; dir. edn. Valley Meml. Hosp., Livermore, 1987-90; asst. prof. Samuel Merritt Coll., Oakland, 1990-92, U. Nev., Reno, 1992—; part time faculty statewide nursing program Calif. State U., Dominguez Hills, Calif., 1987—; per diem staff nurse, IV therapy nurse, relief liaison nurse home health care dept. Mt. Diablo Hosp. Med. Ctr., 1988-89; per diem home health nurse Kaiser Martinez Home Health Dept., 1990-94; rsch. coord. Care Continuation Rsch. Project, Kaiser Martinez Med. Ctr., 1991-94; presenter in field. Contbr. articles to profl. jours. Mem. child health improvement task force Hoover Elem. Sch. Coalition, Oakland, 1990-92; mem. profl. adv. bd. Contra Costa County Home Health Agy., 1990-93; mem. State of Nev. Primary Care Com., 1992—. Recipient Outstanding Achievement award Hosp. Consortium of San Mateo County, 1986, scholarship Calif. Soc. for Nursing Svc. Adminstrs., 1988. Mem. APHA, AAUW, Assn. Cmty. Health Nursing Educators (western states rep.), Calif. Pub. Health Assn., Bay Area Soc. for Healthcare Edn. and Tng. (treas. 1984, 85, award of appreciation 1984, 85), Nev. Nurses Assn. (sec.), U. Calif. San Francisco Alumni Assn., Sigma Theta Tau (Nu Iota and Alpha Gamma chpt., Linda Lee Miller scholarship 1986, Linda Lee Miller rsch. award 1991). Democrat. Office: Univ Nev Reno Orvis Sch Nursing # 134 Reno NV 89557-0052

LYON, RICHARD, mayor, retired naval officer; b. Pasadena, Calif., July 14, 1923; s. Norman Morais and Ruth (Hollis) L.; m. Cynthia Gisslin, Aug. 8, 1975; children—Patricia, Michael, Sean; children by previous marriage—Mary, Edward, Sally, Kathryn, Patrick (dec.), Susan. B.E., Yale U., 1944; M.B.A., Stanford U., 1953. Commd. ensign USN, 1944; advanced through grades to rear adm. SEAL, 1974; served in Pacific and China, World War II; with Underwater Demolition Team Korea; recalled to active duty as dep. chief Naval Res. New Orleans, 1978-81; mayor City of Oceanside, Calif., 1992; mem. Chief Naval Ops. Res. Affairs Adv. Bd., 1978-81; exec. v.p. Nat. Assn. Employee Benefits, Newport Beach, Calif., 1981-90; mem. Bd. Control, U.S. Naval Inst., 1978-81; pres. Civil Svc. Commn., San Diego County, 1990, Oceanside Unified Sch. Bd., 1991. Pres. bd. trustees Children's Hosp. Orange County, 1965, 72. Decorated Legion of Merit. Mem. Nat. Assn. Securities Dealers (registered prin.), Newport Harbor Yacht Club, Rotary Club (Anaheim, Calif. pres. 1966). Republican. Episcopalian. Home: 4464 Inverness Dr Oceanside CA 92057-5052

LYONS, CHERIE ANN, educational administrator, author; b. Denver, Dec. 15, 1948; d. Clair Leroy and Mary Margaret (Benner) Case; m. David Greer Lyons, Aug. 22, 1970; children: Michael Greer, Andrea Christine. BS, U. Colo., 1971, MA, 1975, PhD, 1992. Prof. tchr. cert., adminstr. cert. Colo. Dept. Edn. Tchr. English, Cherry Creek Schs., 1971-76; tchr. English, health edn. Jefferson County Schs., Lakewood, Colo., 1971-76, curriculum writer, 1975-78, project dir. career edn., 1976-81, staff devel. specialist, 1981-87, jr. high sch. principal, 1987-88, coord. prevention programs, 1988-90; exec. dir., dir. grants devel. Jefferson Found., 1990—; cons. Region VII Tng. Ctr., U.S. Dept. Edn., Ctr. Substance Abuse Prevention; dir. Sch. Team Approach to Substance Abuse Prevention, Jefferson County. Coord. Jefferson County Prevention Task Force; exec. dir. of rsch. and resource devel. Jefferson County Schs., 1995; prof. ednl. adminstrn. U. Colo., Denver, 1993; Mem. Am. Assn. Sch. Adminstrs., Colo. Assn. Sch. Execs., Colo Assn. Non-Profit Orgn., Assn. Supervision and Curriculum Devel., Nat. Soc. for Study of Edn., Phi Delta Kappa. Democrat. Author: The Writing Process: A Program of Composition and Applied Grammar, Book 12, 1982. Home: 7584 Taft Ct Arvada CO 80005-3294 Office: Jefferson County Schs 1829 Denver West Dr Bldg 27 Golden CO 80401-3146

LYONS, JANET PEPLOW, career advisor; b. Santa Monica, Calif., Nov. 9, 1951; d. William George and Ava Lucille (Peacock) Peplow; m. Michael Simon Lyons, Aug. 1978 (div. Jan. 1994); children: Carolyn Elizabeth, Emily Christine. BA in Polit. Sci., U. Calif., Santa Barbara, 1974; MBA, Utah State U., Logan, 1980. Cost analyst Thiokol Corp. (formerly Morton-Thiokol), Brigham City, Utah, 1983-84, info. ctr. cons., 1984-85, data systems analyst, 1987-90; instr. Coll. Bus., Utah State U., Logan, 1980-82, 86, 92; asst. dir./advisor career svcs. and coop. edn. Utah State U., Logan, 1992—. Cookie chair Girl Scouts U.S., Logan, 1992, 93; room mother PTA, Logan, 1992, 93. Mem. We. Coll. Placement Assn., Phi Kappa Phi, Beta Gamma Sigma. Democrat. Office: Utah State U Career Svcs Logan UT 84322-4305

LYONS, PAUL M., mechanical engineer; b. Honolulu, June 22, 1963. BS in Physics, U. Hawaii, 1986; MS in Mech. Engring., U. Calif. San Diego, 1988. Sr. engr. Gen. Dynamics, Ontario, Calif., 1989-92; sr. engr. Hughes Missiles Systems Co., Tucson, 1992—. Office: Hughes Missile Systems Co Bldg 840 Nogales Hwy Tucson AZ 85734-1337

LYONS, RICHARD KENT, economics educator; b. Palo Alto, Calif., Feb. 10, 1961; s. J. Richard and Ida (Primavera) L.; m. Barrie Ann Fiske, 1992. BS in Bus. with highest honors, U. Calif., Berkeley, 1982; PhD, MIT, 1987. Rsch. analyst SRI Internat., Menlo Park, Calif., 1983-84; summer intern Orgn. for Econ. Cooperation & Devel., Paris, 1985, Bd. Govs., Fed. Res. System, Washington, 1986; asst. prof. Columbia U., N.Y.C., 1987-91; assoc. prof., 1991-93; asst. prof. U. Calif., Berkeley, 1993—; faculty rsch. fellow Nat. Bur. Econ. Rsch., Cambridge, Mass., 1989—. Assoc. editor Jour. Internat. Fin. Markets, Insts. & Money, Carbondale, Ill, 1989—; contbr. articles to profl. jours. NSF grad. fellow, 1984. Mem. Am. Econ. Assn., Coun. on Fgn. Rels., Phi Beta Kappa, Beta Gamma Sigma, Sigma Alpha Epsilon. Democrat. Office: U Calif 350 Barrows Hall Berkeley CA 94720

LYONS, TERRENCE ALLAN, merchant banking, investment company executive; b. Grande Prairie, Alta., Can., Aug. 1, 1949; s. Allan Lynnwood and Mildred Helen (Smith) L. B.Applied Sci., U. B.C., 1972; MBA, U. Western Ont., 1974. Registered profl. engr., B.C. Gen. mgr. Southwestern Drug Co., Vancouver, B.C., Can., 1975-76; mgr. planning Versatile Corp., Vancouver, 1976-83, asst. v.p., 1983-86, v.p., dir., 1986—; bd. dir. BRL Enterprises, Inc., 1987—, Morgan Fin. Corp.; pres., chief exec. officer FT Capital Ltd., 1990—; bd. dirs. Westbury Can. Life Ins.; pres., dir. B.C. Pacific Capital Corp., 1986—; vice chmn. Westmin Resources Ltd. Author articles on mfg. tech. Office: BC Pacific Capital Corp Royal Ctr, 1632-1055 W Georgia St, Vancouver, BC Canada V6E 3R5

LYOU, KEITH WEEKS (KAY LYOU), editor; b. Los Angeles, Aug. 2, 1930; d. Howard Keith Weeks and Ruth Manson (Day) Wood; m. Joseph Lyou, Mar. 26, 1955 (div. 1972); children: Tracy Ann, Joseph Keith. BS, Lindenwood Coll., 1977, MA, 1979. Cert. community coll. instr., Calif. Editorial asst. Annals of Biomed. Engring., Culver City, Calif., 1971-76; exec. asst. Biomed. Engring. Soc., Culver City, 1974-81; editor Inkslingers, Culver City, 1974—; editor biotechnology lab. UCLA, 1974-81, campus advisor theses and dissertations , 1983-86; exec. asst. Biomed. Engring. Soc., Culver City, 1974-81; instr. adult sch. Culver City Unified Sch. Dist., 1979-81. Mng. editor Am. Intra-Ocular Implant Soc. Jour., Santa Monica, 1982-83. Trustee Culver City Bd. Edn., 1981-89, pres. bd., 1987; counselor Adv. Ctr. for Edn. and Career Counseling, Santa Monica, Calif., 1981-82; mem. project area com. Project and Redevel., Culver City, 1975—, vice chair 1975-77, 85, chair 1979-82; bd. dirs. Culver City Foster Children's Assn., 1981-90; mem. Culver City Coun. PTA (hon. svc. award 1988), sch. attendance rev. bd., Culver City/Beverly Hills Sch. Dists., 1989—, school-age parent and infant devel. adv. com., 1989—, strategic planning com, 1989—; mem. Culver City Youth Health Ctr. Adv. Com., 1986—, Pepperdine U. Cmty. Adv. Com. Tchr. Edn., 1989—; vice chair gen. adv. com. revision of Culver City gen. plan, 1991—. Recipient Citizen Recognition award Culver City C. of C., 1986, Cmty. Arch. (honorable Gwen Moore) 47th Dist. award, 1994, Women of Excellence award Culver City Youth Health Ctr., 1994. Mem. LWV, Bus. and Profl. Women, Biomed. Engring. Soc., Calif. Elected Women's Assn. for Edn. and Research, UCLA Grad. Students Assn. (outstanding adminstrv. award 1970). Democrat. Office: Inkslingers 10827 Arizona Ave Culver City CA 90232-3725

LYTHGOE, DENNIS LEO, newspaper columnist; b. Salt Lake City, Jan. 23, 1939; s. Leo Thomas and Lavinia (Mitchell) L.; m. Marti Lynn Sorensen, Aug. 27, 1965; children: Darrin James, Kelly, David Alan, Charles Edward, Spencer Brent. BA in History, U. Utah, 1964, MA in History, 1966, PhD in History, 1969. Cert. secondary sch. tchr., Utah. Asst. prof. history Bridgewater (Mass.) State Coll., 1969-72, assoc. prof., 1972-76, prof., 1976-89, chair dept. history, 1985-89; adj. prof. U. Utah, Salt Lake City, 1989—; columnist Deseret News, Salt Lake City, 1989—; mem. adv. bd. John F. Kennedy Presdl. Libr., Boston, 1983-89. Author: Let 'Em Holler: Biography of J. Bracken Lee, 1982, Marriage of Equals, 1985, The Sensitive Leader, 1986; mem. editl. bd. Jour. Mormon History, 1977-83, Dialogue Jour., 1976-82; contbr. articles to profl. jours., numerous articles to Mass. and Utah newspapers. Bishop Hingham (Mass.) ward LDS Ch., 1977-82, West Bridgewater (Mass.) ward, 1986-89. Recipient Gov.'s Media award for reporting on women State of Utah, 1991. Mem. Nat. Soc. Newspaper Columnists, Orgn. Am. Historians, Am. Hist. Assn. Democrat. Office: Deseret News PO Box 1257 30 E 1st St S Salt Lake City UT 84110

LYTLE, ROY DOUGLAS, manufacturing executive; b. Spangler, Pa., Sept. 11, 1948; s. John Stuart and Ruby Selinda (Dotts) L.; m. Daphne Christine Lytle, Sept. 28, 1974; 1 child, Bret Christopher. Student, Oreg. State U., 1974-76; AS in Electronics, Chemeketa C.C., 1977; BS in Mgmt. and Comm., Western Bapt. Coll., 1993. Cert. Prodn. and Inventory Mgmt. Electronics technician Tektronix, Inc., 1977-80, mfg. mgr., 1980-83, prodn. and inventory project mgr., 1983-84; mfg. mgr. Photon Kinetics, Salem, Oreg., 1984—. Bd. dirs. Salem Acad. With USAF, 1969-74. Republican. Baptist. Home: 8104 Skyline Rd S Salem OR 97306-9730

LYTTLE, MATTHEW HALDEMAN, chemist; b. Santa Barbara, Calif., July 8, 1953; s. Richard Bard and Jean May (Haldeman) L.; m. Vana Gates Smith, June 25, 1988; children: Lonicera Gates Lyttle, Poppy Chanel Lyttle. BS in Chemistry, U. Calif., Berkeley, 1979, PhD in Chemistry, 1993. Rsch. chemist Biosearch, San Rafael, Calif., 1982-91; sr. scientist Terrapin Techs., South San Francisco, Calif., 1991-93; dir. organic chemistry Terrapin Techs., South San Francisco, 1993—; cons. Millipore Corp., Bedford, Mass., 1991-92. Contbr. articles to profl. jours. Patentee in field. Mem. Am. Chem. Soc. Democrat. Home: 751 B St PO Box 1166 Point Reyes Station CA 94956 Office: Terrapin Techs 750 Gateway Blvd # H South San Francisco CA 94080-7020

MA, FENGCHOW CLARENCE, agricultural engineering consultant; b. Kaifeng, Honan, China, Sept. 4, 1919; came to U.S., 1972; s. Chao-Hsiang and Wen-Chieh (Yang) Ma; m. Fanny Luisa Corvera-Achá, Jan. 20, 1963; 1 child, Fernando. BS in Agr., Nat. Chekiang U., Maytan, Kweichow, China, 1942; postgrad., Iowa State U., 1945-46. Cert. profl. agronomist, Republic of China, 1944; registered profl. agrl. engr., Calif. Chief dept. ops. Agrl. Machinery Operation and Mgmt. Office, Shanghai, China, 1946-49; sr. farm machinery specialist Sino-Am. Joint Commn. on Rural Reconstrn., Taipei, Taiwan, Republic of China, 1950-62; agrl. engring. adviser in Bolivia, Peru, Chile, Ecuador, Liberia, Honduras, Grenada, Bangladesh FAO, Rome, 1962-80; consulting agrl. engr. to USAID projects in Guyana & Peru IRI Rsch. Inst., Inc., Stamford, Conn., 1981-82, 83, 85; chief adviser Com. Internat. Tech. Coop., Taipei, 1984-85; pres. FCM Assocs., Inc., 1962—; short consulting missions to Paraguay, Saudi Arabia, Indonesia, Malawi, Swaziland, Barbados, Dominica, Ivory Coast, Vietnam, Philippines and others. Author papers, studies; contbr. articles to profl. publs. Mem. Am. Soc. Agrl. Engrs. Home: 1004 Azalea Dr Sunnyvale CA 94086-6747 Office: PO Box 70096 Sunnyvale CA 94086-0096

MAAS, DONALD KENNETH, education educator, consultant; b. Orange, Calif., Jan. 14, 1944; s. Richard Kenneth and Mary McClelland (Goodner) M.; m. Cheryl Lynn Corley, Aug. 18, 1967; children: Nathaniel William, Erika Nicole, Lee Kenneth. BA, UCLA, 1966; MEd, SUNY, Buffalo, 1969, EdD, 1971. Cert. secondary and elem. tchr. Demonstration tchr. Fernald Sch., Westwood, Calif., 1966-67; substitute tchr. Buffalo City Schs., 1967-70; coord. EPIS SUNY, Buffalo, 1970-71; from asst. prof. to assoc. prof. U. Guam, Agana, 1971-76; from asst. prof. to prof. Calif. Polytech. U., San Luis Obispo, Calif., 1976—; coord. TRI-Teacher Edn. and Computers, San Luis Obispo, 1982-85. Author: Guamerican Heritage, 1976, Teaching in the Secondary School, 1992, Maintaining Instructional Effectiveness, 1993; author video tape series: Maintaining Teacher Effectiveness, 1990. Pres. San Luis Obispo County Reading Assn., 1978-79; mem. U.S. legis. com. Internat. Reading Assn., Newark, Del., 1982-85. Recipient Print Media award Internat. Reading Assn., 1980-82, Margaret Lynch Exemplary Svc. award Calif. Reading Assn., 1985. Mem. Phi Delta Kappa (life, Outstanding Educator 1986), Alpha Gamma Omega (pres. 1965-66). Home: 3158 Spring Ct San Luis Obispo CA 93401-6014 Office: Calif Polytech U Univ Ctr for Tchr Edn San Luis Obispo CA 93407

MAAS, JOAN LOUISE, training and development consultant; b. San Jose, Calif., Apr. 26, 1961; d. Elmer Alvin Maas and Betty Lu Rowe. BA, Whitman Coll., 1983; MA in Psychology, U.S. Internat. U. Asst. mgr. New Times Clothing Co., Costa Mesa, Calif., 1984-85; bus. analyst Dun and Bradstreet, Long Beach, Calif., 1985-86; intern McDonnell Douglas, Huntington Beach, Calif., 1986; training and personnel asst. Western Digital, Irvine, Calif., 1986-88; instrl. designer Toastmasters Internat., Rancho Santa Margarita, Calif., 1988-91; prin. Maas Tng. and Devel., Mission Viejo, Calif., 1991-92; staff cons. Richard Chang Assocs., Irvine, 1992; orgnl. devel. specialist Anaheim Meml. Hosp., 1992-95. Author Orangespiel newsletter, 1991. Mem. Orange County (Calif.) Young Reps., 1986—, South Orange County Young Reps., 1991. Mem. ASTD (sec. 1992, dir. spl. interest groups 1993, Orange County Merit award 1994), Orange County Nat. Soc. for Performance and Instrn., Toastmasters (v.p. edn. 1991). Home and Office: 4563 Carriage Hill Dr Santa Barbara CA 93110

MAAS, JOHN PAUL, veterinarian, researcher; b. Clinton, Okla., Jan. 13, 1947; s. Victor Herbert and Elsie (Dear) M.; m. Cathy Crowe, Dec. 27, 1968; children: John Travis, Nathan Hartley. BS, Calif. State U., Chico, 1969; DVM, U. Calif., Davis, 1973; MS, U. Mo., 1980. Diplomate Am. Coll. Vet. Nutrition, Am. Coll. Vet. Internal Medicine. Veterinarian in pvt. practice Cottonwood, Calif., 1973-78; prof. vet. medicine U. Idaho, Moscow, 1980-85, Oreg. State U., Corvallis, 1985-88; case supr. Calif. Vet. Diagnostic Lab. System, U. Calif., Davis, 1988-93; extension veterinarian U. Calif., Davis, 1993—. Contbr. numerous chpts. to books, articles to profl. jours. Rsch. grantee. Mem. AVMA, Am. Coll. Vet. Nutrition (pres. 1994-95), Am. Coll. Vet. Internal Medicine, Am. Acad. Vet. Nutrition, Calif. Vet. Med. Assn., others. Office: U Calif Sch Vet Medicine Vet Medicine Extension Davis CA 95616

MAAS, SALLY ANN, newspaper editor, journalist; b. Portage, Wis., Apr. 10, 1947; d. Franklin Arthur and Mabel Gladys (Engen) Maas; m. Robert A. Marshall, Aug. 3, 1973. BJ, U. Wis., 1969. Reporter, The Paper, Oshkosh, Wis., 1969-70; feature writer The Press, Binghamton, N.Y., 1970-71; feature writer The Press-Enterprise, Riverside, Calif., 1971-76, lifestyle editor, 1976-83, feature editor, 1983-85, asst. mng. editor features and art, 1985—. Recipient Outstanding Woman of Achievement award Bus. and Profl. Women's Club, 1981. Mem. Soc. Newspaper Design, Women in Communications, LWV, Sigma Delta Chi. Club: Twin Cities Press (past pres.). Home: 30001 Live Oak Canyon Rd Redlands CA 92373-7940 Office: The Press-Enterprise Co 3512 14th St Riverside CA 92501-3814

MAATSCH, DEBORAH JOAN, trust administrator, compliance officer, paralegal tax specialist; b. Lincoln, Nebr., Mar. 26, 1950; d. Leon F. Forst and Jarolyn J. Hoffman Forst Conrad; m. Gordon F. Maatsch, Mar. 14, 1969; children: Jason, Diana. BS, U. Nebr., 1976. Acct., supr. U.S. Civil Svc., Heidelberg, Ger., 1971-73; paralegal Mattson Rickets Davies et al, Lincoln, Nebr., 1976-87; tax cons. Lincoln and Denver, 1981—; pres. DGJD Inc.-Bleachers, 1993—; paralegal Wade Ash Woods & Hill, P.C., Denver, 1986-94; sr. trust adminstr. Investment Trust Co., Denver, 1994—; compliance officer Nelson, Benson and Zellmer, Inc., 1995—; mem. Denver Trust Officers Assocs., bus. adv. bd. Ponderosa H.S., 1994—; officer The "O" Streeters, Lincoln, 1984-87; spkr., coord. Nebr. Continuing Legal Edn. Seminars, 1976-86. Contbr. articles to profl. jours. Officer The Aurorians Synchronized Swim Team Parents Orgn., Rocky Mt. Spash Parents' Corp.; youth edn. staff Ave Maria Cath. Ch., Parker, Colo., 1990-91; vol., chmn. activities PTSA Ponderosa H.S. Mem. Doane Coll. Alumni Assn. (dir. 1989-93), Rocky Mt. Legal Assts. (dir., sect. chair 1990-94), Am. Soc. Women Accts. (officer, dir.), Nebr. Assn. Legal Assts. (officer, dir. 1976-87), Colo. Bar Assn. (computer probate sect.), Phi Chi Theta (treas. 1988-89). Office: Investment Trust Co 455 Sherman St Ste 180 Denver CO 80203-4400

MABIE, RUTH MARIE, realtor; b. Pueblo, Colo., Feb. 7; d. Newton Everett and Florence Ellen Allen; M.B.A., La Jolla U., 1980, Ph.D., 1981; m. Richard O. Mabie, Nov. 29, 1946; 1 son, Ward A. Mgr., LaMont Modeling Sch., San Diego, 1962; tchr. Am. Bus. Coll., San Diego, 1964-66; fashion modeling, 1960-72; owner, broker Ruth Mabie Realty, San Diego, 1972—; asst. v.p. Skil-Bilt, Inc., 1976—; dir. Mabie & Mintz, Inc. Mem. San Diego Assn. Realtors, Nat. Assn. Female Execs. Republican. Office: 2231 Camino Del Rio S Ste 302 San Diego CA 92108-3612

MABRY, MONTE DEL, geophysicist; b. Dunlap, Tenn., Apr. 18, 1958; s. John D. and Marjorie A. (Metz) M.; m. Jennifer Head, July 15, 1984; children: Laurel, Heather, Sarah, Solomon. BS in Geophysics, Kans. State U., Manhattan, 1980. Geophysicist ARCO Oil & Gas Co., Houston, 1981-85; sr. geophysicist ARCO Alaska, Anchorage, 1986-91, staff geophysicist, 1992—. Mem. Geophys. Soc. Alaska (pres. 1994-95), Am. Assn. Petroleum Geologists, Soc. Exploration Geophysicists, Aircraft Owners and Pilots Assn. Home: 11741 Pinto Cir Anchorage AK 99516-2316 Office: ARCO Alaska 700 G St Anchorage AK 99501-3439

MACALISTER, ROBERT STUART, oil company executive; b. L.A., May 22, 1924; s. Robert Stuart and Iris Grace (Doman) MacA.; m. Catherine Vera Willby, Nov. 15, 1947; children: Rodney James, Sara Marjorie Pfirrmann. Student, Brighton Coll., Sussex, Eng., 1945; BSME, Calif. Inst. Tech., 1947. Registered profl. engr., Tex. Petroleum engr. Shell Oil Co., 1947-56; mgmt. trainee Royal Dutch Shell, The Hague, Netherlands, 1956-57; with exec. staff, mgr. Shell Oil Co., U.S.A., 1957-68; v.p., ops. mgr. Occidental Petroleum Corp., Tripoli, Libya, 1968-71; mng. dir.various subs. London, 1971-76; mng. dir., pres. Occidental Internat. Oil, Inc., London, 1976-78; pres., chmn. bd. Can. Occidental Petroleum Ltd., Calgary Alberta, 1978-81; mng. dir. Australian Occidental Petroleum Ltd., Sydney, 1982-83, Hamilton Bros. Oil & Gas Ltd., London, 1983-86; petroleum cons. Camarillo, Calif., 1986—; exec. U.K. Offshore Operators, London, 1972-78, 83-86. Cubmaster Boy Scouts Am., Larchmont, N.Y., 1964-65, scoutmaster, Houston, 1965-68. Sgt. U.S. Army, 1944-45, ETO. Mem. Am. Assn. Petroleum Geologists, Soc. Petroleum Engrs.,Las Posas Country Club, Gold Coast Srs. Republican. Episcopalian. Home and Office: 78 Lopaco Ct Camarillo CA 93010-8846

MACALLER, NATASHA JEANNETTE, dancer; b. Santa Monica, Calif., Oct. 1, 1961; d. Allan Bruce and Sally Ann (Tupper) MacA. Student, U. Calif., Santa Barbara, 1980-82, Colo. Inst. Art, 1995—. Corps ballerina Koninkiijk Ballet Van Vlaaderen, Antwerp, Belgium, 1979, The Joffrey Ballet, N.Y.C., 1983, Ballet West, Salt Lake City, 1984-85; demi soloist ballerina The Boston Ballet, Boston, 1985-90. Appeared in Phantom of the Opera, N.Y.C., 1990, appeared as Meg in Phantom of the Opera, L.A., 1990-93. Mem. SAG, Am. Guild Musical Artists (Career Transition FOr Dances Scholarship, 1994-95), Actors Equity Assn. Anglican.

MACARTHUR, CAROL JEANNE, pediatric otolaryngology educator; b. Glendale, Calif., Aug. 23, 1957; d. Seth Gerald and Barbara Jeanne (Shaw) MacA.; m. Geoffrey Buncke, Dec. 14, 1990; 1 child, Keith Davis. BS, Occidental Coll., 1979; MD, UCLA, 1984. Diplomate Am. Bd. Otolaryngology. Intern U. Calif., Davis, 1984-85, resident in otolaryngology, 1985-90; fellow in pediatric otolaryngology Boston Children's Hosp., 1990-91; instr. dept. otolaryngology U. Calif.-Davis, Sacramento, 1989-90; clin. fellow in otology and laryngology Harvard U. Med. Sch., Boston, 1990-91; asst. prof., dir. pediatric otolaryngology U. Calif., Irvine, 1991—, asst. prof. dept. pediatrics, 1993-95, program dir. dept. otolaryngology-head and neck surgery, 1992-95. Recipient investigator devel. award Am. Acad. Facial Plastic and Reconstructive Surgery, 1993. Fellow ACS, Am. Acad. Pediatrics; mem. Assn. Women Surgeons, Soc. for Ear, Nose and Throat Advances in Children, Am. Cleft Palate Craniofacial Assn., Am. Acad. Otorhinolaryngology-Head and Neck Surgery, Alpha Omega Alpha. Office: U Calif Med Ctr 101 The City Dr S Bldg 25 Orange CA 92668-3201

MACARTHUR, JOHN REED, physician; b. Santa Barbara, Calif., Nov. 20, 1961; s. Allison Tainter and Virginia Lee (Reed) MacA. BA in Chemistry with distinction, U. Calif., Santa Barbara, 1984; MD, Georgetown U., 1991. Diplomate Am. Bd. Family Practice. Intern and resident family and community medicine U. Calif.-San Francisco/San Francisco Gen. Hosp., 1991-94; fellow health and human rights Harvard U., Cambridge, Mass., 1994—. Human rights researcher Physicians for Human Rights, primary health supr. Internat. Res. Com., Thailand-Burma Border, 1994—. Mem. Am. Acad. Family Practice, Physicians for Human Rights, Physicians for Social Responsibility. Home: 3036 Paseo Del Refugio Santa Barbara CA 93105-2809

MACAULEY, CHARLES CAMERON, media appraiser, consultant; b. Grand Rapids, Mich., Oct. 20, 1923; s. George William and Emma Ann (Hobart) M.; m. Marianne Shirley Johanson, June, 1951; children: Gavin Keith, Alison Jean. BA, Kenyon Coll., Gambier, Ohio, 1949; MS, U. Wis., 1958. Ptnr. Cameron-King Photographers, Gambier, 1946-49; film producer U. Wis., Madison, 1951-58; film producer U. Calif., Berkeley, 1959-63, dir. statewide media ctr., 1964-83; pres. CCM Assocs., El Cerrito, Calif., 1984—; prof. U. Wis., Calif., 1951-83; sr. founding cons. Media Appraisal Cons., El Cerrito, 1986—; instr. film seminar San Francisco Art Inst., 1959-60; awards juror numerous nat. and internat. film and video festivals, 1953—. West coast corr. The Appraiser; producer over 50 motion pictures; contbr. numerous articles, essays and fictional works to publs. With USN, 1943-46. NSF grantee, 1959-64, NEA grantee, 1974, 76, Maurice Falk Med. Fund grantee, 1970; recipient Gold Ribbon award Am. Film and Video Festival, 1991. Mem. Appraisers Assn. Am., Ednl. Film Libr. Assn. (pres. 1973-74), Am. Film and Video Assn. (life), Consortium Coll. and Univ. Media Ctrs. (life), Fossils, Inc., History of Photography Group, Square Riggers Club (historian 1989—, hon. 1989—). Office: CCM Assocs Studio A 731 Seaview Dr El Cerrito CA 94530-3311

MACAUSLAN, IAN JAMES, business development specialist; b. Portland, Maine, Nov. 19, 1961; s. Robert Cubie and Sally Anita (Mirick) MacA.; m. Germaine Annette Hoston, May 30, 1987. Student, Phillips Acad., Andover, Mass., 1980; BA, Johns Hopkins U., Balt., 1985; student, U. London, 1984; M in Pub. Policy, Harvard U., 1987. V.p. Access Informatique, Inc., Balt., 1988-92; internat. policy specialist Nat. Aeronautics and Space Adminstrn., Washington, 1987-92; dir. program devel. Grad. Sch. Internat. Rels. U. Calif., San Diego, 1992—; ptnr. Davis & MacAuslan, San Diego, 1993—; bus. cons. Connect-Russia-Am., Vladivostok, Russia, 1993—, Daiwa Securities, Tokyo, 1993—; participant Devel. Confs. on East-Ctrl. Europe, Inst. for East-West Studies, Prague, Czechoslovakia, 1991. Mem. UN Assn., N.Y.C., 1992—, World Affairs Coun., San Diego, 1992—, Balt., 1987-92. U.S. Presdl. Mgmt. intern, 1987-89; U.S.-USSR Young Leadership Conf. Am. Ctr. for Internat. Leadership, Moscow and Leningrad, USSR, 1990. Mem. Harvard Club of San Diego, World Trade Assn. Democrat. Episcopalian. Home: 8525 Foucaud Way San Diego CA 92129-4123 Office: University of California 9500 Gilman Dr La Jolla CA 92093-5003

MACBRIDE, THOMAS JAMISON, federal judge; b. Sacramento, Mar. 25, 1914; s. Frank and Lotta Kirtley (Little) MacB.; m. Martha Harrold, Nov. 7, 1947; children—Peter, Thomas Jamison, David, Laurie. A.B., U. Calif. at Berkeley, 1936, J.D., 1940. Bar: Calif. 1940. Dep. atty. gen. Calif., 1941-42; pvt. practice Sacramento, 1946-61; U.S. dist. judge Eastern Dist. Calif., Sacramento, 1961-67; chief judge Eastern Dist. Calif., 1967-79, sr. judge, 1979—; mem. U.S. Temporary Emergency Ct. Appeals, 1982-87; mem. Criminal Justice Act Com., U.S. Jud. Conf., 1969-88; mem. U.S. Jud. Conf., 1975-78; chmn. Criminal Justice Act Com. of U.S. Jud. Conf., 1979-88; mem. U.S. Fgn. Intelligence Surveillance Ct., 1979-80. Pres. Town Hall, Sacramento, 1952, N.E. area YMCA, 1960; mem. Calif. Legislature from Sacramento County, 1955-60 mem. Nat. Commn. on Reform Fed. Criminal Laws, 1967-71; bd. dirs. Sacramento YMCA; trustee U. Calif., San Francisco Found., 1982—; bd. dirs. Sacramento Regional Found., 1988—; founding dir. League to Save Lake Tahoe, 1965. Lt. USNR., 1942-46. Mem. ABA, U. Calif. Alumni Assn. (v.p. 1955, 60), Mason (33 deg., Shriner, Jester), Rotarian (pres. 1966-67), Sutter Club, Univ. (pres. 1951-52), Comstock (pres. 1975-76), Senator Outing (sec.-treas.), Kappa Sigma, Phi Delta Phi. Democrat. Office: US Dist Ct US Courthouse 650 Capitol Mall Sacramento CA 95814-4708

MACCALLUM, (EDYTHE) LORENE, pharmacist; b. Monte Vista, Colo., Nov. 29, 1928; d. Francis Whittier and Berniece Viola (Martin) Scott; m. David Robertson MacCallum, June 12, 1952; children: Suzanne Rae MacCallum Barslund and Roxanne Kay MacCallum Batezel (twins), Tracy Scott, Tamara Lee MacCallum Johnson, Shauna Marie MacCallum Bost. BS in Pharmacy U. Colo., 1950. Registered pharmacist, Colo. Pharmacist Presbyn. Hosp., Denver, 1950, Corner Pharmacy, Lamar, Colo., 1950-53; rsch. pharmacist Nat. Chlorophyll Co., Lamar, 1953; relief pharmacist, various stores, Delta, Colo., 1957-59, Farmington, N.Mex., 1960-62, 71-79, Aztec, N.Mex., 1971-79; mgr. Med. Arts Pharmacy, Farmington, 1966-67; cons. pharmacist Navajo Hosp., Brethren in Christ Mission, Farmington, 1967-77; sales agt. Norris Realty, Farmington, 1977-78; pharmacist, owner, mgr. Lorene's Pharmacy, Farmington, 1979-88; tax cons. H&R Block, Farmington, 1968; cons. Pub. Svc. Co., N.Mex. Intermediate Clinic, Planned Parenthood, Farmington; one of the first women registered pharmacist apptd. N.Mex. Bd. Pharm., 1982-92. Author numerous poems for mag. Advisor Order Rainbow for Girls, Farmington, 1975-78. Mem. Nat. Assn. Bds. Pharmacy (com. on internship tng., com. edn., sec., treas. dist. 8, mem. impaired pharmacists adv. com., chmn. impaired pharmacists program N.Mex., 1987—, mem. law enforcement legis. com., chmn. nominating com. 1992), Nat. Assn. Retail Druggists, N.Mex. Pharm. Assn. (mem. exec. coun. 1977-81), Order Eastern Star (Farmington). Methodist. Home and Office: 1301 Camino Sol Farmington NM 87401-8075

MACCAULEY, HUGH BOURNONVILLE, banker; b. Mt. Vernon, N.Y., Mar. 12, 1922; s. Morris Baker and Alma (Gardiner) MacC.; m. Rachael Gleaton, Aug. 30, 1943 (div. May 1980); m. Felice Cooper, Dec. 2, 1980. Student, Rutgers U., 1939-41, Tex. Christian U., 1948-50, U. Omaha, 1957-59. With 102nd Cavalry, Essex Troop N.J. Nat. Guard, 1940-42; commd. 2d lt. U.S. Army, 1943; advanced through grades to col. U.S. Army, USAF, Washington, 1943-73; v.p. Great Am. Securities, San Bernardino, Calif., 1979-94; chmn. bd. Desert Community Bank, Victorville, Calif., 1980—; account exec. Gorian Thornes, Inc., San Bernardino, Calif., 1995—. bd. dirs. Air Force Village West, 1986-88; chmn. bd. and CEO Gen. and Mrs. Curtis E. Lemay Found., 1987—. Decorated Air medal, Legion of Merit. Mem. Daedalian Soc., Rotary. Republican. Presbyterian. Home: 1630 Monroe St Riverside CA 92504-5514 Office: Gorian Thornes Inc 350 W 5th St Ste 103 San Bernardino CA 92401-1327

MACCLEAN, WALTER LEE, dentist; b. Sheridan, Wyo., July 10, 1935; s. Edward Satterlee and Eleanor Elizabeth (Weir) Mac.; m. Nancy Lee Strale, Sept. 4, 1965 (div. 1975); children: David Satterlee, Carrie Lynn. BS with honors, U. Wyo., 1957, postgrad., 1958; DMD, U. Oreg., Portland, 1962. Mil. dental adv. Korean Mil. Adv. Group, Wonju, 1962-63; chief dental svc. Dugway Chem. Testing Ctr., Utah, 1965-68; pvt. dental practice Cheyenne, Wyo., 1968-70; assoc. prof. Sheridan Coll., Wyo., 1970-76; staff dentist VA Hosp. Med. Ctr., Ft. Meade, S.D., 1976—; 1976-93, ret., 1993; cons., lectr. Health Edn. Program Svc., Ft. Meade, 1984-93. With U.S. Army 1962-68. Mem. ADA, Acad. Gen. Dentistry, Elks (Hardin, Mont.), Masons, Phi Mu Alpha. Episcopalian. Home: PO Box 450 Hardin MT 59034-0450

MACCONNELL, ROBERT MONTE, lawyer; b. Dallas, Oct. 18, 1941; s. Frank Montgomery and Helen Victoria (Sauer) MacC.; m. Mary Therese Marriott, Dec. 23, 1966; children: Monte M., Lara T., Michael G., Jacquelyn R. BA, U. Ill., 1963, JD, 1966. Bar: Idaho 1975, U.S. Supreme Ct. 1978, U.S. Ct. Appeals (9th cir.) 1978. Assoc. Arriola, Cushnie & Stevens, Agana, Guam, 1972-74; asst. atty. gen. Atty. Gen. Office, Boise, Idaho, 1974-75, dep. atty. gen., 1975-78; magistrate Boise County, Idaho City, Idaho, 1978-81; contract adminstr. Morrison Knudsen Internat., Inc., Barranquilla, Colombia, 1981-84; pvt. practice Boise, 1984-87; chief counsel Idaho Dept. Law Enforcement, Boise, 1987-90, dep. dir., 1990-95. Mem. La Leche League Internat. Legal Adv. Coun., Schaumberg, Ill., 1981—, Domestic Violence Roundtable, 1988—, Help Abuse Victims Through Edn. Now, Boise, 1994—, Prosecutors Domestic Violence Task Force, Boise, 1994—; instr. Police Officers Standards and Tng. Acad., Meridian, Idaho, 1988—; legal advisor Idaho Spl. Olympics, Boise, 1989—; pres. bd. Anger Control and Abuse Prevention Program, Boise, 1990—. Capt. USMCR, 1966-72, Vietnam. Recipient Svc. award Idaho Network to Stop Violence Against Women, 1990, Dist. Svc. award in Pub. Policy Leadership, Idaho Coun. on Domestic Violence, 1995. Mem. Internat. Assn. Chiefs of Police (vice chair legal office sect. 1989-90), Idaho Bar Assn. Roman Catholic.

MACCORKLE, EMMETT WALLACE, III, insurance agent; b. Portsmouth, Va., Feb. 10, 1942; s. Emmett Wallace and Nelda (Reymann) MacC.; m. Carol Britton, Dec. 27, 1964; children: Jeffrey W., Steven M. BA, Cornell U., 1964. CLU. Agt. Northwestern Mut. Life, San Francisco, 1967-72; dist. agt. Northwestern Mut. Life, San Mateo, 1972-80; pres. MacCorkle Ins. Svcs., San Mateo, 1980—. Mem. Cornell U. Coun., Ithaca, N.Y., 1986-89; mem. Bellarmine Coll. Prep. Bd. Regents, San Jose, Calif., 1988-91; mem. devel. com. Cartoon Art Mus., San Francisco, 1989-90. With USMC, 1964-67, Vietnam. Named Man of Yr., Peninsula Assn. Life Underwriters, San Mateo, 1980. Mem. Bohemian Club (San Francisco), Menlo Circus Club (Menlo Park, Calif.), Cornell Club No. Calif. (pres. 1974). Democrat. Home: 1060 Continental Dr Menlo Park CA 94025-6652 Office: MacCorkle Ins Svcs 1650 Borel Pl Ste 100 San Mateo CA 94402-3507

MACCRACKEN, GORDON STUART, columnist, wire editor; b. Roseburg, Oreg., July 28, 1954; s. Charles Gordon and Aileen Mary (Chamberlain) MacC.; m. Carol Sue Cutting, Aug. 23, 1975; children: Mark Andrew, Julia Anne. BS, U. Oreg., 1976. Reporter The Chronicle, Centralia, Wash., 1976-80; copy editor The Chronicle, Centralia, 1980-81, city editor, 1981-84, news editor, 1984-94, wire editor, 1994—, columnist, 1990—. Coach Centralia (Wash.) Youth Soccer, 1989-90, Centralia (Wash.) Little League Baseball, 1989-92. Recipient various journalism awards Soc. Profl. Journalists, 1983-93. Home: 502 S Oak St Centralia WA 98531-3928 Office: The Chronicle PO Box 580 321 N Pearl St Centralia WA 98531

MACCRACKEN, PETER JAMES, marketing executive, communications exec; b. Trieste, Italy, Dec. 27, 1952; came to U.S., 1956; s. James and Kirsten (Koch) MacC. BA summa cum laude, Albion Coll., 1975; MA, U. Calif., Santa Barbara, 1978. Asst. mgr. GranTree Furniture Rental, San Leandro, Calif., 1979-81; freelance writer San Diego, 1981-82; corp. editor Scripps Meml. Hosps., La Jolla, Calif., 1982-84; sr. v.p. Berkman & Daniels Mktg., San Diego, 1984-89; v.p. Stoorza, Zeigaus & Metzger, Inc., San Diego, 1989-90; pres. MacCracken & McGaugh, San Diego, 1990—. Contbr. over 500 articles, photographs to numerous publs. Recipient 30 bus. comm. awards. Mem. Pub. Rels. Soc. Am. (bd. dirs. 1992—, pres. elect San Diego chpt. 1995), Internat. Assn. Bus. Communicators (pres. San Diego chpt. 1985), Am. Inst. Wine & Food (bd. dirs. 1990—, sec. San Diego chpt. 1995), Phi Beta Kappa. Democrat. Office: 701 B St Ste 2200 San Diego CA 92101-8111

MACDONALD, ALAN HUGH, librarian, university administrator; b. Ottawa, Ont., Can., Mar. 3, 1943; s. Vincent C. and Hilda C. (Durney) MacD.; m. Elizabeth Whalen; children—Eric Paul Henry, Nigel Alan Christopher. B.A., Dalhousie U., Halifax N.S., 1963; B.L.S., U. Toronto, Ont., 1964. With Dalhousie U., 1964-78, law librarian, 1965-67, 69-71, asst. univ. librarian, 1970-72, health sci. librarian, 1972-78; lectr. Sch. Library Services, 1969-78; dir. info. svcs. U. Calgary, Alta., 1988—; dir. libraries U. Calgary, Alta., Can., 1979-92, univ. orator, 1989—; dir. U. Calgary Press, 1984-90; chmn. Alta. Library Network, 1981-89; librarian N.S. Barristers Soc., 1969-74; mem. adv. bd. Nat. Libr. Can., 1972-76, Health Scis. Resource Centre, Can. Inst. Sci. and Tech. Info., 1977-79; mem. Coun. of Prairie Univ. Librs., 1979-92, chair, 1984-85, 89, 91; Bassam lectr. U. Toronto Faculty Info. Studies, 1994. Mem. editorial bd. America: History and Life (ABC-CLIO), 1985-93. Pres. TELED Community Media Access Orgn., Halifax, N.S., 1972-74; mem. Minister's Com. on Univ. Affairs, Alta., 1979-83; bd. dirs. Alta. Found. for Can. Music Ctr., 1985-92; v.p. Can. Inst. for Hist. Microreprodn., 1990-94, treas., 1994—. Council Library Resources fellow, 1975; exec. fellow Univ. Microfilms Internat., 1986; recipient Disting. Acad. Librarian award Can. Assn. of Coll. and Univ. Libraries, 1988. Mem. Can. Libr. Assn. (treas. 1977-79, pres. 1980-81), Atlantic Provinces Libr. Assn. (pres. 1977-78), Libr. Assn. Alta. (v.p. 1988-89, Pres.'s award 1992), Can. Health Libr. Assn. (treas. 1977-79), Can. Assn. Law Librs., Australian Libr. and Info. Assn. (assoc. 1977), N.Z. Libr. Assn., Bibliog. Soc. Can., Foothills Libr. Assn., Can. Assn. Info. Sci. (pres. 1979-80), Can. Assn. Rsch. Librs. (bd. dirs. 1981-86, v.p. 1985-86), Calgary Free-Net Soc. (mem. steering com. 1994—, v.p. 1995—). Office: U Calgary, 2500 University Dr NW A100, Calgary, AB Canada T2N 1N4

MACDONALD, DENNIS RONALD, theology educator; b. Chgo., July 1, 1946; s. James Ronald and Mildred (Friend) MacD.; m. Diane Louise Prosser, June 9, 1973; children: Katya Louise, Julian Peter. AB, Bob Jones U., 1968; MDiv McCormick Theol. Sem., Chgo., 1974; PhD, Harvard U., 1978. Asst. prof. Goshen Coll. (Ind.), 1977-80; asst. prof. N.T., Iliff Sch. Theology, Denver, 1980-83, assoc. prof., 1983-90, prof., 1990—; vis. prof. Harvard Div. Sch., 1985-86, Union Theol. Sem., 1991. Author: The Legend and The Apostle, 1983, Apocryphal Acts of Apostles, 1986, There Is No Male and Female, 1986, The Acts of Andrew and The Acts of Andrew and Matthias, 1990, Christianizing Homer, 1994; also articles in religious jours. Clarence G. Campbell fellow Harvard U., 1975-76; grantee Ind. Council on Humanities, 1978; Young scholar Assn. Theol. Schs., 1983; recipient summer stipend NEH, 1983. Mem. Soc. Bibl. Lit. (v.p. Rocky Mountain region 1983-84, pres. 1984-85). Democrat. Congregationalist. Office: Iliff Sch Theology 2201 S University Blvd Denver CO 80210-4707

MACDONALD, DON, psychotherapist, educator; b. Dowagiac, Mich., Mar. 24, 1950. BA, U. Tex., 1972; MS, Ind. U., 1973; PhD, Mich. State U., 1984. cert. mental health counselor, Wash. Tchr. aide Migrant Edn. Program, Sister Lakes, Mich., 1971-72; resident asst. Ind. U., Bloomington, Ind., 1973; resident dir. Seattle Pacific U., 1973-76; elem. tchr. Northshore Sch. Dist., Kenmore, Wash., 1975-76; grad. asst. Mich. State U., East Lansing, 1976-79; staff psychologist House of Commons, Lansing, Mich., 1977-79; psychology intern Psychological Evaluation & Treatment Ctr., East Lansing, 1977-79; prof. Seattle Pacific U., 1980—; mem. sch. counselor cert. bd. Supt. Pub. Instrn., Olympia, Wash., 1980-87; mem. bd. adv. two pvt. practices, Seattle, 1981-86; editl. cons. Brooks/Cole, Longman, Prentice-Hall, Zondorvan, 1985-94; mem. mental health cert. bd. Dept. Health, Olympia, 1988-93. Co-author: (book) Social and Psychological Foundations of Education, 1986; contbr. articles to profl. jours. Serving elder North Seattle Alliance Ch., 1992-94. Recipient Mental Health Counselors award Wash. Assoc. Mental Health Counselors, 1988; Faculty Rsch. grantee Seattle Pacific U., 1986, 89, Academic Renewal grantee, 1984. Mem. APA, Wash. Counseling Assn., Wash. State Assn. Counselor Educators and Suprs. (pres. 1980-94). Office: Family Psychology Seattle Pacific Univ Seattle WA 98119

MACDONALD, DONALD WILLIAM, federal agency administrator; b. Leadville, Colo., Nov. 19, 1953; s. Donald Lewis Macdonald and Patsy Ruth (Cutbirth) Wellman; m. Miriam Ruth Wall, Oct. 17, 1991. BA, Colo. Coll., 1979. Dir. western slope office U.S. Sen. Gary Hart, Grand Junction, Colo., 1983-85; program mgr. UNC Geotech, Grand Junction, Colo., 1985-90; mgr. Idaho area office RUST Geotech, Idaho Falls, Idaho, 1990-92; mgr. buried waste program U.S. Dept. Energy, Idaho Falls, Idaho, 1992-94, spl. asst. to mgr. Idaho ops., 1994—. Chmn. Lake County Dem. Party, Leadville, Colo., 1981-82, Mesa County Dem. Party, Grand Junction, 1987; candidate Colo. Ho. of Reps., 1986. Home: 437 Renny Ave Idaho Falls ID 83401-3313 Office: US Dept Energy Idaho Ops 850 Energy Pl Idaho Falls ID 83401-1563

MACDONALD, DONALD WILLIAM, architect; b. Calgary, Alta., Can., May 7, 1935; came to U.S., 1957; s. Wallace Harold and Dorothy Louise (DeFaye) MacD.; m. Kerstin Maria Lindberg, July 22, 1965 (div. 1979); children: Pia, Ian, Denise. BArch, U. Okla., 1962; MS, Columbia U., 1963. Registered architect, Calif., Nev., N.Mex., Colo. Archtl. draftsman Bell and McCulloch Architects, Edmonton, Alta., 1955-57; archtl. designer Anshen and Allen Architects, San Francisco, 1965-67; prin. Donald MacDonald Architects, San Francisco, 1967—; assoc. prof. U. Calif.-Berkeley, 1965-66; prof. advisor Cogswell Coll., San Francisco, 1979-81, U. Okla., Norman, 1982—; lectr. archtl. sch. Idaho State U., Pocatello, 1974, Posnan (Poland) Inst. Art and Architecture, 1974, Portsmouth Inst. Tech., Eng., 1974, U. Okla., Norman, 1982, Tex. Tech U., Lubbock, 1984, Auburn (Ala.) U., 1986, Tulane U., New Orleans, 1987, Moscow Inst. Architecture, 1987, U. Calif. Berkeley, 1987, Mich. State U., Lansing, 1988, Ga. Inst. Tech., 1993, San Francisco Inst. Architecture, 1992—, U. Okla. Coll. Architecture, 1992, Archtl. Inst. B.C. Vancouver, 1991, McGill U., 1991, U. Cin., 1991, Woodbury U., Burbank, 1993, Boston Archtl. Sch., 1993, San Jose State U., 1994; lectr. in field; jury mem. Nat. Competition of Plywood Structures, Seattle, 1972, La. AIA Archtl. Design Competition, 1988, Miss. AIA Archtl. Competition, 1988, McGill U., 1991, Northern Calif. Home and Garden, 1991, City Boston Pub. Facilities Dept., 1992, San Diego Housing Commn., 1992; mem. juror panel in field; mem. San Francisco Civil Service Archtl. Selection Com., 1974; examiner Calif. Archtl. Registration Bd., 1979; prof. Calif. Coll. Arts and Crafts, San Francisco, 1988; faculty design studio San Francisco Inst. Architecture, fall 1990; jury chmn. N.C. AIA Archtl. Design Competition, 1988, Alta. Assn. Archs. U. Calgary, 1994, panel mem. 1994; East-West advisor energy conservation in housing Greenpeace, U.S.A.; presenter 9th Ann. Monterey Design Conf., 1989. Author: (with others) Bruce Goff: Toward Absolute Architecture, 1988; guest editor: Architecture and Urbanism, 1978; contbr. articles to profl. and consumer jours., U.S., Eng., Germany, Can., Poland, Russia, China, Italy, Japan. Received recognition through the media ABC, CNN, NBC, Time, People, Internat. Herald Tribune, Der Spiegel, London Observer, etc. for the invention of the City Sleeper, an exptl. environment for the homeless, studio house, and earthquake bed, 1987-91; exhbns. of architectural designs include Royal Inst. British Architects, London, 1985, 92, Contract Design Ctr., San Francisco, 1989, Contemporary Coll. Arts and Crafts, San Francisco, 1989, Contemporary Realist Gallery, San Francisco, 1989, San Francisco chpt. AIA, 1989, Calif. Sch. Bd. Assn., San Jose, Calif., 1989, Philippe Bonnafont Archtl. Drawings, San Francisco, 1990, Columbia U., N.Y.C., 1991, Mill Valley (Calif.) City Hall, 1991, San Mateo (Calif.) County Fair, 1991, Randolph Street Gallery, Chgo., 1991, Portland (Oreg.) chpt. AIA, 1993, San Francisco Examiner Home Buyers and Sellers Fair, 1993, San Francisco Embarcadero Waterfront Competition Exhibit, 1993. Recipient Regolo d'Or award Domas Milan, Italy, 1966, Okla. U. Regent's Disting. Alumni award, 1988, Honor award Calif. Coun. AIA, 1987, Commendation award for Golden Gate Toll Plaza in San Francisco Calif. Counc. AIA, 1987, also for toll booth award of excellence in archtl. conservation Found. for San Francisco Archtl. Heritage, 1989, Community Assistance award for innovative housing Calif. Coun. AIA, 1989, selected projects award Rolex Awards for Excellence, 1990, Fed. Design Achievement award, Presdl. Design awards, Nat. Endowment for Arts, 1991, World Habitat awards, grand prize Bldg. and Social Housing Foundation World Habitat awards, 1990, Gold Nugget awards, Grand award, Merit award Pacific Coast Builders and Sun/Coast ArchitectBuilder mag., 1991, SF mag. and Showplace Sq. Group Designers on Parade award, 1991, Maxwell award of excelence Fannie Mae, 1992, Oakland Orchids award AIA and Oakland Design Advocates, 1992, WorldDesign 92 award City and County of San Francisco, 1992; winner Hon. Mention Am. Plywood Assn., 1986, first place Housing Cost Reduction Co., Mich. State Housing Authority, 1987, No. Calif. Home and Garden mag. DIFFA Design Competition, 1990. Fellow AIA (honor awards San Francisco chpt. 1983, jury mem. San Mateo (Calif.) design awards program 1990); mem. Constrn. Specification Inst., McIntosh Archtl. Soc. Scotland, Columbia Archtl. League N.Y., Archtl. Assn. London. Clubs: St. Andrews Soc. (San Francisco); Chelsea Art (London); Columbia N.Y. Home: 743 Northpoint St San Francisco CA 94109 Office: Donald MacDonald Architects 1620 Montgomery St # 140 San Francisco CA 94111-1016

MACDONALD, GORDON JAMES FRASER, geophysicist; b. Mexico City, July 30, 1929; s. Gordon and Josephine (Bennett) MacD.; m. Marcelline Kuglen (dec.); children: Gordon James, Maureen, Michael; m. Betty Ann Kipniss; 1 son, Bruce; m. Margaret Stone Jennings. A.B. summa cum laude, Harvard U., 1950, A.M., 1952, Ph.D., 1954. Asst. prof. geology, geophysics Mass. Inst. Tech., 1954-55, assoc. prof. geology, geophysics, 1955-58; staff assoc. geophysics lab. Carnegie Inst. Washington, 1955-58; cons. U.S. Geol. Survey, 1955-60; prof. geophysics UCLA, 1958-68; dir. atmospheric rsch. lab., 1960-66, assoc. dir. UCLA (Inst. Geophysics and Planetary Physics), 1960-68; v.p. rsch. Inst. for Def. Analyses, 1966-67, exec. v.p., 1967-68, trustee, 1966-70; vice chancellor for rsch. and grad. affairs U. Calif. at Santa Barbara, 1968-70, prof. physics and geophysics, 1968-70; mem. coun. on Environ. Quality Washington, 1970-72; Henry R. Luce prof. environ. studies and policy, dir. environ. studies program Dartmouth Coll., 1972-79; trustee The MITRE Corp., McLean, Va., 1968-70, 72-77, exec. com., 1972-77; disting. vis. scholar The MITRE Corp., 1977-79, chief scientist, 1979-83, v.p., chief scientist, 1983-90; prof. internat. rels., rsch. dir. U. Calif., San Diego, 1990—; cons. NASA, 1960-70, mem. lunar and planetary missions bd., 1967; mem. Def. Sci. Bd., Dept. Def., 1966-70; cons. Dept. State, 1967-70; mem. Pres.'s Sci. Adv. Com., 1965-69; adv. panel on nuclear effects Office Tech. Assessment, 1975-77. Author: The Rotation of the Earth, 1960; co-author: Sound and Light Phenomena: A Study of Historical and Modern Occurrences, 1978, The Long-Term Impacts of Increasing Atmospheric Carbon Dioxide Levels, 1982, Global Climate and Ecosystem Change, 1990; contbr. articles to sci., tech. jours. Fellow AAAS, Am. Mineral. Soc., Am. Meteorol. Soc., Geol. Soc. Am., Am. Geophys. Union, Am. Acad. Arts and Scis., Am. Philos. Soc.; mem. Am. Math. Soc., Nat. Acad. Scis. (chmn. environ. studies bd. 1970, 72-73, chmn. commn. on natural resources 1973-77), Royal Astron. Soc. (fgn. assoc.), Geochem. Soc. Am., Seismol. Soc. Am., Soc. Indsl. and Applied Math., Coun. Fgn. Rels., Cosmos Club, Sigma Xi. Office: U Calif San Diego Inst Global Conflict Coop 9500 Gilman Dr La Jolla CA 92093-5003

MACDONALD, KATHARINE MARCH, journalist, public relations executive; b. Los Angeles, Nov. 12, 1949; d. Ian G. and Eve (March) M. Grad. high sch., Beverly Hills, Calif.; student, Santa Monica Coll., 1971-73, Whittier Law Sch., Los Angeles, 1975-76. Scheduling asst. Jess Unruh for Gov., Los Angeles, 1969-70; dep. press. sec. Jess Unruh for Mayor, Los Angeles, 1973; polit. cons. various local campaigns, Los Angeles, 1973-78; researcher Washington Post-Los Angeles Bur., 1978-86; spl. corr. Washington Post-Los Angeles Bur., Washington, 1980-86; reporter State Capitol Bur. San Francisco Examiner, 1986-89; press dep. to L.A. City Councilman Zev Yaroslavsky, 1990-94; v.p. Hill and Knowlton, Inc., L.A., 1994—; guest lectr. journalism and polit. sci. various colleges and universities, 1984—. Office: 21st Fl 6500 Wilshire Blvd Fl 21 Los Angeles CA 90048-4920

MACDONALD, KENNETH RICHARD, writer; b. Flint, Mich., June 2, 1912; s. Frederic Vinton and Cora (Muma) MacD.; m. Katherine Fisher; children: Carol, Kenneth Vinton. Reporter Detroit Free Press, Detroit Times, Internat. News Svc., Detroit, UPI, Detroit; freelance writer bus. news, 33 yrs. Democrat. Home: 24 White St San Francisco CA 94109-2610

MACDONALD, NORVAL (WOODROW), safety engineer; b. Medford, Oreg., Dec. 8, 1913; s. Orion and Edith (Anderson) MacD.; m. Elizabeth Ann Clifford, Dec. 8, 1937; children: Linda (Mrs. Bob Comings), Peggy (Mrs. Don Lake), Kathleen (Mrs. Michael Nissenberg). Student, U. So. Calif., 1932-34. Registered profl. safety engr., Calif. Safety engr. Todd Shipyards, San Pedro, Calif., 1942-44, Pacific Indemnity Ins. Co., San Francisco, 1944-50; area safety engrng. chief safety engr. Indsl. Ind., San Francisco, 1950-76; v.p. loss control Beaver Ins. Co., 1982-88; tchr. adult evening classes U. San Francisco, 1960-63, Golden Gate U., 1969—. Contbr. articles to profl. jours.; producer safety training films. Mem. ASME, Am. Soc. Safety Engrs. (pres. 1958, 59), Las Posas Country Club, Masons, Shriners. Methodist. Home: 1710 Shoreline Dr Camarillo CA 93010-6018

MACDONALD, ROBBIN RIECK, clergyman; b. Martins Ferry, Ohio, Oct. 14, 1944; s. Robert Peebles and Wilma Pearl (Henry) MacD.; 1 child, Robbin, Jr. BA, Muskingum Coll., 1966; MDiv, San Francisco Theol. Sem., 1970, DMin, 1972. Asst. pastor First Presbyn. Ch., Modesto, Calif., 1970-72; pastor United Presbyn. ch., Terra Bella, Calif., 1972-78; sr. pastor Bethany Presbyn. Ch., Grandview, Wash., 1978-82, First Presbyn. Ch., Pomona, Calif., 1982-89; interim pastor N.Mex. and Ariz., 1989-91; pastor Shepherd of the Valley Presbyn. Ch., Safford, Ariz., 1991—; adj. instr. Northland Pioneer Coll., Ariz., 1992—, No. Ariz. U., 1992—, Ea. Ariz. Coll., 1992—. Mem. Ariz. Archaeol. Soc. (sec. Coronado chpt. 1993), Gila Valley Ministerial Assn. (pres. 1993-94), Safford Lions Club (v.p. 1993-94, pres. 1994—), Assn. of Presbyn. Interim Ministry Specialists, de Cristo Presbytery. Home: 3433 S Robinson Ave Thatcher AZ 85552-5171 Office: Shepherd of the Valley Presbyn Ch PO Box 827 Safford AZ 85552

MACDONALD, THOMAS JOSEPH, JR., trust company executive; b. Providence, Sept. 17, 1940; s. Thomas J. and Elizabeth (Dion) MacD.; m. Kathleen J. Purnell, Aug. 26, 1961. BA, U. R.I., 1962; MA, Stanford U., 1965. Trust officer Lincoln Rochester (N.Y.) Trust Co., 1968-70; trust officer Hawaiian Trust Co. Ltd., Honolulu, 1970-72, mgr. probate dept., 1973-78, mgr. trust dept., 1979-83, sr. v.p. Client Svcs. Group, 1983-86, exec. v.p., COO, 1986—, pres., 1993—; pres. Bishop Trust Co. Ltd., 1993—, Am. Trust Co., Inc., 1993—. Bd. dirs. YMCA of Honolulu, 1986—; bd. dirs., treas. Aloha United Way, 1987—; bd. dirs., pres. Hawaii Planned Parenthood, 1973-75. Capt. U.S. Army, 1966-68. NDEA fellow, 1962-65. Mem. Am. Bankers Assn. (exec. com. trust divsn.), Internat. Wine and Food Soc. (bd. dirs., pres.), Rotary (bd. dirs. Honolulu 1991—). Home: 4999 Kahala Ave Honolulu HI 96816 Office: Hawaiian Trust Co Ltd PO Box 3170 Honolulu HI 96802-3170

MACDONALD, VIRGINIA BROOKS, architect; b. Denver, July 17, 1918; d. Emmet Earl and Lulu (Gatchel) Stoffel; widowed; m. Russell A. Apple, Oct. 18, 1981; children: Philip Brooks, Anne Brooks Hormann, Bill Brooks, Mike Brooks. BArch, Case Western Res. U., 1946. Registered architect, Hawaii. Dir. Timberline Camp., Honolulu, 1962-67; planner State of Hawaii, Honolulu, 1967-77; pvt. practice architecture Volcano, Hawaii, 1977—. Author: West Hawaii, 1972; (book/report) Na Ala Hele, 1973. Active Volcano Community Assn., 1980—. Recipient Innovative Energy award U.S. Dept. Energy, 1984, Energy Saving award State of Hawaii, 1984, Gov.'s award, 1993. Mem. AIA (past pres. local sect. 1988, dir. state coun., Passive Solar Design award 1994), Sierra Club (past state bd. dirs.), Hawaii Conservation Coun. (past state pres.).

MACDONOUGH, ROBERT HOWARD, consulting engineer; b. Chgo., Jan. 24, 1941; s. John Haaf and Helen Margaret (McWilliams) MacD.; m. Joan Carol Rosecrants, Dec. 28, 1963 (div. Nov. 1975); children: John Haaf, Thomas William, Mark Peter. BS in Engring. Ops., Iowa State U., 1962; MA in Econ., Drake U., 1966. Registered profl. engr., Iowa. Assoc. Mgmt. Sci. Am., Palo Alto, Calif., 1969; mng. assoc. Theo. Barry & Assoc., Los Angeles, 1970-72; mgr. indsl. engring. Advanced Memory Systems, Sunnyvale, Calif., 1972-73; mgr. planning and engring. Signetics, Sunnyvale, 1973-75; pres. Facilities Cons., Mountain View, Calif., 1976—. Mem. Inst. Indsl. Engrs. (sr.), Phi Gamma Delta. Republican.

MACDOUGALL, MALCOLM EDWARD, lawyer; b. Denver, Jan. 26, 1938; s. Malcolm W. and Helen (Harlow) MacD.; m. Phyllis R. Pomrenke, Dec. 20, 1959; children: Barry Malcolm, Christopher Scott (dec.). BS, Colo. State U., 1959; LLD, U. Colo., 1962. Bar: Colo. 1962, U.S. Dist. Ct. Colo. 1962. Law clk. to judge U.S. Ct. Appeals (10th cir.), Denver, 1962-63; atty. Denver Water Bd., 1963-65; assoc. Saunders, Snyder and Ross, Denver, 1965-68; gen. counsel Golden Cycle Corp., Colorado Springs, Colo., 1968-71; ptnr. Geddes, MacDougall and Worley, P.C., Colorado Springs, 1971-91; sole practitioner Colorado Springs, 1991—; bd. dirs. Park State Bank. Mem. Colo. Bar Assn. Republican. Office: 102 N Cascade Ave Ste 400 Colorado Springs CO 80903-1418

MACDOUGALL, WILLIAM RODERICK, lawyer, county official; b. Nevada City, Calif., May 14, 1914; s. William Stewart and Ethel Martha (Hutchison) McDougall; m. Carol Bernie Keane, May 1, 1937; children: Marcia MacDougall Williams, James Stewart. AA, Sacramento City Coll., 1930-32; student U. Calif.-Berkeley, 1933-34; JD, U. of Pacific, 1941. Bar: Calif. 1941, U.S. Dist. Ct. (no. dist.) Calif. 1941, U.S. Supreme Ct. 1950. Library page Calif. State Library, Sacramento, 1932-33; sr. auditor Office of Controller, State of Calif., Sacramento, 1934-37; chief bur. of collections Calif. Social Welfare Dept., Sacramento, 1937-42; gen. counsel County Suprs. Assn. Calif., Sacramento, 1946-70; exec. dir. U.S. Intergovt. Relations Commn., Washington, 1970-75; planning commr. County of Orange, Santa Ana, Calif., 1976-84; chief counsel Calif. Alcoholic Beverage Control Appeals Bd., 1984-92; exec. dir. Calif. County Govt. Edn. Found., 1965-69; chmn. home rule com. Nat. Assn. Counties, 1963-67. Mem. Fed. Public Assistance Adv. Council, 1959-60, Gov.'s Commn. on Met. Problems, Calif., 1960; pres. Laguna Beach Sch. of Art (Calif.), 1983-84. Mem. Am. Planning Assn., Nat. Assn. County and Pros. Attys. (hon.), Calif. County Planning Commrs. Assn. (dir. 1981-84). Republican. Presbyterian.

MACDUFF, NANCY, adult education educator; b. Washington, Dec. 18, 1942; d. Hugh Glen and Elizabeth Jane (Tonge) M.; m. Floyd W. Bunt, Jr., June 18, 1965; children: Laura DeLand Bunt, David Macduff Bunt. BS, Ea. Mich. U., 1964; M. Adult and Continuing Edn., Wash. State U., 1983. Asst. to edn. dir. Boston Ctr. for Adult Edn., 1967-69; exec. dir. Walla Walla (Wash.) Coun. of Camp Fire, 1969-83; community resource coord. dept. social and health svcs. Columbia and Walla Walla County, Walla Walla, 1983-89; pres. Macduff/Bunt Assocs., Walla Walla, 1983—; instr. Concordia Coll., Portland, Oreg., 1991-93; adj. faculty Wash. State U., Pullman, 1985-93, Lewis and Clark Coll., Portland, Oreg., 1993—; adv. bd. Walla Walla Dept. Human Svcs., 1984-88; adv. com. Dept. Social and Health Svcs. Region 2, several ea. Wash. counties, 1974-79. Author: Volunteer Recruiting and Retention: A Marketing Approach, 1985, Building Effective Volunteer Committees, 1986, Slide Shows on a Shoestring, 1987, Designing Programs for the Volunteer Sector, 1989, Episodic Volunteering, 1991; contbr. articles to Vol. Today newsletter, 1985-92; contbr. chpt. to book, articles to profl. jours. Mem. vestry St. Paul's Episcopal Ch., Walla Walla, 1990-91, St. James Episcopal Ch., Milton-Freewater, Oreg., 1985-87. Mem. Assn. for Rsch. on Non-Profits and Vol. Action (sec.-treas. 1989—), NW Adult Edn. Assn. (bd. dirs. 1988-90), Assn. for Vol. Adminstrn. (Diamond award 1988), Am. Assn. Adult and Continuing Edn. Home: 821 Lincoln St Walla Walla WA 99362-3235

MACER, GEORGE ARMEN, JR., orthopedic hand surgeon; b. Pasadena, Calif., Oct. 17, 1948; s. George A. and Nevart Akullian M.; m. Celeste Angelle Lyons, Mar. 26, 1983; children: Christiana Marilu, Marina Lynn, Emily Sue. BA, U. So. Calif., 1971, MD, 1976. Diplomate Am. Bd. Med. Examiners, Am. Bd. Orthopaedic Surgery; cert. surgery of hand. Intern Meml. Hosp. Med. Ctr., Long Beach, Calif., 1976; resident Orthopaedic Hosp./U. So. Calif., 1977-81; pvt. practice hand surgery Long Beach, 1983—; asst. clin. prof. orthopaedics U. So. Calif., Long Beach, 1983-89, 1990—; cons. hand surgery svc. Rancho Los Amigos Hosp. Downey, 1990—; cons. Harbor UCLA Med. Ctr., Torrance, 1983—. Joseph Boyes Hand fellow, 1982; mem. AMA, Calif. Med. Assn., L.A. County Med. Assn., Western Orthopaedic Assn., Am. Soc. for Surgery of Hand, Am. Acad. Orthopaedic Surgery. Republican. Office: 701 E 28th St Ste 418 Long Beach CA 90806-2767

MACGILLIVRAY, MARYANN LEVERONE, marketing consultant; b. Mpls., Oct. 18, 1947; d. Joseph Paul and Genevieve Gertrude (Ozark) Leverone; B.S., Coll. of St. Catherine, St. Paul, 1969; Med. Technologist, Hennepin County Gen. Hosp., 1970; M.B.A., Pepperdine U., 1976; m. Duncan MacGillivray, Apr. 28, 1973; children—Duncan Michael, Catherine Mary and Monica Mary (twins), Andrew John. Med. technologist Mercy Hosp., San Diego, 1970-72; with Diagnostics div. Abbott Labs., South Pasadena, Calif., 1972-79, tech. service rep., 1972-74, sr. tech. service rep., 1974-75, product coordinator, mktg., 1975-77, mktg. product mgr., 1977-79; clin. diagnostic mktg. cons., Sierra Madre, Calif., 1979-88; founder, mktg. dir. Health Craft Internat., Pasadena, Calif., 1988—; elected council woman City of Sierra Madre, 1990-94, mayor, 1994-95, re-elected council women, 1994—. Recipient Pres.'s award Abbott Diagnostics Div., 1975. Mem. Biomed. Mktg. Assn., Am. Assn. Clin. Chemistry, Am. Assn. Clin. Pathologists, Am. Soc. Med. Tech., Calif. Assn. Med. Lab. Technologists, Pasadena Symphony Assn. Roman Catholic. Home: 608 Elm Ave Sierra Madre CA 91024-1245

MACGINITIE, LAURA ANNE, electrical engineer; b. N.Y.C., Aug. 30, 1958; d. Walter Harold and Ruth (Kilpatrick) MacG. MS, MIT, 1982, PhD, 1988. Asst. prof. dept. Engring. Pacific Lutherna Univ., Tacoma, Wash., 1993—. Author: (with others) Mechanistic Approaches to Interaction of Electrical and EM fields, 1987; contbr. articles to profl. jours. Mem. Rails to Trails Conservancy, Washington, 1989—, Tacoma Wheelmen, 1993—. NSF grantee, 1991, 93-95; recipient Fedn. Internat. de Societes de L'Aviron; Gold medal as mem. U.S. Lightweight Rowing Team, 1984. Mem. IEEE, Bioelectromagnetics Soc., Soc. Phys. Regulation Biol. Medicine (coun. mem. 1991-93, chair publs. com.), Orthopaedic Rsch. Soc., Biomed. Engring. Soc. (membership com. 1991), Sigma Xi. Democrat. Office: Pacific Luth Univ Dept Engring Tacoma WA 98447

MACGINITIE, WALTER HAROLD, psychologist; b. Carmel, Calif., Aug. 14, 1928; s. George Eber and Nettie Lorene (Murray) MacG.; m. Ruth Olive Kilpatrick, Sept. 2, 1950; children: Mary Catherine, Laura Anne. B.A., UCLA, 1949; A.M., Stanford U., 1950; Ph.D., Columbia U., 1960. Tchr. Long Beach (Calif.) Unified Sch. Dist., 1950, 1955-56; mem. faculty Columbia U. Tchrs. Coll., 1959-80, prof. psychology and edn., 1970-80; Lansdowne scholar, prof. edn. U. Victoria, B.C., Can., 1980-84; research assoc. Lexington Sch. Deaf, N.Y.C., 1963-69; mem. sci. adv. bd. Ctr. for Study of Reading, 1977-80, chmn. 1979-80. Co-author: Gates-MacGinitie Reading Tests, 1965, 78, 89, Psychological Foundations of Education, 1968; Editor: Assessment Problems in Reading, 1972; co-editor: Verbal Behavior of the Deaf Child, 1969. Life mem. Calif. PTA. Served with USAF, 1950-54. Fellow APA, AAAS, Am. Psychol. Soc., Nat. Conf. Research English, N.Y. Acad. Scis.; mem. Internat. Reading Assn. (pres. 1976-77, Spl. Svc. award 1981), Reading Hall of Fame (pres. 1989-90). Home and Office: PO Box 1789 Friday Harbor WA 98250-1789

MACGREGOR, DONALD LANE, JR., retired banker; b. Duluth, Minn., June 21, 1930; s. Donald Lane and Julia (Waldo) MacG.; m. Mary Jo Rouse, Sept. 27, 1959; children—Jeffrey Lane, Steven Scott, John Rouse. Student, Carleton Coll., 1948-51; B.A. in Econs., Macalester Coll., 1956. Asst. cashier 1st Nat. Bank of Mpls., 1956-61; v.p. United Calif. Bank, San Francisco, 1961-69; pres. Ormand Industries, Dallas, 1969-70; v.p. United Calif. Bank, Los Angeles, 1970-71; pres., COO Am. Security Bank (name now First Interstate Bank of Hawaii), Honolulu, 1972-83, pres., CEO, 1983-91. Hon. trustee Hawaii Army Mus. Soc., Honolulu, 1978-91; vice chmn., bd. regents Chaminade U., Honolulu; trustee Hawaii Conf. Found., 1985-91. Capt. USAF, 1951-55. Mem. Am. Bankers Assn. (leadership del. 1984-92), Hawaii Bankers Assn., Hawaii C. of C. (bd. dirs. 1985-91). Republican. Clubs: Outrigger Canoe, Pacific, Waialae Country (Honolulu).

MACGREGOR, JAMES THOMAS, toxicologist; b. N.Y.C., Jan. 14, 1944; s. James and Phyllis (Bowman) MacG.; m. Judith Anne Anello, July 12, 1969; 1 child, Jennifer Lee. BS in Chemistry, Union Coll., Schenectady, N.Y., 1965; PhD in Toxicology, U. Rochester, 1970. Diplomate Am. Bd. Toxicology. Postdoctoral fellow U. Calif., San Francisco, 1970-72; dir. food safety rsch. USDA, Berkeley, Calif., 1972-88; assoc. prof. U. Calif., Berkeley, 1978-88; pres. Toxicology Consulting Svcs., Danville, Calif., 1988-90; dir. toxicology lab. SRI Internat., Menlo Park, Calif., 1990—; mem. numerous nat. and internat. profl. coms. and working groups. Mem. editorial bd.: Environ. Molecular Mutagenesis, N.Y.C., 1986-88, Mutation Res., Amsterdam, 1989-91, Mutagenesis, Oxford, 1989-93. Recipient Alexander Hollender award, 1995. Mem. Am. Assn. Cancer Rsch., Soc. Toxicology, Environ. Mutagen Soc. (treas. 1986-89, pres. 1992-93), Genetic Environ. Toxicology Assn. No. Calif. (pres. 1982). Office: SRI Internat 333 Ravenswood Ave Menlo Park CA 94025-3453

MACHLEDER, HERBERT IVAN, surgeon, educator; b. N.Y.C., May 10, 1937; m. Karin Machleder; children: Dietrich, Anton. AB, Columbia Coll., 1958; MD, U. Rochester, 1961. Diplomate Am. Bd. Surgery. Intern UCLA, 1962-64, resident in surgery, 1964-65; fellow Mayo Clinic, Rochester, Minn., 1965-68; chief resident in surgery UCLA, 1968-70; prof. Stanford U., Calif., 1970, UCLA, 1988-90; attending surgeon, chief staff UCLA Med. Ctr. Author: Vascular Disorders of the Upper Extremity, 1990. Lt. comdr. USPHS, 1965. Fogarty internat. fellow U.S. Nat. Inst. Health, Bristol, Eng., 1981. Mem. Am. Surg. Assn., Soc. Vascular Surgery. Office: UCLA Sch Medicine Divsn Gen Surgery 10833 Le Conte Ave Los Angeles CA 90024

MACHOSKIE, KATIE HERBERT, fundraising executive. BA in English Lit., UCLA, 1986. Devel. mgr. Canyon Acres Residential Ctr., Anaheim, Calif., 1991-92; chpt. dir. Juvenile Diabetes Found., Irvine, Calif., 1993—. Pub. rels. chair Jr. League of Orange County, Irvine, 1992. Office: Juvenile Diabetes Found 1451 Quail St # 108 Newport Beach CA 92660

MACK, BRENDA LEE, sociologist, public relations consulting company executive; b. Peoria, Ill., Mar. 24; d. William James and Virginia Julia (Pickett) Palmer; m. Rozene Mack, Jan. 13 (div.); 1 child, Kevin Anthony. AA, L.A. City Coll.; BA in Sociology, Calif. State U., L.A., 1980. Ct. clk. City of Blythe, Calif.; partner Mack Trucking Co., Blythe; ombudsman, sec. bus facilities So. Calif. Rapid Transit Dist., L.A., 1974-81; owner Brenda Mack Enterprises, L.A., 1981—; conflict mediator, cultural sensitivity cons.; lectr., writer, radio and TV personality; cons. European community; co-originator advt. concept View/Door Project; pub. News from the United States newsletter through U.S. and Europe; Cultural Sensitivity Cons.; Conflict Mediator. Past bd. dirs. Narcotic Symposium, L.A. With WAC, U.S. Army. Mem. Women For, Calif. State U. L.A. Alumni Assn., World Affairs Coun., German-Am. C. of C., European Community Studies Assn. Home: 8749 Cattaraugus Ave Los Angeles CA 90034-2558 Office: Brenda Mack Enterprises/Mack Media Presents PO Box 5942 Los Angeles CA 90055-0942

MACK, CHARLES DANIEL, III, labor union executive; b. Oakland, Calif., Apr. 16, 1942; s. Charles Daniel and Bernadine Zoe (Ferguson) M.; m. Marlene Helen Fagundes, Oct. 15, 1960; children: Tammy, Kelly, Kerry, Shannon. B.A., San Francisco State Coll., 1964. Truck driver Garrett Freight Lines, Emeryville, Calif., 1962-66; bus. agt. Teamsters Local No. 70, Oakland, 1966-70, sec.-treas., 1972—; legis. rep. Calif. Teamsters Pub. Affairs Council, Sacramento, 1970-71; trustee Western Conf. Teamsters Pension Trust Fund, 1980—, mem. policy com., 1980-82, pres. Teamsters' Joint Council 7, San Francisco, 1982—; mem. Calif. Inst. for Fed. Policy Rsch., 1993—. Bd. dirs. Econ. Devel. Corp. of Oakland, 1980-90, Pvt. Industry Council, Oakland, 1983-84, Children's Hosp. of East Bay, 1981-83, Calif. Compensation Ins. Fund, San Francisco, 1980-86, Alameda County Easter Seals, 1983-85, United Way, 1978-82. Democrat. Roman Catholic. Office: Teamsters' Joint Counc 7 Executive Park Blvd San Francisco CA 94134-3301

MACK, CRISTINA IANNONE, accountant; b. Olean, N.Y., Sept. 25, 1940; d. Angelo M. and Rose M. (Sirianni) Iannone; m. John O. Mack, Nov. 19, 1967; children—Elizabeth, Andrew. B.A. in Math., U. Calif.-Santa Barbara, 1962; postgrad. U. San Francisco, 1978—, Golden Gate U., 1983. Exec. dir. Bar Assn. San Francisco, 1966-68; owner, acct. CIM Assocs., San Francisco, 1978—; pres. Pacific Staff Inc., 1987—. Treas. Mothers Milk Bank, 1977-87; vice-chmn. Rep. County Central Com., 1991-93; San Francisco co-chair Citizens for Law & Order; v.p. Justice for Murder Victims. Coro Found. fellow, 1963. Mem. Calif. Agrl. Assn. (bd. dirs. dist. 1-A 1986—), Nat. Assn. Women Bus. Owners, Chi Omega Sorority (pres. 1962, treas. 1984-93). Roman Catholic. Club: San Francisco Lawyers Wives (pres. 1974, auditor 1978—). Avocations: tennis. Home: 963 Pizarro Ln Foster City CA 94404-2929 Office: 5 Thomas Mellon Cir San Francisco CA 94134-2501

MACK, DONALD, publisher; b. St. Louis, June 23, 1931; s. Herman and Mary (Schvack) M.; divorced; 5 children. B.A., U. Mo., 1967. Constrn. co. owner Ho. of Tomorrow, St. Louis, 1955-60; pres., editor Towerhigh Pub. Inc., L.A., 1960—. Pub. Today's Policeman, 1960—, Today's Fireman, 1960—. Bd. dirs Greater Kansas City Shelter for Mentally Handicapped, 1969-74. With U.S. Army, 1951-54. Office: Towerhigh Pub Inc PO Box 875108 Los Angeles CA 90087-0208

MACK, J. CURTIS, II, civic organization administrator; b. Los Angeles, Dec. 22, 1944; s. James Curtis and Ahli Christina (Youngren) M.; m. Tamara Jo Kriner, Jan. 23, 1988; children: James Curtis III, Robert Lee. BA cum laude, U. So. Calif., 1967, M in Pub. Adminstrn., 1969, MA, 1976. Asst. to regional dir. VA, Los Angeles, 1973-79; exec. dir. Citizens for the Republic, Santa Monica, Calif., 1979-85; asst. sec. oceans and atmosphere U.S. Dept. Commerce, Washington, 1985-88; pres. Los Angeles World Affairs Coun., 1988—; bd. dirs. Brentwood Bank of Calif. Col. USAFR, 1969—. Mem. Nat. Space Club (bd. dirs. 1987-88). Republican. Episcopalian. Office: Los Angeles World Affairs Coun 911 Wilshire Blvd Ste 1730 Los Angeles CA 90017-3409

MACKAY, JOHN, mechanical engineer; b. Stockport, Eng., Mar. 26, 1914; s. Frederick and Annie MacK.; m. Barbara Hinnell, Jan. 11, 1939; 1 child, Penelope; m. Veronica Hwang, Dec. 2, 1960; 1 child, Teresa. Student, Malvern Coll., 1927-31; BS, U. Manchester, 1936. Registered profl. engr., N.Y. Mng. dir. Industrial Gases (Malaya) Ltd., Singapore, 1947-50; dir. Saturn Oxygen Co. Ltd. & Group, London, 1950-52; supt. Am. Cyanamid, New Orleans, 1952-56; project mgr. M.W. Kellogg Co., N.Y.C., 1956-67, Union Carbide, N.Y.C., 1967-70; v.p. Procon Internat., Chgo., 1970-75; mgr. sales Davy Powergas, Houston, 1975-78; pres. Davy Corp. (Korea) Ltd., Seoul, 1978-80; v.p. Davy McKee Overseas Corp., Singapore, 1980-82; regional rep. Davy Corp. Ltd., Singapore, 1980-82; cons. Petronas, Kuala Lumpur, Malaysia, 1982-83; asst. dept. head cryogenics Superconducting Supercollider Lab./U. Rsch. Assocs., Waxahachie, Tex., 1989-93; cons. Lotepro Corp., Valhalla, N.Y., 1993—. Lt. col. Brit. Army, 1939-46. Decorated Brit. Terr. decoration, Chevalier l'Ordre Leopold II avec Palme, Croix de Guerre avec Palme. Mem. ASME (life), Instn. Mech. Engrs., Sports Car Club Am. Republican. Home: 9570 SW 101st Ln Ocala FL 34481-9004

MACKENROTH, JOYCE ELLEN, secondary school educator; b. Portland, Oreg., June 22, 1946; d. Ferrel Adelbert and Ellen Ellenora (Setala) McKinney; m. Glen MacKenroth, Sept. 21, 1968; 1 child, Tonia Lynn. BS, Western Oreg. State Coll., 1968; postgrad, U. Oreg., 1980, 81, 83, 85, Portland State U., 1984. Cert. elem. tchr., Oreg.; cert. reading K-9, health K-9. Tchr. Lincoln County Sch. Dist., Newport, Oreg., 1970—; bd. dirs. Curriculum Coordinating Coun., Newport; computer instr. and coordinator Lincoln County Sch. Dist., 1984-87; mem. various lang. arts and writing coms., 1981—; rep. Avon Co., Toledo, 1974-78; piano, organ tutor, Toledo, 1974-78; mem. dist. instrnl. team, dist. assessment team, area instrnl. team, site council, 1994—. Sec. State Assn. Pageant Bds., Seaside, Oreg., 1984-85; active Miss Lincoln County Scholarship Pageant, Toledo, Oreg., 1979-87; founder, pres. Youth Activities Coun., 1988; chair East Area Cmty. Ctr. Bd. Dirs., Inc., 1994—. Mem. ASCD, Oreg. Assn. Curriculum Devel., Internat. Reading Assn., Oreg. Reading Assn., Seacoast Reading Assn., Oreg. Edn. Assn. (uniserv treas. 1979-81, bd. dirs. 1981-82), Lincoln County Edn. Assn. (sec. 1974, v.p. 1975, pres. 1976, 81), NEA, Bus. and Profl. Women, Beta Sigma Phi (sec. 1983-84, v.p. 1985-86, pres. 1986-88). Democrat. Home: 264 NE 1st St Toledo OR 97391-1505 Office: Toledo Mid Sch 600 SE Sturdevant Rd Toledo OR 97391-2405

MACKENZIE, LINDA ALICE, computer company executive, consultant telecommunications; b. Bronx, N.Y., June 24, 1949; d. Gino Joseph and Mary J. (Damon) Arale; m. John Michael Lassoureille, Aug. 7, 1968 (div. 1975); 1 child, Lisa Marie Lassoureille; m. Donald John Mackenzie, July 2, 1978 (div. 1982). Student Richmond Coll., 1967-68, West L.A. Community Coll., 1978-81. Spl. rep. N.Y. Telephone Co., White Plains, 1968-71; asst. mgr. Paul Holmes Real Estate Inc., Richmond, N.Y., 1974-77; telcom applications specialist engring. Continental Airlines, L.A., 1977-83; data transmission specialist Western Airlines, Los Angeles, 1983-87; owner Computers on Consignment, El Segundo, Calif., 1984-94; cons. Farwest Brokers, L.A., 1984-85, Caleb Feb. Credit Union, Las Vegas, Nev., 1985, Nat. Dissemenators, Las Vegas, 1985, Vega & Assocs. Prodn. Div., 1987, Uptech/Downtech, 1986, Dollar Rent-a-Car, 1987, Pomona Sch. Dist., 1987, Advanced Digital Networks, 1987, State Senate, 1988, Nordstroms, 1988, Flying Tigers, 1988, Fed. Express, 1989, Sita/ITS, 1990-92, Neutrogena, 1991, B & B Computers, 1992; mktg. cons. AT&T, L.A., 1984-85, Creative Bus. Mktg., Manhattan Beach, Calif., 1994—. Author: The World Within, 1983. Active Calif. Lobbyists for Conservation, 1986. Contbr.: Am. Anthology Poetry, 1987, 88., Poetic Voices of America, 1988. Recipient Alexander award Met. Mus. Art, N.Y., 1967. Mem. Nat. Assn. Female Execs., El Segundo C. of C., Mgmt. Assocs. (assoc.). Republican. Clubs: Marina City, Manhattan Beach Women's. Avocations: painting, creative writing, aerobic dance, skiing, travel.

MACKENZIE, PETER SEAN, publications designer, writer; b. L.A., Aug. 25, 1954; s. William Duncan and Patricia Ann (Kronschnabel) Mack; m. Carin Willette, Dec. 28, 1983; 1 child, Liam Reynolds. BA, Western Wash. U., 1976. Bus. editor Skagit Valley Herald, Mount Vernon, Wash., 1976-79; mng. editor Stanwood (Wash.)-Camano News, 1979-84; graphic artist Pacific Media Group, Seattle, 1985-90, editor, 1990-93; prin. MacKenzie Creative Systems, Seattle, 1994—; instr. U. Wash. Exptl. Coll., Seattle, 1990-91. Author: Jumper, 1989; rec. artist LP KEZX Album Project, 1987, Victory Music Vol. # 2, 1988; speaker Viacom Cable Pub. Access TV, Seattle, 1990. V.p. Stanwood, Wash. C. of C., 1983. Recipient 1st place newswriting award Wash. Newspaper Pubs. Assn., 1981, 82, 2d place award for comprehensive coverage, 1982, 3d place awards in newswriting, features and spot news, 1983. Mem. Soc. Profl. Journalists (2d place award for investigative reporting 1982, 3d place award for editls. 1983), Greenpeace, Internat. Assn. Scientologists. Home: 316 NW 86th St Seattle WA 98117-3125 Office: MacKenzie Creative Sys PO Box 9627 Seattle WA 98109-0627

MACKEY, MAUREEN ELISE, rehabilitation medicine physician; b. Teaneck, N.J., Oct. 10, 1943; d. Thomas D. Jr. and Regina (Morley) M. BA with honors, U. Dallas, Irving, 1969; MD, U. Tex., Houston, 1974. Diplomate Am. Bd. Phys. Medicine and Rehab.; cert. expert in diagnosis of drug and alcohol abuse, cert. as examiner for permanent partial disability, cert. as expert witness; lic. physician, Tex., Nev., Mo. Intern USPHS Hosp., New Orleans, 1974-75; resident in phys. medicine and rehab. Parkland Meml. Hosp., Dallas, 1978-80; attending staff Jean Hanna Clark Rehab. Ctr., Las Vegas, 1981-88, 90—; cons. staff Humana Sunrise Hosp., Las Vegas, 1984-88, Valley Hosp., Las Vegas, 1983-88, Univ. Med. Ctr., Las Vegas, 1982-87, 91—; cons. VA Outpatient Clinic, Las Vegas, 1992—. Precinct chair Dem. Party, Dallas, 1978-80, committeewoman, 1978-80, del. to State Conv., 1978-80, committeewoman, Las Vegas, 1981-83; vol. med cons. Salvation Army, Las Vegas, 1983-87, We Care Women's Alcohol Recovery House, Las Vegas, 1983-93; bd. dirs. Sunrise Home Health Svcs., Las Vegas, 1984-87. Surgeon USPHS, 1973-78. Fellow Am. Acd. Phys. Medicine and Rehab., Am. Acad. Disability Evaluating Physicians; mem. AMA, Nev. State Soc. Phys. Medicine and Rehab. (past pres.), Am. Soc. for Addiction Medicine, Nev. State Med. Soc., Clark County Med. Soc. Democrat. Office: Jean Hanna Clark Rehab Ctr 1001 Shadow Ln Las Vegas NV 89106-4124

MACKEY, WAYNE ALLISON, electrical engineer; b. Pitts., Sept. 22, 1955; s. George Allison and Dorothy Jayne (Ross) M.; m. Mary Lou Herbers, Nov. 16, 1984; children: Benjamin Paul, Craig Thomas. BSEE and Econs., Carnegie Mellon U., 1977; MS in Engring., Loyola Marymount U., L.A., 1982. Engr. space and info. systems Raytheon Co., Sudbury, Mass., 1977-78; mem. tech. staff Hughes Aircraft Co., El Segundo, Calif., 1978-84, head tech. sect., 1984-87, sr. scientist, engr., 1987-90, div. sr. scientist, 1990—, team leader event based concurrent engring., 1991—, team leader estimating process improvement, 1992, team leader customer focused quality and orgn. metrics system, 1993, team leader 6 Sigma quality, 1994, team leader RCS supplier devel., 1995; team leader 6 Sigma quality, 1994. Inventor automated environ. tester, universal FLIR tester, automatic bid/spread sheet. Fellow Hughes Corp. Edn. Coun., 1980. Mem. Am. Soc. Quality Control, Assn. Proposal Mgmt. Profls., Tau Beta Pi. Home: 1315 10th St Manhattan Beach CA 90266-6035 Office: Hughes Aircraft Co PO Box 902 E180 El Segundo CA 90245

MACKIE, JERRY, state legislator, business owner; b. Ketchikan, Alaska, Jan. 10, 1962; s. Ralph P. Mackie and Marge (Thompson) Young; divorced; 1 child, John. Grad. high sch., Ketchikan. Chmn. bd. Shaan Seet Inc., Craig, Alaska, 1981-90; comml. fisherman Craig, 1985—; rep. Alaska State Legislature, Juneau, 1990—; owner fishing lodge Craig, 1985—. Bd. dirs. Alaska Fed. Natives, Anchorage. Recipient Pub. Svc. commendation USCG, 1987. Mem. Alaska Native Brotherhood, Moose. Democrat. Home: PO Box 795 Craig AK 99921-0795 Office: Alaska State Legislature State Capital Juneau AK 99801

MACKIE, RICHARD ALLEN, small business owner, publishing company executive; b. L.A., July 8, 1933; s. Stanley Warren and Marjorie Eugenia (Stewart) M.; m. Patricia Ann Bentz, July 14, 1956 (div. Nov. 1978); children: Wendy Kay Mackie Baird, Gerald Bruce, Kenneth Edward; m. Jean Hicks McNeill, Apr. 24, 1983; stepchildren: Mike McNeill, Jane Moses. BS, San Diego State U., 1955; MS, U. Idaho, 1957. C.C. teaching credential, Calif. Agr. insp. San Diego County Dept. Agr., San Diego, 1957-59, pub. health entomologist, 1959-71; chief pub. health officer Guam Dept. Pub. Health, Magnilao, 1971-79; med. mgmt. cons. Health Mgmt. Internat., Calabasas, Calif., 1979-81; mgr. Olsten Corp., San Jose, Calif., 1981-83; v.p. Newton Assocs., Walnut Creek, Calif., 1983-91; owner, pres. R. Mackie Assocs., Concord, Calif., 1991—, Solution Pub., Concord, 1994—; country rep. to WHO, The Philippines, 1972-79; chmn. Guam Health Coordinating Coun., Agana, 1976-79; coord. Operation New Life, Guam, 1975; chmn. Gov.'s White Paper on Health Care, Guam, 1977. Author, pub. Beat the Devil, 1994; author: Take This Job and Sell It, 1994; contbg. author: We Pulled Together and Won, 1993; contbr. articles to profl. jours. French horn player San Diego Youth Symphony, 1948-54, San Diego Symphony, 1954-55. Home and Office: 1790 Ellis St Apt 8 Concord CA 94520-2743

MACKIN, TERRENCE CHRISTIAN, infosystems consultant; b. St. Paul, Minn., July 21, 1947; s. Donald and Laura Ann (Mumm) M.; m. Leah Adrian Amilaner, June 11, 1972 (div. Sept. 1984); children: Aaron Jacob, Sasha Esther; m. Judith Kaye Applen, Sept. 17, 1989; 1 child, Katherine Applen. BS, Hamline U., 1969; postgrad., Syracuse U., 1969-70, U. Minn., 1975-76. Systems mgr. Infinite Graphics, Mpls., 1972-75; computer ops. B. Dalton Bookseller, Mpls., 1975-77, mgr. store systems, 1977-87; computer security analyst N.W. Bank Corp., Mpls., 1977; sr. cons. Peter R. Johnson & Assoc., Richmond, Calif., 1987-91; bus. cons. No. States Power Co., Mpls., 1991-93; mgr. desktop techs. Mervyn's, Hayward, Calif., 1993—. Mem. Planning Dist. 10 St. Paul, Minn., 1979-81. With U.S. Army, 1970-72. Recipient Summer Rsch. Grant Nat. Sci. Found. Macalester Coll., 1968, Grad. Fellowship Nat. Sci Found. Syracuse U., 1969-70. Mem. Res. Officers Assn., IBM POS User Group (bd. dirs. 1985), DTS POS User Group (pres. Minn. 1983). Office: Mervyn's MS M4AY 22301 Foothill Blvd Hayward CA 94541-2709

MACKINNON, ANNE, editor; b. Evanston, Ill., Jan. 19, 1952; d. Cyrus Leland and Helen (Wigglesworth) MacK.; m. Jon Brian Huss, July 5, 1986; 1 child, Theodore MacKinnon Huss. BA, Harvard U., 1973; JD, U. Calif., Berkeley, 1981. Bar: Wyo. Researcher, pub. rels. dept. Courier Jour., Louisville, 1973-75; paralegal Legal Aid Soc., Louisville, 1974; legal rsch. Ea. Ky. Resource Ctr., Jenkins, 1975-76; freelance corres. Mountain Eagle, Whitesburg, 1976; asst. mng. editor Casper (Wyo.) Star Tribune, 1985-90, editor, 1990—; bd. dirs. Wyo. Humanities Coun., Laramie, 1995—; energy and bus. reporter Casper Star Tribune, 1979-85. Bd. assoc. Am. Heritage Ctr., U. Wyo., Laramie, 1992—; ethics com. mem. Wyo. Med. Ctr., Casper, 1992—; emergency mgmt. com. mem. Wyo. Emergency Mgmt. Office, Cheyenne, 1987-89. Recipient Excellence in Media award Planned Parenthood Rocky Mountain, Denver, 1991. Democrat. Office: Casper Star Tribune PO Box 80 170 Star Ln Casper WY 82601

MACKINNON, PEGGY LOUISE, public relations executive; b. Florence, Ariz., June 18, 1945; d. Lacy Donald Gay and Goldie Louise (Trotter) Martin; m. Ian Dixon Mackinnon, Oct. 20, 1973. BA, San Jose State U., 1967, postgrad., 1968. Cert. secondary tchr., Calif. Tchr. Las Lomas High Sch., Walnut Creek, Calif., 1968-69; edn. officer Ormond Sch., Sydney, Australia, 1970-72; tchr. Belconnen High Sch., Canberra, Australia, 1972-73; temp. exec. sec. various orgns., London, 1973-75; mktg. mgr. Roadtown Wholesale, Tortola, British Virgin Islands, 1975-80; sr. v.p., gen. mgr. Hill & Knowlton Inc., Denver, 1981—. Bd. dirs. Rocky Mountain Poison and Drug Found., Denver, 1984-87, Denver C. of C., Boy Scouts Am., Denver coun. Mem. Pub. Relations Soc. Am. (accredited). Home: Apt 21 9200 Cherry Creek South Dr Denver CO 80231-4018 Office: Hill & Knowlton 999 18th St Ste 2450 Denver CO 80202-2424

MACKINNON, STEPHEN R., Asian studies administrator, educator; b. Columbus, Nebr., Dec. 2, 1940; s. Cyrus Leland and Helen (Wigglesworth) MacK.; m. Janice Carolyn Rachie, July 15, 1967; children: Rebecca, Cyrus R. BA, Yale U., 1963, MA, 1964; PhD, U. Calif., Davis, 1971. Acting instr. Chinese U., Hong Kong, 1968-69; dir. Asian Studies, prof. History Ariz. State U., Tempe, 1971—; vis. assoc. Chinese Acad. Social Sci., Beijing, 1979-81, 85; mem. U.S. State Dept. Selection Bd., Washington, 1991, Nat. Com. on U.S.-China Rels., N.Y.C., 1991—; cons. PBS film documentary "Dragon and Eagle" on U.S.-China rels., San Francisco, 1986—. Author: (book) Power/Politics China, 1980; co-author: (books) Agnes Smedley, 1988, China Reporting, 1987; co-editor: (book) Chinese Women Revolution, 1976 (ALA notable book 1976); lectr. on China to local orgns. and TV, 1981—. Commr. Phoenix Sister Cities, 1986-91; treas. Com. on Fgn. Rels., Phoenix, 1988—. Rsch. fellow Am. Coun. Learned Socs., Hong Kong, 1978, Fulbright Found., India, 1977-78; rsch. sr. Com. on Scholarly Com. People's Republic China, Washington-Beijing, 1992. Mem. Assn. Asian Studies (bd. dirs. 1990-91), Am. Hist. Assn. (program com. 1990-91). Office: Ariz State U Ctr for Asian Studies 109 W Hall Tempe AZ 85287-1702

MACKINTOSH, FREDERICK ROY, oncologist; b. Miami, Fla., Oct. 4, 1943; s. John Harris and Mary Carlotta (King) MacK.; m. Judith Jane Parnell, Oct. 2, 1961 (div. Aug. 1977); children: Lisa Lynn, Wendy Sue; m. Claudia Lizanne Flournoy, Jan. 7, 1984; 1 child, Gregory Warren. BS, MIT, 1964, PhD, 1968; MD, U. Miami, 1976. Intern then resident in gen. medicine Stanford (Calif.) U., 1976-78, fellow in oncology, 1978-81; asst. prof. med. U. Nev., Reno, 1981-85, assoc. prof., 1985-92, prof. medicine, 1992—. Contbr. articles to profl. jours. Fellow ACP; mem. Am. Soc. Clin. Oncology, Am. Cancer Soc. (pres. Nev. chpt. 1987-89, Washoe chpt. 1988-90), No. Nev. Cancer Coun. (bd. dirs. 1981-92), No. Calif. Cancer Program (bd. dirs. alt. 1983-87, bd. dirs. 1987-91). Office: Nev Med Group 781 Mill St Reno NV 89502-1320

MACKO, NANCY, artist, educator; b. Oceanside, N.Y., Apr. 29, 1950; d. Emil E.M. and Arline (Walker) Kelly; m. Jan Blair, Dec. 24, 1985. BS in Liberal Arts, U. Wis., River Falls, 1977; MA, U. Calif., Berkeley, 1980, MFA in Painting and Printmaking, 1981, Ma in Edn. Psychology, 1989. Assoc. registrar Asian Art Mus., San Francisco, 1985-86; asst. prof. art

Scripps Coll., Claremont, Calif., 1986-92, assoc. prof. art, 1992—; vis. lectr. U. Calif., Davis, 1983-84; vis. artist, prof. La Corte della Miniera, Urbino, Italy, 1990; adj. prof. Claremont Grad. Sch., 1986-91; dir. Scripps Computer Art Program, 1990—; cons. in field. Mem. exhbn. com. L.A. Ctr. Photographic Studies, 1994. Faculty rsch. grantee, 1986-95; rsch. fellow Scripps Coll., 1989. Mem. Calif. Soc. Printmakers (pres. 1984-85), Coll. Art Assn. N.Y. (bd. dirs. 1994—, exec. bd. 1995—). Democrat. Home: 810 Kodak Dr Los Angeles CA 90026 Office: Scripps Coll 1030 Columbia Ave Claremont CA 91711-3905

MAC LAM, HELEN, editor, periodical; b. N.Y.C., Aug. 17, 1933; d. Forrest Mearl and Bertha Margaret (Herzberger) Keen; m. David Carlyle MacLam, Feb. 7, 1953; children: Timothy David, David Andrew. AB Sociology, Heidelberg Coll., 1961; AMLS, U. Mich., 1967; MA African Am. Studies, Boston U., 1978. Dep. clerk Mcpl. Ct., Tiffin, Ohio, 1962-64; subprofessional asst. Heidelberg Coll. Libr., Tiffin, Ohio, 1964-66; collection devel. libr. social scis. Dartmouth Coll. Libr., Hanover, N.H., 1967-83; social scis. editor Choice Mag., Middletown, Conn., 1983—; cons. in field; spkr. in field. Editorial bd. Multicultural Review, 1992-95; contbr. articles to profl. jours. Bd. dirs. Headrest, 1976-80, Hanover Consumer Coop. Soc., 1969-72. Recipient Grant award Rsch. Program for Ethnic Studies Librarianship Fisk U., 1975. Mem. Nat. Assn. Ethnic Studies (pres. 1985-87, assoc. editor publs. 1980-83), African Studies Assn., Africana Libs. Coun. (exec. bd. 1989-91), Am. Soc. Indexers, Freelance Editorial Assn., Women in Scholarly Publishing, Assn. Coll. and Rsch. Librs. (New England chpt.). Home: RR 2 Box 92 Norwich VT 05055-9724 Office: Choice Mag 100 Riverview Ctr Middletown CT 06457-3401

MACLAUCHLIN, ROBERT KERWIN, communications artist, educator; b. Framingham, Mass., Oct. 8, 1931; s. Charles Lewis and Elinor Frances (Kerwin) MacL.; m. Elizabeth D'Ann Willson, June 13, 1964. BA in Sociology, U. Mass., Amherst, 1954; MEd, Bridgewater State Coll., 1958; MS in Radio and TV, Syracuse U., 1959; PhD in Speech, Radio, TV, Mich. State U., 1969. Personnel trainee Nat. Security Agy., Washington, 1954-55; elem. sch. tchr. Mattapoisett (Mass.) Pub. Schs., 1957-58; asst. prof., dir. programming Maine Ednl. TV Network, Orono, 1959-66; assoc. prof. speech communications, dir. TV-Radio instrn. Colo. State U., Ft. Collins, 1969-76, prof., dir. TV-Radio instrn., 1976—; cons. U. Maine, Orono, 1968, Ft. Collins Presbyn. Ch., 1976-78, Sta. KCOL-AM-FM, Ft. Collins, 1978, Pub. Health Assn., Ft. Collins, 1985; archives program guest Maine Pub. Broadcast, Orono, 1983. Served with inf. U.S. Army, 1955-57. Recipient Excellence in Teaching award Mich. State U., 1969, Friend of Broadcasting award Colo. Broadcasters Assn., 1985; named Disting. Vis. Prof. U. Vt., Burlington, 1983, A Teacher Who Makes A Difference Denver's Rocky Mountain News, KCNC-TV, 1987. Mem. NATA (panel Colo. chpt. 1989—), Broadcast Edn. Assn. (Industry State chmn. 1981-86, panel 1991—, chmn. faculty internship com. 1991—), Colo. Broadcasters Assn. (edn. com. 1972—, Hall of Fame com. 1980—, human resources com. 1991, Friends of Broadcast award 1985, panelist summer conv. 1994, panelist summer conv. 1995), Speech Comm. Assn., Kiwanis (Disting. past pres. 1979-80). Republican. Home: 1407 Country Club Rd Fort Collins CO 80524-1907 Office: Colo State U Dept Speech Communicat Fort Collins CO 80523

MACLEAN, EDNA AHGEAK, language educator, researcher; b. Barrow, Alaska, Nov. 5, 1944; d. Joseph A. and Maria (Brower) Ahgeak; m. Stephen F. MacLean, July 11, 1967 (div. June 1992); children: Stephen, Andrew. BA, Colo. Women's Coll., 1967; cert. in tchg., U. Calif., Berkeley, 1969; MEd, U. Wash., 1991; postgrad., Stanford U., 1991—. Rsch. asst. Naval Arctic Rsch. Lab., Barrow, Alaska, summer 1971; Inupiaq lang. specialist U. Alaska, Fairbanks, 1973-75, asst. prof. Inupiaq-Eskimo, 1976-87; Alaska Native edn. coord. Alaska Dept. Edn., Juneau, 1987-90; Inupiaq curriculum developer North Slope Borough Sch. Dist., Barrow, 1992; mem. steering com. Internat. Cross-Cultural Edn. Seminar Series in the Circumpolar North, 1983—; mem. Inuit Circumpolar Conf. Com. on Edn., 1978-83; mem. com. on arctic social scis., Polar Rsch. Bd., NRC, 1987-91; v.p. for Alaska Inuit Circumpolar Exec. Coun., 1989-92. Author: (with others) Genealogical Record of Barrow Eskimo Families, 1973, Eskimo Languages, Their Present-Day Conditions, 1979; contbr. articles to profl. jours. Mem., pres. North Slope Borough Commn. on History, Lang., and Culture, Barrow, 1973-83. Recipient Shareholder of Yr. award, Ukpeagvik Inupiat Corp., 1982, Cert. of Spl. Recognition, City of Barrow, 1982. Fellow Arctic Inst. N.Am. Home: 1470 Sand Hill Rd # 104 Palo Alto CA 94304-2058

MACLEAN, VICTORIA GRAHAM, journalist, editor; b. Brockville, Ont., Can., June 2, 1948; d. Findlay Barnes and Helen Lois (Graham) MacL.; m. Robert E. Knight, Sept. 29, 1973 (div. Jan. 1985). Student, Trent U. Proofreader, adv. salesman, photo engraver, reporter, editor Brockville Recorder and Times, 1964-72; reporter, columnist, mng. editor St. Albert (Alta., Can.) Gazette, 1976-85; editor Edmonton (Alta.) Sun, 1988—. Columnist Can. Comty. Newspapers, 1980. Home: 8547 80th Ave, Edmonton, AB Canada T6C 0T2 Office: Edmonton Sun, Ste 250, 4990 92d Ave, Edmonton, AB Canada T6B 3A1

MACLEOD, KATHLEEN BROMLEY, internist; b. Oakland, Calif., Mar. 25, 1953; d. LeRoy Alton and Bernice (Doyle) Bromley; m. Glen Earl MacLeod, Dec. 22, 1973. BA in Bacteriology with high honors, U. Calif., Berkeley, 1975; MD, UCLA, 1984. Diplomate Am. Bd. Internal Medicine and Infectious Disease. Staff rsch. assoc. dept. genetics U. Calif., Berkeley, 1976-77; microbiologist bacterial zoonoses br. Bur. Epidemiology, Ctrs. for Disease Control, Atlanta, 1978-80; resident in internal medicine Wadsworth VA Med. Ctr., L.A., 1984-87; fellow in infectious diseases U. Calif.-Irvine Sch. Medicine, Orange, 1987-89; pvt. practice infectious diseases Los Alamitos, Calif., 1989—. Mem. ACP, AMA, Infectious Disease Soc. Am., Am. Soc. Microbiology, Calif. Med. Assn. Home: 6310 E Bay Shore Walk Long Beach CA 90803-5637

MACLEOD, RICHARD PATRICK, foundation administrator; b. Boston, Apr. 2, 1937; s. Thomas Everett and Margaret Gertrude (Fahey) MacL.; m. Sarah Frances Mancari, Sept. 7, 1963; children: Kimberly Margaret Hamelin, Richard Alexander MacLeod. BA in Govt., U. Mass., 1960; MA in Internat. Rels., U. So. Calif., 1968. Instr. polit. sci. USAF Acad., 1968-71; Commd. 2d lt. USAF, 1960, advanced through grades to col., 1981; sr. rsch. fellow The Nat. Def. U., Washington, 1978-79; chief Space Policy Br., dep. chief Plans USAF Aerospace Def. Command, 1979-80; exec. officer to the comdr. in chief USAF Aerospace Def. Command, NORAD, 1980-81; chief of staff NORAD, 1981-84, USAF Space Command, 1982-84; ret. U.S. Space Found., 1985; exec. dir. U.S. Space Found., Colorado Springs, Colo., 1985-88; pres. U.S. Space Found., Colorado Springs, 1988—; bd. dirs. Analytical Surveys, Inc., Colorado Springs, 1985—; space edn. advisor Coll. Engring. Adv. Coun., U. Colo., Colorado Springs. Author: Peoples War in Thailand, Insurgency in the Modern World, 1980. Mem. White House Space Policy Adv. Bd.; bd. dirs. Pike's Peak Coun. Boy Scouts Am., Colorado Springs; past pres. Colorado Springs Symphony Coun.; past dir. World Affairs Coun., Colorado Springs. Fellow Brit. Interplanetary Soc.; mem. AIAA, Air Force Acad. Found. (bd. dirs., trustee), U.S. Space Found. (founding), Aviation Space Writers Assn., Am. Legion, The Co. of Fifers and Drummers. Office: US Space Found 2860 S Circle Dr Ste 2301 Colorado Springs CO 80906-4107

MACLEOD, ROBERT FREDRIC, editor, publisher; b. Chgo., Oct. 15, 1917; s. Ernest F. and Martha W. (Ruzicka) MacL.; children—Merrill, Robert Fredric, E. Jay, Ian. B.A., Dartmouth Coll., 1939. Advt. mgr. Town & Country mag., N.Y.C., 1949; v.p., pub. Harper's Bazaar, N.Y.C., 1950-55, 55-60; v.p., advt. dir. Hearst Mags., N.Y.C., 1960-62; pub. Seventeen mag., N.Y.C., 1962-63; v.p., dir. mktg. Subscription TV Inc., Santa Monica, Calif., 1963-64; editor, pub. 'Teen Mag., Los Angeles, 1965—, now editorial dir., exec. pub.; sr. v.p. Petersen Pub. Co., L.A., 1976-95; ret., 1995, ind. pub. cons. Served to maj. USMC, 1941-46. Named to Football Hall of Fame, 1977. Club: Bel Air Country. Home: 110 Colony Dr Malibu CA 90265

MACLISE, JAMES RAYMOND, educator, writer; b. Newark, Dec. 14, 1935; s. Deming Gerow and Vivian Ruth (Jackson) M.; m. Lura Elizabeth Geyser, Aug. 24, 1968; children: James Deming, Daniel Ross. B.A., U. Calif.-Davis, 1957; M.A., U. San Francisco, 1971. Cert. secondary and community coll. tchr., Calif. Lectr. U. San Francisco, 1971-72; tchr. English, Lodi High Sch., Calif., 1972—. Author radio mystery articles. Served with U.S. Army, 1959-60. Mem. Soc. to Preserve Hist. Radio Program Materials.

MACMASTER, JOHN ARTHUR, state legislative lawyer; b. St. Paul, Minn., Aug. 14, 1943; s. Lawrence G. and Donna M. (Black) MacM.; m. Bonita Rose Revier, Feb. 14, 1969; children: Cary Jon, Dylan Robert, Jack Kiner. BA in Philosophy, U. Minn., 1965, JD, 1968. Legal editor West Pub. Co., St. Paul, 1969-72, Equity Pub. Co., Orford, N.H., 1972-81; staff atty., ho. jud. com., adminstrv. code com. Mont. State Legislature, Helena, 1987—. Author, co-author and editor numerous statutes, codes of law and state court reports for various states. Mem. Mont. State Bar Assn. Home: 3271 Spokane Creek Rd East Helena MT 59635-9740 Office: Mont Legis Coun Rm 138 State Capitol Helena MT 59635

MACMILLAN, CATHERINE COPE, restaurant owner; b. Sacramento, Mar. 3, 1947; d. Newton A. Cope and Marilyn (Jacobs) Combrink; m. Thomas C. MacMillan, Dec. 18, 1967 (div. Jan. 1984); children: Corey Jacobs, Andrew Cope. BA, U. Calif., 1969; MBA, Calif. State U., Sacramento, 1978; JD, McGeorge Sch. Law, 1993. Pub. health microbiologist County of Sacramento, 1969-74; pres., gen. mgr. The Firehouse Restaurant, Sacramento, 1980—; bd. dirs. Westamerica Bank, San Rafael, Calif. Chmn. Sacramento Conv. and Visitors Bur., 1987-88; pres. Old Sacramento Propery Owners Coun., 1987; mem. Sacramento Sports Commn, 1988-89. Mem. Calif. Restaurant Assn. (bd. dirs.), Sacramento Restaurant Assn. (restaurateur of yr. 1983), Old Sacramento Citizens and Merchants Assn. (chmn. bd. dirs. 1984), Sacramento Met. C. of C. (bus. woman of yr. 1992), Calif. State U.-Sacramento Alumni Assn. (sch. of bus. alumna award 1992), Sacramento Capital Club (pres. 1995). Office: The Firehouse Restaurant 1112 2nd St Sacramento CA 95814-3204

MACMILLAN, KIP VAN METRE, foundation executive; b. Evanston, Ill., Dec. 18, 1937; s. Charles Daniel and Janet Marvia (Van Metre) M.; m. Linda Jean Griesbach, Dec. 22, 1962; children: Christopher, Julia. Sgt., lt., div. comdr. Evanston Police Dept., 1961-88; supr. Polio Plus campaign Rotary Found., Evanston, 1988-90, ret., 1990. Bd. dirs. Youth Orgn. Umbrella, Evanston, 1974, McGaw YMCA, Evanston, 1976-89, Shore, Community Svcs. for Retarded Citizens, Evanston, 1986-90; v.p. Teton Youth & Family Svcs.; chmn. Evanston March of Dimes, 1987; mem. adv. com. Cook County Dept. Children and Family Svcs., Chgo., 1987-90; mem. Ill. Coord. System Response Project-Mass Abuse of Children, Springfield, 1987-89; chmn. Wildcat Dist. Com. Boy Scouts Am.; dir., treas. Evanston Sister City Found., 1989-90; vol. Grand Teton Music Festival. Recipient Top Vol. of Yr. award North Shore mag., 1987, Jay Moore award Youth Orgn. Umbrella, 1988, William Harper award McGaw YMCA, 1975. Mem. Nat. Soc. Fundraising Execs., Internat. Assn. Chiefs of Police, Rotary (bd. dirs. Evanston club 1986-89, bd. dirs. Jackson Hole club, pres. Jackson Hole club 1994-95, Outstanding Rotarian Evanston club 1988), Am. Soc. Indsl. Security, Teton County Peace Officers Assn. (chair congressional awards com.). Republican. Episcopalian.

MACMILLAN, ROBERT SMITH, electronics engineer; b. L.A., Aug. 28, 1924; s. Andrew James and Moneta (Smith) M.; BS in Physics, Calif. Inst. Tech., 1948, MS in Elec. Engring., 1949, PhD in Elec. Engring. and Physics cum laude, 1954; m. Barbara Macmillan, Aug. 18, 1962; 1 son, Robert G. Rsch. engr. Jet Propulsion lab. Calif. Inst. Tech., Pasadena, 1951-55, asst. prof. elec. engring., 1955-58; assoc. prof. elec. engring. U. So. Calif., L.A., 1958-70; mem. sr. tech. staff Litton Systems, Inc., Van Nuys, Calif., 1969-79; dir. systems engring. Litton Data Command Systems, Agoura Hills, Calif., 1979-89; pres. The Macmillan Group, Tarzana, Calif., 1989—; treas., v.p. Video Color Corp., Inglewood, 1965-66. Cons. fgn. tech. div. USAF, Wright-Patterson AFB, Ohio, 1957-74, Space Tech. Labs., Inglewood, Calif., 1956-60, Space Gen. Corp., El Monte, Calif., 1960-63. With USAAF, 1943-46. Mem. IEEE, Am. Inst. Physics, Am. Phys. Soc., Sigma Xi, Tau Beta Pi, Eta Kappa Nu. Research in ionospheric, radio-wave, propagation; very low frequency radio-transmitting antennas; optical coherence and statist. optics. Home: 350 Starlight Crest Dr La Canada Flintridge CA 91011-2839 Office: The Macmillan Group 5700 Etiwanda Ave Apt 260 Tarzana CA 91356-2546

MACMILLEN, RICHARD EDWARD, biological sciences educator, researcher; b. Upland, Calif., Apr. 19, 1932; s. Hesper Nichols and Ruth Henrietta (Golder) MacM.; m. Ann Gray, June 12, 1953 (div. 1975); children: Jennifer Kathleen, Douglas Michael; m. Barbara Jean Morgan, Oct. 23, 1980; 1 child, Ian Richard. BA, Pomona Coll., 1954; MS, U. Mich., 1956; PhD, UCLA, 1961. From instr. to assoc. prof. Pomona Coll., Claremont, Calif., 1960-68, Wig Disting. prof., 1965; assoc. prof., then prof. U. Calif., Irvine, 1968—, chair dept. population and environ. biology, 1972-74, chair dept. ecology and evolutionary biology, 1984-90; prof. emeritus, 1993—; mem. award panel NSF, Washington, 1976-80. Contbr. numerous articles to profl. jours. Chair sci. adv. bd. Endangered Habitats League, 1991-93. Recipient rsch. awards NSF, 1961-83; Fulbright-Hays advanced rsch. fellow Monash U., Australia, 1966-67. Fellow AAAS; mem. Am. Soc. Mammalogists (life), Ecol. Soc. Am. (cert. sr. ecologist), Am. Ornithologists Union, Cooper Ornithol. Soc. (life, bd. dirs. 1982-84). Democrat. Home: Rt 1 RK 35 Bishop CA 93514-3030 Office: U Calif White Mtn Rsch Sta Bishop CA 93514

MACMULLEN, DOUGLAS BURGOYNE, writer, editor, retired army officer, publisher; b. Berkeley, Calif., Dec. 26, 1919; s. T. Douglas and Florence (Burgoyne) MacM.; ed. San Francisco State U., 1937-41, Stanford U., U. Calif., Fgn. Svc. Inst., Strategic Intelligence Sch., Indsl. Coll. of the Armed Forces, Air War Coll., Army Mgmt. Sch.; m. Sherry Bernice Auerbach, Mar. 11, 1942; 1 child, Douglas Burgoyne Jr. Commd. 2d lt. F.A. Res. U.S. Army, 1941; advanced through grades to col. M.I., 1967; Army gen. staff Psychol. Ops. Fgn. Svc., PTO; ret., 1972; exec. editor Am. Rsch. Assoc., Sherman Oaks, Calif.; cons. in communication; accredited corr. Def. Dept. Bd. govs. Monte Vista Grove Homes, Pasadena, Calif., Shriners Hosps. for Crippled Children, L.A.; pres. Clan MacMillan Soc. N.Am., 1973-77, trustee, 1975—; mem. L.A. Olympics Citizens Adv. Commn., 1982-84; mem. L.A. Philanthropic Found.; bd. dirs. Masonic Press Club, L.A., 1975, 84-88; mem. steering com. Mayor L.A. Coun. Internat. Visitors and Sister Cities, 1969; chmn. Los Angeles-Glasgow Sister Cities Ad Hoc Com.; former mem. San Francisco Mayor's Mil. and Naval Affairs Com.; mem. wills and gifts com. Shriners Hosp. Crippled Children, Al Malaikah Temple, L.A., 1974-80; cons. com. on pub. info. Masons Grand Lodge of Calif., 1985-86. Decorated Legion of Merit, Army Commendation medal (U.S.), Knight Comdr. Order of Polonia Restituta (Free Poland), Red Cross of Constantine; Royal Order Scotland. Mem. Internat. Inst. Strategic Studies, Nat. Mil. Intelligence Assn., Assn. Former Intelligence Officers (pres. L.A. County chpt.), U.S. Naval Inst., Assn. U.S. Army, Company Mil. Historians, Am. Def. Preparedness Assn., St. Andrew's Soc. Los Angeles (past pres., trustee), Air Force Assn., Stanford U. Alumni Assn., Calif. Newspaper Pubs. Assn., Nat. Def. Exec. Res., Sigma Delta Chi. Republican. Presbyterian. Clubs: Press, Caledonian (London); Army & Navy Club (Washington), San Francisco Press. Lodges: Masons (32 deg.), K.T., Shriners (editor, pub. The Al Malaikahan, former imperial news editor Shrine of N.Am.), Quatuor Coronati C.C. Co-author: Psychological Profile of Cambodia, 1971; author-editor: A Sentimental Journey--The History of the First Hundred Years, 1988; numerous other publs. and articles; radio commentator and newspaper columnist on mil., polit. and internat. affairs. Address: PO Box 5201 Sherman Oaks CA 91413-5201

MACNAUGHTON, ANGUS ATHOLE, finance company executive; b. Montreal, Que., Can., July 15, 1931; s. Athole Austin and Emily Kidder (MacLean) MacN.; children: Gillian Heather, Angus Andrew. Student, Lakefield Coll. Sch., 1941-47, McGill U., 1949-54. Auditor Coopers & Lybrand, Montreal, 1949-55; acct. Genstar Ltd., Montreal, 1955; asst. treas. Genstar Ltd., 1956-61, treas., 1961-64, v.p., 1964-70, exec. v.p., 1970-73, pres., 1973-76, vice chmn., chief exec. officer, 1976-81, chmn. or pres., chief exec. officer, 1981-86; pres. Genstar Investment Corp., 1987—; bd. dirs. Can. Pacific Ltd., Sun Life Assurance Co. Can. Ltd., Barrick Gold Corp., Varian Assocs. Inc., Wolverine Tube Inc., San Francisco Opera; past pres. Montreal chpt. Tax Execs. Inst. Bd. govs. Lakefield Coll. Sch.; past chmn. San Francisco Bay Area coun. Boy Scouts Am. Mem. Pacific Union Club, World Trade Club, Villa Taverna (San Francisco), Mt. Royal Club (Montreal), Toronto Club. Office: Genstar Investment Corp 950 Tower Ln Ste 1170 Foster City CA 94404-2127 also: Am Barrick Resources Corp, 24 Hazelton Ave, Toronto, ON Canada M5R 2E2

MAC NEIL, JOSEPH NEIL, archbishop; b. Sydney, N.S., Can., Apr. 15, 1924; s. John Martin and Kate (Mac Lean) Mac N. BA, St. Francis Xavier U., Antigonish, N.S., 1944; postgrad., Holy Heart Sem., Halifax, N.S., 1944-48, U. Perugia, 1956, U. Chgo., 1964; JCD, U. St. Thomas, Rome, 1958. Ordained priest Roman Cath. Ch., 1948. Pastor parishes in N.S., 1948-55; officialis Chancery Office, Antigonish, 1958-59; adminstrn. Diocese of Antigonish, 1959-60; rector Cathedral Antigonish, 1961; dir. extension dept. St. Francis Xavier U., Antigonish, 1961-69, v.p., 1962-69; bishop St. John, N.B., Can., 1969-73; chancellor U. St. Thomas, Fredericton, N.B., 1969-73; archbishop of Edmonton, Alta., 1973—; chmn. Alta Bishops' Conf., 1973—; chmn. bd. Newman Theol. Coll., Edmonton, 1973—, St. Joseph's Coll. U. Alta., Edmonton, 1973—. Vice chmn. N.S. Voluntary Econ. Planning Bd., 1965-69; bd. dirs. Program and Planning Agy., Govt. of N.S., 1969; exec. Atlantic Provinces Econ. Coun., 1968-73, Can. Coun. Rural Devel., 1965-75; bd. dirs. Futures Secretariat, 1981, Ctr. for Human Devel., Toronto, Ont., Can., 1985—; mem. bd. mgmt. Edmonton Gen. Hosp., 1983-92, Edmonton Caritas Health Group, 1992—; mem. Nat. Com. for Can. Participation in Habitat, 1976. Mem. Canadian Assn. Adult Edn. (past pres. N.S.), Canadian Assn. Dirs. Univ. Extension and Summer Schs. (past pres.), Inst. Research on Public Policy (founding mem.), Can. Conf. Cath. Bishops (pres. 1979-81, mem. com. on ecumenism 1985-91, com. on missions 1991—, mem. permanent coun. 1993—). Address: Archbishop of Edmonton, 8421 101st Ave, Edmonton, AB Canada T6A 0L1

MACNEIL, MICHAEL DAVID, research geneticist; b. Warsaw, N.Y., Aug. 7, 1952; s. Hugh S. and Georgia E. (McGowan) MacN.; m. Betty K. Smith, May 17, 1980; children: Megan, Brendan. BS, Cornell U., 1974; MS, Mont. State U., 1978; PhD, S.D. State U., 1982. Instr. S.D. State U., Brookings, 1979-80; statis. cons. U.S. Meat Animal Rsch. Ctr., Clay Ctr., Nebr., 1980-88; rsch. geneticist USDA-Agrl. Rsch. Svc., Miles City, Mont., 1989—. Contbr. over 100 sci. reports to profl. publs. Orgnl. leader 4-H Club, Miles City, 1990—. Recipient Cert. of Merit, USDA, 1990. Mem. Am. Soc. Animal Sci., Coordinating Com.-Beef Cattle Breeding in Western Region (chmn. 1989). Office: USDA Agrl Rsch Svc RR 1 Box 2021 Miles City MT 59301-9202

MACNEILL, BRIAN F., oil company executive; b. 1939; married; 4 children. B in Comms., Mont. State U., 1965. Acct. Haskins & Sells, San Francisco, 1967, Alta., Can., 1969; mgr. acctg. Home Oil Co. Ltd., 1971, comptr., 1973, v.p. fin., 1976-80; v.p. fin. Scurry-Rainbow Oil Ltd., 1976-80; v.p., treas. Hiram Walker Resources Ltd., 1980-82; v.p. fin., CFO Home Oil Co., Ltd.; also bd. dirs.; pres., CEO Interprovincial Pipe Line, Inc., Edmonton, Alta., Can.; bd. dirs. Scurry Rainbow Oil Ltd., Plains Petroleums Ltd. Mem. Fin. Execs. Inst., CICA, Alta. and Ont. Inst. of Chartered Accts., Metro Toronto Bd. Trade, Calgary Petroleum Club, Canyon Meadows Golf & Country, Cambridge. Office: Interprovincial Pipe Line Inc, 10201 Jasper Ave, Edmonton, AB Canada T5J 2J9

MAC-NOYE, SHIRLEY, public trust executive; b. Sunland, Calif., Aug. 2, 1940; d. Raymond Leonard Smith and Evelyn Shirley (Lawrence) Maldonado; m. Edward Makraczyk, July 26, 1959 (div. 1966); children: Victoria Ann., Edward Ray; m. Harry Robert Noye, Oct. 7, 1978 (dec. Oct. 1993). Owner, mgr. Playmates Pre-Sch., Lake Havasu City, Ariz., 1964-69; broker Lake Havasu City, Ariz., 1969—; founder, exec. sec. Individuals for Havasu Inc., 1984—; tax agt. Advantage 2000, 1990—; pres., chmn. bd. Citizens Island Bridge Co., Ltd., Lake Havasu City, 1992—. Contbr. newsletter The Havasu Citizen, 1992. Pres. Lake Havasu Bd. Realtors, 1978, chmn, 1982; mem. Mohave County Indsl. Devel. Authority, 1990—, Lake Havasu Comprehensive Plan Com., 1985, Ariz. Town Hall, 1983—; dist. II dir. Mohave County Rep. Ctrl. Com., 1991-92; chmn. Lake Havasu Rep. Women. 1990-91. Named Rep. Woman of Yr., 1991. Office: Citizens Island Bridge Co Ltd 1350 Mcculloch Blvd Lake Havasu City AZ 86403-6834

MACON, CAROL ANN GLOECKLER, micro-computer data base management company executive; b. Milw., Mar. 25, 1942; d. William Theodore and Gwendolyn Martha (Rice) Gloeckler; m. Jerry Lyn Macon, Aug. 28, 1981; children: Christian, Marie. BS in Edn. cum laude, U. Wis., Milw., 1969; postgrad., Midwestern State U., Wichita Falls, Tex., 1977, U. Tex., San Antonio, 1978, U. Colo., Colorado Springs. Tchr. Lubbock, Tex.; patient affairs coord. Cardiac Assocs., Colorado Springs; founder, CFO Macon Systems, Inc., Colorado Springs. Artist, Australia, Tex., Colo. Mem. Software Pubs. Assn., Colorado Springs Symphony Coun., Colorado Springs Fine Arts Ctr., Colorado Springs Rose Soc., DaVinci Quartet Assn., Colo. Mountain Club, Phi Kappa Phi, Kappa Delta Pi, Sigma Tau Delta, Psi Chi.

MACON, JAMES BARBOUR, III, neurological surgeon; b. Richmond, Va., Mar. 23, 1947; s. James Barbour and Marion (Pate) M.; m. Caroline Sprague Stewart, Aug. 31, 1972; children: James Barbour IV, Charles Sprague, Peter Randolph. AB magna cum laude, Princeton U., 1968; MD cum laude, Harvard U., 1974. Diplomate Am. Bd. Neurol. Surgery. Intern in surgery Stanford U. Med. Ctr., Palo Alto, Calif., 1974-75; resident in neurosurgery Mass. Gen. Hosp., Boston, 1977-82; practice medicine specializing in neurol. surgery, Louisville, 1982-90. Contbr. articles to profl. jours. Recipient Neurosurgery Resident Research award New Eng. Neurosurg. Soc., 1980, 81, 82; Neurophysiol. fellow NIH, Bethesda, Md., 1975-77; Fulbright scholar, Coll. de France, Paris, 1968-69. Fellow ACS; mem. Am. Pain Soc., Am. Assn. Neurol. Surgeons, Internat. Assn. for Study of Pain, Calif. Med. Assn., Congress Neurol. Surgeons, Mass. Med. Soc., Riverside County Med. Soc. Clubs: Ivy (Princeton, N.J.); Dedham Country (Mass.). Home: 45855 Paradise Valley Rd Indian Wells CA 92210-8455 Office: James B Macon MD Eisenhower Med Ctr Rancho Mirage CA 92270

MACON, JERRY LYN, software company owner, software publisher; b. Okla., Jan. 10, 1941; s. James Westwood and Mary Isabelle (Hankins) M.; m. Carol Ann Gloeckler, Aug. 28, 1981; children: Heather, Scott, Karla. BS in Physics magna cum laude, Colo. Coll., 1963; MS in Physics, MIT, 1966; MBA in Fin., U. Colo., 1980. Physics instr. U.S. Naval Acad., Annapolis, Md., 1966-69; stockbroker Merrill Lynch, Colorado Springs, 1969-71; dir. systems analysis and programming Colorado Springs Pub. Schs., 1971-80; co-founder, pres. Alpine Software, Inc., Colorado Springs, 1980-82, Macon Systems Inc., Colorado Springs, 1981—. Author software: DB Master, 1980, Advanced CB Master, 1981, Advanced DB Master for Windows Version 6.0, 1995. Mem. Colorado Springs Fine Arts Ctr., 1982—, Colorado Springs Symphony Coun., 1985—, Colorado Springs Better Bus. Bur., 1990—. Cmdr. USN, 1966-69, USNR, 1959-63, 69-82. Boettcher Found. scholar, 1959; Woodrow Wilson fellow, 1963; MIT rsch. assistantship, 1964. Mem. Nat. Fedn. Ind. Bus., Software Pubs. Assn., Colo. Springs Rose Soc., Colo. Mountain Club, Phi Beta Kappa. Office: Macon Systems Inc 724 S Tejon St Colorado Springs CO 80903-4042

MACPHERSON, KEVIN DAN, artist; b. Orange, N.J., Apr. 9, 1956; s. James F. and May Rose (McCrink) M.; m. Wanda Lynn Robbins, Oct. 21, 1979. BFA, No. Ariz. U., 1978; student, Scottsdale Artists Sch., 1986-93. Illustrator graphic studio, Phoenix, 1978-80; freelance illustrator, artist, Taos, N.Mex., 1980-90; fine artist Taos, 1987—; tchr. various art guilds countrywide, 1990—. One man shows at Plein Air Painters Am. Show, Avalon, Calif., 1987—, O'Brien's Art Emporium, Scottsdale, Ariz., 1989, 92, Oil Painters of Am., 1992-94, Redfern Gallery, Laguna, Calif., 1994; represented in numerous permanent collections. Stacey scholar Nat. Acad. Western Art, 1990. Mem. Oil Painters Am. (signature mem.), Plein Aire Painters Am. Home and Studio: Rt 1 Box 55 Taos NM 87571

MACUMBER, JOHN PAUL, insurance company executive; b. Macon, Mo., Jan. 21, 1940; s. Rolland Deardorf and Althea Villa (Cason) M.; BA, Cen. Meth. Coll., Fayette, Mo., 1962; Asso. in Risk Mgmt., Ins. Inst. Am., 1978; m. Marilyn Sue Ashe, Nov. 10, 1962; children—Leanne, Cheryl. Casualty underwriter U.S. Fidelity & Guaranty Co., St. Louis, 1962-66; automobile underwriter Am. Indemnity Co., Galveston, Tex., 1966-69; auto casualty underwriter St. Paul Cos., New Orleans, 1969-73; sr. comml. casualty underwriter Chubb/Pacific Indemnity, Portland, Oreg., 1973-75; casualty underwriter Interstate Nat. Corp., L.A., 1975-76, underwriting supr., 1976-78, v.p., br. mgr., Mpls., 1978-82, also v.p. subs. Chgo. Ins. Co.; umbrella/spl. risk supr. Guaranty Nat. Ins. Co., Englewood, Colo., 1982-85;

br. mgr. Burns & Wilcox, Ltd.-West, Salt Lake City, 1985—. With USAF, 1962-68. Nat. Methodist scholar, 1958; named Co. Person of Yr. Profl. Ins. Agts Utah, 1991. Mem. Ins. Assn. Utah (sec.-treas. 1992-93, v.p. 1993-94, pres. 1994-95), Profl. Ins. Agts. Utah, Ind. Ins. Agts. Utah, Surplus Line Assn. Utah (bd. dirs. 1994—), Nat. Assn. Profl. Surplus Lines Offices. Republican. Mem. Unity Ch. of Salt Lake City (v.p., bd. dirs. 1988). Lodges: Optimists (charter pres. 1968) (Friendswood, Tex.); Kiwanis (charter pres. 1979) (Bloomington, Minn.). Clubs: Insurance, Blue Goose (Salt Lake City). Home: 9683 Buttonwood Dr Sandy UT 84092-3245 Office: 185 S State St Ste 840 Salt Lake City UT 84111-1538

MACY, JONATHAN ISAAC, ophthalmologist, educator; b. N.Y.C., Sept. 28, 1950; s. Isaac Glass and Florence Goodblatt; m. Jeannette Meerovich, Nov. 28, 1976; children: Alexandra, Adam. BA magna cum laude, Boston U., 1972, MD, 1976. Diplomate Am. Bd. Ophthalmology, Am. Coll. Surgeons., Nat. Bd. Med. Examiners. Intern LAC-U. So. Calif. Med. Ctr., L.A., 1976-77, resident ophthalmology, 1978-81; rsch. fellow Estelle Doheny Eye Found., L.A., 1977-78; clin. instr. Jules Stein Eye Inst. U. So. Calif., L.A., 1981-84, clin. instr. dept. ophthalmology, 1982-85, asst. clin. prof. Jules Stein Eye Inst., 1984—, asst. clin. prof. dept. ophthalmology, 1985—; chief dept. ophthalmology Midway Hosp. Med. Ctr., L.A., 1986-87, vice chief of staff, 1988-89, chief of staff, 1990-91; Bd. dirs. Midway Hosp. Med. Ctr., 1987—, Myasthenia Gravis Found., 1981—; med. adv. bd. Lions Doheny Eye Bank, 1990—, Myasthenia Gravis Found., 1986—; rsch. assoc. Discovery Fund for Eye Rsch., 1986—. Contbr. articles to numerous profl. jours. Exec. bd. Physicians Who Care, 1986 87; bd. dirs. Found. for the Jr. Blind, 1986—. Fellow Am. Physicians, Am. Acad. Ophthalmology, Am. Coll. Surgeons; mem. Am. Soc. Cataract and Refractory Surgery, Nat. MarfanFound., Calif. Assn. Ophthalmology, Calif. Med. Assn., Internat. Clin. Contact Lenses Soc., Internat., Cornea Soc., Internat. Soc. Refractory Keratoplasty, Lions Eye Found., L.A. County Med. Assn., L.A. Soc. Ophthalmology (Merit award for original rsch.), Pan-Am. Assn. Ophthalmology, World Med. Assn., UCLA Alumni Assn., UCLA Dept. Ophthalmology Assn., U. So. Calif./Doheny Residents Assn., U. So. Calif. Profl. Practice Assn., Sjogrens Found. L.A., Phi Beta Kappa, Psi Chi. Office: Am Eye Inst 8635 W 3rd St # 390W Los Angeles CA 90048-6101

MACY, RICHARD J., state judge; b. Saranac Lake, N.Y., June 2, 1930; m. Emily Ann Macy; children: Anne, Patty, Mark. BS in Bus., U. Wyo., 1955, JD, 1958. Pvt. practice Sundance, Wyo., 1958-85; justice Wyo. Supreme Ct., Cheyenne, 1985—, former chief justice; Crook County atty., 1970-85; mem. Nat. Conf. Commrs. on Uniform State Laws, 1982—. Mem. Sigma Chi (Nat. Outstanding Sig award 1986). Office: Wyo Supreme Ct Supreme Ct Bldg Cheyenne WY 82002*

MADDEN, JAMES COOPER, V, management consultant; b. Glen Cove, N.Y., June 18, 1961; s. James Cooper IV and Linda Marie (Lizza) M.; m. Jill Louise Howenstine, July 27, 1985; 1 child, Jennifer Louise. Student, Webb Inst. Naval Architecture, Glen Cove, 1979-80; BA cum laude, So. Meth. U., 1983, BBA magna cum laude, 1983. Cert. Soc. Naval Architects and Marine Engrs. Cons. Andersen Cons./Arthur Andersen, Houston, 1983-85, sr. cons., 1985-87; mgr. Andersen Cons./Arthur Andersen, L.A., 1987-90, sr. mgr., 1990-91; prin. Booz-Allen & Hamilton, L.A., 1991-93; v.p. mng. dir., c.p. comml. opers. SHL SYSTEMHOUSE, L.A., 1995—; mem. adv. bd. Claremont Grad. Sch., Mgmt. Info. Svcs. Program; mem. UCLA Anderson Sch., I.S. Assocs. Author industry papers. Scholar Webb Inst. Naval Architecture, 1979-80. Home: 41 Bridgeport Rd Newport Coast CA 92657-1015 Office: SHL System House 12750 Center Court Dr S Cerritos CA 90701-4552

MADDEN, JOHN, television sports commentator, former professional football coach; b. Austin, Minn., Apr. 10, 1936; s. Earl and Mary O'Flaherty M.; m. Virginia Madden; children: Mike, Joe. B.S., Calif. Poly. U., 1959, M.A., 1961. Player Phila. Eagles (NFL team), 1959; asst. coach Hancock Jr. Coll., Santa Maria, Calif., 1960-62; head coach Hancock Jr. Coll., 1962-64; defensive coordinator Calif. State U., San Diego, 1964-66; with Oakland Raiders, Am. Football League (now Am. Football Conf., Nat. Football League), 1967-79, linebacker coach, 1967-69, head coach, 1969-79; head coach NFL Pro Bowl team Am. Football Conf., 1971, 73, 74, 75; head coach 6 Western div. Am. Football Conf. championship teams, Super Bowl champions, 1976; sports commentator, football analyst CBS Sports, 1979-93; appears in TV and radio commls.; sports commentator, football analyst Fox Network, 1994—. Author: Hey, Wait a Minute, I Wrote a Book!, 1984; One Knee Equals Two Feet, 1986; developer (software) John Madden Football, 1988, John Madden Football II, 1993. Named Coach of Year Am. Football League, 1969, Sports Personality of the Yr., Am. Sportscasters Assn., 1985; recipient Emmy awards for sports broadcasting, 1982, 83, 85, 86, 87, 88. Office: care Fox Network PO Box 900 Beverly Hills CA 90213-0900

MADDEN, PAUL ROBERT, lawyer; b. St. Paul, Nov. 13, 1926; s. Ray Joseph and Margaret (Meyer) M.; m. Rosemary R. Sorel, Aug. 7, 1974; children: Margaret Jane, William, James Patrick, Derek R. Sorel, Lisa T. Sorel. Student, St. Thomas Coll., 1944; AB, U. Minn., 1948; JD, Georgetown U., 1951. Bar: Ariz. 1957, Minn. 1951, D.C. 1951. Assoc. Hamilton & Hamilton, Washington, 1951-55; legal asst. to commr. SEC, Washington, 1955-56; assoc. Lewis and Roca, Phoenix, Ariz., 1957-59, ptnr., 1959-90; ptnr. Beus, Gilbert & Morrill, Phoenix, 1991-94; ptnr. Chapman & Cutler, Phoenix, 1994—. Sec. Minn. Fedn. Coll. Rep. Clubs, 1947-48; chmn. 4th dist. Minn. Young Rep. Club, 1948; nat. co-chmn. Youth for Eisenhower, 1951-52; mem. Ariz. Rep. Com., 1960-62; past chmn., bd. dirs. Camelback Behavioral Health Svcs., Scottsdale, Ariz.; bd. dirs. Found. Jr. Achievement Ctrl. Ariz., Cath. Community Found., Phoenix, Heritage Hills Homeowners Assn.; past bd. dirs. Camelback Charitable Trust, The Samaritan Found., Phoenix; past bd. dirs., past chmn. Camelback Hosps., Inc., Scottsdale; past bd. dirs., past. pres. Ariz. Club, Phoenix, 1990-93; bd. dirs., past chmn. Found. for Sr. Living, Phoenix; bd. dirs., vice chmn., Cen. Ariz. chpt. ARC; past bd. dirs., past pres. Jr. Achievement Cen. Ariz., Inc. With USNR, 1946-48. Mem. ABA, Ariz. Bar Assn., Maricopa County Bar Assn., Fed. Bar Assn., Fedn. Ins. Counsel, Nat. Health Lawyers Assn., Am. Soc. Hosp. Attys., Nat. Assn. Bond Lawyers, Ariz. Assn. for Indsl. Devel., East Valley Partnership, Phi Delta Phi. Clubs: The Barristers (Washington), Arizona. Home: 5847 N 46th St Phoenix AZ 85018-1234 Office: Chapman & Cutler Two N Central Ave Ste 1100 Phoenix AZ 85004

MADDEN, RICHARD BLAINE, forest products executive; b. Short Hills, N.J., Apr. 27, 1929; s. James L. and Irma (Twining) M.; m. Joan Fairbairn, May 24, 1958; children: John Richard, Lynn Marie, Kathryn Ann, Andrew Twining. B.S., Princeton U., 1951; J.D., U. Mich., 1956; M.B.A., NYU, 1959; PhD (hon.), St. Scholastica Coll., 1994. Bar: Mich. 1956, N.Y. 1958. Gen. asst. treas.'s dept. Socony Mobil Oil Corp., N.Y.C., 1956-57; spl. asst. Socony Mobil Oil Corp., 1958-59, fin. rep., 1960; asst. to pres Mobil Chem. Co.; also dir. Mobil Chems. Ltd. of Eng., 1960-63; exec. v.p., gen. mgr. Kordite Corp.; also v.p. Mobil Plastics, 1963-66; v.p. Mobil Chem. Co., N.Y.C., 1966-68; group v.p. Mobil Chem. Co., 1968-70; asst. treas. Mobil Oil Corp., 1970-71; chmn. Mobil Oil Estates Ltd., 1970-71; pres., chief exec. to chmn., chief exec. officer Potlatch Corp., San Francisco, 1971-94; ret., 1994; bd. dirs. Potlatch Corp., Pacific Gas and Electric Co., Consolidated Freightways, Inc., Pacific Gas Transmission Co., URS Corp.; former bd. dirs. Del Monte Corp., AMFAC Inc., Bank Calif. N.A. and BankCal Tri-State Corp.; from lectr. to adj. assoc. prof. fin. NYU, 1960-63. Bd. dirs. Smith-Kettlewell Eye Rsch. Inst., Nat. Park Found., mem. exec. com., devel. com.; trustee emeritus Am. Enterprise Inst.; bd. govs., mem. exec. com. San Francisco Symphony; mem. Bus.-Higher Edn. Forum, Com. for Econ. Devel. Lt. (j.g.) USNR, 1951-54. Mem. N.Y. Bar Assn., Mich. Bar Assn. Roman Catholic. Clubs: Bohemian (San Francisco); Lagunitas (Ross, Calif.); Metropolitan (Washington).

MADDUX, PARKER AHRENS, lawyer; b. San Francisco, May 23, 1939; s. Jackson Walker and Jeanette Ahrens M.; m. Mathilde G.M. Landman, Mar. 20, 1966; 1 child, Jackson Wilhelmus Quentin. AB, U. Calif., 1961; JD, Harvard U., 1964. Bar: Calif. 1965, U.S. Dist. Ct. (no. so. and ea. dist.) Calif. 1965, U.S. Ct. Appeals (9th cir.) 1972, U.S. Ct. Claims, 1974, N.Y. 1981, U.S. Supreme Ct. 1982, Assoc., Pillsbury, Madison & Sutro, San Francisco, 1965-72, ptnr., 1973—; lectr. in field. Bd. dirs. Friends of Recreation and Parks, San Francisco; trustee Town Sch. for Boys, San Francisco; co-chair San Francisco Open Space Citizens Adv. Com. Fulbright fellow, 1964-65. Mem. ABA, Calif. Bar Assn., San Francisco Bar Assn., St. Francis Yacht (San Francisco) Club, Harvard Club (N.Y.C., San Francisco), Pacific Union Club. Republican. Unitarian. Contbr. articles to profl. jours. Office: Pillsbury Madison & Sutro 225 Bush St San Francisco CA 94104-4207

MADDY, DONALD LEE, computer company executive, software developer; b. Whittier, Calif., Aug. 27, 1949; s. Keith Thomas and Colleen Joanne (Barlow) M.; m. Lynne Louise Juhnke, June 29, 1985; children: Crystal Lynne, Michael Donald. Nuclear weapons, electronics student, Sandia AFB, 1970; BS in Computer Sci., Calif. State U., Sacramento, 1976. Cert. data processor, real estate agt. Nuclear weapons electronics specialist U.S. Army, Istanbul, Turkey, 1970-71; programmer Water Resources Control Bd. Div. Water Quality, Sacramento, 1974-75, Calif. State Coll., Bakersfield, 1976-78; programmer, analyst Sierra Pacific Power Co., Reno, Nev., 1979-80; sr. programmer, analyst State of Idaho Transp. Dept., Boise, 1980-81, United Grocers Warehouse, Oakland, Calif., 1981-84; sr. programming cons. Farmers Savings & Loan, Davis, Calif., 1984-87, Pacific Gas & Electric Co., Avila Beach, Calif., 1987—; pres. Maddy Corp., 1994—. Co-author: Computer Software Security System for Plant Info. Mgmt. System, 1992. With U.S. Army, 1969-72. Mem. Assn. Sys. Mgrs., Data Processing Mgmt. Assn., Assn. Computing Machinery, Am. Nuclear Soc. Republican. Office: The Maddy Corp 1220 16th St Los Osos CA 93402-1422

MADDY, KENNETH LEON, state senator, lawyer; b. Santa Monica, Calif., May 22, 1934; s. Russell T. and Anna M. (Balzer) M.; m. Beverly Ann Chinello, 1957; children—Deanna G., Donald P., Marilyn M.; m.2d, Norma Foster, 1981. B.S., Fresno State Coll., 1957; J.D., UCLA, 1963. Ptnr., Chinello, Chinello, Maddy & Shelton, Fresno, Calif., after 1963; mem. Calif. State Assembly from Dist. 30, 1970-78, now mem. Calif. State Senate. Del. Republican Nat. Conv., 1976, 80, 84, del., 1988, Senate Republican leader, 1987—. Served to 1st lt., USAF, 1957-60; capt. Res. Mem. Calif. Bar Assn., Jaycees, Fresno C. of C., Blue Key, Sigma Nu, Phi Delta Phi. Lodge Rotary. Office: Office of State Senate 2503 W Shaw Ave Ste 101 Fresno CA 93711-3309 Address: 305 State Capitol Sacramento CA 95814

MADDY, PENELOPE JO, philosopher; b. Tulsa, July 4, 1950; d. Richard and Suzanne (Lorimer) Parsons. BA in Math., U. Calif., Berkeley, 1972; PhD in Philosophy, Princeton U., 1979. Asst. prof. U. Notre Dame (Ind.), 1978-83; assoc. prof. U. Ill., Chgo., 1983-87; assoc. prof. U. Calif., Irvine, 1987-89, prof., 1989—, dept. chair, 1991-95; mem. editorial bd. Jour. Philos. Logic, 1985—. Author: Realism in Mathematics, 1990; editor Notre Dame Jour. Formal Logic, 1979-84, editl. bd., 1984—; editl. bd. Jour. Symbolic Logic, 1995—. Fellow AAUW, 1982-83, U. Calif., 1988-89; NSF grantee, 1986, 88-89, 90-91, 94-95, Marshall scholar, 1982-83, Westinghouse Sci. scholar, 1968-72. Mem. Assn. Symbolic Logic (mem. exec. com. 1993—), Am. Philos. Assn. (mem. exec. com.), Philosophy of Sci. Assn. (mem. governing bd. 1993—). Office: U Calif Dept Philosophy Irvine CA 92717

MADER, CHARLES LAVERN, chemist; b. Dewey, Okla., Aug. 8, 1930; s. George Edgar and Naomia Jane (Harer) M.; m. Emma Jean Sinclair, June 12, 1960; 1 child, Charles L. II. BS, Okla. State U., 1952, MS, 1954; PhD, Pacific Western U., 1980. Fellow Los Alamos (N.Mex.) Nat. Lab., 1955—; JIMAR sr. fellow U. Hawaii, Honolulu, 1985-94; pres. Mader Consulting Co., Honolulu, 1985—. Author: Numerical Modeling of Detonation, 1979, Numerical Modeling of Water Waves, 1988, LASL Data Volumes, 1980-82; contbr. numerous articles to profl. jours.; author 70 reports. Scoutmaster Boys Scouts Am., Los Alamos, 1971-85. Fellow Am. Inst. Chemists; mem. Am. Chem. Soc., Combustion Inst., Tsunami Soc. (editor 1985—), Marine Tech. Soc., Sigma Xi, Pi Mu Epsilon, Phi Lambda Upsilon. Methodist. Home: 1049 Kamehame Dr Honolulu HI 96825-2860 Office: Mader Cons Co 1049 Kamehame Dr Honolulu HI 96825-2860

MADER, DOUGLAS PAUL, statistician; b. Brookings, S.D., May 16, 1963; s. Lawrence Harold Mader Jr. and Susan Margaret (Littleton) Burk; m. Darla Sue Hower, Dec. 30, 1991; children: Alyssa, Megan. BS in Engring. Physics, S.D. State U., 1985; MS in Math., Colo. Sch. of Mines, 1990; PhD in Mech. Engring., Colo. State U., 1994. Cert. quality engr. Am. Soc. Quality Control, 1990-93. Quality control engr. Govt. Electronics Group, Motorola, Scottsdale, Ariz., 1985-87; integrated circuit test engr. Semiconductor Products sector, Motorola, Mesa, Ariz., 1987-88; sr. staff engr. Six Sigma Rsch. Inst., Motorola, Schaumburg, Ill., 1990-92, prin. staff scientist, 1992; cons. Rockwell Internat., Cedar Rapids, Iowa, 1992-93; quality engring. mgr. Advanced Energy Industries, Ft. Collins, Colo., 1993-95; instr. stats. and mech. engring. Colo. State U., 1993-94; statistician Hewlett-Packard Co., Greeley, Colo., 1995—. Author: Process Control Methods, 1993 (videotapes) Concurrent Engineering - The Foundation of Six Sigma Quality, 1992; mem. editorial bd. Internat. Jour. of Ops. and Quantitative Mgmt., 1994—. Mem. Am. Statis. Assn., Inst. Indsl. Engrs., Am. Soc. Quality Control (mem. standing rev. and mix media rev. bd. 1992—, mem. editl. bd. for quality engring. 1994—), Inst. Ops. Rsch. and Mgmt. Sci., Decision Scis. Inc. Office: Hewlett-Packard Co 700 71st Ave Greeley CO 80634

MADER, KELLY FORBES, public policy executive, senator; b. Sheridan, Wyo., Jan. 21, 1952; s. Richard August and Ena Cora (Forbes) M.; m. Nancy Gay Murray, Nov. 16, 1975; children: Amy, Angie, Ian. Student, Bob Jones U., 1970-71, Grace Coll., 1971-72, Tex. A&M U. Owner, pres. Kelly F. Mader & Assocs., Gillette, Wyo., 1973—; rep. Wyo. State Legis., Cheyenne, 1982-84, senator, 1984-91; chmn. senate appropriations com., 1989-91; co-chmn. joint appropriations com.; chmn. Senate Rep. Conf., 1988-90. Officer Campbell County Sheriffs Res., Gillette, 1981-91, Campbell County Search and Rescue Team, 1981-91; mem. nat. bd. dirs. Justice Fellowship, 1993—. Named one of Outstanding Young Men of Am., 1982, 85, 89. Mem. Am. Legis. Exch. Coun. (state chmn. 1984-91, nat. bd. dirs. 1991-92, Outstanding Legis. Leader award 1989), NRA. Republican.

MADER, THOMAS H., ophthalmologist; b. San Jose, Calif.. BS in Biology, U. Ariz., 1971, MD, 1975. Diplomate Am. Bd. Ophthalmology. Resident in ophthalmology Fitzsimmons Army Med. Ctr., 1980-83; fellow Emory U. Sch. of Medicine, 1989-90; chief of ophthalmology Madigan Army Med. Ctr., Tacoma, Wash. Author numerous articles & book chpts.

MADERA, MARIE LOUISE, magazine publishing executive; b. Los Angeles, June 11, 1955; d. Leroy James and Helen Jean (Clark) M. BA, Calif. State U., Long Beach, 1978. Art dir. Keyboard World mag., Downey, Calif., 1978-79, Popular Ceramics mag., Glendale, Calif., 1980; mgr. prodn. Creative Age Pubs., Van Nuys, Calif., 1980-86; dir. prodn. High Tech Pubs., Torrance, Calif., 1986; dir. pubs. Family Living Mag., Buena Park, Calif., 1986-93; prodn. mgr. Fancy Publs., Irvine, Calif., 1993—; cons. affluent Target Mktg., La Mirada, Calif., 1986-93; host Theatre Scene local cable TV show. Choreographer community theatres, 1981—. Mem. NAFE, Western Pubs. Assn., Advt. Prodn. Assn. So. Calif., Pubs. Prodn. Mgr. Club So. Calif. NOW. Roman Catholic. Home: 2502 E Willow St Unit 201 Long Beach CA 90806-2231 Office: Fancy Pubs 3 Burroughs Irvine CA 92718-2804

MADIREDDI, MALLAREDDY, physiologist; b. Deveryamjal, India, Apr. 10, 1952; came to the U.S., 1984; s. Narsareddy and Laxmamma (Anthireddigari) M.; m. Sucharitha Ala, Dec. 15, 1983; children: Sunthosh P., Sundeep P. BS, Osmania U., Hyderabad, India, 1974, MSc, 1976, PhD, 1979; Longterm P.G. Electrophysiology, Czechoslovakia Acad. Scis., Prague, 1978-80. Asst. in physiology Inst. Physiology, Ludwig Maxmilions U. Munich, Germany, 1980-83; postgrad. rsch. electrophysiologist U. Calif., Divsn. Biomed. Scis., Riverside, 1984-85, asst. rsch. psysiologist Steps, 1985—, tchr., 1986—; tchr. Osmania U., Hyderabad, 1976-78, vis. scientist, 1983-84; presenter in field. Contbr. articles to profl. jours. Recipient UNESCO and WHO postdoctoral award, 1978-80, UNESCO Travel grant, 1978, U.S. Cystic Fibrosis Found. travel grant, Verona, Italy, 1987, Dallas, 1981, Cystic Fibrosis Found. U.S. Postdoctoral Rsch. award, 1990, Cystic Fibrosis Found. grant, 1990-93, Cystic Fibrosis Inc. rsch. grant, Palo Alto, 1994. Mem. AAAS, Am. Physiol. Soc., Biophys. Soc. Am. Home: 1306 Johns Rd Perris CA 92571-0842 Office: Divsn Biomed Scis Univ Calif Riverside CA 92521

MADIX, ROBERT JAMES, chemical engineer, educator; b. Beach Grove, Ind., June 22, 1938; s. James L. and Marjorie A. (Strohl) M.; children: Bradley Alan, David Eric, Micella Lynn, Evan Scott. BS, U. Ill., 1961; PhD, U. Calif., 1964. NSF postdoctoral fellow Max Planck Inst., Göttingen, Fed. Republic of Germany, 1964-65; asst. prof, chem. engr. Stanford (Calif.) U., 1965-72, assoc. prof., chem. engr., 1972-77; prof. chem. engring. Stanford U., 1977—, chmn., chem. engr., 1983-87, prof. chemistry, 1981—; cons. Monsanto Chem., St. Louis, 1975-84, Shell Oil Co., Houston, 1985-86; Peter Debye lectorship Cornell U., 1985; Eyring lectr. chemistry Ariz. State U., 1990; disting. prof. lectr. U. Tex., Austin, 1980; chmn. Gordon Rsch. Conf. on Reactions on Surfaces, 1995. Assoc. editor Catalysis Rev., 1986—, Catalysis Letters, 1992—, Rsch. on Chem. Intermediates, 1994—; contbr. articles to profl. jours. Recipient Alpha Chi Sigma award Am. Inst. Chem. Engrs., 1990, Paul Emmett award Catalysis Soc. N.Am., 1984, Humboldt U.S. Sr. Scientist prize, 1978; For Found. fellow, 1969-72. Mem. Am. Chem. Soc. (Irving Langmuir Disting. Lectr. award 1981), Am. Phys. Soc., Am. Vacuum Soc., AIChE, Calif. Catalysis Soc. Office: Stanford Univ Dept Chemical Engring Stanford CA 94305

MADNI, ASAD MOHAMED, engineering executive; b. Bombay, Sept. 8, 1947; came to U.S., 1966; s. Mohamed Taher and Sara Taher (Wadiwalla) M.; Gowhartaj Shahnawaz, Nov. 11, 1976; 1 child, Jamal Asad. Gen. cert. edn., U. Cambridge, Bombay, 1964; AAS in Electronics, RCA Insts., Inc., 1968; BS in Engring., UCLA, 1969, MS in Engring., 1972; postgrad. exec. inst., Stanford U., 1984; cert. in engring. mgmt., Calif. Inst. Tech., 1987; PhD in Engring., Calif. Coast U., 1987; sr. exec. program, MIT, 1990. Sr. instr. Pacific States U., L.A., 1969-71; electronics auditor Pertec Corp., Chatsworth, Calif., 1973-75; project engr., sr. engr., program mgr, dir. advanced program Microwave div. Systron Donner, Van Nuys, Calif., 1975-82, dir. engring., 1982-92; gen. mgr. Microwave and Instrument div. Systron Donner, Van Nuys, Calif., 1985-90; chmn., pres., chief exec. officer Systron Donner Corp., 1990-92; pres., CEO Sensors and Controls Group BEI Electronics, Inc., 1992-93; pres., CEO BEI Sensors and Systems Co., Inc., 1993—; vice-chmn. IEEE-MTTS, San Fernando Valley chpt., 1991-92, chmn., 1992-94; tech. advisor Test and Measurement World, Boston, 1982-90; adv. Calif. State U. Northridge. Mem. editorial rev. bd., West coast chmn. Microwave Systems News and Communications Tech., 1982-90; contbr. more than 50 articles to numerous tech. publs.; patentee in field. Mem. AAAS, IEEE (sr.), NRA (life), Assn. Old Crows (life, Gold Cert. Merit 1992), Calif. Rifle and Pistol Assn. (life), MIT Soc. Sr. Execs. (life), UCLA Alumni Assn. (life), MIT Alumni Assn. (life). Home: 3281 Woodbine St Los Angeles CA 90064-4836 Office: BEI Sensors & Systems Co 13100 Telfair Ave Sylmar CA 91342-3573

MADORY, RICHARD EUGENE, lawyer; b. Kenton, Ohio, May 14, 1931; s. Harold Richard and Hilda (Strictland) M.; m. Barbara Jean Madory, Sept. 25, 1955; children—Richard Eugene, Terry Dean, Michael Wesly. B.S. in Edn., Ohio State U., 1952, J.D., Southwestern U., 1961. Bar: Calif., 1961, U.S. Ct. Mil. Appeals, U.S. Supreme Ct., U.S. Dist. Ct. (cen. dist.) Calif. With firm Madory, Booth, Zell & Pleiss, Santa Ana, Calif., 1962—, now pres., v.p., sec.-treas. lectr. Continuing Edn. of Bar State of Calif. Served to col. USMC. Fellow Am. Coll. Trial Lawyers; mem. ABA, Orange County Bar Assn., Los Angeles County Bar Assn., So. Calif. Def. Counsel Assn., Am. Bd. Trial Advs., Nat. Bd. Trial Advocacy. Office: 17822 17th St Ste 205 Tustin CA 92680-2152

MADRIL, LEE ANN, writer; b. Burbank, Calif., Sept. 16, 1944; d. George Mathew McDougall; 1 child, Francis Michael. Student, Granada Hills (Calif.) Coll., 1962. Freelance writer, 1986-90; shoot out artist, life mem. Bad Co., Auburn, Calif., 1990—; writer Idaho State Newspaper, Just Horses, Indian Valley, 1994—; cons. in authenticity, Calif. State Horsemen, Santa Rosea, 1988-90, Bad Co., 1990. Writer Idaho State Newspaper Just Horses; contbr. articles to profl. jours. Vol. Red Cross, Soques, Calif., 1982, Salinas (Calif.) Valley Meml. Hosp., 1979, Greenpeace, Humane Soc. U.S. Recipient Kodak KINSA award, 1989, winner County and State photo awards, 1993. Mem. Calif. State Horseman's Assn. (state champion 1989-90), Silver Spurs. Republican. Roman Catholic.

MADSEN, ELIZABETH KARLENE, librarian; b. Swarthmore, Pa., Aug. 16, 1944; d. Roy Harding and Katharine (Walters) M. BA, Western Wash. State U., 1966; MLS, U. Hawaii, 1972, postgrad.; MA, Stanford U., 1985; postgrad., Fielding Inst., 1994—. Editor Kodiak (Alaska) Daily Mirror, 1967-68; outreach libr. Fairbanks (Alaska) North Star Borough Libr., 1972; asst. libr. A. Holmes Johnson Libr., Kodiak, 1973-74, Bothell Libr. King County, Wash., 1974-76; coll. libr. Matanuska-Susitna Coll. U. Alaska, Palmer, 1976-90; social sci. libr. U. Hawaii, Manoa, 1990-91; libr. dir. Matanuska-Susitna, 1992—; del. Alaska Gov.'s Conf. on Librs., 1979; mem. Western Libr. Network Users Bd., 1993. Contbr. articles to profl. jours. Chmn. steering com. Alaska Collection Devel., 1982—; bd. dirs. Alaska Pub. TV, Anchorage, 1978-80. Named Boss of Yr. Profl. Secs. Internat., 1993. Mem. ALA, Pacific N.W. Libr. Assn., Alaska State Libr. Assn. (chmn. Mat-Su chpt. 1976, state treas. 1979-80), Hawaii Libr. Assn., Internat. Platform Assn., Mensa, Stanford U. Alumni Assn. Republican. Home: PO Box 499 Palmer AK 99645-0499

MADSEN, LINDA ANN, pediatrics nurse; b. Joliet, Ill., Aug. 15, 1961; d. Clarence Robert and Rosemary Eleanor (Vadovicky) M. BS, Tex. Woman's U., 1985. Cert. lactation cons. Staff nurse spl. care nurseries Parkland Meml. Hosp., Dallas, 1985-88; clin. nurse pediatrics unit Alaska Native Med. Ctr., Anchorage, 1988—. Mem. ANA, Nat. Assn. Neonatal Nurses, Sigma Theta Tau. Home: 2104 Roosevelt Dr Apt 6 Anchorage AK 99517

MADSEN, WILLIAM MARSHALL, media specialist; b. L.A., Aug. 15, 1939; s. William Felix Madsen and May Francis (Beattie) Atkins; m. Bettie Wanda Berkes, July 17, 1965 (div. sept. 1974); m. Charleen Joy Kelly, July 18, 1976; children: Synthia, Lesovsky. AA in Mktg., Fresno City Coll., 1963; BA in Radio, TV and Film, Fresno State Coll., 1971. Dir. med. and dental bldg. J. H. Hedrick Co., San Gabriel, Calif., 1977-78; v.p. constrn. sales and mktg. Juo Perkins Co., L.A., 1978-79; account exec. various automotive aftermarket cos., L.A., 1980-85; advt. dir. mag., TV acct. exec. Argus Pubs. Corp., L.A., 1985-93; media dir. Torco Internat. Corp., Santa Fe Springs, Calif., 1994—. Republican. Mem. Assembly of God. Office: Torco Internat Corp 9916 Pioneer Blvd Santa Fe Springs CA 90670-3220

MADSON, JOHN ANDREW, architect; b. Mankato, Minn., Nov. 12, 1920; m. Joyce Helen Madson, Sept. 4, 1949; children: Brian A., David G., Paul J., Thomas R., John E., Tracy Ann. BA, U. Minn., 1949, BArch, 1950. Archtl. draftsman, designer Perry E. Crosier & Son, Mpls., 1950-53; architect-in-tng. Magney Tusler & Setter, Mpls., 1953-55; ptnr., prin. Patch Erickson Madson Watten, Inc., Mpls., 1955-89; chief exec. officer Madson & Assocs., Mpls., 1989—. Capt. USAF, 1944-45, ETO. Corp. mem. AIA. Republican. Lutheran. Home: 17419 N 130th Ave Sun City West AZ 85375-5061

MAEDA, J. A., data processing executive; b. Mansfield, Ohio, Aug. 24, 1940; d. James Shunso and Doris Lucille Maeda; m. Robert Lee Hayes (div. May 1970); 1 child, Brian Sentaro Hayes. BS in Math., Purdue U., 1962, postgrad., 1962-63; postgrad., Calif. State U., Northridge, 1968-75; cert. profl. designation in tech. of computer operating systems and tech. of info. processing, UCLA, 1971. Cons., rsch. asst. computer ctr. Purdue U., West Lafayette, Ind., 1962-63; computer operator, sr. tab operator, mem. faculty Calif. State U., Northridge, 1969, programmer cons., tech. asst. II, 1969-70, supr. acad. applicatons, EDP supr. II, 1970-72, project tech. support coord. programmer II, office of the chancellor, 1972-73, tech. support coord. statewide timesharing tech. support, programmer II, 1973-74, acad. coord., tech. support coord. instrn., computer cons. III, 1974-83; coord. user svcs. info. ctr., mem. tech. staff IV CADAM INC subs. Lockheed Corp., Burbank, Calif., 1983-86, coord. end user svcs., tech. specialist computing dept., 1986-87; v.p., bd. dirs. Rainbow Computing, Inc., Northridge, 1976-85; dir. Aki Tech./Design Cons., Northridge, 1976—; mktg. mgr. thaumaturge Taro Quipu Cons., Northridge, 1987—; tech. cons. Digital Computer Cons., Chatsworth, Calif., 1988; cons. computer tech., fin. and bus. mgmt., sys. integration, 1988-90; tech. customer s/w support Collection Data Sys., Westlake, Calif., 1991; tech. writer Sterling Software Applications Engring. Divsn., 1992—. Author, editor more than 250 user publs., tutorials, ref. manuals, user guides; contbr. articles, papers, and photos to profl. jours.

Mem. IEEE, SHARE, Digital Equipment Computer Users Soc. (DECUS, author papers and presentations 1977-81, ednl. spl. interest group 1977-83, steering com. RSTS/E 1979-82, Sterling Software Silver Achievement award 1993). Office: Sterling Software Applicns Engring Divsn 5900 Canoga Ave Woodland Hills CA 91367-5034

MAEHL, WILLIAM HARVEY, historian, educator; b. Bklyn., May 28, 1915; s. William Henry and Antoinette Rose (Salamone) M.; m. Josephine Scholl McAllister, Dec. 29, 1941; children: Madeleine, Kathleen. BSc, Northwestern U., 1937, MA, 1939; PhD, U. Chgo., 1946. Asst. prof. history St. Louis U., 1941-42, Tex. A&M U., College Sta., 1943, De Paul U., Chgo., 1944-49; historian Dept. of Def., Karlsruhe, Stuttgart, Fed. Rep. Germany, 1950-52; chief briefing office U.S. hdqrs. EUCOM, Frankfurt, Fed. Rep. Germany, 1952-53; chief historian Artillery Sch. Ft. Sill, Okla., 1954, war plans office Hdqrs. NAMAE, USAF, Burtonwood, Eng., 1954-55; assoc. prof. European history Nebr. Wesleyan U., Lincoln, 1955-57, prof., 1958-62, 65-68; prof. German history Auburn (Ala.) U., 1968-81, prof. emeritus, 1981—; vis. prof. U. Nebr., 1962, U. Auckland, New Zealand, 1963-64, Midwestern U., Wichita Falls, Tex., 1965. Author: German Militarism and Socialism, 1968, History of Germany in Western Civilization, 1979, A World History Syllabus, 3 vols., 1980, August Bebel, Shadow Emperor of the German Workers, 1980, The German Socialist Party: Champion of the First Republic, 1918-33, 1986; author monographs, chpts. in books, atomic, biol. and emergency war plans for NAMAE, USAF; contbr. poems to A Question of Balance, Tears of Fire, Distinguished Poets of Am., Best Poems of 1995, Journey of the Mind; contbr. articles to profl. jours. Grantee Nebr. Wesleyan U., 1959, Auburn U., 1969-73, 79-80, Am. Philosophical Soc., 1973-74, Deutscher Akademischer Austauschdienst, 1978. Mem. Am. Hist. Assn., Phi Kappa Phi, Phi Alpha Theta.

MAFNAS, ISABEL IGLESIAS, computer lab specialist, computer consultant; b. Austin, Tex., Sept. 21, 1965; d. Juan Crisostomo and Isabel (Iglesias) M. BA in Statistics, U. Calif., Berkeley, 1987; postgrad., Chabot Coll., 1989-91, Merritt Coll., 1991-92. Stats. tutor, stats. reader U. Calif., Berkeley, 1986-87; stats. reader U. Calif. Extension, Berkeley, 1987-89; instrnl. asst. II Chabot Coll., Hayward, 1988-92, computer lab. specialist, 1992—; tchr. computers Eureka!-Girls Inc., San Leandro, 1993-95. Author: (Software user's guide) Academic Session Time Keeper, 1990, 91, 92, 94. Recipient Newspaper Carrier scholarship Gannett Found., Inc., Guam, 1983, Gannett Spl. scholarship Gannett Found., Inc., Guam, 1983. Office: Chabot College 25555 Hesperian Blvd Hayward CA 94545-2447

MAGALLANES, DEBORAH JEAN, business consulting company executive; b. Gary, Ind., May 22, 1951; d. Ray Daniel and Courtney Ann (Manders) M.; m. Gary Allen DeBardi, 1975. Student pub. schs., Crown Point, Ind. Adminstrv. asst. Fasfax Corp., Nashua, N.H., 1971-75; adminstrv. asst. Advanced Tech. Labs., Bellevue, Wash., 1975, part-time, 1975-77; sales asst. VMC Corp., Woodinville, Wash., 1975-76; cons. personnel Bus. Men's Clearing House, Bellevue, 1976-79; salesperson, gen. mgr. Cypress Steel, Inc., Bellevue, 1979, part-time, 1979-80; pres. Magallanes, Inc., Bellevue, 1979—; cons., project mgr. in field; founder Hug'M Messengers, 1979, Ace Entertainment, 1980; part-time ski instr. Mini-Mountain Sports Ctr., 1992—. Author: (with others) Guide to Better Relationships Through Dealmaking, 1985. Mem. Up With People, 1969—, Seattle-King County Conv. and Visitors Bur.; bd. dirs. Friends of Youth, Renton, Wash., 1984-90, v.p., 1986-90, vol., 1990—, Save the Elephants Campaign, Seattle, 1984-87; mem. Bellevue Leaders, 1982—, bd. dirs., 1983—, pres., 1984, sec./treas., 1990—. Mem. Women's Bus. Exchange (bd. dirs. 1981-85, Networker of Yr. 1983), Profl. Orgn. Ski Instrs. (cert. level I), MIT Alumni Assn. (hon. nat. officer 1984). Club: Hetty Green Partnership (pres. 1986-88, treas. 1988-89). Lodge: Soroptimists (bd. dirs. 1986, 88, 90, corr. sec. 1990, chair ways and means 1991, del. 1992). Avocations: canoeing, fishing, snow skiing, martial arts (1st degree black belt in Chung Moo Doe). Office: 405 114th Ave SE # 375 Bellevue WA 98004-6424

MAGALNICK, ELLIOTT BEN, retail medical supply company executive; b. Cleve., Aug. 19, 1945; s. Joseph Hyman and Ann (Resnick) M.; m. Diane Kerner, May 26, 1968 (div. Feb. 1988); children: Joel A., David A.; m. Judy Banjavic, June 9, 1991; stepchildren: Daniel Banjavic, David Banjavic. BS in Bus. Mgmt., Temple U., 1968. Cert. orthopedic fitter Health Industries Dealer Assn. Retail mgr. Milner Surg. Supply Co., Phila., 1970-72, Colo. Surg. Supply Co., Denver, 1972-73; mgr. non wheelchair retail Wheelchairs, Inc., Englewood, Colo., 1973-77; asst. mgr. ops. Denver Surg. Supply Co., 1977-78; owner, founder The Get Well Shop, Inc., Aurora, Colo., 1978—. Mem. chorus Shir Ami Singers, Denver, 1978-95, Colo. Symphony Orch., Denver, 1986-95; vol. Allied Fedn. Denver, 1984-87; mem. Legion of Merit, Rep. Party, Denver, 1992; donor Belle Bonfils Blood Ctr., 1976—; active Cantor Temple Micah, Denver. Named Disting. Pres., Optimist Internat., 1987. Mem. Colo. Assn. Med. Equipment Suppliers (dealer mem.), Health Industries Dealer Assn. 9cert. oprthopedic fitter), Home Health Care Dealers Coop., Luncheon Optimist Club Windsor Gardens (pres. 1986), Masons (master mason Columbine lodge), Colo. Consistory, El Jebel Temple, Rocky Mountain Cantors Assn. Jewish. Office: The Get Well Shop Inc 12028 E Mississippi Aurora CO 80012

MAGEE, DENNIS, cultural organization administrator; b. Pala, Calif., Oct. 9, 1937; s. Raymond Milton and Prudence Theresa (Golsh) M. BSBA, San Diego State U., San Diego, 1961. Wholesaler Kroshel Industries, San Diego, 1962-69; adminstr. Indian Health Council Inc., Pauma Valley, Calif., 1970—; adv. bd. Masters in Pub. Health Program for Native Americans, U. Calif., Berkeley; bd. trustees Robert F. Kennedy Meml. Found., Washington; bd. dirs. Comprehensive Health Planning Assn. of San Diego, Riverside and Imperial Counties, Nat. Indian Health Bd., Denver; mem. San Diego State U. Athletic Found, San Diego State U. Alumni Assn., San Diego Council of Community Clinics. Bd. dirs. United Way of San Diego County; mem. San Diego County Human Relations Commn.

MAGEE, DONALD EDWARD, national park service administrator; b. Trenton, N.J., Sept. 24, 1937; s. Donald A. and Anna C. (Bocskowics) M.; m. Linda Kimball, June 27, 1964; children: Kevin, Bonnie Magee Burch, Gale. BS in Forestry Mgmt., U. Mass., 1964. Pk. ranger Bryce Canyon (Utah) Nat. Pk., 1966-68; area mgr. Sunset Crater Nat. Monument, Flagstaff, Ariz., 1968-73; mgmt. analyst Nat. Capital Region, Washington, 1973-80; supt. Stones River Nat. Battlefield, Murfreesboro, Tenn., 1980-89, USS Ariz. Meml., Pearl Harbor, Hawaii, 1989—. With USN, 1956-58. Recipient Excellence of Svc. award Dept. of Interior, 1991. Office: USS Ariz Meml 1 Arizona Memorial Rd Honolulu HI 96818-3145

MAGEE, DOUGLAS SCOTT, public relations executive; b. Lincoln, Nebr., Feb. 22, 1952; s. Robert and Leah (Jacoby) M.; m. Mary Therese Hesse, Sept. 10, 1974 (div. Feb. 1984); children: Ashriel, Kylah Nicole. Student, U. Nebr. Lincoln, 1970-72. Bassist Codr Mgmt., Lincoln, Nebr., 1970-75, Creative Mgmt. Cons., Golden, Colo., 1975-78; from interviewer to v.p. Cmty. Response, Inc., Denver, 1978-81; mgr. rsch. Entercom, Inc., Denver, 1981-84; prin. Mgmt. Group, Inc., Denver, 1984-86; dir. rsch. Michael Gaughan and Assocs., Inc., Denver, 1986-87; v.p. rsch. MGA/Thompson, Inc., Denver, 1987—. Water Conservation com. mem. City of Arvada, Colo., 1990—, park adv. com. chair, 1994—, environ. com. mem., 1994—; bd. dirs. Am. Cancer Soc. Colo. Divsn. Recipient Gold Pick award Pub. Rels. Soc. Am. Colo. chpt., 1992, 94. Mem. Am. Mktg. Assn. Colo. chpt. (bd. dirs. 1983-89, treas. 1985-86, pres.-elect 1986-87, pres. 1987-88, pres. adv. coun. 1988—, PEAK award 1988, 94, 95). Republican. Home: 7275 W 62nd Ave Arvada CO 80003-5325 Office: MGA/Thompson Inc 1125 17th St Ste 1800 Denver CO 80202-2033

MAGID, GAIL AVRUM, neurosurgery educator; b. Chgo., Oct. 15, 1934; s. Harry M. and Henrietta (Busch) M.; m. Janet Louise Reinhardt, June 15, 1962 (div.); children: Allison Magid London, Jonathan Alward; m. Roseanne Cipra Muirhead, Sept. 4, 1982. BSc, U. Ill., 1954; MD, Chgo. Med. Sch., 1958. Diplomate Am. Bd. Neurol. Surgery. Intern Cook County Hosp., Chgo., 1958-59; resident, then fellow neurol. surgery Mayo Clinic, Rochester, Minn., 1959-61, 63-65; clin. instr. neurosurgery U. Calif., San Francisco, 1965-70, asst. clin. prof., 1970-79, assoc. prof., 1979—; chmn. Dominican Neurol. Inst., Santa Cruz, Calif., 1975—; bd. dirs. Dominican Found.; cons. neurosurgery U.S. Army, San Francisco Gen. Hosp. Assoc. editor: Clinical Neurosurgery, 1974. Bd. dirs. Santa Cruz Symphony Assn., 1983-85, U. Calif. Friends of Arts, Santa Cruz, 1985-86. Served to lt. comdr. USN, 1961-63. Fellow ACS, Internat. Coll. Surgeons; mem. AMA, Calif. Med. Assn., Internat. Soc. Pediatric Neurosurgeons, Am. Assn. Neurol. Surgeons, Western Neurosurg. Soc., Cong. Neurol. Surgeons, San Francisco Neurol. Soc. (pres.-elect 1991, pres. 1992), St. Francis Yacht Club (San Francisco). Republican. Home: 241 4th Ave Santa Cruz CA 95062-3815 Office: 1661 Soquel Dr Santa Cruz CA 95065-1709

MAGINNITY, GERALD FRANCIS, librarian; b. Boston, Nov. 11, 1950; s. Paul Morris and Mary Ann (Roberts) M.; m. Evelyn Elaine Espinosa, Aug. 16, 1986; children: Paul Edward, Anne Elizabeth, Joseph Dominic. BS, Ohio State U., 1972; MLS, U. Western Ont., London, Can., 1974. Advisor Inst. Tech., Monterrey, Mex., 1974-76; asst. county librarian Lassen County Library, Susanville, Calif., 1977-78; reference coordinator Imperial Valley Serra Coop. Library System, San Diego, 1978-80; Vallejo region librarian Solano County Library, Fairfield, Calif., 1980-82; assoc. county librarian Fresno (Calif.) County Library, 1982-89; coord. Mountain Valley Libr. Sys., Sacramento, 1989—. Mem. ALA, Calif. Libr. Assn. Democrat. Roman Catholic. Office: Mountain Valley Libr System 828 I St Ste 524 Sacramento CA 95814-2508

MAGNER, MARTIN, theatrical producer and director; b. Stettin, Ger., Mar. 5, 1900; came to U.S., 1939, naturalized, 1945; s. Max. and Zerlina (Silberstein) M.; m. Marion Palfi, June 6, 1951. Actor Hamburger kammerspiele, Germany, 1918-20; producer, dir. Nuremberg, Germany, 1921-27, Breslau, Germany, 1928-33, Berlin, 1928-33, Vienna, Austria, 1919-38, Prague, Czechoslovakia, 1933-39; stage dir. Chgo. Opera Co., 1940-41, San Francisco Opera, 1972; producer, dir. NBC, Chgo. and N.Y.C., 1942-49, CBS, N.Y.C., 1950-63; instr., artist-in-residence drama and music U. Chgo., 1941, Northwestern U., 1942-43, Adelphi Coll., 1948, Canisius Coll., 1958; artistic dir. New Theatre Inc., Los Angeles, 1977—. Recipient several documentary awards AMA, Spl. award for maintaining consistently high standards L.A. Drama Critics Circle, 1975, Disting. Lifetime Achievement award L.A. Drama Critics Circle, 1988, Life Time Achievement award Gov. of Calif., 1991; recepient The Cross of merit First Class from the Bundes Repulik of Germany , 1992. Mem. Dirs. Guild Am. Home: 1282 S Burnside Ave Los Angeles CA 90019-2607

MAGNER, RACHEL HARRIS, banker; b. Lamar, S.C., Aug. 5; d. Garner Greer and Catherine Alice (Cloaninger) Harris; m. Fredric Michael Magner, May 14, 1972. BS in Fin., U. S.C., 1972; postgrad. UCLA, 1974, Calif. State U., 1975. Mgmt. trainee Union Bank, L.A., 1972-75, comml. loan officer, 1975-77; asst. v.p. comml. fin. Crocker Bank, L.A., 1978, asst. v.p., factoring account exec. subs. Crocker United Factors, Inc., 1978-81; v.p. comml. services div. Crocker Bank, 1981-82, v.p., sr. account mgr. bus. banking div., 1982-83; v.p. and mgr. corporate banking Office of Pres., Sumitomo Bank Calif., 1983—. Home: 2200 Pine Ave Manhattan Beach CA 90266-2833 Office: Sumitomo Bank Calif 15250 Ventura Blvd Sherman Oaks CA 91403

MAGNES, HARRY ALAN, physician; b. Orange, N.J., Dec. 3, 1948; s. Sam and Shirley (Daniels) M.; m. Patricia Bruce, Mar. 25, 1989; 1 child, Carlos Fontiveros. AB in Biology magna cum laude, Brown U., 1970; MD, Yale U., 1974. Cert. Am. Bd. Internal Medicine. Intern, resident internal medicine U. Iowa Hosps. and Clinics, 1974-77; ptnr., med. dir., pres., CEO Gallatin Med. Clinic, Downey, Calif., 1977—; pres., CEO Gallatin Med. Corp., Downey, Calif., 1992-94; med. dir., bd. dirs. Gallatin Med. Found., Downey, Calif., 1993—; staff physician Downey Cmty. Hosp., 1977—, Presbyn. Intercmty. Hosp., 1992—; bd. dirs. Primehealth of So. Calif.; clin. instr. Rancho Los Amigos Hosp., Downey, 1981-83. Author: Rheumatic Fever in Connecticut, 1974. James Manning scholar Brown U., 1968. Mem. ACPE, Healthcare Assn. So. Calif., Primehealth, Am. Coll. Med. Practice Execs., Unified Med. Group Assocs., Med. Group Mgmt. Assn., Calif. Assn. Healthcare Provider Founds., Sigma Xi, Phi Beta Kappa. Office: Gallatin Med Found 10720 Paramount Blvd Downey CA 90241-3306

MAGNESS, BOB JOHN, telecommunications executive; b. Clinton, Okla., 1924; married. Grad., South Western State Coll., 1949. Chmn. Tele-Communications, Inc., Denver; chmn. Community Tele-Communications, Inc.; bd. dirs. Republic Pictures Corp., WestMarc Communications, United Artists Communications, Inc. Office: Tele-Comm Inc PO Box 5630 Denver CO 80217-5630*

MAGNESS, RHONDA ANN, microbiologist; b. Stockton, Calif., Jan. 30, 1946; d. John Pershing and Dorothy Waneta (Kelley) Wetter; m. Barney LeRoy Bender, Aug. 25, 1965 (div. 1977); m. Gary D. Magness, Mar. 5, 1977; children: Jay D. (dec.), Troy D. BS, Calif. State U., 1977. Lic. clin. lab. technologist, Calif., med. technologist; cert. clin. lab. scientist. Med. asst. C. Fred Wilcox, MD, Stockton, 1965-66; clk. typist Dept. of U.S. Army, Ft. Eustis, Va., 1967, Def. Supply Agy., New Orleans, 1967-68; med. asst. James G. Cross, MD, Lodi, Calif., 1969, Arthur A. Kemalyan, MD, Lodi, 1969-71, 72-77; med. sec. Lodi Meml. Hosp., 1972; lab. aide Calif. State U., Sacramento, 1977; phlebotomist St. Joseph's Hosp., Stockton, 1978-79; supr. microbiology Dameron Hosp. Assn., Stockton, 1980—. Active Concerned Women Am., Washington, 1987—. Mem. AAUW, Calif. Assn. Clin. Lab. Technologists, San Joaquin County Med. Assts. Assn., Nat. Geog. Soc., Nat. Audubon Soc. Baptist. Lodge: Jobs Daus. (chaplain 1962-63). Home: 9627 Knight Ln Stockton CA 95209-1961 Office: Dameron Hosp Lab 525 W Acacia St Stockton CA 95203-2405

MAGNUSON, ALAN DOUGLAS, retired banking executive, real estate broker; b. Valparaiso, Ind., Jan. 22, 1942; s. Douglas Harold and Alice Elizabeth (Burch) M.; m. Rose Becerra, Apr. 25, 1971; children: Lori, Kathi, Juli. Diploma, South Bend Coll. Commerce, 1962. Officer trainee Crocker-Citizens Bank, Los Angeles, 1967-70, ops. officer, 1967-70; ops. officer So. Calif. 1st Nat. Bank, San Diego, 1970-73; loan officer 1st Nat. Bank Nev., Las Vegas, 1973-80; br. mgr. 1st Interstate Nev., Las Vegas, 1980-82, v.p., 1984—; instr. Cmty. Coll. of So. Nev., Las Vegas; spkr. SBA, Las Vegas; mem. spkrs. bur. First Interstate Bank Nev., Las Vegas, Disting. Men of So. Nev. Active Nev. Spkrs. Bur.; bd. dirs. Nev. Child Seekers, 1992—. Sgt. U.S. Army, 1960-63. Mem. Am. Inst. Banking (gov. So. Nev. chpt. 1971-77, plaque 1977), Bank Adminstrn. Inst. (pres. So. Nev. chpt. 1982-83, plaque 1983), Greater Las Vegas Assn. Realtors, Henderson C. of C., Boulder City C. of C. (v.p. 1980-81), North Las Vegas C. of C. (comml. com., chmn. audit com., chmn. fairshow, chmn. funds appropriation subcom., import-export com., chmn. fin. subcom., pub. relations com.), Lions (chmn. Nev. zone 1982-83, sec. Nev. cabinet 1983-84, gov. Nev. dist. 1985-86, chmn. coun. govs. Calif./Nev. 1985-86). Republican. Office: Americana Group Realtors/ Better Homes & Gardens #150 2625 N Green Valley Pkwy Henderson NV 89014

MAGNUSON, DONALD RICHARD (BLAINE NELLINGTON), motion picture and television screenwriter, producer, director; b. Chgo., Apr. 23, 1951; s. Donald Orville and Olive June (O'Keefe) M.; m. Debra Michelle Ruzek, June 9, 1973; children: Jennifer Jean, Erick Richard. Diploma, No. Ill. U., summer 1968; student, Coll. of Du Page, 1971. Tchr. pro-tennis Westside Racquet Club, Oakbrook Terr., Ill., 1971-73; founder, co-chmn. Chicagoland Pictures Ltd.; founder, pres. Magnuson Entertainment Group, Malibu Magnuson Ltd., 1987—; founder, co-chmn. Chicagoland Picture Ltd. Screenwriter: The Taiwan Factor, Another Autumn, Reunion, Black & White, (with Fabiola Sarah Volante) Harry's Harem, Best Medicine, Midnight Internment, Dancer, The Long & Short of It, Retro Warrior, (with Christina Cardan) An Aspen Affair, Love The One You're With (with Deirdre S. Hamilton). Mem. Porsche Club Am., Ferrari Club Am. Roman Catholic. Office: 19866 Ridge Manor Way Yorba Linda CA 92686-6537

MAGNUSON, JON ALLAN, research engineer; b. Albert Lea, Minn., Dec. 10, 1951; s. Erick Joel and Evelyn Arlene (Iams) M.; m. Cheryl Anne Anderson, July 17, 1981. BS in Physics, Idaho State U., 1979; PhD in Physics, Dartmouth Coll., 1985, M Engring., 1986. Journeyman carpenter Mitchell Constrn. Co., Pocatello, Idaho, 1970-75; health physicist Idaho Nat. Engring. Lab., summer 1978; tchrs. asst., rsch. asst. Dartmouth Coll., Hanover, N.H., 1980-86; assoc. fellow Nichols Rsch. Corp., Newport Beach, Calif., 1986—; editor interface control document various cos., El Segundo, Calif., 1992—; cons. IR surveillance sys. L.A. AFB/Space Divsn., El Segundo, 1986—. Dartmouth fellow, Hanover, 1980-86. Mem. IEEE, Am. Def. Preparedness Assn., Internat. Soc. Optical Engrs., Mensa. Lutheran. Office: Nichols Rsch Corp 3919 Westerly Pl Newport Beach CA 92660-2308

MAGNUSSEN, MAX GENE, psychologist; b. Roland, Iowa, Sept. 12, 1927; s. Arthur Christian and Mary E. (Rakard) M.; m. Margaret Anne Hahn, Feb. 2, 1952 (div. Apr. 1985); 1 child, Anne H. BA, U. Iowa, 1952, MA, 1953; PhD, U. Ky., 1958. Lic. psychologist, Pa., N.Mex.; registered health svc. provider in psychology. Staff psychologist VA Hosp., Cin., 1958-59; clin. psychologist, asst. dir., psychol. cons. aircraft nuclear propulsion dept. GE Co., Cin., 1959-60; chief psychologist to dir. Lincoln-Lancaster Child Guidance Ctr., Lincoln, Nebr., 1960-68; chief psychologist to acting dir. Pitts. Child Guidance Ctr., 1968-80; dir. to attending sr. psychologist Programs for Children/U. N.Mex. Med. Ctr., Albuquerque, 1980—; instr. to asst. prof. U. Cin., 1958-60; asst. prof. U. Nebr., 1961-68; assoc. to full prof. U. Pitts., 1968-80; prof. of psychiatry and psychology U. N.Mex., 1980—; vis. prof. Inst. of Psychiatry, London, 1988-89; site vis. Am. Psychol. Assn, Washington, 1972—; field specialist site vis. HEW, 1977—. Contbg. author various books including Individual Versus Family Therapy, 1982, Multiple Impact Therapy, 1982, Development of a Minimal Clinical Data System, 1982, others; author: Pittsburgh Child Guidance Center Data System, 1974, others; contbr. articles to profl. jours. Mem. Health Systems Agy., Southwest Pa., Pitts., 1977-80, monitor, 1977-80. Sgt. U.S. Army, 1946-48. Recipient commendation Calif. Psychol. Assn., 1986—. Fellow APA (site visitor), Am. Orthopsychiat. Assn., Pa. Psychol. Assn. (ins. chmn. 1979), Soc. Personality Assessment; mem. Can. Psychol. Assn. (site visitor, accreditation panel), Nebr. Psychol. Assn. (sec./treas. 1963-66, pres. 1966-67), Am. Psychol. Assn. (grantee 1973, vis. psychologist 1974). Office: U NMex Sch Medicine 2600 Marble Ave NE Albuquerque NM 87106-2721

MAGOWAN, PETER ALDEN, professional baseball team executive, grocery chain executive; b. N.Y.C., Apr. 5, 1942; s. Robert Anderson and Doris (Merrill) M.; m. Jill Tarlau (div. July 1982; children—Kimberley, Margot, Hilary; m. Deborah Johnston, Aug. 14, 1982. BA, Stanford U.; MA, Oxford U., Eng.; postgrad., Johns Hopkins U. Store mgr. Safeway Stores Inc., Washington, 1968-70; dist. mgr. Safeway Stores Inc., Houston, 1970-71; retail ops. mgr. Safeway Stores Inc., Phoenix, 1971-72; div. mgr. Safeway Stores Inc., Tulsa, 1973-76; mgr. internat. div. Safeway Stores Inc., Toronto, Ont., Can., 1976-78; mgr. western region Safeway Stores Inc., San Francisco, 1978-79; chmn. bd., CEO Safeway Stores Inc., Oakland, Calif., 1980-93, chmn. bd., 1980—; pres., mng. gen. ptnr. San Francisco Giants, 1993—; bd. dirs. Chrysler Corp., Vons Cos. Inc., Caterpillar. Office: San Francisco Giants Candlestick Park San Francisco CA 94124

MAGRUDER, THOMAS MALONE, marriage and family therapist; b. Columbus, Ohio, Apr. 26, 1930; s. Thomas Malone and Elizabeth (McCarroll) M.; m. Carol Ann Schnitzer, Aug. 16, 1958; children: Scott D., John T., Ellen L. Bargainer. BA, Coll. Wooster, 1952; MDiv, Ch. Div. Sch. of Pacific, Berkeley, Calif., 1956; PhD, U.S. Internat. U., 1969. Lic. marriage and family therapist; ordained Episcopalian priest. Priest, vicar Holy Trinity Episcopal Ch., Fallon, Nev., 1956-60; adminstrv. asst. to bishop Episcopal Diocese of Nev., Reno, 1960-64; asst. priest St. David's Episcopal Ch., N. Hollywood, Calif., 1969-71; dir. People, Inc., Reno, 1971—; bd. dirs. Crisis Call Ctr., Reno. Columnist Gannett News Svc., 1978-85. Vol. counselor Nev. Women's Prison, Carson City, 1983-90, ct. appointed spl. adv., 1992—. With USN, 1948-49. Mem. Am. Assn. Marriage and Family Therapy-Nev. Div. (Therapist of Yr. 1990). Democrat. Home: 3160 Achilles Dr Reno NV 89512-1334 Office: People Inc 275 Hill St Ste 260 Reno NV 89501-1828

MAGUEN, EZRA, ophthalmologist, researcher; b. Israel, Mar. 5, 1945; came to U.S., 1974; m. Talma Greenhouse, Sept. 23, 1971; children: Shira, Barak, Jonathan. Grad., Faculte de Medecine, Nancy, France, 1968; MD, Tel Aviv U., 1971. Diplomate Am. Bd. Ophthalmology. Rotating internship Beilinson Hosp., Petah Tikva, Israel, 1971-72, internal medicine resident, 1972-73; ophthalmology resident Case Western Res. U., Mt. Sinai Hosp., Cleve., 1974-77; corneal and external disease fellow Estelle Doheny Eye Found., U. So. Calif. Sch. Medicine, L.A., 1977-79, tchr., 1977-85; attending surgeon Cedars-Sinai Med. Ctr., L.A., 1980—; assoc. clin. prof. Jules Stein Eye Inst., L.A., 1985—; prin. Am. Eye Inst., L.A., 1981—; prin. investigator NIH, 1979; clin. instr. U. So. Calif., Sch. Medicine, L.A., 1979-81, asst. clin. prof. ophthalmology, 1981-85; assoc. clin. prof. ophthalmology UCLA Sch. Medicine, 1985—; rsch. assoc. Discovery Fund for Eye Rsch., L.A., 1985—; mem. sci. adv. bd. Lions Dohey Eye Bank, 1988—; lectr. in field. Contbr. articles to profl. jours. Recipient The Factor Found. award, 1986. Mem. ACS, Am. Acad. Ophthalmology, Am.-Israeli Ophthal. Soc., Am. Soc. Cataract and Refractive Surgery, Internat. Coll. Surgeons, Internat. Soc. Optical Engring. (mem. program com. 1994), Internat. Soc. Refractive Keratoplasty (bd. dirs. 1988), Calif. Med. Assn. (sec. sci. adv. panel sect. ophthalmology 1987-89, sect. chmn. sci. adv. panel on ophthalmology 1989-90), L.A. County Med. Assn., L.A. Soc. Ophthalmology, Assn. Rsch. in Vision and Ophthalmology, Max Fine Corneal Assn., Rsch. Study Club in Ophthalmology L.A., Contact Lens Assn. Ophthalmology. Office: Am Eye Inst 8635 W 3rd St Ste 390W Los Angeles CA 90048-6101

MAGUIRE, ALAN EDWARD, economist, public policy consultant; b. Paterson, N.J., Aug. 27, 1954; s. Edward Lawrence and Severna (Arens) M. BS in Econs., Ariz. State U., 1978. Legis. rsch. economist Ariz. State Senate, Phoenix, 1977-80, econ. advisor, 1980-83; chief dep. state treas. Ariz. State Treasury, Phoenix, 1983-87; 1st v.p. Rauscher Pierce Refsnes, Inc., Phoenix, 1987-91; pres. The Maguire Co., Phoenix, 1991—; forecaster Ariz. Blue Chip Econ. Forecast, Tempe, 1985—, Western Blue Chip Econ. Forecast, Tempe, 1988—. Bd. dirs. Ariz. Town Hall, 1994—, Ariz. Rep. Caucus, Phoenix, 1988-94, Ariz. State Bd. of Deposit, Phoenix, 1988—, Ariz. State Retirement System bd., 1987; active Ariz. Property Tax Oversight Commn., Phoenix, 1987—, Project SLIM Steering Com., 1991-92. Mem. Ariz. Econ. Forum (bd. dirs., v.p. 1983—), Ariz. Town Hall, Phoenix Econ. Club. Office: The Maguire Co PO Box 64382 Phoenix AZ 85082-4382

MAGUIRE, EDWARD FRANCIS, hospital administrator; b. Boonton Twp., N.J., Dec. 11, 1944; s. Edward Francis and Sarah (Whitty) M.; m. Christine Elizabeth Chisholm, July 6, 1968; children: Katherine Irene, Theodore Edward. B in Liberal Arts, U. Mont., 1966; M in Health Care Adminstrn., Wash. U., St. Louis, 1971. Asst. to adminstr. Santa Barbara (Calif.) Gen. Hosp., 1971-72, adminstrv. asst., 1972-73, asst. adminstr., 1973-75, assoc. adminstr., 1977-78; asst. adminstr. Santa Barbara County Health Care Services, 1975-77; asst. adminstr. Grossmont Dist. Hosp., La Mesa, Calif., 1978-83, assoc. adminstr., 1983—. Served to 1st lt. U.S. Army, 1969. Mem. Am. Coll. Hosp. Adminstrs. (Regents adv. com.), Assn. Mental Health Adminstrs. (cert.), Calif. Hosp. Assn. (med. rehab. com.), Health Care Execs. Assn. San Diego County (pres. 1983-84), Calif. Assn. Rehab. Facilities (pres. 1984-85, chmn. long range planning com., legis. com. 1980-81), Hosp. Council San Diego and Imperial Counties (medically indigent adult task force 1982—, provider contract com. 1983, mental health task force 1981—). Lodge: Rotary. Home: 1774 Cousino Way El Cajon CA 92019-3833 Office: Edward F Maguire HC Consulting 555 Washington St San Diego CA 92103-2289

MAGUIRE, JAMES HENRY, English language educator; b. Denver, Apr. 2, 1944; s. Joseph Cornelius Jr. and Margaret Louise (Monson) M.; m. Betty Joan Keller, Sept. 8, 1967; children: Emily Ann, Stephen Joseph. BA, U. Colo., 1966; AM, Ind. U., 1969, PhD, 1970. Teaching assoc. Ind. U., Bloomington, 1967-69; asst. prof. Boise (Idaho) State U., 1970-75, assoc. prof., 1975-87, prof. English, 1987—. Author: (booklet) Mary Hallock Foote, 1972; author, editor: (anthology) Literature of Idaho, 1986 (Idaho Libr. Assn. award 1987); sect. editor: A Literary History of the American West, 1987; contbr. chpt. to The Columbia History of the American Novel, 1991; co-editor: Boise State U. Western Writer Series, 1971—, Into the Wilderness Dream: Exploration Narratives of the American West, 1500-1805, 1994. Mem. Zero Population Growth, Washington, 1970—, ACLU, Snake River Alliance, Boise, 1979—. Mem. Western Lit. Assn. (pres. 1981), MLA, Am. Studies Assn., Mark Twain Cir., Hemingway Soc., Henry James Soc., Melville Soc., Emily Dickinson INternat. Soc., Sierra Club. Democrat. Home: 933 Pierce Ct Boise ID 83712-7448 Office: Boise State U English Dept 1910 University Dr Boise ID 83725-0001

MAGUIRE, JOHN DAVID, university administrator, educator, writer; b. Montgomery, Ala., Aug. 7, 1932; s. John Henry and Clyde (Merrill) M.; m.

Lillian Louise Parrish, Aug. 29, 1953; children: Catherine Merrill, Mary Elizabeth, Anne King. A.B. magna cum laude, Washington and Lee U., 1953, Litt.D. (hon.), 1979; Fulbright scholar, Edinburgh (Scotland) U., 1953-54; B.D. summa cum laude, Yale, 1956, Ph.D., 1960; postdoctoral research, Yale U. and U. Tübingen, Germany, 1964-65, U. Calif., Berkeley, 1968-69, Silliman U., Philippines, 1976-77; HLD (hon.), Transylvania U., 1990. Dir. Internat. Student Ctr., New Haven, 1956-58; mem. faculty Wesleyan U., Middletown, Conn., 1960-70; asso. provost Wesleyan U., 1967-68; vis. lectr. Pacific Sch. Religion and Grad. Theol. Union, Berkeley, 1968-69; pres. SUNY Coll. at Old Westbury, 1970-81, Claremont (Calif.) U. Ctr. and Grad. Sch., 1981—. Author: The Dance of the Pilgrim: A Christian Style of Life for Today, 1967; also numerous articles. Mem. Conn. adv. com. U.S. Commn. Civil Rights, 1961-70; participant White House Conf. on Civil Rights, 1966; advisor, permanent trustee and 1st chmn. bd. dirs. Martin Luther King Ctr. for Social Change, Atlanta, 1968—; bd. dirs. Nassau County Health and Welfare Coun., 1971-81, pres., 1974-76; trustee United Bd. Christian Higher Edn. in Asia, 1975-81, Inst. Internat. Edn., 1980-86, The Tomás Rivera Ctr., Claremont, Calif., 1984—, vice chmn., 1987—, Assn. Ind. Calif. Colls. and Univs., 1985—, chmn. 1990-92, mem. exec. com., 1992—, The Calif. Achievement Coun., 1985-94, chmn. 1990-94, Transylvania U. Bingham Trust, 1987—, Lincoln Found. and Lincoln Inst. of Land Policy, Inc., 1987-94, The JL Found., 1988—, The Bus. Enterprise Trust, 1989—, Ednl. Found. for African Ams., 1991—; bd. dirs. Assn. Am. Colls. and Univs., 1981-86, chmn., 1984-85; bd. dirs. Legal Def. and Edn. Fund. NAACP, 1991—, west coast div., 1981—, Thacher Sch., Ojai, Calif., 1982-94, vice chmn., 1986—, Salzburg Seminar, 1992—; mem. Am. Com. on U.S.-Soviet Rels., 1981-92, Blue Ribbon Calif. Commn. on Teaching Profession, 1984-86; mem. governing coun. Aspen Inst. Wye Faculty Seminar, 1984-94; mem. Coun. on Fgn. Rels., 1983—; adv. bd. RAND Ctr. Rsch. Immigration Policy, 1994—; mem. Pres.'s Adv. Coun. to Commn. on Calif. Master Plan for Higher Edn., 1986-87, L.A. Ednl. Alliance for Restructuring Now, 1992—, Calif. Bus. Higher Edn. Forum, 1992—. Recipient Julia A. Archibald High Scholarship award Yale Div. Sch., 1956; Day fellow Yale Grad. Sch., 1956-57; Kent fellow, 1957-60; Howard Found. postdoctoral fellow Brown U. Grad. Sch., 1964-65; Fenn lectr., 7 Asian countries, 1976-77; recipient Conn. Prince Hall Masons' award outstanding contbns. human rights in Conn., 1965; E. Harris Harbison Gt. Tchr. prize Danforth Found., 1968. Fellow Soc. Values Higher Edn. (pres. 1974-81, bd. dirs. 1972-88); mem. Phi Beta Kappa, Omicron Delta Kappa. Democrat. Office: Claremont U Ctr & Grad Sch Office of Pres 160 E 10th St Claremont CA 91711-5909

MAGUIRE, YU PING, oncologist, department director, consultant; b. Hanon, China, May 27, 1947; came to U.S., 1962.; d. Shao Wen and Charlin (Yu) Yen; m. Russell Gene Maguire, June 13, 1968; 1 child, Jennifer Wei-Shing. MS, Rutgers U., 1976, PhD in Food Sci. and Tech., 1978. Pathology fellow U. Wash. Med. Sch., Seattle, 1979-80, hematology, oncology fellow, 1981-84; sr. scientist Tumor Inst. Swedish Hosp., Seattle, 1984-88; dir. tumor diagnostic Baxter Diagnostics, Bartels Div., Issaquah, Wash., 1988-93; dir. clin. oncology Bartels Prognostics, Inc., Issaquah, 1993—; vis. scientist dept. med. pathology U. Naples (Italy) Med. Sch., 1980-81; immunology cons. Oncogene Bristol Meyers, Seattle, 1985-88; biotech. cons. JWM, Inc., Bellevue, Wash., 1993—. Patentee in field. Mem. Am. Assn. Cancer Rsch., Am. Acad. Sci., N.Y. Acad. Scis., Wash. State Biotech. Assn., Women in Cancer Rsch., Sino-Am. Scientist. Avocations: skiing, mountaining, boating, hiking, travel. Home: 500 W Lake Sammamish Pky NE Bellevue WA 98008-4256 Office: Bartels Prognostics Inc 2005 Sammamish Rd Issaquah WA 98027

MAHADEV, RAJESH, strategic marketing professional; b. Madras, India, Apr. 17, 1966; came to U.S., 1988; s. R.K. and Padma (Alwa) M.; m. Ana Elisa Mendes De Oliveira, Jan. 23, 1992. B. Commerce in Acctg., U. Bangalore (India), 1987; MBA in Mktg. and Fin., U. Denver, 1990. Sr. account exec. Communication Workshop, Bangalore, 1987—; turnaround specialist Corriere & Assocs., Inc., Englewood, Colo., 1992-94; assoc. dir. U.S. West, Inc., Englewood, Colo., 1994—; cons. Corriere & Assocs., Inc., Englewood, 1990-92. Educator Jr. Achievement of Denver, 1992; amb. Greater Denver Chamber, 1992—. Mem. Am. Mensa Ltd. Office: US West Inc # 310 6200 S Quebec St Ste 310 Englewood CO 80111-4750

MAHAFFEY, MARCIA JEANNE HIXSON, secondary school administrator; b. Scobey, Mont.; d. Edward Goodell and Olga Marie (Frederickson) Hixson; m. Donald Harry Mahaffey (div. Aug. 1976); 1 child, Marcia Anne. BA in English, U. Wash.; MA in Secondary Edn., U. Hawaii, 1967. Cert. secondary and elem. tchr. and adminstr. Tchr. San Lorenzo (Calif.) Sch. Dist., 1958-59; tchr. Castro Valley (Calif.) Sch. Dist., 1959-63, vice prin., 1963-67; vice prin. Sequoia Union High Sch. Dist., Redwood City, Calif., 1967-77, asst. prin., 1977-91, ret., 1991; tchr. trainer Project Impact Sequoia Union Sch. Dist., Redwood City, 1986-91; mem. supr.'s task force for dropout prevention, 1987-91, Sequoia Dist. Goals Commn. (chair subcom. staff devel. 1988); mentor tchr. selection com., 1987-91; mem. Stanford Program Devel. Ctr. Com., 1987-91; chairperson gifted and talented Castro Valley Sch. Dist.; mem. family svcs. bd., San Leandro, Calif. Vol. Am. Cancer Soc., San Mateo, Calif., 1967, Castro Valley, 1965; Sunday sch. tchr. Hope Luth. Ch., San Mateo, 1970-76; chair Carlmont High Sch. Site Council, Belmont, Calif., 1977-91. Recipient Life Mem. award Parent, Tchr., Student Assn., Belmont, 1984, Svc. award, 1989, Exemplary Svc award Carlmont High Sch., 1989; named Woman of the Week, Castro Valley, 1967, Outstanding Task Force Chair Adopt A Sch. Program San Mateo (Calif.) County, 1990. Mem. AAUW, DAR, Assn. Calif. Sch. Adminstrs. (Project Leadership plaque 1985), Sequoia Dist. Mgmt. Assn. (pres. 1975, treas. 1984, 85), Assn. for Supervision and Curriculum Devel., Met. Mus. Art, Smithsonian Inst., Internat. Platform Assn., Animal Welfare Advocacy, Commonwealth Club of Calif., Delta Kappa Gamma, Alpha Xi Delta.

MAHAN, JAMES CAMERON, lawyer; b. El Paso, Tex., Dec. 16, 1943; m. Eileen Agnes Casale, Jan. 13, 1968; 1 child, James Cameron Jr. BA, U. Charleston, 1965; JD, Vanderbilt U., 1973. Bar: Nev. 1974, U.S. Dist. Ct. Nev. 1974, U.S. Ct. Appeals (9th cir.) 1975, U.S. Tax Ct. 1980, U.S. Supreme Ct. 1980. Assoc. Lee & Beasey, Las Vegas, Nev., 1974-75; mem. firm John Peter Lee Ltd., Las Vegas, 1975-82; sr. ptnr. Mahan & Ellis, Chartered, Las Vegas, 1982—. With USN, 1966-69. Office: Mahan & Ellis Chartered 510 S 9th St Las Vegas NV 89101-7011

MAHARIDGE, DALE DIMITRO, journalist, educator; b. Cleve., Oct. 24, 1956; s. Steve and Joan (Kopfstein) M. Student, Cleve. State U., 1974-75. Free-lance reporter various publs., Cleve., 1976; reporter The Gazette, Medina, Ohio, 1977-78; free-lance reporter Cleve. Plain Dealer, 1978-80; reporter The Sacramento Bee, 1980-91; lectr. Stanford U., Palo Alto, Calif., 1992—. Author: Journey to Nowhere: The Saga of the New Underclass, 1985, And Their Children After Them, 1989 (Pulitzer Prize for gen. non-fiction 1990), The Last Great American Hobo, 1993; contbr. articles to profl. jours. Nieman fellow Harvard U., 1988; grantee Pope Found., 1994, Freedom Forum, 1995. Democrat. Office: Stanford U Dept Comm Bldg 120 Stanford CA 94305

MAHER, CHRISTINE RITA, emergency room nurse, sexual assault specialist; b. Great Lakes, Ill., Jan. 21, 1952; d. Medard and Rita (Kobus) Schronski; m. William J. Maher, Aug. 23, 1986. BS, U. Ill., Chgo., 1973; AS, Los Medanos Coll., Pittsburg, Calif., 1980. RN, Calif.; cert. BLS, ACLS, MICH; cert. emergency nurse, trauma nurse care, secual assault nurse examiner, Calif.; cert. emergency pediatric nurse. Nursing asst. Contra Costa County Hosp., Martinez, Calif., 1974-78, surg. technician, 1978-80, RN, 1980-84; emergency room nurse, educator, com. mem. North Bay Med. Ctr., Fairfield, Calif., 1984-91; co-founder ind. nursing group practice, co-dir. William J. Maher RN, Fairfield, Calif., 1991—. Day camp dir. Benicia (Calif.) Recreation Dept., 1980. Mem. AACN, Emergency Nurses Assn. (cert. TNCC), Nat. Nurses in Bus. Assn. Office: William J Maher RN 906 Hidden Cove Way Suisun City CA 94585-3511

MAHER, JAMES R., laboratory administrator. Pres., ceo Nat. Health Lab. Inc., La Jolla, Calif. Office: National Health Labs Inc 4225 Executive Sq Ste 800 La Jolla CA 92037-1485

MAHER, JOHN FRANCIS, financial executive; b. Berkeley, Calif., Apr. 25, 1943; s. Edward John and Emilia A. (Radovan) M.; m. Ann Elizabeth Breeden (div. 1975); children: Edward John II, Elizabeth Ann; m. Helen Lee Stillman, Mar. 20, 1976; children: Michael Stillman, Helen Cathline. BS, Menlo Coll., 1965; MBA, U. Pa., 1967. Gen. ptnr. Eastman Dillon, N.Y., 1971; 1st v.p. Blyth Eastman Dillon, N.Y., 1972; exec. v.p. Blyth Eastman Dillon, Los Angeles, 1976-79; exec. v.p., chief fin. officer Gt. Western Fin., Beverly Hills, Calif., 1973-76, also bd. dirs.; mng. dir. Lehman Bros. Kuhn Loeb, Los Angeles, 1979-86; pres., chief operating officer Great Western Fin. Corp., Chatsworth, 1986—; bd. dirs. Gt. Western Fin. Corp., Chatsworth, Baker Hughes Inc., Gt. Western Bank. Bd. dirs. L.A. Big Bros., Inc.; nat. bd. trustees Boys and Girls Clubs Am.; overseer art collections and gardens Huntington Libr. Joseph Wharton fellow U. Pa., 1965-67. Mem. Calif. Bus. Roundtable Group. Office: Gt Western Fin Corp 9200 Oakdale Ave Chatsworth CA 91311-6519*

MAHIN, GLENDA GORDON, product development specialist, hydrologist; b. Merced, Calif., Dec. 3, 1950; d. Alvin L. and Velma (Boyer) Gordon; m. Edward Milton Froeliger, Dec. 18, 1970 (dec. Aug. 1975); children: Edward Glen Froeliger, Frances Glen Froeliger Meyer; m. Donald Alan Mahin, Feb. 6, 1988. BS, Calif. State Poly. U., 1973; MS, U. Nev., Reno, 1991. Lic. tchr., Nev. Nutrition cons. Stockton and Martinez, Calif., 1973-82; elem. sch. tchr. Reno, 1982-86; rsch. asst. U. Nev., Reno, 1987-91; rsch. hydrologist Desert Rsch. Inst., Reno, 1990-93; hydrologist, product devel. specialist Vector Environ. Techs., Inc., Sparks, Nev., 1994—; hydrologist Mahin & Assocs., Reno, Nev., 1994—. Contbr. articles to profl. jours. Del. Sierra Nevada coun. Girl Scouts U.S., 1989—; treas., editor Golden Valley Homeowners Assn., Reno, 1984-87. Named Girl Scout Leader of Yr., Sierra Nev. coun. Girl Scouts, 1993; Exxon grantee, 1970, U.S. Agrl. Rsch. grantee U. Nev., Reno, 1988, U.S. Geol. Rsch. grantee, 1988. Mem. ASCE, AAUW, Assn. Gen. Contractors, Am. Meteorol. Soc., Assn. Groundwater Scientists and Engrs., Air and Waste Mgmt. Soc. Home: 2300 Sagittarius Dr Reno NV 89509-8900 Office: Mahin & Assocs. 4790 Caughlin Pkwy #217 Reno NV 89509

MAHLER, DAVID, chemical company executive; b. San Francisco; s. John and Jennie (Morgan) M.; PhC, U. So. Calif., 1932; children: Darrell, Glenn. Pres., United Drug Co., Glendale, Calif., 1934-37, Blue Cross Labs., Inc., Saugus, Calif., 1937—. Active Fund for Animals, Friends of Animals, Com. for Humane Legislations; patron Huntington Hartford Theatre, Hollywood, Calif. Mem. Packaging and Rsch. Devel. Inst. (hon.), Anti-Defamation League, Skull and Daggar, Rho Pi Phi. Office: 26411 Golden Valley Rd Santa Clarita CA 91350-2621

MAHLER, ROBERT LOUIS, soil scientist, educator; b. Huntington Park, Calif., Jan. 7, 1954; s. Robert Alfred and Emily Chonita (Ortega) M.; 1 child, Claudia. BS, Wash. State U., 1976, MS, 1978; PhD, N.C. State U., 1980. Asst. prof., assoc. prof., now prof. soil sci. U. Idaho, Moscow, 1980—, soil fertility researcher, 1980—, extension soil scientist, 1989—, water quality coord., 1990—. Contbr. to profl. publs. Environ. sciences tchr. Knights of Columbus. Mem. Am. Soc. Agronomy, Soil Sci. Soc. Am., Western Soc. Soil Sci., Rotary, Gamma Sigma Delta (pres. 1989-90). Roman Catholic. Office: Soil Sci Div Univ Idaho Moscow ID 83843

MAHMOOD, AAMER, computer system architect; b. Lahore, Pakistan, Jan. 27, 1956; came to U.S., 1979; s. Muhammad Iftikhar Quereshi and Farakh (Sultana) Iftikhar; m. Samira Aftab, June 28, 1985; children: Muhammad Bilal, Umer Ali. BSEE, U. Engring. & Tech., Lahore, 1979; MSEE, Stanford U., 1980, PhD in Elec. Engring., 1986. Lectr. U. Egnring. & Tech., 1979; teaching asst. Stanford (Calif.) U., 1980-82, rsch. asst., 1983-85; mem. tech. staff Rolm Milspec Computers, San Jose, Calif., 1986-88; mgr., tech. leader CPU and memory systems Amdahl/Advanced Systems, Sunnyvale, Calif., 1988-93; mgr. architect network hardware Cisco Systems, San Jose, 1994—. Contbr. articles to profl. jours. Bd. of Secondary Edn. merit scholar, Lahore, 1971, Bd. of Intermediate Edn. talent scholar, Lahore, 1973. Mem. IEEE (sr.), Assn. Computing Machinery, Stanford Alumni Assn. (life). Home: 1098 Cardinal Way Palo Alto CA 94303-3540

MAHONEY, JAMES P., bishop; b. Saskatoon, Sask., Can., Dec. 7, 1927. Ordained priest Roman Cath. Ch., 1952; bishop Saskatoon, 1967—. Office: Chancery Office, 106 5th Ave N, Saskatoon, SK Canada S7K 2N7*

MAHONY, ROGER M. CARDINAL, archbishop; b. Hollywood, Calif., Feb. 27, 1936; s. Victor James and Loretta Marie (Baron) M. A.A., Our Lady Queen of Angels Sem., 1956; B.A., St. John's Sem. Coll., 1958, B.S.T., 1962; M.S.W., Catholic U. Am., 1964. Ordained priest Roman Cath. Ch., 1962, ordained bishop, 1975, created cardinal priest, 1991. Asst. pastor St. John's Cathedral, Fresno, Calif., 1962, 68-73, rector, 1973-80; residence St. Genevieve's Parish, Fresno, Calif., 1964—, adminstr., 1964-67, pastor, 1967-68; titular bishop of Tamascani, aux. bishop of Fresno, 1975-80; chancellor Diocese of Fresno, 1970-77, vicar gen., 1975-80; bishop Diocese of Stockton (Calif.), 1980-85; archbishop Archdiocese of L.A., 1985-91, cardinal priest, 1991—; diocesan dir. Cath. Charities and Social Svc. Fresno, 1964-70, exec. dir. Cath. Welfare Bur., 1964-70; exec. dir. Cath. Welfare Bur. Infant of Prague Adoption Service, 1964-70; chaplain St. Vincent de Paul Soc., Fresno, 1964-70; named chaplain to Pope Paul VI, 1967; mem. faculty extension div. Fresno State U., 1965-67; sec. U.S. Cath. bishops ad hoc com. on farm labor Nat. Conf. Bishops, 1970-75; chmn. com. on pub. welfare and income maintenance Nat. Conf. Cath. Charities, 1969-70; bd. dirs. West Coast Regional Office Bishops Com. for Spanish-Speaking, 1967-70; chmn. Calif. Assn. Cath. Charities Dirs., 1965-69; trustee St. Patrick's Sem., Archdiocese of San Francisco, 1974-75; mem. adminstrv. com. Nat. conf. Cath. Bishops, 1976-79, 82-85, 87-90, com. migration and refugees, 1976—, chmn. com. farm labor, 1981—, com. moral evaluation of deterrence, 1986-88; cons. com., chmn. for ProLife Activities, 1990—; mem. com. social devel. and world peace U.S. Cath. Conf., 1985, chmn. internat. policy sect., 1987-90; com. justice and peace, Pontifical Couns., 1984-89, 90—, pastoral care of migrants and itinerant people, 1986—, social communications, 1989—. Mem. Urban Coalition of Fresno, 1968-72, Fresno County Econ. Opportunities Commn., 1964-65, Fresno County Alcoholic Rehab. Com., 1966-67, Fresno City Charter Rev. Com., 1968-70, Mexican-Am. Council for Better Housing, 1968-72, Fresno Redevel. Agy., 1970-75, L.A. 2000 Com., 1985-88, Fed. Commn. Agrl. Workers, 1987—, Blue Ribbon Com. Affordable Housing City of L.A., 1988; mem. commn. to Draft an Ethics Code for L.A. City Govt., 1989-90; bd. dirs. Fresno Community Workshop, 1965-67; trustee St. Agnes Hosp., Fresno. Named Young Man of Yr. Fresno Jr. C. of C., 1967. Mem. Canon Law Soc. Am., Nat. Assn. Social Workers. Home: 114 E 2nd St Los Angeles CA 90012-3711 Office: Archdiocese of LA 1531 W 9th St Los Angeles CA 90015-1112*

MAHOUR, GHOLAM HOSSEIN, pediatric surgeon, educator; b. Shiraz, Iran, Aug. 3, 1935; came to U.S., 1963; s. Alie and Shariat (Meshkin) M.; m. Barbara Lee Younggren, June 26, 1966; children: Michelle Marie, Elizabeth Victoria. BS, U. Shiraz, 1955, MD, 1959; MS in Surgery, Mayo Grad. Sch. Medicine, 1968. Diplomate Am. Bd. Surgery in gen. surgery, pediat. surgery and surg. critical care. Assoc. in surgery Harvard U. Sch. Medicine, Boston, 1970-71; from asst. prof. surgery to assoc. prof. surgery U. So. Calif., L.A., 1972-84, prof. surgery, 1984—; chief divsn. pediat. surgery Children's Hosp. L.A., 1978-93, dir. trauma program, 1983—, sr. coord. surg. edn., 1993—. Contbr. numerous sci. papers to med. jours. Grantee March of Dimes, 1973-75, 79-80. Fellow ACS, Am. Acad. Pediatrics, Royal Coll. Surgeons Can., Am. Acad. Pediatrics; m. AAUP, Am. Pediat. Surg. Assn. (grantee 1981-90), Am. Assn. for Surgery of Trauma, Soc. Critical Care Medicine, Am. Trauma Soc. (founding mem.), Brit. Assn. Pediat. Surgeons, Pacific Assn. Pediat. Surgeons, Western Surg. Assn., James T. Priestly Surg. Soc. Office: Children's Hosp LA 4650 W Sunset Blvd Los Angeles CA 90027-6016

MAHUTTE, CORNELIS KEES, internist, educator; b. Rotterdam, Holland, May 10, 1944; came to the U.S., 1979; s. Nicolaas Henri and Margareta (Kieboom) M.; m. Gabriele Katherina Pantel, July 13, 1968; 1 child, Neal Gregory. BS, U. Toronto, 1966; MS, U. Waterloo, Ontario, Canada, 1968, PhD, 1971; MD, McMaster U., 1974. Internal med. resident McMaster U., 1974-76, pulmonary fellow, 1977-79; resident Rsch. U., Toronto, 1976-77; asst. prof. medicine U. Calif., Irvine, 1979-86; chief MICU Long Beach (Calif.) VA Med. Ctr., 1979—, chief pulmonary & critical care sect., 1989—; assoc. prof. medicine U. Calif., Irvine, 1986—. Contbr. numerous articles to profl. jours.; patentee for method for continuous cardiac input. Fellow Royal Coll. Physicians, Coll. Chest Physicians. Home: 1371 Gwen Ave Santa Ana CA 92705-3224 Office: Long Beach VA Med Ctr Pulmonary Critical Care 5901 E 7th St Long Beach CA 90822-5201

MAI, HAROLD LEVERNE, retired federal judge; b. Casper, Wyo., Apr. 5, 1928. BA, U. Wyo., 1950, JD, 1952. Bar: Wyo. 1952, U.S. Supreme Ct. 1963. Sole practice, Cheyenne, Wyo., 1953-62, 67-71; judge Juvenile Ct., Cheyenne, 1962-67; U.S. bankruptcy judge, Cheyenne, 1971-93, ret., 1993. Mem. adv. bd. Salvation Army. Wyo. Mem. ABA, Wyo. Bar Assn., Laramie County Bar Assn., Nat. Conf. Bankruptcy Judges.

MAIBACH, HOWARD I., dermatologist; b. N.Y.C., July 18, 1929; s. Jack Louis and Sidonia (Fink) M.; m. Siesel Wile, July 8, 1953; children—Lisa, Ed, Todd. A.B., Tulane U., 1950, M.D., 1955. Diplomate: Am. Bd. Dermatology. Intern William Beaumont Army Hosp., El Paso, Tex., 1955-56; resident, fellow in dermatology USPHS, Hosp. of U. Pa., 1959-61; asst. instr. U. Pa., 1958-61, lectr., 1960-61; practice medicine specializing in dermatology U. Calif. Hosps., San Francisco, 1961—; asst. prof. dermatology U. Calif. Sch. Medicine, San Francisco, 1961-63; asso. prof. U. Calif. Sch. Medicine, 1967-73; research asso. Cancer Research Inst., 1967—; mem. staff U. Calif.-H.C. Moffitt Hosps., 1961—; cons. Laguna Honda Hosp., 1962-66, chief dermatology service, 1963-67; cons. Letterman Gen. Hosp., Calif. Med. Facility, Vacaville, San Francisco Gen. Hosp., Sonoma State Hosp., Eldridge, Calif., Stanford Research Inst., Menlo Park, Calif., Calif. Dept. Public Health, Berkeley, VA Hosp., Research Inst. Fragrance Materials, Inc., David Grant USAF Hosp. of Travis AFB, Naval Hosp., San Diego, Wilford Hall AFB, Tex., Army Environ. Health Agy., Md.; mem. Internat. Contact Dermatitis Research Com. Editor: Animal Models in Dermatology, 1965; co-editor: Dermatotoxicology and Pharmacology, 1977, Skin Microbiology, 1981; bd. editors: Internat. Jour. Dermatology, 1974—; editorial bd.: Contact Dermatitis: Environ. Dermatology, 1974—, Clin. Toxicology, 1976—; internat. editorial bd.: Excerpta Media, 1976—; author, coauthor, editor of over 30 books and 750 publs. Served to capt. M.C. U.S. Army, 1955-58. Recipient awards Soc. Cosmetic Chemists, 1970, 71, 73. Fellow A.C.P.; mem. Am. Acad. Dermatology (award for essay 1961), San Francisco Dermatol. Soc. (pres. 1970-71), Pacific Dermatol. Assn., Soc. Investigative Dermatology, N.Y. Acad. Scis., Calif. Med. Assn., Am. Fedn. Clin. Research, AMA, San Francisco Med. Soc., Am. Dermatol. Assn., Internat. Soc. Tropical Dermatology, Am. Soc. Clin. Pharmacology and Therapeutics, Am. Coll. Toxicology; hon. mem. Swedish Dermatol. Soc., Am. Vet. Dermatol. Assn., Am. Acad. Vet. Dermatology, Danish Dermatol. Soc., German Dermatol. Soc. Office: Univ of Calif Hosp San Francisco CA 94143

MAIER, CORNELL C., aluminum and chemical company executive; b. Herreid, S.D., Jan. 12, 1925; s. Phillip and Ann (Riedlinger) M. B.S. in Engring, U. Calif. at Berkeley, 1949. With Kaiser Aluminum & Chem. Corp., Oakland, Calif., 1949-87; v.p., mgr. European region Kaiser Aluminum Internat., 1963-68; v.p., gen. mgr. European region Kaiser Aluminum Internat. (Mill Products div. parent co.), 1969; v.p., gen. mgr. European region Kaiser Aluminum Internat. (N.Am. aluminum ops.), 1969-70, exec. v.p., 1970-72; corp. gen. mgr. Kaiser Aluminum and Chem. Corp., Oakland, Calif., 1971-72, pres., 1972-82, chief exec. officer, 1972-87, chmn., 1978-87, mem. exec. com., also bd. dirs.; vice chmn., pres. KaiserTech Ltd., Oakland, 1987, cons.; mem. Bus. Roundtable; bd. dirs. Anglesey Aluminum Metal Ltd., London, Bank of Am. N.T. and S.A., Volta Aluminum Co. Ltd., BankAm. Corp. Co-chmn. Calif. Commn. on Campaign Financing; mem. adv. bd. U. Calif. Sch. Bus., Berkeley; bd. dirs., bd. dirs., mem. exec. com. Bay Area Council Inc.; bd. dirs. Calif. Econ. Devel. Corp. Served with USAAF, 1943-45. Named Mfr. of Yr., Calif. Mfrs. Assn., 1983. Mem. Calif. C. of C. (dir.), Aluminum Assn. (chmn. adv. council). Clubs: Round Hill Country, Alamo, Silverado Country, Pacific Union. Office: Kaiser Aluminum & Chem Corp Kaiser Ctr 300 Lakeside Dr Oakland CA 94643-0001

MAIER, GERALD JAMES, natural gas transmission and marketing company executive; b. Regina, Sask., Can., Sept. 22, 1928; s. John Joseph and Mary (Passler) M. Student, Notre Dame Coll. (Wilcox), U. Man., U. Alta., U. Western Ont. With petroleum and mining industries Can., U.S., Australia, U.K.; responsible for petroleum ops. Africa, United Arab Emirates, S.E. Asia; chmn. TransCan. PipeLines, Calgary, 1985-95, also bd. dirs., 1985-95; bd. dirs. BCE Inc., Bank of N.S., TransAlta Utilities Corp., Du-Pont Can. Inc., Alberta Nat. Gas Co., Ltd., Petro-Can.; immediate past chmn. Can. Nat. com. for World Petroleum Congresses, Van Horne Inst. for Internat. Transp.; bd. govs. Bus. Coun. on Nat. Issues. Named Hon. Col. King's Own Calgary Rgt., Resource Man of Yr. Alta. Chamber of Resources, 1990; recipient Can. Engr.'s Gold medal Can. Coun. Profl. Engrs., 1990, Disting. Alumni award U. Alta., 1992, Mgmt. award McGill U., 1993, Centennial award Alta Assn. Engrs., Geologists and Geophysicists. Fellow Can. Acad. Engring.; mem. Assn. Profl. Engrs., Geologists and Geophysicists Alta. (past pres.), Can. Inst. Mining and Metallurgy (Past Pres.'s Meml. medal 1971). Office: TransCan PipeLines Ltd, 530 8th Ave SW, Calgary, AB Canada T2P 3V6

MAIERHAUSER, JOSEPH GEORGE, entrepreneur; b. Yankton, S.D., Mar. 23, 1927; s. Joseph and Angela M. (Jung) M.; m. Reta Mae Brockelsby, Nov. 25, 1948 (div. 1965); 1 child, Joe; m. Martha Helen Kuehn, Dec. 10, 1965. Student, U. S.D., Vermillion, 1946, S.D. Sch. Mines and Tech., Rapid City, 1947. Sales mgr. Black Hills Reptile Gardens, Rapid City, S.D., 1949-54; operator Colossal Cave Park, Vail, Ariz., 1956—; ptnr. Sta. KRNR, Roseburg, Oreg., 1961—. Mem. adv. bd. Salvation Army, Tucson, 1979-86; govs. appointee San Pedro Rparian Nat. Cons. Area Adv. Com., 1989—; past pres. So. Ariz. Internat. Livestock Assn., 1987-88; bd. dirs. Friends of Western Art., Tucson; co-founder Pima County Parklands Found.. With U.S. Navy Air Corps., 1944-45. Mem. Mountain Oyster Club (pres. 1989-91, bd. dirs. 1980-83). Republican. Home: Bear Paw Vail AZ 85641 Office: Colossal Cave Mountain Park PO Box D70 Vail AZ 85641-0070

MAIN, ROBERT GAIL, communications educator, training consultant, television and film producer, former army officer; b. Bucklin, Mo., Sept. 30, 1932; s. Raymond M. and Inez L. (Olinger) M.; m. Anita Sue Thoroughman, Jan. 31, 1955; children: Robert Bruce, David Keith, Leslie Lorraine. BS magna cum laude, U. Mo., 1954; grad. with honors, Army Command and Gen. Staff Coll., 1967; MA magna cum laude in Communications, Stanford U., 1968; PhD, U. Md., 1978. Commd. 2d lt. U.S. Army, 1954, advanced through grades to lt. col., 1968; mem. faculty Army Command and Gen. Staff Coll., 1968-70; chief speechwriting and info. materials div. U.S. Army Info. Office, 1971, chief broadcast and film div., 1972-73; dir. def. audiovisual activities Office of Info. for Armed Forces, 1973-76, ret., 1976; chmn. dept. comml. design, prof. instructional technology Calif. State U., Chino, 1976—; dir. Inst. Digital Electronic Art; tng. cons. Author: Rogues, Saints and Ordinary People, 1988; contbr. articles on computer based tng. and telecoms. to scientific and profl. jours.; producer: Walking Wounded, TV documentary, 1983; producer Army Info. Films, Army Radio Series, 1972-73. Decorated Legion of Merit, Meritorious Service medal, Commendation medal with oak leaf cluster, combat Inf. Badge; Vietnamese Cross of Gallantry; recipient Freedom Found. awards, 1972, 73, 74; Bronze medal Atlanta Film Festival, 1972; Best of Show award Balt. Film Festival, 1973; Creativity award Chgo. Indsl. Film Festival, 1973; Cine gold award Internat. Film Producers Assn., 1974; named an Outstanding Prof. Calif State U., 1987-88. Mem. Phi Eta Sigma, Alpha Zeta, Phi Delta Gamma, Omicron Delta Kappa, Alpha Gamma Rho.

MAINS, STEVE ALAN, lawyer, arbitrator, mediator; b. Ft. McClellan, Ala., Oct. 2, 1946; s. Charles H. and Gwendolyn M.; 1 child, Ursula. BS, Ind. U., 1968; JD, Ind. U., Indpls., 1973; Internat. law cert., City of London Poly., 1970. Bar: Ind. 1974, Colo., Calif. 1989, U.S. Dist. Ct. (so. dist.) Ind. 1974, U.S. Ct. Colo., 1979, U.S. Ct. Appeals (10th cir.) 1990. Sole practitioner Indpls., 1974-78; ptnr. Roper, Mains & Cobb, Boulder, Colo., 1978-87; of counsel Dorr Carson Sloan & Birney, Denver and Boulder, 1989-95; dir. profl. svcs. JAMS/ENDispute Colo. Regional Office, Denver, 1995—. With U.S. Army, 1968-70. Mem. FBA (pres. Colo. chpt. 1994-95), Computer Law Assn. (dir. 1982-87), Colo. Bar Assn., Boulder Bar Assn., Colo. Coun. Mediators, Colo. Sch. Mediation Project (pres. bd. dirs.). ; JAMS/EnDispute 410 17th St Denver CO 80202 Office: Jams/Endispute 410 17th St Denver CO 80202

MAINWARING, WILLIAM LEWIS, publishing company executive, author; b. Portland, Oreg., Jan. 17, 1935; s. Bernard and Jennie (Lewis) M.; m. Mary E. Bell, Aug. 18, 1962; children: Anne Marie, Julia Kathleen, Douglas Bernard. B.S., U. Oreg., 1957; postgrad., Stanford U., 1957-58. With Salem (Oreg.) Capital Jour., 1958-76, editor, pub., 1962-76; pub. Oreg. Statesman, 1974-76; pres. Statesman-Jour. Co., Inc., Salem, 1974-76, Westridge Press, Ltd., 1977—; pres. MediAmerica, Inc., Portland, 1981—, CEO, 1988—. Author: Exploring the Oregon Coast, 1977, Exploring Oregon's Central and Southern Cascades, 1979, Exploring the Mount Hood Loop, 1992. Pres. Salem Beautification Coun., 1968, Marion-Polk County United Good Neighbors, 1970, Salem Social Svcs. Commn., 1978-79, Salem Hosp. Found., 1978-81. 2d lt. AUS, 1958; capt. Res. Ret. Mem. Salem Area C. of C. (pres. 1972-73), Oreg. Symphony Soc. Salem (pres. 1973-75), Salem City Club (pres. 1977-78), Sigma Chi. Republican. Presbyterian (ruling elder). Home: 1090 Southridge Pl S Salem OR 97302-5947 Office: Oreg Bus Mag 610 S W Broadway Ste 200 Portland OR 97205

MAIO, SAMUEL JOSEPH, English language and literature educator; b. Raton, N.Mex., May 16, 1955; s. Ernest James and Norma Sara (Giardino) M.; m. Kathryn Todd, May 29, 1978; children: Arnesti Giacomi, Cristina Mary, Tiara Sara, Nicolina Steffani. BA, U. Utah, 1977, MA, 1979; PhD, U. So. Calif., 1986. Teaching asst. U. Utah, 1978-79; instr. Trinidad (Colo.) State Jr. Coll., 1979-81; asst. lectr. U. So. Calif., 1981-85; lectr. U. Calif., Davis, 1985-90; asst. prof. San Jose State U., 1990-93, assoc. prof., 1993—; coord. creative writing program San Jose State U., 1992—; poetry judge Pacific Internat. Contest, 1992. Author: Creating Another Self: Voice in Modern American Personal Poetry, 1995; author numerous poems, essays and revs. Recipient Acad. Am. Poets prize, 1984; Teaching award U. So. Calif., 1983, Calif. State U. Rsch. award, 1992. Office: San Jose State U Dept English One Washington Sq San Jose CA 95192-0090

MAIROSE, PAUL TIMOTHY, mechanical engineer, consultant; b. Mitchell, S.D., Aug. 4, 1956; s. Joseph E. and Phyllis R. (Glissendorf) M.; m. Connie L. Nickell, Apr. 1, 1989 (dec. June 1992); m. Donna M. Ward, Sept. 10, 1993; 1 child, Carly Jo. BSME, S.D. Sch. Mines and Tech., 1978; postgrad., Tulane U., 1986. Registered profl. engr., Wash. Mech. engr. UNC Nuclear Industries, Richland, Wash., 1979-80, Wash. Pub. Power Supply System, Richland, 1980-85, 89; cons. La. Power & Light Co., New Orleans, 1985-86, Erin Engring. & Rsch. Inc., Walnut Creek, Calif., 1986-87, Sacramento Mcpl. Utility Dist., 1987-89; mech. engr. GE, Portland, Oreg., 1989-90; sr. cons. Rocky Flats Project Cygna Energy Svcs., 1990-91; v.p. mktg. Data Max, 1991—; pvt. practice cons. engr. Vancouver, Wash., 1991—; project engr. Mactec, Inc., Richland, Wash., 1990-91; pres. Project Tech. Mgmt., 1990—; chief engr. S.W. Air Pollution Control Authority, Vancouver, Wash., 1992—. Co-author: Topical Report on Extreme Erosion at Yucca Mountain, Nevada, 1993. Mem. polit. action com. Sacramento Mcpl. Utility Dist., 1988. Mem. ASME (assoc.), ASHRAE (assoc.), Aircraft Owners and Pilots Assn., Profl. Assn. Diving Instrs., Air & Waste Mgmt. Assn., Sierra Club, Bards of Bohemia. Republican. Roman Catholic. Home: 4606 NW 387th St Woodland WA 98674

MAIS, DALE EUGENE, chemist, pharmacologist; b. South Bend, Ind., Mar. 24, 1952; s. Rollin Charles and Violet Maybel (Paine) M.; m. Ellen Maria Barrell, May 9, 1976; children; James Charles, Maryellen Clare. BS in Chemistry, Ind. U., 1974, MS in Organic Chemistry, 1977, PhD in Pharmacology, 1983. Undergrad. rsch. asst. Ind. U., Bloomington, Ind., 1972-74, teaching asst. in chemistry, grad. rsch. asst., 1973-77, 74-77; mgr. organic synthesis Lafayette (Ind.) Pharmacal Inc., 1977-79; teaching asst. anatomy, grad. rsch. asst. Ind. U., Bloomington, 1979-80, 79-83; postdoctoral fellow, asst. prof. Med. U. of S.C., Charleston, 1983-86, 86-89; sr. pharmacologist dept. cardiovascular pharmacology Eli Lilly and Co., Indpls., 1989-92; adj. assoc. prof. Ind. U. Sch. of Medicine, Indpls., 1990-92; sr. rsch. scientist Ligand Pharm., Inc., San Diego, 1992—; expert analyst Organic Chemistry Edition of Chemtracts, 1990—. Editor: Eicosanoids in the Cardiovascular and Renal Systems, 1988; patentee in field; contbr. numerous articles to profl. jours. and chpts. to books. Named Ira E. scholar Ind. U., 1974, Drug Sci. Found. scholar, 1983-86; recipient Grad. Grant-in-Aid, Ind. U., 1982, 83, Nat. Rsch. Svc. award, 1983-86, First Pl. in Postdoctoral Divsn. of Student Rsch. Day Competition, 1984, 85, Louis N. Katz Basic Rsch. award-Finalist, 1985. Mem. Am. Socs. of Pharmacology and Exptl. Therapeutics, Am. Chem. Soc., S.C. Acad. Sic., Sigma Xi. Office: Ligand Pharms 9393 Towne Centre Dr Ste 100 San Diego CA 92121-3016

MAISEL, SHERMAN JOSEPH, economist, educator; b. Buffalo, July 8, 1918; s. Louis and Sophia (Beck) M.; m. Lucy Cowdin, Sept. 26, 1942; children: Lawrence C., Margaret L. A.B., Harvard U., 1939, M.P.A., 1947, Ph.D., 1949. Mem. bd. govs. FRS, 1965-72; economist, fgn. service res. officer Dept. State, 1945-46; teaching fellow Harvard U., 1947-48; asst. prof., assoc. prof., prof. bus. adminstrn. U. Calif. at Berkeley, 1948-65, 72-86; sr. economist Nat. Bur. Econ. Research-West, 1973-78; chmn., bd. dirs. Farmers Savings & Loan, 1986-88; pres. Sherman J. Maisel & Asscs. Inc., 1986—; fellow Fund For Advancement Edn., 1952-53, Inst. Basic Math. with Application to Bus., 1959-60, Center for Advanced Study in Behavioral Scis., 1972; mem. adv. coms. to Bur. Census, FHA, State of Calif., Ford Found., Social Sci. Research Council; mem. bldg. research adv. bd. NRC. Author: Housebuilding in Transition, 1953, Fluctuations, Growth, and Forecasting, 1957, Managing the Dollar, 1973, Real Estate Investment and Finance, 1976, Risk and Capital Adequacy in Commercial Banks, 1981, Macroeconomics: Theories and Policies, 1982, Real Estate Finance, 1987, 2d edit., 1992. Bd. dirs. Berkeley Unified Sch. Dist., 1962-65. Served to capt. AUS, 1941-45. Mem. Am. Fin. Assn. (pres. 1973), Am. Econ. Assn., Am. Statis. Assn. Home: 2164 Hyde St San Francisco CA 94109-1701 Office: U Calif Haas Bus Sch Berkeley CA 94720

MAJERLE, DANIEL LEWIS, professional basketball player, Olympic athlete; b. Traverse City, Mich., Sept. 9, 1965. Student, Ctrl. Mich. Forward Phoenix Suns, 1988—. Mem. Bronze Medal Winning Olympic Team, Seoul, Korea, 1988; mem. NBA All-Defensive second team, 1991, 93; mem. NBA All-Star team, 1992, 93; named to Dream Team II, 1994. Office: Phoenix Suns 201 E Jefferson St Phoenix AZ 85004-2412*

MAJOR, CAROL ANN, perinatologist, obstetrician/gynecologist; b. Berkeley, Calif., Oct. 30, 1959. BA, Stanford U., 1981; MD, Case Western Res. U., 1981-85. Diplomate Am. Bd. Ob-Gyn., Am. Bd. Maternal-Fetal Medicine. Intern U. Calif., San Francisco, 1985-86, resident, 1986-89; fellow U. Calif., Irvine, 1989-91; asst. prof. U. Calif. Irvine Med. Ctr., Orange, 1991—; bd. dirs. Orange County (Calif.) Perinatal Coun. Contbr. articles to profl. jours. Mem. Am. Women's Med. Assn., Orange County Ob-Gyn. Soc.

MAJOR, CLARENCE LEE, novelist, poet, educator; b. Atlanta, Dec. 31, 1936; s. Clarence and Inez (Huff) M.; m. Pamela Ritter, May 8, 1980. BS, SUNY, Albany; PhD, Union Inst. Prof. U. Colo., Boulder, 1977-89, U. Calif., Davis, 1989—. Author: All-Night Visitors, 1969, Dictionary of Afro-American Slang, 1970, No, 1973, Reflex and Bone Structure, 1975, Emergency Exit, 1979, Swallow the Lake, Some Observations of a Stranger at Zune in the Latter Part of the Century, 1989, My Amputations, 1986, Such Was the Season, 1987, Painted Turtle, 1988, Fun and Games, 1990, Parking Lots, 1992, Calling the Wind, 1993, Juba to Jive: A Dictionary of African-American Slang, 1994; poetry: Symptoms & Madness, 1971, Private Line, 1971, The Cotton Club, 1972, Inside Diameter: The France Poems, 1974, Surfaces and Masks, 1988; contbr. articles to Washington Post Book World, L.A. Times Book Rev., N.Y. Times Book Rev., Am. Rev. Recipient Nat. Council on Arts award, Washington, 1970; Western States Book award, Western States Found., Santa Fe, 1986; Fulbright grantee, 1981-83. Office: U Calif Dept of English Sproul Hall Davis CA 95616

MAJOR, KARL BURCE, air force officer; b. Kansas City, Mo., Feb. 13, 1960; s. Schwab Samuel and Wilma Jean (Briscoe) M.; m. Sari Lane, Dec. 9, 1989; 1 child, McKayla Kristen. BSME, Okla. State U., 1982; MSME, Calif. State U., Fresno, 1993. Comd. 2d lt. USAF, 1982, advanced through grades to maj., 1995; pilot 41st Aero. Rescue & Recovery, McClellan AFB, Calif., 1984-87; instr. pilot 1550th Combat Crew Tng. Wing, Kirtland AFB, Calif., 1989-90; experiment test pilot 412th Test Wing, Edwards AFB, Calif., 1990—; investigating officer for aircraft mishap investigation bd. USAF, 1993. Recipient Comendation for Exemplary Svc. in USAF, City of Kansas City, 1990. Mem. AIAA, Soc. Experimental Test Pilots, Phi Kappa Phi. Home: 44910 13th St E Lancaster CA 93535-1104 Office: USAF Test Pilot Sch 220 S Wolfe Ave Edwards CA 93524-6845

MAJOR, MARGUERITE LOUISE, retired magazine editor; b. Kansas City, Mo., Jan. 26, 1929; d. Ray Clark and Celia Marguerite (Fowler) M. AB in Journalism, San Jose State U., 1950. Editorial asst. Norcross Greeting Cards, Inc., N.Y.C., 1950-51; reporter, editor Sunnyvale (Calif.) Standard, 1951-52; alumni dir. San Jose State U., 1953-57; pubs. dir. Santa Clara (Calif.) U., 1957-60, news dir., 1960-78, pub. affairs dir., 1978-83; editor Santa Clara Today, Santa Clara U., 1983-86, Santa Clara mag., Santa Clara U., 1986-91. Mem. Am. Coll. Pub. Rels. (regional dir. 1974-75), Pub. Rels. Soc. Am. (accredited), Coun. Advancement & Support Edn. (trustee 1975-77). Republican. Episcopalian. Office: 912 Cypress Point Loop Ashland OR 97520-3754

MAJUMDAR, DEBAPRASAD (DEBU), physicist, nuclear engineer; b. Calcutta, West Bengal, India, Dec. 10, 1941; came to U.S. 1964; s. Hem Chandra and Amala Bala (Roy) M.; m. Marie Catherine Heery, May 30, 1971; children: Rajeev David, Nikhil Daniel. BSc in Physics, MSc in Physics, Calcutta U., 1961, 63; MS in Physics, U. Pa., 1966; MS in Nuclear Engring., U. Mich., 1973; PhD in Physics, SUNY, Stony Brook, 1969. Registered profl. engr., Idaho. Postdoctoral fellow Syracuse (N.Y.) U., 1969-71; assoc. rsch. scientist and postdoctoral fellow U. Mich., Ann Arbor, 1971-74; nuclear engr. Brookhaven Nat. Lab., Upton, N.Y., 1974-80; program mgr. U.S. Dept. Energy, Idaho Falls, 1980—. Co-editor: Anticipated and Abnormal Plant Transients in Light Water Reactors, 1984, Artificial Intelligence and Other Innovative Computer Applications in Nuclear Industry, 1988; contbr. articles to profl. jours. Active Boy Scouts Am., 1989—. Recipient Gold medals, U. Calcutta, 1961, 63; All India Merit scholar, 1957-63; named Outstanding Vol., Idaho Falls Mayor's Office, 1987. Mem. Am. Nuclear Soc. (sec., chmn. nuclear reactor safety div. program com. 1987-90, chmn. and fellow Idaho sect.), Am. Phys. Soc. Home: 1749 Delmar Dr Idaho Falls ID 83404-7461 Office: US Dept Energy 785 Doe Pl Idaho Falls ID 83401-1562

MAJURE, JOYCE ARLENE, surgeon; b. Kansas City, Mo., May 30, 1951; d. Oliver Davis and Betty Lou (Tucker) M.; m. Christopher Al Moreno, Apr. 14, 1984; children: Thomas Daniel, James Luis, Alana Joy. BA, Yale U., 1973; MD, U. Kans., 1976. Diplomate Am. Bd. Surgery. Resident in surgery U. Colo. Health Scis., Denver, 1976=80, 81-82; rsch. fellow Beth Israel Hosp., Boston, 1980-81; pvt. practice Rifle, Colo., 1982-84; surgeon Ctr. for Plastic and Reconstructive Surgery, Denver, 1984-86; pvt. practice Moscow, Idaho, 1986-87, Lewiston, Idaho, 1987—; cancer liaison physician St. Joseph Regional Med. Ctr., Lewiston, 1988—. Author and editor The Pocket Mentor: A Manual for Surgical Interns and Residents, 1993. Fellow ACS (pres. Idaho chpt. 1994, exec. com. of com. on oper. room environment); mem. Idaho Med. Assn., Assn. Women Surgeons (chmn. comm. com. 1989—, editor newsletter 1989-94, pres.-elect 1995—). Office: 307 Saint Johns Way Ste 11 Lewiston ID 83501-2435

MAK, STANLEY MING, distributor, importer, trading consultant, radio broadcasting management consultant; b. Chengdu, People's Republic of China, Feb. 17, 1949; came to U.S., 1969; s. Fung and Sui-Fun (Yil) M.; m. Suzanne Debra Phelps, June 9, 1971; children: Justin, Kristin, Kathryn. BA in Radio/TV Mgmt., Ea. Washington State U., 1972. Sales agt. Equitable of Iowa, Spokane, Wash., 1972-73; account exec. KREM AM/FM/TV, Spokane, Wash., 1973-77, KING TV, Seattle, 1977-79; local sales mgr. KINK Radio, Portland, Oreg., 1979-80, gen. sales mgr., 1980-81, gen. mgr., 1981-83, v.p., gen. mgr., 1983-87; sr. v.p. King Broadcasting Co., Seattle, 1987-92; pres. Mak Pacific, Inc., Bellevue, Wash., 1993—; sec. Portland Area Radio Coun., 1985-87. Mem. exec. bd. ARC, Oreg. Trail chpt., Portland, 1986-87; mem. exec. bd. Seattle Youth Symphony, 1990-92, bd. dirs., 1988-90. Republican. Home: 16520 NE 132nd St Redmond WA 98052-1112

MAKER, JANET ANNE, author, lecturer; b. Woburn, Mass., Feb. 13, 1942; d. George Walter and Margaret Anna (Kopasz); children: Thomas Walter, Jane McKinley. BA, UCLA, 1963; MS, Columbia U., 1967; PhD, U. So. Calif., 1978. lectr. in devlopmental edn., 1979—. Author: Get It All Together, 1979, Interpretive Reading Comprehension, 1984, Keys to a Powerful Vocabulary, Level I, 1981, 88, 94, Level II, 1983, 90, 94, Keys to College Success, 1980, 85, 90, College Reading, Book 1, 1984, 88, 91, Book 2, 1982, 86, 89, 92, Book 3, 1985, Academic Reading with Active Critical Thinking, 1995. Home and Office: 925 Malcolm Ave Los Angeles CA 90024-3113

MAKI, KAZUMI, physicist, educator; b. Takamatsu, Japan, Jan. 27, 1936; s. Toshio and Hideko M.; m. Masako Tanaka, Sept. 21, 1969. B.S., Kyoto U., 1959, Ph.D., 1964. Research asso. Inst. for Math. Scis., Kyoto U., 1964; research asso. Fermi Inst., U. Chgo., 1964-65; asst. prof. physics U. Calif., San Diego, 1965-67; prof. Tohoku U., Sendai, Japan, 1967-74; vis. prof. Universite Paris-Sud, Orsay, France, 1969-70; prof. physics U. So. Calif., Los Angeles, 1974—; vis. prof. Inst. Lau-Langevin, U. Paris-Sud, France, 1979-80, Max-Plank Inst fur Festkorper Forschung, Stuttgart, Germany, 1986-87, U. Paris-7, 1990, Hokkaido U., Sapporo, Japan, 1993, Centre de Recherche sur Tres Basses Temperatures, Grenoble, France, 1993-94, Instituto de Ciencia de Materiales, Madrid, Spain, 1994. Assoc. editor Jour. Low Temperature Physics, 1969-91; contbr. articles to profl. jours. Recipient Nishina prize, 1972, Alexander von Humboldt award, 1986-87; Fulbright scholar, 1964-65; Guggenheim fellow, 1979-80. Fellow Japan Soc. Promotion of Sci., Am. Phys. Soc.; mem. AAAS, Phys. Soc. Japan. Office: U So Calif Dept Physics Los Angeles CA 90089-0484

MAKI, ROBERT RICHARD, sculptor, draftsman, educator; b. Walla Walla, Wash., Sept. 15, 1938; s. Samuel Eino and Ethel Hildegrad (Busch) M.; m. Dee Ann Engelsen, Feb. 17, 1962; 1 child, Andrea. Student, Clark Jr. Coll., 1956-58; BA in Edn. and Indsl. Arts, Western Wash. Coll., 1962; MFA in Sculpture, U. Wash., 1966; student, San Francisco Art Inst., 1967. Instr. art and indsl. arts Gig Harbor (Wash.) High Sch., 1962-64; mem. hon. art faculty U. Wash., Seattle, 1966-68; artist-in-residence Humboldt State U., Arcata, Calif., fall 1974, N.C. Sch. of the Arts, Winston-Salem, fall 1978, Wake Forest U., Winston-Salem, winter 1979; guest artist Mont. State U., Bozeman, summer 1973, St. Cloud (Minn.) U., fall 1974, Seattle Pacific U., summer 1974; vis. artist, lectr. numerous colls. and univs. One-man shows include Attica Gallery, Seattle, 1967, Richmond Art Ctr., 1967, Richard White Gallery, Seattle, 1969, Michael Walls Gallery, San Francisco, 1969, Portland (Oreg.) Art Mus. Sch., 1970, Western Wash. State U., Bellingham, 1970, Seattle Pacific U., 1971, Seattle Art Mus., 1973, Mont. State U., Bozeman, 1973, Portland Ctr. for Visual Arts, 1974, Humboldt State U., 1974, Reed Coll., Portland, 1975, Dootson/Calderhead Gallery, Seattle, 1976, Evergreen State Coll., Olympia, Wash., 1977, Richard Hines Gallery, Seattle, 1979, 81, Whatcom Mus. History and Art, Bellingham, Wash., 1983, Laura Russo Gallery, 1987, 88, Diane Ferris Gallery, Vancouver, B.C., 1988, Cliff Michel Gallery, Seattle, 1989, Lannon-Cole, Chgo., 1992, Butters Gallery, Ltd., Portland, 1994, Ratner Gallery, Chgo, 1994, Bellevue Botanical Garden Outdoor Sculpture Exbhn., 1995, Wake Forest U., Winston-Salem, N.C., 1995, others; group exhbns. include Seattle Art Mus., 1967, 74, 80, Mus. Art. U. Oreg., Eugene, 1968, L.A. Mcpl. Mus., 1968, Portland Art Mus., 1968, Denver Art Mus., 1979, Nat. Collection Fine Arts, Washington, 1979, Bellevue Art Mus., 1983, 91, Western Wash. State U., 1984, 85, San Jose Mus. Art, 1987, Mona Bismark Estate, Paris, 1988, Ishikawa Prefectural Mus., Japan, 1990, Cliff Michel Gallery, Seattle, 1990, J. Rosenthal Gallery, Chgo., 1992; represented in collections Nat. Coll. Am. Art, Seattle Art Mus., Henry Gallery, Seattle, Stanford U., Wash. U., St. Louis, U. Mont., Bozeman, Pierce Coll., Wash., Western Wash. U., City of Seattle, Security Pacific Bank, U.S. West, Seattle, Federal Home Loan Bank, Seattle, Bogles and Gates, Seattle, Group Health Coop., Seattle, Microsoft, Redmond, Wash., others; subject articles. Bd. dirs. Seattle Acad. Arts and Sci., 1985-87; panelist, juror GSA, Nat. Endowment Art in Architect Program, 1980; juror visual arts fellows Nat. Endowment Arts/New England Regional Fellowship, 1992. Pvt. USAR, 1959-65. Fellow in sculpture Nat. Endowment for Arts and Humanities, Washington, 1968, Sr. fellow in drawing, 1985, Centennial Alumni fellow Western Wash. U., 1993; Rockefeller Residency fellow Wake Forest U., 1979; Materials grantee Weyerhaeuser Co., 1968, Bethlehem Steel Corp., 1979, Sculpture Matching grantee Nat. Endowment for Arts and Wake Forest U., 1979; recipient Sculpture Commn. award GSA, Fed. Bldg., Eugene, 1974, Park and Sculpture Commn. award Westlake Park, Seattle, 1981-88, King County Honors award, 1990, others. Mem. Internat. Sculpture Ctr. Home: 8 Florentia St Seattle WA 98109-1709

MAKINO, CLINT LAWRENCE, neurobiologist; b. East Patchogue, N.Y., July 30, 1958; s. Ray Chiyoto and Chiyoko (Okabayashi) M. BS, Duke U., 1980; PhD, Fla. State U., 1987. Biochemistry technician Nat. Inst. on Aging, Balt., 1980-82; postdoctoral fellow Stanford (Calif.) U., 1987-93, rsch. assoc. in life scis., 1993—. Contbr. articles to profl. jours. Mem. Hawaii Sunsetters, San Mateo, Calif., 1994. Robinson Neurol. Found. grantee; recipient Individual Nat. Rsch. Svc. award Nat. Eye Inst., Rsch. to Prevent Blindness Career Devel. award. Mem. AAAS, Biophys. Soc., Assn. Rsch. in Vision and Ophthalmology, No. Calif. Volleyball Assn. Office: Stanford Univ Dept of Neurobiology Fairchild Bldg D238 Stanford CA 94305

MAKKER, SUDESH PAUL, physician; b. Sargodha, Punjab, India, June 8, 1941; came to U.S., 1966; s. Manohar Lal and Daya Wati (Kharbanda) M.; m. Donna Mae Stohs, Feb. 15, 1969; children: Vishal, Kirin. Fellow of Sci., Panjab U., 1959; MD, All India Inst. med. Scis., New Dehli, 1964. Bd. cert. Am. Bd. Pediatrics, Am. Bd. Pediatric Nephrology. Intern in internal medicine All India Inst. of Med. Scis., New Dehli, 1965, resident in internal medicine, 1966; rotating intern Queens Gen. Hosp., N.Y.C., 1966-67; resident in pediatrics U. Chgo. (Ill.) Hosps., 1967-69; rsch. fellowship in pediatric nephrology Case Western Res. U., 1969-71; fellowship in pediatric nephrology U. Calif., San Francisco, 1971; instr. to asst. prof. pediatrics Case Western Res. U., Sch. Medicine, Cleve., 1971-76, assoc. prof., div. head pediatric nephrology, 1976-83; prof., div. head pediatric nephrology U. Tex. Health Sci. Ctr., San Antonio, 1983-91; prof., sect. chief pediatric nephrology U. Calif., Davis Sch. Medicine, Davis, 1991—; mem. ad hoc com. on nat. standards for dialysis and transplantation in children Am. Soc. Pediatric Nephrology; ad hoc com. on hypertension in the young Am. Heart Assn., N.E. Ohio Chpt.; mem. end stage renal disease program Crippled Children Svcs. State of Ohio; mem. rsch. grants com. and pub. edn. com. Kidney Found. of Ohio; vis. prof. U. Pa. Children's Hosp., Phila., 1981, U. So. Calif., L.A., 1981, U. Calif. Sch. Medicine, San Francisco, 1982, U. Mich., Ann Arbor, 1990, and many others. Editor: (textbook) Pediatric Nephrology, 1992; editorial bd.: Internat. Jour. Pediatric Nephrology, Indian Jour. Pediatrics; contbr. over 80 articles to profl. jours. Mem. AAAS, Am. Acad. Pediatrics, Am. Soc. Nephrology, The Soc. for Exptl. Biology and Medicine, Am. Assn. Immunologists, Soc. for Pediatric Rsch., Am. Pediatric Soc., Sigma Chi, Sigma Xi. Office: Univ Calif Davis Med Ctr Pediatric Nephrology 2516 Stockton Blvd Sacramento CA 95817-2208

MAKKER, VIRENDER KUMAR, engineer, scientist; b. Naushehra, India, Oct. 8, 1943; came to U.S., 1965; s. Manohar Lal and Daya Wati (Kharbanda) M.; m. Madhu Batra, May 15, 1972; children: Vandana, Amit. B-Tech, Indian Inst. Tech., Kanpur, 1965; MS, U. Minn., 1967; PhD, U. So. Calif., 1970. Mem. tech. staff Bell Telephone Labs., Murray Hill, N.J., 1970-75; R&D engr. Hewlett-Packard, Santa Rosa, Calif., 1976—. Home: 1239 Melissa Ct Santa Rosa CA 95409-2525

MAKOWSKI, HEIDI MICHELLE, academic program director; b. Orem, Utah, Nov. 6, 1958; d. Bert William and Betty Gay (Callahan) Wagstaff; m. Edward Dennis Makowski, July 21, 1989. BS, U. Utah, 1983. Asst. to dean Coll. Fine Arts U. Utah, Salt Lake City, 1984-90, dir. of devel. Coll. Fine Arts, 1990—. Mem. NAFE, Utah Soc. of Fund Raisers, Coun. for Advancement and Support of Edn., Jr. League of Salt Lake, Alumni Assn. Bd., Discrimination Complaints Hearing Panel. Democrat. Office: U Utah 250 AAC Coll Fine Arts Salt Lake City UT 84112

MAKOWSKI, PETER EDGAR, hospital executive.; b. Milw., Nov. 21, 1953; s. Edgar Leonard and Patricia Mae (Nock) M.; m. Cynthia Renee Edgerly, Apr. 7, 1979. B.A. in Polit. Sci., Whittier Coll., 1976; M.P.H., UCLA, 1980. Adminstrv. intern Calif. Hosp. Med. Center, Los Angeles, 1977, unit mgr. emergency dept., 1977-78; adminstrv. resident Presbyn. Intercommunity Hosp., Whittier, Calif., 1979-80, adminstrv. dir. support services, 1980-82, v.p. ambulatory/spl. services, 1982-84, v.p. diagnostic/therapeutic services, 1984-85; sr. v.p. Calif. Med. Ctr., Los Angeles, 1985-86; exec. v.p. Queen of the Valley Hosp., West Covina, Calif., 1986—. Mem. adv. council San Gabriel Valley Area Health Edn. Ctr., 1983-84; vice-chmn. adv. com. Trauma Hosp., Los Angeles County, 1987—. Mem. Am. Cancer Soc. (Long Beach SE unit, bd. dirs. 1984-85), Am. Hosp. Assn., Am. Coll. Hosp. Adminstrs. (student assoc.), Health Care Execs. So. Calif., UCLA Hosp. Adminstrn. Alumni Assn., Nat. Honor Soc, Whittier Alumni Assn. (bd. dirs. 1984—). Republican. Roman Catholic. Club: Whittier Host Lions. Home: 18520 Flora Dr Yorba Linda CA 92686-4937 Office: 1115 S Sunset Ave West Covina CA 91790-3940

MALA, THEODORE ANTHONY, physician, consultant; b. Santa Monica, Calif., Feb. 3, 1946; s. Ray and Galina (Liss) M.; children: Theodore S., Galina T. BA in Philosophy, DePaul U., 1972; MD, Autonomous U., Guadalajara, Mex., 1976; MPH, Harvard U., 1980. Spl. asst. for health affairs Alaska Fedn. Natives, Anchorage, 1977-78; chief health svcs. Alaska State Div. of Corrections, Anchorage, 1978-79; assoc. prof., founder, dir. Inst. for Circumpolar Health Studies, U. Alaska, Anchorage, 1982-90; founder Siberian med. rsch. program U. Alaska, Anchorage, 1982, founder Magadan (USSR) med. rsch. program, 1988; commr. Health and Social Svcs. State of Alaska, Juneau, 1990-93; pres. chief exec. officer Ted Mala, Inc., Anchorage, 1993—; pres., ptnr. Mexican-Siberian Trading Co., Monterrey, Mex., 1994—; mem. Alaska rsch. and publs. com. Indian Health Svc., USPHS, 1987-90; advisor Nordic Coun. Meeting, WHO, Greenland, 1985; mem. Internat. Organizing Com., Circumpolar Health Congress, Iceland, 1992-93; chmn. bd. govs. Alaska Psychiat. Inst., Anchorage, 1990-93; cabinet mem. Gov. Walter J. Hickel, Juneau, 1990-93; advisor humanitarian aid to Russian Far East U.S. Dept. State, 1992—; cons. USAID on U.S.-Russian Health Programs, 1994. Former columnist Tundra Times; contbr. articles to profl. jours. Trustee United Way Anchorage, 1978-79; chmn. bd. trustees Alaska Native Coll., 1993—. Recipient Gov.'s award, 1988, Outstanding Svc. award Alaska Commr. Health, 1979, Ministry of Health citation USSR Govt., 1989, Citation award Alaska State Legislature, 1989, 90, 94, Commendation award State of Alaska, 1990, Alaska State Legislature, 1994, Honor Kempton Svc. to Humanity award, 1989, citation Med. Comty. of Magadan region, USSR, 1989; Nat. Indian fellow U.S. Dept. Edn., 1979. Mem. Assn. Am. Indian Physicians, N.Y. Acad. Scis., Internat. Union for Circumpolar Health (permanent sec.-gen. 1987-90, organizing com. 8th Internat. Congress on Circumpolar Health 1987-90). Home: 205 E Dimond Blvd # 544 Anchorage AK 99515 Office: 205 E Dimond Blvd Ste 544 Anchorage AK 99515-1909

MALCOLM, ANDREW HOGARTH, journalist, writer; b. Cleve., June 22, 1943; s. Ralph Monteith and Beatrice Florence (Bowles) M.; m. Connie D'Amelio, Nov. 28, 1981; children: Christopher, Spencer, Emily, Keddy. BJ, Northwestern U., 1966, MJ, 1967. Clk. The N.Y. Times, N.Y.C., 1967-68, met. reporter, 1969-70; nat. corr. The N.Y. Times, Chgo., 1971-73, San Francisco, 1974-75; fgn. corr. The N.Y. Times, Vietnam, Thailand, Guam, 1975, Tokyo, 1975-78, Republic of Korea, 1975-78; bur. chief The N.Y. Times, Toronto, Ont., Can., 1978-82, Chgo., 1982-87; asst. nat. editor The N.Y. Times, N.Y.C., 1987-88, nat. affairs corr., columnist, 1988-93; exec. asst. policy and communications Govs. Office, Helena, Mont., 1993—. Author: Unknown America, 1975, The Canadians, 1985, Final Harvest, 1986, This Far and No More, 1987, Someday, 1991, U.S. 1: America's Original Main Street, 1991, The Land and People of Canada, 1991, Huddle: Fathers, Sons, and Football, 1992. Recipient George Polk award L.I. U., 1975, Page One award N.Y. Newspaper Guild, 1975, 83. Office: Governor's Office State Capitol Helena MT 59620-0801

MALCOLM, GAROLD DEAN, architect; b. Belle Fouche, S.D., Apr. 25, 1940; s. Gifford Garold Malcolm and Ellen Eve Liming; m. Breta Lois Bailey, 1966 (div. 1982); children: Heather Marie, Allison Claire; m. Lucia Eagon Stenson, 1991. BArch, U. Oreg., 1966. Ptnr. McAdoo, Malcolm & Youel, Architects, 1981—. Prin. works include Creston-Nelson Elec. Substation, Seattle (Honor award Wash. Aggregates and Concrete Assn.), Arboretum Visitor's Ctr., Seattle (Honor award Builders Community Awards Program, People's Choice award Seattle chpt. AIA), Des Moines (Wash.) Libr., Queen Anne Swimming Pool, Seattle. Mem. AIA, Matsumura Kenpo Karate Assn. (black belt). Office: McAdoo Malcolm & Youel Architects 1718 E Olive Way Seattle WA 98102-5615

MALCOLM, RICHARD WARD, college administrator, consultant; b. Columbus, Ohio, July 27, 1933; s. Ralph James and Beatrice (Ward) M.; m. Cheryl Wallace, Dec. 26, 1993; 1 child, Gwynn Malcolm Socolich. BS, U. Findlay (Ohio), 1956; MA, Ariz. State U., 1960; MEd, U. So. Calif., 1965, EdD, 1966. Acad. dean Martin Coll., Pulaski, Tenn., 1965-67; dean instruction Arapahoe Community Coll., Littleton, Colo., 1967-71; chair edn. div. Chapman Coll., Orange, Calif., 1971-80; assoc. prof. U. So. Calif., 1976-77; dean instruction Mesa (Ariz.) Community Coll., 1980-91; asst. to provost Chandler (Ariz.)/Gilbert Community Coll., 1991-92, chair divsn. social and behavioral scis., 1993—. Author: Mental Measurement Yearbook, 1972. Pres. Ariz. Rail Pasenger Assn., Phoenix, 1984-93. Mem. Am. Assn. Higher Edn., Ariz. Acad. Adminstrv. Assn. (treas. 1991—), Rotary. Methodist. Office: Chandler/Gilbert Community Coll 2626 E Pecos Rd Chandler AZ 85225-2413

MALCOLM-CALLIS, KATHRYN JANETTE, animal scientist; b. Livingston, Mont., May 29, 1958; d. Orlin Rae and Dorothy Helen (Anderson) Malcolm; m. Quint F. Callis (div.); 1 child, Kaitlyn Sarah. BS in Animal Sci., Mont. State U., 1980; MS, N.Mex. State U., 1986, PhD, 1990. With Pub. Auction Yards, Billings, Mont., 1978-79; intern Colmey Vet. Clinic, Livingston, 1980; rsch. tech. Mont. State U., 1980-84; grad. rsch. and teaching asst. N.Mex. State U., 1985-86, 1987-89; rsch. specialist Clayton (N.Mex.) Livestock Rsch. Ctr., 1990—. Contbr. articles and abstracts to profl. jours. Sunday sch. tchr. Paradise Valley Community Ch. Mem. Am. Soc. Animal Sci., Am. Dairy Sci. Assn. Office: Clayton Livestock Rsch Ctr RR 1 Box 109 Clayton NM 88415-9501

MALCOR, LINDA A., writer, researcher; b. Pasadena, Calif., Feb. 3, 1962; d. Victor Carl and Gloria Gail (Russ) Peterson; m. Daniel Roy Malcor, Dec. 19, 1987. AB in English cum laude, Occidental Coll., 1984; MA, UCLA, 1986, PhD in Folklore and Mythology, 1991. Writing adviser Occidental Coll., L.A., 1982-83; rsch. asst., teaching asst. UCLA, 1985-86, 2d bibliographer, 1987-89; course instr. Learning Tree U., Chatsworth, Calif., 1990-93; freelance rschr., 1985—, freelance writer, 1987—; adj. faculty Antioch U., Marina Del Rey, Calif., 1992-94. Author: the Chalice at the Cross, 1991; co-author: From Scythia to Camelot, 1994; freelance screenwriter Morris, Inc., Torrance, Calif., 1992—; option feature script to high velocity Entertainment, Simi Valley, Calif., 1994; freelance writer for Ency. of Am. Popular Beliefs and Superstitions, L.A., 1989; author articles. Deacon Prsbyn. Ch., Pasadena, 1987-89, Presbyn. Ch., Inglewood, Calif., 1992-94, mem. nursery sch. bd., 1995—; judge Election Bd., L.A., 1990-91, insp., 1992-95. Recipient Victor Gruen award, 1978; UCLA Grad. Div. travel grantee, 1985-87. Mem. Am. Folklore Soc.,Calif. Folklore Soc., So. Calif. Acad. Scis. (Best Paper award 1984, 86, 87), Tugs (skipper 1992-93), Phi Alpha Theta. Republican. Home and Office: 3223 Bagley Ave Apt 101 Los Angeles CA 90034-2971

MALEE, THOMAS MICHAEL, lawyer; b. Omaha, May 25, 1947. BA, Carroll Coll., 1970; JD, U. Mont., 1975. Bar: Mont. 1975, U.S. Dist. Ct. Mont. 1975, U.S. Ct. Appeals (9th cir.) 1986, U.S. Supreme Ct. 1988. Staff atty. State of Mont. Legis. Counsel, Helena, Mont., 1975-76; asst. atty. gen. State of Mont. Dept. Revenue, Helena, 1976; pvt. practice Seattle, Tacoma, Wash., 1977-78, Helena, 1979-82, Billings, Mont., 1982—. Mem. Assn. Trial Lawyers Am., State Bar of Mont. (ins. com. 1988—). Roman Catholic. Office: 1109 N 22nd St Apt 103A Billings MT 59101-0253

MALHOTRA, MANOHAR LAL, metallurgist, metals company executive; b. Multan, West Pakistan, Sept. 12, 1939; came to U.S., 1968, naturalized, 1977; s. Chetan Dass and Prakash Wati (Khanna) M.; m. Usha Kapoor, June 6, 1966; children: Ravi, Arun. BSc with honors in Physics, Delhi (India) U., 1961, MS in Physics, 1963; MS magna cum laude in Physics, Fairleigh Dickinson U., 1970; PhD in Physics, Banaras Hindu U., 1972; PhD in Materials Sci., U.Va., 1974. Scientist, Nat. Phys. Lab., New Delhi, 1965-68; teaching cum research fellow dept. physics Fairleigh Dickinson U., 1968-70; NIH predoctoral research fellow in materials sci. U.Va., 1970-74; NSF postdoctoral research fellow in chem. engring. SUNY, Buffalo, 1974-75; NIH postdoctoral research fellow dept. dental materials U. Mich., 1975-77; dir. rsch. Julius Aderer Inc. and Degussa Dental Inc., L.I.C., N.Y., 1977-86; v.p. tech. Argen Precious Metals, Inc., San Diego, 1987—. Contbr. rsch. articles in field. Mem. Internat. Assn. Dental Rsch., Am. Assn. Dental Rsch., Am. Soc. Metals, Internat. Precious Metals Inst., Am. Def. Preparedness Assn., Sigma Xi. Home: 12634 Brickellia St San Diego CA 92129-3704 Office: Argen Precious Metals Inc 5855 Oberlin Dr San Diego CA 92121-4718

MALHOTRA, VIJAY KUMAR, mathematics educator; b. Punjab, India, Sept. 23, 1946; came to U.S., 1969; s. Anand K. and Swarn Kanta (Chadha) M.; m. Madhu Chadha, Aug. 18, 1973; children: Jaishri, Vaishali, Vivek.. BA, Delhi (India) U., 1965; MA, Meerut U., India, 1968, Pepperdine U., 1970; EdD, Nova Southwestern U., 1994. Cert. instr. community colls., Calif. Head math. dept. Le Lycee de L.A., 1971-78; instr. math. L.A. Trade Tech. Coll., 1978-84; prof. El Camino Coll., Torrance, Calif., 1984—. Mem. Am. Fedn. Tchrs. Office: El Camino Coll 16007 Crenshaw Blvd Torrance CA 90506-0001

MALICK, PETER BENSON, accountant; b. L.A., July 13, 1957; s. David and Barbara Lynn (Schulman) M.; m. Linda Cherry, Aug. 19, 1989. BA in Econ., UCLA, 1980; MS in Tax, Golden Gate U., 1985. CPA, Calif. Para profl. tax dept. Touche Ross & Co., L.A., 1977-78; staff acct. Cohen & Weir, Encino, Calif., 1978-80; sr. staff acct. Ernst & Whinney, Century City, Calif., 1980-82; mgr. tax dept. Nigro, Karlin & Segal, Century City, 1982-89; pvt. practice Woodland Hills, Calif., 1989—; mortgage loan lender Westside Lenders, Inc., Beverly Hills, Calif., 1993—. Mem. AICPA, Calif. Soc. CPAs, Phi Eta Sigma, Omicron Delta Epsilon. Office: Peter Benson Malick CPA 5959 Topanga Canyon Blvd Woodland Hills CA 91367-3648

MALIK, SOHAIL, chemistry educator, researcher, consultant; b. Karachi, Pakistan, Nov. 7, 1958; came to U.S., 1986; s. Bakhtiar Malik and Amna Begum; m. Rubina Sial, Jan. 1, 1990. BSc with honors, U. Karachi, 1980, MS, 1982, PhD, 1986; postgrad., Stanford U., 1986-88. Instr. div. chemistry and nephrology, depts. lab. medicine and medicine U. Wash., Seattle, 1988-89, asst. prof. depts. lab. medicine and medicine, 1989—; head natural products lab. dept. lab. medicine, 1990—; co-dir. div. chemistry, dept. lab. medicine U. Wash., Seattle, 1991—; postdoctoral rsch. assoc. dept. chemistry Stanford (Calif.) U., 1986-88; peer rev. cons. NIH/Alcohol Drug Abuse and Mental Health Adminstrn. Mem. editorial bd. Current Medicinal Chemistry; contbr. articles to profl. jours.; patentee in field. Fellow Am. Inst. Chemists, Stanford U. scholar, 1986-88. Mem. Am. Assn. Advancement Sci., Am. Chem. Soc., Am. Soc. Pharmacognosy, Am. Assn. for Clin. Chemistry, N.Y. Acad. Scis., Internat. Isotope Soc., Acad. Clin. and Lab. Physicians and Scientists. Office: U Wash Div Chemistry Dept Lab Medicine Box 357110 Seattle WA 98195-7110

MALIN, HAROLD MARTIN, JR., sexologist, educator; b. Colorado Springs, Aug. 26, 1945; s. Harold M. and Harriett Anne (Heyer) M.; m. Janice Karen Atkins. BA in Chemistry and Biology, Cornell Coll., 1967; postgrad., U. Iowa Med. Sch., 1968, Nat. Found. Study and Treatment of Pathological Gambling, 1985-86; PhD in Human Sexuality, Inst. for Advanced Study of Human Sexuality, 1986; postgrad., Johns Hopkins U., 1986-87. Diplomate Am. Coll. Sexologists. Clin. sexologist Sexology Assocs., Inc., 1985—; cons. clin. sexologist Johns Hopkins Hosp. Sexual Disorders Clinic Johns Hopkins U. Med. Sch., 1987-89, mgr. Johns Hopkins Hosp. Sexual Disorders Clinic, 1989-91, cons. clin. sexologist Johns Hopkins Hosp. Sexual Disorders Clinic, 1991-92, instr. clin. sexology dept. psychiatry and behavioral scis., 1992-95; assoc. prof. clin. sexology, chair clin. studies dept. Inst. for Advanced Study of Human Sexuality, 1992—; cons. clin. sexologist, corp. sec. Nat. Ctr. for Study and Treatment of Pathol. Gambling, Balt., 1986—; cons. clin. sexologist Nat. Inst. for Study, Prevention and Treatment of Sexual Trauma, Balt., 1991—, Drug and Alcohol Prevention Program, Inc., Ocean City, Md., 1991-95; cons. clin. sexologist for program devel. Nat. Ctr. on Instns. and Alternatives, Alexandria, Va. and Balt., 1991-94; sr. case mgmt. supr. Planned Parenthood Shasta-Diablo, Fairfield, Calif., 1994—. Cons. editor Jour. of Sex and Marital Therapy; peer reviewer Jour. Sex Rsch.; contbr. articles to profl. jours. Mem. Solano County Adolescent Resource Network, Solano County Ryan White Consortium, Solano County Cmty. Health Outreach Sys., Solano Cmty. Svcs. Task Force. Mem. Am. Profl. Soc. on Abuse of Children, Am. Assn. Sex Educators, Counselors and Therapists, Am. Bd. Sexology (bd. clin. examiners, diplomate, cert. sex therapist, cert. clin. supr., cert. sex rschr.), Assn. Sexologists, Am. Acad. Clin. Sexologists (founding life clin. fellow), Soc. for Sci. Study of Sex, Harry Benjamin Internat. Gender Dysphoria Assn., Ctrl. Md. Sexual Abuse and Treatment Task Force, Sex Edn. Coalition Washington, Sloano County Adolescent Resource Network, Solano County Ryan White Consortium, Solano County Cmty. Health Outreach Sys., Solano Cmty. Svcs. Task Force, Inst. Advanced Study of Human Sexuality Alumni Assn. Inc. (pres., bd. dirs.), Intersex Soc. of N.Am. (bd. dirs.). Office: Clinical Sexology Assocs 1525 Franklin St San Francisco CA 94109-9592

MALINS, DONALD CLIVE, biochemistry, researcher; b. Lima, Peru, May 19, 1931; came to U.S., 1947; s. Richard Henry and Mabel (Madeline) M.; m. Mary Louise Leiren, 1962; children: Christopher W., Gregory S., Timothy J. BA, U. Washington, 1953; BS in chem., Seattle U., 1956; PhD in biochemistry, U. Aberdeen, 1967, DSc, 1976. Dir. environ. conservation div. Nat. Marine Fisheries Svc., Seattle, 1974-87; sr. scientific cons. U.S. Dept. Justice, Washington, 1989-91; scientific cons. Nat. Ocean & Atmosphere Adminstrn., 1990-92; head molecular epidemiology program Pacific Northwest Rsch. Found., Seattle, 1992—; rsch. prof. dept. chem. Seattle U., 1972—; affiliate prof. dept. environ. health U. Washington, 1984—, Coll. Ocean & Fishery Scis. U. Washington, 1974-91; editor-in-chief Aquatic Toxicology, 1980—; lectr., speaker in field. Contbr. articles to profl. jours.; inventor in field. Bd. dirs. Am. Oceans Campaign, 1989-91; adv. bd. Internat. Jt. Commn., 1990-91; mem. review bd. Sch. Environ. Scis. U. Sterling, Scotland, 1990. Recipient U.S. Dept. Commerce Golf medal, 1982. Mem. Am. Soc. Biochemistry and Molecular Biology, Am. Chem. Soc., Am. Assn. for Cancer Rsch. Office: Pacific Northwest Rsch Found 720 Broadway Seattle WA 98122

MALISH, DAVID MARC, physician; b. Phila., Dec. 29, 1947; s. Irvin and Esther (Divor) M.; m. Robin, June 16, 1976 (div. 1990); children: jennifer, Scott; m. Shani Boxon, Sept. 26, 1992; 1 child, Jack. BS, Knox Coll., 1969; MD, Hahnmann U., 1973. Diplomate Am. Bd. Internal Medicine, Am. Bd. Allergy and Immunology. Intern Hahnemann Hosp., Phila., 1973-74; internal medicine resident Monmouth Med. Ctr., Long Branch, N.J., 1974-76; fellow in allergy and immunology Kaiser Found. Hosp.-Sunset facility, UCLA Immunodeficiency Clinic, Children's Hosp., L.A., 1976-78; locum tenems Drs. Cenci and Krall, West Hartford and Hartford, Conn., 1978-79; pvt. practice San Jose, Calif., 1979—; staff internist Monte Villa Hosp., Morgan Hill, Calif., 1979-81; med. dir., staff internist Good Samaritan Recovery Ctr., Good Samaritan Hosp., San Jose, 1991-94, med. cons. Samaritan Pain Ctr., San Jose. Bd. dirs. Am. Lung Soc., Santa Clara, 1980—; med. dir. Camp Superstuff-Asthmatic Camp for Children, 1985—; head pediat. asthma sect. Am. Lung Assn., Santa Clara County, 1994—; mem. fin. bd. for physicians Com. to Reelect Congressman Norm Mineta. Fellow Am. Acad. Allergy and Immunology, Am. Coll. Allergy; mem. Am. Acad. Physicians, Calif. Soc. Addiction Medicine (cert.), Santa Clara Med. Assn. Office: 2505 Samaritan Dr Ste 606 San Jose CA 95124

MALLEN, BRUCE, real estate developer, educator, producer, economist, consultant; b. Montreal, Que., Can., Sept. 4, 1937; Came to the U.S., 1978; s. Mitchell and Mary Mallen; m. Carol Klein; children: Howard Eliot, Jay Leslie, Reesa Lynn. BA in Philosophy, B of Commerce, Sir George Williams U., Montreal, 1958; MS, Columbia U., 1959; MBA, U. Mich., 1960; PhD, NYU, 1963; DSC (hon.), Pacific Western U., 1993. Registered fin. planner; cert. realtor; lic. real estate broker, Calif. Sr. cons., dir. econ. and market rsch. P.S. Ross & Ptnrs., Montreal, 1961-64; pres. Bruce Mallen & Assocs., Inc., Montreal, 1964-79; assoc. prof. Concordia U., Montreal, 1964-67, chmn. dept. mktg., 1964-71, prof. mktg., 1967-79, founding chmn. grad. studies commerce, 1968-75, acting dean faculty of commerce and adminstrn., 1970-71; pres. Filmcorp Entertainment Fins., Inc., Montreal, L.A., 1979—; econ. cons. Consulate Gen. Japan, Montreal, 1966-78; vis. prof. mktg. Laval U., 1968-70; vis. scholar Grad. Sch. Mgmt., UCLA, 1978-79; vis. prof. U. So. Calif., 1979-81. Author: The Costs and Benefits of Evening Shopping to the Canadian Economy, 1969, Principles of Marketing Channel Management, 1977; co-author: Marketing Canada, 1968 (2d edit.), Marketing in the Canadian Environment, 1973, Principles of Marketing in Canada, 1979, Distribution of Canadian Feature Films in the U.S. Market, 1979, and others; founder, 1st editor-in-chief The Can. Marketer; mem. editorial rev. bd. The Jour. of Mktg.; mem. editorial bd. Internat. Jour. of Phys. Distbn.; contbr. articles to profl. jours.; developer Filmland Corp. Ctr., Culver City, Calif.; prodr. sev. feature films. Ford Found. fellow, 1961-62; recipient Founders Day award, 1963, Alumni Achievement award for distinction in the entertainment industry, 1990. Mem. Am. Mktg. Assn. (past internat. dir., past pres. Montreal chpt.), Prodrs. Guild Am., Acad. Can. Cinema, Assn. of Indsl. Marketers and Advertisers (past pres. Montreal chpt.), Mktg. and Sales Execs. (past dir.), L.A. Arts Coun.(past dir.), Advt. and Sales Execs., Montreal Club (past dir.), Culver City C. of C. (past dir. entertainment industry coun.), Beverly Hills Bd. Realtors.

MALLISON, ROBERT ANDREW, neurologist; b. St. Mary's, Pa., Apr. 16, 1939; s. Bernard M. and Florence (Geeck) M.; m. Lois Mallison, May 29, 1965; children: Christine, Karen, Denise, Kevin, Brian, Stacey. BA, St. Vincent Coll., 1961; MD, Loyola U., Chgo., 1965. Intern St. Mary's Hosp., San Francisco, 1965-66; resident U. Calif., San Francisco, 1966-69; pvt. practice neurology San Jose, Calif., 1971—; mem. faculty U. Tenn., 1969-71, U. Calif., 1971-76, Stanford U., 1972-90. Chmn. stroke divsn. Santa Clara County Heart Assn., 1971-76. Comdr. USN, 1969-71. Mem. AMA, Calif. Med. Assn., Am. Acad. Neurology. Office: 2505 Samaritan Dr Ste 309 San Jose CA 95124-4011

MALLON, PETER, bishop; b. Prince Rupert, B.C., Dec. 5, 1929; s. Joseph P. and Sheila M. (Keenan) D. Grad., Seminary Christ the King, Burnaby and Mission, B.C. Asst. Holy Rosary Cath., Vancouver, B.C., 1956-64, rector, 1966-82; chancellor Archdiocese Vancouver, 1964-65, dir. religious edn., 1971-73; adminstr. Guardian Angels Parish, Vancouver, 1965-66; pastor St. Anthony's, West Vancouver, 1982-89; bishop Nelson, B.C., 1989—. Address: 813 Ward St, Nelson, BC Canada V1L 1T4

MALLORY, STEVEN REECE, software engineering executive; b. Lynwood, Calif., Nov. 23, 1947; s. Joseph William and Edith Pauline (Robertson) M.; m. Kelly Kay Walsh, Jan. 2, 1977 (div. June 1980); m. Elizabeth Margaret Kuntz, Sept. 1, 1990; 1 child, Lauren Beth. BS in Applied Math., Calif. State Poly. Coll., 1971, MS in Computer Sci., 1976. Mem. tech. staff Hi-Shear Corp., Torrance, Calif., 1971, 73-74, Sci. Applications, Inc., San Diego, 1971-72, Planning Rsch. Corp., San Diego, 1972-73, Universal Analytics, Inc., Westchester, Calif., 1976-77; mgr. tng. applications divsn. Sci. Applications Inc., San Diego, 1977-84; mgr. computer and sys. applications group Photon Rsch. Inc., San Diego, 1984-86; dep. v.p., mgr. engring. ops. Titan Sys. Inc., San Diego, 1986-88; mgr. software devel. engring. IVAC Corp., San Diego, 1988-95; cons. and presenter in field. Author: Software Development and Quality Assurance for the Healthcare Manufacturing Industries, 1994; mem. editorial bd. Med. Device and Diagnostic Industry; contbr. articles to profl. jours. Mem. IEEE, Assn. for the Advancement of Med. Instrumentation, Assn. for Computer Machinery, Soc. for Computer Simulation, Soc. for Inds. and Applied Math., Am. Soc. for Quality Control. Republican. Home: 4918 Amador Dr Oceanside CA 92056-4971 Office: IVAC Corp 4918 Amador Dr Oceanside CA 92056

MALM, ROYCE ELLIOTT, musician; b. Los Angeles, Nov. 22, 1929; s. Albin Nils and Mildred Elizabeth (Aden) M.; Mus.B., U. So. Calif., 1952, M.Mus. in Composition, 1954; m. Enid Elliott Malm; children: Jaime Louise, Lorraine Elise. Tchr. public schs. in Calif., 1957-89; tchr. secondary choral music and music appreciation Burbank (Calif.) Unified Sch. Dist., 1964-89; ret. 1989; mem. Burbank Symphony Assn., 1971-91, pres., 1975-78, exec. dir., 1979—; dir. ch. choirs, 1953—; v.p. Burbank Community Concerts Assn., 1973-75, Symphony League Los Angeles County, 1975-78, Performing Arts Fedn. Burbank, 1977-78; music cons., estate and radio music archivist, recording restoration Cambria Records, 1992—. Composer: Reflections, 1980; others. Served with AUS, 1954-56. Mem. Music Educators Nat. Conf., NEA, Burbank Tchrs. Assn., Calif. Tchrs. Assn., Choral Conductors Guild Calif., So. Calif. Vocal Assn., Pro Musica Sana, Sir Thomas Beecham Soc., Pi Kappa Lambda, Phi Mu Alpha. Democrat. Presbyterian. Home: 5905 Ironwood St Palos Verdes Peninsula CA 90275-1762 Office: Cambria Master Recordings PO Box 374 Lomita CA 90717-0374

MALMGREN, DICK, school principal, teacher; b. Leadville, Colo., Oct. 27, 1940; s. Walter Gustav and Antonia (Peltin) M.; m. Connie Lee Montoya, June 11, 1964 (div. Dec. 1975); children: James, Danielle Malmgren Swenson; m. JoAnne Wright, July 2, 1977. BS in Phys. Edn. & History, U. Colo., 1962; MA in Secondary Adminstrn., Western State Coll., 1967; EdD in Adminstrn./Supervision/Curriculum, U. Colo., 1981. Tchr., coach Leavenworth (Wash.) High Sch., 1962-63, Battle Mountain Jr. Sr. High Sch., 1963-66; prin. Soroco High Sch., 1967-68, Battle Mountain Jr. Sr. High Sch., 1968-75, Nederland Jr. Sr. High Sch., 1975-85; dir., prin. Boulder Valley Community Schs./Dist. Summer Sch., 1985-86; tchr., prin. Fairview High Sch./Dist. Summer Sch., Boulder, Colo., 1986—. Past. pres. Orange Orchard Homeowners; past officer West Vail (Colo.) Water Bd. Mem. NEA, Nat. Assn. Secondary Sch. Prins. (pres. 1980-81), Colo. Assn. Sch. Execs., Colo. Assn. Secondary Sch. Prins. (pres. 1978-79), North Ctrl. Assn. (exec. bd. 1979-82), Colo. Assn. Cmty. Educators, Boulder Valley Prins. Assn., Colo. High Sch. Activities Assn., Colo. Edn. Assn., Wash. Edn. Assn., Nederland C. of C., Rotary, Ski Club Vail, U.S. Ski Assn., Colo. Ski Race Ofcls. (internat. cert.). Home: 4271 Peach Way Boulder CO 80301-1736

MALMGREN, RENÉ LOUISE, educational theater administrator; b. Mpls., Nov. 14, 1938; d. Albert William (dec.) and Hildegarde Ann (Topel) Erickson; m. Donald Elwin Mamlgren, Dec. 27, 1958; children: D. Gustaf, Ericka Susan, Beret Kristina. BA in Theatre, Speech and English, Colo. Women's Coll., 1966; MA in Ednl. Adminstrn and Curriculum Devel., U. Colo., 1981. Cert. supt., Ariz.; cert. type D adminstr., ESL cert., Colo. Cons. creative drama cultural arts program Denver Pub. Schs., 1970-72; tchr. APS Crawford Elem. Sch., Aurora, Colo., 1972-78; instr. Colo. Women's Coll., Denver, 1974-75; ednl. dir. Colo. Children's Theatre Co., Denver, 1977-86; coord. curriculum Aurora Pub. Schs., 1982-85; asst. dir. instrn. fine arts Tucson Unified Sch. Dist., 1985-90; mng. dir. Ariz. Children's Theatre Co., Tucson, 1990—; adminstr. svcs. Tucson Ctr. for Performing Arts, 1992-94; editor dramatic arts curriculum Ariz. Dept. Edn., Phoenix, 1989; rev. panelist Ariz. Commn. on Arts, Phoenix, 1986-87. Co-author satellite TV curriculum, 1987; appeared in premier of play The Only Woman Awake, 1984. Del. Colo. Dem. Conv., Denver, 1980; peacekeeper Take Back the Night March-Rape Assistance and Awareness Program, Denver, 1982-84; mem. policy. com. Tucson Cable Arts Channel, 1986-87; mem. edn. com. Tucson Symphony Orch., 1988-92; bd. dirs. Arts and Creativity Early Childhood, 1990-93, Arts Genesis, 1990-92. Mem. ASCD, Nat. Art Edn. Assn., Ariz. Arts Supervisory Coalition, Ariz. Theatre Educators Assn. (bd. dirs. 1985-89, pres. 1988-89), Phi Delta Kappa. Home: 2612 E La Cienega Dr Tucson AZ 85716-1546

MALMSTROM, PATRICIA ELIZABETH, social service agency administrator, consultant; b. Abbington, Pa., June 28, 1938; d. John Francis and Jean Marie (McCauley) Maxwell; m. Edward J. Malmstrom Jr., June 30, 1962 (div. 1988); children: Carolyn, Diana, Krista, Kelda. BA, Dominican Coll., San Rafael, Calif., 1960; gen. secondary credential, U. Calif., Berkeley, 1961; MA, Calif. State U., Sonoma, 1978. Instr. English and drama Carmel (Calif.) H.S., 1961-62; dir. math. lab. Oxford Elem. Sch., Berkeley, 1970-74; project dir., founder The Twinline of Bananas, Inc., Oakland, Calif., 1978-83; founder, dir. Twin Svcs., Inc., Berkeley, 1983—; editor Twin Svcs. Reporter, Berkeley, 1983—; mem. steering com. Calif. Health Mothers Health Babies Coalition, Oakland, 1987—; mem. adv. com. Calif. Adv. Com. Prevention Preterm Labor, San Francisco, 1987-92; mem. contract process revision adv. com. Maternal Child Health br. Calif. Dept. Health, Sacramento, 1991-92; mem. adv. bd. Ctr. for Loss in Multiple Birth, Palmer, Alaska, 1992—. Bd. dirs. Montessori Sch., Berkeley, 1969-71; vol. Sierra Club, Oakland, 1992—. Recipient Cert. of Commendation Calif. Dept. Social Svcs., 1992, Spl. Recognition award Calif. Health Mothers Health Babies Coalition, 1989, others. Mem. Internat. Soc. for Twin Studies (v.p. 1992—), Internat. Coun. Multiple Birth Orgn. (chair 1992—), Calif. Advocates for Pregnant Women, Calif. Assn. Non Profits, Maternal and Child Health Network for Improved Health Outcomes (charter). Office: Twin Svcs Inc PO Box 10066 Berkeley CA 94709-5066

MALOFF, STEPHEN MARTIN, plastic surgeon; b. Phila., Dec. 21, 1941; s. Abraham and Ruth (Skolkin) M.; m. Joan Fayette Baker; children: Erin, Kerstin. BA, Emory U., 1963; MD, U. Tenn., Knoxville, 1967; degree, U. N.Mex., 1976; student, Grady Meml. Hosp., Atlanta, 1967-68, U. Louisville, 1973-74. Diplomate Am. Bd. Plastic Surgery. Intern Grady Meml. Hosp., Atlanta, 1967-68; resident gen. surgery U. N.Mex. Sch. Medicine, Albuquerque, 1971-72, resident plastic surgery, 1974-76; fellow hand surgery U. Louisville, 1973-74; pvt. practice Pocatello, Idaho, 1976—; adj. staff mem. Idaho State U., Pocatello, 1990—. Maj. USAF, 1969-71, Vietnam. Mem. Am. Soc. Plastic and Reconstructive Surgeons, Rocky Mountain Assn. Plastic Surgeons, Skyline Med. Assn. Office: PO Box 4171 Pocatello ID 83205-4171

MALOHN, DONALD A., manufacturing executive, retired; b. South Bend, Ind., Mar. 26, 1928; s. Harry A. and Opal (Baker) M.; m Myla Claire Lockwood, Feb. 9, 1948; 1 child, Chris. BSEE, Tri-State U., Angola, Ind., 1952. Engr. jet engine div. Studebaker Corp., South Bend, Ind., 1952-54; prodn. rsch. engr. Ford Motor Co., Dearborn, Mich., 1954-61; sr. analytical engr. Solar, San Diego, 1961-62; dept. mgr. Sundstrand Aviation, Denver, 1962-66; sr. dir. engring. Ai Rsch. Mfg. Co., Phoenix, 1966-78; exec. v.p. Tiernay Turbines, Phoenix, 1978-94. Inventor: five patents, 1963; contbr. tech. jours. Mem. ASME, Am.Soc. Metals, Soc. Automotive Engrs., Life Mem. Soc. Republican. Home: 7848 E Sage Dr Scottsdale AZ 85250-7648

MALONE, JOHN C., telecommunications executive; b. 1941; m. Leslie. Attended Yale U., Johns Hopkins U. Formerly pres. Jerrold Electronics Corp.; pres., chief exec. officer Tele-Communications, Inc., Denver; chmn., dir. Liberty Media Corp., Denver. Office: Tele-Comm Inc 5619 Dtc Pky Englewood CO 80111-3017*

MALONE, KARL (THE MAILMAN), professional basketball player; b. Summerfield, La., July 24, 1963. Student, La. Tech. U., 1981-85. Basketball player Utah Jazz, 1985—; mem. U.S. Olympic Basketball Team (received Gold medal), 1992. Mem. NBA All-Star team, 1988-94; recipient NBA All-Star Game MVP award, 1989, 1993; mem. All-NBA first team, 1989-94; mem. All-NBA second team, 1988; mem. NBA All-Defensive second team, 1988; mem. NBA All-Rookie Team, 1986. Office: Utah Jazz Delta Ctr Salt Lake City UT 84180-1105*

MALONE, MICHAEL PETER, academic administrator, historian; b. Pomeroy, Wash., Apr. 18, 1940; s. John Albert and Dolores Frances (Cheyne) M.; m. Kathleen Malone, Apr. 17, 1983; children: John Thomas, Molly Christine. BA in History, Gonzaga U., 1962; PhD in Am. Studies, Wash. State U., Pullman, 1966. Asst. prof. history Tex. A&M U., College Station, 1966-67; asst. prof., prof. history Mont. State U., Bozeman, 1967—, dean grad. studies, 1979-89, v.p. acad. affairs, 1989-90; pres. Mont. State U., 1991—; bd. dirs. Buttrey Food & Drug. Author: The Battle for Butte, 1981 (Sick award 1981), Historians and The American West, 1983, (with others) Montana: A History of Two Centuries, 1976, 2d edit., 1991, The American West: A 20th Century History, 1989, James J. Hill, Empire Builder of the Northwest, 1995. Mem. Western History Assn. Home: 2310 Springcreek Dr Bozeman MT 59715-6035 Office: Mont State U Bozeman MT 59717

MALONE, MICHAEL WILLIAM, electronics executive, software engineer; b. Belmore L.I., N.Y., Mar. 31, 1956; s. Daniel Joseph Malone and Frances Ann (Reilly) Coppersmith; m. Jane Pauline Raese, Aug. 20, 1988. BS in Elec. Engring. and Computer Sci., U. Colo., 1986. Test engr. Catalina Controls, Longmont, Colo., 1984-86; design engr. Inlab, Inc., Broomfield, Colo., 1986-87, mgr. engring., 1987-89; software engr. UMG, Inc., Golden, Colo., 1989-90, sr. software engr., 1990-91, v.p., 1991-94; sr. software engr. RELA, Boulder, Colo., 1994—. Developer software. With USN, 1975-79. Office: UMG Inc 25528 Genesee Trail Rd Golden CO 80401-9366

MALONE, ROBERT JOSEPH, bank executive; b. Sept. 3, 1944. With Bank of Am., 1969-81; chmn., pres., CEO First Interstate Bank Boise, Idaho, 1981-84; pres., CEO First Interstate Bank Denver, 1984-90; chmn., pres., CEO Western Capital Investment Corp. (now First Bank System, Inc.), Denver, 1990-92; chmn., CEO Bank Western/Central Banks (now First Bank System, Inc.), Denver, 1992-93, Colo. Nat. Bank, Denver, 1993—. Office: Colorado Nat Bank 950 17th St Denver CO 80202-2827

MALONEY, DOUGLAS JAMES, lawyer; b. San Francisco, May 26, 1933; s. James Douglas and Loretta (O'Donnell) M.; m. Elenore Hill, Dec. 31, 1976 (div. 1986); children: Lynn, Karen, Douglas Jr., Susan, Pamela; m. Ellen Caulfield, May 14, 1988. BS, Calif. Maritime Acad., 1954; JD, U. San Francisco, 1958. Bar: Calif. 1959, U.S. Dist. Ct. (no. dist.) Calif. 1959, U.S. Ct. Appeals (9th cir.) 1959, U.S. Supreme Ct. 1970. Dep. county counsel Sonoma County, Santa Rosa, Calif., 1959-60, Marin County, San Rafael, Calif., 1960-62; county counsel Marin County, San Rafael, 1962-93; ptnr. Nossaman, Guthner, Knox & Elliott, San Francisco, 1993—. Author (musical satires) Pigmailion, 1979, Electric Politician, 1981, Blazing Ballots, 1983, Scandals of 1933, 1986, Damn Yuppies, 1989. Bd. dirs. Living History Ctr., San Rafael, 1983-86, Buck Ctr. for Rsch. in Aging, San Rafael, 1987—. With U.S. Merchant Marine, 1955-56. Named Citizen of Yr., City of San Rafael, 1986. Mem. ABA, County Counsels Assn., Nat. Assn. County Civic Attys., Irish Am. Bar Assn. Democrat. Roman Catholic. Home: 204 Forbes Ave San Rafael CA 94901-1745 Office: Nossamon Gothner Knox & Elliott 34th Fl 50 California St San Francisco CA 94111-4624

MALONEY, PATSY LORETTA, university official, nursing educator; b. Murfreesboro, Tenn., Feb. 19, 1952; d. Buford Leon Browning and Ina (Bush) Dubose; m. Richard J. Maloney, July 26, 1975; children: Katherine Nalani, Nathaniel Allen, Elizabeth Maureen. BS in Nursing, U. Md., 1974; MA, Cath. U., 1984, MS in Nursing, 1984; EdD, U. So. Calif., 1994. Commd. 1st lt. U.S. Army, 1974, advanced through grades to lt. col., 1989; asst. chief nurse evenings and nights DeWitt Army Hosp., Ft. Belvoir, Va.; chief nurse, tng. officer 85th EVAC Hosp., Ft. Lee, Va.; clin. head nurse emergency rm./PCU Tripler Army Med. Ctr., Honolulu, chief nursing edn.; chief surg. nursing sect. and acute care nursing sect. Madigan Army Med. Ctr., Tacoma, 1991-94; ret., 1994; dir. Ctr. for Continued Nursing Learning, Pacific Luth. U., Tacoma, Wash., 1994—; asst. prof., dir. ctr. for continued nursing learning Pacific Luth. U., Tacoma, 1994—. Mem. Emergency Nurses Assn., Nat. Nursing Staff Devel. Orgn., Assn. Mil. Surgeons, Acad. Med. Surg. Nurses, Sigma Theta Tau, Phi Kappa Phi. Home: 7002 53rd St W Tacoma WA 98467-2214 Office: Pacific Luth U Ctr Cont Nursing Learning Tacoma WA 98467

MALONEY, THOMAS J., anthropologist, educator, writer; b. Arlington, Mass., Nov. 16, 1922; s. Thomas Joseph and Doris Eleanor (Edwards) M.; m. Elizabeth Gartner, Feb. 7, 1948; children: Susan, Margaretha, Elizabeth, Thomas Jefferson. BSChemE, Northeastern U., 1948; STB, Harvard U., 1952; AM in Sociology, Wash. U., St. Louis, 1956; PhD in Anthropology, Wash. U., 1966. Chem. engr. Gen. Aniline & Film Corp., Easton, Pa., 1948, U. Colo. Experiment Sta., Boulder, Colo., 1948-49, Aircraft Gas Turbine divsn. GE, Boston, 1950-52; min. Unitarian Ch., Davenport, Iowa, 1952-53, Quincy, Ill., 1953-56; tech. pers. assoc. Bettis Atomic Power divsn. Westinghouse Electric Corp., Pitts., 1956-57; part-time instr. dept. anthropology U. Colo., Boulder, 1957-59; min. Unitarian Ch., Boulder, 1957-62; asst. prof. N.Mex. Highlands U., Las Vegas, 1962-67; assoc. prof. anthropology and sociology Ripon (Wis.) Coll., 1967-69; prof. anthropology So. Ill. U., Edwardsville, 1969-87, prof. emeritus, 1987—. With U.S. Army, 1942-44, with USMC, 1944-46; 1st lt. USAR, 1949-52. Fellow AAAS, Am. Anthrop. Assn. Address: 1309 City Park Ave Fort Collins CO 80521-4442

MALOOF, GILES WILSON, academic administrator, educator, author; b. San Bernardino, Calif., Jan. 4, 1932; s. Joseph Peters and Georgia (Wilson) M.; m. Mary Anne Ziniker, Sept. 5, 1958 (dec. Oct. 1976); children: Mary Jane, Margery Jo. BA, U. Calif. at Berkeley, 1953; MA, U. Oreg., 1958; PhD, Oreg. State U., 1962. Petroleum reservoir engr. Creole Petroleum Corp., Venezuela, 1953-54; mathematician electronics div. research dept. U.S. Naval Ordnance Rsch. Lab., Corona, Calif., 1958-59; asst. prof. math. Oreg. State U., Corvallis, 1962-68, rsch. assoc. dept. oceanography, 1963-68, vis. prof. math., 1977-78; prof. math. Boise (Idaho) State U., 1968—, head dept., 1968-75, dean grad. sch., 1970-75; project dir. Dept. Energy Citizens' Workshop Energy Environment Simulator for Eastern Oreg., No. Nev. and Idaho, 1976—. Served with Ordnance Corps, AUS, 1950, 54-56. Author, reviewer of coll. textbooks; contbr. to profl. jours. Recipient Carter award, 1963, Mosser prize, 1966, Oreg. State U. Mem. Math. Assn. Am., Am. Math. Soc., Soc. Indsl. and Applied Math., Northwest Coll. and Univ. Assn. for Sci. (dir. 1973—, pres. 1990-92), Northwest Sci. Assn. (trustee 1977-80), Assoc. Western Univs. (mem. edn. and rsch. com. 1993—), Sigma Xi, Pi Mu Epsilon, Phi Kappa Phi. Home: 1400 Longmont Ave Boise ID 83706-3730

MALOTT, DWIGHT RALPH, accountant; b. Medford, Oreg., Mar. 24, 1947; s. Ralph Joseph and Eugenia (Romanchuk) M.; m. Janet Gail Born, June 28, 1975; children: Jennifer, Paul, Michelle. A in Tech Arts, Everett Jr. Coll., 1967; BBA, U. Wash., 1969. CPA, Wash. Acct. Main Hurdman, Everett, Wash., 1973-81; controller Shaffer Crane, Inc., Everett, 1981-83; prin. acct. Dwight Malott & Co., P.S., Arlington, Wash., 1983-88; ptnr. Wintch Tobiason & Co. PS CPA, Everett, Wash., 1988—. Loaned exec. United Way of Snohomish County, Everett, 1977, mem. allocations panel, 1980, 81, 82; bd. dirs. Lions Sight and Hearing Found. of Snohomish County, Everett, 1979-84; mem. acctg. adv. com. Everett C.C., 1979—; bd. dirs. North Puget Sound Ops. Improvement, 1991—, treas., 1992-95. With USAF, 1969-73. Mem. AICPA, Wash. Soc. CPAs (treas. Snohomish chpt. 1991-93), U. Wash. Alumni Assn. (life), Lions (local pres. 1981-82), Beta Alpha Psi, Rotary, Le Tip. Democrat. Office: Wintch Tobiason & Co PS CPA 3802 Colby Ave Everett WA 98201-4940

MALOUF-CUNDY, PAMELA BONNIE, visual arts editor; b. Reseda, Calif., July 9, 1956; d. Jubert George and Marguerite I. (Llido) Malouf. AA in Cinema with honors, Valley Community Coll., 1976. Asst. film editor various film studios including Paramount, 20th Fox, CBS MTM, and others, 1976-80; post prodn. coordinator, supr. David Gerber Co., Culver City, Calif., 1981-82; post prodn. coordinator Paramount TV, Los Angeles, 1982-84; sole proprietor Trailers, Etc., North Hollywood, Calif., 1984-85; film and video editor Paramount Pictures, L.A., 1985-86; film editor Universal Studios, Universal City, Calif., 1987-89; film, video editor New World TV, L.A., 1991-92; associate dir. Tri-Star TV, Studio City, Calif., 1992-93; film and video editor various studios, Studio City, 1993—; owner, mgr. Choice Editing Systems, Northridge, Calif., 1993—. Film and video editor: (TV shows) A Year in the Life, MacGyver, Call to Glory, The Making of Shogun, Nightingales, Mission Impossible, Murder C.O.D., I'll Take Romance, Get a Life, A Fire in the Dark, The Fifth Corner, The Edge, others (movies) Search for Grace, Eyes of Terror, Then There Was One, Sweet Bird of Youth, Without You I'm Nothing, All in the Family, Rockford Files, Is There Life Out There?; asst. film editor: (movies) King of Gypsies, Star Wars, others. Mem. Internat. Alliance of Theatrical Stage Employees and Moving Picture Machine Operators of U.S. and Can., Tri-Network (pres. 1979-80), Acad. Magical Arts, Inc., Am. Cinema Editors, Acad. TV Arts and Scis., Dir.'s Guild of Am. Democrat. Roman Catholic.

MALPHURS, ROGER EDWARD, insurance company executive, chiropractor, biomedical technologist, private commodity trader; b. Lake Worth, Fla., Dec. 15, 1933; s. Cecil Edward and Muriel Thelma (Ward) M.; m. Carolyn Sue Calapp, Feb. 2, 1963(div. 1993); children: Steven, Brian, Darren, Regina, Victoria. BS, U. Utah, 1961; D of Chiropractic, Palmer Coll. Chiropractic West, 1990. Cert. med. technologist; lic. chiropractor, Calif., Ariz. Supr. spl. chemistry Cen. Pathology Lab., Santa Rosa, Calif., 1968-73; mgr. lab. Community Hosp., Santa Rosa, 1973-76; supr. chem., staff asst. Meml. Hosp., Santa Rosa, 1976-85; pres., chief exec. officer R.E. Malphurs Co., Sunnyvale, Calif., 1972—; owner, developer REMCO Mktg. Assocs., Santa Rosa, 1970-71; pvt. commodity trader, 1974—; owner Better Bus. Forms and Typeset, Santa Rosa, 1977-81, commodity pool operator, 1979-80; dept. mgr. immunochemistry Spectra Labs., Fremont, Calif., 1990-95; clin. trials cons. hematology Abbott Diagnostics, Santa Clara, Calif., 1995—. Author: A New, Simple Way to Win at Blackjack, 1972. Served as squadron commdr. CAP USAF Aux., 1982-84. Mem. Am. Chiropractic Assn., Calif. Chiropractic Assn., Optimists Internat. (youth awards chmn. 1969-74), Am. Pub. Health Assn., Toastmasters (sec./treas. 1988-89), Rep. Senatorial Inner Circle. Republican.

MALSON, VERNA LEE, special education educator; b. Buffalo, Wyo., Mar. 29, 1937; d. Guy James and Vera Pearl (Curtis) Mayer; m. Jack Lee Malson, Apr. 20, 1955; children: Daniel Lee, Thomas James, Mark David, Scott Allen. BA in Elem. Edn. and Spl. Edn. magna cum laude, Met. State Coll., Denver, 1975; MA in Learning Disabilities, U. No. Colo., 1977. Cert. tchr., Colo. Tchr.-aide Wyo. State Tng. Sch., Lander, 1967-69; spl. edn. tchr. Bennett Sch. 29J, Colo., 1975-79, chmn. health, sci., social studies, 1977-79; spl. edn. tchr. Deer Trail Sch., Colo., 1979—, chmn. careers, gifted and talented, 1979-87, spl. edn./preschool tchr. 1992—; course cons. Regis Coll., Denver, 1990; mem. spl. edn. parent adv. com. East Central Bd. Coop. Ednl. Services, Limon, Colo. Colo. scholar Met. State Coll., 1974; Colo. Dept. Edn. grantee, 1979, 81; recipient Cert. of Achievement, Met. State Coll., 1993. Mem. Council Exceptional Children, Bennett Tchrs. Club (treas. 1977-79), Kappa Delta Pi. Republican. Presbyterian. Avocations: coin collecting; reading; sports. Home: PO Box 403 Deer Trail CO 80105-0403 Office: Deer Trail Pub Schs PO Box 26J Deer Trail CO 80105-0026

MALTIN, FREDA, retired university administrator; b. Calgary, Alta., Can., June 4, 1923; came to the U.S., 1958; d. Meyers Wolfe and Ida (Kohn) Rosen; m. Manny Maltin, Aug. 25, 1950; 1 child, Richard Allan. Diploma Garbutt's Bus. Coll., Calgary, 1942. Various secretarial and bookkeeping positions, 1951; mem. adminstrv. staff U. So. Calif., 1960-92, asst. to exec. dir. Davidson Conf. Ctr., 1987-92, Grad. Sch. Bus. Adminstrn., 1981-92. Recipient staff achievement award U. So. Calif., 1991. Mem. Exec. Women Internat., U. So. Calif. Staff Club (charter), U. So. Calif. Skull and Dagger (hon.), U. So. Calif. Town and Gown.

MALTZAN, MICHAEL THOMAS, architect; b. Roslyn Heights, N.Y., Oct. 10, 1959; s. William George and Jaqualine (Cain) M.; m. Amy Louise Murphy, Sept. 25, 1988. Student, Wentworth Inst. Tech., 1977-79; BFA, RISD, 1984, BArch, 1985; MArch, Harvard U., 1988. Lic. architect, Calif. Architect The Architects, Glastonbury, Conn., 1978-80, Williamd D. Warner Assocs., Exeter, R.I., 1980-83, Steven Lerner Assocs., Providence, 1983-84, Schwartz/Silver Assocs., Boston, 1984-86, Machado-Silvetti Assocs., Boston, 1986-88, Frank O. Gehry Assocs., L.A., 1988—; instr. RISD, Providence, 1987, Harvard U., Cambridge, Mass., 1988; co-instr. UCLA, 1989; invited jury critic Harvard U., RISD, So. Calif. Inst. Architecture, L.A., Ariz. State U., tempe, Calif. Coll. Arts and Crafts, San Francisco, U. SO. Calif., L.A., UCLA, Iowa State U., Ames, Miami (Ohio) U. Prin. works include Sweat Equity Housing, Hartford, Conn., 1978-80, Unitarian-Universalist Ch., Vernon, Conn., 1979, Providence Riverfront Study, 1982, Harvard Law Sch. Alumni Bldg. Addition, Cambridge, 1984, 330 Congress St. Renovation, Boston, 1985, 280 Summer St. Renovation, Boston, 1986, City of Leonforte, Italy Master Plan, 1987 (Progressive Architecture award), North Park Apt. Complex Renovation, Chevy Chase, Md., 1988, Walt Disney Concert Hall, 1988— (Progressive Architecture award), Culver City (Calif.) Retail Complex Master Plan, 1990, Villa Olympica Retail and Entertainment Complex, Barcelona, Spain, 1992,, U. Toledo Art Sch., 1992 (AIA award), Inner-City Arts Sch., L.A., 1994, various pvt. resdl. bldgs.

MAMALIS, NICK, ophthalmologist, researcher; b. Wyo., Sept. 22, 1955. BA in Biochemistry, Harvard U., 1978; MD, U. Utah, 1982. Diplomate Am. Bd. Ophthalmology. Intern in internal medicine Loyola U. Med. Ctr., Ill., 1983; fellow in opthalmic pathology U. Utah, 1984; lectr. in ophthalmic pathology Loyola U., Maywood, Ill., 1984-87; resident in opthalmology Loyola U. Med. Ctr., 1987; asst. prof. ophthalmology U. Utah, Salt Lake City, 1987-91, dir. ophthalmic pathology, 1988—, dir. Intermountain Ocular Rsch. Ctr., 1988—, assoc. prof. ophthalmology, 1991-95, prof. ophthalmology, 1995—; chief ophthalmology divsn. VA Hosp., Salt Lake City, 1989—; manuscript cons. Jour. Pediat. Ophthalmology and Strabismus, Ophthalmology, Survey of Ophthalmology. Author: Intraocular Lenses: Evolution Design, Complications and Pathology, 1989; author: (with others) Current Therapy in Ophthalmic Surgery, 1988, Management and Care of the Cataract Patient, 1992; assoc. editor Jour. Cataract and Refractive Surgery, 1990—. Ophthalmologic assoc. Rsch. to Prevent Blindness; bd. dirs. Nat. Soc. to Prevent Blindness. Rsch. grantee Am. Intraocular Implant Soc., 1983, U. Utah, 1989, 90. Mem. AMA, Am. Acad. Ophthalmology, Am. Assn. Ophthalmic Pathologists, Am. Soc. of Cataract and Refractive Surgery (grantee 1988), Assn. for Rsch. in Vision and Ophthalmology, Michael Hogan Ophthalmic Pathology Soc. Office: U Utah/John Moran Eye Ctr Dept Ophthalmology 50 N Medical Dr Salt Lake City UT 84132-0001

MAN, LAWRENCE KONG, architect; b. Kowloon, Hong Kong, July 4, 1953; s. Hon-Kwong Man and Sau-Ching Luk. Student, U. Redlands, 1971-72; BArch, U. Oreg., 1977; MArch, Harvard U., 1978. Registered architect, Mass. Designer, project architect Shepley Bulfinch Richardson & Abbott, Boston, 1978-86; project designer, project architect E. Verner Johnson & Assoc., Boston, 1987-91; owner Lawrence Man Architect, Cambridge, Mass., 1992-95, L.A., 1994-95. Prin. works include Tai Pan Restaurant, Cambridge, Mass. (Honor award AIA 1993, New Eng. award Excellence in Architecture 1993, Design Excellence award Nat. Orgn. Minority Architects 1993), Ti-Sales Office, Sudbury, Mass. (Design Excellence award Nat. Orgn. Minority Architects 1993), Dental Clinic, Reading, Mass. (AIA Interior Architecture award 1992, Interior Design Project award Am. Soc. Interior Designers 1991, Boston Exports citation AIA 1990), Mus. Ctr. Union Terminal, Cin. (Reconstrn. award 1991), Ramesses Pavilion Boston Mus. Sci. (Double Vision award/Double Silver Soc. Environ. Graphics 1990), Smithsonian South Quadrangle Mus., Washington (Boston Exports award/citation AIA 1990, Honor award AIA 1989), Pub. Mus. Grand Rapids (Mich.) River Front Devel., U. Vt. Student Ctr., Burlington, Campus Ctr. Study and Libr. addition Franklin & Marshall Coll., Andover (Mass.) Co. Corp. Hdqs., Emerson Hosp., Concord, Mass., pvt. residences, others. Mem. AIA, Am. Assn. Mus., Boston Soc. Architects, Nat. Orgn. Minority Architects. Home: 2158 Valentine Pl San Marino CA 91108

MANARA, JAMES ANTHONY, software executive, consultant; b. Westfield, Mass., Sept. 17, 1945; s. James Anthony and Genevieve Sophia (Chlastawa) M.; m. Sheila Aileen Barry, Sept. 6, 1970; children: Gregory James, Beth Ann. BA, Rutgers U., 1973; MBA, Fairleigh Dickenson U., 1977. Cert. data processing; project mgmt. profl. Programmer AT&T, Bedminster, N.J., 1973-80; v.p. Security Pacific Nat. Bank, Glendale, Calif., 1980-86; mgr. Candle Corp., L.A., 1985-94; dir. 4th Dimension Software, 1994—; sr. instr. UCLA, 1980-93; cons. Sigma Delta Group, Thousand Oaks, Calif., 1986—; speaker in field. Bd. dirs. Hart Pony League Baseball, 1986-89. Sgt. USMC, 1966-70, Vietnam. Republican. Roman Catholic. Office: 4th Dimension Software 11th Fl One Park Plz Irvine CA 92714

MANARY, RICHARD DEANE, manufacturing executive; b. Des Moines, Nov. 11, 1944; s. Robert Claude and Veronica (Cornwell) M.; m. Eileen Cecile, Aug. 16, 1986; children: Erica (dec.), Matthew, Stephen, Lauren. AA in Indsl. Engring., Southwestern Coll., 1976; BA in History, Calif. State U., San Diego, 1967, BS in Edn., 1973; grad., Stanford U. Bus. Ext., 1991; MBA, Nat. U., 1993. Registered profl. engr., Calif.; cert. elem. tchr., Calif. Mfg. engr. Rohr Industries, San Diego, 1967-78; chief R&D div. Rohr Industries, Riverside, Calif., 1978-80, project mfg. mgr., 1980-84; dep. program mgr. Rohr Industries, Wichita, Kans., 1984-87; mgr. Titan 3d, Titan IV missile programs Rohr Industries, Riverside, 1987-89; program mgr. MD-11 Rohr Industries, 1989-91; gen. program mgr. Boing mil. programs Rohr Industries, Chula Vista, Calif., 1991-95; gen. mgr. Space Products Divsn., 1995—. Contbr. articles to profl. jours. Chmn. employee and community assistance program Rohr Industries, Riverside, 1981-85; adv. Riverside chpt. Jr. Achievement, 1978-79. Mem. Soc. Mfg. Engrs. (sr., assoc., chmn. 1978-79), Soc. Automotive Engrs., Soc. Material and Process Engrs., Am. Soc. Metals, Nat. Mgmt. Assn. (chmn. 1980-81), Air Force Assn., KC. Democrat. Roman Catholic. Home: 4098 Martin Canyon Ct Bonita CA 91902-2562 Office: 850 Lagoon Blvd Chula Vista CA 91912-0878

MANASC, VIVIAN, architect, consultant; b. Bucharest, Romania, May 19, 1956; d. Bercu and Bianca (Smetterling) M.; m. William A. Dushenski, Feb. 25, 1984; children: Peter Gabriel, Lawrence Alexander. BS in Architecture, McGill U., Montreal, Que., Can., 1977, BArch, 1979; MBA, U. Alta., Edmonton, 1982. Architectural insp. Transport Can., Edmonton, 1977-79; project architect Bell Spotowski Architects, Edmonton, 1980-82; asst. dir. design constrn. Edmonton Pub. Schs., 1982-84; mgr., prin. Ferguson, Simek, Clark Architects Ltd., Edmonton, 1985-88; mng. dir. FSC Groves Hodgson Manasc Architects Ltd., Edmonton, 1988—. Contbr. articles to profl. jours. Advisor YWCA, Edmonton, 1980-82; mentor RAIC Syllabus Program, Edmonton, 1982-88; bd. dirs. Design Workshop, Edmonton, 1983. Scholar McGill U., 1974. Mem. Royal Archtl. Inst. Can. (chmn. architecture for healthcare com., assoc. regional dir.), Alta. Assn. Archs., Manitoba Assn. Archs., B.C. Assn. Archs., Saskatchewan Assn. Archs., Coun. Edn. Facility Planners, Nat. Coun. Jewish Women (past pres. Edmonton sect.), Jewish Fedn. Edmonton (v.p. planning). Office: FSC Groves Hodgson Manasc, 10417 Saskatchewan Dr, Edmonton, AB Canada T6E 4R8

MANASSERO, WILLIAM JOSEPH, software executive, consultant; b. San Diego, May 26, 1955; s. Albert Joseph and Kathleen Veronica M.; m. Susette Rodriguez Manassero, June 1990; 1 child, Ariana Kathleen Manassero; step children: Jasmine Brooke Jakubowski, Jordan Christopher Jakubowski. AA, Columbia Coll., 1975; BA, Calif. State U., 1981; profl. designation in Pub. Rels., UCLA, 1986. V.p., advt. mgr. US Life Savings and Loan, L.A., 1979-81; pres., CEO Manassero & Assocs., L.A., 1981-88; v.p. Kalman Comm., Santa Monica, 1988-90; v.p., acct. dir. Bob Thomas & Assocs., L.A., 1990-93; sr. v.p. The Spindler Orgn., L.A., 1993-94; exec. dir. Software Coun. of So. Calif., Torrance, 1994—; comm. com. chmn. L.A. Bus. Coun., 1989-90. Contbr. articles to profl. jours. Elected mem. Dem. Ctrl. Com. Tuolumne County, Calif., 1975. Recipient Golden Mirror award Fin. Mktg. Assn., 1985-86. Mem. Pub. Rels. Soc. Am., Christian Businessmen's Com. Republican. Baptist. Office: Software Council So Calif 21041 S Western Ave Ste 160 Torrance CA 90501-1727

MANASSON, VLADIMIR ALEXANDROVICH, physicist; b. Chernovtsy, Ukraine, Mar. 4, 1952; came to U.S., 1991; s. Alexander and Chaya (Finkelsteyn) M.; m. Katrine Kokhanovskaya, Aug. 2, 1975; children: Alexander, Julia. BSEE, Moscow Inst. Electronic Mfg., 1973, MSEE, 1974; PhD in Physics, Chernovtsy U., 1984. Entr. Acad. of Scis. of the Ukraine Material Sci. Inst., 1975-78, sr. engr., 1978-80, jr. rsch. assoc., 1980-85, sr. rsch. assoc., 1985-90; rsch. scientist Phys. Optics Corp., Torrance, Calif., 1991-94, sr. scientist, 1994—. Patentee several photosensitive devices, 1984-90; contbr. articles to profl. jours. NSF grantee, 1993-94, Dept. Transp. grantee, Dept. Def. grantee. Mem. Internat. Soc. Optical Engring., Optical Soc. Am., Lasers and Electro-Optic Soc. of IEEE. Office: Phys Optics Corp 20600 Gramercy Pl Torrance CA 90501-1821

MANATT, JAMES C., JR., oil and gas exploration executive; b. El Paso, Aug. 20, 1948; s. James C. and Norma M. (Kellner) M.; m. Marilyn McMullan, May 5, 1980; children: Claire E., Robert M., Benjamin F. BA in Journalism, N.Mex. State U., 1971. Exec. dir. Rep. Party of N.Mex., Albuquerque, 1973-78; mktg. rep. Permian Exploration Corp., Roswell, N.Mex., 1979-83, v.p. mktg., 1984-89, pres., 1990-94; CEO Providence Tech., Inc., Roswell, 1994—; mem. Petroleum Tech. Transfer Coun., Socorro, N.Mex., 1994—. Chmn. Rep. Party, Chaves County, N.Mex., 1984, Bush for Pres., Chaves County, 1992; chmn. oil and gas divsn. United Way, Chaves County, 1986; pres. Spectacular Airshow N.Mex., Roswell, 1991. 1st lt. U.S. Army, 1971-72. Mem. Soc. Exploration Geophysists, Rotary. Episcopalian. Office: Providence Techs Inc PO Box 392 Roswell NM 88202-0392

MANAYAN, HENRY C., corporate executive; b. N.Y.C., Nov. 3, 1955; s. Henry A. and Lorraine M. BA, Syracuse U., 1979; Reader-in-Law, Oxford U., 1980; JD, Santa Clara U., 1983. Assoc. Hartsell & Caselli, San Jose, Calif., 1983; real estate advisor Park Cen. Investments, Alameda, Calif., 1984; dir. real estate Brugger Corp., Redwood City, Calif., 1985; pres. Advance Data, Inc., San Francisco, Calif., 1986; pres., CEO Transpacific Cos., San Jose, 1990—; chmn. of the bd. Commonwealth Ctrl. Credit Union, San Jose; chmn. polit. action com. San Jose Real Estate Bd. Bd. dirs. Arts Coun., San Jose, 1991—, Milpitas (Calif.) C. of C., 1990—; transp. commr. Santa Clara County Transp. Agy., San Jose, 1991-93; planning commr. Milpitas Planning Commr., 1993—; commr. Community Adv. Com., Milpitas, 1990-93; chmn., dir. San Jose Performing Arts Consortium, 1988-93. Recipient Bus. Leadership award Arts Coun. Santa Clara County, 1991, named Outstanding Businessman of Yr., Chamber of Commerce, San Jose, 1992. Mem. Toastmasters (v.p.), Rotary (bd. dirs.), ABA, Hawaii Bar Assn., Silicon Valley Capital Club. Office: Transpacific Capital Corp 1155 N 1st St Ste 101 San Jose CA 95112-4925

MANCINI, ROBERT KARL, computer analyst, consultant; b. Burbank, Calif., May 13, 1954; s. Alfred Robert and Phyllis Elaine (Pflugel) M.; m. Barbara Diane Bacon, Aug. 4, 1979; children: Benjamin Robert, Bonnie Kathryn, Brandon Peter. BA in Econs., UCLA, 1976; cert. in bibl. studies, Multonmah Sch. of the Bible, 1981; MBA, Santa Clara (Calif.) U., 1987. Process clk. Am. Funds Svc. Co., L.A., 1976-77; exec. asst. Sierra Thrift & Loan Co., San Mateo, Calif., 1977-78; sci. programming specialist Lockheed Missiles & Space Co., Sunnyvale, Calif., 1978-90; mgr. tech. publs. Diversified Software Systems Inc., Morgan Hill, Calif., 1990—; cons. Mancini Computer Svcs., San Jose and Morgan Hill, 1985—; instr. Heald Coll., San Jose, Calif., 1990. Mem. fin. coun. Hillside Ch., 1990-91; mem. blue ribbon budget rev. com. City of Morgan Hill, 1992. Mem. Phi Kappa Sigma (expansion com. 1976-78). Republican. Home: PO Box 1602 Morgan Hill CA 95038-1602

MANCINI, WILLIAM F., diplomat; b. Downey, Calif., Jan. 16, 1959. BA in Polit. Sci., Calif. State U., 1980. Prodn. asst. Winner/Wagner and Assocs., Los Angeles, 1978-83; protocol officer U.S. Dept. of State, Washington, 1983-84; advance rep. for the Pres. The White House, Washington, 1984-85; asst. to the chmn. Com. for the 50th Am. Presdl. Inaugural Galas, Washington, 1984-85; confidential asst. to the dir. Pub. Affairs Agy. U.S. Dept. of Commerce, Washington, 1985-86; pres. Mancini Internat., Newport Beach, Calif., 1986—; hon. consul gen. Sultanate of Oman, L.A., 1991—; cons. Embassy of Oman, Paramount Pictures, Niles Internat., Burbank, Calif., The Greater Alarm Co., Inc., Huntington Beach, Calif., The Challenger Ctr. for space Sci. Edn., Washington, Innovation USA, Newport Beach; advance rep. Whote Ho., 1989—. Patentee in field. Mem. The Big Bros. of Greater Los Angeles and Washington. Mem. Profl. Ski Instrs. Am., Aircraft Owners and Pilots Assn. Office: Mancini Internat 10940 Wilshire Blvd Fl 16 Los Angeles CA 90024-3915

MANCLARK, CHARLES ROBERT, microbiologist, researcher; b. Rochester, N.Y., June 22, 1928; s. Charles and Mary (Powell) M.; m. Doloras Jolly, Dec. 19, 1953; children: Charles Scott, Timothy Brooks. BS in Biology, Calif. Poly. State U., 1953; PhD in Bacteriology, UCLA, 1963. Rsch. and teaching asst. UCLA, 1956-61; asst. prof. Calif. State U., Long Beach, 1961-64; rsch. bacteriologist UCLA, 1963-65; asst. prof. U. Calif., Irvine, 1965-67; chief lab. of pertussis Ctr. for Biologics Evaluation and Rsch., Bethesda, Md., 1967-93; dir. WHO Collaborating Ctr., Bethesda, 1978-93; cons. WHO, UN, Pan. Am. Health Orgn., UNICEF and many fgn. countries worldwide, 1971—. Author of 2 lab. manuals for bacteriology; editor of 9 books on pertussis and pertussis vaccine; contbr. over 100 articles to profl. jours. Patentee in field. Cpl. U.S. Army, 1953-55. Recipient Merit award FDA, 1985, Group Recognition award 1989, medal Institutos de Salud, Lima, Peru, 1980, Disting. Svc. award for biomed. rsch. Dept. HHS, 1992; named Honored Alumnus in Sci. and Math., Calif. Poly. State U., 1992; Univ. fellow in microbiology UCLA, 1960. Fellow Am. Acad. Microbiology; mem. Am. Soc. for Microbiology, Internat. Assn. Biol. Standardization, Sigma Xi, Beta Beta Beta (pres. Epsilon Pi chpt. 1952-53). Home: 3236 Braemar Dr Santa Barbara CA 93109-1067 Office: 3236 Braemar Dr Santa Barbara CA 93109-1067

MANDEL, JEFF, writer, director, composer; b. L.A., May 27, 1952; s. Sheldon Charles and Renee Babette (Donatt) M. BA, U. Calif., L.A., 1973. V.p. Warren Lockhart Productions, L.A., 1980-82; exec. script cons. Ohara/Warner Bros. TV, L.A., 1987-88; supervising producer Superforce (Viacom), L.A., 1990—; advisor Slavko Vorkapich, L.A., 1974-76. Writer and co-writer for TV and cable; writer, co-writer, producer, directed various films; composed musical material for film and TV, 1975—; co-exec. producer Firehead (the series); contbr. articles to profl. jours. Mem. Libertarian Cen. Com., L.A., 1982, 83; patron Museum of Neon Arts, L.A., 1983—. Recipient 4 Crystal Reel awards Fla. Film Commn., 1991-92. Mem. Writers Guild Am., Am Soc. Composers, Authors and Pubs.

MANDEL, MARTIN LOUIS, lawyer; b. L.A., May 17, 1944; s. Maurice S. and Florence (Byer) M.; m. Duree Dunn, Oct. 16, 1982; 1 child, Max Andrew. BA, U. So. Calif., 1965, JD, 1968; LLM, George Washington U., 1971. Bar: Calif. 1969, U.S. Dist. Ct. (cen. dist.) Calif. 1972, U.S. Ct. Claims, 1971, U.S. Tax Ct. 1971, U.S. Supreme Ct. 1972. With office of gen. csl. IRS, Washington, 1968-72; ptnr. Stephens, Jones, LaFever & Smith, L.A., 1972-77, Stephens, Martin & Mandel, 1977-79, Fields, Fehn, Feinstein & Mandel, 1979-83; sr. v.p., gen. counsel Investment Mortgage Internat., Inc., 1983-84; ptnr. Feinstein, Gourley & Mandel, 1984-85, Mandel & Handin, San Francisco, 1985—; pres. The Mandel Group, 1988—; gen. counsel L.A. Express Football Club, 1983-85; instr. corps. U. West L.A., 1973-83. Mem. ABA, L.A. County Bar Assn., L.A. Athletic Club, Phi Delta Phi. Office: 131 Steuart St Ste 700 San Francisco CA 94105-1230

MANDEL, MAURICE, II, lawyer; b. Hollywood, Calif.; s. Maurice and Wynne Mary Mandel. BSBA, U. So. Calif., 1971, MEd, 1972; JD, Western State U., 1979. Bar: Calif. 1980, U.S. Dist. Ct. (ctrl. dist.) Calif. 1982, U.S. Ct. Appeals (fed. and 9th cirs.) 1983, U.S. Dist. Ct. (we. dist.) Tenn. 1987, U.S. Dist. Ct. Ariz. 1990, U.S. Dist. Ct. (so. dist.) Calif. 1991, U.S. Supreme Ct. 1991, U.S. Ct. Appeals (5th cir.) 1995. Tchr. Orange County (Calif.) Sch. Dist., 1972-82; pvt. practice law Newport Beach, Calif., 1982—; instr. C.C., 1987-95, prof., 1995—; prof. law Irvine (Calif.) U. Coll. of Law, 1994—; instr. OCBA Coll. of Trial Advocacy, 1994—; instr. OCBA MCLE Bear Mountain Calif. Ski Sch., 1994; FBA/OCC MCLE provider, 1994—. Counselor Troy Camp, 1969-72; chmn. Legal Edn. for Youth, 1984-86; active Ctr. Dance Alliance, Orange County, 1986—; mem. Friends Am. Ballet Theatre, Opera Pacific Guild, Calypso Soc., World Wildlife Found., L.A. County Mus. Art, Newport Beach Art Mus., Met. Mus. Art, Laguna Beach Mus. Art, Smithsonian Instn., Friends of Joffrey Ballet; assoc. U.S. Ski Team, 1975—; com. assoc. U.S. Olympics, 1988—; mem. alumni and scholarship com. Beverly Hills H.S. Recipient cert. of appreciation U.S. Dist. Ct., L.A., 1985, Thwarted Thwart award Hewport Harbor C. of C., 1989, Tovarich award Kirov Ballet, 1989, 92, Perostroika award Moscow Classical Ballet, 1988-89, 94, Skrisivi Nogi award Bolshoi Ballet, 1990, Marinskii Dance award St. Petersburg, 1993. Mem. ABA, Assn. Trial Lawyers Am., Assn. Bus. Trial Lawyers, Fed. Bar Assn. (pres. Orange County chpt. 1986, nat. del. 1988-90, founder criminal indigent def. panel 1986, mem. numerous other coms., nat. chpt. activity award 1987, nat. membership award 1987, OCC svc. award 1989, nat. regional membership chmn. 1990, spl. appointee nat. membership com. 1991), Calif. Bar Assn. (Pro Bono awards 1985-89), Orange County Bar Assn. (legal edn. for youth com. 1982-90, chmn. 1985, fed. practice com., sports com., mandatory fee arbitration com. 1985—, lawyer's referral svc. com. 1984—, Merit award 1986), Orange County Bar Found. (trustee 1984-87), Women Lawyers of Orange County, U.S. Supreme Ct. Hist. Soc., 9th Jud. Cir. Hist. Soc., Am. Inns of Ct., Calif. Trial Lawyers Assn., Calif. Employee Lawyers Assn., Plaintiff Employee Lawyers Assn., Employees Rights Coun., Bar Leaders Coun. Dist. 8, Amicus Publico, U. So. Calif. Alumni Assn., Mensa. Club: Balboa Yacht. Home: PO Box 411 Bethel Island CA 94511-0411

MANDEL, ROBERT MICHAEL, social sciences educator; b. Washington, Oct. 30, 1949; s. Philip and Alice Grace Mandel; m. Annette Colleen Kelley, Aug. 1, 1981; children: Travis Scott, Laura Diane. AB, Brown U., 1972; MA, Yale U., 1974, MPhil, 1975, PhD, 1976. Intern CIA, Washington, 1974-75; asst. prof. internat. affairs Lewis and Clark Coll., Portland, Oreg., 1976-82; assoc. prof. internat. affairs Lewis and Clark Coll., Portland, 1982-88, prof. internat. affairs, 1988—, dean social sci. divsn., 1990-92, chair internat. affairs, 1994—; acad. assoc. Atlantic Coun., Washington, 1985—; vis. scholar Def. Intelligence Coll., Washington, 1989; adv. bd. mem. Microsoft, Redmond, Wash., 1993—. Author: Perception, Decision Making and Conflict, 1979, Irrationality in International Confrontation, 1987, Conflict Over the World's Resources, 1988; assoc. editor: (jour.) Armed Forces and Society, 1993—. Mem. Am. Polit. Sci. Assn., Internat. Studies Assn., Phi Beta Kappa. Office: Lewis and Clark Coll 0615 SW Palatine Hill Rd Portland OR 97219

MANDELSTEIN, PAUL STANLEY, book publishing executive; b. Bklyn., May 18, 1946; s. Max and Esther (Friedman) M.; m. Cornelia S. Pratt, Feb. 21, 1973 (div. June 1993); children: Zachary, Naomi, Nicolas. Student, Bklyn. Coll., 1965. Pres. Quantum Pub., Mill Valley, Calif., 1984—, The Book Pub. Co., Summertown, Tenn.; mktg. cons. Farm Foods, Summertown, Tenn., 1975—, Solar Electronics, Summertown, 1976—, Shambhala Pubs., 1994—; bus. cons. Audio Scholar, Mendocino, Calif., 1991. Author: The Nightingale and the Wind, 1993, The Lute Player, 1994. Home: 1204 El Cide Ct Mill Valley CA 94941-3401 Office: PO Box 1738 Mill Valley CA 94942-1738

MANDEVILLE, CRAIG H., aircraft company executive, retired military officer; b. Chickasha, Okla., Sept. 22, 1940. BA, Okla. State U., 1963. Commd. 2d lt. U.S. Army, 1963, advanced through grades to lt. col., 1979; battery comdr. Battery A 2d Battalion 320th Field Artillery, 101st AIrborne Divsn. U.S. Army, Vietnam, 1967-68, dep. regimental advisor 15th Inf. Regiment, 9th ARVN Divsn., 1971-72; staff officer, dep. chief of staff ops. and plans, requirements directorate Hdqrs. DA U.S. Army, Washington, 1978-82; battalion comdr. 1st Battalion (LANCE) 12th Field Artillery U.S. Army, Ft. Sill, Okla., 1982-83; ret. U.S. Army, 1983; mgr. C-17 program devel. Douglas Aircraft Co.-McDonnell Douglas Corp., Long Beach, Calif., 1983-89, bus. unit mgr. C-17 program devel., 1989-91, acting gen. mgr. C-17 program exts., 1991, now exec. asst. to C-17 sr. v.p., program mgr. Founder, dir. L.A. Rams Pro-Am Celebrity Tennis Tournament; assisted clubs with tennis clinics, tournaments; instr. tennis. Decorated Silver Star (2), Bronze Star (3), Legion of Merit, Purple Heart (3), Combat Infantryman's Badge, Parachute Badge, others. Mem. U.S. Tennis Assn. Home: 16521 Grunion Apt 200 Huntington Beach CA 92649-3484 Office: McDonnell Douglas Aerospace MDTAMS 54 54 1510 Hughes Way Long Beach CA 90810

MANEA-MANOLIU, ION S., journalist, editor; b. Galati, Romania, Sept. 3, 1925; came to U.S., 1978; s. Solomon I. and Dobrita (Goldemberg) Manes; m. Maria I. Manoliu Manea, Nov. 26, 1968; 1 child, Alex Manea (dec.). MA, U. Bucharest, Romania, 1959, PhD, 1975. Lectr. U. Bucharest, 1948-77; journalist, columnist Romanian Press Agy. and Fgn. Langs., 1946-77; rsch. assoc. U. Calif., Davis and Berkeley, 1979-86; journalist Radio Free Europe, 1980-89; editor Am. Romanian Acad. U. Calif., Davis, 1980—, mem. exec. com. Am. Romanian Acad., 1992—. Author: Suez, 1956, Problema Germanta si Conferinta dela Geneva, 1959, Dosare ale Violentei, 1972; editor: Un Om, O Via, Un Destin, 1990, Homo Religiousus: To Honor Mircea Eliade, 1990, O viata de Om, 1991, Români in Stiinta si Cultura Occidentala, 1992, (jour.) Am. Romanian Acad. Jour., 1980—; contbr. numerous articles on Romanian fgn. policy, polit. life in Ea. and Western Europe and U.S. broadcast on Radio Free Europe to profl. jours. Mem. task force Rep. Party, Calif., 1985—, life mem., 1988—; mem. ARA, Calif., 1980—. Mem. Journalist Assn. Romania (exec. com. 1955-62), Journalists Club in Bucharest (gen. mgr., bd. dirs. 1955-62), Scottish Rite of Freemasonry, Athens Lodge # 228 (officer 1985—), Ben Ali Temple. Orthodox. Office: U Calif Am Romanian Acad Davis CA 95616

MANES, JOHN DALTON, retired hospital administrator, anaesthesiologist; b. Winnipeg, Man., Can., Oct. 29, 1920; s. John Harold and Elizabeth (Dalton) M.; m. Jean Julia Diggins, Aug. 28, 1946 (dec. 1970); children: Maureen Jean, John William; m. Wilda Ann Suffel, Nov. 7, 1975. B.Sc., McGill U., 1948, M.D., C.M., 1951. Anaesthesiologist Holy Cross Hosp., Calgary, Alta., Can., 1954-86, med. dir., 1967-76, exec. dir., 1976-86; exec. dir. Can. Assn. Med. Clinics, 1967-73. Contbr. articles to profl. jours. Capt. Can. Army, 1940-45. Recipient Queen's Silver Jubilee medal Queen Elizabeth II, 1977. Mem. Can. Med. Assn., Can. Anaesthesia Assn. Progressive Conservative. Roman Catholic. Clubs: Calgary Golf and Country, Glencoe. Home: PO Box 369, Sylvan Lake, AB Canada T0M 1Z0 Office: Bentley Gen Hosp, PO Box 30, Bentley, AB Canada T0C 0J0

MANETTA, ALBERTO, gynecologic oncologist; b. Buenos Aires, Feb. 17, 1944; came to U.S., 1968; s. Guido and Rachel (Raquelle) M.; m. Nancy Mosard, Nov. 14, 1969; children: Edward, Katy. BS in Biol. Sci., Liceo San Martin, Buenos Aires, 1962; MD, U. Buenos Aires, 1968. Diplomate Am. Bd. Ob-Gyn. Resident Winthrop U. Hosp., SUNY, Stony Brook, 1968-72; dir. Blair County Prenatal Ctr., 1974-77; attending physician pvt. practice Altoona (Pa.) Hosp. Ob-Gyn, 1972-82; clin. asst. prof. family and cmty. medicine Coll. Medicine Pa. State U., Hershey, 1976-82, asst. prof. ob-gyn divsn. gynecol. oncology Coll. Medicine, 1984-88; attending physician D.C. Gen. Hosp., 1982-84, Univ. Hosp., Milton S. Hershey Med. Ctr., Hershey, 1984-88, U. Calif.-Irvine Med. Ctr., Orange, Calif., 1988—; asst. prof. ob-gyn divsn. gynecol. oncology U. Calif., Irvine, 1988-90, assoc. prof., 1990, assoc. prof. ob-gyn., 1992-93, sr. assoc. dean ednl. affairs, 1993—; cons. staff dept. ob-gyn U. Nev. Sch. Medicine, 1988—; cons. staff dept. surgery City of Hope Nat. Med. Ctr., Duarte, Calif., 1988—; exec. chief proctor Nat. Bd. Med. Examiners, 1992—; presenter in field. Assoc. editor Am. Jour. Ob-Gyn; reviewer jours. in field; contbr. articles to profl. jours., chpts. to books; patentee in field. Recipient 1st Excellence in Teaching award Assn. Profs. Gynecology and Obstetrics, 1992; grantee Am. Cancer Soc., 1987-88, 1992, U.S. Biosci., Phila., 1989, Cetus Corp., 1989, UCI, 1989-90, Wyeth-Ayerst Labs., 1991, Meml. Health Svcs. Grant Com., 1991-92, 93, Nat. Cancer Inst., 1994. Fellow ACS, Am. Coll. Obestricians and Gynecologists (Continuing Med. Edn. award 1989-92, 92—); mem. AMA, Assn. Profs. Gynecologic Oncology, Assn., Assn. Am. Med. Colls. (dean's del. group on ednl. affairs com. 1993—), Soc. Gynecologic Oncologists (found. award 1986), Gynecologic Urology Soc. (charter), Mid-Atlantic Gynecologic Oncology Soc., Am. Soc. Clin. Oncology, Orange County Med. Assn., Western Assn. Gynecologic Oncologists, Am. Assn. Cancer Rsch., Gynecologic Oncology Group (mem. coms.). Office: UCI Med Ctr Divsn Gyn/Oncology 101 The City Dr S Bldg 23 Orange CA 92668-3201

MANFRE, MICHAEL, food products executive; b. 1949. Ptnr. Frank Capurro & Son, Watsonville, Calif., 1970—. Office: Frank Capurro & Son 2250 Salinas Rd Watsonville CA 95076-9232*

MANGAN, TERENCE JOSEPH, police chief; b. Utica, N.Y., Feb. 17, 1938; s. Lawrence and Eloise (Roth) M.; m. Charlotte Mauss, June 19, 1971; children: Sean, Megan. B.A., St. Mary's Coll., Norwalk, Conn., 1961; M.A., St. Albert's Coll., 1965; postgrad. in Pub. Adminstrn., Adminstrn. Justice, U. So. Calif., 1972-76; Grad. FBI Nat. Acad. Cert. Wash. State Criminal Justice Tng. Commn., Calif. Peace Officers Standards and Tng. Commn.; grad. Northwest Law Enforcement Exec. Command Coll., 1986; cert. Gov.'s Rev. Tean Child Abuse Services, 1986. With Seaside (Calif.) Police Dept., 1968-72; with Lakewood (Calif.) Police Dept., 1972-76, chief, dir. community safety, to 1976; chief Bellingham (Wash.) Police Dept., 1976-87; chief Spokane (Wash.) Police Dept., 1987—; chmn. Wash. State Criminal Justice Tng. Commn.; mem. Mgmt. Adv. Group Organized Crime and Narcotics Enforcement; appointed to Death Investigations Coun., Spl. Task Force on Child Abuse, Gov's Criminal Justice Adv. Bd.; master mentor Waspc's Exec. Leadership Inst., coord. Northwest Law Enforcement Exec. Command Coll. Program; lectr. FBI Acad. Mem. archdiocesan steering com. Ann. Catholic Appeal, 1982; chair fund-raising drives Am. Cancer Soc., Am. Heart Assn., Salvation Army, Easter Seal Soc., Assn. for Retarded Citizens; bd. advs. Holy Names Ctr.; exec. bd. Boy Scouts of Am., Inland Empire Coun.; bd. dirs. Spokane Goodwill Industries, United Way, Whatcom County, Calif. Recipient citation U.S. Secret Service, 1969, Congressional Com. Internal Security, 1971, Svc. award City of Seaside, 1972, Disting. Svc. award City of Lakewood, also Wash. Assn. Sheriffs and Police Chiefs, 1978-81, Police Officer of Yr. award Nat. Exchange Club, 1979, Lawman of Yr. award Vets. of Foreign Wars, 1980, Law Enforcement Officer of Yr. award Wash. VFW, 1980, Community Service award Wash. Toastmasters Internat., 1980, Pres. award Pacific Lutheran U., 1981, Paul Harris fellow Rotary Internat., 1986. Mem. Internat. Assn. Chiefs Police, Nat. Council Crime and Delinquency, Wash. Assn. Sheriffs and Police Chiefs (past pres.), Internat. Peace Arch Law Enforcement Council. Roman Catholic. Office: Spokane Police Dept Office of the Chief 1100 W Mallon Ave Spokane WA 99260-2043*

MANGHAM, CHARLES ADLEY, SR., psychiatrist; b. San Antonio, Jan. 17, 1919; s. Arthur Decatur and Emma Evelyna (Flanagan) M.; m. Aileen Muriel Ramberg, Apr. 15, 1944; children: Charles A. Jr., A. Deborah, Joel R. BS, U. Va., 1939, MD, 1942. Diplomate Am. Bd. Psychiatry & Neurology. Intern Virginia Mason Hosp., Seattle, 1942-43; med. officer U.S. Army Med. Corps, 1943-46; resident in medicine Emergency Hosp., Washington, 1946-47; resident in psychiatry Cin. Gen. Hosp., 1947-50; instr. psychiatry U. Wash., Seattle, 1950-51; pvt. practice child psychoanalysis Seattle, 1951—; clin. prof. dept. behavioral scis. U. Wash., 1968—. Mem. Assn. Child Psychoanalysis (pres. 1990-92), Am. Psychoanalytic Assn., Wash. State Med. Assn., King County Med. Assn. Office: 4033 E Madison St Seattle WA 98112-3117

MANGHAM, JOHN RANDALL, information systems professional; b. Oklahoma City, July 19, 1957; s. Clarence Madison and Ola B. (Hodges) M. Student, Okla. State U., 1975-77, 80-81. Night ops. mgr. Citizens State Bank, Liberal, Kans., 1982-83; contract programmer M. David Lowe, Inc., Houston, 1983-84; programmer/analyst Thorpe Corp., Houston, 1984-87, Dairy div. Borden, Inc., Houston, 1987-88, Battle Mountain Gold Co., Houston, 1988-89; sr. programmer/analyst Primeco, Inc., Houston, 1989-90; project leader Auto Parts Club, Inc., San Diego, 1990—. Contbr. articles to profl. jours. Missionary Ch. Jesus Christ LDS, Italy, 1978-80; bishop, bd. dirs. Restoration Fellowship in Jesus Christ, San Diego, 1990—; v.p. Houston Interfaith Alliance, 1987, pres., 1988. Mem. Application Systems Group (bd. dirs. 1992-94, treas. 1993-94), Common. Libertarian. Mormon. Home: PO Box 371728 San Diego CA 92137-1728 Office: Auto Parts Club Inc 5825 Oberlin Dr Ste 100 San Diego CA 92121-3702

MANGIN, RENÉ-MARC, systems physicist; b. Paris, July 11, 1956; came to U.S., 1961; s. Melvyn B. and Jeanne Marie (Bradin) M.; m. Susan Beth Burger; 1 child, Alexandre Marceau. BS in Cell Biology, BS in Environ. Sci., Wash. State U., 1979, MS in Envrion. Toxicology, 1982; postgrad., U. Wash., 1984-85; PhD, Wash. State U., 1989. Writer, editor USDA Coop. Ext., Pullman, Wash., 1979-80; instr. environ. sci. Wash. State U., Pullman, 1980-81, soil scientist, 1981-82, toxicologist, 1983; ecologist, consulting toxicologist U.S. Forest Svc., Missoula, Mont., 1982-83, regional pest control mgr., 1982-87; environ. program mgr. U.S. Dept. Energy, Richland, Wash., 1987-88, spl. cons. to Tri-Party Agreement, 1987-88; ext. prof. polit. sci. Wash. State U., Pullman, 1989-91; conflict resolution cons. Nat. Ctr. Assocs., Tacoma, Wash., 1990—; mgmt. analyst Bonneville Power Adminstrn., Portland, Oreg., 1993—; interim chief regulatory analysis Bonneville Power Adminstrn., Portland, 1992-93, interim chief policy & strategy, 1992-93. Author: Culture Clash: Natural Resource Conflicts in the West, 1994; contbr. articles to profl. jours., chpt. to book. Vol. Habitat for Humanity, Portland, 1992. Boeing Acad. scholar, 1977; recipient Lake Roosevelt Mgmt. Planning grant award N.W. Area Found., 1990; named Ark. Traveler by Gov. Bill Clinton, 1991. Mem. Soc. Profls. in Dispute Resolution, Am. Soc. Pub. Adminstrn., Speech Communication Assn. Home: 1547 NE 51st Ave Portland OR 97213-2701

MANGINI, RICHARD ALAN, religious organization executive; b. Concord, Calif., Oct. 23, 1940; s. Raymond A. and Margaret E. (Levada) M. MDiv, St. Patrick's Sem., 1967; MJ, U. Calif., Berkeley, 1972; MA in Sprituality, U. San Francisco, 1982. Editor The Cath. Voice, Oakland, Calif., 1973-80; adminstr. St. Charles Ch., Livermore, Calif., 1976; pastor St. Leander Ch., San Leandro, Calif., 1976-90; dir. strategic planning Diocese of Oakland, 1990-95. Mem., chair Human Rels. Commn., City of San Leandro, 1980-87, Ecumenical Assn., 1980-87. Recipient Medal of Merit, Govt. of Portugal, 1992. Mem. Commonwealth Club. Democrat. Roman Catholic.

MANGINO, KRISTIN MIKALSON, secondary education educator; b. Spokane, Wash., July 7, 1939; d. Norman Lillard and Mabel Mae (Lewis) Mikalson; m. Paul Angelo Mangino, Aug. 15, 1965; children: Kyle Aaron, Lisan Kristin. Student, Cottey Coll., 1957-58, Ea. Wash. Coll. Edn. (now Ea. Wash. U.), 1958-61; BS in Psychology, Wash. State U., 1961; student, Calif. State U., Fullerton, 1961-66; postgrad., U. Calif., Irvine, 1966; MS in Spl. Edn., Portland State U., 1983. Cert. elem. and secondary tchr., Calif., Wash., Oreg. Tchr. English and reading Jr. High Sch., Anaheim and Monterey, Calif., 1961-68; substitute tchr. Elma (Wash.) Sch. Dist., 1970-71, Evergreen Sch. Dist., Vancouver, Wash., 1974-75; tutor Evergreen Sch. Dist., Vancouver, 1975-84; tutor, substitute tchr. Vancouver and Evergreen Sch. Dists., 1984-88, tutor, 1988—; bd. dirs. Arden Tree Farms; hostess with svc. sales City Welcome Svc., 1986-87; co-pres. Spl. Edn. Adv. Coun., Vancouver, 1986-87; mem. direction svc. bd. Ednl. Svc. Dists. 112, 1980. Sec. Spl. Olympics, Evergreen Sch. Dist., 1989-90; mem. D.D. Parent Coalition of Clark County, 1993—. Mem. Philanthropic Ednl. Orgn. (G.X. chpt. officer), The Arc (bd. dirs. 1992-93), Internat. Rett Syndrome Found., Berg Freunde Ski Club. Presbyterian. Home and Office: PO Box 5542 Vancouver WA 98668-5542

MANGIR, TULIN ERDIM, science educator, consultant; b. Ankara, Turkey, May 3, 1950; d. Ali Riza and Sabahat Erdim; m. Metin S. Mangir, Sept. 19, 1970; children: Alan-Cem, David-Emre. BSEE, UCLA, 1971; attended, U So. Calif., 1973-75, MSEE in Semiconductor Device Physics, 1974, MSEE in Computer Architecture, 1975; PhD in Engring., UCLA, 1981. Engr. Burroughs Western Divsn., Pasadena, Calif., 1974-76; rsch. engr., teaching assoc. UCLA, 1975-81; from sr. staff dir. to v.p. XEROX Microelectronics Ctr., El Segundo, Calif., 1978-81; prof. Computer Engring. UCLA, 1981-86; prin. cons. Advanced Tech. Consulting, West L.A., Calif., 1981-86; tech. acqusition mgr., chief sci., project mgr. TRW, Inc., Redondo Beach, Calif., 1986-92; founding exec. ptnr. The Sci. Alliance, Santa Monica, Calif., 1992—; pres. TM Assocs., Santa Monica, Calif., 1992—; cons. numerous orgns. including European Econ. Commn., Swedish Govt. Microelectronics Program, Nokia, Thompson C.S.F., Aerospace co., NASA, private and pub. co., venture firms, 1981—; lectr. NATO Spl. Studies Inst., 1987-90; rep. U.S. aerospace industry, Japan, 1991-92. contbr. articles to profl. jours., chpts. to books. fund raiser, vol. Westside Dem. Campaign (including Clinton & Gore, Boxer, Feinstein), 1992; vol. sci. instr. Santa Monica Sch. Dist., 1990—; fundraiser Westside Foodbank, City of Hope, AIDS Project, 1988—; chair child devel. com., Santa Monica Sch. Dist., 1991—; reg. v.p. ATAA, 1982-85. Recipient Young Investigator award Internat. Fedn. Info. Processing 1984-86, Service award, 1984-86, Recognition award Swedish Govt., 1984-87, Vol. award Community Action Teams, 1990-92; rsch. grantee, IBM, 1983-86, travel grantee Electronics Rsch. and Sci. Inst., Taiwan, 1985-86. Mem. IEEE (organizing coms. 1980 , referee NSF pubs., proposals 1980—, travel grantee 1984-85, lectr.), Women in Tech. Internat. Office: TM Assocs 536 16th St Santa Monica CA 90402-3002

MANGUM, WILLIAM, management consulting company executive; b. Memphis, Dec. 7, 1931; s. Cary P. and Jennie Elizabeth (Matthews) M.; m. Maria Elena Smith, Apr. 2, 1978 (div.); children: Christopher, Stacy. BS, U. So. Calif., 1954. With Fairchild Camera & Instruments Corp., L.A., 1954-59; pres. Thomas Mangum Co., L.A., 1960—. Author: 99 Minutes to Your Ideal Job, 1995, The Job Search Workbook, 1995. Pres. Save Our Rural Environ., L.A., 1976-82, La Habra Heights Improvement Assn., L.A., 1982; bd. dirs., pres. La Habra Heights Planning Com., 1978-84. Recipient President's award La Habra Heights Improvement Assn., 1984. Mem. AIAA, IEEE, Am. Soc. Quality Control, Soc. Photo-Optical Instrument Engrs., Am. Mgmt. Assn., Calif. Exec. Recruiters Assn., Internat. Assn. Corp. Profl. Recruiters. Office: 500 E Del Mar Blvd Apt 19 Pasadena CA 91101-3607 Office: 2469 Cahvilla Hills Dr Palm Springs CA 92264-8901

MANION, JERRY ROBERT, hotel chain executive; b. Mt. Vernon, Ill., Feb. 27, 1938; s. Frances Manion; m. Salley Trinkle, Dec. 30, 1964; children: Courtney Elizabeth, Patrick Robert. BBA, U. Ill., 1960; MS in Bus. Mgmt., So. Ill.U., 1962. Sr. v.p., franchise dir. Quality Inns Internat., Inc., Md., 1977-80; sr. v.p., dir. ops. Metro Hotels, Inc., Tex., 1980-83; pres. Economy Motor Inns, Inc., Tex., 1983-85; pres. hotel group Ramada Inc., Phoenix, 1985-89; exec. v.p. Motel 6 Ops., Dallas, 1989-93; exec. v.p. devel. Richfield Hotel Mgmt. Inc., Englewood, Colo., 1993-94; bd. trustees Ednl. Inst. Adv. Coun., Hotel Sch. No. Ariz. U. Mem. Am. Hotel & Motel Assn. Office: Manion Investments 2701 E Camelback Rd Ste 450 Phoenix AZ 85016-4326*

MANK, EDWARD WARREN, marketing professional; b. Boothbay Harbor, Maine, Oct. 2, 1962; s. Edward Raymond Jr. and Sandra Gail (Strahan) M. Assoc. in Liberal Arts, C.C. Vt., 1985; cert. ophthalmic technician, Nat. Edn. Ctr., San Francisco, 1992; cert. real estate broker, Am. Sch. Mortgage Banking, Walnut Creek, Calif., 1994. Lic. real estate salesman, Calif.; cert. Am. Bd. Optometry Dispensing. Tng. coord. Burger King Corp., South Burlington, Vt., 1985-87, San Francisco, 1988-89; asst. mgr. Bonanza Family Restaurant, South Burlington, 1987-88; supr. U.S. Census Bur., San Francisco, 1990; sales rep. Viacom Cablevision, San Francisco, 1991; programming researcher NBC, San Francisco, 1992; mktg. cons. Calyx & Corolla, San Francisco, 1993; mktg. rep. Alliance Bancorp, Millbrae, Calif., 1993—. Sustaining mem. Rep. Nat. Com., Washington, 1989—; sponsor Heritage Found., Washington, Cato Inst., Washington. Mem. Acad. Polit. Sci., Coun. Fgn. Rels., World Affairs Coun., Nat. Rifle Assn. (life), Reason Found. Republican. Episcopalian. Home: 205 Palmcrest Dr Daly City CA 94015-1553 Office: Alliance Bancorp 800 El Camino Real Millbrae CA 94030-2010

MANKOFF, ALBERT WILLIAM, cultural organization administrator, consultant; b. Newark, Aug. 24, 1926; s. Albert and Dorothy M.; m. Audrey Emery, Mar. 18, 1972; 1 child, Robert Morgan. BLS, U. Okla., 1967. With Am. Airlines, Inc., 1947-69; mgr. mgmt. tng. and devel. Am. Airlines Inc., 1957-67; mgr. orgn. devel. Am. Airlines, Inc., Tulsa, 1968-69; dir. personnel Peat, Marwick, Mitchell & Co., Chgo., 1969-72; ptnr. Lexicon, Inc. Cons., Raleigh, N.C., 1972-77; Pacific area mgr. safety and tng. Trailways, Inc., L.A., 1978-80; tng. cons. State of Sacramento, Sacramento, 1980-91; pres. Inst. Am. Hist. Tech., Ojai, Calif., 1987—. Author: Trolley Treasures, 4 vols., 1986-87, The Glory Days, 1989, Tracks of Triumph, 1993, Tarnished Triumph, The Edison Paradigm, 1994, Sacramento's Shining Rails, 1995, Trolleys in America: The Long Road Back, 1995; contbr. articles to profl. jours. Bd. dirs., v.p. OASIS; Midwest Centre for Human Potential, Chgo., 1970-72, Tulsa Urban League, 1962-69; v.p., bd. dirs. Meditation Groups Inc., Ojai, Calif., Psychosynthesis Internat., Ojai Internat. Assn. Managerial and Orgnl. Psychosynthesis, Thousand Oaks, Calif. Home and Office: 1223 Gregory St Ojai CA 93023-3038

MANLEY, JOAN A(DELE) DANIELS, retired publisher; b. San Luis Obispo, Calif., Sept. 23, 1932; d. Carl and Della (Weinmann) Daniels; m. Jeremy C. Lanning, Mar. 17, 1956 (div. Sept. 1963); m. Donald H. Manley, Sept. 12, 1964 (div. 1985); m. William G. Houlton, May 31, 1991. BA, U. Calif., Berkeley, 1954; DBA (hon.), U. New Haven, 1974; LLD (hon.), Babson Coll., 1978. Sec. Doubleday & Co., Inc., N.Y.C., 1954-60; sales exec. Time Inc., 1960-66, v.p., 1971-75, group v.p., 1975-84, also bd. dir.; circulation dir. Time-Life Books, 1966-68, dir. sales, 1968-70, pub., 1970-76; chmn. bd. Time-Life Books Inc., 1976-80; vice chmn. bd. Book-of-the-Month Club, Inc., N.Y.C., until 1984; supervising dir. Time-Life Internat. (Nederland) B.V., Amsterdam, until 1984; bd. dirs. Scholastic Inc., Viking Office Products Inc., AON Corp., Sara Lee Corp., BFP Holdings, Inc. Past trustee Mayo Found., Rochester, Minn., Nat. Repertory Orch., William Benton Found.; former mem. adv. coun. Stanford U. Bus. Sch., Haas Sch. Bus. U. Calif.; trustee Vail Valley Inst., Keystone Ctr. Named to Direct Mktg. Hall of Fame, 1993; U. Calif.-Berkeley fellow, 1989. Mem. Assn. Am. Pubs. (past chmn.).

MANLEY, RICHARD WALTER, insurance executive; b. Malone, N.Y., Dec. 26, 1934; s. Walter E. and Ruth (St. Mary) M.; m. Linda Kimberlin, Dec. 18, 1965; children: Stephanie, Christopher. BS in Bus., U. So. Miss., 1960. Cert. real estate broker. Account exec. Colonial Life and Accident, Hattiesburg, Miss., 1960-63; dist. mgr. Colonial Life and Accident, Oklahoma City, 1963-66; regional dir. Colonial Life and Accident, Denver, 1966-76, zone dir., 1976-82; pres. Commonwealth Gen. Group, Denver, 1982-92, Manley Properties Inc., Denver, 1982-90, Richard W. Manley Commonwealth Gen. Grps., Inc., Denver, 1982—; cons. Capitol Am. Life Ins. Co., Cleve., 1987-92; bd. dirs. (merco) Mercy Hosp., Denver, 1982-87. With USAF, 1956-59. Mem. Nat. Life Underwriters, Sertoma, Cherry Hills C. of C., Petroleum Club, Elks, Alpha Tau Omega. Roman Catholic. Home: 6510 E Lake Pl Englewood CO 80111-4411

MANN, BRIAN ROLAND, editor; b. Memphis, Nov. 1, 1964; s. Billy R. and Geraldine L. (Hoffman) M.; m. Bobbie Jean Wescovich. BS in English and Creative Writing, U. So. Miss., 1988. Freelance writer Hattiesburg, 1988-92; packager Silverline, Hattiesburg, Miss., 1989-92; editor Malibu Comics, Calabasas, Calif., 1992—. Author comic series Cat & Mouse, 1989-92 (Top 10 award 1991). Baptist. Home: 17950 Lassen St # 114 Northridge CA 91325-4792 Office: Malibu Comics 26707 Agoura Rd Calabasas CA 91302-1960

MANN, CLARENCE CHARLES, real estate company official; b. Oradell, N.J., Oct. 15, 1929; s. Clarence Theodore and Martha Barbara (Koster) M.; m. Joan Elizabeth Schnoor, Nov. 25, 1951 (div. Jan. 1985); 1 child, Gary John. BA, NYU, 1951; MA, U. Pa., 1958, Am. U., Beirut, Lebanon, 1963. Commd. 2d. lt. U.S. Army, 1951, advanced through grades to col., ret., 1977; def. attache to Jordan, 1959-64; mktg. mgr. Litton Industries, Jordan, Saudi Arabia, 1977-81; mktg. mgr. Mid-East Hughes Aircraft Co., Fullerton, Calif., 1981-91; dir. relocation ERA Gem Realty, Tucson, 1992—. Author: Abu Dhabi: Birth of an Oil Shaikhdom, 1964. Decorated Legion of Merit. Mem. Met. Tucson Conv. and Visitors Bureau, Chamber Mil. Affairs Com., Tucson C. of C.

MANN, CLAUD PRENTISS, JR., retired television journalist, real estate agent; b. Galveston, Tex., June 30, 1925; s. Claud Prentiss and Henrietta Anno (Cline) M.; m. Loris Lea Padgett, Sept. 18, 1948; children: Beatrice Anno, Claudea Padgett, Claud Prentiss III. BS, U. Houston, 1949. Cert. tchr., Calif.; lic. real estate agt., Wash. Fellow Fund for Adult Edn. Mass Media U. Calif., Berkeley, 1958-59; anchor, reporter, writer, prodr., commentator Sta. KTVU-TV, San Francisco, Oakland, Calif., 1962-87; news dir., anchor, prodr. Sta. KTIE-TV, Oxnard, Santa Barbara, Calif., 1987-88; freelance writer, producer, pub. info. specialist, 1988—; journalism instr. Highline and South Seattle Community Colls., 1990-92. Bd. dirs., performer Dramadock Community Theater, Vashon Island, Wash. Recipient No. Calif. Emmy awards for reporting and anchor work, 1975, 76, 77, 79, 81, John Swett award for Edn. Reporting; commendations U.S. State Dept., City of Oakland, City of San Francisco, Calif. State Legis. Mem. Am. Fedn. Radio and TV Artists, Vashon Allied Arts (dir. 1989-91), Nat. Acad. TV Arts and Scis. (Silver Circle), Soc. Profl. Journalists. Home: 25115 122nd Ave SW Vashon WA 98070-7820

MANN, DONALD ROBERT See VALA, ROBERT

MANN, HAROLD W., agricultural products executive; b. 1908. Pvt. practice with father Delano and Salinas, Calif., 1919-45; with Mann Packaging Co., Inc., 1945—, now chmn. bd. Office: Mann Packing Co Inc 1250 Hansen St Salinas CA 93901-4552*

MANN, INEZ KIMIKO, public relations professional, consultant; b. Honolulu, Aug. 10, 1944; s. Yoshio and Florence Matsuko (Shibuya) Ishihara; m. Ronald Philip Mann, May 21, 1966 (div. 1975); 1 child, Elisa Akiko. B.A. cum laude, U. Hawaii, 1966, M.A., 1967. Research asst. editor ERIC/CAPS, U. Mich., Ann Arbor, 1967-69; tech. editor Cyphernetics Corp., Ann Arbor, 1969-70; lectr. Leeward and Honolulu Community Colls., Honolulu, 1976-77; tech. writer Computab, Honolulu, 1974; tech. rep. Proprietary Computer Systems, Honolulu, 1975-76; pub. relations dir. The Habilitat Inc., Kaneohe, Hawaii, 1977, Hosp. Assn. Hawaii, Honolulu, 1978-83; mgr. corporate communications Pacific Health Resources, Los Angeles, 1983-84; pres. McIntyre & Mann, Los Angeles, 1984; mgr. pub. relations Internat. Med. Exchange, Los Angeles; dir. comm. AMI Ambulatory Centres Inc., Culver City, Calif., 1985-86; pres. Mann & Assocs., Pasadena, Calif., 1987—. Author numerous poems. Editor: KAPA, 1966. Mem. Big Sisters Hawaii, 1979-83, Pacific div. Disaster Com. ARC, 1979-81. Recipient Hemingway award for creative writing, 1966. Mem. Pub. Relations Soc. Am. (accredited), Internat. Assn. Bus. Communicators (bd. dirs. Hawaii 1981), Hosp. Publ. Relations Assn. Hawaii (bd. dirs. 1979-82), Mortar Bd., Phi Beta Kappa, Phi Kappa Phi. Home: 1719 Gillette Crescent St South Pasadena CA 91030-4321 Office: Mann & Assocs 200 E Del Mar Blvd Ste 115 Pasadena CA 91105-2551

MANN, KAREN, consultant, educator; b. Kansas City, Mo., Oct. 9, 1942; d. Charles and Letha (Anderson) M. BA, U. Calif.-Santa Barbara, 1964; MPA, Golden Gate U., 1975, PhD, 1994. Cert. lay minister Order of Buddhist Contemplatives. Tchr. Sisters of Immaculate Heart, Los Angeles, 1964-68; group counselor San Francisco and Marin County Probation Depts., parole agt. Calif. Dept. Corrections, Sacramento and San Francisco, 1970-86; researcher and cons. Non-profit Orgnl. Devel., 1986—, Computer Applications for Persons with Disabilities, 1986—; adj. faculty Grad. Theol. Union, Berkeley, 1984—; Compuserve Disabilities Forum, 1988—; asst. forum adminstr.; mem. faculty Golden Gate U., 1990. Co-author: Prison Overcrowding, 1979; Community Corrections: A Plan for California, 1980; sec., bd. dirs. Spirit Rock Meditation Ctr. Active Fellowship of Reconciliation, N.Y., 1970—; co-founder Network Ctr. for Study of Ministry, San Francisco, 1982; pres. San Francisco Network Ministries, 1980-82; mem. Disabled Children's Computer Resource Group, 1988—, Springwater Ctr. for Meditative Inquiry and Retreats, 1986—. Office: PO Box 377 Lagunitas CA 94938-0377

MANN, LESTER PERRY, mathematics educator; b. Milford, Mass., May 30, 1921; s. Lester P. and Viola E. (Tracy) M.; m. Dorothy M. Davis, Oct. 11, 1947; children: Kelly P., Leslie P. BS with high honors, U. Md., 1964; MEd, U. Alaska, Anchorage, 1974; EdD, Boston U., 1983. Cert. elem. tchr., reading specialist and supr., Mass.; cert. elem. tchr., reading specialist, Alaska. Commd. 2nd lt. USAAF, 1941; advanced through grades to maj. USAF, 1954, navigator, weather officer, 1941-64; ret., 1964; resident counselor OEO-Job Corps, 1965-66; flight navigator Südflug, Braniff, Capitol and Japan Air Lines, 1966-73; instr. math., adminstr., curriculum developer U. Alaska, 1974-86, adj. instr., 1987—; instrnl. assoc. Mann Assocs., Applied Lifelong Learning, Anchorage, 1983—; instr. Anchorage Community Coll., 1974-86; asst. prof. Embry-Riddle Aero. U., Anchorage, 1987—, acad. advisor, 1987-90; mem. for remedial reading Alaska Talent Bank; vis. adult educator German Adult Edn. Assn., 1984. Mem. Math. Assn. Am., Nat. Coun. Tchrs. Math., Internat. Reading Assn., Am. Assn. Adult and Continuing Edn. (profl., past mem. nomination and election com.), Am. Meteorol. Soc., Phi Alpha Theta, Phi Kappa Phi. Home and Office: 2304 Turnagain Pky Anchorage AK 99517-1124

MANN, MICHAEL MARTIN, electronics company executive; b. N.Y.C., Nov. 28, 1939; s. Herbert and Rosalind (Kaplan) M.; m. Mariel Joy Steinberg, Apr. 25, 1965. BSEE, Calif. Inst. Tech., 1960, MSEE, 1961; PhD in Elec. Engring. and Physics, U. So. Calif., 1969; MBA, UCLA, 1984. Cert. bus. appraiser, profl. cons., mgmt. cons., lic. real estate broker, Calif. Mgr. high power laser programs office Northrop Corp., Hawthorne, Calif., 1969-76; mgr. high energy laser systems lab. Hughes Aircraft Co., El Segundo, Calif., 1976-78; mgr. E-0 control systems labs. Hughes Aircraft Co., El Segundo, 1978-83, asst. to v.p., space & strategic, 1983-84; exec. v.p. Helionetics Inc., Irvine, Calif., 1984-85, pres., chief exec. officer, 1985-86, also bd. dirs.; ptnr. Mann Kavanaugh Chernove, 1986-87; sr. cons. Arthur D. Little, Inc., 1987-88; chmn. bd., pres., CEO, Blue Marble Devel. Group, Inc., 1988—; exec. assoc. Ctr. Internat. Cooperation and Trade, 1989—; sr. assoc. Corp. Fin. Assocs., 1990—; exec. assoc. Reece and Assocs., 1991—; dir. Reece & Assocs., 1991—; mng. dir. Blue Marble Ptnrs. Ltd, 1991—; chmn. bd. dirs., CEO Blue Marble Ptnrs., 1992—; chmn., CEO, En Compass Techs., Inc., Torrance, Calif., 1994—; mem. Army Sci. Bd., Dept. Army, Washington, 1986-91; chmn. Ballistic Missile Def. Panel, Directed Energy Weapon Panel, Rsch. and New Initiatives Panel; cons. Office of Sec. of Army, Washington, 1986—, Inst. of Def. Analysis, Washington, 1978—, Dept. Energy, 1988—, Nat. Riverside Rsch. Inst., 1990—; bd. dirs. Datum, Inc.,1988—, Fail-Safe Tech., Corp., 1989-90, Safeguard Health Enterprises, Inc., 1988—, Am. Video Communications, Inc., Meck Industries, Inc., 1987-88, Decade Optical Systems, Inc., 1990—, Forum Mil. Application Directed Energy, 1992—, Am. Bus. Consultants, Inc., 1993—; chmn. bd. Mgmt. Tech., Inc. 1991—, Encompass Tech., Inc., 1994—; bd. dirs., mem. adv. bd. Micro-Frame, Inc., 1988-91; chmn. bd. HLX Laser, Inc., 1984-86; bd. dirs. Cons's. Roundtable, 1992—, Am. Bus. Cons., Inc., 1993—; rsch. assoc., mem. extension teaching staff U. So. Calif., L.A., 1964-70; chmn. Ballistic Missile Def. Subgroup, 1989-90, Tactical Directed Energy Weapons Subgroup, 1988-90; chmn., chief exec. officer Mgmt. Tech., Inc., 1991—; dir. Am. Bus. Cons., Inc., 1993—. Contbg. editor, mem. adv. bd. Calif. High-Tech Funding Jour., 1989-90; contbr. over 50 tech. articles to profl. jours.; patentee in field. Adv. com. to Engring. Sch., Calif. State U., Long Beach, 1985—; chmn. polit. affairs Am. Electronics Assn., Orange County Coun., 1986-87, mem. exec. com., 1986-88; adv. com. several Calif. congressmen, 1985—; mem. dean's coun. UCLA Grad. Sch. Mgmt., 1984-85; bd. dirs. Archimedes Circle U. So. Calif., 1983-85, Ctr. for Innovation and Entrepreneurship, 1986-90, Caltech/MIT Venture Forum, 1987-91. Hicks fellow in Indsl. Rels. Calif. Inst. Tech., 1961, Hewlett Packard fellow. Mem. So. Calif. Tech. Execs. Network, IEEE (sr.), Orange County CEO's Roundtable, Pres.' Roundtable, Nat. Assn. Corp. Dirs., Aerospace/Def. CEO's Roundtable, Am. Def. Preparedness Assn., Security Affairs Support Assn., Acad. Profl. Cons. and Advisors, Internat. Platform Assn., Inst. of Mgmt. Cons's., Pres. Assn., Nat. Assn. Corp. Dirs., Cons's. Roundtable, Pres. Assn., King Harbor Yacht Club. Republican. Home: 4248 Via Alondra Palos Verdes Peninsula CA 90274-1545 Office: Blue Marble Partners 406 Amapola Ave Ste 200 Torrance CA 90501-6229

MANN, NANCY LOUISE (NANCY LOUISE ROBBINS), entrepreneur; b. Chillicothe, Ohio, May 6, 1925; d. Everett Chaney and Pauline Elizabeth R.; m. Kenneth Douglas Mann, June 19, 1949 (div. June 1979); children: Bryan Wilkinson, Laura Elizabeth. BA in Math., UCLA, 1948, MA in Math., 1949, PhD in Biostatistics, 1965. Sr. scientist Rocketdyne Div. of Rockwell Internat., Canoga Park, Calif., 1962-75; mem. tech. staff Rockwell Sci. Ctr., Thousand Oaks, Calif., 1975-78; rsch. prof. UCLA Biomath., L.A., 1978-87; pres., CEO, owner Quality Enhancement Seminars, Inc., L.A., 1982—; pres., CEO Quality and Productivity, Inc., L.A., 1987—; curriculum adv. UCLA Ext. Dept. of Bus. and Mgmt., L.A., 1991—; mem. com. on Nat. Statistics, Nat. Acad. Scis., Washington, 1978-82; mem adv. bd. to supt. U.S. Naval Posgrad. Sch., Monterey, Calif., 1979-82. Co-author: Methods for Analysis of Reliability and Life Data, 1974; author: Keys to Excellence, 1985, The Story of the Deming Philosophy, 2d edit., 1987, 3d edit., 1989; contbr. articles to profl. jours. Recipient award IEEE Reliability Soc., 1982, ASQC Reliability Divsn., 1986. Fellow Am. Statis. Assn. (v.p. 1982-84); mem. Internat. Statis. Inst. Office: Quality and Productivity Inc 1081 Westwood Blvd # 217 Los Angeles CA 90024-2911

MANN, RACHEL KRONSTADT, writer, producer; b. Miami, July 11, 1947; d. Leonard Aaron and Sunya (Permutter) K.; m. Arnold Jack Mann, Aug. 20, 1987. BA in Econs., George Washington U., 1968; MA equivalent, U. Colo., 1973. Economist Fed. Govt., 1972; self-employed State of Md., 1973-78; computer sys. cons. PMI, N.Y., 1980-83; computer sys. engr. Chem. Bank, 1983-85; owner Mann-Made Software, 1985—. Author (screenplay) Backtrack, 1987, Block and Tackle; assoc. producer Round Numbers, 1992; patentee in design field. Mem. Writer's Guild Am., Women in Film, Scripts. Home: 12021 Wilshire Blvd # 278 Los Angeles CA 90025-1200

MANNERS, NANCY, mayor; b. Catania, Sicily, Italy; d. Gioacchino Jack and Maria Providenza (Virzi) Marasa; m. George Manners, Dec. 20, 1941; children: Gene David, Nancy Ellen Manners Sieh, Joan Alice. BA in Pub. Adminstrn., U. La Verne, 1979. Asst. city mgr. City of Covina, 1963-74; mcpl. mgmt. cons., 1975-85; mem. city coun. City of West Covina, Calif., 1984—; pres. Ind. Cities Risk Mgmt. Authority, West Covina, 1988; mayor City of West Covina, 1988-89, 92-93; pres. Ind. Cities Assn., 1989-90. Pres. Covina Coord. Coun., 1970-71, Altrusa Club of Covina-West, 1971-72, Ea. San Gabriel Valley Regional Occupation Program, 1974-76, San Gabriel Valley Planning Com., 1986-87, Mid-Valley Mental Health Coun., 1988-89; regional chmn. San Gabriel Valley Lung Assn., 1971-73; trustee Covina-Valley Unified Sch. Dist., 1973-77; foreman pro tem L.A. County Grand Jury, 1980-81; chmn. L.A. County Solid Waste Mgmt. Com., 1986-89; treas., bd. dirs. San Gabriel Valley Commerce and Cities Consortium, 1991, policy and steering com. Nat. League Cities, 1991—; chmn. employee rels. policy com. League Calif. Cities; bd. dirs. L.A. County Sanitation Dist., 1992-94, San Gabriel Valley Coun. of Govts., San Gabriel Valley Mosquito Abatement Dist., 1994—. Named Covina Citizen Yr., 1977, West Covina Citizen Yr., 1983, Woman Yr., Calif. State Legislature, 1990; recipient Woman of Distinction award Today's Woman Forum, 1988, Woman of Achievement award YWCA, 1987, 88, Community Svc. award West Covina C. of C., 1989, and others. Mem. LWV (pres. Asn Gabriel Valley 1978), Am. Heart Assn. (mem. bd. dirs.), Mcpl. Mgmt. Assocs. of So. Calif. (v.p. 1972-73), Queen of the Valley Hosp. 2100 Club (bd. dirs. 1991—), Ind. Cities Assn. (v.p. 1988, pres. 1989), West Covina Historical Soc. (v.p. 1995—), West Covina Rotary Club (bd. dirs.). Home: 734 N Eileen Ave West Covina CA 91791-1042

MANNIK, MART, medical educator; b. Tallinn, Estonia, Jan. 21, 1932; came to U.S., 1950; s. Paul and Martha (Partelpoeg) M.; Zita A. Lundell, Nov. 15, 1976. AB, Ohio No. U., 1955; MD, Western Res. U., 1959. Diplomate Am. Bd. Internal Medicine, subspecialty rheumatology. Med. intern Mass. Gen. Hosp., Boston, 1959-60, asst. resident medicine, 1960-61; guest investigator, asst. physician to hosp. Rockefeller U., N.Y.C., 1961-63; asst. prof. Rockefeller Inst., N.Y.C., 1965-67; clin. assoc. rheumatology br. Nat. Inst. Arthritis and Metabolic Diseases, Bethesda, Md., 1963-65; assoc. prof. medicine U. Wash., Seattle, 1967-73, prof. medicine, 1973—, head divsn. rheumatology, 1967—; cons. Children's Orthopaedic Hosp. and Med. Ctr., Seattle, 1968-75; attending staff Harborview Med. Ctr., Seattle, 1967—; attending physician Univ. Hosp., U. Wash., Seattle, 1967—; assoc. resident physician Rockefeller U. Hosp., N.Y.C., 1965-67; mem. arthritis tng. grants com. Nat. Inst. Arthritis and Metabolic Diseases, 1969-72; co-chmn. rsch. work group Nat. Arthritis Commn., 1975-76; cons. subspecialty com. rheumatology Am. Bd. Internal Medicine, 1975-76, mem. com. on rheumatology, 1976-80; mem. arthritis ctrs. ad hoc study sect. Nat. Inst. Arthritis, Diabetes, Digestive and Kidney Diseases, 1978, 79-80, cons. spl. projects rev. group A, 1981-84; mem. med. adv. bd. Lupus Found. Am., 1983-87; mem. Nat. Arthritis and Musculoskeletal and Skin Diseases adv. coun. NIH, 1987-90, mem. nat. rsch. plan task force, 1991. Mem. editorial bd. Arthritis and Rheumatism, 1970-82, 85-89, Kidney, 1971-74, Inflammation, 1979—, Clin. Aspects of Autoimmunity, 1988-92, Jour. Clin. Immunology, 1989-92, Scandinavian Jour. Immunology, 1991; adv. editor Immunochemistry, 1976-78, Molecular Immunology, 1979-80; contbr. articles to profl. publs. Bd. dirs., bd. govs. Arthritis Found., 1969-75, rsch. com., 1989-91, trustee, 1985-86, mem. evaluation rsch. in rheumatic diseases com., 1972. Recipient Lee Howley prize for rsch. in arthritis Arthritis Found., 1988, Disting. Alumnus award Case Western Res. U. Sch. Medicine, 1989. Fellow AAAS; mem. Am. Coll. Rheumatology (chmn. com. on postgrad. tng. in rheumatology 1967-70, chmn. membership com. 1969-76, chmn. gen. publs. com. 1972-75, mem. various coms.), Harvey Soc., Am. Assn. Immunologists (chmn. adv. bd. Manual on Clin. Immunology 1974-76), Am. Soc. Clin. Investigation (v.p. 1977-78), Western Soc. Clin. Investigation, N.W. Rheumatism Soc. (exec. com. 1969—), Western Assn. Physicians, Assn. Am. Physicians, Alpha Omega Alpha. Office: U Wash Dept Medicine RG-28 Seattle WA 98195

MANNING, ARLENE M., home care administrator; b. Liberty, N.Y., Aug. 14, 1943; d. Mark A. Schmouth and Catherine Sedlacek Schmouth Watson; m. Thomas J. Manning, Sept. 12, 1964; children: Kathleen Marie, Sean Mark. Diploma, Binghampton Gen. Hosp., 1964; BSN, U. Phoenix, 1993. Cert. Oncology. Staff nurse, charge nurse, asst. head nurse Binghamton (N.Y.) Gen. Hosp., 1964-69; staff nurse, head nurse, rehab. coord. supr. River Mede Manor, Binghamton, N.Y., 1969-74; staff nurse, rehab. Read Meml. Hosp., Hancock, N.Y., 1974-76; resident care dir. Susquehanna Nursing Home, Binghamton, N.Y., 1977-78; nurse coord. Read Meml. Hosp., Hancock, N.Y., 1978-79; staff nurse, ICU Phoenixville (Pa.) Hosp., 1980-81; asst. dir. nursing Phoenixville (Pa.) Manor, 1981-83; case mgr. Northern Chester County Nursing Svc., Phoenixville, Pa., 1983-86; staff nurse, intake coord. John C. Lincoln Home Health, Phoenix, Ariz., 1987-88, quality assurance coord., 1988-94; assoc. dir. Home Care So. Ariz., Green Valley, Ariz., 1994-95, area dir., 1995—. Mem. Ariz. Assn. Home Care. Home: 124 El Viento Green Valley AZ 85614

MANNING, CHRISTOPHER ASHLEY, finance educator, consultant; b. L.A., June 26, 1945; s. Ashley and Vivian LaVerne (Wagner) M.; m. Cathy Ann Nichols, July 30, 1977 (div. Sept. 1993). BS, San Diego State U., 1967; MBA, Northwestern U., 1971; PhD, UCLA, 1983. Corp. loan officer Security Pacific Nat. Bank, L.A., 1971-75; v.p. fin. Solitude Ski Resort, Bravo Ski Corp., Salt Lake City, 1975-78; pres. Sequoia Spa Co., L.A., 1976-79; pres. Manning and Co., L.A., 1971-86, Manning's Little Red Piano Shop, L.A., 1971-86; instr. corp. fin. Pepperdine U., L.A., 1979-83; instr. corp. fin. and real estate Long Beach State U. (Calif.), 1983-86; assoc. prof. fin. Loyola Marymount U., L.A., 1986-92, prof. fin., 1992—; mng. prin. Denver office Houlihan Valuation Advisors, 1993-94; founder, mng. prin. Manning Advisors. Mem. editl. bd. Jour. of Real Estate Rsch., 1988-90, 91-93, 94—; contbr. articles to profl. jours. 1st lt. U.S. Army, 1967-70. Decorated Bronze Star medal. Mem. Am. Real Estate Soc. (bd. dirs. 1994—), Beta Gamma Sigma, Phi Eta Sigma. Republican. Episcopalian. Home: 29438 Quailwood Dr Rancho Palos Verdes CA 90275 Office: Manning Advisors 29438 Quailwood Dr Rancho Palos Verdes CA 90275

MANNING, DANIEL RICARDO, professional basketball player; b. Hattiesburg, Miss., May 17, 1966; s. Ed Manning. Student, U. Kans. Basketball player L.A. Clippers, 1988-94, Atlanta Hawks, 1994, Phoenix Suns, 1994—. Recipient Bronze medal U.S. Olympic Basketball Team, 1988; named Most Outstanding Player NCAA Divsn. I Tournament, 1988, Naismith award, 1988, Wooden award, 1988; named to Sporting News NCAA All-Am. first team, 1987, 88, NBA All-Star Team, 1993-94. Office: Phoenix Suns 201 E Jefferson St Phoenix AZ 85004-2412

MANNING, JULIE JONES, public relations executive; b. Vancouver, Wash., May 28, 1957; d. Herman Carpenter and Margaret Janet (Stark) Jones; m. Walter Raymond Manning, Apr. 28, 1984; children: Jackson Jones, Patrick James. BA in Communications with honors, Lewis and Clark Coll., 1979; MS in Journalism, Boston U., 1982. Tchr. journalism and TV Wilson High Sch., Portland, Oreg., 1979-81; editor lifestyle sect. Ind.-Record, Helena, Mont., 1982; asst. press sec. Office of Gov. State of Oreg., Salem, 1982-83; vis. lectr. communications Lewis and Clark Coll., Portland, 1983-85; dir. devel. and cmty. rels. Good Samaritan Hosp., Corvallis, Oreg., 1985—; writing trainer George Austin & Assocs., Portland; mem. alumni bd. Lewis and Clark Coll., 1982-88, 90—; mem. exec. com. Health Acad., 1995—. Mem. Healthcare Communicators Oreg. (sec. 1985—, pres. 1987-88), Am. Soc. Hosp. Mktg. and Pub. Relations, Pub. Rels. Soc. Am. Democrat. Methodist. Office: Good Samaritan Hosp 3600 NW Samaritan Dr Corvallis OR 97330-3737

MANNING, PATRICIA KAMARAS, biochemist, process engineer, research scientist; b. Harlingen, Tex., May 26, 1953; d. Henry Julius and Audrey Marie (Klimas) Kamaras. BS, U. Ariz., 1975, MS, 1978, PhD, 1987. Grad. rsch. asst. U. Ariz., Tucson, 1976-78, sponsor grad.rsch., 1986-88; rsch. scientist Armour Dial, Inc., Scottsdale, Ariz., 1978-79; sr. chemist Armour Rsch. Ctr., Armour Food Co., Scottsdale, Ariz., 1979-86; exec. v.p., tech. dir. Manning, Batson & Assocs., Inc., Seattle, 1986-90; pres. Manning & Assocs., Gilbert, Ariz., 1989—; v.p. Quality Assurance and Rsch. Oceantrawl, Inc., Seattle, 1990—. Inventor in field. Vol. Humane Soc Ariz., 1986—, Humane Soc. Am., 1987—. Mem. Inst. Food Technologists (profl.), Nat. Fisheries Inst. (tech. subcom. 1988—, govt. rels. com. 1988—, com. chmn. Surimi tech. and scientific subcommittee 1992—), Assn. Ofcl. Analytical Chemists, Am. Oil Chemists Soc., Alaska Fisheries Devel. Found. (voting cons. 1986—, rsch & devel. grantee 1986-89), N.Y. Acad. Scis., So. Ariz. Runners Club. Roman Catholic. Office: Oceantrawl Inc 1200 Market Place Tower 2025 1st Ave Seattle WA 98121-2100

MANNING, RICHARD DALE, writer; b. Flint, Mich., Feb. 7, 1951; s. Harold J. Manning and Juanita Mayo; m. Margaret B. Saretsky, June 5, 1971 (div.); 1 child, Joshua; m. Tracy M. Stone, Sept. 8, 1990. AB in Polit. Sci., U. Mich., 1973. News dir. Sta. WATZ, Alpena, Mich., 1975-79; reporter Alpena News, 1977-79; city editor Post-Register, Idaho Falls, Idaho, 1979-81; editor, columnist Wood River Jour., Hailey, Idaho, 1981-82; city editor, columnist Times-News, Twin Falls, Idaho, 1982-85; reporter, columnist Missoulian, Missoula, Mont., 1985-89; John S. Knight fellow in journalism Stanford (Calif.) U., 1994-95. Author: Last Stand: Timber, Journalism and the Case for Humility, 1991, A Good House, 1993, Grassland, 1995. Recipient Blethen award for investigative reporting Allied Newspapers, 1986-87.

MANNINO, J. DAVIS, psychotherapist; b. Patchoque, N.Y., Sept. 27, 1949; s. Joseph I. and Adrienne Adele (Davis) M. BA magna cum laude, SUNY, Stony Brook, 1971; MSW summa cum laude, San Francisco State U., 1974; EdD in Counseling and Ednl. Psychology, U. San Francisco, 1989. Lic. psychotherapist, Calif.; lic. clin. social worker, Calif., marriage, family and child counselor. Instr. U. Malaysia, 1974-76; dir. refugee programs City San Francisco, 1979-82; instr. U. San Francisco, 1979-85; pvt. practice specializing in psychology San Francisco, Sonoma Counties, 1979—; cons. foster care Calif. State Legis., 1980, community rels., San Francisco Police Dept., 1982-87, Hospice Sonoma County, 1990, Sonoma County Mental Health, 1990; forensic task force on AIDS, San Francisco Pub. Health Dept., 1984-85; child abuse investigation supr. City of San Francisco, 1985-88; supr. Reasonable Efforts to Families Unit; project coord. Edna McConnell Clark Found. Family Mediation Demonstration Grant, 1987-88; instr. child growth and devel., death and dying, Intro. to Psychology Santa Rosa Jr. Coll., 1990—; commr. Calif. Bd. Behavioral Sci. Examiners, 1990. Contbr. articles to profl. jours.; local psychology columnist Art of Caregiving, 1986—. Mem. Am. Psychol. Assn., Nat. Assn. Social Workers (diplomate clin. social work), Orthopsychiat. Assn., Am. Assn. Counseling and Devel., Calif. Assn. Marriage Family and Child Therapists, Golden Gate Bus. Assn. (ethics com. 1986, Disting. Svc. award, 1985), Am. Assn. Marriage and Family Therapists, Nat. Register Clin. Social Workers, Lions (Helen Keller Humanitarian award, bd. dirs. San Francisco chpt. 1986). Office: 4597 18th St San Francisco CA 94114 also: PO Box 14031 San Francisco CA 94114-0031

MANNIX, KEVIN LEESE, lawyer; b. Queens, N.Y., Nov. 26, 1949; s. John Warren Sr. and Editta Gorrell M.; m. Susanna Bernadette Chiocca, June 1, 1974; children: Nicholas Chiocca, Gabriel Leese, Emily Kemper. BA, U. Va., 1971, JD, 1974. Bar: Oreg. 1974, U.S. Ct. Appeals (9th cir.) 1976, U.S. Supreme Ct. 1978, Guam 1979. Law clk. to judge Oreg. Ct. Appeals, Salem, 1974-75; asst. atty. gen. Oreg. Dept. Justice, Salem, 1975-77, Govt. of Guam, Agana, 1977-79; judge adminstrv. law Oreg. Workers' Compensation Bd., Salem, 1980-83; assoc. Lindsay, Hart, Neil & Weigler, Portland, Oreg., 1983-86; pres. Kevin L. Mannix Profl. Corp., Salem, 1986—. Chmn. St. Joseph Sch. Bd., Salem, 1981-86; pres. Salem Cath. Schs. Corp., 1985; v.p. Salem Cath. Schs. Foun., 1985-88, pres., 1988-90, 91-94, state rep., 1989—. Mem. Marion Bar Assn., Rotary (bd. dirs. East Salem 1985-89, pres. 1987-88), KC. Democrat. Home: 375 18th St NE Salem OR 97301-4307 Office: 2003 State St Salem OR 97301-4349

MANO, RONALD MAKOTO, accounting educator; b. Ogden, Utah, Aug. 28, 1942; s. Eisaku and Michi (Morio) M.; m. Cheryl Sei Shimizu, Mar. 22, 1969; children: Tiffany Taka, Patrice Michiko, Tisha Misa, Karisa Kazuko, Rhett Makoto, Darin Masao, Taryn Tamiko. BS, U. Utah, 1968, MBA, 1970; PhD, U. Nebr., 1978. CPA, cert. fraud examiner. Staff acct. Hansen, Barnett & Maxwell CPAs, Salt Lake City, 1968-70; audit sr. Ernst & Young, Salt Lake City, 1970-73; instr. acctg. U. Utah, Salt Lake City, 1973-78, asst. prof., assoc. prof., 1978-85; assoc. prof. Weber State U., Ogden, 1985-86; prof. acctg., Willard L. Eccles acctg. fellow Weber State Coll., Ogden, 1986—; vis. prof. Brigham Young U., Provo, summer 1985; Willard L. Eccles vis. prof. Weber State U., 1982-83; vis. asst. prof. U. Nebr., Lincoln, 1976-77; cons., lectr., condr. seminars in field. Contbr. articles to profl. jours. Bd. dirs. Sandy Edn. Found., Utah, 1987—; del. State Rep. Conv., Salt Lake City,1987-88. U. Utah rsch. grantee, 1979-84; Weber State U. grantee, 1982, 85, 86, 87, 88; recipient Outstanding Educator award, Utah Assn. of CPAs, 1992. Mem. AICPA, Utah Assn. CPAs (pres. South Valley chpt.), Am. Acctg. Assn., Inst. Internal Auditors, Nat. Assn. Accts. (dir. publicity 1987-88, v.p. communications 1986-87, dir. manuscripts 1988—), Western Risk and Ins. Assn., Nat. Assn. Cert. Fraud Examiners. Republican. Mormon. Home: 8640 Snowville Dr Sandy UT 84093-1768 Office: Weber State U Coll Bus and Econs Dept Acctg Ogden UT 84408

MANOLAKAS, STANTON PETER, watercolor artist; b. Detroit, July 25, 1946; s. Constantine Stamatios and Angela (Kaloyeropolous) M.; m. Barbara Soldathos, July 25, 1971. Student, Eastman Sch. of Music, 1964-65; BA in Psychology, U. So. Calif., L.A., 1969; postgrad., Calif. State U., Long Beach, 1969-70. Represented by Art Angle's Gallery, Orange, Calif., 1985-94, New Masters Gallery, Carmel, Calif., 1991—; artist Mamone Gallery, San Francisco, Maui, Hawaii, 1994—. Exhibited in group show at Zantman Galleries, Carmel, Calif., 1989, Dossin Great Lakes Mus., 1994; demonstration artist City Art exhibit Millard Sheets Gallery, L.A. County Fair, Pomona, Calif., 1994, L.A. Heritage Sq. Mus., 1994; represented in permanent collections Bechtel Industries, San Francisco, Marriott Hotel Corp., Newton, Mass., Gallagher & Heffernan Inc., San Francisco, The Borovay Group, L.A., Datum Inc., Anaheim, Calif., Tarbell Realty Inc., Costa Mesa, Calif., Wild Wings, Inc. Active AFL-CIO County Fedn. of Labor, L.A., 1982-92; mem. Saint Sophia Cathedral Choir, L.A., 1970-82,

Burbank Symphony Orch., 1973-76, Glendale (Calif.) Symphony Orch., 1975-77. Mem. Am. Fedn. of Musicians (local 47). Republican. Eastern Orthodox. Home: 2500 Las Flores Dr Los Angeles CA 90041-1021

MANOLIU-MANEA, MARIA, linguist; b. Galatz, Romania, Mar. 12, 1934; came to U.S., 1978, naturalized, 1987; d. Ion T. and Ana S. (Codescu) Manoliu; m. Ion S. Manea, Nov. 26, 1968. BA, French Coll., Galatz, 1951; MA, U. Bucharest, Romania, 1955, PhD, 1966. Asst. prof. Romance linguistics U. Bucharest, 1957-61, assoc. prof., 1961-68, prof., 1968-77; prof. linguistics U. Calif., Davis, 1978—; vis. prof. U. Chgo., 1972-74, H. Heine Universitat, Dusseldorf, 1994; cons. NEH, 1980—; mem. adv. bd. Revue Romane, Copenhagen, 1972, Roman Philology, Berkeley, Calif., 1984—, Philologica Canariensia, Spain, 1992—. Author: Sistematica Substitutelor, 1968 (Ministry of Edn. award 1968), Gramatica Comparatâ a limbilor romanice, 1971, El Estructuralismo Lingüístico, 1979, Tipologia e Historia, 1985, Gramaticâ, Pragmasemanticâ si Discurs, 1993, Discourse and Pragmatic Constraints on Grammatical Choices. A Grammar of Surprises, 1994; editor-in-chief Bull. de la S.R.L.R., Bucharest, 1975-78; contbr. articles to profl. jours. Recipient Evenimentul award for Outstanding Contbn. to Romanian Culture, 1991; grantee Internat. Com., Linguists, 1972, Fulbright Found., 1972-74, 91-92, IREX, 1993, U. Calif., 1970-90. Mem. MLA, Am. Romanian Acad. (pres. 1982-95), Academia Românâ (hon.), Soc. de Linguistique Romane, Soc. Roumaine de Linguistique Romane (v.p. 1974-78), Internat. Assn. Hist. Linguistics, Linguistics Soc. Am., Internat. Assn. Pragmatics, Romanian Studies Assn. Am. (pres. 1986-88). Office: U Calif Dept French and Italian 509 Sproul Hall Davis CA 95616

MANOOGIAN, TERRI LAWRENCE, dietitian, food service administrator; b. Las Vegas, Apr. 10, 1956; d. Clifford Jex and Carolyn (Carter) Lawrence; m. Cary Michael Manoogian, May 21, 1983; children: Kristin Nicole, Ashley Lauren. Student, U. Utah, 1974-76; BS, U. Nev., Reno, 1980. Registered dietitian. Clin. dietitian Los Angeles County, L.A., 1982-83; trayline mgr. Morrison's Custom Mgmt., L.A., 1983-84; food svc. dir. Morrison's Hospitality Group, Van Nuys, Calif., 1984-87, Morrison's Health Care Group, Sylmar, Calif., 1987—. Mem. Am. Dietetic Assn., Calif. Restaurant Assn. Office: Morrison's Health Care Grp 14445 Olive View Dr Rm 1c112 Sylmar CA 91342-1438

MANOOGIAN, WILLIAM, lawyer; b. Fresno, Calif., Mar. 29, 1946; s. Morris Anthony and Doris Eunice (Parigian) M.; m. Margaret Ann Solt, Oct. 18, 1975; children: Nicole-Helene, Claire-Louise. BA, Stanford U., 1968; postgrad., U. Paris, 1968-70; JD, Am. U., Washington, 1973. Legis. atty. Rep. Nat. Com., Washington, 1973-75; minority counsel Civil Svc. com. Civic Svc. com. Ho. of Reps., Washington, 1975-83; spl. counsel Dept. of Edn., Washington, 1983-84; counsel to the amb. Dept. of State, Mexico City, 1984-86; cons. to Dr. Armand Hammer Occidental Petroleum, L.A., 1986-87; gen. atty. Criminal divsn., Dept. of Justice, Washington, 1987-89, Immigration and Naturalization Svc., San Diego, 1989—; advisor to William Saroyan, Paris, 1969-70. Contbr. articles to profl. jours. Legal advisor to Rep. campaigns, Washington, 1974. Mem. D.C. Bar Assn., Chi Psi. Armenian Orthodox. Home: 13771 Mercado Dr Del Mar CA 92014-3415 Office: Justice Dept 880 Front St Ste 1234 San Diego CA 92101-8803

MANOS, CHRISTOPHER ALEXANDER, crime prevention specialist; b. Bklyn., Sept. 16, 1956; s. Alexander Christopher and Eleanore H. (Marx) M. AAS in Police Sci., Community Coll. of USAF, 1980; BS in Criminal Justice, Mercy Coll., 1982; MA in Mgmt., Webster U., 1985. Asst. leasing dir. Am. Can Co., Greenwich, Conn., 1980-82; sr. crime prevention officer Arapahoe County Sheriff's Dept, Littleton, Colo., 1982—. Author: Using Magic in Drug and Alcohol Prevention Presentations, 1991 (Sutherland award 1991). Mem. Cherry Creek Community Task Force, Englewood, Colo., 1988-92; mem. CAP, Maxwell AFB, 1968—; adviser Boy Scouts Am., Dallas, 1984-90. With USAF, 1975-79. Mem. Colo. Crime Prevention Assn. (v.p. 1984-92, Practitioner of Yr. 1984, 88, Pres.'s award 1989), Internat. Soc. Crime Prevention Practitioners (com. mem. 1988—, George B. Sunderland Lifetime Achievement award 1991, bd. dirs. and regional dir. 1988—, 2d v.p. 1993—), Am. Soc. for Indsl. Security (com. mem. 1989-90, Office of Yr. 1990), Mile High Magicians Soc. (pres. 1988-91). Home: PO Box 714 Littleton CO 80160-0714 Office: Arapahoe Co Sheriffs Dept 5686 S Court Pl Littleton CO 80120-1205

MANOUGIAN, EDWARD, physician; b. Highland Park, Mich., Apr. 11, 1929; s. George Krikor and Vera Varsen (Jernukian) M. BS, Wayne U., 1951; MD, U. Mich., 1955. Intern San Bernardino County (Calif.) Charity Hosp., 1955-56; house physician Patton (Calif.) State Hosp., 1956-60; NIH postdoctoral fellow in biophysics U. Calif., 1960-62; rsch. assoc. Lawrence Berkeley (Calif.) Lab., 1962-77; house physician Peralta Hosp., Oakland, Calif., 1979-81; assoc. med. dir. Hospice Contra Costa, Pleasant Hill, Calif., 1982-90, med. dir., 1991-92; rschr. Ocular Hazards Divsn. U.S. Army. Contbr. articles to profl. jours. Capt. M.C., U.S. Army, 1957-59; lt. col. USAR, 1985-94, Persian Gulf, 1990-91. Mem. AAAS, Acad. Hospice Physicians, Am. Math. Soc., Alameda Contra Costa County Med. Soc., Calif. Med. Soc. Home and Office: 1517 Summit Rd Berkeley CA 94708-2216

MANOUKIAN, RITA CHAKE, sales executive; b. Manhasset, N.Y., Feb. 14, 1964; d. Aram Manoukian and Astrid Tchalekian Torosian. BS, St. John's U., 1985. Sales system analyst Bristol-Myers Products, N.Y.C., 1987-88, sales devel. asst., 1988-89; sales and promotion devel. mgr. Bristol-Myers Products, Bridgewater, N.J., 1989-90; div. sales devel. mgr. Bristol-Myers Products, Irvine, Calif., 1990, mgr. category devel., 1990-92; dir. key account sales Intactix Internat., Manhattan Beach, Calif., 1992-94; regional v.p. Intactix Internat., Laguna Niguel, Calif., 1994—.

MANSERGH, GORDON DWIGHT, health promotion and health behavior researcher, consultant; b. St. Paul, Aug. 7, 1962; s. Gerald Gordon and Nancy Helen (Stuessy) M. BA, Gustavus Adolphus Coll., 1984; MA, Mich. State U., 1986; MEd, Boston U., 1991; postgrad., U. So. Calif., 1992—. Substance abuse counselor NORCAP Lodge, Foxboro, Mass., 1986-87; asst. dir. student affairs Chamberlayne Coll., Boston, 1987; asst. dir. orientation, off-campus svcs. Boston U., 1987-90, founding dir. Wellness Ctr., 1990-92; rsch. asst. U. So. Calif. Inst. for Prevention Rsch., 1992—; grant writer, program evaluator; cons. EMT Calif. State Drug Prevention Tech. Assistance Project; rsch. asst. Kaiser Permanente So. Calif., 1992—, U.S. Ctrs. Disease Control and Prevention, 1995; co-founder, coord. Pasadena Area Colls. Together in Drug Prevention, 1993—; dir. PREVENT Consortium, 1991-92; drug prevention planning com. U.S. Dept. Edn., 1991-94; dir. Project DART, 1990-92; mem. N.W. Pasadena Health Coalition, L.A. Adolescent HIV Consortium, Mass. Coun. on Compulsive Gambling Prevention Coalition; chair Boston U. Substance Abuse Task Force, 1989-92; founding chair Boston AIDS Consortium Coll. Cmty. Edn. Com., 1988-90. Editor, co-author: The Wellness Resource Book, 1991, Adventures in Prevention, 1992, Wellnews, 1990-92. Vol. community svc. AIDS Action Com. Mass., Calif. AIDS Ride, AIDS Project L.A., Calif. AIDS Ride. Named Outstanding Young Man of Am., 1986-87; recipient Nat. Disting. Svc. Registry award, 1989-90; honoree Guild of St. Ansgar Gustavus Adolphus Coll., 1984; fellow Mich. State U., 1984-85. Mem. Am. Coll. Pers. Assn. (dir. wellness com. 1990-92), Am. Coll. Health Assn., Am. Psychol. Assn., Am. Pub. Health Assn., Soc. for Behavioral Medicine, Pi Lambda Theta.

MANSFIELD, ELAINE SCHULTZ, molecular geneticist, automation specialist; b. Boulder, Colo., Apr. 20, 1954; d. William Varley and Juanita M. (Zingg) M.; m. Gary G. Schultz, Nov. 24, 1983; children: Matthew, Greggory Mark. BA in Molecular Biology, San Jose State U., 1975; MS in Genetics, U. Calif., Berkeley, 1978, PhD in Genetics, 1983. Diplomate Am. Bd. Med. Genetics (fellow), Am. Bd. Clin. Molecular Genetics. Customer cons. IntelliGenetics, Mountain View, Calif., 1980-81; staff scientist Applied Biosys., Foster City, Calif., 1978-80; sr. staff scientist Molecular Dynamics, Sunnyvale, Calif., 1993—; lectr. in the field. Author (with others) Mutations in the Human Genome, 1993; contb. to profl. jours.; patentee in field. U. Calif. grant, Chancellors Patent Fund grant U. Calif. Mem. AAAS, Am. Soc. Human Genetics, Am. Soc. Histocompatibility and Immunogenetics, Women in Sci., Black Masque (pres. 1975). Office: Molecular Dynamics 928 E Arques Ave Sunnyvale CA 94086-4519

MANSFIELD, ROGER LEO, astronomy and space publisher; b. Boston, Feb. 18, 1944; s. Roy D. Sr. and Nellie E. (Venzlowski) M.; m. Alice Lee Waring, Nov. 1, 1969 (div. Mar. 1983); 1 child, Jason Benjamin; m. Karen June Sprout, June 27, 1987. BS in Chemistry with high honors., U. Cin., 1965; MA in Math., U. Nebr., 1972. Chemist Lockheed Missiles & Space Co., Palo Alto, Calif., 1967; orbital analyst USAF, Offutt AFB, Nebr., 1967-73; instr. Dept. of Math. USAF Acad., Colorado Springs, Colo., 1973-74; aerospace engr. Philco-Ford Corp., Palo Alto, 1974-75, Data Dynamics Inc., Mountain View, Calif., 1975-76, Ford Aerospace & Communications Corp., Colorado Springs, 1976-90; prin. engr. Loral Aerospace Corp., Colorado Springs, 1990-95; owner Astron. Data Svc., 1976—. Pub. Skywatcher's Almanac, Local Planet Visibility Report, Photographer's Almanac, Comparative Ephemeris, Space Birds; contbr. articles to profl. jours. Mem. Am. Astron. Soc., Math. Assn. Am., Internat. Planetarium Soc., Rocky Mountain Planetarium Assn. Home and Office: 3922 Leisure Ln Colorado Springs CO 80917-3502

MANSINGHKA, SURENDRA KUMAR, finance educator; b. Kanpur, India, Aug. 3, 1944; came to U.S., 1966; s. Badri Prasad and Parmeshwari (Devi) M.; m. Asha Goel, Dec. 30, 1976; 1 child, Vikash. B. Commerce, U. Calcutta, 1973; MS, UCLA, 1968, PhD, 1971. Asst. prof. U. Calif., Riverside, 1970-75; asst. prof. San Francisco State U., 1975-76, assoc. prof., 1976-80, prof., 1980—; cons. several profit and non-profit corps., 1975—. Contbg. author: Readings in Mergers and Acquisitions. Mem. Am. Fin. Assn., Fin. Mgmt. Assn. Office: San Francisco State U 1600 Holloway Ave San Francisco CA 94132-1722

MANSON, MALCOLM HOOD, educational administrator; b. Melton Mowbray, Leicester, Eng., May 31, 1938; s. James Milne and Williamina (Hood) M.; m. Snowden Sandra Johnston. BA, Oxford U., Eng., 1961, MA, 1964. Tchr. The Choate Sch., Wallingford, Conn., 1961-63, adminstr., 1963-69; headmaster Marin Country Day Sch., Corte Madera, Calif., 1969-82, Ore. Episcopal Sch., Portland, Oreg., 1982-90; canon headmaster Cathedral Sch. for Boys, San Francisco, 1990—. Mem. Calif. Assn. Ind. Schs. (bd. dirs., v.p. 1976-80), Pacific N.W. Assn. Ind. Schs. (pres. 1985-86). Episcopal. Office: Cathedral Sch for Boys 1275 Sacramento St San Francisco CA 94108-1910

MANSOOR, CHRISTINE MARIE-DOMINIQUE, television producer; b. L.A., June 10, 1968; d. Henry and Roxane (Vlahos) M. BA in Radio, TV, Broadcasting, Calif. State U., Northridge, 1991. Producer A Current Affair, L.A., 1989—. Author: The Scandal of the Century - The Mansoor Amarna Expose, 1992. Office: A Current Affair 5746 W Sunset Blvd Los Angeles CA 90028-8588

MANSOOR, JOHN JIRIUS, sports management executive; b. New Ulm, Minn., July 13, 1955; s. Khalil Audi Mansoor and Audre Helen (Woebke) McGranahan. AA, Am. River Jr. Coll., Sacramento, 1975; BA, Ohio State U., 1978; MA, U. Calif., Davis, 1979. Coach U. Calif., Davis, 1979-81; exec. dir. Sacramento Long Distance Running Assn., 1984—; chmn. Pacific Assn./The Athletics Congress, Sacramento, 1980—. Bd. dirs. Am. River Parkway Commn., Sacramento, 1984-85, Save the Am. River Assn., 1986-88. Home: 800 Bonita Dr El Dorado Hills CA 95762

MANSOUR, TAG ELDIN, pharmacologist; b. Belkas, Egypt, Nov. 6, 1924; came to U.S., 1951, naturalized, 1956; s. Elsayed and Rokaya (Elzayat) M.; m. Joan Adela MacKinnon, Aug. 6, 1955; children—Suzanne, Jeanne, Dean. DVM, Cairo U., 1946; PhD, U. Birmingham, Eng., 1949, DSc, 1974. Lectr. U. Cairo, 1950-51; Fulbright instr. physiology Howard U., Washington, 1951-52; sr. instr. pharmacology Case Western Res. U., 1952-54; asst. prof., assoc. prof. pharmacology La. State U. Med. Sch., New Orleans, 1954-61; assoc. prof., prof. pharmacology Stanford U. Sch. Medicine, 1961—, chmn. dept. pharmacology, 1977-91, Donald E. Baxter prof., 1977—; cons. USPHS, WHO, Nat. Acad. Scis.; Mem. adv. bd. Med. Sch., Kuwait U.; Heath Clarke lectr. London Sch. Hygiene and Tropical Medicine, 1981. Contrbr. sci. articles to profl. jours. Commonwealth Fund fellow, 1965; Macy Found. scholar NIMR, London, 1982. Fellow AAAS; mem. Am. Soc. Pharmacology and Exptl. Therapeutics, Am. Soc. Biol. Chemists, Am. Heart Assn., Sierra Club, Stanford Faculty Club. Office: 300 Pasteur Dr Stanford CA 94305-5332

MANSOURI, LOTFOLLAH, opera stage director; b. Tehran, June 15, 1929; arrived in Can., 1976; s. Hassan and Mehri (Jalili) M.; m. Marjorie Anne Thompson, Sept. 18, 1954; 1 child, Shireen Melinda. AB, UCLA, 1953. Asst. prof. UCLA, 1957-60; resident stage dir. Zurich Opera, 1960-65; chief stage dir. Geneva Opera, 1965-75; gen. dir. Can. Opera Co., Toronto, Ont., 1976-88, San Francisco Opera, 1988—; dramatic coach Music Acad. West, Santa Barbara, Calif., 1959; dir. dramatics Zurich Internat. Opera Studio, 1961-65, Centre Lyrique, Geneva, 1967-72; artistic adviser Tehran Opera, 1973-75; opera adviser Nat. Arts Centre, Ottawa, Ont., 1977; v.p. Opera America, 1979—; operatic cons. dir. Yes, Giorgio, MGM, 1981; dir. opera sequence for film Moonstruck (Norman Jewison), 1987. Guest dir. opera cos. including Met. Opera, San Francisco Opera, N.Y.C. Opera, Lyric Opera of Chgo., Houston Grand Opera, La Scala, Covent Garden, Australian Opera, Vienna Staatsoper, Vienna Volksoper, Salzburg Festival, Amsterdam Opera, Holland Festival, Nice (France) Opera, Festival D'Orange, France; co-author: An Operatic Life, 1982 (initiated above-stage projection of Surtitles (a simultaneous transl. of opera) 1983). Mem. Am. Guild Mus. Artists, Can. Actors Equity Assn.

MANTLE, LARRY EDWARD, radio director; b. L.A., Jan. 12, 1959; s. John Randall Mantle and Carole Jean (Hubka) Morse; m. Kristen Hernandez, Aug. 8, 1993. BA, So. Calif. Coll., 1979. Program and news dir. Sta. KPCC-FM, Pasadena, L.A., Calif., 1984—; host Larry Mantle's AirTalk Sta. KPCC-FM, 1985—; moderator, host Sta. KPAS-TV, Pasadena, 1986—; prof. Pasadena City Coll., 1986—; moderator UN Assn., Pasadena, 1987—, Calif. Inst. Tech., Pasadena, 1986—; advisor Radio West, L.A., 1992—. Recipient Award of Excellence, Greater L.A. Press Club, 1982, Gold Medal award Coun. Advancement & Support Edn., 1989, Diamond award So. Calif. Cable Assn., 1990. Mem. Radio & TV News Assn. So. Calif. (dir. 1987—, v.p. 1993—, sec. 1987-89, Cut-In newsletter editor 1989—, Golden Mike awards 1986, 87, 88), Soc. Profl. Journalists, AP Calif. and Nev. (Excellence awards 1981, 82, 87), Radio-TV News Dirs. Assn. Office: Sta KPCC-FM 1570 E Colorado Blvd Pasadena CA 91106-2003

MANTOR-CLARYSSE, JUSTINE CLAIRE, fine arts educator; b. Neenah, Wis., Aug. 12, 1943; d. Jack Allen and Ann Elizabeth (Suchy) Mantor; m. John Allan Wantz, June 18, 1968 (div. 1983); m. Omer T. Clarysse, July 28, 1994. BFA, Sch. Art Inst. Chgo., 1967; MA, No. Ill. U., 1969, MFA, 1971. Assoc. prof. fine arts Loyola U., Chgo., 1971-93, dir. women's studies, 1982-83; represented by Artisimo Gallery, Scottsdale, Ariz.; instr. Coll. of DuPage, Glen Ellyn, Ill., 1971-72, North Shore Art League, Winnetka, Ill., 1972-73, DuPage Art League, Wheaton, Ill., 1972; gallery dir. Water Tower Gallery, Loyola U., Chgo., 1973-82; lectr. Ill. Conf. L.Am. Studies, U. Ill., 1990, Chantanqua Conf. Fgn. Lang. Tchrs., Pheasant Run, Ill., 1991, U. Wis., Madison, 1991, Mid-Am. Coll. Art Assn., Madison, Wis., 1991, 92, Mid-Am. South-East Coll. Art Assn., Birmingham, Ala, 1992, Nat. Coll. Art Assn., Seattle, 1993, N.Y., 94. Solo exhbns. include U. Ill. Med. Ctr., Chgo., 1979, Springfield (Ill.) Art Assn., 1979, John Nelson Bergstrom Art Ctr. and Mus., Neenah, Wis., 1980, Aurora (Ill.) Coll., 1980, Arc Gallery, Chgo., 1981, 83, Illini Union Gallery, Champaign, Ill., 1982, Fountain Hills Cmty. Ctr., Ariz., 1990, Downtown Gallery, Phoenix, 1994, others; permanent collections include Ill. State Mus., Rockford Mus., Kemper Ins. Co., Gillman Gallery, Chgo., Byer Mus., No. Ill. U. Student Ctr. and Fine Arts Dept., Loyola U. Gallery Coll., Chgo., others. Named Best of Show, Fountain Hills Art Fair, Ariz., 1993, 94, Best of Show and 1st Pl. Acrylic, Juried Competition, 1994, Fountain Hills Art Fair; grantee Ill. Arts Coun., 1978, Ill. Art Coun./Mellon Found., 1979, Nat. Humanities Assn., 1980, Ill. Humanities Coun., 1980-81. Mem. AAUP, Nat. Coll. Art Assn. (lectr. 1993), Mid-Am. Coll. Art Assn. (lectr. 1991, 92), Internat. Friends of Transformative Art (co-editor The Transformer newsletter) Fountain Hills Art League, Ariz. Artists' Guild, Chgo. Artists' Coalition, Sch. Art Inst. Chgo. Alumni Assn., Ariz. Women's Caucus for Art (pres. 1994). Democrat. Presbyterian. Office: Loyola U Chgo Crown Ctr Humanities 6525 N Sheridan Rd Chicago IL 60626-5311

MANZ, MICHAEL PAUL, child psychiatrist; b. Mpls., Jan. 8, 1948; s. Paul Otto and Ruth Marie (Mueller) M.; m. Patricia Sue Stanwood, June 19, 1971; children: Erik, David, Rachael. BS, Augsburg Coll., 1970; MD, Baylor U., 1973. Resident in adult psychiatry Pacific Med. Ctr., San Francisco, 1974-76; fellow in child psychiatry U. Oreg. Health Sci. Ctr., Portland, 1977-79; staff child psychiatrist Cmty. Mental Health Ctr., Spokane, Wash., 1980-85; pvt. practice Spokane, 1980—; med. dir. Sacred Heart Med. Ctr., Spokane, 1985—; owner, winemaker Mountain Dome Winery, Spokane. Lutheran. Office: Marycliff Inst 807 W 7th Ave Spokane WA 99204-2808

MANZANARES, DENNIS, lawyer; b. Santa Fe, N.Mex., Sept. 20, 1950; s. Ercilia E. Martinez. BA, Coll. Santa Fe, 1973; JD, Georgetown U., 1976. Bar: N.Mex. 1976, U.S. Dist. Ct. N.Mex. 1976, U.S. Ct. Appeals (10th cir.) 1979, U.S. Supreme Ct. 1981. Asst. pub. defender State of N.Mex., Albuquerque, 1976-79; gen. counsel to state auditor State of N.Mex., Santa Fe, 1979-82; sole practice Santa Fe, 1983-90; town atty. Taos, N.Mex., 1990-94; sole practice, 1994—; of counsel Scott Sanger Law Offices; instr. U. N.Mex., Taos; accident prevention counselor FAA; adj. instr. FEMA, N.Mex. Dept. Pub. Safety; instr. Grad. and Undergrad. Programs U. Phoenix. V.p. N.Mex. Young Dems., 1979-82; judge Marriage Tribunal Archdiocese Santa Fe, 1978-85; air and field coordinator N.Mex. State Police Search and Rescue, 1985-95; mem. jud. council N.Mex. Dem. Party, 1981-85, Santa Fe Airport Adv. Bd., 1985-88. Mem. ABA, N.Mex. Bar Assn. (chmn. pub. advocacy sect. 1983-84, so. regional v.p.), Lawyer-Pilot Bar Assn., Nat. Transp. Bd. Bar Assn., Nat. Dist. Attys. Assn., N.Mex. Civil Air Patrol (comdr., legal officer S.W. region 1983-91, comdr. Santa Fe squadron 1985-87, Outstanding Sr. Mem. award 1983-84, Gill Robb Wilson award 1985, Search & Rescue Find award 1984-85), N.Mex. Pilots Assn. (v.p. 1986-92, Leadership and Safety awards 1985—), N.Mex. Woodworkers Guild (v.p. 1983-85), Young Astronaut Program (chpt. sponsor). Home: 346 Vegas de Taos Circle Taos NM 87571 Office: PO Box 1628 Taos NM 87571-1628

MANZO, ANTHONY JOSEPH, painter; b. Saddle Brook, N.J., Apr. 25, 1928; s. Michael and Jennie (Spinneli) M.; m. Ruth Hendricks, Jan. 27, 1956; children—Kathleen, Joanne. Student NAD, N.Y.C., 1946-49, Phoenix Sch. Design, N.Y.C., 1955-58; studied privately with Salvatore Lascari N.A., 1945-65. Freelance comml. illustrator, 1956-59; painter and sculptor, 1958—; instr. pvt. art classes Renaissance Sch. Art, N.J. Served with U.S. Army, 1950-52. Recipient Ray A. Jones award N.J. Painters and Sculptors Soc., 1976. Roman Catholic. Address: PO Box 2708 Taos NM 87571-2708

MANZOR, LILLIAN, humanities educator; b. Ciego de Avila, Cuba, Dec. 20, 1956; came to U.S., 1968; d. Nelson and Olga (Díaz-Duque) M.; m. Daniel Correa, Dec. 9, 1994. BA, U. Miami, Fla., 1978; MA, U. So. Calif., 1982, PhD, 1988. Vis. prof. Notre Dame U., South Bend, Ind., 1983-85, Purdue U., West Lafayette, Ind., 1985-88; asst. prof. U. Calif., Irvine, 1988—; lit. cons. Internat. Sch. Latin Am. Theater, Havana, Cuba. Author: Borges/Escher, Cobra/Cobra, 1994. Advisor Mecha, U. Calif., Irvine, 1991, mem. Global Peace & Conflict Studies, 1991—; mem. CISPES, Ind., 1983-88. Summer grantee NEH, 1989; residence fellow Humanities Rsch. Inst., Irvine, 1992-93; rsch. grantee SCR-43 Calif. Legis., 1992—; travel grantee Am. Coun. Learned Socs., 1990. Mem. Modern Lang. Assn., Am. Comparative Lit. Assn., Am. Studies Assn., Latin Am. Studies Assn., Nat. Coun. Rsch. Women. Office: U Calif Dept Comparative Lit Irvine CA 92717

MAO, KENT KEQIANG, engineering executive; b. Beijing, People's Republic of China, July 11, 1956; came to U.S., 1984; s. Zhicheng and Shuqing (Dai) M.; m. Yue Zhang, Aug. 20, 1983; children: Jennifer May, Jessica Mary. BCE, Tsinghua U., Beijing, 1982; MS, Colo. State U., 1985, PhD, 1990. Cert. profl. engr., Colo., Wash. High sch. physics tchr. Beijing #32 High Sch., 1975-78; rsch. engr. Inst. Water Conservancy and Hydroelectric Power Rsch., Beijing, 1982-84; water resources engr. Water and Wastewater Utilities, Ft. Collins, Colo., 1986-91; sr. project water resources engr. HDR Engring., Inc., Bellevue, Wash., 1991-93; v.p. KCM, Inc., Seattle, 1993—. Co-author: Environmental Engineer's Handbook; contbr. articles to profl. jours. Pres. Chinese Student Assn., Colo. State U., 1985-86; pres. Tsinghua Alumni Assn. in Am., 1991-94. Named Outstanding Tchr. of Beijing Dept. Edn. of Beijing, 1976; recipient Rsch. Scholarship award Inst. Water Conservancy and Hydroelectric Power Rsch., Beijing, 1984. Mem. ASCE (co-chmn. internat. Asian affairs com. 1992—), Am. Water Resources Assn. (vice chair internat. affairs com.). Home: 17014 NE 38th Pl Bellevue WA 98008-6120 Office: KCM Inc 1917 1st Ave Seattle WA 98101-1010

MAPES, JEFFREY ROBERT, journalist; b. San Francisco, Nov. 21, 1954; s. James Robert and Phyllis June (Bloemker) M.; m. Karen Jane Minkel, Aug. 20, 1978; children: Katharine, James. BA, San Jose State U., 1976. Reporter Napa (Calif.) Register, 1976-79; Washington corr. Scripps League Newspapers, 1979-83; reporter The Oregonian, Portland, 1984-87, chief polit. reporter, 1987—. Office: The Oregonian 1320 SW Broadway Portland OR 97201-3469

MAPLES, JAMES ALFRED, software consultant; b. Somerville, N.J., Apr. 1, 1950; s. Francis Kirby and Lois (Cooley) M.; m. Patricia Anne Levinson, June 15, 1980; children: Elizabeth Anne, Jennifer Lynn. BA magna cum laude, Harvard U., 1972; MS in Elec. Engring., Stanford U., 1980, PhD, 1985. Software design engr. Hewlett-Packard, Avondale, Pa., 1972-75; electronics design engr. Ronan Engring., Woodland Hills, Calif., 1975-77, Hewlett-Packard, Palo Alto, Calif., 1977-78; project mgr. Adept Tech., San Jose, Calif., 1984-87; software cons. Maples & Assocs., Palo Alto, 1988—. Nat. Merit scholar, 1968-72; NSF grad. fellow, 1978-81.

MARAFINO, VINCENT NORMAN, aerospace company executive; b. Boston, June 8, 1930; m. Doris Marilyn Vernall, June 15, 1958; children: Marli Ann, Sheri Louise, Wendi Joan. A.B. in Acctg. and Econs., San Jose State Coll., 1951; M.B.A., Santa Clara U., 1964. Chief acct. Am. Standard Advance Tech. Lab., Mountain View, Calif., 1956-59; with Lockheed Missiles & Space Co., Sunnyvale, Calif., 1959-70, asst. dir. fin. ops., 1968-70; asst. controller Lockheed Corp., Burbank, Calif., 1970-71, v.p., controller, 1971-77, sr. v.p. fin., 1977-83, exec. v.p., chief fin. and administrv. officer, 1983-88, vice chmn. bd., chief fin. and adminstrv. officer, 1988—, also dir.; bd. dirs. Lockheed Missiles & Space Co., Inc.; chmn. bd. dirs. Lockheed Fin. Corp. Trustee Holy Cross Med. Ctr., Mission Hills, Calif. Served with USAF, 1953-55. Mem. Fin. Execs. Inst., AICPAs, North Ranch Country Club. Office: Lockheed Corp 4500 Park Granada Calabasas CA 91399-0001

MARAIS, HENRI JOHN, cardiologist; b. Begobo, Katanga, Zaire, Jan. 3, 1949; naturalized U.S. Citizen, 1984; s. Henri Ernest and Faith (Stevens) M.; m. Deirdre Davies; 1 child, Ryan Alistair John. MB, ChB, Stellenbosch U., Belville, South Africa, 1972. Diplomate Am. Bd. Internal Medicine, Am. Bd. Cardiology, Am. Bd. Critical Care Medicine, Am. Bd. Pacing, Am. Bd. Geriatric Medicine. Rotating intern North York Branson Hosp., Toronto, Can., 1973-74; tropical medicine intern Songa Hosp. and Leprosarium, Zaire, 1974-76; resident internal medicine, clin. fellow Harvard Med. Sch., Brigham & Women's Hosp., Boston, 1976-77, asst. and sr. resident physician, 1977-78; cardiology fellow Beth Israel Hosp., Boston, 1980-82; emergency rm. physician, internist locum tenens Milford & Whitinsville Hosp., Franklin Health Ctr., 1977-79; relif internist Guam Meml. Hosp., Guam, 1979-80; electrocardiology instr. Beth Israel Hosp., Boston, 1981-82; staff cardiologist, family practice cardiology instr., asst. chief cardiology to acting chief cardiology New England Meml. Hosp., Stoneham, Mass., 1982-85; cardiologist Loma Linda Faculty Med. Group, Sun City, Calif., 1985-90; staff cardiologist, assoc. prof. medicine Loma Linda U., Calif., 1987-94; asst. adj. prof. medicine Baylor Coll. Medicine, 1987-94; cons. cardiologist Beaver Med. Group, 1994—; patentee in the field. Contbd. to numerous jours. Fellow Am. Coll. Cardiology, Am. Coll. Chest Physicians; mem. Am. Coll. Physicians., Human Undersea and Hyperbaric Med. Soc. Home: 40070 Pine Bench Rd Oak Glen CA 92399 Office: Loma Linda U Dept Cardiology Loma Linda CA 92354

MARANGI, VITO ANTHONY, SR., claim administrator; b. Utica, N.Y., Jan. 1, 1932; s. Mary Margaret Lokey, Apr. 10, 1960 (div. July 1973); children: Vito Anthony Jr., Vanetta Gayle, Gregory Alan; m. Diann Louise Bunch, Apr. 11, 1987. BS, SUNY, Potsdam, 1958. Asst. regional claims mgr. Hartford Ins. Group, Fresno, Calif., 1958-67; supervising adjuster Underwriters Adjusting Co., Fresno, 1967-70; home office claim supr. Meritplan Ins. Co., Newport Beach, Calif., 1970-71; appeals referee State of Nev., Reno and Carson City, 1971-73, 76-79; br. mgr. Brown Bros. Adjusters, Reno, 1974-87; ind. ins. adjuster Tony Marangi, Adjuster, Carson City, 1987—; vice chmn., bd. trustees Carson-Tahoe Hosp., 1991—. Scout master Boy Scouts Am., Utica, N.Y., Fresno, Calif., Carson City, 1953-85. With USN, 1949-53. Mem. Nev. State Claims Assn. (pres., v.p., treas., sec.), No. Nev. Claims Assn. (pres., v.p., treas., sec.), Nat. Assn. of Adminstrv. Law Judges, Internat. Assn. of Arson Investigators (Nev. chpt.), Carson City Elks Lodge, VFW, Carson City C. of C. (bus. edn. com. 1987—, transp. com. 1987—). Home: PO Box 843 Carson City NV 89702-0843 Office: Carson Tahoe Hosp PO Box 2168 Carson City NV 89702-2168

MARAVICH, MARY LOUISE, realtor; b. Fort Knox, Ky., Jan. 4, 1951; d. John and Bonnie (Balandzic) M. AA in Office Adminstrn., U. Nev., Las Vegas, 1970; BA in Sociology and Psychology, U. So. Calif., 1972; grad. Realtors Inst. Cert. residential specialist. Adminstrv. asst. dept. history U. So. Calif., L.A., 1972-73; asst. pers. supr. Corral Coin Co., Las Vegas, 1973-80; realtor, Americana Group div. Better Homes and Gardens, Las Vegas, 1980-85, Jack Matthews and Co., 1985-93, Realty Execs., Las Vegas, 1993—. Mem. Nev. Assn. Realtors (cert. realtors inst.), Las Vegas Bd. Realtors, Nat. Assn. Realtors, Women's Council of Realtors, Am. Bus. Women's Assn., NAFE, Million Dollar Club, Pres.'s Club. Office: Realty Execs 1903 S Jones Blvd # 100 Las Vegas NV 89102-1260

MARCELYNAS, RICHARD CHADWICK, management consultant; b. New London, Conn., Aug. 21, 1937; s. Anthony F. and Elizabeth A. (Chadwick) M.; m. Betty A. Forray, July 1, 1961; children: Michael R., Thomas R. BA in Bus. Adminstrn., U. Wash., 1961; postgrad. Seattle U., 1971-72. Mgmt. trainee, installation foreman Pacific Bell, Fullerton, Calif., 1964-65; cost acct. Scott Paper Co., Everett, Wash., 1965-68; asst. v.p. personnel and adminstrn. Nat. Pub. Service Ins. Co., Seattle, 1968-77; mgr. indsl. relations Heath Tecna Precision Structures Inc., Kent, Wash., 1978-85; mgmt. con. Pilon Mgmt. Co., Seattle, 1985-90; pers. adminstr. Peninsula Group Olympia, Wash., 1990-94; mgmt. cons., Olympia, 1994—; cons., lectr. Served to maj. USMCR, 1961-77. Decorated commendations for bravery and tech. expertise, 1962, 63, 64; recipient Seattle chpt. Pacific N.W. Personnel Mgrs. Assn. Bd. Dirs. award, 1975. Mem. Am. Soc. Personnel Adminstrs., Pacific N.W. Personnel Mgrs. Assn. (past pres. Tacoma chpt.). Office: 623 Sherman St SW Olympia WA 98502-5454

MARCH, GEORGE PATRICK, retired naval officer; b. Corvallis, Oreg., Jan. 16, 1924; s. George Clayton and Margaret Isobel (Motley) M.; m. Betty Eileen Saum, Dec. 20, 1946; children: Maureen, Terese, Margaret. B.S., U.S. Naval Acad., 1946; M.A., Georgetown U., 1952, Ph.D., 1965. Commd. ensign U.S. Navy, 1946, advanced through grades to rear adm., 1973; staff and command assignments (Atlantic and Pacific fleets); shore duty in Morocco, Cyprus, Germany, Eng. and Japan, 1946-73; asst. dir. (Nat. Security Agy.), Washington, 1973-74; comdr. (Naval Security Group Command), dir. electronic warfare and cryptology div. on staff of chief of naval ops., 1974-78, ret. 1978. Author: Cossacks of the Brotherhood. Decorated Legion of Merit (2). Mem. U.S. Naval Inst., Am. Hist. Assn., Am. Assn. for the Advancement of Slavic Studies, Phi Gamma Delta, Phi Alpha Theta. Address: 3043 Old Port Ln NW Olympia WA 98502

MARCH, JAMES GARDNER, social scientist, educator; b. Cleve., Jan. 15, 1928; s. James Herbert and Mildred (MacCorkle) M.; m. Jayne Mary Dohr, Sept. 23, 1947; children: Kathryn Sue, Gary Clifton, James Christopher, Roderic Gunn. BA, U. Wis., 1949; MA, Yale U., 1950, PhD, 1953; hon. doctorate, Copenhagen Sch. Econs., 1978, Swedish Sch. Econs., 1979, U. Wis., Milw., 1980, U. Bergen, 1980, Uppsala U., 1987, Helsinki Sch. Econs., 1991, Dublin City U., 1994. From asst. prof. to prof. Carnegie Inst. Tech., 1953-64; prof., dean Sch. Social Scis., U. Calif.-Irvine, 1964-70; prof. mgmt., higher edn., polit. sci. and sociology Stanford U., 1970—; adj. prof. U. Bergen, 1989-92; cons. in field, 1954—; Mem. Nat. Council Ednl. Research, 1975-78; mem. Nat. Sci. Bd., 1968-74; mem. sociol.-social psychology panel NSF, 1964-66; social sci. tng. com. NIMH, 1967-68; mem. math. social sci. com. Social Sci. Research Council, 1958-60; mem. Assembly Behavioral and Social Sci., NRC, 1973-79, chmn. com. on aging, 1977-82, chmn. com. on math., sci., tech. edn., 1984-86. Author: (with H.A. Simon) Organizations, 1958, 2nd edit., 1993, (with R.M. Cyert) A Behavioral Theory of the Firm, 1963, 2nd edit., 1992, Handbook of Organizations, 1965, (with B.R. Gelbaum) Mathematics for the Social and Behavioral Sciences, 1969, (with M.D. Cohen) Leadership and Ambiguity, 1974, 2nd edit., 1986, Academic Notes, 1974, (with C.E. Lave) An Introduction to Models in the Social Sciences, 1975, (with J.P. Olsen) Ambiguity and Choice in Organizations, 1976, Aged Wisconsin, 1977, Autonomy as a Factor in Group Organization, 1980, Pleasures of the Process, 1980, Slow Learner, 1985, (with R. Weissinger-Baylon) Ambiguity and Command, 1986, Decisions and Organizations, 1988, (with J.P. Olsen) Rediscovering Institutions, 1989, Minor Memos, 1990, A Primer on Decision Making, 1994, Fornuft og Forandring, 1995, (with J.P. Olsen) Democratic Governance, 1995; contbr. articles to profl. jour. Fellow Ctr. Advanced Study in Behavioral Scis., 1955-56, 73-74; recipient Wilbur Lucius Cross medal Yale U., 1968, Walter P. Gores award Stanford U., 1995. Mem. NAS, Nat. Acad. Edn., Accademia Italiana di Economia Aziendale, Royal Swedish Acad. Scis., Norwegian Acad. of Sci. and Letters, Am. Acad. Arts and Scis., Am. Econ. Assn., Am. Polit. Sci. Assn. (v.p. 1983-84), Am. Psychol. Assn., Am. Sociol. Assn., Acad. Mgmt., Russell Sage Found. (trustee 1985-94, chmn. 1990-93), Finnish Soc. Scis. and Letters, Phi Beta Kappa, Sigma Xi. Home: 837 Tolman Dr Palo Alto CA 94305-1025 Office: Stanford U 509 Ceras Stanford CA 94305-3084

MARCHAND, JOANN, laboratory coordinator, greenhouse manager; b. Cañon City, Colo., June 5, 1941; d. Lawrence Eugene and Helen Lucille (Giem) M. BS, Colo. State U., 1962, MS, 1967. Vol. Peace Corps, Nepal, 1962-64; grad. research asst. Colo. State U., Ft. Collins, 1965-67, lab. technician II biology dept., 1967-93, lab. coord., greenhouse mgr., 1993—; cons. Sci. Tchr.'s Workshop, Kathmandu, Nepal, 1963, cons. for research Mission Hosp., Tansen Palpa, West Nepal, 1963. Contbr. articles to profl. jours. Sponsor, com. mem. Larimer County 4-H Catch-it-Lamb program; vol. Colo. Divsn. Wildlife, Nature Conservancy. Mem. Colo. Assn. Pub. Employees, NRA, Rocky Mountain Bighorn Soc., Colo. Cattlemen's Assn., Nat. Cattlemen's Assn., Rocky Mountain Elk Found., Nature Conservancy (life), Nat. Wildlife Fedn. (life), Sigma Xi, Gamma Sigma Delta. Home: 4908 E County Rd 60 Wellington CO 80549-1609 Office: Colo State U Biology Dept Fort Collins CO 80523

MARCHAND, RUSSELL DAVID, II, fire chief; b. Lafayette, Ind., May 14, 1950; s. Russell David and Mable May (Gean) M.; m. Sandra Green, June 12, 1951 (div. Nov. 1986); 1 child, Russell David III; m. Carol Bella Flashenburg, May 31, 1987. AA in Fire Sci., Clark County Community Coll., Las Vegas, Nev., 1979. Cert. fire service instr., supr. instr. Firefighter North Las Vegas Fire Dept., 1973-78, engr., 1978-82, capt., 1982-95, divsn. chief, officer-in-charge bldg. and constrn., 1990—; pres. Local 1607 Internat. Assn. Fire Fighters, Las Vegas, 1980— (v.p. 1976-80); instr. N. Las Vegas Fire Dept., 1986. Chmn. N. Las Vegas Firefighters Polit. Action Com., 1980—, Muscular Dystrophy Assn., 1980-83, 85. Sgt. USMC, 1968-72, South Vietnam. Named Fireman of Yr., Optimist Club, 1981, Lions Club Nev., 1989, Profl. Ins. Agts. of Am.; received citation of merit Muscular Dystrophy Assn., 1982, commendation City of N. Las Vegas, 1980, 83, 85. Mem. Fed. Firefighters Nev. (received commendation 1982), Nat. Assn. Miniature Enthusiasts, Internat. Assn. Fire Fighters (local 1607 pres. emeritus 1990). Office: 2626 E Carey Ave North Las Vegas NV 89030-6215

MARCHETTI, KAREN J., advertising executive; b. Coronado, Calif., Mar. 2, 1958; d. Salvatore and Frances R. (Piscotty) M. BBA, San Diego State U., 1981, MS in Bus. Adminstrn., 1986. Mktg. intern Am. Airlines, San Diego, 1981-83; mktg. specialist Point Loma FCU, San Diego, 1983-84; asst. product mgr. Home Fed. Bank, San Diego, 1984-86; new product mgr. Security Pacific Fin. Svcs., San Diego, 1986-89; account supr. Rosenfield/Vinson, Inc., San Diego, 1989-90, dir. client svcs., 1990-91; v.p., dir. client svcs. Strategic Mktg. and Advt., Inc., San Diego, 1991—; cons. U.S. Olympic Tng. Ctr., San Diego, 1991, Planning Forum, San Diego, 1992; instr. U. San Diego, U. San Francisco, Calif. State U.-Long Beach, v.p. membership, bd. dirs. U. Calif. San Diego, 1995-96. Contbr. articles to profl. jours. and mags. Mem. Am. Mktg. Assn. (pres. 1994-95), Bank Mktg. Assn., San Diego Direct Mktg. Club (pres. 1995—), Direct Mktg. Club of So. Calif., Computer Electronics Mktg. Assn. Office: Strategic Mktg and Advt Inc 11758 Caminito Missiones San Diego CA 92128

MARCHI, JON, cattle rancher, exporter, former investment brokerage executive; b. Ann Arbor, Mich., Aug. 6, 1946; s. John Robert and Joan Trimble (Toole) M.; m. Mary Stewart Sale, Aug. 12, 1972; children: Aphia Jessica, Jon Jacob. Student Claremont Men's Coll., 1964-65; BS, U. Mont., 1968, MS, 1972. Sec., treas. Marchi, Marchi & Marchi, Inc., Morris, Ill., 1968-69; account exec. D. A. Davidson & Co., Billings, Mont., 1972-75, asst. v.p., office mgr., 1976-77, v.p. mktg. and adminstrn., Great Falls, Mont., 1977—; sec., dir., v.p. fin. svcs. and exec. devel., D. A. Davidson Realty Corp., Great Falls, 1978-85, chmn. rsch. com., 1980; cattle rancher, Polson, Mont., 1985—; bd. dirs. Big Sky Airlines, Billings, Mont., chmn. bd. dirs., 1995; bd. dirs. Energy Overthrust Found., Mansfield Found., Mont. Beverages, Mont. Venture Capital Network, Direct Advantage, Inc., Hamilton, Mont., Mont. Naturals Internat., Inc., Eclipse Techs., Inc., Mont. Small Bus. Investment Corp.; chmn., dir. Devel. Corp. Mont., Helena, 1995. Chmn. Mont. Gov.'s Subcom. for Venture Capital Devel., Mont. Community Fin. Corp., Helena; chmn. investment com., State of Mont. Sci. and Tech. Alliance, 1985—; chmn. seed capital com. State of Mont., bd. dirs. job svc. com. Mem. Mont. Peoples Action; sec.-treas. Valley View Assn., 1987—; trustee sch. dist. # 35, Polson, Mont., 1990—, chmn., 1991—; bd. dirs. Mont. Entrepreneurship Ctr., Missoula, Mont., 1990—; pres., dir., sec./treas. Mont. Pvt. Capital Network, Bozeman, Mont., 1990—, pres., 1992—; chmn., dir. Mont. Naturals Internat., Inc., 1991; dir. Mont. State Rural Devel. Coun., 1992, Mont. SBA Adv. Coun., 1992; dir. Ctr. Econ. Renewal and Tech. Transfer Mont. State U., Bozeman, 1994—; del. to White House Conf. on Small Bus., Washington, 1994-95. With U.S. Army, 1969-71. Mem. Nat. Cattlemen's Assn. (fgn. trade com.), Polson C. of C. (bd. dirs.), Valley View Assn. (bd. dirs.), Mont. Cattle Feeders Assn., Montana Angus Assn., Am. Angus Assn., Western Mont. Stockgrowers Assn., Securities Industry Assn., Mont. Stock Growers Assn., Mont. Ambassadors (dir. 1995), Polson C. of C. (dir.), Leadership Great Falls Club, Ski Club, Mont. Club, Helena Wilderness Riders Club, Rotary. Episcopalian. Home: 7783 Valley View Rd Polson MT 59860-9302 Office: Marchi Angus Ranches 7783 Valley View Rd Polson MT 59860-9302

MARCHINI, JO ANNE, secretary-treasurer; b. Stockton, Calif., June 25, 1949; d. Joseph Hohn and Marianne Frances (Faracias) Marchesotti; m. Ronald Lee Marchini; children: Paul, Dax. BA, U. Pacific, 1971. Sec.-treas. Joe Marchesotti & Co., Inc., Stockton. Office: Joe Marchesotti Co Inc 1201 E Alpine Ave Stockton CA 95204-3502

MARCKWARDT, HAROLD THOMAS, association executive; b. Chgo., May 4, 1920; s. Herman and Carrie (Polachek) M.; AB, U. So. Calif., 1949, AM, 1953; MS, U. Calif., 1970, postgrad, 1970—; m. Patricia Ann Hoffman, Apr. 7, 1945; children: Craig, Diana, Brad, Glenn. Tool and machinery designer Douglas Aircraft, Santa Monica, Cal., 1939-43; playground leader County Los Angeles, 1946-47; community program dir. Hollywood (Calif.) YMCA, 1947-51, dir. community program and bldg., 1952-55; exec. dir. Westchester YMCA, Los Angeles, 1955-63; area dir. Nat. Council YMCA, 1963-66, pres. Western Center Assocs., Los Angeles, 1966—; internat. mgmt. cons., Indonesia, 1985-91, Sri Lanka, 1989; field assoc. Internat. Exec. Service Corps, 1987-93. Exec. dir. Calif. Youth and Govt. Statewide Com., 1965, del. seminar UN, 1959. Colliver lectr. U. Pacific, 1965. Trainer, Leadership Devel. Camp, Los Angeles, 1959; mem. Mayor's Steering Com., 1973-75, chmn. Mayor's Facilitators com. Conf. Children, Youth and Sr. Citizens, 1974; mem. employment and tng. subcom. Los Angeles County Task Force, 1977; mem. Task Force on Equity for Women in Employment, 1976-77. Served to 1st lt., USAAF, 1943-46, USAF (SAC), 1950-52. Recipient One of Hollywood's Top Ten Young Men award, 1954. Mem. Am. Soc. Tool Engrs. (charter mem.), Pacific S.W. Area YMCA Assn. Profl. Dirs. (pres. 1963-66), Orgn. Devel. Network, Airplane Owner's and Pilots Assn., Am. Soc. Tng. and Devel. (v.p. 1979, pres. 1980), Internat. Fedn. Tng. and Devel. Orgns., Pacific Asia Travel Assn. (exec. bd.), Indonesian Bus. Soc., Am. Soc. Travel Agts., Indonesian Trade Mission, World Span-One Club (pres. 1993-94, v.p. 1991-93). Democrat. Author: The Leader Makes The Difference, 1968; Leading Discussion Groups, 1972; How to Make Executive Decisions About Training, 1976; 16 Steps to the Job You Want, 1979; The Quality Circles Kit, 1982. Home: 4216 Colbath Ave Sherman Oaks CA 91423-4210 Office: 4716 Woodman Ave Sherman Oaks CA 91423-2416

MARCO, DAVID DUANE, biomedical engineer; b. Apollo, Pa., Feb. 3, 1951; s. Peter M. and Jean M. (Merlo) M.; m. Nancy Elizabeth Bierman, Nov. 16, 1985; 1 child, Phoebe Elizabeth. BS in Biomed. Engring., Rensselaer Polytechnic Inst., 1973. Operating engr. Shock & Trauma Unit Albany (N.Y.) Med. Ctr., 1973-75; research technician Abcor Inc., Boston, 1975-76; clin. engr. Boston U. Med. Ctr. Hosp., 1975-77; field clin. engr. Arco/Med. Products, San Francisco, 1977-81; sales rep. Siemens-Elema, Oakland, Calif., 1981-85; field clin. engr. Pacesetter, Oakland, 1985—, western field clin. engr. mgr., 1993—. Contbr. articles to profl. jours. Mem. Shiloh Christian Fellowship, Oakland, 1983, dist. dir., 1991—. Mem. N.Am. Soc. Pacing & Electrophysiology. Republican. Office: Pacesetter Inc Ste A150 3470 Mount Diablo Blvd Lafayette CA 94549-3917

MARCOTTE, MICHAEL VINCENT, journalist, public radio executive; b. La Crosse, Wis., July 18, 1956; s. Henry Joseph and Ardis Joy (Denton) M.; m. Valerie Ann Prebo, June 28, 1980; children: Nicholas, Aaron, Trevor. BA in Journalism, U. Ga., 1982, MA, 1984. Radio producer WUOG, Athens, Ga., 1979-83; radio newscaster WGAU/WNGC, Athens, 1982-84; broadcast producer WOSU, Columbus, Ohio, 1984-87; radio instr. Ohio State U., Columbus, 1984-87; news dir. KPLU, Tacoma, 1987-92, asst. program dir./news, 1992—; panelist Voice of Democracy, Columbus, 1985-87; pub. spkr. journalism ethics Pacific Lutheran U. Spkrs. Bur. Creator, dir. Theatre of Sound, 1982; freelance producer radio features for Nat. Pub. Radio, 1987—; author radio plays. Vis. lectr. Bethel and Franklin Pierce Schs., Wash., 1988-92; mem. communication arts adv. bd. Pacific Luth. U., 1992—. With U.S. Army, 1974-77. Recipient 30 awards for documentaries, series, spots, features. Mem. Pub. Radio News Dirs. Assn. (nat. bd. dirs.), Soc. Profl. Journalists, Radio-TV News Dirs. Assn. Home: 310 190th St E Spanaway WA 98387-8311 Office: KPLU-FM 121st and Park Tacoma WA 98447

MARCOVITZ, LEONARD EDWARD, retail executive; b. Bismarck, N.D., Sept. 6, 1934; s. Jacob and Frieda M. Asst. mgr. Greengard's Clothing, Mandan, N.D., 1955-58; mgr. K-G Men's Stores, Inc., Bismarck, 1958-61, Billings, Mont., 1961-69; v.p. store ops. K-G Men's Stores, Inc., 1969-73; pres. Leonard's Men's Stores, Yakima, Wash. and Billings, Mont., 1973-77; chief exec. officer K-G Retail div. Chromalloy Am. Corp., Englewood, Colo., 1977-81; pres. DeMarcos Men's Clothing, Casper, Wyo., 1982—, Idaho Falls, Idaho, 1984—, Billings, Mont., 1986—. Mem. Menswear Retailers Am. (past dir.), Billings Petroleum Club, Order of Demolay (Degree of Chevalier 1952, Internat. Master Councilor 1953, Demolay Dad 1959), Elks. Home: PO Box 23344 Billings MT 59104-3344

MARCUS, CRAIG BRIAN, lawyer; b. Boise, Idaho, May 30, 1939; s. Claude Virgil and Marie Louise M.; m. Lynne Merryweather, Sept. 3, 1960; children: Shawn, Brian, Trent. Student, Boise Jr. Coll., 1958, U. Pa., 1958-59, Mexico City Coll., 1959-60; JD, U. Idaho, 1963. Bar: Idaho 1963, U.S. Dist. Ct. Idaho 1963. Ptnr. Marcus, Merrick & Montgomery, predecessors, Boise, 1963—. Ada County dir. Rep. Congl. Campaigns, Boise, 1964-66; Ada County coord. Rep. Senatorial Campaigns, 1969; chmn. jud. campaign Idaho Ct. of Appeals, 1984, 90. Mem. ABA, Idaho Bar Assn. (peer rev. com. 1971-73), 4th Dist. Bar Assn. (treas. 1967-68, ct. trial porcedural rules com. 1973-74), Lincoln Day Banquet Assn. (pres. 197-), Elks. Home: 7711 Apache Way Boise ID 83703-1903 Office: Marcus Merrick & Montgomery 737 N 7th St Boise ID 83702-5504

MARCUS, DONALD MORTON, psychoanalyst; b. Bklyn., Aug. 29, 1924; s. Phineas and Claire (Ingleson) M.; m. Sylvia Roslyn Kinberg, May 22, 1949; children: Andrea Gayle, Donna Joy, Leslie Rochelle. BS, Ind. U., 1945, MD, 1948; PhD, So. Calif. Psychoanalytic Inst, 1962. Diplomate Am. Bd. Psychiatry and Neurology Psychoanalysis. Cons. L.A. (Calif.) County Probation Dept., 1955-59; assoc. clin. prof. psychiatry U. So. Calif., L.A. (Calif.) County Med. Ctr., 1959-82; faculty So. Calif. Psychoanalytic Inst., Beverly Hills, 1962-85; cons. VA Hosp., Sepulveda, Calif., 1970-73; tng. and supervising analyst Psychoanalytic Ctr. of Calif., L.A., 1985—; pvt. practice psychiatry and psychoanalysis Beverly Hills, 1955—. Contbr. articles to profl. jours. Lt. USNR, 1943-52. Mem. Alpha Omega Alpha, Sigma Xi. Office: #445 9735 Wilshire Blvd Beverly Hills CA 90212

MARCUS, FRANK ISADORE, physician, educator; b. Haverstraw, N.Y., Mar. 23, 1928; s. Samuel and Edith (Sattler) M.; m. Janet Geller, June 30, 1957; children: Ann, Steve, Lynn. BA, Columbia U., 1948; MS, Tufts U., 1951; MD cum laude, Boston U., 1953. Diplomate Am. Bd. Internal Medicine, subspecialty cardiovascular diseases. Intern Peter Bent Brigham Hosp., Boston, 1953-54; asst. resident Peter Bent Brigham Hosp., 1956-57, research fellow in cardiology, 1957-58; clin. fellow in cardiology Georgetown U. Hosp., 1958-59, chief med. resident, 1959-60; chief of cardiology Georgetown U. Med. Service, D.C. Gen. Hosp., Washington, 1960-68; instr. medicine Georgetown U. Sch. Medicine, 1960-63, asst. prof., 1963-68, assoc. prof., 1968; prof. medicine, chief cardiology sect. U. Ariz. Coll. Medicine, Tucson, 1969-82, disting. prof. internal medicine (cardiology), 1982—, dir. electrophysiology, 1982—; cons. cardiology VA Hosp., Tucson, 1969, USAF Regional Hosp., Davis-Monthan AFB, Tucson, 1969; mem. courtesy staffs Tucson Med. Ctr., St. Mary's Hosp., Tucson.; mem. panel drug efficacy study, panel on cardiovascular drugs Nat. Acad. Scis.-NRC, 1967-68; chmn. undergrad. cardiovascular tng. grant com. HEW-NIH, 1970. Editor Modern Concepts of Cardiovascular Disease, 1982-84; mem. editorial bd. Circulation, 1976-81, Current Problems in Cardiology, 1976-80, Cardiocascular Drugs and Therapy, 1986—, New Trends in Arrythmias, 1984—, Jour. Am. Coll. Cardiology, 1984-87, Am. Jour. Cardiology, 1984—, Jour. Cardiovascular Drugs and Therapy, 1994—, Jour. Cardiovascular Pharmacology and Therapeutics, 1994—; contbr. numerous articles to med. jours. Chmn. Washington Heart Assn. High Sch. Heart Program, 1966-68. Served to capt. USAF, 1954-56. Recipient Career Devel. award NIH, 1965, Student AMA Golden Apple award Georgetown U. Sch. Medicine, 1968; Mass. Heart Assn. fellow, 1957-58; John and Mary Markle scholar, 1960-65. Fellow Coun. on Clin. Cardiology Am. Heart Assn., ACP (Ariz. laureate award 1987), Am. Coll. Cardiology (bd. govs. Ariz. 1984-87, asst. sec. 1987-89, trustee); mem. Am. Fedn. Clin. Rsch., Am. Soc. Pharm. and Exptl. Therapeutics, Assn. Univ. Cardiologists, Inc. (v.p. 1989-90, pres. 1990-91), Ariz. Heart Assn. (dir. 1970, v.p. 1972-73, chmn. rsch. com. 1970-72), So. Ariz. Heart Assn. (dir. 1969), N.Am. Soc. for Pacing and Electrophysiology, Alpha Omega Alpha. Home: 4949 E Glenn St Tucson AZ 85712-1212 Office: U Ariz Univ Med Ctr 1501 N Campbell Ave Tucson AZ 85724-0001

MARCUS, HUBERT C., ophthalmologist; b. San Francisco, Mar. 27, 1931; s. Herman and Rose B. (Steinburg) M.; m. Diane F. Libby, Apr. 12, 1959; children: Deborah L., David S., Anne L. BA, U. Calif., Berkeley, 1952; MD, U. Calif., San Francisco, 1955. Diplomate Am. Bd. Ophthalmology. Resident in ophthalmology U. Calif. Sch. Medicine, San Francisco, 1958-61; pvt. practice Peninsula Eye Physicians Med. Group, Inc., San Mateo and Burlingame, Calif., 1961—; assoc. clin. prof. ophthalmology U. Calif., San Francisco, 1961—. Capt. U.S. Army, 1956-58. Mem. Frederick C. Cordes Eye Soc. (pres. 1993-94). Office: Peninsula Eye Physicians 1720 El Camino Real Ste 7 Burlingame CA 94010-3226

MARCUS, JEFFREY HOWARD, electronic security system company executive; b. Albany, N.Y., June 4, 1950; s. Paul and Phyllis (Zippert) M.; m. Carol Ellen Marcus, Aug. 28, 1994. BS in Elec. Engring. and Computer Sci., U. Colo., Denver, 1977; MBA, U. Phoenix, Denver, 1985. Specialist counter intelligence U.S. Army, Washington, 1971-73; v.p. engring. Securus, Inc. (formerly Photo-Scan of Colo.), Denver, 1977-81, pres., 1981—; also bd. dirs. Securus (formerly Photo-Scan of Colo.), Denver; bd. dirs. PSA Fin. Svcs., Inc., Westminster; chmn. bd., tech. com. PSA Security NEtwork, Westminster. Democrat. Office: Securus Inc 12411 E 37th Ave Denver CO 80239-3404

MARCUS, KAREN MELISSA, foreign language educator; b. Vancouver, B.C., Feb. 28, 1956; came to the U.S., 1962; d. Marvin Marcus and Arlen Ingrid (Sahlman) Bishop; m. Jorge Esteban Mezei, Jan. 7, 1984 (div. Mar. 1987). BA in French, BA in Polit. Sci., U. Calif., Santa Barbara, 1978, MA in Polit. Sci., 1981; MA in French, Stanford U., 1984, PhD in French, 1990. Lectr. in French Stanford (Calif.) U., 1989-90; asst. prof. French No. Ariz. U., Flagstaff, 1990—; cons. Houghton Mifflin, 1993, Grand Canyon (Ariz.) Natural History Soc., 1994. Vol., letter writer Amnesty Internat. Urgent Action Network, 1991—; vol. No. Ariz. Aids Outreach Orgn., Flagstaff, 1994—. Recipient medal for outstanding achievement in French, Alliance Francaise, Santa Barbara, 1978; named Scholarship Exch. Student, U. Geneva, Switzerland, 1979-80; doctoral fellow Stanford (Calif.) U., 1981-85. Mem. MLA, Am. Assn. Tchrs. French, Am. Coun. on the Tchg. Fgn. Langs., Am. Literary Translators Assn., Women in French, Coordination Internat. des Chercheurs Sur Les Litteratures Maghrebines, Phi Beta Kappa, Pi Delta Phi, Alpha Lambda Delta. Democrat. Jewish. Office: No Ariz Univ Modern Lang Dept Box 6004 Flagstaff AZ 86011

MARCUS, RUDOLPH ARTHUR, chemist, educator; b. Montreal, Que., Can., July 21, 1923; came to U.S., 1949, naturalized, 1958; s. Myer and Esther (Cohen) M.; m. Laura Hearne, Aug. 27, 1949; children: Alan Rudolph, Kenneth Hearne, Raymond Arthur. BSc in Chemistry, McGill U., 1943, PhD in Chemistry, 1946, DSc (hon.), 1988; DSc (hon.), U. Chgo., 1983, Poly. U., 1986, U. Göteborg, Sweden, 1987, U. N.B., Can., 1993, Queens U., Can., 1993; Oxford U., U.K., 1995. Rsch. staff mem. RDX Project, Montreal, 1944-46; postdoctoral rsch. assoc. NRC of Can., Ottawa, Ont., 1946-49, U. N.C., 1949-51; asst. prof. Poly. Inst. Bklyn., 1951-54, assoc. prof., 1954-58, prof., 1958-64; prof. U. Ill., Urbana, 1964-78; Arthur Amos Noyes prof. chemistry Calif. Inst. Tech., Pasadena, 1978—; hon. fellow University Coll., Oxford, England, 1995—; hon. prof. Inst. of Chemistry/Chinese Acad. of Scis., Beijing, 1995—; mem. Courant Inst. Math. Scis., NYU, 1960-61; trustee Gordon Rsch. Confs., 1966-69, chmn. bd., 1968-69, mem. coun., 1965-68; mem. rev. panel Argonne Nat. Lab., 1966-72, chmn., 1967-68; mem. rev. panel Brookhaven Nat. Lab., 1971-74; mem. rev. com. Radiation Lab., U. Notre Dame, 1975-80; mem. panel on atmospheric chemistry climatic impact com. NAS-NRC, 1975-78, mem. com. kinetics of chem. reactions, 1973-77, chmn., 1975-77, mem. com. chem. scis., 1977-79, mem. com. to survey opportunities in chem. scis., 1982-86; adv. com. for chemistry NSF, 1977-80, external adv. bd. NSF Ctr. Photoinduced Charter Transfer, 1990—; adviser of the Centre for Molecular Scis., Chinese Acad. Scis. and of the State Key Lab. for Structural Chemistry of Unstable and Stable Species, Beijing; vis. prof. theoretical chemistry U. Oxford, Eng., IBM, 1975-76; also professorial fellow Univ. Coll., 1975-76; treas. L.A. Cen. City Assn., 1995. Former mem. editorial bd. Jour. Chem. Physics, Ann. Rev. Phys. Chemistry, Jour. Phys. Chemistry, Accounts Chem. Rsch., Internat. Jour. Chem. Kinetics Molecular Physics, Theoretica Chimica Acta, Chem. Physics Letters; mem. editorial bd. Laser Chemistry, 1982—, Advances in Chem. Physics, 1984—, World Sci. Pub., 1987—, Internat. Revs. in Phys. Chemistry, 1988—, Faraday Trans., Jour. Chem. Soc., 1990—, Progress in Physics, Chemistry and Mechanics (China), 1989—, Perkins Transactions 2, Jour. Chem. Soc., 1992—, Chem. Physics Rsch. (India), 1992—, Trends in Chem. Physics Rsch. (India), 1992—. Alfred P. Sloan fellow, 1960-61, sr. postdoctoral fellow NSF, 1960-61; sr. postdoctoral fellow NSF, 1960-61; sr. Fulbright-Hays scholar, 1972; recipient Sr. U.S. Scientist award Alexander von Humboldt-Stiftung, 1976, Electrochem. Soc. Lecture award Electrochem. Soc., 1979, Robinson medal Faraday divsn. Royal Soc. Chemistry, 1982, Centenary medal Faraday divsn., 1988, Chandler medal Columbia U., 1983, Wolf prize in Chemistry, 1985, Nat. Medal of Sci., 1989, Evans award Ohio State U., 1990, Nobel prize in Chemistry, 1992, Hirshfelder prize in Theoretical Chemistry, U. Wis., 1993, Golden Plate award Am. Acad. Achievement, 1993, Lavoisier medal French Chem. Soc., 1994; named Hon. Citizen, City of Winnipeg, 1994. Fellow AAAS (hon.), Am. Acad. Arts and Scis (hon., exec. com. western sect., co-chmn. 1981-84, rsch. and planning com. 1989-91), Am. Phys. Soc., Internat. Soc. Electrochemistry (hon.), Royal Soc. Chemistry (hon.), Royal Soc. London (hon.), Internat. Acad. Quantum Molecular Sci. (hon.), Royal Soc. Can. (hon.); mem. NAS (hon.), Am. Philos. Soc. (hon.), Am. Chem. Soc./ (past divsn. chmn., mem. exec. com., mem. adv. bd. petroleum rsch. fund, Irving Langmuir award Chem. Physics 1978, Peter Debye award Phys. Chemistry 1988, Willard Gibbs medal Chgo. sect. 1988, S.C. Lind Lecture, East Tenn. sect. 1988, Theodore William Richards medal Northwestern sect. 1990, Edgar Fahs Smith award Phila. sect. 1991, Ira Remsen Meml. award Me.

sect. 1991, Pauling medal Portland, Oreg., and Puget Sound sect. 1991), Internat. Acad. Quantum Molecular Sci., hon. Home: 331 S Hill Ave Pasadena CA405

MARDIAN, DANIEL, construction company director; b. Pasadena, Calif., Apr. 10, 1917; s. Samuel and Akabe (Lekerian) M.; m. Katherine Evkhanian, Jan. 30, 1942; children: Daniel Jr., Tom, John, Paul, Scott. Student, Pasadena City Coll., 1937; diploma, U.S. Army Engring. Sch., Ft. Belvoir, Va., 1944, U.S. Army Command and Gen. Staff Coll., 1961. Commd. U.S. Army, 1942, advances through grades to lt. col., 1962, ret., 1970; ptnr. Mardian Constrn. Co., Phoenix, 1945-47, exec. v.p., 1947-66, pres., 1966-78, also bd. dirs.; past chmn., mem. Nat. Joint Apprenticeship/Tng. Commn. Oper. Engrs., Washington, 1975-78; mem. adv. bd. constrn. programs Ariz. State U., Tempe, 1957—, mem. adv. bd. coll. engring., 1957—; bd. dirs. Citibank, Phoenix, 1962-87. Pres. Am. Coun. Constrn. Edn., Monroe, La., 1991-93; past pres., bd. dirs. Fiesta Bowl, Tempe, 1986-92; gen. campaign chmn. United Way, Phoenix, 1967; pres. Met. Phoenix C. of C., 1967-68. Capt. C.E., U.S. Army, 1942-46, PTO, 1970—. Recipient Hall of Fame Award Ariz. State U., 1990, Excellence in Constrn. Award Am. Subcontractors Assn., 1988, Hall of Fame Award Nat. Football Found., 1987, Brotherhood Award Ariz. chpt. Nat. Conf. Christians and Jews, 1981. Mem. Associated Gen. Contractors Am. (life bd. dirs., chmn. yr. award 1970, mem. manpower tng. com., laborers tng. com., 1969—), Sun Angel Found. (chmn. 1989-91), Ariz. Acad., Phoenix Country Club (bd. dirs., pres. 1985-86), Phoenix Kiwanis Club (past dir.). Republican. Mem. United Ch. Christ. Home: 7215 N 3rd St Phoenix AZ 85020-4904 Office: Perini Building Co 360 E Coronado Rd Phoenix AZ 85004-1524

MARDIAN, ROBERT CHARLES, JR., restaurateur; b. Orange, Calif., Feb. 1, 1947; s. Robert Charles Sr. and Dorothy Driscilla (Denniss) M.; m. Jayne Marie Garvin, June 21, 1970 (div. 1977); 1 child, Robert Charles III; m. Kathleen Frances Dixon, Oct. 13, 1984 (div. 1991); children: Alexandra Quinn, Ashley Michele. BA, Stanford U., 1969; MBA, Pepperdine U., 1986. Gen. mgr. Loft Restaurant, San Jose, Calif., 1969-71; chief exec. officer/chmn. bd. Wind & Sea Restaurants, Inc., Dana Point, Calif., 1971—; bd. dirs. Dana Niguel Bank, cons. U.S. Olympic Com., Colorado Springs, 1984-88. Commr. Dana Point Econ. Devel. Mem. Young Pres. Orgn. Republican. Home: 34699 Golden Lantern St Dana Point CA 92629-2908 Office: Wind & Sea Restaurants Inc 34699 Golden Lantern St Dana Point CA 92629-2908

MAREE, WENDY, painter, sculptor; b. Windsor, Eng., Feb. 10, 1938. Student, Windsor & Maidenhead Coll., 1959; studied with Vasco Lazzlo, London, 1959-62. Exhibited at Windsor Arts Festival, San Bernardino (Calif.) Mus.; exhibited in one woman show Lake Arrowhead (Calif.) Libr., 1989, Amnesty Internat., Washington, 1990, Phyllis Morris Gallery, Many Horses Gallery, L.A., 1990, Nelson Rockefeller, Palm Springs, Calif., 1992, Stewart Gallery, Rancho Palos Verdes, Calif., Petropavlovsk (Russia) Cultural Mus., Kamchatka, Russia, 1993, Nelson Rockefeller Gallery, Palm Springs, Calif., 1994, Coyle-Coyle Gallery, Blue Jay, Calif., 1995, La Quinta Sculpture Park, Calif, 1995; numerous others; represented in pvt. collections His Royal Highness Prince Faisal, Saudi Arabia, Gena Rowlands, L.A., John Cassavetes, L.A., Nicky Blairs, L.A., Guilford Glazer, Beverly Hills, Calif., June Allyson, Ojai, Calif., Amnesty Internat., Washington. Recipient award San Bernardino County Mus., 1988, Gov. Kamchatka of Russia, 1993. Mem. Artist Guild of Lake Arrowhead. Address: 246 Saturmino Dr Palm Springs CA 92262

MAREFAT, MICHAEL M., electrical and computer engineering educator; b. Sept. 21, 1963; came to U.S., 1980; s. Abdolhossein and Akram (Mosavat) M.; m. Ai-Nhi Tran, June 23, 1990. BA in Math. Scis., Rice U., 1986, BS in Elec. and Computer Engring., 1986; MSEE, Purdue U., 1988, PhD in EE, 1991. Registered profl. engr., Tex. Computer programmer Baylor Coll. of Medicine, Houston, 1986; rsch. asst. Purdue Engring. Rsch. Ctr. for Intelligent Mfg., 1987-91; rsch. scientist Schlumberger Lab. for Computer Sci., Austin, Tex., 1990; asst. prof. elec. and computer engring. U. Ariz., Tucson, 1992—, dir. intelligent systems lab., 1992—; proposal referee, panel mem. NSF, Arlington, Va., 1992, 1995; mem. exec. com. Ctr. for Advanced Integration Mfg. Scis. and Techs., Tucson, 1993—. Author: (with others) Handbook of Expert Systems Applications in Manufacturing, 1994; contbr. articles to profl. jours. Mem. IEEE, Am. Assn. for Artificial Intelligence, Assn. for Computing Machinery, Tau Beta Pi, Eta Kappa Nu. Office: U Ariz Dept Elec and Computer Engring 1230 E Speedway Blvd Tucson AZ 85721

MAREI, IBRAHIM, medical technologist; b. Marowe, Sudan, Dec. 6, 1939; s. Hassan and Shafika (Mohamed) M. BS in Chemistry, U. Cairo, 1966; MS in Med. Tech., Calif. State U., 1980. Lic. clinical chemist tech., Calif., clinical lab. tech., Calif. Clinical chemist SmithKline-Beecham, Van Nuys, Calif., 1969-71; supr. ctr. critically ill lab. Hollywood Presbyn. Med. Ctr., L.A., 1971-75; sr. toxicologist, clin. chemist spl. chemistry dept., instr. on the job tng. and edn. new students, tech. staff Reference Labs., Newbury Park, Calif., 1975-88; clin. chemist endochronology dept., med. technologist Smith Kline Biosci. Labs., Van Nuys, Calif., 1988—. Mem. Am. Soc. Clinical Pathologists (cert.), Am. Chem. Soc., Am. Assn. Clinical Chemists (cert.), Am. Pub. Health Assn. Calif. Assn. for Med. Lab. Tech. Home: 7441 Hazeltine Ave Apt 107 Van Nuys CA 91405-1486 Office: Smith Kline Biosci Labs 7600 Tyrone Ave Van Nuys CA 91405-1449

MAREK, TAMMY ANN, banking consultant; b. Chgo., June 11, 1958; d. Chester Stanley and Laura Marie (Arnold) M. BS in Mktg. and Econs., Elmhurst Coll., 1981. Sales coord. GCA/Precision Sci., Chgo., 1982-84; mktg. adminstr. John O. Butler Co., Chgo., 1984-86; cons. Sears Mortgage Corp., Westchester, Ill., 1986-91; pvt. cons. Portland, Oreg., 1991—. Home: 555 NW Park Ave Apt 232 Portland OR 97209-3419

MARESH, NANCY MAE, educational entrepreneur; b. Iowa City, June 27, 1946; d. Gerald Stanley and Ethel (Nelson) M. Grad. high sch., Denver. Chmn. bd. Ednl. Discoveries, Inc. (formerly Quantum Ednl. Discoveries), 1983—. Patentee The Acctg. Game, 1982. Recipient grant St. of Vt., 1978. Home: 3134 6th St Boulder CO 80304-2508 Office: Creative Learning Internat 3134 6th St Boulder CO 80304

MARGESON, DOUGLAS WILLIAM, reporter; b. Seattle, Aug. 23, 1946; m. Apr. 12, 1969; 2 children. BA in Comms., Editorial Journalism, U. Wash., 1968. Pubs. dir. Seattle Pacific U., 1971-73; speech writer Pacific N.W. Bell, Seattle, 1973-75; reporter, editor Lynnwood (Wash.) Enterprise, 1975-78; reporter, feature writer Fournier Newspapers, Renton, Wash., 1978-82; feature writer, investigative reporter Bellevue (Wash.) Jour. Am., 1982—; lectr. at profl. meetings, ednl. instns., 1983-86. With USMC, 1968-70. Recipient 156 Journalism awards for his work from Nat. Press Women Assn., Suburban Newspapers of Am., Wash. Press Assn., Sigma Delta Chi, N.W. Region Soc. Profl. Journalists, Wash. Newspaper Pubs. Assn. Mem. ACLU, Soc. Profl. Joruanlists, Wash. Press Assn., N.W. Screenwriters Alliance, Pacific N.W. Writers Conf., Sigma Delta Chi. Home: 18131 NE 191st St Woodinville WA 98072-8239

MARGO, KENNETH CRAIG, counselor; b. Oklahoma City, Apr. 22, 1953; s. Marvin Kenneth and Bobbie June (Cravens) M.; m. Laura Leslie Brooks, June 19, 1980. BA in Psychology, Centenary Coll., Shreveport, La., 1975; MEd in Counseling Psychology, Ctrl. State U., Edmond, Okla., 1978. Lic. profl. counselor, Okla., Wyo. Staff psychologist Okla. Children's Meml. Hosp., Oklahoma City, 1978-82; psychologist, clinic dir. Lincoln County Guidance Ctr., Chandler, Okla., 1982-84; pvt. practice Oklahoma City, 1984-86, 89-90; staff psychologist Mentla Helath Svcs. So. Okla., Ardmore, 1986-88; therapist, staff devel. coord. St. Joseph's Childrens Home, Oklahoma City, 1988-89; supr. outpatient substance abuse programs Ctrl. Wyo. Counseling Ctr., Casper, 1990—. Mem. Okla. Youth and Suicide Task Force, Oklahoma City, Health Planning Comm., Chandler. Mem. ACA, Am. Mental Health Counselors Assn., Wyo. Mental Health Counselors Assn., Wyo. Counseling Assn., Okla. Assn. Counseling & Devel. (pres. 1989). Office: Ctrl Wyo Counseling Ctr 1200 E 3rd St Ste 330 Casper WY 82601-2933

MARGOLIS, BERNARD ALLEN, library administrator, antique book merchant and appraiser; b. Greenwich, Conn., Oct. 2, 1948; s. Sidney S. and Rose (Birkenfeld) M.; m. Amanda Batey, Nov. 2, 1973. BA in Polit. Sci., U. Denver, 1970, MLS, 1973. Cert. libr., Mich. Libr. asst. Denver Pub. Libr., 1970-72; br. head Virginia Village Libr., Denver Pub. Libr., 1972-73; dep. dir. Monroe County Libr. Sys., Mich., 1973-75; dir. Raisin Valley Libr. Sys., Monroe, 1976-78, S.E. Mich. Regional Film Libr., Monroe, 1976-88, Monroe County Libr. Sys., 1976-88, Pikes Peak Libr. Dist., Colorado Springs, Colo., 1988—; pres. Colo. Ctr. for Books, 1989-92, Colo. Ctr. for the Book, 1993—; cons. in libr. pub. rels., 1976—; founding trustee United Colo. Investment Trust, 1993-95; chmn. Colo. Gov.'s Conf. on Libr. and Info. Svcs., 1990; lectr. Western Mich. U., Kalamazoo, 1978-81; appraiser rare books, Monroe, Colorado Springs, 1970—. Contbr. articles to profl. jours; mem. editl. bd. Bottom Line Mag. Fin. Mgmt. for Librs., 1986—. Bd. dirs. Monroe Sen. Citizens Ctr., 1976-80, Monroe Fine Arts Coun., 1978-81, Am. the Beautiful Centennial Celebration, Inc., 1993, The Libr. Consortium, 1993—, Downtown Colo. Springs, Inc., 1994—, Care & Share, Inc., sec., 1994—, vice chmn., 1995, chmn., 1995—; chmn. Blue Cross-Blue Shield Consumer Coun., Detroit, 1984-88; mem. adv. bd. Access Colo. Libr. and Info. Network (ACLIN), 1991—, Mercy Meml. Hosp., Monroe, 1984-86, 5th Congl. Art Competition Com., 1992—; Dem. candidate for Mich. Senate, 1986; mem. allocations com. Pikes Peak United Way, 1988-91, chmn., 1990-91, bd. dirs., 1990-91, 94—; chmn. Great Pikes Peak Cowboy Poetry Gathering, 1990, 91, 92, 94, 95; del. White House Conf. on Libr. and Info. Scis.; mem. El Paso County, Colo. Retirement Bd., 1995—. Recipient Mayoral Cert. Commendation award Denver, 1972, 73; named Mich. Libr. of Yr., 1985, Colo. Libr. of Yr., 1990; commendation John F. Kennedy Ctr. for Performing Arts, 1993. Mem. ALA (governing coun. 1986—, endowment trustee 1989-93, sr. endowment trustee 1993—, chmn. resolutions com. 1991-92, cons. ann. swap and shop 1979-84, John Cotton Dana award 1977, 91, Libr. Awareness Idea Search award Washington 1982), Colo. Libr. Assn. (mem. legis. com., Intellectual Freedom award 1993), Libr. Adminstrv. Mgmt. Assn., Pub. Libr. Assn. Democrat. Jewish. Home: 10640 Hungate Rd Colorado Springs CO 80908-4380 Office: Pikes Peak Libr Dist PO Box 1579 5550 N Union Blvd Colorado Springs CO 80901-1579

MARGOLIS, DONALD L., mechanical engineering educator, consultant; b. Washington, Nov. 13, 1945; s. Joel and Jeanette (Lowenwirth) M.; children: Scott, David. BSME, Va. Poly. and State U., 1967; MSME, MIT, 1969, PhD, 1972. Instr. dept. mech. engring. MIT, Cambridge, Mass., 1969-72; prof. dept. mech. engring. U. Calif., Davis, 1972—; cons. various industries, nat. labs., U.S., Japan. Author: (textbook) System Dynamics: A Unified Approach, 1990; contbr. over 100 articles to profl. jours. Fellow ASME (Outstanding Teaching award 1980); mem. Soc. Automotive Engrs. (Ralph R. Teeter Ednl. award 1986). Office: U Calif Davis Dept Mech Engring Davis CA 95616

MARGOSIAN, LUCILLE MANOUGIAN (MRS. ERVIN M. MARGOSIAN), artist, educator; b. Highland Park, Mich.; d. George Krikor and Vera Varsenig Manougian; BFA, Wayne State U., 1957, MA, 1958; postgrad. Calif. State U., Fresno, 1959-60, U. Calif. at Berkeley, 1960-61; m. Ervin M. Margosian, Oct. 28, 1960; children: Rebecca L., Rachel L. Juror fine arts and photography exhbns. Carmel Art Festival, 1994. One-man show at Jackson's Gallery, Berkeley, Calif., 1961; exhibited in group shows at Detroit Art Inst., 1958, Oakland (Calif.) Art Museum, 1961, Wayne State U. Community Arts Center, Detroit, 1965, San Francisco Ann. Art Festivals, 1967, 68, 69, Jack London Square Arts Festival, Oakland, 1969, 70, Judah L. Magnes Meml. Mus., Berkeley, 1970, Kaiser Center Gallery, Oakland, 1970, Oakland Mus. Changing Gallery, 1969, Olive Hyde Art Center, Fremont, 1971, 73, Richmond (Calif.) Art Center, 1972, Villa Montalvo Galleries at Phelan Estate, Saratoga, Calif., 1976, others; faculty Peralta Community Colls., Laney campus, Oakland, 1967—, prof. art, 1970—, chmn. dept., 1982-84, 89—. Charter mem. univ. art mus. council U. Calif. at Berkeley, 1965—. Recipient Certificate of Distinguished Achievement, Am. Legion, 1950; Best of Show 1st prize 5th Ann. Textile Exhbn., Fremont, Calif., 1973; Merit award City of Fremont, 1973, Zellerbach Bldg. Gallery, San Francisco, 1975. Mem. Calif. Art Edn. Assn., Oakland Museum Assn., Richmond Art Center, Women of Wayne, Wayne State U. Alumni Assn., East Bay Watercolor Soc., Internat. Platform Assn., Am. Fedn. Tchrs., Peralta Fedn. Tchrs. Office: Laney Coll Art Dept 900 Fallon St Oakland CA 94607-4808

MARGULEAS, HOWARD P., agricultural products executive; b. 1934. U. Calif., Berkeley, 1957. With Heggblade-Marguleas-Tenneco, Bakersfield, Calif., 1957-74, Sun World, Inc., Bakersfield, Calif., 1974—; with Sun World Internat. Corp., 1980—, now chmn. bd., CEO. Office: Sun World International Inc 5544 Cal Ave Ste 280 Bakersfield CA 93309*

MARGULIES, LEE, newspaper editor. Television editor Los Angeles Times, Calif. Office: Los Angeles Times Times Mirror Sq Los Angeles CA 90053

MARIANI, MARK A., food products executive; b. 1952. With Mariani Packaging Co., Inc., 1973—, now pres. Office: Mariani Packing Co Inc 320 Jackson St San Jose CA 95112-3206*

MARIGOLD, LAWRENCE LEE, international energy consultant; b. Tecachapi, Calif., Oct. 14, 1940; s. George Austin and Pauline M. (Vukich) M.; m. Julie Ann Chohon, Sept. 9, 1978; 1 child, Michelle. AA, Contra Costa Coll., 1961; BS, U. San Francisco, 1964; MBA, Golden Gate U., 1967. Mgr. Chevron, San Francisco, 1965-70; group mgr. Unical, Palatine, Ill., 1970-74; dir., corp. rep. Anheuer Busch Inc., St. Louis, 1974-84; pres., CEO Marigold Ventures, Fair Oaks, Calif., 1984-93, 94—; dir. methanol mktg. MG Refining & Mktg., Forest Hill, Md., 1993-94; cons. to Internat. Metallgeshellschaft, Frankfort, Germany, 1984—, ICI, State of Calif., others. Contbr. articles to profl. jours. Spkr. various civic and polit. groups, Calif., 1984—. Roman Catholic. Home and Office: Marigold Ventures 4925 Saint Thomas Dr Fair Oaks CA 95628-5312

MARINACCI, TERESA DENISE, theater director; b. Exeter, Calif., Jan. 31, 1964; d. Elmer Dean Longest and Billie Rae (Hunter) Butler; m. Christopher Marinacci, July 20, 1985. BA in Psychology/BA in Theater Arts, U. Calif., Santa Cruz, 1989; MFA, U. Calif., Davis, 1992. Pvt. instr. in Drama various cities, Calif., 1982—; dir., playwright various theaters, various cities, Calif., 1984—; instr. U. Calif., Davis, 1989-91; artistic dir. King's Ct. Players, San Francisco, 1992-94, TheatreMaker, San Francisco, 1993—; bd. dirs., pres., membership chair Solano County Arts Alliance, Fairfield, Calif. Asst. dir. (play) Redwood Trilogy, 1991, The Queen's Garden, 1992-93 (4 Dramalogue awards), on tour, 1994—, Dell Arte Player's Slapstick, 1994; collaborator Brenda Wong Aoki's Random Acts of Kindness, 1994—; playwright, dir.: Legend of the 5th World, 1992, Tellin' Tall Tales, 1993; playwright, dir., producer: Starving Actors Perform-A Showcase of Music, Dance, Sorrow & Laughter, 1993; dir. co-author (K. Carner's) Wisdom While on my Back (Part I- Surviving College), 1994; author, dir. Love, Romance & Passion for the Oakland Lyric Opera, 1995. Mem. We the People, 1992. Mem. AAUW, Nat. Mus. Women in Arts, Theatre Bay Area, Theatre Comm. Group, Oreg. Shakespeare Festival, Solano County Arts Alliance, Alumni Assn. U. Calif. Santa Cruz, Calif. Aggie Alumni Assn.

MARINE, ROBERT JAMES, nursing administrator, consultant, naval officer, researcher; b. Richmond, Va., Mar. 8, 1951; s. James Edward and Hazel Maxine (Corwin) M. BSN, San Diego State U., 1979; MA in Edn., Stanford U., 1990, postgrad., 1992—. ACLS, BLS, PALS. With Kellogg Co., Battle Creek, Mich., 1969-72; chemist Dexter Midland Corp., Waukegan, Ill., 1973-76; commd., Nurse Corps USN, 1979-93, advanced through grades to lt. comdr., 1979-93; staff nurse, ICU, Int. Med., PARR Naval Hosp., Guam, 1979-83; staff nurse surgery Naval Hosp., Long Beach, Calif., 1985-86, asst. dept. head, div. officer Command Edn. Dept., 1986-88; charge nurse med./surg. Naval Hosp., Long Beach, 1988-89; div. officer life support Command Edn. Dept. Naval Hosp., Oakland, Calif., 1990, head command edn. dept., 1990-93; health plan adminstr. Stanford U., 1994—; cons. Paul Armstrong Assocs., Oakland, 1990-91; total quality mgmt. facilitator Dept. of the Navy, Bethesda, Md., 1991-94; pres., CEO Oak Hill Assocs., Oakland, 1991—, Merritt C.C. Health Care Programs, Oakland, 1990-94; affiliate faculty Am. Heart Assn., ACLS-I/ACLS/BLS-I/BLS/PALS, 1986—; sailing instr. USN/ARC, 1986—; rschr. in tech. in med. edn., 1994—. Co-author (manual) ACLS Instructor/Student Guide, 1987 (Affiliate Faculty of the Yr. 1987); patentee in field. Mem. AACN, Health Care Execs. of No. Calif., East Bay Bus. Assn., Sierra Club. Home: 149 California Ave #A308 Palo Alto CA 94306-1926 Office: Stanford U Total Comp Dept Code 6110 Stanford CA 94305-6110

MARINELLY, RALPH, secondary educator; b. Akron, Ohio, Dec. 28, 1931; s. Ralph and Ruth (Biggie) M.; m. Lori Stanaley, Oct. 13, 1935; children: Michael, Mark, Steven, Jennifer. BA, Calif. State U., 1954, MA, 1960; postgrad., U. Calif., Berkeley, 1960-63. Cert. tchr., adminstr., Calif. Tchr., counselor Oakland (Calif.) Pub. Schs., 1956-64, dir. student activities, adminstrv. asst.; tchr., coord. instrnl. improvement program San Mateo Union H.S. Sch. Dist., 1964—; prin. Am. program U. Stranieri, Perugia, Italy, 1965; coord. gifted program Crestmoor H.S., faculty pres., 1972, 73, mem. faculty senate, 1976, legis. rep., 1974, 75; dept. head social sci. Burlingame H.S., San Mateo H.S. Commr., chmn. Piedmont (Calif.) Park Commn., 1984-90, vice chmn. recycling com., 1991—; pres. Piedmont High Sch. Dad's Club, 1977-79; dir. Piedmont Hist. Soc., 1992—. Recipient Commendation Piedmont City Coun., 1989. Mem. Calif. Tchrs. Assn. (legis. rep. 1956—), NEA. Republican. Roman Catholic. Home: 312 Jerome Ave Piedmont CA 94610-1024

MARINER, WILLIAM MARTIN, chiropractor; b. Balt., Jan. 2, 1949; s. William Joseph and Ellen (Dexter) M. AA, Phoenix Coll., 1976; BS in Biology, L.A. Coll. of Chiropractic, 1980, D Chiropractic summa cum laude, 1980; DD (hon.), Universal Life Ch., Modesto, Calif., 1986. Health food restaurant mgr. Golden Temple of Conscious Cookery, Tempe, Ariz., 1974-75; health food store mgr. Guru's Grainery, Phoenix, 1975; physical therapist A.R.E. Clinic, Phoenix, 1975-76; research dir., founder G.R.D. Healing Arts Ctr., Phoenix, 1974-77; aminstrv. asst., acad. dean L.A. Coll. Chiropractic, Whittier, Calif., 1977-80; faculty Calif. Acupuncture Coll., L.A., 1978-80; ednl. cons. Avanti Inst., San Francisco, 1985-91; found, dir., head clinician Pacific Healing Arts Ctr., Del Mar, Calif., 1980-93, Mt. Shasta, Calif., 1993—; ednl. cons. John Panama Cons., San Francisco, 1991—. Patentee in field. Co-dir. "We Care We Share" Charitable Orgn., San Diego, 1985-86. Named Outstanding Sr., L.A. Coll. Chiropractic, 1980. Mem. San Diego Chiropractic Soc., Calif. Chiropractic Assn., Am. Chiropractic Assn., Internat. Coll. Applied Kinesiology, Holistic Dental Assn., Brit. Homopathic Assn., Rotary. Office: Pacific Healing Arts Ctr PO Box 192 Mount Shasta CA 96067-0192

MARIO, ERNEST, pharmaceutical company executive; b. Clifton, N.J., June 12, 1938; s. Jerry and Edith (Meijer) M.; m. Mildred Martha Daume, Dec. 10, 1961; children: Christopher Bradley, Gregory Gerald, Jeremy Konrad. B.S. in Pharmacy, Rutgers U., 1961; M.S. in Phys. Scis., U. R.I., 1963, Ph.D. in Phys. Scis., 1965. Registered pharmacist, R.I., N.Y. Vice pres. mfg. Smith Kline Corp., Phila., 1975-77; v.p. mfg. ops. U.S. Pharm. Co. (divsn. E. R. Squibb), New Brunswick, N.J., 1977-79; v.p., gen. mgr. chem. div. E. R. Squibb, Princeton, N.J., 1979-81; pres. chem. and engring. div., sr. v.p. Squibb Corp., Princeton, 1981-84; v.p. Squibb Corp., 1984-86; pres., COO Glaxo Inc., 1986-88, chmn., CEO, 1988, chmn., 1989-91; CEO Glaxo Holdings plc, 1989-93, dep. chmn., 1991-93; co-chmn., CEO, Alza Corp., Palo Alto, Calif., 1993—; grad. asst., instr. U. R.I., Kingston, 1961-66; research fellow Inst. Neurol. Diseases, Bethesda, Md., 1963-65. Contbr. articles to profl. jours. Trustee Duke U., Rockefeller U., U. R.I. Found.; mem. president's coun. U. R.I.; chmn. Am. Found. for Pharm. Edn.; bd. dirs. Nat. Found. Infectious Diseases, Antigenics, Pharm. Product Devel., Stanford Health Svcs. Office: Alza Corp 950 Page Mill Rd Palo Alto CA 94304-1012

MARIONI, TOM, artist; b. Cin., May 21, 1937; s. John D. and Jennie (Geiss) M.; m. Kathan Brown, June 14, 1983; children by previous marriage: Marino, Anthony, Miles. MFA, Cin. Art Acad., 1959. Curator, Richmond Art Ctr. (Calif.), 1968-71; founding dir. Mus. Conceptual Art, San Francisco, 1970-84. Exhibited one-man shows: Galeria Foksal, Warsaw, Poland, 1975, DeYoung Mus., San Francisco, 1977, Modern Art Gallery, Vienna, Austria, 1979, Crown Point Press, San Francisco, 1993, Margarete Roeder Gallery, N.Y.C., 1994; group shows include: Tate Gallery, London, 1982, Belca House, Kyoto, Japan, 1982, Mus. Contemporary Art, L.A., 1995; editor, designer Vision, 1975-81. Mem. tech. assistance com. San Francisco Redevel. Agy., 1982—. Served with U.S. Army, 1960-63. W.Ger. Nat. Endowment Arts grantee, 1980; Guggenheim Found. fellow, 1981; Awards in Visual Arts grantee, 1984. Address: 657 Howard St San Francisco CA 94105

MARISCAL ZUNIGA, JOSE LUIS, funding company executive; b. Mascota, Jalisco, Mex., Aug. 19, 1942; came to U.S., 1960, naturalized, 1967; s. Juan José Mariscal Hurtado and Maria Del Rosario Zuñiga; m. Edith Gutstein, Jan. 6, 1966; children: Alicia Conzuelo, Luis Herschel. AA, Merritt Coll., 1965; BA, Calif. State U., Hayward, 1967, MPA, 1969; PhD, Golden Gate U., 1992; cert. factoring specialist, Internat. Factoring Inst., 1994. Cert. factoring specialist. Fellowship Coro Found., San Francisco, 1969-70; adminstrv. asst. County of Santa Cruz, Calif., 1970-71; dir. rsch. and evaluation City of Pitts., 1971-73; dep. dir. U. Health Ctrs. of SJV, Orange Cove, Calif., 1973-75; dir. of planning and devel. N.E. Valley Health Corp., San Fernando, Calif., 1976-79; prof. Inst. of Tech., Tepic, Mex., 1980-82; pres., CEO Green Grow Funding, Oakland, Calif., 1994—; cons. econ. integration of Am. hemisphere, import and export, NAFTA issues, Oakland, 1984—, Health and Human Svcs., Calif., 1970-79, Dept. Econ. Devel., 1980-82, Fruit Growers Assn., State of Nay, Mex., 1979-82. Bd. dirs. Berkeley Coop., 1985; community trainer Pitts. Model Cities, Pittsburg, Calif., 1971-73; cons. community groups, 1970-79. Fellowship Coro Found., 1969-70. Mem. Nat. Assn. of Factoring Profls., Internat. City Mgmt. Assn., Am. Soc. for Pub. Adminstrn., Conf. of Minority Pub. Adminstrs. Democrat. Home: 4365 39th Ave Oakland CA 94619-1612 Office: Green Grow Funding 4365 39th Ave Oakland CA 94619-1612

MARK, ARTHUR, information systems specialist; b. San Francisco, Aug. 1, 1948; s. Bo You and Chew Lin (Oyoung) M.; m. Alice Look, Sept. 1, 1973 (div. Oct. 1987); children: Jennifer, Brandon. BS, Calif. State U., 1971, MS, 1977. Cert. data processing, info. systems auditor, internal auditor. Instr. info. systems Calif. State U., Sacramento, 1978—, Am. River Coll., Sacramento City Coll.; with State of Calif., Sacramento, 1977-85, 88—. Active United Way. Maj. USMC, 1985-88. Mem. MENSA, Inst. Internal Auditors. Republican. Home: 8985 Laguna Place Way Elk Grove CA 95758-5366

MARK, DENIS HUGH, lawyer; b. N.Y.C., May 27, 1951; s. Murray Samuel and Roslyn (Strauchler) M.; m. Laurel Frances Lester, May 15, 1983; children: Joseph Warren, Elizabeth Mary-Lester. BS, Tufts U., 1972; postgrad., Washington U., St. Louis, 1975-76; JD, U. Colo., 1978. Bar: Colo. 1978, U.S. Dist. Ct. Colo. 1978, U.S. Ct. Appeals (10th cir.) 1980, U.S. Tax Ct. 1983, U.S. Ct. Appeals (9th and 6th cirs.) 1985, U.S. Supreme Ct. 1985. Law clk. to presiding judge Colo. Ct. Appeals, Denver, 1978-79; assoc. Wagner, D'Onofrio, Waller & Stouffer, Denver, 1979-80; assoc. Wagner & Waller, P.C., Englewood, Colo., 1980-83, ptnr., 1983-84; ptnr. Waller, Mark & Allen, P.C., Denver, 1985-90, Vinton, Waller, Slivka & Panasci, Denver, 1990-93, Waller and Mark, P.C., Denver, 1993—. Editor: U. Colo. Law Rev., 1978. Del. Colo. State Dem. Assembly, Denver, 1980, 86. Mem. ABA, Colo. Bar Assn., Denver Bar Assn., Nat. Assn. Criminal Def. Lawyers, Assn. Trial Lawyers Am., Colo. Trial Lawyers Assn. (bd. dirs. 1984-88, 90—, chmn. amicus curiae com. 1989-91, mem. exec. com. 1990-91), Order of Coif. Jewish. Home: 7051 S Locust Cir Englewood CO 80112-1575 Office: Waller and Mark PC 1777 S Harrison P200 Denver CO 80210

MARK, MAXINE CATHERINE SCHLIEKER, writer; b. Lisco, Nebr., Dec. 13, 1932; d. Arnold H. and Irene M. (Kummer) Schlieker; m. Thomas R. Mark, July 9, 1953; children: Gregory A., Brian M. BA, Colo. State U., 1954, MA, 1966. Math. and English tchr. Berea (Ohio) Sch. Dist., 1956-57; part-time English prof. Colo. State U., Ft. Collins, 1957-69; honors tchr. Blevins Jr. H.S., Ft. Collins, 1969-79; AP coord., tchr. Rocky Mountain H.S., Ft. Collins, 1979-90; tchr. U. Budapest, Hungary, 1990-91; writer, editor MM Writer/Communications, Ft. Collins, 1991—; ednl. test reader Ednl. Testing Svc., Princeton, N.J., 1985-93; conductor advanced placement seminars Colo. State U., Ft. Collins, summers 1988-92. Devel. and copy editor: Value & Form: Comparative Literature, Painting & Music, 1993, From Concept to Form in Landscape Design, 1993. Newsletter editor Phi Delta Kappa, Ft. Collins, 1991-92; sec. of bd. Alzheimers Assn., Ft. Collins, 1994. Mem. MLA, Rocky Mountain Profl. Publishers Guild. Home and

Office: MM/Writer Communications 1309 Parkwood Dr Fort Collins CO 80525

MARK, RUFUS JAMES, physician, educator; b. Castro Valley, Calif., Dec. 28, 1957; s. Hans Michael and Marion Genevieve (Thorpe) M.; m. Katherine Ann Johnson, Jan. 30, 1988; children: Phillip, Nicholas, Juliette. BS summa cum laude, Yale U., 1981; MD, UCLA, 1986. Diplomate Am. Bd. Radiology. Intern Presbyn. Hosp., Pacific Med. Ctr., 1986-87; resident in radiation oncology UCLA Med. Ctr., 1987-90, asst. clin. prof., 1990—; asst. clin. prof. U. Calif. San Diego Med. Ctr., 1991—; physician radiation oncology Radiation Med. Group, San Diego, 1991-95, Good Samaritan Hosp., L.A., 1995—. Contbr. more than 30 articles to med. jours. Mem. AMA, Am. Cancer Soc., Am. Soc. Therapeutic Radiation Oncology, Calif. med. Assn., N.Y. Acad. Scis., Phi Beta Kappa. Home: 8724 Butano Ct San Diego CA 92129-4438 Office: Good Samaritan Hosp dept Radiation Oncology 1225 Wilshire Blvd Los Angeles CA 90017

MARKARIAN, ALEXIA MITRUS, artist; b. Binghamton, N.Y.; m. Raymond Markarian. Studied with Robert Beverly Hale, Art Students League, N.Y.C. Artist, 1985—; juror 10th Ann. Congressional Arts Caucus, 41st Dist., 1991, Scott Watson Meml. Salon, Soc. Calif. Assn. Camera Clubs, 1991, North County Artist's Coop., Escondido, Calif., 1993, San Diego Art Inst., 1992, lectr. isomata master class, Idyllwild, Calif., 1992; co-originator Photropolis 95 Internat. Photo/Art Exhbn., San Diego, 1995. Solo shows include Fla. So. State Coll. Melvin Art Gallery, Lakeland, 1988, U. Mo. Gallery 210, St. Louis, 1988, Witter Gallery, Storm Lake, Iowa, 1988, Mira Costa Coll. James Crumley Gallery, Oceanside, Calif., 1988, Dietrich Jenny Gallery, San Diego, 1989, Cazenovia (N.Y.) Coll. Chapman Cultural Ctr., 1989, Rogue C.C. Wiseman Gallery, Grants Pass, Oreg., 1989, U. No. Colo. Miriani Gallery, Greeley, Colo., 1989, Memphis State U., 1989, Butte Coll. Coyote Gallery, Oroville, Calif., 1990, Oneiros Gallery, San Diego, 1991, Visual Arts Ctr. Alaska, Ancorage, 1991, Wichita Falls Mus. and Art Ctr., 1991, Edmonton Art Gallery, Alta., Can., 1992, Robertson Ctr. Arts and Scis., Binghamton, N.Y., 1992, Washington and Jefferson Coll., Washington, Pa., 1992, Art Gallery Greater Victoria, B.C., Can., 1993, Kelowna (Can.) Mus., 1993, Red Venus Gallery, San Diego, 1994; exhibited in group shows at Orange County Art Assn. Nat., Brea, Calif., 1985, Internat. Soc. for Airbrush Arts, 1985, Pitts. Ctr. for Arts, 1985, Chautauqua Nat. Exhibit of Am. Art, N.Y., 1985, Touring Group Exhibit "Five Women Artists, 1986, Small Works Nat., N.Y., 1986, San Diego Art Inst. Ann. Nat., 1986, San Diego Mus. Art, 1986, Riverside Art Mus., Calif., 1986, Butler Inst. Am. Art, Youngstown, Ohio, 1985, Calif. Watercolor and Drawing Survery, 1986, Butler Inst. Am. Art, Youngstown, Ohio, 1987, San Diego Art Inst., 1987 (Mid Winter award), Fresno Arts Ctr., 1987, Mus. No. B.C., Prince Rupert, Can., 1987, Elvehjem Mus. Art, Madison, Wis., 1987, Minot (N.D.) Art Gallery, 1987, Coll. Ea. Utah, Price, 1987, Mt. Mercy Coll., Cedar Rapids, Iowa, 1987, Masur Mus. Art, Monroe, La., 1988, Fla. Nat./Fla. State U., Tallahassee, 1988, LaGrange (Ga.) Nat. XIII, 1988 (Purchase award), Tex. A&M U., College Station, 1988, John Thomas Gallery, Fullerton, Calif., 1989, Dietrich Jenny Gallery, San Diego, 1989, San Diego Art Inst., 1990 (award), Artists Union Gallery, Moscow, 1990, San Diego Mus. Art, 1991, Calif. Ctr. for Arts, Escondido, 1993, Central Cultural, X Festival Internacional, Tijuana, Mex., 1994others; represented in pvt. and public collections. Recipient Visual Arts fellowship Calif. Arts Coun., 1989-90, Pub. Art grant Calif. Transp./City Heights Community Devel. Corp., 1993. Home: 4411 Alamo Way San Diego CA 92115-5909

MARKELL, EDWARD KINGSMILL, medical parasitologist, educator; b. N.Y.C., Apr. 14, 1918; s. Edward Louis and Genevieve Janet (Williams) M.; m. Nancy Jean Hiler, Mar. 14, 1953; children: Edward Christopher, Anne Elizabeth. BA in Zoology with high honors, Pomona Coll., 1938; PhD in Zoology, U. Calif., Berkeley, 1942; MD, Stanford U., 1951. Diplomate Am. Bd. Med. Microbiology. Teaching asst. zoology, head teaching asst. parasitology U. Calif., Berkeley, 1938-41, rsch. fellow zoology, 1946; intern medicine Stanford U. Hosps., 1950-51; asst. prof. infectious diseases UCLA, 1951-58, Markle fellow med. sci., 1952-57; mem. dept. internal medicine Permanente Med. Group, Oakland, Calif., 1958-84; clin. assoc. prof. community and preventive medicine Stanford U., 1962-70, clin. prof. family, community and preventive medicine, 1970-84, prof. emeritus, 1984—; clin. prof. medicine and tropical medicine U. Calif., San Francisco, 1985—; cons. parasitology Calif. State Dept. Pub. Health, 1952-58; mem. standards and examination com. Am. Bd. Microbiology, 1960-67; mem. parasitology adv. bd. U.S. Pharmacopeia, 1988—. Author: Diagnostic Medical Parasitology, 1958, Medical Parasitology, 1965, 7th edit., 1992, Parasitologia: Diagnostico, Prevencion y Tratamiento, 1984; author: (with others) Hunter's Tropical Medicine, 1984, 91, Current Therapy of Pediatric Infectious Diseases, 1986, 3d edit., 1993, Parasitic Infections in Pregnancy and the Newborn, 1988, Tropical Medicine/Medical Parasitology, 1989; editorial cons. Dorland's Illustrated Medical Dictionary, 1969-74. Vestry All Souls Episcopal Ch., Berkeley, 1960-63, 76-79, 87-90, sr. warden, 1963, 79. With USNR, 1942-46. Mem. Am. Soc. Tropical Medicine and Hygiene (delegation to China 1978), Am. Soc. Parasitologists (chmn. edn. com. 1976-79, chmn. clin. lab. com. 1980-83, del. clin. lab. standards 1981-83), Calif. Med. Assn., Alameda-Contra Costa County Med. Assn. (mediation com. 1970-91), Royal Soc. Tropical Medicine and Hygiene, Phi Beta Kappa, Sigma Xi, Alpha Omega Alpha. Home and Office: 28 Senior Ave Berkeley CA 94708-2212

MARKEN, WILLIAM RILEY, magazine editor; b. San Jose, Calif., Sept. 2, 1942; s. Harry L. and Emma Catherine (Kraus) M.; m. Marilyn Tonascia, Aug. 30, 1964; children—Catherine, Elizabeth, Michael, Paul. Student, Occidental Coll., 1960-62; B.A., U. Calif.-Berkeley, 1964. Writer, mng. editor, now editor-in-chief and v.p. Sunset Mag., Menlo Park, Calif., 1964—. Bd. dirs. Calif. Tomorrow, 1979-83; pres. League to Save Lake Tahoe, 1994-96. Democrat. Office: Sunset Mag 80 Willow Rd Menlo Park CA 94025-3661

MARKER, MARC LINTHACUM, lawyer, investor; b. Los Angeles, July 19, 1941; s. Clifford Harry and Voris (Linthacum) M.; m. Sandra Yocom, Aug. 29, 1965; children: Victor, Gwendolyn. BA in Econs. and Geography, U. Calif.-Riverside, 1964; JD, U. So. Calif., 1967. Asst. v.p., asst. sec. Security Pacific Nat. Bank, L.A., 1970-73; sr. v.p., chief counsel, sec. Security Pacific Leasing Corp., San Francisco, 1973-92; pres. Security Pacific Leasing Svcs. Corp., San Francisco, 1977-85, dir., 1977-92; bd. dirs., sec. Voris, Inc., 1973-86; bd. dirs. Refiners Petroleum Corp., 1977-81, Security Pacific Leasing Singapore Ltd., 1983-85, Security Pacific Leasing Can. Ltd., 1989-92; lectr. in field. Served to comdr. USCGR. Mem. ABA, Calif. Bar Assn., D.C. Bar Assn., Am. Assn. Equipment Lessors. Republican. Lutheran. Club: Univ. (L.A.). Office: 471 Magnolia Ave # B Larkspur CA 94939-2034

MARKEY, THOMAS ADAM, school business manager; b. Dayton, Ohio, June 12, 1956; s. Paul Robert Markey and Cathleen Wilgus. BA, Ariz. State U., 1980, MBA, 1992. CPA. Fin. analyst Maricopa County Sch. Supt., Phoenix, 1982-84; EDP acct. Maricopa County Fin. Dept., Phoenix, 1984-88, sr. fin. acct., 1988-90, sr. budget analyst, 1990-92; dir. bus. East Valley Inst. Tech., Mesa, Ariz., 1992—. Sustaining mem. SW Assn. Indian Affairs, Santa Fe, N.Mex., 1990; active mem. Intertribal Indian Ceremonial Assn., Gallup, N.Mex., 1990. Mem. AICPA, Ariz. Soc. CPA's, Assn. Govt. Accts. (exec. com. Phoenix chpt. 1992—), Ariz. Assn. Sch. Bus. Ofcls., Western Govtl. Rsch. Assn., Am. Acad. Religion, Beta Gamma Sigma. Democrat. Home: 3421 N 26th Pl Phoenix AZ 85016-7435 Office: East Valley Inst Tech 200 S Center Mesa AZ 85210-1502

MARKHAM, JOHN CHARLES, biologist; b. Hood River, Oreg., Apr. 2, 1943; s. Wilbur A. and Mamie L. (Graybill) M. AB in Biol. Scis., Stanford U., 1965; MA in Biol. Oceanography, Oreg. State U., 1967; PhD in Marine Biology, U. Miami, 1974. Cert. tchr., Oreg. Rsch. assoc. Bermuda Biol. Sta. for Rsch., St. Georges, 1974-79; researcher Centro de Investigaciones de Quintana Roo, Puerto Morelos, Mex., 1986-87; dir. Arch Cape (Oreg.) Marine Lab., 1979—; courtesy rsch. prof. Oreg. State U., Corvallis, 1985—; rschr. systematics and distbn. of isopoda bopyridae. Contbr. articles to profl. jours. Advisor Haystack Rock Awareness Program, Cannon Beach, Oreg., 1985—. Recipient scholarship Stanford U., 1963-64, A.P. Giannini Found. scholarship, 1964-65; Fulbright scholar, 1967-68; rsch. grantee NSF, 1976-79, Christensen Rsch. Found., 1989, Govt. of France, 1991; Robert E. Maytag fellow U. Miami, 1968-71, Exxon Corp. fellow, 1975. Mem. Crustacean Soc., So. Calif. Acad. Scis. (life), Biol. Soc. Wash. Office: Arch Cape Marine Lab 108 W Markham Ave Arch Cape OR 97102-0105

MARKHAM, REED B., education educator, consultant; b. Alhambra, Calif., Feb. 14, 1957; s. John F. and Reeda (Bjarason) M. BA, Brigham Young U., 1982, MA, 1982; BS, Regents Coll., 1981, MA, 1982; MPA, U. So. Calif., 1983; MA, UCLA, 1989; PhD, Columbia Pacific U., 1991. Mem. faculty Brigham Young U., Provo, Utah, 1984; mem. faculty Calif. State U., Fullerton and Long Beach, 1984, Northridge, 1985; mem. faculty El Camino Coll., Torrance, Calif., 1986, Orange Coast Coll., Costa Mesa, Calif., 1986, Pasadena (Calif.) Coll., 1986, Fullerton (Calif.) Community Coll., 1986; instr., mem. pub. rels. com. Chaffey (Calif.) Coll., 1986-87; prof., CARES dir. Calif. State Poly. U., Pomona, 1987—; adj. prof. Calif. State U., L.A., 1992-93; rsch. asst. to pres. Ctr. for the Study of community Coll., 1985; mem. faculty Rivershde (Calif.) Coll., 1989-90, Rio Hondo (Calif.) Coll., 1989-90, English Lang. Inst., 1994, Calif. Poly Summer Bridge, 1989-95; speechwriter U.S. Supreme Ct., Washington, 1980; cons. gifted childrens program Johns Hopkins U./Scripps Coll., Claremont Calif., 1987-88. Author: Power Speechwriting, 1983, Power Speaking, 1990, Public Opinion, 1990, Advances in Public Speaking, 1991, Leadership 2000: Success Shills for Univeristy Students, 1995; editor Trojan in Govt., U. So. Calif., 1983; editorial bd. Edn. Digest, Speaker and Gavel, Innovative Higher Edn., Pub. Rels. Rev., Nat. Forensic Jour., The Forensic Educator, Clearinghouse for the Contemporary Educator, Hispanic Am. Family Mag.; writer for N.Y. Times, Christian Sci. Monitor; ednl. columnist San Bernardino (Calif.) Sun., 1992-95. Pres. bd. trustees Regents Coll., 1986. Mem. Doctorate Assn. N.Y. Scholars, Nat. Assn. Pvt. Nontraditional Colls. (accrediting com. 1989—), Pub. Rels. Soc. Am. (dir.-at-large inland empire 1992-93, faculty advisor). LDS. Home: 801 E Alosta Ave # T-307 Azusa CA 91702-2744 Office: Calif Polytech U Communications Dept 3801 W Temple Ave Pomona CA 91768-2557

MARKHAM, RICHARD GLOVER, research executive; b. Pasadena, Calif., June 18, 1925; s. Fred Smith and Maziebelle (Glover) M.; m. Jonne Louise Pearson, Apr. 29, 1950; children: Janet B., Fred S., Charles R., Richard G., Marilyn A. Student, Stanford U., 1943; BS, Calif. Inst. Tech., Pasadena, 1945; MS, Stanford U., 1947. Pres., owner Aquarium Pump Supply, Prescott, Ariz., 1957-78; 1st v.p., dir. Bank of Prescott, 1981-87; also v.p., bd. dirs. Oxycal Labs., Prescott, 1981—. Mem. Ariz. Dept. Econ. Planning and Devel., 1967-72; treas. Ariz. State Rep. Com., 1970-72; active Ariz. Acad., 1974—; trustee Orme Sch., Mayer, Ariz., 1970-83, Prescott Coll., 1979-83. Office: Oxycal Labs 533 Madison Ave Prescott AZ 86301-2432

MARKKULA, A. C., JR., entrepreneur, computer company executive. Co-founder, former pres., chief exec. officer Apple Computer Inc., now chmn. bd. dirs.; founder, chmn. Echelon, Los Gatos, Calif. Office: Apple Computer Inc 20525 Mariani Ave Cupertino CA 95014-6201*

MARKO, CHRIS EMERY, social services administrator; b. Eugene, Oreg., Aug. 2, 1966; m. Emery Imre and Margit (Lind) M. BA in English and Writing, U. Wash., 1987; MA in Pub. Affairs, U. Oreg., 1992. Mem. cmty. devel. staff Lane County, Eugene, Oreg., 1989-90, intern coord., 1990-91; planning technician Lane Coun. of Govts., Eugene, Oreg., 1990-91; cmty. devel. specialist, weatherization auditor/insp. Cmty. Action Program East Ctrl. Oreg., Pendleton, 1992—. Mem. Affordable Housing Devel. Forum, Pendleton, 1992. Recipient piano Oreg. Competition award, Nat. Piano Tchrs. Guild, 1982; grantee U.S. Forest Svc., 1990, Oreg. Housing and Cmty. Svcs., 1993. Home: 217 SW 6th St Pendleton OR 97801-2022 Office: Cmty Action Program East Ctrl Oreg 721 SE 3rd St Ste D Pendleton OR 97801-3056

MARKOS, LAURA L., risk management professional; b. Chgo., Mar. 15, 1951. BA, N. Ctrl. Coll., Naperville, Ill., 1972; MBA, N. Ill. U., DeKalb, 1975; CPCU, 1980. Plan acct., prodn. estimator, prodn. planner, prodn.; planning supr., staff asst., acting ins. mgr. Container Corp. Am., 1971-78; acct. exec., asst. v.p. Sedgwick James of Ill., 1978-81; RM 54 instr., ins. edn. commn. Ins. Sch. Chgo., 1978-81; avery rish mgr., 1981-84, dir. R.M., 1984-93, v.p. risk mgmt., 1993—; risk mgmt. adv. L.A. Orgn. Com., 1981-84. Author: Risk Control Student Study Guide for RIM Program, 1978, Managing International Risks, Manufacturing Risk and Insurance International Risk Management, 1988; co-author: Risk Financing Student Guide for R.M. Program, 1978. Bd. dirs. ARC. Recipient Student Achievement award Wall Street Jour., 1972. Mem. Risk Mgmt. Rsch. Coun., RIMS (bd. dirs.), RIMS Industry Liaison Com., RIMS Internat. Com. (chmn. 1987-91, vice chair 1991-92), Internat. Fedn. Risk and Ins. Mgmt. Assocs. (dir., treas. 1991-94).

MARKOVICH, PATRICIA, economist; b. Oakland, Calif.; d. Patrick Joseph and Helen Emily (Prydz) Markovich; BA in Econs., MS in Econs., U. Calif.-Berkeley; postgrad. (Lilly Found. grantee) Stanford U., (NSF grantee) Oreg. Grad. Rsch. Ctr.; children: Michael Sean Treece, Bryan Jeffry Treece, Tiffany Helene Treece. Cert. Emergency Mgmt. Planner. pub. rels. Pettler Advt., Inc.; pvt. practice polit. and econs. cons.; aide to majority whip Oreg. Ho. of Reps.; lectr., instr., various Calif. instns., Chemeketa (Oreg.) Coll., Portland (Oreg.) State U.; commr. City of Oakland (Calif.), 1970-74; chairperson, bd. dirs. Cable Sta. KCOM; mem. gen. plan commn. City of Piedmont, Calif.; mem. Oakland Mus. Archives of Calif. Artists. Mem. Internat. Soc. Philos. Enquiry, Mensa (officer San Francisco region), Bay Area Artists Assn. (coord., founding mem.), Berkeley Art Ctr. Assn., San Francisco Arts Commn. File, Calif. Index for Contemporary Arts, Pro Arts, YLEM, Artists Using Sci. and Tech., Nat. Assn. Female Execs., No. Calif. Pub. Ednl. and Govt. Access Cable TV Com. (founding), Triple Nine Soc., Nat. Coord. Coun. Emergency Mgmt., NAFE.

MARKOVITS, ANDREI STEVEN, political science educator; b. Timisoara, Rumania, Oct. 6, 1948; came to U.S., 1960, naturalized, 1971; s. Ludwig and Ida (Ritter) M. B.A., Columbia U., 1969, M.B.A., 1971, M.A., 1973, M.Phil., 1974, Ph.D., 1976. Mem. faculty N.Y.U., 1974, John Jay Coll. Criminal Justice, CUNY, 1974, Columbia U., 1975; rsch. assoc. Inst. Advanced Studies, Vienna, Austria, 1973-74, Wirtschafts und Sozialwissenschaftliches Inst., German Trade U. Fedn., Duesseldorf, Fed. Republic Germany, 1979, Internat. Inst. Comparative Social Rsch., Sci. Ctr. Berlin, 1980; asst. prof. govt. Wesleyan U., Middletown, Conn., 1977-83; assoc. prof. polit. sci. Boston U., 1983-92; prof., chair bd. studies in politics U. Calif., Santa Cruz, 1992—; vis. prof. Tel Aviv U., 1986, Osnabruck U., 1987, Bochum U., 1991; sr. rsch. assoc. Ctr. for European Studies, Harvard U., 1975—. Author, editor books and papers in field; TV and radio commentator. Univ. Pres.'s fellow Columbia U., 1969, B'nai B'rith Found. fellow, 1976-77, Kalmus Found. fellow, 1976-77, Ford Found. fellow, 1979, Hans Boeckler Found. fellow, 1982; N.Y. State scholar Columbia U., 1969. Mem. N.Y. Acad. Scis., Am. Polit. Sci. Assn., Internat. Polit. Sci. Assn., AAUP. Home: 287 Harvard St Cambridge MA 02139-2336 Office: U Calif Merrill Coll Bd Studies in Politics Santa Cruz CA 95064 also: Harvard U Ctr European Studies 27 Kirkland St Cambridge MA 02138-2043

MARKOWITZ, SAMUEL SOLOMON, chemistry educator; b. Bklyn., Oct. 31, 1931; s. Max and Florence Ethel (Goldman) M.; children: Michael, Daniel, Jonah. B.S. in Chemistry, Rensselaer Poly. Inst., 1953; M.A., Princeton U., 1955, Ph.D., 1957; postgrad. Brookhaven Nat. Lab., 1955-57. Asst. prof. chemistry U. Calif.-Berkeley, 1958-64, assoc. prof., 1964-72, prof., 1972—; faculty sr. scientist Lawrence Berkeley Lab., 1958—; vis. prof. nuclear physics Weizmann Inst. Sci., Rehovot, Israel, 1973-74. Mem. Bd. Edn. of Berkeley Unified Sch. Dist., 1969-73, pres. bd., 1971-72. Recipient Elizabeth McFeely D'Urso Meml. Pub. Ofcl. award Alameda County Edn. Assn., 1973; LeRoy McKay fellow Princeton U., 1955; Charlotte Elizabeth Proctor fellow Princeton U., 1956; NSF postdoctoral fellow U. Birmingham, Eng., 1957-58; NSF sr. postdoctoral fellow Faculte des Scis. de L'Universite de Paris a Orsay, Laboratoire Joliot-Curie de Physique Nucleaire, 1964-65. Fellow AAAS; mem. Am. Chem. Soc. (bd. dirs. Calif. sect., chmn. 1991, 93-94), Am. Phys. Soc., Am. Inst. Chemists, N.Y. Acad. Scis., Calif. Inst. Chemists, Sigma Xi. Home: 317 Tideway Dr Alameda CA 94501-3540 Office: U Calif Dept Chemistry Berkeley CA 94720

MARKS, ARNOLD, journalist; b. Phila., Aug. 4, 1912; s. Morris M. and Esther (Joel) M.; m. Isabelle Ruppert, Oct. 3, 1942 (dec.); 1 son, Rupert William Joel (dec.); m. Emi Seligman Simon. B.A., U. Wash., 1935; M.S., Columbia U., 1939. Editor Pasco (Wash.) Herald, 1946; with Oreg. Jour., Portland, 1946-78; drama, TV, entertainment editor Oreg. Jour., 1948-58, entertainment editor, 1958-78, ret., 1978, freelance writer. Served with AUS, 1942-46. Mem. Sigma Delta Chi, Sigma Alpha Mu. Club: University (Portland). Home: PO Box 590 Gleneden Beach OR 97388-0590 also: 2393 SW Park Pl Portland OR 97205-1056

MARKS, PETER AMASA, technical consulting company administrator; b. Passaic, N.J., Dec. 5, 1948; s. Amasa A. and Eunice L. (Irwin) M.; BS in Design Engring., U. Cin., 1972, MA in Media Communications, 1973, postgrad. in human factors engring. Rsch. asst. dept. mech. engring. U. Cin., 1972; sr. engr. Ford Motor Co., Sharonville, Ohio, 1972-75; prin. Design Insight Cin., 1976—; mng. dir. SDRC TEC Services, Milford, Ohio, 1978-84, dir. product planning and devel., SDRC, Inc., Milford, 1981-84; sr. v.p. ops. Automation Tech., Campbell, Calif., 1985-88; CEO, Design Insight, 1988—. lectr., cons. on product design tech. implementation, U.S., Asia, Europe, also for Am. Mgmt. Assns.; co-founder, head bd of judges Am. Product Excellence (APEX) Awards. Grad. fellow; Gen. Motors grantee in design, 1970; winner nat., internat. competitions for tech. programs. Mem. ASME, IEEE, Soc. Mfg. Engrs. Author books, articles and films in field. Office: Design Insight PO Box 37 Los Gatos CA 95031-0037

MARKS, ROBERT ARTHUR, lawyer, attorney general; b. Dayton, Ohio, Oct. 9, 1952; s. Arthur Kenneth and Patricia Marks; m. Victoria Scurlock, Oct. 21, 1978; two sons. BA, U. Wis., 1974; JD, U. Cin., 1977. Bar: Ohio 1977, Hawaii 1978, U.S. Ct. Appeals (6th cir.) Ohio 1977, U.S. Ct. Appeals (9th cir.) Hawaii 1978, U.S. Supreme Ct. 1992. Pvt. practice Honolulu, 1978-84; dep. atty. gen. State of Hawaii, Honolulu, 1984-87, supervisory dept. atty. gen., 1987-92, 1st dep. atty. gen., 1992, atty. gen., 1992—. Office: Hawaii Dept Atty Gen 425 Queen St Honolulu HI 96813-2903

MARKS, ROBERT L. (BOB MARKS), treasurer ex-officio, rancher; b. Clancy, Montana; m. Barbara Marks; 6 children. Student, U. Mont., Mont. State U. Rancher Clancy; mem. Mont. Ho. of Reps., Helena, 1968-89; with State Dept. Adminstrn., Helena, 1993—; treasurer State of Mont., 1993—; minority whip, 1975; minority leader, 1977; speaker of the house, 1981-82, 1987-88; Rep. house leader, 1985-86; served numeous regional, nat. coms. Office: Mont Ho of Reps Sam W. Mitchell Bldg rm 155 State Capitol Helena MT 59620

MARKS, SHARON LEA, primary school educator, nurse; b. Arroyo Grande, Calif., June 12, 1942; d. Donald Elmore and Gertrude (Grieb) Shaffer; m. George Conrad Schmidt, June 23, 1963 (div. 1975); children: Kerrilynn, Robert, Marianne; m. Keith Dalton Marks, June 4, 1978; children: Joseph, Erik, Alice. Diploma, Sch. Nursing Samuel Merritt Hosp., 1963; BS in Nursing, Lewis and Clark State Coll., 1984, BS in Mgmt., 1986. RN, Calif., Wash. Staff nurse Vesper Meml. Hosp., San Leandro, Calif., 1968-74; night nurse supr. Tuolumne Gen. Hosp., Sonora, Calif., 1975; nurse Orleans (Calif.) Search and Rescue Team, 1975-78; instr. nursing Pasadena (Calif.) City Coll., 1978-79; resource coord. learning ctr. div. health sci. Spokane (Wash.) Community Coll., 1979-84; staff nurse Kootenai Med. Ctr., 1979-85; instr. North Idaho Coll., Coeur d'Alene, 1984-85; staff nurse North Idaho Home Health, Coeur d'Alene, 1985-86; coord. br. office Family Home Care, Spokane, 1986-87; devel., dir. Good Samaritan Home Health Plummer, Idaho and Fairfield, Washington, 1987-88; mgr. patient svcs. VNS Seattle-King County, Tukwila, Wash., 1988-89; co-owner, v.p. The Wooden Boat Shop, Seattle, 1989—; primary sch. tchr. Marisposa Sch., 1994—; owner Marks and Assocs., 1994—; instr. in emergency med. tech. Orleans campus Coll. Redwoods, Eureka, Calif., 1977-78; book reviewer Brady Co., Besterfield and Assocs., 1994; film reviewer Olympia Media Info. Mem. Nat. Head Injury Found., Wash. State Head Injury Found. Office: 8023 Park Lawn Ct Fontana CA 92336

MARKS, STANLEY J., international legal and business consultant; b. Chgo., Apr. 26, 1914; s. Samuel and Sarah Marks; m. Ethel Milgrom, Aug. 1, 1936; 1 child, Roberta E. AB, U. Ill., 1934; LLB, JD, John Marshall Law Sch., Chgo., 1937. Bar: Ill. 1939. Pres., chmn. bd. Beauti-Dor, Inc., Chgo., from 1939, Glamour Glass Door, Inc., Chgo., from 1939; legal and bus. practice Calif., from 1964; internat. and nat. legal and bus. cons. L.A., 1964—; lectr. on polit. and social/econ. events worldwide. Author: (with Ethel Marks) The Bear That Walks Like a Man, 1943, Murder Most Foul, 1967, Two Days of Infamy, 1969, Coup d'Etat!, 1970, Through Distorted Mirrors, 1974, Judaism Looks at Christianity, 1986, A Year in the Lives of the Damned, Reagan, Reaganism, 1986, The 1991 U.S. Consumer Market, 1991, Yes, Americans, A Conspiracy Murdered JFK!, 1992, Jews, Judaism, and the U.S., 1992, others; playwright: Two Days of Judgment, 1984; pub. weekly polit. newsletter Diogenes, 1984, 88. Writer Dem. Nat. Com., 1936, 40, 48, 52, 60, 91. With AUS, 1944-46. Recipient various Army decorations. Mem. Am. Acad. Polit. and Social Scis., Soc. Am. Mil. Engrs., Authors League Am., Dramatists Guild (life), Masons, Shriners. Home: 1530 S Saltair Ave Los Angeles CA 90025-2644

MARKS, WILLIAM H., organ transplant program director, pharmacologist; b. Chgo., Aug. 16, 1948; s. Louis M. and Bertha M. (Michaelson) M.; m. Christine M. Marks, Nov. 1971; children: Annika, Daniel, Susie, Julia. BS, Loyola U., Chgo., 1970; MS, U. Ill., Chgo., 1973; MD, Loyola U., 1977; PhD, Lund U., 1983. Instr. U. Mich., Ann Arbor, 1973-85; asst. prof. surgery and biochemistry Loyola U., Maywood, Ill., 1985-87; assoc. prof. surgery Yale U., New Haven, Conn., 1987-93; adj. assoc. prof. pharmacology U. Ill., Chgo., 1987—; dir. organ transplantation Swedish Med. Ctr., Seattle, 1994—; dir. lab. for transplant biology; surg. adv. bd. Smith Kline Beechan, Phila., 1992—; USMLE surg. step II Nat. Bd. Med. Examiners, Phila., 1992—. Editor Resident Surgery, 1992, Plytomedicine, 1994; editl. bd. Resident Surgery, 1992—; contbr. articles to profl. jours.; patentee in field. Mem. exec. com. N.W. Kidney Ctrs., Seattle, 1993. Fellow ACS (SK&F fellowship 1985, 86); mem. Am. Soc. Transplant Surgeons, Am. Soc. Transplant Physicians, Soc. Univ. Surgeons, The Transplant Soc. Office: Organ Transplant Program #400 1120 Cherry St # 400 Seattle WA 98104-2023

MARKS, WILLIAM J., cable television executive; b. Akron, Ohio, May 24, 1944; s. Richard D. and B. Katherine (Duell) M.; m. Patricia Ann Marks (div. 1985); children: William J., Lanetta; m. Donna Morgan, Apr. 25, 1985. BSME, Akron U., 1966; Hon. PhD, Heed U., Hollywood, Fla., 1980. Exec. v.p., owner Am. Video Corp., Ft. Lauderdale, Fla., 1968-75; founder Coral Springs Cablevision, Inc., West Boca CableVision, Inc., Marks Cablevision of Ohio; owner, pres. Planned Cable Systems, Inc., San Francisco, 1975—; owner, operator The Marks Group; bd. dirs. Inisght Comm., Ltd., U.K., 1990— Equitable Banks of Dallas; owner The Marks Group. Mem. Shriners, Masons, Cable Television Pioneers Club. Home: 2755 Fillmore St San Francisco CA 94123-4700

MARKS-KATZ, MARJORIE LOUISE, medical nutrition therapist, writer; b. N.Y.C., Feb. 19, 1949; d. Earle David and Etta (Walkowitz) Marks; m. Paul Joseph Katz, Nov. 7, 1981; children: Eldon, Emily, Jacob. BA, Queens Coll., 1969; MEd, Columbia U., 1978. Registered dietitian. Pediatric nutritionist North Shore Univ. Hosp., Manhasset, N.Y., 1980-85; mgr. nutrition products Practorcare, Inc., San Diego, 1987; positive choice counselor Kaiser Permanente, San Diego, 1988; prenatal nutritionist Nassau County Health Dept., Mineola, N.Y., 1989-90; nutrition edn. coord. C.W. Post Coll., L.I. U., Brookville, N.Y., 1990-91; nutrition cons. in pvt. practice, Tucson, 1991-93; med. nutrition therapist Children's Clincs for Rehab. Svcs., Tucson, 1993—; nutrition/health writer Positive Promotions, Bklyn., 1992—. Scriptwriter, Polished Apple Film Co., 1981; author newspaper column Newsday, 1991, USA Today, 1993; editor-in-chief ADA-Oncology Nutrition Newsletter, 1993, L.I. Dietetic Assn.Newsletter, Bellmore, N.Y., 1990. Vol. Am. Cancer Soc., Tucson, 1994; active Tucson Unified Sch. Dist., 1992, 93. March of Dimes grantee, 1980. Mem. Am. Dietetic Assn., Pediatric Nutrition Practice Group, Dietitians in Devel. Disorders, Dietitians in Nutrition Support, Am. Soc. for Parenteral and Enteral Nutrition. Jewish. Office: Children's Clinics for Rehab Svcs 2600 N Wyatt Dr Tucson AZ 85712

MARLATT, MICHAEL JAMES, lawyer; b. L.A., Jan. 15, 1957; s. James Raymond and Norma Jean (Greenfield) M.; m. Donna Marie Healey, Mar. 13, 1985. BA, Calif. Poly. U., 1981; JD, Pepperdine U., 1984. Bar: Calif. 1984, U.S. Dist. Ct. (ctrl. dist.) Calif. 1985, U.S. Supreme Ct. 1990. Project liaison U. So. Calif., Sch. Medicine, L.A., 1975-78; documentation rschr. NASA-Jet Propulsion Lab., Pasadena, Calif., 1978-81; ptnr. Thompson & Colegate, Riverside, Calif., 1984—; bd. dirs. Assn. So. Calif. Def. Counsel, L.A., U. Calif., Riverside; lectr., spkr. health care ins. cos., 1988—. Mem. ctr. com. Calif. Rep. Party, Sacramento, 1990-93; bd. dirs. U. Calif., Riverside. Mem. So. Calif. Assn. Hosp. Risk Mgrs., Victoria Country Club, Phi Alpha Delta. Roman Catholic. Office: Thompson & Colegate PO Box 1299 3610 14th St Riverside CA 92501-3847

MARLER, LARRY JOHN, private investor; b. Chgo., Sept. 22, 1940; s. Walter William and Lena Inez (Killen) M.; m. Katy Jo Hibbits, Oct. 17, 1962 (div. Apr. 1971); 1 child, Preston Scott; m. Linda Lee Sorg, Sept. 2, 1982. BA, Christian Coll. Am., 1987; MA, Houston Grad. Sch. Theology, 1988; PhD, U.S. Internat. U., San Diego, 1992. Acct. Shell Oil Co., New Orleans and Houston, 1964-73; acctg. supr. We. Geophys. Co. Am., Houston, 1974; payroll supr. Olsen Inc., Houston, 1975-77; corp. credit mgr. Grant Corps., Houston, 1977-82; rschr., student contractor Navy Pers. R&D Ctr., San Diego, 1990-92; entrepreneur Denver, 1992—. Served with USCG, 1959-62. Mem. Am. Psychol. Soc., Am. Soc. Quality Control, Toastmasters Internat. Republican. Protestant.

MARLETT, DE OTIS LORING, retired management consultant; b. Indpls., Apr. 19, 1911; s. Peter Loring and Edna Grace (Lombard) M.; m. Ruth Irene Pillar, Apr. 10, 1932 (dec. Feb., 1969); children: De Otis Neal, Marilynn Ruth; m. Marie Manning Ostrander, May 1, 1970 (dec. Apr. 1982); m. Peggie P. Whittlesey, Jan. 15, 1983 (dec. Oct., 1993); m. Estelle B. Brewer, Sept. 23, 1994. B.A., M.A., U. Wis., 1934; postgrad., Northwestern U., (part time), 1934-39, Harvard U.; postgrad. (Littauer fellow in econs. and govt.), 1946-47. CPA, Wis., 1935. Staff mem. Ill. Commerce Commn., 1934-39; lectr. in econs. and pub. utilities Northwestern U., (part time), 1936-39; staff mem. Bonneville Power Adminstrn., U.S. Dept. Interior, 1939-45, asst. adminstr., 1945-52; acting adminstr. Def. Electric Power Adminstrn., 1950-51; asst. to v.p., gen. mgr. Dicalite and Perlite divs. Great Lakes Carbon Corp., 1952-53; v.p., also gen. mgr. Dicalite, Perlite, Mining and Minerals divs. Gt. Lakes Carbon Corp., 1953-62, v.p. property investment dept., 1962-81; pres., chief exec. officer Great Lakes Properties, Inc., 1981-83, ret., 1983; past pres., dir. Rancho Palos Verdes Corp., G.L.C. Bldg. Corp., Del Amo Energy Co., Torrance Energy Co.; former mem. L.A. arbitration panel N.Y. Stock Exch. Contbr. articles and reports on public utility regulation, operation and mgmt. to profl. jours. Past bd. dirs. United Cerebral Palsy Assn. Los Angeles County; bd. dirs., past co-chmn. So. Calif. region NCCJ, mem. nat. trustee, mem. nat. exec. bd., nat. protestant co-chmn., 1987-90; past mem. Orthopaedic Hosp. Adv. Coun.; past trustee City of Hope; past pres., dir. Los Angeles area coun., past chmn. relationships com., past pres. Sunshine area, pres. Western region Boy Scouts Am., 1978-81, nat. exec. bd., 1978-88, past mem. nat. exec. com., past chmn. properties com., chmn. logistics for world jamboree delegation to Australia, 1987-88; past trustee Nat. Scouting Mus.; mem. internat. com. Baden Powell fellow World Scouting Found., 1984; past mem. Western Govs. Mining Adv. Coun., Calif. State Mining Bd.; bd. govs. Western div. Am. Mining Congress, chmn., 1962-63; incorporator, past pres., bd. dirs. Torrance Meml. Med. Center Health Care Found.; region III dir., mem. corp. adminstrn. and fin. com., Los Angeles United Way. Recipient Disting. Service medal U.S. Dept. Interior, 1952; named knight Order of Crown Belgium; commd. Ky. Col.; recipient Silver Beaver, Silver Antelope, Silver Buffalo awards Boy Scouts Am., 1984. Mem. AIME, AICPA, Fin. Execs. Inst., L.A. World Affairs Coun., Wis. Alumni Assn., Perlit Inst. (past pres., dir.), L.A. C. of C. (past dir., chmn. mining com.), Mining Assn. So. Calif. (past pres., dir.), Calif. Mine Operators Assn. (past dir.), Bldg. Industry Assn. So. Calif., Calif. Club, Portuguese Bend Club (past pres.), Palos Verdes Bay Club (past v.p.), Phi Kappa Phi, Beta Gamma Sigma, Phi Beta Kappa, Beta Alpha Psi, Lambda Alpha Internat. Democrat. Home: 32759 Seagate Dr Apt 204 Rancho Palos Verdes CA 90275

MARMADUKE, ARTHUR SANDFORD, educational administrator; b. Long Beach, Calif., May 29, 1926; s. William Sandford and Nina Belle (Romberger) M.; m. Carolyn Ann Tilden, Aug. 21, 1949; children: Jennifer, Stephen, Scott. AB, Occidental Coll., 1950; MPA, U. Mich., 1952; DPA (hon.), U. Pacific, 1970. Adminstrv. analyst Office Legis. Analyst Calif. State Legis., Sacramento, 1951-55; dir. admissions Occidental Coll., L.A., 1955-60; dir. Calif. Student Aid Commn., Sacramento, 1960-85; exec. dir. Eureka Project, Sacramento, 1986-90; dir. Independent Solution Project, 1989-91; cons. Weingart Found., 1987, Bush Found., 1985; vice chmn. nat. task force on student aid programs KEppel Com., 1974-75; chmn. Coll. Scholarship Svc., Coll. Entrance Examination Bd., 1967-69; mem. planning com., dir. Calif. Higher Edn. Policy Ctr., 1991—. Contbr. author several student aid books. Trustee Sacramento Country Day Sch. Recipient Disting. Service award Calif. Student Fin. Aid Adminstrs., 1982, Raol Wallenberg New Traditional High Sch., San Francisco, 1985, Coll. Bd. Scholarship Service, N.Y.C., 1985. Home: 1516 Del Dayo Dr Carmichael CA 95608-6011

MARMARELIS, VASILIS ZISSIS, engineering educator, author; b. Mytilini, Greece, Nov. 16, 1949; came to U.S., 1972; s. Zissis P. and Elpis V. (Galinos) M. Diploma in elec. and mech. engring., Nat. Tech. U. of Athens, Greece, 1972; MS in Info. Sci., Calif. Inst. Tech., 1973, PhD in Engring. Sci., 1976. Rsch. fellow Calif. Inst. Tech., Pasadena, 1976-78; asst. prof. U. So. Calif., L.A., 1978-83, assoc. prof., 1983-88, prof., 1988—, chmn. biomed. engring., 1990—, also dir. biomed. simulations resource, 1985—, chmn. dept. biomed. engring., 1990—; pres. Multispec Corp., L.A., 1986—. Author: Analysis of Physiological Systems, 1978, Advanced Methods of Physiological Systems Modeling, Vol. I, 1987, Vol. II, 1989, Vol. III, 1994; editor: Annals of Biomed. Engring.; contbr. numerous articles to profl. jours. Mem. IEEE, Internat. Fedn. Automatic Control, N.Y. Acad. Scis., Biomed. Engring.Soc. Office: U So Calif OHE 500 Los Angeles CA 90089-1451

MARMOR, MICHAEL FRANKLIN, ophthalmologist, educator; b. N.Y.C., Aug. 10, 1941; s. Judd and Katherine (Stern) M.; m. C. Jane Breeden, Dec. 20, 1968; children: Andrea K., David J. AB, Harvard U., 1962, MD, 1966. Diplomate Am. Bd. Ophthalmology. Med. intern UCLA Med. Ctr., 1967; resident in ophthalmology Mass. Eye and Ear Infirmary, Boston, 1970-73; asst. prof. ophthalmology U. Calif. Sch. Medicine, San Francisco, 1973-74; asst. prof. surgery (ophthalmology) Stanford (Calif.) U. Sch. Medicine, 1974-80, assoc. prof., 1980-86, prof., 1986—, head. div. ophthalmalogy, 1984-88, chmn. dept., 1988-92, dir. Basic Sci. Course Ophthalmology, 1993—; mem. assoc. faculty program in human biology Stanford U., 1982—; chief ophthalmology sect. VA Med. Ctr., Palo Alto, Calif., 1974-84; mem. sci. adv. bd. No. Calif. Soc. to Prevent Blindness, 1984-92, Calif. Med. Assn., 1984-92, Nat. Retinitis Pigmentosa Found., 1985-95. Editor: The Retinal Pigment Epithelium, 1975, The Effects of Aging and Environment on Vision, 1991; editor-in-chief Doc. Ophthalmologica, 1995—; mem. editl. bd. Healthline, Lasers and Light in Ophthalmology; contbr. more than 175 articles to sci. jours., 25 chpts. to books. Mem. affirmative action com. Stanford U. Sch. Medicine, 1984—. Sr. asst. surgeon USPHS, 1967-70. Recipient Svc. award Nat. Retinitis Pigmentosa Found., Balt., 1981, Rsch. award Alcon Rsch. Found., Houston, 1989; rsch. grantee Nat. Eye. Inst., Bethesda, Md., 1974-94. Fellow Am. Acad. Ophthalmology (bd. councillors 1982-85, pub. health com. 1990-93, rep. to NAS com. on vision 1991-93, Honor award 1984); mem. Internat. Soc. Clin. Electrophysiology of Vision (v.p. 1990—), Assn. Rsch. in Vision and Ophthalmology, Internat. Soc. for Eye Rsch., Macula Soc. (rsch. com.), Retina Soc. Democrat. Office: Stanford U Sch Medcine Dept Ophthalmology Stanford CA 94305

MARONDE, ROBERT FRANCIS, internist, clinical pharmacologist, educator; b. Monterey Park, Calif., Jan. 13, 1920; s. John August and Emma Florence (Palmer) M.; m. Yolanda Cerda, Apr. 15, 1970; children—Robert George, Donna F. Maronde Varnau, James Augustus, Craig DeWald. B.A., U. So. Calif., 1941, M.D., 1944. Diplomate: Am. Bd. Internal Medicine. Intern L.A. County-U. So. Calif. Med. Ctr., 1943-44, resident, 1944-45, 47-48; asst. prof. physiology U. So. Calif., L.A., 1948-49, asst. clin. prof. medicine, 1949-60, assoc. clin. prof. medicine, 1960-65, assoc. prof. medicine and pharmacology, 1965-67, prof. medicine and pharmacology, 1968-90, emeritus, 1990—, prof. emeritus, 1990—; spl. asst. v.p. for health affairs, 1990—; cons. FDA, 1973, Medco Containment Co. Inc., 1991—, State of Calif. Dept. Health Svcs., 1993. Served to lt. (j.g.) USNR, 1945-47. Fellow ACP; mem. Am. Soc. Clin. Pharmacology and Therapeutics, Alpha Omega Alpha. Home: 785 Ridgecrest St Monterey Park CA 91754-3759 Office: U So Calif 2025 Zonal Ave Los Angeles CA 90033-4526

MAROTTA, GEORGE RAYMOND, money manager, research institute fellow; b. Scotia, N.Y., Oct. 6, 1926; s. Giusceppi and Rosa (Fasulo) M.; m. June Alison Mortlock, Aug. 29, 1948; children: Raymond, Paul, David. AB, Syracuse U., 1950, MPA, 1951; cert. fin. planner. Mgmt. officer Dept. State, Washington, 1951-53; planner, coordinator Nat. Security Council, Washington, 1953-61; Univ. relations officer Peace Corps, Washington, 1961-62; internat. security planner Dept. Defense, Washington, 1962-67; foreign service reserve officer Agency Internat. Devel., Washington, 1967-75; pub. affairs coordinator Hoover Instn., Stanford, Calif., 1975-84, research fellow, 1977—; lectr. Stanford U., 1995—; investment portfolio mgr. Marotta and Johnson Asset Mgmt., Inc. Recipient Meritorious Honor award Agency Internat. Devel., 1968, Honorable Achievement award Pub. Relations Soc. Am., 1980. Mem. Internat. Assn. Fin. Planners, Inst. Cert. Fin. Planners, Pub. Relations Soc. Am. (accredited mem.). Office: Stanford U Hoover Instn Stanford CA 94305

MARQUAND, IAN MACDONALD, television producer; b. Denver, June 2, 1956; s. Kenneth Earl and Betty Harlina (Farley) M.; m. Susan Carol MacDonald, July 4, 1982; children: Adrienne Coral, Ashley Elizabeth. BA in Radio/TV with high honors, U. Mont., 1979. News reporter, anchor KPAX-TV, Missoula, Mont., 1978-81, news dir., 1982-84; interim sports dir. Mont. TV Network, Billings, 1984; state capitol bur. chief Mont. TV Network, Helena, 1984-85; news dir. KTVH-TV, Helena, 1986-89, KPAX-TV, Missoula, 1989-92; spl. projects. coord. KPAX/KRTV/KXLF, Missoula, 1992—; v.p. Mont. Freedom of Info. Hotline, Helena, 1988—. V.p. Missoula Advocacy Program for the Disabled, 1980-84; adv. mem. Helena AIDS Task Force, 1988-89, Missoula Habitat for Humanity, 1993-94, Mont. Tobacco Control Coalition, Helena, 1994. Named Mont. TV Broadcaster of Yr., Mont. Broadcasters Assn., 1989, 90, 92, Mont. TV Program of the Yr., Mont. Broadcasters Assn., 1987, 89, 90, 92, Mont. News Enterprise of the Yr., 1988, 89; recipient Silver Gavel award Mont. Bar Assn., 1992. Mem. Soc. Profl. Journalists (state pres. 1988, pres. 1994-95), Japan Kumamoto club of Western Mt., (pres. 1994—). Office: KPAX-TV 2204 Regent St Missoula MT 59801-7941

MARQUARDT, KATHLEEN PATRICIA, association executive; b. Kalispell, Mont., June 6, 1944; d. Dean King and Lorraine Camille (Buckmaster) Marquardt; m. William Wewer, Dec. 6, 1987; children: Shane Elizabeth, Montana Quinn. Purser, Pan Am. World Airways, Washington, 1968-75; info. specialist Capital Systems Group, Kensington, Md., 1979-81; dir. pub. affairs Subscription TV Assn., Washington, 1981-83, exec. dir., 1983-86; pres. Internat. Policy Studies Orgn., 1983-90; pres., designer Elizabeth Quinn Couture; lectr. in field. Chmn. bd. Friends of Freedom, 1982-90, Putting People First, 1990—; bd. dirs. Tex. Sportsman's Legal Fund, 1992—; treas. Yes on Caps, 1994—. Author: Animal Scam-The Beastly Abuse of Human Rights, 1993, (national newpaper column) From the Trenches; contbr. articles to syndicated newspapers and mags.; host Grass Roots radio. Recipient Citizen Achievement award Ctr. fo Def. Free Enterprise, 1992, Gold Medal award Pa. State Fish and Game Protective Assn., 1993. Mem. Outdoor Writers Assn. Am. Home: 533 5th Ave Helena MT 59601-4359 Office: Putting People First 21 N Last Chance Gulch Helena MT 59601

MARQUARDT, ROD LEWIS, probation officer; b. Phoenix, Dec. 11, 1953; s. Philip Walter Marquardt and Jo Ann (Mulvenon) Butcher; m. Sally Louise Happel, June 24, 1978; children: Joseph Philip, Alison Ann. BS in Criminal Justice, Ariz. State U., 1975; MA in Edn. Adminstrn., No. Ariz. State U., 1993. Dep. probation officer Mohave County Probation, Kingman, Ariz., 1976-77, chief probation officer, dir. juvenile ct. svcs., 1977—; assoc. faculty Mohave C.C., Kingman, 1994—; bd. dirs. Am. Probation and Parole, Kingman. Bd. dirs. Kingman Regional Med. Ctr., 1993—; commr. Kingman Econ. Tourism Devel. Commn., 1994. Mem. Ariz. Assn. of Chief Probation Officers (pres. 1984-88), Kingman Rotary Club, Phi Kappa Phi.

MARQUESS, LAWRENCE WADE, lawyer; b. Bloomington, Ind., Mar. 2, 1950; s. Earl Lawrence and Mary Louise (Coberly) M.; m. Barbara Ann Bailey, June 17, 1978; children: Alexander Lawrence, Michael Wade. BSEE, Purdue U., 1973; JD, W.Va. U., 1977. Bar: W.Va. 1977, Tex. 1977, U.S. Dist. Ct. (so. dist.) W.Va. 1977, U.S. Dist. Ct. (no. dist.) Tex. 1977, Colo. 1980, U.S. Dist. Ct. Colo. 1980, U.S. Ct. Appeals (10th cir.) 1980, U.S. Supreme Ct. 1984, U.S. Dist. Ct. (no. dist.) Ohio 1988. Assoc. Johnson, Bromberg, Leeds & Riggs, Dallas, 1977-79, Bradley, Campbell & Carney, Golden, Colo., 1979-82, ptnr., 1983-84; assoc. Stettner, Miller & Cohn P.C., Denver, 1984-85, ptnr., 1985-87; of counsel Nelson & Harding, Denver, 1987-88, Heron, Burchette, Ruckert & Rothwell, 1989-90, Harding & Ogborn, 1990-94, Otten, Johnson, Robinson, Neff & Ragonetti, Denver, 1994—. Mem. faculty Am. Law Inst.-ABA Advanced Labor and Employment Law Course, 1986, 87. Mem. ABA (labor, antitrust and litigation sects.), Colo. Bar Assn. (co-chmn. labor law com. 1989-92), Denver Bar Assn., 1st Jud. Dist. Bar Assn., Sierra Club, Nat. Ry. Hist. Soc., ACLU. Democrat. Methodist. Home: 11883 W 27th Dr Lakewood CO 80215-7000 Office: Otten Johnson Robinson Neff & Raginetti 950 17th St Ste 1600 Denver CO 80202-2828

MARQUEZ, ALFREDO C., federal judge; b. 1922; m. Linda Nowobilsky. B.S., U. Ariz., 1948, J.D., 1950. Bar: Ariz. Practice law Mesch Marquez & Rothschild, 1957-80; asst. atty. gen. State of Ariz., 1951-52; asst. county atty. Pima County, Ariz., 1953-54; adminstrv. asst. to Congressman Stewart Udall, 1955; judge U.S. Dist. Ct. Ariz., Tucson, 1980—. Served with USN, 1942-45. Office: US Dist Ct US Courthouse Rm 327 55 E Broadway Blvd Tucson AZ 85701-1719

MARQUEZ, ANTHONY PHILIP, lawyer; b. L.A., Oct. 10, 1950; s. Tony Marquez and Helen (Ruiz) Frescas. BA, Columbia U., 1972; JD, Harvard U., 1975. Bar: N.Mex. 1976, Calif. 1978, Tex. 1986. Mng. atty. Legal Aid Soc., Albuquerque, 1975-77; legal counsel Legis. Counsel, Sacramento, Calif., 1977-78; asst. atty gen. Atty. Gen. Office, Santa Fe, N.Mex., 1978-82; chief counsel Transp. Dept., Santa Fe, 1982-83, deputy sec., 1983-84; adminstrv. asst. N.Mex. Supreme Ct., Santa Fe, 1984-86; ptnr. Diamond & Marquez, El Paso, Tex., 1986-88; dep. counsel Legis Counsel, Sacramento, 1988-89; chief counsel Joint Legis. Ethics Com., Sacramento, 1989—; contracts com. Nat. Transp. Bd., Washington, 1979-84; supreme ct. liaison, N.Mex. Compilation Commn., Santa Fe., 1984-86; pro tem judge Superior Ct., Sacramento, 1989-93. Editor Harvard Civil Rights-Civil Liberties Law Rev., 1974; staff mem. Harvard Civil Liberties Law Rev., 1973-74. Active Santa Fe City Arts Bd., 1983-86, NEA Local Arts Agys. Panel, 1992-94, State-Local Partnership Panel, 1992-94, NEA Guidelines, Pres.' Initiative on Rural Am., 1992-93, Sacramento Met. Arts Commn., 1991—, chmn. 1992-94; mem. adv. bd. Hidden Gallery, 1989, Bridge Gallery, El Paso, 1986-87; bd. dirs. Calif. Confedn. Arts, 1991-94, sec., 1992-94, Sacramento Light Opera Assn., 1993—. Recipient Outstanding Service award, N.Mex. Supreme Ct., Santa Fe, 1985, Outstanding Young Man award, Jaycees, 1978, Outstanding Service award, Legal Assts. of N.Mex., Albuquerque, 1986. Mem. Ferrari Club Am. Office: Joint Legis Ethics Com 1021 O St Ste A-602 Sacramento CA 95814

MARQUEZ, MARTINA ZENAIDA, elementary education educator; b. Santa Rosa, N.Mex., Nov. 5, 1935; d. Jose Zenon and Adelina (Romero) Sanchez; m. George J. Marquez, June 17, 1972. Student, Mt. St. Scholastica Coll., 1954-56, Regis Coll., 1956-59; BA, Coll. Santa Fe, 1963; MA, U. N.Mex., 1968. Cert. tchr., N.Mex. Elem. tchr. St. Rose Lima Sch., Santa Rosa, 1959-67, Cristo Rey Sch., Santa Fe, 1967-68, Los Lunas (N,Mex.) Consol. Schs., 1975-78, head tchr. adults operation; SER Manpower Devel. Tng. Act, Albuquerque, 1968-71, 73-75; tchr., cons. Regional Resource Ctr., N.Mex. State U., Las Cruces, 1971-72; counselor, coord. Taos (N.Mex.) Career Edn. Program, 1972-73; chpt. I reading tchr. Grants (N.Mex.) & Cibola County Schs., 1978—; chmn. ethics com. Profl. Standards Commn., N.Mex. Dept. Edn., 1986-88. Dir. choir St. Vivian's Ch., Milan, N.Mex., 1978—; del. Dem. Women's Club, Grants, N.Mex., 1981—; v.p. Literacy Vols. Am. of Cibola County. Selected as 1991 Cibola County Woman of Achievement 3rd Ann. Women's Resource Conf. Mem. AAUW (bylaws chmn. 1984, Grants Woman of Yr. award 1988), Internat. Reading Assn. (1st v.p. Malpais coun. 1988-89, pres. 1989-90, state pres. 1992-93, dist. 3 facilitator, Local Literacy award 1986, State Literacy award 1987, state pres. N.Mex. 1992-93), Delta Kappa Gamma (pres. Psi chpt. 1986-88). Democrat. Roman Catholic. Home: PO Box 11 Bluewater NM 87005-0011 Office: Grants-Cibola County Schs Jemez and Del Norte St Grants NM 87020

MARRINGTON, BERNARD HARVEY, retired automotive company executive; b. Vancouver, B.C., Can., Nov. 9, 1928; s. Fredrick George and Constance Marie (hall) M.; m. Patricia Grace Hall, Sept. 3, 1953 (div. 1993); children: Jodie Lynn, Stacey Lee. Student, U. Pitts., 1982, Bethany Coll., W.Va., 1983; BS in Mktg. Mgmt., Pacific Western U., 1985. V.p., sales mgr. W & L of La Mesa, Calif., 1960-66; pres., gen. mgr. W & L of La Mesa, 1966-68; regional mgr. PPG Industries, Inc., L.A., 1977-88, regional mgr. profit ctr., 1988-91; cons. L.A. Unified Sch. Dist., 1972, South Coast Air Quality Mgmt. Dist., El Monte, Calif., 1987-91; adv. com. So. Calif. Regional Occupational Ctr., Torrance, 1978-91. Contbr. articles to profl. jours. Sustaining sponsor Ronald Reagan Presdl. Found., Simi, 1987—; sustaining mem. Rep. Nat. Com., L.A., 1985-92, Rep. Presdl. Legion of Merit, 1986-94; del. Rep. Platform Planning com., L.A., 1992; charter mem. Nat. Tax Limitation Com., Washington, 1988, Jarvis Gann Taxpayers Assn., L.A., 1979-94; sponsor Reagan Presdl. Libr., 1986. Recipient Award for Outstanding Community Support, So. Calif. Regional Occupational Ctr., 1986. Episcopalian.

MARROW, MARVA JAN, photographer, writer, video and multimedia producer; b. Denver, Apr. 22, 1948; d. Sydney and Helen Berniece (Garber) M. Student, Carnegie-Mellon U., 1965-67. Singer, songwriter RCA Records, Italy, 1972-77; pvt. practice photography Italy and U.S., 1976—; dir. acquisitions RAI TV, L.A., 1990-91; mng. agt. Thomas Angel Prodns., L.A., 1991-94; represented by Shooting Star Photo Agy., Agenzia Marka, Agenzia Masi, Italy, Uniphoto Press Internat., Japan; corr., photographer Italian TV Guide, Milan, 1979—; collaborator, photographer for other U.S. and European publs., radio and TV; TV news and documentary prodr. RAI TV, 1990—. Author numerous songs for Italian pop artists including Lucio Battisti, Battiato, Premiata Forneria Marconi (PFM), Patty Pravo, 1972—; author: (photobook) Inside the L.A. Artist, 1988; project dir. Digital Art Mus. (CD-Rom), 1994—; prodr. (CD-Rom) The Kat's Meow, 1995, The Top Dog, 1995; contbr. photographs for covers and articles to nat. and internat. mags. Mem. Motion Picture Assn. of Am., Fgn. Press Assn. Democrat. Home and Studio: 2080 Garfield Ave Altadena CA 91001-2959 Office: Shooting Star Agy PO Box 93368 Los Angeles CA 90093-0368

MARRS, ROY ALONZO, magazine editor, educator; b. Dale, Okla., Nov. 28, 1924; s. Mitchell Siler Marrs and Vida Emily Kerns Marrs Christenson; m. Claudia Ruth Whitford, Feb. 1946 (dec. July 1957); m. Alvina Miller; children: Lucille, Lawrence, Loren, John, Jim. BA, Phillips U., Enid, Okla., 1952; MA, Long Beach (Calif.) State U., 1970. Ordained minister Ch. of God, 7th Day, 1954; cert. h.s. tchr., elem. tchr., Calif. Min., pastor Ch. of God, 7th Day, Okla., Wis., Mo., Oreg., Colo., 1948-56, 83-94; coll. dir. Midwest Bible Coll., Stanberry, Mo., 1953-56; linotype operator Springfield (Oreg.) Daily News, 1958, Bible Advocate Press, Stanberry, 1957-58; elem. sch. tchr. Hawthorne (Calif.) Elem. Sch. Dist., 1958-86; editor-in-chief Bible Advocate Mag., Denver, 1992—; pres. ministerial coun. Gen. Conf. Ch. of God, 7th Day, Denver, 1990-92, v.p. gen. conf., 1991-92. Served with U.S. Army, 1943-46, ETO. Decorated Bronze Star (2). Republican. Home: 102 Mokelumne River Dr Lodi CA 95240-7612 Office: Bible Advocate 330 W 152nd Ave Broomfield CO 80020-9100

MARSDEN, EUGENE DENNIS, SR., bleacher seating manufacturing executive; b. Madison, Wis., June 5, 1930; s. Glenn R. and Frieda Marsden; m. Margot Boice, Apr. 29, 1950; children: Eugene D. Jr., David B. Jeffrey. BS, UCLA, 1954. Pres. Marsden Bros. Inc., Santa Monica, Calif., 1960—. 1st lt. U.S. Army, 1954-56. Republican. Roman Catholic. Office: Marsden Bros Inc 127 Esparta Way Santa Monica CA 90402-2138

MARSH, DAVE RODNEY, writer, publisher, editor; b. Pontiac, Mich., Mar. 1, 1950; s. Oliver Kenneth and Mary A. (Evon) M.; m. Barbara E. Carr, July 21, 1979; stepchildren: Sasha J. Carr, Kristen A. Carr (dec.). Student, Wayne State U., 1968-69. Editor Creem Mag., Detroit and Birmingham, Mich., 1969-73; music critic Newsday, Garden City, N.Y., 1973, 74-75; assoc. editor Rolling Stone Mag., N.Y.C., 1975-78, contbg. editor, 1978-85; contbg. editor The Record, N.Y.C., 1982-84; editor, pub. Rock & Rap Confidential, L.A., 1983—; music critic Playboy, 1985—, Rock Today (syndicated radio), 1987-92; contbg. editor Entertainment Weekly, 1991-93. Author: Born to Run: The Bruce Springsteen Story, 1979, The Book of Rock Lists, 1981, Elvis, 1982, Before I Get Old, 1983, Fortunate Son, 1985, Michael Jackson and the Crossover Dream, 1985, Glory Days: Bruce Springsteen in the 1980s, 1987;The Heart of Rock and Soul, 1989, 50 Ways to Fight Censorship, 1991, Louie, Louie, 1993, Merry Christmas Baby, 1993, The New Book of Rock Lists, 1994; editor: Rolling Stone Record Guide, 1979, The First Rock and Roll Confidential Report, 1985, Pastures of Plenty (Woody Guthrie, Harper and Row), 1990, (with Don Henley) Heaven Is Under Our Feet: Essays for Walden Woods, 1991, Mid-Life Confidential: The Rock Bottom Remainders Tour America, 1994; host Radio Mafia, Finland, 1990—. Trustee Kristen Ann Car Fund; active The Critics Chorus, Rock Bottom Remainders, 1992-94. Office: Rock & Rap Confidential PO Box 341305 Los Angeles CA 90034-9305

MARSH, FRANK RAYMOND, engineering technical writer; b. Waterville, Maine, Aug. 5, 1938; s. Gerald Raymond and Dorothy Marion (Haines) M. B of Gen. Studies, Chaminade U., Honolulu, 1968; BFA, Otis Art Inst., 1971, MFA, 1973; BS in Computer Sci., West Coast U., 1984, MS in Computer Sci., 1986, MIBA, 1987, MMIS, 1988, MSMIS, 1990, BS in Elec. Engring., 1993. Editor, cartographer Thomas Bros. Maps, L.A., 1974-80; engring. writer Singer Co., Glendale, Calif., 1983-87; sr. tech. writer Amperpif Corp., Chatsworth, Calif., 1987-89; prin. engring. writer Litton Data Systems, Van Nuys, Calif., 1990—. One-man shows includes Westwood (Calif.) Art Assn., 1973, Westwood Ctr. of the Arts, 1975, Villa Montalvo, Saratoga, Calif., 1975, Sr. Eye Gallery, Long Beach, Calif., 1979, 81, Studio 1617 Gallery, L.A., 1984; numerous group exhbns. and juried invitationals; permanent collections include Detroit Mortgage Co., Gulf and Western, Homes Savs. and Loan Bank, Otis Art Inst., Palmcrest Ho., United Calif. Bank. Mem. L.A. Art Mus. Graphics Coun., 1976—. With USAF, 1961-69. Mem. AIAA, IEEE, Artists Equity, L.A. Printmaking Soc., Soc. for Tech. Comm., Ann. for Computing Machinery, Math. Assn. of Am., Litton Mgmt. Club. Home: 2800 Lambert Dr Los Angeles CA 90068-2323

MARSH, JAMES ROBERT, federal law enforcement official; b. Grosse Pointe Farms, Mich., June 26, 1947; s. Robert George and Mary Elizabeth (McDonald) M.; m. Nancy Lynn Beaty, Feb. 26, 1982; children: Jason Robert, Matthew James. BS in Police Adminstrn., Mich. State U., 1969; MA in Sociology, U. Detroit, 1974. Supr. Mich. Bell Telephone Co., Lansing, 1968-70; probation officer Oakland County Circuit Ct., Pontiac, Mich., 1970-76; probation officer ea. dist. Mich. U.S. Dist. Ct., Detroit, 1976-82; probation officer no. dist. Tex. U.S. Dist. Ct., Dallas, 1982-84; chief pretrial svcs. officer dist. Nev. U.S. Dist. Ct., Las Vegas, 1984—; regional rep. Chiefs' Mgmt. Coun., Washington, 1990-93; chmn. Pretrial Svcs. Com., Washington, 1990-93; co-chmn. Pretrial Svcs. Supervision Task Force, Washington, 1991—. Contbr. articles to profl. jours. Pres. Oakland County Corrections Assn., Pontiac, 1975; chmn., bd. dirs. Help Ctr. Drug Program, Highland, Mich., 1978. Methodist. Office: US Pretrial Svcs 330 S 3rd St Ste 820 Las Vegas NV 89101-6032

MARSH, JOHN HARRISON, environmental planner, lawyer; b. Auburn, Wash., June 25, 1954; s. F. A. Buzz and Margery Ann (Greene) M.; m. Debra Rose Raniere, June 18, 1977; children: Jenna Rose, Christian John. BS in Fisheries Scis., Oreg. State U., 1977; JD, Lewis & Clark Coll., 1985, cert. natural resources and environ. law, 1985. Bar: Oreg. 1986. Rsch. asst. EPA, Corvallis, Oreg., 1975-77; fisheries biologist Nat. Marine Fisheries Svc., Portland, Oreg., 1977-78, Oreg. Dept. Fish and Wildlife, Astoria, 1978; pub. info. officer Columbia River Inter-Tribal Fish Commn., Portland, 1978-79, fisheries ecologist, 1979-85; system planning coord. N.W. Power Planning Coun., Portland, 1985—; speaker, expert witness in field; guest lectr. Lewis and Clark Coll., 1984, 95. Contbr. articles to profl. publs. Organizer food drive Friends of Seasonal Workers, 1987; chair ann. NPPC food drive Sunshine Divsn., 1987-94; bd. dirs. Panavista Park Homeowners Assn., 1991-93, mem. archtl. rev. com., 1990—, chair, 1991—; Leader, Sunday sch. instr. grades 5-6 Riverwest Ch., 1992—; asst. scoutmaster Boy Scouts Am., 1972-73. Mem. Am. Fisheries Soc. (cert. profl. fisheries scientist, exec. com. Portland chpt. 1981-84, v.p. 1981-82, pres. 1982-83, chair legis. com. Oreg. chpt. 1988-89, program com. 1980-81, riparian com. Western div. 1982-83, convenor various sessions, mem. native peoples fisheries com. 1982-88, chair

1984-86, resolutions com. 1985-86, strategic plan devel com., 1993-95, other coms.), Oreg. State Bar Assn., Native Am. Fish and Wildlife Assn., Knights of the Vine, Great Lovers of Wine Soc. Oreg. (pres. 1988). Office: NW Power Planning Coun 851 SW 6th Ave Ste 1100 Portland OR 97204-1348

MARSH, MALCOLM F., federal judge; b. 1928. BS, U. Oreg., 1952, LLB, 1954, JD, 1971. Ptnr. Clark & Marsh, Lindauer & McClinton (and predecessors), Salem, Oreg., 1958-87; judge U.S. Dist. Ct. Oreg., Portland, 1987—. With U.S. Army, 1946-47. Fellow Am. Coll. Trial Lawyers; mem. ABA. Office: US Dist Ct 114 US Courthouse 620 SW Main St Portland OR 97205-3037

MARSHAK, HARRY, physician, plastic surgeon; b. L.A., Oct. 1, 1961; s. Herbert and Pearl (Engetron) M. BS, U. Calif., Riverside, 1981; MD, UCLA, 1984. Diplomate Am. Bd. Surgery, Am. Bd. Plastic Surgery. Pvt. practice Beverly Hills, Calif., 1991-95. Fellow ACS (hon.), Internat. Coll. Surgeons; mem. Am. Soc. Plastic and Reconstructive Surgeons, Calif. Soc. Plastic Surgery. Republican. Office: 150 N Robertson Blvd Ste 140 Beverly Hills CA 90211

MARSHALL, ANNE CAROLYN, financial services company official; b. Phila., Aug. 9, 1932; d. Albert Greenwood and Margaret (Garton) M. Grad. parochial high sch., Haddonfield, N.J. CLU. Stenographer RCA, Camden, N.J., 1950-66; sec. Conn. Mut. Life Ins. Co., Phoenix, 1968-71, Mass. Mut. Life Ins. Co., Phoenix, 1971-72, Meldman, Davies & Vance, Phoenix, 1972-74; pension adminstr. B.A. Meldman/ERISA, Ltd., Phoenix, 1974-85; asst. to pres. B.A. Meldman/Meldman Fin. Svcs., Ltd., Phoenix, 1985—. Office: Meldman Fin Svcs Ltd 7600 N 16th St Ste 200 Phoenix AZ 85020-4447

MARSHALL, ARTHUR K., lawyer, judge, arbitrator, educator, writer; b. N.Y.C., Oct. 7, 1911. BS, CUNY, 1933; LLB, St. John's U., N.Y.C., 1936; LL.M., U. So. Calif., 1952. Bar: N.Y. State 1937, Calif. 1947. Practice law N.Y.C., 1937-43, Los Angeles, 1947-50; atty. VA, Los Angeles, 1947-50; tax counsel Calif. Bd. Equalization, Sacramento, 1950-51; inheritance tax atty. State Controller, Los Angeles, 1951-53; commr. Superior Ct. Los Angeles County, 1953-62; judge Municipal Ct., Los Angeles jud. dist., 1962-63, Superior Ct., Los Angeles, 1963-81; supervising judge probate dept. Superior Ct., 1968-69, appellate dept., 1973-77; presiding judge Appellate Dept., 1976-77; pvt. practice arbitrator, mediator, judge pro tem, 1981—; acting asst. prof. law UCLA, 1954-59; grad. faculty U. So. Calif., 1955-75; lectr. Continuing Edn. of the Bar; mem. Calif. Law Revision Commn., 1984—, chmn., 1986-87, 92-93; chmn. com. on efficiency and econs. Conf. Calif. Judges, past chmn. spl. action com. on ct. improvement; past chmn. probate law cons. group Calif. Bd. Legal Specialization. Author: Joint Tenancy Taxwise and Otherwise, 1953, Branch Courts, 1959, California State and Local Taxation Text, 2 vols., 1962, rev. edit., 1969, supplement, 1979, 2d edito., 1981, Triple Choice Method, 1964, California State and Local Taxation Forms, 2 vols., 1961-75, rev. edit., 1979, California Probate Procedure, 1961, 5th rev. edit., 1994, Guide to Procedure Before Trial, 1975; contbr. articles to profl. jours. Mem. Town Hall; mem. Com. on Fgn. Affairs. With AUS, 1943-46; lt. col. JAGC Res. (ret.). Named Judge of Yr. Lawyers Club L.A. County, 1975; first recipient Arthur K. Marshall award established by estate planning, trust and probate sect. L.A. Bar Assn., 1981, Disting. Jud. Career award L.A. Lawyers Club, award L.A. County Bd. Suprs., 1981. Fellow Am. Bar Found.; mem. ABA (probate litigation com. real property, probate and trust sect.), Am. Arbitration Assn. (mem. nat. panel of arbitrators), Internat. Acad. Estate and Trust Law (academician, founder, 1st pres., now chancellor), Calif. State Bar (advisor to exec. com. real property, probate and trust sect. 1970-83), Santa Monica Bar Assn. (pres. 1960), Westwood Bar Assn. (pres. 1959), L.A. Bar Assn., Am. Legion (comdr. 1971-72), U. So. Calif. Law Alumni Assn. (pres. 1969-70), Phi Alpha Delta (1st justice alumni chpt.). Office: 300 S Grand Ave Fl 28 Los Angeles CA 90071-3109

MARSHALL, CONRAD JOSEPH, entrepreneur; b. Detroit, Dec. 23, 1934; s. Edward Louis Fedak and Maria Magdalena Berzsenyi; m. Dorothy Genieve Karnafil, Dec. 1, 1956 (div. 1963); children: Conrad Joseph Jr., Kevin Conrad, Lisa Marie; m. Beryle Elizabeth Callahan, June 15, 1965 (div. 1972); children: Brent Jasmer, Farah Elizabeth. Diploma, Naval Air Tech. Tng. Ctr., Norman, Okla., 1952; student, Wayne State U., 1956-59; Diploma, L.A. Police Acad., 1961. Dir. mktg. Gulf Devel., Torrance, Calif., 1980-83; sales mgr. Baldwin Piano Co., Santa Monica, Calif., 1977-80; dir. mktg., v.p. Western Hose, Inc., L.A., 1971-76; city letter carrier U.S. Post Office, L.A., 1969-71; writer freelance L.A., 1966—; police officer L.A. Police Dept., 1961-66; asst. sales mgr. Wesson Oil Co., Detroit, 1958-60; agt. Life Ins. Co. of Va., Wayne, Mich., 1956-58; pres. Am. Vision Mktg., L.A., 1990—, Con-Mar Prodns., L.A., 1983—; sr. v.p. Pacific Acquisition Group, 1992—, Invest. Admin. HealthCom., Int., 1993—; pres. Midway TV Co., 1994—; tech. advisor Lion's Gate Films, Westwood, Calif., 1970-74, Medicine Wheel Prodns., Hollywood, Calif., 1965-75; mng. gen. ptnr. Encino Wireless #1, 1994—; CEO Midway TV Co., 1995. Author: (series) "Dial Hot Line", 1967, (screenplay) "Heads Across the Border", 1968, "The Fool Card", 1970, "Probable Cause", 1972; co-author: The Fedak File, 1995; albums include Song Shark, 1992, Conrad Marshall Quintet, 1991. Campaign vol. Dem. Party, L.A., 1976; vol. Amanda Found., Beverly Hills, Calif., 1992. With USN, 1952-56. Mem. Screen Actors Guild, Internat. Platform Assn. Home: 11853 Kling Ste 17 Valley Village CA 91607 Office: Con-Mar Prodns 11853 Kling St Apt 16 North Hollywood CA 91607-4048

MARSHALL, CONSUELO BLAND, federal judge; b. Knoxville, Tenn., Sept. 28, 1936; d. Clyde Theodore and Annie (Brown) Arnold; m. George Edward Marshall, Aug. 30, 1959; children: Michael Edward, Laurie Ann. A.A., Los Angeles City Coll., 1956; B.A., Howard U., 1958, LL.B., 1961. Bar: Calif. 1962. Dep. atty. City of L.A., 1962-67; assoc. Cochran & Atkins, L.A., 1968-70; commr. L.A. Superior Ct., 1971-76; judge Inglewood Mcpl. Ct., 1976-77, L.A. Superior Ct., 1977-80, U.S. Dist. Ct. Central Dist. Calif., L.A., 1980—; lectr. U.S. Information Agy. in Yugoslavia, Greece and Italy, 1984, in Nigera and Ghana, 1991, in Ghana, 1992. Contbr. articles to profl. jours.; notes editor Law Jour. Howard U. Mem. adv. bd. Richstone Child Abuse Center. Recipient Judicial Excellence award Criminal Cts. Bar Assn., 1992; research fellow Howard U. Law Sch., 1959-60;. Mem. State Bar Calif., Calif. Women Lawyers Assn., Calif. Assn. Black Lawyers, Calif. Judges Assn., Black Women Lawyers Assn., Los Angeles County Bar Assn., Nat. Assn. Women Judges, NAACP, Urban League, Beta Phi Sigma. Office: US Dist Ct 312 N Spring St Los Angeles CA 90012-4701

MARSHALL, JAMES KENNETH, consulting services executive; b. Providence, Dec. 25, 1952; s. James William and Eileen Frances (O'Connell) M.; m. Mary H. Jackson, Mar. 17, 1987. BA in Chemistry, SUNY, Plattsburgh, 1974; MBA in Fin., U. R.I., 1977; postgrad., U. Wash., 1978-79. Fin. instr. U. R.I., Kingston, 1978; teaching assoc. U. Wash., Seattle, 1978-79; asst. dir. facilities mgmt. U. Colo., Boulder, 1979-86, dir. buying and contracting, 1986-90; transp. mgr. Town of Vail, Colo., 1991-92; v.p. Women at the Wheel Automotive Cons. and Consumer Edn. Svc., Avon, Colo., 1990—; honorarium instr. U. Colo., Denver, 1981-85; bd. dirs. Minority Enterprises, Inc., 1988-90. Contbr. chpt. to book on plant administration. Recipient Job Well Done award U. Colo. Boulder Dept. Facilities Mgmt., 1983. Mem. Beta Gamma Sigma, Phi Kappa Phi. Office: Women at the Wheel PO Box 2829 Avon CO 81620-2829

MARSHALL, L. B., medical technologist; b. Chgo., Feb. 10; s. Gillman and Ethel (Robinson) M.; m. Esther Wood, Sept. 28, 1961; children: Lester B. III, Kiti B., Lelani. Student, San Francisco State U., 1950; AA, City Coll. San Francisco, 1957; BS in Podiatric Medicine, U. Puget Sound, 1961; ScD, London Inst., Eng., 1972. Pres., Med. Offices Health Services Group Inc., San Francisco, 1964—. Mem. NAACP. With U.S. Army, 1947-53. Decorated Bronze Star, Med. Combat Badge; recipient Cert. Appreciation Pres. Nixon, 1973, Urban League, 1973, Calif. Dept. Human Resources, 1973. Mem. Am. Calif. Assns. Med. Technologists, Calif. State Sheriff's Assn. (assoc.), Oyster Point Yacht Club, Press Club, Commonwealth Club (San Francisco).

MARSHALL, LUCILLE TAYLOR, educator, receptionist; b. St. Louis, June 23, 1924; d. Harold Densmore and Mildred Colleen (Tennell) Taylor; m. Victor Earl Marshall (dec.); adopted chidren: Anna Marie, Frances Helena. BA in English, U. San Francisco, 1970, tchg. credential, 1971, MA in Writing, 1988. Bus. rep. Office Employees Local 3, San Francisco, 1968-70; tchr. San Francisco (Calif.) Sch. Dist., 1971-85; receptionist St. Rose Acad., San Francisco, St. Dominic's Parish, 1990—; sec. Edn. Action Coun. Vols., San Francisco Unified Sch. Dist., 1992-93. Editor: Informative African-American Profiles, 1994. Summer sch. tchr. Third Bapt. Ch., 1984-93. Recipient U. San Francisco Black Alumni award, 1992, Outstanding Svc. award Third Bapt. Ch., 1992, Unsung Heroes award San Francisco (Calif.) Libr., 1992. Mem. San Francisco Bus. and Profl. Women, Inc. (1st v.p. 1988-92). Roman Catholic. Home: 2770 Pine St Apt 104 San Francisco CA 94115-2542

MARSHALL, MERYL CORINBLIT, television producer, lawyer; b. Los Angeles, Oct. 16, 1949; d. Jack and Nita (Green) Corinblit; BA, UCLA, 1971; JD, Loyola Marymount U., L.A., 1974. Bar: Calif. 1974. Dep. pub. defender County of L.A., 1975-77; sole practice, L.A., 1977-78; ptnr. Markman and Marshall, L.A., 1978-79; sr. atty. NBC, Burbank, Calif., 1979-80, dir. programs, talent contracts bus. affairs, 1980, asst. gen. atty., N.Y.C., 1980-82, v.p., compliance and practices, Burbank, 1982, v.p. program affairs, Group W Prodns., 1987-89, sr. v.p. future images, 1991—, TV producer, Meryl Marshall Prodns., 1991—; pres. Two Oceans Entertainment Group, 1991—. Treas. Acad. T.V. Arts. and Scis., 1985-87, bd. govs., 1989—; chmn., Nat. Women's Polit. Caucus, Westside, Calif., 1978-80; mem. Calif. Dem. Cen. Com., 1978-79; mem. Hollywood Women's Polit. Com., 1988. Mem. Acad. TV Arts and Scis. (treas. 1985, Bd. Govs. 1989), Women in Film. Democrat. Jewish. Home: 4528 Camellia Ave North Hollywood CA 91602-1908 Office: Two Oceans Entertainment Group 15060 Ventura Blvd Ste 400 Sherman Oaks CA 91403

MARSHALL, ROBERT HERMAN, economics educator; b. Harrisburg, Pa., Dec. 6, 1929; s. Mathias and Mary (Bubich) M.; m. Billie Marie Sullivan, May 31, 1958; children: Mellisa Frances, Howard Hylton, Robert Charles. A.B. magna cum laude, Franklin and Marshall Coll., 1951; M.A., Ohio State U., 1952, Ph.D., 1957. Teaching asst. Ohio State U., 1952-57; mem. faculty, then prof. econs. U. Ariz., Tucson, 1957—, head dept., 1967-69; dir. Internat. Bus. Studies Project, 1969-71; research observer Sci.-Industry Program, Hughes Aircraft Co., Tucson, summer 1959. Author: Commercial Banking in Arizona: Structure and Performance Since World War II, 1966, (with others) The Monetary Process, 2d edit, 1980. Bd. dirs. Com. for Econ. Opportunity, Tucson, 1968-69. Faculty fellow Pacific Coast Banking Sch., summer 1974. Mem. Am. Econ. Assn., Phi Beta Kappa, Beta Gamma Sigma, Pi Gamma Mu, Phi Kappa Phi, Delta Sigma Pi. Democrat. Roman Catholic. Home: 6700 N Abington Rd Tucson AZ 85743-9795

MARSHALL, ROBERT WILLIAM, lawyer, rancher; b. L.A., Apr. 12, 1933; s. Kenneth I. and Helen (Putnam) M.; m. Nanette Hollenbeck, June 10, 1965; children: Thomas, Victoria, Rebecca, Kathleen. AB in Pre Law, Stanford U., 1955, JD, 1957. Bar: Calif. 1958, Nev. 1958, U.S. Dist. Ct. (so. dist.) Calif. 1958, U.S. Dist. Ct. Nev. 1958. Assoc. Vargas & Bartlett, Reno, Nev., 1958-64; ptnr. Vargas & Bartlett, Reno, 1964-85, sr. ptnr., 1985-94; chmn. of bd. Marshall, Hill, Cassas & de Lipkau, 1994—. Advisor Explorer Boy Scouts Am., Reno, 1971-76, 87-89, scoutmaster Troop 444 Boy Scouts Am., Reno, 1981-85; state chmn. Nev. Young Reps., 1962-64. Mem. ABA, Nat. Cattlemen's Assn., Calif. Bar Assn., Nev. Bar Assn., Washoe County Bar Assn., Rocky Mountain Mineral Law Inst., No. Nev. Indsl. Gas Users (organizer), No. Nev. Large Power Users (organizer), So. Nev. Large Power Users (organizer), Nev. Cattlemen's Assn., Reno Stanford Club (pres. Reno chpt. 1974). Republican. Mormon. Office: Marshall Hill Cassas et al 333 Holcomb Ave # 300 Reno NV 89502-1648

MARSTON, EDWIN H., newspaper publisher; b. Bklyn., Apr. 25, 1940; s. Jack and Matilda Marston; m. Elizabeth Avice Pilat, Oct. 2, 1976; children: Wendy Meredith, David Michael. BS, CCNY, 1962; PhD in Physics, SUNY, Stony Brook, 1968. Asst. prof. Queens (N.Y.) Coll., 1968-71; assoc. prof. Ramapo Coll. of N.J., Mahwah, 1971-74; pub. North Fork Times, Paonia, Colo., 1975-80, High Country News, Paonia, 1983—. Editor: Western Water Made Simple, 1987, Reopening the Western Frontier, 1989; author: The Dynamic Environment, 1975. Mem. adv. bd. Rocky Mountain Reg. Environ. Def. Fund, Boulder, 1989—; bd. dirs. Pacif Rivers Coun., Eugene, Oreg., 1991—, Delta-Montrose Elec. Assn., Colo., 1983-89, Friends of the Earth, 1988-93. Democrat. Jewish. Home: PO Box 281 4114 Lamborn Hills Paonia CO 81428 Office: High Country News PO Box 1090 119 Grand Ave Paonia CO 81428

MARSTON, MICHAEL, urban economist, asset management executive; b. Oakland, Calif., Dec. 4, 1936; s. Lester Woodbury and Josephine (Janovic) M.; m. Alexandra Lynn Geyer, Apr. 30, 1966; children: John, Elizabeth. BA, U. Calif., Berkeley, 1959; postgrad. London Sch. Econs., 1961-63. V.p. Larry Smith & Co., San Francisco, 1969-72, exec. v.p. urban econ. div., 1969-72; chmn. bd. Keyser Marston Assocs., Inc., San Francisco, 1973-87; gen. ptnr. The Sequoia Partnership, 1979-91; pres. Marston Vineyards and Winery, 1982—, Marston Assocs., Inc., 1982—. Cert. rev. appraiser Nat. Assn. Rev. Appraisers and Mortgage Underwriters, 1984—. Chmn., San Francisco Waterfront Com., 1969-86; chmn. fin. com., bd. dirs., mem. exec. com., treas. San Francisco Planning and Urban Rsch. Assn., 1976-87, Napa Valley Vintners, 1986—, mem. gov. affairs com.; trustee Cathedral Sch. for Boys, 1981-82, Marin Country Day Sch., 1984-90; v.p. St. Luke's Sch., 1986-91; pres. Presidio Heights Assn. of Neighbors, 1983-84; chmn. Presidio Com. 1991—; v.p., bd. dirs., mem. exec. com. People for Open Space, 1972-87, chmn. adv. com., 1988—; mem. Gov.'s Issue Analysis Com. and Speakers Bur., 1966; mem. speakers bur. Am. Embassy, London, 1961-63; v.p., bd. dirs. Dem. Forum, 1968-72; v.p., trustee Youth for Service. Served to lt. USNR. Mem. Napa Valley Vintners, Napa Grape Growers, Urban Land Inst., World Congress Land Policy (paper in field), Order of Golden Bear, Chevalier du Tastevin, Commanderie de Bordeaux, Bohemian Club, Pacific Union Club, Lambda Alpha. Contbr. articles to profl. jours. Home: 3375 Jackson St San Francisco CA 94118-2018

MARSTON, RICHARD ALAN, geography educator, consultant; b. Bethesda, Md., Apr. 6, 1952; s. Alan Douglas and Nancy (Burdick) M.; m. Linda Mary Crowe, July 16, 1977. BA, UCLA, 1974; MS, Oreg. State U., 1976, PhD, 1980. Environ. sci. V.T.N.-Colo., Denver, 1974-76, EPA, Corvallis, Oreg., 1976-77; hydrologist U.S. Forest Service, Waldport, Oreg., 1978-79; asst. prof. geography U. Tex., El Paso, 1980-86; asst. prof. geography U. Wyo., Laramie, 1986-88, assoc. prof., 1988-94, prof., 1994—; cons. environ. geoscis., 1980—; affiliate faculty dept. geology and geological engrs. U. Idaho, 1994—. Contbr. articles to profl. jours. Grantee Ft. Bliss Mil. Reservation, 1981, Horizon Cmtys. Improvement Assn., 1983, Assn. Western Univs., 1984, U.S. Forest Svc., 1988, 93, U.S. Geol. Survey, 1987, Wyo. Water Rsch. Ctr., 1988, Nat. Pk. Svc., 1989-93, NSF, 1995-98, Fulbright Rsch. Commn., France, 1993. Mem. Assn. Am. Geographers (Warren Nystrom award 1981), Am. Geomorphological Field Group, Am. Water Resources Assn., Assn. Geoscientists for Internat. Devel., Royal Geographical Soc., Sigma Xi. Office: U Wyo Dept Geography and Recreation Laramie WY 82071

MARTELL, CHARLES RENNIE, JR., dean, librarian; b. Cambridge, Mass., Sept. 18, 1936; s. Charles Rennie and Dorothy Elizabeth (Hurley) M.; m. Pamela Sue Wells, June 27, 1971 (div. Jan. 1990); children: Ryan Matthew, Jennifer Kristin. BA, Brown U., 1964; MS in Libr. Sci., Syracuse U., 1972; D of Libr. Sci., U. Calif., Berkeley, 1979. Asst. to univ. libr. U. Calif., Berkeley, 1976-80; lectr. sch. libr. and info. studies, edn. psychology libr. U. Calif., 1980-81; acquisitions libr. U. Ill., Chgo., 1981-83; asst. prof. sch. libr. and info. sci. U. Ill., Urbana, 1982-83; assoc. univ. libr. pub. svcs. Calif. State U., Sacramento, 1983-87, dean, univ. libr., 1987—; contract cons. Swedish Nat. Bd. Tech. Devel., Stockholm, 1975-76; cons. office mgmt. studies Assn. Rsch. Librs., Washington, 1981-83; mem. coun. libr. dirs. Calif. State U., 1987—, mem. acad. deans coun., 1987—, mem. acad. senate, 1987—, chair libr. adminstrv. coun., 1987—, mem. various campus coms., chair numerous libr. coms.; assoc. Dougherty & Assocs., Ann Arbor, Mich., 1992—; evaluator Western Assn. Schs. and Colls., Oakland, Calif., 1993—; lectr. in field. Author: A Client Centered Academic Library: An Organizational Model, 1983, Critical Issues in Library Personnel Management, 1989; chair editorial bd. Coll. and Rsch. Librs., 1984-90, editor, 1984-90; mem. editorial bd. Coll. and Rsch. Librs. News, 1984-90; mem. adv. bd. Advances in Librarianship, 1991—; assoc. editor Jour. Acad. Librarianship, 1992-93, editor, 1993—; contbr. articles to profl. jours. Chair Calif. State U. campus chpt. United Way, 1990-91. Staff sgt. U.S. Army, 1958-60. Rsch. grantee U. Calif., 1981, grantee Calif. State U., 1984, Calif. State Libr., 1990-93; Librarianship Doctoral fellow U. Calif., 1972-75; Univ. scholar Brown U. Mem. ALA (mem. com. rsch. 1985-89, chair 1986-88, mem. planning and budget assembly 1986-88, mem. liaison with Japanese librs. ad hoc com. 1990-92, mem. internat. rels. com. 1990-92), Assn. Coll. & Rsch. Librs. (mem. budget and planning com. 1990-94), Libr. Adminstrn. and Mgmt. Assn., Libr. and Info. Tech. Assn. (mem. internat. rels. task force 1990-92, chair internat. rels. com. 1992-93). Office: Calif State U University Library Sacramento CA 95819-6039

MARTELL, WILLIAM CLAISE, screenwriter, film producer, writer; b. Concord, Calif., July 20, 1957; s. Robert Leroy and Margaret (Davis) M. AS in Film Arts, Diablo Valley Coll., Pleasant Hill, Calif., 1975-78. Asst. mgr. Syuffy Theatres, Pleasant Hill, Calif., 1973-75; teaching asst. Diablo Valley Coll., Pleasant Hill, Calif., 1975-78; asst. mgr. Kmart, Pleasant Hill, Calif., 1975-77; mgr. Americana Theatres, San Francisco, 1977-78; journeyman clk. Safeway Stores, Pleasant Hill, Calif., 1978-81; v.p. devel. Movie Media Prop, Oakland, Calif., 1981; shipping/receiving Liquor Barn, Walnut Creek, Calif., 1982-89; journeyman clk. Liquor Barn, L.A., 1991; screenwriter pvt. practice, L.A., 1981—; le grande fromage Rogue Motion Pictures, L.A., 1991—; columnist, Screenwrite Now! Mag. Baldwin, Md., 1991—, Screenwriter Insider, L.A., 1993—. Author: Courting Death, 1981, Deadly Masquerade, 1982, The Secrets of Action Screenwriting, 1994, Advanced Screenwriting, 1995; produced screenplays including Ninja Busters, 1981, Treacherous, 1993, Victim of Desire, 1994, Grid Runners, 1994, Hard Evidence, 1994, Night Hunter, 1995. Named Best Student Film Bay Area Film Assn., San Francisco, 1978, Cable A.C.E. Cable TV Industry, E. San Francisco Bay, 1987. Mem. Mystery Writers Am., Scritpwriters Network, Screenwriters Forum. Democrat. Office: 6440 Bellingham Ave # 155 North Hollywood CA 91606-1402

MARTENS, RICHARD LAWRENCE, lawyer; b. Detroit, Oct. 12, 1943; s. George Frederick and Mildred May (Ruddy) M.; m. Jacinta Taitano, Aug. 10, 1968 (div. Jan. 1983); children: Erin Elizabeth, Anne Marie; m. Emily Ann Ericsen, May 6, 1989. BS, U.S. Naval Acad., 1966; JD, U. Mich., 1970. Bar: Mich. 1971, Wash. 1972, U.S. Dist. Ct. Mich., (ea. and we. dists.) Wash., U.S. Cir. Ct. Appeals (9th cir.). Commd. ensign USN, 1966, advanced through grades to lt. comdr., 1978, trial counsel Judge Advocate Gen. Corp., 1970-74; ptnr. Phillips, Wahlstrom & Martens, Bellvue, Wash., 1974-76, Waitt, Johnson & Martens, Seattle, 1976-90, Johnson & Martens, Seattle, 1990—. Mem. Wash. Bar Assn., Wash. Def. Trial Lawyers, Mich. Bar Assn., Columbia Tower Club, Bear CReek Country Club. Office: Johnson & Martens PS 7400 Columbia Ctr Seattle WA 98104

MARTIN, ALBERT CAREY, architect; b. Los Angeles, Aug. 3, 1913; s. Albert Carey and Carolyn Elizabeth (Borchard) M.; m. Dorothy Virginia Dolde, Nov. 15, 1937; children—Albert Carey III, David Charles, Mary Martin Marquardt, Claire, Charles Dolde. B.Arch. cum laude, U. So. Calif., 1936. Registered architect, Calif. Architect Albert C. Martin and Assocs., Los Angeles, 1937-42; ptnr. Albert C. Martin and Assocs., 1942—; dir. Rancho Los Alamitos Found. Prin. works include Los Angeles Dept. Water and Power, ARCO Twin Towers, St. Basil's Ch., Union Bank Sq. Trustee Los Angeles Orthopaedic Hosp.; bd. dirs. Long Beach Mus. Art Found. Recipient Annual Spirit of Los Angeles award Los Angeles Hdqrs. City Assn., 1980, Brotherhood award NCCJ, 1980, Asa V. Call Achievement award U. So. Calif. Alumni Assn., 1984, Boy Scouts Am. Good Scout award L.A. Area Coun., 1989; named Constrn. Man of Yr. Los Angeles C. of C., 1971. Fellow AIA (past dir., pres. So. Calif. chpt., past v.p. Calif. Coun.); mem. U. So. Calif. Archtl. Guild (advisor, disting. alumnus 1990), L.A. C. of C. (past pres.), Calif. C. of C. (past dir.), Lambda Alpha, Automobile Club of So. Calif. Republican. Roman Catholic. Clubs: California, Jonathan (Los Angeles). Office: Albert C Martin and Assocs 811 W 7th St Los Angeles CA 90017-3408

MARTIN, BOYD ARCHER, political science educator emeritus; b. Cottonwood, Idaho, Mar. 3, 1911; s. Archer Olmstead and Norah Claudine (Imbler) M.; m. Grace Charlotte Swingler, Dec. 29, 1933; children: Michael Archer, William Archer. Student, U. Idaho, 1929-30, 35-36, B.S., 1936; student, Pasadena Jr. Coll., 1931-32, U. Calif. at Los Angeles, summer 1934; A.M., Stanford, 1937, Ph.D., 1943. Rsch. asst. Stanford U., 1936-37, teaching asst., 1937-38; instr. polit. sci. U. Idaho, 1938-39; acting instr. polit. sci. Stanford U., 1939-40; John M. Switzer fellow, summer 1939-40; chief personnel officer Walter Butler Constrn. Co., Farragut Naval Tng. Center, summer 1942; instr. polit. sci. U. Idaho, 1940-43, asst. prof. polit. sci., 1943-44, asso. prof. polit. sci., 1944-47; prof., head dept. social sci., asst. dean coll. letters and sci. U. Idaho, 1947-55, dean, 1955-70, Borah Distinguished prof. polit. sci., 1970-73, prof., dean emeritus, 1973—; vis. prof. Stanford U., summer 1946, spring 1952, U. Calif., 1962-63; affiliate Center for Study Higher Edn., Berkeley, 1962-63; mem. steering com. N.W. Conf. on Higher Edn., 1960-67, pres. conf., 1966-67; mem. bd. Am. Assn. of Partners of Alliance for Progress; chmn. Idaho Adv. Coun. on Higher Edn.; del. Gt. Plains UNESCO Conf., Denver, 1947; chmn. bd. William E. Borah Found. on Causes of War and Conditions of Peace, 1947-55; mem. Commn. to Study Orgn. Peace; dir. Bur. Pub. Affair Rsch., 1959-73, dir. emeritus, 1973—; dir. Martin Peace Inst., 1970—. Author: The Direct Primary in Idaho, 1947, (with others) Introduction to Political Science, 1950, (with other) Western Politics, 1968, Politics in the American West, 1969, (with Sydney Duncombe) Recent Elections in Idaho (1964-70), 1972, Idaho Voting Trends: Party Realignment and Percentage of Voters for Candidates, Parties and Elections, 1890-1974, 1975, In Search of Peace: Starting From October 19, 1980, 1980, Why the Democrats Lost in 1980, 1980, On Understanding the Soviet Union, 1987; editor: The Responsibilities of Colleges and Universities, 1967; contbr. to: Ency. Britannica, 1990, 91; also articles. Mem. Am. Polit. Sci. Assn. (exec. council 1952-53), Nat. Municipal League, Am. Soc. Pub. Adminstrn., Fgn. Policy Assn., UN Assn., AAUP, Western Polit. Sci. Assn. (pres. 1950), Phi Beta Kappa, Pi Gamma Mu, Kappa Delta Pi, Pi Sigma Alpha. Home: 516 N Eisenhower St Moscow ID 83843-9596

MARTIN, CATHERINE ELIZABETH, anthropology educator; b. N.Y.C., Feb. 14, 1943; d. Walter Charles and Ruth (Crucet) Strodt; children: Kai Stuart, Armin Wade. BA, Reed Coll., 1965; MA, UCLA, 1967, PhD, 1971. Cert. C.C. tchr., Calif. From asst. to full prof. anthropology Calif. State U., L.A., 1970—, coord. women's studies, 1979-88, acting dir. acad. advisement, 1992-93, dir. Can. studies, 1991, dir. gen. edn. honors program, 1992—. Contbr. chpts. to books and poetry to profl. publs. Cubmaster, den mother Boy Scouts Am., L.A. and Pasadena, 1982-85; leader Tiger Cubs, Boy Scouts Am., 1983. Recipient Outstanding Tiger Cub Leader award Boy Scouts Am., L.A., 1983, Cub Scout Growth award Boy Scouts Am., L.A., 1984. Mem. Am. Anthropol. Assn., Southwestern Anthropol. Assn., S.W. Mus. Office: Calif State U LA Dept Anthropology 5151 State University Dr Los Angeles CA 90032

MARTIN, CLYDE VERNE, psychiatrist; b. Coffeyville, Kans., Apr. 7, 1933; s. Howard Verne and Elfrieda Louise (Moehn) M.; m. Barbara Jean McNeilly, June 24, 1956; children: Kent Clyde, Kristin Claire, Kerry Constance, Kyle Curtis. Student Coffeyville Coll., 1951-52; AB, U. Kans., 1955; MD, 1958; MA, Webster Coll., St. Louis, 1977; JD, Thomas Jefferson Coll. Law, Los Angeles, 1985. Diplomate Am. Bd. Psychiatry and Neurology. Intern, Lewis Gale Hosp., Roanoke, Va., 1958-59; resident in psychiatry U. Kans. Med. Ctr., Kansas City, 1959-62, Fresno br. U. Calif.-San Francisco, 1978; staff psychiatrist Neurol. Hosp., Kansas City, 1962; practice medicine specializing in psychiatry, Kansas City, Mo., 1964-84; founder, med. dir., pres. bd. dirs. Mid-Continent Psychiat. Hosp., Olathe, Kans., 1972-84; adj. prof. psychology Baker U., Baldwin City, Kans., 1969-84; staff psychiatrist Atascadero State Hosp., Calif., 1984-85; clin. prof. psychiatry U. Calif., San Francisco, 1985—; chief psychiatrist Calif. Med. Facility, Vacaville, 1985-87; pres., editor Corrective and Social Psychiatry, Olathe, 1970-84, Atascadero, 1984-85, Fairfield, 1985—. Contbr. articles to profl. jours. Bd. dirs. Meth. Youthville, Newton, Kans. 1965-75, Spofford Home, Kansas City, 1974-78. Served to capt. USAF, 1962-64, ret. col. USAFR. Oxford Law & Soc. scholar, 1993. Fellow Am. Psychiat. Assn., Royal Soc. Health, Am. Assn. Mental Health Profls. in Corrections, World Assn. Social Psychiatry, Am. Orthopsychiat. Assn.; mem. AMA, Assn. for Advancement Psychotherapy, Am. Assn. Sex Educators, Counselors and Therapists (cert.), Assn. Mental

Health Adminstrs. (cert.), Kansas City Club, Masons, Phi Beta Pi, Pi Kappa Alpha. Methodist (del. Kans. East Conf. 1972-80, bd. global ministries 1974-80). Office: PO Box 3365 Fairfield CA 94533-0587

MARTIN, DAVID LEE, computer scientist; b. Hickory, N.C., Apr. 4, 1953; s. Boyce Neil and Juanita Rose (Warren) M.; m. Barbara Ann Deines, Oct. 5, 1991; 1 child, Douglas Lee. BS in Computer Sci., Calif. State U., Northridge, 1987; MS in Computer Sci., UCLA, 1992. Sr. software engr. Mark V Systems, Encino, Calif., 1986-94; computer scientist SRI Internat., Menlo Park, Calif., 1994—. Calif. Grad. fellow State of Calif., 1988, 89; Ocean Tech. Corp. undergrad. scholar, L.A., 1985, Litton Data Systems Mgmt. Club scholar, L.A., 1986. Mem. IEEE, Assn. Computing Machinery, Am. Assn. Artificial Intelligence, Computer Profls. for Social Responsibility, Behavioral and Brain Scis. (assoc.). Office: SRI Internat 333 Ravenswood Ave Menlo Park CA 94025-3453

MARTIN, DAVID R., oil company executive; b. 1931. BA, UCLA, 1957, MA, 1958. With Mobil Oil Corp., N.Y.C., 1959-61; with Occidental Oil & Gas Corp., 1969—, v.p. Latin Am. ops., 1969-85, pres., 1986—; exec. v.p. Occidental Petroleum Corp., 1986—. Served with USAF, 1950-53. Office: Occidental Oil & Gas Corp 10889 Wilshire Blvd Los Angeles CA 90024-4201

MARTIN, DONALD WALTER, author, publisher; b. Grants Pass, Oreg., Apr. 22, 1934; s. George E. and Irma Ann (Dallas) M.; m. Kathleen Elizabeth Murphy, July, 1970 (div. May 1979); children: Daniel Clayton, Kimberly Ann; m. Betty Woo, Mar. 18, 1985. Enlisted USMC, 1952; advanced through grades to staff sgt. USMC, Japan, Republic of Korea, Republic of China, 1956-61; reporter Blade-Tribune, Oceanside, Calif., 1961-65; entertainment editor Press-Courier, Oxnard, Calif., 1965-69; mng. editor Argus-Courier, Petaluma, Calif., 1969-70; assoc. editor Motorland mag., San Francisco, 1970-88; founder, prin., CEO Pine Cone Press, Inc., Columbia, Calif., 1988—. Author: Best of San Francisco, 1986, 90, 94, Best of the Gold Country, 1987, 92, San Francisco's Ultimate Dining Guide, 1988, Best of Arizona, 1990, 93, Inside San Francisco, 1991, Coming to Arizona, 1991, Best of the Wine Country, 1991, 95, Best of Nevada, 1992, Oregon Discovery Guide, 1993, Northern California Discovery Guide, 1993, The Ultimate Wine Book, 1993, Washington Discovery Guide, 1994, Utah Discovery Guide, 1995; contbr. articles on travel to various publs. Recipient Diane Seely award Ventura County Theatre Council, 1968. Mem. Soc. Am. Travel Writers. Republican. Home and Office: 11362 Yankee Hill Rd PO Box 1494 Columbia CA 95310-1494

MARTIN, DORIS ELLEN, publisher, management consultant; b. Chgo., Oct. 26, 1927; d. John L. and Marie (Miller) Martin; m. Morton Rosenberg, Dec. 15, 1963 (div. 1964). BS, NYU, 1952; MS, Boston U., 1958; EdD, Columbia U., 1964. Instr. Colby Coll., Waterville, Maine, 1952-54; dir. edn. dept. YWCA, Honolulu, 1954-59; dir. The Conf. Ctr., U. Hawaii, Honolulu, 1960-65; dir. spl. projects and assoc. prof. NYU, N.Y.C., 1965-66; dir. of spl. project state plan Dept. Planning/Econ. Devel., State of Hawaii, Honolulu, 1966-69; spl. asst. George Washington U., Washington, 1970; mgmt. cons. Dr. D. Martin Assocs., Wailuku, Hawaii, 1980—; pres., pubr. Martin Mgmt. Books, Wailuku, Hawaii, 1985—. Author 7 books. Mem. Rep. Nat. Com., 1975—. Mem. Pubrs. Mktg. Assn. Home and Office: 2108 Kahekili Hwy Wailuku HI 96793-9207

MARTIN, GEORGE, psychologist, educator; b. L.A., May 8, 1940; s. George Leonard and Margaret (Padigamus) M.; m. Penny Harrell, June 22, 1963 (div. 1984); children: Jeni, Kimberle. BA, UCLA, 1965; MA, Calif. State U., L.A., 1967; MS, Calif. State U., Fullerton, 1994. Systems analyst L.A. Dept. Water & Power, 1965-67; project coord. L.A. Police Dept., 1967-70, edn. cons., 1980-83; alcohol researcher Pomona (Calif.) Coll., 1970-73; tng. systems researcher Lanterman State Hosp., Pomona, 1973-77; prof. psychology Mt. San Antonio Coll., Walnut, Calif., 1970—, dir. rsch., 1986-94. Contbr. articles to profl. jours. Rsch. dir. Orange County Dem. Party, 1985-86. With U.S. Army, 1959-61. Grantee Nat. Inst. Law Enforcement, 1967-70, Nat. Inst. Alcohol, 1970-74. Mem. APA, NSA. Home: 1313 N Grand Ave Ste 326 Walnut CA 91789-1317 Office: Mt San Antonio Coll 1100 N Grand Ave Walnut CA 91789-1341

MARTIN, GEORGE M., pathologist, gerontologist; b. N.Y.C., June 30, 1927; s. Barnett J. and Estelle (Weiss) M.; m. Julaine Ruth Miller, Dec. 2, 1952; children: Peter C., Kelsey C., Thomas M., Andrew C. BS, U. Wash., 1949, MD, 1953. Diplomate Am. Bd. Pathology, Am. Bd. Med. Genetics. Intern Montreal Gen. Hosp., Quebec, Can., 1953-54; resident-instr. U. Chgo., 1954-57; instr.-prof. U. Wash., Seattle, 1957—; vis. scientist Dept. Genetics Albert Einstein Coll., N.Y.C., 1964; chmn. Gordon Confs. Molecular Pathology, Biology of Aging, 1974-79; chmn., nat. res. Plan on Aging Nat. Inst. on Aging, Bethesda, Md., 1985-89; dir. Alzheimer's Disease Rsch. Ctr. U. Wash., 1985—. Editor Werner's Syndrome and Human Aging, 1985; contbr. articles in field to profl jours. Active Fedn. Am. Scientists. With USN, 1945-46. Recipient Allied Signal award in Aging, 1991, Rsch. medal Am. Agy. Assn., 1992, Kleemeier award, 1994; named Disting. Alumnus, U. Wash. Sch. Medicine, 1987; USPHS rsch. fellow dept. genetics, Glasgow U., 1961-62; Eleanor Roosvelt Inst. Cancer Rsch. fellow Inst. de Biologie, PHysiologie, Chimie, Paris, 1968-69; Josiah Macy faculty scholar Sir William Din Sch. Pathology, Oxford (Eng.) U., 1978-79, Humboldt Disting. scientist dept. genetics U. Wurzburg, Germany, 1991. Fellow AAAS, Gerontol. Soc. Am. (chmn. Biol. Sci. 1979, Brookdale award 1981), Tissue Culture Assn. (pres. 1986-88); mem. Inst. Medicine, Am. Assn. Univ. Pathologists (emeritus), Am. Soc. Human Genetics, Am. Soc. Investigative Pathology. Democrat. Home: 2223 E Howe St Seattle WA 98112-2931 Office: U Wash Sch Medicine Dept Pathology Sm # 30 Seattle WA 98195

MARTIN, GORDON EUGENE, electrical engineer; b. San Diego, Aug. 22, 1925; s. Carl Amos and Ruth Marie (Fountain) M.; m. Tricia Jane Totten, June 10, 1949; children: Gloria, Theodore, Kathryn, Susan. BSEE, U. Calif., Berkeley, 1947; MS in Engring., UCLA, 1951; MA in Physics, S.D. State U., 1961; PhD in Elec. Engring., U. Tex., 1966. Elec. engr. Convar (Gen. Dynamics), San Diego, 1947; rsch. physicist Navy Electronics Lab., San Diego, 1947-52, Naval Ocean Systems Ctr., San Diego, 1954-80; acoustics dept. head Systems Exploration Inc., San Diego, 1980-82; pres. Martin Analysis Software Tech., Inc., San Diego, 1982—; cons. USN Hdqrs., Washington, 1954-80, piezoelectric bd. USN, Washington, 1960-80. Patentee of sonar and radio system. Lt. USNR, 1943-45, 52-54. Fellow Acoustical Soc. Am. (chpt. pres.); mem. N.Y. Acad. Scis., Inst. Electronics & Elec. Engring. (com. mem.), Sigma Xi, Sigma Pi Sigma. Office: Martin Analysis Software Tech Inc 3675 Syracuse Ave San Diego CA 92122-3322

MARTIN, HUGO CASILLAS, staff writer; b. San Fernando, Calif., Feb. 20, 1965; s. Pedro and Merecedes (Casillas) M. BA in Govt., Pomona Coll., 1987. Trainee L.A. Times, 1987-90, staff writer, 1990—. Mem. Nat. Assn. of Hispanic Journalists, Calif. Chicano News Media Assn.

MARTIN, JAMES LOWREY, JR., foundation administrator; b. Memphis, Sept. 5, 1954; s. James L. and Martha (Argo) M.; m. Hilma Ann Rowe, July 13, 1974; children: Philip, Michael, Wesley. BA, Memphis State U., 1978; MA, Wheaton (Ill.) Coll., 1986. Ops. mgr., CFO Christian Camping Internat., Wheaton, 1986-91; CEO Calif. Redwoods Christian Assn., Boulder Creek, 1991—. Office: Redwood Christian Park 15000 Two Bar Rd Boulder Creek CA 95006-9766

MARTIN, JOSEPH, JR., lawyer, former ambassador; b. San Francisco, May 21, 1915; m. Ellen Chamberlain Martin, July 5, 1946; children: Luther Greene, Ellen Myers. AB, Yale U., 1936, LLB, 1939. Assoc. Cadwalader, Wickersham & Taft, N.Y.C., 1939-41; ptnr. Wallace, Garrison, Norton & Ray, San Francisco, 1946-55, Pettit & Martin, San Francisco, 1955-70, 73-95; gen. counsel FTC, Washington, 1970-71; ambassador, U.S. rep. Disarmament Conf., Geneva, 1971-76; mem. Pres.'s Adv. Com. for Arms Control and Disarmament, 1974-78; bd. dirs. Astec Industries, Inc. Pres. Pub. Utilities Commn., San Francisco, 1956-60; Rep. nat. committeeman for Calif., 1960-64; treas. Rep. Party Calif., 1956-58; bd. dirs. Patrons of Art and Music, Calif. Palace of Legion of Honor, 1958-70, pres., 1963-68; bd. dirs. Arms Control Assn., 1977-84; pres. Friends of Legal Assistance to Elderly, 1983-87. Lt. comdr. USNR, 1941-46. Recipient Ofcl. commendation for Outstanding Service as Gen. Counsel FTC, 1973, Distinguished Honor award U.S. ACDA, 1973, Lifetime Achievement award Legal Assistance to the Elderly, 1981. Fellow Am. Bar Found. Clubs: Burlingame Country, Pacific Union. Home: 2879 Woodside Rd Woodside CA 94062-2441 Office: 3 Embarcadero Ctr #2280 San Francisco CA 94111

MARTIN, JOSEPH BOYD, neurologist, educator; b. Bassano, Alta., Can., Oct. 20, 1938; s. Joseph Bruce and Ruth Elizabeth (Ramer) M.; m. Rachel Ann Wenger, June 18, 1960; children: Bradley, Melanie, Douglas, Neil. B.Sc., Eastern Mennonite Coll., Harrisonburg, Va., 1959; M.D., U. Alta., 1962; Ph.D., U. Rochester, N.Y., 1971; M.A. (hon.), Harvard U., 1978; ScD (hon.), McGill U., 1994. Resident in internal medicine Univ. Hosp., Edmonton, Alta., 1962-64; resident in neurology Case-Western Res. U. Hosps., 1964-67; rsch. fellow U. Rochester, N.Y., 1967-70; mem. faculty McGill U. Faculty Medicine, Montreal, Que., Can., 1970-78; prof. medicine and neurology, neurologist-in-chief Montreal Neurol. Inst., 1976-78; chmn. dept. neurology Mass. Gen. Hosp., Boston, also Dorn prof. neurology Harvard U. Med. Sch., 1978-89; dean Sch. Medicine U. Calif., San Francisco, 1989-93; chancellor U. Calif., San Francisco, 1993—; mem. med. adv. bd. Gairdner Found., Toronto, 1978-83; adv. council neurol. disorders program Nat. Inst. Neurol., Communicative Disorders and Stroke, 1979-82. Coauthor: Clinical Neuroendocrinology, 1977, The Hypothalmamus, 1978, Clinical Neuroendocrinology: A Pathophysiological Approach, 1979, Neurosecretion and Brain Peptides: Implications for Brain Functions and Neurological Disease, 1981, Brain Peptides, 1983; editor Harrison's Principles of Internal Medicine, Clin. Neuroendocrinology 2d edit., 1987. Recipient Moshier Meml. gold medal U. Alta. Faculty Medicine, 1962, John W. Scott gold med. award, 1962; Med. Research Council Can. scholar, 1970-75. Mem. NAS, Internat. Soc. Neuroendocrinology (coun. 1980—), Am. Neurol. Assn. (pres. 1990), Am. Physiol. Soc. (Bowditch lectr. 1978), Royal Coll. Phys. and Surg. Can., Endocrine Soc., Soc. Neurosci., Am. Soc. Clin. Investigation, Assn. Am. Physicians, Am. Acad. Arts and Scis., Inst. of Medicine, Nat. Adv. Coun., Nat. Inst. Aging. Office: U Calif 513 Parnassus Ave Ste 126 San Francisco CA 94122-2722

MARTIN, JULIA L., public relations account executive; b. Little Rock, Ark., Mar. 21, 1965; d. Robert F. Brewer and Mary Ann (Chrisman) Morden; m. Lawrence M. Martin, Jr., May 30, 1992,. BA in Journalism, U. Cntl. Ark., 1984, MA in English, 1985. Comms. asst. Stephens, Inc., Little Rock, 1986-89; comm. coord. So. Tech. Coll., Little Rock, 1989-90; dir. pub. rels. Coll. Arts, Humanities and Social Scis., U. Ark., Little Rock, 1990-92; spl. events coord. March of Dimes, Nebr., Bebr., 1992-93. Mem. Pub. Rels. Soc. Am. (accredited pub. rels. profl.), Toastmasters.

MARTIN, JULIUS OREN, minister, social services administrator; b. Red Oak, Iowa, Aug. 3, 1936; s. James Jefferson and Violet Celsta (Worm) M.; m. Darlene Roberta Collins, June 30, 1958; children: David, Rachel, Deborah, Timothy, Tabitha, Ruth, Sarah. BA in Religion, N.W. Bible Coll., Minot, N.D., 1962. Ordained to ministry Ch. of God, 1968. State youth dir. Ch. of God, Mont. and Wyo., 1962-66; pastor Ch. of God, Wallace, Idaho, 1966-70, Bisbee, Ariz., 1970-73, Kellogg, Idaho, 1973-75, Winnipeg, Can., 1975-78, Mpls., 1978-81, Las Cruces, N.Mex., 1981-87; exec. dir. Gospel Rescue Mission, Las Cruces, N.Mex., 1987—. Author: Book of Daily Prayer, 1990. Mem. state coun. Ch. of God, Idaho, 1968-70, 74-75, mem. state youth bd., Minn., 1978-81; bd. dirs. Wallace (Idaho) Youth Ctr., 1968-70, Shoshone County Cub Scouts, Boy Scouts Am., 1968-70; mem. Mayor's Task Force for the Homeless, Las Cruces, 1989, N.Mex. Task Force for Educating Homeless Children, Santa Fe, 1991; pres. Evang. Mins. Fellowship, 1989-92. Sgt. U.S. Army, 1955-58. Named Chaplain of Yr. Hennepin County Commrs., 1981. Mem. Internat. Union of Gospel Mission (trustee 1990—), Kiwanis (pres. 1993-94), Gen. Hosp. Chaplains (pres. 1983-89). Republican. Office: Gospel Rescue Mission 1422 S Solano Dr Las Cruces NM 88001-4236

MARTIN, JUNE JOHNSON CALDWELL, journalist; b. Toledo, Oct. 6; d. John Franklin and Eunice Imogene (Fish) Johnson; m. Erskine Caldwell, Dec. 21, 1942 (div. Dec. 1955); 1 child, Jay Erskine; m. Keith Martin, May 5, 1966. AA, Phoenix Jr. Coll., 1939-41; BA, U. Ariz., 1941-43, 53-59; student Ariz. State U., 1939, 40. Free-lance writer, 1944—; columnist Ariz. Daily Star, 1956-59; editor Ariz. Alumnus mag., Tucson, 1959-70; book reviewer, columnist Ariz. Daily Star, Tucson, 1970-94; ind. book reviewer and audio tape columnist, Tucson, 1994—; panelist, co-producer TV news show Tucson Press Club, 1954-55, pres., 1958; co-founder Ariz. Daily Star Ann. Book & Author Event. Contbg. author: Rocky Mountain Cities, 1949; contbr. articles to World Book Ency., and various mags. Mem. Tucson CD Com., 1961; vol. campaigns of Samuel Goddard, U.S. Rep. Morris Udall, U.S. ambassador and Ariz. gov. Raul Castro. Recipient award Nat. Headliners Club, 1959, Ariz. Press Club award, 1957-59, Am. Alumni Council, 1966, 70. Mem. Nat. Book Critics Circle, Jr. League of Tucson, Tucson Urban League, PEN U.S.A. West, Pi Beta Phi. Democrat. Methodist. Club: Tucson Press. Home: Desert Foothills Sta PO Box 65388 Tucson AZ 85728

MARTIN, KEVIN JAY, investment and development executive; b. Wilmington, Del., June 21, 1948; s. Clair Albright and Mary Margurite (Simmons) M.; m. Pamela Jean Bishop, Aug. 24, 1974 (div. Dec. 1990); 1 child, Kimberly Jean Bishop Martin. BS in Mktg. and Fin., San Diego State U., 1972. Gen. mgr. Toys-R-Us, San Jose, Calif., 1972-84; sales rep. Tandy, San Jose, 1985; gen. ptnr. Martin & Miller Constrn., San Diego, 1987-89, Martin & Martin Investment and Constrn., Palm Springs, Calif., 1990—. Mem. Masons. Home and Office: 33-971 Westchester Dr Thousand Palms CA 92276-3901

MARTIN, LINDA GAYE, demographer, economist; b. Paris, Ark., Dec. 17, 1947; d. Leslie Paul and Margie LaVerne (Thomas) M. BA in Math., Harvard U., 1970; MPA, Princeton U., 1972, PhD in Econs., 1978. Dir. mgmt. info. bur. purchased social svcs. for adults City of N.Y., 1972-74; rsch. assoc., rsch. dir. U.S. Ho. of Reps. Select Com. on Population, Washington, 1977-79; rsch. assoc. East-West Population Inst., Honolulu, 1979-89, asst. dir., 1982-84; asst. prof. econs. U. Hawaii, Honolulu, 1979-81, assoc. prof., 1981-89, prof., 1989; dir. com. on population Nat. Acad. Scis., Washington, 1989-93; dir. domestic rsch. divsn., v.p. RAND, Santa Monica, Calif., 1993—; mem. neurosci. behavior and sociology of aging rev. com. Nat. Inst. on Aging, Bethesda, 1991—; chair panel on aging in developing countries NAS, Washington, 1987, mem. com. on population , 1993—. Editor: The ASEAN Success Story, 1987; co-editor: Demographic Change in Sub-Saharan Africa, 1993, Demographic Effects of Economic Reversals in Sub-Saharan Africa, 1993, The Demography of Aging, 1994; author: (monograph) The Graying of Japan, 1989; contbr. articles to profl. jours. Recipient Fulbright Faculty Rsch. award Coun. for Internat. Exch. of Scholars, 1988. Mem. Gerontol. Soc. Am., Internat. Union for Scientific Study Population, Population Assn. Am. (bd. dirs. 1991-93), Japan Am. Soc. So. Calif. (bd. dirs. 1994—). Democrat. Office: Rand PO Box 2138 Santa Monica CA 90407-2138

MARTIN, LOREN WINSTON, physician; b. Albertsville, Ala., Apr. 20, 1938; s. Loren d. and Byrda G. (Crotwell) M.; m. Vivian Elizabeth Sanger Martin, Dec. 29, 1960; children: Lori Ann, Karen Lynn, James Winston. BA in Chemistry, Duke U., 1959; MD, U. Tenn., 1962. Lic. physician, Ariz. Rotating internship Fitzsimons Army Hosp., Denver, 1963; med. residency Honolulu, 1964-67; med. officer U.S. Army, 1962-70; fellowship allergy U. Colo., Denver, 1970-71; pvt. practice Tucson, 1971—. Decorated Bronze Star. Fellow Am. Acad. Allergy & Immunology, Am. Coll. Allergy & Immunology; mem. Pima County Med. Soc. Republican. Office: 5300 E Erickson Dr Ste 120 Tucson AZ 85712-2809

MARTIN, LUCY Z., public relations executive; b. Alton, Ill., July 8, 1941; d. Fred and Lucille J. M. BA, Northwestern U., 1963. Adminstrv. asst., copywriter Batz-Hodgson-Neuwoehner, Inc., St. Louis, 1963-64; news reporter, Midwest fashion editor Fairchild Publs., St. Louis, 1964-66; account exec. Milici Advt. Agy., Honolulu, 1967; publs. dir. Barnes Med. Ctr., St. Louis, 1968-69; communications cons. Fleishman-Hillard, St. Louis, 1970-74; communications cons., chief exec. officer, pres. Lucy Z. Martin & Assocs., Portland, Oreg., 1974—; Speaker Healthcare Assn. Hawaii, 1993, Oreg. Assn. Healthcare, 1992, Healthcare Fin. Mgmt. Assn., 1993, Healthcare Communicators Oreg., 1994; bd. dirs. Am. Mktg. Assn. Oreg. chpt. 1992-93. Featured in Entrepreneurial Woman mag.; contbr. articles to profl. jours. Chmn. women's adv. com. Reed Coll., Portland, 1977-79; mem. Oreg. Commn. for Women, 1984-87; bd. dirs. Ronald McDonald House Oreg., 1986, Oreg. Sch. Arts & Crafts, 1989—, Inst. Managerial and Profl. Women, 1992—, Northwestern U. Alumni Coun., 1992—; chmn. bd. Good Samaritan Hosp. Assocs., 1991—; mem. alumni coun. Northwestern U., 1992—; mem. pub. policy com. YMCA, 1993—; mem. adv. bd. Jr. League, 1994—. Recipient MacEachern Citation Acad. Hosp. Pub. Relations, 1978, Rosey awards Portland Advt. Fedn., 1979, Achievement award Soc. Tech. Communications, 1982, Disting. Tech. Communication award, 1982, Exceptional Achievement award Council for Advancement and Support Edn., 1983, Monsoon award Internat. Graphics, Inc., 1984; named Woman of Achievement Daily Jour. Commerce, 1980. Mem. Pub. Rels. Soc. Am. (pres. Columbia River chpt. 1984, chmn. bd. 1980-84, Oreg. del. 1984-86, judicial panel N. Pacific dist 1985-86, exec. bd. health care sect. 1986-87, mem. Counselors Acad., Spotlight awards 1985, 86, 87, 88, nat. exec. com. 1987-91), Portland Pub. Rels. Roundtable (chmn. 1985, bd. dirs. 1983-85), Assn. Western Hosps. (editorial adv. bd. 1984-85), Best of West awards 1978, 80, 83, 87), Oreg. Hosp. Pub. Relations Orgn. (pres. 1981, chmn. bd. 1982, bd. dirs. 1992-93), Acad. Health Service Mktg., Am. Hosp. Assn., Am. Mktg. Assn. (Oreg. chpt. bd. dirs. 1992-93), Am. Soc. Hosp. Mktg. & Pub. Relations, Healthcare Communicators Oreg. (conf. keynote speaker 1994), Internat. Assn. Bus. Communicators (18 awards 1981-87), Oreg. Assn. Hosps. (keynote speaker for trustee, 1991, speaker, 1993, bd. dirs. 1992-93), Oreg. Press Women, Nat. and Oreg. Soc. Healthcare Planning and Mktg., Women in Communications (Matrix award 1977), Inst. Managerial and Profl. Women (bd. dirs. 1992—), City Club Portland. Office: 1881 SW Edgewood Rd Portland OR 97201-2235

MARTIN, MICHAEL ANTHONY, medical educator; b. Cin., Aug. 17, 1951; s. Peter A. and Lorraine A. (Froelicher) M.; m. Katherine Von Derau, Feb. 28, 1976; children: Michael Jr., Claire Louise. BS in Chemistry cum laude, U. Cin., 1976; MD, Med. Coll. Ohio, 1980. Diplomate Am. Bd. Internal Medicine, Am. Bd. Infectious Diseases, Nat. Bd. Med. Examiners. Intern U. Wis., Madison, 1980-81, resident, 1981-83; fellow infectious diseases U. Iowa, Iowa City, 1984-86, fellow clin. epidemiology, 1986-87; hosp. epidemiologist, assoc. prof. medicine Oreg. Health Scis. U. Editorial reviewer: New Eng. Jour. Medicine, Annals of Internal Medicine, Antimicrobial Agts. and Chemotherapy, Infection Control and Hosp. Epidemiology, Western Jour. Medicine, Jour. Clin. Oncology, Critical Care Medicine; contbg. author to books in field; contbr. articles to profl. jours. Grantee Nat. Found. Infectious Diseases, 1986-87, Xoma Corp., 1989-90, Cutter Biological, Berkeley, Calif., 1991-92, Univax, Rockville, Md., 1992-93, 3M, Mpls., 1993-94, Pfizer/Roerig, N.Y.C., 1993-94. Office: Oreg Health Sci Univ UHN 59 Portland OR 97201-3098

MARTIN, NANCY L., communications exective; b. Phoenix, Dec. 6, 1931; d. Donald Mackenzie and Mary (Wilson) M. BA, U. Calif., 1954. Reporter Phoenix Gazette, 1951-52; creative dir. Modern Advtg., Santa Monica, Calif., 1954-60; publicist Los Angeles, 1960-63; exec. v.p. Ad Mktg., Beverly Hills, Calif., 1963-68; pres. Martin Ptnrs., Inc., Beverly Hills, 1968-75; supr. Sitmar Cruises, Los Angeles, 1975-86, nat. tng. cons., 1986-90; v.p. mktg. and sales Uniglobe Hi Desert Travel, Victorville, Calif., 1990—. Pres. Llano Cmty. Assn., 1995—. Recipient Design Excellence award Type Dirs. Club, 1963. Mem. ASTD. Democrat. Roman Catholic. Home: 31350 157th St E Llano CA 93544-1232

MARTIN, NEIL ALFRED, neurosurgeon; b. Phila., June 5, 1951; s. Alfred Nicholas and Mary (Ziegler) M.; m. Colleen Patricia Cudahy, Sept. 22, 1991; children: Neil Alfred Jr., Nicholas Alexander. BS, Yale U., 1973; MD, Med. Coll. of Va., 1978. Intern U. Calif., San Francisco, 1978-79, resident in neurosurgery, 1979-84; neurovascular fellowship Barrow Neurol. Inst., Phoenix, 1984-85; asst. prof. UCLA Med. Sch., 1985-90, assoc. prof., 1990-95, prof., 1995—, dir. vascular neurosurgery, 1986—, dir. cerebral blood flow lab., 1989—. Contbr. more than 100 articles to profl. jours., chpts. in books in field. Rsch. grantee NIH, 1991-96. Mem. Am. Assn. Neurol. Surgeons, Congress of Neurol. Surgeons, Neurosurgical Soc. Am., Western Neurosurgical Soc. Office: UCLA Sch Medicine 74-140 CHS 10833 Le Conte Ave Los Angeles CA 90024

MARTIN, PAUL, hepatologist, medical educator; b. Dublin, Ireland, July 13, 1954; came to the U.S., 1987; s. Nicholas Colman and Maura Josephine (Bugler) M.; m. Maria Teresa Abreu, Apr. 9, 1994. MD, U. Coll., Dublin, 1978. Cert. Am. Bd. Internal Medicine; cert. gastroenterology. Intern and resident St. Vincent Hosp., Dublin, 1978-82; resident U. Alt., Edmonton, Can., 1982-84; gastroenterology fellow Queen's U., Ont., 1984-86; hepatology fellow U. Toronto, Ont., 1986-87; med. staff fellow NIH, Bethesda, Md., 1987-89; asst. prof. medicine Jefferson Med. Coll., Phila., 1989-92; dir. hepatology UCLA, 1992-95, assoc. prof. medicine, 1995—. Editor: Viral Hepatitis, 1994; contbr. articles to profl. jours. Fellow ACP, Royal Coll. Physicians Can. and Ireland; mem. Am. Assn. for the Study Liver Disease. Democrat. Roman Catholic. Office: UCLA Sch Medicine 77-123 DCHS 10833 Le Conte Ave Los Angeles CA 90024

MARTIN, RICHARD OTTO, medical device company executive; b. Chgo., Jan. 28, 1940; s. Richard and Barbara (Hildner) M.; divorced; children: Michelle Marie, Richard Michael, Bryan Joseph. BS in Elec. Engring., Christian Bros. Coll., Memphis, 1962; MSin Elec. Engring., Notre Dame U., 1964; PhD, Duke U., 1970. Registered prof. engr., Tenn. Research instr. dept. of medicine U. Tenn., Memphis, 1970-75; assoc. prof., head elec. engring. dept. Christian Bros. Coll., 1970-75; dir. U.S. Tech. Ctr. and Adv. Lead Devel. Medtronic, Inc., Mpls., 1975-78; v.p. clin. engring. Intermedics, Inc., Freeport, Tex., 1978-83; exec. v.p. Intermedics, Inc., 1983-85, pres., chief operating officer, 1985-87; pres., chief operating officer Positron Corp., 1988-89; v.p. bus. devel. Cardiovascular Sulzermedica, 1989—. Contbr. articles to profl. jours. NIH fellow, 1967-70. Mem. IEEE (assoc. editor Transactions on Biomed Engring. 1976-87), Am. Soc. Engring. Edn., Assn. for Advancement of Med. Instrumentation, N.Am. Soc. Pacing and Electrophysiology, Tau Beta Pi. Roman Catholic. Office: Physio-Control Corp 11811 Willows Rd NE Redmond WA 98052-2003

MARTIN, ROBERT (TONY MARTIN), environmental geologist; b. Evansville, Ind., Oct. 14, 1962; s. Al A. and Barbara J. (Montanari) M. A in Geology, Fresno City Coll., 1983; B in Geology, Calif. State U., Fresno, 1985. Registered environ. assessor, Calif. Staff geologist Krazan & Assocs., Inc., Fresno, 1987-88, environ. div. mgr., 1988-94, v.p. environ. svcs., 1993-94; sr. geologist Kleinfelder, Inc., Stockton, Calif., 1994—. Mem. task force City of Fresno Little Hoover Commn,. 1991-92; asst. scoutmaster, scoutmaster Boy Scouts Am., Madera, 1980—. Mem. Calif. Groundwater Assn., Assn. Environ. Profls., Fresno Geol. Soc., Am. Assn. Petroleum Geologists, Nat. Assn. Eagle Scouts, Calif. Air and Waste Mgmt. Assn. Republican. Roman Catholic. Home: 1142 Champagne Ln Manteca CA 95337-6815 Office: Kleinfelder Inc 2825 E Myrtle St Stockton CA 95205-4719

MARTIN, ROBERT BURTON, management consultant; b. Takoma Park, Md., Mar. 17, 1935; s. Herbert Lester and Lenora Marie (Sponseller) M.; m. Mary Lou Rushworth, Sept. 7, 1959 (div. Dec. 1982); children: Laurajean, Kenneth, Donna Beth. BEE, Cornell U., 1958; MS, Northwestern U., 1966, PhD, 1967. Dir. mgmt. systems Denver and Rio Grande Western R.R., 1967-71; v.p. Mgmt. Design Assoc., Denver, 1971-79; owner Martin & Assoc., Denver, 1979—; founder Martin Aviation Ltd., Denver, 1993—; treas. Rocky Mountain chpt. Inst. of Mgmt. Sci., Denver, 1968-70; opening speaker AICPAs, Las Vegas, Nev., 1988. Author, pub.: (newsletter) Martin Reports, 1981—, Bob Martin-Chris Frederiksen Marketing and Management Report for CPAs, 1990—. Served to lt. USN, 1958-63. Mem. Inst. Mgmt. Cons., Alpha Pi Mu, Sigma Xi. Home and Office: PO Box 6886 Denver CO 80206-0886

MARTIN, ROBERT GREGORY, chemist; b. Denver, Apr. 24, 1959; s. Harold Gregory and Margaret C. (Mayer) M. BS, U. Denver, 1982. Computer distbr. Tronics Sales Corp., Ft. Worth, 1983; lab. technician Hager Labs., Denver, 1983-84, chem. analyst I, 1984-85, chem. analyst II, 1985-86, chem. analyst III, 1986-87, operator GC/MS, 1987-88; chemist IV, operator GC/MS Rocky Mountain Analyyical Labs, Environ. Svc. Co., Arvada, Colo., 1988-91; chemist V Rocky Mountain Analytical Labs, Environ. Svc. Co., 1991-92; chemist U.S. geol. survey Nat. Water Quality Lab., Arvada,

Colo., 1992—. Recipient Hornbeck award U. Denver, 1982; scholar U. Denver, 1982. Mem. AAAS, Am. Chem. Soc., N.Y. Acad. Sci., Am. Inst. Chemists, The Planetary Soc., Gold Key, Alpha Lambda Delta, Alpha Epsilon Delta. Roman Catholic. Home: 7911 Otis Cir Arvada CO 80003-2309 Office: US Geol Survey Nat Water Quality Labs 5293 Ward Rd # B Arvada CO 80002-1811

MARTIN, ROBERT GROVER, business and computers educator, artist; b. Winston-Salem, N.C., Sept. 26, 1948; s. Frederick and Mary F. (Wentz) M.; m. Sandra J. Mauney, Aug. 3, 1968; children: Robert G. Jr., Thomas K. BSBA, U. Albuquerque, 1980; MBA, N.Mex. Highlands U., 1985. Enlisted man USAF, 1967, mgr., instr., technician, 1967-87; ret., 1987; dir. Muir Tech. Coll., Albuquerque, 1988-90; instr., coord. data processing Computer Career Ctr., Albuquerque, 1991-94; instr. No. Ariz. Inst. Tech., Albuquerque, 1994—; owner Martin & Assocs., Albuquerque, 1975-94. One-man show Albuquerque Dept. Human Svcs., 1993, Albuquerque Pub. Libr., 1994; represented in pvt. collections throughout U.S. Mem., sec.-treas. North Valley Adv. Coun., 1990-94. Mem. N.Mex. Art League (treas. 1993-94). Republican. Home: 1717 Mary Ellen St NE Albuquerque NM 87112-4143 Office: St Catherine's Indian Sch 80 Griffin Santa Fe NM 87501

MARTIN, ROBERT MICHAEL, lawyer; b. N.Y.C., Nov. 28, 1922; s. Charles Augustus and Mary Corcoran (Shannon) M.; m. Monica Maria Schmid, Jan. 22, 1951; children: Tara J., C. Brian, Stacy D. BA, Amherst Coll., 1949; grad. cert., Trinity Coll., Dublin, Ireland, 1950; JD, U. So. Calif., 1965; diploma in law, Nat. D.A. Coll., 1973. Bar: Calif. 1966. Mem. faculty Chadwick Sch., Rolling Hills, Calif., 1952-56; mgmt. Servo-Mechanisms, Torrance, Calif., 1956-58, Systems Devel.Corp., Santa Monica, Calif., 1958-62, Douglas Missile & Space, Santa Monica, Calif., 1962-63; v.p. Automation Svc. Co., Beverly Hills, 1963-65; dep. pub. defender L.A. County, 1965-67, spl. asst. dist. atty., dept. dist atty., 1971-93; chief counsel, exec. officer Calif. Alcohol Beverage Control Bd., 1967-69; state dir. Calif. Dept. of Social Welfare, Sacramento, 1969-71; ptnr. Donahue, Donahue and Martin, Redondo Beach, Calif., 1995—; instr. travel law West L.A. Coll. Author: Automation in Medicine. Sgt. U.S. Army Air Corp., 1942-45. Mem. Calif. Bar Assn., Calif. Dist. Atty. Assn., Irish-Am. Bar Assn., Asia-Pacific Lawyers Assn., Internat. Forum of Travel and Tourism Advocates, Air Force Assn., 454th Bombardment Group Assn., Amherst Coll. Alumni Assn., U. So. Calif. Alumni Assn. Republican. Office: Donahue Donahue and Martin 116 Ave I 2d fl Redondo Beach CA 90277

MARTIN, RONALD GENE, logistics program manager; b. San Bernardino, Calif., Apr. 24, 1954; s. Donald Arthur Sr. and Beverly Jean (Willis) M.; m. Mary Alice Acosta, Oct. 14, 1978 (div. Mar. 1990); 1 child, Natalie Rebecca; m. Desiree Pietzsch, Jan. 9, 1991; 1 stepchild, Tara Brianna. AS, C.C. Air Force, 1981; AA, San Bernardino Valley Coll., 1977; BA, Calif. State U., San Bernardino, 1981, MA, 1989. Cert. acquistion profl. Quality assurance rep. Western Space & Missile Ctr., Vandenberg AFB, Calif., 1984-85; logistics program mgr. Ballistic Missile Office, Norton AFB, Calif., 1985-88; integrated logistics support mgr. Ballistic Systems Divsn., Norton AFB, Calif., 1988-91; dep. dir. logistics Pacific Air Forces, Hickam AFB, Hawaii, 1991-93; sr. logistics mgr. Space & Missile Systems Ctr., L.A. AFB, 1993—; instr. Air Force Inst. Tech., Hickam AFB, Hawaii, 1991-93. With USAFR, 1972-84. Democrat. Home: PO Box 2286 Redlands CA 92373-0761 Office: Space & Missile Systems Ctr (ALK) 2420 Vela Way Ste 1467 A-8 El Segundo CA 90245

MARTIN, SANDRA LEE, molecular biology educator; b. Albuquerque, May 28, 1954; d. Harry Hudson and Margery Ella (Brandes) M.; m. Steven Kent Nordeen, Dec. 30, 1981; 1 child, Claire Anna. BA, Stanford U., 1976; PhD, U. Calif., Berkeley, 1982. Postdoctoral fellow U. N.C., Chapel Hill, 1982-84; scientist Synergen, Inc., Boulder, Colo., 1984-86; asst. prof. U. Colo. Sch. Medicine, Denver, 1986-94, assoc. prof., 1994—; ad hoc reviewer NIH, Washington, 1993-94, Jour. Molecular Evolution, 1990-94, Jour. Molecular Biology, 1994, Mammalian Genome, DNA and Cell Biology, NSF, others. Contbr. articles to profl. jours., chpts. to books. Postdoctoral fellow Jan Coffin Childs Fund, 1981-84; grantee NIH, 1988-93, 94—, Army Rsch. Office, 1992—. Mem. Am. Soc. Microbiology, Molecular Evolution Soc. Office: U Colo Sch Medicine C&S Biology Box B111 4200 E 9th Ave Denver CO 80220-3706

MARTIN, SUNNY, accountant; b. Ft. Bragg, Calif., Mar. 10, 1913; d. John William and Magdalena Wilhelmina (Giesler) Meyer; m. Arthur L. Smith, June 21, 1941 (div. 1951); m. Alphonso Martin, June 28, 1958 (dec. Oct. 1981). Student, Heald Bus. Coll., Oakland, Calif., 1931-33. Acct., office mgr. various cos., 1933-75; founder, sec./treas. Am. Bashkir Curly Register, Ely, Nev., 1971-93; ret. Am. Bashkir Culry Register, Ely, Nev., 1993. Author various cowboy poems, western street skits; editor newsletter, historical photos for Ely Daily Times. Founder Ely Riding Club, 1951, Ely Jr. Riding Club and Gymkhana, 1951; book com. editor Friends of Nev. Northern Railway, 1985-91; del. State Rep. Conv., 1965; active Ret. Sr. Vol. Program (recipient numerous awards). Recipient Golden Rule award for saving Curly Horse breed from extinction in the U.S., J.C. Penney, 1992; named to White Pine High Sch. Hall of Fame, Ely, Nev., 1992. Mem. White Pine Hist. Soc. (past pres. 1979-81, historian 1973-94, editor slide show, 1980, 4-H Club (horsemanship leader). Methodist. Home: PO Box 453 Ely NV 89301-0453

MARTIN, THOMAS HENRY, JR., water resource engineer, software writer; b. Plainfield, N.J., Aug. 3, 1957; s. Thomas Henry Sr. and Audrey May (Goldhammer) M.; m. Lisa Marie Burley, July 1, 1995. BS in Civil Engring., U. Vt., 1981; postgrad., Harvard U., 1988. Registered profl. engr., Maine, Wash.; cert. water distbn. mgr., Wash. Hydropower engr. ind. cons., Fanwood, N.J., 1981; geotech. engr. Geotech Assocs., Fanwood, 1981; water resource engr. Camp Dresser & McKee Inc., Boston, 1982-86, systems engr., 1986-88; software engr. WSI Corp., Billerica, Mass., 1988-90; civil engr. EA Engring., Redmond, Wash., 1991-92; water resource engr. Foster Wheeler Environ. Corp. (formerly Ebasco), Bellevue, Wash., 1992—. Co-author: Vermont Hydro-Logic: Small-Scale Licensing and Governing Issues, 1981, (computer automated weather info. system) WxWindows: Touchscreen System, 1989; engr. removal of dam from East Fork Salmon River, Idaho, 1991; engr. water quality computer model Columbia River System Operation Rev. EIS, 1994. Andrew Mellon Environ. and Natural Resources grantee, Burlington, Vt., 1979. Mem. IEEE, Am. Water Works Assn. Home: 7550 Roosevelt Way NE Seattle WA 98115-4221

MARTIN, VANCE GREGORY, nature conservationist; b. Washington, July 20, 1949; s. Thomas Oliver and Alyce Jean (Dickerson) M.; m. Catherine Elizabeth Corness, Aug. 27, 1977; children: Farren Drew, Felicia Gabriel. BA magna cum laude, W.Va. U., 1971. Co-owner, mgr. Natural Foods Store, Morgantown, W.Va., 1970-74; environ. dir. Findhorn Found., Scotland, 1975-84, gen. mgr., 1978-80; exec. dir. World Wilderness Congress, Ojai, Calif., 1983—; pres. Internat. Wilderness Leadership Wild Found., Ojai, Calif., 1984—; fellow Findhorn Found., Scotland, 1985—; exec. dir. Internat. Ctr. for Earth Concerns; bd. dirs. Conservation Endowment Fund, Calif., Fulcrum Publ., Golden, Colo.; cons. USAID. Editor: Wilderness, 1982, Wilderness—The Way Ahead, 1984 (British Coun. Exemplary book 1984), For the Conservation of Earth, 1988, Arctic Wilderness: 5th WWC, 1995. Vol. Ft. Collins Relief, 1989—. Office: The Wild Found 2162 Baldwin Rd Ojai CA 93023-9704

MARTIN, WILFRED WESLEY FINNY, psychologist, property owner and manager; b. Rock Lake, N.D., Dec. 3, 1917; s. William Isaac and Anna Liisa (Hendrickson-Juntunen) M.; m. Stella Helland, Sept. 25, 1943; children: Sydney Wayne, William Allan. BA, Jamestown Coll., 1940; army specialized tng. program, Hamilton Coll., 1944; MS, EdD, U. So. Calif., 1956. Highsch. prin., coach pub. sch., Nekoma, N.D., 1940-42; contact rep., psychologist VA, L.A., 1946-49, psychologist, chief rehab., 1972-77; from intern to resident Fargo (N.D.) VA Hosp., 1953-58; guidance dir., instr. Concordia Coll., Moorhead, Minn., 1951-53; psychologist VA, Fargo, N.D., 1953-57; assoc. Sci. Rsch. Assoc./IBM, Boulder, Colo., 1957-65; regional dir. Sci. Rsch. Assoc./IBM, L.A., 1966-72; owner, mgr. Martin Investments, Huntington Beach, Calif., 1977—; adjutant U. Miss., Oxford, 1942; trustee Wilfred W. and Stella Martin Trust, Huntington Beach, 1991. Author: Veterans Administration Work Simplification, 1948, 57. Charter mem. Rep. Presdl. Task Force, 1980; adv. sr. ptnrs. bd. dirs. U. Calif. Med. Sch., Irvine, 1990; donor Dr. and Mrs. W.W. Martin Endowment, Jamestown Coll., N.D., 1985. With U.S. Army, 1942-45. Mem. Am. Psychol. Assn., Cardinal & Gold U. So. Calif., Jamestown Coll. Heritage Circle (charter), Suomi Coll. Second Century Soc., Elks. Republican. Lutheran. Home: PO Box 5445 Huntington Beach CA 92615

MARTIN, WILLIAM CHARLES, lawyer; b. Shenandoah, Iowa, May 25, 1923; s. J. Stuart and Chloe Irene (Anderson) M.; m. Marilyn Forbes, Oct. 18, 1947 (div. 1979); children: Ann, James; m. 2d, Kathryn Ann Fehr, Sept. 17, 1979. BA, U. Iowa, 1946, JD, 1947. Bar: Iowa 1947, Oreg. 1948. Sr. ptnr. Martin Bischoff, Templeton, Biggs & Ericsson, Portland, Oreg., 1951-86; mem. Oreg. Bd. Bar Examiners, 1966-69; instr. Lewis and Clark Coll. Law, 1973-75, U. Hawaii-Hilo, West Hawaii, 1989—. Bd. dirs. Eastmoreland Gen. Hosp., Portland, 1960-84, chmn., 1978-81; mem. Lawyers Com. for Civil Rights Under Law, Jackson, Miss., 1965; bd. dirs. Lake Oswego (Oreg.) Pub. Libr., 1981-84, chmn., 1982-84; mem. Kona bd. Am. Cancer Soc. 1st lt. USAAF, WWII. Mem. ABA, Oreg. State Bar, Kona Heavens Assn. (pres. 1994-95), Univ. Club, Kona Outdoor Cir. (Kailua Kona), Keauhou Yacht Club, Phi Delta Phi, Sigma Nu. Democrat. Episcopalian. Home: 73 4825 Anini St Kailua Kona HI 96740-9202

MARTINDALE, JEANIE ARLENE, nursing administrator and educator; b. Valentine, Nebr., Aug. 12, 1956; d. Dale George and Viola Louise (Nollett) Coleman; m. Shelby Ray Martindale, Mar. 2, 1985 (div. July 1994); children: Katherine, William, Margaret. Diploma in Nursing, Bishop Clarkson, Omaha, 1977; BSN, U. Nebr. Med. Ctr. Coll. of Nursing, 1989; postgrad., U. Wyo., 1990—; grad. RN, Wyo., Nebr.; cert. gen. nursing practice. Staff nurse West Nebr. Gen. Hosp., Scottsbluff, Nebr., 1977-79, staff nurse CICU, 1979-82; community clinic supr. Nebr. State Health Dept., Scottsbluff, 1982-89; nursing instr. Laramie County C.C., Cheyenne, Wyo., 1989-93; dir. home care Cmty. Hosp., Torrington, Wyo., 1993—. Mem. ANA, Wyo. Nurses Assn., Sigma Theta Tau. Home: 2535 Main St Torrington WY 82240-1923 Office: Cmty Hosp Home Care Dept 2000 Campbell Dr Torrington WY 82240-1528

MARTINES, KAREN LOUISE, hospital administrator, nurse; b. Paris, Ont., Can., July 24, 1952; d. Norman Walter and Shirley Lorraine (Ford) Watts; m. Lawrence James Martines, Feb. 23, 1980; 1 child, Maria Nicole. BSN, U. Western Ont., London, Can., 1976; MS, Chapman U., 1983. RN Centinela Hosp., Inglewood, Calif., 1976-77, gastroenterology RN III, 1977-83; med./surg. mgr. Flagstaff (Ariz.) Med. Ctr., 1983-87, cluster mgr. med./surg., 1987-89; dir. managed care McKenzie-Willamette Hosp., Springfield, Oreg., 1989-94; dir. quality resource svcs. St. Mary-Corwin Regional Med. Ctr., Pueblo, Colo., 1994—. Mem. NAFE, Profl. Women's Network, Calif. Soc. Gastrointestinal Assts. (v.p. 1981-82, pres. 1982-83), Soc. Gastrointestinal Assts. (by-laws com. 1982-83), Nat. Assn. Quality Assurance Profls., Am. Soc. Health Risk Mgmt. Office: St Mary-Corwin Regional Med Ctr 1008 Minnequa Ave Pueblo CO 81004-3733

MARTINETTI, RONALD ANTHONY, lawyer; b. N.Y.C., Aug. 13, 1945; s. Alfred Joseph and Frances Ann (Battipaglia) M. Student, U. Chgo., 1981-82; JD, U. So. Calif., 1982. Bar: Calif. 1982; U.S. Dist. Ct. (cen. and no. dists.) Calif. 1982, U.S. Dist. Ct. Ariz., 1992; U.S. Ct. Appeals (9th cir.) 1982. Ptnr. Kazanjian & Martinetti, Glendale, Calif., 1986—. Author: James Dean Story, 1995. Vol. trial lawyer Bet Tzedek Legal Svcs., 1987—; judge pro tem L.A. Superior Ct., 1994—. Mem. Calif. Bar Assn. Roman Catholic. Office: Kazanjian & Martinetti 520 E Wilson Ave Glendale CA 91206-4374

MARTINEZ, AL, journalist, screenwriter; b. Oakland, Calif., July 21, 1929; s. Alfredo Martinez and Mary (Larragoite) Lehmann; m. Joanne Cinelli, July 30, 1949; children: Cinthia, Linda, Allen. Student, San Francisco State U., 1949-50, U. Calif., Berkeley, 1952-53, Contra Costa Jr. Coll., Walnut Creek, Calif., 1953-54. Reporter, feature writer Richmond (Calif.) Ind ., 1952-55; reporter, feature writer Oakland Tribune, 1955-71, columnist, 1963-71; profilist, feature writer L.A. Times, 1972-84, columnist, 1984—; screenwriter CBS, ABC, NBC, L.A., 1975—; tech. advisor Lou Grant TV Series, CBS, Los Angeles, 1979-80. Author: Rising Voices, 1974, Jigsaw John, 1976, Ashes in the Rain, 1989, Dancing Under the Moon, 1992, Rising Voices: A New Generation, 1993, City of Angles, 1995; screenwriter TV movie That Secret Sunday, 1988, Out on the Edge, 1990 (nominated for Emmy Best Screenplay 1990), other TV movies, pilots, 1975—. Recipient Nat. Headliner award Atlantic City Press Club, 1987, 88, Best Columnist award Nat. Soc. News Columnist, St. Louis, 1986, Pulitzer prize (shared Gold medal to L.A. Times) Columbia U., 1984, Nat. Ernie Pyle award, 1991. Mem. PEN, Writers Guild Am. Office: Los Angeles Times Editorial Dept Times Mirror Sq Los Angeles CA 90053

MARTINEZ, AMOS DELFIN, health facility administrator, social worker; b. Salt Lake County, Utah, Sept. 9, 1953; s. Jose Delfin and Teresa M.; m. Dana E. Summers, Jan. 17, 1980; 1 child, Mason Delfin Martinez. BA, U. No. Colo., Greeley, 1975; MSW, U. Utah, 1978; M in Criminal Justice, U. Colo., 1987, MPA, 1994. Lic. clin. social work, Colo. Juvenile parole counselor Colo. Dept. Institutions Youth Svcs., Grand Junction, 1975-76; youth counselor Utah Detention Ctr., Salt Lake County, 1977-78; sch. social worker Mesa County Valley Sch. Dist. # 51, Grand Junction, Colo, 1978-80; exec. dir. Nat. Coun. on Alcoholism and Drug Abuse, Grand Junction, Colo., 1981-83; police officer Police Dept., Grand Junction, Colo., 1981-82; police detective Police Dept., Grand Junction, 1982-84, police sgt., 1984-85; criminal investigator Complex Crimes Unit Denver Dist. Atty's. Office, 1985-87; diagnostician, assessment coord. Colo. Dept. Institutions Youth Svcs., 1987-88; investigator Profl. Licensing Bds. Colo. Dept. Regulatory Agys., 1988-89. Contbr. articles to profl. jours. Democrat. Home: 9465 E Tanglewood Rd Franktown CO 80116-9428 Office: Univ Colo 1560 Broadway Ste 1340 Denver CO 80202

MARTINEZ, EDGAR, professional baseball player; b. N.Y.C., Jan. 2, 1963. Student, American Coll., Puerto Rico. Baseball player Seattle Mariners, 1982—. Named. to Am. League All-Star Team, 1992, Am. League Silver Slugger Team, 1992. Office: Seattle Mariners PO Box 4100 411 1st Ave S Seattle WA 98104*

MARTINEZ, ELIZABETH COONROD, Spanish language educator; b. Austin, Tex., June 3, 1954; d. Holmes Thomas Coonrod and Phyllis D (Berry) Gaxiola. BA in English, Portland State U., 1983; MA in Hispanic Civilization, NYU, 1991; PhD in Latin Am. Lit., U. N.Mex., 1995. Pub. info. reporter Portland (Oreg.) State U. Pub. Info., 1981-83; reporter, photographer Woodburn (Oreg.) Ind., 1983-84; reporter The Oregonian, Portland, 1984-86; reporter, asst. editor The New Haven Ind., 1986-89; mng. editor Albuquerque Monthly mag., 1989; anchor, news dir. Sta. KLUZ-TV, Albuquerque, 1989-91; instr. Spanish U. N.Mex., Albuquerque, 1991-95, instr. journalism, 1992-94; asst. prof. Spanish Sonoma State U., Rohnert Park, Calif., 1995—; host Sta. KNME Pub. TV, Albuquerque, 1990, 93; dir., instr. Mex. Summer Abroad Program, U. N.Mex., Albuquerque, 1993, minority H.S. students summer workshop in journalism, 1994. Author: (biographies) Sor Juana, A Trailblazing Thinker, 1993, Henry Cisneros, Mexican-American Leader, 1993, Edward James Olmos, Mexican-American Actor, 1994, (history) Coming to America: The Mexican-American Experience, 1995; contbr. to Christian Sci. Monitor, N.Y. Times, 1989-90. Speaker Cuba (N.Mex.) H.S. Commencement Address, 1990; chair HIV prevention comty. awareness task force, U. N.Mex. Hosp., Albuquerque, 1990-91; mem. centennial pub. rels. com. U. N.Mex., Albuquerque, 1991, panelist comty. and regional planning com., 1993, mem. Grad. Student Assn., 1993-95. Recipient Edtl. Travel award Univision TV, 1990, 1st pl. Opinion Column award Conn. Sigma Delta Chi Press Assn., 1988, Sammy award, 1986, News Feature award Sigma Delta Chi, 1986, Best Editl. Column award, 1986, Investigative Journalism award New Eng. Press Assn., 1987; Challenge Assistantship fellow U. N.Mex., 1993-94; Latin Am. travel rsch. grantee Latin Am. Inst., U. N.Mex., 1993; Teaching fellow Poynter Inst., 1995. Mem. AAUW, MLA, Latin Am. Studies Assn., Rocky Mountain Modern Lang. Assn., S.W. Writers Workshop. Office: Dept Fgn Langs Sonoma State U Rohnert Park CA 94928

MARTINEZ, JOHN STANLEY, entrepreneur; b. Phila., Apr. 14, 1930; s. Joseph Vincent and Helen Leeds (Simpson) M.; m. Britta K. Ponder, Dec. 29, 1987; children: John Jr., Joseph G., Mary Lynn. BChemE, Rensselaer Poly. Inst., 1951; diploma, Oak Ridge Sch. Reactor Tech., 1957; PhD, U. Calif., Berkeley, 1962. Rsch. engr. N.Am. Aviation Co., Santa Susanna, Calif., 1954-55, Jet Propulsion Lab., Calif. Inst. Tech., Pasadena, Calif., 1955-61; rsch. assoc. Livermore (Calif.) Nat. Lab., 1959-61; with TRW Systems Group, Redondo Beach, Calif., 1961-76, mgr. high energy laser bus. area, 1970-76; pres. Physics Internat. Co., San Leandro, Calif., 1976-84, Jamar Enterprises, Moraga, Calif., 1970—, HLX Laser Inc., San Diego, 1986-87, Air-Sea Comm. Corp., San Diego, 1988-89; pres., CEO Jamar Tech. Co., San Diego, 1987-89, Calif. Jamar, Inc., 1989-92; chmn. Surgilase, Inc., Warwick, R.I., 1991-94, Benchmark Industries, Goffstown, N.H., 1991—; CEO and chmn. JMAR Industries, San Diego, 1993—; chmn. Pacific Precision Labs., Inc., Chatsworth, Calif., 1993—; supervisory dir. Pisces Internat., Netherlands, 1982-84; pres., chmn. Hermosa Entertainment Corp., Hermosa Beach, Calif., 1969-72. Contbr. articles to profl. publs.; patentee in field. Chmn. Hermosa Beach City Improvement Commn., 1968-70. Capt. USMC, 1951-54, Korea. AEC fellow, 1958, Ford Found. fellow, 1960. Mem. IEEE, Sigma Xi, Tau Beta Pi. Home: PO Box 1030 Del Mar CA 92014-1030 Office: 3956 Sorrento Valley Blvd San Diego CA 92121-1403

MARTINEZ, MATTHEW GILBERT, congressman; b. Walsenburg, Colo., Feb. 14, 1929; children: Matthew, Diane, Susan, Michael, Carol Ann. Cert of competence, Los Angeles Trade Tech. Sch., 1959. Small businessman and bldg. contractor; mem. 97th-103rd Congresses from 30th (now 31st) Calif. dist., 1982—; mem. edn. and labor com., fgn. affairs com. Mem. Monterey Park Planning Commn., 1971-74; mayor City of Monterey Park, 1974-75; mem. Monterey Park City Council, 1974-80, Calif. State Assembly, 1980-82; bd. dirs. San Gabriel Valley YMCA. Served with USMC, 1947-50. Mem. Congl. Hispanic Caucus, Hispanic Am. Democrats, Nat. Assn. Latino Elected and Apptd. Ofcls., Communications Workers Am., VFW, Am. Legion, Latin Bus. Assn., Monterey Park C. of C., Navy League (dir.). Democrat. Lodge: Rotary. Office: US Ho of Reps 2239 Rayburn Bldg Ofc Washington DC 20515-0005*

MARTINEZ, OSCAR JAQUEZ, educator, author; b. Mex., Mar. 4, 1943; s. Bernardo and Magdalena (Jaquez) M.; children: Jamie, Gabriel, Daniel, David, Andres. BA, Calif. State U., L.A., 1969; MA, Stanford (Calif.) U., 1970; PhD, UCLA, 1975. Prof. of history U. Tex., El Paso, 1975-88, dir. inst. of oral history, 1975-82, dir. ctr. for Inter-Am. and border studies, 1982-87; prof. history U. Ariz., Tucson, 1988—, dir. Latin Am. area ctr., 1994—; vis. prof. Yale U., 1995. Author: Border People, 1994, Troublesome Border, 1988, Border Boom Town, 1978, author, editor: Fragments of the Mexican Revolution, 1983, The U.S. Mexico Borderlands; editor: Across Boundaries, 1986, The U.S.-Mexico Borderlands, 1995. With U.S. Army, 1963-65. Fellowship Ctr. for Advanced Study in the Behavioral Scis., 1981-82. Mem. Assn. for Borderlands Scholars (pres. 1985-87, Achievement award 1992), Latin Am. Studies Assn. (bd. dirs. 1980-82). Office: U Ariz History Dept Tucson AZ 85721

MARTINEZ, PATRICIA ANN, middle school educator, administrator; b. Phoenix, Oct. 12, 1963; d. Jack Leon and Eleanor Jean (Gripman) McMullen; m. Gerald Marc Martinez, Aug. 11, 1984. BA, Calif. State U., 1986, MA magna cum laude, 1994. Cert. tchr. Calif. Tchr. St. Athanasius Elem. Sch., Long Beach, Calif., 1987-93; vice prin. St. Athanasius Elem. Sch., Long Beach, 1990-93; lang. arts specialist Washington Mid. Schs., Long Beach, 1993—; mentor tchr. St. Athanasius Elem. Sch., Long Beach, 1988-90. Mem. ACLU, Greenpeace, 1988—. Mem. ASCD, NEA, Nat. Cath. Edn. Assn., Internat. Reading Assn., Tchrs. Assn. Long Beach, Calif. Tchrs. Assn., Kappa Delta Pi, Phi Kappa Phi. Democrat. Lutheran. Home: 3601 Gardenia Ave Long Beach CA 90807-4303 Office: Washington Mid Sch 1450 Cedar Ave Long Beach CA 90813-1705

MARTINEZ, VIRGINIA MARCELINA, dietitian; b. Denver, June 2, 1942; d. Maxcimo and Maria R. (Salas) M.; m. Jimmy Allen Tanhoff, Nov. 15, 1967 (div. Dec. 1989). MS, Mont. State U., 1990, BS, 1987. Lic. nutritionist Mont. Bd. Med. Examiners; registered dietitian. Sr. acctg. clk. 1st Bank Bozeman, Mont., 1974-80; rsch. asst. Mont. State U., Bozeman, 1984-90; nutritionist County of Big Horn, Hardin, 1992—; part-time instr. Little Big Horn Coll., Crow Agency, Mont., 1991—; part-time women, infants and children program dir. No. Cheyenne Bd. of Health, Lame Deer, Mont., 1992—; with Big Horn Count Health Bd., Hardin, Even Start Adv. Bd., Hardin. With USN, 1960-63. Recipient Outstanding Presentation award U. Minn., 1986; scholar Mont. Pub. Health Assn., Mont. State U. Coll. Edn., Mex. Am. Nat. Women's Assn. Mem. Am. Dietetics Assn. (registered dietitian, scholar), Big Horn Nutrition Coun. Roman Catholic. Home: RR 1 Box 1187 Hardin MT 59034-9719 Office: Big Horn County 809 N Custer Ave Hardin MT 59034-1300

MARTINEZ-LÓPEZ, ENRIQUE, Spanish educator; b. Granada, Spain, Aug. 18, 1928; came to the U.S., 1959, naturalized 1967; s. Francisco and Amparo (Lopez Mesa) M.; m. Maria Teresa Leal, Feb. 10, 1954 (div. 1965); children: Maria Teresa, Maria Isabel, Enrique; m. Natalie Louise Campbell, Nov. 10, 1966. BA, U. Granada, 1947; MA in Romance Philology, U. Madrid, 1952, PhD, 1964. Instr. SPanish and Hispanic Lit. U. da Paraiba, João Pessoa, Brazil, 1954-56, U. do Recife, Brazil, 1956-59; asst. prof. Spanish U. Houston, 1959-63; asst. prof. Spanish U. Calif., Santa Barbara, 1963-66, assoc. prof., 1966-72, chmn. dept. Spanish and Portuguese, 1970-74, prof., 1972—; vis. lectr. U. Wis., Madison, 1966, 67; fellow, rschr. Cervantes INst. Consejo Superior de Investigaciones Cientificas, Madrid, 1952-54; conf. organizer III Ann. So. Calif. Cervantes Symposium, Santa Barbara, 1992. Author: Granada, Paraiso Cerrado, 1971, 89; editor: Camoniana Californiana, 1985; editor: Ency. Britannica Editores, 1962-64. Chair intercultural com. YWCA, Houston, 1960-62; chair com. on culture Alianza Cultural Mexicana, Santa Barbara, 1973-75. 2d lt. Spanish Army, 1953-54. Recipient award Cruz de Caballero, Orden del Merito Civil Govt. of Spain, 1955; grantee Am. Philos. Soc. Inst. Humanities, 1966, 71, 74. Mem. MLA, Am. Assn. Tchrs. Spanish and Portuguese, Internat. Assn. Hispanists, Internat. Inst. Iberoam. Lit., Am. Soc. Sephardic Studies, Internat. Assn. Golden Age Studies, Inst. Brasileiro de Cultura Hispanica (pres. 1956-58). Democrat. Roman Catholic. Home: 503 Miramonte Dr Santa Barbara CA 93109-1400 Office: U Calif Dept Spanish and Portuguese Santa Barbara CA 93106-4150

MARTINI, ROBERT EDWARD, wholesale pharmaceutical and medical supplies company executive; b. Hackensack, N.J., 1932. BS, Ohio State U., 1954. With Bergen Brunswig Corp., Orange, Calif., 1956-92, v.p., 1962-69, exec. v.p., 1969-81, pres., 1981-92, CEO, 1990—; chmn. Bergen Brunswig Corp., Orange, 1992—; chmn. exec. com. Bergen Brunswig Corp. Capt. USAF, 1954. *

MARTINS-GREEN, MANUELA, cell biologist; b. Luso, Moxico, Angola, Dec. 30, 1947; came to U.S., 1973; d. Joaquim P. and Maria Alice (Marques) Martins; m. Harry W. Green, II, May 15, 1975; children: Alice, Harry, Maria Green. BS, U. Lisbon, 1970; MS, U. Calif., Riverside, 1975; PhD, U. Calif., Davis, 1987. Chief scientist EM lab Agronomical Sta., Oeiras, Portugal, 1970-73; electron microscopist, dept. ophthalmology U. Calif., Davis, 1975-82; postdoctoral researcher Lawrence Berkeley Lab., U. Calif., 1987-88, rsch. scientist, 1992-93; adj. asst. prof. Rockefeller U., 1991-92; asst. prof. biology U. Calif., Riverside, 1993—; vis. lectr. U. Wuhan, China, 1988. Contbr. articles to profl. jours., books. Recipient Fulbright Travel grant Internat. Exch. Scholars, Riverside, 1973, dept. fellowship U. Calif., Riverside, 1973-75, Regents fellowship, 1985, NIH traineeship, 1986-87, Nat. Rsch. Svc. award, 1988-91; NIH grantee, 1992—. Mem. Am. Cancer Soc., Am. Soc. for Cell Biology, Am. Soc. Devel. Biology, Elec. Microscopy Soc. of Am., Women for Cell Biology, Wound Healing Soc., Phi Kappa Phi. Office: U Calif Dept Biology Riverside CA 92521

MARTINSON, CONSTANCE FRYE, television program hostess, producer; b. Boston, Apr. 11, 1932; d. Edward and Rosalind Helen (Sperber) Frye; m. Leslie Herbert Martinson, Sept. 24, 1955; 1 child, Julianna Martinson Carner. BA in English Lit., Wellesley Coll., 1953. Dir. pub. relations Coro Found., Los Angeles, 1974-79; producer/host KHJ Dimensions, Los Angeles, 1979-81, Connie Martinson Talks Books, Los Angeles, 1981—; instr. dept. humanities UCLA, 1981—; moderator, instr. Univ. Judaism; celebrity advisor Book Fair-Music Ctr., L.A., 1986; bd. dirs. Friends of English UCLA; TV rep. L.A. Pub. Libr. L.A. Cityview, Sta. WNYE, Channel Am. Author Dramatization of Wellesley After Images, 1974; book editor, columnist Calif. Press Bur. Syndicate, 1986—. Pres. Mayor's adv.

council on volunteerism, Los Angeles, 1981-82; chmn. community affairs dept. Town Hall of Calif., Los Angeles, 1981-85; bd. dirs. legal def. fund NAACP, Los Angeles, 1981-84. Mem. Women in Cable, Am. Film Inst., Jewish TV Network (bd. dirs. 1985-87), PEN, Nat. Book Critics Assn., Wellesley Coll. Club (pres. 1979-81), Mulholland Tennis Club. Democrat. Jewish. Home and Office: 2288 Coldwater Canyon Dr Beverly Hills CA 90210-1756

MARTINSON, JOHN ROBERT, merchant banker; b. Chgo., Sept. 9, 1935; s. Warren Charles Martinson and Jane (Martin) Finlayson; m. Kathryn Hellyer, June 14, 1958 (div. Dec. 1970); children: Kate, John Robert Jr., Johanna; m. Patricia Richardson, Nov. 17, 1973 (div. Sept. 1981); children: Erik, Torgen; m. Jacyln Norwood, Aug. 30, 1986; 1 stepchild, Jack Thomas. BSE, Princeton U., 1957; MBA, Northwestern U., Chgo., 1959. Planning assoc. Mobil Oil Corp., N.Y.C., 1959-62, 65-66, London, 1967-69; stockbroker Kidder Peabody & Co., N.Y.C., 1962-65, Oppenheimer & Co., N.Y.C., 1969-73; owner Hawthorne Exploration Co., N.Y.C., 1973—; Ketchum, Idaho, 1984—; owner MVP, Ketchum, Idaho, 1984-88, also bd. dirs.; owner, mng. dir. Wood Roberts, Inc., Ketchum, 1988—; prin. Martinson, O'Dell & Ogden, LLC, Houston, 1995—; bd. dirs. Latex Resources, Inc., Tulsa. Inventor radio controlled electric load mgmt. Bd. dirs. Boise (Idaho) Philharmonic Assn., 1988-94. Mem. Ind. Petroleum Assn. Am., Vikings of Scandia. Republican. Presbyterian. Home: 161 Laurel Ln Ketchum ID 83340 Office: Wood Roberts Inc Box 1017 Ketchum ID 83340 also: Martinson O'Dell & Ogden 952 Echo Ln Ste 210 Houston TX 77024

MARTINSON, JULIA ELLENOR, health science administrator; b. Paso Robles, Calif., May 1, 1951; d. John Elwyn and Betty Jeanne (Fruehling) M. BA in Journalism, U. Nev., 1973, BA in Phys. Edn., 1976. Store mgr. S. S. White, Reno, 1979, Kelly Dental Supply Co., Reno, 1979-81; office mgr. Fine Arts Dental Studio, Reno, 1981-88; sec., treas. Superior Dental Lab. Inc., Reno, 1988—. Mgr. Reno Royals, 1979—; active Campus Christian Assn., treas. 1986-92, Reno Urban Forestry Commn., 1992—, Reno Park and Recreation Commn., 1993—; commr. Nev. Women's Fastpitch Commn., 1993—. Mem. Women's Softball Alumni Assn. (treas. U. Nev.-Reno chpt. 1983-88, publicity dir. 1993), U. Nev. Boosters (v.p. 1986-88). Democrat. Episcopalian. Home: 1200 Casa Loma Dr Reno NV 89503-3132 Office: Superior Dental Lab Inc 300 Brinkby Ave # 201 Reno NV 89509-4349

MARTORI, ARTHUR J., JR., food products executive; b. 1942. With Martori Bros. Distbg., Glendale, Ariz., 1963-78; pres. Goldmar Inc., Phoenix, Ariz., 1978, Production Farm Mgmt., Glendale, 1979—. Office: Production Farm Management 6205 N 55th Ave Glendale AZ 85301-4518*

MARTORI, JOSEPH PETER, lawyer; b. N.Y.C., Aug. 19, 1941; s. Joseph and Teresa Susan (Fezza) M. BS summa cum laude, NYU, 1964, MBA, 1968; JD cum laude U. Notre Dame, 1967. Bar: D.C. 1968, U.S. Dist. Ct. D.C. 1968, U.S. Dist. Ct. Ariz. 1968, U.S. Ct. Appeals (9th cir.) 1969, U.S. Supreme Ct. 1977. Assoc. Sullivan & Cromwell, N.Y.C., 1967-68, Snell & Wilmer, Phoenix, 1968-69; pres. Goldmar Inc., Phoenix, 1969-71; ptnr. Martori, Meyer, Hendricks & Victor, P.A., Phoenix, 1971-85; ptnr. Brown & Bain, P.A., Phoenix, 1985-94, chmn. corp. banking & real estate dept.; bd. dirs. Firstar, Met. Bank, Phoenix, Red Rock Collection Inc., Phoenix; chmn., pres. ILX Inc. Author: Street Fights, 1987; also articles, 1966-70. Bd. dirs. Men's Arts Council, Phoenix, 1972—; trustee Boys' Clubs Met. Phoenix, 1974—; consul for Govt. of Italy, State of Ariz., 1987—. Mem. ABA, State Bar Ariz., Maricopa County Bar Assn., Lawyers Com. for Civil Rights Under Law (trustee 1976—), Phoenix Country Club, Plaza Club (founding bd. govs. 1979-90). Republican. Roman Catholic. Office: ILX Inc 2777 E Camelback Rd Phoenix AZ 85016-4302

MARTY, LAWRENCE A., magistrate, lawyer; b. Leigh, Nebr., June 17, 1926. Student Wayne State U., 1944-46, Creighton Sch. Law, 1946-48; J.D., U.Wyo., 1954. Bar: Wyo. 1954. Sole practice, Green River, Wyo., 1954-67; ptnr. Mart & Clark, Green River, 1967-74; ptnr. Marty & Ragsdale, Green River, 1975—; judge Green River Mcpl. Ct., 1956-58; U.S. Magistrate Dist. Wyo., 1958—. Alt. del. Rep. Nat. Conv., 1964. Mem. ABA, Wyo. Bar Assn., Sweetwater County Bar Assn. Office: 20 E Flaming Gorge Way Green River WY 82935-4210

MARTZ, JOHN ROGER, lawyer; b. Buffalo, June 13, 1937; s. George Albert and Dorothy (Dinsbier) M.; m. Charlotte Gail Lemberes, July 22, 1966; children: Teresa Gail, Nicole Jackie. BS, U.S. Mil. Acad., 1960; MS in Engring., Purdue U., 1964; JD, U. San Francisco, 1980. Bar: Nev. 1980. Commd. 2d lt. U.S. Army, 1960; nuclear engr. Army Nuclear Power Program, 1964-66; with Spl. Forces in Okinawa, Vietnam, Thailand, Korea, Taiwan,, Philippines, 1966-72; elec. engr. Armed Forces Radiobiology Rsch. Inst. and Def. Nuclear Agy., 1972-75; advisor N.G., Calif. and Nev., 1975-80; ret. U.S. Army, 1980; atty. Henderson & Nelson, Reno, 1980-85; pvt. practice Reno, 1985—. Decorated Bronze Star, Combat Inf. badge; recipient Joint Svc. Commendation medal U.S. Dept. Def., 1975. Mem. Nev. State Bar Assn., Washoe County Bar Assn. Office: 440 Ridge St Reno NV 89501-1718

MARUYAMA, ICHIRO, biologist, educator; b. Tsunan, Nigata, Japan, Nov. 8, 1952; came to U.S., 1991; s. Nihei and Iku Maruyama; m. Hiroko Iketani, Aug. 4, 1982; children: Risa, Gene. BSc, Nigata U., 1975; MS, U. Tokyo, 1977, PhD, 1981. Postdoctoral fellow Nat. Inst. Genetics, Mishima, Japan, 1981-83; mem. sci. staff MRC Lab. Molecular Biology, Cambridge, Eng., 1983-86, MRC Molecular Genetics Unit., Cambridge, 1986-91; asst. prof. cell biology Scripps Rsch. Inst., La Jolla, Calif., 1991—. Mem. AAAS, Am. Soc. Cell Biology, N.Y. Acad. Sci. Office: The Scripps Rsch Inst 10666 N Torrey Pines Rd La Jolla CA 92037-1027

MARVIN, GRACE MARIA, sociology, educator; b. Athens, Greece, Mar. 25, 1950; d. Donald M. and Rickel Barbara (Kehr) M. BA in Philosohy, Coll. of William and Mary, 1972; MS in Sociology, Va. Commonwealth U., 1975; PhD in Sociology, U. Va., 1983. Teaching asst. U. Va., Charlottesville, 1975-76; lectr. Sweet Briar Coll., Va., 1976; instr. sociology U. Va., Charlottesville, 1977-78, U. S.C., Spartanburg, 1979-82; asst. prof. sociology Southwestern U., Memphis, 1982-84; asst. prof. Calif. State U., Chico, 1984-88, assoc. prof. sociology, 1988-94, prof., 1994—. Contbr. articles to profl. jours. Am. Sociol. Assn. scholar, 1979, NEH scholar, 1984, Ctr. Middletown Studies scholar, 1988, U. Tubingen (Germany) scholar, 1991-92, Humboldt U. scholar, 1994. Mem. Am. Sociol. Assn., Pacific Sociol. Assn., Internat. Sociol. Assn., Assn. Humanist Sociology. Office: Calif State U Dept Sociology Chico CA 95929-0445

MARX, JOHANN RUDOLF, psychiatrist; b. Saarbrucken, Germany, Apr. 14, 1910; came to U.S., 1936; s. Leopold and Regina Elsa (Smith) M.; m. Lieselotte Seidel, 1937 (div. 1954); children: Doris, Vera, Sylvia, Ara; m. Joyce Donner; 1 child, John. MD, U. Leipzig, 1935. Diplomate Am. Bd. Psychiatry & Neurology. Intern Bethel-Bielefeld, Germany, 1935-36; resident in psychiatry Hastings State Hosp., Ingleside, Nebr., 1937-40; clin. dir. Hastings State Hosp., 1940-44; fellow in child psychiatry Inst. Juvenile Rsch., Chgo., 1944-46; psychiatrist Boys Tng. Sch., St. Charles, Ill., 1944-46; psychiatrist, then asst. chief VA Hosp. Mental Hygiene Clinic, Denver, 1946-59; from exec. dir. to med. dir. Centennial Mental Health Ctr., Sterling, Colo., 1959—; pvt. practice psychiatry, Denver, 1954—. Fellow Am. Psychiat. Assn. (life), Am. Acad. Child and Adolescent Psychiatry (life), Colo. Psychiat. Soc.; mem. AMA, Orthopsychiat. Assn., Colo. Child & Adolescent Psychiat. Soc., Colo. Med. Soc., Denver Med. Soc. Democrat. Office: 1514 Fairfax St Denver CO 80220-1322

MARX, MICHAEL JOSEPH, market researcher; b. L.A., Dec. 17, 1953; s. Horst Joseph and Marion Ethel (Wolf) M.; m. Reneé Phyllis Resnick, Aug. 17, 1986. BA, U. Calif., Santa Cruz, 1975; MA in Comm., U. Pa., 1977. Telecomm. specialist U.S. Dept. Justice, Washington, 1976-80; account exec. Market Facts Inc., L.A., 1980-83; sr. analyst Clorox Co., Oakland, Calif., 1983-85; v.p. mgr. market rsch. Wells Fargo Bank, San Francisco, 1985—; advisor VISA Market Rsch. Adv. Bd., San Mateo, Calif., 1989—. Mem. Am. Mktg. Assn. Office: Wells Fargo Bank 111 Sutter St 12th Fl San Francisco CA 94104-4504

MARX, WESLEY, writer, environmental educator; b. L.A., Nov. 2, 1934; s. Edward Howard and Kathleen (Woods) M.; m. Judith Ann Mell, Aug. 26, 1962; children: Christopher, Heather, Tyler. BA in Polit. Sci., Stanford U., 1956. Reporter Pasadena (Calif.) Star News, 1960-61; contbg. editor L.A. Magazine, Beverly Hills, Calif., 1961-64; author, lectr. Irvine, Calif., 1966—; mem. NRC coastal sci. and policy panel, 1992, marine monitoring, 1987-88; lectr. social ecology, U. Calif., Irvine; cons. Calif. Coastal Commn., San Francisco. Author: The Pacific Shore, 1974, The Protected Ocean, 1972, Oilspill, 1971, Man and His Environment: Waste, 1971, The Frail Ocean, 1967, Acts of God, Acts of Man, 1977, The Oceans: Our Last Resource, 1981, Pacific Coast, 1988, The Frail Ocean, 1991; contbr. articles to profl. jours. Mem. Calif. Tahoe Reg. Planning Agy., Lake Tahoe, 1981-83, Calif. Atty. Gen.'s Environ. Task Force, 1972-78, Irivne Planning Commn., 1972-73. Mem. Ctr. for Law in Pub. Interest (trustee 1979—), Water Environ. Fedn., Nat. Marine Edn. Assn., Friends of Newport Bay.

MARXMAN, GERALD ALBERT, venture capital executive; b. Rochelle, Ill., Apr. 10, 1933; s. Albert Edward and Helen Margaret (Allaben) M. BA, Monmouth Coll., 1956; BS, Case Western U., 1956, MS, 1959; PhD, Calif. Inst. Tech., 1962. Sr. staff scientist United Technologies Ctr., Sunnyvale, Calif., 1961-65; dir. phys. scis. Stanford Rsch. Inst., Menlo Park, Calif., 1965-71; sr. v.p. Envirodyne Industries, L.A., 1971-79; co-founder, pres. Nepenthe Group, San Francisco, 1979—; co-founder, pres., dir. CommTech Internat., Menlo Park, Calif., 1982—; co-founder, dir Digideck, Inc., Mountain View, Calif., Coloray Display Corp., Fremont, Calif., Amati Comms. Corp., Palo Alto, Calif. Contbr. articles to profl. jours. Ramo Wooldridge fellow Calif. Tech., Pasadena, 1959-61. Office: Commtech Internat Ste 200 535 Middlefield Rd Menlo Park CA 94025-1869

MASAGATANI, ERNESTA, school superintendent; b. Sept. 24, 1937; d. Louis Keahiuaokalani Sr. and Lei Lincoln Collins; children: Jason T.K., Jesse L.K., Jobie M.K. BE, U. Hawaii, 1960, M of Ednl. Adminstrn., 1983. Cert. tchr., Hawaii. Tchr. Aiea High Sch., Kailua High Sch., 1962-66; beginning tchr. supr. Windward Dist. Office, 1966-69, dist. resource tchr., 1971-75; tchr. Kainalu Elem. Sch., 1969-71; vice prin. Kalaheo High Sch., Kailua High Sch., Palisades Elem. Sch., 1975-79; prin. Robert Louis Stevenson Intermediate Sch., 1979-87; dep. dist. supt. Honolulu Dist., 1987-93, dist. supt., 1993—; personnel specialist Personnel Indsl. Rels. Bd. Office of Personnel Svcs., Dept. Edn. State of Hawaii, 1995—. Mem. Liliuokalani Trust Adv. Coun., Pihana Na Mano Adv. Coun., Alii Pauahi Civic Club. Mem. Daus. Hawaii. Mem. Kawaiahao Ch. Address: 3137 Hinano St Honolulu HI 96815-4330

MASI, EDWARD A., computer company executive; b. Medford, Mass., May 7, 1947; s. Joseph Carl and Rita Olivine (Metras) M.; m. Kristine Ann Lauderbach Masi, Jan. 24, 1970. BSME, Tufts U., 1969. Mktg. sales IBM, Boston, 1969-76; commercial analysis IBM, Westchester, N.Y., 1976-78; mktg. mgr. IBM, Bethesda, Md., 1978-80; region mgr. mktg. sales Cray Rsch., Calverton, Md., 1980-87; exec. v.p. mktg. Mpls., 1988-92; corp. v.p. and pres. Intel Corp., Beaverton, Oreg., 1992. Mem. Am. Electronics Assn. (vice chair 1991-92). Office: Intel Scalable Systems Divsn 5200 NE Elam Young Pkwy Beaverton OR 97124

MASKELL, DONALD ANDREW, contracts administrator; b. San Bernadino, Calif., June 22, 1963; s. Howard Andrew Maskell and Gloria Evelyn (Iglesias) White. BA, U. Puget Sound, 1985. Adminstrv. asst. State of Wash., Kent, 1986-87; data analyst Boeing Co., Seattle, 1987-93, engring. contract requirements coord., 1993—, requirements support specialist. Mem. Elks. Republican. Presbyterian.

MASLAND, LYNNE S., university official; b. Boston, Nov. 18, 1940; d. Keith Arnold and Camilla (Puleston) Shangraw; m. Edwin Grant Masland, Stpe. 19, 1960 (div. 1975); children: Mary Conklin, Molly Allison; m. Steven Alan Mayor, July 1, 1995. Student, Mt. Holyoke Coll., South Hadley, Mass., 1958-60; BA, U. Calif., Riverside, 1970; MA, U. Calif., 1971; PhD, U. B.C., Vancouver, Can., 1994. Asst. pub. rels. dir. Inter-Am. U., San German, P.R., 1963-64; asst. to dir. elem. edn. Govt. of Am. Samoa, Pago Pago, 1966-68; project dir., cons. Wash. Commn. for Humanities, Seattle, 1976-80; exec. editor N.W. Happenings Mag., Greenbank, Wash., 1980-84; media specialist Western Wash. U., Bellingham, 1984-88; dir. pub. info. Western Wash. U., 1988—; asst. prof. Fairhaven Coll., 1995—; cons. William O. Douglas Inst., Seattle, 1984, Whatcom Mus. History and Art, Bellingham, 1977; instr. U. Nebr., Omaha, 1972-86, Western Wash. U., 1972-86. Editor: The Human Touch: Folklore of the Northwest Corner, 1979, Proceedings: The Art in Living, 1980, Reports to the Mayor on the State of the Arts in Bellingham, 1980-81; contbr. numerous articles to profl. jours. Pres. LWV, Whatcom County, Bellingham, 1977-79; bd. dirs. N.W. Concert Assn., 1981-83, Wash. State Folklife Coun., 1985-90; docent Nat. Gallery, Washington, 1969; bd. dirs. Sta. KZAZ, nat. pub. radio, Bellingham, 1992-93. Univ. grad. fellow U. B.C., 1990-94. Mem. Am. Comparative Lit. Assn., Nat. Assn. Presswomen, Wash. Press Assn. (pres. 4th Corner chpt. 1987-88, Superior Performance award 1986), Can. Comparative Lit. Assn., Internat. Comparative Lit. Assn., Philological Assn. of Pacific Coast, Coun. for Advancement and Support Edn. (Case Dist. VIII Gold award for Media Rels.), Rotary (bd. dirs. 1992-94). Episcopalian. Office: Western Wash U High St Bellingham WA 98225

MASLIN, HARRY, recording industry executive, producer; b. Phila., Apr. 4, 1948; s. Philip and Sarah (Jacobs) M. Rec. engr. Regent Sound, N.Y.C., 1969-71; chief engr. Hit Factory Studios, N.Y.C., 1971-73, 74-75; rec. engr. Record Plant Studios, N.Y.C., 1973-74; record producer HRM Prodns., Hollywood, Calif., 1975—; co-owner, pres. Image Rec. Studios, Hollywood, 1983—. Recipient 20 gold and platinum records Rec. Industry Assn. of Am. Mem. Nat. Acad. Rec. Arts and Scis., ASCAP, Audio Engring. Soc. Office: Image Rec Studios 1020 N Sycamore Ave Los Angeles CA 90038-2308

MASLINE, RICHARD CHARLES, financial executive; b. N.Y.C., July 12, 1942; s. Charles Andrew and Annabelle Jean (Reed) M.; m. Mary Elizabeth Davis, Mar. 19, 1966; 1 child, Kathryn Ann. AB, Davidson Coll., 1965; MBA, Pepperdine U., 1980; MSCS, West Coast U., 1991. Exec. asst. Anvil Brand, High Point, N.C., 1965-67; programmer Duke Power, Charlotte, N.C., 1967-69; sys. analyst J.P. Stevens, Charlotte, 1969-71; project mgr., DB cons. Burroughs Corp., Detroit, 1971-78; sr. staff, group mgr. Transaction Tech. City Corp., Santa Monica, Calif., 1978-84; mem. tech. staff Jet Propulsion Lab., Pasadena, Calif., 1984-93; exec. v.p. Geo-Capital, Glendale, Calif., 1994—; founder The Geo Group, Valencia, Calif., 1994—; sr. lectr. West Coast U., L.A., 1981-93. Author: Data HAndling Options for Space Station Freedom, 1989. Active Habitat for Humanity, San Fernando, Calif., 1993-94, Homeless Shelter Com., Valencia, 1993-94; area coord. Episcopal Marriage Encounter, L.A. County, 1994; vol. ARC, Santa Clarita, Calif., 1994. Mem. IEEE (L.A. area cons. network), AIAA (Calif. synergistic acquisition transfer), Assn. for Computing Machinery, Orange County IEEE Cons. Network. Republican. Office: Geo-Capital 517 E Wilson Ave Ste 100 Glendale CA 91206-4376

MASLOW, RICHARD EMANUEL, psychology consultant; b. Bklyn., Dec. 20, 1929; s. Louis William and Helen Lillian (Danziger) M.; m. Karen Mae Olson, May 11, 1956; children: Troy Mae, Darcy Sue. BS, Western N.Mex. U., 1952, MS, 1957. Tchr., coach Eddyville High Sch., Nebr., 1955-57; tchr., coach, counselor Quincy High Sch., Calif., 1957-62; psychology instr. San Joaquin Delta Coll., Stockton, Calif., 1963-91; student tchr. supr. Calif. State U., Stanislaus, 1993; stress mgmt. cons.; text book cons. Harper & Row, McGraw Hill, Houghton-Mifflin; basketball ofcl. No. Calif. Coll. Basketball Ofcls., 1979-90. Contbr. articles to profl. jours. Mem. sch. bd. Lincoln Unified Sch. Dist., Stockton, Calif., 1978—, pres. bd., 1980, 85, 88, 91. Served with U.S. Army, 1952-55. Mem. APA, Am. Psychol. Soc., Western Psychol. Assn., San Joaquin County Psychol. Assn. (pres. 1977-78), Calif. Sch. Bd. Assn., Nat. Sch. Bd. Assn. Home and Office: 3788 W Benjamin Holt Dr Stockton CA 95219-3324

MASON, ALBERT ABRAHAM, psychoanalyst, psychiatrist, educator; b. Newark, May 29, 1926; s. Louis and Annie Hinda (Gluckstein) M.; m. Paule Deglon, Aug. 8, 1956; children: Sara Carolyne, Mark Christopher. MB, BS, U. London, Guys Hosp., 1949. Sr. registrar Queen Victoria Hosp., East Grinstead, Surrey, Eng., 1951-53; psychiatrist West London Hosp., 1953-63; rsch. fellow in psychotherapy St. Georges Hosp., London, 1953-54; assoc. clin. prof., psychiatrist Sch. Medicine U. So. Calif., L.A., 1969-72, clin. prof. psychiatry, 1972 . Author: Hypnotism for Medical Practitioners, 1960; contbr. articles to profl. jours. Rsch. fellow Asthma Rsch. Coun. Gt. Britain, 1956-59. Mem. Am. Psychoanalytic Assn., Internat. Psychoanalytic Assn., L.A. Psychoanalytic Assn., Psychoanalytic Ctr. Calif. (pres. 1990-92, 94-96). Office: 450 N Bedford Dr Ste 305 Beverly Hills CA 90210-4307

MASON, CARTER GREGG, government employee; b. Fresno, Calif., Feb. 18, 1935; s. Morley Jack Mason and Viola Louise (Carter) Densmore; m. Betty Jean Manly, 1964 (div. 1973); 1 child, Denver Morley; m. Beverly Ann Libbon, Oct. 19, 1974; children: Michael Dean Libonati, Nicholas Gregg. B in Sociology, Stanislaus State Coll., 1970; MPA, U. So. Calif., L.A., 1974. Asst. mgr. Standard Stas., Yosemite, Calif., 1953-54; mgr. Standard Stas., Yosemite, 1959-61; correctional officer Calif. Dept. Corrections, Jamestown, Calif., 1961-69; parole agt. Calif. Dept. Corrections, San Jose, Calif., 1970-89; spl. agt. Dept. Def., Santa Clara, Calif., 1989—. V.p. Affirmative Action Com. for Dept. of Corrections, So. Calif., 1972-73; spl. liaison Ventura (Calif.) County Corrections, 1973-74; planning commr. Planning Commn., Santa Maria, Calif., 1980-84. 2d class petty officer USN, 1953-59, master chief petty officer USCGR, 1977-95. Mem. Loyal Order Elks, E Clampus Vitus. Republican. Roman Catholic. Home: 1031 Crestview Dr Apt 116 Mountain View CA 94040-3401

MASON, DEAN TOWLE, cardiologist; b. Berkeley, Calif., Sept. 20, 1932; s. Ira Jenckes and Florence Mabel (Towle) M.; m. Maureen O'Brien, June 22, 1957; children: Kathleen, Alison. B.A. in Chemistry, Duke U., 1954, M.D., 1958. Diplomate: Nat. Bd. Med. Examiners, Am. Bd. Internal Medicine (cardiovascular diseases). Intern, then resident in medicine Johns Hopkins Hosp., 1958-61; clin. assoc. cardiology br., sr. asst. surgeon USPHS, Nat. Heart Inst., NIH, 1961-63, asst. sect. dir. cardiovascular diagnosis, attending physician, sr. investigator cardiology br., 1963-68; prof. medicine, prof. physiology, chief cardiovascular medicine U. Calif. Med. Sch., Davis-Sacramento Med. Center, 1968-82; dir. cardiac ctr. Cedars Med. Ctr., Miami, Fla., 1982-83; physician-in chief Western Heart Inst., San Francisco, 1983—; chmn. dept. cardiovascular medicine St. Mary's Med. Ctr., San Francisco, 1986—; co-chmn. cardiovascular-renal drugs U.S. Pharmacopeia Com. Revision, 1970-75; mem. life scis. com. NASA; med. rsch. rev. bd. VA, NIH; vis. prof. numerous univs., cons. in field; mem. Am. Cardiovascular Splty. Cert. Bd., 1970-78. Contbr. numerous articles to profl. publs. Recipient Research award Am. Therapeutic Soc., 1965; Theodore and Susan B. Cummings Humanitarian award State Dept.-Am. Coll. Cardiology, 1972, 73, 75, 78; Skylab Achievement award NASA, 1974; U. Calif. Faculty Research award, 1978; named Outstanding Prof. U. Calif. Med. Sch., Davis, 1972. Fellow Am. Coll. Cardiology (pres. 1977-78), A.C.P., Am. Heart Assn., Am. Coll. Chest Physicians, Royal Soc. Medicine; mem. Am. Soc. Clin. Investigation, Am. Physiol. Soc., Am. Soc. Pharmacology and Exptl. Therapeutics (Exptl. Therapeutics award 1973), Am. Fedn. Clin. Research, N.Y. Acad. Scis., Am. Assn. U. Cardiologists, Am. Soc. Clin. Pharmacology and Therapeutics, Western Assn. Physicians, AAUP, Western Soc. Clin. Research (past pres.), Phi Beta Kappa, Alpha Omega Alpha. Republican. Methodist. Club: El Marcero Country. Home: 44725 Country Club Dr El Macero CA 95618-1047 Office: Western Heart Inst St Mary's Med Ctr 450 Stanyan St San Francisco CA 94117-1079

MASON, ELIZABETH FRYE, violinist, educator; b. Marmet, W.Va., Jan. 28, 1936; d. Forrest Carl and Ruby Irene (Barker) Frye; m. Joseph B. Mason, Feb. 20, 1962 (dec. Mar. 9, 1987); children: Renee Michele, Scott Forrest. MusB in Applied Violin, Piano, U. Cin., 1957; postgrad., U. N.Mex., 1959-60. Violinist Charleston (W.Va.) Symphony Orch., 1948-52, Dayton (Ohio) Philharmonic Orch., 1953-57, Houston Symphony Orch., 1957-58; concert mistress Albuquerque Symphony Orch., 1958-60; violinist Aspen (Colo.) Festival Orch., 1960-61, Indpls. Symphony Orch., 1960-62, Little Orch. of N.Y.C., 1963-64, New Orleans Philharmonic Orch., 1964-69; orch. and band tchr. Spring Branch Ind. Schs., Houston, 1971-73; prin. violin N.Mex. Symphony, Albuquerque, 1973-86; violin and viola N.Mex. Touring Ensemble, Albuquerque, 1973-86; violinist Roswell (N.Mex.) Symphony, 1987—; pvt. instr. violin, Bosque Farms, N.Mex., 1949—. Named NBC Nat. Young Artist, 1952; Coll. Music Cin. scholar, 1953-57, Tanglewood Music Festival scholar, 1955-56; Ford Found. grantee, 1966.

MASON, FRANK HENRY, III, automobile company executive, leasing company executive; b. Paris, Tenn., Nov. 16, 1936; s. Frank H. and Dorothy (Carter) M.; children—Robert C., William C. B.E.E., Vanderbilt U., 1958; M.S. in Indsl. Mgmt., MIT, 1965. With Ford Motor Co., 1965-71, asst. controller Ford Brazil, Sao Paulo, Brazil, 1971-74, mgr. overseas financing dept., Dearborn, Mich., 1974-76, asst. controller engine div., 1976-78, mgr. facilities and mgmt. services, 1978-81; controller Ford Motor Credit Co., Dearborn, 1981-87; dir. finance Ford Fin. Services Group, Dearborn, 1987-89; exec. v.p., chief fin. officer U.S. Leasing, Internat., San Francisco, 1989-92; ret. 1992. Served to lt. USN, 1958-63.

MASON, JAMES ALBERT, museum director, university dean; b. Eureka, Utah, 1929; married, 1956; 3 children. BA, Brigham Young U., 1955, MA, 1957; EdD, Ariz. State U., 1970. Cons., clinician in fine arts, 1955—; former chmn. dept. music Brigham Young U., Provo, dean Coll. Fine Arts and Communications; now dir. Mus. of Art Brigham Young U. vis. prof., lectr. Ind. U., Northwestern U., Cin. Coll.-Conservatory, U. Tex., Central Conservatory, Beijing, Internat. Soc. Music Edn., Warsaw; chmn. nat. symposium Applications of Psychology to the Teaching and Learning of Music; chmn., bd. dirs. The Barlow Endowment for Music Composition; co-founder, 1st pres. Utah Valley Symphony Orch.; past condr. Utah Valley Youth Orch.; bd. trustees Utah Opera Co.; commr. Utah Centennial of Statehood. Editor: The Instrumentalist, Orch. News, Utah Music Educator, Research News column, Jour. Research in Music Edn. Bd. dirs. Presser Found. Mem. Music Educators Nat. Conf. (past nat. pres., council), Nat. Music Council (past bd. dirs.), Am. Music Conf. (past bd. dirs.). Office: Brigham Young U Coll Fine Arts and Communications A410 Harris Fine Arts Ctr Provo UT 84602-1026

MASON, JAMES OSTERMANN, public health administrator; b. Salt Lake City, June 19, 1930; s. Ambrose Stanton and Neoma (Thorup) M.; m. Lydia Maria Smith, Dec. 29, 1952; children: James, Susan, Bruce, Ralph, Samuel, Sara, Benjamin. BA, U. Utah, 1954, MD, 1958; MPH, Harvard U., 1963, DPH, 1967. Diplomate Am. Bd. Preventive Medicine. Intern Johns Hopkins Hosp., Balt., 1958-59; resident in internal medicine Peter Bent Brigham Hosp.-Harvard Med. Service, Boston, 1961-62; chief infectious diseases Latter-day Saints Hosp., Salt Lake City, 1968-69; commr. Health Services Corp., Ch. of Jesus Christ of Latter-day Saints, 1970-76; dep. dir. health Utah Div. Health, 1976-78, exec. dir., 1979-83; chief epidemic intelligence service Ctr. Disease Control, Atlanta, 1959, chief hepatitis surveillance unit epidemiology br., 1960, chief surveillance sect. epidemiology br., 1961, dep. dir. bur. labs., 1964-68, dep. dir. of Ctr., 1969-70; dir. Ctrs. for Disease Control, Atlanta; adminstr. Agy. for Toxic Substances and Disease Registry, 1983-89; acting asst. sec. health HHS, Washington, 1985, asst. sec. for health, acting surgeon gen., 1989-90, asst. sec. for health, 1990-93; asst. prof. dept. medicine and preventive medicine U. Utah, Salt Lake City, 1968-69; assoc. prof., chmn. div. community medicine, dept. family and community medicine U. Utah, 1978-79; v.p. planning, devel., prof. preventive medicine and biometrics Uniformed Svcs. U. Health Scis., 1993-94; 2nd quorum of Seventy LDS Ch., 1994—; physician, cons. to med. services Salt Lake VA Hosp., 1977-83; clin. prof. dept. family and community medicine, U. Utah. Coll. Medicine, 1979-83, clin. prof. dept. pathology, 1980-83; clin. prof. community health Emory U. Sch. Medicine, 1984-86; chmn. joint residency com. in preventive medicine and pub. health Utah Coll. Medicine, 1975-80; mem. Utah Cancer Registry Research Adv. Com., 1976-83; mem. adv. com. Utah Ctr. Health Stats., 1977-79; chmn. bd. Hosp. Coop. Utah, 1977-79; chmn. exec. com. Utah Health Planning and Resource Devel. Adv. Group, 1977-79; chmn. Utah Gov.'s Adv. Com. for Comprehensive Health Planning, 1975-77; mem. recombinant DNA adv. com. NIH, 1979-83; mem. Gov.'s Nuclear Waste Repository Task Force, 1980-83, chmn., 1980-82; bd. dirs. Utah Health Cost Mgmt. Found., 1980-83; mem. adv. com. for programs and policies Ctrs. for Disease Control, 1980; mem. com. on future of local health depts., Inst. Medicine, 1980-82; mem. exec. com., chmn. tech. adv. com. Thrasher Research Found., 1980-89; mem. Robert Wood Johnson Found. Program for Hosp. Initiatives in Long-Term Care, 1982-84; mem. sci. and tech. adv. com. UNDP-World Bank-WHO Spl. Programme for Research and Tng. in Tropical Diseases, 1984-89; mem. Utah Resource for Genetic and Epidemiologic Research, 1982-85, chmn. bd., 1982-83; U.S. rep. WHO Exec. Bd., 1990-93. Author: (with H.L. Bodily and E.L. Updyke) Diagnostic Procedures for Bacterial, Mycotic and Parasitic Infections, 5th edit., 1970; (with M.H. Maxell, K.H. Bousfield and D.A. Ostler) Funding Water Quality Control in Utah, Procs. for Lincoln Inst., 1982; contbr. articles to profl. jours. Mem. nat. scouting com. Boy Scouts Am., 1974-78. Recipient Roche award U. Utah, 1957, Wintrobe award U. Utah, 1958, Disting. Alumni award U. Utah, 1973, Adminstr. of Yr. award Brigham U., 1980, spl. award for outstanding pub. svc. Am. Soc. Pub. Adminstrn. 1984, Disting. Svc. medal USPHS, 1988, LDS Hosp. Deseret Found. Legacy of Life award, 1992, Gorgas Medal and Scroll, 1993. Mem. Inst. Medicine of NAS, AMA, Am. Pub. Health Assn. (task force for credentialing of lab. personnel 1976-78, program devel. bd. 1979-81), Utah State Med. Assn. (trustee 1979-83), Utah Acad. Preventive Medicine (pres. 1982-83), Utah Pub. Health Assn. (pres. 1980-82, Beatty award 1979), Sigma Xi, Alpha Epsilon Delta, Phi Kappa Phi, Alpha Omega Alpha, Delta Omega. Mem. LDS Ch. Lodge: Rotary. Office: LDS ChThe 70 47 E South Temple St Salt Lake City UT 84150 also: Africa Area Adminstrv Office, POBox 1218, Lonehill 2062, South Africa

MASON, JEFFREY DANIEL, theatre educator; b. San Francisco, Aug. 30, 1952; s. Lawrence Albert and Nancy Lavinia (Griffitts) M.; m. Susan Sefton, Aug. 4, 1979; 1 child, Ashley Siobhan. AB in English and Music, Stanford U., 1974, MA in Edn., 1975; MA in Drama, Calif. State U., Sacramento, 1980; PhD in Dramatic Art, U. Calif., Berkeley, 1983. Cert. stage combatant in armed and unarmed techniques, 1983. Assoc. instr. dramatic art U. Calif., Berkeley, 1980-82; instr. performing arts Diablo Valley Coll., 1982; lectr. theatre arts, artistic dir. Madrigal Dinner San Francisco State U., 1983-84; lectr. theatre Calif. State U., Bakersfield, 1984-85, asst. prof., 1985-87, assoc. prof., 1987-92, prof., 1992—, chair fine arts dept., 1991—; artistic dir. Kern Art Theatre, Bakersfield, 1985—. Author: Wisecracks: The Farces of George S. Kaufman, 1988, Melodrama and the Myth of America, 1993, (plays) Sherlock Holmes: The Legend, 1988, Camille, 1989; contbr. articles and revs. to profl. jours.; dir. plays Encore Dinner Theatre, 1985, Musica da Camera, 1985, Kern Art Theatre, 1985-90, Walnut Creek Civic Arts Repertory, 1982, Los Altos Conservatory Theatre, 1982, Foothill Theatre Co., Nevada City, Calif., 1992, Calif. State U., Bakersfield, 1984—; also others; actor various plays. Mem. bd. Foothill Theatre Co., Nevada City. Pearl Hickman fellow, U. Calif., Berkeley, 1979-80, 82-83, Calif. state fellow in edn., 1974-75; grantee Com. on Teaching, U. Calif., Berkeley, 1981, Calif. State U., Bakersfield Univ. Rsch. Coun., 1988-89. Mem. Am. Studies Assn., Am. Theatre and Drama Soc. (mem. bd. 1991-95), Am. Soc. Theatre Rsch., Assn. Theatre in Higher Edn. Office: Calif State U Fine Arts Dept 9001 Stockdale Hwy Bakersfield CA 93311

MASON, JUDITH ANN, freelance writer; b. Newark, Dec. 27, 1945; d. Richard Algie and Mary Ann (Beneck) M. Diploma in legal sci., Spencerian Bus. Coll., 1965; BA, Northeastern Ill. U., 1984. Legal sec. Harney B. Stover, Atty., Milw., 1967-69, Robert P. O'Meara, Atty., Waukegan, Ill., 1969-70; sec. to pres. First Midwest Bank, Waukegan, 1970-72, asst. cashier, 1972-76; legal sec. Eugene M. Snarski, Atty., Waukegan, 1976-81; adminstrv. aide Lake County Forest Preserve Dist., Libertyville, Ill., 1981-89; freelance writer Tucson, 1989—; legal sec., asst. Jeffrey H. Greenberg, Atty.; office mgr. Greenberg & Assocs., Tucson, 1989—; travel rep. Antioch (Ill.) Travel Agy., 1980-89, Advance Travel Agy., Zion, Ill., 1980-89; pub. speaker for various orgns., Lake County, Ill., 1984-89. Author: Why I Remember Yesterday, 1979, Haggadah (play), 1982; editor poetry column: Bank Man Magazine, 1972-75; contbg. article writer Compendum Mag. Tchr. Confraternity Christian Doctrine St. Patrick's Ch., Wadsworth, Ill., 1980-85; lector, eucharistic min. Prince of Peace Ch., Lake Villa, Ill., 1980-89; hospice vol. St. Therese Hosp., Waukegan, 1984; speech writer Grace Mary Stern lt. gubernatorial campaign, Lake County, 1984; voter registrar County of Lake Ill., 1986-89; cons. pub. rels. Lake County Cir. Ct. Judge campaign, 1988, Presdl. Campaign Paul Simon; co-chmn., organizer Women's Exhibit, Evergreen Air Show, 1993. Recipient Brian F. Shehanhan Creative Writing award Am. Inst. Banking, 1972, 1st Place pub. speaking, 1974. Mem. AAUW (pub. rels. chair 1986, pres. Chain O'Lakes br. 1988-89, Ill. Pub. Info. award 1987, pub. rels. chair Tucson br. 1991-92), NAFE, Northeastern Ill. U. Alumni Assn., Soc. Southwestern Authors, Pi Rho Zeta (pres. 1964-65). Democrat. Roman Catholic. Home and Office: 2195 E River Rd Tucson AZ 85718-6586

MASON, MARSHALL W., theater director; b. Amarillo, Tex., Feb. 24, 1940; s. Marvin Marshall and Lorine (Chrisman) M. B.S. in Speech, Northwestern U., 1961. prof. Ariz. State U., 1994; chief drama critic New Times, Phoenix, Ariz., 1994—. Founder, artistic dir. Circle Repertory Co., 1969-87, guest artistic dir., Ctr. Theater Group, 1988; dir. Broadway prodns. Redwood Curtain, 1993, The Seagull, 1992, Solitary Confinement, 1992, Burn This, 1987, As Is, 1985 (Drama Desk award, Tony nomination), Passion, 1983, Angels Fall, 1983 (Tony nomination), Fifth of July, 1981 (Tony nomination), Talley's Folly, 1980, (Pulitzer Prize, N.Y. Drama Critics Circle award, Tony nomination), Murder at the Howard Johnsons, 1979, Gemini, 1977, Knock Knock, 1976 (Tony nomination); Off-Broadway prodns. A Poster of the Cosmos/The Moonshot Tape, 1994, The Destiny of Me, 1992, Sunshine, 1989, Talley and Son, 1985, Childe Byron, 1980, Hamlet, 1979, Serenading Louie, 1976 (Obie award), Knock Knock, 1976 (Obie award), The Mound Builders, 1975 (Obie award), Battle of Angeles, 1974 (Obie award), The Sea Hourse, 1974, The Hot L Baltimore, 1973 (Obie award); dir. numerous prodns. including Who's Afraid of Virginia Woolf?, Tokyo, 1985, Talley's Folly, 1982, London, Home Free! and The Madness of Lady Bright, 1968, London, Nat. Tour Sleuth, 1988, Summer and Smoke, 1988, Whisper in the Mind, 1990; dir. numerous TV prodns. including Picnic, 1986, Kennedy's Children, 1982, The Fifth of July, 1983. Recipient Vernon Rice award, 1975, Drama Desk award, 1977, Margo Jones award, 1977, Outer Critics Circle award, 1978, Theatre World award, 1979, Shubert's Vaughan award, 1980, Obie award for Sustained Achievement, 1983, Inge Festival award for lifetime achievement, 1990. Mem. Soc. Stage Dirs. and Choreographers (pres. 1983-85), Dirs. Guild Am., Actors Equity Assn. Office: care Chandler Warren 7803 W Sunset Blvd Los Angeles CA 90046-3305

MASON, NAOMI ANN, interior designer; b. Kansas City, Mo., Mar. 11, 1934; d. Hugh Fredrick and Lottie Elizabeth (Granstrom) Guilford; m. Ronald A. Mason, May 28, 1954; children: Teresa Elizabeth, Sheryl Lynn, Christina Marie, Ronald Anthony Jr. AA, Kansas City (Mo.) Jr. Coll., 1954; BA, Calif. State U., Long Beach, 1980. Cert. interior designer, Calif. Owner Design Ctr. Interiors, Orange, Calif., 1985—. Co-host (TV show) A Slice of Orange. Mem. Orange Planning Commn., 1982-86; bd. dirs., 2d v.p. Orange C. of C., 1987-92; bd. dirs. Orange Elderly Svcs., 1987-91, Red Ribbon 100, 1987-95; pres., 1st v.p., 2d v.p. Orange Rep. Women Fedn., 1991-95; bd. dirs. Pacific S.W. dist. Mo. Synod Luth. Ch., 1994—. Named Citizen of Yr. City and Chamber, Orange, 1992, Women of Distinction Soroptimist, 1993. Mem. Am. Soc. Interior Designers (bd. dirs. 1986-90), Rotary. Republican. Lutheran. Home and Office: 525 S Arlington Rd Orange CA 92669-5127

MASON, ROBERT (BURT MASON), lawyer; b. Ft. Worth, Aug. 17, 1948; s. Joe Lennard and Eugenia (Moss) M. BS, Tex. A&M U., 1970; MS, U. Ark., 1976; JD, St. Mary's U., San Antonio, 1979. Bar: Tex. 1979, Alaska 1979. Lawyer Pletcher, Slaybaugh, Anchorage, 1979-81, lawyer, prin., 1981-83; sole practitioner Anchorage, 1983-87; ptnr. Mason & Griffin, Anchorage, 1987—; legal advisor Dist 49A Lions Dist. and Found., Anchorage, 1990—. Capt. USAF, 1970-76, S.E. Asia. Mem. VFW, Lions (bd. dirs. 1990-93, chmn. 1984-94, v.p. 1994-95, pres. 1995-96, drug awareness chmn. 1990-95, Dist. Lion of Yr. 1990-91), Elks, Am. Legion. Home: 18642 Stillwater Dr Eagle River AK 99577-7928 Office: Mason & Griffin 1600 A St Ste 101 Anchorage AK 99501-5146

MASON, RONALD LEONARD, architect; b. Winnipeg, Man., Can., June 14, 1938; came to U.S., 1952; s. Arthur Hater and Lillian Eileen (Pennock) M.; m. Joan Louise Irwin, July 19, 1958 (div. 1976); children: Mark, Susan, Jeffrey; m. Kimberly Kay Wood, June 1, 1988. Student, U. Colo., 1958-62. Registered architect, Colo., S.D.; cert. Nat. Coun. Archtl. Registration Bds., value engr. Archtl. draftsman Charles S. Sink Arch., Denver, 1961-70; archtl. draftsman and assoc. ABR Partnership Arch., Denver, 1970-75, John D. Anderson & Assocs., Denver, 1975-80; arch. Anderson Archs., Denver, 1980-85; pres. Anderson Mason Dale, P.C., Denver, 1985—; mem. Creekfront Project adv. com. Denver Partnership, mem. 16th Street Mall sign code com.; spl. design cons. Platte River Greenway Com. Prin. works include Western Wyo. Coll. expansion, Rock Springs Wyoming, Joint Inst. for Lab. Astrophysics bldg. and addition, U. Colo., Boulder, master plan and new visitor facilities Mt. Rushmore Nat. Meml., S.D., Brighton (Colo.) H.S., Scis. and Industries Bldg. and South City Campus expansion Salt Lake C.C., New Meeting Bldg., Denver Botanic Gardens, Biomed. Rsch. Facility, U. Colo. Health Scis. Ctr., Denver, also schs. in Colo. Chmn. urban follies competition Urban Design Forum, Denver, 1991, also bd. dirs. Fellow AIA (Denver city and county design rev. group, mem. design awards jury Dallas 1989, Ky. and Wyo. 1990, Ariz. 1992, chmn. Colo. design conf. 1993). Office: Anderson Mason Dale 1615 17th St Denver CO 80202-1203

MASON, ROSE F., nurse administrator; b. Chinle, Ariz., Nov. 7, 1940; d. Edward and Ida (Hosgan) Francis; m. Richard Mason, June 1, 1963; children: Ralph, Cindy, Cheryl. Diploma, St. Anthony's Sch. Nursing, 1962; BSN, U. N.Mex., 1983. Clin. nurse specialist in adminstrv. nursing svcs. Clin. nurse Albuquerque Indian Hosp., 1971-73; supr. clin. nurse Albuquerque PHS Indian Hosp., 1973-81; clin. nurse Nursing Edn. Ctr., Albuquerque, 1981-83; supr. clin. nurse PHS Indian Health Svcs., Shiprock, N.Mex., 1983-84; clin. nurse Albuquerque PHS Indian Hosp., 1984-85; supr. clin. nurse Chinle (Ariz.) PHS Indian Hosp., 1983-84, Ft. Defiance (Ariz.) Indian Hosp., 1983-84; supr. clin. nurse Albuquerque PHS Indian Hosp., 1985-88, nurse specialist, 1988-91, acting dir. nurses, 1991, nurse specialist, 1992—. Contbr. ednl. video taping Oncology Nursing: Making a Difference, 1993. Bd. dirs. adult day care program Share Your Care Inc., 1993-94; mem. Tb Task Force Com. N.Mex., 1993—; mem. steering com. N.Mex. Cancer Pain Initiative, 1993—. Mem. Assn. Practitioners in Infection Control, Inc. (treas. 1992-93, Edn. Advancement award 1991), N.Mex. Indian Nurses Assn. (bd. dirs.), N.Mex. Assn. Continuity of Care (hon. mention award of excellence 1992). Home: 1325 Sasebo St NE Albuquerque NM 87112-6329

MASON, SARA SMITH, managed healthcare consultant; b. Rochester, N.Y., May 30, 1948; d. Harry F. and Louise S. (Sullivan) Smith; m. Larry S. Mason, Oct. 14, 1972. BA, Lewis and Clark Coll., Portland, Oreg., 1970, MA in Teaching, 1972; MBA, U. Oreg., 1987. Dir. N.W. area Intracorp., Portland, 1979-90; dir. ops. Western region Ptnrs. In Exec. Solutions, Irvine, Calif., 1990-91; asst. v.p. group and casualty svcs. ETHIX Nat., Portland, Oreg., 1992-94; managed care product mgr. Fireman's Fund Ins. Cos., Portland, 1994—. Mem. med. subcom. Worker's Compensation, Salem, Oreg., 1987. Mem. Oreg. Exec. MBA Alumni Bd. (bd. dirs.), Nat. Assn. Rehab. Profl. in Pvt. Sector, Portland City Club (bus. labor com. 1990-91). Office: Firemans Fund Ins Cos 101 SW Main St Ste 710 Portland OR 97204-3215

MASON, TERENCE K., critical care nurse; b. Elgin, Ill., June 10, 1953; s. LeRoy B. and Doris M. (Kelly) M.; m. Cheryl S., Apr. 23, 1989. AA, Phoenix Coll., 1977; BSN, Ariz. State U., 1981, postgrad. RN, Ariz.; cert. critical care nurse, ACLS, BCLS provider and instr. Staff nurse SCU Valley Luth. Hosp., Mesa, Ariz., 1985-86; freelance nurse, Tempe (Ariz.) St. Luke's Hosp., Phoenix, 1989-90; charge nurse coronary ICU, Tempe (Ariz.) St. Luke's Hosp., 1981-85, 86-88; asst. clin. dir. coronary ICU, Tempe (Ariz.) St. Luke's Hosp., Phoenix area, Ariz., 1988-89, 91-95, staff nurse CICU, 1995—. Sgt. U.S. Army, 1971-74. Mem. AACN. Office: Tempe St Luke's Hosp 1500 S Mill Ave Tempe AZ 85281-6630

MASOTTI, LOUIS HENRY, management educator, consultant; b. N.Y.C., May 16, 1934; s. Henry and Angela Catherine (Turi) M.; m. Iris Patricia Leonard, Aug. 28, 1958 (div. 1981); children: Laura Lynn, Andrea Anne; m. Ann Randel Humm, Mar. 5, 1988. AB, Princeton U., 1956; MA, Northwestern U., 1961, PhD, 1964. Fellow Nat. Ctr. Edn. in Politics, 1962; asst. prof. polit. sci. Case Western Res. U., Cleve., 1963-67, assoc. prof., 1967-69, dir. Civil Violence Rsch. Ctr., 1968-69; sr. Fulbright lectr. Johns Hopkins U. Ctr. Advanced Internat. Studies, Bologna, Italy, 1969-70; assoc. prof. Northwestern U., Evanston, Ill., 1970-72, prof. polit. sci. and urban affairs, 1972-83, dir. Ctr. Urban Affairs, 1971-80, dir. Program in Pub. and Not-for-Profit Mgmt., Kellogg Sch. Mgmt., 1979-80, prof. mgmt. and urban devel. Kellogg Sch. Mgmt., 1983-94, dir. Real Estate Research Ctr., 1986-88; cons. to numerous publs., govt. agys. real estate devels. and corps.; vis. assoc. prof. U. Wash., summer 1969; exec. dir. Mayor Jane Byrne Transition Com., Chgo., 1979; vis. prof. Stanford Sch. Bus., 1989-92, UCLA Sch. Mgmt., 1989-92; prof., dir. real estate mgmt. program U. Calif. Grad. Sch. Mgmt., Irvine, 1992—, dir. NHC, Inc., dir. Tucker Properties Corp., 1993; dir. Facilities Mgmt. Internat., 1994—, MCH, Inc., 1993—, Tucker Properties Corp. (REIR), 1993—. Author: Education and Politics in Suburbia, 1967, Shootout in Cleveland, 1969, A Time to Burn?, 1969, Suburbia in Transition, 1973, The New Urban Politics, 1976, The City in Comparative Perspective, 1976, co-editor: Metropolis in Crisis, 1968, 2d edit., 1971, Riots and Rebellion, 1968, The Urbanization of the Suburbs, 1973, After Daley: Chicago Politics in Transition, 1981, Downtown Development, 1985, 2d edit., 1987; editor Edn. and Urban Soc., 1968-71, Urban Affairs Quar., 1973-80; sr. editor Econ. Devel. Quar., 1986-92; vice chmn. bd. Illinois Issues jour., 1986-92. Rsch. dir. Carl Stokes for Mayor of Cleve., 1967; mem. Cleveland Heights Bd. Edn., 1967-69; devel. coordinator for high tech. State of Ill.-City Chgo., 1982-83; advisor to various congl., gubernatorial and mayoral campaigns, Ohio, Ill., N.J., Calif.; cons. urban devel. issues Corps. developers, govt. agys. and news media. Lt. USNR, 1956-59. Fellow Homer Hoyt Inst. for Advanced Real Estate Studies; recipient Disting. Service award Cleve. Jaycees, 1967; numerous fed. and found. research grants, 1963—. Mem. Urban Land Inst., Nat. Coun. Urban Econ. Devel., Internat. Assn. Corp. Real Estate Execs., Internat. Devel. Rsch. Coun., Nat. Assn. Indsl. Office Properties (bd. dirs.), Lambda Alpha Internat. Home: 2810 Villa Way Newport Beach CA 92663-3729

MASOUREDIS, SERAFEIM PANAGIOTIS, pathologist, educator; b. Detroit, Nov. 14, 1922; s. Panagiotis and Lemonia (Moniodis) M.; m. Marion Helen Mykytew, Oct. 1943; children: Claudia, Linus. AB, U. Mich., 1944, MD, 1948; PhD in Med. Physics, U. Calif., Berkeley, 1952. Diplomate Am. Bd. Pathology. Intern U. Calif. Svc./San Francisco Gen. Hosp., 1952-53, asst. resident in medicine, 1954-55; fellow Clinic Hematology/Donner Lab./Univ. Calif., Berkeley, 1953-54; asst. prof., then assoc. prof. pathology U. Pitts. Med. Sch., 1955-59; asst. dir. Cen. Blood Bank Pitts., 1955-59; assoc. prof. preventive medicine U. Calif., San Francisco, 1959-62, assoc. prof. medicine, 1962-67, assoc. prof. clin. pathology, 1966-67; prof. medicine Marquette U., Milw., 1967-69; exec. dir. Milw. Blood Ctr., 1967-69; prof. pathology U. Calif., San Diego, 1969-90, prof. emeritus, 1990—; cons. WHO, Geneva, 1965-67; bd. dirs. Am. Assn. Blood Banks, Washington,1 981-83. Assoc. editor Jour. Transfusion, Washington, 1981-90; contbr. sci. articles and rsch. papers to various publs. Emily Cooley Meml. lectr. Am. Assn. Blood Banks, 1973, recipient Karl Landsteiner Meml. award, 1979. Mem. Am. Assn. Immunologists, Am. Soc. Clin. Investigation, Am. Soc. Hematology, Brit. Soc. Immunology, Am. Assn. Cancer Rsch., Internat. Soc. Blood Transfusion, Western Assn. Physicians. Office: U Calif San Diego Dept Pathology Sch Medicine La Jolla CA 92093-0612

MASOVER, GERALD KENNETH, microbiologist; b. Chgo., May 12, 1935; s. Morris H. and Lillian (Perelgut) M.; m. Bonnie Blumenthal, Mar. 30, 1958 (dec. 1992); children: Steven, Laurie, David; m. Lee H. Tower, Mar. 25, 1995. BS, U. Ill., Chgo., 1957, MS, 1970; PhD, Stanford U., 1973. Registered pharmacist, Calif., Ill. Owner, operator Ropert Pharmacy, Chgo., 1960-68; rsch. assoc. Stanford U. Med. Sch., Palo Alto, Calif., 1974-80; assoc. rsch. cell biologist Children's Hosp., Oakland, Calif., 1980-83; rsch. microbiologist Hana Biologics, Berkeley, Calif., 1983-86; pharmacist various locations, 1970—; quality control sect. head Genentech, Inc., South San Francisco, 1986-90, quality control sr. microbiologist, 1990—. Contbr. articles to profl. jours., chpts. to books. 1st Lt. USAR, 1957-66. NSF predoctoral fellow, 1970-73; NIH rsch. grantee, 1974-78. Mem. Tissue Culture Assn., Internat. Orgn. for Mycoplasmology, Parenteral Drug Assn., Am. Soc. for Microbiology, Sigma Xi. Jewish. Home: 4472 24th St San Francisco CA 94114 Office: Genentech Inc 460 Point San Bruno Blvd South San Francisco CA 94080-4918

MASRI, MERLE SID, biochemist, consultant; b. Jerusalem, Palestine, Sept. 12, 1927; came to U.S., 1947; s. Said Rajab and Fatima (Muneimné) M.; m. Maryjean Loretta Anderson, June 28, 1952 (div. 1974); children: Kristin Corinne, Allan Eric, Wendy Joan, Heather Anderson. BA in Physiology, U. Calif., Berkeley, 1950; PhD in Mammalian Physiology and Biochemistry, U. Calif. Berkeley, 1953. Rsch. asst. Dept. Physiology, Univ. Calif., Berkeley, 1950-53; predoctoral fellow Baxter Labs., Berkeley, 1952-53; rsch. assoc. hematology Med. Rsch. Inst., Michael Reese Hosp., Chgo., 1954-56; sr. rsch. biochemist Agrl. Rsch. Svc., USDA, Berkeley, 1956-87; supervisory rsch. scientist Agrl. Rsch. Svc., USDA, N.D. State U. Sta., Fargo, N.D., 1987-89; pvt. practice as cons. Emeryville, Calif., 1989—; lectr. numerous confs. Contbr. over 130 articles to profl. jours. Recipient Spl. Svc. and Merit awards USDA, 1966, 76, 77, Superior Svc. award USDA, 1977. Fellow Am. Inst. Chemists; mem. AAAS, Am. Chem. Soc., Am. Oil Chemists Soc., Am. Assn. Cereal Chemists, N.Y. Acad. Scis., Sigma Xi. Home: 9 Commodore Dr Emeryville CA 94608-1652

MASSARO, ANTHONY SCOTT, environmental consultant; b. Denver, June 23, 1957; s. Nicholas Ross and Barbara E. (Peila) M.; 1 child, Patrick. BS in Polit. Sci. and Econs., Colo. State U., 1979. Exec. dir. Coloradoans for Recycling, 1981-82; dir. environ. affairs Office of Mayor, Denver, 1983-91; pub. affairs mgr. Eric Group, Inc., 1991-92; sr. ptnr. Rocky Mountain Environ. Strategies, Inc., Denver, 1992—; guest lectr. U. Colo., Denver, U. Denver, Regis Coll., Va. Poly. Inst. and State U. Contbr. articles and papers to profl. jours. Mem. exec. com. Gov.'s Alternative Fuels Task Force, 1990-91, mem. regional air quality coun., 1989-91; chmn. Brown Cloud com. Metro Air Quality Coun., 1985-89; mem. nat. nuclear waste transp. planning com. U.S. Dept. Energy, 1989-91; bd. dirs. Am. Lung Assn. Colo., 1985-87; participant 1st Internat. Conf. for Protection of Mountain Gorilla, Kigali, Rwanda, 1990; founding sponsor Women's Polit. Tng. Inst., 1984; active Vols. for Outdoor Colo., 1992—. Recipient Pub. Svc. award Mayor Federico Peña, 1991, Cert. of Appreciation for Environ. Action, City of Denver, 1991, Environ. Achievement cert. Friends of UN and Renew America, 1991; McCloy fellow, 1990. Mem. Air and Waste Mgmt. Assn., Nat. Assn. Environ. Profls. Democrat. Office: Rocky Mountain Environ Strategies Inc 3047 W 26th Ave Denver CO 80211-4059

MASSEY, DOUGLAS GORDON, physician, educator; b. Clinton, Ont., Can., Oct. 14, 1926; came to U.S., 1973; s. Douglas and Zeralda (Churchill) M.; m. Gisele Fournier, Aug. 27, 1967; children: Anne, Nicole, Jennifer. MD, U. Toronto, 1951; MSc, McGill U., 1964. Intern St. Michaels Hosp., Toronto, 1951-52; resident Sunnybrooke Hosp., Toronto, 1952-53, Leahi Hosp., Honolulu, 1953-55; assoc. prof. U. Sherbrooke (Que., Can.), 1964-73; prof. U. Hawaii, Honolulu, 1973—; dir. inst. rsch. St. Francis Med. Ctr., 1991—. Recipient Palmes Academiques, France. Mem. Alliance Francaise of Hawaii (pres. 1986-92), Fedn. Alliances Francaise (dir., treas. 1993—). Home: 4523 Aukai Ave Honolulu HI 96816-4922 Office: John A Burns Sch Medicine Leahi Hosp 3675 Kilauea Ave Honolulu HI 96816-2333

MASSEY, LEON R., association executive; b. Grand Island, Nebr., Jan. 16, 1930; s. James Moore and Iva Pearl (Richardson) M.; m. Jean M. Nielsen, June 17, 1951; children: Dean R., Maureen L. Student, U. Colo., 1948-49; BA, U. Nebr., 1955; postgrad., N.Y. Inst. Fin., 1963. Salesman consumer products Union Carbide Corp., Memphis, 1956-57, Greenville, Miss., 1957-58, Albuquerque, 1958-61, Dallas, 1962-63; regional sales mgr. GC Electric div. Textron Corp., Dayton, Ohio, 1963-64; account exec. Merrill Turben Co., Dayton, 1964-66; with Nat. Electric Contractors Assn., Dayton, 1967-72, Denver, 1972-83, exec. sec., 1967-83, also bd. dirs. Rocky Mountain chpt.; pres. RLM's Assocs., Englewood, Colo., 1983—; instr. adult edn. Wayne State U., Dayton, 1964-66. City councilman City of Greenwood Village, Colo., 1986-90; pres. Cherry Creek Civic Assn., 1979-80, bd. dirs. 1973-74; bd. dirs. Assn. Operating Rm. Nurses, Cherry Creek Village Water Dist., 1992—; bd. dirs. Goldsmith Gulch Sanitation Dist., 1990—, pres., 1992—; active Dem. Party, 1960. With USAF, 1950-54, Korea. Mem. Am. Soc. Assn. Execs. (cert., bd. dirs.), Colo. Soc. Assn. Execs. (life, pres. 1979), Civitan Club, Masons, Phi Kappa Psi. Office: RLM Assocs 5031 S Beeler St Englewood CO 80111-1313

MASSIE, BARRY MICHAEL, cardiologist; b. St. Louis, May 23, 1944; s. Edward and Felice (Ozerovich) M.; m. Ellen Sue Weisberg, May 29, 1970; children: Jennifer Nicole, Rebecca Elizabeth. BA, Harvard Coll., 1966; MD, Columbia U., 1970. Resident Bellevue Hosp., N.Y.C., 1970-74; prof. medicine U. Calif., San Francisco, 1978-83, assoc. prof., 1983-89, prof., 1989—; dir. coronary care unit, chief hypertension unit VA Med. Ctr., San Francisco, 1978—; staff mem. Cardiovascular Rsch. Inst., San Francisco, 1981—; mem. adv. panel Food & Drug Adminstrn., Rockville, Md., 1992—. Fellow Am. Coll. Cardiology, Am. Heart Assn. (coun. clin. cardiology); mem. Am. Fedn. Clin. Rsch., Western Soc. Clin. Rsch., Western Assn. Physicians. Office: VA Hosp Cadiology 111C 4150 Clement St San Francisco CA 94121-1545

MASSIMINO, ROLAND V., former university basketball coach; b. Hillside, N.J., Nov. 13, 1934; s. Salvatore and Grace (Alberti) M.; m. Mary Jane Reid, Aug. 13, 1958; children—Thomas, Lee Ann, Michele, R.C., Andrew. Degree in Bus., U. Vt., 1956; M.P.E., Rutgers U., 1959; guidance cert., Tufts U., 1969. Asst. coach Cranford High Sch., N.J., 1956-59; coach Hillside High Sch., N.J., 1959-63, Lexington High Sch., Mass., 1963-69; head coach SUNY-Stony Brook, 1969-71; asst. coach U. Pa., 1971-73; head coach Villanova U., Pa., 1973-92, U. Nev., Las Vegas, 1992-95. Winning coach NCAA Nat. Basketball Championship, 1985; named Coach of Yr., Phila. Big 5, 1975 76, 77 78, 81-82, 82-83, 84-85, Eastern Athletic Assn., 1976-77, Eastern 8 Conf., 1978-79, 79-80, Widmer Cup Eastern Coach of Yr., 1981-82, Coach of Yr., Big East Conf., 1981-82, Eastern Basketball Eastern Coach of Yr., 1984-85, Harry Latwick/Herb Good Phila. Mem. Nat. Assn. Basketball Coaches. *

MASSY, PATRICIA GRAHAM BIBBS (MRS. RICHARD OUTRAM MASSY), social worker, author; b. Newbury, Eng., Mar. 21, 1918; came to U.S., 1963, naturalized, 1969; d. Oswald Graham and Dorothy (French) Bibbs; m. Richard Outram Massy, July 22, 1944 (dec. Aug. 1986); children: Patricia Lynn Massy Holmes, Julie Suzanne, Shaun Adele Massy Brink. BA, U. B.C., 1941, MSW, 1962. With B.C. Welfare Field Svc., Vancouver, Kamloops, Abbotsford, 1942-44; social worker Brandon Welfare Dept., Man., Can., 1945; with Children's Aid Soc., Vancouver, 1948-62; supr. Dept. Pub. Social Svc., L.A., 1963-70, staff devel. specialist-mgmt., 1970-77; lectr. colls. and seminars; lectr. Rogue Coll., Grants Pass, 1990; author, publisher: A Study Guide for a Course in Miracles, 1984; One, 1985. Mem. AAUW (treas. 1970), Nat. Assn. Social Workers, Alpha Phi. Mem. Unity Ch. Home: 18936 Upper Cow Creek Rd Azalea OR 97410-9730

MAST, JIM, food executive; b. 1936. BS in Agrl. Econs., U. Ariz., 1959. With Mesa (Ariz.) Citrus Growers, 1959—, now gen. mgr. Office: Mesa Citrus Growers 254 W Broadway Mesa AZ 85210-1510*

MASTERS, ELAINE, educator, writer; b. Kansas City, Kans., Oct. 6, 1932; d. David Shepherd and Stella Frances (Ragan) M.; m. Donald Ramon Masters, Apr. 27, 1951; children: David, Vicki, Jennifer, Kevin. BS in Edn. with honors, U. Mo., Kansas City, 1968. Cert. tchr., Mo., Va. Tchr. Am. Sch., Manila, 1956-57, Escuela Gloria Felix, Caracas, Venezuela, 1960-62, Okinawa Christian Sch., Urasoe, 1968-70, Flint Hill Elem. Sch., Vienna, Va., 1970-73, Bible Inst. Hawaii, Honolulu, 1991-92; children's ministries coord. Kaneohe Corps. Salvation Army, Hawaii, 1991-94; evangelist, Hong Kong, Malaysia, Nigeria, Thailand, Russia; seminar leader on Bible and Christian living, Hong Kong, Malaysia, Nigeria, Thailand; advisor Pentecostal Assemblies of Tribes, Chiang Mai, Thailand, 1991—; lectr. Christian Writers Workshop, 1993—. Author: Ali and the Ghost Tiger, 1967, Teach Us To Pray, 1970, Day Camp and Day Care Handbook, 1989; contbr. articles to mags. and newspapers; inventor cricket transposer tool for musicians. Mem. speakers bur. Alzheimer's Assn., Honolulu, 1991—; young people's sgt. maj. Salvation Army, Kaneohe, Hawaii, 1992-94. Mem. Women's Aglow Fellowship Internat., Nat. Writers Club, Soc. for Children's Book Writers and Illustrators. Home: 1911 Kalakaua Ave Apt 601 Honolulu HI 96815-1809 Office: Salvation Army Kaneohe Corps 45-175 Waikalua Rd Kaneohe HI 96744-2765

MASTERSON, LINDA HISTEN, medical company executive; b. N.Y.C., May 21, 1951; d. George and Dorothy (Postler) Riddell; m. Robert P. Masterson, March 6, 1982; m. William J. Histen, May 24, 1971 (div. 1979). BS in med. tech., U. R.I., 1973; MS in microbiology, U. Md., 1977; student, Wharton U. Pa., Phila., 1988. Med. technologist various hosps.,

1972-78; microbiology specialist Gen. Diagnostics, Warner-Lambert, Morris Plains, N.J., 1978-80; from tech. sales rep. to dir. internat. mktg. Micro-Scan, Baxter Internat., Sacramento, 1980-87; dir. mktg. Ortho Diagnostics, Johnson & Johnson, Raritan, N.J., 1987-89; sr. v.p. mktg/sales GenProbe, San Diego, 1989-92; v.p. mktg./sales Bio Star, Boulder, Colo., 1992-93; exec. v.p. Cholestech Inc., Hayward, Calif., 1994—; bd. dirs. Ethicon Employee Fed. Credit Union, Sommerville, N.J., 1988-89. Tribute to women in industry Young Women's Christian Assn., N.J., 1989. Mem. Biomedical Mktg. Assn., Med. Mktg. Assn., Phi Kappa Phi. Office: Cholestech Inc 5347 Investment Blvd Hayward CA 94541-9999

MASTERSON, WILLIAM A., state judge; b. N.Y.C., June 25, 1931; s. John Patrick and Helen Audrey (O'Hara) M.; m. Julie Dohrmann Cosgrove; children: Mark, Mary, Timothy, Barbara. BA, UCLA, 1953, JD, 1958. Bar: Calif., U.S. Supreme Ct. Assoc. Sheppard, Mullin, Richter & Hampton, L.A., 1958-62; ptnr., 1962-79; ptnr. Rogers & Wells, 1979-83, Skadden, Arps, Slate, Meagher & Flom, 1983-87; judge L.A. Superior Ct., 1987-92, justice Ct. Appeals, 1993—. Author, editor: Civil Trial Practice: Strategies and Techniques, 1986. With inf. U.S. Army, 1953-55. Fellow Am. Coll. Trial Lawyers; mem. Order of Coif. Office: Ct Appeals 300 S Spring St Los Angeles CA 90013

MASTRINI, JANE REED, social worker, consultant; b. Lincoln, Nebr., July 23, 1948; d. William Scott and Ellen (Daly) Cromwell; m. Charles James Mastrini, July 19, 1969. BA, Western State Coll., Gunnison, Colo., 1970; MSW, U. Denver, 1980. Lic. social worker Colo.; cert. alcohol counselor Colo. and nat. Tchr. Flandreau (S.D.) Indian Sch., 1970; social worker S.D. Dept. Welfare, Pierre, 1970-75; child care worker Sacred Heart Home, Pueblo, Colo., 1975-76; counselor Fisher Peak Alcohol Treatment Ctr., Trinidad, Colo., 1976-77; family therapist West Nebr. Gen. Hosp., Scottsbluff, 1980-81; adolescent coord. St. Luke's Hosp., Denver, 1981-86; exec. dir. New Beginnings At Denver, Lakewood, Colo., 1986-90; pres. Counseling Dimensions of Colo., Denver, 1990-92; trainer Mile High Inst., 1987-93; outpatient mgr. Arapahoe House, 1992-94; therapist Kaiser Permanente, Denver, 1994—; cons. Colo. Counseling Consortium, Denver, 1984-90; field work supr. U. Denver, 1983—. Lectr., group leader Colo. Teen Inst., Denver, 1984-85. Mem. NASW (cert.), P.E.O. (pres. 1984-87, 94—), Colo. Counseling Consortium, Colo. Assn. Addiction Treatment Programs (v.p. 1991-92). Democrat. Episcopalian. Home: 11785 W 66th Pl # D Arvada CO 80004-2473 Office: Kaiser Permanente CDTP 360 S Garfield St Ste 4000 Denver CO 80209-3136

MASUDA, YOSHINORI, systems analyst; b. Kasai, Hyogo, Japan, Apr. 6, 1953; came to U.S., 1977, naturalized, 1993; s. Saburo and Mitsuyo (Masuda) M. BL, Kobe U., Japan, 1977; MBA, U. San Francisco, 1980. Gen. mgr. Kotobuki Trading Co., San Francisco, 1980-85; distbn. analyst Kikkoman Internat. Inc., San Francisco, 1986-87, mgr. mgmt. info. system, 1987-88, mgr. electronic data interchange, 1988-93, mgr. distbn./customer svc./electronic data interchange, 1993—. Mem. Japanese C. of C. No. Calif. Govt. Rels., Beta Gamma Sigma. Home: 480 Wellesley Ave Mill Valley CA 94941-3540 Office: Kikkoman Internat Inc 50 California St Ste 3600 San Francisco CA 94111-4760

MASUOKA, SUSAN NAOMI, art historian; b. L.A., Aug. 14, 1949; d. David Takashi and Margaret Sumiko (Funakoshi) M.; m. William A. Orme Jr., Mar. 21, 1980 (div. 1991); 1 child, David Liam. BA, U. Calif., Berkeley, 1971; MA, UCLA, 1975, MFA, 1977, PhD, 1991. Teaching asst. dept. engring. UCLA, 1977, exhbns. asst. Wight Gallery, 1977-78; field investigator Guatemala, 1978-81; rsch. affiliate Ixchel Mus. Maya Costume, Guatemala City, 1979-80; rsch. assoc. Fowler Mus. Cultural History, 1985-89; art programs asst. Voyager Co., Santa Monica, Calif., 1992-93; vis. curator Fowler Mus. Cultural History, 1988-94. Author: En Calavera: The Papier-Maché Art of the Linares Family, 1994; contbr. articles and revs. to profl. jours.; assoc. book rev. editor for Ctrl. Am.: Studies in Latin Am. Popular Culture, 1987-90; contbg. editor: Americas mag., 1985-88. Office: Fowler Mus Cultural History UCLA 405 Hilgard Los Angeles CA 90024

MATA, MICHAEL ANTHONY, religion educator; b. Houston, Aug. 5, 1953; s. Joe G. and Josephine (Arias) M.; m. Kristina Jean Craig, Aug. 18, 1984; 1 child, Diane; foster children: Mary, Jerry. BA in Biblical Lit., Pt. Loma Nazarene Coll., 1975, MA in Religion, 1977; MDiv in Theology, Nazarene Theol. Sem., 1980; M City Planning, U. Calif., Berkeley, 1987. Ordained elder Ch. of the Nazarene, 1984. Instr. in theology Mex. Nazarene Sem., Mexico City, 1983; lectr. in urban studies Bresee Inst., L.A., 1983-93; teaching asst. dept. city and regional planning U. Calif., Berkeley, 1987; minister to youth L.A. First Ch. of Nazarene, 1980-85; assoc. pastor L.A. First Ch. of Nazarene, L.Z., 1983-85, 87—; Mildred M. Hutchinson prof. urban ministry Sch. of Theology at Claremont, Calif., 1993—, dir. Urban Leadership Inst., 1993—; cons. to various non-profit community orgns., L.A., 1989—; adj. faculty mem. in urban ministry Nazarene Theol. Sem., Kansas City, Mo., Mid-Am. Nazarene Coll., Olathe, Mo., Azusa (Calif.) Pacific U. Grad. Sch. Theology, So. Nazarene U., Bethany, Okla., N.W. Nazarene Coll., Nampa, Idaho; program planner Golden Gate Ministries, San Francisco, 1986-87; dir. Bresee Inst., L.A., 1987-93; ch.-based cmty. devel. coord. L.A. World Vision, U.S. Programs, Monrovia, Calif., 1990-93. Mem. ctrl. com. Calif. State Dem. Party, L.A., 1990-93; vice chair 46th Assembly Dist. Com., 1993-94; bd. dirs. West L.A. Cmty. Devel. Corp., 1994—, Affordable Housing Svcs., 1993—, Wilshire Stakeholders, Inc., 1988-93, So. Calif. Adv. Coun. for World Vision, 1992-93, Wilshire Ctr. Cmty. Involvement Assn., Inc., 1981-85, 87-90, P.F. Bresee Found., 1987-90, 93—, John M. Perkins Found. for Reconcillation and Devel., 1991—; mem. City of Berkeley Planning Commn., 1986; sec. bd. dirs. So. Calif. Coalition of Ethnic Religious Leaders, 1992-93; mem. adv. bd. Jimmy Carter L.A. Work Proejct, 1993-95; mem. cabinet Interfaith Coalition to Heal L.A., mem. subcom. econ. devel., 1992—; mem. steering com. Consortium of Urban Leadership Devel. Programs, 1991—; mem. New Ethnic Majority Econ. Task Force, 1990—; mem. steering com. Native Am. Gathering Table, 1988—; mem. adv. bd. Fransican Health Ctr., 1990-92; exec. mem. bd. dirs. Hope-Net, 1988-92; mem. steering com. So. Calif. Interfaith Hunger Coalition, 1988-89, 91-93; mem. regional adv. coun. Hispanic Assn. (Bilingual/Bicultural Ministries), 1993—. Recipient Cert. of Commendation, L.A. City Coun., 1983, Cert. of Appreciation, L.A. City Coun., 1984, 89, 94, Cert. of Recognition for Cmty. Svc., Calif. State Assembly, 1989, Acad. Excellence award Calif. Planning Found., 1987; named Urban Role Model, Urban Family Mag., 1993, Point Loma alumni award, 1994. Mem. Am. Planning Assn., So. Calif. Assn. Non-Profit Housing, Hispanic Assn. Theol. Edn., Nat. Soc. Internships and Exptl. Edn., Am. Planning Assn. Office: Sch Theology 1325 N College Ave Claremont CA 91711-3154

MATARAZZO, HARRIS STARR, lawyer; b. Portland, Oreg., July 24, 1957; s. Joseph Dominic and Ruth Wood (Gadbois) M.; m. Judith Grace Hudson, Jan. 2, 1988. AB in Polit. Sci., Brown U., 1979; JD, Northwestern Sch. Law, Portland, 1983. Bar: Oreg. 1986, U.S. Dist. Ct. Oreg. 1986, U.S. Ct. Appeals (9th cir.) 1986, U.S. Supreme Ct. 1992. With Aitchison, Imperati, Paull, Barnett and Sherwood, Portland, 1986; assoc. Parks & Bauer, Salem, Oreg., 1987-88; pvt. practice Portland, 1988—. Mem. Hist. Preservation League Oreg., Portland, 1984—, Oreg. State Pub. Interest Rsch. Group, Portland, 1985—, The Old Ch. Soc., Portland, 1986—, Pittock Mansion Soc., Portland, 1986; bd. dirs. Bosco Milligan Found., Rape Survivors Inc.; mem. vestry Trinity Episcopal Ch., 1992-95. Mem. ABA, Fed. Bar Assn., Oreg. State Bar Assn., Oreg. Criminal Def. Lawyers Assn., Multnomah County Bar Assn. Office: Bank Am Fin Ctr 121 SW Morrison Ste 1020 Portland OR 97204

MATARAZZO, JOSEPH DOMINIC, psychologist; b. Caiazzo, Italy, Nov. 12, 1925; (parents Am. citizens); s. Nicholas and Adeline (Mastroianni) M.; m. Ruth Wood Gadbois, Mar. 26, 1949; children: Harris, Elizabeth, Sara. Student, Columbia U., 1944; BA, Brown U., 1946; MS, Northwestern U., 1950, PhD, 1952. Fellow in med. psychology Washington U. Sch. Medicine, 1950-51; instr. Washington U., 1951-53, asst. prof., 1953-55; research assoc. Harvard Med. Sch., assoc. psychologist Mass. Gen. Hosp., 1955-57; prof., head med. psychol. dept. Oreg. Health Scis. U., Portland, 1957—; Mem. nursing rsch. and patient care study sect., behavioral medicine study sect. NIH, nat. mental health adv. coun. NIMH; mem. bd. regents Uniformed Svcs. U. Health Scis., 1974-80. Author: Wechsler's Measurement and Appraisal of Adult Intelligence, 5th edit., 1972, (with A.N. Wiens) The Interview: Research on its Anatomy and Structure, 1972, (with Harper and Wiens) Nonverbal Communication, 1978; editor: Behavioral Health: A Handbook of Health Enhancement and Disease Prevention, 1984; editorial bd.: Jour. Clin. Psychology, 1962—; cons. editor: Contemporary Psychology, 1962-70, 80—, Jour. Community Psychology, 1974-81, Behavior Modification, 1976-91, Intelligence: An Interdisciplinary Jour, 1976-90, Jour. Behavioral Medicine, 1977—, Profl. Psychology, 1978—, Jour. Cons. and Clin. Psychology, 1978-85; editor: Psychology series Aldine Pub. Co, 1964-74; psychology editor: Williams & Wilkins Co, 1974-77; contbr. articles to psychol. jours. Ensign USNR, 1943-47; capt. Res. Recipient Hofheimer prize Am. Psychiat. Assn., 1962. Fellow AAAS, APA (pres. 1989-90, divsn. health psychology 1978-89, Coun. Reps. 1982-91, bd. dirs. 1986-90); mem. Western Psychol. Assn., Oreg. Psychol. Assn., Am. Assn. State Psychology Bds. (pres. 1963-64), Nat. Assn. Mental Health (bd. dirs.), Oreg. Mental Health Assn. (bd. dirs., pres. 1962-63), Internat. Coun. Psychologists (bd. dirs. 1972-74, pres. 1976-77), Assn. Advancement of Psychology (trustee 1980-84, chmn. bd. trustees 1983-85). Home: 1934 SW Vista Ave Portland OR 97201-2455 Office: Oreg Health Scis U Sch Medicine 3181 SW Sam Jackson Park Rd Portland OR 97201-3011

MATARÉ, HERBERT F., physicist, consultant; b. Aachen, Germany, Sept. 22, 1912; came to U.S., 1953; s. Josef P. and Paula (Broicher) M.; m. Ursula Krenzien, Dec. 1939; children: Felicitas, Vitus; m. Elise Walbert, Dec. 1983; 1 child, Victor B. BS in Physics, Chemistry and Math., Aachen U. Geneva, 1933; MS in Tech. Physics, U. Aachen, 1939; PhD in Electronics, Tech. U. Berlin, 1942; PhD in Solid State Physics summa cum laude, Ecole Normale Supérieure, Paris, 1950. Asst. prof. physics & electronics Tech. U. Aachen, 1936-45; head of microwave receiver lab. Telefunken, A.G., Berlin, 1939-46; mgr. semincondr. lab. Westinghouse, Paris, 1946-52; founder, pres. Intermetall Corp., Düsseldorf, Fed. Republic Germany, 1952-56; head semincondr. R & D, corp. rsch. labs. Gen. Telephone & Electronics Co., N.Y.C., 1956-59; dir. rsch. semicondr. dept. Tekade, Nürnberg, Fed. Republic Germany, 1959-61; head quantum physics dept. rsch. labs. Bendix Corp., Southfield, Mich., 1961-64; tech. dir., acting mgr. hybrid microelectronics rsch. labs. Lear Siegler, Santa Monica, Calif., 1963-64; asst. chief engr. advance electronics dept. Douglas Aircraft Co., Santa Monica, 1964-66; tech. dir. McDonnell Douglas Missile Div., 1964-69; sci. advisor to solid state electronics group Autonetics (Rockwell Internat.), Anaheim, Calif., 1966-69; pres. Internat. Solid State Electronics Cons., L.A., 1973—; prof. electronics U. Buenos Aires, 1953-54; vis. prof. UCLA, 1968-69, Calif. State U., Fullerton, 1969-70; dir. Compound Crystals Ltd., London, 1989—; cons. UN Indsl. Devel. Orgn. to 15 Indian insts. and semiconductor cos. with conf. talks at India Inst. Tech., New Delhi and Bombay, 1978. Author: Receiver Sensitivity in the UHF, 1951, Defect Electronics in Semiconductors, 1971, Conscientious Evolution, 1978, Energy, Facts and Future, 1989, (with P. Faber) Renewable Energies, 1993; patentee first European transistor, vacuum crystal growth, solid state oscillators, grain boundary transistor, unipolar tunnel transistor, light detection with grain-boundaries, 60 others; contbr. over 100 articles to profl. jours. Fellow IEEE (life); mem. AAAS, IEEE Nuclear Plasma Scis. Soc., IEEE Power Engring. Soc., Inst. for Advancement of Man (hon.), Am. Phys. Soc. (solid state div.), Electrochem. Soc., Am. Vacuum Soc. (thin film div.), Materials Rsch. Soc., N.Y. Acad. Scis. (emeritus). Home: 23901 Civic Center Way Apt 130 Malibu CA 90265-4883 Office: ISSEC PO Box 2661 Malibu CA 90265-7661

MATAS, MYRA DOROTHEA, interior architect and designer, kitchen and bath designer; b. San Francisco, Mar. 21, 1938; d. Arthur Joseph and Marjorie Dorothy (Johnson) Anderson; m. Michael Richard Matas Jr., Mar. 15, 1958; children: Michael Richard III, Kenneth Scott. Cert. interior design, Canada Coll.; cert. interior design, Calif. Owner, operator Miquel's Antiques Co., Millbrae, Calif., 1969-70, Miguel's Antiques & Interiors Co., Burlingame, Calif., 1970-79, Country Elegance Antiques & Interiors Co., Menlo Park, Calif., 1979-84, La France Boutique Co., 1979-84, Myra D. Matas Interior Design, San Francisco, 1984—, Lafayette, La., 1994—; mgr. La France Imports, Inc., 1982-92; pres., gen. contractor Artisans 3 Inc., Burlingame, 1988-92; gen. contractor Matas Constr., Millbrae, 1993—; instr. interior design dept. Canada Coll. Mem. Calif. Coun. Interior Design. Contbr. articles in field to profl. jours.

MATASEJE, VERONICA JULIA, sales executive; b. St. Ann's, Ontario, Can., Apr. 5, 1949; came to U.S., 1985; d. John and Anna Veronica M. Grad. H.S., Smithville, Can. Clk. typist, typesetter Crown Life Ins. Co., Toronto, Can., 1966-70; typesetter Toronto Life/Calendar Mag., 1970-71; typesetter, exec. sec. Cerebrus Prodns. Ltd., Toronto, 1971-74; pres. Veron Prodns. Ltd., Toronto, 1975-81, Acclaim Records Inc., Toronto, 1981-88; pvt. health care provider Las Vegas, Nev., 1989-94; retail sales mgr. Top Cats, Las Vegas, Nev., 1994—. Campaign vol. Dist. Atty., Las Vegas, 1994; vol. pilot Angel Planes, Las Vegas, 1989. Home: 4326 Caliente St Las Vegas NV 89119-5801 Office: Top Cats PO Box 61173 Las Vegas NV 89160-1173

MATEER, DAVID ARTHUR, public relations executive; b. Joliet, Ill., Aug. 31, 1957; s. Arthur George and Pauline (Havira) M. BS in Mktg., Bradley U., 1978; MS in Sports Mgmt., Western Ill. U., 1981. Asst. sports info. dir. DePaul U., Chgo., 1980-82; sports info. dir. Valparaiso (Ind.) U., 1982-87, part-time journalism instr., 1984; dir. communications for athletics U. Ill., Chgo., 1987-92; media coord. Gt. Alaska Shootout Basketball Tournament, 1992—; sports info. dir. U. Alaska, Anchorage, 1992—; adminstrv. asst. NBA pre-draft camp, Chgo., 1988-93; media ctr. chief-yachting Pan Am. Games, Michigan City, Ind., 1987; core com. mem. U. Ill. Chgo. student athlete assistance program, 1991-92. Mem. Coll. Sports Info. Dirs. Am. (NCAA legislation liaison com. 1995—, publs. cert. com. 1988-93, chmn. 1991-93, membership svcs. com. 1994-95, publs. contest com. 1983-88, publs. award publicity com. 1982-83, Best in Dist.-Season Rev. writing contest 1990, 92, 2d in Nation-Season Rev. writing contest 1991, 3d in Nation Season Preview writing contest 1993), U.S. Volleyball Media Assn., U.S. Basketball Writers Assn. Lutheran.

MATELIC, CANDACE TANGORRA, museum studies educator, consultant, museum director; b. Detroit, Aug. 21, 1952; d. Paul Eugene and Madeline Marie (Tangora) M.; m. Steven Joseph Mrozek, Sept. 17, 1983 (div. Sept. 1989); 1 child, Madeline Rose. BA, U. Mich., 1974; MA, SUNY, Oneonta, 1977. Interpretive specialist Living History Farms, Des Moines, 1978-80; mgr. adult edn. Henry Ford Mus./Greenfield Village, Dearborn, Mich., 1981-82, mgr. interpretive tng., 1982-84; dir., prof. mus. studies Cooperstown grad. program SUNY, Oneonta, 1986-94; exec. dir. Mission Houses Mus., Honolulu, 1994—; cons. history mus., 1979—; lectr., tchr. nat. and regional confs., workshops, seminars, 1979—; grant reviewer Nat. Endowment for the Humanities and Inst. for Mus. Svc., Washington, 1982—. Author: (with others) Exhibition Reader, 1992; co-author: A Pictorial History of Food in Iowa, 1980, Survey of 1200-Plus Museum Studies Graduates, 1988; contbr. articles and videos on mus. interpretation and tng., 1979—; author conf. proceedings. Mem. Am. Assn. State and Local History (sec., bd. dirs 1988—, program chmn. ann. meeting 1988), Assn. Living Hist. Farms and Agrl. Mus. (bd. dirs. 1980-88, pres. 1985), Midwest Open Air Mus. Coordinating Coun. (founder, bd. dirs., pres. 1978-80), Am. Assn. Mus. (mus. studies com. 1986—), Internat. Coun. Mus., Nat. Trust for Hist. Preservation. Democrat. Roman Catholic. Office: Mission Houses Mus 553 S King St Honolulu HI 96813

MATERA, FRANCES LORINE, elementary educator; b. Eustis, Nebr., June 28, 1926; d. Frank Daniel and Marie Mathilda (Hess) Daiss; m. Daniel Matera, Dec. 27, 1973; children: Richard William Post, Mary Jane Post Craig. BS in Edn., Concordia Tchrs. Coll., Seward, Nebr., 1956; MEd, U. Oreg., 1963; Luth. tchrs. diploma, Concordia Tchrs. Coll., Seward, 1947. Elementary tchr. Our Savior's Luth. Ch., Colorado Springs, Colo., 1954-57; tchr. 5th grade Monterey (Calif.) pub. schs., 1957-58; tchr. 1st grade Roseburg (Oreg.) Schs., 1959-60; tchr. several schs. Palm Springs (Calif.) Unified Sch. Dist., 1960-73; tchr. 3rd grade Vista del Monte Sch., Palm Springs, Calif., 1973-93; ret., 1993. Named Tchr. of the Yr., Palm Springs Unified Schs. Mem. Kappa Kappa Iota (chpt. and state pres.).

MATHENY, ROBERT LAVESCO, history educator, former university president; b. Lubbock, Tex., Jan. 15, 1933; s. Samuel Worth and Elsie Jane (Jones) M.; m. Sandra Hansen, July 6, 1973; children: Nelda, Monica, Cali. B.A., Eastern N.Mex. U., 1961, M.A., 1962; Ph.D., U. Ariz., 1975. Asst. prof. Eastern N.Mex. U., Portales, 1968-72, assoc. prof., 1972-76, v.p. Clovis campus, 1977-80, exec. v.p., 1981-83, pres., 1983-89, prof. dept. history, 1989—, dir. devel. and govt. rels., 1989—; dean continuing edn. Ft. Hays State U., Hays, Kans., 1980-81. Rockfellow Found. fellow, 1967-68. Mem. Western History Assn. Club: N.Mex. Amigos. Lodge: Rotary (Portales). Office: Ea NMex Univ Office Devel Portales NM 88130

MATHENY, SUSAN KAY, news editor; b. Sleepyeye, Minn., Nov. 21, 1950; d. Harvey B. and Elisabeth Dallmann; m. Ronald Edward Matheny, Sept. 16, 1973; children: Lisa, Marty. BA in English, Oreg. State U., 1975. Sec., receptionist C. Robert Hall, M.D., Corvallis, Oreg., 1975-79; transcriptionist Howard Korn, M.D., Corvallis, Oreg., 1979-80; sec. Ctrl. Oreg. Cmty. Edn. Ctr., Madras, Oreg., 1987-89; news editor Madras Pioneer, 1989—. Contbr. articles to profl. publs. Mem. adv. bd. Ctrl. Oreg. C.C., Madras, 1987—; mem. Oreg. Peaceworks, Madras, 1987-94; jr. H.S. youth group leader United Meth. Ch., Madras, 1992-94, sr. H.S. youth group asst., 1994—. Home: 3010 NE Elm Ln Madras OR 97741-8971 Office: Madras Pioneer Newspaper 241 SE 6th St Madras OR 97741-1635

MATHER, E. COTTON, geography educator; b. West Branch, IA, Jan. 3, 1918; s. Anders Vetti and Alleda (Zwickey) M.; m. Julia Marie Eiler, Dec. 23, 1944; children: Cotton Vetti, J'Lee Alleda. AB, U. Ill., Champaign, 1940, MS, 1941; PhD, U. Wis., Madison, 1950. Geographer Army Map Svc., Washington, 1941; rsch. analyst Office of Strategic Svcs., Washington, 1942-44; instr. U. Wis., Madison, Wis., 1945-46; assoc. to full prof., dept. chmn. U. Minn., Mpls., 1957-85; pres. N.Mex. Geog. Soc., Mesilla, N.Mex., 1985-94; vis. prof. numerous univs. U.S., Can., overseas, 1959-88. Co-editor: Atlas of Kentucky, 1977, (14) International Geographical Guidebooks of North America, 1992; co-author: India, Cultural Patterns and Processes, 1982, Prairie Border Country, 1980, Upper Coulee Country, 1975, St. Croix Border Country, 1968, Beyond the Great Divide, 1992, Registered Places of New Mexico, 1994. Recipient research award, Assn. of Am. Geographers, 1954, Ford Found., 1964, 65. Mem. Assn. Am. Geographers, Pierce County Geog. Soc., Internat. Geog. Union, N.Mex. Geog. Soc., Ctr. Am. Places (dir.), Explorers Club. Home: PO Box 1184 Mesilla NM 88046-1184 Office: NMex Geograph Soc PO Box 1201 Mesilla NM 88046-1201

MATHER, ROBERT LAURANCE, physicist; b. Clarksville, Iowa, Oct. 1, 1921; s. Milo Ghion and Lillie Mabel (Lister) M.; m. F. Isabel Brown, Sept. 29, 1956; children: Anne, David. BS in Physics, Iowa State U., 1942; MA in Physics, Columbia U., 1947; PhD in Physics, U. Calif., Berkeley, 1951. Physicist U.S. Naval Ordnance Lab., Washington, 1942-44; electronic engr. Radio Corp. Am., Harrison, N.J., 1944-46; physicist N.Am. Aviation, Berkeley, Calif., 1950-52, U.S. Naval Radiol. Def. Lab., San Francisco, 1952-69; electronic engr. U.S. Naval Ocean Systems Ctr., San Diego, 1969-85, Computer Scis. Corp., San Diego, 1985-87; retired, 1987; vis. scholar U. Calif., Berkeley, 1991—; mem. physics astronomy coun. Iowa State U., Ames, 1992—. Fellow Am. Physical Soc.; mem. IEEE, AAAS, Sigma Xi. Home: 100 Bay Pl Apt 2110 Oakland CA 94610-4436

MATHERS, EARL FRANK, economic developer; b. Marietta, Ohio, Mar. 26, 1950; s. Earl Frank and Mildred Augusta (Lunsford) M.; m. Kalie Rea Rademacher, Oct. 6, 1980; children: Jonathan, Joshua, Julie, Jena. BA, U. Mont., 1980; MPA, U. Wyo., 1986. Dir. phys. plant Northwest Coll., Powell, Wyo., 1981-85; dir. vocat. svcs. RENEW, Sheridan, Wyo., 1986-88; county devel. dir. Fremont County, Lander, Wyo., 1988-91; exec. dir. Campbell County Econ. Devel. Corp., Gillette, Wyo., 1991-95; CEO Northeast Wyo. Econ. Devel. Coalition, 1995—; cons. adminstr. City of Lander, 1989-90; Am. Advisor to Russia, 1994—. Contbr. articles to profl. jours. Mem. Gillette Campus Bd., 1983—, Gillette Adminstrv. Caucus, 1991; del. Rocky Mountain Trade Corridor, Helena, Mont., 1992. Mem. Am. Econ. Devel. Coun., Wyo. Econ. Devel. Assn., Rotary. Republican. Mem. Ch. of Christ. Home: 7110 Mather Ave Gillette WY 82718-7494 Office: Campbell County Econ Devel PO Box 3948 222 S Gillette Ave #510 Gillette WY 82717-3948

MATHERS, MARGARET, charitable agency consultant, political activist; b. Ada, Okla., Feb. 16, 1929; d. Robert Lee and Josephine Margaret (Reed) Erwin; m. Coleman F. Moss, Sept. 1956 (div. 1966); children: Carol Lee Doria, Marilyn Frances; m. Boyd Leroy Mathers, Apr. 10, 1967. BS in Music, Tex. U., 1950. Svc. rep. Gen. Tel. Co., Santa Monica, Calif., 1955-58; tchr. pvt. sch., Santa Monica, 1958-60; computer program and data analyst System Devel. Corp., Santa Monica, 1961-66; computer programmer Inst. Def. Analyses, Arlington, Va., 1966-70; typist, transcriber, Edgewater, Md., 1971-80; sec. People Assisting the Homeless, 1992-94, bd. dirs., 1985-95; asst. dir. San Juan Cath. Charities, Farmington, N.Mex., 1993—; sec. Cmty. Network Coun., 1992-94, treas. 1994—; pres. San Juan Coun. Cmty. Agys., 1986-87, treas., 1987-89, 92—, sec., 1989-90; pres. Davidsonville-Mayo Health Assn., Edgewater, 1973-76, 77-80; cons. in field, 1983—. Chmn. county Libertarian Party of N.Mex., San Juan County, 1985, sec. ctrl. com., 1988-92, mem. ctrl. com., 1988—; asst. sec. Our Lady of Perpetual Help, Parish Coun., Edgewater, 1979-82, Parish Coun. Sacred Heart, Farmington, 1987, sec., 1988-90, mem. social justice com., 1992; mem. adv. bd. San Juan County DNA Legal Aid, 1992, sec., 1993; sec. River Club Community Assn., Edgewater, 1975-82; mem. selection com. Habitat for Humanity, 1990; mem. San Juan County Task Force on Housing, 1991, Task Force on Transp., 1991; sec. Com. Preserve 2d Amendment Rights, 1994. Mem. Informed Citizens Alliance, Secular Franciscan Order. Roman Catholic. Avocations: nature study, birdwatching, reading, music, Indian studies. Office: San Juan Cath Charities 119 W Broadway Farmington NM 87401-6419

MATHESON, LOU THELMA, mental health counselor, multicultural specialist; b. Seattle, Mar. 8, 1931; d. Albert Lee Stears and Thelma Mamie (Bennett) Brennan; m. Asif Zahir, Dec. 12, 1953 (div. 1967); children: Jeffery, Kim, Tamur, Sheenkai, Zalmai; m. Donald M. Matheson, Oct. 15, 1973; stepchildren: Paul, Charlene, David, Marjorie, Dianne, Donna, Charles. BA in Music, Marylhurst Coll., 1952; MA in Psychology, Antioch West U., 1977. Cert. mental health counselor, Wash. Rehab. supr. Pacific State Hosp., Pomona, Calif., 1954-56; rehab. counselor Fircrest Sch., Seattle, 1966-69; assoc. dir. U. Wash., Seattle, 1972-74; rschr., writer Wash. State Office Indian Affairs, Olympia, 1974-75; mental health profl. Puyallup Tribe, Tacoma, Wash., 1975-80; coord. bi-cultural program Spokane (Wash.) Cmty. Mental Health Ctr., 1980-92; cons., counselor Spokane, 1992—; adj. faculty Gonzaga U., Spokane, 1992—, Antioch West U., Seattle, 1993—, N.W. Indian Coll., Spokane, 1994; workshop and conf. presenter various orgns., 1985—. Author: The People Speak, 1975, (with others) X-Cult Training for Mental Health Professionals, 1983. Bd. dirs. Urban Indian Health Svcs., Spokane, 1982-86; co-founder, mem. Native Am. Polit. Action, Spokane, 1982-88; minority rep. Child Protective Team, Spokane, 1990—; Am. Indian rep. Ethnic Minority Adv. Com., State of Wash., 1980-94. Fellow U. Wash., 1970-71. Mem. Am. Counseling Assn. Democrat.

MATHESON, SUZANNE ADRIE, insurance broker; b. L.A., Feb. 13, 1958; d. Charles Barton and Catherine Isabella (Manley) M.; m. Michael Trifunovic, July 8, 1978 (div. Sept. 1987), 1 child, Joshua Michael. Student, U. So. Calif., L.A., Am. Film Inst., L.A., Brentwood Sch. Fine Art, Santa Monica, Calif. Lic. property/casualty broker; lic. life/health/disability broker. Model Blair Agy., Beverly Hills, Calif., 1976-80; writer AFI, L.A., 1976-80; ins. broker James Econn & Co., L.A., 1976-78; ins. broker Miller & DeCray, L.A., 1978—, Santa Monica, Calif., 1978—. Author: American Anthology of Poetic Writing, 1980; (screenplay) Human Acts, 1982. Mem. Ind. Ins. Agts. Am., Sports Club L.A. Republican. Home: 720 22nd St Santa Monica CA 90402-3124 Office: Miller & DeCray Ins Brokers 1919 Santa Monica Blvd Santa Monica CA 90404-1951

MATHEWS, ANNE JONES, international consultant, library director; b. Phila., Feb. 5, 1928; d. Edmond Fulton and Anne Ruth (Reichner) Jones; m. Frank Samuel Mathews, June 16, 1951; children: Lisa Anne Bingham, David Morgan, Lynne Elizabeth Beitenhader, Alison Fulton Sawyer. AB, Wheaton Coll., 1949; MA, U. Denver, 1965, PhD, 1977. Mem. field staff Intervarsity Christian Fellowship, Chgo., 1949-51; Interviewer supr. Colo. Market Rsch. Svcs., Denver, 1952-64; reference libr. Oreg. State U., Corvallis, 1965-67; program dir. Ctrl. Colo. Libr. System, Denver, 1969-70; inst. dir. U.S. Office of Edn., Inst. Grant, 1979; asst. prof., dir. pub. rels. U. Denver Grad. Sch. Librarianship & Info. Mgmt., 1970-76, dir. continuing edn., 1977-80, assoc. prof., 1977-79, prof., 1979-85; dir. Office Libr. Programs U.S. Dept. Edn., Washington, 1986-91; dir. Nat. Libr. Edn., Washington, 1992-94; cons.

Acad. Ednl. Devel., Washington, 1994—; vis. lectr. Simmons Coll. Sch. Libr. Sci., Boston, 1977; cons. USIA, 1984-85, mem. book and libr. adv. com., 1981-91; faculty assoc. Danforth Found., 1974-84; speaker in field; mem. secondary sch. curriculum com. Jefferson County Pub. Schs., Colo., 1976-78; mem. adv. com. Golden H.S., 1973-77; mem. adv. coun. White House Conf. on Librs. and Info. Svs., 1991; del. Internat. Fedn. Libr. Assns. Author, editor 3 books; contbr. articles to profl. jours., numerous chpts. to books. Mem. rural librs. and humanities program Colo. planning and resource bd. NEH, 1982-83; bd. mgrs. Friends of Denver Pub. Libr., 1976-82; pres. Faculty Women's Club, Colo. Sch. Mines, 1963-64. Mem. ALA (visionary leaders com. 1987-89, coun. mem. 1979-83, com on accreditation 1984-85, orientation com. 1974-77, 83-84, pub. rels. com.), Am. Soc. Info. Sci. (pub. rels. chmn. 1971), Mountain Plains Libr. Assn. (profl. devel. com. 1979-80, pub. rels. and publs. com. 1973-75, continuing edn. com. 1973-76), Colo. Libr. Assn. (pres. 1974, bd. dirs. 1973-75, continuing edn. com. 1976-80), Assn. Libr. & Info. Sci. Edn. (communication com. 1978-80, program com. 1977-78), Cosmos Club (Washington). Home: 492 Mount Evans Rd Golden CO 80401-9626

MATHEWS, BARBARA EDITH, gynecologist; b. Santa Barbara, Calif., Oct. 5, 1946; d. Joseph Chesley and Pearl (Cieri) Mathews; AB, U. Calif., 1969; MD, Tufts U., 1972. Diplomate Am. Bd. Ob-Gyn. Intern, Cottage Hosp., Santa Barbara, 1972-73, Santa Barbara Gen. Hosp., 1972-73; resident in ob-gyn Beth Israel Hosp., Boston, 1973-77; clin. fellow in ob-gyn Harvard U., 1973-76, instr., 1976-77; gynecologist Sansum Med. Clinic, Santa Barbara, 1977—; faculty mem. ann. postgrad. course Harvard Med. Sch.; bd. dirs. Sansum Med. Clinic; dir. ann. postgrad course UCLA Med. Sch. Bd. dirs. Meml. Rehab. Found., Santa Barbara, Channel City Club, Santa Barbara, Music Acad. of the West, Santa Barbara; mem. citizen's continuing edn. adv. council Santa Barbara C.C.; moderator Santa Barbara Cottage Hosp. Cmty. Health Forum. Fellow ACS, Am. Coll. Ob-gyn.; mem. AMA, Am. Soc. Colposcopy and Cervical Pathology (dir. 1982-84), Harvard U. Alumni Assn., Tri-counties Obstet. and Gynecol. Soc. (pres. 1981-82), Phi Beta Kappa. Clubs: Birnam Wood Golf (Santa Barbara). Author: (with L. Burke) Colposcopy in Clinical Practice, 1977; contbg. author Manual of Ambulatory Surgery, 1982. Home: 2105 Anacapa St Santa Barbara CA 93105-3503 Office: 317 W Pueblo St Santa Barbara CA 93105-4355

MATHEWS, KENNETH PINE, physician, educator; b. Schenectady, N.Y., Apr. 1, 1921; s. Raymond and Marguerite Elizabeth (Pine) M.; m. Alice Jean Elliott, Jan. 26, 1952 (dec.); children: Susan Kay, Ronald Elliott, Robert Pine; m. Winona Beatrice Rosenburg, Nov. 8, 1975. A.B., U. Mich., 1941, M.D., 1943. Diplomate Am. Bd. Internal Medicine, Am. Bd. Allergy and Immunology (past. sec.). Intern, asst. resident, resident in medicine Univ. Hosp., Ann Arbor, Mich., 1943-45, 48-50; mem. faculty dept. medicine med. sch. U. Mich., 1950—, assoc. prof. internal medicine, 1956-61, prof., 1961-86, prof. emeritus, 1986—, head div. allergy, 1967-83; adj. mem. Scripps Clinic and Research Found., La Jolla, Calif., 1986—; past chmn. residency rev. com. for allergy and immunology, past chmn. allergy and immunology rsch. com. NIH. Co-author: A Manual of Clinical Allergy, 2d edit, 1967; editor: Jour. Allergy and Clin. Immunology, 1968-72; contbr. numerous articles in field to profl. jours. Served to capt. M.C. AUS, 1946-48. Recipient Disting. Service award Am. Acad. Allergy, 1976; Faculty Disting. Achievement award U. Mich., 1984. Fellow Am. Acad. Allergy (past pres.), A.C.P. (emeritus); mem. Am. Assn. Immunologists (emeritus), Ctrl. Soc. Clin. Rsch. (emeritus), Am. Fedn. Clin. Rsch., Alpha Omega Alpha, Phi Beta Kappa. Home: 7080 Caminito Estrada La Jolla CA 92037-5714 Office: Scripps Clinic & Rsch Found Dept Molecular & Exptl Medicine 10666 N Torrey Pines Rd La Jolla CA 92037-1027

MATHEWS, LARRY ARTHUR, research physical chemist; b. Bremerton, Wash., Mar. 23, 1936; s. Francis Arthur and Ouida Gage (Christian) M.; m. Esther Ellen Donohoe Sires, June 14, 1971 (div. Aug. 1982); children: Sean Arthur, Scott Francis, Staci Elizabeth; m. Linda Evonne Wright, Jan. 9, 1987. BSChemE, U. Wash., 1959; MS in Engring., U. Utah, 1968, PhDChemE, 1969. Technologist Shell Oil Co., Anacortes, Wash., 1959-60; assoc. engr. Boeing Co., Seattle, 1960-61; NDEA fellow U. Utah, Salt Lake City, 1961-64, rsch. and teaching asst., 1965-69; rsch. phys. chemist Naval Weapons Ctr., China Lake, Calif., 1970-93; cons. Gt. Basin Air Pollution Control Dist., Bishop, Calif., 1976-80; mem. Owens Dry Lake Task Force Com., Bishop, 1980-93, Joint Tri-Svcs. Coordinating Group, Smoke and Aerosol Working Group, 1983-93. Contbr. articles to profl. jours.; patentee method of producing cumulus clouds. Carkeek Meml. fellow, 1955-59. Mem. Sigma Xi, Tau Beta Pi, Phi Lambda Upsilon, Zeta Mu Tau. Home: 1012 W Kinnett Ave Ridgecrest CA 93555 Office: Naval Air Weapons Sta Code 823E00D China Lake CA 93555-3043

MATHEWS, TIMOTHY LEROY, military officer; b. Kalamazoo, Mich., June 7, 1957; s. Donald Leroy and Grace Megumi (Ota) M.; m. Barbara Jean Warren, June 7, 1982. BSME, U. N.Mex., 1987. Enlisted USMC, 1976, advanced through ranks to staff sgt., commd. 2d lt., 1987, advanced through grades to capt., 1991; served in Persian Gulf War and Liberation of Kuwait, 1990-91; sr. cryptologic officer in Operation Restore Hope Somalia, 1992-93; signals intelligence and spl. security officer 1st Marine Divsn., Camp Pendleton, Calif., 1991-94; mem. staff comdr.-in-chief Pacific Fleet HQs, Pearl Harbor, Hawaii, 1994—. Participant Project Wildlife, San Diego County, 1993. Decorated Navy Commendation medal, 1990-91; recipient Leadership award Nat. U., San Diego, 1992. Mem. Marine Corps Assn., Armed Forces Comm. and Elec. Assn.

MATHEWS, WILLIAM EDWARD, neurological surgeon, educator; b. Indpls., July 12, 1934; s. Ples Leo and Roxie Elizabeth (Allen) M.; m. Eleanor Jayne Comer, Aug. 24, 1956 (div. 1976); children: Valerie, Clarissa, Marie, Blair; m. Carol Ann. Koza, Sept. 12, 1987; 1 child, William Kyle. BS, Ball State U., 1958; DO, Kriksville Coll. Osteopathic Medicine, 1961; MD, U. Calif., L.A., 1962; student, Armed Forces Trauma Sch., Ft. Sam Houston, Tex., 1967-68. Diplomate Am. Bd. Neurol. and Orthopedic Surgery, Am. Bd. Pain Mgmt., Am. Bd. Indsl. Medicine, Am. Bd. Spinal Surgeons (v.p. 1990-92). Intern Kirksville (Mo.) Osteopathic Hosp., 1961-62; resident neurosurgery Los Angeles County Gen. Hosp., 1962-67; with Brookes Army Hosp., Ft. Sam Houston, 1967-68; with 8th field hosp. U.S. Army Neurosurgeon C.O. & 933 Med. Corp, Vietnam, 1968-69; chief neurosurgery Kaiser Med. Group, Walnut Creek, Calif., 1969-77; staff neurosurgeon Mt. Diablo Med. Ctr., Concord, Calif., 1977—; chief resident neurosugery Los Angeles County Gen. Hosp., 1962-67; chief neurosurgery Kaiser Permanente Med. Group, Walnut Creek, 1969-77; comdg. officer 933d Med. Detachment Vietnam R.V.N., 1968-69; asst. prof. Kriksvelle Coll. Osteopathic Medicine, 1958-62; asst. lecturing prof. Neuroanatomy U. Calif. Coll. of Medicine, 1962-65. Author: (jour./book) Intracerebral Missile Injuries, 1972, Early Return to Work Following Cervical Disc Surgery, 1991; contbr. articles to profl. jours. Mem. adv. com. Rep. Presdl. Selection Com.Maj. U.S. Army, 1967-69, Vietnam. Recipient Disting. Svc. award Internat. Biography, 1987; scholar Psi Sigma Alpha, 1989. Fellow Congress Neurol. Surgeons (joint sect. on neurotrauma), Royal Coll. Medicine, Am. Acad. Neurologic and Orthopedic Surgeons (pres. 1981-82); mem. AMA, Calif. Med. Assn., San Francisco Neurologic, Contra Costa County Med. Soc. Roman Catholic.

MATHEWS, WILMA KENDRICK, public relations executive; b. Danville, Va., Dec. 23, 1945; d. Clarence Blanchard and Tina Collins (Powell) Kendrick; AA, Stratford Coll., 1966, BA, 1970; student East Carolina U., 1966-67, U. Md., European div., 1967-68, Guilford Coll., 1978-80. Asst. editor The Commonwealth Mag., Richmond, Va., 1970-72; news editor The Comml. Appeal, Danville, Va., 1972-73; pub. rels. mgr. Danville C. of C., 1973-74; publs. officer Bowman Gray Bapt. Hosp. Med. Ctr., Winston-Salem, N.C., 1974-78; sr. pub. rels. specialist Western Electric, 1978-82; mgr. pub. rels. AT&T Internat., Basking Ridge, N.J., 1982-84; media rels. mgr. AT&T Network Systems, 1985-87, mgr. pub. rels. field support, 1987-90, pub. rels. adv. dir., 1990-93, cons., 1993—; dir. pub. rels. Ariz. State U., 1995—; sr. pub. rels. adv. N.C. Epilepsy Info. Svc., 1979-80. Co-author: On Deadline: Managing Media Relations, 1985, 94; Inside Organizational Communications, 2d edit., 1985, Marketing Communications, 1987; Mem. Danville Bicentennial Commn., 1972-74; bd. dirs. Nat. Tobacco-Textile Mus., 1973-74; mem. Danville City Beautiful Com., 1973-74, Maplewood Cultural Commn., 1986-87. Fellow Internat. Assn. Bus. Communicators (dir. 1978-81, pres. N.C. chpt. 1977, 78, dir. Found. 1984-87, chmn. Found. 1987-90, accreditation bd. 1983-89, 94—, bd. chmn. 1990-91), Pub. Rels. Soc. Am.; mem. Danville Hist. Soc. (dir. 1973-74), N.C. Zool. Soc., Smithsonian Instn., Internat. TV Assn. (sec. N.C. chpt. 1979-80), Internat. Pub. Rels. Assn., Coun. for Communications Mgmt. (bd. dirs. 1987-89), Friends of Maplewood Libr. (pres. 1985-86), Ahwatukee Foothills C. of C. (bd. dirs. 1994—), Stratford Coll. Alumni Assn., Internat. Order Job's Daus. Republican. Baptist. Home and Office: 14836 S Foxtail Ln Phoenix AZ 85048-4335

MATHIAS, BETTY JANE, communications and community affairs consultant, writer, editor, lecturer; b. East Ely, Nev., Oct. 22, 1923; d. Royal F. and Dollie B. (Bowman) M.; student Merritt Bus. Sch., 1941, 42, San Francisco State U., 1941-42; 1 child, Dena. Asst. publicity dir. Oakland (Calif.) Area War Chest and Community Chest, 1943-46; pub. rels. Am. Legion, Oakland, 1946-47; asst. to pub. rels. dir. Cen. Bank of Oakland, 1947-49; pub. rels. dir. East Bay chpt. of Nat. Safety Council, 1949-51; propr., mgr. Mathias Pub. Rels. Agy., Oakland, 1951-60; gen. assignment reporter and teen news editor Daily Rev., Hayward, Calif., 1960-62; freelance pub. rels. and writing, Oakland, 1962-66, 67-69; dir. corp. communications Systech Fin. Corp., Walnut Creek, Calif., 1969-71; v.p. corp. communications Consol. Capital companies, Oakland, 1972-79, v.p. community affairs, Emeryville, Calif., 1981-84, v.p. spl. projects, 1984-85; v.p., dir. Consol. Capital Realty Svcs., Inc., Oakland, 1973-77; v.p., dir. Centennial Adv. Corp., Oakland, 1976-77; communications cons., 1979—; cons. Mountainair Realty, Cameron Park, Calif., 1986-87; pub. rels. coord. Tuolumne County Visitors Bur., 1989-90; lectr. in field; bd. dirs. Oakland YWCA, 1944-45, ARC, Oakland, So. Alameda County chpt., 1967-69, Family Ctr., Children's Hosp. Med. Ctr. No. Calif., 1982-85, March of Dimes, 1983-85, Equestrian Ctr. of Walnut Creek, Calif., 1983-84, also sec.; adult and publs. adv. Internat. Order of the Rainbow for Girls, 1953-78; communications arts adv. com. Ohlone (Calif.) Coll., 1979-85, chmn., 1982-84; mem. adv. bd. dept. mass communications Calif. State U.-Hayward, 1985; pres. San Francisco Bay Area chpt. Nat. Reyes Syndrome Found., 1981-86; vol. staff Columbia Actors' Repertory, Columbia, Calif., 1986-87, 89; mem. exec. bd., editor newsletter Tuolumne County Dem. Club, 1987; publicity chmn. 4th of July celebration Tuolumne County C. of C., 1988; vol. children's dept. Tuolumne County Pub. Libr., 1993—. Recipient Grand Cross of Color award Internat. Order of Rainbow for Girls, 1955. Order Eastern Star (publicity chmn. Calif. state 1955). Editor East Bay Mag., 1966-67, TIA Traveler, 1969, Concepts, 1979-83. Home: 20575 Gopher Dr Sonora CA 95370-9034

MATHIAS, HARRY MICHAEL, cinematographer, consultant, author; b. London, Aug. 15, 1945; came to U.S., 1949.; s. Eric Manfred and Elsa (Herbst) M.; m. Ann C. Johnston, Oct. 4, 1987; 1 child, Morgan A. AA, San Francisco City Coll., 1965; BA, Calif. State U., 1968, MA, 1974. Dir. photography numerous motion pictures, 1969-88; sr. cons. Panavision Inc., Tarzana, Calif., 1981—; cons. Eastman Kodak Co., Rochester, N.Y., 1982-84; pres. Data Engring., Santa Monica, Calif., 1986—; mem. faculty UCLA, 1984—; lectr. Swedish Film Inst., Am. Film Inst., Stanford U. Author: Electronic Cinematography, 1980; author (with others) Image Quality, 1984, The American Cinematographers Handbook, 1986, HDTV: The Politics, Policies and Economics of Tommorow's Television, 1990; contbr. articles to profl. jours.; dir. photography Solly's Dinner, 1980 (Oscar nomination). Mem. Mus. Contemporary Art, Los Angeles, 1988, Los Angeles County Mus. Art, 1987, 88. Mem. Soc. Motion Picture and TV Engrs., Working Group on High Definition Electronic Prodn. Stds. (chmn. film splty. com.). Democrat. Home: PO Box 3174 Thousand Oaks CA 91359-0174

MATHIAS, LESLIE MICHAEL, electronic manufacturing company executive; b. Bombay, Dec. 17, 1935; came to U.S., 1957; s. Paschal Lawrence and Dulcine (D'Souza) M.; m. Vivian Mae Doolittle, Dec. 16, 1962. BSc, U. Bombay, 1957; BS, San Jose (Calif.) State U., 1961. Elec. engr. Indian Standard Metal, Bombay, 1957; sales engr. Bleisch Engring. and Tool, Mt. View, Calif., 1958-60; gen. mgr. Meadows Terminal Bds., Cupertino, Calif., 1961-63; prodn. mgr. Sharidon Corp., Menlo Park, Calif., 1963-67, Videx Corp., Sunnyvale, Calif., 1967-68, Data Tech. Corp., Mt. View, 1968-69; pres. L.G.M. Mfg., Inc., Mt. View, 1969-83; pvt. practice plating cons. Los Altos, Calif., 1983-87; materials mgr. Excel Cirs., Santa Clara, Calif., 1987-91, 93—, acct. mgr., 1991-93, materials mgr., 1993—. Social chmn. Internat. Students, San Jose, 1958-59. Mem. Nat. Fedn. Ind. Bus., Calif. Cirs. Assn., Better Bus. Bur., Purchasing Assn., U.S. C. of C. Roman Catholic. Home: 20664 Mapletree Pl Cupertino CA 95014-0449

MATHIES, ALLEN WRAY, JR., physician, hospital administrator; b. Colorado Springs, Colo., Sept. 23, 1930; s. Allen W. and Esther S. (Norton) M.; m. Lewise Austin, Aug. 23, 1956; children: William A., John N. BA, Colo. Coll., 1952; MS, Columbia U., 1956, PhD., 1958; MD, U. Vt., 1961. Rsch. assoc. U. Vt., Burlington, 1957-61; intern L.A. County Hosp., 1961-62; resident in pediatrics L.A. Gen. Hosp., 1962-64; asst. prof. pediatrics U. So. Calif., L.A., 1964-68, assoc. prof., 1968-71, prof., 1971—, assoc. dean, 1969-74, interim dean, 1974-75, dean, 1975-85; head physician Communicable Disease Svc. U. So. Calif., Los Angeles, 1964-75; pres., chief exec. officer Huntington Meml. Hosp., Pasadena, Calif., 1985-94; pres., CEO So. Calif. Healthcare Sys., Pasadena, 1992—; bd. dirs. Pacific Mut. Contbr. articles to med. jours. Bd. dirs. Occidental Coll. With U.S. Army, 1953-55. Mem. Am. Acad. Pediatrics, Infectious Disease Soc. Am., Am. Pediatric Soc., Soc. Pediatric Rsch. Republican. Episcopalian. Home: 314 Arroyo Dr South Pasadena CA 91030-1623 Office: Huntington Meml Hosp PO Box 7013 Pasadena CA 91109-7013

MATHIESEN, TIMOTHY ROLLIN, photographer; b. Sacramento, Calif., Nov. 21, 1946; s. Roy Melfred and Marilyn (Kamp) M.; m. Sally Griffin Mathiesen, July 6, 1968; children: Sean David, Daniel Bryan (twins). B Profl. Arts, Brooks Inst. Photography, 1970, postgrad., 1973-75. Photographic systems engr. Skylab and viking programs Martin-Marietta Corp, Denver, 1970-75; tech. rep. Fuji Photo Film USA, Hollywood, 1976-81; tech. mgr. Fuji Photo Film USA, Carson, Calif., 1981-89; mgr. photographic svcs. Fuji Photo Film USA, Cypress, Calif., 1989—; mem. adv. bd. Internat. Photography Hall of Fame, Oklahoma City, Okla., 1993—. Co-author: A Game for All America, 1988, 1992 Profl. Photographers Am. Loan Collection Book, 1992, 1993 Profl. Photographers Am. Loan Collection Book, 1993; photographer: (book) Muscle Aerobics, 1983; contbr. articles to profl. jours.; represented in permanent collection Internat. Photography Hall of Fame, 1993. Recipient Silver Beaver award Boy Scouts Am., 1987, Vigil honor, 1988. Fellow Am. Soc. Photographers (bd. govs. 1994—, gold medal 1993), Profl. Photographers Calif. (pres. 1983-84, svc. award 1987), Cameracraftsmen Am.; mem. Profl. Photographers Am. (photog. exhbn. com. 1993—, photog. craftsman 1976, Master of Photography award 1977, nat. award 1987). Roman Catholic. Home: 7352 Rockmont Ave Westminster CA 92683-6125 Office: Fuji Photo Film USA 6200 Phyllis Dr Cypress CA 90630-5239

MATHIS, JENNIFER, food products executive; b. 1951. BS in Acctg., Calif. State U., Fresno, 1974. Sr. acct. Touche Ross & Co., Fresno, 1974-77; with Valley Fig Growers, Inc., 1977—, now pres. Office: Valley Fig Growers Inc 2028 S 3rd St Fresno CA 93702-4156*

MATHIS, KATHLEEN MARIE, drug abuse counselor; b. Twin Falls, Idaho, Nov. 8, 1953; d. Vernon Leroy and Opal May (Johnson) Bretsch; m. Willie Curtis Mathis, May 24, 1981 (div. Feb. 1994); 1 child, Nicole Marie. Cert. chm. dependency counselor. Counselor The Bonus Plan, Van Nuys, Calif., 1983-93; program dir. Inter-Agy. Drug Abuse Recovery Program, Van Nuys, 1994—; instr., asst. dir. Inst. for Advanced Counseling, Woodland Hills, Calif., 1991—. Mem. sch. bd. San Fernando Valley Acad. Mem. Am. Counseling Assn., San Fernando Valley Bd. Realtors. Home: 18926 Sherman Way Apt 303 Reseda CA 91335-7706 Office: 7400 Van Nuys Blvd Ste 207 Van Nuys CA 91405-1972

MATHISON, THOMAS K., food products executive; b. 1926. Pvt. practice Mathison & Mathison, Wenatchee, Wash., 1951-90; with Stemilt Growers, Inc., Wenatchee, Wash., 1964—. Office: Stemilt Growers Inc Olds Station Warehouse Rd Wenatchee WA 98801*

MATHUR, ASHOK, telecommunications engineer, educator, researcher; b. Gorakhpur, Uttar Pradesh, India; came to U.S., 1979; s. Raj Swarup and Savitri Mathur; m. Jayanti Srivastava, May 31, 1978; children: Menka, Puja. BS, U. Agra, India, 1963, MS, 1965; PhD, U. Southampton, Hampshire, Eng., 1974. Cert. telecommunications engr., Calif.; teaching credential, Calif. Lectr. upper atmospheric physics Kanpur, India, 1965-68; doctoral researcher U. Southampton, 1968-73; postdoctoral research fellow U. Poitiers, Vienne, France, 1973-74; assoc. prof., research supr U. Kanpur, 1974-79; mem. tech. staff telecomms. sci. and engring. divsn. Jet Propulsion Lab. Calif. Inst. Tech., Pasadena, 1979-92; prin. systems engr. applied tech. divsn. Computer Scis. Corp., Pasadena, 1992—. Contbr. numerous publs. to profl. jours.; mem. editorial bd. Acta Ciencia Indica Jour., 1975-78. Recipient 10-Yr. Svc. award Jet Propulsion Lab. Calif. Inst. Tech., 1990, Overseas Students award Brit. Coun., London, 1968, Délégation Générale a la Recherche Scientifique et Technique award, Paris, 1973, cert. of merit for disting. svcs. Internat. Biographical Ctr., Cambridge, Eng., 1988, Group Achievement award NASA, 1991. Mem. IEEE (sr.), AIAA (vice chmn. pub. policy San Gabriel Valley, sec. L.A. 1987-92), The European Phys. Soc., Calif. Inst. Tech. Mgmt. Club, Armed Forces Comms. and Electronics Assn. Home: 1923B Huntington Dr Duarte CA 91010-2637 Office: Jet Propulsion Lab MS 264-829 4800 Oak Grove Dr Pasadena CA 91109-8001

MATIN, ABDUL, microbiology educator, consultant; b. Delhi, India, May 8, 1941; came to U.S., 1964, naturalized, 1983; s. Mohammed and Zohra (Begum) Said; m. Mimi Keyhan, June 21, 1968. BS, U. Karachi, Pakistan, 1960, MS, 1962; PhD, UCLA, 1969. Lectr. St. Joseph's Coll., Karachi, 1962-64; research assoc. UCLA, 1964-71; sci. officer U. Groningen, Kerklaan, The Netherlands, 1971-75; from asst. prof. to prof. microbiology and immunology Stanford U., Calif., 1975—; prof. Western Hazardous Substances Rsch. Ctr. Stanford U.; prof. western hazardous substances Rsch. Ctr., Stanford U.; cons. Engenics, 1982-84, Monsanto, 1984—, Chlorox, 1992—; chmn. Stanford Recombinant DNA panel; lectr. ASM Found.; mem. Accreditation Bd. for Engring. and Tech.; mem. panel Yucca Mountain Microbial Activity, Dept. of Energy; convener of microbiol. workshop and confs. Mem. editorial bd. Jour. of Bacteriology; bd. dirs. Ann. Rev. Microbiol., Rev. of NSF and other Grants; contbr. numerous publs. to sci. jours. Fellow Fulbright Found., 1964, NSF, 1981—, Ctr. for Biotech. Research, 1981-85, EPA, 1981-84, NIH, Coll. Biotech., U.N. Tokten, 1987. Mem. AAAS, AAUP, Am Soc. for Microbiology (Found. lectr. 1991-92), Soc. Gen. Microbiology, Soc. Indsl. Microbiology, No. Soc. Indsl. Microbiology (bd. dirs.), Biophys. Soc. Home: 690 Coronado Ave Stanford CA 94305-1039 Office: Stanford U Dept Microbiology and Immunology Fairchild Sci Bldg Stanford CA 94305-5402

MATISOFF, SUSAN, cultural research organization administrator. Dir. Ctr. East-Asian Studies, Stanford U., Calif. Office: Stanford University Ctr E-Asian Studies 300 Lasuen St Stanford CA 94305-8311

MATLEY, BENVENUTO GILBERT (BEN MATLEY), computer engineer, educator, consultant; b. Monroe, La., Sept. 8, 1930; s. Welcome Gilbert and Lucette Marie (Renaud) M.; m. Patricia Jean McWilliams, June 21, 1959; children: Elizabeth, Katherine, John, Stephen, Richard, David. AB, San Diego State U., 1960; MBA, U. So. Calif., 1964; EdD, Nova U., 1980. Cert. data processor. Mathematician, engr. various data processing and computing firms, San Diego and L.A., 1956-64; sr. computer systems engr. Nortronics div. Northrop Corp., Hawthorne, Calif., 1964-69; prof. data processing and math. Ventura (Calif.) Coll., 1969—; lectr. in mgmt. and computer sci. West Coast U., L.A., 1982—; software cons, ednl. cons., Ventura, 1972—. Author: Principles of Elementary Algebra: A Language and Equations Approach, 1991; sr. author: National Computer Policies, 1988; contbr. chpts. to books, articles to profl. jours. Active Ventura County coun. Boy Scouts Am., 1979-82; cons. Calif. Luth. U., Thousand Oaks, Calif., 1989. Lt. (j.g.) USNR, 1952-55, Europe. Mem. IEEE Computer Soc. (Disting. Visitor 1988-91), Assn. for Computing Machinery. Office: Ventura Coll 4667 Telegraph Rd Ventura CA 93003-3872

MATOSSIAN, JESSE NERSES, physicist; b. L.A., Feb. 2, 1952; s. Hagop Sarkis and Alice Elizabeth (Barsoomian) M. BS in Physics, U. So. Calif., L.A., 1975; MS in Physics, Stevens Inst. Tech., Hoboken, N.J., 1976; PhD in Physics, Stevens Inst. Tech., 1983. Mem. tech. staff Hughes Rsch. Labs., Plasma Physics Lab., Malibu, Calif., 1983-91, sr. mem. tech. staff, sr. rsch. staff physicist, 1992—. Reviewer Jour. Propulsion and Power, 1987-91; contbr. over 45 articles to profl. jours. and tech. publs.; 10 patents, 10 patents pending in field. Patrom mem. L.A. County Mus. of Art; bd. dirs. Graphic Arts Coun. Mem. AIAA, IEEE, Am. Phys. Soc. (life), N.Y. Acad. Scis., Sigma Xi.

MATOVICH, MITCHEL JOSEPH, JR., motion picture producer, executive; b. Watsonville, Calif., Dec. 16, 1927; s. Mitchel Joseph and Mildred Florence (Ingrom) M.; widowed, 1968; divorced, 1983; children: Wayne, Mark, Laura; m. Patte Dee Matovich, 1989. Student, San Jose State U., 1946-49. Mechanical designer Stanford Rsch. Inst., Menlo Park, Calif., 1955-59; rsch. specialist Lockheed Missiles & Space Co., Sunnyvale, Calif., 1959-70; mgr. NASA and Dept. of Def. bus. sect. Engineered Systems Div. FMC Corp., San Jose, Calif., 1970-77; pres. and chief exec. officer Morton Co. Div. of Haycor Corp., Hayward, Calif., 1977-82; pres. Concept Devel. Co., Newark, Calif., 1982-89, Matovich Prodns., Hollywood, Calif., 1987—, Stereotronics Inc., Beverly Hills, Calif., 1988—; co-owner Vagabond Theatre, L.A., 1990-91. Author: The Image Machine, feature length screenplays, stories for screenplays, short stories; producer (feature films) Lightning in a Bottle, 1993 (Gold award Houston Film Festival, Award of Excellence Film Adv. Bd.), I Don't Buy Kisses Anymore, 1992 (named Best Ind. Feature Houston Internat. Film Festival, Award of Excellence Film Adv. Bd., Angel award Excellence in Media, Top Applause award Santa Clarita Valley Internat. Film Festival); co-producer: Social Suicide; co-inventor: Stereotronics 3-D Video System; patentee in field. With USN, 1945-46, 51-52, Korea. Mem. Soc. Motion Picture and TV Engrs., Producers' Guild, Mensa, Intertel. Home: 26727 Oak Garden Ct Santa Clarita CA 91321 Office: Matovich Prodns Inc PO Box 5744 Beverly Hills CA 90209-5744

MATRAY, JAMES IRVING, history educator; b. Evergreen Park, Ill., Dec. 6, 1948; s. Theodore John and Caroline Kathryn (Werstler) M.; m. Mary Karin Heine, Aug. 14, 1971; children: Benjamin Robert, Amanda Jane. BA in European and Am. History, Lake Forest Coll., 1970; MA in Am. History, U. Va., 1973, PhD, 1977. Vis. asst. prof. History N.Mex. State U., Las Cruces, 1980-82, asst. prof. History, 1982-87, assoc. prof. History, 1987-92, prof. History, 1992—; vis. assoc. prof. History U. So. Calif., L.A., 1988-89; disting. vis. scholar grad. inst. peace studies Kyung Hee U., Seoul, Korea, 1990. Author: The Reluctant Crusade: American Foreign Policy in Korea, 1941-1950, 1985, Historical Dictionary of the Korean War, 1991, Korea and the Cold War: Division, Destruction, and Disarmament, 1993; contbr. chpts. to various books, articles to profl. jours., entries in various dictionaries; bd. editors Pacific Historical Review, 1989-92. With Ill. Nat. Guard, 1970-71, USAR, 1971-80. N.Mex. State U. rsch. grantee, 1982, 83, 84, 86, 90, Harry S Truman Found. rsch. grantee, 1975, 82, MacArthur Meml. Libr. rsch. grantee, 1984, NEH grantee, 1985, 90. Mem. Am. Hist. Assn. (Pacific Coast br.), Assn. for Asian Studies, Orgn. of Am. Historians, Soc. for Historians of Am. Fgn. Rels. Democrat. Home: 4426 Echo Canyon Rd Las Cruces NM 88011-7530 Office: NMex State Univ Dept History Box 3H Las Cruces NM 88003

MATSCH, RICHARD P., federal judge; b. 1930. A.B., U. Mich., 1951, J.D., 1953. Bar: Colo. Asst. U.S. atty. Colo., 1959-61; dep. city atty. City and County of Denver, 1961-63; judge U.S. Bankruptcy Ct., Colo., 1965-74, U.S. Dist. Ct. for Colo., 1974—. Served with U.S. Army, 1953-55. Mem. ABA, Am. Judicature Soc. Office: US Dist Ct 1929 Stout St Denver CO 80294-2900*

MATSEN, JOHN MARTIN, pathology educator, microbiologist; b. Salt Lake City, Feb. 7, 1933; s. John M. and Bessie (Jackson) M.; m. Joneen Johnson, June 6, 1959; children: Marilee, Sharon, Coleen, Sally, John H., Martin K., Maureen, Catherine, Carl, Jeri. BA, Brigham Young U., 1958; MD, UCLA, 1963. Diplomate Am. Bd. Pediatrics, Am. Bd. Pathology, Spl. Competence in Med. Microbiology. Intern UCLA, 1963-65; resident L.A. County Harbor/UCLA, Torrance, Calif., 1965-66; USPHS fellow U. Minn., Mpls., 1966-68, asst. prof., 1968-70, assoc. prof., 1971-74, prof., 1974; prof. U. Utah, Salt Lake City, 1974—, assoc. dean, 1979-81, chmn. Dept. of Pathology, 1981-93, v.p. health scis., 1993—; pres. Associated Regional and

Univ. Pathologists, Inc., Salt Lake City, 1983-93, chmn. bd. dirs., 1993—. Author over 200 publs. in field. Recipient Sonnenwirth Meml. award Am. Soc. Microbiology, 1993. Mem. Acad. Clin. Lab. Physicians and Scientists (pres. 1978-79), Assn. of Pathology Chmn. (pres. 1990-92). Mem. LDS Church. Home: 410S 10 W Farmington UT 84025-2203 Office: U Utah Health Scis Ctr 50 N Medical Dr Salt Lake City UT 84132-0001

MATSON, EVA JANE, publisher; b. Tucson, Oct. 3, 1937; d. Stewart Henry and Ada Berniece (Coyner) Robeson; m. Stephen Michael Matson, Aug. 1, 1960; children: Christopher Lee, Michael Aaron. BA in History, N.Mex. State U., 1959, MA in History, 1960. Jr. and sr. high sch. tchr. Gadsden Schs., Anthony, N.Mex., 1960-68; freelance typist and word processor Las Cruces, N.Mex., 1974-88; pub. Yucca Tree Press, Las Cruces, 1988—. Author: It Tolled for New Mexico, 1994; editor: Heroes of Bataan, Corregidor and North Luzon, 1988; pub.: Beyond Courage, 1992 (Zia award 1994). Tchr., chair various groups St. Paul's United Meth. Ch., Las Cruces, 1955—; past pres., newsletter editor, life mem. Friends of T. Branigan Meml. Libr., Las Cruces, 1986—. Recipient Dist. Award of Merit, Boy Scouts Am., 1979. Mem. Rocky Mountain Book Pubs., Mountain and Plains Booksellers Assn. Home: 2130 Hixoll Dr Las Cruces NM 88005-3305 Office: Yucca Tree Press 2130 Hixon Dr Las Cruces NM 88005-3305

MATSUI, JIRO, importer, wholesaler, small business owner; b. Honolulu, Hawaii, Apr. 5, 1919; s. Juro and Tsuta (Murai) M.; m. Barbara Toshiko Tanji; children: Kenneth Jiro, Alan Kiyoshi, Carol Ritsu. BA, U. Hawaii, 1949. Owner Honolulu Aquarium and Pet Supply, Honolulu, 1946-77, Bird House, Honolulu, 1957-61; owner, pres., chmn. Petland, Inc., Honolulu, 1961—, Pets Pacifica, Inc., Honolulu, 1977—, Global Pet Industries, Honolulu, 1975—; organizer, coord. first Pet Consumer Show in U.S., 1979, pres. 1979-82; first Internat. Pet Show; cons. Japan Pet Product Mfr. Assn. Fair, Japan, 1981—. Pres. Waikiki Vets. Club, Kapahulu, Oahu, Hawaii, 1948-66, Waiawa (Oahu) Farmers, 1948-88; sr. adv. com. plants and animals State of Hawaii, 1974—. Sgt. U.S. Army, 1941-46. Decorated with Bronze Star, U.S. Army, 1947. Mem. Am. Pet Soc. (pres. 1979-82, chmn. 1989-92), Western World Pet Supply Assn. (bd. dirs. 1974-93, pres. 1985-90, Edward B. Price award 1982), Honolulu C. of C. (bd. dirs. 1974—). Office: Pets Pacifica Inc 94-486 Ukee St Waipahu HI 96797-4211

MATSUI, ROBERT TAKEO, congressman; b. Sacramento, Sept. 17, 1941; s. Yasuji and Alice (Nagata) M.; m. Doris Kazue Okada, Sept. 17, 1966; 1 child, Brian Robert. AB in Polit. Sci, U. Calif., Berkeley, 1963; JD, U. Calif., San Francisco, 1966. Bar: Calif. 1967. Practiced law Sacramento, 1967-78; mem. Sacramento City Council, 1971-78, vice mayor, 1977; mem. 96th-104d Congresses from 5th Calif. dist., 1979—; ranking minority mem., mem. ways and means subcom. on oversight; chmn. profl. bus. forum Dem. Congl. Campaign Com.; congl. liaison nat. fin. council Dem. Nat. Com.; mem. adv. council on fiscal policy Am. Enterprise Inst. chmn. Profl. Bus. Forum of the Dem. Congl. Co. and Com.; congl. liaison Nat. Fin. Council, Dem. Nat. Com.; mem. Am. Enterprise Inst. Adv. Council on Fiscal Policy. Named Young Man of Yr. Jr. C. of C., 1973; recipient Disting. Service award, 1973. Mem. Sacramento Japanese Am. Citizens League (pres. 1969), Sacramento Met. C. of C. (dir. 1976). Democrat. Clubs: 20-30 (Sacramento) (pres. 1972), Rotary (Sacramento). Office: US Ho of Reps 2311 Rayburn HOB Washington DC 20515-0505*

MATSUMURA, MASAZUMI, research scientist, biochemist; b. Osaka, Japan, Oct. 3, 1952; came to U.S., 1986; s. Masayuki and Sadako (Noda) M.; m. Masako Izuka, Apr. 11, 1982 (div. June 1993); children: Yosuke, Maki. BSc, Osaka U., 1974, MSc, 1976, PhD, 1984. Rsch. assoc. Osaka U., 1979-86; postdoctoral fellow U. Oreg., Eugene, 1986-89; asst. prof. The Scripps Rsch. Inst., La Jolla, Calif., 1989-93; sr. scientist Supragen, Inc., Lakewood, Colo., 1993—. Contbr. articles to profl. jours. Grantee NIH, 1993-94. Mem. AAAS, Am. Soc. Sci., Am. Soc. for Biochemistry and Molecular Biology, Japanese Soc. of Molecular Biology. Home: 5609 S Lansing Way Englewood CO 80111-4105

MATSUMURA, VERA YOSHI, pianist; b. Oakland, Calif.; d. Naojiro and Aguri Tanaka; B.A. in Piano Pedagogy, Coll. of Holy Names, Oakland, 1938; pvt. studies with F. Moss, M. Shapiro, L. Kreutzer, P. Jarrett; m. Jiro Matsumura, Aug. 8, 1942; 1 son, Kenneth N. Staff mem., pianist Radio Sta. KROW, Oakland, 1938-39; numerous concert performances in Far East (Japan, Thailand), 1940—; numerous teaching appointments, 1940—; dir. Internat. Music Council, Berkeley, Calif., 1969—. Named to Hall of Fame, Piano Guild, 1968. Mem. Music Tchrs. Nat. Assn., Music Tchrs. Assn. Calif., Internat. Platform Assn., Alpha Phi Mu. Methodist. Home: 2 Claremont Cres Berkeley CA 94705-2324

MATSUNAGA, GEOFFREY DEAN, lawyer; b. L.A., Sept. 30, 1949; s. Hideo Arthur and Yuri (Yamazaki) M.; m. Masako Inoue, Aug. 20, 1981; children: Ayako, Hideko, Lisa Fumi. BS, USAF Acad., 1971; MBA, U. Calif., Los Angeles, 1972; postgrad., Inter U. Ctr. Japanese Lang. Studies, 1979-80; JD, U. Calif., Berkeley, 1982. Bar: Calif. 1982, U.S. Dist. Ct. (cen. dist.) Calif. 1982, N.Y. 1983, U.S. Dist. Ct. (so. dist.) N.Y. 1983. Jud. extern U.S. Dist. Ct. (cen. dist.), L.A., 1981; atty. Milbank, Tweed, Hadley & McCloy, N.Y.C., 1982-84, Tokyo, 1984-87; atty. Sidley & Austin, Tokyo, 1987-88, L.A., 1988-91; atty. Sheppard, Mullin, Richter & Hampton, L.A., 1991-94, Kagei Briggs & Matsunaga, L.A., 1995—. Founding bd. dirs. Futures Industry Assn., Japan, 1987; counsel East West Players, 1992-95. Lt. USN, 1972-78. Japan Found. fellow, Tokyo, 1979-80. Mem. Japan Bus. Assn. Southern Calif., Japan Am. Soc. So. Calif. (adv. bd. South Bay 1992-95). Episcopalian. Office: Kagei Briggs & Matsunaga 879 W 190th St Los Angeles CA 90248

MATSUOKA, ERIC TAKAO, mathematics educator; b. Honolulu, May 9, 1967; s. Kenneth Tamotsu and Hilda Sumie (Hino) M. BA in Math. with distinction, U. Hawaii, 1987, MA in Math., 1994. Acctg. clk. Wayne Choo, CPA, Honolulu, 1987-88; lab. instr. in math. Leeward Community Coll., Pearl City, Hawaii, 1988-91, lectr. in math., 1989-94; contr. Computronics, Honolulu, 1989-93; instr. math., 1994—. Mem. Math. Assn. Am. (Instnl. award 1987). Office: Leeward CC 96-045 Ala Ike Pearl City HI 96782

MATTATHIL, GEORGE PAUL, communications specialist, consultant; b. Kottayam, India, May 12, 1957; came to U.S., 1985; s. Paul and Annamma M. Bs, U. Kerala (India), 1973-78; MS, Indian Inst. Tech., 1978-82. Project engr. Tekelec, Calabasas, Calif., 1986-89; sr. systems analyst Security Pacific Automation, L.A., 1989-90; sr. design. engr. Telenova, Camarillo, Calif., 1990-91; cons. Raynet, Menlo Park, Calif., 1991, Larse, Santa Clara, Calif., 1991—, NEC, 1992—, Level One Comm., Sacramento, 1994—, DigitalLink, 1994—, Verilink, San Jose, 1994—, Tlelbit, Sunnyvale, 1995—. Nat. Sci. Talent scholar, India, 1975-80. Mem. Assn. Computing Machinery, Software Entrepreneurs Forum, Soc. Telecom. Cons. Office: Silicom Inc PO Box 2264 Cupertino CA 95015-2264

MATTEN, JEFFREY S., quality assurance engineer, computer consultant; b. Newark, Jan. 1, 1953; s. Bernard and Florence Matten. BA, Rutgers U., 1974; MS, Colo. State U., 1993. Owner, mgr. Matten, Newark, 1970-78; ins. broker Mut. of Omaha, Denver, 1978-80; hydrocabon well analyst Continental Labs., Denver, 1980-83; computer scientist C.C. of Aurora, Colo., 1986-87, Met. State Coll., Denver, 1988, Colo. State U., Ft. Collins, 1988, 90-91, U.S. Dept. Agr., Ft. Collins, 1989, U.S. Forest Svc., Ft. Collins, 1991-93, Dataware Techs., Boulder, Colo., 1993—. Floor mgr. Dukakis for Pres. Campaign, Colo. Dem. Conv., Boulder, 1988. Mem. Assn. Computing Machinery. Office: Dataware Tech 5775 Flatiron Pky # 220 Boulder CO 80301

MATTEOLI, RALPH, JR., nursing educator; b. Yreka, Calif., Jan. 30, 1938; s. Ralph Francis and Hazel Grace (McNeal) M. BS, U. Calif., San Francisco, 1962, MS, 1964; EdD, U. San Francisco, 1989. RN; cert. marriage, family and child counselor. Staff nurse Santa Rosa (Calif.) Gen. Hosp., 1962-63; psychiat. nurse Napa (Calif.) State Hosp., 1963-66; asst. prof. Chico (Calif.) State Coll., 1966-70; assoc. prof., coord. psychiat./mental health nursing San Francisco State U., 1970—; cons. Sonoma County Alliance for Mentally Ill, Santa Rosa, Sonoma County AIDS Project, Santa Rosa. Author: (with others) Nursing Assessment, 1969. Vol. AIDS Network, Santa Rosa. Recipient French Medal of Honor, French Consulate, San Francisco, 1957, Cert. of Recognition, Calif. State Senate, 1991; named Outstanding Individual Calif. Human Devel. Corp., 1991. Mem. Am. Psychiat. Nurses Assn. (Native Son Trailblazer award 1992), Nat. Alliance for Mentally Ill, Assn. Am. Indian and Alaskan Native Profs. Democrat. Roman Catholic. Office: San Francisco State U Sch Nursing 1600 Holloway Ave San Francisco CA 94132-1722

MATTESON, SANDRA ANNE, audit manager; b. Eau Claire, Wis., May 12, 1956; d. Ivan Arthur and Benita Arlene (Draeger) Duerkop; m. Steven Lowell Matteson, Apr. 1, 1977; children: Christopher Lee, Wayne Aaron. BA, Evergreen State Coll., 1982, MPA, 1985. CPA, Wash. Accounts payable clk. ARC, Portland, 1978-79; acctg. asst. 2 Wash. State Dept. Social and Health Svcs., Olympia, 1980-81; employer auditor 2 Wash. State Dept. Labor and Industries, Olympia, 1982-84; acct. 2 Wash. State Gambling Commn., Olympia, 1984-86, investigative auditor, 1986-89; audit mgr. Wash. State Gambling Commn., Seattle, 1989—. With U.S. Army, 1974-78. Mem. AICPA, NAFE, Wash. Soc. CPA, Am. Soc. Women Accts. Republican. United Methodist.

MATTEUCCI, DOMINICK VINCENT, real estate developer; b. Trenton, N.J., Oct. 19, 1924; s. Vincent Joseph and Anna Marie (Zoda) M.; BS, Coll. of William and Mary, 1948; BS, Mass. Inst. Tech., 1950. Registered profl. engr., Calif.; lic. gen. bldg. contractor, real estate broker; m. Emma Irene DeGuia, Mar. 2, 1968; children: Felisa Anna, Vincent Eriberto. Owner, Matteucci Devel. Co., Newport Beach, Calif.; pres. Nat. Investment Brokerage Co., Newport Beach. Home: 2104 Felipe Newport Beach CA 92660-4040 Office: PO Box 8328 Newport Beach CA 92658-8328

MATTHAU, CHARLES MARCUS, film director; b. N.Y.C., Dec. 10, 1964; s. Walter and Carol M. BA, U. So. Calif., 1986. Pres. The Matthau Co., L.A., 1986—. Dir. motion picture; Doin' Time on Planet Earth, 1988 (Saturn award Coun. Film Orgns., Silver Scroll award Acad. Sci. Fiction); dir., producer TV show Mrs. Lambert Remembers Love, 1991 (Golden Angel award Best TV spl. 1991, Golden Medal award Best Drama Prodn. 1991, Grand award The Houston Internat. Film Festival); dir., producer motion picture The Grass Harp, 1995; dir. over 50 feature shorts. Nat. spokesperson Am. Lung Assn., L.A., 1989—; active Action on Smoking and Health, Washington, 1986—. Recipient Cine award, Coun. Non-Theatrical Events, Washington, 1985, Golden Seal award, London Amateur Film Festival, 1986. Mem. Dirs. Guild Am., Acad. Sci.-Fiction, Fantasy and Horror Films, Am. Film Inst.

MATTHEW, LYN, art marketing consultant, educator; b. Long Beach, Calif., Dec. 15, 1936; d. Harold G. and Beatrice (Hunt) M.; m. Wayne Thomas Castleberry, Aug. 12, 1961 (div. Jan. 1976); children: Melanie, Cheryl, Nicole, Matthew. BS, U. Calif.-Davis, 1958; MA, Ariz. State U., 1979. Cert. hotel sales exec., 1988, meeting profl. Pres., Davlyn Cons. Found., Scottsdale, Ariz., 1979-82; cons., vis. prof. The Art Bus., Scottsdale, 1982—; pres., dir. sales and mktg. Embassy Stes., Scottsdale, 1987—, bd. trustees Hotel Sales and Mktg. Assn. Internat. Found., 1988—, chmn., 1991-93, mem. exec. com., 1993—; vis. prof. Maricopa C.C., Phoenix, 1979—, Ariz. State U., Tempe, 1980-83; cons. Women's Caucus for Art, Phoenix, 1983-88. Bd. dirs. Rossom House and Heritage Square Found., Phoenix, 1987-88. Author: The Business Aspects of Art, Book I, 1979, Book II, 1979; Marketing Strategies for the Creative Artist, 1985. Mem. Women Image Now (Achievement and Contbn. in Visual Arts award 1983), Women in Higher Edn., Nat. Women's Caucus for Art (v.p. 1981-83), Ariz. Women's Caucus for Art (pres. 1980-82, hon. advisor 1986-87), Ariz. Vocat. Edn. Assn. (sec. 1978-80), Ariz. Visionary Artists (treas. 1987-89), Hotel Sales and Mktg. Assn. Internat. (pres. Great Phoenix chpt. 1988-89, regional dir. 1989-90, bd. dirs. 1985-90), Meeting Planners Internat. (v.p. Ariz. Sunbelt chpt. 1989-91, pres. 1991-92, Supplier of Yr. award 1988), Soc. Govt. Meeting Planners (charter bd. dirs. 1987, Sam Gilmer award 1992, nat. conf. co-chmn. 1993-94), Ariz. Visionary Artists (treas. 1987-88), Ariz. Acad. Performing Arts (v.p. bd. dirs. 1987-88, pres. 1988-89).

MATTHEWS, DAVID FORT, military weapon system acquisition specialist; b. Lancaster, N.H., Sept. 25, 1944; s. Clinton Fort and Mabel Sawin (Oaks) M.; m. Eva Mae Horton, Nov. 10, 1990. BA, Vanderbilt U., 1966; MA, Mid. Tenn. U., 1973. Cert. acquisition mgr. Rsch. and devel. officer U.S. Army Rsch. Inst., Washington, 1974-77; exec. officer 194th Maintenence Battalion-Camp Humphreys, Korea, 1978-79; career program mgr. U.S. Army Mil. Pers. Ctr., Washington, 1979-82; logistics staff officer Dep. Chief of Staff Logistics, Washington, 1982-83; team chief Chief of Staff Army Study Group, Washington, 1983-85; logistics div. chief Multiple Launch Rocket System Project Office, Huntsville, Ala., 1985-88; comdr. Ordanance Program Div., Riyadh, Saudi Arabia, 1988-90; project mgr. Army Tactical Missile System, Huntsville, 1990-94; sr. lectr. weapon systems acquisition Naval Postgrad. Sch., Monterey, Calif., 1994—. Decorated Legion of Merit, Bronze Star; recipient award as project mgr. of yr. Sec. of Army, 1991. Mem. Am. Ordinance Assn., Am. Def. Prepardness Assn., Assn. U.S. Army. Home: 83 High Meadow Ln Carmel CA 93923 Office: Naval Postgrad Sch Monterey CA 93943

MATTHEWS, DONALD ROWE, political scientist, educator; b. Cin., Sept. 14, 1925; s. William Procter and Janet Burch (Williams) M.; m. Margie C. Richmond, June 28, 1947 (div.); children: Mary, Jonathan; m. Carmen J. Onstad, July 7, 1970 (div.); children: Christopher, Amy. Student, Kenyon Coll., 1943, Purdue U., 1944-45; A.B. with high honors, Princeton, 1948, M.A., 1951, Ph.D., 1953; Dr. hon. causa, U. Bergen, 1985. Instr. Smith Coll., Northampton, Mass., 1951-53; asst. prof. govt. Smith Coll., 1953-57; lectr. polit. sci. U. N.C., Chapel Hill, 1957-58; assoc. prof. U. N.C., 1958-63, prof., 1963-70; research prof. Inst. for Research in Social Sci., 1963-70; sr. fellow in govtl. studies Brookings Instn., Washington, 1970-73; prof. polit. sci. and research assoc. Inst. for Research in Social Sci., U. Mich., Ann Arbor, 1973-76; prof. polit. sci. U. Wash., Seattle, 1976—, chmn. dept. polit. sci., 1976-83; guest prof. U. Bergen, Norway, 1980-81, 93; fellow Ctr. for Advanced Study in the Behavioral Scis., 1964-65; cons. to U.S. Commn. on Civil Rights, 1958-60, NBC News, 1966-68, Ford Found., 1967-68, U.S. Ho. of Reps., 1970-72, others; faculty lectr. U. Wash., 1989. Author: The Social Background of Political Decision-Makers, 1954, U.S. Senators and Their World, 1960, (with James Prothro) Negroes and the New Southern Politics, 1966, Perspectives on Presidential Selection, 1973, (with William Keech) The Party's Choice, 1976, (with James Stimson) Yeas and Nays: A Theory of Decision-Making in the U.S. House of Representatives, 1975; Contbr. articles to profl. jours. Served with USNR, 1943-46. Recipient Sr. Award for Research in Govtl. Affairs Social Sci. Research Council, 1962; Ford Found. fellow, 1969-70; Guggenheim fellow, 1980-81. Fellow Am. Acad. Arts and Scis.; mem. Am. Polit. Sci. Assn. (treas. 1970-72, v.p. 1985-86), Pacific N.W. Polit. Sci. Assn. (pres. 1977-78), Western Polit. Sci. Assn. (pres. 1979-80), So. Polit. Sci. Assn., Midwestern Polit. Sci. Assn., Inter-Univ. Consortium for Polit. Research (exec. com. 1970-72). Democrat. Home: Houseboat B 3125 Fairview Ave E Seattle WA 98102-3063 Office: U Wash Polit Sci Do # 30 Seattle WA 98195

MATTHEWS, ESTHER ELIZABETH, education educator, consultant; b. Princeton, Mass., June 20, 1918; d. Ralph Edgar and Julia Ellen (Cronin) M. BS in Edn., Worcester State Coll., 1940; EdM, Harvard U., 1943, EdD, 1960. Tchr. various Mass. schs., 1942-47; guidance dir. Holden (Mass.) Pub. Schs., 1947-53, Wareham (Mass.) Pub. Schs., 1954-57; counselor Newton (Mass.) High Sch., 1957-60, head counselor, 1960-66; assoc. prof. edn. U. Oreg., 1966-70, prof. edn., 1970-80, prof. emerita, 1980—; vis. prof. U. Toronto, Ont., Can., summer 1971; lectr. on edn. Harvard U., 1963-66; cons. in field; lectr. various colls. and univs. Author book chpts.; contbr. numerous articles to profl. jours. and papers to conf. proc. Mem. ACD (Recognition for Contbn. to Promote Human Rights 1987), World Future Soc., Nat. Vocat. Guidance Assn. (pres. 1974-75, chair nat. com. 1966-67, sec. 1967-68, bd. trustees 1968-71, editl. bd. Vocat. Guidance Quar. 1966-68), Oreg. Pers. and Guidance Assn. (Leona Tyler award 1973, Disting. Svc. award 1979), Oreg. Career Devel. Assn. (Disting. Svc. award 1987, Esther E. Matthews Ann. award for outstanding contbn. to career devel. in Oreg. established in her honor 1993). Home: 832 Lariat Dr Eugene OR 97401-6438

MATTHEWS, EUGENE EDWARD, artist; b. Davenport, Iowa, Mar. 22, 1931; s. Nickolas Arthur and Velma (Schroeder) M.; m. Wanda Lee Miller, Sept. 14, 1952; children: Anthony Lee, Daniel Nickolas. Student, Bradley U., 1948-51; BFA, U. Iowa, 1953, MFA, 1957. Prof. fine arts grad. faculty U. Colo., Boulder, 1961—, dir. vis. artists program, 1985—; vis. artist Am. Acad. Rome, 1989. Exhibited in one-man shows U. Wis., Milw., 1960, Brena Gallery, Denver, 1963, 65, 67, 70, 74, 76, 78, 80, 83, 88, Colorado Springs Fine Arts Ctr., 1967, Sheldon Art Gallery, U. Nebr., 1968, Denver Art Mus., 1972, James Yu Gallery, N.Y.C., 1973, 77, Dubins Gallery, L.A., 1981, Galeria Rysunku, Poznan, 1983; exhibited numerous group shows U.S., Europe, Africa, Asia, internat. watercolor exhbn. New Orleans, 1983, Louvre, Paris, Met. Mus. of Art, N.Y.C., Internat. Art Ctr., Kyoto, Japan, Mus. of Modern Art, Rijeka, Yugoslavia, Taipei Fine Arts Mus., Taiwan, Republic of China; represented in permanent collections Nat. Mus. Am. Art, Washington, Denver Art Mus., Butler Inst. Am. Art, Chrysler Art Mus., others. Recipient Penello d'Argento award Acitrezza Internazionale, 1958, S.P.Q.R. Cup of Rome, Roma Olimpionica Internazionale, 1959, Gold medal of honor Nat. Arts Club, N.Y.C., 1969, Bicentennial award Rocky Mountain Nat. Watercolor Exhbn., 1976, Am. Drawings IV Purchase award, 1982, others; fellow in painting Am. Acad. Rome, 1957-60, U. Colo. Creative Rsch. fellow, 1966-67. Mem. Watercolor U.S.A. Honor Soc. (charter). Home: 720 Hawthorn Ave Boulder CO 80304-2140

MATTHEWS, JOHN LOUIS, retired military officer, educator; b. Copperton, Utah, June 27, 1932; m. Darlene Davis, 1956 (dec.); 3 children; m. Janice Holbrook, June 27, 1990. BS in Geology, Brigham Young U., 1955, MEd in Ednl. Adminstrn., 1967; grad. Air War Coll., 1976. Commd. 2d lt. USAF, 1954, advanced through grades to maj. gen., 1984; instr. pilot, Laredo, Tex., 1955-58; with Utah Air N.G., 1959-94, Colo. Air N.G., 1961-62, comdr. 151st Air Refueling Group, adj. gen. State of Utah, 1982-94; prin. Dixon Jr. H.S., Provo, Utah, 1967-73; prin. Timpview H.S., Provo, 1976-79. Mem. Steering Com. Pres. Sixth Quadrennial Rev. of Mil. Compensation, Washington; former chmn. air Res. Forces Policy com.; mem. Res. Forces Policy Bd. Sec. of Def., Washington; commn. on Rolls and Mission of the Armed Forces. Decorated Disting. Svc. medal, Legion of Merit, Vietnam Svc. medal, Nat. Def. Svc. medal, AE Disting. Svc. medal, others. Mem. N.G. Assn. of U.S. (pres. 1992-94), Adjs. Gen. Assn. of U.S. (pres., 1987-89), Commn. on Rolls and Missions, Air Force Assn., Assn. U.S. Army, Rotary.

MATTHEWS, MARILYN ANN, college development director; b. Anderson, Ind., Dec. 28, 1931; d. Fred and Doris Newbert (Denney) Betz; m. Russell T. Matthews, Jan. 13, 1951 (div. June 1992); children: Linda Ann Morgan, Susan Louise Rae. BS in Art Edn., Minot State U., 1968; MA, U. No. Colo., 1974; MEd, Colo. State U., 1983. Cert. tchr. N.D., Colo. Tchr. R2-J Sch. Dist., Loveland, Colo., 1968-78; slide librarian Colo. State U., Ft. Collins, 1978-80; coord. adult edn. Cen. Wyo. Coll., Riverton, 1984-87, dir. higher edn. Ctr. Carbon County Bd. Higher Edn., Rawlins, Wyo., 1987-90; dir. devel. projects San Juan Coll., Farmington, N.Mex., 1991—; adv. bd. mem. Project Read, Farmington, 1991—, ABE Program, Farmington, 1993-94. Exhibited in shows in N.D., Colo., N.Mex., 1968—; contbr. articles to profl. jours. Bd. dirs. Northwest N.Mex. Fine Arts, Farmington, 1992—, San Juan Coll. Fine Arts, Farmington, 1994—. Recipient Art scholarship Quota Club, Minot, N.D., 1965, Kelogg award U. Ga., 1989-90, Women Helping Women award Soropimist Internat., 1990, Partnerships award N.Mex. Orton Dyslexia Assn., 1994; Mott fellow, 1965. Mem. Am. Assn. Adult Continuing Edn. (nat. devel. edn. asst.), N.Mex. Adult Edn. Assn., N.Mex. Vocat. Edn. Assn., Nat. Vocat. Edn. Assn., Orton Dyslexia Soc. Republican. Episcopalian. Home: 1603 E 21st St Farmington NM 87401-4337 Office: San Juan Coll 4601 College Blvd Farmington NM 87402-4609

MATTHEWS, NORMAN SHERWOOD, JR., insurance company executive; b. San Antonio, Tex., Apr. 23, 1944; s. Norman Sherwood and Alice Ann (Hathaway) M.; student Middle Tenn. State U., 1962-64, Ventura Coll., 1965, Calif. State U., 1965-66, U. Md., 1968-70; BBA, U. Tex., 1972; postgrad. U. Hawaii, 1977-79; m. Masayo Nakamura, Sept. 1, 1970; children: Debbie Ann, Scott Tsuyoshi. Research asst. State Farm Ins. Co., Murfreesboro, Tenn., 1963-64; inventory control analyst Minn. Mining & Mfg. Co., Camarillo, Calif., 1964-65; sr. acct. Peat, Marwick, Mitchell & Co., Honolulu, 1973-75; dir. mgmt. analysis Hawaii Med. Service Assn., Honolulu, 1975-89; asst. v.p. mgmt. analysis and security Hawaii Med. Svc. Assn., 1989—. With USAF, 1966-70. Decorated Air medal with 8 oak leaf clusters. CPA, Hawaii; cert. internal auditor. Mem. AICPA, Hawaii Soc. CPAs, Am. Acctg. Assn., Am. Mgmt. Assn., Inst. Mgmt. Accts., Inst. Internal Auditors, Info. Sys. Audit and Control Assn. Home: 2724 Kahoaloha Ln Apt 1903 Honolulu HI 96826-3338 Office: Hawaii Med Svc Assn 818 Keeaumoku St Honolulu HI 96814-2365

MATTHEWS, ROBERT DEAN, urologist; b. Portsmouth, Va., Mar. 24, 1960; s. Joseph Allen and Genevieve Helen (Copeland) M. BS magna cum laude, U. Ala., 1982; MD, Vanderbilt U., 1986. Commd. ensign USN, 1982, advanced through grades to lt. comdr., 1991; with dept. urology Nat. Naval Med. Ctr., Bethesda, Md. Mem. Am. Urological Assn. (pres. 1990—), Am. Coll. Surgeons, Soc. Govt. Svc. Urologists (mem. exec. bd. 1993-94). Office: 2902 Harris Ave Wheaton MD 20902

MATTHEWS, VALERIE JO, development company executive; b. Omaha, June 6, 1947; d. Blaine Leroy and Betty Rae (Peterson) Rish; m. L. D. Matthews (div. 1975); children: Amy Lynne, Timothy Bryan. Grad. high sch., Omaha, 1965. Acct. various firms, Fremont, Nebr., 1967-78; sales assoc. Sunrise Home, Lincoln, Nebr., 1979-81, Lamb Realty, Thousand Oaks, Calif., 1981-82; rep. and mgr. sales Centex Homes, Oklahoma City, 1982-85; div. pres. Oklahoma City and Denver, 1985-87; with Lamb Realty, Thousand Oaks, Calif., 1988; dir. constrn. and land C.R. Wood Devel. Inc., Thousand Oaks, 1987-91; pres. C.R. Wood Devel., Inc., Thousand Oaks, 1991-92, Rish Homes, Inc., Meridian, Idaho, 1992—; owner Sunrise Realty, Meridian, Idaho, 1993—; pres. Learning Dynamics, Meridian, Idaho, 1994—; pvt. practice tax and fin. cons. Vol. YMCA, Fremont, 1972, Vols. in Arts, Oklahoma City, 1985, Make-A-Wish-Found.; active Boys Scouts Am., F.O.P. Mem. Calif. Assn. Realtors, Nat. Assn. Home Builders, Bldg. Industry Assn.

MATTHEWS, WARREN WAYNE, state supreme court justice; b. Santa Cruz, Calif., Apr. 5, 1939; s. Warren Wayne and Ruth Ann (Maginnis) M.; m. Donna Stearns, Aug. 17, 1963; children: Holly Maginnis, Meredith Sample. A.B., Stanford U., 1961; LL.B., Harvard U., 1964. Bar: Alaska 1965. Assoc. firm Burr, Boney & Pease, Anchorage, 1964-69, Matthews & Dunn, Matthews, Dunn and Baily, Anchorage, 1969-77; assoc. justice Alaska Supreme Ct., Anchorage, 1977—, former chief justice. Bd. dirs. Alaska Legal Services Corp., 1969-70. Mem. Alaska Bar Assn. (bd. govs. 1974-77), ABA, Anchorage Bar Assn. *

MATTIA, THOMAS GERARD, public relations executive; b. Newark, Nov. 2, 1948; s. Anthony and Audrey Elizabeth (Murray) M.; m. Christine Wesche, Oct. 22, 1978 (div. Mar. 1988); m. Martha Louise Boone, July 28, 1988; children: Mary Elizabeth, Caitlin Jane, Matthew Jefferson. BA in Journalism, Rutgers U., 1970. Journalist several daily newspapers N.J., Vt. and Conn., 1970-80; various positions IBM, White Plains, N.Y., 1980-84; issues mgr. IBM, Armonk, N.Y., 1985-86; mgr. real estate and constrn. IBM, Stamford, Conn., 1986-87; mgr. sys. and software IBM, White Plains, 1987-89; dir. advanced workers sta. mktg. com. IBM, Stamford, 1989-90; sr. v.p., gen. mgr. Hill and Knowlton/New Eng., Waltham, Mass., 1990-91; exec. v.p., mng. dir. Hill and Knowlton Asia Ltd., Hong Kong, 1991-93; exec. v.p., gen. mgr. Hill and Knowlton/L.A., 1994-95; pres. GCI Jennings, San Francisco, 1994—. Mem. Internat. Assn. Bus. Communicators, Pub. Rels. Soc. Am., Am. C. of C. Hong Kong (gov. 1993-94), L.A. C. of C. Home: 606 Pt Gallinas Rd San Rafael CA 94903 Office: GCI Jennings 131 Steuart St San Francisco CA 94103

MATTICE, JACK SHAFER, electric power research manager; b. Hobart, N.Y., Aug. 25, 1941. BS, SUNY, Stony Brook, 1963; PhD, Syracuse U., 1971. Teaching asst. Syracuse U., 1965-67, rsch. asst., 1967-68, predoctoral fellow, 1968-70; postdoctoral rsch. fellow dept. hydrobiology Inst. Ecology, Warsaw, Poland, 1970-71; rsch. staff mem. Environ. Scis. div. Oak Ridge (Tenn.) Nat. Lab., 1972-81; sr. project mgr. ecol. studies program Elec. Power Rsch. Inst., Palo Alto, Calif., 1981—; adj. asst. prof. Tenn. Technol. U., Cookeville, 1980-81. Author: (with others) Water Chlorination: Environmental Impact and Health Effects, Vol. 1, 1978, Vol. 2, 1978, Vol. 3,

1980, Vol. 5, 1985, Hydropower Engineering Handbook, 1991; editor, author: (with others) Water Chlorination: Environmental Impact and Health Effects, Vol. 4, 1983, Vol. 6, 1990. Mem. AAAS, ASTM, Am. Fisheries Soc., Ecol. Soc. Am., N.Am. Benthological Soc., Soc. Environ. Toxicology and Contamination, Sigma Xi. Office: Elec Power Rsch Inst 3412 Hillview Ave Palo Alto CA 94304-1395

MATTIONI, THOMAS A., physician, electrophysiologist; b. Chgo., Aug. 5, 1955. BS, U. Ill., Chgo., 1977; MD, Northwestern U., Chgo., 1981. Diplomate Am. Bd. Internal Medicine and Cardiovascular Diseases. Instr. of medicine Northwestern U., Chgo., 1987-89; asst. prof. medicine U. Md., Balt., 1989-91; dir. electrophysiology Ariz. Heart Inst., Phoenix, 1991—. Contbr. book chpts. and articles to profl. jours. Fellow ACP, Am. Coll. Cardiology, Am. Coll. of Chest Physicians; mem. Coun. of Clin. Cardiology of Am. Heart Assn., N.Am. Soc. of Pacing and Electrophysiology. Office: Ariz Heart Inst 2632 N 20th St Phoenix AZ 85006-1339

MATTISON, ELISA SHERI, organizational psychologist; b. Grand Rapids, Mich., Apr. 24, 1952; d. Andrew and Loraine R. Wierenga. BS cum laude, Western Mich. U., 1974, MA, 1979; postgrad., Fielding Inst., 1990. Trainer No. Inst., Anchorage, 1980; mgmt. cons., trainer Alaska Assocs. Human Devel. Inc., Anchorage, 1980-82; job devel. specialist Collins, Weed and Assocs., Anchorage, 1982-83; owner, pres. Mattison Assocs. Inc., Anchorage, 1993—; mem. adj. faculty Anchorage Community Coll., 1981-82; work environment and design coord. ARCO Alaska Inc., 1983-86; cons. Employee Assts. Cons. Alaska, Anchorage, 1982; v.p. Human Resource Mgmt. and Mktg. Alaskan Fed. Credit Union, 1986-90; asst. dir. degree completeion program, adult and continuing edn., Alaska Pacific U., 1990-92, adj. faculty, 1990—. Mem. Am. Soc. Tng. and Devel., Soc. Human Resource Mgmt. Contbr. articles to profl. publs. Office: 3910 Iona Circle Anchorage AK 99507-3344

MATTSON, GEORGE ARTHUR, architect; b. Knoxville, Tenn., Oct. 4, 1936; s. Frank Emil and Hildur Augusta (Freeberg) M.; m. Beverly Joanne Bruegger, Feb. 25, 1960; children: Steven, Susan. BArch, Mont. State Coll., 1959. Assoc. Paffard Clay Architect, San Francisco, 1964-70; pvt. practice Bozeman, Mont., 1971-77, 92—; ptnr. Mattson, Prugh & Lenon Architects, Bozeman, 1978-91. Prin. works include Bozeman Pub. Libr., 1980, Bozeman Fire Sta. No. 2, 1984, Mus. of Rockies, 1987. Founding bd. mem. Sweetpea Arts Festival, Bozeman, 1977-86; bd. dirs. Loft Community Theater, Bozeman, 1980-85, Gallatin Performing Arts Ctr., Bozeman, 1989—; founding mem. Beall Park Art Ctr., Bozeman, 1984. Lt. USN, 1960-62. Mem. Quest for Knowledge Club, AIA. Democrat. Home: 47 Hitching Post Rd Bozeman MT 59715-9241 Office: 17 W Main St Bozeman MT 59715-4642

MATZDORFF, JAMES ARTHUR, investment banker; b. Kansas City, Mo., Jan. 3, 1956. BS, U. So. Calif., 1978; MBA, Loyola U., Los Angeles, 1980. Comml. loan officer Bank of Am., Los Angeles, 1976-78; mng. dir. James A. Matzdorff & Co., Beverly Hills, Calif., 1978—. Mem. Rep. Nat. Com., 1980—. Mem. NRA, Am. Fin. Assn., Porsche Car Club, Range Rover Club, Harley Davidson Club, Phi Delta Theta. Office: 9903 Santa Monica Blvd Ste 374 Beverly Hills CA 90212-1671

MAUBAN, RENE AVANZADO, physician; b. San Pablo, Laguna, Philippines, Dec. 15, 1958; came to U.S., 1969; s. Raymundo Soriano and Imelda (Avanzado) M.; m. Eileen Cordero, Mar. 15, 1989; children: Elizabeth, Elaine. BS in Biology, U. Mo., 1981; MD, Perpetual Help Coll. Medicine, Biñan, Philippines, 1986. Diplomate Am. Bd. Family Practice. Resident family practice St. Elizabeth Hosp., Chgo., 1989-92; family physician S.W. Med. Assn., Las Vegas, Nev., 1992-93; dir. family practice S.W. Med. Assn., Las Vegas, 1993—. Mem. AMA, Am. Assn. Family Practice, Nev. Med. Soc., Clark County Med. Soc. Roman Catholic. Home: 9413 Calico Garden Ave Las Vegas NV 89134-0163

MAUGHAN, WILLARD ZINN, dermatologist; b. Riverside, Calif., Apr. 21, 1944; s. Franklin David and Martha Charlotte (Zinn) M.; m. Rona Lee Wilcox, Aug. 20, 1968; children: Julie Anne, Kathryn Anita, Willard Wilcox, Christopher Keith. Student, Johns Hopkins U., Balt., 1962-64; BS, U. Utah, 1968, MD, 1972. Diplomate Am. Bd. Dermatology. Intern Walter Reed Army Med. Ctr., Washington, 1972-73; fellow Mayo Clinic, Rochester, Minn., 1976-79; pvt. practice Ogden, Utah, 1979—. Contbr. articles to profl. jours. Commr. Boy Scouts Am., Weber County, Utah, 1980-84, dist. chmn., 1993-95; pres. Am. Cancer Soc., Weber County, 1985-86. Maj. U.S. Army, 1971-76. Recipient Dist. award of merit Boy Scouts Am., 1985, Silver Beaver award 1994. Fellow ACP, Am. Acad. Dermatology, Royal Soc. Medicine (London); mem. N.Y. Acad. Scis., Kiwanis Club. Republican. Mormon. Home: 2486 W 4550 S Roy UT 84067-1944 Office: 3860 Jackson Ave Ogden UT 84403-1956

MAUK, PAMELA ANNE, marketing and development consultant; b. L.A., Apr. 25, 1953; d. Frederick Henry and Marion (Morris) M.; m. Mark Randolph Cross, Mar. 24, 1990. BA, U. Calif., Long Beach, 1976; MA, U. Washington, 1980. Ins. processor St. Mary Med. Ctr., Long Beach, 1973-77; teaching asst. U. Washington, Seattle, 1977-79; slide libr. Seattle Art Mus., 1978-79, writer, 1980; summer staff lectr. Nat. Gallery Art, Washington, 1979; freelance newsletter editor Seattle, 1981; asst. to dir. Childhaven, Seattle, 1981; pub. rels. and devel. mgr. Ryther Child Ctr., Seattle, 1982-87; dir. mktg. and devel. Snoqualmie (Wash.) Valley Hosp., 1987-90; dir. devel. and community rels. Marianwood, Issaquah, Washington, 1987-89; pres. Pamela Mauk Communications, Redmond, Wash., 1990-95; exec. dir. Family Resource Ctr., Redmond, 1995—; trustee Pub. Rels. Round Table, Seattle, 1983-86, pres. 1985. Commr. Issaquah (Wash.) Arts Commn., 1988-91, chair, 1991; creator, sr. editorial adv. Issaquah Arts, 1989-91; adv. Children's Svcs. of Sno-Valley, Snoqualmie, 1989-90, Citizen's for Better Sch., Snoqualmie, 1989-90; coun. mem. Eastside Ops. Coun. United Way of King County Bellevue, Wash., 1990-92; svc. panel mem. United Way King County, 1990-92. Recipient Award in Art Bank of Am., 1971, two 1st prizes Washington Press Assn., 1984, Commendation Issaquah Sch. Dist., 1989, Pacesetter award Internat. Assn. Bus. Communicators, 1986. Mem. Internat. Assn. Bus. Communicators, Puget Sound Grant Writers Assn., N.W. Devel. Officers Assn. Office: 247 208th Ave NE Redmond WA 98053-6937

MAUL, TERRY LEE, psychologist, educator; b. San Francisco, May 6, 1946; s. Chester Lloyd and Clella Lucille (Hobbs) M.; AB, U. Calif., Berkeley, 1967, MA, 1968, PhD, 1970; student Coll. San Mateo, 1964-65; m. Gail Ann Retallick, June 27, 1970 (div. Dec. 1986); 1 son, Andrew Eliot. Prof. psychology San Bernardino Valley Coll., San Bernardino, Calif., 1970—, chmn. dept., 1979-82; researcher self-actualization. Mem. AAUP (chpt. pres. 1971-73), Am. Psychol. Assn., Audubon Soc., Mensa, Nature Conservancy, Rachel Carson Council, Wilderness Soc., Sierra Club. Democrat. Author: (with Eva Conrad) Introduction to Experimental Psychology, 1981; (with Gail Maul) Beyond Limit: Ways to Growth and Freedom, 1983; contbg. author other psychol. texts. Home: 6155 Bluffwood Dr Riverside CA 92506-4605 Office: San Bernardino Valley Coll 701 S Mount Vernon Ave San Bernardino CA 92410-2705

MAULE, RANDY WILLIAM, information systems specialist, educator, producer; b. Anaheim, Calif., July 20, 1954; s. William Marvin and Nadine Hazel (Clark) M. BBA, Mich. State U., 1978; MA in Communications, U. Fla., 1984, PhD in Edn., 1987; MLS in Info. Sci., U. Calif., Berkeley, 1993. Communications analyst Manufacturers Hanover Trust Co., N.Y.C., 1978-79; mktg. dir. Abbell Communications, Orlando, Fla., 1980-82; instr. San Jose State U., 1985-86; exec. producer Progressive Video Network, Lansing, Mich., 1987—; asst. prof. Cen. Mich. U., Mt. Pleasant, 1987-88, U. Fla., Gainesville, 1988-91; assoc. prof. U. San Francisco, 1991—. Mem. Assn. for Ednl. Comms. and Tech., Internat. Comm. Assn., Internat. Soc. Tech. Edn., Info. Resource Mgmt. Assn.

MAURER, ADAH ELECTRA, psychologist; b. Chgo., Oct. 26, 1905; d. Frank Ulysses and Mary Louise (Meng) Bass; m. Harry Andrew Maurer, June 14, 1937 (div. 1947); children: Douglas, Helen. BS, U. Wis., 1927; MA, U. Chgo., 1957; PhD, Union Inst., 1976. Lic. sch. psychologist, Calif. Tchr. pub. schs. Chgo., 1927-61; psychologist pub. schs. Calif., 1962-71; pvt. practice marriage, family and child counselor Berkeley, Calif., 1965-75; organizer, chief exec. officer End Violence Against the Next Generation, Inc., Berkeley, 1972—; lectr. U. Calif., Davis, 1965-68; bd. dirs. Nat. Ctr. for Study Cpl. Punishment & Alternatives in Schs. Temple U., Phila.; liaison People Opposed to Paddling Students, Houston, 1981—; v.p. Nat. Coalition to Abolish Cpl. Punishment in Schs., Columbus, Ohio, 1987—; cons. Calif. State Dept. Social Svcs., 1988. Author: Paddles Away, 1981, 1001 Alternatives, 1984, (with others) The Bible and the Rod, 1983, Think Twice, 1985; editor: (newsletter) The Last? Resort, 1972—; contbr. numerous articles to profl. jours. Sponsor End Phys. Punishment of Children Worldwide. Recipient Disting. Humanitarian award Calif. State Psychol. Assn., Presdl. award Nat. Assn. Sch. Psychologists, 1988, Donna Stone award Nat. Commn. for Prevention of Child Abuse, 1988, commendation Giraffe Project, 1988, award in recognition of pioneering efforts in banning corporal punishment in nation's schs. Nat. Coalition to Abolish Corporal Punishment in Schs., Achievement award Child, Youth and Family Svcs. Am. Psychol. Assn., 1994. Mem. Am. Psychol. Assn. (Lifetime Career Achievement award 1995), Hemlock Soc. Home and Office: 977 Keeler Ave Berkeley CA 94708-1440

MAURER, JOHN IRVING, psychiatrist; b. Madison, Wis., Sept. 10, 1934; s. Irving John and Kathryn (Fischer) M.; m. Linda Collins, Sept. 17, 1961 (div. Jan. 1982); children: Kathryn, Karen Walker, Paul. Student, U. Wis., 1952-53; BS, Stanford U., 1956, MD, 1960. Cert. Am. Bd. Psychiatry. Intern Hartford (Conn.) Hosp., 1960-61; psychiatric resident Stanford Med. Sch., 1961-62, 64-66; staff psychiatrist Stanford Student Health Svcs., 1966-70; ptnr. Palo Alto Med. Clinic, 1966-70; founding dir. Emanuel Cmty. Health Ctr., Turlock, Calif., 1970-73; program dir., psychiatrist Tuolumne County Mental Health Svcs., 1973-74; staff psychiatrist, cons. Stanislaus County Mental Health Svcs., 1974-76; pvt. practice psychiatrist, 1976—; clin. instr. Stanford Med. Ctr., 1966-70; tchg. faculty in psychiatry Scenic Gen. Hosp., 1978-83; cons. Turlock (Calif.) Sch. Sys, 1979-81-86, Tuum Est Drug Treatment Program, 1981; founding med. dir. Crossroads In-Patient Unit, Meml. South Hosp., Ceres, Calif., 1986-87; founding dir. Eating Disorders In-Patient Unit, Modesto (Calif.) Psychiat. Ctr., 1987-88. Contbr. articles to profl. jours. Bd. dirs. Medic Alert Found. Internat., 1961-85, chmn. bd. 1977-78; mem. steering com. Turlock (Calif.) Counseling Ctr., 1977-81; pres., bd. dirs. Turlock Golf and Country Club, 1977-78; co-founding dir. Alcoholism Coun. Stanislaus County/ Nat. Coun. Alcoholism, 1980-81; mem. Stanislaus County Mental Health Adv. Bd., 1980-82. Capt. USAF, 1962-64. Fellow Acad. Psychosomatic Medicine, Am. Psychiat. Assn.; mem. AMA, Calif. Med. Assn., Stanislaus Med. Soc., Internat. Soc. for Study Multiple Personality Disorders, Ctrl. Calif. Psychiat. Soc. (pres. Modesto/Stockton chpt. 1981, 90, nominating com. 1981, 87, exec. coun. 1982). Office: Therapy Offices of Turlock 600 E Main St Ste 220 Turlock CA 95380-4547

MAURICE, DON, personal care industry executive; b. Peoria, Ill., Aug. 29, 1932; s. Imajean (Webster) Crayton; m. Cindalu Jackson, Aug. 31, 1990. Student, Loma Linda U., 1984-86; cert. paralegal studies, Calif. State U., San Bernardino, 1994. Lic. hair stylist, skin therapist. Owner 2 schs. in advanced hair designs, San Diego, 1962-64, D & M Enterprises, Advt. Agy., 1964-78; now cons. D&M Enterprises Advt. Agy.; dist. mgr. AqRo Matic Co. Water Purification Systems, San Diego, 1972-75; profl. sales educator Staypower Industries, San Diego, 1972-76, 3d v.p., 1975-76; regional bus. cons. Estheticians Pharmacology Rsch., Garden Grove, Calif., 1975-81; owner, operator Don Maurice Hair Designs, Hemet, Calif., 1980-83; dir., operator Hair Sytles by Maurice, Loma Linda, Calif., 1984-88; owner, pres. Grooming Dynamics, Redlands, Calif., 1988—; bus. cons. Yogurt Place, Paradise Valley, Ariz., 1978-79, others; regular guest Channel 6/Channel 8, San Diego, 1968-78; cons. infomercial Pre-Paid Legal Svcs., Inc., 1994—. Author: The New Look For Men, 1967, The Art of Men's Hair Styling, 1968 (accepted by Library of Congress), Baldness, To Be or Not To Be, 1989. Promoter Spl. Olympics, Hemet, 1981. Sgt. U.S. Army, 1950-53, Korea. Decorated Purple Heart, 1952; named Leading Businessman in His Profession, Union and Evening Tribune, 1969. Mem. Internat. Platform Assn., Christian Businessmen's Assn. Office: Grooming Dynamics PO Box 1279 Loma Linda CA 92354-1279

MAURO, RICHARD FRANK, lawyer, investment manager; b. Hawthorne, Nev., July 21, 1945; s. Frank Joseph and Dolores D. (Kreimeyer) M.; m. LaVonne M. Madden, Aug. 28, 1965; 1 child, Lindsay Anne. AB, Brown U., 1967; JD summa cum laude, U. Denver, 1970. Bar: Colo. 1970. Assoc. Dawson, Nagel, Sherman & Howard, Denver, 1970-72; assoc. Van Cise, Freeman, Tooley & McClearn, Denver, 1972-73, ptnr., 1973-74; ptnr. Hall & Evans, Denver, 1974-81, Morrison & Forester, Denver, 1981-84; of counsel Parcel, Mauro, Hultin & Spaanstra, P.C., Denver, 1984—, pres., 1988-90, of counsel, 1992—; pres. Sundance Oil Exploration Co., 1985-88; exec. v.p. Castle Group, Inc., 1992—; adj. prof. U. Denver Coll. Law, 1981-84. Symposium editor: Denver Law Jour., 1969-70; editor: Colorado Corporation Manual; contbr. articles to legal jours. Pres. Colo. Open Space Coun., 1974; mem. law alumni coun. U. Denver Coll. Law, 1988-91. Francis Wayland scholar, 1967; recipient various Am. jurisprudence awards. Mem. ABA, Colo. Bar Assn., Denver Bar Assn., Colo. Assn. Corp. Counsel. (pres. 1974-75), Am. Arbitration Assn. (comml. arbitrator), Order St. Ives, Denver Athletic Club (bd. dirs. 1986-89). Home: 2552 E Alameda Ave No 128 Denver CO 80209-3320 Office: 475 17th St Ste 750 Denver CO 80202-4017

MAUS, JOHN ANDREW, computer systems engineer; b. Whittier, Calif., July 13, 1945; s. Kenneth Waring and Bertha Estella (Eckman) M.; M. Diana Barba, April 16, 1977 (div. May 1, 1983); m. Colette An Moschelle, Nov. 23, 1985; stepchildren: BreAnn, Adam; children: Steven Andrew, Terra An. BA in Physics, U. Calif., Riverside, 1963-67; MS in Physics, San Diego State U., 1967-70. Cert. data processor, 1983. Programmer, analyst San Diego State Found., 1970-72; instr. bus. San Diego State U., 1971-73; systems programmer San Diego State U., San Diego, 1971-74; data processing mgr. M.H. Golden Co., San Diego, 1974-79; computer systems engr. Hewlett-Packard Co., Spokane, Wash., 1979-84, sr. systems engr., 1984-86, network systems engr., 1986-89, sr. tech. cons., 1989—; physics lab. asst. USDA Salinity Lab., Riverside, 1965-67; underwater acoustics programmer Naval Undersea Ctr., San Diego, 1967-70; programmer San Diego Inst. Pathology, 1972-76; adv. com. Computer Sci. Bus. Applications North Idaho Coll., 1989—; mem. career network U. Calif., Riverside, 1990—; dist. tech. com. Nine Mile Falls (Wash.) Sch., 1994—. Author: INTEREX Conference Proceedings, 1989; co-author: Chemical Physics Letters, 1971, Electronic and Atomic Collisions, 1971. Merit badge counselor Spokane chpt. Boy Scouts Am., 1983—. Mem. Assn. Computing Machinery (founder Spokane chpt., chpt. chmn. 1980-82, service award 1981). Home: 12417 W Sunridge Dr Nine Mile Falls WA 99026-9311 Office: Hewlett-Packard Co 1121 N Argonne Rd Ste 121 Spokane WA 99212-2656

MAUTER, WARREN EUGENE, chemist, business development manager; b. Denver, Aug. 27, 1953; s. Jacob Martin and Harriette June (Kaiser) M.; m. Deborah Lee Long, Jan. 22, 1983 (div. 1987). BS in Chemistry, Met. State Coll., 1976; MS in Engring., U. Colo., 1980, MBA, 1986. Rsch. chemist Manville Corp., Denver, 1973-80, group leader, 1980-83; applications mgr. Cardinal Chem., Columbia, S.C., 1983-84; prin. Alpine Cons., Denver, 1984-88; corp. mgr. COBE Labs., Inc., Lakewood, Colo., 1988—; instr. econs. and fin. U. Colo. Coll. Engring, 1987-89; mem. bd. advisors. Shuck Found., 1986-88. Bd. reviewers Jour. Vinyl Tech., 1981-83; contbr. articles to profl. jours. Sci. and Tech. Colo. scholar Met. State Coll., 1972-75. Mem. ASTM, Soc. Plastics Engrs. (bd. dirs. vinyl div. 1982-86), Nat. Sanitation Found. (industry adv. bd. 1980-84), Am. Chem. Soc., Am. Mgmt. Assn., Colo. Mountain Club, U. Colo. Execs. Club (Denver, v.p. 1987, pres. 1988). Republican. Home: 1649 S Marion St Denver CO 80210-2752 Office: COBE Labs Inc 1185 Oak St Lakewood CO 80215-4407

MAUTZ, EDWARD JOHN, professor, public information officer; b. Inglewood, Calif., Aug. 21, 1942; s. Ferdinand Ludwig and Myrtle Margaret (Gillaspie) M.; m. Donna June Kunz, Feb. 2, 1963; children: Felicia Lucette, Edward John II. BA in Pub. Svc. Mgmt., U. Redlands, 1978; MPA, U. San Francisco, 1982; D of Pub. Adminstrn., U. La Verne, 1995. Sgt. L.A. Police Dept., L.A., 1968-93; assoc. dept. Pub. Adminstrn. U. La Verne (Calif.), 1989—; instr. El Camino C.C., Torrance, Calif., 1981-91, L.A. Trade Tech. Coll., 1985-92; lectr. El Camino Coll., 1981-91, L.A. Trade Tech. Coll., 1985-92, U. La Verne, 1989—. Scout master, asst. scout master Boy Scouts Am., L.A., 1977—. Mem. Acad. Criminal Justice Sci., Assn. Pub. Policy and Mgmt., Acad. Polit. Sci., Am. Soc. Law Enforcement Trainers, Am. Soc. Pub. Adminstrs., Internat. City Mgrs. Assn., Internat. Soc. for Gen. Semantics, The Inst. of Mgmt. Sci., Operation Rescue Soc. Am., West & Pacific Assn. Criminal Justice Edn. Republican. Office: U La Verne 2220 3rd St La Verne CA 91750-4917

MAUZY, MICHAEL PHILIP, environmental consultant, chemical engineer; b. Keyser, W.Va., Nov. 14, 1928; s. Frank and Margery Ola (Nelson) M.; m. Nancy Shepherd Watson, Mar. 27, 1949; children: Michael P. Jr., Jeffrey A., Rebecca A. BSChemE, Va. Poly. Inst., 1950; MSChemE, U. Tenn., 1951. Registered profl. engr., Va., Ill. With Monsanto Co., St. Louis, 1951-71, dir. engring. and mfg., 1968-71; mgr. comml. devel. Kummer Corp., Creve Coeur, Mo., 1971-72; mgr. labs. Ill. EPA, Springfield, 1972-73, mgr. water pollution control, 1973-74, mgr. environ. programs, 1974-77, dir., 1977-81; v.p. Roy F. Weston, Inc., West Chester, Pa., 1981-88, Vernon Hills, Ill., 1988-93, Albuquerque, 1993—; also bd. dirs. Roy F. Weston, Inc., West Chester, Pa.; bd. dirs. DeTox Internat. Corp., St. Charles, Ill.; provider Congl. testimony, 1974-81; presenter various workshops, symposia and seminars, 1974—. Contbr. articles on environ. mgmt. to profl. pubis., 1974—. Mem. Ohio River Valley Water Sanitary Commn., Cin., 1976-81. 1st lt. U.S. Army, 1951-53. Recipient Environ. Quality award Region V, U.S. EPA, Chgo., 1976, Disting. Svc. award Cons. Engrs. Coun. of Ill., 1978, Ill. award Ill. Assn. Sanitary Dists., 1979, Clarence W. Klassen award Ill. Assn. Water Pollution Control Ops., 1984. Mem. Am. Pub. Works Assn., Am. Inst. Chem. Engring., Water Pollution Control Assn., Am. Mgmt. Assn.

MAVADY, KAYKHAM, electrical engineer, drafting; b. Savannakhet, Laos, Sept. 15, 1970; came to U.S., 1979; s. Phom and Keo M. Cert., Area Tech. Trade Ctr., 1988; BS, U. the Pacific, 1993. Head tech. asst. U. the Pasific, Stockton, Calif., 1990-93; drafting tech., WAN/LAN adminstr. Honeywell, Las Vegas, Nev., 1993—. Mem. IEEE (v.p. 1992), So. Nev. Auto CAD User Group, Order of the Engr. Republican. Office: City of Las Vegas 407 E Stewart Ave Las Vegas NV 89101

MAWHINNEY, CHARLES HENRY, III, computer science educator; b. Washington, Pa., Apr. 14, 1943; s. Charles Henry Jr. and Margaret Rose (Trembour) M.; m. Mary Lou Bloom, Apr. 3, 1964 (div. Apr. 1974); children: Margaret Lucille Barta, Charles Henry IV; m. Annette M. Lege, Aug. 27, 1982; 1 child, Michael David. Student, U.S. Naval Acad., Annapolis, 1961-64; BS in Math., Carnegie Inst. Tech., 1967; MBA, U. Pitts., 1970, PhD in Bus., 1986. Rsch. asst. B.F. Drakenfeld (Hercules, Inc.), Washington, Pa., 1964-69; lectr. Ahmadu Bello U., Zaria, Nigeria, 1972-73; assoc. prof. Ind. U. of Pa., 1974-86; asst. prof. Bentley Coll., Waltham, Mass., 1986-91; assoc. prof. Met. State Coll. Denver, 1991-95, 1995—; part-time lectr. Robert Morris Coll., Pitts., 1974, U. Pitts., 1971, 74; ptnr. Bear Enterprises, Indiana, Pa., 1983-86, 91—; book reviewer CBS Coll. Pub., N.Y.C., 1986, Wm. C. Brown Pubs., Dubuque, Iowa, 1990, Bus. Media Resources, Corte Madera, Calif., 1991; grant reviewer Yankee Ingenuity Initiative, Conn. Innovations, Inc., Dept. Econ. Devel., 1992, 93; jour. reviewer Jour. of MIS, Comms. of the Assn. of Computing Machinery, Jour. Mgmt. Sys., Jour. of End User Computing. Author: A Modular Approach to dBASE III Plus, 1989, A Modular Approach to dBASE IV-MS DOS Version, 1992; author: (with G. Miller) The Boston SIM Information Management Careers Prototype Videotape, 1990, (with D.R. Callaghan, D.R. Chand and C. Whitcomb) A Modular Approach to DOS, Wordstar 5.5, Lotus 1-2-3 Version 2.2, and dBASE IV, 1992; mem. editl. bd. Jour. Computer Pers. Rsch.; contbr. articles to profl. jours. Bd. dirs. Ken-Caryl Fond., 1993—; mem. hogback fundraising com., 1992—; mem. Bradford Elem. Sch. PTA, 1992—. Mem. Inst. Mgmt. Sci., Assn. for Computing Machinery, Decision Scis. Inst., Soc. for Info. Mgmt., Info Resources Mgmt. Assn., Assn. Computing Educators, Internat. Bus. Schs. Computer Assn., Am. Prodn. and Inventory Control Soc. (v.p. advanced planning Pitts. chpt. 1982-83), Beta Gamma Sigma. Office: Met State Coll Denver PO Box 193362 Campus Box 45 Denver CO 80217

MAXCY, LAWRENCE STAHL, education administrator; b. Rochester, N.Y., May 28, 1935; s. William Frank and Gertrude (Stahl) M.; m. Carol Marie Silvernail, June 1, 1957; children: Ann, Lee, Frank, Paul, Mark. AB, Syracuse U., 1958, MPA, 1960. Administr. NIH, Bethesda, Md., 1960-62; administrv. officer NIH Latin Am. Office, Rio de Janeiro, 1962-66; administr. NIH, Bethesda, Md., 1966-68; asst. to dean U. Calif. Div. Natural Scis., Santa Cruz, Calif., 1968-91. Contbr. articles to popular mags. Pres. Santa Cruz Schs. Pers. Commn., 1975-81; active Santa Cruz Vol. Ctr., 1981-91 (pres. 1987-89), Santa Cruz County Grand Jury, 1988-89; Oreg. coord. publicity & assoc. dist. coord. So. Oreg. Am. Assn. Retired Persons Tax-Aide program, 1995—. Democrat. Home: 221 Dick George Rd Cave Junction OR 97523-9619

MAXEY, DIANE MEADOWS, artist; b. Lufkin, Tex., Feb. 26, 1943; d. Warren Gaston and Jackie (Keen) Meadows; m. William Brant Maxey, Sept. 5, 1964; children: Dananne, Robert Warren. BA in Art and Edn., U. North Tex., 1965; postgrad., U. Tex., Arlington, Tex. Tech U., Lubbock; studied with Al Brouilette, Bud Biggs, Edgar Whitney, Dick Phillips, Robert E. Wood, Rex. Brandt, Milford Zornes. Art tchr. Dallas Pub. Schs., 1965-66; substitute tchr. Arlington Pub. Schs., 1969-72; pvt. classes San Angelo, Tex., 1973-77, Scottsdale, Ariz., 1978-92; owner Maxi Watercolor Studio, Paradise Valley, 1978—, Bandanna Tours, Scottsdale, 1988-91; mem. staff Scottsdale Artist Sch., North Coast Art Ctr., Dillman's Art Center. Exhibited works at The Frame and Design, Nacogdoches, Tex., The Gold Nuggett Art Gallery, Wickenburg, Ariz., Vanier and Roberts Gallery, Scottsdale, Ariz. Dir. visual ministry First So. Bapt. Ch., Scottsdale, 1988-95. Recipient numerous awards; named featured artist in the book Freshening Your Paintings With New Techniques. Mem. Western Fedn. Watercolor Soc. (gen. chmn. 1981-82), Southwestern Watercolor Assn. (signature), Ariz. Artist Guild (pres. 1982-83), Ariz. Watercolor Assn., Tex. Watercolor Assn. (signature), 22 x 30 Profl. Critique Group. Home and Office: Maxi Watercolor Studio 7540 N Lakeside Ln Paradise Valley AZ 85253-2857

MAXFIELD, PETER C., state legislator, law educator, lawyer; b. 1941. AB, Regis Coll., 1963; JD, U. Denver, 1966; LLM, Harvard U., 1968. Bar: Colo. 1966, Wyo. 1969. Trial atty. Dept. Justice, 1966-67; assoc. Hindry, Erickson & Meyer, Denver, 1968-69; asst. prof. U. Wyo. Coll. Law, 1969-72, assoc. prof., 1972-76, prof., 1976—, dean, 1979-87; vis. assoc. prof. U. N.Mex., 1972-73; Raymond F. Rice Disting. prof. U. Kans., 1984; Chapman Vis. Disting. prof., U. Tulsa, 1987; vis. prof. U. Utah, 1992. Coord. Wyo. State Planning, 1988-89; spl. asst. Gov. Wyo. 1989-90; Dem. nominee U.S. Ho. Reps., 1990; mem. Wyo. Environ. Quality Coun., 1991-93; mem. Wyo. Senate, Laramie, 1993—. Mem. Order St. Ives, Omicron Delta Kappa, Pi Delta Phi. Author: (with Bloomenthal) Cases and Materials on the Federal Income Taxation of Natural Resources, 1971, 72, 77; (with Houghton) Taxation of Mining Operations, 1973, 76; (with Trelease and Dietrich) Natural Resources Law on American Indian Lands, 1977. Home: 3501 Grays Gable Rd Laramie WY 82070 Office: U Wyo Coll Law PO Box 3035 Laramie WY 82071-3035

MAXMIN, JODY LEWIS, art educator; b. Phila.; d. Henry Wertheimer and Louise Olga (Strousse) M. BA, Oberlin (Ohio) Coll., 1971; diploma with distinction, Oxford (Eng.) U., 1973, PhD, 1979. Acting asst. prof. Stanford (Calif.) U., 1979-80, asst. prof., 1980-88, assoc. prof., 1988—; undergrad. advisor, chair honors com. art dept. Stanford U., 1989—. Author poems; contbr. articles to profl. jours. Woodrow Wilson Found. fellow, 1971; Danforth Found. fellow, 1971; Leonard and Katherine Woolley fellow Somerville Coll, Oxford U., 1973; Jr. Rsch. fellow Wolfson Coll., Oxford U., 1975-79. Mem. Archaeol. Inst. Am., Coll. Art Assn. (Millard Meiss award 1982), Soc. for Promotion Hellenic Studies, Soc. for Preservation of Greek Heritage, Phi Beta Kappa (Excellence in Teaching award 1991, Excellence in Undergrad. Teaching award 1992). Jewish. Office: Stanford U Dept Art Stanford CA 94305

MAXWELL, DAVID E., academic executive, educator; b. N.Y.C., Dec. 2, 1944; s. James Kendrick and Gertrude Sarah (Bernstein) M.; children: Justin Kendrick, Stephen Edward. BA, Grinnell Coll., 1966; MA, Brown U., 1968, PhD, 1974. Instr. Tufts U., Medford, Mass., 1971-74, asst. prof., 1974-78, assoc. prof. Russian lang. and lit., 1978-89, dean undergrad. studies, 1981-89; pres. Whitman Coll., Walla Walla, Wash., 1989-93; dir. Nat. Fgn. Lang. Ctr., Washington, 1993—; chmn. steering com. Coop. Russian Lang. Program, Leningrad, USSR, 1981-86, chmn. 1986-90; cons. Coun. Internat.

Ednl. Exchange, 1974—, bd. dirs., 1988-92, 93-94, vice chair, 1991-92, cons. Internat. Rsch. Exchanges, 1976—; mem. adv. bd. Israeli Lang. Policy Inst. Contbr. articles to scholarly jours. Fulbright fellow, 1970-71, Brown U., 1966-67, NDEA Title IV, 1967-70; recipient Lillian Leibner award Tufts U., 1979; citation Grad. Sch. Arts & Scis., Brown U., 1991. Mem. MLA, Am. Coun. Edn. (commn. on internat. edn., pres.'s coun. on internat. edn.), Am. Assn. Advancement of Slavic Studies, Am. Assn. Tchrs. Slavic and E. European Langs., Assn. Am. Colls., Am. Assn. Higher Edn., Am. Coun. Tchg. Fgn. Langs., Brown U. Alumni Assn. Democrat. Avocations: tennis, running, music. Office: Nat Fgn Lang Ctr 1619 Massachusetts Ave NW Washington DC 20036-2213

MAXWELL, DONALD STANLEY, publishing executive; b. L.A., May 30, 1930; s. Harold Stanley and Margaret (Trenam) M.; m. Martha Helen Winn, Dec. 5, 1952; children: Sylvia Louise, Cynthia Lynn, Bruce Stanley, Bradley Erl, Walter James, Wesley Richard, Amy Bernice. Student, Long Beach City Coll., 1948-50; BBA, Woodbury Coll., 1956; D of Bus. Adminstrn. (hon.), Woodbury U., 1991. CPA. Ptnr. Robert McDavid & Co. (CPAs), L.A., 1955-61; controller Petersen Pub. Co., L.A., 1961-68; v.p. fin. Petersen Pub. Co., 1969; controller L.A. Times, 1969-79; v.p. Los Angeles Times, 1977-79, v.p. fin., 1979-81; asst. treas. Times Mirror Co., 1971-82, v.p., controller, 1982-87, v.p., chief acctg. officer, 1987-93, v.p., 1993, exec. dir. fin. program, 1993-95; ret., 1995. Trustee Woodbury U., 1981—, chmn. bd. trustees, 1984-87. Served with AUS, 1950-52. Mem. Fin. Execs. Inst. (dir. 1979-82, pres. L.A. chpt. 1973-74), Internat. Newspaper Fin. Execs. (dir. 1978-82, pres. 1980-81), Am. Inst. CPAs, Calif. Soc. CPAs, Am. Horse Council, Internat. Arabian Horse Assn., Arabian Horse Assn. So. Calif., Friendly Hills Country Club. Republican. Baptist. Home: 2160 Le Flore Dr La Habra Heights CA 90631-8020 Office: Times Mirror Co Times Mirror Sq Los Angeles CA 90012-3816

MAXWELL, JEROME EUGENE, electronics company executive; b. Princeton, Ill., June 2, 1944; s. Emmett Eugene and June (Erickson) M.; BSEE, So. Meth. U., 1967, MSEE, 1971; m. Cynthia Jane O'Connell, July 30, 1977; children: Eric Vaughn, Christina Dawn, Jeremy Emmett, Jason Daniel, Nicholas Mark. Maintainability engr. product support div. Collins Radio Co., Richardson, Tex., 1965-67; jr. engr. computer systems div., 1967-70; sr. engr. TRW Electronic Products, Inc., Colorado Springs, 1970-73, mgr. engring., 1973-79, mgr. program mgmt. office, 1979-81, gen. mgr. space electronics mfg. div., 1981-86; pres., chief exec. officer G&S Systems, Inc., Bedford, Mass., 1986-87; pres., chief exec. officer Atec, Inc., Houston, 1987-91; v.p., divsn. dir. Nat. Systems & Rsch. Co., Colorado Springs, Colo., 1992—. Mem. adv. council U. Colo., Colorado Springs, 1973-86, U. So. Colo., Pueblo, 1974-78; Weblo leader, asst. pack leader Boy Scouts Am., 1976-77; fin. chmn. Ascension Luth. Ch., 1981-86; cons. to community edn. coordinator for computer systems and equipment, 1980-86. Mem. AIAA (sr.), Assn. Old Crows (pres. space chpt.). Republican. Patentee in field.

MAXWELL, NEAL A., church official; m. Colleen Hinckley; four children. B in Polit. Sci., M in Polit. Sci., U. Utah, LLD (hon.); LLD (hon.), Brigham Young U.; LittD (hon.), Westminster Coll.; HHD (hon.), Utah State U., Ricks Coll. Legis. asst. U.S. sen. Wallace F. Bennett, Utah; exec. v.p. U. Utah, Salt Lake City; various ch. positions including bishop Salt Lake City's Univ. Sixth Ward, mem. gen. bd. youth orgn., adult correlation com. and one of first Regional Reps. of the Twelve; elder Ch. Jesus Christ Latter Day Sts., Asst. to the Council of Twelve, 1974-76, mem. of Presidency of First Quorum of the Seventy, 1976-81, mem. of Council of Twelve Apostles, 1981—; bd. dirs. Quester Corp., Deseret News Pub. Co. Mem. Quorum of the Twelve Ch. of Jesus Christ of Latter-Day Saints, Salt Lake City. Recipient Liberty Bell award Utah State Bar, 1967; named Pub. Adminstr. of Yr. Inst. Govt. Service Brigham Young U., 1973. Office: LDS Church Quorum of the Twelve 47 E South Temple Salt Lake City UT 84150

MAXWELL, RAYMOND ROGER, accountant; b. Parmer County, Tex., Jan. 7, 1918; s. Frederick W. and Hazel Belle (Rogers) M.; m. Jeanne Hollarn, June 16, 1945 (dec. Dec. 1987); children: Donald R., Bruce Edward, Sabrina G. Spiering Warren Kleinecke. Ed.B., Western Ill. State Tchrs Coll., 1941; MBA in Acctg., U. Fla., 1949; postgrad., UCLA, 1965-68. CPA, Fla., Calif. Asst. to bus. mgr. Western Ill. State Tchrs. Coll., Macomb, 1939-41; apprentice acct. Charles H. Lindfors, CPA, Ft. Lauderdale, Fla., 1946-48; acct./auditor Frederic Dunn-Rankin & Co. CPA, Miami, Fla., 1948-49; CPA staff Charles Costar, CPA, Miami, 1951; resident auditor/CPA prin. Raymond R. Maxwell CPA, Ft. Lauderdale, 1951-56; supt. pub. instrn. Broward County, Ft. Lauderdale, 1956 61; staff asst. in fin North Am. Aviation, Inc., El Segundo, Calif., 1961-65; tchr. Calif. Polytechnic, 1967; acctg. prin. Raymond R. Maxwell, CPA, Whittier, Calif., 1968—; tchr. Calif. State U., Fullerton, 1989; part-time rsch. asst. UCLA, 1965, teaching asst., 1966, 67; instr. Calif. Poly., 1967. Active precinct election bds., Whittier, L.A. County, 1989; 1st reader First Ch. of Christ, Scientist, Whittier, 1990-92, exec. bd., 1989, exec. bd. chmn., 1993, participant Bible Explorations, 1991-92. 1st lt. USAAF, 1942-46. Republican. Office: Unit # C 13217 Whittier Blvd Whittier CA 90602-3050

MAXWELL, RAYMOND SAMUEL, III, history educator; b. Seattle, Dec. 2, 1952; s. Raymond Samuel Maxwell and Barbara E. (Peterson) Paquette; m. Rosemarie Groeneveld, July 14, 1979; children: Raymond Samuel IV, David Leendert Robert, Elisabeth Maria. BA in History, Western Wash. U., 1982; MA in History, U. Wis., Milw., 1984. Lectr. history Cornish Coll. Arts, Seattle, 1986—; grant reviewer Dept. Edn., Washington, 1994. Mem. editl. adv. bd. Collegiate Press, Calif., 1987-88; reader W.C. Brown and Benchmark Pubs., Iowa and Wis., 1992. Fulbright scholar USIA, 1989, M.J. Murdock scholar M.J. Murdock Found. Vancouver, 1991, Fulbright scholar Dept. Edn., 1992. Mem. Fulbright Assn., N.W. Conf. Brit. Studies. Office: Cornish Coll Arts 710 E Roy St Seattle WA 98102

MAXWELL-BROGDON, FLORENCE MORENCY, school administrator, educational adviser; b. Spring Park, Minn., Nov. 11, 1929; d. William Frederick and Florence Ruth (LaBrie) Maxwell; m. John Carl Brogdon, Mar. 13, 1957; children: Carole Alexandra, Cecily Ann, Daphne Diana. B.A., Calif. State U., L.A., 1955; MS, U. So. Calif., 1957; postgrad. Columbia Pacific U., San Rafael, Calif., 1982-86. Cert. tchr., Calif. Dir. Rodeo Sch., L.A., 1961-64; lectr. Media Features, Culver City, Calif., 1964—; dir. La Playa Sch., Culver City, 1968-75; founding dir. Venture Sch., Culver City, 1974—, also chmn. bd.; bd. dirs., v.p. Parent Coop. Preschools, Baie d'Urfe Que., Can., 1964—; del. to Ednl. Symposium, Moscow-St. Petersburg, 1992, U.S./China Joint Conf. on Edn., Beijing, 1992, Internat. Confedn. of Prins., Geneva, 1993, Internat. Conf., Berlin, 1994. Author: Let Me Tell You, 1973; Wet'n Squishy, 1973; Balancing Act, 1977; (as Morency Maxwell) Framed in Silver, 1985; (column) What Parents Want to Know, 1961—; editor: Calif. Preschooler, 1961-74; contbr. articles to profl. jours. Treas. Democrat Congl. Primary, Culver City, 1972. Mem. Calif. Council Parent Schs. (bd. dirs. 1961-74), Parent Coop. Preschools Internat. (advisor 1975—), Pen Ctr. USA West, Mystery Writers of Am. (affiliate), Internat. Platform Assn., Nat. Assn. Secondary Sch. Prins., Libertarian. Home: 10814 Molony Rd Culver City CA 90230-5451 Office: Venture Sch 5333 Sepulveda Blvd Culver City CA 90230-5233

MAXWORTHY, TONY, mechanical and aerospace engineering educator; b. London, May 21, 1933; came to U.S., 1954, naturalized, 1961; s. Ernest Charles and Gladys May (Butson) M.; m. Emily Jean Parkinson, June 20, 1956 (div. 1974); children: Kirsten, Kara; m. Anna Barbara Parks, May 21, 1979. BS in Engring., U. London, 1954; MSE, Princeton U., 1955; PhD, Harvard U., 1959. Research asst. Harvard U., Cambridge, Mass., 1955-59; sr. scientist, group supr. Jet Propulsion Lab., Pasadena, Calif., 1960-67, cons., 1968—; assoc. prof. U. So. Calif., Los Angeles, 1967-70, prof., 1970—, Smith Internat. prof. mech. and aero. engring., 1988—, chmn. dept. mech. engring., 1979-89; cons. BBC Rsch. Ctr., Baden, Switzerland, 1972—, J.P.L., Pasadena, Calif., 1968—; lectr. Woods Hole Oceanographic Inst., Mass., summers 1965, 70, 72, 83; Forman vis. prof. in aeronautics Tech. Haifa, 1986; vis. prof. U. Poly, Madrid, 1988, Inst. Sop. Tech., Lisbon, 1988, E.T.H., Zürich, 1989, E.P.F., Lausanne, 1989—. Mem. editorial bd. Geophys. Fluid Dynamics, 1973-79, 88—, Dynamic Atmospheric Oceans, 1976-83, Phys. Fluids, 1978-81, Zeitschrift fuer Angewandte Mathematik und Physik, 1987—; contbr. articles to profl. jours. Recipient Humboldt Sr. Scientist award, 1981-83; fellow Cambridge U., 1974, Australian Nat. U., 1978, Nat. Ctr. Atmospheric Research, 1976, Glennon fellow U. Western Australia, 1990, Sr. Queen's fellow in Marine Scis., Commonwealth of Australia, 1984, recipient Halliburton award U. So. Calif., 1980, Otto Laporte award Am. Phys. Soc., 1990. Fellow Am. Phys. Soc. (chmn. exec. com. fluid dynamics div. 1974-79); mem. NAE, Am. Meteorol. Soc., Am. Geophys. Union, ASME (fluid mechs. com.), European Geophys. Soc. Office: U So Calif Dept Mech Engring Exposition Park Los Angeles CA 90089-1453

MAY, ADOLF DARLINGTON, civil engineering educator; b. Little Rock, Mar. 25, 1927; s. Adolf Darlington and Inez (Shelton) M.; m. Margaret Folsom, Dec. 23, 1948; children—Dolf, Barbara, David, Larry. B.Sc. in Civil Engring, So. Meth. U., 1949; M.Sc., Iowa State U., 1950; Ph.D., Purdue U., 1955. Asst. prof., then assoc. prof. Clarkson Coll. Tech., 1952-56; assoc. prof. Mich. State U., 1956-59; research engr. Thompson-Ramo Wooldridge, 1959-62; project dir. Ill. Div. Hwys., 1962-65; mem. faculty U. Calif., Berkeley, 1965—, prof. civil engring., 1965-91, prof. emeritus, 1991—; guest prof. numerous univs., 1965—, cons. to industry, 1965—. Contbr. to profl. jours., books. Served with USNR, 1944-47. Recipient Disting. Engring. Alumnus award Purdue U., 1978; Fulbright scholar to Netherlands, 1977; German Humboldt Scholarship awardee, 1980. Mem. ASCE (Turner award 1994), Transp. Rsch. Bd. (Disting. Lectr. award 1994), Nat. Acad. Engring. (Matson Transp. Rsch. award 1992), AAm. Soc. Engring. Edn., Inst. Traffic Engrs., Sigma Xi, Tau Beta Pi. Home: 1645 Julian Dr El Cerrito CA 94530-2011 Office: U Calif Dept of Civil Engring 114 McLaughlin Hall Berkeley CA 94720

MAY, CLIFFORD DANIEL, newspaper editor, journalist; m. Lou Ann Brunwasser; 1 child, Miranda Rose. Cert. in Russian lang. and lit., U. Leningrad, 1972; BA, Sarah Lawrence Coll., 1973; M Journalism, Columbia U., 1975, M Internat. Affairs, 1975. Assoc. editor Newsweek, 1975-78; roving fgn. corr. Hearst Newpapers, 1978-79; sr. editor Am. edit. Geo mag., 1979-80; gen. editor Sunday Mag., Washington corr. N.Y. Times, 1980-89; chief West Africa bur. N.Y. Times, Abidjan, Ivory Coast, 1984; assoc. editor Rocky Mountain News, Denver, 1989—; spl. corr. CBS Radio News, Bill Moyers' Jour./Internat. Report-PBS-TV, 1970's; host, prodr. Roundtable, Sta. KRMA, Colo.; freelance writer, 1979-89. Contbg. editor World Press Rev. Mag.; host, prodr. roundtable Sta. KRMA, Denver, 1994—. Office: Rocky Mountain News 400 W Colfax Ave Denver CO 80204-2607

MAY, EUGENE FRANK, neuro-ophthalmologist; b. New Orleans, Jan. 28, 1961; s. Martin M. and Renate A. (Teichman) M.; m. Patricia A. Shuster, Aug. 26, 1990; children: Allan J., Nathan S. BS in Engring., Tulane U., 1982; MD, U. Chgo., 1987. Diplomate Am. Bd. Psychiatry and Neurology, 1992, Nat. Bd. Med. Examiners. Commd. 2nd lt. U.S. Army, 1987, advanced through grades to maj., 1993; intern Walter Reed Army Med. Ctr., Washington, 1987-88, resident in neurology, 1988-91; neuro-ophthalmologist Madigan Army Med. Ctr., Tacoma, Wash., 1992—. Mem. AMA, Am. Acad. Neurology, Am. Acad. Ophthalmology, N.Am. Neuro-Ophthalmology (assoc.). Office: Madigan Army Med Ctr Neurology Svc Tacoma WA 98431

MAY, GERALD WILLIAM, university administrator, educator, civil engineering consultant; b. Kenya, Jan. 2, 1941; s. William and Ruth (Koch) M.; m. Mary Joyce Pool, July 27, 1963; children: Erica Ruth, Christian William, Heidi Clara. B.S., Bradley U., 1962; M.S., U. Colo., 1964, Ph.D., 1967. Registered profl. engr., N.Mex. Civil engr. Ill. Hwy. Dept., Peoria, summer 1959-63; instr. U. Colo., Boulder, 1964-67; from asst. to prof. engring. U. N.Mex., Albuquerque, 1967-77, prof. of civil engring, 1977—; dean Coll. Engring., U. N.Mex., Albuquerque, 1980-86; pres. U. N.Mex., Albuquerque, 1986-90; dir. accident study program, Albuquerque, 1970-75, cons. to corps., govtl. agys. Contbr. articles to profl. jours., chpts. to books. Recipient Borden Freshman award Bradley U., 1958. Mem. ASCE (pres. N.Mex. sect. 1982-83), Am. Soc. Engring. Edn. (Outstanding Young Faculty award 1973), Nat. Soc. Profl. Engrs., Sigma Xi, Chi Epsilon, Tau Beta Pi, Phi Eta Sigma. Office: Univ N Mex Civil Engring Dept Albuquerque NM 87131

MAY, JOHN STUART, fundraising executive; b. Orange, N.J., Aug. 31, 1956; s. Merrill Ray and Audrey Merril (Kutz) M.; m. Robin Kevin McGraw, Mar. 23, 1987; children: Majken Ariel, Hanna Taylor. Student, U. Ala., Birmingham and Tuscaloosa, 1973-75, 78-80, Oreg. State U., 1980, U. Oreg., 1980-82; BS, U. Oreg., 1988. Asst. mgr. Lucy Devine's Restaurant, Eugene, Oreg., 1980-82; sales rep. Rogers Cablesystems, Portland, Oreg., 1982-84; account exec. King Broadcasting, KGW Radio, Portland, 1984-85; dir. corp. support Oreg. Pub. Broadcasting, Portland, 1985-91; exec. dir. Doernbecher Children's Hosp. Found., Oreg. Health Scis. U., Portland, 1992—; spkr. in field. employment adv. bd. Oreg. Commn. for the Blind, Portland, 1983-86; pub. rels. bd. Planned Parenthood, Portland, 1986-88; pres. Corbett, Terwilliger, Lair Hill Neighborhood Assn., Inc., Portland, 1987-91; bd. mgrs. Metro Family YMCA, Portland, 1988-91. With USN, 1975-78. Recipient PBS Advt. and Promotion award, 1989, PBS Nat. Underwriting award, 1990, PBS cert. of merit Spl. Event/Coffee, Tea and OPB, 1991. Mem. Nat. Soc. Fundraising Execs. (cert. fund raising exec., bd. pres.). Coun. for Advancement Secondary Edn., Willamette Valley Devel. Officers, Kiwanis Internat. Unitarian. Office: Doernbecher Childrens Hosp 1121 SW Salmon St Portland OR 97205-2000

MAY, LAWRENCE EDWARD, lawyer; b. N.Y.C., Aug. 7, 1947; s. Jack and Ann Marie (Schnell) M.; m. Rosalind Marsha Israel, Feb. 3, 1979; children: Jeremy, Lindsey. BA, UCLA, 1969, JD, 1972. Bar: Calif. 1972, N.Y. 1973. Assoc. Paul, Weiss, Rifkind, Wharton & Garrison, N.Y.C., 1972-76, Levine, Krom & Unger, Beverly Hills, Calif., 1976-79, Weissburg & Aronson, L.A., 1979-81, Valensi & Rose, L.A., 1981-83; ptnr. Pollet & May, L.A., 1983-84; prin. Lawrence E. May, P. C., L.A., 1984-95; of counsel Kenoff & Machtinger, 1993—; bd. dirs. Pub. Counsel, treas., 1992-93, sec., 1993-94, v.p., 1994-95, pres., 1995—. Mem. editorial adv. bd. L.A. Jewish Jour., 1985-91, adv. bd. L.A. Area Coun. Boy Scouts Am., 1985—, exec. com. Pacific S.W. Region Anti-Defamation League, 1985—. Mem. State Bar Calif., Los Angeles County Bar Assn. (trustee 1987-88), Beverly Hills Bar Assn. (bd. govs. 1981-90, pres. 1988-89, chmn. bus. law sect. 1984-85). Democrat. Office: 1999 Avenue of Stars Ste 1250 Los Angeles CA 90067

MAY, MICHAEL WAYNE, technical school executive; b. Springhill, La., Mar. 31, 1949; s. Willie Wilmer and Ethel Florene (Sigler) M. Student So. Ark. U., 1968-70, La. Tech. U., 1970-71. Prodn. dir. Sta. KKAM, Pueblo, Colo., 1973-75; quality control dir. Sta. KBOZ, Bozeman, Mont., 1975-78; music dir., dir. rsch., disk jockey Sta. KOOK, Billings, Mont., 1978-80; founder, operator May Tech. Coll., Billings, Great Falls, 1980—; owner Sta. KMAY, Billings, Mont. Mem. Career Coll. Assn. (state capt. for Mont.). Author: Building with the Basics: Radio Personality Development, 1979, Radio Personality Basics, 1992. Home: 80 Skyline Dr Billings MT 59105-3038 Office: PO Box 127 Billings MT 59103-0127

MAY, PHILIP ALAN, sociology educator; b. Bethesda, Md., Nov. 6, 1947; s. Everette Lee and Marie (Lee) M.; m. Doreen Ann Garcia, Sept. 5, 1972; children: Katrina Ruth, Marie Ann. BA in Sociology, Catawba Coll., 1969; MA in Sociology, Wake Forest U., 1971; PhD in Sociology, U. Mont., 1976. NIMH predoctoral fellow U. Mont., Missoula, 1973-76; dir. health statistics and rsch. Navajo Health Authority, Window Rock, 1976-78; asst. prof. U. N.Mex., Albuquerque, 1978-82, assoc. prof., 1982-89, prof., 1989—, dir. Ctr. on Alcoholism, Substance Abuse and Addictions, 1990—; cons. various govt. agys., 1976—; dir. Nat. Indian Fetal Alcohol Syndrome Prevention Program, Alubuquerque, 1979-85; mem. adv. bd. Nat. Orgn. on Fetal Alcohol Syndrome, Wshington, 1990—; rsch. assoc. Nat. Ctr. for Am. Indian and Alaska Native Mental Health Rsch., 1986—; mem. fetal alcohol syndrome study group Inst. of Medicine, NAS, 1994-95. Contbr. chpts. to books and articles to profl. jours. Mem. Ctrl. United Meth. Ch., Albuquerque, 1980-90, First United Meth. Ch., Albuquerque, 1990—. Lt. USPHS, 1970-73. Recipient Spl. Recognition award U.S. Indian Health Svc., 1992, award Navajo Tribe and U.S. Indian Health Svc., 1992, Human Rights Promotion award UN Assn., 1994. Mem. APHA, Am. Sociol. Assn., Population Ref. Bur. Home: 4610 Idlewilde Ln SE Albuquerque NM 87108-3422 Office: U NMex CASAA 2350 Alamo Ave SE Albuquerque NM 87106-3202

MAY, RICHARD PAUL, data processing professional; b. Milw., Oct. 19, 1946; s. Gorden Elliot and Marie Karen (Leidgen) M.; m. Amy Yamashiro, Mar. 5, 1982. BBA, U. Hawaii, 1972; Cert. in Owners/Pres's. Mgmt., Harvard U., 1989; MBA, U. Hawaii, 1990. Customer engr. IBM, Honolulu, 1968; co-founder, chief exec. officer Aloha Tax Svc., Honolulu, 1972-88; founder, pres., chief exec. officer Honolulu Bar Supply Ltd./May Foodsvc., 1972-90; co-founder Indtl. Distbrs., Kahului, Hawaii, 1976-88; mng. ptnr. Data Capture Systems, Kaneohe, Hawaii, 1990—; pres. Rick May, Inc., Honolulu, 1989—. With U.S. Army, 1968-70, Vietnam. Decorated Bronze Star medal, Air medal, 2 Purple Heart medals. Mem. Inst. Indsl. Engrs., Harvard Bus. Sch. Club, C. of C., Hawaii Visitors Bur., Beta Gamma Sigma. Republican. Roman Catholic. Office: Data Capture Systems 46-001 Kamehameha Hwy Ste 317 Kaneohe HI 96744-3711

MAY, SCOTT C., special education educator; b. Seattle, Mar. 21, 1964; s. Kenneth Gordon and Susan Catherine (Carter) M. BS, Syracuse U., 1986, MA in Emotional Disturbance and Autism, 1989; PhD in Edn., U. Melbourne, Australia, 1995. Cert. spl. edn. tchr., N.Y., Hawaii, Alaska, Pa. Resident advisor Syracuse (N.Y.) U.; dir. after sch. program, lead tchr. Jowonio Sch., Syracuse, 1986-90; spl. edn. tchr Lanai High & Elem., Lanai City, Hawaii, 1990-92; rschr. in tchr. tng., 1992-95; mem. U.S. Spl. Edn. Delegation to Russia and the Czechoslovakia Republic. Advocate inclusive environments handicapped students' programs. Mem. ASCD, Assn. for Persons With Severe Handicaps, Coun. for Exceptional Children. Home: 881 Sudden Vly Bellingham WA 98226-4824

MAYA, WALTER, chemistry educator; b. N.Y.C., Oct. 25, 1929; s. Walter and Harriet (Kaplan) M.; m. Karen Greenbaum, June 30, 1985; children: Lynn Maya Fenstermaker, Leslie Maya-Charles, Susan H., Theodore W. Student, Pasadena (Calif.) C.C., 1948-50; BS with honors, UCLA, 1954, PhD, 1958. Rsch. chemist E.I. Du Pont de Nemours & Co., Wilmington, Del., 1958-59, Rocketdyne, Canoga Park, Calif., 1959-70; prof. chemistry Calif. Poly. U., Pomona, 1971—. Contbr. articles to profl. jours.; copatentee on preparation chlorine pentafluoride. With U.S. Army, 1951-52, Korea. DuPont predoctoral fellow UCLA, 1957, Pfizer postdoctoral fellow U. Ill., 1958. Mem. AAAS, Am. Chem. Soc., Sigma Xi. Democrat. Home: 1845 Antioch Rd Claremont CA 91711-2767 Office: Calif Poly U Chemistry Dept Pomona CA 91768

MAYBAY, DUANE CHARLES, recycling systems executive; b. Ft. Dodge, Iowa, Oct. 5, 1922; s. John H. and Florabel (Hibbard) Lungren; m. Mary Tribble Parrish, Dec. 18, 1947 (div. Oct. 1972); children: Tina Biggs, Karen Woodward. BA in Mktg., U. Wis., 1948. Product engr. Gates Rubber Co., Denver, 1948-50; asst. dir. sales & mktg. Hi-C divsn. Hi-C and Snow Crop Divsn. Minute Maid Corp., N.Y.C., 1951-63; mktg. dir. Knudsen Foods, L.A., 1963-70; owner Mountain Foods, Altadena, Calif., 1970-79, Maybay Recycling Sys., Irvine, Calif., 1976-84; ptnr. Resource Recovery Sys., Irvine, 1984—. Served to lt. col. U.S. Army Air Corps, 1943-45, Italy. Home: 104 Pergola Irvine CA 92715-1704 Office: Resource Recovery Sys PO Box 17426 Irvine CA 92713-7426

MAYBERRY, HERBERT SYLVESTER, lawyer; b. Enid, Okla., Jan. 20, 1927; s. Herbert Sylvester and Pearl Wilma (Bridal) M.; m. Gladys Anne Cody, Nov. 21, 1951 (div. Feb. 1974); children: Martha Rebecca, Molly Nanette; m. Joan Wilma Burnette, Dec. 28, 1974. BS in Geology, U. Okla., 1949; JD, U. Denver, 1959. Bar: Colo. 1959, Tex. 1979. Geologist Shell Oil Co., Denver, 1949-58; mgr. Ball Assocs. Ltd., Denver, 1958-65; exec. asst. Western Geophys. Co., Shreveport, La., 1965-66; v.p., gen. counsel, sec. McAlester (Okla.) Fuel Co., 1966-81; assoc. gen. counsel Enstar Corp., Houston, 1977-84; v.p., gen. counsel, sec. Ultramar Oil and Gas Co., Houston, 1985-89; pvt. practice Grand Junction, Colo., 1989—. With USNR, 1945-46. Mem. ABA, Am. Assn. Petroleum Geologists, Am. Inst. Profl. Geologists. Home: 1701 Cortland Ct Grand Junction CO 81502-2294

MAYENKAR, KRISHNA VAMAN, environmental engineer, consultant; b. Bombay, Nov. 16, 1943; came to U.S., 1969; s. Vaman Krishna and Tara Vaman (Deshpande) M.; m. Shobhana Krishna Karnik, Feb. 12, 1967; children: Kiefer, Neelan. BChemE, Indian Inst. Tech., Bombay, 1966; M in Chem. Engring., U. Louisville, 1970. Registered profl. engr., environ. assessor, Calif. Devel. engr. West Coast Paper Mill, India, 1966-69, 71-72; project engr. Roy F. Weston, Inc., Wilmette, Ill., 1973-75; with Harza Engring. Co., Chgo., 1975-85, engr. VI, 1979-81, sect. head, 1982-85; sr. project mgr. EMCON Assocs., San Jose, Calif., 1986-87, exec. mgr., 1987-89, dir. tech. svcs. div., 1990-91, v.p., bd. dirs., 1991-93; bd. dirs. EMCON Associates; v.p. Harza Environ. Svcs., Chgo., bd. dirs. Inventor toxic metal removal process from water and wastewater; contbr. articles to profl. jours. Mem. Rep. Party, Washington, 1980—, mem. presdl. task force, 1988—. mem Am Inst. Chem. Engrs., Nat. Soc. Profl. Engrs., Calif. Soc. Profl. Engrs.

MAYER, ADOLPH, university official; b. Denver, Feb. 16, 1919; s. Adolph and Aimee (Levy) M.; m. Eileen Mayer, Sept. 14, 1943; children: Reed F., Meredith A. BA in Journalism, U. Colo., 1941. Account exec. Max Goldberg Advt. Agy., Denver, 1941-42; reporter Rocky Mountain News, Denver, 1942-44; news editor NBC, San Francisco, 1944-47; news dir. Sta. KFBK, Sacramento, 1947-49; dir. pub. rels. U. Denver, 1949-86, spl. asst. to chancellor, 1986-90; cons. in field. Mem. editorial rev. bd. Pub. Rels. Quar., 1966-89. Bd. dirs. Auraria Cmty. Ctr., Denver, 1954-56, Colo. TB Assn., 1956-58, Found. for Pub. Rels. Edn., 1968-74; v.p. Mile Hi ARC, 1968-72, bd. dirs., 1964-72; mem. Southmoor Pk. Homeowners Assn., 1977—, pres. bd. dirs., 1992; mem. Denver Cmty. Coun., 1963-71. Recipient Disting. award U. Denver, 1992. Mem. Pub. Rels. Soc. Am. (assembly del. 1968-71, 84-87, mem. grievance bd., 1969-72, chmn. Rocky Mountain dist. 1968, pres. Colo. chpt. 1963, Disting. Svc. award Colo. chpt. 1993), Am. Coll. Pub. Rels. Assn. (mem. nat. bd. 1966-72, dist. dir. 1958, 65, chmn. nat. honors competition 1972, named to Hall of Fame 1968), Denver C. of C., Colo. Assn. Commerce and Industry, Cen. City Opera Assn., Denver Press Club, Sigma Delta Chi. Jewish. Home: 3665 S Jersey St Denver CO 80237-1135

MAYER, BARBARA JEAN, critical care nurse; b. Detroit, May 21, 1957; d. Harry Jr. and Helen Ann (Abeli) Rotter; m. Thomas August Mayer, Feb. 25, 1984; 1 child, Christian August. ADN, Palomar Community Coll., 1977; BSN, Statewide Nursing Program, 1986; MSN, San Diego State U., 1992. Cert. ACLS instr. Staff nurse ICU Tri City Med. Ctr., Oceanside, Calif., 1977-79, asst. unit mgr. ICU, 1979-91; clin. instr. allied health Palomar Community Coll., San Marcos, Calif., 1987-89; critical care nurse specialist Alvarado Hosp. Med. Ctr., San Diego, 1991-94, dir. edn., 1994—; speaker in field. Mem. AACN, Nat. Nursing Staff Devel. Orgn., Sigma Theta Tau. Republican. Roman Catholic. Home: 3519 Stockton Pl Carlsbad CA 92008-7044 Office: Alvarado Hosp Med Ctr 6655 Alvarado Rd San Diego CA 92120-5208

MAYER, HERBERT CARLETON, JR., computer consultant; b. Newton, Mass., Aug. 2, 1922; s. Herbert Carleton and Elsie Marie (Hauser) M.; m. Maryetta Brodkord, Aug. 21, 1948; children: Judith Marie, Christine Louise. BS, Parsons Coll., 1943; MS, U. Iowa, 1947; PhD, U. So. Calif., 1975. Instr. math. U. Idaho, Moscow, 1947-48, U. Utah, Salt Lake City, 1949-51; edn. adminstr. Gen. Electric co., Richland, Wash., 1951-59; systems engr., univ. industry specialist IBM, Chgo., 1959-81; assoc. prof. mgmt. info. systems Wash. State U., Pullman, 1980-82; assoc. prof. U. Wis.-Parkside, Kenosha, 1982-85, Eastern Wash. U., Cheney, 1985-90; adj. prof. mgmt. U. Tex., El Paso, 1976-78. Pres. Tri-City Heights Assn., Kennewick, Wash., 1956-58, PTA, Kennewick, 1957-58; v.p. Kennewick Sch. Bd., 1958-59, pres., 1959. Mem. Math. Assn. Am., Internat. Assn. Computing in Edn., Am. Soc. Engring. Edn., Data Processing Mgmt. Assn. (bd. dirs., sec. Spokane chpt. 1988, v.p. edn. Spokane chpt. 1989, v.p. student chpt. 1990), Phi Delta Kappa (found. chmn. Spokane chpt. 1992-94). Home: 3334 S Bernard St Spokane WA 99203-1636

MAYER, NEIL STEPHEN, municipal official; b. Milw., May 13, 1947; s. Arnold M. and Edith I. (Franks) M.; m. Loduskia R. Pierce, Mar. 27, 1983; 1 child, Jeremy Pierce. BA, Harvard U., 1968; PhD, U. Calif., Berkeley, 1978. Analyst Congl. Budget Office, Washington, 1975-77; sr. rsch. assoc. Urban Inst., Washington, 1977-85; cons. Neil S. Mayer and Assocs., Berkeley, 1980-85; dir. econ. devel. City of Berkeley, 1985-91, dir. cmty. devel., 1991-95; pres. Neil Mayer and Assocs., 1995—. Author: Keys to the Growth of Neighborhood Development Organizations, 1981, Neighborhood Organizations and Community Development, 1984; contbr. articles to profl. jours. Mem. Berkeley Planning Commn., 1972-75; chair Bay Area Housing

Support Collaborative, San Francisco, 1991—; mem. no. Calif. adv. bd. Local Initiatives Support Group, San Francisco, 1985—. NSF resident scientist, Berkeley, 1980-82; Nat. Merit scholar, 1964-68. Mem. Am. Econ. Assn., Am. Planning Assn., Nat. Cmty. Devel. Assn. Democrat. Jewish. Home: 1039 Sierra St Berkeley CA 94707-2526 Office: Neil Mayer & Assocs 160 Sansome St Ste # 700 San Francisco CA 94104

MAYER, PATRICIA JAYNE, financial officer, management accountant; b. Chgo., Apr. 27, 1950; d. Arthur and Ruth (Greenberger) Hersh; m. William A. Mayer Jr., Apr. 30, 1971. AA, Diablo Valley Coll., 1970; BSBA, Calif. State U., Hayward, 1975. Cert. mgmt. acct. Staff acct., auditor Elmer Fox Westheimer and Co., Oakland, Calif., 1976; supervising auditor Auditor's Office County of Alameda, Oakland, 1976-78; asst. acctg. mgr. CBS Retail Stores doing bus. as Pacific Stereo, Emeryville, Calif., 1978-79; contr. Oakland Unified Sch. Dist., 1979-84; v.p. fin., chief fin. officer YMCA, San Francisco, 1984—; instr. acctg. to staff YMCA, San Francisco, 1984—, CBS Retail Stores, 1978-79. Draft counselor Mt. Diablo Peace Ctr., Walnut Creek, Calif., 1970-72; dep. registrar of voters Contra Costa County Registrar's Office, Martinez, Calif., 1972-77. Mem. Fin. Execs. Inst. (bd. dirs. San Francisco chpt.), Inst. Mgmt. Accts. (pres.-elect Diablo Valley chpt. 1995, pres. 1995-96), Dalmatian Club No. Calif., Dalmatian Club Am. Democrat. Jewish. Home: 2395 Lake Meadow Cir Martinez CA 94553-5475

MAYER, THOMAS, economics educator; b. Vienna, Austria, Jan. 18, 1927; s. Felix and Helen (Pollatschek) M.; m. Dorothy JoAnne Harmison, Apr. 7, 1963. BA, Queens Coll., 1948; MA, Columbia U., 1949, PhD, 1953. Economist Treasury Dept., 1951-52, Office of Price Stabilization, 1952, Bur. of Mines, 1953; asst. prof. U. Notre Dame, 1954-56; from asst. to assoc. prof. Mich. State U., 1956-61; vis. assoc. prof. U. Calif., Berkeley, 1961-62; prof. U. Calif., Davis, 1962-93, prof. emeritus, 1993—; vis. ast. prof. W.Va. U., 1953-54. Author: Monetary Policy in the United States, 1968, Permanent Income, Wealth and Consumption, 1972; (with D.C. Rowan) Intermediate Macroeconomics, 1972; (with others) The Structure of Monetarism, 1978; (with others) Money, Banking and the Economy, 1981, 2d edit., 1984, 3d edit., 1987, 4th edit., 1990, 5th edit., 1993, Chineses edit., 1988; Revealing Monetary Policy, 1987, Monetarism and Macroeconomic Policy, 1990, Truth Versus Precision in Economics, 1993, Doing Economics: Essays on the Applied Methodology of Economics, 1995; editor: The Political Economy of American Monetary Policy, 1990, Monetary Theory, 1990, (with F. Spinelli) Studies in Macroeconomics and Monetary Policy Issues, 1991; mem. editorial bd. Jour. of Econ. Lit., 1985—, others. Mem. Am. Econ. Assn., Am. fin. Assn., Internat. Network Econ. Method (chmn. 1993—), Western Econ. Assn. (v.p. 1976-77, pres. 1978-79), Royal Econ. Soc. Home: 3054 Buena Vista Way Berkeley CA 94708-2020

MAYES, SHARON SUZETTE, sculptor, educator; b. Sparta, Ind., Apr. 18, 1948; d. Herbert Franklin and Alma Sue (Keller) M.; m. David Allenberg Katzenstein, Dec. 25, 1983; 1 child, Melissa Sanders-Self. BA, Mich. State U., 1969; MPh, Yale U., 1972, PhD, 1974; MA in Clin. Psychology, Wright Inst., Berkeley, Calif., 1982. Asst. prof. U. Md., College Park, 1974-80; assoc. prof. U. Calif., San Diego, 1981-82; writer, sculptor pvt. practice, Berkeley, Calif., 1982-84; assoc. prof. Macalester Coll., St. Paul, Minn., 1984-86; dir., curator Modern Africa Gallery, Menlo Park, Calif., 1989—. Author: Immune, 1988; contbr. numerous articles and short stories to various publs.; sculptor: works included in juried shows, 1994—. Phi Beta Kappa. Home: 435 San Mateo Dr Menlo Park CA 94025-5348

MAYEUX, JERRY VINCENT, biotechnology executive, microbiologist; b. Mamou, La., Apr. 22, 1937; s. Avie and Ida (Fontenot) M.; m. Sally Louise Brown, June 13, 1981; children by previous marriage: Anne Claire, Peter John. B.S., La. State U., 1960, M.Sc., 1961; Ph.D., Oreg. State U., 1965. Nat. Acad. Sci. research fellow NASA, 1965-66; asst. prof. Colo. State U., Ft. Collins, 1966-70; chief life scis. sect. Martin Marietta Aerospace Corp., Denver, 1970-74; dir. research Ferma Gro Corp., Storm Lake, Iowa, 1974-75; chmn. bd., pres. Dawn Corp., Denison, Iowa, 1976-80; founder Burst AgriTech, Inc., Overland Park, Kans., 1980, chmn. bd., 1982-86, pres., 1987—; pres., chief exec. officer Plant Bioregulator Techs., Inc., Corrales, N.Mex. Adv. com. Kans. Tech. Enterprise Corp., 1987, chmn. Biotechnology Steering Com. Silicon Prarie Technology Assn., 1990-92. Served to 1st lt. M.S.C., U.S. Army, 1965. Mem. Am. Soc. Microbiology, Am. Chem. Soc., AAAS, Plant Growth Regulator Soc., Soc. Indsl. Microbiology.

MAYFIELD, SIGNE, curator of exhibitions; b. Woodbury, N.J., Mar. 14, 1942; d. James P. and Helen (Curtis) Shambaugh; m. William B. Mayfield, Jan. 24, 1946; children: Ross D., Kendra. BA, U. Calif., Berkeley, 1965; postgrad., George Washington U. Curator The Art Corridor, Menlo Park, Calif., 1984-87; gallery dir. Miller-Brown Gallery, San Francisco, 1988-89; curator of exhbns. Palo Alto (Calif.) Cultural Ctr., 1989—; bd. dirs. Achenbach Graphic Arts Coun., Art Table, 1994—; mem. adv. coun. Am. Art Study Ctr., M.H. de Young Mus., Fine Arts Mus. San Francisco. Revs., articles and featured exhbns. in Art of Perception (Australia), Artweek, Am. Craft Mag., Fiberworks, Surface Design, Woodturning (Eng.), San Francisco Chronicle, San Jose Mercury; author exhbn. catalogs.

MAYFIELD-KOCH, LORI JAYNE, insurance processor; b. Newport Beach, Calif., Sept. 11, 1955; d. John Vincent and Marilyn Jane (Huish) M. Student Linn-Benton Community Coll., 1973-75, N.W. Coll., 1975-76; AA in Gen. Edn. Saddleback Community Coll., 1993. Gen. ins. cert. Ins. Inst. Am. Cashier Auto Club So. Calif., Anaheim, 1977-80, ins. clk., sec., Fullerton, 1980-81, ins. rep., 1981, field coord., Costa Mesa, Calif., 1981-86; auto. club sales rep., 1986-88; pres. LJM Enterprises; customer svc. rep. Roadway Express, Irvine, Calif., 1989-93; ins. processor Prudential Ins., Laguna Hills, Calif., 1993—. Recipient Outstanding Citizenship award YMCA, Santa Ana, Calif., 1984. Mem. NAFE. Office: Prudential Fin Svcs Ste 115 24036 Avenida De La Carlota # 570 Laguna Hills CA 92653-3121

MAYHEW, LAWRENCE LEE, electronics company executive; b. Santa Paula, Calif., Mar. 17, 1933; s. Paul Donald and Lucille Frances (Winkler) M.; m. Kathleen Joan McCown, Feb. 6, 1955; children: Taryn Lee, Jeffrey Park, Kimberly Anne. BS, Calif. State Poly. U., 1961. Design engr. Tektronix Inc., Beaverton, Oreg., 1961-65; ops. mgr. Tektronix Inc., Netherlands, 1965-69; div. gen. mgr. Tektronix Inc., Beaverton, 1969-73; div. v.p. Tektronix Inc., 1973-78, group v.p., 1978-82; pres., chief exec. officer Data I/O Corp., Redmond, Wash., 1982-90; ret. Lt. USNR, 1953-58. Mem. IEEE (sr.), Am. Electronics Assn. (dir., chmn. 1981). Republican.

MAYNARD, GLENN C., healthcare administrator, counselor; b. Longview, Wash., May 28, 1949; s. Glenn Colan and Anne Therese (Gramlick) M.; m. Jill E. Miller, Aug. 29, 1970; children: Meegan, Katy, Molly. BS in Sociology, Portland State U., 1971; MEd in Counseling, Lewis and Clark Coll., 1977. Lic. profl. counselor, Oreg.; nat. cert. counselor. Caseworker Pub. Welfare/Adult & Family Svcs., Portland, 1972-76; casework supr. Adults & Family Svcs., Portland, 1976-78; mental health specialist Washington County Mental Health, Hillsboro, Oreg., 1978-79; dir. LINC/adult day Clackamas County Mental Health, Gladstone, Oreg., 1979-87; clin. supr., dir. dual diagnosis svcs. Providence Med. Ctr., Portland, 1987-91, dir. addictions/svcs., 1991-94, dir. chem. dependency svc., 1994—; pvt. practice counseling Portland, 1980—; chmn. mental health/chem. dependency com. Providence Health Plans, 1989—. Mem. citizen adv. com. David Douglas Sch. Bd., Portland, 1989-93, chair, 1990. Recipient Meritorious Svc. award Oreg. Mental Health Assn. Mem. Am. Counseling Assn., Am. mental Health Counselor Assn. Office: Providence Chem Dependency 5228 NE Hoyt St Portland OR 97213-3055

MAYNARD, JOHN HERBERT, electronics engineer; b. Glendale, Calif., Mar. 17, 1935; s. Herbert Walter and Marjorie Edna (Orson) M.; m. Diane Parker, Feb. 2, 1957 (div. 1972); childrne: Laurie Loder, Debra Leebolt, John Herbert Jr.; m. Rosalie Ann Kostanzer, Aug. 12, 1977 (div. 1992); m. Norma Jean Sheahan, June 6, 1992. BS, San Diego State U., 1957; MS, U.S. Internat. U., San Diego, 1972; postgrad., UCLA, 1957-66, U. Hawaii, 1972. Electronics engr. Navy Electronics Lab., San Diego, 1957-64, radar br. head, 1967-68, microwave div. head, 1968-76; exchange scientist Admirality Surface Weapons, Portsmouth, Eng., 1965-66; dept. head Naval Ocean Systems Ctr., San Diego, 1977-84, tech. mgr., 1985-92; tech. mgr. Office Naval Rsch., Arlington, Va., 1993; dept. dir. ops. Naval Command Control Ocean Surveillance Ctr., San Diego, 1993—; owner Rojon Enterprises, San Diego, 1980—; lectr. U.S. Naval War Coll., Newport, R.I., 1988-92. Contbr. articles to profl. jours. Mem. San Diego Opera Assn., 1985—, San Diego Mus. Art, 1986—, La Jolla Mus. Contemporary Art, 1986—. Recipient Achievement in Mgmt. award Dept. of Navy, 1975. Mem. IEEE (sr.), Aerospace and Electronic Systems Soc. of IEEE (chmn. 1971-72), San Diego State U. Alumni Assn., San Diego Apt. Assn. Republican. Presbyterian. Home: 5473 Drover Dr San Diego CA 92115-1129 Office: Naval Command Control and Ocean Surveillance Ctr 53570 Silvergate Ave San Diego CA 92152

MAYNARD, KENNETH DOUGLAS, architect; b. Hackensack, N.J., Aug. 16, 1931; s. Douglas Harry and Eva (Whiting) M.; m. Myrna Myrtle James, Feb. 4, 1956; children: Colin, Vivien Regan. Cert. in Architecture, U. Natal, Durban, Republic of South Africa, 1958. Registered architect Alaska. Draftsman Morross & Graff, Johannesburg, Republic of South Africa, 1950-51, Anglo-Am. Corp., Johannesburg, Republic of South Africa, 1951-54, Moir & Llewellyn, Empangeni, Zululand, Republic of South Africa, 1955-57; architect Pearse Aneck-Hahn & Bristol, Johannesburg, 1957-60, Manley & Mayer, Anchorage, 1960-61, FAA, Anchorage, 1961-62, Crittenden Cassetta Wirum & Jacobs, Anchorage, 1962-65; prin. Schultz & Maynard, Anchorage, 1965-68, Kenneth Maynard Assocs., Anchorage, 1968-78; pres. Maynard & Partch, Anchorage, 1978—. Active Western Alaska Coun. Boy Scouts. Am., Anchorage, 1965-84; bd. dirs. Salvation Army Adv. Bd., Anchorage, 1981-87, Anchorage Mus. Assn., 1969-86, Anchorage Opera Co., 1983-90; chmn. Mayor's Comprehensive Homeless Program Strategy Group, 1992-94. Fellow AIA (pres. Alaska chpt. 1969, N.W. regional rep. for nat. com. on design 1976-89); mem. Constrn. Specification Inst. (pres. Cook Inlet chpt. 1993-94), Soc. Am. Mil. Engrs. Republican. Home: 2237 Forest Park Dr Anchorage AK 99517-1324 Office: Maynard & Partch 4007 Old Seward Hwy Ste 800 Anchorage AK 99503-6060

MAYNARD, LYNN MARIE, lawyer; b. Centralia, Wash., Oct. 16, 1952; d. Everett Earl and Ealoha M. (James) M. Student, U. Wash., 1975, JD, 1978. Bar: Wash. 1978, U.S. Dist. (we. dist.) Wash. 1985. Trial counsel Naval Legal Svc. Office, Subic Bay, Philippines, 1979-80; appellate counsel Navy-Marine Corps Appellate Rev. Activity, Washington, 1980-82; command judge advocate USS Hunley (AS-31), Holy Loch, Scotland, 1982-84; trial atty. Enbody & Dugaw, Centralia, 1985—. Lt. USN, 1978-84. Mem. Am. Legion, Wash. State Bar Assn. (young lawyers rep. 1985-86), Centralia Eagles (madam pres. 1987-88). Republican. Office: Enbody & Dugaw PO Box 855 Centralia WA 98531-0855

MAYO, BENJAMIN FRANKLIN, therapist; b. Columbus, Ohio, Mar. 26, 1941; s. Benjamin and Peryle Mae (Kinzer) M.; m. Diana Wilson, June 12, 1959 (div. May 1966); children: Robin, Mark; m. Arlene Hayden, June 6, 1971; children: Staci, Darrell. BFA, Pont Josephine, Worthington, Ohio, 1961; MFA, Ohio U., 1963; PhD, U. Soc. Calif., L.A., 1993. Cert. hypnotherapist; cert. chem. dependency counselor. Spl. edn. tchr. Found. for Jr. Blind; owner Leimert Park Printers and Office Supply; therapist Bear Inst., L.A. Dir. youth activiies Brookins Cmty. AME Ch.; past mem. bd. dirs. Inglewood Pub. Libr.; bd. dirs. Rebuild L.A.; bd. mem. Youth Gangs Svc. Agy. Greater L.A.; mem. Coun. for Aged City of L.A. Named Bus. Man of Yr. Fortune Mag., 1993, Minority Bus. Man of yr., City of L.A., 1992. Mem. ACA, NAACP, Urban League, Am. Mental Health Assn., Assn. Spiritual, Ethical and Religious Values in Counseling, Nat. Assn. Mental Health Specialists, Calif. Assn. Mental Health Specialists, Assn. Black Psychologists. Home: 4320 Monteith Los Angeles CA 90043 Office: Bear Inst 3450 W 43rd St Los Angeles CA 90008-4906

MAYO, CESAR M., neurologist; b. Lipa City, Batangas, Philippines, Feb. 23, 1939; came to the U.S., 1961; s. Bartolome Lantin and Concepcion Reyes Mayo; m. Corazon Ordoveza Gomez, Feb. 17, 1962; children: Bernadette, Maria Christina, Martin. AA in Pre-Medicine, U. Santo Tomas, Manila, 1955, MD, 1960. Diplomate Am. Bd. Psychiatry and Neurology, Am. Bd. Electrodiagnostic Medicine. Intern USAF Hosp. Clark AFB, Pampanga, Philippines, 1959-60; adj. resident internal medicine and neurology Santo Tomas U., Manila, 1960-61; resident neurology U. Louisville (Ky.) Hosps., 1961-62, chief resident neurology, 1963-64; resident neurology Detroit (Mich.) Receiving Hosp., 1962-63; fellow neuropathology Northwestern U. Med. Sch., Chgo., 1964-66, clin. asst. in neurology and psychiatry, 1964-65, instr. neurology, 1965-67, assoc. neurology, 1967-68, asst. prof. neurology, 1968-69; asst. prof. neurology Albany (N.Y.) Med. Coll., 1969-70, assoc. prof. neurology, 1970-71; asst. attending neurologist Albany Med. Ctr. Hosp., 1969-70, attending neurologist, 1970-71; chief neurology svc. VA Hosp., Martinez, Calif., 1971-72; pvt. practice neurology San Jose, Calif., 1972—; pres. Pacific Imaging Svcs., Inc., San Jose; resident coord. neurology svc. VA Hosp., Hines, Ill., 1965-66, sect. chief neurology svc., 1966-69, asst. chief-acting chief neurology svc., 1969; cons. in neurology Elgin (Ill.) State Hosp., 1967-69; attending physician Neurology Clinics, Northwestern U. Med. Sch., Chgo., 1966-69; attending neurologist Hinsdale (Ill.) Hosp. and Sanatorium, 1968-69; chief neurology svc. VA Hosp., Martinez, Calif., 1971-72; ind. med. examiner Ct. of Indsl. Rels., State of Calif., 1980—. Contbr. articles to profl. jours. Fellow ACP, Am. Acad. Neurology, Am. Geriatric Soc.; mem. AMA, Calif. Med. Assn., Am. Assn. Electromyography and Electrodiagnosis, Am. EEG Soc. (assoc.), Am. Acad. Clin. Neurophysiology, Am. Soc. Neuroimaging, Am. Imaging Assn., Am. Fedn. Clinic Rsch., Western Electroencephalography Soc., N.Y. Acad. Scis., Royal Soc. Medicine (affiliate), Santa Clara County Med. Soc. Office: Pacific Imaging Svcs 361 S Monroe St San Jose CA 95128

MAYO, ROBERT N., software engineer; b. Washington, Aug. 23, 1959; s. Robert P. and Marian A. Mayo. BS in Computer Sci., Washington U., St. Louis, 1981; MS in Computer Sci., U. Calif., Berkeley, 1983, PhD of Computer Sci., 1987. Asst. prof. U. Wis., Madison, 1988; software engr. Digital Equipment Corp., Palo Alto, Calif., 1989—. Mem. Assn. Computer Machinery. Office: Digital Equipment Corp 250 University Ave Palo Alto CA 94301-1713

MAYOL, RICHARD THOMAS, advertising executive, political consultant; b. Springfield, Ill., Oct. 30, 1949; s. Richard McFaren and Marjorie (Maddex) M. AA, Springfield Coll., 1969; BS, U. Tulsa, 1972. Co-owner First Tuesday Inc., Phoenix, 1976-85; pres. Mayol and Assocs., Phoenix, 1985—; CEO New West Policy Group, Prescott, Ariz., 1993—; cons. Dem. candidates, Western U.S., Mo. Udall for Congress, Tucson, Mayor Terry Goddard, Phoenix, Senator John Melcher, Mont. Mem. Phoenix Film Commn., 1985—. Mem. Am. Assn. Polit. Cons., Phoenix Grand Prix Commn. Home and Office: Mayol and Assocs 348 Moreland Cir Prescott AZ 86303-4035 also: 223 Union St Prescott AZ 86303-3813

MAYRON, LEWIS WALTER, clinical ecology consultant; b. Chgo., Sept. 20, 1932; s. Max and Florence Minette (Brody) M.; divorced; children: Leslie Hope Mayron Coff, Eric Brian. BS in Chemistry, Roosevelt U., 1954; MS in Biochemistry, U. Ill., 1955, PhD in Biochemistry, 1959. Rsch. assoc. Dept. Biochemistry and Nutrition U. So. Calif., L.A., 1959-61; asst. biochemist Dept. Biochemistry Presby.-St. Luke's Hosp., Chgo., 1961-62; instr. Dept. Biological Chemistry U. Ill., Chgo., 1961-62; biochemistry group leader Tardanbek Labs., Chgo., 1962-63; sr. devel. chemist Abbott Labs., Chgo., 1963-64; asst. attending physician, mem. spl. staff Michael Reese Hosp. and Med. Ctr., Chgo., 1964-66, rsch. assoc. Dept. Allergy Rsch., 1964-66; asst. prof. in biochemistry and physiology Sch. Dentistry Loyola U., Chgo., 1968-71; guest investigator Argonne (Ill.) Nat. Lab., 1973-79; rsch. chemist V.A. Hosp., Hines, Ill., 1968-79; chief clin. radiobiochemist nuclear medicine svc. V.A. Wadsworth Hosp. Ctr., L.A., 1979-83; cons. in clin. ecology, 1980—. Contbr. articles to profl. jours. Mem. Am. Assn. Clin. Chemists, Am. Assn. for the Advancement of Sci., Soc. for Experimental Biology and Medicine, Sigma Xi. Home: 1779 Summer Cloud Dr Thousand Oaks CA 91362-1217

MAYS, JOHN MOLTENO, science educator, consultant; b. N.Y.C., Mar. 11, 1923; s. John Glasscock and Monica Celia (Molteno) M.; m. Luisa Bibiana Noriega, July 29, 1955; children: Christopher Manuel, Claire Marina Mays Poumadère. BS, Calif. Inst. Tech., Pasadena, 1947; PhD, Columbia U., N.Y.C., 1950. Nat. rsch. fellow Harvard U., Cambridge, Mass., 1950-51, AEC fellow, 1951-52; mem. tech. staff Bell Telephone Labs, Murray Hill, N.J., 1952-60; program dir. Nat. Sci. Found., Washington, 1960-66; staff mem. Office Sci. Adviser to Pres., Washington, 1966-72; sci. adviser Nat. Inst. Edn., Washington, 1972-83; cons., 1983—. Co-author: Youth: Transition to Adulthood, 1977. Writer, speaker, cons. Washington, L.A., 1983-90, 1991—. Fellow Nat. Rsch. Coun., Washington, 1950, Atomic Energy Commn. Washington, 1951. Democrat. Home and Office: 21434 Calle del Barco Pacific Palisades CA 90272-4124

MAYS, WILLIE HOWARD, JR. (SAY HEY KID), former professional baseball player; b. Westfield, Ala., May 6, 1931; s. William Howard and Ann M.; m. Mae Louise Allen, Nov. 27, 1971; 1 adopted son, Michael. Baseball player Birmingham Black Barons, 1948-50, Trenton Inter-State League, 1950-51, Mpls. Millers, Am. Assn., 1951, N.Y. Giants, 1951-57, San Francisco Giants, 1958-72, N.Y. Mets, 1972-73; with Bally's Park Place, Atlantic City, 1980—; pub. rels. exec. San Francisco Giants, 1986—. Author: Willie Mays: My Life In and Out of Baseball, 1966, Say Hey: The Autobiography of Willie Mays, 1988. Served with AUS, 1952-54. Named Most Valuable Player Nat. League, 1954, 65; named Player of Yr. Sporting News, 1954, Baseball Player of Decade Sporting News, 1970, Male Athlete of Yr. AP, 1954, Rookie of the Yr., 1951, Most Exciting Playin Sport Sporting News, 1954, All-Star Game, 1954-73; recipient Hickok belt, 1954, Golden Bat award to commemorate 600 home runs, Gold Glove award (12 times), 1st Commissioner's award, 1970, Golden Plate awarded to America's Captains of Achievement by Am. Acad. Achievement, 1976, Spirit of Life award City of Hope, 1988, Sportsman of Decade, Cong. Racial Equality, 1991, Legendary Star award HBO Video; inducted into Ala. Sports Hall of Fame, Baseball Hall of Fame, 1979, Black Hall of Fame, 1973, Calif. Sports Hall of Fame. Office: care San Francisco Giants Candlestick Park San Francisco CA 94124*

MAYTUM, HARRY RODELL, retired physician; b. Alexandria, S.D., Jan. 25, 1913; s. Wellington James and Lillian May (Syferd) M.; m. Louetta Susanna Stoltz, Apr. 27, 1937; children: James, Nancy, Joan. BS magna cum laude, U. Wis., 1936, MD, 1938. Intern Alameda County Hosp., Oakland, Calif., 1938-39, resident in surgery, 1946-47; resident in surgery Merced County Hosp., Merced, Calif., 1939-41; pvt. practice, Merced, 1947-93; ret., 1993; chief staff Mercy Hosp., Merced, Merced County Hosp. Bd. dirs. Merced County Mosquito Abatement Dist., 1954-64. Lt col. M.C., USAAF, 1941-47, ETO. Fellow Am. Geriatric Soc., Am. Acad. Family Practice (charter); mem. AMA, Calif. Med. Assn. (Plessner Meml. award 1992), Merced-Mariposa County Med. Soc. (pres.. 1955), Merced C. of C. (bd. dirs. 1973-77, former chmn. health affairs com., Merced Citizen of Yr. award 1989), Kiwanis (pres. Merced 1953), Elks, Phi Beta Kappa, Alpha Omega Alpha. Republican. Home: 2887 Forist Ln Merced CA 95340-2553

MAZARAKIS, MICHAEL GERASSIMOS, physicist, researcher; b. Volos, Greece; came to U.S., 1966, naturalized, 1980; s. Gerassimos Nikolaos and Anthie Gerassimos (Kappatos) M.; m. Carolyn Seidel, June 30, 1990. BS in Physics, U. Athens, Greece, 1960; MS in Physics, U. Sorbonne, Paris, 1963, PhD in Physics, 1965; PhD in Physics, Princeton U. and U. Pa., 1971; cert. in mgmt., MIT, 1976. Mem. faculty Rutgers U., New Brunswick, N.J., 1971-74; v.p. and dir. exptl. program Fusion Energy Corp., Princeton, N.J., 1974-77, also exec. v.p., 1975-77; research physicist Argonne Nat. Lab., U. Chgo., 1978-81; research physicist Sandia Nat. Lab. Div. 1231, Albuquerque, 1981—. Contbr. articles to profl. jours. Patentee in field. Bd. dirs. Orthodox Ch., Albuquerque, 1981—; Served to maj. Greek Army, 1960-62. Recipient award Italian. Govt., 1956, Greek Govt., 1956-60, French Govt., 1962-65; Yale U. grantee, 1966. Mem. Am. Phys. Soc., IEEE, Alliance Francaise, N. Mex. Mountain Club, N.Y. Acad. Sci., Sigma Xi. Current work: Particle beam physics, accelerator research and development, inertial fusion, pulse power technology, plasma physics. Subspecialty: Nuclear fusion, particle beam physics.

MAZELIS, MENDEL, plant biochemist, educator, researcher; b. Chgo., Aug. 31, 1922; s. Jacob and Anna (Brvarnick) M.; m. Noreen Beimer, Mar. 24, 1969; 1 son, Jacob Russell. B.S., U. Calif.-Berkeley, 1943, Ph.D., 1954. Jr. research biochemist U. Calif.-Berkeley, 1954-55; research assoc., instr. U. Chgo., 1955-57; assoc. chemist Western Regional Research Lab., Albany, Calif., 1957-61; asst. prof. U. Calif.-Davis, 1961-64, assoc. prof., 1964-73, prof., 1973-91, prof. emeritus, 1991—. Served to lt. (j.g.) USN, 1943-46. Mem. Am. Soc. Plant Physiologists, Am. Soc. Biochemists and Molecular Biologists, Biochem. Soc. London, Phytochem. Soc. N.Am., Phytochem. Soc. Europe, Inst. Food Technologists. Office: U Calif Dept Food Sci/Tech 111 Cruess Hall Davis CA 95616

MAZID, MOHAMMED ABDUL, chemist; b. Mymensingh, Bangladesh, Mar. 16, 1950; s. Shafdur Rahman and Jamila Khatoon; m. Sanjida Shahnaz, July 22, 1978; 1 child, Imrul. BS with hons., U. Dhaka, Bangladesh, 1971, MS, 1973; MS, Lakehead U., Thunder Bay, Can., 1978; PhD, U. Ottawa, Can., 1981. Various to rsch. assoc. scientist Export Packers Co., Ltd., Winnipeg, Manitoba, Can., 1983-85; with Inrad Indsl. Rsch. and Devel., Ltd., Winnipeg, 1985-86; rsch. assoc. dept. chemistry U. Alberta, Edmonton, Can., 1986-87; sr. scientist, group leader biochem. devel. Chembiomed Ltd., Edmonton, 1987-91; sr. devel. scientist, mfg. technologies Alberta Rsch. Coun., Edmonton, 1991-92; prin. R & D scientist Glyko Inc., Novato, Calif., 1992-94; project mgr. Sepragen Corp., San Leandro, Calif., 1994—; vis. fellow Nat. Sci. and Engring. Rsch. Coun. Can., 1981-83. Patentee in field; contbr. to profl. publs. Univ. rsch. fellow Lakeheed U., 1976-77, grad. rsch. fellow U. Ottawa, 1978-79. Mem. Am. Chem. Soc., Soc. Biomaterials. Office: Sepragen Corp Glyko Inc 2126 Edison Ave San Leandro CA 94577

MAZUREK, STEPHEN JEROME, foreign language educator; b. Natrona Heights, Pa., Mar. 5, 1951; s. Edward Thaddeus and Hedwig Anne (Nowakowski) M. AB, U. Pitts., 1973; MA, NYU, 1975, U. Calif., Berkeley, 1978; PhD, U. Calif., Berkeley, 1986. Calif. C.C. instr.'s credential for Russian. Tchg. asst. U. Calif., Berkeley, 1976-78, tchg. assoc., 1978-80; various positions Berkeley (Calif.) Unified Sch. Dist., 1983—; instr. Piedmont (Calif.) Adult Edn., 1989-91, Cabrillo Coll., Aptos, Calif., 1991—; presenter in field. Internat. Rsch. and Exch. Bd. grantee, 1992. Mem. MLA, Am. Assn. for the Advancement Slavic Studies, Am. Assn. Tchrs. Slavic and East European Langs., Linguistic Soc. Am., Fgn. Lang. Assn. No. Calif., Oakland-Nakhodka Sister City Assn. Home: 1207A University Ave Berkeley CA 94702-1708

MAZZA, JOHN GAMBLE, financial company executive; b. Trona, Calif., Nov. 8, 1945; s. Harold and Edith (Gamble) M.; m. Toni Swords Ferring, Dec. 31, 1981 (div. Aug. 1985); m. Robby Bertheau Fulton, Aug. 25, 1990. BA, Claremont McKenna Coll., 1967; MBA, U. So. Calif., 1969. Sec., treas., dir., chief fin. officer William O'Neil & Co. Inc., L.A., 1969-84; pres., dir. Drake Holding Co., Santa Monica, Calif., 1984—. Mem. Fin. Analysis Soc., Lincoln Club. Republican. Home: 6613 Zumirez Dr Malibu CA 90265-4312 Office: Drake Capital Inc 1250 4th St Santa Monica CA 90401-1350

MCADAMS, CHARLES MICHAEL, academic administrator; b. Camp Pendleton, Calif., May 8, 1947; s. John and Trudy Mae (Fleming) McA.; m. Barbara M. Austin, Feb. 27, 1995. BA in History, U. The Pacific, 1976; MA in History, John Carroll U., 1978; postgrad. in Edn., U. San Francsico, 1978-82. Regional dir. U. San Francisco, 1978—; cons. in field. Author monographs. Advisor Calif. State Assembly, 1974-78; founder, chair Com. on Higher Edn., Sacramento, 1982-88; foreman U.S. Grand Jury, ea. dist. Calif., 1988-91; bd. dirs. Croatian Scholarship Found., Calif., 1990—. ABA fellow, 1976-77, Sourissea Acad. fellow, 1978-80. Mem. Am. Assn. Advancement Slavic Studies, Croatian Acad. Am., Croatian Studies Found. Australia and New Zealand, Assn. Croatian Studies, El Inst. Croata Latin Am. de Cultura, Phi Alpha Theta.

MCALINDIN, DAVID PETER, municipal employee; b. Newark, Oct. 11, 1950; s. David Peter and Catherine Agnes (Roberts) McA.; m. Kathleen Ann Tisdale, Aug. 24, 1983 (div. Sept. 1992); children: Tyson Dean, Caitlin Marie. BA, Monmouth Coll., 1972; postgrad., San Diego State U., 1972-73; MPA, Boise State U., 1979. Br. mgr. Household Fin. Co., Nampa, Idaho, 1973-77; devel. & data mgr. Div. Econ. & Cmty. Affairs, Boise, 1979-83; spl. asst. Office of Gov., Boise, 1984-86; devel. dir. Idaho Youth Ranch, Boise, 1987; econ. devel. dir. City of Twin Falls, Idaho, 1988—; bd. dirs. 1st Interstate Bank cmty. adv. coun., Twin Falls; sr. staff mem. Idaho Investment Panel, Boise, 1982. Author: Idaho Industrial Rrvenue Bond Handbook, 1983; co-author: County Profiles of Idaho, 4th edit., 1980. Pres. United Way of Magic Valley, Twin Falls, 1993. Mem. Twin Falls C. of C.,

Scottish Rites. Democrat. Roman Catholic. Home: 842 Walnut St N Twin Falls ID 83301-4141 Office: City of Twin Falls 321 2nd Ave E Twin Falls ID 83301-6466

MCALISTER, MAURICE L., savings and loan association executive; b. 1925; married. Pres., dir. Downey Savs. and Loan, Newport Beach, Calif., 1957—, chmn. bd. Office: Downey Savs & Loan Assn PO Box 6000 3501 Jamboree Rd Newport Beach CA 92660-2939*

MCALISTER, MICHAEL HILLIS, architect; b. Bakersfield, Calif., May 22, 1945; s. Doyle R. and Mary E. McAlister. AA, Bakersfield Coll., 1967; BArch, Calif. Polytech. U., 1971. Planning technition Bakersfield City Hall, 1963; carpenter Del Webb Corp., Kern City, Calif., 1964; architectural draftsman Goss & Choy Architects, Bakersfield, 1965-67; architect, v.p. D.G.C. & Assocs., Bakersfield, 1971-80; dir. architecture, v.p. N.B.A. & Assocs., Architects, Bakersfield, 1980-83; architect, pres. Michael H. McAlister, A.I.A., Bakersfield, 1983—; hepthology design cons. for various treatment groups and hosps., 1987—. Commr., architectural advisor Historic Preservation Commn., Bakersfield, 1986-87; bd. dirs. Camp Fire Coun., Kern County, Calif., 1980-84. Recipient Architectural Pub. Bldg. Hist. award Beautiful Bakersfield Com., City of Bakersfield's City Coun. and Hist. Preservation Commn., 1985, 87, Exterior Environ. Design Excellence Bakersfield C. of C., 1988, Comml. Design Excellence award, 1984, Design Excellence and Beautification award City of Taft, Calif., 1989, Design Excellence award State of Nev., 1992. Mem. AIA (Calif. Coun., Golden Empire chpt.). Office: 5030 Office Park Dr Ste B Bakersfield CA 93309-0612

MCALLISTER, BYRON LEON, mathematics educator; b. Midvale, Utah, Apr. 29, 1929; s. Donald Leon and Julia Vilate (Roundy) McA.; m. Kay Marie Keithley, Nov. 29, 1957; children: Marie Elizabeth, Galen Arthur, Tamara Ann. BA, U. Utah, 1951, MA, 1955; PhD, U. Wis., 1966. Asst. prof. to assoc. prof. S.D. Sch. of Mines and Tech., Rapid City, 1958-67; assoc. prof. to prof. Mont. State U., Bozeman, 1967-91, prof. emeritus, 1991—; instr. U. Wis., Menasha, 1961-62. Contbr. articles to profl. jours. With U.S. Army, 1952-54. Mem. Am. Math. Soc., Math. Assn. Am., Mystery Writers of Am.

MCALLISTER, CHASE JUDSON, human resource director; b. Idaho Falls, Idaho, Apr. 23, 1942; s. Charles Thane and Margaret Frances (Witherspoon) McA.; children: Branden Jason, Frances Paige. Student, Idaho State U., 1960-63. Laborer Basic Am. Foods, Blackfoot, Idaho, 1965-66; mechanic Basic Am. Foods, Blackfoot, 1966-67, electrician, 1967-72, personnel mgr., 1972-77, mgr. labor rels., 1977-88, mgr. labor rels., safety and security, 1989, mgr. div. human resources, 1989-90, dir. human resources, 1990—; pension com. mem. Basic Am. Foods, Blackfoot, 1979—. Chmn. Blackfoot United Fund, 1977-78, Bingham County Personnel Adv. Coun., Blackfoot, 1981-83, Bingham Meml. Hosp. Bd. Dirs., 1989-91; pres. Eastern Idaho Am. Soc. for Pers. Adminstrn., Pocatello, 1978-79. Recipient Idaho State Outstanding Personnel Adminstr., 1977. Mem. Rotary, Soc. for Human Resource Adminstrn. (sr. profl. 1992). Episcopalian. Office: Basic Am Foods PO Box 592 Blackfoot ID 83221-0592

MCALLISTER, PETER MICHAEL, healthcare executive; b. Glendale, Calif., Mar. 27, 1938; s. Paul Blanchard and Blanche Isabell (Kirkpatrick) McA.; m. Diane Marie Williams, Feb. 4, 1961; children: Kevin Michael, Paul Scott, Kim Marie, Jeannie Isabella. BS in Indsl. Mgmt., U. So. Calif., 1961. Asst. plant dir. Krasne div. Royal Industries, L.A., 1968-69; dir. mgmt. engring. Am. Medicorp, Inc., L.A., 1970-73; chief oper. officer Sunrise Hosp., Las Vegas, Nev., 1973-82; adminstr. Huntington Park Community Hosp., L.A., 1982-83; cons. McAllister & Assocs., Las Vegas, 1983-84; salesman Americana Group Realtors, Las Vegas, 1984-85, Real Corp., Las Vegas, 1985-86; cons. Adelman & Assocs., Las Vegas, 1986-88; dir. mgmt. svcs. U. Med. Ctr., Las Vegas, 1988—. Capt. USMC, 1961-66, Vietnam. Decorated Air medal, Purple Heart. Mem. Nev. Hosp. Assn. (chmn. so. coun. 1975-76, pres. 1981-82). Home: 7435 Rogers St Las Vegas NV 89139-5750 Office: U Med Ctr 1800 W Charleston Blvd Las Vegas NV 89102-2329

MCALMOND, RUSSELL WAYNE, bank executive; b. Bremerton, Wash., May 26, 1952; s. Philip Hugh and Shirley Jean (Beal) McA.; m. Jacqueline May McReynolds, Oct. 6, 1979; children: Brittney Jon, Kristie Jean. Student, Oreg. State U., 1973-74, Portland State U., 1974-75; grad., Coll. Fin. Planning, 1992. CFP, cert. fund specialist, trust and fin. adviser. Mgr. MP, Inc., Portland, 1975-82; fin. cons. Shearson Lehman Bros., Portland, 1982-84; pres. McAlmond Fin. Mgmt., Portland, 1984-86; asst. v.p. AGFC, L.A., 1986-88, Bank of Calif., Portland, 1988-89; v.p. U.S. Nat. Bank of Oreg., Portland, 1989-94; v.p., mgr. First Interstate Bank of Oreg., 1994—; mem. Estate Planning Coun. Portland. Contbr. articles to profl. jours. Com. United Way of Oreg., Portland, 1989—. Mem. City Club of Portland, Internat. Assn. Fin. Planners (pres. Portland chpt.), Inst. CFP, Oreg. Soc. CFPs, Oreg. Pub. Broadcasting, Internat. Bd. Standards and Practices, Marine Corps Officers Assn., High Desert Mus. Office: 1st Interstate Bank Oreg 900 SW Fifth Ave Portland OR 97208-3459

MCANIFF, EDWARD JOHN, lawyer; b. N.Y.C., June 29, 1934; s. John Edward and Josephine (Toomey); m. Jane Reiss, June 11, 1960; children: John E., Maura T., Anne T., Jane A., Peter J., Kathleen A. AB magna cum laude, Holy Cross Coll., 1956; LLB cum laude, NYU, 1961. Bar: N.Y. 1962, Calif. 1963, D.C. 1976. Law clk. to Justice A.T. Goodwin Supreme Ct. Oreg., Salem, 1961-62; assoc. then ptnr. O'Melveny & Myers, L.A., 1962—; lectr. Stanford U., 1974-75, 94, Boalt Hall Law Sch., 1992—; fgn. law counsel Freehill, Hollingdale & Page, Sydney, Australia, 1981-82; bd. dirs. Mellon Bank Corp. Trustee Mayfield Sr. Sch., 1979—, chmn. bd. trustees, 1980-81; bd. dirs. L.A. Master Chorale, 1979-81, 87—, pres., 1992—; trustee Music Ctr. Los Angeles County, 1992—, mem. exec. com., 1992—; bd. dirs. Music Ctr. Found., 1992—. Capt. USNR, 1956-83. Mem. City Club, Valley Hunt Club. Republican. Home: 3315 San Pasqual St Pasadena CA 91107-5436 Office: O'Melveny & Myers 275 Battery St Ste 2500 San Francisco CA 94111-3338

MCARTHUR, ELDON DURANT, geneticist, researcher; b. Hurricane, Utah, Mar. 12, 1941; s. Eldon and Denise (Dalton) McA.; m. Virginia Johnson, Dec. 20, 1963; children: Curtis D., Monica McArthur Bennion, Denise, Ted O. AS with high honors, Dixie Coll., 1963; BS cum laude, U. Utah, 1965, MS, 1967, PhD, 1970. Postdoctoral rsch. fellow, dept. demonstrator Agrl. Rsch. Coun. Gt. Britain, Leeds, Eng., 1970-71; rsch. geneticist Intermountain Rsch. Sta. USDA Forest Svc., Ephraim, Utah, 1972-75; rsch. geneticist Shrub Scis. Lab., Intermountain Rsch. Sta. USDA Forest Svc., Provo, Utah, 1975-83, project leader, chief rsch. geneticist, 1983—; adj. prof. dept. botany and range sci. Brigham Young U., Provo, 1976—. Author over 250 rsch. papers; contbr. chpts. to books; editor symposium procs. Grantee Sigma Xi, 1970, NSF, 1981, 85, Coop. State Rsch. Svc., 1986, 91. Mem. Soc. Range Mgmt. (pres. Utah sect. 1987), Botan. Soc. Am., Soc. Study Evolution, Am. Genetic Assn., Shrub Rsch. Consortium (chmn. 1983—), Intermountain Consortium for Aridlands Rsch. (pres. 1991—). Mormon. Home: 555 N 1200 E Orem UT 84057-4350 Office: USDA Forest Svc Shrub Scis Lab 735 N 500 E Provo UT 84606-1856

MCATEE, RICHARD EVERETT, chemist, consultant; b. Springfield, Mo., Dec. 14, 1929; s. Eslie Howard and Esther Marie (Rippey) McA.; m. Wande Joyce Houston, Jan. 20, 1952; children: Peggy Jo, Diana Gay, Nancy Beth. BS, Ft. Hayes Kans. State Coll., 1962; MS, U. Idaho, 1964. Spectrochemist Phillips Petroleum Co., Idaho Falls, 1964-68; chemist Idaho Nuclear Corp., Idaho Falls, 1968-71; sr. chemist Allied Chem. Co., Idaho Falls, 1971-78; sci. specialist EG&G, Idaho Inc., Idaho Falls, 1978—; cons. in chem. processing, 1990-94; mem. EPA adv. com. for geothermal sampling, Las Vegas, Nev., 1981. Contbr. articles to profl. jours.; inventor chemical logging of geothermal wells, polyphosphozene membranes and spray forming membranes. Bd. dirs. Atomic Workers Credit Union, Idaho Falls, 1973-82; pres. Idaho Falls Figure Skating Club, 1989. With U.S. Army, 1948-50. Mem. Am. Nuclear Soc., Am. Chem. Soc. (health and safety divsn.), VFW. Republican. Methodist. Home: 646 E 16th St Idaho Falls ID 83404-5950 Office: LITCO PO Box 1625 Idaho Falls ID 83415-0001

MCATEER, JAMES FRANCIS, lawyer; b. Seattle, Feb. 23, 1931; s. George Henry and Irene Mary (Ethier) McA.; m. Joan Francis Fitzpatrick, July 31, 1954 (div. Aug. 1977); children: Maryjeanne, Anne, Patricia, Margaret, Kathleen, Suzanne, Heidi; m. Judith Ann Gautsch, Jan. 24, 1978. Student, Santa Clara U., 1948-51; BS, U. Wash., 1953, JD, 1954. Bar: Wash. 1954, U.S. Supreme Ct. 1976. Asst. U.S. atty. for western dist. Wash., Seattle, 1959-62; ptnr. Lenihan, Ivers & McAteer, 1962-86, Schwabe, Williamson, Ferguson & Burdell, Seattle, 1986—. Mem. Law Rev., U. Wash., 1953-54. Capt. JAGC, U.S. Army, 1954-58. Mem. Wash. State Bar Assn., Seattle-King County Bar Assn., Wash. Athletic Club, Central Park Tennis Club, Order of Coif. Roman Catholic. Home: 2109 E Crescent Dr Seattle WA 98112-3413 Office: Schwabe Williamson Ferguson & Burdell 1420 5th Ave Ste 3400 Seattle WA 98101-2333

MCAULEY, SKEET, artist; b. Monahans, Tex., Mar. 7, 1951; s. George Clifford and Thelma Lee (Martin) McA.; m. Karen Suzanne Gee, June 25, 1994. BA, Sam Houston State U., 1976; MFA, Ohio U., 1978. Instr. photography Spring Hill Coll., Mobile, Ala., 1978-79, Tyler (Tex.) Jr. Coll., 1979-81; assoc. prof. photography U. N.Tex., Denton, 1981-93; featured in numerous articles and publs. One-person exhibits include Christopher Grimes Gallery, Santa Monica, Calif., 1995, Lowinsky Gallery, N.Y.C., 1993, U.S. Golf Assn. Mus., Far Hills, N.J., 1993, Dallas Mus. Art, 1992, Moody Gallery, Houston, 1992, Tyler Mus. of Art, 1992, The Heard Mus., Amherst, Mass., 1991, Calif. Mus. Photography, Riverside, 1991, Etherton/Stern Gallery, Tucson, Ariz., 1991, The Albuquerque Mus., 1990; group exhibits include Cleve. Mus. Art, 1994, Virginia Beach Ctr. for Arts, 1994, others; author: Sign Language: Contemporary Southwest Native Americans, 1989. Grantee Polaroid Copr., 1988, Nat. Endowment for the Arts Individual Artist fellowship, 1984, 86. Mem. Soc. Photographic Education (bd. dirs. 1990-93). Democrat. Office: 3516 Madera Ave Los Angeles CA 90039-1930

MCBEATH, GERALD ALAN, political science educator, researcher; b. Mpls., Sept. 13, 1942; s. Gordon Stanley and Astrid Elvira (Hjelmeir) McB.; m. Jenifer Huang, June 7, 1970; children: Bowen, Rowena. BA, U. Chgo., 1963, MA, 1964; PhD, U. Calif., Berkeley, 1970. Vis. asst. prof. polit. sci. Rutgers Coll., New Brunswick, N.J., 1970-72; asst. prof. John Jay Coll., CUNY, N.Y.C., 1972-74, 75-76; assoc. prof. Nat. Chengchi U., Mucha, Taipei, Taiwan, 1974-75; prof. U. Alaska, Fairbanks, 1976—, acting dean coll. liberal arts, 1991-93, dir. faculty devel., 1990-92; cons. Inst. Social and Econ. Rsch., Anchorage, 1976-77; contract rschr. Alaska Dept. Natural Resources, Alaska Dept. Edn., Nat. Inst. Edn., others; staff dir. task force on internat. trade policy Rep. Conf., U.S. Senate. Sr. author: Dynamics of Alaska Native Self-Government, 1980; author monograph: North Slope Borough Government and Policymaking, 1981; jr. author: Alaska's Urban and Rural Governments, 1984; sr. editor Alaska State Government and Politics, 1987; co-author: Alaska Politics and Government, 1994 (Am. Assn. State & Local History Commendation cert. 1995); editor: Alaska's Rural Development, 1982. Mem. bd. edn. Fairbanks North Star Borough, 1986—, pres. 1989-90, 93-94, treas., 1991-93. Recipient Emil Usibelli Disting. Svc. award 1993; Chiang Ching-Kuo Found. fellow, 1995—; named Outstanding Faculty Mem., Assn. Students U. Alaska, Fairbanks, 1979, Alumni Assn. U. Alaska, Fairbanks, 1981; grantee Nat. Inst. Edn., 1980-83, Alaska Coun. on Sci. and Tech., 1982-84, Spencer Found., 1987-88. Mem. Asian Studies on Pacific Coast (program chmn. 1983, bd. dirs. 1982-83), Assn. Asian Studies, Western Polit. Sci. Assn. (mem. editl. bd. Western Govtl. Rschr.), Am. Polit. Sci. Assn., Am. Soc. Pub. Adminstrn. (v.p. Alaskachpt.), Fairbanks N. Star Borough Bd. Edn. Democrat. Home: 1777 Red Fox Dr Fairbanks AK 99709-6625 Office: U Ala Dept Polit Sci Fairbanks AK 99775

MCBETH, RUBEN JOSE, JR., retired criminal justice administrator; b. St. Louis, May 2, 1945; s. Ruben Andrew McBeth and Doris Augusta (Bell) Sweet; 1 child, Lisa Christine. BS in Criminal Justice, Pacific Western U., Los Angeles, 1980; grad., Nat. Inst. Corrections, FBI Tng. Acad.; postgrad., U. Colo., Denver, 1987—. Cert. instr. self-defense, tactical instr. With Sheriff's Dept. City of Denver, 1970-95, cpl., 1974-75, sgt., 1975-78, lt., 1978-79, capt., 1978-95, tng. capt., 1987-95, ret., 1995; instr. jail ops. Nat. Sheriffs Assn., Alexaddria, Va., 1980—, I.P.A. correctional program specialist, U.S. Dept. Justice; NIC, Nat. Acad. Corrections, Boulder, Colo., 1989-90, 91, Denver Sheriff Dept., Capt. Internal Investigations, NCIC. Served as sgt. USAF, 1965-68; Vietnam. mem. Am. Correctional Assn. (auditor, standards and accreditation com. 1986—, mem. affirmative action com. 1978-80), Am. Jail Assn., Am. Correctional Assn., Nat. Assn. Blacks in Law Enforcement, Nat. Orgn. Black Law Enforcement Execs., Nat. Sheriffs Assn., Colorado Correctional Assn., Colo. Police Protective Assn., Am. Legion. Home: 7156 E Appleton Cir Englewood CO 80112

MCBRIDE, JOYCE BROWNING, accountant; b. Ga., May 28, 1927; d. Eph and Zula (Harden) Browning; grad. So. Bus. U., 1947; children: Jan Burge, Gary McBride, Kandie Van Affelen. Asst. controller Hampton Court Knits, Los Angeles, 1967-78; owner, mgr. McBride & Assocs. Bookkeeping Service, 1978—. Address: 2925 Tyler Ct Simi Valley CA 93063-1742

MCBRIDE, LINDA CARROLL, psychologist; b. Pensacola, Fla., Nov. 12, 1943; d. Carroll James and Helen Katherine (Berchtold) McBride; m. William Marion Gurka, June 4, 1966 (div. Nov. 1980); children: Valerie Lynn, Elaine Melanie. BA in French and German, Purdue U., 1965; MA in French Lit., U. Mo., 1967, MEd in Counseling Psychology, 1987, PhD in Counseling Psychology, 1994. French instr. U. Mo., Columbia, 1966-79, rsch. asst., 1989-93; French instr. Stephens Coll., Columbia, 1967-68; French/German tchr. Columbia Pub. Schs., 1980-88; profl. psychology intern U. Calif. Davis Counseling Ctr., 1993-94; psychol. asst. Davis Ctr. for Psychotherapy, 1994—; outreach presenter stress mgmt., eating disorders, multicultural issues U. Calif., Davis, 1993-94. Soprano Columbia Choral Ensemble, 1980-87, 92-93, Winifred Baker Chorale, San Francisco, 1994-95, Winifred Baker Chamber Chorus, 1994-95, Dans Chorale, 1995—, Sacramento Area Bach Festival, 1995. NEH grantee, 1983. Mem. APA, Sierra Club. Home: 2978 W Portage Bay Ave Apt 180 Davis CA 95616-2836 Office: Davis Ctr Psychotherapy 1621 Oak Ave Ste B Davis CA 95616-1000

MCBROOM, MARY CATHERINE MAHER, public relations executive; b. Salt Lake City, Mar. 18, 1923; d. James Bernard and Julia Marguerite (Hearley) Maher; m. John Keith Lunberg, Nov. 15, 1943 (dec.); m. Ralph Ainsworth McBroom, Mar. 2, 1950; children: Ralph A., James B., Robert J., Mary McBroom Waters, Anne McBroom Flanagan. BA, Cath. U. Am., 1949. Tchr. drama St. Mary of the Wasatch, Salt Lake City, 1969-70; dir. pub. relations Utah council Girl Scouts U.S., Salt Lake City, 1973-75; summer youth coordinator Salt Lake County, Salt Lake City, 1975-80; reporter Intemountain Cath., Salt Lake City, 1980-81; advt. mgr. Island Park (Idaho) Villager, 1982-87, asst. editor, 1987-89; sssoc. editor Yellowstone Gateway Post, Island Park, 1993-95. Designer brochure Nat. Press Women, 1974; contbr. articles to profl. publs. Pres. Cath. Women's League, Salt Lake City, 1967-69, Island Park Hist. Soc., 1992-95. Mem. Idaho Press Women (historian 1985-95), Salt Lake County Bar Aux. (pres. 1966), Pub. Rels. Soc. Am. (accredited pub. rels.), Utah Press Women (v.p. 1973, sec. 1995), Island Park Sportsmen's Assn. (bd. dirs. 1987-89). Democrat. Home: PO Box 244 Island Park ID 83429-0244 Office: Yellowstone Gateway Post HC 66 Box 185 Island Park ID 83429-9701

MCBURNETT, ROBERT KEITH, child and adolescent psychology educator, researcher; b. Brunswick, Ga., Feb. 10, 1953; s. Kenneth Stewart and Betty Jean (Pilgrim) McB. BA, U. Ga., 1976, MS, 1985, PhD with honors, 1989. Lic. psychologist, Calif. Juvenile svc. staff Clarke County Youth Dept. Ct., Athens, Ga., 1974-76; rsch. asst. psychology dept. U. Ga., Athens, 1977-78, 85-87; behavior specialist Elbert County Mental Retardation Ctr., Elberton, Ga., 1979-81, Barrow County Mental Retardation Ctr., Winder, Ga., 1980-87; mental health profl. WPIC ADD program U. Pitts., 1987; psychology intern Rusk Inst., Bellevue Hosp./NYU Med. Ctr., N.Y.C., 1987-88; psychologist Child Devel. Ctr., U. Calif., Irvine, 1989-90; asst. prof. dept. pediatrics U. Calif., Irvine, 1990—, dir. rsch. and clin. tng. div. child devel. pediatrics dept., 1992—; reviewer Leon Lowenstein Found., 1992. Contbr. articles to profl. jours., book chpts. to publs. in field. NIMH grantee, 1991-93; recipient NIMH Rsch. Scientist Devel. award 1993-98. Mem. Am. Psychol. Assn., Am. Psychol. Soc., Assn. for Advancement Behavior Therapy, Soc. Rsch. in Child and Adolescent Psychopathology, Profl. Group for Attention and Related Disorders, Phi Beta Kappa. Office: U Calif Child Devel Ctr 4621 Teller Ave Ste 108 Newport Beach CA 92660-2165

MCBURNEY, GEORGE WILLIAM, lawyer; b. Ames, Iowa, Feb. 17, 1926; s. James William and Elfie Hazel (Jones) McB.; m. Georgianna Edwards, Aug. 28, 1949; children: Hollis Lynn, Jana Lee McBurney-Lin, John Edwards. B.A., State U. Iowa, 1950, J.D. with distinction, 1953. Bar: Iowa 1953, Ill. 1954, Calif. 1985. With Sidley & Austin and predecessor, Chgo., 1953—, ptnr., 1964-1993, counsel, 1994—; resident ptnr. Singapore, 1982-84. Editor-in-chief: Iowa Law Rev., 1952-53. Mem. Chgo. Crime Commn., 1966-84; trustee Iowa Law Sch. Found., 1988—, Old People's Home of City of Chgo., 1968-83, sec., 1967-69, exec. v.p., 1969-74, pres., 1974-82, hon. life trustee, 1983—; hon. life trustee Georgian, Evanston, Ill., trustee, counsel, 1976-82, v.p., 1980-82. Served with inf. AUS, 1944-46. Fellow Am. Coll. Trial Lawyers, Am. Bar Found. (life); mem. ABA, State Bar Calif., Los Angeles County Bar Assn., Fed. Bar Assn., Bar Assn. 7th Fed. Cir., Am. Judicature Soc., Am. Arbitration Assn. (panelist large complex dispute resolution program), Assn. Atty. Mediators (treas. So. Calif. chpt.), Assn. Bus. Trial Lawyers, The Ctr. for Internat. Comml. Arbitration L.A. (bd. dirs., exec. v.p.), Nat. Coll. Edn. (bd. assocs. 1967-84), U.S. C. of C. (govt. and regulatory affairs com. on coun. on antitrust policy 1980-82), L.A. Complex Litigation Inn of Ct., Law Soc. Singapore (hon.), Western Ctr. on Law and Poverty (bd. dirs. 1992—), L.A. Union League Club (vet.), Mid-Day Club Chgo., Law Club (life), Legal Club Chgo., Am. Club, Cricket Club, Town Club Singapore, Phi Kappa Psi, Omicron Delta Kappa, Delta Sigma Rho, Phi Delta Phi. Republican. Presbyterian. Home: Malibu Pacifica 13 3601 Vista Pacifica Malibu CA 90265-4830 Office: Sidley & Austin 555 W 5th St Ste 4000 Los Angeles CA 90013-3000

MCBURNEY, LINDA LEE, health facility administrator; b. Denver, June 10, 1942; d. Maurice J. and Dorothy Mae (Whitman) Mooney; m. Kenneth Robert McBurney, June 16, 1962 (div. 1980); children: Scott Robert, Laura Lynn, Brenda Sue, Valerie Kaye. BS in Bus. Adminstrn., Regis Coll., 1985. Office mgr. electrical company, Lakewood, Colo., 1980; sec. Safeco Ins. Co., Lakewood, 1980-82; office mgr. oil company, Golden, Colo., 1982; from clerical specialist to exec. sec. Cobe Labs., Lakewood, 1982-86; beauty cons. Mary Kay Cosmetics, Lakewood, 1986-87; adminstrv. mgr. Cobe Labs., Lakewood, 1986-89, med. systems mfr., adminstrn. & fin. mgr. worldwide svc. orgn., 1989-90, mgr. customer engring. response ctr., 1990-91; admissions coord. Hospice of Met. Denver, 1992—. Mem. Golden Area Sch. Adv. Com., 1974-80, Jefferson County Sr. High Curriculum Com., 1980; room mother Kyffin Elem. Sch., Golden, numerous years; vol. Luth. Hosp. Med. Ctr., Wheatridge, Colo., 1973-92; pres. Women's Assn. Arvada (Colo.) Presbyn. Ch., 1979. Mem. AAUW, Assn. Field Svc. Mgrs., Hospice of Metro Denver/Colo. Assn. of Home Health Agys., AAUW, Gamma Phi Beta. Republican. Home: 5 Paramount Pky Lakewood CO 80215-6615 Office: 3955 E Exposition Ave Ste 500 Denver CO 80209-5033

MCCABE, ROBERT R., architect, city planner. BArch, U. Calif., Berkeley, 1965; postgrad., Mich. State U., 1967-68; M in Community Planning, U. Cin., 1971. Vol. Peace Corps, Colombia; city planner 5, chief planner model cities physical planning program Cin. City Planning Commn.; prin. Flatow, Moore, Shaffer, McCabe, Inc., Albuquerque, 1984—; instr. U. N.Mex. 1976-79, Grad. Dept. Community Planning, Cin., 1972, Urban Conservation Project, Cin., 1968, Mich. State U., 1968; assoc. prof. community planning Sch. Art, Architecture and Design, U. Cin., 1972. Prin. works include Albuquerque Acad. Mid. Sch., St. Joseph Rehab. Hosp., Vision of Albuquerque, among others. Mem. Environ. Planning Commn., Downtown Action Planning Com., Comprehensive Plan Oversight Com.; v.p. met. affairs, v.p. govtl. affairs, Albuquerque Mus. Found., mem. exec. com.; mem. bus. adv. coun. Gov. Garry Carruthers, chmn. long-range planning task force. Mem. AIA (com. on architecture for health), Am. Planning Assn., Nat. Coun. Archtl. Registration Bds., Greater Albuquerque C. of C. (bd. dirs.). Office: Flatow Moore Shaffer McCabe Inc PO Box 8266 Albuquerque NM 87198-8266

MCCAFFERTY, ROBERT MAURICE, communications and media skills executive, speaker; b. Seattle, Nov. 14, 1937; s. Robert William and Edythe Mae (Young) McC.; m. Valerie Ann Smith, Feb. 24, 1956 (div. Dec. 1972); children: Jeff William, Robert Stephen, Kathryn Marie, Donna Lynn; m. Diane Benita Sheldon. Student, Don Martin Broadcasting, Hollywood, Calif., 1963-65; AA in Social Studies, Cosumnes Jr. Coll., 1975. News dir., anchor Sta. KHSL, Chico, Calif., 1965-67; reporter, anchor, prodr. Sta. KXTV, Sacramento, 1967-71, assignment editor, show host, prodr., 1971-72; mgr. Office Broadcast Svcs. Gov.'s Office, Sacramento, 1972-75; assignment editor Sta. KOVR, Sacramento, 1975-76; media dir. Calif. Legislature, Sacramento, 1976-77; comms. dir. Calif. Employment Devel. Dept., Sacramento, 1977-79; ptnr. Huckaby, McNally & McCafferty, Sacramento, 1979-80; owner, pres. McCafferty and Co., Fair Oaks, Calif., 1980—. Sr. writer bus. subjects Comstock's Mag., 1989—; writer aviation and aerospace subjects Air & Space/Smithsonian, 1988—; prodr., writer TV documentaries on environment, POW wives, alcoholism, 1967-71. Bd. dirs. Calif. Internat. Marathon, Sacramento, 1986-90; mentor, inspirational speaker La Entrada H.S., Sacramento, 1992—. With USAF, 1955-61. Mem. Soc. Profl. Journalists, Aviation/Space Writers Assn., Nat. Speakers Assn. (v.p. comms. 1993-95), Sacramento Pub. Rels. Assn. (pres. 1984-85), Calif. Writers Club, Sunrise Ctr. Toastmasters, Fair Oaks C. of C. (program chmn. 1989-94). Republican. Presbyterian. Home: 4800 Timothy Way Fair Oaks CA 95628-5122 Office: McCafferty and Co Comms 4800 Timothy Way Fair Oaks CA 95628-5122

MCCAIG, JEFFREY JAMES, transportation company executive; b. Moose Jaw, Sask., July 5, 1951; s. John Robert and Anne Shorrocks (Glass) McC.; m. Marilyn Graves, July 7, 1983; children: Robbert Angus, Scott Thomas, Christa Mae. Student, Can. Jr. Coll. Lausanne, Switzerland, 1970; AB, Harvard Coll., 1973; LLB, Osgoode Hall Law Sch., Can., 1976; MSc in Mgmt., Leland Stanford Jr. U., 1984. Assoc. MacKimmie Matthews, 1976-81; owner, sr. officer Jeffery J. McCaig Profl. Corp., 1981-83; v.p. planning and corp. devel. Trimac Ltd., Calgary, Alta., Can., 1983-87, exec. v.p., 1987-90; pres. Trimac Ltd., Clagary, Alta., Can., 1990-94, pres., CEO, 1994—; chmn. Bovar, Inc., Calgary, 1994—; bd. dirs. Bovar Inc., chmn.; bd. dirs. Trimac Ltd., Greyhound Lines Can. Ltd., 20/20 Fin. Group, Alberta Spl. Waste Mgmt. System, Richland Petroleum Corp., Conf. Bd. Can., ATA Found., Inerta. Mem. Law Soc. Alta., Young Pres.'s Orgn., Calgary Golf and Country Club, Calgary Petroleum Club, Glencoe Club, 400 Club. Home: 1201 Riverdale Ave SW, Calgary, AB Canada T2S 0Z1 Office: Trimac Ltd, 800 5 Ave SW Ste 2100, Calgary, AB Canada T2P 3T6

MCCAIG, JOHN ROBERT, transportation executive; b. Moose Jaw, Sask., Can., June 14, 1929; m. Ann McCaig; children: Jeffrey, JoAnn, Melanie. Grad. pub. sch., Moose Jaw. Various positions Maccam Transport Ltd., 1947-52, gen. mgr., 1952-60; pres. Trimac Transp. Ltd. and H.M. Trimble & Sons Ltd., 1961-68, Westburne Internat. Industries Ltd., 1969-70; chmn. Trimac Ltd., Calgary, Alta., Can., 1970-72, 80—; pres. Trimac Ltd., Calgary, Alta., 1972-80, CEO, 1972-94; chmn. Trimac Ltd., Calgary, 1994—; bd. dirs. Banister Found., Inc., Chauvco Resources Ltd., Computalog, Inc., Pan-Alta Gas Ltd., Cameco Corp., Vencap Equities. Past pres. Jr. Achievement So. Alta, Calgary; campaign chmn. Western Orthopaedic and Arthritis Found., Calgary. Mem. Calgary Petroleum Club, Ranchmen's Club, Calgary Golf and Country Club, Glencoe Club. Office: Trimac Ltd, 800 5 Ave SW Ste 2100, Calgary, AB Canada T2P 3T6

MCCAIN, JOHN SIDNEY, III, senator; b. Panama Canal Zone, Aug. 29, 1936; s. John Sidney and Roberta (Wright) McC.; m. Cindy Hensley, May 17, 1980; children: Doug, Andy, Sidney, Meghan, Jack, Bridget. Grad. U.S. Naval Acad., 1958; grad., Nat. War Coll., 1973-74. Commd. ensign U.S. Navy, 1958, capt., navy pilot, 1977; prisoner of war Hanoi, Vietnam, 1967-73; dir. Navy Senate Liaison Office, Washington, 1977-81; mem. 98th-99th Congress from 1st Ariz. Dist.; U.S. senator from Ariz., 1987—. Bd. dirs. Community Assistance League, Phoenix, 1981-82. Decorated Legion of Merit; decorated Silver Star, Bronze Star, Purple Heart, D.F.C., Vietnamese Legion of Honor. Mem. Soc. of the Cin., Am. Legion, VFW. Republican. Episcopalian. Office: US Senate 111 Russell Senate Office Washington DC 20510*

MCCAIN, NANCY SCHLOERKE, library director; b. Highland Park, Mich., Feb. 25, 1950; d. Wallace C. and Janice E. (Fletcher) Schloerke; m. Jeffrey W. McCain; children: Zebulon S., Starr D., Ewan S. BFA, U. Iowa, 1972; MLS, Emporia State U., 1993. Bookmobile driver Park County Libr.

Sys., Hartsel, Colo., 1982-86; br. mgr. Park County Libr. Sys., Fairplay, Colo., 1986-93; dir. Lake County Pub. Libr., Leadville, Colo., 1993—. Mem. ALA, Colo. Libr. Assn. Office: Lake County Pub Libr 1115 Harrison Ave Leadville CO 80461-3324

MCCALL, FRANCEEN KAY, social services administrator; b. Scottsbluff, Nebr., Aug. 10, 1950; d. Francis Leroy and Wauneta Mae (Unzicker) Pecht; m. Donald Gene Kelley, Nov. 22, 1970 (div. 1983); children: Jodi Kay, Jill Allison. AA, Nebr. Western Coll., 1970; BS, Chadron State Coll., 1972, MA, 1988. Social worker Nebr. State Dept. Social Svcs., Gering, 1978-82; elem. tchr. St. Agnes Elem. Sch., Scottsbluff, 1982-87; counseling/advising specialist Western Nebr. C.C., Scottsbluff, 1987-89; exec. dir. House of Neighborly Svc., Loveland, Colo., 1990—; bd. dirs. Friends Inc., Scottsbluff; mem. State Foster Care Rev. Bd., Scottsbluff, 1985; mem. FEMA bd. County of Larimer, Fort Collins, Colo., 1990—. Author: A Handbook for Disenfranchised Women, 1989, The Searing Desert, 1990, (newsletter) The Neighbor, 1990—. Mem. Chi Sigma Iota, Phi Theta Kappa.

MCCALL, LAURA, education educator, writer; b. Ill., Nov. 8, 1951; d. Richard Joseph and Corinne (Durava) McC. Cert. in French Lang. and Lit., U. Geneva, 1971; BA in History, Northwestern U., Evanston, Ill., 1973; MA in History, U. Mich., 1980, PhD, 1988. History tchr., womens basketball coach Shattuck Prep. Sch., Faribault, Minn., 1976-78; tchr. Gunnison (Colo.) H.S., 1979-86; history teaching fellow U. Mich., Ann Arbor, 1980-82; history instr. U. Mich., Dearborn, 1980-82; from instr. to asst. prof. history Western State Coll., Gunnison, 1982-90, asst. chair dept. history, politics and econs., 1987-90, chair dept., 1990; asst. prof. history Met. State Coll., Denver, 1990—; chair athletic coun. Met. State Coll., Denver, 1991—, promotion and tenure com. history dept., 1990—, com. on internat. edn., 1991—; chair dept. history, politics and econ. Western State Coll., Colo., 1990, asst. chair, 1987-90, chair Livermore Scholarship, 1988-90, student adv. corps., gen. edn. com., 1989-90; faculty athletic rep. NCAA, Denver, 1993—; adj. prof. liberal arts and internat studies Colo. Sch. Mines, Golden, spring 1992. Mem. editorial bd. Jour. of the Early Republic, 1988-95; contbr. articles to profl. jours. Host, lectr. for advanced placement history students Adams County H.S., 1991; Arbor Day participant Lake Elem. Sch., 1990; pub. sch. vol. Blackstocks Elem. Sch., 1989-90; Colo. Knowledge Bowl sponsor Gunnison H.S., 1985-86. Teaching fellow U. Mich., 1980-82, John D. Pierce fellow, 1982, Program in Am. Instn. fellow, 1986-87, Newberry Libr. Chgo. fellow, 1986-87; NEH grantee, 1989. Mem. Soc. for Historians the Early Republic, Orgn. Am. Historians, Rocky Mountain MLA, Colo. History Group, Northwestern Alumni Assn., Sierra Club, World Wildlife Fund, Nature Conservancy, Phi Beta Kappa, Phi Alpha Theta (host, organizer Regional Conf. 1988, faculty sponsor 1987-90, Best Chpt. award 1991, Best Sponsor award 1995), Alpha Lambda Delta, Delta Kappa Gamma. Office: Met State Coll PO Box 173362 Denver CO 80217-3362

MCCALL, NELDA DUNN, economist; b. Dayton, Ohio, Nov. 28, 1945; d. Wilson Alexander and Marie Geraldine (Fanning) McC.; m. Steven Snyder, June 6, 1970. BA in Econs., Cath. U. Am., 1967; MA in Econs., Georgetown U., 1971. Assoc. programmer Fed. Systems div. IBM, Gaithersburg, Md., 1967-70; rsch. assoc. Palo Alto (Calif.) Med. Rsch. Found., 1970-77; sr. analyst Control Analysis Corp., Palo Alto, 1977; founder, dir. health policy rsch. SRI Internat., Menlo Park, Calif., 1977-88; pres. Laguna Rsch. Assocs., San Francisco, 1988—; mem. Nat. Ctr. for Health Svcs. Rsch., Health Svcs. Devel. Grants Rev. Subcom. Study Sect., 1984-88; mem. Calif. Health Policy and Data Adv. Com., 1985-87. Contbr. articles on financing and delivery of med. care to profl. jours. Mem. Am. Pub. Health Assn. (governing council), Am. Econ. Assn., Assn. for Health Services Rev., Assn. Social Services and Health. Office: Laguna Rsch Assocs 455 Market St Ste 1190 San Francisco CA 94105-2430

MCCALL, ROBERT H., oil and chemical company executive; b. 1938. Attended, U. Colo. With McCall Oil & Chem. Corp., Portland, Oreg., 1961—, pres., 1967—, now also chief exec. officer. With USAF, 1959-60. Office: McCall Oil & Chem Corp 808 SW 15th Ave Portland OR 97205-1907

MCCALL, STEPHEN SHAWN, philanthropist; b. Balt., July 29, 1950; s. Henry David and Olivia Genevieve (Gunkel) McC.; m. Irene Takeko Kitagawa, Feb. 24, 1985; children: Emily Teiko, Stephen Hideo. BS, Towson State U., 1972. Educator Balt. City Pub. Sch. System, 1972-79; trainer, tech. writer Hawaii Med. Svcs. Assn., Honolulu, 1990—; founder, pres. Johanna Hawkins Meml. Inst. for the Humanities, Inc., Honolulu, 1984—. Mem. Am. Mensa Ltd. Democrat. Home: 3249 Hoolulu St Honolulu HI 96815-3840 Office: Johanna Hawkins Meml Inst Humanities Inc 3249 Hoolulu St Honolulu HI 96815-3840

MCCALL, SUSAN ELIZABETH, small business owner; b. Ogden, Utah, Nov. 21, 1945; d. Edward George and Virginia Alene (Davis) Mester; children: Melissa M., Ian E. Spencer. BFA, Utah State U., 1975. Office mgr. Sewing Dist., Phoenix, Ariz., 1969-70; art tchr. North Ogden City Schs., 1970-71; graphic arts Permaloy Corp., Ogden, 1972-74; regional purchasing agt. USDA Forest Service, Ogden, 1976; owner, mgr. The Flower Co., Albuquerque, 1976-89; dir. dist. 8-J Florists Transworld Delivery Assn., 1988-89; mgr. Spring Flowers, Sydney, 1990-91; owner, mgr. Floral Arts Design Sch. N. Mex., 1994—. Recipient First Place award Utah Soc. Art, 1964. Mem. West Tex. Florist Assn., N.Mex. Floral Assn., Albuquerque Vis.' Conv. (mktg. com. 1986-90), Fla. Transworld Delivery Assn. (dir. Dist. 8-J, 1988), Profl. Women in Bus. Office: The Flower Co 3716 Edith Blvd NE Albuquerque NM 87107

MCCALL, WILLIAM CALDER, oil and chemical company executive; b. Hoquiam, Wash., Feb. 1, 1906; s. Dougall Hugh and Hughena (Calder) McC.; m. Marian Hall, Mar. 22, 1946; children—Ernest, Robert. Student U. Oreg., 1924-28; LHD Lewis & Clark Coll., 1992. Asst. sales mgr. Anaconda Sales Co., Chgo., 1932-39; chmn. McCall Oil & Chem. Corp., Portland, Oreg., 1939—, Gt. Western Chem. Co., Portland, 1975—; dir. Oreg. Bank, Portland, King Broadcasting Co., Seattle. Pres. Oreg. Art Mus., Portland; trustee Lewis and Clark Coll., Portland; exec. v.p. Oreg. Symphony Soc.; dir. Oreg. Health Scis. Found., Good Samaritan Hosp. Found., Portland. Republican. Episcopalian. Clubs: Eldorado Country (Indian Wells, Calif.) (pres. 1978-79); Arlington (Portland); Pacific-Union (San Francisco); Los Angeles Country, Vintage (Palm Desert, Calif.), Waverley Country, Rainier (Seattle). Office: McCall Oil and Chem Corp 808 SW 15th Ave Portland OR 97205-1907

MCCALLISTER, WREN VANCE, building services company executive; b. Seattle, Aug. 14, 1969; s. Warren Vance and Sandra Jean (Hansen) McC. AA, Shoreline C.C., 1992. Founder Titan Maint. Co., Seattle, 1988-90; chmn., chief exec. officer Eastlake Bldg. Maint., Inc., Seattle, 1990-94. Mem. Bldg. Svc. Contrs. Assn. Internat. (selected to svc. on 1991 membership com.), Cleaning Mgmt. Inst. Republican. Office: Eastlake Bldg Maint Inc 19924 Aurora Ave N # 152 Seattle WA 98133-3526

MCCAMLY, JERRY ALLEN, secondary education educator; b. Battle Creek, Mich., Mar. 15, 1940; s. Derrol John and Adelee (Harding) McC.; m. Janet Aileen Pulatie, Aug. 25, 1962; children: Ty A., Jodi. BS in Edn., Ariz. State Coll., 1963; MA in Edn., Azusa Pacific Coll., 1978. Tchr. Casa Grande (Ariz.) High Sch., 1963-64, Whittier (Calif.) High Sch., 1964-65, Norwalk (Calif.)-LaMirada Unified Sch. Dist., 1965—; cons. WASC Accrediting Assn., Burlingame, Calif., 1978—. Contbr. articles to profl. publs. Recipient Hon. Svc. award Norwalk Sch. PTA, 1986, Tchr.'s Medal Freedoms Found., 1977. Mem. L.A. Continuation Assn. (pres. 1980-81), Calf. Continuation Assn. (pres. 1981-82), World Future Soc. Republican. Methodist. Home: 25630 Sierra Calmo Ct Moreno Valley CA 92551-2162 Office: John Glenn High Sch 13520 Shoemaker Ave Norwalk CA 90650-4521

MC CANDLESS, ALFRED A. (AL MC CANDLESS), congressman; b. Brawley, Calif., July 23, 1927; s. Max T. and Fleta (Beaty) Mc C.; m. Gail W. Glass, Nov. 26, 1982; children: Cristina, Alfred A., Craig, Blaine, Ward. B.A. in Polit. Sci. and Pub. Adminstrn., UCLA, 1951. Mem. Riverside County Bd. Suprs., Calif., 1971-82, chmn. bd., 1971-72, 80-81; founder McCandless Motors, Indio, Calif., 1953-75; mem. 98th-103rd Congresses from 37th (now 44th) dist. Calif., 1983—. Founding mem. South Coast Air Quality Mgmt. Dist.; founding mem. Sunline Transit Agy.; founder Coachella Valley Assn. Govts.; exec. com., dir. County Suprs. Assn. Calif.; bd. dirs. Coachelle Valley Housing Coaltion. Served to capt. USMC, 1945-46, 50-52. Mem. Indio Co. of C. (hon. life), Greater Riverside C. of C. Lodge: Indio Rotary (past pres.). Office: US Ho of Reps 2422 Rayburn Bldg Ofc B Washington DC 20515-0005*

MCCANN, BARBARA ANN, school director; b. Pendleton, Oreg., Sept. 27, 1951; d. John Gordon Bensel and D. Lois (Carey) Bohlender; m. James Noel McCann, Aug. 6, 1982 (div. 1987); children: Sage, David. Cert., Fla. Inst. Tech., 1969; BA, Western Wash. U., 1974; cert. in manual interpretation, Blue Mountain Coll., 1987; MS in Edn., Lewis and Clark Coll., 1988. Cert. tchr., Wyo.; cert. interpretor, domestic violence counselor, Oreg.; cert. fed. contract specialist, Wash. Housing and employment commr. City of Bellingham, Wash., 1970-74; contract specialist U.S. Forest Svc., Seattle, 1974-76; ind. contract cons. Seattle and Tacoma, 1976-78; loan specialist Island Savs. and Loan, Mt. Vernon, Wash., 1978-80; materials specialist Umatilla County Edn. Svc. Dist., Pendleton, Oreg., 1980-87; specialist for hearing impaired Fremont County Sch. Dist. 1, Lander, Wyo., 1988-91; instr. sign lang. and edn. Cen. Wyo. Coll., Riverton, 1988—; dir. Title VII and V programs and curriculum Wyo. Indian Schs., Ethete, 1991—; mem. north ctrl. accreditation team Wyo. Indian Schs., 1991—; English instr. Blue Mountain C.C.; drama dir. Lander Dist. 1. Author, illustrator sign lang. edn. materials. Mem. Fairhaven com. Fairhaven Coll., Bellingham, 1970-71, advocate, 1970-72; mem. Bellingham Landlords' Assn., 1970-74; rep. Pioneer Sq. Assn., Seattle, 1976-78; vol. counselor Domestic Violence Svcs., Pendleton, Oreg., 1982-87; vol. sign lang. interpreter various orgns., Wyo., 1988—. Named Outstanding Vol., Domestic Violence Svcs., Pendleton, 1986; recipient Exceptional Svc. award United Way Umatilla County, 1986, Outstanding Instr. award Ctrl. Wyo. Coll., 1990. Mem. ASCD, NEA, Nat. Indian Edn. Assn., Nat. Assn. Bilingual Edn., Wyo. Speech and Hearing Assn., Conv. Am. Instrs. of Deaf, Ethete Ednl. Assn., Wyo. Edn. Assn. Home: 609 S 7th St Lander WY 82520-3219 Office: Wyo Indian Sch 636 Blue Sky Hwy Ethete WY 82520

MCCANN, JACK ARLAND, former construction and mining equipment company executive, consultant; b. Chestnut, Ill., Apr. 16, 1926; s. Keith Ogden and Miriam Imogene McC.; m. Marian Adele Gordon, Mar. 31, 1956; 1 son, Christopher John. A.B., Bradley U., 1950. Mgr. Washington Office, R.G. LeTourneau Inc., 1950-53; mgr. def. and spl. products Westinghouse Air Brake Co., 1958-64, mgr. nat. accounts, 1964-67, mng. dir. Belgian plant and European mktg., 1967-70; gen. sales mgr. WABCO div. Am. Standard Inc., Peoria, Ill., 1970-73, v.p. mktg., 1973-80, v.p. staff, 1980-82; ret., 1982; now cons. With USNR, 1944-46. Decorated chevalier Ordre de la Couronne (Belgium). Mem. Nat. Def. Transp. Assn. (life), U.S. C. of C., Am. Legion, Bradley Chiefs Club, Country Club Green Valley (pres., dir.), Green Valley Rep. Club (bd. dirs.), Shriners, Masons.

MCCANN, RICHARD JAMES, economist, consultant; b. Grand Rapids, Mich., Apr. 30, 1958; s. John J. McCann and Helen Jane Matekel; m. Ellen Moratti, Feb. 23, 1992. BS Polit. Economy of Natural Resources, U. Calif., Berkeley, 1981; M of Pub. Policy, U. Mich., 1985; MS in Agrl. & Resource Econs., U. Calif., Berkeley, 1990; postgrad., U. Calif., 1990—. Staff economist Dames & Moore, San Francisco, 1985-86; sr. rsch. assoc. QED Rsch. Inc., Palo Alto, Calif., 1986-88; grad. student researcher, teaching asst. U. Calif., Berkeley, 1989-92; sr. economist Foster Assocs./Spectrum Econs., San Francisco, 1989-92; econ. and policy cons., ptnr. M. Cubed, West Sacramento, Calif., 1993—. Contbr. articles to profl. jours. Mem. Housing and Cmty. Devel. Adv. Commn., Yolo County, Calif., 1993-94; mem. Overall Econ. Devel. Plan Task Force, Yolo County, West Sacramento, 1994. Mem. Am. Agrl. Econs. Assn., Assn. Environ. and Resource Economists, Am. Econs. Assn., Western Econs. Assn. Internat., Am. Water Resources Assn., Assn. Environ.Profls., Track and Field Writers Assn., Phi Beta Kappa. Office: M Cubed 2876 Pekins Ct West Sacramento CA 95691-4438

MC CARDLE, RANDALL RAYMOND, real estate developer; b. Phila., Sept. 2, 1931; s. Russell Henry and Ruth Hertha (Snyder) McC.; m. Yong Suk Yi; 1 child, Mark. AA, Orange Coast Coll., 1956; BA, Chapman Coll., 1958, MA, 1966; PhD, Colo. U., 1974; Real estate broker, Newport Beach, Calif., 1953-95; founder, pres. The Real Estaters, Orange County, Calif., 1961—, Treeco Escrow Co., Inc., Costa Mesa, Calif., 1971—; founder Bank of Costa Mesa, 1972, dir. bus. devel., 1973—; also newspaper columnist, lectr., investment counselor. Fund-raising chmn. Boys' Club of Am., Harbor area, 1979-80; bd. dirs. Boys Club Harbor Area; mem. adv. com. Orange Coast Coll., 1964—, Golden West Coll., 1969—; dir. Harbor Ridge Masters, 1990-95; mem. St. Andrews Presbyn. Ch. With USN, 1950-53. Decorated Nat. Def. Svc. medal, UN Svc. medal, Korean Svc. ribbon with 2 stars; recipient Appreciation award Bd. Realtors, 1967, 68, 70, 76, 80, UN citation; inducted into Orange Coast Coll. Hall of Fame, 1983; named Realtor of Yr., 1989. Mem. Calif. Assn. Realtors (state dir. 1963-67), Calif. Assn. Real Estate Tchrs. (state dir. 1966-80), Orange County Coast Assn. (dir. 1974—), C. of C., Nat. Assn. Real Estate Appraisers, Bd. Realtors (pres. 1966-67 long-range planning com. 1981), U. So. Calif. Faculty Assn., Red Baron Flying Club, Big Canyon Country Club, Mason, Shriner. Contbr. articles to profl. jours. Home: 12 Geneve Newport Beach CA 92660-6813 Office: 1000 Quail St Ste 260 Newport Beach CA 92660-2721

MCCARTHY, BEA, state legislator; b. Great Falls, Mont., Apr. 17, 1935; d. Robert Joseph and Rose Mary (Krier) McKenna; m. Edward Joseph McCarthy, June 27, 1959; children: Colleen, Mary, Edward Jr., Patrick, John. BS in Elem Edn., Mont. State U., 1957. Tchr. 1st grade Anaconda, Mont., 1968—; rep. dist. 66 Mont. State Legis., 1994—. Mem. Mont. Bd. Regents, 1983-90, Mont. Bd. Edn., 1983-90. Mem. AAUW, Am. Legion Aux., Ladies Ancient Order Hibernians (past pres.), Phi Beta Phi, Delta Kappa Gamma. Democrat. Roman Catholic. Home: 1906 Ogden St Anaconda MT 59711-1706

MCCARTHY, BRIAN NELSON, marketing and distribution company executive; b. Detroit, May 24, 1945; s. Andrew Nelson and Ruth Elizabeth (Hill) McC.; married, 1974 (div. 1991); children: Amanda Lang, Kelly Elizabeth, Meghan Virginia; m. Shannon Headley, Sept. 7, 1991; 1 child, Conner Michael. BS in Engring. Sci., Oakland U., Rochester, Mich., 1966; MBA, Harvard U., 1972. Engr. Gen. Motors Corp., Pontiac, Mich., 1965-67; co-owner Sound Wave Systems, Costa Mesa, Calif., 1971-78; chief fin. officer, controller A&W Gershenson Co., Farmington, Mich., 1972-75; chief op. officer Devel. Group, Southfield, Mich., 1975-81; chief exec. officer Brichard & Co., San Francisco, 1982-87; pres., chief exec. officer Watermark Corp., Sausalito, Calif., 1987-89; chief exec. officer Indian Wells Water Co., Inc., 1989—. Lt. USNR, 1967-70, Rear Adm. supply corps, Res. Decorated Navy Commendation medal with gold star, Meritorious Svc. medal with two gold stars, Def. Meritorious Svc medal with oak leaf cluster. Mem. Navy Supply Corps Assn. (bd. dirs. 1987—), Internat. Bottle Water Assn., Calif. Bottle Water Assn., Harvard Bus. No. Calif. Club, Commonwealth Club. Republican. Office: Indian Wells Water Co 45 Koch Rd Corte Madera CA 94925-1232

MCCARTHY, CHARLOTTE MARIE, microbiologist, educator; b. Watford City, N.D., Sept. 7, 1937; d. Walter James and Mildred Christine (Johnson) McC. BS, Idaho State U., 1958; MS, Oreg. State U., 1961; PhD, U. Wash., 1967. Microbiologist Park-Davis & Co., Detroit, 1958-59, Nat. Jewish Hosp., Denver, 1968-71; microbiologist, instr. U. Oreg. Dental Sch., Portland, 1961-63; asst. prof. microbiology N.Mex. State U., Las Cruces, 1972-75, assoc. prof. microbiology, 1975-83, prof. microbiology, 1983—; reviewer NIH, Bethesda, Md., 1985—, Ford Found., Washington, 1993-95, USDA, Washington, 1990—. NIH grantee, 1970-87, 87-90, 89-93. Mem. AAAS, Am. Soc. Microbiology (chair elect. divsn. U 1986, chair 1987), N.Mex. Network of Women in Sci. and Engring. (sec. 1984), Sigma Xi. Office: NMex State U Biology Dept 3 AF Las Cruces NM 88003-0001

MCCARTHY, GLENN, information systems administrator; b. N.Y.C., Nov. 13, 1949; s. Randolph and Pauline Cecilia (Burns) McC.; m. Rebecca Sue Schreiner, Oct. 6, 1988; children: Lisa Marie, Nelse Carl, Kate Michelle. Student, Fresno City Coll., 1969-70, Fresno State U., 1970-72. Sr. programmer/analyst Hewlett Packard, no. Calif., 1978-88; mgr. MIS Melco Industries, Westminster, Colo., 1988-93, Wright & McGill Co., Denver, 1993—. Mem. Data Processing Mgmt. Assn. Office: Wright & McGill Co 4245 E 46th Ave Denver CO 80216-3219

MCCARTHY, LAURENCE JAMES, physician, pathologist; b. Boston, Aug. 11, 1934; s. Theodore Clifford and Mary Barrett (Moran) McC.; m. Cynthia Marion DeRoch, Aug. 28, 1978; children: Laurence J. Jr., Jeffrey A., Karen E., Patrick K., Ryan N. BA, Yale U., 1956; student, Georgetown U. Sch. Med., 1956-58; MD, Harvard U., 1960; MS, U. Minn., 1965. Cert. Am. Bd. Pathology, 1965. Intern Boston City Hosp., 1960-61; resident in pathology Mayo Clinic, Rochester, Minn., 1961-65; pathologist Honolulu Heart Program, 1965-67; chief pathology Kelsey-Seybold Clinic, Houston, 1967-68; clin. asst. pathologist M.D. Anderson Hosp., Houston, 1967-68; chief pathology Straub Clinic, Honolulu, 1968-72; assoc. pathologist Wilcox Hosp., Lihue, Hawaii, 1972-74; chief pathology A.R. Gould Hosp., Presque Isle, Maine, 1975-78; assoc. pathologist Kuakini Med. Ctr., Honolulu, 1978—. Med. dir. USPHS, 1965-67. Fellow Coll. Am. Pathologists, Am. Soc. Clin. Pathologists; mem. AMA, Hawaii Soc. Pathologists (pres. 1970), Am. Acad. Forensic Sci., Hawaii Med. Assn., Honolulu County Med. Soc. (del. 1982-83). Roman Catholic. Home: 249 Kaelepulu Dr Kailua HI 96734-3311 Office: Kuakini Med Ctr 347 N Kuakini St Honolulu HI 96817-2372

MCCARTHY, MARIE GERALDINE, program director, coordinator; b. San Francisco, Nov. 7, 1940; d. Emmett Francis and Marie Delores (Costello) McC.; children: Peter, Robert, Todd Brockman. BA, Lone Mountain Coll., 1962; MA, Dominican Coll., San Rafael, Calif., 1972. Gen. secondary credential; cert. cmty. coll. chief adminstrv. officer, supr., history, basic edn., spl. edn., profl. edn. educator, counselor. Coord., counselor Work Incentive Program, Employment Devel. Dept., Marin County, Calif., 1970-72; coord., instr. Neighborhood Youth Corps Program, Marin County, Calif., 1972-74; coord. Marin City Project Area Com., Marin County, Calif., 1978-79; coord. basic skills program Coll. of Marin, Kentfield, Calif., 1973-79, edn. cons., 1980-83, pres. acad. senate, 1993—, coord. Disabled Students Program, 1984—; faculty advisor Challenged Students Club, Coll. of Marin, Kentfield, 1983—, exec. coun. United Profs. of Marin, Local 1610, 1984-92, mem. staff devel. com., 1986-88, event coord. ann. student fundraiser for students with disabilities, 1985—, dist. psychol. disabilities task force, 1994—, dist. councilmem. Faculty Assn. Calif. C.C.s, 1994—, dist. budget com., 1994—, dist. master planning com., 1994—, mem. crisis intervention team, 1990—, editor DPS Forum, 1995—. Author: How To Learn To Study: Bridging the Study Skills Gap, 1982, The Faculty Handbook on Disabilities, 1993. Bd. dirs., v.p. CENTERFORCE, 1992—; bd. dirs. Marin Coalition, Marin Athletic Found., 1992—, Marin Ctr. for Ind. Living, 1994—, EXODUS, 1992—, sec.; past v.p. Bay Faculty Assn.; founder Youth Helping Homeless, 1990—; mem. Alliance for the Mentally Ill., 1994—, JERICHO, 1994—; founding bd. dirs. INSPIRIT, 1984—. Recipient Spl. Achievement award Calif. Youth Soccer Assn., 1980, Marin County Mother of Yr. award, 1984, Spl. Recognition awards The Indoor Sports Club for Physically Handicapped, 1984, 88-90, 92-93, Mom Makes the Difference honoree Carter Hawley Hale Stores, Inc., 1994, Cert. of Recognition, Marin Human Rights Commn., 1994, Hayward award, 1995. Mem. AAUW, Calif. Assn. Post-secondary Educators for the Disabled, Faculty Assn. Calif. C.C.s, Commonwealth Club Calif., U.S. Soccer Fedn. Home: 6004 Shelter Bay Ave Mill Valley CA 94941-3040 Office: Coll of Marin College Ave Kentfield CA 94904

MCCARTHY, MARY ANN BARTLEY, electrical engineer; b. Drummond, Okla., Nov. 27, 1923; d. William Clifford and Estella Florence (Williams) Bartley; m. Joseph Manderfield McCarthy, Aug. 23, 1946 (dec. 1983); 1 child, Mary Ann McCarthy Morales. BEE, B of Material Sci., U. Calif., Berkeley, 1976. Aircraft radio technician U.S. Civil Svc., San Antonio and Honolulu, 1942-46; salesperson Sears Roebuck & Co., Enid, Okla., 1954-56; specialist reliability engring. Lockheed Corp., Sunnyvale, Calif., 1977-82, program responsible parts engr., 1986-93; rsch. engr. Lockheed Corp., Austin, Tex., 1982-86; presenter 9th Internat. Conf. Women Engrs. and Scientists U. Warwick, Eng., 1991. Contbr. articles to profl. jours. Vol. sci. coord. U. Calif. Berkeley Ext.-4H Series Excel, 1991—, bd. dirs. sci. and youth, 1994—. Fellow Soc. Women Engrs. (sr. life mem., pres. S.W. Tex. chpt. 1984, counsel reps. sec. 1985, pres. Santa Clara Valley chpt. 1986-87, nat. v.p. 1987-88, 88-89, chmn. nat. career guidance 1988-89, coord. 1990-91, counsel sect. rep. 1991-92, coord. Resnik Challenger medal 1990-91, 91-92, 92-93); mem. AAUW (life, com. chmn. 1984, co-chmn. literacy com. 1984), Toastmasters (Vanderhoof award 1992). Republican. Roman Catholic. Home: 6103 Edenhall Dr San Jose CA 95129-3006

MCCARTHY, MARY FRANCES, hospital foundation administrator; b. Washington, Apr. 16, 1937; d. Joseph Francis and Frances (Oddi) McGowan; m. Charles M. Sappenfield, Dec. 14, 1963 (div. June 1990); children: Charles Ross, Sarah Kathleen; m. Daniel Fendrick McCarthy, Jr., Aug. 25, 1990. BA, Trinity Coll., Washington, 1958; cert. in bus. adminstrn., Harvard U.-Radcliffe Coll., 1959; MA, Ball State U., Muncie, Ind., 1984. Systems engr. IBM, Cambridge, Mass., 1959-61; editorial asst. Kiplinger Washington Editors, 1961-63; feature writer pub. info. dept. Ball State U., 1984-85, coll. editor Coll. Bus., 1985-86, coord. alumni and devel., 1986-88, dir. major gift clubs and donor rels., 1988-90; dir. devel. Sweet Briar (Va.) Coll., 1990-91; adminstr. St. Mary's Hosp. and Med. Ctr. Found., Grand Junction, Colo., 1991—. Editor: A History of Maxon Corporation, 1986, Managing Change, 1986, Indiana's Investment Banker, 1987; assoc. editor Mid-Am. Jour. Bus., 1985-86. Participant Leadership Lynchburg, 1990, Jr. League; mem. Sr. Companions Bd., Grand Junction, 1992—; mem. Mesa County Healthy Communities Steering Com., 1992—; mem. Mesa County Health Assessment, 1994—; mem. steering com. Channel 18, 1995. Recipient Golden Broom award Muncie Clean City, 1989; svc. of distinction award Ball State U. Coll. Bus., 1990. Mem. Coun. for Advancement and Support of Edn., Assn. of Healthcare Philanthropy (regional 9 cabinet 1992—), Nat. Soc. Fundraising Execs. (cert., Colo. chpt. bd. dirs. 1994—). Republican.

MC CARTHY, PATRICIA MARGARET, retreat house administrator, social worker; b. L.A., Mar. 2, 1943; d. Alphonsus Martin and Margaret (Kroutil) Mc C. BA, Dominican Coll., San Rafael, Calif., 1964; MSW, U. So. Calif., 1967. Lic. clin. social worker, Calif. Community organizer Holy Name Parish Archdiocese L.A., 1980-82; social worker St. Anne's Maternity Home, L.A., 1967-73, Holy Family Adoption Svc., L.A., 1973-78, Stanford Home, Sacramento, 1982-84; info. specialist Info. & Referral Svc. L.A. County, El Monte, Calif., 1984-87; exec. dir. Holy Spirit Retreat Ctr., Encino, Calif., 1987—. Mem. Jericho, L.A., 1988; inc. mem. Sisters of Social Svc. L.A., 1978—. Named Outstanding Citizen L.A. City Coun., 1982. Mem. NASW, Retreats Internat. (so. Calif. area rep. 1990-93). Democrat. Roman Catholic. Office: Holy Spirit Retreat Ctr 4316 Lanai Rd Encino CA 91436-3617

MCCARTHY, WILLIAM JAMES, research psychologist, consultant, psychology educator; b. Paris, May 20, 1951; came to U.S. 1969; s. John Robert and Helen Ruth (House) McC.; m. Angela Wong, Mar. 23, 1974 (div. 1984); m. Bambi Batts Young, Aug. 7, 1988; 1 child, Jordan Robert. BA, Columbia U., 1973; MA, U. Ill., 1976; PhD, Yale U., 1980. Vis. asst. prof. Hampshire Coll., Amherst, Mass., 1978-79; instr. Pepperdine U., Los Angeles and Malibu, Calif., 1979; asst. research psychologist UCLA, 1980—, adj. asst. prof., 1987—; dir. sci. Pritikin Systems, Inc. (subs. Quaker Oats Co.), 1992—; cons. Am. Heart Assn. of Los Angeles, 1982-83; cons., bd. dirs. Am. Cancer Soc. Coastal, Los Angeles, 1982—, v.p. pub. issues, 1989-93, pres. 1993-95; bd. dirs. Calif. divsn., Am. Lung Assn. of Los Angeles, 1983-90, Internat. Chem. Workers' Union, Akron, Ohio, 1984-85, Nat. Cancer Inst., Bethesda, Md., 1986-92, Calif. Dept. Health, Sacramento, 1986, Karl Lorimar Video Prodns., 1986-87, Los Angeles County Dept. Health Services, 1986-88. Editor: So. Calif. Language and Gender Interest Group Newsletter, 1980-88, Psychology of Women Quarterly, 1986-89; consulting editor: Health Psychology, 1992-93. Bd. dirs. So. Calif. Skeptics, Pasadena, 1986-88; mem. L.A. Year 2000 Program; mem. grants review bd. Am. Lung Assn. Los Angeles County, 1984-89, Healthy Mothers Healthy Babies Coalition Los Angeles, 1985-88. Mem. Coalition for Clean Air, Santa Monica, Calif. Consulting editor Health Psychology. Grantee NIH, 1980-84, Am. Lung Assn., 1982, Nat. Cancer Inst., 1985, 86, 87-92, tobacco-related disease program U. Calif., 1990-93; recipient Fitness Leadership award L.A. County,

Calif., 1994, Capitol Dome Pub. Svc. award Am. Cancer Soc., 1994. Mem. AAAS, APHA, Am. Psychol. Soc., Am. Cancer Soc. (mem. smoking cessation subcom. 1984-89, nutrition subcom., 1990—), Soc. Behavioral Medicine. Democrat. Home: 2050 Newell Rd Malibu CA 90265-2938 Office: UCLA Psychology Dept 1282 Franz Hall Los Angeles CA 90024 also: Pritikin Longevity Ctr 1910 Ocean Front Walk Santa Monica CA 90405

MCCARTNEY, PATRICK KEVIN, newspaper reporter; b. L.A., Sept. 9, 1948; s. Warren Phil and Mildred Pauline (Weiler) McC. BA, U. San Diego, 1970; MA, U. So. Calif., 1983. Statis. analyst L.A. County Probation Dept., Downey, Calif., 1973-79; writer Free Venice (Calif.) Beachhead, 1984-88; editor, reporter Westchester (Calif.) Jour., 1987-88; reporter Blade-Citizen newspaper, Solana Beach, Calif., 1988-89; staff writer Press-Courier, Oxnard, Calif., 1990-91; corr. L.A. Times, Ventura, Calif., 1991—. Contbr. articles to newspapers. Pres. Venice Town Council, 1984-86, Coalition Concerned Communities, L.A., 1986-87; bd. dirs. Not Yet N.Y., L.A., 1986-87; candidate for L.A. City Coun., 1987. Mem. San Diego Press Assn., Venice Hist. Soc. (co-founder, bd. dirs. 1986-88), Encinitas Hist. Soc. (bd. dirs. 1989), Ventura County Press Club (co-founder, bd. dirs. 1991—). Home: 930 Tahoe Blvd # 349 Incline Village NV 89451

MCCLAIN, RICHARD STAN, cinematographer; b. Los Angeles, Oct. 7, 1951; m. Kim Girard, Nov. 7, 1987. Founder Pasadena Camera Sys., Inc. Aerial cameraman: (feature films) The Client, I Love Trouble, Lightning Jack, Tombstone, Falling Down, Heart and Soul, So, I Married an Axe Murderer, The Good Son, Made in America, This Boy's Life, Fearless, Passenger 57, Wind, At Play in the Fields of the Lord, The Right Stuff, The Iceman, Rambo, Firebirds, Wind, Basic Instinct, Innerspace, Buster, U2 Rattle and Hum, Crazy People, The Hunt for Red October, The Doors, Flatliners, Nell, Murder in the First, Drop Zone, Get Shorty, The Money Train; (TV shows) Magnum P.I., Airwolf. Recipient Best Cinematography award London Internat. Advt. Awards, 1993, Telly award (2), 1993, (1), 1994. N.Y. Festival Silver award, 1993, Telly award (2) 1994, (4) 1995. Mem. Internat. Photographers, Screen Actors Guild, Dirs. Guild Am.

MCCLAIN, ROGER ALLEN, aerospace industry executive; b. Anderson, S.C., Nov. 17, 1943; s. Robert McClain and Francis Lorene (Jefferson) Beatty; children: Teresa McClain-Gabinger, Deborah White, Karen Kittelson. BS, Clemson U., 1965; MS, AFIT, 1967; M in Divinity, United Theol. Sem., 1976. Commd. 2d lt. USAF, 1965, advanced through grades to col., 1984, ret., 1990; dir. Loral, Pasadena, Calif., 1990—. Editor: Command & Staff Review Canadian Forces College, 1978. Active Leukemia Soc. Am., Nat. Parkinson Found. Decorated Legion of Merit; named one of Outstanding Young Men Am., 1972. Mem. Air Force Assn. (life). Methodist. Home: 1659 Henrietta St Redlands CA 92373-7256

MCCLANAHAN, CLARENCE EDWARD, academic administrator. BA in English, William Paterson Coll., 1973; MA in English, NYU, 1977, PhD in Comparative Lit., 1981. Prof. City Coll. San Francisco, 1980-84, Armstrong U., Berkeley, Calif., 1988-90; cons. San Francisco Corps., 1985-87; adminstr. U.S.-Japan Tech. Mgmt. Ctr. Stanford (Calif.) U., 1991—; mem. com. for art, Stanford U., 1994—. Author: European Romanticism, 1990; contbr. articles, essays to profl. publs. Recipient cert. Goethe Inst., 1979. Mem. Elks. Home: 360 Hyde St Apt 202 San Francisco CA 94109-8020 Office: Stanford U US Japan Ctr 322 McCullough Bldg Stanford CA 94305

MCCLANAHAN, MICHAEL NELSON, systems analyst; b. Cin., Oct. 28, 1953; s. Roland Nelson and Jeanne Ann (Stevens) McC.; m. Tina Rosanne Swiecki, Mar. 8, 1986; 1 child, Sean Gabriel. Student, U. Cin., 1972-73, Goldenwest Coll., 1979-80, Riverside Community Coll., 1980-83, 90-92. Pres. Riverside (Calif.) Mktg., 1983-88; digital systems analyst Wyle Labs., Norco, Calif., 1988-93; systems analyst Ctr. for Environ. Rsch. and Tech. U. Calif., Riverside, 1993—. Author: (software) SDAS, 1989, HCSS DAS System, 1990, (book) HCSS Systems Operation, 1990, (manual) Software Quality Assurance, 1991. Recipient Svc. award Wyle Labs., 1991. Mem. IEEE, Assn. Computing Machinery, Instrument Soc. of Am. Address: U Calif Riverside CE-CERT 1200 Columbia Ave Riverside CA 92507 Office: 1200 Columbia Ave Riverside CA 92507

MCCLANE, ANGELA DAWN, marriage, family and child counselor; b. Fort Benning, Ga., Mar. 7, 1961; d. Victor Lee and Lucerne Cordelia (Parks) Weber; m. George Eddington McClane, May 14, 1994. BS, Ill. State U., Normal, 1983; MA, Trinity Divinity Sch., Deerfield, Ill., 1989. Recreation therapist F. Edward Herbert Hosp., New Orleans, 1984-86; rsch. asst. Alex Masterson, M.D., Loma Linda, Calif., 1989-90; marriage, family & child counseling intern Loma Linda Behavioral Med. Ctr., 1990-91, Riverside (Calif.) Psychiat. Med. Group, 1991-94; psychiat. emergency team Knollwood Hosp., Riverside, 1992-94. Mem. Am. Counseling Assn., Calif. Assn. Marriage & Family Therapists.

MCCLARD, RONALD WAYNE, chemist; b. Aug. 12, 1951. BA, Cen. Coll., Pella, Iowa; PhD, UCLA, 1978. Postdoctoral rsch. assoc. U. N.C., 1979-82; asst. prof. chemistry Boston Coll., 1982-84; asst. prof. chemistry and biochemistry Reed Coll., Portland, Oreg., 1984-87, assoc. prof. chemistry and biochemistry, 1988-94, prof. chemistry and biochemistry, 1994—; vis. assoc. prof. biochemistry Oreg. Health Scis. U., 1990-91; adj. asst. prof. chemistry Oreg. Grad. Ctr., 1984-87. Contbr. articles to profl. jours.; patentee in field. Recipient So. Calif. Edison award for Disting. Achievement in the Scis., 1968, Bank of Am. Achievement award, 1969, Nat. Rsch. Svc. award 1979, 81, New Investigator Rsch. award Nat. Cancer Inst., 1982; rsch. grantee Juv. Diabetes Found., 1984, Med. Rsch. Found. of Oreg., 1986, 95, Rsch. Corp., 1987, Am. Cancer Soc., 1987, Am. Diabetes Assn., 1987, Camille and Henry Dreyfus Found. Tchng. and Rsch. fellowship, 1988, NSF, 1991, others. Office: Reed Coll Arthur F Scott Chemist Portland OR 97202

MCCLATCHY, JAMES B., editor, newspaper publisher; b. Sacramento; s. Carlos K. and Phebe (Briggs) McC.; m. Susan Brewster; children: Carlos F., William B. B.A., Stanford U.; M.S., Columbia U. Reporter Sacramento Bee; reporter, editor Fresno Bee, Calif.; pub. McClatchy Newspapers, Sacramento. Dir. French Am. Bilingual Sch. Pilot USAFR, 1945-57. Mem. InterAm. Press Assn. (dir.), Calif. Nature Conservancy (dir.), Am. Press Inst. Office: McClatchy Newspapers 21st & Q Sts Sacramento CA 95813

MCCLAUGHERTY, JOE L., lawyer, educator; b. Luling, Tex., June 1, 1951; s. Frank Lee and Elease (Terrell) McC. BBA with honors, U. Tex., 1973, JD with honors, 1976. Bar: Tex. 1976, N.Mex. 1976, U.S. Dist. Ct. N.Mex. 1976, U.S. Ct. Appeals (10th cir.) 1976, Colo. 1988, U.S. Supreme Ct. 1979. Assoc. firm Rodey, Dickason, Sloan, Akin & Robb, P.A., Albuquerque, 1976-81, ptnr., dir., 1981-87, resident ptnr., Santa Fe, 1983-87, mng. ptnr., 1985-87, ptnr. Kemp, Smith, Duncan & Hammond, P.C., 1987-92, resident ptnr., Santa Fe, 1987-92, mng. ptnr., 1987-92; ptnr. McClaugherty, Silver & Downes, P.C., 1992—; adj. prof. law U. N.Mex., Albuquerque, 1983—; faculty Nat. Inst. Trial Advocacy, so. regional, So. Meth. U. Law Sch., 1983—, Rocky Mt. regional, U. Denver Law Sch., 1986—, nat. session U. Colo. Law Sch., 1987; faculty Hastings Ctr. for Trial and Appellate Advocacy, 1985—; bd. dirs. MCM Corp., Raleigh, N.C., Brit.-Am. Ins. Co., Ltd., Nassau, The Bahamas, 1985-91. Mem. N.Mex. Bar Assn. (bd. dirs. trial practice sect. 1976-85, chairperson 1983-84, dir. young lawyers div. 1978-80), N.Mex. Assn. Def. Lawyers (pres. 1982-83, bd. dirs. 1982-85). Office: McClaugherty Silver & Downes PC PO Box 8680 Santa Fe NM 87504-8680

MCCLEERY, RICHARD GRIMES, retired pathologist; b. Washington, Iowa, May 7, 1928; s. Richard Hamilton and Sara Lois (Grimes) McC.; m. Patsy Ruth Hollister, Aug. 11, 1950 (div. Apr. 1964); children: Mark, Michael, Scott; m. Patricia Lee Foreman, Aug. 7, 1965; 1 child, Andrew. BA, The Colo. Coll., 1950; MD, U. Iowa, 1954. Diplomate Am. Bd. Pathology. Pathologist Meml. Hosp. of Laramie County, Cheyenne, Wyo., 1960-85, D. Paul Hosp., Cheyenne, 1960-85; con. pathologist VA Hosp., Cheyenne, 1960-85; officer, trustee Clin. Lab., Cheyenne, 1970-85, ret., 1985. Bd. dirs. Cheyenne Family YMCA, 1962-63; allocations com. United Way, Cheyenne, 1963. Capt. USAF, 1957-59. Rsch. fellowship Am. Cancer Soc., 1959. Fellow Coll. Am. Pathologists (emeritus); mem. Wyo. State Med. Soc. (pres. 1981), Am. Soc. of Clin. Pathologists (emeritus), Cheyenne Young Men's Lit. Club (pres. 1990). Presbyterian.

MCCLELLAN, BENNETT EARL, producer; b. Sedalia, Mo., Nov. 20, 1952; s. G. Earl and Ruth E. (McQueen) McC.; m. Gail Jones, Sept. 5, 1981; children: Ian Michael, Elizabeth Gayle. MBA, Harvard U., 1981; MFA in Film and TV, UCLA, 1989. Writer, dir. Old Globe Theater, San Diego, 1973-76; artistic dir. Genesis Theater, San Diego, 1977-79; cons. McKinsey & Co., L.A., 1981-87, Arthur D. Little Media & Entertainment Group, Cambridge, Mass., 1987-89; prodn. exec. Hanna-Barbera Prodns., 1990-91; gen. mgr. L.A. Philharmonic Assn., 1992-94, Nicktoons/Games Animation, Studio City, Calif., 1994—. Producer: (TV series) Good News, Bad News, 1988. Paramount fellow Paramount Pictures, 1989; named Outstanding Grad. Student UCLA Alumni Assn., 1990. Mem. Hollywood Radio and TV Soc. (Internat. Broadcasting award 1989), Acad. TV Arts and Scis. Office: Nickelodeon 4040 Vineland Ave Studio City CA 91604-3350

MCCLELLAN, CRAIG RENE, lawyer; b. Portland, Oreg., June 28, 1947; s. Charles Russell and Annette Irene (Benedict) McC.; m. Susan Armistead Nash, June 7, 1975; children: Ryan Alexander, Shannon Lea. BS in Econs., U. Oreg., 1969; JD magna cum laude, Calif. We. U., 1976. Bar: Calif. 1976, U.S. Dist. Ct. (so. dist.) Calif. 1976, U.S. Dist. Ct. (ea., ctrl., no. dists.) Calif. 1991, U.S. Supreme Ct. 1991. Compliance specialist Cost of Living Coun. and Price Commn., Washington, 1972-73, dir. Oil Policy subcom., 1973; ptnr. Luce, Forward, Hamilton & Scripps, San Diego, 1976-87; owner McClellan & Assocs., San Diego, 1987—. Chmn. annual fundraising auction KPBS, 1984. Capt. USMC, 1969-72. Mem. Assn. Trial Lawyers Am., Am. Bd. Trial Advocates, Am. Inns of Ct (master), Calif. State Bar Assn., San Diego County Bar Assn., Calif. Trial Lawyers Assn. (bd. govs. 1985-87), San Diego Trial Lawyers Assn. (bd. dirs. 1983-90), Nat. Forensics League, Phi Gamma Delta, Phi Alpha Delta. Presbyterian. Office: McClellan & Assocs 1144 State St San Diego CA 92101-3529

MCCLELLAND, KAMILLA KURODA, news reporter, proofreader, book agent; b. Boseman, Mont., June 16, 1964; d. Yasumasa and Alice (Kassis) Kuroda; m. Craig Alexander McClelland, June 25, 1989. BA in Asian Studies, U. Calif., Berkeley, 1987; MS in Print News, U. Ill., Champaign-Urbana, 1989. Legis. aide Hawaii State Ho. of Reps., Honolulu, 1987; grad. asst. U. Ill. Dept. Journalism, Champaign, 1987-89; asst. op-ed editor The Daily Illini, Champaign, 1988-89; reporter AP, Seattle, 1989, Tacoma News Tribune, 1989-90; bus. news reporter The Olympian, Olympia, Wash., 1990—; proofreader Minerva Rsch., Inc., Honolulu, 1982—. Vol. Am.-Arab Anti Disc Com., Berkeley, Calif., 1984-87, Capital City Marathon, Olympia, 1993-94; active Japanese Am. Citizens League, Honolulu, 1983-89. Recipient Recognition awards for newswriting Gannett, 1991, 92, 1st pl., Best of Gannett award for Bus. and Consumer Reporting, 1994. Mem. Asian Am. Journalists Assn. Office: The Olympian PO Box 407 Olympia WA 98507-0407

MCCLENDON, IRVIN LEE, SR., technical writer and editor; b. Waco, Tex., June 12, 1945; s. Irvin Nicholas and Evelyn Lucile (Maycumber) McC.; divorced; children: Michael Boyd, Irvin Lee Jr., Laura Ann, Paul Nicholas, Richard Lester. Student El Camino Coll., 1961-63, U. So. Calif., 1962-66; BA in Math., Calif. State U.-Fullerton, 1970, postgrad. in bus. adminstrn., 1971-76; cert. nat. security mgmt. Indsl. Coll. Armed Forces, 1974; postgrad. in religion Summit Sch. Theology, 1982-84. Engring. lab. asst. Rockwell Internat. Corp., Anaheim, Calif., 1967-68, test data analyst, 1968, assoc. computer programmer, 1968-70, mem. tech. staff, 1970-82; systems programmer A-Auto-trol Tech. Corp., Denver, 1982-84, sr. tech. writer, 1984-86; sr. tech. writer, editor Colo. Data Systems, Inc., Englewood, Colo., 1986-87; engring. writer III CalComp subs. Lockheed Co., Hudson, N.H., 1987; sr. tech. writer CDI Corp., Arvada, Colo., 1987-88; staff cons. CAP GEMINI AM., Englewood, 1989; sr. tech./instrnl. writer & editor Tech. Tng. Systems, Inc., Aurora, Colo., 1990—. Sec. of governing bd. Yorba Linda Libr. Dist., 1972-77; trustee Ch. of God (Seventh Day), Bloomington, Calif., 1979-81, treas., 1980-81, mem. Calif. State U. and Coll. Statewide Alumni Coun., 1976-77; 2d v.p. Orange County chpt. Calif. Spl. Dists. Assn., 1976, pres., 1977; mem. Adams County Rep. Cen. Com., 1984-90, mem. Denver County Republican Ctrl. Com., 1992—; charter mem. Harmony: A Colo. Chorale, 1991— (treas., bd. dirs. 1992—). With USAFR, 1967-71. USAF Nat. Merit scholar, 1963-67. Mem. Calif. Assn. Libr. Trustees and Commrs. (exec. bd., So. Calif. rep. 1976-77), Nat. Eagle Scout Assn. (life), Scottish-Am. Mil. Soc., St. Andrew Soc. Colo., Am. Coll. Heraldry, Calif. State U.-Fullerton Alumni Assn. (dir. 1975-77). Republican. Office: 3131 S Vaughn Way Ste 300 Aurora CO 80014-3503

MCCLENNEN, MIRIAM J., former state official; b. Seattle, Sept. 16, 1923; d. Phillip and Frieda (Golub) Jacobs; m. Louis McClennen, Apr. 25, 1969; stepchildren: Peter Adams, James C.A., Helen, Persis, Crane, Emery. BA, U. Wash., 1945; MBA, Northwestern U., 1947. Exec. trainee Marshall Field & Co., Chgo., 1945-47; asst. buyer Frederick & Nelson (subs. of Marshall Field), Seattle, 1947-49; buyer Frederick & Nelson (subs. of Marshall Field), 1949-57; fashion coordinator, buyer Levy Bros., Burlingame/San Mateo, Calif., 1957-63; buyer Goldwaters, Phoenix, 1963-67; adminstrv. asst. to pres. Ariz. State Senate, Phoenix, 1973-76; dir. publs. Office of Sec. of State, Phoenix, 1976-87; chairwoman legis. subcom. adminstrv. procedure Ariz. State Legislature, Phoenix, 1984-85. Original compiler, codifier, editor publ. Ariz. Adminstrv. Code, 1973-87, Ariz. Adminstrv. Register, 1976-87. Bd. dirs., mem. Phoenix Art Mus. League, 1972-90, Phoenix Symphony Guild, 1970-88; bd. dirs., sec. Combined Metro. Phoenix Arts and Scis., 1974-90, mem. adv. bd., 1990—; bd. dirs. Phoenix Arts Coun., Master Apprentice Programs, 1980-83; bd. dirs., mem. exec. com. Heard Mus., 1982-88, 90—, chmn. publs. com., 1982-88, chmn. exhibit and edn. com., 1990-93; mem. Ariz. State Hist. Records Adv. Bd., 1987-90, Ariz. Commn. on Arts, 1989—, Phoenix Art Mus., 1972—. Recipient Disting. Svc. award Atty. Gen. Ariz., 1987, Outstanding Svc. to People, Ariz. State Senate, 1987, Nat. Assn. Secs. of State award, 1987. Mem. English Speaking Union, Nat. Soc. Arts and Letters, Charter 100 (bd. dirs. 1981-85), Phoenix County Club, Ariz. Club. Home: 5311 N La Plaza Cir Phoenix AZ 85012-1415

MCCLOSKEY, LAWRENCE A., management consultant, author; b. Albany, Oreg., Sept. 24, 1949; s. Harold Steven and Charmion Kathleen (Hood) McC.; m. Susan Elizabeth Gale, June 19, 1971; children: Erin, Rebecca. BS in Humanities, Western Oreg. State Coll., 1972. Police detective Benton County Sheriff's Office, Corvallis, Oreg., 1972-91; pres. Investigative Rsch., Albany, Oreg., 1989—. Author: TQM, A Basic Text, 1993, Selling with Excellence, 1994. Office: IRC PO Box 1462 Albany OR 97321-0448

MCCLUNE, MICHAEL MARLYN, real estate asset management company executive; b. Denver, July 12, 1950; s. Raymond Earl and Lorraine Elva (Bohm) McC.; m. Elizabeth Ann Butler, Sept. 18, 1982; children: Kristin Elizabeth, Michael Ryan. BSCE magna cum laude, U. So. Calif., 1972, MBA, 1974. Lic. real estate broker, Calif. Real estate investment broker Vistar Fin., Marina del Rey, Calif., 1979-81; program bus. mgr. Hughes Aircraft Co., El Segundo, Calif., 1981-85; v.p. LaSalle Ptnrs. Ltd., L.A., 1985-93; pres., CEO, New Am. Asset Mgmt. Svcs., Long Beach, Calif., 1993—; pres. New Am. Cons. Svcs., Long Beach, 1994—; pres., bd. dirs. Indsl. Complex Camarillo, Calif., 1988-93; founder, ptnr. CyberLease, Costa Mesa, Calif., 1990-92. Capt. USAF, 1974-79. Mem. Bldg. Owners and Mgrs. Assn. Greater L.A. (bd. dirs. 1994—, chmn. bd. 1995—, President's award 1993), Long Beach Mgrs. Assn. (v.p. 1988-90), Long Beach C. of C., Rotary, Tau Beta Pi. Office: New Am Asset Mgmt Svcs 4510 E Pacific Coast Hwy Long Beach CA 90804-3282

MCCLUNG, MICHAEL ROY, physician, medical educator, researcher; b. Louisville, June 19, 1943; s. Roy C. and Juyne Genelle (Bucklew) McC.; 1 child, Daniel ;m. Betsy Claire Willims, June 5, 1993. BA in Biology, Rice U., 1965; MD, U. Tex. S.W. Med. Sch., 1969. Diplomate Am. Bd. Internal Medicine, Am. Bd. Endocrinology and Metabolism. Intern Parkland Meml. Hosp., Dallas, 1969-70, resident, 1970-72; fellow in endocrinology NIH, Bethesda, Md., 1972-75; asst. prof. medicine Oreg. Health Scis. U., Portland, 1976-80, assoc. prof. medicine, 1980—; chief sect. endocrinology VA Med. Ctr., Portland, 1980-86; asst. dir. dept. med. edn. Providence Med. Ctr., Portland, 1987—, dir. Ctr. for Metabolic Bone Disorders, 1987—; dir. dept. diabetes, metabolism and endocrinology Chiles Rsch. Inst., Portland, 1988—; cons. endocrinology VA Med. Ctr., Portland, 1977-81, staff physician, 1980-87; dir. Endocrinology Clinic, Univ. Hosp., Portland, 1977-81, dir. Bone and Mineral Clinic, 1981-87, dir. Osteoporosis Ctr., 1985-87. Contbr. numerous articles, abstracts to profl. jours., chpts. to books. Recipient Edwin H. Carey Meml. award, 1966, Dean's Scholarship award U. Tex. S.W. Med. Sch., 1966-69, Chief Residents Tchg. award, 1981. Mem. Am. Fedn. Clin. Rsch. (Western sect. program com. 1977, chmn. endocrinology subsplty. session 1977), Am. Soc. Bone and Mineral Rsch., Am. Thyroid Assn. (travel grantee 1980), The Endocrine Soc. (program com. 1977, clin. day program com. 1989-90, chmn. program com. 1991), Oreg. Med. Assn., Multnomah County Med. Soc., Alpha Omega Alpha. Office: Providence Med Ctr 5050 NE Hoyt St Ste 651 Portland OR 97213-2996

MCCLURE, JAMES A., lawyer, retired senator; b. Payette, Idaho, Dec. 27, 1924; s. W. R. and Marie McC.; m. Louise Miller; children: Marilyn, Kenneth, David. JD, U. Idaho, 1950; DL (hon.), Coll. Idaho, 1986. Mem. Idaho State Senate, 1961-66; asst. majority leader, 1965-66; city atty. City of Payette, Idaho; pros. atty. Payette County, Idaho; mem. 90th-92nd Congresses 1st Idaho Dist., 1967-73; senator Idaho, 1973-90; chmn. Energy and Natural Resources Com., 1981-86; mem. Com. on Rules and Adminstrn., Com. on Appropriations; pres. McClure, Gerard & Neuenschwander, Inc., Washington, 1990—; ptnr. Givens, Pursley, & Huntley, Boise, Idaho, 1990—. Trustee Kennedy Ctr., Meth. Ch. Mem. Elks, Masons, Kiwanis, Phi Alpha Delta. Methodist. Office: McClure Gerard & Neuenschwander Inc 801 Pennsylvania Ave NW Washington DC 20004-2615 also: Givens Pursley & Huntley Ste 200 Park Pl 277 N 6th St Boise ID 83701

MCCLURE, THOMAS FULTON, artist, retired educator; b. Pawnee City, Nebr., Apr. 17, 1920; s. Clate Ray and Virginia Ann (Carden) McC.; m. Roberta Lucille Estey, Mar. 14, 1942; children: Colleen Elaine Kotila, James Ray. BFA, U. Nebr., 1941; postgrad., Wash. State Coll., 1941; MFA, Cranbrook Acad. of Art, 1947. Tech. illustrator Boeing Aircraft Co., Seattle, 1942-45, Pontiac (Mich.) Motor Co., 1946; instr. Sch. for Am. Craftsmen, Alfred (N.Y.) Univ., 1947-48; asst. prof. art Univ. Okla., Norman, 1948-49; prof. of art Univ. Mich., Ann Arbor, 1949-81. Exhibited in Pa. Acad. of Fine Arts, 1958, Neon & Kinetic Art Mus. of Neon Art, L.A., 1987, and others; represented in many pub. collections including, Seattle Art Mus., Detroit Inst. Arts, Syracuse Mus. Fine Arts; work illustrated in books, Sculpture Casting, Plastics in Sculpture, Public Art-New Directions, American Artists, An Illustrated Survey. Recipient many comissions for works and many prizes in sculpture and drawing. Home: 2406 Pine Cove Rd Prescott AZ 86301-4054

MCCLURE, WILLIAM OWEN, biologist; b. Yakima, Wash., Sept. 29, 1937; s. Rexford Delmont and Ruth Josephine (Owen) McC.; m. Pamela Preston Harris, Mar. 9, 1968 (div. 1979); children: Heather Harris, Rexford Owen; m. Sara Joan Rorke, July 27, 1980. BSc, Calif. Inst. Tech., 1959; PhD, U. Wash., 1964. Postdoctoral fellow Rockefeller U., N.Y.C., 1964-65; rsch. assoc. Rockefeller U., 1965-68; asst. prof. U. Ill., Urbana, 1968-75; assoc. prof. U. So. Calif., L.A., 1975-79; prof. biology, prof. neurology U. So. Calif., 1979—; v.p. sci. affairs Nelson Rsch. & Devel. Co., Irvine, Calif., 1981-82; acting v.p. rsch. & devel. Nelson Rsch. & Devel. Co., 1985-86; dir. program. neurol. info. sci. U. So. Calif., 1982-92, dir. program in psychobiology, 1991—; dir. cellular biology U. So. Calif., 1979-81, dir. neurobiology, 1982-88, dir. prog. psychobiology, 1991—; cons. in field; dir. Marine & Freshwater Biomed. Ctr., U. So. Calif., 1982-83; co-dir. Baja Calif. Expedition of the R/V Alpha Helix, 1974, others; chmn. Winter Conf. on Brain Rsch., 1979, 80, others; lectr. in field; sci. adv. bd. Nelson R & D, 1972-91; mem. bd. commentators Brain and Behavioral Scis., 1978—. Editor or author 3 books; co-editor: Wednesday Night at the Lab; patentee in field; mem. editorial bd. Neurochem. Rsch., 1975-81, Jour. Neurochemistry, 1977-84, Jour. Neurosci. Rsch., 1980-86; contbr. over 100 articles to profl. jours. Bd. dirs. San Pedro and Peninsula Hosp. Found., 1989—, Faculty Ctr., U. So. Calif., 1991-95, San Pedro Health Svcs., 1992—. Scripps Inst. fellow, 1958, NIH fellow, 1959-64, 64-65, Alfred P. Sloan fellow, 1972-76, others; recipient rsch. grants, various sources, 1968—; Intersci. Rsch. Inst. fellow, 1989. Mem. AAAS, Am. Soc. Neurochemistry, Soc. for Neurosci., Am. Soc. Biol. Chemistry and Molecular Biology, Interant. Soc. Neurochemistry, Assn. Neurosci. Depts. and Programs, Univ. Park Investment Group, Bay Surgical Soc., N.Y. Acad. Scis. Republican. Presbyterian. Home: 30533 Rhone Dr Palos Verdes Peninsula CA 90275-5742 Office: U So Calif Dept Biol Scis Los Angeles CA 90089

MCCLUSKEY, LOIS THORNHILL, photographer; b. Boston, Apr. 7, 1945; d. Fred S. and Mary (Evans) T.; BA, Middlebury Coll., 1966; postgrad. U. St. Thomas, Houston, 1967-69; MA, NYU, 1971; cert. in graphic design U. Calif.-Santa Cruz, 1983; m. Edward J. McCluskey, Feb. 14, 1981. Research technician dept. virology Baylor Sch. Medicine, Houston, 1966-68; with Kelly Girls, Palo Alto, 1971-72; slide curator dept. art Stanford (Calif.) U., 1972-80; founder, pres. Stanford Design Assocs., Palo Alto, 1981—; cons. copy and museum photography; designer, producer custom lecture slides. Mem. Smithsonian Assos. Home: 895 Northampton Dr Palo Alto CA 94303-3434 Office: PO Box 60451 Palo Alto CA 94306-0451

MCCOLL, CAROL ANN, financial executive, educator; b. Arlington Heights, Ill., June 10, 1953; d. Charles Richard and Jean (Gore) Barton; m. Donald Bruce McColl, Dec. 6, 1975 (div. July 1984); 1 child, Donald Daniel. BA, Colo. Coll., 1974; MBA, U. Colo., 1987. Office mgr. Worksafe, Inc., Denver, 1979-83; divsn. adminstr. Dysan Corp., Colorado Springs, 1984-86; exec. dir. Tech. Assistance Ctr., Denver, 1987-90; v.p. fin. and adminstrn. McRel, Aurora, Colo., 1990—; adj. instr. Regis U., Denver, 1992—. Mem. fin. com. Archdiocese of Denver, 1993—; vice chair, bd. dirs. Metro Denver Gives, 1989-90; sec., bd. dirs. Colo. Lawyers for the Arts, Denver, 1991; vol. Tech. Assistance Ctr., Denver, 1990—. Mem. Beta Gamma Sigma. Roman Catholic. Office: McRel 2550 S Parker Rd Ste 500 Aurora CO 80014-1678

MCCOLLUM, ALVIN AUGUST, real estate company executive; b. L.A., Jan. 20, 1920; s. Nile Clarkson and Ida Martha (Kuhlman) McC.; m. Maxine Eleanor Seeberg, July 29, 1944; children: Robert Michael, James Alan, Patricia Kathleen. BA, UCLA, 1941; postgrad., U.S. Naval Acad., 1946, Southwestern U., 1949-50. Exec. v.p., dir. Strout Realty, N.Y.C., 1948-61, Del E. Webb Corp., Phoenix, 1961-67; pres., dir. Sahara Nev. Corp., Las Vegas, 1964-67, Devel. Svcs., Inc., Scottsdale, Ariz., 1967-69; pres., chmn. Recreation Leisure Land, Inc., Scottsdale, 1969-71; asst. pres., dir. A.J. Industries, Inc., L.A., 1971-74; pres., dir. Carefree (Ariz.) Ranch, Inc., 1974-76; pres., bd. dir. Cons. Internat., Scottsdale, 1976—; chmn. CEO Greenway Environmental Svs., Inc., Gilbert, Ariz., 1992—; pres., bd. dirs. Combined Assets, Inc., Westlake Village, Calif., First Realty Fin., Inc., L.A., Corp. Capital Resources, Inc., Westlake Village. Bd. dirs. Admiral Nimitz Found., Fredericksburg, Tex., 1970—, Boys Club Las Vegas, 1964-68, United Fund, Las Vegas, 1966; co-chmn. Nat. Conf. Christians and Jews, Las Vegas, 1966; elder Presbyn. Ch. USA, 1954—. Lt. USN, 1943-48, PTO. Mem. Masons, Shriners, Am. Legion, Mt. Shadows Country Club (bd. dirs. 1962-64). Republican. Home: 4118 N 87th Way Scottsdale AZ 85251-2940 Office: Greenway Environ Svcs Inc 644 E Southern Ave # 204 Mesa AZ 85204-4934

MCCOMAS, MICHELLE RAE, cell biologist, biochemist; b. Coco Beach, Fla., Jan. 1, 1968; s. Henry Neal and Carole Virginia (Dudley) Anderson; m. Brian Keith McComas, Apr. 8, 1989. Student, Calif. Poly. State U., San Luis Obispo, 1986-89; BS, SUNY, New Paltz, 1993. Biochem. prodn. technologist Ortho Diagnostic Systems Inc. a J&J Co., Carpenteria, Calif., 1990-93; rsch. assoc. Amgen Inc., Thousand Oaks, Calif., 1994—, Boulder, Colo. Mem. AAAS. Republican. Baptist. Office: Amgen Inc AB-5A 3200 Walnut St Boulder CO 80301

MCCOMB, RONALD GRAEME, rolfer; b. Burns, Oreg., Jan. 6, 1938; s. Oliver Graham and Melba Viettta (Oard) McC.; m. Annie Bernice Duggan, Nov. 1968 (div.); 1 child, Siobhan Ariel Duggan. Student, Portland Art Mus. Sch., 1957-61; Cert., Rolf Inst., Boulder, Colo., 1971. Cert. rolfer. Artist, 1961-66; film maker Union Light Co., N.Y.C., 1966-70, Am. Film Inst., Hollywood, Calif., 1970; rolfer pvt. practice Portland, Seattle, 1971—. Contbr. articles to profl. jours. Mem. Rolf Inst. Office: 311 1st Ave S Seattle WA 98104

MCCONKEY, MAX, association executive; b. Altoona, Pa., Mar. 14, 1945; s. Robert Paul and Ruth Lenora (Moyer) McC.; m. Judith Elizabeth Colvin, Mar. 28, 1965 (div. 1980); children: Lisa Christine, Aaron Thoreau; m. Anne Maley, Aug. 29, 1987. BA, Pa. State U., 1967; postgrad., U. Mass., 1976. Tchr., dept. chair William Penn Sr. High Sch., York, Pa., 1967-69; cartoonist Lancaster (Pa.) Ind. Press, Liberation News Svc., 1968-72; reporter, desk editor The Gazette & Daily, York, 1968-69; tchr., dept. chair Mt. Anthony Union High Sch., Bennington, Vt., 1969-72; reporter, columnist The Bennington Banner, 1970-71; dir. The Network, Inc., Andover, Mass., 1972-92; exec. dir. Nat. Dissemination Assn., Tucson, Ariz., 1981—; dir. Ariz. office Far West Lab., San Francisco, 1992—; cons., pub. speaker in field. Editor, writer, pub. (newsletter) The Update, 1982—; editorial cartoonist Lawrence Eagle newspaper, 1979-85; collage artist. Del. Dem. Nat. Conv., 1968. Mem. Am. Ednl. Rsch. Assn. (chair nat. outreach com. 1993—). Office: Nat Dissemination Assn 4732 N Oracle Rd Ste 217 Tucson AZ 85705

MCCONKIE, OSCAR WALTER, lawyer; b. Moad, Utah, May 26, 1926; s. Oscar Walter and Margaret Vivian (Redd) M.; m. Judith Stoddard, Mar. 17, 1951; children: Oscar III, Ann, Daniel, Gail, Clair, Pace Jefferson, Roger James, Edward. BS in Polit. Sci., U. Utah, 1949, JD, 1952. Bar: Utah 1952, U.S. Ct. Appeals (10th cir.) 1952, U.S. Supreme Ct. 1981. County atty. Summit County (Utah), 1959-63; instr. bus. law Stevens Henager Coll., Salt Lake City, 1952-67; ptnr. Kirton & McConkie, Salt Lake City, 1967—. Served with USN, 1944-46. Mem. Utah House of Reps., 1955-57; pres. Utah State Senate, 1965-66; chmn. Utah Bd. Edn., 1983-85. Mem. Utah Bar Assn., Salt Lake County Bar Assn. Democrat. Mormon. Author: The Kingdom of God, 1962; God and Man, 1963; The Priest in the Aaronic Priesthood, 1964; Angels, 1975; Aaronic Priesthood, 1977; She Shall Be Called Woman, 1979. Home: 1954 Laird Dr Salt Lake City UT 84108-1823 Office: 1800 Eagle Gate Tower 60 E South Temple Salt Lake City UT 84111-1004

MCCONN, DONAVON J., engineer; b. Minot, N.D., Feb. 24, 1944; s. Gordon Anthony and Myrtle M. (Young) McC.; m. Diane Carol Martinson, Aug. 11, 1966; children: Donavon J. II, Eric Michael. Ariz. State U., 1965-69. Lic. steam engr., real estate agt.; cert. fire safety dir. Chief engr., ops. mgr. EDM Investments, San Francisco, 1974-84; chief engr. Tishman Office Ctr., 1984-86; supr. engr. East Bay Properties, 1986-89; regional engr. mgr. Allegiance Realty Group, San Francisco, 1989-94, Insignia Comml. Group, 1994—. With U.S. Army, 1962-65. Mem. Bldg. Owners & Mgrs. Assn., Am. Inst. Plant Engrs., Nat. Assn. Power Engrs., Nat. Fire Protection Assn., The Assn. Profl. Energy MGrs. Office: Insignia Comml Group 71 Stevenson St Ste 1600 San Francisco CA 94105-2938

MCCONNEL, RICHARD APPLETON, aerospace company official; b. Rochester, Pa., May 29, 1933; s. Richard Appleton Sr. and Dorothy (Merriman) McC.; m. Mary Francis McInnis, 1964 (div. 1984); children: Amy Ellen, Sarah Catherine; m. Penny Kendzie, 1993. BS in Naval Engring., U.S. Naval Acad., 1957; MS in Aerospace Engring., USN Postgrad. Sch., 1966. Commd. ensign USN, 1957; naval aviator Operation ASW, 1959-63, 68-71, 75-79; asst. prof. math. U.S. Naval Acad. 1966-68; program mgr. P3C update Naval Air Devel. Ctr., 1971-75; range program mgr. Pacific Missile Test Ctr., 1979-82; ret. USN, 1982; program mgr. Electromagnetic Systems div. Raytheon Co., Goleta, Calif., 1982-87; sr. engr. SRS Techs., Inc., Camarillo, Calif., 1987-92, High Tech. Solutions, Inc., Camarillo, Calif., 1992—. Mem. Internat. Test and Evaluation Assn., Assn. Old Crows. Republican. Office: High Tech Solutions 1000 Paseo Camarillo # S120 Camarillo CA 93010-6021

MCCONNELL, CALVIN DALE, clergyman; b. Monte Vista, Colo., Dec. 3, 1928; s. Roy and Leota Fern (Taylor) McC.; m. Mary Caroline Bamberg, Sept. 2, 1952 (dec. Apr. 1986); children: David William, Mark Andrew; m. Velma Duell, Dec. 17, 1988. B.A., U. Denver, 1951; M.Div., Iliff Sch. Theology, 1954; S.T.M., Andover Newton Theol. Sem., 1967. Ordained to ministry United Meth. Ch.; pastor Meth. Ch., Williams, Calif., 1955-58, 1st United Meth. Ch., Palo Alto, Calif. and Stanford U. Wesley Found., 1958-61; chaplain and asst. prof. religion Willamette U., Salem, Oreg., 1961-67; pastor Christ United Meth. Ch., Denver, 1968-72; pastor 1st United Meth. Ch., Boulder, Colo., 1972-79, Colorado Springs, Colo., 1979-80; bishop United Meth. Ch., Portland Area, 1980-88, Seattle Area, 1988—. Trustee U. Puget Sound, Iliff Sch. Theology; pres. United Meth. Ch. Bd. Higher Edn. and Ministry. Office: 2112 3rd Ave Ste 301 Seattle WA 98121-2310

MCCONNELL, PATRICIA LYNN, vocational consultant; b. Denver, Feb. 20, 1956; d. James Donald and Joyce Clemence (Wortman) McC.; m. Roger Tribble, 1989. BS, U. No. Colo., 1979. Mental health worker Arapahoe Mental Health Ctr., Littleton, Colo., 1977-79; work adjustment cons. recycling ctr. City of El Cerrito (Calif.), 1980-83; job developer, ind. contractor with Dept. of Rehab., Pleasant Hill, Calif., San Pablo, Vallejo, Calif., 1983-87; vocat. rehab. cons. Guitterez & Co., Oakland, Calif., 1987-89; owner, vocat. cons. JobPerfect, Berkeley, Calif., 1989—; owner, fundraiser Community Svcs. Mktg., Oakland; workshop leader Calif. Dept. of Rehab., Pleasant Hill, 1983-87, San Pablo, 1989. Author: (workbook) Job Search for the Disabled, 1985, Job Perfect Job Search Manual Datebook and Organizer, 1995; dir., producer (video) JobPerfect, 1992, How To Improve Your Communication and Interview Skills, 1994, Job Perfect, Job Search, 1995, Legacies, 1995. Mem., fundraiser No. Calif. Recyclers Assn., Berkeley, 1982-87, Calif. Marine Mammal Ctr., Marine Headlands, Calif., 1987-90, Bay Area Cmty. Svcs., 1993—. Recipient Dance award Englewood High Sch., Colo., 1974, Appreciation award Regional Occupational Program, San Pablo, 1989. Mem. Calif. Assn. for Rehab. Profls., Nat. Rehab. Assn. (bd. dirs. 1983-85). Office: JobPerfect at BFTI 2236 Derby St Berkeley CA 94705-1018

MC CONNELL, ROBERT EASTWOOD, architect, educator; b. Spokane, Wash., July 15, 1930; s. Robert Ervie and Alma (Eastwood) Mc C.; m. Beverly Ann Vincent, Sept. 12, 1953; children: Kathleen Ann, Karen Eileen, Terri Lynn. B in Archtl. Engring., Wash. State U., 1952; MArch, Mass. Inst. Tech., 1954. Project architect John W. Maloney (Architect), Seattle, 1956-62; asst. prof. architecture Ariz. State U., Tempe, 1962-66; asso. prof. Ariz. State U., 1966-67; prof. U. Kans., Lawrence, 1967-69; prof., head dept. art and architecture U. Idaho, Moscow, 1969-71; prof. U. Ariz., Tucson, 1971-92; dean Coll. Architecture U. Ariz., 1971-92; prof. emeritus, dean emeritus U. Ariz., Tucson, 1992—, acting assoc. dean, 1994; partner McConnell & Peterson, Architects, Tempe, 1963-66; pvt. practice architecture, 1962—. Author, project dir.: Land Use Planning for Ariz., Ariz. Acad, 1974; Contbr. articles to profl. jours. Chmn. Idaho Gov.'s Awards Program in Arts and Humanities, 1970; project dir. Rio Salado Conceptual Study, Phoenix, 1966; bd. dirs. Tucson Regional Plan, 1972-79. Served with USAF, 1954-56. Fellow AIA (awards 1969, 76, pres. So. Ariz. chpt. 1975-76, bd. dirs. 1971-77); mem. AAUP, Ariz. Town Hall, Ariz. Soc. Architects (mem. coun. of dels. 1971-77, chmn. honor awards jury 1975), Phi Kappa Phi, Scarab, Tau Beta Pi, Sigma Tau. Home: 7001 N Edgewood Pl Tucson AZ 85704-6924 Office: U Ariz Coll Architecture Tucson AZ 85721

MCCONNELL, ROSS FERGUSON, engineering executive; b. Huntington, W.Va., June 22, 1939; s. Ross William McConnell and Bess L. (Ferguson) Jones; m. Latricia Brown, Dec. 18, 1961 (div. Aug. 1973); children: Ross Ferguson II, Dwain Elliott; m. Maureen Edwardson, Oct. 28, 1974; 1 child, Maegan Anne. BSEE, Howard U.; postgrad., U. Calif. Cert. environ. engr. Pres., CEO Integrated Environmental Engring., Altadena, Calif., 1993—. Youth dir. Trinity Luth. Ch., Pasadena, Calif., 1992-94, ch. coun., 1982, 92.Capt. U.S. Army, 1963-65. Mem. NSPE, Kappa Alpha Psi. Lutheran. Office: Integrated Environ Engring 406 Wapello St Altadena CA 91001-1610

MCCOOEY, EVERETT DAVID, JR., construction company executive; b. N.Y.C., Dec. 7, 1935; s. Everett David Sr. and Mary Gertrude (Ennis) McC.; m. Patricia Kathleen Quinn, Feb. 27, 1960; children: Mark, David, Daniel, Everett III. MCE, Cornell U., 1958. From field engr., asst. supt. to cost engr. Turner Constrn. Co., N.Y.C., 1958-61; from estimating engr. to project engr. Turner Constrn. Co., Boston, 1961-68; from project mgr. to chief estimator Turner Constrn. Co., Houston, 1978-84; ops. mgr. Turner Constrn. Co., Somerset, N.J., 1984-88; project exec. Turner Constrn. Co., Seattle, 1988—; project mgr. Turner Internat. Ind., N.Y.C., 1975-78. Chmn. Planning Bd., Holliston, Mass., 1973-75; active Sch. Bldg. Com., Holliston, 1973-75, Ch. Bldg. Com., Spring, Tex., 1982-84. Recipient Outstanding Bld. Projects awards Assn. Gen. Contractors, Houston, 1983, Seattle, 1991. Mem. Am. Numismatic Assn., Meridian Valley Country Club. Republican. Roman Catholic.

MCCORD, THOMAS B., geophysicist, educator; b. Elverson, Pa., Jan. 18, 1939; s. Thomas M. and Hazel Violet (Bard) M.; m. Carol S. Bansner, Dec. 20, 1962. BS, Pa. State U., 1962; MS, Calif. Inst. Tech., 1964, PhD, 1968. From asst. to assoc. prof. (tenured) MIT, Boston, 1969-77; sr. research scientist Ctr. for Space Research, MIT, Boston, 1977-86; prof. planetary scis., depts. geology and geophysics, and physics and astronomy U. Hawaii, Honolulu, 1976—; vis. assoc. Planetary Sci., Calif. Inst. Tech., 1969-72; dir. George R. Wallace Jr. Astrophys. Obs., MIT, Boston, 1970-77; asst. dir. Inst. for Astronomy, U. Hawaii, Honolulu 1976-79; chmn. div. planetary sci. Hawaii Inst. Geophysics U. Hawaii, 1979-90; co-founder, chmn. chief sci. SETS Inc., Honolulu, 1978—; mem. NASA teams on 6 past and current space missions, positions included team leader Comet Rendezvous Asteroid Flyby Project and team mem. Galileo, Cassini and Mars 96 mission. Pres. Pacific Space Ctr., 1988-90. With USAF 1958-62. Named Research Fellow in Planetary Sci., Calif. Inst. Tech., 1968; recipient numerous research grants from various govt. and private agencies including NASA, Jet Propulsion Lab., Nat. Oceans and Atmospheres Adminstrn., and NSF, 1980-87, W.M. Keck Found. grant, 1986, Honolulu City and County award; asteroid discovered in 1985 named for him. Fellow Am. Geophys. Union (pres. planetary sect. 1986-90), AAAS; mem. Am. Astron. Soc. (pres. divsn. planetary sect. 1980-82), Internat. Astron. Union, European Geophys. Soc., Explorers Club. Office: U Hawaii Hawaii Inst Geophysics and Planetology Honolulu HI 96813 also: SETS Inc Tech Mililani Tech Pk 300 Katielu Ave Mililani HI 96789

MCCORKINDALE, CAROLYN CHRISTINE, dietitian; b. Berkeley, Calif., Oct. 18, 1962; d. John McCorkindale and Joan (Roth) Finnie. BS, Calif. Poly., 1984; MPH, San Jose State U., 1989. Registered dietitian, Calif.; cert. diabetes educator. Nutritionist San Francisco Gen. Hosp., 1989-91; clin. dietitian Laguna Honda Hosp., San Francisco, 1991-95; clin. dietitian, diabetes educator Palo Alto (Calif.) Med. Clinic, 1995—. Mem. Am. Diabetes Assn., Am. Dietetic Assn. (author jour. 1990, Huddleson award 1991), Am. Assn. Diabetic Educators, Calif. Dietetic Assn. Democrat. Home: 555 W Middlefield #E301 Mountain View CA 94043 Office: Palo Alto Med Clinic 319 Homer Ave Palo Alto CA 94301

MCCORKLE, ROBERT ELLSWORTH, agribusiness educator; b. Salinas, Calif., Apr. 3, 1938; s. Stanley Harold and Muriel Eugenia (Vosti) McC.; m. Mary E. McCorkle, June 26, 1965; children: Bonnie Kathleen, Robyn Krystyna. BSc in Farm Mgmt., Calif. Poly. State U., San Luis Obispo, 1960; MSc in Agrl. Econs., U. Calif., Davis, 1962; postgrad., U. Wis., 1969, Oreg. State U., 1966. Rsch. statistician U. Calif., Davis, 1960-62; asst. prof. agrl. bus. Calif. Poly. State U., San Luis Obispo, 1962-66, dir. internat. edn., 1970-74, asst. prof. agrl. mgmt., 1969-76, prof. agribus., 1976—; chief farm mgmt. officer Ministry Agr., Lusaka, Zambia, 1967-69; dir., owner McCorkle Farms, Inc., Willows, Calif., 1970—; vis. prof. Mich. State U., U.S. AID, Washington, 1984-85; dir., owner McCorkle Trucking, Glenn, Calif., 1988—; agrl. economist U.S. AID-Redso ESA, Nairobi, Kenya, 1984-85. Author: Guide for Farming in Zambia, 1968. Pres. Cabrillo Property Owners Assn., Los Osos, Calif., 1976-78; vol. Atty. Gen.'s Adv. Com., Calif., 1972-74. U.S. Peace Corps strategy grantee, Washington, 1976—. Mem. Am. Agrl. Econs. Assn., Western Agrl. Econs. Assn., Calif. Poly. Farm Mgmt. Club, Calif. Poly. Alumni Assn., Blue Key, Alpha Zeta (sr. advisor Delta chpt., nat. high coun. chronicler, bd. dirs., v.p. found.). Republican. Episcopalian. Office: Calif Poly State U San Luis Obispo CA 93407

MCCORMAC, BILLY MURRAY, physicist, research institution executive, former army officer; b. Zanesville, Ohio, Sept. 8, 1920; s. Samuel Dennis and Phyllis (Murray) M.; m. Dorothy Boros, 1948; children: Norene Leslie, Candace Elizabeth, Lisbeth Phyllis; m. Diana Root, 1968; children: Billy Murray II, Samuel Dennis Root. B.S., Ohio State U., 1943; M.S., U. Va., 1956, Ph.D. in Nuclear Physics, 1957. Commd. 2d lt. U.S. Army, 1943; advanced through grades to lt. col.; physicist U.S. Army (Office Spl. Weapons Devel.), 1957-60; scientist U.S. Army (Office of Chief of Staff), 1960-61; physicist U.S. Army (Def. Atomic Support Agy.), 1961-62, chief electromagnetic br., 1962-63; ret., 1963; sci. advisor rsch. inst. Ill. Inst. Tech., 1963, dir. div. geophysics rsch. inst., 1963-68; sr. cons. scientist Lockheed Rsch. Labs., Palo Alto, Calif., 1968-69, mgr. Radiation Physics Lab., 1969-74, mgr. Electro-optics Lab., 1974-76, mgr. solar and optics physics, 1976-89, staff exec. physical and electronic scis., 1989-92; Chmn. radiation trapped in earth's magnetic field Adv. Study Inst., Norway, 1965, chmn. aurora and airglow, Eng., 1966, Norway, 1968, Can., 1970, chmn. physics and chemistry of atmospheres, France, 1972, Belgium, 1974, chmn. earth's particles and fields, Germany, 1967, Calif., 1969, Italy, 1971, Eng., 1973, Austria, 1975; chmn. Shuttle Environment and Ops.-I, Washington, 1983, -II, Houston, 1985; chmn. Space Station in 21st Century, Reno, 1986, Space Station I, Washington, 1988. Editor: Jour. Water, Air and Soil Pollution, Geophysics and Astrophysics Monographs; editor-in-chief Natural Sinks CO2, 1992, Quantification of Sinks and Sources, 1993. Fellow AIAA (assoc., mem. publ. com. 1981—, v.p. publs. 1987-91); mem. AAAS, Am. Astron. Soc. (sr.), Am. Phys. Soc., Am. Geophys. Union, Marine Tech. Soc. Home: 696 Village Blvd Apt 9 Incline Village NV 89451-9017

MC CORMAC, WESTON ARTHUR, retired educator and army officer; b. Tacoma, Mar. 3, 1911; s. Jesse Carney and Jessie (Myron) McC.; B.A., Golden Gate U., M.B.A., 1968; diploma Nat. War Coll., 1956; M.P.A., U. So. Calif., 1972; M.A., Calif. Poly. State U., 1975. m. Mary Jeanne Rapp, Sept. 5, 1940. Account exec. Merrill, Lynch, Pierce, Fenner & Beane, Tacoma, Seattle, 1929-40; commd. lt. U.S. Army, 1940, advanced through grades to col., 1946; asst. chief of staff 7th Army G 1, 1952-54; comdg. officer 35th F.A. Group, Germany, 1956-58; dep. chief of staff V Corps, 1958-60, asst. chief of staff G 1, Pacific, 1962-65; ret., 1966; prof. bus., dept. chmn. Calif. Poly. State U., San Luis Obispo, 1968-80, ret., 1980. Decorated Legion of Merit with 2 oak leaf clusters, Silver Star, Bronze Star medal, Commendation medal with oak leaf cluster. Fellow Fin. Analysts Fedn.; mem. Los Angeles Soc. Fin. Analysts. Home: 16732 Lew Allen Cir Riverside CA 92518-2909

MCCORMACK, DENNIS K., clinical psychologist; m. Nancy K. McCormack; children: Kelly, Karen. BA in Math., Calif. Western U., 1969; MA, U.S. Internat. U., 1971, PhD in Leadership and Human Behavior, PhD in Psychology, 1974, 78. Diplomate Internat. Council Profl. Counseling and Psychotherapy, Am. Inst. Counseling and Psychotherapy, Internat. Acad. Health Care Profls. Pvt. practice family therapist Coronado, Calif.; chief family therapy Winn Army Cmty. Hosp.; guest spkr. at numerous clubs, lodges and local orgns. Contbr. articles to profl. jours. Mem. Sr. Citizen Adv. Com., 1982—, Land Use Adv. Com., Coronado, 1979-80; chmn. Coronado Planning Commn., 1978-83, St. Paul's United Meth. Ch., 1978-81, personnel com., 1978-81, mem. adminstrv. bd., 1983—; pres. Coronado Coordinating Council, 1983—; mem. adv. bd. Mil. Affairs Com., 1984—; bd. dirs. Vietnam Vets. Leadership Program, 1984—, Coronado Hosp. Found., 1988—; mem. Southbay Chember Exec. Com., 1986—, Coronado Visitor Promotion Bd., 1986—. Fellow Internat. Council of Sex Edn. and Parenthood of Am. U., Am. Bd. Med. Psychotherapists (clin. assoc.), S.D. Acad. Psychologists (chmn. membership com. 1988—), Coronado C. of C. (pres. 1986—). Office: PO Box 577 Richmond Hill GA 31324-0577

MC CORMACK, FRED ALLEN, state social services administrator; b. Bklyn., June 10, 1930; s. Frank J. and Rhea (Del Castro) Mc C.; m. Ellen Anne Lockwood, June 19, 1954 (div.); children: Mary Lee, Lynn Anne, Rosemarie, Fred A., Julie Ellen, Rhea Michelle, Claire Eileen; m. Elin Howe, Jan. 1994. BS, Seton Hall U., 1953; MSW, U. Conn., 1955. Social worker Montrose (N.Y.) VA Hosp., 1955-61; adminstr., dir. Tappan Zee Mental Health Ctr., North Tarrytown, N.Y., 1957-62; supr. social worker Orange County Mental Health Clinic, Goshen, N.Y., 1961-62; dir. Sweetwater Counseling Svc., Rock Springs, Wyo., 1962-65; asst. supt., dir. geriatric program Manteno (Ill.) State Hosp., 1965-68; dir. Tacoma Comprehensive Mental Health Ctr., 1968-69; cons. Dept. Instns. Wash., 1968-69, Laurel Haven Sch., Ballwin, Mo., 1977-78; supt. W.G. Murray Children's Ctr., Centralia, Ill., 1969-71, Elisabeth Ludeman Ctr., Park Forest, Ill., 1971-76; dir. San Luis Valley Mental Health Ctr., Alamosa, Colo., 1976-77, Monroe Devel. Ctr., Rochester, N.Y., 1977-80, Suffolk Devel. Ctr., Melville, N.Y., 1980-85; assoc. commr. N.Y. State Office Mental Retardation and Devel. Disabilities, Albany, 1985-93; ret., 1993; part-time tchr. Western Wyo. Jr. Coll., 1963-65, Prairie State Coll., Chicago Heights, Ill., 1965-68, Green River C.C., 1968-69; instr. Adams State Coll., Alamosa, 1977; cons. Snohomish Community Action Coun., Everett, Wash., 1969. Past mem. citizens adv. bd. Sch. Dist. 162, Matteson, Ill.; chmn. Park Forest Sr. Citizens Commn.; past bd. dirs. Gavin Found., Park Forest; bd. dirs. Jones Community Ctr., Chicago Heights; chmn. State Employees Federated Appeal, United Way Rochester, 1979-80, L.I., 1984-85. Recipient cert. of merit Nat. Assn. Physically Handicapped, Dir. of Yr. award N.Y. State Family Care Providers Assn., 1984. Fellow Am. Assn. Mental Deficiency (pres. Ill. chpt. 1972); mem. NASW, Acad. Cert. Social Workers. Home: 1408 Myers Holw Prescott AZ 86301-5145

MCCORMICK, ALMA HEFLIN, writer, retired educator, psychologist; b. Winona, Mo., Sept. 2, 1910; d. Irvin Elgin and Nora Edith (Kelley) Heflin; m. Archie Thomas Edward McCormick, July 14, 1942 (dec.); children: Thomas James, Kelly Jean. BA, Ea. Wash. Coll., 1936, EdM, 1949; PhD, Clayton U., 1977. Originator dept. severely mentally retarded Tri-City Public Schs., Richland, Wash., 1953, Parkland, Wash., 1955; co-founder, dir. Adastra Sch. for Gifted Children, Seattle, 1957-64; author profl. publs., novels; contbr. articles to various publs., 1937—. Mem. Am. Psychol. Assn., OX 5 Aviation Pioneers, Kappa Delta Pi. Republican. Roman Catholic. Editor: Cub Flyer, Western Story Mag., Wild West Weekly; assoc. editor: Mexico City Daily News (English sect. of Novedades). One of the first Am. woman test pilot's, 1942. Home and Office: 11437 Chimayo Rd Apple Valley CA 92308-7754

MCCORMICK, BETTY LEONORA, accountant; b. Missoula, Mont., July 18, 1961; d. George Oliver and Betty June (Dolton) W. BBA, U. Mont., 1983. CPA, Mont. Staff acct. Ellis & Assocs., Boise, Idaho, 1984; acct. Glacier Electric Coop., Cut Bank, Mont., 1984-86, office mgr., 1986—; income tax cons. Mem. AICPA, Beta Gamma Sigma. Democrat. Roman Catholic. Avocations: skiing, sewing, reading, hunting. Office: Glacier Electric Coop Inc 410 E Main St Cut Bank MT 59427-3012

MCCORMICK, FLOYD GUY, JR., agricultural educator, college administrator; b. Center, Colo., July 3, 1927; s. Floyd Guy and Gladys (Weir) McC.; m. Constance P. Slane, Sept. 18, 1965; children: Angela Lynn, Craig Alan, Kim Ann, Robert Guy. BS, Colo. State U., 1950, MEd, 1959; PhD, Ohio State U., 1964. Tchr. vocat. agr. State of Colo., 1956-62; asst. prof. agrl. edn. Ohio State U., 1964-67; mem. com. agr. edn. com. edn. in agr. and natural resources Nat. Acad. Scis., 1967-69; prof. agrl. edn., head dept. U. Ariz., 1967-89, prof. emeritus, dept. head emeritus, 1990—; cons. in-svc. edn., div. vocat. edn. Ohio Dept. Edn., 1963-64; vis. prof. Colo. State U., 1973, U. Sierra Leone, Njala Univ. Coll., 1989; external examiner U. Sierra Leone, 1984, 85, 87; adv. trustee Am. Inst. Cooperatives, Washington, 1985-88; mem. Nat. Coun. Vocat. and Tech. Edn. in Agr., Washington, 1985-88. Co-author: Teacher Education in Agriculture, 1982, Supervised Occupational Experience Handbook, 1982; author: The Power of Positive Teaching, 1994, also instrl. units, tech. bulls., articles in profl. jours.; spl. editor: Agrl. Edn. mag., 1970-74. Trustee Nat. FFA Found. Served with USNR, 1945-46. Named hon. state farmer Colo., 1958, Ariz., 1968, Am. farmer, 1972; recipient Centennial award Ohio State U., 1970, E.B. Knight award NACTA Jour., 1980, Regional Outstanding Tchr. award Nat. Assn. Coll. Tchrs. Agr., 1989, also fellow, 1988, VIP citation Nat. FFA Assn., 1990, Diamond Anniversary award Ohio State U., 1992. Mem. Am. Vocat Assn. (mem. policy com. agrl. edn. divsn. 1976-79, v.p. divsn. 1985-88, chmn. membership com. 1980-83, sec. agrl. edn. divsn. 1983-86, pres. 1985-88, outstanding svc. awrd 1989), Nat. Vocat. Agr. Tchrs. Assn. (life, Outstanding Svc. award Region I 1974, 83), Am. Assn. Tchr. Educators in Agr. (disting. lectr. 1984, editor newsletter 1975-76, pres. 1976-77, Disting. Svc. award 1978, 88, Rsch. award western region rsch. 1988), Alpha Zeta, Alpha Tau Alpha (hon.), Gamma Sigma Delta, Phi Delta Kappa, Epsilon Pi Tau. Home: 6933 E Paseo San Andres Tucson AZ 85710-2203

MCCORMICK, FRANK EDWARD, economist; b. Elmira, N.Y., Oct. 3, 1939; s. John Michael and Sara Theresa (Sweeney) McC.; m. Judith Mary Klink, July 2, 1966; children: Erin Marie, Daniel Francis. BS in Physics, Villanova U., 1961; PhD in Econs., U. Calif., Berkeley, 1971. Qualified to operate nuclear reactor AEC. Asst. prof. econs. U. Calif., Riverside, 1971-75; economist Fed. Res. Bd., Washington, 1975-79; v.p., sr. economist Bank of Am., San Francisco, 1979—. Contbr. articles to sci. jours. Lt. USN, 1961-66. Mem. Am. Econs. Assn., Nat. Assn. Bus. Economists, Western Econs. Assn. Home: 506 Monarch Ridge Dr Walnut Creek CA 94596-2935 Office: Bank of Am Econs Dept # 3015 Box 37000 San Francisco CA 94137

MCCORMICK, RICHARD DAVID, telecommunications company executive; b. Fort Dodge, Iowa, July 4, 1940; s. Elmo Eugene and Virgilla (Lawler) McC.; m. Mary Patricia Smola, June 29, 1963; children: John Richard, Matthew David, Megan Ann, Katherine Maura. B.S. in Elec. Engring., Iowa State U., 1961. With Bell Telephone Co., 1961-85; N.D. v.p., chief exec. officer Northwestern Bell Telephone Co., Fargo, 1974-77; asst. v.p. human resources AT&T, Basking Ridge, N.J., 1977-78; sr. v.p. Northwestern Bell, Omaha, 1978-82, pres., chief exec. officer, 1982-85; exec. v.p. U.S. West Inc., Englewood, Colo., 1985-86, pres., chief oper. officer, 1986-90, pres., chief exec. officer, 1990-91, chmn., pres., chief exec. officer, 1992 ; bd. dirs. Super Valu Stores, Norwest Corp. Mem. Phi Gamma Delta. Office: US West Inc 7800 E Orchard Rd Ste 300 Englewood CO 80111-2533*

MCCOWN, LINDA JEAN, medical technology educator; b. Pitts., Mar. 18, 1953; d. William Earnest and Mary Elizabeth McC. BS, Pa. State U., 1975; MS, U. Pitts., 1979. Cert. med. technologist, clin. lab. scientist. Microbiology aide Pa. State U., University Park, 1973-74; med. technologist, asst. supr., rsch. technologist Children's Hosp. of Pitts., 1975-80; asst. prof. med. tech., assoc. program dir. Ctrl. Wash. U., Ellensburg, 1980—; critique, insp. Nat. Accreditation Agy. for Clin. Lab. Scis., Chgo., 1984—; test item writer Nat. Cert. Agy., Washington, 1989—; recruiter Am. Soc. Clin. Pathologists, Chgo., 1988—. Contbr. articles to profl. jours. Stephen ministry, deacon First Presbyn. Ch., Yakima, Wash., 1992—; bd. dirs. The Campbell Farm, Wapato, Wash., 1990—; rally chmn. Heifer Project Internat., Wapato, 1991-94. Mem. Am. Soc. for Med. Tech. (mem. commn. on accreditation 1988-91), Wash. State Soc. for Med. Tech. (conv. chair 1992, edn. chair 1986-94, pres. 1994-95, Pres.'s award 1992), Columbia Basin Soc. Clin. Lab. Sci. (pres.-elect 1993-94, pres. 1994-95), Omicron Sigma. Avocations: photography, hiking, tennis, travel, music. Home: 1305 Jefferson Ave Yakima WA 98902-2528 Office: Ctrl Wash U Ctr Med Tech 1114 W Spruce Ste 37 Yakima WA 98902

MCCOY, EUGENE LYNN, civil engineer; b. Ridgefield, Wash., Apr. 9, 1926; s. Eugene Victor McCoy and Thelma Lucinda (Ayres) Martin; m. Marcia Helen Schear, Sept. 14, 1955 (div. 1974); children: Thomas Edwin, Susan Lynn, Molly Kay (dec.). AS, Lower Columbia Coll., 1948; BS, Wash. State U., 1950; MS, U. Wash., 1955. Registered profl. engr., Wash. Successively civil engr. soils, chief soils engr. sect., chief geotech. br. Portland (Oreg.) dist., chief geotech. br. North Pacific div. U.S. Army Corps. Engrs., 1955-85; staff cons. Shannon and Wilson, Portland, 1985-88, Cornforth Cons. Inc., Tigard, Oreg., 1988—; tech. specialist delegation for design of Longtan Dam, U.S. Army Corps. Engrs., Beijing, 1981, People to People's delegation Dams and Tunnels, 1987. Contbr. articles to profl jours. Active camp com. Campfire Girls, 4-H Clubs, Oregon City; vol. Loaves and Fishes, Oreg. State U. Ext., AARP Tax Aid. Radio officer U.S. Merchant Marine, 1944-46; with U.S. Army, 1950-52. Mem. ASCE, U.S. Com. Large Dams, Oreg. Master Gardener. Democrat. Unitarian. Home: 20551 S Fischers Mill Rd Oregon City OR 97045-9646 Office: Cornforth Cons Inc 10250 SW Greenburg Rd Ste 111 Portland OR 97223-5460

MC COY, FRANK MILTON, concert pianist, educator, lecturer; b. El Centro, Calif., s. Henderson C. and Annie (Lee) McC.; A.B. (Rotary scholar), San Francisco State Coll., 1949, MA, 1960; postgrad. U. Wash., 1952-53, U. Calif. at Santa Barbara, 1957-58, U. So. Calif., 1961-65, U. Valencia (Spain), summer 1967; PhD Walden U., 1980; studied piano under Jean Le Duc, 1947-49, Madame Berthe Poncy-Jacobsen, 1952-53, Amparo Iturbi, 1960-62. Grad. asst. Sch. Music, U. Wash., Seattle, 1952-53; tchr. music edn. San Diego City Schs., 1953-54, El Centro Pub. Schs., 1954-57; counselor Social Service Center, Calexico, Calif., 1955-59; prof. piano and English Compton Coll., 1971-73; chmn. dept. music Portola Jr. H.S., L.A., 1985;

personal rep. Odyssey Internat. Attractions. Piano, soloist All Am. Chorus tour 1956; 1st Am. to concertize on islands of St. Pierre and Miguelon, 1960; made concert tours Europe, Can., Latin Am., U.S., North Africa, Carribean, Middle East, USSR, China, Hong Kong; TV appearance CBC, 1965; appeared in Ebony mag., Sepia mag.; music critic Gilmore Piano Festival, Kalamazoo, Mich., 1994; adjudicator piano div. Southwestern Youth Music Festival, 1964; mem. bd. adjudicators Nat. Piano Playing Auditions, 1965; music-drama critic Post-Press Newspapers; founder, chmn. Annie Lee McCoy-Chopin Meml. Piano Award, 1975—; Mem. Founders Ch. of Religious Sci.; master tchr. in music L.A. City Schs., 1983-84. Bd. dirs. El Centro Cmty. Concert Assn. Recipient Leona M. Hickman award U. Wash., 1953, Mayor Tom Bradley commendation, 1991. Mem. Music Educators Nat. Conf., Nat. Guild Piano Tchrs., Am. Guild Mus. Artists, Music Critics Assn. North Am., Southeast Symphony Assn. (bd. dirs.), Internat. Platform Assn., Greater L.A. Press Club. Author: Black Tomorrow: A Portrait of Afro-American Culture, 1976; Playlet: Music Masters, Old and New, 1966, We, Too, Are Americans, 1977; music critic L.A. Sentinel, 1988—. Home: 234 S Figueroa St Apt 431 Los Angeles CA 90012-2509

MCCOY, JAMES HENRY, oil company executive; b. Evanston, Ill., July 7, 1947; s. James Henry and Helen (Johnson) McC. BSChemE, Mich. Technol. U., 1968. Registered profl. engr., Ill., Mich. Chief startup engr. process div. UOP, Des Plaines, Ill., 1972-78, project engr., 1978-80; mng. engring. Total Petroleum Inc., Alma, Mich., 1980-85, refinery mgr., 1985-87; v.p. wholesale mktg. and supply Total Petroleum Inc., Denver, 1987-89, v.p. refining, 1989-91, sr. v.p. refining and transp., 1991—. Office: Total Petroleum Inc 999 18th St Denver CO 80202-2440

MCCOY, JAMES M., data processing, computer company executive; b. Cheyenne, Wyo., 1946. Grad., San Jose St. U., 1969. With Internat. Bus. Machines Corp., 1968-73; v.p. mktg. Verbatim Corp., 1973-78; with Shugart Assocs., 1978-80; with Quantum Corp., 1980-81; pres., CEO Maxtor Corp., 1982—, chmn. bd., 1986-94; Bd. dirs. Centigram Corp., Exabyte Corp. Office: Maxtor Corp 211 River Oaks Pky San Jose CA 95134-1913*

MC COY, LOIS CLARK, emergency services professional, retired county official, magazine editor; b. New Haven, Oct. 1, 1920; d. William Patrick and Lois Rosilla (Dailey) Clark; m. Herbert Irving McCoy, Oct. 17, 1943; children: Whitney, Kevin, Marianne, Tori, Debra, Sally, Daniel. BS, Skidmore Coll., 1942; student Nat. Search and Rescue Sch., 1974. Asst. buyer R.H. Macy & Co., N.Y.C., 1942-44, assoc. buyer, 1944-48; instr. Mountain Medicine & Survival, U. Calif. at San Diego, 1973-74; cons. editor Search & Rescue Mag., 1975; cons. editor, Rescue Mag., 1988—; editor Press On Newsletter, 1992—. coord. San Diego Mountain Rescue Team, La Jolla, Calif., 1973-75; exec. sec. Nat. Assn. for Search and Rescue, Inc., Nashville and La Jolla, 1975-80, comptr., 1980-82; disaster officer San Diego County, 1980-86, Santa Barbara County, 1986-91, ret. Contbr. editor Rescue Mag., 1989—, editor-in-chief Response! mag., 1982-86; editor Press On! Electronic mag., 1994—; mem. adv. bd. Hazard Montly, 1991—; cons. law enforcement div.; Calif. Office Emergency Svcs., 1976-77; pres. San Diego Com. for Los Angeles Philharmonic Orch., 1957-58. Bd. dirs. Search and Rescue of the Californias, 1976-77, Nat. Assn. for Search and Rescue, Inc., 1980-87, pres., 1985-87, trustee, 1987-90, mem. Calif. OES strategic com., 1992—; pres., CEO Nat. Inst. For Urban Search & Rescue, 1989—; mem. Gov.'s Task Force on Earthquakes, 1981-82, Earthquake Preparedness Task Force, Seismic Safety Commn., 1982-85. Recipient Hal Foss award for outstanding service to search and rescue, 1982. Mem. IEEE, Armed Forces Comm. and Electronics Assoc., Nat. Assn. for Search & Rescue (life, Svc. award 1985), San Diego Mountain Rescue Team (hon. life), Santa Barbara Amateur Radio Club. Episcopalian. Author: Search and Rescue Glossary, 1974; contbr. to profl. jours. Office: PO Box 91648 Santa Barbara CA 93190-1648

MCCOY, WALLY WARREN, tax consultant; b. Weston, Oreg., Feb. 28, 1936; s. Ashby W. and Mildred (Knechtley) McC.; m. Jeanne August, Feb. 20, 1964 (div. 1973); children: Timothy, Shaun, Geoffrey. BSBA, Portland State U., 1965. Lic. tax cons. Ins. salesman Standard Ins., Portland, Oreg., 1965-66; fin. cons. Internat. Securities, Portland, 1966-68; tax. cons. Portland, 1967—, real estate salesman, 1970-82. Editor, pub. newsletter The Enlightened Investor, 1991—. With U.S.Army, 1959-61. Mem. Computer Users Group of Am. Assn. Ind. Investors, Preg. Assn. Tax Cons., Oreg. Soc. Tax Cons., Alpha Kappa Psi (pres. PSU chpt. 1964-65). Republican. Home and Office: 2515 SE Division St Portland OR 97202-1250

MCCRACKEN, EDWARD R., electronics executive; b. Fairfield, Iowa, 1943. BSEE, Iowa State U., 1966; MBA, Stanford U., 1968. With Hewlett Packard Co.; pres., CEO Silicon Graphics, Inc., 1984—, chmn., CEO, 1994—; dir. Digital Rsch., Inc. Home: 11 Angela Dr Los Altos CA 94022-3003 Office: Silicon Graphics Inc PO Box 7311 2011 N Shoreline Blvd Mountain View CA 94043-1321*

MCCRACKEN, JOHN HARVEY, painter, sculptor; b. Berkeley, Calif., Dec. 9, 1934; s. John H. and Marjorie (Strain) McC.; m. Gail Barringer, May 4, 1991; children: David Gordon, Patrick Daniel. BFA, Calif. Coll. Arts & Crafts, 1962, postgrad., 1962-65. Tchr., U. Calif., Irvine, 1965-66, L.A., 1966-68, Santa Barbara, 1974-85, Sch. Visual Arts, N.Y.C., 1968-69, Hunter Coll., N.Y.C., 1970-71, U. Nev., Reno, 1971-72, Las Vegas, 1972-75. One man shows include: Robert Elkon Gallery, N.Y.C., 1966, 67, 68, 72, 73, Galerie Ileana Sonnabend, Paris, 1969, Sonnabend Gallery, N.Y.C., 1970, Ace Gallery, L.A., 1985, PS 1, Long Island City, N.Y., 1986, Newport Harbor Art Mus., Calif., 1987, Contemporary Arts Mus., Houston, 1989, HoffmanBorman Gallery, Santa Monica, Calif., 1988, Konrad Fischer Gallery, Düsseldorf, Fed. Republic Germany, 1989, Lisson Gallery, London, 1990, Galerie Nordenhake, Stockholm, 1990, Fred Hoffman Gallery, L.A., 1990, Galerie Froment & Putman, Paris, 1991, Sonnabend Gallery, N.Y.C., 1992, Louver Gallery, L.A., 1993, 94, Galerie Xavier Hufkens, Brussels, 1993, Galerie Art & Public, Geneva, 1994, Galerie Tanit, Munich, 1995, Hochshule Fur Angwandte Kunst, Vienna, 1995, Kunsthalle Basel, Switzerland, 1995; group exhbns. include: Solomon R. Guggenheim Mus., N.Y.C., 1967, Saatchi Gallery, London, 1985, Venice (Italy) Biennale, 1986, Centro de Arte Reina Sofia, Madrid, 1987, Musee St. Pierre Art Contemporain, Lyon, France, 1988, Solomon R. Guggenheim Mus., N.Y.C., 1989-90, Carnegie Internat., Carnegie Mus. Art, Pitts., 1991; represented in mus. collections including: Art Inst. Chgo., Solomon R. Guggenheim Mus., N.Y.C.; Mus. Modern Art, N.Y.C., San Francisco Mus. Art, Whitney Mus. Am. Art, N.Y.C., Mus. Contemporary Art, L.A., L.A. County Mus. Art. Grantee, NEA, 1968.

MC CRACKEN, PHILIP TRAFTON, sculptor; b. Bellingham, Wash., Nov. 14, 1928; s. William Franklin and Maude (Trafton) McC.; m. Anne MacFetridge, Aug. 14, 1954; children—Timothy, Robert, Daniel. B.A. in Sculpture, U. Wash., 1954. Asst. to Henry Moore Eng., 1954. One-man shows: Willard Gallery, N.Y.C., 1960, 65, 68, 70, Seattle Art Mus., 1961, Wash. State Capitol Mus., Olympia, 1964, Art Gallery of Greater Victoria, B.C., 1964, LaJolla (Calif.) Mus. Art, 1970, Anchorage Hist. and Fine Arts Mus., 1970, Tacoma Art Mus., 1980, Kennedy Galleries, N.Y.C., 1985, Lynn McAllister Gallery, Seattle, 1986, 89, Valley Mus. N.W. Art, La Conner, Wash., 1993, Whatcom Mus., Bellingham, Wash., 1994, others; group shows include: Mus. Art, Ogunquit, Maine, 1957, Chgo. Art Inst., 1958, Detroit Inst. Arts, 1958, Pa. Acad. Fine Arts, 1958, Contemporary Art Gallery, Houston, 1958, DeYoung Meml. Mus., San Francisco, 1960, Los Angeles Mcpl. Art Mus., 1960, Galerie Claude Bernard, Paris, 1960, Phillips Gallery, Washington, 1966, Corcoran Gallery, 1966, Mus. Art, Akron, 1967, Finch Coll., N.Y.C., 1968, Rutgers U., 1968, Whitney Mus. Art, 1978, Portland Art Mus., 1976, Mont. State U., Bozeman, 1979, Brigham Young U., 1980, Bellvue (Wash.) Art Mus., 1986, Lynn McAllister Gallery, 1986, Am. Acad. Arts and Letters, N.Y.C., 1986, Schmidt Bingham Gallery, N.Y.C., 1987, Wash. State Capital Mus., 1987, 89, Cheney-Cowles Mus., Spokane, Wash., 1988, Smithsonian Instn., 1991—, Nat. Mus., Ottawa, Can., 1991-92, Gallery Three-Zero, N.Y.C., 1993, Seattle Art Mus., 1994, others; sculptures represented: Norton Bldg., Seattle, Kankakee (Ill.) State Hosp., Swinomish Indian Tribal Center, LaConner, UN Assn., N.Y.C., King County King Dome, Seattle, City Hall, Everett, Wash., others. (Recipient numerous prizes, awards). Address: 401 Guemes Island Rd # B Anacortes WA 98221-9534

MCCRACKEN, ROBERT DALE, anthropologist, writer; b. Fairplay, Colo., Aug. 8, 1937; s. Robert Gerald McCracken and Martha Lucile (Grice) Foster; m. Susan Shihadeh Cline, June 24, 1967 (div. Oct. 1974); 1 child, Bambi Michelle McCracken Metscher. BA in Psychology, U. Colo., 1962, MA in Anthropology, 1965, PhD in Anthropology, 1968; postgrad., Washington U., St. Louis, 1972. Instr. extension ctr. U. Colo., Grand Junction, 1965; instr. dept. anthropology Met. State Coll., Denver, 1966; instr. Colo. Women's Coll., Denver, 1966-67; asst. prof. anthropology Calif. State U., Long Beach, 1968-69; asst. prof. Memphis State U., 1976-79; asst. prof. Sch. Pub. Health UCLA, 1969-71; postdoctoral fellow dept. psychology Washington U., St. Louis, 1971-72; freelance writer, 1972-74; dir. rsch. Colo. Migrant Coun., Denver, 1974-76; asst. prof. U. Tenn., Knoxville, 1979-80; ind. social sci. cons. RDM Assocs., Las Vegas, 1980—; rsch. and field experience at Navajo Urban Relocation Project, U. Colo., Boulder, 1964-67, Navajo Reservation, summers, 1966-71; cons., researcher, presenter in field; dir. rsch. and new programs Colo. Migrant Coun., 1974-75. Contbr. articles to profl. pubs. Mem. Nev. Town History Project, Nye County, 1987—; active with Sioux, Ute, Hopi, Shoshoni, Navajo Native Ams., 1965—, with migrant farmworkers, Colo., 1974-76; educator on sch. nutrition and learning performance West L.A., 1970-71. Mem. Anthropological Assn. Home: PO Box 1232 Tonopah NV 89049-1232 Office: 3930 Swenson St Apt 810 Las Vegas NV 89119-7271

MCCRACKEN, STEVEN CARL, lawyer; b. Artesia, Calif., Oct. 29, 1950; s. Glenn A. and Helen V. (Fears) McCracken; m. Susan Lee Waggener, July 29, 1979; children: Casey James, Scott Kevin. BA magna cum laude, U. Calif., Irvine, 1972; JD, U. Va., 1975. Bar: Calif. 1975, U.S. Dist. Ct. (cen. dist.) Calif. 1975, U.S. Ct. Appeals (9th cir.) 1976, U.S. Dist. Ct. (no. dist.) Calif. 1977, D.C. 1979, U.S. Supreme Ct. 1985, U.S. Dist. Ct. (so. dist.) Calif. 1990. Assoc. Gibson, Dunn & Crutcher, L.A., 1975-82; ptnr. Gibson, Dunn & Crutcher, Irvine, Calif., 1983-94; v.p., sec. and gen. counsel Callaway Golf Co., Carlsbad, Calif., 1994—; lawyer rep. Ninth Cir. Jud. Conf., 1989-91. Editor Va. Law Rev., 1973-75, mng. bd. 1974-75, bd. editors The Computer Lawyer, 1984—. Mem. ABA (antitrust sect.), Orange County Bar Assn. (bd. dirs. 1988-90, chmn. fed. ct. com. 1988-89, chmn. bus. litigation sect. 1990, sec. 1991, treas. 1992, pres.-elect 1993, pres. 1994). Democrat. Office: Callaway Golf Co 2285 Rutherford Rd Carlsbad CA 92008-8815

MCCRAVEN, CARL CLARKE, health service administrator; b. Des Moines, May 27, 1926; s. Marcus Henry and Buena Vista (Rollins) McC.; BS in Elec. Engring., Howard U., 1950; MS in Health Svcs. Adminstrn., Calif. State U.-Northridge, 1976; m. Eva Louise Stewart, Mar. 18, 1978; 1 child, Carl B. Radiation physicist Nat. Bur. Standards, 1951-55; rsch. engr. Lockheed Calif. Co., 1955-63; mem. tech. staff TRW Systems, 1963-72; assoc. adminstr. Pacoima Meml. Hosp., Lake View Terrace, Calif., 1972-74; founder, chief exec. officer Hillview Mental Health Ctr., Inc., Lake View Terrace, 1974—; asst. prof. Calif. State U., Northridge, 1976-78. Regent Casa Loma Coll.; bd. dirs. San Fernando Valley Girl Scout Council, Pledgerville Sr. Citizens Villa, ARC; treas. San Fernando Valley Mental Health Assn. Recipient citation Calif. Senate, 1971, 88, Resolution of commendation, 1988, Calif. Assembly, 1971, 88, commendation, 1989, City of Los Angeles, 1971, 78, 88, commendation, 1989, County of Los Angeles, 1988, commendation, 1989, Mayor of L.A. commendation, 1989; developer, mgr. Hillview Village Housing Project. Fellow Assn. Mental Health Adminstrs.; mem. Am. Pub. Health Assn., Am. Mgmt. Assn., Nat. Assn. Health Svcs. Execs., NAACP (pres. so. area Calif. conf. 1967-71, nat. dir. 1970-76), North San Fernando Valley Rotary (pres. 1983), Sigma Pi Phi. Home: 17109 Nanette St Granada Hills CA 91344-1410

MCCRAVEN, EVA STEWART MAPES, health service administrator; b. L.A., Sept. 26, 1936; d. Paul Melvin and Wilma Zech (Ziegler) Stewart; m. Carl Clarke McCraven, Mar. 18, 1978; children: David Anthony, Lawrence James, Maria Lynn Mapes. ABS magna cum laude, Calif. State U., Northridge, 1974, MS, Cambridge Grad. Sch. Psychology, 1987; PhD, 1991. Dir. spl. projects Pacoima Meml. Hosp., 1969-71, dir. health edn., 1971-74; asst. exec. dir. Hillview Community Mental Health Center, Lakeview Terrace, Calif., 1974—; past dir. dept. consultation and edn. Hillview Ctr., developer, mgr. long-term residential program, 1986-90; former program mgr. Crisis Residential Program, Transitional Residential Program and Day Treatment Program for mentally ill offenders, dir. mentally ill offenders svcs.; former program dir. Valley Homeless Shelter Mental Health Counseling Program; dir. Integrated Services Agy., Hillview Mental Health Ctr., Inc., 1993—; Former pres. San Fernando Valley Coordinating Coun. Area Assn., Sunland-Jujunga Coordinating Coun.; bd. dirs. N.E. Valley Health Corp., 1970-73, Golden State Community Mental Health Ctr., 1970-73. Recipient Resolution of Commendation award State of Calif., 1988, Commendation award, 1988, Spl. Mayor's plaque, 1988, Commendation awards for community svcs. City of L.A., 1989, County of L.A., 1989, Calif. State Assembly, 1989, Calif. State Senate, 1989, award Sunland-Tujunga Police Support Coun., 1989, Woman of Achievement award Sunland-Tujunga BPW, 1990. Mem. Assn. Mental Health Adminstrs., Am. Pub. Health Assn., Valley Univ. Women, Health Services Adminstrn. Alumni Assn. (former v.p.), Sunland-Jujunga Bus. and Profl. Women, LWV. Office: Hillview Community Mental Health Ctr 11500 Eldridge Ave San Fernando CA 91342-6523

MCCRAW, LESLIE G., engineering and construction company executive; b. Sandy Springs, S.C., Nov. 3, 1934; s. Leslie Gladstone and Cornelia (Milam) McC.; m. Mary Earle Brown; children: Leslie Gladstone III, James B., John. BSCE, Clemson U., 1956. Registered profl. engr., Del. Design engr. Gulf Oil Corp., Phila., 1956-57; various engring. and constrn. positions E.I. DuPont Co., Wilmington, Del., 1960-75; v.p., mgr. div. Daniel Constrn. Co., Greenville, S.C., 1975-82, pres., 1982-84; pres., chief exec. officer Daniel Internat., Greenville, 1984-86, Fluor Daniel, Greenville and Irvine, Calif., 1986-88; pres. Fluor Corp., Irvine, 1988-90, vice chmn., chief exec. officer, 1990-91, chief exec. officer, chmn. bd. dirs., 1991. Bd. dirs. Allergan and Multimedia Inc., Orange County Performing Arts Ctr., Calif. Econ. Devel. Corp., U.S.-China Bus. Coun.; trustee Hampden-Sydney Coll., Va.; mem. adv. bd. rsch. found., mem. pres.' adv. coun. Clemson U.; mem. bd. visitors U. Calif. Grad. Sch. Mgmt. Mem. Bus. Roundtable, Constrn. Industry's Pres.'s Forum, Nat. Assn. Mfrs. (bd. dirs.), Calif. Bus. Roundtable Palmetto Bus. Forum. Republican. Presbyterian. Office: Fluor Corp Inc 3333 Michelson Dr Irvine CA 92715

MCCRAY, CURTIS LEE, university president; b. Wheatland, Ind., Jan. 29, 1938; s. Bert and Susan McCray; m. Mary Joyce Macdonald, Sept. 10, 1960; children: Leslie, Jennifer, Meredith. B.A., Knox Coll., Galesburg, Ill., 1960; postgrad. U. Pa., 1960-61; Ph.D., U. Nebr., 1968. Chmn. dept. English, Saginaw Valley Coll., University Center, Mich., 1972-73, dean arts and scis., 1973-75, v.p. acad. affairs, 1975-77; provost, v.p. acad. affairs Govs. State U., Chgo., 1977-82; pres. U. North Fla., Jacksonville, 1982-88, Calif. State U., Long Beach, 1988-93, Millikin U., Decatur, Ill., 1993—. Bd. dirs., 1982-88, campaign chmn. Jacksonville United Way, 1987; bd. dirs. Sta. WJCT Channel 7 and Stereo 90, Jacksonville, 1982-88, Jacksonville Art Mus., 1983-88, Meml. Med. Ctr., Jacksonville, 1983-88, Jacksonville Community Council, Inc., 1982-88, Arts Assembly Jacksonville, 1984-88, Jacksonville Urban League, 1985-88; hon. dir. Jacksonville Symphony Assn., 1983; mem. Dame Point Bridge Commn., Jacksonville, 1982; mem. Jacksonville High Tech Task Force, 1982; chmn. SUS High Tech. and Industry Council, 1986-88; mem. state relations and undergrad. edn. com. Am. Assn. State Colls. and Univs., 1985-88. Woodrow Wilson fellow, 1960; Johnson fellow, 1966; George F. Baker scholar, 1956; Ford Found. grantee, 1969; recipient Landee award for excellence in teaching Saginaw State Coll., 1972. Mem. AAUP. Club: Torch. Office: Millikin U 1184 W Main St Decatur IL 62522-2039

MCCREA, PETER, oil company executive; b. San Francisco, Nov. 4, 1939; s. Frederick Hoyt and Eleanor Knox (Wheeler) McC.; m. Willinda McClung, Nov. 14, 1964; children: Frederick Hoyt, Sarah Frances. BS, Dartmouth Coll., 1961, BCE, 1962. Engr. Arabian Am. Oil Co., Dhahran, Saudi Arabia, 1964-69; engr. Chevron Corp., San Francisco, 1969-72, various positions, 1972-79; exec. Chevron Chem. Corp., San Francisco, 1979-89; sr. v.p. Chevron Internat. Oil Co., San Francisco, 1990-92; v.p. Chevron USA Products Co., San Francisco, 1992—; pres. San Francisco Pub. Utilities Commn, 1980-83. Chmn. The Fertilizer Inst., Washington, 1987-88; pres. Stony Hill Vineyard, St. Helena, Calif. Mem. Bohemian Club. Office: Chevron USA Products Co 575 Market St San Francisco CA 94105-2823

MCCREADY, ERIC SCOTT, academic administrator, educator; b. 1941. BS in Gen. Sci., U. Oreg., 1963; BA in History, U. Pavia (Italy), U. Oreg., 1965; MA in Art History, U. Oreg., 1968; PhD in Art History, U. Del., 1972. Vis. lectr. in Art History U. Victoria (B.C., Can.), 1968-69; asst. prof. Art, asst. coord. acad. program devel. Bowling Green (Ohio) State U., 1972-75; asst. prof. History, dir. Elvehjem Mus. Art U. Wis., Madison, 1975-79; dir. Archer M. Huntington ARt Gallery U. Tex., Austin, 1979-89, assoc. prof. Art, 1979-80, sr. lectr. Art, 1980-89; dir. Charles Cowles Gallery, N.Y.C., 1989-90; assoc. prof. Art, assoc. dir. maj. gifts program U. Oreg., Portland, 1990—; mem. adv. bd. Mus. Natural History U. Oreg., 1988-94; bd. dirs. Crow's Shadow Inst., 1993—. Author: The Nebraska State Capitol: Its Design, Background and Influence, 1974; contbr. articles to prof. jours.; lectr. in field. Trustee Portland Art Mus., 1994—. NEA fellow, 1985-86, 86-87. Mem. Soc. Archtl. Historians,. Office: U Oreg 720 SW 2nd Ave Portland OR 97204-3102

MCCRELESS, THOMAS GRISWOLD, nuclear engineer; b. San Antonio, Aug. 20, 1927; s. Thomas G. Sr. and Laura (Sparks) McC.; m. Nancy Ament, June 1, 1951; children: Cynthia M. Tate, Nancy M. Klein. BS in Engring., U.S. Naval Acad., 1951; MS in Nuclear Engring., U. Md., 1965, PhD in Nuclear Engring., 1977. Staff engr. AEC, Bethesda, Md., 1960-75; br. chief Adv. Com. Reactor Safeguards U.S. Nuclear Regulatory Commn., Washington, 1975-80, asst. exec. dir., 1980-88; pres. Cyprus Cove Community Assn., San Clemente, Calif., 1989-92, also bd. dirs. Author: Nuclear Interactions, 1965. Capt. USMC, 1951-60, Korea. Mem. Am. Nuclear Soc. (emeritus), Sigma Xi. Republican. Methodist. Home: 3817 Calle De Las Focas San Clemente CA 92672-4538

MC CRONE, ALISTAIR WILLIAM, university president; b. Regina, Sask., Can., Oct. 7, 1931; came to U.S., 1953, naturalized, 1963; s. Hugh McMillan and Kathleen Maude Tallent (Forth) McCrone; m. Judith Ann Saari, May 8, 1958; children: Bruce, Craig, Mary. B.A., U. Sask., 1953; M.S. (Shell fellow), U. Nebr., 1955; Ph.D., U. Kans., 1961. Instr. geology NYU, 1959-61, asst. prof., 1961-64, assoc. prof., 1964-69, prof., 1969-70; chmn. dept. geology N.Y. U., 1966-69; assoc. dean NYU Grad. Sch. Arts and Scis., 1969-70; acad. v.p. U. of Pacific, Stockton, Calif., 1970-74; prof. geology U. of Pacific, 1970-74; pres., prof. geology Humboldt State U., Arcata, Calif., 1974—; lectr. geology CBS-TV network, 1969-70. Contbr. articles to profl. jours. Trustee Pacific Med. Center, San Francisco, 1971-74; mem. Calif. Council for Humanities., 1978-82. Recipient Erasmus Haworth Honors award U. Kans., 1957; named Danforth Assos. convenor N.Y. U., 1966-68, Outstanding Educator of Am., 1975. Fellow AAAS, Geol. Soc. Am., Calif. Acad. Sci.; mem. Am. Assn. Univ. Adminstrs. (bd. dirs. 1986-89), Am. Auto Assn. (bd. dirs. 1990-93), Calif. State Auto Assn. (bd. dirs. 1988—), Assn. Am. Colls. (bd. dirs. 1989, chair 1991), St. Andrews Soc. of N.Y., Sigma Xi. Lodge: Rotary. Office: Humboldt State U Univ Campus Arcata CA 95521

MCCUAIG, IAN CARRUTHERS, fundraising consultant; b. Orillia, Ont., Can., Mar. 5, 1962; came to U.S., 1992; s. Alan Hayes and Elizabeth Louise (Bonnell) McC.; m. Sarah Elizabeth Robertson, July 2, 1994. Student, Royal Conservatory of Music, Toronto, Ont., 1983; BA in Internat. Rels., U. Toronto, 1990. Devel. cons. UN Assn., Toronto, 1988-89; account exec. Gordon L. Goldie Co., Ltd., Toronto, 1989-92; cons. Marts & Lundy, Inc., San Francisco, 1992—. Contbr. articles to profl. publs. Nat. sec. Amnesty Internat. Can., Ottawa, Ont., 1986-88; chair human rights com. UN Assn., Toronto, 1988-89; elder Timothy Eaton Meml. Ch., Toronto, 1984-92; deacon Calvary Presbyn. Ch., San Francisco, 1992—; mem. Dem. Nat. Com. Mem. World Affairs Coun., Nat. Soc. Fundraising Execs. (cert.), Am. Prospect Rsch. Assn., Nat. Com. on Planned Giving, Can.-Am. C. of C., Nat. Yacht Club, Commonwealth Club of Calif. Office: Marts & Lundy Inc 1280 Wall St W Lyndhurst NJ 07071-3517

MCCULLOCH, ALEXANDER THOMAS, JR., plastic surgeon; b. Cleve., May 3, 1951; s. Alexander Thomas and Helen Irene McC.; m. Carole Jean Sullivan, Aug. 2, 1979; children: Elizabeth, Lauren, Katie, Lexi, Alex, Garrett. BS, Bowling Green U., 1972, MS, 1974; MD, Med. Coll. Ohio, Toledo, 1978. Diplomate Am. Bd. Plastic Surgery. Resident Rush Presbyn. St. Luke, Chgo., 1983; Pvt. practice plastic surgery Colorado Springs, Colo., 1983—; attending plastic surgeon Meml. Hosp., Colo. Springs, 1983, Penrose Hosp., Colo. Springs, 1883—. Fellow Am. Coll. Surgeons; mem. Am. Assn. for Hand Surgery, Am. Soc. Maxillofacial Surgeons. Home: 3585 Van Teylingen Colorado Springs CO 80917 Office: 3585 Van Teylingen Dr Ste B Colorado Springs CO 80917-4872

MCCULLOCH, TERRI, secondary school educator; b. Salt Lake City, Sept. 18, 1957; d. Hilton Clair and Ranae (Brown) McCulloch; m. John Carl Stoughton, July 28, 1989. BS, Weber State U., Ogden, Utah, 1979; MBA, Utah State U., 1987, adminstr. and supervisory endorsement, 1993. Night mgr. Dee's, Ogden, 1973-78; with Smith's Food King, Clearfield, Utah, 1978-89; smoking cessation instr. Humana Hosp., Layton, Utah, 1987-91; tchr. Ogden Sch. Dist., 1979—, secondary math. specialist, 1992—; tutor Ogden, 1990-92; workshop presenter Utah Bd. Edn., Ogden, 1979—. Bd. dirs. Cath. Cmty. Svcs., 1987-89, Utah Election Law Task Force, 1989-92; mem. Atty. Gen.'s Cmty. AGREE Team. Named Tchr. of the Yr., Ogden Sch. Dist., 1988-89, Woman of the Yr., YWCA, Ogden, 1986, Focus on Excellence award, Ogden Sch. Dist., 1988, Golden Apple award, 1988. Mem. ASCD, Tchr. Acad. for Math., AAUW, Utah LWV (state pres. 1989-92, dir. resource devel. 1992-95), Weber County LWV (local pres. 1985-89, treas. 1993—), Delta Kappa Gamma, Phi Delta Kappa. Democrat. Mem. LDS Ch. Home: 1369 Orchard Ave Ogden UT 84404-5853 Office: Ben Lomond H S 800 Jackson Ave Ogden UT 84404

MCCULLOUGH, GAYLE JEAN, graphic artist, publisher; b. Mare Island, Calif., Feb. 7, 1943; d. Earl Martin and Dorothy Clare (Vincent) Hoos; m. Norris Henry Hill; m. James Arthur McCullough, Feb. 19, 1979; children: Kareena Jean, Michael Earl, Michelle Lin. AA in Graphic Arts, Sacramento City Coll., 1970. Composing operator Cal-West Life Ins., Sacramento, 1972-75; sr. graphic artist Dept. Social Svcs. State of Calif., Sacramento, 1975—; mem. AOA implementation team State COSS, Sacramento, 1993—, mem. equal employment opportunity disabled adv. bd., 1986-87. Author, illustrator: Feud for Thought, 1993; author: Everything Hearing People Know About Deafness, 1994, What's Next?, 1994; author, illustrator, pub. (mag.) Life After Deafness, 1993-94. V.p. cmty. coun. NorCal Ctr. on Deafness, Sacramento, 1993-94. Recipient Swimming and Diving Champion award Sacramento City and County, 1957-59, Gold Keys for Art award Brueners & Hallmark Cards, 1959, 60; grantee Bank of Am., 1970. Mem. Calif. Assn. Late Deafened Adults (bd. dirs. 1993-94), Assn. Late Deafened Adults Sacramento (pres., founder 1990—). Home: 6773 Starboard Way Sacramento CA 95831-2413 Office: COSS MS 7-182 744 P St Sacramento CA 95814-6413

MCCULLOUGH, WILLIAM EDWARD, metrologist; b. Anacortes, Wash., Apr. 25, 1941; s. Ray Edward and Florence Sadie (Torpey) McC.; m. Sharon Lea Lenhart, Dec. 21, 1968; children: Shaunna, Debra. AGS, Western Nev. C.C., Carson City, 1991; BS in Mgmt., Calif. Coast U., 1994. Calibration technician Philco Tech., Vanderberg AFB, Calif., 1963-65; field svc. engr. Lockheed, Sunnyvale/Vanderberg AFB, and Kodiak, Alaska, 1965-68; metrology engr. Ford Aerospace (Philco Ford), Palo Alto, Calif., 1968-75; metrology mgr. Bently Nevada, Minden, Nev., 1975—; del. Nat. Conf. Standards Labs., Boulder, Colo., 1975—;. Founding mem. United We Stand Am., Dallas, 1993-94. With USN, 1959-63. Home: 1936 June Cir Carson City NV 89706-2625 Office: Bently Nevada Corp PO Box 157 Minden NV 89423

MCCUNE, ELLIS E., retired university system chief administrator, higher education consultant; b. Houston, July 17, 1921; s. Ellis E. and Ruth (Mason) McC.; m. Hilda May Whiteman, Feb. 8, 1946; 1 son, James Donald. Student, Sam Houston State U., 1940-42; B.A., UCLA, 1948, Ph.D., 1957; LHD, Golden Gate U., 1994. Teaching asst. UCLA, 1949-51; from instr. to assoc. prof. polit. sci. Occidental Coll., Los Angeles, 1951-59; chmn. applied politics and econs. curriculum Occidental Coll., 1951-56; asst. prof. Calif. State U., Northridge, 1959-61, assoc. prof., chmn. dept. polit. sci., 1961-63, prof., 1963, dean letters and sci., 1963; dean acad. planning Calif. State Univs. and Colls., 1963-67; pres. Calif. State U., Hayward, 1967-90, pres. emeritus, 1991—; acting chancellor The Calif. State U. System, 1990-91, ret., 1991; cons. govtl. units and agys.; lectr., panelist; mem. Calif. State Scholarship and Loan Commn., 1964-68, chmn., 1967-68; pres. Govtl. Adminstrn. Group Los Angeles, 1959; chair planning com., mem. exec. com., bd. dirs. Eden Med. Ctr. Found., 1994—, pres.-elect, 1995—. Chmn. univs. and colls. div. United Bay Area Crusade, 1969-70, 73-74; bd. dirs. Oakland (Calif.) Museum Assn., 1974-77, 86-88; vice chmn. higher edn. div., East Bay United Way, 1989-90; mem. arts adv. council, 1986-87, devel. com., 1988-89, Bay Area Urban League, bd. trust Calif. Coun. Econ. Edn. No. sect., Emergency Shelter Program Adv. Coun., Hayward Area Hist. Assn., NAACP Hayward chpt.; trustee Calif. Council Econ. Edn.; sec. bd. dirs. Eden Community Found., 1978-79; rsch. fellow Haynes Found, 1957. With USAAF, 1942-46. Mem. Am. Coun. Edn. (adv. com. 1970-72, inst. coll. & univ. adminstrs. 1973-74, bd. dirs. 1985-86), Western Assn. Schs. and Colls. (accrediting commn. sr. colls. and univs. 1974-78, chmn., 1978-82, pres. 1979-81), N.W. Assn. Schs. and Colls. (commn. colls. 1974-80), Assn. Am. Colls. (bd. dirs. 1972-75, vice chmn. 1975-76), Assn. Western Univs. (bd. dirs.), Coun. Postsecondary Accreditation (bd. dirs. 1977-88, exec. com. 1979-88, chmn. 1985-87, immediate past chmn., 1988-89, chmn. com. recognition 1982-84), Am. Assn. State Colls. and Univs. (chmn. accreditation com. 1983-86, com. acad. pers. and acad. freedom 1987-88, com. on acad. affairs 1988-91), Calif. Coun. Edn. (trustee), Western Polit. Sci. Assn. (exec. coun. 1958-61), Hayward C. of C. (dir. 1968-71, 73-76, 77-80, 82-85, 86-90), Regional Assn. East Bay Colls. and Univs. (exec. com. 1974-90, sec. 1975-76, 87-88, vice chmn. 1976-77, 84-85, chmn. 1977-79, 85-86), Rotary, Phi Beta Kappa, Pi Gamma Mu, Pi Sigma Alpha. Club: Bohemian (San Francisco). Home: 17577 Parker Rd Castro Valley CA 94546-1227 Office: Calif State U Pres Emeritus LI 3167 Hayward CA 94542-3053

MC CUNE, JOHN FRANCIS, III, retired architect; b. New Castle, Pa., Oct. 23, 1921; s. John Francis and Alice (Miles) McC.; m. Jeanne Ramsay, Sept. 28, 1946; children—Morgan R., Martha (Mrs. Dennis L. Maddox), David M., William S. Student, Vanderbilt U., 1938-40; B.S. in Architecture, U. Mich., 1943. Draftsman firm Walter E. Bort (Architect), Clinton, Iowa 1946-47; firm Pope & Kruse (Architects), Wilmington, Del., 1947-54; asso. Pope & Kruse (Architects), 1955-60; partner firm Pope, Kruse & McCune (Architects), Wilmington, 1961-72; owner McCune Assos. (Architects), Wilmington, 1972-81; v.p., prin. architect Diamond/McCune (Architects & Engrs.), Wilmington, 1981-88. Projects include Gander Hill Correctional Facility; renovation of Wilmington Public Bldg, all Wilmington; historic preservation projects include Presbyn. Ch, New Castle, Old Court House, New Castle, Barrett's Chapel, Frederica, Del., Old State House, Dover, Del., Loockerman Hall, Dover. Mem. Hist. Area Commn., New Castle, Del., 1974-88. Mem. AIA (pres. Del. chpt. 1970-71, mem. nat. com. historic resources 1975-88, state preservation coordinator Del. 1975-88), Soc. Archtl. Historians, Assn. for Preservation Tech., ASTM (com.), Nat. Trust Hist. Preservation, Del. C. of C., Nat. Fire Protection Assn. (com. libraries, museums and hist. bldgs. 1975-88), Kappa Sigma. Home: 14011 Antelope CT Sun City West AZ 85376

MCCUNE, SARA MILLER, foundation executive, publisher; b. N.Y.C., Feb. 4, 1941; d. Nathan M. and Rose (Glass) M.; m. George D. McCune, Oct. 16, 1966 (dec. May 1990). BA, Queens Coll., 1961. Asst. to v.p. sales Macmillan Pub. Co., N.Y.C., 1961-63; sales mgr. Pergamon Press Ltd., Oxford, England, 1963-64; pres., pub. Sage Publs. Inc., N.Y.C., 1965-66, Beverly Hills, Calif., 1966-83; pub., chmn. Sage Publs. Inc., Newbury Park, Calif., 1984—; bd. dirs. Sage Publs. Ltd., London, chmn., 1990—; bd. dirs. Sage Publs. India, New Delhi; pres. McCune Found., Newbury Park, Calif., 1990—; mem. bd. dirs. UCSB Comm. Dept. Adv. Bd., Santa Barbara, Calif., 1994—, USCB Bd. Trustees, 1994—, The Fielding Inst., 1994—, Am. Acad. Pol. Scis., Phila., 1994—. Mem. Am. Evaluation Assn. (spl. award for disting. contbns. 1988). Office: Sage Publications Inc 2455 Teller Rd Newbury Park CA 91320-2218

MCCUSKEY, ROBERT SCOTT, anatomy educator, researcher; b. Cleve., Sept. 8, 1938; s. Sidney Wilcox and Jeannette M. (Scott) M.; m. Rebecca Woodworth, July 19, 1958 (div.); children: Geofrey, Gregory, Michael; m. Margaret A. Krasovich, Apr. 17, 1993. A.B., Western Res. U., 1960, Ph.D., 1965. Instr. anatomy U. Cin., 1965-67, asst. prof., 1967-71, assoc. prof., 1971-75, prof., 1975-78; prof., chmn. anatomy W.Va. U., Morgantown, 1978-86; prof., head dept. cell biology and anatomy U. Ariz., Tucson, 1986—, prof. physiology, 1987—; vis. prof. U. Heidelberg, Fed. Republic Germany, 1981-83, 87-88, 93-95; cons. Hoffmann-La Rouche, N.J., 1972-75, Procter & Gamble Co., Cin. 1966-86. Recipient NIH Rsch. Career Devel. award, 1969-74; Humboldt Sr. U.S. Scientist prize, Fed. Republic Germany, 1982, Nishimaru award Japan Microcirculatory Soc., 1987; grantee NIH, NSF, 1966—. Mem. AAAS, Microcirculatory Soc., Am. Assn. Anatomists, Am. Assn. Study Liver Diseases, Rsch. Soc. on Alcoholism, Internat. Soc. Exptl. Hematology. Mem. editorial bd. Microvascular Rsch., 1974-84, Shock, 1993—, Am. Jour. Physiology, 1995—; contbr. numerous articles to profl. jours. Office: Ariz Health Scis Ctr Dept Cell Biology and Anatomy 1501 N Campbell Ave Tucson AZ 85724-0001

MCCUTCHEN, EDNA ELIZABETH, counselor; b. Washington, Iowa, Sept. 6, 1914; d. Charles Sanford and Gertrude Josephine (Swift) Ragan; m. Carl Richard McC., July 3, 1938; children: Evelyn Hitchcock, Carl Richard III, Charles. BA cum laude, Calif. State U., Long Beach, 1971. Researcher State Univ. System, Iowa, 1953-62, Gallup Poll, Palos Verdes (Calif.) Estates, and Iowa, 1954-68, Palos Verdes Estates, 1960-69; counselor for family svc. Long Beach, 1971-73; social worker L.A. County, 1973-83; pvt. practice in counseling Long Beach, 1983—; vol. Gov.'s Study of Aged State of Iowa, 1960-69; lectr. St. Bartholomew's, Long Beach. Insp. election bds., Los Angeles County, Long Beach, 1964—; crew leader U.S. Census, Washington County, Iowa, 1950; Eucharistic min. St. Bartholomew's Ch. Recipient Commendation Community Svc. award Family Svc., Long Beach, 1972. Mem. LWV, AAUW, Nat. Social Workers, Consumer's Union-Consumer's Rsch., DAR (sec. 1948-49), Dau. Am. Colonists, Friends of Library, Phi Kappa Phi. Home: 3435 E 1st St Long Beach CA 90803-2658

MCCUTCHEON, JAMES MILLER, history and American studies educator; b. N.Y.C., Oct. 31, 1932; s. James Cochrane and Katharine (Miller) McC.; m. Elizabeth Douglas North, Apr. 4, 1959; children: Ian North, Eric James. BA summa cum laude, Hobart Coll., Geneva, N.Y., 1954; MS, U. Wis., 1955, PhD, 1959. Grad. asst. U. Wis., Madison, 1954-59; Fulbright fellow U. London, 1959-60; asst. prof. history Simpson Coll., Indianola, Iowa, 1960-61; asst. prof. history and Am. studies U. Hawaii Manoa, Honolulu, 1961-66, assoc. prof., 1966-72, prof., 1972—, chair Am. studies, 1984-88; sr. Fulbright fellow Beijing Fgn. Studies U., 1981-82; spl. asst. pres. U. Hawaii Manoa, Honolulu, 1979, program coord. coll. opportunity, 1971-72; mem. selection com. Community Scholarships, Honolulu, 1973-85; prin. scholar Hawaii Commn. for Humanities, Honolulu, 1973—. Author: China and America: Bibliography, 1972. Recipient Clopton Community Svc. award U. Hawaii Manoa, Honolulu, 1978. Mem. Am. Hist. Assn., Orgn. Am. Historians, Am. Studies Assn., Urban Studies Assn., World History Assn., Phi Beta Kappa. Episcopalian. Home: 3618 Woodlawn Terrace Pl Honolulu HI 96822-1475 Office: U Hawaii Manoa Am Studies Dept 1890 E West Rd Honolulu HI 96822-2318

MCCUTCHEON, RANDALL JAMES, educator; b. Salem, Oreg., Mar. 4, 1949; s. James Vale and Delores (Bertholsen) McC. BS in Secondary Edn., U. Nebr., 1971. Announcer KRFS Radio, Superior, Nebr., 1966-67, KFMQ Radio, Lincoln, Nebr., 1968-75; grad. teaching asst. U. Nebr., Lincoln, 1971-73; tchr. East High Sch., Lincoln, 1975-85, Milton (Mass.) Acad., 1985-88, Valley High Sch., West Des Moines, Iowa, 1988-89, Albuquerque Acad., 1989—. Author: Get Off My Brain, 1985, Can You Find It?, 1989 (Ben Franklin Book of Yr. 1990); co-author: Communication Matters, 1993. Named Dale E. Black Outstanding Young Speech Tchr. of Yr. Nebr. Speech Communication Assn., 1979, Nebr. Tchr. of Yr. Dept. Edn., 1985. Mem. Speech Communication Assn., Nat. Forensic League (Nat. Coach of Yr. 1987), Cath. Forensic League (diocesan dir. 1990—). Office: Albuquerque Acad 6400 Wyoming Blvd NE Albuquerque NM 87109-3843

MCDANIEL, BRUCE ALAN, economist, educator; b. Warsaw, Ind., June 12, 1946; s. Maurice M. and Hattie M. (Stidham) McD.; m. Darcy L. Stouder, Dec. 29, 1972; children: Rachel L., Nathan A., Jordan J. BS, Manchester Coll., 1968; MA, Ball State U., 1972; PhD, Colo. State U., 1979. Instr. Colo. State U., Fort Collins, 1975-79; asst. prof. Ind. U., Indpls., 1979-82, Marquette U., Milw., 1982-85; pres., owner Prairieland, Atwood, Ind., 1985—; asst. prof. U. No. Colo., Greeley, 1992—. Contbr. articles to profl. jours. Mem. Assn. for Social Econs. (midwest regional dir. 1986-92, exec. coun. 1983-92, Helen Potter award 1983), Phi Kappa Phi, Omicron Delta Epsilon. Office: U No Colo Dept Econs Greeley CO 80639

MCDANIEL, GARY ALLAN, geologist; b. Enid, Okla., Oct. 14, 1931; s. William Taylor and Golda Mae (Bell) McD.; m. Elizabeth Marie Vacin, June 15, 1951 (div. 1980); children: Mark, Gari Lynn, Dana, Lance, Lisa; m. Linda R. LaMascus, Mar. 4, 1987. BSc in Geology, U. Okla., 1953, MSc in Geology, 1959. Geologist, Shell Oil Co., 1959-62; advanced geologist Skelly Oil Co., 1962-66; geologist Midwest Oil Co., Oklahoma City, Okla., 1966-68; dist. geologist Champlin Petroleum Co., Oklahoma City, 1968-70; div. geologist Clarcan Petroleum Corp., Oklahoma City, 1970-74; v.p. May Petroleum Co., Dallas, 1974-75; cons., Oklahoma City, 1975-89; chief geologist Bradmar Petroleum Corp, Oklahoma City, 1990-92; cons., 1992—. Contbr. articles to profl. publs. Served to 1st lt. USMC, 1953-56. Mem. Am. Assn. Petroleum Geologists (chmn. publicity com. 1974-75, award of Merit 1975), Oklahoma City Geol. Soc. (pres. 1972-73, award of Recognition 1969, 73, 78, award of Appreciation 1971), Am Inst. Profl. Geologists (pres. Okla. sect. 1980, award of Recognition 1980), Sigma Xi, Sigma Gamma Epsilon (E.L. McCullough award 1959), Phi Kappa Psi. Home: 4057 Lupine Dr Vail CO 81657-4816

MCDANIEL, JOSEPH CHANDLER, lawyer; b. Covington, Va., Mar. 24, 1950; s. Everts Hardin and Betty (Chandler) McD.; m. Sandra Lee Bonds, Dec. 27, 1976; children: Sean Kenneth, Caitlin Bonds. BA in Philosophy, Ariz. State U., 1974, JD, 1980. Bar: Ariz. 1980, U.S. Dist. Ct. Ariz. 1981. Law clk. U.S. Bankruptcy Ct., Phoenix, 1980-82; pvt. practice Phoenix, 1982-84; ptnr. McDaniel and Jaburg, P.C., Phoenix, 1984-89, McDaniel and Lee, Phoenix, 1989-91, McDaniel & Gan, P.C., 1991-93, McDaniel & Kamp, P.C., 1993-94, Lerch, McDaniel & Kamp, P.L.C., 1994—; mem. Scriveners Com. Local Rules of Ct. for Dist. of Ariz. Bankruptcy Cts., Phoenix, 1980. Author: A Guide to Researching Bankruptcy Law, 1980; editor: (with others) Arizona Civil Remedies, 1982. Bd. dirs. St. Patrick's Day Parade, 1988-89, Irish Cultural Assn. Phoenix, 1988-89. Mem. ABA (gen. practice sect. bankruptcy com., chmn., dep. chmn. membership com.pubs. bd.), Ariz. Bar Assn. (lectr., co-chmn. continuing legal edn. com., bankruptcy sect. 1987-88, chmn. 1988-89, co-chmn. jud. rels. com. 1990-92), Maricopa County Bankruptcy Practitioners (chmn.), Ariz. Bankruptcy Coalition (bd. dirs. 1986—), Maricopa County Bar Assn., Am. Bankruptcy Inst. Democrat. Roman Catholic. Office: Lerch McDaniel & Kamp PLC 3636 N Central Ave Ste 990 Phoenix AZ 85012-1939

MCDANIEL, PAUL WILLIAM, physicist, researcher; b. Robards, Ky., Jan. 1, 1916; s. Leslie Elbert and Lillie (Ligon) McD.; m. Loreen Webb, June 4, 1937 (div. Aug. 1975); m. Kathryn Mitchell, Aug. 16, 1975. BS, Western Ky. U., 1936; MA, Ind. U., 1938, PhD, 1941. Dep. dir. rsch. AEC, Washington, 1950-60, dir. rsch., 1960-72; pres. Argonne U. Assn., Washington and Argonne, Ill., 1973-75, ret., 1975. Maj. U.S. Army, 1942-45. Home: 4295 Warren Way Reno NV 89509-8215

MCDANIEL, RICKEY DAVID, senior living executive; b. Rochester, Minn., Apr. 10, 1946; s. Malcolm David and Elaine (Lee) McD.; m. Shelley Ann Sorenson, May 10, 1980; children: Michael, Mathew, Joseph. AA, Rochester Jr. Coll., 1966; BA, Winona State U., 1969. Clin. mgr. St. Mary's Hosp., Rochester, Minn., 1971-74; long term care adminstr. Roderick Enterprises, Inc., Portland, Oreg., 1974-78; regional dir. Roderick Enterprises, Inc., Portland, 1978-80, v.p. ops., 1980-84; pres. Health Sys. Mgmt. and Devel., L.A., 1984-86; ops. dir. Brim Enterprises, Inc., Portland, 1987-88, v.p., 1988-92, sr. v.p., 1992-93; pres. Brim Sr. Living, Inc., Portland, 1993—; bd. dirs. Brim Homestead, Inc., Portland, Dominican Life Care Svcs., Portland, Belmar, Inc., Portland, also v.p. 1989—; pres. Care Mgmt., Inc., A Fla. Employee Leasing Corp., 1991—. Cpl. USMC, 1969-71. Republican. Lutheran. Home: 16492 S Arrowhead Dr Oregon City OR 97045-9287 Office: Brim Inc 305 NE 102nd Ave Portland OR 97220-4170

MCDANIEL, WILLIAM J., career military officer; b. Muskogee, Okla., Feb. 26, 1943; s. L.B. Allen and Vera Juanita (Purdom) McD.; m. Judy Siebert, May 30, 1964 (div. Apr. 1967); m. Shirley Blair, Dec. 13, 1969; children: Valerie Park, Natalie Park, Tara. MD, U. Okla., 1968. Commd. ensign USN, advanced through grades to rear adm., 1989; orthopedic resident Oakland Naval Hosp., Calif., 1973-77; chief of orthopedics Naval Hosp., Rota, Spain, 1977-80; orthopedics dept. Naval Acad., Annapolis, Md., 1980-83, Nat. War Coll., Washington, 1983-84; fleet surgeon Seventh Fleet, Yokosuka, Japan, 1984-86; commanding officer Naval Hosp., Oak Harbor, Wash., 1986-88, Charleston, S.C., 1988-90, Portmouth, Va., 1992—. Team Physician U.S. Olympic Team, L.A., 1984, cons., Colorado Springs, Colo., 1981—. Inducted Okla. State U. Alumni Hall of Fame, 1994. Mem. Am. Acad. Orthopedic Surgery. Republican. Office: Naval Med Ctr Portsmouth VA 23708

MCDAVID, DOUGLAS WARREN, systems consultant; b. San Francisco, Feb. 25, 1947; s. James Etheridge and Elizabeth Rae (Warren) McD.; m. Nancy Kathleen Somers, June 1968 (div. 1982); 1 child, Amy Kemp; m. Carleen Ann Richmond, Feb. 14, 1987; 1 child, Amanda Claire. BA in Sociology, U. Calif., Santa Cruz, 1969; MA in Libr. Sci., San Jose State U., 1972. Libr. Palo Alto (Calif.) City Libr., 1969-81; systems analyst Tymnet (Tymshare), Cupertino, Calif., 1981-84; mgr. systems architecture Tymnet McDonnell Douglas, San Jose, Calif., 1984-86; data modeling cons. Fireman's Fund Ins., Terra Linda, Calif., 1986-87, Bank of Calif., San Francisco, 1988; systems cons. Pacific Bell, San Ramon, Calif., 1989-93; prin. Integrated Info., 1994—; dir. Computer Resources Group, San Francisco; spkr. Entity/Relationship Conf. Internat., Burlingame, Calif., 1991, DAMA Internat. Conf., 1994; sr. cons. in bus. semantic modeling for object-oriented applications IBM Corp., 1994—. Mem. IEEE, Assn. for Computing Machinery, Data Adminstrn. Mgmt. Assn. (San Francisco bd. dirs. 1987-91, Sacramento bd. dirs. 1992, speaker 1991, 92), Data Processing Mgmt. Assn. (speaker 1992), Am. Assn. Artificial Intelligence (speaker 1993). Home and Office: 8611 Kingslynn Ct Elk Grove CA 95624

MCDERMOTT, DAVID (JOHN), artist, writer, photographer; b. Wrangell, Alaska, Apr. 8, 1958; s. A.W. and Margaret (Price) McD.; m. Rebeca Reyna, Dec. 29, 1978; children: Amy, Rachel, Kelly. Student, Seattle Pacific Coll., 1976-77. Nat. registered and cert. emergency med. technician; cert. instr. NRA. Pres., owner Mut. Devel. Co., Ketchikan, 1980—; fireman, emergency med. technician Ketchikan Vol. Fire Dept., 1989-91; contbg. cons. bodybldg. books and mags., 1986—; feature article Musclemag Internat. mag., 1990. Artist ltd. edit. art print series, 1977—. Recipient Expert Rifleman award U.S. Govt., 1973, 1st, 2d & 3d Profl. Painting prizes Arts Guild Show, 1995. Mem. NEA (del. state/nat. governing assemblies), Ketchikan Edn. Assn. (exec. bd. 1992—, pres. 1994—), Nat. Assn. EMTs, Nat. Soc. EMT-Paramedics, Nat. Soc. EMS Adminstrs., Soc. EMT Tech. Instr./Coords. Home: 626 Anderson Dr Ketchikan AK 99901-5404 Office: Mut Devel Co 627 Carlanna Ketchikan AK 99901-5620

MCDERMOTT, JAMES A., congressman, psychiatrist; b. Chicago, Ill., Dec. 28, 1936; children: Katherine, James. BS, Wheaton Coll., 1958; MD, U. Ill., 1963. Intern Buffalo Gen. Hosp., 1963-64; resident in adult psychiatry U. Ill. Hosps., Chgo., 1964-66; resident in child psychiatry U. Wash. Hosps., Seattle, 1966-68; asst. clin. prof. dept. psychiatry U. Wash., Seattle, 1970-83; mem. Wash. Ho. of Reps., 1971-72, Wash. Senate, 1975-87; regional med. officer U.S. Fgn. Svc., 1987-88; mem. 101st-104th Congresses from 7th Wash. dist., 1989—; former chmn. stds. of ofcl. conduct com., mem. ways and means com., ranking minority mem., mem. stds. of ofcl. conduct com.; mem. exec. and edn. com. Nat. Conf. State Legislatures. Mem. Wash. State Arts Commn., Wash. Coun. for Prevention Child Abuse and Neglect; Dem. nominee for gov., 1980. Lt. comdr. M.C., USN, 1968-70,. Mem. Am. Psychiat. Assn., Wash. State Med. Assn., King County Med. Soc. Democrat. Episcopalian. Office: US Ho of Reps 2349 Rayburn HOB Washington DC 20515*

MCDERMOTT, LUCINDA MARY, minister, teacher, philosopher, poet, author; b. Lynwood, Calif., June 3, 1947; d. R. Harry and Cathrine Jaynne (Redmond) Boand. BA, U. So. Calif., L.A., 1969; MS, Calif. State U., Long Beach, 1975; PhD, Saybrook Inst., 1978. Pres. Environ. Health Systems, Newport Beach, Calif., 1976-90, Forerunner Publs., Newport Beach, 1985—; founder, pres. Life-Skills Learning Ctr., Newport Beach, 1985—; founder, dir. Newport Beach Ecumenical Ctr., 1993—; bd. dirs. Key Mgmt., The Boand Family Found.; founder, dir. Newport Beach (Calif.) Ecumenical Ctr., 1993—. Author: Bridges to Another Place, 1972, Honor Thy Self Vol. I and II, 1973, Hello-My-Love-Good Bye, 1973, Life-Skills for Children, 1984, Myrika-An Autobiographical Novel, 1989, White Knights and Shining Halos: Beyond Pair Bonding, 1995. Mem. APA, Alpha Kappa Delta, Kappa Kappa Gamma.

MCDERMOTT, ROSE MARIE JOAN, investment company executive; b. Bryn Mawr, Pa., Apr. 11, 1961; d. Patrick and Joan (Peake) McD. MBA, Drexel U., 1987. Project specialist The Vanguard Group, Wayne, Pa., 1983-91; asst. v.p. and officer Hawaiian Trust Co., Honolulu, 1991—; bd. dirs. Downtown Exchange Club, 1992-94. Chairperson Neighborhood, Alewa Heights, 1993—. Mem. Chartered Fin. Anaylst. Office: Hawaiian Trust Co 130 Merchant St Honolulu HI 96812

MCDEVITT, CHARLES FRANCIS, state supreme court justice; b. Pocatello, Idaho, Jan. 5, 1932; s. Bernard A. and Margaret (Hermann) McD.; m. Virginia L. Heller, Aug. 14, 1954; children: Eileen A., Kathryn A., Brian A., Sheila A., Terrence A., Neil A., Kendal A. LLB, U. Idaho, 1956. Bar: 1956. Ptnr. Richards, Haga & Eberle, Boise, 1956-62; gen. counsel, asst. sec. Boise Cascade Corp., 1962-65; mem. Idaho State Legislature, 1963-66; sec., gen. counsel Boise Cascade Corp., 1965-67, v.p. sec., 1967-68; pres. Beck Industries, 1968-70; group v.p. Singer Co., N.Y.C., 1970-72, exec. v.p., 1973-76; pub. defender Ada County, Boise, 1976-78; co-founder Givens, McDevitt, Pursley & Webb, Boise, 1978-89; justice Idaho Supreme Ct., Boise, 1989—, chief justice, 1993—; served on Gov.'s Select Com. on Taxation, Boise, 1988-89. Home: 4940 Boise River Ln Boise ID 83706-5706 Office: Idaho Supreme Ct 451 W State St Boise ID 83702-6006

MCDEVITT, JOHN ALFRED, program manager, military officer, retired; b. Woburn, Mass., Dec. 16, 1951; s. William Richard and Inez Demetrie (Ireland) McD.; m. Patricia Ann Walsh, June 23, 1973; children: Jennifer Kristen, Michelle Christine, Sean Patrick. BS, USAF Acad., 1973; MBA in Mgmt., Rensselaer Poly. Inst., 1980. Commd. 2d lt. USAF, 1973, advanced through grades to lt. col., 1982; radar navigator, wing staff officer Griffiss AFB, N.Y. and Pease, N.H., 1973-82; program mgr. Combat Identification System Program Office, Wright-Patterson AFB, Ohio, 1982-85, Office of Asst. Sec. of Air Force for Acquisition, 1985-89; sr. project lead Hqrs. Air Force Space Command, 1989-93; ret. USAF, 1993; mgr. TASC, Colorado Springs, Colo., 1993—. Mem. Armed Forces Comm. Electronics Assn., Am. Def. Prepardness Assn., Assn. Grads. Office: TASC Ste 106 1150 Academy Park Loop Colorado Springs CO 80910

MCDONALD, ALAN ANGUS, federal judge; b. Harrah, Wash., Dec. 13, 1927; s. Angus and Nell (Britt) McD.; m. Ruby K., Aug. 22, 1949; children: Janelle Jo, Saralee Sue, Stacy. BS, U. Wash., 1950, LLB, 1952. Dep. pros. atty. Yakima County, Wash., 1952-54; assoc. Halverson & Applegate, Yakima, 1954-56; ptnr. Halverson, Applegate & McDonald, Yakima, 1956-85; judge U.S. Dist. Ct. (ea. dist.) Wash., Yakima, 1985—. Fellow Am. Coll. Trial Lawyers; Yakima C. of C. (bd. dirs.). Clubs: Yakima Country, Royal Duck (Yakima). Office: US Dist Ct PO Box 2706 Yakima WA 98907-2706

MC DONALD, BARBARA ANN, psychotherapist; b. Mpls., July 15, 1932; d. John and Georgia Elizabeth (Baker) Rubenzer; B.A., U. Minn., 1954; M.S.W., U. Denver, 1977; m. Lawrence R. McDonald, July 27, 1957 (dec. Sept. 1993); children—John, Mary Elizabeth. Diplomate Am. Bd. Social Work; lic. psychotherapist. Day care cons. Minn. Dept. Public Welfare, St. Paul, 1954-59; social worker Community Info. Center, Mpls., 1959-60; exec. dir. Social Synergistics Co., Littleton, Colo., 1970—; cons. to community orgns., Indian tribes. Family therapist , 1979—. Bd. dirs. Vol. Bur. Sun Cities, Ariz., 1988, 89, 90. Named 1 of 8 Women of Yr. and featured on TV spl. Ladies Home Jour., 1974; Clairol scholar, 1974; Am. Bus. Women's Assn. scholar, 1974; Alpha Gamma Delta scholar, 1974. Mem. Minn. Pre-Sch. Edn. Assn. (hon. life), AAUW, Nat. Assn. Social Workers, Ariz. Assn. Social Workers, Assn. Clin. Social Workers, Am. Bus. Women's Assn., U. Minn. Alumni Club (sun cities chpt.), Alpha Gamma Delta (Disting. Citizen award 1975). Club: Altrusa (hon.). Author: Selected References on the Group Day Care of Pre-School Children, 1956; Helping Families Grow: Specialized Psychotherapy with Hearing Impaired Children and Their Families, 1984. Office: 13720 W Franciscan Dr Sun City West AZ 85375-5219

MCDONALD, DANIEL ROBERT, senator; b. Seattle, Feb. 4, 1944; s. Robert William and Josephine Dorothy (Quigley) McD.; m. Norah Jane Cornwall, Dec. 28, 1966; children: Tod Robert, Evan Daniel. BSME, U. Wash., 1965, MA in Econs., 1975. Registered profl. engr., Calif., Wash. Mem. Wash. Ho. of Reps., Olympia, 1979-83, floor leader, 1983; mem. Wash. Senate, Olympia, 1983—, floor leader, 1985-86, chmn. Ways and Means Com., 1988-92; mem. revenue forecast coun. Olympia, 1984—, chmn. 1984-85; mem. legis. evaluation and accountability program, Olympia, 1983-90; commr. exec. bd. Western Interstate Com. on Higher Edn., 1983-87; mem. State Investment Bd. Mem. Seattle/King County Drug Commn., 1978-79, Mcpl. League, Seattle, 1979—. Served to lt. (j.g.) USN, 1966-69, Vietnam. Mem. Am. Pub. Works Assn., Am. Waterworks Assn., Bellevue (Wash.) C. of C. Republican. Presbyterian. Lodge: Rotary. Home: 4650 92nd Ave NE Bellevue WA 98004-1335 Office: Wash State Senate Institutions Bldg Rm 202 Olympia WA 98504

MCDONALD, HARRY ALONZO, JR., school counselor; b. Abilene, Tex., June 17, 1943; s. Harry Alonzo and Mary (Boggs) mcD.; m. Janie Lynn Zimmerman, June 11, 1967; 1 child, Tiffany Lynne. B in Music Edn., U. Colo., 1968; MA in Music, Western State Coll., 1973, MA in Counseling, 1987. Lic. profl. counselor, Colo.; cert. profl. sch. counselor, Colo. Band dir. Montrose (Colo.) Sch. Dist., 1969-87, counselor, 1987—; pvt. practice Montrose, 1987—. Author: Content Parenting, 1992, (manual) Parent Support for Love Manual, 1987. Moderator, chmn. bd. Hillcrest United Ch. of Christ, Montrose, 1994, spiritual dir., 1985-92, guest speaker, 1985—. With USAF, 1962-66. Mem. ACA, Am. Sch. Counselor Assn., Colo. Counselor Assn., Colo. Sch. Counselors Assn. (rep. 1992-93, Hats Off award 1992, 93, middle level Counselor of the Yr., 1995). Democrat. Home: 16098 6765 Rd Montrose CO 81401-7473 Office: Columbine Mid Sch PO Box 1328 Montrose CO 81402-1328

MCDONALD, IAN MACLAREN, psychiatrist, educator; b. Regina, Sask., Can., May 20, 1928; s. George and Alexandrina Sutherland (MacLaren) McD.; m. Margaret Anne McGavin, Nov. 21, 1953; children: David, Bruce, Catherine, Susan, Shelagh. M.D., U. Man., Can., 1953. Intern Vancouver Gen. Hosp., B.C., 1952-53; resident Crease Clinic, Essondale, B.C., Can., 1953-54, Munroe Wing, Regina Gen. Hosp., Can., 1954-55; fellow in neurology U. Hosp. Saskatoon, Can., 1956; resident Colo. Psychopathic Hosp., Denver, 1956-57; lectr. U. Colo., Denver, 1957-58; asst. prof. U. Sask., Saskatoon, Sask., Can., 1958-62, assoc. prof., 1962-68, prof. coll. medicine, 1968—, dean of medicine, 1983-93; vis. prof. Harvard U., 1992. Fellow U. Edinburgh, 1967-68; recipient Spl. Recognition award Can. Mental Health Assn., 1983. fellow Royal Coll. Physicians Can., Am. Psychiat. Assn. (life); mem. Can. Med. Assn., Can. Psychiat. Assn. Presbyterian. Office: Royal U Hosp, Dept Psychiatry, Saskatoon, SK Canada S7N OW8

MCDONALD, JEANNE GRAY (MRS. JOHN B. MCDONALD), television producer; b. Seattle, Sept. 10, 1917; d. George Patrick and Mary Edna (Gray) Murphy; m. John B. Mc Donald, June 30, 1951; children: Gregory Roland Stoner, Jeanne Eve. Student, Columbia U., 1940, Art Students League, 1940-43, Nat. Acad. Dramatic Art, 1945. Radio producer, commentator The Woman's Voice Sta. KMPC, L.A., 1947-50; TV producer, commentator, writer The Woman's Voice Sta. KTTV-CBS, L.A., 1950-51; TV producer, commentator The Jeanne Gray Show Sta. KNXT-TV CBS, L.A., 1951-53; West Coast editor Home Show NBC, L.A., 1955-56; TV film producer documentaries and travelogues Virgonian Prodns., L.A., 1953—. Author: The Power of Belonging, 1978. Women's chmn. Los Angeles Beautiful, 1971; mem. Women's Aux. St. John's Hosp.; trustee Freedoms Found. at Valley Forge, 1966—, founder, pres. women's chpt., Los Angeles County chpt., 1965-66, Western dir. women's chpt., 1967-68, nat. chmn. 1968-71, nat. chmn. women vols., 1973-75, hon life mem. Recipient Francis Holmes Outstanding Achievement award, 1949, Silver Mike award, 1948, Emmy award Acad. TV Arts and Scis., 1951, Lulu award Los Angeles Advt. Women, 1952, Genii award Radio and TV Women, 1956, George Washington Honor award Freedoms Found. Valley Forge, 1967, honor cert., 1972, Morale award Christians and Jews for Law and Morality, 1968, Exceptional Service award Freedoms Found., 1975, Liberty Belle award Rep. Women's Club, 1975, Leadership award Los Angeles City Schs., 1976, Theodore Roosevelt award USN League, 1986. Mem. Am. Women in Radio and TV, Radio and TV Women So. Calif. (hon., life, founder, 1st pres. 1952), Footlighters (v.p. 1958-59), Los Angeles C. of C. (bd. dirs. women's div. 1948-54, exec. bd., women's div. 1954-66, pres. women's div. 1963-64, hon. past pres. women's div. 1979), L.A. Orphanage Guild, DAR, Les Dames de Champagne, Bel Air Garden Club, Calif. Yacht Club. Home: 910 Stradella Rd Los Angeles CA 90077

MCDONALD, JOHN GREGORY, financial investment educator; b. Stockton, Calif., 1937; m. Melody McDonald. BS, Stanford U., 1960, MBA, 1962, PhD, 1967. Mem. faculty Grad. Sch. Bus. Stanford U., Calif., 1968—; now The IBJ prof. fin. Grad. Sch. Bus. Stanford U.; vis. prof. U. Paris, 1972, Columbia Bus. Sch., 1975, Harvard Bus. Sch. 1986; vice chmn., bd. govs. NASD/NASDAQ Stock Market, 1989-90; mem. adv. bd. InterWest Venture Capital; dir. Investment Co. of Am., New Perspective Fund, Inc., Scholastic Corp., Varian, EuroPacific Growth Fund. Contbr. articles to profl. jours. Bd. overseers vis. com. Harvard U. Bus. Sch., Cambridge, Mass., 1994—. Fulbright scholar, Paris, 1967-68. Office: Stanford U Grad Sch Bus Stanford CA 94305

MCDONALD, JOHN PETER, management consultant; b. Boston, June 23, 1940; s. Peter A. and Monica A. McDonald; m. Barbara G. McDonald, Nov. 7, 1959; children: Peter, Ian, Kevin, Christine. AA, Santa Ana (Calif.) Coll., 1966; JD, Pepperdine U., 1970. Bar: Calif. 1973, U.S. Supreme Ct. 1973. Sys. analyst O.C. Orange County Supreme Ct., Santa Ana, 1968-71; trial atty. Cohen, Stokke, Owen & Davis, Santa Ana, 1971-73; exec. dir. Legal Aid Soc. Orange County, Santa Ana, 1973-79; dir. mgmt. devel. and tng. Legal Svcs. Corp., Washington, 1979-82, dir., 1979-82; owner McDonald Assocs., Laguna Beach, Calif., 1982-87; v.p. Orion, San Diego, 1987-89; pres. Profl. Advisers, Inc., Carlsbad, Calif., 1989—. Recipient Franklin C. West award, Orange County Bar Assn., 1973. Mem. Assn. for Psychol. Type. Home: 1552 Madrid Dr Vista CA 92083 Office: Profl Advisors Inc 2111 Palomar Airport Rd Ste 160 Carlsbad CA 92009-1419

MCDONALD, JOSEPH LEE, insurance broker; b. Bremerton, Wash., Aug. 15, 1931; s. Joseph Okane and Ida Elizabeth (Finholm) McD.; m. Glorietta Maness, Jan. 22, 1954 (dec. 1984); children: Holly Ann Chaffin, Andrew Lee McDonald; m. Beverly Mae Falkner, June 22, 1986. BS, U. Wash., 1954. Various mgmt. positions AT&T, 1956-62; broker, ptnr. McDonald & McGarry Co., Seattle, 1962-84; ptnr., exec. McDonald Ins. Group, Kirkland, Wash., 1984—; v.p., bd. dirs. Chimayo Inc., Seattle, 1990—, Santa Fe Food Corp., Seattle, 1991—. City councilman City of Bellevue, 1971-75; commr. Water Dist. #97, Bellevue, 1967-71, Lake Hills Sewer Dist., Bellevue, 1965-71; pres. Wash. State Assn. of Sewer Dists., Seattle, 1969. With U.S. Army, 1954-56. Mem. Coll. Club of Seattle, Overlake Golf and Country Club, Western Assn. of Ins. Brokers, Ind. Ins. Agts. Assn., Seattle Master Builders Assn., Apt. Assn. of Seattle and King County, Roche Harbor Yacht Club. Home: 7235 91st Pl SE Mercer Island WA 98040-5803 Office: McDonald Ins Group 416-6th St South Kirkland WA 98033

MC DONALD, LEE CAMERON, political science educator; b. Salem, Oreg., Feb. 22, 1925; s. O. Lyman and Mabel (Duncan) McD.; m. Claire Elizabeth Kingman, Aug. 17, 1946; children: Mary, Alison, Julia, Devon (dec.), Thomas, Paul. Student, U. Oreg., 1942-43; B.A., Pomona Coll., 1948; M.A., UCLA, 1949; Ph.D., Harvard U., 1952. Teaching asst. UCLA, 1948-49; teaching fellow Harvard U., 1950-52; mem. faculty Pomona Coll., Claremont, Calif., 1952—; prof. govt. Pomona Coll., 1962—, Thompson prof. govt., 1980—, emeritus, 1990—, dean coll., 1970-75; Chmn. com. faculty interests, dept. higher edn. Nat. Council Chs., 1966-69; mem. adv. council Danforth Found. Assocs. Program, 1964-67; mem. Commn. on Liberal Learning Assn. Am. Colls., 1974-76; adj. prof. The Claremont Grad. Sch., 1991—. Author: Western Political Theory: The Modern Age, 1962, Western Political Theory: Origins to the Present, 1968; editor: Human Rights and Educational Responsibility, 1979; editorial bd.: Western Polit. Quar, 1963-66, 68-70, Claremont Quar, 1960-64; contbr.: Reformed Faith and Economics, 1989, Three Beginnings: Revolution, Rights and the Liberal State, 1994. Served with USAAF, 1943-45. Recipient Harbison Distinguished Teaching award Danforth Found., 1963; NEH fellow, 1982-83. Mem. Am. Polit. Sci. Assn., Western Polit. Sci. Assn. (exec. council 1972-74), So. Calif. Polit. Sci. Assn. (pres. 1969-70), Am. Soc. Polit. and Legal Philosophy, Am. Conf. Acad. Deans (dir. 1973-76), Phi Beta Kappa, Pi Sigma Alpha. Democrat. Presbyterian (elder 1958-60, 72-74, 92—). Home: 239 W 11th St Claremont CA 91711-3804

MCDONALD, MALCOLM GIDEON, education educator; b. Boise, Idaho, Mar. 22, 1932; s. Gideon L. and Annette (Connell) McD.; m. Glenda S. Yarbrough, Nov. 23, 1962; children: Ronald, Steven, Michael. AA, Boise Jr. Coll., 1951; BA, Wash. State U., 1954, MA, 1972; EdD, U. Idaho, 1991. Prof. North Idaho Coll., Coeur d'Alene, Idaho, 1977-78; exec. dir. Spokane Higher Edn. Office, 1978-84; dir. CAREERS, Eastern Wash. U., 1984-86; dir. continuing edn. Eastern Wash. U., Cheney, Wash., 1986-89, asst. prof. dept. comm. studies, 1989-94. Ret. lt. col. U.S. Army. Recipient Legion of Merit award, Bronze stars (2), Air medals (11), Meritorious Svc. medal, Commendation medal (5), Vietnam medal of Gallantry, 1954-76. Presbyterian. Home: 2841 Spalding Dr Las Vegas NV 89134-7555

MCDONALD, MARIAN RICHIE, nurse epidemiologist; b. Davenport, Iowa, Jan. 5, 1944; d. Reeder McHaney and Mary Elizabeth (Fox) Porterfield; m. James Richie, May 18, 1962 (div. May 1971); children: Victory Fox, Bert; m. John A. McDonald, Nov. 26, 1993. BA in Edn., Harris-Stowe Coll., St. Louis, 1965; AA in Nursing, Santa Rosa Jr. Coll., 1976; BSN, Sonoma State U., Rohnert Park, Calif., 1983. RN, Calif.; cert. infection control. Night charge nurse Ukiah (Calif.) Gen. Hosp., 1976-78; staff nurse ICU and CCU, Cmty. Hosp. Sonoma County, Santa Rosa, Calif., 1978-83; nursing supr. Sonoma (Calif.) Valley Hosp., 1986-87, infection control nurse, 1983-87; nurse epidemiologist U. Calif. San Francisco-Mt. Zion Med. Ctr., 1987—, co-chmn. TB exposure control plan task force, 1994—. Contbg. author: APIC Curriculum on Infection Control Practice, 1994. Chmn. disaster action team ARC, San Francisco, 1988-92, chmn. disaster health svcs., 1989-92, vol., 1983—. Mem. Assn. for Profls. in Infection Control (chpt. pres. 1991, v.p. Calif. coordinating coun. 1992). Office: U Calif-Mt Zion Med Ctr 1600 Divisadero St San Francisco CA 94115-3010

MCDONALD, MARIANNE, classicist; b. Chgo., Jan. 2, 1937; d. Eugene Francis and Inez (Riddle) McD.; children: Eugene, Conrad, Bryan, Bridget, Kirstie (dec.), Hiroshi. BA magna cum laude, Bryn Mawr Coll., 1958; MA, U. Chgo., 1960; PhD, U. Calif., Irvine, 1975, doctorate (hon.) Am. Coll. Greece, 1988, hon. diploma Am. Archaeological Assn. Teaching asst. classics U. Calif., Irvine, 1974, D Litt (hon.) U. Athens, Greece, 1994, U. Dublin, 1994. instr. Greek, Latin and English, mythology, modern cinema, 1975-79, founder, rsch. fellow Thesaurus Linguae Graecae Project, 1975—; bd. dir. Centrum. Bd. dirs. Am. Coll. of Greece, 1981-90, Scripps Hosp., 1981; Am. Sch. Classical Studies, 1986—; mem. bd. overseers U. Calif. San Diego, 1985—; nat. bd. advisors Am. Biog. Inst., 1982—; pres. Soc. for the Preservation of the Greek Heritage, 1990—; founder Hajime Mori Chair for Japanese Studies, U. Calif., San Diego, 1985, McDonald Ctr. for Alcohol and Substance Abuse, 1984, Thesaurus Linguarum Hiberniae, 1991—; vis. prof. U. Dublin, 1990—; adj. prof. theatre U. Calif., San Diego, 1990, prof. theatre and classics, 1994. Recipient Ellen Browning Scripps Humanitarian award, 1975; Disting. Svc. award U. Calif.-Irvine, 1982, Irvine medal, 1987, 3rd Prize Midwest Poetry Ctr. Contest, 1987; named one of the Community Leaders Am., 1979-80, Philanthropist of Yr., 1985, Headliner San Diego Press Club, 1985, Philanthropist of Yr. Honorary Nat. Conf. Christians and Jews, 1986, Woman of Distinction Salvation Army, 1986, Eleventh Woman Living Legacy, 1986, Woman of Yr. AHEPA, 1988, San Diego Woman of Distinction, 1990, Woman of Yr. AXIOS, 1991; recipient Bravissimo gold medal San Diego Opera, 1990, Gold Medal Soc. Internationalization of Greek Lang, 1990, Athens medal, 1991, Piraeus medal, 1991, award Desmoi, 1992, award Hellenic Assn of Univ. Women, 1992, Academy of Achievement award AHEPA, 1992, Woman of Delphi award European Cultural Ctr. Delphi, 1992, Civis Universitatis award U. Calif. San Diego, 1993, Hypatia award Hellenic U. Women, 1993, Am.-Ireland Fund Heritage award, 1994, Contribution to Greek Letters award Aristotle U. Thessaloniki, 1994, Order of the Phoenix, Greece, 1994. Vol. Decade Women's International Ctr., 1994. Mem. MLA, AAUP, Am. Philol. Assn., Soc. for the Preservation of the Greek Heritage (pres.), Libr. of Am., Am. Classical League, Philol. Assn. Pacific Coast, Am. Comparative Lit. Assn., Modern and Classical Lang. Assn. So. Calif., Hellenic Soc., Calif. Fgn. Lang. Tchrs. Assn., Internat. Platform Assn., Greek Language Found., Royal Irish Acad., Greece's Order of the Phoenix (commdr. 1994), KPBS Producers Club, Hellenic Univ. Club (bd. dir.). Author: Terms for Happiness in Euripides, 1978, Semilemmatized Concordances to Euripides' Alcestis, 1977, Cyclops, Andromache, Medea, 1978, Heraclidae, Hippolytus, 1979, Hecuba, 1984, Hercules Furens, 1984, Electra, 1984, Ion, 1985, Trojan Women, 1988, Iphigenia in Taurus, 1988, Euripides in Cinema: The Heart Made Visible, 1983; translator: The Cost of Kindness and Other Fabulous Tales (Shinichi Hoshi), 1986, (chpt.) Views of Clytemnestra, Ancient and Modern, 1990, Classics and Cinema, 1990, Modern Critical Theory and Classical Literature, 1994, A Challenge to Democracy, 1994, Ancient Sun/Modern Light: Greek Drama on the Modern Stage, 1990; contbr. numerous articles to profl. jours. Avocations: karate, harp (medieval), skiing, diving. Home: PO Box 929 Rancho Santa Fe CA 92067-0929 Office: U Calif at San Diego Dept Theatre La Jolla CA 92093

MCDONALD, PENNY S(UE), educational administrator; b. Portland, Oreg., May 1, 1946; d. Norman James and Edna (Kaufmann) McD. BA, Oreg. State U., 1968, MEd, 1974; EdD, Portland State U./U. Oreg., 1981, Harvard U., summer 1987. Tchr. English, Fleming Jr. High Sch., Los Angeles, 1968-69; tchr. lang. arts and social studies Highland View Jr. High Sch., Corvallis, Oreg., 1970-72; tchr. English, dir. student activities Crescent Valley High Sch., Corvallis, 1973-78; grad. asst. Portland State U., Oreg., 1978-80; evaluation intern N.W. Regional Edn. Lab., Portland, 1980; Nat. Inst. Edn. assoc., edn. policy fellow Nat. Commn. on Excellence in Edn., Washington, 1981-83; prin. Inza R. Wood Middle Sch., West Linn Sch. Dist., Wilsonville, Oreg., 1983-88; adminstr. in residence for ednl. adminstrn. Lewis & Clark Coll., Portland, 1988-91; prin. Adams Traditional Alternative Elem., Eugene (Oreg.) Sch. Dist., 1991—; cons. Oreg. Dept. Edn., 1980-81; sr. counselor Oreg. Assn. Student Councils Camps, 1976-78, 80; adj. prof. ednl. adminstrn. Lewis & Clark Coll., 1987-88. Coord., com., adminstr. Oreg. Mentorship Program, 1986-87. Named to Outstanding Young Woman Am., U.S. Jaycees; AFL-CIO scholar Oreg. State U., Corvallis, 1964; Univ. scholar Oreg. State U., 1965-68; nat. Alpha Delta Pi scholar Oreg. State U., 1967-68; Delta Kappa Gamma scholar Portland State U./U. Oreg. 1979-81. Mem. Nat. Assn. Student Councils, Oreg. Assn. Activities Advisors (chmn. 1976-77, bd. dirs. 1977-78), Oreg. Assn. Student Councils, Confedn. Oreg. Sch. Adminstrs. (curriculum commn. 1985-86, asst. chmn., sec. 1986-87, chmn. 1987-88, ex-officio mem. exec. bd. 1987-88), Nat. Assn. Secondary Sch. Prins., N.W. Women in Ednl. Adminstrn. (Oreg. bd. dirs., pres. elect), Delta Kappa Gamma (chpt. rec. sec.), Phi Delta Kappa. Democrat. Office: Adams Trad Alternative Elem Sch 950 W 22nd Ave Eugene OR 97405-2119

MCDONALD, ROSA NELL, federal research and budgets manager; b. Boley, Okla., Feb. 12, 1953; d. James and Beatrice Irene (Hayes) McD. BS, Calif. State U., Long Beach, 1975; MBA, Calif. State U., Dominquez Hills, 1980 also postgrad; BS computer information systems, Chapman Coll, 1988. Acct., The Aerospace Corp., El Segundo, Calif., 1976-77; analytical accountant, 1977-79, budget analyst, 1979-81, sr. budget analyst, 1981-84, budget adminstr., 1984-86, mgr. indirect budgets, 1986-91, head budgets and pricing dept., 1991—. Vol., Youth Motivation Task Force, El Segundo, 1980—, Holiday Project, El Segundo, 1984, 85. Recipient Adminstrn. Group Achievement award The Aerospace Corp., 1985, Robert Herndon Image award, 1988; named Woman of Yr, Aerospace Corp., 1987, NAACP Legal Def. Fund Woman of Achievement, 1988. Mem. Am. Bus. Woman's Assn., Nat. Assn. Female Execs., Beta Gamma Sigma. Democrat. Avocations: dancing; aerobics; reading; contests. Office: 2350 E El Segundo Blvd # M1 400 El Segundo CA 90245-4609

MCDONALD, THOMAS EDWIN, JR., electrical engineer; b. Wapanucka, Okla., June 19, 1939; s. Thomas Edwin and Rosamond Bell (Enoch) McD.; m. Myrna Kay Booth, Sept. 10, 1961; children: Stephen Thomas, Jennifer Kay, Sarah Lynn. BSEE, U. Okla., 1962, MSEE, 1963; PhDEE, U. Colo., 1969. Asst. prof. elec. engring. U. Okla., Norman, 1969-70; planning engr. Okla. Gas and Electric Co., Oklahoma City, 1970-72; staff mem. Los Alamos (N.Mex.) Nat. Lab., 1972—, group leader, 1974-80, program mgr., 1980-92; program mgr. Centurion program Los Alamos (N.Mex.) Nat. Lab., Los Alamos, 1986-90; dep. program dir. inertial confinement fusion program Los Alamos (N.Mex.) Nat. Lab., 1990-92, program coord. mine detection and laser tech., 1992-93; project mgr. Nat. Ctr. for Advanced Mfg. Tech., 1993—; adj. prof. elec. engring. U. Okla., 1970-72; cons. Los Alamos Tech. Assocs., 1980—, mgr. design sect., 1980-81. Researcher: Inertial Confinement Fusion; Contbr. articles to profl. jours. Bd. dirs., mem. United Ch. Los Alamos, 1987—, chmn. bd. elders, 1992. Served to capt. U.S. Army, 1963-67. Mem. IEEE (chmn. Los Alamos sect.), AAAS, Los Alamos Gymnastics Club (treas., bd. dirs. 1980-88), SIE, SPIE, Rotary (sec. Los Alamos club, v.p.), Sigma Xi, Etta Kappa Nu. Republican. Home: 4200 Ridgeway Dr Los Alamos NM 87544-1956 Office: Los Alamos Nat Lab PO Box 1663 MS 0406 Los Alamos NM 87544-0600

MCDONALD, TIM, professional football player; b. Fresno, Calif., Jan. 6, 1965. Student, U. So. Calif. With St. Louis Cardinals, 1987; safety Phoenix Cardinals (formerly St. Louis Cardinals), 1988-92; with S.F. 49ers, 1993—. Named defense back The Sporting News All-America team, 1985. Office: San Francisco 49ers 4949 Centennial Blvd Santa Clara CA 95054-1229*

MCDONNEL, WILLIAM GEORGE, chemical instrumentation executive; b. Rabat, French Morocco, May 10, 1952; came to U.S., 1953; s. Harold Albert and Anna (Yoos) McD.; BS in Chemistry/Biochemistry, Calif. State U., Fullerton, 1974, MBA Pepperdine U., 1987; m. Nancy Ann Hopwood, Aug. 27, 1977; children: Melissa, Allison Roe. Product specialist Process Instruments div. Beckman Instruments, Inc., Fullerton, 1974; sr. tech. specialist ion selective electrodes Lab. Products div. Orion Research Inc., Cambridge, Mass., 1975-87; region mgr. Milton Roy Inc., 1988-91; gen. mgr. Southwest Sci., Inc., 1991—; speaker in field. Mem. Am. Chem. Soc., Am. Electroplaters Spc., Phi Kappa Tau. Republican. Home: 27412 Cenajo Mission Viejo CA 92691-1418

MC DONNELL, LORETTA WADE, lawyer; b. San Francisco, May 31, 1940; d. John H. and Helen M. (Tinney) Wade; m. John L. McDonnell, Jr., Apr. 27, 1963 (div.); children: Elizabeth, John L. III, Thomas. BA, San Francisco Coll. for Women, 1962; MA, Stanford U., 1963; grad. Coro Pub. Affairs Tng. Program for Women, 1976; JD Golden Gate U., 1989. Bar: Calif. 1990. High sch. tchr. East Side Union High Sch. Dist., San Jose, Calif., 1962-63; project coordinator Inter Agency Collaboration Effort, Oakland, Calif., 1977; legal asst. Pacific Gas and Electric Co., 1980-89, coord., 1989—. Bd. dirs. Carden Redwood Sch., 1975-77, St. Paul's Sch., 1974-75; budget panelist United Way of Bay Area, 1975-77; community v.p. Jr. League, 1976-77, nat. conv. del., 1976; bd. dirs. Alameda County Vol. Bur., 1973-74; chmn. speakers panel Focus on Am. Women, 1973-74. Mem. Jr. League of Oakland-East Bay, Inc., Stanford Alumni. Democrat. Roman Catholic. Clubs: Stanford San Francisco Luncheon, Commonwealth. Assoc. editor The Antiphon, 1971-74.

MCDONOUGH, PATRICIA M., education educator; b. Boston, Sept. 24, 1952; d. William Francis and Winifred Elizabeth (Donovan) McD. BA, U. Mass., 1974; MA, George Washington U., 1980, Stanford (Calif.) U., 1991; PhD, Stanford (Calif.) U., 1992. Co-founder edn. dir. Washington Ctr., 1975-80; policy analyst Nat. Manpower Inst., Washington, 1980-81; cdn. dir. Bus. and Profl. Women's Fedn., Washington, 1981-82; faculty coord. Stanford (Calif.) Linear Accelerator Ctr., 1983-85; dir. upward bound Stanford U., 1986-87, rsch. asst., 1987-91; asst. prof. Grad. Sch. of Edn., UCLA, 1991—; cons. Office of the Pres., U. Calif., 1991, Far West Labs., San Francisco, 1991. Predoctoral fellowship Nat. Inst. Mental Health/Stanford Ctr. for Orgns. Rsch., 1987-89. Mem. Am. Ednl. Rsch. Assn., Assn. for Study of Higher Edn., Am. Sociol. Assn. Office: UCLA Grad Sch Edn 405 Hilgard Ave Los Angeles CA 90024-1521

MCDOUGALL, DONALD BLAKE, retired government official, librarian; b. Moose Jaw, Sask., Can., Mar. 6, 1938; s. Daniel Albert and Donela (McRae) McD.; m. Norma Rose Peacock, May 19, 1962. B.A., U. Sask., 1966, B.Ed., 1966; B.L.S., U. Toronto, 1969, M.L.S., U. Alta., 1983. Classroom tchr., Regina Bd. Edn., Sask., 1960-63, vice prin., 1963-68; asst. chief libr. Stratford Pub. Library, Ont., Can., 1969, chief. libr., 1970-72; supr. info. svcs. Edmonton Pub. Library, Alta., Can., 1972, head pub. svcs., 1973-74; legislature libr. Province of Alta., Edmonton, 1974-87; asst. dep. min., legis. libr. Legis. Assembly Alta., 1987-93, ret., 1993. Editor microfilm: Alberta Scrapbook Hansard, 1906-1964, 1976, editor Book: A History of the Legislature Library, 1979, Princess Louise Carline Alberta, 1988, Lieutenant-Governors of the Northwest Territories and Alberta, 1876-1991, 1991, Premiers of the Northwest Territories and Alberta, 1897-1991, 1991. Govt. Sask. scholar, 1965; recipient Queen's Silver Jubilee medal Govt. Can., 1977; named Hon. Clk.-At-The-Table, Legis. Assembly Alberta, 1987. Mem. Alta. Govt. Libraries Council (chmn. 1975), Assn. Parliamentary Librarians in Can. (pres. 1980-82), Edmonton Library Assn., Hist. Soc. Alta. (v.p. Edmonton chpt. 1987), Library Assn. Alta., Can. Library Assn., Inst. Pub. Adminstrn. Can., Beta Phi Mu. Presbyterian. Clubs: Edmonton Jaguar Drivers, Edmonton Scottish Soc. Home: 209 Rhatigan Rd W, Edmonton, AB Canada T6R 1A2

MCDOUGALL, IAIN ROSS, nuclear medicine educator; b. Glasgow, Scotland, Dec. 18, 1943; came to U.S., 1976; s. Archibald McDougall and Jean Cairns; m. Elizabeth Wilson, Sept. 6, 1968; children: Shona, Stewart. MB, ChB, U. Glasgow, 1967, PhD, 1973. Diplomate Am. Bd. Nuclear Medicine (chmn. 1985-87), Am. Bd. Internal Medicine (gov. 1984-86). Lectr. in medicine U. Glasgow, 1969-76; fellow Harkness-Stanford Med. Ctr., 1972-74; assoc. prof. radiology and medicine Stanford (Calif.) U., 1976-84, prof. radiology and medicine, 1985—. Contbr. numerous articles to sci. jours. Fellow Royal Coll. Physicians (Glasgow), Am. Coll. Physicians; mem. Am. Thyroid Assn., Soc. Nuclear Medicine, Western Assn. for Clin. Research. Office: Stanford U Med Ctr Divsn Nuclear Medicine Stanford CA 94305

MCDOUGALL, JACQUELYN MARIE HORAN, therapist; b. Wenatchee, Wash., Sept. 24, 1924; d. John Rankin and Helen Frampton (Vandivort) Horan; m. Robert Duncan McDougall, Jan. 24, 1947 (div. July 1976); children: Douglas, Stuart, Scott. BA, Wash. State U., 1946. Lic. therapist, Wash.; cert. nat. addiction counselor II. Pres. oper. bd. Ctr. for Alcohol/Drug Treatment, Wenatchee, 1983-85; sec. Wash. State Coun. on Alcoholism, 1988-89, supr. out-patient svcs., 1989-90; case mgmt. counselor Lakeside Treatment Ctr., East Wenatchee, Wash., 1991-92; ret., 1994. Treas. Allied Arts, Wenatchee, 1984; pres. Rep. Women, Wash., 1969-70.

MCDOWELL, DAVID E., pharmaceutical executive; b. 1942. AA, Orange Coast Jr. Coll., 1962; MS, Stanford U., 1978. V.p., gen. mgr. quality control Internat. Bus. Machines, Armonk, N.Y., 1962-91; pres., COO, bd. dirs. McKesson Corp., 1991—. Office: McKesson Corp 1 Post St San Francisco CA 94104-5203*

MCDOWELL, JEFFREY STEVEN, corporate information executive; b. Eugene, Oreg., Oct. 30, 1954; s. Howard G. and Jean B. McDowell. BA, U. Mont., 1979, postgrad., 1984-85. Reporter Tobacco Valley News, Eureka, Mont., 1979-80, asst. editor, 1980-82; sports editor Lewistown (Mont.) News-Argus, 1982-84; sr. editor Mont. Kaimin, Missoula, 1984; legis. corr. Mont. Kaimin, Helena, 1985; night editor Ravalli Rep., Hamilton, Mont., 1985; corp. info. mgr. Ribi ImmunoChem Rsch., Inc., Hamilton, 1985—. Asst. scoutmaster Boy Scouts Am., Missoula, 1972-76. Mem. Soc. Profl. Journalists (bd. dirs. 1983-85, v.p. 1985-86, pres. 1986-87), Mont. Press Women (bd. dirs. 1983-84), Bitterroot Valley C. of C. (bd. dirs. 1989-92). Office: Ribi ImmunoChem Rsch Inc 533 Old Corvallis Rd Hamilton MT 59840-3131

MCDOWELL, JENNIFER, sociologist, composer, playwright, publisher; b. Albuquerque; d. Willard A. and Margaret Frances (Garrison) McD.; m. Milton Loventhal, July 2, 1973. BA, U. Calif., 1957; MA, San Diego State U., 1958; postgrad., Sorbonne, Paris, 1959; MLS, U. Calif., 1963; PhD, U. Oreg., 1973. Tchr. English Abraham Lincoln High Sch., San Jose, Calif., 1960-61; free-lance editor Soviet field, Berkeley, Calif., 1961-63; rsch. asst. sociology U. Oreg., Eugene, 1964-66; editor, pub. Merlin Papers, San Jose, 1969—, Merlin Press, San Jose, 1973—; rsch. cons. sociology San Jose, 1973—; music pub. Lipstick and Toy Balloons Pub. Co., San Jose, 1978—; composer Paramount Pictures, 1982-88; tchr. writing workshops; poetry readings, 1969-73; co-producer radio show lit. and culture Sta. KALX, Berkeley, 1971-72. Author: (with Milton Loventhal) Black Politics: A Study and Annotated Bibliography of the Mississippi Freedom Democratic Party, 1971 (featured at Smithsonian Instn. spl. event 1992), Contemporary Women Poets: An Anthology of California Poets, 1977, Ronnie Goose Rhymes for Grown-ups, 1984; co-author: (plays off-off Broadway) Betsy and Phyllis, 1986, Mack the Knife Your Friendly Dentist, 1986, The Estrogen Party To End War, 1986, The Oatmeal Party Comes To Order, 1986, (plays) Betsy Meets the Wacky Iraqi, 1991, Bella and Phyllis, 1994; contbr. poems, plays, essays, articles, short stories, and book revs. to lit. mags., news mags. and anthologies; rschr. women's autobiog. writings, contemporary writing in poetry, Soviet studies, civil rights movement, and George Orwell, 1962—; writer: (songs) Money Makes a Woman Free, 1976, 3 songs featured in Parade of Am. Music; co-creator mus. comedy Russia's Secret Plot To Take Back Alaska, 1988. Recipient 8 awards Am. Song Festival, 1976-79, Bill Casey Award in Letters, 1980; doctoral fellow AAUW, 1971-73; grantee Calif. Arts Coun., 1976-77. Mem. Am. Sociol. Assn., Soc. Sci. Study of Religion, Poetry Orgn. for Women, Dramatists Guild, Phi Beta Kappa, Sigma Alpha Iota, Beta Phi Mu, Kappa Kappa Gamma. Democrat. Office: care Merlin Press PO Box 5602 San Jose CA 95150-5602

MCDOWELL, KAREN ANN, lawyer; b. Ruston, La., Oct. 4, 1945; d. Paul and Opal Elizabeth (Davis) Bauer; m. Gary Lee McDowell, Dec. 22, 1979. BA, N.E. La. U., 1967; JD, U. Mich., 1971; diploma, John Robert Powers Sch., Chgo., 1976, Nat. Inst. Trial Advocacy, 1990. Bar: Ill. 1973, Colo. 1977, U.S. Dist. Ct. (so. dist.) Ill. 1973, U.S. Dist. Ct. Colo. 1977. Reference libr. assoc. Ill. State Library, Springfield, 1972-73; asst. atty. gen. State of Ill., Springfield, 1973-75; pvt. practice Boulder, Colo., 1978-79, Denver, 1979—. Mem. So. Poverty Law Ctr. Mem. ABA, DAR, Amnesty Internat., Colo. Bar Assn. (com. alcohol and related problems), Denver Bar Assn., Colo. Women's Bar Assn. (editor newsletter 1982-84), Colo. Soc. Study Multiple Personality and Dissociation, Survivors United Network (legal coord. 1992-93), Survivors United Network Profls. (exec. com. 1992), Internat. Platform Assn., Mensa (local sect. Ann Arbor, Mich. 1968), Colonial Dames, Nat. Soc. Magna Carta Dames, Phi Alpha Theta, Sigma Tau Delta, Alpha Lambda Delta. Office: 428 E 11th Ave Ste 100 Denver CO 80203-3207

MCDOWELL, MARION, state agency director. BA in Sociology, U. Ariz.; MA in Pub. Personnel Adminstrn., George Washington U. Mem. grad. faculty for pub. personnel mgmt. Coll. Notre Dame, Belmont, Calif.; dep. supt. personnel svcs. Sequoia Union High Sch. Dist., 1988-95; pres. Calif. State Bd. of Edn., 1995—. Mem. Civil Svc. Commn. for San Mateo County, 1987—. Mem. Am. Soc. Personnel Adminstrn., Am. Assn. for Sch. Personnel Adminstrn., Calif. Ednl. Placement Assn., Assn. Calif. Sch. Adminstrs., No. Calif. Human Resources Coun. Office: State Bd of Edn Rm 532 721 Capitol Mall Sacramento CA 95814*

MCDOWELL, ROBIN SCOTT, physical chemist; b. Greenwich, Conn., Nov. 14, 1934; s. James Duffil and Aimee Marguerite (Lavers) McD.; m. Arlene R. Egertsen, Nov. 23, 1963; children: Jennifer Ellen, Allison Elizabeth. BA, Haverford Coll., 1956; PhD, MIT, 1960. Mem. staff Los Alamos (N.Mex.) Nat. Lab., 1960-81, asst. group leader, 1981-82, fellow, 1983-91; sr. chief scientist in chem. structure and dynamics program Battelle Pacific N.W. Labs, Richland, Wash., 1991—. Contbr. articles to profl. jours. and encyclopaedias. Chmn. Los Alamos County Libr. Bd., 1981-82; mem. bd. Mid-Columbia Symphony, 1994—. Mem. AAAS, Am. Chem. Soc., Optical Soc. Am., Coblentz Soc. Inc. (pres. 1987-89), Soc. Applied Spectroscopy, Sigma Xi. Office: Battelle Pacific NW Labs Richland WA 99352

MCDUFFIE, ANNIE LAURA, special needs educator; b. Jan. 17, 1936; d. Robert Frederick and Annie Belle (Bean) Cannon; m. Ralph Arthur McDuffie, Aug. 27, 1965; children: Shirley, Shelby, Patrice, Ralph Jr.,

Keith. BA in English, Calif. State U., Dominguez Hills, 1980, MA in English summa cum laude, 1991. Student tchr. Carson (Calif.) H.S., spring 1981, Carnegie Jr. H.S., Carson, spring 1982; tchr. Hawthorne (Calif.) Christian Sch., spring 1983, Exceptional Children's Found., L.A., spring 1984; rehab. specialist Willing Worker's Inc., L.A., 1984—. Democrat. Baptist. Home: 3120 W 110th St Inglewood CA 90303-2308

MCELIGOT, DONALD MARINUS, thermal scientist, engineering educator; b. Passaic, N.J.; s. Maurice Joseph Benedict and Shirley Irene (Gambling) McE.; m. Julimae Albright; children: Kim, Kyle, Sean. BS in Mech. Engring., Yale U.; MS in Engring., U. Wash., postgrad.; PhD, Stanford U. Registered profl. engr., N.J. Assoc. prof. U. Ariz., Tucson, 1963-68, prof., 1968-85, prof. emeritus, 1985—; thermohydromechanics scientist, mgr. Gould Ocean Systems Divsn. (name changed to Westinghouse Naval Systems Divsn.), Middletown, R.I., 1984-91; prin. thermal scientist Idaho Nat. Engring. Lab., Idaho Falls, 1991—; vis. staff Imperial Coll. Sci. and Tech., London, 1969-70; guest prof. U. Karlsruhe, Germany, 1975-76, 79, Max Planck Institut fuer Stroemungsforschung, Goettingen, Germany, 1982-84; adj. prof. mech. engring. U. R.I., West Kingston, 1986-91. Lt. (j.g.) USN; capt. USNR-Ret. Lt. (j.g.) USN; Capt. USNR-Ret. Recipient Gold badge for soaring with 2 diamonds Fedn. Aeronautique Internat., 1971, 78, Calif. State Altitude Gain record (15m sailplane), 1978, Abzeichen fuer Truppendienst in Silber, Bundeswehr, Germany, 1976, 83, Charles H. Jennings Meml. award Am. Welding Soc., 1992; Yuba Consol. Industries fellow Stanford U., AEC Sci. and Engring. fellow U. Wash., Stanford U.; sr. Fulbright Rsch. scholar U.S.-Deutschland Fulbright Commn., 1982-83; U. Ariz. Outstanding Prof. award for excellence in teaching, 1983; grantee NSF, ONR, ARO-D, USA MERDC. Fellow ASME (chmn. heat transfer gen. papers com. 1981-82, assoc. tech. editor J. Heat Transfer 1986-92, gas turbine heat transfer com., Cert. Appreciation award 1992), Am. Phys. Soc., U.S. Naval Inst., Tucson Soaring Club (treas. 1972-73), Yale Club of Tucson (sec.-treas. 1967-69), Tin Can Sailors Assn., Idaho Falls Ski Club, Sigma Xi, Tau Beta Pi.

MCELROY, LEO FRANCIS, communications consultant, journalist; b. Los Angeles, Oct. 12, 1932; s. Leo Francis and Helen Evelyn (Silliman) McE.; m. Dorothy Frances Montgomery, Nov. 3, 1956 (div. 1981); children: James, Maureen, Michael, Kathleen; m. Judith Marie Lewis, May 30, 1992. BS in English, Loyola U., L.A. 1953. News dir. KFI, KRLA, KABC Radio, L.A., 1964-72; pub. affairs host Sta. KCET, Pub. TV, L.A., 1967-74; v.p. Sta. KROQ AM/FM, L.A., 1972-74; polit. editor Sta. KABC-TV, L.A., 1974-81; pres. McElroy Communications, L.A. and Sacramento, 1981—; pres. sec. Lt. Gov.'s Office, Sacramento, 1983-84; chmn. Calif. AP Broadcasters, 1972-74; cons. State Office Migrant Edn., Sacramento, 1974, Californians for Water, L.A. , 1982, Calif. Water Protection Coun., Sacramento, 1982, Planning and Conservation League, Sacramento, 1984—, Common Cause, Sacramento, 1988—. Author: Uneasy Partners, 1984; author plays: Mermaid Tavern, 1956, To Bury Caesar (Christopher award 1952), 1952, Rocket to Olympus, 1960, The Code of Whiskey King, 1995. State del. Western Am. Assembly on Prison Reform, Berkeley, Calif., 1973; chmn. State Disaster Info. Task Force; Calif., 1973-74; campaign media cons. statewide issues, various candidates, Sacramento, L.A., 1981—; bd. dirs. Vols. in Victim Assistance, Sacramento, 1984, Rescue Alliance, Sacramento, 1987—, Mental Health Assn., Sacramento, 1985-89, Leukemia Soc., 1992—. Recipient Gabriel award Cath. Archdiocese, L.A., 1972, Golden Mike award Radio-TV News Assn., L.A., 1973; Hon. Resolution, Calif. State Assembly, Sacramento, 1981. Mem. ASCAP, AFTRA, Screen Actors Guild, Am. Assn. Polit. Cons. Republican. Roman Catholic. Home: 8217 Oakenshaw Way Orangevale CA 95662-2953 Office: McElroy Comm 2410 K St Ste C Sacramento CA 95816-5002 also: 6363 Wilshire Blvd Ste 129 Los Angeles CA 90048-5701

MC ELROY, WILLIAM DAVID, biochemist, educator; b. Rogers, Tex., Jan. 22, 1917; s. William D. and Ora (Shipley) McE.; m. Nella Winch, Dec. 23, 1940 (div.); children—Mary Elizabeth, Ann Reed, Thomas Shipley, William David; m. Marlene A. DeLuca, Aug. 28, 1967; 1 son, Eric Gene. B.A., Stanford, 1939; M.A., Reed Coll., 1941; Ph.D., Princeton U., 1943; D.Sc., U. Buffalo, 1962, Mich. State U., 1970, Loyola U., Chgo., 1970, U. Notre Dame, 1975, Calif. Sch. Profl. Psychology, 1978; D.Pub. Service, Providence Coll., 1970; LL.D., U. Pitts., 1971, Johns Hopkins U., 1977. War research, com. med. research OSRD, Princeton, 1942-45; NRC fellow Stanford, 1945-46; instr. biology dept. Johns Hopkins, 1946, successively asst. and asso. prof., prof. biology, 1951-69, chmn. biology dept., 1956-69; also dir. McCollum-Pratt Inst., 1949-64; dir. NSF, Washington, 1969-71; chancellor U. Calif., San Diego, 1972-80, prof., from 1980, now prof. emeritus. Author textbook.; Editor: (with Bentley Glass) Copper Metabolism, 1950, Phosphorus Metabolism, 2 vols, 1951, 52, Mechanism of Enzyme Action, 1954, Amino Acid Metabolism, 1955, The Chemical Basis of Heredity, 1957, The Chemical Basis of Development, 1959, Light and Life, 1961, Cellular Physiology and Biochemistry, 1961, (with C.P. Swanson) Foundations of Modern Biology series, 1961-64. Mem. Sch. Bd. Baltimore City, 1958-68. Recipient Barnett Cohen award in bacteriology, 1958; Rumford prize Am. Acad. Arts and Scis., 1964. Mem. AAAS (pres. 1976, chmn. 1977), Am. Inst. Biol. Scis. (pres. 1968), Am. Chem. Soc., Nat. Acad. Sci., Am. Soc. Biol. Chemists (pres. 1963-64), Soc. Gen. Physiology (pres. 1960-61), Soc. Naturalists, Soc. Zoologists, Am. Acad. Arts and Scis., Am. Soc. Bacteriologists, Am. Philos. Soc.,Sigma Xi, Kappa Sigma. Office: U Calif at San Diego La Jolla CA 92093

MC ELWAIN, LESTER STAFFORD, lawyer; b. San Mateo, Calif., Jan. 1, 1910; s. George Walter and Ethel (Dickson) McE.; m. Loretta F. Barksdale, July 12, 1977; children from previous marriage: Roderick, Malcolm, Douglas. BA, Stanford U., 1931, JD, 1934. Bar: Calif. 1934, U.S. Supreme Ct. 1955. Assoc. Donahue, Richards & Hamlin, Oakland, Calif., 1934-41; pvt. practice, Oakland, 1946—. Past pres. Alameda County Rep. Assembly. With USN, 1941-46, to comdr. USNR. Mem. ABA, Calif. Bar Assn., Alameda County Bar Assn., Assn. Trial Lawyers Am., Am. Arbitration Assn., Ret. Officers Assn. (past pres.), Phi Alpha Delta, Phi Sigma Kappa, Jr. C. of C. (state v.p. 1940). Clubs: Athenian-Nile. Lodges: Kiwanis (past lt. gov.), Masons (33d degree, past grand master), Elks. Home: 4557 Mayfield Ct Fremont CA 94536-6731 Office: 436 14th St Oakland CA 94612-2703

MCELWEE, DENNIS JOHN, lawyer, pharmaceutical company executive; b. New Orleans, July 30, 1947; s. John Joseph and Audrey (Nunez) McE.; m. Nancy Lu Travis, Sept. 3, 1976. BS, Tulane U., 1970; JD., U. Denver, 1992, Hague Acad. Internat. Law, 1990-91. Clean room and quality control analyst Sci. Enterprises Inc., Broomfield, Colo., 1975-76; analytical chemist in toxicology Poisonlab. Inc., Denver, 1977; analytical chemist, then dir. analytical quality control program Colo. Sch. Mines Rsch. Inst., 1977-79; dir. quality control, then dir. compliance Benedict Nuclear Pharms. Co., Golden, Colo., 1979-84; pres. MC Projections, Inc., Morrison, Colo., 1985-86, dir. regulatory affairs, Electromedics Inc., Englewood, Colo., 1986-91; pvt. practice 1992—. Author: Mineral Research Chemicals, Toxic Properties and Proper Handling, 2d edit., 1979; contbr. articles to profl. jours. Mem. Colo. Bar Assn. Recipient Sutton prize in internat. law, 1991. Home: PO Box 56 Morrison CO 80465-0056 Office: 2009 Wadsworth Blvd Ste 200 Lakewood CO 80215-2031

MCELWEE, JEANETTE GAYE, management and program consultant; b. New Castle, Pa., Sept. 23, 1950; d. George Thomas McElwee and Bernice Elaine (Welker) Haines. BS in Music Edn., Ea. Nazarene Coll., 1972; MusM, Kent State U., 1976; postgrad., UCLA, 1980. Tchr. New Kensington (Pa.) Pub. Schs., 1972-74; asst. prof. Edinboro (Pa.) State U., 1976-77, Oberlin (Ohio) Coll. Conservatory of Music, 1977-79; dir. external and cmty. affairs Carter Hawley Hale Stores, 1981-92; prin. Jan McElwee Kensington Assocs., Burbank, Calif., 1993—; vis. lectr. S.N.D.T. U., Bombay, India, 1978, pres., co-founder Arts, Inc.; pres. Aman Internat. Music & Dance Co. Mem. Mayor's Task Force on Volunteerism, L.A.; commn. on arts edn. Calif. Dept. Edn.; mem. strategic planning com. L.A. United Way; mem. Getty Fund for Visual Arts, Calif. Cmty. Found.; mem. multicultural arts com. L.A. 2000. Mem. So. Calif. Assn. for Philanthropy (chair), Asia Soc./So. Calif. Ctr., Am. Women for Internat. Understanding, Cmty. Ptnrs. Office: Kensington Assocs PO Box 887 Burbank CA 91503-0887

MCELYEA, ULYSSES, JR., veterinarian; b. Ft. Collins, Colo., Oct. 29, 1941; s. Ulysses and Hazel (Hall) McE.; m. Rexanna Bell, Dec. 29, 1975 (div. 1980). BS in Pharmacy, U. N.Mex., 1963; DVM, Colorado State U., 1967, MS, 1968. Diplomate Am. Bd. Vet. Practicioners; cert. in companion animals. Owner Alta Vista Animal Clinic, Las Cruces, N.Mex., 1970—; bd. dirs. N.Mex. Acad. Vet. Practice, Albuquerque, bd. dirs. state of N.Mex. Bd. Vet. Examiners, v.p., 1989-92, vice chair, 1992, chair, 1992—, Bank of the Rio Grande. Pres. Las Cruces Community Theater, 1974; founder, bd. dirs. Dona Ann Arts Coun., Las Cruces, 1976-80. Capt. U.S. Army, 1968-70. Mem. AVMA, Am. Pharm. Assn., Am. Assn. Feline Practitioners, Am. Soc. Vet. Ophthalmologists, N.Mex. Vet. Med. Assn. (bd. dirs. 1976-82), So. N.Mex. Vet. Assn. (pres. 1974, 84), N.Mex. State U. Athletic Assn. 9bd. dirs. 1976—, pres.-elect 1992-93, pres. 1993-94), N.Mex. State U. Pres.'s Assn. 9bd. dirs. 1988-91), U. N.Mex. Alumni Assn. (bd. dirs. 1976-80). Democrat. Home: 2635 Fairway Dr Las Cruces NM 88011-5044 Office: Alta Vista Animal Clinic 725 S Solano Dr Las Cruces NM 88001-3244

MCENTEE, JAMES PATRICK, SR., human relations executive; b. Oakland, Calif., Apr. 9, 1931; s. James and Mary (Kelly) McE.; m. Ann J. Mainland, Aug. 18, 1973; children: Mona, Jesse, Maria Elena, Dianne, James, Chinecy, Amy K., Peter M. BA, St. Joseph's Coll., 1957; MDiv., St. Patrick's Sem., 1973; AA, San Jose City Coll., 1979. Pastoral assoc. Roman Catholic Archdiocese of San Francisco, 1957-73; exec. dir. Vol. Action Ctr., San Jose, Calif., 1973-76; dir. human rels. County of Santa Clara, San Jose, Calif., 1976—; counselor A&J Assoc., San Jose, 1974-94. Pres. Calif. Assn. Human Rights Orgn., 1986-90; chairperson Mexican Am. United for Progress, Morgan Hill, Calif., 1969-73. Recipient Commendation award NAACP, 1990, Commendation award Asian Law Alliance, 1984, Commendation award Am. Indian Ctr., 1989; named Family of Yr. B'Hai Cmty., San Jose, 1994. Democrat. Roman Catholic. Office: Office of Human Rels County Santa Clara 70 W Hedding St San Jose CA 95110-1705

MCEVERS, DUFF STEVEN, lawyer; b. L.A., Apr. 21, 1954; s. Milton Stoddard and Virginia Mary (Tongue) McE.; m. Jeannine Marie Matthews, July 14, 1984; children: Tay Colleen, Reily Maureen. BA, U. So. Calif., 1976; JD, Western State U., 1980. Bar: Calif. 1981, U.S. Dist. Ct. (so. dist.) Calif. 1993, U.S. Dist. Ct. (ctrl. dist.) Calif. 1982, U.S. Ct. Appeals 99th cir.) 1988. Assoc. Donald B. Black Inc., Laguna Beach, Calif., 1981-85; pvt. practice Laguna Beach and Newport Beach, Calif., 1985-88, Assoc. Law Office of Terry J. Coniglio, Inc., Long Beach, Calif., 1988-89; with Barclay Law Corp., 1989-91; pvt. practice Newport Beach and Sonoma, Calif., 1992—; of counsel Walker Law Firm, P.C., Newport Beach, Calif., 1992—. Editor: Law Review, 1979. Mem. Calif. Bar Assn., Orange County Bar Assn., Breakfast Club Newport Beach, St. Timothy's Men's Club. Office: 1301 Dove St Newport Beach CA 92660-2412

MC EVILLY, THOMAS VINCENT, seismologist; b. East Saint Louis, Ill., Sept. 2, 1934; s. Robert John and Frances Nathalie (Earnshaw) Mc E.; m. Dorothy K. Hopfinger, Oct. 23, 1970; children: Mary, Susan, Ann, Steven, Joseph, Adrian. BS, St. Louis U., 1956, PhD, 1964. Geophysicist California Co., New Orleans, 1957-60; engring. v.p. Sprengnether Instrument Co., St. Louis, 1962-67; asst. prof. seismology U. Calif., Berkeley, 1964-68, assoc. prof., 1968-74, prof., 1974—, chmn. dept. geology and geophysics, 1976-80, asst. dir. seismographic sta., 1968-90; dir. earth sci. div. Lawrence Berkeley Lab., 1982-93; chmn. bd. dirs. Inc. Research Instns. for Seismology, 1984-86; cons. numerous govt. agys., geotech. cos. Contbr. numerous articles to profl. jours. Mem. Am. Geophys. Union, Royal Astron. Soc., Seismol. Soc. Am. (editor bull. 1976-85), Soc. Exploration Geophysicists, AAAS, Phi Beta Kappa. Office: Univ Calif Dept Geology and Geophysics Berkeley CA 94720

MCEVOY, NAN TUCKER, publishing company executive; b. San Mateo, Calif., July 15, 1919; s. Nion R. and Phyllis (de Young) Tucker; m. Dennis McEvoy, 1948 (div.); 1 child, Nion Tucker McEvoy. Student, Georgetown U., 1975. Newspaper reporter San Francisco Chronicle, 1944-46, N.Y. Herald Tribune, N.Y.C., 1946-47, Washington Post, 1947-48; rep. in pub. rels. John Homes, Inc., Washington, 1959-60; spl. asst. to dir. U.S. Peace Corps, Washington, 1961-64; mem. U.S. delegation UNESCO, Washington, 1964-65; dir. Population Coun., Washington, 1965-70; co-founder, dep. dir. Preterm, Inc., Washington, 1970-74; chmn. bd. Chronicle Pub. Co., San Francisco, 1975—. Mem. nat. bd. dirs. Smithsonian Instn., Washington, 1994—; mem. Brookings coun. Brookings Instn., Washington, 1994—; commr. Nat. Mus. Art, Washington; mem. U. Calif. San Francisco Found., 1993—; formerly arbitrator Am. Arbitration Assn., Washington. Named Woman of Yr., Washingtonian Mag., 1973. Mem. Am. Art Forum, Burlingame Country Club, The River Club, Commonwealth Club of Calif., World Affairs Coun., Villa Taverna. Office: The Chronicle Pub Co 655 Montgomery St Ste 1430 San Francisco CA 94111

MCEWAN, WILLARD WINFIELD, JR., lawyer, judge; b. Evanston, Ill., Dec. 26, 1934; s. Willard Winfield Sr. and Esther (Sprenger) McE.; children: Michael, Elizabeth, Allison. BS, Claremont Men's Coll., 1956; LLB, U. Calif., San Francisco, 1959. Bar: Calif. 1960, U.S. Dist. Ct. (no. and so. dists.) Calif. 1960, U.S. Supreme Ct. 1974. Commd. U.S. Army, 1956, advanced through grades to capt., 1965, resigned, 1968; dep. legis. counsel. City of Sacramento, Calif., 1960-61; asst. city atty. City of Santa Barbara, Calif., 1961-62; sole practice Santa Barbara, 1962—; judge U.S. Magistrate Ct., Santa Barbara County, 1973—; atty. Goleta Water Dist., 1986-87; lectr. Santa Barbara Adult Edn. Program. Founder, bd. dirs., officer, gen legal coun. Santa Barbara Coun. for Retarded, 1962-72; active WORK Workshop for Handicapped, Assn. Retarded Citizens, Santa Barbara City Landmarks Adv. Com., 1967-73; v.p. Santa Barbara Harbor Pageants and Exhibits Com., 1964; chmn. Citizens Save our Shoreline Com., 1964, Citizens Community Master Plan Com., 1964, YMCA Membership Drive, 1964, Citizens Adv. Com. on Sch. Dist. Tax Needs, 1965; commr. Santa Barbara City Water Commn., 1965, City of Santa Barbara Recreation Commn., 1970-73. Recipient Disting Svc. award Santa Barbara Jaycees, 1965; named Santa Barbara's Young Man of Yr. Sanata Barbara C. of C. 1983. Mem. Am. Heart Assn. (pres. Santa Barbara County chpt. 1981-82), Santa Barbara Heart Assn. (bd. dirs., pres. bd. dirs. 1981-82, chmn. Heart Sunday 1973, 75), Santa Barbara Malacological Soc., Santa Barbara Kiwanis (pres. 1967), C. of C. (com. on local govt., state legisaltion com., bd. dirs., past v.p. bd. dirs., pres. bd. dirs. 1981-82, chmn. several coms.). Republican. Roman Catholic. Office: US Courthouse 8 E Figueroa St Ste 210 Santa Barbara CA 93101-2720

MCEWEN, JOAN E., researcher, microbiology educator; b. Lawrence, Kans., July 3, 1952; d. William Edwin and Miriam Kellogg (Sherman) McE.; m. Philip Alfred Kern, June 12, 1974; children: Leslie McEwen Kern, Emily McEwen Kern. BA summa cum laude, Tufts U., 1974; MS, Albert Einstein Coll. Medicine, 1976, PhD, 1980. Postdoctoral fellow U. Colo., Boulder, 1980-84; asst. prof. U. Calif., L.A., 1984-93; assoc. rsch. scientist Beckman Rsch. Inst. of City of Hope Med. Ctr., Duarte, Calif., 1993—. Contbr. articles to profl. jours. Grantee NIH, Am. Heart Assn. Mem. AAAS, Am. Soc. for Microbiology, Genetics Soc. Am., Am. Soc. Biochemistry and Molecular Biology, Phi Beta Kappa. Democrat. Office: Beckman Rsch Inst Dept Molecular Genetics 1450 Duarte Rd Duarte CA 91010-3011

MCFADDEN, BRUCE ALDEN, biochemistry educator; b. La Grande, Oreg., Sept. 23, 1930; s. Eugene Field and Mary Elizabeth (McMaster) McF.; m. Roberta Ray Wilson, June 14, 1958; children: Paul, David, John. AB in Chemistry with honors, Whitman Coll., 1952, DSc (hon.), 1978; PhD in Biochemistry, UCLA, 1956. From instr. to prof. chemistry Wash. State U., Pullman, 1956-66, prof. biochemistry, 1974—, dir. sci. devel., 1974-78, chmn. dept. biochemistry, 1978-84; vis. prof. U. Leicester, Eng., 1972-73, U. Florence, Italy, 1980, Tech. U., Munich, 1980-81; vis. scientist Minority Instns. (FASEB), 1988; mem. study sect. NIH, Bethesda, Md., 1978-79, 82; panelist rsch. grants U.D. Dept. Energy, 1983, 91; panelist Frasch grants Am. Chem. Soc., 1982-87; cons. to numerous jours. and agys., Pullman, 1966—. Editor Archives Microbiology, 1977-83; contbr. articles to profl. jours.; patentee in field. Pres. Sunnyside Sch. PTA, Pullman, 1972; chmn 1984 and Beyond Citizens' com., Pullman Sch. Bd., 1983-84. Recipient Disting. Sr. U.S. Scientist award Humboldt Found. Tech. U. Munich, 1980-81; fellow Guggenheim Found., 1972-73, NIH, 1954-56, 63-69, 73; grantee in field. Fellow AAAS; mem. Am. Chem. Soc. (pres. Wash.-Idaho Border sect. 1963-64), Am. Soc. Biol. Chem. & Molecular Biol., Am. Soc. Microbiologists, Pacific Slope Biochem. Soc. (pres. 1973-74), Am. Soc. Plant Physiologists, Sigma Xi, Phi Kappa Phi, Phi Lambda Upsilon (pres. 1955). Democrat. Home: 1465 SW Wadleigh Dr Pullman WA 99163-2048 Office: Wash State U Biochemistry Dept Pullman WA 99164

MCFADDEN, JO BETH, oil company executive; b. Tucumcari, N.Mex., Oct. 26, 1938; d. Ernest and Oveta (Barnes) Hogan; m. Gerald B. McFadden, Oct. 15, 1965. BS, Regis U., Denver, 1983. Adminstrv. asst. Gov. State N.Mex., Santa Fe, 1967-71; com. coord. Taxation and Revenue State N.Mex., Santa Fe, 1971-78; budget adminstr. Canterra Petroleum, Denver, 1979-84; v.p., corp. sec.-treas. Sharon Resources, Inc., Englewood, Colo., 1984—; also dir. Named Good Citizen of Yr., DAR, Tucumcari, 1955. Mem. Am. Assn. Ret. Persons, Rocky Mountain Mineral Law Found., 40 Plus of Colo., Nat. Notary Assn., Nat. Writer's Club. Home: 7233 S Vine St Littleton CO 80122-1626

MCFADDEN, LEON LAMBERT, artist, inventor; b. St. Paul, Apr. 19, 1920; s. Frank Grover and Irene Manilla Lambert McF.; m. Karyn Flannery, Nov. 6, 1986. Student, several colls., univs., art insts. Prin. McFadden Commercial Studios, 1946-50; with McFadden-Kaump Art Service, 1952-54; pres. McFadden Advt. (merger with Sundial Services, Inc.), 1954-70; mktg. dir. Kinelogic Corp., Mountain View, Calif., 1965-70; dir. rsch. and devel. proprietary patents Sundial Svcs., Inc., 1968-70; art instr. various Calif. community colls., 1972-74; minority bus. cons. VISTA/ACTION, 1974-75; pres., CEO Prometheus Project, Inc., Yreka, Calif., 1975—. Inventor, patentee 18 mechanical tools and devices; prin. artistic works include large assemblage painting of liberty, found image works (represented in White House spl. collection). Served with USN, 1942-46, PTO. Mem. AAAS, Mensa, Artists Equity Assn. Inc., Artists Equity Assn. N.Y., Siskiyou Artists Assn., Sierra Club. Home: 551 N Main St Yreka CA 96097-2524 Studio: Liberty Painting Corp 6725 Old Highway 99 S Yreka CA 96097-9760

MCFARLAND, JOHN BERNARD, economist, legal assistant, writer; b. Cambridge, Mass., Jan. 16, 1943; s. William Anthony and Louise Marie (Bagdasarian) McF. BS, MIT, 1964; MA, Johns Hopkins U., 1974; postgrad., Harvard U., 1964-66. Economist FRS, Washington, 1970-71, AMA, Chgo., 1972-74, Am. Hosp. Assn., Chgo., 1975-76, U.S. Dept. Energy, FEA, Seattle, 1976-81; legal asst. Bassett and Morrison, Seattle, 1986-92, Gaitan & Cusack, Seattle, 1993, Le Gros, Buchanan & Paul, Seattle, 1994—; freelance writer various publs., 1973—. Author: The Exploding Frog, 1981; contbr. articles on econs. and journalism to various jours., also fiction. Mem. Am. Econ. Assn., Soc. Children's Book Writers and Illustrators. Home: 2320 10th Ave E Apt 5 Seattle WA 98102-4076

MCFARLAND, JON WELDON, county commissioner; b. Wenatchee, Wash., Aug. 23, 1938; s. Charles Edward and Maud Elizabeth (Brennan) McF.; m. Kay Annette Erbes, Apr. 5, 1956; children: Colleen, Michael, Heather. BS in Edn., Eastern Wash. State U., 1961; MS in Personnel Adminstrn., George Washington U., 1966; Grad., Command and Gen. Staff Coll., Fort Leavenworth, Kans., 1970, U.S. Army War Coll., Carlisle Barracks, Pa., 1980. Commd. U.S. Army, 1961, advanced through grades to col., 1981, retired, 1988; ops. officer European Hdqtrs. U.S. Army, Heidelberg, Fed. Republic Germany, 1980-83; commdr. 16th mil. police brigade U.S. Army, Fort Bragg, N.C., 1983-85, provost marshal 18th Airborne Corps, 1983-85; asst. commandant, commdr. of troops U.S. Army Mil. Police Sch., Fort McClellan, Ala., 1985-88; county commr. Columbia County, Wash., 1989—; dir., owner Mr. Mc's Direct Mktg. Svcs., 1992—; owner, dir. Spectro-Optics of Ea. Wash., Dayton, 1994—; vice chmn. Southeastern Emergency Med. and Trauma Coun., Wash., 1990-94, chmn., 1995—; chmn. Columbia County Bd. Commrs., 1990, 93; bd. dirs. Emergency Mgmt. Svcs., Columbia County. Author: History of Civil Disturbance 1960-68, 1969. Bd. dirs. Columbia County Pub. Health Dist., Dayton, 1989—, chmn., 1995—; bd. dirs. Project Timothy Pub. Svcs., Columbia County Health Found., 1989—; vice chmn. Palouse Econ. Devel. Corp., 1990-92, chmn., 1993-95. Decorated Legion of Merit, Bronze Star, numerous others. Mem. Assn. U.S. Army, Wash. State Assn. Counties, U.S. Army War Coll. Found., Kiwanis (bd. dirs. Dayton 1990—). Democrat. Roman Catholic. Home: RR 3 Box 248 Dayton WA 99328-9792 Office: Columbia County 341 E Main St Dayton WA 99328-1361

MC FARLAND, NORMAN FRANCIS, bishop; b. Martinez, Calif., Feb. 21, 1922; student St. Patrick's Sem., Menlo Park, Calif.; J.C.D., Cath. U. Am. Ordained priest Roman Catholic Ch., 1946, consecrated bishop, 1970; titular bishop of Bida and aux. bishop of San Francisco, 1970-74; apostolic adminstr. Diocese of Reno, 1974-76; bishop Diocese of Reno-Las Vegas, 1976-87, Diocese of Orange, Calif., 1987—. Office: Marywood Ctr 2811 E Villa Real Dr Orange CA 92667-1999

MCFARLAND, TIMOTHY ANDREW, artist, artisan-craftsman; b. Morenci, Ariz., Jan. 8, 1953; s. John Robert and Ruth (Frauenfelder) McF. BFA, Ariz. State U., 1976, MFA, 1992. Constrn. foreman M & M Court Sys., Rutherford Constrn. Co., L.A., 1976-79; woodworker, furniture maker, artist Tempe, Ariz., 1979-82; resident carpenter, furniture maker Chuang Yen Monastery, Carmel, N.Y., 1982-85; supr., woodcarver P. L. Custom Woodworking, Tempe, 1985-87; sculptor, artist Tempe, 1987—. Sculptures in various pub. and pvt. collections, 1990—. Mem. Phi Kappa Phi. Home and Studio: 6524 S Jentilly Ln Tempe AZ 85283-3810

MCFARLAND-ESPOSITO, CARLA RAE, nursing executive; b. Cin., July 20, 1957; d. Jay Crawford McFarland and Stella (Herndon) O'Donnell; m. S. Esposito; 1 child, Jayson Vicenso Esposito. BSN, Ea. Ky. U., 1979. RN, Calif.; cert. pub. health nurse. Charge nurse St. Elizabeth Med. Ctr., Covington, Ky., 1980-82; traveling nurse various cities, 1983-86; nurse recruiter Med. Recruiters of Am., Culver City, Calif., 1987; nurse recruiter, liaison nurse, br. mgr. traveling nurse program NSI Svcs., Inc., Beverly Hills, Calif., 1987-90; dir. traveling nurse network, dir. nursing acute care Associated Health Profls. Inc., Culver City, 1990-91; dir. traveling profls., dir. bus. devel. NSI Svcs., Inc., Beverly Hills, 1991-92; clin. dir. ultra care and med. surg. units Westside Hosp., L.A., 1992-94, dir. admitting, dir. utilization rev., 1994—, mem. case mgmt. team, 1992—; mem. utilization rev. com. Associated Physicians of St. John's, 1994. Vol. pediatric assessments, immunizations Oscar Romera Clinic., L.A., 1991—. Mem. NAFE, AACN, Assn. Nurse Execs., Networking Orgn. Democrat. Home: 411 Whitegate Rd Thousand Oaks CA 91320 Office: Westside Hosp 910 S Fairfax Ave Los Angeles CA 90036-4419

MCFARLANE, WILLIAM F., wholesale nut company executive. Vice chmn., dir. Calif. Almond Growers Exchange, Sacramento. Office: Calif Almond Growers Exch 1802 C St Sacramento CA 95814-1010

MCGAGH, WILLIAM GILBERT, financial consultant; b. Boston, May 29, 1929; s. Thomas A. and Mary M. (McDonough) McG.; m. Sarah Ann McQuigg, Sept. 23, 1961; children: Margaret Ellen, Sarah Elizabeth. BSBA, Boston Coll., 1950; MBA, Harvard U., 1952; MS, MIT, 1965. Fin. analyst Ford Motor Co., Dearborn, Mich., 1953-55; mem. staff treas. office Chrysler Corp., Detroit, 1955-64; compt., treas. Canadian div. Chrysler Corp., Windsor, 1965-67; staff exec.-fin. Latin Am. ops. Chrysler Corp., Detroit, 1967-68, asst. treas., 1968-75, treas., 1975-76, v.p., treas., 1976-80; sr. v.p. fin. Northrop Corp., Los Angeles, 1980-88; owner McGagh Assocs., Beverly Hills, Calif., 1988—; bd. dirs. Pacific Am. Income Shares, Inc., Western Asset Trust, Inc., Chrysalis. Board dirs. Greater L.A. Zoo Assn., John Tracy Clinic (pres. 1994—), Mt. St. Mary's Coll. With USAF, 1952-53. Sloan fellow MIT, 1965. Mem. fin. Execs. Inst. (pres. Detroit chpt. 1979-80), Harvard Bus. Sch. Assn. So. Calif. (bd. dirs.). Clubs: Orchard Lake Country; Harvard (N.Y.C. and Boston); Beach (Santa Monica, Calif.); Los Angeles Country, California (Los Angeles), Eastward Ho Country. (Chatham, Mass.). Home: 2189 Century Hl Los Angeles CA 90067-3516 Office: McGagh Assocs 9601 Wilshire Blvd Ste 623 Beverly Hills CA 90210-5208

MCGANN, JOHN MILTON, real estate executive; b. Omaha, Mar. 18, 1948; s. John Byron and Donna M. (Rehnquist) McG.; m. Barbara June Scott, June 2, 1978. BSBA, cert. real estate, U. Nebr., Omaha, 1971. Property mgr. Boetel & Co., Omaha, 1971-73; asst. office bldg. mgr. The Irvine Co., Newport Beach, Calif., 1973-74; property mgr. Harbor Investment Co., Corona Del Mar, Calif., 1974-76, Robert A. McNeil Corp., Santa

Ana, Calif., 1976-78; gen. mgr. Daon Mgmt., Newport Beach, 1978-80; v.p. August Mgmt. Inc., Long Beach, Calif., 1980-82, Calif. Fed. Asst. Mgmt., L.A., 1982-83; pres. Wespac Mgmt. Realty Corp., Newport Beach, 1983-87; v.p., dir. asset mgmt., pres. CalFed Asset Mgmt. Co., L.A., 1987-90; v.p. com. ops. Pinnacle Realty (formerly Sovereign/Ring), Santa Monica, 1990—. Mem. Inst. Real Estate Mgmt. (L.A. chpt., cert. property mgr.), Internat. Coun. Shopping Ctrs. (cert. shopping ctr. mgr.), Lambda Chi Alpha, Delta Sigma Pi, Rho Epsilon (pres.). Republican. Mem. Christian Sci. Ch. Home: 1009 4th St Hermosa Beach CA 90254-4802 Office: Pinnacle Realty Mgmt Co 501 Santa Monica Blvd # 610 Santa Monica CA 90401-2411

MCGAVIN, JOCK CAMPBELL, airframe design engineer; b. L.A., Sept. 14, 1917; s. Campbell and Irene (LeMarr) McG.; m. Catherine Marcelle Glew, Jan. 12, 1952; 1 child, James Campbell. AA, L.A. City Coll., 1950; AB, U. So. Calif., 1970, MS, 1975; PhD, Calif. Coast U., 1989. Airframe design engr. Rockwell Internat. Corp., L.A., 1946-82; ret., 1982; sr. design engr. X-15 airplane, Apollo Command Module, space shuttle, others. Vol. mem. pub. involvement subcom. Puget Sound Water Quality Authority, Seattle, 1987-89; commd. Ky. Col., ETO svc., 1994. Capt. C.E. U.S. Army, 1940-46, ETO. Recipient Apollo Achievement award NASA, 1969; named to Honorable Order of Ky. Colonels. Mem. Soc. for History Astronomy, Izaak Walton League Am. (pres. Greater Seattle chpt. 1991-93, vol. worker environ. projects 1985—), U. So. Calif. N.W. Alumni Club (pres. 1987-89). Home: 12939 NE 146th Pl Woodinville WA 98072-4632

MCGEAN, KELLY KENNISON, corporate executive; b. N.Y.C., Jan. 11, 1946; s. Douglas Fredwill Winnek and Jean (Phillips) McG.; m. Lois Jeanne Hutto, May 27, 1967 (wid. Nov. 1971); children: Kendra Lois (dec.), Michael Christopher (dec.); m. Annick Mireille Todd-Le Douarec, June 16, 1989. MA, Stanford U., 1972; MSM, Fla. Internat. U., 1976; MBA, Wesleyan U., 1974, PhD, 1978. Regional dir. of sales Bestline Pharms., Inc., Miami, 1971-73; v.p. of mktg. Hansen Music & Books, Inc., Miami, 1973-76; exec. dir. Kern County Profl. Standards Rev. Orgn., Bakersfield, Calif., 1976-78; pres., CEO Vantage Mgmt., Inc., Palo Alto, Calif., 1978-82; lead instr. Sml. Bus. Devel. Ctr./Lane C.C., Eugene, Oreg., 1984-91; pres., CEO Camarata Group, Inc., Eugene, 1982—; adj. prof. U. Miami, 1972-74, U. Oreg., 1983-84, 90-92, Linfield Coll., McMinnville, Oreg., 1991—; cons. U.S. Dept. HEW, Washington, 1976-81; co-founder, bd. dirs. Am. Gramophone, inc., L.A. Composer: (musical compositions) Symphony #1 Heritage, 1966, Symphony #2 Gettysburg, 1974, Symphony #3 American, 1981, Requiem and Gloria, 1987 (Best New Work 1988), Symphony #4 Oregon, 1990, various choral works, 1964—, (operas) Calico, 1971, Ilarus, 1979, Calypso, 1987; author: Book Management in An International Context, 1976, 1989, Strategy Traps, 1985, New Paradiems in Management, 1990; contbr. articles to profl. jours. Chmn. Found. for the Performing Arts, San Francisco, 1980-83; comm. mem. Comm. for Healthcare Reform, State Dept. of Health Svcs., Sacramento, 1978-80; v.p. Young Reps. Orgn., Palo Alto, Calif., 1977; bus. advisor Bus. Assistance Team, Eugene, 1984-91; bd. dirs. Goodwill Industries, Eugene, 1988-91, Am. Founds. for Med. Care, Sacramento, 1976-88. Lt. USN, 1965-71, Vietnam. Recipient Outstanding Svc. award U.S. Dept. HEW, Washington, 1978; named Composer of Yr., Phi Mu Alpha Sinfonia, Chgo., 1967. Mem. Internat. Assn. Composers and Dirs. (pres. 1975-77, Composer of Yr. 1989), Am. Mktg. Assn., Lane C.C. Edn. Assn. (v.p. 1990-91), Oreg. Edn. Assn. (bd. dirs. 1987-90), NEA, Am. Assn. Health Care Execs. (pres. 1978-79, Man of Yr. 1980). Republican. Methodist. Office: Camarata Group Inc PO Box 41304 Eugene OR 97404-0329

MCGEE, LINDA JEANNE DANNER, school counselor; b. St. Louis, Sept. 21, 1948; d. George Julues and Vera Margaret (Purnell) Danner; m. Kenneth Allen McGee, Sept. 7, 1968; children: Jennifer Lyn and Stephanie Jeanne (twins). BS in Elem. Edn., U. Mo., 1970, MEd in Counseling and Student Pers. Svcs., 1973; postgrad., Va. Poly. Inst., 1977-84, Seattle Pacific U., 1986-88. Cert. tchr., Mo., Wash., counselor, prin., Wash. Rsch. asst. agrl. chemistry dept. U. Mo., Columbia, 1968-70; elem. sci. tchr. Jefferson City (Mo.) Pub. Schs., 1970-72; counselor, tchr. Congl. Schs. Va., Falls Church, 1972-81, headmistress elem. div., 1981-84; counselor McLoughlin Middle Sch., Vancouver, Wash., 1984—; dist. testing com. mem. Vancouver Sch. Dist., 1984-87, guidance/counseling steering com. mem., 1984-88, bldg. leader team guidance/counseling com. McLoughlin Middle Sch., 1986—, parent edn. workshop, 1986-90, parent workshop transitions, 1990—, adv. planning com., 1989-90, adv. coord. McLoughlin, 1988-90; com. mem. Commn. on Student Learning, Olympia, Wash., 1994; presenter in field. Contbr. articles to profl. jours. Pres. No. Va. Counselor Assn., 1982-83, exec. bd. dirs., 1978-84, treas., 1979-80; active PTA. Named Chpt. Member of Yr. No. Va. Counselors Assn., 1983. Mem. NEA, Am. Sch. Counselor Assn. (middle/jr. high v.p. 1991-93, named Middle Sch. Counselor of Yr. 1994), Am. Counseling Assn., Nat. Middle Sch. Assn., Wash. Edn. Assn., Vancouver Edn. Assn., Washington Sch. Counselor Assn. (pres. 1989-91, conf. chair 1989-91, nominations/elections chair 1990-91, bylaws chair 1992-93, named Middle Sch. Counselor of Yr. 1994), Washington Counseling Assn. (pres. 1994—, exec. bd. dirs. 1989-90), Kappa Delta Kappa, Phi Delta Kappa, Phi Lambda Theta. Home: 13210 NE 6th Ct Vancouver WA 98685-2664 Office: McLoughlin Mid Sch 5802 Macarthur Blvd Vancouver WA 98661

MCGEE, MICHAEL JAY, fire marshal, educator; b. Ft. Worth, June 9, 1952; s. Cecil Carl McGee and Helen Ruth (Peeples) McGee-Furrh; m. Carol Lee Garbarino, Sept. 18, 1982; children: Megan Rose, John Michael, Molly Caitlin. Student, U. Tex., 1970-73, Western Oreg. State U., 1983; AAS in Fire Protection Tech., Colo. Mountain Coll., 1990. Lic. fire suppression systems insp., Colo., vocat. educator, Colo.; cert. hazardous materials technician, Colo., 1992, EMT, Colo.; cert. fire safety hazardous materials instr., evaluator. Driver Massengale Co., Austin, Tex., 1970-73; gen. mgr. Sundae Palace, Austin, 1973-74; staff mem. Young Life, Colorado Springs, Colo., 1970-75; mgr. Broadmoor Mgmt. Co., Vail, Colo., 1974-76; technician Vail Cable Communications, 1976-77; fire marshal Vail Fire Dept., 1977—; instr. Colo. Mountain Coll., 1980—; dist. rep. Joint Coun. Fire Dist. Colo., 1983-85; co-chmn. Eagle County Hazardous Materials, 1984-85, mem. planning com., 1987-90; mem. accountability com. Eagle County Sch. Dist., 1991—, mem. budget rev. com., 1991-93, vice chair accountability com. 1992-93, chmn. accountability com., 1993—, mem. policy rev. com., 1993—, bldg. coord., team coach Odyssey of the Mind at Eaglevale Elem. Sch., 1995. Chmn. Eagle County chpt. ARC, 1980-83, disaster chmn., 1977-80; tng. officer Eagle Vol. Fire Dept., 1988-90; mem. parish coun. St. Mary's Parish, Eagle County, 1989-90; mem. citizen's adv. com. Colo. Mountain Coll., 1990-91, bd. dirs. 1990; bldg. coord., team coach Oddessey of the Mind, Eagle Valley Elem. Sch., 1994-95. Mem. Internat. Assn. Arson Investigators (Colo. chpt.), Internat. Platform Assn., Nat. Fire Protection Assn., Colo. State Fire Marshals Assn., Colo. State Fire Chiefs Assn. Office: Vail Fire Dept 42 W Meadow Dr Vail CO 81657-5705

MCGEE, MIKE JAMES, gallery director, writer; b. Ft. Lee, Va., Mar. 2, 1955; s. Lloyd James and Sylvia L. (Mounts) McG. BA, Calif. State U., Fullerton, 1978; MFA, U. Calif.-Irvine, 1980. Dir. The Edge Gallery, Fullerton, 1982-85; programs coord. Laguna Art Mus., Laguna Beach, Calif., 1986-88; writer, educator various instns., 1988—; art gallery dir. Orange Coast Coll., Costa Mesa, Calif., 1989-91; art forum lecture series head Rancho Santiago Jr. Coll., Santa Ana, 1991—; art gallery dir., asst. prof. Calif. State U., Fullerton, 1992—. Pres. bd. trustees Orange County Ctr. for Contemporary Art, Santa Ana, 1990—; arts com. chair Orange County Arts Alliance, Santa Ana, 1982; bd. dirs. Arts Orange County, 1995—. Mem. Am. Assn. Museums. Home: PO Box 3154 Fullerton CA 92634-3154 Office: Calif State U Fullerton CA 92634-9480

MCGEE, REX ALAN, motion picture screenwriter; b. Cleburne, Tex., Nov. 22, 1951; s. Theo Rex and Ella Lucille (Clark) McG.; m. Sandra Marie Pace, Dec. 31, 1992. BBA, U. So. Calif., 1975. Personal asst. to film dir. Billy Wilder L.A. and Munich, 1974, 77; journalist Am. Film, Playboy, L.A. and TV Guide, 1979-82; motion picture story analyst United Artists/The Ladd Co., L.A., 1977-80; screenwriter, 1981—; Intern for dir. Am. Film Inst., L.A., 1974. Author: (motion picture) "Pure Country", 1992. Mem. Leadership Cleburne, Tex., 1992; advisor Main Street Project, Cleburne, 1993; trustee Johnson County Com. on Aging, Cleburne, 1994. Mem. Writers Guild of Am. West. Home: 305 N Pendell St Cleburne TX 76031-3529 Office: 9507 Santa Monica Blvd Ste 206 Beverly Hills CA 90210-4542

MCGEE, SAM, laser scientist; b. Louisville, Mar. 4, 1943; s. Walter R. and Sue (Burchett) McG. BA, Vanderbilt U., 1965. Mktg. dir. Brown-Forman Corp., Louisville, 1966-73; pres. FYI Corp., L.A., 1973-75; sr. v.p., gen. mgr. Brady Enterprises, East Weymouth, Mass., 1979-82; pres. Laser Images, Inc., L.A., 1982-85; pres., owner Starlasers, L.A., 1985—; mgmt. cons. L.A., 1976-78; cons. in field; bd. dirs. various cos. Mem. Hon. Order Ky. Cols. Office: Starlasers 13156 Leadwell St North Hollywood CA 91605-4117

MCGEE, WILLIAM DEAN (WILLIE MCGEE), professional baseball player; b. San Francisco, Nov. 2, 1958. Student, Diablo Valley Coll., Pleasant Hill, Calif. Baseball player N.Y. Yankees, 1977-81, St. Louis Cardinals, 1981—, Oakland Athletics, 1990, San Francisco Giants, 1990—. Mem. Nat. League All-Star Team, 1983, 85, 87-88; recipient Gold Glove Award, 1983, 85-86; named Nat. League Most Valuable Player, Basball Writers Assoc. of Am., 1985; Sporting News Nat. League Player of the Year, 1985; recipient Silver Slugger award, 1985; Nat. League Batting Champion, 1985, 90. Office: San Francisco Giants Candlestick Park San Francisco CA 94124-3998*

MCGETTIGAN, CHARLES CARROLL, JR., investment banker; b. San Francisco, Mar. 28, 1945; s. Charles Carroll McGettigan and Molly (Fay) McGettigan Pedley; m. Katharine Havard King, Nov. 1, 1975 (div. 1981); m. Meriwether Lewis Stovall, Aug. 6, 1983; 1 child, Meriwether Lewis Fay. AB in Govt., Georgetown U., 1966; MBA in Fin., U. Pa., 1969. Assoc., asst. v.p., v.p. Blyth Eastman Dillon, N.Y.C., 1970-75, 1st v.p., 1975-78, sr. v.p., San Francisco, 1978-80; sr. v.p. Dillon, Read & Co., San Francisco, 1980-83; gen. ptnr. Woodman Kirkpatrick & Gilbreath, San Francisco, 1983-84; prin. corp. fin. Hambrecht & Quist, Inc., San Francisco, 1984-88, mng. dir, founder McGettigan, Wick & Co., Inc., San Francisco, 1988—; gen. ptnr., founder Proactive Ptnrs. L.P., San Francisco, 1990—, Proactive Investment Mgrs., L.P., 1991—; gen. ptnr. Fremont Proactive Ptnrs., L.P., 1991—; bd. dirs. Digital Dictation, Inc., Vienna, Va., NDE Environ. Corp., Austin, PMR Corp., San Diego, I.-Flow Corp., Irvine, Calif., Sonex Rsch., Inc., Annapolis, Md., Modtech, Inc., Perris, Calif., Wray-Tech Instruments, Inc., Stratford, Calif.; chmn. Onsite Energy Corp., Carlsbad, Calif.; adv. dir. Chesapeake Ventures, Balt., 1984-94. Trustee St. Francis Meml. Hosp., San Francisco, 1980-86; mem. United San Francisco Rep. fin. com., 1983—, steering com., 1986—; adv. bd. dirs. Leavey Sch. Bus. Adminstrn., Santa Clara U., Calif., 1984-1990. With USN, 1966. Named Confrerie des Chevaliers du Tastevin, 1991. Mem. The Brook, Racquet and Tennis Club (N.Y.), The Pacific Union Club, Bohemian Club (San Francisco), San Francisco Golf Club, Burlingame Country Club (Hillsborough, Calif.), Calif. Club (L.A.), Boston Club (New Orleans), Piping Rock Club (Locust Valley, N.Y.). Republican. Roman Catholic. Home: 3375 Clay St San Francisco CA 94118-2006 Office: McGettigan Wick & Co Inc 50 Osgood Pl San Francisco CA 94133-4617

MCGHAY, JON DAVIES, engineer; b. Enid, Okla., June 7, 1959; s. Donald L. and E. Marie (Davies) McG. BS in Geology, Okla. State U., 1982, MBA, 1988. Owner Lightning Lectr. Notes Inc., Stillwater, Okla., 1984-86; mgr., bd. dirs. TLT Inc., Stillwater, Okla., 1981-88; fin. analyst Lomas Mortgage USA, Dallas, 1988-89; account mgr. Texaco Refining and Mktg. Inc., Dallas, 1989-90; lubrication engr. Texaco Refining and Mktg. Inc., Phoenix, 1990—. Mem. Am. Assn. Petroleum Geologists, Soc. of Tribiologists and Lubrication Engrs., Okla. State U. Alumni Assn. (bd. dirs. Ariz. chpt. 1993—). Home: 1901 E Osborn Rd Apt 136 Phoenix AZ 85016-7263

MCGIBBON, WILLIAM ALEXANDER, rancher, photographer; b. Evanston, Ill.; s. Edmund L. and Catherine (Klink) M.; m. Nancy Hornaday, Aug. 27, 1966; children: Heather M., Andrew W. BA, U. Pa., 1966; postgrad., U. Ariz., 1970-71. Pres., chief exec. officer Santa Rita Ranch, Inc., Green Valley, Ariz., 1970—; adv. com. Coll. Agr., U. Ariz., Tucson. Photographer: photographs pub. in numerous agrl. and livestock publs., 1980--. Mem. Continental Sch. Bd. Green Valley, 1976-84, pres., 1978-84; mem. Ariz. Bd. Pesticide Control, Phoenix, 1983-86; bd. dirs. Green Valley Community Fund, 1988--. Mem. Ariz. Cattlemen's Assn. (bd. dirs.), Nat. Cattlemen's Assn., Green Valley Rotary Club (pres. 1986, v.p. Green Valley Rotary Club Found. 1988--), So. Ariz. Cattlemen's Assn. (pres.), Cattle Growers Assn. (v.p., pres.-elect), Freelance Photographers Orgn. Republican. Home and Office: Santa Rita Ranch Inc 8200 E Box Canyon Rd PO Box 647 Green Valley AZ 85622-0647

MCGIHON, MICHAEL EDWIN, sheet metal manufacturing executive; b. Long Beach, Calif., July 31, 1949; s. Alvin Frances and Edna Lona (Windes) McG.; m. Phyllis Rachel Tiner, Aug. 15, 1970; 1 child, Scott Del. Student, Long Beach C.C., 1971. Apprentice McGihon Sheet Metal, Long Beach, 1967-71, journeyman, foreman, 1971-91, pres., 1991—, cons. R&D, 1985—. Mem. Aircraft Owners and Pilots Assn., Long Beach Ski Club (asst. v.p. 1992-93). Democrat. Lutheran. Home: 2901 N Heather Rd Long Beach CA 90815-1052

MCGILLICUDDY, JOAN MARIE, psychotherapist, consultant; b. Chgo., June 23, 1952; d. James Neal and Muriel (Joy) McG. BA, U. Ariz., 1974, MS, 1976. Cert. nat. counselor. Counselor ACTION, Tucson, 1976; counselor, clin. supr. Behavioral Health Agy. Cen. Ariz., Casa Grande, 1976-81; instr. psychology Cen. Ariz. Coll., Casa Grande, 1978-83; therapist, co-dir. Helping Assocs., Inc., Casa Grande, 1982—, v.p., sec., 1982—; cert. instr. Silva Method Mind Devel., Tucson, 1986—; presenter Silver Mind Control Internat., 1988-91. Mem. Mayor's Com. for Handicapped, Casa Grande, 1989-90, Human Svcs. Planning, Casa Grande, 1985-90. Named Outstanding Am. Lectr. Silva Midn Internat., 1988-95. Mem. AACD. Office: Helping Assocs Inc 1901 N Trekell Rd Casa Grande AZ 85222-1706

MCGILLIVRAY, KAREN, elementary school educator; b. Richland, Oreg., Aug. 24, 1936; d. Kenneth Melton and Catharina (Sass) McG. BS in Edn. cum laude, Ea. Oreg. State Coll., 1958; MRE, Pacific Sch. Religion, 1963. Cert. tchr., Oreg. 4th grade tchr. Salem (Oreg.)-Keizer Pub. Schs.; ret., 1995. Contbr. articles, stories to ednl. mags. U.S. Govt. grantee. Mem. NEA (rep. assembly), Oreg. Edn. Assn. (rep. assembly), Oreg. Ret. Educators Assn., Salem Edn. Assn. (officer), Oreg. Ret. Tchrs. Assn., Phi Delta Kappa (officer), Delta Kappa Gamma (officer, state bd. mem.). Methodist. Home: 325 Cedarwood Ave Mcminnville OR 97128

MCGILVERY, LAURENCE, book publisher, dealer; b. L.A., May 21, 1932; s. Neil Lee and Joan (Girard) McG.; m. Geraldine Malloy, July 5, 1955; children: Lynette, Lise, Erin, Justin. BA, Pomona Coll., 1954. Engr. Walter Dorwin Teague Assocs., Pomona, Sunnyvale, Calif., 1954-60; owner, bookseller Nexus, La Jolla, Calif., 1960-66; antiquarian book dealer La Jolla, 1966—. Mem. ACLU, Antiquarian Booksellers Assn. Am. (pres. So. Calif. chpt. 1987), Art Librs. Soc. N.Am., San Diego Booksellers Assn. (bd. dirs.). Democrat. Office: PO Box 852 La Jolla CA 92038-0852

MCGINN, SUSAN FRANCES, musician; b. Detroit, May 26, 1961; d. Michael Thomas and Bernice Frances (DePollo) McG. MusB, U. Mich., 1983; MusM, U. Ill., 1985; postgrad., Ind. U., 1985-89. Co-prin. flute L.A. Philharm. Inst., 1985, Nat. Repertory Orch., Keystone, Colo., 1987, Nat. Orchestal Inst., College Park, Md., 1989, Schleswig-Holstein Musik Festival, Salzau, Germany, 1988, 89; prin. flute, flutist wind quintet Canton (Ohio) Symphony Orch., 1989-90, Honolulu Symphony Orch., 1990—; grad. teaching asst. U. Ill., Urbana, 1983-85; assoc. instr. Ind. U., Bloomington, 1986-89; flutist spring wind quinted Chamber Music Hawaii, Honolulu, 1990-92. Scholar U. Ill., 1983-85; fellow Ind. U., 1985-86, scholar, 1986-89. Office: Hawaii Symphony Orch 444 Hobron Ln Ste V-ib Honolulu HI 96815-1229

MCGINNES, JAMES MARC, lawyer, lecturer; b. Murray, Utah, Sept. 27, 1941; s. Alfred James and Fern (Furner) McG.; m. Seyburn Zorthian, Sept. 4, 1982; children: Skye McGinnes, Zachary McGinnes. BA in History, Stanford U., 1963; JD, U. Calif., Berkeley, 1966. Bar: Calif. 1967. Lawyer Thelen, Marrin, Johnson and Bridges, San Francisco, 1967-69, Westwick, Collison and Talaga, Santa Barbara, Calif., 1969-71; pvt. practice Santa Barbara, 1971-77; founder, exec. dir., counsel Environ. Def. Ctr., Santa Barbara, 1977—; lectr. in environ. studies U. Calif., Santa Barbara, 1971—; founding pres. Cmty. Environ. Coun., Inc., Santa Barbara, 1970-74. Author: Principles of Environmental Law, 1980. Dir. Congress on Optimum Population and Environment, Chgo., 1970-72, Earth Island Inst., San Francisco, 1986-88; founder, dir. Peaceful Resolutions Inst., Santa Barbara, 1986—. Found. fellow Rotary Internat., France, 1966-67. Mem. Calif. Bar Assn., Santa Barbara County Bar Assn. Office: U Calif Environ Studies Santa Barbara CA 93106

MCGINNIS, DEBORAH CHERYL, county official; b. Oak Park, Ill., Feb. 2, 1955; d. Victor and Wanda Ann (Konieczy) Kaminski; m. Danny Allyn McGinnis, Feb. 14, 1973 (div. Sept. 1986); children: Brandy Lyn, Jonathan Dylan. Grad., high sch., 1972. Cert. document examiner. Title searcher Safeco Title Ins., San Bernardino, Calif., 1978-79, title examiner, 1979-80; dep. examiner San Bernardino Recorder, 1980-90, rec. supr., 1990—; guest speaker to various orgns.; liaison between local real estate orgns. Active in local politics. Christian.

MCGINNIS, MICHAEL PATRICK, psychotherapist; b. Madison, Wis., Oct. 4, 1950; s. James and Patricia Jane (Cole) McG.; m. Carol Ann Bailey, Aug. 8, 1982; children: Arielle Dominque, Chandra Eden. Student, U. Wis., 1968-69, U. Maine, 1971-73; BA, Sonoma State U., 1980, MA, 1984. Cert. marriage, family and child counselor, Calif. Offset printer Portland (Maine) Printing Co., 1970-71, Pronto Prints, Madison, 1972-74; mental health specialist Sheltered Workshop, Madison, 1975-77; mental health worker social svc. dept. Treatment Alternatives to Street Crimes, Santa Rosa, Calif., 1977-79; counselor Nat. Coun. on Alcoholism, Santa Rosa, 1978-79, exec. dir. Sonoma County, 1979-81; counselor, trainer Sonoma County Family Svc. Agy., Santa Rosa, 1981-86; pvt. practice, Healdsburg, Calif., 1985—; trainer, cons. domestic violence treatment Calif. Dept. Mental Health, 1979-84, YWCA Women's Emergency Shelter, Santa Rosa, 1980-86. Mem. Calif. Assn. Marriage and Family Therapists (clin.), Am. Profl. Soc. on Abuse on Children (clin.), Calif. Profl. Soc. on Abuse of Children (clin.). Democrat. Home and Office: 610 Alta Vista Dr Healdsburg CA 95448-4651

MCGINNIS, SCOTT GEORGE, cruise line executive; b. McKeesport, Pa., Nov. 8, 1950; s. George Franklin and Alice Yvonne (Proch) McG.; m. Carol Lee Poulos, Oct. 7, 1972 (div. Jan. 1985); children: Patrick Scott, Shannon Lee; m. Barbara Lee Beck, June 19, 1985; 1 child, Seth Connor. BS in Bus. Mgmt., Pa. Mil. Coll., 1972. Sales rep. Procter & Gamble, Lancaster, Pa., 1975-77; asst. account exec. SSC & B, n.Y.C., 1977-78; account exec. Ketchum, MacLeod & Grove, Pitts., 1978-81; sr. supr. PPG Industries, Pitts., 1981-83; v.p., account supr. Cole, henderson, Drake, Atlanta, 1983-89; v.p. pres., mktg. Royal Viking Line, Miami, 1989-91; v.p. mktg. and sales Windstar Cruises, Seattle, 1991—. Lt. USN, 1972-75. Mem. Cruise Line Internat. Assn. (mktg. com. 1991—, mng. com. 1991—). Republican. Lutheran. Home: 3002 35th Ave W Seattle WA 98199-2619 Office: Windstar Cruises 300 Elliott Ave W Seattle WA 98119-4122

MCGINTY, BRIAN DONALD, lawyer, author; b. Santa Barbara, Calif., June 22, 1937; s. Donald Bruce and Natalia Vallejo (Haraszthy) M. AB, U. Calif.-Berkeley, 1959, JD, 1962. Bar: Calif. 1963. Assoc. Twohig, Weingarten & Haas, Seaside, Calif., 1962-63; ptnr. Weingarten & McGinty, Seaside, 1963-70; sole practice, Monterey, Calif., 1970-73, San Francisco, 1973-83; writer, editor Matthew Bender & Co., San Francisco and Oakland, Calif., 1984-93. Author: Haraszthy at the Mint (Calif. Trials Series), 1975; The Palace Inns, 1978, We the People, 1987; contbg. author: The Craft of the Essay, Historical Times Illustrated Encyclopedia of the Civil War, Portrait of America, 5th edit., 1990, California Real Estate Law and Practice, California Legal Forms, California Insurance Law, California Public Agency Law and Practice, California Wills and Trusts; editor: Napa Wine (Rounce and Coffin Club award 1975), 1974; contbr. numerous articles to profl. jours. Recipient Excellence in Writing award Nat. Hist. Soc., 1976. Mem. Calif. Hist. Soc.

MCGLASHAN, TERESA DUANE, environmentalist; b. Santa Ana, Calif., Nov. 19, 1962; d. William Earl and Christney McGlashan; m. Timothy Patrick Duane, Sept. 9, 1989. BA, Yale U., 1985; MSc, London Sch. Econs., 1988. Legis. asst. Congressman Don Bonker, Washington, 1985-87; internat. coord. Earth Day 1990, Palo Alto, Calif., 1989-90; N.Am. coord. and Asia liaison EarthAction Network, Oakland, Calif., 1991-94. Co-founder Yale-Moscow State Undergrad. Confs., Yale U., 1985. Home: 1061 Monterey Ave Berkeley CA 94707

MCGLAUGHLIN, THOMAS HOWARD, publisher, retired naval officer; b. Cin., Jan. 12, 1928; s. George Godden and Cordelia (Herrlinger) McG.; m. Moana Maharam-Stone, Jan. 4, 1984. BS in Elec. Engring., U.S. Naval Acad., 1950. Lic. master mariner. Commd. ensign U.S. Navy, 1950, advanced through grades to capt., 1970; White House aide to Pres. John F. Kennedy, Washington, 1960-63; exec. officer USS Prichett, Long Beach, Calif., 1963-65; comdg. officer USS Maddox, Long Beach, 1965-67; exec. officer USS Boston, Boston, 1967-70; chief naval ops. Comdr.-in-Chief, Pacific, Honolulu, 1970-74; chief of staff Mil. Sealift Command, N.Y.C., 1974-79; ret. U.S. Navy, 1979; pres. Falmouth Press, Honolulu, 1983—; marine surveyor R.W. Dickieson Internat., Inc., Honolulu, 1982—; master M.V. Rella Mae, Honolulu, 1981-90, Royal Taipan, Cebu, Philippines, 1990. Hon. police chief Boston Police Dept., 1969. Decorated Bronze Star; recipient medal for Outstanding Svc., Am. Legion, Pitts., 1942. Mem. Nat. Def. Transp. Assn., VFW (life), U.S. Naval Acad. Alumni Assn. (life), The Retired Officers Assn. Republican. Presbyterian. Home: The Royal Iolani #1702 581 Kamoku St Honolulu HI 96826 Office: RW Dickieson Internat Inc 46-208 Kahuhipa St Kaneohe HI 96744-3905

MCGLONE, DAVID ANTHONY JOSEPH, publishing executive; b. Castle AFB, Calif., Feb. 28, 1952; s. Willard Estel and Joan Marianne (Legrande) M.; m. Carolyn Frances Illig, July 30, 1973 (div. 1976); m. Deborah Snavely, May 1, 1977. Student, San Diego State U., 1970-72. Cook various restaurants, San Diego, Riverside, Calif., 1972-77; keypunch operator Mrs. Keypunch, San Francisco, 1977-78; messenger, dispatcher Bradford Security Trust Co., San Francisco, 1978-81; with customer support dept. Tymshare, Sunnyvale, Calif., 1983; tech., software developer Tandem Computers, Cupertino, Calif., 1984-92; pres. Lambda Software Pub., Eugene, Oreg., 1988—. Editor, pub. The Z-Letter, 1988—, Eagle Computer User Group NL, 1987-90, Kirjasto, 1982-84; author: (software) LPascal, 1992-93. Contbr. So. Poverty Law Ctr., 1985—. SSG. USAR, 1976-82. Mem. Hist. Computer Soc., Amnesty Internat., ACLU, Soc. for Creative Anachronism (Order of Laurel 1976, Order of Pelican 1979). Democrat. Home and Office: 149 W Hilliard Ln Eugene OR 97404-3057

MCGLYNN, BETTY HOAG, art historian; b. Deer Lodge, Mont., Apr. 28, 1914; d. Arthur James and Elizabeth Tangye (Davey) Lochrie; m. Paul Sterling Hoag, Dec. 28, 1936 (div. 1967); children: Peter Lochrie Hoag, Jane Hoag Brown, Robert Doane Hoag; m. Thomas Arnold McGlynn, July 28, 1973. BA, Stanford U., 1936, MA, U. So. Calif., 1967. Cert. secondary tchr., Calif. Rsch. dir. So. Calif. Archives of Am. Art, L.A., 1964-67, Carmel (Calif.) Mus. Art, 1967-69; dir. Triton Mus. Art, Santa Clara, Calif., 1970; archivist, libr. San Mateo County (Calif.) Hist. Soc. Mus., 1972-74; cons. Monterey Peninsula Mus. Art, Calif., 1964—; tchr. art extension Monterey Peninsula Coll., Calif., 1970, San Jose City Coll., 1971; lectr. in field. Author: The World of Mary DeNeale Morgan, 1970, Carmel Art Association: A History, 1987; contbg. author: Plein Air Painters of California, The North, 1986, Orchid Art and the Orchid Isle, 1982, Hawaiian Island Artists and Friends of the Arts, 1989; editor, author of jours. La. Peninsula, 1971-75, Noticias, 1983-88; author of booklets; contbr. articles to profl. jours. Appraiser art work City of Carmel, 1967, City of Monterey, 1981; mem. Friends of Harrison Meml. Libr., Carmel, Friends of Sunset Found., Carmel, Pacific Grove Art Ctr., Monterey Bay Aquarium. Mem. Butte (Mont.) Arts Chateau, Carmel Art Assn. (hon.), Carmel Heritage Soc., Carmel Found., Carmel Residents Assn., Chinese Hist. Soc., Monterey History and Art Assn. (art cons.), Monterey Peninsula Mus. Art (acquisitions bd.), Monterey County Geneal. Soc., Gallatin County Hist. Soc. (Mont.), Stanford Alumni Assn., Robinson Jeffers Tor House Found. (art cons.), Hawaiian Hist. Soc., Mont. Hist. Soc., Nat. Mus. of Women in Arts, The Westerners, P.E.O., Book Club of Calif. Republican. Home and Office: PO Box 7189 Carmel CA 93921-7189

MCGOVERN, DOUGLAS EDWARD, mechanical engineer; b. Schenectady, N.Y., Apr. 15, 1946; s. Arthur Douglas and Virginia Seibert McGovern; divorced; children: Thomas A., Robert D., Joanna M. BS with distinction, Northwestern U., 1968; MS in Elec. Engring., U. N.Mex., 1972;

MS in Mech. Engring., Stanford U., 1969, PhD, 1975. Design engr., project leader Sandia Nat. Labs., Albuquerque, 1969-82; mgr. Dallas Devel. Lab. Gearhart Industries, Inc., Ft. Worth, 1982-83; unit mgr., staff engr. Govt. Comm. Systems, RCA, Camden, N.J., 1983-85; project leader Sandia Nat. Labs., Albuquerque, 1985-89, dep. mgr., 1989—. Contbr. articles to profl. jours.; patentee in field. Mem. Sigma Xi, Tau Beta Pi, Sigma Tau, Pi Tau Sigma, Phi Eta Sigma. Home: 6621 Orphelia Ave NE Albuquerque NM 87109-3752

MCGOVERN, RICKY JAMES, architect, educator; b. Tacoma, June 16, 1948; s. James Patrick and Betty Irene (Baxter) McG.; m. Kathleen Joy Kerrone, June 14, 1968; children: Jamie Francis, Brandon James. BArch, Wash. State U., 1973, BS, 1973. Registered architect, Wash. Architect Burr Assocs., Tacoma, 1973-79, Erickson-Hogenson Architects, Tacoma, 1979-81; ptnr. Erickson-McGovern Architects, Tacoma, 1981-94, Erickson McGovern Peterson Storaasli Archs., Tacoma and Chelan, Wash., 1995—; instr. Tacoma C.C., 1979-85; vocat. advisor Bethel Sch. Dist., Spanaway, Wash., 1981—; sec. Avitar Inc., Tacoma, 1980—; bd. dirs. Sound Ventures, Inc., Plaza Hall. Co-chmn. Clearwood Cmty. Assn., Pierce County, Wash., 1976-82; designer Bethel Cmty. Daffodil Float, Spanaway, 1983-84. Recipient appreciation award Clearwood Cmty. Assn., 1982; named Citizen of Yr., 1988. Mem. AIA, Council Ednl. Facilities Planning, Soc. Am. Value Engrs. (bd. dirs. 1982-83), Shelter Industry Coalition (vice chmn. 1983-90), Parkland-Spanaway C. of C. (chmn. Cmty. Days 1984, 90-94, pres. 1987-88, Citizen of Yr. award 1985, 86, 91), Winner's Circle (v.p. 1983-90). Clubs: Plaza Hall (bd. dirs. 1985-92) City. Lodge: Kiwanis (pres. 1984-85, Kiwanian of Yr. award 1982, 83, 84, Citizen of Yr. 1988). Office: Erickson McGovern Peterson Storaacsli Archs 120 131st St S Tacoma WA 98444-4804

MC GOVERN, WALTER T., federal judge; b. Seattle, May 24, 1922; s. C. Arthur and Anne Marie (Thies) McG.; m. Rita Marie Olsen, June 29, 1946; children: Katrina M., Shawn E., A. Renee. B.A., U. Wash., 1949, LL.B., 1950. Bar: Wash. 1950. Practiced law in Seattle, 1950-59; mem. firm Kerr, McCord, Greenleaf & Moen; judge Municipal Ct., Seattle, 1959-65, Superior Ct., Wash., 1965-68, Wash. Supreme Ct., 1968-71, U.S. Dist. Ct. (we. dist.) Wash., 1971—; chief judge, 1975-87; mem. subcom. on supporting personnel Jud. Conf. U.S., 1981-87, chmn. subcom., 1983, mem. adminstrn. com., 1983-87, chmn. jud. resources com., 1987-91. Mem. Am. Judicature Soc., Wash. State Superior Ct. Judges Assn., Seattle King County Bar Assn. (treas.), Phi Delta Phi. Club: Seattle Tennis (pres. 1968). Office: US Dist Ct US Courthouse 5th Fl 1010 5th Ave Seattle WA 98104-1130

MCGOWAN, JOHN JOSEPH, energy manager; b. Phila., Nov. 28, 1950; s. Daniel Joseph and Catherine Theresa (Durkin) McG.; m. Judy Eileen Reed, June 3, 1978; children: Dustin, Kendall. BS, Temple U., 1975; MA, U. N.Mex., 1980. Cert. energy mgr.; cert. corgenation profl.; cert. lighting efficiency profl. Tchr. Zuni Indian Reservation, 1975-79; energy mgr. Haufler Inc., Phila., 1981-83; asst. dir. of energy Svc. Mdse. Corp., Nashville, 1983-86; v.p. Automation Mgmt. Systems, Kansas City, 1986-87; mgr. systems Honeywell, Albuquerque, 1987-91; dir. N.Mex. Energy Conservation Div., Santa Fe, 1991-92; mgr. market develop. Honeywell, Albuquerque, 1992-94; tech. support mgr. Burke Engring., Albuquerque, 1994—; chmn. tech. sessions World Energy Engring. Congress, 1985, 89, 90-92; tech. adv. bd. Energy User News Mag., Radnor, Pa., 1992—; prof. U. N.Mex., U. Phoenix; speaker in field and seminar presenter. Author: Networking for Building Automation Systems, 1991, Energy Management for Buildings, 1989, Energy Management and Control Systems, 1988, Direct Digital Control Systems, 1994; contbg. author: New Mexico State Energy Policy, 1992; editl. bd. Strategic Planning for Energy and Environ., 1990—; contbr. articles to profl. jours. Managed pub. agy. N.Mex. State Energy Office, 1991. Mem. ASHRAE, Assn. of Energy Engrs. (v.p. 1992, Energy Profl. Yr. 1991, nat. v.p. 1993—), Assn. of Profl. Energy Mgrs. Office: Burke Engring 3330 Vassar Dr NE Albuquerque NM 87107-2024

MCGOWAN, JOSEPH ANTHONY, JR., news executive; b. Sheridan, Wyo., May 16, 1931; s. Joseph Anthony and Eda B. (Harris) McG.; m. Patricia Donnette Mitchell, June 7, 1958 (div. 1980); children—Joseph Howard, Colleen Diane; m. Catherine Doris Netick, June 12, 1982. B.S., U. Wyo. Newsman AP, Miami, Fla., 1960-64; bur. chief AP, New Delhi, India, 1965-68, Lima, Peru, 1968-70, Indpls., 1970-75, Boston, 1975-78, Denver, 1978—; lectr. U. Denver, 1978—, Colo. U., Boulder, 1978—, Northeastern U., Boston, 1975-78. Scoutmaster Boy Scouts Am., Sudbury, Mass., 1977-78. Served with USNR, 1953-55. Named Disting. Alumnus, U. Wyo., 1992; Knight Internat. Press fellow to Pakistan, 1995. Mem. Denver Press Club (bd. dirs. 1989-92), Press Club Boston, Colo. Assn. Commerce and Industry (communications council 1986-89), Sigma Delta Chi (Big Hat award 1983). Republican. Office: AP 1444 Wazee St Ste 130 Denver CO 80202-1326

MCGOWAN, MITCHELL JOSEPH, director, stage manager; b. Nebraska City, Nebr., Aug. 20, 1964; s. Ward Allan and Karen Rae McG.; m. Cynthia Lynne Cox, Sept. 6, 1982. BFA, U. Victoria, B.C., Can., 1987. Dir. The Lion In Winter, Empire Builder, My Cup Ranneth Over, Grey Matters, Drought, Passion, Poison and Petrifaction, My Daughter, My Son; prodn. stage mgr. Twelfth Night; state mgr. Age of Wonders, Shenandoah, A Little Night Music, And The Soul Shall Dance, The Tempest, As You Like It, Machinal, Kitty-Kitty/Last Supper, Rodgers & Hart, The Trojan Women; appeared in The Grapes of Wrath, A Midsummer Night's Dream, Man of La Mancha, Tintypes, The Eunuch, Sweet Charity, Philadelphia, Here I Come, Sleeping Beauty, The Good Doctor, The Rainmaker, The Boyfriend. Home: 14058 NE 181st St Apt F-304 Woodinville WA 98072-6853

MCGOWAN, THOMAS RANDOLPH, religious organization executive; b. Balt., Apr. 19, 1926; s. Robert and Mary (Miller) McG.; m. Bernice A. Bernard, May 20, 1967 (dec. Nov. 1981); children: Howard, James, Terry; m. Roedean Olivia Oden, Feb. 9, 1985; children: Karen White, Kevin, Kurt. AA, Oakland Jr. Coll., 1964; postgrad., San Francisco State Coll., 1964-68; BS, U. Md., 1978. Lt. security police Oakland (Calif.) Army Base, 1955-60; chief motor pool San Francisco Procurement Agy., Oakland, 1960-64, contract specialist, 1964-68; contract specialist Harry Diamond Labs., Washington, 1968-79, br. chief procurement divsn., 1972-79; chief procurement directorate Yuma (Ariz.) Proving Ground, 1979-82; dir. ecumenism Roman Cath. Diocese of Oakland, 1983—; dir. African Am. Cath. Pastoral Ctr., Diocese of Oakland, 1991—. Convener Interreligious Coun. of Oakland, 1988—; trustee Greater Oakland Interfaith Newtork, 1989-92; mem. East Oakland Renewal Task Force, 1990—; bd. dirs. Columbia (Md.) Found., 1972-74, chmn., 1975-79; dir. Bd. Cons., Graymoor, N.Y., 1990—; bd. dirs. Thea Bowman Manor, Oakland, 1989—. With U.S. Army, 1944-46. Mem. Knights of Peter Claver, Rotary. Democrat. Home: 139 Pinto Dr Vallejo CA 94591-8451

MCGRADY, CORINNE YOUNG, design company executive; b. N.Y.C., May 6, 1938; d. Albert I. and Reda (Bromberg) Young; m. Michael Robinson McGrady; children: Sean, Siobhan, Liam. Student, Bard Coll., Annandale-on-Hudson, N.Y., 1960, Harvard U., 1968-69. Founder, pres. Corinne McGrady Designs; designer Corinneware (joint venture of Corinne McGrady Designs and Boston Warehouse Trading Corp. 1990), East Northport, N.Y., 1970—. Acrylic works exhibited in group shows at Mus. Contemporary Crafts, N.Y.C., 1969-70, Smithsonian Instn., 1970-71, Pompidou Ctr., Paris, 1971, Mus. Sci. and Industry, 1970; sculpture exhibited at Guild Hall Show, Southampton, N.Y., 1968, Hecksher Mus., 1968. Vice pres. Woman's Internat. League for Peace and Freedom, Huntington, N.Y., 1971. Recipient Design Rev. award Indsl. Design, 1969, 70; Instant Supergraphic Indsl. Design Rev. award, 1971. Patentee cookbook stand. Home and Office: PO Box 27 Lilliwaup WA 98555-0027

MCGRATH, DANIEL BERNARD, newspaper editor; b. Chgo., Apr. 9, 1950; s. James Joseph and Margaret Mary (Mackey) McG.; m. Jo-Anna Marie Grannon, Nov. 27, 1971; children—Megan, Matthew. Grad., Marquette U., 1972. Sports editor Freeport Jour. Standard, Ill., 1972-75; sports writer, columnist Nev. State Jour., Reno, 1975-77; sports editor Sacramento Union, 1977-79, San Francisco Chronicle, 1979—. Editor: "Super Season" San Francisco 49ers, 1984, 1984. Recipient Nev. Sportswriter of Yr. award Nat. Assn. Sportswriters, Sportscasters, 1976-77; Best Sports Sect. award Calif. Newspaper Pubs. Assn., 1978; Best sports Story award San Francisco Press Club, 1983. Mem. AP Sports Editors. Democrat. Roman Catholic. Home: 194 Ashland Dr Daly City CA 94015-3406 Office: The Sacramento Bee 21st & Q Sts PO Box 15779 Sacramento CA 95852

MCGRATH, PATRICK JOSEPH, bishop; b. Dublin, Ireland, July 11, 1945; came to U.S., 1970; Grad., St. John's Coll. Sem., Waterford, Ireland; student, Lateran U., Rome. Ordained priest Roman Cath. Ch., 1970, titular bishop of Allegheny. Aux. bishop Archdiocese San Francisco, 1989—. Office: Archdiocese San Francisco Chancery Office 445 Church St San Francisco CA 94114-1720*

MCGRAW, SUSAN CATHERINE, interior designer; b. Long Beach, Calif., Apr. 16, 1945; d. Thomas Printis and Mary Ruth (Reese) Gregg; m. Don George McGraw, Nov. 21, 1964; children: DeAnna Coulombe, Katrina Daymude. Dental assistant diploma, Career Tng. Inst., 1964. Cert. interior designer, 1993. Ptnr., buyer The Corner, Garden Grove, Calif., 1971-79; interior designer Kris Noel & Assoc., Huntington Beach, Calif., 1980-85; owner, designer A.I. Designs, Huntington Beach, Calif., 1986-94; ptnr., designer Ross-McGraw Studio, Huntington Beach, Calif., 1994—. Bd. dirs. Parent Help USA, Huntington Beach, 1992; sec. Seacliff Home Owners Assn., Huntington Beach, 1992-93; v.p. way and means Huntington Youth Shelter Guild, Huntington Beach, 1994—. Mem. Am. Soc. Interior Design (profl. mem.).

MCGREGOR, JAMES ALLEN, obstetrician/gynecologist; b. Hawkesbury, Ont., Can., Aug. 2, 1944; came to U.S., 1947; s. James Duncan and Margaret Eleanor (Moyle) McG.; children: Alison, Andrew, Margaret. AB, Dartmouth Coll., 1966; MDCM, McGill U., 1970. Diplomate Am. Coll. Obstetricians and Gynecologists. Prof. obstetrics and gynecology U. Colo. Sch. Medicine, Denver, 1977—. Bd. dirs. Planned Parenthood, Denver, 1985-88. Office: U Colo Health Scis Inst Obstetrics and Gynecology 4200 E 9th Ave Denver CO 80220-3706

MCGROGAN, MICHAEL PATRICK, molecular and cell biologist; b. San Francisco, Apr. 4, 1947; s. John Thomas and Venetia Almeta (Wideman) McG.; m. Sharol Kay Hudson, Sept. 13, 1969; 1 child, Melissa Catherine. Student, U. Mo., St. Louis, 1965-67; BA in Microbiology, U. Mo., Columbia, 1969; student, St. Louis U., 1971-73; PhD in Molecular and Cell Biology, Wash. U., St. Louis, 1977. Postdoctoral rschr. Wash. U. Med. Sch., St. Louis, 1977-78; NCI postdoctoral fellow dept. bio. scis. Stanford (Calif.) U., 1978-81; scientist, rsch. group leader molecular biology dept. Cetus Corp., Emeryville, Calif., 1981-85; sr. scientist, rsch. group leader molecular biology dept. InVitron Corp., Redwood City, Calif., 1985-90; dir., sr. staff scientist Dept. of Gene Expression, Berlex Biosci., Alameda, Calif., 1990-93; chief scientific officer Sierra BioSource, Gilroy, Calif., 1993—; project leader Interleukin 2 (IL-2) Cetus Corp., 1982-84; primary investigator Protease Nexin, InVitron Corp., Redwood City, 1986-88; rsch. leader for granulocyte proteins project, 1988-90. Contbr. articles to profl. jours.; patentee in field. Fellow NDEA, St. Louis U., 1971; rsch. grantee NIH, Wash. U., 1973. Mem. AAAS, Am. Soc. of Microbiology. Office: Sierra BioSource 1180 Day Rd # C Gilroy CA 95020-9308

MC GUIGAN, FRANK JOSEPH, psychologist, educator; b. Oklahoma City, Dec. 7, 1924. BA, UCLA, 1945, MA, 1949; PhD, U. So. Calif., 1950. Instr. Pepperdine Coll., 1949-50; asst. prof. U. Nev., 1950-51; rsch. assoc. Psychol. Corp., 1950-51; rsch. scientist, sr. rsch. scientist, acting dir. rsch. Human Resources Rsch. Office, George Washington U., 1951-55; prof. psychology (Hollins Coll.), Roanoke, Va., 1955-76; chmn. dept. (Hollins Coll.), 1955-76; rsch. prof. (Grad. Sch.); prof. dept. psychology, dep. psychiatry and behavioral scis. (Sch. Medicine); dir. Performance Rsch. Lab., Inst. Advanced Study, U. Louisville, 1976-83; prof. psychology, dir. Inst. Stress Mgmt. U.S. Internat. U., San Diego, 1983—; adj. prof. psychiatry and behavioral scis. U. Louisville Sch. Medicine, 1986—; adj. rsch. prof. N.C. State U., 1970-72; vis. prof. U. Hawaii, summer 1965, U. Calif., Santa Barbara, 1966, Hiroshima Shudo U., 1984; Nat. Acad. Scis. vis. scientist, Hungary, 1975, Bulgaria, 1987; sr. rsch. fellow Naval Health Rsch. Ctr., summer 1991. Author: numerous books in field including The Biological Basis of Behavior, 1963, Contemporary Studies in Psychology, 1972, Cognitive Psychophysiology - Principles of Covert Behavior, 1978, Experimental Psychology: Methods of Research, 6th edit., 1993, Psychophysiological Measurement of Covert Behavior—A Guide for the Laboratory, 1979, Calm Down—A Guide for Stress and Tension Control, 2d edit., 1992, Stress and Tension Control: Procs. of Internat., Interdisciplinary Conf. on Stress and Tension Control, 1980, vol. 2, 1984, vol. 3, 1989; (with Edmund Jacobson) cassettes Self-Directed Progressive Relaxation Training Instructions, 1981, Critical Issues in Psychology, Psychiatry and Physiology, 1986, Biological Psychology--A Cybernetic Science, 1994; editor numerous works in field.; editor, Internat. Jour. Stress Mgmt.; contbr. articles to profl. jours.; mem. editorial bd. Archiv fur Arzneitherapie, Biofeedback and Self-regulation, Activitas Nervosae Superioris. Served with USNR, 1942-46. Recipient award for outstanding contbns. to edn. in psychology Am. Psychol. Found., 1973, Blue medal of honor Union Scientists Bulgaria, 1980, medal of Sechenov USSR Acad. Med. Scis., 1983, medal of Anohkin, 1984, Pres.'s medal U. Hiroshima-Shudo, 1982, medal Okayama U., 1987, medal Tbilisi (USSR) Inst. Physiology, 1989, Edmund Jacobson award for stress mgmt., 1995, Gold medal award for lifetime achievement in application of psychology Am. Psychol. Found., 1995. Fellow APA, Internat. Soc. Rsch. on Aggression; mem. Am. Assn. Advancement of Tension Control (now Internat. Stress Mgmt. Assn.) (exec. dir. 1973-82, pres. 1985-89, exec. dir. 1992—, chmn. bd. dirs.), Pavlovian Soc. (mem. exec. bd. 1973—, pres. 1975-86, editor, chmn. publ. bd. Pavlovian Jour. Biol. Sci.), Am. Physiol. Soc., Biofeedback Soc. Am., Internam. Soc. Psychology, Internat. Congress of Applied Psychology, Psychonomic Soc., Soc. Psychophysiol. Rsch., Bulgarian Soc. for Psychiatry (hon.), Sigma Xi. Office: US Internat U Inst for Stress Mgmt 10455 Pomerado Rd San Diego CA 92131-1717

MCGUINNESS, MARGARET ELIZABETH, pharmacist; b. Christchurch, Canterbury, New Zealand, Oct. 22, 1956; came to U.S., 1989; d. John Southward and Gloria Shirley (Whiteacre) McG. Diploma in pharmacy, Cen. Inst. Tech., Wellington, New Zealand, 1978; postgrad. diploma in hosp. pharmacy, U. Sydney, Australia, 1980; PharmD, Mercer U., 1991. Pharmacist North Canterbury Hosp. Bd., Christchurch, 1977-80, Dodds Pharmacy, Christchurch, 1980-82; lectr. pharmacy practice Cen. Inst. Tech. Sch. Pharmacy, 1982-86, 87-89; pharmacist N.W. Thames Regional Health Authority, London, 1986, 87, rsch. pharmacist, 1986-87, drug info. pharmacist, 1989-90, 90-91; resident in clin. pharmacy (internal medicine) U. Tex. Health Sci. Ctr., San Antonio, 1991-92, fellow in clin. scis. (internal medicine), 1992-94; asst. prof. Coll. Pharmacy Oreg. State U., Portland, 1994—; lectr. pharmacology New Zealand Inst. Med. Reps., 1982-89; cons. pharmacist Consumer mag., N.Z., 1984-86. Author: Pharmacology for Medical Representatives, 1984, 2d edit., 1989; also articles. Dean's and internat. scholar Mercer U., 1989-91. Mem. Pharm. Soc. New Zealand (coord. continuing edn. 1982-84, 88-89, pres. Wellington br. 1985, J.R. Robertson scholar 1980, grantee Edn. and Rsch. Found. 1989), Royal Pharm. Soc. Gt. Britain, Hosp. Pharmacists Assn. New Zealand, Am. Soc. Hosp. Pharmacists, Am. Pharm. Soc., Phi Kappa Phi, Phi Delta Chi. Office: Oreg State Univ Coll Pharmacy GH 212 3181 SW Sam Jackson Park Rd Portland OR 97201-3011

MCGUIRE, DIANA HARMAN, dietitian, educator; b. Blackfoot, Idaho, Mar. 18, 1950; d. Thomas Carl and Ruby Gertrude (Ward) Harman; m. William Kent McGuire, Mar. 12, 1976; children: Kristina, William Jr., Robert, Natalie, Julianne. BS in Clin. Dietetics, Brigham Young U., 1974, MS in Nutrition Sci., 1976. Registered dietitian; cert. nutrition support dietitian. Clin. dietitian Utah Valley Hosp., Provo, 1976; instr. dept. nutrition U. Utah, Salt Lake City, 1978; dietitian WIC, Farmington, Utah, 1978; clin. dietitian Davis North Hosp., Layton, Utah, 1979; cons. dietitian Tanner Med. Clinic, Layton, 1979-88; clin. dietitian McKay-Dee Hosp., Ogden, Utah, 1980-88; clin. instr. nutrition and food sci. dept. Utah State U., Logan, 1986-88; clin. instr. food sci. and nutrition dept. Brigham Young U., Provo, 1988—. Contbg. author: Handbook of Clinical Dietetics, 2d edit., 1976, 5th edit., 1986, 6th edit., 1994. Precinct sec. Rep. Party, Fruit Hts., Utah, 1993-94; mem. cmty. coun. Knowlton Elem. Sch., Farmington, 1993—; active Boy Scouts Am., 1990—, 4-H, 1985-88, 94—. Named to Outstanding Young Women of Am., 1979; Am. Dietetic Assn. scholar, 1973, 75; Brigham Young U. scholar, 1968. Mem. Am. Dietetic Assn., Utah Dietetic Assn. (found. dir. 1993-95, scholarship com. 1994, nominating com. 1987-88), Utah Nutrition Coun. Mormon. : Brigham Young U Food Sci and Nutrition Dept 2218 Sflc Provo UT 84602-1041

MCGUIRE, JAMES CHARLES, aircraft company executive; b. St. Louis, Aug. 8, 1917; s. John Patrick and Anna Beulah (Erbar) McG.; A.B., Washington U., St. Louis, 1949, M.A. (Univ. fellow), 1953, Ph.D., 1954; m. Eunice Leota Sloop, Mar. 21, 1942 (div. June 1948); 1 child: Judith Lynn; m. Ingrid Elisabeth Getreu, Sept. 16, 1954. Research assoc. Ohio State U., 1953-56; rsch. psychologist Aeromed. Lab., Wright-Patterson AFB, Ohio, 1956-59; group supr. Boeing Airplane Co., Seattle, 1959-61; dept. mgr. Internat. Electric Corp., Paramus, N.J., 1961-62; sr. human factors scientist System Devel. Corp., Santa Monica, Calif., 1962-67; v.p. Booz-Allen Applied Rsch., Saigon, Vietnam, 1967-72; v.p. Assoc. Cons. Internat., Saigon, 1972-75, Bethesda, Md., 1975-78; br. chief Human Factors, System Tech. Devel., 1978-82; prin. staff engr. tech. modernization methodology Douglas Aircraft Co., Long Beach, Calif., 1982-85; program mgr. cockpit automation tech. program, Northrop Aircraft div., Hawthorne, Calif., 1985-87; sect. mgr. aircraft programs human factors engring. dept. Douglas Aircraft Co., Long Beach, 1987—, sr. staff engr. Crew Systems Tech., 1990-93; prin. engr. tech. McDonnell Douglas Aerospace Transport Aircraft, 1993-94; prin. engr.-scientist, crew sys. tech., advanced transport aircraft devel., McDonnell Douglas Aerospace, 1995—; lectr. Nat. Def. Coll., Vietnamese Armed Forces, Saigon, 1971. Served with AUS, 1940-46. Decorated Bronze Star medal with oak leaf cluster; recipient Tech. Svc. First Class medal Republic South Vietnam Armed Forces, 1968. Mem. Am. Psychol. Assn., IEEE, Computer Soc. of IEEE, Human Factors Soc., Am. Assn. Artificial Intelligence, Phi Beta Kappa, Sigma Xi. Republican. Home: 23201 Mindanao Cir Monarch Beach CA 92629-3625 Office: McDonnell Douglas Aerospace Advanced Transport Aircraft Devel 1510 Hughes Way Mail Code 71-11 Long Beach CA 90810-1870

MCGUIRE, JOSEPH SMITH, physician; b. Logan, W.Va., Apr. 19, 1931; s. Joseph Smith and Ruby Kellogg (Rose) McG.; m. Margaret Michael, June 5, 1954 (div. 1966); children: Mary Elizabeth, Joseph Smith III, Alison Litz, D. Thompson; m. Mary Lake Polan, 1979, Joshua Lake, Lindsay Kellogg, Scott Hunter. AB, W.Va. U., 1952; MD, Yale U., 1955. Clin. assoc. NIH, Bethesda, Md., 1956-59; asst. prof. dermatology Yale U., New Haven, 1961-64, assoc. prof., 1964-72; prof., 1972-90; Carl Herzog prof. dermatology, pediatrics Stanford (Calif.) U., 1990—. Sr. asst. surgeon USPHS, 1956-59. Mem. Am Soc. Clin. Investigation, Am. Soc. Cell Biology, Soc. Investigative Dermatology (pres. 1988-89), Am. Dermatol. Assn., Am. Acad. Dermatology, Pacific Dermatology Assn. Office: Stanford U Dept Dermatology MSLS P-204 Stanford CA 94305-5486

MCGUIRE, MICHAEL FRANCIS, plastic and reconstructive surgeon; b. St. Louis, Oct. 4, 1946; s. Arthur Patrick and Virginia Claribel (Gannon) McG. BA, Columbia U., 1968, D of Medicine, 1972. Diplomate Am. Bd. Surgery, Am. Bd. Plastic Surgery. Intern UCLA, 1972-73, resident in gen. surgery, 1973-77, resident in plastic surgery, 1978-80; fellow in plastic surgery rsch. Stanford (Calif.) U., 1977-78; traveling fellow in plastic surgery Gt. Britain, 1980; chief plastic surgery L.A. County-Olive View Med. Ctr., Sylmar, Calif., 1980-85; pvt. practice Santa Monica, Calif., 1980—; bd. dirs. Calif. Med. Rev., Inc.; pres. Pacific Coast Plastic Surgery Ctr., Inc., Santa Monica, 1987—; asst. clin. prof. surgery UCLA, 1980—, mem. exec. com., 1993—; vice chmn. plastic surgery St. John's Hosp., Santa Monica, 1987-91, chmn. plastic surgery, 1992—; dir. cleft palate team L.A. County-Olive View Med. Ctr., 1986—; mem. ops. com. Med. Profl. Group, 1995. Charter patron L.A. Music Ctr. Opera, 1983—, sponsoring patron L.A. County Art Mus., 1986—, patron Colleague Helpers in Philanthropic Svc., Bel Air, Calif., 1987, 93, 95. Fellow ACS, Royal Soc. Medicine; mem. Am. Soc. Plastic and Reconstructive Surgeons, Inc., Am. Assn. for Accreditation of Ambulatory Surgery Facilities (legis. chmn. 1995, mem. ops. com. 1995), L.A. County Med. Assn. (v.p. 1995-96), Calif. Soc. Plastic Surgery (exec. com., auditor 1988-89, program chmn. 1990, exec. coun. 1991-94, treas. 1994—), Calif. Med. Assn. (del. 1992, 93, 94, 95), Alpha Omega Alpha. Democrat. Episcopalian. Office: 1301 20th St Ste 460 Santa Monica CA 90404-2050

MC GUIRE, MICHAEL JOHN, environmental engineer; b. San Antonio, June 29, 1947; s. James Brendan and Opal Mary (Brady) McG.; BS in Civil Engring., U. Pa., 1969; MS in Environ Engring., Drexel U., 1972, PhD in Environ. Engring., 1977; diplomate Am. Acad. Environ. Engring.; m. Deborah Marrow, June 19, 1971; children: David, Anna. San. engr. Phila. Water Dept., 1969-73; rsch. assoc. Drexel U., Phila., 1976-77; prin. engr. Brown & Caldwell Cons. Engrs., Pasadena, Calif., 1977-79; water quality engr. Met. Water Dist. of So. Calif., L.A., 1979-84, water quality mgr., 1984-86, dir. water quality, 1986-90, asst. gen. mgr., 1990-92; pres. McGuire Environ. Cons., Inc., Santa Monica, Calif., 1992—; cons. to subcom. on adsorbents, safe drinking water com. Nat. Acad. Scis., 1978-79; cons. mem. Techs. Workgroup USEPA, DBP Reg Neg, 1992-93. Registered profl. engr., Pa., N.J., Calif. Mem. Am. Water Works Assn. (Acad. Achievement award 1978, edn. div. chmn. 1982-83, chair taste and odor com. 1993—, Calif.-Nev. sect., chmn. water quality and resources div. 1982-83, governing bd. 1984-87, 89—, exec. com. 1989—, chmn. 1991-92, nat. dir. 1993—, trustee Research Found. 1983-86, nat. v.p. 1994—, nat. exec. com. 1994—, Fuller award, 1995), Am. Chem. Soc., ASCE, Internat. Water Supply Assn., Internat. Assn. on Water Quality (specialist group on taste and odor control 1982—, chmn. organizing com. 1991, off-flavor symposium 1987-91), Internat. Ozone Assn. (internat. bd. dirs. 1992—), Sigma Xi, Sigma Nu, Sigma Tau. Editor: (with I.H. Suffet) Activated Carbon Adsorption of Organics From the Aqueous Phase, 2 vols., 1980; Treatment of Water by Granular Activated Carbon, 1983; contbr. articles to profl. jours. Office: McGuire Environ Cons Inc 469 25th St Santa Monica CA 90402-3103

MCGUIRE, SONDRA LEE, automotive executive; b. Columbus, Ohio, Nov. 9, 1941; d. Charles Richard Whitehurst and LaVerne Adele (Harlow) Battelle; m. Brandt B. Shumate, June 2, 1958 (div. Dec. 1978); children: Raymond Murl, Russell James; m. Clyde Leon McGuire, May 29, 1982. Student, U. Ariz., 1975-76, Pima Coll., 1977-81. Sales audit, payroll Levy's Dept. Store, Tucson, 1960-61; office mgr. Shumate's Custom Interiors, Tucson, 1962-78; chief exec. officer Auto Trimmer's Supply, Tucson, 1978—; cons. curriculum Sunnyside High Sch., Tucson, 1983. Contbr. articles to profl. jours. Mem. Exec. Women's Coun., So. Ariz., 1980; dir. Girls in Action, Sabino Rd. Bapt. Ch.; asst. dir. Girls in Action Catalina Assn. 65 chs. Recipient Cert. of Appreciation award Beacon Found., 1984. Mem. Auto Service Industry Assn. (program chmn. 1985, exec. bd. dirs. Auto Trim div.1981-88, chairperson 1987, 88, cert. of appreciation award 1985, 87, Hall of Fame plaque 1987), Tucson C. of C. Republican. Baptist. Home: 4351 N Summer Set Loop Tucson AZ 85715 Office: Auto Trimmers Supply Inc 2958 E 22nd St Tucson AZ 85713-2010

MCGUIRE, THOMAS ROGER, distribution company executive; b. Marshfield, Wis., Aug. 29, 1943; s. James Gilbert and Gene Elizabeth (Connor) McG.; m. Patricia Mae Ainsworth, Aug. 25, 1962; children: Elizabeth Anne, Amy Lynn. Chief exec. officer, chmn. bd. dirs. Coast Fabrication, Inc., San Jose, Calif., 1964-83, Coast R.V., Inc., San Jose, 1977—. Republican. Methodist. Home: 1480 Calaveras Ave San Jose CA 95126-2502 Office: Coast Distbn System 1982 Zanker Rd San Jose CA 95112-4216

MCGULPIN, ELIZABETH JANE, nurse; b. Toledo, Oct. 18, 1932; d. James Orville and Leah Fayne (Helton) Welden; m. David Nelson Buster, Apr. 9, 1956 (div. Nov. 1960); children: David Hugh, James Ray, Mark Stephen; m. Fredrick Gordon McGulpin, Oct. 7, 1973. AA in Nursing, Pasadena City Coll., 1968. RN, Wash. Lic. nurse Las Encinas Hosp., Pasadena, Calif.; nurse Hopi Indian Reservation HEW, Keams Canyon, Ariz., 1969-70; nurse, enterostomal therapist Pasadena Vis. Nurse Assn., 1972-74; nurse Seattle King County Pub. Health, 1977-81; home care nurse Victorville, Calif., 1983-85; nurse Adult Family Home, Woodinville, Wash., 1986—; vol. nurse, counselor Child Protective Svcs., Victorville, 1984; realtor Century 21, Lynden, Wash., 1993—. Vol. nurse Am. Cancer Soc., Pasadena, 1973-75, United Ostomy Assn., Los Angeles, Victorville, 1973-84. Am. Cancer Soc. grantee. Mem. Nat. Assn. Realtors, Wash. Assn. Realtors, Whatcom County Assn. Realtors, Vis. Nurse Assn. (Enterostomal Therpay grantee 1973). Home: 106 Kale St Everson WA 98247-9660

MCGWIRE, MARK DAVID, professional baseball player; b. Pomona, Calif., Oct. 1, 1963; s. John and Ginger McGwire; m. Kathy McGwire; 1 child, Matthew. Student, U. So. Calif. With Oakland Athletics, 1984—; player World Series, 1988, 89, 90. Named Am. League Rookie of Yr. Baseball Writers' Assn. Am., 1987, Sporting News, 1987; recipient Gold Glove award, 1990; named to All-Star team, 1987-92; recipient Silver Slugger Award, 1992; Am. League Home Run Leader, 1987; mem. U.S. Olympic Baseball Team, 1984. Office: Oakland Athletics Oakland-Alameda County Coliseum 7000 Coliseum Way Oakland CA 94621-1945*

MCHARDY, JOHN ALEXANDER, lawyer; b. Mpls., Apr. 17, 1933; s. John Alexander and Marjorie Jean (Kehr) McH.; m. Gail Frances Gustafson, Mar. 27, 1955; children: Heather, Scott, Stuart, Gregor, Fiona, Megan. BSL, U. Minn., 1955, JD, 1957. Bar: Minn. 1957, Colo. 1987. Atty. Burkhardt & Dunlap, Plainview, Minn., 1957-67; commd. 2d lt. U.S. Army, 1967, advanced through grades to lt. col.; judge advocate U.S. Army, worldwide, 1967-87; ret. U.S. Army, 1987; legal access atty. Colo. Dept. Corrections, Canon City, 1992—; bd. dirs. Pueblo West Met. Dist., 1991—. County atty. Wabasha County, Wabasha, Minn., 1964-67. Decorated Bronze Star. Mem. Assn. U.S. Army, Ret. Officers Assn., Am. Legion, VFW. Republican. Mormon. Home: 382 S Escalante Plz Pueblo West CO 81007-2212

MCHENRY, PATRICIA ROSE, state agency administrator; b. Burbank, Calif., Mar. 24, 1950; d. Clarence U. and Neota Etta (Common) Benton. BA with distinction, U. N.Mex., 1977. Office mgr. S.W. Cable TV, Espanola, N.Mex., 1978-79; exec. asst. Baha'i' Internat. Ctr., Haifa, Israel, 1980-83; exec. mgmt. analyst N.Mex. Dept. Fin. and Adminstrn., Santa Fe, 1979, exec. budget analyst, 1983-85; sr. fiscal analyst N.Mex. Legis. Fin. Com., Santa Fe, 1985-88; dep. dir. adminstrv. svcs. div. N.Mex. Dept. Corrections, Santa Fe, 1988-89; adminstr. data processing N.Mex. Human Svc. Dept., Santa Fe, 1990-92; dep. dir. property control div. N.Mex. Gen. Svc. Dept., Santa Fe, 1992—. Mem. Baha'i' Faith. Office: NMex Gen Svc Dept Property Control Divsn 1100 S Saint Francis Dr Santa Fe NM 87505-4147

MCHUGH, BETSY BALDWIN, sociologist, educator, business owner; b. Concord, N.H.; d. Walter Killenbeck and Elizabeth Alice (Hunt) Slater; m. Michael Joseph McHugh, Dec. 19, 1954; children: Betsy, Michael. MusB in Vocal Music, Syracuse (N.Y.) U., 1954; grad. student, Cornell U. Tchr. pub. schs. Juneau, Alaska, 1966-85; owner/founder Cashé Pub. Co., Nikish Ki Lodge and Youth Camps, Baldwin Enterprises. Named one of Alaska's Outstanding Educators, Gov. Alaska Woman's Commn., 1985, Una of Yr., 1993, 94, Internat. Una of Yr., 1993, 94, one of 2000 Most Notable Women, Woman of Yr. 1994, Better Profl. Women, 1993, 94. Mem. Can. Nat. Libr., Bus. Assn. N.Y. State, Libr. of Congress, Can. Bus. D.C. C. of C., Mex. C. of C., Sigma Delta Chi. Office: Cashé Pub Co PO Box 22031 Juneau AK 99801

MCHUGH, JAMES JOSEPH, retired naval officer, retired associate dean; b. Phila., Aug. 12, 1930; s. James Joseph and Patience Mary (McGowan) McH.; m. Rita Marie Huber, May 21, 1960; children: Margaret Marie, James Joseph IV. B.A. (with honors), U. Pa., 1951, LL.B., 1954; M.S. in Internat. Relations, George Washington U., 1972. Bar: Pa. 1955. Commd. ensign U.S. Navy, 1955, advanced through grades to rear adm., 1980; legal officer Naval Air Station, Point Mugu, Calif., 1955-58; staff officer Office Judge Adv. Gen., Washington, 1959-63; staff instr. U.S. Naval Justice Sch., Newport, R.I., 1963-65; counsel Bur. Naval Personnel, Washington, 1965-68; asst. fleet judge adv. to comdr. in chief U.S. Pacific Fleet, 1968-71; spl. counsel to chief naval ops. Washington, 1972-76; officer in charge Naval Legal Service Office, San Francisco, 1976-78; asst. judge adv. gen. Washington, 1978-80; dep. judge adv. gen. Alexandria, Va., 1980-82, judge adv. gen., 1982-84; asst. dean McGeorge Sch. Law, Sacramento, 1984-86, assoc. dean, 1987-93. Decorated D.S.M., Legion of Merit (2), Meritorious Svc. medal (2), Navy Commendation medal. Mem. ABA, Order of Coif (hon.), Phi Beta Kappa. Republican. Roman Catholic. Home: 4704 Olive Oak Way Carmichael CA 95608-5663

MC HUGH, MARGARET ANN GLOE, psychologist; b. Salt Lake City, Nov. 8, 1920; d. Harold Henry and Olive (Warenski) Gloe; m. William T. McHugh, Oct. 1, 1943; children: Mary Margaret McHugh-Shuford, William Michael, Michelle. BA, U. Utah, 1942; MA in Counseling and Guidance, Idaho State U., 1964; PhD in Counseling Psychology, U. Oreg., 1970. Lic. psychologist; nat. cert. counselor . Tchr. kindergarten, Idaho Falls, Idaho, 1951-62, tchr. high sch. English, 1962-63; counselor Counseling Center, Idaho State U., Pocatello, 1964-67; instr. U. Oreg., Eugene, 1967-70; asst. prof. U. Victoria, B.C., Can., 1970-76; therapist Peninsula Counseling Center, Port Angeles and Sequim, Wash., 1976-81, McHugh & Assocs. Counseling Center, 1981—. Served with WAVES, 1943-44. Mem. APA, ACA, Am. Assn. Marriage and Family Therapy, Wash. Psychol. Assn. (rsch. women issues, rels's., depression and women, sexual abuse, adults with childhood and abuse). Home: 1175 Cameron Rd Sequim WA 98382-9437

MCILVAINE, WILLIAM BROWN, JR., pediatric anesthesiologist; b. Lake Forest, Ill., Apr. 8, 1952; s. William Brown McIlvaine Sr. and Adele Ellis (Arrowsmith) Douglas; m. Stephan Barnes Parsons, Oct. 30, 1946; children: Julia Margaret Fenno, William Brown III. BA with honors, Stanford U., 1974; MD, CM, McGill U., Montreal, Can., 1978. Diplomate Am. Bd. Anesthesiology, Nat. Bd. Med. Examiners. Intern Queen Elizabeth Hosp., Montreal, 1978-79; resident in anaesthesia McGill U., Montreal, 1979-82; fellow in pediat. anesthesia Children's Meml. Hosp. & Northwestern U., Chgo., 1982-83; asst. prof. anesthesiology Health Scis. Ctr. U. Colo., Denver, 1983-85, asst. clin. prof. anesthesiology, 1985—, dir. pediat. anesthesia Univ. Hosp., 1983-85, med. dir. operating rms. Univ. Hosp., 1983-85; mem. staff Children's Hosp., Denver, 1985—, Littleton (Colo.) Hosp., 1989—; mem. courtesy staff Aurora (Colo.) Regional Med. Ctr., 1990—, Rose Med. Ctr., Denver, 1990—, Porter Meml. Hosp., Englewood, Colo., 1993—, Swedish Med. Ctr., Englewood, 1993—; mem. active staff Presbyn.-St. Luke's Med. Ctr., Denver, 1990—, St. Joseph's Hosp., Denver, 1990—; assoc. examiner Am. Bd. Anesthesiology, 1988—; vis. prof. pediat. anesthesia Richland Meml. Hosp. and U. S.C., Columbia, 1989; presenter Hosp. for Sick Children, Toronto, 1983, Children's Hosp., Denver, 1983; presenter numerous confs. Author: (with others) Ocular Therapeutics and Pharmacology, 1985, Textbook of Paediatric Anesthetic Practice, 1989, Clinical Practice of Regional Anesthesia, 1991, Acute Pain: Mechanisms and Management, 1992; contbr. articles to profl. jours. Fellow Royal Coll. Physicians and Surgeons (Can.), Am. Acad. Pediat.; mem. Am. Soc. Anesthesiologists, Can. Anesthetists' Soc., Colo. Med. Soc., Denver Med. Soc., Internat. Anesthesia Rsch. Soc., Soc. for Pediat. Anesthesia. Home: 191 University Blvd Ste 314 Denver CO 80206-4613 Office: Pediat Anesthesia Cons PO Box 18248 Denver CO 80218-0248

MCINNIS, SCOTT STEVE, congressman, lawyer; b. Glenwood Springs, Colo., May 9, 1953; s. Kohler McInnis and Carol Kreir; m. Lori McInnis; children: Daxon, Tessa, Andrea. BA, Ft. Lewis Coll., 1975; JD, St. Mary's Law Sch., 1980. Atty. Delaney & Balcomb P.C., Glenwood Springs, Colo., 1981—; mem. Colo. Ho. of Reps., 1984-93; majority leader, 1990-93; mem. 103d-104th Congresses from 3d Colo. Dist., 1993—; chmn. agrl. livestock and natural resources com., 1986-90, mem. rules com. Recipient Florence Sabin award, 1984, Guardian of Small Bus. award Nat. Fed. Ind. Bus., 1990, Lee Atwater Leadership award, 1991, and various awards from United Vets. Commn.; named Legislator of Decade and Legislator of Yr by Colo. Ski Country and Colo. Wildlife Fund. Mem. Elks, Rotary, Phi Delta Phi. Republican. Roman Catholic. Office: US Ho of Reps 215 Cannon HOB Washington DC 20515-0603*

MCINNIS, SUSAN MUSÉ, corporate communications specialist; b. Seattle, July 22, 1955; d. Emmett Emory Jr. and Florence Howardine (McAteer) McI. BSBA, U. Denver, 1977; cert. in environ. design, UCLA, 1985; MA in Journalism, Calif. State U., Fullerton, 1992. Researcher Denver Gen. Hosp., summer 1973; mktg. coord. 3M Bus. Products, Emeryville, Calif., 1978-79; spl. libr. Reel Grobman & Assocs., L.A., 1981-83; tchr. Mayfield Sr. Sch., Pasadena, Calif., 1985-87; advt. coord. Reynolds Advt., 1987; cmty. and employee rels. mgr. Calif.-Am. Water Co. (oper. co. Am. Water Works), San Marino, Calif., 1988—. Mem. Am. Water Works Assn. (cert. water distbn.), Pub. Rels. Soc. Am., Kiwanis (pres. Duarte, Calif. chpt. 1994-95).

MCINTOSH, GARY LYNN, theology educator, consultant, writer; b. Colorado Springs, Colo., Feb. 9, 1947; s. William Vance and Billie Colleen (Thompson) McI.; m. Carol Ann Kurylow, June 21, 1968; children: Gary Lynn II, Aaron James. BA, Rockmont Coll., 1970; MDiv, Western Bapt. Sem., 1975; DMin, Fuller Sch. Theology, 1982. Sr. pastor Grace Bapt. Ch., San Bernardino, Calif., 1976-83; v.p. consulting svcs. Ch. Growth Inc., Pasadena, Calif., 1983-86; dir. DMin program, prof. practical theology Talbot Sch. Theology, La Mirada, Calif., 1986—. Co-author: Finding Them; Keeping Them, 1992, The Issachar Factor, 1994; author: (with others) Handbook of Practical Theology, Vol. 2, 1994; author: Three Generations, 1995, The Exodus Principle, 1995; editor (newsletter) Church Growth Network, 1989—. Mem., bd. dirs. Conservative Bapts. Assn., Anaheim, Calif., 1980-83; founder, dir. The Ch. Growth Network, San Bernardino, 1989—; chmn., bd. dirs. Christian H.S., San Bernardino, 1991-94. Mem. Am. Soc. Ch. Growth (pres. 1995—), Assn. Doctor Min. Dirs. (pres. 1995—). Office: Talbot Sch Theology 13800 Biola Ave La Mirada CA 90639-0002

MCINTOSH, GREGORY STEPHEN, artist; b. Ojai, Calif., May 7, 1946; s. Donald Frederick James and Hedwig Marie (Berend) McI. BA, Santa Clara U., 1968, MA, 1971. Cert. secondary tchr. history and fine arts, Calif. Teaching asst. fine arts Santa Clara (Calif.) U., 1967-70; instr. fine arts, asst. prof. history St. Patrick's Coll., Mountain View, Calif., 1971-72; profl. artist Ojai, Calif., 1973—. Exhibited works at shows in Ventura County Hist. Mus., 1982-84, Ojai Art Ctr., 1985—, Long Beach Mus. Art, 1987, Vizcaya Mus., Miami, 1988, Tampa (Fla.) Mus. Art, 1988, Ft. Lauderdale (Fla.) Mus. Art, 1988, Crocker Ctr., Boca Raton, Fla., 1988, Walt Disney Corp., Orlando, Fla., 1989, Alliance for the Arts, Guilford, Conn., 1990, Artist-in-Residency, Paris, 1991, City of Miami Beach, 1992, Lipsett Gallery NIH, Washington, 1993, New Eng. Fine Arts Inst., Boston, 1993; represented in permanent collections at Library of Congress, Washington, Calif. Palace of Legion of Honor, San Francisco, San Francisco Mus. of Modern Art, L.A. County Mus. of Art, The Oakland Mus., Muskegon (Mich.) Mus. of Art. Maestro grantee Calif. Arts Coun., 1983. Mem. Pastel Soc. Am. Office: PO Box 961 Ojai CA 93024-0961

MCINTOSH, JAMES ALBERT, lawyer; b. Long Beach, Calif., Nov. 2, 1933; s. James H. and Grace I. (Greenwell) McI.; m. Earlene Rae Bagley, June 22, 1956; children: Richard, Robert, Debra, Bruce, Linda, Sheri, Diane. BS, U.S. Mil. Acad., 1955; JD, U. Utah Law Sch., 1961. Bar: Utah 1961. Law clk. to justice Utah Supreme Ct., 1960-61; dep. county atty. Salt Lake County, 1962-66; legal adv. flood control and storm drainage matters Bd. Salt Lake County Commrs., 1967-73; prin. James A. McIntosh & Assocs., Salt Lake City, 1974-77; pvt. practice, Salt Lake City, 1961-74, 1984-85; v.p., ptnr. McMurray & McIntosh, 1977-84; officer, pres. James A. McIntosh & Assocs. P.C., 1985—. Trustee, U.S. Bankruptcy Ct. Utah, 1962-69. 1st lt. airborne artillery U.S. Army, 1955-58. Recipient Am. Jurisprudence award, 1961, Jumpmaster Badge, U.S. Army Ranger Tab. Mem. Utah State Bar, Utah Trial Lawyers Assn., Salt Lake County Bar Assn., Phi Delta Phi, Exchange Club (dist. pres. 1980-81). LDS. Office: James A McIntosh & Assocs PC Intrade Bldg S 1399 S 700 E Ste 17 Salt Lake City UT 84105-2149

MCINTURFF, KIM, design engineer, mathematician; b. Spokane, Wash., June 13, 1948; s. Don R. and Mae (Lancaster) McI.; m. Denise E. Lockhart, July 17, 1976; children: Ian, Margo. BS in Math., Stanford U., 1971; MA in Math., U. Calif., Santa Barbara, 1976, MSEE, 1986. Software engr. E Systems, Goleta, Calif., 1978-82; design engr. Raytheon ESD, Goleta, Calif., 1983—. Contbr. articles on antenna design and analysis to profl. jours.; copatentee multibeam antenna system. Mem. Math. Assn. Am. Home: 5433 Thames Ct Santa Barbara CA 93111-1074 Office: E Systems 6380 Hollister Ave Goleta CA 93117

MCINTYRE, GARY ALLEN, plant pathology educator; b. Portland, Oreg., July 16, 1938; s. John H. and Onie Marie (Meihoff) McI.; m. Loene Beneva, Sept. 1, 1963; children: Paula Lynn, Laura Ann. BS, Oreg. State U., 1960, PhD, 1964. Asst. prof. botany and plant pathology U. Maine, Orono, 1963-68, assoc prof., 1968-73, prof., 1973-75, chmn. botany, plant pathology dept., 1969-75; prof., chmn. botany, plant pathology Colo. State U., Ft. Collins, 1975-84, prof., head plant pathology and weed sci. dept., 1984—; Coordinator Western Regional Integrated Pest Mgmt. program, 1979—. Mem. Am. Phytopathol. Soc., Potato Assn., Phi Kappa Phi, Phi Sigma Soc., Soc. Sigma Xi, Gamma Sigma Delta. Office: Colo State U Dept Plant Pathology/ Weed Sci Fort Collins CO 80523

MCINTYRE, GUY MAURICE, professional football player; b. Thomasville, Ga., Feb. 17, 1961. Student, U. Ga. Offensive guard San Francisco 49ers, 1984-94; played in Super Bowl XIX, 1984, XXIII, 1988, XXIV, 1989. *

MCINTYRE, HUGH BAXTER, neurology educator; b. Jacksonville, Fla., June 26, 1935; s. Hugh Baxter and Helen (Watson) McI.; m. Patricia Ann Bowne, July 11, 1959; children: Anne Louise, Hugh Cameron. BS, U. Fla., 1957, MD, 1962; PhD, UCLA, 1972. Diplomate Am. Bd. Psychiatry and Neurology, Am. Bd. Qualification in Electroencephalography; lic. med. examiner, Calif., Fla. Intern straight medicine UCLA Med. Ctr., 1962-63, resident I medicine, 1963-64, resident I neurology, 1964-65, resident II neurology, 1965-66, sr. resident neurology, 1966-67; spl. rsch. fellow Nat. Inst. Nervous Disorders Harbor-UCLA Med. Ctr., 1969-72, staff physician, chief div. neurophysiology, 1972—; asst. prof. neurology in residence UCLA Sch. Medicine, 1972-74, adj. assoc. prof. neurology, adj. prof. neurology, 1972—; adj. prof. biomed. scis. U. Calif., Riverside, 1983—; assoc. chair dept. neurology Harbor-UCLA Med. Ctr., 1990—; bd. dirs. Harbor/UCLA Med. Found., Inc., 1986—; assoc. examiner Am. Bd. Psychiatry and Neurology, 1974—, Am. Bd. Clin. Neuophysiology, 1975—; civilian cons., lectr. neurology U.S. Naval Hosp., Long Beach, Calif., 1970-85; acad. cons. St. Mary Med. Ctr., Long Beach, 1982—, Long Beach Meml. Hosp., 1973—; chmn. Orange Coast Coll. Electro-Diagnostic Technician Adv. Com., 1973—; site visit team mem. Joint Rev. Com. on Edn. in EEG Tech. and Div. Allied Health and Accreditaiton of AMA, 1976—. Editor-in-chief Bull. Clin. Neuroscis., 1976-92; author: The Primary Care of Seizure Disorders, 1982, Primary Care: Symposium on Clinical Neurology, Vol. II, 1984; contbr. articles to profl. jours. Lt. comdr., M.C., USNR, 1967-69. Recipient Certs. of Appreciation, San Diego County Epilepsy Soc., 1968, Orange Coast Coll., 1989. Fellow ACP, Am Acad. Neurology, Am. EEG Soc. (com. on guidelines in EEG); mem. Am. Acad. Neurology, L.A. Soc. Neurology and Psychiatry (pres. 1979), Fedn. Western Soc. Neurol. Sci., L.A. County Med. Assn., Western Electroencephalographic Soc. (pres. 1994), Internat. Soc. Neuroendocrinology, Am. Epilepsy Soc., Calif. Epilepsy Soc. (bd. dirs., 2nd v.p. 1982-86, svc. award 1985). Republican. Presbyterian. Office: Harbor UCLA Med Ctr 1000 W Carson St Torrance CA 90502-2004

MC INTYRE, JAMES A., diversified financial services executive; b. 1932. BS, U. So. Calif., 1954. With Ernst & Ernst, L.A., 1958-63; pres. Fremont Indemnity Co., 1963-80; pres., CEO Fremont Gen. Corp., Santa Monica, Calif., 1980—. Office: Fremont Gen Corp 2020 Santa Monica Blvd Santa Monica CA 90404-2023*

MCINTYRE, NORMAN F., petroleum industry executive; b. Pangman, Sask., Can., Oct. 21, 1945; s. Donald and Jean (Cruickshank) McI.; m. Lana Jean, June 10, 1967; children: Jason Lee, Spencer James. BSc in Petroleum Engring., U. Wyo., 1971; MS in Mgmt., MIT, 1991. Various positions with Mobil Oil, U.S., Can., to 1982; group mgr. engring. offshore divsn. Petro-Can., 1982-83, gen. mgr. frontier devel. offshore divsn., 1983, v.p. frontier devel., 1983-86, v.p. prodn. devel., 1986-89; sr. v.p. western region Petro-Can. Products, 1989-90; pres. Petro-Can. Resources, Calgary, Alta., Can., 1990—; exec. v.p. Petro-Can., 1995—; dir. Panarctic Oils Ltd., Petroleum Transmission Co. Office: Petro-Canada, 150-6th Ave SW PO Box 2844, Calgary, AB Canada T2P 3E3

MCINTYRE, ROBERT MALCOLM, utility company executive; b. Portland, Oreg., Dec. 18, 1923; s. Daniel A. and Bessie W. (Earsley) McI.; m. Marilyn Westcott, Aug. 27, 1949; 1 child, Julie. BA, UCLA, 1950; postgrad., UCLA, U. So. Calif., Columbia U. With So. Calif. Gas Co. (subs. Pacific Enterprises), L.A., 1952-67, gen. sales mgr., 1967-70, v.p., 1970-74, sr. v.p., 1974-80, pres., 1980-85, chmn., chief exec. officer, 1985-88; also bd. dirs. So. Calif. Gas Co. (subs. Pacific Enterprises); regent's prof. U. Calif., Irvine. Mem. Korean Am. Centennial Commn., Huntington Libr. Soc. Fellows, L.A. Olympic Citizens Adv. Commn.; mem. bus. coun. Newport Harbor Art Mus.; mem. steering com. Orange County Bus. Com. for Arts; mem. ad hoc com. on city fin., L.A.; bd. dirs. NCCJ, Calif. Coun. Environ. and Econ. Balance, Calif. Found. Environment and Economy, L.A. United Way, Hoag Meml. Hosp.; trustee UCLA Found., L.A. Orthopaedic Hosp., mem. exec. com.; pres. Hoag Hosp. Found., L.A. Chamber Assocs. Lt. USN, 1942-46. Decorated Order of the Rising Sun with Gold Rays and Ribbon (Japan); recipient Outstanding Svc. award Mex. Am. Legal Def. Fund, 1981, Humanitarian award NCCJ, Roy Wilkins award L.A. chpt. NAACP, others. Mem. Pacific Coast Gas Assn. (past dir., 49er Club award 1979), Am. Gas Assn., Inst. Gas Tech. (trustee), U.S.-Mex. C. of C., L.A. C. of C. (past chmn. Medici award), Calif. Club, 100 Club, Big Canyon Country Club, Center Club, Pacific Club, The Lakes Country Club, Phi Kappa Psi. Republican. Presbyterian. Office: So Calif Gas Co 555 W 5th St Los Angeles CA 90013-1010

MCINTYRE, ROBERT WHEELER, conservation organization executive; b. Chgo., Aug. 26, 1936; s. Henry Langenberg and Winifred (Wheeler) McI.; m. Emily Beardsley Taylor, Oct. 12, 1961 (div. 1985); children: W. Burley, Nancy T., Oliver W., Shanna L., Amanda K.; m. Miriam de Jesus Zarate, June 23, 1990. AB in Sociology, Stanford U., 1959; MBA, Harvard U., 1964. Loan analyst Wells Fargo Bank, San Francisco, 1964-65; supr. budget analysis Ford Aerospace, Palo Alto, Calif., 1965-69; controller Allied Life Scis., San Leandro, Calif., 1969-70; ptnr. Diplomat Mfg. Co., Palo Alto, 1970-71; staff cons. Opportunity Through Ownership, San Francisco, 1971-72; gen. mgr. Quality Metal Finishers, San Francisco, 1972-73; sr. v.p., chief fin. officer The Trust for Pub. Land, San Francisco, 1973—. Adv. bd. Peninsula Open Space Trust, Menlo Park, 1978—, Resource Renewal Inst., Sausalito, 1988—, Wter Heritage Trust, Sausalito, 1988—, Dorothy Erskine Open Space Fund, San Francisco, 1978—; bd. dirs. Environ. Vols., Palo Alto, 1980—; bd. dirs., treas. Robert C. Wheeler Found., Palo Alto, 1965—. Lt. (j.g.) USNR, 1959-62. Recipient Presdl. Citation award, The Trust for Pub. Land, 1988, Spl. Svc. award, Environ. Vols., 1989. Mem. Harvard Club of N.Y., Harvard Club of Boston, Sundown Tennis Club (San Mateo). Office: The Trust for Public Land 116 New Montgomery St 4th Fl San Francisco CA 94105-3607

MCJONES, PAUL ROBERT, computer scientist, software engineer; b. Inglewood, Calif., July 6, 1949; s. Robert Wayne and Norma Jeane (Prater) McJ.; m. Raquel Atkinson, Feb. 20, 1970. BS in Engring. Math., U. Calif., Berkeley, 1971. Computer programmer Athena Programming, Redondo Beach, Calif., 1967, U. Calif., Berkeley, 1967-72, Virtual Memory Sys., Orinda, Calif., 1973-74; rsch. staff mem. IBM San Jose (Calif.) Rsch. Lab., 1974-76; cons. mem. programming staff Xerox Corp., Palo Alto, Calif., 1976-81; software designer Tandem Computers Inc., Cupertino and Austin, 1981-85; cons. software engr. Digital Equipment Corp./Sys. Rsch. Ctr., Palo Alto, 1985—. Contbr. articles to profl. jours. Fellow Assn. for Computing Machinery. Home: 710 View St Mountain View CA 94041-2151 Office: DEC Sys Rsch Ctr 130 Lytton Ave Palo Alto CA 94301-1044

MCKASSON, CHERI ANN, winery executive; b. Rockford, Ill., Dec. 27, 1964; d. Richard Kern and Andrea (Rusch) McK. BA, San Diego State U., 1987. Ter. mgr. Kelley-Clarke, Inc., Diamond Bar, Calif., 1987-88, schematics specialist, 1988-89, dist. mgr., 1989-90, divsn. mgr., 1990; regional chain mgr. Vintners Internat., Gonzales, Calif., 1990-92, regional mgr. juice and wine, 1992-93; bus. mgr. Monsieur Henri Wines, Ltd., Century City, 1993-94; v.p. Franciscan Wine Merchants, Rutherford, Calif., 1994—. Treas. Christenson Found., Irvine, Calif., 1990—, v.p., 1994, pres., 1995; wine coord. City of Hope-Harvest Ball, Duarte, Calif., 1993-95. Mem. Orange County Wine Soc. Office: Franciscan Wine Merchants 20462 Graystone Ln Huntington Beach CA 92646-5332

MC KAUGHAN, HOWARD PAUL, linguistics educator; b. Canoga Park, Calif., July 5, 1922; s. Paul and Edith (Barton) McK.; m. Barbara Jean Budroe, Dec. 25, 1943; children: Edith (Mrs. Daniel Skene Santoro), Charlotte (Ms. Charlotte Barnhart), Patricia (Mrs. Stephen B. Pike), Barbara (Mrs. Ronald Chester Bell), Judith (Mrs. Frank L. Achilles III). AB, UCLA, 1945, MTh, Dallas Theol. Sem., 1946; MA, Cornell U., 1952, PhD, 1957. Mem. linguistic research team Summer Inst. Linguistics, Mexico, 1946-52; asso. dir. Summer Inst. Linguistics, Philippines, also assoc. dir. summer sessions U. N.D., 1952-57, dir. Philippine br., 1957-61; research asst. prof. anthropology U. Wash., 1961-62; research assoc. prof., 1962-63; assoc. prof. linguistics U. Hawaii, 1963-64, prof. linguistics, 1964-88, prof. emeritus, 1988—, chmn. dept., 1963-66, dir. Pacific and Asian Linguistics Inst., 1964, 1966-69, assoc. dean grad. div., 1965-72, dean grad. div., dir. research, 1972-79, acting chancellor, 1979, interim vice chancellor acad. affairs, 1981-82, acting dir research, 1982-84, acting dean grad. div., 1982-83, dean, 1984-87, dir. research relations, 1987-88; lectr. linguistics U. Philippines, summers, 1954, 60; Fulbright vis. prof. Philippine Normal Coll.-Ateneo De La Salle Consortium, Philippines, 1977, De La Salle U., Philippines, 1992; vis. prof. lingustics Bukidnon State Coll., Malaybalay, Philippines, 1993, 94; prin. Wycliffe Sch. Linguistics, summers 1953, 61; vis. prof. Australian Nat. U., Canberra, 1970; adj. prof. linguistics U. Okla., summers 1984, 85, 86; vis. prof., head dept. linguistics Payap U., Chiang Mai, Thailand, 1989-90. Sr. scholar East-West Ctr., Honolulu, 1964; NDEA Maranao-Philippines research grantee, 1963-65; Office of Edn. Hawaii English grantee, 1965-66; NSF Jeh Language of South Vietnam grantee, 1969-70, Maranao Linguistic Studies, 1971-72, numerous other research grants. Mem. linguistic socs. Am., Philippines, Western Assn. Grad. Schs. (pres. 1978), Hawaii, Linguistic Circle N.Y., Philippine Assn. Lang. Tchrs., Hawaii Govt. Employees Assn., Phi Beta Kappa, Phi Kappa Phi. Author (with B. McKaughan): Chatino Dictionary, 1951; (with J. Forster) Ilocano: An Intensive Language Course, 1952; The Inflection and Syntax of Maranao Verbs, 1959; (with B. Macaraya): A Maranao Dictionary, 1967. Editor: Pali Language Texts: Philippines, 21 vols., 1971; The Languages of the Eastern Family of the East New Guinea Highlands Stock, 1973, Maranao Stories, 1995, Stories from the Darangen, 1994; contbr. articles, chpts. to books, sci. jours. Home: 420 S Hill Rd Mcminnville OR 97128

MCKAY, ALICE VITALICH, school system administrator; b. Seattle, Sept. 6, 1947; d. Jack S. and Phyllis (Bourne) Vitalich; m. Larry W. McKay, Aug. 14, 1973 (div. Jan. 1983). BA, Wash. State U., 1969; MEd, U. Nev., Las Vegas, 1975; EdD, U. Nev., Reno, 1986. High sch. tchr. Clark County Sch. Dist., Las Vegas, 1972-77, specialist women's sports, 1977-80, high sch. counselor, 1980-84, high sch. asst. prin., 1984—; pres. Lotus Profit, Inc., Las Vegas, 1985-86. Mem. Am. Assn. Counseling and Devel. (committee on women 1985—), Nev. State Counseling and Devel. (pres. 1985-86), Nat. Assn. Female Execs., AAUW, Phi Delta Kappa (exec. bd. 1980-82). Office: Washoe County Sch Dist 425 E 9th St Reno NV 89512-2800

MCKAY, FLOYD JOHN, journalist, educator; b. Bottineau, N.D., Oct. 18, 1935; s. Harold S. and Maude (Steinmeier) McK.; m. Dixie Ann Johnson, Mar. 29, 1957; children: Karen LeAnn McKay Wolf, David Scott. BA, Linfield Coll., 1957, MA, U. Md., 1990. Reporter Springfield (Oreg.) News, 1958-60, The Oreg. Statesman, Salem, 1960-70; news analyst Sta. KGW-TV, Portland, Oreg., 1970-86; adminstv. asst. to gov. State of Oreg., Salem, 1987-89; sr. fellow The East-West Ctr., Honolulu, 1989; assoc. prof. journalism Western Wash. U., Bellingham, 1990—; mem. steering com. Reporters' Com. for Freedom of the Press, Washington, 1980-87; cons. Ctr. for Fgn. Journalists, Washington, 1989-90. Trustee Linfield Coll., McMinnville, Oreg., 1972-78, The Catlin Gabel Sch., Portland, 1976-81. Nieman fellow Harvard U., 1967-68; recipient DuPont-Columbia Broadcast award Columbia U., 1977. Mem. Sigma Delta Chi. Office: Western Wash U Dept Journalism Bellingham WA 98225

MCKAY, KATHRYN L., historian; b. N.Y.C., May 3, 1958; d. Robert Budge and Sara Kate (Womack) McK.; m. Bryan Wane Nichols, July 7, 1990. BA in Classics, Williams Coll., 1980; MA in Am. History, U. Del., 1985. Archeol. technician Flathead Nat. Forest, Kalispell, Mont., 1988-91; owner Kathryn L. McKay, Consulting Historian, Columbia Falls, Mont., 1991—. Adv. bd. Cultural and Aesthetics Projects, Helena, Mont., 1991—; long-range planning com. Flathead County Libr., Kalispell, 1995—. Eleutherian Mills-Hagley fellow, 1983-85. Mem. Mont. Wilderness Assn.,

Mont. Preservation Alliance (sec., bd. dirs.), Mont. Hist. Soc., Soc. Indsl. Archaelogy, Save Old Main Assn. (founder). Address: 491 Eckelberry Dr Columbia Falls MT 59912-9224

MCKAY, MICHAEL DENNIS, lawyer; b. Omaha, May 12, 1951; s. John Larkin and Kathleen (Tierney) McK.; m. Christy Ann Cordwin, Apr. 22, 1978; children: Kevin Tierney, Kathleen Lindsay, John Larkin. BA in Polit. Sci. with distinction, U. Wash., 1973; JD, Creighton U., 1976. Bar: Wash. 1976, U.S. Dist. Ct. (we. dist.) Wash. 1978, U.S. Dist. Ct. (ea. dist.) Wash. 1982, U.S. Ct. Appeals (9th cir.) 1982, U.S. Supreme Ct. 1993. Sr. dep. pros. atty. King County, Seattle, 1976-81; ptnr. McKay & Gaitan, Seattle, 1981-89; U.S. atty. we. dist. Wash. Seattle, 1989-93; ptnr. Lane Powell Spears Lubersky, Seattle, 1993-95, McKay, Chadwell & Matthews PLLC, Seattle, 1995—. Bd. dirs. Mental Health North, Seattle, 1982-85, St. Joseph Sch. Bd., 1984-87, Our Lady of Fatima Sch. Commn., 1994—, Creighton U., 1988-90; mem. stadium adv. bd. Seattle Kingdome, 1987-89; state vice chmn. George Bush for Pres., 1988; mem. U.S. Atty. Gen. Adv. Com., 1991-93, vice chmn., 1992. Mem. Creighton U. Alumni Assn. (pres. 1988-90, nat. alumni bd. 1988-92), Wash. Athletic Club, Columbia Tower Club. Republican. Roman Catholic. Office: McKay Chadwell & Matthews 7201 Columbia Ctr 701 5th Ave Seattle WA 98104

MCKAY, MONROE GUNN, federal judge; b. Huntsville, Utah, May 30, 1928; s. James Gunn and Elizabeth (Peterson) McK.; m. Lucile A. Kinnison, Aug. 6, 1954; children: Michele, Valanne, Margaret, James, Melanie, Nathan, Bruce, Lisa, Monroe. B.S., Brigham Young U., 1957; J.D., U. Chgo., 1960. Bar: Ariz. 1961. Law clk. Ariz. Supreme Ct., 1960-61; assoc. firm Lewis & Roca, Phoenix, 1961-66; ptnr. Lewis & Roca, 1968-74; assoc. prof. Brigham Young U., 1974-76, prof., 1976-77; judge U.S. Ct. of Appeals (10th cir.), Denver, 1977—, chief judge, 1991—. Mem. Phoenix Community Council Juvenile Problems, 1968-74; pres. Ariz. Assn. for Health and Welfare, 1970-72; dir. Peace Corps, Malawi, Africa, 1966-68; bd. dirs., pres. Maricopa county Legal Aid Soc., 1972-74. Served with USMCR, 1946-48. Mem. ABA, Ariz. Bar Assn., Maricopa County Bar Assn., Am. Law Inst., Am. Judicature Soc., Order of Coif, Blue Key, Phi Kappa Phi. Mem. Ch. Jesus Christ of Latter-day Saints. Office: US Ct Appeals 6012 Fed Bldg 125 S State St Salt Lake City UT 84138-1102*

MC KEE, ALLEN PAGE, investment company executive; b. L.A., July 26, 1941; s. Norman C. and Eleanor (Page) McK.; BA in Econs., U. Mich., 1964; MBA, U. Calif.-Berkeley, 1971. Area relations officer internat. div. Bank of Am., San Francisco, 1967-70; investment officer BankAm. Internat. Fin. Corp., San Francisco, 1971-73; v.p. and dir. internat. investments Union Bank, San Francisco, 1973-74; pres. Montgomery Assocs., Inc., San Francisco, 1975—, dir., 1977—; mng. dir. Fal N.V., 1979-87, Willhurst Co. N.V., 1980—; dir. Hawaiian Plantations, Inc., 1981-83, Dynodata, Inc., 1983—, Analytical Products, Inc., 1984—. Served to lt. USN, 1964-67, Vietnam. Mem. World Affairs Council No. Calif., Western Assn. Venture Capitalists, Soc. Calif. Pioneers, Calif. Bus. Alumni Assn., Delta Kappa Epsilon. Republican. Club: Commonwealth of Calif. Home: 23 Turtle Rock Ct Belvedere Tiburon CA 94920-1301 Office: 505 Montgomery St Ste 680 PO Box 2230 San Francisco CA 94126

MCKEE, BYRON DUNCAN, livestock broker; b. Denver, June 24, 1935; s. B. Duncan and Adeline Janet (O'Neal) McK.; children: B. Duncan III, James John, Carole Anne. Laborer Nat. Commn. Co., 1955-56; laborer, bookkeeper John O'Dea Livestock Commn. Co., 1956-57; advt. profl. Denver Dry Goods, 1954-55; clk. and asst. store mgr. Safeway Stores, 1957-59; fat and feeder cattle buyer Armour & Co., 1959-61; feedlot mgr. Wilhelm/Mancini Feedlots, 1961-62; dir. livestock purchase and sales McKee Cattle Co., 1962-67; mgr. feedlots, purchase and sales of livestock Farr Farms Co., 1967-80; pres., founder Front Range Cattle Co., Livestock Corp. and Consulting, Greeley, Colo., 1980—. Home: 1832 26th Ave Greeley CO 80631-4915 Office: Front Range Livestock Corp 1832 26th Ave Greeley CO 80631-4915

MC KEE, JOHN ANGUS, oil company executive; b. Toronto, Ont., Can., Aug. 31, 1935; s. John William and Margaret Enid (Phippen) McK.; m. Susan Elizabeth Harley, May 30, 1970; children: John Andrew, Mary Susan. Student, U. Toronto, 1954-58, Upper Can. Coll., Port Hope, Ont., Trinity Coll. Sch., Port Hope, Ont. With Dominion Securities Corp. Ltd., Toronto, 1958-60; mng. dir. Patino Mining Group, Toronto and London, Eng., 1960-71; pres. J. Angus McKee & Assoc., 1971-83; pres., chief exec. officer Can. Occidental Petroleum Ltd., 1983-93; bd. dirs., CEO, pres., chmn. Gulfstream Resources Canada, Ltd., Calgary, Alta., 1993—; dir. Stone & Webster Can. Ltd., Big Rock Brewery Ltd., Gerling Global Ins. Group, Stone & Webster, Inc. Bd. govs. Trinity Coll. Sch.. Mem. Toronto Club, York Club, Badminton and Racquet Club, Ranchmen's Club, Calgary Petroleum Club, Knickerbocker Club (N.Y.C.), Craigleith Ski Club, Internat. Order of St. Hubert, Goodwwod Club, Alpha Delta Phi (bd. govs. and dir.). Office: Gulfstream Resources Canada Ltd, 855 2d St SW 34th Fl, Calgary, AB Canada T2P 4J8

MCKEE, MARGARET CRILE, pulmonary medicine and critical care physician; b. Cleve., Jan. 12, 1945; d. Richard List and Florence Mae (Johnson) McK. BA, Coll. Wooster, 1967; M in Regional Planning, Cornell U., 1971; MD, SUNY, Stony Brook, 1976. Diplomate Am. Bd. Internal Medicine, Pulmonary Medicine and Critical Care. Social planner Model Cities, Binghamton, N.Y., 1970-71; resident internal medicine Harlem Hosp., N.Y.C., 1976-79; physician Health Ins. Plan, Bedford-Williamsburg, N.Y., 1979-80; pulmonary fellow Columbia Presbyn. Med. Ctr., N.Y.C., 1980-82; chief of medicine Phoenix Indian Med. Ctr., 1983-92; pvt. practice Ariz. Med. Clinic, Sun City, Ariz., 1992—. Mem. Am. Coll. Chest Physicians, Am. Thoracic Soc., Soc. of Critical Care Medicine, Union of Concerned Scientists, Sierra Club. Methodist. Office: Ariz Med Clinic 13640 N Plaza Del Rio Blvd Peoria AZ 85381-4848

MCKEE, MELISSA MARIE, animator, artist; b. Santa Rosa, Calif., Nov. 25, 1964; d. Rodney Park McKee and Marian Esther (Taylor) McKee-Roberts; children: Misty Marie, Micheal David Christopher. Student, Hartnell Coll., Salinas, Calif., 1985-87, Colo. Inst. Art, Denver, 1987, Front Range C.C., 1992-93. Artist Good Decal, Denver, 1987-90, Sachs Lawlor, Denver, 1991, Exec. Design, Denver, 1991; owner Graphic Connection, Denver; mem. Hanes Group Microenterprizing, Denver, 1991—. Bd. dirs. Child Opportunity Program, Head Start, 1992—; bd. dirs. Colo. State Parent Tchr. Assn., Parent Edn. Commn., 1991-94. Mem. Colo. State Parents Assn. (pres., bd. dirs. region VIII 1992-93), People for Children Coun. (treas. 1988-91, Top Vol. 1992). Home and Office: 2401 Newton St Denver CO 80211-4444

MCKEE, PENELOPE MELNA, library director; b. New Liskeard, Ont., Can., Dec. 31, 1938; d. Melvin Hugh and Violet Mary (Hooton) Olimer; m. Arthur Donald McKee, Mar. 5, 1960 (div. 1985); children: Suzanne, Carolyn, Stephen. BA with honors, U. Toronto, Can., 1960, BLS, 1961, MLS, 1980; diploma, Coll. Applied Arts and Tech., 1976. Cert. mcpl. mgr., Ont. Mcpl. Mgmt. Devel. Bd. Fine arts libr. North York Pub. Libr., Ont., Can., 1961-63, reference libr., 1969-74; reference libr. Toronto Montessori Schs., Thornhill, Ont., 1974-76; cons. Grolier Pub., Toronto, 1976; libr. supr. Toronto Pub. Libr., 1977-80; dir. Aurora Pub. Libr., Ont., Can., 1980-86, Peterborough Pub. Libr., Ont., Can., 1986-90, Edmonton Pub. Libr., Alta., Can., 1990—; adj. assoc. prof. U. Alta., Edmonton, 1992—; cons. Edmonton Cath. Sch. Bd., 1992. Contbr. articles to profl. jours. Vice chmn. Project Hostel, Aurora, 1986-89; bd. dirs. Friends of Trent Severn Waterway, Peterborough, 1990; active Edmonton Centennial Celebrations Com., 1992. Russell scholar U. Toronto, 1956. Mem. Canadian Libr. Assn., Ontario Libr. Assn. (pres.), Libr. Assn. Alta., Alta. Pub. Libr. Dirs. Coun. (chair), Rotary Club of Downtown Edmonton (pub. rels. chmn.). Office: Edmonton Pub Libr, 7 Sir Winston Churchill Sq, Edmonton, AB Canada T5J 2V4

MC KEE, RAYMOND WALTER, accountant; b. Joplin, Mo., Dec. 24, 1899; s. Charles Edward and Sarah Ellen (Epperson) McK.; m. Frances Ida Howe, Nov. 1, 1947; children: Michael, David, Roderick, Duncan, Malcolm, Brude. Student pub. schs., Joplin. CPA, Calif. Acct., Price, Waterhouse & Co., 1923-25, Haskins & Sells, 1925-26; pvt. practice acctg., La Puente, Calif., 1964—; lectr. St. Louis U., 1923-24; v.p. Richfield Oil Corp., Pan Am. Petroleum Corp., 1928-30; sec. West Coast Air Transport, 1926-30; sec.-treas. West Coast div. Anchor Hocking Corp.; pres. Cross Water Co. Co-founder Nat. Paraplegia Found. (name now Nat. Spinal Cord Found.), 1927. Mem. Petroleum Accts. Soc. (co-founder, life). Club: Lions. Author: Accounting for Petroleum Industry, 1925; Petroleum Accounting, 1938; Saludos California, 1947; Book of McKee, 1959. Home and Office: 738 S 3rd Ave La Puente CA 91746-2735

MCKEE, ROGER CURTIS, federal magistrate judge; b. Waterloo, Iowa, Feb. 11, 1931; s. James A. and Leonace (Burrell) McK.; m. Roberta Jeanne Orvis, Sept. 3, 1954; children: Andrea Jane, Brian Curtis, Paul Robert. BA, State Coll. of Iowa, 1955; MA, U. Ill., 1960; JD, U. San Diego, 1968. Bar: Calif. 1970, U.S. Dist. Ct. (so. dist.) Calif. 1969, U.S. Ct. Appeals (9th cir.) 1971. Telegrapher, agt. Ill. Cen. R.R., 1950-55; tng. asst. No. Ill. Gas Co., Aurora, 1959-60; with indsl. rels. dept. Convair div. Gen. Dynamics Corp., San Diego, 1960-68; contract adminstr. and supr. Datagraphix div. Gen. Dynamics Corp., San Diego, 1968-69, asst. counsel, 1969-70; ptnr. Powell & McKee, San Diego, 1970-75, Millsberg, Dickstein & McKee, San Diego, 1975-83; magistrate judge U.S. Dist. Ct. for So. Dist. Calif., San Diego, 1983—; presiding magistrate judge, 1993—. Bd. trustees So. Calif. Presbyn. Homes, L.A., 1979-81; moderator Presbytery of San Diego, 1980. Capt. USNR, 1949-85. Mem. Calif. Bar Assn., Fed. Magistrate Judges Assn., Navy League U.S., Naval Res. Officers Assn., Res. Officers Assn., Dixieland Jazz Soc. (bd. dirs. San Diego chpt. 1984—). Republican. Office: US Cts Bldg 940 Front St San Diego CA 92101-8994

MCKEE, SUZANNE PESHETTE, optics scientist; b. Vallejo, Calif., May 19, 1941; d. Eugene Wilfred and Margaret Helen (Lundblad) Peshette; m. Christopher Fulton McKee, June 20, 1965; children: William Arthur, Christopher Eugene, Maria Helene. AB, Vassar Coll., 1963; PhD, U. Calif., Berkeley, 1970. Instr. St. Mary's Coll., Moraga, Calif., 1969-70, Calif. State U./Calif. Poly. Inst., L.A./Riverside, 1970-71; scientist Polaroid Corp., Cambridge, Mass., 1971-74; asst. rsch. physiologist U. Calif., Berkeley, 1974-81; sr. scientist Smith-Kettlewell Eye Rsch. Inst., San Francisco, 1981-90, assoc. dir., 1990—; chair com. on vision NRC, Washington, 1989-91. Assoc. editor Perception, London, 1985—; author numerous rsch. reports, articles and book chpts. NSF fellow, 1963-68. Mem. Assn. for Rsch. in Vision and Ophthalmology (trustee 1994—), Optical Soc. Am. (fellow, 1994), Psychonomic Soc., Phi Beta Kappa. Democrat. Roman Catholic. Office: Smith-Kettlewell Eye Rsch 2232 Webster St San Francisco CA 94115-1821

MCKEEVER, JEFFREY D., computer company executive; b. Marion, Ind., 1942. Grad., U. Ariz., Tucson, 1965; MBA, U. Ariz., 1973. Chmn., CEO, dir. Microage Inc., Tempe. Office: Microage Inc 2308 S 55th St Tempe AZ 85282-1824

MCKELLAR, JAMES LOUIS, publisher; b. L.A., Nov. 23, 1940; s. Francis Matthew and Muriel Dorothy (Swensen) McK.; m. Judith Lynn Davis, Dec. 17, 1964; children: Lindsey Christina, Matthew James, Randal William. BS, San Jose State U., 1963. Pres. McKellar Publs. Inc., Glendale, Calif., 1963—; bd. dirs. Pacific Coast Builders Conf., Sacramento. With U.S. Army. Office: McKellar Publs Inc 333 E Glenoaks Blvd Ste 204 Glendale CA 91207-2074

MCKENNA, JEANETTE ANN, archaeologist; b. N.Y.C., Aug. 6, 1953; d. Edward Patrick and Ann Jeanette (O'Brien) McKenna; children: Stephanie Jane, Daniel Glen Edward. AA in Phys. Edn., Mount San Antonio Jr. Coll., 1974-84; BA in Anthropology, Calif. State U., Fullerton, 1977, MA in Anthropology, 1982; postgrad., Ariz. State U., 1981-84. Field archaeologist Archaeol. Rsch., Inc., Costa Mesa, Calif., 1976-79; rsch. asst. Calif. State U., 1979; lab. dir. Environ. Rsch. Archaeologists, L.A., 1978-79; staff archaeologist Ariz. State U., Tempe, 1979-82; rsch. archaeologist Soil Systems, Inc., Phoenix, 1982-84, Sci. Resource Surveys, Huntington Beach, Calif., 1984-87; co-owner, prin. Hatheway & McKenna, Mission Viejo, Calif., 1987-89; owner, prin. McKenna et al., Whittier, Calif., 1989—. Contbr. numerous articles to profl. jours. and reports. Bd. dirs. Whittier Conservancy, 1987—, interim treas., 1994, pres., 1994-95. Mem. Soc. Profl. Archaeologists (bd. dirs. 1993—), Archaeol. Inst. Am., Am. Soc. Conservation Archaeology, Am. Mus. Natural History, Soc. Am. Anthropology, Ariz. Archaeol. Coun., Ariz. Hist. Found., Calif. Hist. Soc., Nat. Arbor Day Found., Nat. Parks and Conservation Assn., Nat. Trust for Historic Preservation, Soc. Calif. Archaeology, Soc. Hist. Archaeology, S.W. Mus. Assn., Wilderness Soc., Whittier Conservancy, Southwestern Anthrop. Assn., Gene Autry Western Heritage Mus. Assn., Nature Conservancy, Smithsonian Assocs., Sierra Club, otehrs. Democrat. Roman Catholic. Home: 6008 Friends Ave Whittier CA 90601 Office: McKenna et al 6008 Friends Ave Whittier CA 90601

MC KENNA, MARIAN CECILIA, historian; b. Scarsdale, N.Y., July 3, 1926; d. John Francis and Marguerite (Hanfling) McK. BS, Columbia U., 1949, MA, 1950, PHD in History (Am. Philos. Soc. Penrose award 1952-53, Erb fellow), 1953. Instr. Hunter Coll., CUNY, 1953-59; assoc. prof. Manhattanville Coll., Purchase, N.Y., 1959-66; prof. Am . history U. Calgary, Alta., Can., 1966—; cons. Nat. Endowment for Humanities. Author: Borah, 1960, Pictorial History of Catholicism, 1961, Myra Hess: a Portrait, 1976, Tapping Reeve and the Litchfield Law School, 1986, Canadian and American Constitutions in Comparative Perspective, 1993. Recipient Can. Coun. award, 1967, 68, 69, 72, 76, Social Scis. and Humanities Rsch. Coun. Can. award, 1989, 90, Faculty of Social Sci. Disting. Tchr. award U. Calgary, 1993; Danforth fellow, 1965. Mem. Orgn. Am. Historians, Am. Hist. Assn., Am. Soc. Legal History. Roman Catholic. Home: 3343 Upton Pl NW, Calgary, AB Canada T2N 4G9 Office: U Calgary, History Dept, 2500 University Dr NW, Calgary, AB Canada T2N 1N4

MCKENZIE, MICHAEL CARTER, seminary educator; b. Medford, Oreg., July 29, 1956; s. Dale Farrell and Maxine Grace (Carter) McK. BA, Ctrl. Wash. U., 1981; MA summa cum laude, Simon Greeleaf Law Sch., 1985; MA in Religion, Westminster Theol. Sem., 1988; PhD, U. So. Calif., 1992. Instr. in Greek Cathedral Bible Coll., Escondido, Calif., 1986; asst. lectr. U. So. Calif., 1991-92; adj. prof. theology Northwest Coll., 1992, 93; adj. prof. theology Faith Evang. Sem., Tacoma, 1993, asst. prof. ethics and apologetics, 1993-94; guest spkr. Trinity Luth. Ch., Anaheim, Calif., 1994; guest Sta. KGNW. Contbr. articles to profl. jours. Mem. Evang. Theol. Soc. Home: 4303 SW 102nd Seattle WA 98146

MCKENZIE, RICHARD ELVIN, aerospace engineer; b. San Rafael, Calif., Sept. 27, 1951; s. Cecil L. and Estelle B. McKenzie; m. Iris V. Cavazos, Apr. 28, 1972; children: Jacqueline Nicole, Alexander Scott. BS, U. Tex., 1975, MS, 1976. Consulting engr. Pollak & Skan, Dallas, 1981-85; sr. staff scientist Merit Tech., Inc., Dallas, 1985-89; sr. staff engr. Geodynamics Corp., Denver, 1989—; co-founder The Computer Coll., Dallas, 1982-85; cons. System Specialists, Dallas, 1981-85. Patentee for A Terrain Avoidance Algorithm. Pres. Ramshorn Coop., Austin, 1969-70. Sr. mem. AIAA; mem. Sigma Gamma Tau. Home: 165 Wuthering Heights Dr Colorado Springs CO 80921-2571

MCKEON, HOWARD P. (BUCK MCKEON), congressman, former mayor; b. Los Angeles; m. Patricia; 6 children. BS, Brigham Young U. Mem. Coun. City of Santa Clarita, Calif., 1987-92, mayor, 1987-88; mem. 103rd Congress from 25th Calif. dist., 1993—; founding dir., chmn. Valencia Nat. Bank; co-owner Howard & Phil's Western Wear, Inc. Hon. chmn. Leukemia Soc. Celebrity program, 1990, Red Cross Community Support Campaign, 1992; active Dist. Com. Boy Scouts Am.; chmn., trustee William S. Hart Sch. dist., 1979-87; chmn., dir. Henry Mayo Newhall Meml. Hosp., 1983-88; mem. Calif. Rep. State Ctrl. Com., 1988-92; bd. dirs. Santa Clarita Valley Sml. Bus. Devel. Ctr., 1990-92, Canyon Country C. of C., 1988-92. Office: US Ho of Reps 307 Cannon Ho Ofc Bldg Washington DC 20515*

MCKIBBEN, HOWARD D., federal judge; b. Apr. 1, 1940; s. James D. and Bernice McKibben; m. Mary Ann McKibben, July 2, 1966; children: Mark, Susan. B.S., Bradley U., 1962; M.P.A., U. Pitts., 1964; J.D., U. Mich., 1967. Assoc. George W. Abbott Law Office, 1967-71; dep. dist. atty. Douglas County, Nev., 1969-71, dist. atty., 1971-77; dist. ct. judge State of Nev., 1977-84; judge U.S. Dist. Ct. Nev., Reno, 1984—. Mem. ABA, Nev. Bar Assn., Am. Inns of Ct. (pres. Nev. chpt. 1986-88). Methodist. Home: PO Box 588 Verdi NV 89439-0588 Office: US Dist Ct 300 Booth St Rm 5137 Reno NV 89509-1356

MCKIM, HARRIET MEGCHELSEN, education educator; b. Keokuk, Iowa, Oct. 17, 1919; d. Herbert John and Florence Josephine (Ottowa) Megchelsen; m. Lanier McClure, Nov. 1, 1944 (div. 1948); 1 child, Janet Gray; m. L.A. McKim, July 28, 1950 (div. 1968). BA, Calif. State U., Sacramento, 1952; MA, U. So. Calif., 1963, EdD, 1979. Tchr., prin. Cumberland County Schs., Crossville, Tenn., 1939-42; sec. Tenn. Valley Authority, Oak Ridge Def. Plant, Mare Island Naval Shipyard and Cal-West Ins., 1942-52; tchr., vice-prin., reading specialist, dir. ESEA I various pub. schs., Oxnard, Orcutt, Sacramento, Edwards AFB, Calif. and Spokane, Wash., 1950-64; coord. Yuba City and Yuba County Schs., 1964-70; cons. Calif. Dept. Edn., 1970-83; part-time instr. Alan Hancock Community Coll., Santa Maria, Calif., Polytech. U., San Luis Obispo, Calif., U. Calif., Davis, Santa Barbara, 1960-70; supr. student tchrs. Calif. State U., Sacramento, 1984; adj. prof. edn. Nat. U., Sacramento, 1986-88; rep. Child Devel. Assocs., 1992—. Vol. tchr. ARC parenting classes, Sacramento, 1984-85; docent, spkr. Crocker Art Mus.; vol. Loaves and Fishes; bd. dirs. Sacramento Internat. Students' coun., Friends of Libr. Calif. State U., Elderhostel Calif. State U.; docent Sacramento History Ctr.; deacon Fremont Presbyn. Ch.; v.p. Sacramento World Affairs Coun. Mem. AAUW, Nat. Assn. Edn. Young Children, Calif. Ret. Tchrs., Am. Assn. Ret. Persons, Profs. of Early Childhood Edn., Sacramento Affiliates, Amnesty Internat., World Affairs Coun. (adminstrv. v.p.), Sierra Club, Delta Kappa Gamma, Phi Delta Kappa. Address: 5332 State Ave Sacramento CA 95819-1738

MCKINLEY, JOSEPH WARNER, health science facility executive; b. Champaign, Ill., Jan. 9, 1943; s. Lyle Warner and Eloise M. (Coleman) McK. BS, Georgetown U., 1968; MBA, George Washington U., 1973. Asst. adminstr. Weiss Meml. Hosp., Chgo., 1973-75; assoc. v.p. Rockford (Ill.) Meml. Hosp., 1975-78; v.p. ops. Phoenix Meml. Hosp., 1978-84, exec. v.p., chief exec. officer, 1984-88; exec. v.p. St. Francis Med. Ctr., Lynwood, Calif., 1988-90; CEO Meridian Point Rehab. Hosp., Scottsdale, Ariz., 1990-95, St. Agnes Med. Ctr./Nazareth Hosp., Phila., 1995—. Capt. U.S. Army, 1968-71, Vietnam. Mem. Am. Coll. of Healthcare Execs., Ariz. Club, Plaza Club. Republican. Episcopalian. Home: 6 Colonia Miramonte Paradise Valley AZ 85253

MCKINLEY, LOREN DHUE, museum director; b. Tillamook, Oreg., Feb. 1, 1920; s. Henry Raymond and Flora (Phillips) McK.; m. Mary Eileen Sessions, May 22, 1942; children: Candace Eileen, Scott Dhu, Kevin Loren, Laurie Lee, Maris Colleen. Student, Oreg. State U., U. Oreg.; D.Sc., U. Portland, 1973. Advt. mgr. Headlight Herald, Tillamook, 1946; partner Kenwood Press, Tillamook, 1949; dir. Oreg. Mus. Sci. and Industry, Portland, 1960-78; chief exec. officer Oreg. Mus. Sci. and Industry, 1978—; bd. dirs. Fred Hutchinson Cancer Rsch. Ctr. Found.; Portland ops. mgr. Office of Devel. Oreg. State U. Mayor of Tillamook, 1954-60; pres. Leukemia Assn. Oreg. Inc., 1983—; bd. dirs. St. Mary's Acad., 1993—; mem. Oreg. State U Found. Served with AUS, World War II, ETO, MTO. Decorated Bronze Star with oak leaf cluster; named 1st Citizen of Oreg., 1951; recipient award Oreg. Mus. Sci. and Industry, 1965, Elsie M.B. Naumberg award as outstanding sci. mus. dir., 1968, citation for outstanding svc. Oreg. Acad. Sci., 1971, Aubrey Watzek award Lewis and Clark Coll., 1973. Mem. Assn. Sci. and Tech. Ctrs. Am. (pres. 1973—), League Oreg. Cities (past pres.), Kappa Sigma. Republican. Home and Office: 11925 SW Belvidere Pl Portland OR 97225-5805

MC KINNEY, ROBERT MOODY, newspaper editor and publisher; b. Shattuck, Okla., Aug. 28, 1910; s. Edwin S. and Eva (Moody) McK.; married, 1943; 1 child, Mrs. Meade Martin; m. Marie-Louise de Montmollin, May 7, 1970. AB, U. Okla., 1932; LLD, U. N.Mex., 1964. Investment analyst Standard Stats. Co., Inc. (now Standard and Poor's Co.), 1932-34; ptnr. Young-Kolbe & Co., 1934-38, Robert R. Young & Co., 1938-42; exec. v.p., treas. Pathe Film Co., 1934-39, Allegheny Corp., 1936-42, Pittston Corp. and subs., 1936-42; v.p. Fremkir Corp., 1937-50, Allan Corp., 1937-50; exec. v.p., treas. Mo. Pacific R.R., 1938-42; ptnr. Scheffmeyer, McKinney & Co., 1945-50; editor, pub. Santa Fe New Mexican, 1949—; chmn. bd. The New Mexican, Inc., 1949—; profl. corp. dir. 10 N.Y.S.E. cos., 1934-86; chmn. Robert Moody Found.; chmn. N.Mex. Econ. Devel. Commn. and Water Resources Devel. Bd., 1949-51; asst. sec. U.S. Dept. Interior, 1951-52; chmn. panel to report to Congress on impact of Peaceful Uses of Atomic Energy, 1955-56; permanent U.S. rep. to Internat. Atomic Energy Agy., Vienna, 1957-58; U.S. rep. Internat. Conf. Peaceful Uses Atomic Energy, Geneva, 1958; U.S. ambassador to, Switzerland, 1961-63; exec. officer Presdl. Task Force on Internat. Investments, 1963-64; chmn. Presdl. Commn. on Travel, 1968; chmn. bd. visitors U. Okla., 1968-72; U.S. rep. Internat. Centre Settlement Investment Disputes, Washington, 1967-74. Author: Hymn to Wreckage: A Picaresque Interpretation of History, 1947, The Scientific Foundation for European Integration, 1959, On Increasing Effectiveness of Western Science and Technology, 1959, The Red Challenge to Technological Renewal, 1960, Review of the International Atomic Policies and Programs of the United States, 1960, The Toad and the Water Witch, 1985, Variations on a Marxist Interpretation of Culture, 1986. Served from lt. (j.g.) to lt. USNR, 1942-45. Recipient Disting. Service medal U.S. Dept. Treasury, 1968, Disting. Service medal U. Okla., 1972. Mem. Am. Soc. Newspaper Editors, Coun. Fgn. Rels., Newspaper Assn. of Am., Phi Beta Kappa, Phi Gamma Delta. Democrat. Episcopalian. Clubs: Chevy Chase (Md.); F Street, Metropolitan (Washington); University, Brook, Century, Links, Knickerbocker, River (N.Y.C.). Home: Wind Fields 39850 Snickersville Tpke Middleburg VA 22117-3002 Office: PO Box 1705 Santa Fe NM 87504-1705

MC KINNON, CLINTON D., editor, former congressman; b. Dallas, Feb. 5, 1906; s. John C. and Tennie Clifdell (Hawkins) McK.; m. Lucille Virginia McVey, Oct. 15, 1932; children—Clinton Dan, Michael, Connie. A.B., U. Redlands, Calif., 1930, L.H.D. (hon.), 1967; postgrad., U. Geneva, Switzerland, 1930. Reporter, editor, advt. mgr. on various So. Calif. newspapers, 1931-35; pres., gen. mgr. Valley News Corp., North Hollywood, Calif., 1935-43; established San Fernando Valley Times, 1935, Los Angeles Aircraft Times, 1940, Long Beach Shipyard Times, 1941; established San Diego Daily Jour., 1944, editor, pub. and owner, 1944-48; co-owner Coronado Jour., 1953-72; owner Radio Sta. KSDJ (Columbia affiliate), San Diego, 1945-48; pres., editor and pub. Los Angeles Daily News, 1954; pres., gen. mgr. Alvarado Television Co., Inc., KVOA-TV, Tucson and KOAT-TV, Albuquerque, 1955-63; chmn. San Diego North Shores Pub. Co., San Diego, 1953-72, Sentinel Savs. and Loan Assn., 1963-69, San Diego Transit Co., 1966-71; sec. South Tex. Telecasting Co. Inc., 1963-79; Chmn. Indsl. Devel. Commn., San Diego, 1964-66, Econ. Devel. Corp., San Diego County, 1966-67, San Diego Urban Coalition, 1967-69; mem. Gov.'s Bus. Adv. Council, Calif. Bd. dirs. U. Calif., San Diego Sch. Medicine, 1979—; bd. dirs. Cancer Center Research Bd., U. Calif., San Diego, 1981—; Mem. 81st-82d Congresses from Calif.; vice chmn. Democratic State Central Com. of Calif., 1952-54. Recipient San Diego Golden Man and Boy award, 1968; San Diego Mayor's award of merit, 1971; named to San Diego Transit Hall Fame, 1987. Clubs: Rotarian, San Diego Yacht. Home: 1125 Pacific Beach Dr Apt 401 San Diego CA 92109-5155 Office: 945 Hornblend St San Diego CA 92109-4057*

MCKINNON, JAMES BUCKNER, real estate sales executive, writer, researcher; b. Tacoma, Dec. 5, 1916; s. James Mitchell and Rochelle Lenore (Buckner) McK.; m. Mary C. Corbitt, Dec. 1961 (div. June 1963); 1 child, James H.C.; m. Marylyn Adelle Coote, Mar. 12, 1967 (div. May 1977); 1 child, Michelyn; m. Martha Sackmann, June 12, 1977. BA in Internat. Studies, U. Wash., 1983, H.M. Jackson Sch. Police detective Los Angeles Police Dept., 1946-50; bn. security officer 1st med. bn. 1st Marine div. Fleet Marine Force, 1950-53; owner, operator, mgr., dir. promotional sales The Saucy Dog Drive-In, Venice, Calif., 1953-63; salesman new car sales and leasing Burien Mercury, Seattle, 1963-66; real estate salesman and appraiser various firms Seattle, 1966—; instr., lectr. U.S. Naval Support Activity, Sandpoint, Wash., 1964-74; mem., lectr. NRC 11-8, Naval Postgrad. Sch., Monterey, Calif., 1975-76; Burien Mercury announcer KOMO TV. Author: (poetry) On the Threshold of a Dream, Vol. III, 1992, Best Poems of the 90's, 1992; contbr. to anthologies: Where Words Haven't Spoken, 1993, Fire From Within, 1994; contbr. articles to various newspapers and mil. jours. Mem. br. adv. com. Seattle YMCA, Seattle, 1994—, treas., 1986-94, mem. so. dist. fin. bd., 1989-93, 94, 95-96. With USN, 1939-53, PTO,

Korea. Recipient Wilmer Culver Meml. award Culver Alumni Fictioneers, Seattle, 1979, Silver Poet award World of Poetry Press, 1986, Golden Poet award, 1987-92, Best Poet of the 90's Nat. Libr. of Poetry, 1992; Occidental Coll. scholar, 1935; named to Honorable Order Ky. Cols., 1976; named One of Best New Poets, Am. Poetry Assn. Anthology, 1988. Mem. Internat. Soc. Authors and Artists, Internat. Platform Assn., U.S. Naval Inst. (life), Internat. Soc. Poets (life), N.W. Writers Conf., Ret. Officers Assn. (life), Mensa, Acad. Am. Poets, KP, Masons. Republican. Home: 2312 41st Ave SW Seattle WA 98116-2060

MCKINSTRY, WILLIAM A., judge; b. San Francisco, Apr. 5, 1944; s. James J. and Helen (Bernau) McK. BS, St. Mary's Coll., Moraga, Calif., 1965; JD, Hastings Coll. Law, 1968. Dep. dist. atty. Alameda County, Oakland, Calif., 1969-85; judge Mcpl. Ct., Oakland, 1985-89; judge superior ct. Alameda Cts., 1989—; pres. Alameda County Bar Assn., Oakland, 1982; chair Governing Com. Continuing Edn. of the Bar, Berkeley, Calif., 1987. Office: Superior Ct 1225 Fallon St Oakland CA 94612-4218

MCKITTRICK, JOSEPH TERRENCE, school administrator, educator; b. Memphis, Aug. 30, 1935; s. Joseph Terrence and Grace Louise (Werner) McK.; m. Donna J. Newman, Aug. 22, 1963 (div. 1964); m. Nancy Joan Christopher, July 3, 1965; children—Michele Tresa, Christopher William. B.A. in Philosophy, Quincy Coll., 1960; M.A. in Edn., Calif. Coast U., 1977, Ph.D. in Edn., 1979. Tchr., coach Cath. High Sch., Memphis, 1960-63; tchr., coach, counselor Dinuba High Sch., Calif., 1963-74; prin. Lovell High Sch., Orosi, Calif., 1974-89; instr. Calif. State U.-Fresno, 1980—; v.p. El Monte Sch., Orosi, 1989—. Chmn. Dinuba Planning Commn., 1972-75; candidate Dinuba City Council, 1980. Recipient Tchr. in Politics award, 1974; Disting. Pres.'s pin and award Kiwanis Internat., 1980; Cert. of Merit for Outstanding Service in Sch. Dist., 1982; Nat. Appreciation award Soc. Disting. Am. High Sch. Students, 1982. Mem. Calif. Continuation Edn. Assn. (pres. 1976-77, plaque 1978), Assn. Calif. Sch. Adminstrs., Western Assn. Schs. and Coll., State Continuation Adv. Bd. (cert. of appreciation 1978), Phi Delta Kappa. Democrat. Methodist. Home: 636 E Davis Dr Dinuba CA 93618-3047 Office: El Monte Sch 41855 Road 128 Orosi CA 93647-2008

MCKNIGHT, GARY LEE, biochemist, researcher; b. Grants Pass, Oreg., Aug. 30, 1954; s. Raymond Leroy and Betty Louise (Sparks) McK.; m. Therese Anne Tutino, July 29, 1984 (div. Feb. 1994); m. Claire Joan Laush, Apr. 24, 1994. BS, Oreg. State U., 1976; MS, U. Rochester, 1979, PhD, 1981. Postdoctoral fellow U. Wash., Seattle, 1981-83, rsch. assoc., 1983-84; sr. scientist ZymoGenetics, Inc., Seattle, 1984—. Contbr. articles to profl. jours. Mem. Am. Diabetes Assn. Office: ZymoGenetics Inc 1201 Eastlake Ave E Seattle WA 98102-3702

MCKNIGHT, LENORE RAVIN, child psychiatrist; b. Denver, May 15, 1943; d. Abe and Rose (Steed) Ravin; m. Robert Lee McKnight, July 22, 1967; children: Richard Rex, Janet Rose. Student, Occidental Coll., 1961-63; BA, U. Colo., 1965, postgrad. in medicine, 1965-67; MD, U. Calif., San Francisco, 1969. Diplomate Am. Bd. Psychiatry and Neurology. Cert. adult and child psychiatrist Am. Bd. Psychiatry. Intern pediatrics Children's Hosp., San Francisco, 1969-70; resident in gen. psychiatry Langley Porter Neuropsychiat. Inst., 1970-73, fellow child psychiatry, 1972-74; child psychiatrist Youth Guidance Center, San Francisco, 1974-74; pvt. practice medicine specializing in child psychiatry, Walnut Creek, Calif., 1974-93; asst. clin. prof. Langley Porter Neuropsychiat. Inst., 1974—; former clin. assoc. in psychiatry U. Calif. Med. Sch., Davis; asst. clin. prof. psychiatry U. Calif. San Francisco Med. Ctr. Internat.; med. dir. CPC Walnut Creek (Calif.) Hosp., 1990-93. Insts. Edn. fellow U. Edinburgh, 1964; NIH grantee to study childhood nutrition, 1966. Fellow Am. Acad. Child and Adolescent Psychiatry; mem. Am. Psychiat. Assn., Am. Coll. Physician Execs., Psychiat. Assn. No. Calif., Am. Med. Women's Assn., Internat. Arabian Horse Assn., Diablo Arabian Horse Assn. Avocation: breeding Arabian Horses. Office: Kaiser Martinez Inpat Psych 200 Muir Rd Martinez CA 94553-4614

MCKNIGHT, STEVEN LANIER, molecular biologist; b. El Paso, Tex., Aug. 27, 1949; s. Frank Gillespie and Sara Elise (Stevens) McK.; m. Jacquelynn Ann Zimmer, Sept. 16, 1978; children: Nell, Grace, Frances, John Stevens. BA, U. Tex., 1974; PhD, U.Va., 1977. Postdoctoral fellow Carnegie Instn. Washington, Balt., 1977-79, staff assoc., 1979-81, mem. staff, 1984-92; co-founder, dir., dir. rsch. Tularik Inc., 1991—. Contbr. articles to jours. in field. With U.S. Army, 1969-71, Vietnam. Decorated ARCOM medal; recipient Eli Lilly prize Am. Soc. Microbiology, 1987, Newcomb-Cleveland prize Sci. mag., 1989, NAS Molecular Biology award Nat. Acad. Sci., 1991. Fellow Carnegie Inst. (Washington, hon.); mem. Nat. Acad. Scis., Am. Acad. Arts and Scis., Am. Soc. for Biochemistry and Molecular Biology, Am. Soc. for Cell Biology, Japanese Biochem. Soc. (hon.). Democrat. Home: 530 Roehampton Rd Hillsborough CA 94010-6854 Office: Tularik Inc 270 Grand View Ave San Francisco CA 94114-3152

MC KNIGHT, WILLIAM WARREN, JR., publisher; b. Normal, Ill., June 9, 1913; s. William Warren and Isabel Alida (Travis) McK.; m. Alice McGuire, Oct. 30, 1937; children: William Warren, III, Michael Joe, John James. B.S. in Bus. Adminstrn., Northwestern U., 1938. With McKnight Pub. Co., Bloomington, Ill., 1938-83; sec.-treas. McKnight Pub. Co., 1949-56, pres., 1956-67, chmn. bd., 1968-79; bd. dirs. Gen. Telephone Co. Ill., Champion Fed. Savs. & Loan Assn., chmn. bd. Pres. Bloomington Rotary Club, 1952, Bloomington C. of C., 1954; mem. Ill. Commn. Higher Edn., 1956-60; chmn. Bloomington-Normal Airport Authority, 1965-70, CETA Pvt. Industry Council Ill. Balance of State, 1979-81. Served with USNR, 1942-46. Recipient Disting. Service award Bloomington Kiwanis Club, 1963, Disting. Service award Normal C. of C., 1973; Good Govt. award Bloomington Jaycees, 1970; Edn. Constrn. award Edn. Council Graphic Arts Industry, 1974; Disting. Alumni award Ill. State U., 1978; Disting. Service award Spirit of McLean County, 1982; Disting. Service citation Epsilon Pi Tau, 1983; award of Merit Am. Vocat. Assn., 1990; disting. assoc. award Coun. on Tech. Tchr. Edn., 1995. Mem. Graphic Arts Edn. Assn., Internat. Tech. Edn. Assn., Nat. Assn. Indsl. and Tech. Tchrs. Educators, Ill. C. of C. (dir. 1964-69), Ill. Mfrs. Assn. (dir. 1954-62). Republican. Presbyterian. Clubs: Coll. Alumni, Bloomington Country. Home: 401 W Vernon Ave Normal IL 61761-3542 Home (winter): 7788 E Stallion Rd Scottsdale AZ 85258-3485

MCKUSICK, MARSHALL KIRK, computer scientist; b. Wilmington, Del., Jan. 19, 1954; s. Blaine Chase and Marjorie Jane (Kirk) McK.; domestic ptnr. Eric P. Allman. BSEE with distinction, Cornell U., 1976; MS in Bus. Adminstrn., U. Calif., Berkeley, 1979, MS in Computer Sci., 1980, PhD in Computer Sci., 1984. System designer Hughes Aircraft Co., 1977-79; software cons., 1982—; rsch. computer scientist U. Calif., Berkeley, 1984-93. Author: The Design and Implementation of the 4.3BSD UNIX Operating System, 1989, translated into German, 1990, Japanese, 1991, The Design and Implementation of the 4.3BSD UNIX Operating System Answer Book, 1991, translated into Japanese, 1992; contbr. to profl. publs. Mem. IEEE, Usenix Assn. (Lifetime Achievement award 1992, past pres. 1990-92, bd. dirs. 1986-92), Assn. Computing Machinery. Democrat. Office: 1614 Oxford St Berkeley CA 94709-1608

MCLAREN, ARCHIE CAMPBELL, JR., marketing executive; b. Atlanta, Sept. 25, 1942; s. Archie Campbell and Virginia Lynn (Sides) McL.; m. Georgia Mae Blunt, 1969 (div. 1971); 1 child, Leslie Michelle. BA, Vanderbilt U., 1964; JD, Memphis State U., 1968. Clk. FBI, Memphis, 1965-66; tchr., tennis coach Memphis U. Sch., 1966-68; tchr. Hunt High Sch., Columbus, Miss., 1968-69; tennis coach Miss. State U., Starkville, Miss., 1968-69; concierge The Roosevelt Hotel, New Orleans, 1969-70; sales rep. West Pub. Co., St. Paul, 1970-84, adminstr. internat. mktg. The Orient, 1985-90; freelance wine cons., 1985—; cons. Calif. Ctrl. Coast Wine Growers Assn., Santa MAria, 1987-91; lectr. advanced wine appreciation Calif. Poly. U. Extended Edn., San Luis Obispo, 1986-90; dir. KCBX Ctrl. Coast Wine Classic, San Luis Obispo, 1985—, KHPR Wine Classic, Honolulu, 1987-91, Winesong, Ft. Bragg, Calif., 1987—, WETA Washington Wine Classic, 1989-90, KCRW Summerday, 1991; auction cons. Am. Inst. of Wine and Food, 1994—. Host talk show Pub. Radio Sta. KCBX, San Luis Obispo, 1984—; columnist (newspaper) San Luis Obispo Telegram-Tribune, 1992-95, New Times San Luis Obispo, 1995—; contbg. writer: Adventures in Dining, 1994—. Bd. dirs. Avila Beach County Water Dist., 1992-95, pres., 1992-94; bd. dirs. San Luis Obispo (Calif.) Mozart Festival, 1988-92, pres., 1991-92; dir. Internat. Festival Champagne and Sparkling Wine, 1992—, Santa Barbara Wine Auction, 1992-94; mem. Avila Valley Adv. Coun., 1993—; bd. dirs. Guild South County Ctr. for Performing Arts, 1993-94. Mem. Calif. Cen. Coast Wine Soc. (pres. 1985), Am. Soc. Wine Educators, German Wine Soc. Honolulu, Vintners Club San Francisco, Avila Bay Wine Soc., Cen. Coast Chaine des Rotisseurs (chpt. pres. 1987, 88, 89), Marin County Food and Wine Soc., Internat. Food, Wine & Travel Writers' Assn., Austrian Wine Brotherhood, Avila Bay Club, Pismo Beach Athletic Club. Office: PO Box 790 Avila Beach CA 93424-0790

MCLAREN, M(ALCOM) BRUCE, library director; b. Detroit, Nov. 17, 1940; s. Cameron G. and Pearl M. (Baker) McL.; m. Karlene M. Lamberton, Jan. 29, 1965; children: Cameron B., Kathleen M., Sean M. BA, Western Mich. U., 1963; MEd, Wayne State U., 1968. Libr., tchr. history Holly (Mich.) High Sch., 1963-65; resource ctr. coord. Waterford (Mich.) Mason Jr. High Sch., 1965-67; libr./media specialist Oakland County Ind. Sch. Dist., Mich., 1967-68; curriculum resource ctr. developer, asst. prof. edn. L.I. (N.Y.) U., 1968-71; dist. dir. media svcs. Wayne-Westland Schs., Mich., 1971-76; dir. Toles Learning Ctr. N.Mex. Mil. Inst., 1976—; vis. prof. Eastern Mich. U., 1975-76; vis. lectr. Eastern N.Mex. U., 1977-80; ednl. cons. U.S. Merchant Marine Acad., N.Y., 1980-81, Doyle & Assoc., Mich., 1973-76, The Baker & Taylor Co., N.Y., 1969-76, Lamar U., Tex., 1977-78, N.Mex. Ednl. Stds. Com., 1976-77, N.Mex. Commn. on Pub. Broadcasting, 1979-83. Contbr. articles to profl. jours. Chmn. Roswell Parks and Recreation Commn.; bd. dirs. Eastern N.Mex. Med. Ctr. Found., Am. Cancer Soc.; chief of staff N.Mex. State Def. Force; host family Fgn. Exch. Student, 1992. Recipient Commendation award, 1985, 90, Meritorious Svc. award, 1985, Sch. Media Specialist Teamwork award, 1985, CLSI Online recognition, 1985, Seven Seals award U.S. Dept. Def., 1989, Svc. award, 1991, Centennial Commn. recognition, 1991; named Outstanding Mem. of Roswell Cmty. by RISD Bilingual Program, 1989. Mem. Assn. for Ednl. Comm. and Tech., Cmty. Coll. Assn. for Instrn. and Tech. (pres.), Broadcast Edn. Assn., Am. Assn. Cmty. Colls., Nat. Coun. Learning Resources and Instrnl. Telecomm. Consortium, Internat. TV Assn. Office: N Mex Mil Inst 101 W College Blvd Roswell NM 88201-5174

MCLARNAN, DONALD EDWARD, banker, corporation executive; b. Nashua, Iowa, Dec. 19, 1906; s. Samuel and Grace (Prudhon) McL.; m. Virginia Rickard, May 5, 1939; children: Marilyn, Marcia, Roxane. A.B., U. So. Calif., 1930; grad., Southwestern U. Law Sch., 1933; postgrad., Cambridge U. Trust appraiser, property mgr. Security-Pacific Nat. Bank, Los Angeles, 1935-54; regional dir. SBA for, So. Calif., Ariz., Nev., 1954-61; area adminstr. SBA for, Alaska, Western U.S., Hawaii, Guam, Samoa, U.S. Trust Terr., 1969-73; pres. Am. MARC, Inc. (offshore oil drillers and mfr. diesel engines), 1961-63, Terminal Drilling & Prodn. Co., Haney & Williams Drilling Co., Western Offshore, 1961-63; v.p., dir. Edgemar Dairy, Santa Monica Dairy Co., 1954-70; founder, pres., chmn. bd. Mission Nat. Bank, 1963-67; pres. Demco Trading Co., Mut. Trading Co.; dir. Coast Fed. Savs. & Loan; cons. numerous corps.; guest lectr. various univs. Contbr. articles on mgmt. and fin. to profl. jours. Chmn. fed. agys. div. Community Chest, 1956; nat. pres. Teachers Day, 1956; bd. councillors U. So. Calif.; founder, chmn., pres. Soc. Care and Protection Injured Innocent; adv. bd. Los Angeles City Coll.; bd. dirs. Calif. Easter Seal Soc.; nat. chmn. U. So. Calif. Drug Abuse Program. Recipient Los Angeles City and County Civic Leadership award, 1959. Mem. Nat. Assn. People with Disabilities (pres.); Mem. Skull and Dagger, Delta Chi. Clubs: Mason (Los Angeles) (K.T., Shriner), Los Angeles (Los Angeles), Jonathan (Los Angeles). Home: 135 S Norton Ave Los Angeles CA 90004-3916 Office: 1111 Crenshaw Blvd Los Angeles CA 90019-3112

MCLAUGHLIN, CALVIN STURGIS, biochemistry educator; b. St. Joseph, Mo., May 29, 1936; s. Calvin Sturgis and Agnes Jane McLaughlin; m. Chin Helen Moy, Sept. 7, 1960; children—Heather Chin Chu, Christine Leng Oy, Andrew Calvin Moy. BS, King Coll., 1958; postgrad., Yale U., 1958-59; PhD, MIT, 1964. Postdoctoral fellow Institut de Biologie Physico-Chimique, Paris, 1964-66; prof. biochemistry U. Calif., Irvine, 1966—, dir. Cancer Research Inst., 1981-83; vis. prof. Sch. Botany Oxford U., Eng., 1976, 80; mem. peer rev. panels Am. Cancer Soc., NSF, NIH, VA. Contbr. numerous articles to profl. jours.; mem. editorial bds. Jour. Bacteriology, 1975-80, Exptl. Mycology, 1980-86; reviewer profl. jours. Bd. dirs. Am. Cancer Soc., Orange County, 1980-89; mem. Traffic Affairs Com., Newport Beach, Calif., 1972-78. Named Outstanding Tchr. U. Calif.-Irvine, 1978, Gabriel Lester Meml. Lectr. Reed Coll., 1979; fellow Rockefeller Found., 1958-59, Upjohn Found., 1959-60, Nutrition Found., 1960-61, NIH, 1961-64, Am. Cancer Soc., 1964-66. Mem. Genetics Soc. Am., Am. Soc. Biol. Chemistry, Am. Soc. Microbiology, Am. Soc. Mycology, Am. Soc. for Cell Biology, Yeast Genetics and Molecular Biology Soc. Am. (co-chair 1986-88). Presbyterian. Office: U Calif-Irvine Dept Biol Chemistry Irvine CA 92717

MCLAUGHLIN, CONSTANCE NETHKEN, science educator; b. Elkins, W.Va., Feb. 3, 1949; d. Ralph David and Helen Irene (Shreve) Nethken; m. Terry Walthall McLaughlin, May 23, 1970; 1 child, Veronica McLaughlin Mercure. BS in Chemistry, W.Va. U., 1971; MA in Sci. Edn., U. No. Colo., 1980; cert. in Ednl. Adminstrn., U. Denver, 1988. Cert. tchr., Colo. Tchr. Jefferson County Schs., Golden, Colo., 1982—; participant Process Consultation Cadre Jefferson County Schs., Jefferson County Life Sci. Cadre. Recipient Outstanding Tchr. award Colo. Awards Com. Mem. Colo. Biology Tchrs. Assn., NEA, Colo. Assn. Sch. Execs., Alpha Delta Kappa. Methodist.

MCLAUGHLIN, FRANK E., nursing educator; b. Bklyn., Mar. 27, 1935; s. Edward Patrick and Anna (Barr) McL. BS, Adelphi U., 1959; MA, NYU, 1961; PhD, U. Calif., Berkeley, 1968. Lecturer U. Calif., San Francisco, 1968-69, asst. prof., 1969-70, coord. rsch. grad. programs, 1970-72, chief rsch. in clin. nursing, 1972-81, assoc. clin. prof., 1975—; asst. clin. prof. U. Calif., Davis, 1972-84; assoc. prof. San Francisco State U., 1981-84, vice chmn. dept. nursing, 1984-87, prof., 1984—, grad. coord. Sch. Edn., 1990-94; assoc. dir. grad. program Sch. Nursing Coll. Health and Human Svcs., San Francisco State U., 1995—. Author: Advanced Nursing and Health Care Research, 1990 (Book of Yr. award Am. Jour. Nursing 1990). V.p. bd. trustees Cen. City Hospitality House, San Francisco, 1975-78; chmn. Mental Health Adv. Bd. San Francisco, 1979-85; bd. dirs. San Francisco Mental Health Assn., 1985-88. Recipient Outstanding Nurse Leadership award Golden Gate Nurses Assn., 1986. Fellow Am. Acad. of Nursing; mem. ANA, Sigma Theta Tau.

MC LAUGHLIN, HERBERT E., architect; b. Chgo., June 15, 1934; s. Herbert and Corinne (Brewer) McL.; m. Eve Pell, Apr. 1960 (div. June 1970); children—Daniel, Peter, John. B.Arch., Yale U., 1956, M.Arch., 1958. Architect, Skidmore Owings Merrill, 1961-62; ptnr. Ellis Kaplan, San Francisco, 1962-63; ptnr.-in-charge of design Kaplan/McLaughlin/Diaz, San Francisco, 1963—; vis. lectr. various univs.; speaker. Contbr. articles to profl. jours. Bd. dirs. Soc. San Francisco Planning and Urban Renewal, Soc. Archtl. Heritage; mem. ad hoc adv. com. architecture U.S. Dept. Justice. Served to 1st lt. USAF, 1958-61. Recipient numerous awards, including Honor award Napa chpt. AIA for Cronan House, 1966; award of recognition Am. Hosp. Assn., 1968; Honor award for Martin Luther King Sq., San Francisco, AIA, 1972; Honors award No. Calif. chpt. AIA for Tomales Bay Housing, Calif., 1974, Martin Luther King Sq., San Francisco, 1974 (also Nat. Honors award); Record Houses Award, 1976; ACA/AIA Merit award for Contra Costa Detention Facility, 1978; Record Houses award, 1979; Pacific Coast Builders Gold Nugget award (2), 1979, 83; spl. citation S.W. Wash. chpt. AIA for St. Peter Hosp., Olympia, 1980; Outstanding Project award Nat. Concrete Masonry Assn., 1982; cert. of nat. recognition HUD, 1983; Merit award Calif. Hist. Preservation Conf., 1983; Merit award Builder's Choice, 1983, Grand award, 1983; Merit award No. Calif. chpt. Am. Concrete Inst., 1983. Mem. AIA (chmn. nat. task force). Home: 2315 Broadway St San Francisco CA 94115-1233 Office: Kaplan/McLaughlin/Diaz 222 Vallejo St San Francisco CA 94111-1522

MCLAUGHLIN, JAMES DANIEL, architect; b. Spokane, Wash., Oct. 2, 1947; s. Robert Francis and Patricia (O'Connel) McL.; B.Arch., U. Idaho, 1971; m. Willa Kay Pace, Aug. 19, 1972; children: Jamie Marie, Robert James. Project architect Neil M. Wright, Architect, AIA, Sun Valley, Idaho, 1971-74, McMillan & Hayes, Architects, Sun Valley, 1974-75; now pres., prin. McLaughlin Architects Chartered, Sun Valley. Prin. works include Oakridge Apts., Moscow, Idaho (Excellence in Design award AIA), Walnut Ave. Mall, Ketchum, Idaho (Excellence in Design award AIA, 1987), McMahan Residence, Sun Valley (Excellence in Design award AIA, 1987). Chmn., Ketchum Planning and Zoning Commn., Ketchum Planning Commn., Ketchum Zoning Commn.; chmn. Sun Valley Planning and Zoning Commn.; vice-chmn. Idaho Archtl. Licensing Bd. Served to 1st lt. U.S. Army. Registered architect, 10 states including Idaho. Mem. AIA , Nat. Coun. Archtl. Registration Bds., Nat. Home Builders Assn., Ketchum-Sun Valley C. of C. (dir.). Roman Catholic. Club: Rotary. Prin. archtl. works include James West Residence, First Fed. Savs., Fox Bldg. Rehab., Walnut Ave. Mall, First St. Office Bldg. Home: PO Box 6 Lot # 5 Red Cliffs Subdivsn Ketchum ID 83340-0006 Office: McLaughlin Architects Chartered PO Box 479 Sun Valley ID 83353-0479

MCLAUGHLIN, LINDA LEE HODGE, federal judge; b. 1942. BA, Stanford U., 1963; LLB, U. Calif., Berkeley, 1966. With Keatinge & Sterling, L.A., 1966-70, Richards, Martin & McLaughlin, Beverly Hills and Newport Beach, Calif., 1970-73, Bergland, Martin & McLaughlin, Newport Beach, 1973-76, Bergland & McLaughlin, Costa Mesa, Calif., 1976-80; judge North Orange County Mcpl. Ct., Fullerton, Calif., 1980-82, Orange County Superior Ct., Santa Ana, Calif., 1982-92, U.S. Dist. Ct. (ctrl. dist.) Calif., Santa Ana, 1992—; mem. adv. com. jud. forms Jud. Coun., 1978—, mem. adv. com. gender bias in cts., 1987-90. Active Edgewood Sch. Parents Assn., Cate Sch. Parents Aux.; mem. governing bd. Victim-Witness Assistance Program Orange County. Mem. Nat. Assn. Women Judges, Calif. State Bar Assn. (mem. com. profl. ethics 1976-80, disciplinary referee dist. 8 1978-80), Calif. Women Lawyers (gov. dist. 8 1978-80), Calif. Judges Assn. (chair civil law and procedure com. 1985-86), Orange County Bar Assn. (mem. com. adminstrn. justice 1975-78, client rels. com. 1978-80, com. jud. appointments 1979-80), Orange County Women Lawyers, Boalt Hall Alumni Assn., Stanford U. Alumni Assn., Cap and Gown Hon. Soc. *

MCLAUGHLIN, STEVEN PAUL, botany educator; b. Tacoma, Wash.; s. Winfred Lorne and Gloria Grace (Dunlap) McL.; m. Diane Elizabeth Peel, June 12, 1971 (div. Aug. 1977); m. Janice Emily Bowers, Jan. 17, 1990. BS, U. Wash., 1972; PhD, U. Ariz., 1978. Rsch. assoc. U. Ariz., Tucson, 1978-86, asst. prof., 1986-93, asst. rsch. scientist Office of Arid Lands Studies, 1987, assoc. prof., 1993—; adj. prof. plant scis. dept. U. Ariz., Tucson, 1987—, mem. publs. rev. com. Office of Arid Lands Studies, 1980—, instrn. com., 1987—, tenure and promotion guidelines com., 1990, mem. arid lands resource scis. com., 1988—, dean's ad hoc com. on herbarium, 1988, chmn. Hatch-Act proposal rev. coms., 1990, 94; lectr. and workshop leader in field. Manuscript reviewer: Jour. Ariz.-Nev. Acad. Scis., Econ. Botany, Jour. Range Mgmt., Ecology, Jour. Ethnobiology, Jour. Vegetation Sci., others; contbr. chpts. to books, articles and monographs to profl. jours. Chmn. adv. com. Ariz. State Parks, Phoenix, 1991—. Mem. AAAS, Soc. for Econ. Botany (assoc. editor Sci. 1982-94), Am. Inst. Biol. Scis., Bot. Soc. Am., Calif. Bot. Soc., Phi Beta Kappa. Office: U Ariz Office of Arid Lands Study 845 N Park Ave Tucson AZ 85719-4816

MCLEAN, HUGH ANGUS, management consultant; b. Salt Lake City, Feb. 19, 1925; s. George Mark and Rose (Powell) McL.; m. Martha Lane Green, Nov. 23, 1949; children: Michael Hugh, Merrie Smithson. Student, U. Kans., 1943-44; BSME, Iowa State U., 1946; postgrad., U. Utah, 1946, 61-66. Registered profl. engr., Utah. With Utah Oil Refining Co., Boise, Idaho, Twin Falls, Idaho and Salt Lake City, 1953-61, Am. Oil Co., Salt Lake City and 11 western states, 1961-66; cons. Standard Oil (Ind.), Chgo., 1966-69; v.p. Mahler Assocs., Midland Park, N.J., 1969-76; pres. McLean Mgmt. Systems, Wyckoff, N.J., 1976-84, Heber City, Utah, 1984—. Author: There Is a Better Way to Manage, 1982, Developmental Dialogues, 1972, Career Planning Program, 1975; creator, host (TV) live shows and commls., 1956-57; creator stewardship mgmt. system, 1987. Rep. election judge, Salt Lake City, 1964, Operation Eagle Eye, Chgo., 1968; pub. communications dir. Ch. Jesus Christ Latter-Day Saints, N.Y. metro area, 1981-84; introduced SAFE HOMES in county and state, 1987; chmn. bd. dirs. Town Hall Playhouse, 1990; served to lt. (j.g.) USNR, 1943-46. Recipient Silver award Am. Petroleum Inst., 1957. Mem. Am. Soc. Tng. Devel. (chmn. N.Y. metro chpt. field trips 1972-74). Home: PO Box 251 Heber City UT 84032-0251 Office: McLean Mgmt Systems PO Box 251 Heber City UT 84032-0251

MCLEAN, IAN SMALL, astronomer, physics educator; b. Johnstone, Scotland, U.K., Aug. 21, 1949; s. Ian and Mary (Small) McL.; (div.); 1 child, Jennifer Ann; m. Janet Wheelans Yourston, Mar. 4, 1983; children: Joanna, David Richard, Graham Robert. BS with hons., U. Glasgow, 1971, PhD, 1974. Rsch. fellow Dept. Astronomy U. Glasgow, Scotland, 1974-78; rsch. assoc. Steward Observatory U. Ariz., Tucson, 1978-80; sr. rsch. fellow Royal Observatory U. Edinburgh, Scotland, 1980-81, sr. scientific officer Royal Observatory, 1981-86; prin. scientific officer Joint Astronomy Ctr., Hilo, Hawaii, 1986-89; prof. Dept. Physics and Astronomy UCLA, 1989—. Author: Electronic and Computer-Aided Astronomy: From Eyes To Electronic Sensors, 1989; contbr. articles to profl. jours. Recipient Exceptional Merit award U.K. Serc, Edinburgh, 1989; NSF grantee, 1991. Fellow Royal Astron. Soc.; mem. Internat. Astron. Union (pres. com. Paris chpt. 1988-91, v.p. 1985-88), Inst. Physics, Am. Astron. Soc. Office: UCLA Dept Astronomy 405 Hilgard Ave Los Angeles CA 90024-1301

MCLEAN, ROBIN JENNIFER, marketing, advertising professional; b. Denver, Dec. 15, 1960; d. Robert Earl and Marjorie Lee (Worland) McL. BA, U. Denver, 1983, postgrad., 1986—. Prodn. asst. Sta. KOA, Denver; advt. intern Colle & McVoy, Englewood, Colo.; advt. sales rep. Dow Jones & Co., Inc., Englewood, 1983-85; acct. exec. Univ. Graphics, Inc., Englewood, 1985-86; v.p. Columbine Mktg., Denver, 1986-90; acct. exec. Century Media, 1990-91; dir. advertising, mktg. Cherry Creek Locale, Denver, 1992—; owner Cherry Creek Law Bldg., 1994; advisor U. Denver, 1985—; mktg. and pub. rels. cons. U.S. West, Inc. Mem. Denver Mus. of Natural History, Denver Botantical Gardens. Republican. Roman Catholic. Home: 270 Glencoe St Denver CO 80220-5716

MCLELLON, RICHARD STEVEN, aerospace engineer, consultant; b. Lawton, Okla., May 28, 1952; s. Robert Nelson and Jane (Warriner) McL. BSME, Old Dominion U., 1979. Aerospace engr. Naval Engring. Support Office, Norfolk, Va., 1979-82, U.S. Army Aviation Systems Commd., Ft. Eustis, Va., 1982-86; lead dynamicist Martin Marietta Astronautics Group Launch Systems (now Lockheed Martin Techs. Inc. Space Launch Sys.), Denver, 1986—; cons. Aircraft Devel., Inc., Englewood, Colo., 1991—. Mem. Soc. Naval Archs. and Marine Engrs., Rocky Mountain Aerobatic Club. Office: Aircraft Devel Inc PO Box 814 Englewood CO 80151-0814

MCLEOD, BRUCE ROYAL, electrical engineering educator, consultant; b. Greeley, Colo., Jan. 17, 1939; s. Royal and Alma McLeod; m. Peggy Sue Hubbard, Sept. 30, 1961; children: Robert Royal, Cathryn Elaine McLeod McAllister. BSEE, Colo. State U., 1961; MSEE, U. Colo., 1965, PhD in Elec. Engring., 1968. Elec. engr. light mil. electronics dept. GE Co., Utica, N.Y., 1961-64; rsch. engr. Boeing Aerospace Group, Seattle, 1968-70; asst. prof. elec. engring. Mont. State U., Bozeman, 1970-74, assoc. prof., 1974-79, prof., 1979-89, 90—; owner, operator Spear Lazy U Ranch, Wilsall, Mont., 1989-90; pres. Life Resonances Inc., Bozeman, 1987—, cons., 1990—; vis. rsch. scientist Columbia Presbyn. Hosp., N.Y.C., VA Hosp., U. Ky. Med. Ctr., 1981-82; cons. Devel. Tech. Corp., Bozeman, 1972, Infosystems, Bozeman, 1972, La Jolla (Calif.) Tech. Inc., 1983-85, Finnegan, Henderson, Farabow, Garret & Dunner, Washington, 1983, 85-86, IatroMed Inc., Phoenix, 1989-90. Contbr. over 30 articles to profl. jours. and books; presenter over 35 abstracts at nat. & internat. meetings; invited spkr. in field; holder of 23 U.S. patents, 8 Australian patent, 2 Can. patent, 1 Japanese patent. Pres. Park County Legis. Assn., Livingston, Mont., 1988-90. Mem. IEEE (sr., chmn. Mont. sect. 1983-84), AAAS, Bioelectromagnetics Soc. (program com.), Bioelec. Repair and Growth Soc. (program com. 1985-86, chmn. program com. 1988-90, coun. 1986-88, pres.-elect 1990, pres. 1991), Nat. Cattleman's Assn., Park County Stockgrowers Assn., Masons, Shriners, Sigma Xi (v.p. Mont. State U. chpt. 1979-80, pres. 1980-81), Sigma Tau, Eta Kappa Nu, Kappa Mu Epsilon, Sigma Xi. Office: Montana State University Electrical Engring Dept Bozeman MT 59717-0378

MCLEOD, JENNIFER GAIL, English language educator; b. Downey, Calif., Mar. 30, 1955; d. David Edwin and Rosemary Ann (Klecman)

Cripps; m. Colin Campbell McLeod, Oct. 31, 1984;; 1 child, Eric. BA in English, Calif. State U., Chico, 1991, postgrad., 1991—. K-12 teaching credential, Calif. Musician, singer various bands, 1976-84; activity leader Victorian Guest Home, Chico, 1988-90; tchr. English, Chico Jr. H.S., 1992; writing tutor Writing Ctr., Calif. State U., 1987-90, teaching asst. in English, 1994—. Contbr. articles and poetry to profl. jours. Vol. with schizophrenics Cmty. Action Vols. in Edn., Chico, 1990; vol. with elderly St. John's Cath. Ch., Chico, 1992-93. Jean Nedrow Kutz scholar, 1990, Helen Elizabeth Stansell scholar, 1992-93. Mem. Phi Kappa Phi. Democrat.

MCLEOD, JOHN HUGH, JR., mechanical and electrical engineer; b. Hattiesburg, Miss., Feb. 27, 1911; s. John Hugh and Martha (Caldwell) McL.; m. Suzette Boutell, June 23, 1951; children: John Hugh III, Robert Boutell. BS, Tulane U., 1933. Registered profl. engr., Calif. Engr. various firms, 1933-39; field engr. Taylor Instrument Co., Rochester, N.Y., 1940-42; rsch. and devel. engr. Leeds & Northrup Co., Phila., 1943-47; sect. head guidance systems and guided missiles U.S. Naval Air Missile Test Ctr., Point Mugu, Calif., 1947-56; design specialist Gen. Dynamics/Astronautics, San Diego, 1956-63, cons., 1963-64; pvt. practice mech. and elec. engring. cons., La Jolla, Calif., 1964—; disting. vis. prof. Calif. State U. Chico, 1975; mem. exec. com. Fall Joint Computer Conf. Am. Fedn. Info. Processing Socs., 1965. Co-founder San Diego Symposium for Biomed. Engring., 1961. Author: Simulation: The Dynamic Modeling of Ideas and Systems with Computers, 1968, Computer Modeling and Simulation: Principles of Good Practice, 1982; editor, pub.: Simulation Council Newsletter, 1952-55; editor: Simulation, 1963-74; assoc. editor Instruments & Control Systems, 1955-63, Behavioral Sci., 1973—; tech. editor Simulation in the Service of Soc., 1971—; co-author: Large-Scale Models for Policy Evaluation, 1977. With USN, 1942-43. Recipient Sr. Sci. Simulation award Electronic Assocs., Inc., 1965, TIMS award Inst. Mgmt. Scis., 1986; NEH, NSF grantee, 1983; McLeod Inst. Simulation Sci. named in his honor Calif. State U., Chico, 1991, other ctrs. located U. Calgary, Can., U. Ottawa, Can., U. Ghent, Belgium, Istituto per la Recerca, Naples, Italy. Mem. IEEE, AAAS, Soc. Computer Simulation (chmn. com. on profl. ethics, publs. advisor, John McLeod award 1987). Home: 8484 La Jolla Shores Dr La Jolla CA 92037-3019 Office: Soc Computer Simulation PO Box 17900 San Diego CA 92177-7900

MCLEOD, MALCOLM STEWART, financial executive; b. Gloucester, Mass., May 21, 1941; s. Malcolm Stewart and Mary Evelyn (Keane) McL.; m. Stephanie Green, May 29, 1994; children: Karen Lee, Kristin Sinset. BA, U. Mass., 1966; MA, U. Hawaii, 1968. State trans. economist State of Hawaii, Honolulu, 1975-86; pres. Ctr. for Psycho Social Rsch., Honolulu, 1986-90; v.p. Abel Appraisers and Bus. Valuations, Honolulu, 1990—; mem. faculty Hawaii Pacific U. Sch. Bus., 19866; mem. adv. com. Royal State Ins. Co., Honolulu. 1986-92; com. mem. Nat. Rsch. Coun., Washington, 1986-95; dir. Investors Fin., 1994. Contbr. articles to profl. jours. Conv. del. Hawaii Govt. Employees Assn., Honolulu, 1987-93. With USAF, 1959-63. Recipient Cert. of Nat. Merit U.S. Dept HUD, 1985. Mem. Am. Econ. Assn., ESOP Assn., Inst. of Bus. Appraisers, Hawaii Yacht Club, Omicron Delta Epsilon. Office: Abel Appraiser/Bus Valuation 1188 Bishop St Ste 911 Honolulu HI 96813-3304

MCLEOD, SUSAN MARGARET, English language educator; b. Shreveport, La., Nov. 27, 1942; d. Milton Frederick and Margaret Ellis Herminghaus; m. Douglas B. McLeod, Dec. 28, 1965; children: Alison Marie, Jonathan Mark. BA, Principia Coll., 1964; MA, U. Wis., 1965, PhD, 1972. Lectr. Haile Selassie I U., Addis Ababa, Ethiopia, 1966-68; instr. San Diego State U., 1974-79, 81-86; assoc. prof. Wash. State U., Pullman, 1986-92, prof. English, assoc. dean, 1992—; mem. exec. com. Conf. on Coll. Composition and Comm., 1990-92, Coun. of Writing Program Adminstrs.; bd. cons. Nat. Network Writing Across the Curriculum Programs. Editor: Strenghthening Programs for WAC, 1988, Writing About the World, 1991, 2d edit., 1994, WAC: A Guide to Developing Programs, 1992. Recipient Tchg. Excellence award Burlington No., 1989. Mem. Rocky Mountain MLA (pres. 1989-90). Office: Wash State U Coll of Liberal Arts Pullman WA 99164-2630

MCLESKEY, CHARLES HAMILTON, anesthesiology educator; b. Phila., Nov. 8, 1946; s. W. Hamilton and Marion A. (Butts) McL.; m. Nanci S. Simmons, June 3, 1972; children: Travis, Heather. BA, Susquehanna U., 1968; MD, Wake Forest U., 1972. Diplomate Am. Bd. Anesthesiology. Intern Maine Med. Ctr., Portland, 1972-73; resident in anesthesiology U. Wash. Sch. Medicine, Seattle, 1973-76, NIH rsch. trainee, 1974-75; clin. teaching assoc. dept. anesthesiology U. Calif., San Francisco, 1976-78; asst. prof. anesthesiology Wake Forest U. Bowman Gray Sch. Medicine, Winston-Salem, N.C., 1978-83, assoc. prof., 1983-84; assoc. prof. U. Tex. Med. Br., Galveston, 1985-87; assoc. prof. anesthesiology U. Colo. Health Sci. Ctr., Denver, 1987-91, prof., 1991-93, dir. acad. affairs, 1987-93; prof., chmn. dept. anesthesiology Tex. A&M U., 1993—; chmn. dept. anesthesiology Scott and White Clin. and Meml. Hosp., Temple, Tex., 1993—; cons., lectr. Janssen Pharmaceutica, Piscataway, N.J., 1980—, Alza Corp., Palo Alto, Calif., 1986—; cons. Glaxo-Wellcome Co., Research Triangle Park, N.C., Abbott Labs., Chgo., Marion Merrill Dow, Kansas City, Kans.; lectr. to over 500 nat. and state med. orgns., 1982—; examiner Am. Bd. Anesthesiology. Assoc. editor Anesthesiology Rev.; editor Geriatric Anesthesiology, 1989; contbr. numerous articles to med. jours. Mem. choir Friendswood (Tex.) Meth. Ch., 1983-87, mem. Friendswood Fine Arts Commn., 1985-87. Lt. comdr. M.C., USN, 1976-78. Woodruff-Fisher scholar, 1964-68. Mem. Internat. Platform Assn., Assn. U. Anesthetists, Am. Soc. Anesthesiologists (del. 1983-85, 88—), Soc. for Edn. in Anesthesia (v.p.), Colo. Soc. Anesthesiologists (pres.), Oenophile Soc., Nat. Speakers Assn., Evergreen Newcomers, Alpha Omega Alpha. Republican. Presbyterian.

MC LURE, CHARLES E., JR., economist; b. Sierra Blanca, Tex., Apr. 14, 1940; s. Charles E. and Dessie (Evans) McL.; m. Patsy Nell Carroll, Sept. 17, 1962. B.A., U. Kans., 1962; M.A., Princeton U., 1964, Ph.D., 1966. Asst. prof. econs. Rice U., Houston, 1965-69, assoc. prof., 1969-72, prof., 1972-79, Allyn R. and Gladys M. Cline prof. econs., 1973-79; exec. dir. for research Nat. Bur. Econ. Research, Cambridge, Mass., 1977-78, v.p., 1978-81; sr. fellow Hoover Instn., Stanford U., 1981—; dep. asst. sec. Dept. Treasury, 1983-85; sr. staff economist Coun. Econ. Advisers, Washington, 1969-70; vis. lectr. U. Wyo., 1972; vis. prof. Stanford U., 1973; cons. U.S. Treasury Dept., Labor Dept., World Bank, UN, OAS, Tax Found., Com. Econ. Devel., IMF, govts. Can., Colombia, Malaysia, Panama, Jamaica, Bolivia, Indonesia, New Zealand, Trinidad and Tobago, Venezuela, Guatemala, Peoples Republic China, Egypt, Malawi, Mex., Bulgaria, Brazil, Russia, Ukraine, Kazakhstan, South Africa. Author: Fiscal Failure: Lessons of the Sixties, 1972, (with N. Ture) Value Added Tax: Two Views, 1972, (with M. Gillis) La Reforma Tributaria Colombiana de 1974, 1977, Must Corporate Income Be Taxed Twice?, 1979, Economic Perperspectives on State Taxation of Multijurisdictional Corporations, 1986, The Value Added Tax: Key to Deficit Reduction, 1987; co-author: Taxation of Income from Business and Capital in Colombia, 1989; also numerous articles on econs. and public finance. Ford Found. faculty research fellow, 1967-68. Mem. Am. Econ. Assn., Nat. Tax Assn., Beta Theta Pi. Home: 250 Yerba Santa Ave Los Altos CA 94022-1609 Office: Stanford U Hoover Instn Stanford CA 94305-6010

MCLURKIN, THOMAS CORNELIUS, JR., lawyer; b. L.A., July 28, 1954; s. Thomas Cornelius and Willie Mae (O'Connor) McL.; m. Charmaine Bobo. BA, U. So. Calif., 1976, MPA, 1980, PhD in Pub. Adminstrn., 1995; JD, U. LaVerne, 1982. Bar: Calif. 1984, U.S. Dist. Ct. (ctrl. dist.) Calif. 1984, U.S. Dist. Ct. Hawaii 1984, U.S. Ct. Appeals (9th cir.) 1984, U.S. Dist. Ct. (ea., no. and so. dists.) Calif. 1985, U.S. Tax Ct. 1988, U.S. Ct. Mil. Appeals 1989, U.S. Army Ct. Mil. Rev. 1993, U.S. Supreme Ct., 1995. Law clk. Dept. Water and Power City of L.A., 1979-82; jud. clk. U.S. Dist. Ct. (cen. dist.) Calif., L.A., 1982-83; law clk. Office City Atty., L.A., 1983-84, Dep. City Atty., 1984—. Author (with others): Facts in American History, 1968, 2nd edit. 1989, Eagle Scout, 1970. Mem. L.A. World Affairs Coun., 1980—, Smithsonian Assocs.; bd. dirs. L.A. Area coun. Boy Scouts Am., Hillsides Homes for Children; provisional patron Tournament of Roses Assn., Pasadena, 1994—; mem. Verdugo Hills Area coun. Boy Scouts Am. Mem. ABA, ALA, L.A. County Bar Assn., Assn. Trial Lawyers Am., Langston Law Assn. L.A., Am. Soc. Pub. Adminstrs., U. So. Calif. Gen. Alumni Assn. (bd. govs. exec. bd. 1986-90), U. So. Calif. Black Alumni Assn.-Ebonics (pres. 1988-89), U. So. Calif. Pres.'s Cir., Elks, Phi Alpha Delta, Kappa Alpha Psi. Republican. United Methodist. Office: LA City Atty Office 111 N Hope St Los Angeles CA 90012-5701

MCMAHAN, CELESTE TINA, architect, construction and real estate project manager; b. Denver, Jan. 4, 1948; d. Frank McMahan and Jean Dolores (Graves) Kauno; m. George Cardinal Richards, Dec. 2, 1977. BS in Urban Studies, U. Colo., 1976, MS in Urban and Regional Planning, 1977, postgrad. in architecture, 1977. Lic. real estate sales rep. Colo. Housing sales coordinator Gt. Western United, Colorado City, Colo., 1970-74; dir. parks and recreation City of Edgewater, Colo., 1975-76; intern WICHE, 1976; intern planner City of Aurora, Colo., 1976-77; project mgr./architect Stanford U., Calif., 1977-79; designer, facilities planner Sacramento Savs., 1979-80; project mgr. Crocker Bank, San Francisco, 1980-81, Bank of Am., San Francisco, 1981-85, team mgr. No. Calif. project devel., 1985—; owner McMahan Assocs., Vallejo, Calif., 1979—. Author: A Market Analysis of Downtown, 1976; Housing Market and Population Projections, 1976; Tales From the Old Country, 1984. Photographer. Mem. archtl. com. San Francisco Traditional Jazz Found., 1985; commr. Archtl. Rev. Bd., Menlo Park, Calif., 1978; mem. com. Gov.'s Housing Policy Com., Rural Subcom. on Housing Legis., Social Concerns Legis. Com., Denver, liason com. to form Aurora Community Devel. Corp., 1976; bd. dirs. Bay Area Lawyers for the Arts (now Calif. Lawyers For the Arts); mem., trustee, mem. congl. council Grace Cathedral, 1987-88, 89—, devel. com., 1986-87; bd. dirs. San Francisco Friends of Arts, 1984-88, QUEST: Grace Cathedrals' Search for Spiritual Wholesness, 1988—, Inst. for Study of Natural Systems, 1987-88; chmn. Michaelmas Faire, 1987-88, 89—, art com. Grace Cathedral. Recipient 1st place award Music Educators Assn. Ensemble Festival, 1965; ednl. grantee U. Colo., 1974-77. Mem. Orgn. Women Architects, AIA, Nat. Assn. Women in Constrn., Women Evening Orgn. (v.p.), Nat. Assn. Corp. Real Estate Execs., Downtown Aurora Mchts. Assn. (hon.), Internat. Acad. Lymphology (Cert.)., Internat. Platform Assn., Stanford U. Alumni Assn., Commonwealth Club (San Francisco). Home: PO Box 1152 Vallejo CA 94590-0115 Office: Bank of Am Corporate Real Estate Dept 560 Davis St San Francisco CA 94111-1902

MCMAHON, JAMES PATRICK, ecologist, science association administrator; b. Chgo., July 10, 1951; s. James Patrick and Helen Margaret (Walter) McM.; m. Alice Anne Oakes, Sept. 8, 1989; children: J. Emrys, Jacqueline Anne. BS in Ecology, U. Ill., 1974; postgrad., Cen. Wash. U., 1975-76, Naropa Inst., Boulder, 1993-94. Owner Seattle Recycling, Inc., 1976-79; program planner City of Seattle, 1979-80; divsn. mgr. Fibres Internat., Bellevue, Wash., 1980-85; owner Environ. Enhancement Group, Lynnwood, Wash., 1985-88; regional mgr. 20:20 Recycle Ctrs., Inc., L.A., 1987-88; nat. mktg. dir. May Mfg., Denver, 1990-94; ptnr. Agua Fria Enterprises, Prescott, Ariz., 1992—; project dir. Nature Conservancy, 1994—; sr. fellow Independence Inst., Golden, Colo., 1990-93, The Gallatin Inst., Bozeman, Mont., 1994—; participant 50 for Colo. leadership program Colo. Assn. Commerce and Industry, 1993; condr. numerous bus. seminars; developer original recycling strategy City of Seattle; expatriot in Saint Martin, French West Indies, 1989. Exec. prodr. (video) Recycling in Washington State, 1985; contbr. many articles on Western pub. lands, natural resources, Philippine Eagle recovery, logging and men's issues to newspapers, mag. and other publs., U.S. and London; frequent radio commentator. Mem. survey and nat. conf. coms. Dept. Ecology, 1985-86; bd. dirs. Nat. Recycling Coalition, 1983-86. Mem. Wash. State Recycling Assn. (v.p. 1984-85), Nature Conservancy, Greater Seattle C. of C., Rocky Mountain Angling Club, Trout Unltd. Home and Office: 1383 Ironwood Ln Dewey AZ 86327

MCMATH, CARROLL BARTON, JR., past college administrator, retired army officer; b. Godfrey, Wash., Sept. 18, 1910; s. Carroll Barton and Grace Jenness (Matthews) McM.; BS, Oreg. State U., 1932; MS (A. Olson Research scholar), N.Y. U., 1936; m. Betty Ruth Thompson, Nov. 26, 1937; children: Robert Thompson, Carol. With Sacramento Bee Newspaper, 1932-35; jr. exec. Lord & Taylor, N.Y.C., 1936-39; head dept. bus. Boise (Ida.) Jr. Coll., 1939-40; Res. officer on active duty U.S. Army, 1940-46, assigned gen. staff War Dept., 1943-45; commd. capt. regular U.S. Army 1947, advanced through grades to lt. col., assigned Joint Chiefs of Staff, 1951-53, Office Sec. of Army, 1953-55, ret., 1963; campaigns include Okinawa, Korea, Vietnam; mem. faculty U. Hawaii, Honolulu, 1964-77, asst. to dir. research, profl. adviser to faculty on rsch., 1964-77; faculty Indsl. Coll. of Armed Forces, Washington, 1945-46; asst. prof. retailing N.Y. U., N.Y.C., 1946-47. Mem. Assn. U.S. Army, AAAS, AAUP, Ret. Officers Assn., Honolulu Acad. Arts, Hawaiian Hist. Soc., Am. Theatre Organ Soc., Hawaii Found. History and Humanities, Scabbard and Blade, Alpha Delta Sigma, Alpha Kappa Psi, Eta Mu Pi, Elk, Koa Anuenue. Democrat. Home: 1624 Kanunu St Honolulu HI 96814-2747

MCMEEKIN, KAREN ANN, air force officer; b. Plainfield, N.J., Sept. 19, 1962; d. Samuel G. and Linda J. (Cutting) McM. BA in French, Rutgers U., 1984; MPA, U. West Fla., 1992. Air weapons contr. Commd. 2d lt. USAF, 1984, advanced through grades to capt., 1988; weapons assignment officer N.W. Air Def. Sector, McChord AFB, Wash., 1985-88; sr. air def. contr. Air Forces Iceland, Keflavik Naval Air Sta., 1988-89; air weapons contr. instr. 331st Tech. Tng. Squadron, Tyndall AFB, Fla., 1989-93; combat crew comdr. 10th Air Def. Squadron, Wheeler Army Air Field, Hawaii, 1993—, squadron pub. affairs rep., chief exercises, 1993—; squadron tng. officer Air Forces Iceland Command Post, Keflavik Naval Air Sta., 1988-89; squadron plans officer 325 Weapons Contr. Tng. Squadron, Tyndall AFB, Fla., 1989-92, squadron intro officer, 1989-91. Contbr. articles to newspapers. Big Sister, vol. Big Bros./Big Sisters Am., New Brunswick, N.J. and McChord AFB, Wash., 1981-82, 86-88; escort, vol. Spl. Olympics, McChord AFB, Wash. and Tyndall AFB, Fla., 1987, 90; vol. United Svcs. Orgn., Honolulu, 1993—. Mem. Am. Soc. Pub. Adminstrn., Women of the Moose, Hickam AFB Officers Club, Hickam AFB Co. Grade Officers Coun., Air Force Assn., Women in Mil. Svc. for Am. Meml. Found., Pi Alpha Alpha. Democrat. Methodist.

MCMICHAEL, DONALD EARL, lawyer; b. Denver, Aug. 8, 1931; s. Earl L. and Charlotte F. McM.; m. Zeta Hammond, July 6, 1955; children: Lauren A. McMichael Gleason, Thomas D., Susan E. McMichael Markle. AB, Dartmouth Coll., 1953; LLB, U. Colo., 1956. Bar: Colo. 1956, U.S. Dist. Ct. Colo. 1956, U.S. Ct. Appeals (10th cir.) 1956. Assoc. Holme Roberts & Owen, 1956-58; pres. Corp. Ins. Assocs., 1958-70; dir. trust devel. Central Bank Denver, 1970-72; ptnr. Brenman, Sobol & Baum, Denver, 1972-74; ptnr. McMichael, Burlingame, Multz & Lipton (formerly McMichael, Benedict & Multz), Denver, 1974—. Chmn. Denver Cen. YMCA, 1971-73. Capt. USAR, 1956-64. Named Layman of Yr. Denver Metro Cen. YMCA, 1973, 89, named to Denver Metro YMCA Hall of Fame, 1989. Mem. Colo. Bar Assn., Denver Bar Assn., Denver Estate Planning Council (sec. 1971-73). Republican. Methodist. Office: 1580 Lincoln St Denver CO 80203-1501

MCMILLAN, JOHN A., retail executive; b. 1931. BA, U. Wash., 1957. With Nordstrom Inc., Seattle, 1957—, exec. v.p., 1975—, pres., 1989—, co-chmn., 1991—. Office: Nordstrom Inc 1501 5th Ave Seattle WA 98101-1603

MCMILLEN, DARRYL CHARLES, architect; b. Los Angeles, Feb. 1, 1941; s. Charles Henry and Yvonne (Genevieve Ehrgott) McM.; m. Mary Elaine Crandell, June 14, 1964; children—Lainie, Jesse, Genevieve. B.Arch., U. So. Calif., 1966; student Los Angeles City Coll., 1958-61. Designer/planner Walt E. Disney Enterprises, Glendale, Calif., 1966-67; design draftsman Harold Levitt, Architect, Beverly Hills, Calif., 1967-68; project architect David J. Flood Assocs., Los Angeles, 1968-71; resident architect Sun Valley Co., Sun Valley, Idaho, 1971-73; prin. McMillen & Hayes, Sun Valley, 1973-75; owner Darryl C. McMillen, Sun Valley, 1975—. Chmn. Sun Valley Planning and Zoning Com., 1979-81, Elkhorn Archtl. Environ. Control Com., 1983-84. Served with U.S. Army, 1960-62. Mem. AIA. Republican. Lodge: Rotary (pres. 1983-84). Home: 209 Broadway Blvd Ketchum ID 83340 Office: Darryl C McMillen AIA Sun Valley Mall PO Box 1068 Sun Valley ID 83353

MCMILLIN, ANNE, public affairs officer. BA in Internat. Rels. and French, U. Calif., Davis, 1987. Asst. pub. affairs officer Naval Air Sta., Moffett Field, Calif., 1988-94; pub. affairs officer Naval Air Sta., Fallon, Nev., 1994—. Mem. Pub. Rels. Soc. Am. (accredited pub. rels.). Office: USN Pub Affairs Office Naval Air Sta Fallon NV 89496

MC MILLION, JOHN MACON, retired newspaper publisher; b. Coffeyville, Kans., Dec. 25, 1929; s. John Dibrell and Mattie Anna (Macon) McM.; m. Melanie Ann McMillion; children: John Thomas, Johanna, Jennifer, Amanda. Student, Vanderbilt U., 1947-49; B.S. in Journalism, U. Kans., 1956. Police reporter Amarillo (Tex.) Globe-News, 1956; sports editor, telegraph editor Grand Junction (Colo.) Daily Sentinel, 1956-58; mng. editor Alliance (Nebr.) Times-Herald, 1958-59, Clovis (N.Mex.) Jour., 1959-62; gen. mgr. Pasadena (Tex.) Citizen, 1962; bur. mgr. UPI, 1962-66; exec. editor Albuquerque Jour., 1966-69; bus. mgr. Albuquerque Pub. Co., 1971-75; pub. Herald and News-Tribune, Duluth, Minn., 1975-86, Akron (Ohio) Beacon Jour., 1986-90, ret.; campaign mgr. gubernatorial campaign, 1969-71. Served with USN, 1950-54. Address: 12404 Royal Oak Ct NE Albuquerque NM 87111-6237

MCMULLIN, JOYCE ANNE, general contractor; b. Tulsa, Jan. 6, 1952; d. Junior Lawrence Patrick and Carol Anne (Morris) McM.; m. David Lawrence Tupper, Jan. 1, 1980 (div. May 1982). BFA, Calif. Coll. Arts and Crafts, 1973. Interior designer Design Assocs., Oakland, Calif., 1974; interior designer, sales rep. Sullivan's Interiors, Berkeley, Calif., 1975; supr. bldg. maintenance Clausen House, Inc., Oakland, 1975-82; owner New Life Renovation, Lafayette, Calif., 1981—. Contbr. articles to mags., newspapers. Mem. Contra Costa Coun., Nat. Trust Historic Preservation. Mem. AAUW, NAFE, Bus. and Profl. Women, Contra Costa County Women's Network, Self-Employed Tradeswomen (sec. 1984), Contra Costa Coun., Leads Club.

MCMURDO, C(HARLES) GREGORY, state official, lawyer; b. Klamath Falls, Oreg., Apr. 30, 1946; s. Charles Andrew and Juanita Berniece (Bell) McM.; B.A., Oreg. State U., 1968; J.D., Lewis and Clark Coll., 1972. Bar: Oreg. 1972, U.S. Dist. Ct. Oreg. 1975, U.S. Ct. Appeals (9th cir.) 1980, U.S. Supreme Ct. 1984. Legal counsel Oreg. Ho. of Reps., Salem, 1972-76; asst. sect. state State of Oreg., Salem, 1976-81, dep. sec. state, 1981-85; mem. Workers Compensation Bd., 1985-88; dir of govt. rels, Metro, Portland, 1988-90; dep. supt. of pub. instrn., State of Oreg., 1990—. Mem. Oreg. State Bar. Republican. Episcopalian. Office: Oreg Dept of Edn Pub Srvc Bldg 255 Capitol St NE Portland OR 97310

MCMURTY, JUDY JEAN, school counselor; b. Denver, Apr. 5, 1939; d. Lonnie G. and Veva H. (Corlett) Pippin; m. Ray McMurty, Dec. 21, 1958; children: Jerry, Patricia, Michael, Suzan. BA, Adams State Coll., 1963; MA, Calif. State U., 1991. Cert. counselor, Calif. Tchr. Colo. Christian Schs., Denver, 1975-78; libr. media ctr. dir. Melodyland Schs., Anaheim, Calif., 1979-80, adminstrv. asst., 1980-85; counselor So. Calif. Christian Schs., Orange, 1985-88; tchr. Val Verde Unified Sch. Dist., Perris, Calif., 1988-91, counselor, 1991—, mem. crisis intervention team, 1993-94; adj. prof. Azusa (Calif.) Pacific U., summers 1992, 93; counseling dept. chair Vista Verde Mid. Sch., Moreno Valley, Calif., 1991-94; mem. grad. com. Rancho Verde H.S., Moreno Valley, 1991. Worship team instrumentalist Mission Cmty. Ch., Riverside, Calif., 1993-94, Christian Life Ctr., Riverside, 1991-93. Mem. Am. Counseling Assn., Calif. Sch. Counselors Assn., Riverside/San Bernardino County Counselors Assn., Am. Assn. Christian Counselors (charter). Republican. Office: Vista Verde Mid Sch 25777 Krameria Moreno Valley CA 92551

MCNAIR, NORMA DIANE, nurse; b. Berkeley, Calif., July 1, 1953; d. Norman David and Shirley Claire (Grady) McNair. BSN, Calif. State U., 1976; MSN, Yale U., 1985. Staff nurse Sutter Gen. Hosp., Sacramento, Calif., 1976-79, U. Calif., Sacramento, 1979-80, The Nat. Hosp., London, 1980-81, Sutter Gen. Hosp., Sacramento, 1982-83, Hosp. St. Raphael, New Haven, Conn., 1984; clin. nurse specialist, trainee Veteran's Adminstrn., West Haven, 1984-85; clin. nurse specialist Hermann Hosp., U. Tex. Med. Sch., Houston, 1986-89, Mercy Gen. Hosp., Sacramento, 1989-91, UCLA Med. Ctr., 1991—. Cultural Affairs, Am. Red Cross, Houston, 1987-88. Mem. ANA, AACN, Am. Assn. Neuroscience Nurses (bd. dirs. 1988-90). Democrat. Presbyterian.

MCNALL, BRUCE, professional sports executive, numismatist; m. Jane Cody; children: Katie, Bruce. Student, UCLA. Founder, chmn. bd. Numismatic Fine Arts, Inc., L.A.; owner, chmn. bd. Summa Stable, Inc.; chmn. bd. Gladden Entertainment Corp.; former ptnr. Dallas Mavericks NBA; co-owner L.A. Kings, 1986-87, sole owner, 1988-94, co-owner, 1994—; owner Toronto Argonauts, 1991—. Office: LA Kings 3900 W Manchester Blvd Inglewood CA 90305-2200*

MCNALL, LESTER RAY, chemist, horticultural specialist; b. Gaylord, Kans., Oct. 28, 1927; s. Webster and Bertha Katherine (Heide) McN. BS in Chemistry, U. Wis., 1950; PhD in Chemistry, UCLA, 1955. Rsch. chemist Esso Rsch. & Engring. Co., Linden, N.J., 1955-56; head chem. rsch. PaperMate Mfg. Co. div. Gillette Co., Santa Monica, Calif., 1956-65; tech. dir. Leffingwell Chem. Co., Brea, Calif., 1965-76; gen. mgr. Leffingwell div. Thompson-Hayward Chem. Co., Brea, 1976-84; pres. Nutrient Techs., Inc., La Habra, Calif., 1984—. Mem. Am. Chem. Soc., Am. Soc. for Hort. Sci. Home: 311 E Country Hills Dr La Habra CA 90631-7625 Office: Nutrient Techs Inc PO Box 903 Dinuba CA 93618-0903

MCNALLY, BRIAN CRAIG, creative director, philosopher, publisher; b. Culver City, Calif., Dec. 16, 1965; s. John Larry and Marcia Ann (Younkin) McN. AA in Philosophy, Cerritos Coll., Norwalk, Calif., 1987; BA in Philosophy, Calif. State U., Fullerton, 1990; MA in Philosophy, U. Calif., Riverside, 1991. Philosophy tchg. asst. Calif. State U., Fullerton, 1989-90, U. Calif., Riverside, 1990-91; master rendering painter, bus. owner, mgr. McNally Art Enterprises West, Bellflower, Calif., 1991-92; sculptor, castor technician In Svc. Miniatures, Lakewood, Calif., 1991-92; writer, artist Freman Publs., Chatsworth, Calif., 1992—; founder, pres., CEO, creative dir., gen. mgr. Praxis Publs., Inc., Huntington Beach, Calif., 1993—; guest lectr. Calif. State U., Fullerton, 1992, symposium spkr., 1992; spkr. Oriel Coll., Oxford (Eng.) U., 1990-91; highlighted artist, instr. Game Mfrs. Assn., Dallas, 1991-92. Artist numerous paintings and sculptures. Mem. sch. bd. dirs. Bellflower Unified Sch. Dist., 1982-83; vol., polit. advisor Campaign for Diane Finestein, Riverside, Calif., 1990-91, Campaign for Roy McNally, Redondo Beach, Calif., 1991-92. Recipient scholarship Lions Club, 1994-95. Mem. Huntington Beach C. of C. (amb. 1993-94), Orange County Dasein Assn. (speaker 1993-94). Democrat. Office: Praxis Publs Inc 16892 Bolsa Chica St Ste 203 Huntington Beach CA 92649-3578

MCNALLY, JAMES HENRY, physicist, defense consultant; b. Orange, N.J., Dec. 18, 1936; s. James Osborne and Edith Maude (Jones) McN.; m. Nancy Lee Eudaley, July 4, 1976. B. in Engring. Physics, Cornell U., 1959; PhD in Physics, Calif. Inst. Tech., 1966. Staff mem. program mgr. Los Alamos (N.Mex.) Nat. Lab., 1965-74; asst. dir for laser and isotope separation tech. AEC/ERDA, Washington, 1974-75; assoc. div. leader, dep. for inertial fusion, asst. for nat. sec. issues Los Alamos Nat. Lab., 1975-86; dep. asst. dir. Arms Control and Disarmament Agy., Washington, 1986-88; dir. office staff Los Alamos Nat. Lab., 1988-90, Washington Inst., 1990-94; cons., 1990—; U.S. del. Geneva Conf. on Disarmament, 1969, 73, 74, Threshold Test Ban Treaty, Moscow, 1974, Nuclear Testing Talks, Geneva, 1986-88. Bd. dirs. Wilson Mesa Met. Water Dist., 1976-88; v.p. Mountain Canine Corps, 1994—. Mem. AAAS, Am. Phys. Soc., Internat. Inst. Strategic Studies. Home and Office: 550 Rim Rd Los Alamos NM 87544-2931

MCNAMARA, BRENDA NORMA, secondary education educator; b. Blackpool, Lancashire, Eng., Aug. 8, 1945; came to U.S., 1946; d. Milford Hampson and Nola (Welsby) Jones; m. Michael James McNamara, July 19, 1969. BA in History, Calif. State U., Long Beach, 1967; postgrad., Calif. State U., various campuses, 1967—. Cert. secondary tchr. and lang. devel. specialist, Calif. Tchr. history West High Sch., Torrance, Calif., 1968—, dept. chair, 1989—; cons. in field. Co-author: World History, 1988. Western Internat. Studies Consortium grantee, 1988. Mem. Calif. Tchrs. Assn., Calif. Coun. for Social Studies, Torrance Tchrs. Assn. (bd. dirs. 1992—), South Bay Coun. for Social Studies, Nat. Tchrs. Assn., Nat. Coun. for Social Studies. Office: West High Sch 20401 Victor St Torrance CA 90503-2255

MCNAMARA, E. MICHAEL, cosmetics executive. V.p. mktg. Noxele Corp., Hunt Vanley, Md. Office: DEP Corp 2101 E Via Arado Compton CA 90220-6113

MCNAMARA, JOHN STEPHEN, artist, educator; b. Cambridge, Mass., Feb. 16, 1950; s. John Stephen and Mary (Adams) McN. BFA in Painting, Mass. Coll. Art, Boston, 1971, MFA in Painting, 1977. Tchr. Mus. Fine Arts Sch., Boston, 1983; undergrad. and grad. painting tchr. Mass. Coll. Art, Boston, 1988; undergrad. painting tchr. Boston Archtl. Ctr., Boston, 1977; color fundamentals tchr. Mass. Coll. Art, Boston, 1987, undergrad. drawing, 1975-88; vis. lectr. San Francisco Art Inst., 1992, 93, U. Calif., Berkeley, 1993, 94, 95. One-man shows include Starvaridis Gallery, Boston, 1985, Bess Cutler Gallery, 1986, Mass. Coll. Art, 1986, Honolulu Acad. Fine Art, 1987, Nielson Gallery, 1990, 92, Miller Block Gallery, Boston, 1995; exhibited in group shows at Boston Collects, Mus. Fine Arts, Stavaridis Gallery, 1986, Bess Cutler Gallery, N.Y.C., 1987, Am. Painters and Sculptors, Met. Mus. Art, N.Y.C., 1988, Resonant Abstraciton, Fuller Mus. Art, Brockton, Mass., 1989-90. Mass. Art and Humanities grantee, 1980, 83, 86, 89, Award in the Visual Arts grantee, 1982, Nat. Endowment Arts grantee, 1981. Home: 1150 Sanchez St San Francisco CA 94114-3857

MC NAMARA, JOSEPH DONALD, researcher, retired police chief, novelist; b. N.Y.C., Dec. 16, 1934; s. Michael and Eleanor (Shepherd) McN.; divorced; children: Donald, Laura, Karen. BS, John Jay Coll., 1968; fellow, Harvard Law Sch., 1970; DPA (Littauer fellow), Harvard U., 1973. Served to dep. insp. Police Dept., N.Y.C., 1956-73; police chief Kansas City, Mo., 1973-76, San Jose, Calif., 1976-91; rsch. fellow Hoover Instn., Stanford U., 1991—; adj. instr. Northeastern U., 1972, John Jay Coll., 1973, Rockhurst Coll., 1975-76, San Jose State U., 1980; cons. U.S. Civil Rights Commn., 1978; lectr., appearances on nat. TV; apptd. nat. adv. bd. U.S. Bur. Justice Stats., 1980, U.S. Drug Control Policy Office, 1993; commentator Pub. Broadcasting Radio. Author: (non-fiction) Safe and Sane, 1984, (novel) The First Directive Crown, 1985, Fatal Command, 1987, The Blue Mirage, 1990; contbr. articles to profl. publs. Bd. dirs. Drug Policy Found., Washington; active NCCJ. Served with U.S. Army, 1958-60. Named one of 200 Young Am. Leaders Time mag., 1975; recipient disting. alumni award John Jay Coll., 1979, Pres.'s award Western Soc. Criminology1979, Morrison Gitchoff award Western Soc. Criminology, 1992, H.B. Spear award Drug Policy Found., 1992; Kansas City police named Best in Country by Nat. Newspaper Enterprises, 1974, San Jose Police Dept. named Nat. Model U.S. Civil Rights Commn., 1980; named Law Enforcement Officer of Yr., Calif. Trial Lawyers Assn., 1991. Mem. Internat. Assn. Chiefs of Police, Calif. Police Chiefs Assn., Calif. Peace Officers Assn., Major Cities Police Chiefs Assn., Police Exec. Research Forum (dir.). Office: Hoover Instn Stanford CA 94305

MCNAMARA, KAY COPELAND, publishing executive; b. San Antonio, July 4, 1946; d. Joseph Bryson and Gladys (Ware) Copeland; m. Landon Schultz, Oct. 1, 1973 (div. Apr. 1975); m. Stephen McNamara, June 10, 1978; children: Christopher, Morgan. BA in Math. and Psychology, U. Tex., 1970; MPH, U. Tex., Houston, 1971. Alcohol and drug abuse adminstr. Tex. Dept. Mental Health and Mental Retardation, Austin, 1971-75; v.p. Marin Sun Printing, Inc., Mill Valley, Calif., 1978-93, Marin Solar Village Corp., Mill Valley, Calif., 1978—; gen. ptnr. Sunrise Investment Co., Mill Valley, Calif., 1980—; circulation mgr., prodn. mgr., advt. mgr., assoc. publisher Pacific Sun Pub., Mill Valley, 1990—. Treas. parent bd. Marin Country Day Sch., Corte Madera, Calif., 1989; mem. parent bd. San Francisco U. H.S., 1994—. Mem. Scott Valley Swim and Tennis Club, Chi Omega. Democrat. Home: 384 Tennessee Ave Mill Valley CA 94941-3840 Office: Pacific Sun Pub 21 Corte Madera Ave Mill Valley CA 94941

MCNAMARA, STEPHEN, newspaper executive; b. Chgo., July 9, 1934; s. Robert Charles McNamara Jr. and Susan (Deuel) Shattuck; m. Hanne Morgensen Petterson, Feb. 21, 1960 (div. Aug. 1968); children: Lise, Natalie, Kevin; m. Kay Copeland, June 10, 1978; children: Christopher, Morgan. AB in Am. History, Princeton U., 1955. Reporter Winston-Salem (N.C.) Jour., 1955-57; sports writer Miami Herald, 1957-59; contbg. European editor Car & Driver, N.Y.C., 1960; asst. news editor, exec. sports editor, Sunday editor San Francisco Examiner, 1961-67; CEO, editor, pub. Pacific Sun, Mill Valley, Calif., 1967—; co-pub. The Ark, Tiburon, Calif., 1987—; pres. Marin Sun Printing Co., Mill Valley, 1967-93; mng. gen. ptnr. Sunrise Investment Co., Mill Valley, 1980—; vis. lectr. San Francisco State U., 1967; mem. innovation and planning commn. Calif. Dept. Edn., Sacramento, 1980; co-founder, pres. Marin Solar Village Corp., Mill Valley, 1976—, Marin Cmty. Video, Mill Valley, 1973-78. Mem. Soc. Profl. Journalists, Nat. Assn. Alternative Newsweeklies (pres. 1978-81), Calif. Assn. Alternative Newsweeklies (pres. 1990-92), Calif. Soc. Newspaper Editors (pres. 1985-86, bd. dirs. 1983-93), Calif. Newspaper Pubs. Assn. (bd. dirs. 1989-93), San Francisco Press Club (1st place newspaper writing award 1967, 3-2d place awards), Cap and Gown Club (Princeton U.), Scott Valley Swimming and Tennis Club. Democrat. Home: 384 Tennessee Ave Mill Valley CA 94941-3840 Office: Pacific Sun Publ Co 21 Corte Madera Ave Mill Valley CA 94941-1800

MCNAMEE, STEPHEN M., federal judge; b. 1942. B.A., U. Cinn., 1964; M.A., J.D., U. Ariz., 1969. U.S. atty. Dist. of Ariz., Phoenix, 1985-90; judge U.S. Dist. Ct. Ariz., Phoenix, 1990—. Office: 1400 US Courthouse 230 N 1st Ave Phoenix AZ 85025-0230*

MC NEAL, MARTHA VON OESEN, landscape architect; b. Wilmington, N.C., May 16, 1952; d. Henry Martin and Martha Alice (Applewhite) von Oesen; m. Clyde Otis McNeal, Sept. 3, 1983 (div. 1995); stepchildren: Kimberly, Doug. BA cum laude, Randolph-Macon Women's Coll., 1974; M Landscape Architecture, U. Ga., 1979. Planner Henry von Oesen & Assocs., Inc., Wilmington, 1974-75; landscape architect Kilday & Assocs., Inc., West Palm Beach, Fla., 1979-80; sr. landscape architect Gee & Jenson, E.A.P., Inc., West Palm Beach, 1980-88; environ. coordinator Fla. Power & Light Co., Juno Beach, 1988-92; EMF program dir. Pacific Gas and Elec., San Francisco, 1992-95; owner McNeal Consulting, Inc., West Palm Beach, Fla., 1995—; mem. Palm Beach County 208 Com., 1983-85; mem. Electric and Magnetic Fields task force Edison Electric Inst., Washington, 1988-95, chmn., 1991-93; mem. task force Fla. Electric Power Coord. Group, Tampa, 1988-92; mem. Electric Power Rsch. Inst., Electric and Magnetic Fields Task Force, 1994-95. Bd. dirs. Dreher Park Zoo, West Palm Beach, 1985-91; mem. Palm Beach County Planning Congress, West Palm Beach, 1981-85, 95—. Mem. NAFE, Am. Soc. Landscape Architects, Jr. League Palm Beaches. Democrat. Lutheran. Home and Office: 2334 Saratoga Bay Dr West Palm Beach FL 33409

MC NEALY, SCOTT, computer company executive; b. 1954. BA, Harvard U., 1976; MBA, Stanford U., 1980. Chmn., pres., chief exec. officer Sun Microsystems Inc., Mountain View, Calif.; with Rockwell Internat. Corp., Troy, Mich., 1976-78, sales engr.; staff engr. FMC Corp., Chgo., 1980-81; dir. ops. Onyx Systems, San Jose, Calif., 1981-82; with Sun Microsystems Inc., Mountain View, Calif., 1982—, now chmn. bd., pres., chief exec. officer, also dir. Office: Sun Microsystems Inc 2550 Garcia Ave Mountain View CA 94043-1109*

MCNEIL, JOHN STUART, publisher; b. L.A., Oct. 17, 1935; s. Murray Charles and Helen Katherine (Curtis) McN.; divorced; children: Elizabeth Ann, Kenneth John, Karen Lynn. BS, San Jose State U., 1962. Asst. dean for fiscal affairs U. Hawaii Sch. Medicine, Honolulu, 1968-72; fiscal officer Postgrad. Med. Edn. Program for Ryukyus, Honolulu, 1968-72; bus. mgr. Ann. Revs., Inc., Palo Alto, Calif., 1962-68, chief exec. officer, 1973-81; sec.-treas. Ann. Revs., Palo Alto, 1973—, pub., 1981—; lectr. on econs. sci. book pub., 1973—; mem. adv. coun. Astron. Soc. Pacific, 1991—; trustee Soc. for Promotion Sci. and Scholarship, 1982—. Vol. United Way Santa Clara County, San Jose, 1988—. With USN, 1954-56. Mem. Internat. Group Sci., Tech. and Med. Pubs., Bookbuilders West. Democrat. Office: Ann Revs Inc PO Box 10139 Palo Alto CA 94303-0139

MCNEIL, ROBERT DUELL, family businesses consultant; b. Chehalis, Wash., Sept. 16, 1935; s. Robert Maxwell Donahoe and Alice Julia (Duell) McN.; m. Lila G. Davis, Sept. 5, 1958 (div. 1961); children: Katrina, Kathleen; m. Virginia Allen, June 1964 (div. 1966); children: Mark, Marceline; m. Rita Camille Grove, June 29, 1972. Student, U. Oreg., 1954. Mgr. retail sales Standard Oil Calif., Santa Monica, 1956-63; dist. mgr. Questor Corp., 1963-65; regional sales mgr. Perfection Gear Co., L.A., 1965-66; gen. mgr. San Diego Tool Co., 1966-68; pres. F. Mohling Co., San Diego, 1968-70; with Midas Internat., Inc., L.A., Chgo., 1970-72; pres. Muffco, Inc., Lakewood, Colo., 1972-78; v.p. devel. Glassrock Med. Co., Atlanta, 1978-80; prin. R.D. McNeil & Assocs., Scottsdale, Ariz., 1981-86; mng. ptnr. Vaughn-McNeil & Assocs., Denver, 1986-89; prin. R.D. McNeil & Assocs., Littleton, Colo., 1990—. Home and Office: 7040 W Fairview Dr Littleton CO 80123-5425

MCNEILL, DOUGLAS ARTHUR, priest; b. Bklyn., Mar. 6, 1942; s. Daniel Patrick and Elizabeth (Gallagher) McN. Student, Sacred Heart Sem., 1965, MTh, 1968; MS in Edn., Fordham U., 1973. Founder St. Bonaventure Indian Missions, Thoreau, N.Mex., 1974; CEO Gallup Diocese Cath. Charities, Inc., Gallup, N.Mex., 1994—; chmn. Diocesan Pers. Bd., Gallup, N.Mex., 1975-81, Greater Thoreau (N.Mex.) Found., 1986—; founder Blessed Kateri Tekakwitha Acad., Thoreau, 1980; Episcopal vicar McKinley Vicariate, Gallup, 1985—. Candidate N.Y. State Assembly, Bklyn., 1972, Gallup-McKinley Sch. Bd., Gallup, 1976; mem. N.W. N.Mex. Drug Coun., Gallup, 1990—; exec. bd. dirs. S.W. Indian Found., Gallup, 1976-82; mem. Thoreau Water & Sanitation Bd., 1976-86. Mem. Diocesan Pastoral Coun., Diocesan Presbyteral Coun., Nat. Cath. Devel. Conf., Diocesan Religious Edn. (bd. dirs. Gallup chpt. 1973-86), Propagation of the Faith Soc. (bd. dirs. Gallup chpt. 1980—), K.C. (chaplain 1987—). Republican. Roman Catholic. Home: PO Box 218 Gallup NM 87305-0218 Office: Catholic Charities Bldg 506 W 66 Ave Gallup NM 87301

MCNEILL, WILLIAM, environmental scientist; b. Evanston, Ill., Jan. 1, 1930; s. John and Ebba Katrina (Hansen) McN.; m. Caryl Mook, June 15, 1951 (dec. 1969); children: Elizabeth Marie, Charles Craig, Margaret Ruth; m. Caecilia Cinquanto, Oct. 10, 1970. BA, Colgate U., 1951; MA, Temple U., 1955, PhD, 1961. Chief phys. chemistry br. Frankford Arsenal U.S. Army, Phila., 1955-70, dir. applied sci., 1970-75; chief scientist, environ. mgr. Rocky Mountain Arsenal U.S. Army, Denver, 1975-80, dir. tech. ops., 1980-85; gen. mgr. Battelle Denver Ops., 1985-88; sr. tech. adviser Sci. Applications Internat. Corp., Golden, Colo., 1989-92; dir. tech. devel. Sci. Applications Internat. Corp., Oak Ridge, Tenn., 1992—; mem. materials adv. bd. ceramics Nat. Acad. Sci./Nat. Rsch. Coun., Washington, 1966; mem. Gov.'s Task Group on Rocky Mountain Arsenal, 1976, Colo. Pollution Prevention Adv. Bd., Denver, 1991—. Contbr. articles to Jour. Che. Physics, Applied Physics Letters, other profl. publs. Mem. Am. Chem. Soc.,Hazardous Material Control Rsch. Inst., Air and Waste Mgmt. Assn. Home: 319 Cliffrose Ct Lafayette CO 80026

MCNUTT, STEPHEN RUSSELL, volcanologist, geophysical scientist; b. Hartford, Conn., Dec. 21, 1954; s. Elmer Ellsworth and Leona (LaPointe) McN. BA, Wesleyan U., Middletown, Conn., 1977; MA, Columbia U., 1982, MPhil, 1984, PhD, 1985. Sr. seismologist Calif. Div. Mines and Geology, Sacramento, 1984-91; rsch. prof. U. Alaska, Fairbanks, 1991—; cons. U. Costa Rica, San José, 1982—. Contbr. articles to profl. jours. Mem. Seismol. Soc. Am., Am. Geophys. Union, Internat. Assn. Volcanology and Chemistry of Earth's Interior, Buffalo Chips Running Club (Sacramento, bd. dirs. 1986-90). Democrat. Roman Catholic. Office: U Alaska Geophys Inst Alaska Volcano Obs PO Box 757320 Fairbanks AK 99775-7320

MCPEAK, WILLIAM JOHN, science and technical author, consultant; b. Glendale, Calif., Dec. 8, 1948; s. John Joseph and Grace Marie (Mosley) McP.; m. Yvette Sheree Richardson, Mar. 17, 1979; 1 child, Logan William. BA in Atmospheric Sci., U. Calif., L.A., 1971; MA in History of Sci., Pepperdine U., 1977. Cert. Calif. coll. instrnl.-engring. and history. Meteorologist USAF Air Weather Svc., Omaha, 1972-76; mem. tech. staff Hughes Aerospace, Long Beach, Calif., 1978—; grant reviewer sci., soc. and tech. program NSF, Washington, 1992—. Contbg. author encys. and periodicals. With USAF, 1972-76. Mem. Am. Geophys. Union (atmospheric sect.), Inst. for Hist. Study, Nat. Coalition Ind. Scholars, History of Sci. Soc. (book reviewer 1990—).

MCPHADEN, MICHAEL JAMES, oceanographer, educator; b. Buffalo, N.Y., Oct. 22, 1950; s. William Francis and Irene (Scholl) McP.; m. Elisabeth Boice, Aug. 14, 1982; 1 child, Megan Boice. BS magna cum laude, SUNY, Buffalo, 1974; PhD in Phys. Oceanography, U. Calif., San Diego, 1980. Postdoctoral fellow Nat. Ctr. for Atmospheric Rsch., Boulder, Colo., 1980-82; rsch. asst. prof. Sch. Oceanography U. Wash., Seattle, 1984-86, from affiliate asst. prof. to affiliate assoc. prof., 1988-93, affiliate prof., 1993—; oceanographer NOAA-Pacific Marine Environ. Lab., Seattle, 1986—; dir. Tropical Atmosphere Ocean Array project office, Seattle, 1992—; vis. rsch. scientist Joint Inst. Study of Atmosphere and Ocean U. Wash., 1982-84; mem./chmn. various nat. and internat. sci. coms. overseeing ocean climate rsch. Contbr. numerous sci. articles to profl. publs. Mem. Am. Geophys. Union, Am. Meteorol. Soc., The Oceanography Soc., Phi Beta Kappa. Office: Pacific Marine Environ Lab 7600 Sand Point Way NE Seattle WA 98115-6349

MCPHEE, W. R. (BOB MCPHEE), orchestra managing director; b. Winnipeg, Man., Jan. 22, 1956; s. William Ross and Iona (Chisholm) McP.; m. Sandra Kathleen Brown, Aug. 29, 1981. BEd, U. Man., 1978; grad. in Arts Adminstrn., Grant MacEwan Coll., 1982; grad. sch. mgmt., Banff Sch. Fine Arts, 1984. Dir. devel. Calgary (Alta.) Philharm. Orch., 1984-85; asst. gen. mgr. Orch. London, Ont., 1986-88, gen. mgr., 1988-89; gen. mgr. Edmonton (Alta.) Symphony Orch., 1989—; mng. dir. Edmonton Concert Hall Found., 1992—; lectr. Grant MacEwan Coll., Edmonton, Mount Royal Coll., Calgary, Assn. Can. Orchs., Performing Arts Publicist Assn. Mem. Olympic Arts Festival Com., 1984-88. Recipient Alta. Achievement award Province of Alta., Rose Bowl from Man. Music Fest, Syncrude Bus. in the Arts award, 1994. Office: Edmonton Symphony Orch, N Alb Jub Aud 10160-103 St, Edmonton, AB Canada T5J 0X6

MCPHERSON, JAMES WILLIS, III, health care public affairs director; b. Canton, Ohio, Aug. 9, 1956; s. James Willis Jr. and Bea (Shaheen) McP. BA in Pub. Adminstrn., Miami U., Oxford, Ohio, 1978; MA in Pub. Adminstrn., Ohio State U., 1981. Transp. planner Mid-Ohio Regional Planning Commn., Columbus, 1979-81; asst. project dir. Triad Am. Corp., Salt Lake City, 1983-86; mktg. coord. FHP Health Care, Salt Lake City, 1987, pub. affairs dir., 1987—; pres., mem. FHP Health Care PAC, 1987—. Author: History of Hartville, Ohio, 1976. Active Ariz. Affordable Healthcare Found., 1991—; comm. chmn. Ariz. Assn. Managed Care Plans, 1992—; dir. Ariz. Partnership for Infant Immunization, 1992—, Ariz. Preservation Found., 1992—. Named Outstanding Vol., Utah Heritage Found., 1988. Mem. Pub. Rels. Soc. Am., Miami U. Alumni Assn. (pres. Utah chpt. 1988-91), Ohio State U. Alumni Assn., Alpha Tau Omega, Pi Sigma Alpha.

MC PHERSON, ROLF KENNEDY, clergyman, church official; b. Providence, Mar. 23, 1913; s. Harold S. and Aimee (Semple) McP.; m. Lorna De Smith, July 21, 1931 (dec.); children—Marlene (dec.), Kay. Grad., So. Cal. Radio Inst., 1933; D.D. (hon.), L.I.F.E. Bible Coll., 1944; LLD (hon.), L.I.F.E. Bible Coll., Los Angeles, 1988. Ordained to ministry Internat. Ch. Foursquare Gospel, 1940. Pres. Internat. Ch. Foursquare Gospel, L.A., 1944-88, dir., 1944-92; dir. emeritus, 1992—; pres., dir. L.I.F.E. Bible Coll., Inc., L.A., 1944-88. Mem. Echo Park Evangelistic Assn. (pres. 1944—). Office: Internat Ch Foursquare Gospel 1910 W Sunset Blvd Ste 200 Los Angeles CA 90026-3247

MCQUARRIE, TERRY SCOTT, technical director; b. Springville, Utah, Dec. 27, 1942; s. Evan Dain and Fay (Torkeldsen) McQ.; m. Judith Lynn Lewellen, June 20, 1970; children: Devin Daniel, Melanie Fay. BA, U. Oreg., 1966; MA, San Jose State U., 1977. Production mgr. Lunastran Co., San Jose, Calif., 1974-76; group leader Koppers Co., Inc., Pitts., 1978-79, industry mgr., 1980-87; v.p., tech. dir. Glasforms, Inc., San Jose, Calif., 1987—, also bd. dirs.; bd. dirs. Glasforms, Inc. Contbr. articles to profl. publs. Mem. ASTM, Soc. Plastics Industry (Composites Inst., chmn. pultrustion industry coun. 1988-90, vice chmn. panel coun. 1986-87). Republican. Mem. LDS Ch.

MCQUERN, MARCIA ALICE, newspaper publishing executive; b. Riverside, Calif., Sept. 3, 1942; d. Arthur Carlyle and Dorothy Louise (Krupke) Knopf; m. Lynn Morris McQuern, June 7, 1969. BA in Polit. Sci., U. Calif., Santa Barbara, 1964; MS in Journalism, Northwestern U., 1966. Reporter The Press-Enterprise, Riverside, 1966-72, city editor, 1972-74, capitol corrs., 1975-78, dep. mng. editor news, 1984-85, mng. editor news, 1985-87, exec. editor, 1988-94, pres., 1992—, editor, pub., 1994—; asst. metro editor The Sacramento Bee, 1974-75; editor state and polit. news The San Diego Union, 1978-79, city editor, 1979-84; juror Pulitzer Prize in Journalism, 1982, 83, 92, 93. Mem. editorial bd. Calif. Lawyer mag., San Francisco, 1983-88. Bd. advisors U. Calif.-Berkeley Grad. Sch. Journalism, 1991—, U. Calif.-Riverside Grad. Sch. Mgmt., 1994—. Recipient Journalism award Calif. State Bar Assn., 1967, Sweepstakes award Twin Counties Press Club, Riverside and San Bernardino, 1972. Mem. Am. Soc. Newspaper Editors (bd. dirs. 1992—), Calif. Soc. Newspaper Editors (bd. dirs. 1988-95), Calif. Newspaper Pubs. Assn. (bd. dirs. 1992—), Soc. Profl. Journalists, U. Calif.-Santa Barbara Alumni Assn. (bd. dirs. 1983-89). Home: 5717 Bedford Dr Riverside CA 92506-3404 Office: Press-Enterprise Co 3512 14th St Riverside CA 92501-3814

MCQUIDDY, MARIAN ELIZABETH, publisher, editor; b. Los Angeles, Mar. 21, 1952; d. Arthur Robert and Aleen Frampton (Hinkle) McQ. B.J., Purdue U., 1974; postgrad. in press photography Northwestern U., 1973; postgrad. in comparative psychotherapy Webster Coll., 1981, postgrad. in math. and computer sci., N.Mex. State U., 1983-85, postgrad. in Edn. N. Mex. State U., 1995—. Summer editorial intern Chgo. Daily News, 1973; new dir. Sta. KSVP, Artesia, N.Mex., 1974; police reporter, polit. editor Roswell (N.Mex.) Daily Record, 1974-77; night editor, sports and feature editor UPI, Des Moines, 1977-79; editor Mt. Vernon (Iowa) Democrat, 1979; news editor Cadillac (Mich.) Evening News, 1979-80; tchr. adult edn. Pine River High Sch., LeRoy, Mich., 1979-80; editor Portage (Wis.) Daily Register, 1980-81; pub., editor Los Lunas (N.Mex.) Village Voice, 1981-82; police and ednl. writer Alamogordo Daily News, 1982-85, sports editor, 1985—. Bd. dirs. Cadillac Area Arts Council, Community Theater, United Way, Portage, Alamogordo Music Theater, White Sands Press Club, Alamogordo Press Club, Alamogordo Century Club, Otero County Boys and Girls Club, Big Brothers/Big Sisters of Otero County, Sertoma Club of Alamogordo, Sertoma Scholarship Pageant; mem. campaign cabinet United Way. Recipient journalism award N.Mex. Press Assn., N.Mex. Farm Bur., service awards Roswell Library, Optimists, Boy Scouts Am., Portage Jaycees, Wis. Newspaper Assn. Mem. Nat. Fedn. Press Women, Women in Communications, Alamogordo C. of C., Alamogordo Ambassadors, Eagles Auxiliary, Associated Press Sports Editors, Assn. Women Sports Editor, Jr. League, Sigma Delta Chi. Methodist. Home: 3245 E University #709 Las Cruces NM 88001 Office: Alamo Daily News 518 24th St Alamogordo NM 88310-6104

MCQUILLIN, CYNTHIA ANN, music publishing company executive; b. Santa Monica, Calif., July 25, 1953; d. John and Betty McQ. AA, City Coll. State U., Long Beach, Calif., 1976. Singer Calif., 1972—; rsch. asst. Richard C. Spurney, Long Beach, Calif., 1974-77; drafter R.E. Pearsalls, Long Beach, Calif., 1978-79; asst. office mgr. Compex, Inc., Culver City, Calif., 1981-84; shift supr. Etak, Inc., Menlo Pk., Calif., 1984-86; head of client liaison Compex, Inc., San Francisco, 1987-88; recording artist, producer Off Centaur Publs., El Cerrito, Calif., 1980-89; geographic tech. Etak, Inc., Menlo Pk., 1989-90; owner, operator Unlikely Publs., Berkeley, Calif., 1985—; Ind. recording artist, co-producer with Flowinglass Studios, Berkeley, Calif., 1991—, Wail Songs, Oakland, Calif., 1992—, Dag Prodns., L.A., 1991—, Thor Records, L.A., 1992-95. Contbr. stories and poetry to profl. publs.; composer of over 200 recorded songs. Mem. BMI, Sci. Fiction and Fantasy Writers of Am., Horror Writers Am., Authors Guild. Office: Unlikely Publs PO Box 8542 Berkeley CA 94707-8542

MCQUILLIN, RICHARD ROSS, management consultant; b. Elyria, Ohio, Oct. 15, 1956; s. Wayne Rupp and Frana Rose (Romp) McQ.; m. Riko K. McQuillin; 1 child, Richard K. Quillin. BS, Ohio State U., 1979; MS, U. So. Calif., L.A., 1983; MBA, UCLA, 1990. Sr. staff mem. TRW Inc., Redondo Beach, Calif., 1979-88; sr. cons. Deloitte & Touche, L.A., 1990-91; project mgr. NetBase Computing, Torrance, Calif., 1993—. Treas., controller Patio Creek Homeowners Assn., Torrance, Calif., 1986-91, pres. 1991—; pres. TRW Investment Club, Redondo Beach, 1984-87. UCLA fellow, 1989. Mem. IEEE, Beta Gamma Sigma. Home: 19028 Entradero Ave Torrance CA 90503-1360 Office: NetBase Computing Inc 3625 Del Amo Blvd Ste 220 Torrance CA 90503

MCQUISTON, STEVAN LOY, electronics engineer; b. Long Beach, Calif., Jan. 19, 1947; s. Edwin Ernest and Bonnie Dell (Lockwood) McQ.; m. A. T. Lane, Aug. 30, 1971; 1 child, Kennon Sean. BS, Long Beach State U., 1974; MBA, Calif. State U., Fullerton, 1980. Assoc. engr. Calcomp, Anaheim, Calif., 1968-71, engr., 1971-74, sr. engr., 1974-79; mem. tech. staff Hughes Aircraft-Fullerton, Fullerton, Calif., 1980-82, sr. staff engr., 1982-86; mgr. quality strategy Hughes Aircraft-SSSD, Fullerton, Calif., 1987-88; mgr. components and materials engring. Hughes Aircraft-Fullerton, Fullerton, Calif., 1989-92, mgr. components engring., 1992—. Mem. Phi Kappa Phi.

MCRAE, HAMILTON EUGENE, III, lawyer; b. Midland, Tex., Oct. 29, 1937; s. Hamilton Eugene and Adrian (Hagaman) McR.; m. Betty Hawkins, Aug. 27, 1960; children: Elizabeth Ann, Stephanie Adrian, Scott Hawkins. BSEE, U. Ariz., 1961; student, USAF Electronics Sch., 1961-62; postgrad., U. Redlands, Calif., 1962-63; JD with honors and distinction, U. Ariz., 1967; LHD (hon.), Sterling Coll., 1992; vis. fellow, Darwin Coll., Cambridge (Eng.) U. Bar: Ariz. 1967, U.S. Supreme Ct. 1979; cert. real estate specialist, Ariz. Elec. engr. Salt River Project, Phoenix, 1961; assoc. Jennings, Strouss & Salmon, Phoenix, 1967-71, ptnr., 1971-85, chmn. real estate dept., 1980-85, mem. policy com., 1982-85, mem. fin. com., 1981-85, chmn. bus. devel. com., 1982-85; ptnr. and co-founder Stuckey & McRae, Phoenix, 1985—; co-founder, chmn. bd. Republic Cos., Phoenix, 1985—; magistrate Paradise Valley, Ariz., 1983-85; juvenile referee Superior Ct., 1983-85; pres., dir. Phoenix Realty & Trust Co., 1970—; officer Indsl. Devel. Corp. Maricopa County, 1972-86; instr. and lectr. in real estate; officer, bd. dirs. other corps.; adj. prof. Frank Lloyd Wright Sch. Architecture, Scottsdale, Ariz., 1989—; instr. Ariz. State U. Coll. Architecture and Environ. Design; lead instr. ten-state-bar seminar on Advanced Real Estate Transactions, 1992; evaluation com. for cert. real estate specialist Ariz. Bar, 1994—; mem. state bar com. for selecting real estate specialists, 1994—. Exec. prodr. film documentary on relief and devel. in Africa, 1990; contbr. articles to profl. jours. Elder Valley Presbyn. Ch., Scottsdale, Ariz., 1973-75, 82-85, chair evangelism com. 1973-74, corp. pres., 1974-75, 84-85, trustee, 1973-75, 82-85, chmn. exec. com., 1984, mem. mission com. 1993—; trustee Upward Found., Phoenix, 1977-80, Valley Presbyn. Found., 1982-83, Ariz. Acad., 1971—; trustee, mem. exec. com. Phi Gamma Delta Ednl. Found., Washington, 1974-84; trustee Phi Gamma Delta Internat., 1984-86; bd. dirs. Archon, 1986-87; founder, trustee, pres. McRae Found., 1980—; bd. dirs. Food for Hungry Inc. (Internat. Relief), 1985-95, exec. com., 1986—, chmn. bd. dirs., 1987-92; chmn. bd. dirs. Food for Hungry Internat., 1993-95; pres. adv. coun., 1995—; trustee, mem. exec. com. Ariz. Mus. Sci. and Tech., 1984—, 1st v.p., 1985-86, pres., 1986-88, chmn. bd. dirs., 1988-90; Lambda Alpha Internat. Hon. Land Econs. Soc, 1988—; sec.-treas. Ariz. State U. Coun. for Design Excellence, 1989-90, bd. dirs. 1988—, pres. 1990-91; mem. Crisis Nursery Office of the Chair, 1988-89, Maricopa Community Colls. Found., 1988—, sec. 1990-91, 2d v.p. 1993-94, 1st v.p. and pres. elect 1994-95, pres. 1995—, Phoenix Cmty. Alliance, 1988-90, Interchurch Ctr. Corp., 1987-90, Western Art Assocs., bd. dirs., 1989-91, Phoenix Com. on Fgn. Rels., 1988—, U. Ariz. Pres.'s Club, 1984—, chmn., 1991-92; bd. dirs. Econ. Club of Phoenix, 1987— , sec.-treas., 1991-92, v.p., 1992-93, pres. 1993-94; bd. dirs. Ctrl. Ariz. Shelter Svcs., 1995—; mem. adv. bd. Help Wanted USA, 1990-92; vol. fund raiser YMCA, Salvation Army, others; bd. dirs. Frank Lloyd Wright Found., 1992—; mem. Taliesin Coun., 1985—; founding mem. Frank Lloyd Wright Soc., 1993—; mem. fin. com. Kyl for Congress, 1985-92, bd. dir. campaign bd. Kyl for U.S. Senate, 1993-94; Senator Kyl Coun., 1995—; campaign com. Symington for Gov. '90, 1989—, mem. gubernatorial adv. bd., 1990-91; mem. Gov.'s Selection Com. for State Revenue Dir., 1993; mem. bond com. City of Phoenix, 1987-88; mem. Ariz. State U. Coun. of 100, 1985-89, investment com., 1985-89; bd. govs. Twelve Who Care Hon Kachina, 1991; mem. adv. coun. Maricopa County Sports Authority, 1989-93; mem. Ariz. Coalition for Tomorrow, 1990-92; founding mem., bd. dirs. Waste Not Inc., 1992-94, pres., 1990-92, chmn., 1992-94. 1st lt. USAF, 1961-64,. Recipient various mil. award. Mem. ABA, AIEE, AIME, Ariz. Bar Assn., Maricopa County Bar Assn., U. Ariz. Alumni Assn., Nat. Soc.

Fund Raising Execs., Clan McRae Soc. N.Am. Phoenix Racquet Club, Teton Pines Country Club, Tau Beta Pi. Republican. Home: 8101 N 47th St Paradise Vly AZ 85253-2907 Office: Republic Cos 2425 E Camelback Rd Ste 900 Phoenix AZ 85016-4215

MCREE, DUNCAN EVERETT, molecular biologist, researcher; b. San Francisco, Feb. 5, 1957; s. John Everett and Joan Marie (Kilburn) McR.; m. Janice Anne Yuwiler, May 15, 1983; children: Alexander Marc, Kevin Lawrence. BS, U. Calif., Davis, 1978; PhD in Biochemistry, Duke U., 1984. Helen Hay Whitney fellow The Scripps Rsch. Inst., La Jolla, Calif., 1985-89, asst. mem., 1989—. Author: Practical Protein Crystallography, 1993, (software) Xtal View, 1992. Calif. State scholar, 1975-77; NIH grantee, 1990-95. Office: The Scripps Rsch Inst MB4 10666 N Torrey Pines Rd La Jolla CA 92037-1027

MCREYNOLDS, BARBARA, artist; b. Omaha, May 5, 1956; d. Zachariah Aycock and Mary Barbara (McCulloh) McR.; m. Stephen Dale Dent, Mar. 12, 1983 (div. Dec. 30, 1992); children: Madeleine Barbara, Matthew Stephen; m. Ross Coleman, Oct. 16, 1993; 1 child, Marie Jeanne Coleman. Student, U. N.Mex., 1979, MA in Community and Regional Planning, 1984. Artist, 1986-92; lectr. U. N.Mex. Sch. of Architecture, Albuquerque, 1979-82, 91—; assoc. planner, urban designer City of Albuquerque Planning Div., 1982-84; city planner, urban designer City of Albuquerque, N.Mex. Redevel. Div., 1984-88; cons. City of Albuquerque Redevel. Dept., 1987-88; urban design cons. Southwest Land Rsch., Albuquerque, 1991. Columnist for "Kids and Art", 1990-92; author: Coors Corridor Plan (The Albuquerque Conservation Assn. urban design award 1984), Electric Facilities Plan, Downtown Core Revitalization Strategy and Sector Development Plan; contbg. author: Anasazi Architecture and American Design, 1994; contbr. articles to profl. publs.; exhibited in shows at Dartmouth St. Gallery, Brandywine Galleries, Albuquerque, Laurel Seth Gallery, Santa Fe, Chimayo (N.Mex.) Trade and Mercantile, Ruby Blakeney Gallery. Vol. art tchr. Chaparral Elem. Sch., Albuquerque, 1989-92. Recipient First Pl. for Pastels, 20th Ann. Nat. Small Painting Exhibition, N.Mex. Art League, 1991, Best of Show awards Pastel Soc. of N.Mex., 1990, Award of Merit, Pastel Soc. of S.W., 1989, TACA award for Urban Design, 1984. Mem. Pastel Soc. of Am., Pastel Soc. N.Mex. (pres. 1991-92). Democrat. Episcopalian. Office: U NMex Sch Architecture Univ Of New Mexico NM 87131

MC REYNOLDS, MARY BARBARA, retired secondary school educator, community volunteer; b. Los Angeles, Feb. 18, 1930; d. Clyde C. and Dorothy (Slaten) McCulloh; m. Zachariah A. McReynolds, Feb. 9, 1952 (dec.); children: Gregg Clyde, Barbara, Zachariah A.; m. John Richard Street, May 7, 1994. BA, U. N.Mex., 1951, MA, 1972, Edn. Specialist, 1975, postgrad., 1981—. Dept. sec. USAF Intelligence, Wiesbaden, W. Ger., 1953-54; tchr. Annandale (Va.) Elem. Sch., 1962-65, supr. adult edn., 1965-66; tchr. Albuquerque High Sch., 1968-77, 79-91, social studies curriculum dir., 1973-75; instr. U. N.Mex., Albuquerque, 1975-76, acad. decathlon coach Albuquerque High Sch., 1986-91; evaluator N. Central Assn., 1970-81, dir. Cultural Awareness Workshop, 1976, 79; coord. Sex Equality, 1979, 80. Bd. dirs. Greater U. N.Mex. Fund, 1978-79, 79-80, fund raiser, 1976-81, pres. club, 1977-80; campaign mgr. state senatorial campaign, 1976; exec. sec. Civic Assn., 1958-60; sponsor Black Student Union, 1978-80; sponsor Boys and Girls State, 1968-75; rep. Am. Fedn. Tchrs., 1982-91; sponsor Close-Up, 1987—; precinct chmn. Democratic Party, Albuquerque, 1985-86; mem. exec. bd. Albuquerque Rehab. Ctr., 1993—; vol. Cancer Soc., KKM; mem. fin. and pub. rels. coms. RCI Bd. Indian research and tuition edn. grantee, 1971; grantee U. N.Mex., 1975-76, others. Mem. Assn. Supervision and Curriculum Devel., Nat. Social Studies Council, N.Mex. Social Studies Council, Phi Kappa Phi, Phi Delta Kappa, Pi Alpha Theta, Kappa Kappa Gamma. Democrat. Episcopalian. Clubs: N.Mex. Democratic Women, Air Force Officers Wives, Kappa Kappa Gamma Alumni (pres. 1991-93, chmn. ways and means com. 1994, Outstanding Alumna award 1994). Condr. research in field. Home: 749 Tramway Ln NE Albuquerque NM 87122-1601

MCREYNOLDS, ROCHELLE SHARON, broadcast executive; b. Orange, Calif., Jan. 23, 1950; d. Buren Kenneth and Bernice Geneva (Thomas) Smith. BFA, U. Calif., Irvine, 1975; postgrad., Emerson Coll., 1981-82. Former profl. dancer, actress, singer; adminstr., mem. faculty Boston Conservatory, 1982-87; devel. officer Boston Ballet, 1985-86, dir. major gifts, 1986-90; dir. devel. Laguna Art Mus., Laguna Beach, Calif., 1990-91; dir. bus. devel. KOCE-TV Pub. TV, Orange County, Calif., 1991—; speaker in field; adj. faculty mem. Sch. Bus. and mgmt. U. Calif., Urvine, 1994—; v.p., bd. dirs. Nat. Soc. Fundraising Execs. Bd. dirs. Orange County coun. Girl Scouts U.S.A., Laguna Playhouse; mem. Planned Giving Roundtable, Orange County; chair Nat. Philanthrophy Day, Orange County, 1994. Recipient Emmy nomination, Nat. Acad. TV Arts and Scis., 1994; named Outstanding Profl. of Yr. for Orange County, 1995. Office: KOCE-TV 15751 Gothard St Huntington Beach CA 92647-3057

MCREYNOLDS, STEPHEN PAUL, lawyer; b. Sacramento, Oct. 16, 1938; s. Leslie N. and Mary C. McR.; m. Chodi D. Greeno, Sept. 29, 1970. A.B., U. Calif.-Davis, 1969, J.D., 1972. Bar: Calif. 1972. Sole practice, Sunnyvale, Calif., 1972—. Served with U.S. Navy, 1956-62. Mem. Mensa Internat. Office: 1111 W El Camino Real # 326 Sunnyvale CA 94087-1056

MCSHIRLEY, SUSAN RUTH, gift industry executive, consultant; b. Glendale, Calif., July 31, 1945; d. Robert Claude and Lillian Dora (Mable) McS. BS, U. Calif.-Berkeley, 1967. Nat. sales dir. McShirley Products, Glendale, Calif., 1967-71, Viade Products, Camarillo, Calif., 1972-80; pres. SRM Press, Inc., L.A., 1980—; nat. sales cons. Warner Bros. Records, Burbank, Calif., 1985. Author: Racquetball: Where to Play, USA, 1978; patentee picture pen; creator novelty trademarks including The Pig Pen, The Road Hog, DFZ/Drug Free Zone, Tobacco Free Zone, Protect Our Planet. Mem. Calif. Alumni Assn., Alpha Omicron Pi. Avocations: travel, photography, tennis, foreign languages. Home: 15947 Temecula St Pacific Palisades CA 90272-4239 Office: SRM Press Inc 4216 Glencoe Ave Marina Del Rey CA 90292

MCSORLEY, CISCO, lawyer; b. Albuquerque, July 8, 1950; s. Frank N. and Virginia E. (Norton) McS. BA, U. N.Mex., 1974, JD, 1979; postdoctoral sch. govt., Harvard U., 1986. Bar: N.Mex. 1980, U.S. Dist. Ct. N.Mex. 1980. Tchr. Academia Cotopaxi, Quito, Ecuador, S. Am., 1973-76; sole practice Albuquerque, 1980—. State rep. N.Mex. Ho. Reps., Albuquerque, 1984—. Mem. ABA, N. Mex. Bar. Assn., N. Mex. Trial Lawyers Assn., Assn. Trial Lawyers Am. Democrat. Mem. Soc. of Friends.

MCSPEDON, EDWARD, engineering company executive; b. Yonkers, N.Y., May 20, 1951; s. Edward and Esther V. (Peterson) McS.; m. JoAnn Catherine Scully; 1 child, Karen Ann. B of Civil Engring., Manhattan Coll., 1973, M of Civil Engring., 1978; grad. profl. mgmt. program, U. So. Calif., L.A., 1989. Registered profl. engr., N.Y., Calif. Civil engr. N.Y.C. Transit Authority, 1973-78; program mgr. U.S. Dept. of Transp., N.Y.C., 1978-82; sr. project engr., office mgr. Gibbs & Hill Inc., N.Y.C. and Beverly Hills, Calif., 1982-85; pres. rail constrn. corp. L.A. Met. Trans. Authority, 1985-94; v.p. HNTB Corp., L.A., 1995—; mem. airline passenger safety task force City of L.A. Mayor's Office, 1992. Contbr. articles to profl. jours. Mem. Castle Peak Homeowners, West Hills, Calif., 1990—. Recipient Chmn.'s Spl. award for urban design L.A. Bus. Coun., 1993, Leadership Achievement award Cen. City Assn., 1994. Fellow Inst. for Advancement of Engring. (life, Outstanding Engring. Merit award 1993); mem. ASCE (mem. editl. bd. engring. mgmt. jour. 1990—), Am. Pub. Transit Assn. (chmn. constrn. com. 1994-97), Constrn. Mgmt. Soc. Am. (Engring. Project Advancement award 1993, Project Achievement award 1990), Constrn. Industry Think Tank, L.A. Athletic Club. Home: 7252 Elmsbury Ln West Hills CA 91307-3828 Office: HNTB Corp Rail Constrn Corp 665 S Oxford Ave Los Angeles CA 90005

MC TAVISH, HUGH ELSER, biochemist, researcher; b. Mpls., June 22, 1962; s. John Elser and Johne (Thornberry) Mc T. BA, CArleton Coll., Northfield, Minn., 1984; MS, Brown U., 1986; PhD, U. Minn., 1992. Rschr. Solar Energy Rsch. Inst., Golden, Colo., 1987-88; postdoctoral fellow U. Minn., St. Paul, 1988-93, Oreg. State U., Corvallis, 1993—. Author: Ending War in Our Lifetime, 1994; contbr. articles to profl. jours. Home: 1215 Englewood Ave Saint Paul MN 55104-1412 Office: Oreg State U Dept Botany 2082 Cordley Hall Corvallis OR 97331-8530

MCTIGUE, BERNARD FRANCIS, curator, consultant; b. N.Y.C., June 24, 1946; s. Bernard Francis and Eileen Marie (Lillis) McT. B.A., Columbia U., 1973, M.S., 1974; M.A., Hunter Coll., 1980. Librarian N.Y. Pub. Library, N.Y.C., 1974-81; curator Arents Collections, N.Y. Pub. Library, N.Y.C., 1981-90, keeper of rare books, 1988-90; chmn. dept. spl. collections U. Fla., Gainesville, 1990-93; curator spl. collections Knight Libr. U. Oreg., Eugene, 1993—. Author: A Child's Garden of Delight, 1987, Treasures of the New York Public Library, 1988, Nature Illustrated, 1989; editor Am. Book Collector, 1985-88, Bull. Bibliography, 1991—; Am. corr. Bull. du Bibliophile, 1992-94. Home: 3210 Kinsrow Ave Eugene OR 97401-8822 Office: U Oreg Knight Libr Eugene OR 97403

MCVAY, JOHN EDWARD, professional football club executive; b. Bellaire, Ohio, Jan. 5, 1931; s. John A. and Helen (Andrews) McV.; m. Eva Lee; children: John R., James P., Timothy G. B.S. in Edn., Miami U., Oxford, Ohio, 1953; M.A. in Sch. Adminstrn., Kent (Ohio) State U., 1963. Asst. football coach, instr. phys. edn. Mich. State U., 1962-65; head coach, dir. athletics U. Dayton, Ohio, 1965-74; head coach, gen. mgr. Memphis in World Football League, 1974-76; head football coach New York Giants, Nat. Football League, 1976-78; dir. player personnel San Francisco 49ers, Nat. Football League, 1979-80, dir. football ops., 1980-81, v.p. adminstrn., 1981-83, gen. mgr., v.p., 1983-89, v.p. FB ops., 1990—. Exec. dir. Catholic Youth Council, Canton, Ohio, 1959-62. Named to Miami U. Athletic Hall of Fame, named NFL exec. of the year, 1989. Mem. Sigma Chi (Significant Sig award), Phi Epsilon Kappa, Phi Delta Kappa. Office: care San Francisco 49ers 4949 Centennial Blvd Santa Clara CA 95054-1229

MCVEIGH, BYRON JOSEPH, economist; b. Cheyenne, Wyo., May 14, 1956; s. William Patrick and Carolyn Irene (Hoover) McV.; m. Lucy Ann Freeman, Aug. 29, 1987; children: Hayden Michael, Myles Taylor. AA, Laramie County C.C., Cheyenne, 1974-76; BS, U. Wyo., 1979. Agrl. statistician Dept. Agr., State of Wyo., Cheyenne, 1980-85; economist Dept. Adminstrn., State of Wyo., Cheyenne, 1985-88, sr. economist, 1988-94; mgmt. info. system adminstr. State Auditor's Office State of Wyo., Cheyenne, 1994—; economist Consensus Revenue Estimating Group, Cheyenne, 1985-94; chair Socio-Econ. Rsch. Coordinating Com., Cheyenne, 1991-92; mem. Cmty. Assessment Team-Econ. Devel., Cheyenne, 1989-91. Author: Equality State Almanac, 1993, Wyoming in Economic Forecast Report, 1993, 94, Wyoming Gross State Product Report, 1988, 91, Wyoming Sales and Use Tax Revenue Report, 1986-94; editor: Wyoming Data Handbook, 1985, 87, 89, 91. Bd. dirs. Laramie County C.C. Golden Eagles Club, Cheyenne, 1986-87; mem. adv. bd. DePaul Health and Fitness Inst., Cheyenne, 1990-91. Named to Outstanding Young Men of Am., 1980-81. Mem. Sigma Chi (life). Republican. Roman Catholic. Home: 2319 Van Lennen Ave Cheyenne WY 82001-3121 Office: State of Wyo State Auditor's Office Cheyenne WY 82002

MCVEIGH-PETTIGREW, SHARON CHRISTINE, communications consultant; b. San Francisco, Feb. 6, 1949; d. Martin Allen and Frances (Roddy) McVeigh; m. John Wallace Pettigrew, Mar. 27, 1971; children: Benjamin Thomas, Margaret Mary. B.A. with honors, U. Calif.-Berkeley, 1971; diploma of edn. Monash U., Australia, 1975; M.B.A., Golden Gate U., 1985. Tchr., adminstr. Victorian Edn. Dept., Victoria, Australia, 1972-79; supr. Network Control Ctr., GTE Sprint Communications, Burlingame, Calif., 1979-81, mgr. customer assistance, 1981-84, mgr. state legis. ops., 1984-85, dir. revenue programs, 1986-87; communications cons. Flores, Pettigrew & Co., San Mateo, Calif., 1987-89; mgr. telemarketing Apple Computer, Inc., Cupertino, Calif., 1989-94; prin. The Call Ctr. Group, San Mateo, Calif., 1995—; telecomm. cons. PPG Svcs., 1994—; telecomm. spkr. Dept. Consumer Affairs, Sacramento, 1984. Panelist Wash. Gov.'s Citizens Council, 1984; founding mem. Maroondah Women's Shelter, Victoria, 1978; organizer nat. conf. Bus. Women and the Polit. Process, New Orleans, 1986; mem. sch. bd. Boronia Tech. Sch., Victoria, 1979. Recipient Tchr. Spl. Responsibilities award Victoria Edn. Dept., 1979. Mem. Women in Telecommunications (panel moderator San Francisco 1984), Am. Mgmt. Assn., Peninsula Profl. Women's Network, Am. Telemktg. Assn. (bd. dirs. 1992), Women's Econ. Action League. Democrat. Roman Catholic.

MCVICAR, SHERRY FISHER, human resources executive; b. N.Y.C., Sept. 17, 1952; d. William Sidney and Beverly (Harris) Miller; m. Allan A McVicar III, July 28, 1986. BA, Hofstra U., 1973; MS, Queens Coll., 1976. With Cox & Co., Inc., N.Y.C., 1973-76; mgr. tng. and labor rels. Quantor Corp., Mountain View, Calif., 1976-78; v.p. human resources Qume Corp., San Jose, Calif., 1978-87, Convergent, Inc., San Jose, 1987-91; group v.p. human resources Unisys Network Computing Group, San Jose, 1989-90; v.p. human resources Unisys Computer Systems Product Group, San Jose, 1990-91, Read-Rite Corp., Milpitas, Calif., 1991—; cons. in field; speaker on labor rels. Recipient of 1992 YWCA Twin award. Mem. Am. Arbitration Assn. Office: READ-RITE Corp PO Box 6685 345 Los Coches St Milpitas CA 95035-5428

MCWHIRTER, JOAN BRIGHTON, psychologist; b. Urbana, Ill., July 10, 1954; d. Gerald David and Lois (Robbins) Brighton; m. Richard Eugene McWhirter, Aug. 13, 1976. BA in Sociology, So. Ill. U., 1974; MA in Psychology, U. Nev., 1982. VISTA vol. Oper. Life, Las Vegas, 1974-75; grad. asst. U. NEv., Las Vegas, 1978-80; psychologist So. Nev. Adult Mental Health Svcs., Las Vegas, 1984-92; vocational rehab. counselor State Indsl. Ins. System, Las Vegas, 1992—. Treas. Spiritual Assembly of Baha'is, North Las Vegas, 1977-92; vice chmn. Baha'is, Sunrise Manor, 1993—. Pres. scholar So. Ill. U., 1971-74. Mem. Nat. Alliance for Mentally Ill, Nat. Wildlife Fedn., Nat. Wildlife Fund, Nev. Alliance for Mentally Ill (liaison 1986-89), State of Nev. Employee's Assn., Amnesty Internat., Sierra Club (Toiyabe chpt.), Habitat for Humanity, Phi Kappa Phi, Psi Chi. Home: 3648 Rochester Ave Las Vegas NV 89115-0229 Office: State Indsl Ins System 1700 W Charleston Blvd Las Vegas NV 89102-2335

MCWHORTOR, PATRICK SEAN, lobbyist, consultant; b. South Bend, Ind., Jan. 10, 1965; s. William Frank and Velma Darnell (Morford) McW.; m. Ronda Louise Hall, June 22, 1985; children: Nathan Patrick, Joshua David. Cert. broadcast, Bailie Sch. Broadcast, 1984; BA in Polit. Sci., Ariz. State U., 1988. News dir. Sta. KATO-KXKQ, Safford, Ariz., 1984-85, Sta. KFMM, Safford, 1985; video prodn. cons. Phoenix, Ariz., 1986—; intern Ariz. Ho. of Reps., Phoenix, 1988; programs coord. Gov.'s Office of Drug Policy, Phoenix, 1989-90; comty. programs cons. Phoenix, 1991—; legis. liaison Ariz. Audubon Coun., Phoenix, 1992—; exec. dir. Ariz. Student's Assn., Tempe, 1992—; student regent Ariz. Bd. Regents, Phoenix, 1988-89. Prevention Outreach specialist Mesa (Ariz.) Project, 1990-91; chmn. dist. 6 Ariz. State U. Alumni Assn. Network, Phoenix, 1992—; bd. dirs. Tempe Little Theatre, 1991-93, pres., 1991-92; chmn. Phoenix Fights Back, 1990-92. Leadership scholar Student Found., 1987. Democrat. Methodist. Home and Office: 16421 S 33rd St Phoenix AZ 85044-7845

MCWILLIAMS, MARGARET ANN, home economics educator, author; b. Osage, Iowa, May 26, 1929; d. Alvin Randall and Mildred Irene (Lane) Edgar; children: Roger, Kathleen. BS, Iowa State U., 1951, MS, 1953; PhD, Oreg. State U., 1968. Registered dietitian. Asst. prof. home econs. Calif. State U., L.A., 1961-66, assoc. prof., 1966-68, prof., 1968-92, prof. emeritus, 1992—, chmn. dept., 1968-76; pres. Plycon Press, 1978—. Author: Food Fundamentals, 1966, 6th edit., 1995, Nutrition for the Growing Years, 1967, 5th edit., 1993, Experimental Foods Laboratory Manual, 1977, 4th edit., 1994, (with L. Kotschevar) Understanding Food, 1969, Illustrated Guide to Food Preparation, 1970, 7th edit., 1995, (with L. Davis) Food for You, 1971, 2d edit., 1976, The Meatless Cookbook, 1973, (with F. Stare) Living Nutrition, 1973, 4th edit., 1984, Nutrition for Good Health, 1974, 2d edit., 1982 (with H. Paine), Modern Food Preservation, Fundamentals of Meal Management, 1978, 2d edit., 1993, Foods: Experimental Perspectives, 1989, 2d edit., 1993. Chmn. bd. Beach Cities Symphony, 1991-94. Recipient Alumni Centennial award Iowa State U., 1971, Profl. Achievement award, 1977; Phi Upsilon Omicron Nat. Founders fellow, 1964; Home Economist in Bus. Nat. Found. fellow, 1967; Outstanding Prof. award Calif. State U., 1976. Mem. Am. Dietetic Assn., Inst. Food Technologists, Phi Kappa Phi, Phi Upsilon Omicron, Omicron Nu, Iota Sigma Pi, Sigma Delta Epsilon, Sigma Alpha Iota. Home: PO Box 220 Redondo Beach CA 90277-0220

MCWILLIAMS, ROBERT HUGH, federal judge; b. Salina, Kans., Apr. 27, 1916; s. Robert Hugh and Laura (Nicholson) McW.; m. Catherine Ann Cooper, Nov. 4, 1942 (dec.); 1 son, Edward Cooper; m. Joan Harcourt, Mar. 8, 1986. A.B., U. Denver, 1938, LL.B., 1941. Bar: Colo. bar 1941. Colo. dist. judge Denver, 1952-60; justice Colo. Supreme Ct., 1961-68, chief justice, 1969-70; judge U.S. Ct. Appeals (10th cir.), Denver, 1970—. Served with AUS, World War II. Mem. Phi Beta Kappa, Omicron Delta Kappa, Phi Delta Phi, Kappa Sigma. Republican. Episcopalian. Home: 137 Jersey St Denver CO 00220 Office: Byron White US Courthouse 823 Stout St Rm 216 Denver CO 80257

MEACHAM, CHARLES P., consulting firm executive; b. Susanville, Calif., Apr. 29, 1947; m. Charlene D. Heriot, 1969; 3 children. BS, Humboldt State U., 1969, MS in Fisheries, 1971. Comml. fisherman Bristol Bay, Alaska, 1963-66; with Bumble Bee Seafoods, Bristol Bay, S.E. Alaska, 1967-69; fisheries cons. Winzler & Kelly Engring., Eureka, Calif., 1970; seafood insp. U.S. Army Med. Dept., Ft. Richardson, Alaska, 1971-74; staff biologist Alaska Dept. of Fish and Game, Juneau, Alaska, 1974-75; rsch. biologist Artic Char investigations Alaska Dept. of Fish and Game, Dillingham, Alaska, 1975-77; Bristol Bay rsch. project leader Alaska Dept. of Fish and Game, Anchorage, 1978-81, regional rsch. supr., 1981-89, mgr. fishery program divsn. of oil spill impact assessment and restoration, 1990-91; dep. commr. Alaska Dept. of Fish and Game, Juneau, 1991-95; pres. Capital Consulting, 1995—; affiliate faculty U. Alaska, 1983-87; mem. Bering Sea/Aleutians plan team N. Pacific Fisheries Mgmt. Council, 1989, Alaska Regional Marine Rsch. Bd., 1992—, Pacific Fisheries Mgmt. Coun., 1991—; commr. Pacific States Marine Fisheries Commn., 1991—; presidential appointment as commr. for Pacific Salmon Commn., 1991—. Mem. Mayor's Task Force on Fisheries, Anchorage, 1988-89, Alaska Tourism Coordinating Commn., 1992—; mem. review team Alaska Sci. & Tech. Found., 1989; alt. mem. Exxon Valdez Oil Spill Trustee Coun., 1992—. Mem. NAS, OSB (fisheries com., 1992, 95), Am. Fisheries Soc. (life, v.p. Alaska chpt. 1975, pres. elect 1977, pres. 1978), Am. Inst. of Fishery Rsch. Biologists. Home: 533 Main St Juneau AK 99801-1153

MEAD, BEVERLY MIRIUM ANDERSON, author, educator; b. St. Paul, May 29, 1925; d. Martin and Anna Mae (Oshanyk) Anderson; m. Jerome Morton Nemiro, Feb. 10, 1951 (div. May 1975); children: Guy Samuel, Lee Anna, Dee Martin; m. William Isaac Mead, Aug. 8, 1992. Student Reed Coll., 1943-44; BA, U. Colo., 1947; postgrad., U. Denver. Tchr., Seattle Pub. Schs., 1945-46; fashion coord., dir. Denver Dry Goods Co., 1948-51; fashion model, Denver, 1951-58, 78—; fashion dir. Denver Market Week Assn., 1952-53; free-lance writer, Denver, 1958—; moderator TV program Your Preschool Child, Denver, 1955-56; instr. writing and communications U. Colo. Denver Ctr., 1970—, U. Calif., San Diego, 1976-78, Met. State Coll., 1985; dir. pub. relations Fairmont Hotel, Denver, 1979-80; free lance fashion and TV model; author, co-author: The Complete Book of High Altitude Baking, 1961, Colorado a la Carte, 1963, Colorado a la Carte, Series II, 1966, (with Donna Hamilton) The High Altitude Cookbook, 1969, The Busy People's Cookbook, 1971 (Better Homes and Gardens Book Club selection 1971), Where to Eat in Colorado, 1967, Lunch Box Cookbook, 1965, Complete Book of High Altitude Baking, 1961, (under name Beverly Anderson) Single After 50, 1978, The New High Altitude Cookbook, 1980. Co-founder, pres. Jr. Symphony Guild, Denver, 1959-60; active Friends of Denver Libr., Opera Colo. Recipient Top Hand award Colo. Authors' League, 1969, 72, 79-82, 100 Best Books of Yr. award N.Y. Times, 1969, 71; named one of Colo.'s Women of Yr., Denver Post, 1964. Mem. Am. Soc. Journalists and Authors, Colo. Authors League (dir. 1969-79), Authors Guild, Authors League Am., Friends Denver Library, Rotary, Sigma Delta Chi, Kappa Alpha Theta. Address: 23 Polo Club Dr Denver CO 80209-3309

MEAD, SEDGWICK, physician; b. Guymon, Okla., July 2, 1911; s. Redmond Boyd and Bertha Mabel (Hunter) Corbett; m. Marjorie Frances Chick, Sept. 22, 1940 (dec.); children: Sedgwick Jr., Marshall; m. Mary Adelaide Abbott, May 8, 1995. Student, U. Ariz., 1930-31; SB cum laude, Harvard U., 1934, MD, 1938. Diplomate Am. Bd. Phys. Medicine and Rehab. Baruch fellow Harvard Med. Sch., Boston, 1946-47; assoc. prof. Sch. of Medicine Washington U., St. Louis, 1948-54; med. dir. Kaiser Found. Rehab. Ctr., Vallejo, Calif., 1954-69; ast. clin. prof. Sch. of Medicine Stanford (Calif.) U., 1955-60; clin. prof. U. Calif., Davis, 1969-72; chief neurology Kaiser-Permanente Med. Ctr., Vallejo, 1969-77; med. dir. Easter Seal Rehab. Ctr., Oakland, Calif., 1983-93; intern Mass. Gen. Hosp., 1938-40, resident pathology, 1940-41, resident neurology, 1941-42; cons. coun. on med. physics AMA, Chgo., 1950-54; pres. Assn. Rehab. Ctrs., 1953, Am. Acad. Cerebral Palsy, Richmond, Va., 1967. Chmn. governing bd. Retired Physicians Assn. Perm Med. Group, Oakland, 1989-90; trustee Costra Costa County Mosquito Abatement Dist., Concord, Calif., 1970-93; mem. White House Conf. on Health, Washington, 1953. With AUS, 1942-45, col. USAR, ret. 1971. Scholar Harvard Coll., 1932. Mem. AMA, World Med. Assn., Mass. Med. Soc., Am. Acad. Neurology, Am. Acad. Cerebral Palsy (pres. 1967), Faculty Club U. Calif. Berkeley, Harvard Club San Francisco. Unitarian.

MEAD, TERRY EILEEN, clinic administrator, consultant; b. Portland, Oreg., Mar. 14, 1950; d. Everett L. and Jean (Nonken) Richardson; divorced; 1 child, Sean Wade Adcock. AA, Seattle U., 1972; postgrad., U. Wash., 1971, USAF Acad., Colorado Springs. Project mgr. Assoc. Univ. Physician, Seattle, 1971-74; pathology supr. Swedish Hosp., Seattle, 1974-77; svcs. supr. Transamerica, Seattle, 1977-78; various mgmt. positions Providence Hosp., Seattle, 1978-83; adminstr. Evergreen Surg. Ctr., Kirkland, Wash., 1983-86; bus. mgr. Ketchikan (Alaska) Gen. Hosp., 1986—; instr. U. Alaska, Ketchikan, 1990; adminstr. Bethel (Alaska) Family Clinic, 1994—; sec. S.E. adv. bd. U. Alaska, Ketchikan, 1987—; cons. to hosps. and physicians, Wash., Alaska, 1980-89; mgr. Practice Mgmt. Cons., Seattle, 1982-83. Mem. City Charter Rev. Com., Ketchikan, 1990, High Sch. Facilities Com, Ketchikan, 1990; S.E. dir. search com U. Alaska, Ketchikan, 1990; treas. Calvary Bible Ch., Ketchikan, 1989-91; bd. dirs. S.E. Alaska Symphony, 1992—, Jr. Achievement, 1992-93; mem. fin. com. City of Bethel; chmn. Alaska dist. 39 Republican Party. Mem. Rotary Internat. Home: PO Box 2221 Bethel AK 99559-2221 Office: PO Box 1796 Bethel AK 99559-1796

MEAD, TRAY C., museum administrator; b. Mesa, Ariz., Apr. 1, 1950; s. Norman Wesley and Peggy Lee (Barrows) M.; Barbara Celaya, Feb. 9, 1981; children: Michael Adam, Kristiana Nicole. BA in Edn., Ariz. State U., 1973. Cert. tchr., Ariz. Publisher Ariz. Northland Mag., Flagstaff, 1973-77; mus. dir. Mesa Southwest Mus., 1977—; founding dir. Ariz. Fed. Credit Union, Phoenix, 1980-85. Author: Mesa, Beneath the Superstitions, 1988, Sirrine House Story, 1992; editor: Mesa Grande, 1979, Capturing the Canyon, 1987; field editor Ariz. White Mountain Mag., 1965—; contbg. editor Tonto Trails Mag., 1970—. Founding dir. Mesa Conv. and Tourism Bureau, 1989—; founding chmn. S.W. Svc. Corp., Phoenix, 1981-85; bd. dirs., founding pres. Arts in Mesa, 1980—. Recipient Excellence award Centennial Com., 1978, Golden Quill award Caligraphic Soc. Ariz., 1987, Native Am. Heritage award U.S.M.C. Netherlands, 1991; named Hon. Medicine Man, Ft. Apache Tribe, 1973, Hon. Chmn. Mesa Parade, Mayor City of Mesa, 1980. Mem. Nat. Trust Hist. Preservation, Am. Assn. State and Local Histories, Am. Assn. Mus., Mus. Assn. Ariz. (founding mem., v.p. 1982—), Ctrl. Ariz. Mus. Assn. (founding pres. 1978—), Mesa C. of C. (com. chmn. 1979-89). Home: 370 E Pinon Way Gilbert AZ 85234-4573 Office: Mesa Southwest Museum 53 N Macdonald Mesa AZ 85201-7325

MEADE, KENNETH JOHN, realty company owner, broker; b. N.Y.C., Nov. 25, 1925; s. John Joseph and Blanche (Woodworth) M.; m. Alice Elizabeth (Steinmann), Nov. 8, 1952; children: Steven, Janet, Patricia. Student, N.Y. Inst. Fin., 1960-62. Cert. real estate residential broker. Sales broker Del Webb Devel., Sun City, Ariz., 1974-82; mgr. Mull Realty Inc., Sun City, Ariz., 1982-83; broker, owner 6 offices Ken Meade Realty Inc., Sun City, Ariz., 1983—; dir., treas. Sun City Bd. Realtors, 1988—. Bd. dirs., v.p. Sun City Ambs., 1988—. With USN, 1942-45. Mem. Nat. Assn. Realtors, Ariz. Assn. Realtors, Dale Carnegie Club (past instr. sales course, Outstanding Achievment 1964). Republican. Lutheran. Home: 13306 W Meeker Blvd Sun City West AZ 85375-3815 Office: Ken Meade Realty Inc 17001 N Del Webb Blvd Sun City AZ 85373-1804

MEADER, WILLARD LINGEL, health maintenance organization executive; b. LaPorte, Ind., Nov. 23, 1933; s. Robert Paul and Julia Louise

(Lingel) M.; m. Sharon Sue Inman, Jan. 21, 1961; children: Richard P., Dana L. Albion Coll., 1954, MD; Temple U. Sch. Med., Phila., 1958; MPH, U. Calif., 1965; postgrad., Indsl. Coll. Armed Forces, Ft. McNair, DC, 1975. Commd. USAF, 1959, advanced through grades to brig. gen.; various med. positions to comdr. 377th Dispensary USAF, Tan Son Nhut Airfield, Vietnam, 1967-68; comdr. USAF, Clinic RAF, Wethersfield, Great Britain, 1968-70; dir. of aero med. & deputy surgeon Hdqrs. 2d Air Force, Barksdale AFB, La., 1970-71; cmmdr. USAF, Clinic RAF, Bentwaters, Great Britain, 1971-74; dir. of biotech. & dep. surgeon hdqrs. Air Force Systems Command USAF, Andrews AFB, Md., 1975-78; hosp. cmmdr. USAF, Nellis AFB, Nev., 1978-80; command surgeon hdqrs. Pacific Air Forces USAF, Hickam AFB, Hawaii, 1980-83; command surgeon hdqrs. Air Force Logistics Command USAF, Wright-Patterson AFB, Ohio, 1983-89; retired USAF, 1989; pres. Hanford Environ. Health Found., Richland, Wash., 1989-93; v.p. Group Health Northwest, Kennewick, Wash., 1993—; preceptor aerospace med. HQ 2nd Air Force Barksdale, 1971-72, assoc. clinical prof. Wright State U. Sch. of Med. Dayton, 1984—, Sch. Pub. Health and Community Medicine U. Wash., 1989—. Fellow Am. Coll. Preventive Medicne, Am. Coll. Physician Execs., Am. Coll. Occupl. and Environ. Medicine, Aerospace Med. Assn.; mem. AMA, Am. Mgmt. Assn., Soc. USAF Flight Surgeons (pres. 1980-81). Methodist. Home: 2013 Greenview Dr Richland WA 99352-9698 Office: 3311 W Clearwater Ave Ste 1010 Kennewick WA 99336-2710

MEADOR, BILLIE COOEETTA, nurse. Diploma, Kaiser Found Sch. Nursing, 1970; AA in Nursing, Contra Costa Coll., 1970; BSN, Sonoma State U., 1976; MS in Physiologic Nursing, U. Calif., San Francisco, 1978. RN, Calif., Tex., Ariz.; cert. BCLS and ACLS instr., ACLS affiliate faculty. Staff nurse, charge nurse, acting head nurse Kaiser Permanente Med. Ctr., San Francisco, 1970-74; staff nurse, relief charge nurse Santa Rosa (Calif.) Meml. Hosp., 1974-76; student teaching asst. in phys. assessment and physiology Sonoma State U., Rohnert Park, Calif., 1975-76; staff nurse med. ICU St. Mary's Hosp. and Med. Ctr., San Francisco, 1976-77; lectr. continuing edn. and phys. assessment U. Calif., San Francisco, 1977-78; critical care instr. VA Med. Ctr., Martinez, Calif., 1978-79; clin. specialist med. intensive care unit VA Med. Ctr., San Diego, 1979-81; staff nurse critical care Calif. Nurses Bur., San Diego, 1981-85; teaching asst. U. Tex. Sch. Nursing, Austin, 1985-86; staff nurse ICU St. David's Community Hosp., Austin, 1986-88; edn. coord., staff nurse United Western Med. Ctr., Orange, Calif., 1988-90; clin. nurse specialist critical care St. John's Hosp. and Health Ctr., Santa Monica, Calif., 1990—; lectr. San Diego (Calif.) C.C., 1980-83, Consortium of State Colls. and Univs., 1983-85, San Diego (Calif.) State U., 1983-85; presenter in field. Mem. editorial bd.: RN Mag., 1984-86; author: Critical Care Review and Update, Critical Care Self Assessment; contbr. articles to profl. jours. Mem. AACN (CCRN, initiating mem. San Francisco chpt. 1972, treas. 1972-73, corr. sec. 1973-74, pres.-elect Alameda-Contra Coast chpt. 1978-79, pres. 1979-80, mem. Greater Long Beach-Orange County chpt. 1989-91), Am. Heart Assn. (ACLS subcom., com. for continuing edn. for nurses San Diego chpt. 1983-85), Am. Lung Assn. (profl. edn. com. 1989-90), Sigma Theta Tau, Kappa Delta Pi. Home: 855 Coriander Dr Torrance CA 90502-3016 Office: St Johns Hosp & Health Ctr 1328 22nd St Santa Monica CA 90404-2032

MEADOR, JAMES PARNELL, toxicologist; b. Long Beach, Calif., June 23, 1952; s. James Gene and Alice (Martin) M.; m. Susan Jean Picquelle, Sept. 19, 1981. BA in Zoology, Humboldt State U., 1975; MS in Biology and Physiology, San Diego State U., 1981; PhD in Aquatic Toxicology, U. Wash., 1988. Staff rsch. assoc. Scripps Inst. Oceanography U. Calif., San Diego, 1975-81; sr. rsch. biologist Computer Scis. Corp., San Diego, 1982, analyst, 1983; predoctoral rsch. asst. U. Wash., Seattle, 1983-88; sr. assoc. scientist Envirosphere Co., Seattle, 1988-89; rsch. assoc. Nat. Rsch. Coun., 1989-90; rsch. fisheries biologist Nat. Marine Fisheries, NOAA, 1990—; instr. Centro de Investigacion Cientifica y de Educacion Superior de Ensenada, Baja Calif., Mex., 1982; predoctoral teaching asst. Sch. of Oceanography and Sch. of Fisheries, U. Wash., 1984-87. Contbr. articles to profl. jours. Geil Meml. Scholarship, 1986, Egtvedt Scholarship, 1985, Summer Rsch. Scholarship, Sch. of Fisheries, U. Wash., 1986, 88; Nat. Rsch. Coun. Associateship, 1989-90. Mem. Soc. of Environ. Toxicology and Chemistry (bd. mem. Pacific Northwest chpt.), Western Soc. Naturalists, Pacific Estuarine Rsch. Soc.

MEADOWS, DONALD FREDERICK, librarian; b. Regina, Sask., Can., Jan. 13, 1937; s. Frederick John and Doris Eileen (Willock) M.; m. Ruth Susan Cochran, June 10, 1960; children—Scott Frederick, George Edward. B.A., U. Sask., 1962; B.L.S., U. B.C., 1968. Library cons. Sask. Provincial Library, Regina, 1968-69; asst. provincial librarian Sask. Provincial Library, 1969-70, provincial librarian, province of Sask., 1970-81; dir. Met. Toronto Library, 1981-86; dir. Vancouver Island Regional Library, Nanaimo, B.C., Can., 1986—, also bd. dirs. Mem. Canadian Library Assn., ALA, B.C. Library Assn. Mem. United. Ch. Can. Office: Vancouver Island Regional Library, PO Box 3333, Nanaimo, BC Canada V9R 5N3

MEADOWS, JOHN FREDERICK, lawyer; b. Manila, Philippines, Mar. 7, 1926; s. Grover Cleveland and Millie M.; m. Karen Lee Morris, Nov. 17, 1962; children—Ian Joseph, Marie Irene. A.A., U. Mich., 1944; B.A. (Freshman Alumni Scholar, 1943), U. Calif., Berkeley, 1948, LL.B., Boalt Hall, 1951. Bar: Calif. 1952, U.S. Dist. Ct. (no. dist.) Calif 1952, U.S. Ct. Apls. (9th cir.) 1952, U.S. Sup. Ct. 1958. Assoc. Wallace, Garrison, Norton & Ray, San Francisco, 1952-56; atty. advisor Maritime Adminstrn., U.S. Dept. Commerce, Washington, 1956; trial atty. Admiralty and Shipping Sect., U.S. Dept. Justice, West Coast Office, San Francisco, 1956-64, atty. in charge, 1964-72; sr. resident ptnr. Acret & Perrochet, San Francisco, 1972-76; sr. ptnr. Meadows, Smith, Lenker, Sterling & Davis, San Francisco, Long Beach, Calif., Seattle, 1976-93, mng. ptnr. west coast Kirlin, Campbell, Meadows & Keating, 1993; ptnr. Jedeikin, Green Meadows & Schneider, Francisco, 1994—. cons. maritime law, UN, lectr. seminar Taipei, Taiwan, 1968; Served to lt. M.I. AUS, 1944-46. Mem. ABA, Assn. Def. Counsel, Maritime Law Assn., San Francisco Bar Assn.; Republican. Roman Catholic. Clubs: Merchants Exchange. Assoc. editor Am. Maritime Cases; author: Preparing a Ship Collision Case for Trial; contbr. articles to legal publs. Home: 205 The Uplands Berkeley CA 94705-2818 Office: Ste 450 300 Montgomery St San Francisco CA 94104-1906

MEAGHER, MICHAEL, radiologist; b. New Rochelle, N.Y., Oct. 24, 1942; s. Joseph Aloysius and Elizabeth (Ahern) M.; m. Martha Batten Mitchell, 1968; children: Kelly, Courtney. Student, Rensselaer Poly. Inst., 1960-62; AB with distinction, U. Rochester, 1964; MD, Stanford U., 1969. Diplomate Am. Bd. Radiology, Nat. Bd. Med. Examiners. Intern in medicine Cornell U., N.Y. Hosp., 1969-70; jr. asst. resident in diagnostic radiology U. Wash., Seattle, 1970-71, sr. asst. resident diagnostic radiology, 1973-74, resident diagnostic radiology, 1974-75; active staff mem. dept. radiology Queen's Med. Ctr., Honolulu, 1975—, Leahi Hosp., Honolulu, 1981—, Kahuku (Hawaii) Hosp., 1988—; pres. Radiology Assocs., Inc., 1978, 81-84, 90; chmn. dept. radiology Queen's Med. Ctr., 1979-80, 82-86, 88-90, dir. dept. radiology, 1985-91, dir. magnetic resonance imaging, 1991—, chmn. cancer com., 1980-82; mem. med. staff Hawaii Health Tech. Magnetic Resonance Imaging Facility, Honolulu, 1986—, chief of staff, 1978; clin. instr. dept. radiology U. Hawaii Sch. Medicine, 1983-89, clin. assoc. prof., 1989-93, clin. prof., 1993—, asst. rsch. prof. Cancer Rsch. Ctr. Hawaii, 1989—; clin. asst. prof. dept. radiology U. Wash. Sch. Medicine, 1980-88; presenter in fld. Contbr. articles to profl. publs. Chmn. high tech. adv. com. State Health Planning and Devel. Agy., 1983—; bd. dirs. Friends of Hawaii Pub. TV, 1979-81; pres., CEO Queen's Health Care Plan, Honolulu, 1985-89, chmn. bd. dirs., 1989-91; bd. dirs. Managed Care Mgmt., Inc., Honolulu, 1990; v.p. bd. dirs. Hawaii Opera Theatre, 1990-91, treas., 1991—. Lt. comdr. USN, 1971-73. NIH fellow, 1966; Kaiser Found. grantee, 1967. Fellow Am. Coll. Radiology; mem. AMA, Hawaii State Radiol. Soc. (sec.-treas. 1978-79, v.p. 1979-80, pres. 1980-81), Radiol. Soc. N.Am., Soc. Computer Applications in Radiology (charter), Am. Roentgen Ray Soc. Home: 1234 Maunawili Rd Kailua HI 96734-4642 Office: Queen's Med Ctr Dept Radiology Honolulu HI 96813

MEALEY, ANNE ROE, mental health nurse, educator, consultant; b. Butte, Mont., Mar. 4, 1928; d. James and Katherine Louise (Porter) Roe; divorced; children: Patrick, Cornelius, Katherine, Brian, Megan, Honore. Diploma, Sisters of Charity Hosp., Butte, 1948; BS in Nursing Edn., St. Louis U., 1951; MEd, Gonzaga U., Spokane, 1973; PhD, U. Wash., 1983; postdoctoral study, U. Calif., San Francisco, 1987. Advanced Registered Nurse Practitioner, Wash.; cert. clin. specialist in adult psychiat. and mental health nursing. Staff nurse St. James Hosp., Butte, 1948-49, Desloge Hosp., St. Louis, 1949-51; instr. Mont. State Coll., Butte, 1951-53, Bozeman, 1961-63; instr. Sacred Heart Sch. Nursing, Spokane, 1969-73; asst. prof. Intercollegiate Ctr. for Nursing Edn. Wash. State U., Spokane, 1973-82, assoc. prof., mem. grad. faculty, 1982-93, prof., 1994—; rsch. assoc. U. Wash., Seattle, 1982; cons. emotional care unit Lake Chelan (Wash.) Hosp., 1989-91; cons. psychiat. unit Sacred Heart Med. Ctr., 1983. Contbr. chpt. to book, articles to profl. jours. Recipient various awards. Mem. ANA, Wash. State Nurses Assn., Inland Empire Nurses Assn. (treas. 1989-92), Coun. on Psychiat./Mental Health Nursing, Sigma Theta Tau, Gamma Pi Epsilon. Roman Catholic. Office: ICNE 2917 W Ft Wright Dr Spokane WA 99204

MEANS, JAMES ANDREW, engineer; b. Heavener, Okla., Oct. 11, 1937; s. Edward Andrew and Lorena (Nobles) M.; Therese Louise Zimmermann, Feb. 21, 1959; children: James A. Jr., William R., Charles E., Vicky M. Locken. BSEE, U. Ariz., 1962, MSEE, 1966; PhD, U. Calif., Santa Barbara, 1972; MS in Computer Sci., Chapman U., Orange, Calif., 1988. Engr. Pacific Missile Test Ctr., Pt Mugu, Calif., 1962-72; engr. mgr. Pacific Missile Test Ctr., 1972-79; tech. dir. Space & Missile Test Orgn., Vandenberg AFB, Calif., 1979-89; sr. tech. advisor SRI Internat., Menlo Park, Calif., 1990—; cons. Agri-Craft, Camarillo, Calif., 1968-70, Astro-Geo-Marine, Ventura, Calif., 1972-74. Patentee in field. Mem. Internat. Found. for Telemetering (pres. 1988—), Internat. Test and Evaluation Assn. Democrat. Baptist. Home: 284 St Andrews Way Lompoc CA 93436-1355 Office: SRI Internat 333 Ravenswood Ave Menlo Park CA 94025-3453

MEANY, DAVID WILLIAM, civil engineer; b. Sydney, Australia, Oct. 26, 1937; m. Maire Meany; m. Jan. 1967. BSc in Civil Engring., U. NSW, 1964; MSc in Civil Engring., World Open U., 1979; MBA in Fin., Golden Gate U., 1980; MA in Internat. Econs., U. San Francisco, 1981; MBA in Info. Systems, Golden Gate U., 1983; diploma in Fin. Mgmt., U. New England, 1989; BS in Acctg., SUNY, Albany, 1994. Project mgr. Foster Engring., San Francisco, 1989-90; resident engr. City of Tracy, Calif., 1990-92; water resources engr. Zone 7 Water Agy., Pleasanton, Calif., 1992—. Mem. ASCE, ASME, NSPE, Instn. Civil Engring. (U.K.), Instn. Profl. Engrs. New Zealand. Home: 7744 Creekside Dr Pleasanton CA 94588-3687 Office: Zone 7 Water Agy 5997 Parkside Dr Pleasanton CA 94588-5127

MEAUX, ALAN DOUGLAS, facilities technician, sculptor; b. Joliet, Ill., Sept. 10, 1951; s. Berry Lee and Luella Ann (Ferguson) M.; m. Letta Sue Nygaard, Sept. 15, 1984; children: Ashley Nicole, Lacey Marie. Student, Joliet Jr. Coll., 1969-71, Bradley U., 1971-72, U.S. Dept. Agr. Grad. Sch., 1972, Skagit Valley Coll., 1983-85. Photographer J.J.C. Blazer, Joliet Herald News, Joliet, 1969-71; auto mechanic Pohanka Olds and Fiat, Hillcrest Heights, Md., 1972-74, Hoffman Olds and Rolls Royce, Hartford, Conn., 1974-75; carpenter Klappenbach Constrn. Co., Moscow, Idaho, 1975-79; property mgr. Olympic Builders, Oak Harbor, Wash., 1979-86; maintenance technician Troubleshooters Inc., Oak Harbor, 1986-87; facilities technician Island County Govt., Coupeville, Wash., 1987—; bronze sculptor Ronin Art Prodns., Oak Harbor, 1979—; appraiser class A Mid-Am. Appraisers Assn., Springfield, Mo., 1986—; bd. dirs. North West Token Kai, U. Wash., Seattle, 1989—, lectr., 1985; contbr. Nanka Token Kai, L.A., 1985—. Author: Japanese Samurai Weapons, 1989; prin. works exhibited at Mini Guild Children's Orthopedic Show, Ballard, Wash., 1986, Worldfest/Ethnic Heritage Coun., Seattle, 1988, 89, 90, Stanwood (Wash.) Invitational Art Show, 1988. Mem. NRA (life), Japanese Sword Soc. U.S. (life), N.W. Token Kai (charter, bd. dirs. 1989-91), Western Mus. Conf., Wash. Mus. Assn., Ethnic Heritage Coun., Nanka Token Kai, Japan Soc. Inc., Wash. Arms Collectors Assn., North Whidbey Sportmen's Assn. (chmn. range com.), Cen. Whidbey Sportmen's Club. Office: Ronin Art Prodns PO Box 1271 Oak Harbor WA 98277-1271

MEBRAHTU, YEMANE BERHAN, medical microbiologist, entomologist, researcher; b. Men-Defera, Seraye, Eritrea, July 12, 1950; came to U.S., 1992; s. Mebrahtu Hagos and Leteberhan G. Michael; m. Lula A. Asmelash, May 14, 1978; children: Jonathan Yemane, Fanuel Yemane. BS in Biology, Chemistry, Haile Sellaisie I U., Addis Ababa, Ethiopia, 1972; MS in Med. Entomology, Nairobi U., Kenya, 1984, PhD in Med. Microbiology, 1991. Assoc. rsch. scientist Ctrl. Lab. and Rsch. Inst., Addis Ababa, 1972-77; lectr. (part-time) Addis Ababa U., 1977-79; head vector control div. Ctrl. Lab. and Rsch. Inst., Addis Ababa, 1977-80; sr. rsch. officer U.S. Army Med. Rsch. Unit, Nairobi, 1981-93, Biomed. Scis. Rsch. Ctr., Kenya Med. Rsch. Inst., Nairobi, 1983-93; vis. asst. rsch. scientist U. Ariz., Tucson, 1993—. Reviewer Sinet, Ethiopian Jour. of Sci., 1976-80; contbr. articles to profl. jours. Recipient grant WHO, Kenya, 1980-83, grant Walter Reed Army Inst. Rsch., 1988-91, grant Commn. of European Community, The Netherlands, 1989. Mem. Am. Soc. Tropical Medicine and Hygiene, Am. Mosquito Control Assn., Am. Assn. Advancement of Sci., Nat. Geographic Soc., Haile Sellasie I U. Biology Assn. (sec. 1970-71, pres. 1971-72). Home: 555 E Limberlost Dr Apt 1077 Tucson AZ 85705-2883 Office: Univ Ariz Dept Entomology Forbes Bldg # 410 Tucson AZ 85721

MECHAM, GLENN JEFFERSON, lawyer, mayor; b. Logan, Utah, Dec. 11, 1935; s. Everett H. and Lillie (Dunford) M.; m. Mae Parson, June 5, 1957; children: Jeff B., Scott R., Marcia, Suzanne. BS, Utah State U., 1957; JD, U. Utah, 1961; grad. Air Command and Staff Coll., Air War Coll., 1984. Bar: Utah 1961, Supreme Ct. U.S., U.S. Ct. Appeals (10th Cir.), U.S. Dist. Ct. Utah, U.S. Ct. Claims. Gen. practice law, 1961-65; atty. Duchesne County, Utah, 1962, City of Duchesne, 1962; city judge Roy City, Utah, 1963-66; judge City of Ogden, Utah, 1966-69, mayor, 1992—; lectr. law and govt. Stevens-Henager Coll., Ogden, 1963-75; asst. U.S. dist. atty. State of Utah, 1969-72; ptnr. Mecham & Richards, Ogden, Utah, 1972-82; pres. Penn Mountain Mining Co., South Pacific Internat. Bank, Ltd.; mem. Bur. Justice Stats. Adv. Bd., U.S. Dept. Justice, U.S. Conf. Mayors. Chmn. Ogden City Housing Authority; chmn. bd. trustees Utah State U., Space Dynamics Lab. Utah State U.; mem. adv. coun. Fed. Home Loan Bank; pres. Utah League Cities and Towns, 1981-82. Col. USAF, 1957. Mem. ABA, Weber County Bar Assn. (pres. 1966-68), Utah Bar Assn., Am. Judicature Soc., Weber County Bar Legal Svcs. (chmn. bd. trustees 1966-69), Utah Assn. Mcpl. Judges (sec.), Sigma Chi, Phi Alpha Delta. Home: 1715 Darling St Ogden UT 84403-0556 Office: City of Ogden 2484 Washington Blvd # 300 Ogden UT 84401

MECKLENBURG, KARL BERNARD, professional football player; b. Seattle, Sept. 1, 1960; s. Fred and Marjory Mecklenburg; m. Kathi Mecklenburg; 1 child, Luke. Student, Augustana Coll.; BS in Biology, U. Minn. Linebacker Denver Broncos, 1983—. Office: Denver Broncos 13655 E Davies Pl Englewood CO 80112-4004*

MECKLER, MILTON, engineering consultant; b. Long Branch, N.J., Dec. 29, 1932; s. Morris and Irma (Hering) M.; m. Marlys Enid Alpert, Aug. 15, 1959; children: Ilyce Bonnie, Reneé Barbara. BS in Engring. with distinction, Worcester Poly. Inst., 1954; MS in Engring., U. Mich., 1955. Registered profl. engr., Calif., 15 others; lic. gen. bldg. and engring. contractor, Calif., diplomate Nat. Acad. Forensic Engrs. Sr. mech. engr. Daniel, Mann, Johnson & Mendenhall, L.A., 1963-65; ptnr. Silver, Meckler & Assocs., L.A., 1965-69; prin. Hellman, Silver, Lober & Meckler, Hollywood, Calif., 1969-71; pres. Meckler Assocs., L.A., 1971-74, Envirodyne Energy Svcs., Long Beach, Calif., 1974-76, The Energy Group, Century City, Calif., 1976-78; pres., chief exec. officer The Meckler Group, Encino, Calif., 1978—. Author: Energy Conservation in Buildings and Industrial Plants, 1980, Innovative Energy Design for the 90's, 1992; author, editor: Retrofitting of Commercial, Industrial, and Institutional Buildings for Energy Conservation, 1984, Indoor Air Quality Design Guidebook, 1990, Retrofitting Buildings for Energy Conservation, 2d edit., 1994; contbr. over 200 tech. publs. Dir. Bus. Coun. on Indoor Air, 1988—. Fellow Am. Soc. Mech. Engrs., Am. Inst. Chemists, Am. Soc. Heating, Refrigeration and Air Conditioning Engrs. (Crosby Field award 1990, Best Symposium Paper award 1990, Disting. Svc. award 1993), Environ. Engrs. and Mgrs. Inst. (Environ. Profl. of Yr. award 1992), Assn. Energy Engrs., Nat. Acad. Forensic Engrs.; mem. Encino Chamber of Commerce (dir. 1982-83, v.p. 1983), Am. Inst. Constructors, Sigma Xi, Tau Beta Pi. Office: The Meckler Group 17525 Ventura Blvd Encino CA 91316-3836

MEDAVOY, MIKE, motion picture company executive; b. Shanghai, China, Jan. 21, 1941; came to U.S., 1957, naturalized, 1962; s. Michael and Dora Medavoy; 1 child, Brian. B.A., UCLA, 1963. With Casting dept. Universal Studios, 1963; agt. Bill Robinson Assos., Los Angeles, 1963-64; v.p. motion picture dept. GAC/CMA Co., 1965-71, IFA Co., 1971-74; sr. v.p. United Artists Corp., 1974-78; one of founders, exec. v.p. Orion Pictures Co., Burbank, Calif., 1978-82; exec. v.p. Orion Pictures Corp. (formerly Orion Pictures Co.), Burbank, 1982-90; chmn. Tri-Star Pictures, Inc., Burbank, 1990—, Phoenix Pictures Corp., 1995; bd. dirs. Sony Pictures Corp. Mem. vis. com. Boston Museum Fine Arts.; chmn. Ctr. Internat. Strategic Affairs, UCLA, Com. to Cure Cancer through Immunization UCLA; co-chmn. Olympic Sports Fedn. Com., Music Ctr. Unified Fund Campaign; bd. govs. Sundance Inst., 1980-86; bd. dirs. Calif. Mus. Sci. and Industry, 1984-87. Recipient Academy award for One Flew Over the Cuckoo's Nest, Rocky, Annie Hall, Amadeus, Platoon, Dances With Wolves, Silence of the Lamb. Mem. Acad. Motion Picture Arts and Scis. (gov. 1977-81), UCLA Found., UCLA Chancellors Assocs.

MEDDLETON, DANIEL JOSEPH, health facility administrator; b. July 11, 1936. AA in Bus. Adminstrn., Broome Tech. Community Coll., Binghamton, N.Y., 1959; BSBA, Mich. Technol. U., 1964; M in Health Care Adminstrn., Univ. Minn., 1966. Asst. adminstr. Univ. Cin. Med. Ctr., 1968-70; assoc. adminstr. Providence Hosp., Anchorage, Alaska, 1970-76; exec. v.p. Benedictine Hosp., Kingston, N.Y., 1976-82; dir. Div. Planning, Policy and Prog. Evaluation State of Alaska/Dept. Health and Social Svcs., 1983-84; owner Kits Cameras, Juneau, Alaska, 1984-90; adminstr. Juneau Pioneers' Home, 1988-93, Alaska Psychiat. Hosp., 1993—. Bd. dirs. Alaska Econ. Devel. Adv. Coun.; steering com. Southeast Alaska Regional Econ. Devel. Inst., 1987; bd. dirs. Big Bros./Big Sisters, others. Fellow Am. Coll. Health Care Execs.; mem. No. N.Y. Met. Hosp. Assn. (past bd. dirs.), Mid Hudson Health Systems Agy. (past bd. dirs.), Rotary, others. Home: 3820 Resurrection Dr Anchorage AK 99504-4719

MEDEL, REBECCA ROSALIE, artist; b. Denver, Mar. 26, 1947; d. Natividad and Josefa (Apodaca) M. BFA, Ariz. State U., 1970; MFA, UCLA, 1982. Art instr. 9-12 Tucson Sch. Dist., Santa Rita H.S., 1973-78; substitute tchr. Alameda and Richmond Sch. Dists., Calif., 1978-79; weaving asst. to Yoshiko Wada Berkeley, 1979; asst. Tomasello Fabric Showroom, L.A., 1979-81; rsch. ast. Hunter Coll., N.Y. and Pasadena, 1981-83; asst. prof. fibers dept. head Tenn. Technol. U., Smithville, 1983-88; lectr. Dept. of Design, UCLA, 1989-91; studio artist, 1991—; lectr. N.C. State U., Raleigh, San Diego State U., SUNY, Purchase, 1992, Penland Sch. Asheville, N.C., Textile Study Group, N.Y.C., Calif. Coll. of Arts & Crafts, Oakland, Calif., San Jose State U., Am. Ctr., Kyoto, Japan, City Ctr., Sapporo, Japan, 1986; vis. artist U. N.D., 1985. One-woman shows include Neuberger Mus. of Art, Purchase, N.Y., 1992-93, Bellas Artes Gallery, N.Y.C., 1991, N.D. Mus. Art, Grand Forks, 1985, Maya Behn Galerie, Zurich, 1984, UCLA, 1982; two-person exhbns. include Heath Gallery, Atlanta, 1987, Maya Behn Gallerie, 1986; group shows include Bellas Artes Gallery, Santa Fe, N.Mex., 1992, N.C. State U. Gallery, 1992, Portland Art Mus., 1995, Madison (Wis.) Art Ctr., 1995, Santa Monica (Calif.) Art Gallery, 1995, Maya Behn Gallerie, 1991, Mus. Van Bommel-Van Dam, Venlo, Netherlands, 1990, Palo Alto Cultural Ctr., 1990, many others. Fellowship Nat. Endowment for the Arts Visual Artist, 1986, 88, fellowship for emerging visual artists So. Arts Fedn. NEA, 1985; scholarship to Arcosanti Nat. Endowment for the Arts, 1976; recipient Bronze medal Triennial of Tapestry, 1985. Home: 7134 Potomac St Riverside CA 92504-3936

MEDINA, DANIEL ANDREW, banker; b. Monterey Park, Calif., Nov. 23, 1957; s. Andrew and Maria (Barboa) M.; m. Laura Martin, July 16, 1983; 1 child, Andrew Martin. AB, Harvard Coll., 1979, MBA, 1983. Assoc. Salomon Bros. Inc., N.Y.C. and L.A., 1983-86; v.p. Bear, Stearns & Co. Inc., L.A., 1986-90; mng. dir. mcht. banking Union Bank, L.A., 1992—. Mem. adv. bd. Broadway Fed. Savs. and Loan Assn., 1993—. Home: 1825 W Haven Rd San Marino CA 91108-2567 Office: Union Bank Mcht Banking Dept 445 S Figueroa St Los Angeles CA 90071-1602

MEDINA-PUERTA, ANTONIO, scientist; b. Almeria, Spain, Jan. 20, 1956; s. Antonio and Maria Mar (Puerta) Medina; m. Mary Medina-Puerta, Sept. 20, 1986. MS, U. Politecnica, Madrid, 1979, MIT, 1982; OD, U. Complutense, Madrid, 1979; diploma Electrical Engring., MIT, 1981; PhD, U. Politecnica, Madrid, 1983. Optometrist Centro de Vision Luz, Almeria, 1978-79; engr. Philips, Eindhoven, Holland, 1979-80; rsch. asst. MIT, Cambridge, Mass., 1981-83; sci. assoc. Eye Rsch. Inst., Boston, 1983-88; task mgr. Calif. Inst. Tech., Pasadena, 1988-91; adviser NASA, Washington, 1988—, USN, 1989—. Contbr. articles to profl. publs.; patentee in field. Fellow Christ's Coll., Cambridge Univ., Eng. Fellow Acad. Applied Sci.; mem. IEEE, Optical Soc. Am., Soc. Photo-optical Instrumentation Engrs., Biomed. Soc. Roman Catholic. Home and Office: 281 E Colorado Blvd # 1002 Pasadena CA 91101-1903

MEDINE, PETER ERNEST, literature educator; b. DeKalb, Ill., Mar. 30, 1941; s. Ernest Glenn and Ann Margaret (Marshal) M.; m. Patricia Jean Davis (div. 1976); children: Eric Joseph, David Eric. BA, Northwestern U., 1963; MA, U. Wis., 1965, PhD, 1970. Asst. prof. English U. Ariz., Tucson, 1969-75, assoc. prof., 1975-93, prof., 1993—. Editor: Horace: His Art, 1972, De satyrica Graecorum poesi, 1973, Art of Rhetoric, 1994; author: Thomas Wilson, 1986. Chair bd. govs. St. Michael's Day Sch., Tucson, 1989-94. Mem. MLA, Spenser Soc. Am., Milton Soc. Am. Democrat. Mem. Anglican Ch. Home: 2804 E 2nd St Tucson AZ 85716-4109 Office: U Ariz Tucson AZ 85721

MEDITCH, JAMES STEPHEN, electrical engineering educator; b. Indpls., July 30, 1934; s. Vladimir Stephen and Alexandra (Gogeff) M.; m. Theresa Claire Scott, Apr. 4, 1964; children: James Stephen Jr., Sandra Anne. BSEE, Purdue U., 1956, PhD, 1961; SM, MIT, 1957. Staff engr. Aerospace Corp., Los Angeles, 1961-65; assoc. prof. elec. engring. Northwestern U., 1965-67; mem. tech. staff Boeing Sci. Research Labs., Seattle, 1967-70; prof. U. Calif., Irvine, 1970-77; prof. U. Wash., Seattle, 1977—, chmn. dept. elec. engring., 1977-85, assoc. dean engring., 1987-90. Author: Stochastic Optimal Linear Estimation and Control, 1969; co-editor: Computer Communication Networks, 1984. Fellow IEEE (Disting. mem. control systems soc., 1983, editor Proceedings 1983-85, Centennial medal 1984). Office: U Wash Dept Elec Engring Ft # 10 Seattle WA 98195

MEDOFF, MARK HOWARD, playwright, screenwriter, novelist; b. Mt. Carmel, Ill., Mar. 18, 1940; s. Lawrence Ray and Thelma Irene (Butt) M.; m. Stephanie Thorne, June 24, 1972; children: Debra, Rachel, Jessica. B.A., U. Miami, Fla., 1962; M.A., Stanford U., 1966; D.H.L., Gallaudet Coll., 1981. Instr. English and drama N.Mex. State U., 1966-79, dramatist in residence, 1974—, head dept. drama, 1978-87, prof. drama, 1979-93, artistic dir., 1982-87; artistic dir. Am. S.W. Theatre Co., 1984-87. Author: (plays) When You Comin' Back, Red Ryder?, 1974, The Wager, 1975, The Kramer, 1975, The Halloween Bandit, 1978, The Conversion of Aaron Weiss, 1978, Firekeeper, 1978, The Last Chance Saloon, 1979, Children of a Lesser God, 1980 (Soc. West Theatres best play award 1982), The Majestic Kid, 1981, The Hands of Its Enemy, 1984, Kringle's Window, 1985, The Heart Outright, 1986 (novel) Dreams of Long Lasting; (films) When You Comin' Back, Red Ryder?, 1979, Off Beat, 1986, Apology, 1986, Children of a Lesser God, 1986, Good Guys Wear Black, 1978, Clara's Heart, 1988, The Majestic Kid, 1988, City of Joy, 1992, Homage, 1995; workers appear in Best Plays, 1973-74, 74-75, 79-80, Best Short Plays, 1975, The Homage that Follows, 1987; plays Stumps, 1989, Stefanie Hero, 1990. Guggenheim fellow, 1974-75; recipient Obie award, Drama Desk award, Outer Critics Circle award, Media award Pres.'s Com. Employment Handicapped, Tony award; Oscar award nominee for Best Screenplay for Children of A Lesser God, 1987. Mem. Dramatists Guild, Writers Guild Am., Actors Equity Assn., Screen Actors Guild Pen. Office: PO Box 3072 Las Cruces NM 88003-3072

MEDUSKI, JERZY WINCENTY, nutritionist, biochemist; b. Kalusz, Poland, Oct. 29, 1918; s. Dobieslaw Antoni and Katarzyna (Barbowska) M.; came to U.S., 1962, naturalized, 1969; M.D., Warsaw (Poland) Med. Sch., 1946; Ph.D. in Biochemistry, U. Lodz (Poland), 1951; 1 child, Jerzy Dobieslaw. Organizer, chief pharmacology labs. Polish Nat. Inst. Hygiene, Warsaw, 1945-52, organizer, head lab. of intermediary metabolism, 1952-59; assoc. prof. biochemistry Warsaw Med. Sch., 1955-59; asst. prof. neurology U. So.

Calif. Sch. Medicine, Los Angeles, 1973—; pres. Nutritional Cons. Group, Inc. Mem. Los Angeles County Bd. Suprs. Task Force on Nutrition. WHO fellow, Holland, Scotland, 1948-49; research grantee, USSR, 1956. Mem. Polish Acad. Sci. (sci. sec. biochem. com. 1952-59), Polish Med. Assn. (sci. sec. nat. bd. 1958-59), Polish Biochem. Soc. (founding mem.), Biochem. Soc. London, Royal Soc. Chem. London, Internat. Soc. on Toxinology, AMA, Am. Soc. Microbiology, Internat. Soc. on Oxygen Transport to Tissues, Sigma Xi. Author 3 books on biochemistry; contbr. more than 80 articles to internat. jours.; author textbook on nutritional biochemistry, 1977. Home: 1066 S Genesee Ave Los Angeles CA 90019-2448 Office: U So Calif Sch Medicine 2025 Zonal Ave Los Angeles CA 90033-4526

MEDVIN, EVELYN ANNE, geophysicist; b. Bronx, N.Y., Aug. 4, 1958; d. Marshall Jerome and Frieda (Panken) Grossbard; m. Roger William Medvin, July 1, 1984; children: Sara Joy, Seth David. BS, U. Okla., 1980. Geophysicist Cities Svc. Oil Co., Houston, 1980-83, Occidental Petroleum, Bakersfield, Calif., 1983-91; sr. geophysicist OXY USA Inc., Bakersfield, 1991—. Vol. Am. Cancer Soc., Bakersfield, 1987-92; tchr. Bakersfield Unified Religious Sch., 1993—. Mem. Am. Assn. Petroleum Geologists (award 1980), Soc. Exploration Geophysicists. Jewish. Office: OXY USA Inc 1200 Discovery Dr Bakersfield CA 93309-7007

MEE, JOY ANNE, city planning executive; b. Verona, N.J., Sept. 30, 1946; d. Irving Jones and Lorene Ada (Weissenborn) Greenslade; m. William Robert Mee, Jr., Oct. 9, 1970; children: Christopher Stanton, Nathan Frederick. BA, Principia Coll., Elsah, Ill., 1968; M of Urban Planning, U. Ill., 1970. Planner City of Phoenix, 1971-79, prin. planner, 1979-84, asst. planning dir., 1984—; mem. planning adv. cou., dept. urban and regional planning U. Ill., Urbana, 1985—. Author: (govt. document) Phoenix Housing Element, 1975. Mem. citizens adv. coun. Madison Sch. Dist., Phoenix, 1985—, mem. fin. oversight com., 1990—. Mem. Am. Inst. Cert. Planners (cert.; mem. accreditation team 1990—), Ariz. Planning Assn., Soroptimist Internat. (vice chair Ariz. Women's Townhall 1994). Home: 2550 E Denton Ln Phoenix AZ 85016-3641 Office: City of Phoenix Planning Dept 200 W Washington Phoenix AZ 85003

MEECHAM, WILLIAM CORYELL, engineering educator; b. Detroit; s. William Edward and Mabel Catherine (Wilcox) M.; m. Barbara Jane Brown, Sept. 4, 1948 (dec.); children: Janice Lynn, William James; m. Della Fern Carson,. BS, U. Mich., 1948, MS, 1948, PhD in Physics, 1954. Head acoustics lab. Willow Run Labs., Ann Arbor, Mich., 1959-60; asst. prof. U. Mich., Ann Arbor, 1958-60; prof. U. Minn., Mpls., 1960-67; prof. fluid mechanics and acoustics UCLA, 1967—, chmn. dept. mechanics and structures, 1972-73; cons. Aerospace Corp., El Segundo, Calif., 1975-80, Rand Corp., Santa Monica, Calif., 1964-74, Bolt, Beranek and Newman, Cambridge, Mass., 1968-73, Arete Assocs., Encino, Calif., 1976—, CRT Corp., Chatsworth, Calif., 1985—. Author: (with R. Lutomirski) Lasar Systems, 1973; author 120 papers on fluid mechanics and acoustics. Treas. Unitarian Ch., Ann Arbor, Mich., 1958-60; advisor U.S. Congress Com. on Pub. Works, Congl. Record Report N.J., 1972; mem. Calif. Space and Def. Council, U.S. Congress, 1982—. Served with U.S. Army, 1944-46. Mich. Alumni scholar 1942-44, Donovan scholar U. Mich., 1944-45; UCLA senate rsch. grantee, 1968—, NASA rsch. grantee, 1971—, Office Naval Rsch. grantee, 1977-85; recipient Disting. Svc. award U.S. Army. Fellow Acoustical Soc. Am. (gen. chmn. meeting 1973), AIAA (assoc. fellow); mem. com. aeroacoustics 1972-75); mem. Am. Phys. Soc. (fluid dynamics div.), Inst. Noise Control Engring., Sigma Xi, Tau Beta Pi. Home: 927 Glenhaven Dr Pacific Palisades CA 90272-2202 Office: UCLA Sch Engring & Applied Sci Los Angeles CA 90024

MEECHAM, WILLIAM JAMES, ophthalmologist; b. Ann Arbor, Mich., Nov. 30, 1958; s. William Coryell and Barbara (Brown) M. AB in Zoology, U. Calif., Berkeley, 1980, MA in Biophysics, 1983; MD, U. Calif., San Francisco, 1987. Diplomate Nat. Bd. Med. Examiners, Am. Bd. Ophthalmology. Med. intern Cabrini Med. Ctr., N.Y.C., 1987-88; resident in ophthalmology U. Calif., San Francisco, 1988-91, ocular oncology fellow, 1991-92, clin. asst. prof., 1991—, ocular plastics fellow, 1992-93; attending physician San Francisco Gen. Hosp., 1991—; career physician Kaiser Permanente, San Rafael, 1993—. Contbr. articles to profl. pubs.; editor-in-chief U. Calif.-San Francisco Synapse, 1984-85. Mem. Am. Acad. Ophthalmology. Office: 99 Montecillo Rd San Rafael CA 94903-3300

MEEHAN, EILEEN R., communications educator; b. San Francisco, Aug. 3, 1951; d. James Anthony and K. (McGroary) M.; m. Alfred J. Babbitt, Aug. 15, 1978. BA in Social Sci., San Francisco State Coll., 1973; MA, U. Pa., 1975; PhD, U. Ill., 1982. From lectr. to asst. prof. dept. comm. U. Iowa, Iowa City, 1982-89; asst. prof. dept. media arts U. Ariz., Tucson, 1989-93, assoc. prof. dept. media arts, 1993—; assoc. prof. comparative culture & lit.; vis. asst. prof. dept. comm. arts U. Wis., Madison, 1992; spkr. Univ. Bus. and Profl. Womens Assn., Tucson, 1991, Ariz. Bus. & Profl. Womens Assn., 1992, Tucson Cmty. Cable Corp., 1994. Mem. editl. bd. Comm. Perspectives, 1978-85; contbr. articles to profl. jours. Panelist LWV, Tucson, 1993. Grantee U. Ariz., 1992, 94, U. Wis., 1992. Mem. Union for Dem. Comm. (consultative group mem. 1990-94, chair steering com. 1984-89), Internat. Assn. for Comm. Rsch., Speech Comm. Assn. (newsletter editor 1985-86). Democrat. Office: Univ Ariz Dept Media Arts Harvill Bldg Tucson AZ 85721

MEEK, GERRY, library director. Dir. Calgary (Alta.) Pub. Libr., Can. Office: Calgary Pub Libr, 616 Macleod Trail SE, Calgary, AB Canada T2G 2M2*

MEEKS, CHRISTOPHER NELSON, writer; b. Mpls., Sept. 13, 1953; s. George Nelson Meeks and Sidney (Young) Wear; m. Carol Anne Fuchs, May 26, 1985; 1 child, Zachary Edward Meeks. BA in Mass Comm./Psychology, U. Denver, 1976; MFA in Profl. Writing, U. So. Calif., L.A., 1983. Freelance writer various publs. including N.Y. Times, Writer's Digest, others, 1982—; book reviewer The L.A. Herald-Examiner, 1985-86; writing cons. The Annenberg Sch. of Comms., U. So. Calif., 1986-87; sr. editor Prelude Press, 1983-87; nationally syndicated columnist Personal Computers jour., 1985—; theatre critic Daily Variety, 1989—; inst. writer, editor-in-chief CalArts/Current jour. The Calif. Inst. of the Arts, 1987—, faculty mem., 1994—; owner Inherit the Earth Technologies, 1990—. Author: Roald Dahl/Reaching Your Goal Series, 1993, Arnold Schwarzenegger/Reaching Your Goal Series, 1993, Skydiving, 1991, Japan: World Partner, 1990, The Personal Computer Book (with Peter McWilliams), 1990, On Being A Writer, 1989, others; playwright: Suburban Anger, 1993. Recipient 1st place U. So. Calif.'s Playwright's Festival/Fiveplay, 1983, Donald Davis Dramatic Writing award/Henry's Room, 1982. Mem. Dramatists Guild, PEN Ctr. USA West. Office: Inherit the Earth Tech # 326 1800 S Robertson Blvd # 326 Los Angeles CA 90035-4352

MEES, BUDDIE PETRUSKE, retail executive; b. Benton Harbor, Mich., Apr. 5, 1930; d. Gustav and Kathleen (Coburn) P. BS, U. Mich., 1951, MS, 1953, PhD, 1974. Merchandiser intimate apparel Halle Bros. Co., Cleve., 1960-69; owner, founder, CEO Sugar Plum, Inc., Idaho Springs, Colo., 1968—; mgr. ESPIAL, Englewood, Colo., 1994—. V.p., co-founder Listen Found., 1968, Foresees - Colo. Citizens for Ctrl. City., 1968-74. Mem. Internat. Platform Assn. Home: Box 1329 1845 Miner Idaho Springs CO 80452 Office: Sugar Plum Inc Idaho Springs CO 80452

MEGALOS, BILL, film director; b. N.Y.C., Oct. 30, 1953; s. Arthur Christopher and Malamo (Corniotes) M.; m. Judie Lee Hammond, Sept. 25, 1983; children: Elena, Sultana. BA, Columbia Coll., 1977; MFA, Columbia U., 1981. Tech. dir. Nikolais Dance Theatre, N.Y.C., 1974-75; prodn. stage mgr. Eliot Feld Ballet Co., N.Y.C., 1975-76; lighting designer various rock groups, 1976-80; freelance dir. cameraman, 1980—; adj. prof. Sch. Visual Arts, N.Y.C., 1984-88. Dir./producer: (TV features) Jack Benny: Comedy in Bloom, Ultimate Challenge, Moving Pictures, Springsteen, Take Back American/Jerry Brown for President 1992, Leadership '92, Strange Turf; dir./cameraman: (music videos) D.R.I., Kate and Anna McGarrigle, Dianne Reeves, A.C. Black, Rebel Pebbles, others. (commls.) Alpo, Broadway Bound, Bide-A-Wee Home, Yes on Six, Red Cross Water Safety PSA, Family Planning in Bangladesh, (others) Into the Woods, The Secret Garden, Showscan 'Space Race', more. Recipient Canon Cinematography award 1976, Best Cinematography, WHO, Beijing, 1984, Acad. award 1987, Acad. award nomination 1993, Emmy award 1990.

MEGDAL, SHARON BERNSTEIN, economics educator, consultant; b. Newark, Apr. 4, 1952; d. William B. and Ann (Kopatonsky) Bernstein; m. Ronald G. Megdal, Aug. 18, 1974, 1 child. AB in Econs., Rutgers U., 1974; MA in Econs., Princeton U., 1977, PhD in Econs., 1981. Asst. prof. econs. U. Ariz., Tucson, 1979-87, pres., owner MegEcon Cons., 1987—; vis. assoc. prof. No. Ariz. U., 1987-88; commr. Ariz. Corp. Commn., 1985-87; exec. dir. Santa Cruz Valley Water Dist., 1991-94; speaker, panelist in field. Chairwoman Ariz. Joint Select Com. on State Revenues and Expenditures, 1989; mem. Ariz. State Treansp. Bd., 1991—, vice chair, 1995—; bd. dirs. Tucson Electric Power Co., Inc., 1989-91, So. Ariz. Water Resources Assn., 1991—, pres. 1994—; bd. dirs. United Way, 1989-92; chmn. bd. trustees Tucson Med. Ctr.; bd. trustees Tucson Med. Ctr., 1990-95, chmn., 1993-95; bd. trustee TMcare Healthpartners of So. Ariz., 1993—; bd. dirs. Ariz. Hosp. & Healthcare Assn., 1995—, So. Ariz. Water Resources Assn., 1991—, pres. 1994—; mem. Tucson Airport Authority, Gov.'s Regional Airport Adv. Com., bd. regents Commn. on Status of Women, First Leadership Am. Class; participant Econ. Conf. of Pres.-elect, Little Rock, Dec., 1992; mem. Transp. and Econ. Devel. Com., Transp. Rsch. Bd., Nat. Rsch. Coun. Contbr. articles on econs. to profl. jours. Vol. United Way of Greater Tucson, 1982-85, 87-88. Richard D. Irwin fellow, 1977-78; fellow Princeton U., 1974-78, Sloan Found., 1976-78; U. Ariz. Rsch. grantee, 1982, 83, Figgle Corp. grantee, 1984. Mem. Am. Econs. Assn. (com. on status of women 1983—), Women Execs. in State Govt., Nat. Assn. Regulatory Utility Commrs. (com. on electricity), Phi Beta Kappa, Beta Gamma Sigma. Democrat.

MEHALCHIN, JOHN JOSEPH, entrepreneur, financial executive; b. Hazleton, Pa., Aug. 8, 1937; s. Charles and Susan (Korba) M.; divorced; 1 child, Martin. BS with honors (1st in class), Temple U., 1964; MBA, U. Calif., Berkeley, 1965; postgrad., U. Chgo., 1964; Supr. costs Winchester-Western, New Haven, Conn., 1965-67; mgmt. cons. Booz-Allen & Hamilton, N.Y.C., 1967-68; mgr. planning TWA, N.Y.C., 1968-69; officer Smith, Barney, N.Y.C. and Paris, 1970-74; chief fin. officer, pres. leasing co. Storage Tech. Corp., Louisville, 1974-79; sr. v.p. Heizer Corp., 1979; pres., founder Highline Fin. Svcs., Inc. and fgn. subs. Boulder, Colo., London, Paris, and Frankfurt, 1979—. With AUS, 1958-61. U. Calif. fellow, Berkeley, 1964, 65; U. Chgo. scholar, 1964. Mem. Fin. Execs. Inst., Equipment Leasing Assn., Beta Gamma Sigma, Omicron Delta Epsilon. Home and Office: Highline Fin Svcs Inc 1881 9th St # 300 Boulder CO 80302-5148

MEHDIZADEH, PARVIZ, insurance company executive; b. Tehran, Iran, Sept. 15, 1934; came to U.S., 1981; s. Alexander and Sedigheh (Siavooshy) M.; m. Manijeh Sadri, Sept. 12, 1961; children: Sheida, Peyman, Pejman. BS, Forestry Sch., Tehran, 1958; MS, N.C. State U., 1963, PhD, 1966. Pres. Research Inst. Natural Resources, Tehran, 1968-73; assoc. prof. U. Tehran, 1973-74; prof. environ. sci. U. Tabriz, Iran, 1974-76; chmn. resolution com. FAO, Rome, 1976-77; chmn. natural resources Cen. Treaty Orgn., Ankars, Turkey, 1977-78; spl. adviser to sec. Ministry of Agr., Tehran, 1978-79; dist. mgr. Am. Family Life Assurance Co., Beverly Hills, Calif., 1981—; v.p. Point Internat. Corp. Inc., Los Angeles, 1986—; cons. Ministry of Sci., Tehran, 1972-75, UN U., Tokyo, 1975-76; chmn. bd. dirs. Active Universal Corp., Inc.; gen. agent AFLAC, 1995. Author: Flowering Plants of Semi-Arid Regions, 1976, Economizing of Water Use in Agriculture, 1977; editor Khandamhayeh Hafteh, 1979. Mem. U.S. Senatorial Club, Washington, 1984; charter mem. Rep. Presdl. Task Force, Washington, 1984. Mem. Life Underwriters Assn. (L.A. chpt., Health Ins. Quality award 1985, 88, 89), Rotary (chmn. dist. 5280 1992, Paul Harris Fellow award 1989). Office: Am Family Life Assurance 9301 Wilshire Blvd Ste 508 Beverly Hills CA 90210-5412

MEHLIG, DONALD HOMER, insurance broker; b. Torrance, Calif., Feb. 3, 1935; s. John Homer Mehlig and Melita Evelyn (Hawkins) Wolford; m. Patricia Ann Nield, Mar. 19, 1954; children: Steven, Sharon, Susan. BA, UCLA, 1957. CLU, ChFC. Ins. agt. Provident Mut., L.A., 1957-62; pres. Cal-Surance Benefits Plans, Inc., Torrance, 1962—; bd. dirs. M Life Ins. Co., mem. adv. bd., 1993; nat. speaker CLU Inst., U.S., 1992—. Bd. dirs. Little Co. Mary Hosp., Torrance, 1987—; bd. trustees Am. Coll., Bryn Mawr, Pa., 1989—. Named Outstanding Life Ins. Man, Leader's Mag., 1978, 88; recipient William G. Farrell award L.A. Life Underwriting Assn., 1985. Mem. Life Ins. and Trust Coun., Am. Soc. CLUS (bd. dirs., past pres.), Christian Businessmen's Com. (bd. dirs. 1987—), Million Dollar Round Table (life), Palos Verdes Golf Club, Del Amo Rotary Club. Republican. Office: Cal Surance Benefit Plans PO Box 3459 Torrance CA 90510-3459

MEHLMAN, LON DOUGLAS, information systems specialist; b. Los Angeles, Apr. 29, 1959; s. Anton and Diane Mehlman. BA, UCLA, 1981; MBA, Pepperdine U., 1983. Systems programmer Ticom Systems Inc., Century City, Calif., 1978-81; systems analyst NCR Corp., Century City, 1981-83; sr. systems analyst Tandem Computers Inc., L.A., 1983-91; sr. computer scientist Computer Scis. Corp., El Segundo, Calif., 1991—. Mem. Am. Mgmt. Assn., Assn. for Info. and Image Mgmt., Armed Forces Communications and Electronics Assn., Sierra Club, Phi Delta Theta. Office: Computer Scis Corp 2100 E Grand Ave El Segundo CA 90245-5024

MEHLUM, DAVID L., otolaryngologist; b. Phoenix, Sept. 10, 1950; s. Charles J. and Jessaline (V.) M.; m. Mary Jo Mills, June 17, 1972; children: N. Eric, Kristen M. AA, Phoenix Coll., 1970; BS, U. Ariz., 1972; MD, U. Tex., Dallas, 1976. Diplomate Am. Bd. Otolaryngology. Intern U. Tex. Southwestern Affiliated Hosp., Dallas, 1976-77, resident, 1977-80; med. staff mem. Group Health Coop., Seattle, 1983—; cons. Indian Health Svc., Ariz., Nev., 1981-83; clin. asst. prof. otolaryngology U. Calif., San Francisco, 1981-83; clin. instr. otolaryngology U. Wash. Med. Sch., Seattle, 1984—; chief of otolaryngology Group Health-Cen., Seattle, 1987-90. Contbr. articles to profl. jours. Lt. comdr. USNR, 1980-83. Recipient Medallion of Merit, Ariz. State U., 1970. Mem. ACS, Am. Acad. Otolaryngology, Am. Assn. Facial Plastic and Reconstructive Surgery, Nat. Ski Patrol (bd. dirs. ski acres patrol 1989—, nat. appointment 1992, asst. patrol dir. 1992—). Lutheran. Office: Group Health Coop Dept Otolaryngolgy 125 16th Ave Seattle WA 98122-5610

MEHLUM, JOHAN ARNT, banker; b. Trondheim, Norway, Nov. 11, 1928; came to U.S., 1950, naturalized, 1955; s. Hans Aage and Olga (Nygaard) M.; diploma Norwegian Bus. Coll., 1946, postgrad. Rutgers U., 1971; m. Ladona Marie Christensen, May 30, 1951 (dec. 1983); children: Ann Marie, Katherine, Susan Jane, Rolf Erik; m. Emel Hekimoglu, Sept. 27, 1986. Clk. Forretningsbanken, Trondheim, 1946-50, First Nat. Bank Oreg., Astoria and Corvallis, 1952-57; cashier, mgr. Bank of Shedd, Brownsville, Oreg., 1958-63; pres., chmn. Siuslaw Valley Bank, Florence, Oreg., 1963—; chmn. bd. Community Bank Creswell (Oreg.), 1970-79; founding dir., pres. Western Banker Svc. Corp., 1983-84; dir. Siuslaw Valley Plaza, Inc., 1966—. Mayor, Dunes City, Oreg., 1973-75. Trustee Lane Community Coll. Found., 1971-78; founding chmn., bd. dirs. N.W. Intermediate Banking Sch., Lewis and Clark Coll., Portland, Oreg., 1975-77; trustee, past chmn. Western Lane County Found., 1976-82. With Royal Norwegian Army, 1948-49. Named Jr. First Citizen, Astoria, 1955, First Citizen, Brownsville, 1962; recipient internat. rels. award U.S. Jr. C. of C., 1960; inducted Oreg. Bankers Hall of Fame, 1988. Mem. Norwegian/Am. C. of C., Western Ind. Bankers (mem. exec. coun. 1970-74), Am. Bankers Assn. (mem. exec. com. community bankers div. 1976-78, governing coun. 1982-84), Oreg. Bankers Assn. (exec. coun. 1977-83, pres. 1981-82), Western States Bankcard Assn. (bd. dir. 1987—), Florence Area C. of C. (pres. 1970), Banking Profession Polit. Action Com. (state chmn. 1973-76), Sons of Norway, Elks, Rotary (pres. 1967-68), Norsemen's League (pres. 1954). Home: PO Box 131 Florence OR 97439-0005 Office: PO Box 280 Florence OR 97439-0280

MEHNER, WILLIAM MICHEL, financial company executive; b. Ada, Okla., Aug. 5, 1943; s. Dors Jenkins and Minnie (Brooks) Snyder; m. Bonnie Lee Hackett, May 31, 1965; children: Bethany Anne, Whitney Alison. BA, Alaska Meth. U., 1965; postgrad., Stanford U., 1983, U. Nebr., 1995. Mgr. Alaska div. Equitable Fin. Co., Anchorage, 1969-89, Mut. of Omaha, Anchorage, 1989-93; real estate agent Jack White Co., Anchorage, 1993—. Contbr. mgmt. and mktg. articles to newspapers and mags. Bd. dirs. Western coun. Boy Scouts Am., Anchorage, 1980-87, Glacier Creek Acad., Girdwood, Alaska, 1985-94, Chugach Elec. Assn., 1994-95; chmn., moderator Humana Hosp., 1990-91, Alaska Regional Hosp., 1994—; pres. Alaska Conservatory Music, Anchorage, 1985-87; del. Anchorage Rep. Com., 1988. 1st lt. U.S. Army, 1965-69. Mem. Alaska Assn. Life Underwriters (pres. 1983-84, bd. dirs. 1982-85), So. Alaska Life Underwriters (bd. dirs. 1972-85), Internat. Assn. Fin. Planners, Gen. Agts. and Mgrs. Assn. (pres. 1986-87, life qualified mgmt. award), Equitable Regional Mgrs. Assn. (pres. 1985), Rotary. Home: 2295 Arcadia Dr Anchorage AK 99517 Office: Jack White Co 3201 C St Ste 400 Anchorage AK 99503-3934

MEHRA, PANKAJ, computer scientist, researcher; b. New Delhi, Dec. 3, 1964; came to U.S., 1986; s. Kamal Narain and Motia (Arora) M.; m. Ranjana Srivastava, Dec. 3, 1989; 1 child, Charulata. BTech. in Computer Sci. and Engring., Indian Inst. Tech., 1986; PhD in Computer Sci., U. Ill., 1992. Rsch. asst. U. Ill., Urbana, 1986-92; computer scientist Recom Techs., Moffett Field, Calif., 1993—. Editor: Artificial Neural Networks: Concepts and Theory, 1992. Mem. IEEE, Assn. Computing Machinery, Tau Beta Pi. Office: Recom Technologies Nasa Ames Rsch Ctr M S # 269 3 Moffett Field CA 94035-1000

MEHRING, CLINTON WARREN, engineering executive; b. New Haven, Ind., Feb. 14, 1924; s. Fred Emmett and Florence Edith (Hutson) M.; m. Carol Jane Adams, Mar. 9, 1946; children—James Warren, Charles David, John Steven (dec.), Martha Jane. B.S., Case Inst. Tech., 1950; M.S., U. Colo., 1956. Registered profl. engr., Wyo., Colo., Nev. Design engr. U. S. Bur Reclamation, Denver, 1950-56; design engr. Tipton & Kalmbach, Denver, 1956-58; asst. resident engr. Tipton & Kalmbach, Quito, Ecuador, 1959-61; asst. chief design engr. Tipton & Kalmbach, Lahore, Pakistan, 1962-65; v.p. Tipton & Kalmbach, Denver, 1966-73, exec. v.p., 1973-79, pres., 1979—, also bd. dirs. Served with AUS, 1943-45. Recipient Theta Tau award as outstanding grad. Case Inst. Tech., 1950. Fellow ASCE (life); mem. Am. Cons. Engrs. Coun., U.S. Com. on Large Dams, Am. Concrete Inst., U.S. Com. Irrigation and Drainage (life), Sigma Xi, Tau Beta Pi, Theta Tau, Sigma Chi, Blue Key. Methodist. Club: Denver Athletic. Home: 1821 Mt Zion Dr Golden CO 80401-1733 Office: 1331 17th St Denver CO 80202-1566

MEHTA, ZUBIN, conductor, musician; b. Bombay, India, Apr. 29, 1936; came to U.S., 1961; s. Mehli Nowrowji and Tehmina (Daruvala) M.; m. Nancy Diane Kovack; children: Zarina, Merwan. Student, St. Xavier's Coll., Bombay, 1951-53, State Acad. Music, Vienna, Austria, 1954-60; LL.D., Sir George Williams U., Montreal, 1965; D.Mus. (hon.), Occidental Coll.; hon. doctorate, Colgate U., Brooklyn Coll., Westminster Choir Coll., Juilliard Sch., Weizmann Inst. Sci. (Israel). Music dir., Montreal (Can.) Symphony Orch., 1961-67, Los Angeles Philharmonic Orch., 1962-78; mus. dir.: Israel Philharmonic, from 1969, appointed dir. for life, 1981; music dir., N.Y. Philharmonic, 1978-91, guest condr., Met. Opera, Salzburg (Austria) Festival, Vienna Philharmonic, Berlin Philharmonic, La Scala, Milan, Italy, music dir., Maggio Musicale Florence, Italy, rec. artist for, Decca, CBS, RCA, New World Records, (recipient 1st prize Liverpool (Eng.) Condrs. Competition 1958). Decorated Padma Bhushan India, 1967, commendatore of Italy. Office: Israel Philharm Orch, 1 Huberman St Box 11292, 61112 Tel Aviv Israel also: Orch Maggio Musicale, Teatro, Comunale Via Solferino 15, I-50123 Florence Italy

MEIBERT, CATHERINE WELCH, secondary school educator, administrator; b. Miami, Ariz., Feb. 6, 1933; d. Arthur George and Anna Louise (Curtis) Welch; m. Virgil E. Meibert, Aug. 13, 1955 (div. Oct. 1965); children: Kenneth Arthur, David Francis. BA in Edn., Ariz. State U., 1954, MA in Edn., 1963. Cert. secondary educator, Ariz., Calif., sch. adminstr., jr. coll. educator, Ariz. Tchr. English and journalism Tolleson (Ariz.) Unified High Sch., 1954-55; tchr. English Rosary High Sch., San Diego, 1955-56, Good Shepherd Sch., Phoenix, 1957; tchr. English, journalism Xavier High Sch., Phoenix, 1957-59, Tennyson Unified High Sch., Haward, Calif., 1961-66, Amador Valley Joint Unified High Sch., Pleasanton, Calif., 1966-67, South Mountain High Sch., Phoenix, 1967-92; asst. prin. Seton Cath. High Sch., Chandler, Ariz., 1992—. Editor The State Press, 1954. Sch. bd. mem. Mount Carmel Sch., Tempe, Ariz., 1994—. Mem. Nat. Cath. Edn. Assn. Democrat. Roman Catholic. Office: Seton Cath High Sch 1150 N Dobson Rd Chandler AZ 85224-4004

MEIER, ROBERT JOHN, secondary education educator; b. Glendale, Calif., July 8, 1956; s. Robert Walter and Mary Jane (Pellizzer) M. AA, Glendale C.C., 1975; BA, Calif. State U., Northridge, 1978; MS, U. La Verne, 1989. Educator, counselor Rogers High Sch., Van Nuys, Calif., 1983—. Mem. AFTRA, Nat. Assn. Biology Tchrs., Nat. Sci. Tchrs. Assn., Calif. Continuation Edn. Assn. (treas. 1992-95, pres. 1995—), United Tchrs. L.A., Actors Equity Assn., Screen Actors Guild. Office: Will Rogers High School 15141 Lemay St Van Nuys CA 91405-4529

MEIERAN, EUGENE STUART, material scientist; b. Cleve., Dec. 23, 1937; s. Elias and Rae (Linetsky) M.; m. Rosalind Berson, Mar. 25, 1962; children—Sharon Elizabeth, Andrew Marc. B.S. in Metallurgy, Purdue U., 1959; M.S. in Metallurgy, MIT, 1961, Sc.D. in Material Sci., 1963. Sr. mem. tech. staff Fairchild R & D, Palo Alto, Calif., 1963-73; engring. mgr. Intel Corp., Santa Clara, Calif., 1973-77, sr. mgr. quality assurance, 1977-84, Intel fellow, 1984—, mgr. AI lab., 1989—; dir. rsch. LFM program MIT, 1993—; vis. lectr. Technion, Haifa, Israel, 1970-71, H.H. Wills Physics Lab., Bristol, Eng., 1970-71. Contbr. articles to profl. jours. Mem. adv. bd. Lawrence Berkeley Lab., 1984—. AEC fellow, 1960; recipient Internat. Reliability awards, 1970, 79, 85.; appt. Disting. Engring. Alumnus Purdue U., 1988. Mem. AIME (chmn. electronic material symposium 1973—), Electron Microscope Soc. U.S.A., Tau Beta Pi, Phi Lambda Upsilon. Democrat. Jewish. Home: 5421 E Camello Rd Phoenix AZ 85018-1910 Office: Intel Corp 5000 W Chandler Blvd Chandler AZ 85226-3601

MEIGEL, DAVID WALTER, musician, military officer; b. Chgo., Feb. 27, 1957; s. Thomas Arent and Annie Elizabeth (Thomas) M. Diploma, USAF NCO Leadership Sch., Chanute AFB, Ill., 1981, USAF/CAP SQD Officer Sch., 1987, USAF NCO Acad., Norton AFB, Calif., 1991. Enlisted USAF, 1976; commd. staff sgt. to 2d lt. CAP, Travis AFB, Calif., 1986; advanced through grades to tech. sgt. USAF, 1989; percussionist 724th USAF Band, McChord AFB, Wash., 1976-78, 752d USAF Band, Elmendorf AFB, Alaska, 1978-80, 505th USAF Band, Chanute AFB, Ill., 1980-84, 504th USAF Band, Travis AFB, 1984-90; prin. percussionist, chief of adminstrn. Am.'s Band in Blue, USAF, Travis AFB, 1990-92. Prin. percussionist San Diego (Calif.) Civic Orch., 1973-76, Poway (Calif.) High Sch. Band, 1974-75; percussionist Anchorage (Alaska) Civic Opera, 1979-80, Anchorage (Alaska) Scottish Soc., 1979-80, Fairfield Civic Theatre, Fairfield, Calif., 1984—; communications officer USAF Civil Air Patrol, Travis AFB, 1986—. Recipient Gov.'s medal Youkon Internat. Invitational Scottish Games, Whitehorse City Council, B.C., 1980; decorated USAF Achievement medal 1989, 93, Comdrs. Commendation medal; named one of Outstanding Young Men Am., 1988, 92. Mem. Percussive Arts Soc., CAP USAF Aux. Home: 1427 Phoenix Dr Apt 24 Fairfield CA 94533-5356 Office: Americas Band in Blue 271 Dixon Ave Travis AFB CA 94535-2867

MEIGHAN, STUART SPENCE, hospital consultant, internist, writer; b. Glasgow, Scotland, Jan. 30, 1923; came to U.S., 1962; s. Stuart Spence and Annie Louise (Brown) M; m. Anne Stewart Henderson, Nov. 4, 1952 (div. 1968); children: Jane Spence, Stuart Spence; m. Louise Rhys McGregor, July 7, 1985. MB, U. Glasgow, 1945. Registrar, sr. registrar Nat. Health Svc., U.K., 1948-57; sr. staff mem. Allan Blair Meml. Clinic, Regina, Sask., Can., 1957-62; internist Cleland Clinic, Oregon City, Oreg., 1962-64; dir. med. affairs Good Samaritan Hosp., Portland, Oreg., 1964-78; pres. Spence Meighan and Assocs., Portland, 1978—; cons. several hosps. and orgns. Contbr. over 100 articles to profl. jours. Lt. Royal Navy, 1946-48. Recipient Disting. Svc. award Am. Soc. Internal Medicine. Fellow Am. Coll. Physicians, Royal Coll. Physicians. Home and Office: 408 NW Rainier Ter Portland OR 97210-3347

MEIKLEJOHN, ALVIN J., JR., state senator, lawyer, accountant.; b. Omaha, June 18, 1923; B.S., J.D., U. Denver, 1951; m. Lorraine J. Meiklejohn; children: Pamela Ann, Shelley Lou, Bruce Ian, Scott Alvin. Mem. Colo. Senate from 19th dist., 1976—, chmn. com. edn.; mem. Edn. Commn. of States, 1981—, chmn. Colo. Commn. on Ach. in Edn., 1995;

chmn., 1993—. Mem. Jefferson Sch. Dist. No. R-1 Bd. Edn., 1971-77, pres., 1973-77; commr. Commn. on Uniform State Laws, 1988—. Served to capt. U.S. Army, 1940-46; to maj. USAF, 1947-51. Mem. Colo. Soc. CPA's, Arvada C. of C. Republican. Clubs: Masons, Shriners. Home: 7540 Kline Dr Arvada CO 80005-3732 Office: Jones & Keller PC 1625 Broadway Ste 1600 Denver CO 80202-4730

MEIKLEJOHN, (LORRAINE) MINDY JUNE, political organizer, realtor; b. Staunton, Colo., June 9, 1929; d. Edward H. and Erna E. (Schwabe) Mindrup; m. Alvin J. Meiklejohn, Apr. 25, 1953; children: Pamela, Shelley, Bruce, Scott. Student Ill. Bus. Coll., 1948, Red Rocks C.C., 1980-81. Pvt. sec. Ill. Liquor Commn., 1948-51, David M. Wilson, Ill. Sec. of State's Office, 1951-52; flight attendant Continental Airlines, 1952-53, pvt. sec. to mgr. flight svcs. office, 1953-54; organizational dir. Colo. Rep. Party, Denver, 1981-85, mem. Cen. Com., 1987—; campaign coord. Hank Brown's Exploratory Campaign for Gov., 1985, mgr. Hank Brown for Congress, 1985-86; dep. campaign dir. Steve Schuck for Gov., 1985-86; vice chmn. 2d Congl. Cen. Com. Colo.; active campaigns; del., alt. to various, county, state, dist. and nat. assemblies and convs.; Colo. chmn. Citizens for Am., 1987—; realtor, sales assoc. Metro Brokers, Inc.; mem. polit. action com. Jefferson County Bd. Realtors. Apptd. trustee Harry S. Truman Scholarship Found., 1991; mem. Jefferson County Hist. Commn., Colo., 1974-82, pres., 1979; vol. Jefferson County Legal Aid Soc., 1970-74; vice chmn. Jefferson County Rep. Party, 1977-81, exec. com., 1987; vice chmn. Colo. State Rep. Party, 1981-85; chmn. Rep. Nat. Pilot Project on Volunteerism, 1981; mem. adv. coun. U.S. Peace Corps, 1982-84; sect. chmn. Jefferson County United Way Fund Drive; mem. exec. bd. Colo. Fedn. Rep. Women; pres. Operation Shelter, Inc., 1983—; state chair Citizens for Am., 1987—; bd. dirs. Scientific and Cultural Facilities dist. 1989-94, Jefferson County chpt. Am. Cancer Soc., 1987-91, Jefferson Found., 1991—. Mem. Jefferson County Women's Rep. (edn. chmn. 1987-91). Lutheran. Home: 7540 Kline Dr Arvada CO 80005-3732

MEINDL, ROBERT JAMES, English language educator; b. Wausau, Wis., Sept. 17, 1936; s. George Martin and Adeline Emilie (Goetsch) M.; m. Victoria Lynn Chavez; children: Karin Rose, George Andrew, Damian Kurt, Erika Wittmer, Christopher Smith, Gabrielle Remelia. BS, U. Wis., 1958; MA, U. Conn., 1960; PhD, Tulane U., 1965. Teaching asst. U. Conn., Storrs, 1958-60; teaching fellow Tulane U., 1960-62; lectr. U. Wis., Green Bay, 1963-65; from asst. to full prof. English Calif. State U., Sacramento, 1965—. Translator: Studies in John Gower, 1981; book rev. editor: Studia Mystica Jour., 1984-89; contbr. numerous articles to profl. jours. With USNR, 1953-61, 79—, PTO, ETO. Mem. MLA, Medieval Acad. Am., Sacramento Turn Verein (v.p. 1976-77, sec. 1977-79), New Chaucer Soc., John Gower Soc., Medieval Assn. of the Pacific, Early English Text Soc. Home: 2301 Pennland Dr Sacramento CA 95825-0329 Office: Calif State U 6000 J St Sacramento CA 95819-2605

MEINEL, MARJORIE PETTIT, optical engineer; b. Pasadena, Calif., May 13, 1922; d. Edison and Hannah (Steele) Pettit; m. Aden Baker Meinel, Sept. 5, 1944; children: Carolyn, Walter, Barbara, Elaine, Edward, Mary, David. BA, Pomona Coll., Claremont, Calif., 1943; MA, Claremont Coll., 1944. Rsch. assoc. Calif. Inst. Tech., Pasadena, 1944-45, U. Ariz., Tucson, 1974-83; mem. tech. staff Jet Propulsion Lab., Pasadena, 1985—; vis. faculty Nat. Cen. U., Chung-Li, Taiwan, 1978-80; commr. Ariz. Solar Energy Commn., Phoenix, 1975-81; mem. office tech. assessment U.S. Congress, Washington, 1974-79. Author: Applied Solar Energy, 1977, Sunsets, Twilights and Evening Skies, 1983; patentee in field. Recipient Exceptional Svc. medal Nat. Aeronautics and Space Adminstrn., Kingslake medal. Fellow Internat. Soc. Optical Engrng. Lutheran.

MEIS, JEANETTE KAY, elementary educator; b. Greeley, Colo., July 16, 1959; d. Gerald Martin and Kathryn Ella Jean (Chessmore) M. BA, U. No. Colo., 1980, MA, 1986. Cert. elem. tchr., Colo. Tchr. kindergarten Hugo (Colo.) Pub. Sch., 1981, tchr. 4th grade, 1981-82; tchr. Greeley Pub. Schs., 1982-83, tchr. 2d grade, 1983-88, tchr. kindergarten, 1988—; activity coord. Colo. Camp Cherith, Woodland Park, 1978-88, dir., 1988—. Mem. Alpha Delta Kappa. Baptist. Home: 1622 14th Ave Greeley CO 80631-5302

MEISFJORD, ERIC PALMER, newspaper editor; b. Salem, Oreg., Mar. 14, 1955; s. Palmer Alexander and Maryellen Harriet (Lobdell) Mesford; m. Kathlyn Diana Lasswell, Sept. 1, 1984; children: Thomas Palmer, Maryalice Amelia. BA in History, Gonzaga U., 1977; MA in Comm., U. Portland, 1983. Tchr. music St. Joseph Sch., Salem, 1979; announcer, copywriter Sta. KCCS-AM, Salem, 1980-82; grad. asst. U. Portland, Oreg., 1982-83; editor CC Publs., Tualatin, Oreg., 1983-84; reporter, media cons. Inland Register, Spokane, Wash., 1984-85, editor, 1985—. Mem. Cath. Press Assn. (mem. liaison com. with Cath. News Svc. 1992—). Office: Inland Register 1023 W Riverside Ave Spokane WA 99201-1103

MEISSNER, LOREN PHILLIP, JR., systems analyst; b. Fontana, Calif., May 12, 1953; s. Loren P. and Peggy Louise (Pritchard) M. BA in English, San Francisco State U., 1981, MBA, 1984. Sales asst. IBM Corp., San Francisco, 1983; systems analyst Pacific Bell, San Francisco, 1984; software purchasing agt. ComputerLand USA, Hayward, Calif., 1985; computer analyst/programmer State of Wash., Olympia, 1986-90; sys. analyst/programmer U. Wash., Seattle, 1990—. With USN, 1971-74. Office: U Wash Mail Stop 359104 Seattle WA 98195

MEISTER, JOHN EDWARD, JR., systems analyst, technical educator; b. Elgin, Ill., Nov. 17, 1956; s. John Edward and Marilyn Barbara (Futter) M.; m. Rebecca Marie Buehner, Nov. 15, 1975; children: Christine Marie, Mark Christopher. AA, Cen. Tex. Coll., 1979, U. Md., 1980; BS cum laude, U. Md., 1981; postgrad., Western Conservative Baptist Sem., 1982-83. Enlisted U.S. Army, 1974, advance through grades to staff sgt., 1980; electronics technician Frankfurt, Fed. Republic of Germany, 1974-77; maintenance supr. Darmstadt, Fed. Republic of Germany, 1978-81; transferred from 232d Signal Co. Telecommunications, 1981; instr. U.S. Army Signal Sch., Ft. Gordon, Ga., 1981-82; resigned U.S. Army, 1982; sr. electronics instr. ITT Tech. Inst., Portland, Oreg., 1982-83; equipment engrng. and engrng. svcs. technician Intel Corp., Aloha, Oreg., 1983-85; dealer AMSOIL Dealer, Snohomish, Wash., 1983—; electronic designer Boeing Electronics Co., Everett, Wash., 1985-89; systems analyst Boeing Comml. Airplanes, Everett, 1989—; instr. computing Boeing Off-Hour Tng., 1994—; electronics engr. Innovative Designs and Electronic Sys. Techs., Portland, 1982-85. Bd. dirs. Machias Ridge East Homeowner's Assn., 1988-91; fin. advisor Jr. Achievement, Everett High Sch., 1988-89. Mem. NRA, Pacific N.W. 4-Wheel Dr. Assn. Republican. Baptist. Home: PO Box 1737 Snohomish WA 98291-1737 Office: Boeing Comml Airplane Co M/S ØL-CR PO Box 3707 Seattle WA 98124-2207

MEISTER, VERLE MARTIN, management recruiter; b. Moville, Iowa, Mar. 16, 1937; s. Otto John Fred and Ruth Louise (Hughes) M.; m. Connie Margaret Sturm, May 11, 1968; 1 child, John Martin. BA in Bus. and Econs., Wartburg Coll., 1964. Employment interviewer J.I. Case Co., Bettendorf, Iowa, 1964-65; employment mgr. J.I. Case Co., Terre Haute, Ind., 1966-68, Am. Air Filter Co., Moline, Ill., 1965-66; adminstrv. asst. to pres. Vindale Corp., Dayton, Ohio, 1968-75; mgr. labor rels. Robbins & Myers, Springfield, Ohio, 1975-78; pres. Mgmt. Recruiters Cheyenne, Wyo., 1978—; del. White House Conf. on Small Bus., 1986. Chmn. spl. events Am. Cancer Soc., Cheyenne, 1979-80. With U.S. Army, 1960-63. Mem. Am. Soc. Pers. Adminstrs. (pres. 1986), Small Bus. Coun. (chmn. 1987-89, bd. dirs. 1989-92), Cheyenne C. of C. (pres. 1991), Kiwanis (pres. 1991, 92, lt. gov. 1993-94). Home: 123 Longs Peak Dr Cheyenne WY 82009-3550 Office: Mgmt Recruiters Cheyenne 1008 E 21st St Cheyenne WY 82001-3910

MEITZLER, NEIL, artist; b. Pueblo, Colo., Sept. 14, 1930; s. Herbert Claussen and Virginia (Fellar) M.; m. Darlene Dinwiddie, Oct. 1, 1951 (div. 1965); children: Kenneth Neil Palmore, Charlotte Meitzler Engelhart, Carrie Meitzler Leonard. MFA, U. Wash., 1957. Represented in permanent collections Seattle Art Mus., County Mus. Art, Hagerstown, Md., Memphis Acad. Art, Emperor of Japan, Tokyo. Recipient Kathrine Baker award Seattle Art Mus., 1958; grantee Nat. Endowment for Arts, 1967. Home and Studio: 637 Pleasant St Walla Walla WA 99362-3367

MEL, HOWARD CHARLES, biophysics educator; m. Nancy Helene Shenon, June. 18, 1949; children—Amélie Catherine, Stéphanie Frances, Bartlett Woolsey. Student electronics and physics, Bowdoin Coll., 1945; student humanities and music, U. Geneva., Conservatoire de Musique, Geneva., 1946-47; B.S. with honors, U. Calif.-Berkeley, 1948, Ph.D. in Phys. Chemistry, 1953; postgrad., U. Brussels, 1953-55. Traffic mgr. Calo Pet Food Co., Oakland, 1948-50; instr. chemistry U. Calif.-Berkeley, 1955, USPHS fellow, lectr. med. physics, 1955-60, asst. prof., assoc. prof. biophysics, 1960-74, prof. biophysics, 1974-93, prof. emeritus, 1993—, dir. Lawrence Hall of Sci., 1981-82; faculty sr. scientist Lawrence Berkeley Lab. U. Calif. Berkeley, 1960—; dir. U. Calif. Study Ctrs., Bordeaux, Pau, Poitiers, France, 1986-89; dir. tng. grants Nat. Inst. Gen. Med. Scis., 1972-82; maître de recherche INSERM, U. Paris, 1974-75. Organizer, editor: Aharon Katchalsky Meml. Symposium, 1977; editor for biophysics: Ency. Sci. and Tech., 4th edit., 1977; mem. editorial bd.: Blood Cells, 1974—, Cell Biophysics, 1978—, Rev. Sci. Instruments, 1975-78, Jour. Math. Biology, 1974-82; contbr. numerous articles to profl. jours.; patentee in field; researcher in cell membrane biophysics, hematopoiesis, biophys. instrumentation, and thermodynamic theory; inventor, developer stable-flow free-boundary method for analytical characterization & preparative separation of live cells and other particles, and of resistive pulse spectroscopy for characterization of geometrical, rheological, membrane-osmotic properties of cells, especially red blood cells. Former dir., mem. exec. com., chmn. music com. Oakland Symphony Orch. Assn.; v.p. Berkeleans for Acad. Excellence, 1970, Inverness Properties, Inc., 1965-75; bd. dirs. Pine Acres Homeowners Assn., 1983-86. Served to lt (j.g.) USNR, 1943-46. Recipient Prix du Rayonnement de la Langue Francaise Acad. Francais, 1993; Fulbright fellow to Brussels, 1953-55; NSF sr. postdoctoral fellow, 1965-66. Fellow AAAS, Assn. Claude Bernard, Sigma Xi; mem. Biophys. Soc. (coun. 1969-71, founding), Am. Chem. Soc., Am. Inst. Physics, Am. Assn. Physics Tchrs., Soc. Gen. Systems Rsch., Internat. Soc. Biorheology, Internat. Union Pure and Applied Biophysics, Assn. Sci. Tech. Ctrs., Phi Beta Kappa, Sigma Phi Epsilon. Clubs: Faculty U. Calif.-Berkeley (dir. 1979-80); Bohemian (San Francisco), Sierra (San Francisco); Amphion (Berkeley), Mosswood Investment (Berkeley) (pres. 1958). Office: U Calif MCB-CDB Donner Lab Berkeley CA 94720-3206

MELDMAN, BURTON ALAN, insurance salesman; b. Milw., Sept. 5, 1933; s. Edward Harry and Rose (Bortin) M.; m. Margery Scholl, June 11, 1955; children: Sharon, Michael, Debra. BBA, U. Wis., 1955; JD, Marquette U., 1958. CLU, Chartered Fin. Cons. Life ins. salesman Mass. Mut. Life, Springfield, Mass., 1956—; registered rep. Integrated Resources Equity Corp., N.Y.C., 1979-87, MML Investors Svcs., Inc., Springfield, Mass., 1988—; pres., chief exec. officer ERISA, Ltd., Phoenix, 1975-85; chief exec. officer Meldman Fin. Svcs., Ltd., 1985—. Mem. Nat. Assn. Life Underwriters, Phoenix Assn. Life Underwriters, Million Dollar Roundtable. Office: Mass Mutual Cos 7600 N 16th St Ste 200 Phoenix AZ 85020-4447

MELEHAN, JOSEPH P., food products executive; b. 1925. With Mayfair Packing Co. Inc., San Jose, Calif., 1946—. Office: Mayfair Packing Co Inc 2070 S 7th St San Jose CA 95112-6010*

MELENDEZ, JAMES PATRICK, editor; b. Albuquerque, Oct. 2, 1966; s. James Patrick and M.C. (Roybal) M. BA, U. N.Mex., 1992; postgrad., St. Mary's U. of Minn., 1994—. Coord. comms. ctr. U. N.Mex. Cancer Ctr., Albuquerque, 1988-93; assoc. editor dept. English U. N.Mex., Albuquerque, 1993-94; mng. editor Am. Literary Realism, Albuquerque, 1993-94, Blue Mesa Rev., Albuquerque, 1993-94. Mem. Am. Polit. Sci. Assn., Am. Sociol. Assn., SIGGraph. Democrat. Roman Catholic.

MELICH, DORIS S., public service worker; b. Salt Lake City, Apr. 8, 1913; d. Edward Harrison and Marie Cushing Snyder; m. Mitchell Melich, June 3, 1935; children: Tanya Marie Melich Silverman, Michael E., Nancy Lynne, Robert Allen. BA in Western History, U. Utah, 1934. Mem. Nat. Commn. Arthritis and Related Musculoskeltal Diseases, 1974-76, Nat. Arthritis Adv. Bd., 1977-84, 86-90; Utah del. Nat. Ho. of Dels. Arthritis Found., 1982-87; pres. Utah Arthritis Found. Bd., 1975-78, v.p., 1968-69, 73-74; Utah rep. Arthritis Found. Govt. Affairs, 1983—. Leader, founder 1st Girl Scouts Lone Troop U.S., Moab, Utah, 1947, regional selections com., 1958-67; active Utah Ballet Guild, Salt Lake Art Ctr., Utah Arts Coun., 1988—, Utah State Rep. Women, YWCA; trustee emeritus Arthritus Found. Recipient Pyramid award Nat. Arthritis Found., 1986, Utah Girl Scouts Regional award, 1987, Thanks Badge, 1963, Merit Honor award U. Utah Emeritus Club, 1978, Minute Man award Utah N.G., 1985; named to Nat. Women's Wall of Fame, Seneca Falls, N.Y., 1993. Mem. AAUW, Nat. Assistance League of Salt Lake City (charter mem.), Utah Women's Forum, Order Ea. Star, Alpha Delta Pi, Beta Sigma Phi (sponsor). Home: 900 Donner Way Apt 708 Salt Lake City UT 84108-2112

MELICH, MITCHELL, lawyer; b. Bingham Canyon, Utah, Feb. 1, 1912; s. Joseph and Mary (Kalembar) M.; m. Doris M. Snyder, June 3, 1935; children: Tanya (Mrs. Noel L. Silverman), Michael, Nancy, Robert A. LL.B., U. Utah, 1934. Bar: Utah 1934. Pvt. practice Moab, 1934-63, city atty., 1934-55; county atty. Grand County, 1940-42; sec., dir. Utex Exploration Co., Moab, 1953-62; pres., dir. Uranium Reduction Co., Moab, 1954-62; cons. to pres. Atlas Minerals, div. Atlas Corp., 1962-67; dir., treas. New Park Mining Co., 1962-65; assoc. Ray, Quinney & Nebeker, 1973—; solicitor Dept. Interior, Washington, 1969-73;. Mem. of Colorado River Com. of Utah, 1945-47; mem. Utah Water and Power Bd., 1947; chmn. Citizens Adv. Com. on Higher Edn., 1968; mem. nat. adv. council U. Utah, 1976—; Mem. Utah Senate, 1942-50, minority leader, 1949-50; mem. Utah Legislative Council, 1949-54; del. Republican Nat. Conv., 1952-72; mem. Rep. Nat. Com. for Utah, 1961-64; Rep. candidate for gov., 1964; cons. on staff Congressman Sherman P. Lloyd, Utah, 1967-68; bd. dirs. St. Marks Hosp., 1973-87; bd. regents U. Utah, 1961-65, also mem. devel. fund com., mem. nat. adv. council, 1968-73, 76—; mem. Utah Statewide Health Coordinating Coun., 1985; mem. Utah Fusion Energy Coun., 1989—. Recipient Disting. Alumni award U. Utah, 1969, Man of Yr. award, Arthritis Found., 1991. Mem. Am. Bar Assn., Utah State Bar, Utah Mining Assn. (pres. 1962-63), Kappa Sigma. Republican. Club: Alta Salt Lake Country (Salt Lake City). Lodges: Masons; Shriners. Home: 900 Donner Way Apt 708 Salt Lake City UT 84108-2112 Office: 400 Deseret Bldg 79 S Main St Salt Lake City UT 84111-1901

MELING, ERIC M., food executive; b. 1953. Grad., Calif. State U., Fresno, 1975. With Wilshire & Doss, CPA, Hanford, Calif., 1975-77, County of Tulare, Visalia, Calif., 1977-79, M. Green & Co. Accountancy Corp., Visalia, 1979-87, Westbrook Bastrire Accountancy Corp., Visalia, 1987-91; CFO, treas. Klink Citrus Assn., Ivanhoe, Calif., 1991—. Office: Klink Citrus Assoc 32921 Road 159 Ivanhoe CA 93235-1455*

MELLON, WILLIAM KNOX, foundation executive, consultant; b. Houston, Oct. 20, 1925; s. William Knox and Zelma (Cochran) M.; m. Josselyn Bale, Aug. 6, 1948 (div. 1968); children: Lesley, Andrea, Frederick; m. Carlotta Herman, June 8, 1972. BA, Pomona Coll., 1950; MA, Claremont Grad. Sch., 1952, PhD, 1972. Prof. history Mt. San Antonio Coll., Walnut, Calif., 1955-60, Immaculate Heart Coll., L.A., 1960-75; dir. State Office Hist. Preservation, State of Calif., Sacramento, 1975-83, state hist. preservation officer, 1977-83; dir. Mission Inn Found., Riverside, Calif., 1986—; adj. prof. history, U. Calif., Riverside, 1987—; pres. Mellon & Assocs., hist preservation cons., Riverside, 1986—. Editor: Development of Civilization, 1960, Like It Is, Like It Was: Readings in Western Civilization, 1972. Pres. Sam and Alfreda MaLoof Found. for Arts and Crafts, 1994—; Dem. nominee for U.S. Ho. of Reps., 1962; dir. orgn. Brown for Gov. Campaign, L.A., 1974. Recipient Hist. Preservation award Calif. Hist. Soc., 1978, Calif. Preservation Found., 1984, Annual Historic Preservation award. Home: 4631 Ladera Ln Riverside CA 92501-2013 Office: Mission Inn Found 3696 N Main St Riverside CA 92501-2839

MELLOW, JUDITH ELIZABETH, lawyer; b. South Bend, Ind., Aug. 29, 1935; d. Joseph and Mary (Dechter) M.; m. Gerald S. Gotterer, Sept. 2, 1956 (div. Apr. 1978); children: Elizabeth Gotterer, Rebecca Gotterer. AB, Bryn Mawr Coll., 1957; MA, U. Md., 1969, JD, 1978. Bar: Md. 1979, N.Mex. 1983. Tchr. English Bryn Mawr Sch., Balt., 1969-75; asst. states atty. Balt. (Md.) City, 1979-83; reporter Santa Fe (N.Mex.) Reporter, 1987-88, Rio Grande Sun, Espanola, N.Mex., 1989; spl. asst. atty. gen. N.Mex. Motor Vehicle Divsn., Santa Fe, 1990—. Office: DWI Legal Sect PO Box 1028 Santa Fe NM 87504-1028

MELNICK, ALICE JEAN (AJ MELNICK), counselor; b. St. Louis, Dec. 25, 1931; d. Nathan and Henrietta (Hausfater) Fisher; BJ, U. Tex., Austin, 1952; MEd, U. North Tex., 1974; m. Harold Melnick, May 24, 1953; children—Susan, Vikki, Patrice. Lic. profl. counselor. Reporter, San Antonio Light, 1952-53; instr. journalism project Upward Bound, So. Meth. U., Dallas, 1967-71; instr. writing El Centro Dallas County Community Coll., Dallas, part time 1972-74; instr. human devel. Richland Community Coll., Dallas, part-time 1974-79; tchr. English, journalism and psychology Dallas Ind. Sch. Dist., 1969-81; counselor Ursuline Acad., 1981-94; part-time instr. human devel. Sante Fe C.C. Freelance photographer. Mem. N.Mex. Counseling Assn., Assn. Humanistic Edn., Dallas Sports Car Club. Jewish. Home: 10 Baya Rd Santa Fe NM 87505-8703

MELOAN, TAYLOR WELLS, marketing educator; b. St. Louis, July 31, 1919; s. Taylor Wells and Edith (Graham) M.; m. Anna Geraldine Leukering, Dec. 17, 1944 (div. 1974); children: Michael David, Steven Lee; m. Jane Innes Bierlich, Jan. 30, 1975. B.S. cum laude, St. Louis U., 1949; M.B.A., Washington U., St. Louis, 1950; D of Bus. Admin., Ind. U., 1953. Advt. mgr. Herz Corp., St. Louis, 1941-42; sales promotion supr. Liggett & Myers Tobacco Co., St. Louis, 1942-43; asst. prof. mktg. U. Okla., Norman, 1953; asst., then assoc. prof. mktg. Ind. U., Bloomington, 1953-59; prof., chmn. dept. mktg. U. So. Calif., Los Angeles, 1959-69, prof. mktg., 1969-92, Robert E. Brooker prof. mktg., 1970-79, Robert E. Brooker prof. mktg. emeritus, 1991—; dean Sch. Bus. Adminstrn. U. So. Calif., 1969-71, assoc. v.p. acad. adminstrn. and research, 1971-81; prof. bus. adminstrn. U. Karachi, Pakistan, 1962; vis. prof. mktg. Istituto Post U. Per Lo Studio Dell Organizzazione Aziendale, Turin, Italy, 1964, U. Hawaii, 1993, Madrid Bus. Sch., 1993; disting. vis. prof. U. Witwatersrand, Johannesburg, 1978, U. Hawaii, 1993; editl. advisor bus. adminstrn. Houghton Mifflin Co., Boston, 1959-73; cons. to industry and govt., 1953%; bd. dirs Inst. Shipboard Edn. Author: New Career Opportunities, 1978, Innovation Strategy and Management, 1979, Direct Marketing: Vehicle for Department Store Expansion, 1984, Preparing the Exporting Entrepreneur, 1986, The New Competition: Dilemma of Department Stores in the 1980's, 1987, Franchise Marketing: A Retrospective and Prospective View of a Contractual Vertical Marketing System, 1988; co-author: Managerial Marketing, 1970, Internationalizing the Business Curriculum, 1968, Handbook of Modern Marketing, contbg. author, 1986; co-author, co-editor: International and Global Marketing: Concepts and Cases, 1994; bd. editors Jour. Mktg., 1965-72. Trustee World Affairs Coun. Orange County, 1994—. Lt. (j.g.) USMS, 1943-46. Mem. Am. Mktg. Assn. (pres. L.A. chpt. 1963-64), Order of Artus, Beta Gamma Sigma, Delta Pi Epsilon, Calif. Yacht Club, Univ. Club, Rotary. Home: 59 Lakefront Irvine CA 92714-4683 Office: U So Calif Los Angeles CA 90089-1421

MELOSH, HENRY JAY, IV, planetary science educator; b. Paterson, N.J., June 23, 1947; s. Henry Jay III and Eleanor (Wilde) M.; m. Marie Randal Bergquist, June 15, 1983 (div.); children: Nicholas Alexander, Gregory Scott; m. Ann Marie Vickery, June 13, 1984; 1 child, Caroline Melissa. AB, Princeton U., 1969; MS, Calif. Tech., 1971, PhD, 1973. Vis. scientist CERN, Geneva, 1971-72; rsch. assoc. U. Chgo., Chgo., 1972-73; instr. Geophysics and Planetary Sci. Calif. Tech, Pasadena, 1973-75, from asst. prof. to assoc. prof. Planetary Sci., 1976-79; assoc. prof. Geophysics SUNY, Stony Brook, 1979-82; prof. Planetary Sci. U. Ariz., Tucson, 1982—; cons. Los Alamos (N.Mex.) Nat. Lab., 1980-85, Sandia Nat. Labs., Albuquerque, 1983-85. Author: (book) Impact Cratering: A Geologic Process, 1989. Fellow Meteoritical Soc., Geolog. Soc. Am., Am. Geophysical Union. Office: Lunar & Planetary Lab U Ariz Tucson AZ 85721

MELOTT, RONALD K., fire protection engineer, consultant; b. Hillsboro, Oreg., May 8, 1939; s. Quinlin W. and Alma (Doern) M.; m. Marilyn R. Volz, Feb. 3, 1961; children: Pamela S. Heathman, Carla M., Daniel W. BS, Portland State U., 1970. Profl. engr. Oreg., Calif., Wash. Fire fighter Portland (Oreg.) Bur. Fire, 1961-64, fire insp., 1964-68, fire lt., 1968-69, staff lt., 1969-72; chief fire prevention spec. Nat. Fire Protection Assn., Boston, 1972-77; fire protection cons., owner Melott and Assocs., Inc., Beaverton, Oreg., 1977—. Contbr. author, editor: Fire Inspection Manual; co-author: Flammable Liquids Code Handbook; co-developer audio-visual tng. program. Treas. Roth Scholarship Found., Portland. With U.S. Army, 1961-63. Named Fireman of Yr. Internat. Assn. Fire Chiefs, 1965-66. Mem. Soc. Fire Protection Engrs., Nat. Fire Protection Assn. (MAC region vice-chair), Fire Marshals Assn. N.Am. (exec. sec. 1974-77), Internat. Soc. Fire Svc. Instrs., Internat. Assn. Arson Investigators, Am. Soc. Mech. Engrs., Nat. Soc. Profl. Engrs. Republican. Baptist. Office: Melott & Assocs Inc 11650 SW Bel Aire Ln Beaverton OR 97008-5908

MELROSE, ALBERT JOSEPH, investor relations professional; b. Santa Monica, Calif., June 13, 1926; s. Norris Albert and Marguerita Josephine (Menegus) M.; m. Jean Frances Wade, Feb. 14, 1953 (div. Feb. 1987); children: Mark, Dana; m. Marilyn Rausa Jones, May 21, 1987; children: Judith, Malcolm, Barton. AA, Santa Monica City Coll., 1948; AB, U. So. Calif., 1951. From flight test coord. to customer liaison Douglas Aircraft, Santa Monica, 1952-55; from contracts mgr. to mktg. adminstr. Ampex Corp., Santa Monica/Redwood City, Calif., 1955-60; mktg. mgr. Eitel-McCullough Inc., San Carlos, Calif., 1960-62; mktg. rep. Ryan Electronics, San Diego, 1962-63; mktg. analyst Autonetics, Anaheim, Calif., 1963-64; from mktg. mgr. to dir. investor rels. Litton Industries, San Carlos, Beverly Hills, Calif., 1964-79; dir. investor rels. Lockheed Corp., Burbank, Calif., 1979-81; v.p. corp. comms. Kaiser Steel Corp., Fontana, Calif., 1981-83; v.p. internat. mktg. Seidler Amdec Securities, L.A., 1983-88; dir. investor rels. AST Computer, Irvine, Calif., 1988-94; cons. in field, Newport Beach, Calif., 1994—; instr. U. Calif., Irvine, 1978-79; corp. advisor Calif. State U., Fullerton, 1991, UCLA Grad. Bus. Sch., 1982. Author: Investor Relations Executive Briefings, 1993. Served in U.S. Navy, 1944-46, Pacific/Asia. Home and Office: 1048 Irvine Ave Ste 189 Newport Beach CA 92660-4602

MELSHEIMER, HAROLD, obstetrician/gynecologist; b. Legenfeld, Germany, June 11, 1927; came to U.S., 1955; naturalized, 1960; s. Louis and Hella Leonie (Schwehr) Peterman; m. Norma Sykes Sabrina, Nov. 27, 1967; children: Laura, Linda. BS, Marburg U., West Germany, 1951, MD, 1954. Diplomate Am. Bd. Ob-Gyn. Intern Baden County Hosp., West Germany, 1954-55, St. Mary's Hosp. Med. Ctr., Long Beach, Calif., 1955-56; resident Queens Hosp. Med. Ctr., Honolulu, 1956-57, Calif. Hosp. Med. Ctr., L.A., 1957-59; pvt. practice ob-gyn. Encino, Calif., 1959-87; ret.; former dept. chief, now hon. staff mem. Am. Med. Internat. Med. Ctr., Tarzana, Calif., Encino Hosp.; founder Technion Inst. of Tech. Contbr. articles to profl. jours. Operational mem. USCG Aux., 1971. Recipient cert. of honor Wisdom Soc.; named Hon. Citizen, Rep. of Korea, 1966. Fellow ACS (life), Am. Coll. Ob-Gyn., Internat. Coll. Surgeons; mem. AMA, Calif. Med. Assn., L.A. County Med. Assn., Am. Physicians Fellowship for Israel Med. Assn., N.Y. Acad. Scis., Braemar Country Club. Home: 25660 Deertrail Dr Tehachapi CA 93561-9140

MELTON, CHERYL ANN, special education educator, small business owner; b. Bklyn., Jan. 5, 1949; d. Raymond Franklin and Irene Louise (Cotton) Blair; m. Gilbert Edmund Melton, Aug. 26, 1972; children: Byron Adrian, Brandie Alicia. BS in Edn., Ohio State U., 1971; MS in Edn., Nazareth Coll., Rochester, N.Y., 1976. Prof. clear multiple subject teaching credential, Calif. Elem. tchr. N.Y.C. Bd. Edn., Bklyn., 1971-72, Rochester City Sch. Dist., 1973-84; elem. tchr. Long Beach (Calif.) Unified Sch. Dist., 1984-90, lang. arts specialist, 1990—, reading recovery tchr., 1992—; v.p. sales and mktg., Orange County M2 Solutions, 1992—; mem. Sch. Program Improvement Leadership Team, Long Beach, 1990—; adv. bd. Scholastic, Inc.-Literacy Place, 1994-95; summer facilitator trainer Early Literacy In-service Course, 1995. Chmn. membership devel. Jr. League Long Beach, 1991-92, mem. by-laws task force, 1992-93, adv. future planning, 1989—, selected mentor, 1991—, sustaining advisor placement com., 1994-95, sustainer coun. mem., 1995—; chosen del. Jr. League Dallas. Scholar Calif. literature project Calif. State U., Dominguez Hills, 1992. Mem. Tchrs. Assn. Long Beach, Nat. Coun. Tchrs. English, Nat. Coun. Negro Women, Links (Orange County chpt. Inc., co-chair 1st model initiative youth project 1994, 95, co-chair Journey into Possibilities, Rochester chpt., charter), Jack and Jill of Am. (charter Long Beach chpt.), Internat. Reading Assn., Reading

Recovery Coun. N.Am., Beach Cities Reading Assn., Calif. Reading Assn., Delta Sigma Theta (charter, Long Beach alumnae). Democrat. Baptist. Home: 4508 Hazelnut Ave Seal Beach CA 90740-2918

MELTZOFF, ANDREW N., psychologist, educator; b. N.Y.C., Feb. 9, 1950; s. Julian and Judith (Novikoff) M. BA, Harvard U., 1972; PhD, Oxford U., Eng., 1976. Rsch. instr. U. Wash., Seattle, 1977-80, rsch. asst. prof., 1980-84, assoc. prof., 1984-88, prof., 1988—, adj. prof. psychiatry and behavioral scis., 1988—. Contbr. articles to profl. jours.; mem. editorial bd. Infant Behavior and Devel. Grantee NSF, 1983, NIH, 1986; MacArthur Found. grantee, 1984; recipient James McKeen Cattell award, 1990. Fellow AAAS, Am. Psychol. Assn., Am. Psychol. Soc.; mem. Soc. Rsch. and Child Devel., N.Y. Acad. Scis., Western Psychol. Assn., Phi Beta Kappa. Office: U Wash Dept Psychology # Wj-10 Seattle WA 98195

MELTZOFF, JULIAN, psychologist; b. N.Y.C., Feb. 16, 1921; s. Nathan G. and Sadie L. (Marcus) M.; m. Judith Novikoff (div. 1975); children: Andrew, Nancy; m. Antonia Ratensky, Oct. 16, 1976. BS, CCNY, 1941; MLitt, U. Pitts., 1946; PhD, U. Pa., 1950. Lic. psychologist, Calif. Clin. psychologist U.S. Army, 1942-46; asst. NYU Testing & Advisement Unit, N.Y.C., 1946; clin. psychology trainee VA Regional Office Mental Hygiene Clinic, Phila., 1946-50, asst. chief psychology, 1950-53; chief psychology sect. VA Hosp., Phila., 1953-54; chief psychology svc. VA Outpatient Clinic, Bklyn., 1954-77; prof., dir. rsch. Calif. Sch. Profl. Psychology, San Diego, 1979—. Author: Day Treatment Center: Principles, Application & Evaluation, 1966, Research in Psychotherapy, 1970; also articles. Staff sgt. U.S. Army, 1942-46, ETO. Fellow APA, Am. Psychol. Soc. Home: 7056 Vista Del Mar Ave La Jolla CA 92037-5339

MELVIN, JAY WAYNE, computer programmer; b. Oak Park, Ill., Feb. 3, 1946; s. Kendred Wayne and Margarita Alice (Pérez) M.; m. Linda Hansen, Dec. 10, 1980. MA in Urban Studies, Claremont (Calif.) Grad. Sch., 1975, postgrad., 1977. Hot line/prodn. mgr. Forth, Inc., Hermosa Beach, Calif., 1981-85; sr. software engr. Maxtor Corp., San Jose, Calif., 1986-88; computer programmer Tracor-Ultron Labs., San Jose, 1988-90, Comtech Labs., Palo Alto, Calif., 1990-92; programmer, team leader, mgr. software devel. lab. Omnipoint Corp., Colorado Springs, Colo., 1992—; cons. phenomenoLogic, La Honda, Calif., 1985-92, InfoPath, La Honda, 1990—. Contbr. articles to profl. jours. Peace corps vol. U.S. State Dept., Begal, India, 1966-68; fire dept. vol. Calif. Dept. Forestry, Kings Mountain, 1986-88; fire dept. lt. Vol. Fire Brigade, La Honda, San Mateo, 1988-94; radio operator Mil. Affiliate Radio Svc., Jackson, Miss., 1962-64. Recipient Award Beyond War, 1987; grad. fellowship Law Enforcement Adminstrn. Assn., 1975-77. Mem. Am. Radio Relay League (life, radio amateur), Amateur Satellite Corp. (life), Forth Interest Group, Assn. of Computing Machinery, Pi Sigma Alpha. Home and Office: 111 Scenic Dr La Honda CA 94020-0123

MEMEL, SHERWIN LEONARD, lawyer; b. Buffalo, Mar. 28, 1930; s. Maurice Memel and Nellie (Munshen) Katz; m. Iris C. Gittleman, Aug. 17, 1952; children: Jana Sue, Steven Keith, David Scott, Mara Jean. BA, UCLA, 1951, JD with honors, 1954. Bar: Calif. 1955, U.S. Ct. Appeals (9th cir.) 1955, U.S. Dist. Ct. (cen. dist.) Calif. 1959, U.S. Supreme Ct. 1963, D.C. 1979. Sr. ptnr. Memel & Ellsworth (formerly Memel, Jacobs, Pierno & Gersh and Memel, Jacobs, Pierno, Gersh & Ellsworth), Los Angeles, 1975-87; ptnr., chmn. health law dept. Manatt, Phelps & Phillips, Los Angeles, 1987—; instr. health law USC Sch. Pub. Adminstrn.; former instr. health UCLA; former mem. Fed. Health Ins. Benefit Adv. Coun.; cons. to major indsl. corps. on health bus. matters; lectr. in field. Contbr. numerous articles on health law to profl. jours. Chmn. Los Angeles Arts Council, 1986-87; vice chmn. Dem. Bus. Council, Washington, 1985-86; past pres. Calif. Bd. Med. Quality Assurance. Recipient Disting. Service award Fedn. Am. Hosps., 1970. Mem. ABA (forum com. health law), Am. Hosp. Assn. (life, Award of Honor 1971), Am. Acad. Hosp. Attys., Am. Soc. Law and Medicine, Nat. Health Lawyers Assn., Calif. Soc. for Healthcare Attys. (pres. 1983). Democrat. Office: Manatt Phelps & Phillips 11355 W Olympic Blvd Los Angeles CA 90064

MENARD, MICHAEL JOSEPH, museum director; b. Saginaw, Mich., Sept. 25, 1948; s. Louis Raymond and Dorothy Cicelia (Rable) M.; m. Nora Webb, Apr. 3, 1971; children: James T., Karla A. BA, Mich. State U., 1974, MA, 1976. Archivist State of Mich., Lansing, 1975-76; curator archives Mus. We. Colo., Grand Junction, 1977-80; dir. mus. Ft. Caspar Mus., Casper, Wyo., 1981-87; hist. sites adminstr. London Town Publik House and Garden, Edgewater, Md., 1987-92; mus. dir. Koshare Indian Mus., La Junta, Colo., 1992—. Sgt. USAF, 1968-72, Vietnam. Mem. Am. Assn. Mus. (cons. mus. assessment 1986—), Am. Assn. State and Local History, Mid-Atlantic Assn. Mus., Mountain Plains Mus. Assn. (state rep.), Colo.-Wyo. Assn. Mus. (vice chmn. bd. dirs. 1984-87), C. of C. for Annapolis and anne Arundel County. Office: 2217 Claudia Ct # A Grand Junction CO 81503-1124

MENDELSOHN, HAROLD, sociologist, educator; b. Jersey City, Oct. 30, 1923; s. Louis and Bessie (Yulinsky) M.; m. Irene Sylvia Gordon, Apr. 10, 1949; 1 dau., Susan Lynn. B.S., CCNY, 1945; M.A., Columbia U., 1946; Ph.D., New Sch. Social Research, 1956. Sr. survey analyst U.S. Dept. State, Washington, 1951-52; research assoc. Bur. Social Sci. Research, Am. U., Washington, 1952-56; assoc. mgr. mktg. communications McCann-Erickson Advt., N.Y.C., 1956-58; assoc. dir. Psychol. Corp., N.Y.C., 1958-62; prof. dept. mass communications U. Denver, 1962-89, prof. emeritus, 1989—, chmn., 1970-78, dean faculty social scis., 1984-86, spl. asst. to chancellor, 1986-88; Morton vis. disting. prof. Ohio U., spring 1981; cons. FTC, Denver Rsch. Inst., U.S. Consumer Product Safety Commn., The Gallup Orgn., Ford Found., Fedn. Rocky Mountain States, CBS, ABC, Children's TV Workshop. (Emmy award Nat. Acad. TV Arts Scis. 1968, Gold Camera award U.S. Indsl. Film Festival 1972); Author: Mass Entertainment, 1966, (with David H. Bayley) Minorities and the Police: Confrontation in America, 1969, (with Irving Crespi) Polls, Television and the New Politics, 1970, (with others) Television and Growing Up: The Impact of Televised Violence, 1972, (with Garrett O'Keefe) The People Choose a President, 1976; editor: Mass Communications series, 1967-69; contbr. articles to profl. jours. Mem. Denver Coun. Pub. TV, 1970-78; mem. U.S. Surgeon Gen.'s Sci. Adv. Com. on TV and Social Behavior, 1969-71; bd. dirs. Nat. Safety Coun., 1963-69; mem. pub. affairs adv. bd. Air Force Acad. Found., 1972-76; mem. cancer control and rehab. adv. com. Nat. Cancer Inst., 1976-81; mem. adv. coun., prevention div. Nat. Inst. Alcoholism and Alcohol Abuse, 1977-82; trustee Colo. Med. Svc., Inc., 1973-78. Recipient award TV Bur. Advt., 1962, Met. Life award Nat. Safety Council, 1967; Gold Eagle award, 1973; Silver award Internat. Festival Film and TV, 1974. Fellow Am. Psychol. Assn., Am. Sociol. Assn.; mem. Am. Assn. Pub. Opinion Research (pres. 1973-74), AAAS, N.Y. Acad. Scis., Sigma Delta Chi, Omicron Delta Kappa. Club: Chicago Press. Home: 1451 E Cornell Pl Englewood CO 80110-3013 Office: U Denver Dept Mass Communications Denver CO 80208

MENDELSON, STEVEN EARLE, lawyer; b. Los Angeles, Mar. 24, 1948; s. Robert Alexander and Nell Earle (Jacobs) M.; m. Katherine Grace Endicott; children: Carolyn, Laurel. BA, U. Calif., Santa Cruz, 1971; JD, Golden Gate U., 1975. Bar: Calif. 1975, U.S. Dist. Ct. (no. dist.) Calif. 1975. Assoc. Law Offices Robert A. Mendelson, Los Angeles, 1975-76, Law Offices Paul A. Eisler, San Francisco, 1976-77; sole practice Oakland, Calif., 1977-84; ptnr. Mendelson & Mendelson, Oakland, 1985—. Founding sponsor Civil Justice Found., 1986. Mem. Assn. Trial Lawyers Am., Calif. Trial Lawyers Assn. (speaker), Alameda Contra Costa Trial Lawyers Assn., Calif. Applicant Atty's Assn., Am. Back Soc. (workshop dir., speaker, bd. dirs. com. on programs and interprofl. relations, incorporator, legal counsel 1981—). Office: Mendelson & Mendelson 120 11th St Oakland CA 94607-4806

MENDENHALL, JACK L., artist, educator; b. Ventura, Calif., Apr. 7, 1937; s. Boyd Albert and Francis Florine (Dugan) M.; m. Kim Wolfman, June 21, 1981; 1 child, Blake. MFA, Calif. Coll. Arts & Crafts, Oakland. Home: 5824 Florence Ter Oakland CA 94611-2104

MENDEZ, C. BEATRIZ, obstetrician/gynecologist; b. Guatemala, Apr. 21, 1952; d. Jose and Olga (Sobalvarro) M.; m. Mark Parshall, Dec. 12, 1986. BS in Biology and Psychology, Pa. State U., 1974; MD, Milton Hershey Coll. Medicine, 1979. Diplomate Am. Bd. Ob-gyn. Resident in ob-gyn. George Washington U., Washington, 1979-83; pvt. practice Santa Fe, 1985—; chair perinatal com. St. Vincent's Hosp., Santa Fe, 1986-89, quality assurance mem., 1986—, chief ob-gyn, 1992-94; bd. dirs. Milton S. Hershey Coll. Medicine, Hershey, Pa., 1977-82. With USPHS, 1983-85. Mosby scholar Mosby-Hersey Med. Sch., Hershey, 1979. Fellow Am. Coll. Ob-Gyn. (Continuing Med. Edn. award 1986—); mem. AMA (Physician Recognition award 1986—), Am. Assn. Gynecol. Laparascopists, Internat. Soc. Gynecol. Endoscopy, Am. Fertility Soc., Am. Soc. Colposcopy and Cervical Pathology, N.Mex. Med. Soc., Santa Fe Med. Soc., Residents Assn. George Washington U. (co-founder 1981-83). Democrat. Office: Gallisteo Ob-gyn 539 Harkle Rd Santa Fe NM 87505-4748

MENDEZ, CELESTINO GALO, mathematics educator; b. Havana, Cuba, Oct. 16, 1944; s. Celestino Andres and Georgina (Fernandez) M.; came to U.S., 1962, naturalized, 1970; BA, Benedictine Coll., 1965; MA, U. Colo., 1968, PhD, 1974, MBA, 1979; m. Mary Ann Koplau, Aug. 21, 1971; children: Mark Michael, Matthew Maximilian. Asst. prof. maths. scis. Met. State Coll., Denver, 1971-77, assoc. prof., 1977-82, prof., 1982—, chmn. dept. math. scis., 1980-82; adminstrv. intern office v.p. for acad. affairs Met. State Coll., 1989-90. Mem. advt. rev. bd. Met. Denver, 1973-79; parish outreach rep. S.E. deanery, Denver Cath. Cmty. Svcs., 1976-78; mem. social ministries com. St. Thomas More Cath. Ch., Denver, 1976-78, vice-chmn., 1977-78, mem. parish council, 1977-78; del. Adams County Rep. Conv., 1972, 74, elected del., 1994, Colo. 4th Congl. Dist. Conv., 1974, Colo. Rep. Conv., 1982, 88, 90, 92, Douglas County Rep. Conv., 1980, 82, 84, 88, 90, 92, 94; alt. del. Colo. Rep. Conv., 1974, 76, 84, 5th Congl. dist. conv., 1976, mem. rules com., 1978, 80, precinct committeeman Douglas County Rep. Com., 1976-78, 89—, mem. cen. com., 1976-78, 89—; dist. 29 Rep. party candidate Colo. State Senate, 1990; Douglas county chmn. Rep. Nat. Hispanic Assembly, 1989—; bd. dirs. Rocky Mountain Better Bus. Bur., 1975-79, Rowley Downs Homeowners Assn., 1976-78, Douglas County Rep. Leadership Program, 1989-90, Rep. Leadership Program, 1990—; mem. exec. bd., v.p. Assoc. Faculties of State Inst. Higher Edn. in Colo., 1971-73; trustee Hispanic U. Am., 1975-78; councilman Town of Parker (Colo.), 1981-84, chmn. budget and fin. com. 1981-84; chmn. joint budget com. Town of Parker-Parker Water and Sanitation Dist. Bds., 1982-84; commr. Douglas County Planning Commn., 1993—. Recipient U. Colo. Grad. Sch. excellence in teaching award, 1965-67; grantee Benedictine Coll. , 1964-65, Math. Assn. Am. SUMMA grantee Carnegie Found. N.Y., 1994, NSF, 1995—. Mem. Math. Assn. Am. (referee rsch. notes sect. Am. Math. Monthly 1981-82, gov. Rocky Mountain section 1993—, investment com. 1995—, devel. com. 1995—, task force on reps. 1994—, commr.), Am. Math. Soc., Nat. Coun. Tchrs. of Math., Colo. Coun. Tchrs. of Maths. (bd. dirs. 1994—), Colo. Internat. Edn. Assn., Assoc. Faculties of State Insts. Higher Edn. in Colo. (v.p. 1971-73). Republican. Roman Catholic. Assoc. editor Denver Metro. Jour. Math. and Computer Sci., 1993—; contbr. articles to profl. jours. including Am. Math. Monthly, Procs. Am. Math. Soc., Am. Math. Monthly, Jour. Personalized Instruction, Denver Met. Jour. Math. and Computer Sci., and newspapers. Home: 11482 S Regency Pl Parker CO 80134-7330 Office: PO Box 173362 Denver CO 80217

MENDIUS, PATRICIA DODD WINTER, editor, educator, writer; b. Davenport, Iowa, July 9, 1924; d. Otho Edward and Helen Rose (Dodd) Winter; m. John Richard Mendius, June 19, 1947; children: Richard, Catherine M. Graber, Louise, Karen M. Chooljian. BA cum laude, UCLA, 1946; MA cum laude, U. N.Mex., 1966. Cert. secondary edn. tchr., Calif., N.Mex. English teaching asst. UCLA, 1946-47; English tchr. Marlborough Sch. for Girls, L.A., 1947-50, Aztec (N.Mex.) High Sch., 1953-55, Farmington (N.Mex.) High Sch., 1955-63; chair English dept. Los Alamos (N.Mex.) High Sch., 1963-86; sr. technical writer, editor Los Alamos Nat. Lab., 1987—; adj. prof. English, U. N.Mex., Los Alamos, 1970-72, Albuquerque, 1982-85; English cons. S.W. Regional Coll. Bd., Austin, Tex., 1975—; writer, editor, cons. advanced placement English test devel. com. Nat. Coll. Bd., 1982-86, reader, 1982-86, project equality cons., 1985-88; book selection cons. Scholastic mag., 1980-82. Author: Preparing for the Advanced Placement English Exams, 1975; editor Los Alamos Arts Coun. bull., 1986-91. Chair Los Alamos Art in Pub. Places Bd., 1987-92; chair adv. bd. trustees U. N.Mex., Los Alamos, 1987-93; pres. Los Alamos Concert Assn., 1972-73, 95—; chair Los Alamos Mesa Pub. Libr. Bd., 1990-94, chair endowment com., 1995—. Mem. Soc. Tech. Communicators, AAUW (pres. 1961-63, state bd. dirs. 1959-63, Los Alamos Coordinating Coun. 1992-93, pres. Los Alamos br. 1993-94), DAR, Order of Ea. Star, Mortar Bd., Phi Beta Kappa (pres. Los Alamos chpt. 1969-72), Phi Kappa Phi, Delta Kappa Gamma, Gamma Phi Beta. Home: 124 Rover Blvd Los Alamos NM 87544-3634 Office: Los Alamos Nat Lab Diamond Dr Los Alamos NM 87544

MENDONÇA, MARIA LUISA, video producer, educator; b. Rio de Janeiro, Brazil, Mar. 8, 1962; came to U.S., 1989; d. Aramis Marengo and Suely Rocha (Ferreira) M. Student, Estacio de Sá, Rio de Janeiro, 1983, San Francisco State U., 1990. Tchr. asst. Estacio de Sá U., Rio de Janeiro, 1982-84; prodr. videos Olhar Electronico, São Paulo, Brazil, 1984-89; mem. core faculty New Coll. Calif., San Francisco, 1990—; artist in residency The Banff Ctr. for the Arts, Can., 1992. Prodr. video documentary, exptl. video; prodr., dir. exptl. video, multimedia presentation. Panelist grants program dept. cultural affairs City of L.A., 1990; bd. dirs. Cine Acción, San Francisco, 1991—. Recipient Best Video award Festival Internat. Cinema and Video Rio de Janeiro, 1987, Best Documentary award Rio Cine Festival and Festival Internat. de Havana, 1987, Video Brazil Festival and Festrio, 1988. Fellow Brazil Action Solidarity Exch., Lilith Video Collective (prodr. 1985-88), Olhar Electronico Found.; mem. Bay Area Video Coalition (educator 1991), Film Arts Found. (educator 1991), Alliance for Cultural Democracy. Office: New Coll Calif 766 Valencia St San Francisco CA 94110-1735

MENEFEE, MERRITT MARIE, interior designer; b. Wheeling, W.Va., Sept. 29, 1970; d. Stephen Arvis and Marcia Ann (Whipkey) M. BS, Sch. Art & Design, 1992. Project designer Facilitec, Inc., Tempe, 1992—. Mem. DAR, Am. Soc. Interior Designers (allied), Pi Beta Phi. Republican. Presbyterian. Home: 200 E Southern Ave Apt 232 Tempe AZ 85282-5157 Office: Facilitec Inc 1860 W University Dr Ste 110 Tempe AZ 85281-3247

MENIKOFF, BARRY, English language educator; b. Bklyn., Jan. 2, 1939; s. Frank and Blanche (Goldman) M.; m. Michael Eastus, Aug. 20, 1966 (div. Oct. 1974); children: Carrie, Alec, Aaron. BA, Bklyn. Coll., 1960; MS, U. Wis., 1962, PhD, 1966. Asst. prof. English U. Hawaii, Honolulu, 1965-69; Fulbright lectr. U. Santiago (Spain), 1968-69; assoc. prof. English U. Hawaii, Honolulu, 1969-83, prof. English, 1983—; vis. assoc. prof. U. So. Calif., L.A., 1976-78, vis. prof. English, 1985-86; vis. prof. English U. Victoria, B.C., 1992. Author: R.L. Stevenson & Beach of Falesa, 1984, The Short Story, 1969, 75, R.L. Stevenson: Tales from the Prince of Storytellers, 1993; contbr. chpts. to books and articles to profl. jours. Rsch. fellow U. Coll. London, 1992; fellow NEH-Huntington Libr., San Marino, Calif., 1984, Newberry Libr., Chgo., 1981, Clark Libr., L.A., 1983; grantee Am. Philos. Soc., 1978, 81. Mem. MLA, AAUP. Home: 2729 Peter St Honolulu HI 96816-2015 Office: U Hawaii Dept English 1733 Donaghho Rd Honolulu HI 96822-2315

MENJO, HIROSHI, management consultant; b. Tokyo, Feb. 11, 1954; came to U.S., 1991; s. Takashi and Toyoko (Watanabe) M.; m. Mikako Tamiya, Feb. 10, 1980. BS in Chemistry, U. Tokyo, 1976, MS Phys. chemistry, 1978; MS in Electronic Materials, MIT, 1985. Rsch. staff Konica Corp., Tokyo, 1978-83, sr. rsch. staff, 1986-87; cons. The Boston Cons. Group, Tokyo, 1988-91; dir. AZCA, Inc., Redwood City, Calif., 1991-94; prin. Regis McKenna Inc., Palo Alto, Calif., 1994—; vis. scientist microsystems tech. lab. MIT, Cambridge, 1985-86, mem. Stanford venture lab. Patentee color photographic film, 1980-82; contbr. articles to profl. jours. Active Plan Internat., Warwick, R.I., 1988—. Mem. MIT Club No. Calif., Pacific Club, Sigma Xi. Office: Regis McKenna Inc 1755 Embarcadero Rd Palo Alto CA 94303-3304

MENKE, JAMES MICHAEL, chiropractor; b. Greenville, Ohio, Oct. 1, 1951; s. Stewart Hume and Elizabeth Janette (Amburn) M. Student, U. Cin., 1970-71, 1983-84; BS summa cum laude, Wright State U., 1975, MA, 1978; D of Chiropractic Medicine, Palmer U., 1987. Pvt. practice Menke Clinic, Los Altos, Calif., 1987—; cons. Found. Chiropractic Edn. Rsch., Washington, 1987-91, Ford Motor Co., Batavia, Ohio, 1983-84; lectr. U. Cin., 1983-84; adj. faculty Palmer U., Sunnyvale, Calif., 1987—. Contbr. articles to profl. jours. Wright State U. scholar Dayton, Ohio, 1975. Mem. APHA, Am. Chiropractic Scoliosis Found., Profl. Chiropractic Assn., Inst. Advancement Health, Calif. Chiropractic Assn., Am. Mensa, Rotary. Office: Menke Clinic Menke Clin 27 Second St # 3 Los Altos CA 94022

MENKE, TIMM REINER, German language educator; b. Oldenburg, Germany, Sept. 24, 1946; came to the U.S., 1963; m. Anne Critchfield, Aug. 30, 1982. BA, Lawrence U., 1972; MA, U. Wash., 1980, PhD, 1983. Lectr. German lang. U. Minn., 1985-87, Macalester Coll., St. Paul, 1987-88; assoc. prof. Portland (Oreg.) State U., 1988—; dir. Deutsche Sommerschule am Pazifik, Portland, 1991, 92; vis. scholar U. Cambridge, 1994-95. Contbr. articles to profl. jours, scholarly books. Fulbright scholar, 1971-72; NEH grantee, 1988. Office: Portland State U Dept Fgn Langs Portland OR 97207

MENKIN, CHRISTOPHER (KIT MENKIN), leasing company executive; b. Manhattan, N.Y., Jan. 1, 1942; s. Lawrence and Columbia (Riland) M.; children: Dashiel, Tascha, Ashley. Student, Julliard Sch. of Music, 1960, Santa Monica Coll., 1959-61, UCLA, 1961-64. News editor, dir. Sta. KRFC Radio, San Francisco, 1964-67; adminstrv. asst. to assemblyman Leo J. Ryan South San Francisco, 1967-68; mng. editor Sta. KGO TV News, San Francisco, 1968-69; news producer west coast Sta. ABC TV, Los Angeles, 1969; city mgr. City of San Bruno (Calif.), 1970; owner Menkin & Assocs., Santa Clara, Calif., 1971—; sr. ptnr. Am. Leasing, Santa Clara, 1971—; ptnr. Medallon Leasing, Santa Clara, 1974-80; pres. Monte Sereno Wine Co., Santa Clara, 1978—; dir. Meridian Nat. Bank, 1982-84. Chmn. nominating com. San Jose (Calif.) Symphony, 1988—; sec. Salvation Army, Santa Clara, 1968—, bd. dirs., 1990—, bd. dirs. San Jose chpt., 1990, vice chmn. county adv. bd., 1992; bd. dirs. Cmty. Against Substance Abuse, Los Gatos, Calif., 1988—, Valley Inst. of Theater Arts, Saratoga, Calif., 1987-88, San Jose Trolley, 1988—. Mem. United Assn. Equipment Leasing (regional chmn. 1992-95, membership chmn. 1994—), Santa Clara Valley Wine Soc. (pres. 1988), Credit Profls. Santa Clara Valley (pres. 1990-91), Assn. Credit Grantors (past pres.), Credit Women Internat. (1st male pres.), Santa Clara C. of C. (pres. 1973-76), Bay Area Exec. Club (sec.), Confrerie de la Chaine de Rotisseurs (charge de presse 1992-95), Royal Rose Soc. Gt. Britain (rep. No. Calif. 1990—). Democrat. Office: Am Leasing 348 Mathew St Santa Clara CA 95050-3114

MENNELLA, VINCENT ALFRED, automotive manufacturing and airplane company executive; b. Teaneck, N.J., Oct. 7, 1922; s. Francis Anthony and Henrietta Vernard (Dickson) M.; B.A. in Acctg., U. Wash., 1948; m. Madeleine Olson, Aug. 18, 1945; children—Bruce, Cynthia, Mark, Scott, Chris. Sales and bus. mgmt. positions Ford div. Ford Motor Co., 1949-55; founder, pres. Southgate Ford, Seattle, 1955-80; pres. Flightcraft, Inc., Seattle, 1973-86; chmn. bd. Stanley Garage Door Co., 1981-86, Zman Magnetics, 1990—. Former chmn. March of Dimes. Served to capt. USNR, 1942-45. Republican. Roman Catholic. Clubs: Rainier Golf, Seattle Tennis, Rotary (past pres.). Home: 1400 SW 171st Pl Seattle WA 98166-3453

MENNIS, EDMUND ADDI, investment management consultant; b. Allentown, Pa., Aug. 12, 1919; s. William Henry and Grace (Addi) M.; m. Selma Adinoff, Sept. 25, 1945; children: Ardith Grace, Daniel Liam. B.A., CCNY, 1941; M.A., Columbia U., 1946; Ph.D., NYU, 1961. Security analyst Eastman, Dillon & Co., N.Y.C., 1945-46; sr. research asst. Am. Inst. Econ. Research, Great Barrington, Mass., 1946-50; security analyst Wellington Mgmt. Co., Phila., 1950-61; dir. research Wellington Mgmt. Co., 1958-61, v.p., mem. investment com., 1958-66, economist, 1953-66; sr. v.p., chmn. trust investment com. Republic Nat. Bank, Dallas, 1966-72; sr. v.p., chmn. investment policy com. Security Pacific Nat. Bank, Los Angeles, 1973-81; pres., dir. Bunker Hill Income Securities, Inc., 1973-81; chmn. bd. Security Pacific Investment Mgrs., Inc., 1977-81; ind. cons. to investment mgmt. orgns., 1982—; Tech. cons. Bus. Council, Washington, 1962-66, 72-77, 79-81; econ. adviser sec. commerce, 1967-68; mem. investment adv. panel Pension Benefit Guaranty Corp., 1981-83. Assoc. editor: Financial Analysts Jour., 1960-88; editor: C.F.A. Digest, 1971-86, Bus. Econs., 1985—, Bank Funds Mgmt. Report, 1993—; author or editor books, chpts., numerous articles in field of econs. and investments. Trustee Fin. Analysts Research Found., 1981-86. Served to 1st lt. USAAF, 1942-45; to capt. USAF, 1951-53. Fellow Nat. Assn. Bus. Economists (coun. 1967-69), Fin. Analysts Fedn. (dir. 1970-72, Graham and Dodd award 1972, Molodovsky award 1972); mem. Am. Econ. Assn., Am. Fin. Assn., N.Y. Soc. Security Analysts, L.A. Soc. Fin. Analysts, Conf. Bus. Economists (vice chmn. 1977, chmn. 1978), Inst. Chartered Fin. Analysts (pres. 1970-72, trustee 1968-74, C. Stewart Sheppard award 1978). Home: 721 Paseo Del Mar Palos Verdes Estates CA 90274 Office: PO Box 1146 Pls Vrds Est CA 90274-7946

MENOHER, PAUL EDWIN, JR., army officer; b. West Palm Beach, Fla., July 20, 1939; s. Paul E. and Gladys (Bingaman) M.; m. Kay I. Craddock; 1 child, Scott A.; m. Bebe Doris Etzler, Aug. 21, 1980. BA in Polit. Sci., U. Calif., Berkeley, 1961; MS in Internat. Rels., George Washington U., 1972. Commd. 2d lt. U.S. Army, 1961, advanced through grades to lt. gen.; student USN Coll. Command and Staff, Newport, R.I., 1971-72, U.S. Army War Coll., Carlisle, Pa., 1977-78; chief plans br. Hdqrs. U.S. Army Forces Command, Ft. McPherson, Ga., 1978-79, chief combat intelligence div., 1979-81; chief collection div. Hdqrs. U.S Army Europe, Heidelberg, Fed. Republic Germany, 1981-82; G2 VII Corps, Stuttgart, Fed. Republic Germany, 1982-84; comdr. 501st Mil. Intelligence Brigade, Seoul, Republic of Korea, 1984-86; dir. U.S. Army Intelligence and Electronic Warfare Master Plan, Washington, 1986-89; comdg. gen. U.S. Army Intelligence Agy., Washington, 1987-89, U.S. Army Intelligence Ctr., Ft. Huachuca, Ariz., 1989-93, U.S. Army Intelligence and Security Command, Ft. Belvoir, Va., 1993-94; dep. chief of staff for intelligence Dept. Army, Washington, 1994—. Mem. Assn. U.S. Army, Armed Forces Comms. and Electronics Assn., Assn. Old Crows. Office: Dept Army Hdqs The Pentagon Washington DC 20310*

MENSH, IVAN NORMAN, medical psychology educator; b. Washington DC, Oct. 30, 1915; s. Shea Jacob and Rose (Clayman) M.; m. Frances Levitas. AB, George Washington U., 1940, AM, 1942; PhD, Northwestern U., 1948. Diplomate Am. Bd. Clin. Psychology; lic. psychologist, Calif. Prof., head med. psychology, dept. psychiatry Washington U., St. Louis, 1948-58; prof., head div. med. psychology, dept. psychiatry UCLA, 1958-86, prof. emeritus, 1986—. Author 2 text books; contbr. chpts. to books and numerous articles to profl. jours. Capt. USNR, 1943—. Recipient Certs. of Appreciation, Office Naval Rsch., Am. Bd. Profl. Psychology, Jour. Med. Edn., NIH. Fellow APA (past pres., past sec.); mem. Calif. Psychol. Assn. (past treas., past bd. chair, Silver Psi award), Assn. Am. Med. Colls., Assn. Am. Profs. Med. Psychology, Assn. Behavioral Scis. and Med. Edn., N.Y. Acad. Scis., Western Psychol. Assn. Office: UCLA Dept Biobehavioral Scis 760 Westwood Plz Los Angeles CA 90024-8300

MENSINGER, PEGGY BOOTHE, retired mayor; b. Modesto, Calif., Feb. 18, 1923; d. Dyas Power and Margaret (Stewart) Boothe; m. John Logan Mensinger, May 25, 1952; children: John B., Stewart I., Susan B. AB in Polit. Sci, Stanford U., 1944. Reporter San Francisco Red Cross Chpt. News Bur., 1944; acting mgr. Boothe Fruit Co., Modesto, Calif., 1945; asst. dir. Stanford (Calif.) Alumni Assn., 1947; exec. sec. pub. exercises com. Stanford U., 1949-51; mem. Modesto City Council, 1973-79, mayor, 1979-87; ret., 1987; Mem. adv. bd. Agrl. Issues Ctr. U. Calif., 1988-94. Bd. dirs. Nat. coun. Girl Scouts U.S.A., 1978-87, Calif. Planning and Conservation League, 1980—; adv. bd. U. Calif. Agricultural Issues Ctr., 1988-94; Friends Outside Nat. Bd., 1991-93; chmn. Citizens Com. for Internat. Students, 1965-70; pres. Modesto PTA Coun., 1967-69, Modesto chpt. Am. Field Svc., 1969-70, Stanislaus County Hist. Soc., 1970-71; mem. state bd. Common Cause, 1973-75; chmn. Modesto City Cultural Comm., 1968-73; del. White House Conf. on Families, L.A., 1980; chmn. Stanislaus Area Assn. Govts., 1976-77; chmn. air quality subcom. U.S. Conf. Mayors, 1985-87. Recipient Woman of Yr. award VFW Aux., 1980, Man of Yr. award Am. Legion, 1987, State of Calif. Legislature Women of Yr. Mem. Nat. League Am. Pen Women (assoc.), Stanford Assocs. (pres. 1985-87), Soroptimist (hon., Women Achievement award 1980), Phi Beta Kappa, Gamma Phi Beta. Unitarian. Home: 1320 Magnolia Ave Modesto CA 95350-5250

MERCEREAU, JAMES EDGAR, educator, physicist; b. Sharon, Pa., Apr. 3, 1930; s. James T. and S. Francis (Festermaker) M.; m. Gabriella Lengyel, Dec. 23, 1967; children: James A., Michael D., Steven F. B.A., Pomona Coll., 1953, Sc.D. (hon.), 1968; M.S., U. Ill., 1954; Ph.D., Calif. Inst. Tech., 1959. Research physicist Hughes Research Lab., 1954-59; asst. prof. physics Calif. Inst. Tech., 1959-62, prof., 1969—; prin. scientist Ford Sci. Lab., 1962-65; mgr. Ford Cryogenic Labs., 1965-69; Dir. R.A.I. Corp.; Mem. adv. com. NASA; mem. Nat. Acad. Com. Adv. to Nat. Bur. Standards. Contbr. articles profl. jours. Named one of America's 10 Outstanding Young Men U.S. Jr. C. of C., 1965; recipient achievement award in physics Am. Acad. Achievement, 1966. Fellow Am. Phys. Soc. Home: 24652 El Camino Capistrano Dana Point CA 92629-3012 Office: 1201 E California Blvd Pasadena CA 91125-0001

MERCHANT, JUDITH MIRIAM, state agency administrator, educator, counselor; b. Burlington, Iowa, Aug. 27, 1940; d. Arnold Walter and Dorothy Lulu (Kretzschmar) Schmidt; m. Richard Ival Merchant, Dec. 19, 1961; children—Michael Brian, David Bradley. B.A. Summa cum laude, U. Iowa, 1962; M.A., Ball State U., 1974; cert. advanced grad. study Boston U., 1976. Adminstr. alcohol program Wash. Dept. Social and Health Services, Olympia, 1977-79, mgr. day care services, 1978-80, dir. bur. alcohol and substance abuse, 1980-81, exec. asst. to dept. sec. and chief intergovtl. relations, 1981-82, dir. div. income assistance, 1982-86; dep. dir. Mich. Dept. Social Services, 1986; dep. dir. Wash. Dept. of Fisheries, 1986-93; dir. Wash. State Energy Office Gov. Cabinet, 1993—; adminstr. alcohol and drug services, also educator secondary edn. Dept. Def., Fed. Republic of Germany, 1971-76; dep. dir. Wash. State Dept. Fisheries, 1986—. Ch. council Lutheran Ch. of Good Shepherd, Olympia, 1979-82; adv. com. Community Vol. Med. Program for Low-Income Families, Olympia, 1982—; bd. dirs. Wash. State Employees Credit Union, Olympia, 1983—. Recipient Service award VIIth Corps Hdqrs. U.S. Army, Fed. Republic of Germany, 1975. Mem. Nat. Assn. State Alcohol and Drug Dirs. (exec. bd. 1980-81), Am. Pub. Welfare Assn. (exec. bd.), Pacific Fisheries Mgmt. Coun., N. Pacific Mgmt. Coun., 1987-93, Nat. Assn. State Energy Officials (vice chair), We. Interstate Energy Bd. (mem. exec. com. 1994), European Congress Am. Parents and Tchrs. (v.p. 1972-74), Exec. Women in State Govt., Phi Beta Kappa. Home: 3724 Pifer Ct SE Olympia WA 98501-4160 Office: Energy Office PO Box 43165 Olympia WA 98504-3165

MERCHANT, ROLAND SAMUEL, SR., hospital administrator, educator; b. N.Y.C., Apr. 18, 1929; s. Samuel and Eleta (McLymont) M.; m. Audrey Bartley, June 6, 1970; children—Orelia Eleta, Roland Samuel, Huey Bartley. BA, NYU, 1957, MA, 1960; MS, Columbia U., 1963, MSHA, 1974. Asst. statistician N.Y.C. Dept. Health, 1957-60, statistician, 1960-63; statistician N.Y. TB and Health Assn., N.Y.C., 1963-65; biostatistician, adminstrv. coord. Inst. Surg. Studies, Montefiore Hosp., Bronx, N.Y., 1965-72; resident in adminstrn. Roosevelt Hosp., N.Y.C., 1973-74; dir. health and hosp. mgmt. Dept. Health, City of N.Y., 1974-76; from asst. adminstr. to adminstr. West Adams Community Hosp., L.A., 1976; spl. asst. to assoc. v.p. for med. affairs Stanford U. Hosp., Calif., 1977-82, dir. office mgmt. and strategic planning, 1982-85, dir. mgmt. planning, 1986-90; v.p. strategic planning Cedars-Sinai Med. Ctr., L.A., 1990-94; cons. Roland Merchant & Assocs., L.A., 1994—; clin. assoc. prof. dept. family, community and preventive medicine Stanford U., 1986-88, dept. health rsch. and policy Stanford U. Med. Sch., 1988-90. Served with U.S. Army, 1951-53. USPHS fellow. Fellow Am. Coll. Healthcare Execs., Am. Pub. Health Assn.; mem. Am. Hosp. Assn., Nat. Assn. Health Services Execs., N.Y. Acad. Scis. Home: 27335 Park Vista Rd Agoura Hills CA 91301-3639

MERCHEY, RUTH ANN, artist, designer; b. Bell, Calif., Feb. 26, 1947; d. Charles Wesley and Esther (Rogers) Lester; m. Morton Donald Merchey, Aug. 19, 1971 (div. Sept. 1991); children: Jason Aaron, Kelly Leigh. BA, Woodbury U., L.A., 1971; postgrad., UCLA, 1972-73. Designer Regal Rugs, Inc., Beverly Hills, Calif., 1968-75; designer, artist Ruth Merchey Designs, Downey, Calif., 1975-90; artist, builder Ruth Merchey Designs, Big Bear City, Calif., 1990—; owner R&S Designs, Downey, 1980-91. Author: (play) 12 Steps for 12 and Under, 1988 (spl. recognition award 1989); exhibited in group shows L.A. County Fair, 1978 (Best of Show), Valley Art Guild, Encino, Calif., 1989, 90 (1st place 1989, Best of Show award 1990), Costa Mesa Art Guild, 1991, San Bernardino County Art Mus., Redlands, Calif., 1991. Fundraiser L.A. County Med. Assn. Aux., Downey, 1975-80, City of Hope, Downey; officer Downey Elem. Sch., Downey Mid. Sch., Downey High Sch., 1979—; chmn. election campaign Downey Unified Sch. Bd., 196-88; cons., vol. S.E. Coun. on Alcohol Abuse, Downey, 1986-89, Polonaise Ball, Beverly Hills, Calif., 1985—. Recipient hon. award City of Hope, 1976, 80, 84. Mem. Redlands Art Assn., Taos Art Assn., Fine Arts Inst., Bear Valley Art Assn. Republican.

MERCIER, MICHAEL ANTHONY, advertising executive; b. Inglewood, Calif., Nov. 7, 1959; s. Terrence Joseph and Patricia Marie (Rodriguez) M.; m. Oct. 1, 1989 (div. 1991); 1 child, Scott T. BA in Polit. Sci., Calif. State U., Long Beach, 1982; MBA, U. So. Calif., 1992. Field rep. Assemblyman Chet Wray, Garden Grove, Calif., 1982-83; cons. assembly selcect com. Assemblyman Bruce Young, Norwalk, Calif., 1983-84; sr. account exec. Cerrell Assocs., 1984-85; v.p. Englander/Adler & Droz, Newport Beach, Calif., 1985-88; ptnr. Mercier/Kukurin, Beverly Hills, Calif., 1985-88; dir. non-profit fundraising div. Mailing & Mktg., Orange, Calif., 1988-90; exec. v.p. Pacific Admail, Fountain Valley, Calif., 1991-94, pres., COO, 1994; pres. M & M Cons., Santa Ana, Calif., 1994—. Contbr. articles to profl. jours. Chair Youth Commn., Buena Park, Calif., 1979-80; mem. Rent Arbitration bd., Norwalk, Calif., 1983. Recipient Gold Ink award Printing Tech. Mag., 1989, Gold Pioneer award Dirdouble Mktg. Creative Guild, 1990. Mem. Am. Mktg. Assn., Nat. Soc. Fundraising Cons., Direct Mktg. Guild, Acad. for Health Svcs. Mktg., Internat. Assn. Polit. Cons. Office: 3441 W Macarthur Blvd Santa Ana CA 92704-6805

MERCURIO, EDWARD PETER, natural science educator; b. Orange, Calif., Dec. 28, 1944; s. Peter Amadeo and Jeanne (Monteleone) M.; m. Jeanne Roussel Gable, Oct. 18, 1980 (div. Dec. 1984); 1 child, Katherine Roussel; m. Patricia Ann Kahler, Apr. 12, 1987; children: Peter Edward, Rose Sierra. BA, UCLA, 1967, MA, 1970, CPhil, 1978. Research asst. UCLA, 1971, teaching asst., 1968-71; instructional assoc. Golden West Coll., Huntington Beach, Calif., 1972-73; cons. Monterey County Planning Dept., Salinas, Calif., 1980; prof. Hartnell Coll., Salinas, Calif., 1973—; photographer in field, Calif., 1961—; lectr. in field, Calif., 1970—; cons. in field, 1980—. Fellow Woodrow Wilson Nat. Fellowship Found., 1967. Mem. AAAS, Sierra Club. Democrat. Home: 647 Wilson St Salinas CA 93901-1346 Office: Hartnell Coll 156 Homestead Ave Salinas CA 93901-1628

MERCURIO-MUICO, LUISA, critical care nurse; b. Caloocan, Manila, Philippines, Nov. 17, 1955; d. Amado B. and Eustaquia (Buenavista) Muico; m. Wilfred Tongson Mercurio, Dec. 28, 1974; children: Elyjah Matthew, Kristoffer Ross, Mercurio. ADN, Harbor City Coll., 1978; BSN, Calif. State U., 1989, postgrad., 1992—. Cert. ACLS instr., BLS instr; CCRN; cert. pub. health nurse. Staff nurse ICU Long Beach (Calif.) Meml. Med. Ctr., 1978-80; staff nurse CVT/ICU Cedar Sinai Med. Ctr., L.A., 1980-84; staff nurse ICU, critical care unit, emergency rm., cath. lab. Long Beach Community Hosp., 1982-86; ICU, CCU coord. Pioneer Hosp., Artesia, Calif., 1986-87; staff nurse CSU Kaiser-Permanente, L.A., 1988-90, pub. health nurse, 1990, asst. dept. adminstr., 1990-92; asst. dept. adminstr. Kaiser-Permanente, Sunset and Bellflower, Calif.; cardiovascular/thoracic surgery nurse coord. Kay Med. Group/Hosp. Good Samaritan, L.A., 1992—; staff nurse critical care unit UCLA, 1994—; nursing faculty Pacific Coast Coll., 1994—. Named to Dean's list Harbor City Coll., 1976-78, Dean's list Calif. State U., 1978—. Mem. AACN (cert.), NRA, Nat. Golden Key Honor Soc., Nursing Honor Soc., Sigma Theta Tau (Nu Mu chpt.). Republican.

MERGL, BETTY MAE, senior center executive director; b. Omaha, Nebr., Aug. 30, 1931; d. Edward Sedlacek and Agnes Marie (Skavril) Swirczek; m. Aldrich Norbert Mergl, Feb. 9, 1951; children: Christine, Kenneth, Gerald, Allan, Brian, Meredith. Grad. h.s., Omaha. Bookkeeping First Nat. Bank, Omaha, 1950-51; claims sec. Lloyd's of London, Tacoma, Wash., 1951-53; payroll supr. Western Paving Co., Denver, 1958-68; exec. dir. Tri Valley Sr. Citizens Assn., Deer Trail, Colo., 1977—; adv. bd. Arapahoe County Transp. Svc., Denver, 1981-84, Arapahoe County C.S.B.G. Funds, Denver, 1983-84. Sch. bd. mem. Deer Trail Sch., Colo., 1979-84; mem. Colo. Congress of Sr. Orgns., Denver, 1982; del. Gov.'s Conf. on Aging, State of Colo., 1980; mem. Sr. Ctrs. of colo., 1982—; adv. bd. mem. Arapahoe Regional Libr., Denver, 1981-84, Gov.'s Vol. Citizen Bd., Denver, 1981-85; mem. Adams County Coun. of Older Ams., Arapahoe County Coun. for Sr. Citizens, Srs. and Lawmen Together-Adams County Sheriff's dept. Recipient Cert. of Appreciation ARC, 1983, 84, Tri County Health, State of Colo., 1979, award HUD, 1995. Mem. I-70 Corridor C. of C. Home: PO Box 83 665 4th Ave Deer Trail CO 80105 Office: Tri Valley Sr Citizens Assn PO Box 233 665 4th Ave Deer Trail CO 80105

MERIFIELD, PAUL M., geologist, consultant; b. Santa Monica, Calif., Mar. 17, 1932; m. Ruth Ann Friend. BA, UCLA, 1954, MA, 1958; PhD, U. Colo., 1963. Rsch. scientist Lockheed Aircraft Corp., Burbank, Calif., 1962-64; cons. geologist L.A., 1964—; adj. prof. UCLA, 1970—. Mem. Assn. Engring. Geologist, Geol. Soc. Am.

MERIGAN, THOMAS CHARLES, JR., physician, medical researcher, educator; b. San Francisco, Jan. 18, 1934; s. Thomas C. and Helen M. (Greeley) M.; m. Joan Mary Freeborn, Oct. 3, 1959; 1 son, Thomas Charles III. BA with honors, U. Calif., Berkeley, 1955; MD, U. Calif., San Francisco, 1958. Diplomate: Am. Bd. Internal Medicine. Intern in medicine 2d and 4th Harvard med. services Boston City Hosp., 1958-59, asst. resident medicine, 1959-60; clin. assoc. Nat. Heart Inst., NIH, Bethesda, Md., 1960-62; asso. Lab. Molecular Biology, Nat. Inst. Arthritis and Metabolic Diseases, NIH, 1962-63; practice medicine specializing in internal medicine and infectious diseases Stanford, Calif., 1963—; asst. prof. medicine Stanford U. Sch. Medicine, 1963-67, assoc. prof. medicine, 1967-72, head div. infectious diseases, 1966-92, prof. medicine, 1972—, George E. and Lucy Becker prof. medicine, 1980—; dir. Diagnostic Microbiology Lab., Univ. Hosp., 1966-72, Diagnostic Virology Lab., 1969—, Ctr. AIDS Rsch. Stanford U., 1988—; hosp. epidemiologist, 1966-88; mem. microbiology rsch. tng. grants com. NIH, 1969-73, virology study sect., 1974-78; cons. antiviral substances program Nat. Inst. Allergy and Infectious Diseases, 1970—, mem. AIDS clin. drug devel. commn., 1986-94; mem. Virology Task Force, 1976-78, bd. sci. counselors, 1980-85; mem. U.S. Hepatitis panel U.S. and Japan Coop. Med. Sci. Program, 1979-90, AIDS subcom. Nat. Adv. Allergy and Infectious Diseases Coun., 1988-89; co-chmn. interferon evaluation Group Am. Cancer Soc., 1978-81; mem. vaccines and related biol. products adv. com. Ctr. for Drugs and Biols., FDA, 1984-88; mem. internat. adv. com. on biol. sci. Sci. Council, Singapore, 1985-88; mem. adv. com. J.A. Hartford Found., 1979-84; mem. Albert Lasker awards jury, 1981-84; mem. peer review panel U.S. Army Med. Rsch. and Devel. Com., 1986-88; nat. com. to rev. current procedures for approval New Drugs for Cancer and AIDS, 1989-90; mem. Com. to Study Use of Coms. within FDA, 1991-92. Contbr. numerous articles on infectious diseases, virology and immunology to sci. jours.; editor: Antivirals with Clinical Potential, 1976, Antivirals and Virus Diseases of Man, 1979, 2d edit., 1984, 3d edit., 1990, Regulatory Functions of Interferon, 1980, Interferons, 1982, Interferons as Cell Growth Inhibitors, 1986; assoc. editor: Virology, 1975-78, Cancer Research, 1987-91; co-editor: monograph series Current Topics in Infectious Diseases, 1975—, Cytomeglovirus Infect and Ganciclovir, 1988, Focus on Didanosine (ddI), 1990, Practical Diagnosis of Viral Infection, Textbook of AIDS Medicine, 1993; editorial bd.: Archives Internal Medicine, 1971-81, Jour. Gen. Virology, 1972-77, Infection and Immunity, 1973-81, Intervirology, 1973-85, Proc. Soc. Exptl. Biology and Medicine, 1978-87, Reviews of Infectious Diseases, 1979-89, Jour. Interferon Research, 1980-89, Antiviral Research, 1980-86, Jour. Antimicrobial Chemotherapy, 1981-91, Molecular and Cellular Biochemistry, 1982-89 , AIDS Research and Human Retroviruses, 1983—, Jour. Virology, 1984-89, Biotechnology Therapeutics, 1988—, Jour. Infectious Diseases, 1989—, Drug Investigation, 1989—, HIV: Advances in Research and Therapy, 1990—, Internat. Jour. Antimicrobial Agts. 1990—, The AIDS Reader, 1991—, AIDS, 1993, Clinical Immunotherapeutics, 1994—. Recipient Borden award for Outstanding Rsch., Am. Assn. Med. Colls., 1973, Merit award, Nat. Inst. Allergy and Infectious Diseases, 1988, Maxwell Finland award Infectious Diseases Soc. Am., 1988; Guggenheim Meml. fellow, 1972. Mem. Assn. Am. Physicians, Western Assn. Physicians, Am. Soc. Microbiology, Am. Soc. Clin. Investigation (coun. 1977-80), Am. Assn. Immunologists, Am. Fedn. Clin. Rsch., Western Soc. Clin. Rsch., Soc. Exptl. Biology and Medicine (publ. com. 1985-89), Infectious Diseases Soc. Am., Am. Soc. Virology, Inst. Medicine, Pan Am. Group for Rapid Viral Diagnosis, AMA, Internat. Soc. Interferon Rsch. (coun. 1983-89), Calif. Med. Assn., Santa Clara County Med. Soc., Cacad. Medicine, Royal Soc. Medicine, AAAS, Alpha Omega Alpha. Home: 148 Goya Rd Menlo Park CA 94028-7307 Office: Stanford U Sch Medicine Div Infectious Diseases Stanford CA 94305

MERKLE, ALAN RAY, lawyer; b. Boise, Idaho, Oct. 14, 1947; s. John William and Arlene June (Hawkins) M.; m. Diane M. Martin, June 15, 1973 (div. 1978); m. Linda Jo Todd, Mar. 15, 1980; children: Amanda, Lindsay. AS, Boise State U., 1967; BSME, U. Idaho, 1970, MBA, 1971; JD, Lewis & Clark Coll., 1982. Bar: Oreg. 1983, Wash. 1983, U.S. Dist. Ct. (Oreg.) 1983, U.S. Dist. Ct. (we. dist.) Wash. 1984; registered profl. engr. Wash., Oreg., Idaho. Field engr. GE, N.Y., Oreg., Wash., other location, 1971-74; svc. specialist GE, Seattle, 1974-77; svc. mgr. steam turbines GE, Portland, Oreg., 1977-80; mgr. hydro ops. GE, 1980-82; assoc. Stoel, Rives, Boley, Jones & Grey, Portland, 1982-86, ptnr., 1987—. Author: Construction Law, Licensing and Registration, 1988, Damages, Liability of Architects and Engineers, 1989, 93, Public Contracting in Washington, 1992, 93, 94, Washington Lien Law, 1992, Defending Claims Against the Owner, 1994. Recipient Cornelius honor award. Mem. ABA, Oreg. State Bar Assn., Wash. State Bar Assn., Fed. Energy Bar Assn. (chair pub. procurement, pvt. law sect., associated gen. contractors, legal affairs com.). Democrat. Office: Stoel Rives Boley Jones & Grey 3600 One Union Sq 600 University St Seattle WA 98101-1129

MERLO, HARRY ANGELO, forest products executive; b. Stirling City, Calif., Mar. 5, 1925; s. Joseph Angelo and Clotilde (Camussa) M.; 1 son, Harry A. BS, U. Calif.-Berkeley, 1949, postgrad., 1949. Vice pres. Rockport Redwood Co., Cloverdale, Calif., 1967; v.p. No. Calif. div. Ga.-Pacific Corp., Samoa, Calif., 1967-69; v.p. Western lumber div. Ga.-Pacific Corp., Portland, Oreg., 1969-71, exec. v.p. Western timber, plywood and lumber operations, 1971-73; pres., chmn. bd. La.-Pacific Corp., Portland, 1973—; bd. dirs. World Forestry Ctr. Mem. Pres.'s Coun., Columbia Pacific coun. Boy Scouts Am.; former mem. nat. adv. coun. Salvation Army; trustee Hugh O'Brian Youth Found., Oreg. Mus. Sci. and Industry, Goodwill Industries; past chmn. bd. Am. Acad. Achievement; former western fin. chmn. U.S. Olympic commn.; past chmn., adv. bd. Salvation Army, Oreg.; past bd. dirs. Marshall U. Soc. Yaeger Scholars. Lt. USMCR. Named Man of Year Ga.-Pacific Corp., 1969; recipient Golden Plate award Am. Acad. Achievement, 1974; Horatio Alger award, 1980, Gold award for forest products industry The Wall St. Transcript, 1982, 83, 94, Disting. Svc. award La. Tech. U., 1984, Aubrey Watzek award Lewis and Clark Coll., 1984, Citizen of Merit award Assoc. Builders and Contractors, 1986, Piemontese Del Munde award, 1986, Merit award Calif. Parks & Recreation Soc., 1988, John J. Mulrooney award N.Am. Wholesale Lumber Assn., 1989, Hope award Nat. Multiple Sclerosis Soc., 1993. Mem. Calif. Redwood Assn. (past pres., bd. dirs.), Horatio Alger Assn. (pres., chmn.), Founders Club (bd. dirs.), Waverly Country Club, Multnomah Athletic Club, Ingomar Club, Knight of the Vine. Office: La-Pacific Corp 111 SW 5th Ave Portland OR 97204-3604

MERRELL, ARTHUR N., psychiatrist; b. Tulsa, Jan. 13, 1943; s. Ira Nelson and Rita Noriene (Harris) M.; m. Caro Arlene Merrell, Apr. 22, 1966; children: Kelly, Joshua, Adam, Jacob. BA, Colo. Coll., 1963; MD, U. Colo., 1967. Diplomate Am. Bd. Psychiatry and Neurology. Med. dir. S.E. Wyo. Mental Health Ctr., Cheyenne, 1974—. Col. Wyo. Air Nat. Guard, 1983—. Methodist. Office: 2526 Seymour Ave Cheyenne WY 82001-3159

MERRELL, CYRUS WALBRIDGE, JR., artist, rancher; b. St. Louis, June 13, 1929; s. Cyrus Walbridge and Frances (Spink) M.; m. Katharina Falsen Moller, May 5, 1989; 1 child, Leslie Drayton Merrell Zimmerman. BA, U. Va. Rancher, Victor, Mont. Lt. (j.g.) USN, 1952-56. Mem. Royal St. George Golf Club (Sandwich, Eng.). Republican. Episcopalian. Address: PO Box 818 Victor MT 59875-0818

MERRICK, NICHOLAS GREGORY, photographer; b. Detroit, Apr. 11, 1954; s. Thano and Esther (Lambros) M.; m. Shaun Gilmore, Feb. 27, 1982; children: Athan Gilmore, Benjamin Gilmore, Cole Gilmore. BFA, U. Mich., 1976; MFA, Sch. Art Inst. of Chgo., 1980. Adj. faculty Triton Coll., Riverwoods, Ill., 1977-78; asst. photographer Hedrich-Blessing, Chgo., 1977-79, photographer, 1979-84, ptnr. and prin., 1984—; workshop instr. Santa Fe (N.Mex.) Photo Workshops, 1993; lectr. on photography, 1980—; photograph for archaeol. expdn., Cyrene, Libya, 1973-75, 78-79; photography illustrated various pubs. including Architecture, Archtl. Lighting, Archtl. Record, Chgo. Arch. Ann., Country Home, Designer, Interiors, Interior Design, Iowa Architect, Nikkei Architect, Perspective, Progressive Architecture, Texas Architect, Victoria, Inland Arch., El Croquis, Corporate Design, Corporate Design and Realty, others. One man shows of photographs include Shade Gallery, Lansing, Mich., 1976, The Studio Gallery, Kirkland, Fine Arts Ctr., Decatur, Ill., 1982, Photographer's Gallery, Tarrant C.C., Dallas, 1984, Sill Gallery; group shows include Ypsilanti, Mich., 1976, N.A.M.E. Gallery, Chgo., 1976, Art Inst. Chgo., 1977, 83, Ctr. for Creative Studies, Detroit, 1978, Gilbert Gallery, Chgo., 1980, The Studio, San Francisco, 1980, others. Adj. mem. Galisteo (N.Mex.) Vol. Fire and Rescue Dept., 1992—. Home: Hedrich-Blessing HC 75 Box 118 Galisteo NM 87540-9752

MERRILL, FRANK HARRISON, data processing executive, consultant; b. Pitts., June 20, 1953; s. Edgar Frank and Harriet Margaret (Gallagher) M.; m. Rita Alice Mae Murray, May 27, 1977; 1 child, Laura Dawn. BSMetE, Colo. Sch. Mines., 1971-76; M of Computer Info. Systems, U. Denver, 1988. Cert. sys. profl., computer programmer; cert. PICK profl.; cert. computer profl. Metall. engr. Inspiration Copper Co., Miami, Ariz., 1979-80, Cominco Am., Inc., Bixby, Mo., 1980-81; programmer, analyst M.L. Foss, Inc., Denver, 1981-83, Titsch & Assocs., Denver, 1983; data processing mgr. PBI/BAXA, Inc., Denver, 1983-86; owner (systems cons.) Dynamic Solutions, Denver, 1986—; cons. in field, Denver, 1985—; instr. continuing edn. User's Group, Denver, 1985—; instr. computer info. sys. U. Denver, 1990—; mem. grad. computer info. sys. faculty Colo. campus, U. Phoenix, 1991-94; bd. dirs. Inst. for Cert. of Computer Profls. Adult leader Boy Scouts Am., Denver and Globe, Ariz., 1973-88; mem. Marriage Encounter Interfaith Bd., Denver, 1985-89, chair, 1988-89; mem. coun. Rocky Mtn. Aldersgate Marriage Encounter, 1986—, exec. couple, 1990-94; mem. Volksmarch Steering Com. Lakewood on Parade, 1990—; mem. St. Andrew's Soc. Colo.; nominating com. Free Meth. Ch., 1989-92, ch. bd. property and fin., 1992-94. 2d lt. U.S. Army, 1977-79. Named to PICK Industry Accreditation Coun., 1990; recipient God and Svc. award Free Meth. Ch., 1984, Recognition award Assn. for Systems Mgmt., 1991, Merit award, 1993. Mem. SAR, Assn. Sys. Mgmt. (profl. sec. Mile-Hi chpt. 1989-91, v.p. 1991-92, pres. 1992-93, liaison com. mem. internat. cert. 1993—, mem. divsn. 17 coun. 1994—, vice chmn. divsn. 17 coun. 1995—, Recognition award 1991, Merit award 1993), Colo. Pick Users' Group (edn. chmn. 1984—, chmn. internat. cert. com. 1994—), Info. Sys. Security Assn., Scottish-Am. Mil. Soc. (charter, post contbr. Post 100 Colo.), Falcon Wanderers Club, Cheyenne High Plains Wanderers Club. Republican. Mem. Free Methodist Ch.

MERRILL, ROBERT EDWARD, special machinery manufacturing company executive; b. Columbus, Ohio, Oct. 21, 1933; m. Donna Rae Bernstein, Mar. 19, 1967; children: Robert Edward, Aaron Jay, Jonathan Cyrus, Raquel Naomi. MBA, Pepperdine U. Pres. PSM Corp., San Jose, Calif., 1974—. Author: The ABC's of Small Business Money. Served with AUS, 1950-51; Korea. Patentee in pneumatic applications for indsl. press machinery. Home: 858 Fieldwood Ct San Jose CA 95120-3311

MERRILL, RONALD THOMAS, geophysicist, educator; b. Detroit, Feb. 5, 1938; s. Robert Able and Freda (Havens) M.; m. Nancy Joann O'Byrne, Sept. 1, 1962; children: Craig Elliot, Scott Curtis. BS in Math., U. Mich., 1959, MS in Math., 1961; PhD in Geophysics, U. Calif., Berkeley, 1967. Asst. prof. oceanography U. Wash., Seattle, 1967-72, assoc. prof. geophysics and oceanography, 1972-77, prof. geophysics and geol. sci., 1977—, chmn. dept. geophysics, 1985-92. Author: (with M.W. McElhinny) The Earth's Magnetic Field, 1984; contbr. numerous articles to profl. jours. Recipient numerous rsch. grants from NSF, other founds. Fellow Am. Geophys. Union (pres. geomagnetism and paleomagnetism sect. 1988-90); mem. AAAS, Soc. Geomagnetism (Japan). Office: U Wash Dept Geophysics AK-50 Seattle WA 98195

MERRILL, STEVEN WILLIAM, research and development executive; b. Oakland, Calif., Aug. 6, 1944; s. David Howard and Etha Nadine (Wright) M. BA in Chemistry, Calif. State U., 1986. Lic. pyrotechnic, Calif. Apprentice Borgman Sales Co., San Leandro, Calif., 1960-64; assembler Calif. Fireworks Display, Rialto, Calif., 1970; pyrotechnician Hand Chem. Industries, Milton, Ont., Can., 1972-74; dir. R&D Pyrospectaculars, Rialto, 1988—; owner, dir. Merrill Prodns. Ordnance, Crestline; experimenter in field, 1958—; chief chemist Baron Blakesly Solvents, Newark, Calif., 1987-88; court expert San Francisco Superior Ct., 1971, Victorville (Calif.) Superior Ct. Counselor Xanthos, Inc., Alameda, Calif., 1970. Mem. AAAS, Am. Chem. Soc., Am. Stats. Assn., Am. Bd. Forensic Examiners, Internat. Platform Assn. Home: PO Box 676 Crestline CA 92325-0676 Office: Merrill Prodns PO Box 3327 Crestline Rd Crestline CA 92325

MERRILL, THOMAS M., produce executive; b. 1929. With Merrill Farms, 1945—, now pres., CEO. Office: Merrill Farms 1067 Merrill St Salinas CA 93901*

MERRILL, THOMAS ST. JOHN, medical photographer; b. Jersey City, N.J., Feb. 21, 1946; s. Willard St. John and Frances Minnie (Havlieck) M.; m. Marie Knoetig, Mar. 19, 1967; children: Monica Marie-Rose, Michelle St. John. Student, Fairleigh Dickenson U., 1963-64, Germain Sch. Photography, 1967-68; AA, Saddleback Coll., 1990; student, Mt. San Antonio Coll., 1990-92; BA in bus. adminstrn., U. Phoenix, 1995. Cert. retinal angiographer. Photography asst. VA Hosp., N.Y.C., 1968; dept. head, photography Manhatten Eye, Ear and Throat Hosp., N.Y.C., 1968-69; med. photographer Don Allen Studio, N.Y.C., 1969-71; sr. ophthalmic photographer Mt. Sinai Sch. Medicine, N.Y.C., 1971-76; ophthalmic photographer U. Calif., Irvine, 1976-86; photographer Allergan Inc., Irvine, 1986-89; owner, pres. The Med. Image, Chino, Calif., 1983—; sr. med. photographer St. Joseph Med. Ctr., Burbank, Calif., 1991—. Mem. Luth. Hour Rose Float Com., Pasadena, Calif. With U.S. Army, 1964-67, Vietnam. Mem. Biol. Photographic Assn. (fellow 1991, chmn. so. Calif. chpt. 1990-92), Ophthalmic Photographers' Soc., VFW (life), AMVETS. Home: 4395 Goldenrod Ct Chino CA 91710-1618 Office: St Joseph Med Ctr 501 S Buena Vista St Burbank CA 91505-4809

MERRILL, WILLIAM DEAN, architect, medical facility planning consultant; b. Portland, Oreg., June 1, 1915; s. Charles O. and Grace (Ruhl) M.; m. Bernice E. Wickham, Apr. 19, 1943; 1 child, Sue Ann Merrill Boardman. Student in Fine Arts and Forestry, Oreg. State U., 1936-38; student in Architecture, U. Oreg., 1939-42. Registered architect, Oreg., Calif. Prin. W.D. Merrill, Architect, Portland, 1959-64; architect, ptnr. Bissell & Merrill, Architects, Stockton, Calif., 1964-68; architect Kaiser Found. Hosps. design and constrn., 1968-81; pvt. practice hosp. design and constrn., residential design and constrn., Bay Area, 1981-91; hosp. constrn. insp. State of Calif., 1984-93. Served as lt. (j.g.) USN, 1942-44, PTO. Mem. AIA (emeritus). Republican. Address: 14349 SE Sieben Pky Clackamas OR 97015-6319

MERRILL, WILLIAM DICKEY, architect; b. Honolulu, Mar. 21, 1909; s. Arthur Merton and Grace (Dickey) M.; m. Evelyn Gregory Selfridge, Oct. 23, 1936; children: Elizabeth, Thomas Selfridge. BA, U. Calif., Berkeley, 1930; MArch, Harvard U., 1932; PhD, Edinburgh U., 1974. Staff achitect Am. Schs. Oriental Rsch., Jerusalem, 1933-35; assoc. C.W. Dickey, architect, Honolulu, 1936-42; ptnr. Merrill, Simms and Roehrig, architects, Honolulu, 1942-60; pres. Merrill, Roehrig, Onodera and Kinder, Inc., Honolulu, 1960-65; cons. architect Honolulu, 1965-81; mem. affiliate grad. faculty U. Hawaii, 1971. Prin. works include Neill Blaisdell Concert Hall, campus Mid-Pacific Inst., campus Kamehameha Elem. Sch., class rm. bldg. Kamehameha Girls Sch., Foremost Dairies, TH-3 Hawaii Housing Authority, other comml., indsl., ednl. and mil. structures, hosps. in Hawaii. Mem. com. mgmt. Armed Svcs. YMCA, 1952-69; bd. dirs. Hawaiian Humane Soc., 1954-65, Hawaiian Mission Children's Soc., 1945-64. Fellow AIA (past pres. Hawaii, mem. emeritus). Home: 8545 Carmel Valley Rd Carmel CA 93923-9556

MERRIN, JAMES STEVEN, internist; b. La Crosse, Wis., Mar. 30, 1954; s. Irving and Verna Mae (Borovoy) M.; m. Theresa Suzanne Drapkin, Feb. 23, 1992; 1 child, Abigail Rose. BS, U. Wis., 1976, MS, 1979; MD, La. State U., 1989. Diplomate Am. Bd. Internal Medicine. Resident Cedars Sinai Med. Ctr., L.A., 1989-93; physician Briarwood Ind. Physicians Assn., Thousand Oaks, Calif., 1993—. Eagle Scout, 1969. Named Chancellor's scholar U. Wis., 1972, Mary Shine Peterson scholar in Biochemistry, U. Wis., 1975; recipient Rsch. scholarship Epilepsy Found. of Am., 1987. Mem. AMA, Am. Coll. Physicians, Sierra Club. Office: Briarwood IPA 299 W Hillcrest Dr Thousand Oaks CA 91360-4264

MERRITT, ALAN EDWIN, environmental professional; b. Denison, Tex., Sept. 22, 1952; s. Edwin Herald and Dorothy May (Dooley) M.; m. Cheryl Fields, June 6, 1980. BS, East Tex. State U., 1975, MS, 1980; MBA, Amber U., 1986. Chemist, biologist North Tex. Mcpl. Water Dist., Wylie, 1980-85; field and quality control chemist Laidlaw Environ. Svcs., Clearwater, Fla., 1989-91; environ. scientist State of Idaho Idaho Nat. Engring. Lab. Oversight Program, Idaho Falls, 1991—. Field support vol. NRA, Idaho Falls, 1992—; pres. libr. bd. Sachse (Tex.) Pub. Libr., 1984-85. Served with U.S. Army, 1975-77. Mem. Sigma Xi (assoc.). Republican. Office: State of Idaho INEL Oversight Program 900 N Skyline Dr Idaho Falls ID 83402-1718

MERRITT, BRUCE GORDON, lawyer; b. Iowa City, Iowa, Oct 4, 1946; s. William Olney and Gretchen Louise (Kuever) M.; m. Valerie Sue Jorgensen, Dec. 28, 1969; children: Benjamin Carlyle, Alicia Marie. AB magna cum laude, Occidental Coll., 1968; JD magna cum laude, Harvard U., 1972. Bar: Calif. 1973. Assoc. Markbys, London, 1972-73; assoc. Nossaman, Krueger & Marsh, L.A., 1973-79, ptnr., 1979-81; asst. U.S. atty., L.A., 1981-85; ptnr. Hennigan & Mercer, L.A., 1986-88; ptnr. Debevoise & Plimpton, L.A., 1989—. Fellow Am. Coll. Trial Lawyers; mem. Calif. State Bar Assn. (exec. com. litigation sect. 1992—), L.A. County Bar Assn. (del. state bar conf. 1984-86), Phi Beta Kappa. Office: Debevoise & Plimpton 601 S Figueroa St Ste 3700 Los Angeles CA 90017-5742

MERSEL, MARJORIE KATHRYN PEDERSEN, lawyer; b. Manila, Utah, June 17, 1923; d. Leo Henry and Kathryn Anna (Reed) Pedersen; AB, U. Calif., 1948; LLB, U. San Francisco, 1948; m. Jules Mersel, Apr. 12, 1950; 1 son, Jonathan. Admitted to D.C. bar, 1952, Calif. bar, 1955; Marjorie Kathryn Pedersen Mersel, atty., Beverly Hills, Calif., 1961-71; staff counsel Dept. Real Estate State of Calif., Los Angeles, 1971—. Active L.A.-Guangzhou Sister City. Mem. Beverly Hills Bar Assn., L.A. County Bar Assn., Trial Lawyers Assn., So. Calif. Women Lawyers Assn. (treas. 1962-63), L.A.-Guangzhou Sister City Assn., Beverly Hills C. of C., World Affairs Coun., Current Affairs Forum, L.A. Athletic Club, Sierra Club. Home: 13007 Hartsook St Sherman Oaks CA 91423-1616 Office: Dept Real Estate 107 S Broadway Los Angeles CA 90012

MERSENSTEIN, GERALD BURTON, pediatrician, educator; b. Pitts., Feb. 14, 1941; s. Morris and Sarah (Shrinsky) M.; m. Barnetta Maryn, Aug. 21, 1960. BS, U. Pitts., 1962, MD, 1966. Diplomate Am. Bd. Pediatrics; lic. physician, Calif., Colo. Intern then resident Fitzsimons Gen. Hosp., Aurora, Colo., 1966-69; fellow Children's Hosp. San Francisco, 1969-71; program dir. neonatal-perinatal fellowship Fitzsimons Army Med. Ctr., Aurora, Colo., 1975-86, chmn. dept. pediatrics, 1979-86; dir. Lubchenco Perinatal Ctrs. U. Colo./Children's Hosp., Denver, 1986—, acting chmn. dept. pediatrics, 1988-90, dir. child health assoc. program, physician asst., 1994—. Co-editor: Handbook of Neonatal Intensive Care, 1985, 2d edit., 1989, 3d edit., 1993, Handbook of Pediatrics, 16th edit., 1991, 17th edit., 1994. Bd. dirs. Nat. Cert. Corp., Chgo., 1988—; mem. steering com. March of Dimes, White Plains, N.Y., 1990-93. Col. U.S. Army, 1966-86. Named Outstanding Man of Yr., Denver Jaycees, 1974. Fellow Am. Acad. Pediatrics (chair com. fetus and newborn 1989-93); mem. Am. Pediatric Soc., Assn. Pediatric Program Dirs. (exec. com., councilor), Alpha Omega Alpha. Democrat. Jewish. Office: U colo Health Scis Ctr C219 Denver CO 80262

MERTA, PAUL JAMES, cartoonist, photographer, engineer, restauranteur, real estate developer; b. Bakersfield, Calif., July 16, 1939; s. Stanley Franklin and Mary Ann (Herman) M.; AA, Bakersfield Jr. Coll., 1962; BS in Engring., San Jose State Coll., 1962. Cartoonist nat. mags., 1959—; civilian electronics engr. Air Force/Missiles, San Bernardino, Calif., 1962-65; electronics countermeasures engr., acquisition program mgr. Air Logistics Command, Sacramento, 1965-90; ret.; TV film, video animator, producer, owner Merge Films, 1965—; photographer, owner The Photo Poster Factory, Sacramento, 1971—; owner restaurant La Rosa Blanca, Sacramento, 1979-91; ptnr. Kolinski and Merta Hawaiian Estates, 1981—; polit. cartoonist Calif. Jour., 1958-59, Sacramento Union Newspaper, 1974-94, Sacramento Legal Jour., 1979. Home: 4831 Myrtle Ave Apt 8 Sacramento CA 95841-3621 Office: 1005 12th St Sacramento CA 95814-3920

MERTON, EGON STEPHEN, English literature educator; b. N.Y.C., Nov. 26, 1912; s. Leslie Rudolph and Fanny (Schor) M. BA, Columbia U., 1933, MA, 1935, PhD, 1949. Instr. Colo. Coll., Colorado Springs, Colo., 1939-42; asst. prof. Coll. of William and Mary, Williamsburg, Va., 1943-46; instr. Cornell U., Ithaca, N.Y., 1946-50; prof. CUNY, 1950-75; prof., chmn. English dept. U. Cairo, 1957-58; prof. emeritus CUNY, 1975—. Author: Science and Imagination, 1949, reprint 1969, Skyscrapers and Pyramids, 1965, Mark Rutherford, 1967; contbr. articles to profl. jours. Grantee U.S. govt., Taiwan, 1965.

MERWIN, EDWIN PRESTON, educator; b. Revere, Mass., Oct. 13, 1927; s. George Preston and Edith Charlotte (Miller) M.; m. Marylynn Joy Bicknell, Nov. 3, 1979; 1 son by previous marriage, Ralph Edwin; stepchildren: Charles John Burns, Patrick Edward Burns, Stephen Allen Burns. BS, U. So.Calif., 1955, postgrad. Law Sch., 1955-57; postgrad., San Fernando Valley State Coll., 1965-66; M in Pub. Health (USPHS fellow), U. Calif. at Berkeley, 1970; PhD, Brantridge Forest (Eng.), 1971. Tng. officer Camarillo (Calif.) State Hosp., 1961-66; asst. coord. Mental Retardation Programs, State of Cal., Sacramento, 1966-67; project dir. Calif. Council Retarded Children, Sacramento, 1967-69; asst. dir. Golden Empire Comprehensive Health Coun., Sacramento, 1970-76, health care cons., 1976-77; gen. ptnr. EDRA Assocs., 1976—; cons. Calif. Dept. Health, 1977-78; cons. Calif. Office Statewide Health Planning and Devel., 1978-79; chief Health Professions Career Opportunity Program State of Calif., Sacramento, 1979-81; chief Health Personnel Info. and Analysis Sect., Office of Statewide Health Planning and Devel., 1981-82, asst. div. chief div. Health Professions Devel., 1982-84, asst. dep. dir., 1984-86; project dir. Alzheimers Disease Insts., Calif., 1986-87; chief Demonstration Project Sect. div. Health Projects and Analysis, 1987-89, chief Policy Analysis and Professsions Devel. Sect., 1989-93; tchr. Ventura (Calif.) Coll., 1962-66, Merritt Coll., Oakland, Calif., 1969; sr. adj. prof. Golden Gate U., 1976—; lectr. continuing edn. program U. Calif. at Berkeley; instr. Los Rios C.C. Dist., 1982—; mem. Task Force for New Health Care Sys. in Macedonia; mem. adv. com. Health Faculty, Golden Gate U., 1995—; cons.. NIMH, HEW, Calif. Assn. Health Facilities. Mem. Health Adv. Council San Juan Sch. Dist., 1972-73; treas. Calif. Camping and Recreation Council, 1972-73. Bd. dirs. Sacramento Rehab. Facility, 1970-86, v.p., 1973-76, bd dirs. Sacramento Vocational Svcs., 1986-93. Recipient Pres.'s award Golden Gate U., 1982. Mem. Am. Assn. Mental Deficiency, Calif. Pub. Health Assn., Sacramento Mental Health Assn., Sacramento Assn. Retarded (life mem., dir., svc. award 1984), Nat. Assn. for Retarded Children, DAV (life), Am. Legion, Marines Meml. Assn. (life), AAAS, SCAPA Praetors U. So. Calif., Miles Merwin Assn. Founder, editor: T. Patrick Heck Meml. Case Series, 1982; co-author textbook: (with Dr. Fred Heck) Written Case Analysis, 1982; founder, cons. Internat. U. Am., 1995—; contbr. articles to profl. lit. Home: 8008 Archer Ave Fair Oaks CA 95628-5907 Office: Golden Gate U 3620 Northgate Blvd Ste 100 Sacramento CA 95834-1619

MESAROS, KENNETH LEE, rancher, state senator; b. Great Falls, Mont., June 17, 1950; s. Albert and Hilda (Heiman) M.; m. Rebecca Lynn Mesaros; children: Mathew, Michael, Scot, Kimberly. BS in Agr. Edn., Mont. State U., 1973. Owner, operator Mesaros Ranch, Cascade, Mont., 1969—; senator State of Mont., Helena, 1992—; dir. Am. Inst. Cooperatives, Mpls., 1978; chmn., dir. Foothill Livestock Assn., Cascade County, Mont., 1982-88, Equity Co-op Assn., Ulm, Mont., 1977-84. Sch. bd. chmn. Sch. Dist. # 95, Deep Creek, Mont., 1986-90. Staff sgt. Mont. Air N.G., 1969-75. Mem. Mont. Stockgrowers Assn. (dir. 1990-94), Cascade Lions Club, Great Falls Elks Club. Republican. Roman Catholic.

MESCHKOW, JORDAN MARK, lawyer; b. Bklyn., Mar. 25, 1957; s. Gerald Meschkow and Florence Y. (Katz) Silverman; m. Susan G. Scher, Aug. 10, 1980; children: Sasha Hayley, Alisha Sadie. BS in Biology, SUNY, Stony Brook, 1979; JD, IIT, 1982. Bar: Ariz.z 1982, Fla. 1983; registered U.S. Patent and Trademark Office 1983. Assoc. James F. Duffy, Patent Atty., Phoenix, Ariz., 1982; ptnr. Duffy & Meschkow, Phoenix, 1983-84; sole practice Phoenix, 1984-92; sr. ptnr. Meschkow & Gresham, Plc., Phoenix, 1992—; frequent talk radio guest and spkr. at seminars on patent, trademark and copyright law. Contbr. article series to profl. jours.; patentee in field. Mem. Am. Intellectual Property Law Assn., State Bar Ariz. (intellectual property sect. 1982—), Maricopa County Bar Assn. Office: 320 E McDowell Rd Ste 110 Phoenix AZ 85004-4515

MESERVE, BRUCE ELWYN, mathematics educator; b. Portland, Maine, Feb. 2, 1917; s. Walter Joseph and Bessie Adelia (Bailey) M.; m. Gertrude Morey Holland, June 7, 1941 (div. 1961); children: Arthur, Virginia, Donald; m. Dorothy Spencer Tucker, Aug. 5, 1961. AB, Bates Coll., Lewiston, Maine, 1938; MA, Duke U., 1941, PhD, 1947. Tchr. Moses Brown Sch., Providence, R.I., 1938-41; from instr. to asst. prof. U. Ill., Champaign, 1946-54; from assoc. prof. to prof., chmn. math. dept. Montclair State Coll., Upper Montclair, N.J., 1954-64; prof. U. Vt., Burlington, 1964-83, prof. emeritus, 1983—; co-chmn. Internat. Study Group on Rels. Between History and Pedagogy of Math., 1980-84. Author: Fundamental Concepts of Algebra, 1951, Fundamental Concepts of Geometry, 1955, and others; contbr. articles to profl. jours.; editor several books. Moderator Town of Fairfax, Vt., 1976-84. Fellow AAAS; mem. Am. Math. Soc., Math. Assn. Am., Nat. Coun. Tchrs. Math. (pres. 1964-66, bd. dirs. 1958-67), Phi Beta Kappa, Sigma Pi Sigma. Home: 521 S Paseo Del Cobre Green Valley AZ 85614-2321

MESINA, DENNIS G., lawyer; b. Davao City, The Philippines, Nov. 28, 1953; came to U.S., 1984; s. Fermin R. and Gloria (Francisco) M. AB in Philosophy cum laude, U. Philippines, Quezon City, 1976, LLB, 1981; LLM, U. Pa., 1985. Bar: Philippines 1982, Calif. 1988. Lectr. philosophy U. Philippnes, Quezon City, 1980-82; assoc. Siguion Reyna, Montecillo and Ongsiako, Philippines, 1982-84, 86-87, Popella, Allard, McCowan & Jones, San Jose, Calif., 1988-89, Thoits, Hershberger et al, Palo Alto, Calif., 1989-91; pvt. practice San Francisco, 1991—; v.p. Filipino Bar Assn. No. Calif., San Francisco, 1990-91, pres., 1991-92. Founder, steering com. mem. Philippine Environ. & Support Network, Burlingame, Calif., 1990—; v.p. Fil-Am. Coun. of San Francisco, 1992-94. Mem. Fil-Am. C. of C., of San Francisco, Yerba Buena Ctr. for Arts, San Francisco Mus. Modern Art, Sierra Club. Office: 580 California St Fl 16 San Francisco CA 94104-1000

MESKIN, ESTELLE ROSE, college/vocational counselor, educational consultant; b. Detroit, Apr. 16, 1939; d. Julius and Helen (Krolik) R.; m. Larry Meskin, Aug. 23, 1959; children: Scott, Sarah. BS, U. Minn., 1974; MA, U. Colo., 1986. Nat. cert. counselor; registered dental hygienist. Pvt. practice dental hygiene Detroit, 1960-75; instr. dental hygiene NormanDale C.C., Mpls., 1970-74; instr. health occupations Mpls. Area Vo/Tec-Mpls. Pub. Schs., 1975-79; health educator Pilot City Health Ctr./Mpls. Pub. Schs., 1979-81; career resource specialist Arapahoe-Douglas Area Vocat., Littleton, Colo., 1981-90; edn. cons. Santa Fe C.C., 1990-91; vocat. counselor Arapahoe-Douglas Area Vocat. Sch., Littleton, 1989-92; health educator Denver Sch.-Based Health Ctrs., 1992—; ednl. cons. U.S. West Pathways Program, Denver, 1987-90; health edn. adv. bd. Denver Pub. Schs., 1992-94; scholarship com. Pres.'s Leadership Class, U. Colo., Boulder, 1990—. Bd. dirs. Jewish Family and Childrens Svc., Denver, 1994—. Recipient Health Edn. grant March of Dimes, 1992-94; recipient Award of Excellence for Spl. Programs, Colo. C.C. and Occupational Edn., 1986, Vocat. Edn. Policy fellow, 1989, 90, Women's Leadership Inst. fellow, 1990-91. Mem. Colo. Career Devel. Assn. (pres.-elect 1991-92, pres. 1992-93), Colo. Counseling Assn., Am. Counseling Assn., Nat. Career Devel. Assn., Colo. Vocat. Assn., Am. Vocat. Assn., Nat. Assn. Coll. Admissions Counselors. Jewish.

MESLOH, WARREN HENRY, civil and environmental engineer; b. Deshler, Nebr., Mar. 17, 1949; s. Herbert Frederick and Elna Florence (Petersen) M.; m. Barbara Jane Anderson, Sept. 7, 1969; children: Christopher Troy, Courtney James. BS, U. Kans., 1975; postgrad., Kans. State U., 1976-77. Registered profl. engr. Colo., Kans., Nebr. Project mgr. Wilson & Co. Engrs., Salina, Kans., 1975-80, process design dir., 1980-82; engring. dir. Taranto, Stanton & Tagge, Fort Collins, Colo., 1982-85; pres. The Engring. Co., Fort Collins, Colo., 1985—; mem. civil engring. adv. bd. Kans. U., Lawrence, 1982—. Contbg. author (book) Pumping Station Design, 1989, (water pollution control manual) Manual of Practice No. OM-2, 1991; contbr. articles to profl. jours. Cub master Boy Scouts Am., Salina, 1980-81; active Luth. Ch., 1982—; vol. Paralyzed Vets. Orgn., Fort Collins, 1985—; pres. Foothills Green Pool Assn., Fort Collins, 1987-88. Sgt. U.S. Army, 1971-73, Germany. Named Outstanding Engr.-In-Tng. NSPE, 1978. Mem. Am. Pub. Works Assn., Am. Water Works Assn., Water Pollution Control Fedn., Fort Collins Country Club. Republican. Office: The Engring Co 2310 E Prospect Rd Fort Collins CO 80525

MESQUITA, ROSALYN ANAYA, artist, educator; b. Belen, N.Mex., Aug. 21, 1935; d. Trinidad Jose and Margaret Oliva (Aragon) Anaya; m. Theodore Richard Mesquita, Jan. 14, 1956 (div.); children: John, Richard, Larry, Thresa. BA, Calif. State U., Northridge, 1974; MFA, U. Calif., Irvine, 1976. Cert. community coll. credential, Calif. Curator State of N.Mex., Santa Fe, 1968-72; lectr. L.A. Hist. Soc., 1978—; prof. Pasadena (Calif.) City Coll., 1981—; lectr. Non-Govtl. Orgn. UN Planning Com., Nairobi, Kenya, and N.Y., 1985—; curator, participant Am. Women in Art, UN World Conf., Nairobi, 1985; curator Mus. Natural History, L.A., 1978; mem. planning com. worldwide women's conf. Global Focus, Beijing, 1995. Lectr. L.A. BiCentennial and 1985 Olympic Com., 1976-84; mem. Santa Monica Art Commn., 1991—. Recipient Col.-Aide-De Camp award Gov. David F. Cargo, 1972; Ford Found. fellow, 1975. Mem. Coll. Art Assn., Nat. Women's Caucus for Art (affirmative action officer 1980-83, honorarium 1983), Hispanic Faculty Assn. (treas. 1980-90), Assn. Latin Am. Artists (pres. 1982-90), L.A. La Raza Faculty Assn. (sec. 1979-85, v.p. 1988-89). Democrat. Roman Catholic. Home: 13426 Vanowen St Van Nuys CA 91405-4329 Office: Pasadena City Coll 1370 Colorado Blvd Pasadena CA 90405-1628

MESROBIAN, EDMOND, computer scientist, researcher; b. Constansa, Romania, May 9, 1960; came to U.S., 1966; s. Ovanes and Aneta (Moshigian) M. BS in Computer Sci., UCLA, 1982, MS in Computer Sci;., 1986, PhD in Computer Sci., 1992. Tchg. assoc. in computer sci. UCLA, 1983-87, rsch assoc. in computer sci., 1987-90, prin. devel. engr., 1993—; sr. scientist Perceptronics, Inc., Woodland Hills, Calif., 1990-92. Contbr. articles to profl. jours. Mem. IEEE, Assn. Computing Machinery, Optical Soc. Am., Soc. for Computer Simulation. Home: 1014 N Alexandria Ave Los Angeles CA 90029 Office: UCLA Dept Computer Sci 4810 Boelter Hall Los Angeles CA 90024

MESSENGER, GEORGE CLEMENT, engineering consultant; b. Bellows Falls, Vt., July 20, 1930; s. Clement George and Ethel Mildred (Farrar) M.; m. Priscilla Betty Norris, June 19, 1954; children: Michael Todd, Steven Barry, Bonnie Lynn. BS in Physics, Worcester Poly. U., 1951; MSEE, U. Pa., 1957; PhD in Engring., Calif. Coast U., 1986. Rsch. scientist Philco Corp., Phila., 1951-59; engring. mgr. Hughes Semicondr., Newport Beach, Calif., 1959-61; div. mgr. Transitron Corp., Wakefield, Mass., 1961-63; staff scientist Northrop Corp., Hawthorne, Calif., 1963-68; cons. engr., Las Vegas, Nev., 1968—; lectr. UCLA, 1969-75; v.p., dir. Am. Inst. Fin., Grafton, Mass., 1970-78; gen. ptnr. Dargon Fund, Anaheim, Calif., 1983—; v.p., tech. dir. Messenger and Assoc., 1987—, registered investment adviser, 1989—. Co-author: The Effects of Radiation on Electronic Systems, 1986; contbg. author: Fundamentals of Nuclear Hardening, 1972; contbr. numerous articles to tech. jours.; patentee microwave diode, hardened semicondrs. Recipient Naval Rsch. Lab. Alan Berman award, 1982; Best Paper award HEART Conf., 1983, Spl. Merit award HEART Conf., 1983; fellow IEEE, 1976, annual merit award 1986, Pete Haas award. HEART Conf., 1992. Mem. Rsch. Soc. Am., Am. Phys. Soc. Congregationalist. Home and Office: 3111 Bel Air Dr Apt 7F Las Vegas NV 89109-1510

MESSENGER, RON J., health facility administrator; b. 1944. MBA, U. So. Calif., 1968. Engr. CASH, L.A., 1968-73; v.p. Nat. Med. Enterprises, Santa Monica, Calif., 1973-84; pres. L.A. Cmty. Hosp., 1984—, Hollywood (Calif.) Cmty. Hosp., 1984—; pres., sec., CEO Paracelsus Healthcare Corp., Pasadena, Calif., 1984—. Office: Paracelsus Healthcare 155 N Lake Ave Ste 1100 Pasadena CA 91101-1857

MESSERLI, DOUGLAS, author, publisher; b. Waterloo, Iowa, May 30, 1947; s. John H. and Lorna (Caspers) M.; companion Howard N. Fox. BA in English, U. Md., 1972, MA in English, 1974, PhD in English, 1979. Admissions coord. U. Wis., Madison, 1967-69; asst. head protocol Columbia U., N.Y.C., 1969-70; grad. asst., tchr., coord. interns U. Md., 1973-77; pub. Sun & Moon Press, L.A., 1976—; prof. dept. English Temple U., Phila., 1979-84; dir. The Contemporary Arts Ednl. Project, Inc., 1983—; part-time faculty mem. Calif. Inst. Tech., Pasadena, 1987-89, Otis-Parsons Sch. Arts, L.A., 1989. Author: (poetry) Dinner on the Lawn, 1979, Some Distance, 1982, River to Rivet: A Manifesto, 1985, River to Rivet: A Poetic Trilogy, 1985, Maxims from My Mother's Milk/Hymns to Him: A Dialogue, 1988, An Apple, A Day, 1993, (drama) Silence All Round Marked: An Historical Play in Hysteria Writ, 1992, (as Kier Peters) The Confirmation, 1993, (fiction/film/poetry) Along Without: A Fiction in Film for Poetry, 1993; editor: From the Other Side of the Century: A New American Poetry 1960-1990, 1994, The Sun & Mood Guide to Eating Through Literature and Art, 1994, 50: A Celebration of Sun & Moon Classics, 1995. Recipient Carey-Thomas award Pubs. Weekly, 1987, Harry Ford Editor's award Nat. Poetry Series, 1994. Mem. MLA, Am. Booksellers Assn. Office: Sun & Moon Press 6026 Wilshire Blvd Los Angeles CA 90036

MESSINGER, J. HENRY, lawyer; b. N.Y.C., Sept. 7, 1944; s. Benjamin and Edna (Balser) M.; m. Karen Gilbert D'Abo, Feb. 5, 1977 (div.); 1 son, Alan Toby. B.A., Union Coll., 1965; J.D., NYU, 1968, M.A., 1969. Bar: N.Y. 1968, N.Mex. 1973, U.S. Tax Ct. 1973. Sole practice, Woodstock, N.Y., 1970-72; assoc. Stephen Natelson, Esq., Taos, 1972-73; ptnr. Natelson & Messinger, Taos, 1974-75; sole practice, Taos, 1976-94, Albuquerque, 1994—. Bd. dirs. Taos Sch. Music, 1982—; bd. dirs. R.C. Gorman Found., 1986—, Taos Valley Sch., 1979-82, pres. 1980-81. Mem. ABA, Am. Polit. Sci. Assn., Law and Soc. Assn. Office: 809 Branding Iron St SE Albuquerque NM 87123-4207

MESTAD, ORVILLE LAVERNE, bank executive; b. Decorah, Iowa, Mar. 22, 1923; s. Clarence Benjamen and Edna Belinda (Larson) M.; m. Shirley Gail Matthews, July 20, 1948; children: Cynthia Mestad Johnson, Ronald Matthew. BS, U. So. Calif., 1949, DDS with honors, 1953. Pvt. practice dentistry Arcadia, Calif., 1953-83; instr. clin. dentistry U. Soc. Calif., Los Angeles, 1953-57; organizer, chmn. Foothill Ind. Bank, Glendora, Calif., 1973—; chmn. Foothill Ind. Bancorp, Glendora, 1986-92. Trustee Foothill Presbyn. Hosp., Glendora, 1972-90, 91—, chmn., 1987-89, 93—; mem. exec. com. Citrus Coll. Found., Glendora, 1982-89. Decorated Bronze Star; named Citizen of Yr., City of Glendora, 1990. Mem. ADA, Arcadia Lions Club, Alpha Tau Epsilon. Republican. Presbyterian. Home: 1144 Indian Springs Dr Glendora CA 91741-2334 Office: Foothill Ind Bancorp 510 S Grand Ave Glendora CA 91741-4207

MESTRIL, RUBEN, biochemist, researcher; b. N.Y.C., Jan. 21, 1951; s. Fernando and Renee (Casanova) M.; m. Ilona Erika Brelewski, Dec. 16, 1984; 1 child, Sebastian. BA in Chemistry summa cum laude, St. Thomas U., 1981; PhD in Biochemistry, U. Miami, Coral Gables, Fla., 1986. Postdoctoral fellow German Cancer Rsch. Ctr., Heidelberg, 1986-88; asst. rsch. biochemist U. Calif., San Diego, 1988-92, asst. adj. prof., 1992—. Reviewer Circulation jour., San Diego, 1991—; contbr. revs., articles to profl. jours., chpts. to books. Grantee NSF, 1980, Am. Heart Assn., 1991, NIH, 1994. Mem. AAAS, Am. Inst. Chemists, Am. Soc. Biochemistry and Molecular Biology, Am. Heart Assn. (basic sci. coun. 1991—), Internat. Soc. Heart Rsch. Democrat. Office: U Calif San Diego Med Ctr 200 W Arbor Dr Bldg 8412 San Diego CA 92103-1911

METCALF, EUGENE MAX, artist, educator; b. Wellington, Kans., Apr. 22, 1927; s. Lloyd Everett Metcalf and Lenore Marietta Ray Dolven; m. Norma Dean Crouch, Aug. 23, 1953; children: Steven Allen, Kevin Eugene, Jill Stephanie Stafford. Art dir. Melrose Outdoor Advt. Co., Hollywood, Calif., 1954-56, L.A. Outdoor Advt. Co., Baldwin Park, Calif., 1956-66; self employed artist, 1966—. Author: Calligraphy Techniques and Uses. Recipient numerous awards in design, for watercolors, others. Mem. Soc. Calligraphers, L.A. Soc. Illustrators. Home: 1006 E Rosewood Ave Orange CA 92666-2832

METCALF, SCOTT, computer company executive. Dir. materials Sun Microsys., Inc.; pres. Dynabook, 1990; v.p. of portable products group Unisys Corp., 1990-91; pres., COO, acting CEO Hal Computer Sys., Inc., 1991—. Office: Hal Computer Systems Inc 1315 Dell Ave Campbell CA 95008-6609*

METCALF, VIRGIL ALONZO, economics educator; b. Branch, Ark., Jan. 4, 1936; s. Wallace Lance and Luella J. (Yancey) M.; m. Janice Ann Maples, July 2, 1958; children: Deborah Ann, Robert Alan. BS in Gen. Agr., U. Ark., 1958, MS in Agrl. Econs., 1960; Diploma in Econs., U. Copenhagen, 1960; PhD in Agrl. Econs., U. Mo., 1964. Asst. prof. U. Mo., Columbia, 1964-65, asst. to chancellor, 1964-69, assoc. prof., 1965-69, prof., exec. asst. to the chancellor, 1969-71; prof. econs., v.p. adminstrn. Ariz. State U., Tempe, 1971-81, prof. Sch. Agribus. and Natural Resources, 1981-88, prof. internat. bus. Coll. of Bus., 1988—; asst. to the chancellor U. Mo., 1964-69, coord. internat. programs and studies, 1965-69, mem. budget com., 1965-71, chmn., co-chmn. several task forces; cons. Ford Found., Bogota, Colombia, 1966-67; mem. negotiating team U.S. Agy. for Internat. Devel., Mauritania, 1982, cons., Cameroon, 1983, agrl. rsch. specialist, India, 1984, agribus. cons., Guatemala, 1987, 88, asst. dir. Reform Coops. Credit Project, El Salvador, 1987-90; co-dir. USIA univ. linkage grant Cath. U., Bolivia, 1984-89; cons. World Vision Internat., Mozambique, 1989. Contbr. numerous articles to profl. jours. Mem. City of Tempe U. Hayden Butte Project Area Com., 1979; bd. commrs. Columbia Redevel. Authority; mem. workable project com. City of Columbia Housing Authority. Econs. officer USAR, 1963, econ. analyst, 1964-66. Fulbright grantee U. Copenhagen, 1959-60, U. Kiril Metodij, Yugoslavia, 1973. Mem. Am. Assn. Agrl. Economists, Soc. for Internat. Devel., Samaritans (chmn. 1976, bd. dirs. 1976, mem. task force of health svc. bd. trustees 1974, health svc. 1974-78, chmn. program subcom. 1975), Kiwanis, Blue Key, Gamma Sigma Delta, Alpha Zeta, Alpha Tau Alpha. Democrat. Home: 1508 W Brooks St Chandler AZ 85224-2645 Office: Ariz State U Tempe AZ 85287

METROPOLIS, NICHOLAS CONSTANTINE, mathematical physicist; b. Chgo., June 11, 1915; s. Constantine Nicholas and Katharine (Ganas) M.; m. Patricia Hendrix, Oct. 15, 1955 (div. 1977); children: Katharine, Penelope, Christopher. BS, U. Chgo., 1936, PhD, 1941. Staff mem. Manhattan Project U. Chgo., 1942, asst. prof., 1946-48, prof., 1957-64; group leader Los Alamos Sci. Lab, Los Alamos, N.Mex., 1943-46, 1948-57, sr. fellow, 1965-85, emeritus, 1985—; cons. nat. labs. U. Ill. at Champaign-Urbana, 1970—; mem. com. for rsch. NSF, Washington, 1974-76; mem. tech. mission UN, Calcutta, India, 1961; mem. US-USSR Exch. State Dept., USSR, 1976; mem. 70th anniversary celebration Internat. Conf. on Quantum, Monte Carlo; J.R. Oppenheimer Meml. Lectr., Los Alamos, 1992; speaker 50th anniversary celebration Los Alamos Nat. Lab., 1993. Editor: J.R. Oppenheimer, 1984, The Los Alamos 40th Anniversary Vol.: New Directions in Physics; editor-author: History of Computing, 1980, Essays in Applied Math., 1976; editor, contbr. MIT publ. Daedalus, 1993; mem. editl. bds. profl. jours., 1970—; contbr. articles to profl. jours. Mem. J.R. Oppenheimer Meml. Com., Los Alamos, 1965—; trustee Santa Fe Inst., 1985-88, bd. advisors, 1988—; sec., bd. dirs. Global Pursuits, Inc., 1986—. U. Chgo. fellow, 1938-41; recipient Computer Pioneer medal IEEE, 1984. Fellow Am. Phys. Soc.; mem. AAAS, Am. Math. Soc., Soc. Indsl. and Applied Math., Am. Acad. Arts and Scis. (contbr. to Daedalus 1992). Home: 71 Loma Vista St Los Alamos NM 87544-3090 Office: Los Alamos Nat Lab Mail Stop B210 Los Alamos NM 87545

METROS, MARY TERESA, librarian; b. Denver, Nov. 10, 1951; d. James and Wilma Frances (Hanson) M. BA in English, Colo. Women's Coll., 1973; MA in Librarianship, U. Denver, 1974. Adult svcs. libr. Englewood (Colo.)

Pub. Libr., 1975-81, adult svcs. mgr., 1983-84; libr. systems cons. Dataphase Systems, Kansas City, Mo., 1981-82; circulation libra. Westminster (Colo.) Pub. Libr. 1983; pub. svcs. supr. Tempe (Ariz.) Pub. Libr., 1984-90, libr. adminstr., 1990—. Mem. ALA, Pub. Libr. Assn., Ariz. Libr. Assn, Libr. Adminstrn. and Mgmt. Assn. Democrat. Home: 11860 E Purdue Ave Scottsdale AZ 85259-5963 Office: Tempe Pub Libr 3500 S Rural Rd Tempe AZ 85282-5405

METSKER, THOMAS CHARLES, map company executive; b. Tacoma, May 24, 1927; s. Charles Thomas and Emily Rose (Fleming) M.; m. Patricia Jeanne Rossiter; children: Mark F., Thad C., Kimberly J., Ty Thomas. BA in Bus., U. Puget Sound, 1951. Pres. Metsker Map Co., Tacoma, 1942—. Del. Wash. state convs. Rep. Party, 1960-70. With USN, 1945-47. Roman Catholic. Home: 3012 N Narrows Dr Unit 6 Tacoma WA 98407-1556 Office: Metsker Map Co 9616 40th Ave SW Tacoma WA 98499-4302

METTLER, LEEMAN, food executive; b. 1936. Produce insp. USDA, Stockton, Calif., 1958-72; field foreman Demont Packing Co., Victor, Calif., 1973-76; with Delta Packing Co. of Lodi (Calif.), 1976—. Office: Delta Packing Co of Lodi 5950 E Kettleman Ln Lodi CA 95240-6410*

METZ, MARY SEAWELL, university dean, retired college president; b. Rockhill, S.C., May 7, 1937; d. Columbus Jackson and Mary (Dunlap) Seawell; m. F. Eugene Metz, Dec. 21, 1957; 1 dau., Mary Eugena. BA summa cum laude in French and English, Furman U., 1958; postgrad., Institut Phonetique, Paris, 1962-63, Sorbonne, Paris, 1962-63; PhD magna cum laude in French, La. State U., 1966; HHD (hon.), Furman U., 1984; LLD (hon.), Chapman Coll., 1985; DLT (hon.), Converse Coll., 1988. Instr. French La. State U., 1965-66, asst. prof., 1966-67, 1968-72, assoc. prof., 1972-76, dir. elem. and intermediate French programs, 1966-74, spl. asst. to chancellor, 1974-75, asst. to chancellor, 1975-76; prof. French Hood Coll., Frederick, Md., 1976-81, provost, dean acad. affairs, 1976-81; pres. Mills Coll., Oakland, Calif., 1981-90; dean of extension U. Calif., Berkeley, 1991—; vis. asst. prof. U. Calif.-Berkeley, 1967-68; mem. commn. on leadership devel. Am. Coun. on Edn., 1981-90, adv. coun. Stanford Rsch. Inst., 1985-90, adv. coun. Grad. Sch. Bus., Stanford U.; assoc. Gannett Ctr. for Media Studies, 1985—; bd. dirs. PG&E, Pacific Telesis, PacTel & PacBell, Union Bank, Longs Drug Stores, S.H. Cowell Found. Author: Reflets du monde francais, 1971, 78, Cahier d'exercices: Reflets du monde francais, 1972, 78, (with Helstrom) Le Francais a decouvrir, 1972, 78, Le Francais a vivre, 1972, 78, Cahier d'exercices: Le Francais a vivre, 1972, 78; standardized tests; mem. editorial bd.: Liberal Edn., 1982—. Trustee Am. Conservatory Theater. NDEA fellow, 1960-62,, 1963-64; Fulbright fellow, 1962-63; Am. Council Edn. fellow, 1974-75. Mem. Western Coll. Assn. (v.p. 1982-84, pres. 1984-86), Assn. Ind. Calif. Colls. and Univs. (exec. com. 1982-90), Nat. Assn. Ind. Colls. and Univs. (govt. rels. adv. coun. 1982-85), So. Conf. Lang. Teaching (chmn. 1976-77), World Affairs Coun. No. Calif. (bd. dirs. 1984-93), Bus.-Higher Edn. Forum, Women's Forum West, Women's Coll. Coalition (exec. com. 1984-88), Phi Kappa Phi, Phi Beta Kappa. Address: PO Box 686 Stinson Beach CA 94970-0686

METZ, RICHARD ALAN, medical administrator; b. N.Y.C., July 23, 1949; s. Robert J. and Anna S. Metz. BA in Sociology, Case Western Reserve U., 1971; MHA, Cornell U., 1973. Transplant coord. U. Miami Sch. Medicine, 1973-74, adminstr. Renal Transplant Program, 1974-84; adminstrv. dir. Phoenix Transplant Ctr., 1987-90; adminstrv. dir. Ariz. Organ and Tissue Banks, Phoenix, 1991-92, pres., CEO, 1992-94; nat. accounts mgr. Cryolife, Inc., Phoenix, 1994—. Author (with L. Burnett) Organ Procurement and Transplantation, A View from the Front Lines, 1988. Mem. Am. Mgmt. Assn., Assn. Organ Procurement Orgns., Healthcare Fin. Mgmt. Assn., Am. Assn. Tissue Banks, Coalition of Ariz. Bicyclists (chmn.), Ariz. Bicycle Club (bd. dirs.).

METZ, ROBERT ALLEN, mining geologist; b. Cleve., Dec. 22, 1932; s. Allen Andrew and Beatrice Marie (Schlitter) M.; m. Victoria Eugenia Hopper, Dec. 17, 1961 (div. Feb. 1972); children: James A., Thomas C., Lori A., David A.; m. Sarah Jocelyn Wallace, Dec. 23, 1973 (div. Mar. 1987); m. Helen Lee Hart, Jan. 23, 1993. Degree in Geol. Engring., Colo. Sch. Mines, 1955. Registered profl. geologist. Asst. geologist Kennecott Copper Corp., Santa Rita, N.Mex., 1955-59; div. geologist Ray Mines div. Hayden, Ariz., 1959-68; chief mine geologist Duval Sierrita Corp., Tucson, 1968-69, sr. geologist, 1969-70, dist. geologist, 1970-78, mgr. evaluation sect., 1978-85; sr. geologist evaluation Battle Mountain Exploration Co., Tucson, 1985-91; sr. geologist Phelps Dodge Mining Co., 1991-92; cons. mining geologist, 1992—. Author: Arizona Geological Society Guidebook III, 1968, SPOT Simulations Applications Handbook, 1985, Geology of the Porphyry Copper Deposits of Southwestern North America, 1966; editor Applied Mining Geology: Problems of Sampling and Grade Control, 1985. Mem. Soc. for Mining, Metallurgy and Exploration of AIME (chmn. Tucson sect. 1984, chmn. Western region sect. reps. 1986, v.p. Western region 1993—), Soc. Econ. Geologists, Ariz. Geol. Soc. (treas. 1972), N.Mex. Geol. Soc., Mining Club S.W. (1st v.p. 1989, pres. 1990), Aircraft Owners and Pilots Assn (pvt. pilot), NRA, Tucson Rod and Gun Club, People for the West!, Ariz. Pilots Assn. Republican. Lodge: Elks. Home and Office: 675 N Houghton Rd Tucson AZ 85748-1927

METZ, STEVEN WILLIAM, small business owner; b. Inglewood, Calif., Nov. 30, 1946; s. Glenn Ludwig and Kathleen Martha (Peterson) M.; m. Michelle Marie McArthur, Aug. 11, 1989; 1 child, Glenn Christian. Student, Fullerton Coll., Calif. Supt. Oahu Interiors, Honolulu, 1969-71, Hackel Bros., Miami, Fla., 1971-73; exec. v.p. Tru-Cut Inc., Brea, Calif., 1974-82; gen. mgr. The Louvre', Grass Valley, Calif., 1983-85; mfg. engring. mgr. Rexnord Aerospace, Torrance, Calif., 1986-87; pres., founder Metz/Calcoa Inc., Torrance, Calif., 1987—; mfg. rep. consul Orange County Spring, Anaheim, 1987—, Alard Machine Products, Gardena, Calif., 1988—, TALSCO, 1994—, Precision Resources, 1994—, GEMTECH, 1994—. Charter mem. Rep. Presdl. Task Force, 1991—; mem. L.A. Coun. on World Affairs, 1991-92. With U.S. Army, 1966-68. Recipient Appreciation awards DAV, 1968, Soc. Carbide & Tool Engrs., 1981, Soc. Mfg. Engrs., 1991. Fellow Soc. Carbide Engrs.; mem. Soc. Carbide & Tool Engrs. (chpt. pres. 1980-82), Rep. Presdl. Legion of Merit.

METZGER, VERNON ARTHUR, management educator, consultant; b. Baldwin Park, Calif., Aug 13, 1918; s. Vernon and Nellie C. (Ross) M.; BS, U. Calif., Berkeley, 1947, MBA, 1948; m. Beth Arlene Metzger, Feb. 19, 1955; children: Susan, Linda, 1 step-son, David. Estimating engr. C. F. Braun & Co., 1949; prof. mgmt. Calif. State U. at Long Beach, 1949-89, prof. emeritus, 1989—, founder Sch. Bus.; mgmt. cons., 1949-89. Mem. Fire Commn. Fountain Valley, Calif., 1959-60; pres. Orange County Dem. League, 1967-68; mem. State Dept. mgmt. task force to promote modern mgmt. in Yugoslavia, 1977; mem. State of Calif. Fair Polit. Practices Commn., Orange County Transit Com. Served with USNR, 1942-45. Recipient Outstanding Citizens award Orange County (Calif.) Bd. Suprs. Fellow Soc. for Advancement of Mgmt. (life; dir.); mem. Acad. Mgmt., Orange County Indsl. Rels. Rsch. Assn. (v.p.), Beta Gamma Sigma, Alpha Kappa Psi, Tau Kappa Upsilon. Home: 1938 Balearic Dr Costa Mesa CA 92626-3513 Office: 1250 N Bellflower Blvd Long Beach CA 90840-0006

METZINGER, TIMOTHY EDWARD, lawyer; b. L.A., Aug. 21, 1961; s. Robert Cole and Mary Jean (Cusick) M.; m. Cynthia Lee Stanworth, Nov. 16, 1991. BA, UCLA, 1986; JD, U. San Francisco, 1989. Bar: Calif. 1989, U.S. Dist. Ct. (ctrl., so., ea. and no. dists.) Calif. 1989, U.S. Ct. Appeals (9th cir.) 1989, U.S. Supreme Ct. 1994. Assoc. Bronson, Bronson & McKinnon, L.A., 1989-93, Price, Postel & Parma, Santa Barbara, Calif., 1993—. Mem. Santa Barbara County Bar Assn., Santa Barbara Barristers Club (dir.), Order of Barristers. Office: Price Postel & Parma 200 E Carrillo St Santa Barbara CA 93101-2118

METZNER, JEFFREY LEE, psychiatrist, educator; b. Hagerstown, Md., Mar. 15, 1950; married. BS, U. Md., 1972; MD, U. Md., Balt., 1975. Diplomate Am. Bd. Psychiatry and Neurology, Am. Bd. Forensic Psychiatry; cert. correctional health profl. Intern U. Colo. Health Scis. Ctr., Denver, 1975, resident in psychiatry, 1975-79, chief resident psychiat. liaison div., 1978-79, clin. instr. dept. psychiatry, 1978-81, asst. clin. prof., 1981-89, assoc. clin. prof., 1989—, assoc. dir. forensic psychiatry fellowship program, 1992—; pvt. practice Denver, 1979—; chief psychiatry div. forensic psychiatry Colo. State Hosp., 1978; com. mem. Gov's. Criminal Insanity Task Force, 1978-79; lectr.-in-law U. Denver Coll. of Law, 1984-86; co-chmn. Civil Commitment Task Force, 1987-90; examiner Am. Bd. Psychiatry and Neurology, Inc., 1988—; examiner Am. Bd. Forensic Psychiatry, Inc., 1989—, mem. written exam. com., 1989-93, bd. dirs. 1992—, chmn. oral exam. com., 1992-93; chairperson expert panel psychiat. disorders and comml. drivers U.S. Dept. Transp., 1990-91. author: (with others) Psychiatric Decision Making, 1984, Undestanding and Managing Child Sexual Abuse, 1990, Principles in Practice of Forensic Psychitry, 1994; contbr. articles to profl. jours.: reviewer Child Abuse and Neglect: The Internat. Jour., 1986—, Hosp. Community Psychiatry, 1993—. Fellow Am. Psychiat. Assn. (mem. task force on psychiat. svcs. in correctional facilites, 1985-89, mem. coun. on psychiatry and the law 1989-94, vice chmn., 1993-94, mem. task force on sexually dangerous offenders, 1993—); mem. Am. Correctional Health Svcs. Assn. (also Rocky Mountain chpt.), Am. Acad. Psychiatry and the Law (active numerous coms., editor newsletter), Am. Correctional Assn., Am. Coll. Legal Medicine, Am. Acad. Forensic Scis., Colo. Psychiat. Soc.,.

METZNER, RICHARD JOEL, psychiatrist, psychopharmacologist, educator; b. L.A., Feb. 15, 1942; s. Robert Gerson and Esther Rebecca (Groper) M.; children: Jeffrey Anthony, David Jonathan; m. Leila Kirkley, June 26, 1993. BA, Stanford U., 1963; MD, Johns Hopkins U., 1967. Intern, Roosevelt Hosp., N.Y.C., 1967-68; resident in psychiatry Stanford U. Med. Center, 1968-71; staff psychiatrist div. manpower and tng. NIMH-St. Elizabeths Hosp., Washington, 1971-73; chief audiovisual edn. system VA Med. Center Brentwood, L.A., 1973-79, chmn. VA Dist. 26 Ednl. Task Force, 1976-78; asst. prof. psychiatry UCLA Neuropsychiat. Inst., 1973-80, assoc. clin. prof., 1980—, lectr. Sch. Social Welfare, 1975-84; pvt. practice medicine specializing in psychiatry, Bethesda, Md., 1972-73, L.A., 1973—; dir. Western Inst. Psychiatry, L.A., 1977—; pres. Psychiat. Resource Network, Inc., 1984—; Served with USPHS, 1968-71. Recipient 6 awards for film and videotape prodns., 1976-80; diplomate Am. Bd. Psychiatry and Neurology (cons. 1974-78, producer audiovisual exam. programs 1975-77). Fellow Am. Psychiat. Assn.; mem. So. Calif. Psychiat. Soc., Mental Health Careerists Assn. (chmn. 1972-73), Phi Beta Kappa. Democrat. Jewish. Contbr. numerous articles to profl. publs., 1963—; producer, writer numerous ednl. films and videotapes, 1970—. Office: 9911 W Pico Blvd Ste 1570 Los Angeles CA 90035-2716

MEULI, MINDY DENISE, clinical dietitian; b. Tulsa, June 22, 1963; d. R. Larry and A. Victoria (Parker) M.; m. Bryan F. Clerkin, May 2, 1992. BS in Zoology, U. Wyo., 1985, MS in Food Sci. & Human Nutrition, 1987. Registered dietitian; cert. diabetes educator. Ext. nutrition asst. Expanded Foods and Nutrition Edn. Program, Laramie, Wyo., summer 1986; lab. asst. nutrition lab. U. Wyo., Laramie, 1987; asst. food svc. mgr. U. Wyo. Food Svc., Laramie, 1987-88; clin. dietitian Freeport (Ill.) Meml. Hosp., 1988-89; cons. dietitian Bethesda Care Ctr., Laramie, 1989-93; clin. dietitian Ivinson Meml. Hosp., Laramie, 1989—; mem. Albany County Ext. Adv. Com., Laramie, Albany County Comty. Health Awareness Com., Albany County Nutrition Coun., chair comty. benefits coun.; mem. bd. dirs. nom. com. Albany County Heart Assn. Co-author: (video) Centsible Nutrition, 1986. Bd. dirs. Ivinson Meml. Hosp. Found., Laramie, 1994-96. Mem. Am. Dietetic Assn., Wyo. Dietetic Assn. (legis. network coord. 1990-94, bd. dirs., Recognized Young Dietitian 1994), Soroptimist Internat. Republican. Presbyterian. Office: Ivinson Meml Hosp 255 N 30th St Laramie WY 82070

MEYER, AUGUST CHRISTOPHER, JR., broadcasting company executive, lawyer; b. Champaign, Ill., Aug. 14, 1937; s. August C. and Clara (Rocke) M.; m. Karen Haugh Hassett, Dec. 28, 1960; children: August Christopher F., Elisabeth Hassett. BA cum laude, Harvard U., 1959, LLB, 1962. Bar: Ill. 1962. Ptr. Meyer, Capel, Hirschfeld, Muncy, Jahn and Aldeen, Champaign, Ill., 1962-77, of counsel, 1977—; owner, dir., officer Midwest TV, Inc., Sta. KFMB-TV-AM-FM, San Diego, Sta. WCIA-TV, Champaign, Ill. , Sta. WMBD-TV-AM, WMXP, Peoria, Ill., 1968—; pres. Sta. KFMB-TV-AM-FM, San Diego, Sta. WCIA-TV, Champaign, Ill. , Sta. WMBD-TV-AM, WMXP, 1976—; bd. dirs. BankIll.; spl. asst. atty. gen. State of Ill., 1968-76. Chmn. bd. trustees Carle Found. Hosp., Urbana, Ill. Mem. Ill. Bar Assn., Champaign County Bar Assn. Club: Champaign Country. Home: 1408 S Prospect Ave Champaign IL 61820-6837 Office: Midwest TV Inc PO Box 777 509 S Neil St Champaign IL 61820-5219 also: Sta KFMB PO Box 85888 7677 Engineer Rd San Diego CA 92111-1515

MEYER, C. RICHARD, architect. BArch, U. Calif., Berkeley, 1968. Registered architect, Wash. With The Callison Partnership, Seattle, 1977—, dir. quality assurance; mem. adv. bd. cert. program project mgmt. U. Wash.; contracts rev. panelist Soc. Archtl. Adminstrs.; mem. faculty Pacific real estate symposium N.W. Real Estate Inst.; guest lectr. Archtl. Registration Exam. Seminar; guest lectr. coll. architecture and urban planning U. Wash.; guest panelist Internat. Conf. of Bldg. Ofcls. Nat. Conf., 1991. Mem. AIA (treas. Seattle chpt., mem. steering com. Pacific NW regional conf., vice-chair nat. risk mgmt. com., mem. steering com. nat. practice com., liaison to Am. Arbitration Assn.), Nat. Inst. Bldg. Scis. Office: The Callison Partnership Ltd 1420 5th Ave Ste 2400 Seattle WA 98101-2333

MEYER, CARL BEAT, chemical consultant, lawyer; b. Zurich, Switzerland, May 5, 1934; came to U.S., 1960; s. Karl and Alice (Wegenstein) M.; m. Elizabeth Anne Cousins, Feb. 26, 1960; 1 child, Birgit Franziska. Matura, Kantonsschule, Zuerich, Switzerland; PhD in Chemistry, U. Zurich, 1960; JD, Calif. Western Sch. Law, 1988. Bar: Nev. 1988, Calif. 1989. Postdoctoral fellow U. Calif., Berkeley, 1961-64; from asst. prof. to prof. chemistry U. Wash., Seattle, 1964-86; cons. San Diego, 1986—, pvt. practice, 1988—; cons. Lawrence Berkeley Lab., U. Calif., Berkeley, 1964-88, U.S. Consumer Product Safety Commn., Washington, 1980-83. Author: Sulfur, Energy and Environment, 1976, Urea-Formaldehyde Resins, 1978, Indoor Air Quality, 1984; contbr. 118 articles to profl. jours. Recipient Nathan Burkan Meml. Competition award ASCAP, 1988. Fellow Am. Inst. Chemistry; mem. ASTM (vice-chair com. D-22.05 1986—), ABA, Am. Chem. Soc., Am. Phys. Soc., Calif. Bar Assn., Nev. Bar Assn. Office: Kapsa & Meyer 325 S 3rd St Ste 3 Las Vegas NV 89101-6007

MEYER, CHRISTOPHER HAWKINS, lawyer; b. Springfield, Mo., Sept. 29, 1952; s. Richard DeWitt and Nancy (Hawkins) M.; m. Karen Anne Adams, Aug. 8, 1987; 1 child, C. Andrew Meyer. BA in Econs. magna cum laude, U. Mich., 1977, JD cum laude, 1981. Bar: D.C. 1981, U.S. Ct. Appeals (D.C. cir.) 1982, U.S. Ct. Appeals (9th cir.) 1983, Colo. 1985, U.S. Ct. Appeals (10th cir.) 1985, Idaho, U.S. Ct. Appeals (8th cir.). Counsel water resources program Nat. Wildlife Fedn., Washington, 1981-84; assoc. prof. adjoint, counsel Rocky Mountain Natural Resources Clinic Nat. Wildlife Fedn., Boulder, Colo., 1984-91; ptnr. Givens Pursley & Huntley, Boise, 1991—. Contbr. articles to profl. publs. Mem. steering com. Idaho Environ. Profls.; bd. dirs. Idaho Food Bank. Recipient Lawyer of Yr. award Environ. Policy Inst., 1984, Water Conservationist of Yr. Nebr. Wildlife Fedn., 1989. Mem. Phi Beta Kappa. Democrat. Roman Catholic. Home: 2460 E Bergeson St Boise ID 83706-6012 Office: Givens Pursley & Huntley 277 N 6th St Ste 200 Boise ID 83702-7720

MEYER, DANIEL KRAMER, real estate executive; b. Denver, July 15, 1957; s. Milton Edward and Mary (Kramer) M. Student, Met. State Coll., Denver, 1977-78, U. Colo., 1978-80. Ptnr., developer RM & M II (Ltd. Partnership), Englewood, Colo., 1981-87; pres. Centennial Mortgage and Investment, Ltd., Englewood, Colo., 1984-87; prin. Capriole Properties, Greenwood Village, Colo., 1983—. Alumni mem. bd. trustees Kent Denver Country Day Sch., 1981-83; sec. dist. 37 ctrl. and vacancy com. Colo. Ho. of Reps., 1991-92. Recipient Pamela Davis Beardsley devel. award Kent Denver Sch., 1995. Mem. Greenwood Athletic Club. Republican.

MEYER, EDMOND GERALD, energy and natural resources educator, resources scientist, entrepreneur, former chemistry educator, university administrator; b. Albuquerque, Nov. 2, 1919; s. Leopold and Beatrice (Ilfeld) M.; m. Betty F. Knobloch, July 4, 1941; children: Lee Gordon, Terry Gene, David Gary. B.S. in Chemistry, Carnegie Mellon U., 1940, M.S., 1942; Ph.D., U. N.Mex., 1950. Chemist Harbison Walker Refractories Co., 1940-41; instr. Carnegie Mellon U., 1941-42; asst. phys. chemist Bur. Mines, 1942-44; chemist research div. N.Mex. Inst. Mining and Tech., 1946-48; head dept. sci. U. Albuquerque, 1950-52; head dept. chemistry N.Mex. Highlands U., 1952-59; dir. Inst. Sci. Rsch., 1957-63; dean Grad. Sch., 1961-63; dean Coll. Arts and Sci., U. Wyo., 1963-75, v.p., 1974-80, prof. energy and natural resources, 1981-87, prof. and dean emeritus, 1987—; exec. cons. Diamond Shamrock Corp., 1980; bd. dirs. Carbon Fuels Corp., First Nat. Bank, Laramie; pres. Coal Tech. Corp., 1981—; cons. Los Alamos Nat. Lab., NFS, HHS, GAO, Wyo. Bancorp.; contractor investigator Rsch. Corp., Dept. of Interior, AEC, NIH, NSF, Dept. Energy, Dept. Edn.; Fulbright exch. prof. U. Concepcion, Chile, 1959. Co-author: Chemistry-Survey of Principles, 1963, Legal Rights of Chemists and Engineers, 1977, Industrial Research & Development Management, 1982; contbr. articles to profl. jours.; patentee in field. Lt. comdr. USNR, 1944-46, ret. Recipient Disting. Svc. award Jaycees; rsch. fellow U. N.Mex., 1948-50. Fellow AAAS, Am. Inst. Chemists (pres. 1992-93, chmn. 1994—); mem. Assoc. Western Univs. (chmn. 1972-74), Am. Chem. Soc. (councilor 1962-90), Biophys. Soc., Coun. Coll. Arts and Scis. (pres. 1971, sec.-treas. 1972-75, dir. Washington office 1973), Laramie C. of C. (pres. 1984), Laramie Regional Airport Bd. (chair 1989-93, treas. 1994—), Sigma Xi. Home: 1058 Colina Dr Laramie WY 82070-5015 Office: U Wyo Laramie WY 82071-3825

MEYER, GREG CHARLES, psychiatrist; b. Bismarck, N.D., Aug. 17, 1935; s. Oscar Clarence and Agnes Josephine (Pearson) M. Degree in profl. engring., Colo. Sch. Mines, 1958, Alexander Hamilton Bus. Inst., 1960; MME, U. So. Calif., 1965; MD, Marquette U., 1970. Diplomate Am. Bd. Psychiatry and Neurology. Engr. Minuteman-Thiokol, Brigham City, Utah, 1958-61; sr. engr. Saturn S-II N.Am. Aviation, Downey, Calif., 1962-65; design specialist Titan-Martin, Denver, 1965-66; rotating intern Weld Country Gen. Hosp., Greenly, Colo., 1970-71; psychiatric resident Ariz. State Hosp., Phoenix, 1971-74, psychiatrist, 1974-76; pvt. practice Mesa, Ariz., 1975-94; psychiatrist Ariz. Ctrl. Med. Ctr., 1994—; psychiatrist Ariz. Ctrl. Med. Ctr.; chmn. psychiatry Desert Samaritan Hosp., Mesa, 1982-86, 90-94, chmn. joint mental health, 1981-83, mem. edn. com., 1979-82, quality assurance com., 1979; mem. exec. com. Desert Vista Hosp., Mesa, 1988-94, chief of staff, 1989; chmn. psychiatry Mesa Luth. Hosp., 1984-85, mem. exec. com., 1984-85; mng. ptnr. Desert Samaritan Med. Bldg. II, Mesa, 1985-86; rsch., edn. com. East Valley Camel Back Hosp., 1989-90, quality assurance com., 1985; psychiatrist Ctrl. Ariz. Med. Ctr., 1995. Co-discoverer Larson-Meyer Transform. Coach Pop Warner Football, 1974. With USMCR, 1953-59. Mem. AMA, Am. Psychiatric Assn., Ariz. Med. Assn., Ariz. Psychiatric Assn., Phoenix Psychiatric Coun., Maricopa Country Med. Assn., Christian Med./Dental Assn., Triple Nine Soc. Republican. Lutheran.

MEYER, GREGORY TOBIN, city official, public administration executive; b. L.A., June 12, 1942; s. Glenn Harold and Kathryn Gertrude (Lyons) M.; m. Susan L. Rehshaw, Aug. 27, 1971 (div. 1992). BA in Pub. Adminstrn., Calif. State U., L.A., 1964; MS in Pub. Adminstrn., 1967; cert. in Urban mgmt., MIT, Cambridge, 1977. Cert. cmty. coll. tchr., Calif. Adminstrn. intern City of Pasadena, Calif., 1963-64; adminstrn. aide City of Alhambra, Calif., 1965-66; asst. to city mgr. City of Pasadena, Calif., 1966-72; deputy city mgr. City of Torrance, Calif., 1972-79; city mgr. City of Coachella, Calif., 1979-81, City of Hermosa Beach, Calif., 1981-87; deputy adminstr. Cmty. Redevelelopment Agy., City of L.A., 1987—. Author: Toptal Compensation Costing in California Cities, 1976, Orienting Elected Officials in California Cities, 1977. Pres. Greater Pasadena (Calif.) Kiwanis, 1970; pres., exec. dir. Nat. Coun. on Sexual Addiction and Compulsivity, Tucson, 1990-91; pres. Men's Guild, St. George's Episc. Ch., Hawthorne, 1994-95, Episc. lay eucharist min.. Staff sgt. U.S. Army, 1966-71. Named Com. Chmn. of Yr. Pasadena (Calif.) Jaycees, 1969. Mem. Bus. Profl. Assn. L.A., Gay Fathers, Lambda Alumni UCLA and USC, South Coast Chorale. Home: 1515 Prospect Ave Hermosa Beach CA 90254-3334

MEYER, HARRY MARTIN, JR., retired health science facility administrator; b. Palestine Tex., Nov. 25, 1928. s. Harry Martin and Marjory Isabel (Griffin) M.; m. Mary Jane Martin, Aug. 19, 1949 (div. 1966); children: Harry, Mary, David; m. Barbara Story Chalfort, Nov. 21, 1966. BS Hendrix Coll., 1949, MD U. Ark., 1953; Diplomate Am. Bd. Pediatics, 1960. instr. biology Little Rock Coll., 1949, intern. Walter Reed Army Hosp., Washington, 1953-54, med. officer dep. virus and rickettsial diseases, Walter Reed Army Inst. Rsch., 1954-57, asst. resident dep. pediatrics, N.C. Meml. Hosp., Chapel Hill, 1957-59, head virology sect. div. biologics standards, NIH, Bethesda, Md., 1959-64, chief lab. of viral immunol., div. biologics standards, NIH, 1964-72, dir. bur. biologics FDA, Bethesda, 1972-82, dir. Ctr. for Drugs & Biologics, Rockville, Md., 1982-86, pres. med. research div. Am. Cyanamid Co., Pearl River, N.Y., 1986-93; retired 1993. Served to rear admiral USPHS, 1959-86, capt. U.S. Army, 1953-57. Mem. AMA, Am. Epidemiol. Soc., Am. Acad. Pediatrics, Am. Pediatric Soc. Protestant. Avocations: sailing, scuba diving, skiing, back packing. Conbr. articles to profl. jours.; patentee in field.

MEYER, JAROLD ALAN, oil company research executive; b. Phoenix, July 28, 1938; s. Lester M. and Anita (Walker) M.; m. Diane Louise Wheeler; children: Ronald Alan, Sharon Lynne. BSChemE, Calif. Inst. Tech., 1960, MS, 1961. Mgr. process devel. Chevron Rsch., Richmond, Calif., 1978-82; tech. mgr. Chevron U.S.A., El Segundo, Calif., 1982-84; v.p. process rsch. Chevron Rsch., Richmond, 1984-86, pres., 1986—; sr. v.p. Chevron Rsch. and Tech., Richmond, 1990-93; ret., 1993; prin. J.A. Meyer Assocs., Martinez, Calif., 1993—; bd. dirs. Solvent Refined Coal Internat., Inc., San Francisco; mem. adv. bd. Surface Sci. and Catalysis Program Ctr. for Advanced Materials, Lawrence Berkeley Lab., 1988-91; mem. adv. coun. Lawrence Hall Sci., 1989-94; indsl. advisor Accreditation bd. for Engring. and Tech. Inventor petroleum catalysts; contbr. articles to profl. jours. Bd. visitors U. Calif., Davis, 1986-93, trustee found., 1989—. Mem. Nat. Acad. Engring., Am. Chem. Soc., Nat. Petroleum Refining Assn., Indsl. Rsch. Inst., Conf. Bd. Internat. Rsch. Mgmt. Coun., Accreditation Bd. for Engring. and Tech. Indsl. Advisor, Sigma Xi, Tau Beta Pi. Home and Office: 849 Corte Briones Martinez CA 94553-5950

MEYER, JEROME J., diversified technology company executive; b. Caledonia, Minn., Feb. 18, 1938; s. Herbert J. and Edna (Staggemeyer) M.; m. Sandra Ann Beaudoin, June 18, 1960; children—Randall Lee, Lisa Ann, Michelle Lynn. Student, Hamline U., 1956-58; B.A., U. Minn., 1960. Devel. engr. Firestone Tire & Rubber Co., Akron, Ohio, 1960-61; v.p., gen. mgr. Sperry Univac, St. Paul, 1961-79; group v.p. Honeywell, Inc., Mpls., 1979-84; pres., chief operating officer Varian Assocs., Palo Alto, Calif., 1984-86, also bd. dirs.; pres., chief exec. officer Honeywell Inc., 1986-90; from pres. to CEO, CFO Tektronix Inc., Beaverton, Oreg., 1990—; dir. Magnetic Data Inc., Mpls., Keycom Electronic Pub. Co., Chgo., Honeywell Erickson Devel. Co., Anaheim, Calif. Bd. dirs. YMCA, West St. Paul, Minn., 1977. Clubs: Southview Country (West St. Paul) Palo Alto Hills Country, Mission Viejo Country. Office: Tektronix Inc PO Box 1000 26600 S W Pky Wilsonville OR 97070*

MEYER, JOHN MICHAEL, judge; b. San Francisco, Apr. 7, 1947; s. Julian John and Anne L. Meyer; m. Susan L. Johnson, Oct. 26, 1968; children: Jennifer, Erika. BA, U. Wash., 1968; JD, U. Calif., San Francisco, 1975-95. Bar: Calif. 1972, Wash. 1973, U.S. Dist. Ct. (we. dist.) Wash. 1976, U.S. Ct. Appeals (9th cir.) 1979. Staff atty. FPC, Washington, 1973-75; ptnr. Gilbert & Meyer, Mt. Vernon, Wash., 1975—; dist. judge, 1995—. Pres. Skagit Valley YMCA, Mt. Vernon, 1977-79, Skagit Valley Coll. Found., Mt. Vernon, 1986-88; trustee Skagit Valley Coll., 1993—. 1st lt. Q.M.C. 1971-73. Mem. U. Wash. Alumni Assn. (bd. dirs., treas.), Skagit County Bar Assn. (pres. 1993-94), Rainier Club. Lutheran. Office: 600 S 3d St Mount Vernon WA 98273

MEYER, JOSEPH B., state attorney general; b. Casper, Wyo., 1941; m. Mary Orr; children: Vincent, Warren. Student, Colo. Sch. Mines; BA, U. Wyo., 1964, JD, 1967; postgrad., Northwestern U., 1968. Dep. county atty. Fremont County, Wyo., 1967-69; assoc. Smith and Meyer, 1968-71; asst. dir. legis. svc. office State of Wyo., Cheyenne, 1971-87, atty. gen., 1987—; conductor numerous govt. studies on state codes including Wyo. probate, criminal, state adminstrn., banking, domestic rels., game and fish, state instn., employment security, worker's compensation, motor vehicle, others; conductor legis. rev. of adminstrv. rules; negotiator with Office of Surface Mining for Wyo. state preemption; instr. Wyo. Coll. Law, fall 1986; lectr. Rocky Mountain Mineral Law Found., 1977; chmn. Conf. Western Atty. Gen., 1992-93; mem. exec. com. Nat. Assn. Attys. Gen. Bd. dirs. Cheyenne Jr. League, 1982-85, Jessup PTO, 1980-81; instr. Boy Scouts Am. Mem.

Rotary. Congregationalist. Office: Office of Atty Gen 123 Capitol Bldg Cheyenne WY 82002

MEYER, LEE GORDON, lawyer, energy company executive; b. Washington, Oct. 22, 1943; s. Edmond Gerald and Betty (Knobloch) M.; children: Veronica, Victoria, David. BS in Chemistry, U. Wyo., 1966, MBA, 1969, JD (hon.), 1973; M in Tech. Mgmt., U. Denver, 1994. Bar: Wyo. 1973, Tex. 1973, Ohio 1981, Ky. 1982, Colo. 1985, U.S. Patent Office, U.S. Supreme Ct. Patent atty. Texaco Corp., Austin, Tex., 1974-77; chief patent and trademark counsel Alcan Aluminum Co., Cleve., 1977-79; gen. counsel Donn, Inc., Cleve., 1979-81; asst. gen. counsel Diamond Shamrock Co., Lexington, Ky., 1981-83; v.p. fin. and adminstrn. Fort Union Coal Co., Denver, 1983-84; pres., chief exec. officer Carbon Fuels Corp., Denver, 1984—. Patentee in field. Mem. ABA, Am. Mgmt. Assn., Am. Chem. Soc., Licensing Exec. Soc., Ops. Rsch. Soc., Denver C. of C. Republican. Home: 12706 E Pacific Dr # 201 Aurora CO 80014-5323 Office: Carbon Fuels Corp 5105 Dtc Pky # 317 Englewood CO 80111-2600

MEYER, MADELINE ANNA, librarian; b. Great Bend, Kans., Mar. 26, 1948; d. George Albert and Anna Millicent (Noel) M. Student, Cambridge U., Eng., 1967-68; BA, Valparaiso U., 1970; MA, U. Denver, 1981. Libr. Denver Pub. Library, 1971-76; lease records mgr. Vantage Cos., Dallas, 1976-77; libr. Lytham-St. Annes Coll., St. Annes-on-Sea, Lancashire, Eng., 1977-78; lease records asst. J. Grynberg & Assocs., Denver, 1978-79; travel cons. Free Spirit Travel, Aurora, Colo., 1979-82; libr. Aurora Pub. Library, 1982-83; customer svc. rep. Western Air Lines, Denver, 1983-85; libr. Mesa (Ariz.) Pub. Library, 1985-87, Scottsdale (Ariz.) Pub. Library, 1987—. Dep. registrar Election Com., Phoenix, 1985—. Mem. Ariz. State Library Assn., Nat. Mgmt. Assn., Cen. Ariz. Tall Soc. Democrat. Lutheran. Office: Scottsdale Pub Libr 3839 N Civic Center Blvd Scottsdale AZ 85251-4405

MEYER, MICHAEL EDWIN, lawyer; b. Chgo., Oct. 23, 1942; s. Leon S. and Janet (Gorden) M.; m. Catherine Dieffenbach, Nov. 21, 1982; children: Linda, Mollie, Patrick, Kellie. BS, U. Wis., 1964; JD, U. Chgo., 1967. Bar: Calif. 1968, U.S. Supreme Ct. 1973. Assoc. Lillick & McHose, L.A., 1967-73, ptnr., 1974-90, mng. ptnr., 1986-87; ptnr. Pillsbury Madison Sutro, 1990—, mem. mgmt. com., 1990-92; judge pro tem Beverly Hills Mcpl. Ct., Calif., 1976-79, Los Angeles Mcpl. Ct., 1980-86; lectr. in field. Bd. dirs. Bldg. Owners and Mgrs. Assn. of Greater L.A., L.A. Coun. Boy Scouts Am., United Way Greater L.A. Recipient Good Scout award L.A. coun. Boy Scouts Am., 1992. Mem. ABA, Am. Arbitration Assn. (arbitrator), Calif. Bar Assn., L.A. Bar Assn., U. Chgo. Alumni Assn. So. Calif. (pres. 1980-82), Calif. Club, U. L.A. Club (dir. 1979-85, pres. 1984-85), L.A. Country Club. Jewish. Home: 4407 Roma Ct Marina Dl Rey CA 90292-7702 Office: Pillsbury Madison Sutro 725 S Figueroa St Los Angeles CA 90017-5524

MEYER, PAUL J., food products executive; b. 1947. BA, Stanford U.; MBA, U. Calif., Berkeley, 1969. With Continental Ill. Nat. Bank, Chgo., 1969-71, Bank of Am., San Francisco, 1971-81, Itel Corp., San Francisco, 1981-83, Victoria Sta., Inc., San Francisco, 1983-84; exec. v.p. Maui Land & Pinapple Co., Inc., Kahului, Hawaii, 1984—. Office: Maui Land & Pineapple Co Inc 120 Kane St # 187 Kahului HI 96732*

MEYER, RICHARD ERWIN, English language educator; b. Evanston, Ill., Sept. 20, 1939; s. Erwin Conrad and Florence Nettie (Wussow) M.; m. Lotte Norvig Larsen, Sept. 10, 1983; 1 child, Anne Elizabeth. BA summa cum laude, Northwestern U., 1965; MA, U. Wash., 1969; postgrad., U. Oreg., 1974-75. Dir. liberal arts seminars, asst. dean continuing edn. U. Wash., Seattle, 1965-69; prof. English/Folklore Western Oreg. State Coll., Monmouth, 1969—; cons. Office Hist. Preservation, State of Hawaii, Honolulu, 1987, Nat. Register Hist. Places, Washington, 1992. Author, editor: Cemeteries and Gravemakers: Voices of American Culture, 1989, (with others) A Sense of Place: Essays in American Regional Culture, 1990, Ethnicity and the American Cemetery, 1993, The Revival Styles in American Memorial Art, 1994; editor: Markers the Jour. of the Assn. for Gravestone Studies; contbr. articles to profl. jours. Sgt. U.S. Army, 1959-62. Mem. Am. Folklore Soc., Am. Culture Assn. (chmn. cemeteries and gravemarkers sect. 1984—), Pacific N.W. Am. Studies Assn., Oreg. Folklore Soc. (pres. 1975-76), Coun. of Editors of Learned Jours., Phi Kappa Phi. Democrat. Episcopalian. Home: 407 19th St NE Salem OR 97301-4304 Office: Western Oreg State Coll English Dept Humanitie Dv Monmouth OR 97361

MEYER, ROBERT ALLEN, human resource management educator; b. Wisconsin Rapids, Wis., May 31, 1943; s. Charles Harold and Viola Bertha (Stoeckmann) M.; 1 child, Timothy Charles. BA, Valparaiso (Ind.) U., 1966; MA, Mich. State U., 1967, PhD, 1972, postgrad., 1981. Asst. prof. Muskingum Area Tech. Coll., Zanesville, Ohio, 1972-74; adj. prof. U. Fla., Gainesville, 1974-80; dean acad. affairs Santa Fe Community Coll., Gainesville, 1974-80; asst. prof. Purdue U., W. Lafayette, Ind., 1982-84, Ga. State U., Atlanta, 1985-89; assoc. prof., program coord. U. N. Tex., Denton, 1989-91; Fulbright profl. scholar, Bangkok, 1991-92; coord. travel, tourism, hotel, restaurant mgmt. program U. Hawaii Manoa Campus, Honolulu, 1992—; investor, asst. mgr. LaSiene Restaurant, Ann Arbor, Mich., 1970-72; investor, cons. Cafe Brittany St. Thomas, U.S. V.I., 1974-80, owner, operator, Houston, 1980; pres. RTM Cons., Honolulu, Hawaii, 1989—; educator World Tourism Orgn., 1993—; mem. vis. ind. coun. C. of C., 1993—; club mgr. Assn. Am., 1994—. Contbr. articles to profl. jours. Recipient White House Commendation for Partnerships with Industry and Higher Edn.,1984, George Washington Medal of Honor for innovations in higher edn., Freedoms Found., 1985, 86, Achievement award in hospitality edn. Coun. of Hotel, Restaurant & Instl. Edn., 1987. Mem. Tarrant County Hotel and Motel Assn., Dallas Hotel Assn., Am. Soc. Tng. and Devel., Travel Ind. Assn. Tex., Hotel Sales & Mktg. Assn. (bd. dirs. 1985-89), Coun. of Hotel, Restaurant and Instl. Edn. (grad. com. 1989-90). Home: 2611 Ala Wai Blvd Apt 1608 Honolulu HI 96815-3907 Office: U Hawaii Manoa Campus 2560 Campus Rd Honolulu HI 96822-2217

MEYER, ROBERT LEE, secondary education educator; b. St. Joseph, Mo., July 9, 1952; s. Robert James and Jerry Lee (Patterson) M.; m. Barbara Anita Stickles, Aug. 2, 1986. BS in Edn., Mo. Western State Coll., 1974; MA in Edn., U.S. Internat. U., 1988. Cert. tchr., Calif., Mo.; cert. specialist learning handicapped, resource specialist cert., adminstr., Calif. Spl. edn. tchr., learning handicapped Mann Jr. High Sch., San Diego, 1978-80, Serra High Sch., San Diego, 1980-84, Morse High Sch., San Diego, 1984-85; magnet seminar tchr. Bell Jr. High Sch., San Diego, 1985-91; project resource tchr., dir. student activities Serra High Sch., San Diego, 1991-94, resource specialist, 1994—; chmn. resource com. Western Assn. Schs. & Colls. accreditation Serra High Sch., San Diego, 1995, sch. site coun., 1992-95, gov. team mem., 1992-95, chair spl. edn. dept., 1983, mem. sch. leadership team, 1992-95, sr. class advisor, 1994-95; monitor City Schs. Race Human Rels. Monitoring Team, 1991-92; restructuring coord. Senate Bill 1274 Grant, 1993-95, resource specialist, 1994—. Contbr.: (book) History of Andrew Meyer Family, 1989. Alternate del. Dem. Party 6th Dist. and State Conventions, Holt County, Mo., 1976. Mem. Calif. Assn. for Dirs. of Activities, Neighborhood House, Delta Chi Frat. Democrat. Roman Catholic.

MEYER, ROGER JESS CHRISTIAN, pediatrics educator; b. Olympia, Wash., May 14, 1928; s. Paul Eugene and Martha Bell Rogers Meyer; m. Joyce Langley, Mar. 14, 1959; children: Paul, John, William, Douglas, Nancy, Liz. BS in Chemistry, U. Wash., Seattle, 1951; MD, Washington U., St. Louis, 1955; MPH, Harvard U., 1959. Cert. pediatric bds. eligible rehab., preventive medicine, family practice. Instr. pediatrics Harvard Med. Sch., Boston, 1959-62; asst. prof. U. Vt. Coll. Medicine, Burlington, 1962-65; assoc. prof. U. Va. Sch. Medicine, Charlottesville, 1965-68; assoc. prof. pediatrics Northwestern U., Chgo., 1968-76; asst. dean U. Ill. Sch. Pub. Health, Chgo., 1974-76; prof. pediatrics and pub. health Sch. Medicine U. Wash., Seattle, 1976—; with U.S. Army Res. Med. Corps, 1982; advanced through grades to col. U.S. Army, 1986; chair, bd. dirs. community pediatrics sect. Am. Acad. Pediatrics, Evanston, Ill., 1973-74; pres. Child and Family Health Found., 1976—; bd. dirs. Nat. Com. Prevention Child Abuse, Chgo., 1974-76. Author 140 books and articles. Bd. dirs. N.W. orgn. ARC, Miller Bay Estates and Indianola Land Trust; v.p. Unitarian Universalist Ch., Bremerton; chief pub. health Pacific Rim, U.S. Army Med. Corps 364 Civil Affairs, 1986-93; staff Madigan Army Med. Ctr.; faculty Def. Dept. JMRTC. Decorated Army Achievement medal (2) for disting. svc. 1988-89; recipient NIMH Social Sci. in Medicine award Harvard U., 1961, Children's Hosp. Ann. award, Boston, 1959; Shaller scholar U. Wash., 1950-51, NIMH Health scholar U. Rochester, 1957-58; Oxford fellow, 1992. Mem. APHA, Am. Acad. Pediat. (sect. on child devel., ethics, pediat. mil.), Marine Sci. Soc. of the Pacific N.W. (N.W. global epidemiology com.), N.W. Pediat. Soc., Res. Officers Assn., Harvard U. Alumni Assn., Washington U. Alumni Assn. Home: 22125 Apollo Dr NE Poulsbo WA 98370-7719

MEYER, ROGER PAUL, physician; b. Atlanta, Mar. 30, 1950; s. Leonard Arthur and Janet Elanor (Miller) M.; children: Seth E., Hilary R. BA in Psychology with honors, U. N.C., 1972; MD, Med. Coll. Ga., 1976; postgrad., U. N.Mex., 1980. Physician in pvt. practice Carson Med. Group, Carson City, Nev., 1980—; chief of staff Carson Tahoe Hosp., 1986-87, chmn. dpt. ob-gyn., 1990-91; v.p. Nev. Physicians Rev. Orgn., 1987; dir. Physicians Managed Care IPO. Fellow Am. Coll. Ob-Gyn. (Nev. legis. liaison 1991); emm. Am. Fertility Soc., Am. Coll. Physician Execs. Democrat. Jewish. Office: Carson Med Group 1200 N Mountain St Carson City NV 89703-3824

MEYER, RUDOLF X., engineering educator, retired space technology executive; b. Rapperswil, Switzerland, Jan. 13, 1922; came to U.S., 1947; s. Carl and Alice A. (Muller) M.; m. Jeanne A. Meyer, Feb. 8, 1947; children: Jacqueline C. Meyer-Donaher, Dorothy A. Works. Diploma Engr., Swiss Inst. Tech., Zurich, 1945; D of Engring, Johns Hopkins U., 1955. Engr. De Laval Steam Turbine Co., Trenton, N.J., 1947-48; asst. prof. aeronautics U.S. Naval Postgrad. Sch., Annapolis, Md., 1948-52; project mgr. The Hydrofoil Corp., Annapolis, 1952-55; dept. head The Ramo-Wooldridge Corp., L.A., 1955-60; from assoc. dir. phys. rsch. lab. to gen. mgr./chief engr. The Aerospace Corp., L.A., 1960-87; adj. prof. Sch. Engring. UCLA, 1987—; mem. adv. bd. Dept. Def., Washington, 1980-81; invited lectr. MIT, Naval Postgrad. Sch., Naval. Acad., U. So.Calif. Assoc. editor AIAA, 1975-80; contbr. more than 70 articles to profl. jours.; patentee in field. Served with Swiss Army, 1942-45. Recipient Air Force Space div. Excellence awrd USAF, 1985; Regents lectr. U. Calif., 1987. Fellow AIAA. Republican. Roman Catholic. Home: 16966 Livorno Dr Pacific Palisades CA 90272 Office: UCLA MANE Dept M 405 Hilgard Ave Los Angeles CA 90024-1301

MEYER, STEVEN JOHN, electrical engineer; b. Glendale, Calif., Mar. 17, 1961; s. Albert John and Diane (Whitehead) M.; m. Wendy Dawn Fullmer, Apr. 23, 1988; children: Joshua David, Trevor John. BSEE, Brigham Young U., 1987; MSEE, Calif. State U., Northridge, 1991. Elec. engring. intern Radio Free Europe, Radio Liberty, Lisbon, Portugal, 1984; elec. engr. Weapons divsn. Naval Air Warfare Ctr., China Lake, Calif., 1987—. Contbr. articles to profl. jours.; patent pending in field. Asst. scoutmaster Boy Scouts Am., Ridgecrest, Calif., 1989-95, scoutmaster, 1995—. Mem. Mercury Amateur Radio Assn., Sierra Amateur Radio Club. Republican. Mem. LDS Ch. Office: Naval Air Warfare Ctr Weapons Divsn Code 543400D China Lake CA 93555

MEYER, SUSAN THERESA, business and training industry consultant; b. Ames, Iowa, Mar. 29, 1950; d. Robert William Keirs and Jeanne Marion (Thomas) Kaufer; m. John Allen Meyer, Dec. 18, 1972; children: Katherine Jeanne, Robert John. BS cum laude, U. Wis., 1972; MBA, Ea. Mich. U., 1982. Cert. spl. edn. tchr., Wis., Va. Spl. edn. tchr. Prince George (Va.) Pub. Schs., 1972-73; acct. DEMPUBCO Printing Co., Colorado Springs, Colo., 1973-74; adminstr., dir. EEO Dept. of Army, Frankfurt, Fed. Rep. of Germany, 1974-77; program coordinator Wake Up La., New Orleans, 1977-78; buyer Ford Motor Co., Dearborn, Mich., 1978-81; fgn. procurement specialist Ford Motor Co., Dearborn, 1981-85; pres. Mgmt. Recruiters of No. Del., Wilmington, 1985-91, The Obermeyer Group Ltd., Fort Collins, Colo., 1991—; dir. Small Bus. and Internat. Devel. Ctr., Ft. Collins, Colo., 1993-94; adj. prof. mktg. U. No. Colo., 1991—, Colo. State U., 1992—; cons. Fed. Women's Program, Frankfurt, 1974-77. Adv. bd. Women's Devel. Coun./Women Bus. Owners, Ft. Collins, 1993—, Ft. Collins Chamber Bus. Assistance Ctr., Ft. Collins, 1992—; mem. adv. bd. Comty. Involvement for Bank One, Ft. Collins, 1993—. Mem. Wilmington Women in Bus., Nat. Assn. Female Execs. Republican. Roman Catholic. Home: 6465 Hidden Springs Rd Fort Collins CO 80526-6511 Office: The Obermeyer Group Ltd PO Box 270711 Fort Collins CO 80527-0711

MEYER, WILLIAM TRENHOLM, defense company official, real estate executive, former army officer; b. Ancon, C.Z., May 28, 1937; s. Trenholm Jones and Virginia Blanche (Morgan) M.; m. Erna Charlotte Albert, Dec. 14, 1961; children: Cynthia L., Bonnie A., Christopher T., Tori L. BS, U. Nebr., 1965; grad. U.S. Army Command and Gen. Staff Coll., 1973. 2d lt. U.S. Army, 1961, advanced through grades to lt. col., 1976, ret., 1981; sr. engr. ManTech Internat. Corp., Sierra Vista, Ariz., 1981-82; mgr. field ops. RCA, Sierra Vista, 1982-86; chief exec. officer MYCO, 1989; gen. ptnr., dir. Southwestern Investment Ltd. Partnership, Sierra Vista, 1983-89; mgr. advanced devel. GE, 1986—. Sustaining mem. Republican Nat. Com., 1983—, GE 1986-93, Martin Marietta, 1993—. Mem. Assn. Old Crows (regional dir. 1984-87, chpt. pres. 1983-84, 89-91, v.p. 1992—, Internat. Electronic Warfare-Intelligence medal 1983, Electronic Warfare special medal 1991), Armed Forces Communications and Electronics Assn., Ret. Officers Assn., Assn. U.S. Army. Roman Catholic. Clubs: Kings Tennis (pres. 1980, 87, 88), Aquatic (pres. 1981) (Sierra Vista). Home: 1902 N San Diego Cir Sierra Vista AZ 85635-9521 Office: Martin Marietta 2700 E Fry Blvd Ste 3B Sierra Vista AZ 85635-2826

MEYEROWITZ, BASIL RALPH, surgeon; b. Johannesburg, South Africa, Sept. 14, 1929; came to U.S., 1960, natuaralized, 1965; m. Miriam Lewinsky, Nov. 1963; children: Robin Marie, Eric Lloyd, Lisa Ann, Jennifer Ray. MB, BCh, Witwatersrand U., 1952. Intern Johannesburg Gen. Hosp., 1953-55; resident Hammersmith Hosp. Postgrad. Sch. of Medicine, 1955-60, Royal Infirmary, Leicester, Eng., 1956-57; spl. fellow, instr. in surgery Albert Einstein Coll. Medicine, 1960-62, asst. prof. surgery, 1962-67; dir. of the Stanford Surg. Svc. San Mateo County Gen. Hosp., 1967-70, chief of surg. svc., 1970-80; clin. assoc. prof. surgery Stanford U. Sch. Medicine, 1967—; assoc. vis. surgeon Bronx Mcpl. Hosp. Ctr., 1967; asst. attending surgeon Mount Sinai Hosp. Divsn. at Elmhurst Hosp., 1967; chief of staff Mills Hosp., 1982-88; chmn. dept. surgery, 1975-77, 90-92, chmn. continuing edn. com., 1974-80, chmn. interdisciplinary com., 1980, chmn. D.R.G. com., 1987-88; chief of staff Chope Community Hosp., San Mateo, 1974-75; hosp. staff Mills Hosp., San Mateo County Gen. Hosp. Contbr. numerous articles to profl. jours. Fellow ACS (No. Calif. chpt.); mem. Royal Coll. of Surgeons (Eng.), Calif. Med. Assn., Assn. for Acad. Surgery, Soc. for Surgery of the Alimentary Tract, San Francisco Surg. Soc., Calif. Acad. of Medicine, Am. Soc. Bariatric Surgery (founder), San Mateo County Med. Soc. (bd. dirs. 1976-79, 79-82, del. to Calif. Med. Assn. 1979-80, 80-83, many coms.), Calif. Med. Assn. (hosp. surveyor 1980—). Office: 101 S San Mateo Dr Ste 307 San Mateo CA 94401-3844

MEYEROWITZ, ELLIOT MARTIN, biologist, educator; b. Washington, D.C., May 22, 1951; s. Irving and Freda (Goldberg) M.; m. Joan Agnes Kobori, June 17, 1984; 2 children. AB, Columbia U., 1973; MPhil, Yale U., 1975, PhD, 1977. Rsch. fellow Stanford U., Calif., 1977-79; asst. prof. biology Calif. Inst. Tech., Pasadena, 1980-85, assoc. prof. 1985-89, prof., 1989—. Mem. editl. bd. Trends in Genetics, Current Biology, Cell Devel.; contbr. articles to profl. jours., 1978—. Jane Coffin Childs Meml. Fund fellow, 1977-79, Sloan Found. fellow, 1980-82. Fellow AAAS; mem. NAS, Am. Acad. Arts and Scis. (Pelton award), Botanical Soc. Am. (Gibbs medal), Am. Soc. Plant Physiologists, Botanical Soc. Am., Am. Soc. Plant Physiology, Genetics Soc. Am. (bd. dirs.), Internat. Soc. Developmental Biology (bd. dirs.), Internat. Soc. for Plant Molecular Biology (pres.). Office: Calif Inst Tech Div Biology Pasadena CA 91125

MEYERS, ALBERT IRVING, chemistry educator; b. N.Y.C., Nov. 22, 1932; s. Hyman and Sylvia (Greenberg) M.; m. Joan Shepard, Aug. 10, 1957; children—Harold, Jill, Lisa. BS, NYU, 1954, PhD, 1957. Rsch. chemist Cities Svc. Oil Co., Cranbury, N.J., 1957-58; asst., assoc. prof., prof. La. State U., New Orleans, 1958-70, Boyd prof., 1969; prof. Wayne State U., Detroit, 1970-72; prof. Colo. State U., Fort Collins, 1972—, disting. prof., 1986—, John K. Stille prof. chemistry, 1993—; spl. postdoctoral fellow Harvard U., Cambridge, 1965-66; cons. G.D. Searle Co., Skokie, Ill., 1972-84, Mid-West Rsch. Inst., Kansas City, Mo., 1974-77, Bristol-Myers Squibb Co., 1983—, NIH, Bethesda, Md., 1977-79, 85-89, Syntex Co., 1989—, Smith Kline Beecham Co., 1994—. Assoc. editor Jour. Am. Chem. Soc., 1980-85; editl. bd. Jour. Organic Chemistry, 1990-94, Tetrahedron, 1990—, Jour. Chem. Soc., 1993—; contbr. over 400 articles to profl. jours. Recipient Alexander von Humboldt award Fed. Republic of Germany, 1984, Disting. Alumni award NYU, 1990; named Man of Yr., New Orleans Jaycees, 1968, Boyd Prof. La. State U., 1969. Fellow AAAS, Nat. Acad. Sci.; mem. Royal Soc. Chemistry (silver medalist 1982), Phila. Organic Chemistry Soc. (Allan Day award 1987). Home: 1500 Hepplewhite Ct Fort Collins CO 80526-3822 Office: Colorado State Univ Dept Chemistry Fort Collins CO 80523

MEYERS, ANN SIPL, hotel and casino owner operator; b. Krindia, Yugoslavia, Apr. 26, 1943; came to U.S., 1951; d. Joseph and Magdalena Sipl; m. Leon Paul Meyers, Mar. 2, 1963 (div. 1972); children: Bridgett Ann, Leah Marlene. Student, Kent State U., 1963, 66, 67,, Kent State U., 68, 69, Ohio State U., 1975, 76. Head teller in charge of vault City Bank, Kent, Ohio, 1966-68; head interior decorator Schottensteins Dept. Stores, Columbus, 1972-74; owner, operator Casbah Hotel, Las Vegas, 1986-89, Queen of Hearts Hotel, Las Vegas, 1986—; owner Nev. Hotel and Casino, Las Vegas, 1992—; dir. Down Town Progress Assn., Las Vegas, 1976-90. Vol. Las Vegas C. of C., 1976-90. Recipient Women of Achievement award Las Vegas C. of C., 1991. Mem. Toastmasters (sgt. of arms 1982, 83, 88, 89). Office: Queen of Hearts Hotel 19 Lewis Ave Las Vegas NV 89101-6306

MEYERS, CAROLE TERWILLIGER, writer; b. San Francisco; married; 2 children. BA in Anthropology, San Francisco State U.; Teaching Credential, Fresno State U. Editor, pubr. Family Travel Guides Catalogue, 1986—; pub. Carousel Press, 1975—; columnist: San Francisco Examiner, 1989-91, San Jose Mercury News, 1978-79, 89-90, Parents' Press, 1980-90, San Francisco Focus, 1988-90, Calif. Mag., 1981-88, Goodlife Mag., 1983, Calif. Travel Report, 1982-83, Oakland Mag., 1980, Adventure West Mag., 1994—; contbr. numerous articles to mags. including Parenting, Family Fun, Diablo, Family Cir., Parents, Motorland. Author: How to Organize a Babysitting Cooperative and Get Some Free Time Away from the Kids, 1976, Getting in the Spirit: Annual Bay Area Christmas Events, 1979, Eating Out with the Kids in San Francisco and the Bay Area, 1976, 3d edit. 1985, Weekend Adventures for City-Weary People: Overnight Trips in Northern Calif., 1977, 5th edit. 1993, San Francisco Family Fun, 1990, Miles of Smiles: 101 Great Car Games and Activities, 1992; editor: The Family Travel Guide: An Inspiring Collection of Family-Friendly Vacations, 1995. Bd. advisors San Francisco Internat. Toy Ctr. and Mus., 1986-91. Recipient 1st place in self-published travel book category (for Weekend Adventures) Travel Pub. News Awards, 1990. Mem. Internat. Food, Wine and Travel Writers Assn., Bay Area Travel Writers, Northern Calif. Book Publicists Assn. Office: PO Box 6061 Albany CA 94706-0061

MEYERS, DENNIS JAY, economist; b. San Bernardino, Calif., Apr. 23, 1957; s. Robert Allen and Ila Fay (Hood) M.; m. Charlotte Delaire, 1975; children: Benjamin Allen, Abraham Martin. BA in Econs., Calif. State U., Sacramento, 1983, MA in Econs., 1987. Stock broker TIS Inc., Sacramento, 1984; economist ADM Assocs., Rancho Cordova, Calif., 1985; inventory mgmt. specialist Dept. of Def., Sacramento, 1985—; econs. instr. Consumnes River Coll., Sacramento, 1988—; econ. rsch. analyst Calif. Integrated Waste Mgmt. BRD, Sacramento, 1988-90, econ. rsch. mgr., 1990—. Cons. Jr. Achievement, Sacramento, 1988; vol. Playground Pals, Elk Grove, Calif., 1994. With U.S. Army, 1974-80. Mem. Toastmasters Internat. (Trash Talkers chpt.), Nat. Assn. of Bus. Econs. (Sacramento Econs. Roundtable). Democrat. Home: 5341 Spring Creek Way Elk Grove CA 95758-4724 Office: Calif Integrated Waste Mgmt Bd 8800 Cal Center Dr Sacramento CA 95826

MEYERS, GENE HOWARD, computer scientist; b. Chgo., Dec. 6, 1942; s. Charles S. and Sara (Miller) M.; m. Carole Esther Terwilliger, May 2, 1971; children: David, Suzanne. BS, U. Ill., 1964; PhD, U. Calif., Berkeley, 1969. Sci. programmer Kaiser Aluminum, Pleasanton, Calif., 1969-77, sr. system analyst, 1977-81, staff system analyst, 1981-88, mgr. computer sci., 1988—. Mem. Assn. Computing Machinery. Democrat. Jewish. Office: Kaiser Aluminum 6177 Sunol Blvd Pleasanton CA 94566-7769

MEYERS, HERBERT, geophysicist; b. N.Y.C., Nov. 15, 1931; s. Sam and Pauline M.; m. Ethel V. Knight; children: David, Greg, Karen, Tiffany. BS in Geology, CCNY, 1958; postgrad., Am. U., 1959-64. Geophysicist Coast and Geodetic Survey, Washington, 1958-63, chief. spl. projects, 1963-66; chief earth scis. Environ. Data Service NOAA, Washington, 1966-72; chief solid earth Nat. Geophysics Data Ctr. NOAA, Boulder, Colo., 1972-95; dir. World Data Ctr. for Solid Earth, Boulder, 1979-95; cons. geophys. dates, 1995—. Served to capt. USAF, 1952-55. Mem. Am. Geophys. Union, Soc. Exploration Geophysicists, Sigma Xi. Home: 986 Mcintire St Boulder CO 80303-2725 Office: NOAA 325 Broadway St Boulder CO 80303-3337

MEYERS, HOWARD CRAIG, lawyer; b. Chgo., Nov. 15, 1951; s. Spencer M. and Joyce L. (Dresdner) M. BA in English, Ariz. State U., 1973, JD, 1977. Bar: Ariz. 1977; cert. bus. bankruptcy specialist Am. Bankruptcy Bd. Cert., cert. bankruptcy specialist State Bar Ariz. Of counsel Burch & Cracchiolo, P.A., Phoenix, Ariz. Mem. ABA, Comml. Law League of Am., Am. Bankruptcy Inst., State Bar Ariz., Maricopa County Bar Assn., Internat. Council of Shopping Ctrs., Plaza Club. Republican. Home: 6711 E Camelback Rd Unit 65 Scottsdale AZ 85251-2067 Office: PO Box 16882 702 E Osborn Rd Ste 200 Phoenix AZ 85011

MEYERS, MARLENE O., hospital administrator; m. Eugene Meyers; children: Lori, Lisa, Dean. BSc, U. Sask., 1962; MSc, U. Calgary, Alta., Can., 1976. Instr., chair Mount Royal Coll. Allied Health, Calgary, 1969-82; asst. exec. dir. Rockyview Hosp., Calgary, 1982-85; v.p. patient svcs. Calgary Gen. Hosp., 1985-91, pres., CEO, 1991-95; pres., CEO Meyers and Assocs. Health Care Mgmt. Cons., Calgary, 1995—; surveyor Can. Coun. on Health Facilities Accreditation, 1986—. Named Calgary Woman of Yr., 1982. Mem. Alta. Assn. RNs. Office: Meyers and Assocs, 139 Coleridge Rd NW, Calgary, AB Canada T2K 1X5

MEYERS, PIETER, JR., chemist; b. Oostkapelle, Zeeland, Netherlands, July 10, 1941; came to U.S., 1968; s. Pieter Sr. and Jacomina Cornelia (Daamen) M.; m. Alida Lubertha Van Den Brink, Sept. 24, 1965. Student, U. Amsterdam, Netherlands, Doctorandus, 1965, PhD, 1968. Rsch. assoc. Inst. for Nuclear Physics Rsch., Amsterdam, 1965-68, Brookhaven Nat. Lab., Upton, N.Y., 1968-69; vis. prof. Am. U., Cairo, 1969-70; rsch. collaborator Brookhaven Nat. Lab., 1970-85; rsch. chemist Met. Mus. Art, N.Y.C., 1970-76; sr. rsch. chemist Met. Mus. Art, 1976-81; sr. rsch. chemist L.A. County Mus. of Art, 1981-85, head conservation, 1985—; adj. prof. art history dept. Columbia U., N.Y.C., 1981. Fellow Internat. Inst. for Conservation of Hist. and Artistic Works, Am. Inst. Conservation (pres. 1982-84); mem. Am. Assn. Mus., Internat. Coun. of Mus. Office: LA County Mus of Art Conservation Ctr 5905 Wilshire Blvd Los Angeles CA 90036-4523

MEYERS, RANDAL CURTIS, sculptor; b. Salt Lake City, June 23, 1961; s. C. LaMar and LaRaine (Curtis) M. AAS in Fashion Design, Parsons Sch. Design, 1983; A in Bus. Mgmt. summa cum laude, Salt Lake C.C., 1988; BFA in Sculpture and Painting, U. Utah, 1995. Window designer ZCMI Dept. Store, Salt Lake City, 1978-79, Bergdorf Goodman, N.Y.C., 1979-80; collection designer Geoffrey Beene, N.Y.C., 1983-84; women's collection designer Perry Ellis, N.Y.C., 1984-86; haute couture designer Hanae Mori Paris, 1986-87; women's sportswear designer Hanae Mori, Tokyo, 1987-88; freelance artist, sculptor Salt Lake City, 1988—; instr. drawing Visual Art Inst., Salt Lake City, 1990-91. Author: Fashion Designers Inspired by Painters, 1982; filmmaker (video) ANIMA, 1994; artist/sculptor represented in one-person and group shows at various locations, 1992-94. Recipient Parson Sch. of Design and Fashion Inds. Gold Thimble award, 1983, U. Utah Pres. award, 1991-92, 92-93; Florence Ware scholar Coll. Fine Arts U. Utah, 1992-93, Coll. Fine Arts Adv. Bd. scholar, 1994-95; rsch. grantee U. Utah, 1994. Democrat. Home: 4207 Panorama Dr Salt Lake City UT 84124-2810 Office: R C Meyers Studio 1075 Harvard Ave Salt Lake City UT 84105-1834

MEYERS, ROBERT ALLEN, scientist, publisher; b. L.A., May 15, 1936; s. Jack B. Meyers and Pearl (Cassell) Sorkin; m. Roberta Lee Hart, June 24, 1961 (div. 1976); children: Tamara, Robert Jr.; m. Ilene Braun, Feb. 27, 1977; children: Jennifer, Jacelyn. BA, San Diego State U., 1959; PhD, UCLA, 1963. Mem. faculty Calif. Inst. Tech., Pasadena, 1963-64; rsch. scientist Bell & Howell Rsch. Ctr., Sierra Madre, Calif., 1965; project mgr. TRW Def. & Space, Redondo Beach, Calif., 1966-81; bus. area mgr. TRW Energy Group, Redondo Beach, 1981-86; mgr. process devel. TRW Def. & Space, Redondo Beach, 1986-88, mgr. new projects devel., 1988-95; pres. Ramtech Ltd., Tarzana, Calif., 1995—; del. U.S.-USSR Working Group, Washington and Moscow, 1973-80; chmn. adv. bd. Guide to Nuclear Power Tech., N.Y.C., 1982-84; mem. adv. coun. chemistry dept. UCLA, 1991—. Author: Coal Desulfurization, 1977; editor: Coal Handbook, 1981, Coal Structure, 1982; editor-in-chief Ency. of Phys. Sci. and Tech., 1987, 92, Ency. of Modern Physics, 1990, Ency. of Lasers and Optics, 1991, Molecular Biology and Biotech., 1995, Ency. of Molecular Biology and Molecular Medicine, 1995. Mem. Am. Chem. Soc., Am. Inst. Chem. Engrs. Home: 3715 Gleneagles Dr Tarzana CA 91356-5622 Office: Ramtech Ltd One Space Pk 3715 Gleneagles Dr Ste 100 Tarzana CA 91356-5622

MEYERS, ROGER JOSEPH, telegram company executive; b. Kansas City, Mo., Feb. 15, 1955; married; 2 children. BFA, NYU, 1977. Founder, chief exec. officer Am. Telegram, Beverly Hills, Calif., 1986—. Address: 270 N Canon Dr # 1167 Beverly Hills CA 90210-5323

MEYERS, THEDA MARIA, textile company executive; b. Bremen, Germany, Feb. 16, came to U.S. 1937, d. Johann-Friedrich and Christophina E.L.J. (Fentrohs) Ficke; m. Laurence Jay Meyers, Oct. 2, 1960 (div. 1970); 1 child, Jayson Bennett. Dipl., U. Bremen, 1956; student, Fashion Inst. Tech., N.Y.C., 1960. Artist-stylist Rosewood Fabrics, N.Y.C., 1960-62; textile stylist Belding Corticelli, N.Y.C., 1962-65; chief designer Jerry Mann of Calif., L.A., 1969-74; fashion designer Sunbow Ltd., Prisma Corp., L.A., 1974-81, Frig & Frag Inc., L.A., 1981-83, Jonathan Martin, L.A., 1983-85; textile stylist, v.p. design E.M.D.A.Y., Inc., L.A., 1985-92; cons. Theda Meyers Consultancy, L.A., 1993—; part-time tchr. Fashion Inst. of Design & Merchandising, L.A., to 1974; part-time judge Trade Tech. Coll., L.A. to 1981; textile designer extensive nat. and internat. experience in womenswear apparel design and textile design. designer Calif. apparel. Mem. NAFE.

MEYR, SHARI LOUISE, computer consultant, computer company executive; b. San Diego, Dec. 6, 1951; d. Herchell M. and Etta Louise (Bass) Knight; m. William Earl Groom, Oct. 22, 1977 (div. Sept. 1989), Herbert Carl Meyr Jr., Feb. 23, 1990. AS in Fire Scis., San Diego Mesa Coll., 1976. T.O.S.S. specialist Spectrum Scis. & Software, Mountain Home AFB, 1989-94; equestrian instr. Summerwind Ctr., Mountain Home, 1979-91; Chow Chow breeder Meyr Kennels, Mountain Home, 1990—; multimedia P.C. cons., CEO Access to Answers, Mountain Home, 1990—; seasonal zoo keeper Soco Gardens Zoo, Maggie Valley, N.C., 1995. Mem. U.S. Ski Assn. (competition lic., alpine ofcl., profl. coach, master's alpine racer 1991—), Summerwind Riding Club (founder, pres. 1981-89), Mountain Home Ski Club (founder, bd. dirs. 1991—), Bogus Basin Ski Club, Sun Valley Ski Club, Amateur Trapshooting Assn. (life), Mensa. Home: 570 E 16th N Mountain Home ID 83647-1717

MEZEY, ROBERT, poet, educator; b. Phila., Feb. 28, 1935; s. Ralph and Clara (Mandel) M.; m. Olivia Simpson (div.); children: Naomi, Judah, Eve. Student, Kenyon Coll., 1951-53; BA, U. Iowa, 1959; postgrad., Stanford U., 1960-61. Lectr. Western Res. U., Cleve., 1963-64, Franklin & Marshall Coll., Lancaster, Pa., 1965-66; asst. prof. Fresno (Calif.) State U., 1967-68, U. Utah, Salt Lake City, 1973-76; prof., poet-in-residence Pomona Coll., Claremont, Calif., 1976—. Author: (poems) White Blossoms, 1965, The Lovemaker, 1960 (Lamont award), The Door Standing Open, 1970, Selected Translations, 1981, Evening Wind, 1988 (Bassine citation, PEN prize 1989); editor: Naked Poetry, 1968, Collected Poems of Henri Coulette, 1990. With U.S. Army, 1953-55. Fellow Ingram Merrill, 1973, 89, Guggenheim Found., 1977, Stanford U., 1960, NEA, 1987; recipient Poetry prize Am. Acad. Arts and Letters, 1982. Home: 1663 Chattanooga Ct Claremont CA 91711-2917 Office: Pomona Coll Dept English 140 W 6th St Claremont CA 91711

MIAN, GUO, electrical engineer; b. Shanghai, Feb. 6, 1957; came to U.S., 1987; s. Wenseng Mian and Guorong Sun; m. Ann Wang, Nov. 1, 1989. BS in Physics, Shanghai U. Sci. & Tech., 1982; MS in Physics, Western Ill. U., 1989; DSc in Elec. Engring., Washington U., 1992. Mgr. Rec. Media Lab. Magnetic Rec. Ctr., Shanghai (China) Ctrl. Chem. Ltd., 1982-85; vis. scientist materials sci. lab. Keio U., Yokohama, Japan, 1985-87; sr. rsch. elec. engring. Quantum Corp., Milpitas, Calif., 1992-93, Conner Peripherals, San Jose, Calif., 1993-95; sr. mgr. HDD R&D Ctr. Samsung Info. Sys. Am., San Jose, Calif., 1995—. Contbr. articles to Jour. Materials Sci., IEEE Trans. Magnetics, Jour. Magnetism & Magnetic Materials, Jour. Applied Physics, Japanese Jour. Applied Physics, Jour. Japanese Magnetic Soc. Recipient C & C Promotion award Found. for C & C Promotion, Tokyo, 1986. Mem. IEEE, IEEE Magnetics Soc., IEEE Computer Soc., Am. Phys. Soc. Home: 105 Serra Way # 362 Milpitas CA 95035-5206

MICHAEL, ERNEST ARTHUR, mathematics educator; b. Zurich, Switzerland, Aug. 26, 1925; came to U.S., 1939; s. Jakob and Erna (Sondheimer) M.; m. Colette Verger Davis, 1956 (div. 1966); children: Alan, David, Gerard; m. Erika Goodman Joseph, Dec. 4, 1966; children: Hillary, Joshua. B.A., Cornell U., 1947; M.A., Harvard U., 1948; Ph.D., U. Chgo., 1951. Mem. faculty dept. math. U. Wash., Seattle, 1953—; asst. prof. U. Wash., 1953-56, assoc. prof., 1956-60, prof., 1960-93, prof. emeritus, 1993—; mem. Inst. for Advanced Study, Princeton, 1951-52, 56-57, 60-61, 68, Math. Research Inst., E.T.H., Zürich, 1973-74; vis. prof. U. Stuttgart, Ger., 1978-79, U. Munich, Fed. Republic Germany, 1987, 88, 92-93. Editor: Procs. Am. Math. Soc., 1968-71, Topology and Its Applications, 1972-94; contbr. articles to profl. jours. Served with USNR, 1944-46. Grantee AEC; Grantee Office Nav. Research; Grantee NSF; Grantee Guggenheim Found.; Grantee Humboldt Found. Mem. Am. Math. Soc., Math. Assn. Am., ACLU, Amnesty Internat. Jewish. Home: 16751 15th Ave NW Seattle WA 98177-3842

MICHAEL, GARY G., retail supermarket and drug chain executive; b. 1940; married. BS in Bus., U. Idaho, 1962. Staff acct. Ernst & Ernst, CPA's, 1964-66; with Albertson's, Inc., Boise, Idaho, 1966—, acct., 1966-68, asst. controller, 1968-71, controller, 1971-72, v.p., controller, 1972-74, sr. v.p. fin., treas., 1974-76, exec. v.p., 1976-84, vice chmn., CFO, corp. devel. officer, 1984-91, chmn., CEO, 1991—; also dir. Albertson's, Inc. Served to 1st lt. U.S. Army, 1962-64. Office: Albertson's Inc PO Box 20 Boise ID 83726-0020*

MICHAEL, GARY LINN, architect; b. Portland, Oreg., Apr. 27, 1934; s. Donald Glenn and Ida Marie (Luoto) M.; m. Sandra Ann Schori, Sept. 16, 1956 (div. 1982); children: Brian Russell, Laura Joy, Jesse Daniel. B.Arch., U. Oreg., 1957; M.Arch., Yale U., 1965. Partner Campbell, Michael, Yost, Portland, 1965-68; prin. Architects & Planners Gary L. Michael, Portland, 1969-74; pres. Michael & Kuhns, Architects, Portland, 1974—; mem. Oreg. Bd. Architect Examiners, 1978-84; guest archtl. design critic Portland State U., U. Oreg.; guest lectr. pub. schs., colls., tchr. tng. seminars. Works include Mentor Graphics Child Development Center, Wilsonville, Oreg., 1991, Zach Studio and Residence, Elmira, Oreg., 1969, Cowles Bldg, Portland, 1973, Unthank Plaza Pub. Housing, Portland, 1977, Duniway Ctr., Portland, 1982, student housing at Wash. State U., U. Wash., U. Alaska, Portland State U., The Evergreen State Coll., So. Oreg. State Coll. Mem. Portland Sch. Dist. Eco-Aesthetics Bd., 1972-74; mem. citizens coordinating com. Oreg. Hwy. Div., 1973; chmn. Sensible Transp. Options for People, Portland, 1974; mem. Downtown Housing Adv. Com., 1978-81; chair adv. com. Milw. Riverfront Devel., 1987-89. Ion Lewis Traveling fellow, 1957. Fellow AIA (11 local design awards 1960-80, nat. design award 1973, pres. Portland chpt. 1972). Home: 11907 SE 19th Ave Milwaukie OR 97222-7801 Office: Michael & Kuhns Archs PC 421 SW 6th Ave Portland OR 97204

MICHAEL, JAMES DANIEL, computer scientist; b. Peoria, Ill., May 27, 1957; s. Thomas Proctor and Mary Lou (Wagner) M.; m. Judith Ann O'Donnell, June 23, 1979. BS in Psychology, U. Calif., Davis, 1978. Teller Bank of Am., Davis, 1978-79, Fresno, Calif., 1979; computer operator Fresno County Computer Svcs., 1979-81; computer programmer Gesco Corp., Fresno, 1981-83, systems programmer, 1983-89; supr. operating systems support Calif. State U., Fresno, 1989—. Co-author: The Porter Tract - An Historical and Architectural Survey, 1990; contbr. articles to profl. publs. Mem. Fresno City and County Hist. Soc., 1989—; founding mem. Landmarks Preservation Coun., Fresno, 1991—, Tree Fresno, 1987—; mem. Fresno Zool. Soc. Mem. Assn. for Computing Machinery, Nat. Systems Programmer Assn. Democrat. Office: Calif State U CCMS 2225 E San Ramon Ave Fresno CA 93740-8029

MICHAELIS, GEORGE H., securities executive; b. 1937. BS in Engring. with honors, UCLA, 1958; MBA with distinction, Harvard Bus. Sch., 1960. V.p. Hohneberg & Assocs., Inc., 1969-71; sr. v.p. Source Capital, Inc., L.A., 1971-76, pres., dir., 1978—; sr. v.p. CMB Investment Counselors, 1976-78; exec. v.p. Paramount Mutual Fund, Inc., L.A.; chmn. bd., CEO First Pacific Advisors, Inc. Office: First Pacific Advisors Inc 11400 W Olympic Blvd Los Angeles CA 90064-1550*

MICHAELS, JEREMY DANIEL, judge; b. N.Y.C., July 26, 1954; s. Martin and Rose (Feldman) M.; m. Deborah Downey, June 2, 1984. AB, Colgate U., 1975; JD, Case Western Res. U., 1978. Bar: Wyo. 1978, U.S. Dist. Ct. Wyo. 1978, U.S. Ct. Appeals (10th cir.) 1978, U.S. Supreme Ct. 1978, U.S. Tax. Ct. 1981, U.S. Ct. Mil. Appeals 1981, N.Y. 1988, Colo. 1988, U.S. Ct. Claims 1988, U.S. Ct. Internat. Trade 1988, U.S. Ct. Appeals (fed. cir.) 1988. Legal advisor to sheriff Campbell County Sheriff's Dept., Gillette, Wyo., 1978-81; dep. county and prosecuting atty. Campbell County Atty.'s Office, Gillette, 1978-84; pvt. practice, Gillette, 1978-84; judge county ct. State of Wyo., Gillette, 1984-89, commr. county ct., 1989—, commr. dist. ct., 1984—; ptnr. Michaels & Michaels, Gillette; instr. Sheridan (Wyo.) Coll., 1979-81; pres. jud. div. County Ct., Cheyenne, 1986-88; faculty advisor gen. jurisdiction Nat. Jud. Coll., 1988; bd. dirs. EnergyShare of Wyo. Bd. dirs. Gillette Abuse Refuge Found., 1980-83, Power River Arts Coun., 1982-85. Mem. ABA (ho. of dels. 1986-88), Jud. Conf. County Ct. (chmn. 1986-88), Am. Judicature Soc., Masons. Republican. Home: 1202 Hilltop Ct Gillette WY 82718-5625 Office: 222 S Gillette Ave Ste 702 Gillette WY 82716-3746

MICHAELS, PATRICK FRANCIS, broadcasting company executive; b. Superior, Wis., Nov. 5, 1925; s. Julian and Kathryn Elizabeth (Keating) M.; AA, U. Melbourne, 1943; BA, Golden State U., 1954; PhD, London U., 1964; m. Paula Naomi Bowen, May 1, 1960; children—Stephanie Michelle, Patricia Erin. War corr. CBS; news editor King Broadcasting, 1945-50; war corr. Mid-East Internat. News Service, 1947-49; war corr. MBS, Korea, 1950-53; news dir. Sta. WDSU-AM-FM-TV, 1953-54; fgn. corr. NBC, S. Am., 1954-56; news dir. Sta. KWIZ, 1956-59; commentator ABC, Los Angeles, 1959-62; fgn. corr. Am. News Services, London, 1962-64; news commentator McFadden Bartell Sta. KCBQ, 1964-68; news commentator ABC, San Francisco, 1968-70; news dir. Sta. KWIZ, Santa Ana, Calif., 1970-74, station mgr., 1974-81; pres. Sta. KWRM, Corona, Calif., Sta. KQLH, San Bernardino, Calif., 1981-88; chmn. Michaels Media, Corona del Mar, Calif., 1988—. Bd. dirs. Econ. Devel. Corp. Mem. Nat. Assn. Broadcasters (bd. dirs.), Calif. Broadcasters Assn. (v.p.), Am. Fedn. TV and Radio Artists, Orange County Broadcasters Assn. (pres.), Sigma Delta Chi (ethics com.). Republican. Clubs: Rotary, Balboa Bay (bd. govs.), South Shore Yacht, Internat. Yachting Fellowship of Rotarians (staff commodore). Home: 2214 Vista Hogar Newport Beach CA 92660-4030

MICHAELS, STACEY QUALLS, recording engineer; b. Las Vegas, Feb. 3, 1964; d. George Michael and Mary Darlene (Harrison) Qualls; m. Robert Nik Michaels, Sept. 3, 1982 (div. Apr. 1986). Student, U. Nev., 1982. Engr. Dick Orkins Radio Ranch, Hollywood, Calif., 1988; freelance engr. Hollywood, Calif., 1988-91, Waves Recording, Hollywood, Calif., 1991-92, Hollywood Recording, Hollywood, Calif., 1992—; instr. U. Sound Arts, Hollywood, 1983; sound designer The Groundlings Theater, L.A., 1984, others. Various svc. roles Al-Anon, L.A. Mem. Sierra Club. Office: Hollywood Recording Svcs 6565 Hollywood Blvd Los Angeles CA 90028-6241

MICHALIK, JOHN JAMES, legal association executive; b. Bemidji, Minn., Aug. 1, 1945; s. John and Margaret Helen (Pafko) M.; m. Diane Marie Olson, Dec. 21, 1968; children: Matthew John, Nicole, Shane. BA, U. Minn., 1967, JD, 1970. Legal editor Lawyers Coop. Pub. Co., Rochester, N.Y., 1970-75; dir. continuing legal edn. Wash. State Bar Assn., Seattle, 1975-81, exec. dir., 1981-91; asst. dean devel. & cmty. rels. Sch. of Law U. Wash., 1991-95; exec. dir. Assn. Legal Adminstrs., 1995. Mem. Am. Soc. Assn. Execs., Nat. Assn. Bar Execs., Am. Mgmt. Assn., Nat. Trust Hist. Preservation, Ninth Jud. Cir. Hist. Soc., Univ. Faculty Club, Coll. Club Seattle. Lutheran. Office: Assn Legal Adminstrs 175 E Hawthorn Pky Vernon Hills IL 60061-1428

MICHALKO, JAMES PAUL, library association administrator; b. Cleve., May 13, 1950; s. Paul James and Lillian (Fanta) M.; 1 child, Alexandra. BA, Georgetown U., 1971; MLS, MBA, U. Chgo., 1974. Asst. to v.p., adminstrn. Technicare Inc. (formerly BCC Industries), Cleve., 1971-72; asst dir., adminstrn. U. Pa. Librs., Phila., 1974-80; dir. bus. and fin. Rsch. Librs. Group, Stanford, Calif., 1980-85, v.p. fin. and adminstrn., 1985-87, acting pres., 1988-89; pres. Rsch. Librs. Group, Mountain View, Calif., 1989—. Contbr. to Libr. Quar., Coll. & Rsch. Librs.; reviewer for Libr. Quar., Coll. & Rsch. Librs., Acad. of Mgmt. Rev., Jour. Acad. Librarianship, Jour. Libr. Adminstrn. Office: Rsch Librs Group Inc 1200 Villa St Mountain View CA 94041-1106

MICHALS, LEE MARIE, retired travel agency executive; b. Chgo., June 6, 1939; d. Harry Joseph and Anna Marie (Monaco) Perzan; children: Debora Ann, Dana Lee, Jami. BA, Wright Coll., 1959. Cert. travel specialist and cons., destination specialist. Internat. travel sec. E.F. MacDonald Travel, Palo Alto, Calif., 1963-69; pres. Travel Experience, Santa Clara, Calif., 1973-88; ptnr. Cruise Connection, Mountain View, Calif., 1983-85; with Allways Travel, Sunnyvale, Calif. Mem. Am. Soc. Travel Agts., Inst. Cert. Travel Agts., Bay Area Travel Assn., Pacific Area Travel Agts., San Jose Women in Travel (organizing pres. 1971, 1st v.p. 1989). Office: Allways Travel 139 S Murphy Ave Sunnyvale CA 94086-6113

MICHAUD, MICHAEL GREGG, publishing executive, writer; b. Augusta, Maine, Aug. 22, 1955; s. Homer Joseph Jr. and Marion Gloria (Hodgson) M. AA, So. Maine U., 1975. Pres. MGM Press, L.A., 1987—. Author: The World of Mirth, 1988, The Sea Within, 1988, Silly Me, 1989, Christmas Carols, 1989, New Snow on Old Ice, 1990, Lion Tales, 1991, The World According to Natasha, 1991, The Land of Open Hands, 1991, Cardinal Winds, 1992, Flames of Hate in the City of Angels, 1992, Moribundo, 1992, Uncle Mike's Totally Cool Way Excellent Tasty Sweet and Real Fattening Heirloom Dessert Recipes in No Particular Order and Some Candy Recipes Too, Cookbook, 1993, Giraffes on Horseback Salad, 1994; editor: The Cats of Shambala, 1992, Touching Certain Things, 1992; contbr. numerous articles to profl. jours. Bd. dirs. Roar Found., Acton, Calif., 1991—. Mem. Pen Ctr. West. Home: 442 S Kenmore Ave Los Angeles CA 90020-2488

MICHEL, VICTOR JAMES, JR., retired librarian; b. St. Louis, Feb. 2, 1927; s. Victor James and Bernadette (Fox) M.; m. Margaret A. Renaud, Feb. 3, 1951; children: Dennis W., Daniel J., Catherine A., Denise M.; student St. Louis U., 1946-48. Asst. librarian McDonnell Aircraft Corp., St. Louis, 1948-55; mgr. Anaheim (Calif.) Information Center, Electronics Ops., Rockwell Internat. Corp., 1955-84; pres. V.J. Michel Inc., Grass Valley, Calif., 1986—; sec. Placentia Devel. Co., 1964-71. Charter mem. Placentia-Tlaquepaque Sister City Orgn., 1964-84; founder, pres. Placentia chpt. St. Louis Browns Fan Club. Planning commr., Placentia, Calif., 1957-60, city councilman, 1960-70, vice-mayor, 1960-64, mayor, 1964-68. Trustee Placentia Library Dist., 1970-79, pres., 1974-79; city historian, Placentia, 1976-84, city treas., 1980-84; chmn. Placentia Fine Arts Commn., 1978-80. Served from pvt. to staff sgt. AUS, 1945-46. Named Placentia Citizen of Yr., 1979. Mem. Placentia C. of C. (v.p. 1960), Placentia Jaycees (hon. life), Calif., Orange County (pres. 1976) library assns. Democrat. Roman Catholic. Club: West Atwood Yacht (hon. yeoman emeritus with citation 1970, ship's librarian). Author: Pictorial History of the West Atwood Yacht Club, 1966; Placentia—Around the World, 1970; also articles in profl. jours. Home: 909 Jack Rabbit Ct Saint Peters MO 63376-5921

MICHELS, ELIZABETH FRANCES, international economist; b. Fayetteville, N.C., Mar. 16, 1959; d. John Henry and Helen Faye (Kondracki) McMinn; 1 child, Christopher Patrick. BS in Fgn. Svc., Georgetown U., 1979; MA in Internat. Econs., Johns Hopkins U., Washington, 1985. Internat. economist U.S. Internat. Trade Adminstrn., U.S. Dept. Commerce, Washington, 1985-86, U.S. Dept. Treasury, Washington, 1986-87; industry economist IRS, San Francisco, 1988-89; study abroad advisor City Coll. San Francisco, 1990-93; economist Bank of Am., San Francisco, 1993—; admissions interviewer, recruiter Georgetown U., Washington and San Francisco, 1988—; cons. Accent Internat. Edn. Programs Abroad, Ltd., San Francisco, 1991-92. Instr. religion St. Gabriel's Parish, San Francisco, 1990-93; career advisor Alumnae Resources, San Francisco, 1992—. Recipient award for sustained superior performance U.S. Civil Svc., Goeppingen, Germany, 1981; scholar Nat. Spanish Contest, 1974; fellow Army Officers Wives Club Greater Washington Area, 1983. Mem. Am. Econ. Assn., Nat. Assn. Bus. Economists, World Affairs Coun. No. Calif., Georgetown U. Alumni Club. Roman Catholic. Home: 1606 Graystone Ln Daly City CA 94014-3454

MICHELSEN, ARI MONTGOMERY, economist, educator; b. Oslo, Aug. 10, 1954; s. Arve and Frances Michelsen; m. Miriam A. Cook; 1 child, Sonja. BS in Conservation Resource Mgmt., U. Md., 1976; MS in Econs., Colo. State U., 1983, PhD in Agrl. and Resource Econs., 1988. Rsch. assoc. Jack Faucett Assocs., Inc., Chevy Chase, Md., 1976-80; rsch. and teaching asst. Colo. State U., 1982-88; v.p., prin. Coal Network Assocs., Inc., Fort Collins, Colo., 1983-87; sr. assoc. environment and resource group RCG/Hagler, Bailly, Inc., Boulder, Colo., 1987-89; assoc. prof. dept. agrl. econs. U. Wyo., Laramie, 1989-94, assoc. dir. tech. and info. transfer water resources ctr., 1989-93; asst. prof. dept. econs. Wash. State U., Vancouver, 1994—. Contbr. articles and revs. to profl. jours.; editor: Water Resources Rsch., 1992—, Wyo. Hydrogram, Rsch. Briefs, Water Issues, 1989-93, Water Resources Update, 1991. Active natural resources adv. bd. City of Fort Collins, Colo., 1985-90, chair, 1987-89; mem. adv. com. Colo. River Basin Severe and Sustained Drought Study, 1990-91. Grantee U.S. Geol. Survey, 1993-94, UN Dept. Econ. and Social Devel., 1991-94, U.S. Geol. Survey and Wyo. Water Resources Ctr., 1991-93, 90-93, Wyo. Dept. Environ. Quality, 1990-91, Wyo. Water Resources Ctr., 1991-93. Mem. Am. Econ. Assn., Am. Water Resources Assn., Am. Water Works Assn., Assn. Environ. and Resource Econs., Internat. Assn. Energy Econs., Western Agrl. Econs. Assn. Office: Wash State U Vancouver Campus 1812 E Mcloughlin Blvd Vancouver WA 98663-3509

MICHELSON, SONIA, music educator, author; b. L.A., Feb. 14, 1928; d. Maurice and Elizabeth (Jacobs) Saeta; m. Irving Michelson, Apr. 4, 1954 (div. Aug. 1982); children: Ann Michelson Shoham, Louis E., Hadassah Zelman, Zahava Waldman, Elisheva Levin, Eliyahu Michaeli, Jack. BA, U. Calif., Berkeley, 1949. Instr. in guitar Suzuki Music Acad. of Chgo., 1980-81, Music Arts Sch., Highland Park, Ill., 1973-82; dir. in classical guitar Michelson Classic Guitar Studio, Chgo., 1973-88; dir. Michelson Classic Guitar Studio, L.A., 1988—; cons. Music Educators Nat. Conf., Atlantic City, N.J., 1976; columnist Guitar Found. of Am., L.A., 1984—. Author: Easy Classic Guitar Solos, 1977, Classical Guitar Study, 1982, New Dimensions in Classical Guitar for Children, 1984, Young Beginner's First Repertoire for Classical Guitar, 1995; contbr. articles to profl. jours. Mem. Am. String Tchrs. Assn. (spl. cons. 1977-85), Chgo. Classical Guitar Soc. (pres. 1978-88), Guitar Found. of Am. (mem. editorial bd. 1972—), Suzuki Assn. Am., Nat. Music Tchrs. Assn., Music Tchrs. Assn. Calif. Democrat. Jewish. Home: 1465 Reeves St Los Angeles CA 90035-2945

MICKEL, BUCK, construction company executive; b. Elberton, Ga., Dec. 17, 1925; s. James Clark and Reba (Vaughn) M.; m. Minor Herndon, May 2, 1946; children: Minor M. Shaw, Buck Alston, Charles Clark. BSCE, Ga. Inst. Tech., 1947; PhD (hon.), Erskine Coll., 1975. With Daniel Internat. Corp., Greenville, S.C., from 1948, chmn., from 1974; pres. Fluor Corp., Irvine, Calif., 1984-86; vice chmn. Fluor Corp., Irvine, from 1986, also dir.; vice chmn. U.S. Shelter Corp., Greenville, also bd. dirs.; chmn., bd. dirs. R.S.I. Corp., Greenville, 1978—; chmn., chief exec. officer Delta Woodside Industries Inc.; bd. dirs. Textile Hall Corp., Duke Power Co., Charlotte, C&S Corp., Atlanta, Monsanto Co., St. Louis, Liberty Corp., Greenville, Nat. Intergroup, Pitts., J.P. Stevens & Co., N.Y.C. Life trustee Converse Coll., 1964—, Clemson U., S.C., 1975—; mem. adv. bd. U. S.C. Bus. Sch., Columbia, S.C. Found. Ind. Colls., Columbia, James F. Brynes Internat. Ctr., Columbus, 1984—; bd. dirs. S.C. Bus. Week, S.C., 1985. Served to lt. C.E., U.S. Army; Korea. Named Citizen of Yr. Wofford Coll., Spartanburg, S.C., 1978; Disting. Salesman, Sales & Mktg. Execs., Greenville, 1975; inducted into S.C. Bus. Hall of Fame, 1986; First Institutional Advancement award Clemson U., 1986. Mem. S.C. State C. of C. (Businessman of Yr. 1983), U. S.C. Alumni Assn. (hon.). Republican. Baptist. Clubs: Augusta Nat. Golf; Collins Creek Gun., Commerce, Cotillion; Greenville Country, Green Valley Country (Greenville). Home: 415 Crescent Ave Greenville SC 29605-2818 Office: US Shelter Corp PO Box 1089 Greenville SC 29602-1089

MICKELSON, ALAN ROLF, electrical engineering educator, optoelectronics researcher; b. Westport, Conn., May 2, 1950; s. Siegfried Thor and Maybelle (Brown) M.; m. Ann Karin Sumstad; 1 child, Lars S. BSEE, U. Tex., 1973; MS, Calif. Inst. Tech., 1974, PhD, 1978. Postdoctoral fellow Calif. Inst. Tech., Pasadena, 1978-79; vis. scientist Byurakan (Armenian S.S.R.) Obs., 1979-80; research scientist, electronics lab. Norwegian Inst. Tech., Trondheim, 1980-83; asst. prof. elec. engring. U. Colo., Boulder, 1984-86, assoc. prof., 1986—. Author 2 textbooks; contbr. numerous articles to profl. jours. Mem. IEEE (hon. mention for best paper from Antennas & Propagation Soc. 1979, chmn. Denver sect. Lasers & Electrophysics Soc. 1992-94), AAAS, Optical Soc. Am. (chmn. Rocky Mtn. chpt. 1992-93), Nat. Radio Sci. Union (sec. commn. D 1992—), Internat. Soc. Hybrid Microelectronics, Caltech Alumni Assn. (Rocky Mtn. chpt. chmn. 1994—). Office: U Colo Elec Engring Dept Campus Box 425 Boulder CO 80309-0425

MICKELSON, GREG R., commerical real estate broker; b. Torrance, Calif., Mar. 14, 1962; s. Rodney D. and Patricia A. Mickelson; m. Laura K. Curran, Oct. 21, 1989. BA in Econs., U. Calif., 1984. Comml. real estate broker Ashwill-Schneider, Newport Beach, Calif., 1985-87, Grubb & Ellis Co., Newport Beach, Calif., 1987—; cons. IMAX Theatres, Toronot, Ont., Can., 1990-93. Pres., bd. dirs. U. Calif. Athletic Found., Irvine, 1992—; bd. dirs. Bren Events Ctr., Irvine, 1991—. Mem. Internat. Coun. of Shopping Ctrs., Comml. Indsl. Devel. Assn., U. Calif. Alumni Assn. (v.p., fin. 1993—), Orange County Sigma Chi Alumni (pres. 1990-91). Office: Grubb & Ellis Co 4000 Macarthur Blvd Ste 1500 Newport Beach CA 92660-2517

MICKELSON, H(ERALD) FRED, electric utility executive; b. Pratt, Kans., Oct. 4, 1938; s. Herald E. and Arvilla (Knight) M.; m. D. Joan Mickelson, Feb. 21, 1958; children: Mikel Tod, Janet Lynn. BS in Mgmt. Sci., Pepperdine U., 1974; postgrad. Mgmt. Policy Inst., U. So. Calif., 1978. Dist. mgr. So. Calif. Edison, Santa Ana, 1982-84; mgr. corp. communications So. Calif. Edison, Rosemead, 1984-85; div. ops. mgr. So. Calif. Edison, Santa Ana, 1985-86, San Bernardino, 1986-87; mgr. mktg. So. Calif. Edison, Rosemead, 1987-91; regional v.p. So. Calif. Edison, Santa Ana, 1992—. Officer, bd. dirs. Calif. divsn. Am. Cancer Soc., chmn. bd. Calif. divsn., 1993-94, nat. bd. dirs.; officer, mem. exec. com., bd. dirs. United Way of Orange County, chmn. bd., 1995, chmn. bd., 1995; bd. dirs. ARC of Orange County, St. Joseph's Hosp. of Orange; chmn. Orange County Econ. Devel. Commn., 1993-94; adv. bd. St. Jude's Hosp. of Fullerton, Sch. Bus. and Econs. Chapman U.; officer, bd. dirs. Nat. Conf. Christians and Jews, presiding co-chmn., 1994—; officer, bd. dirs. Orange County Bus. Com. for the Arts, Orgn. Unified Concerned Homeowners; bd. govs. Orange County Human Rels. Com.; mem. Indsl. League Orange County, Orange County Transp. Coalition. Recipient Field Svcs. Builder award Am. Cancer Soc., 1992, Humanitarian award Orange County Human Rels. Commn., 1993, Comty. Leadership award Orange County Black C. of C., 1994; named one of Top 25 Bus. Leaders in Orange County, Orange County Bus. Jour., 1993-95. Mem. Edison Electric Inst. (customer svc. and mktg. bd. dirs.), Pacific Coast Electric Assn. (customer svc. and mktg. exec. com.), Orange County C. of C. (bd. dirs., exec. com., chmn. bd. 1994). Republican. Mem. Evangelical Free Ch. Office: So Calif Edison Co 1325 S Grand Ave Santa Ana CA 92705-4406

MICKELSON, SIG, broadcasting executive, educator; b. Clinton, Minn., May 24, 1913; s. Olaf and Harriet (Reinholdson) M.; m. Maybelle Brown,

June 8, 1940 (dec. Apr., 1985); children: Karen Ann (Mrs. Christiaan De Brauw), Alan; m. Elena Mier y Teran, June 14, 1986. B.A., Augustana Coll., 1934, LLD, 1987; M.A., U. Minn., 1940. With CBS, N.Y.C., 1943-61; pres. CBS News, 1954-61; v.p., dir. Time-Life Broadcast, Inc., N.Y.C., 1961-70, Ency. Brit. Ednl. Corp., Chgo., 1970-72; prof., chmn. editorial dept. Medill Sch. Journalism, Northwestern U., Evanston, Ill., 1972-75; pres. RFE/RL, Inc., Washington, 1975-78; Disting. vis. prof. San Diego State U., 1978-79, exec. dir. Ctr. for Communications, 1979-82, adj. prof, 1984-90, Van Deerlin prof. communications, 1989-90; pres. San Diego Communications Coun., 1989-90; Manship prof. journalism La. State U., 1991-93, disting. prof. comm., 1994—; research fellow Hoover Instn., 1981—; advisor Nat. News Council, 1973-80; ex-officio Bd. Internat. Broadcasting, 1975-78; dir. Stauffer Communications Inc. Author: The Electric Mirror, 1972, America's Other Voice, 1983, The First Amendment: The Challenge of New Technology, 1989, From Whistle Stop to Sound Bite, 1989, The Northern Pacific Railroad and the Selling of the West, 1993. Bd. regents Augustana Coll., 1993-95. Mem. Radio TV News Dirs. Assn. (founder; v.p. 1946-48, pres. 1948-49), Internat. Inst. for Comm. (founder; chmn. 1970-71, chmn. exec. com. 1967-70, 71-73), Coun. on Fgn. Rels., Soc. Profl. Journalists. Clubs: Century Assn. (N.Y.C.); Cosmos (Washington). Home: 6443 Pasatiempo Ave San Diego CA 92120-3823

MIDANEK, DEBORAH HICKS, portfolio manager, director; b. N.Y.C., Nov. 30, 1954; d. Frederick Stevens and Mary Leavenworth (Barnes) H.; m. James Ira Midanek, Sept. 29, 1985; children: Benjamin Abraham, Thomas Hicks. AB, Bryn Mawr Coll., 1975; MBA, U. Pa., 1980. Asst. dir. admissions Bryn Mawr (Pa.) Coll., 1975-78; asst. v.p. Bankers Trust, N.Y.C., 1980-84; v.p. Drexel Burnham Lambert, N.Y.C., 1984-90; CEO Solon Asset Mgmt. Corp., 1990—; mng. dir. mutual funds Montgomery Asset Mgmt., San Francisco, 1992-93; bd. dirs. Drexel Burnham Lambert Group, 1990-92, Std. Brands Paint Co., chmn. compensation com., 1993—, chmn. of the bd., 1995—. Trustee, treas. New St. Found., 1992-94; bd. dirs. Pelham (N.Y.) Art Ctr., 1989-91, Mgmt. Decision Lab. Stern Sch. Bus., NYU, 1990-93, United Way of Pelham, 1990-93; mem. exec. bd. exploring divsn. Greater N.Y. coun. Boy Scouts Am., 1991-93; trustee Warren Wilson Coll., Asheville, N.C., 1993—. Mem. N.Y. Soc. Securities Analysts, Bryn Mawr Coll. Club of N.Y. (pres. 1991-93), Econ. Club of N.Y. Republican. Home: 375 La Casa Via Walnut Creek CA 94598-4842 Office: Solon Asst Mgmt LP 1981 N Broadway Ste 325 Walnut Creek CA 94596-3852

MIDDLEBROOKS, DELORIS JEANETTE, nurse, retired; b. Cedar Rapids, Iowa, Apr. 9, 1931; d. Harland R. and Rosa V. (Anderson) Hickey; m. Johnnie L. Middlebrooks, Apr. 25, 1963 (dec.); children: James, Kathleen. Diploma, Evang. Hosp. Sch. Nursing, 1956; BSN, State U. Iowa, 1958; MS in Nursing, U. Calif., San Francisco, 1960; EdD, U. Nev., Las Vegas, 1985. Instr., coord. Nev. State Hosp. Sch. Practical Nursing, Sparks, 1963-66; staff nurse St. Mary's Hosp., Reno, 1968; instr., coord. Reno VA Sch. Practical Nursing, 1968-72; instr,. coord. health occupations Wooster High Sch., 1972-73; nursing faculty Truckee Meadows C.C., 1973-94, retired, 1994; intermittent staff nurse VA Hosp., 1984-86; instr., review course Stanley Kaplan Ednl. Ctr., 1987-89; clin. nursing faculty Western Nev. C.C., Carson City, 1987, Northern Nev. C.C., Elko, 1979-93; guest assoc. prof. nursing Lewis-Clark State Coll., Lewiston, Idaho, 1989; cons. Irish Bd. Nursing, Dublin, Ireland, 1985. Nominated Nev. Voc. Tchr. of Yr., 1975, 79, 88, 89; Recipient March of Dimes Community Leadership award, 1990. Mem. ANA, Am. Voc. Assn., Western Inst. Nursing, Western Soc. Rsch. Nursing, Nev. Nurses Assn., Nev. Voc. Assn., Sigma Theta Tau, Phi Kappa Phi. Home: 1385 Ebbetts Dr Reno NV 89503-1918

MIDDLETON, ANTHONY WAYNE, JR., urologist, educator; b. Salt Lake City, May 6, 1939; s. Anthony Wayne and Dolores Caravena (Lowry) M.; m. Carol Samuelson, Oct. 23, 1970; children: Anthony Wayne, Suzanne, Kathryn, Jane, Michelle. BS, U. Utah, 1963; MD, Cornell U., 1966. Intern, U. Utah Hosps., Salt Lake City, 1966-67; resident in urology Mass. Gen. Hosp., Boston, 1970-74; practice urology Middleton Urol. Assos., Salt Lake City, 1974—; mem. staff Primary Children's Hosp., staff pres., 1981-82; mem. staff Latter-Day Saints Hosp., Holy Cross Hosp.; assoc. clin. prof. surgery U. Utah Med. Coll., 1977—; vice chmn. bd. govs. Utah Med. Self-Ins. Assn., 1980-81, chmn. 1985-87. Bd. dirs. Utah chpt. Am. Cancer Soc., 1978-86; bishop, later stake presidency Ch. Jesus Christ Latter-day Saints; vice chmn. Utah Med. Polit. Action Com., 1978-81, chmn., 1981-83; chmn. Utah Physicians for Reagan, 1983-84; mem. U. Utah Coll. Medicine Dean's Search Com., 1983-84; bd. dirs. Utah Symphony, 1985—. editor (monthly pub.) AACU-FAX, 1992—. Capt. USAF, 1968-70. Mem. ACS, Utah State Med. Assn. (pres. 87-88), Am. Urologic Assn. (socioecons. com. 1987—, chmn. western sect. 1989—, western. sect. health policy com. chmn., 1990—), AMA (alt. del. to House of Dels. 1989-92, 94), Salt Lake County Med. Assn. (sec. 1965-67, pres. liaison com. 1980-81, pres.-elect 1981-83, pres. 1984), Utah Urol. Assn. (pres. 1976-77), Salt Lake Surg. Soc. (treas. 1977-78), Am. Assn. Clin. Urologists (bd. dirs. 1989-90, nat. pres. elect 1990-91, pres. 1991-92, nat. bd. chmn. urologic polit. action com. UROPAC, 1992—), Phi Beta Kappa, Alpha Omega Alpha, Beta Theta Pi (chpt. pres. Gamma Beta 1962). Republican. Contbr. articles to profl. jours. Home: 2798 Chancellor Pl Salt Lake City UT 84108-2835 Office: 1060 1st Ave Salt Lake City UT 84103-4147

MIDDLETON, MICHAEL JOHN, civil engineer; b. N.Y.C., May 14, 1953; s. Vincent Aloysius and Mary Hilda (Lehane) M. BS in Civil Engring., U. Calif., Davis, 1975. Registered profl. engr., Calif., Wash., Hawaii. Project mgr. G.A. Fitch & Assoc., Concord, Calif., 1975-78, v.p., 1978-80; project mgr. Santina & Thompson, Inc., Concord, 1980-83, dir. engring., 1983-88, sr. v.p., 1988—. scholar, Calif. Scholarship Fedn., 1971. Mem. ASCE, Nat. Soc. Profl. Engrs., Soc. Am. Mil. Engrs. Roman Catholic. Home: 1409A Bel Air Dr Concord CA 94521-2802 Office: Santina & Thompson Inc 1355 Willow Way Ste 280 Concord CA 94520-5728

MIDDLETON, RICHARD GEORGE, urologist, educator; b. Salt Lake City, May 7, 1933; s. Richard Palmer and Lucy Jane (Rose) M.; m. Jayne G. Middleton, Sept. 24, 1957; children: Elizabeth, William, Amy. BA, U. Utah, 1955; MD, Cornell U., 1958. Prof. surgery, chmn. divsn. urology U. Utah Sch. Medicine, Salt Lake City, 1968—. Home: 1424 Circle Way Salt Lake City UT 84103-4432 Office: U Utah Sch Medicine 50 N Medical Dr Salt Lake City UT 84132

MIDDLEWOOD, MARTIN EUGENE, technical communications specialist, writer, consultant; b. Galesburg, Ill., Mar. 21, 1947; s. Martin and Bernetta Maxine (Henderson) M.; m. Mona Marie Jarmer, Sept. 10, 1971; children: Erin, Martha, Emily, Margaret. BA, Ea. Wash. U., 1973, MA, 1980. Writer tech. manuals Tektronix, Inc., Beaverton, Oreg., 1976-77, tech. writer, 1977-79, sr. tech. writer, 1979-82, sup. pub. rels., 1982-84, mgr. pub. rels., 1984-85; mgr. mktg. communications Tektronix, Inc., Vancouver, Wash., 1985-87; account supr. Waggener Edstrom, Portland, Oreg., 1987—; pub. Cognizer Report, Portland, Oreg., 1990-94; chmn. adv. bd. sci. and tech. writing, Clark Coll., Vancouver, 1984—; owner communications cons. firm, Vancouver, 1978—. Author: (ednl. brochure series) Oscilloscope Measurements, 1979 (award of excellence Willamette Valley chpt. Soc. Tech. Communication, 1980); contbr. articles to profl. jours. Served with USMC, 1967-70. Recipient Cert. Recognition Clark Coll., Vancouver, 1984, 86, 89, 92; award of Excellence Pacific N.W. chpt. Internat. Assn. Bus. Communicators, 1985. Mem. Soc. Tech. Communication (sr., pres. Willamette Valley chpt. 1983-85, award of recognition 1986, chpt. pub. achievement award 1985, 2 awards of distinction 1981). Home: 1107 SE 98th Ave Vancouver WA 98664-4119 Office: Waggener Edstrom 6915 SW Macadam Ave Ste 300 Portland OR 97219-2300

MIDKIFF, DONALD WAYNE, program manager; b. Post, Tex., Sept. 26, 1940; s. Colvert Crockett Midkiff and Judy M. (Poss) Hinckley; m. Olga Maria Androvitch, June 21, 1961 (div. 1968); m. Manbeth Jean Crowell, Apr. 29, 1979. BS in Tech. Mgmt., Denver Tech. Coll., 1988; MS in Mgmt., Colo. Tech. Coll., 1994. With USAF, 1960, advanced through grades to sgt., 1968; electronics supr. Lockheed Aircraft, Jidda, Saudi Arabia, 1969-71; site mgr. Kentron Hawaii, Ltd., Pleiku, South Vietnam, 1971-73; supr. Kentron, Kwajalein, Marshall Islands, 1973-80, range ops. engr., 1980-84; ops. supr. Kentron PRC, Maui, Hawaii, 1984-85; ops. mgr. Kentron PRC, Colorado Springs, Colo., 1985-87; div. security mgr. PRC, Colorado Springs, Colo., 1987-89; program mgr. PRC Inc., Colorado Springs, Colo., 1989—; advisor Denver Tech. Coll., Colorado Springs, 1991—. CPR instr. Am. Red Cross, 1980-86; pres. Kwajalein Dive Club, 1981-83, Kwajalein Tennis Club, 1978-80. Recipient Group Achievement award NASA, 1992. Mem. AFCEA, Mensa, Nat. Contract Mgmt. Assn., Profl. Assn. Diving Instrs. (dive master). Republican. Office: PRC Inc 985 Space Center Dr Ste 200 Colorado Springs CO 80915-3638

MIECH, ALLEN C., financial services company executive; b. 1939. Attended, U. Wis., 1960. With Transamerica Fin. Group. Inc., L.A., 1962—, br. mgr., 1965-68, dist. mgr., 1968-77, area mgr., 1977-79, asst. to pres., gen. mgr. br. Sys Lyon Moving & Storage, 1979-81, regional v.p., 1981-83, chief credit officer, 1983-84; exec. v.p. sales & mktg. ops., then pres. TransAmerica Fin. Svcs. Calif., L.A., 1984—, pres., CEO. With USNG, 1960-62. Office: TransAmerica Fin Svcs Calif 1150 S Olive St Los Angeles CA 90015-2211*

MIEL, GEORGE JOSEPH, computer scientist; b. Paris, Sept. 7, 1943; s. Joseph and Josephine (Modlinska) M. BS, U. Ill., 1964, MS, 1965; PhD, U. Wyo., 1976. Mem. tech. staff Bellcomm, 1967-69, NASA, 1967-69; cons. Siemens A.G., Munich, 1969-70; computer scientist Applied Rsch. Labs., Ecublens, Switzerland, 1970-73; assoc. prof. U. Nev., Las Vegas, 1978-85; researcher Hughes Aircraft Co., Malibu, Calif., 1985—; prof. U. Nev., Las Vegas, 1991—; cons. on computer modeling Las Vegas, 1994—; vis. asst. prof. U. Calgary, Can., 1976-78; vis. assoc. prof. Ariz. State U., Tempe, 1983-84; cons. on computer modelling, Las Vegas, 1994—. Contbr. numerous articles to profl. jours. Recipient numerous rsch. grants, Chauvenet prize Math. Assn. Am., 1986. Mem. IEEE, AIAA (vice chmn. com. on software sys. 1993—), Aerospace Industries Assn. (chmn. computational sci. com. Washington 1989-91), soc. Indsl. Applied Math. (cons. and researcher). Office: PO Box 72226 Las Vegas NV 89170-2226

MIEL, VICKY ANN, municipal government executive; b. South Bend, Ind., June 20, 1951; d. Lawrence Paul Miel and Virginia Ann (Yeagley) Hernandez. BS, Ariz. State U., 1985. Word processing coordinator City of Phoenix, 1977-78, word processing adminstr., 1978-83, chief dep. city clk., 1983-88, city clk. dir., 1988—; assoc. prof. Phoenix Community Coll., 1982-83, Mesa (Ariz.) Community Coll., 1983; speaker in field, Boston, Santa Fe, Los Angeles, N.Y.C. and St. Paul, 1980—. Author: Phoenix Document Request Form, 1985, Developing Successful Systems Users, 1986. Judge Future Bus. Leaders Am. at Ariz. State U., Tempe, 1984; bd. dirs. Fire and Life Safety League, Phoenix, 1984. Recipient Gold Plaque, Word Processing Systems Mag., Mpls., 1980, Green Light Productivity award City of Phoenix, 1981, Honor Soc. Achievement award Internat. Word Processing Assn., 1981, 1st Ann. Grand Prize Records Mgmt. Internat. Inst. Mcpl. Clks., 1990, Olsten Award for Excellence in Records Mgmt., 1991, Tech. Award of Excellence, 1995. Mem. Assn. Info. Systems Profls. (internat. dir. 1982-84), Internat. Inst. Mcpl. Clks. (cert., Tech. award of excellence 1995), Am. Records Mgrs. Assn., Assn. Image Mgmt., Am. Soc. Pub. Adminstrs., Am. Mgmt. Assn. Office: City of Phoenix 200 W Washington St Ste 1500 Phoenix AZ 85003-1611

MIELE, ANTHONY WILLIAM, retired librarian; b. Williamsport, Pa., Feb. 12, 1926; s. Harry John and Louise Casale (Troyano) M.; m. Ruth Cassidy, Jan. 29, 1955; children—Terri Ann, Anthony William, Robert John, Elizabeth Ann. B.S. in Bus. Adminstrn, Marquette U., Milw., 1951; M.L.S., U. Pitts., 1966. Partner, mgr. restaurant Williamsport, 1960-66; dir. Elmwood Park (Ill.) Pub. Libr., 1967-68; asst. dir. Oak Park (Ill.) Pub. Libr., 1968-70; asst. dir. tech. services Ill. State Libr., Springfield, 1970-75; state librn. Ala. Pub. Libr. Service, Montgomery, 1975-86; coord. Libr. Svcs. and Constrn. Act, 1986-87; dir. library extension div. Ariz. Dept. Libr., Archives and Pub. Records, Phoenix, 1987-95; ret.; exec. dir. Ill. Nat. Libr. Week, 1970, ALA Nat. Libr. Week Commn., 1971-74; mem. Pub. Printer's Adv. Coun. Depository Librs., 1975-78, vice chmn., 1977-78; mem. CLSI Nat. Adv. Com., 1983-87; reader NEH, 1987; exhibits chair for confs. Mountain Plains Libr. Assn., Ariz. State Libr. Assn., Ariz. Edn. Media Assn., 1992; co-chair ASLA/AEMA Annual Conf., 1993. Assoc. editor Govt. Publs. Rev., 1974-85; contbr. articles to profl. publs. Mayor Arrowhead Community, 1984; bd. dirs. Amigos Libr. Network, 1990-94. Recipient cert. of appreciation Am. Libr. Trustee Assn., 1986. Mem. ALA (chmn. govt. documents round table 1974-76, chair state libr. agy. sect. 1992-93, mem. coun. 1994—), Ill. Libr. Assn., Ala. Libr. Assn. (Exceptional svc. citation 1986), Ariz. State Libr. Assn. (Pres. award of recognition 1993), Nat Microfilm Assn., Spl. Libr. Assn., Chief Officers State Libr. Agys. (sec. 1978-80), Beta Phi Mu. Roman Catholic.

MIELKE, PAUL WILLIAM, JR., statistician; b. St. Paul, Feb. 18, 1931; s. Paul William and Elsa (Yungbauer) M.; m. Roberta Roehl Robison, June 25, 1960; children: William, Emily, Lynn. BA, U. Minn., 1953, PhD, 1963; MA, U. Ariz., 1958. Teaching asst. U. Ariz., Tucson, 1957-58; teaching asst. U. Minn., Mpls., 1958-60, statis. cons., 1960-62, lectr., 1962-63; from asst. to assoc. prof. dept. statistics Colo. State U., Fort Collins, 1963-72, prof. dept. statistics, 1972—. Contbr. articles to Am. Jour. Pub. Health, Jour. of Statis. Planning and Inference, Ednl. and Psychol. Measurement, Biometrika, Earth-Sci. Revs. Capt. USAF, 1953-57. Fellow Am. Statis. Assn.; mem. Am. Meteorol. Soc. (Banner I. Miller award 1993), Biometric Soc. Home: 736 Cherokee Dr Fort Collins CO 80525-1517 Office: Colo State U Dept Stats Fort Collins CO 80523

MIGDEN, CAROLE, county official; b. N.Y.C., Aug. 14, 1948. BA, Adelphi U., 1970; M in Psychology, Sonoma State U., 1976. Exec. dir. Operation Concern, San Francisco, 1981-89; mem. bd. suprs. City of San Francisco, 1991—; vice-chair San Francisco (Calif.) County Transp. Authority, 1994—; former commr. Calif. State Health Commn. Former chair San Francisco Dem. Party; chair Calif. Dem. Party Platform Com.; platform com. mem. Dem. Nat. Com.; past bd. mem. United Way, Lyon-Martin Women's Health Svcs., Hadassah, Western States Legal Found., San Francisco Women's Bldg. Recipient numerous cmty. awards. Jewish. Office: Bd Suprs City Hall Rm 308 401 McAllister St San Francisco CA 94102

MIGDEN, CHESTER L., association executive; b. N.Y.C., May 21, 1921; s. Albert and Louise (Jawer) M.; m. Dina Vohl, July 22, 1944; children: Barbara, Ann, Amy. B.A., CCNY, 1941; LL.B., Columbia U., 1947. Bar: N.Y. State 1947. Atty. NLRB, N.Y.C., 1947-51; various positions Screen Actors Guild Inc., Hollywood, 1952-81; nat. exec. sec. Screen Actors Guild Inc., 1973-81; v.p. Internat. Fedn. Actors, 1973-81, Calif. Labor Fedn., 1974-81, Associated Actors and Artistes Am., 1973-81; exec. dir. Assn. Talent Agts., 1982-94; ret., 1994; officer, trustee Producers-Screen Actors Guild pension, welfare plans, 1960-81; v.p. Motion Picture and TV Fund, 1975—; instr. extension program UCLA. Contbr. articles to profl. jours. Mem. Acad. Motion Picture Arts and Scis., Am. Arbitration Assn. (arbitrator), Labor Rels. Cons. Democrat.

MIGUEL DESOUSA, LINDA J., critical care nurse, nursing educator; b. Honolulu, Dec. 6, 1946; d. Gregory and Irene N. (Calasa) Furtado; children: Joseph H. Miguel Jr., Brett A. Miguel. ADN, Maui Community Coll., Kahului, Hawaii, 1980; BSN, U. Hawaii, 1987, MS, 1990. RN, Hawaii. Charge nurse ICU-CCU Maui Meml. Hosp., Wailuku; nursing instr. Maui Community Coll., Kahului; unit supr.-coronary care Straub Clinic and Hosp., Honolulu; nursing instr. Kapiolani Community Coll., Honolulu; edn. dir. Waianae Health Acad.; researcher in field. Contbr. articles to profl. jours. Outer Island Students Spl. Nursing scholar, 1988-90, Rsch. scholarship, 1989. Mem. AACN, Hawaii Nurses Assn., Hawaii Soc. for Cardiovascular and Pulmonary Rehab., Sigma Theta Tau. Home: 98-402 Koauka Loop #1202 Aiea HI 96701

MIHALIC, DAVID ANTHONY, national park administrator; b. Litchfield, Ill., July 10, 1946; s. John Anthony and Geraldine Emily (Mills) M.; m. Jeri Lynn Andrews, June 25, 1988; children: Emily Victoria, Nicholas Charles. BS, So. Ill. U., 1968; MS, Mich. State U., 1974; grad. with distinction, Fed. Law Enforcement Tng. Ctr., Glynco, Ga., 1976. Environ. planner U.S. Army C.E., Ft. Worth, 1969-72; park ranger Glacier Nat. Park Nat. Park Svc., Mont., 1972-74; recreation planner Bur. Land Mgmt., Fairbanks, Alaska, 1974-76, Denver, 1977-78; dist. ranger Yellowstone Nat. Park Nat. Park Svc., Old Faithful, Wyo., 1978-81; supt. Yukon-Charley Rivers Nat. Res. Nat. Park Svc., Eagle City, Alaska, 1981-85; asst. supt. Great Smoky Mountains Nat. Park Nat. Park Svc., Tenn. and N.C., 1985-88; supt. Mammoth Cave Nat. Park, Nat. Park Svc., Ky., 1988-93; chief Office of Policy Nat. Park Svc. Hdqrs., Washington, 1993-94; supt. Glacier Nat. Park, West Glacier, Mont., 1994—; spl. advisor Barren River Area Devel. Dist., Bowling Green, Ky., 1988-94; instr. Albright Tng. Acad., Grand Canyon, Ariz., 1989—; adv. dir. Cave City Conv. Ctr., 1990-94; dir. Caveland Sanitation Authority, Cave City, Ky., 1988-94; dir. Flathead Basin Commn., 1994—, Flathead Vis. and Conv. Assn., 1994—. Contbr. articles to profl. jours. Scoutmaster Boy Scouts Am., Ft. Worth, 1971; mem. bldg. com. Our Lady of The Caves Ch., Horse Cave, Ky., 1990; councilman Eagle City, Alaska, 1984. Capt. U.S. Army, 1968-72. Named Supt. of Yr., Nat. Park Svc., 1994; named to Hon. Order Ky. Cols., 1988. Mem. Assn. Nat. Pk. Rangers (charter, regional rep. 1979-80, svc. award 1979, 89), Employee and Alumni Assn. Nat. Pk. Svc., Internat. Assn. Natural Resource Pilots, Rotary, Kiwanis (v.p. Gatlinburg, Tenn. club 1987). Roman Catholic. Office: Glacier Nat Park West Glacier MT 59936

MIHAN, RALPH GEORGE, lawyer; b. San Francisco, Mar. 30, 1941; s. Ralph William and Norma Rose (Holmes) M.; m. Eleanor Mae Green, Sept. 24, 1966; children: Gregory Scott, Jeffrey Matthew. BA, St. Mary's Coll., 1963; JD, U. San Francisco, 1966. Bar: Calif. 1966, U.S. Dist. Ct. (no. dist.) Calif. 1967, U.S. Ct. Appeals (9th cir.) 1967. Atty. U.S. Dept. Interior, San Francisco, 1967-74, field solicitor (area counsel) Office of the Solicitor, 1974—; lectr. Nat. Park Svc. Rangers Acad., 1976—. Dir. coach St. Raphael's Cath. Youth Orgn. Basketball Program, San Rafael, 1977-88, San Rafael Youth Soccer League, 1978-88, San Rafael Little League, 1979-89; commr. City San Rafael Pk. and Recreation Commn., 1982—. Recipient Outstanding Community Svc. award Calif. Pk. and Recreation Soc., 1983. Mem. San. Francisco Bar Assn., Fed. Bar Assn. (pres. San Francisco chpt. 1974-75, exec. com. 1976—, Outstanding Contbn. award 1977). Office: US Dept Interior Office of the Solicitor 600 Harrison St Ste 545 San Francisco CA 94107-1370

MIHAN, RICHARD, dermatologist; b. L.A., Dec. 20, 1925; s. Arnold and Virginia Catherine (O'Reilly) M.; student U. So. Calif., 1945; MD, St. Louis U., 1949. Rotating intern Los Angeles County Gen. Hosp., 1949-51, resident in dermatology, 1954-57; practice medicine specializing in dermatology, Los Angeles, 1957—; emeritus clin. prof. dept. medicine, dermatology and syphilology U. So. Calif. Served as lt. (j.g.) M.C., USNR, 1951-53, ret. as lt. comdr. Diplomate Am. Bd. Dermatology. Fellow ACP; mem. Internat. Soc. Dermatology, Soc. Investigative Dermatology, Pacific Dermatologic Assn. (exec. bd. 1971-74), Calif. Med. Assn. (chmn. dermatologic sect. 1973-74), AMA, Los Angeles Dermatol. Soc. (pres. 1975-76), Am. Acad. Dermatology, L.A. Acad. Medicine (pres. 1988-89), Calif. Club. Roman Catholic. Office: 1245 Wilshire Blvd Los Angeles CA 90017-4810

MIILLÉ, CAROL ANN, counselor; b. Lincoln, Nebr., Nov. 14, 1945; d. Roy Everet Jr. and Twila Isabell (Terril) Hinsley; m. Gary Nieland Miillé, Nov. 30, 1963 (div. Apr. 1988); children: Gary Neiland Jr., Danielle Denene Miillé Rainville; m. Gil Julian Thomas, Sept. 25, 1993. AS, Clackamas C.C., 1982; BA, Portland State U., 1984; MA, Lewis & Clark Coll., 1987. Lic. profl. counselor, Oreg.; cert. hypnotherapist. Clin. dir. Counseling Interventions, Portland, Oreg., 1987-89; clin. supr. Morrison Ctr., Portland, 1989-91; pvt. practice mental health therapist Milw., 1990—; mem. N.W. Women's Therapy Project, Portland, 1987-94; pvt. practice supr. for counselors, Milw., 1989—; chem. dependence instr. Project Stop, Portland, 1989-91; cons. to therapists, Portland Met. area, 1989—; guest lectr. Portland State U., 1990. Mem. Nat. Counseling Assn., Oreg. Counseling Assn., Milw. Bus. Assn. Democrat. Roman Catholic. Office: PO Box 1376 9136 SE St Helens St Clackamas OR 97015-1376

MIKALOW, ALFRED ALEXANDER, II, deep sea diver, marine surveyor, marine diving consultant; b. N.Y.C., Jan. 19, 1921; m. Janice Brenner, Aug. 1, 1960; children: Alfred Alexander, Jon Alfred. Student Rutgers U., 1940; MS, U. Calif., Berkeley, 1948; MA, Rochdale U. (Can.), 1950. Owner Coastal Diving Co., Oakland, Calif., 1950—, Divers Supply, Oakland, 1952—; dir. Coastal Sch. Deep Sea Diving, Oakland, 1950—; capt. and master rsch. vessel Coastal Researcher I; mem. Marine Inspection Bur., Oakland. marine diving contractor, cons. Mem. adv. bd. Medic Alert Found., Turlock, Calif., 1960—. Lt. comdr. USN, 1941-47, 49-50. Decorated Purple Heart, Silver Star. Mem. Divers Assn. Am. (pres. 1970-74), Treasury Recovery, Inc. (pres. 1972-75), Internat. Assn. Profl. Divers, Assn. Diving Contractors, Calif. Assn. Pvt. Edn. (no. v.p. 1971-72), Authors Guild, Internat. Game Fish Assn., U.S. Navy League, U.S. Res. Officers Assn., Tailhook Assn., U.S. Submarine Vets. WWII, Explorer Club (San Francisco), Calif. Assn. Marine Surveyors (pres. 1988—), Soc. Naval Archs. and Marine Engrs. (assoc.), Masons, Lions. Author: Fell's Guide to Sunken Treasure Ships of the World, 1972; (with H. Rieseberg) The Knight from Maine, 1974. Office: 320 29th Ave Oakland CA 94601-2104

MIKEL, THOMAS KELLY, JR., laboratory administrator; b. East Chicago, Ind., Aug. 27, 1946; s. Thomas Kelly and Anne Katherine (Vrazo) M.; BA, San Jose State U., 1973; MA, U. Calif.-Santa Barbara, 1975. Asst. dir. Santa Barbara Underseas Found., 1975-76; marine biologist PJB Labs., Ventura, Calif., 1976-81; lab. dir. CRL Environ., Ventura, 1981-88; lab. dir. ABC Labs, Ventura, 1988—; instr. oceanography Ventura Coll., 1980-81. With U.S. Army, 1968-70. Mem. Assn. Environ. Profls., Soc. Population Ecologists, ASTME (rsch. contbr. 10th ann. symposium 1986). Biol. coord.Anacapa Underwater Natural trail U.S. Nat. Park Svc., 1976; designer ecol. restoration program of upper Newport Bay, Orange County, Calif., 1978; rsch. contbr. 3d Internat. Artificial Reef Conf., Newport Beach, Calif., 1983, Ann. Conf. Am. Petroleum Inst., Houston. Democrat.

MIKESELL, RICHARD LEO, computer programmer; b. Charleston, W.Va., Oct. 31, 1958; s. Leo Ross and Virginia Elaine (Bowman) M.; Debra Ann Lozowski, Mar. 31, 1979; 1 child, Justin Richard. BS, Calif. State U., Fullerton, 1994. Asst. mgr. Kmart Corp., Bellflower, Calif., 1979-81, Covina, Calif., 1981, Industry, Calif., 1981-82, Tucumcari, N.Mex., 1982-83, Farmington, N.Mex., 1983-84, Ft. Worth, 1984-85; merchandise mgr. Kmart Corp., Richardson, Tex., 1985-88; merchandiser Kmart Corp., Huntington Beach, Calif., 1988-94; computer programmer Pacific Decision Sci. Corp., Tustin, Calif., 1994—; cons. IBM-Pennant, Lexington, Ky. and Dallas, 1994. Republican. Home: Lakeside Dr S Garden Grove CA 92640 Office: Pacific Decision Sci Corp 12341 Newport Ave Santa Ana CA 92705-3289

MIKESELL, RICHARD LYON, lawyer, financial counselor; b. Corning, N.Y., Jan. 29, 1941; s. Walter Ray and Clara Ellen (Lyon) M.; m. Anna May Creese, Mar. 16, 1973; 1 child, Joel. BSChemE, U. Calif., Berkeley, 1962; LLB, Duke U., 1965; BA in Liberal Studies, UCLA, 1967. Bar: U.S. Supreme Ct., Ohio, Calif., U.S. Ct. Appeals (9th and 2d cirs.), U.S. Patent Office. Patent atty. Procter & Gamble, Cin., 1965-66, Rocketdyne divsn. N.Am. Aviation, L.A., 1966-69; pvt. practice law L.A., 1969-81; prin. Law Offices of R.L. Mikesell, L.A., 1981—; fin. counselor L.A. Police Dept., 1986—; arbitrator Am. Arbitration Assn., L.A., 1980—. Pres. San Fernando Valley Fair Housing Coun., L.A., 1969-72, Valley Women's Ctr., L.A., 1990; line res. officer L.A. Police Dept., 1969-72. Named Res. Officer of Yr. L.A. Police Dept., 1990. Office: 14540 Hamlin St Ste B Van Nuys CA 91411-1626

MIKHAIL, MARY ATTALLA, computer systems development executive; b. Cairo, Egypt, Apr. 2, 1945; came to U.S., 1980.; d. Attalla Shehata and Soad (Kamel) Abd-El-Malek; m. Ibrahim Fahmy Mikhail, May 1 ,1967; 1 child, Ireny. BS in Math. and Physics, U. Assiut, Egypt, 1965; MS in Math. and Computer Sci., U. Clausthal, Fed. Republic Germany, 1973; PhD in Math., U. Tuebingen, Fed. Republic Germany, 1976. Lectr. Math. Inst., Assiut, Egypt, 1965-67; from instr. to asst. prof. Math. Inst., Tuebingen, Fed. Republic Germany, 1973-78; cons., project mgr. Datel, Fed. Republic Germany, 1978-80; planner, systems analyst C.F. Braun, Alhambra, Calif., 1980-82; optic dept. mgr. Burroughs Corp., City of Industry, Calif., 1982-87; project mgr. continuous transaction processing Unisys Corp., Mission Viejo, Calif., 1987-88, project mgr. systems software devel. Open Systems Interconnectivity, 1988-92, program mgr. Open/OLTP, 1992—. Contbr. articles to profl. jours. Mem. IEEE (standards for software error, faults and failures com., standards for quality metrics com.), Am. Mgmt. Assn. Mem. Coptic Orthodox Ch.

MILAN, JOHN MAURICE, engineering executive; b. Miami, Ariz.; s. C.M. and Ethel (Jackson) M.; m. Diane Neville, June 28, 1968; children: Andrew,

Jeannine. BSEE, U. Ariz., 1967; MSEE, Stanford U., 1968; PhD, UCLA, 1990. Design engr. ITT Gilfillan, Van Nuys, Calif., 1968—, dir. design engr., 1989, v.p. & dir. of engring., 1993. Patentee in field. Mem. IEEE (sr.), Radar Systems Panel. Office: ITT Gilfillan 7821 Orion Ave Van Nuys CA 91406-2027

MILANDER, HENRY MARTIN, community college president; b. Northampton, Pa., Apr. 17, 1939; s. Martin Edward and Margaret Catherine (Makovetz) M.; children: Martin Henry, Beth Ann. BS summa cum laude, Lock Haven U., Pa., 1961; MA, Bowling Green (Ohio) State U., 1962; EdS (Future Faculty fellow 1964), U. No. Iowa, 1965; EdD, Ill. State U., Normal, 1967. Instr. Wartburg Coll., Waverly, Iowa, 1962-64; asst. prof. Ill. State U., 1966-67; dean instrn. Belleville (Ill.) Area Coll., 1967-69; v.p. acad. affairs Lorain County Community Coll., Elyria, Ohio, 1969-72; pres. Olympic Coll., Bremerton, Wash., 1972-87, Northeastern Jr. Coll., Sterling, Colo., 1988—; pres. Bremers, Inc., 1986-87. Contbr. articles to profl. jours. Pres. Kitsap County Comprehensive Health Planning Council, 1975-76; pres. Logan County Colo. United Way, 1992-93. Recipient Faculty Growth award Wartburg Coll., 1963, Community Service award, 1975, Chief Thunderbird award, 1985. Mem. Am. Assn. C.C., Am. Assn. Sch. Adminstrs., N.W. Assn. Cmty. and Jr. Colls., Wash. Assn. C.C. (pres. 1984-85), Wash. C.C. Computing Consortium (chmn. bd. dirs. 1985-87), Puget Sound Naval Bases Assn. (pres. 1982-86), Wash. Assn. C.C. Pres. (pres. 1984-85), Bremerton Area C. of C. (pres. 1977-78), Colo. Assn. C.C. Pres. (pres. 1993-94), Rotary (pres. Sterling Club 1992-93), Kappa Delta Pi, Phi Delta Kappa. Lutheran. Home: 302 Delmar St Sterling CO 80751-3904 Office: Northeastern Jr Coll 100 College Dr Sterling CO 80751-2344

MILANFAR, PEYMAN, research engineer; b. Teheran, Mar. 1, 1966; came to U.S., 1984; BS, U. Calif., Berkeley, 1988; MS, MIT, 1991, EE, 1992, PhD, 1993. Support engr. Hewlett Packard, Cupertino, Calif., 1988-89; mem. tech. staff Alphatech Inc., Burlington, Mass., 1993-94; rsch. engr. SRI Internat., Menlo Park, Calif., 1994—. Author tech. articles. Pres.'s undergrad fellow U. Calif., Berkeley, 1988; Clement Vaturi fellow MIT, 1992, 93. Mem. IEEE, Math. Assn. Am., Sigma Xi. Office: SRI Internat Mailstop 409-44 333 Ravenswood Ave Menlo Park CA 94025-3453

MILANOVICH, NORMA JOANNE, occupational educator, training company executive; b. Littlefork, Minn., June 4, 1945; d. Lyle Albert and Loretta (Leona) Drake; m. Rudolph William Milanovich, Mar. 18, 1943; 1 child, Rudolph William Jr. BS in Home Econs., U. Wis., Stout, 1968; MA in Curriculum and Instrn., U. Houston, 1973, EdD in Curriculum and Program Devel., 1982. Instr. human svcs. dept. U. Houston, 1971-75; dir. videos project U. N.Mex., Albuquerque, 1976-78, dir. vocat. edn. equity ctr., 1978-88, asst. prof. tech. occupational edn., 1982-88, coord. occupational vocat. edn. programs, 1983-88, dir. consortium rsch. and devel. in occupational edn., 1984-88; pres. The Alpha Connecting Tng. Corp., Albuquerque, 1988—; adj. instr. Cen. Tng. Acad., Dept. Energy, Wackenhut; mem. faculty U. Phoenix; mem. adj. faculty So. Ill. U., Lesley Coll., Boston. Author: Model Equitable Behavior in the Classroom, 1983, Handbook for Vocational-Technical Certification in New Mexico, 1985, We, The Arcturians, 1990, Sacred Journey to Atlantis, 1991, The Light Shall Set You Free, 1995, A Vision for Kansas: Systems of Measures and Standards of Performance, 1992, Workplace Skills: The Employability Factor, 1993; editor: Choosing What's Best for You, 1982, A Handbook for Handling Conflict in the Classroom, 1983, Starting Out. . .A Job Finding Handbook for Teen Parents, Going to Work. . .Job Rights for Teens. Bd. dirs. Albuquerque Single Parent Occupational Scholarship Program, 1984-86; del. Youth for Understanding Internat. Program, 1985-90; mem. adv. bd. Southwestern Indian Poly. Inst., 1984-88; com. mem. Region VI Consumer Exch. Com., 1982-84; tour dir. internat. study tours to Japan, Austria, Korea, India, Nepal, Mex., Eng., Greece, Egypt, Australia, New Zealand, Fed. Republic Germany, Israel, Guatemala, Peru, Bolivia, Chile, Easter Island, Tibet, China, Hong Kong, Turkey, Italy, 1984-95. Grantee N.Mex. Dept. Edn., 1976-78, 78-86, 83-86, HEW, 1979, 80, 81, 83, 84, 85, 86, 87, JTPA Strategic Mktg. Plan. Mem. ASTD, Am. Vocat. Assn., Vocat. Edn. Equity Coun., Nat. Coalition for Sex Equity Edn., Am. Home Econs. Assn., Inst. Noetic Scis., N.Mex. Home Econs. Assn., N.Mex. Vocat. Edn. Assn., N.Mex. Adv. Coun. on Vocat. Edn., Greater Albuquerque C. of C., NAFE, Phi Delta Kappa, Phi Upsilon Omicron, Phi Theta Kappa. Democrat. Roman Catholic.

MILANT, JEAN ROBERT, art dealer; b. Milw., Dec. 27, 1943; s. Jacques Jean and Virginia (Zeller) M. BFA, U. Wis., Mils., 1965; cert. master printer, Tamarind Lithography Workshop, L.A., 1969; MA, U. N.Mex., 1970. Tchr. lithograophy U. Calif., Long Beach, 1970; owner, dir. Cirrus Editions Ltd., L.A., 1970—, Cirrus Gallery; lectr., presenter numerous seminars in field, including Art Ctr. Coll. Design, Pasadena, Calif., Otis Art Inst., Alta. Coll. Art, Calgary, Can., San Francisco Mus. Contemporary Art, Santa Barbara (Calif.) Mus. Contemporary Graphics Ctr., others;. Exhibition of Circus at L.A. County Mus of Art, 1995-96. Bd. dirs. Contemporary Art Publs., 1980-83. Mem. Mus. Contemporary Art L.A. (founding), L.A. County Mus. Art, L.A. Inst. Contemporary Art (bd. dirs. 1971-78), New Mus., L.A. Visual Arts (bd. dirs. 1981-85).

MILES, DON CLIFFORD, architect; b. Ft. Knox, Ky., Sept. 17, 1942; s. Don and Kathrine Eva (Gray) M.; m. Pamela Wait, Aug. 6, 1972; children: Katherine Wait, Lesley Gray, Nicole Conel. BArch with honors, U. Wash., 1966; MArch, M of City Planning in Urban Design, Harvard U., 1971. Registered architect, Wash. Assoc. ptnr. Zimmer, Gunsul, Frasca Partnership, Seattle; cons., lectr. numerous orgns., cities, corps. Prin. projects include Pedestrian Corridor, Major Pub. Open Spaces, CBD Transit Ctr., Bellevue, Wash., Banfield Light Rail Project, Portland, Boise (Idaho) Downtown Major Pub. Open Space, Street Improvements and Transit Malls, Honolulu Rapid Transit Project, Revitalization of State St., Chgo., Midway Corridor Project, Mpls., High Capacity Transit Project, Seattle, Ctrl. Orange County Aerial Fixed Guideway, Mission Valley West Extension Light Rail Project, San Diego, Master Plan for Capitol of State of Wash., Seattle Union Sta. Redevel. Plan, Weyerhauser Corp. Campus, Quadrant Corp. site, Lake Union, Seattle, Whitman Coll. Bd. dirs., founder Project for Pub. Spaces, 1975—; bd. dirs. Seattle Children's Mus., 1978-82; trustee Queen Ann Community Coun., 1978-80. Fellow AIA, Inst. Urban Design. Home: 611 W Comstock St Seattle WA 98119-3422 Office: Zimmer Gunsul Frasca 1191 2nd Ave Ste 800 Seattle WA 98101-2933

MILES, GORDON HUGH, restaurant company executive, lawyer; b. 1940. Bar: Nebr. 1964, U.S. Supreme Ct. 1964. With Walsh, Walentine and Miles, until 1977; chmn. Vicorp Restaurants, Inc., 1977-86; chmn., dir. Rusty Pelican Restaurants, Inc.; chmn. Green Leaf Ventures, Inc. and Papa Gino's Holdings, Inc., San Diego. Office: Green Leaf Ventures Inc 6610 Convoy Ct San Diego CA 92111-1009

MILES, OWEN PHILIPS, JR., retired consulting geologist; b. Freeport, Ill., June 15, 1928; s. Owen Philips and Helen (Minard) M.; m. Madelyn Larsen, Sept. 2, 1951; children—Lisa, Aimie. B.S., Beloit Coll., 1950; postgrad. U. Colo.-Boulder, 1950-51. Jr. geologist Magnolia Petroleum Co., Oklahoma City, 1950, Mobil Producing Co., Big Piney and Basin Wyo., 1951-53; instr. U.S. Army Petroleum Product Analysis Sch., Ft. Lee, Va., 1953-55; sr. geologist Mobil Oil Co., Casper, Wyo., 1955-64; self-employed cons. geologist, Casper, 1964-93, ret. 1993. Author: (guidebook) Kummerfeld Field, 1963; co-author Bur. Mines report. Mem. Am. Assn. Petroleum Geologists, Am. Inst. Profl. Geologists (pres. Wyo. sect. 1965-67), Wyo. Geol. Assn. Republican. Home: 3803 Alpine Dr Casper WY 82601-5947

MILES, RICHARD ROBERT, art historian, writer; b. Tokyo, Apr. 1, 1939; s. Robert Henri and Eleanor Alfrida (Child) Perreau-Saussine. BA, UCLA, 1972. Novelist, screenwriter various, 1965-72; dir. Meilinki Enterprises Ltd., 1980—; pres. Burbank (Calif.) Tchrs. Assn., 1984-85; bd. dirs. Balcom Trading Co., Tokyo, 1979-82. Author: That Cold Day in the Park, 1965 (Dell Book award 1965), Angel Loves Nobody, 1967 (Samuel Goldwyn award UCLA, 1969); (art history) Prints of Paul Jacoulet, 1982, Elizabeth Keith-The Prints, 1989, The Watercolors of Paul Jacoulet, 1992, others. Mem. Internat. Soc. of Fine Art Appraisers, New Eng. Appraisers Assn., Writers Guild of Am. West, Acad. of Am. Poets. Office: Meilinki Enterprises Ltd 214 N Bowling Green Way Los Angeles CA 90049-2816

MILES, SAMUEL ISRAEL, psychiatrist; b. Munich, Mar. 4, 1949; came to U.S., 1949; s. Henry and Renee (Ringel) M.; m. Denise Marie Robey, June 26, 1977; children: Jonathan David, Justin Alexander. BS, CCNY, 1970; MD, N.Y. Med. Coll., 1974; PhD, So. Calif. Psychoanalytic Inst., 1986. Diplomate Am. Bd. Psychiatry and Neurology with added qualifications in forensic psychiatry. Intern D.C. Gen. Hosp., Washington, 1974-75; resident in psychiatry Cedars-Sinai Med. Ctr., Los Angeles, 1975-78; practice medicine specializing in psychiatry Los Angeles, 1978—; ind. med. examiner Calif. Dept. Indsl. Relations, 1984-91, qualified med. examiner, 1991—; asst. clin. prof. psychiatry UCLA Sch. Medicine, 1978—; attending psychiatrist Cedars-Sinai Med. Ctr., 1978—, co-chmn. util. rev./qual. assurance com. dept. psychiatry, 1984-89, chmn. qual. assurance com. dept. psychiatry, 1990-91, mem. in-patient adv. com., 1983-85, 87-90, 95—, psychiatry adv. com., 1984-86; attending psychiatrist Brotman Med. Ctr., Culver City, Calif., 1978—; faculty mem. Soc. Calif. Psychoanalytic Inst., 1986—; mem. psychiat. panel Superior Ct., L.A. County, 1990—, Fed. Ct., 1990—. Fellow Am. Acad. Psychoanalysis, Am. Orthopsychiat. Assn.; mem. Acad. Psychiatry and the Law, Calif. Psychiat. Assn. (manage and care com. 1991—), So. Calif. Psychiat. Soc. (coun. rep. 1985-88, 92-95, chair pvt. practice com. 1988-92, sec. 1991-92, worker's compensation com. 1992—), Am. Coll. Legal Medicine, So. Calif. Psychoanalytic Inst. (pres. clin. assocs. orgn. 1981-82, mem. admissions com. 1988-93, ethics stds. com. 1991-92, chair 1993—, exec. com. 1993—). Jewish. Office: 8631 W 3rd St Ste 425E Los Angeles CA 90048-5908

MILES, SHEILA LEE, artist, consultant; b. Indpls., Aug. 10, 1952; d. Robert Evan and Elizabeth Louise (Marcum) Miles; 1 child, Paris Miles Brenden. BA, Purdue U., 1973, MA, 1974. Dir. Provincetown Art Assn. & Mus., Provincetown, Mass., 1975-77; instr. art Ea. Mont. Coll., Billings, 1980-85; artist-in-the-schs. Mont. Arts Coun./Custer County Art Ctr., Miles City, Mont., 1982-83; gallery dir. Ea. Mont. Coll., 1984-85; gallery dir./instr. Mont. State U., Bozeman, 1985-86; curator Yellowstone Art Ctr., Billings, 1986-90; instr. U. Mont., Missoula, 1995. Panel mem. Mont. Arts Coun., Helena, 1986—, peer cons.; cons. Deaconess Hosp., Billings, 1989—, ACLU, 1986—. Mont. arts Coun. fellow, 1984. Home: 508 E Front St Missoula MT 59802-4712

MILFORD, PEGGY R., communications executive; b. Fairmont, Minn., Oct. 1, 1945; d. Glenn E. and Truma (Niss) M. BA, St. Olaf Coll., 1967; MBA, U. Minn., 1983. V.p. quality assurance U.S. West, Denver. Mem. Nat. Women's Polit. Caucus, Washington. Office: US West Communications 188 Inverness Dr W Englewood CO 80112-5207

MILGRIM, DARROW A., insurance broker, recreation consultant; b. Chgo., Apr. 30, 1945; s. David and Miriam (Glickman) M.; m. Laurie Stevens, Apr. 15, 1984; children: Derick, Jared, Kayla. BA, Calif. State U., San Bernardino, 1968; postgrad., U. So. Calif., 1972. Accredited ins. adv.; cert. ins. counselor; cert. sch. adminstr. Tchr. Rialto (Calif.) Unified Sch. Dist., 1969-70, Las Virgines Unified Sch. Dist., Westlake Village, Calif., 1970-78; instr. Calif. State U., Northridge, Calif., 1980-84; ins. broker, v.p. Speare Ins. Brokers, Blade Ins. Svcs., Brentwood, Calif., 1984—; dir. Calamigos Star C Ranch Summer Camp, Malibu, Calif., Calamigos Environ. Edn. Ctr., Malibu. Editor: Legislation and Regulations for Organized Camps, 1987. Pres. Calif. Camping Adv. Coun., Long Beach, 1985-87; bd. dirs. Calif. Collaboration for Youth, Sacramento, 1985—, Camp Ronald McDonald for Good Times, 1989—; commr. dept. parks and recreation City of Agoura Hills, Calif., 1987-93; cons. So. Calif. Children's Cancer Svcs., L.A., 1986—. Mem. Am. Camping Assn. (bd. dirs. So. Calif. sect., chmn. nat. legis. com. Martinsville, Ind., 1980—, nat. bd. dirs. 1990-95, legis. liaison, regional honor 1986). Office: Speare and Co Ins Brokers PO Box 250024 Los Angeles CA 90025-9524

MILHOLLAND, DAVID MARION, writer, editor; b. Greeley, Colo., Oct. 19, 1946; s. Delbert Martin and Alice Olene (Luvaas) M.; m. Theresa Marquez; children: Zachary O., Lola Maria Marquez. BA, Lewis and Clark Coll. Peace corps vol. Peace Corps-Guatemala, Aguacatan, 1968-70; rsch. coord. Yaden & Assocs., Portland, Oreg., 1971-75; filmmaker David Milholland & Assocs., Portland, Oreg., 1971-85; mgr., co-owner Clinton St. Theatre, Portland, Oreg., 1979-85; editor, art dir. Clinton St. Quar., Portland, Seattle, 1979-91; prodn. mgr. Nature's Fresh N.W.!, Portland, 1991-93; edn. dir. Oregon Tilth, Portland, 1993-94; ptnr. Crackerjack Mktg./Pacific Green, Portland, 1993—. Filmmaker including feature documentaries Blackjack's Family, 1974 (Best of N.W. Film Video festival 1974), The Thorne Family Film, 1977 (N.Y. Film Festival award 1977); editor Clinton St. Quar., 1979-91. Bd. dirs. Media Project, Portland, 1972-77; pres. Local Sch. Adv. Group, Jefferson H.S., Portland, 1988-92, Oreg. Cultural Heritage Commn., 1988-94; mem. Christic Inst., N.W., Wash., 1989-92. Recipient First Pl. in Editorial Writing, Sigma Delta Chi Soc. Profl. Journalists (N.W. chpt.), 1981-88. Mem. PEN Internat. Office: PO Box 3588 Portland OR 97208-3588

MILHOUS, ROBERT E., advertising executive; b. 1937; married. BS, Purdue U., 1960. Advt. salesman Gen. Telephone Co., Calif., 1960-63; with B&B Advt. Co., Stanton, Calif., 1963-68; now chmn. bd. dirs., chief exec. officer Treasure Chest Advt. Co., Glendora, Calif., also bd. dirs. Served U.S. Army, 1958-60. Office: Treasure Chest Advt Co Inc 511 W Citrus Edge St Glendora CA 91740-5006

MILLAR, MICHAEL WILLIAM, trombonist; b. N.Y.C., June 22, 1953; s. W. Llewellyn and Janet Josephine (Dean) M.; m. Lisa Rochelle Branch, July 30, 1983 (dec. Aug. 1987); m. Dava Grace Smart, June 25, 1989; children: Emily Ellyn, Matthew Ian. MusB in Performance, U. Colo., Boulder, 1976; MA in Performance Music, Calif. State U., L.A., 1980; studied with George Roberts, Roy Main, Charlie Shoemake. Trombonist Ollie Mitchell's Sunday Band, 1979-85, Harry James Orch., 1980-85, Les Hooper Grand Band, 1983—; mem. faculty U. Colo., Denver, 1987; has appeared with various brass quintets, brass choirs, trombone choirs, trombone jazz bands, big bands, symphony orchs. and other mus. groups; performed in TV and radio jingles for Sta. KCBS-TV Action News, Budweiser, Toyota, Anheuser Busch, Mountain Dew, 1-800-COLLECT, Gt. Western Bank, Texaco, Am. Express, Home Shopping Network, Honda, Delta Airlines, Spray 'n Wash, Qantas, Word Perfect, New Eng. Tel., Sunny Delight, Disney World, AT&T, numerous others. Albums include Blast Off, 1981, Anything Goes, 1989, Singin' With the Big Bands, 1994; appeared in films Hot to Trot, Sing, For the Boys, The Doors, on TV in Hull High; performed with Steven Allen, Ray Anthony, Tex. Beneke Orch., George Burns, Ray Charles Orch., Warren Covington and Pied Pipers, Rosemary Clooney, Colo. Music Festival Orch., Buddy Greco, Merv Griffin, Jerry Lewis, Shari Lewis, Rich Little, Gordon MacRae, Mills Bros., Helen O'Connell, Patti Page, Debbie Reynolds, The Smothers Brothers, numerous others. Mem. NARAS, Rec. Musicians Assn., Am. Fedn. Musicians. Democrat. Presbyterian. Home: 25430 Via Impreso Valencia CA 91355-2709

MILLAR, ROBERT, artist; b. L.A., Mar. 6, 1958; s. Thomas A. and Josephine E. (Alford) M. BA, Calif. State U., Northridge, 1980. Exhibited work at L.A. Metro Rail Sta., 1990 (progressive Arch. citation 1992), Newport Harbor Art Mus., 1991, Rose Theatre Site, London, 1992, S.D. Alvarado Filtration Plant, 1993. Arts commr. City of Manhattan Beach, Calif., 1985-94; mem. pub. art adv. com. Calif. Arts Coun., 1992. Grantee Pollock-Krasner Found., 1989. Studio: PO Box 515 Manhattan Beach CA 90267-0515

MILLARD, DEREK, organizational development consultant; b. Cortez, Colo., Feb. 6, 1954; s. Arthur Randall and Mildred Mae Millard; m. Janet Marie Klun Lanigan, Feb. 14, 1972 (div. July 1977). Student, U. So. Colo., 1969-70, Lawrence U., Appleton, Wis., 1971-72; degree, U. Wis., Oshkosh, 1976; MS in Human Resource Devel., Am. U., Washington, 1982. Mgr. Culbreath Schs., Colorado Springs, Colo., 1970-71; indsl. engr. Thilmany Pulp and Paper divsn. Hammermill Papers, Kaukauna, Wis., 1971-75; v.p. ops. Rosenow XYZ Corp., Appleton, 1975-76; founder, owner Remarket Industries, Appleton, 1976-79; prin., owner Facilitating Change, Houston, 1979-89, Derek Millard Assocs., San Francisco, 1990—; orgnl. devel. cons. Levi Strauss & Co., San Francisco, 1990-95; cons. Honeywell Corp., Houston, 1988-90, Human Affairs Internat. divsn. Aetna, Houston, 1989-90; cons. and assoc. Designed Learning, Plainfield, N.J., 1993—. Mem. chem. abuse adv. com. Houston-Galveston Area Coun., 1980-84; state co-founder, state chmn. Libertarian Party, Appleton, Wis., 1971-75. Mem. Orgnl. Devel. Network, Am. U./NTL Assn. Libertarian. Home and Office: 308 Shields St San Francisco CA 94132

MILLARD, ESTHER LOUND, foundation administrator, educator; b. Metaline, Wash., June 10, 1909; d. Peter S. and Emily Christine (Dahlgren) Lound; m. Homer Behne Millard, Apr. 25, 1951 (dec. May 1962). BA, U. Wis., 1933, MA, 1935. Cert. tchr., Oreg., Wis. Instr. U. Hawaii, Honolulu, 1938-43; joined USN, 1943, advanced through ranks to lt. commdr., resigned, 1952; dir. Millard Sch., Bandon, Oreg., 1954-81; pres. Millard Found., Bandon, 1984—. Trustee Falcon Found., Colorado Springs, Colo., 1986—; established scholarship fund for med. sch. students, U. Wis. Mem. Bascom Hill Soc. (U. Wis.), Phi Beta Kappa. Republican. Home: 52 Tom Smith Rd Bandon OR 97411-9311

MILLARD, GEORGE RICHARD, bishop; b. Dunsmuir, Calif., Oct. 2, 1914; s. George Ellis and Constance (Rainsberry) M.; m. Mary Louise Gessling, June 29, 1939; children: George, Martha, Joseph. A.B., U. Calif.-Berkeley, 1936; B.D., Episcopal Theol. Sch., Cambridge, Mass., 1938; S.T.M., Pacific Sch. Religion, 1958; D.D., Ch. Div. Sch. Pacific, 1960; M.A., U. Santa Clara, 1983. Ordained to ministry Episcopal Ch. as priest 1938. Asst. in Episc. Ch., N.Y.C., 1938-39, Waterbury, Conn., 1930-40; rector in Episc. Ch., Danbury, Conn., 1940-50, Alameda, Calif., 1951-59; suffragan bishop Episc. Diocese Calif., 1960-76; bishop of San Jose, 1969-76; exec., venture in mission program, exec. council Episc. Ch., 1977-78; bishop in charge Am. Chs. in Europe, 1978-80, bishop in charge ch. divinity sch. pacific exec. office for alumni/ae affairs, 1978-80; dean Convocation of Oakland, Calif., 1957-60; chmn. dept. missions Diocese Calif., 1958-60; mem. Joint Commn. on Structure, Episc. Ch., 1967-76. Chmn. Maria Kip Orphange; chmn. devel. program U. Calif. at Berkeley Student Coop. Assn., 1966; coord. Ch. Div. Sch. Pacific Alumni Affairs, 1986-88. Mem. U.S. Club of Rome.

MILLARD, MALCOLM STUART, retired lawyer; b. Highland Park, Ill., Mar. 22, 1914; s. Everett L. and Elizabeth (Boynton) M.; m. Joanne T. Blakeman; 1 child, Anne W. Benjamin. BA, Harvard U., 1936; JD, Northwestern U., 1939. Bar: Ill. 1939, Calif. 1951. Ptnr. Farr & Millard, Carmel, Calif., 1951-55, Millard, Tourangeau, Morris & Staples, P.C., Carmel, 1955-91; ptnr. Millard, Morris & Staples, Carmel, 1991-94, ret., 1994; dir. Leslie Salt Co., 1975-81. Trustee Community Hosp. of Monterey Peninsula, 1982-88, Monterey Inst. Fgn. Studies, 1955-76, Community Found. Monterey County, 1988—; pres. Community Chest of Monterey Peninsula, 1958. Served to lt. USN, 1943-46. Mem. Monterey Inst. Internat. Relations (hon. lifetime trustee 1982—, hon. DHL 1991), Ill. State Bar, Calif. State Bar, Monterey County Bar Assn. (pres.), Old Capital Club, Harvard Club.

MILLARD, NEAL STEVEN, lawyer; b. Dallas, June 6, 1947; s. Bernard and Adele (Marks) M.; m. Janet Keast, Mar. 12, 1994; 1 child, Kendall Layne. BA cum laude, UCLA, 1969; JD, U. Chgo., 1972. Bar: Calif. 1972, U.S. Dist. Ct. (cen. dist.) Calif. 1973, U.S. Tax Ct. 1973, U.S. Ct. Appeals (9th cir.) 1987, N.Y. 1990. Assoc. Willis, Butler & Schiefly, Los Angeles, 1972-75; ptnr. Morrison & Foerster, Los Angeles, 1975-84, Jones, Day, Reavis & Pogue, Los Angeles, 1984-93, White & Case, L.A., 1993—; instr. Calif. State Coll., San Bernardino, 1975-76; lectr. Practising Law Inst., N.Y.C., 1983-90, Calif. Edn. of Bar, 1987-90; adj. prof. USC Law Ctr., 1994—. Citizens adv. com. L.A. Olympics, 1982-84; trustee Altadena (Calif.) Libr. Dist., 1985-86; bd. dirs. Woodcraft Rangers, L.A., 1982-90, pres., 1986-88; bd. dirs. L.A. County Bar Found., 1990—; mem. Energy Commn. of County and Cities of L.A. Mem. ABA, Calif. Bar Assn., N.Y. State Bar Assn., L.A. County Bar Assn. (trustee 1985-87), Pub. Counsel (bd. dirs. 1984-87, 90-93), U. Chgo. Law Alumni Assn. (bd. dirs. So. Calif. chpt. 1981—), Calif. Club, Phi Beta Kappa, Pi Gamma Mu, Phi Delta Phi. Office: White & Case 633 W 5th St Ste 1900 Los Angeles CA 90071-2017

MILLER, ALLEN TERRY, JR., lawyer; b. Alexandria, Va., Sept. 19, 1954; s. Allen Terry and Eleanor Jane (Thompson) M.; m. Maureen Ann Callaghan, June 22, 1985; children: Brendan Allen, Patrick Joseph, Brigit Eleanor. BA, U. Va., 1977; JD, Seattle U., 1982. Bar: Wash. 1982, U.S. Dist. Ct. (we. dist.) Wash. 1982, U.S. Ct. Appeals (9th cir.) 1985, U.S. Dist. Ct. (ea. dist.) Wash. 1986, U.S. Dist. Ct. (no. dist.) N.Y. 1990, U.S. Dist. Ct. (we. dist.) Mich. 1990, U.S. Supreme Ct. 1990, U.S. Ct. Appeals (2d and 6th cirs.) 1991. Legis. asst. Congressman Paul N. McCloskey Jr., Washington, 1978-79; asst. atty. gen. State of Washington, Olympia, 1982-92; prin. Connolly, Holm, Tacon & Meserve, Olympia, 1992—; adj. prof. environ. law U. Puget Sound, 1991—. Commr. Olympia Planning Commn., 1987-92, vice chair, 1991, chair, 1992; mem. N. Capitol Campus Heritage Pk. Devel. Assn., 1989—, sec., 1989-90, pres., 1991-94; pres. Olympia Chorale and Light Opera Co., 1984-85; mem. St. Michael's Sch. Bd., 1993—, chair, 1994-96. Recipient Am. Jurisprudence award Lawyer Coop. Pub. Co., 1980, Merit award Am. Planning Assn., 1989, 92. Mem. ABA, Wash. Bar Assn. (mem. environ. law sect. 1984—, ct. rules com. 1985-89, jud. recommendation com. 1991-94, Govt. Bar Assn., legis. com. 1994—), Thurston County Bar Assn., Leadership Thurston County. Democrat. Roman Catholic. Home: 1617 Sylvester St SW Olympia WA 98501-2228 Office: Heritage Bldg Heritage Bldg 5th and Columbia Olympia WA 98501-1114

MILLER, ANNE KATHLEEN, training company executive, technical marketing consultant; b. Denver, Sept. 15, 1942; d. John Henry and Kathryn Elizabeth (Doherty) Meyer; m. Edgar Earle Miller, Aug. 20, 1966 (div. Aug. 1976); children: Sheila Anne, Rebecca Elizabeth; m. Warren Ross Landry, Dec. 11, 1982 (dec. Oct. 1990). BS in Chemistry, St. Mary Coll., Leavenworth, Kans., 1964. Cert. jr. coll., secondary tchr., Calif. Lectr. San Jose (Calif.) State U., 1978-82; product mgr. Jasco Chem., Mountain View, Calif., 1979-82; v.p., gen. mgr. Micropel, Hayward, Calif., 1982-84; product mgr. Cambridge Instruments, Santa Clara, Calif., 1984-86; product mktg. mgr. KLA Instruments, Santa Clara, 1986-87; pres., owner Meyland Enterprises, Redwood City, Calif., 1987—, Semiconductor Svc. Tng. Orgn., Redwood City, Calif., 1988—. Inventor formation of optical film. Mem. Soc. Photo Optical Instrumentation Engrs., Am. Chem. Soc., Semiconductor Industry Equipment Materials Internat., Am. Electronics Assn. Office: Meyland/Semiconductor Svcs 735 Hillcrest Way Redwood City CA 94062-3428

MILLER, BARBARA DARLENE, art educator; b. Jarbidge, Nev.; d. Herbert Beard and Gerra Vanetten (Carncross) Beard; 2 children. BA, U. Wash., 1955; MEd, U. Hawaii, 1974. Cert. secondary tchr. Occupational therapist N.D. State Hosp. for Mental Illness, Jamestown, 1954-55; art tchr. Dept. Edn. Hilo (Hawaii) High Sch., 1957-58; art specialist Elem. Intermediate Sch., Kahului, Hawaii, 1964-65; art instr. Maui Community Coll., Kahului, 1965—; art dir. Sta. KHVH-TV, Honolulu, 1962-63. One-woman shows include County Bldg., 1985, 87-90, MCC Libr., 1987, 90, exhibited in group shows at Am. Fac Pla., 1980, 91, Hawaii State Libr., 1980, Honolulu Acad. Arts; commd. numerous portraits. Visual Arts chairperson Maui Community Arts Coun., 1972-80; bd. dirs., past pres. Hui Noeau Art Soc., 1966-90; v.p. Maui Weavers Guild, 1976; planning com., bd. dirs. Art Maui '80-'84, 1979-84; bd. dirs. Maui Symphony Orch., 1984-87; mayor's adv. coun. for culture and the arts Archtl. Art Com., 1986-87; Maui rep. on budget com. Hawaii State Found. on Culture and the Arts, 1991. Recipient Certificate of Appreciation for Beautification of Maui County Council of Maui. Mem. NEA, AAUP, Maui Aikido Ki Soc. Office: Maui Community Coll 310 W Kaahumanu Ave Kahului HI 96732-1617

MILLER, BARBARA STALLCUP, development consultant; b. Montague, Calif., Sept. 4, 1919; d. Joseph Nathaniel and Maybelle (Needham) Stallcup; m. Leland F. Miller, May 16, 1946; children: Paula Kay, Susan Lee, Daniel Joseph, Alison Jean. B.A., U. Oreg., 1942. Women's editor Eugene (Oreg.) Daily News, 1941-43; law clk. to J. Everett Barr, Yreka, Calif., 1943-45; mgr. Yreka C. of C., 1945-46; Northwest supr. Louis Harris and Assocs., Portland, Oreg., 1959-62; dir. pub. relations and fund raising Columbia River council Girl Scouts U.S.A., 1962-67; pvt. practice pub. relations cons., Portland, 1967-72; adviser of student publs., asst. prof. communications U. Portland, 1967-72, dir. pub. relations and info., asst. prof. communications, 1972-78, dir. devel., 1978-79, exec. dir. devel., 1979-83; assoc. dir. St. Vincent Med. Found., 1983-88; dir. planned giving Good Samaritan Found., 1988-95; planned giving cons., 1995—. Pres. bd. dirs. Vols. of Am. of Oreg., Inc.,

1980-84, pres. regional adv. bd., 1982-84; chmn. bd. dirs. S.E. Mental Health Network, 1984-88; nat. bd. dirs. Vols. of Am., Inc., 1984—; pres., bd. dirs. Vol. Bur. Greater Portland, 1991-93; mem. U. Oreg. Journalism Advancement Coun., 1991—; named Oasis Sr. Role Model, 1992. Recipient Presdl. Citation, Oreg. Communicators Assn., 1973, Matrix award, 1976, 80, Miltner award U. Portland, 1977, Communicator of Achievement award Oreg. Press Women, 1992, Willamette Valley Devel. Officers award, 1992 (Barbara Stallcup Miller Profl. Achievement award, 1992), Mem. Nat. Soc. Fundraising Execs., Nat. Planned Giving Coun, Women in Comm. (NW regional v.p. 1973-75, Offbeat award 1988), Nat. Fedn. Press Women, Oreg. Press Women (dist. dir.), Pub. Rels. Soc. Am. (dir. local chpt., Marsh award 1989), Oreg. Fedn. Womens Clubs (communications chmn. 1978-80), Alpha Xi Delta (found. trustee, editor 1988-95). Unitarian. Clubs: Portland Zenith (pres. 1975-76, 81-82). Contbr. articles to profl. jours. Home and Office: 1706 Boca Ratan Dr Lake Oswego OR 97034-1624

MILLER, BILL, management and marketing consultant; b. Jersey City, Mar. 6, 1933; Children: Valerie, Lynn, Lori, Michael, Billy Joe. MBA, La Jolla U., 1980. Cert. (life) coll. level tchr. psychology, bus. mgmt. and mktg., mgmt. orgn. and human relations, Calif. Enlisted USMC, 1948, ret., 1967; instr. karate, judo and mob control N.J. and Calif. Police Depts.; owner, pres. Bill Miller and Assocs., Inc., 1976—, Mgmt. Dynamics; cons. to mgmt. in healthcare, exec. search; presenter mgmt. seminars; instr. psychology, bus. mgmt. and mktg., mgmt. orgn. and human relations U. Calif.-La Jolla and Nat. U., San Diego. Home: 12696 Pacato Cir N San Diego CA 92128-2370

MILLER, BURTON LEIBSLE, sales executive; b. L.A., July 17, 1944; s. Kenneth Wilbur and Dorothy (Leibsle) M.; m. April Suydam, Dec. 22, 1969 (div. 1983); children: Brandon, Gregory; m. Linda L. Reynolds, Aug. 11, 1990. BSCE, San Jose State U., 1968; MS in Engring., U. So. Calif., 1977. Civil engr. USN, San Bruno, Calif., 1968-74; cost engr. Bechtel Corp., L.A., 1974-79; supr. Bechtel Corp., Saudi Arabia, 1979-81; project mgr. Bechtel Corp., San Francisco, 1981-84, Bay Area Contractors, San Francisco, 1984—; dist. sales mgr. ISC, San Francisco, 1994—; cons. KMD/Kimco Mgmt. Co., San Francisco, 1989-90. Mem. World Affairs Coun., San Francisco, 1991, C. of C., San Francisco, 1986. Recipient Commendation, V.P. Dan Quayle, 1992, Cert. of Appreciation, Pres. George Bush, 1989, Cert. of Appreciation, Congressman Bob Mitchel, 1991. Mem. Commonwealth Club of Calif., Olympic Club, Project Mgmt. Inst. Republican. Home: 1035 Cabrillo St San Francisco CA 94118 Office: 634 28th Ave San Francisco CA 94121

MILLER, CARL DUANE, transportation company executive; b. Tulare, Calif., Aug. 24, 1941; s. Carl D. and Ida Ferne (Martin) M.; m. Cheryl Rae Henard, Mar. 29, 1961; children: Kelli R. Walker, Lori Leigh Elmore, Craig D. Student, Coll. of Sequoias, 1959-60, Am. Inst. Banking, 1964-69. Ops. supr. Crocker Citizens Nat. Bank., Tulare, 1964-69, Am. Nat. Bank, Tulare, 1969-70; Modesto terminal mgr. Kings County Truck Lines, 1970-75; Fresno outbound supr. Calif. Motor Express, 1975-77; terminal mgr. System 99 Transport, Tulare, 1977-80; pres., CEO Cal-Western Transport, Tulare, 1980-90, Daystar Transp., Tulare, 1990—; dir. Silver Arrow Express, Regency Transport Inc.; cons. Calif. Milk Producers, Artesia, Calif., 1990; transp. cons. Calif. Coop. Creamery, Petaluma, Calif., 1990; speaker world govt. and world monetary system various svc. clubs. Mem. City Coun., City of Tulare, 1979-83, mayor, 1983-87, Bd. Pub. Utilities, 1978; bd. mem. Nat. Coun. for Drugs and Alcohol, Tulare, 1980—; mem. exec. bd. Tulare County Econ. Devel.; transp. com. League of Calif. Cities. With USAF, 1960-64; v.p. Little League Baseball, Babe Ruth Baseball. Louis Pasteur fellow Scripps Clinic Rsch. Coun. Mem. NRA, AMVETS, Am. Legion, Am. Mgmt. Assn., Elks, Lions (v.p.). Republican. Home and Office: Daystar Transp Inc 2511 E Vassar Ct Visalia CA 93292-5666

MILLER, CARL VOSBURGH, artist; b. Waterbury, Conn., Feb. 13, 1932; s. Carl Vosburgh Miller; m. Catherine L. Webb, Aug. 22, 1956; children: Craig, Cari. Student, Grand Canyon Coll., Ariz. State Coll. Cert. tchr., Calif. Exhibited watercolor paintings in numerous shows including Adirondacks, N.Y., 1992, West Conn. Watercolor Soc., 1992, Western Colo. Watercolor Soc., 1991, 94, Nat. Watercolor Soc., 1991, Watercolor West, 1986, 87, 88, 90, San Diego Internat., 1988, 90, Rocky Mountain Nat., 1990, many others. Recipient Pauline Mintz award Audubon Artists, 1989, Gold medal award, 1990, Merit award West Conn. Watercolor Soc., 1992, Mary S. Litt medal Am. Watercolor Soc., 1993, Award of Achievement and Contbns. to Arts Stockton Arts Commn., 1994. Mem. Watercolor West, Midwest Watercolor Soc., Am. Watercolor Soc. Home: 334 Paragon Ave Stockton CA 95210-1315

MILLER, CAROLE ANN LYONS, editor, publisher, advertising specialist; b. Newton, Mass., Aug. 1; d. Markham Harold and Ursula Patricia (Foley) Lyons; m. David Thomas Miller, July 4, 1978. BA, Boston U., 1964; bus. cert., Hickox Sch., Boston, 1964; cert. advt. and mktg. profl. UCLA, 1973; cert. retail mgmt. profl. Ind. U., 1976. Editor Triangle Topics, Pacific Telephone, L.A.; programmer L.A. Cen. Area Speakers' Bur., 1964-66; mng. editor/mktg. dir. Teen mag., L.A. and N.Y.C., 1966-76; advt. dir. L.S. Ayres & Co., Indpls., 1976-78; v.p. mktg. The Denver, 1978-79; founder, editor, pub. Clockwise mag., Ventura, Calif., 1979 85; mktg. mgr., mgr. pub. rels. and spl. events Robinson's Dept. Stores, L.A., 1985-87, exec. v.p., dir. mktg. Harrison Svcs., 1987-93; pres. divsn. Miller & Miller Carole Ann Lyons Mktg., Camino, Calif., 1993—; instr. retail advt. Ind. U., 1977-78. Recipient Pres.'s award Advt. Women of N.Y., 1974; Seklemian award 1977; Pub. Svc. Addy award, 1978. Mem. Advt. Women N.Y., Fashion Group Internat., Bay Area Integrated Mktg., San Francisco Fashion Group, San Francisco Direct Mktg. Assn. UCLA Alumni Assn. Editor: Sek Says, 1979. Home: 3709 Carson Rd Camino CA 95709-9593

MILLER, CHARLES DALY, lumber company executive; b. Hartford, Conn., 1928; married. Grad., Johns Hopkins U. Sales and mktg. mgr. Yale & Towne Mfg. Co., 1949-59; assoc. Booz, Allen & Hamilton, 1959-64; with Avery Internat. Corp., Pasadena, Calif., 1964—; v.p., mng. dir. Materials Europe, 1965-68; v.p. Fasson Internat. Ops., 1968; group v.p. materials group Avery Internat. Corp., Pasadena, 1969-75, pres., bd. dirs., COO, 1975-77, pres., CEO, 1977-83; chmn., CEO Avery Dennison Corp. (formerly Avery Internat. Corp.), Pasadena, 1983—. Office: Avery Dennison Corp PO Box 7090 Pasadena CA 91109-7090

MILLER, CLARA BURR, education educator; b. Higganum, Conn., July 19, 1912; d. Eugene Orlando and Mabel (Clark) Burr; m. James Golden Miller, Sept. 19, 1942; children: Clara Elizabeth, Eugenia Manelle. BA, Mt. Holyoke Coll., 1933; MA, Columbia U., 1942. Cert. tchr., Conn., N.Y., Pa., Ariz. Tchr. Suffield (Conn.) Jr. High Sch., 1934-36, Rockville (Conn.) High Sch., 1936-41, Buckeley High Sch., Hartford, Conn., 1941-42, Pitts. Schs., 1952-55, Winchester-Thurston Sch., Pitts., 1955-58, Vail-Deane Sch., Elizabeth, N.J., 1959-69, Kingman (Ariz.) High Sch., 1971-76; mem. res. faculty Mohave C.C., Kingman, 1978-94; pres. bd. edn., clk. Mohave Union H.S. Dist. 30, 1983-91, bd. dirs., 1983-94; bd. dirs. Mohave Mental Health Clinic, v.p. bd. dirs., 1988, pres. bd. dirs., 1989-90. Author: Trails, Rails and Tales, 1981, (with others) Short Stories, 1984. Bd. dirs. No. Ariz. Comprehensive Guidance Ctr., Flagstaff, 1985-90, Kingman Aid to Abused People; sec. Good Samaritan Assn., Inc., Kingman, 1979—; pres. Ch. Women United, 1972-74, Presbyn. Women, 1987; elected elder session Kingman Presbyn. Ch., 1986—; mem. Mohave County Cmty. Action Bd., Western Ariz. Coun. Govts.; coord. League Friendship Indians and Ams., 1981—; co-chmn. Women Making History Com., 1992-94. Recipient Nat. Community Svc. award Mohave County Ret. Tchrs. Assn., 1987, Leta Glancy/Cecil Lockhart-Smith award No. Ariz. Comprehensive Guidance Ctr., 1990; named one of Women Making History Kingman Multi-Club Com., 1985. Mem. NEA, AAUW (pres. 1979-81), Ariz. Edn. Assn., Ariz. Sch. Bds. Assn., Soc. Profl. Journalists, Mohave County Ret. Tchrs. Assn. (v.p. 1991-93, pres. 1993-93), Footprinters. Democrat. Home: 2629 Mullen Dr Kingman AZ 86401-4264

MILLER, CLIFFORD ALBERT, merchant banker, business consultant; b. Salt Lake City, Aug. 6, 1928; s. Clifford Elmer and LaVeryl (Jensen) M.; m. Judith Auten, Sept. 20, 1976; 1 child, Courtney; children by previous marriage, Clifford, Christin, Stephanie. Student, U. Utah, 1945-50, UCLA, 1956. Pres. Braun & Co., L.A., 1955-82, chmn., 1982-87; exec. v.p. Gt. Western Fin. Corp., Beverly Hills, Calif., 1987-91; chmn. Clifford Group, Inc., bus. cons., 1992—; mng. dir. Shamrock Holdings, Inc., 1992—, Shamrock Capital Advisors, L.P., 1992—; bd. dirs. First Am. Corp., First Am. Bankshares, Inc., Washington, Shamrock Broadcasting, Inc., Burbank, Calif., L.A. Gear, Inc., Santa Monica, Calif.; cons to White House, 1969-74. Trustee Harvey Mudd Coll., Claremont, Calif., 1974—, chmn. bd. trustees, 1991; chmn. bd. dirs. L.A. Master Chorale, 1989-93, chmn. emeritus, 1993; mem. chmn.'s coun. Music Ctr. Unified Fund Campaign. Mem. UCLA Chancellor's Assocs., Skull and Bones, The Lakes Country Club, Calif. Club, Wilshire Country Club, Jeremy Golf and Country Club, Pi Kappa Alpha. Office: Shamrock Holdings Inc 4444 W Lakeside Dr Burbank CA 91505-4054

MILLER, CLIFFORD JOEL, lawyer; b. L.A., Oct. 31, 1947; s. Eugene and Marian (Millman) M.; m. Coco Ando, Apr. 9, 1990. BA, U. Calif., Irvine, 1969; JD, Pepperdine U., 1973. Bar: Calif. 1974, Hawaii 1974, U.S. Dist. Ct. Hawaii 1974. Ptnr. Rice, Lee & Wong, Honolulu, 1974-80, Goodsill Anderson Quinn & Stifel, Honolulu, 1980-89, McCorriston, Miho, Miller & Mukai, Honolulu, 1989—. Mem. ABA, Calif. Bar Assn., Hawaii Bar Assn., Am. Coll. Real Estate Lawyers. Office: McCorriston Miho Miller & Mukai 5 Waterfront Pla 500 Ala Moana Blvd Honolulu HI 96813-4920

MILLER, DANIEL NATHAN, communications executive; b. Sharon, Pa., Sept. 23, 1954; s. Francis P. and Shirley R.; m. Semadar Barzel, Mar. 21, 1983; children: Joshua Moses, Lillian Chelsea. BA in History and Journalism, Hampshire Coll., 1977; MBA in Fin., Columbia U., 1980. Dir. Link Resources Corp., N.Y.C., 1980-83; v.p. mktg. Warner-Littletext, Inc., Sunnyvale, N.Y., 1983-86; pres. OPUS Rsch., Inc., San Francisco, 1986—; past mem. Assn. Computer-Telephone/Applicational Suppliers, Washington; pub. Telemedia News and Views, 1993—. Editor: The Kelsey Report, 1994. Office: OPUS Rsch Inc 345 Chenery St San Francisco CA 94131-3069

MILLER, DAVID CRAIG, cardiovascular surgeon; b. San Francisco, Dec. 3, 1946; s. Charles Miller; m. Elsann Laws. Student, Dartmouth Coll., 1965-68; BA in Basic Med. Scis., Stanford U., 1969, MD, 1972. Diplomate Am. Bd. Surgery, Am. Bd. Thoracic Surgery, Am. Bd. Gen. Vascular Surgery. Resident in gen. surgery Stanford U. Med. Ctr. and Affiliated Hosps., 1972-75; chief resident in peripheral vascular surgery Stanford U. Med. Ctr., 1975-76, chief resident in cardiovasc. surgery, 1976-77, chief resident in thoracic surgery, 1977, program dir. peripheral vascular surgery residency, 1985-93; chief cardiac surgery section Palo Alto VA Med. Ctr., 1978-86; clin. asst. prof. cardiovasc. surgery sch. medicine Stanford U., 1978, asst. prof., 1978-83, assoc. prof., 1983-89, prof., 1989—; dir. Cardiovasc. Surg. Physiology Rsch. Labs.; staff surgeon cardiac surgery sect. Palo Alto DVA Med. Ctr.; mem. various coms. Stanford U.; mem. dean's com. Palo Alto VA Med. Ctr., 1980-88; co-chmn. external rev. com. on cardiac surgery U. Calif. Davis Med. Ctr., 1981-83; mem. strategic planning and mktg. com. and exec. steering subcom. Faculty Practice Plan, 1987-92, bd. dirs., 1989-90, mem. fin. exec. com., 1992-93; mem. VA Rsch. Merit Rev. Bd. Surgery, 1988-91, chmn., 1990-91; presenter in field. Mem. editl. bd. Jour. Cardiac Surgery, 1985—, Jour. Surg. Rsch., 1990-94, Circulation 1991-93, Jour. Heart Valve Disease, 1992—, others; ad hoc referee Circulation, Jour. Clin. Investigation, Jour. Thoracic and Cardiovasc. Surgery, others; contbr. articles to profl. jours. Lt. comdr. M.C., USNR. Grantee Searle Family Found., 1979-82, Upjohn Pharms. Co., 1982-85, NIH, 1983—. Mem. AAAS, ACS (mem. cardiovasc. surgery com. 1986-88, mem. exec. com. 1987-88), AMA, Am. Surg. Assn., Am. Assn. Thoracic Surgery, Am. Coll. Cardiology (mem. sci. abstract rev. com. 1986, 90, mem. peripheral vascular disease com. 1994-95), Am. Coll. Chest Physicians, Am. Fedn. Clin. Rsch., Am. Heart Assn. (bd. dirs. Santa Clara County chpt. 1980-82, mem. rsch. com. 1981-83, mem. exec. com. coun. cardiovasc. surgery 1985—, mem. program com. 1988-92, chmn. 1989-92, mem. optimal resources for vascular surgery com. 1985-89, co-chmn. com. sci. sessions program 1992-93, grantee Calif. affiliate 1980-82, grantee 1981-83, 91-93), Sociedad Colombiana de Cirugia, Sociedad Chilena de Cardiologia y Cirugia Cardiovascular, Cardiac Soc. Australia and New Zealand (corr.), Calif. Med. Assn., No. Calif. Vascular Soc., San Francisco Surg. Soc., Soc. Clin. Surgery, Santa Clara County Med. Soc. (mem. ethics com. 1980-82), Soc. Univ. Surgeons (mem. publs. com. 1982-85), Soc. Vascular Surgery, Western Thoracic Surg. Assn. (mem. program. com. 1983-88, chmn. 1986-88, sec. 1989-93, v.p. 1993-94, pres. 1994-95), Soc. Thoracic Surgeons, Assn. Acad. Surgery, Western Vascular Soc., Internat. Soc. Cardiovasc. Surgery (mem. program com. 1984-87), Pacific Coast Surg. Assn., Soc. Clin. Vascular Surgery, Soc. Thoracic Surg. Edn., Sociedad de Cardiocirujanos (pres. 1987-88), Pan-Pacific Surg. Assn., Stanford U. Med. Sch. Alumni Assn. (bd. govs. 1983-89), Cardiac Surgery Biology Club. Office: Stanford U Sch Medicine Falk Cardiovascular Rsch Ctr Stanford CA 94305-5247

MILLER, DAVID FOSTER, academic administrator, educator; b. Cleve., Nov. 2, 1940; s. Thomas Theodore and Mildred D. (Seitz) M.; m. Koyce J. Morgan, Aug. 5, 1961; children: David Scott, Michael Thomas. BA, We. Bapt. Coll., El Cerrito, Calif., 1963; BD, San Francisco Bapt. Sem., 1966, ThM, 1968; ThD, Grace Sem., Winona Lake, Ind., 1977. Ordained to ministry Bapt. Ch., 1966. Prof. Bibl. studies We. Bapt. Coll., Salem, Oreg., 1966—, pres., 1991—; pastor, founder Valley Bapt. Ch., Perrydale, Oreg., 1974-91. Contbr. articles to profl. jours. Bd. dirs. KIDS Inc., Dallas, Oreg., 1979-87. Republican. Home: 5270 Woodscape Dr SE Salem OR 97306-1003 Office: We Bapt Coll 5000 Deer Park Dr SE Salem OR 97301-9330

MILLER, DAVID WAYNE, construction inspector, coordinator; b. Yuba City, Calif., June 23, 1949; s. Lloyd Wayne and Beverly Lorene (Ryan) M.; children: Quinlan Kenneth, Erin Patricia, Justin Michael Francis. AA in Constrn. Tech., Delta, 1985; BA in Art, Calif. State U., Hayward, 1989. Cert. tech. transfer and commercialization Internat. Conf. Bldg. Ofcls./Internat. Assn. Plumbing and Mech. Ofcls. Uniform Plumbing Code. Plumber/fitter local 492 United Assn. Pipe Trades, Stockton, Calif., 1972—; plumber/fitter Lawrence Livermore Nat. Lab., Livermore, Calif., 1983-87, estimator, 1987-90; owner Moon Studios, 1976-80, Moonraker, 1991—. Author: (short story) Morgan's Tide, 1982, (Fremont C. of C. lit.) History of Fremont, 1982—; contbr. articles to CitySports, 1982. Sgt. U.S. Army, 1969-71, Vietnam. Mem. Lawrence Livermore Armed Force Vets. Assn., (founder, pres. 1986), Toastmasters.

MILLER, DIANE DORIS, executive search consultant; b. Sacramento, Calif., Jan. 18, 1954; d. George Campbell and Doris Lucille (Benninger) M. BA, U. Pacific, 1976, Golden Gate U., 1985, MBA, 1987. Mgr., A.G. Spanos, Sacramento, 1977-81, Lee Sammis, Sacramento, 1981-83; v.p. Consol. Capital, San Francisco, 1983-86; ptnr. Wilcox, Bertoux and Miller, Sacramento, 1986—. Bd. dirs. Sacramento Symphony En Corps, 1982-84, Sacramento Ballet, 1983-84, 86—, Sacramento Symphony Assn., 1988—, Oakland Ballet, Calif., 1984-85. Named Vol. of Yr., Junior League, 1983, Bus. Vol. in the Arts, Sacramento C. of C., 1989. Mem. U. Pacific Alumni Assn. (bd. dirs. 1978-85). Republican. Avocations: ballet, water sports.

MILLER, DIANE WILMARTH, human resources director; b. Clarinda, Iowa, Mar. 12, 1940; d. Donald and Floy Pauline (Madden) W.; m. Robert Nolen Miller, Aug. 21, 1965; children: Robert Wilmarth, Anne Elizabeth. AA, Colo. Women's Coll., 1960; BBA, U. Iowa, 1962; MA, U. No. Colo., 1994. Cert. tchr., Colo.; vocat. credential, Colo.; cert. sr. profl. in human resources. Sec.-counselor U. S.C., Myrtle Beach AFB, 1968-69; instr. U. S.C., Conway, 1967-69; tchr. bus. Poudre Sch. Dist. R-1, Ft. Collins, Colo., 1970-71; travel cons. United Bank Travel Svc., Greeley, Colo., 1972-74; dir. human resources Aims Community Coll., Greeley, 1984—; instr. part-time Aims Community Coll., Greeley, 1972—. Active 1st Congl. Ch., Greeley. Mem. Women's Investment Group Soc., Questers, Coll. Univ. Pers. Assn., Coll. Univ. Pers. Assn. Colo., No. Colo. Human Resources Assn., Soc. Human Resource Mgmt., Philanthropic Ednl. Orgn. (pres. 1988-89), Women's Panhellenic Assn. (pres. 1983-84), Scroll and Fan Club (pres. 1985-86), WTK Club. Home: 3530 Wagon Trail Pl Greeley CO 80634-3405 Office: Aims Community Coll 5401 20th St Greeley CO 80634-3002

MILLER, DONALD GABRIEL, chemist; b. Oakland, Calif., Oct. 29, 1927; s. Nathan Harry and Edith Eileen (Levy) M.; m. Miriam G. Cohen, Aug. 14, 1949; children: Nancy Gail, Lynne Sandra. BS in Chemistry with honors, U. Calif., Berkeley, 1949; PhD in Phys. Chemistry, U. Ill., 1953. Asst. prof. U. Louisville, Ky., 1952-54; postdoctoral fellow Brookhaven Nat. Lab., Upton, N.Y., 1954-56; chemist Lawrence Livermore (Calif.) Nat. Lab., 1956—; adj. prof. Tex. Christian U., Ft. Worth, 1991—; guest prof. Technische Hochschule, Aachen, Germany, 1985, 88; vis. prof. U. Naples, Italy, 1983, 85, 87, 90, 93. Contbr. articles to profl. jours. and chpts. to books. Planning commr. City of Livermore, 1966-68, councilman, 1968-76, mayor, 1973-74; grand juror County of Alameda, 1992-93. Mem. Am. Chem. Soc., Math. Assn. Am., NRA (life), Nat. Muzzle Loading Rifle Assn. (life), Sigma Xi. Home: 2862 Waverly Way Livermore CA 94550-1740

MILLER, DONALD WESLEY, JR., cardiac surgeon; b. Honolulu, Aug. 5, 1940; s. Donald Wesley and Charlotte W. (Williams) M.; m. Nell Bowen, May 12, 1968 (div. Aug. 1977); children: James, Elizabeth; m. Linda Lutes Costello, Dec. 27, 1986; children: Michael Daniel. AB, Dartmouth Coll., 1962, B. Med. Scis., 1963; MD, Harvard U., 1965. Diplomate Am. Bd. Surgery, Am. Bd. Thoracic Surgery. Intern The Roosevelt Hosp., N.Y.C., 1965-66, resident in gen. surgery, 1966-70; resident in cardiac and thoracic surgery Columbia-Presbyn. Med. Ctr., Harlem Hosp., N.Y.C., 1972-74; pvt. practice Seattle Heart Surgery Inc., Seattle, 1974-75; asst. prof. Cardiothoracic Surgery U. Wash. Sch. Medicine, Seattle, 1975-78, assoc. prof. Cardiothoracic Surgery, 1978-80, clin. assoc. prof. Cardiothoracic Surgery, 1980—; pvt. practice, Seattle, 1980—; mem. staff Swedish Med. Ctr., Seattle, 1974—, U. Wash. Med. Ctr., Seattle, 1975—, Providence Hosp., 1986—, Overlake Hosp. Med. Ctr., Seattle, 1975—. Author The Practice of Coronary Artery Bypass Surgery, 1977; co-author: Atlas of Cardiac Surgery, 1983; contbr. chpt. Clinical Essays on the Heart, vol. 2, 1983; contbr. articles to profl. jours. Bd. dirs. Seattle Symphony Orch., 1983-87; trustee Seattle Opera Assn., 1984—, Seattle Chamber Music Festival, 1986-94; mem. devel. adv. bd. U. Wash. Coll. Arts and Scis., 1985-88. Lt. comdr. M.C., USNR, 1970-72. Mem. ACS, Am. Assn. Thoracic Surgery, Am. Coll. Cardiology, King County Med. Soc., North Pacific Surg. Assn., Seattle Surg. Soc., Soc. Thoracic Surgery, Western Thoracic Surg. Soc., Boylston Soc. Republican. Presbyterian. Home: 12064 Lakeside Pl NE Seattle WA 98125-5957

MILLER, EDMUND SEVERN, JR., professional land surveyor; b. Balt., Jan. 5, 1950; s. Edmund Severn and Nancy Bell (Wilson) M.; m. Beverly Christine Johnson, Oct. 14, 1984; children: Anne Christine, Rachael Abbe. Registered profl. land surveyor, Calif. Surveyor City of Long Beach, Calif., 1980-90; chief surveyor Port of Long Beach, 1990—. Mem. Am. Congress on Surveying and Mapping, Calif. Land Surveyors Assn. Mem. Assemblies of God. Office: Port of Long Beach 925 Harbor Plz Long Beach CA 90802-6411

MILLER, ERIC NATHAN, neuropsychologist; b. Oceanside, Calif., Nov. 21, 1955; s. David Wesley and Nancy Norland (Guinand) M.; 1 child, Bryan Scott. BA in Psychology, U. Va., 1977; MS in Psychology, U. Wis., 1981, PhD of Clin. Psychology, 1986. Lic. clin. psychologist, Calif. Fellow neuropsychology UCLA, 1986-88, asst. rsch. neuropsychologist, clin. prof., 1988—; owner, proprietor Norland Software, L.A., 1983—; project dir. Divsn. Epidemiology, UCLA, 1987—. Contbr. articles to profl. jours.; consulting editor Psychol. Assessment; reviewer jours. in field. Fellow Ittleson Consulting, Wis. Alumni Rsch. Fund. Mem. APA, Internat. Neuropsychol. Soc., Phi Beta Kappa. Office: UCLA Neuropsychiat Inst 760 Westwood Plz Rm C8-747 Los Angeles CA 90024-8300

MILLER, FRANKLIN EMRICK, software engineer, project engineer; b. Greenville, Ohio, Aug. 12, 1946; s. Rollin Linde and E. Evelyn (Emrick) M.; m. Sandra Lewis, Dec. 20, 1969; children: William Rollin, Rose Mary. BS in Math. and Physics, Otterbein Coll., 1969; MEd in Ednl. Psychology and Counseling, Wayne State U., 1975; PhD in Ednl. Psychology, Computer Stats., U. Denver, 1984. Lic. pvt. pilot FAA. Commd. U.S. Air Force, 1969, advanced through grades to capt.; space surveillance officer SLBM, Maine, 1970-71, BMEWS Thule, Greenland, 1971-72; chief instr./systems analyst, Correlation Ctr. 440L, McGuire AFB, N.J., 1972-73; site space surveillance officer, Aviano, Italy, 1973-75; chief Defense Support Program support programming unit, Colo., 1975-79; chief applications support programming DSP, South Australia, 1979-81, ret., 1988; software engr. Aerojet Electro Systems Corp., Aurora, Colo., 1981-88. Bd. dirs., Aurora Community Mental Health Ctr., 1976-79; vol. counselor Comitis Crisis Ctr., YMCA, Aurora, 1976-78. Mem. Am. Psychol. Assn. (div. Applied Experimental and Engring. Psychologists), Denver Astron. Soc. (sec.), Phi Delta Kappa. Republican. Author: The Preliminary Online Rorschach Test Manual, 1980; contbr. article to profl. jour. Office: The Aerospace Corp Buckley Ang Base 18300 E Crested Butte Ave Aurora CO 80011-9518

MILLER, GARY ALAN, commercial banker; b. Phoenix, Ariz., July 4, 1943; s. Lawrence Joseph and Marjorie (McGlone) M.; m. Bonnie Jean Welch; children: Karyn, Matthew, Christopher. BA, Ariz. State U., 1965, MA, 1967; M in int. mgmt. (hons.), Thunderbird Grad. Sch., Phoenix, 1972. Analyst First Nat. Bank of Albuquerque, New Mex., 1972-74; training program Export Import Bank of U.S., Washington, 1974; asst. v.p. Bank of Am., L.A., Chgo., 1975-79; v.p. Nat. Westminister Bank, Chgo., 1979-83; sr. v.p. NatWest Markets, L.A., 1983—; instr. mktg. Elmhurst (Ill.) Coll., 1975-79. Pres. British Am. Bus. Coun., Washington, 1991; active com. Fgn. Rels., L.A., 1994—. 1st lt. U.S. Army, 1967-71, Vietnam. Decorated Bronze Star U.S. Army, 1970, Army Commendation medal, 1970. Mem. British Am. C. of C. Republican. Presbyterian. Office: NatWest Markets 350 S Grand Ave Ste 39 Los Angeles CA 90071-3459

MILLER, GEORGE, mayor; b. Detroit; m. Roslyn Girard; 4 children. BA, U. Ariz., 1947, MEd, 1952. Tchr. high schs., owner, prin. painting contracting co., until 1989; mayor City of Tucson, 1991—. Active mem. Dem. Party So. Ariz., 1960—, treas. Pima County div., state chmn. Presdl. Del. Selection Reform Commn.; bd. dirs. Tucson Jewish Community Ctr., Anti-Defamation League of B'nai B'rith; councilman Tucson City Coun., 1977-91, also vice mayor. With USMC, WWII. Decorated Purple Heart; recipient recognition award United Way, Community Svcs. Support award Chicanos Por La Causa (2), cert. appreciation San Ignacio Yaqui Coun., Old Pasqua, Man of Yr. award So. Ariz. Home Builders Assn. Office: Office of Mayor PO Box 27210 Tucson AZ 85726-7210*

MILLER, GEORGE, congressman; b. Richmond, Calif., May 17, 1945; s. George and Dorothy (Rumsey) M.; m. Cynthia Caccavo, 1964; children: George, Stephen. B.A., San Francisco State Coll., 1968; J.D., U. Calif., Davis, 1972. Legis. counsel Calif. senate majority leader, 1969-73; mem. 94th-104th Congresses from 7th Calif. dist., 1975—; chmn. subcom. on oversight and investigations, 1985—, chmn. subcom. on labor stds., 1981-84, chmn. select com. on children, youth and families, 1983-91, chmn. com. on natural resources, 1991-94; mem. com. on edn. and lab., dep. majority whip, 1989-94; vice chair Dem. Policy Com., 1995—. Mem. Calif. Bar Assn. Office: House of Representatives 2205 Rayburn Bldg Washington DC 20515-0005

MILLER, GORDON HOLMAN, chemical, nuclear and environmental engineering consultant; b. Kansas City, Mo., Jan. 12, 1916; s. Mervin Thurmond and Alice Henshaw (Snively) M.; m. Marjorie Jane Trimble, Feb. 14, 1942. AS, Kansas City Jr. Coll., Mo., 1934; BSChemE, U. Kans., Lawrence, 1936; MSChemE, Pa. State U., 1939; PhD in Nuclear Engring., U. Mich., 1962. Chemist, Kansas City Testing Labs., Mo., 1936; chief chemist Certain-Teed Products Corp., Kansas City, 1937; from chemist to supr. Texaco Inc., Port Arthur, Tex., 1939-56, sr. engr. radiation research, Beacon, N.Y., 1956-62, environ. coordinator, Denver, 1974-82; research assoc. Texaco Experiment Inc., Richmond, Va., 1962-74; cons. chem., nuclear and environ. engring. Texaco Inc., Littleton, Colo., 1982-84; pvt. cons. chem., nuclear and environ. engring., Littleton, 1982—. Patentee in field. Recipient Thiokol award Am. Rocket Soc., 1959. Mem. Am. Chem. Soc. (sect. chmn. 1955-56), N.Y. Acad. Scis. (Boris Pregel award 1962), AAAS, Am. Forestry Assn., Research Soc. Am. (sec. chmn. 1962), Sigma Xi, Tau Beta Pi, Sigma Tau, Pi Mu Epsilon. Home and Office: 1321 E Costilla Ave Littleton CO 80122-1300

MILLER, GREGORY STEWART, civil engineer; b. Seattle, Mar. 15, 1946; s. Eskridge Sherman and Margaret Ann (Stewart) M.; children: Nikolaos Stewart, Ioanna Margaret. Student civil engring., U. Wash., 1969, Ga. Inst. Tech., 1977. Commd. U.S. Army, 1969-93, advanced through grades to lt. col.; dir. for installation support Ft. Benjamin Harrison, Indpls., 1990-93; engr. mgr. Washington County, Hillsboro, Oreg., 1994—. Leader, Boy

Scouts Am., Heidelberg, Germany, 1987-90, Troop 157, Indpls., 1990-93.. Mem. Am. Pub. Works Assn., Soc. Am. Mil. Engrs. Orthodox Christian Ch. Home: 824 SE 60th Ave Hillsboro OR 97123-5802 Office: Washington County 155 N 1st Ave Hillsboro OR 97124-3072

MILLER, HAROLD WILLIAM, nuclear geochemist; b. Walton, N.Y., Apr. 21, 1920; s. Harold Frank and Vera Leona (Simons) M. BS in Chemistry, U. Mich., 1943; MS in Chemistry, U. Colo., 1948, postgrad. Control chemist Linde Air Products Co., Buffalo, 1943-46; analytical research chemist Gen. Electric Co., Richland, Wash., 1948-51; research chemist Phillips Petroleum Co., Idaho Falls, Idaho, 1953-56; with Anaconda (Mont.) Copper Co., 1956; tech. dir., v.p. U.S. Yttrium Co., Laramie, Wyo., 1956-57; tech. dir. Colo. div. The Wah Chang Co., Boulder, Colo., 1957-58; analytical chemist The Climax (Colo.) Molybdenum Co., 1959; with research and devel. The Colo. Sch. of Mines Research Found., Golden, 1960-62; cons. Boulder, 1960—; sr. research physicist Dow Chem. Co., Golden, 1963-73; bd. dirs. Sweeney Mining and Milling Corp., Boulder; cons. Hendricks Mining and Milling Co., Boulder; instr. nuclear physics and nuclear chemistry Rocky Flats Plant, U. Colo. Contbr. numerous articles to profl. jours. Recipient Lifetime Achievement award Boulder County Metal Mining Assn., 1990. Mem. Sigma Xi. Home and Office: PO Box 1092 Boulder CO 80306-1092

MILLER, HARRIET SANDERS, art center director; b. N.Y.C., Apr. 18, 1926; d. Herman and Dorothy (Silbert) S.; m. Milton H. Miller, June 27, 1948; children—Bruce, Jeffrey, Marcie. B.A., Ind. U., 1947; M.A., Columbia U., 1949; M.S., U. Wis., 1962, M.F.A., 1967. Dir. art sch. Madison Art Ctr., Wis., 1963-72; acting dir. Center for Continuing Edn., Vancouver, B.C., 1975-76; mem. fine arts faculty Douglas Coll., Vancouver, 1972-78; exec. dir. Palos Verdes Arts Center, Calif., 1978-84; dir. Junior Arts Center, Los Angeles, 1984—; one woman exhibits at Gallery 7, Vancouver, 1978, Gallery 1, Toronto, Ont., 1977, Linda Farris Gallery, Seattle, 1975, Galerie Allen, Vancouver, 1973. Mem. Calif. Art Edn. Assn., Museum Educators of So. Calif., Arts and Humanities Symposium. Office: Junior Arts Ctr 4814 Hollywood Blvd Los Angeles CA 90027-5302

MILLER, JEAN RUTH, librarian; b. St. Helena, Calif., Aug. 4, 1927; d. William Leonard and Jean (Stanton) M. BA, Occidental Coll., 1950; MLS, U. So. Calif., Los Angeles, 1952. Base librarian USAF, Wethersfield, Eng., 1952-55; post librarian USMC Air Sta., El Toro, Calif., 1955-63; data systems librarian Autonetics (Rockwell), Anaheim, Calif., 1963-65; mgr. library services Beckman Instruments, Inc., Fullerton, Calif., 1966-93; mem. adv. com. Library Technician Program, Fullerton Coll., 1969—. Author: (bibliography) Field Air Traffic Control, 1965, Electrical Shock Hazards, 1974. Chair Fullerton Are U. So. Calif. Scholarship Alumni Interview Program, Fullerton, 1974—. Mem. IEEE, So. Calif. Assn. Law Libraries, Med. Library Group of So. Calif., Spl. Libraries Assn. (pres. So. Calif. chpt. 1975-76, chair Sci./Tech. Div. 1985-86). Republican. Home: 3139 E Chapman Ave Apt 9C Orange CA 92669-3743

MILLER, JEFFREY ROBERT, mayor, insurance planner; b. Cleve., Dec. 18, 1941; s. Donal Harry and Elizabeth (Jackson) M.; m. Mary Ann Greenway, July 26, 1969; children: Jennifer Lynn, Christopher Jeffrey. BTh, N.W. Christian Coll., 1969; MDiv, Tex. Christian U., 1972. Ordained minister Christian Ch., 1969. Assoc. min. 1st Christian Ch., Lebanon, Oreg., 1972-73; min. 1st Christian Ch., Eugene, Oreg., 1974-78, Allison Park Christian Ch., Eugene, 1978-86; ins. planner Lincoln Nat. Life Ins., Eugene, 1987-89; ins. agt., ptnr. Russell, Miller & Assocs., Eugene, 1990—; mayor City of Eugene, 1988—. Mem. City Coun., Eugene, 1985-88; trustee N.W. Christian Coll., Eugene, 1990—. With U.S. Army, 1965-64. Recipient Robert P. Connelly medal for life saving Kiwanis Internat., 1989, appreciation award for life saving City of Springfield, Oreg., 1989. Mem. Oreg. Life Underwriters, Rotary. Democrat.

MILLER, JEREMY, law educator. BA, Yale U., 1976; JD cum laude, Tulane U., 1980; LLM, U. Pa., 1981. Bar: Mass., 1980. Law clk. Chief Justice Supreme Ct. State Colo., 1982; dean, prof. law Sch. Law Chapman U., 1992-93; editor-in-chief Orange County Lawyer Mag., 1994—; prof. Western State U., 1983-94; adj. prof. Fleming's Fundamentals of Law Bar Review, 1992—; Calif. State U., 1987-91; arbitrator Am. Arbitration Assn., 1993-94; legal cons. Editor: Flemings Fundamentals of Law, 1991—; contbr. articles to profl. jours. Named Best Tchr. Calif. State U., 1991, Best Tchr. Western State U., 1988, 89, 90, 91, 92, 93; named Outstanding Young Man of Am., 1989. Mem. ABA, AAUP, Orange County Bar Assn., Calif. Task Force Testing Profl. Responsibility. Home: 8008 E Deerfield Ln Orange CA 92669 Office: Chapman U Sch of Law Ste 200 1240 S State College Blvd Anaheim CA 92806

MILLER, JOANNE LOUISE, middle school educator; b. Milton, Mass., Apr. 4, 1944; d. Joseph Louis and Marion Theresa (Saulnier) Fasci; m. William Frederick Miller, Dec. 4, 1962; 1 child, Robert Joseph. BS, U. Oreg., 1972, MS in Curriculum and Instrn., 1973; EdD, Brigham Young U., 1980; postgrad., Oreg. State U., 1995. Lic. counselor, tchr., adminstr., Oreg. Tchr. South Lane Sch. Dist., Cottage Grove, Oreg., 1973—, lang. arts div. chairperson, 1975-78, 89-90, reading coord., 1978-79, 7th grade block chairperson, 1982-92, mid. sch. talented and gifted coord., 1992-93, counselor, 1991-93; mem. Oreg. State Assessment Content Panel Reading, Salem, 1987-88; mem. Oreg. Lang Arts Curriculum Devel. Com., Salem, 1985-87; del. to Citizen Amb. Program of People to People Internat. 1st U.S.-Russia Joint Conf. on Edn., Moscow, 1994. Vol. Am. Cancer Soc., Am. Diabetes Assn., 1990—. Mem. ACA, NEA, Internat. Reading Assn., Am. Sch. Counselor Assn., Oreg. Counseling Assn., Oreg. Edn. Assn., South Lane Edn. Assn., Oreg. Reading Assn., Delta Kappa Gamma, Alpha Rho State (v.p. 1995—). Democrat. Roman Catholic. Home: 85515 Appletree Dr Eugene OR 97405-9738 Office: Lincoln Mid Sch 1565 S 4th St Cottage Grove OR 97424-2955

MILLER, JOHN LAURENCE, professional golfer; b. San Francisco, Apr. 29, 1947; s. Laurence O. and Ida (Meldrum) M.; m. Linda Strouse, Sept. 17, 1969; children: John Strouse, Kelly, Casi, Scott, Brent, Todd. Student, Brigham Young U., 1965-69. Profl. golfer, 1969—; Pres. Johnny Miller Enterprises, Inc. Author: Pure Golf, 1976, Johnny Miller's Golf for Juniors, 1987. Named PGA Player of Yr., 1974. Office: PO Box 2260 Napa CA 94558-0060*

MILLER, JOHN NELSON, banker; b. Youngstown, Ohio, Sept. 15, 1948; s. W. Frederic and Julia Elizabeth (Lohman) M.; MusB in Cello, Westminster Coll., 1970; MBA in Fin., Wharton Sch. Fin., U. Pa., 1974; m. Judy Congleton, Aug. 18, 1980. Asst. br. mgr. Mahoning Nat. Bank, Youngstown, 1970-72; asst. dir. fin. services dept. Mellon Bank N. Am., Pitts., 1974-76; v.p., head cash mgmt. div. Md. Nat. Bank, Balt., 1976-78; v.p., mgr. corp. cash mgmt. div. N.Y. Bank of Am., N.Y.C., 1978-80; dir. cash mgmt., strategic planning, product mgmt. and tng. Bank of Am. S.F., 1980-81; v.p., global account officer for utilities/telecommunications S.E. unit Bank of Am., N.Y.C., 1981-84; team leader, chief fin. officer, corp. payment div. large corp. sales, 1984-87; mgr. credit preparation and analysis unit N. Am. Div., N.Y.C., 1987-88; v.p., eastern region mgr. cash mgmt. div. Wells Fargo Bank N.Y., 1988-90; v.p., div. mgr. Eastern, Midwestern, Rocky Mountain, Pacific and nat. fin. instns., 1990-93; v.p. and group sales mgr., Bank of Am. NT & SA Foreign Currency Svcs., San Francisco, 1993-94; v.p. & regional sales mgr. Bank of Am. Global Payment Svcs. Bank of Am., 1994—; lectr. Wharton Grad. Sch., Am. Mgmt. Assn. cash mgmt. seminars, Bank Adminstrn. Inst., others; speaker Payment Systems Inc., Corp. EFT Seminar, Atlanta, Nat. Conv. Treasury Mgmt. Assn.; mem. Corp. Payment Task Force, N.Y.C., Corp. EFT Cost-Benefit Task Force. Chmn. ann. giving program Wharton Grad. Sch., 1977-79. Mem. Wharton Grad. Alumni Assn. (pres., local club, rep., nat. dir., mem. exec. com.), Bank Adminstrn. Inst. (mem. subcom. interindustry commn.), Am. Nat. Standards Inst. (sub com. on interindustry optical scan standards), Cash Mgmt. Inst. (dir.), Omicron Delta Kappa. Clubs: Mchts. (Balt.); University (Pitts.); Rotary (San Francisco). Office: Bank of Am NT & SA Foreign Currency Svcs 3068 Two Embarcadero San Francisco CA 94111

MILLER, JONATHAN LEWIS, lawyer, computer consultant; b. Boston, Dec. 9, 1947; s. Harold Irving and Maida (Rosenberg) M.; m. Arleen Garfinkle, Nov. 2, 1985; 1 child, Jonah Maxwell. BA in Sociology, Colby Coll., 1973; BS in Physics, U. Washington, 1980; JD, U. Denver, 1994. Bar: Colo. 1994. Proprietor, cons. J. Miller & Assoc., Colo., 1982-85; pres., atty. J. Miller & Assoc., Inc., Boulder, Colo., 1985-95; assoc. Martin & Mehaffy LLC, Boulder, 1995—. Editor: Transp. Law Jour., 1992-94; author: Rocky Mountain Land Use Technical Servia Report, 1994, Orange County Lawyer, 1994. Home: 173 Wild Tiger Rd Boulder CO 80302-9263

MILLER, JOSEPH ARTHUR, manufacturing engineer, educator, consultant; b. Brattleboro, Vt., Aug. 28, 1933; s. Joseph Maynard and Marjorie Antoinette (Hammerberg) M.; m. Ardene Hedwig Barker, Aug. 19, 1956; children: Stephanie L., Jocelyn A., Shana L., Gregory J. BS in Agrl., Andrews U., Berrien Springs, Mich., 1955; MS in Agrl. Mechs., Mich. State U., 1959; EdD in Vocat. Edn., UCLA, 1973. Constrn. engr. Thornton Bldg. & Supply, Inc., Williamston, Mich., 1959-63, C & B Silo Co., Charlotte, Mich., 1963-64; instr. and dir. retraining Lansing (Mich.) Community Coll., 1964-68; asst. prof./prog. coord./coop coord. San Jose State U., 1968-79; mfg. specialist Lockheed Missiles & Space Co., Sunnyvale, Calif., 1979-81, rsch. specialist, 1981-88, NASA project mgr., 1982-83, staff engr., 1988—, team leader Pursuit of Excellence award winning machine tool project, 1990—, coord. flexible mfg. system simulation project, 1994—, team mem. federally funded AIMS Agile Mfg. project, 1995—; agrl. engrng. cons. USDA Poultry Expt. Sta., 1960-62; computer numerical control cons. Dynamechtronics, Inc., Sunnyvale, 1987-90; machining cons. Lockheed, Space Sys. Div., 1986—; instr. computer numerical control DeAnza Coll., Cupertino, Calif., 1985-88, Labor Employment Tng. Corp., San Jose, Calif., 1988-93; instr. computer-aided mfg. and non traditional machining San Jose (Calif.) State U., 1994—. Author: Student Manual for CNC Lathe, 1990; contbr. articles to profl. jours. Career counselor Pacific Union Coll., Angwin, 1985-92. UCLA fellow, 1969-73. Mem. Soc. Mfg. Engrs. (sr. 1980-92, chmn. edn. com. local chpt. 98 1984-85, career guidance counselor 1986-88), Nat. Assn. Indsl. Tech. (pres. industry divsn. 1987-88, bd. cert. 1991-92, chmn. accreditation visitation team 1984—), Calif. Assn. Indsl. Tech. (pres. 1974-75, 84-85), Am. Soc. Indsl. Tech. (pres. 1980-81). Seventh-day Adventist. Home: PO Box 190 Berry Creek CA 95916-0190 Office: Lockheed Missiles & Space 1111 Lockheed Way Sunnyvale CA 94089-1212

MILLER, JUDITH JUNTURA, artist; b. Ontario, Oreg., Jan. 31, 1939; d. Ben and Hazel Adeline (Richie) Jones; m. Jerry Wayne Miller, Feb. 19, 1956; children: Jeffrey, Andrew. AA with honors, Canada Coll., Redwood City, Calif., 1973, postgrad., Y; BA with honors, San Jose State U., 1976; BFA, San Francisco Art Inst., 1980. guest lectr. Cabrillo Coll. Auditorium, Aptos, Calif., 1991; guest lectr. mixed media work Santa Cruz Mus. Art, Cabrillo Coll. Gallery, 1991. One-woman shows include City Hall Gallery, Sunnyvale, Calif., 1982, So. Exposure Gallery, San Francisco, 1985, Pacific Grad. Sch. Psychology, Palo Alto, Calif., 1989, Stanford (Calif.) U., 1990, Branner Spangenberg Gallery, Palo Alto, 1991, Cabrillo Coll. Gallery, 1991, Art F/X, 1994; group shows include San Francisco Art Inst., 1985, Seipp Gallery, Palo Alto, 1986, 92, San Jose Mus. Art, 1988, 92, Clara Kott Von Storch Gallery, Dexter, Mich., 1994, Gallery 57, Fullerton, Calif., River Gallery, Chattanooga, San Diego Art Inst., Triton Mus. of Art, Santa Clara, Calif., One West Contemporary Art Ctr., Ft. Collins, Colo., Gallery 206, St. Joseph, Mo., 1995, Palo Alto Cultural Ctr., 995, ACAC Gallery, Sutter Creek, Calif., 995, Richard Summer, Palo Alto, 1995, Ralston Fine Art, Johnson City, Tenn., 1995, Galeria Tonantzin, San Juan Bautista, Calif., 1995, Univ. Art Gallery, N.E. Mo. State U., Kirksville, 1995. Recipient Cert. of Excellence, Internat. Art Competition, Metro Art, N.Y., 1986, Best of Show award Aesthetics "89," Friendship Hall Gallery, McPherson, Kans., Patron's award No. Nat. Juried Art Exhibit, LRC Gallery, Nicolet Coll., Rhinelander, Wis., 1989, Cert. of Merit, 87th Open Juried Exhbn., Long Beach (Calif.) Art Assn., 1991, Merit award Calif. Works, Calif. State Fair, Sacramento, 1991, Gold and Silver Discovery awards Art of Calif., 1992. Mem. South Bay Area Women's Caucus for Art (founding, v.p. slide registry 1990), Women's Caucus for Art (v.p. membership 1991-92, coord. Art Reach 1990-91, guest lectr. 1991), Calif. Soc. of Printmakers, L.A. Printmaking Soc., The Print Consortium. Home and Studio: 4141 Old Trace Rd Palo Alto CA 94306-3728

MILLER, KATHERINE TOY, writer; b. Taft, Calif., Jan. 9, 1955; d. John Jasper and Betty Irene (Harkleroad) M. BA in English, U. Redlands, 1977; MFA, U. Ariz., 1983. Newspaper reporter Daily Midway Driller, Taft, 1978-80; instr. English and com. Norwich U., Northfield, Vt., 1984-86; instr. English Muskingum Coll., New Concord, Ohio, 1987-88; writing fellow Fine Arts Work Ctr., Provincetown, Mass., 1988-89; part time instr. Calif. State U., Bakersfield, 1989; instr. U. Calif. Santa Barbara, 1990. Contbr. numerous articles to profl. publs. Home: 543 Front St Taft CA 93268-3407

MILLER, KENNETH EDWARD, mechanical engineer, consultant; b. Weymouth, Mass., Dec. 24, 1951; s. Edward Francis and Lena Joan (Trotta) M.; m. Florence Gay Wilson, Sept. 18, 1976; children: Nicole Elizabeth, Brent Edward. BSME, Northeastern U., 1974; MS in Systems Mgmt., U. So. Calif., 1982. Registered profl. engr., N.Y., N.H., Ariz., Nev.; registered land surveyor, Ariz. Test engr. Stone & Webster Engring., Boston, 1974-76; plant engr. N.Y. State Power Authority, Buchanan, 1976-80; maintenance engr. Pub. Service Co. of N.H., Seabrook, 1980-82; cons. engr. Helios Engrng. Inc., Litchfield Park, Ariz., 1982-87; sr. supervisory service engr. Quadrex Corp., Coraopolis, Penn., 1987-89; cons. engr. Helios Engring., Inc., Litchfield Park, Ariz., 1989—. Republican. Roman Catholic. Office: 360 Ancora Dr S Litchfield Park AZ 85340-4639

MILLER, KEVIN LANE, software engineer/architect, consultant; b. Wichita Falls, Tex., Feb. 2, 1970; s. Dave Lane Miller and Sharon Kay Nixon Silva; m. Victoria J. Weightman, Oct. 4, 1991. BA, Hampden-Sydney Coll., 1991; postgrad., U. Phoenix, 1994—. Info. systems adminstr. Amity, Inc., Tucson, 1992; software engr. Midak Internat., Tucson, 1992-93; sr. software engr./architect Scottsdale (Ariz.) Ins., 1993—; chief cons. scientist Fionn Enterprises, Scottsdale, 1993—; dir. rsch. Coun. for Energy Rsch., Tucson, 1990-93; mem. bd. publs. Hampden-Sydney, Va., 1990-91. Editor: Wittgenstein's Tractatus Logico-Philosophicus, 1991; author/architect: (software product) Helpdesk, 1993; editor The New Environ. Herald, 1992. Hampden-Sydney Coll. grantee in philosophy, 1990. Mem. IEEE, Phi Beta Kappa, Eta Sigma Phi, Theta Alpha Kappa. Republican. Home: 11772 E Clinton Scottsdale AZ 85259

MILLER, KUBY SUSIE, dance and modeling school owner; b. Romal, Italy, May 14, 1954; d. Stephen and Josette (Jorma) Kuby; m. Lyle G. Miller, Nov. 14, 1988. Grad. high sch., Madison, Wis. Dancer Royal Ballet, London, 1964-70; model Lynette Berit, Paris, 1967-69; dancer Ballet Repertoire, N.Y.C., 1970-75, Southeast Dancing Co., N.Y.C., 1975-76, Bultcr Jazz Co., Salt Lake City, 1976-77, Music Ctr., Salt Lake City, 1977-78, Utah Ballet Co., Salt Lake City, 1979-85; model Channel Runway, Paris, 1986-87; dancer Musical Theater Fine Arts, Salt Lake City, 1988-89, TCG Theatre Group, 1993-94, Accop Arts USA, 1994—. Bd. dirs. Mus. Theaters, Salt Lake City, 1988-89, Ballet Dept., Sale Lake City, 1989-90, Susie's Dancing Co., Salt Lake City, 1990—, Susie's Modeling Co., Salt Lake City, 1990-92; mem. Wake Adoption, North Falmouth, 1991, Nat. Abortion Rights Action League, Salt Lake City, 1990, Nat. Wildlife Fedn., Salt Lake City, 1991. Mem. Theatre Critics (honor 1991), N.Y. Theatre. Home and Office: 273 East 2100 South Salt Lake City UT 84115

MILLER, LARRY H., professional sports team executive, automobile dealer; b. Salt Lake City; m. Gail Miller; 5 children. Formerly with auto parts bus., Denver and Salt Lake City; now owner auto dealerships, Salt Lake City, Albuquerque, Denver and Phoenix; part-owner Utah Jazz, NBA, Salt Lake City, 1985-86, owner, 1986—. Office: care Utah Jazz 301 W South Temple Salt Lake City UT 84101-1216*

MILLER, LEROY BENJAMIN, architect; b. Cleve., Dec. 24, 1931; s. Harry Simon and Carol Jane (Goldberg) M.; m. Sue Firestone, July 1, 1956; children: Laurie, Janet, David, Matthew. BArch, U. Mich., 1956. Registered architect, Calif. From assoc. to v.p. Daniel Dworsky & Assocs., L.A., 1958-66; prin., pres. Leroy Miller Assocs., L.A., Santa Monica, Calif., 1966—; tchr. Calif. State Poly. Coll., Pomona, 1971-72. Exhibited in group shows, 1976, 84, 94. Pres. Leo Baeck Temple, L.A., 1991-93. Cpl. U.S. Army, 1956-58. Fellow AIA (Design awards L.A. chpt. 1966, 69, 72, 89). Democrat. Jewish. Office: Leroy Miller Assocs 2800 Olympic Blvd Santa Monica CA 90404-4119

MILLER, LESTER LIVINGSTON, JR., librarian, researcher; b. Portland, Oreg., June 5, 1930; s. Lester Livingston Sr. and Alice Jane (Howell) M.; m. Velma Grace Ross, Sept. 1, 1961; 1 child, Michelle Freia-Anne. BS, Portland State U., 1963; MEd, U. Oreg., 1965. Cert. secondary edn. tchr., libr., Wash. With U.S. CIA, 1958-60; sch. libr. Tigard (Oreg.) Pub. Schs., 1964-66; instr. Continuation Ctr. U. Oreg., Portland, 1966; sch. libr. U.S. Naval Sta., Guantanamo Bay, Cuba, 1966-68, Jefferson High Sch., Portland, 1968-70; asst. libr. Acad. Library, Ft. Benjamin Harrison, Ind., 1972-74; reference libr. U.S. Army Field Artillery Sch., Ft. Sill, Okla., 1974-78, adminstrv. libr., 1978-88; chief exec. officer Les Miller Enterprises Rsch. Svcs., Centralia, Wash., 1988—. Bibliographer for numerous periodical articles; editor biographical sketches; indexer mil. periodicals; author numerous poems. Sgt. USAF, 1949-56. Named Boss of Yr., Lawton (Okla.)-Ft. Sill Toastmistress, Inc.; recipient Decoration for Meritorious Civilian Svc., 1974-88. Mem. VFW (Lewis comdr. 1990-92), Masons. Democrat. Episcopalian. Home and Office: 1316 W Main St Centralia WA 98531-1338

MILLER, LIZ RODRIGUEZ, public library system director, librarian; b. Tucson, Feb. 22, 1954; d. Tony S. Martinez and Maria (Corral) Rodriguez; m. Marc Alan Miller, Nov. 5, 1972; children: Andrea Eve, Matthew Luke, Meredith C. BA in Spanish, U. Ariz., 1976, MLS, 1978. Unit mgr. S. Tuscon Libr., 1978-80; activities coord. community cable com. City of Tuscon, 1980; info./reference mgr. Tuscon Pub. Libr., 1981-84, agy. mgr., 1984-85, regional mgr., 1985-87, asst. dir. pub. svcs., 1987-89; dep. exec. dir. divsn. ALA Libr. Adminstrn. & Mgmt. Assn., Chgo., 1990; dep. dir. Tuscon Pima Libr., 1990-91, libr. dir., 1991—. Co-editor: Great Library Propotion Ideas V, 1990; contbr. articles to profl. jours. Mem. adv. bd. libr. power grant Tuscon Unified Sch. Dist., 1992—; bd. dirs. Tuscon area Literacy Coalition, 1992—; active Hispanic Profl. Action Com., 1992—. Mem. ALA (mem. pres. program com. 1987, mem. nominating com. 1991-93), REFORMA (chair elections com. 1983-84, 85, chair conf. program 1987, pres. 1987-88), Am. Soc. Pub. Adminstrn., Libr. Adminstrn. and Mgmt. Assn. (mem. cultural diversity com. 1991-92, chair 1992-93, mem. nominating com. 1992-93), Pub. Libr. Assn. (mem. Pub. Libr. Assn.-Libr. Adminstrn. and Mgmt. Assn. cert. com. 1991-92, chair 1992-93, chair Allie Beth Martin Award com. 1987-88, mem. 1989), Ariz. State Libr. Assn. (chair svcs. to Spanish-speaking Roundtable 1980-82, pres. pub. libr. divsn. 1984-85, chair ann. conf. 1986), U. Ariz. Hispanic Alumni Assn., Beta Phi Mu. Office: Tucson Pima Library PO Box 27470 101 N Stone Ave Tucson AZ 85726-7470

MILLER, LOUISE DEAN, writer, retired journalist; b. Lubbock, Tex., Dec. 10, 1921; d. Arlie David and Ludie Lee (Hart) Dean; m. Mickey Lester Miller, Aug. 30, 1946; children: Linda Miller Kelly, Lee Miller Parks, Lynne Miller Carson. BA in Journalism, Tex. Woman's U., 1943, BS in Journalism, 1943. Gen. reporter Vernon (Tex.) Daily Record, 1943-4; feature gen. reporter Tinker AFB Paper, Oklahoma City, 1944-46; women's editor Albuquerque Tribune, 1946-48; writer Albuquerque Pub. Schs., 1967-68; program dir. Young Women's Christian Assn., Albuquerque, 1970-72; newspaper columnist Albuquerque Jour., 1972-87. Author, editor: The Book of Windows, 1990; co-author, editor: Administration of Secondary Athletics, 1991. Sec.-treas. El Vado (N.Mex.) Cabin Owners Assn., 1977-95. Mem. AAUW (pres. 1964-66, sec. N.Mex. div. 1989-93), Soc. Profl. Journalists, Women in Communications Inc. (pres. 1968-70). Democrat. Methodist. Home: 1201 Richmond Dr NE Albuquerque NM 87106-2023

MILLER, M. JOY, financial planner, real estate broker; b. Enid, Okla., Dec. 29, 1934; d. H. Lee and M.E. Madge (Hatfield) Miller; m. Richard L.D. Berlemann, July 21, 1957 (div. Nov. 1974); children: Richard Louis, Randolph Lee. BSBA, N.Mex. State U., 1956. Cert. fin. planner; grad. Realtors Inst. Tchr. of bus. and mathematics Alamogordo (N.Mex.), Las Cruces (N. Mex.) and Omaha Pub. Schs., 1956-63; tchr., dir. Evelyn Wood Reading Dynamics Southern N.Mex. Inst., 1967-68; registered rep. Westamerica Fin. Corp., Denver, 1968-76; gen. agt. Security Benefit Life, Topeka, 1969—, Delta Life & Annuity, Memphis, 1969—; registered rep. Am. Growth Fund Sponsors, Inc., Denver, 1976—; pres., broker Fin. Design Corp. R.E., Las Cruces, 1977—; official goodwill ambassador of U.S. Treasury, U.S. Savs. Bond Div., Washington, 1968-70. Contbr. articles to profl. jours. Vice pres. Dona Ana County Fedn. Rep. Women. Recipient Top Sales Person award Investment Trust and Assurance, 1976-77. Fellow Life Underwriting Tng. Coun.; mem. Nat. Assn. Realtors, Nat. Assn. Life Underwriters, Internat. Bd. CFP's, Internat. Assn. Registered Fin. Planners, S.W. N.Mex. Assn. Life Underwriters (treas. 1990-91, pres.-elect 1991-92, pres. 1992-93), Las Cruces City Panhellenic, Altrusa, Order Fa. Star, Delta Zeta. Presbyterian. Home: 1304 Wolf Trl Las Cruces NM 88001-2357 Office: Fin Design Corp PO Box 577 Las Cruces NM 88004-0577

MILLER, MARC DOUGLAS, airline pilot; b. New Orleans, Oct. 28, 1953; s. Harold and Juliette (Graff) M.; m. Denice Kaye Duchemin, Apr. 24, 1983; children: Catherine Rachael, Audrey Rose. BS, Tulane U., 1975, MS, 1976. Lic. FAA airline transport pilot; cert. flight instr. Regional airline capt. Scheduled Skyways, Inc., Fayetville, Ariz., 1983-85; nat. airline capt. Am. West Airlines, Phoenix, 1985—. Percussionist Mesa (Ariz.) Symphony Orch., 1985—. Served to lt. USN, 1976-82; lt. comdr. USNR, 1983—. Mem. Aircraft Owners and Pilots Assn. Republican. Jewish. Home: 15 W Vinedo Ln Tempe AZ 85284-1323 Office: Am West Airlines 222 S Mill Ave Tempe AZ 85281-2869

MILLER, MARY ANNE, marketing professional; b. Denver, Nov. 4, 1958; d. Frank Sheldon and Mary Jane (Kokel) Marshall; m. Robert J. Miller, Oct. 10, 1992. BS, U. Colo., 1981, MBA, 1986. Cons. Summit Mktg., Denver, 1983-87; mktg. rep., mktg. mgr. Elitch Gardens Amusement Park, Denver, 1983-94, mktg. dir., 1994—. Mem. Denver Advt. Fedn. Republican. Roman Catholic. Office: Elitch Gardens Amusement Pk 1675 Broadway Ste 2500 Denver CO 80202

MILLER, MAUREEN DENICE, pediatrics nurse; b. Calif., Mar. 16, 1966; d. John Arthur and Betty (Slegers) M. BSN, Point Loma Nazarene Coll., 1988; M in Nursing Pediatric Nurse Practitioner, UCLA, 1995. RN, Calif. Pre-registered nurse aide U. Calif. San Diego Med. Ctr., 1987-88; staff RN pediatrics/womans health care Pres. Intercommunity Hosp., Whittier, Calif., 1988-92; pub. health RN Vis. Nurses Assn., Long Beach, Calif., 1991—; RN pediatric ICU Long Beach Meml. Med. Ctr.-Miller Children's Hosp., 1991—; mem. edn. com., transport com. Long Beach Meml. Med. Ctr.-Miller Children's Hosp., 1991—. Mem. Point Loma Nazarene Coll. Nursing Honor Soc., Sigma Theta Tau Internat. Republican. Home: 5453 Twin Lakes Dr Cypress CA 90630-5945 Office: Long Beach Meml Med Ctr 2801 Atlantic Ave Long Beach CA 90806-1737

MILLER, MAYNARD MALCOLM, geologist, educator, research foundation director, explorer, state legislator; b. Seattle, Jan. 23, 1921; s. Joseph Anthony and Juanita Queena (Davison) M.; m. Joan Walsh, Sept. 15, 1951; children: Ross McCord, Lance Davison. BS magna cum laude, Harvard U., 1943; MA, Columbia U., 1948; PhD (Fulbright scholar), St. John's Coll., Cambridge U., Eng., 1957; student, Naval War Coll., Air War Coll., Oak Ridge Inst. Nuclear Sci.; D of Sci. (hon.), U. Alaska, 1990. Registered profl. geologist, Idaho. Asst. prof. naval sci. Princeton (N.J.) U., 1946; geologist Gulf Oil Co., Cuba, 1947; rsch. assoc., coordinator, dir. Office Naval Rsch. project Am. Geog. Soc., N.Y.C., 1948-52; staff scientist Swiss Fed. Inst. for Snow and Avalanche Rsch., Davos, 1952-53; instr. dept. geography Cambridge U., 1953-54, 56; assoc. producer, field unit dir. film Seven Wonders of the World for Cinerama Corp., Europe, Asia, Africa, Middle East, 1954-55; rsch. assoc. Lamont Geol. Obs., N.Y.C., 1955-57; sr. scientist dept. geology Columbia U., N.Y.C., 1957-59; asst. prof. geology Mich. State U., East Lansing, 1959-61, assoc. prof., 1961-63; prof. Mich. State U., Lansing, 1963-75; dean Coll. Mines and Earth Resources U. Idaho, Moscow, 1975-88, prof. geology, dir. Glaciological and Arctic Scis. Inst., 1975—; dir., state geologist Idaho Geol. Survey, 1975-88; elected rep. Legislature of State of Idaho, Boise, 1992—; prin. investigator, geol. cons. sci. contracts and projects for govt. agys., univs., pvt. corps., geographic socs., 1946—; geophys. cons. Nat. Park Svc., NASA, USAF, Nat. Acad. Sci.; organizer leader USAF-Harvard Mt. St. Elias Expdn., 1946; chief geologist Am. Mt. Everest Expdn., Nepal, 1963; dir. Nat. Geographic Soc. Alaskan Glacier Commemorative Project, 1964-74; organizer field leader Nat. Geographic Soc. Joint U.S.-Can. Mt. Kennedy Yukon Meml. Mapping Expdn., 1965, Muséo Argentino de Ciencias Naturales, Patagonian expdn. and glacier study for Inst.. Geologico del Peru & Am. Geog. Soc., 1949-50, participant adv. missions People's Republic of China, 1981, 86, 88, geol. expdns. Himalaya, Nepal, 1963, 84, 87, USAF mission to Ellesmere Land and Polar Sea, 1951; organizer, ops. officer USN-LTA blimp geophysics flight to North Pole area for Office Naval Rsch., 58; prin. investigator U.S. Naval Oceanographic Office Rsch. Ice Island T-3 Polar Sea, 1967-68, 70-73; dir. lunar field sta. simulation program USAF-Boeing Co., 1959-60; co-prin. investigator Nat. Geographic Soc. 30 Yr. Remap of Lemon & Taku Glaciers, Juneau Icefield, 1989-92; exec. dir. Found. for Glacier and Environ. Rsch., Pacific Sci. Ctr., Seattle, 1955—, pres., 1955-85, trustee, 1960—, organizer, dir. Juneau (Alaska) Icefield Rsch. Program (JIRP), 1946—; cons. Dept. Hwys. State of Alaska, 1965; chmn., exec. dir. World Ctr. for Exploration Found., N.Y.C., 1968-71; dir., mem. adv. bd. Idaho Geol. Survey, 1975-88; chmn. nat. coun. JSHS program U.S. Army Rsch. Office and Acad. Applied Sci., 1982-89; sci. dir. U.S. Army Rsch. Office-Nat. Sci. and Humanities Symposia program, 1991—; disting. guest prof. China U. Geoscis., Wuhan, 1981-88, Changchun U. Earth Scis., People's Republic of China, 1988—; affiliate prof. U. Alaska, 1986—. Author: Field Manual of Glaciological and Arctic Sciences; co-author books on Alaskan glaciers and Nepal geology; contbr. over 200 reports, sci. papers to profl. jours., ency. articles, chpts. to books, monographs; producer, lectr. 16 mm. films and videos. Past mem. nat. exploring com., nat. sea exploring com. Boy Scouts Am.; mem. nat. adv. bd. Embry Riddle Aero. U.; bd. dirs. Idaho Rsch. Found.; pres. state divsn. Mich. UN Assn., 1970-73; mem. Centennial and Health Environ. Commns., Moscow, Idaho, 1987-94. With USN, 1943-46, PTO. Decorated 11 battle stars; named Leader of Tomorrow Seattle C. of C. and Time mag., 1953, one of Ten Outstanding Young Men U.S. Jaycees, 1954; recipient commendation for lunar environ. study USAF, 1960, Hubbard medal (co-recipient t. Everest expdn. team) Nat. Geographic Soc., 1963, Elisha Kent Kane Gold medal Geog. So. Phila., 1964, Karo award Soc. Mil. Engrs., 1966, Franklin L. Burr award Nat. Geog. Soc., 1967, Commendation Boy Scouts Am, 1970, Disting. Svc. commendation plaque UN Assn. U.S.A., Disting Svc. commendation State of Mich. Legislature, 1975, Outstanding Civilian Svc. medal U.S. Army Rsch. Office, 1977, Outstanding Leadership in Minerals Edn. commendations Idaho Mining Assn., 1985, 87; recipient numerous grants NSF, Nat. Geographic Soc., others, 1948—. Fellow Geol. Soc. Am., Arctic Inst. N.Am., Explorers Club; mem. councilor AAAS (Pacific divsn. 1978-88), AIME, Am. Geophys. Union, Internat. Glaciological Soc. (past councilor), ASME (hon. nat. lectr.), Am. Assn. State Geologists (hon.), Am. Assn. Amateur Oarsmen (life), Am. Alpine Club (past councilor, life mem.), Alpine Club (London), Appalachian Club (hon. corr.), Brit. Mountaineering Assn. (hon., past v.p.), The Mountaineers (hon.), Cambridge U. Mountaineering Club (hon.), Himalyan Club (Calcutta), English Speaking Union (nat. lectr.), Naval Res. Assn. (life), Dutch Treat Club, Circumnavigators Club (life), Adventurers Club N.Y. (medalist), Am. Legion, Harvard Club (N.Y.C. and Seattle), Sigma Xi, Phi Beta Kappa (pres. Epsilon chpt. Mich. State U. 1969-70), Phi Kappa Phi. Republican. Methodist. Home: 514 E 1st St Moscow ID 83843-2814 Office: U Idaho Coll Mines & Earth Resources Mines Bldg Rm 204 Moscow ID 83843 also: House of Reps Idaho State House Boise ID 83720 also: Found for Glacier & Environ Rsch 4470 N Douglas Hwy Juneau AK 99801-9403

MILLER, MICHAEL PATIKY, lawyer; b. Huntington, N.Y., Apr. 16, 1944; s. George J. and Alida (Patiky) M.; m. Dorothy Denn, Dec. 25, 1966; children: Lauren M. Golubtchik, Jonathan M., Rachel B. AB, Rutgers U., 1965; JD, NYU, 1968. Bar: N.J. 1968, U.S. Dist. Ct. N.J. 1968, Calif. 1975, U.S. Dist. Ct. (no. dist.) Calif. 1975, U.S. Tax Ct. 1977, U.S. Ct. Appeals (9th cir.) 1977, U.S. Ct. Appeals (fed. cir.) 1984, U.S. Dist. Ct. (cen. dist.) Calif. 1982, U.S. Supreme Ct. 1983, U.S. Claims Ct. 1986. Atty. Electric Power Research Inst., Palo Alto, Calif., 1974-77; assoc. Weinberg, Ziff & Kaye, Palo Alto, 1977-78; ptnr. Weinberg, Ziff & Miller, Palo Alto, 1978—; lectr. on tax and estate planning U. Calif. Extension, 1980—. Author: Creditor Rights in Proceedings Outside Estate Adminstrn., 1995; contbg. author: California Wills and Trusts, 1991; author: Creditor Rights in Proceedings Outside Estate Administration, 1995; contbr. articles to profl. jours. Treas. No. Calif. region United Synagogue Am., 1985-89, pres. 1992-95. Capt. U.S. Army, 1968-74, Vietnam, Ethiopia. Recipient Lion of Judah award, 1984, Cert. Merit U. Judiasm, 1992. Mem. ABA (chmn. region VI pub. contract law sect. 1975-78, commn. tax practice in small law firms, com. on taxation of trusts, estates, taxation sect. 1986—), N.J. State Bar, State Bar of Calif. (commr. tax law adv. commn. 1989-92, 93-95, chair 1994-95, mem. bd. legal specialization 1994-95), Santa Clara County Bar Assn. (chmn. estate planning, probate and trust sect. 1982, trustee 1983-84). Office: Weinberg Ziff & Miller 400 Cambridge Ave Palo Alto CA 94306-1507

MILLER, MILTON ALLEN, lawyer; b. Los Angeles, Jan. 15, 1954; s. Samuel C. and Sylvia Mary Jane (Silver) M.; m. Mary Ann Toman, Sept. 10, 1988; 1 child, Mary Ann. AB with distinction and honors in Econs., Stanford U., 1976; JD with honors, Harvard U., 1979. Bar: Calif. 1979, U.S. Ct. Appeals (9th cir.) 1979, U.S. Dist. Ct. (cen., no. and so. dists.) Calif., U.S. Supreme Ct. 1989. Law clk. U.S. Ct. Appeals (9th cir.), Sacramento, 1979-80; assoc. Latham & Watkins, L.A., 1979-87, ptnr., 1987—. chmn. ethics com. Latham & Watkins. Author: Attorney Ethics; articles editor Harvard Law Rev., 1978-79. Mem. Am. Cancer Soc., L.A. Mem. ABA, Calif. State Bar Assn. (com. on profl. responsibility), L.A. County Bar Assn. (chmn. profl. responsibility and ethics com.), Assn. Trial Lawyers Am., Phi Beta Kappa. Office: Latham & Watkins 633 W Fifth St Ste 4000 Los Angeles CA 90071

MILLER, MONA JOY DEUTSCH, lawyer; b. Coral Gables, Fla., Feb. 9, 1953; d. Irvin and Freda (Smukler) Deutsch; m. Steven Jeffrey Miller, Aug. 21, 1977; 1 child, Thaïs Helene. AB with distinction, Cornell U., 1973; JD, Stanford U., 1977. Bar: Calif. 1977, U.S. Dist. Ct. (cen. dist.) Calif. 1978, U.S. Dist. Ct. (so. dist.) Calif. 1994, U.S. Supreme Ct. 1994. Assoc. McKenna, Conner & Cuneo, Los Angeles, 1977-83, ptnr., 1983-89; of counsel Blanc, Williams, Johnston & Kronstadt, L.A., 1990—. Mem. Univ. Synagogue, Brentwood, Calif., 1980—, sisterhood co-v.p. for programming, 1990-93. Mem. Los Angeles County Bar Assn. (real property and comml. law and bankruptcy sects.), Calif. Attys. Fed. Credit Union (bd. dirs. 1982), Phi Beta Kappa. Jewish.

MILLER, NEIL ALLEN, police agent; b. Lincoln, Nebr., Dec. 5, 1952; s. Royce Jordan Miller and Norma Jean (Kahlbau) Poucher; m. C. Susan Wright; 1 child, Sarah Louise. AS, Pikes Peak C.C., 1979; BS in Criminology, Met. St. Coll., 1990. Security guard St. Francis Hosp., Colorado Springs, 1977-81; police officer U. Colo. Med. Ctr. Police Dept., Denver, 1981-83, Broomfield (Colo.) Police Dept., 1983-90; police agt. Lakewood (Colo.) Police Dept., 1990—; team watch mem. USN Res., Aurora, 1991—. Coach spl. olympics Fletcher-Miller Sch., Lakewood, 1991—. Sgt. USMC, 1971-78. Recipient Svc. to Handicap award Internat. Toastmasters Club, 1993, World Bench Press Record 198# USPF/World Police-Fire Athletic Assn., 1993, Nat. Bench Press Records 198# NASA Drug Free Assn., 1993, Colo. State Powerlifting Record 198# NASA and Colo. Police and Fire Athletic Assn., 1986-93. Mem. Vietnam Vets of Am., VFW, Am. Legion, Fraternal Order of Police, Am. Fedn. of Police, Lakewood Police Athletic League. Home: 2958 Will Ave Cir Broomfield CO 80020 Office: Lakewood Police Dept 445 S Allison Pky Lakewood CO 80226-3106

MILLER, NICOLE GABRIELLE, clinical psychologist; b. N.Y.C., Apr. 19, 1962; d. Michael David and Merle Judith (Jablin) M. BA in Psychology, U. Pacific, 1984, MA in Psychology, 1988; PhD in Clin. Psychology, Calif. Sch. Profl. Psychology, 1990. Therapist various clinics, Stockton, Calif., 1984-86; psycholog. trainee Calif. Men's Colony State Prison, San Luis Obispo, 1987, Dept. Health, Fresno, Calif., 1987-88; intern VA Med. Ctr., Loma Linda, Calif., 1988-89; psycholog. technician and consultant VA Med. Ctr., Martinez, Calif., 1989-90, researcher, 1990, clin. psychologist, 1990—; clin. instr. psychiatry Sch. Medicine, U. Calif., Davis, 1991—, clin. dir. outpatient substance abuse program, 1990—. Mem. APA. Democrat. Office: VA Med Ctr Psychology Svcs 150 Muir Rd # 116B Martinez CA 94553-4612

MILLER, NORMAN CHARLES, JR., newspaper editor; b. Pitts., Oct. 2, 1934; s. Norman Charles and Elizabeth (Burns) M.; m. Mollie Rudy, June 15, 1957; children—Norman III, Mary Ellen, Teri, Scott. B.A., Pa. State U., 1956. Reporter Wall Street Jour., San Francisco, 1960-63; reporter Wall Street Jour., N.Y.C., 1963-64; bur. chief Wall Street Jour., Detroit, 1964-66; Washington corr. Wall Street Jour., 1966-72, Washington Bur. chief, 1973-83; nat. editor Los Angeles Times, 1983—. Author: The Great Salad Oil Swindle, 1965. Served to lt. (j.g.) USN, 1956-60. Recipient Disting. Alumnus award Pa. State U., 1978; George Polk Meml. award L.I. U., 1963; Pulitzer Prize, 1964. Roman Catholic. Club: Gridiron (Washington). Office: Los Angeles Times Times Mirror Sq Los Angeles CA 90012

MILLER, O'MALLEY MURRAY, lawyer; b. Sept. 25, 1951; m. Ann W. (Wapple) Miller; children: Brendan, Kevin, Brian, Grady. BA with distinction, Stanford U., 1973; JD, U. So. Calif., 1976. Bar: Calif. 1976. Ptnr. Allen, Matkins, Leck, Gamble & Mallory, 1981-92, Munger, Tolles & Olson, L.A., 1992—. Contbr. articles to profl. jours. Mem. ABA, Am. Coll. Real Estate Laywers, Calif. Bar Assn. (exec. com. real property law sect. 1989-90), L.A. County Bar Assn. (exec. com. real property sect. 1980—, chair, 1991-92). Office: Munger Tolles & Olson 355 S Grand Ave Fl 35 Los Angeles CA 90071-1560

MILLER, RALPH MENNO, minister, religious organization administrator; b. Hubbard, Oreg., Mar. 22, 1925; s. Samuel S. and Catherine (Hooley) M.; m. Evelyn Irene Whitfield, Feb. 23, 1947; children: Judith Karen, Donna Joyce. D of Ministry, Internat. Bible Inst. and Sem., 1985. Owner, operator M & M Logging, Sweet Home, Oreg., 1952-56; support person Children's Farm Home, Palmer, Alaska, 1956-58; pastor North Pole (Alaska) Assembly of God, 1959-68, Sitka (Alaska) Assembly of God, 1968-78; pioneer pastor Sand Lake Assembly of God, Anchorage, 1978-84; sec., treas. Alaska Dist. Assemblies of God, Anchorage, 1978—, presbyter, 1964—; gen. presbyter Gen. Council Assemblies of God, Springfield, Mo.; exec. presbyter Alaska Assemblies of God, Anchorage, 1978—; exec. dir. Alaska Ch. Builders, 1984—, Revolving Loan Fund, Anchorage, 1984—, Little Beaver Camp, Big Lake, Alaska, 1984-90. Pres. PTA, North Pole, 1964-66. Republican. Home: 12630 Galleon Cir Anchorage AK 99515-3652 Office: Alaska Dist Assemblies of God 1048 W Internat Airport Rd # 101 Anchorage AK 99518

MILLER, RICHARD ALAN, agricultural consultant; b. Everett, Wash., Mar. 16, 1944; s. John Harrison and Katheryn Ada (Nelson) M.; m. Patricia Merz, June 30, 1964 (div. 1972); 1 child, Paula Anne. BS in Physics, Washington State U., 1966; Degree in Fluidics (hon.), MIT, 1967; MS in Physics, U. Del., 1968; engr. in tng./profl. engr., U. Wash., 1969. Cert. biophysicist, 1972, hypnotherapist. Physicist instruments products div. Dupont, Wilmington, Del., 1966-68; physicist The Boeing Co./MASD, Seattle, 1968-71; biophysicist dept. anesthesiology U. Wash., Seattle, 1971-73; owner, mgr. The Beltane Corp., Inc., Seattle, 1973-80; ltd. ptnr. Western Herb Farms/Country Spice, Seattle, 1980-82; owner, mgr., writer Orgn. Advancement of Knowledge, Grants Pass, Oreg., 1983—; owner, mgr., broker Northwest Bots., Inc., Grants Pass, 1987—; ptnr., sales mgr. Coltsfoot, Inc., Grants Pass, 1986—; advisor Ariz. Herb Growers Assn., Phoenix, 1988—; mem. New Crops Devel. Oreg. Dept. Agriculture; cons. in field; lectr. in field. Author: The Potential of Herbs as a Cash Crop, 1985, The Magical and Ritual Use of Herbs, 1985, The Magical and Ritual Use of Aphrodisiacs, 1987, The Magical and Ritual Use of Perfumes, 1989, Native Plants of Commercial Importance, 1989, Forest Farming, 1990, The Mordern Alchemist, 1994; contbr. articles to profl. jours. Amb. All Am. City, Grants Pass, 1987—. Small Bus. Innovative Rsch. grantee USDA, 1986, Neighborhood Devel. grantee SBA, 1977, USDA grant, 1994. Mem. Am. Coun. Hypnotist Examiners, Masons. Home and Office: Northwest Botanicals Inc 2185 SE Portola Dr Grants Pass OR 97526-3943

MILLER, RICHARD FRANKLIN, educational consultant, researcher; b. San Francisco, Sept. 9, 1927; s. Henry G. and Hulda M. M. AB, San Francisco State U., 1950; MA, U. Calif.-Berkeley, 1964, EdD, 1970. Cert. secondary tchr., gen. supr. Calif. With San Francisco Unified Sch. Dist., 1956-89, tchr. bus. edn., econs. and social studies Mission H.S., 1967-89, adminstr. career edn. program, 1970-80; ednl. cons., 1989—. Mem. San Francisco Symphony, Fine Arts Mus. Soc. Served to sgt., U.S. Army, 1952-54. Fellow in edn. U. Calif.-Berkeley, 1974-75. Mem. ASCD, United Educators San Francisco, Phi Delta Kappa. Democrat. Unitarian.

MILLER, RICHARD SHERWIN, legal educator; b. Boston, Dec. 11, 1930; s. Max and Mollie (Kroger) M.; m. Doris Sheila Lunchick, May 24, 1956; children: Andrea Jayne Armitage, Matthew Harlan. B.S.B.A., Boston U., 1951, J.D. magna cum laude, 1956; LL.M., Yale U., 1959. Bar: Mass. 1956, Mich. 1961, Hawaii 1977. Pvt. practice law Boston, 1956-58; assoc. prof. law Wayne State U., Detroit, 1959-62, prof., 1962-65; prof. Ohio State U., Columbus, 1965-73, dir. clin. and interdisciplinary program, 1971-73; prof. U. Hawaii, Honolulu, 1973-95, prof. emeritus, 1995—, dean, 1981-84; vis. prof. law USIA/U. Hawaii, Hiroshima U., Japan, fall 1986, Victoria U., Wellington, N.Z., spring 1987; del. Hawaii State Jud. Conf., 1989-92. Author: Courts and the Law: An Introduction to our Legal System, 1980; editor: (with Roland Stanger) Essays on Expropriations, 1967; editor-in-chief: Boston U. Law Rev., 1955-56; contbr. articles to profl. jours. Mem. Hawaii Substance Abuse Task Force, 1994—. 1st lt. USAF, 1951-53. Sterling-Ford fellow Yale U., 1958-59; named Lawyer of Yr. Japan-Hawaii Lawyers Assn., 1990. Mem. ABA, Hawaii State Bar Assn., Hawaii ACLU, Am. Inn of Ct. IV (founding mem.,master of the bench), Am. Law Inst., Honolulu Community-Media Coun. (chair 1994—). Office: U Hawaii Richardson Sch Law 2515 Dole St Honolulu HI 96822-2328

MILLER, ROBERT DAVID, forensic psychiatrist; b. Chapel Hill, N.C., Sept. 4, 1941; s. Augustus Taylor and Adeline Helen (Porombovics) M. BS cum laude, Davidson Coll., 1964; PhD in Biochemistry, Duke U., 1972, MD, 1973. Cert. Am. Bd. Psychiatry and Neurology, Am. Bd. Forensic Psychiatry. Resident in psychiatry Duke U., Durham, N.C., 1973-76; with psychiatry dept. Duke U., Durham, 1976-82; staff psychiatrist John Umstead Hosp., Butner, N.C., 1976-78, dir. admissions, 1978-80, resident tng. dir., 1980-82; dir. forensic tng. Mendota Mental Health Inst., Madison, 1982-91; prof. psychiatry U. Colo., 1991—; lectr. in law U. Denver Law Sch., 1993—. Contbr. articles to profl. jours. Fellow Am. Acad. Forensic Scis. (program chmn. 1985, sec. psychiat. sect. 1987), Am. Psychiat. Assn.; mem. Am. Acad. Psychiatry and Law (exec. coun. 1986, sec. Midwest chpt. 1985-91, v.p., pres. 1988), Internat. Acad. Law and Mental Health. Democrat. Jewish. Home: 8190 E Tempest Ridge Way Parker CO 80134-5866 Office: Colo Health Scis Ctr Box C-249-27 4200 E 9th Ave Denver CO 80220-3706

MILLER, ROBERT G., retail company executive; b. 1944. With Albertson's Inc., 1961-89, exec. v.p. retail ops., 1989-91; chmn. bd., CEO Fred Meyer Inc., Portland, Oreg., 1991—. Office: Fred Meyer Inc 3800 SE 22nd Ave Portland OR 97202-2918*

MILLER, ROBERT JENNINGS, medical board administrator; b. Battle Creek, Mich., Nov. 26, 1949; s. Mary Margaret (Jennings) M.; m. Shereen Ann Lerner, Jan. 16, 1982; children: Alyssa Josephine, Benjamin Jennings. BA, Western Mich. U., 1973, MA summa cum laude, 1976; PhD, Ariz. State U., 1981. Teaching asst. sociology dept. Western Mich. U., Kalamazoo, 1973, teaching asst. anthropology dept., 1973-75, instr., 1975; instr. social sci., anthropology Mesa (Ariz.) Community Coll., 1980-85; assoc. dir. rsch. Ariz. Emergency Med. Systems, Phoenix, 1981-82, dep. dir., 1982-84, exec. dir., 1984-89; pres. Advanced Emergency Med. Svc., Phoenix, 1984-85; v.p. med. svc. S.W. Med. Svcs., Phoenix, 1989-90; exec. dir. Ariz. Bd. Osteo. Med. Examiners, Phoenix, 1990—; adjunct faculty Ariz. State U., 1994—; faculty Nat. Symposium on Trauma Care, Phoneix, 1984; rsch. asst. Ariz. State U., Tempe, 1977-78, Ariz. State U., U.S. Forest Svc. Nat. Sci. Found., 1979-80, others; project supr. Auckland Mus. Ariz. State U., 1978; cons. Cen. Ariz. Health Systems Agy., Phoneix, 1984, Northland Rsch., Inc., Tempe, 1989-90, Saferide Svcs., Inc., 1990; cons. program devel. evaluation People-to-People Health Found., San Jose, Costa Rica, 1990. Contbr. articles to profl. jours. Chair Design Rev. Bd., Tempe, 1985-93; bd. dirs. Tri City Jewish Cmty. Ctr., Tempe, 1988-93, treas., 1990-92; mem. Rover Sch. Adv. Com., Tempe, 1992—; v.p. Adminstrs. in Medicine, 1993—. John L. and Helen Kellogg Found. scholar, 1968, 69, Bd. dirs. scholar Western Mich. U., 1970, 71, Tuition scholar Ariz. State U., 1976, 77; rsch. grantee U.S. Forest Svc., 1979. Mem. Am. Pub. Health Assn., Am. Osteopathic Assn., Fedn. State Med. Bds., Adminstrs. in Medicine. Office: Ariz Bd Osteo Examiners 141 E Palm Ln Ste 205 Phoenix AZ 85004-1555

MILLER, ROBERT JONATHAN, science/technology educator; b. Beaver Falls, Pa., Dec. 9, 1953; s. George Vernon and Fredrica Catherine (Smith) M. BS in Environ. Policy Studies, U. Calif., Davis, 1976; MA in Edn., U. San Francisco, 1989. Cert. ednl. supervision and adminstrn., Calif. Rschr. Stanford U., Palo Alto, Calif., 1978-80; tchr. sci., math. and tech., coord. Monterey (Calif.) Peninsula Unified Sch. Dist., 1981—; trainer of tchrs. space sci. NASA, Sunnyvale, Calif., 1984-88; trainer of tchrs. marine biology Monterey Bay Aquarium, 1984-88; prof. Grad. Sch., Nat. U., San Jose, 1989; adv. bd. Yosemite (Calif.) Insts., 1994—. Author: Principal's Handbook, 1989, (sch. curriculum) Mainstreaming Exceptional Students, 1979. Area coord. Beyond War, Monterey Peninsula, Calif., 1984-88; pres. bd. dirs. Lyceum of Monterey Peninsula, 1983-86; charter vol. asst. Monterey Bay Aquarium, 1984-93. Mem. NEA, Calif. Sci. Tchrs. Assn., Calif. Edn. Leadership Acad. (sr. assoc.), Calif. Tchrs. Assn., Lifespring, Inc. (life), Computer Users Assn. (presenter), Earthwatch, Nature Conservancy, Diver Alert Network, U. Calif. Alumni Assn., U. San Francisco Alumni Assn., Reef Environ. Ednl. Found., Sierra Club, Greenpeace, World Wildlife Fedn. Democrat. Home: Box 3533 Carpenter and 2d St Carmel by the Sea CA 93921 Office: Monterey Peninsula USD PO Box 1031 Monterey CA 93942-1031

MILLER, ROBERT JOSEPH, governor, lawyer; b. Evanston, Ill., Mar. 30, 1945; s. Ross Wendell and Coletta Jane (Doyle) M.; m. Sandra Ann Searles, Oct. 17, 1949; children: Ross, Corrine, Megan. BA in Polit. Sci., U. Santa Clara, 1967; JD, Loyola U., Los Angeles, 1971. First legal advisor Las Vegas (Nev.) Met. Police Dept., 1973-75; justice of the peace Las Vegas Twp., 1975-78; dep. dist. atty. Clark County, Las Vegas, 1971-73, dist. atty., 1979-86; lt. gov. State of Nev., 1987-89, acting gov., 1989-90, gov., 1991—. Chmn. Nev. Commn. on Econ. Devel., Carson City, 1987-91, Nev. Commn. on Tourism, Carson City, 1987-91; mem. Pres. Reagan's Task Force on Victims of Crime, 1982; chmn. Nev. divsn. Am. Cancer Soc., 1988-90. Mem. Nat. Dist. Atty.'s Assn. (pres. 1984-85), Western Govs. Assn. (chair-elect 1992-93, chmn. 1993-94), Nat. Govs. Assn. (past chmn. com. on justice and pub. safety, chmn. legal affairs com. 1992-94, lead gov. on trasp. 1992—) Nev. Dist. Atty.'s Assn. (pres. 1979, 83). Democrat. Roman Catholic. Home: Gov Mansion 606 N Mountain St Carson City NV 89703-3955 Office: State of Nev Office of Gov Capitol Bldg Carson City NV 89710

MILLER, ROBERT LEWIS, consulting firm executive; b. Uniontown, Pa., Oct. 14, 1946; s. Robert Ralph and Alice Estella (Lewis) M.; life ptnr. Nancy Jo Sauder; 1 ward, Rachael Lee. AA, Calif. State Coll., 1976; BS, U. Pitts., 1974. Cons. to beef supr. Sterling Beef, Denver, 1977-82; beef supr. Excel Corp., Ft. Morgan, Colo., 1977-82; cons. to safety supr. ConAgra, Longmont, Colo., 1982-86; cons. to plant mgr. Unitog, Greeley, Colo., 1986-92; pres., CEO Condustry Enterprises, Kansas City, Mo., 1989—; instr. OSHA/N.I.O.S.H., Denver, 1982—. Author: The Live Bait Purist, 1992. Instr. Colo. Divsn. of Wildlife, State of Colo., 1985—. Capt. USMC, 1964-89. Decorated Bronze star, Republic of Vietnam, Cross of Gallantry, Purple Heart. Mem. Nat. Assn. of Hunter Safety Coords., Am. Legion. Republican. Lutheran.

MILLER, ROBERT LINDSEY, bishop; b. Eagle Grove, Iowa, June 24, 1933; m. Doris Mandsager; children: Tedd, Darrell, Diane. BA, St. Olaf Coll., 1966. Pastor Luth. congregations, St. Louis Park, Minn., Riverside and Santa Barbara, Calif., First Luth. Ch., Fullerton, Calif.; bishop Pacifica Synod, Evang. Luth. Ch. in Am., Yorba Linda, Calif., 1988—. Office: Evang Luth Ch in Am 23655 Via Del Rio Yorba Linda CA 92687-2718*

MILLER, ROBERT REUBEN, political science educator; b. Tel Aviv, Sept. 30, 1949; came to U.S., 1977; s. Kalman and Nadia (Davidov) M.; m. Esther F. Farkas, June 22, 1986; children: Nurit S., Adiv K. BA in History and Philosophy, Tel Aviv U., 1976; MA in History, U. Bridgeport, 1979; MA in Internat. Studies, U. Denver, 1982, PhD, 1987. Data analyst Inst. Ct. Mgmt., Denver, 1982; editorial intern U. Denver, 1982-86; asst. prof. U. Colo., Denver, 1990—; rsch. assoc. Abbott Assoc., Inc., Springfield, Va., 1986-87; vis. prof. Old Dominion U., 1988-89, U. No. Colo., 1989-90; instr. Metro. State Coll., Denver, 1981-93, U. Colo., Boulder, 1981-82, St. Francis Coll., Denver, summer, 1982, U. Denver, 1981-86; computer rsch. asst. Grad. Sch. Internat. Studies/U. Denver., 1981-86; cons. Risk Mgmt. Internat., Denver, 1987-88, Moran, Stahl and Boyer, Inc., Boulder, 1985-86; guest lectr. USAF War Coll., Montgomery, Ala., 1994, Air Force Res. Officer Corps., Greeley, 1989, Army-Air Force Ctr. for Low Intensity Conflict, Langley, 1989; presenter in field. Contbr. articles to profl. jours. Sgt. Israel Army, 1967-71. Weinberg fellow Tel Aviv U., 1973, Dr. Irving Vinnick fellow, 1993; Dr. James Halsey internat. scholar U. Bridgeport, 1977; travel grantee Denver U., 1985. Mem. Am. Polit. Sci. Assn. (rsch. travel grantee 1983), Can. Assn. for Security and Intelligence. Home: 520 S Poplar Way Denver CO 80224-1557

MILLER, ROBERT RYAL, history educator; b. Lake Andes, S.D., Oct. 3, 1923; s. John Carroll and Hazel C. (Peck) M.; m. Penelope Handsaker, June 12, 1955. AB, U. Calif., Berkeley, 1948, MA, 1951, PhD, 1960. Asst. prof. history U. Southwestern La., Lafayette, 1959-60; asst. to assoc. prof. N.Mex. State U., Las Cruces, 1960-68; prof. history Ind. U. Southeast, New Albany, Ind., 1970; prof. history Calif. State U., Hayward, 1970-80, prof. emeritus, 1980—; vis. prof. San Marcos U., Lima, Peru, 1966. Author: For Science and National Glory, 1968, Mexico: A History, 1985, Shamrock and Sword, 1989; editor: Mexican War Jour., 1991. Sgt. U.S. Army Air Corps, 1942-46, Med. Mem. Conf. on Latin Am. History, Calif. Hist. Soc.

MILLER, ROBERT SCOTT, mental health professional, social worker; b. Seattle, Dec. 12, 1947; s. Bert Lester and Carol Theresa (Gustafson) M.; m. Karen Ann Staake, Nov. 12, 1977; children: Sarah, Megan, Emily. BA in Sociology cum laude, Seattle Pacific U., 1970; AM in Social Work, U. Chgo., 1972; MA in Human Resources Mgmt., Pepperdine U., 1977. Cert. social worker, Wash. Br. supr. Wash. State Dept. Social and Health Svcs., Oak Harbor and Anacortes, 1975-78; supr. casework Wash. State Dept. Social and Health Svcs., Everett, 1973-75; lectr., coord. rural community mental health project U. Wash., Seattle, 1978-83; exec. dir. Armed Svcs. YMCA, Oak Harbor, 1984-86; area dir. United Way of Island County, Oak Harbor, 1986-88, exec. dir., 1988-92; exec. dir. Saratoga Community Mental Health, Coupeville, Wash., 1992-93; outpatient therapist, attention-deficit/hyperactivity disorder mental health specialist Cath. Community Svcs. Northwest, Oak Harbor, Wash., 1993—; part-time instr. sociology Chapman U., Orange, Calif., 1988—; mem. adv. bd. Island Family Health Ctr., Oak Harbor, 1990-91. Contbr. articles to profl. jours. Bd. dirs. Puget Sound chpt. Huntington's Disease Soc. Am., 1989-93, pres., 1991, fundraising chmn., 1989-91, v.p., 1990; adv. bd. United Ways Washington, 1991-92; chmn. Island County bd. emergency food and shelter program Fed. Emergency Mgmt. Agy.; vice chair Community Resource Network, Oak Harbor, 1991; steering com. Greater Oak Harbor Econ. Summit, 1991; mem. strategic planning com. Whidbey Gen. Hosp., Coupeville, 1992-93; exec. com. Mt. Baker Coun. Boys Scouts Am., 1993; bd. dirs. The Opportunity Coun., Bellingham, 1993-94; v.p., bd. dirs. Concerts on the Cove, Coupeville, 1993—; mem. citizen's comprehensive plan task force City of Oak Harbor, 1994. Recipient outstanding svc. award Armed Svcs. YMCA of U.S., Dallas, 1985, two program merit awards McDonald's Corp., Oak Harbor, 1986; named Alumni of a Growing Vision, Seattle Pacific U., 1991, Diplomat of Yr. Greater Oak Harbor C. of C., 1991. Mem. NASW (bd. dirs. Wash. chpt. 1982-85), Wash. Assn. Social Welfare (pres. 1975-76), Acad. Cert. Lutheran. Home: 2450 S Rocky Way Coupeville WA 98239-9610 Office: Cath Community Svcs NW 5047 50th St NW Oak Harbor WA 98277-4021

MILLER, ROBERT STEVEN, educational association administrator; b. Van Nuys, Calif., Aug. 9, 1963; s. Frederick Earl and Mary (Brash) M. AA, L.A. Valley Coll., 1984; BSBA, Calif. State U., 1987, MA in History, 1990. Cert. substitute tchr., 1993—. Study group leader, study skills researcher Ednl. Opportunity Program Calif. State U., L.A., 1989-93, faculty mem. History Dept., lectr., 1990-92; sec., treas. Agate/Amethyst World, Inc., Van Nuys, Calif., 1986-91, v.p., 1992—; with Summer Bridge Program Calif. State U., L.A., 1994—. Mng. editor (jour.) Perspectives, 1990, editor-in-chief, 1991. Jake Gimbel scholar, 1989. Mem. Am. Historians Assn., The Soc. for Historians of Am. Fgn. Rels., Phi Alpha Theta (v.p. 1990, pres. 1991, Eta Xi chpt., Ledeboer Family scholar 1989), Pi Sigma Epsilon (v.p. 1986-87, pres. 1988 Phi chpt.), Mu Kappa Tau (pres. and founder 1989), Calif State U. LA chpt.). Democrat. Roman Catholic. Home: 13750 Runnymede

St Van Nuys CA 91405-1515 Office: Agate Amethyst Imports 7712 Gloria Ave Ste 8 Van Nuys CA 91406-1802

MILLER, ROBERT STEVENS, JR., finance professional; b. Portland, Oreg., Nov. 4, 1941; s. Robert Stevens and Barbara (Weston) M.; m. Margaret Rose Kyger, Nov. 9, 1966; children: Christopher John, Robert Stevens, Alexander Lamont. AB with distinction, Stanford U., 1963; LLB, Harvard U., 1966; MBA, Stanford U., 1968. Bar: Calif. bar 1966. Fin. analyst Ford Motor Co., Dearborn, Mich., 1968-71; spl. studies mgr. Ford Motor Co., Mexico City, 1971-73; dir. fin. Ford Asia-Pacific, Inc., Melbourne, Australia, 1974-77, Ford Motor Co., Caracas, Venezuela, 1977-79; v.p., treas. Chrysler Corp., Detroit, 1980-81, exec. v.p. fin., 1981-90, vice chmn., 1990-92; sr. ptnr. James D. Wolfensohn, Inc., N.Y.C., 1992-93; chmn. bd. dirs. Morrison Knudsen Corp., 1995—; bd. dirs. Fed.-Mogul, U.S. Bancorp, Fluke, Polk & Talbot, Coleman, Symantec.

MILLER, ROBERT VICTOR, scientific research administrator; b. Batavia, N.Y., Apr. 30, 1936; s. James Joseph and Josephine (Brunovsky) M.; m. Mildred Rose Canne, June 8, 1956; children: Stephen, Cheryl, Eric, Elizabeth. BS, Cornell U., 1958, PhD, 1964; MS, U. Ark., 1961. Rsch. asst. prof. U. Md., Solomons, 1963-65; systematic zoologist U.S. Bureau Comml. Fisheries, Miami, Fla., 1965-71; leader marine mammal rsch. program U.S. Nat. Marine Fisheries Svc., Washington, 1971-80; dep. dir. NOAA/Nat. Marine Fisheries Svc. Nat. Marine Mammal Lab, Seattle, 1980—; mem. affiliate faculty U. Miami, Fla., 1966-71, Fla. Atlantic U., Miami, 1966-71, U. Wash. Sch. Fisheries, Seattle, 1983—; U.S. chair U.S.-Russia Marine Mammal Project, 1973—. Author nat. reports to internat. orgns., papers in field. Coord. blood donor drives NOAA campus Puget Sound Blood Ctr., Seattle, 1990—. Mem. Am. Soc. Ichthyologists and Herpetologists, Am. Soc. Mammalogists, Am. Inst. Fisheries Rsch. Biologists, Soc. Marine Mammalogists, Soc. for Preservation and Encouragement of Barber Shop Quartet Singing in Am. (sec. 1989—). Office: Nat Marine Mammal Lab 7600 Sand Point Way NE Bldg 4 Seattle WA 98115-6349

MILLER, RONALD GRANT, journalist; b. Santa Cruz, Calif., Feb. 28, 1939; s. Fred Robert and Evelyn Lenora (Mosher) M.; m. Darla-Jean Irene Rode, Nov. 2, 1963. AA, Monterey Peninsula Coll., 1958; BA, San Jose State U., 1961. Reporter Santa Cruz (Calif.) Sentinel, 1959-62; reporter, chief news bur. San Jose (Calif.) Mercury News, 1962-77, editor T.V., 1977—; syndicated TV columnist Knight Ridder Syndicate, 1978—; commentator, critic Sta. KLOK, San Jose, 1981-83; panelist, guest speaker various orgns., 1978—; nat. judge Cableace awards, 1987. Author: (forward) Les Brown's Encyclopedia of Television, 1992; contbr. articles, short fiction to various mags. Recipient Nat. Spot News Photo award Sigma Delta Chi, 1961, Outstanding Alumnus award San Jose State U. Dept. Journalism and Mass Comm., 1985, Nat. Headline award Press Club Atlantic City, 1994. Mem. TV Critics Assn. (nat. pres. 1981). Democrat. Home and Office: 1554 Arbor Ave Los Altos CA 94024-5913

MILLER, SONJA GLAASER, social worker; b. Coos Bay, Oreg., Oct. 16, 1953; d. Edward Glaaser and Gwendolyn (Elrod) Michael; m. David Weston Miller, Oct. 8, 1988; children: Benjamin Frank, Nicolas Johan. BS in Bus. Fin., U. Oreg., 1978; MA in Counseling/Psychology, Lewis & Clark Coll., 1994. Personal property appraiser Lane County Assessors, Eugene, Oreg., 1979; residential appraiser Jackson County Assessor, Medford, Oreg., 1979-82; camp dir., asst. dir. Silver Sage Girl Scout Coun., Boise, Idaho, summer 1983, 84; young program dir. Ch. of the Good Samaritan, Corvallis, Oreg., 1983-84; youth program cons. Corvallis, Oreg., 1983-86; alcohol and drug abuse counselor DePaul Adolescent Treatment Program, Portland, Oreg., 1987-88; social worker White Shield Ctr., Salvation Army, Portland, Oreg., 1994—. Author: The Director's Handbook for Youth Conferences, 1983. Mem. youth commn. Diocese of Oreg., Portland, 1980-84, chair, 1984-86, program and budget com., 1993—, convocation rep., 1995—; youth dir. vol. St. Mark's Ch., Medford, 1979-83; counselor vol. William Temple House, Portland, 1994; co-pres. MOMS Club Portland, 1993-94; sr. warden St. Michael All Angels Ch., Portland, 1993, mem. vestry, 1990-93, convener women's group, 1994—. Mem. ACA, Oreg. Counseling Assn. Democrat. Episcopalian.

MILLER, STANLEY LLOYD, chemistry and biochemistry educator; b. Oakland, Calif., Mar. 7, 1930; s. Nathan Harry and Edith (Levy) M. BS, U. Calif., Berkeley, 1951; PhD, U. Chgo., 1954. F.W. Jewett fellow Cal-Tech., Pasadena, Calif., 1954; asst. prof. Coll. Physicians and Surgeons, N.Y.C., 1955-60; from asst. to full prof. U. Calif., San Diego, 1960—. Mem. Am. Chem. Soc., Am. Soc. Biol. Chemists, Nat. Acad. Scis., Internat. Soc. for the Study of the Origin of Life (pres. 1986-89). Office: Univ Calif San Diego Dept Chemistry 9500 Gilman Dr La Jolla CA 92093-5003

MILLER, STEPHEN HERSCHEL, surgery educator; b. N.Y.C., Jan. 12, 1941; s. Morris Louis and Mildred Lily (Beller) M.; m. Carol Susan Shapiro, Dec. 18, 1965; children: Mark, David. BS, UCLA, 1960, MD, 1964. Diplomate Am. Bd. Surgery, Am. Bd. Plastic Surgery (mem. exec. com. 1985—, chmn. written examination sect. 1985—, bd. dirs. 1984—, chmn. 1989-90). Asst. prof. surgery U. Calif., San Francisco, 1973-74; from asst. prof. to prof. surgery Milton S. Hershey Med. Ctr., Hershey, Pa., 1974-78; chief div. plastic surgery Oreg. Health Scis. U., Portland, 1979-88, Staff Scripps Clinic, La Jolla, Calif., 1988—; clin. prof. surgery U. Calif., San Diego, 1989—. Editor-in-chief Yearbook of Plastic, Reconstructive and Aesthetic Surgery, 1988-95. Physician advisor Boy Scouts Am., dist. chmn. scoutmaster exec. coun., 1983-84; bd. dirs. Temple Beth Israel, Portland, 1984-86. Recipient Physician Recognition award, 1976; grantee Med. Rsch. Found. of Oreg., 1980, Oreg. Health Scis. U., 1980. Mem. ACS (chmn. program com. 1983-87), Am. Soc. Plastic and Reconstructive Surgery (bd. dirs. 1980-89, v.p. 1985-86, pres.-elect 1986-87, pres. 1987-88, grantee 1976), Am. Assn. Plastic Surgeons (chmn. rsch. com. 1983-84, trustee 1988-91, sec. 1990-93, pres. 1994-95), Assn. Acad. Chmn. Plastic Surgery (sec./treas. 1985—). Home: 6555 Caminito Northland La Jolla CA 92037-5823 Office: Scripps Clinic 10666 N Torrey Pines Rd La Jolla CA 92037-1027

MILLER, STEVE, television director, producer; b. L.A., Sept. 13, 1951; s. Nathan H. and Shirley Ann (Watstein) M.; m. Lee Keiter, June 22, 1975; children: Jeffrey, Brian, David. BA in Telecommunications, U. So. Calif., 1973. Producer, dir. TV program: The Love Report, Eye on Hollywood, Entertainment Tonight, Christmas Eve at the Music Ctr., Dads, The Car Man, Together with Shirley and Pat Boone, Summer Faire, The Voyager Spacecraft Meets Saturn; dir. home videos Shape Up with Arnold Schwarzenegger, Mickey, Donald, Goofy & Friends, How to Use Your IBM PC; dir., producer commls. and corp. videos, contbr. articles to profl. jours. Mem. Dirs. Guild Am., Acad. TV, Arts and Scis.

MILLER, SUSAN WISE, career counselor, consultant; b. Cambridge, Mass., Feb. 1, 1941; d. Joseph and Madeline (Komar) Wise; m. Joseph Monte Miller, Dec. 29, 1963; children: Joanne Wise, Emily Wise. BS, Wheelock Coll., 1963; MA in Counseling Psychology, U. Calif., Berkeley, 1965; postgrad., UCLA, Loyola Marymount U., 1974-76. Nat. cert. career counselor, cert. vocat. evaluator; diplomate Am. Bd. Vocat. Experts. Career couseling, cons. Vocat. Tng. Consulting Svcs., L.A., 1975—; pvt. career counselor, 1977—; cons. Career and Vocat. Unit Calif. State Dept. Edn., Sacramento, 1974-90, assoc. project. dir. TIDE Project Career and Vocat. Unit, 1982-90; cons. UCLA Office Spl. Pers. Programs, 1980, 83, mem. ext., 1979—; speaker Am. Assn. Matrimonial Lawyers, 1989, L.A. Employee Relocation Coun., 1989; workshop leader Conciliation Ct. Conf., 1979—; instr. Mchts. and Mfrs. Assn., 1983—; mem. vocat. edn. div. Nev. State Dept. Edn.; adj. prof. U. Judaism, 1983-86, U. San Francisco, 1987—; on-line career counselor Times-Link, 1994—. Area rep. Career Planning and Adult Devel. Network, 1982—; bd. dir. Nat. Network Adv. Bd., catalyst, 1981-85; adv. bd. dir. L.A. County Career Guidance Ctr., 1979-80; commr. L.A. Sch. Dist. Commn. for Sex Equity, 1980-83. Recipient Appreciation award L.A. County Commn. on the Status Women, 1978. Mem. ASTD (Appreciation award 1989), Beverly Hills Bar Assn. (adj. mem. 1983—), San Fernando Valley Bar Assn. (assoc. 1990—), Am. Vocat. Assn., Calif. Assn. Counseling and Devel., Calif. Career Guidance Assn.

MILLER, TERRENCE CLARK, software engineer; b. New Rochelle, N.Y., June 2, 1947; s. John Francis and Henrietta (Clark) M.; m. Denise Eleanor Sullivan, Aug. 6, 1977. BS in Engring. & Applied Sci. cum laude, Yale U., 1969, MS in Computer Sci., 1974, MPhil in Computer Sci., 1975, PhD in Computer Sci., 1978. Applications programmer Informatics Inc., College Park, Md., 1972; tchg. asst. in computer sci. Yale U., 1974-75; asst. prof. elec. engring. computer sci. dept. U. Calif., San Diego, 1977-79; mem. tech. staff Hewlett Packard Labs., Hewlett Packard Co., Palo Alto, Calif., 1979-83; project mgr. Hewlett Packard Labs., Hewlett Packard Co., 1983-85, dept. mgr., 1985-86; staff engr. Sun Microsystems, Mt. View, Calif., 1986-89; sr. staff engr. Sun Microsystems, 1989—. Contbr. articles to profl. jours.; patentee in field. Lt. (j.g.) USNR, 1969-72. Mem. IEEE, Assn. Computing Machinery, Tau Beta Phi. Office: SunSoft M/S 12-33 2550 Garcia Ave Mountain View CA 94043-1109

MILLER, THOMAS ALBERT, entomology educator; b. Sharon, Pa., Jan. 5, 1940; s. Stephen Andrew and Amelia (Gorence) Miller (Chmeliar); m. Hollace Lee Gruhn, Dec. 18, 1965 (div. Nov. 1988); children: Remembrance L., Honor C.; m. Soo-ok Johnson, Dec. 13, 1991. BA in Physics, U. Calif., Riverside, 1962, PhD in Entomology, 1967. Rsch. assoc., NIH postdoctoral fellow U. Ill., Urbana, 1967-68; NATO postdoctoral fellow U. Glasgow, Scotland, 1968-69, vis. prof. zoology dept., 1973; NIH fellow U. Calif., 1964-67, asst. prof. entomology, 1969-72, assoc. prof., 1972-76, prof., entomologist, 1976—, acting head div. toxicology and physiology, 1979-80, head div., 1984-86; cons. in residence Wellcome Rsch. Labs., Berkhamsted, Eng., 1973-74, Australian Cotton Growers Rsch. Assn., 1983-84; vis. prof. U. Ariz., 1990; overseas cons. Wellcome Found., London, 1990-93; cons. AID, Ariz. Dept. Agr., Ciba-Geigy, Dow Chem. Co., DuPont Chem. Co., Food Machinery Corp., U. Calif., Berkeley, numerous others; organizer Symposium on Advances in Insect Neurobiology, Entomol. Congress, Hamburg, 1984, organizer, chmn. Symposium on Insect Autonomic Nervous System, Vancouver, 1988. Author: Insect Neurophysiological Techniques, 1979; editor 16 books; founder 2 book series; contbr. over 130 articles and revs. to sci. jours. and proc., including Jour. Analytical Chemistry, Annals Entomol. Soc. Am., Archives Insect Biochem. Physiology, Jour. Econ. Entomology, Jour. Neurochemistry, Pesticide Sci., also chpts. in books. Sgt. Calif. N.G., 1956-62. NAS exch fellow, Hungary, 1978-79, Czechoslovakia, 1986; grantee Nat. Inst. Neurol. Diseases and Stroke, 1967-72, Rockefeller Found., 1970-76, Nat. Inst. Environ. Health Scis., 1972-84; numerous others. Mem. AAAS, Entomol. Soc. Am., Am. Chem. Soc. Office: Entomology Dept U Calif Riverside CA 92521-0134

MILLER, THOMAS CECIL, private investigator, forensic examiner, lawyer; b. L.A., Jan. 27, 1951; s. Thomas Cecil Miller and Oetta Elizabeth (Buckman) Harrison; m. Michele Marie Austin, Aug. 23, 1986; two children. BA in History and Journalism, Metro State Coll., 1974; BA in Classical Langs., U. Denver, 1985; MA in English, Middlebury Coll., 1985; JD, U. Denver, 1992. Bar: Colo. 1993. Freelance writer, journalist Denver; prin. Investigative Reporting Services, Inc., Denver, 1983—; tchr. creative writing and mag. editing Arapahoe Community Coll., 1985-88, 92—, Met. State Coll., 1987-88, leal investigations Denver Paralegal Inst., 1993—; lectr. in investigation U. Denver, 1991—; founder Pearl St. Press, 1988. Author numerous poems. Mem. Profl. Pvt. Investigators Assn. Colo. (bd. dirs. 1988, 89, 90, pres. 1992-93), World Assn. of Detectives, Colo. Press Assn., Rocky Mountain Graphology Assn., Am. Handwriting Analysis Assn. Roman Catholic. Office: Investigative Reporting Svcs PO Box 10844 Denver CO 80250

MILLER, THOMAS ROY, computer company executive; b. Washington, Apr. 12, 1957; s. Roy Samuel and Lucille Irene (Beck) M.; m. Karen Louise Sheehan, Oct. 7, 1989; 1 child, David Theodore Roy Miller. BA in Econs. cum laude, BS in Info and Computer Scis. cum laude, U. Calif., Irvine, 1979; MBA in Fin., U. Chgo., 1981. V.p. Samor Mgmt., Evanston, Ill., 1981-82; ops. analyst RR Donnelley, Chgo., 1982-86; mgr. RR Donnelley, Lisle, Ill., 1986-87, project mgr., 1987-89; controller Advanced Electronic Packaging, Huntington Beach, Calif., 1989-90; v.p. ops. Advanced Electronic Packaging, Huntington Beach, 1990-91; prin. Orange Coast Cons., Westminster, Calif., 1991—; chmn. Excalibur Security Ltd., Westminster; bus. and tech. counselor Accelerate, Irvine, Calif., 1992—. Active U. Chgo. Bus. Sch. Alumni Activities, Boy Scouts Am., 1977—, USCG Aux., 1987—. Named Eagle Scout Boy Scouts Am., 1973. Mem. Info. Industry Assn. (steering com. Chgo. chpt. 1984-89, program chair 1988-89), Orange County Venture Forum (adv. bd. 1991—). Republican. Lutheran. Home: 13242 Chestnut St Westminster CA 92683-2604 Office: 4199 Campus Dr Ste 240 Irvine CA 92715-2698

MILLER, TIMOTHY ALDEN, plastic and reconstructive surgeon; b. Inglewood, Calif., Dec. 11, 1938; s. Henry Bernard and Florence Algena (Maddock) M.; 1 child, Matthew Christopher. Student, U. Calif., Berkeley; MD, UCLA, 1963. Diplomate Am. Bd. Surgery, Am. Bd. Plastic Surgery (bd. dirs. 1991—). Intern Vanderbilt U. Hosp., Nashville, 1963-64; resident in surgery, dept. surg. pathology UCLA, 1966-67, resident, then chief resident gen. and thoracics sugery, 1967-69, acting asst. prof., 1969-70, prof. surgery, 1981—; asst. surg. resident John Hopkins Hosp., 1967; fellow plastic and reconstructive surgery U. Pitts., 1970-72; chief plastic surgery West L.A. VA Med. Ctr., 1973—; dir. Am. Bd. Plastic Surgery, 1991—. Author: (novel) Practice to Deceive, 1991; assoc. editor Jour. Plastic & Reconstructive Surgery, 1987-93, co-editor, 1994—. Trustee Children's Inst. Internat., 1995—. Capt. U.S. Army, 1964-66, Vietnam. Decorated Bronze Star; recipient Thomas Symington award Pitts. Acad. Medicine, 1971. Mem. Am. Soc. for Plastic Surgery (chmn. jud. coun. 1991—), Am. Soc. for Aesthetic Plastic Surgery (bd. dirs. 1990-92), Plastic Surgery Ednl. Found. (bd. dirs. 1991—). Office: UCLA Med Ctr 200 Medical Plz Ste 669 Los Angeles CA 90095-6960

MILLER, VIRGINIA LEE, business owner; b. Columbus, Ohio, Oct. 26, 1941; d. Theodore Irving and Georgiana Mae (Reed) Jones; m. Arthur R. Miller II, Nov. 26, 1960; children: Elizabeth Ann Lilly, William Theodore Miller, Arthur III. Student, Columbus Coll. & Art & Design, 1959-60, Ohio State U., 1960-61. Clerical Sears, Tuscon, Ariz., 1976-84; computer imput Sears, Las Vegas, 1984—; sec., owner business Las Vegas, 1989—. Active Weep, Las Vegas, 1992-93; bd. dirs. Luth. Ch., Las Vegas., 1987-94; social events sec. Youth for Internat. Understanding, Las Vegas, 1991-94; active Cheyene H.S. Booster Club, Las Vegas, 1992-94; com. mem. Boy Scouts of Am., advancement chair., 1993-94, sec., 1991-94, com. chair. 1989-90, social chmn., 1991-93; com. mem., parent adv., Girl Scouts of Am., 1972-75; com. mem. Cub Scouts, 1984-89; worship com. Holy Spirit Lutheran Ch., 1986-94, youth coord., 1993—. Recipient Amb. of Faith award ELCA Luth. Ch., Phoenix, 1993-94. Republican. Office: Sears 4000 Meadows Ln Las Vegas NV 89107-3108

MILLER, WARREN EDWARD, political scientist; b. Hawarden, Iowa, Mar. 26, 1924; s. John Carroll and Mildred Ovedia (Lien) M.; m. Ruth S. Jones, May 1981; children by previous marriage: Jeffrey Ralph, Jennifer Louise. B.S., U. Oreg., 1948, M.S., 1950; Ph.D., Maxwell Sch. Citizenship and Public Affairs, Syracuse U., 1954; Ph.D. (hon.), U. Goteborg, Sweden, 1972. Asst. study dir. Survey Research Ctr., Inst. Social Research, U. Mich., 1951-53, study dir., 1953-56, research assoc., 1956-59, program dir., 1959-68, research coordinator polit. behavior program, 1968-70, prin. investigator nat. election studies, 1977—; dir. Ctr. Polit. Studies, Inst. Social Research, 1970-81; program dir. Ctr. Polit. Studies, 1982-93; asst. prof. polit. sci. Ctr. Polit. Studies, Inst. Social Research, 1956-58, asso. prof., 1958-63, prof., 1963-93, Arthur W. Bromage prof. polit. sci., 1981-82; prof. polit. sci. Ariz. State U., 1981—; fellow Ctr. Advanced Study in Behavioral Scis., 1961-62; exec. dir. Inter-univ. Consortium for Polit. and Social Rsch., 1962-70, assoc. dir., 1978—; vis. prof. U. Tilburg, Netherlands, 1973, U. Geneva, 1973, European U. Inst., Florence, Italy, 1979; vis. Disting. prof. Ariz. State U., 1981; trustee Inst. Am. Univs., 1970—; Regents' prof., Ariz. State U., 1988—. Author: (with others) books including The Voter Decides, 1954, American Voter, 1960, Elections and the Political Order, 1966, (with T.E. Levitin) Leadership and Change: Presidential Elections from 1952-1976, 77, (with M.K. Jennings) Parties in Transition, 1986, Without Consent, 1988, (with others) The American National Election Studies Data Sourcebook, 1952-1978, 80, The American National Election Studies Data Sourcebook, 1952-86, 89; contbr. (with others) articles to profl. publs.; editorial bd.: (with others) Am. Polit. Sci. Rev., 1966-71, Computers and the Humanities, 1969-71, Social Science History, 1976-91, Social Science Rev., 1973; editorial adv. bd.: (with others) Sage Electoral Studies Yearbook, 1974. Served with USAAF, 1943-46. Recipient Disting. Alumnus award Maxwell Sch. Citizenship and Public Affairs, Syracuse U., 1974, Disting. Faculty Achievement award U. Mich., 1977; honored in the creation of the Warren E. Miller award for Intellectual Accomplishment and Svc. Am. Polit. Sci. Assn. sect. on Elecions, Pub. Opionion and Voting Behavior, 1995, creation of the Warren E. Miller award for Meritorious Svc. to Social Scis. Inter-Univ. Consortium for Polit. and Social Rsch., 1993. Fellow Am. Acad. Arts and Scis.; mem. AAAS, Am. Polit. Sci. Assn. (pres. 1979-80), Internat. Polit. Sci. Assn. (coun. 1969-73), M.W. Polit. Sci. Assn., Internat. Soc. Polit. Psychology, So. Polit. Sci. Assn., Social Sci. History Assn. (pres. 1979-80), Norwegian Acad. Sci. and Letters. Office: Ariz State U Dept Polit Sci Tempe AZ 85287

MILLER, WILLIAM CHARLES, architect, educator; b. San Francisco, May 11, 1945; m. Beverly Jean McConnell, Dec. 22, 1968; children: Britt A., David A. BArch, U. Oregon, 1968; MArch, U.Ill., 1970. Registered architect, Ariz., Kans., Utah; cert. Nat. Coun. Archtl. Registration Bd. Project architect Don L. McKee, Architect, Anacortes, Wash., 1968-69, Enteleki-Architects, San Francisco, 1973-74; asst. prof. U. Ariz., Tucson, 1970-73, 74-77; assoc. prof. Kans. State U., Manhattan, 1977-86, prof., 1986-92, head of dept. of architecture, 1990-92; prof., dean Grad. Sch. Architecture U. Utah, Salt Lake City, 1992—; lectr. various orgns., 1976—; guest juror at architecture schs., 1976—. Author: Alvar Aalto: An Annotated Bibliography, 1984; co-author: Architecture of the in Between, 1990, Architecture...Back...to...Life, 1991; editl. bd. Jour. Archtl. Edn., 1984-88; contbr. articles to profl. jours. Bd. dirs. Assist, Inc., 1992—. Grantee U. Ariz. 1976, NEH, 1985, Am. Scandinavian Found., 1985, Graham Found. 1989; fellow U. Ill., 1970. Mem AIA (treas. Utah 1992-95), Assn. Collegiate Schs. of Architecture (west ctrl. region dir. 1988-91, bd. dirs. 1988-91), Soc. Archtl. Historians, Contemporary Artists Group (bd. dirs. 1992—), Salt Lake Art and Design Bd., Tau Sigma Delta. Office: U Utah Grad Sch Architecture Salt Lake City UT 84112

MILLER, WILLIAM ELWOOD, mining company executive; b. Bend, Oreg., May 9, 1919; s. Harry Adelbert and Sarah (Heyburn) M.; B.A., Stanford, 1941, M.B.A., 1947; m. Constance Alban Crosby, July 2, 1955; children: William, Constance, Harold, Mary, Sarah Crosby, Charles Crosby, Helen, Harry. Owner and operator Central Oregon Pumice Co., Bend, 1948—; pres. The Miller Lumber Co., Bend, The Miller Ranch Co., Bend, Miller Tree Farm. Commr., City of Bend, 1959-62, mayor, 1960. Bd. dirs. Central Oreg. Coll.; pres. Central Oreg. Coll. Found., 1956-57; dir. Central Oregon Coll. Area Ednl. Dist., 1961-65, chmn., 1964-65; bd. govs. Ore. Dept. Geology and Mineral Industries, 1971-75. Served with A.C., USNR, 1942-45. Decorated D.F.C., Air medal. Mem. Central Oreg. (v.p. 1954), Bend (pres. 1954) C. of C., Bend Golf Club, Rotary (dir. Bend 1955-56), Kappa Sigma. Republican. Episcopalian. Home: 527 NW Congress St Bend OR 97701-2509 Office: 1 NW Greenwood Ave Bend OR 97701-2028

MILLER, WILLIAM FREDERICK, research company executive, educator, business consultant; b. Vincennes, Ind., Nov. 19, 1925; s. William and Elsie M. (Everts) M.; m. Patty J. Smith, June 19, 1949; 1 son, Rodney Wayne. Student, Vincennes U., 1946-47; BS, Purdue U., 1949, MS, 1951, PhD, 1956; D.Sc., 1972. Mem. staff Argonne Nat. Lab., 1955-64, assoc. physicist, 1956-59, dir. applied math. div., 1959-64; prof. computer sci. Stanford U., Palo Alto, Calif., 1965—; Herbert Hoover prof. pub. and pvt. mgmt. Stanford U., 1979—, assoc. provost for computing, 1968-70, v.p. for research, 1970-71, v.p., provost, 1971-78; mem. Stanford Assocs., 1972—; pres., chief exec. officer SRI Internat., Menlo Park, Calif., 1979-90; chmn. bd., chief exec. officer SRI Devel. Co., Menlo Park, David Sarnoff Research Ctr., Inc., Princeton, N.J.; profl. lectr. applied math. U. Chgo., 1962-64; vis. prof. math. Purdue U., 1962-63; vis. scholar Ctr. for Advanced Study in Behavioral Scis., 1976; bd. dirs. Varian Assocs. Inc., 1st Interstate Bancorp, 1st Interstate Bank Calif., Pacific Gas and Electric Co., Regis McKenna, Inc., Scios-Nova, Inc.; mem. adv. coun. BHP Internat.; mem. computer sci. and engring. bd. Nat. Acad. Sci., 1968-71; mem. Nat. Sci. Bd., 1982-88; mem. corp. com. computers in edn. Brown U., 1972-79; mem. policy bd. EDUCOM Planning Coun. on Computing in Edn., 1974-79, chmn., 1974-76; ednl. adv. bd. Guggenheim Meml. Found., 1976-80; com. postdoctoral and doctoral rsch. staff NRC, 1977-80, mem. computer sci. and telecommunications bd., Nat. Inst. Standards Tech. bd. assessment; mem. internat. adv. panel Nat. Sci. and Tech. Bd., Singapore. Assoc. editor: Pattern Recognition Jour, 1968-72, Jour. Computational Physics, 1970-74. Served to 2d lt. F.A. AUS, 1943-46. Recipient Frederic B. Whitman award United Way Bay Area, 1982. Fellow IEEE, Am. Acad. Arts and Scis., AAAS; mem. Am. Math. Soc., Am. Phys. Soc., Soc. Indsl. and Applied Math., Assn. Computing Machinery, Nat. Acad. Engring., Sigma Xi, Tau Beta Pi. Office: Stanford U Grad Sch Bus Stanford CA 94305

MILLER, WILLIAM HUGHES, theoretical chemist, educator; b. Kosciusko, Miss., Mar. 16, 1941; s. Weldon Howard and Jewel Irene (Hughes) M.; m. Margaret Ann Westbrook, June 4, 1966; children: Alison Leslie, Emily Sinclaire. B.S., Ga. Inst. Tech., 1963; A.M., Harvard U., 1964, Ph.D., 1967. Jr. fellow Harvard U., 1967-69; NATO postdoctoral fellow Freiburg (Germany) U., 1967-68; asst. prof. chemistry U. Calif., Berkeley, 1969-72, assoc. prof., 1972-74, prof., 1974—, dept. chmn., 1989-93; fellow Churchill Coll., Cambridge (Eng.) U., 1975-76; hon. prof. Shandong U., People's Republic of China, 1994. Alfred P. Sloan fellow, 1970-72; Camille and Henry Dreyfus fellow, 1973-78; Guggenheim fellow, 1975-76, Christensen fellow St. Catherine's Coll., Oxford, 1993; recipient Alexander von Humboldt-Stiftung U.S. Sr. Scientist award, 1981-82, Ernest Orlando Lawrence Meml. award, 1985. Fellow AAAS, Am. Acad. Arts and Scis., Am. Phys. Soc. (Irving Langmuir award 1990); mem. NAS, Am. Chem. Soc. (theoretical chemistry award 1994), Internat. Acad. Quantum Molecular Sci. (Ann. prize 1974). Office: U Calif Dept Chemistry Berkeley CA 94720

MILLER, WILLIAM J., computer company executive; b. 1946. Exec. v.p., pres. info. svcs. Control Data Corp.; CEO Quantum Corp., 1992—. Office: Quantum Corp 500 Mccarthy Blvd Milpitas CA 95035-7908*

MILLER, WILLIAM J., village official; b. Phillipsburg, N.J., Feb. 19, 1940; s. Peter P. and Anna C. (Chapman) M.; m. Stella Charles, May 5, 1961; children: Charles Peter, Doris Ann. Grad., Hillside (N.J.) H.S., 1958. Mil. policeman U.S. Army, 1959-62; commd. USAF, advanced through grades to master sgt., ret., 1980; advisor Dot Lake (Alaska) Village Coun., 1980-84, coun. pres., 1984—; planner Tanana Devel. Corp., Tok, Alaska, 1983-85; land mgr., adminstr. Dot Lake (Alaska) Native Corp., 1983—; exec. dir. United Crow Band, Inc., Tok, 1989—. Mem. sch. bd. Village of Dot Lake, 1981-86; mem. adv. com. Upper Tanana/40 Mile Fish and Game, Tok, 1983-90; mem. adv. bd. subregional TCC, 1983-86; advisor Tanana Basin Area Plan, 1984-85; vice chmn. Alaska Gateway Regional Sch. Bd., Tok, 1986-91; active Rural Edn. PAC, 1984-86. Home: Box 2262 Dot Lake AK 99737 Office: United Crow Band Inc Box 131 Tok AK 99780

MILLER, ZOYA DICKINS (MRS. HILLIARD EVE MILLER, JR.), civic worker; b. Washington, July 15, 1923; d. Randolph and Zoya Pavlovna (Klementinovska) Dickins; m. Hilliard Eve Miller, Jr., Dec. 6, 1943; children: Jeffrey Arnot, Hilliard Eve III. Grad. Stuart Sch. Costume Design, Washington, 1942; student Sophie Newcomb Coll., 1944, New Eng. Conservatory Music, 1946, Colo. Coll., 1965; grad. Internat. Sch. Reading, 1969. Instr. Stuart Summer Sch. Costume Design, Washington, 1942; fashion coord. Julius Garfinckel, Washington, 1942-43; fashion coord., cons. Mademoiselle mag., 1942-44; star TV show Cowbelle Kitchen, 1957-58, Flair for Living, 1958-59; model mags. and comml. films, also nat. comml. recs., 1956—; sr. devel. officer Webb-Waring Lung Inst., Denver, 1973—. Contbr. articles, lectures on health care systems and fund raising. Mem. exec. com., bd. dirs. El Paso County chpt. Am. Lung Assn., Colo., 1954-63; mem. exec. com. Am. Lung Assn. Colo., 1965-84, bd. dirs. 1965-87, chmn. radio and TV coun., 1963-70, mem. med. affairs com., 1965-70, pres., 1965-66, procurer found. funds, 1965-70; developer nat. radio ednl. prodns. for internat. use Am. Lung Assn., 1963-70, coord. statewide pulmonary screening programs Colo., other states, 1965-72; chmn. benefit fund raising El Paso County Cancer Soc., 1963; co-founder, coord. Colorado Springs Debutante Ball, 1967—; coord. Nat. Gov.'s Conf. Ball, 1969; mem. exec. com. Colo. Gov.'s Comprehensive Health Planning Coun., 1967-74, chmn., 1971-72; chmn. Colo. Chronic Care Com., 1969-73, chmn. fund raising, 1970-72, chmn. spl. com. congl. studies on nat. health bills, 1971-73; mem. bd. Colo.-Wyo. Regional Med. Program Adv. Coun., 1969-73; mem. Colo. Med. Found. Consumers Adv. Coun., 1972-78; mem. decorative arts com. Colorado Springs Fine Arts

Ctr., 1972-75; founder, state coord. Nov. Noel Pediatrics Benefit Am. Lung Assn., 1973-87; founder, state pres. Newborn Hope, Inc., 1987—; mem. adv. bd. Wagon Wheel Girl Scouts, 1991—, Cmty. in Schs., 1995. Zoya Dickins Miller Vol. of Yr. award established Am. Lung Assn. of Colo., 1979; recipient James J. Waring award Colo. Conf. on Respiratory Disease Workers, 1963, Nat. Pub. Rels. award Am. Lung Assn., 1979, Gold Double Bar Cross award, 1980, 83, Jefferson award Am. Inst. Pub. Svc., 1991, Recognition award So. Colo. Women's C. of C., 1994, Silver Spur Community award Pikes Peak Range Riders, 1994; named Humanitarian of Yr., Am. Lung Assn. of Colo., 1987, One of 50 Most Influential Women in Colorado Springs by Gazette Telegraph Newspaper, 1990, One of 6 Leading Ladies Colo. Homes & Lifestyles Mag., 1991. Lic. pvt. pilot. Mem. Colo. Assn. Fund Raisers, Denver Round Table for Planned Giving, Nat. Soc. Fund Raising Execs., Nat. Cowbell Assn. (El Paso county pres. 1954, TV chmn., chmn. nat. Father of Yr. contest Colo. 1956-57), Broadmoor Garden Club. Home: 74 W Cheyenne Mountain Blvd Colorado Springs CO 80906-4336

MILLER-HOUCK, NANCY JOAN, nurse, psychotherapist, consultant, educator; b. Newton, Mass., May 20, 1947; d. Harold Max and Selma Irma (Finkelstein) Gerrish; divorced, 1974; m. Douglas Houck, July 13, 1991. BA in Sociology, C. W. Post Coll. L.I. U., 1968; postgrad., Mich. State U., 1969; RN diploma, Jackson Meml. Hosp., 1977; MS in Mental Health Counseling, Barry U., 1989. Cert. psychiat. RN, specialist in adult mental health nursing, substance abuse counselor, State of Hawaii. Social worker Suffolk (N.Y.) County Social Svcs., 1968-71; social worker, counselor Met. Dade County, Miami, Fla., 1971-74; charge nurse Newton Wellsley Hosp., Newton Upper Falls, Mass., 1977-78; head nurse substance abuse Humana Hosp. Biscayne, Miami, Fla., 1978-80; charge nurse Mt. Zion Hosp., San Francisco, 1980-81; staff nurse mental health unit Marin Gen. Hosp., Greenbrae, Calif., 1981-84; clin. coord. Humana Hosp. Biscayne, Miami, Calif., 1984-86; head nurse, dir. treatment svcs. addiction Victoria Hosp., Miami, 1986-87; per diem nurse Highland Park Hosp., Miami, 1987-89; staff nurse med./surg. Blue Hill (Maine) Meml. Hosp., 1989; pvt. practice Blue Hill, 1989-91, Lahaina, Hawaii, 1992—. HIV/AIDS Teaching grantee State of Maine, 1990, Social Svcs. Program grantee State of Fla., 1974. Mem. AACD, ANA (cert. psychiat. nurse, clin. nurse specialist). Office: PO Box 11348 181-K Lahainaluna Rd Lahaina HI 96761-6348

MILLER-TIEDEMAN, ANNA LOUISE, counselor, writer; b. Huntington, W.Va., Sept. 21, 1934; d. Elmer and Pearl (Todd) Miller; m. David Valentine Tiedeman, Jan. 6, 1973. BBA, Marshall U., 1963, MA, 1967; PhD, Ohio U., 1973. Cert. counselor/nat. bd.; cert. tchr., Ill.; standard designated svcs. cert., Calif. Mgr. sta. merger Chesapeake and Ohio Railroad, Huntington, 1957-66; resident dir. Ohio U., Athens, 1967; human rels. specialist Inst. for Regl. Devel., Athens, 1968; housing specialist Action, Inc., Huntington, 1969; real estate salesperson Massey Reality, Huntington, 1968-71; assoc. edn. devel. specialist Appalachian Edn. Lab., Charleston, W.Va., 1970-71; self-employed writer Palo Alto, Calif., 1971-72; counselor San Mateo (Calif.) City Sch. Dist., 1971-73; vis. lectr. The Johns Hopkins U., Balt., 1984-86, C.W. Post Coll./L.I. U., 1987; spl. issue co-editor Jour. of Career Edn., Columbia, Mo., 1982-84. Author: How Not to Make It . . . And Succeed: Life On Your Own Terms, 1989 (Ben Franklin award finalist 1990), Lifecareer: The Quantam Leap Into a Process Theory of Career, 1988; contbg. author: Developmental Counseling and Teaching, 1980. Prodn. asst. Hollywood (Calif.) Bowl Easter Svcs., 1987; dir. press desk Fourth Ann. International Wilderness Congress, Denver, 1987. Recipient Outstanding Rsch. award Am. Personnel and Guidance Assn., Washington, 1981; co-leader Nat. Assembly to Advance Career, Nat. Inst. for Advancement of Career Edn., L.A., 1983, George E. Hill Disting. Alumnae award Ohio U., Athens, 1986. Mem. Am. Counselor Assn. (Spl. Writing award 1975, 78), Nat. Career Devel. Assn. Home: 1078 La Tortuga Dr Vista CA 92083-6441 Office: Lifecareer Ctr 1078 La Tortuga Dr Vista CA 92083-6441

MILLETT, MERLIN LYLE, aerospace consultant, educator; b. East Moline, Ill., Dec. 29, 1923; s. Merlin Lyle Sr. and Erie Lucille (Hyland) m.; m. Glendola Mae Westlic, Feb. 23, 1945 (dec. 1968); 1 child, Debra Sue; m. Esther Lee Dayhuff, Aug. 21, 1970. BS, Iowa State Coll., 1945, MS, 1948, PhD, 1957. Registered profl. engr., Iowa. Draftsman Am. Machine and Metals, East Moline, Ill., 1941-42; instr. Iowa State Coll., Ames, 1946-48, asst. prof. aerospace engring., 1952-57, assoc. prof., 1957-61; prof. Iowa State U., Ames, 1961-75; flight test engr. Douglas Aircraft Co., Santa Monica, Calif., 1948-52; dean of faculty Parks Coll. St. Louis U., Cahokia, Ill., 1975-78; mgr. fighter aircraft Boeing Mil. Airplanes, Wichita, 1978-89; adj. prof. Okla. State U., Stillwater, 1979-94; design cons. Architects Associated, Des Moines, 1970-72; aeronautical cons. Iowa Aeronautics Commn., Des Moines, 1972-74; co-prin. investigator U.S. Dept. Transp., Ames, 1973-75; power plant engr. Fed. Aviation Agy., Ames, 1971-75; cons. City of Ames, 1973. Patentee low cost drone. Pres. bd. dirs. Suntree East Home Owners Assn., 1993-94; pres. Scottsdale Ranch Cmty. Assn., 1993—95, mem. architecture com., 1989—, bd. dirs., 1989—. Lt. USNR, ret. Fellow AIAA (assoc., dep. dir. 1986-94). Home: 10515 E Fanfol Ln Scottsdale AZ 85258-6032

MILLEY, JOHN ROSS, neonatologist, educator; b. Hartford, Conn., Oct. 10, 1946; s. Chesley Ross and Muriel Frances (Potter) M.; m. Donna Beatrice Scholts, June 11, 1968; 1 child, Jeffrey Ross. BA in Chemistry, Ill. Wesleyan U., 1967; PhD in Chemistry, U. Chgo., 1974, MD, 1975. Diplomate Am. Bd. Pediats., Neonatal Perinatal Medicine, Nat. Bd. Med. Examiners; lic. physician, Md., Pa., Utah. Intern in pediats. Johns Hopkins U., Balt., 1975-76, resident in pediats., 1976-78, fellow in perinatal medicine, 1978-80, asst. in pediats., 1979-80; from asst. prof. to assoc. prof. ob-gyn. U. Pitts. Sch. Medicine, 1980-88; mem. med. staff Primary Children's Med. Ctr., Salt Lake City, 1988—, U. Utah Med. Ctr., Salt Lake City, 1988—; assoc. prof. pediats. U. Utah Sch. Medicine, Salt Lake City, 1988—; dir. neonatal fellowship program U. Pitts., 1987-88, U. Utah, Salt Lake City, 1988—; mem. med. staff Johns Hopkins Hosp., Balt., 1979-80, Children's Hosp. Pitts., 1980-88, Children's Home of Pitts., 1985-88, LDS Hosp., Salt Lake City, 1988—, Magee-Womens Hosp., Pitts., 1980-88, mem. quality assurance com., 1985-88, perinatal morbidity and mortality com., 1984-88; vis. prof. dept. pediatrics U. Cin. Sch. Medicine, 1987; mem. instnl. rev. bd. Primary Children's Med. Ctr., Salt Lake City, 1989—, chmn. instnl. rev. bd., 1991—; mem. ad hoc subcom. for decentralized lab. testing U. Utah Sch. Medicine, Salt Lake City, 1990—; prin. investigator numerous grants, programs Nat. Inst. Child Health and Human Devel. Ad hoc reviewer: Pediats. Rsch., Diabetes, Am. Jour. Physiology; contbr. articles to profl. publs. Mem. med. adv. com. Pitts. Planned Parenthood, 1982-86. Rsch. grantee Children's Hosp. Pitts., 1980-85, Magee-Womens Hosp. Rsch. Fund, 1980-81, 81-84, 82-85, 84-85, 86-87, Ann Ricketson Loftberg Fund, 1981-85, Western Pa. Heart Assn., Inc., 1981-82, Ross Labs., 1984-86, 84-88, U. Utah Sch. Medicine, 1988-89. Fellow Am. Acad. Pediats. (dist. VIII perinatal sect. 1988—), Am. Physiol. Soc., Intermountain Pediat. Soc., Soc. for Pediat. Rsch., Perinatal Rsch. Soc., Utah Perinatal Assn., Study Group for Complications of Perinatal Care. Office: Univ Utah Sch Medicine 50 N Medical Dr Salt Lake City UT 84132-0001

MILLIGAN, GATEWOOD CARLISLE, physician, retired; b. Shannon, Miss., July 23, 1907; s. Martin Gatewood and Johnnie Carlisle (McCown) M.; m. Maxine Louise Redeker, Apr. 1, 1933; children: Jociele Aline Nordwall, Jonanna Lee Dilsaver. Student, Park Coll., 1924-26, Hastings Coll., 1927, U. Wyo., 1927-28; MD, U. Colo., 1929-33. Lic. to practice medicine Colo. 1933, Tex., 1935. Pvt. practice Denver, 1934-36; partner C.W. Bixler & G.C. Milligan, Erie, Colo., 1935, Drs. Alldredge & Milligan, Englewood, Colo., 1935-46, Drs. Milligan & Hogan, Englewood, 1946-52, Drs. Milligan & Miner, Englewood, 1952-69, Drs. Milligan, Miner & Langstaff, Englewood, 1957-60; ob.-gyn. pvt. practice Englewood, 1969-84; pres. Arapohoe county Med. Soc., Englewood, 1940-41, Colo. Med. Soc., Denver, 1957-58; pres. med. staff Porter Hosp., Denver, 1944-45, Swedish Hosp., Englewood, 1960-61. Mem. Englewood City Coun., 1954-58, Colo. Commn. on Aging, Denver, 1964-72, Colo. State Bd. Health, Denver, 1977-86, Elsie Malley Sr. Recreation Ctr. Adv. Bd., Englewood, 1975-81; chmn. bd. trustees Malley Trust Fund, Englewood, 1983—. Recipient Outstanding Svc. award Arapahoe Med. Soc., Englewood, 1973-74, Cert. of Svc. award Colo. Med. Soc., Denver, 1957, 66, 78, Excellence award U. Colo. Med. Alumni, Denver, 1986, Humanitarian award Rocky Mt. Conf. United Meth. Ch., Denver, 1990. Mem. AMA (hon.), Arapahoe County Med. Assn. (hon.), Colo. Med. Assn. (hon.), Englewood Rotary (Compassion award dist. 5450 1992), Englewood United Meth. Ch. Democrat. Methodist. Home: 3975 S Fox St Englewood CO 80110-4560

MILLIKEN, JOHN GORDON, research economist; b. Denver, May 12, 1927; s. William Boyd and Margaret Irene (Marsh) M.; m. Marie Violet Machell, June 13, 1953; children: Karen Marie, Douglas Gordon, David Tait, Anne Alain. BS, Yale U., 1949, BEng, 1950; MS, U. Colo., 1966, PhD, 1969. Registered profl. engr., Colo. Engr. U.S. Bur. Reclamation, Denver, 1950-55; asst. to plant mgr. Stanley Aviation Corp., Denver, 1955-56; prin. mgmt. engr., dept. mgr. Martin-Marietta Aerospace Div., Denver, 1956-64; mgmt. engr. Safeway Stores, Inc., Denver, 1964-66; sr. rsch. economist, prof., assoc. div. head U. Denver Rsch. Inst., 1966-86; pres. Univ. Senate, 1980-81; prin. Milliken Chapman Rsch. Group, Inc., Littleton, Colo., 1986-88, Milliken Rsch. Group, Inc., Littleton, 1988—; vis. fellow sci. policy rsch. unit U. Sussex, Eng., 1975-76; bd. dirs. Sci. Mgmt. Corp.; cons. mgmt. engr. Author: Aerospace Management Techniques, 1971, Federal Incentives for Innovation, 1974, Recycling Municipal Wastewater, 1977, Water and Energy in Colorado's Future, 1981, Metropolitan Water Management, 1981, Technological Innovation and Economic Vitality, 1983, Water Management in the Denver, Colorado Urban Area, 1988, Benefits and Costs of Oxygenated Fuels in Colorado, 1990, Water Transfer Alternatives Study, 1994, Colorado Springs Water Resources Plan Alternative Assessment Study, 1995; contbr. articles to profl. jours. Bd. dirs. Southeast Englewood Water Dist., 1963—, South Englewood San. Dist., 1965—; bd. dirs. South Suburban Park and Recreation Dist., 1971—, chmn., 1990-92; chmn. Dem. Com. of Arapahoe County, 1969-71, 5th Congl. Dist. Colo., 1972-73, 74-75; mem. exec. com. Colo. Faculty Adv. Coun., 1981-85; mem. Garrison Diversion Unit Commn., 1984; trustee Colo. Local Govt. Liquid Asset Trust, 1986—, chmn., 1991-93; bd. dirs. Colo. Spl. Dist. Assn. Property and Liability Pool, 1989—. With M.C. U.S. Army, 1945-46. Recipient Adlai E. Stevenson Meml. award, 1981, hon. title "Amicus Universitatis," U. Denver, 1994. Mem. Acad. Mgmt., Nat. Assn. Bus. Economists, Yale Sci. and Engring. Assn., Am. Water Works Assn., Sigma Xi, Tau Beta Pi, Beta Gamma Sigma, Sigma Iota Epsilon. Congregationalist. Home and Office: 6502 S Ogden St Littleton CO 80121-2561

MILLMAN, PAUL RICHARD, fundraiser; b. Hartford, Conn., Nov. 5, 1959; s. Richard B. and Marion (Kopcych) M. BA, U. Hartford, 1981. Projects coord. ORMC Found., Orlando, Fla., 1981-83; assoc. dir. ann. giving Rollins Coll., Winter Park, Fla., 1983-86; dir. ann. giving Art Ctr. Coll. of Design, Pasadena, Calif., 1986-89; dir. ann. fund U. Ctrl. Fla., Orlando, 1989-91; devel. dir. PUENTE Learning Ctr., L.A., 1991—. Recipient Fund Raising Improvement award CASE, 1988. Mem. Nat. Soc. Fund Raising Execs. (chair fund raising com. 1994, bd. dirs. Greater L.A. chpt. 1994, Mem. of Month award 1994). Democrat. Office: PUENTE Learning Ctr 501 S Boyle Ave Los Angeles CA 90033-3816

MILLS, ALAN BENJAMIN, insurance company executive; b. Tacoma, June 1, 1945; s. Benjamin Franklin and Guinevere (Crouch) M.; m. Vickie Lynn, June 26, 1976; adopted children: James Edward, James Wayne, Pamela Jane. BA, U. Calif., Berkeley, 1967. Claims rep. Farmers Ins. Group, Oakland and Concord, Calif., 1970-86; br. claims supr. Farmers Ins. Group, Salinas, Calif., 1986-89, Oakland, 1989-92; claim rep. Farmers Ins. Group, Pleasanton, 1992—. Republican. Office: Farmers Ins Group 11533 Dublin Canyon Rd Pleasanton CA 94588-2816

MILLS, BASIL E., food products executive. Attended, U. Colo., 1948-50. Broker Walter S. Markham Co., Salinas, Calif., 1953-55; with Royal Packing Co., Salinas, 1955-58; pres. Mills Distributing Co., Salinas, 1958—; ptnr. MIVCO Packing Co., Salinas, 1973—. With U.S. Army, 1951-53. Office: Mills Distributing Co 375 W Market St Salinas CA 93901-1423*

MILLS, CAROL MARGARET, business consultant, public relations consultant; b. Salt Lake City, Aug. 31, 1943; d. Samuel Lawrence and Beth (Neilson) M.; BS magna cum laude, U. Utah, 1965. With W.S. Hatch Co., Woods Cross, Utah, 1965-87, corp. sec., 1970-87, traffic mgr., 1969-87, dir. publicity, 1974-87; cons. various orgns., 1988—; dir. Hatch Service Corp., 1972-87, Nat. Tank Truck Carriers, Inc., Washington, 1977-88; bd. dirs. Intermountain Tariff Bur. Inc., 1978-88, chmn., 1981-82, 1986-87; bd. dirs. Mountainwest Venture Group. Fund raiser March of Dimes, Am. Cancer Soc., Am. Heart Assn.; active senatorial campaign, 1976, gubernatorial campaign, 1984, 88, congl. campaign, 1990, 92, 94, vice chair voting dist., 1988-90, congressional capmpaing, 1994; chmn. 1990-92, chmn. party caucus legis. dist.; witness transp. com. Utah State Legislature, 1984, 85; apptd. by gov. to bd. trustees Utah Tech. Fin. Corp., 1986—, corp. sec., mem. exec. com., 1988—. Recipient service awards W. S. Hatch Co., 1971, 80; mem. Pioneer Theatre Guild, 1985—; V.I.P. capt. Easter Seal Telethon, 1989, 90, recipient Outstanding Vol. Svc. award Easter Seal Soc. Utah, 1989, 90. Mem. Nat. Tank Truck Carriers, Transp. Club Salt Lake City, Am. Trucking Assn. (public relations council), Utah Motor Transport Assn. (dir. 1982-88), Internat. Platform Assn., Beta Gamma Sigma, Phi Kappa Phi, Phi Chi Theta. Home and Office: 77 Edgecombe Dr Salt Lake City UT 84103-2219

MILLS, CELESTE LOUISE, hypnotherapist, professional magician; b. L.A., May 16, 1952; d. Emery John and Helen Louise (Bradbury) W.; m. Robert Richardson Feigel, Apr. 11, 1971 (div. 1973); m. Peter Alexander Mills, June 12, 1991. (div. 1992). BBA, Western State U., Doniphan, Mo., 1987; PhD in Religion, Universal Life Ch. Univ., 1987; grad., Hypnotism Tng. Inst., Glendale, Calif., 1990. Cert. hypnotherapist. Credit mgr. accounts receivable Gensler-Lee Diamonds, Santa Barbara, Calif., 1973-74, Terry Hinge and Hardware, Van Nuys, Calif., 1975-78; credit mgr., fin. analyst Peanut Butter Fashions, Chatsworth, Calif., 1978-82; personal mgr. Charter Mgmt. Co., Beverly Hills, Calif., 1982-83; co-owner, v.p. Noreen Jenney Communicates, Beverly Hills, 1983-85; corp. credit mgr., fin. analyst Cen. Diagnostic Lab., Tarzana, Calif., 1985-89; credit mgr., fin. analyst Metwest Clin. Lab., Inc., Tarzana, Calif., 1989-90; pvt. practice, 1990—; cons. Results Now, Inc., Tarzana, 1986-87. Prodr., host (TV) Brainstorm, 1993—. Mem. NAFE, Nat. Assn. Credit Mgmt., Credit Mgrs. Assn. So. Calif., Credit Ednl. Found., Nat. Humane Ednl. Found., Credit Mgrs. Assn. Trade Groups (bd. govs. 1988-89), Nat. Clin. Lab. Trade Group (chmn. 1988-89), Med. and Surg. Suppliers Trade Group (vice-chmn. 1988-89, chmn. 1989-90), Soc. Am. Magicians, Acad. Magical Arts, Internat. Brotherhood of Magicians, Assn. Advanced Ethical Hypnosis, Am. Coun. Hypnotist Examiners.

MILLS, DON HARPER, pathology and psychiatry educator; b. Peking, Republic of China, July 27, 1927; came to U.S., 1928; s. Clarence Alonzo and Edith Clarissa (Parrett) M.; m. Lillian Frances Snyder, June 11, 1949; children: Frances Jo, Jon Snyder. BS, U. Cin., 1950, MD, 1953; JD, U. So. Calif., 1958. Diplomate Am. Bd. Law in Medicine. Intern L.A. County Gen. Hosp., 1953-54, admitting physician, 1954-57, attending staff pathologist, 1959—; pathology fellow U. So. Calif., L.A., 1954-55, instr. pathology, 1958-62, asst. clin. prof., 1962-65, assoc. clin. prof., 1965-69, clin. prof., 1969—, clin. prof. psychiatry and behavioral sci., 1986—; asst. in pathology Hosp. Good Samatarian, L.A., 1956-65, cons. staff, 1962-72, affiliating staff, 1972-91; dep. med. examiner Office of L.A. County Med. Examiner, 1957-61; instr. legal medicine Loma Linda (Calif.) U. Sch. Medicine, 1960-66, assoc. clin. prof. humanities, 1966—; cons. HEW, 1972-73, 75-76, Dept. of Def., 1975-80; bd. dirs. Am. Bd. Law in Medicine, Inc., Chgo., 1980-86; med. dir. Profl. Risk Mgmt. Group, 1989—. Column editor Newsletter of the Long Beach Med. Assn., 1960-75, Jour. Am. Osteopathic Assn., 1965-77, Ortho Panel, 1970-78; exec. editor Trauma, 1964-88, mem. editorial bd., 1988—; mem. editorial bd. Legal Aspects of Med. Practice, 1972-90, Med. Alert Communications, 1973-75, Am. Jour. Forensic Medicine and Pathology, 1979-87, Hosp. Risk Control, 1981—; contbr. numerous articles to profl. jours. Bd. dirs. Inst. for Med. Risk Studies, 1988—. Fellow Am. Coll. Legal Medicine (pres. 1974-76, bd. govs. 1970-78, v.p. 1972-74, chmn. malpractice com. 1973-74, jour. editorial bd. 1984—), Am. Acad. Forensic Scis. (pres. 1986-87, v.p. 1984-85, exec. com. 1971-74, gen. program chmn. 1966-67, chmn. jurisprudence sect. 1966-67, 73-74, jour. editorial bd. 1965-79); mem. AMA (jour. editorial bd. 1973-77), Calif. Med. Assn., L.A. County Med. Assn., AAAS, ABA, L.A. County Bar Assn., Am. Judicature Soc., Am. Soc. Hosp. Attys., Calif. Soc. Hosp. Attys. Home: 700E Ocean Blvd Unit 2606 Long Beach CA 90802-5039 Office: 911 N Studebaker Rd Ste 250 Long Beach CA 90815-4900

MILLS, JONATHAN A., microbiologist, educator; b. Columbus, Ohio, May 10, 1960; s. Paul Wynce and Rosemary A. (Vowell) M.; m. Sharon Kay Baird, Feb. 11, 1984; children: Taylor Katherine, Brooke Paterson. BS in Microbiology, Colo. State U., 1982; MS in Biology, Cath. U. Am., 1988, PhD in Biology, 1992. Lab. tech. U.S. Army, Utah, 1983; rsch. assoc. Walter Reed Army Inst. Rsch., Washington, 1984-91; postdoctoral fellow and instr. Colo. State U., Ft. Collins, 1992-94; sr. rsch. sci. Gen-Probe, San Diego, 1995—. Contbr. articles to profl. publs. With U.S. Army, 1984-87. Mem. AAAS, Am. Soc. Microbiology, Delta Upsilon. Republican. Episcopalian. Office: Gen-Probe Dept Therapeutics 9880 Campus Point Dr San Diego CA 92121-1514

MILLS, JOSEPH LOREN, vascular surgeon, educator; b. San Francisco, May 26, 1955; s. Loren F. and Margaret (Griesser) M.; m. Margaret Schneider, Jan. 25, 1954; children: Joseph Jr., Daniel, Andrew. BS cum laude, Georgetown U., 1977, MD cum laude, 1981. Diplomate Nat. Bd. Med. Examiners, Am. Bd. Surgery, cert. spl. qualifications gen. vascular surgery Am. Bd. Surgery, cert. added qualifications surg. critical care Am. Bd. Surgery; lic. physician, Fla., Oreg., Ariz. Intern in gen. surgery Wilford Hall USAF Med. Ctr., Lackland AFB, Tex., 1981-82, resident in gen. surgery, 1982-85, chief resident gen. surgery, 1985-86; resident in vascular surgery Oreg. Health Scis. U., Portland, 1986-87; asst. chief vascular surgery Wilford Hall USAF Med. Ctr., Lackland AFB, 1987-89, chief vascular surgery, 1989-92, asst. chmn. dept. gen. surgery, 1991-92; chief vascular surgery James A. Haley Vets. Hosp., Tampa, Fla., 1992—, Tampa Gen. Hosp., 1992-94; chief vascular surgery, fellowship program dir. U. Ariz., Tucson, 1994—; asst. clin. prof. surgery F. Edward Hebert Sch. Medicine, Uniformed Svcs. Sch. Health Scis., Bethesda, Md., 1988-91, assoc. prof. surgery, 1991-92; dir. quality assurance program Peripheral Vascular Lab., Wilford Hall USAF Med. Ctr., 1987-92, mem. ultrasound com., 1990-92; assoc. prof. surgery U. South Fla. Sch. Medicine, 1992-94, Ariz. Coll. Medicine, 1994—; mem. grad. edn. selection bd., cons. peripheral vascular surgery USAF, 1989-92; mem. utilization rev. com. James A. Haley VA Hosp., 1992—; mem. pharmacy and therapeutics com. Tampa Gen. Hosp., 1992—. Guest editor: Seminars in Vascular Surgery, 1993; contbg. editor: Year Book of Vascular Surgery, 1993; contbr. chpts. to books, articles to profl. jours. Maj. USAF, 1981-92. Recipient Surgeon Gen.'s award, 1985, clin. surgeon's award, 1987, award for excellence for clin. rsch., 1987; Edwin J. Wylie traveling fellow, 1993-94. Fellow ACS (mem. Fla. chpt.), Southwestern Surg. Congress; mem. AMA, Internat. Soc. for Cardiovascular Surgery, So. Assn. for Vascular Surgery, Soc. Vascular Surgery, Soc. Air Force Clin. Surgeons, Mil. Vascular Surgery Soc., Peripheral Vascular Surgery Soc. (councilor at large 1991-94, program com. 1990-93, pres.-elect 1994), Assn. for Acad. Surgery, San Antonio Vascular Surgery Soc. (treas. 1988-91), San Antonio Surg. Soc., Hillsborough County Med. Assn., Sigma Xi, Alpha Omega Alpha. Republican. Roman Catholic. Home: 4201 N Circulo Manzanillo Tucson AZ 85715-1881 Office: Univ Ariz Health Sci Ctr 1501 N Campbell Ave Tucson AZ 85724-0001

MILLS, LAWRENCE, lawyer, business and transportation consultant; b. Salt Lake City, Aug. 15, 1932; s. Samuel L. and Beth (Neilson) M. BS, U. Utah, 1955, JD, 1956. Bar: Utah 1956, ICC 1961, U.S. Supreme Ct. 1963. With W.S. Hatch Co. Inc., Woods Cross, Utah, 1947-89, gen. mgr., 1963-89, v.p., 1970-89, also dir.; bd. dirs. Nat. Tank Truck Carriers, Inc., Washington, 1963—, pres., 1974-75, chmn. bd., 1975-76; mem. motor carrier adv. com. Utah State Dept. Transp., 1979—; keynote speaker Rocky Mountain Safety Suprs. Conf., 1976. Contbr. articles to legal publs. Del. to County and State Convs., Utah, 1970-72; v.p. Utah Safety Coun., 1979-82, bd. dirs., 1979—, pres., 1983-84; mem. Utah Gov's Adv. Com. on Small Bus.; capt. Easter Seal Telethon, 1989, 90; state vice chmn. High Frontier, 1987—; mem. adv. com. Utah State Indsl. Commn., 1988—, chmn. com. studying health care cost containment and reporting requirements 1990—. Recipient Safety Dir. award Nat. Tank Carriers Co., 1967, Outstanding Svc. and Contbn. award, 1995, Trophy award W.S. Hatch Co., 1975, Disting. Svc. award Utah State Indsl. Commn., 1992, Outstanding Svc. award Utah Safety Coun., 1994. Mem. Salt Lake County Bar Assn., Utah Motor Transport Assn. (dir. 1967—, pres. 1974-76, Outstanding Achievement Award 1989), Utah Hwy. Users Assn. (dir. 1981—), Indsl. Rels. Coun. (dir. 1974—), Salt Lake City C. of C., U.S. Jaycees (life Senator 1969—, ambassador 1977—, pres. Utah Senate 1979-80, Henry Giessenbier fellow 1989), Nat. Petroleum Coun., Utah Associated Gen. Contractors (assoc. 1975-77, 88—), Silver Tank Club. Home and Office: 77 Edgecombe Dr Salt Lake City UT 84103-2219

MILLS, PAUL CHADBOURNE, museum director; b. Seattle, Sept. 24, 1924. Student, Reed Coll., 1945-48; BA, U. Wash., 1953; MA, U. Calif., Berkeley, 1961; PhD (hon.), Calif. Coll. Arts and Crafts, 1971. Reporter Bellevue Am., Wash., 1948-51; asst. curator Henry Gallery, U. Wash., 1952-53; curator art Oakland Mus., Calif., 1953-70; v.p. Western Mus. Conf., 1956, 59; dir. Santa Barbara Mus. Art, 1970-82, New Glory Bicentennial Flag Hist. and Design Project, 1974-77; exec. dir. Santa Barbara Flag Project, 1977—; bd. dirs. Santa Barbara Trust for Hist. Preservation, 1992—, 1st v.p., 1994. Author: The New Figurative Art of David Park, 1988, David Park Scroll, 1989; art editor: O, California!, 1988, 89; publisher The California Missions of Edwin Deakin, 1966, Colonial and Revolutionary Era Flags, 1975, (with Mark Adams), 1984. Bd. dirs. Santa Barbara Downtown Orgn., 1990—; Air Fair Flags ptnr., Santa Barbara, 1983—. Ford Found. fellow, 1960-61; grantee Spain, 1977-79. Mem. Am. Assn. Mus., Am. Assn. Art Mus. Dirs. (hon. mem., trustee 1971-72, sec. 1973), N.Am. Vexillological Assn., Western Assn. Art Mus. (v.p. 1956-57, treas. 1971-72, trustee 1979), Heraldry Soc., Santa Barbara Hist. Soc., Santa Barbara Geneal. Soc. Home: 314 E Figueroa St Santa Barbara CA 93101-1413

MILLS, ROGER E., food products executive; b. 1935. Exec. v.p. Mills Distbg. Co., Inc., Salinas, Calif., 1958—; ptnr. Mivco Packing Co., Salinas, Calif., 1973—. Office: Mills Distributing Co Inc 375 W Market St Salinas CA 93901-1423*

MILLS, SHERRY RAE, training and conference planner; b. Colorado Springs, Colo., Apr. 3, 1940; d. Ray Edwin and Lorena Marguerite (Ferguson) Gregory; m. Ronald Keith Mills, July 22, 1962; children: Tracy Rae, Darren Keith. B in Music Edn., U. Colo., 1962; MA, U. Colo., Colorado Springs, 1979. Tchr. Harrison Dist. 2, Colorado Springs, 1962-66; music tchr. Rocky Mountain Rehab. Ctr., Colorado Springs, 1969-72; music specialist Colorado Springs Dist. 11, Colorado Springs, 1972-75; pres., exec. dir. Colo. Arts for the Handicapped, Colorado Springs, 1975-85; owner, gen. ptnr. Creative Tng. Assocs., Colorado Springs, 1985—; presented papers Colo. State Conf. of the Coun. for Exceptional Children, 1976, 77, 78, 79, 80, Chgo., 1976; conducted numerous workshops for Mile High Consortium, Denver, 1976, Head Start, Colorado Springs, 1977, Nat. Assn. of Music Therapy, Anaheim, Calif., 1977, Butte (Mont.) Silverbow Anti-Poverty Coun.-Head Start, 1978, Nat. Conf. for Citizens with Down Syndrome, Boston, 1976, St. Louis, 1978, Washington, 1987, Fla. Learning Resource Sys., Pensacola, 1980, Pueblo Sch. Dist. 60 Music Tchrs., 1979, Internat. Conf. Coun. Exceptional Children, Dallas, 1979, Phila., 1980, Houston, 1982; instr. U. Colo., Colorado Springs, Chapman Coll., Pikes Peak C.C., Adams State Coll., Ft. Lewis Coll., Morgan C.C., Trinidad State Jr. Coll., Mesa State Coll., Aurora U., New Berlin, Wis.; leader workshops nat. leadership conf. Am. Soc. Tng. and Devel., 1991, 92; presenter in field. Author: Fun with Instruments: An Instrumental Method for the Special Child, 1976-78, A Source Guide for the Special Child: Learning Activities and Music, 1978; contbr. articles to profl. jours. Vol. grant writer Colo. Springs Police Dept. Grantee Colo. Coun. for Exceptional Children Dept. Edn., 1980-81, 81-82, Found. for Exceptional Children, 1981, Arts for the Handicapped program. Mem. ASTD, ASCD, ASTD (treas. 1988, v.p. 1989, pres. 1990, 91, chair region VI conf. 1991, rep. region VI coun. 1991, 92, region VI rep. nat chpt. award com. 1993, nat. awards com. 1994, asst. regional dir. Train Am.'s Workforce program 1992, v.p. membership 1994, 95, Nat. Staff Devel. Coun., Meeting Planners and Conf. Suupliers of So. Colo., Meeting Planners Assn. Colorado Springs (treas. 1989, pres. 1990, immediate past pres. 1991, conf. chair 1990-91, 1st v.p. 1992, pres. 1993, 2d v.p. 1994, Meeting Planner of Yr. award 1990), Coun. for Exceptional Children (sec. chpt. 403 1976-77, pres. elect 1977-78, pres. 1978-79, membership chair 1984-88; state chmn. com. for direct svc. to children 1977-79, v.p. Colo. fedn., 1979-80, pres. elect 1980-81, pres. 1981-82, immediate past pres. 1982-83, chmn. grants com. 1983-86), Down Syndrome Congress, Am. Assn. Mental Deficiency, Found. for Exceptional Children, Internat. Platform Assn., Music Edn. for Handicapped. Baptist. Home: 2220 Glenwood Cir

Colorado Springs CO 80909-1555 Office: Creative Tng Assocs PO Box 25806 Colorado Springs CO 80936-5806

MILLS, THOMAS COOKE, psychiatrist; b. San Francisco, Nov. 24, 1955; s. Willard Cooke and Billie Dee (Hunt) M. BS, MIT, 1977; MD, U. Ill., Chgo., 1981; MPH, U. Calif., Berkeley, 1991. Diplomate Am. Bd. Psychiatry and Neurology. Resident in psychiatry U. Calif., San Francisco, 1981-85, asst. clin. prof., 1985-91, assoc. clin. prof., 1991—; med. dir. Jail Psychiat. Svcs., San Francisco, 1985-88; pvt. practice San Francisco, 1985-88; staff psychiatrist Dept. Vets. Affairs, San Francisco, 1988-93, psychiat. authorizing physician, 1991-93; postdoctoral fellow U. Calif., Berkeley, 1990-91. Fellow NIMH, 1990-91. Mem. Am. Psychiat. Assn., No. Calif. Psychiat. Soc. Office: PO Box 460520 San Francisco CA 94146-0520

MILLSAPS, RITA RAE, elementary school educator; b. Magdalena, N.Mex., Jan. 14, 1937; d. Samuel Thomas Martin and Geneva Opal (Nicholson) Martin Freeman; m. Daryl Ray Millsaps, June 26, 1955; children: Michael (dec.), Kathleen, Marian, Larry. Student, Delta Community Coll., 1981-82; BA, Calif. State U., Sacramento, 1986, MEd in Curriculum and Instrn., 1993. Cert. elem. educator, Calif. Mem. ASCD, Internat. Reading Assn. Home: PO Box 1413 San Andreas CA 95249-1413

MILNER, JOE W., journalism educator; b. Winnsboro, Tex., Jan. 2, 1929; s. O.K. and Annie (Boyd) M.; children: Derek Jeffrey, Brent Martin. BS, East Tex. State U., 1954; MA, U. Okla., 1955; EdD, U. Wyo., 1963. Reporter Commerce (Tex.) Daily Jour., 1947-49; reporter Dallas Times Herald, 1949-51, Greenville (Tex.) Herald, 1953-54; journalism instr. Eastern N.Mex. U., Portales, 1955-57; head journalism dept. Miss. State Coll. for Women, Columbus, 1957-58; prof. U. Wyo., Laramie, 1960-67; dir. Journalism Sch. Ariz. State U., Tempe, 1970-79, prof., 1967—; vis. prof. Angelo State U., San Angelo, Tex., 1992-93. Editor Wyo. Press, Laramie, 1960-67, Journalism Roundtable, 1965-73. Recipient Disting. Newspaper Advisor award, Nat. Coun. Coll. Advisors, 1965. Mem. Soc. Profl. Journalists, Nat. Conf. Editl. Writers. Home: 2095 E Manhatton Dr Tempe AZ 85282-5967 Office: Sch of Journalism Ariz State U Tempe AZ 85287

MILNES, ROBERT WINSTON, artist, educator; b. Washington, DC, Apr. 1, 1948; s. James Earl and Virginia Rose (Murphy) M.; m. Karen Sidney Greenebaum, May 22, 1988. BA, Claremont Men's Coll., Claremont, Calif., 1970; MFA, U. Wash., 1974; PhD, U. Pitts., 1987. Instr. ceramics Cornish Sch. of Allied Arts, Seattle, 1971-74; prof. Art Dept. Edinboro (Pa.) U., Pa., 1974-87; chmn. Art Dept. Edinboro (Pa.) U., 1980-86; dir. Sch. of Art La. State U., Baton Rouge, 1987-90; dir. Sch. of Art and Design, San Jose (Calif.) State U., 1990—; cons. Arts. Coun., Baton Rouge, 1989; higher edn. rep. Pa. Art Edn. Assn., Harrisburg, 1987. One-man show Exhbn. Cross Creek Gallery, L.A., 1986, Theo Portnoy Gallery, N.Y.C., 1980, Baton Rouge Gallery, 1990. Chmn. steering com. City Nat. Bank Coll. Art Competition, Baton Rouge, 1989; panelist for grants La. Divsn. Arts, Baton Rouge, 1988, Office Cultural Affairs, San Jose, 1994. Mem. Nat. Assn. Schs. of Arts and Design (accreditation commn. 1990—), Coll. Art Assn., Nat. Coun. Art Adminstrs. (pres. 1991-93), Arts Coun. Santa Clara County (v.p. 1993—). Democrat. Episcopalian. Home: 1426 Camino Robles Way San Jose CA 95120

MILONE, ANTHONY M., bishop; b. Omaha, Sept. 24, 1932. Grad., North American Coll. (Rome). Ordained priest Roman Catholic Ch., 1957. Ordained titular bishop of Plestia and aux. bishop Diocese of Omaha, 1982; apptd. bishop Mont. Diocese, Great Falls-Billings, 1987—. Office: PO Box 1399 121 23rd St S Great Falls MT 59403*

MILONE, EUGENE FRANK, astronomer, educator; b. N.Y.C., June 26, 1939; arrived in Can., 1971; s. Frank Louis and Vera Christine (Joeckle) M.; m. Helen Catherine Louise (Ligor), Mar. 1, 1959; children: Bartholomew Vincenzo Llambro, Marie Christina Milone Jack. AB, Columbia U., 1961; MSc, Yale U., 1963, PhD, 1967. Astronomer space sci. div. rocket spectroscopy br. Naval Rsch. Lab., Washington, 1967-84; asst. prof. Gettysburg (Pa.) Coll., 1968-71; asst. prof. dept. physics and astronomy U. Calgary, Alta., Can., 1971-75, assoc. prof., 1976-81, prof., 1981—; co-dir. Rothney Astrophys. Obs., 1975—; Organizer Internat. Symposium on the Origins, Evolution and Destinies of Binary Stars in Clusters, U. Calgary, June 1995; chair rsch. grants com. U. Calgary, 1995—. Author: Infrared Extinction and Standardization, 1989, Challenges of Astronomy, 1991; editor: Light Curve Modeling of Eclipsing Binary Stars, 1993; contbr. over 150 articles to profl. jours. Elected mem. com. for coll. and univ. svcs. Evang. Luth. Ch. in Can., Synod of Alberta and the Territories, Edmonton, Alta., 1989-93. Operating and Equipment grantee Natural Scis. and Engring. Rsch. Coun. Can., 1972—; Killam Resident fellow Killam Found. U. Calgary, 1982, 88. Mem. Internat. Astron. Union (mem. organizing com., commn. 25 1985-91, 94—), Am. Astron. Soc. (chmn. local organizing com. Calgary meeting 1981), Can. Astron. Soc., Sigma Xi (pres. U. Calgary chpt. 1979-80). Democrat. Lutheran. Home: 1031 Edgemont Rd NW, Calgary, AB Canada T3A 2J5 Office: U Calgary Dept Physics and Astronomy, 2500 University Dr NW, Calgary, AB Canada T2N 1N4

MILOS, MARILYN FAYRE, health organization administrator; b. San Mateo, Calif., Mar. 22, 1940; d. Edgar Wilson and Eleanor Grace (Zimmerman) Mumford; m. Joseph Paul Edmiston, Jan. 30, 1958 (div. 1964); children: Michael Paul, Troy Christian, Kate JoAnn; m. Matthew John Milos, Apr. 7, 1979 (dec.); 1 child, Timothy Mark. AS, Coll. Marin, 1979. RN. Charge nurse Marin Gen. Hosp., Greenbrae, Calif., 1979-80, staff nurse, 1980-85; exec. dir. Nat. Orgn. Circumcision Info. Resource Ctrs., San Anselmo, Calif., 1986—; coord. 1st, 2d and 3d Internat. Symposium on Circumcision, Anaheim, Calif., San Francisco, College Park, Md., 1989, 91, 94. Author, producer, dir. (videotape) Informed Consent, 1982; author: Circumcision Why?, 1985, Answers to Your Questions About Your Young Son's Intact Penis, 1994, also other articles; editor: (documentary) Crimes of Genital Mutilation, (newsletter) NOCIRC Newsletter. Bd. dirs. In Spirit, Woodacre, Calif., 1986-95. Recipient Maureen Ricke award Calif. Nurses' Assn., 1988. Mem. NOW, Internat. Childbirth Edn. Assn., Assn. Pre- and Perinatal Psychology and Health, World Assn. Perinatal Medicine. Office: NOCIRC Resource Ctrs PO Box 2512 San Anselmo CA 94979-2512

MILOSZ, CZESLAW, poet, author, educator; b. Lithuania, June 30, 1911; came to U.S., 1960, naturalized, 1970; s. Aleksander and Weronika (Kunat) M. M Juris, U. Wilno, Lithuania, 1934; LittD (hon.), U. Mich., 1977; honoris causa, Harvard U., 1989, Jagellonian U., Poland, 1989, U. Rome, Italy, 1992. Programmer Polish Nat. Radio, 1935-39; diplomatic service Polish Fgn. Affairs Ministry, Warsaw, 1945-50; vis. lectr. U. Calif., Berkeley, 1960-61; prof. Slavic langs. and lits. U. Calif., 1961-78, prof. emeritus, 1978—. Author: The Captive Mind, 1953, Native Realm, 1968, Post-War Polish Poetry, 1965, The History of Polish Literature, 1969, Selected Poems, 1972, Bells in Winter, 1978, The Issa Valley, 1981, Separate Notebooks, 1984, The Land of Ulro, 1984, The Unattainable Earth, 1985, Collected Poems, 1988, Provinces, 1991, Beginning With My Streets, 1992, A Year of the Hunter, 1994, Facing the River, 1995. Recipient Prix Littéraire Européen Les Guildes du Livre, Geneva, 1953, Neustadt Internat. prize for lit. U. Okla., 1978, citation U. Calif., Berkeley, 1978, Nobel prize for lit., 1980, Nat. Medal of Arts, 1990; Nat. Culture Fund fellow, 1934-35; Guggenheim fellow, 1976. Mem. AAAS, Am. Acad. Arts and Scis., Am. Acad and Inst. Arts and Letters, Polish Inst. Letters and Scis. in Am., PEN Club in Exile. Office: U Calif Dept Slavic Langs Lits Berkeley CA 94720

MILTON, HENRY BENFORD HOLLIS, automotive executive; b. River Rouge, Mich., Nov. 28, 1961; s. Samuel Byron Jr. and Veronica Joyce (Hollis) M. AB in Philosophy, U. Mich., 1984; MBA in Mktg., Atlanta U., 1986. Minority peer advisor U. Mich., Ann Arbor, 1983-84; adminstrv. intern Milton Cmty. Hosp., River Rouge, 1984-85, CEO, 1986-88; acctg. and bus. comm. instr. Pontiac (Mich.) Bus. Inst., 1987-88; customer svc. rep. Ford Motor Co., Milpitas, Calif., 1988-89; parts and svc. zone mgr. customer svc. divsn. Ford Motor Co., Pleasanton, Calif., 1989—; ski instr. Blizzard Ski Sch., Bloomfield Hills, Mich., 1980-88. Vol. Glide Meml. Meth. Ch., San Francisco, 1994; bd. dirs. Metro Detroit Hosp. Svcs., Inc., 1986-88, Milton Cmty. Hosp., River Rouge, 1986-88. Mem. Alpha Phi Alpha (treas. 1983-84, historian, fin. sec. 1982-83). Democrat. Roman Catholic. Home: 1458 Madison St Apt 305 Oakland CA 94612-4333 Office: FCSD San Francisco PO Box 9010 Pleasanton CA 94566-9010

MIMS, EDWARD TROW, electronics industry executive; b. Pittsburgh, Calif., Feb. 29, 1948; s. Arthur Trow and Marjorie (Fisher) M.; m. Verna Lynne Daubert, Jan. 23, 1981; 1 child, Matthew Edward. Student, U. Tex., 1966-70. Profl. baseball player Houston Astros Sports Assn., 1970-75; dist. mgr. Team Electronics, Mpls., 1976-80; regional mgr. Bose Corp., Framingham, Mass., 1980-85, mgr. nat. field sales, 1985-86, mgr. nat. accounts, 1986-90, dir. spl. markets, 1990-91, dir. sales N.Am., 1991-93; dir. sales N.Am. Cerwin-Vega! Inc., Simi Valley, Calif., 1993—.

MINAMI, ROBERT YOSHIO, artist, graphic designer; b. Seattle, May 1, 1919; s. Kichitaro and Suma (Fujita) M.; m. Shizu Tashiro, May 30, 1953; 1 child, Ken. Artist; student, Art Inst., Chgo., 1957, Am. Acad. Art, Chgo., 1980-81. Graphic artist Filmack Studios, Chgo., 1945-48, S. Taylor & Leavitt Assocs., Chgo., 1949-50; head graphic designer NBC-TV, Chgo., 1950-82; fine artist Robert Minami's Studio, Oceanside, Calif., 1983—; artist Goodman Theatre Design, Chgo., 1955-56. Active Supporters for City Couns., Oceanside, 1984—. Recipient Merit award Artist Guild Chgo., 1956, People's Choice award Carlsbad Oceanside Art League, 1986, Dick Blick award, 1992, 1st place award Mixed Media Collage, 1993, Nat. Watercolor award Watercolor West, 1994. Mem. San Diego Watercolor Soc., United Scenic Artists (life), Am. Fine Art Connection, San Diego Art Inst., Nat. Watercolor Soc. (assoc.), Watercolor West Juried Assn.

MINARD, EUGENE WATKINS, retired psychiatrist; b. Villisca, Iowa, Mar. 28, 1924; s. Jess Ernest and Iva Eda (Watkins) M.; m. Joyce Almira Smith, Dec. 13, 1947 (div. May 1966); children: Diane, Scott, Kurt, Mark, Elizabeth; m. Doris Marie Cameron-Minard, July 6, 1982. BA, Stanford (Calif.) U., 1946, MD, 1949; MPH, U. Calif., Berkeley, 1956. Diplomate Am. Bds. Preventive Medicine, Psychiatry and Neurology; lic. Calif., Oreg., Wash. Rotating intern San Francisco City and County Hosp., 1948-49; psychiatric resident VA Hosp., Palo Alto, Calif., 1949-50; with U.S. Army, 1943-46, capt. psychiatrist and preventive medicine officer, 1951-53; public health resident San Joaquin Local Health Dist., Stockton, Calif., 1953-55; asst. dir. pub. health County San Bernardino, 1956-59; pvt. practice San Bernardino, 1959-60, 63-70; staff psychiatrist, psychiatric resident Patton State Hosp., San Bernardino, Calif., 1960-63; pvt. practice San Diego, 1970-80; staff psychiatrist Northwest Permanente, Portland, Oreg., 1980-82; psychiatrist II Western State Hosp., Ft. Steilacoom, Wash., 1982; staff psychiatrist Dammasch State Hosp., Wilsonville, Oreg., 1982-84; pvt. practice Portland, 1983-86, Salem, Oreg., 1985-89; supervising and staff psychiatrist Dammasch State Hosp., 1989-94; cons. State Vocat. Rehab. Dept., Family Svcs. Agy., Calif. Medi-Cal Program, Mental Health Assn., San Bernardino, 1963-70; part-time San Diego County Mental Health Svcs., Douglas Young Clinic, State of Calif. Medi-Cal, 1970-80; mem. mental health adv. bd. Oreg. Advocacy Ctr., Portland, 1986-89; mem. provider panel Capitol health Care, Salem. Disability Determinations, Oreg. and Wash. Presenter and author in field. Capt. USAF, 1951-53. Mem. Am. Psychiatric Assn., Am. Neuropsychiatric Assn., Am. Acad. of Psychaitry and the Law, Am. Assn. Community Psychiatrists, World Psychiatric Asns., World Fedn. for Mental Haleth, Oreg. Psychiatric Assn., North Pacific Soc. for Neurology and Psychaitry, Oreg. Med. Assn., Clackamas County Med. Assn., Amnesty Internat., Internat. Physicians for Prevention of Nuclear War.

MINDELL, EARL LAWRENCE, nutritionist, author; b. St. Boniface, Man., Can., Jan. 20, 1940; s. William and Minerva Sybil (Galsky) M.; came to U.S., 1965, naturalized, 1972; BS in Pharmacy, N.D. State U., 1963; PhD in Nutrition, Pacific We. U., 1985; m. Gail Andrea Jaffe, May 16, 1971; children: Evan Louis-Ashley, Alanna Dayan. Pres. Adanac Mgmt. Inc., 1979—, Compact Disc-Count, Inc.; instr. Dale Carnegie course; lectr. on nutrition, radio and TV. Mem. Beverly Hills, Rancho Park, Western Los Angeles (dir.) regional chambers commerce, Calif., Am. pharm. assns., Am. Acad. Gen. Pharm. Practice, Am. Inst. for History of Pharmacy, Am. Nutrition Soc., Internat. Coll. Applied Nutrition, Nutrition Found., Nat. Health Fedn., Am. Dieticians Assn., Orthomolecular Med. Assn., Internat. Acad. Preventive Medicine. Clubs: City of Hope, Masons, Shriners. Author: Earl Mindell's Vitamin Bible, Parents Nutrition Bible, Earl Mindell's Quick and Easy Guide to Better Health, Earl Mindell's Pill Bible, Earl Mindell's Shaping Up with Vitamins, Earl Mindell's Safe Eating, Earl Mindell's Herb Bible, Newsletter Joy of Health Earl Mindell's Food as Medicine, Earl Mindell's Soy Miracle, 1995; columnist Let's Live mag., The Vitamin Supplement (Can.), The Vitamin Connection (U.K.), Healthy N' Fit; contbr. articles on nutrition to profl. jours. Home: 244 S El Camino Dr Beverly Hills CA 90212-3809 Office: 10750 Beverly Dr Beverly Hills CA 90212-3020

MINDEN, R. DOYLE, university administrator; b. Storm Lake, Iowa, May 7, 1933; s. Clarence and Alma (Sievers) M.; m. Marilyn L. Anderson, Aug. 16, 1953; children: Steven, Sandra, Constance. BJ, U. Mo., 1957. News editor Laurens (Iowa) Sun, 1957-59; assoc. editor Northwestern Banker, Des Moines, 1959-64, Underwriters Rev., Des Moines, 1959-64; dir. pub. rels. Drake U., Des Moines, 1964-68; dir. univ. rels. U. of the Pacific, Stockton, Calif., 1968—. Author, editor: Management by Objectives for Public Relations, 1972. Del. Rep. Party, Des Moines, 1966. Cpl. U.S. Army, 1953-55. Mem. Pub. Rels. Soc. Am. (accredited), Sacramento Pub. Rels. Soc. Am. (pres. 1970-71), Oakland-East Bay Pub. Rels. Soc. Am. (v.p. 1980-81), Rotary Internat. (bd. dirs. 1981-85, Rotarian of Yr. 1984). Home: 3308 Riverton Way Stockton CA 95219-3136 Office: U of the Pacific 3601 Pacific Cir Stockton CA 95211-0110

MINELLA, DAVID A., investment company executive; b. 1953. Nat. sales mgr., contr. Putnam Group, Boston, 1975-87; pres. GT Global Fin. Svcs., San Francisco, 1987—. Office: GT Global Fin Svcs 50 California St Fl 27 San Francisco CA 94111*

MINER, JOHN EDWARD, city manager; b. Wabash, Ind., Feb. 6, 1937; s. Carlos Monroe and Mary Rebecca (Hoover) M.; m. Sharon Rose Craft, Mar. 24, 1961; children: Clarla Marie, Carla Marie Crowfoot, Heather Lynet. BS, Manchester Coll., North Manchester, Ind., 1962, Ind. U., 1972; MPA, Ind. U., 1978. Reg. adminstr. Ind. Criminal Justice, Lafayette, Ind., 1970-73; chief rsch. Allen County Sheriff's Dept., Ft. Wayne, Ind., 1973-75; city adminstr. City of Wabash, Ind., 1976-79; exec. budget analyst State of Ariz., Phoenix, 1980; prof. pub. adminstrn. Western Internat. U., Phoenix, 1981-83; city mgr. City of Benson, Ariz., 1981-84; pres., chief exec. officer Municipal MegeTrends, 1984—; govt./environ. affairs specialist Laurent Bouillet-Howard, Phoenix, Paris, 1985-90; city mgr. City of Quartzsite, Ariz., 1990-93; cmty. devel. dir. Town of Camp Verde, Ariz., 1993—. With USMC, 1957-59. Gov.'s fellow in pub. adminstrn., State of Ind., 1976-78; recipient Award of Excellence in Energy Conservation, Govt., State of Ariz., 1983. Mem. Masons, Elks, Am. Criminal Justice Assn. Home: 2311 W Tuckey Ln Phoenix AZ 85015-1041

MINER, JOHN RONALD, bioresource engineer; b. Scottsburg, Ind., July 4, 1938; s. Gerald Lamont and Alice Mae (Murphy) M.; m. Betty Katheron Emery, Aug. 4, 1963; children—Saralena Marie, Katherine Alice, Frederick Gerald. B.S. in Chem. Engring, U. Kans., 1959; M.S.E. in San. Engring, U. Mich., 1960; Ph.D. in Chem. Engring. and Microbiology, Kans. State U., 1967. Lic. profl. engr., Kans., Oreg. San. engr. Kans. Dept. Health, Topeka, 1959-64; grad. research asst. Kans. State U., Manhattan, 1964-67; asst. prof. agrl. engring. Iowa State U., 1967-71, assoc. prof., 1971-72; assoc. prof. agrl. engring. Oreg. State U., 1972-76, prof., 1976—, head dept., 1976-86, acting assoc. dean Coll. Agrl. Sci., 1983-84, assoc. dir. Office Internat. Research and Devel., 1986-90, extension water quality specialist, 1991—; environ. engr. FAO of UN, Singapore, 1980-81; internat. cons.; cons. to livestock feeding ops., agrl. devel. firms. Co-author book on livestock waste mgmt.; author 3 books of children's sermons; contbr. numerous articles on livestock prodn., pollution control, control of odors associated with livestock prodn. to profl. publs. Mem. Am. Soc. Agrl. Engrs. (bd. dirs. 1985-87), Water Pollution Control Fedn., Sigma Xi, Gamma Sigma Delta, Alpha Epsilon, Tau Beta Pi. Presbyterian. Office: Oreg State U Dept Bioresource Engring Corvallis OR 97331

MINES, MICHAEL, lawyer; b. Seattle, May 4, 1929; s. Henry Walker and Dorothy Elizabeth (Bressler) M.; m. Phyllis Eastham, Aug. 24, 1957; children: Linda Mines Elliott, Sandra, Diane Paull, Michael Lister. Student Whitman Coll., 1947-49; BA, U. Wash., 1951, JD, 1954. Bar: Wash. 1954, U.S. Dist. Ct. (we. dist.) Wash. 1957, U.S. Dist. Ct. Mont. 1970, U.S. Ct. Appeals (9th cir.) 1961, U.S. Supreme Ct. Assoc. Skeel, McKelvy, Henke, Evenson & Uhlman, Seattle, 1956-66, ptnr., 1966-68, Hullin, Roberts, Mines, Fite & Riveland, Seattle, 1968-75, Skeel, McKelvy, Henke, Evenson & Betts, Seattle, 1975-79, Betts, Patterson & Mines, Seattle, 1978—. Moderator Wash.-No. Idaho conf. United Ch. of Christ, 1975-76. With U.S. Army, 1954-56. Mem. ABA, Wash. State Bar Assn., Seattle-King Bar Assn., Am. Coll. Trial Lawyers (state chair 1982-83, Internat. Assn. Def. Counsel, Wash. Assn. Def. Counsel (pres. 1971-72), Internat. Acad. Trial Lawyers (bd. dirs. 1991—), Def. Rsch. Inst., U. Wash. Law Sch. Alumni Assn. (trustee, pres. bd. dirs. 1995—). Home: 2474 Crestmont Pl W Seattle WA 98199-3714 Office: Betts Patterson Mines PS 800 Financial Ctr 1215 4th Ave Seattle WA 98161-1001

MINETA, NORMAN YOSHIO, congressman; b. San Jose, Calif., Nov. 12, 1931; s. Kay Kunisaku and Kane (Watanabe) M.; m. Danealia; children: David, K., Stuart S. B.S., U. Calif.-Berkeley, 1953; D of Pub. Svc., Santa Clara U., 1989; HHD (hon.), Rust Coll., 1993. Agt./broker Mineta Ins. Agy., San Jose, 1956-89; mem. adv. bd. Bank of Tokyo in Calif., 1961-75; mem. San Jose City Council, 1967-71; vice mayor City of San Jose, 1969-71, mayor, 1971-75; mem. 94th-104th Congresses from 13th (now 15th) Calif. dist., 1975—; subcom. surface transp., 1989-92, former dep. Dem. whip, ranking minority mem. transp. and infrastructure com.; chmn. fin. com. Santa Clara County (Calif.) Council Chs., 1960-62; commr. San Jose Human Relations Commn., 1962-64, San Jose Housing Authority, 1966—. Precinct chmn. Community Theater Bond Issue, 1964; mem. spl. gifts com. Santa Clara County council Boy Scouts Am., 1967; sec. Santa Clara County Grand Jury, 1964; bd. dirs. Wesley Found., San Jose State Coll., 1956-58, Pacific Neighbors, Community Council Cen. Santa Clara County, Japan Soc., San Francisco, Santa Clara County chpt. NCCJ, Mexican Am. Community Services Agy.; mem. exec. bd. No. Calif.-Western Nev. dist. council Japanese Am. Citizens League, 1960-62, pres. San Jose chpt., 1957-59; bd. regents Smithsonian Instn., 1979—; chmn. Smithsonian vis. com. for Freer Gallery, 1981—; mem. bd. regents Santa Clara U. Served to lt. AUS, 1954-56. Mem. Greater San Jose C. of C., Nat. Assn. Indsl. Ins. Agts., Calif. Assn. Indsl. Ins. Agts., San Jose Assn. Ind. Ins. Agts. (dir. 1960-62), North San Jose Optimists Club (pres. 1956-58), Jackson-Taylor Bus. and Profl. Assn. (dir. 1963). Methodist. Office: US Ho of Reps 2221 Rayburn HOB Washington DC 20515*

MINGER, TERRELL JOHN, management company executive; b. Canton, Ohio, Oct. 7, 1942; s. John Wilson and Margaret Rose M.; m. Judith R. Arnold, Aug. 7, 1965; 1 child, Gabriella Sophia. BA, Baker U., 1966; MPA, Kans. U., 1969; Urban Exec. Program, MIT, 1975; Loeb fellow Harvard U., 1976-77; Exec. Devel. Program, Stanford U., 1979; MBA, U. Colo., 1983. Asst. dir. admissions Baker U., 1966-67; asst. city mgr. City of Boulder, Colo., 1968-69; city mgr. City of Vail, Colo., 1969-79; pres., chief exec. officer Whistler Village Land Co., Vancouver, B.C., Can., 1979-81; v.p., gen. mgr. Cumberland S.W. Inc., Denver, 1981-83; exec. asst., dep. chief of staff to Gov. Colo., 1983-87; pres., chief exec. officer Sundance (Utah) Inst. for Resource Mgmt., 1986—; pres., chief exec. officer Sundance Enterprises Ltd., 1988-91; adj. prof. grad. sch. pub. affairs U. Colo., 1983—, Sch. Bus. U. Denver, 1992—; bd. dirs. Colo. Open Lands, Inc., 1986—; participant UN Conf. on Environment and Devel., Rio de Janeiro, 1992; chmn. environ. adv. bd. Wal-Mart, Inc., 1990—. Editor: Greenhouse/Glasnost—The Global Warming Crisis, 1990. Spl. del. UN Habitat Conf. Human Settlements, spl. rep. to UN Environment Program, 1992, coord. UN Global Youth Forum, 1993, 94, co-chmn. conf. on environment and marketing, N.Y.C., 1993; founder Vail Symposium; co-founder, bd. dirs. Colo. Park Found., 1985—; founding mem. Greenhouse/Glasnost U.S./USSR Teleconf. with Soviet Acad. Scis., 1989—; mem. pres. task force Commn. on Sustainable Devel., 1994—; co-chmn. Golf and Environ. Conf., Pebble Beach, Calif., 1995. Nat. finalist White House Fellowship, 1978; named one of B.C.'s Top Bus. Leaders for the '80's, 1980. Mem. Urban Land Inst., Colo. Acad. Pub. Adminstrn. (charter, founding mem. 1988), Colo. City Mgmt. Assn., Internat. City Mgrs. Assn. (Mgmt. Innovation award 1974-76), Western Gov.'s Assn. (staff coun., chmn. adv. com. 1985-86), Flatirons Athletic Club. Editor: Vail Symposium Papers, 1970-79; author, editor: Growth Alternatives for Rocky Mountain West, 1976; Future of Human Settlements in the West, 1977. Home: 785 6th St Boulder CO 80302-7416 Office: Ctr for Resource Mgmt 1410 Grant St Ste 307C Denver CO 80203-1846

MINK, MAXINE MOCK, real estate executive; b. Lakeland, Fla., Jan. 17, 1938; d. Idus Frank and Elizabeth (Warren) Mock; student Fla. So. Coll.; children: Lance Granger, Justin Chandler. With Union Fin. Co., Lakeland, Fla., 1956-62; ptnr./owner S & S Ent. & Arrow Lake Mobile Home Pk., Lakeland, 1957-66; head bookkeeper Seaboard Fin., Lakeland, 1964-68; ptnr. Custom Chem., Inc., Lakeland, 1968-75, Don Emilio Perfumers, Newport Beach, Calif., 1978-79; owner Maxine Mink Public Relations, Newport Beach, 1978-83; fine homes and relocation specialist Merrill Lynch Realty, Newport Beach, 1985-90, Tarbell Realtors, Newport Beach, 1990-93, Prudential Calif. Realty, Newport Beach, 1993—. Bd. dirs. Guild of Lakeland Symphony Orch., 1972-75; mem. Lakeland Gen. Hosp. Aux., 1974-76, Mus. Modern Art. Mem. NAFE, Newport Beach C. of C., Hoag Hosp. Aux., Orange County Music Center Guild. Republican. Clubs: Balboa Bay, Sherman Library and Gardens, The 552. Office: PO Box 1262 Newport Beach CA 92659-0262

MINK, PATSY TAKEMOTO, congresswoman; b. Paia, Maui, Hawaii, Dec. 6, 1927; d. Suematsu and Mitama (Tateyama) Takemoto; m. John Francis Mink, Jan. 27, 1951; 1 child, Gwendolyn. Student, Wilson Coll., 1946, U. Nebr., 1947; BA, U. Hawaii, 1948; LLD, U. Chgo., 1951; DHL (hon.), Chaminade Coll., 1975, Syracuse U., 1976, Whitman Coll., 1981. Bar: Hawaii. Pvt. practice Honolulu, 1953-65; lectr. U. Hawaii, 1952-56, 59-62, 79-80; atty. Territorial Ho. of Reps., 1955; mem. Hawaii Ho. of Reps., 1956-58, Ter. Hawaii Senate, 1958-59, Hawaii State Senate, 1962-64, 89th-94th Congresses from 2nd Hawaii dist., 101st-104th Congresses from 2d dist. Hawaii, 1989—; mem. econ. and ednl. opportunity com., mem. budget com.; mem. U.S. del. to UN Law of Sea, 1975-76, Internat. Woman's Yr., 1975, UN Environ. Program, 1977, Internat. Whaling Commn., 1977; asst. sec. of state U.S. Dept. State, 1977-78. Charter pres. Young Dem. Club Oahu, 1954-56, Ter. Hawaii Young Dems., 1956-58; del. Dem. Nat. Conv., 1960, 72, 80; nat. v.p. Young Dem. Clubs Am., 1957-59; v.p. Ams. for Dem. Action, 1974-76, nat. pres., 1978-81; mem. nat. adv. com. White House Conf. on Families, 1979-80; mem. nat. adv. coun. Federally Employed Women. Recipient Leadership for Freedom award Roosevelt Coll., Chgo., 1968, Alii award 4-H Clubs Hawaii, 1969, Nisei of Biennium award, Freedom award Honolulu chpt. NAACP, 1971, Disting. Humanitarian award YWCA, St. Louis, 1972, Creative Leadership in Women's Rights award NEA, 1977, Human Rights award Am. Fedn. Tchrs., 1975, Feminist of Yr. award Feminist Majority Found., 1991, Margaret Brent award ABA, 1992. Office: US Ho of Reps 2135 Rayburn HOB Washington DC 20515*

MINNERLY, ROBERT WARD, headmaster; b. Yonkers, N.Y., Mar. 21, 1935; s. Richard Warren and Margaret Marion (DeBrocky) M.; m. Sandra Overmire, June 12, 1957; children: Scott Ward, John Robert, Sydney Sue. AB, Brown U., 1957; MAT, U. Tex., Arlington, 1980. Tchr., coach Rumsey Hall Sch., Washington, Conn., 1962-64; tchr., coach Berkshire Sch., Sheffield, Mass., 1964-70, asst. head, 1969-70, headmaster, 1970-76; dir. Salisbury (Conn.) Summer Sch. Reading and English, 1970; prin. upper sch. Ft. Worth Country Day Sch., 1976-86; headmaster Charles Wright Acad., Tacoma, Wash., 1986—; cons. Tarrant County Coalition on Substance Abuse, 1982-84; mem. mayor's task force Tacoma Edn. Summit, 1991-92. Contbr. articles to profl. jours. Bd. dirs. Tacoma/Pierce County Good Will Games Art Coun., 1989; mem. exec. com. Am. Leadership Forum, 1991-95; mem. Broadway Ctr. for Performing Arts, Tacoma, 1988-94, mem. exec. com., 1990-93. Named Administr. of Yr. Wash. Journalism Edn. Assn., 1991. Mem. Pacific N.W. Assn. Ind. Schs. (chmn. long-range planning com. 1989-92, exec. com. 1990-92, 91, v.p. 1994). Republican. Presbyterian. Home: 4214 39th Avenue Ct NW Gig Harbor WA 98335-8029 Office: Charles Wright Acad 7723 Chambers Creek Rd W Tacoma WA 98467-2099

MINNICH, JOSEPH EDWARD, tourist railway consultant; b. Swanton, Ohio, Sept. 13, 1932; s. Charles and Leila (Gaiman) M.; m. Frances Katherine Searcy, Feb. 6, 1977; children: Christopher, Susan, Teresa. Student, U. Toledo, 1956-58, Am. U., 1969. Ins. broker Wright Russell & Bay Co., Toledo, 1961-67; ch. adminstr. St. Paul's Luth. Ch., Toledo, 1968-

80; pres. Toledo Lake Erie & Western R.R., 1978-81, Heritage R.R. Co., 1981-83; exec. v.p. Centennial Rail, Ltd., Denver, 1981—; v.p. Airpower West Ltd., 1992—. Author: Steam Locomotives in the United States, 1985, Historic Diesels in the United States, 1988; editor Trainline mag., 1979—. V.p. Airpower West, Ltd., 1992—. Sgt. USAF, 1951-55. Nat. Assn. Ch. Bus. Adminstrs. fellow, 1971. Mem. Tourist Ry. Assn. (bd. dirs. 1984—, Disting. Svc. award 1991), Colo. Ry. Mus. Republican. Lutheran. Home: 3641 S Yampa St Aurora CO 80013-3527 Office: Centennial Rail Ltd PO Box 460393 Aurora CO 80046-0393

MINNIE, MARY VIRGINIA, social worker, educator; b. Eau Claire, Wis., Feb. 16, 1922; d. Herman Joseph and Virginia Martha (Strong) M. BA, U. Wis., 1944; MA, U. Chgo., 1949, Case Western Reserve U., 1956. Lic. clin. social worker, Calif. Supr. day care Wis. Children Youth, Madison, 1949-57; coordinator child study project Child Guidance Clinic, Grand Rapids, Mich., 1957-60; faculty, community services Pacific Oaks Coll., Pasadena, Calif., 1960-70; pvt. practice specializing in social work various cities, Calif., 1970-78; ednl. cons. So. Calif. Health Care, North Hollywood, Calif., 1978—; med. social worker Kaiser Permanente Home Health, Downey, Calif., 1985-87; assoc. Baby Sitters Guild, Inc., 1987-94; cons. Home Health, 1987-90; pres. Midwest Assn. Nursery Edn., Grand Rapids, 1958-60; bd. dirs., sec. So. Calif. Health Care, North Hollywood; bd. dirs., v.p. Baby Sitters Guild Inc., South Pasadena, 1986-94; cons. project Head Start Office Econ. Opportunity, Washington, 1965-70. Mem. Soc. Clin. Social Workers, Nat. Assn. Social Workers, Nat. Assn. Edn. Young Children (1960-62). Democrat. Club: Altrusa (Laguna Beach, Calif.) (pres. 1984-87). Home and Office: 2225 Silver Oak Way Hemet CA 92545-8126

MINNIS, JOHN MARTIN, state legislator, protective services official; b. Garden City, Kans., Dec. 14, 1953; s. Elbert William and Helen R. Logerwell) M.; m. Karen Marie Bartrug, Oct. 14, 1972; children: Steven, Michael, Jennifer. Student, Portland State U. Machinist-apprentice Bingham-Willamette Co., Portland, Oreg., 1973-74; rsch. dep. sheriff Multnomah County, Oreg., 1976; police officer Portland Police Dept., 1976-92, detective, 1992—; mem. Oreg. Ho. of Reps., Salem, 1985—, minority whip, 1989, asst. majority leader, 1991; also co-chmn. joint ways and means com. Sgt. USAF and Oreg. Air Guard, 1972-78. Mem. Am. Legis. Exch. Coun., Nat. Conf. State Legislatures (vice chmn. com. on fed. budget and taxation), Am. Profl. Soc. on Abuse of Children. Home: 23765 NE Holladay St Troutdale OR 97060-2903

MINOR, LARRY J., food products executive; b. 1945. With Agri-Empire, pres. Office: Agri-Empire 630 W 7th St San Jacinto CA 92583-4015*

MINOT, MARK MORTON, engineering executive; b. L.A., Dec. 26, 1958; s. Robert M. and Marcia Minot; m. Katharine Minot, 1982; children. BSEE, U. Calif., 1981, MSEE, 1982, PhD, 1990; postgrad., Pepperdine U., 1992—. Con. engr. Spotered Films Inc., Santa Barbara, Calif., 1979-82; cons. engr. ECS, Santa Barbara, Calif., 1979-82; sr. design engr. Avantek Microwave Inc., Santa Clare, Calif., 1982-85; cons. engr. ECS, Irvine, Calif., 1985-91; engring. mgr. R&D Baxter Healthcare, Irvine, Calif., 1991—. Contbr. articles to profl. jours. Mem. IEEE, Am. Vacuum Soc., Optical Soc. Am., Assn. Advancement Med. Instrumentation, Soc. Photometric Instrumentation Engrs. Office: Baxter Healthcare 17221 Red Hill Ave Irvine CA 92714-5627

MINTS, GRIGORI EFROIM, operations research specialist; b. Leinigrad, USSR, June 7, 1939; s. Efroim B. and Lea M. (Novick) M.; m. Maryanna Rozenfeld, July 21, 1987; 1 child, Anna. Diploma, Leinigrad U., 1961, PhD, 1965, ScD, 1989. Rsch. assoc. Steklov Inst. Math., Leningrad, 1961-79; with Nauka Pubs., Leningrad, 1979-85; sr. rsch. assoc. Inst. Cybernetics, Tallinn, Estonia, 1985-91; prof. dept. philosophy Stanford (Calif.) U., 1991—; mem. adv. bd. Jour. Symbolic Logic, 1987-90; mem. editorial bd. Jour. Symbolic Computation, 1983—, Jour. of Functional Programming, 1990—; mem. program orgn. com. Logic in Computer Sci., 1991-94, Conf. on Automated Deduction, Logic Programming and Automated Reasoning. Editor: Mathematical Investigation of Logical Deduction, 1967, COLOG-88, 1989, Journal of Logic and Computation, 1991—; contbr. articles to profl. jours. Mem. Assn. Symbolic Logic (coun. mem. 1990-93), Internat. Union History and Philosophy and Sci. (assessor 1991—), Annals of Pure and Applied Logic (mem. edit. bd. 1980-89).

MINTY, KEITH LARRY, medical services corporation executive; b. Roseburg, Oreg., Mar. 1, 1933; s. John Raymond and Vivian Melba (Adams) M.; m. Mary Louise Davis, May 4, 1953; children: Ronald, Karen, Gary. Enlisted airmen USAF, 1952—, advanced to master sgt., ret., 1978; bus. mgr. Nev. MRI Assocs., L.P., Las Vegas, 1987—, Palomino-Tonopah Assocs., Las Vegas, 1987—; ptnr., treas. Nev. MRI Assocs., Inc., Las Vegas, 1986—, also bd. dirs.; ptnr. Nev. MRI Assocs. Ltd. Partnership, Las Vegas, 1987—; COO Taylor Knudson & Lum Profl. Assn., Las Vegas, Nev., 1993—; dir., treas. Nev. MRI Assocs., Inc., Las Vegas, 1987—; mgmt. com., mem. Palomino-Tonopah Assocs., Las Vegas, 1987—; mem. Nev. Baptist Convention (exec. bd. 1990-94, pres. 1994—). Decorated Air Force Commendation medal with 2 oak leaf clusters, Bronze Star. Republican. So. Baptist. Office: Taylor Knudson & Lum PA 2020 Palomino Ln # 100 Las Vegas NV 89106-4812

MINTZ-BINDER, RONDA DEBRA, nursing educator, counselor; b. L.A., Mar. 28, 1960; d. Nathan and Charlotte (Siegel) Mintz; m. Richard Allen Binder, Sept. 9, 1989. BA in Biology, U. Calif., Riverside, 1980; BSN, UCLA, 1982, M Nursing, 1985. RN, Calif.; cert. for psychiatric nurses in pvt. practice Bd. Registered Nursing. Clin. nurse Neuropsychiat. Inst., L.A., 1982-85; insvc. educator Del Amo Psychiat. Hosp., Torrance, Calif., 1985-86; project dir. play therapy Calif. Med. Ctr., 1987-88; lectr. UCLA Sch. Nursing, 1988—; pvt. practice counseling, Santa Monica and Beverly Hills, Calif., 1985—; expert witness on malpractice to law firms, L.A., 1988—; lectr. Nursing Rev. '90, 1989-90. Contbg. author: Psychiatric and Mental Health Nursing, 1989; author, speaker videotape Sexual Abuse of Children, 1985. Mem. Psychiat. Nurses in Pvt. Practice, Chironians, Sigma Theta Tau. Office: UCLA Sch Nursing 10833 Le Conte Ave # 3 952 Los Angeles CA 90024

MINUDRI, REGINA URSULA, librarian, consultant; b. San Francisco, May 9, 1937; d. John C. and Molly (Halter) M. B.A., San Francisco Coll. for Women, 1958; M.L.S., U. Calif.-Berkeley, 1959. Reference librarian Menlo Park (Calif.) Pub. Library, 1959-62; regional librarian Santa Clara County (Calif.) Library, 1962-68; project coordinator Fed. Young Adult Library Services Project, Mountain View, Calif., 1968-71; dir. profl. services Alameda County (Calif.) Library, 1971, asst. county librarian, 1972-77; library dir. Berkeley Pub. Library, 1977-94; lectr. U. San Francisco, 1970-72, U. Calif., Berkeley, 1977-81, 91-93; lectr. San Jose State U., 1994—; cons., 1975—; adv. bd. Miles Cutter Ednl., 1992—. Bd. dirs. Cmty. Memory, 1989-91, Berkeley Cmty. Fund, 1994—, chair youth com., 1994—; mem. bd. mgrs. cen. br. Berkeley YMCA, 1988-93. Recipient proclamation Mayor of Berkeley, 1985, 86, 94, Citation of Merit Calif. State Assembly, 1994; named Woman of Yr. Alameda County North chpt. Nat. Women's Polit. Caucus, 1986, Outstanding Alumna U. Calif. Sch. Library and Info. Scis., Berkeley, 1987. Mem. ALA (pres. 1986-87, exec. bd. 1980-89, council 1979-88, 90-94, Grolier award 1974), Calif. Library Assn. (pres. 1981, council 1965-69, 79-82), LWV (dir. Berkeley chpt. 1980-81). Author: Getting It Together, A Young Adult Bibliography, 1970; contbr. articles to pubs. including School Library Jour., Wilson Library Bulletin. Office: Reality Mgmt 836 The Alameda Berkeley CA 94707-1916

MINZNER, DEAN FREDERICK, aviation company executive; b. Winchester, Mass., July 20, 1945; s. Frederick Louis and Winifred (Hughes) M.; B.A., Franklin and Marshall Coll., 1967; M.B.A., Columbia U., 1972. Dist. exec. Greater N.Y. councils Boy Scouts Am., N.Y.C., 1972-76; sales exec. Coast Avia, Long Beach, Calif., 1976-78, Performance Aircraft, Inc., Hayward, Calif., 1978; owner, pres. Western Aviation Consultants, Inc., Hayward, 1978-82, Cal-Pacific Assocs., Inc., Hayward, 1979—, Cal-Pacific Enterprises, Hayward, 1982—. Mem. Assn. M.B.A. Execs., Columbia U. Grad. Sch. Bus. Alumni Assn., Aircraft Owners and Pilots Assn. Office: PO Box 6206 Hayward CA 94540-6206

MIR, MARILYN, retired educator; b. Upland, Ind., Dec. 9, 1927; d. Robert Heavin Thompson and Lenora Hults; m. Hashem Robert Mir-Afzali, May 12, 1957 (div. 1976); children: Michael Robert Mir-Afzali, Susan Marie Farrell. BS, Ball State U., 1947; postgrad., U. Colo., 1948; MS, Ind. U., 1950; postgrad., U. Wash., 1951, U. Calif., 1952-53, San Francisco State U., 1984-85. Tchr. bus. Ind., 1947-50, Wenatchee (Wash.) High Sch., 1950-52; exec. sec. Fritzi of Calif., San Francisco, 1958-63; engring. sec. Div. of Westinghouse, San Francisco, 1963-68; tchr. bus. and English San Francisco Unified Schs., 1968-85, attendance coord., 1985-87, cons., 1987-90. Vol. libr. Grossmont High Sch. Dist., El Cajon, Calif., 1990—, San Carlos Pub. Libr., San Diego, 1985; ednl. missionary Utah Presbyn. Schs., 1985, N.Mex. Presbyn. Schs., 1987, N.C. Presbyn. Schs., 1989. Mem. AAUW, San Carlos Women's Club (edn. com.). Democrat. Presbyterian. Home: 7912 June Lake Dr San Diego CA 92119-3120

MIRANTE, KATHLEEN MARIE, cardiologist; b. Seattle, Apr. 8, 1940; d. Dominic and Frances (Drew) M. BS, Coll. Notre Dame, 1967; MD, Med. Coll. Pa., 1971. Diplomate Am. Bd. Internal Medicine, Am. Bd. Cardiovascular Disease. Resident Montefiore Hosp. & Med. Ctr., Bronx, N.Y., 1971-73, Mercy Hosp. & Med. Ctr., San Diego, 1973-74; fellow in cardiology Pacific Med. Ctr., San Francisco, 1974-76; attending physician Kaiser Found. Hosp., Fontana, Calif., 1976—; dir. cardiac rehabilitiation Kaiser Found. Hosp., Fontana, 1978—, dir. CCU, 1994. Named Physician of Yr. Soc. Calif. Permanente Med. Group, Fontana, 1987. Fellow Am. Coll. Cardiology, Am. Coll. Chest Physicians. Office: Kaiser Hosp Dept Cardiology 9981 Sierra Ave Fontana CA 92335-6720

MIRICH, DAVID GAGE, secondary education language educator; b. Rock Springs, Wyo., June 17, 1956; s. John Jack and Kay Marie (Garvin) M. Student, U. de Filologia, Sevilla, Spain, 1981-82; BA in Psychology, Dakota Western U., 1981; teaching cert., U. Colo., 1989; postgrad., U. de Complutense, Madrid, 1991, Universidad de Salamanca, Spain, 1993; MA in Bilingual/Spl. Edn., U. Colo., 1995; postgrad., 1994—. Pvt. practice tchr., interpreter Sevilla, 1981-83; tchr. bilingual Horace Mann Middle Sch., Denver (Colo.) Pub. Schs., 1989-92; tchr. bilingual/ESOL coord. North High Sch., Denver (Colo.) Pub. Schs., 1992—; tchr. on spl. assignment, secondary bilingual and ESOL edn. Founder, chmn. Boulderiety Conv., Boulder, Colo., 1989-92; candidate Boulder Valley Sch. Bd., 1989; founder, pres. Front Range Children's Orthodontic Fund, Denver, 1991-92. With USN, 1974-75. Named Vol. of Week., Vol. Boulder (Colo.) County, 1987, Hero of the Week, Rocky Mountain News, 1994. Mem. Nat. Assn. Bilingual Edn. (Nat. Bilingual Tchr. of the Yr. 1994) Colo. Assn. Bilingual Edn. (v.p. 1993-95, Colo. Bilingual Tchr. of the Yr., 1994). Home: 2224 Hooker St Denver CO 80211 Office: Denver Pub Schs Dept Bilingual and ESOL Edn 900 Grant St Denver CO 80203

MIRIKITANI, JOHN MASA, foundation administrator; b. Honolulu, Nov. 24, 1962; s. Clifford Kunio and Helene M. AB, U. Calif., Berkeley, 1985; JD, U. Mich., 1990; postgrad., U. Hawaii. Policy analyst intern Sloan Found. for Pub. Policy and Mgmt./U. Calif., Berkeley, 1984; policy analyst legis. bus. devel. com. State of Hawaii, Honolulu, 1988-89; founder, pres. John and Clifford Mirikitani Found., Honolulu, 1988—; sponsor Mirikitani Lectrs. in law and econs. edn., U. Hawaii, Manoa, Honolulu, 1989—. Candidate for State Bd. Edn., State Hawaii, 1992, 94. Recipient scholarship to Harvard Kennedy Sch. of Govt., 1985. Mem. Am. Law and Econs. Assn., Phi Beta Kappa. Home: 2336 Oahu Ave Honolulu HI 96822-1965

MIRISOLA, LISA HEINEMANN, air quality engineer; b. Glendale, Calif., Mar. 25, 1963; d. J. Herbert and Betty Jane (Howson) Heinemann; m. Daniel Carl Mirisola, June 27, 1987; 1 child, Ian Cataldo. BSME, UCLA, 1986. Cert. engr.-in-tng., Calif. Air quality engr. South Coast Air Quality Mgmt. Dist., Diamond Bar, Calif., 1988—. Chancellor's scholar UCLA, 1981. Mem. ASME, NSPE, Soc. Women Engrs. Office: South Coast Air Quality Mgmt Dist 21865 Copley Dr Diamond Bar CA 91765-4178

MIRK, JUDY ANN, elementary educator; b. Victorville, Calif., June 10, 1944; d. Richard Nesbit and Corrine (Berghoefer) M. BA in Social Sci., San Jose (Calif.) State U., 1966, cert. in teaching, 1967; MA in Edn., Calif. State U., Chico, 1980. Cert. elem. edn. tchr., Calif. Tchr. Cupertino (Calif.) Union Sch. Dist., 1967-95; lead tchr. lang. arts Dilworth Sch., San Jose, 1988-90, mem. supt.'s adv. team, 1986-90, mem. student study team, 1987-95; mem. student study team, 1987-95; mem. Dilworth Sch. Site Coun., 1981-95. Mem. Calif. Tomorrow. Mem. ASCD, Calif. Assn. Counseling and Devel., Daytime Drama Guild (charter), Phi Mu. Republican. Home: 4132 Valerie Dr Campbell CA 95008-3728 Office: Cupertino Union Sch Dist 10301 Vista Dr Cupertino CA 95014-2040

MIRKOVICH, THOMAS REID, business information educator; b. Redwood City, Calif., May 9, 1954; s. Samuel Adams and Helen (Bokan) M.; m. Mary Kathleen Clark, May 1, 1976; children: Samuel Reid, Lara. BA, U. Wash., 1982, MLS, 1988. Info. asst. Price Waterhouse, Seattle, 1987-88; head reference libr. Carson City (Nev.) Libr., 1989-90; bus. & hotel libr. U. Nev., Las Vegas, 1990-93; asst. collection devel. libr. U. Nev., 1994—; chair Nev. Coll. & Rsch. Librs. Com., Carson City, 1993—. Editor (column) High Roller, 1990-93. Del. Gov.'s Conf. on Librs., Las Vegas, 1989. Recipient History award U. Wash., 1981-82. Mem. ALA, Nev. Libr. Assn., Nev. Hotel Assn., Spl. Libr. Assn. Home: 528 8th St Boulder City NV 89005-3038 Office: U Nev Libr 4505 S Maryland Pky Las Vegas NV 89154-9900

MIRSKY, PHYLLIS SIMON, librarian; b. Petach Tikva, Israel, Dec. 18, 1940; d. Allan and Lea (Prizant) Simon; m. Edward Mirsky, Oct. 21, 1967; 1 child, Seth. BS in Social Welfare, Ohio State U., 1962; postgrad., Columbia U., 1962-63; AMLS, U. Mich., 1965. Caseworker field placement Children's Aid Soc., N.Y.C., 1962-63; hosp. libr. hosp. and instns. divsn. Cleve. Pub. Libr., 1963-64; reference libr. UCLA Biomed. Libr., 1965-68, reference/acquisitions libr., 1968-69, head cons./continuing edn. Pacific S.W. Regl. Med. Libr. Sv., 1969-71, asst. dir. Pacific S.W. Regl. Med. Libr. Sv., 1971-73, faculty coord. Biomed. Libr. program Cen. San Joaquin Valley Area Health Edn. Ctr., 1973-77, assoc. dir. Pacific S.W. Regl. Med. Libr. Sv., 1973-79; head reference sect., coord. libr. assoc. program Nat. Libr. of Medicine, Bethesda, Md., 1979-81; asst. univ. libr., scis. U. Calif.-San Diego, La Jolla, 1981-86, acting univ. libr., 1985, 92-93, asst. univ. libr. adminstrv. and pub. svcs., 1986-87, assoc. univ. libr. adminstrv. and pub. svcs., 1987-92, assoc. univ. libr., 1993—; guest lectr. Libr. Schs. UCLA and U. So. Calif., 1967-78, Grad. Sch. Libr. Sci. Cath. U., Washington, 1980, Grad. Sch. Libr. and Info. Sci. UCLA, 1984; mem. task force on role of spl. libr. nationwide network and coop. programs Nat. Commn. on Libr. and Info. Svcs./Spl. Libr. Assn., 1981-83; facilitator AASLD/MLA Guidelines Scenario Writing Session, L.A., 1984; mem. users coun. OCLC Online Computer Libr. Ctr., Inc., 1991-94; U. Calif.-San Diego rep. Coalition for Networked Info., 1992—; instr. Assn. Rsch. Librs., Office Mgmt. Studies, Mgmt. Inst., 1987; peer reviewer Coll. Libr. Tech. and Cooperation Grant Program U.S. Dept. Edn., 1988—; cons. Nat. Libr. Medicine, Bethesda, Md., 1988, San Diego Mus. Contemporary Art Libr., La Jolla, Calif., 1993—, Salk Inst., 1995. Contbr. articles to profl. jours. and bulls. NIH fellow Columbia U., 1962-63; sr. fellow UCLA/Coun. on Libr. Resources, 1987. Mem. ALA (site visitors panel com. on accreditation 1990-92, libr. adminstrn. and mgmt. assn. 1990-92), Med. Libr. Assn. (bd. dirs. 1977-80), Med. Libr. Group Soc. Calif. and Ariz. (sec. 1970-71, v.p. 1971-72, pres. 1972-73), Documentation Abstracts, Inc. (bd. dirs. 1985-90, vice chair bd. dirs. 1988-90), Med. Libr. Assn. (pres. 1984-85), U. Mich. Sch. Libr. Sci. Alumni Assn. Office: U Calif-San Diego Univ Libr 0175G 9500 Gilman Dr La Jolla CA 92093-5003

MISA, KENNETH FRANKLIN, management consultant; b. Jamaica, N.Y., Sept. 24, 1939; s. Frank J. and Mary M. (Soszka) M.; BS cum laude in Psychology, Fairfield U., 1961; MS in Psychology, Purdue U., 1963; PhD in Psychology (Fellow 1963-66), St. John's U., 1966. Staff psychologist Rohrer, Hibler & Replogle, Los Angeles, 1966-67; assoc. A.T. Kearney, Inc., Los Angeles, 1968-71, sr. assoc., 1972-74, prin., 1975-78, v.p., partner, 1979-86; pres. HR Cons. Group, 1987—. Cert. mgmt. cons.; lic. psychologist, Calif. Mem. Am. Psychol. Assn., Am. Psychol. Soc., Calif. State Psychol. Assn., Soc. for Human Resources Mgmt., Human Resources Planning Soc., Indsl. Rels. Rsch. Assn., Soc. for Indsl. and Organizational Psychology, World Affairs Coun. of L.A., Town Hall of So. Calif., Glendale C. of C., Jonathan Club. Republican. Roman Catholic. Home: 924C S Orange Grove Blvd Pasadena CA 91105-1741 Office: HR Cons Group 100 N Brand Blvd Ste 200 Glendale CA 91203-2614

MISCHE, KURT ANDREW, broadcast executive; b. Boone, Iowa, Feb. 2, 1956; s. Sterling H. and Darlene G. (Reike) M.; m. Carla Jean Griffiths, July 16, 1978 (div. May 11, 1984); m. Judy Elise Costanza, Sept. 6, 1986; children: Daniel Bruce, Elise Annjeanette. BS, So. Ill. U., 1978. CRMC Designation, Radio Advt. Bur., 1981, CRSM Designation, 1993. Announcer Stas. WCIL AM/FM, Carbondale, Ill., 1974-75; announcer, salesman Sta. WGGH-AM, Marion, Ill., 1975-78; asst. sales mgr. Sta. WYBR-FM, Rockford, Ill., 1978; sta. mgr. Sta. WEBQ AM/FM, Harrisburg, Ill., 1978-79; sales mgr. Sta. WQHK-AM Radio, Ft. Wayne, Ind., 1979-83; gen sales mgr. Sta. WXUS-FM Radio, Lafayette, Ind., 1983-84; nat. and regional sales mgr. Stas. WQHK/WMEE, Ft. Wayne, 1984-88; dir. sales devel. Stas. WCOA/WJLQ, Pensacola, Fla., 1988-90; gen. sales mgr. Sta. WZEZ-FM, Nashville, 1990-91; cons. in-sta. sales tng. Boston, 1991-92; gen. sales mgr. Sta. KRLV-FM, Las Vegas, 1992-94, v.p., gen. mgr., 1994—; speaker in field. Contbr. articles to profl. jours. Chmn. Peace Luth. Ch., Ft. Wayne, 1986-88; bd. dirs. Pensacola Beach C.C., Gulf Breeze, Fla., 1989—, Ft. Wayne Assoc. Chs., 1987; bd. elders First Good Shepherd Luth. Ch., 1992—; mem. Friends of Channel 10, 1993—, sec., 1994. Mem. West Fla. Ad Assn. Mobil Ad Fedn., So. Nev. Radio Assn., Pensacola C. of C., So. Ill. U. Alumni Assn. Lutheran. Home: 1832 Somersby Way Henderson NV 89014 Office: KRLV-FM 1064 E Sahara Ave Las Vegas NV 89104-3220

MISCHER, DONALD LEO, television director and producer; b. San Antonio, Mar. 5, 1940; s. Elmer Frederick and Lillian Alma. B.A., U. Tex., 1961, M.A., 1963. Mem. faculty U. Tex., 1962-63; producer/dir. USIA, Washington, 1965-68; with Charles Guggenheim Prodns., 1969-71; pres. Don Mischer Prodns., pres. Mischer Enterprises, Inc., Beverly Hills, Calif., prodr., dir., and program packager for network television programs, 1971—. Television programs include: The Kennedy Center Honors: A Celebration of the Performing Arts (Emmy Awards 1981,87); The Tony Awards (Emmy Awards 1987-88); Michael Jackson's Super Bowl XXVII Halftime Show; Baryshnikov by Tharp (Emmy Award 1985); Gregory Hines, Tap Dance America; Carnegie Hall: Live at 100; It's Garry Shandling's Show; Mowtown 25: Yesterday, Today, Tomorrow (Emmy Award 1983); The Muppets Celebrate Jim Henson; Motown Returns to the Apollo (Emmy Award 1985); Baryshnikov in Hollywood, Goldie and Liza Together, Shirley MacLaine—Illusions, Making Television Dance with Twyla Tharp, An Evening with Robin Williams, Am. Film Inst. Salute to Gene Kelly; producer additional programs with Bob Hope (Bob Hope: The First 90 Years - Emmy award Outstanding Variety, Music or Comedy Special, 1993), Barbara Walters, Goldie Hawn, others. Recipient: Primetime Emmy awards (10), Director's Guild awards for Outstanding Directorial Achiement (8), NAACP Image awards (3), Peabody award, Golden Rose of Montreux award, Gabriel award, Ohio State award. Mem. Dirs. Guild Am., Nat. Acad. TV Arts and Scis. Gov., Am. Film Inst. Office: Brillstein-Grey Entertainment 9150 Wilshire Blvd Ste 350 Beverly Hills CA 90212-3430

MISHKIN, MARJORIE WONG, aviation and marketing consultant; b. Los Angeles, Oct. 28, 1940; d. Thomas A. and Mayme M. (Moe) Wong; children: Barbara Joanne, Cynthia Anne; m. David Gordon Mishkin, Jan. 6, 1991. BA, Goucher Coll., 1962; MA, U. Calif. at Berkeley, 1965. Research economist Fed. Reserve Bank San Francisco, 1964-65; bus. cons., travel industry, 1968-74; marketing analyst The Flying Tiger Line Inc., Los Angeles, 1974-76, systems analyst, 1976-77, mgr. mgmt. reporting and performance analysis, 1977-78; dir. passenger pricing and fare devel. Continental Airlines, 1978-80, dir. internat. pricing, 1980-83; aviation and mktg. cons. Chen & Assocs., 1983—, dir. practice devel. Greenberg, Glusker, Fields, Claman & Machtinger, 1989-90; fin. cons. Shearson Lehman Hutton; bd. dirs. Continental Fed. Credit Union. Trustee, chmn. devel. Marlborough Sch.; trustee, deacon 1st Congl. Ch. of Los Angeles; mem. evaluation com. Am. Heart Assn. Danforth Found. assoc., 1968-79. Mem. Nat. Mgmt. Assn. (membership chmn.), World Affairs Council L.A., L.A. Libr. Assn. (v.p., treas.), Town Hall Calif., U. Calif. Alumni Assn., Marlborough Alumni Assn. Republican. Home: 640 N June St Los Angeles CA 90004-1012

MISIASZEK, JOHN J., psychiatrist; b. London, Dec. 10, 1948; came to U.S., 1951; s. Walter Peter and Maria Elizabeth (Smagula) M.; m. Jenifer Davis George; children: Julie, Michael. BS with distinction, U. Ariz., 1971, MD, 1975. Diplomate Nat. Bd. Med. Examiners; bd. cert. psychiatry; lic. psychiatrist, Ariz.; cert. controlled substances registration. Intern in medicine Santa Barbara (Calif.) Gen. Hosp., 1975-76; resident in psychiatry Ariz. Health Scis. Ctr., Tucson, 1976-79; coord. consultation-liaison svc. dept. psychiatry U. Ariz., Tucson, 1978; asst. prof. psychiatry dept. psychiatry Ariz. Health Scis. Ctr.-U. Ariz., Tucson, 1979-85, dir. consultation-liaison svc., 1979-90, clin. asst. prof. psychiatry, 1985, assoc. prof. clin. psychiatry, 1985—; dir. med. psychiatry Outpatient Clinic, Tucson, 1993—; cons. psychiatrist VA Hosp., Tucson, So. Ariz. Mental Health Ctr., Tucson. Contbr. articles to med. and sci. jours. Fellow Am. Psychiat. Assn.; mem. Assn. for Academic Psychiatry, Acad. Psychosomatic Medicine. Office: Ariz Health Scis Ctr 1501 N Campbell Ave Tucson AZ 85724-0001

MISNER, CHARLOTTE BLANCHE RUCKMAN, community organization administrator; b. Gifford, Idaho, Aug. 30, 1937; d. Richard Steele and Arizona (Hill) Ruckman; m. G. Arthur Misner, Jr., Aug. 29, 1959; children: Michelle, Mary, Jennifer. BS in Psychology, U. Idaho, 1959. Vol. numerous orgns. India, Mexico, The Philippines, 1962-70; sec., v.p., pres., trustee St. Luke's Hosp., Manila, 1970-84; founding mem., 3d v.p., pres. Am. Women's Club of Philippines, 1980-84; exec. adminstr. Friends of Oakland (Calif.) Parks and Recreation, 1986-92, exec. dir., 1992—. Active Lincoln Child Ctr., Oakland, 1984—. Recipient Vol. Svc. award Women's Bd. St. Luke's Hosp., 1977, Mid. Sch. Vol. award Internat. Sch.-Manila, 1980. Me. Alpha Gamma Delta (alumnae treas., pres. East Bay 1985-89, province dir. alumnae 1989—), Cum Laude Soc. (hon.). Home: 481 Ellita Ave Oakland CA 94610-4808 Office: Friends of Oakland Parks & Recreation 1520 Lakeside Dr Oakland CA 94612-4521

MISNER, GERVASE ARTHUR, personnel administrator; b. Lewiston, Idaho, Nov. 21, 1935; s. Gervase A. and Blenda (Westerlund) M.; m. Charlotte B. Ruckman, Aug. 29, 1959; children: Michele, Mary, Jennifer. BS in Agr. with high honors, U. Idaho, 1958; B Fgn. Trade, Am. Inst. for Fgn. Trade, 1960; MBA cum laude, U. Ams., Mexico City, 1970; postgrad., Laney Coll., 1990. Pres. Philippines Rohm and Haas Co., Phila., 1971-78, area dir. East Asia, 1976-80, area dir. South Asia, 1981-83; v.p. Corp. Fin. Assocs., Atlanta, 1984-86; co-founder UCAM Corp., San Jose, Calif., 1987-89; pers. adminstr. City of Oakland, Calif., 1990—; bd. dirs. Envirozone Techs., Inc., Tracy, Calif. Mem. Ateneo de Manila (prof., chmn. exec. com. 1976-77), Rotary Club (pres. 1975-76), Lake Merritt Breakfast Club. Home: 481 Ellita Ave Oakland CA 94610-4808 Office: City of Oakland 505 14th St Oakland CA 94612-1406

MISSAL, JOSHUA MORTON, composer, conductor; b. Hartford, Conn., Apr. 12, 1915; s. Joseph I. and Rose R. (Bayer) M.; m. Pegge McComb, July 16, 1944; children: Sonya Anne, Stephen Joseph. MusB, Eastman Sch. of Music, Rochester, N.Y., 1937, MusM, 1938; MusD (hon.), London Coll. of Music, 1972. Violist Rochester Philharmonic Orchestra, 1935-40; conductor Albuquerque Philharmonic, 1940-42; chief warrant officer/band leader 608th AAF Band, Tyndall, Fla., 1942-46; head of instrumental dept. Danfelser Sch. of Music, Albuquerque, 1946-50; lectr. U. N.Mex., Albuquerque, 1946-50; head of music edn. dept. So. Miss. U., Hattiesburg, 1950-52; assoc. prof., chmn. music theory/composition dept. Wichita (Kans.) State U., 1952-70; chmn., music dept. Tunxis Community Coll., Farmington, Conn., 1972-76; assoc. conductor Wichita Symphony, 1954-70; conductor Hartford Civic Orchestra, 1972-76, Scottsdale (Ariz.) Civic Orchestra, 1979-85; co-dir. Missal Art Gallery, Farmington and Scottsdale, 1970-86. Composer pub. compositions for band, orchestra, chorus and small ensembles. Mem. ASCAP, Music Tchrs. Nat. Assn., Music Educators Nat. Conf., Am. String Tchrs. Assn. Home: 1343 E Enrose Cir Mesa AZ 85203-5709

MISSETT, KATHRYN MCANDREW, public relations expert; b. Suffolk, Va., Mar. 9, 1949; d. William Joseph and Kathryn Rose (McAndrew) M.; m. Randall T. Cox, July 16, 1983; 1 child, Matthew. BA, U. Wyo., 1973. Editor Wyo. Issues mag. U. of Wyo., Laramie, 1979-82; asst. editor Wyo. Game & Fish, Cheyenne, 1983-85; pub. rels. coord. Campbell County Pub.

Libr., Gillette, 1993—; v.p. editl. affairs High Country News, Paonia, Colo., 1985-87, bd. dirs. Mem. Wyo. C.C. Commn., Cheyenne, 1986-92, Wyo. Commn. on Women, Cheyenne, 1984-86; bd. dirs. Johnson County Children's Ctr., Buffalo, Wyo., 1987-88, Johnson County Pub. Libr., Buffalo, 1989-92. Mem. Nat. Fedn. Press Women, Wyo. Media Profls. Office: Campbell County Pub Libr 2101 4-J Rd Gillette WY 82718

MITCHELL, BETTIE PHAENON, religious organization administrator; b. Colorado Springs, Colo., June 6, 1934; d. Roy William and Laura Lee (Costin) Roberts; m. Gerald Mitchell, May 3, 1952; children: Michelle Smith, Laura Sweitz, Jennie Grenzer, Mohammad Bader. BS in Edn., Lewis & Clark Coll., 1954; postgrad., Portland State U., 1962-72; MA in Religion summa cum laude, Warner Pacific Coll., 1979. Cert. counselor, Oreg. Elem. tchr. Quincy Sch. Dist., Clatskanie, Oreg., 1955-56; substitute tchr. Beaverton (Oreg.) and Washington County Schs., 1956-77; tchr. of the Bible Portland (Oreg.) C.C., 1974-92; counseling and healing ministry, 1977-79; founder, exec. dir. Good Samaritan Ministries, Beaverton, 1979-88; founder, internat. exec. dir. Good Samaritan Ministries, 1988—; tchr. Christian Renewal Ctr. Workshops, 1977-85; speaker, presenter in field; leader tours in the Mid. East. Author: Who Is My Neighbor? A Parable, 1988, The Power of Conflict and Sacrifice, A Therapy Manual for Christian Marriage, 1988, Good Samaritan Training Handbook, 1989, Be Still and Listen to His Voice, The Story of Prayer and Faith, 1990, A Need for Understanding - International Counselor Training Manual, 1993. Mem. Israel Task Force, Portland, 1974-80; Leader Camp Fire Internat., 1962-73, elem. sch. coord., 1962-68; asst. dir. Washington County Civil Def., 1961-63; precinct committeewoman Rep. Party, 1960; bd. dirs. Beaverton Fish, 1966-74; v.p. NCCJ, Portland, 1983-85; chmn., speaker's bur. Near East Task Force for Israel; chmn. fire bond issue campaign City of Beaverton; mgr. mayoral campaign, 1960; sunday sch. tchr., speaker, organizer Sharing and Caring program Bethel Ch., 1974-79. Mem. ACA, Christian Assn. for Psychol. Studies, Oreg. Counseling Assn. Republican. Home: 6550 SW Imperial Dr Beaverton OR 97008 Office: Good Samaritan Ministries 7929 SW Cirrus Dr # 23 Beaverton OR 97008

MITCHELL, BETTY JO, writer, publisher; b. Coin, Iowa, May 2, 1931; d. Edith Darrah McWilliams; B.A., S.W. Mo. State U., Springfield; M.S.L.S., U. So. Calif. Asst. acquisitions librarian Calif. State U., Northridge, 1967-69, librarian for personnel and fin., 1969-71, acting asso. library dir., 1971-72, asso. dir. univ. libraries, 1972-81; owner Viewpoint Press, Tehachapi, Calif.; cons. Western Interstate Commn. for Higher Edn. USOE Inst. for Tng. in Staff Devel. Problem Solving; participant workshops in field. Bd. dirs. San Fernando Valley council Girl Scouts U.S.A., 1974-77, employed personnel com., 1979-81; bd. dirs. Bear Valley Springs Condominium Owners Assn., 1978, Empyrean Found., 1978-81. Mem. Assn. Women in Computing (bd. dirs. 1987-89), ALA (mem., chmn. various coms.), Nat. Library Assn., Calif. Library Assn., Assn. Calif. State U. Profs. (sec., exec. com., 1971-72), AAUP, Pi Beta Chi, Alpha Mu Gamma. Author: ALMS: A Budget Based Library Management System, 1982, The Secret of Hilhouse: An Adult Book for Teens; co-author: Cost Analysis of Library Functions: A Total System Approach, 1978, How to See the U.S. on $12 a Day; speaker profl. confs.; contbr. writings to profl. publs.; editor Staff Development column in Special Libraries, 1975-76. Home: 29650 Starland Star Route 3 Box 4600-7 Tehachapi CA 93561 Office: PO Box 1090 Tehachapi CA 93581-1090

MITCHELL, BRIAN JOHN, financial planner; b. N.Y.C., Nov. 13, 1951; s. Clifford V. and Rita M. (McBreen) M. BA summa cum laude, Ohio U., 1973; Cert. Spl. Studies in Adminstrn., Harvard U., 1985. Sr. analyst Colo. Legislature, Denver, 1976-83; dir. legis. affairs New Eng. Coun., Boston, 1984-86; pres. TMS Mgmt. Corp., Stamford, Conn., 1987-90; fin. analyst Asset Mgmt. Group, Englewood, Colo., 1991—. Bd. dirs. Irish-Am. Cultural Inst., Denver, 1994—. Recipient environ. merit award EPA, 1985; scholar Ohio U., 1969. Mem. Ohio U. Alumni Assn. (bd. dirs. Denver chpt. 1993—). Office: Asset Mgmt Group 6312 S Fiddlers Green Cir Englewood CO 80111-4943

MITCHELL, CARL JACK, medical entomologist, research scientist; b. Sallisaw, Okla., Dec. 3, 1936; s. George and Vera (Walters) M.; m. Barbara M. Williams, Dec. 14, 1961; children: Katherine Ann, Samuel Joseph, Thomas Owen. BS, Northeastern State U., Tahlequah, Okla., 1959; MS, U. Hawaii, 1963; ScD, Johns Hopkins U., 1966. Postdoctoral fellow NIH, Hamilton, Mont., 1966-67; chief Tex. activities U.S. CDC, Plainview, 1967-70; project leader WHO, Taipei, Taiwan, 1970-72; scientist, biologist WHO, Geneva, Switzerland, 1972-73; extension entomologist U. Calif., Davis, 1973-75; rsch. entomologist U.S. CDC, Ft. Collins, Colo., 1974-85, chief Vector Virology Lab., 1984-89, chief med. entomology-ecology br., 1989—; entomologist U.S. Antarctic Rsch. Project, McMurdo Sound, 1961-62; cons. Pan Am. Health Orgn., Dominican Republic and Argentina, 1977, 84, WHO, Geneva, 1986, U.S. AID, Kathmandu, Nepal, 1989; mem. joint Soviet/U.S.A. expdns. to western Siberia, 1990, 91. Author or co-author book chpts. and numerous sci. articles. Recipient Antarctic Svc. medal Dept. Def., 1962, Meritorious Citation, Republic of China, 1972. Mem. Am. Mosquito Control Assn. (editorial bd.), Am. Soc. Tropical Medicine and Hygiene, Soc. for Vector Ecology, Entomol. Soc. Am. Office: US CDC PO Box 2087 Fort Collins CO 80522

MITCHELL, DAVID, environmental research executive; b. 1945. PhD, U. Wyo., 1976. Supr. Metro Lab., Seattle; now v.p. Analytical Resources, Inc., Seattle. Office: Analytical Resources Inc 333 9th Ave N Seattle WA 98109-5122*

MITCHELL, DAVID CAMPBELL, corporate executive; b. Sacramento, Dec. 11, 1957; s. Alan Campbell and Lorraine May (Grant) M.; m. Noreen Peterson, May 8, 1988 (dec.); children: Kendal Raymond (dec.), Brian Jerry, Mark Reid, David Kirk, Joshua Grant (dec.); m. Lanette Pearson; children: Travis, Holly Ann. Student, U. Utah, 1973-74, Brigham Young U. Rsch. dir. Flex Inc., Williston, N.D., 1976-78; with Deseret Industries, Salt Lake City, 1978-81; head R&D Pro Biotiks Labs., Ogden, Utah, 1981—, Meleleuca, Idaho Falls, Idaho, 1987-89; pres., chmn. David C. Mitchell Med. Rsch. Inst., Salt Lake City, 1980—; rsch. cons. U. Utah Rsch. Park, Salt Lake City, 1981—; environ. cons. Hi-Valley Chem., Salt Lake City, 1988—; v.p. Mitchell Products, Orem, Utah, 1989—. Inventor, patents in biochemistry. Vol. Freeman Inst., Salt Lake City, 1980-87; vol. supr. Granite Bakery (Feed the Poor), Salt Lake City, 1982-87; active rehab. handicapped Deseret Industries, Salt Lake City, 1978-81; pres., young adults rep. Latter-day Saints Ch., Salt Lake City, 1977-78. Scholar NSF, 1973; named one of Outstanding Young Men of Am., 1989. Fellow AAAS. Home and Office: 7919 S Thornton Cir Sandy UT 84093

MITCHELL, DAVID E., petroleum company executive; b. Calgary, Alta., Can.. Registered profl. engr., Alta. With Great Plains Devel. Co. Can. Ltd., 1950-75, pres., chief exec. officer, 1964-75; pres. Alta. Energy Co. Ltd., Calgary, Alta., 1975—. Mem. Ind. Petroleum Assn. Can. (past pres.), Oilfield Tech. Soc. (past pres.). Office: Alberta Energy CoLtd, 10707 100 Ave NW Ste 1200, Edmonton, AB Canada T5J 3M1

MITCHELL, DAVID GLEN, research aerospace engineer; b. Malvern, Ark., July 26, 1954; s. Jewell Delois Mitchell and Ruby Rachel (Reid) Moore; m. Holly Ann Gretsch, June 17, 1984. BS in Engring., UCLA, 1977; MS in Aerospace Engring., Northrop U., 1987. Aerospace engring. trainee NASA Dryden Flight Research Ctr., Edwards, Calif., 1973-76; staff engr. Systems Tech. Inc., Hawthorne, Calif., 1977-93; tech. dir. Hoh Aeronautics Inc., Lomita, Calif., 1993—; lectr. Calif. Poly. U., Pomona, 1987—, chmn. aerospace action coun., 1993—. Contbr. articles to profl. jours. Assoc. fellow AIAA; mem. AAAS, Aircraft Owners and Pilots Assn., Am. Helicopter Soc. Office: Hoh Aeronautics Inc 2075 Palos Verdes Dr N Ste 217 Lomita CA 90717-3726

MITCHELL, GENEVA BROOKE, hypnotherapist; b. Ringgold, Tex., Feb. 15, 1929; d. Roy Banks and Willie Jewel (Lemons) Shaw; m. Roy David Mitchell, Nov. 30, 1947; children: Ronald, Donald, Joel, Pamela, Annette. Cert. master hypnotist Hypnosis Tng. Inst., L.A., 1980, cert. hypnotherapist, 1983; cert. in advanced investigative and forensic hypnosis Tex. A&M U., 1982; D. Clin. Hypnosis, Am. Inst. Hypnotherapy, Calif., 1989. Chiropractic asst. Alamogordo, N.Mex., 1962-79; hypnotherapist Alamogordo Hypnosis and Counseling Ctr., 1980-92; mgr. Shaw Mobile Home Park, 1986—; mng. ptnr. Shaw, Mitchell & Mallory, Albuquerque, 1986, mgr., 1987-88; hypnotherapist M&M Horses Corp., Tularosa, N.Mex., 1985-92; owner A New Image Hypnosis Ctr., Albuquerque, retired, 1992; pres. N.Mex. Chiropractic Aux., 1984-85; mem. Am. Council Hypnotist Examiners, 1980-85; hypnotist for tape series; instr. New Forever Trim Life Loss Program. Author: Take The Power, 1991. Charter pres. La Sertoma, Alamogordo, 1957; pres. Oregon sch. PTA, Alamogordo, 1958, La Luz Sch. Parents Club, N.Mex., 1962; sec. N.Mex. Jr. Rodeo Assn., 1964; co-founder Pre-Sch. La Luz, 1969; mem. N.Mex. Gov.'s Council on Youth, 1969; bd. dirs. Otero County Jr. Rodeo Assn., N.Mex., 1968; dir. self-hypnosis sch.; speaker Am. Bd. Hypnotherapy Conv., 1991. Recipient Speakers award Life Found., 1984. Mem. Am Assn. Profl. Hypnotherapists, Ladies for Life (Appreciation award 1984, 90), N.Mex. Ladies Life Fellowship (pres. 1983, bd. dirs. 1985), S.W. Hypnotherapy Examining Bd., Internat. Chiropractic Assn. Aux. (pres. 1994—, conv. chmn. 1993), Ladies for Life Chiropractic Orgn. (pres. elect 1993). Avocations: golf, painting, swimming, martial arts, writing.

MITCHELL, HERBERT EUGENE, management consultant, marketing specialist; b. Elkhart, Ind., July 25, 1929; s. Charles Nathaniel and Beulah Mae (McDonald) M.; m. Roberta Marie Blesie, Oct. 22, 1949; children: Robert, Debra, Kimbra, Candi, Melissa. BS, Iowa State U., 1949. Cert. mgmt. cons. Retail bus. owner J.W. Rodgers Florist, Dayton, Ohio, 1949-65; dir. product devel. The John Henry Co., Lansing, Mich., 1965-67; dir. wholesale mktg. Harry & David/Jackson & Perkins, Newport Beach, Calif., 1967-69; v.p. mktg. Teleflora div. D&B, Redondo Beach, Calif., 1969-75; pvt. practice cons. Creative Mktg., Newport Beach, 1975—. Author: The Fundamentals of Visual Presentation, 1987, Design With Flowers Premier Edition, 1991; editor-in-chief Teleflora Spirit, 1965-67, Design for Profit, 1981-84, The Profl. Floral Designer, 1984-91, Design With Flowers, 1991-92; sr. editor Floriculture Directions, 1975-91. Elder, St. Andrew's Presbyn. Ch., Newport Beach, 1975-78. Recipient Floriculture Hall of Fame award Soc. Am. Florists, 1984. Fellow Am. Inst. Floral Designers (bd. dirs. 1976-78, pres. 1978-80, award of disting. svc. 1983); mem. Inst. Mgmt. Cons. Republican. Office: Creative Mktg & Mgmt Specialists 1308 Mariners Dr Newport Beach CA 92660-4928

MITCHELL, JAMES HERBERT, public relations consultant; b. Tacoma, Wash., May 11, 1946; s. Emmett George and Marvel (Carscadden) M.; children: Ryan James, Claire Therese, Rose Catherine. BA, U. Portland, 1968; postgrad., U. Wash., 1969-70. Pub. rels. mgr./No. Calif. Div. Georgia-Pacific Corp., Fort Bragg, Calif., 1973-79; ednl. svcs. mgr. Georgia-Pacific Corp., Portland, Oreg., 1979-82; v.p. Bacon & Hunt, Inc., Portland, 1983-86; pres. Mitchell, Hagley, Malek, Inc., Portland, 1986-92; practice devel. dir. Lane Powell Spears Lubersky, Portland, 1992—; instr. pub. rels., Marylhurst Coll. Co-author: The Attorneys' Complete Guide to Practice Development: How to Build Your Practice and Career, 1991; contbr. articles to profl. jours. 1st lt. U.S. Army, 1971-73. Mem. Tualatin Hills Dive Club (bd. dirs. 1987-93, pres. 1989-92), Pub. Rels. Soc. Am. (cert., bd. dirs. Columbia River chpt. 1984-89, pres. 1988), Oreg. State Bar (pub. svc. and info. com. 1987-92). Republican. Roman Catholic. Home: 17775 NW Park View Blvd Portland OR 97229-3438 Office: Lane Powell Spears Lubersky 520 SW Yamhill St Portland OR 97204-1335

MITCHELL, JOHN HENDERSON, retired army officer, management consultant; b. Atlanta, Sept. 9, 1933; s. William Lloyd and Jessie (Henderson) M.; m. Joan Ann Cameron, Apr. 8, 1961; children—John Cameron, Christopher Lloyd, Colin MacKenzie. BA in Bus. Adminstrn., St. Bonaventure U., 1956, PhD in Sci., 1991; MA in Pub. Adminstrn., Shippensburg State U., 1973. Commd. 2d lt. U.S. Army, 1956, advanced through grades to maj. gen., 1982; comdr. 8th Battallion, 6th Arty., 1st Infantry div. U.S. Army, Vietnam, 1968; chief officer assignments, field arty. br., Officer Personnel Directorate U.S. Army, Washington; chief of staff 8th div. U.S. Army, 1973-75; asst. dept. chief of staff for personnel, Hdqrs. U.S. Army Europe and 7th Army U.S. Army, Heidelberg, Fed. Republic Germany, 1975-77; div. arty. comdr., chief of staff, 1st Inf. Div. U.S. Army, Ft. Riley, Kan., 1977-79; comdr., Field Command, Def. Nuclear Agy. U.S. Army, Kirtland AFB, N.Mex., 1979-81; dir. Human Resources Devel. Office, dept. chief staff for pers. U.S. Army, Washington; U.S. comdr. Berlin, 1984-88; ret., 1989; pres. Intersystems, Inc., Englewood, Colo., 1989-93, POM Enterprises, Inc., Colo. Springs, Colo., 1994. Bd. dirs. Nat. Safety Council, 1982-84. Decorated D.S.M. with oak leaf cluster, Legion of Merit with oak leaf cluster, D.F.C. with oak leaf cluster, Bronze Star with oak leaf cluster and V., Air medals. Mem. Assn. U.S. Army, VFW, Army Navy Club, Army War Coll. Alumni, Soc. of First Inf. Div. Republican. Roman Catholic. Home: 375 Hidden Creek Dr Colorado Springs CO 80906-4386 Office: POM Enterprises Inc PO Box 60171 Colorado Springs CO 80960-0171

MITCHELL, JOHN NOYES, JR., electrical engineer; b. Pownal, Maine, Dec. 16, 1930; s. John Noyes and Frances (Small) M.; m. Marilyn Jean Michaelis, Sept. 1, 1956; children: Brian John, Cynthia Lynn Mitchell Tumbleson, Stephanie Lee Mitchell Judson. BSEE, Milw. Sch. Engring., 1957. Registered profl. engr., Ohio. Elec. rsch. engr. Nat. Cash Register Co., Dayton, Ohio, 1957-65; sr. engr. Xerox Corp., Rochester, N.Y., 1965-70, area mgr., 1970-73; area mgr. Xerox Corp., Dallas, 1973-76; area mgr. Xerox Corp., El Segundo, Calif., 1976-79, tech. program mgr., 1979-85, competitive benchmarking mgr., 1985-92, quality mgr., 1992—. With USN, 1949-53. Mem. IEEE, Mason. Republican. Episcopalian. Home: 11300 Providencia St Cypress CA 90630-5351 Office: Xerox Corp ESC1-1600 101 Continental Blvd El Segundo CA 90245-4806

MITCHELL, JOHN WILLIAM, economist; b. New Haven, Conn., July 13, 1944; s. Frank Sprague and Martha Louise (Bridge) M.; m. Susan Catherine Lewis, Aug. 27, 1966 (div. 1983); children: Heather, Kiandra; m. Carol Diane Overlund, Sept. 11, 1988. BA in Econs., Williams Coll., Williamstown, Mass., 1966; MA in Econs., U. Oreg., 1968, PhD in Econs., 1970. Prof. econs. Boise (Idaho) State U., 1970-83; chief econ. U.S. Bancorp, Portland, Oreg., 1983—; prin. M&H Econ. Cons., Boise, 1973-83. Chmn. leadership coun. N.W. Policy Ctr., Seattle, 1990-91; active Emanuel Found. Bd., Portland, 1989—. Mem. Nat. Assn. Bus. Econs. (chmn.), Oreg. Coun. Econs. Advisors, Phi Beta Kappa. Office: US Bancorp 111 SW 5th Ave Portland OR 97204-3604

MITCHELL, JOSEPH PATRICK, architect; b. Bellingham, Wash., Sept. 29, 1939; s. Joseph Henry and Jessie Delila (Smith) M.; student Western Wash. State Coll., 1957-59; BA, U. Wash., 1963, BArch, 1965; m. Marilyn Ruth Jorgenson, June 23, 1962; children: Amy Evangeline, Kirk Patrick, Scott Henry. Assoc. designer, draftsman, project architect Beckwith Spangler Davis, Bellevue, Wash., 1965-70; prin. J. Patrick Mitchell, AIA & Assoc./Architects/Planners/Cons., Kirkland, Wash., 1970—. Chmn. long range planning com. Lake Retreat Camp, 1965-93; bldg. chmn. Northshore Baptist Ch., 1980—, elder, 1984-90; mem. bd. extension and central com. Columbia Baptist Conf., 1977-83; Northshore Bapt. Ch. del. Bapt. World Alliance 16th Congress, Soul Korea, 1990, 17th Cong., Buenos Aires, Argentina, 1995; trustee Bakke Libr./Cultural Ctr., 1994—; vice moderator Columbia Baptist Conf., 1995—. Recipient Internat. Architectural Design award St. John Vianney Parish, 1989. Cert. Nat. Council Archtl. Registration Bds. Mem. AIA, Constrn. Specification Inst., Interfaith Forum Religion, Art, and Architecture, Nat. Fedn. Ind. Bus., Christian Camping Internat., Wash. Farm Forestry Assn., Rep. Senatorial Inner Circle, Woodinville C. of C., Kirkland C. of C. Republican. Office: 12620 120th Ave NE Ste 208 Kirkland WA 98034-7511

MITCHELL, KATHLEEN ANN, illustrator, graphic designer; b. Cin., July 27, 1948; d. Gerald Paige and Velma Alice (Bleier) Clary; m. Terence Nigel Mitchell, Feb. 2, 1977; children: Jessica Rose, Alexander Christien. BSc in Design, U. Cin., 1971. Graphic designer Lippincott & Margulies, N.Y.C., 1971, Allied Internat., London, 1972, Moura-George Briggs, London, 1973-75; art dir., photographer Phonograph Record Mag., L.A., 1976-77; ptnr. Walter Morgan Assocs., Santa Monica, Calif., 1977-80; illustrator Artists Internat., L.A. and N.Y.C., 1983—. Illustrator: (book) Once Upon a Cat, 1983, Jane Eyre, 1983, Alice in Wonderland, 1986, The Wizard of Oz, 1987, The Secret Garden, 1987, Kittens, Kittens, Kittens, 1987, My Bible Alphabet, 1987, The Christmas Story, 1989, Silent Night, 1989, The First Christmas, 1992, Aladdin and the Magic Lamp, 1993, Cinderella, 1993, Cats, 1994, Friendship, 1994, Thoughts, 1994, Beauty and the Beast, 1995, Joseph and the Dream Coat, 1995, Dogs, 1995, My Little Flower, 1995, Jaina and the Hanadak, 1995. Democrat. Home: 1040 22nd St Santa Monica CA 90403-4518

MITCHELL, KEN, retired government executive, insurance agent; b. Adams County, Colo., May 14, 1931; s. Harold and Gene Mitchell; m. Dorothy Mitchell, Mar. 1, 1951; children: Gail Lyn, Sandra Kay. Grad, high sch., Brighton Colo., 1949. Formerly with Dept Def. Mem. Brighton (Colo.) City Coun., 1964-94, mayor, 6 yrs.; chair Brighton Planning Commn.; chair Adams County Bd. Adjustment; chair Adams County Coun. Govt., 1994. Mem. Elks, Masons. Democrat. Home: 141 S 17th Avenue Dr Brighton CO 80601-2317

MITCHELL, LAURA ELLEN, adult critical care and high-risk/critical care obstetrics nurse; b. Boston, July 5, 1959; d. Milton G. and Bruce (Bowman) Campbell; m. Edward L. Mitchell, Apr. 12, 1987; 1 child, Amy. ADN, Palomar Coll., 1988; BSN, Calif. State U., Dominguez Hills, 1994. CCRN, cert. in med.-surg. perinatal nursing. Staff nurse Nurse Care Plus, Oceanside, Calif., Tri-City Med. Ctr., Oceanside; clin. nurse II U. Calif. Med. Ctr., Irvine; clin. nurse U. Calif. San Diego Med. Ctr. With U.S. Army, 1977-81. Mem. AACN, AAUW, ANA (practice couns. advanced practice and acute care), Assn. Women's Health, Obstetric and Neonatal Nursing, Jacobs Inst. Women's Health. Home: PO Box 4915 Oceanside CA 92052-4915

MITCHELL, LINDELL MARVIN, financial planner; b. Hagerman, N.Mex., July 11, 1937; s. Marvin P. and Lillie (Collom) M.; children: Lisa A. Purdy, Leah J. Student, N.Mex. State U., 1954-61. CFP; CLU; ChFC; registered rep., investment advisor. Owner, ins. broker, fin. planner, investment advisor Lindell M. Mitchell & Assocs., Albuquerque, 1971—; broker dealer Brokers Transaction Svcs., Inc., Dallas, Tex. Mem. N.Mex. Life Underwriters Assn. (pres. 1977-90), N.Mex. Soc. of Inst. Cert. Fin. Planners (founding pres.), Nat. Assn. Life Underwriters, Million Dollar Round Table. Republican. Home: 8800 Osuna Rd NE Albuquerque NM 87111-2142 Office: 5907 Alice Ave NE Ste F Albuquerque NM 87110-6560

MITCHELL, LYNN LEE, secondary education educator; b. Scottsbluff, Nebr., Feb. 18, 1945; s. Robert A. and Maxine M. (Holm) M.; m. Gertrude W. Wahl, Aug. 27, 1966; children: Anthony M., Robert L. Degree in Metall. Engring., Colo. Sch. Mines, 1968; M in Vocat.-Tech. Edn., Colo. State U., 1972. Metall. engr. Youngstown Steel, East Chgo., Ind., 1968-71; tchr. math. Baker (Oreg.) H.S., 1972-78; tchr. math. and sci. Seisen Internat. Sch., Tokyo, 1978-83; tchr. sci. Hood River (Oreg.) Valley H.S., 1983—. Named NSF chem. tchr., U. Wash., Seattle, summer 1988; recipient Presdl. Citation for instrn. & profl. devel. Oreg. Edn. Assn., 1990, OMSI & Tektronix Excellence in Teaching award, 1995. Mem. Oreg. Sci. Tchrs. Assn., Oreg. Coun. Tchrs. Math., Hood River Edn. Assn. (pres. 1992-95), Mt. Hood UNISERV (officer 1990—). Office: Hood River High Sch 1220 Indian Creek Rd Hood River OR 97031-9624

MITCHELL, MARGARETTA KUHLTHAU, photographer; b. Bklyn., May 27, 1935; d. Conrad William and Margaretta (Rice) Kuhlthau; m. Frederick Cleveland Mitchell, May 23, 1959; children: Margaretta Anne, Kate Davison, Julia Warren. BA, Smith Coll., 1957; MA, U. Calif., Berkeley, 1985. Rsch. asst. to Dr. Edwin Land Polaroid Corp., Cambridge, Mass., 1957-59; established darkroom U. Calif., Berkeley, 1960, worker darkroom facility, 1964-66; instr. Head-Royce evening program Head-Royce Sch., Oakland, Calif., 1971-76; instr. U. Calif. Ext. Program, San Francisco, Berkeley, 1976-78; tchr. Associated Students of U. Calif., Vista Coll., 1977-80; instr. Civic Arts Program, Walnut Creek, Calif., 1980-84, Calif. Coll. Arts and Crafts Ext. Program, 1985-87, Friends of Photography Workshop, San Francisco, 1988, Acad. of Art, San Francisco, 1990-95; lectr. in field. Author: (book) Gift of Place, 1969, To a Cabin, 1973, After Ninety, 1977, Recollections: Ten Women of Photography, 1979, Contemporary Photographers, 1982, Rising Goddess, 1982, Dance for Life, 1985, Ruth Bernhard-The Eternal Body-A Collection of Fifty Nudes, 1986, 94, The Gledhills: Portraits, 1988, Flowers, 1991; illustrator in field for various mags., jours. and books; one-woman shows include The Athenaeum, Boston, 1959, The Gallery, San Francisco, 1980, 81, Yuen Lui Gallery, Seattle, 1980, 86, Mount Vernon Coll., Washington, 1981, UPB Gallery, Berkeley, Calif., 1985, Sandra Berler, Washington, 1986, The Gallery at Lincoln Ctr., N.Y.C., 1986, War Meml. Opera House, San Francisco, 1986, Gump's Gallery, San Francisco, 1991, 92, Sandra Berler Gallery, Washington, 1994; exhibited in group shows at Friends of Photography Gallery, 1968, Focus Gallery, San Francisco, 1974, San Francisco Mus. Modern Art, 1978, The Dulin Gallery of Art, Knoxville, Tenn., 1980, Grand Rapids (Mich.) Art Mus., 1980, Smith Coll. Mus. Art, Northampton, Mass., 1980, Met. Mus. and Art Ctr., Coral Gables, Fla., 1980, William Rockhill Nelson Gallery and Atkins Mus. of Fine Art, Kansas City, Mo., 1980, Marcuse Pfeifer Gallery, N.Y., 1981, 86, Munson-Williams-Proctor Inst., Utica, N.Y., 1981, Gibbes Art Ballery, Charleston, S.C., 1981, Ark. Art Ctr., Little Rock, 1981, New Orleans Mus. Art, 1981, Mary and Leigh Block Gallery Evanston, Ill., 1982, Salt Lake Art Ctr., Salt Lake City, 1982, Presentation House, North Vancouver, B.C., Can., 1985, The Copley Soc., Boston, 1986, Mt. Holyoke Coll., South Hadley, Mass., 1988, Shapiro Gallery, San Francisco, 1989, 94, Witkin Gallery, N.Y., 1991, 94, Pepper Gallery, Boston, 1993, Pepper Gallery, Boston, 1993; represented in permanent collections San Francisco Mus. Modern Art, UCLA, Princeton U., N.Y. Public Library, Internat. Ctr. of Photography, Royal Print Collection, numerous other pub. and pvt. collections. Grantee Calif. Coun. for Humanities, 1980, 1984-85, In Dulci Jubilo Found., 1981, L. J. and Mary C. Skaggs Found., 1981, Calif. Coun. for the Arts, 1981-82, Polaroid Found., 1984, Polaroid Worldwide Creative Svcs., 1989. Mem. Am. Soc. Media Photographers (v.p. No. Calif. chpt. 1988-90, pres. 1990-92), Inst. for Hist. Study, Friends of Photography, Camerawork, Smith Coll. Alumnae Assn. (nat. alumnae admission com. 1986-89, chmn., bd. dirs. 1991-94), Fotoforum, San Francisco Mus. Modern Art, Smith Club (pres. 1989-90). Home and Studio: 280 Hillcrest Rd Berkeley CA 94705-2844

MITCHELL, MARTHA L., library director; b. Oregon City, Oreg., Nov. 4, 1958; d. James M. and Betty L. (Sampsel) Manning; m. Byron D. Mitchell, Sept. 26, 1981; children: Aaron Lee Mitchell, Ashley Marie Mitchell. Student, Portland State U., 1976-78, Columbia Christian Coll., Portland, 1978-79. Security K-Mart, Tualatin, Oreg., 1976-77; ins. coder Farmers Ins., Tigard, 1977-79; nanny Rafter Q Cattle Co., Paulina, Oreg., 1979-81; mainstream facilatator Umatilla E.S.D., Pendleton, Oreg., 1989-92; libr. dir. Helix (Oreg.) Pub. Libr., 1992—. Vol. aide in schs., Helix, 1990-94; coach Little League Baseball, Helix, 1991-94; mem. Helix Park and Recreation Bd., 1991-93. Republican. Mem. Christian Ch. Office: Helix Pub Libr PO Box 324 Helix OR 97835-0324

MITCHELL, MAUREEN, clinical dietitian, consultant; b. Bad Hersfeld, Germany, Apr. 7, 1960; came to U.S., 1962; d. Willis Charles and Frances Vernon (Murphy) M. BS, Viterbo Coll., La Crosse, Wis., 1983. Registeted dietitian; cert. diabetic educator. Dietitian, mgr. Meml. Med. Ctr., Ashland, Wis., 1983-85; clin. dietitian, asst. dept. mgr. Havasu Samaritan Regional Hosp., Lake Havasu City, Ariz., 1985—; speaker in field. Dir. Food Festival, Am. Heart Assn. Cmty. Program, Lake Havasu City, 1992, 93; mem. Nat. Coun. Against Health Fraud, 1993, 94; mem. Nat. Kidney Found., 1993, 94. Recipient Cert. of Recognition, Am. Heart Assn., 1992. Mem. Am. Dietetic Assn. (clin. dietetic support group), Ariz. Dietetic Assn., Am. Diabetes Assn. Office: Havasu Samaritan Reg Hosp 101 Civic Center Ln Lake Havasu City AZ 86403-5607

MITCHELL, MICHAEL, pediatric urologist, educator; b. Montclair, N.J., Apr. 11, 1943; s. William Alexander and Ruth (Cobbey) M.; m. Constance Wormser, June 25, 1967; children: Michael, Emily, Nicole, Hallie. BS, Princeton U., 1965; MD, Harvard U., 1969. Diplomate Am. Bd. Urology. Chief pediatric urology Ind. U., Indpls., 1984-89, prof. urology, 1985-89; chief pediatric urology, prof. urology U. Wash., Seattle, 1989—; sec. faculty Ind. Med. Sch., Indpls., 1988. Contbr. articles to profl. jours. Fellow Am. Acad. Pediatrics, Am. Coll. Surgeons; mem. Am. Urol. Soc., Genito Urinary Surgeons, Soc. Pediatric Urology (sec./treas. 1993—), Soc. Pediatric Urologis Surgeons. Office: Childrens Hosp and Med Ctr Box C5371 Seattle WA 98105

MITCHELL, MICHAEL KIEHL, elementary and secondary education educator, minister; b. Phila., Pa., Oct. 27, 1932; s. Robert Bartow and Louise

Room (Keyser) M.; m. Gloria (Nell) Wilburn, Nov. 12, 1960; children: Donald Kiehl, Robert Alan. B in Edn., U. Miami, 1955; MEd, Tex. A&M U., 1975, PhD, 1978; grad., Internat. Sch. Christian Comm. Cert. elem. and secondary edn., Fla., Tex., Alaska; lic. comml. pilot. Tchr. math. Dade County Pub. Schs., Miami Springs, Fla., 1955-60; tchr. elem. Greenwood Sch. Dist., Midland, Tex., 1961-63; from tchr. social studies, English to tng. coord. Midland (Tex.) Sch. Dist., 1963-75; prin. rsch. investigator Tex. A&M U., College Station, 1977-78; project dir. Edn. Profl. Devel. Consortium, Richardson, Tex., 1978-79; sr. rsch. scientist Am. Airlines, Dallas, 1979-83; pres. North Rsch. Inc., Anchorage, Alaska, 1983-84; vocat. edn. curriculum specialist Anchorage Sch. Dist., 1984-87; sci. tchr., dept. head McLaughlin Youth Ctr. Anchorage (Alaska) Sch. Dist., 1987—; adj. prof. U. Alaska, Anchorage, 1987-89; evaluation team N.W. Accreditation Assn., Anchorage, 1985; asst. min. United Meth. ch., 1990-94; min. Christian Comty. Fellowship, 1994—; instr. Flight and Ground Sch. Dir., v.p. Anchorage Comty. Theater, 1984-89; marriage commr. 3d Jud. Dist. Alaska, Anchorage, 1989-93; vol. United Way, Anchorage, 1984-90, Tony Knowles for Gov. Campaign, Anchorage, 1990, 94, Mark Begich for Mcpl. Assembly Campaign, 1991, Cheryl Clementson for Mcpl. Assembly Campaign, 1993. With U.S. Army, 1946-47. Tex. Edn. Agy. fellow, Austin, 1975, Ednl. Profl. Devel. fellow, 1975-78. Mem. Am. Correctional Edn. Assn., Alaska Airmans Assn. (bd. dirs. 1983-89), Screen Actors Guild, Mensa, Am. Legion, Clowns of Am., Nat. Sci. Tchrs. Assn., Alaska Sci. Tchrs. Assn., Alaskan Aviation Safety Found., Tex. Assn. Aerospace Tchrs., Phi Delta Kappa, Phi Kappa Phi. Home: 6626 Foothill Dr Anchorage AK 99504-2620 Office: McLaughlin Youth Cen High 2600 Providence Dr Anchorage AK 99508-4613

MITCHELL, RIE ROGERS, psychologist, counseling educator; b. Tucson, Feb. 1, 1940; d. Martin Smith and Lavaun (Peterson) Rogers; student Mills Coll., 1958-59; B.S., U. Utah, 1962, M.S., 1963; postgrad. San Diego State U., 1965-66; M.A., UCLA, 1969, Ph.D., 1969. Registered play therapist; cert. sandplay therapist; diplomate Am. Bd. Psychology, 1992; m. Rex C. Mitchell, Mar. 16, 1961; 1 child, Scott Rogers. Tchr., Coronado (Calif.) Unified Sch. Dist., 1964-65; sch. psychologist Glendale (Calif.) Unified Sch. Dist., 1968-70; psychologist Glendale Guidance Clinic, 1970-77; asst. prof. ednl. psychology Calif. State U., Northridge, 1970-74, asso. prof., 1974-78, prof., 1978—, chmn. dept. ednl. psychology, 1976-80, acting exec. asst. to pres., 1981-82; acting exec. asst. to pres. Calif. State U., Dominguez Hills, 1978-79; cons. to various Calif. sch. dists.; pvt. practice psychology, Calabasas, Calif. Recipient Outstanding Educator award Maharishi Soc., 1978; Woman of Yr. award U. Utah, 1962, Leadership award Western Assn. Counselor Edn., 1990. Mem. Calif. Assn. Counselor Edn., Supervision and Adminstrn. (dir. 1976-77), Western Assn. Counselor Edn. and Supervision (officer 1978-82, pres. 1980-81, profl. leadership award, 1990), Assn. Counselor Edn. and Supervision (dir. 1980-81, program chmn. 1981-82, treas. 1983-86, Presdl. award 1986, Leadership award 1987), UCLA Doctoral Alumni Assn. (pres. 1974-76), Am. Psychol. Assn., Am. Ednl. Research Assn., Calif. Women in Higher Edn. (pres. chpt. 1977-78), Calif. Concerns (treas. 1984-86), Pi Lambda Theta (pres. chpt. 1970-71, chairwoman nat. resolutions 1971-73). Author: Sandplay: Past Present & Future, 1994; contbr. numerous articles on group process, sandplay, counselor edn. to profl. jours. Home: 4503 Alta Tupelo Dr Calabasas CA 91302-2516 Office: Calif State U Northridge CA 91330

MITCHELL, ROBERT, province official; b. Preeceville, Sask., Can., Mar. 29, 1936; s. Charles Stuart M. and Beda Annette Abrahamson; m. Sandra Gail Stolson, Oct. 18, 1968; children: Janet Maureen, Roberta June, Stephanie Arbonna, Shannon Elizabeth, Donna Gailynn, Alison T. Marie. BA, U. Sask., 1957, LLB, 1959. Assoc. Salloum & Hagemeister, 1961-64; ptnr. Pierce, Hleck, Kanuka, Mitchell & Thuringer, 1964-70; dir. legal svcs. and legis. rsch. Labour Can., 1970-72; dir. legal svcs. Dept. of Regional Economic Expansion, 1973; labor rels. expert Internat. Labour Orgn., 1973-74; dep. min. Sask. Labour, 1974-79; sr. ptnr. Mitchell Taylor Mattison Ching, 1979-91; mem. Sask. Legis. Assembly, 1986; re-elected, 1991; Min. of Justiceand Atty. Gen. Province of Sask., Saskatoon, Can., 1991—; Provincial Sec. and Min. Human Resources, Labour and Employment Province of Sask., Can., 1991-92; now Min. of Indian and Metis Affairs Province of Sask., Regina, Can.; opposition critic Trade & Investment; chmn. Bd. of Inquiry, 1979-81; chief fed. negotiator Inuit Land Claim, 1980-82; cons. Labour Legis. Govt. of Yukon, 1981-84, province of Man., 1984; auditor gen. adv. com. Labrador, Can., 1984; del. to C.P.A. Registration Seminar, P.E.I., 1988. Author: Mega-Projects, 1981. Mem. United Ch. Mem. law Soc. of Sask. NDP. Office: Dept of Justice, 1874 Scarth St, Regina, SK Canada S4P 3V7 Home: 70 Degeer Cres, Saskatoon, SK Canada S7H 4P7

MITCHELL, ROBERT CAMPBELL, nuclear consultant; b. West Point, N.Y., Mar. 28, 1940; s. Herbert V. and Beatrice Cheeseman (Campbell) M.; m. Mardeene Burr, Aug. 19, 1963 (div. Dec. 1983); children: Wendolyn, Dawnelle; m. Patricia Johnson, Aug. 17, 1987. B of Engring., Stevens Inst. Tech., 1962; MEE, Rensselaer Poly. Inst., 1965. Registered profl. engr., Calif. Design engr. Knolls Atomic Power Lab., Schenectady, N.Y., 1962-65, sr. reactor operator, 1965-67; prin. tng. engr. Nuclear Energy Div. Gen. Electric Co., San Jose, Calif., 1967-72, project engr., 1972-75, mgr. advanced projects, 1975-77, project mgr., 1977-87, licensing mgr., 1987-95; cons. in field, 1995—. Contbr. articles to profl. jours. Nominee White House fellow Gen. Electric Co., San Jose, 1973. Mem. Elfun Soc. Republican. Episcopalian. Home and Office: 5188 Meridian Ave San Jose CA 95118

MITCHELL, ROBIN, artist, educator; b. L.A., Sept. 29, 1951; d. Lee and Libby (Besser) M. Student, Calif. State U., Northridge, 1968-70, UCLA, 1970-71; BFA, Calif. Inst. of Arts, 1972, MFA, 1974. Lectr. Calif. State U., Northridge, 1977-80; lectr. Sch. Fine Arts U. So. Calif., L.A., 1981—; lectr. Claremont (Calif.) Grad. Sch., 1979-80, U. So. Calif., 1981—, U. Calif., Irvine, 1987-92, Santa Barbara, 1991, 93-94, 94—. One-woman shows include Jan Baum Gallery, L.A., 1984, 83, 93, Baum-Silverman Gallery, L.A., 1981, Comsky Gallery, L.A., 1994; exhibited in group shows at Selby Gallery of Ringling Sch. of Art and Design, 1994, U. Calif. Santa Barbara, 1993, Susan Landau Contemporary Art, West L.A., 1992, Otis Sch. Art and Design Gallery, L.A., 1992, Michael Himovitz Gallery, Sacramento, 1992, Dorothy Goldeen Gallery, Santa Monica, Calif., Jan Turner Gallery, L.A., 1991, Sant Barbara Comtemporary Arts Forum, 1995. Grantee Nat. Endowment for Arts, 1987. Home: 2614 Euclid St Apt E Santa Monica CA 90405-4735

MITCHELL, TERENCE EDWARD, materials scientist; b. Haywards Heath, Sussex, Eng., May 18, 1937; came to U.S., 1963, naturalized, 1978; s. Thomas Frank and Dorothy Elizabeth (Perrin) M.; m. Marion Wyatt, Dec. 5, 1959; children: Robin Norman, Jeremy Neil. BA, St. Catharine's Coll., Cambridge (Eng.) U., 1958, MA, 1962, PhD in Physics, 1962; ScD, U. Cambridge, 1994. Research fellow Cavendish Lab., Cambridge, 1962-63; asst. prof. metallurgy Case Inst. Tech., 1963-66; assoc. prof. Case Western Res. U., 1966-75, prof., 1975-87, adj. prof., 1987—, chmn. dept., 1983-86, dir. high voltage electron microscopy facility, 1970-82, co-dir. materials research lab., 1982-83; vis. scientist NASA at Ames Lab., Stanford U. and Electric Power Research Inst., Palo Alto, Calif., 1975-76; scientist Ctr. Materials Sci. Los Alamos (N.Mex.) Nat. Lab., 1987—, lab fellow, 1991—; lab fellows chair Los Alamos (N.Mex.) Nat. Lab., 1993—; chmn. steering com. Electron Microscopy Ctr. Argonne (Ill.) Nat. Lab., 1979-83; cons. in field; mem. vis. com. metals and ceramics div. Oak Ridge Lab., 1987-91; vis. com. solid state scis. div. Ames Lab., 1987-89; sci. adv. com. Sci. and Tech. Ctr. for Superconductivity, 1989-93. Materials sci. editor Microscopy Rsch. and Technique, 1986—; sr. editor North Am., 1994—; contbr. articles to profl. jours. Pres. Cleve. Ethical Soc., 1970-72; bd. dirs Am. Ethical Union, 1972-74; steward Los Alamos Unitarian Ch., 1992-94; mem. policy com. Univ. Materials Coun., 1986-89; mem. policy com. Argonne Electron Microscopy Steering Com., chmn. 1978-82. Electric Power Research Inst. fellow, 1975-76; NSF grantee, 1966-88; Dept. Energy grantee, 1970-86, 87—; NIH grantee, 1969-72; NASA grantee, 1974-77, 81-87; USAF Office Sci. Research grantee, 1974-85; U.S. Army Research Office grantee, 1970-75, 79-83, EPRI grantee, 1986-89. Fellow Am. Soc. Metals, Am. Phys. Soc., Am. Ceramics Soc. (assoc. editor jour.), Los Alamos Nat. Lab.; mem. Metall. Soc. (editl. bd. 1981—), Electron Microscopy Soc. Am. (program chmn. 1981-82, dir. 1984-86, pres.-elect 1994, pres. 1995), Materials Rsch. Soc., Soc. Francaise de Microscopie Electronique (sci. com. 1982-90). Office: Los Alamos Nat Lab Ctr Materials Sci Ms # K-765 Los Alamos NM 87545

MITCHELL, THOMAS EDWARD, JR., communications cabling executive; b. Sacramento, Apr. 12, 1946; s. Thomas Edward and Violet Mae (Southall) M.; m. Terri Kathleen Vance, Apr. 20, 1969; children: Anthony E., Brian C. BA, Nat. U., 1987, MBA, 1988. Enlisted USMC, 1966, advanced through grades to maj., 1980, retired, 1989; sr. exec. Nat. Decision Sys., Encinitas, Calif., 1989-90, Equifax Mktg. Decision Sys., San Dieto, 1990-93; pres., COO Holocomm Sys. Inc., San Diego, 1993—; bd. dirs. Cal-Pacific Steel Structure Inc., Hawaii, Calif. Contbr. articles to profl. jours.; patentee in field. Dir. Toys for Tots, L.A./ORange Counties, Calif., 1974-77. Recipient Silver Star medal U.S. Pres., 1968, Meritorious Svc. medal, Joint Chiefs of Staff Commendation medal, others. Mem. World Trade Assn. (assoc. 1989—), Am. Legion, Internat. Platform Assn. Home: 3264 Chase Ct Oceanside CA 92056-3809 Office: Holcomm Sys Inc 6640 Lusk Blvd Ste D-211 San Diego CA 92121

MITCHELL, THOMAS GEORGE, real estate company executive; b. July 2, 1944; s. Charles Henry and Loraine (Hauber) M.; divorced; 1 child, Erik. BBA, U. Cin., 1967; postgrad., U. Cin., Santa Clara U. Corp. acct., computer systems mktg. exec. Litton Industries, Cin., 1970-73, Burroughs Corp., Cin., 1973-75; founder, mng. gen. pgnr. Mitchell & Co. Real Estate, Inc., 1979-89; pres. Elite Properties Inc., 1989—; pres. PRD Realty Group, Inc. Author: The Commercial Lease Guidebook; Learn how to win the leasing game!, 1992, (software) Real Estate Devel. System, 1984. Home: 3870 Mahinahina St Lahaina HI 96761-9346 Office: PO Box 5273 Lahaina HI 96761-5273

MITCHELL, WAYNE LEE, health care administrator; b. Rapid City, S.D., Mar. 25, 1937; s. Albert C. and Elizabeth Isabelle (Nagel) M.; m. Marie Galletti; BA, U. Redlands (Calif.), 1959; MSW, Ariz. State U., 1970, EdD, 1979. Profl. social worker various county, state, and fed. agys., 1962-70, Bur. Indian Affairs, Phoenix, 1970-77, USPHS, 1977-79; asst. prof. Ariz. State U., 1979-84; with USPHS, Phoenix, 1984—. Bd. dirs. Phoenix Indian Cmty. Sch., 1973-75, ATLATL, 1995; bd. dirs. Phoenix Indian Ctr., 1974-79, Cmty. Svc. award, 1977; mem. Phoenix Area Health Adv. Bd., 1975; mem. Community Behavioral Mental Health Bd., 1976-80; lectr. in field. Bd. dirs. Cen. Ariz. Health Systems Agy.; mem. Fgn. Rels. Com. Phoenix. Served with USCG, 1960-62. Recipient Community Service award Ariz. Temple of Islam, 1980. Mem. NASW, UN Assn., Am. Orthopsychiat. Assn., NAACP, Internat. Platform Assn., Asia Soc., U.S.-China Assn., Kappa Delta Pi, Phi Delta Kappa, Chi Sigma Chi, Nucleus Club. Congregationalist. Democrat. Contbr. articles to publs. Home: PO Box 9592 Phoenix AZ 85068-9592 Office: 3738 N 16th St Phoenix AZ 85016-5947

MITRA, WILLIAM E., video game producer; b. Orange, Calif., May 6, 1966; s. James E. and Michael Ann (Mitchell) M. BA, Reed Coll., 1987; BS, Calif. Inst. Tech., 1989. Computer programmer Apple Computer, Cupertino, Calif., 1989-91; freelance writer, New Orleans, 1991-92; prodr. video games Crystal Dynamics, Inc., Palo Alto, Calif., 1992—. Office: Crystal Dynamics Inc 87 Encina Ave Palo Alto CA 94301-2322

MITCHISON, TIMOTHY JOHN, cell biologist, pharmacology educator; b. Edinburgh, Scotland, July 20, 1958; came to U.S., 1980; s. Avrion and Lorna (Martin) M. BA in Biochemistry, Oxford (Eng.) U., 1980; PhD in Biochemistry, U. Calif., San Francisco, 1984. Asst. prof. U. Calif., San Francisco, 1987-92, assoc. prof., 1992—. Contbr. numerous sci. articles to profl. publs. Rsch. grantee NIH, 1987—; fellow Packard Found., Searle Found. Mem. Am. Soc. Cell Biology. Office: U Calif Dept Pharmacology San Francisco CA 94143-0450

MITHUN, ROBERT JAMES, physician; b. Seattle, June 4, 1949; s. Omer Lloyd Mithun and Ruth Eleanor (Trueblood) Klopfer; m. Anne Kimi Fukutome, Apr. 7, 1984; children: Paul, Julie, Lisa. BA, Stanford U., 1971; MD, U. Colo., 1975. Diplomate Am. Bd. Internal Medicine. Owner Mithun Electronics, Denver and San Francisco, 1971-84; intern in medicine Children's Hosp., San Francisco, 1975-76, resident in medicine, 1976-78; rsch. fellow Vets. Hosp., Martinez, Calif., 1978-79; internist French Health Plan, San Francisco, 1979-88, med. dir., 1983-88; internist Permanente Med. Group, San Francisco, 1988—, asst. chief of medicine, 1991—; cons. Biofeedback Inst. of San Francisco, 1976-83, Children's Hosp. Health Plan, San Francisco, 1978-79, Richmond (Calif.) Hosp., 1978-79. Mem. ACP, San Francisco Med. Co., Calif. Med. Assn. Office: Permanente Med Group 2200 Ofarrell St San Francisco CA 94115-3357

MITIO, JOHN, III, state agency administrator; b. Michigan City, Ind., Jan. 15, 1950; s. John Mitio Jr. and Bonnie Gloria (Pence) Morse; stepson of Eugene A. Morse; m. Judy Sena, Nov. 25, 1971 (div. 1985); m. Gail Stefl, Sept. 5, 1987 (div. 1995); 1 child, Kevin Michael. AA in Liberal Arts, N.Mex. State U., Alamogordo, 1976; BA in Anthropology, N.Mex. State U., Las Cruces, 1979. Engr. aide U.S. Civil Service, Alamogordo, 1974-75, Dynalectron Corp., Alamogordo, 1976; law enforcement campus police N.Mex. State U., Las Cruces, 1977-79; eligibility worker human svcs. dept. State of N. Mex., Albuquerque, 1984-86; medicaid planner human svcs. dept. State of N. Mex., Santa Fe, 1986—. Sgt. USAF, 1969-73, 1st lt., 79-83. Decorated Nat. Def. Svc. medal, Armed Forces Expeditionary medal, Air Force Overseas Svc. medal, Air Force Good Conduct medal. Mem. Planetary Soc., World Future Soc., Nat. Space Soc. Republican. Roman Catholic. Home: PO Box 16094 Santa Fe NM 87506 Office: Human Svcs Dept PO Box 2348 2500 Cerrillos Rd Santa Fe NM 87504-2348

MITRA, SANJIT KUMAR, electrical and computer engineering educator; b. Calcutta, West Bengal, India, Nov. 26, 1935; came to U.S., 1958; MS in Tech., U. Calcutta, 1956; MS, U. Calif., Berkeley, 1960, PhD, 1962; D of Tech. (hon.), Tampere (Finland) U., 1987. Asst. engr. Indian Statis. Inst., Calcutta, 1956-58; from teaching asst. to assoc. Univ. Calif., Berkeley, 1958-62; asst. prof. Cornell U., Ithaca, N.Y., 1962-65; mem. tech. staff Bell Telephone Labs., Holmdel, N.J., 1965-67; prof. U. Calif., Davis, 1967-77; prof. elec. and computer engring. U. Calif., Santa Barbara, 1977—, chmn. dept. elec. and computer engring., 1979-82; dir. Ctr. for Info. Processing Rsch., 1993—; cons. Lawrence Livermore (Calif.) Nat. Lab., 1974—; cons. editor Van Nostrand Reinhold Co., N.Y.C., 1977-88; mem. adv. bd. Coll. Engring. Rice U., Houston, 1986-89; mem. adv. coun. Rsch. Inst. for Math. and Computing Sci., U. Groningen, The Netherlands, 1995—. Author: Analysis and Synthesis of Linear Active Networks, 1969, Digital and Analog Integrated Circuits, 1980; co-editor: Modern Filter Theory and Design, 1973, Two-Dimensional Digital Signal Processing, 1978, Miniaturized and Integrated Filters, 1989, Multidimensional Processing of Video Signals, 1992, Handbook for Digital Signal Processing, 1993. Named Disting. Fulbright Prof., Coun. for Internat. Exch. of Scholars, 1984, 86, 88, Disting. Sr. Scientist, Humboldt Found., 1989. Fellow AAAS, IEEE (Edn. award Crcts. and Systems Soc. 1988, disting. lectr. Crcts. and Systems Soc. 1991—), Internat. Soc. Optical Engring.; mem. Am. Soc. for Engring. Edn. (F.E. Terman award 1973, AT&T Found. award 1985), European Assn. for Signal Processing. Office: Univ Calif Dept Elec Computer Eng Santa Barbara CA 93106

MITRANY, DEVORA, marketing consultant, writer; b. Oak Park, Ill., Mar. 20, 1947; d. John Joseph and Frances Elizabeth (Kirke) Lang; m. Douglas Allen Braun, Sept. 16, 1967 (div. Sept. 1976); m. Stanton Mitrany, Feb. 7, 1988 (div. July 1994). BA cum laude, Beloit Coll., 1969; postgrad., Boston U., 1971-72. Elem. and presch. tchr., Oak Park, Ill. and Boston, 1969-72; regional adminstr. TRW Fin. Systems, Wellesley, Mass., 1972-76; mgr. mktg. communications Computer Sharing Svcs., Denver, 1976-82; dir. corp. communications Corp. Mgmt. Systems, Denver, 1982-85; sr. copywriter On-Line Software Internat., Fort Lee, N.J., 1985-86; mgr. corp. communications Health Mgmt. Systems, N.Y.C., 1986-89; dir. pub. rels. Am. Sephardi Fedn., 1989-92; pres. The Mitrell Group, 1992-94; U.S. mktg. dir. The Best of Israel, 1994—; press release chmn. Nassau Region Hadassah, 1992-94. Warden, vestry mem. Trinity Ch., Wrentham, Mass., 1974-76; mem. vestry St. Philip and St. James Episcopal Ch., Denver, 1983; vol. Hospice of Holy Spirit, Lakewood, Colo., 1980-83; bd. dirs. Talia Hadassah, 1986-94, copres., 1990-92; v.p. edn. Long Beach Hadassah, 1992-94; dir. pub. rels. Bus. Roundtable on Nat. Security, Colo., 1983-84. Recipient Nat. Leadership award, Long Beach Hadassah, 1991-92, Nat. Leadership award Talia Hadassah, 1993-94; named Woman of Yr. Talia Hadassah, 1993. Mem. Denver Advt. Fedn. (bd. dirs. 1981-83, Alfie award 1984), Colo. Conf. Communicators (Denver Advt. Fedn. liasion 1981-84), Am. Sephardi Fedn. (edn. com. 1987-89). Jewish. Democrat.

MITTELSTAEDT, RICK H., technical communicator; b. Salt Lake City, Apr. 10, 1966; s. Richard H. Mittelstaedt and Linda Kaye (McReynolds) Cook; m. Gillian Dianne Gawne, Aug. 4, 1991; 1 child, Sawyer Douglas. BA in Tech. Comm., U. Wash., 1994. Tech. communicator Snohomish County PUD, Everett, Wash., 1991-93, Attachmate Corp., Bellevue, Wash., 1993—. Mem. IEEE, Scientific and Tech. Comm. (newsletter editor 1993-94), Usability Profls. Assn., Profl. Comm. Soc., Nat. Assn. Investors Corp. Home: 1725 174th Pl SE Mill Creek WA 98012-6491 Office: Attachmate Corp 3617 131st Ave SE Bellevue WA 98006-1330

MITTERMEIER, JANICE, commercial airport executive. Airport dir. John Wayne Airport, Costa Mesa, Calif. Office: John Wayne Airport Orange County 3151 Airway Ave Bldg K-101 Costa Mesa CA 92626-4607*

MITTON, MICHAEL ANTHONY, corporate executive; b. Bremen, Fed. Republic Germany, Mar. 13, 1947; came to U.S., 1948 (parents Am. citizens); s. Ralph Walter and Aniela (Pilarz) M.; m. Lisa Van der Veer, Mar. 7, 1986 (div. 1991); m. Marilyn Kay Bowen, Sept. 18, 1993. BS, U. Wyo., 1970. Asst. mgr. ops. Moller Steamship Co., N.Y.C., 1970-72; investment analyst Moller Industries, N.Y.C., 1972-73; internal auditor Corning (N.Y.) Glass Works, 1973-75, supr. acctg., 1975-76; dir. acctg. Autotrain Corp., Washington, 1977-78; pres. RMA Ltd., Ft. Collins, Colo., 1978-81; contr. Purecycle Corp., Boulder, Colo., 1981-83; pres., chief exec. officer, treas. Synthetech Inc., Albany, Oreg., 1983-90, bd. dirs., chmn., 1990—; pres., CEO Chemical Biosensors, Inc., Beaverton, Oreg., 1992—; co-chmn. Oreg. Biotech. Industry Coun., 1989-90; mem. Gov.'s Task Force Tech. Transfer, 1992—. Mem. Gov.'s Task Force Tech. Transfer, 1992-94. Fellow Am. Leadership Forum; mem. Soaring Soc. Am., Oreg. Biotech. Assn. (bd. dirs., chmn. 1990-91, pres. 1991-92), Multnomah Athletic Club. Home: PO Box 982 Lincoln City OR 97367-0982 Office: Chemical Biosensors Inc PO Box 1120 Beaverton OR 97075-1120

MITZE, CLARK HAROLD, retired arts administrator; b. Cedar Falls, Iowa, Mar. 28, 1918; s. George H. and Alace (Brown) M.; m. Verla Marie Diekman, May 20, 1941; children: Thomas, Michael Terry, Robert. BA, No. Iowa U., 1939; MA, U. Iowa, 1947. Asst. prof. Washngton U., St. Louis, 1951-67; dir. Mo. Arts Coun., St. Louis, 1965-68, Calif. Arts Coun., Sacramento, 1976-78; dir. state community Nat. Endowment for Arts, Washington, 1968-76; dir. Ill. Arts Coun., Chgo., 1978-81; ret., 1981; vis. prof. arts adminstrn. San Francisco State U., 1981-84; music reviewer Sacramento Pub. Radio, 1984—. Lt. col. USAAF, 1941-46. Recipient Disting. Alumni award No. Iowa U., 1979. Home: 626 Rivercrest Dr Sacramento CA 95831-1121

MIYAHIRA, SARAH DIANE, college dean, psychologist, educator; b. Wailuku, Maui, Hawaii, May 13, 1948; d. Ronald Takayoshi and Bertha Asae (Nagagaki) M.; m. Justin Masakatsu Koizumi, Sept. 7, 1974; 1 child, Jason Miyahira Koizumi. BA, U. Hawaii, 1970; MA, Ohio State U., 1973, PhD, 1976. Lic. psychologist, marriage, family and child counselor, Calif. Postdoctoral trainee L.A. Dept. Mental Health, 1977; staff psychologist counseling svcs. U. So. Calif., L.A., 1978-81; lectr. L.A., 1978-80; assoc. dir. counseling svcs. U. So. Calif., L.A., 1981-83, dir., 1983-85; dean student svcs. Honolulu Community Coll., 1985-88; dean student affairs and open grants East-West Ctr., Honolulu, 1988-94; assoc. dir. of edn. Pacific Ctr. for PTSD, 1994—; psychotherapist, orgnl. behavior cons., L.A., 1979-85; mem. bd. behavioral sci. examiners State of Calif., 1981-84, mem. accreditation team postsecondary edn. com., 1981; mem. adv. com. Ctr. for Non-Profit Mgmt., L.A., 1984-85; mem. commn. on status of women U. Hawaii, Honolulu, 1987, mem. com. human studies, 1994—, mem. clin. studies program adv. bd. dept. psychology, 1994—. Mem. steering com. Asian Pacific Women's Network, L.A., 1980; bd. dirs. Asian Pacific Am. support group U. So. Calif., 1983-85; mem. scholarship com. Japanese Am. Citizens League, San Francisco, 1984-85; mem. nominating com. YWCA, Honolulu, 1986-88. Mem. APA (bd. ethnic minority affairs 1986-88, chmn. 1988, mem. ethics com. 1989-90, com. on women in psychology 1992-95, chmn., 1994, chair divsn. 35 continuing edn. com. 1993—, mem. women's work group, rural health svcs. delivery task force 1995—), Soc. for Study Ethnics and Minority Issues, Nat. Assn. Fgn. Student Advisors, Nat. Assn. for Internat. Educators, Asian Am. Psychol. Assn., Women in Higher Edn. Adminstrn., Hawaii Network, Pacific and Asian Affairs Coun., Honolulu Com. on Fgn. Rels. Office: 1132 Bishop St Ste 307 Honolulu HI 96813-2830

MIYAMOTO, CRAIG TOYOKI, public relations executive; b. Joliet, Ill., Oct. 14, 1944; s. Robert Mitsuo and Dorothy Toyoko (Okumura) M.; BBA, Woodbury Coll., 1967; MA, U. So. Calif., 1972; m. Diana Chie Ueda, Mar. 24, 1966; children: James Anthony Kazuyuki, Carleton Alan Yasuo. Reporter, Alhambra (Calif.) Post-Advocate, 1968-70; editor Monterey Park Californian, 1970-71; mng. editor So. Calif. Pub. Co., 1971-72; dep. pub. rels. dir. Honolulu Bd. Water Supply, 1972-76, pub. rels. dir., 1976-77; pres. Miyamoto Advt./Pub. Relations, Honolulu, 1977-87; v.p. Profl. Communications, Inc., 1987-92; exec. v.p., 1995—; asst. prof. U. Hawaii, 1992-95; Pineapple Post, Honolulu, 1977—, Aura Publs., Honolulu, 1980-83, instr. pub. rels. U. Hawaii, 1978-80. Pres., Honolulu Jaycees, 1975-76; mem. exec. com. 50th State Fair, 1974-76; dir. pub. rels. Hawaii Jaycees, 1974-75, Monterey Park C. of C., 1970-71; bd. dirs. San Gabriel Valley YMCA, 1971-72, Garfield Community Sch. Bd., 1971-72; mem. Jaycees Internat. Senate, 1976—; treas. Alzheimer's Assn. of Hawaii, 1991-92; bd. dirs. Am. Heart Assn. Hawaii affiliate. Named Man of Yr., Honolulu, 1974; recipient John Armbruster award, 1974, State Svc. award Hawaii Jaycees, 1974, Gregg Perry Pub. Rels. Profl. of the Year, Hawaii, 1992. Fellow Pub. Rels. Soc. Am. (accredited, bd. dirs. Hawaii chpt., pres., v.p., sec. Hawaii chpt., chmn. South Pacific dist., sec. environ. sect.); mem. Am. Advt. Fedn., Nat. Assn. Environ. Communicators, Assn. Edn. in Journalism and Mass Comm., Internat. Acad. Bus. Disciplines, Hawaii Advt. Fedn. (bd. dirs.), Mensa, Am. Philatelic Soc., Am. Topical Assn., Internat. Soc. for Japanese Philately, Bur. Issues Assn., Hawaiian Philatelic Soc., Hawaii Stamp and Coin Dealers Assn. (pres., v.p.). Democrat. Author: How to Earn $2,000 or More Without Hardly Working At All, 1979, The Pineapple Post Catalogue, 1984, Environmental Public Relations: A Primer on the Hottest Growth Area of the 90's, 1991, U.S. Corporate Environmental Policy: Philosophy vs. Practice at the Dawnof a New Millenium, 1995. Office: Pacific Tower 19th Fl 1001 Bishop St Honolulu HI 96813

MIYAMOTO, OWEN, state agency administrator. Airport adminstr. Hawaii State Dept. of Transp., Honolulu, HI. Office: Honolulu Internat Airport 400 Rodgers Blvd Ste 700 Honolulu HI 96819-1880

MIYASAKI, GEORGE JOJI, artist; b. Kalopa, Hawaii, Mar. 24, 1935. BFA, Calif. Coll. Arts and Crafts, 1957, MFA, 1958. Asst. prof. art Calif. Coll. Arts and Crafts, Oakland, 1958-64; mem. faculty dept. art U. Calif., Berkeley, 1964-94; prof. emeritus U. Calif. John Hay Whitney fellow, 1957-58; Tamarind printing fellow, 1961; Guggenheim fellow, 1963-64; Nat. Endowment for Arts fellow, 1980-81, 85-86. Mem. Nat. Acad. of Design. Home: 2844 Forest Ave Berkeley CA 94705-1309

MIYATA, KEIJIRO, culinary arts educator; b. Tokyo, Mar. 8, 1951; came to U.S., 1967; s. Yataro Miyata and Hekkiken (Liu) Choy; m. Connie Joyce Nelson, Mar. 8, 1976; children: Michelle, Kelly, Adam. Assoc. in Occupational Study, Culinary Inst. Am., Hyde Park, N.Y., 1972, cert. of nutrition, 1991; cert., Seattle Wine Sch., 1991. Cert. exec. chef; cert. culinary educator. Garde mgr. Mid-Pacific Country Club, Kailua, Hawaii, 1972; working chef Waikiki Yacht Club, Honolulu, 1972-74, Sagano Japanese Restaurant, New Rochelle, N.Y., 1974-76; asst. pastry chef Rye Town (N.Y.) Hilton Hotel, 1976-77; working chef The Copper Kettle, Everett, Wash., 1977-79; exec. chef Holiday Inn, Everett, 1979-81, Mill Creek (Wash.) Country Club, 1981; culinary art instr. Everett Community Coll., 1981-85, North Seattle (Wash.) Community Coll., 1985-90, Seattle Cen. Community Coll., 1990—; cons. Chalon Corp., Redmond, Wash., Chiang-Mai Restaurant, Mukilteo, Wash., 1988, Holiday Inn Crown Plaza, Seattle. Recipient Gold awards Am. Culinary Fedn., Oreg. State Chef's Assn., Portland, 1983, Gold and Bronze medals World Culinary Olympic, Frankfurt, Germany, 1984, 88, Grand Champion award U.S. Nat. Ice Carving Contest, N.Y.C., 1986, 2d place award All Japan Ice Carving Assn., Asahikawa, 1988, Ednl. Excellence award Oreg. and Wash. Community Coll. Couns. Wash. Fedn. of Tchrs. & Am. Fedn. of Tchrs., AFL-CIO, 1988, 89; ACF Seafood Challenge State finalist, Charlotte, N.C., 1989, New Orleans, 1990; 1st place Pacific Rim

Invitational World Ice Sculpting Classic, 1989; 1st place Seymour Ice Sculpting Competition, 1991; 1st place 3d Ann. Internat. Ice Sculpting Competition, Lake Louise, Alta., Can., 1993, Award of Excellence Wash. Fedn. Tchrs./Am. Fedn. Tchrs./AFL-CIO, 1993, 1st place Wash. State Seafood Festival Recipe Contest, Shelton, Wash., 1993, Grand Cahmpion, 1994, 1st place ICE ART'94 Ice Sculpting Competition, Fairbanks, Alaska, 1994. Mem. Wash. State Chefs Assn. (bd. dirs. 1982, 83, 86, 87, 88, cert. chmn. 1986-92, Chef of Yr. 1986), Am. Acad. Chefs. Office: Seattle Cen Community Coll 1701 Broadway Seattle WA 98122-2413

MIZER, RICHARD ANTHONY, technology consultant; b. San Francisco, Jan. 7, 1952; s. Conrad Xavier and Sally Jo (Hagan) M. BA in Bioengring. and Econs., U. Calif., San Diego, 1977. Founding ptnr. Microdoctors, Palo Alto, Calif., 1974—; mgr., ptnr. K-Family Corp. dba Harlow's Night Club, Fremont, Calif., 1977-79, Restaurants Unique Inc., Mountain View, Calif., 1980-83; mgr. engring. Pacific Bell, San Ramon, Calif., 1983-89; tech. cons. advanced techs. Pacific Bell, 1989—; developer Advanced Video Svcs., 1989-92, project mgr., 1992-93, tech. mgr., 1993—. Exec. in charge of prodn. Cinema of the Future; assoc. prodr. Soccer Fest: World Cup Soccer Final in HDTV to Europe and U.S. theaters from Pasadena Rose Bowl, 1994; exec. prodr. HDTV prodn. of 50th Anniversary of Signing of UN Charter, 1995. Mem. security staff Republican Task Force, San Francisco, 1984, tech. staff U.S. Olympic Com., Los Angeles, 1984. Mem. IEEE, Nat. Assn. Broadcasters, Soc. Motion Picture and TV Engrs. Roman Catholic. Office: Pacific Bell 2600 Camino Ramon # 15300 San Ramon CA 94583-5041

MIZRAHI, YVES, retail executive; b. Paris, France, Nov. 22, 1934, came to U.S., 1959; s. Maurice and Fanny (De Leon) M.; m. Deborah Anne Mizrahi, May 20, 1978; children: Lauren, Amanda. BA in Biology, U. Wash., 1977; MBA in Fin., U. Puget Sound, 1980. Registered real estate broker, Wash. Pers. officer U. Wash., Seattle, 1977-80; sr. treasury analyst ENI Exploration Co., Seattle, 1980-81; sr. fin. analyst Seafirst Bank, Seattle, 1981-83; sr. econ. cons. The NBBI Group, Seattle, 1983-85; sr. investment analyst Composite Rsch., Seattle, 1985-86; v.p. Wahl & Assocs., Seattle, 1986-88; v.p. real estate Starbucks Coffee, Seattle, 1988—. Mem. com. Downtown Seattle Assn., 1983-85; mem. fin. com. Villa Acad., Seattle, 1992-93. Mem. Internat. Conf. Shopping Ctrs., NACORE. Home: 3803 43rd Ave NE Seattle WA 98105-5446 Office: P O Box 34067 2203 Airport Way S Seattle WA 98124-1067

MIZUNO, NOBUKO SHIMOTORI, biochemist; b. Oakland, Calif., Apr. 20, 1916; d. Shinichiro and Kii (Niyomura) S.; m. Walter M. Mizuno, Mar. 20, 1942 (dec. 1946). AB, U. Calif.-Berkeley, 1937, MA, 1939; PhD, U. Minn., 1956. Rsch. asst. U. Calif., Berkeley, 1939-41; instr. Macalester Coll., St. Paul, 1943-51; rsch. assoc. U. Minn., St. Paul, 1956-62; rsch. biochemist VA Med. Ctr., Mpls., 1962-79; ret. Contbr. articles to profl. jurs. NSF fellow, 1956. Mem. AAAS, Am. Inst. Nutrition, Am. Soc. Biochemistry and Molecular Biology, Iota Sigma Pi (historian 1970-72). Home: 3628 Loma Way San Diego CA 92106-2034

MOBERLY, DAVID LINDSEY, foundation executive; b. Irvine, Ky., Apr. 25, 1929; s. Earl and Blanche (Finney) M.; m. Peggy Compton, Dec. 30, 1951; children—Kent, Lynn. A.B., U. Ky., 1951; postgrad., Am. U., 1950; M.A., U. Ky., 1953; Ph.D., Kent State U., 1965. Tchr. Jefferson County Bd. Edn., Louisville, 1951-54; dean of boys Jefferson County Bd. Edn., 1954-55, asst. prin., 1955-57; ednl. adv. AID, U.S. State Dept., Tripoli, Benghazi, Libya, 1957-61; edn. program officer, research and survey team AID, U.S. State Dept., Nairobi, Kenya, 1961-62; instr., resident project coordinator in Tanzania Kent State U., 1962-65; supt. schs. Bd. Edn., Tallmadge, Ohio, 1966-67, Warren, Ohio, 1967-71, Cleve. Heights, 1971-74; supt. schs. Evanston (Ill.) Twp. High Sch., 1974-76, Seattle Sch. Dist. 1, 1976-81; pres. Seattle Found., 1981-84; nat. edn. mgr. Deloitte, Hoskins & Sells, 1984-89; asst. state supt. State of Wash., 1989—; spl. participant documentary on problems in edn. ABC-TV, 1976. Area chmn. Ohio's Right-to-Read project, 1969-71; chmn. alumni com. for edn. com. Kent State U., 1968-71; mem. nat. adv. bd. Corp. for Pub. Broadcasting; U.S. del. to World Orgn. of Teaching Profession in, Rome, Italy, 1958; Mem. Seattle council Boy Scouts Am.; bd. dirs. Jr. Achievement; trustee Pacific Sci. Center Found., Seattle; mem. Pvt. Sector's Initiative Bd., Seattle. Mem. NEA, Am. Assn. Sch. Adminstrs., Wash. Assn. Sch. Adminstrs., Mcpl. League, Seattle C. of C., Kappa Delta Pi, Phi Delta Kappa. Club: Rotarian. Home: 3045 44th Ave W Seattle WA 98199-2401

MOBERLY, LINDEN EMERY, educational administrator; b. Laramie, Wyo., Jan. 4, 1923; s. Linden E. and Ruth (Gathercole) M. BS, Coll. Emporia, 1952; MS, Kans. State Tchrs. Coll., 1954; m. Viola F. Mosher, Apr. 29, 1949. Tchr. sci., Florence, Kans., 1952-54, Concordia, Kans., 1954-56, Grand Junction, Colo., 1957-60; asst. prin. Orchard Mesa Jr. High Sch., Grand Junction, 1960-66, prin., 1967-84; field cons. Nat. Assn. Secondary Sch. Prins., 1985—. Sgt. USMC, 1941-46. Recipient Outstanding Secondary Prin. award Colo. Assn. Sch. Execs., 1978. Mem. NEA, VFW, Nat. Assn. Secondary Prins. (bd. dir. 1979-83), Colo. Edn. Assn. (bd.dir. 1968-71), Colo. North Central Assn. Colls. and Secondary Schs., Colo. Assn. Secondary Sch. Prins. (bd. dir. 1974-77), Lions, Sons of the Revolution, Marine Corps League (life), VFW (life), Masons (award of Excellence 1990). Home: 2256 Kingston Rd Grand Junction CO 81503-1221

MOBERLY, MICHAEL DEAN, lawyer; b. Webster City, Iowa, Nov. 21, 1956; s. Maurice Dean and Elaine Adele (DeArmond) M.; m. Jeanine Ann Biggins, Aug. 6, 1977; children: Daniel Philip, Chelsea Jean, Thomas Stephen. BBA with high distinction, U. Iowa, 1979, JD with high distinction, 1983. Bar: Ariz. 1983, U.S. Dist. Ct. Ariz. 1983, U.S. Ct. Appeals (9th cir.) 1983, U.S. Ct. Appeals (8th cir.), U.S. Ct. Appeals (D.C. cir.) 1987, U.S. Supreme Ct. 1986. Ptnr. Ryley, Carlock & Applewhite, Phoenix, 1983—. Editor The Ariz. Labor Letter. Vice chmn. Ariz. Agrl. Employment Rels. Bd. Recipient Am. Jurisprudence awards. Mem. ABA, Ariz. Bar Assn., Maricopa County Bar Assn., Order of Coif, Beta Alpha Psi. Republican. Roman Catholic. Home: 2619 S Evergreen Rd Tempe AZ 85282-3038 Office: Ryley Carlock & Applewhite 101 N 1st Ave Phoenix AZ 85003-1902

MOBLEY, CHARLES MURRAY, archaeologist; b. Paulding, Ohio, Feb. 18, 1954; s. Charles Richard and Theresa (Bradley) M.; divorced; 1 child, Charles Ottar Carlson Mobley. BA in Anthropology, Case Western Res. U., 1974; MA in Conservation Archaeology, So. Meth. U., 1978, PhD in Anthropology, 1981. Cert. Soc. Profl. Archeologists. Prof. anthropology Sheldon Jackson Coll., Sitka, Alaska, 1986-88; dir. Exxon Cultural Resource Program, Anchorage, 1989-90; pres. Charles M. Mobley & Assocs., Anchorage, 1982—; adj. prof. U. Alaska, Anchorage, 1982, 83, 85, 91; guest lectr. Crystal Cruises, L.A., 1990. Author: The Campus Site: A Prehistoric Camp, 1991; contbr. articles to profl. jours. Grantee Inst. for Study of Earth and Man, 1978, Alaska Hist. Commn., 1983, 84, Sheldon Jackson Coll., 1986, 87; Geist Fund grantee U. Alaska Mus., 1982. Mem. Soc. for Am. Archaeology, Alaska Anthrop. Assn., Soc. Profl. Archaeologists. Office: Charles M Mobley & Assocs 200 W 34th Ave # 534 Anchorage AK 99503-3942

MOBLEY, KAREN RUTH, art gallery director; b. Cheyenne, Wyo., Aug. 26, 1961; d. David G. and Marlene G. (Franz) M. BFA, U. Wyo., 1983; MFA, U. Oka., 1987. Sales assoc. Morgan Gallery, Kansas City, Mo., 1984-85; grad. asst. U. Okla. Mus. Art, Norman, 1985-87; dir. Univ. Art Gallery N.Mex. State U., Las Cruces, 1988-93; exec. dir. Nicolaysen Art Mus., Casper, Wyo., 1993—; guest artist Okla. City Community Coll., 1986. Paintings exhibited in numerous exhbns. including Phoenix Triennial, 1990, New Am. Talent, Laguna Gloria Art Mus., Austin, Tex., 1992, Adair Margo Gallery, El Paso, 1992, 93, 94, Wyo. Arts Coun. Gallery and Casper Coll., 1995. Wyo. Arts Coun. Individual Artist grantee 1994; named Outstanding Young Women Am. Mem. Am. Assn. Mus., Mountain Plains Mus. Assn., N.Mex. Mus Assn., Coll. Art Assn., Phi Beta Kappa, Phi Kappa Phi. Home: PO Box 1574 Casper WY 82602-1574 Office: Nicolaysen Art Mus 400 E Collins Dr Casper WY 82601-2815

MOBLEY, LUCILLE JOHANNA, real estate broker; b. Albuquerque, Aug. 16, 1944; d. Vernon Theodore Mobley and Esther May Beckstrom; divorced; children: Leah Rae, Sarah Renee, Debrah Rebecca Bonn. AA, Phoenix Coll., 1962. Bldg. mgr. Murdock Mgmt. Co., Phoenix, 1969-81; real estate salesperson Century 21/John Noble Real Estate, Scottsdale, Ariz., 1988-90, Realty Execs., Phoenix, 1990-92, Terra Comml. Property Svcs., Phoenix, 1992-93; owner, broker Comml. Property Svcs., Phoenix, 1993—. Vol. St. Luke's Hosp., Phoenix, 1986-88, also various polit. campaigns, fund raiser Tavan Sch., Phoenix, 1987, 88, Easter Seals, Phoenix, 1990. Mem. Phoenix Bd. Realtors (edn. chair 1992, mktg. meeting chair 1991-92), Cen. Ariz. CCIM (sec., bd. dirs. 1992), Optimists, DAR. Republican. Home: 4902 E Osborn Rd Phoenix AZ 85018-5539 Office: Comml Property Svcs 4902 E Osborn Rd Phoenix AZ 85018-5539

MOCK, STANLEY CLYDE, financial planner, investment advisor; b. Seattle, Nov. 7, 1946; s. Darrell O. and Elsie (Broeckel) M.; m. Deloris J. Weis, June 4, 1967; children: Shannon Mock Frohardt, Kristin Ann. Student, Columbia Basin U., 1965-67; CFP, Coll. Fin. Planning, 1987. CFP; registered fin. advisor, investment advisor. Agt. Met. Life Ins. Co., Eugene, Oreg., 1969-73; sales mgr. Met. Life Ins. Co., Spokane, 1973-76; advanced underwriting advisor Met. Life Ins. Co., Bellevue, Wash., 1976; dist. sales mgr. Met. Life Ins. Co., Boise, Idaho, 1976-78; gen. agt. Ohio Nat. Cos., Boise, 1978—; fin. planner Fin. Planning Svcs., Boise, 1978—. Author: Life Insurance Selling, 1992; contbr. articles to mags. With USNR, 1967-69. Named One of Best Fin. Planners in Am., Money Mag., 1987. Mem. Internat. Assn. Fin. Planning (pres. 1988-89), Distributive Edn. Club Am. (pres. 1965), Rotary. Republican. Home: 10246 W Cranberry Ct Boise ID 83704-1999 Office: Fin Planning Svcs 3050 N Lakeharbor Ln Ste 200 Boise ID 83703-6243

MOCKARY, PETER ERNEST, clinical laboratory scientist, researcher; b. Zghorta, Lebanon, Jan. 6, 1931; came to U.S., 1953; s. Ernest Peter and Evelyn (Kuddo) M.; m. Yvette Fadlallah, Aug. 27, 1955; children: Ernest, Evelyn, Paula, Vincent, Marguerite. BA in Philosophy, Coll. des Freres, Tripoli, Lebanon, 1948; BA in Medicine, Am. U. Beirut, 1950, postgrad., 1950-52. Cert. clin. lab. technologist, Calif.; cert. clin. lab. scientist Nat. Certification Agy. Chief hematology unit VA Wadsworth Med. Ctr., West Los Angeles, Calif., 1956-81; CEO Phoenicia Trading Co., 1981-88; dir. Coagulation Lab., Orthopaedic Hosp., L.A., 1988—; lab. supr. Westside Hosp., L.A., 1964-79; lectr. hematology UCLA, West Los Angeles, 1970-78. Pres. World Lebanese Cultural Union, L.A., 1978-79. With U.S. Army, 1954-56. Recipient outstanding performance award lab. svc. VA Wadsworth Med. Ctr., 1972-76. Republican. Roman Catholic. Home: 3103 Gilmerton Ave Los Angeles CA 90064-4319 Office: Orthopaedic Hosp 2400 S Flower St Los Angeles CA 90007-2629

MOCKLER, ESTHER JAYNE, state legislator; b. Jackson, Wyo., Sept. 21, 1957; d. Franklin and Nancy (Fisher) Mockler. BA in Polit. Sci., Wellesley Coll., 1980. Mem. Wyo. Ho. of Reps., 1992—. Office: PO Box 2036 Cheyenne WY 82003-2036

MOE, ANDREW IRVING, veterinarian; b. Tacoma, Jan. 2, 1927; s. Ole Andrew and Ingeborg (Gordham) M.; BS in Biology, U. Puget Sound, 1949; BA, Wash. State U., 1953, DVM 1954; m. Dorothy Clara Becker, June 25, 1950; children: Sylvia Moe McGowan, Pamela Moe Barker, Joyce. Meat cutter Art Hansen, Tacoma, 1943-48; gen. practice as veterinarian Baronti Vet. Hosp., Eugene, Oreg., 1956-57; veterinarian, regulatory Calif. Animal Health br. Calif. Dept. Food and Agr. Resident veterinarian II, Modesto, Calif., 1957-64, acting veterinarian-in-charge Modesto Dist. Office (veterinarian III), 1976-77, ret., 1990—. Watersafety instr. ARC, 1958-61. Capt., Vet. Corps., 1954-56, 62; comdr. 417th Med. Svc. Flight Res. (AFRES), 1965-66, 71-73; lt. col. Biomed. Scis. Corps USAF, ret., 1982. Recipient Chief Veterinarian badge, 1975. Mem. VFW (life), AVMA, Calif. Vet. Med. Assn., No. San Joaquin Vet. Med. Assn. (pres. 1979), Calif. Acad. Vet. Medicine (charter), Res. Officers Assn. (life), Ret. Officers Assn. (life), Assn. Mil. Surgeons U.S. (life), U.S. Animal Health Assn., Sons of Norway, Shriners (bd. dirs.), Masons (Illustrious Master Modesto chpt. 1983, Allied Masonic degrees, pres. Modesto Masonic Luncheon Club 1991, Meritorious Svc. medal 1992), Internat. Order of the Rainbow for Girls, Theta Chi. Alpha Psi. Lutheran (del. 102d Synod 1961). Home: 161 Norwegian Ave Modesto CA 95350-3542 Office: Field Vets Emeritus 1620 N Carpenter Rd Ste 48D Modesto CA 95351-1153

MOE, ORVILLE LEROY, racetrack executive; b. Spokane, Wash., Nov. 26, 1936; s. Clarence Orville and Georgia Maria (Lombard) M.; m. Deonne Wesley Schultz, Jan. 11, 1953; children: Susan Marie, Terry Ann. Co-owner Moe's Sudden Svc. Fuel Co., Spokane, Wash., 1956-74; sec. Gold Res. Mining Corp., Spokane, 1973-89, Bonanza Gold Corp., Spokane, 1973-85; pres., founder Spokane Raceway Park, Inc., 1971—; regional v.p. Am. Hot Rod Assn., Kansas, Mo., 1968-84, mktg. dir., 1978-84; co-producer Internat. Car Show Assn., Spokane, 1969-90. Co-producer Spokane Auto Boat Speed Show, 1964—. Mem. Nat. Rep. Senatorial Com., 1984—; mem., trustee Rep. Presdl. Task Force, mem. 1992 Presdl. Trust Rep. Nat. Com. Mem. ISCA, Eagles, Am. Hot Rod Assn. (exec. v.p. Spokane, Wash. 1986—), Internat. Footprint Assn., Am. Auto Racing Assn. (regional v.p.). Republican. Office: Spokane Raceway Park Inc 101 N Hayford Rd Spokane WA 99204-9510

MOE, STANLEY ALLEN, architect, consultant; b. Fargo, N.D., May 28, 1914; s. Ole Arnold and Freda Emily (Pape) M.; m. Doris Lucille Anderson, May 25, 1937; children: Willa Moe Crouse, Myra Moe Parsons. BArch, U. Minn., 1936; D of Engring. (hon.), U. N.D., 1993. lic. architect several states; NCARB cert. Project architect several firms in Midwest, 1936-42; project architect U.S. Army Corps Engrs., Africa, 1942-43; ptnr. H.S. Starin, Architects & Engrs., Duluth, Minn., 1943-47; sr. ptnr. Moe & Larsen, Architects & Engrs., L.A., 1947-54; ptnr., gen. mgr., exec. v.p. Daniel, Mann, Johnson & Mendenall, L.A., 1954-71, corp. v.p., 1972-79; prin. Stanley A. Moe, AIA, L.A., 1979—; dir. design of major mil. projects in Eritrea, Sudan, Egypt, Yemen for Allied Forces, 1942-43; chmn. control com. DMJM & Assocs., designer of prototype, tng. and operational facilities for Titan I Ballistic Missile program for USAF, 1958-63; project dir. Space Shuttle facilities Kennedy Space Ctr., 1973; project dir. for design of aircraft maintenance complex Iranian Aircraft Industries, 1978; project mgr. for design of major med. facility program Min. of Def. and Aviation, Saudi Arabia, 1975-76; project mgr. design of Boufarik Internat. Airport, Algeria, 1983. Pres. San Fernando Valley Young Reps., 1952, Van Nuys (Calif.) Jaycees, 1950. Recipient Dsiting. Svc. award for cmty. svc. Van Nuys Jaycees, 1949, Sioux award U. N.D. Alumni Assn., 1985, Trustees Soc. award U. Minn., 1992. Mem. AIA (Calif. coun.), Delta Tau Delta. Republican. Presbyterian. Home and Office: 447 S Plymouth Blvd Los Angeles CA 90020-4706

MOEL, STEVEN ALLEN, ophthalmologist; b. Charleston, W.Va., Sept. 18, 1943; s. Harry and Ruth (Lee) M.; m. Susan Gayle Dill, Aug. 13, 1981; children: Andrew, Erin. AB, U. Miami, Fla., 1965; MD, W.Va. U., 1970. Diplomate Am. Bd. Ophthalmology. Intern Gen. Rose Meml. Hosp., U. Colo., Denver, 1970-71; resident in ophthalmology La. State U., New Orleans, 1971-75; research fellowship in ophthalmology U. Ill. Eye and Ear Infirmary, Chgo., 1973-74; pvt. practice medicine specializing in ophthalmology Monterey Park, Calif., 1980—; v.p. acquisitions and mergers, bd. dirs. Akorn Inc., New Orleans; pres. Redwood Inc., 1986—; pres., chmn. SEN Enterprises, 1986-88; chmn. bd. Grudzen Devel. Corp., 1991—, Paradigm Techs., Inc., 1991—. Contbr. articles to profl. jours. Fellow Am. Acad. Ophthalmology. Office: 500 N Garfield Ste 100 Monterey Park CA 91754

MOELLER, JAMES, state supreme court justice; b. Valley, Nebr., Nov. 14, 1933; s. Hans and Marie Grace (Shumaker) M.; m. Nancy Lee Kiely, Dec. 16, 1961; children: Amy Jo, Linda Anne. BA, Nebr. Wesleyan U., 1954; JD with high distinction, George Washington U., 1959. Bar: Ariz. 1959, U.S. Dist. Ct. Ariz. 1959, U.S. Ct. Appeals (9th cir.) 1961. Assoc. Lewis and Roca, Phoenix, 1959-64, ptnr., 1964-70; ptnr. Moeller Hover Jensen & Henry, Phoenix, 1970-77; judge Maricopa County Superior Ct., Phoenix, 1977-87; assoc. justice Ariz. Supreme Ct., Phoenix, 1987-92, vice chief justice, 1992—. Editor-in-chief George Washington U. Law Rev., 1958-59. Bd. dirs. Found. for Blind Children, Scottsdale, Ariz., 1964-70, Ariz. Found. Prevention of Blindness, Phoenix, 1966-70; Rep. committeeman, Phoenix and Scottsdale, 1965-69. Served with U.S. Army, 1954-56. Mem. ABA, Am. Judicature Soc., Ariz. Bar Assn., Maricopa County Bar Assn. Methodist. Office: Ariz Supreme Ct 432 Ariz Courts Bldg 1501 W Washington Phoenix AZ 85007

MOELLER, RONALD SCOTT, mechanical engineer; b. Teaneck, N.J., Nov. 12, 1963; s. Dennis Edward Moeller and Joyce (Anderson) Berger. AAS, County Coll. of Morris, Randolph, N.J., 1986; BSME, N.J. Inst. Tech., 1988. Devel. engr. I Lytel Corp., Somerville, N.J., 1986-88; engring. mgr. Ortel Corp., Alhambra, Calif., 1988—. Republican. Office: Ortel Corp 707 S Raymond Ave Alhambra CA 91803-1535

MOELLER, WALTER EUGENE, management consultant; b. Spokane, Wash., Mar. 4, 1944; s. William Fredrick and Chlorene (Myers) M.; children: Jeffrey William, Jonathan Edward, Jennifer Marie. AA, Maple Woods Cmty. Coll., Kansas City, Mo., 1973; BBA, U Mo., 1975, MBA, 1978. Sr. mgr. Arthur Young, 1985-89; regional mgr. Axiom Info. Cons., Inc., 1990-91; pres., sr. cons. Walter E. Moeller Consulting, Inc., Concord, Calif., 1992—; dir. Marcus Software Designs, Davis, Calif., 1991—; founder, pres. San Francisco Case Users Group, 1987-88; founding bd. mem. Internat. Case User's Group; co-founder San Francisco Entity Relationship Diagrammers Group. Contbr. articles to profl. jours. Mem. San Francisco Data Adminstr. Mgmt. Assn. (past pres. 1986-88). Office: W E Moeller Cons Inc 4390 N Weeping Spruce Ct Concord CA 94521-4444

MOERBEEK, STANLEY LEONARD, lawyer; b. Toronto, Ont., Can., Nov. 12, 1951; came to U.S., 1953; s. John Jacob and Mary Emily (Giroux) M.; m. Carol Annette Mordaunt, Apr. 17, 1982; children: Sarah, Noah. BA magna cum laude, Calif. State U., Fullerton, 1974; student, U. San Diego-Sorbonne, Paris, 1977; JD, Loyola U., 1979. Bar: Calif. 1980. From law clk. to assoc. McAlpin Doonan & Seese, Covina, Calif., 1977-81; assoc. Robert L. Baker, Pasadena, Calif., 1981-82, Miller Bush & Minnott, Fullerton, 1982-83; prin. Law Office of Stanley L. Moerbeek, Fullerton, 1984—; judge pro tem Orange County Superior Ct., Calif., 1984—; notary pub., lt. gov. 9th cir. law student divsn. ABA, 1979. Mem. Heritage Found., Washington, 1989—. Calif. Gov.'s Office scholar, 1970; recipient Plaque of Appreciation, Fullerton Kiwanis, 1983. Mem. Calif. Assn. Realtors (referral panel atty. 1985—), Orange-L.A. County Bar Assns., L.A. Consumer Atty. Assn., Phi Kappa Phi. Roman Catholic. Office: 1370 N Brea Blvd Ste 210 Fullerton CA 92635-4128

MOFFATT, HUGH MCCULLOCH, JR., hospital administrator, physical therapist; b. Steubenville, Ohio, Oct. 11, 1933; s. Hugh McCulloch and Agnes Elizabeth (Bickerstaff) M.; m. Ruth Anne Colvin, Aug. 16, 1958; children: David, Susan. AB, Asbury Coll., 1958; cert. in phys. therapy, Duke U., 1963. Lic. in phys. therapy and health care adminstrn., Alaska. Commd. officer USPHS, 1964, advanced through grades to capt.; therapist USPHS, N.Y.C., 1964-66, Sitka, Alaska, 1970-72; therapist cons. USPHS, Atlanta, 1968-70; clinic adminstr. USPHS, Kayenta, Ariz., 1972-73; hosp. dir. USPHS, Sitka, 1973-78; therapist cons. Idaho Dept. Health, Boise, 1966-68; contract health officer USPHS, Anchorage, 1978-89, ret., 1989; phys. therapy cons. Ocean Beach Hosp., Ilwaco, Wash., 1989—, Harbors Home Health Svcs., Aberdeen, Wash., 1990—; therapist cons. Our Lady of Compassion Care Ctr., Anchorage, 1979—, Alaska Native Med. Ctr., Anchorage, 1988—. With U.S. Army, 1955-57. Mem. Am. Phys. Therapy Assn., Commd. Officers Assn. USPHS, Res. Officers Assn., Ret. Officers Assn., Am. Assn. Individual Investors, Am. Assn. Ret. Persons, Eagles.

MOFFATT, ROBERT HENRY, accountant, publisher, writer, consultant; b. Montreal, Que., Can., June 30, 1930; came to U.S., 1968, naturalized, 1973; s. James Bigelow and Edwige Edith M.; m. Hannelore Mann, Jan. 7, 1989. Student Loyola Coll., Montreal, Que., 1948-52, Acadia U., 1962, UCLA, 1970, 72. Lic. in air navigation, Can.; enrolled agt., Dept. Treasury. Mng. editor, pub. Kings-Annapolis Wings, 1961-66; pres., Valley Pubs. Ltd., Kingston, N.S., Can., 1961-67 exec. dir. Maritime Motor Transport Assn. and editor Maritime Truck Transport Rev., Moncton, N.B., Can., 1967-68; dir. spl. products div. Wolf-Brown Inc., Los Angeles, 1968-77; newsletter pub, writer, 1980—; pvt. practice tax acctg., Los Angeles, 1970—; noetic ethicist. Columnist, author editorials in mags. Clk., author constn. Village of Greenwood, N.S., 1961-63; chmn. bd. commrs., 1963-66; publicity chmn. Voluntary Econ. Planning Program, province N.S., 1965-66. Served to lt. Can. Air Force, 1954-60. Mem. Nat. Assn. Enrolled Agts. (newsletter editor, bd. dirs.), Nat. Soc. Pub. Accts (accredited in taxation), Calif. Soc. Enrolled Agts. Home and Office: 7509 W 88th St Los Angeles CA 90045-3408

MOFFEIT, TONY ARCHIE, poet, librarian; b. Claremore, Okla., Mar. 14, 1942; s. Archie and Virginia Ruth (Bell) M.; m. Diana Lee Black, Apr. 28, 1964 (div. 1977); 1 child, Miles. BS in Psychology, Okla. State U., 1964; MLS, U. Okla., 1965. Asst. dir. libr. svcs. U. So. Colo., Pueblo, 1979-87, dept. chair libr. svcs., 1988—, poet in residence, 1987—, honors faculty, 1991—; dir. Pueblo Poetry Project, 1980—; performance poet., 1985—. Author: Pueblo Blues, 1986 (Jack Kerouac award 1986), Luminous Animal, 1989, Dancing with the Ghosts of the Dead, 1992, Neon Peppers, 1992, Poetry is Dangerous, the Poet is an Outlaw, 1995; editor: Prairie Smoke, 1990. Fellow U. So. Colo., 1991, Nat. Endowment for Arts, 1992; Colo. Coun. Arts and Humanities grantee, 1992. Mem. ALA, Colo. Libr. Assn. (div. chmn. 1981-83). Home: 1501 E 7th St Pueblo CO 81001-3235 Office: U So Colo 2200 Bonforte Blvd Pueblo CO 81001-4901

MOFFETT, FRANK CARDWELL, architect, civil engineer, real estate developer; b. Houston, Dec. 9, 1931; s. Ferrell Orlando and Jewell Bernice (Williams) M.; BArch, U. Tex., 1958; m. Annie Doris Thorn, Aug. 1, 1952 (div.); children: David Cardwell (dec.), Douglas Howard; m. Darlene Adele Alm Sayan, June 7, 1985 (div.). Architect with archtl. firms, Seattle, Harmon, Pray & Detrich, Arnold G. Gangnes, Ralf E. Decker, Roland Terry & Assocs., 1958-64; ptnr. Heideman & Moffett, AIA, Seattle, 1964-71; chief architect Wash. State Dept. Hwys., Olympia, 1971-77, Wash. State Dept. Transp., 1977-87; owner The Moffett Co., Olympia, 1974—; founder, treas. TAA, Inc., Olympia, 1987-90, pres., 1991—; advisor Wash. State Bldg. Code Council, 1975-95; instr. civil engring. tech. Olympia Tech. Community Coll., 1975-77; adv. mem. archtl. barriers subcom. Internat. Conf. Building Ofcls.; archtl. works include hdqrs. Gen. Telephone Directory Co., Everett, Wash., 1964; Edmonds Unitarian Ch., 1966; tenant devel. Seattle Hdqrs. Office, Seattle-First Nat. Bank, 1968-70; Wash. State Dept. Transp. Area Hdqrs. Offices, Mt. Vernon, Selah, Raymond, Colfax and Port Orchard 1973-87; Materials Lab., Spokane, Wash., 1974; Olympic Meml. Gardens, Tumwater, Wash., 1988, City Anacortes emergency power stas., 1989, L. Albert Residence, 1990, F. Gasperetti Residence, 1991; archtl. barriers cons. State of Alaska, 1978, State of Wash., 1992-94. Chmn. Planning Commn. of Mountlake Terr., Wash., 1963, 64, mem., 1961-67; mem. State of Wash. Gov.'s Task Force on Wilderness, 1972-75, Heritage Park Task Force, Olympia, Wash., 1986—; trustee Cascade Symphony Orch., 1971; incorporating pres. United Singles, Olympia, 1978-79; lt. CAP, pub. affairs officer Olympia Squadron. With USN, 1951-54. Registered architect, Alaska, Calif., Wash., profl. engr., Wash.; cert. Nat. Council Archtl. Registration Bds., U.S. Dept. Def., Fallout Shelter Analysis, environ. engring. Mem. AIA (dir. S.W. Wash. chpt. 1980-82, pres.-elect 1985, pres. 1986, dir. Wash. council 1986, architects in govt. nat. com. 1978-87, chmn. N.W. and Pacific region conf. 1991), Am. Public Works Assn., Inst. Bldgs. and Grounds, ASCE, Constrn. Specifications Inst., Am. Arbitration Assn. (invited panelist), Gen. Soc. Mayflower Descs. (gov. Wash. Soc. 1982-83), Nat. Huguenot Soc. (pres. Wash. Soc. 1981-83, 85-87, 95—), Olympia Geneal. Soc. (pres. 1978-80), SAR (state treas. 1984-85), SCV, Sons and Daus. of Pilgrims, (gov. Wash. Soc. 1984), Order of Magna Charta, Aircraft Owners' and Pilots' Assn., Rotary (pres. Edmonds, 1969-70), Olympia, Coll. Club of Seattle, Olympia Country and Golf Club. Co-author: An Illustrated Handbook for Barrier-Free Design, 2d edit., 1984, 3d edit., 1987, 4th Edit., 1989, Accessibility Design for All, 1992. Republican. Unitarian. Home and Office: PO Box 2422 Olympia WA 98507-2422

MOFFITT, DONALD EUGENE, transportation company executive; b. Terre Haute, Ind., May 22, 1932; s. James Robert and Margaret Mary (Long) M.; m. Billie Duffy, Feb. 21, 1989; 1 child, Jaime. BA, Ind. State U., 1954; postgrad., Ind. U., 1956; grad., Advanced Mgmt. Program, Harvard U., 1972. Acct. Foster Freight Lines, Indpls., 1955-56; with Consol. Freightways Inc., San Francisco, 1956-88, v.p. planning, 1961-69; v.p. fin., motor carrier subs. Consol. Freightways Corp. Del., 1969-75; v.p. fin., treas. parent co. Consol. Freightways Inc., San Francisco, 1975-81; exec. v.p. Consol. Freightways Inc., Palo Alto, Calif., 1981-86; vice chmn. parent co. bd. Consol. Freightways, Inc., Palo Alto, Calif., 1986-88; chmn., CEO Circle Express, Indpls., 1988-90; pres., CEO Consol. Freightways, Inc., Palo Alto,

Calif., 1990—, chmn., CEO, 1995—, also bd. dirs.; chmn. bd. dirs. all subsidiaries Consolidated Freightways, Inc., 1990—. Bd. dirs. Bay Area Coun., Calif. Bus. Roundtable, Conf. Bd., Boy Scouts Am., ARC; bd. dirs., exec. com. Hwy. Users Fedn.; bd. trustees Automotive Safety Found.; bus. adv. coun. Northwestern U. Transp. Ctr. Mem. Nat. C. of C. (Washington) (bd. dirs.). Office: Consol Freightways Inc 3240 Hillview Ave Palo Alto CA 94304-1201

MOFFITT, KEVIN DAVID, food products executive; b. Portland, Oreg., Apr. 23, 1957. BSBA, U. Oreg., 1980. Mgr. new product Dole Food Co., San Francisco, 1981-86; sales mgr. Agrl. Mktg. and Devel., Florence, N.J., 1986-88; internat. mktg. svcs. mgr. Sun Diamond Growers of Calif., Pleasant, Calif., 1988-89; v.p. internat. mktg. Oreg.-Wash.-Calif. Pear Bur., Portland, 1989—. Contbr. articles to profl. jours. Mem. Moffat Clan Soc. N.Am., Chi Psi (bd. dirs. undergrad. 1978-79). Office: Oreg-Wash-Calif Pear Bur 813 SW Alder St Ste 601 Portland OR 97205-3114

MOFFITT, PHILLIP WILLIAM, magazine editor; b. Kingsport, Tenn., Sept. 11, 1946; s. Wallace and Claire Matilda (Allen) M. BS, U. Tenn., 1968, MS, 1971. Co-founder 13-30 Pub. (now Whittle Communications), Knoxville, Tenn., 1971, editor, 1971-79, pres., 1976—; editor-in-chief 13-30 Publs. Group, Knoxville, Tenn., 1979-86; editor, pres. Esquire Magazine, N.Y.C., 1979-84, editor-in-chief, pres., 1984-86; chmn. Light Source Computer Images, Inc., 1989—. Co-author: The Power to Heal, 1990, Medicine's Great Journey, 1992; contbr. columns to Esquire Mag., 1979-88. Bd. dirs. C.J. Jung Found. Mem. Mag. Pubs. Assn. (bd. dirs. 1984—). Home and Office: 1 Pelican Point Rd Belvedere Tiburon CA 94920-2456*

MOGG, DONALD WHITEHEAD, chemist; b. La Grange, Ill., Feb. 11, 1924; s. Harold William and Margaret (Whitehead) M.; B.S., Allegheny Coll., 1944; postgrad. Harvard U., 1946-47. Asst. chemist Gt. Lakes Carbon Corp., Morton Grove, Ill., 1947-48, chemist, 1948-53, research chemist, 1953-56, project supr., 1956-59, sect. head, 1959-63; sect. head Gt. Lakes Research Corp., Elizabethton, Tenn., 1963-66; research and devel. mgr. bldg. products div. Grefco, Inc., Torrance, Calif., 1966-68, corp. research and devel. mgr., 1968-72, group mgr., 1972-81, sr. research assoc., 1981-82. Served with U.S. Army, 1944-46. Mem. Am. Chem. Soc., AAAS, Phi Beta Kappa, Phi Kappa Psi. Presbyterian. U.S. and fgn. patentee in field of bldg. products. Home: 3823 Ingraham St Apt B202 San Diego CA 92109-6436

MOGHADAM, AMIR, engineering educator, consultant. BSME, U. London, 1983; PhD in Aeronautical Engring., U. Cambridge, 1987. Rsch. asst. Cambridge U., 1983-87; rsch. assoc. U. Calif., Santa Barbara, 1987-88; asst. prof. Northrop U., L.A., 1988-92, v.p. faculty senate, 1990-91; assoc. prof. Northrop-Rice Aviation Inst. of Tech., Inglewood, Calif., 1992-94; dir. engring. tech., 1994—; pres., CEO Aeronautics Innovation Inc., Marina del Rey, Calif., 1993—; ind. cons., Woodland Hills, Calif., 1988-93. Contbr. articles to profl. jours. Mem. AIAA, ASME, Soc. Automotive Engrs., Am. Soc. Engring. Edn., Sigma Xi, Tau Alpha Pi, Tau Beta Pi, Sigma Gamma Tau. Office: Northrop-Rice Aviation InstTech 8911 Aviation Blvd Inglewood CA 90301

MOHAMED, SHAMIM P., computer science educator; b. Mangalore, Karnataka, India, Dec. 29, 1964; came to U.S., 1986; s. Habeeb and Zulekha (Manippady) M. BTech, Indian Inst. of Tech., 1986; MS, U. Ariz., 1988, PhD, 1993. Rsch. assoc. U. Ariz., Tucson, 1989-93; asst. prof. Idaho State U., Pocatello, 1993—. Mem. Assn. for Computing Machinery (referee Transactions on Computer Sys., 1990—, Transactions on Computer Human Interaction, 1993—). Office: Idaho State U Box 8085 Math Pocatello ID 83209

MOHAN, D. MIKE, transportation company executive; b. Chico, Calif., Apr. 10, 1945; s. Alfred and Velda June (Clark) M.; m. Dixie Watson, June 21, 1969; children—Laurel, Patrick, Christopher. B.A., U. Calif.-Berkeley, 1967, M.B.A., 1968; A.M.P., Harvard U., 1983. With So. Pacific Transp. Co., 1968—; asst. to pres. So. Pacific Transp. Co., San Francisco, 1981-82; v.p.-maintenance So. Pacific Transp. Co., 1982-83, exec. v.p., 1983-88, also dir.; pres., chief oper. officer So. Pacific Transp. Co., San Francisco, Denver & Rio Grande Western R.R., 1988—; bd. dirs. Rio Grande Industries. Mem. Nat. Freight Traffic Assn., Assn. Am. R.Rs (bd. dirs.). Office: So Pacific Transp Co 1 Market Plz San Francisco CA 94105

MOHANTY, BIBHU PRASAD, electrical engineer; b. Cuttack, Orissa, India, May 21, 1961; came to U.S., 1987; s. Padma Charan and Basant (Das) M.; m. Yana Zilberberg. BTech with honors, Indian Isnt. Tech., Kharangpur, 1982; M of Engring., McMaster U., Hamilton, Ont., Can., 1987; PhD in Elec. Engring., U. Mass., 1993. Engr. Ops. Rsch. Group, Baroda, India, 1982-85; rsch. asst. McMaster U., 1985-87, U. Mass., Amherst, 1987-93; sr. engr. Qualcomm Inc., San Diego, 1993—; vis. lectr. M.S. U., Baroda, 1982-84. Contbr. articles to profl. jours. Clifton Sherman fellow McMaster U., 1987. Mem. IEEE. Office: Qualcomm Inc 6455 Lusk Blvd San Diego CA 92121-2779

MOHR, ANTHONY JAMES, judge; b. L.A., May 11, 1947; s. Gerald Leonard and Rita Lenore (Goldstein) M. BA in Govt. cum laude with honors, Wesleyan U., 1969; JD, Columbia U., 1972; diploma with honors Faculté Internationale pour l'Enseignement du Droit Comparé, 1975. Bar: Calif. 1972, U.S. Dist. Ct. (cen. dist.) Calif. 1973, U.S. Ct. Appeals (9th cir.) 1974, D.C. 1976, U.S. Supreme Ct. 1981. Law clk. to judge U.S. Dist. Cent. Dist. Calif., 1972-73; assoc. Schwartz Alschuler & Grossman (now Alschuler Grossman & Pines), 1973-75; pvt. practice, L.A., 1976-94; judge L.A. Mcpl. Ct., 1994—; faculty atty. asst. tng. program UCLA, 1982—, bd. dirs. internat. student ctr., 1986—. Del., White House Conf. on Youth, 1971; nat. adv. coun. Ctr. for Study of Presidency, 1974—; mem. L.A. Dist. Atty.'s Adv. Coun., 1976-82; hearing officer L.A. County Employees Retirement Assn., 1986-94. Mem. Beverly Hills Bar Assn. (bd. govs. 1975-80, chmn. litigation sect. 1983-85, chair resolutions com. 1991-92, dist. svc. award 1992), Barristers of Beverly Hills Bar Assn. (pres. 1979-80), Am. Judicature Soc. (dir.), ABA, L.A. County Bar Assn. (editorial bd. L.A. Lawyer Mag. 1989-94), Phi Beta Kappa, Phi Delta Phi. Contbr. articles to profl. jours.; editorial bd. Calif. Bar Jour., 1979-80. Office: LA Mcpl Ct 110 N Grand Ave Los Angeles CA 90012

MOHR, JOHN LUTHER, biologist, environmental consultant; b. Reading, Pa., Dec. 1, 1911; s. Luther Seth and Anna Elizabeth (Davis) M.; m. Frances Edith Christensen, Nov. 23, 1939; children: Jeremy John, Christopher Charles. A.B. in Biology, Bucknell U., 1933; student, Oberlin Coll., 1933-34; Ph.D. in Zoology, U. Calif. at Berkeley, 1939. Research asso. Pacific Islands Research, Stanford, 1942-44; rsch. assoc. Allan Hancock Found., U. So. Calif., 1944-46, asst. prof., 1946-47, asst. prof. dept. biology, 1947-54, asso. prof., 1954-57, prof., 1957-77; chmn. dept., 1960-62, prof. emeritus, 1977—; vis. prof. summers U. Wash. Friday Harbor Labs., 1956, '57; marine borer and pollution surveys harbors So. Calif., 1948-51, arctic marine biol. research, 1952-71; chief marine zool. group U.S. Antarctic research ship Eltanin in Drake Passage, 1962, in South Pacific sector, 1965; research deontology in sci. and academia; researcher on parasitic protozoans of anurans, crustaceans, elephants; analysis of agy. and industry documents, ethics and derelictions of steward agy., sci. and tech. orgns. as they relate to offshore and coastal onshore oil activities, environ. effects of oil spill dispersants and offshore oil industry discharges and naturally occurring radioactive material NORMs. Active People for the Am. Way; mem. Biol. Stain Commn., 1948-80, trustee, 1971-80, emeritus trustee, 1981—, v.p., 1976-80. Recipient Guggenheim fellowship, 1957-58. Fellow AAAS (coun. 1964-73), So. Calif. Acad. Sci., Sigma Xi (exec. com. 1964-67, 68, 69, chpt. at large bd. 1968-69); mem. Am. Micros. Soc., Marine Biol. Assn. U.K. (life), Am. Soc. Parasitologists, We. Soc. Naturalists (pres. 1960-61), Soc. Protozoologists, Am. Soc. Tropical Medicine and Hygiene, Am. Soc. Zoologists, Ecol. Soc. Am., Planning and Conservation League, Calif. Native Plant Soc., Am. Inst. Biol. Scis., Save San Francisco Bay Assn., Ecology Ctr. So. Calif., Assn. Forest Svc. Employees Environ. Ethics, Common Cause, Huxleyan, Sierra Club, Phi Sigma, Theta Upsilon Omega. Democrat. Home: 3819 Chanson Dr Los Angeles CA 90043-1601

MOHR, SELBY, retired ophthalmologist; b. San Francisco, Mar. 11, 1918; s. Selby and Henrietta (Foorman) M.; AB, Stanford U., 1938, MD, 1942; m. Marian Buckley, June 10, 1950; children—Selby, John Vincent, Adrianne E., Gregory P. Asst. resident in ophthalmology U. Calif. Hosp., 1942-43; pvt. practice ophthalmology, San Francisco, 1947-88; mem. past pres. med. staff Marshall Hale Meml. Hosp.; mem. staff Mt. Zion Hosp., St Francis Meml. Hosp. Dir. Sweet Water Co., Mound Farms, Inc., Mound Farms Oil & Gas; Inc. Lt. (j.g.) USNR, 1943-46; PTO. Diplomate Am. Bd. Ophthalmology. Fellow Am. Acad. Ophthalmology and Otolarngology; mem. AMA, Calif., San Francisco Med. Socs., Pan-Pacific Surg. Soc., Pan-Am. Assn. Ophthalmology, Pacific Coast Oto-Ophthalmol. Soc., Pan-Am. Med. Soc. Home: 160 Sea Cliff Ave San Francisco CA 94121-1125 Office: 450 Sutter St San Francisco CA 94108-4206

MOHRDICK, EUNICE MARIE, nurse, health educator; b. Alameda, Calif.; d. Walter William and Eunice Marie (Connors) M. BS in Nursing Edn., U. San Francisco, 1955; MA in Edn. spl interest, San Francisco State Coll., 1967; Pub. Health Cert., U. Calif., San Francisco, 1968; EdD, Western Colo. U., 1977. RN, Calif. Supr. oper. rm. St. John's Hosp., Oxnard, Calif., 1947-50, supr. maternity, delivery and nursery rms., 1950-53; nurse, supr. St. Mary's Hosp., San Francisco, 1943-45, supr., instr., 1955-60, 62-65; asst. dir. nursing, tchr. nursing history St Mary's Coll. of Nursing, San Francisco, 1953-55; tchr. home nursing Mercy High Sch., San Francisco, 1960-61; tchr. Health, Family Life San Francisco Unified Schs., 1968-83; tchr. holistic health Contra Costa Coll., 1981-86; cons. pvt. practice Albany, Calif., 1986—; tchr. El Cerrito (Calif.) Senior Ctr., 1986-88. Author: Elementary Teacher Handbook, How to Teach Sex Education, Grades, 4,5,6, 1977. Mem. Madonna Guild, San Francisco, 1986—, v.p., 1989—; mem. Half Notes' Singing Club to Sick and Spl. Needy, 1970—. Recipient Title I Grant U. Calif. San Francisco, 1968, Workshop Grant for Culture Inter-relationship Study, Singapore, UNESCO, Washington U., St. Louis, 1973. Mem. AAUW, San Francisco State U. Alumna, U. San Francisco Nursing Alumni (charter mem., bd. dirs. 1974-88), Mensa. Republican. Roman Catholic. Home & Office: 555 Pierce St Apt 129 Albany CA 94706-1011

MOJAS, KATHLEEN MARIE, psychologist; b. Santa Monica, Calif., July 1, 1961; d. Peter William and Mary Elizabeth (Simpson) M. BA in Comms., UCLA, 1987; PhD in Clin. Psychology, Calif. Grad. Inst., 1992. Lic. psychologist, Calif., 1994. Intern, tutor, counselor Dr. Gardner Child Psychologist, Brentwood, Calif., 1988-90; psychol. asst. Calif. Grad. Inst. Counseling Ctr., L.A., 1988-89; psychol. asst. Options Counseling Ctr., Beverly Hills, Calif., 1989-94, seminar leader, spkr., writer, 1989—; rsch. asst. UCLA, 1987, Artists and Educators for Self-Esteem, L.A., 1987-89, Dick Clark Prodns., L.A., 1987; behavior edn. counselor Nutrisys., Northridge, Calif., 1986-87; media psychologist nat. talk, news shows. Contrb. articles to profl. jours., mags. Assoc. mem. APA, Golden Key. Democrat. Office: 420 Beverly Dr #100 Beverly Hills CA 90212

MOLDANADO, SWARNALATHA ADUSUMILLI, nursing educator, researcher; b. Vijayawada, Andhra, India; came to U.S., 1977; d. Punnaih and Nagaratna (Chintapally) A.; m. Alexander Moldanado, Dec. 23, 1979; 1 child, Arjun. RN, and midwife, Ill, Calif. Lectr. Postgrad. Inst. of Medical Edn. and Research, Chandigarh, India, 1971-77; research assoc., teaching asst. U. Ill. Coll. of Nursing, Chgo., 1977-81; tchr. practice Rush U. Coll of Nursing, Chgo., 1981-82; assoc. prof., chmn. dept. nursing Rockford Coll., Ill., 1982-85; prof., Calif. State U., San Bernardino, 1985-87; prof. San Francisco State U., 1988—. Mem. Voice for Choice Campaign of San Mateo County Planned Parenthood. Mem. Am. Pub. Health Assn., Sigma Xi Research Soc., Sigma Theta Tau Internat. Avocations: music, gardening. Office: San Francisco State Univ 1600 Holloway Ave San Francisco CA 94132-1722

MOLDAW, STUART G., venture capitalist, retail clothing stores executive; b. 1927. Student, Syracuse U. With Allied Stores, N.Y.C., 1949-51, G. Fox Co., Hartford, Conn., 1951-55; founder Foxmoor Casuals, 1959; co-founder U.S. Venture Ptnrs., 1981; chief exec. officer Ross Store Inc., Newark, Calif., from 1987, chmn. bd., 1988—. Office: Ross Stores Inc PO Box 728 8333 Central Ave Newark CA 94560-3440

MOLENKAMP, CHARLES RICHARD, physicist; b. San Francisco, Aug. 26, 1941; s. Charles and Sophia Henrietta (Lappinga) M.; m. Margaret Joyce Wattron, Aug. 26, 1967; children: Robin Christine, William Charles. BS, Calvin Coll., 1963; MS, U. Ariz., 1967, PhD, 1972. Physicist Lawrence Livermore (Calif.) Nat. Lab., 1972—. Contbr. articles to profl. jours. Mem. Am. Meteorol. Soc., Am. Sci. Affiliation, Am. Assn. for Aerosol Rsch., Phi Beta Kappa. Office: Lawrence Livermore Nat Lab PO Box 808 Livermore CA 94551-0808

MOLINA, RAFAEL ANTONIO, investment company executive; b. Sept. 5, 1963; s. Rafael Antonio and Rosa Isabel (Villacorta) M.; m. Maria Asuncion Cornejo, Sept. 28, 1985; children: Elisa Maria, Rafael Augusto, Cristia Adolfo, Leonardo Paolo. AA, Sacramento City Coll., 1983; BS, Golden Gate U., 1994. Cert. adminstr. Calif. State Auto Assn. CFO MVM Investments, Sacramento, 1983-85; adminstr. State of Calif., Sacramento, 1985-93; CEO, mng. dir. C & T Investments, Dixon, Calif., 1988—; dir. MAM Co., Sacramento, 1985—; CEO, dir. Del Sol Investments, Dixon, 1989—. Mem. Calif. State Employees Assn., Sacramento, 1985, Am. Mgmt. Assn., Sacramento, 1991; pres. St. Peter's Ch., Dixon, 1992. Recipient Outstanding Achievement award Calif. Dept. Health Svcs., 1988, Primary Clinics, 1990. Mem. Am. Mgmt. Assn., Network Profl. Assn., Tele-Comms. Assn., Calif. Microcomputers Users. Roman Catholic. Office: C & T Investments Co PO Box 671 Dixon CA 95620-0671

MOLINARO, DAVID, design engineer; b. Ketchikan, Alaska, Mar. 31, 1962; s. David Whitney and Gail Ellen (Tuininga) M.; m. Debra Louise Steele, Feb. 25, 1989; 1 child, Brianna Michelle. BA in Econs., Claremont McKenna Coll., 1986. Sr. product specialist Lodestar Systems, Claremont, Calif., 1984-86; telemarketer 1st Securities Group Calif., Beverly Hills, 1986-87; mktg. cons. A.G. Industries, Upland, Calif., 1987-88; design engr. Acorn Engring. Co., Industry, Calif., 1988-91; sr. design engr. Whitehall Mfg. Inc., Industry, Calif., 1991—. Inventor in field. Vol. Habitat for Humanity, San Gabriel Valley, Calif., 1993—. Mem. NSPE. Office: Whitehall Mfg Inc 15125 Proctor Ave La Puente CA 91746-3327

MOLINSKY, BERT, tax consultant; b. Bronx, N.Y., Feb. 25, 1938; s. Joseph and Ida G. (Rosenberg) M.; m. Donna L. Thurman, June 26, 1964; children: Avery, Lucy, Lois, Sarah. Student, U. Ariz., 1956-61, Diablo Valley Coll., 1986-88, Calif. State U., Hayward, 1988-92. CFP; CLU; ChFC; Enrolled Agt. Field supt. INA Life, Phoenix, 1968-72; regional life mgr. Sentry Life Ins. Co., Oklahoma City, 1972-73, Mpls., 1973-75, San Francisco, 1975-78; mgr. Acacia Mutual Life, Oakland, Calif., 1978-80; gen. agt. Am. United Life, Concord, Calif., 1980-82; owner East Bay Triple Check Tax Svcs., Walnut Creek, Calif., 1982—, Triple Check Income Tax Shoppe, Peoria, Ariz., 1993—; instr. Golden Gate U. CPD, San Francisco, 1983-93, Mt. Diablo Sch. Dist., Concord, 1986-93; faculty Coll. for Fin. Planning, Denver, 1983—; bd. dirs. Triple Check Licensee Coun. Contbr. articles to profl. jours. Nat. dir. U.S. Jaycees, Phoenix, 1967; pres. Bnai Brith Coun. of Lodges, San Francisco, 1986. With USNR, 1955-72. Named Jaycee of Yr. Ariz. Jaycees, 1967. Mem. Enrolled Agts., East Bay Assn. Life Underwriters (pres. 1985-86), Nat. Assn. Enrolled Agts. Office: 8466 W Peoria Ave 4 Peoria AZ 85345-6548 also: PO Box 100 Peoria AZ 85380-0100 also: Triple Check-Tucson 2301 E Broadway Blvd Ste 100 Tucson AZ 85719-6024

MOLLETT, DAVID L., artist; b. Portland, Oreg., Mar. 5, 1950; s. Donald Lee and Shirley (Gordon) M.; m. Nina Dee Schectman, Nov. 3, 1976 (div.); 1 child, Tobin Lee. Student, N.Y. Studio Sch., N.Y.C., 1970-71; BA, Reed Coll., Portland, Oreg., 1975. Instr. studio art courses U. Alaska, Fairbanks, 1985—; curator paintings from the Arctic Refuge Civic Ctr. Gallery, Fairbanks, 1991. Exhibited in one-man shows at Anchorage Hist. and Fine Arts Mus., 1981, 89, Alaska State Mus., Juneau, 1991, Civic Ctr. Gallery, Fairbanks, 1980, 85, 94, Alaska Pacific U., Anchorage, 1994, Espace Reduit Gallerie, Cassis, France, 1992, Stonington Gallery, Anchorage, 1987, 92; exhibited in group shows at Chaffey Coll., Rancho Cucamonga, Calif., 1994, Norway-L.A. Print Exch. Exhbn., Oslo, 1993. Panelist for grants and budgets Alaska State Coun. on the Arts, 1990, 94. Resident fellow Camargo Found., Cassis, 1992; Alaska State Coun. on Arts fellow, 1982, 88. Mem. N.W. Print Coun., L.A. Printmaking Soc. Democrat. Office: Site 250 Fine Art 250 Cushman St Ste 2A Fairbanks AK 99701-4665

MOLLING, CHARLES FRANCIS, lawyer; b. Grafton, Wis., Jan. 5, 1940; s. Frank Joseph and Gertrude Catherine (Tillmann) M.; m. Gretchen Arlene Lundberg, Sept. 27, 1961. BA magna cum laude, U. Mo., 1973; JD, Loyola U., Chgo., 1977. Bar: Colo. 1977, Ill. 1977, U.S. Dist. Ct. Colo. 1979, U.S. Dist. Ct. (no. dist.) Ill. 1979, U.S. Ct. Appeals (7th and 10th cirs.) 1979, U.S. Ct. Claims 1979. Claims and bond underwriting positions various ins. cos., Milw. and other locations, 1961-76; assoc. state counsel Pioneer Title Ins. Co., Denver, 1976-77; assoc. Boatright & Deuben, Wheat Ridge, Colo., 1977-78, McNeela & Griffin, Chgo., 1979; ptnr. Boatright Molling & Ripp, Wheat Ridge, 1980-88; pvt. practice law Denver, 1988—. Author: Public Trustee Foreclosures in Colorado--A Systems Approach, 1983; (computer software) MicroLawyer, 1985. Cpl. USMC, 1960-61. Mem. Colo. Bar Assn., Denver Bar Assn., 1st Jud. Dist. Bar Assn., POETS. Office: 4704 Harlan St Ste 300 Denver CO 80212-7418

MOLLMAN, JOHN PETER, book publisher, consultant electronic publishing; b. Belleville, Ill., Feb. 8, 1931; s. Kenneth John and Maurine (Farrow) M.; m. Jane Michael Kendall, Aug. 22, 1953; children—Sarah Chase, Eric Cleburne. B.Arts, Washington U., St. Louis, 1952. Advt. specialist Gen. Electric Co., Schenectady and Boston, 1952-54; mgr. Enterprise Printing Co., Millstadt, Ill., 1956-66; gen. mgr. Monarch Pub. Co., N.Y.C., 1966-67; dir. prodn. Harper & Row Pubs., N.Y.C., 1967-74; pub. Harper's Mag. Press, N.Y.C., 1971-74; v.p. prodn. Random House Inc., N.Y.C., 1974-81; sr. v.p. World Book-Childcraft Inc., Chgo., 1981-88; pres. World Book Pub., 1988-91; pub. cons., 1991-92; dir. intellectual property devel. Multimedia Publishing Microsoft, 1992—. Chmn. graphics standards rsch. com. NEH; mem. vis. com. Washington U., pub. com. Art Inst. of Chgo. With U.S. Army, 1954-56. Mem. Assn. Am. Pubs., Siwanoy Club (Bronxville, N.Y.), Sigma Delta Chi, Omicron Delta Kappa. Unitarian. Home: 4511 103rd Ln NE Kirkland WA 98033-7639 Office: Microsoft 1 Microsoft Way Redmond WA 98052-8300

MOLLNER, FREDERICK RICHARD, director publications, graphic designer; b. L.A., Aug. 21, 1946; m. Virginia Donahoo, Jan. 6, 1973. BA, Calif. State U., L.A., 1971, MA, 1972; postgrad., Art Ctr. Coll. Design, L.A. Graphic designer Calif. State U., L.A., 1972-77; art dir. Amb. Coll., Pasadena, Calif., 1977-78; art dir. Pepperdine U., Malibu, Calif., 1978-80, creative dir., 1980-84, dir. pubs., 1984—; tchr. Calif. State U., 1983-84, Pepperdine U., 1988; freelance graphic designer. Mem. Coun. for Advancement and Support of Edn., Univ. and Coll. Designers Assn. (sec. 1980), Advt. Club Ventura County, Art Dir. Club L.A., Am. Inst. Graphic Artists. Office: Pepperdine U 24255 Pacific Coast Hwy Malibu CA 90263-0001

MOLTON, PETER MICHAEL, waste conversion researcher, consultant; b. Wolverhampton, Eng., Aug. 21, 1943; came to U.S., 1971; s. Cuthbert Joseph and Fay (Hudson) M.; m. Elizabeth Eirwen Carrington, Nov. 17, 1964 (div. Feb. 1971); m. Marion Elizabeth Glock, Feb. 25, 1971 (div. June 1995); children: Sharon Elizabeth, Ivan Robert, Kerrin Amy. BSc with honors, U. Manchester, Eng., 1964; PhD in Organic Chemistry, U. London, 1967, MPhil in Microbiology, 1971, Diploma in Space Physics, 1971. NAS postdoctoral fellow NASA-Ames, Moffett Field, Calif., 1971-72; rsch. assoc. U. Md., College Park, 1972-74; sr. rsch. scientist Battelle-N.W. Lab., Richland, Wash., 1975—. Contbr. articles to profl. jours.; inventor sludge to oil reactor system; patentee tritum polymer lights. Ward treas. Chiswick Conservative Party, London, 1969-70. Recipient R & D 100 award R & D mag., 1988, Excellence in Tech. Transfer award Fed. Lab. Consortium, 1988. Fellow Brit. Interplanetary Soc.; mem. Am. Chem. Soc., Internat. Soc. for Study Origin of Life, Alpha Chi Sigma. Republican. Home: Apt E203 425 N Columbia Center Blvd Kennewick WA 99336-7706 Office: Battelle-Pacific NW Lab Battelle Blvd K7-97 Richland WA 99352

MOLTZAN, NICOLINE G., nurse, administrator; b. Morehead City, N.C., Dec. 7, 1940; d. Nils George Christiansen and Stella Amelia (Smith) Christiansen Martinez; m. William J. Moltzan, Oct. 5, 1963 (dec.). Diploma, Beth El Sch. Nursing, Colorado Springs, Colo., 1963; BS, Coll. St. Francis, Joliet, Ill., 1982, MS in Health Adminstrn., 1988. Head nurse ICU-CCU Penrose Hosp., Colorado Springs, staff nurse ICU-CCU; staff nurse ICU-CCU Evans Army Community Hosp., Ft. Carson, Colo., evening and night supr. Mem. AACN. Office: PO Box 60386 Colorado Springs CO 80960-0386

MOMENT, JOAN, artist, educator; b. Sellersville, Pa., Aug. 22, 1938; d. Robert Joseph and Margaret Velma (Adams) Ingham; m. Roger Lloyd Moment, May 27, 1962 (div. 1970); 1 child, Benjamin Robert. BS and RN, U. Conn., 1960; MFA, U. Colo., 1970. Psychiat. nurse Yale Med. Ctr., New Haven, 1960-61; pub. health nurse Vis. Nurse Assn., New Haven, 1961-62; grad. assistantship U. Colo., Boulder, 1968-69; lectr. U. Colo., Denver, 1970; from asst. prof. to full prof. Calif. State U., Sacramento, 1970—; vis. assoc. prof. East Carolina U., Greenville, N.C., 1984; vis. artist, lectr. Syracuse (N.Y.) U., 1985, U. N.C., Chapel Hill, 1986, Princeton U., 1987; guest lectr. Crocker Art Mus., 1994. One woman shows include Candy Store Gallery, Folsom, Calif., 1973, Wenger Gallery, San Francisco, 1974, La Jolla, 1975, 82, Whitney Mus. Am. Art, N.Y.C., 1974, La Jolla, 1975, 82, Galerie Simonne Stern, New Orleans, 1979, Crocker Art Mus, Sacramento, 1981, Quay Gallery, San Francisco, 1982, Southeastern Ctr. for Contemporary Art, Winston Salem, N.C., 1984, Gray Art Gallery, E. Carolina U., Greenville, N.C., 1984, Rena Bransten Gallery, San Francisco, 1985, Calif. State U., Sacramento, 1985, Galerie Hirondelle, N.Y.C., 1987, Jennifer Pauls, 1978, 89, Solomon Dubnick Gallery, Sacramento, 1992; group exhbns. include Calif. State U., Sacramento, 1971, 76, 88, 94, San Francisco Art Inst., 1972, Oakland Mus., 1972, 83, 92, 94, Crocker Mus., 1972, 85, 88, 91, 94, 95, Whitney Mus. of Am. Art, N.Y.C., 1973, Walnut Creek Civic Arts Gallery, Calif., 1977, Portland Ctr. Visual Arts, Oreg., 1977, L.A.C.E., L.A., 1979, Palo Alto Cultural Ctr., Calif., 1979, San Jose Mus. Art, 1981, Quay Gallery, San Francisco, 1981-84, Long Beach Mus. Art, Long Beach, Ca., 1982, Chan Elliot Gallery, 1983, San Francisco Arts Commn. Gallery, 1983, Auckland Mus., Chapel Hill, N.C., 1987, Fresno Art Mus., Calif., 1987, Jennifer Pauls Gallery, 1988, CSU, Long Beach, Calif., 1989, Richard Nelson Gallery, U. Calif. Davis, 1990, 94, 95, San Francisco Mus. Modern Art Rental Gallery, 1990, U. Colo. Art Mus., 1991, Pence Gallery, 1991, 94, Ctr. for Contemporary Art, Sacramento, Calif., 1991, William Sawyer Gallery, 1993, Bergen Mus. Art, Paramus, N.J., 1993, Alza Corp., Vacaville, Calif., 1991, Oakland Mus., 1992, 94, Somona State U., Rohnert Park, Calif., 1995, Temporary/Contemporary, Las Vegas, 1995, others; collections include Crocker Art Mus., U. Colo., Boulder, Oakland Mus., N.Y. State Devel. Corp., Allen Meml. Art Mus., Oberlin, Ohio, others. Juror selection panelist Art in Pub. Places Meml. Auditorium, Sacramento, 1991; juror Calif. Exposition and State Fair, Sacramento, 1991. Recipient Meritorious Performance award Calif. State U., 1986; Rockefeller artist-in-residency fellow, 1984. Mem. Coll. Artists Assn. Home: 306 Dunbarton Cir Sacramento CA 95825-6811 Office: Calif State Univ Dept Art 6000 J St Sacramento CA 95819-2605

MOMMSEN, KATHARINA, retired German language and literature educator; b. Berlin, Sept. 18, 1925; came to U.S., 1974, naturalized, 1980; d. Hermann and Anna (Johannsen) Zimmer; m. Momme Mommsen, Dec. 23, 1948. Dr.phil., U. Tübingen, 1956; Dr. habil., Berlin Free U., 1962. Collaborator Acad. Scis., Berlin, 1949-61; assoc. prof. Free U., Berlin, 1962-70; prof. German Carleton U., Ottawa, Can., 1970-74; Albert Guerard prof. lit. Stanford U., 1974-95, ret., 1995; vis. prof. U. Giessen, Tech. U. Berlin, 1965, State U. N.Y., Buffalo, 1966, U. Calif., San Diego, 1973. Author over 150 publs. on 18th-20th century German and comparative lit.; editor: Germanic Studies in America. Mem. Internat. Assn. Germanic Langs. and Lit., Goethe Soc., Schiller Soc. Home: 980 Palo Alto Ave Palo Alto CA 94301-2223

MONACO, DICK STEVEN, mail order vendor; b. San Diego, Oct. 12, 1956; s. Louis Antonio and Judith Ann (Frank) M.; m. Anne Raylene Hoover, Sept. 26, 1989; children: Teresa Anne, Michele Dawn. BA in Journalism, Nat. U., 1990. Copywriter, artist Interstate Mktg., San Diego, 1979-93; owner Dicks of Am., San Diego, 1986—; cons. computer graphics, San Diego, 1990-94. Author: I Love Peanut Butter Cookbook, 1985 (Best Self Pub. award Am. Bookdealer's Exch. 1987), Dick Liquers, 1994. Office: Dicks of Am PO Box 600782 San Diego CA 92160-0782

MONACO, FERDINAND ROGER, mathematics educator; b. Pitts., Oct. 2, 1940; s. Charles Anthony and Bertha Ann (Grove) M.; m. Roberta Denise Karl, Jan. 30, 1987. BA, Calif. State U., Long Beach, 1979, MA, 1982; PhD, Walden U., 1989. Prof. emeritus L.A. Community Coll. Dist., 1982—; adj. prof. math. Linfield Coll., McMinnfield, Oreg.; cons., prin. Learning Resources Co., McMinnville, 1985—. Author: (textbooks) Intro Microwave Technology, 1989, Essential Mathematics for Electronics Technicians, 1990, FCC Licensing, 1990, Resources in Mathematics for Electronics, 1990, Laboratory Activities in Microwave Technology, 1990, Interactive Software: Math for Physics, 1993, Applied Math, 1993. Mem. Am. Math. Assn., Am. Math. Assn. Two Yr. Colls., Phi Kappa Phi, Phi Delta Kappa. Home: 15500 SW Dusty Dr Mcminnville OR 97128-8500

MONACO, PAUL, academic administrator, educator, artist, writer; b. Niskayuna, N.Y., Sept. 11, 1942; s. Angelo M. and Birdena (O'Melia) M.; m. Victoria O'Donnell, 1993. BS, Columbia U., 1965; MA, U. N.C., 1966; PhD, Brandeis U., 1974. Asst. prof. hist. Brandeis U., Waltham, Mass., 1973-75; prof. arts and humanities U. Tex., Dallas, 1975-85, dir. grad. studies arts and humanities, 1976-80; dept. head, prof. media and theatre arts Mont. State U., Bozeman, 1985—; bd. dirs. U. Film and Video Assn., 1988-91, 95—, Bozeman Film Festival, 1985— (pres. 1987-90); mem. Hist. Preservation Com., Bozeman, 1988-90, Mont. Com. for Humanities, Missoula, 1989-93; regional coord. Nicholls Screenwriting Awards, 1989-91. Author: Cinema and Soc., Modern Europe Culture..., 1983, Ribbons in Time, 1988 (ALC 10 best award 1988); prodr., dir.: Montana: 2nd Century, 1990-96 (Mont. broadcasters award 1991); prodr., dir., co-writer: Home to Montana, 1988; dir. Women, War and Work, 1994, Way of the Trout, 1994, I Often Thought of Berlin, 1989. Bd. mem. Mont. Ballet Co., Bozeman, 1986-90. Recipient Fulbright Prof. award U.S., Germany, 1982-83, 92. Home: 290 Low Bench Rd Gallatin Gateway MT 59730-9741

MONAHAN, RITA SHORT, nursing educator; b. Waterloo, Iowa, Sept. 16, 1954; d. Andrew T. and Lillian R. (Weber) Short; m. W. Gregory Monahan, Jr., June 2, 1976; children: Andrew G., Catherine R. BSN, U. Iowa, 1976; MS in Nursing, Duke U., 1980; EdD, W.Va. U., 1986. Cert. gerontology clin. nurse specialist. From instr. to asst. prof. sch. nursing W.Va. U., Morgantown, 1981-86; assoc. prof. sch. nursing Oreg. Health Scis. U., LaGrande, 1986—. Contbr. articles to profl. jours. Mem. ANA, AAUW, Am. Diabetes Assn., Oreg. Nurses Assn., Sigma Theta Tau. Office: Oreg Health Scis U Sch Nursing 1410 L Ave La Grande OR 97850-2807

MONARCHI, DAVID EDWARD, management scientist, information scientist, educator; b. Miami Beach, Fla., July 31, 1944; s. Joseph Louis and Elizabeth Rose (Muller) M.; BS in Engring. Physics, Colo. Sch. of Mines, 1966; PhD (NDEA fellow), U. Ariz., 1972; 1 child by previous marriage, David Edward. Asst. dir. of Bus. Rsch. Divsn., U. Colo., Boulder, 1972-75, asst. prof. mgmt. sci./info. systems, 1972-75, assoc. prof. mgmt. sci. and info. systems, 1975—; assoc. dir. Bus. Rsch. Divsn., 1975-80, dir. Divsn. Info. Sci. Rsch., 1982-84; prin. investigator of socio-econ. environ. systems for govtl. agys., and local govt. orgns., State of Colo., also info. systems for pvt. firms, 1972-77. Mem. Gov.'s Energy Task Force Com., 1974. Mem. IEEE, Inst. for Mgmt. Sci., Assn. Computing Machinery, Am. Assn. Artificial Intelligence. Contbr. numerous articles on socio-econ. modeling, object-oriented systems and artificial intelligence to profl. jours. Home: 32 Benthaven Pl Boulder CO 80303-6210 Office: U Colo Grad Sch Bus Boulder CO 80309-0419

MONCHARSH, PHILIP ISAAC, lawyer; b. N.Y.C., May 27, 1948; s. Bernard J. and Betty R. (Chock) M.; m. Karen L. Fellows, Nov. 1, 1981; children: Rachael, Anna. BA, Yale U., 1970; JD, Columbia U., 1973. Bar: Calif. 1973, U.S. Dist. Ct. (cen. dist.) Calif. 1979, U.S. Ct. Appeals (9th cir.) 1981. Trial dep. L.A. County Pub. Defender, L.A., 1973-78; assoc. Strote & Whitehouse, Beverly Hills, Calif., 1978-81, Ghitterman, Hourigan, et al, Ventura, Calif., 1981-86, Heily & Blase, Ventura, Calif., 1986-87; of counsel Hecht, Diamond & Greenfield, Pacific Palisades, Calif., 1988; ptnr. Benton, Orr, Duval & Buckingham, Ventura, 1988-89, Rogers & Sheffield (now Rogers Sheffield & Herman), Santa Barbara, Calif., 1989—; arbitrator, judge pro tem Superior and Mcpl. Cts., Ventura and Santa Barbara, 1986—. Pres. Ojai Valley (Calif.) Land Conservancy, 1988-94. Mem. Calif. Trial Lawyers Assn., Santa Barbara Trial Lawyers Assn., Ventura Trial Lawyers Assn., L.A. Trial Lawyers Assn., Assn. Trial Lawyers Am., Consumer Attys. of Calif., Consumer Attys. of L.A., Yale Club Santa Barbara, Ventura and San Luis Obispo Counties (pres.). Office: Rogers Sheffield & Herman 427 E Carrillo St Santa Barbara CA 93101-1401

MONDA, MARILYN, quality improvement consultant; b. Paterson, N.J., Aug. 11, 1956; d. Thomas John and Lydia Mary (Dal Santo) M.; m. Lawrence G. Gifford, Jr., Aug. 25, 1984. BA, San Diego State U., 1980; MA, Baylor U., 1984. Math. statistician Navy Personnel Rsch. and Devel. Ctr., San Diego, 1984-86; quality engr. Info. Magnetics, Inc., San Diego, 1986-87; mgmt. cons. Process Mgmt. Inst., Inc., Mpls., 1987-89; staff assoc. Luftig & Assocs., Inc., Detroit, 1989-92; founder Quality Disciplines, San Diego, 1992—; bd. dirs. Deming Users Group, San Diego, 1985-87; lecturer in the field. Contbr. articles to profl. jours. Mem. San Diego Deming Users Group, Am. Soc. Quality Consultants, Am. Statistical Assn., Phi Beta Kappa.

MONDAVI, ROBERT GERALD, winery executive; b. Virginia, Minn., June 18, 1913; s. Cesare and Rosa (Grassi) M.; m. Marjorie Declusin, 1940 (dec.); children: Robert, Timothy, Marcia; m. Margrit Biever, 1980. BA, Stanford U., 1936. Dir. Sunny St. Helena Wine Co., St. Helena, Calif., 1937-45; v.p., gen. mgr., Charles Krug Winery, St. Helena, 1943-66; pres. Robert Mondavi Winery, Oakville, Calif., 1966—, now chmn. bd. Office: Robert Mondavi Winery PO Box 106 Oakville CA 94562-0106

MONDAVI, ROBERT MICHAEL, vintner; b. 1943. Grad., Santa Clara U. Prin. Robert Mondavi Winery; pres., CEO Robert Mondavi Corp., Oakville, Calif. Office: Robert Mondavi Corp 7801 St Helena Hwy Oakville CA 94562*

MONDAY, JOHN CHRISTIAN, manufacturing company executive; b. West Bend, Wis., June 29, 1925; s. Leo John and Emilie Suzanne (Klapper) M.; m. Alyce S. Riesch, Aug. 20, 1949 (div. Jan. 1981); children: Linda Lee Monday Orlando, John Scott; m. Virginia M. Clayton, Jan. 29, 1981. BA in Math. and Econs., Ripon Coll., 1949; BSBA, MIT, 1951; MBA, U. Wis., 1954. Dir. research Hevi Duty Elec. Co., 1951-54, div. mgr., 1954-59; v.p., gen. mgr. Hubbard Aluminum Products Co., Pitts. and Abingdon, Va., 1959-65; pres. Am. Vitrified Products Co., Cleve., 1965-69; exec. v.p., bd. dirs. Intermark Inc., La Jolla, Calif., 1969-91; pres., chmn. Specialties Engring. Corp, San Diego, 1991—; pres., bd. dirs. Specon Inc.; pres., chmn. bd. dirs. Spltys. Engring. Corp., 1976—, San Diego; pres. Specon Inc., La Jolla, 1981—. Author: Radiography of Copper Casting, 1951. Mem. Com. of 25, Washington, 1967-69; Trustee Johnston Meml. Hosp., 1963-65, Va. Highlands Found., 1963-65; dir. Street and Hwy. Safety Lighting Bur., 1959-65; regional chmn. ednl. council M.I.T., 1969-82. Served with AUS, 1943-46. Mem. ASTM (mem. D 33 com., subcom. chmn., steel structures painting coun.), Nat. Elec. Mfrs. Assn., Am. Mgmt. Assn., Clay Pipe Assn. (vice chmn. 1965-69), Nat. Assn. Corrosion Engrs., La Jolla Country Club (San Diego), Baillage La Chaine des Rotisseurs (Bailli of La Jolla). Republican. Presbyterian. Home: 5192 Chelsea St La Jolla CA 92037-7908

MONEY, ARTHUR L., electronics executive; b. Stockton, Calif.; m. Sharon Money; children: Jennifer, David. BSME, San Jose State Coll., 1965; MSME, U. Santa Clara, 1970. Data analysis of space and missile sys. Lockheed Missiles and Space Co., 1962-72; engr., then mgr. and dir. various units ESL Inc., Sunnyvale, Calif., 1972-84, v.p., gen. mgr. signals, analysis and sys. divsn., 1984-89, v.p. advanced programs and devel., 1989-90, pres., 1990—. Chmn. United Way campaign Santa Clara County, 1993; bd. dirs. Valley Med. Ctr. Found., Am. Leadership Forum, Santa Clara County Mfg. Group, Silicon Valley Art Fund, San Jose U. Sch. Engring. Mem. AIAA, Am. Electronics Assn., Navy League Am., Assn. Old Crows, Planetary Soc., Am. Def. Preparedness Assn., Security Affairs Support Assn. Office: ESL Inc PO Box 3510 495 Java Dr Sunnyvale CA 94088-3510

MONFERRATO, ANGELA MARIA, entrepreneur, investor, writer; b. Wissembourg, Alsace-Loraine, France, July 19, 1948; came to U.S., 1950; d. Albert Carmen and Anna Maria (Vieri) M. Diplomate, Pensionnat Florissant, Lausanne, Switzerland, 1966-67; BS in Consumer Related Studies, Pa. State U., 1971, postgrad., 1971-72. Simultaneous translator fgn. langs. Inst. for Achievement of Human Potential, Phila., 1976-78; art dir. The Artworks, Sumneytown, Pa., 1975-76; asst. productionist Film Space, State College, Pa., 1976; real property mgr. Pla. 15 Condominium, Ft. Lauderdale, Fla., 1979-80; legal asst. Ft. Lauderdale, Fla., 1981-85; owner Rising Sun the Real Estate Corp. South Fla., Ft. Lauderdale, 1986—; pres. Kideos Video Prodns., 1985—; designer Colo. Remodel & Design, 1988-92; owner, designer Monferrato Designs, 1993-95. Office: Monferrato Designs Telluride 200 Front St Placerville CO 81430

MONGOLD, MICHAEL RAY, psychologist; b. Fresno, Calif., Aug. 18, 1951; s. Elton Conway and Carol (McKinsey) M.; m. Kathleen Washburn, July 17, 1987; children: Michael David, Sarah Michelle, Allison Carol. BA in Recreation Therapy, Calif. State U., Fresno, 1973; MA in Counseling, Pepperdine U., 1976; MA in Clin. Psychology, Calif. Sch. Profl. Psychology, 1981, PhD in Clin. Psychology, 1983. Lic. psychologist, Calif. Dir./therapist 8th Jud. Ct. of Conciliation, Great Falls, Mont., 1977-79; psychology intern Youth City Am., Mariposa, Calif., 1979-80, U. Calif. Davis Med. Ctr., Sacramento, 1980-81; crisis worker Valley Med. Ctr., Fresno, Calif., 1981-82; predoctoral intern in clin. and cmty. psychology Shasta County Mental Health Svcs., Redding, 1982-83, crisis intervention coord., 1985-86, program mgr., 1986-87; exec. dir., staff psychologist Mat-Su Cmty. Counseling Ctr., Wasilla, Alaska, 1983-85; pvt. practice clin. psychology Redding, 1985, 87—; dir. psychiat. programs Redding (Calif.) Specialty Hosp., 1990-92, dir. psychol. svcs., 1992—; mem. staff Valley Hosp., Palmer, Alaska, 1985, Shasta Psychiat. Hosp., Redding, 1986—, Mercy Med. Ctr., Redding, 1990—, Redding Med. Ctr., 1990—, Redding Specialty Hosp., 1991—; tchr. U. San Francisco, 1986-88, Mat-Su C.C., 1984-85; clin. supr. social work, counseling psychology and psychiat. nurse students U. Alaska, Anchorage, 1983-85; clin. supr. Mat-Su Cmty. Counseling Ctr., Wasilla, 1984-85, Shasta County Mental Health Svcs., 1986-88, Redding Specialty Hosp., 1991—. Mem. adv. bd. No. Valley Cath. Social Svcs.; active Shasta Symphony Orch., Redding Symphony Orch., Shasta County Performing Arts Soc. Capt. USAF, 1973-77. Mem. APA, Calif. State Psychol. Assn., Shasta County Psychol. Assn. (chair hosp. practice com., Outstanding Psychologist of Yr. 1992). Office: Redding Specialty Hosp 2801 Eureka Way Redding CA 96001-0222

MONK, DIANA CHARLA, artist, stable owner; b. Visalia, Calif., Feb. 25, 1927; d. Charles Edward and Viola Genevieve (Shea) Williams; m. James Alfred Monk, Aug. 11, 1951; children: Kiloran, Sydney, Geoffrey, Anne, Eric. Student, U. Pacific, 1946-47, Sacramento Coll., 1947-48, Calif. Coll. Fine Arts, San Francisco, 1948-51, Calif. Coll. Arts & Crafts, Oakland, 1972. Art tchr. Mt. Diablo Sch. Dist., Concord, Calif., 1958-63; pvt. art tchr. Lafayette, Calif., 1963-70; gallery dir. Jason Aver Gallery, San Francisco, 1970-72; owner, mgr. Monk & Lee Assocs., Lafayette, 1973-80; stable owner, mgr. Longacre Tng. Stables, Santa Rosa, Calif., 1989—. One-person shows include John F. Kennedy U., Orinda, Calif., Civic Arts Gallery, Walnut Creek, Calif., Vallery Art Gallery, Walnut Creek, Sea Ranch Gallery, Gualala, Calif., Jason Aver Gallery, San Francisco; exhibited in group shows at Oakland (Calif.) Art Mus., Crocker Nat. Art Gallery, Sacramento, Le Salon des Nations, Paris. Chair bd. dirs. Walnut Creek (Calif.) Civic Arts, 1972-74, advisor to dir., 1968-72; exhibit chmn. Valley Art Gallery, Walnut Creek, 1977-78; juror Women's Art Show, Walnut Creek, 1970, Oakland Calif. Art. Home and Office: Longacre Tng Stables 1702 Willowside Rd Santa Rosa CA 95401-3922

MONK, JANICE JONES, women's studies researcher, university program administrator; b. Sydney, Australia, Mar. 13, 1937; came to U.S., 1961; d. Harold Frederick and Edith Emily (Collins) J.; m. David Monk, July 31, 1964. BA with honors, U. Sydney, 1958; MA, U. Ill., 1963, PhD, 1972. Instr. geography U. Ill., Urbana, 1967-72, asst. prof., 1972-80; assoc. dir. S.W. Inst. for Rsch. on Women U. Ariz., Tucson, 1980-83, exec. dir., 1983—; cons. Nat. Geog. Soc., 1979-81, 86, 87; mem. U.S. Nat. Com. Internat. Geog. Union, Washington, 1980-88, vice chairperson gender study group, 1988-92, Commn. on Gender, 1992—; bd. dirs. Ctr. for Geography in Higher Edn., Oxford, England. Co-editor: Women and the Arizona Economy, 1987, The Desert is No Lady, 1987, Western Women: Their Land, Their Lives, 1988, Full Circles: Geographies of Women over the Life Course, 1993; contbr. articles to various publs. Mem. rsch. com. nat. bd. YWCA, N.Y.C.; bd. dirs. Prescott Coll., 1990—. Mem. Assn. Am. Geographers (councilor 1978-81, meritorious svc. award perspectives on women group 1988, honors award 1992), Nat. Coun. Geog. Edn. (sec. 1984-86, bd. dirs. 1980-83), Soc. Woman Geographers (Washington, nat. councilor 1987-90). Office: U Ariz SW Inst Rsch Women 102 N Douglas Cir Tucson AZ 85711-2814

MONKS, CARON LORRAINE, marketing specialist; b. Preston, Eng., June 1, 1961; came to U.S., 1968; d. Raymond and Brenda (Moss) M.; m. Scott Charles Foulk, Nov. 7, 1987 (div. Sept. 1992). BA in Pub. Rels. and Advt., Western Wash. U., 1984. Pub. rels. specialist Pay'n Save Corp., Seattle, 1984-85; acct. coord. Goodrich & Snyder Pub. Rels., Bellevue, Wash., 1987-88; pub. rels./mktg. cons. Monks Comm., Kirkland, Wash., 1985-89; mktg. coord. Geo Engrs., Redmond, Wash., 1989-91, HDR Engring., Bellevue, 1992-93; mktg. dir. Phinney Design, Seattle, 1993; acct. exec./mktg. specialist Technigraphic Sys. Inc., Edmonds, Wash., 1993—. Editor: Klipsun mag., 1983. Mem. NAFE, Am. Mktg. Assn. Office: Technigraphic Sys Inc 111 James St Edmonds WA 98020-3589

MONKS, KAREN ELIZABETH, nursing educator; b. Grand Rapids, Mich., Nov. 3, 1936; d. Louis Francis and Evelyn Anne (Hammerschmidt) McGough; m. Patrick Joseph Monks, Nov. 26, 1966; children: Laura Anne, Joseph Patrick. Diploma in nursing Mercy Central Sch. Nursing, Grand Rapids, 1956; BSN, Marquette U., 1965; MSN, U. Tex. Med. Br., Galveston, 1984. RN, Mich., Wis., Ariz. Staff nurse St. Mary's Hosp., Grand Rapids, 1957-58; staff nurse, then head nurse Kent County Hosp., Grand Rapids, 1958-62; staff nurse part-time St. Joseph's Hosp., Milw., 1962-65, head nurse, 1965-66; staff nurse, then house supr. Yuma Regional Med. Ctr. (Ariz.), 1966-72; nursing instr. Ariz. Western Coll., Yuma, 1972—, div. chmn. human services, 1984-92; case mgr. Olsten Kimberly Quality Care, 1991—; bd. dirs. Yuma Regional Med. Ctr., 1980-91, chmn. 1989, sec./treas., 1987, vice-chmn., 1988, chmn. personnel/nominations, 1981-84; chmn. Ariz. Council Assoc. Drgree Nursing Programs, 1985-86; co-chmn. Ariz. Council on Nursing Edn., 1985-86. Mem. Nat. League Nursing (bd. rev. 1990—, accreditation visitor, 1985—), Toastmasters Internat. (able toastmaster). Democrat. Roman Catholic. Home: 1946 S London Dr Yuma AZ 85364-5023 Office: Ariz Western Coll PO Box 929 Yuma AZ 85366-0929

MONROE, KEITH, writer, consultant; b. Detroit; s. Donald and Gladys Violet (Wiley) M. Student, Stanford U., 1934-35, UCLA, 1936-38. Suburban corr. N.Y. Times, N.Y.C., 1930-33; mng. editor Teaneck (N.J.) Post, 1933-34; rschr. Foote Cone & Belding, L.A., 1938-39; copy chief Advt. Counselors, Phoenix, 1940-41; asst. dir. pub. rels. Ryan Aero. Co., San Diego, 1942-45; freelance writer and cons., L.A., 1946-58; copywriter Fuller & Smith & Ross, L.A., 1958-61; exec. editor N.Am. Rockwell, El Segundo, Calif., 1963-70; writer, cons., L.A., 1970—; cons. Govt. of Pakistan, Karachi, 1949-50, Govt. of Guatemala, Guatemala City, 1954-55, Bank Am., L.A., 1955-58; editor RAND Corp., Santa Monica, Calif., 1970-71. Author: (book and film) Be Prepared, 1953, (book) How To Succeed in Community Service, 1962, City for Sale—A History of Century City, 1965; contbr. over 150 articles to Fortune, Life, N.Y. Times Mag., Harper's, New Yorker, also others. V.p. Family Svc. Assn., L.A., 1955-58; mem. exec. bd. Adoption Inst., L.A., 1957-60; dist. chmn. Welfare Planning Coun., L.A., 1959-61; mem. health and safety com. Boy Scouts Am., Irvine, Tex., 1978-91. Recipient Silver Beaver award Boy Scouts Am., 1958. Mem. Authors Guild, Am. Soc. Journalists and Authors, Rotary (sec. Santa Monica 1986-87). Home and Office: 11965 Montana Ave Los Angeles CA 90049-5037

MONROE, MARY-LYNNE, computer consultant, special education educator; b. Chgo., Sept. 30, 1954; d. Clarence Anthony and Edna Ruth (Waleski) M.; m. Richard Neilan McPartland, Nov. 19, 1994; 1 child, Alyssa Joy McPartland. BS in Edn., Ill. State U., Normal, 1977; MS in Edn., Portland (Oreg.) State U., 1991. Cert. tchr., Oreg., Ill. Spl. educator Higbee Jr. H.S., Pittsfield, Ill., 1977-78, Bloomington (Ill.) Alternative Sch., 1978-83, Woodstock Sch., Portland, Oreg., 1983-84; spl. educator Franklin H.S., Portland, 1984-91, English educator, 1992-93; computer coord. Am. Internat. Sch., Cairo, Egypt, 1991-92; computer cons. Matrix Cons., Wilsonville, Oreg., 1994—. Mem. Fellowship of Reconciliation, Portland, 1990—; PAL, speaker Cascade AIDS Project, Portland, 1989—; local rep. UN NGO Forum on Women, Beijing, 1995. Mem. NEA, Oreg. Edn. Assn., Portland Assn. Tchrs., Women's Internat. League for Peace and Freedom.

MONSON, ARVID, food products executive; b. 1941. With Munson & Son Cattle Co., Sunnyside, Wash., 1959-84; pres. Munson Ranches, Inc., Outlook, Wash., 1984—. Office: 2330 Outlook Rd Outlook WA 98938-9200*

MONSON, BEVERLY PARRY, dietitian; b. Denver, Oct. 18, 1961; d. Robert Alvarus and Ruth Ivy (Wagner) Parry; m. Rodney Hal Monson, Sept. 9, 1988; 1 child, Joshua. BS in Med. Dietetics, Brigham Young U., 1988. Registered dietitian. Clin. dietitian ARA Svcs./Holy Cross Hosp., Salt Lake City, 1988-89, chief clin. dietitian, 1989-92; consulting dietitian IV Plus/Foothill Family Clinic, Salt Lake City, 1992-93, Palo Alto, Calif., 1993—; instr. low-fat cooking Granite Sch. Dist., Salt Lake City, 1991-92; low-fat chef/nutrition specialist KSL-TV, Eyewitness News at Noon, Salt Lake City, 1992-93; adj. faculty Utah State U., Brigham Young U., Logan, Utah, Provo, 1990-92. Mem. Am. Dietetic Assn., Calif. Dietitc Assn. (San Jose chpt.). Mem. LDS Ch. Home: Escondido Village # 112B Stanford CA 94305

MONSON, JAMES EDWARD, electrical engineer, educator; b. Oakland, Calif., June 20, 1932; s. George Edward and Frances Eleanor (Fouche) M.; m. Julie Elizabeth Conzelman, June 25, 1954; children—John, Jamie, Jennifer. BSEE, Stanford U., 1954, MSEE, 1955, PhD in Elec. Engring., 1961. Mem. tech. staff Bell Telephone Labs., Murray Hill, N.J., 1955-56; devel. engr. Hewlett-Packard Co., Palo Alto, Calif., 1956-61; Robert C. Sabini prof. engring. Harvey Mudd Coll., 1961—. Mem. governing bd. Claremont Unified Sch. Dist., 1966-71, pres., 1969-70; pres. Claremont Civic Assn., 1974-75; bd. dirs. Claremont YMCA, 1978-82. NSF fellow, 1954-55; Fulbright research grantee, 1975-76; Fulbright sr. lectr., 1980; Japan Soc. Promotion of Sci. fellow, 1984. Mem. AAUP, IEEE, Magnetics Soc. Japan, Phi Beta Kappa, Sigma Xi, Tau Beta Pi. Home: 353 W 11th St Claremont CA 91711-3806 Office: Harvey Mudd Coll 301 E 12th St Claremont CA 91711-5901

MONSON, JANET MARLENE, biochemist; b. Mondovi, Wis., July 31, 1944; d. Sigvald and Velma Lillian (Nyre) M. BS in Chemistry, Gonzaga U., 1969; PhD in Biochemistry, U. Wash., 1974. Postdoctoral fellow U. Wash., Seattle, 1974; Eidgenössische Techische Hochschule U. Zurich, ETH Molecular Biology Inst., Honggerberg, Switzerland, 1975; postdoctoral fellow U. Calif., San Francisco, 1975-78; postgrad. rsch. scholar, 1978; asst. rsch. biochemist U. Calif., San Francisco, 1979-82; sr. rsch. scientist, project leader Zymos Corp., Seattle, 1982; vis. scientist U. Wash. and Fred Hutchinson Cancer Rsch. Inst., Seattle, 1982-83; asst. prof. dept. surgery Mcill U., Montreal, Que., 1983-89; freelance writer Hayward, Calif. Contbr. articles to profl. jours. Cmty. chair biohazard com. U. Calif., San Francisco, 1975-78; sr. biohazard safety officer USPHS, San Francisco, 1975-78. Recipient Individual Postdoctoral fellowship Am. Cancer Soc., 1975, Nat. Rsch. Svc. award, Individual Postdoctoral fellowship USPHS, 1975-78, Sr. Scientist award Fonds de la recherche en sante du Quebec, 1984-87, Sr. Scientist award Med. Rsch. Coun. Can., 1984-89; USPHS grantee, 1979-82, Med. Rsch. Coun. Can., grantee, 1984-89. Mem. AAAS, Phi Lambda Upsilon.

MONSON, THOMAS SPENCER, church official, publishing company executive; b. Salt Lake City, Aug. 21, 1927; s. George Spencer and Gladys (Condie) M.; m. Frances Beverly Johnson, Oct. 7, 1948; children—Thomas L., Ann Frances, Clark Spencer. BS with honors in mktg, U. Utah, 1948; MBA, Brigham Young U., 1974, LLD (hon.), 1981. With Deseret News Press, Salt Lake City, 1948-64; mgr. Deseret News Press, 1962-64; mem. Council Twelve Apostles, Ch. of Jesus Christ of Latter Day Saints, 1963-85, mem. first presidency, 1985—, bishop, 1950-55; pres. Canadian Mission, 1959-62; chmn. bd. Deseret News Pub. Co., 1977—; dir. Deseret Mgmt. Corp.; pres. Printing Industry Utah, 1958; bd. dirs. Printing Industry Am., 1958-64; mem. Utah exec. bd. U.S. West Communications. Mem. Utah Bd. Regents; mem. nat. exec. bd. Boy Scouts Am.; trustee Brigham Young U.. With USNR, 1945-46. Recipient Recognition award, 1964, Disting. Alumnus award U. Utah, 1966; Silver Beaver award Boy Scouts Am., 1971; Silver Buffalo award, 1978; Bronze Wolf award World Orgn. of the Scout Movement, 1993. Mem. Utah Assn. Sales Execs., U. Utah Alumni Assn. (dir.), Salt Lake Advt. Club, Alpha Kappa Psi. Club: Exchange (Salt Lake City). Office: LDS Ch 47 E South Temple Salt Lake City UT 84150 also: Deseret News Pub Co PO Box 1257 30 E 1st St Salt Lake City UT 84110

MONTAG, DAVID MOSES, computer company executive; b. Los Angeles, Apr. 30, 1939; s. Gustave and Esther (Kessler) M.; student UCLA, 1957-61; children: Daniel Gershon, Esther Yael, Michael Menachem; m. Olga Volozova, June 18, 1992. Tech. writer L.H. Butcher Co., Los Angeles, 1961; phys. sci. lab. technician East Los Angeles Coll., Monterey Park, 1961—, planetarium lectr., 1963-78; owner EDUCOMP, Monterey Park, Calif., 1980—; ptnr. David M. Montag & Assocs., Monterey Park, 1993—; pres. Aquinas Computer Corp.; ednl. cons. for computer-assisted instrn. pres., dir. Or Chadash, Inc., Monterey Park, 1968—; v.p., bd. dirs. Coll. Religious Conf., 1968-92. Mem. Assn. of Orthodox Jewish Scientists, Laser Inst. Am., AIAA. Home and Office: PO Box 384 Monterey Park CA 91754-0384

MONTAGNE, ERNEST, operations analyst; b. Galveston, Tex., Dec. 3, 1937; s. Ernest R. and Mary Louise (Howard) M.; m. Elizabeth Ann Bartlett, Aug. 22, 1959 (div. Apr. 1983); children: Michael Leigh, Laura Louise Montagne Magee; m. Sarah Eleanor Brown, Jan. 1, 1991. BA in Geology, Rice U., 1959; MS in Indsl. Engring., Ariz. State U., 1968; DSc in Ops. Rsch., George Washington U., 1981. Cert. profl. ski instr. Commd. 2d lt. U.S. Army, 1959, advanced through grades to lt. col., ret., 1981; sr. scientist CACI-Fed., Inc., 1981-83; prin. staff mem. ANSER, 1983-85, Royal Dutch/Shell, 1985-87, BDM Internat., Inc., 1987—. Contbr. articles to profl. jours. Vestry St. Margaret's Ch., Woodbridge, 1981-85, search com. chair, 1990-91. Mem. Ops. Rsch. Soc. of Am., Mil. Ops. Rsch. Soc., Internat. Test and Evaluation Assn., Armed Forces Comm. Electronics Assn., Omega Rho, Sigma Gamma Epsilon. Home: 2540 S Player Ave Sierra Vista AZ 85635-5204 Office: BDM Fed PO Box 2290 Sierra Vista AZ 85636-2290

MONTAGNE, JOHN, geology educator, consulting geologist; b. White Plains, N.Y., Apr. 17, 1920; s. Henry and Ella Tappey (Spurgeon) de la Montagne; m. Phoebe Morris Corthell, Dec. 23, 1942; children: Clifford, Mathew Hagen. BA, Dartmouth Coll., 1942; MA, U. Wyo., 1951, PhD, 1955. Cert. profl. geologist. Instr., Colo. Sch. Mines, Golden, 1953-55, asst. prof., 1955-57; asst. prof. Mont. State U., Bozeman, 1957-60, assoc. prof., 1960-63, prof. dept. earth scis., 1963-83, prof. emeritus, 1983—; chmn. Internat. Snow Sci. Workshop, Bozeman, 1981-82. Pres. Mont. Wilderness Assn., 1965; pres. bd. Bridger Bowl Ski Area, Inc., Bozeman, 1973. Served to capt. U.S. Army, 1942-46, MTO. Named Rotarian of Yr., 1989; recipient Gold and Blue award Mont. State U., 1987. Fellow Geol. Soc. Am. (sr., chmn. Rocky Mountain sect. 1982); mem. Am. Assn. Petroleum Geologists, Internat. Glaciol. Soc., Am. Inst. Profl. Geologists, Am. Assn. Avalanche Profls. (pres. 1991-94). Lodge: Rotary (pres. Bozeman 1967-68, dist. gov. 1979). Home: 17 Hodgeman Canyon Dr Bozeman MT 59715-9527 Office: Mont State U Dept Earth Scis Bozeman MT 59717

MONTAGUE, GARY LESLIE, newspaper advertising executive; b. Mullan, Idaho, Apr. 4, 1939; s. William Bryan and Gladys Viola (Finkbeiner) M.; m. Dorothy Barclay, Feb. 14, 1959 (div. 1973); children: Teresa Montague Scofield, Douglas; m. Mikael Jones, Mar. 13, 1982. Grad., Am. Press Inst. Columbia U., 1973; postgrad., Cen. Wash. U., 1977. Classified advt. rep. The Wenatchee World, 1957-71, classified advt. mgr., 1971—; sr. ptnr. Leslie/Bryan/Jones, Wenatchee, 1992—; cons., lectr. arts adminstrn. Chmn. Wash. State Arts Commn., Olympia, 1985-88, commr., 1974-78, 82-88; trustee Wash. State Arts Alliance Found., 1981-88, Western States Arts Found., Santa Fe, N.M., 1982-88; pres. Cen. Wash. Hosp. Found., Wenatchee, 1987-88, Wenatchee Area Visitor and Conv. Bur., 1980-81, Allied Arts Coun. of North Cen. Wash., 1973-74, Music Theater of Wenatchee, 1970-71, Wenatchee Valley Dance Found., Gallery '76 art gallery Wenatchee Valley Coll.; commr. City of Wenatchee Arts Commn., 1975-78; exec. com. Wash. State Rep. Cen. Com., 1975-77; dir. Better Bus. Bur.,

1993—. Mem. Assn. Newspaper Classified Advt. Mgrs., Western Classified Advt. Assn. (pres. 1990-91), Pacific N.W. Assn. of Newspaper Classified Advt. Mgrs. (pres. 1981-82), Wenatchee Area C. of C. (pres. 1978-79). Mem. Unity Ch. Lodge: Rotary. Home: 2142 Sunrise Cir Wenatchee WA 98801-1047 Office: World Pub Co 14 N Mission St Wenatchee WA 98801-2250 also: Leslie/Bryan/Jones PO Box 4644 Wenatchee WA 98807-4644

MONTAGUE, SIDNEY JAMES, real estate developer; b. Denver, Oct. 3, 1950; s. Jerome Edward and Donna Sherrill (Nixon) M.; m. Mary Francis Terry, Dec. 26,1987; stepchildren: Jonathan Ramsey Shockley, Britt Elizabeth Shockley; children: Noah Reimer. BA in Econs., Midland Luth. Coll., Fremont, Nebr., 1972. Loan counselor Am. Nat. Bank, Denver, 1972-74; loan officer First Nat. Bank Denver, 1974-79; exec. v.p. Buell Devel. Corp., Denver, 1979-84; v.p. The Writer Corp., Denver, 1985-86; pres. Mondevco Inc., Littleton, Colo., 1986-87; devel. mgr. Perini Land & Devel. Co., Phoenix, 1987-91; v.p. Perini Land & Devel. Co., San Francisco, 1991-94; prin. Farrmont Realty Group, Inc., 1994—. Republican.

MONTALBANO, WILLIAM DANIEL, foreign correspondent, novelist; b. N.Y.C., Sept. 20, 1940; s. Vincent Francis and Gertrude (Reilly) M.; m. Kathleen Feeney, June 18, 1964 (div. 1977); children: Dennis, Andrea; m. Rosanna Mary Bell-Thomson, Dec. 3, 1977; children: Tiva, Teresa, Daniel. BA, Rutgers U., 1960; MS in Journalism, Columbia U., 1962; Nieman fellow, Harvard U., 1970. Reporter Newark (N.J.) Star-Ledger, 1960-62; editor Patriot Ledger, Quincy, Mass., 1962-63, Buenos Aires Herald, 1964-65, United Press Internat., N.Y.C., 1965-67; corr., editor Miami (Fla.) Herald, 1967-79, chief of corrs., 1981-83; Peking (China) bur. chief Knight Ridder Newspapers, Miami, Fla., 1979-81; El Salvador bur. chief L.A. Times, 1983-84, Buenos Aires bur. chief, 1984-85, Rome bur. chief, 1987-95, London bur. chief, 1995—. Author: Powder Burn, 1981, Trap Line, 1983, Death in China, 1984, Sinners of San Ramon, 1989. Recipient Ernie Pyle award Scripps Howard Newspapers, 1974, 75, Maria Moors Cabot prize Columbia U., 1974. Office: 150 Brompton Rd, London SW3 1HX, England

MONTALI, LAWRENCE RICHARD, JR., religious newspaper editor; b. Somerset, Bermuda, Nov. 30, 1962; s. Lawrence Richard and Sammie Louise (Brocato) M.; m. Veronica Bavestrello, Aug. 10, 1991; children: Lorenzo Antonio and Stefano Samuel (twins). Student, U. Exeter, Eng., 1983-84; BA in Psychology, U. Calif., San Diego, 1985; MS in Mag. Journalism, Syracuse U., 1989. Founder, dir. Project Rainbow-Newton Coll., Lima, Peru, 1989-91; editor The Southern Cross, San Diego, 1991—; freelance writer, photographer Nat. Cath. Register, Encino, Calif., 1993—, Our Sunday Visitor, Huntington, Ind., 1994—. Exhbn. photographs Grove Gallery, San Diego. Recipient Best Story award NCCJ, 1993. Mem. San Diego Press Club (Best Story award 1994, Best Feature Story award 1994), Cath. Press. Assn. Roman Catholic. Office: The So Cross PO Box 81869 San Diego CA 92138-1869

MONTANA, MONTIE, JR., performing arts producer; b. Los Angeles, Dec. 28, 1934; s. Montie Montana Sr. and Louise A. (Archer) M.; m. Joan Dorothy Dunn, Dec. 27, 1957 (div. Nov. 1971); children: Kelly, Jess, Dorothy. BS in Animal Sci., U. Calif., Davis, 1957. Performer in rodeos and other shows U.S. and Can., 1938-1965; producer of western shows internationally, 1965-1971; producer Buffalo Bill's Wild West, 25 countries, 1971—. Spokesman Rep. Gov's. campaign, Montana, 1964; campaign chmn. Reagan for Gov., Calif., 1965. Served to 1st lt. cav. U.S. Army, 1957-59. Named Visit U.S.A. Ambassador, U.S. Dept. Commerce, 1974. Mem. Internat. Assn. Fairs & Expositions, Internat. Assn. Auditorium & Arena Mgrs., Internat. Assn. Amusement Parks & Attractions. Office: PO Box 1060 Springville CA 93265-1060

MONTANDON, ARTHER RONALD, city attorney; b. San Diego, Oct. 11, 1952; s. Francis Hammond and Sayoko (Kutazume) M.; m. Cathleen Elizabeth Conway, Aug. 20, 1977 (div. July 1981); m. Carol Lynn McCraw, Dec. 25, 1950; 1 child, Matthew Arthur; stepchildren: Michael Balais, Debra Michelle Hawley, Amber Balais-Montandon, Amy Montandon. BS in Bus. Mgmt., San Diego State U., 1975; JD, U. Pacific, Sacramento, 1979. Bar: Calif. 1979. Assoc. McLean & McLean, San Diego, 1980-82; asst. city atty. City of Gardena, Calif., 1982-84; dep. city atty. City of Santa Maria, Calif., 1984-85, city atty., 1985—; city atty. City of Atascadero, Calif., 1989—. Editor: California Municipal Law Handbook, 1993. Mem. Ethnic Minority Rels. Com. of State Bar, San Francisco, 1991-94, Santa Barbara County Pvt. Industry Coun., 1991-93. Recipient Excellence in Practice of Pub. Law award Santa Barbara County Judges, 1992. Mem. U.S. Jr. C. of C. (amb.). Office: City Hall 204 E Cook St Santa Maria CA 93454-5136

MONTEAU, NORMAN KEITH, gemologist; b. Balt., Dec. 20, 1957; s. Milton Keith and Vieva Regina (Williams) M.; m. Sandra Lynn Staub, Dec. 7, 1987. Cert. diamond grading, Gemol. Inst., 1981, cert. colored stone grading, 1982, cert. gem identification, 1982. Owner, founder Monteau Gemol. Svcs., Woodland Hills, Calif., 1987-91, pres., 1992—; owner, pres. Am. Internat. Gemologists, Beverly Hills, Calif., 1993—; mng. ptnr. The William Staub Co., L.A., 1994—; appraiser to Archdiocese of L.A. Cath. Ch., 1993—; arbitrator State Farm Ins. Co., 1993—; lectr. nat. retail jewelry store chains, 1992—; master gemologist for banks, law enforcement agys., ins. cos., 1991—; cons., advisor to Calif. ins. carriers for earthquake property damage assessment and evaluation for over 40 million dollars worth of property, 1994. Contbr. articles to profl. jours. Recipient Excellence award Aetna Ins. Co., 1992. Mem. Nat. Assn. Jewelry Appraisers, Am. Soc. Appraisers, Gemol. Inst. Am. (mem. Pres.'s Cir. 1992—), Calif. Jewelers Assn., Alumni Assn. Gemol. Inst. Am. (charter), Jewelers Bd. of Trade, Woodland Hills C. of C. Office: Monteau Gemol Svcs Ste 203 21250 Califa St Woodland Hills CA 91367

MONTERO, DARREL MARTIN, sociologist, social worker, educator; b. Sacramento, Mar. 4, 1946; s. Frank and Ann Naake; m. Tara Kathleen McLaughlin, July 6, 1975; children: David Paul, Lynn Elizabeth, Laura Ann, Emily Kathryn. AB, Calif. State U., 1970; MA, UCLA, 1972, PhD, 1974. Postgrad. researcher Japanese-Am. Research Project UCLA, 1971-73, dir. research, 1973-75; assoc. head Program on Comparative Ethnic Studies, Survey Research Ctr. UCLA, 1973-75; asst. prof. sociology Case Western Res. U., Cleve., 1975-76; asst. prof. urban studies, research sociologist Pub. Opinion Survey, dir. urban ethnic research program U. Md., College Park, 1976-79; assoc. prof. Ariz. State U., Tempe, 1979—; cons. rsch. sect. Viewer Sponsored TV Found., Los Angeles, Berrien E. Moore Law Office, Inc., Gardena, Calif., 1973, Bur. for Social Sci. Research, Inc., Washington, Friends of the Family, Ltd., Nat. Sci. Found. Author: Japanese Americans: Changing Patterns of Ethnic Affiliation Over Three Generations, 1980, Urban Studies, 1978, Vietnamese Americans: Patterns of Resettlement and Socioeconomic Adaptation in the United States, 1979, Social Problems, 1988; mem. editorial bd. Humanity and Society, 1978-80; contbr. articles to profl. jours. Served with U.S. Army, 1966-72. Mem. Am. Sociol. Assn., Am. Assn. Pub. Opinion Research (exec. council, standards com.), Am. Ednl. Research Assn., Council on Social Work Edn., Soc. Study of Social Problems, D.C. Sociol. Soc., Am. Soc. Pub. Adminstrn., Nat. Assn. Social Workers, Pacific Sociol. Assn. Office: Sch Social Work Ariz State U Tempe AZ 85281

MONTERROSA, JOSÉ NAPOLEÓN, bilingual school psychologist; b. San Vicente, El Salvador, Feb. 5, 1953; came to U.S., 1972; s. Napoleon and Elia (Roque) M. BA in Philosophy, Don Bosco Coll., 1978; MA in Counseling & Guidance, Loyola Marymount U., L.A., 1984, MA in Ednl. Psychology, 1985, MA in Sch. Adminstrn., 1990. Tchr. St. John Bosco High Sch., Bellflower, Calif., 1978-81, Daniel Murphy High Sch., L.A., 1982-84; counselor L.A. City Coll., 1983-84; specialist Found. for Jr. Blind, L.A., 1985-86; instr. Don Boaso Tech. Inst., Rosemead, Calif., 1988; bilingual sch. psychologist L.A. Unified Sch. Dist., 1986—, pub. rels. media cons., in-svc. cons., 1988—; college counselor West Los Angeles City Coll., 1992-93; edn. cons. Gestión Y Control de Calidad, Valencia, Spain, 1992-93. Mem. Nat. Assn. Sch. Psychologists, Calif. Assn. Psychologists, Am. Psychol. Assn. (assoc.). Mailing: PO Box 3134 Huntington Park CA 90255-2034 Office: Psychol Svcs 2151 N Soto St Los Angeles CA 90032-3629

MONTES, RAMON G., pediatric gastroenterologist, career officer; b. San Juan, P.R., Apr. 7, 1955; s. Ramon G. and Carmen J. (Garces) M.; m. Elizabeth Rodriguez, Dec. 16, 1978; children: Daniel, David, Darren. BS magna cum laude, U. P.R., San Juan, 1974, MD, 1978. Diplomate Nat. Bd. Med. Examiners, Am. Bd. Pediatrics. Resident in pediatrics U. P.R., Caguas, 1978-81; chief resident in pediatrics Caguas Regional Hosp., 1980, med. dir. ICU, 1981-82, chmn. dept. pediatrics, 1982-85, dir. pediatrics residency program, 1982-85; pvt. practice San Juan, 1982-86; med. dir. health dept. City of Bayamon, P.R., 1985-86; commd. capt. USAF, 1986, advanced through grades to lt. col., 1993; staff pediatrician USAF Hosp., Davis-Monthan AFB, Ariz., 1986-87; chief pediatrics svc. 836 Air Divsn. Hosp., Davis-Monthan AFB, 1987-89; gastroenterology fellow Johns Hopkins U., Balt., 1989-92; chief pediatric gastroenterology and nutrition David Grant USAF Med. Ctr., Travis AFB, Calif., 1992-95; chief pediatric gastroenterology Rockford (Ill.) Clinic, 1995—; clin. instr. U. P.R., 1981-86, mem. curriculum com. sch. medicine, 1982-85; clin. examiner P.R. State Bd. Med. Examiners, San Juan, 1981-85; clin. instr. U. Md., 1989-92, U. Calif., Davis, 1992—; liaison officer for Johns Hopkins U. USAF, Balt., 1990. Author: (with others) Textbook of Gastroenterology, Pediatrics, Pediatric Gastrointestinal Disease; question writer Am. Bd. Pediatrics Certifying Exam., 1993-94; contbr. articles to profl. jours. Active Community Coun. Child Abuse, Caguas, 1982-83. Decorated Commendation medal. Fellow Am. Acad. Pediatrics (keyperson com. nutrition); mem. AMA, Am. Gastroent. Assn., N.Am. Soc. Pediatric Gastroenterology and Nutrition, Alpha Omega Alpha. Roman Catholic. Office: David Grant USAF Med Ctr Rockford Clinic 2300 N Rockton Ave Rockford IL 61103

MONTGOMERY, CARROLL ANN., law educator; b. New Orleans, Nov. 28, 1946; d. Herbert Eugene Watson and Mary May (LeCompte) Leathers; m. Daniel G. Montgomery; children: Robert A. Sinex, Jr., Stacie Bateman, Joy Montgomery. JD, San Francisco Law Sch., 1980. Bar: Calif. 1980. Pvt. practice Santa Rosa, Calif., 1980-85; child custody mediator Sonoma County Superior Ct., Santa Rosa, 1985-86; chief dep. county counsel Butte County Counsel, Oroville, Calif., 1986-87; chief dep. dist. atty. Butte County Dist. Atty., Oroville, 1987-94; referee Shasta County Superior Ct., Redding, Calif., 1995—; dean faculty, law prof. Calif. No. Sch. of Law, Chico, 1987—. Commr. Yuba County Juvenile Justice and Delinquency Prevention Commn., Marysville, Calif., 1993-94. Fellow Lawyers in Mensa. Office: Shasta County Superior Ct 1431 Market St Redding CA 96001

MONTGOMERY, JAMES FISCHER, savings and loan association executive; b. Topeka, Nov. 30, 1934; s. James Maurice and Frieda Ellen (Fischer) M.; m. Diane Dealey; children: Michael James, Jeffrey Allen, Andrew Steven, John Gregory. BA in Acctg., UCLA, 1957. With Price, Waterhouse & Co., C.P.A.'s, Los Angeles, 1957-60; controller Conejo Valley Devel. Co., Thousand Oaks, Calif., 1960; asst. to pres. Gt. Western Fin. Corp., Beverly Hills, Calif., 1960-64; pres. United Financial Corp of Calif., Los Angeles, 1964-75; chmn., c.e.o. Great Western Financial Corp., Chatsworth, Calif., 1975—; fin. v.p., treas. United Fin. Corp., Los Angeles, 1964-69, exec. v.p., 1969-74, pres., 1975; pres. Citizens Savs. & Loan Assn., Los Angeles, 1970-75. Served with AUS, 1958-60. Office: Gt Western Fin Corp 9200 Oakdale Ave Chatsworth CA 91311-6519*

MONTGOMERY, JOHN ALAN, surgeon; b. L.A., Jan. 24, 1944; s. Milford Jefferson and Ilah Claudine (Whitely) M.; m. Jean Nishita, Mar. 28, 1970; children: Maggie Mae, Max Alan. BA, UCLA, 1965; MD, U. So. Calif., 1969. Diplomat Am. Bd. Surgery. Intern Los Angeles County-U. So. Calif. Med. Ctr., L.A., 1969-70, resident in surgery, 1970-74; pvt. practice Fortuna, Calif., 1976—; clin. prof. Los Angeles County-U. So. Calif. Med. Ctr.,1 982—; chief of staff Redwood Meml. Hosp., 1990-91. Maj. USAF, 1974-76. Fellow ACS; mem. Calif. Med. Assn., Grad. Soc. Surgeons Los Angeles County Gen. Hosp., Internat. Soc. Philos. Enquiry, Triple 9 Soc., Mensa, Skull and Dagger Honor Soc./U. So. Calif. Home: 4175 Mill St Fortuna CA 95540-9201 Office: 3301 Renner Dr Fortuna CA 95540-3119

MONTGOMERY, MICHAEL BRUCE, lawyer, consultant; b. Santa Barbara, Calif., Sept. 12, 1936; s. Clair Gruwell Montgomery and Florence Louise (Moran) Quigley; m. Carmen Luisa Montalvan, June 16, 1990; children by previous marriage: Michael, Megan. BS, UCLA, 1960; LLB, U. So. Calif., 1963. Bar: Calif. 1963, Hawaii 1985, Fla. 1985. Staff atty. div. hwys. State of Calif., Sacramento and L.A., 1965; assoc. Martin & Flandrick, San Marino, Calif., 1965-66; owner, pres. Michael B. Montgomery, L.C., Pasadena, Calif., 1966—; agy atty. Huntington (Calif.) Park Redevel. Agy., 1988-93, Walnut (Calif.) Imprevement Agy., 1988-92; spl. counsel County of San Bernardino, Calif., 1988-89; city atty. Diamond Bar, Calif., 1993—; U.S. rep. Atlantic Tuna Commn., Madrid, 1985-94. Contbr. numerous articles to profl. jours. Chmn. Calif. Rep. Party, 1977-79; mayor City of South Pasadena, 1980-81; chmn. Calif. Electoral Coll., Sacramento, 1980; commr. Calif. Fair Polit. Practices Commn., 1985-89. Sgt. U.S. Army, 1954-57, ensign USNR, 1960. Mem. Calif. Bar Assn., Fla. Bar Assn., Hawaii Bar Assn., United Sport Fishermen Internat. (pres. 1987-92), Jonathan, Plaza. Office: 10501 Valley Blvd Ste 121 El Monte CA 91731-2403

MONTGOMERY, RICHARD ALAN, sales executive; b. Arlington Heights, Ill., Sept. 5, 1949; s. Charles Gaylord and Luva (Snider) M. BS in Communications, U. Tenn., 1974. Account exec. John M. Rose Advt., Knoxville, Tenn., 1974-75, Metcalfe-Cook & Smith Advt., Nashville, 1975-77, Sta. WTVF-TV, Nashville, 1977-78; div. mgr. Showbiz, Inc., Nashville, 1978-81; sales supr. Multimedia Program Prodns., Nashville, 1981-83; v.p., western regional mgr. Paramount TV, Los Angeles, 1983—. Served with USNG, 1970-78. Mem. Nat. Assn. TV Program Execs., Jr. C. of C. Republican. Methodist. Office: Paramount TV Los Angeles CA 90038

MONTGOMERY, ROBERT F., state legislator, retired surgeon, cattle rancher; b. Ogden, Utah, May 13, 1933; s. William Floyd and Adrianna (Van Zweden) M.; m. Jelean Skeen, June 24, 1953; children: Lance, Dana, Kristen, Keri, Tanya. AS, Weber State U., 1953; BS, Brigham Young U., 1957; MD, U. Utah, 1961. Pvt. practice Anaheim, Calif., 1966-88; senator Utah State Senate, 1992—; chief surgery Anaheim Gen. Hosp., 1970, Anaheim Meml. Hosp., 1972-74. Rep. chmn. Weber County, Utah, 1991-93; pres. Am. Cancer Soc., Salt Lake City, 1992—. Sgt. U.S. Army, 1953-55, Korea. Mem. Rotary, Utah Elephant Club, Travelor's Century Club. Mormon. Home: 1825 Mountain Rd Ogden UT 84414-2903

MONTGOMERY, ROBERT LOUIS, chemical engineer; b. San Francisco, Nov. 20, 1935; s. Louis Clyde and Fay Elythe (Myers) M.; m. Patricia Helen Cook, Mar. 17, 1962; children: Cynthia Elaine, Jeanette Louise, Cecilia Irene, Howard Edwin. BS in Chemistry, U. Calif., Berkeley, 1956; PhD in Phys. Chemistry, Okla. State U., 1975. Registered profl. engr., Kans., Tex., Colo. Phys. chemist U.S. Bur. Mines, Reno, 1956-62; NSF predoctoral fellow Okla. State U., Stillwater, 1963-66; sr. engr. Boeing Co., Wichita, Kans., 1966-75; postdoctoral fellow Rice U., Houston, 1975-77, sr. research assoc., 1982-84; tech. data engr. M.W. Kellogg Co., Houston, 1977-82; staff engr. Martin Marietta, Denver, 1984-94. Contbr. articles to profl. jours. Mem. Am. Chem. Soc., Am. Soc. for Metals, Profl. Engrs. Colo., Sigma Xi. Home: 9933 Fairwood St Littleton CO 80125-8811

MONTGOMERY, SETH DAVID, retired state supreme court chief justice; b. Santa Fe, Feb. 16, 1937; s. Andrew Kaye and Ruth (Champion) M.; m. Margaret Cook, Oct. 29, 1960; children: Andrew Seth, Charles Hope, David Lewis. AB, Princeton U., 1959; LLB, Stanford U., 1965. Bar: N.M. 1965. Ptnr. Montgomery & Andrews, P.A., Santa Fe, 1965-89, of counsel, 1994—; justice N.Mex. Supreme Ct., 1989-94, chief justice, 1994; adj. prof. law, instr. U. N.Mex. Sch. Law, Albuquerque, 1970-71; chmn. N.Mex. adv. coun. Legal Svcs. Corp., Santa Fe, 1976-89. Bd. visitors Stanford U. Sch. Law, 1967-70, 82-85; pres., chmn. Santa Fe Opera, 1981-86; pres. Santa Fe Opera Found., 1986-89; chmn., vice chmn. Sch. Am. Rsch., Santa Fe, 1985-89; bd. dirs. New Vistas, Santa Fe, 1986-89, First Interstate Bank of Santa Fe, 1977-89, Old Cienega Village Mus., 1980-89. Lt. (j.g.) USN, 1959-62. Named Citizen of Yr., Santa Fe C. of C., 1986, Sunwest Bank of Santa Fe, 1994; recipient Disting. Cmty. Svc. award Anti-Defamation League, 1991, Western Area Outstanding Achievement award Nat. Multiple Sclerosis Soc., 1992, award for advancement of law N.Mex. Trial Lawyers, 1994, Award for Outstanding Judge Albuquerque Bar Assn., 1994. Fellow Am. Coll. Trial Lawyers, Am. Coll. Trust and Estate Counsel, Am. Bar Endowment, N.Mex. Bar Assn. (bd. bar commrs. 1986-89, sec., treas. 1988-89, Professionalism award 1993); mem. ABA, Am. Judicature Soc. Democrat.

MONTONE, KENNETH ALAN, art director, creative director, consultant; b. Chgo., Aug. 30, 1938; s. George Joseph and Beatrice Mabel (Calcott) M.; m. Patricia Joan Klapperich, Feb. 1, 1964; children: James Paul, Ian Andrew, Paul Matthew, Anne Elizabeth. BFA with honors, U. Ill., 1963. Graphic designer U. Ill. Press, Champaign, 1962-63; staff graphic designer ABC-TV, Chgo., 1963-65; art dir. McCann-Erickson, Inc., Sydney, Australia, 1965-67; staff graphic designer CBS-TV, Chgo., 1967-69; syndicated cartoonist, "Kiwi" Chgo. Tribune-N.Y. News Syndicate; art dir. McCann-Erickson, Inc., Portland, Oreg., 1969-80; creative dir. Morton Advt., Portland, 1980-84, Ken Montone & Assocs., Portland, 1984—. Art dir.: "Celebrate" series, 1980. With USN, 1956-59. Recipient Reata Howard Trombley award Portland Ad Fedn., 1983, Art Dirs. Club award N.Y. Ad, 1983, Best in West award Am. Advt. Fedn., 1983. Mem. Advt. Industry Emergency Fund (bd. dirs.), Portland Ad Fedn., Advt. Museum. Home and Office: Ken Montone & Assocs 165 NW 95th Ave Portland OR 97229-6303

MONTOYA THOMPSON, VELMA, federal agency administrator; b. L.A., Apr. 9, 1938; d. Jose Gutierrez and Consuelo (Cavazos) Montoya; m. Earl A. Thompson; 1 child, Bret L. Thompson. BA in Diplomacy and World Affairs, Occidental Coll., 1959; MA in Internat. Rels., Fletcher Sch. of Law and Diplomacy, 1960; MS in Econs., Stanford U., 1965; PhD in Econs., U. Calif., L.A., 1977. Asst. prof. Econs. Calif. State U., L.A., 1965-68; vis. assoc. prof. U. So. Calif., 1979; instr. U. Calif., L.A., 1981-82; staff economist The Rand Corp., Santa Monica, Calif., 1973-82; asst. dir. for strategy, White House Office of Policy Devel. Exec. Office of the Pres., 1982-83; expert economist, Office of Regulatory Analysis, Occupational Safety and Health Adminstrn. U.S. Dept. of Labor, 1983-85; dir. of Studies in Pub. Policy and Assoc. Prof. of Political Economy, Sch. of Bus. Mgmt. Chapman U., 1985-87; adj. prof., Sch. of Bus. Mgmt. Pepperdine Univ., 1987-88; pres. Hispanic-Am. Pub. Policy Inst., 1984-90; assoc. prof. of Fin., Sch. of Bus. Adminstrn. Calif. State Polytechnic Univ., Pomona, 1988-90; commr. Occupational Safety and Health Review Commn., 1990—; cons. Urban Inst., 1974, Mexican-Am. Study Project UCLA, 1966, Graduate and Profl. Fellowships to the Office of Post Secondary Education, U.S. Dept. of Edn.; editorial referee Contemporary Policy Issues, Economic Inquiry, Policy Analysis, The Journal of Economic Literature; discussion leader Am. Assembly on Rels. Between the U.S. and Mex.; pres. del. White House Conf. on Aging, 1981; reader of 1988 proposals for the U.S. Dept of Edn. for the Improvement and Reform of Schs. and Teaching; research participant U.S. Dept. of Edn. Delphi Assessment of Drug Policies for Use in Minority Neighborhoods, 1989; mem. hispanic adv. panel Nat. Commn. for Employment Policy, 1981-82; lectr. Brookings Inst. Seminars for U.S. Bus. Leaders; bd. adv. Close-Up Found., 1982-83; discussant Western Economic Assn. Meetings, 1985, 93; bd. adv. Nat. Rehab. Hosp., 1991-94; mem. nat. exec. adv. bd. Harvard Jour. of Hispanic Policy, 1993-95. Bd. regents U. Calif., 1994—; mem. adv. com. U.S. Senate Rep. Conf. Task Force on Hispanic Affairs, 1991—. Named One of the 100 U.S. Hispanic Influentials Hispanic Bus. Mag., 1982, 90, Woman of the Yr. Mex.-Am. Oportunity Found., 1983, The East L.A. Com. Union, 1979, Marshall scholar, Fulbright scholar; recipient Freedom Found. at Valley Forge Honor Econ. Edn. Excellence Cert., 1986, Univ. fellow Stanford Univ., Internat. Rels. fellow Calif. PTA, John Hay Whitney Opportunity fellow; Calif. State Univ. Found. Faculty Rsch. grantee. Mem. ASTM (com. on rsch. and tech. planning 1985-87), Am. Econ. Assn. (session chair ann. meetings 1995), Nat. Coun. of Hispanic Women, State Bar of Calif., Calif. State Bar Ct. (exec. com. 1987-89, disciplinary bd. 1986-89), Western Econ. Assn., Indsl. Rsch. Inst. for Pacific Nations (adv. bd. 1988-89), Salesian Boys and Girls Club (bd. dirs 1989—), Vets. in Com. Svc. (adv. com. 1989-94), Phi Beta Kappa, Omicron Delta Epsilon, Phi Alpha Theta. Home: 6970 Los Tilos Rd Los Angeles CA 90068

MONTROSE, DONALD W., bishop; b. Denver, May 13, 1923. Student, St. John's Sem., Calif. Ordained priest Roman Cath. Ch., 1949. Aux. bishop Roman Cath. Ch., Los Angeles, 1983; bishop Diocese of Stockton, Calif., 1985—. Office: Diocese of Stockton PO Box 4237 1105 N Lincoln St Stockton CA 95203-2410*

MOODY, CHARLES RUSSELL, medical sales and marketing professional; b. Phoenix, Oct. 16, 1956; s. Dean Dalby and Barbara Ann (Peabody) M.; m. Barbie Lynne Gercke, Sept. 21, 1979; children: Nicole, Charles, Chelsea, Alexandria. Student, U.S. Naval Acad., 1974-76, Ariz. State U., 1976-79. Consumer sales Procter & Gamble Dist. Co., Cin., 1979-81; unit mgr. Procter & Gamble Dist. Co., Phoenix, 1981-83; med. sales rep. Johnson & Johnson, Phoenix, 1983-95, Chiron Corp., Phoenix, 1995—. Pres. Intrafraternity Coun., 1978-79; dep. registrar Maricopa County (Ariz.) Voter Registration, 1987—; precinct capt. Maricopa County Democrats, Phoenix, 1987—; chmn. bd. Children in Need Found., Phoenix, 1988—; big brother Valley Big Bros., Phoenix, 1976-79; mem. Semper Fidelis Soc., Annapolis, 1975-76; mem. Active 20/30 Internat., 1983-89 (Man of Yr. 1987), pres. Phoenix #99, 1986-87 (Regular Man of Yr. 1987); nat. pres. Active 20/30 U.S. & Can., 1987-88 (Best Nat. Pres. 1987-88); Am. regional chmn. World Coun., 1988-89. With USN 1974-76. Mem. Am. Legion, Sigma Phi Epsilon. Democrat. Episcopalian.

MOODY, HELEN F., training and consulting company executive, writer; b. Palo Alto, Calif., Feb. 6, 1949; d. Dwight L. and Bobbie J. (Naugher) M.; m. Richard A. Borthwick, Oct. 1, 1988; 1 child from a previous marriage: Amy Stroud Jackson. BA with honors, San Jose State U., 1971; PhD, U. Calif., Berkeley, 1981. Dir. ops. Comm. Strategies, Inc., Albuquerque, 1980-84; pres. Comm. Strategies, Inc., Corrales, N.Mex., 1984—; cons. Albuquerque C. of C., 1986, U. N.Mex., Albuquerque, 1987. Author: The Debate of the Rose, 1981, Good Grammar, Good Style, 1994, Writing by Design, 1995. Mem. Village Planning Task Force, Corrales, 1988. Grantee Ford Found., 1974. Mem. Nat. Soc. Performance and Instrn. (pres. N.Mex. chpt. 1995), Medieval Acad. Am., Soc. Tech. Comm. Office: Comm Strategies Inc PO Box 2578 Corrales NM 87048

MOOG, MARY ANN PIMLEY, lawyer; b. Havre, Mont., May 29, 1952; d. Orville Leonard and Della Mae (Cole) Pimley; m. Daren Russell Moog, Apr. 15, 1978; children: Eric John, Keith Cole, Trygg Orville. BS, Mont. State U., 1975; JD, U. Mont., 1981; LLM, NYU, 1983. Bar: Mont. Law clk. Mont. Supreme Ct., Helena, 1981-82; assoc., ptnr., staff atty. Bosch, Kuhr, Dugdale, Martin & Kaze, Havre, 1984—. Recipient Am. Jurisprudence Book award Lawyers Coop. Publ. Co., 1980-81, Tax award Prentice Hall, Inc., 1981, Northwestern Union Trust Co. award, 1981. Mem. ABA, Mont. Bar Assn., 12th Jud. Bar Assn. (pres. 1987-88), Phi Delta Phi. Democrat. Roman Catholic. Home: 925 Wilson Ave Havre MT 59501-4331 Office: Bosch Kuhr Dugdale Martin & Kaze PO Box 7152 Havre MT 59501-7152

MOON, RONALD T. Y., state supreme court chief justice; b. Sept. 4, 1940; m. Stella H. Moon. B in Psychology and Sociology, Coe Coll., 1962; JD, U. Iowa, 1965. Bailiff, law clk. to Chief Judge Martin Pence U.S. Dist. Ct., 1965-66; dep. prosecutor City and County of Honolulu, 1966-68; assoc. Libkuman, Ventura, Ayabe, Chong & Nishimoto (predecessor firm Libkuman, Ventura, Moon & Ayabe), Honolulu, 1968-72, ptnr., 1972-82; judge 9th div. 1st cir., Cir. Ct., State of Hawaii, Honolulu, 1982-90; assoc. justice Supreme Ct., State of Hawaii, Honolulu, 1990-93; chief justice Supreme Ct., State of Hawaii, 1993—; apptd. to ct. annexed arbitration program com., 1985-90; apptd. chairperson of study for judiciary's automation application transfer team, 1985; apptd. arbitration judge 1st cir. cir. ct., 1986-90; apptd. to bd. advisors Ctr. for Alternative Dispute Resolution, 1989; lectr. and guest spkr. numerous events. Mem. ABA, Hawaii Bar Assn., Hawaii Trial Lawyers Am., Am. Bd. Trial Advocates (pres. 1986-93, nat. sec. 1989—), Am. Inns of Cts. IV (bencher 1983-90), Am. Judicature Soc., Hawaii State Trial Judges' Assn. (seminar orgn. com. 1987, exec. com. 1985-90, liaison supreme ct. 1990). Office: Supreme Ct Hawaii 417 S King St Aliiolani Ha Honolulu HI 96813-2912

MOON, WAYNE, health facility administrator. With Kaiser Foundation Hospital, Oakland, Calif., 1969—, v. pres., regional manager, 1978-85, pres., coo, 1988—. Office: Kaiser Foundation Health of NW 1 Kaiser Plz Oakland CA 94612-3610

MOONEY, CATHERINE LEE, real estate broker; b. Newark, Mar. 29, 1953; d. Robert Edward Lee and Catherine Mary (Sorrentino) Gosnell; m. Marvin Granville Coleman, May 20, 1972 (div. 1978); m. Jerome Henri

Mooney, May 3, 1986; 1 child, Stephen Lloyd Coleman. Student, Strayer Coll., 1972. Cert. residential specialist; lic. real estate agt., broker, Utah, Fla. Legal sec., 1976-82; mktg. asst. BSD Med. Corp., Salt Lake City, 1983; dir. investor rels. Kenman Corp., Salt Lake City, 1983-85; realtor, 1986-88; owner, broker Mooney Real Estate, Salt Lake City, 1988—. Del. Dem. Cen. Com., Salt Lake City, 1989. Mem. Women's Coun. Realtors (edn. chair 1991, Utah state treas. 1994), Residential Sales Coun., Nat. Assn. Realtors, Salt Lake Bd. Realtors (equal opportunity com. 1989, edn. com. 1989, realtor svcs. exec. com. 1992-94), Utah Assn. Realtors. Roman Catholic. Home: 3066 Plateau Dr Salt Lake City UT 84109-2359 Office: Mooney Real Estate 1617 SE 15th St Fort Lauderdale FL 33316-2722

MOONEY, JEROME HENRI, lawyer; b. Salt Lake City, Aug. 7, 1944; s. Jerome Henri and Bonnie (Shepherd) M.; m. Carolyn Lasrich, Aug. 10, 1965 (div. Dec. 1978); 1 child, Dierdre Nicole; m. Catherine Lee, May 3, 1986 (div. Apr. 1995). BS, U. Utah, 1966, JD, 1972. Bar: Utah 1972, U.S. Ct. Appeals (10th cir.) 1974, U.S. Supreme 1984. Sole practice Salt Lake City, 1972-75, 79-83; sr. ptnr. Mooney, Jorgenson & Nakamura, Salt Lake City, 1975-78, Mooney & Smith, Salt Lake City, 1983-87, Mooney & Assoc., Salt Lake City, 1987-94, Mooney Law Firm, Salt Lake City, 1995—; bd. dirs. Mooney Real Estate, Salt Lake City. Mem. Gov.'s Coun. on Vet. Affairs, Salt Lake City, 1982-89; trustee Project Realty, Salt Lake City, 1976—; FDA sponsor Project Reality, 1994—; vice chair State Mil. Acad. Assoc., 1992-93. Mem. ABA (criminal justice sect. U.S. Sentencing Commn. com.), Utah Bar Assn. (chmn. criminal bar sect. 1987-88), Utah NG Assn. (trustee 1976), 1st Amendment Lawyers Assn. (v.p. 1986-88, pres. 1988-89), Nat. Assn. Criminal Def. Lawyers, VFW. Democrat. Jewish. Home: 128 I St Salt Lake City UT 84103-3418 Office: Mooney Law Firm 4th Floor 50 W Broadway Salt Lake City UT 84101-2006

MOONEY, MARK ALVIN, systems manager; b. East Liverpool, Ohio, Mar. 12, 1963; s. Kenneth Harold and Dorothy Ann (Sanford) M. B. Profl. Studies, Barry U., 1993. Radar sys. specialist USAF, Avon Park, Fla., 1981-85; test engr. Harris Corp., Melbourne, Fla., 1985-87; optical sys. specialist Martin Marietta Aerospace, Orlando, Fla., 1987-88; integration specialist Computer Scis. Raytheon, Patrick AFB, Fla., 1988-93; sys. mgr. City of Salem, Oreg., 1993—. With USAF, 1981. Mem. Instrumentation Soc. Am. Democrat. Methodist. Home: 4842 Liberty Rd S Apt 76 Salem OR 97306-2442 Office: City Salem Oreg 1410 20th St SE Bldg 2 Salem OR 97302-1209

MOONEY, PATRICIA KATHRYN, business owner; b. Galesburg, Ill., July 1, 1955; d. Joseph Edmond and Magi (Richard) M.; m. Mark Levon Schulze, July 23, 1987. Student, Mich. State U., 1973-75, Mueller Coll. of Massage, San Diego, 1980. Cert. massage therapist. Office mgr. REGAIN, San Diego, 1977-81; pvt. practice massage therapy San Diego, 1981-82; owner, pres. A-Action Profl. Typing, San Diego, 1983-86; co-owner, v.p. Crystal Pyramid Prodns., San Diego, 1982—, New and Unique Videos, San Diego, 1985—; office coord. Svc. Employees Internat. Union Local 535, San Diego, 1987-94. Author: (video script) Ultimate Mountain Biking, 1989, Great Mountain Biking, Battle at Durango, Massage for Relaxation, Full Cycle: A World Odyssey; co-author: (video script) John Howard's Lessons in Cycling, 1991. Treas. Evonne Schulze for Coll. Bd., San Diego, 1988-92, Coalition of Labor Union Women, San Diego, 1990-92; vol. Lynn Schenk for Congress, San Diego, 1992. Recipient 1st place San Diego Reader, 1978, 1st place poetry Calif. Press Women, 1979, N.Y. Film and TV Festival, 1990, 92, Silver Telly, 1990, 92, Silver medal Houston Internat. Film and TV, 1993. Mem. ACLU, Nat. Off-Road Bicycle Assn., Planned Parenthood, Cousteau Soc., Toastmasters. Democrat. Home and Office: 2336 Sumac Dr San Diego CA 92105-4651

MOONEY, STEVE, food products executive; b. 1957. With Mooney Constrn. and Farms, Chico, Calif., 1978-88; ptnr. Mooney Farms, Chico, Calif., 1988—. Office: Mooney Farms 1220 Fortress St Chico CA 95926-9029*

MOOR, WILLIAM CHATTLE, industrial engineering educator; b. St. Louis, Jan. 17, 1941; s. William A. and M. Carmen (Cross) M.; m. Marilyn E. Nichols, Sept. 19, 1964; children: Kathryn E., William E. BS in Indsl. Engring., Washington U., St. Louis, 1963, MS, 1965; PhD, Northwestern U., 1969. Indsl. engr. GSA, St. Louis, 1963-64; assoc. prof. Ariz. State U., Tempe, 1968—. Contbr. articles to profl. jours. Bd. dirs. Mesa (Ariz.) Bowling Assn., 1977-80, 89—. Mem. Isnt. Indsl. Engrs. (sr.), Am. Soc. for Engring. Mgmt. (charter), Am. Soc. for Engring. Edn., Internat. Assn. for Mgmt. Tech. Methodist. Office: Ariz State U Dept Indsl Engring Tempe AZ 85287-5906

MOORE, BETTY JO, legal assistant; b. Medicine Lodge, Kans., July 10; d. Joseph Christy and Helen Blanche (Hubbell) Sims; m. Harold Frank Moore, June 19, 1941; children: Terrance C., Harold Anthony, Trisha Jo. Cert., U. West L.A., 1978; student, Wichita (Kans.) U., 1940-41. Cert. legal asst./escrow officer. Sec. UCLA, 1949-59; escrow officer Security Pacific Nat. Bank, L.A., 1959-62, Empire Savs. & Loan Assn., Van Nuys, Calif., 1962-64; escrow supr. San Fernando Valley Bank, Van Nuys, 1964; escrow officer Heritage Bank, Westwood, Calif., 1964-66; escrow coord. Land Sys. Corp., Woodland Hills, Calif., 1966-67; escrow officer/asst. mgr., real estate lending officer Security Pacific Nat. Bank, L.A., 1967-80; real estate paralegal Pub. Storage, Pasadena, 1980-81; asst. mgr. escrow dept. First Beverly Bank, Century City, Calif., 1982-84; escrow trainer/officer Moore's Tng. Temps Inc., Canoga Park, Calif., 1984—; participant People to People Ambassador Program/Women in Mgmt. to USSR, 1989; observer Internat. Fedn. Bus. and Profl. Women's Congress, Washington, 1965, 81, Nassau, Bahamas, 1989, Narobi, Kenya, 1991. Adv. bd. escrow edn. Pierce Coll., Woodland Hills, Calif., 1968-80. Recipient Cert. of Appreciation, Pierce Coll., 1979, Calif. Fedn. Bus. and Profl. Women, 1989. Mem. Nat. Fedn. Bus. and Profl. Women's Clubs, Calif. Fedn. Bus. and Profl. Women (pres. dist. 1987-88, Calif. found. chmn. 1988-89), Woodland Hills Bus. and Profl. Women (pres. 1991-92, 94-95), Tri Valley Dist. Bus. and Profl. Women (legis. chair 1992-93, exec./corr. sec. 1993-94, 94-95), Internat. Fedn. Bus. and Profl. Women, Nat. Women's Polit. Caucus (coord., sec. San Fernando Valley caucus 1986-87, legis. co-chair 1991-92, 92-93), Women's Orgn. Coalition San Fernando Valley (sec. 1992), San Fernando Valley Escrow Assn. (bd. dirs. 1962-64), Woodland Hills C. of C. (assoc.), San Fernando Valley Bd. Realtors, L.A. Women's Legis. Coalition, U. West L.A. Alumni Assn. Democrat. Methodist.

MOORE, BEVERLY ANN, librarian; b. Evanston, Wyo., Mar. 17, 1934; d. James H. and Louise M. (Miller) Barrett; m. James O. Moore, Oct. 6, 1957 (div. 1966); children: Louis Barrett, Ann Louise Cushman. AA, Hutchinson (Kans.) Jr. Coll., 1954; BA, U. No. Colo., 1957; MA in Libr. Sci., Denver U., 1970. Br. libr. Pueblo (Colo.) Libr. Dist., 1966-70; documents libr. U. So. Colo., Pueblo, 1970-74, head cataloger, 1974-76, libr. dir., 1976—. Editor: Colo. Academic Libr. Master Plan, 1988. Mem. ALA, Pueblo AAUW, Colo. AAUW (coll. and univ. rep.), Colo. Libr. Assn. (pres. 1985), Colo. Acad. Libr. Com., Pueblo LWV, Colo. Women in Higher Edn. Adminstrn. (state coord. 1990-92), Beta Phi Mu. Democrat. Congregationalist. Office: U So Colo 2200 Bonforte Blvd Pueblo CO 81001-4901

MOORE, BONNIE LEE, secondary school educator; b. Redding, CA, June 24, 1942; d. Ralph O. and Virginia (Smith) Olsen; m. Thomas Wahner, Apr. 22, 1970 (div. July 1975); children: Eric V., Mark Alden. BA in Social Sci., San Diego State U., 1964. Cert. standard secondary tchr., lang. devel. specialist. Tchr. L.A. Sch. Dist., South Gate, Calif., 1965-68, Chino (Calif.) Unified Sch. Dist., 1976—; com. mem. Chino Valley Partnership for Unity in Diversity, 1993—. Campaign mem. to elect sch. bd. mem., Chino, 1992; vol. Republican Party, Chino, 1992. Mem. DAR (vice regent, v.p. 1993-94), Westerners Club.

MOORE, CARLETON BRYANT, geochemistry educator; b. N.Y.C., Sept. 1, 1932; s. Eldridge Carleton and Mabel Florence (Drake) M.; m. Jane Elizabeth Strouse, July 25, 1959; children—Barbara Jeanne, Robert Carleton. BS, Alfred U., 1954, DSc (hon.), 1977; PhD, Cal. Inst. Tech., 1960. Asst. prof. geology Wesleyan U., Middletown, Conn., 1959-61; mem. faculty Ariz. State U., Tempe, 1961—; prof., dir. Ctr. for Meteorite Studies Ariz. State U., Regents' prof., 1988—; vis. prof. Stanford U., 1974; Prin. investigator Apollo 11-17; preliminary exam. team Lunar Receiving Lab., Apollo, 12-17. Author: Cosmic Debris, 1969, Meteorites, 1971, Principles of Geochemistry, 1982, Grundzügeder Geochemie, 1985; editor: Researches on Meteorites, 1961, Jour. Meteoritical Soc.; contbr. articles to profl. jours. Fellow Ariz.-Nev. Acad. Sci. (pres. 1979-80), Meteoritical Soc. (life hon., pres. 1966-68), Geol. Soc. Am., Mineral. Soc. Am., AAAS (council 1967-70); mem. Geochem. Soc., Am. Chem. Soc., Am. Ceramic Soc., Sigma Xi. Home: 507 E Del Rio Dr Tempe AZ 85282-3764 Office: Ariz State U Ctr for Meteorite Studies Tempe AZ 85287

MOORE, CHARLES AUGUST, JR., psychologist; b. Medford, Oreg., Feb. 22, 1944; s. Charles August and Bernadine (Newlun) M. BS, Lewis and Clark Coll., 1965; MA, U. Colo., 1967, PhD, 1972. Lic. psychologist, Calif., Oreg. Teaching asst. U. Colo., Boulder, 1965-66, 70-71, rsch. asst., counselor, practicum supr., 1966-67, 71-72; asst. psychologist State Home and Tng. Sch., Grand Junction, Colo., 1967; intern in psychology Camarillo (Calif.) State Hosp., 1968-69; psychology assoc., program psychologist Camarillo Drug Abuse Program (The Family), 1969-70; intern in psychology Oxnard (Calif.) Mental Health Ctr., 1969; clin. psychologist, dir. intern tng. Rural Clinics, Reno, 1972; clin. psychologist Kern County Mental Health Svcs., Bakersfield, Calif., 1972-74; clin., cons. psychologist San Diego County Mental Health Svcs., 1974-88; pvt. practice La Jolla (Calif.) Clinic, 1976-78; August Ctr., Chula Vista, Calif., 1978-85; staff psychologist Dept. Vet.'s Affairs Domiciliary, White City, Oreg., 1988—; guest lectr. Calif. State Coll., Bakersfield, 1973-74; mem. Health Systems Agy. Mental Health Task Force, 1979; mem. doctoral dissertation com. U.S. Internat. U., 1975-76; mem. mental health task force San Diego County Bd. Suprs., 1979. Contbr. articles to profl. jours. Mem. Univ. City Community Coun., San Diego, 1976-78; bd. dirs. Pub. Employees Assn., 1976-77. Recipient Experiment in Internat. Living European Study award Lewis and Clark Coll., 1962; USPHS fellow, 1967-68; U. Colo. Grad. Sch. Rsch. grantee, 1971; recipient Hands and Heart award Dept. Vets. Affairs, 1989-90, Domiciliary Spl. Contbn. and Outstanding Performance awards, 1990, 91. Mem. APA, Am. Psychology and Law Soc., Calif. Psychol. Assn., Western Psychol. Assn., San Diego County Psychol. Assn., Assn. County Clin. Psychologists San Diego, San Diego Psychology and Law Soc., San Diego Soc. Clin. Psychologists. Office: Dept VA Domiciliary Psychology Svc 8495 Crater Lake Hwy White City OR 97503-3011

MOORE, DAN STERLING, insurance executive, sales trainer; b. Lincoln, Nebr., June 27, 1956; s. Jack Leroy and Carolyn Marie (Bachman) M.; m. Marla Janine Collister, June 2, 1979; children: Tyler David, Anna Rose. Student, Red Rocks Coll., 1977. Lic. ins. exec. Asst. mgr. European Health Spa, Englewood, Colo., 1975-78; sales mgr. Colo. Nat. Homes, Westminster, 1979-80; sales assoc. Dale Carnegie, Denver, 1981; sales mgr. Paramount Fabrics, Denver, 1981-84; sales assoc. Mighty Distbg., Arvada, Colo., 1984-87; divsn. mgr. Nat. Assn. for Self Employed/United Group Assn., Englewood, Colo., 1987—; dist. mgr. Communicating for Agr. Assn., 1993—. Leader, trainer Alpine Rescue Team, Evergreen, Colo., 1971-74; minister Jehovah's Witnesses, 1972—. Home: 892 Nob Hill Trl Franktown CO 80116-8716 Office: Nat Assn Self Employed/United Group 6551 S Revere Pky Ste 135 Englewood CO 80111-6410

MOORE, DANIEL ALTON, JR., state supreme court justice; b. 1933. BBA, U. Notre Dame, 1955; JD, U. Denver, 1961. Dist. ct. magistrate judge Alaska, 1961-62; pvt. practice law, 1962-80; judge 3d Jud. Dist. Superior Ct., 1980-83; justice Alaska Supreme Ct., Anchorage, 1983-92, chief justice, 1992—. Office: Alaska Supreme Ct 303 K St Anchorage AK 99501-2013

MOORE, DAVID AUSTIN, pharmaceutical company executive, consultant; b. Phoenix, May 8, 1935; s. Harry Theodore and Helen Ann (Newport) M.; m. Emily J. McConnell, Jan. 26, 1991; children by previous marriage: Austin Newport, Cornelia Christina, Christopher Robinson. Grad. high sch., Glendale, Ariz.; study opera and voice with Joseph Lazzarini, 1954, 55, 57-64; studied opera and voice, Italy, 1955-56; study with Clarence Loomis, 1958-60; D Naturopathy, Clayton Sch. Natural Healing, Birmingham, Ala., 1994. Pres., owner David A. Moore, Inc., Phoenix, 1969-71, Biol. Labs. Ltd., Phoenix, 1972-78; pres., co-owner Am. Trace Mineral Rsch. Corp., Phoenix, 1979-83; pres., owner Biol. Mineral Scis., Ltd., Phoenix, 1979-82; rsch. dir., pres., owner Nutritional Biols. Inc., Phoenix, 1979-83; nutritional dir.-owner Nutritional Biol. Rsch. Co., Phoenix, 1984-85; rsch. dir., product formulator, owner Nutrition and Med. Rsch., Scottsdale, Ariz., 1986—; biochem. cons. Nutripathic Formulas, Scottsdale, 1975-88; introduced di Calcium Phosphate free concept and 100 percent label disclosure, 1979-83. Pub. NMR Newsletter. Inventor first computerized comprehensive hair analysis interpretation, 1976. Recipient Plaque Am. Soc. Med. Techs., 1982, Mineralab Inc., 1976. Home and Office: PO Box 98 Barnesboro PA 15714-0098

MOORE, DAVID LEWIS, trade association executive; b. Arvin, Calif., Aug. 22, 1931; s. John Chessher and Bonnie (Carter) M.; m. Priscella Jane Martin, Aug. 1, 1953; children: John, Leslie, David, Elizabeth, Andrew. BS, U. So. Calif., 1954. Owner, operator White Wolf Potato Co., 1956-87; chmn. Western Growers Assn., Irvine, Calif., 1984-87, pres., chief exec. officer, 1987—; apptd. Fed. Res. Bd., 1992—; mem. Coun. on Calif. Competitiveness, 1992, Eximbank Adv. Com., 1990—, Agrl. Policy Adv. Com. for Trade, 1987—, Calif. Econ. Devel. Corp., 1987—, Calif. Fgn. Market Devel. Export Incentive Com., 1986-87, Kern County Water Resources Bd., 1978-87; pres. Arvin Co-op Gin, 1968-75, Arvin-Edison Water Storage Dist., 1971-87; vice chmn. Cal-Cot, 1971-76. Former vestryman St. Paul's Episc. Ch., Bakersfield, Calif.; trustee Bakersfield Coll. Found., 1986-87; founder presdl. assocs. U. So. Calif., L.A. Capt. USAF, 1954-56. Republican. Home: 4507 Roxbury Rd Corona Del Mar CA 92625-3126 Office: Western Growers Assn 17620 Fitch Irvine CA 92714-6022

MOORE, DEBORAH, environmental scientist and advocate; b. Charlottesville, Va., June 27, 1963; d. Oliver Semon Moore and Dina Downing DuBois; m. Adam Cheney Dawson, Aug. 13, 1988. BA in Physics, Reed Coll., 1985; MS in Energy and Resources, U. Calif., Berkeley, 1989. Rsch. asst. dept. epidemiology Sloan-Kettering Meml. Hosp., N.Y.C., 1982; asst. mgr. Metaresearch Inc., Portland, Oreg., 1983; instr. dept. physics Reed Coll., Portland, 1983-85; rsch. assoc. dept. biology Brookhaven Nat. Labs., Upton, N.Y., 1985-86; staff scientist Environ. Def. Fund, Oakland, Calif., 1986—. Editor The Water Calendar, 1988-89; contbr. articles to newspapers and jours. Vol. Exploratorium Sci. Mus., San Francisco, 1987—. Mem. Am. Water Resources Assn., Internat. Secretariat for Water (bd. mem.). Office: Environ Def Fund 5655 College Ave Ste 304 Oakland CA 94618-1583

MOORE, DERRITH RACHELLE, environmental specialist; b. Flagstaff, Ariz., Feb. 5, 1964; d. Leo Chester Sr. and Pauline Mae (Yellowhair) Watchman; m. Henry Kee Moore, June 12, 1992; children: Chantal, Callan, Cheyenne. BS in Animal Sci., Colo. State U., 1986. Extension agt. The Navajo Nation Dept. Agrl., Window Rock, Ariz., 1988; environ. specialist The Navajo Nation, EPA, Window Rock, 1988-92; asst. dir., site assessment mgr. all Indian Pueblo coun. Pueblo Office Environ. Protection, Albuquerque, 1992—. Recipient scholarship Am. Indian Sci. and Engring. Soc., Boulder, Colo., 1984; named Outstanding Young Women of Am., 1988. Democrat. Roman Catholic. Home: PO Box 207 Navajo NM 87328-0207 Office: Pueblo Office Environ Protection PO Box 3256 Albuquerque NM 87190-3256

MOORE, DIANNE LEA, recording studio owner; b. North Tonawanda, N.Y., Jan. 30, 1949; d. Donald Robert and Dorothy (Ghise) Wilke; m. William Lewis Tremont, Aug. 21, 1966 (div. Apr. 1973); children: Eric, Michelle; m. Allen Charles Moore, July 11, 1981. AA, Scottsdale C.C., 1978; student, Ariz. State U., 1978-81. Powder paint troubleshooter McGraw Edison, Phoenix, 1980-81; v.p., mgr. Cereus Recording, Tempe, Ariz., 1981—; adminstrv. asst. McKesson, Phoenix, 1982-83; owner, mgr. Cereus Letter Processing, Tempe, 1983-93. Mem. Nat. Fedn. Ind. Businessmen, Better Bus. Bur., Steinway Soc., Tempe C. of C., Ariz. Rd. Racers (bd. dirs.). Democrat. Office: Cereus Rec 1733 E Mckellips Rd Ste 107 Tempe AZ 85281-1372

MOORE, DONALD WALTER, academic administrator, school librarian; b. Culver City, Calif., June 9, 1942; s. Raymond Owen and Jewel Elizabeth (Young) M.; m. Dagmar Ulbrich, Mar. 28, 1968; 1 child, Michael. AA, L.A. Valley Coll., 1967; BA in History, Calif. State U., Northridge, 1970; MA in Learning Disability, Calif. State U., 1973; MLS, U. So. Calif., 1974. Part time librarian L.A. Pierce Coll., Woodland Hills, Calif., 1974—; instr. vocat. edn. act program L.A. Trade Tech. Coll., 1978-80, pres.'s staff asst., 1983-87; instr. learning skills L.A. City Coll., 1987-88, dir. amnesty edn., 1988-92, dir. Citizenship Ctr., 1992—. Author: Cavalrymen, 1983; contbr. fiction, articles, revs. to various publs. Mem. Edn. Writers Am., Co. Mil. Historians, Nat. Indian Wars Assn., Little Big Horn Assn. Republican. Roman Catholic. Office: Citizenship Program LA City Coll 855 N Vermont Ave Los Angeles CA 90029-3500

MOORE, ELIZABETH JANE, banker; b. Long Branch, N.J., Dec. 14, 1940; d. Robert William and Ruth Elizabeth (Dunphy) Marton; m. Gerard George Moore, Mar. 3, 1962; children: Christine Marie, Stephanie Ann, Gerard Marton, Paul Henry George, Barbara Jean. BBA, U. Phoenix, 1987. Charge card specialist Valley Nat. Bank, Phoenix, 1971-74, corp. trust specialist, 1974-80; trust specialist Valley Nat. Bank, Prescott, Ariz., 1980-84, 84-86, trust adminstr., trust officer, 1986-89, asst. v.p., 1989-93; v.p. Bank One, Phoenix, 1993—; sr. trust officer Bank One Ariz. Advantage Trust, Phoenix, 1994—. Bd. dirs. Ctrl. Yavapai County (Ariz.) Fire Dist., 1988-89, clk., 1989—, chmn. bd., 1990-91; bd. dirs. Yavapai Humane Soc., 1989-91, 1st v.p., treas., 1990-91; bd. dirs. Vol. Firefighters Relief and Pension Fund, 1989-91; chmn. bd. dirs. Ctrl. Yavapai Pub. Safety Pers., 1991. Recipient 1st Place Photo Contest award Parade mag., 1992. Mem. Yavapai County Legal Secs. Assn. (treas. 1983-85, gov. 1985-86, Legal Sec. of Yr. 1984), U. Phoenix Network for Profl. Devel. (chartered), Friday Club, Phoenix Pub. Libr. Office: Bank One Ariz Advantage Trust PO Box 71 Phoenix AZ 85001-0071

MOORE, GEORGE W(ILLIAM), geologist; b. Palo Alto, Calif., June 7, 1928; s. George Raymond and Grace Amy (Hauch) M.; m. Ellen Louise James, Nov. 27, 1960; children: Leslie Ann, Geoffrey. BS, Stanford U., 1950, MS, 1951; PhD, Yale U., 1960. Geologist U.S. Geol. Survey, Menlo Park, Calif., 1951-94; courtesy prof. geology, Oreg. State U., Corvallis, 1987—; geologist in charge La Jolla (Calif.) Marine Geology Lab., 1966-75; rsch. assoc. Scripss Instn. Oceanography, La Jolla, 1972-75; participant Deep Sea Drilling Project, Japan, 1977; chmn. arctic panel Circum-Pacific Map Project, 1979—; invited lectr. USSR Acad. Scis., 1980, Indonesian Marine Geol. Inst. and Nat. Petroleum Co., 1986, City of Corvallis Da Vinci Days, 1989-95; rapporteur UN com. for coordination of offshore prospecting, Peoples Republic of China, 1985; advisor Calif. Coastal Commn., 1970-75; chmn. Earth and Space Scis. Awards, Internat. Sci. Fair, 1978. Author: Speleology, 1978 (Sci. Book Club award 1978); editor Geodynamic Map of the Circum-Pacific Region, 1990, Plate-Tectonic Map of the Circum-Pacific Region, 1992. Exhibit com. mem. San Diego Natural History Mus., 1968-75. Fellow AAAS, Geol. Soc. Am.; mem. Nat. Speleol. Soc. (hon., pres. 1963), Am. Assn. Petroleum Geologists (com. chmn. 1977), Am. Geophys. Union, Palo Alto Hist. Assn., Peninsula Geol. Soc. (pres. 1986). Democrat. Home: 3324 SW Chintimini Ave Corvallis OR 97333-1529 Office: Dept Geoscinces Oreg State U Corvallis OR 97331-5506

MOORE, GORDON E., electronics company executive; b. San Francisco, Jan. 3, 1929; s. Walter Harold and Florence Almira (Williamson) M.; m. Betty I. Whittaker, Sept. 9, 1950; children: Kenneth, Steven. BS in Chemistry, U. Calif., 1950; PhD in Chemistry and Physics, Calif. Inst. Tech., 1954. Mem. tech. staff Shockley Semicondr. Lab., 1956-57; mgr. engring. Fairchild Camera & Instrument Corp., 1957-59, dir. research and devel., 1959-68; exec. v.p. Intel Corp., Santa Clara, Calif., 1968-75; pres., chief exec. officer Intel Corp., 1975-79, chmn., chief exec. officer, 1979-87, chmn., 1987—; bd. dirs. Varian Assocs. Inc., Transamerica Corp. Fellow IEEE; mem. Nat. Acad. Engring., Am. Phys. Soc. Office: Intel Corp 2200 Mission College Blvd Santa Clara CA 95054-1537

MOORE, JANET ELLEN, cartographer; b. Portland, Oreg., July 27, 1947; d. Howard James and Clara Alvina (Nelson) Slonecker; m. Michael James Moore (div. Feb. 1994). BA, Wash. State U., 1970; MBS, U. Colo., Colorado Springs, 1994; postgrad., U. Denver, 1994. Planning technician City of Pueblo, Colo., 1991—; freelance cartographer, Beulah, Colo., 1994—. Cartographer: Bicycle Routes and Recreational Trails in the Pueblo Area, 1991, Pueblo Mountain Park, 1993, Pueblo Urbanized Area Year 2015 Transportation Plan, 1994, Boulder Hiking Trails, 1995. Mem. planning group Geographic Info. Sys., City of Pueblo, 1994, Telecom. Pueblo County, 1994; mem. Colo. Hist. Soc., 1992—, Nature Conservancy, 1994—. Mem. Am. Soc. for Photogrammetry and Remote Sensing, Urban and Regional Info. Sys. Assn. Home: PO Box 4 Beulah CO 81023-0004 Office: City of Pueblo Dept Planning and Devel 211 E D St Pueblo CO 81003-3418

MOORE, JOHN D., consultant; b. Mt. Pleasant, Iowa, Apr. 7, 1937; s. Burris P. and Esther I. (Copenhaver) M.; m. Karen K. Kriegel, June 19, 1957; children: Charles A., Michael J., Susan K., David J. AB, Muscatine Community Coll., 1961; BBA, Augustana Coll., 1966; postgrad. U. Iowa, 1966-68. Office mgr. Stanley Engring., Muscatine, Iowa, 1956-64; pers. mgr. Oscar Mayer & Co., Davenport and Perry, Iowa, 1964-68; Midwest regional mgr. A. S. Hansen, Lake Bluff, Ill., 1968-73; legal adminstr. Gardner, Carton & Douglas, Chgo., 1973-78, Heller Ehrman White & McAuliffe, San Francisco, 1978-84; v.p. and dir. Hildebrandt, Inc., Walnut Creek, Calif., 1984-90; pres. Moore Cons. Inc., 1990—. Pres., Libertyville (Ill.) High Sch. Bd., 1974, Libertyville Ecumenical Council, 1975; bd. dirs. Libertyville YMCA, 1969-71. Recipient Muscatine Distinguished Service award, 1963; named Outstanding State V.P., Iowa Jaycees, 1964; Outstanding Nat. Dir., U.S. Jaycees, 1965. Mem. Assn. of Legal Adminstrs. (regional v.p. 1977-78, nat. v.p. 1979-81, nat. pres. 1982-83), Found. Assn. of Legal Adminstrs. (pres. 1986-88), Golden Gate Assn. Legal Adminstrs. Republican. Methodist. Home and Office: 2632 Quiet Place Dr Walnut Creek CA 94598-4440

MOORE, JOHN PORFILIO, federal judge; b. Denver, Oct. 14, 1934; s. Edward Alphonso Porfilio and Caroline (Carbone) Moore; m. Joan West, Aug. 1, 1959 (div. 1983); children—Edward Miles, Joseph Arthur, Jeanne Kathrine; m. Theresa Louise Berger, Dec. 28, 1983; 1 stepchild, Katrina Ann Smith. Student, Stanford U., 1952-54; BA, U. Denver, 1956, LLB, 1959. Bar: Colo. 1959, U.S. Supreme Ct. 1965. Asst. atty. gen. State of Colo., Denver, 1962-68, dep. atty. gen., 1968-72, atty. gen., 1972-74; U.S. bankruptcy judge Dist. of Colo., Denver, 1975-82; judge U.S. Dist. Ct. Colo., Denver, 1982-85, U.S. Ct. Appeals (10th cir.), Denver, 1985—; instr. Colo. Law Enforcement Acad., Denver, 1965-70, State Patrol Acad., Denver, 1968-70; guest lectr. U. Denver Coll. Law, 1978. Committeeman Arapahoe County Republican Com., Aurora, Colo., 1968; mgr. Dunbar for Atty. Gen., Denver, 1970. Mem. ABA. Roman Catholic. Office: US Ct Appeals Byron White US Courthouse 1823 Stout St Denver CO 80257-0001

MOORE, JOSEPH MARK, secondary education educator; b. Galion, Ohio, June 7, 1942; s. Mark and Helen Elizabeth (Huff) M.; m. Gail Janette Harp, Dec. 18, 1971 (dec. Apr. 1987); children: Edward, Teresa, Melanie, Julia. BA, SUNY, 1982; MS, Nat. U., 1990. Cert. tchr., Calif. Enlisted USN, 1960; social studies educator Tracy (Calif.) Joint Union H.S., 1989—. Co-treas. Tracy High Parents Group, 1992; v.p. Tracy Secondary Educators Assn., 1993, polit. action com. mem., 1992. Recipient Achievement medal USN, 1983. Mem. VFW, Nat. Coun. for Social Studies, Calif. Coun. for Social Studies, U.S. Naval Inst., Fleet Res. Assn., Am. Legion. Home: 1265 Doubles Ct Tracy CA 95376-4918 Office: Tracy Joint Union HS 315 E 11th St Tracy CA 95376-4017

MOORE, JUDITH LYNN, animal scientist; b. Pitts., May 3, 1946; d. Carl Emil Joseph and Edris Christine (Ott) Hoffmann; m. James Lynn Moore, Dec. 28, 1968; children: Aaron, Jeremy. BS in Zoology, Colo. State U., 1968; MS in Environ. Comm., U. Wis., 1969. Editor U. Wis., Madison, 1969-70; pvt. practice horse and dog trainer Oregon, Wis., 1970-76, Buena Vista, Colo., 1976—; co-owner Insolar Homes, Inc., 1979—; animal control officer Chaffee County Govt., Colo., 1977-78. Editor: Wisconsin's Recreation-Tourism Industry: An Annotated Bibliography, 1970; author Chaffee County animal control ordinances. Founder, dir. Pet Assistance League, Chaffee County, 1978. Home and Office: 17900 Vista Dr Buena Vista CO 81211-9618

MOORE, JUSTIN EDWARD, data processing executive; b. West Hartford, Conn., June 17, 1952; s. Walter Joseph and Victoria Mary (Calcagni) M. BS in Mgmt. Sci., Fla. Inst. Tech., 1974. Systems assoc. Travelers Ins., Hartford, Conn., 1974-77; data processing programmer R.J. Reynolds Inc.,

Winston-Salem, N.C., 1977-78; programmer/analyst Sea-Land Svc., Elizabeth, N.J., 1978-79; mgr. market analysis Sea-Land Svc., Oakland, Calif., 1979-82; asst. v.p., dir. application systems Fox Capital Mgmt. Corp., Foster City, Calif., 1982-86; mgr. bus. svcs. dept mktg. and pricing Am. Pres. Cos., Ltd., Oakland, 1987-88, dir. mktg. and pricing systems, 1988-89; dir. systems devel. The Office Club, Concord, Calif., 1989-91; dir. MIS Revo, Inc., Mountain View, Calif., 1992-93; account mgr. Imrex Computer Systems, Inc., South San Francisco, 1993-94; project mgr. Exigent Computer Group, Inc., San Ramon, Calif., 1994—. Democrat. Roman Catholic. Home: 5214 Jomar Dr Concord CA 94521-2343 Office: Exigent Computer Group Inc 4000 Executive Pky San Ramon CA 94583-4257

MOORE, KATHLEEN GREEN, educational administrator; b. Elizabeth, N.J., Nov. 12, 1934; d. Oliver and Myrtle Lee (Johnson) Green; m. Donald Leslie Moore, Aug. 1, 1959; children: Donald Leslie Jr., Gaylynn. BS, N.J. State Coll., 1956; MS, Calif. State U., 1975; PhD, U.S. Internat. U., 1979. Tchr. East Brunswick (N.J.) Schs., 1956-59, Hudson Sch. Dist., La Puente, Calif., 1961-65; tchr. Bonita Unified Sch. Dist., San Dimas, Calif., 1966-70, counselor, 1970-77; counselor L.A. County Office Edn., Downey, Calif., 1977-82; dir. career/vocat. edn. and partnership acads. Pasadena (Calif.) Unified Sch. Dist., 1982-94; CEO Pasadena Adult Devel. Ctr., 1994—; assoc. coord. state equity insvc. tng. Calif. Dept. Edn., Sacramento, 1976-91, cons. joint statewide equity adv. com., 1991—; cons. L.A. L.A. County Human Rels. Commn., 1985, U.S. Dept. Edn., 1977, Commn. on Status of Women, Pasadena, 1984. Bd. dirs. Pasadena Planned Parenthood, 1985-91. Mem. Am. Vocat. Edn. Assn., Assn. Pasadena Adminstrn. (chair vocat. edn.), Delta Sigma Theta (1st v.p. 1985-86, chair social action 1988—). Methodist. Home: 1868 N Fernridge Dr San Dimas CA 91773-1308 Office: Pasadena Adult Devel Ctr 789 N Altadena Dr Pasadena CA 91107

MOORE, MARIANNA GAY, law librarian, consultant; b. La Grange, Ga., Sept. 12, 1939; d. James Henry and Avanelle (Gay) M. AB in French, English, U. Ga., 1961; MLS, Emory U., 1964; postgrad., U. Ga., 1965-66, U. Ill., 1967-68. Asst. law libr. U. Ga., Athens, 1964-66; asst. libr. Yavapai Coll. Libr., Prescott, Ariz., 1969-72; libr. U. Ill. Law Libr., Urbana, 1966-68; law libr. Leva, Hawes, Symington, Washington, 1972-75; libr. project coord. Wash. Occupational Info. Svc., Olympia, 1976-80, Wash. State Health Facilities Assn., Olympia, 1981-82; mgr. Wash. State Ret. Tchrs. Assn., Olympia, 1982-83, exec. dir., 1984-89; exec. dir. Wash. State Retired Tchrs. Found., Olympia, 1986-89; law libr. Solano County Law Libr., Fairfield, Calif., 1989—; libr. LIBRARY/USA N.Y. World's Fair, N.Y.C., 1965; consulting law libr. Dobbins, Weir, Thompson & Stephenson, Vacaville, Calif., 1989—; law libr. cons. Coconino County Law Libr., Flagstaff, Ariz., 1968-70. Author: Guide to Fin. Aid for Wash. State Students, 1979; tng. package to introduce librs. to Wash. State Info. Svc., 1980. Bd. dirs. Thurston County Sr. Ctr., Olympia, 1976-84, Thurston-Mason Nutrition Program, Olympia, 1977-79, Wash. Soc. Assn. Execs., Edmonds, 1987-89. Mem. Am. Assn. Law Librs., No. Calif. Assn. Law Librs., Calif. Coun. of County Law Librs., Wash. Soc. Assn. Execs. Office: Solano County Law Libr Hall of Justice 600 Union Ave Fairfield CA 94533-6324

MOORE, MARTIN DALE, software specialist, environmental policy analyst; b. Safford, Ariz., Apr. 3, 1963; s. Loryn Dale and Lille Ann (Reed) M.; m. Joanne Elizabeth Engler, July 26, 1985; children: Jessica, Spencer, Aubrey, Melissa. BA, No. Ariz. U., 1988, postgrad., 1988—. Rsch. asst. No. Ariz. Coun. Govts., Flagstaff, 1987-88, Ariz. Hospitality Rsch. and Resource Ctr., Flagstaff, 1988-90, Ctr. for Colo. Plateau Studies, Flagstaff, 1990-91; tchg. asst., instr. No. Ariz. U., Flagstaff, 1991-93; mem. data processing and planning staff Apache County (Ariz.), St. Johns, 1993-94; dir. county devel. and cmty. svcs. Apache County, St. Johns, Ariz., 1994—; chair resource com. Eastern Ariz. Counties Orgn., 1994—. Contbr. articles to profl. publs. Founder, chair grad. student adv. coun. No. Ariz. U., 1989-90; exec. sec. LDS Ward, Flagstaff, 1988-90, pres. LDS men's orgn., 1986-89; project coord. Flagstaff Housing Authority, 1986-87. Mem. ASPA, Am. Polit. Sci. Assn., Soil and Water Conservation Soc., Policy Studies Orgn. Republican. Home: 970 S Horseshoe Ln Box 151 Saint Johns AZ 85936 Office: Apache County 75 W Cleveland Saint Johns AZ 85936

MOORE, MARY FRENCH (MUFFY MOORE), potter, community activist; b. N.Y.C., Feb. 25, 1938; d. John and Rhoda (Teagle) Walker French; m. Alan Baird Minier, Oct. 9, 1982; children: Jonathan Corbet, Jennifer Corbet, Michael Corbet. BA cum laude, Colo. U., 1964. Ceramics mfr., Wilson, Wyo., 1969-82, Cheyenne, Wyo., 1982—; commr. County of Teton (Wyo.), 1976-83, chmn. bd. commrs., 1981, 83, mem. dept. pub. assistance and social svc., 1976-82, mem. recreation bd., 1978-81, water quality adv. bd., 1976-82. Bd. dirs. Teton Sci. Sch., 1968-83, vice chmn., 1979-81, chmn., 1982; bd. dirs. Grand Teton Music Festival, 1963-68, Teton Energy Coun., 1978-83, Whitney Gallery of Western Art, Cody, Wyo., 1995—; mem. water quality adv. bd. Wyo. Dept. Environ. Quality, 1979-83; Dem. precinct committeewoman, 1978-81; mem. Wyo. Dem. Cen. Com., 1981-83; vice chmn. Laramie County Dem. Cen. Com., 1983-84, Wyo. Dem. nat. committeewoman, 1984-87; chmn. Wyo. Dem. Party, 1987-89; del. Dem. Nat. Conv., 1984, 88, mem. fairness commn. Dem. Nat. Com., 1985, vice-chairwoman western caucus, 1986-89; chmn. platform com. Wyo. Dem. Conv., 1982; mem. Wyo. Dept. Environ. Quality Land Quality Adv. Bd., 1983-86; mem. Gov.'s Steering Com. on Troubled Youth, 1982, dem. nat. com. Compliance Assistance Commn., 1986-87; exec. com. Assn. of State Dem. Chairs, 1989; mem. Wyo. Coun. on the Arts, 1989-95, chmn., 1994-95, Dem. Nat. Com. Jud. Coun., 1989—; legis. aide for Gov. Wyo., 1985, 86; project coord. Gov.'s Com. on Childrens' Svcs., 1985-86; bd. dirs. Wyo. Outdoor Coun., 1984-85; polit. dir., dep. mgr. Schuster for Congress, 1994-95. Recipient Woman of Yr. award Jackson Hole Bus. and Profl. Women, 1981, Dem. of Yr. Nellie Tayloe Ross award, Wyo. Dems., 1990. Mem. Alden Kindred of Am., Jackson Hole Art Assn. (bd. dirs., vice chmn. 1981, chmn. 1982), Assn. State Dem. Chairs, Soc. Mayflower Descendents, Pi Sigma Alpha. Home: 8907 Cowpoke Rd Cheyenne WY 82009-1234

MOORE, MATTHEW EMERSON, environmental program planning management specialist; b. Tuscaloosa, Ala., Aug. 5, 1964; s. Charles Thomas Moore Sr. and Annabel (Owens) Moore Allen; m. Anne Goldthwaite Dorr, March 20, 1993. BS, No. Ariz. U., 1987; MA, Claremont Grad. Sch., 1989. Mem. policy clinic team Ctr. for Politics and Policy, Claremont (Calif.) Grad. Sch., 1987-89; rsch. asst. Rose Inst. State and Local Govt., Claremont, 1989; analyst, asst. planner LSA Assocs., Inc., Irvine, Calif., 1989-90; project mgr. Urban Vision, Irvine, 1991-93; regional water quality mgmt. planning coord. Ariz. Dept. Environ. Quality, Phoenix, 1994; sr. air quality analyst Idaho Divsn. Environ. Quality, Boise, 1994—; mem. Sch. Renewable Natural Resources master's thesis com. U. Ariz., Tucson, 1994. Author: Lead Agency CEQA Procedures Survey Results, 1991; co-author: Taxes, Trees and Transit: California's Response to CO2-Induced Climate Change, 1990, Curbing Air Pollution in the South Coast Air Basin, 1989; editor-at-large: Multiple Resource Mgmt. Plan for El Cipres, Ensenada, Mex. Founding pres. Explorer Post 477, Boy Scouts Am., Tempe, Ariz., 1980-82; interpretive specialist Walnut Canyon Nat. Monument, Flagstaff, Ariz., 1987; mem. drought planning adv. bd. City of Claremont, 1988-89. Mem. Am. Planning Assn., Am. Polit. Sci. Assn., Nat. Assn. Environ. Profls., Internat. Assn. Impact Assessment. Methodist.

MOORE, OMAR KHAYYAM, experimental sociologist; b. Helper, Utah, Feb. 11, 1920; s. John Gustav and Mary Jo (Crowley) M.; m. Ruth Garnand, Nov. 19, 1942; 1 child, Venn. BA, Doane Coll., 1942; MA, Washington U., St. Louis, 1946, PhD, 1949. Instr. Washington U., St. Louis, 1949-52; teaching assoc. Northwestern U., Evanston, Ill., 1950-51; rsch. asst., prof. sociology Tufts Coll., Medford, Mass., 1952-53; researcher Naval Rsch. Lab., Washington, 1953-54; asst. prof. sociology Yale U., New Haven, 1954-57, assoc. prof. sociology, 1957-63; prof. psychology Rutgers U., New Brunswick, N.J., 1963-65; prof. social psychology, sociology U. Pitts., 1965-71, prof. sociology, 1971-89, prof. emeritus, 1989—; scholar-in-residence Nat. Learning Ctr.'s Capital Children's Mus., Washington, 1989-90; pres. Responsive Environ. Found., Inc., Estes Park, Colo., 1962—; assessor of rsch. projects The Social Scis. and Humanities Rsch. Coun. Can., 1982—; adj. prof. U. Colo., Boulder, 1992—. Contbg. editor Educational Technology; contbr. numerous articles to profl. jours.; patentee in field; motion picture producer and director. Recipient Award The Nat. Soc. for Programmed Instruction, 1965, Award Doane Coll Builder Award, 1967, Ednl. Award Urban Youth Action, Inc., 1969, Award House of Culture, 1975, Cert. of Appreciation, 1986, Cert. of Appreciation D.C. Pub. Schs., 1987, da Vinci Award Inst. for the Achievement of Human Potential, 1988, Cert. of Appreciation Capital Children's Museum, 1988, award Jack & Jill of America Found., 1988, Cert. of Appreciation U.S. Dept. of Edn., 1988, Cert. of Appreciation D.C. Pub. Schs., 1990, Person of Yr. in Ednl. Tech. award Ednl. Tech. mag., 1990. Mem. AAAS, Am. Math. Soc., Am. Psychol. Assn., Internat. Sociol. Assn., Am. Sociol. Assn., Assn. for Symbolic Logic, Assn. for Anthrop. Study of Play, Philosophy Sci. Assn., Psychonomics Soc., Soc. for Applied Sociology, Soc. for Exact Philosophy, Math. Assn. Am. Republican. Home and Office: 2341 Upper High Dr PO Box 1673 Estes Park CO 80517

MOORE, RICHARD ALAN, landscape architect; b. St. Louis, Jan. 17, 1930; s. Ira Mack and Helen Adoline (Fakes) M.; m. Patricia Ruth Burke, Mar. 15, 1952 (div. 1967); children: Sheryl Louise, Richard Dennis, Sara Lynn, Sandra Lee. BS, U. Mo., 1951; MLA, U. Oreg., 1957. Registered landscape architect, Calif., Hawaii. Asst. prof., head dept. landscape architecture Calif. State Poly. Coll., Pomona, 1957-61; assoc. prof., head dept. landscape architecture N.C. State U., Raleigh, 1962-67; pvt. practice landscape architecture Pomona, Calif., 1957-61; dir. land devel. and planning Oceanic Properties Inc., Honolulu, 1967-69; pvt. practice Honolulu, 1969-70, 79—; dir. ops. Eckbo, Dean, Austin & Williams, Honolulu, 1970-71, v.p. ops., 1971-73; pres. EDAW, Inc., San Francisco, 1973-76, chmn. bd., 1976-78; prof. landscape architecture Tex. A&M U., Bryan, 1977-79. Prin. works include Whispering Pines Motor Lodge, N.C., 1964 (award of merit N.C. chpt. AIA 1964), North Shore Devel. Plan, Kauai, Hawaii, 1973, Comprehensive Zoning Ordinance, County of Kauai, 1973 (Am. Soc. Landscape Architects honor award 1973, HUD honor award 1974), Lihue Devel. Plan, Kauai, 1975, Koloa, Poipu, Kalaheo Devel. Plan, Kauai, 1978, Gen. Plan Update, Kauai, 1982, Mililani Town Devel. Plan, 1967-69 (Am. Soc. Landscape Architects merit award 1970), Lanai Land Mgmt. and Devel. Study, 1969 (Am. Soc. Landscape Architects merit award 1970), Wailea Master Devel. Plan, 1971, Kukuiula Devel. Plan, 1983, Lanai Project Dist. Master Plan, 1983-89, Maliu Ridge Devel. Plan, North Kohala, 1985, Mililani Mauka Devel. Plan, 1988, Devel. Plan, Lanai City Comml. Dist., 1990, Dandan Golf Course, Guam, 1991. 1st lt. U.S. Army, 1951-53, Korea. Fellow Am. Soc. Landscape Architects; mem. Masons.

MOORE, ROBERT HORTON, physician; b. Jonesboro, Ark., Dec. 29, 1924; s. Robert Horton and Macie Terra (Galloway) M.; m. Joan Brown, Mar. 27, 1954; children: Robert Harold, Pamela Ann. BA, Vanderbilt U., 1947, MD, 1951. Diplomate Am. Bd. Preventive Medicine, Occupational Medicine. Resident in internal medicine Northwestern U., 1956; chief, admitting svc. VA Rsch. Hosp., Chgo., 1956-60; pvt. practice Decatur, Ill., 1960-65; asst. med. dir. Pacific Mut. Life Ins. Co., L.A., 1965-68; v.p. Hanford Environ. Health Found., Richland, Wash., 1968-78; dir. U.S. Uranium Registry, Richland, 1978-88; v.p. Northwest Health Svc., Richland, 1988-89; occupational physician USN, San Diego, Calif., 1989—. Editor: (proceedings) Biokinetics and Analysis of Uranium in Man, 1984; contbr. articles to Health Physics jour., 1978-88. d. dirs. Am. Coll. Occupation and Envrion. Med., Chgo., 1989-92, del. 1972-89. With U.S. Army inf., 1943-45, ETO. Fellow Am. Acad. Occupational Medicine, Am. Occupational Med. Assn.; mem. AMA. Presbyterian. Home: 1258 Santa Barbara St San Diego CA 92107-3960

MOORE, ROGER ALBERT, JR., archaeologist; b. Tampa, Fla., Dec. 18, 1946; s. Roger Albert Moore and Frieda E. (Heil) Hutchison; m. Susan Kay Waters, Sept. 8, 1978; children: Tabitha Rose, Roxie Ann. BA in Anthropology, Ohio State U., 1972; student, U. Tenn., 1974-75; MA in Anthropology, Ea. N.Mex. U., 1981. Lic. archael. surveyor, N.Mex., Colo., Utah. Crew chief, field foreman U. Tenn., Knoxville, 1973-74, excavator, lab. asst., 1974-75; excavator, lab. asst. Cahokia Mounds State Park, Collinsville, Ill., 1974; lithic analyst Ea. N.Mex. U., Portales, 1975-78; lab. dir. U. Colo., Cortez, 1978-79; field dir. ESCA-Tech, Inc., Ridgeway, Colo., 1980; lab. dir. Navajo Nat. Archaeology Dept., Farmington, N.Mex., 1980-82; supervisory archaeologist San Juan County Mus. Assn., Bloomfield, N.Mex., 1982-88; owner, prin. investigator Moore Anthropol. Rsch., Aztec, N.Mex., 1988—; instr. San Juan Coll., Farmington, 1983. Co-author: Old Dallas Historical Archaeology Project, 1987; contbr. articles to profl. jours. Vol. Portales (N.Mex) Food Coop., 1976-78, Salmon Ruin Mus., Bloomfield, 1982-88, Bonds for Books Plus Com., Aztec, 1994; mem. lithic dictionary com. N.Mex. Archaeol. Coun., Albuquerque, 1989—; chmn. com. B.L.M. Cultural Adv. Group, Farmington, 1991—. With U.S. Army, 1967-69. Mem. Soc. Am. Archaeology (life), N.Mex. Archaeol. Coun., Archaeol. Soc. N.Mex. (cert., Archaeol. Achievement award 1994), Ariz. Archael. and Hist. Soc., Tenn. Anthropol. Assn. (life), San Juan County Mus. Assn. (bd. dirs. 1993—), Nat. Trust for Hist. Preservation, Phi Kappa Phi. Republican. Presbyterian. Office: Moore Anthropol Rsch PO Box 1156 102 N Main Aztec NM 87410

MOORE, S. CLARK, judge; b. Norfolk, Va., Aug. 28, 1924; s. Samuel Clark and Mary Elizabeth (Pate) M.; m. Lynette Anita Gladd, Dec. 20, 1974. BA, San Diego State Coll., 1949; JD, U. So. Calif., L.A., 1957, LLM, 1960. Bar: Calif. 1957, U.S. Dist. Ct. (cen. dist.) Calif. 1957, U.S. Ct. Appeals (9th cir.) 1960. Dep. atty. gen. Calif. State Atty. Gen., L.A., 1957-72, asst. atty. gen., 1972-75, sr. asst. atty. gen., 1975-82, chief asst. atty. gen., 1982-83; judge Santa Anita Mcpl. Ct., 1984-94, Pomona Mcpl. Ct., Calif., 1995—; mem. Fed. cts. practice standards com., 1981-84, countywide criminal justice coord. com., 1989-90, courthouse security task force, 1989-90. With U.S. Army, 1943-46. Decorated European Theater medal, Asiatic Pacific medal, Am. Theater medal, Victory medal, Good Conduct medal, Philipine Liberation medal. Mem. L.A. Bar Assn. (former chmn. criminal justice sect., exec. com. bar delegation 1982-84), L.A. Mcpl. Cts. Judges Assn. (sec. 1989, vice chair 1988-89, chair 1989-90, exec. com. 1987-88, 90-91), Presiding Justices Assn. Republican. Office: Pomona Mcpl Ct 350 W Mission Pomona CA 91766-1607

MOORE, SHERYL STANSIL, nursing educator; b. Birmingham, Ala., May 17, 1963; d. Willie Caesar and Irene (Fisher) Stansil; m. Kyle R. Moore; children: Tyler Christina Lowe, Danladi Moore, William Moore. BSN, Dillard U., 1987; MSN in Trauma Nursing, U. Ala. in Birmingham, 1992. Staff nurse Nursefinders, Colorado Springs, Colo., 1994—, Progressive Care Ctr., Terrace Gardens, Colo.; instr. clin. nursing Beth-El Coll. Nursing. Named one of Outstanding Young Women of Am., 1988. Mem. ANA, AACN, State Nurses Assn., Sigma Theta Tau. Home: 1985 Mittenwald Dr #102 Colorado Springs CO 80918

MOORE, SHIRLEY BEAHAM, real estate professional, civic worker; b. Tucson, July 28, 1934; d. Thomas Graham and Virginia (Ruthrauff) Beaham; m. Jack K. Moore, Jr., June 30, 1956 (div. June 1969); children: Catherine Lee Puccetti, Alan Graham. BA, Scripps Coll., 1956. Exec. dir. Pima chpt. Ariz. Kidney Found., Tucson, 1977-81; organizer, participant Southwestern Sch. Behavioral Health Studies, Tucson, 1977-78. Civic worker, Tucson, 1958—; bd. dirs. Planned Parenthood So. Ariz., 1959-65, v.p., 1962, pres., 1963-64; bd. dirs. Jr. League Tucson, 1962-73, Alcoholism Coun. Tucson, 1977-87; bd. dirs. St. Luke's in Desert, Inc., 1975-86, 1990—; mem. planning com., 1984—; area chmn. ARC, 1964; bd. dirs. St. Luke's Bd. Visitors, 1968-78, v.p., 1974, pres., 1975; bd. dirs. Tohono Chul Pk., 1990—; co-chmn. U.S. Senate Campaign, Pima County, 1972; mem. Ariz. Acad., 1975-84, rep. alumnae Scripps Coll., 1979-84. Mem. U. Ariz. Pres.'s Club, PEO. Episcopalian.

MOORE, TERRY WAYNE, management consultant; b. North Kingston, R.I., Feb. 26, 1957; s. Robert Wendell and Marilyn (Rose) M. BS in Engring., U. Fla., 1981; MBA, U. San Diego, 1993. Cert. Project Mgmt. Profl. Sr. materials engr. U.S. Dept. Def., Alameda, Calif., 1981-85, program mgr., 1985-87; staff engr., scientist Gen. Atomics, La Jolla, Calif., 1987-89, project mgr., 1989-92, mktg. program mgr., 1992-93; owner Moore Consulting Co., San Diego, 1994—; entrepreneur Venture Mgmt., Moore Cons. Co., San Diego, 1990—; new high tech. ventures cons. for emerging growth and start up cos., 1991—; mem. Team Dennis Conner's Am.'s Cup Syndicate, 1995, crew mem. Stars and Stripes; mem. San Diego Regional Tech. Alliance, Calif. State Office Strategic Tech. Devel. Judge San Diego Sci. Fair, 1989—; rep. Neighborhood Watch, La Costa, Calif., 1989—; vol. fund raiser Am. Cancer Soc., Epilepsy Soc., United Way. Selected for 1st Annual Def.-High Tech. Entrepreneurship Program U. Calif. San Diego-Connect Office, 1993—. Mem. Am. Soc. for Materials Internat. (sec.-treas. 1990-92, bd. dirs. 1989—, nat. chpt. ops. com., chmn. computer subcom. 1991—, chmn. 1994-95), Project Mgmt. Inst. (sec. 1993-94, treas. 1994-95, bd. dirs. 1993—), Soc. Advancement of Material and Process Engring., Venture Mgmt. Group, MIT Enterprise Forum, San Diego Yacht Club. Republican. Presbyterian. Home: 905 Orchid Way Carlsbad CA 92009-4830 Office: Solar Turbines Inc PO Box 85376 2200 Pacific Hwy San Diego CA 92186-5376

MOORE, WALTER DENGEL, rapid transit system professional; b. Chgo., Sept. 16, 1936; s. Walter D. and Velma Louise (Rhode) M.; m. Sandra M. Stetzel, Jan. 23, 1965 (div. 1980); children: Thomas, Timothy. BA in Liberal Arts and Scis., U. Ill., 1958; BSEE, Ill. Inst. Tech., 1972. Supt. maintenance of way Chgo. Transit Authority, 1963-89; supr. of rail activation and rail tech. support Met. Transp. Assn. Los Angeles County, L.A., 1989—. Mem. L.A. County Transit Commn.'s Rail Constrn. Corp. Users Group, 1990—. With U.S. Army, 1958-60. Mem. Am. Pub. Transp. Assn. (vice chmn. power com. 1974-75), Am. Ry. Engring. Assn. (vice chmn. subcom. on power signals and comm. 1990—), Underwater Soc. Am. (N.Am. record in spear-fishing 1988), Calif. Pub. Utilities Commn. (gen. order 1995), Nat. Rsch. Coun., NAS (transp. rsch. bd.), Nat. Acad. Engrs. Home: 12741 Andy St Cerritos CA 90703-6044 Office: Met Transp Assn L A County 320 Santa Fe Ave Los Angeles CA 90013

MOORE, WILLIAM HOWARD, history educator, writer; b. Harriman, Tenn., June 26, 1942; s. Lonnie Henry and Goldie Myrtle (Williams) M.; m. Mary Elizabeth Galvan, Sept. 27, 1969 (div. 1980); 1 child, Adam William; m. June Uvalda Vialpando, Mar. 8, 1986. BS, U. Tenn., 1964, MA, 1965; PhD, U. Tex., 1971. Instr. Southwest Tex. State U., San Marcos, 1971-72; asst. prof. Ohio U., Athens, 1972-73; from asst. prof. to prof. U. Wyo., Laramie, 1973—, chair dept. history, 1992—; cons. Harper Collins Pubs., N.Y.C., 1991-92, McGraw Hill Pubs., N.Y.C., 1992. Author: Kefauver Committee, 1974, Company Town, 1989; article referee Jour. American History, Bloomington, Ind., 1989; mem. editorial adv. bd. Annals of Wyoming, Cheyenne, 1990—; contbr. articles to profl. jours. Cons. Albany County Sch. Bd., Laramie, 1989, 91. Grantee Nat. Endowment Humanities, 1977, 90, Eisenhower World Affairs Inst., 1990, Hoover Pres. Libr. Assn., 1992. Mem. Orgn. Am. Historians, Ctr. Study Presidency. Home: PO Box 103 Laramie WY 82070-0103 Office: U Wyo Dept History PO Box 3198 Laramie WY 82071-3198

MOORE, WILLIS HENRY ALLPHIN, history and geography educator; b. N.Y.C., Dec. 14, 1940; s. Carl Allphin and Mary Catherine (Moody) M.; children: Patrick Kakela, Michael Kirby, Catherine Malia. BA Letters, U. Okla., 1962; MEd in Adminstrn., U. Hawaii, 1971. Teaching asst. dept. history U. Hawaii, 1962-64; dir. edn. Bernice P. Bishop Mus., Honolulu, 1967-76; pres. Hawaii Geog. Soc., Honolulu, 1976-78, exec. sec., editor, 1978—; mem. Hawaii Com. for Humanities, 1976-78; producer, narrator film-lecture programs Nat. Audubon Soc. and travelogue forums; instr. in history, geography and polit. sci. Chaminade U. of Honolulu, 1986—; lectr. elderhostel U. Hawaii, Hawaii Pacific U.. Co-author/co-editor: Hawaii Parklands, Sociological History of Honolulu, Total Solar Eclipse over Hawaii, 1991; contbr. articles to Honolulu Advertiser, Pacific Daily News, Guam, Pacific Mag., Honolulu Star-Bull. Lay reader St. Andrew's Cathedral; active Nat. Mus. Am. Indian. Mem. Internat. Map Trade Assn., Am. Assn. State & Local History, Am. Mus. Assn., Pacific Sci. Assn., Hawaii Mus. Assn. (pres. 1972-74), Pacific Asia Travel Assn., Hawaii Pub. Radio, Am. Guild Organists, Sierra Club (chmn. Hawaii chpt. 1973-75), Hawaiian Hist. Soc., Nat. Soc. of Arts and Letters. Office: PO Box 1698 Honolulu HI 96806-1698

MOORE, WILLSON CARR, JR., lawyer; b. Honolulu, Nov. 24, 1928; s. Willson Carr and Jenna Vee (McMillan) C.; m. Sally Churchill, Apr. 25, 1952; children: Willson C. III, Brian C., Sharon Moore Fink. BA, U. Calif., Berkeley, 1950; JD, U. Calif., San Francisco, 1953. Law clk. to Hon. Jon Wiig U.S. Dist. Ct., Honolulu, 1953-54; dep. atty. gen. State of Hawaii, 1955-59; pvt. practice Moore & Moore, Honolulu, 1959-64; with Rush, Moore, Craven, Sutton, Morry & Beh, Honolulu, 1965—; bd. dirs. Hawaii Def. Lawyers, 1990-94, Def. Rsch. Inst., 1989-93. Col. USAR, 1950-81. Fellow Am. Coll. Trial Lawyers; mem. ABA, Am. Bd. Trial Lawyers (adv.), Am. Judacature Soc., Assn. Def. Trial Attys. (pres. 1989-90, mem. exec. coun. 1983-91), Phi Alpha Delta. Office: Rush Moore Craven Sutton Morry & Beh 745 Fort Street Mall Ste 2000 Honolulu HI 96813-3820

MOORHEAD, CARLOS J., congressman; b. Long Beach, Calif., May 6, 1922; s. Carlos Arthur and Florence (Gravers) M.; m. Valery Joan Tyler, July 19, 1969; children: Theresa, Catharine, Steven, Teri, Paul. BA, UCLA, 1943; JD, U. So. Calif., 1949. Bar: Calif. 1949, U.S. Supreme Ct. 1973. Pvt. practice law Glendale, Calif., 1949-72; dir. Lawyers Reference Service, Glendale, 1950-66; mem. 93d-104th Congresses from 22d (now 27th) Dist. Calif., 1973—; mem. judiciary com., chmn. subcom. on cts. and intellectual property, vice chmn. commerce com., mem. subcom. on energy & power, subcom. on telecomm. & fin.; dean Calif. Congl. Rep. Delegation; apptd. to Fed. Cts. Study Com. Pres. Glendale Hi-Twelve Club; mem. Verdugo Hills council Boy Scouts Am.; mem. Calif. Assembly, 1967-72; mem. Calif. Law Revision Commn., 1971-72; pres. 43d Dist. Republican Assembly, Glendale Young Republicans; mem. Los Angeles County Rep. Central Com., Calif. Rep. Central Com.; pres. Glendale La Crescenta Camp Fire Girls, Inc. Served to lt. col. AUS, 1942-46. Recipient Man of Yr. award USO, 1979. Mem. Calif. Bar Assn. L.A. County Bar Assn., Glendale Bar Assn. (past pres.), Glendale C. of C., Masons, Shriners, Lions, Moose, VFW. Presbyterian. Office: US House of Representatives 2346 Rayburn House Office Bldg Washington DC 20515

MOORHOUSE, MARY FRANCES, rehabilitation nurse; b. Seattle, Sept. 13, 1947; d. Francis E. and Frances L. (Ranus) McGlothlin; m. Jan G. Moorhouse, Feb. 3, 1968; children: Paul, Jason. Diploma, Beth El Sch. Nursing, Colorado Springs, Colo., 1968. CRRN; cert.. forensic nurse. Patient care coord. critical care Penrose Community Hosp., Colorado Springs, 1974-79; dir. nursing Nurses PRN of Denver, Inc., Colorado Springs, 1985; owner, cons. TNT-RN Enterprises, Colorado Springs, 1985—; nurse cons. Fortis Corp., Colorado Springs, 1989-92. Author: Nursing Care Plans: Nursing Diagnosis in Planning Patient Care, 3d edit., 1993, The Nurses' Pocket Guide: Nursing Diagnosis with Interventions, 5th edit., 1993, Care Plans for Critical Care, 1987. Recipient Outstanding Book of Yr. award Nursing, 1984, AJN Book of Yr. award, 1989; named Nurse of Yr., Colo. Nurses Assn., 1987; So. Colo. Woman of Yr. in Health Field, 1988, honored for sustained contbn. to nursing profession, 1992. Mem. AACN, Colo. Nurses Assn. (honored for sustained contbn. to nursing profession 1992 and for improvement of health status and well-being of citizens of Colo. 1994), Nat. League for Nursing, N.Am. Nursing Diagnosis Assn., Nursing Found. Colo., Assn. Rehab. Nurses, Internat. Assn. Forensic Nurses. Home and Office: 1219 E Bijou St Colorado Springs CO 80909-5515

MOORMAN, LAWRENCE ALAN, humanities educator; b. San Francisco, Feb. 28, 1940; s. Charles Carroll and Margaret (Gormlu) M.; m. Marilyn Petanatti Jones, Apr. 3, 1969 (div. June 1976). AA in English, St. Josephs Coll., Menlo Park, Calif., 1961; BA, St. Patricks Coll., Menlo Park, Calif., 1963; MA in Humanities, San Francisco State U., 1966. Instr. humanities Yuba C.C., Marysville, Calif., 1966—; instr. Core Coll., 1971-73. Author: Value Sources, 1974, Synthesis, 1985; one-man shows include San Francisco State U., 1983, 92, Sacramento State U., 1984, Consumes River Coll., 1989, Sonoma State U., 1988. Singer with Sacramento Symphony all Beethoven concert, 1991, Christmas concert, 1990, 92. Mem. Pioneer Art Gallery. Roman Catholic. Home: 862 Clark Ave Yuba City CA 95991-3815 Office: Yuba C C 2088 N Beale Rd Marysville CA 95901-7605

MOORS, LEONARD JERALD, JR. (JERRY MOORS), musician; b. Santa Rosa, Calif., Oct. 10, 1939; s. Leonard Jerold and Vera Geraldine (Fitzgerald) M.; m. Suzanne Stoughton, June 1994; children : Leland, Megan, Lenny, Daniel, Lauren. Student, Eastman Sch. Music, 1957-59; BA, Sonoma State U., 1967; postgrad., U. Calif., Davis, 1967-69. Freelance arranger, band leader, and pianist Sonoma County, Calif., 1960-65, Santa Rosa, Calif., 1969-73; pianist Ray Anthony Band, 1973-74; pianist, arranger Johnny Russell Orch., Reno, 1975-78; orch. leader, conductor various hotels, Lake Tahoe, Nev., 1978-80; mus. dir., pianist Sonny King Show, Las Vegas, 1980-84; freelance pianist Reno, 1985-88; pianist, mus. advisor Eagle House,

Eureka, Calif., 1989; pianist BenBow Inn, Calif., 1990; freelance pianist San Francisco Bay area, 1991—; pianist Contra Costa Ballet Ctr., Marin Ballet. Composed numerous mus. pieces including Sonatina for Brass Quintet, 1958, Quest, 1977, Ocean Suite, 1957. Recipient Delius Composition award U. Fla., 1977; named ShowCase Artist of Year For the Love of Jazz Soc., 1978. Democrat. Hindu. Home: 32 Atherton Ave Crockett CA 94525-1508

MOOSBURNER, NANCY, nutritionist; b. Houston, Tex., Apr. 6, 1943; d. Henry Fenno and Shirley Louise (McCandless) Laughton; m. Stephen Weinert, Nov. 1964 (div. Nov. 1974); children: Catherine, Jeffery; m. Otto Moosburner, Feb. 7, 1976; 1 child, Brian. BS, U. Nevada Reno, 1979, MS, 1982. Registered dietitian. Edn. specialist Nev. Dept. of Edn., Carson City, 1980-83, state dir., 1983-84; sch. nutrition program supr. Douglas Co. Sch. Dist., Minden, Nev., 1987-93; dir. sch. nutrition St. Helens (Oreg.) Sch. Dist., 1993-94; instr. Truckee Meadows C.C., Reno, Nev., 1982-83, Portland C.C., St. Helens, 1993-94; child nutrition program supr. Auburn (Wash.) Sch. Dist., 1994—; state pres Nev. Sch. Food Svc. Assn., Minden, 1992-93. Contbr. articles to profl. jours. Recipient Excellence in Food Svc. award U.S. Dept. Agri., 1989; named Outstanding Women of Am., 1977. Mem. Am. Dietetic Assn., Am. Sch. Food Svc. Assn. (west region dir. 1991-93, exec. bd.), Oreg. Sch. Food Svc. Assn. (pub. communication 1993-94), Am. Home Econs. Assn., Soc. for Nutrition Edn. Democrat. Home: PO Box 2628 Longview WA 98632-8665

MORA, DAVID RICHARD, city manager; b. L.A., Feb. 18, 1945; s. David Mora and Bessie Saavedra; m. Judith Anne Crawford, June 10, 1972; children: Teresa, Gabriela. BA, Calif. State U., L.A., 1967; MPIA, U. Pitts., 1971. Vol. U.S. Peace Corps, Philippines, 1967-70; planning chief Jobs for Progress, Inc., L.A., 1972-73; community rels. dir. City of Santa Barbara, Calif., 1973-77, dep. city adminstr., 1977-80; town mgr. Town of Los Gatos, Calif., 1981-85; city mgr. City of Oxnard, Calif., 1985-90, City of Salinas, Calif., 1990—. Contbg. author (book) Reflections of Local Government Professionals, 1987. Chair govt. campaign United Way, Salinas, 1993. Fellow Nat. Acad. Pub. Adminstrn.; mem. Itnerant. City Mgmt. Assn. (pres. ICMA Hispanic Network 1990-92, chair ICMA Coun.-Mgr. Task Force 1992-94, mem. ICMA-Cmty. Oriented Police Svcs. Adv. 1994—, mem. Model City charter com. 1986-88), Calif. City Mgrs. Dept. (pres. 1991-92). Office: City of Salinas 200 Lincoln Ave Salinas CA 93901-2639

MORALES, CYNTHIA TORRES, clinical psychologist, consultant; b. L.A., Aug. 13, 1952; d. Victor Jose and Lupe (Pacheco) Torres; m. Armando Torres Morales, June 30, 1989. BA, UCLA, 1975, M in Social Welfare, 1978, D in Counseling Psychology, 1986. Lic. psychologist, Calif. Clin. social worker VA, Brentwood, Calif., 1977-78; med. social worker Harbor-UCLA Med. Ctr., Carson, Calif., 1978-79; psychotherapist San Fernando Valley Child Guidance Clinic, Northridge, Calif., 1979-80; psychiat. social worker L.A. County Dept. Mental Health, 1980-81; child welfare worker L.A. County Dept. Children's Svcs., 1981-86; cons. psychologist, organizational devel. mgr. UCLA, 1986—; pvt. practice and consultation, 1992—; cons. Dept. Children Svcs., Health Svcs. Divsn., 1994—; cons. Hispanic Family Inst., L.A., 1989—, U. Calif., Calif. Youth Authority, Project Info.; mem. diversity com. UCLA, 1988—, mem. mental health emergency task force, 1986-89. Mem. Centro de Ninos Bd. Dirs., L.A., 1984-88; lobbyist self devel. people United Presbyn. Ch. Synod, L.A., 1982-88; chair Inner City Games Acad. Contest Hollenbeck Police Bus. Coun., L.A., 1992; co-chair Inner City Games Acad. Essay Contest, 1993; commr. L.A. County Commn. Children and Family Svcs., 2nd Supervisorial Dist. Recipient Cert. of Appreciation, Children's Bapt. Home, 1984, Cert. of Appreciation, Hollenbeck Police Bus. Coun. 1992, Spl. Recognition award Fed. Judge Takasugi, Pro Bono Bar Rev. and L.A. City Atty. 1993, Cert. of Appreciation, Hollenbeck Youth Ctr., 1992. Mem. APA, L.A. County Psychol. Assn. Office: 1100 Glendon Ave Ste 1701 Los Angeles CA 90024-3521

MORALES, JULIO K., lawyer; b. Havana, Cuba, Jan. 17, 1948; came to U.S., 1960; s. Julio E. and Josephine (Holsters) M.; m. Suzette M. Dussault, May 31, 1970 (div. 1978); children: Julio E., Karel A.; m. Barbara A. Miller, July 14, 1979 (div. 1988); 1 child, Nicolas W. BA, Carroll Coll., 1969; JD, U. Mont., 1972. Bar: Mont. 1972, U.S. Dist. Ct. Mont. 1972, U.S. Ct. Mil. Appeals 1972, U.S. Ct. Appeals (9th cir.) 1980. Law clk. to presiding justice Mont. Supreme Ct., Helena, 1972; sole practice Missoula, Mont., 1973-78, 88—; sr. ptnr. Morales & Volinkaty, Missoula, 1978-88; pvt. practice law Morales Law Office, 1988—. Author: Estate Planning for the Handicapped, 1975. Pres. Rockmont, Inc., Missoula, 1985—. Served to 2d lt. U.S. Army, 1972. Named Boss of the Yr., Missoula chpt. Mont. Assn. Legal Secs., 1988. Mem. ABA (dist. rep. 1975-79, exec. coun. young lawyer divsn. 1977-79), Mont. Bar Assn. (chmn. law day 1974, 75, 77), Am. Judicature Soc., Assn. Trial Lawyers Am., World Assn. Lawyers, Missoula Soccer Assn. (pres. 1983-85), Mont. Sailing Assn. (bd. dirs. 1994—), Nat. Exch. Club (bd. dirs. Yellowstone dist. 1987-88, pres. 1990-91), Missoula Exch. Club, Phi Delta Phi. Roman Catholic. Office: PO Box 9311 430 Ryman St Missoula MT 59802-4208

MORALES, MARGO MELINDA, government analyst; b. Pomona, Calif., Nov. 2, 1958; d. Roman Montes and Nancy Ruth (Sloan) M.; m. Kenneth Clark Brown; stepchildren: Gregory Brown, Leslie Brown. BA in Polit. Sci., Calif. State Poly. U., Pomona, 1982. Loan processor Crocker Nat. Bank, El Segundo, Calif., 1983-86; rehab. specialist Los Angeles County Community Devel. Commn., Monterey Park, Calif., 1986-87, mktg. specialist, 1987-88, environ. specialist, 1988-89; mgmt. analyst Chief Adminstrv. Office, LA County, 1989—; mem. L.A. Means Bus. Task Force, 1992-93; chair Drug Diversion Task Force, L.A., 1991; mem. Calif. Perservation Found., San Francisco, 1988-89. Editor newsletter Calif. State U. Alumni Coun. News and Notes, 1991-92. Team handball support svcs. coord. Olympic Festival, L.A., 1988-91; mem. Calif. State U. Alumni Coun., 1991—; vol. various local, state and fed. campaigns, Los Angeles County, 1980—; bd. dirs. Fair Housing Found., Long Beach, Calif., 1993—. Named to Outstanding Young Women of Am., 1983. Mem. Calif. State Poly. U. Pomona Alumni (hon. life, bd. dirs. 1989—, v.p. 1989). Democrat. Roman Catholic. Office: Los Angeles County Chief Adminstrv Office 500 W Temple St Rm 723 Los Angeles CA 90012-2713

MORAN, RACHEL, lawyer, educator; b. Kansas City, Mo., June 27, 1956; d. Thomas Albert and Josephine (Portillo) M. AB, Stanford U., 1978; JD, Yale U., 1981. Bar: Calif. 1984. Assoc Heller, Ehrman, White & McAuliffe, San Francisco, 1982-83; prof. law U. Calif., Berkeley, 1984—; vis. prof. UCLA Sch. Law, 1988, Stanford (Calif.) U. Law Sch., 1989; ann. civil rights lectr. Creighton U. Sch. Law, Omaha, 1989; Pirsig lectr. William Mitchell Coll. St. Paul, 1989, others; mem. steering com. Nat. Resource Ctr., Berkeley, 1988-89; chair Chicano/Latino Policy Project, 1993—. Contbr. numerous articles to profl. jours. Grantee Joseph and Polly Harris Trust Inst. Govtl. Studies, Berkeley, 1987-89, Faculty Devel. U. Calif., Berkeley, 1985-86; recipient Disting. Tchg. award U. Calif. Mem. ABA, AAUP, Calif. Bar Assn., Phi Beta Kappa. Democrat. Unitarian. Office: U Calif Sch Law Boalt Hall Berkeley CA 94720

MORAN, THOMAS FRANCIS, writer; b. Phila., Dec. 5, 1943; s. George Francis and Alice (Foulk) M.; m. Marilyn Groch, June 24, 1978; children: Rachel Louise, Michael Thomas. BSME, Calif. State Poly. Inst., San Luis Obispo, Calif., 1965; MSME, Calif. State U., Long Beach, 1968. Engr. Jet Propulsion Lab., Pasadena, 1966-71; coun. aide City of L.A., 1975-79; editor Ocean Front Weekly, Marina del Rey, Calif., 1979-80; tech. writer Xerox Electro-Optical, Pasadena, 1982-83; specialist Rockwell Internat., Lakewood, Calif., 1983-92, G&H Tech., Santa Monica, Calif., 1992—; instr. tech. writing Calif. State U., Dominquez Hills, Calif., 1990—; instr. writing L.A. Harbor Coll., Wilmington, 1989—. Author: The Photo Essay, 1974, Fantasy by the Sea, 1979, The Bicycle Motocross Racing, 1986, The U.S. Army, 1990, Los Angeles International Airport, 1993. Bd. dirs. Venice Hist. Soc., 1988-89; bd. advisors Beyond Baroque Found., Venice, 1980-83. Named Citizen of the Yr., Bd. Realtors, Marina del Rey; Apollo Achievement awardee, NASA. Mem. Soc. Tech. Communication. Office: 218 Howland Canal Venice CA 90291-4511

MORAN, THOMAS HARRY, university administrator; b. Milw., Oct. 21, 1937; s. Harry Edward and Edna Agnes Moran; BS, U. Wis., 1964, MA, 1972, PhD, 1974; m. Barbara Ellen Saklad, June 10, 1969; children: David Thomas, Karen Ellen. Dir. capital budgeting Wis. Dept. Adminstrn., 1962-64; exec. dir. Wis. Higher Ednl. Aids Bd., 1964-69; spl. cons. tax policy Wis. Dept. Revenue, 1973-74; dep. dir. Wis. Manpower Coun., Office of Gov., 1974-76; v.p. bus. and fin., treas. U. Detroit, 1976-78; exec. assoc. v.p. health affairs U. So. Calif., L.A., 1979-87; v.p. bus. affairs, 1988—. USN fellow, 1957-59; U.S. Office Edn. rsch. fellow, 1973. Mem. Am. Assn. Higher Edn., Phi Kappa Phi. Office: U So Calif 200 Town & Gown University Park Los Angeles CA 90007

MORAND, BLAISE E., bishop; b. Tecumseh, Ont., Can., Sept. 12, 1932. Ordained priest Roman Cath. Ch., 1958. Ordained coadjutor bishop Diocese of Prince Albert, Sask., Can., 1981, bishop, 1983—. Office: Diocese of Prince Albert, 1415 4th Ave W, Prince Albert, SK Canada S6V 5H1*

MORANG, DIANE JUDY, writer, television producer, business entrepreneur; b. Chgo., Apr. 28, 1942; d. Anthony Thomas Morang and Laura Ann Andrzejczak. Student, Fox Bus. Coll., 1959-60, UCLA, 1967-69. Staff Drury Ln. Theatre, Chgo., 1961-62; chair, mem. judging panel Regional Emmy awards, 1989, judge 2 categories, 1985. Author: How to Get into the Movies, 1978; author, creator: The Rainbow Keyboard, 1991. Bd. dirs., mem. scholarship com. Ariz. Bruins UCLA Alumni Assn. Mem. Nat. Acad. TV Arts and Scis. (Emmy-award winning team 1971), Ariz. Authors Assn. (bd. dirs.), Westworld Polo Club. Roman Catholic.

MORAVCSIK, JULIUS MATTHEW, philosophy educator; b. Budapest, Hungary, Apr. 26, 1931; came to U.S., 1949; s. Julius and Edith (Fleissig) M.; m. Marguerite Germain Truninger, Sept. 14, 1954; children: Adrian Clay, Peter Matthew. BA, Harvard U., 1953, PhD, 1959. Asst. prof. U. Mich., Ann Arbor, 1960-66, assoc. prof., 1966-68; prof. Stanford (Calif.) U., 1968—. Author: Understanding Language, 1973, Thought and Language, 1990, Plato and Platonism, 1992. Recipient Sr. Humanist prize Humboldt Found., 1983; fellow Ctr. Advanced Studies Behavioral Scis., 1986-87, Inst. Advanced Studies, 1988. Mem. Am. Philos. Assn. (pres. Pacific divsn. 1987-88), Am. Soc. Aesthetics (trustee 1988-92), Soc. Ancient Greek Philosophy (pres. 1989-91). Office: Stanford U Dept Of Philosophy Stanford CA 94305

MOREHART, THOMAS BERTON, academic administrator; b. Henderson, Tex., Nov. 17, 1942; s. William Franklin and Marian Louise (Pugh) M.; m. Kaaren Lee Forkner, Mar. 21, 1964; children: Jennifer Lee Morehart Hartin, Jeffrey William Morehart. BS in Math., N.Mex. State U., 1964; MS in Computer Info. Systems, Colo. State U., 1971; PhD in Bus. Adm., Ga. State U., 1976. Mathematician White Sands (N.Mex.) Missile Range, 1966, 1968-70; grad. asst. Colo. State U., Ft. Collins, 1970-71; instr. Western Ill. U., Macomb, 1971-72; asst. to the dean Ga. State U., Atlanta, 1972-74, instr., 1974-75; asst. prof. Ariz. State U., Tempe, 1975-80, assoc. prof., 1980-86; assoc. dean N.Mex. State U., Las Cruces, 1986—; cons. Tempe, Ariz., 1976-86, Las Cruces, N.Mex., 1986—; bd. dirs. Bd. of Pensions PC USA, Phila., 1982-89. Author: Personal Financial Management, 1980; contbr. articles profl. jours. 1st lt. U.S. Army, 1966-68. Mem. Am. Risk and Ins. Assn., Am. Soc. CLUs and Chartered Fin. Cons., Am. Soc. CPCUs, Phi Kappa Phi, Beta Gamma Sigma. Presbyterian. Home: 2420 Desert Dr Las Cruces NM 88001-1609 Office: N Mex State U Coll Bus Adminstrn & Econs PO Box 30001 Dept 3AD Las Cruces NM 88003

MOREHOUSE, CARL EDWARD, land use planner; b. Louisville, Aug. 9, 1951; s. Alan L. and Marjorie Ellen (Holt) M.; m. Felicia C. Tiritilli, Aug. 17, 1977 (div. Dec. 1979). BA, Purdue U., 1973; MPA, Ind. U., 1980. Asst. dir. City-County Planning Commn., Henderson, Ky., 1975-77; housing rsch. asst. Dept. Met. Devel., Indpls., 1980; hist. preservation planner City Planning Dept., Paso Robles, Calif., 1984; asst. planner Community Devel. Dept., Santa Barbara, Calif., 1985-86; from planner I to planner III Resource Mgmt. Agy., Ventura County, Calif., 1986-89, planner IV, 1989—. Mem. Am. Planning Assn., Calif. chpt. Am. Planning Assn., Am. Inst. Cert. Planners.

MOREL-SEYTOUX, HUBERT JEAN, civil engineer, educator; b. Calais, Artois, France, Oct. 6, 1932; came to U.S., 1956; s. Aimé and Suzanne Claire (Rousseau) M.-S.; m. Margery K. Keyes, Apr. 16, 1960; children: Aimée, Claire, Sylvie, Marie-Jeanne. BS, Ecole St. Genevieve, Versailles, France, 1953; MS, Ecole Nationale des Ponts et Chaussées, Paris, 1956; PhD, Stanford U., 1962. Research engr. Chevron Oil Field Research Co., La Habra, Calif., 1962-66; prof. Colo. State U., Ft. Collins, 1966-91, prof. emeritus, 1991—; chargé de recherches U. Grenoble, France, 1972-73; maitre de recherches Ecole des Mines de Paris, Fontainebleau, France, 1982; directeur de recherches ORSTOM, Montpellier, France, 1991—; cons. hydrology Atherton, Calif., 1992—; cons. AID, Dakar, Senegal, 1985-86, 88, Ministry of Agriculture and Water, Riyadh, Saudi Arabia, 1978-83, City of Thornton, Colo., 1986-88, King Abdulaziz U., Jeddah, Saudi Arabia, 1987, 89—, Ford Found., India, 1976, 79, South Fla. Water Mgmt. Dist., West Palm Beach, 1991—, Battelle Pacific Northwest Labs., Richland, Wash., 1991—, City of Paris, France, 1992—, Agence de l'Eau Seine-Normandie, 1992—, Utah State U., Logan, 1994—, Reservoir Engring. Rsch. Inst., Palo Alto, 1994—; vis. prof. Ecole Polytechnique Federale de Lausanne, 1987; vis. scholar Stanford U., 1992—; adj. prof. U. Colo., Boulder, 1992—; lectr. U. Calif., Berkley, 1993. Editor: Hydrology Days, 1981—, 3d Internat. Hydrology Symposium, 1977, Unsaturated Flow in Hydrologic Modeling, 1989. Pres. Internat. Ctr., Ft. Collins, 1984-86. Served to lt. French Army Marine Corps Engrs., 1959-62. Sr. Fulbright scholar, France, 1972-73; recipient Abell Faculty Rsch. award Colo. State U. Coll. Engring., 1985. Mem. Am. Geophys. Union, ASCE, Soc. Petroleum Engrs., Am. Meteorol. Soc., Am. Soc. Agrl. Engrs. Home: 57 Selby Ln Atherton CA 94027-3926 Office: Hydrology Days Publs 57 Selby Ln Atherton CA 94027-3926

MORENO, GUILLERMO FERNANDEZ, minister; b. San Antonio, Aug. 28, 1948; s. Willie Luna and Frances (Fernandez) M.; m. Delia Guerra, June 6, 1971; 1 child, Guillermo. BA, U. Calif., L.A., 1976, MA, 1978; MA, Bob Jones U., 1981, PhD, 1988. Ordained to ministry Christian Ch. Min. Latin Am. Coun. of Christian Chs., Brownsville, Tex., 1967—; pastor Latin Am. Coun. of Christian Chs., Brownsville, 1969—, Latin Am. Coun. of Christian Chs. Galilea, L.A., 1988—; instr. Cladic Sem., L.A., 1969—; choir dir. Cladic Sem., L.A., 1967-79; evangelist Latin Am. Coun. Christian Chs., U.S.A., summers 1968—; vis. instr. Clases Biblicas, Monterrey, Mex., summers, 1975—; mgr. Cladic Bible Book store, L.A., 1984-86; exec. editor Expositor Dominical Cladic, 1993—. Author Bible Doctrine seminar; contbr. articles to profl. jours. Mem. Sigma Delta Pi Spanish Honor Soc. (lifetime), Bob Jones U. Alumni Assn. Republican. Home: 1255 Watson Ave Wilmington CA 90744-2853

MORENO, MANUEL D., bishop; Educator U. of Calif., L.A., St. John's Sem., Camarillo, Calif. Ordained priest Roman Cath. church, 1961. Ordained aux. bishop of Los Angeles, titular bishop of Tanagra, 1977; installed as bishop of Tucson, 1982—. Office: PO Box 31 192 S Stone Ave Tucson AZ 85702

MORENO, PAUL MICHAEL, media relations manager; b. Napa, Calif., Oct. 22, 1962; s. Angelo M. Moreno and Joan Geraldine (La Rocque) Martin. AA, Napa Valley (Calif.) C.C., 1983; BA, Calif. State U., Chico, 1987. Staff writer Paradise (Calif.) Post, 1987; editor Chico (Calif.) Press-Gazette, 1987-88; bur. chief The Appeal- Democrat, Marysville, Calif., 1988-90; media rels. mgr. Calif. Med. Assn., San Francisco, 1990—. Feature story named Best of Month, Apr., 1989, Assoc. Press. Fellow Pub. Rels. Soc. Am. Home: PO Box 377 Rutherford CA 94573-0377 Office: Calif Med Assn PO Box 7090 San Francisco CA 94120-7090

MOREY, CHARLES LEONARD, III, theatrical director; b. Oakland, Calif., June 23, 1947; s. Charles Leonard Jr. and Mozelle Kathleen (Milliken) M.; m. Mary Carolyn Donnet, June 10, 1973 (div. 1975); m. Joyce Miriam Schilke, May 29, 1982; 1 child, William. AB, Dartmouth Coll., 1969; MFA, Columbia U., 1971. Artistic dir. Peterborough (N.H.) Players, 1977-88, Pioneer Theatre Co., Salt Lake City, 1984—; adj. asst. prof. theatre U. Utah, Salt Lake City, 1984—. Actor: N.Y. Shakespeare Festival, Playwrights Horizons, New Dramatists, ARK Theatre Co., Ensemble Studio Theatre, Cubiculo, Folger Theatre, Syracuse Repertory Theatre, Theatre by Sea, others; over 150 plays acted in or directed; guest dir. Ensemble Studio Theatre, ArK Theatre, Am. Stage Festivel, McCarter Theatre, Pioneer Theatre Co., PCPA Theatrefest, The Repertory Theater of St. Louis, Meadow Brook Theatre; author new adaptations Alexander Dumas' The Three Musketeers, Bram Stoker's Dracula, Charles Dickens' A Tale of Two Cities, Victor Hugo's The Hunchback of Notre Dame; TV appearances include: Young Maverick, Edge of Night, World Apart, Our Town. Trustee Utah Arts Endowment, Inc. Mem. Soc. Stage Dirs. and Choreographers, AEA, SAG, AFTRA, Salt Lake City C. of C. (Honors in the Arts award 1991), Utah Assn. Gifted Children (Community Svc. award 1991), Peterborough Players (Edith Bond Stearns award 1990). Democrat. Episcopalian. Home: 1803 Yale Ave Salt Lake City UT 84108-1837 Office: Pioneer Theatre Co U Utah Salt Lake City UT 84112

MOREY, ROBERT HARDY, communications executive; b. Milw., Sept. 5, 1956; s. Lloyd W. and Ruby C. (McElhaney) M. AA, Ricks Coll., 1978; BA, Brigham Young U., 1983. Program dir. Sta. KABE-FM, Orem, Utah, 1982-83, sales mgr., 1983; nat. mgr. ops. Tiffany Prodns. Internat., Salt Lake City, 1983-84; account exec. Osmond Media Corp., Orem, 1984; corp. sec., bd. dirs. Positive Communications, Inc., Orem, 1984—, chief exec. officer, 1987—; gen. mgr. Sta. KSRR, Orem, 1985—; pres. K-Star Satellite Network, Orem, 1986—, Broadcast Media Svcs., Orem, 1989-93; gen. mgr. Sta. KMGR, Salt Lake City, 1993; ops. mgr. KQMB-FM, Salt Lake City, 1994—; guest lectr. various colls. and univs., 1981—. Chmn. Rep. voting dist., Orem, 1984. Recipient Community Service award Utah Valley Community Coll., 1983; named one of Outstanding Young Men in Am. U.S. Jaycees, 1983. Mem. Rotary. Mormon. Home: PO Box 828 Orem UT 84059-0828 Office: Sta KSRR Ventura Media Ctr 1240 E 800 N Orem UT 84057-4318

MORFORD, JAMES WARREN, international health care executive; b. Duluth, Minn., Feb. 22, 1945; s. James Andrew and Christine (Warner) M.; m. Pamela Ann Carlson, July 20, 1974; children: James Warren II, Melissa Lynn. AA, U. Minn., 1965; BS, U. Ariz., 1969. Asst. account exec. Tathum, Laird and Kudner Advt., Chgo., 1969; salesman Guest Pac Corp., Mt. Vernon, N.Y., 1970; v.p. Student Service Directory, Mt. Vernon, 1970-71; dir. mktg. Doctors Diagnostic Labs., Mpls., 1971-76, pres., 1976-78; pres., CEO Lab. Cons. Internat., Mpls., 1977-80; COO Morford Clin., Ltd., Mpls., 1980-88; pres. Morford Properties, Inc., Mpls. and Tucson, 1980—; COO Foothills Women's Ctr., Tucson, 1988—; pres., chmn., bd. dirs. Sistemas de Salud Panamericanos, S.A., Centro Panamericano de Diagnostico pro Imagenes, S.A., Mexico City, 1991—. Mem. Med. Group Mgmt. Assn., Ariz. Med.Group Mgmt. Assn., Minn. Med. Group Mgmt. Assn., Aircraft Owners and Pilots Assn., Chi Phi. Republican. Methodist. Home: 5081 N Camino Sumo Tucson AZ 85718-6053 Office: PanAm Health Sys 5081 N Camino Real Tucson AZ 85718-5925

MORGAN, AUDREY, architect; b. Neenah, Wis., Oct. 19, 1931; d. Andrew John Charles Hopfensperger and Melda Lily (Radtke) Anderson; m. Earl Adrian Morgan (div); children: Michael A., Susan Lynn Heiner, Nancy Lee, Diana Morgan Lucio. BA, U. Wash., 1955. Registered architect, Wash., Oreg.; cert. NCARB. Project mgr. The Austin Co., Renton, Wash., 1972-75; med. facilities architect The NBBJ Group, Seattle, 1975-79; architect constrn. rev. unit Wash. State Divsn. Health, Olympia, 1979-81; project dir., med. planner John Graham & Co., Seattle, 1981-83; pvt. practice architecture, Ocean Shores, Wash., 1983—, also health care facility cons., code analyst. Contbg. author: Guidelines for Construction and Equipment of Hospitals and Medical Facilities; Co-editor: Design Consideration for Mental Health Facilities; contbr. articles to profl. jours. and govt. papers; prin. works include quality assurance coord. for design phase Madigan Army Med. Ctr., Ft. Lewis, Wash.; med. planner and code analyst Rockwood Clinic, Spokane, Wash., Comprehensive Health Care Clinic for Yakima Indian Nation, Toppenish, Wash.; code analyst S.W. Wash. Hosps., Vancouver; med. planner Pacific Contract & Lazer Inst. Chehalis & Kennewick, Wash; med. planner facilities for child, adult, juvenile and forensic psychiatric patients., States of Wash. and Oreg. Cons. on property mgmt. Totem council Girl Scouts U.S.A., Seattle, 1969-84, troop leader, cons., trainer, 1961-74; mem. Wash. State Bldg. Code Coun., tech. adv. group for non-residential bldgs., Barier Free Com. Tech. adv. group for Ams. with Disabilties Act; assoc. mem. Wash State Fire Marshals Tech. Adv. Group. Mem. AIA (nat. acad. architecture for health 1980—, subcoms. codes and standards, chair mental health com., 1989-92, and numerous other coms., founding mem. Wash. council AIA architecture for health panel 1981—, recorder 1981-84, vice chmn., 1987, chmn. 1988, bd. dirs. S.W. Wash. chpt. 1983-84), Nat. Fire Protection Assn., Soc. Am. Value Engrs., Am. Hosp. Assn., Assn. Western Hosps., Wash. State Hosp. Assn., Wash. State Soc. Hosp. Engrs. (hon.), Seattle Womens Sailing Assn., Audubon Soc., Alpha Omicron Pi. Lutheran. Clubs: Coronado 25 Fleet 13 (Seattle) (past sec., bull. editor); GSA 25 Plus. Home and Office: PO Box 1990 Ocean Shores WA 98569-1990 also: 904 Falls Of Clyde Loop SE Ocean Shores WA 98569-9542

MORGAN, CAROL LOUISE, home care manager, nurse; b. Gauhati, India, Nov. 25, 1951; came to U.S. 1968; d. George Simon and Dorothy Louise (Drotz) Johnson; m. Tom D. Morgan, Aug. 25, 1973; children: Matthew, Samuel, Noah. BSN, Seattle Pacific U., 1973. RN, Wash., Oreg., Idaho. Nurse emergency rm. Group Health, Seattle, 1973-74; nurse Peace Corps, Colombia, 1974-75, Vis. Nurse Soc., Phila., 1976-79, Geneva Ctr. Camp, Rochester, Ind., summers 1978-79, Greater Albany (Oreg.) Pub. Schs., 1979-84; RN dir. Home Care Network, Albany, 1984—; mem. sr. disabled svc. adv. com., Corvallis, Oreg., 1986-89. Mem. Oreg. Assn. for Home Care (bd. dirs. 1987-89, mem. reimbursement com. 1985—), Oreg. Hospice Assn. Democrat. Office: Home Care Network 1046 6th Ave SW Albany OR 97321-1916

MORGAN, CHARLES EDWARD PHILLIP, bank executive; b. Wichita, Kans., Nov. 3, 1916; s. Wells C. Morgan and Mary E. (Brown) Allredge; m. Elizabeth Ann Brown, Oct. 14, 1943 (div. Dec. 1972); children—Valerie Donahue, Renee Tompkins. Student U. Wichita, 1935; student bus. adminstrn., U. Calif.-Berkeley, 1963. Teller First Nat. Bank, Santa Fe, 1938-42; safety officer Libby-McNeil-Libby, Sacramento, 1946-48; from teller to v.p./br. mgr. Wells Fargo Bank, Sacramento, 1948-76; sr. v.p. Capitol Bank of Commerce, Sacramento, 1976-86. Served to 1st lt. USAF, 1942-45. Democrat. Mem. Christian Ch. Lodges: Masons, Shriners, Elks. Home: 1111 Alvarado Ave Apt F362 Davis CA 95616

MORGAN, DAVID FORBES, minister; b. Toronto, Ont., Can., Aug. 3, 1930; came to U.S., 1954; s. Forbes Alexander and Ruth (Bamford) M.; m. Delores Mae Storhaug, Sept. 7, 1956; children—Roxanne Ruth, David Forbes II. BA, Rocky Mt. Coll.; ThB, Coll. of the Rockies, MDiv; postgrad. Bishop's Sch. Theology; LittD (hon.), Temple Coll., 1956, D.C. Nat. Coll. Ordained priest. Pres., Coll. of the Rockies, Denver, 1960-73; founder and rector Prior Order of Christ Centered Ministries, Denver, 1973—; canon pastor St. John's Cathedral, Denver, 1982—; bd. dir. Alpha Inc., Denver, 1981—. Author: Christ Centered Ministries, A Response to God's Call, 1973; Songs with A Message, 1956. Clubs: Oxford, Denver Botanic Garden. Home: 740 Clarkson St Denver CO 80218-3204 Office: St Johns Cathedral 1313 Clarkson St Denver CO 80218-1806

MORGAN, GARY B., journalism educator; b. San Diego, Nov. 5, 1943; s. Howard Wilson and Loyola Elizabeth (Heiberger) M.; m. Sharon Kay Traylor, June 16, 1965 (div. 1974); children: Stephen William Laurence, David Nathan Robert. BA, N.Mex. Highlands U., Las Vegas, 1966; MA, Colo. State U., 1968; DA, U. No. Colo., 1990. So. Calif. prep sports editor L.A. Examiner, 1959-61; sports editor Star-News, National City, Calif., 1960-61; announcer KFUN Radio, Las Vegas, N.Mex., 1963-66; sports info. dir. New Mex. Highlands U., 1964-66; grad. teaching asst. dept. English Colo. State U., 1966-68; info. dir. Mt. Plains Intercollegiate Athletic Assn., 1968-71, 74-76; asst. dir. info. svc. U. No. Colo., 1968-77; asst. prof. journalism Met. State Coll., Denver, 1977-84; prof. journalism Oxnard Coll., Calif., 1984—. Author: Yes You Can, 1990, The Georgetown Loop, 1976, Sugar Tramp, 1975, Three Foot Rails, 1970, There Was So Much Laughter, 1984; contbr. articles to profl. jours. Recipient Mark Dever award for excellence in teaching, Oxnard Coll., 1985-86. Mem. Nat. Collegiate Baseball Writers Assn. (pres. 1976), Coll. Sports Info. Dirs. Am. (bd. dirs.), Journalism Assn. Community Colls. (state pres. 1989-90, So. Calif. pres. 1988-89), Community Coll. Journalism Assn. (nat. pres. 1992, pres.-elect 1991), Assn. for Edn. in Journalism and Mass Communication, Calif. Newspaper Pubs. Assn. Office: Oxnard College 4000 S Rose Ave Oxnard CA 93033-6699

MORGAN, JACK M., lawyer; b. Portales, N.Mex., Jan. 15, 1924; s. George Albert and Mary Rosana (Baker) M.; BBA, U. Tex., 1948; LLB, 1950; m. Peggy Flynn Cummings, 1947; children: Marilyn, Rebecca, Claudia, Jack. Admitted to N.Mex. bar, 1950; sole practice law, Farmington, N.Mex., 1956—; mem. N.Mex. State Senate, 1973-88 . Served with USN, 1942-46. Mem. Am. Bar Assn., N.Mex. Bar Assn., S.W. Regional Energy Council (past chmn.), Kiwanis, Elks. Republican. Office: PO Box 2151 Farmington NM 87499-2151

MORGAN, JAMES EARL, librarian, administrator; b. Wheeling, W.Va., June 30, 1941; s. James H. L. and Ethel Irene (Goodwin) M.; m. Carman H. Head, Dec. 23, 1966; 1 child, Scott Andrew. B.S. in Edn., Ariz. State Coll., 1965; M.S.L.S., Fla. State U., 1966. Reference asst. social scis. Fla. State U., Tallahassee, 1965-66; head pub. services Ga. Coll., Milledgeville, 1967-69; dir. pub. services U. Tex. Med. Br., Galveston, 1969-73; dir. libraries U. Conn. Health Ctr., Farmington, 1973-76, Oreg. Health Sci. U., Portland, 1976—. Contbr. articles to profl. jours. Grantee Nat. Library Medicine, 1974-76, 78-81. Mem. ALA (life), Med. Library Assn. (chmn. Pacific NW chpt. 1981), Oreg. Health Scis. Libraries Assn., Pacific NW Library Assn., Spl. Library Assn., Oreg. Library Assn., Portland Area Spl. Librarians Assn., Assn. Coll. and Research Libraries. Democrat. Office: Oreg Health Scis Univ Library Biomedical Info Comm Ctr 3181 SW Sam Jackson Park Rd Portland OR 97201-3011

MORGAN, JAMES FORREST, physician; b. Salt Lake City, Oct. 14, 1951; s. David Nyle Morgan and Ernadene Huber (Oleson) Bascomb; m. Maureen Sun, Nov. 27, 1982; children: Mary Caitlin, Michael James, Elizabeth Dene. AB cum laude, Harvard Coll., 1973; MD, Boston U., 1980. Diplomate Am. Bd. Family Practice. Residency U. Wyo., Casper, 1980-83; rsch. asst. Boston Biomedical Rsch. Inst., Boston, 1975; chief resident U. Wyo., Casper, 1982; staff physician, chief of staff Crook County Meml. Hosp., Sundance, Wyo., 1983-85, Converse County Meml. Hosp., Douglas, Wyo., 1985-94. Steering com. Wyo. Intergrated Network, 1993—. Site investigator G.U.S.T.O. trial New Eng. Jour. Medicine, 1993. Fellow Am. Acad. Family Physicians; mem. Wyo. Medical Soc. Office: 111 S 5th St Ste 3 Douglas WY 82633-2434

MORGAN, JIM LEE, retired business educator; b. Little Rock, Apr. 14, 1943; s. James Charles and Lois Marie (McPherson) M.; BS/BA, U. Ark., 1961, MEd, 1968. Asst. city mgr. City of Beverly Hills, Calif., 1972-74; dir. Human Service Planning, Simi Valley, Calif., 1975-76; prof. bus. and mgmt. West Los Angeles Coll., 1975-91, prof. emeritus, 1991—, pres. acad. senate, 1975—; lectr. in field. dir. info. svcs. U. So. Calif. Traffic Safety Center, 1974-75; bd. dirs. Beverly Hills Chamber Orch., 1973-75, West Los Angeles chpt. ARC, 1972-75; founder, hon. chmn. Ann. Festival of Arts, City of Beverly Hills, 1972-75; founding mem. Research Coordinating Forum of Ventura County, 1976—; v.p. dist. senate Los Angeles C.C., 1978-80, pres. senate, 1980; treas. Acad. Senate, Calif. Community Colls., 1980-81, fin. task force commn. Chancellor's Office, 1980-91. Served to capt. USAF, 1967-72. Decorated Air Force medals; honored by Jim Lee Morgan Day, City of Beverly Hills, Apr. 14, 1974; named Air Force Systems Command Personnel Officer of the Yr., 1970. Mem. Internat. City Mgrs. Assn., So. Calif. Assn. Human Resources Dirs., Am. Soc. Planning Ofcls., Am. Mgmt. Assn., Phi Delta Kappa, Blue Key, Beta Gamma Sigma. Author: Social Planning for the City, 1975, Business of Management, 1982, Study Guide to Management, 1982-95, Instructional Telecourse Study Guide to Business and Management, 1982-95; editor Community Services Newsletter, 1974-75, Customer Relations: Policy and Procedures, 1975, Human Services Directory, City of Simi Valley, 1976, Rev. mag., 1972-74. Home and Office: 9201 Kanis Rd Ste 14-A Little Rock AR 72205

MORGAN, JOE LEONARD, investment company executive, former professional baseball player; b. Bonham, Tex., Sept. 19, 1943. Student, Oakland City (Ind.) Coll., Calif. State U.-Hayward. Infielder Houston Astros, 1962-71, 2d baseman, 1980-81; 2d baseman Cin. Reds, 1971-80, San Francisco Giants, 1981-82, Phila. Phillies, 1982-83, Oakland A's, 1983-84; pres. Joe Morgan Investments Inc., Oakland, 1984—; player World Series, 1972, 75-76, 83. Named Most Valuable Player Tex. League, 1964; Rookie of Yr. in Nat. League Sporting News, 1965; Most Valuable Player Nat. League 1975, 76; Maj. League Player of Year. Sporting News, 1975, 76; named to Nat. League All-Star Team, 1970, 72-79, Nat. League Comeback Player of the Year Sporting News, 1982, Nat. League Player of the Year Sporting News, 1975, Nat. League All Star Team Sporting News, 1972, 73-77; recipient Silver Slugger award Sporting News, 1982; elected to Baseball Hall of Fame, 1990. Office: Joe Morgan Investments Inc 3650 Hayman St Hayward CA 94544*

MORGAN, JOHN ADRIAN, physicist; b. Louisville, Feb. 18, 1952; s. John Tramble and Lois Meredith (Hodgson) M.; m. Ann Elizabeth Wehrle, June 26, 1983; 1 child, Eileen. BS, Calif. Tech., 1974; MS, Rice U., 1977, PhD, 1979. Rsch. fellow Astronomy Ctr., Sussex U., Falmer, U.K., 1979-82; staff scientist solar physics Calif. Tech., Pasadena, 1982-84; mem. tech. staff Aerospace Corp., El Segundo, Calif., 1984-89, engring. specialist, 1989—. Original rsch. pub. in Nucleosynthesis Theory and Physics of the Early Universe, 1977-83; contbr. tech. reports, monographs on space-based remote sensing to sci. publs. Fellow Royal Astron. Soc.; mem. Am. Phys. Soc., Am. Astron. Soc., Internat. Astron. Union. Office: Aerospace Corp MS M4/041 PO Box 92957 Los Angeles CA 90009-2957

MORGAN, KAT C., political activist; b. Bklyn., Aug. 4, 1963; d. David Morgan and Cordelia Katherine (Wagner) Reimers. BA in Women's Studies, U. Colo., 1988; MSW, U. Denver, 1992. Resource specialist Prevention Ctr., Boulder, Colo., 1988-91; cmty. support program coord. SafeHouse for Battered Women, Denver, 1992; exec. dir. Gay, Lesbian & Bisexual Cmty. Svcs. Ctr. of Colo., Denver, 1993-94; program dir. Shelter Against Violent Environments, Fremont, Calif., 1995—; trainer Valuing Diversity Project, Boulder, 1992-94. Bd. editors Empathy jour., Columbia, S.C., 1990—. Bd. dirs. Chinook Fund, Denver, 1992-94, Cmty. Shares of Colo., Denver, 1993-94; founder, pres. Equal Protection Coalition, Boulder, 1985-87. Recipient Making a Difference award Colo. Gay and Lesbian Task Force, 1990. Dean Emil Sunley award U. Denver Grad. Sch. Social Work, 1992, Susan B. Anthony award Boulder NOW, 1993; day named in her honor, Boulder, 1995. Mem. NASW.

MORGAN, LANNY, musician; b. Des Moines, Mar. 30, 1934; s. Harold Ira and Ruth (Maddick) M.; m. Marty Shelton Morgan; children: Breck, Wynter. Student, L.A. (Calif.) City Coll., 1952. instr. Stanford U. Summer Jazz Workshops, L.A. Jazz Workshop, Grove Sch. Music, Many others; guest artist, instr. at coll., high schs. throughout U.S.; played on recordings, films, TV; guest solo U.K. clubs, festivals. Played lead alto saxophone with Rey De Michele Orch., Oliver Nelson, Bill Holman Band, Bob Florence Band, Supersax; appeared, recorded Steely Dan, Natalie Cole, Diane Schurr, Shirley Horn, Andy Williams, Mel Torme, Frank Sinatra, Julie Andrews, and many others; lead quartet/quintet in L.A. With U.S. Army, 1957-59. Home: 6470 Gaviota Ave Van Nuys CA 91406-6401

MORGAN, LYNDA M., state legislator; d. Tommy and Grace (Arviso) Murphy; married; children: Kelly, Russell, Jacob. AA in Elem. Edn., U. N.Mex., Gallup, 1985; BS in Pub. Adminstrn., No. Ariz. U., 1987. Adminstrv. asst. Navajo Skill Ctr. Inc., Crownpoint, N.Mex., 1979-81, acting exec. dir., 1981-83, tng. instr., 1983-84; program mgr. Dept. Youth Svcs., Crownpoint Agy., The Navajo Nation, Crownpoint, N.Mex., 1987-89; mem. N.Mex. Ho. of Reps. Chairwoman Health, Phys., Edn. & Recreation Program Adv. Com., Gallup, N.Mex., 1988—. Home: PO Box 705 Crownpoint NM 87313-0705 Office: N Mex Ho of Reps State Capitol New Mexico State Capitol NM 87503

MORGAN, LYNN JAMES, computer engineer; b. Buffalo, Jan. 18, 1954; d. Roberta Morgan. Student, Waylan Bapt. U., Norfolk State U., Old Dominion U. Data processing technician Fed. Svc., Norfolk, Va., 1973-76, supply clk., 1977-79, computer aid, 1979, computer operator, 1979-80, computer programmer, 1981-85, computer sys. analyst, 1985-86; sr. analyst Integrated Sys. Control, Inc., Norfolk, 1986-93; sr. field engr. Tiburon Sys. Inc., Honolulu, 1993—, San Jose, Calif., 1993—. With USN, 1973. Mem. IEEE.

MORGAN, MARILYN, federal judge; b. 1947; 1 child, Terrence M. Adamson. BA, Emory U., 1969, JD, 1976. Bar: Ga. 1976, Calif. 1977. Ptnr. Morgan & Towery, San Jose, Calif., 1979-88; bankruptcy judge U.S. Bankruptcy Ct. (no. dist.) Calif., 1988—; mem. bankruptcy adv. com. U.S. Dist. Ct., 1984-88; law rep. 9th Cir. Jud. Conf., 1987-88. Mem. adv. bd. Downtown YMCA, 1984-88; dir. The Women's Fund, 1987-88. Mem. Santa Clara County Bar Assn. (chmn. debtor and creditor and insolvency com. 1979, 81, treas. 1982, pres. 1985-86), Santa Clara County Bar Assn. Law Found. (trustee 1982, 86-88, pres. 1985, law related edn. trustee 1986-88), Nat. Assn. Bankruptcy Trustees (founding mem., v.p., sec. 1981-88), Rotary Club San Jose (bd. dirs. 1992—), Nat. Assn. Bankruptcy Trustees (founder). Office: US Bankruptcy Ct 280 S 1st St Rm 3035 San Jose CA 95113-3010*

MORGAN, MARK QUENTEN, astronomer, astrophysics educator; b. Topeka, Dec. 27, 1950; s. Walter Quenten and Barbara Gene (Haynes) M. BA in Astronomy, San Diego State U., 1972; PhD in Astronomy, U. Addison, Ont., Can., 1976. Jet engine and power plant engr. N.Am. Aviation, Palmdale, Calif., 1966-68; astron. observer San Diego State U., 1970-74; engr., solar observer U. Md.-Clark Lake Radio Obs., Borrego Springs, Calif., 1978-82; engr., lectr. Sci. Atlanta, San Diego, 1979—. Inventor continuous wave laser, 1965, high intensity sound acoustic screening system, 1979. Mem. Inst. Environ. Scis., Acoustic Soc. Am., Astrophys. Soc. Am., Union Concerned Scientists, Planetary Soc. Office: Sci Atlanta PO Box 4254 San Diego CA 92164-4254

MORGAN, MEREDITH WALTER, optometrist, retired educator; b. Kingman, Ariz., Mar. 22, 1912; s. Meredith Walter and Florence (Forsyth) M.; m. Ida Marcia Engelking, Mar., 7, 1937 (dec. Nov. 1990); 1 child, Linda Morgan-Outhisack. AB, U. Calif., Berkeley, 1934, MA, 1939, PhD, 1942; DOS (hon.), Ill. Coll. Optometry, 1968; DSc, So. Calif. Coll. Optometry, 1974, Pa. Coll. Optometry, 1976, SUNY, 1989. Pvt. practice optometry Richmond, Calif., 1934-60; from instr. to prof. U. Calif., 1942-75, dean Sch. Optometry, 1960-73, prof. and dean emeritus, 1975—; vis. prof. U. Waterloo, Ont., 1974, U. Ala., Birmingham, 1977; mem. const. rev. com. USPHS, Washington, 1964-65, Nat. Adv. Coun. on Med., Dental, Optometric and Podiatric Edn., 1966-67; mem. adv. coun. Nat. Eye Inst., NIH, Washington, 1969-71; adminstrv. cons. SUNY, 1976. Author: Optics of Ophthalmic Lenses, 1978; co-editor: Vistion and Aging, 1986, rev. edit., 1993, Pediatric Optometry, 1990; contbr. articles to sci. jours. Pres., mem. West Contra Costa County YMCA, Richmond, Calif., 1940-70, Meml. Youth Ctr. Bd., Richmond, 1950-68, Union High Sch. Bd., Richmond, 1950-55, Bd. Edn., Richmond, 1954-61. Fellow Am. Acad. Optometry (life, awards com., pres. 1953-54, Prentice medal 1967); mem. Am. Optometric Assn. (Apollo medal 1975), Sons in Retirement, Rotary. Democrat. Presbyterian. Home: 1217 Skycrest Dr # 4 Walnut Creek CA 94595-1811 Office: U Calif Sch Optometry Berkeley CA 94720

MORGAN, MICHAEL BREWSTER, publishing company executive; b. L.A., Dec. 30, 1953; s. Brewster Bowen and Eleanor (Boysen) M.; m. Debra Hunter, July 20, 1986. BA, Conn. Coll., 1975. Coll. sales rep. Addison Wesley Pub. Co., Chapel Hill, N.C., 1977-81; sponsoring editor Addison Wesley Pub. Co., Reading, Mass., 1981-84; chief exec. officer Morgan Kaufmann Pubs., San Francisco, Calif., 1984—. Mem. Am. Assn. for Artificial Intelligence, Assn. for Computing Machinery. Office: Morgan Kaufmann Pubs 340 Pine St San Francisco CA 94104-3205

MORGAN, MIRIAM RAE, journalist; b. L.A., June 24, 1958; d. Irving and Vivian (Gillman) Porath; m. Richard Brent Morgan, June 20, 1970; children: Daniel, Joanna. BA, U. Calif., Berkeley, 1970; MA, U. Ariz., 1976. Tchr. Franklin Jr. H.S., Vallejo, Calif., 1971-72; tchr., newspaper advisor Canyon Del Oro H.S., Tucson, 1972-78; food writer and editor The Times, San Mateo, Calif., 1979—. Contbg. author: The Mother's Book, 1979, Gault Millau--Best of San Francisco, 1994. Vol. adv. bd. Second Harvest Food Bank, San Mateo, 1991—. Mem. Assn. Food Journalists (Writing award 1993), San Francisco Profl. Food Soc., Soc. Profl. Journalists. Office: The Times 1080 S Amphlett Blvd San Mateo CA 94402-1802

MORGAN, ROBERT HALL, lawyer; b. San Jose, Calif., Oct. 14, 1950; s. William Robert and Willa June (Hall) M.; m. Susan Kay Meyer, June 16, 1972; children: Robert Scott, Ryan William, Cory Benjamin, Nathan Thomas, Katherine Linn. BA, U. Oreg., 1974; MBA, U. Santa Clara, 1975, JD summa cum laude, 1978. Bar: Calif. 1978, U.S. Dist. Ct. (no. dist.) Calif. 1978. Legal extern Supreme Ct. Calif., San Francisco, 1978; pvt. practice law, 1978—; counsel Better Bus. Bur. Santa Clara Valley, Ltd., San Jose, 1980-86. Bd. dirs. Youth Sci. Inst., 1987-92, pres. 1990-92; prin. Morgan Law Offices. Mem. Santa Clara County Bar Assn., Assn. Trial Lawyers Am. Democrat. Office: Morgan Law Offices 1501 The Alameda San Jose CA 95126-2311

MORGAN, RONALD WILLIAM, sales executive; b. Redlands, Calif., May 9, 1951; s. Liberty W. and Eleanor L. (Creech) M.; m. Debra Ann Lein, Nov. 30, 1991. AA in Machine Shop, Valley Coll., 1973; BA in Bus., Calif. State U., San Bernardino, 1977. Sales mgr. Combined Ins., Redlands, 1976-77; ter. sales mgr. Bullard Safety, L.A., 1977-79; sales engr. H.E.S. Machine Tool, Whittier, Calif., 1979-81, Machinery Sales, L.A., 1981-89; regional mgr. Ingersoll Rand Water Jet, Yorba Linda, Calif., 1989-91; ter. sales mgr. Machinery Sales, L.A., 1991-93; dist. mgr. Ellison Machinery, L.A., 1993-94; regional mgr. Daewoo Machinery, L.A., 1995—. With USCGR. Mem. Soc. Mfg. Engrs., Sons Am. Revolution.

MORGAN, STANLEY CHARLES, plastic and reconstructive surgeon; b. Phoenix, July 23, 1935; s. Fred Charles and Hazel (King) M.; m. Doris Anne Duke, Sept. 8, 1956; children: Pamela Anne, Cheryl Lynn, Mark Thomas. BS, U. Ariz.; MD, St. Louis Sch. Medicine. Diplomate Am. Bd. Plastic Surgery. Intern UCLA Ctr. Health Svcs., 1961-62, resident plastic surgery, 1966-68; resident gen. surgery Wadsworth Vets. Hosp., L.A., 1962-66; practice medicine specializing in plastic surgery Pasadena, Calif., 1970—; asst. clin. prof. U. So. Calif. Sch. Medicine, Los Angeles, 1981—, UCLA Ctr. Health Scis., 1970-81. Lt. col. U.S. Army, 1968-70. Fellow ACS, Am. Soc. Plastic and Reconstructive Surgeons, Am. Soc. Aesthetic Plastic Surgery, Calif. Soc. Plastic Surgeons. Office: 10 Congress St Ste 407 Pasadena CA 91105-3023

MORGAN, STEPHEN CHARLES, academic administrator; b. Upland, Calif., June 2, 1946; s. Thomas Andrew and Ruth Elizabeth (Miller) M.; m. Ann Marie McMurray, Sept. 6, 1969; 1 child, Kesley Suzanne. BA, U. La Verne, 1968; MS, U. So. Calif., 1971; EdD, U. No. Colo., 1979. Devel. officer U. La Verne, Calif., 1968-71, asst. to pres., 1971-73, dir. devel., 1973-75, v.p. devel., 1975-76, pres., 1985—; dir. devel. U. So. Calif., L.A., 1976-79; exec. dir. Ind. Colls. No. Calif., San Francisco, 1979-85; dir. Ind. Colls. So. Calif., L.A., 1985—. Bd. dirs. Mt. Baldy United Way, Ontario, Calif., 1988—, McKinley Home for Children, San Dimas, Calif., 1989—; chair nat. com. on higher edn. Ch. of Brethren, Elgin, Ill., 1988-90; dir. Pomona Valley Hosp. Med. Ctr., Inter Valley Health Plan, 1992—. Mem. Assn. Ind. Calif. Colls. and Univs. (exec. com. 1989—), L.A. County Fair Assn., Western Coll. Assn. (exec. com. 1992—), Pi Gamma Mu. Home: 2518 N Mountain Ave Claremont CA 91711-1579 Office: U of LaVerne Office of Pres 1950 3rd St La Verne CA 91750-4401

MORGAN, THOMAS MICHAEL, computer software engineer; b. Pasadena, Calif., Mar. 10, 1953; s. Robert Lester and Janet Mary (Jewett) M. BS, U. So. Calif., 1975; PhD, U. Calif., Berkeley, 1982. Engr. Jet Propulsion Lab., Pasadena, Calif., 1975; software designer Rational Software Corp., Santa Clara, Calif., 1982—. Mem. IEEE, Assn. for Computing Machinery. Home: 445 Mountain Laurel Ct Mountain View CA 94043-5505 Office: Rational Software Corp 2800 San Tomas Expy Santa Clara CA 95051-0951

MORGAN, THOMAS OLIVER, bishop; b. Jan. 20, 1941; s. Charles Edwin and Amy Amelia (Hoyes) M.; m. Lillian Marie Textor, 1963; three children. BA, U. Sask., Can., 1962; BD, King's Coll., London, 1965; DD (hon.), Coll. of Emmanuel and St. Chad, Sask., 1986. Curate Ch. of the Saviour, Blackburn, Lancashire, Eng., 1966-69; rector Ch. of the Good Shepherd, Porcupine Plain, Sask., Can., 1969-73; rector Ch. of the Saviour, Kinistino, 1973-77, Shellbrook, 1977-83; Archdeacon Sask., 1983-85; bishop Diocese of Sask., Prince Albert, 1985-93, Diocese of Saskatoon, Sask., 1993—. Office: Diocese of Saskatoon, PO Box 1965, Saskatoon, SK Canada S7K 3S5

MORGAN-FADNESS, CORRINA MAY, staff charge nurse; b. Longview, Wash., Jan. 12, 1963; d. Arthur Dallas and Dorothy Irene (Ellis) Miller; 1 child, Michael Patrick. AA, Lower Columbia Coll., 1982; BSN, U. Portland, 1987. RN, Wash. Staff nurse Centralia (Wash.) Gen. Hosp., 1987; charge nurse Walker Care Ctr., Centralia, 1987-89, Park Royal Med. Ctr., Longview, Wash., 1987, 89; house supr. WHCC Riverside, Centralia, 1989-92; staff nurse Auburn (Wash.) Gen. Hosp., 1992—, Morton (Wash.) Long Term Care, 1994—, Morton (Wash.) Long-Term Care, 1994—; IV cons. on-call Evergreen Pharms., Inc., 1990—; unit mgr. Oakhurst Convalescent Ctr., Elma, Wash., 1992-93; patient care coord. Rehab. Sharon Care Ctr., Centralia, Wash., 1993—; staff nurse Morton (Wash.) Long Term Care, 1994—. Home: 403 2nd Ave NE Napavine WA 98565

MORGANROTH, MELVIN LEE, internist, educator; b. Detroit, Dec. 7, 1952; s. Ben and Grace (Greenfield) M.; m. Jacqueline Goldfaden, Aug. 30, 1990; children: Amanda, Pam, Samantha, Matthew. BS with high distinction, U. Mich., 1974, MD cum laude, 1978. Diplomate Am. Bd. Internal Medicine, Am. Bd. Pulmonary Disease, Am. Bd. Critical Care Medicine, Nat. Bd. Med. Examiners. Intern Yale U., New Haven, 1978-79, resident in medicine, 1979-81; fellow in pulmonary medicine U. Colo. Health Scis. Ctr., Denver, 1981-84; asst. prof. internal medicine div. pulmonary-critical care U. Mich. Med. Ctr., Ann Arbor, 1984-90, asst. dir. critical care medicine unit, 1984, dir., 1985-90, co-program dir. critical care fellowship tng. program, 1989-90; pvt. practice, Portland, 1990—; clin. assoc. prof. internal medicine Oreg. Health Scis. U., Portland, 1990—; reviewer Jour. Clin. Investigation, Jour. Applied Physiology, Am. Rev. Respiratory Disease, Chest, Jour. Intensive Care Medicine, Jour. Leukocyte Biology, Am. Jour. Physiology; vis. prof. med. ctrs., hosp., med. socs., univs., 1987—, incluuding Med. Coll. Ohio, Toledo, 1988, St. Louis U., 1988, Yale U., 1989, Rsch. Med. Ctr., Kansas City, Kans., 1989, Ohio Soc. Critical Care, 1990. Author: (with L.A. Boxer) Disorders of Granulocyte Function, 1987; editor: Mechanical Ventilation, 1988; contbr. numerous articles and abstracts to Am. Jour. Physiology, Conn. Medicine, Progress in Clin. and Biol. Rsch., Archives Internal Medicine, Jour. Applied Physiology, Prostaglandins, Am. Rev. Respiratory Disease, Chest, Progress in Respiratory Rsch., Lab. Investigation, Wiener Klinische Wochenschrift, Blood, Am. Jour. Pathology, Jour. Intensive Care Medicine, also others, also chpts. Grantee U. Mich., 1987, 88-89, Am. Lung Assn., 1986-88, Am. Heart Assn. Mich., 1985-92, NIH, 1985-95. Fellow Am. Coll. Chest Physicians; mem. ACP, AMA, Am. Thoracic Soc., Am. Fedn. Clin. Rsch., Am. Physiol. Soc., Cen. Soc. Clin. Rsch. (award 1988), Am. Heart Assn. (coun. on circulation), Mich. Thoracic Soc., Colo. Trudeau Soc., Phi Beta Kappa, Alpha Omega Alpha, Phi Eta Sigma. Home: 5532 SW Hamilton St Portland OR 97221-2068 Office: The Thoracic Clinic Pc 507 NE 47th Ave Portland OR 97213-2236

MORGENROTH, EARL EUGENE, entrepreneur; b. Sidney, Mont., May 7, 1936; s. Frank and Leona (Ellison) M.; m. Noella Nichols, Aug. 2, 1958; children: Dolores Roxanna, David Jonathan, Denise Christine. BS, U. Mont., 1961. From salesman to gen. mgr. Sta. KGVO-AM Radio, Missoula, Mont., 1958-65; sales mgr. Stas. KGVO-TV, KTVM-TV and KCFW-TV, Missoula, Butte, Kalispell, Mont., 1965-66, gen. mgr., 1966-68; gen. mgr. Sta. KCOY-TV, Santa Maria, Calif., 1968-69; v.p., gen. mgr. Western Broadcasting Co., Missoula, 1966-69, gen. mgr., pres., 1969-81; gen. mgr., pres. numerous cos., Mont., Calif. Idaho, P.R., Ga., 1966-84; pres., chmn. Western Broadcasting Co., Missoula, 1981-84, Western Communications, Inc., Reno, 1984-90; prin. Western Investments, Reno, 1984—; chmn. Western Fin., Inc., Morgenroth Music Ctrs., Inc., Mont., Mont. Band Instruments, Inc.; chmn. E & B Music Inc. Mem. Mont. Bank Bd., Helena; commencement speaker U. Mont., 1988; bd. dirs. U. Mont. Found., 1985—. With U.S. Army, 1954-57. Named Boss of Yr. Santa Maria Valley J.C.s, 1968. Mem. U. Mont. Century Club (pres.), Missoula C. of C. (pres.), Rocky Mountain Broadcasters Assn. (pres.), Craighad Wildlife-Wildlands Inst. (bd. dirs.), Boone and Crockett Club (bd. dirs., v.p. comm.), Grizzly Riders Internat. (bd. dirs., v.p.). Republican. Methodist. Home: 3525 Brighton Way Reno NV 89509-3871

MORGENSEN, JERRY LYNN, construction company executive; b. Lubbock, Tex., July 9, 1942; s. J.J. and Zelline (Butler) M.; m. Linda Dee Austin, Apr. 17, 1965; children: Angela, Nicole. BCE, Tex. Tech U., 1965. Area engr. E.I. Dupont Co., Orange, Tex., 1965-67; div. engr. E.I. Dupont Co., La Place, La., 1967-73; project mgr. Hensel Phelps Constrn. Co., Greeley, Colo., 1973-78, area mgr., 1978-80, v.p., 1980-85, pres., 1985—. Office: Hensel Phelps Constrn Co 420 Sixth Ave PO Box O Greeley CO 80632*

MORGENSTERN, LEON, surgeon; b. Pitts., July 14, 1919; s. Max Samuel and Sarah (Master) M.; m. Laurie Mattlin, Nov. 27, 1967; 1 son, David Ethan. Student, CCNY, 1936-37; B.A. magna cum laude, Bklyn. Coll., 1940; M.D., N.Y. U., 1943. Diplomate: Am. Bd. Surgery. Intern Queens Gen. Hosp., Jamaica, N.Y., 1943-44; fellow, asst. resident in pathology Queens Gen. Hosp., 1947-48, resident in surgery, 1948-52; practice medicine, specializing in surgery Los Angeles, 1953-59, 60—, Bronx, N.Y., 1959-60; dir. surgery Cedars of Lebanon Hosp., Los Angeles, 1960-73; dir. surgery Cedars-Sinai Med. Center, Los Angeles, 1973-88, emeritus dir. surgery, 1989—; dir. Bioethics Program Cedars-Sinai Med. Ctr., L.A., 1995—; clin. prof. surgery UCLA Sch. Medicine, 1973-85, prof. in residence, 1985—; asst. prof. surgery Albert Einstein Coll. Medicine, N.Y.C., 1959-60. Assoc. editor Mount Sinai Jour. Medicine, 1984-88; contbr. articles to profl. publs. Served to capt. M.C. U.S. Army, 1944-46. Mem. Soc. for Surgery Alimentary Tract, Soc. Am. Gastrointestinal Endoscopic Surgeons (hon.), Am. Gastroent. Assn., L.A. Surg. Soc. (pres. 1977), ACS (sec.-treas. 1976-77, pres. 1978, bd. dirs. So. Calif. chpt. 1976-78, gov.-at-large), Internat. Soc. Surgery, Western Surg. Assn., Pacific Coast Surg. Assn., AMA, Calif. Med. Assn., Los Angeles County Med. Assn., Am. Surg. Assn., others. Home: 5694 Calpine Dr Malibu CA 90265-3812

MORGENSTERN, NORBERT RUBIN, civil engineering educator; b. Toronto, Ont., Can., May 25, 1935; s. Joel and Bella (Skornik) M.; m. Patricia Elizabeth Gooderham, Dec. 28, 1960; children: Sarah Alexandra, Katherine Victoria, David Michael Gooderham. BASc, U. Toronto, 1956, DEng h.c., 1983; DIC, Imperial Coll. Sci., 1964; PhD, U. London, 1964; DSc h.c., Queen's U., 1989. Research asst., lectr. civil engring. Imperial Coll. Sci. and Tech., London, 1958-68; prof. civil engring. U. Alta., Edmonton, Can., 1968-83, Univ. prof., 1983—, chair dept. civil engring., 1994—; cons. engr., 1961—. Contbr. articles to profl. jours. Bd. dirs. Young Naturalists Found., 1977-82, Edmonton Symphony Soc., 1978-85. Athlone fellow, 1956; recipient prize Brit. Geotech. Soc., 1961, 66, Huber prize ASCE, 1971, Legget award Can. Geotech. Soc., 1979, Alta. order of Excellence, 1991. Fellow Royal Soc. Can., Can. Acad. Engring.; mem. U.S. Nat. Acad. Engring. (fgn. assoc.), Cancian Geosci. Coun. (pres. 1983), Can. Geotechnical Soc. (pres. 1989-91), Internat. Soc. for Soil Mechanics and Found. Engring. (pres. 1989-94), Royal Glenora Club, Athenaeum (London), various other profl. assns. Home: 106 Laurier Dr, Edmonton, AB Canada T5R 5P6 Office: U Alta, Edmonton, AB Canada T6G 2G7

MORGENTHALER, ALISA MARIE, lawyer; b. St. Louis, June 3, 1960; d. Gerald Thomas and Mary Louise (Neece) M. BA, S.W. Mo. State U., 1982; JD, Cornell U., 1985. Bar: N.Y. 1986, D.C. 1988, Calif. 1990. Law clk. City of Springfield, Mo., 1981; bd. govs. FRS, Washington, 1984; staff atty. Fed. Res. System, Washington, 1985-86; assoc. Kirkpatrick & Lockhart, Washington, 1986-88, Stroock & Stroock & Lavan, Washington, 1988-89, Christensen, White, Miller, Fink & Jacobs, L.A., 1989—. Mem. ABA, Calif. Bar Assn., D.C. Bar Assn., N.Y. Bar Assn., Los Angeles County Bar Assn., Beverly Hills Bar Assn., Century City Bar Assn., Order of Omega, Phi Alpha Delta, Rho Lambda, Phi Kappa Phi, Pi Sigma Alpha, Gamma Phi Beta. Office: Christensen White Miller Fink & Jacobs 2121 Avenue Of The Stars Fl 18 Los Angeles CA 90067-5010

MORGENTHALER, JOHN HERBERT, chemical engineer; b. Cleve., Jan. 5, 1929; s. Frederick Herman and Anna Margarethe (Welke) M.; m. Kathleen Ann Merriman, June 23, 1956 (dec. Oct. 1986); children: John David, Jennifer Ann, Jeffrey Paul; m. Susan Kay Braaten, Dec. 27,

1988. SB, MIT, 1951, SM, 1952; PhD, U. Md., 1965. Group leader Procter & Gamble Co., Cin., 1954-58; project mgr. Atlantic Rsch. Corp., Alexandria, Va., 1958-62; sr. staff engr. Applied Physics Lab. Johns Hopkins U., Silver Spring, Md., 1962-65; project scientist Marquardt's Gen. Applied Sci. Labs., Westbury, N.Y., 1965-67; rsch. dir. Textron's Bell Aerospace Co., Buffalo, 1967-74; sect. mgr. Stauffer Chem. Co., Richmond, Calif., 1974-77; mgr. comml. ventures Bechtel Corp., San Francisco, 1977-78; pres. JHM Assocs., Tacoma, Wash., 1978—; cons. Moore Rsch. Labs., Inc., Bethesda, Md., 1959-65; mem. adv. bd. U. Tenn. Space Inst., Tullahoma, 1967-68, Assn. Bay Area Govts., Oakland, Calif., 1976-77; chmn. membership com. Nat. Capitol sect. Am. Inst. Chem. Engrs., 1959-61; treas. Buffalo sect. AIAA, 1974. Contbr. articles to Internat. Jour. Heat and Mass Transfer, Jour. Fluids Engring., Jour. Spacecraft and Rockets. Chmn. Joe Berg Sci. Soc., Niagara Falls, N.Y., 1967-71, com. chair Lewiston (N.Y.) Cub Scouts., 1970-71, Walnut Creek (Calif.) Boy Scouts, 1980-82; v.p. Homeowners Assn., Walnut Creek, 1983-85. 1st lt. chem. corps U.S. Army, 1952-54. Scholar Westinghouse Corp., 1947, MIT, 1947-51. Mem. AAAS, Elks, Sigma Xi, Kappa Kappa Sigma (hon.). Republican. Unitarian. Home and Office: 46 Bonney St Steilacoom WA 98388-1502

MORGRIDGE, HOWARD HENRY, architect; b. Pasadena, Calif., May 29, 1919; s. George Burton and Hazel (Hill) M.; m. Alice C. Best, Feb. 1, 1947; children: Sarah, Susan, Shan. BArch, U. So. Calif., 1942. Registered architect, Calif. Ptnr. Marsh, Smith & Powell, Los Angeles, 1947-55, Smith, Powell & Morgridge, Los Angeles, 1955-65; pres. Powell, Morgridge, Richards & Coghlan, Inc., Los Angeles, 1965-72, Morgridge, Bader, Richards & Coghlan, Inc., Los Angeles and Newport Beach, Calif., 1972-78; pres. Howard H. Morgridge FAIA & Assoc., Inc., Tustin, Calif., 1978-86, Balboa, Calif., 1987—, pres. Calif. State Bd. Archtl. Examiners, Sacramento, 1975. Paintings exhibited Stary-Sheets Fine Arts Galleries, Irvine, Calif. Bd. dirs. Pasadena Beautiful, 1965-71; bd. dirs. Planning and Conservation League, San Francisco, 1968-70; mem. art commn. City of Newport Beach, Calif., 1975-77; chmn., exec. com. Nat. Council Archtl. Regulatory Bds. Western States, 1975-76. Served with U.S. Army, 1944-46, PTO. Artist watercolor landscape permanent collection displayed City of Newport Beach Art Festival, Purchase award, 1985, 86. Fellow AIA (pres. so. Calif. chpt. 1963, pres. Calif. council 1967, 1st Honor award 1949, 54). Republican. Congregationalist. Clubs: Newport Harbor, Yacht (Newport Beach). Office: Howard H Morgridge & Assocs 919 Bayside Dr Apt A2 Newport Beach CA 92660-7407

MORI, ALLEN ANTHONY, university dean, consultant, researcher; b. Hazleton, Pa., Nov. 1, 1947; s. Primo Philip and Carmella (DeNoia) M.; m. Barbara Epoca, June 26, 1971; 1 child, Kirsten Lynn. BA, Franklin and Marshall Coll., Lancaster, Pa., 1969; MEd, Bloomsburg U. Pa., 1971; PhD, U. Pitts., 1975. Spl. edn. tchr. White Haven (Pa.) State Sch. and Hosp., 1969-70, Hazleton Area Sch. Dist., 1970-71, Pitts. Pub. Schs., 1971-74; supr. student tchrs. U. Pitts., 1974-75; prof. spl. edn. U. Nev., Las Vegas, 1975-84; dean coll edn. Marshall U., Huntington, W.Va., 1984-87; dean sch. edn. Calif. State U., L.A., 1987—; hearing officer pub. law 94-142 Nev. Dept. Edn., Carson City, 1978—; mem. Nev. Gov.'s Com. on Mental Health and Mental Retardation, 1983-84; cons. Ministry Edn., Manitoba, Can., 1980-82; pres. Tchr. Edn. Coun. State Colls. and Univs., 1993-94. Author: Families of Children with Special Needs, 1983; co-author: Teaching the Severely Retarded, 1980, Handbook of Preschool, Special Education, 1980, Adapted Physical Education, 1983, A Vocational Training Continuum for the Mentally and Physically Disabled, 1985, Teaching Secondary Students with Mild Learning and Behavior Problems, 1986, 93; contbr. numerous articles, book revs. and monographs to profl. jours. Bd. dirs. Assn. Retarded Citizens San Gabriel Valley, ElMonte, 1989-94. Recipient grants U.S. Dept. Edn., 1976-91, Nev. Dept. Edn., W.Va. Dept. Edn., Calif. State U. Chancellor's Office. Mem. Assn. Tchr. Educators, Coun. for Exceptional Children (div. on Career Devel. exec. com. 1981-83), Nat. Soc. for Study of Edn., Kiwanis, Phi Beta Delta, Phi Delta Kappa, Pi Lambda Theta. Office: Calif State U 5151 State University Dr Los Angeles CA 90032-4221

MORIARTY, BRUCE JOSEPH, oil industry executive; b. Stamford, Conn., Mar. 19, 1950; s. William James and Eileen Marie (Nevins) M.; m. Cynthia Barbara Carey, Dec. 16, 1989; 1 child, Laura Frances. BA cum laude, Colgate U., 1972; postgrad., U. S.C., 1972. Sr. geophysicist Vinocon, Inc., Brookfield, Conn., 1978-81; processing geophysicist Sefel Geophysical, Denver, 1981-82; v.p. Grundy, Moriarty & Assoc., Denver, 1982-87; v.p. exploration New Zealand O & G Inc., Denver, 1988-92, Kiwi Am. Energy, Inc., Denver, 1992—; pres. Digitec Seismic Inc., Denver, 1993—. Contbr. papers to books and jours. Mem. Am. Assn. Petroleum Geologists (cert. petroleum geologist), Soc. Exploration Geophysicists (bd. mem. 1985), Denver Geophys. Soc. (continuing edn. chmn. 1983-85, pres. 1985), Rocky Mountain Assn. Geologists. Home: 11863 W 84th Pl Arvada CO 80005-5161 Office: Kiwi Am Energy Inc 6401 N Broadway Unit T Denver CO 80221

MORIARTY, DONALD PETER, II, engineering executive, military officer; b. Alexandria, La., Jan. 26, 1935; s. Donald P. and Catherine G. (Stafford) M.; children by previous marriage: Erin, Donald P. III; m. Diana Mary Blackburn, Feb. 4, 1984. BS, La. State U., 1957; MA, Fla. Atlantic U., 1973; diploma, U.S Army Comdr. and Gen. Staff Coll., 1977. Commd. 2d lt. U.S. Army, 1957, advanced through grades to lt. col., 1978; artillery officer U.S. Army, various, 1957-74; head tactical plans sect. Army Air Def. Command, Darmstadt, Federal Republic of Germany, 1975-77; dir. C3I divsn. Army Air Def. Ctr., Ft. Bliss, Tex., 1977-80; retired Army Air Def. Ctr., 1980; sr. system engr. Hughes Aircraft Co., Fullerton, Calif., 1980-82, mgr. engr. design dept., 1982-84, project mgr., 1984-90; mgr. advanced systems programs, 1990--; U.S. Army Rep. to Tactical Airpower Com. NATO hdqrs., Brussels, 1977-79, Tri-Service Group on Air Def., NATO, 1978-80, Air Def. Electronic Equipment Com., NATO, 1978-80; lead systems engr. Hughes Aircraft Co., Fullerton, 1980-83; Strategic Def. Initiative Program Coordinator Systems Divsn. Hughes Aircraft Co., 1985-87; mgr. Tac Def. and Tac Command Control Program, Systems Divsn., GSG, Hughes Aircraft Co., 1987—. Author: The U.S. Army Officer as Military Statesman, 1973; author genealogical articles. Parade chmn. South Fla. Fair Assn., West Palm Beach, 1971; staff commr. Boy Scouts Am., Kaiserslautern, Fed. Republic of Germany, 1974-76; sr. warden Episcopal Ch., Kaiserslautern, 1975, Wiesbaden, Fed. Republic of Germany, 1977, Placentia, Calif., 1985-88; pres. Episcopal Synod of Am., 1993—; nat. trustee St. Jude's Ranch for Children, 1994—. Decorated Vietnamese Cross of Gallantry with Palm, Air medal with two oak leaf clusters, Bronze Star with one oak leaf cluster, Legion of Merit; recipient Wood Badge award Boy Scouts Am., Newburgh, N.Y., 1969. Fellow Am. Coll. Genealogists; mem. AIAA, Assn. U.S. Army, Armed Forces Com.-Elect Assn., Am. Electronics Assn., SAR, Gen. Soc. Mayflower Descendants, Phi Alpha Theta, Acacia. Republican. Home: 626 E Riverview Ave Orange CA 92665-1336 Office: Hughes Aircraft Co 2175 Park Pl El Segundo CA 90245

MORIARTY, JOHN, opera administrator, artistic director; b. Fall River, Mass., Sept. 30, 1930; s. John J. and Fabiola Marie (Ripeau) M. MusB summa cum laude, New Eng. Conservatory, 1952; D.M. New England Conservatory, 1992. Artistic adminstr. Opera Soc. of Washington, 1960-62, Santa Fe Opera, N.Mex., 1962-65; dir. Wolf Trap Co., Vienna, Va., 1972-77; chmn. opera dept. Boston Conservatory , 1973-89; chmn. opera dept. New Eng. Conservatory, 1989—; prin. condr. Central City Opera, Denver, 1978—, artistic dir., 1982—; panelist Nat. Inst. Music Theater, 1985, 86, 87, Conn. Arts Council, 1982, 84; adjudicator various contests including Met. Opera auditions, 1965—. Author: Diction, 1975. Trustee Boston Concert Opera. Recipient Frank Huntington Beebe award, Boston, 1954, Disting. Alumni award New Eng. Conservatory Alumni Assn., 1982, Gold Chair award Cen. City Opera House Assn., 1988. Mem. Nat. Opera Assn., Sigma Alpha Iota, Delta Omicron, Pi Kappa Lambda. Office: New Eng Conservatory 290 Huntington Ave Boston MA 02115-5018 also: Cen City Opera House Assn 621 17th St Ste 1601 Denver CO 80293-1601

MORIE, G. GLEN, manufacturing company executive, corporate lawyer. BA, Bowdoin Coll., 1964; LLB, U. Pa., 1967. Bar: Wash. 1968. Pvt. practice law Wash., 1970-73; asst. counsel PACCAR, Inc., Bellevue, Wash., 1973-79, asst. gen. counsel, 1979-82, gen. counsel, 1983-85, v.p., gen. counsel, corp. sec., 1985—. Office: PACCAR Inc PO Box 1518 Bellevue WA 98009-1518

MORIKAWA, TOM, political science educator; b. Gunma, Japan, Dec. 21, 1955; came to U.S., 1982; m. Yukiko Morikawa, Dec. 16, 1980; 1 child, Kazan. BA in pol. sci., Waseda U., Tokyo, 1979; MA in pol. sci., Boston U., 1984; MA in internat. studies, U. Oregon, 1993, PhD in pol. sci., 1993. Program officer United Nations Devel. Programme, N.Y., 1988-90; adviser Permanent Mission of Japan to the United Nations, N.Y., 1990-92; instr. Oreg. State U., Corvallis, 1993; asst. prof. Lewis-Clark State Coll., Lewiston, Idaho, 1993—, dir. Pacific Rim studies program, 1993—. Author: Internal Procedures Manual for the United Nations Revolving Fund for Natural Resources Exploration, 1990. Mem. Am. Pol. Sci. Assn., Pi Gamma Mu. Office: Lewis-Clark State Coll Social Scis Div Lewiston ID 83501

MORIMOTO, CARL NOBORU, computer system engineer, crystallographer; b. Hiroshima, Japan, Mar. 31, 1942; came to U.S., 1957, naturalized, 1965; s. Toshiyuki and Teruko (Hirano) M.; m. Helen Kiyomi Yoshizaki, June 28, 1969; children: Matthew Ken, Justin Ray. BA, U. Hawaii, 1965; PhD, U. Wash., 1970. Research assoc. dept. chemistry Mich. State U., East Lansing, 1970-72; postdoctoral fellow dept. biochemistry and biophysics Tex. A&M U., College Station, 1972-75; sr. sci. programmer Syntex Analytical Instruments Inc., Cupertino, Calif., 1975-78; prin. programmer analyst, software engring. mgr. Control Data Corp., Sunnyvale, Calif., 1978-83; mem. profl. staff GE Aerospace, San Jose, Calif., 1983-93; prin. engr. GE Nuclear Energy, San Jose, 1993—. Mem. Am. Crystallographic Assn., Assn. Computing Machinery, Am. Chem. Soc., Sigma Xi. Am. Baptist. Home: 4003 Hamilton Park Dr San Jose CA 95130-1223

MORIN, ROBERT WARNER, civil engineer; b. Middletown, Conn., Dec. 23, 1959; s. Robert Richard Morin and Charlotte (Carlson) Stetson; m. Leah Marie Jacoby, Apr. 10, 1986; children: Amanda Sue, Robert Thomas. AS, Hartford State Tech. Coll., 1980; BS, Lawrence Inst. Technology, Detroit, 1984. Registered profl. civil engr., Calif. Project mgr. Long Beach (Calif.) Naval Shipyard, 1984-86; asst. civil engr. The City of Oceanside, Calif., 1986-88, assoc. civil engr., 1988—. Mem. Am. Pub. Works Assn. Republican. Mem. Christian Ch. Home: 30378 Red River Cir Temecula CA 92591-3868 Office: The City of Oceanside 300 N Hill St Oceanside CA 92054-2824

MORITA, JOHN TAKAMI, artist; b. Honolulu, Apr. 10, 1943; s. Takaichi and Miyako (Shiraishi) M. BA in History, Chaminade Coll., Honolulu, 1965; BFA in Photography, San Francisco Art Inst., 1974; MA in Printmaking, San Francisco State U., 1976. Lectr. in art U. Hawaii-Manoa, Honolulu, 1982-83, Windward C.C., Kaneohe, Hawaii, 1991-92. Exhibited in one-man shows at Galerie Marina Dinkler, Berlin, 1978, San Francisco Mus. Modern Art, 1979, Contemporary Art Ctr., Honolulu, 1982, Soker/Kaseman Gallery, San Francisco, 1983, Alternative Mus., N.Y.C., 1987, Intergrafic 90, Berlin, 1990, Print Club, Phila., 1990, Honolulu Acad. Arts, 1977; group exhbns. include Intergrakif, Berlin, 1984, 87, 90, Alternative Mus., N.Y.C., 1988, 90, 91, Wakayama Internat. Print Biennial, Japan, 1989, 93, Varna (Bulgaria) Internat. Print Biennale, 1991-93; represented in collections. Bd. dirs., mem. program adv. bd. Kapiolani C.C., Honolulu, 1992-94. Served with U.S. Army, 1966-69, West Germany. Recipient 1st prize Internat. Print Triennial, Berlin, 1987, Print Club Selection award Print Club, Phila., 1988; NEA fellow in printmaking, 1986, other awards. Mem. Honolulu Printmaking Workshop (bd. dirs. 1992-94, v.p. 1994—), N.W. Print Coun., L.A. Printmaking Soc. Democrat. Home: 1640 Ahihi St Honolulu HI 96819-3773

MORITA, TOSHIYASU, technical institute administrator; b. Boerne, Tex., Feb. 8, 1967; s. Hiroshi and Fusako (Ishikawa) M. Grad. high sch., 1985. Programmer Origin Systems, Inc., Austin, Tex., 1987; engr. Cyclops Electronics, Boerne, 1988-90; programmer Taito R&D, Bothell, Wash., 1990; mgr. new tech. Lucas Arts Entertainment, San Rafael, Calif., 1990-93; tech. dir. Sega Tech. Inst., Redwood City, Calif., 1993-94, Sega of Am., Redwood City, 1994—. Mem. IEEE Computer Soc. (affiliate), Mensa.

MORITZ, TIMOTHY BOVIE, psychiatrist; b. Portsmouth, Ohio, July 26, 1936; s. Charles Raymond and Elisabeth Bovie (Morgan) M.; m. Joyce Elizabeth Rasmussen, Oct. 13, 1962 (div. Sept. 1969); children: Elizabeth Wynne, Laura Morgan; m. Antoinette Tanasichuk, Oct. 31, 1981; children: David Michael, Stephanie Lysbeth. BA, Ohio State U., 1959; MD, Cornell U., 1963. Diplomate Am. Bd. Psychiatry and Neurology. Intern in medicine N.Y. Hosp., N.Y.C., 1963-64, resident in psychiatry, 1964-67; spl. asst. to dir. NIMH, Bethesda, Md., 1967-69; dir. Community Mental Health Ctr., Rockland County, N.Y., 1970-74, Ohio Dept. Mental Health, Columbus, Ohio, 1975-81; med. dir. psychiatry Miami Valley Hosp., Dayton, Ohio, 1981-82; med. dir. N.E. Ga. Community Mental Health Ctr., Athens, Ga., 1982-83, Charter Vista Hosp., Fayetteville, Ark., 1983-87; clin. dir. adult psychiatry Charter Hosp., Las Vegas, Nev., 1987—; pvt. practice psychiatry Las Vegas, Nev., 1987—; prof. Wright State U., Dayton, Ohio, 1981-82; asst. prof. Cornell U., N.Y.C., 1970-73; cons. NIMH, Rockville, Md., 1973-83. Author: (chpt.) Rehabilitation Medicine and Psychiatry, 1976; mem. editorial bd. Directions in Psychiatry, 1981—. Dir. dept. mental health and mental retardation Gov.'s Cabinet, State of Ohio, Columbus, 1975-81. Recipient Svc. award Ohio Senate, 1981, Svc. Achievement award Ohio Gov., 1981. Fellow Am. Psychiat. Assn. (Disting. Svc. award 1981); mem. AMA, Nev. Assn. Psychiat. Physicians, Nev. State Med. Assn., Clark County Med. Soc., Cornell U. Med. Coll. Alumni Assn. Office: Timothy B Moritz MD 3815 S Jones Blvd # 7 Las Vegas NV 89103-2289

MORIZUMI, SHIGENORI JAMES, applied mathematician; b. San Francisco, Nov. 13, 1923; s. Mohei and Hatsue (Kawaharada) M.; m. Hiroko Kimura, Nov. 20, 1956; 1 child, Miachel N. BS, U. Calif., Berkeley, 1955; MS, Calif. Inst. Tech., 1957; PhD, UCLA, 1970. Sr. aerodynamicist Douglas Aircraft, Santa Monica, Calif., 1955-60; sr. staff engr. TRW Space Tech. Lab., Redondo Beach, Calif., 1960-81; dir. HR-Textron, Irvine, Calif., 1981-82; sr. scientist Hughes Aircraft, El Segundo, Calif., 1982-89. Author: An Investigation of Infrared Radiation by Vibration-Rotation Bands of Molecular Gases, 1970; speaker, presenter in field; contbr. articles to AIAA Jour., Jour. of Quantitative Spectroscopy and Radiative Transfer, Jour. of Spacecraft and Rockets. Mem. Sigma Xi. Home: 29339 Stadia Hill Ln Palos Verdes Estates CA 90274

MORK, DANIEL NEIL, biologist, councilman; b. Seattle, July 13, 1957; s. Barry Vincent and Lee Arlene (McLauchlan) M.; m. Kathryn Lynn Farnham Mork, June 2, 1977; children: Seth Daniel, Sara Kathryn. BS, Ecotun Washington U., 1987. Applicator CI2M, Spokine, Wash., 1975-77, Acoustical Spray and Fireproofing, Spokane, Wash., 1977-79; biologist Bayer Corp, Spokane, Wash., 1979—; dir., v.p. Indsl. Devel. Corp., Spokane, Wash., 1984—. Pres. Zion Luth. Ch., Spokane, Wash., 1994-95. Mem. Internat. Soc. Particle Engr., Spokane Tennis Assn. Republican. Lutheran. Office: Miles Allergy Products 3525 N Regal St Spokane WA 99207-5788

MORLOCK, WALTER O'MALLEY, marketing professional; b. Aurora, Ill., Mar. 22, 1965; s. David and Katherine (O'Malley) M.; m. Kirsten K. Stone, Sept. 1, 1990. Grad., N. Ctrl. Coll., 1987. Mktg. dir. Paramount Arts Ctr., Aurora, 1989-92, Cerritos (Calif.) Ctr. for Performing Arts, 1992—. Mem. Internat. Soc. Performing Arts Adminstrs., Am. Mktg. Assn., Assn. Performing Arts Presenters, Western Assn. Arts Adminstrs. Office: Cerritos Ctr Performing Art 12700 Center Court Dr S Cerritos CA 90701-4552

MORONEY, MICHAEL JOHN, lawyer; b. Jamaica, N.Y., Nov. 8, 1940; s. Everard Vincent and Margaret Olga (Olson) M.; children: Sean, Megan, Matthew. BS in Polit. Sci., Villanova U., 1962; JD, Fordham U., 1965; Police Sci. (hon.), U. Guam, 1976. Bar: Hawaii 1974, U.S. Dist. Ct. Hawaii 1974, U.S. Ct. Appeals (9th cir.) 1974, Guam 1976, U.S. Dist. Ct. (Guam dist.) 1976, U.S. Ct. Claims 1976, U.S. Tax Ct. 1976, U.S. Ct. Mil. Appeals 1977, U.S. Supreme Ct. 1977, High Ct. Trust Ters. 1977, U.S. Dist. Ct. (No. Mariana Islands) 1983. Spl. agt. FBI, Memphis and Nashville, 1965-67, Cleve. and Elyria, Ohio, 1967-71; spl. agt., prin. legal advisor FBI, U.S. Dept. Justice, Honolulu, 1971—; bar examiner and applications rev. com. Supreme Ct. Hawaii, 1980—; pres. Hawaii State Law Enforcement Adminstrn., 1985-86; mem. and del. to congress Gov.'s Task Force on Hawaii's Internat. Role, 1988. Mem. gov.'s task force, del. gov.'s congress on Hawaii's Internat. Role, 1988—. Recipient Govs. Award for Outstanding Contbns. to Law Enforcement, Gov. of Guam, 1974, 76, cert. of appreciation Supreme Ct. Hawaii, 1981, cert. of appreciation Honolulu Police Commn., 1984, 86; named Fed. Law Enforcement Officer of Yr., State of Hawaii, 1992. Mem. ABA, Fed. Bar Assn., Hawaii Bar Assn., Guam Bar Assn., Assn. Trial Lawyers Am., Inst. Jud. Adminstrn., Hawaii State Law Enforcement Ofcls. Assn. (law enforcement officer of yr. 1992), Internat. Assn. Chiefs of Police, Hilo Yacht Club. Address: 7858 Makaaoa Pl Honolulu HI 96825-2848 Office: US Dept Justice PO Box 50164 Honolulu HI 96850

MOROZ, ANDREW, chemical engineer; b. Warsaw, Poland, Sept. 13, 1949; came to U.S., 1988; s. Wlodzimierz and Nina (Karmelit) M.; m. Eva Anna Paczesna, Feb. 15, 1975 (div. June 20, 1987); children: Sylvia, Anna; m. Bozena Krystyna Bekasiewicz, Nov. 21, 1987. BSChemE, Poly. Warsaw, 1973; MSChemE, Tech. U., Lodz, Poland, 1977. Prof. asst. Poly. Warsaw, 1971-73; rsch. engr., lab supr. Polski Fiat/Fiat Corp., Warsaw, 1973-83; prodn. mgr. Poltrade Fgn. Trade Co., Warsaw, 1983-87; pilot plant supr. Borzynski Rsch. Inst., Houston, 1987-90; chief chemist Appropriate Technologies II, Chula Vista, Calif., 1990-92; lab dir. Southland Labs, Inc., National City, Calif., 1992-94; prin. Andrew Moroz Consulting, San Diego, 1992-94; Moroz Labs., Inc., San Diego, 1994—; cons. Polcargo, Warsaw, 1977-81; gen. dir. advisor Polski Fiat, Warsaw, 1981; vis. scientist Bayer Rsch. Ctr., Leverkusen, Germany, 1979, Fiat Rsch. Ctr., Torino, Italy, 1980. Contbr. articles to profl. jours. Pres. Solidarnośc, Warsaw, 1980-81; v.p. Auto Club SKM, Warsaw, 1976-80. Mem. Am. Chem. Soc. Democrat. Roman Catholic. Home and Office: 1242 River Glen Row Apt 39 San Diego CA 92111-7414

MORRELL, JUNE ELIZABETH, elementary educator; b. Yakima, Wash., June 20, 1925; d. Robert Enoch Faw and Birdie Ethel Nead; m. Lawrence Reed Morrell, June 22, 1947; 1 child, Janice Ellen. BA in Edn., Ea. Wash. U., 1969. Tchr. Twisp (Wash.) Pub. Sch., 1969-70; substitute tchr. Springdale and Loon Lake (Wash.) pub. schs., 1971-73; tchr. presch. June's Pre-sch., Springdale, Wash., 1979-81; prin., tchr. Camas Valley Christian Sch., Springdale, 1981—. Home: 4972 Bowler Rd Springdale WA 99173-9726

MORRELLI, GINO J., yacht designer; b. El Paso, Tex., Mar. 19, 1957; s. George Wes and Carlene A. (Bachechi) M.; m. Laura A. Fitzpatrick, Sept. 6, 1988; children: Giovanni, Renetta. Diploma, Univ. H.S., Irvine, Calif., 1975. Sailmaker Reynolds Sails, Newport Beach, Calif., 1975-76; mem. staff parts dept. Hobie Cat, Irvine, 1976-77; owner Climax Catamarans, Huntington Beach, Calif., 1977-81; 1st mate charter cat Hyatt Regency, Maui, Hawaii, 1981-82; owner Morrelli Design, Huntington Beach, 1982-92; ptnr. Morrelli & Melvin Design & Engring., Newport Beach, 1992—; mem. crews for numerous yachting races, 1984—. Designer Stars & Strips yacht (winner Am.'s Cup, 1988), numerous others. Mem. Ocean Racing Catamaran Assn., U.S. Sailing (PHRF multi hull rating chair 1993—). Office: Morrelli & Melvin Design& Engring 177 Riverside Ave Newport Beach CA 92663-4032

MORRIN, THOMAS HARVEY, engineering research company executive; b. Woodland, Calif., Nov. 24, 1914; s. Thomas E. and Florence J. (Hill) M.; m. Frances M. Von Ahn, Feb. 1, 1941; children: Thomas H., Diane, Linda, Denise. BS, U. Calif., 1937; grad., U.S. Navy Grad. Sch., Annapolis, Md., 1941. Student engr. Westinghouse Electric Mfg. Co., Emeryville, Calif., 1937; elec. engr. Pacific Gas & Electric Co., 1938-41; head microwave engring. div. Raytheon Mfg. Co., Waltham, Mass., 1947-48; chmn. elec. engring. dept. Stanford Research Inst., 1948-52, dir. engring., research, 1952-60, gen. mgr. engring., 1960-64, vice pres. engring., sci., 1964-68; pres. University City Sci. Inst., Phila., 1968-69; pres., chmn. bd. Morrin Assos., Inc., Wenatchee, Wash., 1968-72. Trustee Am. Acad. Transp. Served as officer USNR, 1938-58, comdr. USN, 1945-48. Decorated Bronze Star; recipient Bank Am. award for automation of banking during 1950's, 1992. Fellow IEEE, AAAS; mem. Sci. Research Soc. Am., U.S. Naval Inst., Navy League, Marine Meml. Club (San Francisco). Address: 654 23rd Ave San Francisco CA 94121-3709

MORRIN, VIRGINIA WHITE, retired educator; b. Escondido, Calif., May 16, 1913; d. Harry Parmalee and Ethel Norine (Nutting) Rising; BS, Oreg. State Coll., 1952; MEd, Oreg. State U., 1957; m. Raymond Bennett White, 1933 (dec. 1953); children: Katherine Anne, Marjorie Virginia, William Raymond; m. 2d, Laurence Morrin, 1959 (dec. 1972). Social caseworker Los Angeles County, Los Angeles, 1934-40, 61-64; acctg. clk. War Dept., Ft. MacArthur, Calif., 1940-42; prin. clk. USAAF, Las Vegas, Nev., 1942-44; high sch. tchr., North Bend-Coos Bay, Oreg., 1952-56, Mojave, Calif., 1957-60; instr. Antelope Valley Coll., Lancaster, Calif., 1961-73; ret., 1974. Treas., Humane Soc. Antelope Valley, Inc., 1968—. Mem. Nat. Aero. Assn., Calif. State Sheriffs' Assn. (charter assoc.), Oreg. State U. Alumni Assn. (life). Address: 3153 Milton Dr Mojave CA 93501-1329

MORRIS, ALVIN LEE, retired consulting corporation executive, meteorologist; b. Kim, Colo., June 7, 1920; s. Roy E. and Eva Edna (James) M.; BS in Meteorology (U.S. Weather Bur. fellow), U. Chgo., 1942; MS, U.S. Navy Postgrad. Sch., 1954; m. Nadean Davidson, Jan. 16, 1979; children: Andrew N., Nancy L., Mildred M., Ann E., Jane C. Meteorologist Pacific Gas and Electric Co., San Francisco, 1947-50; commd. U.S. Navy, 1942, advanced through grades to capt., USNR, 1962, assignments including staff, comdr. 7th Fleet; dir. rsch. Navy Weather Research Facility, Norfolk, Va., 1958-62; facilities coord., mgr. sci. balloon facility, Nat. Ctr. for Atmospheric Rsch. Boulder, Colo., 1963-75; pres. Ambient Analysis Inc., Internat. Cons., Boulder, 1975-86. Treas. Home Hospitality for Fgn. Students Program, U. Colo., 1969-70; del. People to People Del. on Environment; Peoples Republic of China, 1984. Served with USN, 1942-46, 50-58. Mem. Am. Meteorol. Soc. (cert. cons. meteorologist), Am. Geophys. Union, ASTM, Ret. Officers Assn., N.Y. Acad. Scis., The Planetary Soc., Boulder County Knife and Fork Club. Editor Handbook of Scientific Ballooning, 1975; assoc. editor Jour. Oceanic and Atmospheric Tech., 1984-88; contbr. articles to profl. jours.; convenor, editor proceedings ASTM conf. Home: 880 Sunshine Canyon Dr Boulder CO 80302-9727

MORRIS, BRUCE DORIAN, technical writer, scholar, educator; b. San Francisco, July 10, 1947; s. William and Helen S. (Jorgensen) M. AA, Coll. San Mateo, Calif., 1968; BA in English and Linguistics, San Francisco State Coll., 1969; MA in English Lit., San Francisco State U., 1972; PhD, U. Denver, 1977. Grad. teaching fellow dept. English U. Denver, 1973-77; asst. instr. Pacific Crest Outward Bound Sch., Portland, Oreg., 1978; jr. tech. writer Harris-Farinon, San Carlos, Calif., 1979-82; sr. tech. writer Verilink Corp., San Jose, Calif., 1985-88, Tektronix Corp., Mountain View, Calif., 1988-90, MorComm Tech. Writing Svcs., Palo Alto, Calif., 1991—. Author: (with David Caunt) A Sport Climber's Guide to the Castle Rock Area, 1992; editor: Arthur Symons: Letters to Yeats, 1989. Recipient grad. fellowships. Mem. MLA, Soc. for Tech. Comm., Irish-Am. Cultural Inst., Am. Alpine Club, Access Fund, Alpha Gamma Sigma. Home: 443 Ventura Ave Apt 3 Palo Alto CA 94306-3498 Office: MorComm Tech Writing Svcs 443 Ventura Ave Ste 3 Palo Alto CA 94306-4816

MORRIS, DAVID JOHN, mining engineer, consultant, mining executive; b. Seattle, May 6, 1945; s. Jack Abraham and Alice Jean (Hanson) M.; m. Melania F. Kearney, July 28, 1978; children: Whitney Elizabeth, Benton James, Sienna Elise. BA in Math. and Physics, Whitman Coll., 1968; BS in Mining Engring., Columbia U., 1968. Registered profl. engr., Colo., Utah, Wash. Mining engr. Union Oil of Calif., Los Angeles, 1968-69; mining engr. John T. Boyd Co., Denver, 1974-76, sr. mining engr., 1976-78, v.p., mgr., 1978-87; mng. ptnr. Palmer Coaking Coal Co., Black Diamond, Wash., 1976-82, 90—; pres. Pacific Coast Coal Co., Black Diamond, Wash., 1992—, Pacific Hydropower Devel., Inc., Black Diamond, Wash., 1995—. Mem. Bd. Overseers Whitman Coll., Walla Walla, Wash., 1986—, vice chair, 1993—, chmn. Rep. camapign for Whitman, Denver, 1985; coach youth athletics. Served as lt. USN, 1969-74, Vietnam. Henry Krumb scholar Columbia U., N.Y.C., 1967-68. Mem. NSPE, Soc. Mining Engrs. (admissions com. 1985-88, Howard Eavenson award com. 1984-87, Woomer award com. 1990-93, chair 1993—, Ramsay award com. 1992—, chair 1995—), Nat. Coal Assn. (bd. dirs. 1990-93, exec. com. 1993-94), Nat. Coal Coun. (appointed by Sec. of Energy 1992, 94), Nat. Mining Assn. (bd. dirs. 1995—), Seattle C. of C. (chmn. energy com. 1991-94), Western Rugby Football Union (sec. 1980), Broadmoor Golf Club, Rotary. Republican. Home: 3711 E Madison St Seattle WA 98112-3838 Office: Pacific Coast Coal Co Inc 900 4th Ave Ste 3625 Seattle WA 98164-1001

MORRIS, DEANNA RUTH, mathematics tutor; b. Shelbyville, Tenn., Nov. 21, 1943; d. Henry Franklin and Dorothy Ann (Evans) Shriver; m. Dwight Eduard Morris, June 18, 1967; children: Gregory Dwight, Melody Deanna, Holly Michelle, Gerald R. S. BA, Adams State Coll., 1964, MA in Sec. Edn., History & Math, 1965. Math. tchr. Fairbanks (Alaska) NOrth Star/Borough Schs., 1965-68, homebound tutor, 1987-93, substitute tchr., 1989-94, spl. edn. tutor for expelled students, 1993—; census worker U.S. Census Bur., Fairbanks, 1990. Election worker State of Alaska, Fairbanks, 1992—; precinct chmn. North Star Borough/City of Fairbanks. Named Homemaker of Yr., Tanana Valley Homemakers, Fairbanks, 1974, State Homemaker of Yr., Alaska Homemakers Assn., 1974; recipient Blue Ribbon Svc. award Tanana Valley State Fair Assn., Fairbanks, 1986. Mem. Order Ea. Star (sec. 1989—), Order of Amaranth (treas. 1984—), Grand Ct. Order of Amaranth (treas. 1992—), Grand Assembly Alaska (grand mother 1989-90, 93-94, Grand Cross Color 1990), Internat. Order Rainbow for Girls (adult mem., advisor). Presbyterian. Home: 206 Slater Dr Fairbanks AK 99701-3430

MORRIS, DEBRA LOUISE, secretary; b. Denver, July 17, 1960; d. Wayne Leroy and Margaret Louise (Pyle) M.; 1 child, Zackary David. AAS in computer info. svcs., Denver Tech., 1992. Jr. acct. Restaurant Acctg. Systems, Inc., Denver, 1979-86; dancer, entertainer various show clubs, nationwide, 1986-89; freelance writer Albuquerque, 1986—; receptionist, secretary Shoemaker Landscape Maintenance, Albuquerque, 1989—; owner Angel's Custom Svcs., Computer Svcs. & Metaphysical Gifts and Poems, 1992—; mem. Mgmt. Tng. & Colo. Mountain States Employers Coun., 1989. Author: (poems) Life's Little Treasures, (Am. Poetry Assn. award 1986), Destiny (Golden Poet award 1990, Hon. Mention award World of Poetry, 1990); entertainer South III Show Club, (1st runner up pagent, 1988, Miss April, 1988). Mem. North Shore Animal League. Home and Office: 5001 San Mateo Ln NE Apt 3 Albuquerque NM 87109-2458

MORRIS, DONALD CHARLES, real estate developer; b. Iowa City, Nov. 15, 1951; s. Lucien Ellis and Jean (Pinder) M.; m. Barbara Louise Small, Apr. 28, 1973 (div. Apr. 1980); m. Jana Susan Moyer, Aug. 28, 1982; children: Alexander Charles, Elisa Jean. Student, Cantab Coll., Toronto, Can., 1970-71; BSC, U. Guelph, Can., 1974; MSC, U. Guelph, 1975; PhD, U. B.C., Vancouver, 1978. Instr. U. B.C., Vancouver, 1975-77; pres. Morley Internat., Inc., Seattle, 1976-81; self-employed Comml. Investment Real Estate, Seattle, 1981-83; v.p., regional mgr. DKB Corp., Seattle, 1983-86; pres. Morris Devel. Svcs., Inc., Seattle, 1986—, Washington Group, Inc., Seattle, 1986—. Bd. dirs. Preservation Action, Washington, 1985-90; mem. Nat. Trust for Historic Preservation. Mem. Nat. Assn. Realtors, Wash. Assn. Realtors, Pioneer Square Assn. Seattle, Pioneer Square Property Owners Assn. Seatte, Meydenbauer Yacht Club. Office: Wash Group Morris Devel PO Box 4584 Rollingbay WA 98061-0584

MORRIS, EDWARD J(AMES), JR., insurance agent, small business owner; b. Jersey City, Jan. 9, 1936; s. Edward James Sr. and Mary Alice (Carr) M.; m. Joan M. O'Keefe, Sept. 17, 1955; children: Edward James III, Glenn D., Gary J. Student, Drakes Bus. Coll., 1953; cert. ins. broker, Vale Tech. Inst., 1962. CLU, Chartered Fin. Cons. Part-time salesperson Stanley Home Products, Jersey City, 1958-60; selector Am. Stores, South Kearny, N.J., 1957-62; owner Ed Morris State Farm Agy., Jersey City, 1962-72; owner, mgr., restauranteur E&J Morris Enterprises, Inc., New Bern, N.C., 1972-79; owner, mgr. Morris Ins. Agy., Jackson, N.J., 1979-82; spl. agt., reg. rep. Morris Fin. and Ins. Agy., Matawan, N.J., 1982-92; owner, mgr. Sunset Selections, Scottsdale, Ariz., 1992—; agt. emeritus Prudential Ins. Cos., Scottsdale, 1992—. Contbr. articles to profl. jours. Mem. com. Boy Scouts Am., Jersey City, 1966-72; basketball coach Our Lady of Mercy Ch., Jersey City, 1967-69; treas., basketball coach Coll. Little League, Jersey City, 1966-71; mcpl. chmn. Citizens for Goldwater, Jersey City, 1963-64. Sgt. USMC, 1954-57.

MORRIS, ELIZABETH TREAT, physical therapist; b. Hartford, Conn., Feb. 20, 1936; d. Charles Wells and Marion Louise (Case) Treat; BS in Phys. Therapy, U. Conn., 1960; m. David Breck Morris, July 10, 1961; children: Russell Charles, Jeffrey David. Phys. therapist Crippled Children's Clinic No. Va., Arlington, 1960-62, Shriners Hosp. Crippled Children, Salt Lake City, 1967-69, Holy Cross Hosp., Salt Lake City, 1970-74; pvt. practice phys. therapy, Salt Lake City, 1975—. Mem. nominating com. YWCA, Salt Lake City. Mem. Am. Phys. Therapy Assn., Am. Congress Rehab. Medicine, Nat. Speakers Assn., Utah Speakers Assn., Salt Lake Area C. of C., Friendship Force Utah, U.S. Figure Skating Assn., Toastmasters Internat., Internat. Assn. for the Study Pain, Internat. Platform Assn., World Confederation Phys. Therapy, Medart Internat. Home: 4177 Mathews Way Salt Lake City UT 84124-4021 Office: PO Box 526186 Salt Lake City UT 84152-6186

MORRIS, HENRY MADISON, III, software manufacturing executive, minister; b. El Paso, Tex., May 15, 1942; s. Henry Madison and Mary Louise (Beach) M.; m. Janet Deckman, July 25, 1964; children: Henry M., Scotta Marie. BA summa cum laude, Christian Heritage Coll., 1976; MDiv, Luther Rice Sem., 1977, DMin, 1978; MBA Pepperdine U., 1989. Ordained to ministry Bapt. Ch., 1968. Regional mgr. Integon Ins. Co., Greenville, S.C., 1969-75; pastor Hallmark Bapt. Ch., Greenville, 1969-75; assoc. prof. Bible, Christian Heritage Coll., El Cajon, Calif., 1977-78, adminstrv. v.p., 1978-80; pastor First Bapt. Ch., Canoga Park, Calif., 1980-86; chief adminstrv. officer, CFO SunGard Fin. Systems Inc., Canoga Park, 1986-94, v.p. adminstrn. and mktg., 1994—; lectr. in field. Served with U.S. Army, 1959-66. Republican. Author: Baptism: What is It?, 1977; Explore the Word, 1978; Churches: History and Doctrine, 1980. Office: SunGard Fin Svcs Inc 22134 Sherman Way Canoga Park CA 91303-1126

MORRIS, JOHN THEODORE, planning official; b. Denver, Jan. 18, 1929; s. Theodore Ora and Daisy Allison (McDonald) M.; BFA, Denver U., 1955; m. Dolores Irene Seaman, June 21, 1951; children: Holly Lee, Heather Ann, Heidi Jo, Douglas Fraser. Apprentice landscape architect S.R. DeBoer & Co., Denver, summer 1949, planning technician (part-time), 1954-55; sr. planner and assoc. Trafton Bean & Assocs., Boulder, Colo., 1955-62; prin. Land Planning Assocs., planning cons., Boulder, 1962-65; planning dir. and park coord. Boulder County, 1965-67; sch. planner Boulder Valley Sch. Dist., 1967-84, also dir. planning and engring., 1967-84, supt. facility improvement program, 1969-84; pvt. sch. planning cons., 1984—; cons. U. Colo. Bur. Ednl. Field Svcs., 1974. Bd. dirs. Historic Boulder, 1974-76; mem. parks and recreation adv. com. Denver Regional Coun. Govts., 1975-84. Served with USCG, 1950-53. Mem. Am. Inst. Cert. Planners, Am. Planning Assn., Coun. of Ednl. Facility Planners Internat., Longmont Artist Guild. Home and Office: 7647 32nd St Boulder CO 80302-9327

MORRIS, MICHAEL H., computer company executive; b. 1948. BA, Northwestern U., 1970; JD, U. Mich., 1974. Ptnr. DeFrancesco & Morris, St. Joseph, Mich., 1977-79; gen. coun., sec. ROLM Corp., 1979-86, US Teleceters Corp., 1986-87, Sun Microsystems, Inc., Mountain View, Calif., 1987—. Office: Sun Microsystems Inc MS PAL-1-521 2550 Garcia Ave Mountain View CA 94043-1109

MORRIS, RICHARD WARD, nonprofit organization administrator, author; b. Milw., June 16, 1939; s. Alvin Harry and Dorothy Lydia (Wissmueller) M. BS, U. Nev., 1962, PhD, 1968; MS, U. N.Mex., 1964. Exec. dir. COSMEP, Inc., San Francisco, 1968—. Author: Poetry Is a Kind of Writing, 1975, Light, 1979, The End of the World, 1980, The Fate of the Universe, 1982, Evolution and Human Nature, 1983, Dismantling the Universe, 1983, Time's Arrows, 1985, The Nature of Reality, 1987, The Edges of Science, 1990, Assyrians, 1991, (with others) The Word and Beyond, 1982, Cosmic Questions, 1993. Office: COSMEP Inc PO Box 420703 San Francisco CA 94142-0703

MORRIS, RUSTY LEE, administrative executive; b. Glenwood Springs, Colo., Nov. 28, 1940. Student, York Christian Coll., 1974-75, U. Nebr., 1975-76, Mesa State Coll., 1992-95, Colo. Christian U., 1995—. Specialist comm. security Martin-Marietta Corp., Larson AFB, 1962-63; communications security specialist classified def. project Boeing Aerospace Div., Larson AFB, Wash., 1963-64; with F.W. Sickles div. Gen. Instrument Corp., Chicopee, Mass., 1965-68; adminstr. judicial affairs J. Arthur Hickerson, Judge, Springfield, Mass., 1969-71; researcher Mont. United Indian Assn., Helena, 1970-72; adminstrv. asst. Vanderbilt U. Hosp., Nashville, 1980-82; paid bus. supr. Sears Svc. Ctr., Grand Junction, Colo., 1987-89; founder, chief exec. officer Vast Spl. Svcs., Grand Junction, 1988—; courier U.S. Census Bur., Grand Junction, 1990; spl. program coord. Colo. Dept. Parks and Recreation, Ridgway, 1990-91; acad. athletic program founder/coord. Mesa State Coll., 1992-93, math. and sci. rep., student govt., 1992—, athletic coun., 1993—, student health ctr. com., 1993—, faculty search com., 1993; founder, chief exec. officer Rolling Spokes Assn. Vol. Easter Seals Soc., 1964-67, vol. instr. Adult Literacy Program, 1984-87; vol. T.V. host Muscular Dystrophy Assn. Am., 1975-94; bd. dirs. Independent Living Ctr., 1985-87, Handicap Awareness Week, 1989; trails com. Colo. State Parks and Outdoor Recreation, 1988—; condr. seminars Ams. With Disabilites Act, 1989—; cons. Bur. Reclamation, 1988—, Bur. Land Mgmt., 1989—; staff trainer Breckenridge Outdoor Recreation Ctr., 1989-90; emergency svcs. officer Colo. Civil Air Patrol, Thunder Mountain Squadron, 1989—; bd. dirs. Handicap Awareness, 1989; dir. com. Colo. State Trails Commn., 1989-90; mem. Dem. Nat. Com., 1991—; dist. com. Grand Junction Sch. Dist., 1992—; mem. Restore the Com., Avalon, 1993—; bd. dirs., presenter No. Colo. chpt. Colo. Orgn. of Victim Assistance; with victim assistance Mesa County Sheriff's Dept., 1993—. Recipient Hometown Hero award, 1993. Mem. Handicap Scholarship Assn. (bd. dirs. 1994, award 1993), Nat. Orgn. Victim Assistance (presenter 1988—), Nat. Coun. Alcoholism and Drug Abuse (vol. 1987—), Mother's Against Drunk Driver's (bd. dirs. Mesa County chpt., v.p. 1985—), Concerns of Police Survivors, Club 20 of Western Colo. (mem. com. status), Great Outdoor Colo., Grand Junction C. of C., Grand Junction Symphony, Mus. Western Colo., Mesa State Coll. Geology Club, Toastmasters (Able Toastmaster, winner speech contests 1985-87). Home and Office: Vast Spl Svcs 612 N 15th St Grand Junction CO 81501-4422

MORRIS, SARAH PUREFOY, archaeologist, educator; b. Durham, N.C., Oct. 15, 1954; d. Donald Robert Morris and Sylvia (Stallings) Lowe; m. John K. Papadopoulos, Dec. 1, 1991. BA, U. N.C., 1976; PhD, Harvard U., 1981. Asst. prof. Yale U., New Haven, 1981-86, assoc. prof., 1986-89; assoc. prof. UCLA, 1989-93, prof., 1993—. Author: The Black and White Style, 1984, Daidalos and the Origins of Greek Art, 1992 (James Wiseman Book award award Archael. Inst. Am., 1993, Outstanding Book, Choice mag., 1993). Precinct capt. Dem. Party, L.A., 1992. Rsch. grantee Am. Coun. Learned Socs., 1988. Mem. Am. Philol. Assn., Archael. Inst. Am., Am. Sch. Classical Studies Alumni Assn. (mem. admissions com. 1990-94). Episcopal. Office: UCLA Dept Classics 405 Hilgard Ave Los Angeles CA 90024-1301

MORRIS, STEPHEN BLAINE, clinical psychologist; b. Logan, Utah, Aug. 22, 1951; s. Blaine and Helen (Bradshaw) Morris, Jr.; m. Marilyn Smith, Sept. 12, 1974; children: David Stephen, Angela, Michael Andrew. BA magna cum laude, Utah State U., 1976; MA, Brigham Young U., 1979; PhD, U. Utah, 1986. Lic. psychologist, Utah. Psychol. cons. U. Utah Speech and Hearing Clinic, 1982-83; psychology intern Primary Children's Med. Ctr., Salt Lake City, 1983-86; postdoctoral resident in clin. psychology Comprehensive Psychol. Svcs. of Utah, Salt Lake City, 1986, clin. psychologist, 1988-89; dir. children's program Charter Summit Hosp., Midvale, Utah, 1989-90; cons. children's program Charter Summit Hosp., Midvale, 1991-93; clin. psychologist and dir. outpatient child and family svcs Charter Counseling Ctr., Midvale, 1990; clin. psychologist in pvt. practice Salt Lake City, 1990—; instr. dept. psychology U. Utah, summer 1986; lectr. in field. Contbr. articles to profl. jours. Mem. APA, Utah Psychol. Assn. (sec.-treas. div. hosp. practice 1989-92, pres. practice divsn. 1992-93), Assn. of Mormon Counselors and Psychotherapists, Phi Kappa Phi, Phi Eta Sigma. LDS. Office: 1414 E 4500 S # 4 Salt Lake City UT 84117-4208

MORRIS, SYLVIA MARIE, university official; b. Laurel, Miss., May 6, 1952; d. Earlene Virginia (Cameron) Hopkins Stewart; m. James D. Morris, Jan. 29, 1972; children: Cedric James, Taedra Janae. Student, U. Utah, 1970-71. From adminstrv. sec. to adminstrv. mgr. mech. engring. U. Utah, Salt Lake City, 1972—. Mem. Community Devel. Adv. Bd., Salt Lake City, Utah, 1984—; nom. chmn. and del. to Dem. Mass Meeting, 1988. Recipient Presdl. Staff award, 1994. Mem. NAACP, NAFE, Consortium Utah Women in Higher Edn. Baptist. Home: 9696 Pinebrook Dr South Jordan UT 84095 Office: U Utah 3209 MEB Mech Engr Dept Salt Lake City UT 84112

MORRIS, TAMI CANTUA, public relations and communications consultant; b. Glenwood Springs, Colo., Sept. 24, 1958; m. Guy Richard Morris, Feb. 29, 1980; children: J. Taylor, Jessica Randahl. BS in Pub. Rels. and Journalism, U. So. Colo., 1979; MA in Mass Comm., Tex. Tech. U., 1981. Cert. Am. Soc. for Healthcare Pub. Rels. and Mktg.; accredited Pub. Rels. Soc. Am. Reporter Pueblo (Colo.) Star Jour. and Chieftain, 1979; advt. dir. HUB Times Texas Instruments, Inc., Lubbock, Tex., 1980; cons./mng. editor HUB Mag., Lubbock, 1981; dir. pub. rels. and vol. svcs. Cmty. Hosp. Lubbock, Tex., 1981-82; spl. projects/comm. mgr. Texas Instruments, Inc., Lubbock, 1982-83; v.p. pub. rels. North Bay Healthcare Corp., Fairfield, Calif., 1984-88; dir. corp. comm. Cath. Healthcare West, San Francisco, 1988-89; prin. Comm. Strategies, Oakland, Calif., 1989—; profl. devel. coord. surviving career trauma Soc. for Healthcare Pub. Rels. and Mktg. No. Calif., Napa and Walnut Creek, Calif., 1992, 93. Cmty. newspaper writer East Bay Jour./Orinda News, 1993. Mem. Pub. Rels. Soc. Am. (exec. com. health acad. 1987—, pub. affairs dir. East Bay chpt. 1992-94), Calif. Writers' Club, Mystery Writers Am. Office: Comm Strategies 6114 La Salle Ave Ste 400 Oakland CA 94611-2802

MORRISON, BRADFORD CARY, oil and gas industry executive; b. Fergus Falls, Minn., Feb. 5, 1944; s. Clifford Byron and Bessie Caroline (Danielson) M.; m. Brenda Kay Perry, Nov. 15, 1969; children: Ashley Marie, Devon Lane. BA, Augustana Coll., 1966; MA, U. Wis., 1968. Geologist Shell Oil, New Orleans, 1968-74, Sherwood Exploration, Denver, 1974-75, Fluor Oil & Gas, Denver, 1975-78, Patrick Petroleum, Denver, 1978-80; v.p. United Resources, Denver, 1980-83; ptnr., geologist Banner Oil & Gas, Denver, 1983-85; geologist Ultramar Oil & Gas, Denver, Houston, 1985-88; v.p. Chuska Energy Co., Denver, 1988-91; owner Terrafocus, Ltd., Denver, 1991—. Mem. Am. Assn. Petroleum Geologists (cert., del.), Rocky Mountain Assn. Geologists (v.p. 1991), Houston Geological Soc., New Orleans Geological Soc. Home: 9728 S Ashleigh Ln Highlands Ranch CO 80126

MORRISON, DAVID LEE, librarian, educator; b. New London, Conn., Aug. 28, 1948; s. Samuel and Beatrice (Kinslinger) M. BA in Classics with highest honors, U. Calif., Santa Barbara, 1979; MLS, U. Ariz., 1986. Documents libr. Marriott Libr., U. Utah, Salt Lake City, 1987—, instr. libr. literacy course, 1990—; workshop presenter in field; guest lectr. U. Ariz. Grad. Libr. Sch., fall 1988-94; participant confs. in field. Fay and Lawrence Clark Powell scholar U. Ariz., 1983. Mem. ALA (Govt. Docs. Round Table info. tech. com. 1987-89), Utah Libr. Assn. (GODORT bylaws com. 1987-88, 91-92, chmn. nominating com. 1987-88, mem. continuing edn. com. 1987-89, vice chmn., chmn.-elect 1992-93, chmn. GODORT 1993-94), Patent and Trademark Depository Libr. Assn. (fin. com. 1988-95, sec.-treas. 1989-90, 92-95), Patent Documentation Soc. Home: 859 So Blair St Salt Lake City UT 84111 Office: U Utah Documents Div Marriott Libr Salt Lake City UT 84112

MORRISON, GLADYS MAE, pilot training firm executive; b. Balmorhea, Tex., Jan. 5, 1928; d. James Henry and Alice Vivian (Totter) Walk; m. James Martin Morrison, Nov. 25, 1957 (dec. June 1988). Cert. master aviation instr. Pntr., mgr. Davis Flying Svc., Concord, Calif., 1946-56, Desert Air Oasis, Thermal, Calif., 1957-62; asst. mgr. flight dept. Beechcraft West, Van Nuys, Calif., 1962-64; dir. publs. Fowler Aeronautics, aviation textbook pubs., Burbank, Calif., 1964-65; owner-mgr. Aviation Tng., Prescott, Ariz., 1965—; chief-pilot North-Aire, Inc., Prescott, 1974-86, pres., 1988—, bd. dirs.; instr. FAA approved flight engring. sch. Fowler Aeronautics, Burbank, 1964-65. Author aviation text books; contbr. articles to newspapers and mags. Named Nat. Flight Instr. of Yr. FAA, 1982, FAA Western-Pacific Flight Instr. of Yr., 1982, Ariz. Flight Instr. of Yr. FAA, 1982; recipient Cert. of Recognition, Fedn. Aero Nautique Internat., Paris, 1982. Mem. Aircraft Owner & Pilot Assn. (Master Flight Instr. award 1983), Nat. Assn. Flight Instrs. (Flights Inst. of Yr. 1982), Ninety-Nines, Inc., Silver Wings Fraternity, Alpha Eta Rho (hon.). Republican. Office: North-Aire Inc Prescott Mcpl Airport 6500 Maccurdy Dr Ste 7 Prescott AZ 86301-6135

MORRISON, JAMES IAN, research institute executive; b. Irvine, Scotland, Dec. 22, 1952; came to U.S., 1985; s. James Morrison and Janet Miller (McCondach) Munro; m. Nora Cadham, Dec. 6, 1980; children: David, Caitlin. BPhil, U. Newcastle-upon-Tyne, Eng., 1976; MA, U. Edinburgh, Scotland, 1974; PhD, U. B.C., Can., 1985. Isntr. B.C. Inst. Tech., Vancouver, 1980-85; rsch. assoc. U. B.C., Vancouver, 1980-85; rsch. fellow Inst. for the Future, Menlo Park, Calif., 1985-86, dir. health care rsch. program, 1986—, pres., 1990—; bd. dirs. Interim Svcs., Ft. Lauderdale, Fla.; mem. corp. adv. bd. Bristol-Myers Squibb, Princeton, N.J., 1992—; mem. UNIS Press Adv. Bd., 1990—. Co-author: Looking Ahead at American Health Care, 1988, Directing the Clinical Laboratory, 1990, System in Crisis: The Case for Health Care Reform, 1991, Reforming the System: Containing Health Care Costs in an Era of Universal Coverage, 1992, Future Tense: The Business Realities of the Next Ten Years, 1994; contbr. articles to profl. jours. Mem. environ. scanning com. United Way of Am., 1990—. Social Sci. Rsch. Coun. scholar U. Newcastle-upon-Tyne, 1974-76. Office: Inst for the Future 2744 Sand Hill Rd Menlo Park CA 94025-7020

MORRISON, JOHN CARL, ophthalmologist, educator; b. Portland, Oreg., July 13, 1951; s. Carl Vincent and Dorothy Grace (Nafus) M.; m. Lynne Lorraine Hubbell, Aug. 24, 1974; children: Steven, Elizabeth. BA, U. Oreg., 1973; MD, U. Oreg., Portland, 1977. Diplomate Am. Bd. Ophthalmology, Nat. Bd. Med. Examiners. Intern U. Calif. Davis Med. Ctr., Sacramento, 1977-78; emergency rm. physician St. Vincent Hosp., Portland, Oreg., 1978-80; resident in ophthalmology Oreg. Health Scis. U., Portland, 1982-85, pre-residency fellow, 1980-82, fellow in glaucoma, 1985-86; fellow in glaucoma Johns Hopkins Med. Ctr., Balt., 1986-88; asst. prof. ophthalmology Oreg. Health Scis. U., 1988-93, assoc. prof., 1993—. Contbr. chpts. to books, articles to Am. Jour. Ophthalmology, Ophthal. Surgery, Current Opinion in Ophthalmology, others; patentee microneedle for injecting ocular vessels. Recipient Miriam and Benedict Wolfe award Rsch. to Prevent Blindness, 1991; NIH grantee, 1991, 93. Mem. Am. Acad. Ophthalmology (honor award 1994), Assn. for Rsch. in Vision and Ophthalmology, Oreg. Acad. Ophthalmology, Am. Glaucoma Soc., West Coast Glaucoma Soc., Friedenwald Glaucoma Soc. (charter mem.), Phi Beta Kappa, Alpha Omega Alpha. Office: Casey Eye Int 3375 SW Terwilliger Blvd Portland OR 97201-4146

MORRISON, JOHN GILL, communications executive; b. Upham, N.D., Feb. 22, 1914; s. Claude Collins and Ann Louise (Gill) M.; m. Mary Lou Thompson, Aug. 17, 1940; children: Randolph, Malcolm, Mark, Timothy. BA, U. N.D., 1939, BS, 1940; MD, U. Chgo., 1942. Chmn. bd. Calif. Blueshield, San Francisco, 1960-63; pres. Alameda/Contra Costa Med. Assn., Oakland, Calif., 1961-62, Calif. Med. Assn., San Francisco, 1968-69; council Am. Med. Assn., Chgo., 1970-76; pres., chief exec. officer Audio Digest Fdn., Glendale, Calif., 1973-86; bd. dirs. Am. Sound and Video Corp., Detroit, 1981—; cons. in field. Lt. USN, 1942-48. Mem. Carmel Golf and Country Club. Republican. Home and Office: 450 Hampton Rd Piedmont CA 94611-3317

MORRISON, JOHN STUART, technology company executive; b. St. Louis, Jan. 21, 1947; s. John Gracie and Annebelle (Gordon) M.; m. Patricia Ann Myers, Dec. 3, 1971; children: James, Thomas, Geoffrey. BA in Psychology, Wash. U., St. Louis, 1969; MS, Naval Postgrad. Sch., Monterey, Calif., 1980. Commd. 2d lt. USAF, 1969, advanced through grades to lt. col., 1986; intelligence officer 388 TFW, Korat, Thailand, 1970-71, HW, Strategic Air Command, Omaha, 1971-73; dir. air intelligence RAF Alconbury, U.K., 1974-77; command control and coms. mgr. Tactical Air Forces Interoperability Group, Hampton, Va., 1980-83; joint C3 advisor U.S. Mil. Tng. Mission, Riyadh, Saudi Arabia, 1983-85; dir. plans Nat. Test Bed, Boston, 1985-88; dir. systems engring. and devel. Nat. Test Bed, Colorado Springs, 1988-91; ret. USAF, 1991; pres. Transnat. Techs. Inc., Colorado Springs, Colo., 1991—; cons. Boeing, Martin Marietta, UN, USAF, Rockwell Internat., NCR, 1991-92. Author: Software Reuse in Japan, 1984; contbr. articles to profl. jours. Mem. IEEE, Assn. of Computer Mfrs. Office: Transnational Techs Inc 6736 War Eagle Pl Colorado Springs CO 80919-1634

MORRISON, JOY SOUTH, journalist; b. Montpelier, Idaho, June 3; d. Edward Marshall and Ruth Eldora (Heath) South; m. Thomas Lamar Morrison, Mar. 25, 1950; 1 child, Michele Ann Morrison Heuser. Student, Idaho State U., 1941-43; BA in Journalism, U. Wis., 1946; postgrad., U. Utah, 1951, U. Mo., 1983. Office mgr. Uncle Ray's Mag., Cleve., 1947; journalism tchr. East High Sch., Salt Lake City, 1952--53; copywriter KWIK Radio, Pocatello, 1952-55; editor Idaho State Jour., Pocatello, entertainment and family living editor, 1955—. Chmn. publicity com. Am. Heart Assn., Bannock, Idaho, Pocatello High Sch. Found. Recipient numerous state and nat. awards including Penney-Mo. award, 1987, 88, 1st place family living pages award AP, 1983-90, Athena award, Cmty. Svc. award Gate City Rotary, Paul Harris award Pocatello Rotary, Disting. Svc. award Soroptimist. Mem. Idaho Press Women (editor newsletter, v.p., sec.), Idaho State U. Alumni Assn. (Friend of Idaho State U., Bartz Svc. award). Home: 1015 E Elm St Pocatello ID 83201-3953 Office: Idaho State Jour 305 S Arthur Ave Pocatello ID 83204-3306

MORRISON, MARCY, state legislator; b. Watertown, N.Y., Aug. 9, 1935; m. Howard Morrison; children: Liane, Brenda. BA, Queens Coll., 1957; student, Colo. Coll., U. Colo. Mem. Colo. Ho. of Reps., awd, 1992—; mem. judiciary, health, environ., welfare and instns. coms. Mem. Manitou Springs (Colo.) Sch. Bd., 1973-83, pres., 1980-82, County Park Bd., 1976-83, State Bd. Health, 1985-93, pres., 1988-90, Mountain Scar Commn., 1989, Future Pub. Health, 1989-90, Health Policy Commn., 1990-92; commr. El Paso County, 1985-92, chmn., 1987-89; active Citizens Goals, United Way. Named Outstanding Sch. Bd. Mem., Pikes Peak Tchrs. Assn., 1978, Woman of Spirit, Penrose-St. Francis Hosp. Sys., 1991. Mem. LWV, Health Assn. Pikes Peake Area, Women's Edn. Assn., El Paso Mental Health Assn. Republican. Jewish. Home: 302 Sutherland Pl Manitou Springs CO 80829-2722 Office: Colo Ho of Reps State Capitol Denver CO 80203

MORRISON, MARTHA KAYE, photolithography engineer; b. San Jose, Calif., Oct. 5, 1955; d. Myrle K. and Arthena R. Morrison; 1 child, Katherine A. AA, West Valley Coll., Saratoga, Calif., 1978. Prodn. worker Signetics Co., Sunnyvale, Calif., 1973-75, equipment engr., 1976-78, 79-80, prodn. supr., 1978-79; expediter Monolithic Memories, Sunnyvale, 1975-76; photolithography engr. KTI Chems., 1980-81; founder, chief engr., CEO Optalign, Inc., Livermore, Forest Ranch, Calif., 1981—; participant West Valley Coll. Tennis Team # 1 Singles and Doubles, 1976-78; regional profl. ranking NCTA Opens Singles/Doubles, 1982-85, 93, 94, rankings 15-20 singles/6-8 doubles; instr. tennis Chico Racquet Club, 1994, Butte Creek Country Club, 1995—; participant exhbn. tennis match with Rosie Cosals and Billie Jean King, 1994. Dir. benefit Boys & Girls Club of Chico. Named Champion Chico Open Finalist Woodridge Open, 1994, 1993 #2 NCTA Women's Open Doubles, Doubles #3, 1994. Mem. USPTA (cert.). Office: PO Box 718 Forest Ranch CA 95942-0718

MORRISON, MICHELLE WILLIAMS, nursing educator, administrator, author; b. Reno, Nev., Feb. 12, 1947; d. Robert James and Dolores Jane (Barnard) Williams; m. Harrison Russell Morrison, Dec. 29, 1974. BSN, U. Nev., Reno, 1973; M Health Svc., U. Calif., Davis, 1977. RN, Oreg. Staff nurse VA Hosp., Reno, 1973-77; family nurse practitioner Tri-County Indian Health Svc., Bishop, Calif., 1977-78; instr. nursing Roque C.C., Grants Pass, Oreg., 1978-82; psychiat. nurse VA Hosp., Roseburg, Oreg., 1982; dir. edn. Josephine Meml. Hosp., Grants Pass, 1983-84; geriatric nurse practitioner Hearthstone Manor, Medford, Oreg., 1984-86; chmn. nursing dept. Roque Community Coll., Grants Pass, Oreg., 1986-89; prin. Health and Ednl. Cons., Grants Pass, 1989—; dir. nursing Highland House Nursing Ctr., Grants Pass, 1990; bd. dirs. Tri-County Indian Health Svc.; cons. for nursing svcs. in long term care facilities. Author: Professional Skills for Leadership; contbr. Basic Skills for Nursing. Mem. Josephine County Coalition for AIDS, Grants Pass, 1990. With USN, 1965-69. Mem. NAFE, Nat. League Nursing, Oreg. Ednl. Assn., Oreg. State Bd. Nursing (re-entry nursing com. 1992-93). Office: PO Box 89 Williams OR 97544-0089

MORRISON, MURDO DONALD, architect; b. Detroit, Feb. 21, 1919; s. Alexander and Johanna (Macaulay) M.; BArch, Lawrence Inst. Tech., 1943; m. Judy D. Morrison; children from previous marriage—Paula L., Reed A.,

Anne H. Individual practice architecture, Detroit, 1949, Klamath Falls, Oreg., 1949-65, Oakland, Calif., 1965-78; ptnr. Morrison Assocs., San Francisco, 1978-85, Burlingame, Calif., 1985-89, Redwood City, Calif., 1989—; v.p. Lakeridge Corp., 1968—; chmn. Oreg. Bd. Archtl. Examiners, 1961-65, chmn., 1964. Mem. Town Council Klamath Falls, 1955-57; co-chmn. Oakland Pride Com., 1968-77; mem. Redwood City Gen. Plan Com., 1986, Redwood City Design REv. Com., 1991—, Emerald Hills Design Rev. Bd., 1990—. Served with USN, 1943-46. Recipient Progressive Architecture award, 1955, Alumni of Yr. award Lawrence Inst., 1965. Mem. AIA (treas. East Bay, chmn. Oakland chpt.). Presbyterian. Architect: Gilliam County Courthouse (Progressive Architecture design award), 1955, Chiloquin (Oreg.) Elem. Sch., 1963, Lakeridge Office Bldg., Reno, 1984, Provident Cen. Credit Union Bldg., Monterey, Calif., 1986, Embarcadero Fed. Credit Union, San Francisco, 1991, others. Home and Office: 3645 Jefferson Ave Redwood City CA 94062-3137

MORRISON, PERRY DAVID, librarian, educator; b. Mpls., Nov. 30, 1919; s. Arthur D. and Vera Mae (Perry) M.; m. Catherine Jean Gushwa, Apr. 22, 1946 (dec. Oct. 1991). A.A., Pasadena City Coll., 1940; A.B., Whittier Coll., 1942, M.A., 1947; B.L.S., U. Calif., Berkeley, 1949, D.L.S., 1961. Asst. Huntington Library, San Marino, Calif., 1947-48; asst. univ. librarian, head social sci. librarian U. Oreg., Eugene, 1949-63; prof. Sch. Librarianship U. Oreg., 1967-82, prof. emeritus, 1982—, dean Sch. Librarianship, 1970-73, coordinator library research, univ. library, 1978-82, part-time reference librarian, 1982-89, acting asst. univ. librarian, 1979-80; coll. librarian, dir. library sci. program Sacramento State Coll., 1963-65; assoc. prof. U. Wash. Sch. Librarianship, 1965-67; cons. Monash U. Library, Australia, 1973-76, Central Oreg. Community Coll., 1977, Victoria State Coll. Toorak, Melbourne St. Coll., Kevin Grove St. Coll., Australia, 1980, Portland Community Coll., 1981, Treaty Oak Ednl. Dist., Oreg., 1983; dir. various Office Edn. Insts., 1968-75; mem. grant award appraisal panels Office Edn., Washington, 1972-74. Author: Career of the Academic Librarian, 1969; contbr. numerous articles, revs. to profl. jours.; editorial bd. Serials Libr., 1978-92, Social and Behavioral Scis. Libr., 1978-92; issue editor: Libr. Trends. 1981; compiler: A Journey Through Time: The Oregon Library Association, 1940-90. Mem. adv. bd. Lane County Law Libr., 1986-92; treas. Residents Assn. Cascade Manor, Eugene, Oreg., 1993-95; active U. Oreg. Learning in Retirement Program Com., 1993-94. Capt. U.S. Army, 1942-46. Mem. ALA (life), Spl. Librs. Assn. (hon. life, pres. Oreg. chpt. 1974-75), Oreg. Libr. Assn. (hon. life, pres. 1961-62), Pacific N.W. Libr. Assn. (editor and bus. mgr. jour. 1967-71), Assn. Coll. and Rsch. Librs. Assn. (coms.), Lane County Assn. Oreg. Pub. Employees Retirement System (pres. 1985-86), U. Oreg. Ret. Profs. Assn., Faculty Club U. Oreg. (treas. 1981-82). Democrat. Mem. United Ch. of Christ. Home: 65 W 30th Ave Apt 416 Eugene OR 97405-3373 Office: Library U Oreg Eugene OR 97403

MORRISON, RALPH EVANS, state agency administrator; b. Salt Lake City, Feb. 22, 1959; s. Richard Lee and Carol (Evans) M.; m. Dian Cannon, Apr. 21, 1983; children: Jennifer, Ryan, Spencer. BS in Fin., BS in Mgmt., U. Utah, 1982; MBA, Utah State U., 1983. Cert. fin. planner. Security agt. Envirowest Inc., 1977-78; ch. missionary Rome, 1978-80; asst. cross country coach Olympus High Sch., 1980; polit. intern Utah State Legislature, 1981; intern. to tech. staff Datanow Inc., 1983; instr. in computer techniques Utah State U., 1983; systems engr. IBM, Salt Lake City, 1983-86; info. analyst Utah Retirement Systems, Salt Lake City, 1986-90, purchasing agt., 1990-91, asst. dir. defined contbn. plans, 1990—; cons. Found. for Advanced Rsch., Manhattan Beach, Calif., 1980—; adj. faculty mem. LDS Bus. Coll., 1987; instr. Utah Tech. Coll., 1985. Named State Chess Champion, 1973-74, one of Outstanding Young Men of Am., 1982. Home: 2596 Evergreen Ave Salt Lake City UT 84109-3070

MORRISON, ROBERT LEE, physical scientist; b. Omaha, Nov. 22, 1932; s. Robert Alton and Lulu Irene (Ross) M.; m. Sharon Faith Galliher, Feb. 19, 1966; children: Dennis, Karyn, Cheryl, Tamara, Traci. BA, U. Pacific, Stockton, Calif., 1957, MS, 1960. Chief chemist Gallo Winery, Modesto, Calif., 1957-66; rsch. scientist Lawrence Livermore Nat. Lab., Livermore, Calif., 1966-69, sr. rsch. scientist, 1973-93; pres. Poolinator, Inc., Gardena, Calif., 1970-72; owner R.L. Morrison Techs., Modesto, 1993—; cons., speaker, presenter in field. Contbr. numerous articles to profl. jours.; patentee in field. Recipinet Excellence in Nuclear Weapons award U.S. Dept. Energy, 1990, others. Mem. Am. Chem. Soc. Home: 1117 Spring-creek Dr Modesto CA 95355-4820

MORRISON, ROBERT THOMAS, engineering consultant; b. Manson, Iowa, June 4, 1918; s. Charles Henry and Ida Magdeline (Fuessley) M.; m. Callie Louise Warren, July, 25, 1942; children: Linda Ann, Allan Charles, Janis Lou. BS in Mech. Engring., Iowa State U., 1942; MS in Engring., U. Calif., Los Angeles, 1961. Engr. Gen. Elecric Co., Schenectedy, N.Y., 1942-45; sales engr., inventory supr. Gen. Electric Supply Corp., Omaha, 1945-50; pres. Morrison Mfg. Co., Omaha, 1950-52; elec. system designer Douglas Aircraft, Long Beach and Santa Monica, Calif., 1952-58; system engr., proposal mgr. Rockwell Internat., Downey, Seal Beach, Anaheim, Calif., 1958-81; freelance cons. Garden Grove, Calif., 1981—; originator, coord. system engring. program West Coast U., L.A., 1963-71, assoc. dir. devel., 1972; moderator Rockwell System Engring. Seminar, 1964. Author: Proposal Manager's Guide, 1972, Proposal Style Guide, 1988, Proposal Publications Guide, 1988. Lay minister Crystal Cathedral, Garden Grove, 1980—, dir. New Hope Telephone Counseling Ctr., 1990—; Garden Grove Energy Commn., 1982-85, Garden Grove Planning Commn., 1960-61; com. chmn. March of Dimes, Orange County, 1973-75; pres. Meth. Men, Garden Grove, 1964, 65. Recipient Apollo Achievement award NASA, 1970, Apollo-Soyuz Test Project award NASA, 1975, Space Shuttle Approach and Landing Test award NASA, 1978, Profl. Achievement citation in Engring. Iowa State U., 1984. Mem. Assn. Profl. Cons., World Future Soc., Inst. Mgmt. Scis., Ops. Rsch. Soc. Am., Assn. Proposal Mgmt. Profls., Tech. Mktg. Soc. Am., Masons, Toastmasters, Palm Springs Tennis Club. Republican.

MORRISON, ROBERT TOWNSEND, nephrologist; b. Boston, Dec. 26, 1951; s. Robert Stier and Marie Day (Townsend) M.; m. Margaret Lou Dougherty, July 10, 1976; children: Sarah Marie, Samuel Thomas. BS, Rensselaer Poly. Inst., 1976; student, Columbia U., 1981; MD, Albany Med. Coll., 1985. Assoc. Herbert F. Gold and Assocs., Brookline, Mass., 1976; ins. claims adjuster GAB Adjustment Corp., Boston, 1976-78; lab. technician Rockefeller U., N.Y.C., 1980-81; resident in internal medicine USAF Med. Ctr., Wright-Patterson AFB, Ohio, 1985-88; fellow in nephrology Wilford Hall USAF Med. Ctr., Lackland AFB, Tex., 1988-90; chief nephrology svc. 13th Air Force Med. Ctr., Republic of Philippines, 1990-91, David Grant USAF Med. ctr., Travis AFB, Calif., 1991—; asst. clin. prof. medicine U. Calif. at Davis, Sacramento, 1991—; nephrology cons. to Pacific Air Command, USAF, Clark AB, Philippines, 1990-91; instr. Uniformed Svcs. U. Health Scis., 1988-90. Author jour. articles and abstracts. Co-chair combined fed. campaign United Way of Solano County, 1993-94; chmn. drives ARC, Albany, N.Y., 1982-83; chmn. Hunger Task Force of Riverside Ch., 1979-81. Maj. USAF, 1985—. Mem. ACP, Nat. Kidney Found., Soc. Air Force Physicians, Am. Soc. Nephrology, Sigma Chi (pres. chpt. 1975-76). Democrat. Home: 126 W North College St Yellow Springs OH 45387-1563 Office: SGHM/Dept Internal Medicine 101 Bodin Cir Travis AFB CA 94535-1801

MORRISON, ROGER BARRON, geologist; b. Madison, Wis., Mar. 26, 1914; s. Frank Barron and Elsie Rhea (Bullard) M.; BA, Cornell U., 1933, MS, 1934; postgrad. U. Calif., Berkeley, 1934-35, Stanford U., 1935-38; PhD, U. Nev., 1964; m. Harriet Louise Williams, Apr. 7, 1941 (deceased Feb. 1991); children: John Christopher, Peter Hallock and Craig Brewster (twins). Registered profl. geologist, Wyo. Geologist U.S. Geol. Survey, 1939-76; vis. adj. prof. dept. geoscis. U. Ariz., 1976-81, Mackay Sch. Mines, U. Nev., Reno, 1984-86; cons. geologist; pres. Morrison and Assocs., Ltd., 1978—; prin. investigator 2 Landsat-1 and 2 Skylab earth resources investigation projects NASA, 1972-75. Fellow Geol. Soc. Am.; mem. AAAS, Internat. Union Quaternary Rsch. (mem. Holocene and paleopedology commns., chmn. work group on pedostratigraphy), Am. Soc. Photogrammetry, Am. Soc. Agronomy, Soil Sci. Soc. Am., Internat. Soil Sci. Soc., Am. Quaternary Assn., Am. Water Resources Assn., Colo. Sci. Soc., Sigma Xi, Colorado Mountain Club. Author 2 books, co-author one book, co-editor 2 books; editor: Quaternary Nonglacial Geology, Conterminous U.S., Geol. Soc. Am. Centennial Series, vol. K-2, 1991; mem. editorial bd. Catena, 1973-88; contbr. over 150 articles to profl. jours. Research includes Quaternary geology and geomorphology, hydrogeology, environ. geology, neotectonics, remote sensing of Earth resources, paleoclimatology, pedostratigraphy. Office: PO Box 146 Shoshone CA 92384-0146

MORRISON, WILLIAM FOSDICK, business educator, retired electrical company executive; b. Bridgeport, Conn., Mar. 14, 1935; s. Robert Louis and Helen Fosdick (Mulroney) M.; m. E. Drake Miller, Dec. 14, 1957 (div. Sept. 1972); children: Donna Drake, Deanne Fosdick, William Fosdick; m. Carol Ann Stover, Nov. 20, 1972. BA in Econs., Trinity Coll., 1957. Mgr. purchasing dept. Westinghouse Electric Co., Lima, Ohio, 1960-68; mgr. mfg. Westinghouse Electric Co., Upper Sandusky, Ohio, 1969; gen. mgr. Westinghouse Electric Co., Gurabo, P.R., 1970-71; mgr. tng. Westinghouse Electric Co., Pitts., 1972-84; program mgr. Westinghouse Electric Co., Sunnyvale, Calif., 1984-89, procurement project dir., 1990-94; prof. San Jose State U., Calif., 1993—, Golden Gate U., San Francisco, 1995—; negotiation cons. and trainer, 1969—. Author: The Pre-Negotiation Planning Book, 1985, The Human Side of Negotiations, 1994; contbr. articles to profl. jours. Bd. dirs. Valley Inst. of the Theatre Arts, Saratoga, Calif., 1986-90, Manhattan Playhouse, 1989-94; chmn. Sensory Access Found. Golf Tournament, 1995—. Served to capt. USAFR, 1958-64. Named Man of the Yr. Midwest Lacrosse Coaches Assn., 1983, recipient Service award U.S. Lacrosse Assn., 1982. Mem. Nat. Assn. Purchasing Mgmt. (pres. Lima chpt. 1966-67, dir. nat. affairs 1967-68, dist. treas. 1968-70). Club: Sunnyvale Golf Assn. (vice-chmn. 1985, chmn. 1986, 93, handicap scorer 1992-93). Lodge: Elks. Home: 3902 Duncan Pl Palo Alto CA 94306-4550 Office: San Jose State U Coll of Bus 1 Washington Sq San Jose CA 95192-0070

MORRISSEY, JOHN CARROLL, lawyer; b. N.Y.C., Sept. 2, 1914; s. Edward Joseph and Estelle (Caine) M.; m. Eileen Colligan, Oct. 14, 1950; children: Jonathan Edward, Ellen (Mrs. James A. Jenkins), Katherine, John, Patricia, Richard, Brian, Peter. BA magna cum laude, Yale U., 1937, LLB, 1940; JSD, N.Y. U., 1951; grad., Command and Gen. Staff Sch., 1944. Bar: N.Y. State 1940, D.C. 1953, Calif. 1954, U.S. Supreme Ct. 1944. Asso. firm Dorsey and Adams, 1940-41, Dorsey, Adams and Walker, 1946-50; counsel Office of Sec. of Def., Dept. Def., Washington, 1950-52; acting gen. counsel def. Electric Power Adminstrn., 1952-53; atty. Pacific Gas and Electric Co., San Francisco, 1953-70; assoc. gen. counsel Pacific Gas and Electric Co., 1970-74, v.p., gen. counsel, 1975-80; individual practice law San Francisco, 1980—; dir. Gas Lines, Inc. Bd. dirs. Legal Aid Soc. San Francisco, Presidio Preservation Assn., 1995—; chmn. Golden Gate dist. Boy Scouts Am., 1973-75; commr. Human Rights Commn. of San Francisco, 1976-89, chmn., 1980-82; chmn. Cath. Social Svc. of San Francisco, 1966-68; adv. com. Archdiocesan Legal Affairs, 1991—; regent Archdiocesan Sch. of Theology St. Patrick's Seminary, 1994—. Decorated Bronze star, Army Commendation medal. Mem. NAS, AAAS, ABA, Calif. State Bar Assn., Fed. Power Bar Assn., N.Y. Acad. Scis., Calif. Conf. Pub. Utility Counsel, Pacific Coast Electric Assn., Pacific Coast Gas Assn., Econ. Round Table of San Francisco, World Affairs Council, San Francisco C. of C., Calif. State C. of C., Harold Brunn Soc. Med. Rsch., Electric Club, Serra Club, Commonwealth Club, Yale Club of San Francisco (pres. 1989-90), Pacific-Union Club, Sometimes Tuesday Club, Sovereign Mil. Order Malta, Phi Beta Kappa. Roman Catholic. Home: 2030 Jackson St San Francisco CA 94109-2840 Office: PO Box 77000 123 Mission St Rm 1709 San Francisco CA 94177

MORROW, BRIAN R., publishing executive; b. Summit, N.J., Dec. 25, 1945; s. John and Martha (Sloan) M.; m. Karen Barnett, April 21, 1971; children: BrianJohn, Cheryl Anne, Matthew John, Madelyn Jean. BS, U. Colo., 1967, MS, 1970. Asst. sales Horseman Edge Mag., Denver, 1971-75, assoc. sales, 1975-80, mgr. sales, 1980-86; owner, pres. HorseBeat U.S.A., Flagstaff, Ariz., 1986—. Mem. Am. Mag. Assn. (bd. dir. 1994—), Colo. Mag. Soc. (sec. 1993, pres. 1994), Phi Delta Phi. Democrat. Roman Catholic. Office: Werik Pub 523 N Beaver St Flagstaff AZ 86001-3042

MORROW, JAMES THOMAS, financial executive; b. Seattle, Apr. 24, 1941; s. James Elroy and Helen Margaret (Helzer) M.; B.S. in Elec. Engring. and B.S. in Gen. Sci., Oreg. State U., 1964; Ph.D., U. Santa Clara, 1973, M.B.A., 1966; 1 child, Shannon F. Registered profl. engr.; registered investment advisor. Engr. Gen. Electric Co., San Jose, Calif., 1964-66; engring. mgr. Beckman Instruments, Inc., Palo Alto, Calif., 1966-69; pres. MSA Cons., Inc., Portland, Oreg., 1969-75; asst. prof. U. Portland, 1969-75; mgr. A.T. Kearney, Inc., San Francisco, 1975-78; v.p. mktg. Pierce Pacific Mfg., Portland, 1978-79; chmn., chief exec. officer Lanco Internat., Inc., Clackamas, Oreg., 1979-81; regional mgr., v.p. Case & Co., Portland, 1981-82; chmn. bd., exec. v.p. Morley Fin. Svcs., Inc., 1982-94; exec. v.p., chmn. bd. Biojet, Inc., 1985-94; ptnr. WAM Ptnrship., 1987—; sec.-treas. Environ. Waste of Am., Inc., Seattle, 1992-94; chmn., pres., CEO Capital Devel. Group, Inc., Portland, 1994—; chmn., CEO USA/China Design and Mfg. Inc., Tianjing, China, 1994—; bd. dirs. Accucom Data Network, Inc., Pierce Pacific Mfg., Lanco Internat., Energy Guard, Inc., G&R Devel. Co., Inc., MSA Cons., Inc., Inc. sec.-treas. Everybody's Record Co., Inc. Bd. dirs. Found. for Oreg. Research and Edn., Jr. Achievement, First August Fin., Inc., Met. Youth Symphony; chmn. steering com. R.S. Dow Neurol. Scis. Inst. Republican. Congregationalist. Contbr. articles to profl. jours., chpts. to textbooks; patentee Biojector Needleless Syringe. Home: 2616 NW 81st Pl Portland OR 97229-4104 Office: Capital Devel Group Inc 111 SW 5th Ave Ste 4075 Portland OR 97204-3643

MORROW, MARK JAY, neurologist, educator; b. Methuen, Mass., May 13, 1959; s. Hugh III and Marlen Patricia (McAuliffe), M ; m. Valerie Minna Dessau, Apr. 19, 1986; children: Keith Michael, Kendra Margaret. BA, Boston U., 1982, MD, 1982. Intern internal medicine U. So. Calif. L.A. (Calif.) County Med. Ctr., 1982-83; resident neurology UCLA Med. Ctr., L.A., 1983-85, chief resident neurology, 1985-86; clin. and rsch. fellow neuro-ophthalmology The Toronto (Ont.) Hosp., 1986-89; acting chief dept. neurology Olive View/UCLA Med. Ctr., Sylmar, 1989-90, chief dept. neurology, 1990—; asst. prof. UCLA Sch. Medicine, L.A., 1989—; cons. physician UCLA Med. Ctr., L.A., 1989—, Sepulveda (Calif.) VA Med. Ctr., 1989—. Contbr. to various med. texts and articles to profl. jours. Recipient Nat. Rsch. Svc. award NIH/Nat. Eye Inst., Bethesda, 1987-89, F.I.R.S.T. award NIH/Nat. Eye Inst., Bethesda, 1994—; Rsch. Seed grantee Olive View Edn. and Rsch. Inst., Sylmar, 1990-92; Acad. Senate grantee UCLA Sch. Medicine, L.A., 1991-93. Mem. Am. Acad. Neurology, Soc. for Neuroscience, Assn. for Rsch. in Vision and Opthalmology, N.Am. Neuro-Ophthalmology Soc., Olive View Profl. Staff Assn. (pres. 1994—). Office: Olive View/UCLA Med Ctr 14445 Olive View Dr Sylmar CA 91342-1438

MORROW, WINSTON VAUGHAN, financial executive; b. Grand Rapids, Mich., Mar. 22, 1924; s. Winston V. and Selma (von Egloffstein) M.; m. Margaret Ellen Staples, June 25, 1948 (div.); children: Thomas Christopher, Mark Staples; m. Edith Burrows Ulrich, Mar. 2, 1990. AB cum laude, Williams Coll., 1947; JD, Harvard U., 1950. Bar: R.I. 1950. Assoc. atty. Edwards & Angell, Providence, 1950-57; exec. v.p., asst. treas., gen. counsel, bd. dirs. Avis, Inc. and subs., 1957-61; v.p., gen. mgr. Rent A Car div. Avis, Inc., 1962-64, pres., bd. dirs., 1964-75; chmn., chief exec. officer, bd. dirs. Avis, Inc. and Avis Rent A Car System, Inc., 1965-77; chmn., pres., bd. dirs. Teleflorists Inc. and subs., 1978-80; pres. Westwood Equities Corp., L.A., 1981-95, CEO, 1984-95, also bd. dirs.; chmn., pres., chief exec. officer Ticor Title Ins. Co., 1982-91, also bd. dirs.; chmn. TRTS Data Svcs. Inc., 1985-91; bd. dirs. AECOM Tech. Corp., L.A., 1990—; dir. William & Scott, Inc., 1994—; mem. Pres.'s Industry and Govt. Spl. Travel Task Force, 1968, travel adv. bd. U.S. Travel Svcs., 1968-76, L.A. City-wide Airport Adv. Com., 1983-85; co-chmn. L.A. Transp. Coalition, 1985-91. Mem. juvenile delinquency task force Nat. Coun. Crime and Delinquency, 1985-86, L.A. Mayor's Bus. Coun., 1983-86, Housing Roundtable, Washington, 1983-85; chmn., pres. Spring St. Found., 1991—; bd. dirs. Police Found., Washington, 1983-91; trustee Com. for Econ. Devel., Washington, 1987-91. Decorated Stella Della Solidarieta Italy, Gold Tourism medal Austria). Mem. Fed. Bar Assn., R.I. Bar Assn., Car and Truck Rental and Leasing Assn. (nat. pres. 1961-63), Am. Land Title Assn. (bd. govs. 1989-90), L.A. Area C. of C. (bd. dirs. 1983-90), The Huntington (fellow), Bald Peak Colony Club, Williams Club, L.A. Tennis Club, Phi Beta Kappa, Kappa Alpha. Home: 4056 Farmouth Dr Los Angeles CA 90027-1314 also: Meadowview Farm Cushing Corners Rd Freedom NH 03836-0221

MORSBERGER, ROBERT EUSTIS, English language educator; b. Balt., Sept. 10, 1929; s. Eustis Espey and Mary Virginia (Burgess) M.; m. Katharine Miller, June 17, 1955; 1 child, Grace Anne. BA, Johns Hopkins U., 1950; MA, U. Iowa, 1954, PhD, 1956. Instr., asst. prof. Miami U., Oxford, Ohio, 1956-59; asst. prof. English Utah State U., Logan, 1959-61; asst. prof., assoc. prof. Mich. State U., East Lansing, 1961-68; assoc. prof., dept. head U. Nigeria, Nsukka, 1964-66; prof. English Eastern Ky. U., Richmond, 1968-69; assoc. prof., prof. English, dept. head Calif. State Polytech U., Pomona, 1969—. Author: James Thurber, 1964, (with wife) Lew Wallace: Militant Romantic, 1980; editor: Steinbeck, ZAPATA, 1993; co-editor: American Screenwriters, 1984, vol. 2, 1986; contbr. articles, books and short stories. Chmn. bd. dirs. Claremont (Calif.) Playhouse, 1978-81; bd. dirs. CAMASU, Claremont, 1992—. Mem. Modern Lang. Assn., Internat. John Steinbeck Soc. (edit. bd. 1970—, Burkhardt award Outstanding Contbn. 1991), Am. Assn. 18th Century Studies. Democrat. Home: 1530 Berea Ct Claremont CA 91711-3505 Office: Calif State Polytech U 3801 W Temple Ave Pomona CA 91768

MORSE, JACK CRAIG, lawyer; b. Evanston, Ill., Aug. 11, 1936; s. Leland Robert and Pauline (Pettibone) M.; children by past marriage: David Leland, Katherine Malia. BA, Beloit Coll., 1958; JD, Northwestern U., 1965. Bar: Hawaii 1967, U.S. Dist. Ct. Hawaii 1969, U.S. Ct. Appeals (9th cir.) 1977. Legal staff Bishop Estate, Honolulu, 1966-68; dep. atty. gen. State of Hawaii, Honolulu, 1968-71; ptnr. Saunders & Morse, Honolulu, 1971-73; assoc. Chuck & Wong, Honolulu, 1974-75; officer, dir. Morse, Nelson & Ross, Honolulu, 1976-85; mem. Hawaii Med. Claim Conciliation Panel, Honolulu, 1977—, chmn., 1980—; mem. panel of arbitrators First Judicial Cir., Hawaii, 1986—. Lt. USN, 1959-62. Hardy scholar Northwestern U., 1962. Mem. Am. Judicature Soc., Assn. Trial Lawyers Am., Omicron Delta Kappa. Office: 700 Richards St Apt 1706 Honolulu HI 96813-4619

MORSE, JOHN MOORE, architect, planner; b. Brookline, Mass., Aug. 23, 1911; s. Arthur Moore and Helen (Stearns) M.; m. Emily Hall (dec. 1988); children: David Hall, Catherine Morse Wikkerink; m. Helen Taverniti, Aug. 5, 1989. AB, Harvard U., 1934, MArch, 1940. Registered architect, Wash. Tchr. Loomis Sch., Windsor, Conn., 1934-36; ptnr. Bassetti & Morse, Seattle, 1947-62; prin. John Morse & Assocs., Seattle, 1962-78; ptnr. Morse Stafford Ptnrship., Seattle, 1978-85; prin. John Morse Architect & Planner, Seattle, 1985—. Mem. King County (Wash.) Planning Commn., 1965-70, Design Rev. Bd., Mill Creek, Wash., 1987-89; chmn. Seattle Urban Design Bd., 1966; bd. dirs. Cornish Coll. Arts, Seattle, 1974-80. Fellow AIA (pres. Seattle chpt. 1969, various local and nat. awards). Democrat. Office: 7027 32nd NE Seattle WA 98115

MORSE, JUDY, science foundation administrator. Ceo Arboretum Foundation, Los Angeles County Arboreta and Botanic Gardens, Arcadia, Calif. Office: Los Angeles County Arboretum Found 301 N Baldwin Ave Arcadia CA 91007

MORSE, LOWELL WESLEY, banking and real estate executive; b. West Palm Beach, Fla., May 1, 1937; s. Alton and Blanche (Yelverton) M.; B.S., U. Santa Clara, 1968; grad. Def. Lang. Inst., Monterey, Calif., 1959; m. Vera Giacalone, June 22, 1958; children: Lowell Wesley, Stephen D., Michael S. Russian linguist U.S. Army Security Agy., 1957-60; asst. city mgr. City of Pacific Grove (Calif.), 1961-66; city mgr. Town of Los Altos Hills (Calif.), 1967-69; chmn. Morse & Assos., Inc., Portland, Oreg., 1972—; founder, dir. Comerica Bank Calif., San Jose, 1979—; chmn. Cypress Ventures Inc., Portland, The Bagel Basket, Inc.; bd. trustees Regent U. Served with U.S. Army, 1957-60. Home: 21042 SW Wyndham Hill Ct Tualatin OR 97062-7711 Office: 5335 Meadows Rd Ste 365 Lake Oswego OR 97035-3114

MORSE, MICHAEL DAVID, chemistry educator, researcher; b. New Martinsville, W.Va., Oct. 6, 1952; s. Harold Lane and Opal Geneva (Nichols) M.; m. Cynthia Jo Brandt, Nov. 26, 1983. BS, Haverford Coll., 1974; MS, U. Chgo., 1977, PhD, 1980. Vis. asst. prof. Rice U., Houston, 1981-83, rsch. assoc., 1983-84; asst. prof. U. Utah, Salt Lake City, 1985-90, assoc. prof., 1990-93; prof., 1993—. Contbr. articles to profl. jours. Fellow AAAS; mem. Am. Phys. Soc., Am. Chem. Soc. Office: Univ Utah Dept Chemistry Salt Lake City UT 84112

MORSE, RICHARD, social scientist; b. Boston, Oct. 12, 1922; s. Stearns and Helen Ward (Field) M.; m. Romola Thomas Chowdhry, June 23, 1949; children: Ashok Daniel, Martha Sunita Kelly. A.B., Dartmouth Coll., 1946; postgrad., Banaras Hindu U., Aligarh Muslim U., Gokhale Inst. Politics and Econs., India, 1947, Columbia, 1950; A.M., ABD, Harvard, 1958. Edn. officer ECA, Burma, 1950-53; asst. rep. Ford Found., Burma, 1954-56; sr. internat. economist Stanford Research Inst., Menlo Park, Calif., 1958-64, 66-69; cons. Ford Found., India, 1964-66; indsl. devel. cons. Andover, Mass., 1969-74; rsch. assoc., sr. fellow, co-coord. Participatory Devel. Group East West Ctr., Honolulu, 1974-94; sr. fellow emeritus East West Ctr., Honolulu, 1994—; study dir. Nat. Acad. Sci. and Nat. Acad. Engring. Internat. Panel on Internat. Industrialization Inst., 1972-73; chmn. bd. govs. Inst. Current World Affairs, 1972-74, trustee, 1988-91; bd. dirs. Inst. World Affairs, 1988-91, mem. adv. coun., 1992—; co-founder, dir. Hawaii Entrepreneurship Tng. and Devel. Inst., 1977—; mem. adv. com. Immigrant Ctr. Enterprise Project, Honolulu, 1992—. Co-author: Modern Small Industry for Developing Countries, 1965; (with Eugene Staley) Village Voices in Rural Development and Energy Planning, 1987; co-editor: Grassroot Horizons: Connecting Participatory Development Initiatives East and West, 1995. Served with AUS, 1942-45. Fellow Inst. Current World Affairs, 1946-49; recipient certificate of honor Hawaii Ho. of Reps., 1994. Mem. Am. Econ. Assn., Am. Agrl. Econs. Assn., Am. Assn. Asian Studies, Economists Allied for Arms Reduction, Nitrogen Fixing Tree Assn., Soc. for Internat. Devel. Home: 1621 Halekoa Dr Honolulu HI 96821-1126 Office: 1777 E West Rd Honolulu HI 96822-2323

MORSE, RICHARD JAY, human resources and organizational development consultant, manufacturers' representative company executive; b. Detroit, Aug. 2, 1933; s. Maurice and Belle Rosalyn (Jacobson) M. BA, U. Va., 1955; MA in Clin. Psychology, Calif. State U., L.A., 1967. Area pers. adminstr. Gen. Tel. Co. of Calif., Santa Monica, 1957-67; sr. v.p. human resources The Bekins Co., Glendale, Calif., 1967-83; pvt. cons. human resources and orgn. devel. Glendale, 1983—. Contbr. articles to profl. jours. Fund raiser various orgns., So. Calif., 1970—. Mem. Nat. Soc. Performance and Instrn. (founding mem. 1958—). Republican. Jewish. Home and Office: 6410 Cambria Pines Rd Cambria CA 93428-2009

MORTENSEN, ARVID LEGRANDE, lawyer; b. Bremerton, Wash., July 11, 1941; s. George Andrew and Mary Louise (Myers) M.; m. Elaine Marie Mains, Aug. 2, 1968; children: Marie Louise, Anne Catherine, Joseph Duncan. BS in English and Psychology, Brigham Young U., 1965, MBA in Mktg. and Fin., 1967; JD cum laude, Ind. U., 1980. Bar: Ind. 1980, U.S. Supreme Ct. 1983, Mo. 1985, D.C. 1985, FCC lic. amateur radio operator, 1994—; CLU. Agt. Conn. Mut. Life Ins. Co., Salt Lake City, 1967-68, agt. and br. mgr., Idaho Falls, Idaho, 1968-74; with Rsch. and Rev. Svc. Am., Inc./Newkirk Assocs., Inc., Indpls., 1974-83, sr. editor, 1975-79, mgr. advanced products and seminars, 1979-80, sr. mktg. exec., 1980-83; tax and fin. planner, Indpls., 1980-85, St. Louis and Chesterfield, Mo., 1985-90, Tampa Bay, Fla., 1990-91, Orange County, Calif., 1991—. mem. sr. mgmt. com., v.p. Allied Fidelity Corp., 1983-85, Allied Fidelity Ins. Co., 1983-85, Tex. Fire and Casualty Ins. Co., 1983-85; v.p., bd. dirs. Gen. Am. Ins. Co., St. Louis, 1985-86; v.p. Gen. Am. Life Ins. Co., St. Louis, 1985-90; pvt. practice law, Indpls., 1980-85, St. Louis, Chesterfield and Bridgeton, Mo., 1985-90, Tampa Bay, 1990-91, Orange County, 1991—; active with Ch. Jesus Christ of Latter-day Saints, Denver, Idaho Falls, Idaho, Indpls., St. Louis, Chesterfield, Tampa Bay Area and Orange County, Calif., Profl. Assn. Diving Instrs. cert. Divemaster, 1989—. Mem. Assn. Advanced Life Underwriting, Mo. Bar Assn., Bar Assn. Met. St. Louis, D.C. Bar Assn., Ind. Bar Assn., Am. Soc. CLU's, Nat. Assn. Life Underwriters, Orange County,. Author: Employee Stock Ownership Plans, 1975, Fundamentals of Corporate Qualified Retirement Plans, 1975, 78, 80, Buy-Sell Agreements, 1988, The Key Executive Sale, 1989, (with Norman H. Tarver) The IRA Manual, 1975-87 edits., (with Norman H. Tarver) The Keogh Manual, 1975, 77, 78, 80 edits., (with Norman H. Tarver) The Section 403 (b) Manual, 1975, 77, 78, 80, 84, 85, 87 edits., sole author 1991,93 , 94, edit., (with Leo C. Hodges) The Life Insurance Trust Handbook, 1980; contbr. articles to profl. jours.; editor-in-chief various tax and fin. planning courses; bd. editors Ind. Law Rev., 1977-78. Avocation: lic. amateur radio operator. Office: 620 Newport Center Dr Ste 1100 Newport Beach CA 92660-8011 Also: PO Box 6362 Laguna Niguel CA 92607-6362

MORTENSEN, CARL EVAN, oil company owner; b. Alamosa, Colo., Sept. 21, 1949; s. Grant Curtis and Anne Louise (Crowther) M.; m. Debora Carlene Beggs, Feb. 29, 1968; children: Tyanya, Ky, Naticia, Vanessa, Tysen, Mikasa, Shayla. BA, Adams State Coll., 1973. Owner Arrowhead Sales, Sanford, Colo., 1973—; owner Chiefs Texaco, La Jara, Colo., 1984—, Alamosa, 1994—; owner Arrowhead Jewelry, Sanford, 1973—, Arrowhead Trailers, Sanford, 1993—. Author: The Healing of America, 1993; inventor combination metric and std. Dir. ch. pageant Settlement of West, 1979-93; founders Friends of Ben, Sanford, 1989; scoutmaster Boy Scouts Am., 1982—. Recipient 30 Eagle Scouts Boy Scouts Am., 1992. Mem. Am. Fastener Distbrs., Nat. Assn. of Convenience Stores. Mem. Ch. LDS. Office: Chiefs Texaco PO Box 194 Alamosa CO 81101-0194

MORTENSEN, GLEN ALBERT, chemical engineer; b. Moscow, Idaho; s. William A. and Frances (Nicholson) M; m. Patricia L. Harkness; children: Keith, Wayne, Hans, Mark. BSChemE, U. Idaho, 1955; PhD, U. Calif., Berkeley, 1963. Student Oak Ridge Sch. Reactor Tech., 1956; engr. Atomic Energy Commn., 1956-58, Nat. Reactor Test Sta., 1963-75, Intermountain Techs. Inc., 1975-86; prin. engr. Idaho Nat. Engring. Lab., Idaho Falls, 1986—. Mem. Am. Nuclear Soc., Assn. Computer Machinery. Home: 2975 Balboa Dr Idaho Falls ID 83404-7499 Office: INEL PO Box 1625 Idaho Falls ID 83415-3808

MORTENSEN, GORDON LOUIS, artist, printmaker; b. Arnegard, N.D., Apr. 27, 1938; s. Gunner and Otillia Ernestine (Reiner) M.; m. Phoebe Hollis Hansen, Apr. 10, 1965 (div. 1968); m. Linda Johanna Sisson, Dec. 7, 1969. B.F.A., Mpls. Coll. Art and Design, 1964; postgrad., U. Minn., 1969-72. Exhibited one-man shows, Minn. Mus., St. Paul, 1967, Sioux City Art Ctr., Iowa, 1968, Plains Art Mus., Moorhead, Minn., 1976, 78, 80, 82, 83, Assoc. Am. Artists, Phila., 1979, Mary Ryan Gallery, N.Y.C., 1983, Concept Art Gallery Pitts., 1981, 83, 85, 87, 89, 91, 93, Louis Newman Gallery, Beverly Hills, 1983, C.G. Rein Galleries, Mpls., 1978, 80, 85, 89, 91; group shows, Miami U., Oxford, Ohio (1st place award 1977), Phila. Print Club (George Bunker award 1977), 12th Nat. Silvermine Guild Print Exhbn., New Canaan, Conn., 1976, 78, 80, 83, 86, 94 (Hearsh Mag. award 1978, Purchase award 1983, 86), 4th Miami Internat. Print Biennial (4th place award 1980), Rockford Internat. 1981, 85 (Juror's award 1981), Mpls. Inst. Arts Biennial, 1963, 67, Bklyn. Mus., 1976, Boston Printmakers Nat. Exhbn., 1977, 79, 80, 81, 83 (purchase award 1977, 79, 83); represented permanent collections, Achenbach Foun. Graphic Arts at Palace of Legion of Honor, San Francisco, Bklyn. Mus., Phila. Mus. Art, Library of Congress, Minn. Mus. Art, Met. Mus. and Art Ctr., Miami, Fla., Mus. Am. Art, Washington, Art Inst. Chgo., Mus. Art at Carnegie-Mellon Inst., Pitts., Walker Art Ctr., Mpls., Dulin Gallery Art, Knoxville, Tenn., numerous corp. collections; profiled in numerous art jours. Served with USMC, 1957-60. Mem. Boston Printmakers, Phila. Print Club, Artists Equity, Albany Print Club. Home and Office: 4153 Crest Rd Pebble Beach CA 93953-3052

MORTENSEN, RICHARD EDGAR, engineering educator; b. Denver, Sept. 29, 1935; s. Edgar Steele and Frieda Amalie (Boecker) M.; m. Sarah Jean Raulston, Oct. 12, 1974 (div. 1978). BSEE, MIT, 1958, MSEE, 1958; PhD, U. Calif., Berkeley, 1966. Co-op. engr. GE Co., Schenectady, N.Y., 1955-57; mem. tech. staff Space Tech. Labs., L.A., 1958-61; rsch. asst. U. Calif., Berkeley, 1961-65; prof. engring. UCLA, 1965-91, prof. emeritus, 1991—; cons. TRW, Inc., Redondo Beach, Calif., 1966-70, Aerojet-Gen. Corp., Azusa, Calif., 1970-72, Applied Sci. Analytics, Inc., Canoga Park, Calif., 1980-82; guest lectr. Indian Inst. Sci., Bangalore, India, 1991. Author: Random Signals and Systems, 1987; contbr. to profl. publs. Team mem. Beyond War, Topanga, Calif., 1986-89; alcoholism counselor. Grantee NSF, 1987-90. Mem. IEEE, Soc. Indsl. and Applied Math., Sigma Xi, Tau Beta Pi, Eta Kappa Nu. Office: Dept Elec Engring 405 Hilgard Ave Los Angeles CA 90024-1301

MORTENSEN, RICHARD HAROLD, data processing executive; b. St. Anthony, Idaho, Oct. 23, 1953; s. Richard and Wanda Rae (Green) M.; m. Marva Dawn Storer; children: Kimberli, Dane, Erik. BS in Math./Computer Sci., U. Idaho, 1977. Programmer Billing Computer Corp., Provo, Utah, 1977-79; programmer/sr. analyst HEW, Boise, Idaho, 1979-82; data processing mgr. Bosie Cascade Corp., Boise, 1982—; computer cons. Computer Ptnrs. Inc., Boise, 1982. Author software GS-STAT, Master, 1989. Coach Little League Baseball, Boise, 1989-93, umpire, 1994. Mem. Data Processing Mgmt. Assn. Home: 11807 W Dason Ct Boise ID 83713-1755 Office: Boise Cascade Corp 1 Jefferson Sq Boise ID 83728-0001

MORTENSEN, WILLIAM S., banking executive; b. 1932. Chmn. bd., pres., CEO 1st Fed. Bank Calif., Santa Monica, 1955—, now CEO. Office: 1st Fed Bank Calif 401 Wilshire Blvd Santa Monica CA 90401-1416*

MORTIMER, WENDELL REED, JR., lawyer; b. Alhambra, Calif., Apr. 7, 1937; s. Wendell Reed and Blanche (Wilson) M.; m. Cecilia Vick, Aug. 11, 1962; children: Michelle Dawn, Kimberly Grace. AB, Occidental Coll., 1958; JD, U. So. Calif., L.A., 1965. Bar: Calif. 1966. Trail atty. Legal div. State of Calif., L.A., 1965-73; assoc. Thelen, Marrin, Johnson & Bridges, L.A., 1973-76, ptnr., 1976-93; pvt. practice law San Marino, Calif., 1994—; judge pro tem L.A. Superior Ct., settlement officer. Active San Marino Community Ch. With U.S. Army, 1960-62. Mem. ABA (litigation sect.), Am. Arbitration Assn. (arbitrator), State Bar Calif., L.A. County Bar Assn. (jud. appointments com. 1990-92), Pasadena Bar Assn., Legion Lex., U. So. Calif. Alumni Assn., San Marino City Club. Home and office: 1420 San Marino Ave San Marino CA 91108-2042

MORTIMER, WILLIAM JAMES, newspaper publisher; b. Provo, Utah, June 26, 1932; s. William Earl and Margaret (Johnson) M.; m. Paula Ann Deline, Sept. 17, 1956; children: Jeffrey, David, Gregory, Bradley, Judy, William James II, Jennifer. BS, Utah State U., 1954; MS, Columbia U., 1957. Reporter Deseret News, Salt Lake City, 1957-59, pres., pub., 1985—; sales mgr. Deseret News Press, Salt Lake City, 1959-63; gen. mgr. Deseret News Press, 1979-80, Deseret Book Co., Salt Lake City, 1966-79; sr. account exec. Wheelwright Lithographing, Salt Lake City, 1963-66; dir. LDS Ch. Printing Svcs., Salt Lake City, 1980-85; v.p., dir. Newspaper Agy. Corp., Salt Lake City, 1985—; pres. Printing Industries of Utah, 1964-65, Utah Retail Mchts. Assn., Salt Lake City, 1977-79. Author: How Beautiful Upon the Mountains, 1963. Campaign chmn. Salt Lake Area United Way, 1987; hon. col. Utah N.G.; chmn. Utah Partnership Ednl. and Econ. Devel.; mem. exec. com. Salt Lake Conv. and Visitors Bur.; chmn. bd. Pioneer State Theatre, 1990-93; pres. Utah Arts Endowment; bd. dirs. Utah Symphony. 1st lt. U.S. Army, 1954-56, Korea. Named Alumnus of Yr. Utah State U., Logan, 1985. Mem. Utah-Idaho-Spokane AP Assn. (pres. 1993-94), Utah Press Assn. (pres. 1994-95), Salt Lake Area C. of C. (chmn. bd. 1988-89), Alta Club. Mem. LDS Ch. Home: 8763 Kings Hill Dr Salt Lake City UT 84121-6135 Office: Deseret News Pub Co PO Box 1257 Salt Lake City UT 84110-1257

MORTON, LAUREL ANNE, elementary education educator; b. Cin., July 27, 1954; d. James William and Rosemary (Danner) M. BA in Social Sci., Calif. State U.-Stanislaus, Turlock, 1978; teaching credential, Calif. State Polytech U., Pomona, 1986; MA in Edn., Calif. State Poly. U., Pomona, 1992. Cert. tchr., Calif., Colo. Sr. loan clk. Shearson Am. Express Mortgage Corp., Newport Beach, Calif., 1978-82; adminstrv. asst. Investco Corp., Santa Barbara, Calif., 1982-83; supr. loan servicing dept. County Savs. Bank, Santa Barbara, 1983-84; comm. asst. Fuller Theol. Sem., Pasadena, Calif., 1984-85; elem. tchr. Howard Sch., Ontario, Calif., 1986-91; tchr. Bon View Elem. Sch., Ontario, 1992—, 4th grade team leader, 1993-94. Mem. Nat. Honor Soc., Phi Kappa Phi, Zeta Tau Alpha. Home: 1919 Stonehouse Rd Sierra Madre CA 91024-1409 Office: Bon View Elem Sch 1515 S Bon View Ave Ontario CA 91761-4408

MORTON, LINDA, mayor; b. Dec. 7, 1944; married; 2 children. BA with honors, U. Nebr., 1966. Lic. real estate broker. Tchr. Sunnyvale (Calif.) Elem. Sch., 1967-69, Jefferson County (Colo.) Sch. Dist., 1966-67, 69-70; real estate agt. Crown Realty, Lakewood, Colo., 1979-82, Van Schaack & Co., Lakewood, 1982-83, Re-Max Profls., Lakewood, 1983-91. Mem. city council City of Lakewood, 1981-91, now Mayor, Lakewood, Colo., 1991—; represented Lakewood on Bd. Denver Regional Council of Govts., from 1981, chairwoman, 1986-87; chmn. Jefferson City C. of C., 1989-90; appointed by Gov. Colo. to Met. Air Quality Council, 1985; bd. dirs. Nat. Assn. Regional Coun. Govts., 1986-90, CML, 1993—. Office: City of Lakewood 445 S Allison Pky Lakewood CO 80226-3106

MORTVEDT, JOHN JACOB, soil scientist; b. Dell Rapids, S.D., Jan. 25, 1932; s. Ernest R. and Clara (Halvorson) M.; m. Marlene L. Fodness, Jan. 23, 1955; children: Sheryl Mortvedt Jarratt, Lori Mortvedt Klopf, Julie Mortvedt Stride. BS, S.D. State U., 1953, MS, 1959; PhD, U. Wis., 1962. Soil chemist TVA, Muscle Shoals, Ala., 1962-87, sr. scientist, 1987-92, regional mgr. field programs dept., 1992-93; extension soils specialist Colo. State U., Ft. Collins, 1994—. Editor: Micronutrients in Agriculture, 1972, 2d edit., 1991; contbr. articles to profl. jours. 1st lt. U.S. Army, 1953-57. Fellow AAAS, Soil Sci. Soc. Am. (pres. 1988-89, editor-in-chief 1982-87, Profl. Svc. award 1991), Am. Soc. Agronomy (exec. com. 1987-90); mem. Internat. Soil Sci. Soc., Colombian Soil Sci. Soc. (hon.), Exch. Club (pres. Florence, Ala. chpt. 1987-88), Toastmasters (pres. Florence chpt. 1964-65), Phi Kappa Phi. Office: Colo State U Dept Soil and Crop Scis Fort Collins CO 80523

MOSBY, DOROTHEA SUSAN, municipal official; b. Sacramento, Calif., May 13, 1948; d. William Laurence and Esther Ida (Lux) M. AA in Sociology, Bakersfield (Calif.) Coll., 1966-69; BS in Recreation, San Jose State U., 1969-72; MPA, Calif. State U. Dominguez Hills, Carson, 1980-82. Asst. dept. pers. officer San Jose Pks. and Recreation Dept., 1972-73, neighborhood ctr. dir., 1973-74; sr. recreation leader Santa Monica Recreation and Pks. Dept., 1974-76, recreation supr., 1976-83; head bus. divsn. Santa Monica Recreation and Parks Dept., 1983-88; bus. adminstr. Santa Monica Cultural & Recreation Svcs., 1988-91; dir. pks. and recreation City of South Gate, Calif., 1991—; bd. dirs., officer Santa Monica City Employees Fed. Credit Union, 1980-89, pres. 1986-87; mem. citizens adv. com. L.A. Olympic Organizing Com., 1982-84. Mem. choir, flute soloist Pilgrim Luth. Ch., Santa Monica, 1974—, treas. Luth. ch. coun., 1984-86; vol. driver XXIII Olympiad, Los Angeles, 1984; contbr. local housing assistance U.S. Olympic Com., Los Angeles, 1984; mem. adv. com. Windsor Sq. Hancock Park Hist. Soc., Los Angeles, 1983, dir. Christmas carolling, 1980—, chmn. Olympic com., 1984, bd. trustees, 1984-90, chmn. pub. programs, 1985, co-chmn. pub. programs, 1986, co-vice chair, 1987, chmn., 1988, 89—; L.A. Philharm. Bus. & Profl. Com.; mem. Samuel C. May Grad. Student Rsch. Paper Judging Com., Western Govt. Rsch. Assn., 1994. Recipient Outstanding Profl. of Yr. award Los Angeles Basin Pk. and Recreation Commrs. and Bd. Mems., 1993. Mem. Calif. Pk. and Recreation Soc. (bd. dirs. 1979-82, 86, mem. Calif. bd. pk. and recreation pers. 1990-92, Scholarship Found. Bd., 1992—, dist. 10 v.p. 1994), Nat. Recreation and Pk. Assn., Mgmt. Team Assocs. (sec., treas. 1979-83), L.A. World Affairs Coun., Western Govtl. Rsch. Assn., South Gate C. of C., Kiwanis Club, Chi Kappa Rho (pres. 1986), Pi Alpha Alpha, Nat. Assn. Univ. Women. Home: 9329 Elm Vista Dr Apt 103 Downey CA 90242-2992 Office: City of South Gate Dept Pks and Recreation 4900 Southern Ave South Gate CA 90280-3462

MOSEBAR, DONALD HOWARD, professional football player; b. Yakima, Wash., Sept. 11, 1961. Student, U. So. Calif. Center L.A. Raiders, 1983—. Named NFL All-Pro team center, The Sporting News, 1991, Played in Super Bowl XVIII, 1983. Office: L.A. Raiders 332 Center St El Segundo CA 90245-4047*

MOSELEY, DAVID HERRON, public administrator; b. Mobile, Ala., May 13, 1947; s. Fred Baker and Lily Gay (Lord) M.; m. Juanita Alece Cox, May 1, 1971 (div. July 1984); m. Joan Anne Fennessy, Sept. 23, 1989. BA in Polit. Sci., Willamette U., 1969; MDiv in Counseling, Golden Gate Theol. Sem., 1972; cert., Harvard U., 1986. Dir. Telegraph Ave. Comty. Ctr., Oakland, Calif., 1970-74; project mgr., social svc. coord. comty. accountability prog. City of Seattle, 1974-78, dir. divsn. youth svcs., 1979-81; dir. coll. rels. Seattle Ctrl. C.C., 1982-84; dir. dept. comty. devel. City of Seattle, 1984-90; staff dir. speaker's office Ho. Reps., Washington, 1984-90; town adminstr. Town of Steilacoom, Wash., 1992—; com. mem. Transp. Coordinating Com., Pierce County, Wash., 1993—. Agy. coord. United Way, Pierce County, 1993-94; presdl. appointee Nat. Adv. Com. for Juvenile Justice and Delinquency Prevention, 1979-81. Recipient Affirmative Action award Seattle Urban League, 1981. Mem. Steilacoom C. of C., Rotary Club Lakewood. Democrat. Office: 1715 Lafayette St Steilacoom WA 98388-1327

MOSER, C. THOMAS, lawyer; b. Seattle, Aug. 10, 1947; s. Carl Thomas and Helen Louise (Felton) M.; m. Debbie J. St. Clair, Sept. 25, 1976; children: Nichole, Lauren. BA, Cen. Wash. U., 1972; M in Pub. Adminstrn., George Washington U., 1974; JD, Gonzaga U., 1976. Bar: Wash. 1977; U.S. Dist. Ct. (we. dist.) Wash. 1977, U.S. Dist. Ct. (ea. dist.) Wash. 1980, U.S. Ct. Appeals (9th cir.) 1980, U. S. Supreme Ct. 1981. Dep. pros. atty. Skagit County Pros. Atty., Mount Vernon, Wash., 1976-77, chief civil dep., 1979-80, pros. atty., 1980-86; pros. atty. San Juan County Pros. Atty., Friday Harbor, Wash., 1977-79; pvt. practice Mount Vernon, 1987—; hearing examiner pro tem Skagit County, 1992—. Author: Gonzaga Law Review, 1975. Bd. dirs. Wash. Environ. Coun., Seattle, 1971-72, Padilla Bay Found., Skagit County, Wash., 1988; bd. trustees Wash. Assn. County Officials, Olympia, 1983; exec. bd. North Pacific Conf. Evang. Covenant Ch., vice sec. 1991—. Sgt. U.S. Army, 1967-69, Korea. Recipient Silver Key award ABA Student Law Div., 1976, Legion of Honor award Internat. Order DeMolay, Kansas City, Mo., 1982, Chevalier award 1982. Mem. ATLA, Nat. Coll. Advocacy (advocate), Wash. State Trial Lawyers Assn. (bd. govs. 1990-92), Wash. Assn. Pros. Attys. (bd. dirs. 1983-85), Kiwanis Club Mt. Vernon, Affiliated Health Svc. (ethics com.), Christian Legal Soc. Democrat. Evangelical. Office: 411 Main St Mount Vernon WA 98273-3837

MOSER, DEAN JOSEPH, accountant; b. San Francisco, Apr. 5, 1942; s. Joseph Edward and Velma Ida (Cruz) M.; BS, U. San Francisco, 1964, postgrad. Law Sch., 1964-66; MA in taxation, Golden Gate U., 1988; m. Michele Patrice Cicerone, June 16, 1963; children: Jay, Lynele, Todd. CPA, Calif.; cert. fin. planner; lic. real estate broker, Calif. Owner, acct. DJM Bookkeeping Svc., 1962-65; asst. contr. Dymo Industries, Internat., Berkeley, Calif., 1965-67; mgr. taxes Arthur Andersen & Co., San Francisco, 1967-76; owner, mgr. Contadora Ltd., Novato, Calif., 1981—, Esprit Realty Co., Novato, 1981—; Dean J. Moser Accountancy Corp., Novato, 1981—, Stellar Properties; gen. mgr. Hal C. Aguirre Co.; founding dir., treas., CFO Novato Nat. Bank, NorthBay Bancorp. Asst. scout master Boy Scouts Am.; past bd. dirs. Novato Human Needs Center. Mem. AICPA, Calif. Soc. CPAs. Republican. Roman Catholic. Club: Rotary (Paul Harris fellow, past pres. Ignacio, Marin pres.'s coun., dust. area rep.). Office: 1450 Grant Ave Novato CA 94945-3119

MOSER, SARAH GUNNING, manufacturing engineer, small business owner; b. Seattle, Sept. 17, 1953; d. Harvey Dade and Grace Wills (Bell) Gunning; m. Lawrence Herman Moser, May 18, 1985; children: Grace Elizabeth, Gregory Edward. BA in Archtl. Planning, Evergreen State Coll., Olympia, Wash., 1975; mfg. engring. cert., Boeing Mfg. Engring. Sch., Everett, Wash., 1980. Asst. variety dept. mgr., clk. The Safeway Corp., Seattle, 1977-79; mfg. engr. Boeing Co., 747/767 div., Everett, 1980-82; mfg. engr., sr. mfg. engr. McDonnell Douglas Helicopter Co., Mesa, Ariz., 1982-87; co-owner Moser Design Assocs., Vashon, Wash., 1988—, Moser Design Svcs., Vashon, Wash., 1989-90; bus. mgr. for opera singer Patricia S. Lott, Vashon, 1989-90; engring. trainer McDonnell Douglas Helicopter Co., Mesa, 1986-87, procedure writer, 1986-87; procedure writer The Boeing Co., Everett, 1981. Cmty. outreach speaker Alcohol Pub. Info. Com., Wash., 1976-80, 88-89; coord. Women's Ctr., Evergreen State Coll., 1973-74; trainer, bd. dirs. Sta. KAOS-FM, Olympia, 1972-74; soloist Unity Ch. of Truth, Seattle, Everett, 1978-82; guest soloist various chs.; co-chmn. Vashon-Maury Island Babysitting Coop., 1988-89, chmn., 1989; coord. Island Home Educators, 1991-92, publicist, 1992-94; sec. Vashon Island Cmty. Ch., 1995—. Recipient Cost Savs. awards Boeing Co., 1980-82. Office: Moser Design Assocs PO Box 1406 Vashon WA 98070-1406

MOSES, ELBERT RAYMOND, JR., speech and dramatic arts educator; b. New Concord, Ohio, Mar. 31, 1908; s. Elbert Raymond Sr. and Helen Martha (Miller) M.; m. Mary Miller Sterrett, Sept. 21, 1933 (dec. Sept. 1984); 1 child, James Elbert (dec.); m. Caroline Mae Entenman, June 19, 1985. AB, U. Pitts., 1932; MS, U. Mich., 1934, PhD, 1936. Instr. U. N.C., Greensboro, 1936-38; asst. prof. Ohio State U., Columbus, 1938-46; assoc. prof. Ea. Ill. State U., Charleston, 1946-56; asst. prof. Mich. State U., E. Lansing, Mich., 1956-59; prof. Clarion (Pa.) State Coll., 1959-71, chmn. dept. speech and dramatic arts, 1959—, emeritus prof., 1971—; Fulbright lectr. State Dept. U.S. Cebu Normal Sch., Cebu City, Philippine Islands, 1955-56; vis. prof. phonetics U. Mo., summer 1968; hon. sec.'s advocate dept. of aging State of Pa., Harrisburg, 1980-81. Author: Guide to Effective Speaking, 1957, Phonetics: A History and Interpretation, 1964, Three Attributes of God, 1983, Adventure in Reasoning, 1988, Beating the Odds, 1992; poems included in Best Poems of the 90s, 1992; contbr. articles to profl. jours. Del. 3d World Congress Phoneticians, Tokyo, 1976; mem. nat. adv. com. fng. students and tchrs. HEW; del. to Internat. Congress Soc. Logopedics and Phoniatre, Vienna, 1965; liaison rep. to Peace Corps; pres. County Libr. Bd.; past exec. dir. Clarion County United Way; commr. Boy Scouts Am., 1976-77; pres. Venango County Adv. Coun. for Aging, 1978-79. Maj. AUS, 1942-46, lt. col. AUS, ret. Recipient Ret. Sr. Vol. Program Vol. of Yr. award No. Ariz. Coun. Govts., 1989, Spl. award Speech Comm. Assn., 1989, Endowment Benefactor award, 1991; 6 Diamond Pin of Melvin Jones Found., Internat. Lions, Best Male Songwriter, Poet of Yr. awards Entertainer Network Nashville, 1994, Disting. Achievement in Entertainer Indi-Assn. as Most Consistent Golden Poet of Nashville, 1995. Fellow United Writers Assn.; mem. Ariz. Comm. Support System, Quarter Century Wireless Assn., Soc. Wireless Pioneers, Mil. Affiliate Radio System, Hospitalier Order of St. John of Jerusalem, Knights Hospitalier, Knightly and Mil. Order of St. Eugene of Trebizond (chevalier), Soverign and Mil. Order of St. Stephen the Matyr (comdr.), Knightly Assn. of St. George the Matyr, Ordre Chevaliers du Sinai, Hist. File, VFW (comdr.), Am. Legion (comdr.), Rotary (pres. 1966-67, dist. gov. 1973-74), Order of White Shrine of Jerusalem, Niadh Nask (Marshall of Kilbonane), Internat. Chivalric Inst., Confedn. of Chivalry (life, mem. grand coun.), Ordre Souverain et Militaire de la Milice du Saint Sepulcre (chevalier grand cross), Sovereign World Order of White Cross (lord of knights, dist. commdr. Ariz.), Prescott High Twelve Club (pres. 1990), Morse Telegraph Club, Inc., Phi Delta Kappa (Svc. Key 1978). Republican. Methodist. Home: 2001 Rocky Dells Dr Prescott AZ 86303-5685

MOSES, JAMES ANTHONY, JR., neuropsychologist; b. San Francisco, Feb. 25, 1947; s. James Anthony and Lucille M. M. BA magna cum laude, San Francisco State U., 1968; MS, San Jose State U., 1970; MA, U. Colo., 1971, PhD, 1974. Diplomate Am. Bd. Profl. Psychology. From clin. instr. psychiatry to clin. assoc. prof. Stanford (Calif.) U. Med. Sch., 1975-94, clin. prof., 1994—; rsch. psychologist Palo Alto (Calif.) VA Med. Ctr., 1977—, clin. neuropsychologist, 1974—; jujitsu instr. Stanford U. Athletic Dept., Palo Alto, 1981—; assoc. editor Internat. Jour. of Clin. Neuropsychology, Madison, Wis., 1985-91; mem. editorial adv. bd. Archives of Clin. Neuropsychology, 1986—; bd. dirs. Am. Bd. Profl. Neuropsychology, 1989-91. Author: Interpretation of the Luria-Nebraska Neuropsychological Test Battery, 1983; co-author: Interpretation of the Halstead-Reitan Neuropsychological Battery, 1982; contbr. articles to more than 175 profl. publs. Named Nat. Acad. Neuropsychology fellow, 1984. Fellow Am. Psychol. Soc., Am. Acad. Clin. Psychology; mem. APA, Internat. Neuropsychol. Soc., Soc. Personality Assessment, Masons, Shriners. Republican. Home: 177 Westlawn Ave Daly City CA 94015-1029 Office: VA Med Ctr 3801 Miranda Ave Palo Alto CA 94304-1207

MOSHER, KIRK A., marketing director; b. Newport Beach, Calif., June 14, 1961; s. Robert E. Mosher and Neva L. Akin. BA in Econs., U. Calif., Berkeley, 1983; MBA, Stanford U., 1987. Cons. KAM Mgmt. Group, Palo Alto, Calif., 1983-85; channel devel. specialist Apple Computer, Cupertino, Calif., 1986-87, channel devel. mgr., 1987-89, market devel. mgr., 1989-91, product mktg. mgr., 1991-93; Macintosh product line mgr. Microsoft, Redmond, Wash., 1993-94; mktg. dir. Bull Info. Sys., Phoenix, 1994—. Home: 5122 E Shea Blvd #2074 Red Rock AZ 85245

MOSHER, SALLY EKENBERG, lawyer; b. N.Y.C., July 26, 1934; d. Leslie Joseph and Frances Josephine (McArdle) Ekenberg; m. James Kimberly Mosher, Aug. 13, 1960 (dec. Aug. 1982). MusB, Manhattanville Coll., 1956; postgrad., Hofstra U., 1958-60, U. So. Calif., 1971-73; JD, U. So. Calif., 1981. Bar: Calif., 1982. Musician, pianist, tchr., 1957-74; music critic Pasadena Star-News, 1967-72; mgr. Contrasts Concerts, Pasadena Art Mus., 1971-72; rep. Occidental Life Ins. Co., Pasadena, 1975-78; v.p. James K. Mosher Co., Pasadena, 1961-82, pres., 1982—; pres. Oakhill Enterprises, Pasadena, 1984—; assoc. White-Howell, Inc., Pasadena, 1984—; real estate broker, 1984—; harpsichordist, lectr., 1994—. Contbr. articles to various publs. Bd. dirs. Jr. League Pasadena, 1966-67, Encounters Concerts, Pasadena, 1966-72, U. So. Calif. Friends of Music, L.A., 1973-76, Arroyo Seco Coun., 1991—; bd. dirs. Pasadena Arts Coun., 1986—, pres., 1989-92, chair adv. bd., 1992-93; v.p., bd. dirs. Pasadena Chamber Orch., 1986-88, pres., 1987-88; mem. Calif. 200 Coun. for Bicentennial of U.S. Constn., 1987-90; commr. Endowment Adv. Commn, Pasadena, 1988-90; bd. dirs. Calif. Music Theatre, 1988-90, Pasadena Hist. Soc., 1989-91, I Cantori, 1989-91; bd. dirs. Foothill Area Cmty. Svcs., 1990—, treas., 1991, vice-chair, 1992-94, chair, 1994—. Manhattanville Coll. hon. scholar, 1952-56. Mem. ABA, Calif. Bar Assn., Assocs. of Calif. Inst. Tech., Athenaeum, Kappa Gamma Pi, Mu Phi Epsilon, Phi Alpha Delta. Republican. Home: 1260 Rancheros Rd Pasadena CA 91103-2759 Office: 711 E Walnut St Ste 407 Pasadena CA 91101-4403

MOSING, LISA, nutritionist, dietitian; b. Summit, N.J., Apr. 26, 1959; d. Lionell Waddell and Lois Abigail (Simonson) M. BA, St. Olaf Coll., 1981; MS, Calif. State U., Long Beach, 1983. Registered dietitian. Nutrition instr. Saddleback Coll., Mission Viejo, Calif., 1980-81, Cypress (Calif.) Coll., 1988-91; clin. dietitian Fairview St. Hosp., Costa Mesa, Calif., 1983-85; nutrition dir. Chgo. Health Club, 1985-87; nutrition cons. Care More Med. Group, Orange and L.A. Counties, 1982-94; nutrition educator Brea (Calif.) Hosp.; corp. nutritionist Lucky Stores, Inc., Buena Park, Calif., 1987-94; owner Nutrition Works, Fullerton, Calif., 1983—; speaker, presenter in field. Author: Sharpening Your Image: How To Get, Keep and Expand A Health Care Business, 1992, Nutrition Works Series, 1993, Low Fat Living Class Series 1994, The ABC's of Weight Control Class Series, 1994; interviewed for various periodicals and TV programs. Active soup kitchen assn. Newport Harbor Luth. Ch., Santa Ana, Calif. Mem. Calif. Dietetic Assn. (program chair, coord. 1991-92, mem. mktg. com. 1989—, bd. dirs., vol. recognition and nominating chair Orange dist. 1987-94), Orange Dietetic Assn., Cons. Nutritionists, Dietitians in Bus. and Comms., Am. Dietetic Assn., Am. Coll. Sports Medicine (cert. instr.), Am. Cancer Soc., Am. Heart Assn., Omicron Nu. Office: Nutrition Works 20251 Bancroft Cir Huntington Beach CA 92646-4722

MOSK, RICHARD MITCHELL, lawyer; b. L.A., May 18, 1939; s. Stanley and Edna M.; m. Sandra Lee Budnitz, Mar. 21, 1964; children: Julie, Matthew. AB with great distinction, Stanford U., 1960; JD cum laude, Harvard U., 1963. Bar: Calif. 1964, U.S. Supreme Ct. 1970, U.S. Ct. Mil. Appeals 1970, U.S. Dist. Ct. (no., so., ea., and cen. dists.) Calif 1964, U.S. Ct. Appeals (9th dist.) 1964. Mem. staff Pres.'s Commn. on Assassination Pres. Kennedy, 1964; research clk. Calif. Supreme Ct., 1964-65; ptnr. Mitchell, Silberberg & Knupp, L.A., 1965-87; prin. Sanders, Barnet, Goldman, Simons & Mosk, P.C., L.A., 1987—; spl. dep. Fed. Pub. Defender, L.A., 1975-76; instr. U. So. Calif. Law Sch., 1978; arbitrator Iran-U.S. Claims Tribunal, 1981-84, substitute arbitrator, 1984—; mem. Los Angeles County Jud. Procedures Commn., 1973-82, chmn., 1978; bd. dirs. Internat. Arbitration Commn.; mem. adv. coun. Asia/Pacific Ctr. for Resolution Internat. Trade Disputes, 1986—; chmn. Motion Picture Assn. Classification and Rating Adminstrn., 1994—. Contbr. articles to profl. jours. Mem. L.A. City-County Inquiry on Brush Firs, 1970; bd. dirs. Calif. Mus. Sci. and Industry, 1979-82, Vista Del Mar Child Ctr., 1979-82; trustee L.A. County Law Libr., 1985-86; bd. govs. Town Hall Calif., 1986-91; mem. Christopher Commn. on L.A. Police Dept., 1991; mem. Stanford U. Athletic Bd., 1991—. Served with USNR, 1964-75. Hon. Woodrow Wilson fellow, 1960; recipient Roscoe Pound prize, 1961. Fellow Am. Bar Found.; mem. ABA (coun. internat. law sect. 1986-90), FBA (pres. L.A. chpt. 1972), L.A. County Bar Assn., Beverly Hills Bar Assn., L.A. Assn. Bus. Trial Lawyers, Internat. Bar Assn., Am. Arbitration Assn. (comml. panel, large complex case panel, Asia/Pacific panel), Hong Kong Internat. Arbitration Ctr. (mem. panel

1986—), Am. Film Mktg. Assn. (arbitration panel), L.A. Ctr. Internat. Comml. Arbitration, B.C. Internat. Arbitration Ctr. (mem. panel), World Intellectual Property Orgn. (mem. arbitration panel), Ctr. Pub. Resources (mem. arbitration panel), Phi Beta Kappa. Office: Sanders Barnet Goldman Simons & Mosk 1901 Avenue Of The Stars Los Angeles CA 90067-6078

MOSK, STANLEY, state supreme court justice; b. San Antonio, Sept. 4, 1912; s. Paul and Minna (Perl) M.; m. Edna Mitchell, Sept. 27, 1937 (dec.); 1 child, Richard Mitchell; m. Susan Hines, Aug. 27, 1982 (div.); m. Kaygey Kash, Jan. 15, 1995. Student, U. Tex., 1931; Ph.B., U. Chgo., 1933; postgrad., U. Chgo. Law Sch., 1934; JD, Southwestern U., 1935; postgrad., Hague Acad. Internat. Law, 1970, U. Pacific, 1970; LLD, U. San Diego, 1971, U. Santa Clara, 1976, Calif. Western U., 1984, Southwestern U., 1987, Whittier Coll. Law, 1993, Pepperdine U., 1995, Western State U., San Diego, 1995. Bar: Calif. 1935, U.S. Supreme Ct. 1956. Practiced in Los Angeles, until 1939; exec. sec. to gov. Calif., 1939-42; judge Superior Ct. Los Angeles County, 1943-58; pro tem justice Dist. Ct. Appeal, Calif., 1954; atty. gen. Calif., also head state dept., justice, 1959-64; justice Supreme Ct. Calif., 1964—; mem. Jud. Council Calif., 1973-75, Internat. Commn. Jurists. Chmn. San Francisco Internat. Film Festival, 1967; mem. Dem. Nat. Com., Calif., 1960-64; bd. regents U. Calif., 1940; pres. Vista Del Mar Child Care Service, 1954-58; bd. dirs. San Francisco Law Sch., 1971-73, San Francisco Regional Cancer Found., 1980-83. Served with AUS, World War II. Recipient Disting. Alumnus award U. Chgo., 1958, 93. Mem. ABA, Nat. Assn. Attys. Gen. (exec. bd. 1964), Western Assn. Attys. Gen. (pres. 1963), Calif. Bar Assn., L.A. Bar Assn., San Francisco Bar Assn., Am. Legion, Manuscript Soc., Calif. Hist. Soc., Am. Judicature Soc., Inst. Jud. Adminstrn., U. Chgo. Alumni Assn. No. Calif. (pres. 1957-58, 67), Order of Coif, B'nai B'rith, Hillcrest Country Club (L.A.), Commonwealth Club, Golden Gateway Tennis Club (San Francisco), Beverly Hills Tennis Club. Office: Supreme Ct Calif 303 2nd St San Francisco CA 94107-1366

MOSKOWITZ, ROBERT ARTHUR, publishing executive; b. Newark, Oct. 27, 1946; m. Francine Reese Levy, June 30, 1968; children: Jake, Alex. B of Am. Civilization, U. Pa., 1968; postgrad., New Sch. Social Rsch., 1969-71. Editorial dir.exec. reports divsn. Prentice Hall Pub., Englewood Cliffs, N.J., 1968-70; freelance writer, 1970-75; pres. Personal Productivity Ctr., Phila., 1975-83; sr. cons. Hill and Knowlton, L.A., 1983-84; sr. acct. supr. Madison Fielding Pub. Rels., L.A., 1984-87; pres. Crown Communications Group, Woodland Hills, Calif., 1981—, Key Publs., Woodland Hills, Calif., 1991—. Author: How to Organize Your Work and Yout Life, 1981, Parenting Your Aging Parents, 1991, The Small Business Computer Book-A Guide to Plain English, 1993, Out On Yout Own-Everything You Need to Know Before, During and After Leaving the Nest, 1994. Mem. Am. Telecommuting Assn., Authors Guild, Ind. Writers So. Calif., PEN.

MOSQUEIRA, CHARLOTTE MARIANNE, dietitian; b. L.A., July 26, 1937; d. Leo and Magdalene Tollefson; children: Mark, Michael. BS, St. Olaf Coll., 1959; postgrad. U. Oreg. Med. Sch., 1959-60; MA, Central Mich. U., 1980. Registered dietitian. Chief clin. dietitian, asst. dir. food svc. Queen of Angels Hosp., Los Angeles, 1968-70; asst. dir. food svc. Presbyn. Hosp. Ctr., Albuquerque, 1970-73; dir. food svc. Holy Cross Hosp., Salt Lake City, 1973-77; dir. dietetics Riverside Meth. Hosp., Columbus, Ohio, 1977-79; dir. nutrition and food svc. Fresno (Calif.) Community Hosp. and Med. Ctr., 1980-91; mem. faculty Dept. Enology and Food Sci., Calif. State U., Fresno, 1984-93; dir. nutritional svc. Emanuel Med. Ctr., Turlock, Calif., 1991—. Mem. Am. Dietetic Assn., Calif. Dietetic Assn. Lutheran.

MOSS, CHARLES NORMAN, physician; b. L.A., June 13, 1914; s. Charles Francis and Lena (Rye) M.; A.B., Stanford U., 1940; M.D., Harvard U., 1944; cert. U. Vienna, 1947; M.P.H., U. Calif.-Berkeley, 1955; Dr.P.H., UCLA, 1970; m. Margaret Louise Stakias; children—Charles Eric, Gail Linda, and Lori Anne. Surg. intern Peter Bent Brigham Hosp., Boston, 1944-45, asst. in surgery, 1947; commd. 1st lt. USAF, M.C., USAAF, 1945, advanced through grades to lt. col., USAF, 1956; Long course for flight surgeon USAF Sch. Aviation Medicine, Randolph AFB, Tex., 1948-49, preventive medicine div. Office USAF Surgeon Gen., Washington, 1955-59; air observer, med., 1954, became sr. flight surgeon 1956; later med. dir., Los Angeles div. North Am. Rockwell Corp., Los Angeles; chief med. adv. unit Los Angeles County, now ret. Decorated Army Commendation medal (U.S.); Chinese Breast Order of Yun Hui. Recipient Physicians Recognition award AMA, 1969, 72, 76, 79, 82. Diplomate in aerospace medicine and occupational medicine Am. Bd. Preventive Medicine. Fellow Am. Pub. Health Assn., AAAS, Am. Coll. Preventive Medicine, Royal Soc. Health, Am. Acad. Occupational Medicine, Western Occupational Med. Assn., Am. Assn. Occupational Medicine; mem. AMA, Mil. Surgeons U.S., Soc. Air Force Flight Surgeons, Am. Conf. Govt. Hygienests, Calif. Acad. Preventive Medicine, (dir.), Aerospace Med. Assn., Calif., Los Angeles County med. assns., Assn. Oldetime Barbell and Strongmen. Research and publs. in field. Home: 7714 Cowan Ave Los Angeles CA 90045-1135

MOSS, DEBRA LEE, school counselor; b. L.A., June 15, 1952; d. Boris and Mildred Rose (Volk) Elkin; divorced; children: Ryan Adam, Lauren Nicole, Rebecca Anne. BA in Psychology, UCLA, 1973; MA in Spl. Edn., Calif. State U., L.A., 1977. Cert. elem. tchr. severely handicapped, learning handicapped and jr. coll. tchr., Calif. Tchr. spl. edn. UCLA Neuropsychiat. Inst., 1972-75, demonstration tchr., curriculum coord., 1975-78; edn. specialist Harbor Regional Ctr. for Developmentally Disabled, Torrance, Calif., 1978-82; ednl. cons. North L.A. Regional Ctr. for Developmentally Disabled, Panorama City, Calif., 1982-87; behavior specialist L.A. Unified Sch. Dist., 1987-91, program specialist, 1991-92, support staff spl. edn. mid. schs., 1992-93; inclusion facilitator, 1993—; hon. lectr. West Valley Occupational Ctr., 1986—; tutor spl. edn., L.A., 1973—; behavior specialist to families, 1985—. Contbr. articles to profl. jours. Mem. Am. Assn. on Retardation, Nat. Assn. for Autistic Children and Adults, Coun. for Exceptional Children. Democrat. Office: LA USD West Valley Spl Edn Svc Unit 6505 Zelzah Ave Reseda CA 91335-6221

MOSS, DOUGLAS MABBETT, military officer, aerospace executive; b. Washington, Mar. 21, 1954; s. Lon Harold and Mildred (Mabbett) M. BS in Nuclear Engring., Ga. Inst. Tech., 1976, MS in Mech. Engring., 1981; MBA, U. Phoenix, 1994. Commd. 2d lt. USAF, 1976, advanced through grades to maj., 1988; instr. pilot 71st Flying Tng. Wing USAF, Vance AFB, Okla., 1977-82; F-15 fighter pilot 18th Tactical Fighter Wing USAF, Kadena AFB, Japan, 1982-84; test pilot 6510 Test Wing USAF, Edwards AFB, Calif., 1984-88; tactical weapons officer USAF, Osan AFB, Korea, 1988-89; instr. test pilot USAF Test Pilot Sch., Edwards AFB, Calif.; exptl. test pilotMD-80/MD-90 McDonnell Douglas Corp., Long Beach, Calif., 1990—; project test pilot T-46 Test Force, Edwards AFB, 1986-87; project mgr. Advanced Tactical Fighter, Edward AFB, 1985-88. Mem. Soc. of Exptl. Test Pilots, Martin-Baker Tie Club. Home: 3203 Carolwood Ln Torrance CA 90505 7113 Office: McDonnell Douglas Corp 3855 N Lakewood Blvd Long Beach CA 90846-0003

MOSS, ELIZABETH LUCILLE (BETTY MOSS), transportation company executive; b. Ironton, Mo., Feb. 13, 1939; d. James Leon and Dorothy Lucille (Russell) Rollen; m. Elliott Theodore Moss, Nov. 10, 1963 (div. Jan. 1984); children: Robert Belmont, Wendy Rollen. BA in Econs. and Bus. Adminstrn., Drury Coll., 1960. Registrar, transp. mgr. Cheley Colo. Camps, Inc., Denver and Estes Park, 1960-61; office mgr. Washington Nat. Ins. Co., Denver, 1960-61; sec. White House Decorating, Denver, 1961-62; with Ringsby Truck Lines, Denver, Oakland, Calif., and L.A., 1962-67, System 99 Freight Lines, L.A., 1967-69; terminal mgr. System 99 Freight Lines, Stockton, Calif., 1981-84; with Yellow Freight System, L.A., 1969-74, Hayward, Calif., 1974-77; ops. mgr. Yellow Freight System, Urbana, Ill., 1977-80; sales rep. Calif. Motor Express, San Jose, 1981; regional sales mgr. Schneider Nat. Carriers, Inc., No. Calif., 1984-86; account exec. TNT-Can., Nev. and Cen. Calif., 1986-88; mgr. Interstate-Intermodal Divs. HVH Transp., Denver, 1988-89; regional sales mgr. MNX, Inc., Northern Calif., 1989-91; dir. sales Mountain Valley Express, Manteca, Calif., 1992—; chmn. op. coun. for San Joaquin and Stanislaus Counties Calif. Trucking Assn., 1983-84; planning adv. com. Truck Accident Reduction Projects, San Joaquin County, 1987-88. Mem. Econ. Devel. Coun. Stockton C. of C., 1985-86; active Edison High Sch. Boosters, 1982-88. Mem. Nat. Def. Transp. Assn. (bd. dirs. 1986-87), Stockton Traffic Club (bd. dirs. 1982-84, Trucker of Yr.), Ctrl. Valley Traffic Club, Oakland Traffic Club, Delta Nu Alpha (bd. dirs. Region 1 1982-84, v.p. chpt. 103 1984-85, pres. 1985-86, chmn. bd. 1985-87, regional sec. 1987-88, Outstanding Achievement award 1986, 88). Methodist. Home: 455 E Ocean Blvd Apt 602 Long Beach CA 90802-4940

MOSS, ERIC OWEN, architect; b. L.A., July 25, 1943. BA, UCLA, 1965; MArch with honors, U. Calif., Berkeley, 1968, Harvard U., 1972. Prof. design So. Calif. Inst. Architecture, 1974—; prin. Eric Owen Moss Archs., Culver City, Calif., 1975—; Eliot Noyes chair Harvard U., Cambridge, Mass., 1990; Eero Saarinen chair Yale U., New Haven, 1991; lectr. Hirshhorn Mus. Symposium, Washington, 1990, Nat. AIA Conv., 1990, Mus. Contemporary Art, L.A., 1991, N.Y. Archtl. League, 1991, Archtl. Assn. Ireland, Dublin, Archtl. Assn., London, 1991, Royal Coll. Art, London, 1991, Smithsonian Inst., Washington, 1992, U. Calif., Berkeley, 1992, Osterreichiaches Mus. fur Angewandte Kunst, Vienna, Austria, 1992, UCLA, 1992, Royal Danish Acad. Fine Arts, Copenhagen, 1993, U. Lund, Sweden, 1993, Mus. Finnish Architecture, Helsinki, 1993, Royal Acad. Arts, London, 1993, U. Pa., Phila., 1994, others; tchr. U. Tex., Austin, 1983, Wash. U., St. Louis, 1984, U. Ill., Chgo., 1985, Tulane U., New Orleans, 1985, U. Minn., Mpls., 1985, Columbia U., N.Y.C., 1986, Rice U., Houston, 1988; participant various confs. Exhbns. of work include World Biennial of Architecture, Sofia, Bulgaria, 1989, Salle des Tirages du Credit Foncier de France, Paris, 1990, Bartlett Sch. Architecture and Urban Design, London, 1991, Gallery of Functional Art, Santa Monica, Calif., 1992, GA Gallery, Tokyo, 1992, Mus. fur Gestaltung Zurich, Switzerland, 1993, Santa Monica (Calif.) Mus. Art, 1993, Fonds Regional D'Art Contemporain du Centre, 1993, Aspen (Colo.) Art Mus., 1993, Centro de Arte y Comunicacion, Buenos Aires, 1993, Contemporary Arts Ctr., Cin., 1993, Philippe Uzzan Galerie, Paris, 1993, Contemporary Arts Ctr., Tours, France, 1993, Internat. Exhbn. Contemporary Architecture, Havana, Cuba, 1994, others. Recipient Progressive Architecture Design award, 1978, 92, Winning Interior Archtl. Record award, 1984, Interiors Design award, 1991. Fellow AIA (L.A. awards 1977, 79, 83, 88, 90, Calif. Coun. awards 1981, 86, 88, L.A. Honor awards 1991, Nat. Honor awards 88, 89, Calif. Coun. Urban Design/Adaptive Re-Use awards 1991, Nat. Interior Design awards 1992, 94, L.A. Design awards 1992, 93). Office: 8557 Higuera St Culver City CA 90232-2535

MOSS, JACK, print shop executive, textile chemist, consultant; b. Bklyn., Aug. 29, 1928; s. Sol and Rose (Cohen) M.; m. Phyllis Y. Resnick, June 29, 1952; children: William, Michael A. BS in Chemistry, U. Mass., 1951. Plant supt. Vitromar Piece Dye, Paterson, N.J., 1951-58; supt. Sudamtex de Uruguay, Colonia, Uruguay, 1958-61; rsch. chemist GAF Corp., Easton, Pa., 1961-66; tech. rep. Sandoz, Inc., East Hanover, N.J., 1966-70, Ventron Corp., Beverly, Mass., 1970-77; cons. Whittaker Textiles, Marysville, N.B., Can., 1977-78; sales mgr., asst. to pres. Apex Chem Corp., Elizabeth, N.J., 1975-77; pres. Jack-B-Quick, Inc., Millburn, N.J., 1978-92; ret., 1992; chmn. bd. JBQ Printing Svcs., Inc., Livingston, N.J., Mikie's Inc., Redmond, Wash.; cons. in field. Contbr. material on disperse dyes, fiber blends to Chem. Encyc., 1965. Mem. Nat. Assn. Quick Printers, N.J. Assn. Quick Printers (sec., advt. mgr.), C. of C., Masons (master of lodge 1992). Office: Mikies Inc 16640 Redmond Way Redmond WA 98052-4434

MOSS, MYRA E. See ROLLE, MYRA MOSS

MOSS, RICHARD B., pediatrician; b. N.Y.C., Oct. 30, 1949. MD, SUNY, Downstate, 1975. Intern Children's Meml. Hosp., Chgo., 1975-76, resident, 1976-77; resident Stanford (Calif.) U. Med. Sch., 1980-81; now pediatrician Lucile Salter Packard Children's Hosp., Palo Alto, Calif.; prof. pediats. Stanford U. Med. Sch. Office: Stanford U Sch Med Ctr Dept Pediats Stanford CA 94305-5119*

MOSS, STANLEY W., orthopedic surgeon; b. Salt Lake City, Apr. 20, 1949; s. Lee W. and Loraine (Law) M.; m. Diane Gillespie, May 30, 1973; children: Brian, Eric, Mark, Lisa, Craig. BS in Med. Biology, U. Utah, 1971, MD, 1973. Diplomate Am. Bd. Orthopedic Surgery. Straight surg. intern U. Calif., San Diego, 1973-74; resident in orthopaedic surgery U. Utah Med. Ctr., Salt Lake City, 1977-81; pvt. practice, Boise, Idaho, 1981—. Capt. M.C., U.S. Army, 1974-77. Fellow Am. Acad. Orthopedic Surgery, Western Orthopedic Assn. Office: 333 N 1st St Ste 240 Boise ID 83702-6132

MOSS, STEVEN WALTER, air force officer; b. San Rafael, Calif., Apr. 12, 1957; s. James Teddy and Carla Margaret (Stich) M.; div.; children: Benjamin Thomas, Jennifer Robyn, Kimberly Danielle. BSBA in Fin., Calif. State U., Northridge, 1983; BS in Aero. Engring., Air Force Inst. Tech., 1985; MS in Aerospace Engring., U. Tenn. Space Inst., 1991. Ride operator, ride foreman, then ops. supr. Six Flags Magic Mountain, Valencia, Calif., 1976-82; commd. 2d lt. USAF, 1983, advanced through grades to maj.; wind tunnel test engr. NASA Langley Rsch. Ctr., Langley AFB, Va., 1985-87; facility mgr. prop wind tunnels Arnold Engr. Devel. Ctr., Arnold AFB, Tenn., 1987-89, nat. aerospace plane test project mgr., 1989-91; test and integration br. chief Sec. Air Force Office Spl. Project, L.A. AFB, 1991-93; dep. program mgr. Global Positioning Sys. Program Office, L.A. AFB, 1993—. Pack treas. Boy Scouts Am., San Pedro, Calif., 1993, asst. den leader, 1994, cubmaster, 1995; coach Ft. MacArthur T-Ball League, San Pedro, 1994. Office: SMC/CZSS 2435 Vela Way Ste 1613 Los Angeles CA 90245

MOSS, SUSAN JEAN, interior designer; b. Milw., Nov. 3, 1949. BS in Interior Design, Iowa State U., 1972. Pres. Susan Moss Interiors, Kauai, Hawaii, 1977-85; project designer Richard Crowell Assocs., Honolulu, 1985-90; pres. Trans-Pacific Design, Kamuela, Hawaii, 1991—. Vol. ARC, 1982, mass care vol., 1992; mem. design com. and cmty. rels. North Hawaii Cmty. Hosp., Kamuela, 1993-94. Mem. Am. Soc. Interior Designers (dir., pres. Hawaii chpt., v.p., treas. 1984-91, co-chair design awards 1994, Design Excellence award 1994, 95, Merit award 1987, Fred Harper Cmty. Svc. award 1993, Presdl. citation 1986), AIA (affiliate), Jr. League Honolulu, North Hawaii Rotary Club. Office: Trans-Pacific Design PO Box 190 Kamuela HI 96743

MOSSMAN, ALBERT PRUITT, chemist, consultant; b. Ft. Benning, Ga., June 5, 1937; s. Albert Patterson and Allene (Pruit) M.; m. Martha G. Soto (div.); 1 child, Sabrina A. BS, St. Mary's Coll., 1966. Chemist, Western Regional Rsch. Ctr. USDA, Albany, Calif., 1964—. Author: chpt. on Rice in the Tropics in Handbook of Tropical Foods, 1983; contbr. articles to profl. jours. Mem. Am. Assn. Cereal Chemists, Rice Tech. Working Group. Office: Western Regional Rsch Ctr USDA 800 Buchanan St Berkeley CA 94710-1105

MOSTELLER, JAMES WILBUR, III, data processing executive; b. Ft. Riley, Kans., June 21, 1940; s. James Wilbur, Jr., and Ruth Renfro (Thompson) M.; B.S. in Econs., Rensselaer Poly. Inst., 1962; M.B.A., Temple U., 1971; m. Sandra Josephine Stevenson, Oct. 13, 1962; children—Margaret, Steven, Michael. Data processing systems analyst, Philco-Ford, Ft. Washington, Pa., 1966-69; data processing analyst and supr., Merck Sharp & Dohme, West Point, Pa., 1969-75, dir. mgmt. info. systems KELCO div. Merck and Co., San Diego, 1975-87; dir. info. mgmt. Advanced Systems div. United Technologies, San Diego, 1987-88; computer scientist Navy Personnel Research and Devel. Ctr., San Diego, 1988—. Bd. dirs. New Horizons Montessori Sch., Ft. Washington, Pa., 1974-75; leader youth programs North County YMCA, 1977-81; mem. San Diego Research Park Com., 1978-86; 1st. v.p., mem. exec. com. San Diego Space and Sci. Found., 1985-92. With USN, 1962-66, capt. Res., 1966-93. Cert. in data processing. Mem. Data Processing Mgmt. Assn., Assn. Systems Mgmt., Naval Res. Assn. (life), U.S. Naval Inst. (life), Beta Gamma Sigma, Sigma Alpha Epsilon (chpt. pres. 1961-62). Office: Navy Pers R & D Ctr San Diego CA 92152-6800

MOSZKOWSKI, LENA IGGERS, secondary school educator; b. Hamburg, Mar. 8, 1930; d. Alfred G. and Lizzie (Minden); m. Steven Alexander, Aug. 29, 1952 (div. Oct. 1977); children: Benjamin Charles, Richard David, Ronald Bertram. BS, U. Richmond, 1948; MS, U. Chgo., 1953; postgrad., UCLA, 1958. Tchr. Lab. asst. U. Chgo. Ben May Cancer Research Lab., Chgo., 1951-53; biology, sci. tchrs. Bishop Conaty High Sch., Los Angeles, 1967-68; chemistry, sci. tchr. St. Paul High Sch., Santa Fe Springs, Calif., 1968-69; chemistry, human ecology tchr. Marlborough Sch., Los Angeles, 1969-71; tchr. biology and sci. ecology L.A. Unified Sch. Dist., 1971—. Author: Termite Taxonomy Cryptotermes Haviland and C. Krybi, Madagascar, 1955, Ecology and Man, 1971, Parallels in Human and Biological Ecology, 1977, American Public Education, An Inside Journey, 1991-92. Founder, adminstr., com. mem. UCLA Student (and Practical Assistance Cooperative Furniture), Los Angeles, 1963-67; active participant UCLA Earth Day Program, Los Angeles, 1970. Recipient Va. Sci. Talent Search Winner Va. Acad. of Sci., 1946; Push Vol. Tchr. award John C. Fremont High Sch., Los Angeles, 1978. Mem. NEA, Calif. Tchrs. Assn., United Tchrs. L.A., Sierra Club. Democrat. Jewish. Home: 3301 Shelburne Rd Baltimore MD 21208-5626

MOTAMEDI, MANOUCHEHR EDWARD, electrical engineer, scientist; b. Esfahan, Iran; came to U.S., 1963; s. Mahmood and Batool (Shams) M.; divorced; children: F. Cherissa, F. Michael; m. Fariba Allmozafar, Aug. 24, 1992. MSEE, Northwestern U., 1965, PhD in Elec. Engring., 1971. Prof. Rensselaer Poly. Inst., Troy, N.Y., 1974-80; program mgr. Rockwell Internat. Sci. Ctr., Thousand Oaks, Calif., 1980—. Author: (with others) Microsensors, 1990; editor jour. Acoustic Sensors, 1987; contbr. more than 70 articles to profl. jours. Recipient Murphy award 1966. Mem. IEEE (sr., Achievement award, 1988; tech. program com. 1981—), Soc. Photo-Optical Instrumentation Engring. (tech. program com. 1990—), Internat. Soc. Optical Engring. Office: Rockwell Internat Sci Ctr 1049 Camino Dos Rios Thousand Oaks CA 91360-2362

MOTE, CLAYTON DANIEL, JR., mechanical engineer, educator, administrator; b. San Francisco, Feb. 5, 1937; s. Clayton Daniel and Eugenia (Isnardi) M.; m. Patricia Jane Lewis, Aug. 18, 1962; children: Melissa Michelle, Adam Jonathan. BSc, U. Calif., Berkeley, 1959, MS, 1960, PhD, 1963. Registered profl. engr., Calif. Asst. specialist U. Calif. Forest Products Labs., 1961-62; asst. mech. engr., 1962-63; lectr. mech. engring. U. Calif., Berkeley, 1962-63, asst. prof., 1967-69, asst. research engr., 1968-69, assoc. prof., assoc. research engr., 1969-73, prof., 1973—, vice chmn. mech. engring. dept., 1976-80, 83-86, chmn. mech. engring. dept., 1987-91, vice chancellor univ. rels., FANUC chair mech. systems, 1991—; research fellow U. Birmingham, Eng., 1963-64; asst. prof. Carnegie Inst. Tech., 1964-67; vis. prof. Norwegian Inst. Wood Tech., 1972-73, vis. sr. scientist, 1976, 78, 80, 84, 85; cons. in engring. design and analysis; sr. scientist Alexander Von Humboldt Found., Fed. Republic Germany, 1988, Japan Soc. for Promotion of Sci., 1991; mem. adv. bd. for mech. engring. Ga. Inst. Tech., Carnegie Mellon U.; pres. U. Calif. Berkeley Found.; trustee Behring-Hofmann Ednl. Inst. Mem. editl. bd. Soma Jour. Sound and Vibration, Machine Vibration; contbr. articles to profl. jours.; patentee in field. NSF fellow, 1963-64; recipient Disting. Teaching award, U. Calif., 1971, Pi Tau Sigma Excellence in Teaching award, U. Calif., 1975, Humboldt Prize, Fed. Republic Germany, 1988, Frederick W. Taylor Rsch. medal. Soc. Mfg. Engrs., 1991, Hetenyi award Soc. Exptl. Mechanics, 1992. Fellow NAE, AAAS, ASME (Blackall award 1975, v.p. environ. and transp. 1986-90, nat. chmn. noise control and acoustics 1980-84, chmn. San Francisco sect. 1978-79, Disting. Svc. award 1991, Charles Russ Richards award 1994, Rayleigh lectr. 1994), Internat. Acad. Wood Sci., Acoustical Soc. Am.; mem. ASTM (com. on snow skiing F-27 1984-87, chmn. new projects subcom.), Am. Acad. Mechanics, Am. Soc. Biomechanics, Orthopaedic Rsch. Soc., Internat. Soc. Skiing Safety (v.p., sec. 1977-85, bd. dirs. 1977—, chmn. sci. com. 1985—), Sigma Xi, Pi Tau Sigma, Tau Beta Pi. Office: U Calif 2440 Bancroft Way Berkeley CA 94704-1603

MOTE, KARL WILLIAM, mining engineer; b. Plainview, Nebr., Mar. 27, 1927; s. Ross Allan and Louise (Ebinger) M.; m. Lois Jean Kirchoff, July 23, 1947 (div. Jan. 1974); children: Karen Quinn, Kristine Mote, Kathy Motelamp, Karl William, Kelly; m. Elva June Harlan Dike, June 20, 1981. MetE, Colo. Sch. Mines, 1949. Registered profl. engr., Utah. Various mgmt. positions U.S. Steel, various locations, 1949-70; gen. mgr. Vanguard Exploration, Spokane, 1970-73; asst. to mgr. exploration N/L Industries, Golden, Colo., 1973-74, St. Joseph Exploration, Toronto, 1975; exec. dir., v.p. Northwest Mining Assn., Spokane, 1976—; mem. Fed. Emergency Mgmt.-Minerals, U.S. Dept. Interior, Washington, 1988—. Author book chpt. Address: 10 N Post St Ste 414 Spokane WA 99201-0705

MOTT, JUNE MARJORIE, school system administrator; b. Faribault, Minn., Mar. 8, 1920; d. David C. and Tillie W. (Nelson) Shifflett; m. Elwood Knight Mott, Oct. 18, 1958. BS, U. Minn., 1943, MA, 1948. Tchr. high schs. in Minn., 1943-46, 48-53, 54-57; script writer, Hollywood, Calif., 1953-54; tchr. English, creative writing and journalism Mt. Miguel High Sch., Spring Valley, Calif., 1957-86, chmn. English dept., 1964-71, chmn. Dist. English council, 1967-68; mem. Press Bur., Grossmont (Calif.) High Sch. Dist., 1958-86; elected to Grossmont Union High Sch. Governing Bd., 1986, clk. sch. bd., 1989, v.p. governing bd., 1989-90, 93, pres. sch. bd., 1991-92, v.p., 1992-93, pres. governing bd., 1993-94; scriptwriter TV prodn. Lamp Unto My Feet, Jam Dandy Corp.; free-lance writer, cons. travel writer, photographer; editor, publ Listening Heart, 1989. Author, editor in field. Vice chmn. polit. action San Diego County Regional Resource Ctr., 1980-81; mem. S.D. Bd. of Alcohol and Drug Abuse Prevention, 1990—, Curriculum Com. Grossmont Dist., 1990—, Site Facilities Com., Master Planning Com., 1992—, East County Issues and Mgmt. Com., 1990—, East County Women in Edn.; apptd. del. Calif. Sch. Bds. Assn., 1992—, del. assembly, 1992—, elected to region 17 del. assembly, 1993—; v.p., pub. rels. chmn. Lemon Grove Luth. Ch., 1962-78, 89—, v.p., 1993, pres. 1994. Writing project fellow U. Calif., San Diego, 1978; named Outstanding Journalism Tchr., State of Calif., Outstanding Humanities Tchr., San Diego County, Tchr. of Yr. for San Diego County, 1978; U. Cambridge scholar, 1982; Woman of Yr. Lemon Grove Soroptimists, 1990. Mem. ASCD, NEA, AAUW, Nat. Council Tchrs. English, Nat. Journalism Assn., Calif. Assn. Tchrs. English, Calif. Tchrs. Assn., So. Calif. Journalism Assn., Calif. Sch. Bds. Assn. (elected del. region 17, del. assembly 1993—), Calif. Elected Women's Assn. for Edn. Rsch. (ednl. cons. 1990), San Diego County Journalism Educators Assn. (pres. 1975-76), Grossmont Edn. Assn. (pres. 1978-80), Greater San Diego Council Tchrs. English, Nat. Writers Club, Am. Guild Theatre Organists, Calif. Retired Tchrs. Assn. (membership chairwoman 1986-89, pres. chpt. # 69 1989-94, parlimentarian 1992-93), Lemon Grove C. of C. (mem. econ. devel. com. 1994—), Nat. Sch. Bds. Assn., Order Ea. Star, Kiwanis (pres. elect Lemon grove chpt. 1992, program chmn., pres. 1993-94), Sigma Delta Chi, Delta Kappa Gamma (pres. Theta Gamma chpt. 1993—). Democrat. Home and Office: 2885 New Jersey Ave Lemon Grove CA 91945-2826

MOTTELER, ZANE CLINTON, computer science educator; b. Wenatchee, Wash., July 4, 1935; s. Roy Huling and Elizabeth Ann (Stanford) M.; m. Marilynn Rae Ginsbach, June 25, 1960; children: Clinton, Cara, Renee, Scth. BS, Stanford U., 1957, MS, 1962, PhD, 1964; MS, Mich. State U., 1981. Mem. staff Los Alamos (N.Mex.) Nat. Lab., 1957-65; from asst. prof. to prof. math. Gonzaga U., Spokane, Wash., 1965-72, chmn. dept., 1966-71; prof. math. Mich. Tech. U., Houghton, 1972-82, head dept., 1972-80; prof. computer sci., engr. Calif. Poly. State U., San Luis Obispo, 1982-93, prof. emeritus, 1993—, coord. computer engring., 1991-93; sr. computer scientist/math. programmer Livermore (Calif.) Nat. Lab., 1993—; vis. lectr. computer sci. Mich. State U., East Lansing, 1980-81; cons. Los Alamos Nat. Lab., 1965-69; cons., sr. analyst IBM Corp., San Jose, Calif. and Austin, Tex., 1983-86; sr. computer scientist/summer, Livermore (Calif.) Nat. Lab., 1986-91, Chevron Corp., San Francisco, 1983. Author: Introduction to Ordinary Differential Equations, 1972, Introduction to Complex Analysis, 1975; coauthor: Assembler Language for Univac 1110, 1982; translator: Partial Differential Equations of Elliptic Type, 1970. Fellow NSF, U. Minn., 1957-58, NASA, Am. Soc. Engring. Edn., Langley, Va., 1982. Mem. IEEE, Assn. Computing Machinery, Computer Scis. Accreditation Commn., Sigma Xi, Phi Beta Kappa, Phi Kappa Phi. Democrat. Roman Catholic. Home: 7792 Oak Creek Ct Pleasanton CA 94588-4841 Office: Lawrence Livermore Nat Lab 7000 East Ave L-472 Livermore CA 94550

MOTTRAM, ROBERT HUGH, journalist; b. Yonkers, N.Y., June 12, 1940; s. John Wilbur and Fay (Burak) M.; m. Karen Ann Melick, Aug. 7, 1962; children: Cheryl Ann, Dianna Marie, John Forrest. BS, S.D. State U., 1962. State editor Rapid City (S.D.) Daily Jour., 1963-66; reporter, corres. Associated Press, 1966-73; reporter, chief editorial writer, outdoor writer, columnist The News Tribune, Tacoma, Wash., 1973—. Author: Saltwater Salmon Angling, 1989 (Excellence in Craft award 1990). Recipient Inspirational award Wash. State Sportsmen's Coun., 1990, Spl. award Trout Unltd., 1993. Mem. N.W. Outdoor Writers Assn. (pres. 1993-94, chmn. bd. 1994-95). Office: News Tribune PO Box 11000 Tacoma WA 98411-0008

MOTULSKY, ARNO GUNTHER, geneticist, physician, educator; b. Fischhausen, Germany, July 5, 1923; came to U.S., 1941; s. Herman and Rena (Sass) Molton; m. Gretel C. Stern, Mar. 22, 1945; children: Judy, Harvey, Arlene. Student, Cen. YMCA Coll., Chgo., 1941-43, Yale U., 1943-44; BS, U. Ill., 1945, MD, 1947, DSc (hon.), 1982, MD (hon.), 1991. Diplomate Am. Bd. Internal Medicine, Am. Bd. Med. Genetics. Intern, fellow, resident Michael Reese Hosp., Chgo., 1947-51; staff mem. charge clin. investigation dept. hematology Army Med. Service Grad. Sch., Walter Reed Army Med. Ctr., Washington, 1952-53; research assoc. internal medicine George Washington U. Sch. Medicine, 1952-53; from instr. to assoc. prof. dept. medicine U. Wash. Sch. Medicine, Seattle, 1953-61, prof. medicine, prof. genetics, 1961—; head div. med. genetics, dir. genetics clinic Univ. Hosp., Seattle, 1959-89; dir. Ctr. for Inherited Diseases, Seattle, 1972-90; attending physician Univ. Hosp., Seattle; cons. Pres.'s Commn. for Study of Ethical Problems in Medicine and Biomed. and Behavioral Research, 1979-83; cons. various coms. NRC, NIH, WHO, others. Editor Am. Jour. Human Genetics, 1969-75, Human Genetics, 1969—. Commonwealth Fund fellow in human genetics Univ. Coll., London, 1957-58; John and Mary Markle scholar in med. sci., 1957-62; fellow Ctr. Advanced Study in Behavioral Scis., Stanford U., 1976-77, Inst. Advanced Study, Berlin, 1984. Fellow ACP, AAAS; mem. NAS, Internat. Soc. Hematology, Am. Fedn. Clin. Research, Genetics Soc. Am., Western Soc. Clin. Research, Am. Soc. Human Genetics, Am. Soc. Clin. Investigation, Am. Assn. Physicians, Inst. of Medicine, Am. Acad. Arts and Scis. Home: 4347 53rd Ave NE Seattle WA 98105-4938 Office: U Wash Div Med Genetics RG-25 Seattle WA 98195

MOUCH, THOMAS NORMAN, aerospace engineering educator; b. Toledo, Ohio, Sept. 30, 1955; s. Norman Vincent and Beatrice Barbara (Bialecki) M.; m. Denise Marie, Suchala, Mar. 14, 1980; children: Megan, Erica, Benjamin. BS in Aerospace Engring., U. Notre Dame, 1977, MS in Aerospace Engring., 1981; PhD in Aerospace Engring., U. Kans., 1993. Commd. 2d lt. USAF, 1977; advanced through grades to lt. col., 1994; aircraft comdr. 92nd Bomb Wing, Fairchild AFB/Spokane, Wash., 1979-83; chief/evaluation pilot 376th Strategic Wing, Kadena AB/Okinawa, Japan, 1983-86; asst. prof. USAF Acad., Colorado Springs, 1987-90, dir. Aeronautics Lab., 1993—. Mem. AIAA (sr.), Sigma Gamma Tau, Tau Beta Pi.

MOUDON, ANNE VERNEZ, urban design educator; b. Yverdon, Vaud, Switzerland, Dec. 24, 1945; came to U.S., 1966; d. Ernest Edouard and Mauricette Lina (Duc) M.; m. Dimitrios Constantine Seferis, Dec. 30, 1982; children: Louisa Moudon, Constantine Thomas. BArch with honors, U. Calif., Berkeley, 1969; DSc, Ecole Poly. Fed., Lausanne, Switzerland, 1987. Fed. Register of Swiss Architects. Rsch. assoc. Bldg. Systems Devel., Inc., San Francisco, 1969-70; sr. project planner J. C. Warnecke and Assocs., N.Y.C., 1973-74; archtl. cons. McCue, Boone & Tomsick, San Francisco, 1974-76; asst. to assoc. prof. architecture MIT, Cambridge, Mass., 1975-81, Ford internat. career chair, 1977-79; sec. Assn. Collegiate Schs. Arch., 1978-80; assoc. prof. urban design U. Wash., Seattle, 1981-87, prof. architecture, landscape architecture, urban design and planning, 1987—, dir. urban design program, 1987-93, assoc. dean acad. affairs Coll. Arch. & Urban Planning, 1992-95; dir. Cascadia Cmty. and Environ. Inst., Seattle, 1993—; lectr. in architecture U. Calif., Berkeley, 1973-75; sr. rschr. Kungl Tekniska Hogskolan, Sch. of Architecture, Stockholm, 1989. Author: Built for Change, 1986; editor: Public Streets for Public Use, 1987, 91, (monograph) Master-Planned Communities, 1990; contbr. articles to profl. jours. Recipient seven rsch. grants Nat. Endowment for the Arts, Washington, 1976-89, individual fellowship, 1986-87, Applied Rsch. award Progressive Architecture, 1983, two rsch. grants Wash. State Dept. Transp., Seattle, 1991-92. Fellow Inst. for Urban Design; mem. Internat. Assn. for the Study of People in Their Phys. Surroundings, Orgn. Women Architects, Tau Sigma Delta. Home: 3310 E Laurelhurst Dr NE Seattle WA 98105-5336 Office: U Wash Urban Design Gould Hall JO-40 Gould Hall Seattle WA 98195

MOULAKIS, ATHANASIOS, philosopher, educator; b. Athens, Greece, July 11, 1945; came to U.S., 1986; s. Michael and Frosso (Nassiakou) M.; m. Eleanor Gail Durham, July 9, 1969; 1 child, Anne. PhD, Ruhr U., Bochum, Germany, 1969, habilitation, 1979. Instr. U. Cologne, Germany, 1969; asst. prof. Ruhr U., Bochum, 1970-78; lectr. London Sch. Econs., 1978-79; prof. European Univ. Inst., Florence, Italy, 1979-86; guest prof. U. Calif., San Diego, 1986-87; rsch. assoc. Harvard U., Cambridge, Mass., 1988; tutor St. John's Coll., Annapolis, Md., 1988-89; Herbst prof. of Humanities, dir. Herbst program U. Colo., Boulder, 1989—. Author: Homonoia, 1972, Simone Weil, Die Politik der Askese, 1981, Beyond Utility, 1993 (Choice Outstanding Book of Yr., Ness Book prize Am. Assn. Colls. and Univs.); editor: The Promise of History, 1986. Vice chmn. bd. advisers Am. Sch., Florence, Italy, 1981-83. Named Olin Disting. Lectr. in Philosophy of Free Instns., Harvard U., 1981. Mem. Inst. Internat. de Philosophie Polit. (bd. dirs.), Hellenic Philosophic Soc. (corr.), Circolo dell' Unione, Florence. Mem. Greek Orthodox Ch. Home: 600 Cascade Ave Boulder CO 80302-7428 Office: Univ Colo Campus Box 422 Boulder CO 80309

MOULE, WILLIAM NELSON, electrical engineer; b. Highland Park, Mich., Sept. 13, 1924; s. Hollis Creager and Kate Dette (Hill) M.; m. Brarbara Ann Bagley, June 27, 1953;children: Janice Louise, Robert Hollis (dec.), Linda Anne, Nancy Lynn Moule Moles. BSEE, Mich. State U., 1949; MSEE, U. Pa., 1957. Reg. profl. engr., N.J. Design engr. Radio Corp. of Am., Camden, N.J., 1949-59; sr. design engr. Radio Corp. of Am., Moorestown, N.J., 1959-67; sr. engr. Emerson Elec. Co., St. Louis, 1967-70, Emerson Elec. Rantec Divsn., Calabasas, Calif., 1970; sr. staff engr. Raytheon Co., Santa Barbara, Calif., 1970-73, ITT Gilfillan, Van Nuys, Calif., 1973, Jet Propulsion Lab., Pasadena, Calif., 1973-79; sr. rsch devel. engr. Lockheed Advanced Devel. Co., Burbank, Calif., 1979—. Patentee numerous inventions, 1956—. Dir. nat. alumni bd. Mich. State U., East Lansing, 1984-87; pres. Big Ten Club of So. Calif., L.A., 1992. Staff sgt. USAF, 1943-46. Mem. IEEE (sr. mem., chmn. 1990-91), Antenna and Propagation Soc., 305th Bombardment Group Meml. Assn. (life). Democrat. Presbyn. Home: 5831 Fitzpatrick Rd Calabasas CA 91302 Office: Lockheed Adv Devel Co 1011 Lockheed Wy Palmdale CA 93599

MOUNDS, LEONA MAE REED, educational administrator; b. Crosby, Tex., Sept. 9, 1945; d. Elton Phillip and Ora Lee (Jones) Reed; m. Aaron B. Mounds Jr., Aug. 21, 1965 (div.); 1 dau., Lisa Nichelle. BS in Elem. Edn., Bridgewater State Coll., 1973; MA in Mental Retardation, U. Alaska, 1980. Cert. tchr. Alaska, Colo., Tex., Mass., cert. adminstrv. prin. Tchr., Sch. Dist.# 11, Colorado Springs, Colo., 1973-75; tchr. Anchorage Sch. Dist., 1976-78, 80—, mem. maths. curriculum com., reading contact tchr., mem. talent bank. Tchr. Del Valle (Tex.) Sch. Dist., 1979-80; adminstrv. prin. intern Anchorage Sch. Dist., 1989-90; asst. prin. Spring Hill Elem. Sch., Anchorage, 1990-91; elem. prin. intern.; asst. prin. Ptarmigan Elem. Sch., Anchorage, 1991-93, prin., 1993-94; with Child in Transition Homeless Project Title I Anchorage Sch. Dist., Anchorage, Alaska; 1994—. Bd. dirs. Urban League, 1974; 1st v.p. PTA, Crosby, Tex.; del. Tex. Dem. Conv., 1980; chmn. dist. 13 Dem. Party; mem. Alaska Women Polit. Caucus; bd. dirs. C.R.I.S.I.S. Inc.; tchr. religious edn., lay Eucharist minister St. Martin De Pores Roman Cath. Ch., St. Patrick's Ch.; pres. Black Educators of Pike Peak Region, 1974; mem. social concerns commn. Archidiocese of Anchorage, Coun. for Exceptional Children. With USAF, 1964-66. Alaska State Tchr. Incentive grantee, 1981, Ivy Lutz scholar, 1972. Mem. NEA (human rels. coord. Alaska chpt., region 6 bd. dirs., bd. dirs Alaska chpt., vice-chmn. women's caucus), NAACP, LWV, Anchorage Edn. Assn. (minority chmn. 1982—, mem. black caucus polit. action com., v.p. programs 1986-88), Anchorage Edn. Assn. (v.p. programs com. 1986-87, women's caucus), Assn. Supervision and Curriculum Devel., Alaska Women in Adminstrn., Prins. Assn.

MOUNT, MARSHA LOUISE, management consultant; b. Newark, May 26, 1962; d. Huston Ellis and Katherine Ellery (Lyman) M. BA, Columbia U., 1984, MBA, 1990. Rsch. asst. Gen. Bd. Global Ministries, N.Y.C., 1984-85; analyst Bristol-Myers, N.Y.C., 1986-88; assoc. staff analyst N.Y.C. Dept. Transp., 1990-94, dep. dir. analytical svcs., 1992-94; mgmt. cons. George S. May Internat. Co., San Jose, Calif., 1994—. Mem. Nat. Mus. Women in Arts, Washington. Recipient Cert. of Merit Nat. Merit Scholarship Corp., 1980, Cert. of Distinction Barnard Coll., N.Y.C., 1984. Mem. NAFE, Am. Soc. Quality Control, Nat. Honor Soc., Beta Gamma Sigma. Home: # K8 206 Lilly Rd NE Apt K8 Olympia WA 98506-5020

MOURY, JOHN DAVID, developmental biologist; b. Johnson City, Tenn., Sept. 21, 1960; s. John Evert and Margie Lois (Kitzmiller) M. BS, East Tenn. State U., 1981, MS, 1983; PhD, U. Tex., 1988. Lectr. dept. zoology U. Tex., Austin, 1988-90; instr. dept. biol. sci. East Tenn. State U., Johnson City, 1990-91; instr. dept. environ., population, organismic biology U. Colo., Boulder, 1991, postdoctoral rsch. assoc., 1991-93; postdoctoral fellow sch. medicine U. Utah, Salt Lake City, 1993-94; instr. dept. biology Westminster Coll., Salt Lake City, 1995—. Contbr. articles to profl. jours. Mem. AAAS, Am. Assn. of Anatomists, Am. Inst. Biol. Scis., Am. Soc. Zoologists, Fedn. of Am. Socs. for Exptl. Biology, Soc. for Devel. Biology, Phi Kappa Phi, Pi Gamma Mu, Kappa Delta Pi, Beta Beta Beta. Home: 326 4th Ave # A Salt Lake City UT 84103-2671 Office: Westminster Coll Dept Biology Salt Lake City UT 84105

MOUSEL, CRAIG LAWRENCE, lawyer; b. St. Louis, July 22, 1947; s. George William and Charlotte (Howard) M.; m. Polly Deane Burkett, Dec. 21, 1974; children: Donna, Dennis, D'Arcy. AB, U. So. Calif., 1969; JD, Ariz. State U., 1972. Bar: Ariz. 1973, U.S. Dist. Ct. Ariz. 1973, U.S. Ct. Appeals (9th cir.) 1973, Colo. 1993. Adminstrv. asst. to Hon. Sandra O'Connor Ariz. State Senate, Phoenix, 1971-72; asst. atty. gen. Ariz. Atty. Gen.'s Office, Phoenix, 1973-75; ptnr. Sundberg & Mousel, Phoenix, 1975—; spl. counsel City of Chandler, 1991; varsity baseball coach Valley Luth. H.S. Hearing officer Ariz. State Personnel Bd., 1976-80, spl. appeals counsel, 1978—; hearing officer Ariz. Outdoor Recreation Coordinating Commn., 1975; dep. state land commr. Ariz. State Land Dept., 1978; precinct capt. Rep. Com. Fellow Ariz. Bar Found.; mem. ABA, Ariz. Bar Assn., Assn. Trial Lawyers Am., Internat. Platform Assn., Ariz. Club. Office: Sundberg & Mousel 934 W Mcdowell Rd Phoenix AZ 85007-1730

MOUSSEUX, MARC CHRISTIAN, tree-salvage company executive; b. Santa Barbara, Calif., Sept. 26, 1964; s. Edouard Bosc and Renate Marguerite (Müller) M.; m. Sylvia Corrine Kulic, Oct. 4, 1986; 1 child, Natacha. MSME, Ariz. State U., 1988. Grad. rsch. asst. Ariz. State U., Tempe, 1987-91, grad. tchg. asst., 1989; summer rsch. experimentalist NASA Langley (Va.) Rsch. Ctr., 1989; computer sys. mgr., sheet-metal inspector Precise Metal Products, Phoenix, 1991-92; fluid dynamics engr. Orbital Scis. Corp., Chandler, Ariz., 1992-94; mgr., foreman Desierto Verde, Tempe, 1994—; computational fluid dynamics cons. Orbital Scis. Corp., 1994. Contbr. articles to profl. publs. Mem. AIAA. Home: 330 E Minton Dr Tempe AZ 85282-6952

MOVIUS, ALICE WHITNEY BURTON, writer, educator, speaker; b. Billings, Mont., Apr. 4, 1945; d. William Robert and Alice Whitney (Burton) Movius; divorced; children: David Lindley, Elisabeth Whitney. BA, U. Calif., Berkeley, 1967. Staff mem. Campus Crusade for Christ, various locations, 1967-78; dir. The Happy Place Nursery Sch., Ann Arbor, Mich., 1978-80; curriculum writer, children's songwriter, seminar speaker Ann Arbor, Mich., 1976-85; founder, owner pub. co. Whitney Works!, La Jolla, Calif., 1985-95; writer, founder, pres. Abuse Edn. Network, La Jolla, 1992-95. Author: (workbook, lectures) The Challenge of Being a Woman, 1976, Knowing You Are Loved, 1995; writer 1500 children's songs. Named to Outstanding Young Women of Am., 1978. Office: Whitney Works! PO Box 13338 La Jolla CA 92039-3338

MOWER, WILLIAM REX, medical educator, researcher; b. Ogden, Utah, Jan. 16, 1956; s. William R. Jr. and Paula (Blanch) M. BS in Math. and Physics, U. Utah, 1977, M in Engring., 1979, MD, 1985; MS, UCLA, 1994. Diplomate Am. Bd. Med. Examiners, Am. Bd. Emergency Medicine. Sci. analyst, programmer Hercules, Inc., Salt Lake City, 1979-81; tech. analyst, programmer BSL Techs., Salt Lake City, 1981-83; resigent in surgery U. Utah, Salt Lake City, 1985-87; resident in emergency medicine UCLA Emergency Medicine Ctr., 1987-90; cons. specialist Olive View Med. Ctr., L.A., 1990-92; rsch. fellow in emergency medicine UCLA Sch. Medicine, 1990-92, asst. prof. medicine and emergency medicine, 1992—. Contbr. articles to med. jours. Recipient various awards. Mem. Am. Coll. Emergency Physicians, Soc. Acad. Emergency Medicine, Alpha Omega Alpha. Christian. Office: UCLA Emergency Medicine Ctr 10833 Le Conte Ave Los Angeles CA 90024

MOY, RONALD LEONARD, dermatologist, surgeon; b. Stuttgart, Germany, June 10, 1957; s. Howard Leonard Stephen and Jenny (Yee) M.; m. Lisa Wing Lan Lin, Aug. 10, 1986; children: Lavren, Erin. Grad., Rensselaer Poly. Inst., 1977, Albany Med. Coll., 1981. Dir. Mohs micrographic surgery div. dermatology UCLA, 1988-93, dir. dermatologic surgery div. dermatology, 1988-93, co-chief div. dermatology, 1992-93, chief dermatologic surgery, 1993—. Author: Atlas of Cutaneous Flaps and Grafts, 1990; editor: Principle and Practice of Dermatologic Surgery, 1993; contbr. articles to profl. jours. Bd. dirs. L.A. Costal unit Am. Cancer Soc., 1988. Recipient J. Lewis Piplan award in dermatology Nat. Student Rsch. Forum, 1981, Henry Christian award Am. Fedn. Clin. Rsch., T-cell and Cytolcine Patterns in Skin Cancer award NIH, 1992. Fellow Am. Acad. Dermatology (Gold award 1986); mem. Am. Soc. Dermatologic Surgery (bd. dirs. 1993—), Am. Coll. Mohs Micrographic Surgery and Cutaneous Oncology (bd. dirs. 1992-95), Assn. Acad. Dermatologic Surgeons (bd. dirs. 1992-95). Roman Catholic. Office: UCLA Div Dermatology 100 Ucla Medical Plz # 590 Los Angeles CA 90024-6970

MOYA, PATRICK ROBERT, lawyer; b. Belen, N.Mex., Nov. 7, 1944; s. Adelicio E. and Eva (Sanchez) M.; m. Sara Dreier, May 30, 1966; children: Jeremy Brill, Joshua Dreier. AB, Princeton U., 1966; JD, Stanford U., 1969. Bar: Calif. 1970, Ariz. 1970, D.C. 1970, U.S. Dist. Ct. (no. dist.) Calif. 1970, U.S. Ct. Claims 1970, U.S. Tax Ct. 1970, U.S. Ct. Appeals (D.C. cir.) 1970, U.S. Supreme Ct. 1973. Assoc. Lewis and Roca, Phoenix, 1969-73, ptnr., 1973-83; sr. ptnr. Moya, Bailey, Bowers & Jones, P.C., Phoenix, 1983-84; ptnr., mem. nat. exec. com. Gaston & Snow, Phoenix, 1985-91; ptnr., Ariz. legal practice coord. Quarles & Brady, Phoenix, 1991—; instr. sch. of law Ariz. State U., 1972; bd. dir. Bobby McGee's U.S.A., Inc., 1982-86. Mem. Paradise Valley Bd. Adjustment, 1976-80, chmn., 1978-80; mem. Paradise Valley Town Coun., 1980-82; bd. dirs. Phoenix Men's Arts Coun., 1973-81, pres., 1979-80; bd. dirs. The Silent Witness, Inc., 1979-84, pres., 1981-83; bd. dirs. Enterprise Network, Inc., 1989-94, pres., 1991-92; bd. dirs. Phoenix Little Theatre, 1973-75, Interfaith Counseling Svc., 1973-75; precinct committeeman Phoenix Rep. Com., 1975-77; dep. voter registrar Maricopa County, 1975-76; mem. exec. bd. dirs. Gov.'s Strategic Partnership for Econ. Devel.; pres. GSPED, Inc.; mem. of Steering Com. for Sonora Ariz. Joint Econ. Plan; mem. Gov.'s Adv. Com., Ariz. and Mex., Ariz. Corp. Commn. Stock Exch. Adv. Coun., Ariz. Town Hall. Mem. ABA, Nat. Hispanic Bar Assn., Los Abogados Hispanic Lawyers Assn., Nat. Assn. Bond Lawyers, Ariz. Bar Assn., Maricopa County Bar Assn., Paradise Valley Country Club, Univ. Club. Office: Quarles & Brady 1 E Camelback Rd Ste 400 Phoenix AZ 85012-1668

MOYA, RITA BECKER, public affairs executive; b. Hastings, Neb., Dec. 24, 1949; d. Paul David and Anna (Ulmer) Becker; m. Steven Oscar Moya. BA, U. Neb., 1972; postgrad., U. Vienna, Austria, 1971; MA in Urban Planning, Va. Poly. Inst., 1974. Project adminstr. State of Calif. Citizens Adv. Council, 1974-78; assoc. dir. United Way, Inc., Los Angeles, 1978-79; engr. GTE Corp., Santa Monica, Calif., 1979-80, market analyst, 1980-81, mgr. and dir. community relations, 1981-85; dir. pub. affairs systems GTE Corp., Thousand Oaks, Calif., 1985-90; pres., CEO Nat. Health Found., L.A., 1991—; pres., CEO Healthcare Data Info. Corp., L.A.; adj. faculty U. Redlands (Calif.), 1977-83. Author (guidebook) Citizen Participation Handbook for Mental Health Bds., 1975. Regent Loyola Marymount U. Mem. Assn. of Health Svcs. Rsch., Internat. Women's Forum.

MOYA, SARA DREIER, municipal government official; b. N.Y.C., June 9, 1945; d. Stuart Samuel and Hortense (Brill) Dreier; m. P. Robert Moya, May 30, 1966; children: J. Brill, Joshua D. BA, Wheaton Coll., Norton, Mass., 1967; postgrad., Mills Coll., Oakland, Calif., 1967-68, Ariz. State U., 1992—. Mem. Paradise Valley (Ariz.) Town Coun., 1986—, vice mayor, 1990-92; chmn. Gov.'s Homeless Trust Fund Oversight Com., 1991—; pres. Ctr. for Acad. Precosity, Ariz. State U., Tempe, 1987—; bd. dirs. Ariz. Assn. Gifted and Talented; participant 3d session Leadership Am., 1990. Mem. Citizens Adv. Bd. Paradise Valley Police Dept., 1984-86, Valley Citizens League Task Force on Edn.; chair Maricopa Assn. Govts. Task Force on Homeless, 1989-92; mem. FEMA bd. Maricopa County and Ariz., 1989—; bd. dirs. Valley Youth Theater, 1990—, Maricopa County Homeless Accomodation Sch., 1991—. Mem. ASPA, Ariz. Women in Mcpl. Govt. (sec. 1988-89, bd. dirs. 1986—, pres. 1989-90), Maricopa Assn. Govts. (regional coun. 1988—, vice-chmn. mag. regional devel. policy com. 1989-91, chair 1992—, mag. joint econ. devel./human resources subcom., mag. youth policy com. 1994—), Maricopa Assn. Govts. (air quality policy com. 1994—), Ariz. Acad., Paradise Valley Country Club, Phi Kappa Phi. Republican. Home: 5119 E Desert Park Ln Paradise Valley AZ 85253-3055 Office: Town Paradise Valley 6401 E Lincoln Dr Paradise Valley AZ 85253-4328

MOYER, ALAN DEAN, retired newspaper editor; b. Galva, Iowa, Sept. 4, 1928; s. Clifford Lee and Harriet (Jacques) M.; m. Patricia Helen Krecker, July 15, 1950; children: Virginia, Stanley, Glenn. BS in Journalism, U. Iowa, 1950. Reporter, copy editor Wis. State Jour., Madison, 1950-53; reporter, photographer Bartlesville (Okla.) Examiner-Enterprise, 1953; telegraph editor Abilene (Tex.) Reporter-News, 1954-55; makeup editor Cleve. Plain Dealer, 1955-63; mng. editor Wichita (Kans.) Eagle, 1963-70; exec. editor Wichita Eagle and Beacon, 1970-73; mng. editor Phoenix Gazette, 1973-82, Ariz. Republic, 1982-89; ret., 1989; pres., dir. Wichita Profl. Baseball, Inc., 1969-75; mem. jury Pulitzer Prizes, 1973-74, 85, 86, 88. Mem. AP Mng. Editors Assn. (dir. 1973-78), Am. Soc. Newspaper Editors, Wichita Area C. of C. (dir. 1970-72), Sigma Delta Chi. Office: Phoenix Newspaper Inc 120 E Van Buren St Phoenix AZ 85004-2227

MOYER, ALBERT J., company executive, financial analyst; b. Pitts., Dec. 8, 1943; s. C. Joseph and Mary Moyer; m. Jean E. Moyer, Mar.18, 1977; children: Bret, Adam, Ryan. BBA, Duquesne U., 1965. Controller, officer Nat. Semiconductor Corp., Santa Clara, Calif., 1977-79, v.p., chief fin. officer, 1981-83; exec. v.p. Nat. Advanced Systems, Mountain View, Calif., 1979-81; pres., chief exec. officer Enhansys Inc., Cupertino, Calif., 1983-86; v.p. fin., chief fin. officer Western Digital Corp., Irvine, Calif., 1986—. Bd. dirs., treas. Nat. Commn. Indsl. Innovation, Los Angeles, 1983. Mem. Fin. Execs. Inst., Sports Car Club of Am. Republican. Roman Catholic. Home: 29882 Hillside Ter San Juan Capistrano CA 92675-1534 Office: Western Digital Corp PO Box 19665 2445 Mccabe Way Irvine CA 92714-6244

MOYER, ANN ELIZABETH, historian; b. Monroe, Mich., June 14, 1955; d. John Raymond and Elizabeth Ann (Reber) M.; m. Martin Joseph Burke, Jan. 30, 1993. BA, Mich. State U., 1977; AM, U. Mich., 1980, PhD, 1987. Asst. prof. Rhodes Coll., Memphis, 1987-88; Mellon instr. U. Chgo., 1988-91; asst. prof. U. Calif., Santa Barbara, 1992—; vis. asst. prof. U. Oreg., Eugene, 1991-92. Author: Musica Scientia: Musical Scholarship in the Italian Renaissance, 1992. Mem. Sch. of Hist. Studies, Inst. for Advanced Study, 1994-96. Mem. Am. Hist. Assn., Renaissance Soc. Am., Soc. for Sixteenth Century Studies, Soc. for Italian Hist. Studies (Helen and Howard Marraro book award 1993). Office: U Calif Dept History Santa Barbara CA 93106

MOYER, CRAIG ALAN, lawyer; b. Bethlehem, Pa., Oct. 17, 1955; s. Charles Alvin and Doris Mae (Schantz) M.; m. Candace Darrow Brigham, May 3, 1986; 1 stepchild, Jason; 1 child, Chelsea A. BA, U. So. Calif., 1977; JD, U. Calif., L.A., 1980. Bar: Calif. 1980, U.S. Dist. Ct. (cen. dist.) Calif. 1980. Assoc. Nossaman, Krueger et al, L.A., 1980-83, Finley, Kumble et al, Beverly Hills, Calif., 1983-85; ptnr. Demetriou, Del Guercio, Springer & Moyer, L.A., 1985—; instr. Air Resources Bd. Symposium, Sacramento, 1985—, U. Calif., Santa Barbara, 1989—; lectr. Hazmat Conf., Long Beach, Calif., 1986—, Pacific Automotive Show, Reno, Nev., 1989—; lectr. hazardous materials, environ. law UCLA; lectr. environ. law U. Calif., Santa Barbara; lectr. hazardous materials regulatory framework U. Calif., Santa Barbara. Co-author: Hazard Communication Handbook: A Right to Know Compliance Guide, 1990, Clean Air Act Handbook, 1991; contbr. articles to profl. jours. Pres. Calif. Pub. Interest Rsch. Group, L.A., 1978-80. Mem. ABA (natural resources sect.), Calif. Bar Assn., L.A. County Bar Assn. (environ. law sect., chmn. legis. rev. com., mem. exec. com.), Tau Kappa Epsilon (pres. L.A. chpt. 1975-76, Outstanding Alumnus 1983). Republican. Office: Demetriou Del Guercio Springer & Moyer Chase Plz 801 S Grand Ave Fl 10 Los Angeles CA 90017-4613

MOYER, LINDA LEE, artist, educator; b. Niles, Mich., Feb. 11, 1942; d. Roy Delbert and Estelle Leona (Beaty) Moyer; m. Brock David Williams Dec. 3, 1994; 1 child from previous marriage, Matin Ata Gunsay. Student, Occidental Coll., 1959-61; BA, UCLA, 1964; MA, Calif. State U., Long Beach, 1977, MFA, 1980. Cert. tchr. secondary edn., cert. instr. C.C., Calif. Instr. art. Huntington Beach (Calif.) Union High Sch., 1967-81, Calif. State U., Long Beach, 1981-85, Saddleback Coll., Mission Viejo, Calif., 1986-88, Fullerton (Calif.) Coll., 1990, 94, Goldenwest Coll., Huntington Beach, 1990; artist in residence St. Margaret's Episcopal Sch., San Juan Capistrano, 1993; lectr., workshop presenter Santa Barbara (Calif.) C.C., 1992; series lectr. Rancho Santiago Coll., 1985, 90; lectr. Cypress Coll., 1986, Watercolor West, 1987, 94, others. One-woman shows include Laguna Beach (Calif.) Mus. Art, 1982, Orlando Gallery, Sherman Oaks, Calif., 1983, Long Beach City Coll., 1983, Orange County Ctr. Contemporary Art, 1982, 85, Cerritos Coll., Norwalk, Calif., 1986, Louis Newman Galleries, Beverly Hills, 1986, 88, 90, Westmont Coll., Santa Barbara, Calif., 1992; exhibited in group shows at Owensboro (Ky.) Mus. Fine Arts, 1979, Burpee Art Mus., Rockford, Ill., 1981, Newport Harbor Art Mus., Newport Beach, Calif., 1981, Nat. Acad. Galleries, N.Y.C., 1982, Leslie Levy Gallery, Scottsdale, Ariz., 1983, Art Inst. So. Calif., 1984, Saddleback Coll., Mission Viejo, Calif., 1988, Riverside (Calif.) Art Mus., 1989, Ch. of Jesus Christ of LDS Mus. Art and History, Salt Lake City, 1988, 91, others; represented in permanent collections Home Savings Bank of Am., Nat. Bank of La Jolla, Greenburg Deposit Bank, Ashland, Ky., INMA Gallery, Saudi Arabia, pvt. collectors. Recipient Gold Medal of Honor, Am. Watercolor Soc., 1982, Walser S. Greathouse medal, 1988, Gold Medal of Honor for watercolor Allied Artists Am., 1982, cash merit award Ch. of Jesus Christ Latter Day Saints Mus. Art and History, 1991. Signature mem. Nat. Watercolor Soc., Watercolor West (1st award 1984), West Coast Watercolor Soc.; mem. Women Painters West. Mormon.

MOYERS, WILLIAM TAYLOR, artist; b. Atlanta, Dec. 11, 1916; s. William Taylor and Sarah Frances (McKinnon) M.; m. Neva Irene Anderson, Mar. 20, 1943; children: Joanne, William Taylor, Charles, John. BA, Adams State Coll., Alamosa, Colo., 1939; postgrad., Otis Art Inst., L.A., 1939; Dr. (hon.), Adams State Coll., 1992. Artist Walt Disney Prodns., Burbank, Calif., 1939-40; free lance illustrator, 1946-62. One man show Nat. Cowboy Hall of Fame, 1973; group show Phoenix Art Mus., CAA Shows, 1973-90. Bd. dirs. Albuquerque Arts Bd., 1985, Adams State Coll. Found., 1974—, Cowboy Artists of Am. Mus., Kerrville, Tex., 1984-89. Capt. U.S. Army, 1942-46. Recipient illustration award Ltd. Edits. Club, N.Y.C., 1945, sculpture awards Cowboy Artists Am., 1968-84, silver medal for watercolor, 1989, 91, gold medal for watercolor, 1993; named Artist of Yr., Tucson Festival Soc., 1991. Mem. Cowboy Artists of Am. (pres. 1971-72, 83-84, 88-89). Presbyterian. Home: 1407 Morningside Dr NE Albuquerque NM 87110-5639

MOYES, TERENCE E., publishing executive; b. London, Apr. 22, 1942; came to U.S., 1963; s. Ronald A. and Eileen E.R. (Knight) M.; m. Irene Spencer, Sept. 25, 1942; children: Douglas, Stuart. Classified advt. mgr. George Newnes Ltd., London, 1960-63; advt. dir. Camping Jour., N.Y.C., 1965-70; advt. dir. World Tennis mag. CBS Mags., N.Y.C., 1978-79; advt. dir. Ski Mag. Times Mirror Mags., N.Y.C., 1970-77, 79-81, pub. Popular Sci. Mag., 1981-86; v.p. advt. Ski Bus. Mag., Darien, Conn., 1986-89; v.p., gen. mgr. Ski Racing Internat., Waitsfield, Vt., 1989-91; v.p., gen. mgr./part owner Jaywalker Publs., Santa Fe, N.Mex., 1992—; pub. cons. N.Y.C., 1986-89. Office: Jaywalker Publs 1547 S Saint Francis Dr Santa Fe NM 87505-4039

MOZENA, JOHN DANIEL, podiatrist; b. Salem, Oreg., June 9, 1956; s. Joseph Iner and Mary Teresa (Delaney) M.; m. Elizabeth Ann Hintz, June 2, 1979; children: Christine Hintz, Michelle Delaney. Student, U. Oreg., 1974-

79; B in Basic Med. Scis., Calif. Coll. Podiatric Medicine, D in Podiatric Medicine, 1983. Diplomate Am. Bd. Podiatric Surgery. Resident in surg. podiatry Hillside Hosp., San Diego, 1983-84; pvt. practice podiatry Portland, Oreg., 1984—; dir. residency Med. Ctr. Hosp., Portland, 1985-91; lectr. Nat. Podiatric Assn. Seminar, 1990, Am. Coll. Gen. Practitioners, 1991, Am. Coll. Family Physician, 1995. Cons. editor Podiatry Mgmt. mag., 1994—; contbr. articles to profl. jours.; patentee sports shoe cleat design, 1985. Podiatric adv. coun. Oreg. Bd. Med. Examiners. Fellow Am Coll. Ambulatory Foot Surgeons, Am. Coll. Foot Surgeons. Republican. Roman Catholic. Office: Town Ctr Foot Clinic 8305 SE Monterey Ave Ste 101 Portland OR 97266-7728

MRACKY, RONALD SYDNEY, marketing management and media consultant; b. Sydney, Australia, Oct. 22, 1932; came to U.S., 1947, naturalized, 1957; s. Joseph and Anna (Janousek) M.; m. Sylvia Frommer, Jan. 1, 1960; children: Enid Hillevi, Jason Adam. Student, English Inst., Prague, Czechoslovakia, 1943-47; grad., Parsons Sch. Design, N.Y.C., 1950-53; postgrad., NYU, 1952-53. Designer D. Deskey Assocs., N.Y.C., 1953-54; art dir., designer ABC-TV, Hollywood, Calif., 1956-57; creative dir. Neal Advt. Assocs., L.A., 1957-59; pres. Richter & Mracky Design Assocs., L.A., 1959-68; pres., CEO Richter & Mracky-Bates div. Ted Bates & Co., L.A., 1968-73, pres., CEO Regency Fin., Internat. Fin. Svcs., Beverly Hills, Calif., 1974-76; sr. ptnr. Sylron Internat., L.A., 1973—; mgmt. dir. for N.Am. Standard Advt.-Tokyo, L.A., 1978-91; CEO Standard/Worldwide Cons. Group, Los Angeles and Tokyo, 1981-87; officer, bd. dirs. Theme Resorts, Inc., Denver, 1979—; prin., officer Prodn. Travel & Tours, Universal City, 1981—, Eques Ltd., L.A., 1988—; mng. ptnr. GO! Pubs., 1993—; cons. in field; exec. dir. Inst. for Internat. Studies and Devel., L.A., 1976-77. Contbr. articles to profl. jours. With U.S. Army, 1954-56. Recipient nat. and internat. awards design and mktg. Mem. Am. Mktg. Assn., African Travel Assn. (amb.-at-large, pres. So. Calif. chpt.), L.A. Publicity Club, Pacific Asia Travel Assn., S.Am. Travel Assn., Am. Soc. Travel Agents. Office: 10554 Riverside Dr Toluca Lake CA 91602-2441

MUCH, KATHLEEN, editor; b. Houston, Apr. 30, 1942; d. C. Frederick and Ortrud V. (Lefevre) M.; m. W. Robert Murfin, Aug. 17, 1963 (div. 1981); children: Brian C., Glen M.; m. Paul Stanley Peters Jr., Jan. 1, 1988. BA, Rice U., 1963, MA, 1971, postgrad., 1978. Tchr. Kinkaid H.S., Houston, 1964-66; editor Rice U., 1969—; freelance writer, Calif., 1971—; dir. info. Meth. Hosp., Houston, 1981-84; sr. editor Addison-Wesley Pub. Co., Menlo Park, Calif., 1984-86; editor Ctr. for Advanced Study in Behavioral Scis., Stanford, Calif., 1986—; dir. Tex. Wordworks, Inc., Assn. Rice Alumni. Active Houston Ballet Guild, Rice U. Fund Coun., Friends of Stanford String Quartet, Stanford Music Guild. Mem. Internat. Assn. Bus. Communicators, Soc. Tech. Communication, Phi Beta Kappa. Editor, contbr. profl. jours. Office: Ctr for Advanced Study 202 Junipero Serra Blvd Palo Alto CA 94305-8006

MUECKE, CHARLES ANDREW (CARL MUECKE), federal judge; b. N.Y.C., Feb. 20, 1918; s. Charles and Wally (Roeder) M.; m. Claire E. Vasse; children by previous marriage: Carl Marshall, Alfred Jackson, Catherine Calvert. B.A., Coll. William and Mary, 1941; LL.B., U. Ariz., 1953. Bar: Ariz. 1953. Rep. AFL, 1947-50; reporter Ariz. Times, Phoenix, 1947-48; since practiced in Phoenix; with firm Parker & Muecke, 1953-59, Muecke, Dushoff & Sacks, 1960-61; U.S. atty. Dist. Ariz., 1961-64, U.S. dist. judge, 1964—, now sr. judge.; mem. 9th cir. Jud. Coun. com. review local dist. Ct. Rules. Mem. Phoenix Planning Commn., 1955-61, chmn., 1960; chmn. Maricopa County Dem. Party, 1961-62; trustee U. San Diego Coll. Law. Maj. USMC, 1942-45, USMCR, 1945-60. Mem. Fed. Bar Assn., Ariz. Bar Assn., Maricopa Bar Assn., Am. Trial Lawyers Assn., Dist. Judges Assn. Ninth Circuit, Phi Beta Kappa, Phi Alpha Delta, Omicron Delta Kappa. Office: US Dist Ct US Courthouse & Fed Bldg 230 N 1st Ave Ste 7015 Phoenix AZ 85025-0007

MUEHLEISEN, GENE SYLVESTER, retired law enforcement officer, state official; b. San Diego, Dec. 28, 1915; s. Adolph and Vesta C. (Gates) M.; m. Elsie Jane Conover, Sept. 14, 1940; 1 son, John Robert. Student, San Diego State Coll., 1935-39, San Diego Jr. Coll., 1957. U.S. park ranger Yosemite Nat. Park, summers 1936-39, 79-84; with San Diego Police Dept., 1940-60, dir. tng., 1957-59, comdg. officer patrol div., capt., 1958-60; exec. dir. Commn. on Peace Officer Standards and Tng., Calif. Dept. Justice, Sacramento, 1960-65, 67-76; assoc. dir. Pres.'s Commn. on Law Enforcement and Adminstrn. of Justice, Nat. Crime Commn., 1965-67; chmn. police sci. adv. com. San Diego Jr. Coll., 1957-60, police sci. faculty, 1957-60; staff instr. San Diego Police Acad., 1954-60; guest instr. police adminstrn. Sacramento State Coll., 1964; grad. FBI Nat. Acad. 51st Session, 1953, pres. of class, guest faculty, 1963-66; cons. Ford Found. Internat. Assn. Chiefs of Police Project, 1964-67; cons. U.S. Nat. Park Svc., 1965-84, spl. asst. to regional dir. Western region, 1977-79; adviser Royal Can. Mounted Police, 1961—; guest lectr., 1960—. Mem. tng. com. Internat. Assn. Chiefs of Police, 1963—; mem. adv. com. on police tng. Ford Found., 1964—; U.S. rep. Interpol Symposium on Police Edn. and Tng., Paris, 1965; chmn. Atty. Gen.'s Com. on Law Enforcement Standards, 1957-59; vice chmn. Calif. Commn. Peace Officer Standards and Tng., 1959-60; chmn. police services task force Calif. Council Criminal Justice, 1968-78 ; mem. Atty. Gen.'s Commn. Police-Community Relations, 1971—; mem. adv. com. FBI, 1972—; mem. Gov.'s Pub. Safety Planning Council, 1974—; Pres. San Diego Police Officers Assn., San Diego Police and Fire Retirement System; bd. dirs. San Diego Hist. Soc. Served to capt. USNR, World War II. The Gene Muehleisen Nature Area, Valley Oak Park, Sacramento dedicated, 1992. Mem. Nat. Conf. Police Assns. (com. chmn.), Calif. Peace Officers Assn. (com. chmn.), Peace Officers Research Assn. Calif. (pres. 1959-60, com. chmn.), Am. Soc. Pub. Adminstrn. (dir. San Diego County chpt.), Nat. Assn. State Dirs. Law Enforcement Tng. (pres. 1972-73), Am. Corrections Assn., Calif. Assn. Adminstrn. of Justice Educators, Park Rangers Assn. of Calif., Internat. Police Assn. (life, v.p. region 29 USA), Internat. Assn. Chiefs of Police (life), Calif. Parks and Recreation Soc. (Citizen of Yr. 1992), Sacramento Tree Found. (tech. adv. com. 1983—). Clubs: Kiwanis, San Diego Ski (pres.). Home and Office: 4221 Corona Way Sacramento CA 95864-5301

MUELLER, CARL RICHARD, theater arts educator, author; b. St. Louis, Oct. 7, 1931; s. Anton John and Bonita Blanche (Lacy) M. BS, Northwestern U., 1954; MA, UCLA, 1960, PhD, 1967; cert., Freie U., Berlin, 1961. Prof. theater dept. Sch. Theater, Film and Television UCLA, 1967—; dramaturg New Theatre, Inc., L.A., 1975—; cons. U. Calif. Press, 1972—. Translator plays published include Buechner: Complete Plays, 1963, Brecht: The Visions of Simone Machard, 1965, Brecht: The Measures Taken, 1977, Hauptmann: The Weavers, 1965, Hebbel: Maria Magdalena, 1962, Strindberg: A Dream Play and The Ghost Sonata, 1966, Schnitzler: La Ronde and Game of Love, 1964, Hofmannsthal: Electra, 1964, Wedekind: The Marquis of Keith, 1964, Wedekind: The Lulu Plays, 1967, Zuckmayer: The Captain of Koepenick, 1972; translator plays produced include Anon: The Puppet Play of Dr. Johannes Faustus, Hauptmann: The Beaver Coat, Schnitzler: Dr. Bernhardi, Schnitzler: Anatol, Sternheim: The Underpants, Brecht: Mother Courage, Brecht: Caucasian Chalk Circle, Brecht: The Trial of Joan of Arc, Brecht: In the Jungle of Cities, Brecht: Man is Man, Brecht: He Who Says Yes, Brecht: He Who Says No, Brecht: The Exception and the Rule, Brecht: Round Heads, Peaked Heads, Brecht: Schweyk in the Second World War, Kleist: The Broken Jug, 1992, Lessing: Nathan the Wise, 1993, Toller, The Blind Goddess, 1993, Sophokles, Elektra, 1994, Zweig, Volpone, 1995; gen. editor Visual Resources, Inc., 1976—; theater editor Mankind mag., 1975-82; editor New Theater/Teatro Nuevo, 1985-87; author catalogue and slides A Visual History of European Theater Arts, 1978, A Visual History of European Experimental Theater, 1983, Greek and Roman Classical Theatre Structures and Performance Iconography, 1991, Medieval Theater and Performance Iconography, 1991, The Theater of Meyerhold, 1992, Stanislavsky and the Moscow Art Theater, 1992, The Commedia dell'Arte, 1992, Russian Scene and Costume Design, vols. 1 and 2, 1993, The Baroque Stage, 1993, 18th and 19th Cen. European Theater Structures, Performance Ionography and Costume Designes, 1994, Renaissance Theater Structures, Performance Ionography and Costume Designs, 1994; dir.: (plays) Spring's Awakening, Endangered Species, Hedda Gabler, My Body, Frankly Yours, Hamlet, Macbeth. Served with U.S. Army, 1954-56. Recipient Samuel Goldwyn Creative Writing award Goldwyn Found., 1959; Fulbright exchange grantee Berlin, 1960-61. Mem. Internat. Arthur Schnitzler Research Assn., UCLA Center for Medieval and Renaissance Studies (mem. adv. com. 1980-83). Democrat. Office: UCLA Dept Theater Sch Theater Film and TV 102 E Melnitz Box 951622 Los Angeles CA 90095-1622

MUELLER, DONALD DEAN, food company executive; b. Columbus, Nebr., Sept. 12, 1937; s. Emil J. and Hulda M. (Cattau) M.; m. JoAnn Ferris, Aug. 17, 1963; children: Bradford Paul, Bartley Brandon. Student U. Nebr., 1956-58, 62-63; BBA, U. Denver, 1965. CPA, Colo. Acct., Ernst & Ernst, Denver, 1965-69; treas. Monfort of Colo., Greeley, 1969-72; v.p. fin. Spencer Foods, Iowa, 1972-79; group v.p. fin. svcs. Monfort, Inc., 1979-83, group v.p. fin. svcs. and lamb ops., 1983-89; exec. v.p. fin. and adminstrn. ConAgra Red Meats, 1989-92, pres. Mapelli Food Distbn. Co., 1990-94; exec. v.p. ConAgra Red Meats, 1994—; bd. dirs. 1st Nat. Bank Greeley, 1989—, Purdue Valley Bank, Ft. Collins, Colo., 1993—, Weld Broadcasting Co., 1992—. Bd. dirs. Econ. Devel. Action Partnership, Greeley, Weld County, 1984-92, pvt. industry coun., Greeley, 1985-90, chmn. EDAP, 1990, bd. trustees N.C. Med. Ctr., 1992—, pres., 1993-94, bd. dirs., 1993—. Mem. AICPA, Nat. Assn. Accts., Colo. Soc. CPAs, Greeley Country Club. Republican. Lutheran. Avocations: church activities, singing, sports. Office: ConAgra Red Meats PO Box G Greeley CO 80632-0350

MUELLER, ELIZABETH SUZANNE, physical education educator; b. Garden Grove, Calif., May 23, 1962; d. Robert Lee and Carol Sue (Caspari) M. AA in Gen. Edn., Palomar Coll., 1982; BA in Phys. Edn., San Diego State U., 1985; MA in Phys. Edn., Azusa Pacific U., 1990. Jr. varsity softball coach San Marcos H.S., 1984; instrnl. aide, swimming instr. Fulton Elem. Sch., 1985; jr. varsity volleyball coach San Pasqual H.S., 1986; student tchr. phys. edn., coach Vista H.S., 1986-87; vol. coach USMC, 1987-88; instr. phys. edn., coach Mira Costa Coll., Oceanside, Calif., 1987-90; phys. edn. tchr., strength coach, volleyball and track coach Orange Glen H.S., Escondido, Calif., 1989-92; volleyball and track & field coach Escondido H.S., 1991-95; instr. Calif. Poly. Phys. Edn. Workshops, San Luis Obispo, 1990, 91, 92, 93; speaker Nat. Strength and Conditioning Assn. Nat. Strength Conf., 1991; curriculum writer Escondido Union Sch.Dist., 1989; guest speaker All-Star Sports Camp, 1989-91; instr. Calif. Phys. Edn. Workshops, San Luis Obispo, 1990-91. Olympic Trialist U.S.A. Track n Field, 1984, 88; nat. team mem. U.S.A. Track n Field, 1987. Mem. Nat. Strength and Conditioning Assn. (women's com. 1989-91, Cert. strength and conditioning specialist). Office: Escondido HS 1535 N Broadway Escondido CA 92026-2015

MUELLER, GAIL DELORIES, forensic chemist, toxicologist; b. Chgo., Sept. 30, 1957; d. Roger George and Delories B. (Reppert) Johnson; m. Joseph E. Mueller, Jan. 26, 1991. BS in Chemistry, No. Ill. U., 1980. Quality control chemist Standard Pharmacal Corp., Elgin, Ill., 1980; forensic chemist Ill. Racing Bd. Lab., Elgin, 1980-82, Analytical Techs., Inc., Tempe, Ariz., 1982-84; analytical chemist Nichols Inst., San Juan Capistrano, Calif., 1985-87; forensic chemist, toxicologist, GC/MS group leader Damon Reference Labs., Rancho Cucamonga, Calif., 1987-94; forensic chemist, toxicologist Associated Pathologists Labs., Las Vegas, Nev., 1994—. Fellow Am. Inst. Chemists; mem. Am. Chem. Soc., Calif. Assn. Toxicologists. Office: APL Toxicology Dept 4230 S Burnham Ave Ste 250 Las Vegas NV 89119

MUELLER, GERHARD G(OTTLOB), accounting educator; b. Eineborn, Germany, Dec. 4, 1930; came to U.S., 1952, naturalized, 1957; s. Gottlob Karl and Elisabeth Charlotte (Hossack) M.; m. Coralie George, June 7, 1958; children: Kent, Elisabeth, Jeffrey. AA, Coll. of Sequoias, 1954; BS with honors, U. Calif.-Berkeley, 1956, MBA, 1957, PhD, 1962; D Econs. (hon.), Swedish Sch. Econs. and Bus. Adminstrn., 1994. CPA, Wash. Staff accountant FMC Corp., San Jose, Calif., 1957-58; faculty dept. accounting U. Wash., Seattle, 1960—; assoc. prof. U. Wash., 1963-67, prof., 1967—, chmn. dept., 1969-78, dir. grad. profl. acctg. program, 1979-90, sr. assoc. dean, 1990-95, acting dean, 1994; Hughes M. Blake prof. internat. bus. mgmt. U. Wash., Seattle, 1992—; dir. Seattle Menu Specialists, Inc., U. Wash. Acctg. Devel. Fund, Overlake Hosp. Med. Ctr., Bellevue, chmn. bd. trustees, 1991-93; cons. internat. tax matters U.S. Treasury Dept., 1963-68; cons. Internat. Acctg. Rsch., 1964—; vis. prof. Cranfield Sch. Mgmt., Eng., 1973-74, U. Zurich, Switzerland, 1973-74; lectr. in field. Author: International Accounting, 1967; co-author: Introductory Financial Accounting, 3d edit., 1991, A Brief Introduction to Managerial and Social Uses of Accounting, 1975, International Accounting, 1978, 2nd edit., 1992, Accounting: An International Perspective, 1987, 3rd edit., 1994; editor: Readings in International Accounting, 1969, Accounting-A Book of Readings, 2d edit., 1976, A New Introduction to Accounting, 1971, A Bibliography of Internat. Accounting, 3d edit., 1973, Essentials of Multinational Accounting—An Anthology, 1979, Frontiers of International Accounting, 1986, AACSB Curriculum Internationalization Resource Guide, 1988; contbr. numerous articles to profl. jours. Expert legal witness, IRS, 1991-93. Recipient U. Wash. Disting. Teaching award, 1983, Disting. Service award, 1984; Price Waterhouse internat. accounting research fellow, 1962-64; Ford Found. fellow, 1958-59. Fellow Acad. Internat. Bus.; mem. AICPAs (internat. practice exec. com. 1972-75, exec. coun. 1987-89), Am. Acctg. Assn. (pres. 1988-89, acad. v.p. 1970-71, chmn. adv. bd. internat. acctg. sect. 1977-79, Wildman medal 1986, Nat. Outstanding Educator 1981, Disting. Internat. Lectr. in Black Africa 1987, Outstanding Internat. Acctg. Educator 1991), Fin. Execs. Inst., Wash. Soc. CPAs (pres. 1988-89, Outstanding Educator award 1985, Pub. Svc. award 1995), Acctg. Edn. Change Commn. (chmn. 1994—), Beta Alpha Psi (Acad. Acct. of Yr. 1987), Beta Gamma Sigma (Disting. scholar 1978-79), Alpha Gamma Sigma. Home: 9660 NE 34th St Bellevue WA 98004-1827 Office: U Washington Mackenzie Hall Dj # 10 Seattle WA 98195

MUELLER, HENRIETTA WATERS, psychologist, artist, painter, printmaker; b. Pitts., Apr. 13, 1915; d. William Sidney and Helen Losey (Kirkwood) Waters; m. Werner A. Mueller, June 15, 1940; children: Christopher Bradford, Richard Kirkwood. BFA with honors, Art Inst. of Chgo., 1938; MA, U. Wyo., 1948, MEd, 1960, studied with Ad Reinhardt, Ilya Bolotowsky, George McNeil, 1990; studied with Helen Frankenthaler, Santa Fe Inst., 1990. Tchr. art U. Nebr., Lincoln, 1956-57; summer art tchr. U. Wyo., Laramie, 1956-62; tchr. art Boulder (Colo.) Valley Sch., 1969-75; sch. clin. psychologist Jefferson County Sch. Dist., Lakewood, Colo., 1973-75; dir. speech and lang. clinic U. Wyo., Laramie, 1976; ednl. cons. Natrona County Sch. Dist., Casper, Wyo., 1976-85; prof. printmaking, art edn. U. of the Pacific, Stockton, Calif., summers 1970-71. Solo exhbns. One West, 1992, 10,000 Plus Exhbn. Sch. of the Art Inst., Chgo., 1994. Mem. One West Gallery, Ft. Collins, Colo. Marshall grantee Cummington (Mass.) Found., 1953; recipient purchase awards U. N.C., 1958, U. Wyo. Mus. Art, 1975. Mem. Rule Contemporary Gallery (Denver); mem. Internat. Zonta, Alpha Chi Omega. Democrat. Presbyterian. Home: 520 Mapleton Ave Boulder CO 80304-3986 Studio: 1309 Steele St Laramie WY 82070-4724

MUELLER, MICHELLE MARIE, management executive; b. Madison, Wis., June 15, 1954; d. Neil Edward and Maura Kay (Smith) M.; m. Michael Gault, Sept. 7, 1984; 1 stepchild, Gina Marlena. BA, Eastern Mich. U., 1974; MA, Morehead State U., 1975; postgrad., U. Mich., 1977-78; MBA, Syracuse U., 1985. Radio-TV/Producer Stas. WEMU-FM, WUOM-FM, Ann Arbor, Mich., 1972-78; instr. U. Mich., Ann Arbor, 1976-78; mgr. tech. comm. Bendix Co., Southfield, Mich., 1978-81; dir. advt. and pub. relations E.F. Hutton Life Ins., La Jolla, Calif., 1981-83; v.p. pub. rels. Knoth & Meads Advt./Pub. Rels., San Diego, Calif., 1983-85; asst. v.p. ops. support services M/A-COM Govt. Systems, San Diego, 1985-90; asst. v.p. adminstrn. The Titan Corp., 1990-94, v.p., 1994—; instr. San Diego State U., U. Calif.-San Diego, 1981—; instr. U. Mich., Easter Mich. U., Morehead State U., San Diego State U., 1974—; promotions dir. Artrain, San Diego, 1983. Author cookbook Recipes by the Dozen, 1987; contbr. articles to profl. jours. Mem. Women in Communications (v.p. programs 1983, pres. 1984, v.p. profl. devel. 1981, Woman of Achievement award 1984)), Pub. Rels. Soc. Am. (v.p. promotion 1983, v.p. profl. devel. 1984, sec. 1985, recipient Eva Irving award San Diego chpt. 1990), San Diego C. of C., Oceanside Econ. Devel. Coun., Calif. Jaycees (Outstanding Young Californian), San Diego Jaycees (Outstanding Young Citizen of San Diego), Pub. Rels. Club San Diego (Pub. Rels. Profl. of Yr. 1993), Soc. for Tech. Communications (Outstanding Presentation award 1980), Phi Kappa Phi, Alpha Epsilon Rho. Roman Catholic. Office: 3033 Science Park Rd San Diego CA 92121-1101

MUFTIC, FELICIA ANNE BOILLOT, consumer relations professional; b. Muskogee, Okla., Feb. 27, 1938; d. Lowell Francois and Geneva Margaret (Halstead) Boillot; m. Michael Muftic, Sept. 6, 1961; children: Tanya Muftic-Streicher, Theodore B., Mariana C. BA, Northwestern U., 1960. Exec. dir. Metro Dist. Atty.'s Consumer Office, Denver, 1973-79; talk show host KNUS, Denver, 1981-83; clk., recorder City and County of Denver, Colo., 1984-91; spl. projects dir. Consumer Credit Counseling, Denver, 1991-95; cons. consumer affairs pvt. practice, Denver, 1995—; pres. Muftic and Associates, Denver, 1980-83; commr. Uniform Consumer Credit Code, Colo., 1991—. Author: Colorado Consumer Handbook, 1982. Candidate for mayor, Denver, 1979. Named Media person of Yr., NASW, Colo., 1982; recipient Outstanding Contbrn. in Consumer Affairs award Denver (Colo.) Fed. Exec. Bd., 1982. Mem. Nat. Soc. Fundraising Execs., Inst. Internat. Edn. (bd. mem. 1980—). Democrat. Home and office: 3671 S Pontiac Way Denver CO 80237-1326

MUGLER, LARRY GEORGE, regional planner; b. Chgo., June 22, 1946; s. Warren Franklin and Elaine Mae (Mittag) M.; m. Judy Ann Allison, Aug. 3, 1968; children: Jonathan, Allison. BSCE, Northwestern U., 1968; postgrad., Evang. Theol. Sem., 1968-70; MS in Urban and Regional Planning, U. Wis., 1972. Planning analyst State of Wis., Madison, 1970-72; dir. community devel. Cen. Okla. Econ. Devel. Dist., Shawnee, 1972-74; planner Denver Regional Council of Govts., 1974-80, dir. environ. services, 1980-83, dir. devel. services, 1983—. Contbr. chpt. on pub. works mgmt. to book. Pres. bd. dirs. Leawood Met. Recreation and Park Dist., Littleton, Colo., 1978—; chair planning and rsch. com. Rocky Mountain Conf. The United Meth. Ch. Named one of Outstanding Young Men in Am., Jaycees, 1974; Lasker Found. fellow, 1971; recipient Disting. Svc. award Spl. Dist. Assn. of Colo., 1989. Mem. Am. Planning Assn. (sec. Colo. chpt.), ASCE (subcom. chmn. 1985-86, 88-91, div. exec. com. 1991—), Urban Land Inst. Republican. Methodist. Office: Denver Regional Coun Govts 2480 W 26th Ave Ste 200B Denver CO 80211-5503

MUHAMMAD, KHALEEDAH, entrepreneur, sales and marketing consultant; b. Berkeley, Calif., Nov. 2, 1943; d. Samuel Taylor Odom and Robbie Lee (Taylor) Gordon; m. O.B. Britt, Jan. 2, 1963 (div. 1972); children: Raymie, Jamal; m. Ansar El Muhammad, June 12, 1974; children: Tamishi, Ansar El II. BA, Los Angeles State Coll., 1965; postgrad., Calif. State, Hayward, 1971-72. Caseworker Pacoima (Calif.) Child Guidance Clinic, 1965-68; probation officer Los Angeles Probation Dept., 1968-72; ednl. opportunity program counselor U. Calif., Berkeley, 1974-79; community cons. YWCA, Richmond, Calif., 1979-81; owner, sales mgr. Touch of Class Boutique, Richmond, 1981-84; owner, mktg. cons. Nature's Co., Richmond, 1982-84; owner Unique Home Services, Richmond, 1984—; partowner, mktg. cons. Cora's Kitchen, Oakland, Calif., 1987—, Halal Mktg. Services, Oakland, 1987—; sales, mktg. cons. The Fox Factory, Richmond, 1985-87. Author: (pamphlet) It's Not Easy Being a Parent, 1979. Vice chairperson Unity Orgn., Richmond, 1979-83; founder People United For Coops., Richmond, 1983; bd. dirs. Richmond chpt. Reading Is Fundamental, 1979-83, Minority Arts Network, Contra Costa, Calif., 1987; ct. apptd. spl. rep. Adv. for Wards of the Ct., 1990-91; co-founder Loving Care Inc.; exec. dir. Ansari House Residential Treatment Facility for Teenage Girls. Mem. Nat. Assn. Female Execs. Democrat. Islam.

MUHLBACH, ROBERT ARTHUR, lawyer; b. Los Angeles, Apr. 13, 1946; s. Richard and Jeanette (Marcus) M.; m. Kerry Eldene Mahoney, July 26, 1986. BSME, U. Calif., Berkeley, 1967; JD, U. Calif., San Francisco, 1976; MME, Calif. State U., 1969; M in Pub. Adminstrn., U. So. Calif., 1976. Bar: Calif. 1976. Pub. defender County of Los Angeles, 1977-79; assoc. Kirtland & Packard, Los Angeles, 1979-85, ptnr., 1986—. Chmn. Santa Monica Airport Commn., Calif., 1984-87. Served to capt. USAF, 1969-73. Mem. ABA, AIAA, Internat. Assn. Def. Counsel, Am. Bd. Trial Advs. Office: Kirtland & Packard Ste 2600 1900 Avenue Of The Stars Los Angeles CA 90067-4507

MUHS, ELIZABETH MAE, marriage and family therapist; b. Boulder, Colo., Oct. 27, 1965; d. William Frederick and Joan Marie (Mauck) M. BA in Spanish, U. Mont., 1988; MS in Marriage and Family Therapy, Mont. State U., 1994. Intern, adminstr. Human Devel. Clinic Mont. State U., Bozeman, 1992-93, tchg. asst., 1992-93, counseling intern Counseling and Psychol. Svcs., 1994-95; therpist, pvt. practice Belgrade (Mont.) Counseling Clinic, 1994—; mgr. yard care svc., Bozeman, 1990-94. Vol. Battered Women's Network, Bozeman, 1990-92; instr. Active Parenting Class, Bozeman, 1992. Exploring Relationships scholar Mont. State U., 1994. Mem. Am. Counseling Assn., Mont. Counseling Assn., Internat. Assn. Marriage and Family Therapists. Office: Belgrade Counseling Clinic 103 W Jefferson Ave Ste A Belgrade MT 59714-4404

MUILENBURG, ROBERT HENRY, hospital administrator; b. Orange City, Iowa, Apr. 29, 1941; s. Henry W. and Anna (Vander Zwaag) M.; m. Judith Ann Gebauer, Jan. 1, 1959; children: Ronald, Eric, Matthew. B.A., U. Iowa, 1964, M.A., 1966. Adminstrv. asst. Ill. Masonic Med. Ctr., Chgo., Ill., 1966-67; asst. adminstr. Ill. Masonic Med. Ctr., Chgo., Ill., 1967-68; assoc. adminstr. Ill. Masonic Med. Ctr., Chgo., Ill., 1968-71; assoc. adminstr. U. Utah Hosp., Salt Lake City, 1971-75, adminstr., 1975-78; adminstr. U. Wash. Med. Ctr., Seattle, 1978-84; clin. assoc. prof. health services adminstrn. and planning U. Wash., Seattle, 1978—; exec. dir. U. Wash. Med. Ctr., 1984—. USPHS trainee, 1966. Fellow Am. Coll. Hosp. Adminstrs.; mem. Am. Hosp. Assn. (del. 1984-88, chmn. metro. hosp. sect. 1987, bd. dirs. 1992-94), Wash. State Hosp. Assn. (bd. dirs. 1982-84, 89-94), Seattle Area Hosp. Coun. (pres. 1983). Home: 10019 49th Ave NE Seattle WA 98125-8131 Office: U Wash Med Ctr RC-35 1959 NE Pacific St Seattle WA 98195-0004

MUIR, WILLIAM KER, JR., political science educator; b. Detroit, Oct. 30, 1931; s. William Ker and Florence Taylor (Bodman) M.; m. Paulette Irene Wauters, Jan. 16, 1960; children: Kerry Macaire, Harriet Bodman. B.A., Yale U., 1954, Ph.D., 1965; J.D., U. Mich., 1958. Bar: N.Y. 1960, Conn. 1965. Instr. U. Mich. Law Sch., 1958-59; assoc. firm Davis Polk & Wardwell, N.Y.C., 1959-60; lectr. in polit. sci. Yale U., 1960-64, 65-67; from assoc. to ptnr. Tyler Cooper Grant Bowerman & Keefe, New Haven, 1964-68; prof. polit. sci. U. Calif.-Berkeley, 1968—, dept. chmn., 1980-83; speechwriter v.p. U.S., 1983-85; columnist Oakland (Calif.) Tribune, 1992-93; writer Gov. of Calif., Sacramento, 1994; sr. cons. Calif. State Assembly, Sacramento, 1975-76; cons. Oakland (Calif.) Police Dept., 1970-72; vis. prof. polit. sci. Harvard U., summers 1976, 79. Author: Prayer in the Public Schools, 1967, later republished as Law and Attitude Change, 1974, Police: Streetcorner Politicians, 1977, Legislature: California's School for Politics, 1982, The Bully Pulpit: The Presidential Leadership of Ronald Reagan, 1993. Mem. Berkeley (Calif.) Police Rev. Commn., 1981-83; chmn. New Haven Civil Liberties Coun., 1965-68. Recipient Hadley B. Cantril Meml. award, 1979, Disting. teaching award U. Calif., Berkeley, 1974, Phi Beta Kappa No. Calif. Assoc. Excellence In Teaching award, 1994. Mem. Am. Polit. Sci. Assn. (Edward S. Corwin award 1966). Republican. Presbyterian. Home: 59 Parkside Dr Berkeley CA 94705-2409 Office: Dept Polit Sci U Calif Berkeley CA 94720

MUKHOPADHYAY, BIMAL, environmental scientist, consultant; b. Calcutta, India, July 15, 1944; s. Kamakshya and Monorama (Bhattacharya) M.; m. Dipti Bhattacharya Mukhopadhyay, Aug. 15, 1972; children: Priya, Bejay. BSc with honors, Presidency Coll., Calcutta, 1964; MSc, U. Calcutta, 1966; Phd, U. N.Mex., 1974. Cert. groundwater profl., profl. geologist. Post-doctoral rsch. assoc. U. N.Mex., Albuquerque, 1974-75; rsch. scientist Conoco, Inc., Ponca City, Okla., 1975-79; rsch. supr., prin. geologist ARCO, Plano, Tex., 1979-85; sect. mgr. BPMD Battle Meml. Inst., Columbus, 1986-88; sr. project mgr. Ray F. Weston, Inc., Albuquerque, 1988-92; sr. cons., bus. cons. Dames & Moore, Inc., San Francisco, 1992-93; group leader Lawrence Livermore (Calif.) Nat. Lab., 1993-94; prin. Environ. Sci. & Tech. Internat., Walnut Creek, Calif., 1994—. Contbr. articles to profl. jours. Recipient Rotary Club scholar, Calcutta, 1960-63, Rsch. scholar U. Calcutta, 1967-68; Rsch. fellow Couns. of Sci. & Indsl. Rsch., 1968-70; Rsch. Fund award Am. Chemical Soc., 1971-74. Mem. Am. Soc. Pet. Geologists, Geol. Soc. Am., Nat. Groundwater Assn. Home: 297 Tamarisk Dr Walnut Creek CA 94598

MULASE, MOTOHICO, mathematics educator; b. Kanazawa, Japan, Oct. 11, 1954; came to U.S., 1982; s. Ken-Ichi and Mieko (Yamamoto) M.; m. Sayuri Kamiya, Sept. 10, 1982; children: Kimihico Chris, Paul Norihico, Yurika. BS, U. Tokyo, 1978; MS, Kyoto U., 1980, DSc, 1985. Rsch. assoc. Nagoya (Japan) U., 1980-85; JMS fellow Harvard U., Cambridge, Mass., 1982-83; vis. asst. prof. SUNY, Stony Brook, 1984-85; Hedrick asst. prof. UCLA, 1985-88; asst. prof. Temple U., Phila., 1988-89; assoc. prof. U. Calif., Davis, 1989-91, prof., 1991—, vice chair for undergraduate affairs, 1995—; mem. Math. Scis. Rsch. Inst., Berkeley, Calif., 1982-84, Inst. for Advanced Study, Princeton, N.J., 1988-89; vis. prof. Max-Planck Inst. for Math., Bonn, Germany, 1991-92. Contbr. articles to profl. jours. Treas. Port of Sacramento Japanese Sch., 1990-91. Mem. Math. Soc. Japan, Am. Math. Soc. (com. on internal affairs 1993—). Office: U Calif Dept Math Davis CA 95616

MULCHEY, RONALD DOUGLAS, hospital administrator; b. Toronto, Ont., Can., Aug. 1, 1937; s. William and Rena Katherine (Hilts) M.; m. Heather Elizabeth Spence, Aug. 12, 1967; children: Elizabeth Anne, Ian Douglas. BA, U. Sask., Saskatoon, Can., 1960; Theology Diploma, U. Toronto, 1963, MDiv, 1969, Diploma in Hosp. Adminstrn., 1975. Min. St. Andrews Presbyn. Ch., Thompson, Man., Can., 1963-65, Knox Presbyn. ch., Weyburn, Sask., 1965-69; asst. min. Glenview Presbyn. ch., Toronto, 1969-70; cons. in ch. and univ. The Presbyn. Ch. in Can, Don Mills, Ont., 1970-74; adminstrv. resident Sunnybrook Med. Ctr., Toronto, 1974-75, adminstrv. asst. spl. svcs., 1975-76, dir. support svcs., 1976-78, 80-81, dir. devel., 1978-80, asst. adminstr. planning and spl. svcs., 1981-83, acting exec. dir., 1983, exec. v.p., COO, 1983-87; pres., CEO St. Paul's Hosp., Vancouver, B.C., Can., 1987—; Mem., cons. nat. staff Presbyn. Ch. in Can., exec. sec. com. on ch. and univ.; chmn. computer adv. com. B.C. Ministry of Health; chmn. oper. com. Coun. Univ. Teaching Hosps., B.C.; lectr. Dept. Health Adminstrn. Faculty Medicine U. Toronto, Dept. Health Care and Epidemiology U. B.C. Recipient G. Harvey Agnew award U. Toronto, 1974. Mem. B.C. Health Assn. (bd. dirs. 1987-92, past chmn.), Health Employers Assn. B.C., (bd. dirs. 1991—, past chmn.), Can. Coll. Health Svc. Execs., Shaughnessy Golf and Country Club (Vancouver). Home: 1281 20th St, West Vancouver, BC Canada V7V 3Z4 Office: St Paul's Hosp, 1081 Burrard St, Vancouver, BC Canada V6Z 1Y6

MULDARY, PATRICK FARRELL, manufacturing company executive; b. Ft. Wayne, Ind., Sept. 26, 1951; s. George A. and Mary L. (Suelzer) M.; m. Melanie S. Volkert, May 19, 1979; children: Heather N., Megan T. BS in Aero. Engring., Purdue U., 1973; MS in Engring. Mechanics, U. Minn., 1975, MBA in Fin., 1981. Design engr. Chevron U.S.A., San Francisco, 1975-77; project mgr. Gould Inc.-ABD, St. Paul, 1977-79; mgr. engring. Gould Inc.-PBD, St. Paul, 1979-80, plant mgr., 1980-82; mgr. engring. and quality assurance Nichols-Homeshield, Rice Lake, Wis., 1982-90; dir. mfg. Milgard Mfg., Tacoma, Wash., 1990-91; pres. PFM Enterprises, Inc., Sumner, Wash., 1991—. Inventor steam quality measurement device, 1975. Pres. United Way of Rice Lake, Wis., 1983-90. Mem. ASME, Assn. Mfg. Excellence, Am. Archtl. Mfrs. Assn. (dir. 1991-92). Home: 19806 Island Pky E Sumner WA 98390-9011 Office: PFM Enterprises Inc PO Box 8174 Bonney Lake WA 98390-0885

MULDER, ELDON PAUL, state legislator, real estate agent; b. Sioux Center, Iowa, Aug. 28, 1957; s. Theron John and Marcia Arlene (Schut) M.; m. Wendy Anne Chamberlain, Aug. 1, 1985; children: Corey Anne, Mackenzie Anne. BA, Ctrl. Coll., Pella, Iowa, 1980; MA, U. Colo., 1982. Lic. real estate agt., Alaska. Campaign mgr. Rep. Congl. Campaign from 6th Dist., Sioux Center, 1983-84; legis. aide Alaska State Senate, Juneau, 1985-92; owner Mulder gfmt. Svcs., Anchorage, Alaska, 1989—; real estate agt. Penco Devel., Anchorage, 1993-94; mem. Alaska Ho. of Reps., Juneau, 1993—; appraiser trainee Appraisal Co. Alaska, 1994—. Bd. dirs. Armed Svcs. YMCA, Anchorage, 1992—, Alaska Spl. Olympics, Anchorage, 1993—. Mem. NRA, Anchorage Sports Assn., Assn. U.S. Army, Nat. Rep. Legis. Assn., Alaska Golf Assn., Kenai River Sportfish Assn. Home: PO Box 140711 Anchorage AK 99514-0711 Office: Alaska State Ho of Reps State Capitol Rm 116 Juneau AK 99801

MULDOON, WILLIAM HENRY, III, newspaper publisher; b. San Antonio, June 14, 1935; s. Wilfrid Edward and Laurie Elizabeth (Battersby) M.; m. Nancy Achning, Aug. 23, 1958; children: William Henry IV, Shevaun Elaine. BA, Dartmouth Coll., 1957; postgrad., U. Tex., 1957-58, Oceanside Carlsbad Coll., 1959-60. Pres. V.I. Printing Corp., St. Thomas, 1961-72, Mountain Top Estates, St. Thomas, 1965-76; pub. St. Thomas Jour., 1972-76, Commerce (Tex.) Jour., Harte-Hanks Co., 1976-85, Copperas Cove (Tex.) Leader Press, 1986-87; mktg. dir. Tex. Weekly mag., Harte-Hanks Co., San Antonio, 1985-86; pub. Augusta (Kans.) Daily Gazette, 1987-90, Jour.-Advocate, Sterling, Colo., 1990—; regional dir. Graphic Arts Tech. Found., St. Thomas, 1966-73. Mem. bd. presdl. advisors East Tex. State U., Commerce, 1978-85; chmn. United Way, Commerce, 1978; dist. chmn. Boy Scouts Am., Commerce, 1980; bus. chmn. San Antonio Symphony Soc., 1986; pres. Commerce C. of C., 1985. Capt. USMC, 1958-62. Recipient Silver Beaver award Boy Scouts Am., 1982; named Ky. Col., State of Ky., 1974-91. Mem. Nat. Newspaper Assn., Newspaper Assn. Am., Inter-Am. Press Assn., Colo. Press Assn. (CPA treas.), NRA (life, master shooter), Marine Corps League, 1st Marine Divsn. Assn., U.S. Marine Corps Combat Corr. Assn., VFW, Am. Legion, San Antonio Country Club, Elks, Rotary, Dartmouth Club (Colo.). Republican. Episcopalian. Home: 9218 County Road 35 Sterling CO 80751-8531 Office: Jour-Adv PO Box 1272 504 N 3rd St Sterling CO 80751

MULKEY, SHARON RENEE, gerontology nurse; b. Miles City, Mont., Apr. 14, 1954; d. Otto and Elvera Marie (Haglof) Neuhardt; m. Monty W. Mulkey, Oct. 9, 1976; children: Levi, Candice, Shane. BS in Nursing, Mont. State U., 1976. RN, Calif. Staff nurse, charge nurse VA Hosp., Miles City, Mont., 1976-77; staff nurse obstetrics labor and delivery Munster (Ind.) Community Hosp., 1982-83; nurse mgr. Thousand Oaks Health Care, 1986-88; unit mgr. rehab. Semi Valley (Calif.) Adventist Hosp., 1988-89, DON TCU, 1989-91; DON Pleasant Valley Hosp. Extended Care Vacility and Neuro Ctr., 1991-93; dir. nurses Victoria Care Ctr., Ventura, Calif., 1993—. Mem. ANA, Nat. Gerontol. Nursing Assn., Internat. Platform Assn., Alpha Tau Delta (pres. 1973-75), Phi Kappa Phi. Home: 3461 Pembridge St Thousand Oaks CA 91360-4565

MULLARKEY, MARY J., state supreme court justice; b. New London, Wis., Sept. 28, 1943; d. John Clifford and Isabelle A. (Steffes) M.; m. Thomas E. Korson, July 24, 1971; 1 child, Andrew Steffes Korson. BA, St. Norbert Coll., 1965; LLB, Harvard U., 1968; LLD (hon.), St. Norbert Coll., 1989. Bar: Wis. 1968, Colo. 1974. Atty.-advisor U.S. Dept. Interior, Washington, 1968-73; asst. regional atty. EEOC, Denver, 1973-75; 1st atty. gen. Colo. Dept. Law, Denver, 1975-79, solicitor gen., 1979-82; legal advisor to Gov. Lamm State of Colo., Denver, 1982-85; ptnr. Mullarkey & Seymour, Denver, 1985-87; justice Colo. Supreme Ct., Denver, 1987—. Recipient Alumni award St. Norbert Coll., De Pere, Wis., 1980, Alma Mater award, 1993. Fellow ABA Found., Colo. Bar Found.; mem. ABA, Colo. Bar Assn., Colo. Women's Bar Assn. (recognition award 1986), Denver Bar Assn., Thompson G. Marsh Inn of Ct. (pres. 1993-94). Office: Supreme Ct Colo 2 E 14th Ave Denver CO 80203-2115

MULLEN, ROD GORDEN, nonprofit organization executive; b. Puyallup, Wash., Aug. 2, 1943; s. Charles Rodney and Grace Violet (Fritsch) M.; m. Lois Fern Tobiska, May 3, 1963 (div. Jan. 1977); children: Cristina, Charles, Moneka; m. Naya Arbiter, Oct. 17, 1978. Student, U. Idaho, 1961-63; AB in Polit. Sci., U. Calif., Berkeley, 1966; postgrad., San Francisco Art Inst., 1968. Dir. Oakland (Calif.) facility Synanon Found., Inc., Badger, 1971-73; dir. San Francisco facility Synanon Found., Inc., 1972-73, dir. Tomales Bay (Calif.) facility, 1976-78, dir. Synanon edn. programs, 1973-76; treatment dir. nat. programs Vision Quest, Inc., Tucson, 1981-82; dir. resources and devel. Amity, Inc., Tucson, 1982-84, exec. dir., 1984—; mem. Nat. Adv. Com. on Substance Abuse Prevention, 1990-92, 93—; mem. sci. adv. bd. Ctr. for Therapeutic Cmty. Rsch., Narcotic and Drug Rsch., Inc., N.Y.C., 1991—; program mgr. Drug Abuse Treatment Waiting Period Reduction Program, 1990-91; dir. Coop. Program between Amity, Inc. and Pima County Probation Dept., 1990-92; cons. Calif. Office Criminal Justice Planning, Sacramento, 1993; prin. investigator program Nat. Inst. on Drug Abuse, 1990-93. Contbr. numerous articles to profl. publs., chpts. to books. Mem. Internat. Coun. on Alcoholism and Addictions, Am. Jail Assn., Am. Psychol. Soc., Nat. Assn. Perinatal Addiction Rsch. and Edn., Nat. Assn. State Alcohol and Drug Abuse Dirs., World Fedn. Therapeutic Comtys., U.S.-Mex. Border Health Assn., Nat. Coun. La Raza, Therapeutic Comtys. of Am. (exec. coun. 1988—), Ariz. Assn. Alcohol, Drug and Mental Health Programs, Ariz. Coalition for Human Svcs., Ariz. Coun. Ctrs. for Children and Adolescents. Office: Amity Inc PO Box 32200 Tucson AZ 85751-2200

MULLENIX, TRAVIS H., food products company executive; b. 1931. BA, Univ. of Texas, 1956. With Ralston-Purina Co., 1956-84, group v.p.; with Tri-Valley Growers, 1984—, exec. v.p., chief operating officer, then pres., 1985—. Office: Tri/Valley Growers Inc 1255 Battery St San Francisco CA 94111-1101

MULLER, DAVID WEBSTER, architectural designer; b. Norwich, Conn., Aug. 25, 1956; s. Richard Johnson and Barbara Alice (Reading) M.; m. Susan Akers, Dec. 31, 1989; 1 stepchild, Shannon. BA in Polit. Sci., George Washington U., 1978. Rsch. assoc. Rep. Nat. Com., Washington, 1978-80, dep. dir. spl. projects, 1981-83; western field dir. Nat. Rep. Congl. Com., Washington, 1983-85; v.p. Russo Watts & Rollins, Sacramento, Calif., 1985-86; campaign mgr. Chavez for U.S. Senate, Silver Spring, Md., 1986; v.p. Russo Watts & Rollins, Sacramento, 1987-89; cons. Sacramento, 1989, pvt. investor, 1990—; archtl. design and restoration Muller/West, 1990—. Home and Office: Muller/West 4385 Hale Ranch Ln Fair Oaks CA 95628-6466

MULLER, JEROME KENNETH, photographer, art gallery director, editor; b. Amityville, N.Y., July 18, 1934; s. Alphons and Helen (Haberl) M.; m. Nora Marie Nestor, Dec. 21, 1974. BS, Marquette U., 1961; postgrad., Calif. State U., Fullerton, 1985-86; MA, Nat. U., San Diego, 1988; postgrad., Newport Psychoanalytic Inst., 1988-90. Comml. and editorial photographer N.Y.C., 1952-55; mng. editor Country Beautiful mag., Milw., 1961-62, Reprodns. Rev. mag., N.Y.C., 1967-68; editor, art dir. Orange County (Calif.) Illustrated, Newport Beach, 1962-67, art editor, 1970-79, exec. editor, art dir., 1968-69; owner, CEO Creative Svcs. Advt. Agy., Newport Beach, 1969-79; founder, CEO Mus. Graphics, Costa Mesa, Calif., 1978—; tchr. photography Lindenhurst (N.Y.) High Sch., 1952-54; tchr. comic art U. Calif., Irvine, 1979; guest curator 50th Anniversary Exhbn. Mickey Mouse, 1928-78, The Bowers Mus., Santa Ana, Calif., 1978; organized Moving Image Exhbn. Mus. Sci. and Industry, Chgo., Cooper-Hewitt Mus., N.Y.C., William Rockhill Nelson Gallery, Kansas City, 1981; collector original works outstanding Am. cartoonists at major mus. One-man shows include Souk Gallery, Newport Beach, 1970, Gallery 2, Santa Ana, Calif., 1972, Cannery Gallery, Newport Beach, 1974, Mus. Graphics Gallery, 1993; Author: Rex Brandt, 1972; contbr. photographs and articles to mags. Served with USAF, 1956-57. Recipient two silver medals 20th Ann. Exhbn. Advt. and Editorial Art in West, 1965. Mem. APA, Am. Assn. Profl. Hypnotherapists, Newport Harbor Art Mus., Mus. Modern Art (N.Y.C.), Met. Mus. Art, Art Mus. Assn. Am., Laguna Beach Mus. Art, L.A. Press Club, Newport Beach Tennis Club, Alpha Sigma Nu. Home: 2438 Bowdoin Pl Costa Mesa CA 92626-6304 Office: PO Box 10743 Costa Mesa CA 92627-0234

MULLETT, MELINDA FAE, computer scientist; b. New Martinsville, W.Va., Nov. 2, 1960; d. Michael Larry and Shirley Kay (Athey) M. BS in Computer Sci., U. Wyo., 1986; M in Computer Info. Systems, U. Denver, 1989, cert. of data processing mgmt., 1989. Clk./data entry Univ. Wyo., Laramie, Wyo., 1981-82; pvt. practice computer cons. various cities, 1982-87; programmer/analyst NDL, Internat., Denver, 1987-88; staff cons. Analyst Internat. Corp., Denver, 1988-90; sys. analyst Metro Wastewater Reclamation Dist., Denver, 1990-93; cons. AACCESS, Denver, 1991—, Ciber, Inc., Denver, 1993—; instr. Front Range C.C., Westminster, Colo., 1993—. Mem. Boulder Chpt. Assn. Computing Machinery (chmn. 1990—), IEEE, Math. Assn. Am., NAFE. Home: 11109 Melody Dr Denver CO 80234-3933

MULLIN, CHRIS(TOPHER) PAUL, professional basketball player; b. N.Y.C., July 30, 1963. Student, St. John's U., 1981-85. Basketball player Golden State Warriors, 1985—; mem. U.S. Olympic Team (received Gold medal), 1984, 92. Recipient Wooden award, 1985; named to Sporting News All-Am. First Team, 1985, NBA All-Star team, 1989-93, NBA First Team, 1992.. Office: Golden State Warriors Oakland Coliseum Arena 7000 Coliseum Way Oakland CA 94621-1945*

MULLIN, CONSTANCE HAMMOND, performing arts organization administrator; b. Annapolis, Md., May 31, 1939; d. Jacques Redway and Louise Hopkins (Kemp) Hammond; m. Michael Mahlon Mullin; Dec. 29, 1964; children: Stepeh Joseph, Keith Alan, Laura Anne. AB, Radcliffe Coll., 1961; MA, San Diego State U., 1966. Tchr. Dana Hall Sch., Wellesley, Mass., 1962-64; lectr. San Diego State U., 1966-68; editorial asst. Bioplymers John Wiley & Sons, La Jolla, Calif., 1971-81; writer Sea World, San Diego, 1984-85; founder, dir. Classical Performing Artists Mgmt., La Jolla, 1985—. Chmn. Early Childhood Edn., La Jolla Elem., 1974-76; pres. Friends, La Jolla Chamber Music Soc., 1978-80; concert mgr. Physicians for Social Responsibility, La Jolla, 1982; bd. dirs. The Athenaeum, La Jolla, 1990—. Mem. Assn. Calif. Symphony Orchs., Opera Am. Democrat. Episcopalian. Office: Classical Performing Artists Mgmt 7758 Ludington Pl La Jolla CA 92037-3806

MULLINS, RUTH GLADYS, nurse; b. Westville, N.S., Can., Aug. 25, 1943; d. William G. and Gladys H.; came to U.S., 1949, naturalized, 1955; student Tex. Womans U., 1961-64; BS in Nursing, Calif. State U.-Long Beach, 1966; MNursing, UCLA, 1973; m. Leonard E. Mullins, Aug. 27, 1963; children: Deborah R., Catherine M., Leonard III. Pub. health nurse, L.A. County Health Dept., 1967-68; nurse Meml. Hosp. Med. Center, Long Beach, 1968-72; dir. pediatric nurse practitioner program Calif. State U., Long Beach, 1973—, asst. prof., 1975-80, assoc. prof., 1980-85, prof., 1985—; health svc. credential coord. Sch. Nursing Calif. State U., Long Beach, Calif., chmn., 1979-81, coord. grad. programs, 1985-92; mem. Calif. Maternal, Child and Adolescent Health Bd., 1977-84; vice chair Long Beach/Orange County Health Consortium Divsn. Nursing, 1984-85, chair 1985-86. Tng. grantee HHS, Calif. Dept. Health; cert. pediatric nurse practitioner. Fellow Nat. Assn. Pediatric Nurse Assocs. and Practitioners (exec. bd., past pres.), Nat. Fedn. Nursing Specialty Orgns. (sec. 1991-93); mem. Am. Pub. Health Assn., Nat. Alliance Nurse Practitioners (governing body 1990-92), Assn. Faculties Pediatric Nurse Practitioner Programs, L.A. and Orange County Assn. Pediatric Nurse Practitioners and Assocs., Am. Assn. U. Faculty, Ambulatory Pediatric Assn. Democrat. Methodist. Author: (with B. Nelms) Growth and Development: A Primary Health Care Approach; contbg. author: Quick Reference to Pediatric Nursing, 1984; asst. editor Jour. Pediatric Health Care. Home: 6382 Heil Ave Huntington Beach CA 92647-4232 Office: Calif State U Dept Nursing 1250 N Bellflower Blvd Long Beach CA 90840-0006

MULLIS, KARY BANKS, biochemist; b. Lenoir, N.C., Dec. 28, 1944; s. Cecil Banks Mullis and Bernice Alberta (Barker) Fredericks; children: Christopher, Jeremy, Louise. BS in Chemistry, Ga. Inst. Tech, 1966; PhD in Biochemistry, U. Calif., Berkeley, 1973. Lectr. biochemistry U. Calif., Berkeley, 1972; postdoctoral fellow U. Calif., San Francisco, 1977-79, U. Kans. Med. Sch., Kansas City, 1973-76; scientist Cetus Corp., Emeryville, Calif., 1979-86; dir. molecular biology Xytronyx, Inc., San Diego, 1986-88; cons. Specialty Labs, Inc., Amersham, Inc., Chiron Inc. and various others, Calif., 1988—; chmn. StarGene, Inc., San Rafael, Calif. Contbr. articles to profl. jours.; patentee in field. Recipient Preis Biochemische Analytik award German Soc. Clin. Chem., 1990, Allan award Am. Soc. of Human Genetics, 1990, award Gairdner Found. Internat., 1991, Nat. Biotech. award, 1991, Robert Koch award, 1992, Chiron Corp. Biotechnology Rsch. award Am. Soc. Microbiology, 1992, Japan prize Sci. and Tech. Found. Japan, 1993, Nobel Prize in Chemistry, Nobel Foundation, 1993; named Calif. Scientist of Yr., 1992, Scientist of Yr., R&D Mag., 1991. Mem. Am. Chem. Soc., Am. Acad. Achievement, Inst. Further Study (dir. 1983—). Office: 6767 Neptune Pl Apt 5 La Jolla CA 92037-5924*

MULTHAUP, MERRELL KEYES, artist; b. Cedar Rapids, Iowa, Sept. 27, 1922; d. Stephen Dows and Edna Gertrude (Gard) Keyes; m. Robert Hansen Multhaup, Apr. 7, 1944; children: Eric Stephen, Robert Bruce. Student fine art, State U. of Iowa, 1942-43; student color theory, Rice U., 1971. Mem. teaching faculty Summit (N.J.) Art Assn., 1956-60; art instr. studio classes Springfield, N.J., 1954-55, Bloomfield (N.J.) Art Group, 1955-56, Westport, Conn., 1962-63; mem. teaching faculty Hunterdon Art Ctr., Clinton, N.J., 1985-92. Exhibited in group shows at Nat. Assn. Women Artists, N.Y.C., 1957-93 (awards in figure painting), Hartford (Conn.) Athanaeum Mus., 1961 (1st prize), Highgate Gallery, N.Y.C., Waverly Gallery, N.Y.C., Leicester Gallery, London, Silvermine Gallery, Conn., Pendut Gallery, Tex., Benedict Gallery, Sidney Rothman Gallery, N.J., Stamford (Conn.) Mus., Bridgeport (Conn.) Mus., Montclair (N.J.) Mus., Newark Mus., Coriell Gallery, Albuquerque. Bd. dirs., exhbn. chmn. Summit Art Assn., 1950-60, Silvermine Guild of Art, New Canaan, Conn., 1960-64; bd. dirs. Artist's Equity of N.J., 1977-84, chmn. state-wide event, 1983, 86; artist's adv. coun. Hunterdon Art Ctr., Clinton, 1988-92. Recipient awards in juried exhbns. in Iowa, Pa., N.J., Conn., N.Y.C. Mem. Nat. Mus. for Women in the Arts, Nat. Assn. Women Artists Inc. (awards for figure painting 1957, 80, 89), Albuquerque United Artists. Home and Studio: 1321 Stagecoach Rd SE Albuquerque NM 87123-4320

MULTZ, CARTER VICTOR, rheumatologist; b. Billings, Mont., June 4, 1934; s. Victor William and Charlotte Deneice (Waddeu) M. BS, Gonzaga U., 1955; MD, Loyola U., Chgo., 1959. Diplomate Am. Bd. Internal Medicine. Intern St. Mary's Hosp., San Francisco, 1959-60, resident, 1960-61; fellow, clin. asst. medicine Robert Breck Brigham Hosp., Boston, 1961-62; fellow Lanhey Clinic, Boston, 1962-63; pvt. practice San Jose, 1963-66, 68—; asst. chief rheumatology Walter Reed Gen. Hosp., Washington, 1966-68; clin. assoc. medicine dir. Syntex Rsch., Palo Alto, Calif., 1968-85; med. dir. DDI Pharm., Inc., Mountain View, Calif., 1985-88; pres., med. dir. Personal Choice Med. Group, Inc., San Jose, 1987—; mem. active staff O'Connor Hosp., San Jose; mem. courtesy staff Santa Clara Valley Med. Ctr., San Jose, Good Samaritan Hosp., San Jose, San Jose Hosp.; chmn. utilization rev. com. O'Connor Hosp., 1974, chmn. profl. activities com., 1975, mem. staff exec. com., 1975, 77, chmn. arthritis com., 1985-87; dir. Santa Clara Valley Profl. Standards Rev. Com., 1975-78, chmn., 1977; dir. O'Connor Physician's Assn., 1986-88; dir., chmn. quality assurance com. Silicon Valley Med. Group, 1986-88, v.p., 1988-89; dir. San Jose Med. Group, 1994—; presenter in field. Contbr. numerous articles to profl. jours. Mem. med. and sci. com. No. Calif. chpt. Arthritis Found., 1965-85, chmn. med. adv. com. Santa Clara County br., 1985-87, chmn. adv. bd. 1988—, dir. San Jose br., 1976-84; dir. Calif. Arthritis Inst., 1981-83. Fellow Am. Coll. Physicians, Am. Coll. Rheumatology; mem. Am. Coll. Physician Execs., Calif. Soc. Internal Medicine (membership com. 1986-88, trustee 1990—), Santa Clara County Soc. Internal Medicine (sec., treas. 1985-87, pres. 1987-90). Office: Arthritis Care Ctr Inc 1835 Park Ave San Jose CA 95126-1650

MULVANEY, JANELLE WILLIAMS, securities trader; b. Billings, Mont., July 20, 1959; d. John F. Williams and N. Karen (Young) Musgrave; 1 child, Jason; m. Doug Mulvaney, July 24, 1993. BSBA with honors in Bus. Adminstrn., Ea. Mont. Coll., 1993. Asst. mgr. Size 5.7.9 Shop, Billings, 1977-78; retail mgr. Satin Garter, Billings, 1978-79; night mgr. lounge Dos Machas, Billings, 1979-81; sales rep. US West Communications, Billings, 1981-90; program devel. coord. Ea. Mont. Coll., Billings, 1990-92; stockbroker Dean Witter Reynolds, Billings, 1992—; team leader fund drive Ea. Mont. Coll. Found. Achievement, 1992, 93. Mem. telethon com. Arthritis Found., Billings, 1986-87; sec. bd. dirs. Billings Citizens advocacy, 1987-91; dir. spl. events summer games Mont. Spl. Olympics, Billings, 1987-88; mem. Spl. Olympics outreach program, 1988-90; mem. 1977 reunion com. Billings West High Sch., 1986-90; mem. Ea. Mont. Coll. Ivy Honor Guard, 1991—. Named 1991 CASE Dist. VIII Student del. Mem. NAFE, U.S. West Women, Mont. Devel. Officers Assn., Am. Bus. Womens Assn. (charter Billings chpt., treas., chmn. ednl. scholarship com., mktg. com., program com.), Ea. Mont. Coll. Alumni Assn. (amb. edn. 1994, chair alumni awards program 1994-95). Republican. Methodist. Home: 2918 Silverwood St Billings MT 59102-0652 Office: Dean Witter Reynolds Inc 401 N 31st St Ste 900 Billings MT 59101-1200

MULVIHILL, PETER JAMES, fire protection engineer; b. Honolulu, Jan. 24, 1956; s. James H. and Jane A. (Norton) M. BSCE, Worcester (Mass.) Poly. Inst., 1978. Sr. engr. Indsl. Risk Insurers, San Francisco, 1978-84; fire protection engr. Aerojet Gen. Corp., Sacramento, 1984-87, Reno (Nev.) Fire Dept., 1987-93; fire protection engr., battalion chief Boise (Idaho) Fire Dept., 1993—; part-time instr. univ. extension U. Calif., Davis, 1993—, Truckee Meadows Community Coll., Reno, 1988-93. Commr. Gov.'s Blue Ribbon Commn. to Study Adequacy of State Regulations Concerning Highly Combustible Materials, Carson City, Nev., 1988. Mem. Soc. Fire Protection Engrs., No. Nev. Fire Marshal's Assn. (pres. 1992-93), Nat. Fire Protection Assn., Internat. Assn. Fire Chiefs, Idaho Fire Chiefs Assn., Calif. Fire Chiefs' Assn. (fire prevention officers sect. No. divsn.), Fire Marshals' Assn. N. Am. Office: Boise Fire Dept 625 W Idaho St Boise ID 83702-5900

MUMFORD, CHRISTOPHER GREENE, corporate financial executive; b. Washington, Oct. 21, 1945; s. Milton C. and Dorothea L. (Greene) M.; B.A., Stanford U., 1968, M.B.A., 1975. Cons., Internat. Tech. Resources Inc., 1974; asst. v.p. Wells Fargo Bank, San Francisco, 1975-78; v.p., treas. Arcata Corp., San Francisco, 1978-82, v.p. fin., 1982-87, exec. v.p. fin., 1987-94. gen. ptnr. Scarff, Sears & Assocs., San Francisco, 1986-95, v.p. bd. dirs. Triangle Pacific Corp., Dallas, 1986-88, Norton Enterprises Inc., Salt Lake City, 1988-90; bd. dirs. Community Home Med. Enterprises, Inc., Grass Valley, Calif., Crown Pacific Ltd., Portland, Oreg., Union Security Mortgage, Inc., Santa Ana, Calif., 1993-94. Office: Arcata Corp 601 California St Ste 1800 San Francisco CA 94108-2823

MUMFORD, PATRICIA RAE, religious organization administrator; b. Oklahoma City, Feb. 25, 1932; d. Raymond William and Mildred Louise (Wisdom) Gallagher; m. Donald Earl Mumford, April 6, 1951; children: Raymond Scott, Kenneth Earl, Robert Paul. Columnist The Sapulpan, Sapulpa, Okla., 1949-51; continuity writer Sta. KRMG, Tulsa, 1951-52; with continuity and production TV stas., Phoenix, Las Vegas, Denver, 1953-57; continuity and traffic radio stas. KPOI and KKUA, Honolulu, 1965-71; part-time program asst. Hawaii Council of Chs., Honolulu, 1972-80, assoc. dir., acting dir., 1980-85, exec. coordinator, 1986-87; exec. dir. Hawaii Council of Chs., Kailua, Hawaii, 1987-94, ret., 1994. Contrib. articles to newspapers, newsletters and mags. Bd. dirs. UNA-Hawaii, Meml. Soc. of Hawaii, Vol. Leadership Devel. program, Hawaii Pub. Broadcasting Authority Adv. Bd., Honolulu, 1978-82; mem. Hawaii State Commn. on Martin Luther King Jr. Holiday, 1988—. Named Outstanding Woman of Yr., City and County of Honolulu, 1982. Mem. Nat. Assn. Ecumenical Staff (svc. award 1987, 92), Ch. Women United (local and state pres., mem. nat. coun. 1965-72). Democrat. Mem. Christian Ch., United Presbyn. Ch.

MUNCH, WILLIAM DAVID, information systems consultant; b. Jamaica, N.Y., Mar. 21, 1938; s. William F. and Madeline (Eisenbarth) M.; m. Sigrid M. Loffler, Oct. 9, 1960; children: Lilo, William K., Kurt E. BBA in Indsl. Mgmt., Adelphi U., 1960. Mem. internat. banking group Bankers Trust, N.Y.C., 1974-79; v.p., mgr. br. on-line banking Wells Fargo, San Francisco, 1979-82; info. systems cons. in pvt. practice, Pleasant Hill, Calif., 1982—. Mem. Assn. for Systems Mgmt. (bd. dirs. 1985-88, exec. com. 1989-94, internat. pres. 1993-94, Meritorious Svc. award 1994, Systems Profl. of Yr. award 1984, 86). Home and Office: 178 Devon Ave Pleasant Hill CA 94523-2529

MUNCK, MICHAEL GEORGE, fundraising executive; b. Newcastle, Wyo., Aug. 11, 1954; s. Elroy Delbert and Mary Pauline (Blyholder) M.; m. Kathrine Ann Anderson, Aug. 30, 1986; children: Christian Michael, Aislinn Heather. BA in English, Carroll Coll., 1976. English tchr. Harlem (Mont.) H.S., 1976-77, Hays-Lodgepole (Mont.) H.S., 1978-79; counselor Intermountain Children's Home, Helena, Mont., 1979-81, cottage coord., counselor, 1981-87, asst. dir. devel., 1987-91; exec. v.p. St. Peter's Hosp. Found., Helena, Mont., 1991—. Founder com. Festival of Trees, Helena, 1988, mem. exec. com., 1988-92; mem. alumni divsn. Carroll Coll. Mem. Assn. for Healthcare Philanthropy, Helena Advt. Fedn. (vice chair elect 1990), Helena Estate Planning Coun. (founding), Kiwanis (co-chair Helena chpt. Toys for Tots program 1993, 94), Helena C. of C. (pres.'s club 1992—). Home: 827 12th Ave Helena MT 59601-3767 Office: St Peters Cmty Hosp Found 2475 E Broadway St Helena MT 59601-4928

MUND, GERALDINE, bankruptcy judge; b. L.A., July 7, 1943; d. Charles J. and Pearl (London) M. BA, Brandeis U., 1965; MS, Smith Coll., 1967;

JD, Loyola U., 1977. Bar: Calif. 1977. Bankruptcy judge U.S. Cen. Dist. Calif., 1984—. Past pres. Temple Israel, Hollywood, Calif. Mem. ABA, L.A. County Bar Assn. Office: Roybal Bldg 255 E Temple St Los Angeles CA 90012-3334

MUNDT, JONEL, marketing educator, consultant; b. Denison, Iowa, Aug. 11, 1950; d. John P. and Evelyn A. (Hollrah) M. BA, Hiram Scott Coll., 1971; MBA, U. S.D., 1975; PhD, U. Okla., 1989. Asst. prof. Coll. Bus. Colo. State U., Ft. Collins, 1988-89; vis. asst. prof. Coll. Bus. Adminstrn. U. Okla., Norman, 1989-91; asst. prof. Sch. Bus. and Pub. Adminstrn. U. of the Pacific, Stockton, Calif., 1991—; cons. product-related comm. Comm. Consulting, Norman, 1988—. Author: (book chpt.) Marketing Exchange Relationships, Transactions, and Their Media, 1994; contbr. articles to profl. jours. Consortium fellow U. Okla., 1986. Mem. Am. Mktg. Assn. Office: U of the Pacific 3601 Pacific Cir Stockton CA 95211-0110

MUNERA, GERARD EMMANUEL, manufacturing company executive; b. Algiers, Algeria, Dec. 2, 1935; s. Gabriel and Laure (Labrousse) M.; m. Paule A. Ramos, July 28, 1959; children: Catherine, Philippe, Emmanuelle, Jean-Marie. M in Math., M in Physics, M in Chemistry, Ecole Polytechnique, Paris, 1956; CE, Ecole des Ponts et Chaussees, Paris, 1959. Chief county engr. Dept. Rds. and Bridges, South Algiers, 1959-62; cons. French Ministry Fgn. Affairs, Argentina, 1962-66; sr. v.p. fin. Camea Group Pechiney Ugine Kuhlmann, Buenos Aires, 1966-70, chmn. bd., chief exec. officer, 1976-77; exec. v.p. Howmet Aluminum Corp., Greenwich, Conn., 1976-77, pres., chief operating officer, 1977-79, pres., chief exec. officer, 1980-83; corporate v.p. nuclear fuels Pechiney, Brussels, 1983-85; vice chmn., chief exec. officer Union Minière, Brussels, 1985-89; head corp. planning and devel. RTZ, London, 1989-90; pres., CEO Minorco USA, Englewood, Colo., 1990-94, also bd. dirs.; chmn. and CEO Latin Am. Gold, Inc., N.Y.C., 1994—; bd. dirs. Arcadia Inc., Synergex Inc., Scaltech Inc. Patentee low-income housing system. Served with French Air Force, 1956-57. Decorated Legion of Honor. Roman Catholic. Office: Latin Am Gold Inc 245 Park Ave New York NY 10167-0002

MUNGER, EDWIN STANTON, political geography educator; b. LaGrange, Ill., Nov. 19, 1921; s. Royal Freeman and Mia (Stanton) M.; m. Ann Boyer, May 2, 1970; 1 child, Elizabeth Stanton Gibson. B.Sc., U. Chgo., 1948, M.Sc., 1949, Ph.D., 1951. Fulbright fellow Makerere U., 1949-50; research fellow U. Chgo.; field assoc. Am. Univs. Field Staff, 1950-60; faculty Calif. Inst. Tech., Pasadena, 1961—; prof. polit. geography Calif. Inst. Tech., 1960—; research fellow Stellenbosch U., 1955-56; vis. prof. U. Warsaw, 1973. Author books including Afrikaner and African Nationalism, 1968, The Afrikaners, 1979, Touched by Africa: An Autobiography, 1983, Ethnic Chess Sets, 1992; editor books including Munger Africana Library Notes, 1969-82; contbr. numerous articles to profl. jours., chpts. to books. Evaluator Peace Corps, Uganda, 1966, Botswana, 1967; chmn. State Dept. Evalustion Team South Africa, 1971; trustee African-Am. Inst., 1956-62; acting pres. Pasadena Playhouse, 1966; chmn. bd. trustees Crane Rogers Found., 1979-82, fellow, 1950-54; mem. exec. com. NAACP, Pasadena, 1979—, nat. del., 1984, 85; trustee Leakey Found., 1968—, pres., 1971-84; pres. Cape of Good Hope Found., 1985—; pres. Internat. Vis. Coun., L.A., 1991-93, bd. dirs., 1979-93. Recipient Alumni Citation award for pub. svc. U. Chgo., 1993. Fellow South African Royal Soc., Royal Soc. Arts, African Studies Assn. (founding bd. dirs. 1963-66); mem. PEN USA West (v.p.), Coun. Fgn. Rels., Cosmos Club, Athenaeum Club, Twilight Club. Office: Calif Inst Tech Div Humanities and Social Scis 1201 E California Blvd Pasadena CA 91125-0001

MUNITZ, BARRY, university administrator, English literature educator, business consultant; b. Bklyn., July 26, 1941; s. Raymond J. and Vivian L. (LeVoff) M.; m. Anne Tomfohrde, Dec. 15, 1987. BA, Bklyn. Coll., 1963; MA, Princeton U., 1965, PhD, 1968; cert., U. Leiden, Netherlands, 1962. Asst. prof. lit. and drama U. Calif., Berkeley, 1966-68; staff assoc. Carnegie Commn. Higher Edn., 1968-70; mem. presdl. staff, then assoc. provost U. Ill. System, 1970-72, acad. v.p., 1972-76; v.p., dean faculties Central campus U. Houston, 1976-77, chancellor, 1977-82, chmn. coordinating bd. faculty workload, 1976-80; chmn. Tex. Long Range Planning, 1980-82; pres., COO Federated Devel. Co., 1982-91; vice chmn. Maxxam Inc., L.A., 1982-91; chancellor Calif. State U. System, Long Beach, Calif., 1991—; prof. English lit. Calif. State U., L.A., 1991—; bd. dirs. Sta. KCET-TV, Am. Coun. on Edn., Calif. Econ. Devel. Corp., SunAmerica Inc., SallieMae; cons. in presdl. evaluation and univ. goverance. Author: The Assessment of Institutional Leadership, 1977, also articles, monographs. Mem. task force NSF. Recipient Disting. Alumnus award Bklyn. Coll., 1979, U. Houston Alumni Pres.'s medal, 1981; Woodrow Wilson fellow, 1963. Mem. Young Pres. Orgn., Heritage Club, Phi Beta Kappa. Office: Calif State U System Office of Chancellor 400 Golden Shore St Long Beach CA 90802-4209

MUNN, WILLIAM CHARLES, II, psychiatrist; b. Flint, Mich., Aug. 9, 1938; s. Elton Albert and Rita May (Coykendall) M.; student Flint Jr. Coll., 1958-59, U. Detroit, 1959-61; M.D., Wayne State U., 1965; m. Deborah Lee Munn, 1983; children by previous marriage—Jude Michael, Rachel Marie, Alexander Winston. Intern David Grant USAF Med. Center, Travis AFB, Calif., 1965-66; resident in psychiatry Letterman Army Hosp., San Francisco, 1967-70; practice medicine, specializing in psychiatry, Fairfield, Calif., 1972—; chief in-patient psychiatry David Grant Med. Center, 1970-71, chmn. dept. mental health, 1971-72; psychiat. cons. Fairfield-Suisun Unified Sch. Dist., 1971—, Fairfield Hosp. and Clinic, 1971, N. Bay Med. Ctr.(formerly Intercommunity Hosp.), Fairfield, 1971—, Casey Family Program, 1980—, Solano County Coroner's Office, 1981; asst. clin. prof. psychiatry U. Calif., San Francisco, 1976—; cons. Vaca Valley Hosp., Vacaville, Calif., 1988—, VA Hosp., San Francisco, 1976, David Grant USAF Hosp., 1976. Served to maj., M.C., USAF, 1964-72, flight surgeon, chief public health, chief phys. exam. center McGuire AFB, N.J., 1966-67. Diplomate Am. Bd. Psychiatry and Neurology (examiner). Mem. Am. Psychiat. Assn., No. Calif. Psychiat. Soc., E. Bay Psychiat. Assn. Office: 1245 Travis Blvd Ste E Fairfield CA 94533-4842

MUNNINGER, MICHAEL JOSEPH, architect; b. Albany, N.Y., Aug. 24, 1948; s. Karl Otto and Margaret Josephine (Craugh) M.; children: John Karl, Michael, Suzanne, Paul, Mark. BArch, U. Tex., 1971; postgrad., Ariz. State U., Phoenix, 1976-77. Registered architect, Ariz., Calif., N.Mex. Founder, ptnr. Archtl. Alliance, Phoenix, 1974—. Contbr. articles to mags., newspapers. Active Hunter Safety Instr. Program, Nat. Trust Hist. Preservation; past chmn. City of Phoenix Visual Improvement Com.; past bd. dirs. Boys Club Met. Phoenix, Ariz. Recipient 2nd prize Art by Architects, 1982, Most Beautiful Home award, Phoenix mag., 1982, Visual Improvement award, City of Phoenix, 1984, Am. Concrete Inst. award, 1989, AIA award of merit Homes of Yr., 1989, City of Tempe Beatification award, 1990. Home: 10001 N 132nd St Scottsdale AZ 85259-5401

MUNOZ, JOHN JOSEPH, transportation company executive; b. Salinas, Calif., Jan. 18, 1932; s. John Fernando and Naomal (Smith) M.; m. Phyllis Taylor, Feb. 6, 1961 (div. 1978); children: Sam, Kathy, Toni; m. Rachel Canales, Nov. 24, 1979; children: Michelle, Monique. AA, Allan Hancock Coll., 1956; student, San Jose State U., 1981, Western Sierra Law Sch. Ops. mgr. So. Pacific Milling Co., Santa Maria, Calif., 1971-77; cons. Govt., Venezuela, 1977-78; fleet supt. Granite Rock Co., San Jose, Calif., 1978-80; plant mgr. Granite Constrn. Co., Greenfield, Calif., 1980-85; mgr. transpn. Ball, Ball. & Brosmer Inc., Danville, Calif., 1985-86; ops. mgr., bd. dirs. Sorrento Ready Mix Co., Del Mar, Calif., 1986-89; trans. cons. Greenfield, Calif., 1991—; cons. Dept. Agrl. Devel., Maricaibo, Venezuela, 1976—. Commr. Planning Commn., Greenfield, Calif., 1982-85; mem. fund raising com. Broccoli Festival, Greenfield, 1983-85; dir. Soledad Prison Vocat. Tng., 1982-85. Lt. 11th Ranger Airborne, U.S. Army, 1950-52, Korea. Mem. Am. Concrete Inst., Calif. Trucking Assn., Los Californianos, Rotary, Lions, Elks. Republican. Home: PO Box 3654 Greenfield CA 93927-3654 Office: PO Box 3654 Greenfield CA 93927-3654

MUÑOZ, RICARDO FELIPE, psychology educator; b. Lima, Peru, Apr. 30, 1950; came to U.S., 1961; s. Luis Alberto and Clara Luz (Valdivia) M.; m. Pat Marine, Mar. 31, 1979; children: Rodrigo Alberto, Aubrey Elizabeth Luz. AB, Stanford U., 1972; MA, U. Oreg., 1975, PhD, 1977. Asst. prof. psychology U. Calif., San Francisco, 1977-83, assoc. prof., 1983-89, prof., 1989—; dir. depression clinic San Francisco Gen. Hosp., 1985-90, chief psychologist, 1987—, deputy chief acad. affairs, 1991—; dir. UCSF Clin. Psychology Tng. Program, 1992—; bd. dirs. div. health promotion and disease prevention, Inst. Medicine, NAS, Washington. Co-author: Control Your Depression, 1986, How to Control Your Drinking, 1982, Prevention of Depression: Research and Practice, 1993; editor: Depression Prevention: Research Directions, 1987; co-editor: Social and Psychological Research in Community Settings, 1979. Recipient Health Promotion award Nat. Coalition Hispanic Mental Health and HumanSvcs. Orgn., 1984, Dr. Martin Luther King Jr. award U. Calif., San Francisco, 1991, Lela Rowland Prevention award Nat. Mental Health Assn., 1994. Fellow Am. Psychol. Assn.; mem. AAAS, Nat. Hispanic Psychol. Assn., Am. Assn. for Artificial Intelligence, Phi Beta Kappa. Office: U Calif 1001 Potrero Ave Ste 7M San Francisco CA 94110-3518

MUÑOZ-SANDOVAL, ANA F., linguist; b. Chillan, Chile, Jan. 31, 1947; came to U.S., 1970; d. Washingtón del Carmen Muñoz Canales and Alicia del Carmen Sandoval de Muñoz; m. Frederick Mitronovas, Feb. 24, 1971 (div. Feb. 1988); m. Richard W. Woodcock, June 14, 1991. Student, Tribhuvan U., Katmandu, Nepal, 1979-80, Goethe-Inst., Poona, India; BA in Anthropology, SUNY, Buffalo, 1982, MS in Student Pers. Adminstrn., 1984; EdD in Intercultural/Internat. Edn., U. So. Calif., 1992. Developer, implementer Spanish lang. manual and tapes Buffalo Student Health Clinic, 1982-84; bilingual social svcs. worker Puerto Rican/Chicano Cmty. Svcs. Ctr., Buffalo; tchr. Spanish U. Ariz., 1986-88, U. So. Calif., 1989-91; with Measurement/Learning/Conss., Tolovana Park, Oreg., 1987—. Home: University Village # 1302 2401 Old Ivy Rd Charlottesville VA 22903-4853 Office: Measurement/Learning/Conss PO Box 161 Tolovana Park OR 97145-0161

MUNRO, MALCOLM GORDON, obstetrician/gynecologist, educator; b. Woodstock, Ontario, Can., Mar. 22, 1952; came to U.S., 1991; s. Charles Gordon and Maribelle (Logie) M.; m. Sandra June Brander-Smith, Nov. 17, 1990; 1 child, Tyler Gordon. MD, U. Western Ontario, London, Ontario, 1975. Diplomate Am. Bd.Ob.-Gyne.; fellow Royal Coll. Surgeons, Can., Ob.-Gyn. Intern Royal Columbian Hosp., New Westminster, B.C., 1975-76; resident ob.-gyn, U. Western Ontario, Londong, 1976-77, U. Britich Columbia, London, 1978-80; clin. fellow gyneolgic. oncology U. B.C., Vancouver, 1980-81, clin. instr. ob-gyn., 1981-83, asst. cln. prof., 1983-89, assoc. clin. prof., 1988-92; assoc. prof. UCLA, 1991-95, prof., 1995—, assoc. chmn. dept. ob/gyn., 1994—; chmn. B.C. Med. Assn. sect. ob/gyn., Vancouver, 1984-88, Gynecologic Sstudies Group, Phila., 1993— (founder); cons. Cancer Control Agy., B.C., 1981-91; chmn. Rsch. Coordinating Com., Grace Hosp., Vancouver; cons. Ethicon Endosuture Core Cons. Group, 1992—. Author: (book) Gynecology, A Practical Approach, 1990; contbr. articles to profl. jours., chpts. to books; inventor laparoscopic loop electrodes, 1993; mem. editl. bd. Treating the Female Patient, 1988-94, Jour. of Gynecologic Technique, 1993—; reviewer Obstetrics and Gynecology, Fertil Steril; mem. ad hoc rev. com. Jour. Am. Assn. Gynecologic Laparoscopists, 1994—. Med. dir. Planned Parenthood, Vancouver, B.C., Can., 1980-85; founding dir. Multidisciplinary Osteoporosis Clinic, U. Hosp., Vancouver, 1987-91. Recipient Appreciatiation cert. Planned Parenthood of British Columbia, 1991; grantee: Vancouver Found., 1988, P.W. Woodward Found., 1988, Ethicon Endosurgery, 1992, NIH/NIAID, 1992. Fellow Am. Coll. Ob-Gyn., Soc. Obstetricians and Gynecologists, Can.; mem. Canadian Fertility and Andrology Soc., Am. Fertility Soc., Am. Assn. Gynecologic Laparoscopists. Office: UCLA 22-262 CHS Los Angeles CA 90095-1740

MUNROE, DONNA SCOTT, marketing executive, healthcare and management consultant, educator; b. Cleve., Nov. 28, 1945; d. Glenn Everett and Louise Lennox (Parkhill) Scott; m. Melvin James Ricketts, Dec. 23, 1968 (div. Aug. 1979); 1 child, Suzanne Michelle; m. Peter Carlton Munroe, Feb. 14, 1981. BS in Sociology, Portland (Oreg.) State U., 1976, BS in Philosophy, 1978, MS in Sociology, 1983. Lectr. Portland State U., 1977-79; writing, editorial cons. Worth Pubs., N.Y.C., 1978-79; statis. cons. health scis. U. Oreg., Portland, 1979-82; statis. cons. Morrison Ctr. for Youth and Family Svcs., Portland, 1979-82; writer Equitable Savs. & Loan, Portland, 1981-82; mgr. acct. and projects. Electronic Data Systems, Portland, 1982-87; exec. dir. corp. mktg. and planning CMSI, Portland, 1987—; v.p. mktg. CerikaCorp, Vancouver, Wash., 1993—. Mem. Am. Mgmt. Assn., Am. Mktg. Assn., Am. Soc. for Quality Control, City Club of Portland, Sigma Xi. Democrat. Episcopalian. Home: 536 SW Cheltenham St Portland OR 97201-2602 Office: CerikaCorps 13912 NE 20th Ave Ste 204 Vancouver WA 98686-1465

MUNROE, MARY HILLS, preschool/daycare operator; b. Nantucket Island, Mass., Dec. 11, 1931; d. Isaac III and Hilda Susan Hills; m. Willard Noble Munroe, June 28, 1952 (div. 1975); children: Susan Willard, David, Bruce, Elizabeth. AA, Pima C.C., Tucson, Ariz., 1976. Real estate broker. Co-owner, operator Green Harbor Village, West Yarmouth, Mass., 1955-69; real estate assoc./broker Richard H. Huff, Tucson, 1971-76; founder, dir. Mis Hijitos Presch., Tucson, 1976-94; founder, owner La Palomita de Patagonia, Patagonia, Ariz., 1993—; adv. bd. Ariz. Dept. Health, Phoenix, 1984, Ariz. Dept. Edn. Security, Phoenix, 1980—. Bd. dirs. Community Action Com., Tucson, 1983; mem. panel/polit. interviews C. of C., Tucson, 1992-94. Mem. Ariz. Child Care Assn. (pres. 1978-83, bd. dirs. 1983-93), Patagonia Community Assn.

MUNSON, LUCILLE MARGUERITE (MRS. ARTHUR E. MUNSON), real estate broker; b. Norwood, Ohio, Mar. 26, 1914; d. Frank and Fairy (Wicks) Wirick; R.N., Lafayette (Ind.) Home Hosp., 1937; A.B., San Diego State U., 1963, student Purdue U., Kans. Wesleyan U.; m. Arthur E. Munson, Dec. 24, 1937; children—Barbara Munson Papke, Judith Munson Andrews, Edmund Arthur. Staff and pvt. nurse Lafayette Home Hosp., 1937-41; indsl. nurse Lakey Foundry & Machine Co., Muskegon, Mich., 1950-51, Continental Motors Corp., Muskegon, 1951-52; nurse Girl Scout Camp, Grand Haven, Mich., 1948-49; owner Munson Realty, San Diego, 1964—. Mem. San Diego County Grand Jury, 1975-76, 80-81, Calif. Grand Jurors Assn. (charter). Office: 2999 Mission Blvd Ste 102 San Diego CA 92109-8070

MUNSON, RAY EUGENE, judge; b. Leavenworth, Wash., Sept. 10, 1927; s. Will Keller and Jessie May (Tyler) M.; m. Christine A. Parr, Nov. 13, 1954; children: Mark P., Bradley W., Scott E., Cristofer R. BBA, U. Wash., 1952, JD, 1954. Bar: Wash. 1954, U.S. Dist. Ct. (ea. dist.) Wash. 1957. Spl. agt. FBI, 1954-55; dep. pros. atty. Yakima (Wash.) County Pros. Atty. Office, 1956-57, pros. atty., 1957-61; assoc. Halverson, Applegate, McDonald, Yakima, 1962-65; judge Superior Ct. Wash., Yakima, 1965-69; judge Wash. Ct. Appeals Div. III, Yakima, 1969—, presiding chief judge, 1978, chief judge, 1971-73, 77-79, 83-85, 89. With USN, 1945-48. Home: 821 N 48th Ave Yakima WA 98908-2405 Office: Wash Ct Appeals 500 N Cedar St Spokane WA 99201-1905

MUNSTERTEIGER, KAY DIANE, speech-language pathologist; b. Newcastle, Wyo., June 2, 1956; d. Donald Francis and Janice Mathilda (Emerson) M. BS, U. Wyo., 1978; MS, U. Nev., Reno, 1980. Speech lang. pathologist No. Nev. Speech lang. Clinic, Reno, 1980-82, Washakie County Sch. Dist. 1, Worland, Wyo., 1982—; pvt. practice speech pathologist Worland, 1982—; speech lang. pathologist, cons. Washakie County Sch. Dist. 2, Tensleep, Wyo., 1984-85; speech lang. pathologist Spl. Touch Presch., Worland, 1985-86, 89-93, Rehab Visions, 1995—; pres. bd. examiners Speech Pathology and Audiology, 1988-93. Mem. Pub. Sch. Caucus. Mem. NEA, State Edn. Assn., Am. Speech Lang. Hearing Assn., Wyo. Speech Lang. Hearing Assn., Nat. Stuttering Project, Pub. Sch. Caucus, Assn. Childhood Edn. Internat., Phi Kappa Phi. Democrat. Roman Catholic. Office: Washakie County Sch Dist # 1 1200 Culbertson Ave Worland WY 82401-3520

MURAOKA, DENNIS DEAN, economics educator; b. Santa Barbara, Calif., Nov. 9, 1952; s. Masa and Leora Violet (Macomber) M.; m. Mildred Meredith McKittrick, Dec. 18, 1976. BA, U. Calif., Santa Barbara, 1974, MA, 1976, PhD, 1981. Adminstrv. analyst City of Oxnard, Calif., 1975-79; lectr. Ventura (Calif.) Coll., 1977-80, Oxnard Coll., 1977-80, U. Calif., Santa Barbara, 1979-90, Santa Barbara City Coll., 1979-83; rsch. assoc. Community Orgn. and Rsch. Inst., Santa Barbara, 1980; prof. Calif. State U., Long Beach, 1981—. Co-author: Offshore Lands, 1985; author: (software) Microeconomics Study Wizard Version 1, 1990, Version 2, 1992, Version 3, 1994, Macroeconomics Study Wizard Version 1, 1990, Version 2, 1992, Version 3, 1994; contbr. articles to profl. jours. Mem. Sigma Xi. Home: 129 Loureyro Rd Santa Barbara CA 93108-2911 Office: Calif State U Dept Econs Long Beach CA 90840

MURASE, TERUO, computer executive; b. 1945. With Fujitsu Ltd., Tokyo, 1966-90; v.p., COO Fujitsu Computer Pack, San Jose, Calif., 1991—. Office: Fujitsu Computer Packing Tech 3811 Zanker Rd San Jose CA 95134-1402*

MURASZKO, MICHAEL ROMAN, public relations executive; b. Franklin, N.H., Mar. 11, 1955; s. Frank Michael and Rosemary Catherine (Schneider) M.; m. Judith Ildiko Molnar, Jan. 4, 1992. Summer studies program, Univ. Ibero Americana, Mexico City, 1976; BS in Fgn. Svc., Georgetown U., Washington, 1977. Account exec. Fraser Assocs., Washington, 1977-82; account supr. A.R. Busse & Assocs., Houston, 1982-85; v.p. Manning, Selvage & Lee, Dallas, L.A., 1985—. Vol. mktg., advisor Multiple Sclerosis Soc., L.A., 1991, 92; pub. rels., mktg. cons. vol. Constitutional Rights Found., L.A., 1991-93; vol. mktg. cons. Calif. Dept. Transp., L.A., 1993-94. Mem. PRSA (counselors group L.A. chpt., chmn. membership com. 1993-94, Silver Anvil award 1994), Aero Club Washington, Transp. Rsch. Forum, Nat. Press Club. Roman Catholic. Office: Manning Selvage & Lee 6500 Wilshire Blvd Ste 1900 Los Angeles CA 90048

MURATORE, MARILYN ANN, contractor; b. San Francisco, June 26, 1941; d. Thomas James and Camille Catherine (Bacigalupi) Dennison; m. Richard Peter Muratore, Oct. 25, 1959; 1 child, Tamara Ann. Treas. Peter D. Scatena, Inc., San Francisco, 1974-84; v.p., sec. Muratore Corp., San Francisco, 1985-91, chmn. bd., sec., 1991—. Active Com. to Reelect Dick Claire for Mayor, Redwood City, Calif., 1991. Mem. Am. Bldg. Contractors Assn. (bd. dirs. 1992—), San Francisco C. of C. Office: Muratore Corp 635 Texas St San Francisco CA 94107-2940

MURCH, ANNA VALENTINA, artist, lecturer; b. Dunbarton, Scotland, Dec. 7, 1948; came to U.S., 1976; naturalized, 1977; d. Norman Robbins and Valentina (Gordikova) M. B.A., Leicester Poly. Eng. 1971; M.A., Royal Coll. Art, London, 1973; grad. diploma Archtl. Assn., London, 1974. Vis. lectr. Salisbury Coll. Art, Wiltshire, Eng., 1974, Epson Coll. Art, Surrey, Eng., 1974-75, architecture dept. Calif. Poly. Inst., San Luis, Obispo, 1983-86, art dept. Univ. Calif.-Berkeley, 1984-86, Coll. San Mateo, 1986—. One-man shows include 80 Langton Street Installation, 1981, Kaiser Ctr. Sculpture Gallery, Oakland, 1981, Mills Coll., 1982, Ctr. Contemporary Arts, Santa Fe, 1985, Khiva Gallery, San Francisco, 1986, Kala Inst., Berkeley Art Commn. Annex, San Francisco, 1986, San Francisco Mus. Modern Art, 1987, Fesno Arts Ctr. & Mus., 1989, Mincher Wilcox Gallery, 1989, installations in downtown Oakland, 1983. Mem. San Francisco Art Inst. (artists and exhbns. com.), Orgn. Women Architects and Design Profs. Home: 499 Alabama St Studio 306 San Francisco CA 94110

MURDOCH, PAUL ALLAN, architect; b. Phila., Nov. 6, 1956; s. Roderick Graeme and Mae Ellen (Helfrich) M.; m. Milena Iancovici, Sept. 2, 1985; children: Tess, Graham. BS in Architecture, U. Va., 1978; MArch, UCLA, 1984. Registered architect, Calif., Ariz. Designer Geddes Brecher Qualls & Cunningham, Phila., 1981-82, Urban Innovations Group, 1983; designer, project mgr., architect Arthur Erickson Architects, L.A., 1984-91; founder, owner Paul Murdoch Architects, L.A., 1991—; Mem. L.A. Eco-Cities Coun., Design Profls. Coalition Steering Com., Rebuild L.A. Urban Planning Task Force, Environ. Design Group City L.A.; guest critic Undergrad. Design Studio, Sch. Architecture and Urban Planning, Ahmedabad, India, 1979, U. So. Calif., 1993, 94, Grad. Design Studio, UCLA, 1990, 91, 92; teaching asst., initiator grad. seminar UCLA, 1983; teaching asst. grad. design studio UCLA, 1984; UCLA rep. Internat. Lab. Architecture and Urban Design, Siena, Italy, 1983. Contbg. author: Man and His House in the Himalaya, 1981; contbg. architect: Growth and Integration, 1984, Architecture California, 1982, LA Architect, 1981, GA Houses 33, Tokyo, 1992, House & Garden, N.Y.C., 1992, GA Houses 35, Tokyo, 1992; prin. projects include Donald Bruce Kaufman Brentwood Br. Libr., L.A., Wilson Student Ctr., UCLA Sch. Medicine, Biol. Scis. Bldg. U. Calif., Irvine, Civic Ctr. Metrorail Sta., L.A., Pershing Square Metrorail Sta., L.A., others. UCLA Found. fellow, 1982, 83, 84, UCLA traveling fellow, 1983, McGuire fellow UCLA, 1983, AIA Found. fellow UCLA, 1983; UCLA grad. rsch. grantee, 1982. Mem. AIA. Office: Paul Murdoch Architects 1250 S Lucerne Blvd Los Angeles CA 90019-6805

MURDOCK, DAVID H., diversified company executive; b. Kansas City, Apr. 10, 1923; m. Maria Ferrer, Apr., 1992. LLD (hon.), Pepperdine U., 1978; LHD (hon.), U. Nebr., 1984, Hawaii Loa Coll., 1989. Sole proprietor, chmn., chief exec. officer Pacific Holding Co., L.A.; chmn., chief exec. officer Dole Food Co. (formerly Castle & Cooke, Inc.), L.A., 1985—, also bd. dirs. Trustee Asia Soc., N.Y.C., L.A.; founder, bd. dirs. Found. for Advanced Brain Studies, L.A.; bd. visitors UCLA Grad. Sch. Mgmt.;bd. govs. Performing Arts Coun. of Music Ctr., L.A.; bd. govs. East-West Ctr., L.A.; patron Met. Opera, N.Y.C. With USAAC, 1943-45. Mem. Regency Club (founder, pres.) Bel-Air Bay Country Club, Sherwood Country Club (founder, pres.), Met. Club (N.Y.C.). Office: Dole Food Co Inc 31355 Oak Crest Dr Westlake Village CA 91362 also: Pacific Holding Co 10900 Wilshire Blvd Ste 1600 Los Angeles CA 90024-6536*

MURDOCK, PAMELA ERVILLA, wholesale travel company executive, retail travel company executive; b. Los Angeles, Dec. 3, 1940; d. John James and Chloe Conger (Keefe) M.; children: Cheryl, Kim. BA, U. Colo., 1962. Pres., Dolphin Travel, Denver, 1972-87; owner, pres. Mile Hi Tours, Denver, 1973—, MH Internat., 1987—, Mile-Hi Advt. Agy., 1986— . Named Wholesaler of Yr., Las Vegas Conv. and Visitors Authority, 1984. Mem. NAFE, Am. Soc. Travel Agts., Colo. Assn. Commerce and Industry, Nat. Fedn. Independent Businessmen. Republican. Home: 5565 E Vassar Ave Denver CO 80222-6239 Office: Mile Hi Tours Inc 2120 S Birch St Denver CO 80222-5018

MURDOCK, ROBERT MCCLELLAN, military officer; b. Montclair, N.J., Sept. 27, 1947; s. George Rutherford and Mary (Newell) M.; m. Ann Marie Wingo, Aug. 20, 1977; 1 child, Kristen. BA, Davis and Elkins Coll., 1969; MA, Ctrl. Mich. U., 1979; postgrad., Armed Forces Staff Coll., 1983; student, U.S. Army War Coll., 1988. Lic. command pilot, USAF. Aide, chief of staff The Pentagon, Washington, 1980-82; chief current ops. 60 Airlift Wing, Travis AFB, Calif., 1983; ops. officer 22 Airlift Squadron, Travis AFB, Calif., 1984, comdr., 1985-87; dep. inspector gen. Hdqs. European Command, Stuttgart, Germany, 1988-90; vice comdr. 436 Airlift Wing, Dover AFB, Del., 1990-92; nat. def. fellow The Atlantic Coun., Washington, 1992-93; comdr. Air Force Inspection Agy., Kirtland AFB, N.Mex., 1993—. Decorated D.F.C., Air medal. Mem. Air Force Assn., The Airlift and Tanker Assn., Order of Daedalians. Methodist. Home: 7523 Rio Salado Ct NW Albuquerque NM 87120-5323 Office: Air Force Inspection Agy 9700 G Ave SE Kirtland AFB NM 87117

MURI, JOHN IMRE, mechanical engineer; b. Szerencs, Hungary, Aug. 20, 1964; came to U.S., 1987; s. Istvan and Julia (Toth) M. MSME, Budapest Tech. U., 1987. Chief design engr. Accudyne Engring., Bell Gardens, Calif., 1988-90; devel. engr. Alcon Surgical, Irvine, Calif., 1990-92; sr. engr. Birtcher Medical Systems, Irvine, Calif., 1992-95; cons. R&D Med. Devices Orgn., Irvine, 1993—, Internat. Bus., Budapest, 1992—. Inventor in field. Pres. Youth Dance Club, Budapest, 1987. Mem. Soc. Plastic Engrs. Roman Catholic.

MURIAN, RICHARD MILLER, book company executive; b. East St. Louis, Ill., Sept. 17, 1937; s. Richard Miller Jr. and Margaret Keyes (Gregory) M.; m. Judith Lee, Aug. 11, 1961 (dec. Apr. 1992); 1 child, Jennifer Ann. BA, U. Calif., Davis, 1969; MLS, U. Calif., Berkeley, 1972; MA, Calif. State U., Sacramento, 1975; MDiv, Trinity Evang., 1977. Cert. history instr., libr. sci. instr., Calif. History reader Calif. State U., Sacramento, 1965-66; history reader U. Calif., Davis, 1966-68, philosophy researcher, 1968-69; bibliographer Argus Books, Sacramento, 1970-71; rsch. dir. Nat. Judical Coll., Reno, 1971-72; libr. Calif. State U., Sacramento, 1972-76; tv talk show host Richard Murian Show, L.A., 1979-80; pres. Alcuin Books, Ltd., Phoenix, 1981—; bd. mem. Guild of Ariz. Antiquarian

Books; pres. East Valley Assn. Evangs., Mesa, Ariz., 1984-86; cons. Ariz. Hist. Soc., 1993—. Contbr. articles to profl. jours. Active U. Calif. Riverside Libr., 1981-83, KAET (PBS), 1988—, Ariz. State U., 1989—, Am. Assn. Mus., Ariz. Preservation Found., Grand Canyon Nature Assn.; cons. Ariz. Hist. Soc. Recipient Sidney B. Mitchell fellowship U. Calif., Berkeley, 1971. Mem. Am. Assn. Museums, Ariz. Preservation Found., Grand Canyon Nature Assn., Internat. Platform Assn., Phi Kappa Phi. Democrat. Presbyterian. Office: Alcuin Books Ltd 115 W Camelback Rd Phoenix AZ 85013-2519

MURILLO, VELDA JEAN, social worker, counselor; b. Miller, S.D., Dec. 8, 1943; d. Royal Gerald and Marion Elizabeth (Porter) Matson; m. Daniel John Murillo, June 25, 1967 (div. Dec. 1987); 1 child, Damon Michael. BS, S.D. State U., 1965; MA, Calif. State U., Bakersfield, 1980. Cert. marriage, family and child counselor. Social worker adult svcs. Kern County Dept. Welfare, Bakersfield, 1965-78, social worker child protective svcs., 1978-84; asst. coord. sexual abuse program Kern County Dist. Atty., Bakersfield, 1985-91, coord. sexual abuse program, 1991—; Mem. Calif. Sexual Assault Investigators, 1982-84, Kern Child Abuse Prevention Coun., Bakersfield, 1982-84; co-developer, presenter Children's Self Help Project, Bakersfield, 1982-87; cons. mem. Sexual Assault Adv. Com., Bakersfield, 1991—. Mem. Soroptimist Internat. Democrat. Office: Kern County Dist Atty 1215 Truxtun Ave Bakersfield CA 93301

MURJEE, TARA BONITA, choreographer, dance educator; b. Jersey City, Apr. 26, 1959. BA in Dance and Politics, Mt. Holyoke Coll., 1981; MA in Dance Edn., Columbia U., 1992; credential in edn. and profl. prep., San Jose (Calif.) U., 1994. Dance instr. mid. and h.s. students Northfield-Mt. Hermon Sch., East Northfield, Mass., 1980; dance instr. adults Columbia U. "Alternatives", 1983; guest artist, tchr. Phyllis Rose Dance Co./N.Y. pub. and ind. schs., 1981-83; faculty in dance lower sch. Berkeley-Carroll Sch., Bklyn., 1985-88; faculty in dance K-12 The Chapin Sch., N.Y.C., 1988-91; dance/fitness instr. adults Mid-Peninsula YWCA, Palo Alto, Calif., 1991-92; dance instr. adults and children DanceVisions, Palo Alto, 1993-94; artist, educator The Calif. Arts Project, 1994; adj. instr. dance for adults The Erick Hawkins Studio, N.Y.C., 1986-88; choreographer Larry Richardson's Dance Gallery, N.Y.C., 1985, Robert Yohn Dance Studio, N.Y.C., 1986, The Open Ctr., N.Y.C., 1988, St. Peter's Ch. at Citicorp Ctr., N.Y.C., 1990, Mid. Collegiate Ch. Theater, N.Y.C., 1991, 92, Mountain View Ctr. for Performing Arts, 1993, Cubberly Theater, Palo Alto, 1993.

MURKOWSKI, FRANK HUGHES, senator; b. Seattle, Mar. 28, 1933; s. Frank Michael and Helen (Hughes) M.; m. Nancy R. Gore, Aug. 28, 1954; children: Carol Victoria Murkowski Sturgulewski, Lisa Ann Murkowski Martell, Frank Michael, Eileen Marie Murkowski Van Wyhe, Mary Catherine Murkowski Judson, Brian Patrick. Student, Santa Clara U., 1952-53; BA in Econs, Seattle U., 1955. With Pacific Nat. Bank of Seattle, 1957-58, Nat. Bank of Alaska, Anchorage, 1959-67; asst. v.p., mgr. Nat. Bank of Alaska (Wrangell br.), 1963-66; v.p. charge bus. devel. Nat. Bank of Alaska, Anchorage, 1966-67; commr. dept. econ. devel. State of Alaska, Juneau, 1967-70; pres. Alaska Nat. Bank, Fairbanks, 1971-80; mem. U.S. Senate from Alaska, Washington, D.C., 1981—; chmn. Com. on Energy and Natural Resources; mem. Com. on Fin., Vets Affairs Com., Indian Affairs Com., Japan-US Friendship Com.; senate amb. UN Gen. Assembly, 1994-95; Rep. nominee for U.S. Congress from Alaska, 1970. Former v.p. B.C. and Alaska Bd. Trade. Served with U.S. Coast Guard, 1955-57. Mem. Am. Legion, Polish Legion Am. Vets., AMVETS, Ducks Unltd., NRA, Res. Officer's Assn., Pioneers of Alaska, Shilla Club, Internat. Alaska Nippon Kai, Capital Hill Club, Alaska Geographic Soc., Army Athletic Club, Alaska World Affairs Coun., Congl. Staff Club, AAA, Fairbanks Hist. Preservation Found., Coalition Am. Vets., Alaska Native Brotherhood, Diamond Athletic Club, Nat. Wildlife Fedn., Nat. Mining Hall of Fame, Naval Athletic Assn., Am. Bankers Assn, Alaska Bankers Assn. (pres. 1973), Young Pres.'s Orgn., Young Pres.'s Club, Washington Athletic Club, Alaska C. of C. (pres. 1977), Anchorage C. of C. (dir. 1966), B.C. C. of C., Fairbanks C. of C. (dir. 1973-78). Clubs: Elks, Lions, Washington Athletic. Office: US Senate 706 Hart Senate Bldg Washington DC 20510

MURO, VINCENT, author; b. Apr. 25, 1936; m. Anthea R.S. Muro; children: Czarina, Raymond. BS in Commerce. Prin. Am. Bus. Guides, 1992—. Author: World Banking Handbook, 1984, Handbook of Financial Analysis, 1991.

MUROTAKE, THOMAS HISASHI, emergency medicine technologist; b. Denison, Iowa, July 30, 1955; s. Thomas Hisashi and Nancy May (Morrow) M. EMT. Store mgr. Radio Shack, Van Nuys, Calif., 1980-81; EMT Snyder Ambulance, Van Nuys, Calif., 1981; sales mgr. Radio Shack, Canoga Park, Calif., 1981-82; teletype operator Credit Reports Inc., West L.A., 1982-83; self-employed EMT Event Med. Svcs., Los Alamitos, Calif., 1989—; platoon sgt. emergency treatment NCO CoC, 240th Support Bn., Calif. Army Nat. Guard, Long Beach, Calif., 1989—; corp. support svcs. mgr. Informative Rsch., Garden Grove, Calif., 1983-93; notary public State of Calif., 1990—, Murotake Mobile Notary Svc., 1994-95, A Time to Sign, 1995—, MAGNet, 1995—. Author: Recollections, 1991, Collected Works, 1991. Vol. EMT Maryland City (Md.) Vol. Fire Dept., 1978-80, asst. publicity chmn. 1979-80, SOS Free Med. Clinic, 1993—. With U.S. Army, 1973-80. Recipient Calif. Commendation medal State of Calif. Mil. Dept., 1991, 95, Achievement medal U.S. Army, 1994, Humanitarian Svc. medal U.S. Army, 1994, Counter-Drug Task Force ribbon State of Calif. Mil. Dept., 1995, State Svc. ribbon, 1995; named Non-Commd. Office of Yr. 240th Support Bn., 1991. Mem. Nat. Notary Assn., Am. Legion. Republican. Episcopalian. Home: 6881 Homer St Apt 45 Westminster CA 92683-3741

MURPHY, BRIAN ARTHUR, insurance executive. BSBA, U Nev., 1979; M of Internat. Mgmt., Am. Grad. Sch. Internat. Mgmt., 1980. Ops./property and casualty underwriting mgr. CIGNA Bahamas, 1985; country mgr. CIGNA Guatemala, 1985-91; bus. devel. mgr., team leader S.W. region CIGNA Worldwide Ins. Co., 1991-92; bus. devel. mgr. Midwest/S.W., mgr. advantage unit CIGNA Worldwide Ins. Co., Chgo., Houston, 1992; bus. devel. mgr. S.w. CIGNA Worldwide Ins. Co., 1992—. Office: CIGNA Worldwide Ins Co 5055 Wilshire Blvd Los Angeles CA 90036-6100

MURPHY, DAVID HAZLETT, geologist; b. Ann Arbor, Mich., Sept. 11, 1954; s. Richard J. and Janice (Kerlin) M. B.A., Albion Coll.; M.S., U. Mich. Lic. profl. geologist, Wyo. Geologist, Amoco Prodn. Co., Houston, 1978-81, Mobil Oil Corp., Denver, 1981-86; consulting geologist, Denver, 1986-89; geologist The Mark Group, Pleasant Hill, Calif., 1989; cartographer Def. Mapping Agy., 1989-91; geologist U.S. Bur. Land Mgmt., 1991—. Asst. scoutmaster, Boy Scouts Am., Aurora, Colo., 1981-84, scoutmaster, 1984-87, unit commr., Winnemucca, Nev., 1992, dist. commr., 1993-94, coun. commr., Reno, 1995—. Recipient Dist. Award of Merit, Boy Scouts Am., 1993. Mem. Am. Assn. Petroleum Geologists, Nev. Petroleum Soc., Geothermal Resources Coun., Sigma Gamma Epsilon.

MURPHY, DENNIS ROBERT, state motor vehicle technical coordinator; b. Denver, Sept. 14, 1940; s. William John and Virginia (LaFleur) M.; m. Audrey M., Oct. 20, 1984; children: John, Patrick, Virginia, Lisa, Michelle, Katherine. BS in Bus., U. Colo., 1978. Dir. ops. RF/Broomfield (Colo.), 1979-82; data base adminstr. Luth. Hosp., Wheatridge, 1982-84; programmer Colo. Dept. Revenue, Denver, 1984-92; system mgr. Driver Lic. Sect., Denver, 1992-93; motor vehicle tech. coord. Denver, 1993—. Mem. BPOE. Home: 384 S Balsam St Lakewood CO 80226-3036 Office: 140 W 6th Ave Rm 104 Denver CO 80204-5109

MURPHY, FRANCIS SEWARD, journalist; b. Portland, Oreg., Sept. 9, 1914; s. Francis H. and Blanche (Livesay) M.; BA, Reed Coll., 1936; m. Clare Eastham Cooke, Sept. 20, 1974. With The Oregonian, Portland, 1936-79, TV editor, Behind the Mike columnist, 1952-79. Archeol. explorer Mayan ruins, Yucatan, Mex., 1950—, mem. Am. Quintana Roo Expdn., 1965, 66, 68. With AUS, 1942-46. Author: Dragon Mask Temples in Central Yucatan, 1988. Mem. Royal Asiatic Soc., City Club (bd. govs. 1950, 64-66), Explorers Club, Am. Club of Hong Kong, Oreg. Hist. Soc. Democrat. Congregationalist. Home: 4213 NE 32nd Ave Portland OR 97211-7149

MURPHY, GERALD D., food and agriculture chemicals manufacturing company executive; b. Ames, Iowa, 1928; BA Harvard U., 1952, MBA, 1954. Chmn., CEO Early Calif. Industries Inc.; chmn. Am. Rice, Inc. (bd. dirs.), Pinkertons Internat., Inc. Office: Erly Industries Inc 10990 Wilshire Blvd Los Angeles CA 90024-3913

MURPHY, GERALD W., construction executive. With Aetna Casualty Co., St. Louis, Mo., 1959-71, McCarthy Brothers Co., St. Louis, Mo., 1971-79; pres., CEO McCarthy We. Constructors, Inc., Phoenix, 1979—. Office: McCarthy Western Constructors Inc 120 N 44th St Phoenix AZ 85034-1822*

MURPHY, LINDA SUE, city official; b. Lynchburg, Va., June 7, 1948; d. Carter P. and Dorothy L. (Clark) Tucker; m. Daniel K. Murphy, Mar. 25, 1972; 1 child, Krystal Grace. Student, Longwood Coll., 1966-68. Exec. sec. First Nat. Bank of Anchorage, Seward, Alaska, 1976-80; clk. of ct., asst. magistrate Alaska Ct. System, Seward, 1980-81; city clk., pers. officer City of Seward, 1981—. Sec., Seward Concert Assn., 1982; chmn. Seward Sch. Adv. Bd., 1983; v.p. bd. dirs. Seward Life Action Coun., 1983-84, pres. bd. dirs., 1984-86; chmn. Seward-Obihiro Sister City Com., 1984; active Lt. Gov. Transition Team, 1995; chmn. local United Way, 1995. Named Alaska Mcpl. Official of Yr., 1992. Mem. Internat. Inst. Mcpl. Clks. (bd. dirs. 1992-95, 2d v.p. 1995—), Alaska Assn. Mcpl. Clerks (sec. 1984-85, v.p. 1985-86, pres. 1986-87), Alaska Women in Govt. (v.p. 1985-87), Bus. and Profl. Women's Club (v.p. 1988-89, pres. 1989-90), Rotary (bd. dirs. 1989—, treas. 1991-92, v.p. 1992-93, pres. 1994-95). Democrat. Home: Nhn Salmon Rd Seward AK 99664 Office: Seward City Hall PO Box 167 Seward AK 99664-0167

MURPHY, MARY ANN, human services administrator; b. Salt Lake City, Feb. 13, 1943; d. Wallace L. and Irene (Hummer) Matlock; m. Robert A. Glatzer, Dec. 31, 1977; children: Gabriela, Jessica, Nicholas. BA, U. Wash., 1964; MS, Ea. Wash. U., 1975. House counselor Ryther Child Ctr., Seattle, 1966-67; tchr. presch. Head Start, L.A. and Seattle, 1967-70; tchr. presch. Children's Orthopedic Hosp., Seattle, 1970-71, Washington, 1971-72; mem. faculty Ea. Wash. U., Cheney, 1973-82; exec. dir. Youth Help Assn., Spokane, Wash., 1983-88; mgr. regional ctr. for child abuse and neglect Deaconess Med. Ctr., Spokane, 1988—; pres. Wash. State Alliance for Children, Youth and Families, Seattle, 1985-87; chairperson Gov.'s Juvenile Justice Adv. Commn., Olympia, Wash., 1987—, Spokane Prevention of Child Abuse and Neglect Coun., Spokane, 1988—. Mem. Nat. Coun. on Juvenile Justice, 1994. Recipient Alumni Achievement award Ea. Wash. U., 1994; named Outstanding Women Leader in Health Care, YWCA, 1992. Home: 1950 W Clarke Ave Spokane WA 99201-1306 Office: Deaconess Med Ctr 604 W 6th Ave Spokane WA 99204-2708

MURPHY, MICHAEL JOSEPH, county official; b. Seattle, May 24, 1947; s. John Anthony and Helen Elizabeth (Domick) M.; m. Theresa Ann Smith. BA in History, Seattle U., 1969; MBA, Pacific Luth. U., 1978. Chief adjudicator vet.'s program Office of the State Treas., Olympia, Wash., 1972-75, adminstr. pub. deposit protection commn., 1975-81, internal auditor to state treas., 1981-87; treas. Thurston County, Olympia, 1987—; mem. adv. bd. asset/liability com. Twin County Credit Union, Olympia, 1987—; instr. profl. orgns., govt. Treas. Thurston County Dems., 1973-77. Mem. Wash. Assn. County Treasurers (bd. dirs., officer 1987—, legis. coord. 1989—, Pres. award 1994), Wash. Assn. County Officials (bd. dirs. 1989-90), Wash. Mcpl. Treasurers Assn. (bd. dirs. 1990—, Cert. Excellence for investment policy 1992), Wash. Fin. Officers Assn. (profl. fin. officer 1988-94), Olympia Yacht Club, Olympia Country and Golf Club, Valley Athletic Club. Roman Catholic. Home: PO Box 1342 Olympia WA 98507-1342 Office: Thurston County Treas 2000 Lakeridge Dr SW Olympia WA 98502-6045

MURPHY, PHILIP EDWARD, broadcast executive; b. Chgo., May 11, 1945; s. Edward Curtis and Mary Francis (D'Incecco) M.; m. Carol Jean Sefton, Mar. 11, 1967 (div. 1985); children: Mandy Jean, Patrick Jeffrey. BS, Ind. U., 1967. Prodn. mgr. Sta. WFIU-FM, Bloomington, Ind., 1968; news reporter, photographer, editor Sta. WTHR TV, Indpls., 1969, sr. account exec., 1970-80; account exec. Blair TV, L.A., 1980-81; pres. Am. Spot Cable Corp., Hollywood, Calif., 1981-82; v.p. tech. ops. for United Paramount Network, combined Viacom and Paramount TV markets Paramount Pictures TV, Hollywood, 1982—; spkr. film preservation, in field; advisor Libr. of Congress, Washington, Nat. Archives, Washington. Lighting designer Civic Theatre, Indpls., 1979; tech. dir. Footlite Mus., Indpls., 1970-78; bd. dirs. Cathedral Arts, Indpls., 1978-80. Mem. Assn. Moving Image Archivists, Gay and Lesbian Alliance Against Defamation L.A., Hollywood Supports Assn., Soc. Motion Picture and TV Engrs. Office: Paramount Pictures TV 5555 Melrose Ave Stage # 3/212 Los Angeles CA 90038-3197

MURPHY, SARA JO, library director; b. St. Louis, Nov. 20, 1942; d. Richard O. and Helen F. (Cross) Colvin; m. Dennis R. Murphy, Sept. 5, 1964; children: Thomas R., JoEllen, Andrew R. BA, Emporia State U., 1964. Self-employed ins. agt. Webster Ins., La Veta, Colo., 1978-88; real estate agt. Spoon River Real Estate, La Veta, 1979-88; columnist Huerfano World, Walsenburg, Colo., 1987-90; dir. Carnegie Pub. Libr., Trinidad, Colo., 1990—. County chmn. Rep. Party, Huerfano, Colo., 1988-90. Mem. ALA, Colo. Libr. Assn., Santa Fe Trail Assocs. (Mountain br. bd. dirs. 1994—). Office: Carnegie Public Library 202 N Animas St Trinidad CO 81082-2643

MURPHY, THOMAS JOSEPH, archbishop; b. Chgo., Oct. 3, 1932; s. Barthomew Thomas and Nellie M. AB, St. Mary of the Lake Sem., 1954, STB, 1956, MA, 1957, STL, 1958, STD, 1960. Ordained priest Roman Cath. Ch., 1958. Various positions with Archdiocese of Chgo.; bishop of Great Falls-Billings Mont., 1978-87; coadjutor archbishop of Seattle, 1987-91, archbishop of Seattle, 1991—. Office: Archdiocese of Seattle 910 Marion St Seattle WA 98104-1274*

MURPHY, TIM, food products executive; b. 1954. With USDA Farmers Adminstrn, 1975-79; now pres., treas. APIO Inc., Guadalupe, Calif. Office: APIO Inc 4575 W Main St Guadalupe CA 93434-1659*

MURPHY, WARREN CHARLES, rector; b. Phila., May 6, 1944; s. Warren N. and Frances (Stanley) M.; m. Katharine Linde, June 24, 1977; children: Aaron, Malcolm. BA, Bridgewater Coll., 1967; MDiv, Episc. Grad. Sch., 1972; cert., St. George's Coll., Jerusalem, 1987. Community organizer VISTA, Buffalo and Lackawanna, N.Y., 1967-68; legis. asst. U.S. Sen. Birch Bayh, Washington, 1970-71; exec. dir., founder Compass House, Buffalo, 1972-75; dir. community rels. Cambridge (Mass.) Econ. and Opportunity Commn., 1975-76; rector Little Snake River Episc. Ch., Dixon, Wyo., 1977-82, Trinity Episc. Ch., Lander, Wyo., 1982-89, Christ Episc. Ch., Cody, Wyo., 1989—; rector, priest-in-charge Shoshone Episc. Ch., Ft. Washakie, Wyo., 1985-89; chmn. Wyo. Ch. Coalition, Laramie, 1988-92; dep. Gen. Convention Episc. Ch., 1988, 91, 94. Contbr. articles to newspapers, mags.; author nature booklet Under the Firmament, 1989. Bd. dirs. Ring Lake Ranch, Dubois, Wyo., 1984-90; mem. nat. adv. bd., 1990—; organizer Orgn. of Orgns., Lackawanna, 1967-68; vol. Bayh for Pres., Boston, 1976; mem. Dixon Town Coun., 1979-82; mem. psychiat. adv. bd. Pine Ridge Hosp., Lander, 1984-88; bd. dirs. Crisis Intervention Ctr. of Cody, 1991—, Wyo. Coun. for theHumanities, 1993—, pres. elect. 1995. Mem. Cody Ministerial Assn. Office: Christ Episc Ch 825 Simpson Ave # 1718 Cody WY 82414-4140

MURPHY, WILLIAM ARTHUR, city manager; b. Boston, Apr. 3, 1939; s. John Sebastian and Mary Anastasia (Nolan) M.; m. Davie Joy O'Hair, Sept. 27, 1958; children: Teresa Joy, William Andrew. BA, Chico State Coll., 1965; MA, Calif. State U., Chico, 1973. News writer Chico-Enterprise Record, 1965-66; asst. to pres. Calif. State U., 1966-67, adminstr., mem. faculty, 1972-80; adminstrv. asst. City of Chico, 1967-72; pub. mgmt. cons. Wm. Murphy & Assocs., Chico, 1980-83; mgr. Tahoe Transp. Dist., South Lake Tahoe, Calif., 1983-85; city mgr. City of Anderson, Calif., 1985—; dir. Superior Calif. Devel. Coun., Redding, 1993—. Mem. Chico City Coun., 1975-79, Local Agy. Formation Commn., Butte County, Calif., 1977-79, Tahoe Regional Planning Agy. Adv. Planning Commn., 1983-85; dir. Cmty. Housing Improvement Pro., Chico, 1979-82. With USAF, 1956-60. Named Bus. Person of Yr., Anderson C. of C., 1989. Mem. Internat. City and County Mgrs. Assn. (20 Yrs. Svc. to Local Govt. award 1993), Calif. Pub. Employees Labor Rels. Assn. Home: 3442 Riverside Dr Anderson CA 96007-3822 Office: City of Anderson 1887 Howard St Anderson CA 96007-3340

MURRAY, CONNEL LYLE, advertising and public relations executive, consultant; b. Lompoc, Calif., Feb. 22, 1928; s. Connel Victor and Mary Mandilla (Hostetler) M.; m. June Louise White, Jan. 9, 1954; children: Corinne Louise, Erin Lucille, Connel Raymond, Alison Reita. Student, Lewis and Clark Coll., 1945, 47; BA, San Francisco State Coll., 1954. Pub. relations account exec. Fred Gray & Assocs., San Francisco, 1954-55; v.p., owner Mitchell, Murray & Horn Pub. Relations, San Francisco, 1955-57; newswriter KRON-TV, San Francisco, 1957; account exec. various advt. cos., Calif., 1957-68; pres. Murray/Bradley Advt. and Pub. Relations, Anchorage, 1968-86, The Murray Group, Inc., Seattle, 1986--; cons. Bradley Advt., Anchorage, 1986--. Pres. YMCA, Anchorage, 1976; mem. found. bd. Evergreen State Coll., Olympia, Wash., 1987--. With USN, 1945-47. Recipient North Star award Alaska Visitors Assn., Juneau, 1976. Mem. Am. Assn. Advt. Agys. (Wash. chmn. 1986), Pub. Relations Soc. Am. (accredited, bd. govs. 1972--), Anchorage Yacht Club. Libertarian. Office: The Murray Group 3837 13th Ave W Ste 201 Seattle WA 98119-1354

MURRAY, DONALD EUGENE, plasic surgeon; b. Dillon, Mont., May 30, 1937; s. Ned Charles and Ruth Adelaide (McFarland) M.; m. Charla Leavens Murray, June 18, 1961; children: Thomas Allan, Carol Ann. BS in Quantitative Biology, MIT, 1959; MD, Stanford Sch. of Medicine, 1964. Diplomate Am. Bd. Plastic Surgery, Nat. Bd. Med. Examiners; lic. Mont. Straight surgery internship Palo Alto-Stanford Med. Ctr., Calif., 1964-65; asst. resident gen. surgery Stanford U. Sch. of Medicine, Palo Alto, Calif., 1965-66, fellow in rehabilitaion surgery, 1966-67, resident gen. surgery, 1967-68, chief resident plastic and reconstructive surgery, 1969-70; chief resident gen. surgery San Mateo Gen. Hosp./Stanford U. Sch. of Medicine, Calif., 1968; chief resident head and neck surgery Roswell Park Meml. Inst., Buffalo, N.Y., 1969; fellow plastic and reconstructive surgery Royal Melbourne Hosp., Australia, 1970-71; honorary plastic and reconstructive surgeon Middlemore Hosp., Auckland, New Zealand, 1971; pvt. practice Missoula, Mont., 1971—; chief of surgery Missoula Cmty. Hosp., 1974, St. Patrick's Hosp., 1977; trainee in VRA summer Clin. Tng. Program Rehab. Medicine Stanford Med. Ctr., 1962; clin. clk. St. Thomas' Hosp. Cardiovasc. Surgery, London, England, 1963; mem. Mont. State Comprehensive Health Planning Coun., Mont. Fedn. for Med. Care (instl. rev. steering com. 1976-86, bd. dirs. 1982-88), Mont. Physicians' Svc. Adjudication Com., 1979, Mont. Medicare Adv. Com., 1992—; surgery com. Missoula Cmty. Hosp., 1973, 86, surgery com. St. Patrick's Hosp., 1975-78, 88-89, pres. elect med. staff, 1981, pres. med. staff, 1982, quality assurance com., 1981 (chmn. 1983), by-laws revision com., 1985; chmn. Health Facilities Com. State of Mont. Dept. of Health & Environ. Scis., 1973-75, credentials com. St. Patrick's Hosp., 1986-88; faculty affiliate Dept. Comm. Sci. & Disorders U. Mont., 1975-90; adv. com. Missoula Tech. Ctr., 1977; orgnl. com. Mont. Health Sys. Agy., 1977; burn chmn. Western Mont. Emergency Med. Svcs. Coun., 1978; assoc. mem. Am. Soc. of Clin. Hypnosis, 1982. Mem. Missoula Symphony Assn. (bd. dirs. 1980-87, pres. 1986). Fellow ACS (com. on applicants 1980—); mem. AMA, Am. Soc. of Plastic and Reconstructive Surgeons (annotated bibliography com. 1979-82), Am. Cleft Palate Assn., Northwest Soc. of Plastic Surgeons, Rocky Mountain Assn. of Plastic and Reconstructive Surgeons (nominating com. 1979, pres. elect 1989, pres. 1990), Mont. Cleft Palate Assn. (pres. 1974), Mont. Med. Assn. (joint med. legal panel 1976-78, malpractice panel 1978, profl. liability com. 1980-86), Western Mont. Med. Soc. (v.p. 1974, pres. elect 1975, pres. 1976). Office: 614 W Spruce St Missoula MT 59802-4002

MURRAY, JAMES ALAN, urban and environmental consultant, investor; b. Evansville, Ind., Oct. 2, 1942; s. William Dewey and Dorothy Marie (Gleason) M.; BS, U. N.Mex., 1964; MBA, Harvard U., 1969; MA (NDEA fellow), U. Oreg., 1971, PhD, 1972; children: Heidi Lynn, Paul Alan, Kendra Leigh. Dir. fin. City of Boulder (Colo.), 1972-73, dir. adminstrv. svcs., 1973-74; v.p. Briscoe, Maphis, Murray & Lamont, Inc., Boulder, 1974-78, pres., 1978-84, also dir.; dir. fin. City and County of Denver, 1984-86, chief exec. officer, 1986-87, asst. to mayor, 1987-89; pres., dir. Murray Lamont & Assocs., Inc., 1990—; pres., dir. Colo. Scientific Investments, Inc., 1993—; chmn. Kunshan Murray Clothing Co., Ltd., China, 1994—; adj. assoc. prof. Grad. Sch. Public Affairs, U. Colo., Boulder, 1972-80, Denver, 1985-91. Mem. open space adv. com. City of Boulder, 1972-74; bd. dirs. Met. Denver Sewage Authority, 1984-85; chmn. Colo. Baseball Commn., 1989-93. Mem. ASPA, Am. Econ. Assn., Western Econ. Assn., Water Pollution Control Fedn., Denver Athletic Club, Kappa Mu Epsilon, Pi Alpha Alpha. Home: 99 S Downing St Apt 602 Denver CO 80209-2407 Office: 1660 Wynkoop St Ste 1060 Denver CO 80202-1146

MURRAY, J(AMES) EDWARD, retired newspaper editor, publisher; b. Buffalo, S.D., Apr. 16, 1915; s. George Edward and Eleanor Lillian (Burshek) M.; m. Miriam Irene Virtanen, Dec. 6, 1940; children: Judith Michaela, James Virtanen. BA in Philosophy, Journalism, U. Nebr., 1938, LLD (hon.), 1974. Reporter UPI, Chgo., 1938-42; war corr., fgn. corr. UPI, London, Rome, Paris, 1943-48; mng. editor L.A. Mirror, 1948-60, Ariz. Republic, Phoenix, 1960-71; assoc. editor, editor Knight News Svc. Detroit Free Press, 1971-75; pres., pub. Daily Camera, Boulder, Colo., 1976-82; ret., 1982; pres. AP Mng. Editors Assn., 1961, Am. Soc. Newspaper Editors, 1972-73; lectr., cons., trainer Nepal, India, Bangladesh, Indonesia, Sri Lanka, Malaysia, New Guinea, Philippines, Fiji, Turkey, Nigeria, Sierra Leone, Kenya, 1982-90; lectr. for World Press Freedom Com., Internat. Exec. Svc. Corps., U.S. Info. Svc., Ctr. Fgn. Journalists, Asia Found., East-West Ctr. Recipient John Peter Zenger award for freedom of press U. Ariz., Tucson, 1969. Democrat. Unitarian.

MURRAY, JAMES MICHAEL, librarian, law librarian, legal educator, lawyer; b. Seattle, Nov. 8, 1944; s. Clarence Nicholas and Della May (Snyder) M.; m. Linda Monthy Murray; MLaw Librarianship, U. Wash., 1978; JD, Gonzaga U., 1971. Bar: Wash., 1974. Reference/reserve libr. U. Tex. Law Libr. Austin, 1978-81; assoc. law libr. Washington U. Law Libr. St. Louis, 1981-84; law libr., asst. prof. Gonzaga U. Sch. Law, Spokane, 1984-91; libr. East Bonner County Libr., 1991—; cons. in field. Author: (with Gasaway and Johnson) Law Library Administration During Fiscal Austerity, 1992. Bd. dirs. ACLU, Spokane chpt., 1987-91; Wash. Vol. Lawyers for the Arts, 1976-78. Mem. ABA, Idaho Libr. Assn., Wash. State Bar Assn (law sch. liaison com., 1986-88). Mem. state adv. bd. National Reporter on Legal Ethics and Professional Responsibility, 1982-91; author: (with Reams and McDermott) American Legal Literature: Bibliography of Selected Legal Resources, 1985; editor Texas Bar Jour. (Books Appraisals Column), 1979-82; contbr. numerous articles and revs. to profl. jours., acknowledgements and bibliographies in field. Home: 921 W 29th Ave Spokane WA 99203-1318 Office: East Bonner County Libr 419 N 2nd Ave Sandpoint ID 83864-1501

MURRAY, JAMES PATRICK, newspaper columnist; b. Hartford, Conn., Dec. 29, 1919; s. James and Molly (O'Connell) M.; m. Geraldine Norma Brown, Oct. 20, 1945 (dec. Apr. 1984); children: Theodore, Anthony, Pamela, Eric (dec.). AB, Trinity Coll., Hartford, 1943, LittD honoris causa, 1981; LLD honoris causa, Pepperdine U., 1987. Mem. staff New Haven Register, 1943, Los Angeles Examiner, 1944-48, Time, Inc., 1948-61; sports columnist Los Angeles Times, 1961—. Author: The Best of Jim Murray, 1965, The Sporting World of Jim Murray, 1968, The Jim Murray Collection, 1988, Jim Murray: An Autobiography, 1993. Recipient Sportswriter of Yr. award Nat. Assn. Sportscasters and Sportswriters, 1964, 66-77, 79, Headliners Club award, 1965, 76, Alumni medal Trinity Coll., 1972, J.G. Taylor Spink award Baseball Hall of Fame, Cooperstown, N.Y., 1988, Pulitzer prize for disting. commentary, 1990. Mem. Time-Life Alumni Assn., L.A. Press Club (v.p. 1953), PGA West Club, Riviera Country Club, Bel Air Country Club. Office: Los Angeles Times Times Mirror Sq Los Angeles CA 90012

MURRAY, JOHN FREDERIC, physician, educator; b. Mineola, N.Y., June 8, 1927; s. Frederic S. and Dorothy Murray; m. Diane Lain, Nov. 30, 1968; children—James R., Douglas S., Elizabeth. A.B., Stanford, 1949, M.D., 1953; D.Sc. (hon.), U. Paris, 1983. From instr. to assoc. prof. medicine U. Calif. at Los Angeles, 1957-66; mem. sr. staff Cardiovascular Research Inst., U. Calif., San Francisco, 1966—; asso. prof. medicine Cardiovascular

Research Inst., U. Calif. (Sch. Medicine), 1966-69, prof., 1969—; chief chest service San Francisco Gen. Hosp., 1966-89; Vis. prof. Brompton Inst. for Diseases of the Chest, London, 1972-73; Macy faculty scholar Inst. Nat. de la Santé et de la Recherche Medicale, Paris, 1979-80; mem. adv. council and pulmonary disease adv. com. Nat. Heart, Lung and Blood Inst.; mem. clin. studies panel NRC.; bd. govs. Am. Bd. Internal Medicine, Am. Bd. Emergency Medicine. Author: The Normal Lung, 1976, 2d edit., 1986; co-author: Diseases of the Chest, 5th edit., 1980; co-editor: Textbook of Respiratory Medicine, 1988, 2d edit., 1994; editor: Am. Rev. Respiratory Disease, 1973-79; contbr. articles to profl. jours. Chmn. Internat. Union Against Tb and Lung Disease. Served with USNR, 1945-46. Sr. Internat. fellow Fogarty Inst. Fellow Royal Coll. Physicians; mem. Assn. Am. Physicians, Am. Soc. Clin. Investigation, Am. Physiol. Soc., Western Soc. Clin. Research, Western Assn. Physicians, Am. Thoracic Soc. (pres. 1981-82), Académie Nationale de Médecine Francaise. Home: 24 Edith St San Francisco CA 94133-2913 Office: U Calif PO Box 0841 San Francisco CA 94143

MURRAY, JOHN ROBERTS, physicist; b. Camp White, Oreg., Aug. 8, 1943; s. John Lewis and Cherry Mary (Roberts) M.; m. Gwynedd Morgan Davis, July 1976; children: David James, Catherine Ann. SB, MIT, 1965, PhD, 1970. Laser devel. physicist Lawrence Livermore (Calif.) nat. Lab., 1972—. Divsnl. editor: Applied Optics, 1992—, editor-in-chief, 1994—. Capt. U.S. Army, 1970-72. Fellow Optical Soc. Am. Home: 605 Camino Amigo Danville CA 94526-2305 Office: Lawrence Livermore Nat Lab PO Box 5508 Livermore CA 94551-5508

MURRAY, KEVIN REID, lawyer; b. Vernal, Utah, Sept. 25, 1957; s. Leland P. and Theda (Reid) M.; m. Deon Anne Dunn, Aug. 28, 1987. BA cum laude, Brigham Young U., 1981, JD cum laude, 1984. Bar: Tex. 1984, Utah 1990. Instr. Brigham Young U., Provo, Utah, 1982-84; assoc. Childs, Fortenbach, Beck & Guyton, Houston, 1984-85, Winstead, McGuire, Sechrest & Minick, Dallas, 1985-87, Jones, Day, Reavis & Pogue, Dallas, 1987-89, Berman & O'Rorke, 1989-90, Parry Murray, Salt Lake City, 1990—. Dist. chmn. Boy Scouts Am., Dallas, 1985-87, scoutmaster, 1985—; active bishopric Ch. of Jesus Christ of Latter-Day Saints, Dallas, 1988-89. Mem. ABA, Tex. Bar Assn., Dallas Bar Assn., Utah State Bar, Urban Land Inst. Republican. Home: 1360 Skyline Dr Bountiful UT 84010-1311 Office: Parry Murray Ward & Moxley 1270 Eagle Gate Tower Salt Lake City UT 84111

MURRAY, PATTY, senator; b. Seattle, Wash., Oct. 11, 1950; d. David L. and Beverly A. (McLaughlin) Johns; m. Robert R. Murray, June 2, 1972; children: Randy P., Sara A. BA, Wash. State U., 1972. Sec. various cos., Seattle, 1972-76; citizen lobbyist various ednl. groups, Seattle, 1983-88; legis. lobbyist Orgn. for Parent Edn., Seattle, 1977-84; instr. Shoreline Community Coll., Seattle, 1984—; mem. Wash. State Senate, Seattle, 1989-92; U.S. senator from Washington, 1993—; ranking minority mem. Appropriations Legis. Branch; vice-chmn. Senate Dem. Policy Com.; mem. Com. on Banking, Housing, & Urban Affairs, Budget Com., Senate Dem. Tech. & Comms. Com. Mem. bd. Shoreline Sch., Seattle, 1985-89; mem. steering com. Demonstration for Edn., Seattle, 1987; founder, chmn. Orgn. for Parent Edn., Wash., 1981-85; 1st Congl. rep. Wash. Women United, 1983-85. Recipient Recognition of Svc. to Children award Shoreline PTA Coun., 1986, Golden Acorn Svc. award, 1989; Outstanding Svc. award Wash. Women United, 1986, Outstanding Svc. to Pub. Edn. award Citizens Ednl. Ctr. NW, Seattle, 1987. Democrat. Office: US Senate 111 Russell Senate Office Bldg Washington DC 20510-4704*

MURRAY, ROBERT HENRY, technical manager; b. San Antonio, Aug. 15, 1955; s. Robert H. and Fay C. (Temple) M.; m. Virginia E. Price, Aug. 20, 1975 (div. Aug. 1990); m. Marion McGarrity, Aug. 24, 1990; children: Nicola J., Craig T. BSc in Math., U. Houston, 1982. With CSX (formery Tex. Gas Exploration Corp.), Houston, 1982-86; pvt. cons. PT Badak NGL Co., Bontang, Indonesia, 1986-89, PT Cal Tex, Jakarta, Indonesia, 1989-90, Eczacibi Bilgi Illetim, Istanbul, Turkey, 1990, Brit. Steel, plc, Glasgow, Scotland, 1990, Panhandle Ea. Corp., Houston, 1990-91, Cell-Tech, Houston, 1991, ARCO Alaska, Inc., Anchorage, 1991-93, LGL Alaska Rsch. Assocs., Anchorage, 1993-94; sr. software engr. Computer Task Group, Inc., Anchorage, 1994—; ptnr. Wilkinson Murray & Assocs., Anchorage, 1993—; bd. dirs. CRX Internat. Ltd., Edinburgh, Scotland. Author computer program Inventory Simulation for Maintenance and Repair Operations and Disposal Economics, 1993, 94. Mem. Inst. Data Processing Mgmt. Republican. Episcopalian. Home: 9410 Swan Cir Eagle River AK 99577-8664 Office: Computer Task Group Inc 440 E 36th Ave Ste 400 Anchorage AK 99503-4136

MURRAY, ROBERT MICHAEL, telecommunications executive; b. N.Y.C., Jan. 5, 1961; s. Thomas Patrick and Ida Michelle (Di Persia) M.; m. Heidi Kristine Kingston, June 25, 1988; 1 child, Erin Taylor. BS, U. So. Calif., 1983. CPA, Calif. Acct. Ernst & Young, L.A. and San Diego, 1983-87; account rep. Digital Equipment Corp., San Diego, 1987-90; regional mktg. officer Bank of Am., San Diego, 1990-92; v.p., gen. mgr. PageNet Inc., San Diego, 1992—. Office: PageNet Inc 9360 Towne Centre Dr San Diego CA 92121-3030

MURRAY, STEPHEN O., sociologist consultant; b. St. Paul, Minn., May 4, 1950; s. Omer K. M. and Una C. Peterson; m. Keelung Hong, July 15, 1981. BA, Michigan State U., 1972; MA, U. Ariz., 1975; PhD, U. Toronto, Ont., Can., 1979. Cons. Social Network Conss., San Francisco, 1978-80; postdoctoral fellow U. Calif., Berkeley, 1980-82; rsch. dir. El Instituto Obregón, San Francisco, 1982—. Author: Theory Groups and the Study of Language, 1994, Latin American Male Homosexualities, 1995; co-author: Taiwanese Culture, Taiwanese Society, 1994; editl. bd. Journal of Homosexuality, 1987—, History of Sociology, 1985—, Encyclopedia of Homosexuality, 1986-89, 95—. Bd. dirs. Life Ctr., San Francisco, 1992. Recipient theory devel. award Internat. Gay Acad. Union, 1982. Mem. Am. Sociol. Assn., Am. Anthropol. Assn., Am. Ethnol. Soc., Sociologists' Lesbian and Gay Caucus (editor 1977-79), Soc. Lesbian and Gay Anthropologists (editor 1989-92). Office: El Instituto Obregón 1360 De Haro San Francisco CA 94107

MURRAY, WILLIAM WALLACE, electrical engineer; b. Pipestone, Minn., Apr. 20, 1962; s. Robert A. and Marian D. (Grey) M.; m. Bethann Callis, July 3, 1986; children: Amy E., Brittany D., Paul M. BSEE, S.D. Sch. Mines, 1985. Design support engr. Texas Instruments, McKinney, Tex., 1985-86; elec. design engr. Texas Instruments, Lewisville, Tex., 1986-90; project engr. AlliedSignal-Global Wulfsberg, Prescott, Ariz., 1990-92; sr. project engr. AlliedSignal-Global Wulfsberg, Prescott, 1992—. Editor: (newsletter) The Signal-Yavapai Amateur Radio, 1993-94. Sys. operator KB7FRV Amateur Radio BBS, Prescott, 1994. Mem. Yavapai Amateur Radio Club (pres. 1993-94, bd. mem. 1994—). Home: PO Box 11572 Prescott AZ 86304-1572 Office: AlliedSignal Avionics Inc 6400 Wilkinson Dr Prescott AZ 86301-6164

MURREN, DOUGLAS EDWARD, pastor; b. Wenatchee, Wash., July 16, 1951; s. Virgil Edward and Gloria Mae (Humphres) M.; m. Debra Jean Landin, Mar. 27, 1971; children: Matthew Douglas, Raissa Anne. BA in Religion, Seattle Pacific U., 1973; DD (hon.), Internat. Ch. of the Foursquare Gospel, 1991. Lic. pastor Internat. Ch. Foursquare Gospel. Asst. pastor Bethesda Christian Ctr., Wenatchee, 1974-79; founding pastor Eastside Christian Communion, Bellevue, Wash., 1979-80, Eastside Foursquare Ch., Kirkland, Wash., 1981—; conf. speaker, cons. various orgns., Poland, USSR, Norway, Fed. Republic Germany, Haiti, and U.S.; adj. guest faculty Fuller Theol. and Regent Coll., Vancouver; supt. div Foursquare Gospel Ch., N. King County, Wash., 1985-91. Author: Iceman, 1986, Is It Real When It Doesn't Work?, 1990, Baby Boomerang, 1990, Keeping Your Dreams Alive When They Steal Your Coat, 1993, Leadershift, 1994; host (radio show) Growing Together; columnist Ministries Today, Worship Leader. Office: Eastside Foursquare Ch PO Box 536 Kirkland WA 98083-0536

MURRY, FRANCIE ROBERTA, special education educator; b. Waukegan, Ill.. BA, Ctrl. Wash. U., 1980, MEd, 1988; PhD, U. Va., 1991. Cert. tchr., Wash. Spl. edn. tchr. Adna (Wash.) Sch. Dist., 1980-81; itinerant spl. edn. tchr. Ellensburg Sch. Dist., Kittitas, Wash., 1981-85; dist. cons., spl. edn. tchr. Ellensburg (Wash.) Sch. Dist., 1985-86, at-risk project cons./coord., 1987-88; dist. cons., spl. edn. tchr. Yelm (Wash.) Sch. Dist., 1986-87; grad. asst. Commonwealth Ctr. Edn. of Tchrs., Va. Behavior Disorders, Charlottesville, Va., 1988-89; grad. instr. U. Va., Charlottesville, 1990, grad. intern, 1990; asst. prof. U. Wyo., Laramie, 1991-93, U. No. Colo., Greeley, 1993—; adj. instr. Ctrl. Wash. U., Ellensburg, 1987-91; cons. Ellensburg Sch. Dist., 1987, Yelm Sch. Dist., 1989, Hampton (Va.) City Schs., 1989, U. Va., Behavior Disorders Project, 1990, Auburn (Ala.) U., 1991, Niobrara Sch. Dist., 1991, 92, 93; in-svc. presenter; nat. and internat. conf. speaker. Contbr. articles to profl. jours. Mem. North Ctrl. Evaluation Team, Wyoming Indian High Sch., 1992. Grantee N.W. Spl. Edn., 1980, Vocat. Edn. Spl. Project, 1982, Title VI-B, 1982, Wash. Edn. Rsch. Assn., 1988, Wash. Mental Health, 1988, Region 10, Va. Commonwealth Div., 1989; Dean's fellow, Curry Sch. Edn., U. Va., 1990, U. Va. Deptl. fellow, 1989; recipient Outstanding scholarship Assn. Colls. and Schs. Edn. in State Univs. and Land Grant Colls., 1992. Mem. ASCD, Am. Ednl. Rsch. Assn., Coun. for Exceptional Children (Va. chpt. v.p. 1990), Coun. for Exceptional Children with Behavior Disorders (pres., Wyo. rep. 1992, 93), Coun. for Exceptional Children with Devel. Delays, Tchr. Educators of Children with Behavior Disorders (pres. 1992, v.p. 1993), Ea. Ednl. Rsch. Assn., Phi Delta Kappa. Office: 310 McKee Hall U of No Colo Greeley CO 80639

MURTHY, VEERARAGHAVAN KRISHNA, medical educator; b. Pudukottah, India, Feb. 27, 1934; came to U.S., 1964; naturalized citizen; s. Veeraraghavan and Lakshmi Krishnaswamy; m. Anjana Murthy, May 17, 1964 (div. 1977); children: Gayathri, Sakthi, Hari; m. Eileen Ann Hogan, May 26, 1990. BS, U. Madras, India, 1953; MS, U. Bombay, 1960, PhD, 1964. Rsch. assoc., rsch. fellow U. Fla., Gainesville, 1964-68; instr. Banting Inst., U. Toronto, Ont., Can., 1968-74; asst. prof. medicine, then assoc. prof. medicine U. Nebr. Med. Ctr., Omaha, 1974-86; assoc. adj. prof. medicine U. Calif.-San Francisco, Fresno, 1986—; rsch. investigator VA Med. Ctr./U. Calif.-San Francisco, Fresno, 1987—; prof. biology Calif. State U., Fresno, 1991—; cons. to diabetes svc. Valley Med. Ctr. Fresno, 1986—; speaker at nat. and internat. sci. confs. Author numerous rsch. publs. Fellow Royal Soc. Chemistry London; mem. Am. Diabetes Assn., Am. Physiol. Soc. Office: Diabetes Svc Valley Med Ctr 445 S Cedar Ave Fresno CA 93702-2907

MUSGRAVE, RICHARD ABEL, economics educator; b. Königstein, Germany, Dec. 14, 1910; came to U.S., 1933, naturalized, 1940; s. Curt Abel and Charlotte (Pruefer) M.; m. Peggy Brewer Richman, May 7, 1964. Diploma, U. Heidelberg, 1933; MA, Harvard U., 1936, PhD, 1937; LLD (hon.), Allegheny Coll., 1980; Doktor der Wirtschaftswissenschaften honoris causa, U. Heidelberg, Fed. Republic Germany; Doctoris Oeconomiae honoris causa, Cath. U., Milan, 1989; LLD honoris causa, U. Mich., 1991. Tutor, instr. econs. Harvard, 1936-41; research economist Bd. Govs. Fed. Res. System, Washington, 1941-47; lectr. econs. Swarthmore Coll., 1947-48; prof. econs. U. Mich., 1950-59; prof. polit. economy Johns Hopkins, 1959-62; prof. econs. and pub. affairs Princeton, 1962-65; H.H. Burbank prof. polit. econ. Harvard U., faculty arts and scis. and Law Sch., 1965-81, prof. emeritus, 1981—; adj. prof. U. Calif., Santa Cruz, 1980—; chief economist Internat. Bank Mission to Columbia, 1949; chief ECA Fiscal Mission to Germany, 1951; pres. Colombian Tax Reform Commn., 1968-69; dir. Bolivian Fiscal Reform Mission, 1976-77; at various times cons. bd. govs. Fed. Res. System, Treasury Dept., Council Econ. Advisers, Commn. on Money and Credit. Author: Theory of Public Finance, 1959, Fiscal Systems, 1969, Public Finance in Theory and Practice, 1973; editor Quar. Jour. Econs., 1970-75, Public Finance in a Democratic Soc., 1986; contbr. profl. jours. Recipient Frank E. Seidman award in polit. economy, 1981. Fellow Am. Acad. Arts and Scis.; disting. fellow Am. Econ. Assn. (exec. com. 1956-59, v.p. 1962); hon. mem. Nat. Tax Assn.; mem. NAS, Internat. Seminar in Pub. econs., Internat. Inst. Pub. Fin. (hon. pres. 1978). Home: 760 Western Dr Santa Cruz CA 95060-3033 Office: U Calif Social Sci I Santa Cruz CA 95064

MUSICK, WILLIAM C., bank systems manager; b. Orlando, Fla., Sept. 18, 1954. BS, USAF Acad., 1976; MBA, Stanford U., 1984. Engr. Ford Motor Co., Detroit, 1979-80; project mgr. Gen. Electric Co., San Jose, Calif., 1980-82; systems and programming mgr., analyst Wells Fargo Bank, San Francisco, 1984-88, v.p., mgr. systems integration, 1988-91; sr. operation and fin. analyst Calif. Pacific Med. Ctr., San Francisco, 1991-94, dir. bus. ops., 1994—. pres. San Francisco AIDS Found., 1985-87; participant Leadership San Francisco, 1986-87. Mem. Golden Gate Bus. Assn. (outstanding community service award 1986). Served to lt. USAF, 1976-78. Home: PO Box 868 131 Arbor Ln Moss Beach CA 94038 Office: Calif Pacific Med Ctr 3700 California St San Francisco CA 94118-1618

MUSIHIN, KONSTANTIN K., electrical engineer; b. Harbin, China, June 17, 1927; s. Konstantin N. and Alexandra A. (Lapitsky) M.; m. Natalia Krilova, Oct. 18, 1964; 1 child, Nicholas; came to U.S., 1967, naturalized, 1973; student YMCA Inst., 1942, North Manchurian U., 1945, Harbin Poly. Inst., 1948. Registered profl. engr., Calif., N.Y., Pa., Ill., Wash. Asst. prof. Harbin Poly. Inst., 1950-53; elec. engr. Moinho Santista, Sao Paulo, Brazil, 1955-60; constrn. project mgr. Caterpillar-Brazil, Santo Amaro, 1960-61; mech. engr. Matarazzo Industries, Sao Paulo, 1961-62; chief of works Vidrobras, St. Gobain, Brazil, 1962-64; project engr. Brown Boveri, Sao Paulo, 1965-67; sr. engr. Kaiser Engrs., Oakland, Calif., 1967-73; sr. engr. Bechtel Power Corp., San Francisco, 1973-75; supr. power and control San Francisco Bay Area Rapid Transit, Oakland, 1976-78; chief elec. engr. L.K. Comstock Engrng. Co., San Francisco, 1978-79; prin. engr. Morrison Knudsen Co., San Francisco, 1979-84; prin. engr. Brown and Caldwell, Cons. Engrs., Pleasant Hill, Calif., 1984-85; cons. engr. Pacific Gas and Electric Co., San Francisco, 1986-89; sr. engr. Bechtel Corp., San Francisco, 1989—. Mem. IEEE (sr.), Nat., Calif. socs. profl. engrs., Instituto de Engenharia de Sao Paulo. Mem. Christian Orthodox Ch. Clubs: Am.-Brazilian, Brit.-Am. Home: 320 Park View Ter Apt 207 Oakland CA 94610-4653

MUSSEHL, ROBERT CLARENCE, lawyer; b. Washington, May 1, 1936; s. Chester Carl and Clara Cecelia (Greenwalt) Mussehl; children: Debra Lee, David Lee; spouse: Misook Chung, Mar. 22, 1987. BA, Am. U., 1964, JD, 1966. Bar: Wash. 1967, U.S. Dist. Ct. (we. dist.) Wash. 1967, U.S. Ct. Appeals (9th cir.) 1968, U.S Supreme Ct. 1971. Sr. ptnr. Thom, Mussehl, Navoni, Hoff, Pierson & Ryder, Seattle, 1967-78, Neubauer & Mussehl, Seattle, 1978-80, Mussehl & Rosenberg, Seattle, 1980—; speaker law convs. and other profl. orgns.; moot ct. judge Nat. Appelate Advocacy Competition, San Francisco, 1987; panel mem. ABA Symposium on Compulsory Jurisdiction of World Ct., San Francisco, 1987; chmn. bd., chief exec. officer The Seattle Smashers profl. volleyball club, 1976-80. Contbr. numerous articles to legal publs. Mem. Wash. Vol. Lawyers for Arts, 1976-80; statewide chair Lawyers for Durning for Gov., 1976; mem. task force on the single adult and ch. Ch. Coun. Greater Seattle, 1976-78; bd. dirs. Wash. State Pub. Interest Law Ctr., 1976-81; founder, chmn., exec. com., bd. dirs. Wash. State Lawyers' Campaign For Hunger Relief, 1991—. Fellow Am. Bar Found., Am. Acad. Matrimonial Lawyers; mem. ABA (ho. of dels. 1979-91, spl. adv. com. on internat. activities 1989-91, chair marriage and family counseling and conciliation com. family law sect. 1981-83, mem. world order under law standing com. 1983-89, chair, 1986-89, chair ad hoc com. on the assembly 1986-89, mem. assembly resolutions com. 1979-91, mem. blue ribbon com. for world ct. 1987-88, mem. standing com. on dispute resolution, 1992-93; exec. coun. sect. dispute resolution 1993-95, others, Achievement award), Wash. State Bar Assn. (exec. com. family law sect. 1973-75, chmn. internat. law com. 1974-76, sec.-treas., exec. com. world peace through law sect. 1980—, chair 1981-82, mem. edit. bd. Family Law Deskbook 1987-89), Wash. State Trial Lawyers Assn., Seattle-King County Bar Assn. (family law sect. 1971-90, other coms. 1970—, chmn. young lawyers sect. 1971-72, sec. 1972-73, trustee), Am. Arbitration Assn. (panel arbitrators), World Assn. Lawyers of World Peace Through Law Ctr. (founding mem.), Heritage Club YMCA Greater Seattle (charter 1977—), UN Assn. U.S.A. (bd. dirs. Seattle chpt. 1989-91). Home: 2250 NW 58th St Apt 405 Seattle WA 98107-5402

MUSSELMAN, DARWIN B, artist, educator; b. Selma, Calif., Feb. 16, 1916; s. Laban C. and Lola Belle (Banks) M.; m. Ethel Laura Walker, Aug. 30, 1940; children: Ronald Lee, Carol Sue Musselman Woods, Steven Earl. BA, Fresno State Coll., 1938; MFA, Calif. Coll. Arts & Crafts, 1950; MA, U. Calif., Berkeley, 1952; PhD, Calif. State U., 1966. Artist, tchr., art dir. Thomas Advt. Agy., Fresno, Calif., 1945-46; tchr. Fresno State Coll., 1945-46, Fresno City Sch., 1946-48; dir. Sch. of Edn. Calif. Coll. Arts & Crafts, Oakland, 1948-53; freelance artist, illustrator, 1953-63; prof. Calif. State U., Fresno, 1953-78, ret., 1978. Exhibitor numerous oil and watercolors regional and statewide shows, 1935—, also one-man and invitational shows U.S., Europe and Mex. Mem. Am. Watercolor Soc., Nat. Watercolor Soc., Am. Soc. Portrait Artists (bd. dirs. 1988—). Republican. Home: 2550 Pecho Valley Rd Los Osos CA 93402-4104

MUSSELMAN, ROBERT CARL, plant physiologist; b. Sioux City, Iowa, June 12, 1942; s. Clarence A. and Verdna S. (Scott) M.; m. Andrea M. Foelske, June 15, 1969; children: Rebecca, Elizabeth, Sarah. BS, Iowa State U., 1964, MS, 1967; PhD, U. Wis., 1972. Rsch. specialist N.Y. State Agrl. Experiment Sta., Geneva, 1973-76; rsch. assoc. N.Y. State Agrl. Experiment Sta., 1976-80; rsch. plant physiologist Air Pollution Rsch. Ctr., U. Calif., Riverside, 1980-88; plant physiologist USDA Forest Svc., Rocky Montain Sta., Fort Collins, Colo., 1988—. With U.S. Army, 1967-69. Recipient George M. Darrow award Am. Soc. Horticulture Sci., 1983. Mem. AAAS, Air and Waste Mgmt. Assn. Lutheran. Home: 717 Scenic Dr Fort Collins CO 80526-5103 Office: USDA Forest Svc Rocky Mountain Forest & Range Expt Sta 240 W Prospect Rd Fort Collins CO 80526-2002

MUSSER, C. WALTON, physical scientist, consultant; b. Mt. Joy, Pa., Apr. 5, 1909; s. Ezra Nissley and Cora Grace (Weidman) M.; m. Edna Mae Hoak, June 23, 1937; children: Lila Darle (Mrs. Richard Hackman), Yvonne Duane (Mrs. Harold Graham), Stanley Walton (dec.). Student, Chgo. Tech. Coll., 1926-28, Leavitt Sch. Psychology, 1928-29, Wharton Sch. Fin. and Commerce, 1929-30, U. Pa., 1930-32, MIT, 1957. Chief engr. product devel. Indsl. Improvement Corp., Phila., 1936-41; rsch. adviser Dept. Def., 1941-56; pres., dir. rsch. Sci. Rsch., Inc., Glenside, Pa., 1945-52; pvt. practice cons., adviser in rsch. and devel., 1930—. Holder of over 162 U.S. Patents in 32 different classes and more than 60 patents in over 28 countries. Recipient Exceptional Civilian Service award for First Working Recoilless Weapon, Sec. of War, 1945; John C. Jones medal for Disting. Svc., Am. Ordnance Assn., 1951; Machine Design award ASME, 1968; named to Ordnance Hall of Fame, 1976. Mem. Acad. Applied Scis., Am. Def. Preparedness Assn. (hon. life), Nat. Soc. Profl. Engrs., Sigma Xi. Address: 1206 Lela Ln Santa Maria CA 93454-6642

MUSSMAN, WILLIAM EDWARD, lawyer, oil company executive; b. Mpls., Feb. 10, 1919; s. William Edward and Vera Marie (Chamberlain) M.; m. Janet Jonn Skittone, Dec. 19, 1948; children: William Edward III, Ann C. BS in Law, U. Minn., 1941, JD, 1946. Bar: Minn. 1946, Calif. 1950, U.S. Supreme Ct. 1960. Asst. prof. law U. Minn., 1946-49; vis. prof. U. Calif., Berkeley, 1949; assoc. firm Pillsbury, Madison & Sutro, San Francisco, 1949-56; partner Pillsbury, Madison & Sutro, 1956-74; v.p., legal, dir. Standard Oil Co. of Calif., San Francisco, 1974-84; ptnr. Carr & Mussman, San Francisco, 1984—. Served with USMCR, 1942-45. Decorated D.F.C. Fellow Southwestern Legal Found.; mem. ABA, Am. Arbitration Assn., Chevron Retirees Assn. (area v.p.). Office: 3 Embarcadero Ctr Ste 1060 San Francisco CA 94111-4056

MUSSMAN, WILLIAM EDWARD, III, lawyer; b. San Francisco, Jan. 31, 1951; s. William Edward and Janet Jonn (Skittone) M.; m. Carol Lynne Johnson, Jan. 9, 1988; children: Katherine Ann, Laura Lynne; BS cum laude, Stanford U., 1973; JD, U. Calif.-San Francisco, 1976. Bar: Calif. 1976, U.S. Dist. Ct. (no. dist.) Calif. 1976,, U.S. Dist. Ct. (cen. dist.) Calif. 1982, U.S. Supreme Ct., 1986, U.S. Ct. Appeals (9th cir.) 1987. Assoc. Lasky, Haas, Cohler & Munter, San Francisco, 1980-82, Pillsbury, Madison & Sutro, San Francisco, 1982-84, Carr & Mussman, San Francisco, 1984-91, ptnr., 1991—. Missionary Ch. Jesus Christ Latter Day Sts., Tokyo, 1977-78. Contbr. articles to profl. jours. Mem. Calif. State Bar Assn. (litigation sect., law practice mgmt. sect., mem. ADR subcom.), San Francisco Bar Assn., Stanford Alumni Assn. (life), Tau Beta Pi. Office: Carr & Mussman 3 Embarcadero Ctr Ste 1060 San Francisco CA 94111-4056

MUSTACCHI, PIERO, physician, educator; b. Cairo, Egypt, May 29, 1920; came to U.S., 1947; naturalized, 1962; s. Gino and Gilda (Rieti) M.; m. Dora Lisa Ancona, Sept. 26, 1948; children: Roberto, Michael. BS in Humanities, U. Florence, Italy, 1938; postgrad. in anatomy, Eleve Interne, U. Lausanne, Switzerland, 1938-39; MB, ChB, Fouad I U., Cairo, Egypt, 1944, grad. in Arabic lang. and lit., 1946; D Medicine and Surgery, U. Pisa, 1986; D Honoris Causa, U. Aix-Marseilles, France, 1988; hon. degree, U. Alexandria, Egypt, 1985. Lic. physician, Egypt, Italy; diplomate Am. Bd. Internal Medicine; qualified med. evaluator, Calif., 1994. House officer English Hosp., Ch. Missionary Soc., Cairo, Egypt, 1945-47; clin. affiliate U. Calif., San Francisco, 1947-48; intern Franklin Hosp., San Francisco, 1948-49; resident in pathology U. Calif., San Francisco, 1949-51; resident in medicine Meml. Ctr. Cancer and Allied Diseases, N.Y.C., 1951-53; rsch. epidemiologist Dept. HEW, Nat. Cancer Inst., Bethesda, Md., 1955-57; cons. allergy clinic U. Calif., San Francisco, 1957-70, clin. prof. medicine and preventive medicine, 1970-90, clin. prof. medicine and epidemiology, 1990—, head occupational epidemiology, 1975-90, head div. internat. health edn. dept. epidemiology and internat. health, 1985-90; med. cons., vis. prof. numerous edn. and profl. instsn., including U. Marseilles, 1981, 82, U. Pisa, Italy, 1983, U. Gabon, 1984, U. Siena, Italy, 1985, work clinic U. Calif., 1975-84, Ctr. for Rehab. and Occupational Health, U. Calif., San Francisco, 1984-93; qualified med. evaluator Divsn. Indsl. Accidents, State of Calif., 1990; cons. numerous worldwide govtl. agys. Contbr. chpts. to books, articles to profl. jours. Editorial bd. Medecine d'Afrique Noire, Ospedali d'Italia. Served with USN, USPHS, 1953-55. Decorated Order of Merit (Commander) (Italy), Ordre de la Legion d'Honneur (France), Medal of St. John of Jerusalem, Sovereign Order of Malta, Order of the Republic (Egypt); Scroll, Leonardo da Vinci Soc., San Francisco, 1965; award Internat. Inst. Oakland, 1964; Hon. Vice Consul. Italy, 1971-90. Fellow ACP, Am. Soc. Environ. and Occupational Health; mem. AAAS, Am. Assn. Cancer Rsch., Calif. Soc. Allergy and Immunology, Calif. Med. Assn., San Francisco Med. Soc., West Coast Allergy Soc. (founding), Mex. Congress on Hypertension (corr.), Internat. Assn. Med. Rsch. and Continuing Edn. (U.S. rep.), Villa Taverna Club, Acad. Italiana della Cucina. Democrat. Home: 3344 Laguna St San Francisco CA 94123-2208 Office: U Calif Parnassus Ave San Francisco CA 94143

MUSTAFA, MOHAMMAD GHULAM, biochemistry educator; b. Dhaka, Bangladesh, Mar. 1, 1940; came to U.S., 1963, naturalized, 1978; s. Mohammad and Quamerunnesa Yaseen; m. Sultana Begum Mustafa, Nov. 6, 1969; 1 child, George E. BS, Dhaka U., 1960, MS summa cum laude, 1962; MA, U. Calif., Berkeley, 1966; PhD, SUNY, Albany, 1969. Asst. research biochemist U. Calif., Davis, 1969-73, asst. adj. prof., 1973-75; adj. asst. prof. UCLA, 1975-78, assoc. prof. in residence, 1978-79, assoc. prof., 1979-84, prof. environ. and occupational health sci., 1984—. Co-editor: Biomedical Effects of Ozone, 1983; mem. editorial bd. Toxicology and Indsl. Health, Princeton, N.J., 1984—; contbr. articles to profl. jours. Recipient Research Career Devel. award NIH, 1976-81; grantee NIH, 1970—. Mem. Am. Chem. Soc., Am. Coll. Toxicology, Air Pollution Control Assn., AAAS, N.Y. Acad. Sci., Sigma Xi. Democrat. Muslim. Home: 10534 Louisiana Ave Los Angeles CA 90025-5918 Office: UCLA Sch Pub Health 405 Hilgard Ave Los Angeles CA 90024-1772

MUSZYNSKI, L. JANE, interior designer; b. Memphis, Dec. 4, 1950; d. George Logan and Laura (Wall) Sullivan; m. Jerry Muszynski, Aug. 23, 1975; children: Logan, Jaclyn. BA in Interior Design and Home Econs., Calif. State U., 1973. Profl. status Nat. Coun. Interior Design Qualification, 1986; cert. Calif. Coun. Interior Design, 1993. Graphic designer Stewart Woodard Arch., Irvine, Calif., 1973-74; interior designer Interior Space Design, Newport Beach, Calif., 1974-76; office mgr. purchasing Lockheed Marine Lab., Diablo Canyon, Calif., 1976-77; realtor assoc. Century 21 Real Estate, Los Osos, Calif., 1977-79, Sierra Madre, Calif., 1979-80; v.p. mktg., designer S.K. Young Assocs., Tustin, Calif., 1979-88; sales acct. exec. Entouch Bus. Interiors, Rancho Cucamonga, Calif., 1988-89; sr. interior designer Disneyland Design Studio, Anaheim, Calif., 1989—; mktg. exec., owner Staffease & Advance Concepts, Walnut, Calif., 1991—; realtor, sales assoc. Anthony Real Estate, Santa Maria, Calif., 1977—; instr. Mt. San Antonio Coll., Walnut, 1985, 87, Calif. Poly. U., Pomona, 1988-89, adv. bd. interior design, 1988-90; chmn. nominating com. Bus. Devel. Assn. Orange County, Irvine, 1988-89. Mem. host program Bear Mountain Ski Resort, Big Bear, Calif., 1993, 94; cookie chmn. Girl Scouts Am., Walnut, 1993. Mem. Am. Soc. Interior Designers, Network Exec. Women in Hospitality.

Office: Advance Concepts Employer Svcs 709 Brea Canyon Rd #11 Walnut CA 91789

MUTOMBO, DIKEMBE (DIKEMBE MUTOMBO MPOLONDO MUKAMBA JEAN JACQUE WAMUTOMBO), professional basketball player; b. Kinshasa, Zaire, June 25, 1966. Student, Georgetown U. Center Denver Nuggets, 1991—. Office: Denver Nuggets McNichols Sports Arena 1635 Clay St Denver CO 80204-1799*

MUTSCHLER, HERBERT FREDERICK, retired librarian; b. Eureka, S.D., Nov. 28, 1919; s. Frederick and Helena (Oster) M.; m. Lucille I. Gross, Aug. 18, 1945; 1 dau., Linda M. B.A., Jamestown Coll., 1947; M.A., Western Res. U., 1949, M.S., 1952. Tchr. history high sch. Lemmon, S.D., 1947-48; asst. librarian Royal Oak (Mich.) Libr., 1952-55; head librarian Hamtramck (Mich.) Libr., 1955-56; head public svcs. Wayne County Libr. System, Wayne, Mich., 1956-59; asst. county librarian Wayne County Libr. System, 1960-62; dir. King County Libr. System, Seattle, 1963-89; library bldg. cons. Wayne County Libr., 1956-62, Wash. State Libr., 1966—; cons. Salt Lake County Libr., Pierce County Libr., North Olympic Libr.; lectr. U. Wash. Sch. Librarianship, 1970-71; bldg. cons. Hoquiam (Wash.) Libr., Olympic (Wash.) Regional Libr., Camas (Wash.) Pub. Libr., N. Cen. (Wash.) Regional Libr., Spokane (Wash.) County Libr., Enumclaw (Wash.) Libr., Puyallup (Wash.) Pub. Libr., Kennewick (Wash.) Pub. Libr., Lopez Island (Wash.) Libr. Contbr. articles profl. jours. Served with AUS, 1941-45; to capt. 1950-52. Decorated Silver Star, Bronze Star with cluster, Purple Heart, Presdl. Unit Citation. Mem. ALA (councilor at large 1965-69, chpt. councilor 1971-75, pres. library adminstrv. div. 1974-75), Pacific N.W. Library Assn., Wash. Library Assn. (exec. bd. 1964-65, 69-71, pres. 1967-69). Republican. Lutheran. Club: City, Municipal League. Lodge: Kiwanis. Home: 5300 128th Ave SE Bellevue WA 98006-2952

MUTTART, SUSAN CHAMBLESS, corporate communications manager; b. Tallahassee, Aug. 3, 1957; d. Henry I. and Carrie L. (Anderson) Chambless; m. Daniel H. Muttart, Oct. 9, 1982. BS in Journalism, Fla. A&M U., 1979. Account exec. Manning, Selvage & Lee, Inc., N.Y.C., 1980-81, Lobsenz-Stevens, Inc., N.Y.C., 1982-83; dir. mktg. The Achieve Group divsn. Zenger-Miller, Inc., Mississauga, Ont., Can., 1985-86; mgr. pub. rels. Zenger-Miller, Inc., San Jose, Calif., 1986-90, mgr. publ. rels. & client comms., 1990-93, mgr. corp. comms., 1993—. Vol. mktg. cons. Bay Area Homeless Vets. Rehab. Program, Menlo Park, Calif., 1988-89. Mem. Pub. Rels. Soc. Am., No. Calif. Songwriters Assn., Gospel Music Assn. (assoc.), San Francisco Jr. C. of C. (v.p. adminstrn. 1987-88), N.Y. Jr. C. of C. (dir. publicity and spl. events 1981-82, Outstanding Publicity Support award 1981). Presbyterian.

MUZILA, THOMAS WALTER, marital arts and karate educator, consultant; b. Cleve., June 15, 1949; s. Paul and Stella (Sowa) M.; m. Susan Marie Caron, Sept. 21, 1986; children: Kasha, Kayden. BA in Asian rels., Calif. State U., 1977. Dir. Spl. Forces Investigators, Bellflower, Calif., 1975—; head instr. Martial Arts Security Co., Santa Ana, Calif., 1981—, Calif. State U., Fullerton, 1981-85, Shotokan Karate of Paramount, Paramount, Calif., 1984—; owner Bodyguard Elite, L.A., 1988—; owner and adv. Phenoix Prodns., L.A., 1986—; head instr. and owner Bodyvolving, L.A., 1980—; bd. dirs. Shotokan Karata Am., L.A., 1990; instr. self-defense, guns and knife defense, L.A. Police Dept., Long Beach Police Dept., Santa Ana Police Dept. and others; cons., adv. for films, TV and video tapes. Appeared in films including Above the Law, Hard to Kill, Under Siege; choreographer (film) The Power of One, Deadfall, Brilliant Disguise; appeared in numerous videos on self-defense; author: Optimum Training Systems, 1993; contbr. articles to profl. jours. Sgt. U.S. Army Green Berets, 1970-73. Named Nat. Man of Yr. Shotokan Karate Am., 1981, Man of Yr. West, 1976; numerous athletic world records in karate; named to U.S. Karate Team, 1983, 84. Home: 16922 Virginia Ave Bellflower CA 90706-5636 Office: U S Training Ctr 2024 N Broadway Ste 205 Santa Ana CA 92706-2623

MUZYKA-MCGUIRE, AMY, marketing professional, nutrition consultant; b. Chgo., Sept. 24, 1953; d. Basil Bohdan and Amelia (Rand) Muzyka; m. Patrick J. McGuire, June 3, 1977; children: Jonathan, Elizabeth. BS, Iowa State U., 1975, postgrad., 1978—; registered dietitian, St. Louis U., 1980. Cert. dietitian. Home economist Nat. Livestock and Meat Bd., Chgo., 1975-77; dietary cons. various hosps. and nursing homes, Iowa, 1978-79; supr. foodsvc. Am. Egg Bd., Park Ridge, Ill., 1980-83; assoc. dir., mgr. foodsvc. Cole & Weber Advt., Seattle, 1984-85; prin., owner Food and Nutrition Comms., Federal Way, Wash., 1986—. Co-author: Turkey Foodservice Manual, 1987; editor: (newsletter) Home Economists in Business, 1975-77, Dietitians in Business and Industry, 1982-85; Food Net on Internet, 1995—; contbr. articles to profl. jours. Active Federal Way Women's Network, 1986-87. Named Outstanding Dietitian of Yr. North Suburban Dietetic Assn., 1983. Mem. Am. Dietetic Assn., Internat. Foodsvc. Editorial Coun., Consulting Nutritionists, Vegetarian Nutrition, Home Economists in Bus. Roman Catholic. Home: 5340 SW 315th St Federal Way WA 98023-2034

MYBECK, RICHARD RAYMOND, lawyer; b. Chgo., Dec. 5, 1928; s. Walter Raymond and Genevieve Lucille (Carlsten) M.; m. Betty Jane Engle, Aug. 23, 1952; children: Walter R. II, Wendy Sue, Lucinda Jeanne, Amanda Jane (dec.), Candace Christine, Sara Melinda. BChE, Purdue U., 1950, BS in Engring. Law, 1953; JD, Ind. U., 1953. Bar: Ind. 1953, Wis. 1954, Ill. 1962, Ariz. 1973; registered U.S. patent atty., patent agt., Can. Patent trainee, atty. Allis Chalmers Mfg. Co., West Allis, Wis., 1953-57, patent atty., 1957-62; atty. Koehring Corp., Milw., 1957; patent atty. Armour and Co., Chgo., 1962-71; sr. patent atty. Greyhound Corp., Chgo., Phoenix, 1971-77; sr. counsel Armour Pharmaceutical Co., Phoenix, Scottsdale, Ariz., 1977-81; pvt. practice Scottsdale, 1981—; pres., bd. dirs. Farmakeia, Inc., Scottsdale, Hoosier Investment Co., Scottsdale. Councilman Town of Paradise Valley, Ariz., 1988-92, commr., chmn. planning and zoning commn., 1981-88, mem. chmn. bd. adjustment, 1974-81; lay speaker United Meth. Ch., 1954—. Named to Hall of Fame Oak Park (Ill.) Youth Baseball, 1987; recipient Degentesh award Forest Park (Ill.) VFW, 1969. Mem. ABA, Ariz. Bar Assn. (chmn. various sects.), Ill. Bar Assn., Wis. Bar Assn., Intellectual Property Assn. Chgo., Ariz. Patent Law Assn., Purdue Alumni Assn. (dir. region 15 1993—), Elks, Masons, Tau Kappa Epsilon, Sigma Delta Kappa. Methodist. Home: 4901 E Tomahawk Trl Paradise Vly AZ 85253-2030 Office: Mybeck Law Office 8010 E Morgan Trl Ste 10 Scottsdale AZ 85258-1234

MYER, JON HAROLD, engineering physicist; b. Heilbronn, Germany, Sept. 29, 1922; came to U.S., 1947; naturalized, 1953; s. Oscar Nathan and Greta Cecilie (Wolf) M.; m. Gerda R. Simson, Apr. 20, 1948; children: Gary D., Eric J., Karen B., Kenneth B. BEE, Hebrew Tech. Coll., Haifa, Israel, 1941. Instrument maker Anglo Iranian Oil Co., Abadan, Iran, 1942-44; instrument designer Hebrew Tech. Coll., 1944-46; engring. cons. Haifa, 1946-47; instrumentologist dept. chemistry U. So. Calif., L.A., 1947-53; with Hughes Aircraft Co., L.A., 1953-91; sr. scientist radar systems div. Hughes Aircraft Co., L.A., 1991-92; invention cons. Hughes Rsch. Labs., Malibu, Calif., 1991—; lectr. sci. and tech. in adminstrn. of justice Calif. Luth. Coll., Moorpark, 1979-81. Patentee in engring., physics, magnetics, optics. Pioneering team splty. Explorer program Orange Empire coun. Boy Scouts Am., 1961-66. Recipient Silver Beaver award Boy Scouts Am., 1965. Mem. IEEE, Am. Phys. Soc., Optical Soc. Am., Rsch. Soc. Am., Tau Beta Pi. Home: 22931 Gershwin Dr Woodland Hills CA 91364-3827

MYER, PETER LIVINGSTON, artist, educator; b. Dzone Park, N.Y., Sept. 19, 1934; s. Percy Livingstone and Martha Angeline (MacPherson) M.; m. Ila Marie Lytle, June 4, 1955; children: Sara Danae, Marc Damon, Seth Jamison, Paul Darius, Aaron Lytle, Amie Rachel. BA, Brigham Young U., 1956; MFA, U. Utah, 1959. Tchr. Cen. Jr. High Sch., Parsippany, N.J., 1956-57; asst. prof. art Carbon Jr. Coll., Price, Utah, 1959-62; assoc. prof., chmn. art dept. U. Nev., Las Vegas, 1962-72; gallery dir. Brigham Young U., Provo, Utah, 1972-78, prof. art, 1978—; dir. Paris Ctr. Brigham Young U. semester abroad, 1978; assoc. dir. London Ctr. study abroad, 1990. One-man shows include Springville (Utah) Mus. Art 1979, Salt Lake Art Ctr., 1980 (purchase prize for self portrait sculpture 1975), Kimball Art Ctr., Park City, Utah, 1985, Brigham Young U., 1994; exhbns. include Nat. Art Roundup, 1966 (frist prize 1966, best in show award 1965). Chmn. Allied Arts Council, Las Vegas, 1964-65; regional dir. Experiments in Art and Tech., Nev., 1968-72; bd. dirs. Las Vegas Symphony, 1971-72; judge Sterling Scholar awards, Utah, 1973-86. Served to sgt. U.S. Army, 1957-58. Republican. Mormon. Home: 1425 Oak Cliff Dr Provo UT 84604-3706

MYERS, AL, realtor, property manager, mayor; b. Oakland, Calif., Aug. 6, 1922; s. Alvi A. and Emma (Thoren) M.; student Oreg. Inst. Tech., 1940-41; m. Viola Doreen Wennermark, Sept. 11, 1954; children: Susan Faye, Pamela Ann, Jason Allen. Supt.'s asst. Aluminum Co. Am., Troutdale, Oreg., 1942-44; asst. mgr. Western Auto Supply Co., Portland, 1944-46; owner, operator Al Myers Auto & Electric, Gresham, Oreg., 1946-53; realtor, broker Al Myers Property Mgmt., 1954—; v.p., sec. Oreg. Country, Inc.; faculty Mt. Hood Community Coll. Chmn., Indsl. and Econ. Devel. Com. for Multonomah County, Oreg. Real Estate Ednl. Program, 1961. Mayor Gresham, Oreg., 1972-83. Pres. East Multonomah County Dem. Forum, 1965—, mem. exec. com., 1958—. With AUS, 1943. Mem. Portland Realty Bd., Nat. Assn. Real Estate Bds., Christian Bus. Men's Com. Internat., Internat. Platform Assn., Rho Epsilon Kappa (pres. Oreg.). Mem. Evang. Ch. (trustee, treas.). Home: 935 NW Norman Ave Gresham OR 97030-6966 Office: 995 NE Cleveland Ave Gresham OR 97030-5707

MYERS, CHRISTOPHER CHARLES, interior designer, sales associate; b. Watsonville, Calif., Sept. 16, 1958; s. Charles Benjamin Jr. and Nancy Ann (Mathews) M. BFA in Interior Design, Calif. State U., Long Beach, 1987. Interior design asst. Sheridan-Zimmerman MacGillivray, West Hollywood, Calif., 1987-88; jur. interior designer Murphy-Roth Interior Design, Redondo Beach, Calif., 1988-90; design sales assoc. Stylus Furniture, Huntington Beach, Calif., 1990-92; sales assoc. Robinsons-May, Beverly Hills, Calif., 1992—; design asst. Whittier (Calif.) Design Showcase, 1987, Sandpipers Design Showcase, Palos Verdes Estates, Calif., 1987, Little Co. of Mary Hosp. Design Showcase, Palos Verdes Estates, 1989. Mem. Am. Soc. Interior Designers (student mem. 1987). Democrat. Home: 733 N Kings Rd Apt 201 Los Angeles CA 90069-5912

MYERS, DOUGLAS GEORGE, zoological society administrator; b. L.A., Aug. 30, 1949; s. George Walter and Daydeen (Schroeder) M.; m. Barbara Firestone Myers, Nov. 30, 1980; children: Amy, Andrew. BA, Christopher Newport Coll., 1981. Tour and show supr. Annheuser-Busch (Bird Sanctuary), Van Nuys, Calif., 1970-74, mgr. zool. ops., 1974-75, asst. mgr. ops., 1975-77, mgr. ops., 1977-78; gen. services mgr. Annheuser-Busch (Old Country), Williamsburg, Va., 1978-80, park ops. dir., 1980-81; gen. mgr. wild animal park Zool. Soc. San Diego, 1981-83, dep. dir. ops., 1983-85, exec. dir., 1985—; cons. in field. Bd. dirs. San Diego Conv. and Visitors Bur.; mem. adv. com. of pres.' assn. Am. Mgmt. Assn. Fellow Am. Assn. Zool. Parks and Aquariums (profl.), Internat. Union Dirs. Zool. Gardens; mem. Internat. Assn. Amusement Parks and Attractions, Calif. Assn. Zoos and Aquariums, Mus. Trustee Assn. Lodge: Rotary. Office: San Diego Zoo PO Box 551 San Diego CA 92112-0551

MYERS, ELIZABETH ROUSE, management consultant; b. Grand Island, Nebr., July 14, 1923; d. William Wayne Rouse and Lulu Zella Trout; m. Richard Roland Myers, June 25, 1943; children: Diane Marie Berndt, Richard Wayne. Student, Kearny State Tchrs. Coll., Nebr., 1942-43. Draftsman Borg-Warner Corp., Kalamazooo, 1944; acct. CFI Steel Corp., Pueblo, Colo., 1950-52; sec., treas. Standard Paint, Yakima, Wash., 1954-86; pres. Pied Piper Childrens Books, Yakima, Wash., 1985—; federal oil leases, 1980—; docent Yakima Valley Mus. & Gilbert House, Wash. 1984—. Editor: H.S. Paper. Tchr., supt. First Presbyn. Ch., Yakima, Wash., 1958-70; mem. bd. Parent Tchrs.; bd. dirs., teen chmn. YWCA; pres. Gilbert House. Mem. Yakima Valley Mus. (awarded Doll 1985, Show 1986, vol. of yr. 1994). Republican. Presbyterian. Home: 106 N 25th Ave Yakima WA 98902-2807

MYERS, ELMER, psychiatric social worker; b. Blackwell, Ark., Nov. 12, 1926; s. Chester Elmer Myers and Irene (Davenport) Lewis; widowed; children: Elmer Jr., Keith, Kevin. BA, U. Kans., 1951, MA, 1962; student, U. Calif., Santa Barbara, 1977-78. Psychiat. social worker Hastings (Nebr.) State Hosp., 1960-62; psychiat. social worker State of Calif., Sacramento, 1962-75, supr. psychiat. social worker, 1975-80; supr. psychiat. social worker Alta Calif. Regional Ctr., Sacramento, 1980-85; exec. dir. Tri-County Family Services, Yuba City, Calif., 1966-69; cons. to 3 convalescent Hosps., Marysville, Calif., 1969-71; lectr. Yuba Coll., Marysville, 1971-76; assoc. prof. Calif. State U., Chico, 1972-73; cons. in field, Marysville, 1985—. Juror Yuba County Grand Jury, Marysville, 1965, 87-88; sec. Y's Men's Club, Yuba City, 1964-65; chmn. Tri-County Home Health Agy., Yuba City, 1974-76; vice-chmn. Gateway Projects, Inc., Yuba City, 1974-75; bd. dirs. Christian Assistance Network, 1993, Habitat for Humanity, 1993, Yuba County Truancy Bd., Marysville, 1964-67, Golden Empire Health Sys. Agy., Sacramento, 1972-76, Youth Svcs. Bur., Yuba City, 1967, Bi-County Mental Retardation Planning Bd., Yuba City, 1972, Yuba County Juvenile Justice Commn., Marysville, 1982-90, Am. Cancer Soc., Marysville, 1985-92, Yuba County Rep. Ctrl. Com., 1983-90, Salvation Army, 1990, facilitator care project, 1992; asst. dir. Marysville Adult Activity Ctr., 1990; active Yuba-Sutter United Way, 1971-73, 91—, Tri-County Ethnic Forum, sec. 1991—; steering com. mem. Marysville Sr. Ctr. Assn., 1992; mem. Yuba County Cmty. Svcs. Commn., 1994; v.p. Yuba-Sutter Gleaners, 1995—. Recipient Cert. Spl. Recognition Calif. Rehab. Planning Project, 1969, Cert. Spl. Recognition State of Calif., 1967; Cert. Spl. Recognition Alta Calif. Regional Ctrs., 1985. Mem. Nat. Assn. Social Workers (cert.), Kern County Mental Health Assn. (chmn. 1978-79). Lodge: Rotary (bd. dirs. Marysville club 1975-76). Home and Office: 3920 State Highway 20 Marysville CA 95901-9003

MYERS, GREGORY EDWIN, aerospace engineer; b. Harrisburg, Pa., Jan. 1, 1960; s. Bernard Eugene and Joyce (Calhoun) M.; m. Susan Ann Hayslett, Dec. 30, 1983; children: Kimberly, Benjamin. BS in Aerospace Engring., U. Mich., 1981; MS in Aerospace Engring., Air Force Inst. Tech., 1982. Aerospace engr. Sperry Comml. Flight Systems group Honeywell, Inc., Phoenix, 1987-90; sr. project engr. satellite systems ops. Honeywell, Inc., Glendale, Ariz., 1990-92; sr. project engr. air transport systems Honeywell, Inc., Phoenix, 1992-93, prin. engr., 1993—; presenter in field. Contbr. articles to profl. jours. Mem. Aviation Week Rsch. Adv. Panel, 1990-91. Recipient Certs. of Recognition and Appreciation Lompoc Valley Festival Assn., Inc., 1983, Arnold Air Soc. (comdr. 1979), Cert. of Appreciation Instrument Soc. Am., 1991. Mem. AIAA (sr.). Lutheran. Office: Honeywell Air Transport Systems Divsn 21111 N 19th Ave Phoenix AZ 85027-2708

MYERS, HELEN DEE, small business owner; b. Denver. Student in med. tech., U. Colo., 1953-55. Cert. meeting profl. Owner Preferred Sales, Inc., Las Vegas, Nev., 1962-81, Creative Convs., Las Vegas, Nev., 1978—; small bus. advocate Ctr. for Bus. Advocacy & Svcs. State of Nev., 1995—; dir. Office of Small Bus. State of Nev., 1989-95. Author, publisher: (book) The Business of Seminars, 1982. Coordinator Mary Gojack for Congress, Nev., 1982, Elect Bob Miller, Las Vegas, 1986; chmn. Women Bus. Owners Polit. Action Com., 1987-88; chmn. Gov.'s Small Bus. Coun., 1989—. Mem. Nat. Assn. Women Bus. Owners (sec. 1985-86, bd. dirs. 1983-89), Nat. Assn. of Women Bus. Advocates, Am. Arbitration Assn.. Democrat. Home and Office: 2304 Windjammer Way Las Vegas NV 89107-2361

MYERS, HOMER SAMUEL, technology company executive; b. Salina, Kans., Feb. 20, 1916; s. Clarence Benton and Mary Maude (Booth) M.; m. Marie Alma Beauchamp, Dec. 23, 1939 (div. Dec. 1965); children: Booth Richard, Mary Elizabeth, Gertrude Jane, Homer Samuel Jr. Student, Kans. Wesleyan U., 1934-35; BS, Kans. State U., 1942, MS, 1942. Staff mem. radiation lab. MIT, Cambridge, Mass., 1943-46; group leader Engring. Rsch. Inst. U. Mich., Ann Arbor, 1946-48; pres. Radioactive Products, Inc., Detroit, 1948-54, Solvex Corp., Louisville, 1964-78, Fibrex Corp., Humacao, P.R., 1967-78, Easco, Inc., Mt. Juliet, Tenn., 1983-86, Advanced Cooling Tech., Inc., Lexington, Ky., 1988—; exec. v.p. Tracerlab, Inc., Boston, 1954-62; v.p. Spindletop Rsch. Inst., Lexington, 1962-64; cons. U.S. AEC, Washington, 1959-63, mem. isotope and radiation devel. adv. com., 1959-63, mem. labor-mgmt. adv. com., 1961-63. Patentee in field. Home: 2100 Skycrest Dr Apt 9 Walnut Creek CA 94595-1827

MYERS, JAMES ROBERT, plant geneticist; b. Columbus, Ind., June 26, 1954; s. Richard Frey and Esther Lee (Joyner) M.; m. Diana Lee, June 20, 1979; children: Liatris Anne, Rosa Lee. MS, U. Wis., 1981, PhD, 1984. Postdoctoral fellow Dept. Agronomy, U. Ky., Lexington, 1984-85, rsch. specialist, 1985-87; asst. prof. Dept. Plant Sci., U. Idaho, Kimberly, 1987-93, assoc. prof., 1993—. Contbr. articles to profl. jours. mem. AAAS, Am. Soc. Agronomy, Crop Sci. Soc. Am., Am. Soc. Hort. Sci., Idaho Acad. Sci., Sigma Xi (pres. 1991), Gamma Sigma Delta. Office: Rsch Ext Ctr U Idaho 3793 N 3600 E Kimberly ID 83341-5076

MYERS, JEROME BARTHOLOMEW, physician, pathologist; b. Mason City, Iowa, Jan. 30, 1955; s. Roy William and Dorothy Faye (Long) M.; m. Lisa M. Amato, May 3, 1987; 1 child, Olivia Frances. BS, U.S. Mil. Acad., 1977; PhD in Pathology, Boston U., 1990, MD, 1990. Diplomate Nat. Bd. Med. Examiners; lic. physician, Pa. Commd. 2d lt. U.S.Army, 1977, advanced through grades to maj., 1990; test officer U.S. Army Tropic Test Ctr., Ft. Clayton, Republic of Panama, 1980-82; action officer U.S. Army Armor Sch., Ft. Knox, Ky., 1983; resident in pathology Tripler Army Med. Ctr., Honolulu, 1990—. Contbr. articles to profl. jours. Decorated Meritorious Svc. medal; Charles E. Culpeper fellow, 1986, Boston U. Sch. Medicine fellow, 1987. Mem. AMA, Am. Soc. Clin. Pathologists, Coll. Am. Pathologists, Mass. Med. Soc., Hawaii Soc. Pathologists. Roman Catholic. Office: Dept Anatomic Pathology Tripler Army Med Ctr Tripler Army Medical Center HI 96859

MYERS, JOSEPH JOHN, graphic designer; b. Indpls.; s. Robert Louis and Rose Mary (Peifer) M.; m. Paula Lynn Moreschi, Nov. 11, 1984. BA, U. Wash., 1978. Graphic designer Joe Myers Design, Seattle, Wash., 1978—. Office: Joe Myers Design 1819 17th Ave Ste 901 Seattle WA 98122-2762

MYERS, KATHERINE DONNA, writer, publisher; b. L.A., Nov. 10, 1925; d. John Allen Myers and Eulah Caldwell (Myers) Harris; m. Thomas Miller, Feb. 2, 1944 (div. 1963); children: Kathleen JoAnn Content, David Thomas. Teaching credential in bus. edn., U. So. Calif., L.A., 1975; postgrad., Loyola U., Paris, 1980. Cert. pub. adminstr. Dep. field assessor L.A. County Tax Assessor, L.A., 1944-60; sec. L.A. Unified Sch. Dist., 1960-70; br. sec. bank Crocker Nat. Bank, L.A., 1970-78; instr. legal sec. Southland Coll., L.A., 1975-78; exec. sec. ABC, L.A., 1978-89; v.p. spl. projects Glendale (Calif.) TV Studios, 1990-92; writer, publisher Eagles Wings Publishing Co., L.A., 1992—; owner, pres. Success Secretarial Seminar, L.A., 1980-84; pub., author Eagle's Wings Pub. Co., L.A., 1992—; wedding cons., counselor Crenshaw United Meth. Ch., L.A., 1993—. Author, pub.: Wedding Bells, A New Peal, 1994; (instrnl. book) Productivity Guide, Bilingual Special Education, 1980; (biography) The Eagle Flies on Friday, 1988, (hist. newsletter) Eagle Reader's Newsletter, 1993; author: (tech. booklet) Ronnie Knows about Sickle Cell, 1973 (Founder's award 1973). Troop leader, adminstr. Girl Scouts Am., L.A., 1956; chmn. sickle cell com. MLK Hosp. Guild, L.A., 1974; den mother Boy Scouts Am., 1960; lifetime mem. PTA, L.A., 1960. Recipient THANKS badge Girl Scouts Am., 1959, Founder's award MLK Jr. Hosp. Guild, 1974. Mem. Photo Friends Ctrl. Libr., Wilshire C. of C. (bd. dirs. 1980). Democrat. United Methodist. Home: # 122 4215 W Slauson Ave Apt 122 Los Angeles CA 90043-2831 Office: Eagles Wings Publishing Co PO Box 361263 5350 Wilshire Blvd Los Angeles CA 90036

MYERS, MARK D., petroleum geologist, researcher; b. Monroe, Wis., Apr. 24, 1955; s. Rhea Bowman and Ardelle Ione (Van Matre) M.; m. Alice Reding Myers, April 30, 1983; children: Justine Alice, Nathan Mark. BS in Geology and Geophysics with honors, U. Wis., 1977, MS in Geology, 1981; PhD in Geology, U. Alaska, 1994. Petroleum geologist ARCO Oil & Gas, Lafayette, La., 1981-83, ARCO Alaska, Inc., Anchorage, 1983-87, divsn. of oil & gas, State of Alaska, Anchorage, 1988—. Contbr. articles to scientific jours. lt. USAF, 1979-80. Mem. Am. Assn. Petroleum Geologists (del. 1992—), Alaska Geological Soc. (v.p 1993, mem. bd. dirs. 1993—), Soc. Sedimentary Geology, Eagle River Presbyn. Ch. (mem. bd. trustees 1993—). Office: State of Alaska-divsn oil & gas 3601 C St 3601 C St Ste 1380 Anchorage AK 99503-5948

MYERS, R. DAVID, library director, dean; b. Hutchinson, Kans., Mar. 27, 1949; s. William Raymond and Elizabeth (Haas) M.; m. Barbara Jean Burridge, Sept. 15, 1973; 1 child, John David. BA, U. No. Colo., 1972, MA, 1974; ABD, U. Mich., 1976; MA, U. Denver, 1979. Manuscript curator Western History Collection, Denver, 1976-79; rsch. assoc. Colo. Legis. Coun., Denver, 1979-81; reference specialist Libr. of Congress, Washington, 1981-84, reference supr., 1984-88; libr. dir. State Hist. Soc. of Wis., Madison, 1988-94; assoc. dean univ. libr. N.Mex. State U., Las Cruces, 1994—; editor Am. history Macmillan Pub., N.Y.C., 1991-94; cons. history of medicine dept. U. Wis., Madison, 1993-94. Author bibliographies for Libr. of Congress, 1987, 88. Mem. ALA, Am. Hist. Assn., Orgn. Am. Historians, Wis. Libr. Assn. Office: N Mex State U Dept 3475 PO Box 3006 Las Cruces NM 88003-3006

MYERS, RHONDA JAN, allergist; b. North Hollywood, Calif., Feb. 15, 1954; d. Seymour Leslie and Charlotte Sara (Fradin) M.; m. Klaus Peter Rosebrock, May 14, 1986; children: Laina Emily Myers, Daniel Thomas Myers. BSc, UCLA, 1975; PhD, U. Edinburgh, Scotland, 1980; MD, Albany Med. Coll., 1984. Postdoctoral fellow U. Conn., Farmington, 1979-80, U. Calif., Irvine, 1989-91; pvt. practice Irvine, 1991—. Fellow ACP, Am. Coll. Allergy, Asthma and Immunology; mem. Am. Acad. Allergy and Immunology, Sigma Xi. Office: 4902 Irvine Center Dr Ste 108 Irvine CA 92714-3334

MYERS, ROLLAND GRAHAM, investment counselor; b. St. Louis, Aug. 30, 1945; s. Rolland Everett and Lurilien (Graham) M. Diploma, St. Louis Country Day Sch., 1963; AB cum laude in History and Lit., Harvard U., 1966; postgrad. Faculties of Social Scis. and Law, U. Edinburgh, Scotland, 1966-67; postgrad. Fondation Nationale des Sciences Politiques and Faculte de Lettres et des Sciences Humaines, U. Paris, 1967-68. Trainee global credit dept. The Chase Manhattan Bank, N.A., N.Y.C., 1968-69, mem. 32nd spl. devel. program, 1969, strategic planner internat. dept., 1969-70, securities analyst, mktg. rep., fiduciary investment dept., 1970; assoc. Smith, Barney & Co., Inc., N.Y.C., 1971, account exec. N.Y. sales dept., 1971-72, instl. account exec. N.Y. internat. sales dept., 1972-74, 2nd v.p., stockholder, 1975-76; v.p., stockholder Smith Barney, Harris Upham & Co., Inc. (subs. SBHU Holdings, Inc.), N.Y.C., 1976-78; prin. W.H. Graham & Sons, family investment office, 1977-82, investment counsel, 1982—; ltd. ptnr. Croke Patterson Campbell, Ltd., Denver, 1975—; joint founder, gen. ptnr. Mansion Disbursements, Denver, 1979—; pres., chmn. exec. com., bd. dirs. Fifty-Five Residents Corp., N.Y.C., 1980-84; bd. dirs. Fifty-Six Danbury Rd. Assn., Inc., New Milford, Conn. Trustee, mem. corp. Bishop Rhinelander Found. (Episcopal Chaplaincy at Harvard and Radcliffe Colls.), Cambridge, 1973-75; v.p., treas., bd. dirs. The Whitehill Graham Found., St. Louis, 1976—; bd. dirs. fin. com., bylaws com., mem. corp. Eliot Pratt Edn. Ctr., Inc., The Pratt Ctr.: Your Connection with the Natural World, New Milford, 1987-94; bd. dirs., mem. corp. Kent (Conn.) Land Trust, Inc., 1989—, treas., 1989-93; project financier Restoration of 1851 Samuel Curtiss Hosford House, Nat. Register Historic Dist., Falls Village, Conn., 1984-86; commr. Housatonic River Commn., Warren, Conn., 1985-93, vice chmn., 1986-87, chmn., 1988-92; commr., vice chmn. Conservation, Inland Wetlands and Watercourses Commn., Kent, 1988-92; mem. schs. and scholarships com., Office of Admissions and Fin. Aid, Harvard and Radcliffe Colls., 1991—. Mem. Cum Laude Soc., Mary Inst. and St. Louis Country Day Sch. Alumni Assn., Harvard Alumni Assn., Capitol Hill Club (Washington), Harvard Club (N.Y.C.), Hasty Pudding-Inst. of 1770 (Cambridge), Wyoming Heritage Found. Republican. Episcopalian. Office: W H Graham & Sons Investment Counsel 1818 Evans Ave Ste 207 Cheyenne WY 82001-4664

MYERS, WILLIAM LORING, computer scientist, software engineer; b. Missoula, Mont., Aug. 15, 1957; s. William Mackie and Vera Marie (Tozzer) M.; m. Karen Marie Schneider, June 28, 1992. BA in Math. and French, Dartmouth Coll., 1980; MA in Math., U. Wash., 1982; postgrad., U. Colo., 1992—. Math. instr. U. Mont., Missoula, 1983; sys. analyst SRI Internat., Menlo Park, Calif., 1983-84; software engr. Coop. Inst. for Rsch. in Environ. Scis., Boulder, Colo., 1985-86; pvt. practice cons. Sydney, Australia, 1986-87; software engr. Nat. Ctr. for Atmospheric Rsch., Boulder, 1987—. Inventor in field. Mem. Assn. for Computing Machinery (spl. interest group on computer graphics). Office: Nat Ctr Atmospheric Rsch 3450 Mitchell Ln Boulder CO 80301

MYERSON, ALAN, director, film and television writer; b. Cleve., Aug. 8, 1936; s. Seymour A. and Vivien I. (Caplin) M.; m. Irene Ryan, June 2, 1962; 1 son, Lincoln; m. Leigh French, Apr. 15, 1977; children—Sierra Jasmine French, Darcy Anna French-Myerson. Student, Pepperdine Coll., 1956-57, UCLA, 1957. mem. acting faculty U. Calif., Berkeley, 1966, San Francisco State U., 1967. Dir. N.Y. and Off Broadway Prodns., 1958-64, including This Music Crept By Me Upon the Waters, The Committee; dir.: Second City, N.Y.C. and Chgo., 1961, 62; founder, producer, dir. The Committee, San Francisco, L.A. and N.Y., 1963-74; dir.: (films) Steelyard Blues, 1972, Private Lessons, 1981, Police Academy 5, 1988; numerous TV shows, 1975—, including Laverne and Shirley, Rhoda, Bob Newhart Show, Welcome Back, Kotter, Fame, Crime Story, Dynasty, Miami Vice, Hunter, Sisters, Picket Fences, The Larry Sanders Show, Frazier, Friends; TV films The Love Boat, 1976, Hi, Honey, I'm Dead, 1991, Bad Attitudes, 1991; writer It's Showtime. Active in civil rights, anti-war, anti-nuclear power movements, 1957—. Mem. Dirs. Guild Am., Writers Guild Am. West.

MYERSON, RAYMOND KING, investment counseling company executive; b. Chgo., Oct. 21, 1917; s. Harry J. and Minnie (King) M.; m. Natalie Salter, Feb. 20, 1943; children: Bette Kay, Toby Salter. BA, U. Chgo., 1940. Gen. sales mgr. Helene Curtis Industries Inc., Chgo., 1946-60; v.p., dir. mktg. Solo Cup Co., Chgo., 1961-62; v.p. internat. div. Max Factor & Co., Hollywood, Calif., 1963-69; pres., chief exec. officer Myerson Van Den Berg & Co., Santa Barbara, Calif., 1969—. Trustee, treas. Santa Barbara Mus. Natural History, 1975—; bd. dirs., treas. Rec. for Blind, Santa Barbara, 1975-90, U. Calif.-Santa Barbara affiliates, 1990—. treas., active various local polit. campaigns. Lt. USNR, 1942-45. Republican. Office: 3336 Campanil Dr Santa Barbara CA 93109-1017

MYHREN, TRYGVE EDWARD, communications company executive; b. Palmerton, Pa., Jan. 3, 1937; s. Arne Johannes and Anita (Blatz) M.; m. Carol Jane Enman, Aug. 8, 1964; children: Erik, Kirsten, Tor; m. 2d Victoria Hamilton, Nov. 14, 1981; 1 stepchild, Paige. BA in Philosophy and Polit. Sci., Dartmouth Coll., 1958, MBA, 1959. Sales mgr., unit mgr. Procter and Gamble, Cin., 1963-65; sr. cons. Glendinning Cos., Westport, Conn., 1965-69; pres. Auberge Vintners, 1970-73; exec. v.p. Mktg. Continental, Westport, 1969-73; v.p., gen. mgr. CRM, Inc., Del Mar, Calif., 1973-75; v.p. mktg. Am. TV and Communications Corp., Englewood, Colo., 1975-78, sr. v.p. mktg. and programming, 1978-79, exec. v.p., 1980, pres., 1981, chmn. bd., chief exec. officer, 1981-88; v.p. then exec. v.p. Time Inc., N.Y.C., 1981-88; treas., vice chmn. then chmn. bd. dirs., mem. exec. com. Nat. Cable TV Assn., Washington, 1982-91; mem. adv. com. on HDTV, FCC, 1987-89; bd. dirs. Advanced Mktg. System, Inc., LaJolla, Citizens Bank Corp., Providence; pres. Myhren Media, 1989—, Greenwood Cable Mgmt., 1989-91, Providence Jour. Co., 1990—; pres. CEO King Broadcast Co., 1991—. Vice chmn. Pub. Edn. Coalition; mem. Colo. Forum, 1984-91, chmn. higher edn. com., 1986; bd. dirs., founder Colo. Bus. Com. for the Arts, 1985-91; mem. exec. coun. Found. for Commemoration U.S. Constn., 1987-90; mem. Nat. GED Task Force, 1987-90, Colo. Baseball Commn., 1989-91, Colo. Film Comm., 1989-91; trustee Nat. Jewish Hosp., 1989—, R.I. Hosp., 1991-95, Lifespan Health Sys., 1994—; chmn. Looc 1995 NCAA Hockey Championship. Lt. (j.g.) USNR, 1959-63. Recipient Disting. Leader award Nat. Cable TV Assn., 1988. Mem. Cable TV Adminstrn. and Mktg. Soc. (pres. 1978-79, Grand Tam award 1985, One of a Kind award 1994), Cable Adv. Bur. (founder 1978), Chrons and Colitis Found. Am. (trustee Rocky Mountain chpt.). Episcopalian.

MYLAR, WILLIAM See **ADELMAN, WILLIAM JAMES**

MYLES, WINNFORT JOSEPH, project engineer, real estate broker; b. Gonzales, La., Feb. 6, 1960; s. Victoria Ann M.; m. Deborah F. (Meeks) Myles, May 31, 1982; children: Wallisa Shipp, Antwan Shipp, LaResse Shipp. BS in Physics, So. U. A&M, Baton Rouge, 1981; Real Estate Broker's Lic., Priminer Schs., Culver City, Calif., 1989. Component engr. Hughes Aircraft Co., L.A., 1981-87, supr., 1987-88, project engr., 1988—; real estate agt. Century 21 Cal-West Realty, Carson, Calif., 1989-91; real estate broker Myles Realty 2001, Carson, Calif., 1991—. Sch. coord. Youth Motivation Task Force (YMTF), L.A., 1981— (Radar Sys. Vol. award 1994); mem. Hughes Hiking Club, L.A., 1988—. Recipient Samaritan award Pac-Tel Cellular, 1193. Fellow Inst. for Advancement of Engring.; mem. IEEE (sr.), Calif. Assocs. of Realtors (broker). Home: 1847 E Abbottson St Carson CA 90746-2901 Office: Hughes Aircraft Co 2000 E Imperial Hwy El Segundo CA 90245-3571

MYLNECHUK, LARRY HERBERT, financial executive; b. Littlefork, Minn., Mar. 9, 1948; s. William and Marjorie (Raco) M.; m. Sandy L. Henderson, Mar. 14, 1970; children: Kendra Elizabeth, Scott William. BA, Lewis & Clark Coll., Portland, 1970; JD, Lewis & Clark Coll., 1974. Legal specialist Oreg. Dept. Edn., Salem, 1976-82; sr. v.p., dir. Morley Capital Mgmt. Inc., Portland, 1982-89; founder, pres. Integra Assocs., Inc., Lake Oswego, Oreg., 1989—; exec. dir. The GIC Assn., Inc., Lake Oswego, 1990—; cons. Hueler Analytics, Inc., Mpls., 1989—; conf. chmn. GIC Nat. Forum Conf., Washington, 1993, 94. Contbr. articles to profl. jours. Mem. Portland Com. on Fgn. Rels., 1976—, bd. dirs., 1993-95; mem. Gov.'s Commn. on Adminstrv. Hearings, State of Oreg., 1988-89; trustee St. Francis of Assisi Endowment Fund, 1993; founder Woodstock Neighborhood Assn., 1975; mem. Multnomah County Charter Rev. Commn., 1978; mem. Tualatin (Oreg.) City Coun., 1980-84. NEH fellow, 1979; Edn. Policy Leadership Program fellow, 1980-81. Mem. Western Pension Conf., Assn. Soc. Execs., World Affairs Coun. Oreg., Citizen Amb. Program to Western Europe, SAR (v.p. Lewis and Clark chpt.), Gen. Soc. The War of 1812, Soc. Colonial Wars, Sons and Daus. of Pilgrims. Democrat. Episcopalian. Office: GIC Stable Value Assn Inc PO Box 1594 Lake Oswego OR 97035-0013

MYRIN, N. ALARIK, senator, rancher, investor; b. Salt Lake City, Apr. 30, 1946; s. F.A. and Katherine (Hall) M.; m. Beth Dart, Jan. 1, 1966; children: Alarik, Lisa, April, Annette, Teresa, Deborah, Nils. BS, Utah State U., 1968, MS, 1979. Owner Myrin Ranch, Altamont, Utah, 1968—; mem. Utah Legislature, 1981-86; state senator from Utah, 1987—; owner Sleeping Lion Ranch, Inc., Toponas, Colo., 1979—; chmn. Utah Agrl. Adv. com., 1979-80; senate chmn. Transp. and Pub. Safety Com., 1987-92, Natural Resources, Energy and Agriculture Com., 1993—. Named Outstanding Legislator of 1981 VFW, 1981. Mem. Utah Cattlemen's Assn. (pres. 1978-80), Duchesne Cattlemen's Assn. (named Outstanding Cattleman of the Year 1975, recipient svc. award 1980), Alta Club. Home: HC65 Box 30 Altamont UT 84001-9703 Office: Office of the State Senate State Capital Salt Lake City UT 84114

NACHBAR, JAMES MILTON, plastic surgeon, computer programmer; b. Chgo., Mar. 22, 1956; s. Milton Max Nachbar and Elizabeth Joan Nelson; m. Joyce Ann Irwin, Apr. 16, 1986. BA in Biology, U. Chgo., 1976; MD, Washington U., St. Louis, 1980. Diplomat Am. Bd. Surgery, Am. Bd. Plastic Surgery. Surg. resident U. Ariz., Tucson, 1980-85; plastic surg. resident U. Va., Charlottesville, 1985-88; asst. prof. plastic surgery U. N.Mex., Albuquerque, 1988-91, chief plastic surgery, 1991—. Author: (chpts.) Congenital Craniofacial Malformations, 1991, Postoperative Parotitis, 1995; author: (computer programs) Impair, 1989, PSEF, 1991-94, Computerized In-Service Review, 1991-94; contbr. articles to profl. jours. Recipient grant Plastic Surgery Ednl. Found., 1990. Mem. AMA, Am. Soc. Plastic & Reconstructive Surgeons, Plastic Surgery Rsch. Coun., Assn. for Computing Machinery, Assn. Acad. Chmn. of Plastic Surgery, Greater Albuquerque Med. Assn., Am. Cleft Palate-Craniofacial Assn. Office: Univ NMex Dept Surgery 2211 Lomas Blvd NE Albuquerque NM 87106-2745

NACHBAR, JOYCE IRWIN, critical care nurse; b. Feb. 23, 1951; d. Charles Wayne and Dorothy Mae (Kearns) Irwin; m. James Milton Nachbar, Apr. 19, 1986. Student, Community Hosp. Sch. Nursing, 1972; BS in Health Sci. Adminstrn., U. Phoenix, 1985. Cert. ACLS. Staff nurse postanesthesia care unit Lovelace Med. Ctr., Albuquerque; staff nurse coronary care unit Martha Jefferson Hosp., Charlottesville, Va.; staff nurse post anesthesia care unit Tucson Med. Ctr., staff cardiac surg. intensive care; staff cardiac surg. intensive care Christ Hosp., Cin. Co-author: (manual) Recovery Room Orientation, 1983. Danny Calloway nursing scholar. Mem. ACCN, Am. Soc. Post Anesthesia Nurses, Post Anesthesia Nurses Assn. ... Home: 11333 N 92nd St Apt 1104 Scottsdale AZ 85260

NACHMAN, GERALD WEIL, columnist, critic, author; b. Oakland, Calif., Jan. 13, 1938; s. Leonard Calvert and Isabel (Weil) N.; m. Mary Campbell McGeachy, Sept. 3, 1966 (div. 1979). Student, Merritt Coll., 1955-57; BA in Journalism, San Jose State U., 1960. TV and humor columnist San Jose (Calif.) Mercury, 1960-63; feature writer N.Y. Post, N.Y.C., 1963-66; drama critic Oakland (Calif.) Tribune, 1966-71; syndicated humor columnist N.Y. Daily News, 1973-79; critic and columnist San Francisco Chronicle, 1979-93; author, 1995—; juror Pulitzer Prize Com. to choose best play, 1991. Author: The Portable Nachman, 1960, Playing House, 1978, Out on a Whim, 1983, The Fragile Bachelor, 1989; contbr. to (book) Snooze, 1986; contbr. articles to newspapers, mags.; author, co-lyricist (revues) Quirks, 1979, Aftershocks, 1992. Recipient Page One award N.Y. Newspaper Guild, 1965, Deems Taylor award ASCAP, 1989. Home: 281 Juanita Way San Francisco CA 94127-1744

NACHMANOVITCH, STEPHEN, violinist, composer, author and educator. BA, Harvard U., 1971; PhD in History of Consciousness, U. Calif., Santa Cruz, 1975. violinist performing internationally, numerous appearances on radio, TV and at music and theater festivals. Author: Free Play: Improvisation in Life and Art, 1990; author compositions: The Four Zoas, 1978, Doors of Perception, 1979, Music From Before the Beginning, 1980, Minding the Earth, 1981, Blake's Vision, 1982, Earth's Answer, 1982, Training the Mind Ox, 1984, Path of Light, 1986, First Life, 1986, Music for Rachel's Brain, 1987, Music for Death Valley Jour., 1988, The Magic Number 7, 1992, also recordings; composer computer music software: The World Music Menu, Visual Music. Office: PO Box 265 Pacific Palisades CA 90272-0265

NACHT, DANIEL JOSEPH, architect; b. Chgo., Sept. 22, 1915; s. George Carl and Hattie (Zaylor) N.; m. Mary Alice Belcher, Nov. 19, 1960; 1 dau., Pamela Jean. B.S., U. Ill., 1940. Mem. faculty U. Ill., 1940-42; with Skidmore, Owings & Merrill, Chgo., 1946-53; designer Rogers Engring. Co., San Francisco, 1953-55; architect Starks, Jozens & Nacht, Sacramento, 1956-70, Nacht & Lewis, 1970. Prin. works include Consumnes River Coll, Sacramento County Courthouse. Mem. Capitol Bldg. and Planning Commn., 1959-67; mem. Core Area Com., 1962-64; mem. adv. bd. Salvation Army Sacramento area. With USNR, 1942-46. Fellow A.I.A.; mem. Crocker Art Gallery, Alpha Chi Rho. Club: Mason (Shriner). Home: 7604 Pineridge Ln Fair Oaks CA 95628-4855 Office: 7300 Folsom Blvd Sacramento CA 95826-2622

NACHT, SERGIO, biochemist; b. Buenos Aires, Apr. 13, 1934; came to U.S., 1965; s. Oscar and Carmen (Scheiner) N.; m. Beatriz Kahan, Dec. 21, 1958; children: Marcelo H., Gabriel A., Mariana S., Sandra M. BA in Chemistry, U. Buenos Aires, 1958, MS in Biochemistry, 1960, PhD in Biochemistry, 1964. Asst. prof. biochemistry U. Buenos Aires, 1960-64; asst. prof. medicine U. Utah, Salt Lake City, 1965-70; rsch. scientist Alza Corp., Palo Alto, Calif., 1970-73; sr. investigator Richardson-Vicks Inc., Mt. Vernon, N.Y., 1973-76; asst. dir., dir. rsch. Richardson-Vicks Inc., Mt. Vernon, 1976-83; dir. biomed. rsch. Richardson-Vicks Inc., Shelton, Conn., 1983-87; sr. v.p. rsch. and devel. Advanced Polymer Systems, Redwood City, Calif., 1987-93, sr. v.p. sci. and tech., 1993—; lectr. dermatology dept. SUNY Downstate Med. Ctr., Blkyn., 1977-87. Contbr. articles to profl. jours.; patentee in field. Mem. Soc. Investigative Dermatology, Soc. Cosmetic Chemists (award 1981), Dermatology Found., Am. Physiological Soc., Am. Acad. Dermatology. Democrat. Jewish. Home: 409 Wembley Ct Redwood City CA 94061-4308

NACHT, STEVE JERRY, geologist; b. Cleve., July 8, 1948; s. Max and Elfrida (Kamm) N.; m. Patricia Katherine Osicka, Aug. 3, 1976; 1 child, David Martin. BS in Geology, Kent State U., 1971, MS in Geology, 1973; MS in Urban Studies, Cleve. State U., 1979. Registered geologist, S.C., Va., Wyo.; environ. assessor, Calif.; cert. geologist, Ind.; lic. drinking water treatment class II, Ohio; cert. environ. mgr., Nev. Geologist Cleve. Utilities Dept., 1974-78; geologist, hydrologist Dalton, Dalton & Newport, Cleve., 1979-82; prin. scientist Lockheed-Emsco, Las Vegas, Nev., 1983-86; sr. geologist, project mgr. Earth Tech. Inc., Long Beach, Calif., 1986-87, The MARK Group, Las Vegas, 1987-90; dir. waste tech., sr. geologist Reynolds Elec. & Engring. Co., Las Vegas, 1990-92, chief environ. remediation sect., 1992—; Registered geologist, S.C., Va., Wyo.; environ. assessor, Calif; cert. geologist, Ind.; lic. drinking water treatment class III, Ohio; cert. environ. mgr., Nev. Contbr. articles to profl. jours. Mem. AAAS, ASTM (groundwater com., past chmn. sect., well maintenance, rehab. and decommissioning sect.), Am. Inst. Profl. Geologists (cert.), Assn. Ground Water Scientists and Engrs., Assn. Engring. Geologists, Project Mgmt. Profl. (cert.), Project Mgmt. Inst. Home: 4184 Del Rosa Ct Las Vegas NV 89121-5011 Office: Reynolds Elec & Engring Co PO Box 98521 Las Vegas NV 89193-8521

NADEL, ANN HONIG, sculptor, educator; b. San Francisco, May 9, 1940; d. Louis and Miriam (Anixter) Honig; m. Joseph Nadel, June 10, 1962; children: Marcia, David. BA in Humanities, San Francisco State U., 1962, M in Edn., 1970; studied with Peter Voulkos, 1976. One woman shows include Judy Kay, Burlingame, 1978, Irene Drori Gallery, L.A., 1979, Bluxome Gallery, San Francisco, 1983, 85, Temple Emanu-El, San Francisco, 1988, Grad. Theol. Union, Berkeley, Calif., 1988, Earl McGrath Gallery, L.A., 1988, 90, 92, Jewish Mus., San Francisco, 1994; exhibited in group shows at Am. Crafts Coun., Kitchen Show, San Francisco, 1976, Gump's Gallery, San Francisco, 1981, No. Calif. Craft Exhbn., Mendocino (Calif.) Art Ctr., 1982, The San Francisco Arts Festival, 1983, San Francisco Internat. Airport Commn. Exhbn., 1985, Frederick Weisman Found. of Art, 1986, Cedars-Sinai Med. Ctr., L.A., 1986, Judah L. Magnes Mus., Berkeley, 1987, Jewish Cmty. Mus., San Francisco, 1987, Bluxome Gallery, San Francisco, 1987, Earl McGrath Gallery, N.Y.C., 1992; represented in permanent collections at Residence of U.S. Vice Pres., Washington, Frederick Weisman Found. of Art, Advanced Micro Devices Corp., Hewlett-Packard Co., Fireman's Fund Ins., Koll Co., Steefel, Levitt & Weiss, Folger & Levin, Cedars-Sinai Med. Ctr., Pacific-Telesis, Coudert Bros., Grad. Theol. Sem., DiCarl Ejerassi, Palo Alto, Calif.

NADEL, JAMES OLIVER, musician, music educator; b. St. Louis, Mar. 4, 1950; s. Eli M. and Ruthe G. Nadel. BA, Stanford (Calif.) U., 1972; MNA, U. San Francisco, 1994. Dir. Stanford Jazz Workshop, 1973—; lectr. Stanford U., 1985—; free-lance musician, San Francisco, 1973—. Fellow Washington, 1976. Home: PO Box 11291 Palo Alto CA 94309-1291

NADELL, ANDREW THOMAS, psychiatrist; b. N.Y.C., Nov. 3, 1946; s. Samuel Tyler and Bertha Elaine (Trupine) N.; m. Eleanore Edwards Ramsey, July 24, 1993. MA, Columbia U., 1968; MSc, U. London, 1973; MD, Duke U., 1974. Diplomate Am. Bd. Psychiatry and Neurology. Resident in psychiatry U. Calif., Davis, 1974-77; clin. instr. psychiatry Stanford (Calif.) U. Sch. Medicine, 1979-84, clin. asst. prof. psychiatry, 1984-93. Trustee Calif. Hist. Soc., 1989—. Fellow Royal Soc. Medicine; mem. Am. Psychiat. Assn., Am. Assn. History Medicine, Am. Osler Soc., Calif. Med. Assn., Bay Area History Medicine Soc. (sec. 1984-88, v.p. 1988-90, pres. 1990-92, bd. govs. 1992—), Soc. Social History Medicine, Assn. Internat. de Bibliphilie, Soc. Internat. d'Histoire de la Medicine, Stanford U. Librs. Assocs. (adv. coun. 1988-94), Univ. Club, Olympic Club (San Francisco), Grolier Club (N.Y.C.), Roxburghe Club, Colophon Club, Book Club of Calif. (San Francisco). Office: 1828 El Camino Real Burlingame CA 94010-3103

NADER, LAURA, anthropology educator; b. Winsted, Conn., Sept. 30, 1930; m. Norman Milleron, Sept. 1, 1962; 3 children. B.A., Wells Coll., 1952; Ph.D., Radcliffe Coll., 1962. Mem. faculty U. Calif.-Berkeley, 1960—, now prof. anthropology; vis. prof. Yale Law Sch., New Haven, fall 1971; Henry R. Luce prof. Wellesley Coll., Mass., 1983-84; field work in Mex., Lebanon, Morocco; mem. adv. com. NSF, 1971-75; mem. cultural anthropology com. NIMH, 1968—, chmn. to 1971, chmn. social scis. research tng. rev. com., 1976-78; mem. NAS-NRC assembly behavioral and social scis., 1969-71, 73-75, 75—; mem. com. Nuclear and Alternative Energy Forms, NAS , 1976-77. Editor: Law in Culture and Society, 1969; The Disputing Process, 1978, No Access to Law-Alternatives to the American Judicial System, 1980, Harmony Ideology, 1990; contbr. articles to profl. jours.; author ednl. films; mem. editorial com. Law and Society Rev., 1967—. Mem. Calif. Council for the Humanities, 1975-79; mem. Carnegie Council on Children, 1972-77; active Coun. Librs. at Libr. of Congress, Washington, 1988—. Radcliffe Coll. grantee, 1954-59; Thaw fellow Harvard U., 1955-56, 58-59; Peabody Mus. grantee, 1954-59; Am. Philos. Assn. grantee, 1955; Mexican Govt. grantee, 1957-58; Milton Fund grantee, 1959-60; fellow Ctr. Advanced Study in Behavioral Scis., Stanford, Calif., 1963-64; NSF grantee, 1966-68; Wenner Gren Found. grantee, 1964, 66, 73; Carnegie Corp. grantee, 1975; Woodrow Wilson fellow, 1979-80; Wells Coll. Alumnae award, 1980; Radcliffe Coll. Alumnae award, 1984. Mem. AAAS, Am. Acad. Arts and Scis., Am. Anthrop. Assn. (planning and devel. com. 1968-71, 75-76), Social Sci. Research Council, Law and Soc. Assn. (trustee 1967-72), Ctr. for Study of Responsive Law (trustee 1968—), Soc. Women Geographers. Office: U Calif Dept Anthropology 313 Kroeber Hall Berkeley CA 94720

NADY, JOHN, electronics company executive; b. Agfalva, Hungary, Feb. 13, 1945; came to U.S., 1951; s. John and Hermine Nady. BSEE, Calif. Inst. Tech., 1965; MSEE, U. Calif., Berkeley, 1968. Elec. engr. Lawrence Radiation Lab., Livermore, 1966-71, Westinghouse Corp., Oakland, Calif., 1971-72; owner, chief exec. officer Nady Systems, Inc., Oakland, Calif., 1976—, Calif. Concerts, Inc., Oakland, Calif., 1985-93. Patentee in field. Mem. Nat. Assn. Broadcasters, Audio Engring. Soc., Nat. Assn. Music Merchants. Office: Nady Systems Inc 6701 Bay St Emeryville CA 94608-1023

NAEF, WESTON JOHN, museum curator; b. Gallup, N.Mex., Jan. 8, 1942; s. Weston John and Kathleen Winifred (Skerry) N.; m. Mary Dawes Meanor, Apr. 4, 1964; children: Edward Weston, Ella Dawes. B.A., Claremont Men's Coll., 1964; M.A., Ohio State U., 1966; postgrad., Brown U., 1966-69. Vis. scholar Boston Pub. Library, 1968; dir. art gallery Wheaton Coll., Mass., 1969; staff dept. prints and photographs Met. Mus. Art, N.Y.C., 1970-84; asst. curator Met. Mus. Art, 1971-81, curator, 1981-84; curator photographs J. Paul Getty Mus., Malibu, Calif., 1984—; cons. in field. Author, exhbn. dir. Behind the Great Wall of China, 1971, The Painterly Photograph, 1973, The Truthful Lens: A Survey of Victorian Books Illustrated with Photographs, 1974, Era of Exploration, The Rise of Landscape Photography in the American West 1860-1885, 1975, Pioneer Photographers of Brazil 1839-1914, 1976, The Collection of Alfred Stieglitz, 1978, Georgia O'Keeffe by Alfred Stieglitz, 1978, Eliot Porter, The Intimate Landscapes, 1979, After Daguerre: Masterworks of 19th Century French Photography from the Bibliotheque Nationale, Paris, 1980, Counterparts: Form and Emotion in Photographs, 1982, Whisper of the Muse: Photographs by Julia Margaret Cameron, 1986, Edward Weston in Los Angeles: The Home Spirit and Beyond, 1986, Rare States and Unusual Subjects: Photographs by Paul Strand, Andre Kertesz and Man Ray, 1987, Capturing Shadows: Notable Acquisitions, 1985-1990, 1990; August Sander: Faces of the German People, 1991; Atget's Magical Analysis; Photographs, 1915-27, 91, Two Lives: O'Keeffe by Stieglitz, 1917-23, 1992, Being and Becoming: Photographs by Edmund Teske, 1993, André Kutész: A Centennial Tribute, 1994, Palette of Light: Handcrafted Photographs, 1898-1914, 1994, Frederick Sommer: Poetry and Logic, 1994, Hidden Witness: African Americans in Early Photography, 1995, Carrie Mae Weems Reacts to Hidden Witness, 1995, Alfred Stieglitz: Seen and Unseen, 1995. Kress fellow, 1968. Club: Grolier (N.Y.C.). Office: J Paul Getty Mus Dept Photographs 17985 Pacific Coast Hwy Malibu CA 90265-5708

NAFZIGER, JAMES ALBERT RICHMOND, lawyer, educator; b. Mpls., Sept. 24, 1940; s. Ralph Otto and Charlotte Monona (Hamilton) N.; BA, U. Wis., 1962, MA, 1969; JD, Harvard U., 1967. Bar: Wis. 1967. Law clk. to chief judge U.S. Dist. Ct. (ea. dist.) Wis., 1967-69; fellow Am. Soc. Internat. Law, Washington, 1969-70, adminstrv. dir., 1970-74; exec. sec. Assn. Student Internat. Law Socs., 1969-70; lectr. Sch. Law, Cath. U. Am., Washington, 1970-74; vis. assoc. prof. Sch. Law, U. Oreg., 1974-77; vis. prof. Nat. Autonomous U. Mex., 1978; assoc. prof. law Coll. Law, Willamette U., Salem, Oreg., 1977-80, prof., 1980-95, Thomas B. Stoel prof., 1995—, assoc. dean, 1985-86, dir. China program, 1984—; scholar-in-residence Rockefeller Found. Ctr., Bellagio, Italy, 1985; lectr., tutor Inst. Pub. Internat. Law and Internat. Relations, Thessaloniki, Greece, 1982; cons. Adminstrv. Conf. U.S., 1988-90; mem. bd. advisors Denver Jour. Internat. Law and Policy, Am. Jour. Comparative Law (bd. dirs. 1985—); bd. dirs. N.W. Regional China Coun., 1987-89. Served to 1st lt. U.S. Army, 1962-64. Recipient Burlington No. Faculty Achievement award, 1988. Mem. ABA (legal specialist ctrl. and east European law initiative 1992—), Am. Soc. Internat. Law (exec. coun. 1983-86, 92—, exec. com. 1994—, chmn. ann. meeting 1988, chmn. nominating com. 1989), Am. Soc. Comparative Law (bd. dirs. 1985—), Internat. Law Assn. (rapporteur cultural heritage law commn. 1990—, v.p. 1994—, Am. br. exec. com. 1986—, co-dir. studies 1991-95, chmn. human rights com. Am. br. 1983-88), UNA-USA (pres. Oreg. divsn. 1987-90, bd. govs., nat. coun. 1990—, exec. com. coun. chpt. and divsn. pres., v.p. 1990-94), Washington Fgn. Law Soc. (v.p. 1973-74), Internat. Studies Assn. (exec. bd. 1974-77, internat. law sect.), ACLU (pres. chpt. 1980-81, mem. state bd. 1982-88, sec. 1983-87), Assn. Am. Law Schs. (chmn. law and arts sect. 1981-83, 89-91, chmn. immigration law sect. 1990-91, chmn. internat. law sect. 1984-85, com. on sects. and ann. meeting 1995—, chmn. internat. law workshop, 1995), Am. Law Inst., Oreg. Internat. Coun. (pres. 1990-92), Internat. Sports Law Assn. (v.p. 1992—), Phi Beta Kappa, Phi Kappa Phi. Editor Procs. of Am. Soc. Internat. Law, 1977; Am. author: Conflict of Laws: A Northwest Perspective, 1985, International Sports Law, 1988; contbr. articles to profl. jours. Home: 3775 Saxon Dr S Salem OR 97302-6041 Office: Willamette U Coll Law Salem OR 97301

NAFZIGER, PATTIE LOIS, state legislator; b. Phoenix; married; 4 children. Attended, Colo. Coll., 1947-48, U. Ariz., 1948-50, Ariz. State U., 1967-70, Coll. So. Idaho, 1970-72. Former ptnr. Sunshine Farms; mem. Idaho Ho. of Reps., 1990—. Asst. leader 4-H; active Jr. League of Phoenix. Home: 996 E Riverpark Ln Boise ID 83706-4098 Office: Idaho Ho of Reps State Capitol Boise ID 83720

NAGAO, MIKE AKIRA, horticulturist, county administrator; b. Hilo, Hawaii, Oct. 23, 1947. BA, U. Hawaii, 1969, MS, 1971; PhD, U. Mass., 1975. From asst. to assoc. prof. U. Hawaii, Hilo, 1975-81; from asst. to horticulturist U. Hawaii, Honolulu, 1981—, county adminstr., 1991—. Contbr. articles to profl. jours. Mem. Am. Soc. Hort. Sci. Office: Univ of Hawaii Beaumont Rsch Sta 461 W Lanikaula St Hilo HI 96720-4037

NAGAO, NORRIS SADATO, political science educator, consultant; b. Sacramento, June 9, 1954; s. Sadao and Misao (Iwahashi) N. AA, Sacramento City Coll., 1973; AB, U. Calif., Berkeley, 1975; MA, Columbia U., 1979, EdM, 1980. Legis. aide Calif. State Assembly, Sacramento, 1976-77; exec. dir. N.Y.-Tokyo-Beijing Nanshiki Baseball Friendship Series, N.Y.C., 1981-84; exec. sec. N.Am.-Japan Promotions, Inc., N.Y.C., 1986-89; pres. Mediagenesis Inc., L.A., 1988-91; prof. polit. sci. ethnic studies/history Southwestern Coll., Chula Vista, Calif., 1991—. Mem. bd. libr. commrs. City of San Diego; mem. Mayor Susan Golding's Gay and Lesbian Adv. Bd., San Diego; chmn. selection com. The Harvey Milk/Tom Homann Scholarship Fund; bd. dirs. Ctr. for Social Svcs., Inc., Asian Pacific Ams. in Higher Edn., Calif. Rep. League, Gay and Lesbian Alliance Against Defamation, Goldwater Reps., KPBS TV/FM; mem. Friends of the San Diego Pub. Libr., Citizens in Action for Local Librs. Mem. NEA, Alumni Fedn. of Columbia U., Assn. Asian Am. Studies, Calif. Libr. Assn., Calif. Tchrs. Assn., C.C. Assn., Japan Am. Soc. of So. Calif., Japanese Am. Hist. Soc. San Diego, Log Cabin Club, Media Action Network for Asian Americans, Popular Culture Assn., Sacramento City Coll. Alumni Assn., San Diego-Yokohama Sister City Soc., Southwestern Coll Edn. Assn., Uptown Dist. Owners' Assn., Kappa Delta Pi. Office: PO Box 3643 San Diego CA 92163-1643

NAGASAMY, VIJAY, mechanical and aerospace engineer; b. Thane, Maharashtra, India, Apr. 3, 1961; s. S. and Parvathi (Swamy) N.; m. Kamala Tyagarajan, Mar. 31, 1993; 1 child, Priya. B.Tech. in Mech. Engring., Indian Inst. Tech., Bombay, 1982; MS in Mech. and Aerospace Engring., Rutgers U., 1985, PhD in Mech. and Aerospace Engring., 1988. Rsch. and teaching asst. in mech. and aerospace engring. Rutgers U., 1982-88; sr. engr., project leader LSI Logic Corp., Milpitas, Calif., 1988-91, staff engr. in software R&D divsn., 1991—. Contbr. articles to profl. jours.; patentee methodology for deriving executable low-level structural descriptions and valid physical implementations of circuit and systems from semantic specifications and descriptions thereof. Merit scholar Bd. of Edn., Govt. of India, 1971. Mem. IEEE, Am. Soc. Mech. Engrs., Tau Beta Pi. Home: 34361 Zircon Ter Fremont CA 94555 Office: LSI Logic Corp 1501 McCarthy Blvd MS E-199 Milpitas CA 95035

NAGEL, DARYL DAVID, retail executive; b. Arlington, Minn., Apr. 13, 1939; s. Paul Charles and Frieda L. (Oldenburg) N.; m. Joan Clare Dacey, Dec. 23, 1961; children: Kelly, Andrew, Maureen. BME, U. Minn., 1962; diploma in Advanced Mgmt. Program, Harvard U., 1978. Asst. mdse. mgr. Res. Supply Co., Mpls., 1962-65; mdse. mgr. Reserve Supply Co., Mpls., 1965-66, v.p., gen. mgr., 1966-69; v.p. area gen. mgr. United Bldg. Ctrs., Winona, Minn., 1969-78, exec. v.p., chief ops. officer, 1978-84, pres., chief exec. officer, 1984-87; pres., CEO Lanoga Corp., Seattle, 1987—; bd. dirs. Lanoga Corp., Seattle, 1987—, Badger Foundry, Winona, 1984-87. Bd. dirs. United Way, Winona, 1978-84. Mem. Home Ctr. Leadership Coun., C. of C. (bd. dirs. 1964-69, 73, 78), Sahalee Country Club. Republican. Lutheran. Office: Lanoga Corp 17946 NE 65th St Redmond WA 98052-4963

NAGEL, JEROME KAUB, architect; b. Denver, Dec. 26, 1923; s. Fritz Andrew and Josephine (Gaylord) N.; m. Cynthia Fels, Sept. 1, 1951; children—Peter Barry, James Gaylord. B.Arch., Yale U., 1949. Registered architect, Colo. Prin. J.K. Nagel Architect, Denver, 1953-61, Rogers & Nagel, Denver, 1961-66, Rogers, Nagel, Langhart, Architects, 1966-77, Interplan Inc., 1969-77; pres. Nagel Investment Co.; dir. Bank Western, Denver, Field Devel. Corp., Denver. Mem. Colo. Hwy. Commn., chmn., 1982-83; bd. dirs. Planned Parenthood Fed. Am. Inc., N.Y.C., 1974-78, Rocky Mountain Planned Parenthood, Denver, 1972-76, Colo. chpt. ARC, 1957-60, 80-81, Denver Santa Claus Shop, 1987-91; mem. panel arbitrators Am. Arbitration Assn., 1962—; chmn. Colo. Bicycling Adv., Denver Bicycling Adv. Bd. Served to 1st lt. AC U.S. Army, 1943-45. Decorated D.F.C., Air medal with 11 oak leaf clusters. Mem. AIA (nat. life; sec. chpt. 1960-61, pres. 1962-63), Denver Country (bd. dirs. 1983-86), University (bd. dirs. 1962-66) Mile High, Denver Rotary Club Found. (pres. 1992-93), Denver Athletic Club. Episcopalian. Home: 67 Eudora St Denver CO 80220-6311

NAGEL, PATRICIA JO, state legislator, consultant, lawyer; b. Billings, Mont., Sept. 24, 1942; d. Robert Mark and Evelyn Margaret (Lipsack) McKeown; m. Robert Wells Nagel, Aug. 18, 1963; children: Stacia, Susanna. BA in Polit. Sci., N.Mex. State U., 1965; JD, U. Wyo., 1983. Bar: Wyo. 1984. Interior designer Nassif's Interiors, Cedar Rapids, Iowa, 1965-67, Cedar Rapids Paint, 1973-74; law clk. to presiding justice 7th jud. dist., Casper, Wyo., 1983-84; sole practice Casper, 1984-88; dir. Wyo. Futures Project, Casper, 1986-88; ptnr. Nagel & Nix, Casper, 1988—; mem. Wyo. Ho. of Reps., 1992—. Sr. editor Land and Water Law Rev., 1982-83. Vice chair Wyo. Community Devel. Authority; mem. planning commn. City of Casper, 1980; pres., bd. dirs. Friends of the Libr., Casper, 1980; pres. Meadowlark Montessori Sch., Casper, 1979; sec. Casper Bicentennial Com., 1976; v.p. Nicolaysen Art Mus., Casper, 1985-86; sec., bd. dirs. Hospice Cancer Treatment Ctr., Casper, 1985-86. Republican. Presbyterian. Home: 1105 S Durbin St Casper WY 82601-4327

NAGEL, STANLEY BLAIR, construction and investment executive; b. Bklyn., Mar. 19, 1928; s. Robert Arthur and Renee Ann Nagel; children: Scott Alan, Robert Arthur. BBA, U. Oreg., 1950. With constrn. dept. Nagel Investment, Portland, Oreg., 1955-58, pres., 1956—; pres. R.A. Constrn., Portland, 1956—; buyer May Co., Portland, 1958-72; gen. mgr. Portland Outdoor Store, 1972-75; owner Nagels Nursery & Greenhouses, Portland, 1975—; pres. E & S Distbrs., Portland, 1982—. Co-inventor pizza machine (patent pending). 2d lt. U.S. Army, 1952-55. Republican. Jewish. Home and Office: 5353 SW Martha St Portland OR 97221-1840

NAGLE, ROBERT DAVID, therapist, educator, author; b. Gowanda, N.Y., Sept. 13, 1935; s. Carl and Sarah (Zabatinsky) N.; m. Eugenia S. Karabacz, Nov. 20, 1956; children: Carl, Sonya, Paula. BA, N.Mex. Highlands U., 1960, MA, 1961; PhD, Union U., 1977. Cert. addictions specialist Am. Acad. Health Scis. Providers Addictive Disorders; cert. clin. hypnotherapist. Psyciat. therapist N.Mex. State Hosp., Las Vegas, 1961-63; grad. fellow U. Nebr., Lincoln, 1963-64, U. Miami, Fla., 1964-65; prof. Inst. of Discourse, Kansas City, Mo., 1967—, pres., 1968—; prof. emeritus Northwest Mo. State U., Maryville, 1965-85; dir. ednl. programming Acad. for Counseling and Change, Kansas City, 1981—, dir. profl. hypnotherapy svcs., 1992-93; prof., therapist Ottowa U., Overland Park, Kans., 1987—. Author: When Moses Last in the Dooryard Laughed, 1978, Men Freeing Men, 1985; contbr. poetry to revs. and collections. Bd. dirs. Ariz. Addiction Treatment Program, 1993. Fellow Rader Inst., 1992. Mem. AACD, ACLU, Soc. Philosophy and Psychology, Am. Philos. Assn., Henry Miller Lit. Soc., Mo. Assn. Counseling and Devel., Am. Assn. Profl. Hypnotherapists, Soc. Advanced Philos. Rsch., Inst. Advanced Philos. Rsch. (coun. advisors), The Cousteau Soc., Ariz. State Poetry Soc. (pres. 1995). Home: 3106 E 80th St Kansas City MO 64132-3638 Office: 525 W Southern Ave Ste 11 Mesa AZ 85210-5009

NAGLER, MICHAEL NICHOLAS, classics and comparative literature educator; b. N.Y.C., Jan. 20, 1937; s. Harold and Dorothy Judith (Nocks) N.; m. Roberta Ann Robbins (div. May 1983); children: Jessica, Joshua. BA, NYU, 1960; MA, U. Calif., Berkeley, 1962, PhD, 1966. Instr. San Francisco State U., 1963-65; prof. classics, comparative lit. dept. U. Calif., Berkeley, 1966-91, prof. emeritus, 1991—. Author: Spontaneity and Tradition, 1974, America Without Violence, 1982; co-author: The Upanishads, 1987; contbr. articles to profl. publs. Pres. bd. dirs. METTA Ctrs. for Nonviolence Edn. Fellow Am. Coun. Learned Socs., NIH; MacArthur Found. grantee, 1988. Mem. Am. Philolog. Soc. (editor Oral Tradition). Office: U Calif Classics Dept Berkeley CA 94720

NAGLER, STEWART GORDON, insurance company executive; b. Bklyn., Jan. 30, 1943; s. Henry and Mary N.; m. Bonnie Lawrence, Aug. 9, 1964; children: David, Ellen. B.S. summa cum laude, Poly. U., 1963. With Met. Life Ins. Co., N.Y.C., 1963—, exec. v.p., 1978-85, sr. exec. v.p., 1985—. Fellow Soc. Actuaries, Am. Acad. Actuaries. Office: Met Life Ins Co 1 Madison Ave New York NY 10010-3603

NAGLESTAD, FREDERIC ALLEN, legislative advocate; b. Sioux City, Iowa, Jan. 13, 1929; s. Ole T. and Evelyn Elizabeth (Erschen) N.; student (scholar) U. Chgo., 1947-49; m. Beverly Minnette Shellberg, Feb. 14, 1958; children—Patricia Minnette, Catherine Janette. Pub. affairs, pub. relations, newscaster, announcer KSCJ-radio, Sioux City, Iowa, 1949-51; producer, dir., newscaster, announcer WOW-TV, Omaha, 1953-57; program mgr. WCPO-TV, Cin., 1957-58; mgr. KNTV-TV, San Jose, Calif., 1958-61; owner Results Employment Agy., San Jose, 1961-75; legis. advocate Naglestad Assocs., Calif Assn. Employers, Calif. Automotive Wholesalers Assn., Air Quality Products, Calif. Assn. Wholesalers-Distbrs., State Alliance Bd. Equalization Reform, Quakemaster, many others, 1969—. Pres. Calif. Employment Assn., 1970-72. Asst. concertmaster Sioux City Symphony Orch., 1945-47. Sgt. AUS, 1951-53. Recognized for outstanding contbn. to better employment law, Resolution State Calif. Legislature, 1971. Office: 3991 Fair Oaks Blvd Sacramento CA 95864-7254

NAGY, STEPHEN MEARS, JR., physician, allergist; b. Yonkers, N.Y., Apr. 1, 1939; s. Stephen Mears and Olga (Zahoruiko) N.; m. Branda Yu Nagy, 1966; children: Catherine, Stephen III. BA, Princeton U., 1960; MD, Tufts U., 1964. Diplomate Am. Bd. Internal Medicine, Am. Bd. Allergy and Immunology. Pvt. practice Sacramento, Calif., 1971-95; prof. Sch. Medicine U. Calif., Davis, 1974-95. Author, editor Evaluation & Management of Allergic and Asthmatic Diseases, 1981; mem. editl. bd. Clinical Reviews in Allergy; creator Famous Teachings in Modern Medicine-Allergy Series slide collection. Capt. U.S. Army, 1966-68, Vietnam. Fellow Am. Acad. Allergy, Am. Coll. Allergy; mem. AMA, Sacramento-El Dorado Med. Soc. (bd. dirs. 1971-95). Office: 4801 J St Ste A Sacramento CA 95819-3746

NAHMAN, NORRIS STANLEY, electrical engineer; b. San Francisco, Nov. 9, 1925; s. Hyman Cohen and Rae (Levin) N.; m. Shirley D. Maxwell, July 20, 1968; children: Norris Stanley, Vicki L., Vance W., Scott T. B.S. in Electronics Engring, Calif. Poly. State U., 1951; M.S.E.E., Stanford U., 1952; Ph.D. in Elec. Engring, U. Kans., 1961. Registered profl. engr., Colo. Electronic scientist Nat. Security Agy., Washington, 1952-55; prof. elec. engring., dir. electronics rsch. lab. U. Kans., Lawrence, 1955-66; sci. cons., chief pulse and time domain sect. Nat. Bur. Standards, Boulder, Colo., 1966-73; chief time domain metrology, sr. scientist Nat. Bur. Standards, 1975-83, group leader field characterization group, 1984-85; v.p. Picosecond Pulse Labs, Inc., Boulder, 1986-90; cons. elec. engr., 1990—; prof., chmn. dept. elec. engring. U. Toledo, 1973-75;; prof. elec. engring. U. Colo., Boulder, 1966—; Disting. lectr., prin. prof. Ctr. Nat. d' Etude des Telecomm. Summer Sch., Lannion France, 1978; disting. lectr. Harbin Inst. Tech., Peoples Republic China, summer 1982; mem. faculty NATO Advanced Study Inst., Castelvecchio, Italy, 1983, Internat. Radio Sci. Union/NRC; chmn. Internat. Intercomm. Group Waveform Measurements, 1981-90, chmn. Commn. A, 1985-86; affiliate Los Alamos Nat. Lab., 1990—. Contbr. rsch. articles profl. jours.; patentee in field. Asst. scoutmaster Longs Peak coun. Boy Scouts Am., 1970-73, 75-89. With U.S. Mcht. Marine, 1943-46, U.S. Army, 1952-55. Ford Found. faculty fellow MIT, 1962; Nat. Bur. Standards sr. staff fellow, 1978-79; recipient Disting. Alumnus award Calif. Poly. State U., 1972, Order of Arrow Boy Scouts Am., 1976. Fellow IEEE (life), Internat. Sci. Radio Union; mem. Instrumentation and Measurement Soc. of IEEE (admstrv. com. 1982-84, editorial bd. Trans., 1982-86, Andrew H. chi Best Tech. Paper award 1984, Tech. Leadership and Achievement award 1987), Am. Assn. Engring. Edn., U.S. Mcht. Marine Veterans World War II, Am. Legion, Calif. Poly. State U. Alumni Assn. (life), Stanford U. (life), U. Kans. (life), Am. Radio Relay League Club (life), Sigma Pi Sigma, Tau Beta Pi, Eta Kappa Nu, Sigma Tau, Sigma Xi.

NAHMIAS, VICTOR JAY, architect; b. Woodside, N.Y., May 2, 1951; s. Leon and Judith (Haupt) N.; m. Michal Caspi, June 24, 1975; children: Ariel, Tamar. BA, U. Pa., 1973; BArch, U. B.C., Vancouver, 1977. Registered profl. architect. Carpenter's asst. Weir Constrn., Vancouver, 1973; designer, draftsman Kenn Butts, Northridge, Calif., 1977-78; project mgr. B. Robert Axton, Sherman Oaks, Calif., 1978-79, Howard R. Lane, Woodland Hills, Calif., 1979-81; project architect Rochlin & Baran Assocs., Los Angeles, 1981-84; area architect Kaiser Permanente, Pasadena, 1984-90; ptnr. Wendland-Nahmias AIA & Assocs., Westlake Village, Calif., 1990—; bd. dirs. Kosmic Kids. Bd. dirs., past pres. Cameo Woods Home Owners Assn.; co-convener L.A. City Coun. 8th Dist. West Area Assembly; past chmn. Purim Carnival, libr. com. Temple Israel; mem. Nature Conservancy, World Wildlife Fund, Statue of Liberty/Ellis Island Found., L.A. County Mus. Art, Natural History Mus. of L.A. Mem. AIA (co-chmn. L.A. com. on govt. rels., mem. com. on health), AIA/L.A. Calif. Coun. (past mem. bd. dirs., steering com., past legis. rev. com.), Cmty. Assns. Inst., Am. Philatelic Soc., Nat. Trust for Hist. Preservation, Nat. Audubon Soc., Sierra Club, Conejo Valley C. of C., Westlake Village C. of C. Democrat. Jewish. Home: 3647 Kalsman Dr Apt L Los Angeles CA 90016-4447 Office: 5706 Corsa Ave Thousand Oaks CA 91362-4057

NAHM-MIJO, TRINA, social science educator, dancer, choreographer; b. Honolulu, Sept. 4, 1949; d. Matthew Mai Tai and Elizabeth (Whang) Nahm; m. Jerry Lee Nahm-Mijo, Nov. 18, 1976; children: Rengé, Shayne. BA in Psychology, U. Hawaii, 1969, MEd in Ednl. Psychology, 1971; MPH in Community Mental Health, U. Calif., Berkeley, 1974, PhD in Counseling Psychology, 1979. Dir. dance U. Hawaii, Hilo, 1976-80; lectr. psychology Hawaii Community Coll., Hilo, 1978-79, prof. psychology and sociology, 1979—, chairperson Gen. Edn. and Pub. Svc. div., 1988-91; exchange instr. psychology Santa Monica (Calif.) City Coll., 1985-86; mem. adj. faculty Vt. Coll. of Norwich U., Montpelier, 1987—; coun. chairperson U. Hawaii, Hilo, 1984-85, equal employment opportunity/affirmation action officer, 1991-93. Choreographer (dance/film) Wheels, 1979 (finalist U.S.A. Film Festival 1981, short documentary finalist Acad. Awards 1981). Pres. Family Crisis Shelter, Inc., Hilo, 1987—; mem. adv. bd. Kalani Honua Culture and Conf. Ctr., Kalapana, Hawaii, 1980—; bd. dirs. Kamanawa Sch. Personel Devel., Hilo, 1990-93.. Recipient Leadership in the Arts award YWCA, Hilo, 1984; travel grantee Pres.'s Adv. Com., U. Hawaii, 1990, Humanities grantee NEH, Washington, 1990. Mem. Hawaii State Dance Coun. (grantee 1977, 91), U. Hawaii Commn. on Status of Women (1987-91, 94), Dance 'O Hawaii (founding). Office: U Hawaii Hawaii Community Coll Gen Edn and Pub Svc Div Hilo HI 96720-4091

NAIDORF, LOUIS MURRAY, architect; b. Los Angeles, Aug. 15, 1928; s. Jack and Meriam (Abbott) N.; m. Dorise D. Roberts, June 1948 (div.); children: Victoria Beth Naidorf-Slifer; m. Patricia Ann Shea, June 1, 1968 (div.); m. Patricia Ruth Allen, Dec. 6, 1992. BA, U. Calif., Berkeley, 1949, MA, 1950. Registered architect, Calif. Designer Welton Becket Assocs., L.A., 1950-51, Pereira and Luckman, L.A., 1951-52; project designer Welton Becket Assocs., L.A., 1952-55, sr. project designer, 1955-59, v.p. asst., dir. design, 1959-70, sr. v.p., dir. rsch., 1970-73; sr. v.p., design prin. Ellerbe Becket Assocs., L.A., 1973-95; dean Sch. Architecture and Design Woodbury U., L.A., 1990—; mem. peer rev. panel Nat. Endowment Arts, 1995—; vis. lectr. Calif. Poly. Sch. Architecture, San Luis Obispo, 1975-82; instr. UCLA Sch. Architecture, 1985, UCLA Landscape Archtl. Program, 1980-85, Otis-Parsons, L.A., 1986—. Prin. works include Capitol Records Bldg., Century City, Los Angeles, Hyatt Regency, Dallas, Restoration Calif. State Capitol Bldg. Bd. dirs. Inst. for Garden Studies, L.A., 1986—. Recipient Honor award Nat. Trust for Hist. Preservation, 1985. Fellow AIA (bd. dirs. Los Angeles chpt. 1977-79, Silver Medal 1950, Nat. Honor award 1985). Office: Ellerbe Becket 2501 Colorado Ave Santa Monica CA 90404-3550

NAITO, LISA HEATHER, state legislator; b. Portland, Oreg., May 25, 1955; d. Per Hugo and Christine Annalise (Oertel) Sjogren; m. Steve Lorne Naito; children: Kirsten, Alex. BA, Rice U., 1977; JD, U. Oreg., 1981. Bar: Oreg. Dep. dist. atty. Multnomah County Dist. Atty., Portland, 1981-83; sole practice Portland, 1984-86; atty. Preston, Thorgrimson, Ellis & Holman, Portland, 1988-90; mem. Oreg. Ho. of Reps., Salem, 1991—, vice-chair natural resources subcom. environment and energy, vice chair judiciary subcom. juvenile justice; mem. judiciary subcom. civil law and jud. adminstrn. Oreg. Ho. of Reps.; asst. minority leader Oreg. Ho. of Reps., Salem, 1993; policy coord. Ho. Dem. Caucus. Mem. Child Care Commn., Salem, 1993—; vice chair House children & families com., 1993; mem. alcohol & drug task force, 1993-94, mem. commerce com., bus. com., 1991, 93, mem. energy & environment com., 1991; bd. dirs. Albertina Kerr, 1992—, Delauney Mental Health Ctr., 1984-86. Mem. Oreg. Womens Polit. Caucus. Democrat. Home: 3505 SE Ankeny St Portland OR 97214-2046 Office: Legislative Assembly State St # 492 Salem OR 97301-3648

NAJJAR, TAMARA LITCHFIELD, mail order business owner; b. Elgin, Ill., June 2, 1958; d. Kelmar Thomas and Betty Joan (Light) Litchfield; m. Idris M. Najjar, Jan. 5, 1986; children: Zakariya, Suraya, Ali. AS, We. Ky. U., Bowling Green, 1983. Lic. cosmetologist. Asst. supr. Opryland USA Inc., Nashville, 1983-86; asst. mgr. Hitachi Am., Nashville, 1986-91; owner, mgr. TJ Designs, Riverside, Calif., 1993—. Author, pub.: Beauty Shop in A Book, 1993. Fundraising chair Islamic Acad., Riverside, 1993-94, yearbook organizer, 1993. Mem. Mosque of Riverside. Democrat. Muslim. Home and Office: 273 Newell Dr Riverside CA 92507-3106

NAKABAYASHI, NICHOLAS TAKATERU, retired retail executive; b. Honolulu, Feb. 25, 1920; s. Denji and Ume (Teraoka) N. BS, Utah State U., 1949; MS, U. Ill., 1953, PhD, 1959. Rsch. asst. U. Ill., Urbana, 1953-59; jr. rsch. physiologist UCLA, 1959-61, asst. rsch. physiologist, 1961-64; rsch. fellow Calif. Inst. Tech., Pasadena, 1961-64; sec.-treas. Underwater Rsch. Corp., L.A., 1962-64; rsch. asst. dept. ob/gyn U. Mich. Med. Ctr., Ann Arbor, 1964-70; biologist VA Hosp., Wadsworth, 1971-72; instr. San Gabriel Adult Sch., Calif., 1971-78; supr. serology VA Hosp., Long Beach, Calif., 1972-74; owner Regent Liquor Store, L.A., 1974-79; pres., treas. Regent Liquor, Inc., L.A., 1979-85; ret. NIH grantee, 1967, 69. Mem. N.Y. Acad. Sci., 100th Inf. Battalion Vets. Club. Home: 516 Kamoku St Apt 302 Honolulu HI 96826-5102

NAKAGAWA, ALLEN DONALD, radiologic technologist; b. N.Y.C., Mar. 14, 1955; s. Walter Tsunehiko and Alyce Tsuneko (Kinoshita) N. BS in Environ. Studies, St. John's U., Jamaica, N.Y., 1977; MS in Marine Biology, C.W. Post Coll., 1980. Cert. radiologic technologist, in fluoroscopy, Calif.; cert. Am. Registry Radiol. Technologists. Research asst. environ. studies St. John's U., 1976-78; lab. asst. Bur. Water Surveillance, Nassau Co. of Health Dept., Wantaugh, N.Y., 1978; clin. endocrinology asst. U. Calif. VA Hosp., San Francisco, 1981-83; student technologist St. Mary's Hosp., San Francisco, 1985-86; radiologic technologist Mt. Zion Hosp., San Francisco, 1986-88; sr. radiologic technologist U. Calif., San Francisco, 1989—, urosurg. radiologic technologists, 1988-89. Recruiting chmn. hunger project C.W. Post Coll., 1979; participant 33d Annual Radiology Conf., San Francisco, 1990. Mem. AAAS, Calif. Soc. Radiologic Technologists, Marine Mammal Ctr., Calif. Acad. Scis., Japanese-Am. Nat. Mus., World Affairs Coun. San Francisco, ACLU, Sigma Xi. Democrat. Methodist.

NAKAHATA, TADAKA, retired consulting engineer, land surveyor; b. Kauai, Hawaii, Nov. 24, 1924; s. Tadao and Yae (Ohta) N.; BS in Civil Engring., U. Hawaii, 1951; m. Clara S. Sakanashi, June 23, 1956; children—Leanne A. Nikaido, Holly E. Chung, Merry Y. Ifuku. Engr./surveyor B.H. McKeague & Assos., Honolulu, 1951-55, Harland Bartholomew & Assos., Honolulu, 1955-56, Paul Low Engring. Co., Honolulu, 1956-59, Nakahata, Kaneshige, Imata & Assos., 1959-63; owner T. Nakahata, Honolulu, 1964-83, ret., 1983; mem. Hawaii Bd. Registration of Architects, Engrs. and Land Surveyors, 1980-83. With AUS, 1946-47. Mem. ASCE, Am. Congress Surveying and Mapping, Nat. Soc. Profl. Engrs. Mem. Makiki Christian Ch.

NAKANISHI, HIROSHI, chemist, educator; b. Hakodate, Japan, May 26, 1953; came to U.S., 1982; s. Tomeo and Kayoko (Ida) N.; m. Banka Djordjevic, July 3, 1988. BS, U. Tokyo, 1979, MS, 1981; PhD, Marquette U., 1986. Rsch. assoc. U. Mo., Kansas City, 1986-88, U. Ill., Chgo., 1988-91; staff scientist Synaptic Pharm., Paramus, N.J., 1991-92; sr. scientist Molecumetics, Bellevue, Wash., 1992—; asst. prof. U. Wash., Seattle, 1994—. Contbr. articles to profl. publs. Home: 8315 127th Pl SE Renton WA 98056-9155 Office: Molecumetics Inst 2023 120th Ave NE Ste 400 Bellevue WA 98005-2134

NAKANO-MATSUMOTO, NAOMI NAMIKO, social worker; b. Salt Lake City, May 3, 1960; d. Rokuro George and Miyuki (Tashima) N.; m. Robert Hideo Matsumoto. BS in Sociology and Social Work, Weber State Coll., Ogden, Utah, 1982; MSW, U. Denver, 1986. Lic. social worker, Calif.; lic. clin. social worker, Calif.; cert. social svc. worker, Utah. Student counselor Parkview Community Corrections Ctr., Ogden, 1981-82; caseworker Children's Aid Soc. of Utah, Ogden, 1982-85; intern in social work Asian-Pacific Devel. Ctr., Denver, 1985-86, social worker, 1987; social worker Denver Pub. Schs., 1988-91, Asian-Ams. for Community Involvement, San Jose, Calif., 1991-94; program mgr. Asian Am. Recovery Svcs., Inc., 1994—. Mem. Task Force Monitoring Violence Against Asians, Denver, 1986, com. Japanese - Am. Comty. Grad. Program, Denver, 1989, 92, Nat. JACL Conf. Workshop, 1990, 91; mem. adv. bd. after sch. program Oasis, Ogden, 1985; bd. dirs. Asian Edn. Adv. Coun. Denver Pub. Schs., 1989-91, Yu AiKai Japanese-Am. Comty. Sr. Ctr., 1993—, Am. Inst. for Asian Am. Families, 1994—; vol. friend Denver Girls, Inc., 1990. Named One of Outstanding Young Women in Am., 1988, Outstanding Vol.-Denver Girls, Inc., 1990. Mem. NASW, Nat. Assn. Asian-Pacific-Am. Edn., Asian-Am. Psychol. Assn., Asian Women Advocating for Rights & Empowerment, Asian Pacific Islanders for Choice, Coalition for Multicultural Mental Health Svcs., Asian Human Svcs. Assn., Coalition of Asian Pacific Islander Youth. Democrat. Buddhist.

NAKASHIMA, MITSUGI, state agency administrator. Chmn. Edn. divsn., Honolulu. Office: Education Dvsn PO Box 2360 Honolulu HI 96804-2360

NAKATANI, HENRY MASATOSHI, structural engineer; b. Honolulu, Feb. 23, 1942; s. Minoru and Teruko (Mizusaki) N.; divorced; 1 child, Janice Masako. BS, U. Hawaii, 1964, MS, 1966; postgrad., San Jose State U., 1967-68. Registered profl. engr., Hawaii. Tech. staff mem. Sandia Corp., Livermore, Calif., 1966-69; structural engr. Shimazu, Shimabukuro, Fukuda Inc., Honolulu, 1969-71; structural engr. State of Hawaii Pub. Wks., Honolulu, 1971-78, 81-90, engring. mgr., 1990—; stadium engr. Aloha Stadium, Honolulu, 1978-81; lectr. U. Hawaii, Honolulu, 1980—. Author: Comparison of Wind Induced Vibrations of Structures Using Real and Pseudo Wind Records, 1966. Vice-pres. Parents Without Ptnrs., Honolulu, 1994-95. Recipient Achievement award State of Hawaii, 1989, 93, Outstanding Civil Engring. Sr., ASCE, 1964. Mem. Am. Pub. Wks. Assn. (awards chmn. 1990—), Structural Engrs. Assn. Hawaii, Phi Kappa Phi, Omicron Delta Kappa, Chi Epsilon. Office: State of Hawaii Public Wks 1151 Punchbowl St Honolulu HI 96813-3007

NAKAYAMA, RANDALL SHIGE, English language educator; b. Oakland, Calif., Aug. 20, 1957; s. Shigenobu and Helen (Wada) N. AB in English, U. Calif., Berkeley, 1979, MA in English, 1982, PhD in English, 1986. Vis. asst. prof. San Jose (Calif.) State U., 1988-90; asst. prof. English San Francisco State U., 1991—. Author introduction, editor: The Life and Death of Mrs. Mary Frith, 1993. Mem. Phi Beta Kappa. Home: 314 Garces Dr San Francisco CA 94132-2137 Office: San Francisco State U Dept English San Francisco CA 94132

NAKRA, NARESH KUMAR, food products executive; b. New Delhi, India, Jan. 8, 1946; came to U.S. in 1967; s. Tilak Raj and Eimla K. (Kalra) N.; m. Kavita Nakra, Aug. 16, 1971; children: Neal, Navin. BSME, U. Delhi, India, 1967; MSME, U. Iowa, 1970, PhD, 1975. Sr. process engr. Quaker Oats, Chgo., 1973-78, mgr. env. and energy, 1978-80, mgr. ops. pkg., 1980-84, mgr. engring., 1984-86; v.p. engring. Sunshine Biscuits, Inc., Woodbridge, N.J., 1986-88, v.p. plant ops., 1988-89, sr. v.p. ops., 1989-91; COO Gruma Corp., L.A., 1991-93, pres., CEO, 1993—. Cmty. Leadership, L.A., 1995. Mem. ASME, Packaging Inst. Office: Gruma Corp 5750 Grace Pl Ste 3A Los Angeles CA 90022-4121

NALDER, ERIC CHRISTOPHER, investigative reporter; b. Coulee Dam, Wash., Mar. 2, 1946; s. Philip Richard and Mibs Dorothy (Aurdal) N.; m. Jan Christiansen, Dec. 20, 1968; 1 child, Britt Hillary. BA in Communications, U. Wash., 1968. News editor Whidbey News-Times, Oak Harbor, Wash., 1971; reporter Lynnwood (Wash.) Enterprise, 1972, Everett Herald, Lynnwood, 1972-75; gen. assignment reporter Seattle Post-Intelligencer, 1975-78, edn. writer, 1977-78, investigative reporter, 1978-83; chief investigative reporter Seattle Times, 1983—. Author: Tankers Full of Trouble, 1994. Recipient Edn. Writers Assn. award Charles Stewart Mott Found., 1978, Hearst Community Svc. award, 1978, C.B. Blethen awards (12), Outstanding Govt. Reporting award Seattle Mcpl. League, Pub. Svc. in Journalism award Sigma Delta Chi, 1987, Edward J. Meeman award Scripps Howard Found., 1987, Thomas Stokes award, Washington Journalism Ctr., 1990, Pulitzer prize for nat. reporting, 1990, Nat. Headline award, 1991, Pub. Svc. award AP Mags. Editors Assn., 1992, Goldsmith prize for investigative reporting, 1992, Worth Bingham prize for investigative reporting, 1992, Headliner award, 1992, Investigative Reporters and Editors award, 1992. Mem. Investigative Reporters and Editors, Pacific N.W. Newspaper Guild. Office: Seattle Times Fairview Avenue St N Seattle WA 98109

NAMEN, ANTHONY EUGENE, biochemist, immunologist; b. Helena, Mont., Aug. 3, 1943; s. Anthony James and Kathryn Marie (Morris) N. BS, Mont. State U., 1977, MS, 1979; PhD, Wash. State U., 1984. Sr. staff scientist Immunex Corp., Seattle, 1984—. Contbr. articles to profl. jours. Served with U.S. Navy, 1965-70, Egypt. Mem. N.Y. Acad. Sci. Democrat. Roman Catholic. Home: 1135 4th Ave E Kalispell MT 59901-5818

NANCE, ROBERT LEWIS, oil company executive; b. Dallas, July 10, 1936; s. Melvin Renfro Nance and Ruth Natlie (Seibert) Nowlin; m. Penni Jane Warfel; children: Robert Scott, Amy Louise, Catherine Leslie. BS, So. Meth. U., 1959; LLD (hon.), Rocky Mountain Coll., 1989. V.p. geology Oliver & West Cons., Dallas, 1960-66; ptnr. Nance & Larue Cons., Dallas, 1966-69; pres., CEO Nance Petroleum Corp., Billings, Mont., 1969—; bd. dirs. First Interstate Bank Commerce, MDU Resources, Rocky Mountain Coll., Billings, chmn., 1986-91; mem. Nat. Petroleum Coun., 1992-94. Coun. pres. Am. Luth. Ch., Billings, 1980; trustee, chmn. Deaconess Med. Ctr., Billings; chmn. Deaconess Billings Clinic Healty Sys. Recipient Hall of Fame award Rocky Mountain Coll. Alumni, 1987, Disting. Svc. Trusteeship, Assn. Governing Bds. Univs. Colls., 1988. Mem. Am. Assn. Petroleum Geologists, Ind. Petroleum Assn. Am. (exec. com., v.p. Mont. chpt.), Ind. Petroleum Assn. Mountain States (v.p. Mont. 1977-79), Mont. Petroleum Assn., Hilands Golf Club, Billings Petroleum Club. Office: Nance Petroleum Corp PO Box 7168 550 N 31st St Billings MT 59103

NANDAGOPAL, MALLUR R., engineer; b. Kolar, Karnataka, India, May 14, 1938; came to U.S., 1976; s. M. Ramanuja Iyengar and Garudammal; m. Sreedharani K. Ramamurthy; children: Radha, Meena, Sudha. BS, Cen. Coll., Bangalore, India, 1958; B of Tech., Indian Inst. Tech., Bombay, 1962;

ME, Indian Inst. Sci., Bangalore, 1963, PhD, 1974. Registered profl. engr., Wash. Mem. faculty Indian Inst. Sci., 1963-77; engr. City of Spokane, Wash., 1977—; coord. summer sch. Indian Inst. Sci., 1974-75. Contbr. articles to profl. jours. Mem. restoration adv. bd. Fairchild AFB. Mem. IEEE (sr.), Inst. Sci. (sec. Staff Club 1972-74), Fed. Emergency Mgmt. Agy. (mitigation com.). Hindu. Home: 410 E Shiloh Hills Dr Spokane WA 99208-5819

NANTO, ROXANNA LYNN, career planning administrator, consultant; b. Hanford, Calif., Dec. 17, 1952; d. Lawson Gene Brooks and Bernice (Page) Jackson; m. Harvey Ken Nanto, Mar. 23, 1970; 1 child, Shea Kiyoshi. A. Gen. Studies, Chemeketa Community Coll., 1976; BBA, Idaho State U., 1978. PBX operator Telephone Answer Bus. Svc., Moses Lake, Wash., 1965-75; edn. coord. MimiCassia Community Edn., Rupert, Idaho, 1976-77; office mgr. Lockwood Corp., Rupert, Idaho, 1977-78; cost acct. Keyes Fibre Co., Wenatchee, Wash., 1978-80; acctg. office mgr. Armstrong & Armstrong, Wenatchee, Wash., 1980-81; office mgr. Cascade Cable Constrn. Inc., East Wenatchee, Wash., 1981-83; interviewer, counselor Wash. Employment Security, Wenatchee, 1983-84; pres. chief exec. officer Regional Health Care Plus, East Wenatchee, 1986-88; dist. career coord. Eastmont Sch. Dist., East Wenatchee, 1984-90; prin. Career Cons., 1988-90; exec. dir. Wenatchee Valley Coll. Found., 1990-91; ednl. cons. Sunbelt Consortium, East Wenatchee, 1991-93; cons. CC Cons. Assocs., 1993—; ptnr. Cmty. Devel. Mktg. and Mgmt. Resource Group, Wenatchee, Wash., 1994—; also bd. dirs. Cmty. Devel. Mktg. and Mgmt. Resource Group, Wenatchee; speaker North Cen. Washington Profl. Women, Wenatche, 1987, Wen Career Women's Network, Wenatchee, 1990, Wenatchee Valley Rotary, 1990, Meeting the Challenge of Workforce 2000, Seattle, 1993; cons., speaker Wash. State Sch. Dirs., Seattle, 1987; speaker Wenatchee C. of C., 1989; sec. Constrn. Coun. of North Cen. Washington, Wenatchee, 1981-83; bd. dirs. Gen. Vocat. Adv. Bd., Wenatchee, 1986-88, Washington Family Ind. Program, Olympia, 1989—; mem. econ. devel. coun. Grant County, 1992—. Mem. at large career Women's Network, 1984—, mem. Econ. Devel. Coun. of No. Cen. Washington; mem. Steering Com. to Retain Judge Small. Grantee Nat. Career Devel. Guidelines Wash. State, 1989; named Wenatchee Valley Coll. Vocat. Contbr. of Yr., 1991. Fellow Dem. Women's Club; mem. Nat. Assn. Career Counselors, Nat. Assn. Pvt. Career Counselors, Nat. Coun. Resource Devel., NCW Estate Planning Coun. Home: 704 Larch Ct Wenatchee WA 98802-5052 Office: CC Cons Assn 704 Larch Ct Ste B East Wenatchee WA 98802-5052

NAPIER, MAUREEN JILL, critical care nurse; b. Ipswich, Eng., July 17, 1940; came to U.S., 1960; d. Roy Bacon and Phyllis (Elizabeth) Pickering; m. Jim D. Napier, Mar. 27, 1960; children: Tracey, Mark. ASN with honors, Bakersfield (Calif.) Coll., 1982; BSN with honors, Calif. State U., Bakersfield, 1990. RN, Calif.; CCRN. Staff nurse ICU and CCU San Joaquin Community Hosp., Bakersfield. Mem. AACCN, Nightingale Soc.

NAPLES, CAESAR JOSEPH, public policy educator, lawyer, consultant; b. Buffalo, Sept. 4, 1938; s. Caesar M. and Fannie A. (Occhipinti) N.; children: Jennifer, Caesar; m. Sandra L. Harrison, July 16, 1983. AB, Yale U., 1960; JD, SUNY, 1963. Bar: N.Y. 1963, Fla. 1977, Calif. 1988, U.S. Supreme Ct. 1965. Assoc. Moot & Sprague, Buffalo, 1965-69; asst. dir., employee rels. N.Y. Gov. Office, Albany, 1969-71; asst. v. chancellor SUNY, Albany, 1971-75; vice chancellor Fla. State U. System, 1983-92; v. chancellor Calif. State U. System, Long Beach, 1983-92; vice chancellor emeritus Calif. State U., 1992—; prof. law and fin. Calif. State U. System, Long Beach, 1983—; cons. Govt. of Australia, U. Nev. Sys., Assn. Can. Colls. and Univs., Que., also other univs. and colls. Contbr. articles to profl. jours.; co-author: Romanov Succession, 1989 with J.Victor Baldridge. Mem. Metlife Resources Adv. Bd., 1986—, chmn., 1992—; mem. heart bd. Long Beach Meml. Hosp., 1993—. Capt. U.S. Army, 1963-65. Mem. Acad Pers. Administrn. (founder), Nat. Ctr. for Study Collective Bargaining Higher Edn. (bd. dirs.). Office: 816 N Juanita Ave Ste B Redondo Beach CA 90277-2200

NAPOLIELLO, DANIEL ANDREW, nursing administrator; b. Omaha, Sept. 27, 1944; Ceasare Dan and Therese Mary (Sierszynski) N.; m. Sally Ann Rodak, Jan. 7, 1967; children: John, Ann Marie, Michael. Diploma in nursing, St Joseph Hosp., Omaha, 1965; BS in Nursing, U. S.C., 1975; MEd, Chapman Coll., 1977. Commd. 2nd lt. U.S. Army, 1964; advanced through grades to commdr. Nurse Corps U.S. Army, 1994; chief nurse 8th combat support hosp. Nurse Corps U.S. Army, Fort Ord, Calif., 1975-77, resigned, 1977; commd. officer USPHS, 1977-94, advanced through grades to comdr., 1988; dir. nursing Indian Hosp. USPHS, Rosebud, S.D., 1977-78, Winnebago, Nebr., 1984-87; assoc. hosp. dir. nursing edn. USPHS, Balt., 1978-81, evening supr. nursing, coord. quality assurance, 1981-84; retired, 1994; area hosp. nursing cons. Phoenix Area Indian Health Svc., 1987-94; nurse cons. Glendale, 1994—; mem. USPHS Nursing Continuing Edn. Rev. Com., Rockville, Md., 1979-81, 88-92, Indian Health Svc. Nursing Prof. Splty. Group, Rockville, 1984-90, Ind. Health Svc. Coun. of Nursing Svcs., 1987-94, chmn., 1988-92. Contbr. articles to profl. jours. Asst. scoutmaster Sioux coun. Boy Scouts Am., 1977-78, scoutmaster Balt. coun., 1978-81, asst. dist. commr. Prairie Gold area coun., 1982-87, Theodore Roosevelt coun., 1987-93, chmn. dist. health and safety com., 1978-81, mem. health careers subcom. nat. exploring com., 1989—, dist. commr. Grand Canyon coun., 1993—; instr. CPR, ARC, 1982-87; mem. Hebr. Hist. Soc., Union Pacific R.R. Hist. Soc. Recipient citation USPHS, 1987, commendation medal, 1989, Chief Nurse Office award, 1991, Outstanding Svc. medal, 1992, Nursing Excellence award for Nursing Practice, 1991, Wood Badge Boy Scouts Am., 1981, St. George Emblem, 1982, 3 Bead Wood Badge, 1989, Disting. Commr. award, 1991, Silver Beaver award, 1992, Surgeon Gen.'s Exemplary Svc. medal and Outstanding Svc. medal USPHS, 1992, 93, Dirs. award for Excellence and EEO Excellence award Indian Health Svc., Phoenix, 1994. Mem. ANA, Nebr. Nurses Assn., Balt. Chpt. Commd. Officers Assn. of USPHS (nurse officers rep. 1980, v.p. 1981), Aberdeen Area Coun. on Nursing (pres. 1986-87), Nat. Model Railroaders Assn., Nat. Scout Collectors Soc., Camerail Club, Commd. Officers Assn. (sec.-treas. Phoenix chpt. 188-89, v.p. Phoenix chpt. 1990-91, pres. 1991-92, nat. del. 1987, 88, 92). Democrat. Roman Catholic. Home: 10031 N 47th Ave Glendale AZ 85302-2502

NAPOLITANO, GRACE F., state legislator; b. Brownsville, Tex., Dec. 4, 1936; d. Miguel and Maria Alicia Ledezma Flores; m. Frank Napolitano, 1982; 1 child, Yolando M., Fred Musquiz Jr., Edward M., Michael M., Cynthia M. Student, Cerritos Coll., L.A. Trade Tech, Tec Southwest Coll. Mem. Calif. Assembly, 1993—. Councilwoman City of Norwalk, Calif., 1986-92, mayor, 1989-90; active Cmty. Family Guidance. Mem. Cerritos Coll. Found., Lions Club. Democrat. Roman Catholic. Home: 12946 Belcher St Norwalk CA 90650-3328 Office: Calif Assembly State Capitol Sacramento CA 95814-4906 also: PO Box 942849 Sacramento CA 94249-0001

NARAMORE, JAMES JOSEPH, family practice physician, educator; b. Gillette, Wyo., Nov. 29, 1949; s. Kenneth Chester and Joan (Biggerstaff) N.; m. Karen Rae Buttermore, July 9, 1972; children: Lindsay, Marissa, Jessica, Marcus. BA with highest achievement in Biology, John Brown U., Siloam Springs, Ark., 1972; MD with family practice honors, U. Utah, 1977. Diplomate Am. Bd. Family Practice. Resident in family practice U. Nebr., Omaha, 1977-80, chief resident; pvt. practice, Gillette, 1981—; mem. staff Campbell County Meml. Hosp., Gillette, 1980—, chief staff, 1986, chief dept. family practice, 1990-91; instr. dept. human medicine U. Wyo., 1983-86, clin. assoc. prof. family practice, 1986—; ptnr., co-founder Med. Arts Lab., Gillette, 1981—; med. dir. Campbell County Detention Ctr., 1988—; med. dir. Pioneer Manor Nursing Home, Gillette, 1989—; aviation med. examiner FAA, Oklahoma City, 1986—; cons. on occupational medicine to numerous industries, Campbell County, 1986—. Charter mem. Gillette Area Leadership Inst., 1986-87; chmn. missions com. Grace Bible Ch., Gillette, 1983—, chmn. bd. elders, 1989—. Mem. Am. Acad. Family Physicians, Wyo. Med. Soc., Campbell County Med. Soc. (pres. 1983-84), Gillette C. of C. (bd. dirs. 1987-90), Toastmasters (pres. Gillette 1992, Competent Toastmaster award 1986—). Republican. Home: 1214 Hilltop Ct Gillette WY 82718-5625 Office: Family Health 407 S Medical Arts Ct Ste D Gillette WY 82716-3372

NARATH, ALBERT, laboratory administrator; b. Berlin, Mar. 5, 1933; came to U.S., 1947; s. Albert Narath and Johanna Agnes Anne (Bruggeman) Bruckmann; m. Worth Haines Scattergood (div. 1976); children: Tanya, Lise, Yvette; m. Barbara Dean Camp (div. 1983); 1 child, Albert; m. Shanna S. Lindeman. BS in Chemistry, U. Cin., 1955; PhD in Phys. Chemistry, U. Calif., Berkeley, 1959. Mem. tech. staff, mgr. phys. sci. Sandia Nat. Labs., Albuquerque, 1959-68, dir. solid state sci., 1968-71, mng. dir. phys. sci., 1971-73, v.p. rsch., 1973-82, exec. v.p. rsch. and adv. weapons sys., 1982-84, pres., 1989—. Contbr. sci. articles to profl. jours. Fellow AAAS, Am. Phys. Soc. (George E. Pake prize 1991); mem. NAE. Office: Sandia Nat Labs MS 0101 PO Box 5800 Albuquerque NM 87185-0101

NARAYANAMURTI, VENKATESH, research administrator; b. Bangalore, Karnataka, India, Sept. 9, 1939; came to U.S., 1961; s. Duraiswami and Janaki (Subramaniam) N.; m. Jayalakshmi Krishnayya, Aug. 23, 1961; children: Arjun, Ranjini, Krishna. BSc, MSc, St. Stephen's Coll., Delhi, India, 1958; PhD, Cornell U., 1965. Instr., rsch. assoc. Cornell U., Ithaca, N.Y., 1965-68; mem. tech. staff AT&T Bell Labs., Murray Hill, N.J., 1968-76, dept.head, 1976-81, dir., 1981-87; v.p. rsch. Sandia Nat. Labs., Albuquerque, 1987-92; dean engring. U. Calif., Santa Barbara, 1992—; chmn. adv. bd. Coll. of Elec. Engring., Cornell U., 1989-90, sci. bd. and regional coun. Santa Fe Inst., 1987-90, microelectric bd., Jet Propulsion Lab., Pasadena, Calif., 1988-90, sci. bd. Stanford Synchroton Lab., Stanford, Calif., 1989-92; mem. IUPAP Commn. on Physics for Devel.; engring. directrorate adv. bd. NSF, 1992—; Fermi award com. Dept. of Energy, 1992—; chair Dept. of Energy Inertial Confinement Fusion Adv. Com., 1992—. Author more than 100 publs.; patentee in field. Fellow IEEE, AAAS, Am. Phys. Soc., Indian Acad. Scis.; mem. NAE, Royal Swedish Acad. Engring. Scis. (fgn.). Office: U Calif Engring Santa Barbara CA 93106

NARODICK, KIT GORDON, lawyer, consultant; b. Seattle, Nov. 29, 1937; s. Philip H. and Blanche G. (Gordon) N.; m. Sally Gould, Apr., 1970; children: Lisa Ann, Philip H. BA, U. Wash., 1960, MBA, 1962; PhD, Columbia U., 1967. JD, U. Puget Sound, 1987; Prof. econs. NYU, 1967-73; dir. Boeing Comml. Airplane Co., Seattle, 1973-85; of counsel, Bogle & Gates, Seattle, 1988—; vis. prof. Columbia U., N.Y.C., 1967-69. Bd. dirs. Seattle Repertory Theatre, 1978-85; chmn. Wash. State Com. on Tourism, Olympia, 1984. Mem. Puget Sound Air Transp. Com., 1990-93; bd. trustees Mus. Flight, 1994—. Mem. ABA, Am. Mktg. Assn., Wash. State Bar Assn., King County Bar Assn., Lawyer-Pilots Bar Assn., Transp. Research Forum, Transp. Research Bd., European Soc. Market Research, Travel and Tourism Research Assn. (dir. 1979-83, pres., 1983-84), Pacific Area Travel Assn. (dir. 1980-84, chmn. 1984-85). Jewish. Clubs: Wash. Athletic, Rainier (Seattle), Columbia Tower, Bellevue Athletic. Home: 4513 54th Ave NE Seattle WA 98105-3834 Office: Bogle & Gates 2 Union Square 601 Union St Seattle WA 98101-2327

NARULA, MOHAN LAL, realtor; b. Ferozepur, India, Feb. 2, 1939; came to U.S., 1962; s. Ram Dyal and Pemeshwari Narula; m. Sylvia Conway, Aug. 31, 1968; children: Rabinder, Rajinder. BS, Panjab U., India, 1960; BSME, Calif. Poly. State U., San Luis Obispo, 1965; MS in Engring., Calif. State U., Northridge, 1970. Engr. Abex Corp., Oxnard, Calif., 1965-69; salesman, realtor Walker & Lee, Oxnard, Calif., 1970-73; owner, realtor Narula Co. Realtors, Oxnard, Calif., 1973—. Mem. Cert. Comml. Investment Mem. (designate 1979), Oxnard Harbor Bd. Realtors (mem. profl. standard com. 1980-89), Los Angeles Cert. Comml. Investment Mem. (bd. dirs., treas. 1985). Home: 2830 W Hill St Oxnard CA 93035-2522 Office: Narula Co Realtor 3201 Samuel Ave Ste 7 Oxnard CA 93033-5334

NASH, CLARICE ALDINE HAYES, family nurse practitioner, critical care nurse; b. Chgo., May 12, 1952; d. Clarence Jesse and Beatrice Ann (Bevers) Hayes; m. Robert James Nash, Aug. 8, 1981; children: Christopher Robert, Jesse Daniel, Sara April. BSN, U. Tex., El Paso, 1974; MSN, U. South Ala., 1991; FNP, Miss. U. for Women, 1991. RN, Tex., Calif., Miss., Wash.; cert. FNP, ANCC. Staff nurse Sun Towers Hosp., El Paso, Tex., 1974-76; head nurse CCU, St. Joseph Hosp., El Paso, 1976-77; staff nurse MICU/SICU Grossmont Dist. Hosp., La Mesa, Calif., 1984-86; staff nurse CCU, Sharp Meml. Hosp., San Diego, 1984-86, Gulf Coast Community Hosp., Biloxi, Miss., 1987-89; staff nurse critical care Analytical Med. Enterprises, Gulfport, Miss., 1991; nurse practitioner Kitsap County Health Dist., Bremerton, Wash., 1991-93; family nurse practitioner Peninsula Family Med. Ctr., Gig Harbor, Wash., 1994—; clin. preceptor grad. nursing programs U. Wash. and Pacific Lutheran U., 1994; adj. faculty ADN program Olympic Coll., Bremerton, 1991-94; clin. preceptor grad. nursing programs U. Wash., Pacific Luth. U. With Nurse Corps USN, 1977-83, comdr. USNR. Mem. ANA, AACN, Wash. Nurse's Assn., Nat. League for Nursing, Am. Acad. Nurse Practitioners, Assn. Mil. Surgeons of U.S. Lutheran. Office: Peninsula Family Med Ctr 4700 Point Fosdick Dr NW Gig Harbor WA 98335-1706

NASH, CYNTHIA JEANNE, journalist; b. Detroit, Dec. 24, 1947; d. Frederick Copp and Carolyn (Coffin) N.; 1 child, Lydia Anne Maza; m. Richard Zahler, July 22, 1994. BA, U. Mich., 1969. Reporter, Detroit News, 1970-75, sports columnist, 1975-77, Life Style columnist, 1977-79, Life Style editor, 1979-82; news features editor Seattle Times, 1983, asst. mng. editor Sunday Seattle Times, 1983-86, assoc. mng. editor, 1986—. Mem. Harbor Sq. Club. Office: Seattle Times PO Box 70 Fairview Ave N & John St Seattle WA 98111-0070

NASH, REFORD BROOKS, minister; b. Chickasha, Okla., June 17, 1944; s. Cheston Alfred and Gladys Marion (Brooks) N.; m. Rosemarie Benziger, Mar. 20, 1971 (div. Sept. 1983); 1 child, Aaron Alfred; m. Marilyn Carol Konkol, Aug. 31, 1984; children: Trevor James McLellan, Shelley Elizabeth. BA, Okla. Bapt. U., 1966; MDiv, San Francisco Theol. Sem., 1969; ThM, Princeton Theol. Sem., 1978; D of Ministry, McCormick Theol. Sem., 1985. Ordained, 1969. Assoc. pastor Pasadena (Calif.) Presbyn. Ch., 1969-71, First Presbyn. Ch., Oceanside, Calif., 1971-74; chaplain, chair religion dept. The Hun Sch., Princeton, N.J., 1975-78; pastor First Presbyn. Ch., Grapevine, Tex., 1978-80, West Side Presbyn. Ch., Wichita, Kans., 1980-88; sr. pastor Federated Cmty. Ch., Flagstaff, Ariz., 1988—; mediator Superior Ct., Flagstaff, Ariz., 1994—, Ariz. Atty. Gen., Flagstaff, 1989—; com. on ministry mem. Grand Canyon Presbytery, Ariz., 1993—; commr. Presbyn. Synod of Southwest, Phoenix, 1994. Bd. dirs. Cath. Social Svc., Flagstaff; mem. adv. bd. Grand Canyon Coun. Boy Scouts Am., Phoenix, 1992—. Mem. N.Am. Acad. Liturgy (assoc.), Acad. Family Mediators (cert. mediator), Flagstaff Rotary Club (dir. internat. svc.). Home: 2315 W Lantern Ln Flagstaff AZ 86001-1134 Office: Federated Cmty Ch PO Box 1802 Flagstaff AZ 86002

NASH, RICHARD EUGENE, aerospace engineer; b. San Diego, Feb. 18, 1954; s. Clifford Arthur Jr. and Dorothy Fay (Johnson) N.; m. Lynn Elora Martin, Aug. 5, 1978. BSCE, U. Ky., 1981; MCE, U. So. Calif., 1988. Registered profl. civil engr., Calif.; cert. profl. mgr. Mem. tech. staff Rockwell Internat., Downey, Calif., 1982—, lead engr. space shuttle propulsion systems, 1986-88; engr. Nat. Aero-Space Plane, Long Beach, Calif., 1988-89, orbiter project engr., 1989—; pvt. practice civil engring., Buena Park, Calif., 1985—. Scoutmaster Boy Scouts Am., Covington, Ky., 1972-74, Williamstown, Ky., 1976-82, asst. scoutmaster, Ft. Hood, Tex., 1975-76. Sgt. U.S. Army, 1976. Recipient Eagle Scout award Boy Scouts Am., 1972; named to Hon. Order of Ky. Cols. 1985. Mem. NSPE, Nat. Mgmt. Assn., Nat. Eagle Scout Assn. (advisor 1983), Masons (32 degree, sr. deacon), Chi Epsilon. Republican. Office: Rockwell Internat Space Transp and Systems Div 12214 Lakewood Blvd Downey CA 90242-2655

NASH, STELLA B., government nutrition administrator; b. Gould, Ark., Nov. 3, 1942; d. Virgil and Lessie B. (Bonner) Riley; m. Solomon Nash, Mar. 31, 1973; children: Chad, Jereme. BS, Ark. AM & N Coll., 1964; MA, NYU, 1970; postgrad., Pa. State U., 1973-74, U. Mo., 1974-75. Nutritionist/spl. asst. to the dir. Ark. Office on Aging, Little Rock, 1975-76; supr. child nutrition Ark. State Dept. Edn., Little Rock, 1976-79; supr. Coop. Extension Svc. USDA, Denver, 1979-85; regional nutrition dir. Mountain Plains region USDA Food and Nutrition Svc., Denver, 1985—; home mgmt. specialist U. Ark. Coop. Extension, Pine Bluff, 1972-73; nutritionist N.J. Coll. Medicine and Dentistry, Newark, 1970-72; dietitian King County Hosp., Bklyn., 1964-66. Co-author: (coloring book) Nutrition Education, 1972; contbr. newspaper articles to Rocky Mountain News, 1992; author (jour.) Ill. Tchr., 1974. State v.p., dist. pres. New Home Makers Am., Ark., 1958-59; mem. Montbello Optimist Club, Denver, 1987-89, Far NE Neighbors Assn., Denver, 1985—; chairperson worship United Ch. of Montbello, Denver, 1989—. Recipient Nutrition Edn. award Western Dairy Coun., 1986; named Outstanding Educator of Am., Outstanding Educators of Am., 1973, Outstanding Young Woman of Am., Outstanding Young Women of Am., 1976. Mem. Am. Dietetic Assn. (registered dietitian), Colo. Dietetic Assn. (scholarship chairperson 1990-91, pub. rels. 1983-84) Soc. Nutrition Edn., Ark. Gerontol. Soc. (charter), Delta Sigma Theta (undergrad. chpt. sponsor 1972-73). Home: 4743 Chandler Ct Denver CO 80239-4971

NASH, WILLIAM KELLY, lawyer; b. Preston, Idaho, Mar. 10, 1959; s. William Isaac and Lois Jean (Meyers) N.; m. Karen Lynn Fox, June 24, 1984; children: Amanda Lynn, Lindsay Katherine, Erika Jean, William Brady. BS, Brigham Young U., 1983, JD, 1986. Bar: Utah 1986, U.S. Dist. Ct. Utah 1986. Summer assoc. Jones, Waldo, Holbrook & McDonough, Salt Lake City, 1985, assoc., 1987-90; ptnr. Holme Roberts & Owen, 1990—; jud. clk. U.S. Dist. Ct., Salt Lake City, 1986-87; judge pro tem small claims div. 5th Cir. Ct., Murray, Utah, 1988—. Mormon missionary Kobe/Osaka, Japan, 1978-80. Brigham Young U. scholar, 1977-78, J. Reuben Clark Law Sch. scholar, 1984-86. Mem. Utah Bar Assn. (young lawyers and litigation sect., chmn. membership support com.), Profl. Ski Instrs. Assn. (cert. instr.). Republican. Home: 1709 Haven Chase Ln Salt Lake City UT 84121-6517 Office: Holme Roberts & Owen 111 E Broadway Ste 1100 Salt Lake City UT 84111-5233

NASON, DOLORES IRENE, computer company executive, counselor, eucharistic minister; b. Seattle, Jan. 24, 1934; d. William Joseph Lockinger and Ruby Irene (Church) Gilstrap; m. George Malcolm Nason Jr., Oct. 7, 1951; children: George Malcolm III, Scott James, Lance William, Natalie Joan. Student, Long Beach (Calif.) City Coll., 1956-59; cert. in Religious Edn. for elem tchrs., Immaculate Heart Coll., 1961, cert. teaching, 1962, cert secondary teaching, 1967; attended, Salesian Sem., 1983-85. Buyer J. C. Penney Co., Barstow, Calif., 1957; prin. St. Cyprian Confraternity of Christian Doctrine Elem. Sch., Long Beach, 1964-67; prin. summer sch. St. Cyprian Confraternity of Christian Doctrine Elem. Sch., Long Beach, 1965-67; pres. St. Cyprian Confraternity Orgn., Long Beach, 1967-69; dist. co-chmn. L.A. Diocese, 1968-70; v.p. Nason & Assocs., Inc., Long Beach, 1978—; pres. L.A. County Commn. on Obscenity & Pornography, 1984—; eucharistic minister St. Cyprian Ch., Long Beach, 1985—; bd. dirs. L.A. County Children's Svcs., 1988—; part-time social svcs. counselor Disabled Resources Ctr., Inc., Long Beach, 1992—; vol. Meml. Children's Hosp., Long Beach, 1977—; mem. scholarship com. Long Beach City Coll., 1984-90, Calif. State U., Long Beach, 1984-90. Mem. adv. bd. Pro-Wilson 90 Gov., Calif., 1990; mem. devel. bd. St. Joseph High Sch., 1987—; pres. St. Cyprian's Parish Coun., 1962—; mem. Long Beach Civic Light Opera, 1973—, Assistance League of Long Beach, 1976—. Mem. L.A. Fitness Club, U. of the Pacific Club, K.C. (Family of the Month 1988). Republican. Roman Catholic.

NASR, SEYYED VALI REZA, political science educator; b. Tehran, Iran, Dec. 20, 1960; came to U.S., 1979; s. Seyyed Hossein and Soussan (Daneshvari) N.; m. Darya Ahyaie, Jan. 20, 1987; 1 child, Amir-Ali. BA, Tufts U., 1983; MALD, Fletcher Sch. Law & Diplomacy, 1984; PhD, MIT, 1991. Archivist Found. for Iranian Studies, Bethesda, Md., 1987-91; asst. prof. political sci. U. San Diego, 1992—; vis. asst. prof. Tufts U., Medford, Mass., 1991. Author: The Vanguard of the Islamic Revolution, 1994, Shi'ism: Doctrines, Thought..., 1988, Expectation of the Millenium, 1989; contbr. articles to profl. jours. Recipient Social Sci. Rsch. Coun., 1992, James T. Irvine Found., 1994, Am. Inst. of Pakistan Studies, 1989-90. Office: U San Diego Dept Pol Sci 5998 Alcala Park San Diego CA 92110-2429

NASSIKAS, JAMES ACHILLES, hotel executive; b. Concord, N.H., Sept. 15, 1927; s. Achilles John and Christine (Recoutes) N.; m. Helen McClelland Horner, Aug. 23, 1952; children: William John , Christine Fair. BS in Hotel Adminstrn., U. N.H., 1952; certs. Svc., Cuisine, Ecole Hotelier Soc Suisse, Lausanne, Switzerland, 1954. Dir. food and svc. Plaza Hotel, Mayflower Hotel, N.Y.C., Washington, 1960-65; v.p., gen. mgr. Royal Orleans Hotel Hotel Corp. Am., New Orleans, 1965-69; pres., mng. ptnr. The Stanford Ct. Hotel, Sa Francisco, 1969-89; pres. Deer Valley Resort Co., Park City, Utah, 1978-89; pres., ptnr. Stancourt Corp., Bellevue, Wash., 1989—; adj. prof. U. N.H. Sch. Hotel Adminstrn., Durham, 1984-89; stammvater Stammtisch Ecole Hotelier de la SSH, western div., San Francisco, 1984-88; com. de patronage Ecole Hotelier de la SSH, Lausanne, 1968-82; disting. vis. prof. Johnson and Wales U., Providence, R.I., 1989; lectr. Cornell U., U. N.H., Culinary Inst. of Am. Contbr. numerous articles to profl. jours. and popular pubs. Chmn., pres., New Orleans Hotel and Motorhotel Assn., 1969-70; bd. visitors U. of Calif., Davis Sch. of Medicine, 1982-86; bd. overseers Hanover Inn, Dartmouth Coll., 1991-93. Recipient Silver Spoon award Food Arts Mag., 1991, numerous others; scholar San Francisco Profl. Food Soc., 1989; named Ind. Hotelier of World, Hotels Internat. Mag., 1986, Nat. Gourmet of Yr., Soc Bacchus, 1970, Hon. Mem., Les Clefs d'Or, 1986, Les Maitres-Conseils en Gastronomie, Francaise, 1984. Mem. Am. Inst. Wine and Food (founder, nat. exec. com. 1983—), Cornell Soc. Hotelman (assoc.), Culinary Inst. Am. (life mem.), Commanderie de Bordeaux, Confrerie de la Chaine des Rotisseurs, Marin Wine and Food Soc., New Eng. Innkeepers Assn. (hon. life mem.). Republican. Mem. Greek Orthodox Ch. Home and Office: 9 Marsh Dr Mill Valley CA 94941-1022

NAST, CAROL ANN, laboratory executive; b. Champaign, Ill., Nov. 8, 1945; d. Christian Anthony and Lelia Mae (Glover) N. BS, M.S., Tex. Christian U. Med.technologist Harris Hosp., Ft. Worth, 1967-72; diploma bus. exec. program Stanford U., 1994; chief med. technologist Presbyn. Hosp., Dallas, 1972-73; mfg. dir. Nuclear Med. Labs., Dallas, 1973-85; ops. mgr. Bio Rad Labs., Hercules, Calif., 1985-89; dir. ops Syva Co., Cupertino, 1989; adv. bd. Women in Sci. Program U. Tex., Arlington; adv. bd. Golden Gate U.; adv. editor Med. Device & Diagnostic Industry. Recipient Hon. Tribute to Women in Industry award YWCA. Mem. Am. Prodn. and Inventory Control Soc. (cert. in prodn. and inventory mgmt.), Am. Soc. Clin. Pathologists (asso. mem., cert. med. technologist), Am. Mgmt. Assn., Nat. Purchasing Mgmt. Assn., Sierra Club, Tamalpa Runners, Mensa. Home: 1117 Hamilton Ave Palo Alto CA 94301-2217 Office: 20400 Mariani Ave Cupertino CA 95014-2036

NASVIK-DENNISON, ANNA, artist; b. St. Paul; d. Peter Olson and Hattie Mathilda (Swenson) Nasvik; m. Roger Bennett, Nov. 7, 1936; children: Lynne, Kristin. Student, Coll. of St. Catherine, St. Paul, 1925, St. Paul Sch. of Art, 1927, Art Student's League, 1932. Tchr. art St. Joseph's Acad., St. Paul, 1926-30; freelance fashion illustrator N.Y.C., 1930-64; artist syndicated page The Fashion Syndicate, N.Y.C., 1934-38; mem. nat. art bd. Nat. League Am. Pen Women, 1990-92. One woman shows include Colbert Galleries, Sherbrooke St., Mont., Can., 1979, Gallery Milhalis, Sherbrooke St., Mont., 1984, T. Eaton Foyer des Arts, Mont., 1982-87, Venable-Neslage Gallerie, Washington, 1979-84, Lido Galleries, Scottsdale, Ariz., 1988, Hilltop Galleries, Nogales, Ariz., 1991 (top painting award, People's Choice award), 1995, Maiden Ln. Gallery, San Francisco, 1991, Hilltop Gallery, Nogales, 1995 (hon. mention Tubac Ctr. of Arts 1995). Named Woman of Art, Foyer des Arts, 1982; winner 3 top awards Ariz. juried show, Nat. League Am. Pen Women, 1989; recipient 3 People's Choice award Hilltop Galleries, 1991. Mem. Nat. Mus. Women in Arts, Santa Cruz Valley Art Assn., Lakeshore Assn. of Art, Nat. League of Pen Women (3 Top awards 1989, nat. bd. dirs. 1990—), Pen Women Sonora Desert. Home and Office: 231 W Paseo Adobe Green Valley AZ 85614-3462

NATARAJAN, RAMA, research scientist; b. Bangalore, India, June 30, 1952; came to U.S., 1980; d. Jayaraman Narayaswamy and Kameswari (Natesan) Narayanaswamy; m. Rajan Natarajan, June 27, 1979; 1 child, Pradeep. BS, Bangalore U., 1971, MS, 1973; PhD, Indian Inst. Sci., 1977. Sci. Rsch. Coun. rsch. assoc. Salford (Eng.) U., 1979-80; rsch. assoc. U. So. Calif. Med. Sch., L.A., 1980-87, asst. prof. rsch. medicine, 1987-90; asst. rsch. scientist City of Hope Med. Ctr., Duarte, Calif., 1990—. Contbr. rev. articles to profl. jours. Mem. grant rev. study sect. Am. Heart Assn., L.A., 1994, 95. Recipient R29 1st award NIH, 1993—, Losartan award in rsch. DuPont Merck, 1992, Young Investigator award Am. Heart Assn., 1992. Mem. Endocrine Soc., Am. Diabetes Assn., Am. Fedn. Clin. Rsch. (Henry Christian award for excellence rsch. 1991). Office: City of Hope Med Ctr 1500 Duarte Rd Duarte CA 91010-3012

NATH, ROBERT HENRY, high technology company executive; b. Mpls., July 15, 1936; s. Henry John and Berita Marsella (Dillion) N.; m. Sylvia Ruth Turner, Aug. 22, 1959 (div. 1973); children: Heather Anne, Sarah Turner. BME, U. Minn., 1959. With mktg. dept. internat. bus. Caterpillar Tractor Co., Peoria, Ill., 1960-80; dep. asst. sec. U.S. Dept. Commerce, Washington, 1980-81; v.p. Arco Solar, Inc., Los Angeles, 1981-83; chmn. bd. Cyclean, Inc., Austin, Tex., 1983—; chmn. Quatrosonics Inc., Albuquerque, 1993—; bd. dir. Consol. Dynamics, Seattle. Inventor asphalt recycler, 1983, vibratory compactor, 1986, microwave electromagnetic pulse system, 1988. Mem. Transp. Research Bd., Nat. Asphalt Paving Assn., Asphalt Reclaiming and Recycling Assn., Microwave Power Inst. Club: Algonquin (Boston). Office: Quatrosonics 4209 Balloon Park Rd NE Albuquerque NM 87109-5802

NATHAN, ADELE MARCIA, research director; b. N.Y.C., July 19, 1960; d. M. David and Myra (Lerner) N. Student, Queens Coll., 1978-84, De Anza Coll., 1989, Santa Monica Coll., 1994. Sales asst. Seltel, N.Y.C., 1984-85; buying asst. Botway Libov, N.Y.C., 1985-86; sr. broadcast negiotiator, data syss. coord. Grey Advt., N.Y.C., 1986-89; customer svc. mgr. Mktg. Resources Plus, Palo Alto, Calif., 1989-90; rsch. mgr. Galavision, L.A., 1990-93; rsch. dir. KWHY-TV, L.A., 1993-94; pres. A.M.N. Graphic Solutions, L.A., 1993—. Mem. Am. women in Radio and Television, Am. Mktg. Assn., L.A. Television Sta. Rsch. Com., Ad-Club L.A., Hollywood Radio and Television Soc. Office: 564 Venice Blvd #1 Venice CA 90291

NATHAN, LAWRENCE CHARLES, chemistry educator; b. Corning, Calif., Nov. 26, 1944; s. Jules Morris and Mildred (Wood) N.; m. Frieda Ruth Bjornson, Aug. 29, 1966 (div. Dec. 1987); children: Kristine M., Cheryl L.; m. Linda Lou Hartman Crabb, June 17, 1988; stepchildren: Anthony W. Crabb, Tammy J. Crabb. BA, Linfield Coll., 1966; PhD, U. Utah, 1971. From asst. prof. to assoc. prof. Santa Clara (Calif.) U., 1970-88, prof., 1988—, chmn. chemistry dept., 1992—; vis. assoc. prof. U. Utah, Salt Lake City, 1976, 77. Contbr. articles to profl. jours. Recipient Disting. Faculty awd. Santa Clara U., 1979. Mem. Am. Chem. Soc., Sigma Xi. Office: Santa Clara U Chemistry Dept Santa Clara CA 95053

NATHAN, LEONARD EDWARD, writer, educator; b. Los Angeles, Nov. 8, 1924; s. Israel and Florence (Rosenberg) N.; m. Carol Gretchen Nash, June 27, 1949; children: Andrew Peter, Julia Irene, Miriam Abigail. Student, Ga. Tech., 1943-44, UCLA, 1946-47; BA summa cum laude, U. Calif.-Berkeley, 1950, MA, 1952, PhD, 1961. Instr. Modesto (Calif.) Jr. Coll., 1954-60; prof. dept. rhetoric U. Calif., Berkeley, 1960-91, ret., 1991, chmn. dept., 1968-72. Author: Western Reaches, 1958, The Glad and Sorry Seasons, 1963, The Matchmaker's Lament, 1967, The Day The Perfect Speakers Left, 1969, The Tragic Drama of William Butler Yeats, 1963, Flight Plan, 1971, Without Wishing, 1973, The Likeness, 1975, Coup, 1975, Returning Your Call, 1975, The Transport of Love: The Meghaduta by Kalidasa, 1976, Teachings of Grandfather Fox, 1977, Lost Distance, 1978, Dear Blood, 1980, Holding Patterns, 1982, Carrying On: New and Selected Poems, 1985; also record Confessions of a Matchmaker, 1973, De Meester van Het Winterlandschap, Selected Poems in Dutch transl. by Cees Nooteboom, Uitgeverij de Arbiedspers, Amsterdam, 1990; translator: Songs of Something Else, 1982, Grace and Mercy in Her Wild Hair, 1982, (with Czeslaw Milosz) Happy As a Dog's Tail: Poems by Anna Swir, 1985, (with Czeslaw Milosz) With the Skin: Poems of Aleksander Wat, 1989, (with Arthur Quinn) The Poet's Work: Study of Czeslaw Milosz, 1991. With U.S. Army, 1943-45, ETO. Recipient Phelan award, 1955; Longview prize, 1961; award in lit. Nat. Inst. Arts and Letters, 1971; Poetry medal Commonwealth Club, 1976, 81; U. Calif. Creative Arts fellow, 1961-62, 73-74; U. Calif. Humanities research fellow, 1983-84; Am. Inst. Indian Studies fellow, 1966-67; Guggenheim fellow, 1976-77. Mem. Assn. of Lit. Scholars and Critics. Home: 40 Beverly Rd Kensington CA 94707-1304

NATHAN, ROBERT A., allergist, educator; b. Miami, Fla., Aug. 11, 1948; m. Leslie Lewis, July 2, 1970; children: Brett Andrew, Douglas Adam. BA cum laude, Tulane U., 1970; MD, U. Miami, 1974. Diplomate Nat. Bd. Med. Examiners, Am. Bd. Internal Medicine, Am. Bd. Allergy and Immunology. Intern dept. medicine Jackson Meml. Hosp. and U. Miami Affiliated Hosps., 1974-75, asst. resident, 1975-76, sr. resident, 1976-77; fellow in allergy and clin. immunology Nat. Jewish Hosp. and Rsch. Ctr., Denver, 1977-79; pvt. practice Asthma & Allergy Assocs., P.C., and Rsch. Ctr., Colorado Springs, Colo., 1979—; mem. courtesy staff Penrose/St. Francis Healthcare Sys., 1979-82, mem. active staff, 1982—; mem. courtesy staff Meml. Hosp., 1979-86, mem. active staff, 1986; clin. instr. divsn. allergy and immunology, dept. internal medicine U. Colo. Health Scis. Ctr., Denver, 1981-83, asst. clin. prof., 1983-90, assoc. clin. prof., 1990—; dir. W.C. Service Allergy and Asthma Rsch. Found., Inc., 1981—; chmn. pharmacy com. Penrose Hosp., 1984-86; pres. So. Colo. Med. Practice Assoc., 1985-89; mem. interspecialty adv. panel Physicians Payment Rev. Commn., 1991; mem. reimbursement com. and non-govt. programs subcom. Joint Coun. Allergy and Immunology, 1991-93; mem. Wellpoint Nat. Pharmacy and Therapeutics Com., 1994—; presenter in field. Author: (with others) Understanding Asthma, A Blueprint for Breathing, 1989; mem. editl. bd. The New Eng. and Regional Allergy Procs., 1982-86, Jour. Asthma, 1991—, Allergy Procs., 1994—; contbr. articles to profl. jours. Vol. physician Champ Camp Colo., 1985—; trustee Temple Shalom, 1987-94, pres., 1990-92; bd. dirs. Colo. Found. Med. Care, 1990-94, El Paso County Med. Soc. Found., 1991—, pres., 1991—. Fellow ACP, Am. Coll. Chest Physicians, Am. Coll. Allergy, Asthma, and Immunology (chmn. local, state and regional allergy socs. 1984-86, vice-spkr. ho. of dels. 1988-91, spkr. 1991-94, mem. bd. regents 1991-94), Am. Acad. Allergy and Immunology (bd. govs. Fedn. SLR Socs. 1992—, chmn. physicians pub. svc. coun. 1994—), Am. Assn. Clin. Immunology and Allergy, Am. Assn. Cert. Allergists; mem. AMA, Am. Lung Assn. of Colo. (chmn. com. profl. edn. Pikes Peak regional coun. 1984-87, v.p. 1985-87, pres. 1987-89, bd. dirs. nat. assn. 1987-93, mem. exec. coun. 1990-92, treas. 1991-92, Pres. award 1990, Asthma Rsch. and Vol. Svcs. award Pikes Peak chpt. 1993), Colo. Med. Soc. (mem. jud. coun. 1987-89, bd. dirs. 1989—), Colo. Allergy Soc. (mem. exec. coun. 1981-85, sec./treas. 1981-82, pres. 1982-84), Western Soc. Allergy and Immunology (mem. exec. coun. 1987-95, sec./treas. 1989-90, 94-95, pres.-elect 1990-92, pres. 1992-93), El Paso County Med. Soc. (alt. del. to Colo. Med. Soc., 1981-83, del. 1984-87, mem. exec. coun. 1989—, chmn. med./legal com. 1989-90, chmn. credentials com. 1990-91, v.p. 1990-91, pres.-elect 1991-92, chmn. physicians/nurse collaborative com. 1992-93, pres. 1992-93), Medallion Soc., Phi Delta Epsilon, Phi Beta Kappa. Home: 312 Lake Ave Colorado Springs CO 80906 Office: 2709 N Tejon St Colorado Springs CO 80907

NATHAN, RONALD G., psychiatrist; b. Buffalo, N.Y., Jan. 7, 1938; s. George and Mary J. (Muehlberger) N.; m. Patricia A. Mersmann, Aug. 4, 1962; children: Ronald J., Robert G. BA, U. Toronto, Ont., Can., 1959; MD, SUNY, Buffalo, 1963. Diplomate Am. Bd. Psychiatry, Am. Bd. Neurology (examiner 1980, 84, 89). NIMH Tng. fellow U. Colo., 1964-68; Rensselaer County unit chief Capital Dist. Psychiat. Ctr., Albany, N.Y., 1970-79; clin. dir. Samaritan Mental Health, Troy, N.Y., 1972-79; outpatient dir. So. Ariz. Mental Health, Tucson, 1979-88, med. dir., 1988-90; med. dir. Paritial Hosp. Tucson Gen., 1991—; pvt. practice psychiatrist Tucson, 1990—; mem. faculty Albany Med. Coll., Union U., 1978-79, Coll. Medicine, U. Ariz., Tucson, 1979—. Contbg. author: Aftercare for 80: New Directions, 1983. Major U.S. Army, 1964-70. NIMH Rsch. fellow SUNY, Buffalo, 1961-62. Fellow Am. Psychiat. Assn. (sec. 1988-90, ethics com. 1992-94). Roman Catholic. Office: 2310 N Wyatt Dr Tucson AZ 85712-2166

NATHANSON, JOSEPH S., public relations professional, writer; b. N.Y.C., June 23, 1930; s. Abraham I and Rachel (Holtzberg) N.; divorced; 1 child, Julie. BA, Hobart Coll., Geneva, N.Y., 1952; postgrad., Oxford U., 1953, UCLA, 1970-93. Reporter, editor Reuters Ltd., N.Y.C., UN and London, 1952-57; pub. info. and pub. rels. profl. N.Y. Stock Exch., N.Y.C., 1957-59; account exec., v.p., dir. West Coast ops. Ruder & Finn, N.Y.C. and L.A., 1959-75; chmn. Working Press, Inc., Santa Monica, Calif., 1975—. Mem. Pub. Rels. Soc. Am., L.A. Press Club, Los Angeles County Mus. Art, B'nai B'rith, French Am. C. of C. Office: Working Press Inc 2525 Main St Santa Monica CA 90405-3538

NATHANSON, THEODORE HERZL, aeronautical engineer; architect; b. Montreal, Que., Can., Apr. 20, 1923; came to U.S., 1949; naturalized, 1983; s. Henry and Minnie (Goldberg) N.; student McGill U., 1940-42; SB in Aero. Engring., MIT, 1944; MArch, Harvard U., 1955. Research engr. Noorduyn Aviation Ltd., Montreal, 1944-45; stress engr. Canadair Ltd., Montreal, 1945-46; structural engr. A.V. Roe (Can.) Ltd., Malton, Ont., 1946-47; with Mies van der Rohe, Chgo., summer 1949, R. Buckminster Fuller, Forest Hills, N.Y., summer 1951; cons. engr. and architect, Montreal, Boston, Los Angeles, 1955—; mem. tech. staff Rockwell Internat., 1979-92, structural analysis and advanced design Space Transp. Systems div., Downey, Calif., 1979-86, mission ops. and advanced concepts Space Sta. Systems div., 1986-87, space sta. elec. power system Rocketdyne div., Canoga Park, Calif., 1987-92; cons. Aerospace Engr., L.A., 1992—; lectr. architecture, McGill U., 1967-68. Fellow Brit. Interplanetary Soc.; mem. Order Engrs. Que., Order Architects Que., Soc. Am. Registered Architects, Nat. Soc. Profl. Engrs., AIAA, AIA (assoc.), Royal Archtl. Inst. Can., Nat. Mgmt. Assn., Copley Soc. of Boston, MIT Club of So. Calif. (bd. govs.), Can. Soc. (Los Angeles). Projects and models included in group shows: Mus. Fine Arts, Springfield, Mass., 1961, N.Y. World's Fair, 1965, Winterfest, Boston, 1966, Boston Artists' Project '70. Jewish. Home and Office: 1200 Western Ave Apt 708 Seattle WA 98101-2928

NATHWANI, BHARAT NAROTTAM, pathologist, consultant; b. Bombay, Jan. 20, 1945; came to U.S., 1972; s. Narottam Pragji and Bharati N. (Lakhani) N. MBBS, Grant Med. Coll., Bombay, 1969, MD in Pathology, 1972. Intern Grant Med. Coll., Bombay U., 1968-69; asst. prof. pathology Grant Med. Coll., 1972; fellow in hematology Cook County Hosp., Chgo., 1972-73; resident in pathology Rush U., Chgo., 1973-74; fellow in hematopathology City of Hope Med. Ctr., Duarte, Calif., 1975-76, pathologist, 1977-84; prof. pathology, chief hematopathology U. So. Calif., L.A., 1984—. Contbr. numerous articles to profl. jours. Recipient Grant awards Nat. Libr. Medicine, Bethesda, Md., Nat. Cancer Inst., 1991. Mem. AAAS, Internat. Acad. Pathology, Am. Soc. Clin. Pathology, Am. Soc. Hematology, Am. Soc. Oncology. Office: U So Calif Sch Medicine HMR 204 2025 Zonal Ave Los Angeles CA 90033-4526

NAUGHTEN, ROBERT NORMAN, pediatrician; b. Stockton, Calif., Oct. 13, 1928; s. Norman Stafford and Junetta (Doherty) N.; m. Ann Louise Charkins, June 26, 1954; children: Robert James, Annette Marie Naughten-Dessel, Patricia Louise. AA, San Jose City Coll., San Jose, Calif., 1948; BA, U. Calif., Berkeley, 1950; MA, Stanford U., 1955; MD, Hahnemann U., 1959. Lic. physician and surgeon, Calif. Intern Highland-Alameda County Hosp., Oakland, Calif., 1959-60; rsch. fellow Nat. Cancer Inst., Stanford, Calif., 1960-61; resident pediatrics Stanford Med. Ctr., 1961-63; pvt. practice pediatrics Los Gatos, Calif., 1963—; instr. Santa Clara Valley Med. Ctr., San Jose, 1963—, Dept. of Pediatrics, Stanford, 1963-73; cons. drug abuse San Jose Police Dept., 1963-68; cons. child abuse Dist. Atty., San Jose, 1984—; cons. dept. social svcs. State of Calif., 1989—. Contbr. articles to profl. jours. Bd. dirs., v.p. Outreach and Escort, Inc., San Jose, 1985-88. Named Alumnus of Yr. San Jose City Coll., 1967, Chef of the West Sunset Mag., 1989; fellow Coll. of Physicians, Phila., 1986. Mem. AMA, Calif. Assn., Santa Clara Med. Assn. (v.p. 1986-88), Am. Acad. Pediatrics, Am. Acad. Allergy and Clin. Immunology, Calif. Alumni Assn. (Berkeley), Stanford Alumni Assn., Commonwealth Club (San Francisco), Soc. of the Sigma Xi. Democrat. Roman Catholic. Home: 13601 Riverdale Dr Saratoga CA 95070-5229 Office: 777 Knowles Dr Ste 14 Los Gatos CA 95030-1417

NAUMAN, RUTH EILEEN, author; b. San Diego, May 24, 1946; d. James Earl and Ruth May (Cramer) Gent; m. David Gene Nauman, June 16, 1973. Grad., British Inst. Homeopathy, 1994, 94. Homeopathic practitioner pvt. practice, Cottonwood, Ariz., 1970—; freelance writer Cottonwood, Ariz., 1980—; adj. prof. Union Inst., 1992—; tchr. British Inst. Homeopathy, London, 1992—. Author: Interpreting Your Novien Moon, 1979, The American Book of Nutrition and Medical Astrology, 1980, Colored Stones and Their Meaning, 1990, Medical Astrology, 1992, Soul Recovery and Extraction, 1992, Bach Flower Remedies and Astrology, 1992, Homeopathy: 21st Century Medicine, 1993, numerous romance novels. Firefighter West Point (Ohio) Vol. Fire Dept., 1983-86. With USN, 1964-67. Mem. Am. Fedn. Astrologers. Office: Blue Turtle Publishing PO Box 2513 Cottonwood AZ 86326-2513

NAURATH, DAVID ALLISON, engineering psychologist, researcher; b. Houston, Mar. 11, 1927; s. Walter Arthur and Joy Frances (Bradbury) N.; m. Barbara Ellen Coverdell; children: Kathleen Ann, David Allen, Cynthia Ellyn, Randall Austin. BA, Simpson Coll., Indianola, Iowa, 1948; MA, Southern Meth. U., 1949; postgrad., U. Denver, 1955-57. Job analyst U.S. Air Force, San Antonio and Denver, 1951-55; rsch. psychologist U.S. Air Force, Lowry AFB, Colo., 1955-60, Navy, Life Scis. & Systems div., Point Mugu, Calif., 1960-76; engring. psychologist Navy Systems Engring., Point Mugu, 1976-83; ret.; presenter at profl. socs. and orgns. in field. Contbr. articles to Jour. Engring. Psychology, jour. Soc. for Info. Display, jour. Soc. Photo-optical Instrument Engrs. With USAAF, 1944-46. Mem. AAAS (life), IEEE (sr.), Am. Psychol. Assn., Human Factors Soc. (panel mem. Certification of Human Factors Engrs. 1976), Soc. Engring. Psychologists, Soc. for Info. Display (life). Methodist. Home: 5633 Pembroke St Ventura CA 93003-2200

NAVA, CYNTHIA D., state legislator. BS, Western Ill. U.; MA, Ea. Ill. U. Dir. spl. edn. Godsden Pub. Sch.; mem. N.Mex. Senate; mem. edn. and rules com. Home: 3002 Broadmoor Dr Las Cruces NM 88001-7501 Office: NMex Senate State Capitol New Mexico State Capitol NM 87503

NAVAJAS, GONZALO, foreign language educator; b. Barcelona, Spain, May 14, 1946; came to U.S., 1970; s. Jose and Carmen (Navarro) N.; 1 child, Paul. PhD, UCLA, 1975. Prof. SUNY, Stony Brook, 1980-83, Tulane U., New Orleans, 1983-85; prof. dept. Spanish and Portuguese U. Calif., Irvine, 1985—; lectr., mem. editorial bd. various jours. in field. Author 7 books; contbr. articles to profl. pubs. Mem. Modern Assn. Am., Internat. Assn. Hispanists. Office: U Calif Dept Spanish Irvine CA 92711

NAVARRO, MANUEL, protective services official; b. Oakland, Calif.. AA in Fire Sci., BA in Pub. Adminstrn. Cert. master fire instr., Colo. Fire fighter, 1966-67, Lawrence Radiation Lab. Fire Dept., 1967-72; various positions to asst. chief Oakland (Calif.) Fire Dept., 1972-93; fire chief Colorado Springs (Colo.) Fire Dept., 1993—; mem. FEMA Urban Search and Rescue Mgmt. and Control Com. Mem. Mex.-Am. Polit. Assn. (chairperson). Office: Colorado Springs Fire Dept 31 S Weber St Colorado Springs CO 80903*

NAVE, THOMAS GEORGE, lawyer; b. Medford, Oreg., Mar. 12, 1950; s. Edward Clements and Marjorie May (Donahoe) N.; m. Susan Debra Cox, Sept. 8, 1984; children: Julia, Peter. BS, Oreg. State U., 1972; JD, Lewis and Clark U., 1976. Bar: Alaska 1977. Assoc. Douglas L. Gregg, Juneau, Alaska, 1977, Peter M. Page, Juneau, 1978; asst. pub. defender State of Alaska, Fairbanks, 1979; dep. dir. Alaska Pub. Defender's AGy., Juneau, 1980-85; ptnr. Gullufsen and Nave, Juneau, 1985-90; pvt. practice, 1990—. Mem. ATLA, Alaska Bar Assn., Alaska Jud. Coun. Democrat. Roman Catholic. Home: 1120 Fritz Cove Rd Juneau AK 99801-8501 Office: 227 7th St Juneau AK 99801-1117

NAVONE, BERT, agricultural products executive; b. 1929. Sec. Auvil Fruit Co., Inc., Orondo, Wash., 1957—. Office: Auvil Fruit Co Inc Hwy 97 Orondo WA 98843*

NAVRATIL, GREG ALLAN, artist, screenprinter; b. Denver, Oct. 14, 1946; s. Hans and Mollie (Scheel) N.; m. Judith Winifred Leonard, Jan. 2, 1986. BFA, Met. State Coll., Denver, 1974. Former signpainter, screenprinter, book illustrator, art dir. One-man shows Nat. Ctr. for Atmospheric Rsch., Boulder, Colo., 1993; 2-person show The Lincoln Ctr., Ft. Collins, Colo., 1993; exhibited in over 30 group shows, including Nat. Arts Festival, Louisville, Colo., 1991, Arts for Parks, Jackson Hole, Wyo., 1991, 93, Colo. State Fair, Pueblo, 1992, 93, Fremont Ctr. for Arts, Canon City, Colo., Contemporary Realism V, Scottsdale, Ariz., Conflience, Ingram, Tex., 1994, Salon Internat., Jackson, Miss., 1994; represented in numerous corp. and pvt. collections, including Texaco; represented by Saxon Mountain Gallery, 1/1 Gallery. With U.S. Army, 1963-66. Recipient hon. mention 7-State Regional, Cheyenne, 1990, best of show and hon. mention, 1991, 2d place and hon. mention, 1992; merit award Nat. Arts Festival, 1991, purchase award Am. Realism 91, 1992, jurors award 45th Ann., Central City, Colo., 1992, jurors choice award 46th Ann., 1993, hon. mention Santa Fe Trail Art Show, Trinidad, Colo., 1991, meritorious award Colo. State Fair, 1991, 3d place and People's Choice awards Fremont Ctr. for Arts, 1993, purchase award 33d Ann., 1993, Top award Artist's Mag., 1993; also others. Home and Studio: 3321 W 30th Ave Denver CO 80211-3615

NAVRATIL, JAMES DALE, chemist, researcher; b. Denver, Jan. 20, 1941; s. Hans and Mollie (Schell) N.; .m Sylvia Jane Tascher, Dec. 11, 1967; children: Julie Kornman, Kim Sundstrom, James, Nicole. BA in Chemistry, U. Colo., 1970, MS in Chemistry, 1972, PhD in Chemistry, 1975. Rsch. chemist Dow Chem. Co., 1970-75; with Rockwell Internat., 1975-87, 91-94, group leader, 1978-79, 81-87; sr. scientist Rockwell Internat., Canoga Park, Calif., 1991-94; 1st officer IAEA, 1978-81; head dept. mineral processing, extractive metallurgy U. N.S.W., 1987-90; sr. project mgr. Chem. Waste Mgmt., Geneva, Ill., 1990-91; chief scientist Rust Federal Svcs., Golden, Colo., 1994—; postdoctoral rsch. assoc. U. Colo., 1975-76, instr., 1976-77; adj. prof. Colo. Sch. Mines, 1985-87. 2lt. U.S. Army, 1964-70. Named Rockwell Engr. of the Yr., 1977, R&D 100 awards, 1983, 85; Dow Chem. scholar, 1968-70. Fellow AAAS, Royal Australian Chem. Inst.; mem. Am. Chem. Soc. (Colo. sect. award 1984). Roman Catholic. Office: Rust Fed Svcs 1597 Cole Blvd Ste 350 Golden CO 80401-3414

NAY, SAMUEL WESLEY, retired mechanical engineer; b. Steamboat Springs, Colo., May 29, 1914; s. Samuel W. and Josephine L. (Bartz) N.; m. Edythe L. Winberg, May 31, 1942; 1 child: Samuel III (dec.). BS in Engring., Calif. State U., L.A., 1967. Registered profl. engr., Calif. Tooling engr. Lockheed Aircraft, Burbank, Calif., 1940-47; mech. engr. assoc. design and constrn. Dept. Water and Power, L.A., 1947-78; instr. Calif. U. Extension, L.A., 1978-82; cons. engr. S.W. Nay Assocs., Glendale, Calif., 1979-91; ret., 1991. Editor tech. publ. The Flame, 1978-81. Mem. Town Hall, L.A., 1992—. Sgt. USAF, 1942-45. Fellow Inst. for the Advancement Engring. (bd. dirs., treas. 1978-92); mem. ASME (life), L.A. Coun. Engring. (v.p., bd. dirs. 1978—, pres. 1990-91), L.A. Coun. Engrs. and Scientists (past pres.), Soc. Fire Protection Engrs. (life, past pres.). Home: 813 Palm Dr Glendale CA 91202-2143

NAYLOR, BRUCE GORDON, museum director; b. Midale, Sask., Can., Aug. 19, 1950; s. John Raymond Naylor and Mary Lynn (Frisby) Redeberg; m. Marlene Johnstone, Dec. 19, 1981 (dec. July 1992); m. Judith Jeune, June 11, 1994. BS with high honors, U. Sask., 1972; PhD, U. Alta., 1978. Postdoctoral fellow U. Toronto, Ont., 1978-80; lectr. U. Calif., Berkeley, 1979; asst. prof. U. Alta., Edmonton, 1980-82; curator Tyrrell Mus., Drumheller, Alta., 1982-86; asst. dir. Royal Tyrrell Mus., Drumheller, 1986-92, dir., 1992—; adj. prof. U. Alta., 1983—; sen. U. Calgary, Alta., 1989-90. Assoc. editor Jour. Vertebrate Paleontology, 1991-92; contbr. articls to sci. publs. Operating grantee Nat. Sci. & Engring. Rsch. Coun., Ottawa, 1981-82. Fellow Geol. Assn. Can.; mem. Soc. Vertebrate Paleontology, Rotary Club Drumheller. Office: Royal Tyrrell Mus, Box 7500, Drumheller, AB Canada T0J 0Y0

NAYLOR, GEORGE LEROY, lawyer, rail transportation executive; b. Bountiful, Utah, May 11, 1915; s. Joseph Francis and Josephine Chase (Wood) N.; student U. Utah, 1934-36; student George Washington U., 1937; J.D. (Bancroft Whitney scholar), U. San Francisco, 1953; m. Maxine Elizabeth Lewis, Jan. 18, 1941; children: Georgia Naylor Price, RoseMaree Naylor Hammer, George LeRoy II. Bar: Calif. 1954, Ill. 1968. V.p., sec., legis. rep. Internat. Union of Mine, Mill & Smelter Workers, CIO, Dist. Union 2, Utah-Nevada, 1942-44; examiner So. Pacific Co., San Francisco, 1949-54, chief examiner, 1955, asst. mgr., 1956-61; carrier mem. Nat. R.R. Adjustment Bd., Chgo., 1961-77, chmn., 1970-77; atty. Village of Fox River Valley Gardens, Ill., 1974-77; practice law, legal cons., Ill. and Calif., 1977—, ret. from pvt. practice, 1991; gen. counsel for Can-Veyor, Inc., Mountain View, Calif., 1959-64; adj. instr. dept. mgmt. U. West Fla., 1981. Active Rep. Nat. Com., 1992-93. Served with AUS, World War II. Mem. ABA, Ill. Bar Assn., Calif. Bar Assn., Chgo. Bar Assn., San Francisco Bar Assn. Mormon. Author: Defending Carriers Before the NRAB and Public Law Boards, 1969, Choice Morsels in Tax and Property Law, 1966, Underground at Bingham Canyon, 1944; National Railroad Adjustment Board Practice Manual, 1978. Home and Office: Virginia Lee Rd RR 1 Box 570 Cotter AR 72626

NAYLOR-JACKSON, JERRY, public relations consultant, entertainer, producer; b. Chalk Mountain, Tex., Mar. 6, 1939; s. William Guy and Mary Bernice (Lummus) Jackson; m. Pamela Ann Robinson, Jan. 30, 1966; children: Geoffrey K. Naylor, Kelli A. Naylor, Gregory K. Naylor. Grad., Elkins Electronics Inst., Dallas, 1957; student, U. Md., Fed. Republic of Germany, 1957-58. Life first class radio/TV engring. lic. FCC. Broadcaster various local TV and AM radio stas., San Angelo, Texas, 1955-57; mem. Buddy Holly and the Crickets, 1957-65, lead singer, 1960-65; solo entertainer, performer, recording artist and producer, 1965-83; sr. v.p. corp. devel. Newslink Internat. Satellite Broadcast Comms. Co., Inc., Washington, 1986-88; pres. Internat. Syndications, Inc. subs. Newslink, Inc., Washington, 1986-88; pres., CEO, owner The Jerry Naylor Co., Inc., Agoura, Calif., 1984—; pres., CEO Media Unlimited/Naylor Prodns., Inc., 1983—; v.p. capital programs, sr. cons. Calif. Luth. Univ., Thousand Oaks, 1990-92; sr. cons., dir. ann. fund Calif. Luth. Univ., 1989-90; polit./media cons. various Rep. candidates and orgns., 1968—; spl. cons. to Violeta Barrios de Chamarro, Pres. of Republic of Nicaragua, 1990-92; disc jockey Sta. KHEY-AM, Sta KINT-AM, El Paso, Tex., 1959; on-air personality Sta. KRLA-AM, Sta. KDAY-AM, L.A., 1960, on-air disc jocky/air personality/celebrity host, KLAC-AM, L.A., Calif., 1974-83; on-camera and voice-over spokesman for Safeway Stores, Inc., Avis Rent-a-Car, Mutual of Omaha, Wrigley Co., 1968-83; U.S. presdl. appointee, chmn. Job Tng. Partnership Act work group/youth at risk subcom. Nat. Commn. for Employment Policy, 1985-92; nat. dir. spl. events Reagan For Pres., 1979-81; apptd. mem. commn. for employment policy Pres. Ronald Reagan, 1985-91. Recording artist maj. labels including CBS Records, Motown Records, Warner Bros. Records, EMI Records, 1965-84; host weekly nat. and internat. radio program Continental Country (Number 1 syndicated country music radio show in Am., Billboard Mag., Country Music Assn., 1974, 77). Active presdl. task force Rep. Nat. Com.; nat. dir. spl. events Reagan for Pres., 1975-76, 79-80; sr. cons. to White House, 1981-88, 89-92. With U.S. Army, 1957-58, Fed. Republic of Germany. Named to Top 40 Male Vocalists of Yr., Billboard Mag., 1970, named #1 Rock Group (Crickets), Billboard Mag./New Musical Express Mag., 1958, 62. Mem. NARAS, Am. Film Inst., Country Music Assn., Acad. Country Music (Telly award for TV Documentary 1991, 92), Phi Kappa Phi (alumni). Home and Office: Jerry Nalor Co Inc 5308 Ambridge Dr Agoura Hills CA 91301

NAZAIRE, MICHEL HARRY, physician; b. Jérémie, Haiti, Sept. 29, 1939; s. Joseph and Hermance N.; m. Nicole N., Dec. 28, 1968 (div.); children: Hanick and Carline (twins). Grad., Coll. St. Louis de Gonzague, 1959; MD Faculty of Medicine and Pharmacology, State U. Haiti, 1966. Intern, State U. Hosp., Port-Au-Prince, Haiti, 1965-66; resident physician Sanitarium, Port-Au-Prince, Haiti, 1966-68; practice medicine specializing in pneumophysiology, Port-Au-Prince, 1966—; physician fellow Klinik Havelhohe, West Berlin, 1969-70, 89-91; attending physician Sanitarium, Port-Au-Prince, 1976-91. Dep. mem. Internat. Parliament for Safety and Peace; envoy-at-large Internat. State Parliament; mem. global environ. technol. network Who. Contbr. articles to Jour. Indsl. Hygiene, Pneumology and Respiratory Protection. Fellow Internat. Soc. for Respiratory Protection, Am. Coll. Chest Physicians (assoc.); mem. Am. Pub. Health Assn., Am. Conf. Govtl. Indsl. Hygienists, Internat. Union Against Tuberculosis. Address: 1030 S Whitman Apt 2205 Tacoma WA 98465

NAZZARO, DAVID ALFRED, sales executive; b. Malden, Mass., Sept. 15, 1940; s. Alfred Anthony and Louise (Cunningham) N.; m. Jane Valentine, June 26, 1971; one child, David Thomas. BME, U.S. Mcht. Marine Acad., 1962; MS, Columbia U., 1965; MBA, Pepperdine U., 1975. Regional mgr. Turbo Power and Marine Systems divsn. United Techs., Hardford, Conn., 1965-74; mgr. bus. devel S & Q Corp., San Francisco, 1974-78; v.p. and gen. mgr. Con-Val, Oakland, Calif., 1978-85; pres. and chief exec. officer Dasa Controls, Belmont, Calif., 1985-87; mgr. bus. devel Johnson Yokogawa Corp., San Francisco, 1987-94; ptnr. Nazzaro and Assocs., Mgmt. Cons., 1994—. Contbr. papers to profl. publs. Bd. dirs. Clearview Homeowners

Assn., San Mateo, 1976; pres. St. Bartholomew's Parish Council, San Mateo, 1986. Lt. USNR, 1963-69. Sr. Mem. Instrument Soc. Am. (pres. No. Calif. Sec. 1987-88); mem. ASME, Am. Water Works Assn., Elks, Jaycees, St. Bartholomew's Mens Club (pres. 1977). Home: 30 Tollridge Ct San Mateo CA 94402-3730

NEAL, JAMES MADISON, JR., editor; b. Oklahoma City, Aug. 6, 1925; s. James Madison and Tillie Belle (Milliken) N.; m. Caroline Dorothy Becker (dec. Dec. 1974); children: Charles, James W., Jody, Carolyn. BA, U. Colo., 1949; MA, S.D. State U., 1970. Editor various newspapers, Colo., Nebr. and Okla., 1949-59; wire editor Rapid City Journal, Rapid City, S.D., 1959-67; instr. S.D. State U., Brookings, S.D., 1967-71; asst. prof. U. Nebr., Lincoln, 1971-73, assoc. prof., 1973-90; S.D. chmn. AP Mng. Editors Assn., 1962-64. Mem. Soc. Profl. Journalists, Investigative Reporters and Editors, ACLU (bd. dirs. Nebr. chpt. 1979-82), VFW. Unitarian. Home: 4700 N Kolb Rd Apt 7207 Tucson AZ 85715-6187

NEAL, JERRY EUGENE, controller; b. Columbus, Ohio, Nov. 17, 1941; s. Levert and Anna (Weaver) N.; m. Judith Ann Lehnert; children: Brian, Jeffrey, Timothy. BS, Ohio State U., 1965. Controller Mattel Toys Inc., Hawthorne, Calif., 1979—. Office: Mattel Toys Inc 333 Continental Blvd El Segundo CA 90245-5032

NEAL, MICHAEL RENN, software engineer; b. Augusta, Ga., June 15, 1960; s. James Allen and Grace (Runyan) N.; m. Teresa Jean Schreibeis, Apr. 7, 1990; 1 child, Rianna Michele. BS in Computer Sci., U. S.C., 1983. Sr. software engr. Lockheed Corp., Burbank, Calif., 1983-90, Auto-trol Tech., Thornton, Colo., 1992-93; sr. applications engr. Template Graphics Software, San Diego, 1990-92; project dir. software devel. CogniSeis Devel., Boulder, Colo., 1993—; instr. Xhibition Conf., San Jose, Calif., 1993-94. Contbr. articles to profl. jours. State treas. S.C. Young Reps., 1980; chmn. Lexington County (S.C.) Young Reps., 1980. Mem. Assn. for Computing Machinery (spl. interest group on graphics 1987—, spl. interest group on human computer interface 1993—, course organizer and instr. SIGGRAPH Conf. 1994). Office: CogniSeis Devel 4775 Walnut St Ste 2A Boulder CO 80301-2579

NEAL, PHILIP MARK, diversified manufacturing executive; b. San Diego, Aug. 28, 1940; s. Philip Mark and Florence Elizabeth (Anderson) N.; children: Brian, Kevin. B.A., Pomona Coll., 1962; M.B.A., Stanford U., 1964. Mgr. financial planning and analysis CBS, Hollywood, 1964-66; cons. McKinsey & Co., Los Angeles, 1966-73; v.p., controller Avery Internat. Corp., Los Angeles, 1974-78; sr. v.p. fin. Avery Internat. Corp., Pasadena, 1979-88, group v.p. materials group, 1988-90; exec. pres. Avery Internat. Corp., 1990, pres., chief operating officer, 1990—; bd. dirs. Ind. Colls. of So. Calif. Trustee Pomona Coll; gov. Town Hall of Calif. Bd. Govs. Mem. Fin. Execs. Inst. Republican. Episcopalian. Office: Avery Dennison Corp PO Box 7090 Pasadena CA 91109-7090

NEAMAN, BRYCENE ALLEN, museum curator; b. Toppenish, Wash., Apr. 7, 1955; s. Lee Allen and Lucille (Albert) N.; m. Beverly W. Dogsleep (div. Apr. 1986); children: Coral Rose Neaman. Gen. studies, Brigham Young U., Provo, UT, 1973-75; music-art, UT State U., Logan, UT, 1978-83. Pub. sch. liaison Adult Edn. Program, Toppenish, Wash., 1978-79; museum curator trainee Yakima Nation Cultural Ctr., Toppenish, Wash., 1980, 84; intake office worker Alcoholism Outreach Program, Toppenish, Wash., 1984-88; museum tech. Yakima Nation Cultural Ctr., Toppenish, Wash., 1988; curator Yakima Indian Nation Cultural Heritage Ctr., Toppenish, Wash., 1988—; coord. Wash. Centennial Com., Olympia, Wash., 1988-89; art commr. State Wash.-Wash. State Arts Commn. Coord. Brochure Art of the Yakima Ind. Art Exhibit, 1989. Exec. officer Wash. State Arts Com. Recipient Art of Y.I.N. An Exhibit of Contemporary Vision, Wash. Centennial Com., 1988-89; Wash. Humanities Art of the Yakima, 1988-89. Mem. Wash. Museum Assn., Western Museum Assn., Nat. Trust for Hist. Pres., Yakima Indian Nation. Mem. LDS. Home and Office: Yakima Nation Mus PO Box 151 Toppenish WA 98948-0151

NEARY, PATRICIA ELINOR, ballet director; b. Miami, Fla.; d. James Elliott and Elinor (Mitsitz) N. Corps de ballet Nat. Ballet of Can., Toronto, Ont., 1957-60; prin. dancer N.Y.C. Ballet, 1960-68; ballerina Geneva Ballet (Switzerland), 1968-70, ballet dir., 1973-78; guest artist Stuttgart Ballet, Germany, 1968-71; asst. ballet dir., ballerina West Berlin Ballet, 1970-73; ballet dir. Zurich Ballet (Switzerland), 1978-86, La Scala di Milano ballet co., Italy, 1986-88; tchr., Balanchine ballets, Balanchine Estate, 1987—.

NEBEKER, STEPHEN BENNION, lawyer; b. Salt Lake City, Feb. 21, 1929; s. Acel Hulme and Lora (Bennion) N.; m. June Wilkins, June 18, 1951; children: Jeanne N. Jardine, Mary N. Larson, Stephen W., Ann W. Wilkinson. JD, U. Utah, 1954. Bar: Utah 1957, U.S. Dist. Ct. Utah 1957, U.S. Ct. Appeals (10th cir.) 1957. Assoc. Ray Quinney & Nebeker, Salt Lake City, 1957-63, ptnr., 1963—, mem. exec. com., 1972—, pres., 1992—. Bd. editors Utah Law Rev., 1953-54. Mem. S.J. and Jessie Quinney Found., Salt Lake City, 1982—; chmn. nat. adv. coun. U. Utah; trustee Ray Quinney & Nebeker Found., Salt Lake City, 1982—. 1st lt. U.S. Army, 1954-57. Recipient Disting. Alumnus award U. Utah, 1992, named Lawyer of Yr. by Law Sch., 1988. Fellow Am. Coll. Trial Lawyers (mem. bd. regents 1984-87), Am. Bd. Trial Advs., Internat. Assn. Ins. Counsel, Fedn. Ins. Counsel, Am. Bar Found., Utah Bar Found. (trustee), Utah State Bar (Outstanding Lawyer of Yr. 1986, Trial Lawyer of Yr. 1994), Legal Aid Soc., Am. Inn of Ct. II (pres. 1982-83), Alta Club, Rotary, Salt Lake City Area C. of C. (mem. bd. govs. 1986-89), U. Utah Law Sch. Alumni Assn. (pres. 1985-86). Republican. Mormon. Home: 746 16th Ave Salt Lake City UT 84103-3705 Office: Ray Quinney & Nebeker 400 Deseret Bldg Salt Lake City UT 84111

NEBELKOPF, ETHAN, psychologist; b. N.Y.C., June 13, 1946; s. Jacob and Fannie (Carver) N.; m. Karen Horrocks, July 27, 1976; children: Demian David, Sarah Dawn. BA, CCNY, 1966; MA, U. Mich., 1969; PhD, Summit U., 1989. Social worker Project Headstart, N.Y.C., 1965; coord. Project Outreach, Ann Arbor, 1968-69; program dir. White Bird Clinic, Eugene, Oreg., 1971-75; counseling supr. Teledyne Econ. Devel. Corp., San Diego, 1976-79; dir. planning and edn. Walden House, San Francisco, 1979-89, dir. tng., 1990—; adj. prof. Dept. Social Work, San Francisco State U., 1982-87; cons. Berkeley Holistic Health Ctr., Berkeley, 1979-84, Medicine Wheel Healing Co-op, San Diego, 1976-79; alternate del. Nat. Free Clinic Coun., Eugene, Oreg., 1972-74. Author: White Bird Flies to Phoenix, 1973, The New Herbalism, 1980, The Herbal Connection, 1981, Hope Not Dope, 1990. Mem. Mayor's Task Force on Drugs, San Francisco, 1988; mem. treatment com. Gov.'s Policy Coun. on Drugs, Sacramento, 1989; task force Human Svcs. Tng., Salem, Oreg., 1972; organizer West Eugene Bozo Assn., 1973; founder Green Psychology, 1993. Named Outstanding Young Man of Am., U.S. Jaycees, 1980; recipient Silver Key, House Plan Assn., 1966. Fellow Am. Orthopsychiat. Assn.; mem. Calif. Assn. Family Therapists, World Fedn. of Therapeutic Communities, Nat. Writer's Club, N.Y. Acad. Scis., Internat. Assn. for Human Rels. Lab. Tng., Calif. Assn. of Drug Programs and Profls. (pres. 1988-90), Phi Beta Kappa. Office: 6641 Simson St Oakland CA 94605-2220

NECHIS, BARBARA, artist; b. Mt. Vernon, N.Y., Sept. 25, 1937; d. Rudolph and Anna (Sincoff) Friedman; m. Malvin Nechis, June 22, 1958 (div. 1982); children—Barry, Steven, Sharon; m. Andrew D'Anneo, Oct. 22, 1988. B.A., U. Rochester, 1959; M.S., Alfred U. Mem. faculty Parsons Sch. Design, N.Y.C., 1980-92; condr. watercolor workshops for museums, arts groups and colls including Pratt Inst., N.Y., U. Alaska, Am. Acad. Art, Chgo.; juror Watercolor West, Mid-West Watercolor, Nat. Arts Club, Am. Watercolor Soc. Exhibited one-woman shows including: New Sch.-Parsons Sch. Design, 1984; group shows include: Am. Watercolor Soc., Canton Mus., Ohio, 1985; represented in permanent collecion Butler Inst. Am. Art. Author: Watercolor, The Creative Experience, 1979, Watercolor From the Heart, 1993. Mem. Am. Watercolor Soc. (bd. dirs. 1983-86) Lena Newcastle award 1985. Home and Studio: 1085 Dunaweal Ln Calistoga CA 94515-9799

NECKELS, JACK, park superintendent; b. Watford City, N.D., Mar. 3, 1938; s. Elmer C. and Bessie M. (Miller) N.; m. Jolene K. Neckels, Oct. 25, 1958; children: Bill, Jackie, Nancy. A in Bus. Adminstrn., N.D. Sch. [illegible] A in Forestry; BS in Biology, Dickinson State U. Seasonal park ranger Theodore Roosevelt Nat. Park, N.D., 1960-62; park ranger Blue Ridge Pkwy., N.C., 1963-66, Fire Island Nat. Seashore, N.Y., 1966-67; park mgr. Sagamore Hill NHS, N.Y., 1967-71; trainee Dept. Interior Nat. Park Svc., Washington, 1971-73; dir. N.D. Planning Divsn. State of N.D., Bismarck, 1973-75; assoc. dir. park ops. SW Regional Office, Sante Fe, 1980-84; dep. regional dir. Rocky Mt. Regional Office, Denver, 1984-91; asst. supt. Grand Teton Nat. Park, Jackson, Wyo., 1975-80, supt., 1991—. dir. N.D. State Planning Divsn., 1993—. Mem. Rotary Club. Office: Nat Park Svc PO Box 170 Moose WY 83012-0170

NEE, CHRISTOPHER CHI-HUANG, computer software engineer; b. Taipei, Taiwan, Apr. 4, 1951; came to U.S., 1994; s. Yen-Yuan and Shu-Yuan (Cheng) N.; m. Pauline B. Jaw, June 6, 1991; 1 child, Jasmine. BS in Chemistry, Nat. Chung-Hsing U., 1974; MS in Organic Chemistry, Wash. State U., 1979; postgrad., Ohio State U., 1983; MS in Computer Sci., Tex. A&M U., 1985. Patent exam. officer Organic Synthesis divsn. Nat. Bur. Patents, Taipei, 1974-77; software sys. engr. Columbia Presbyn. Med. Ctr., N.Y.C., 1985-87, Commodore Electronics Ltd., Taipei, 1987-89; sr. software engr. Chroma Ate Inc., Taipei, 1989-91, Leegood Automatic Sys. Inc., Taipei, 1991-94; founder, ind. cons. SESC, Santa Clara, 1004—. Author: Introductin to DCS, 1987. Chinese cultural and natural sci. scholar Republic of China Govt., 1975. Office: 2537 Rose Way Santa Clara CA 95051-5331

NEEB, MARTIN JOHN, media executive; b. Austin, Texas, Aug. 16, 1933; s. Martin Jacob and Vera (Basilius) N.; m. Barbara Ann Brauer, Aug. 25, 1956; children: Douglas Martin, John Martin, Kristina Joy. BA, Concordia Theol. Sem, St. Louis, 1955, MDiv in Theology, 1958; MA, St. Louis U., 1959; PhD, Northwestern U., 1967; grad. exec. mgmt. program, U. Pa., 1983. Gen. mgr. sta. WNUR-FM, Northwestern U., Evanston, Ill., 1965-67; dir. pub. rels., assoc. prof. speech Concordia Coll., Chgo., 1959-67; exec. sec. and gen. mgr. Luth. TV, St. Louis, 1967-78; dir. broadcast divsn. Franciscan Comm. Ctr., L.A., 1978-81; gen. mgr. Sta. KPLU-FM, Pacific Luth. U., Tacoma, 1981—. Former bd. dirs. City Club of Tacoma, founding bd. 1984, West Coast Pub. Radio, Luth. Film Assocs., Templeton Found. Adv. Com., Arthritis Found., U.S. Cath. Conf. Comm. Com.; bd. dirs. Tacoma Art Mus., Broadway Ctr. Performing Arts. Finalist White House fellowship, 1966, fellow Northwestern U., 1965-66, recipient Nat. TV Emmy Awards, 1974, 77, Gabriel awards, various other media awards from N.Y. Film and TV Festival, Columbus Film Festival, TV Bur. Advt., Freedoms Found., San Francisco Internat. Film Festival, Am. Film Festival, Advt. Club of L.A., Faith and Freedom award Religious Heritage Am., 1985; named One of Outstanding Young Men Am., Jr. C. of C., 1967. Mem. Religious Pub. Rels. Assn., Internat. TV Assn., Pub. Rels. Soc. Am., Nat. Protestant Broadcasters (pres. 1982), South County Coun. C. of C. (past pres., past bd. dirs.), City Club Tacoma (program chmn. 1984). Lutheran. Home: 18109 28th Ave E Tacoma WA 98445-4354 Office: Pacific Luth U Tacoma WA 98447

NEEDLER, MARTIN CYRIL, university dean, political science educator; b. Manchester, Eng., Mar. 23, 1933; came to U.S., 1948; s. Thomas Anthony and Beatrice Rebecca (Rosenberg) N.; m. Eva Lore Heyman, Mar. 16, 1955 (div. Mar. 1976); children: Stephen, Daniel; m. Jan Knippers Black, July 23, 1976. AB magna cum laude, Harvard U., 1954, PhD, 1960. Instr. Dartmouth Coll., Hanover, N.H., 1959-60; instr. U. Mich., Ann Arbor, 1960-63, asst. prof., 1963-65; rsch. assoc. Harvard Ctr. for Internat. Affairs, Cambridge, Mass., 1965-66; with U. N.Mex., Albuquerque, 1966-90, dir. div. Inter-Am. affairs, 1966-80, prof. polit. sci. and sociology, 1976-90; dean Sch. Internat. Studies U. Pacific, Stockton, Calif., 1990—; vis. sr. rsch. fellow U. Southampton, Eng., 1974; vis. prof. U. Pitts., 1988; sr. assoc. mem. St. Antony's Coll., Oxford, Eng., 1971; postdoctoral fellow UCLA, 1962. Author: Political Development in Latin America, 1968, Politics & Society in Mexico, 1971, The Problem of Democracy in Latin America, 1987, The Concepts of Comparative Politics, 1991; assoc. editor jour. Armed Forces & Soc., 1983—; contbr. articles to profl. jours. Lectr. Fgn. Svc. Inst., 1967, 80, 81; co-founder N.Mex. Ptnrs. of the Americas, 1969, Border State Univs. Consortium, 1971; founder Internat. Com. for Advanced Latin-Am. Studies, 1974. With U.S. Army, 1954-56. Mem. Latin-Am. Studies Assn. (chmn. program com. 1972-73, exec. coun. 1973-75), Consortium Latin-Am. Studies Program (chmn. steering com. 1970), Am. Polit. Sci. Assn. (comparative politics award com. 1977), Western Polit. Sci. Assn. (exec. coun. 1981-84), Phi Beta Kappa, Phi Kappa Phi. Democrat. Jewish. Office: U Pacific Sch Internat Studies Stockton CA 95211

NEELD, MICHAEL EARL, legislative staff administrator; b. Portland, Oreg., May 13, 1955; s. Carl Eugene and Frances Karlene (Riggers) N. BA in Journalism and Polit. Scis., U. Oreg., 1977. Advt. rep. Post Publs., Camas, Wash., 1977; chpt. cons. Kappa Sigma Internat. Fraternity, Charlottesville, Va., 1977-79; fundraising dir. Am. Cancer Soc., Richmond, Va., 1979-80; news editor, polit. rep. Sta. KYXI, Portland, 1980-84; comms. dir. Moshofsky for Congress, Portland, 1984; pub. info. officer Wash. State Ho. of Reps., Olympia, 1984-85; comms. dir. Paulus for Gov., Portland, 1985-86; Rep. staff coord. Wash. State Ho. of Reps., Olympia, 1991—; founder, ptnr. Pacific N.W. Advocates Pub. Affairs Cons., Olympia, 1989—; instr. polit. strategy, tactics, fundraising and media Wash. State Rep. Party, Tukwila, 1991-92; campaign dir. House Rep. Orgnl. Com., Olympia, 1991-92. Recipient Best Coverage of Breaking News award Oreg. AP/Broadcast, 1982. Mem. U. Oreg. Alumni Assn., Trumpeters, City Club of Portland, Fremont Grove Soc. (founder), Indian Summer Golf and Country Club, Kappa Sigma (alumni, housing corp. bd. dirs. 1980-84). Presbyterian. Home: 3206 Carpenter Hills Loop SE Lacey WA 98503-3900 Office: Wash Ho of Reps 409 John L O'Brien Bldg Olympia WA 98504

NEELY, ALFRED WILLIAM, electrical engineer, marketing professional; b. Chgo., May 26, 1917; s. John Rosboro and Grace (Grougan) N.; m. Eloise Layton, May 31, 1947; children: A. William, Hilarie Neely Job. BSEE, U. Ill., 1943; postgrad., UCLA, 1944-45. Elec. engr. Douglas Aircraft, Santa Monica, Calif., 1944-45; owner, pioneered tape recording Magnetic Recorders Co., L.A., 1946-56; developer and marketer tape dictation machine Comptometer Corp., Chgo., 1956-59; product mgr. home entertainment electronics Warwick Corp, Chgo., 1959-62; v.p. new products devel. Gen. Dynamics Corp., Rochester, N.Y., 1962-63; v.p. import export mfg. home entertainment electronics Trans. Am. Corp., Chgo., 1963-67; owner, pres. CDM Products Co., Chgo., Mission Viejo, Calif., 1967—; cons. import/export and mktg. of home entertainment electronics, Toyomenka Am., N.Y.C., Chgo., 1967-79; cons. product devel. mktg., Universal Power Supply, 1990—. Bd. trustees, deacon Village Presbyn. Ch., Northbrook, Ill.; bd. Boy Scouts Am., Northbrook. Mem. IEEE, Mission Viejo Country Club. Republican. Home and Office: 25872 Quevedo Ln Mission Viejo CA 92691

NEEPER, FREDERIC ALLEN, advertising copywriter; b. Cleve., Apr. 23, 1946; s. Darle Emerson and Mary Lucile (LaMar) N.; m. Mary Lilian Bayliss, Aug. 11, 1970 (div. 1977). BA, Hiram (Ohio) Coll., 1968. Copywriter Pacific Stereo, Emeryville, Calif., 1973-77; sr. tech. writer JBL, Northridge, Calif., 1978-81, communications mgr., 1981-85; copywriter Foote, Cone & Belding, Santa Ana, Calif., 1985-88, sr. copywriter, 1988—. With U.S. Army, 1968-72. Mem. Sierra. Home: 2221 E 1st St Apt I Long Beach CA 90803-2413 Office: Foote Cone & Belding 4 Hutton Centre Dr Santa Ana CA 92707-5770

NEERHOUT, JOHN, JR., petroleum company executive; b. 1931. BSME, U. Calif., 1953. With Bechtel Petroleum, Inc. (now Bechtel, Inc.), San Francisco, 1966—; pres. Bechtel Petroleum, Inc. (now Bechtel, Inc.), 1983-86, also dir. Bechtel Group, Inc. Office: Bechtel Group Inc 50 Beale St San Francisco CA 94105-1813

NEFF, FRANCINE IRVING (MRS. EDWARD JOHN NEFF), former federal government official; b. Albuquerque, Dec. 6, 1925; d. Edward Hackett and Georga (Henderson) Irving; m. Edward John Neff, June 7, 1948; children: Sindle, Edward Vann. A.A., Cottey Coll., 1946; B.A., U. N.Mex., 1948. Div. and precinct chmn. Republican Party, Albuquerque, 1966-71; mem. central com. Bernalillo County (N.Mex.) Republican Party, 1967-74, mem. exec. bd., 1968-70; mem. N.Mex. State central com. Republican Party, 1968-74, 77-82, mem. exec. bd., 1970-74, 81-83; Rep. nat. committeewoman State of N.Mex., 1970-74; also mem. exec. com.; Treas. of U.S. U.S. Dept. Treasury, Washington, 1974-77; nat. dir. U.S. Savs. Bonds, 1974-77; mktg. v.p. Rio Grande Valley Bank, Albuquerque, 1977-81; dir. Hershey Foods Corp., Pa., E-Systems Inc., Dallas, La.-Pacific Corp., Portland, Oreg., D.R. Horton, Inc., Arlington, Tex. N.Mex. state adviser Teenage Reps., 1967-68; del. Rep. Nat. Conv., Miami, 1968, 72; campaign coordinator Congressman Lujan of N.Mex., 1970; pres. Albuquerque Federated Rep. Women's Club, 1977; Leader Camp Fire Girls, Albuquerque, 1957-64; pres. Inez (N.Mex.) PTA, 1961; den mother Cub Scouts Am., Albuquerque, 1964-65; former mem. exec. bd. United Way of Albuquerque; former mem. adv. council Mgmt. Devel. Center, Robert O. Anderson Grad. Sch. Bus. and Adminstrv. Scis., U. N.Mex.; former mem. Def. Adv. Com. on Women in the Services, 1980-83; trustee Cottey Coll., Nevada, Mo., 1982-89. Recipient Exceptional Service award Dept. Treasury, 1976, Horatio Alger award, 1976. Mem. P.E.O. (pres. Albuquerque chpt. 1958-59, 63-64), Albuquerque City Panhellenic Assn. (pres. 1959-60), Greater Albuquerque C. of C. (bd. dirs. 1978-81), Alpha Delta Pi, Sigma Alpha Iota, Phi Kappa Phi, Pi Lambda Theta, Phi Theta Kappa. Episcopalian.

NEFF, JOHN, recording engineer, producer; b. Birmingham, Mich., Mar. 13, 1951; s. Robert Leslie Joseph and Mary Therese (McElvarr) N.; m. Nancy Louise Boocks, Aug. 29, 1987; children: Jennifer Lyn Neff, Bryan C. Groves, Kenneth John Neff. Student, Oakland Community Coll., Auburn Hills, Mich., 1970-72. Freelance recording artist, session musician Detroit, 1965-73; freelance record producer Toronto, Phoenix, L.A., 1974-79; radio announcer, engr. Stas. KVIB, KHEI, KMVI, KLHI, KAOI, 1981-88; record producer Maui Recorders, Kula, Hawaii, 1986-92; cons. studio design Roadrunner Audio Svcs., Glendale, Ariz., 1993—; rec. engr. for Walter Becker, Donald Fagen (Steely Dan), Buffy Ste Marie, Willie Nelson, Sagan Lewis; touring musician Detroit, Toronto, Phoenix, L.A., 1969-79. Recipient Grammy award nomination for Kamakiriad, 1994. Mem. ASCAP, Audio Engrng Soc. (cert.), Am. Fedn. Musicians. Home and Office: Roadrunner Audio Svcs 23846 N 38th Dr Glendale AZ 85310-4113

NEFF, JOHN MICHAEL, health facility administrator, educator, dean; b. Gudalajara, Mex., Dec. 26, 1932; s. Clarence Alvin Neff and Priscilla (Holton) Fenn; m. Lee Cuninggim, Aug. 20, 1961; children: Michael Merriman, Heidi Holton, Joseph Daniel. BA, Pomona Coll., 1955; postgrad., UCLA, 1955-57; MD, Harvard U., 1960. Intern, then resident in pediatrics Sch. Medicine Johns Hopkins U., Balt., 1960-63; epidemic intelligence svc. officer Ctr. for Disease Control USPHS, Atlanta, 1963-65; chief resident in pediatrics Sch. Medicine Johns Hopkins U., Balt., 1965-66, from asst. to assoc. prof. dept. pediatrics, 1968-81, from asst. dean to assoc. dean, 1968-75; fellow in infectious diseases Med. Sch. Harvard U. Children's Hosp., Boston, 1966-68; chief pediatrics Balt. City Hosp., 1975-81; v.p., med. dir. Children's Hosp. Med. Ctr., Seattle, 1981—; prof. pediatrics, assoc. dean Sch. Medicine U. Wash., Seattle, 1981—; founding mem., bd. trustees Broadmead Life Time Care Ctr., Balt., 1975-81; mem. tech. adv. com. Robert Wood Johnson Med. Health Program, 1979-81. Editor: Jour. Infectious Diseases-Evaluation of Smallpox Vaccine, 1977; contbr. articles to profl. jours. Lt. comdr. USPHS, 1963-65. Fellow Infectious Disease Soc. Am.; mem. Soc. Pediatric Rsch., Am. Acad. Pediatrics, Soc. for Epidemiologic Rsch. Office: Children's Hosp Med Ctr 4800 Sandpoint Way NE PO Box C5371 Seattle WA 98105

NEFT, MICHAEL WILLIAM, critical care nurse; b. Pitts., Oct. 5, 1961; s. Harris R. and Fannie R. (Farber) N. Diploma, Mercy Hosp., Pitts., 1983; BS in Nursing, La Roche Coll., Pitts., 1986; MHA, Baylor U., 1993; grad. basic course, officer advanced course, combined arms and svcs. staff sch. Phase I, U.S. Army Med. Dept., 1993. Cert. in critical care nursing. Commd. 2d lt. Nurses Corps U.S. Army, 1985; staff nurse med. ICU Allegheny Gen. Hosp., Pitts., 1985-86; staff-charge nurse med. ICU Fitzsimons Army Med. Ctr., Aurora, Colo., 1986-87; staff-charge nurse intensive care-coronary care unit U.S. Army Nurses Corps, DeWitt Army Hosp., Ft. Belvoir, Va., 1987-90; adminstrv. resident Walter Reed Army Med. Ctr., Washington, 1992-93; head nurse PACU KW Bliss Army Cmty. Hosp., Ft. Huachuca, Ariz., 1993—; head nurse mil. intelligence Primary Care Clinic Raymond W. Bliss Army Cmty. Hosp., Ft. Huachuca, Ariz., head nurse med.-surg. same day surgery PACU. Capt. Nurse Corps, U.S. Army. Mem. ANA, AACN, Am. Coll. Healthcare Execs., Am. Soc. Post Anesthesia Nurses, Am. Acad. Med. Adminstrs., Soc. for Critical Care Medicine, Internat. Assn. Mil. Surgeons of U.S., Sigma Theta Tau. Home: 1167A S Plaza Maria Sierra Vista AZ 85635-4320 Office: USA MEDDAC MCXJ DN-PACU Fort Huachuca AZ 85635

NEHLS, ROBERT LOUIS, JR., school system administrator; b. Berkeley, Calif., Dec. 27, 1944; s. Robert Louis and Inda May (Kean) N.; m. Diana Jean Smith, June 17, 1967; 1 child, Patrick Robert. AA, Coll. Marin, 1965; BS, San Jose State U., 1967, MA, 1976; EdD, U. San Francisco, 1991. Cert. tchr., sch. adminstr., Calif. Tchr. Diablo Valley Coll., Pleasant Hill, Calif., 1979-86; acct. Kelly and Tama, CPAs, Walnut Creek, Calif., 1978-79; tchr. Pleasanton (Calif.) Unified Sch. Dist., 1970-78, 79-81, dir. fiscal svcs., 1981-83; dep. supt. San Leandro (Calif.) Unified Sch. Dist., 1983-87, 90—; asst. supt. Acalanes Union High Sch. Dist., Lafayette, Calif., 1987-89; supt. Orinda (Calif.) Union Sch. Dist., 1989-90; exec. adv. com. Calif. Found. Improvement of Employee/Employer Relationships, Sacramento, 1992—. Contbr. articles to profl. jours. Mem. Assn. Calif. Sch. Adminstrs. (comptroller 1992-95, pres.-elect 1995—), Calif. Assn. Sch. Bus. Ofcls. (bd. dirs. no. sect. 1984-89), No. Calif. Sch. Bus. Ofcls. (past pres.), Acad. of Sci., Phi Kappa Phi. Home: 1004 Leland Dr Lafayette CA 94549-4130 Office: San Leandro Unified Sch Dist 14735 Juniper St San Leandro CA 94579-1222

NEIDERT, KALO EDWARD, accountant, educator; b. Safe, Mo., Sept. 1, 1918; s. Edward Robert and Margaret Emma (Kinsey) N.; m. Stella Mae Vest, June 22, 1952; children—Edward, Karl, David, Wayne, Margaret. B.S. in Bus. Adminstrn. with honors, Washington U., St. Louis, 1949, M.S. in Bus. Adminstrn, 1950; postgrad., U. Minn., 1950-54. CPA, Nev. Mem. faculty U. Minn., 1950-54; mem. faculty U. Miss., 1954-57, U. Tex., Austin, 1957-61, Gustavus Adolphus Coll., St. Peter, Minn., 1961-62, U. Nev., Reno, 1962—; prof. acctg. and info. systems U. Nev., 1962-90, prof. emeritus, 1990—; auditor Washoe County Employee Fed. Credit Union, 1969-82, dir., treas., 1982-86. Author: Statement on Auditing Procedure in Decision Tree Form, 1974. Asst. scoutmaster local Boy Scouts Am.; Bd. dirs. Tahoe Timber Trails, 1980-82, treas., 1981-82, v.p. fin., 1982-84; Bd. dirs. St. Johns Child Care Center, 1982-84; cen. com. mem. Washoe County Rep. Party, Reno, 1986-88, 90—. Mem. AICPA, Assn. System Mgmt. (treas. Reno chpt. 1984—), Am. Acctg. Assn., Am. Econ. Assn., Am. Fin. Assn., Fin. Mgmt. Assn., Nev. Soc. CPAs, Western Fin. Assn., Oddfellows, Beta Alpha Psi, Beta Gamma Sigma. Presbyterian. Office: U Nev Coll Bus Adminstrn Reno NV 89557

NEILL, WILLIAM ALEXANDER, magazine editor; b. Atlanta, Feb. 17, 1957; s. William A. and Sara Ann Neill. BA in English, Wesleyan U., 1979. Editor Car Audio and Electronics, Woodland Hills, Calif., 1989—. Office: Avcom Pub 21700 Oxnard St Ste 1600 Woodland Hills CA 91367-3670

NEIMAN, JERI ANNE, therapist; b. Berkeley, Calif., Jan. 20, 1951; d. Alfred D. Wallace and Marjorie E. (Nordheim) Stevens; m. Roy A. Neiman, June 12, 1969 (div. Aug. 1977); children: Lorien, Arwen. AA, Palomar Jr. Coll., 1977; BA in Psychology with distinction, Calif. State U., Long Beach, 1979, MA in Psychology with distinction, 1981; postgrad. Human Sexuality Program, UCLA, 1991-92. Lic. marriage, family, child therapist, Calif.; cert. community coll. instr., counselor; cert. sex therapist. Rsch. asst. Calif. State U., 1978-82; tchr. Artesia (Calif.)-Bellflower-Cerritos Unified Sch. Dist., 1982-83; dir. Am. Learning Corp., Huntington Beach, Calif., 1983-85; social worker Los Angeles County Children's Protective Svcs., Long Beach, 1986-88; sr. social worker Orange County Social Svc. Agy., Orange, Calif., 1988-90; therapist Cypress Mental Health, Cypress, Calif., 1988—, cons., 1990—; cons., 1990—; group chair, leader Adults Abused as Children, Los Altos Hosp., Long Beach, 1991—, Coll. Hosp., Cerritos, 1993—; speaker, presenter in field. Mem. Child's Sexual Abuse Network, Orange, 1988—; mem. legis. com. Child Abuse Coun. of Orange County, 1988. Women's League scholar, 1980-81. Mem. AAUW, Am. Assn. Marriage, Family Therapists, Calif. Assn. Marriage, Family Therapists, Am. Profl. Soc. for Abused Children, Calif. Profl. Assn. for Abused Children, Phi Kappa Phi, Psi Chi. Republican. Methodist. Office: Cypress Mental Health 5300 Orange Ave Ste 216 Cypress CA 90630-2972

NEIMAN, TANYA MARIE, lawyer; b. Pitts., June 28, 1949; d. Max and Helen (Lamaga) N. AB, Mills Coll., 1970; JD, U. Calif. Hastings Coll. of Law, San Francisco, 1974. Bar: Calif. 1975. Law assoc. Boalt Hall U. Calif., Berkeley, 1974-76; pub. defender State of Calif., San Francisco, 1976-81; assoc. gen. counsel, dir. vol. legal services Bar Assn. San Francisco, 1982—; bd. dirs. Jack Berman Advocacy Ctr. Tanya Neiman Day proclaimed in her honor by Mayor of San Francisco, 1991; recipient Disting. Citizen award Harvard Club San Francisco, 1995. Mem. ABA (mem. ABA Commn. on Homelessness 1993—, speaker 1985—, Harrison Tweed award 1985), Calif. Bar Assn. (exec. com. 1984—, legal svcs. sect., chair steering com. State Bar Legal Corps), Golden Gate Bus. Assn. Found. (v.p. grant making 1985—), Nat. Conf. Women and Law (speaker 1975—), Nat. Lawyers Guild. Office: Bar Assn San Francisco 685 Market St San Francisco CA 94105-4200

NEIMANN, ALBERT ALEXANDER, statistician; b. Torrington, Wyo., Nov. 29, 1939; s. Alexander and Lydia (Temple) N.; m. Barbara Jean Maw, May 6, 1962; children: Debbie, Todd, Amy, Kelly,. BA, Willamette U., 1967. Mathematician Keyport (Wash.) Naval Torpedo Sta., 1968-70; math. statistician Concord (Calif.) Naval Weapons Sta., 1970-85, engring. statistician, 1985-94. Mgr. Little League Baseball, Antioch, Calif., 1977-84, Little League Softball, Antioch, 1984-87; Sunday sch. tchr. Grace Bapt. Ch., 1979-90; statistician Antioch High Sch., 1985-89. Recipient Performance award Concord Naval Weapons Sta., 1978, 88-94. Mem. Am. Statis. Assn., Math. Assn. Am., Am. Soc. for Quality Control, Nat. Coun. Tchrs. Math.

NEINAS, CHARLES MERRILL, athletic association executive; b. Marshfield, Wis., Jan. 18, 1932; s. Arthur Oscar and Blanche Amelia (Reeder) N.; children: Andrew, Toby. B.S., U. Wis., 1957. Asst. exec. dir. Nat. Collegiate Athletic Assn., Kansas City, Mo., 1961-71; commr. Big Eight Conf., Kansas City, 1971-81; exec. dir. Coll. Football Assn., 1981—; Dr. Patricia L. Pacey prof. econs. U. Colo., Boulder, 1981—, econ. cons., 1981—. Served with USNR, 1952-54. Home: 4977 Idylwild Trl Boulder CO 80301-3651 Office: College Football Assoc 6688 Gunpark Dr Boulder CO 80301-3372

NEISWANDER, LAUREL ANN, interior designer; b. Pasadena, Calif., Jan. 15, 1954; d. Robert South and Margaret Florance (Bridle) N.; m. Douglas Burns Rowe, Sept. 21, 1984 (div. Mar. 1990). BA, U. Calif., San Diego, 1976; AA, San Diego Mesa Coll., 1983. Cert. interior designer, Calif. Interior design sales Artistic Eye Interiors, Santa Monica, Calif., 1977-79; interior design sales mgr. Gavin Interiors, San Diego, 1979-82; interior designer, mgr. Wurts Interiors, San Diego, 1982-91; interior designer Glabman Furniture and Interior Design, Woodland Hills, Calif., 1991-93; sole proprietor Neiswander Interiors, Tarzana, Calif., 1993—. Mem. Am. Soc. Interior Designers, Nat. Orgn. Women Bus. Owners, L.A. Conservancy, Architectural Fdn. of L.A. Office: Neiswander Interiors 19437 Collier St Tarzana CA 91356-3012

NELDNER, HELMUT M., telecommunications industry executive; b. Lodz, Poland, Oct. 22, 1938; m. Marion Riske. B in Comm., U. Alta., Can., 1964; grad. advanced mgmt. program, Harvard U., 1984. Joined AGT Ltd. (formerly Alta. Govt. Telephones), 1964, various positions, 1964-74, comptr., 1977-80, v.p. fin., chmn. pension bd., 1980-83, v.p. corporate planning and engring., 1983-84, pres., 1984-87, CEO, 1987-90, now dep. chmn., CEO; pres., CEO Telus Corp., Edmonton, Alta., Can., 1990—; Mem. bus. adv. coun. U. Atla.; bd. dirs. Can. Utilities, Suncor Inc. Office: Telus Corp, 10020-100 St 31st fl, Edmonton, AB Canada T5J 0N5

NELIPOVICH, SANDRA GRASSI, artist; b. Oak Park, Ill., Nov. 22, 1939; d. Alessandro and Lena Mary (Ascareggi) Grassi; m. John Nelipovich Jr., Aug. 19, 1973. BFA in Art Edn., U. Ill., 1961; postgrad., Northwestern U., 1963, Gonzaga U., Florence, Italy, 1966, Art Inst. Chgo., 1968; diploma, Accademia Universale Alessandro Magno, Prato, Italy, 1983. Tchr. art Edgewood Jr. High Sch., Highland Park, Ill., 1961-62, Emerson Sch. Jr. High Sch., Oak Park, 1962-77; batik artist Calif., 1977—; illustrator Jolly Robin Publ. Co., Anaheim, Calif., 1988—; supr. student tchrs., Oak Park, 1970-75; adult edn. tchr. ESL, ceramics, Medinah, Ill., 1974; mem. curriculum action group on human dignity, EEO workshop demonstration, Oak Park, 1975-76; guest lectr. Muckenthaler Ctr., Fullerton, Calif., 1980, 92, Niguel Art Group, Dana Point, Calif., 1989, Carlsbad A.A., 1990, ARt League, Oceanside Art Group, 1992; 2d v.p. Anaheim Hills Women's Club, 1990-91, rec. sec. 1991-92; fabric designer for fashion designer Barbara Jax, 1987. One-woman shows include Lawry's Calif. Ctr., L.A., 1981-83, Whittier (Calif.) Mus., 1985-86, Anaheim Cultural Ctr., 1986-88, Ill. Inst. Tech., Chgo., 1989, Muckenthaler Cultural Ctr., Fullerton, 1990; also gallery exhibits in Oak Brook, 1982, La Habra, Calif., 1983; represented in permanent collections collections McDonald's Corp., Oak Brook, Glenkirk Sch., Deerfield, Ill., Emerson Sch., Oak Park, galleries in Laguna Beach, Calif., Maui, Hawaii, Mich., N.J.; poster designer Saratoga Fine Arts; illustrator The Magic Vineyard, 1995. Active Assistance League, Anaheim, Calif., 1992—, chmn. ways & means com., 1995—. Recipient numerous awards, purchase prizes, 1979—; featured in Calif. Art Rev., Artists of So. Calif., Vol. II, Nat. Artists' Network, 1992. Mem. AAUW (hospitality chmn. 1984-85), Assistance League Anaheim, Oak Park Art League, Orange Art Assn. (jury chairperson 1980), Anaheim Art Assn., Muckenthaler Ctr. Circle, Anaheim Hills Women's Club. Roman Catholic. Home and Office: 5922 E Calle Cedro Anaheim CA 92807-3207

NELLAMS, JANE HARRIS, communications director, journalist; b. Chgo., May 13, 1955; d. Edward Calvin Harris and Bettejane (Morrow) Kirkpatrick; m. Robert Lee Nellams, Oct. 10, 1987; 1 child, André. BA in Journalism, U. Oreg., 1978. Reporter Seattle Post-Intelligencer, Seattle, 1978-80, Bremerton (Wash.) Sun, 1980-81, Jour.-Am., Bellevue, Wash., 1981-84; pub. info. officer Bellevue Community Coll., 1984-90, dir. coll. rels., 1990-91; dir. pub. rels. North Seattle Community Coll., 1991—. Mem. Jr. League of Seattle, 1988—; precinct chair Dem. Party of Wash., Bellevue, 1988. Mem. Nat. Coun. Mktg. and Pub. Rels., U. Oreg. Alumni Assn., Sigma Kappa. Office: North Seattle Community Coll 9600 College Way N Seattle WA 98103-3514

NELLES, MERICE TILMAN, business development consultant; b. Buffalo, Dec. 1, 1932; s. Maurice and Cecelia Mae (Nelson) N.; B.S., Pa. State U.; M.B.A., U. Pa.; C.P.A., U. Ill.; m. Mary Elizabeth Ambrosius, Aug. 6, 1955; 1 dau., Erika Lynn. Commd. ensign U.S. Navy, 1954, advanced through grades to comdr., 1968; comdg. officer at sea and on shore, 9 yrs.; dir. magnetic surveys and degaussing ops., Western Pacific, 1966-67; designer-dir. (with U.S. Army) disaster recovery tng. systems, 1969-73; designer-dir. welding sch., Phila., 1973-77; systems analyst and planner Sun Petroleum Products Co., Phila., 1979-81; sr. venture investments analyst Sun Co., 1981-83; adj. econ. bus. faculty Delaware County Community Coll., 1987-91; instr. Ctr. for Profl. Edn., Phila., 1986-88, dir. devel., 1990-93. Decorated Meritorious Service medal, Navy Commendation medal, Army Commendation medal; cert. data processor Inst. Certification of Computer Profls. Mem. Am. Inst. C.P.A.s., Calif. Soc. CPA's. Contbr. to profl. jours. and manuals. Home: 5522 Rutgers Rd La Jolla CA 92037-7821

NELLINGTON, BLAINE See **MAGNUSON, DONALD RICHARD**

NELSEN, CRAIG JOSEPH, mining company executive, geologist; b. Harlan, Iowa, Sept. 8, 1951; s. Newmark Brondt and Cleopha Ann (Schwery) N.; m. Jackie Birer, Oct. 9, 1980; children: Matthew, Kate. BA, U. Mont., 1975; MS, U. N.Mex., 1980. Geologist Bur. Land Mgmt., Albuquerque, 1977-79, Noranda Exploration Inc., Anchorage, 1979; project geologist Conoco, Albuquerque, 1980-82; sr. geologist Getty Mining Co., Salt Lake City, 1982-84; exploration mgr. USA LAC Minerals Inc., Reno, Nev., 1984-89; v.p. exploration USA LAC Minerals Inc., Denver, 1990; sr. v.p. exploration LAC Minerals Ltd., Toronto, 1991-94; pres., CEO Metallica Resources, Inc., Toronto, 1994—. Mem. Soc. Econ. Geologist, Can. Inst. Mining, N.W. Mining Assn. Home and Office: 7728 S Grape Ct Littleton CO 80122-3810

NELSON, ALAN CURTIS, government official, lawyer; b. Oakland, Calif., Oct. 18, 1933; s. Albert C. and Martha (Peters) N.; m. JoAnn Wallen, Jan. 31, 1960; children: Kristine Ann, Kathryn Donna, Karin Martha. BS, U. Calif., Berkeley, 1955, JD, 1958. Bar: Calif. 1959, U.S. Dist. Cts. Calif. 1959, U.S. Supreme Ct. 1984. Atty. Rogers, Clark & Jordan, San Francisco, 1959-64; dep. dist. atty. Alameda County (Calif.), 1964-69; asst. dir. State of Calif. Human Resource Dept., Sacramento, 1969-72; dir. State of Calif. Dept. Rehab., Sacramento, 1972-75; gen. atty. Pacific Telephone & Telegraph, San Francisco, 1975-81; dep. commr. Immigration and Naturalization Service, Washington, 1981-82, commr., 1982-89; cons. fed. Am. immigration reform U.S. Dept. Justice, Washington, 1989-90, 91-94; gen. counsel employment devel. dept. State of Calif., 1990-91; atty. and cons. on immigration Sacramento, 1994—; adj. prof. McGeorge Sch. Law, U. Pacific. Chmn. Calif. Gov. Com. for Employment of Handicapped, 1981-82. Recipient Alumnus of Yr. award Tau Kappa Epsilon, 1987; Border Patrol Sta., Imperial Beach, Calif. dedicated to Commr. Nelson, 1988. Mem. State Bar Calif., Assn. Calif. Tort Reform (dir.), Bar Assn. San Francisco, Legal Aid Soc. San Francisco (dir.), Assn. Fed. Investigators (pres. 1987). Republican. Club: Commonwealth. Office: Law Offices of Alan Nelson 835 Shoreside Dr Sacramento CA 95831-1422

NELSON, ALLEN F., investor relations and proxy solicitation company executive; b. Portland, Oreg., Oct. 17, 1943; s. Roy August and Mildred Mary (Jensen) N.; BS, U. Iowa, 1965, MA, 1968; m. Johanna Molenaar, Dec. 8, 1973. V.p. Shareholder Communications Corp., N.Y.C., 1970-72, Trafalgar Capital Corp., N.Y.C., 1973; pres. Nelson, Lasky & Co., Inc., N.Y.C., 1974-76; account exec. Corp. Communications Inc., Seattle, 1976-77; pres. Allen Nelson & Co., Inc., Seattle, 1977—, Can. Corp. Shareholder Svcs. Assn. Mem. Fin. Analysts Fedn., Nat. Investor Relations Inst., Nat. Security Traders Assn., Practising Law Inst., Pub. Relations Soc. Am., Am. Soc. Corporate Secs., Can. Soc. Corp. Secs. Clubs: Rainier. Home: 4400 Beach Dr SW Seattle WA 98116-3937 Office: Allen Nelson & Co Inc PO Box 16157 Seattle WA 98116-0157

NELSON, ARJAY JOHN, naval aviator; b. San Francisco, May 9, 1967; s. Roy John Nelson and Joyce Virginia (Bizzi) Babbel. AA, Diablo Valley Coll., 1987; BA, U. Calif., Santa Barbara, 1990. Mover, warehouseman UC Moving Svcs., Oakland, Calif., 1982-88; mktg. asst., mgr. U. Calif., Santa Barbara, 1989-90; naval aviator USN, 1991—. Named one of Outstanding Young Men Am., 1990. Mem. Assn. Naval Aviation, Res. Officers Assn., Total Quality Leadership, Sigma Phi Epsilon Alumni Assn. Republican. Presbyterian. Home: 120 Rubicon Ct Martinez CA 94553-5033

NELSON, BARRY VERNON, engineering executive; b. Glendale, Calif., Apr. 8, 1939; s. Vernon Herbert and Jean Leona (Rulifson) N.; m. Nancy Joyce Cooper, Sept. 14, 1963 (div. Nov. 1984); children: Rodney Norman, Florean Marie, Robert Arthur; m. Nancy Ann Murphy, Dec. 1, 1984. BA, Occidental Coll., 1961; MS, Calif. State U., Northridge, 1973. Project engr. Kurz and Root Co., Anaheim, Calif., 1959-64, Teledyne Corp., Gardena, Calif., 1964-65; project staff engr. Rockwell Corp., Downey, Calif., 1965-67; engr., scientist specialist McDonnell Douglas Corp., Huntington Beach, Calif., 1967-68; adminstrv. asst. Santa Barbara Rsch. Corp., Goleta, Calif., 1968-74; info. systems data mgr. Comprehensive Health Planning Agy., San Diego, 1974-75; data processing mgr. Lucky Stores, Inc., San Diego, 1975-77; CFO Hosp. Mgmt. Svcs., Fullerton, Calif., 1977-80; systems analysis supr. Martin Marietta Corp., Santa Maria, Calif., 1980-82; tech. dir. Sci. Applications Internat. Corp., San Bernardino, Calif., 1982-85; ops. mgr. Frontier Engring. Inc., Concord, Calif., 1985-92; ops. dir. Mgmt. Assistance Corp. of Am., Concord, Calif., 1992—. Office: Mgmt Assistance Corp Am 2715 Lone Tree Way Antioch CA 94509-4960

NELSON, BRYAN H(ERBERT), educational association administrator; b. Yakima, Wash., July 3, 1956; s. Herbert B. and Marilyn A. (Cupper) N.; m. Sandra Exley, June 11, 1993; children from previous marriage: Christofer A., Bryanne E. BEd, Ea. Wash. U., 1977, MS in Speech Pathology, 1978. Speech pathologist Ednl. Svc. Dist. 101, Spokane, Wash., 1978-83, coord. speech pathology, 1983-84, coord. inservice tng., 1985; processor fruit broker Herb Nelson Inc., Yakima, 1985-88; coord. early childhood and spl. edn. programs Selah (Wash.) Sch. Dist., 1989-92, coord. spl. edn., 1989-92; dir. New Directions, EPIC, 1992—; gen. ptnr. Nelson Perkins Assocs., Yakima, 1990—; dir. New Directions-Epic, Yakima, Wash., 1992—; guest lectr. Ea. Wash. U., Cheney, 1984-85; chmn. very spl. arts festival Ednl. Svc. Dist 101, 1985, on-site coord. IDEAS conv., 1983. Bd. dirs., chairperson citizens adv. bd. Yakima Vocat. Skill Ctr., 1988-89; mem. gen. adv. com. Yakima Vocat. Coop.; mem. allocation panel United Way, Yakima, 1974, loaned exec., 1990; mem. exec. com. Yakima County Birth to Six, 1989—. Home: 7303 Perry St Yakima WA 98908-2013 Office: New Directions-Epic PO Box 9279 Yakima WA 98909-0279

NELSON, BURKE EDWARD, engineering executive; b. Hastings, Nebr., Jan. 16, 1938; s. Duane Irving and Hazel Virginia (Yager) N.; m. Ivonne Ingvarsson, Aug. 22, 1980; children: Mark O., Jill L., Burke E. Jr., Megan J. BS in Mech. Engring. with honors, Mich. State U., 1959; MSE in Aeronautics and Astronautics, U. Wash., 1963; PhD in Materials Sci., Drexel U., 1972. Registered profl. engr., Pa. Research engr. The Boeing Co., Seattle, 1959-66; systems engr., research and devel. General Electric Co., Phila., 1966-71; assoc. dir. research optical group Perkin-Elmer Corp., Wilton, Conn., 1971-81; exec. dir. ASME, N.Y.C., 1981-82; dir. engring. spectroscopy div. Perkin-Elmer, Ridgefield, Conn., 1982-84; dir. programs Logicon/RDA, Albuquerque, 1984—; trustee Engring. Info., Inc., N.Y.C., 1981-85. Contbr. articles to profl. jours.; patentee in field. Mem. ASME (congl. fellow 1975), AIAA, Soc. Photo-Optical Instrument Engrs., Triangle Frat., Sigma Xi, Tau Beta Pi (disting.), Pi Tau Sigma. Republican. Roman Catholic. Home: 11201 Oakland Ave NE Albuquerque NM 87122-4158 Office: Logicon/RDA PO Box 9377 Albuquerque NM 87119-9377

NELSON, CRAIG ALAN, management consultant; b. San Rafael, Calif., July 11, 1961; s. Kenneth Alfred and Anne Catherine (Laurie) N. BS in Fin., San Diego State U., 1984. Loan assoc. Union Bank, San Diego, 1984-85, comml. loan officer, 1985-86, corp. banking officer, 1986-87, asst. v.p., 1987-89, v.p. corp. banking, 1989-93; v.p. Alexander & Alexander, San Diego, 1993—. Corp. recruiter United Way, San Diego, 1988; community group chair San Diego chpt. Am. Cancer Soc., 1989; mem. com. Juvenile Diabetes Assn.; bd. dirs. San Diego State Found., 1989—. Mem. San Diego State U. Young Alumni Assn. (pres. 1988-89, bd. dirs. emeritus 1989). Home: 1233 San Dieguito Dr Encinitas CA 92024-5116 Office: Alexander and Alexander 9255 Towne Centre Dr Ste 225 San Diego CA 92121-3035

NELSON, CRAIG STUART, lawyer; b. Greenbrae, Calif., June 20, 1964; s. Gary Dennis Nelson and Sydney Patricia (Jones) Funamura; m. Elizabeth Leanore Mohun, July 18, 1992. BS, BA, Calif. State U., Chico, 1987; JD, Hastings Coll. Law, 1990; ML in Criminal Law, U. San Diego, 1994. Bar: Calif. 1990. Clk. extern 9th Cir. Ct. Appeal, San Francisco, 1989; assoc. atty. Bowles and Verna, Walnut Creek, Calif., 1990-93; dep. atty. gen. Calif. Dept. Justice, San Diego, 1994—. Note editor Constitutional Law Quarterly, 1988-89. Mem. State Bar Calif., Zoological Soc. San Diego, Hastings Alumni Assn. Republican. Office: Calif Dept Justice 110 W A St San Diego CA 92186-2566

NELSON, DANIEL ALAN, editor, columnist; b. Ripon, Wis., Apr. 20, 1966; s. James Lee and Diana Shirley (Lemberg) N. BA in History and Polit. Sci., Wash. State U., 1989. Reporter Pierce County Herald, Puyallup, Wash., 1989-91; editor Signpost for NW Trails Mag., Seattle, 1991—; author Foghorn Press, San Francisco, 1994—; graphic designer Earth-Share of Wash., Seattle, 1992-94. Freelance columnist Am. Hiking mag., Wash., 1993—, Western Angler, Linders, Wyo., 1993—; outdoor columnist The News Tribune, Tacoma, 1994—. Bd. mem. Pierce County Trails Adv. Ctr., Tacoma, 1992-94; adv.-evaluator trail/pks. projects Wash. State Interagency Com. for Outdoor Recreation, Olympia, 1993-94. Mem. Outdoor Writers Assn. Am., Soc. Profl. Journalists. Democrat. Office: Signpost for NW Trails Mag 1305 4th Ave Ste 512 Seattle WA 98101-2401

NELSON, DANIEL R., bank executive; b. Spokane, Wash., 1938. Wash. State U., 1962; Postgrad., U. Wash. With Ranier Bank, Seattle, 1962-84; pres. West One Bank Corp., Boise, Idaho, 1986-93, CEO, 1986—, chmn. bd. dirs., 1993—. Office: West 1 Bancorp PO Box 8247 Boise ID 83733-8247*

NELSON, DARRYL JAMES, small business owner; b. Detroit, Nov. 9, 1950; s. Herschell James Burns and Madeline Veronica Zidick; m. Jennifer Nelson. Student, Whittier Coll. Warehouseman E.D. Bullard & Co., City of Industry, Calif., 1969-72, C Hagar & Sons Hinge Mfg. Co., City of Industry, 1972-73; mgr. shipping, receiving Rutland Tool & Supply Co., Pico Rivera, Calif., 1974-76, mgr. wholesale traffic, 1983—; owner, mgr. Reno (Nev.) Prospector's Supply Co., 1984—. Mem. Nev. Prospectors, Comstock Prospectors, Motherlode Miners, E Clampus Vitus, Reno C. of C., Winners Circle Breakfast Club (bd. dirs., chmn. Welcome Com.). Office: 315 Claremont St Reno NV 89502-2529

NELSON, DAVID SAMUEL, public relations executive; b. LaGrande, Oreg., Dec. 20, 1941; s. Roy K. and Anne Cecila (Barkman) N.; m. Leah Marie Thom, Nov. 7, 1969; children: Barry, Molly, Amy. BA in Agrl., Oreg. State U., 1964, BSBA, 1967. Field rep. Oreg. Farm Bur. Fedn., Salem, 1967-69, exec. v.p., 1969-75; v.p. Agrl. Commodity Promotions, Salem, 1975-77; pres. Dave Nelson & Assocs., Inc., Salem, 1977—; co-founder, v.p. Agro-Comp, Inc., Salem, 1979-82; mem. adv. com. Workmans Compensation Bd., Salem, 1973-83. Mem. Turner (Oreg.) Elem. Sch. Bd., 1974-82, chmn., 1978. Named Seedsmen of Yr. Oreg. Seed Coun., Salem, 1991. Mem. Am. Quarter Horse Assn., Oreg. Quarter Horst Racing Assn. (chmn. 1974—), Capitol Club. Republican Methodist. Office: Dave Nelson & Assocs 1193 Royvonne Ave SE Ste 11 Salem OR 97302-6501

NELSON, DOROTHY WRIGHT (MRS. JAMES F. NELSON), federal judge; b. San Pedro, Calif., Sept. 30, 1928; d. Harry Earl and Lorna Amy Wright; m. James Frank Nelson, Dec. 27, 1950; children: Franklin Wright, Lorna Jean. B.A., UCLA, 1950, J.D., 1953; LL.M., U. So. Calif., 1956; LLD honoris causa, Western State U., 1980, U. So. Calif., 1983, Georgetown U., 1988, Whittier U., 1989, U. Santa Clara, 1990; LLD (honoris causa), Whittier U., 1989. Bar: Calif. 1954. Research assoc. fellow U. So. Calif., 1953-56; instr., 1957, asst. prof., 1958-61, assoc. prof., 1961-67, prof., 1967, assoc. dean., 1965-67, dean., 1967-80; judge U.S. Ct. Appeals (9th cir.), 1980—; cons. Project STAR, Law Enforcement Assistance Adminstrn.; mem. select com. on internal procedures of Calif. Supreme Ct., 1987—; co-chair Sino-Am. Seminar on Mediation and Arbitration, Beijing, 1992; dir. Dialogue on Transition to a Global Soc., Weinacht, Switzerland, 1992. Author: Judicial Adminstration and The Administration of Justice, 1973; Contbr. articles to profl. jours. Co-chmn. Confronting Myths in Edn. for Pres. Nixon's White House Conf. on Children, Pres. Carter's Commn. for Pension Policy, 1974-80, Pres. Reagon's Madison Trust; bd. visitors U.S. Air Force Acad., 1978; bd. dirs. Council on Legal Edn. for Profl. Responsibility, 1971-80, Constnl. Right Found., Am. Nat. Inst. for Social Advancement; adv. bd. Nat. Center for State Cts., 1971-73; chmn. bd. Western Justice Ctr., 1986—; mem. adv. com. Nat. Jud. Edn. Program to promote equality for woman and men in cts. Named Law Alumnus of Yr. UCLA, 1967; recipient Profl. Achievement award, 1969; named Times Woman of Yr., 1968; recipient U. Judaism Humanitarian award, 1973; AWARE Internat. award, 1970; Ernestine Stalhut Outstanding Woman Lawyer award, 1972; Pub. Svc. award Coro Found., 1978, Pax Orbis ex Jure medallion World Peace thru Law Ctr., 1975, Hollzer Human Rights award Jesish Fedn. Coun. L.A., 1988, Medal of Honor UCLA, 1993; Lustman fellow Yale U. 1977. Fellow Am. Bar Found., Davenport Coll., Yale U.; mem. Bar Calif. (bd. dirs. continuing edn. bar commn. 1967-74), Am. Judicature Soc. (dir., Justice award 1985), Assn. Am. Law Schs. (chmn. com. edn. in jud. adminstrn.), Am. Bar Assn. (sect. on jud. adminstrn., chmn. com. on edn. in jud. adminstrn. 1973-89), Phi Beta Kappa, Order of Coif (nat. v.p. 1974-76), Jud. Conf. U.S. (com. to consider standards for admission to practice in fed. cts. 1976-79). Office: US Ct Appeals Cir 125 S Grand Ave Ste 303 Pasadena CA 91105-1652

NELSON, DREW VERNON, mechanical engineering educator; b. Elizabeth, N.J., Oct. 11, 1947; s. Andrew K. and Myra G. (Kempson) N. BSME, Stanford U., 1968, MSME, 1970, PhDME, 1978. Research asst. Stanford U., Calif., 1971-74, asst. prof., 1978-83, assoc. prof., 1983—; engr. Gen. Electric Co., Sunnyvale, Calif., 1975-76, sr. engr., 1977-78; cons. in field. Co-editor: Fatigue Design Handbook, 1989; contbr. articles to profl. jours. Recipient Spergel Meml. award for Most Outstanding Paper, 32nd Internat. Wire and Cable Symposium, 1984. Mem. ASTM, Soc. Automotive Engrs., Soc. for Exptl. Mechanics, Sigma Xi, Tau Beta Pi. Home: 840 Cabot Ct San Carlos CA 94070-3464 Office: Stanford U Dept Mech Engring Stanford CA 94305-4021

NELSON, EDWARD HUMPHREY, architect; b. Winchester, Mass., Sept. 2, 1918; s. Richard MacDonald and Evelyn Miller (Humphrey) N.; m. Lois Whitaker Renouf, Sept. 24, 1948 (dec.); children: Susan, David, Sarah; m. Miriam P. Ketcham, Jan. 2, 1988. Grad., Lenox Sch., 1936; B.Arch., Yale, 1950. Pvt. archtl. practice Tucson, 1953-61; sr. v.p. CNWC Architects, Tucson, 1961-88, pres., 1989-94; bd. dirs. CNWC & Steppe Archs.; mem. adv. com. U. Ariz. Coll. Arch., 1984-93. Works include: design for Tucson Community Ctr. Pres. Tucson Cmty. Coun., 1969-71, Tucson Art Ctr., 1960, Tucson Housing Found., 1969-92; bd. dirs. Tucson Trade Bur., 1976-91, pres., 1984; bd. dirs. Tucson Symphony, 1977-84, Tucson United Way, 1980; trustee Green Fields Sch., 1960-74, Tucson Art Mus.; vestry St. Philips Episc. Ch., 1967-69, sr. warden, 1987-90, parish warden, 1993-94; convenor Episcopal Interparish Coun., 1990-92; mem. Episcopal Diocese of Ariz., W.W. Regional Parish. Served to capt. AUS, 1940-41, WWII, ETO. Decorated Bronze Star with oak leaf cluster, Purple Heart; recipient Disting. Citizen award U. Ariz., 1981. Fellow Am. Inst. Architects (pres. So. Ariz. chpt. 1962, chmn. Ariz. fellows 1986-90); mem. Ariz. Soc. Architects (pres. 1963). Democrat. Episcopalian. Clubs: Yale (Tucson) (pres. 1962, 83, dir. 1979—); U. Ariz. Pres.'. Home: 2020 E 4th St Tucson AZ 85719-5114

NELSON, FRANCES PATRICIA, food service executive; b. Denver, Jan. 15, 1948; d. Wilbur Jordan and Margaret Emma Anna (Kruger) Cannon; m. Kenneth Roy Nelson, Sept. 2, 1972; children: Krista, Erin, Michael. BS, Colo. State U., 1970; MA, U. No. Colo., 1981. Asst. dir. child nutrition Colo. Dept. Edn., Denver, 1971-77; dir. nutrition svc. Denver Head Start, 1981-83; dir. food svc. Englewood (Colo.) Pub. Schs., 1988-91, Jefferson County Schs., Golden, Colo., 1991—; cons. Wildwood Child Care, Englewood, 1984-88, Mile High Child Care Assn., Denver, 1981-83, Colo. Dept. Edn., Denver, 1976, Denver Pub. Schs., 1979. Contbr. articles to profl. jours. Leader Girl Scouts Am., Denver, 1982-88, Boy Scouts Am., 1991; team adminstr. Aurora (Colo.) Soccer Club, 1981-88. Mem. Am. Dietetic Assn., Am. Sch. Food Svc. Assn., Colo. Sch. Food Svc. Assn. (pres.-elect 1991-92, pres. 1992-93). Home: 6227 S Netherland Cir Aurora CO 80016-1323 Office: Jefferson County Pub Schs 1829 Denver West Dr # 27 Golden CO 80401-3146

NELSON, GARY, county councilman, engineer; b. Spokane, Wash., Apr. 11, 1936; s. Nels Alfred and Laura Marie (Winberg) Nelson; m. JoAnne Laura Knudson, Nov. 27, 1959; children: Grant, Geoffrey, Gregory. BSEE, Wash. State U., 1958; MSEE, U. Wis., 1963. Engr. RCA, Camden, N.J., 1958-59; officer USAF, Madison, Wis., 1959-62; mgr. U.S. West, Seattle, 1963-90; pvt. practice Edmonds, Wash., 1990-94; bd. dirs. Stevens Hosp. Found., Edmonds, Olympic Ballet, Snohomish County Health Dist., 1994—, United Way of Snohomish County, Everett, 1986-92; Wash. State Legislator, 1972-94. planning commn. City of Edmonds, 1964-67, city coun., 1968-74. Capt. USAF, 1959-62. Mem. Sons of Norway, Rotary. Republican. Lutheran. Home: 9710 Wharf St Edmonds WA 98020-2363 Office: Snohomish County Coun 3000 Rockefeller M/S 609 Everett WA 98201

NELSON, HAROLD BERNHARD, museum director; b. Providence, R.I., May 14, 1947; s. Harold B. and Eleanor (Lavina) N. BA, Bowdoin Coll., 1969; MA, U. Del., 1972. Rsch. fellow NMAA Smithsonian Inst., Washington, 1976-77; curator Am. art Mus. Art & Archeol., U. Mo., Columbia, 1977-79; registrar Solomon R. Guggenheim Mus., N.Y.C., 1979-83; exhibition program dir. Am. Fedn. Arts, N.Y.C., 1983-89; dir. Long Beach (Calif.) Mus. of Art, 1989—; juror Annual Art Exhibition Mus. Art, Sci. & Industry, Bridgeport, Conn., 1988, Annual Art Exhibition, Clark County Dist. Libr., Las Vegas, Nev., 1984; speaker Am. Assn. Mus. Annual Conf., Detroit, 1985, annual meeting Western Mus. Conf., Portland, Oreg., 1987, Grantmakers in Art Symposium, N.Y.C., 1986, annual meeting Western Mus. Conf., Salt Lake City, 1985; mem. adv. com. APA, Assn. Sci. and Tech. Ctrs.; panelist Aid to Spl. Exhibitions, NEA, Washington, 1986; participant Am. Legal Assn., ABA Conf., San Francisco, 1986; observer, respondent Mus. Symposium, NEA, Dallas, 1985. Author: Sounding the Depths: 150 Years of American Seascape, 1989. Office: Long Beach Mus Art 2300 E Ocean Blvd Long Beach CA 90803-2442

NELSON, HARRY, journalist, medical writer; b. Interlachen, Fla., Apr. 18, 1923; s. Knut Alfred and Edith Farr (Wilkes) N.; m. Diane Gabriella Meerschaert, Aug. 29, 1948 (div. 1977); children—Tanya Ann, Lawrence Stephen, Ronald Gerard, James Anthony, John Christopher; m. Gita Doris Wheelis, Jan. 29, 1984. B.A., U. So. Calif., 1949. Reporter, photographer Bakersfield Press, Calif., 1949; reporter, photographer Bakersfield Community Chest, Calif., 1949; promotion writer Los Angeles Times, 1949-57, reporter, 1957-58, med. writer, 1958-88, sr. writer, 1977-80; freelance med. writer, 1988—; med. writer Milbank Meml. Fund, 1993—. Charter mem. bd. dirs. Los Angeles County Comprehensive Health Planning Assn., Los Angeles, 1968-69. Served with USAAF, 1941-45. Recipient spl. commendation AMA, 1974, John Hancock award John Hancock Ins. Co., 1978, Journalism award Am. Acad. Pediatrics, 1979, Disting. Svc. by non-physician award Calif. Med. Assn., 1988, Lifetime Achievement in med. writing award AMA, 1988, Peter Lisagor award for exemplary journalism Chgo. Headliners Club, 1988. Mem. Nat. Assn. Sci. Writers (pres. 1966). Address: Med Writers Internat PO Box N 14016 Yellowstone Dr Frazier Park CA 93222

NELSON, HELEN MARTHA, retired library director; b. Anaconda, Mont., Dec. 20, 1929; d. Ole Bertin and Caroline Helen (Massey) N. BA with honors, U. Mont., 1951; MLS, U. Wash., 1960. Asst. documents and serials libr. U. Mont., Missoula, 1951-52; tchr. English and history, libr. Laurel H.S., 1952-54; tchr. English, libr. Beaverhead County H.S., 1954-56; tchr. English, journalism Anaconda Sr. H.S., 1956-59; libr., adminstr. U.S. Army, 1960-68; libr. dir. Oceanside (Calif.) Libr., 1968-94; chmn. Serra Coop. Libr., 1973-74, 84-85, 90-91; mem. coun. Serra Coop. Sys., 1969-94. Chmn. Christian Sponsors, Oceanside, 1975; congl. pres. King of Kings Luth. Ch., Oceanside, 1974, 77, 84, mem. coun. 1971-77, 82-84, 92-94; bd. dirs. Oceanside/Carlsbad ARC, 1970-71; del. Calif. Gov.'s Conf. Librs. and Info. Sci. Mem. ALA, AAUW, LWV, Mont. Libr. Assn., Calif. Libr. Assn. (coun. 1978-80, v.p. Palomar chpt. 1978), Pub. Libr. Execs. of So. Calif., Oceanside C. of C., Calif. Inst. Libr. (bd. dirs. 1978-80).

NELSON, IVORY VANCE, university president; b. Curtis, La., June 11, 1934; s. Elijah H. and Mattie (White) N.; m. Patricia Robbins, Dec. 27, 1985; children: Cherlyn, Karyn, Eric Beatty, Kim Beatty. BS, Grambling (La.) State U., 1959; PhD, U. Kans., 1963. Assoc. prof. chemistry So. U., Baton Rouge, 1963-67, head div. sci., 1966-68; prof. chemistry Prairie View (Tex.) A&M U., 1968-83, asst. acad. dean, 1968-72, v.p. rsch., 1972-82, acting pres., 1982-83; exec. asst. Tex. A&M U. System, College Station, 1983-86; chancellor Alamo C.C. Dist., San Antonio, 1986-92; pres. Cen. Wash. U., Ellensburg, 1992—; DuPont teaching fellow U. Kans., 1959; rsch. chemist Am. Oil Co., 1962; sr. rsch. chemist Union Carbide Co., 1969; vis. prof. U. Autonomous Guadalajara, Mex., 1966, Loyola U., 1967; Fulbright lectr., 1966; cons. evaluation coms. Oak Ridge (Tenn.) Assoc. Univs., NSF, Nat. Coun. for Accreditation Tchr. Edn., So. Assn. Colls. and Schs.; mem. regional policy coms. on minorities Western Interstate Com. on Higher Edn., 1986-88; mem. exec. com. Nat. Assn. State Univs. and Land Grant Colls., 1980-82. Contbr. articles to profl. jours. Bd. dirs. Target 90, Goals San Antonio, 1987-89, Commn. on Student Learning, Wash., 1992—, United Way San Antonio, 1987-89, Alamo Area coun. Boy Scouts Am., 1987-89, San Antonio Symphony Soc., 1987-91, Key Bank of Wash.; mem. com. fir jud. reform State of Tex., 1991; mem. edn. adv. bd. Tex. Rsch. Park, 1987-89; bd. givs. Am. Inst. for character Edn., Inc., 1988-91; mem. adv. com. Tex. Ho. of Reps., 1978; chmn. United Way Campaign Tex. A&M U. System, 1984, others. Staff sgt. USAF, 1951-55, Korea. T.H. Harris scholar Grambling State U., 1959; fellow Nat. Urban League, 1969. Mem. AAAS, Am. Chem. Soc., Tex. Acad. Sci., NAACP, Phi Beta Kappa, Sigma Xi, Phi Lambda Upsilon, Beta Kappa Chi, Alpha Mu Gamma, Kappa Delta Pi, Sigma Pi Sigma, Omega Psi Phi, Sigma Pi Phi, Phi Kappa Phi. Home: 211 E 10th Ave Ellensburg WA 98926-2911 Office: Office of Pres Cen Wash U Ellensburg WA 98926

NELSON, JAMES ALONZO, radiologist, educator; b. Cherokee, Iowa, Oct. 20, 1938; s. Joe George and Ruth Geraldine (Jones) N.; m. Katherine Metcalf, July 16, 1966; children: John Metcalf, Julie Heaps. AB, Harvard U., 1961, MD, 1965. Asst. prof. radiology U. Calif. San Francisco, 1972-74; assoc. prof. U. Utah, Salt Lake City, 1974-79, prof., 1979-86; prof. U. Wash., Seattle, 1986—; dir. radiol. rsch. U. Calif.-San Francisco/Ft. Miley VAH, 1973-74, U. Utah, 1984-85, U. Wash., 1986—. Contbr. articles to Aj. Jour. Roentgeneology, Radiology, Investigative Radiology, others; contbr. chpts. to books. Capt. USAF, 1967-69. John Harvard scholar, 1957-61, James Picker Found. scholar, 1973-77; recipient Mallinkrodt prize Soc. Body Computerized Tomagraphy, 1990, Roscoe Miller award Soc. Gastrointestinal Radiology, 1991. Fellow Am. Coll. Radiology (diplomate); mem. Radiol. Soc. N.Am., Assn. Univ. Radiology. Office: U Wash Dept Radiology SB-05 Diagnostic Imaging Sci Ctr Seattle WA 98195

NELSON, JAMES AUGUSTUS, II, real estate executive, architect, banker; b. Damrascotta, Maine, July 26, 1947; s. Robert Maynard and Margret Rebbeca (Harmision) N.; m. Linda Ray, Aug. 15, 1975 (div. 1985); m. Tina Nides, Oct. 22, 1986 (div. 1991); 1 child, Jennifer Alexandria. BArch, Columbia U., 1973, MBA, 1974. Resident v.p. Citibank, N.Y.C., 1974-77; group v.p. Bank of Am., San Francisco, 1977-82; assoc. John Portman and Assocs., Atlanta, 1983-85; pres. J.A. Nelson and Assocs., L.A., 1986-88; dir. real estate planning and devel. MCA Devel. Co., L.A., 1988-94; founder Mother Co., Hollywood, Calif., 1995. Author: Banker's Guide to Construction, 1978, Doing Business in Saudi Arabia, 1979. Chmn. Laurel Canyon Coalition, L.A.; bd. dirs. Laurel Canyon Area Assn., Hollywood Heritage, Hillside Fedn., L.A., Lookout Mountain Assocs., L.A. Home: 8306 Grandview Dr West Hollywood CA 90046-1918 Office: Mother Co 8306 Grandview Dr Los Angeles CA 90046-1918

NELSON, JIM, chemicals executive; b. 1942. Degree, U. Utah. Prof. U. Utah, Salt Lake City; pres. Datacem Labs., Salt Lake City, 1972—. Office: Datacem Labs 960 Levoy Dr Salt Lake City UT 84123-2500*

NELSON, JOHN D., JR., village administrator; b. Dillingham, Alaska, Aug. 19, 1960; s. John D. Sr. and Mary (Newyaka) N. Pres., adminstr. Kokhanok (Alaska) Village Coun., 1977—. Chmn. Kokhanok Sch. Bd., 1986-88; bd. dirs. Bristol Bay Area Health Corp, Dillingham, Alaska, 1989—. Mem. Kokhanok Dog Mushers Club (pres. 1978-86). Russian Orthodox. Home: Kokhanok Village General Delivery Kokhanok AK 99606-9999

NELSON, JON R., music educator; b. Okmulgee, Okla., Aug. 24, 1936; m. Raymond E. and J. Jane (Winn) N. MusB, U. Tulsa, 1955, MusM, 1956; PhD in Hist. Musicology, U. Wash., 1978. Cert. tchr. music history, Calif. Prof. music Phillips U., Enid, Okla., 1960-83; prof. music and chair music dept. Santa Rosa (Calif.) Jr. Coll., 1983—; lectr., staff Nat. Pedagogy Conf., Santa Rosa, 1992; performer many concerts, recitals, orch. appearances, U.S., Europe, 1960-93. With U.S. Army, 1956-58. Presser Found. grantee; Chandler scholar. Mem. All Faculty Assn., Music Assn. of Calif. Cmty. Colls. Republican. Jewish. Home: 1320 North St # 12 Santa Rosa CA 95404-3443 Office: Santa Rosa Junior College 1501 Mendocino Ave Santa Rosa CA 95401-4332

NELSON, KENNETH ARTHUR, electrical engineer; b. Coeur d'Alene, Idaho, Apr. 18, 1942; s. Elton Arthur and Maxine Edna (Barnes) N.; m. Sharon Fay Paynter, Sept. 2, 1962; children: Neva Kenine, Krena Krista, Kelina Kara, Kimberly Kay. BSEE, U. Idaho, 1965; cert., Alexander Hamilton Inst., 1970. Registered profl. engr., Calif., Idaho. With GE, various locations, 1965-75; sr. mfg. engr. Jenn-Air Corp., Indpls., 1975-79; plant engr. A.O. Smith Corp., Newark, Calif., 1979-82; dir. facilities Memorex Corp., Santa Clara, Calif., 1982-88; with Scenic Mgmt. Corp., Tracy, Calif., 1988—; instr. Profl. Engring. Inst., San Carlos, Calif., 1985-88; founder Scenic Mgmt., Livermore, Calif., 1985—. Inventor in field. Mem. IEEE, Am. Soc. Metals Internat. Republican. Lutheran. Home: 1585 Hoot Owl Ct Tracy CA 95376-4396

NELSON, KIM ALEXANDER, construction company executive, consultant; b. Pacatello, Idaho, June 5, 1952; s. Charles Albert and Norma (Kinghorn) N.; m. Lois Ann Forbes, June 24, 1952; children: Rebecca, Sarah. BA in Comm., Brigham Young U., 1978; MS in Counseling, Seattle Pacific U., 1994. Mgmt. cons. WMI Corp., Bellevue, Wash., 1978-81; v.p. Pacific Constrn. Sys., Bellevue, 1981—; constrn. cons. Nelson Enterprises, Bellevue, 1988-94; mem. alumni adv. bd. Marriott Sch. Bus., Brigham Young U., 1994. counselor LDS Social Svcs., Renton, Wash., 1992-94; participant Redmond (Wash.) Devel. Coun., 1993-94. Office: Pacific Constrn Sys Inc 2275 116th Ave NE Bellevue WA 98004-3032

NELSON, LEANN LINDBECK, small business owner; b. McCook, Nebr., Jan. 27, 1937; d. Clifford Roy Lindbeck and Elizabeth J. (Downs) Rollstin; m. Lawrence L. Nelson, June 21, 1958; children: Glen Lindbeck, Todd Alan. BS in Dietetics, U. Tex., 1960. Dietitian Parkview Bapt. Hosp., Yuma, Ariz., 1960-61; instr. foods and nutrition Jefferson County Schs., Lakewood, Colo., 1969-71; dir. education and consumer programs, cons. nutrition Dairy Coun., Inc., Denver, 1971-74; coord. low-income foods and nutrition programs Emily Griffith Opportunity Sch., Denver, 1974-76; dir., asst. dir. edn./info. and product publicity Am. Sheep Prodrs. Coun., Denver, 1976-83; pres. Natural Accents, Denver, 1983-90; cons. fixed income counseling program City of Denver, Denver County, 1975-76, comm. cons., 1989—; pres., owner LeAnn Nelson Presents, 1988—; co-chairperson Home Econs. Nat. Task Force on Profl. Unity and Identity, 1992-93; prof. home econs., mem. adv. com. Coll. Applied Human Scis., Colo. State U., 1994—. Author: Accessories... What a Finish!, 1988. Chmn. home econs. adv. com. U. No. Colo., 1980-82; v.p. Clock Tower Mchts. Assn., Denver, 1983-85; chmn., buyer Denver Symphony Guild Gift Shop, 1984-87; mem. adv. bd. State Bd. Cmty. Colls. Occupational Edn., Home Econ. Tech. Adv. Com., 1986—, Coll. Applied Human Scis. Colo. State U., Ft. Collins, 1986-87. Named Colo. Home Economist of Yr. Colo. Home Econs. Assn., 1979, Colo. Bus. Home Economist of Yr. Colo. Home Econs. Assn., 1980; recipient Leadership award Colo. Home Econs. Assn. Mem. Nat. Assn. Women Bus. Owners, Home Economists in Bus. (nat. chmn.-elect 1981-82, nat. chmn. 1982-83, Nat. Bus. Home Economist of Yr. 1986), Colo. Assn. of Profl. Saleswomen, Profl. Aux. Assistance League of Denver, Denver Fashion Group (regional dir. 1984-86), Am. Women in Radio & TV (treas. Denver chpt. 1978-79). Clubs: Penrose, Executive. Home and Office: 1250 Humboldt St Apt 1001 Denver CO 80218-2416

NELSON, MARGARET ROSE, public relations consultant; b. Juneau, Alaska, Apr. 18, 1958; d. James M. and Ruth I. (Gray) N. Student, U. Santa Clara, 1976-77, U. Bridgeport, 1977-78; BA, U. Alaska, 1980. Reporter Fairbanks (Alaska) Daily News Miner, 1980-86; communications cons. Fairbanks, 1985-86; pub. information officer Alaska Fedn. of Natives, Anchorage, 1986; spl. asst. to exec. dir., corp. communications officer Alaska Housing Fin. Corp., Anchorage, 1986-94; pres. Nelson Communications, 1994—; bd. dir Goldbelt, Inc. 1991-94. Mem. Pub. Rels. Soc. of Am., Am. Mktg. Assn., Advertising Fedn., Am. Indian Bus. Assn.

NELSON, MARY CARROLL, artist, author; b. Bryan, Tex., Apr. 24, 1929; d. James Vincent and Mary Elizabeth (Langton) Carroll; m. Edwin Blakely Nelson, June 27, 1950; children: Patricia Ann, Edwin Blakely. BA in Fine Arts, Barnard Coll., 1950; MA, U. N.Mex., 1963. Juror Am. Artist Golden Anniversary Nat. Art Competition, 1987, Don Ruffin Meml. Art Exhbn., Ariz., 1989, N.Mex. Arts and Crafts Fair, 1989; guest instr. continuing edn. U. N.Mex., 1991; conf., organizer Affirming Wholeness, The Art and Healing Experience, San Antonio, 1992, Artists of the Spirit Symposium, 1994. Group shows include N.Mex. Mus. Fine Arts Biennial, 1987, N.Mex. Lightworks, 1990, Level to Level, Ohio Layering, 1987, Artist as Shaman, Ohio, 1990, The Healing Experience, Mass., 1991, A Gathering of Voices, Calif., 1991, Art is for Healing, The Universal Link, San Antonio, Tex., 1992, Biennial, Fuller Lodge Art Ctr. Los Alamos, N.Mex., 1993, Layering, Albuquerque, 1993, Crossings, Bradford, Mass., 1994, The Layered Perspective, Fayetteville, Ark., 1994; represented in pvt. collections in: U.S., Fed. Republic of Germany, Eng. and Australia; author: American Indian Biography Series, 1971-76, (with Robert E. Wood) Watercolor Workshop, 1974, (with Ramon Kelley) Ramon Kelley Paints Portraits and Figures, 1977, The Legendary Artists of Taos, 1980, (catalog) American Art in Peking, 1981, Masters of Western Art, 1982, Connecting, The Art of Beth Ames Swartz, 1984, Artists of the Spirit, 1994, (catalog) Layering, An Art of Time and Space, 1985, (catalog) Layering/Connecting, 1987; contbg. editor Am. Artist, 1976-91, Southwest Art, 1987-91; editor (video) Layering, 1990; arts correspondent Albuquerque Jour., 1991-93. Mem. Albuquerque Arts Bd., 1984-88. Mem. Soc. Layerists in Multi-Media (founder 1982). Home: 1408 Georgia St NE Albuquerque NM 87110-6861

NELSON, NANCY ELEANOR, pediatrician, educator; b. El Paso, Apr. 4, 1933; d. Harry Hamilton and Helen Maude (Murphy) N. B.A. magna cum laude, U. Colo., 1955, M.D., 1959. Intern, Case Western Res. U. Hosp., 1959-60, resident, 1960-63; pvt. practice medicine specializing in pediatrics, Denver, 1963-70; clin. prof. U. Colo. Sch. Medicine, Denver, 1988—, asst. dean Sch. Medicine, 1982-88, assoc. dean, 1988—. Mem. Am. Acad. Pediatrics, AMA (sect. med. schs. governing coun. 1994—), Denver Med. Soc. (pres. 1983-84), Colo. Med. Soc. (bd. dirs. 1985-88, judicial coun. 1992—). Home: 1265 Elizabeth St Denver CO 80206-3241 Office: 4200 E 9th Ave Denver CO 80220-3706

NELSON, NEVIN MARY, interior designer; b. Cleve., Nov. 5, 1941; d. Arthur George Reinker and Barbara Phyllis (Gunn) Parks; m. Wayne Nelson (div. 1969); children: Doug, Brian. BA in Interior Design, U. Colo., 1964. Prin. Nevin Nelson Design, Boulder, Colo., 1966-70, Vail, Colo., 1970—; program chmn. Questers Antique Study Group, Boulder, 1969. Coord. Bob Kirscht for Gov. campaign, Eagle County, Colo., 1986; state del. Rep. Nat. Conv., 1986-88; county coord. George Bush for U.S. Pres. campaign, 1988, 92; chmn. Eagle County Reps., 1989-93. Mem. Am. Soc. Interior Designers. Episcopalian. Home: PO Box 1212 Vail CO 81658-1212 Office: 2498 Arosa Dr Vail CO 81657-4276

NELSON, PAUL WILLIAM, real estate broker; b. Mpls., Mar. 7, 1952; s. William H. and Jean (Darrington) N.; m. Jill Brownson, Oct. 18, 1986 (dec. Nov. 1990); 1 child, Emily J. BS, U. Colo., 1974. Lic. real estate broker, Colo. Advt. dir. Denver Beechcraft, 1976-77; real estate broker Coldwell Banker, Grand Junction, Colo., 1977—; bd. dirs. Colo. Assn. Realtors, Denver, 1981-83. Mem. Grand Junction City Coun., 1985-93, also mayor pro tem; mem. Downtown Devel. Authority, Grand Junction, 1985-91; bd. dirs. Mesa County Planning Commn., Grand Junction, 1980-85, Colo. Nat. Monument Assn., 1989-91, Grand Junction Visitors and Conv. Bur., 1993—, Club 20 (20 counties west of continental divide) Lobbying Group; mem. Mesa County Uranium Mill Tailings Removal Citizens Com.; mem., co-chmn. Mesa County Riverfront Commn.; mem. dist. resource adv. coun. Bur. Land Mgmt., 1990-93, Grand Junction Visitors and Convention Bureau bd. dirs, 1992—. Recipient Citizen Svc. award Mesa County, 1985. Mem. Grand Junction Bd. Realtors (bd. dirs. 1981-83), Rotary. Republican. Office: Coldwell Banker PO Box 3117 Grand Junction CO 81502-3117

NELSON, PAULA MORRISON BRONSON, educator; b. Memphis, Mar. 26, 1944; d. Fred Ford and Julia (Morrison) Bronson: m. Jack Marvin Nelson, July 13, 1968; children: Eric Allen, Kelly Susan. BS, U. N.Mex., 1967; MA, U. Colo., Denver, 1985. Physical edn. tchr. Grant Union Sch. Dist., Sacramento, 1967-68; physical edn. tchr. Denver Pub. Schs., 1968-74, with program for pupil assistance, 1974-80, chpt. 1 reading specialist, 1983—; tchr. ESL Douglas County Pub. Schs., Parker, Colo., 1982-83; demonstration tchr. Colo. Edn. Assn., 1970-72; mem. curriculum com. Denver Pub. Schs., 1970-72; mem. Douglas County Accountability Com., Castle Rock, Colo., 1986-92; mem. educators rev. panel Edn. for Freedom; computer trainer Denver Pub. Schs. Tech. Team, 1992—. Co-author: Gymnastics Teacher's Guide Elementary Physical Education, 1973, Applauding Our Constitution, 1989; editorial reviewer G is for Geography, 1993, Children's Literature and the Five Themes. 1993; producer slide shows Brotherhood, 1986, We the People...Our Dream Lives On, 1987, Celebration of Cultures, 1988. Named Pub. Edn. Coalition grantee, Denver, 1987, 88, 89, 90, grantee Rocky Mountain Global Edn. Project, 1987, Wake Forest Law Sch., Winston-Salem, N.C., 1988, 89, 90, 92; recipient chpt. II grant, 1991, Tech. grant, 1993, Three R's of Freedom award State Dept. Edn., 1987, Nat. Recognition award Commn. on Bicentennial of Constitution., 1987, Distinguished Tchr. award City of Denver, 1994. Mem. Windstar Found., Colo. Coun. Internat. Reading, Internat. Reading Assn., Nat. Soc. for Study of Edn., Colo. Coun. for the Social Studies, Tech. in Edn., Am. Fedn. Tchrs., Denver Fedn. Tchrs. Republican. Methodist. Home: 10488 E Meadow Run Parker CO 80134-6220

NELSON, RANDALL ERLAND, surgeon; b. Hastings, Nebr., Dec. 28, 1948; s. Marvin Erland and Faith Constance (Morrison) N.; m. Carolyn Joy Kaufman, Feb. 28, 1976. BS in Chemistry cum laude, So. Nazarene U., 1971; MD, U. Nebr., 1975; MS in Surgery, U. Ill., Chgo., 1979. Diplomate Nat. Bd. Med. Examiners, Am. Bd. Surgery. Intern in gen. surgery Strong Meml. Hosp., Rochester, N.Y., 1975-76; resident in gen. surgery U. Rochester Affiliated Hosps., 1976-78, Rush-Presbyn.-St. Luke's Med. Ctr., Chgo., 1978-81; gen. surgeon Surg. Group San Jose, Calif., 1981—; instr. gen. surgery U. Rochester Sch. Medicine and Dentistry, 1975-78, Rush Med. Coll., Chgo., 1978-80; adj. attending surgeon Rush-Presbyn.-St. Luke's Med. Ctr., 1980-81. Mem. Rep. Nat. Com., Washington, 1984—. Fellow ACS, Southwestern Surg. Congress; mem. Calif. Med. Assn., Santa Clara County Med. Soc., San Jose Surg. Soc., U.S. C. of C., Circle-K Club, Phi Delta Lambda. Republican. Office: Surg Group of San Jose 2101 Forest Ave Ste 124 San Jose CA 95128-1424

NELSON, RAYMOND MILFORD, surgeon; b. Loma Linda, Calif., Oct. 10, 1928; s. Hiram Milford Nelson and Eunice Frances Manning Smithwick; m. Carole L. Sundean, Mar. 19, 1932 (dec. 1986); children: Cherie, Cynthia, Kathi, Michael; m. Joni LaVern Denman, May 29, 1988. BS, Pacific Union Coll., 1949; MD, Loma Linda U., 1953. Intern Balboa Naval Hosp., San Diego, 1953-54; resident gen. surg. White Meml. Hosp., L.A., 1957-62; gen. surgeon Belle Vista Mission Hosp., Mayaguez, P.R., 1962-70; pvt. practice surgery Santa Cruz, Calif., 1970—. Lt. USN, 1952-57. Fellow aCS; mem. AMA, Calif. Med. Assn. Home: 520 High St Santa Cruz CA 95060-2643 Office: 602 Frederick St Santa Cruz CA 95062-2203

NELSON, ROBERT E., public relations executive, political consultant; b. Jefferson, Wis., Oct. 25, 1951; s. Clifford H. and Mary Ann (Lundquist) N.; m. Heidi Nelson. Fiscal svcs. officer Orange (Calif.) County Med. Ctr., 1968-73; exec. asst. Orange County Bd. Suprs., Santa Ana, 1973-75; sr. assoc. Butcher-Forde Cons., Newport Beach, Calif., 1976-77; chmn., CEO Nelson Comm. Group, Irvine, Calif., 1979—. dep. asst. dir. pub. outreach presdl. transition, Little Rock, 1993; presdl. appointee U.S. Competitiveness Policy Coun., Washington, 1994—. Recipient Rocky Mountain regional Emmy award TV. advt., 1986. Mem. Internat. Assn. Polit. Cons. (bd. dirs. 1992—), Young Pres. Orgn. (bd. dir.s 1994—), Pacific Club. Office: Nelson Comm Group 18401 Von Karman Ave Ste 120 Irvine CA 92715-1542

NELSON, ROBERT EARL, mental health counselor; b. Hardtnar, Kans., Sept. 13, 1952; s. Robert and Elsie (Brennon) N.; m. Mary K. Burton, Apr. 24, 1976; children: Nathan, Heber, Rebekah, David. BS, Brigham Young U., 1976, MEd, 1985; PhD, Calif. Coast U., 1994. Cert. mental health counselor, Wash. Fin. mgr. Southwestern Investment Co., Amarillo, Tex., 1978-80; officer USMC, 1980-84; sch. counselor Elk Grove (Calif.) H.S., 1985; crisis counselor Sacramento (Calif.) Cmty. Mental Health, 1985-87; chaplain U.S. Army, 1987-92; mental health profl. Columbia River Mental Health, Vancouver, Wash., 1993—; pvt. practice counseling, Vancouver, 1992—; adv. bd. Parents Anonymous, Vancouver, 1993. Author: W.I.N.N. Against Suicide, 1993; contbr. articles to profl. jours. Vol. The Share House, Vancouver, 1993—; mentor The Homeless Coun., Vancouver, 1994; chmn. precinct com. Dem. Party, Vancouver, 1993—; participant Leadership Clark County C. of C. Program, Vancouver, 1994; bd. trustees Cascade Disability Resources, Inc. Mem. ACA, Internat. Brotherhood of Magicians, Am. Mental Health Counselors Assn., Nat. Eagle Scout Assn., The Augustine Soc., Toastmasters Internat. (club pres., area gov. 1992—). Mormon. Home and Office: Nelson Counseling & Cons 1211 Manzanita Way Vancouver WA 98661

NELSON, ROBERT WILLIAM, real estate executive; b. Eugene, Oreg., May 29, 1942; s. Roy Robert and Alta (Peterson) N.; 1 child, Erin Michele; m. René O'Bryant. BS in Mgmt., Oreg. State U., 1965; MBA in Real Estate, U. Oreg., 1972. Lic. real estate investment broker; Cert. Comml. Investment Mem. Real estate investor Nelson, Taylor & McCulley, Inc., Eugene, 1968-72; instr. real estate Lane Community Coll., Eugene, 1972—; pres., broker Robert W. Nelson, Real Estate Cons., Inc., Eugene, 1974—; expert witness to value Oreg. Tax Ct. and Lane County Circuit Ct., 1979—; ptnr., broker, exchange cons. PACWEST Real Estate Investments, 1984—; dir. Oreg. Assn. Realtors, 1992 –; pres. Eugene Assn. Realtors, 1994. Author: Real Estate Law, 1974, Real Estate Finance, 1974, Real Estate Practices, 1974, Tax Deferred Exchanges, 1977, 87, 91, 93. Active Bus. Adv. Counsel, Lane Community Coll., 1975—. Lt. USN, 1965-68. Named Realtor of Yr. Eugene Bd. Realtors, 1983. Mem. Brokers Million Dollar Club (pres. 1986, 89), Comml. Investment Div. (pres. 1972). Methodist. Office: PACWEST Real Estate Investments 59 E 11th Ave Ste 100 Eugene OR 97401-3510

NELSON, RUSSELL MARION, surgeon, educator; b. Salt Lake City, Sept. 9, 1924; s. Marion C. and Edna (Anderson) N.; m. Dantzel White, Aug. 31, 1945; children: Marsha Nelson McKellar, Wendy Nelson Maxfield, Gloria Nelson Irion, Brenda Nelson Miles, Sylvia Nelson Webster, Emily Nelson Wittwer (dec.), Laurei Nelson Marsh, Rosalie Nelson Ringwood, Marjorie Nelson Helsten, Russel Marion Jr. BA, U. Utah, 1945, MD, 1947; PhD in Surgery, U. Minn., 1954; ScD (hon.), Brigham Young U., 1970; DMS (hon.), Utah State U., 1989; LHD (hon.), Snow Coll., 1994. Diplomate: Am. Bd. Surgery, Am. Bd. Thoracic Surgery (dir. 1972-78). Intern U. Minn. Hosps., Mpls., 1947; asst. resident surgery U. Minn. Hosps., 1948-51; first asst. resident surgery Mass. Gen. Hosp., Boston, 1953-54; sr. resident surgery U. Minn. Hosps., Mpls., 1954-55; practice medicine (specializing in cardiovascular and thoracic surgery), Salt Lake City, 1959-84; staff surgeon Latter-day Saints Hosp., Salt Lake City, 1959-84; dir. surg. research lab. Latter-day Saints Hosp., 1959-72, chief cardiovascular-thoracic surg. div., 1967-72, also bd. govs., 1970-90, vice chmn., 1979-89; staff surgeon Primary Children's Hosp., Salt Lake City, 1960; attending in surgery VA Hosp., Salt Lake City, 1955-84, Univ. Hosp., Salt Lake City, 1955-84; asst. prof. surgery Med. Sch. U. Utah, Salt Lake City, 1955-59, asst. clin. prof. surgery, 1959-66, asso. clin. prof. surgery, clin. prof., 1966-69, research prof. surgery, 1970-84, clin. prof. emeritus, 1984—; staff services Utah Biomed. Test Lab., 1970-84; dir. tng. program cardiovascular and thoracic surgery at Univ. Utah affiliated hosps., 1967-84; mem. policyholders adv. com. New Eng. Mut. Life Ins. Co., Boston, 1976-80. Contbr. articles to profl. jours. Mem. White House Conf. on Youth and Children, 1960; bd. dirs. Internat. Cardiol. Found.; bd. govs. LDS Hosp., 1970-90, Deseret Gymnasium, 1971-75, Promised Valley Playhouse, 1970-79. lst lt. to capt. M.C., AUS, 1951-53. Markle scholar in med. scis., 1957-59; Fellowship of Medici Publici U. Utah Coll., 1967; Gold Medal of Merit, Argentina, 1974; named Hon. Prof. Shandong Med. U., Jinan, People's Republic of China, 1985; Old People's U., Jinan, 1986; Xi-an (People's Republic of China) Med. Coll., 1986, Legacy of Life award, 1993. Fellow A.C.S. (chmn. adv. council on thoracic surgery 1973-75), Am. Coll. Cardiology, Am. Coll. Chest Physicians; mem. Am. Assn. Thoracic Surgery, Am. Soc. Artificial Internal Organs, AMA, Dirs. Thoracic Residencies (pres. 1971-72), Utah Med. Assn. (pres. 1970-71), Salt Lake County Med. Soc., Am. Heart Assn. (exec. com. cardiovascular surgery 1972, dir. 1976-78, chmn. council cardiovascular surgery 1976-78), Utah Heart Assn. (pres. 1964-65), Soc. Thoracic Surgeons, Soc. Vascular Surgery (sec. 1968-72, pres. 1974), Utah Thoracic Soc., Salt Lake Surg. Soc., Samson Thoracic Surg. Soc., Western Soc. for Clin. Research, Soc. U. Surgeons, Am., Western, Pan-Pacific surg. assns., Inter. Am. Soc. Cardiology (bd. mgrs.), Phi Beta Kappa, Sigma Xi, Alpha Omega Alpha, Phi Kappa Phi, Sigma Chi. Mem. Ch. of Jesus Christ of Latter-day Saints (pres. Bonneville Stake 1964-71, gen. pres. Sunday sch. 1971-79, regional rep. 1979-84, Quorum of the Twelve Apostles 1984—). Home: 1347 Normandie Cir Salt Lake City UT 84105-1919 Office: 47 E South Temple Salt Lake City UT 84150

NELSON, SCOTT HAVILAND, psychiatrist, administrator; b. Cleve., July 31, 1940; s. Albert S. and Jane (Sutton) N.; children: Todd, Riley, Chad. BA, Yale U., 1962; MD, Harvard U., 1966, MPH, 1970. Diplomae Am. Bd. Psychiatry and Neurology (examiner 1981—). Mental health dir. Job Corps. Dept. Labor, Washington, 1970-72, med. dir., 1972-73; dir. planning and evaluation Alcohol, Drug Abuse and Mental Health Adminstrn., Rockville, Md., 1973-76; dir. mental health divsn. Dept Hosps. and Isntns. State of New Mex., Santa Fe, 1976-78; dir. behavioral health divsn. Dept. Health and Environment State of New Mex., Santa Fe, 1978-80; dept. sec. and commr. of mental health Dept. Pub. Welfare, State of Pa., Harrisburg, 1980-87; chief mental health, social svcs. Indian Health Svc., Albuquerque, New Mex., 1987—; clin. prof. psychiatry U. N. Mex., dept. psychiatry, Albuquerque, 1990—; reviewer Hosp. and Cmty. Psychiatry, 1982—; mem. editorial bd. Cmty. Mental Health Jour., 1984-88, invited reviewr, 1988—; cons. NIMH for Medicare Survey, 1978-84; psychiat. cons. Santa Fe Indian Hosp., Taos, Santa Clara and Dulce Health Clinics. Author: A Collector's Guide to Van Briggle Pottery, 1986; contbr. chpts. to books, monographs for sci. meetings and articles to profl. jours. Pres., past v.p., Los Arroyos Home Owners Assn., Santa Fe, 1992—. Capt. USPHS, 1970—. Recipient Pres.' award Pa. Assn. of Mental Health/Mental Retardation Providers, Harrisburg, 1986, commendation Pa. Alliance for the Mentally Ill, Harrisburg, 1986. Fellow Am. Psychiat. Assn. (mem. many coms. including chmn. task force on involuntary commitment 1979-81, Gold award 1991); mem. Nat. Assn. State Mental Health Dirs. (many coms. and offices including pres. 1981-83), Psychiat. Med. Assn. N.Mex. (pres. 1993-94).

NELSON, STEVEN DWAYNE, lawyer; b. Austin, Minn., Jan. 30, 1950; s. Dwayne Ronald and Verna Nathelle (Larick) N.; m. Vicky L. Staab, July 6, 1990. BA in English, SUNY, Buffalo, 1972; JD, U. Mont., 1978. Bar: Mont. 1978, U.S. Dist. Ct. Mont. 1978. Sole practice Bozeman, Mont., 1978—; city prosecutor City of Bozeman, 1979-82; city atty. City of Ennis (Mont.), 1980-82; assoc. prof. Coll. of Great Falls, Mont., 1990—. Mem. ABA, Mont. State Bar Assn., Phi Delta Phi. Home and Office: PO Box 1962 Bozeman MT 59771-1962

NELSON, THOMAS G., federal judge; b. 1936. Student, Univ. Idaho, 1955-59, LLB, 1962. Ptnr. Parry, Robertson, Daly and Larson, Twin Falls, Idaho, 1965-79, Nelson, Rosholt, Robertson, Tolman and Tucker, Twin Falls, from 1979; judge U.S. Cir. Ct. (9th cir.), San Francisco, Calif., 1990—. With Idaho Air N.G., 1962-65, USAR, 1965-68. Mem. ABA (ho. of dels. 1974, 86-88), Am. Bar Found., Am. Coll. Trial Lawyers, Idaho State Bar (pres., bd. commrs.), Idaho Assn. Def. Counsel, Am. Bd. Trial Advocates (pres. Idaho chpt.), Phi Alpha Delta, Idaho Law Found., Internat. Assn. Def. Counsel. Office: US Ct Appeals 9th Circuit PO Box 1339 Boise ID 83701-1339

NELSON, WALTER WILLIAM, computer programmer, consultant; b. Seattle, May 7, 1954; s. Arne A. and Helen R. (Truitt) N.; m. Paula E. Truax, Dec. 21, 1985. BA in Zoology, U. Wash., 1976, BS in Psychology, 1977; PhC in Psychology, U. Minn., 1982. Systems analyst Dept. of Social and Health Svcs., State of Wash., Seattle, 1986-89; computer info. cons. Dept. of Health, State of Wash., Seattle, 1989-90; pres. Data Dimensions, Inc. (name now Nelson Consulting, Inc.), Seattle, 1990—; cons. The Heritage Inst., Seattle, 1989—; pres. Tech Alliance, Renton, Wash., 1990-91. Contbr. articles to profl. jours. Mem. Tech Alliance, Berkeley Macintosh Users Group, Seattle Downtown Macintosh Bus. Users Group, 4th Dimension Spl. Interest Group (founder, pres. 1990—).

NELSON, WARREN JAMES, III, oil company executive, accountant; b. L.A., Sept. 16, 1950; s. Warren James Jr. and Mary Louise (Simmons) N.; m. Maria Louise Stuebinger, Jan. 5, 1980; 1 child, Trevor Carl. BS in Acctg. with honors, Calif. Poly., San Luis Obispo, 1972; MBA, U. Calif., Berkeley, 1974. CPA, Calif., Tex. Audit mgr. Price Waterhouse, Newport Beach, Calif., 1974-82; acting CFO, chief acctg. officer, contr. Smith Internat., Inc., Houston, 1982-90; exec. v.p., CFO, Everest & Jennings Internat., Ltd., Camarillo, Calif., 1990-92, Huntway Ptnrs., L.P., Newhall, Calif., 1993—. Treas. Salem Luth. Ch., Orange, Calif., 1985-88; treas. troop 0775 Boy Scouts Am., Thousand Oaks, Calif., 1993—. Mem. AICPA, Calif. Soc. CPA's. Republican. Presbyterian. Office: Huntway Ptnrs LP 25129 The Old Rd # 322 Newhall CA 91381

NELSON, WILLARD GREGORY, veterinarian, mayor; b. Lewiston, Idaho, Nov. 21, 1937; s. Donald William and Eve Mae (Boyer) N.; m. Mary Ann Eklund, Apr. 3, 1965 (div.); children: Elizabeth Ann, John Gregory. BS in Premedicine, Mont. State U., 1959; DVM, Wash. State U., 1961. Lic. veterinarian, Wash., Oreg., Idaho, Mont. Pvt. practice vet. medicine, Kuna, Idaho, 1963-66; asst. to dir. Idaho Dept. Agr., Boise, 1966-78; asst. chief Idaho Bur. Animal Health, 1978-80, chief, 1980-81; adminstr., state veterinarian Idaho Div. Animal Industries, 1981-90; dir. Idaho Dept. Agr., 1990—; mayor City of Kuna (Idaho), 1984—; chmn. Idaho Gov.'s Human and Animal Health Consortium, 1983-90. Kuna city councilman, 1964-68, pres. Planning and Zoning Commn., 1968-72; mem. bd. trustees Joint Sch. Dist. 3, 1970-71, pres., 1972-76; mem. adv. bd. Mercy Med. Hosp., Nampa, Idaho, 1986—; mem. adv. com. Wash., Oreg., Idaho Coll. Vet. Medicine, 1983—; mem. ADA Planning Assn., 1986—, vice chmn., 1991-92, chmn. 1993-94; mem. Western U.S. Trade Assn., 1990—, treas., 1992, v.p. 1993, pres. 1994; mem. Idaho Emergency Response Commn., 1992—, Idaho Export Coun., 1992—, Idaho Rural Devel. Coun., 1992—, vice-chair, 1993, chair 1994; bd. dirs S.W. Idaho Rsch. and Devel., 1993—. Served as capt. U.S. Army Vet Corps, 1961-63; lt. col. Idaho Army N.G., 1979-88, col., 1988—. Mem. Idaho Vet. Med. Assn. (v.p. 1987, pres.-elect 1988, pres. 1989, Idaho Veterinarian of Yr. 1989), S.W. Idaho Vet. Med. Assn., U.S. Animal Health Assn. (chmn. anaplasmosis com. 1987-90), AVMA (mem. coun. on pub. health and regulatory medicine 1988-94, chmn. 1993, pres. nat. assembly 1988), Western States Livestock Assn., USDA (nat. damage control adv. com. 1992-94, nat. dir. animal welfare coalition 1992—), Am. Legion. Lutheran. Club: Lions (Kuna). Home: 793 W 4th St Kuna ID 83634-1941 Office: 2270 Old Penitentiary Rd Boise ID 83712-8266

NELSON, WILLIAM RANKIN, surgeon; b. Charlottesville, Va., Dec. 12, 1921; s. Hugh Thomas and Edith (Rankin) N.; m. Nancy Laidley, Mar. 17, 1956 (div. 1979); children: Robin Page Nelson Russel, Susan Kimberly Nelson Wright, Anne Rankin Nelson Cron; m. Pamela Morgan Phelps, July 5, 1984. BA, U. Va., 1943, MD, 1945. Diplomate Am. Bd. Surgery. Intern Vanderbilt U. Hosp., Nashille, 1945-46; resident in surgery U. Va. Hosp., Charlottesville, 1949-51; fellow surg. oncology Meml. Sloan Kettering Cancer Ctr., N.Y.C., 1951-55; instr. U. Colo. Sch. Medicine, Denver, 1955-57; asst. clin. prof. U. Colo. Sch. Medicine, 1962-87, clin. prof. surgery, 1987—; asst. prof. Med. Coll. Va., Richmond, 1957-62; mem. exec. com. U. Colo. Cancer Ctr.; mem. nat. bd., nat. exec. com. Am. Cancer Soc. Contbr. articles to profl. jours. and chpts. to textbooks. Capt. USAAF, 1946-48. Recipient Nat. Div. award Am. Cancer Soc., 1979. Fellow Am. Coll. Surgeons (bd. govs. 1984-89); mem. AMA, Internat. Soc. Surgery, Brit. Assn. Surg. Oncology, Royal Soc. Medicine (U.K.), Soc. Surg. Oncology (pres. 1975-76), Soc. Head and Neck Surgeons (pres. 1986-87), Am. Cancer Soc. (pres. Colo. div. 1975-77, exec. com., nat. bd. dirs., del. dir. from Colo. div. 1975—), Am. Soc. Clin. Oncology, Western Surg. Assn. Colo. Med. Soc., Denver Med. Soc., Denver Acad. Surgery, Rocky Mt. Oncology Soc., Univ. Club, Rotary. Republican. Presbyterian.

NELSON-HANEY, JULIANN DOROTHEA, wire products company executive; b. Portland, Oreg., May 16, 1957; d. Louis Eugene and Jessie Irene (Pease) Nelson; m. John Paul Crimmins, Jan. 24, 1982 (div. Nov. 1984); 1 child, Erin Ella; m. Robert Edward Haney, July 19, 1986; children: Joelle Burch, Robert J., Andrea Therease. Student, Linfield Coll., 1987-88; BS in Orgn. Psychology, Western Oreg. State Coll., 1990. Adminstrn. employment staff Shugart Corp., Santa Clara, Calif., 1984-85; student-supr. Pacific Restaurant Corp., Portland, Oreg., 1985-87; editor, columnist Western Star News, Monmouth, Oreg., 1988-90; MIS adminstr., cons. Temple Beth Israel Synagogue, Portland, 1990-91; contr. Custom Wire Products, Gresham, Oreg., 1991—, CFO, CEO, 1992—, owner, 1993—. Editor, author Western Star News, 1990 (Best Editorial award). Mem. C. of C., Amnesty Internat. Democrat.

NEMAN, EDWARD LOUIS, III, hospital administrator; b. Land O'Lakes, Wis., Mar. 16, 1951; s. Edward Louis Jr. and Helen Eusibia (Lawler) N.; m. Nancy Mitchell Fleming, Sept. 27, 1980. BA in Journalism, Marquette U., 1973, BA in Polit. Sci., 1973, MA in Journalism, 1975; MA in Habitational Resources, U. Wis., Menomonie, 1979. Cert. alcoholism and substance abuse counselor, Ariz. News anchor/producer WITI TV-6, Milw., 1972-74; news dir. WRIT Newsradio, Milw., 1974-76; counselor Pasar, Inc., Tucson, 1979-81; mgr. Thanet Hotel, London, 1981-82; anchor/talk show host KNST Newstalk Radio, Tucson, 1982-84; dir. pub. rels. Owens Advt., Tucson, 1984; pub. rels. dir. Miles Advt. & Pub. Rels., Tucson, 1985; owner, exec. v.p. Lauer-Newman Advt., Tucson, 1986-88; owner, pres. Media Plus Advt. and Pub. Rels., Tucson, 1986-88; psychiat. program dir. Kino Hosp., Tucson, 1988-91; pres. Quality Enhancement Assocs., Inc., Scottsdale, Ariz., 1992—; program cons. Chrysalis Shelters Victims of Domestic Violence, Phoenix, 1993-94; crisis counselor Terros, Inc., Phoenix, 1994—; supervisory mem. King Improvement Coun., Kino Hosp., 1990-91, chmn. comm. coun., 1991; cert. instr. W. Edwards Deming-Theories of Mgmt. Tng., Tucson, 1989-91. Editor, writer, producer documentary film for AMA, 1974; food editor Tucson Mag., 1984-86; food/restaurant critic Am. Restaurant Rev., 1978. Vice chmn. Democrats of Greater Tucson, 1983; dep. voter registrar Pima County, Ariz., Tucson; fundraising chair United Way Pima County, Tucson, 1989, 90; mem. Sunsounds of Ariz.; dep. voter registrar Maricopa County, Ariz.; precinct committeeman, Scottsdale; candidate Ariz. State Ho. of Reps., 1992. Recipient Gov.'s Cup Best Newscast Ariz. Press Club, 1984; named Outstanding Citizen of the Yr. Goodwill Industries, Milw., 1974. Mem. Tucson Press Club, London Press Club, Milw. Press Club (gov. 1976-78), Sigma Delta Chi (pres. 1972-73). Democrat. Home: 4354 N 82nd St Apt 109 Scottsdale AZ 85251-2742 Office: Terros Inc 320 E Virginia Phoenix AZ 85004

NEMAZEE, MAHMOUD, emergency medicine physician, internist, surgeon; b. Shiraz, Fars, Iran, July 16, 1950; came to U.S., 1970; s. Aziz and Parvin Nemazee. BS, U. Iowa, 1974; MS, U. N.H., 1977; MD, Univ. Mundial, Santo Domingo, Dominican Republic, 1984. Pediat. intern Mt. Sinai Med. Ctr., Cleve., 1986-87; resident in internal medicine Greater Balt. Med. Ctr., 1988-91; physician emergency dept. U.S. Army Weed Army Cmty. Hosp., Calif., 1992-95; physician emergency rm. Naval Med. Ctr., Oakland, Calif., 1995—. Mem. AMA, Am. Coll. Physicians, Calif. Med. Assn., L.A. County Med. Assn. Home and Office: 757 Ocean Ave Apt 201 Santa Monica CA 90402-2653

NEMETZ, PETER NEWMAN, policy analysis educator, economics researcher; b. Vancouver, B.C., Can., Feb. 19, 1944; s. Nathan Theodore and Bel Nemetz; m. Roma E.S. Kellock, July 16, 1994; 1 stepchild, Fiona Susan. BA in Econs. and Polit. Sci., U. B.C., 1966; AM in Econs., Harvard U., 1969, PhD in Econs., 1973. Teaching fellow, tutor Harvard U., Cambridge, Mass., 1971-73; lectr. Sch. Planning, U. B.C., Vancouver, 1973-75, asst. prof., assoc. prof. policy analysis, 1975—, chmn., 1984-90; non-resident faculty Green Coll., 1993-94, 95—; postdoctoral fellow Westwater Research Centre, Vancouver, 1973-75; vis. scientist, dept. med. stats. and epidemiol. Mayo Clinic, 1986-88, sr. visiting scientist Dept. of Health Scis. Research Mayo Clinic, 1988—; cons. consumer and corp. affairs, Can., 1977-80; program chmn. The Vancouver Inst., 1990—; mem. rsch. mgmt. com. Ctr. Health Svcs and Policy Rsch., U. B.C., 1990—, mgmt. com. Ctr. Southeast Asian Rsch., 1992—; bd. dirs. U. B.C. Press, 1993—; faculty assoc. Ctr. Japanese Studies, U. B.C., 1992—, faculty mem. resource mgmt. and environ. studies dept., 1979—; selection com. U. B.C. Rhodes Scholarship, 1991-95; assoc. Ctr. Pacific Basin Monetary and Econ. Studies, Econ. Rsch. Dept., Fed. Reserve Bank of San Francisco, 1991—. Mem. bd. mgmt. BC-Yukon divsn. Can. Nat. Inst. for Blind., 1992-94. Editor Jour. Bus. Adminstrn., 1978—. Contbr. articles to sci. jours. Grantee Natural Scis. and Engring. Research Council Can., 1976-92, Consumer and Corp. Affairs Can., 1978-80, Econ. Council of Can., 1979-80, Max Bell Found., 1982-84. Mem. Am. Econ. Assn., AAAS, Assn. Environ. and Resource Economists, Internat. Epidemiol. Assn. Liberal. Jewish. Clubs: Harvard of B.C. (pres. 1986-94), Vancouver Club. Avocations: swimming; photography. Office: Univ British Columbia, Faculty of Commerce, Vancouver, BC Canada V6T 1Z2

NEMIR, DONALD PHILIP, lawyer; b. Oakland, Calif., Oct. 31, 1931; s. Philip F. and Mary (Shavor) N. AB, U. Calif., Berkeley, 1957, JD, 1960. Bar: Calif. 1961. Pvt. practice, San Francisco, 1961—; pres. Law Offices Donald Nemir. Mem. ABA, ATLA, Calif. State Bar Assn., Phi Delta Phi. Home: PO Box 1089 Mill Valley CA 94942-1089 Office: One Sansome St Ste 2000 San Francisco CA 94104

NEMIROFF, MAXINE CELIA, art educator, gallery owner, consultant; b. Chgo., Feb. 11, 1935; d. Oscar Bernard and Martha (Mann) Kessler; m. Paul Rubenstein, June 26, 1955 (div. 1974); children: Daniel, Peter, Anthony; m. Allan Nemiroff, Dec. 24, 1979. BA, U. So. Calif., 1955; MA, UCLA, 1974. Sr. instr. UCLA, 1974-92; dir., curator art gallery Doolittle Theater, Los Angeles, 1985-86; owner Nemiroff Deutsch Fine Art, Santa Monica, Calif.; leader of worldwide art tours; cons. L'Ermitage Hotel Group, Beverly Hills, Calif., 1982—, Broadway Dept. Stores, So. Calif., 1979—, Security Pacific Bank, Calif., 1978—, Am. Airlines, Calif. Pizza Kitchen Restaurants; art chmn. UCLA Thieves Market, Century City, 1960—, L.A. Music Ctr. Mercado, 1982—; lectr. in field. Apptd. bd. dirs. Dublin (Calif.) Fine Arts Found., 1989; mem. Calif. Govs. Adv. Coun. for Women, 1992. Named Woman of Yr. UCLA Panhellenic Council, 1982, Instr. of Yr. UCLA Dept. Arts, 1984. Mem. L.A. County Mus. Art Coun., UCLA Art Coun., UCLA Art Coun. Docents, Alpha Epsilon Phi (alumnus of yr. 1983). Democrat. Jewish.

NEMKO, BARBARA GAIL, academic director; b. Bronx, N.Y., Jan. 24, 1945; d. Herbert and Leona (Beder) Padrid; m. Martin Nathan Nemko, Dec. 26, 1976; 1 child, Amy Helene. BA, Queens Coll., 1964, MS, 1972; PhD, U. Calif.-Berkeley, 1981. Dir. of evaluation (partnership) U. Calif.-Berkeley, 1978-80; project dir. Calif. State Dept. Edn., U. Calif.-Davis, 1979—; cons. Berkeley Unified Sch. Dist., 1974-75, Sonoma State U., Rohnert Park, Calif., 1983—, Calif. State U.-Sacramento, 1983—, Calif. State U.-Los Angeles, 1985—, Calif. Poly. U., Pomona, 1986—; mem. regional action team State Dept. Edn., Sacramento, 1984—; co-host Schooltalk program Sta. KALW, San Francisco. Author: Resources, Strategies, and Directions to Better Serve Disadvantaged Students in Career-Vocational Programs, 1983; (with M. Nemko) How to Get Your Child a Private School Education in a Public School. Mem. Calif. Assn. Vocat. Educators, Am. Vocat. Assn. Jewish. Avocations: tennis, theatre, music, reading. Home: 5936 Chabolyn Ter Oakland CA 94618-1914 Office: Nappa County Office Edn 1015 Kaiser Rd Napa CA 94558

NEOS, PERI FITCH, painting contractor, small business owner; b. San Pedro, Calif., Apr. 27, 1938; d. William Roosevelt Fitch and Adele (Russell) Kane; m. Thomas Harold Holston, May 27, 1957 (div. 1969); children: Kevin T. Russell, Kelly J. Russell, Adele H. Breedlove; m. Konstantinos Demetrios Neos, July 3, 1981. BSL, Western State U. Coll. Law, 1975, JD, 1976. Process piping designer The Fluor Corp., L.A., 1965-68; sr. designer CF Braun, L.A., 1968-70; sr. designer, contractor various enginr./constrn. firms L.A., 1970-81; painting contractor, owner El Greco Painting, Hanford, Calif., 1981—; substitute tchr. Kings and Tulare County Sch. Dists., 1992—. Mem. Kings County Citizens Adv. Bd. on Alcohol and Other Drug Programs, Hanford, 1991—; mem. City of Hanford Hist. Resources Commn., 1994—. With USN, 1956-58. Mem. AAUW, Nat. Assn. Women in Constrn., Hanford C. of C., Mensa. Home and Office: El Greco Painting 293 E Adrian Way Hanford CA 93230-1233

NEPPE, VERNON MICHAEL, neuropsychiatrist, author, educator; b. Johannesburg, Transvaal, Rep. South Africa, Apr. 16, 1951; came to U.S., 1986; s. Solly Louis and Molly (Hesselsohn) N.; m. Elisabeth Selima Schachter, May 29, 1977; children: Jonathan, Shari. BA, U. South Africa, 1976; MB, BCh, U. Witwatersrand, Johannesburg, 1973, diploma in psychol. medicine, 1976, M in Medicine, 1979, PhD in Medicine, 1981; MD, U.S., 1982. Diplomate Am. Bd. Psychiatry and Neurology, Am. Bd. Geriatric Psychiatry, Am. Bd. Forensic Psychiatry; registere psychiatry specialist U.S., Rep. S. Africa, Can. Specialist in tng. dept. psychiatry U. Witwatersrand, Johannesburg, 1974-80; sr. cons. U. Witwatersrand Med. Sch., Johannesburg, 1980-82, 83-85; neuropsychiatry fellow Cornell U., N.Y.C., 1982-83; div. dir. U. Wash. Med. Sch., Seattle, 1986-92; dir. Pacific Neuropsychiat. Inst., Seattle, 1992—; mem. clin faculty dept. psychiatry and behavioral Scis. U. Wash. Med. Sch.; adj. prof. of psychiatry St. Louis U. Sch. of Medicine, dept. psychiatry and human behavior; attending physician N.W. Hosp.; neuropsychiatry cons. S. African Brain Rsch. Inst., Johannesburg, 1985—; chief rsch. cons. Epilepsy Inst., N.Y.C., 1989; mem. faculty lectr. Epilepsy: Refining Medical Treatment, 1993—. Author: The Psychology of Déjà, 1983, Innovative Psychopharmacotherapy, 1990, (text) BROCAS SCAN, 1992, (with others) 31 book chpts.; editor 14 jours. issues; contbr. articles to profl. jours. Recipient Rupert Sheldrake prize for rsch. design (2nd prize) award New Scientist, 1983, Marius Valkhoff medal S. African Soc. for Psychical Rsch., 1982, George Elkin Bequest for Med. Rsch. U. Witwatersrand, 1980; named Overseas Travelling fellow, 1982-83. Fellow Psychiatry Coll. South Africa (faculty), Royal Coll. Physicians of Can., North Pacific Soc. for Neurology, Neurosurgery and Psychiatry, Coll. Internat. Neuropharmacologicum; mem. AMA, Parapsychologic Assn., Am. Psychiatric Assn. (U.S. transcultural collaborator diagnostic and statis. manual 1985-86, cons. organic brain disorders 1988—), Am. Epilepsy Soc., Soc. Biol. Psychiatry, Can. Psychiat. Assn., Soc. Sci. Exploration, Am. Soc. Clin. Psychopharmacology. Jewish. Office: Pacific Neuropsychiat Inst 10330 Meridian Ave N Ste 380 Seattle WA 98133-9463

NEROD, STEVE (SCHEZEPAN ALEXANDER NEROD), entrepreneur, designer; b. Anchorage, June 15, 1952; s. Steve (Schezepan) and Eleanor (Maytak) Nierodzik. Student, U. Wash., 1970-72, U. Alaska, 1978-82, U. Calif., Berkeley, 1983-85. Owner Eldorado Placers, Eldorado Creek, Alaska, 1970-83, Nerod & Assocs. Apparel, San Francisco, Seattle, N.Y., 1971-82, Nerod Orthopedics, San Francisco and Seattle, 1982—, DoNots ATV, 1991—, RadGear Bicycles, 1992—, VAS-Comp, Hong Kong, 1993—, OrthoSys, Everett, Wash., 1994—, N.A.S.T.I., Everett, 1994—; cons. OrthoTech, San Leandro, Calif., Orthopedic Systems, Hayward, Calif., Med. Device Engring., Hayward, Israel Med. Products Devel., Tel Aviv, 1991—. Patentee in field. Mem. Am. Acad. Cosmetic Surgery, Am. Soc. Plastic and Reconstructive Surgery, Am. Orthopedic and Prosthetic Assn., Am. Assn. Orthopaedic Medicine, Am. Acad. Orthopaedic Surgeons, Alaska Miners Assn. Office: PO Box 5461 Everett WA 98206-5461

NESBITT, PAUL EDWARD, historian, author, educator; b. Balt., Dec. 25, 1943; s. William Ervin and Margaret Caroline (Shaw) N.; m. Donna Jean Coppock, Aug. 15, 1966 (dec. 1972); children: Erik-Paul A., Janelle M., m. Pamela Jean Lichty, May 25, 1974 (div. 1983); m. Anita Louise Wood, Dec. 8, 1984 (div. 1989); m. Paula Jane Sawyer, May 7, 1994. AB, U. Wash., 1965; MA, Wash. State U., 1968, PhD (hon.), 1970; PhD, U. Calgary, 1972. Reader in Anthropology, U. Wash., 1965, grad. research-tchr. Wash. State U., 1966-68, instr., Tacoma Community Coll., Wash., 1968-69; grad. research-tchr. U. Calgary, Alta., Can., 1969-71; exec. Hudson's Bay Co., Calgary, 1971; prof. Western Oreg. U., Monmouth, 1971-74; state historian State of Calif., Sacramento, 1974—; dir. Am. Sch. of Interior Design, San Francisco, 1974, HBC Bow Fort Rsch., Morley, Atla., 1970-71; instr. Am. River Coll., Sacramento, 1980-86; exec. mgr. Calif. State Govt. United Way Campaign, 1986, 87, also bd. dirs., mem. fiscal and communication coms., El Dorado County and Sacramento chpts., 1988—; designer, cultural rsch. cons. pvt. contracts western states, 1960—; exec. dir. Heritage Areas Assn., 1993—, pres. bd. dir., 1994—. Contbr. articles to prof. jours. Fellow Am. Anthropl. Assn.; mem. Calif. Hist. Soc., Am. Inst. of Interior Designers (profl. 1974-77, bd. dirs. energy planning and devel. cos.), AIA (Cen. Valley chpt. 1975-77), Rotary. Office: PO Box 942896 Sacramento CA 94296-0001

NESTER, ROBBI LYNNE KELLMAN, writing and literature educator; b. Phila., Oct. 26, 1953; d. Morris David and Lydia Gertrude (Horvitch) Kellman; m. Richard Harrison Nester, May 30, 1976; 1 child, Jeremy Leigh. BA in English, Hollins Coll., 1975, MA in English, 1976; MFA in Creative Writing, U. Calif., Irvine, 1982, PhD in Comparative Lit., 1993. Career libr. U. Mass., Amherst, 1978-80; instr. composition Calif. State U., Long Beach, 1982-83; tchg. asst., assoc., instr. U. Calif., Irvine, 1980-89, 95; tutor Hyperlearning, Irvine, 1993—; tutor, freelance editing, 1976—; co-editor: GradTimes, U. Calif., Irvine, 1986; speaker in field. Publs. include book revs., L.A./The Agitator, 1987, Prodigal Sun, Irvine, 1984, The Greenfield Review, Greenfield, N.Y., others. Sec. Cousin's Club, Irvine, 1988-89; mem. New Jewish Agenda, Irvine, 1986-88. Travel grantee U. Calif., Irvine, 1988. Mem. Vladimir Nabakov Soc., MLA. Democrat. Jewish. Home: 196 Streamwood Irvine CA 92720-1933

NESTY, GLENN ALBERT, manufacturing executive; b. Muncie, Ind., Dec. 23, 1911; s. William Harry and Esther (Peakman) N.; m. Iona Martha Brooks, July 3, 1936; children: Philip, Gregory. BA, DePauw U., 1934; PhD, U. Ill., 1937. Rsch. chemist Allied Chem. Corp., N.Y.C., 1937-42, group leader, 1942-44; asst. dir. cen. rsch. Allied Chem. Corp., Morristown, N.J., 1944-46, assoc. dir. cen. rsch., 1946-55; v.p. R & D Allied Chem. Corp., N.Y.C., 1955-68, bd. dirs., 1957-68; v.p. R & D Internat. Paper Co., N.Y.C., 1968-76, ret., 1976; cons. Internat. Paper Co., N.Y.C., 1976—; bd. dirs. Toth Aluminum Corp., Vacherie, La. Patentee in field. Mem. NSF Study of Industry, Govt. and Univs., Republic of China, 1968; chmn. Dirs. of Indsl. Rsch., 1968, Textile Rsch. Inst., 1964; chmn. rsch. and adv. com. Inst. Paper Chemistry, 1972. DePauw U. scholar, 1930-34; Chem. Found. fellow U. Ill., 1937. Fellow N.Y. Acad. Scis.; mem. AAAS, TAPPI, Am. Chem. Soc. Republican. Methodist. Home: 870 Morningside Dr Apt G125 Fullerton CA 92635-3566

NESWITZ, MARGYE FULGHAM, newspaper columnist; b. Brownsboro, Tex., Oct. 15, 1920; d. Ivy Thomas and Nannie Savannah (Brewer) Fulgham; m. David Ross Thompson, Sept. 11, 1942 (dec.); children: Ivy Victor, (twins) Rhonda Ruth and Dennis Manning (dec.); m. Philip Neswitz, Apr. 9, 1955. AA, Lon Morris Coll., 1939; BA, Baylor U., 19428. Clk. Lockheed, San Diego, 1942-44; prof. drama Lon Morris Coll., Jacksonville, Tex., 1947; tchr. Oxnard (Calif.) H.S., 1949-52; theater critic Chgo. newspapers, 1963-69; freelance travel writer Chgo., 1959—; society columnist Monterey (Calif.) County Herald; society editor KSBW-TV, Monterey; past adv. bd. Ctr. for Performing Arts, Monterey Bay. Chair Art al Fresco of Monterey Peninsula, Pebble Beach, Calif., East Meets West, Pebble Beach. Recipient Monterey County benefactor award Cultural Coun. Monterey County, 1993, disting. alumni award Lon Morris Coll., 1994, spl. commendations: March of Dimes, ARC, Am. Diabetes Assn., Am. Heart Assn., Quota Club Monterey/Pacific Grove, Monterey County United Vol. Svc. Mem. Soroptimists, Monterey County Symphony Guild. Home and Office: PO Box 1131 Pebble Beach CA 93953-1131

NETHERTON, JANE, bank executive; b. Boston, Dec. 5, 1945. With Crocker Nat. Bank, 1967-74; sr. v.p., CFO Harbor Bank, 1974-86; pres., CEO Internat. City Bank NA, Long Beach, Calif., 1986—; mem. bd. govs. Calif. State U., Long Beach, 1990—, chmn. bd. govs., 1992—, mem. univ. extension svcs. adv. bd., 1985-91, mem. sch. bus. adv. bd., 1987—; mem. women's health adv. bd. St. Mary's Med. Ctr., 1988-92; bd. dirs. Long Beach Cmty. Partnership. Bd. dirs. Conservation Corps Long Beach, 1988—, chmn. bd. dirs., 1988-91; active Gov.'s Coun. Calif. Competitiveness, 1991-92, Queen Mary Adv. Com., 1991-92, Pvt. Industry Coun. Long Beach, 1989-92; bd. dirs. Leadership Long Beach, 1991-94, NCCJ, 1991-93, Los Alamitos Med. Ctr., 1992—, Long Beach Youth Ctrs.; mem. adv. bd. YWCA, 1991-92, Long Beach Children's Mus., 1986-88; mem. commissioning com., fin. chairperson USS Curtis Wilbur, 1993-94, co-chair apptd. leadership task force Long Beach Civic Light Opera Mayoral, 1994—. Mem. Long Beach C. of C. (bd. dirs. 1984-95, CFO 1988-89, chair 1990-92), Calif. Bankers Assn. (chmn. ops. com. 1987-89, bd. dirs. 1989-94), Nautical Heritage Soc. (bd. dirs. 1994-95), Long Beach Rotary. Address: Internat City Bank NA 780 Atlantic Ave Long Beach CA 90813-4511

NETHING, MELISSA ANN, human resources representative; b. Jamestown, N.D., Nov. 29, 1965; d. David E. and Marjorie J. Nething. BBA, U. N.D., 1988; MA in Indsl. Rels., U. Minn., 1990. Receptionist Georgia Pope Atty., Jamestown, N.D., 1981-84; cosmetic clk. White Drug Store, Jamestown, 1983-84; ins. clk. Old Republic Cos., Jamestown, 1985-87; personnel intern Minnkota Power Coop., Grand Forks, N.D., 1987-88; personnel officer N.D. Dept. Human Svcs., Bismarck, N.D., 1988; rsch. asst. U. Minn. Indls. Rels. Program, Mpls., 1988-89; human resources intern Exxon Chemical, Baytown, Tex., 1989; v.p. Sector Group Inc., Jamestown, 1989—; employee rels. rep. United Techs.-Otis Elevator Co., Chgo., 1990-92; human resources rep. Weyerhaeuser Co., Enumclaw, Wash., 1992—. Employment Mgmt. Assn. scholar, 1989-90, Grad Sch. Tuition scholar U. Minn., 1988-90; recipient Wall St. Jour. Student Achievement award U. N.D., 1988. Mem. Soc. Human Resource Mgmt., Soc. Human Resource Profls., Human Resources Mgmt. Assn. Chgo., U. N.D. Mgmt. Club (sec.-treas. 1986-88), Iota Rho Chi. Republican. Presbyterian.

NETT, LOUISE MARY, nursing educator, consultant; b. Sept. 25, 1938. Diploma, St. Cloud Sch. Nursing, 1959; cert. in therapy program, Gen. Rose Hosp., Denver, 1967. Staff nurse med. unit Mt. Sinai Hosp., Mpls., 1959-60; staff nurse nursing registry San Francisco, 1960-61; emergency rm. staff nurse Colo. Gen. Hosp., Denver, 1961-62; head nurse Outpatient Clinic Charity Hosp., New Orleans, 1962-64; dir. respiratory care U. Colo. Health Scis. Ctr., Denver, 1965-85, pulmonary program specialist Webb-Waring Lung Inst., 1985-89; rsch. assoc. Presbyn./St. Luke's Ctr. for Health Scis. Edn., Denver, 1989—; clins. assoc. prof. nursing U. Colo. Sch. Nursing, Denver; adj. asst. prof. U. Kans. Sch. Allied Health; instr. medicine pulmonary divsn. U. Colo. Sch. Medicine, Denver, 1980-89; mem. Nat. Heart, Lung, and Blood Inst. adv. coun., NIH, 1979-82, mem. safety and data monitoring bd. for early intervention for chronic obstructive pulmonary disease, lung divsn., 1985-91; mem. clin. practice guidelines for smoking cessation and presentation panel Agy. for Health Care Policy and Rsch., 1994; dir. numerous courses, confs. in field; worldwide lectr. assns., symposia, confs., TV, convs., meetings, workshops; internat. cons. hosps., health depts., 1975—; local, regional lectr. through med. programs Am. Lung Assn., Am. Cancer Soc. Colo., cmty. hosps., businesses. Author: (with T.L. Petty) For Those Who Live and Breathe with Emphysema and Chronic Bronchitis, 1967, 2d edit., 1971, Enjoying Life with Emphysema, 1984, 2d edit., 1987 (Am. Jour. Nursing Book of Yr. award 1987), Rational Respiratory Therapy, 1988; mem. editl. bd. Heart and Lung Jour., 1972-87, Respiratory Times Newsletter, 1986-88, Jour. Home Health Care Practice, 1988; contbr. articles to profl. jours., chpts. to books. Mem. subcom. on nursing Am. Lung Assn., 1975-76; mem. exec. bd. dirs. Colo. divsn. Am. Cancer Soc., 1984—, chairperson pub. edn. com., 1985-86; mem. exec. com. Am. Stop Smoking Intervention Study, 1991-94, mem. alliance bd. Recipient Rocky Mountain Tobacco Free Challenge Regional award for treatment of nicotine addiction program, 1989, award for ednl. seminars, 1989, award in profl. end., 1992, award for outstanding work in developing and promoting smoking cessation, 1992, profl. educator award, 1993, award for nicotine treatment network, 1993. Mem. ANA, Am. Assn. for Respiratory Care (health promotion com. 1987—, internat. liaison com. 1987-90, Charles H. Hudson Pub. Respiratory Health award 1991), Am. Assn. of Cardio Vascular and Pulmonary Rehab., Am. Thoracic Soc. (ad hoc com. role of non-physician in respiratory care 1972, respiratory therapy com. 1972-74, program planning com. 1989), Behavioral Medicine Soc., Colo. Trudeau Soc. (v.p. 1981, pres.-elect 1982, pres. 1983), Colo. Pub. Health Assn., Internat. Oxygen Club, Internat. Soc. for Humor Studies, Soc. of European Pnemonology. Office: Presbyn/St Lukes Ctr Health Clin Rsch Divsn 1719 E 19th Ave Denver CO 80218-1235

NETTLESHIP, LOIS E., history educator; b. Bklyn., June 14, 1942; d. Charles and Ethel (Bernstein) Shankman; m. William. A. Nettleship, Aug. 14, 1966; children: Elizabeth, Anna. BA, Sarah Lawrence Coll., 1964; MA, Columbia U., 1966; DPhil., U. Sussex, Eng., 1976. Mem. faculty Johnson County Community Coll., Overland Park, Kans., 1975-91, Fullerton (Calif.) Coll., 1991—; dir. Johnson County Ctr. for Local History, Overland Park, Kans., 1983-91; tchr. Great Plains and Western U.S. history Columbia U., summer 1990. Author numerous books on local Kans. history, 1986—; contbr. articles to profl. jours. Mem. Johnson County Bicentennial Commn., 1987-88. Woodrow Wilson Found. fellow 1964, NEH fellow 1980, 82; named Innovator of Yr. League for Innovation, 1984. Mem. Kans. Com. for the Humanities (bd. dirs. 1987—), Kans. Hist. Tchrs. Assn. (pres. 1987-88), Kans. State Hist. Soc. (editorial com. 1988—). Home: 526 Pinehurst Ave Placentia CA 92670-4450

NETZEL, PAUL ARTHUR, fund raising management executive, consultant; b. Tacoma, Sept. 11, 1941; s. Marden Arthur and Audrey Rose (Jones) N.; BS in Group Work Edn., George Williams Coll., 1963; m. Diane Viscount, Mar. 21, 1963; children: Paul M., Shari Ann. Program dir. S. Pasadena-San Marino (Calif.) YMCA, 1963-66; exec. dir. camp and youth programs Wenatchee (Wash.) YMCA, 1966-67; exec. dir. Culver-Palms Family YMCA, Culver City, Calif., 1967-73; v.p. met. fin. devel. YMCA Met. Los Angeles, 1973-78, exec. v.p. devel., 1979-85; pres. bd. dirs. YMCA Employees Credit Union, 1977-80; chmn. N.Am. Fellowship of YMCA Devel. Officers, 1980-83; adj. faculty U. So. Calif. Coll. Continuing Edn., 1983-86, Loyola Marymount U., L.A., 1986-90, Calif. State U., L.A., 1991—, UCLA Extension, 1991—; chmn., CEO Netzel Assocs., Inc., 1985—; pvt. practice cons., fund raiser. Chmn. Culver-Palms YMCA, Culver City, 1991-93, chmn. 1989-91, bd. mgrs. 1985—; pres. bd. Culver City Guidance Clinic, 1971-74; mem. Culver City Bd. Edn., 1975-79, pres., 1977-78; mem. Culver City Edn. Found., 1982-91; bd. dirs. Los Angeles Psychiat. Svc., 1971-74, Goodwill Industries of So. Calif., 1993—; mem. Culver City Council, 1980-88, vice-mayor, 1980-82, 84-85, mayor, 1982-83, 86-87; mem. Culver City Redevel. Agy., 1980-88, chmn., 1983-84, 87-88, vice chmn, 1985-86; bd. dirs. Los Angeles County Sanitation Dists., 1982-83, 85-87, Western Region United Way, 1986-93, vice chmn, 1991-92; chmn. bd. dirs. Calif. Youth Model Legislature, 1987-92; mem. World Affairs Coun., 1989—. Recipient Man of Yr. award Culver City C. of C., 1972. Mem. Nat. Soc. Fund Raising Execs. (nat. bd. dirs. 1989-91, vice chmn. 1994, v.p. bd. dirs. Greater L.A. chpt. 1986-88, pres. bd. dirs. 1989-90, Profl. of Yr. 1983), Calif. Club, Rotary (L.A. # 5, pres. 1992-93, treas. L.A. found. 1995—), Mountain Gate Country. Address: Netzel Assocs Inc 9696 Culver Blvd Ste 204 Culver City CA 90232-2753

NEU, CARL HERBERT, JR., management consultant; b. Miami Beach, Fla., Sept. 4, 1937; s. Carl Herbert and Catherine Mary (Miller) N.; BS, MIT, 1959; MBA, Harvard U., 1961; m. Carmen Mercedes Smith, Feb. 8, 1964; children—Carl Bartley, David Conrad. Cert. profl. mgmt. cons. Indsl. liaison officer MIT, Cambridge, 1967-69; coord. forward planning Gates Rubber Co., Denver, 1969-71; pres., co-founder Dyna-Com Resources, Lakewood, Colo., 1971-77; pres., founder Neu & Co., Lakewood, 1977—; mng. dir. Pro-Med Mgmt. Systems, Lakewood, 1981—; lectr. Grad. Sch. Pub. Affairs, U. Colo. Denver, 1982-84. Mem. exec. coun. Episcopal Diocese Colo., 1974; mem. Lakewood City Coun., 1975-80, pres., 1976; chmn. Lakewood City Charter Commn., 1982, Lakewood Civic Found., Inc., 1986—; pres. Lakewood on Parade, 1978, bd. dirs., 1978-80; pres. Classic Chorale, Denver, 1979, bd. dirs., 1978-83; pres. Lakewood Pub. Bldg. Authority, 1983—; bd. dirs. Metro State Coll. of Denver Found., 1990—, treas., 1994—; bd. dirs. Kaiser Permanente Health Adv. Com., 1990—. With U.S. Army, 1961-67. Decorated Bronze Star medal, Army Commendation medal; recipient Arthur Page award AT&T, 1979; Kettering Found. grantee, 1979-80. Mem. World Future Soc., Internat. City Mgrs. Assn., Lakewood-So. Jefferson County C. of C. (bd. dirs. 1983-89, chmn. 1988, chmn. 1987-88), Jefferson County C. of C. (chmn. 1988). Republican. Episcopalian. Contbr. articles to profl. jours. Home: 8169 W Baker Ave Denver CO 80227-3129

NEUDECKER, STEPHEN K., marine ecologist, museum professional. BS in Zoology, U. Ky., 1974; MS in Biology, U. Guam, 1978; PhD in Marine Ecology, U. Calif., Davis, 1982; grad. Mus. Mgmt. Inst., U. Calif., Berkeley, 1993. Project scientist U. Guam Marine Lab., Mangilao, 1975-77; marine environ. cons. Santa Fe Engrs. and Yamada Engrs., Guam and Tokyo, 1977-78, Dames and Moore, Inc., San Francisco, 1983; cons., sr. scientist Ecol. Analysts, Inc., Concord and Lafayette, Calif., 1979-80, 82-84; sr. scientist, lab. coord. Lockheed Engring. and Mgmt. Svcs. Co., Las Vegas, 1984; cons., sr. project mgr. Henwood Energy Svcs., Sacramento, 1985-86; prin. Environ. Cons. Svcs., Davis and Bonita, Calif., 1984—; exec. dir. Bayfront Conservancy Trust, Chula Vista, Calif., 1984—. Contbr. numerous articles to profl. jours. Mem. AAAS, Am. Assn. Mus., Am. Assn. Zool. Parks and Aquaria, Ecol. Soc. Am. (cert. sr. ecologist), Am. Soc. Icthyologists and Herpetologists, Bonita Sunrise Rotary (pres.), Internat. Wine and Food Soc. (past pres. Chula Vista chpt.), Sigma Xi. Office: Chula Vista Nature Ctr Interpretive Ctr 1000 Gunpowder Point Dr Chula Vista CA 91910-1201

NEUGROSCHL, GAIL E. (PENNY NEUGROSCHL), geriatrics nurse, educator; b. Chgo., May 27, 1938; d. Rudolph and Leona (Zurakov) Edelstein; m. J. Gilston Neugroschl, Dec. 27, 1959; children: Cynthia, Scott, Lori Jo. Diploma, Los Angeles Pierce Coll., Woodland Hills, Calif., 1978; BS, Boston U., 1959; MS, U. La Verne, Calif., 1985. Cert. gerontological nurse, BCLS instr. Charge nurse West Valley Community Hosp., Encino, Calif., 1978-79; head nurse Canoga Park (Calif.) Hosp., 1979-80; instr. nursing Valley Coll. of Med.-Dental Careers, North Hollywood, Calif., 1980-82; dir. insvc. Jewish Home for the Aging, Grancell Village, Reseda, Calif., 1982-85; instr. nursing Pacific Coast Coll., West Los Angeles, Calif., 1985-89; asst. dir. nursing edn. Concorde Career Inst. Valley Coll. Campus, North Hollywood, Calif., 1989-92; dir. nursing Country Villa Wilshire, L.A., 1992, West L.A. Pavillion, 1992; dir. edn. Cmty. Hospice Care, L.A., 1993-95; dir. nursing Nicksan Home Healthcare, L.A., 1995—. Pres., Jewish Marriage Enhancement So. Calif. Home: 21900 Marylee St Apt 245 Woodland Hills CA 91367-4821

NEUGROSCHL, SCOTT ALEXANDER, software engineer; b. Whittier, Calif., Oct. 30, 1962; s. J. Gilston and Gail (Edelstein) N.; m. Susan Lynn Ruda, June 26, 1988; children: Sara Lindsay, Robin Ariel. BA in Computer Sci., U. Calif., Santa Cruz, 1984. Software engr. Litton Data Systems, Van Nuys, Calif., 1984—. Nat. Merit scholar Wash. U., St. Louis, 1980-82. Mem. Assn. Computing Machinery.

NEUHARTH, DANIEL J., II, psychotherapist; b. Sioux Falls, S.D., Nov. 10, 1953; s. Allen Harold and Loretta Faye (Helgeland) N. BA, Duke U., 1975; MS in Journalism, Northwestern U., 1978; MA, John F. Kennedy U., 1988; PhD in Clin. Psychology, Calif. Sch. Profl. Psychology, 1992. Lic. marriage, family and child counselor. Reporter USA Today, Washington, 1982-83; lectr. San Diego State U., 1983-84; talk show host KSDO-AM, San Diego, 1983-84; pres. Dialogues, San Francisco, 1987—; psychotherapist pvt. practice, San Francisco, 1992—; vis. prof. U. Fla., Gainesville, 1980-81, U. Hawaii, Honolulu, 1981-82; adj. faculty U. San Francisco, 1989—; nat. adv. com. Freedom Forum Media Studies Ctr. Columbia U. Host, producer radio talk show Saturday Night People, 1984; contbg. author: Confessions of an S.O.B., 1989. Office: Dialogues PO Box 1022 Fairfax CA 94978-1022

NEUMAN, B. CLIFFORD, computer scientist; b. N.Y.C., Sept. 27, 1963; s. Peter H-X. Neuman and Barbara Diane (Allen) Gordon. BS, MIT, 1985; MS, U. Wash., 1988, PhD, 1992. With MIT Project Athena, Cambridge, Mass., 1985-86; rsch. assoc. U. Wash., Seattle, 1987-91; scientist U. So. Calif. Info. Scis. Inst., Marina Del Rey, 1991—; rsch. asst. prof. U. So. Calif., L.A., 1992—; participant Internet Rsch. Task Force, 1991—, Internet Engring. Task Force, 1991—. co-designer Kerberos computer security system, designer Prospero distributed computer system, NetCheque elec. payment system; contbr. articles to profl. jours. Mem. King County (Wash.) Search and Rescue, 1987-91. Mem. IEEE, Assn. for Computing Machinery, Internet Soc., Usenix Assn., Am. Radio Relay League, Aircraft Owners and Pilots Assn. Office: U So Calif Info Scis Inst 4676 Admiralty Way Marina Del Rey CA 90292

NEUMAN, JAMES BURTON, land company executive; b. Concord, Calif., Dec. 11, 1943; s. Charles and Virginia Lee (Jones) N. BS, U. Calif., Berkeley, 1966, MBA, 1968. Pres. Mobil Oil Redwood, Redwood City, Calif., 1969-78, Western Internat. Properties, Portland, Oreg., 1979-88, Stanly Land Co., Napa, Calif., 1989—. Bd. dirs. Napa Valley Coll. Found., Napa, Calif., Napa Valley Econ. Devel. Corp., Napa, Napa Valley Opera House, Napa. Mem. Univ. Club, Napa Valley C. of C. Office: Stanly Land Co 1451 Stanley Ln Napa CA 94559-9760

NEUMANN, CHARLES AUGUST, regional drainage engineer; b. Walla Walla, Wash., Apr. 10, 1935; s. Elmer Henry Neumann and Thelma Viola (Ostrom) Burgess; m. Mary Martha Havens, June 4, 1960; children: Mary, Bob, Alan, Kelly, Chris, Thomas, Martha. BS in Agrl. Engring., Wash. State U., Pullman, 1957. Tool engr. Boeing Airplane Co., Seattle, 1957-58; hydraulic engr. Bur. of Reclamation, Ephrata, Wash., 1958-59, 60-70, Warden, Wash., 1959-60; chief drainage design br. Bur. of Reclamation, Othello, Wash., 1970-77, 85-87; chief drainage design br. Bur. of Reclamation, Ephrata, 1977-85, regional drainage engr., 1987—. Contbr. articles to profl. jours. Lt. U.S. Army, 1958. Mem. Am. Soc. Agrl. Engrs. (chmn. drainage of irrigated lands com. 1985-88), Res. Officers Assn. (chpt. sec. 1976-93, chpt. pres. 1994—). Free Methodist. Home: 952 S Juniper Dr Moses Lake WA 98837-2250 Office: Bur of Reclamation 32 C St NW Ephrata WA 98823-1636

NEUMANN, HERMAN ERNEST, elementary and special education educator; b. Winona, Minn., Nov. 11, 1931; s. Herman Ferdinand and Dena Matilda (Peterson) N.; m. Juanita Evelyn, Sept. 11, 1954; children: Mary Evelyn, Herman Ernest Jr., Martin Andrew, Amy Louise. BS, Winona State U., 1961; MA, Calif. State U., Bakersfield, 1976; postgrad., San Jose U., 1977, Calif. State U., San Barbara, 1978. Cert. early childhood, spl. edn., elem. edn., ESL instr. Classroom tchr. grades K-6, resource specialist Bakersfield (Calif.) City Schs.; classroom tchr. Kern County, Bakersfield; resource specialist Bakersfield (Calif.) City Schs. Contbr. articles to profl. jours. 1st class airman USAF, 1952-56. NSF fellow, 1966, Internat. Biog. Assn. fellow, Cambridge, Eng., 1993; named to Hall of Fame Teaching Excellence Kern County, 1990, Tchr. of Yr., 1990. Mem. NEA (grantee 1969), Bakersfield Elem. Tchrs. Assn., ASCD, Calif. Tchrs. Assn. Home: 5219 Cedarbrook Ln Bakersfield CA 93313-2719

NEUMANN, NORBERT PAUL, immunochemist; b. Chgo.. BS in Chemistry cum laude, St. Peter's Coll., Jersey City, 1953; MS in Biochemistry, Okla. State U., 1955; PhD in Biochemistry, U. Wis., 1958. Teaching asst., rsch. asst. Okla. State U., 1953-55; rsch. asst. U. Wisc., 1955-58; rsch. assoc. The Rockefeller Inst. for Med. Rsch., N.Y.C., 1958-61; from rsch. assoc. to asst. prof. Inst. Microbiology, Rutgers, The State U. N.J., 1961-64, 64-67; asst. prof. exptl. medicine, assoc. dir. tchg. labs. U. Medicine and Dentistry of N.J., Rutgers Med. Sch., 1967-69; sr. scientist immunol. devel. Ortho Diagnostic Sys., Inc., Raritan, N.J., 1969-70; dir. biochemistry Ortho Diagnostic Sys., Inc., Raritan, 1970-74, asst. dir. rsch., 1974-80, prin. scientist clin. immunology, 1980-81, dir. immunol. rsch., 1981-82; dir. biology The Purdue Frederick Co., Norwalk, Conn., 1982-85; dir. product devel. Allergy and Immunotechnology, Inc., Newport Beach, Calif., 1987-88; rsch. assoc. Reagent Applications, Inc., San Diego, 1988-90; sr. immunochemist Internat. Enzymes, Inc., Fallbrook, Calif., 1990—. Contbr. articles to profl. jours. Mem. AAAS, Am. Chem. Soc., Am. Men Sci., N.Y. Acad. Scis., Soc. for Complex Carbohydrates, Soc. Human Genetics, Parenteral Drug Assn., Phi Lambda Upsilon, Sigma Xi. Office: Internat Enzymes 772 F N Twin Oaks Valley Rd N San Marcos CA 92069

NEUMANN, PETER GABRIEL, computer scientist; b. N.Y.C., Sept. 21, 1932; s. J.B. and Elsa (Schmid) N.; 1 child, Helen K. AB, Harvard U., 1954, SM, 1955; Dr rerum naturarum, Technisch Hochschule, Darmstadt, Fed. Republic Germany, 1960; PhD, Harvard U., 1961. Mem. tech. staff Bell Labs, Murray Hill, N.J., 1960-70; Mackay lectr. Stanford U., 1964, U. Calif., Berkeley, 1970-71; computer scientist SRI Internat., Menlo Park, Calif., 1971—. Author: Computer-Related Risks, 1995. Fulbright fellow, 1958-60. Fellow IEEE, Assn. for Computing Machinery (editor jour. 1976-93, chmn. com. on computers and pub. policy 1985—); mem. AAAS (mem.-at-large sect. com. on info., computing and comms. 1991-95). Office: SRI Internat EL-243 333 Ravenswood Ave Menlo Park CA 94025-3453

NEUMANN, RENÉE ANNE, marketing professional; b. Bklyn., Aug. 12, 1951; d. Charles René and Margaret M. (Hoehn) Schmidt. Student, Wagner Coll., 1969-72, Richmond Coll., 1973. Asst. to dir. pub. rels. Nat. Assn. Ins. Agts., N.Y.C., 1972-73; asst. editor S.I. (N.Y.) Register, 1973-74; advt. sales rep. The Staten Islander, 1974-76; outside sales rep. Aamco Transmissions, N.Y., Calif., 1976-81; account exec. UARCO, San Diego, 1982-83; computer sales and mktg. profl. Micro Age of La Jolla (formerly P.C. Specialists), La Mesa, Calif., 1984; self employed, mktg. specialist, automotive aftermarket svcs. San Diego, 1985—; active Women Synergy, 1981-83, Nat. Assn. Profl. Saleswomen, 1983-85, NAFE, 1984-86, San Diego Career Women, 1989-90. Contbr. poetry to lit. mag., columns and articles to gen. interest publs. Winner ann. nationwide pub. rels. contest Gibraltar Transmissions, 1987. Mem. NOW, Am. Humanist Assn., Sierra Club, Mensa (bd. dirs., chair pub. rels. San Diego chpt. 1982-83). Democrat. Buddhist/Wiccan. Office: 15949 Avenida Venusto Apt 1331 San Diego CA 92128-3325

NEUMANN, RITA, lawyer; b. New Brunswick, N.J., Apr. 23, 1944; d. Arno Otto and Florence (Alligier) N. BA in Math., Trenton State Coll., 1965; MS in Math., Stevens Inst. Tech., 1970; JD, Seton Hall U., 1976; LLM in Tax Law, U. San Diego, 1983. Bar: D.C. 1984, U.S. Tax Ct. 1984, N.Y. 1985, N.J. 1986, U.S. Supreme Ct. 1989, Mont. 1990, U.S. Ct. Appeals (9th cir.) 1991. Instr. math. Middlesex County Coll., Edison, N.J., 1971-74; tax cons. Evan Morris Esq. Offices, Woodland Hills, Calif., 1975-85; asst. to editor Jour. Taxation, N.Y.C., 1985-86; pvt. practice law New Brunswick, 1986-94, Las Cruces, N.Mex., 1994—; mcpl. prosecutor Manville, N.J., 1987; adj. instr. bus. law and fin. L.A. C.C. Dist., 1976-82; adj. instr. law and bus. calculus Ventura (Calif.) C.C. Dist., 1977-82; adj. prof. bus. calculus Calif. State U., Northridge, 1981-83; adj. instr. internat. law Laverne U. and San Fernando Valley Coll. Law, 1983-85; disting. lectr. in law and mgmt. Troy State U., Holloman AFB/White Sands Missile Range. Co-author: Doing Business in North America, 1994; contbr. articles to profl. publs. Vol. to farm workers ctr., Moorpark, Calif., 1979; instr. community extension ctr. for women, Calif., 1980; vol. atty. for N.J. Vietnam Vets., 1986; organizer 10-kilometer run to benefit ill children, Manville, N.J., 1986; guest lectr. taxes Second Ann. Bus. Seminar for Vets. and Non-Vet. Am. Indians of N.W. U.S., Billings, Mont., 1988; candidate for freeholder, Middlesex County, 1988; active with numerous Am. Indian tribes thoughout the U.S. in bus. devel. and Indian rights. Fellow Nat. Sci. Found., 1968-71. Mem. Kappa Delta Phi.

NEUMEYER, PETER FLORIAN, English language educator; b. Munich, Aug. 4, 1929; s. Alfred and Eva Maria (Kirchheim) N.; m. Helen Snell, Dec. 28, 1952; children: Zachary, Christopher, Daniel. BA, U. Calif., Berkeley, 1951, MA, 1955, PhD, 1963. Asst. prof. English and edn. Harvard U., Cambridge, Mass., 1963-69; assoc. prof. English SUNY, Stony Brook, 1969-75; prof., chmn. dept. English West Va. U., Morgantown, 1975-78; prof. English San Diego State U., 1978—; disting. vis. prof. English, Chico State U., Calif., 1982; vis. Nat. Endowment for Humanities fellow, Princeton U., 1984. Author: (children's books) Why We Have Day and Night, 1970, The Faithful Fish, 1971, Phantom of the Opera, 1988, The Annotated "Charlotte's Web", 1994, (poetry) Homage to John Clare, 1980. Recipient Internat. Youth Libr. stipend, 1985; SUNY Rsch. Found. grantee, 1970, 74, Swedish Bicentennial grantee, 1992; NEH Vis. fellow, 1984. Home: 7968 Windsor Dr La Mesa CA 91941-7808

NEURATH, HANS, biochemist, educator; b. Vienna, Austria, Oct. 29, 1909; came to U.S., 1935; s. Rudolf and Hedda (Samek) N.; m. Hilde Bial, June, 1935 (div. 1960); 1 child, Peter Francis; m. Susi Ruth Spitzer, Oct. 11, 1960. PhD, U. Vienna, Austria, 1933; DSc (hon.), U. Geneva, Switzerland, 1970, U. Tokushima, Japan, 1977, Med. Coll. Ohio, 1989, U. Montpellier, France, 1989, Kyoto U., Japan, 1990. George Fisher Baker fellow Cornell U., Ithaca, N.Y., 1936-38; prof. biochemistry Duke U., Durham, N.C., 1938-50; prof. biochemistry U. Wash., Seattle, 1950—, chmn. dept. biochemistry, 1950-75, prof. emeritus biochemistry, 1980—; sci. dir. Fred Hutchinson Cancer Rsch. Inst., Seattle, 1976-80; dir. German Cancer Research Ctr., Heidelberg, Fed. Republic Germany, 1980-81; hon. prof. U. Heidelberg, 1980—; fgn. sci. mem. Max Planck Inst. for Exptl. Medicine, Goettingen, Fed. Republic Germany, 1982—; cons. Battelle Meml. Inst., Columbus, 1970-75. Editor: (compendium) The Proteins (3 edits.), 1953-79; editor Biochemistry Jour., 1962-91, Protein Sci., 1991—; contbr. numerous articles to sci. publs. Advisor NIH, Bethesda, Md., 1954-70; mem. med. adv. bd. Howard Hughes Med. Inst., Miami, Fla., 1969-79, Virginia Mason Rsch. Ctr., Seattle, 1982—. Guggenheim fellow, 1955; named hon. mem. Japanese Biochem. Soc., 1977; recipient Disting. Alumnus award Duke U. Med. Sch., 1970, Stein and Moore award Protein Soc., 1989. Fellow AAAS; mem. NAS (nat. bd. grad. edn. 1971-75); sr. mem. Inst. of Medicine . Home: 5752 60th Ave NE Seattle WA 98105-2036 Office: U Wash Dept Biochemistry Seattle WA 98195

NEUTRA, DION, architect; b. Los Angeles, Oct. 8, 1926; s. Richard Joseph and Dione (Niedermann) N.; children: Gregory, Wendy, Haig, Nicholas. Student, Swiss Inst. Tech., 1947-48; B.Arch. cum laude, U. So. Calif., 1950. With Richard J. Neutra (architect), Los Angeles, 1942-55; assoc. Neutra & Alexander, Los Angeles, 1955-60; asso. Robert E. Alexander, Los Angeles, 1960-62; prin. Dion Neutra and Assos., Los Angeles, 1962-65; ptnr. Richard & Dion Neutra, Architects and Assos., Los Angeles, 1965—; pres. Richard J. Neutra, Inc., 1970—; exec. cons. Inst. for Survival Through Design, L.A.; lectr. Calif. State U., L.A., Sacramento City Coll., Mira Costa State U., Cabrillo State U., Soka U., Tokyp, San Diego City Coll., Germany, Switzerland, Eng., Austria; vis. prof. Calif. State U.-Pomona 1970, 85-86; vis. lectr. USC. Prin. works include various residential, ednl., religious and instnl. facilities including Am. Embassy Karachi, Pakistan, Gettysburg Meml., Simpson Coll. Libr., Adelphi Coll. Libr., Libr. and Resource Ctr. for City of Huntington Beach, Calif., Treetops Townhouses, 1980; exhbns. "View from Inside", 1984, 86, 92, "Visions & Exiles", Vienna, 1995. Mem. Silver Lake-Echo Park Dist. Plan Adv. Com., Master Plan City of Los Angeles, 1970-71; mem. Citizens to Save Silver Lake, 1973-76; Dir. Child Care and Devel. Services, 1970-71. Served with USNR, 1944-46. Neutra Place a street named in firm's honor in Silverlake, the site of 10 Neutra designs, 1992; Neutra Centennial named in his honor, 1992. Mem. AIA, Nat. Council Archtl. Registration Bds., Alpha Rho Chi. Studio: Richard & Dion Neutra 2440 Neutra Pl Los Angeles CA 90039-4205

NEUTS, MARCEL FERNAND, statistician, educator; b. Ostend, Belgium, Feb. 21, 1935; came to U.S., 1958; s. Achille Jan and Marceline (Neuts) N.; m. Olga Alida Topff, June 27, 1959; children: Chris, Myriam, Catherine, Debbie. Lic. in math., U. Louvain, Belgium, 1956; MS in Stats., Stanford U., 1959, PhD in Stats., 1961. Instr. Lovanium U., Leopoldville, Zaire, 1956-57; researcher U. Louvain, 1960-62; asst. prof. Purdue U., 1962-64, assoc. prof., 1964-68, prof., 1968-76; vis. prof. Cornell U., 1968-69; Unidel prof. U. Del., 1976-85; prof. systems and indsl. engring. U. Ariz., Tucson, 1985—; lectr. math. scis. Johns Hopkins U., Balt., 1979. Author: Probability, 1973, Matrix-Geometric Solutions in Stochastic Models - An Algorithmic Approach, 1981, Structured Stochastic Matrices of M/G/1 Type and Their Applications, 1989, Algorithmic Probability: A Collection of Problems, 1995; editor: Algorithmic Methods in Probability, 1977; contbr. articles to profl. jours.; coord. editor Jour. Applied Probability and Advances Applied Probability, 1982—; editor in chief, founding editor: Stochastic Models, 1983—. Fellow Commn. Relief Belgium, 1958-60. Recipient Sr. U.S. Scientist award Alexander von Humboldt Found., Fed. Republic of Germany, 1983; Rsch. fellow Ctr. Advanced Study U. Del., 1980-81. Fellow Inst. Math. Stats.; mem. Math. Assn. Am. (Lester R. Ford award 1969), Ops. Rsch. Soc. Am. (Rsch. Excellence prize computer sci. tech. sect. 1989), Ops. Rsch. Soc. Israel, Am. Statis. Assn., Internat. Statis. Inst., Bernoulli Soc., Belgian Soc. Stats. (hon.), Alumnus Assn. Fondation Universitaire Belgium, Alumnus Assn. Founds. Nat. Recherche Scientifique Belgium, Sigma Xi, Omega Rho (hon.). Home: 925 N Smoketree Cir Tucson AZ 85745-9666 Office: U Ariz Dept Systems & Indsl Engring Tucson AZ 85721

NEVILLE, MONICA MARY, state assembly program executive; b. Phila., Jan. 4, 1949; d. Edward Joseph and Mary Monica (Auletta) N.; m. William H. Pickens III, May, 1993; children: Jennifer Kathryn Gamber, John Blair Gamber, Jr. Student, Rutgers U., 1967-69; AB, U. Calif., Berkeley, 1977. Intern Gov.s' Office, Sacramento, Calif., 1976-77; press asst. Gov. Edmund G. Brown, Jr., Sacramento, 1977-80; pub. info. officer Protection and Adv., Inc., Sacramento, 1980-81; asst. press sec. Calif. Assembly Speaker Willie L. Brown, Jr., Sacramento, 1981-84; press sec. Speaker Willie L. Brown, Jr., Sacramento, 1984-86, spl. asst., 1986-88; prin. cons. Assembly Floor Analysis Unit, Sacramento, 1988-91; dir. Calif. Assembly Fellows Program, Sacramento, 1991—; coord. Calif. Assembly Intern Program, Sacramento, 1991—. Editor: Jesse Marvin Unruh Assembly Fellowship Jour., 1991—. Mem. Calif. Studies Assn., Sacramento, Sacramento (Calif.) Symphony Assn. Mem. Sacramento Press Club, U. Calif. Berkeley Alumni Assn. (life mem.). Home: 9706 Mira Del Rio Dr Sacramento CA 95827-1321 Office: Assembly Fellow Program Legis Office Bldg 1020 N St Ste 402 Sacramento CA 95814-5624

NEVIN, DAVID WRIGHT, real estate broker, mortgage broker; b. Culver City, Calif., July 27, 1947; s. Wilbur D. and Anita J. (Hulderman) N.; m. Shirley Grimes, Nov. 12, 1977; children: Jenny, David Wright Jr. BA, Calif. State Poly. U., 1974. Rural manpower asst. employment devel. State Calif., Riverside, 1970-74; pers. mgr. Lindsay Olive Growers, Calif., 1974-79; employee rels. mgr. Morton Salt Co., Newark, Calif., 1979-80; real estate salesman Valley Realty, Fremont, Calif., 1980, The Property Profls., Fremont, Calif., 1980-85; owner Nevin & Nevin, Inc., 1984-88, CitiDesign, 1989—; co-owner Brokers Exch., Inc., 1985-86; dir., officer CitiBrokers Real Estate, Inc., 1986-94; owner Nevin Fin/Mortgage Exchange 1992—; br. mgr. Brandt Property Mgmt. Group, 1994-95. Sustaining mem. Rep. Nat. Com.,

Washington, 1984; mem. Presdl. Task Force, Washington, 1984, Fremont Cmty. Ch. Served with U.S. Army, 1967-69. Mem. Realtors Nat. Mktg. Inst. (real estate brokerage coun.), Internat. Real Estate Fedn., So. Alameda County Bd. Realtors (local govt. rels. com. 1983-86). Address: PO Box 3191 Fremont CA 94539-0319

NEVINS, KEITH PATRICK, city supervisor; b. Leavenworth, Kans., Aug. 11, 1936; s. Lloyd William and Dorothy Helen (Weatherford) N.; m. Marilyn Ann Gottschalk, Jan. 29, 1941; children: David Scott, Kristine Koy, Jill Colleen. BA in Math., St. Benedict's Coll., Atchison, Kans., 1957; BS in Civil Engring., Kans. State U., 1960. Registered profl. engr., Wash. Assoc. John W. Smith, cons. engrs., Hays, Kans., 1960-63; asst. city engr. City of Walla Walla, Wash., 1963-65; city engr., dir. pub. works City of Moses Lake, Wash., 1965-69; dir. pub. works City of Auburn, Wash., 1969-85; city engr., city supr. City of Oak Harbor, Wash., 1985—; past pres. Auburn Credit Union; legis. rep. City Engrs. Assn. and Assn. Washington Cities. Contbr. articles to profl. jours. mem. Oak Harbor Sch. Dist. Cmty. Budget Adv. Com.; bd. dirs. Island County Econ. Devel. Coun. Named Pub. Employee of Yr. Island County Econ. Devel. Coun., 1993. Mem. NSPE, Internat. City Mgmt. Assn., Wash. City Mgmt. Assn., Wash. Soc. Profl. Engrs., Navy League, Greater Oak Harbor C. of C., Am. Pub. Works Assn. (pres., v.p., sec.-treas., bd. dirs. 1961—, James Robertson award Wash. state chpt. 1981, one of top 10 pub. works leader in U.S. and Can. 1982), Inst. Adminstrv. Mgmt. (past pres.). Roman Catholic. Home: 4510 425th Ave W Oak Harbor WA 98277-2434 Office: City of Oak Harbor 3075 300 Ave W Oak Harbor WA 98277-3013

NEVIUS, LLOYD L., air industry services executive; b. 1926. Teamster San Francisco, 1962-78; mgr. Airport Drayage, San Francisco, 1962-78; loader Transwest Air Express, Oakland, Calif., 1978-79; pres. Ontario (Calif.) Aircraft Svc. Inc., 1979—. Office: Ontario Aircraft Service Inc Air Cargo Facty Ontario CA 91764*

NEVLING, HARRY REED, health care human resources executive; b. Rochester, Minn., Sept. 15, 1946; s. Edwin Reid and Ruth Margaret (Mulvihill) N.; m. Joanne Carol Meyer, Nov. 26, 1976; 1 son, Terry John. AA, Rochester Community Coll., 1973; BA cum laude, U. Winona, 1974; MBA, U. Colo., 1990. Pers. rep. Rochester Meth. Hosp., 1974-75; dist. mgr. Internat. Dairy Queen Corp., 1975-76; with David Realty Corp., Littleton, Colo., 1976-83, v.p., 1979-83, gen. mgr., 1981-83, Longmont (Colo.), United Hosp., 1977—; pers. dir., 1977-87, dir. human resources, 1988-95, v.p. human resources; cons. Front Range Community Coll. of Denver, 1983-85; prin. Harry R. Nevling-Broker, 1983-85; v.p. Realty Mart Internat., Inc., 1985-93, Dist. chmn. Am. Party, 1973-74, St. Vrain Valley Sch. Dist., Health Occupations Adv. Com. 1977—, chmn. 1979-85, Vocat. Edn. Adv. Coun. 1986-91, pres. 1986-91; mem. exec. com. Nat. Health Care Skills Stds. Project, 1993-95. Served to capt. U.S. Army, 1965-72; Vietnam. Decorated D.F.C., Bronze Star with oakleaf cluster, Air medal (22, valor device); recipient Rescue citation for lifesaving Boeing Co., 1969, Helping Hand award United Way, 1974, Outstanding Service award, 1979, cert. of appreciation, 1982, Disting. Young Alumni award Winone State U., 1989. Mem. VFW (past post comdr.), Longmont Area Human Resources Assn., Boulder Area Human Resource Assn., Colo. Healthcare Assn. for Human Resource Mgmt. (sec. 1980, pres. 1981-82, exec. com. 1986—), Am. Soc. for Healthcare Human Resources Adminstrn. (ann. meeting chmn. 1985-86, regional dir. 1986-90, legis. and labor liaison 1988-90, chpt. rels. com. 1990-91, pres. elect 1991-92, pres. 92-93, immediate past pres. 1993-95, mem. orgnl. transition task force 1994-95), Soc. for Human Resource Mgmt. (sr. profl., mem. exec. com. 1991-95, chmn. bilaws com. 1994-95, chmn. nominating com. 1994-95, chmn. conflict of interest com. 1994-95), Human Resource Cert. Inst. (sr. profl.). Home: 1432 Brookfield Dr Longmont CO 80501-6709 Office: Longmont United Hosp 1950 Mountain View Ave Longmont CO 80501-3129

NEWACHECK, DAVID JOHN, lawyer; b. San Francisco, Dec. 8, 1953; s. John Elmer and Estere Ruth Sybil (Nelson) N.; m. Dorothea Quandt, June 2, 1990. AB in English, U. Calif., Berkeley, 1976; JD, Pepperdine U., 1979; MBA, Calif. State U., Hayward, 1982; LLM in Tax, Golden Gate U., 1987. Bar: Calif. 1979, U.S. Dist. Ct. (no. dist.) Calif. 1979, U.S. Ct. Appeals (9th cir.) 1979, U.S. Supreme Ct. 1984, Washington D.C. 1985. Tax cons. Pannell, Kerr and Forster, San Francisco, 1982-83; lawyer, writer, editor Matthew Bender and Co., Oakland, 1983—; instr. taxation Oakland (Calif.) Coll. of Law, 1993—; tax cons., Walnut Creek, Calif., 1983—; bd. dirs. Aztec Custom Co., Orinda, Calif., 1983—; cons. software Collier Bankruptcy Filing Sys., 1984. Author/editor: (treatises) Ill. Tax Service, 1985, Ohio State Taxation, 1985, N.J. Tax Service, 1986, Pa. Tax Service, 1986, Calif. Closely Held Corps., 1987, Texas Tax Service, 1988; author: (software) Tax Source 1040 Tax Preparation, 1987, Texas Tax Service 1988, California Taxation, 1989, 2d edit., 1990, Bender's Federal Tax Service, 1989, Texas Litigation Guide, 1993, Family Law: Texas Practice & Procedure, 1993, Texas Transaction Guide, 1994, Ohio Corporation Law, 1994, Michigan Corporation Law, 1994, Massachusetts Corporation Law, 1994. Mem. youth com. Shepherd of the Valley Luth. Ch., Orinda, 1980-85, ch. coun., 1980-82. Mem. ABA, State Bar Assn. Calif., Alameda County Bar Assn., U. Calif. Alumni Assn., U. Calif. Band Alumni Assn., Mensa. Republican. Club: Commonwealth (San Francisco). Home: 5141 Vannoy Ave Castro Valley CA 94546-2558 Office: 5141 Vannoy Ave Castro Valley CA 94546-2558

NEWALL, JAMES EDWARD MALCOLM, manufacturing company executive; b. Holden, Alta., Can., Aug. 20, 1935; 3 children. B.Comm., U. Sask., 1958. With Du Pont Can., Inc., 1957—; v.p. mktg. Du Pont Can., Inc., Montreal, Que., 1975; exec. v.p. Du Pont Can., Inc., 1975-78, dir., 1976-78, pres., 1978-89, chief exec. officer, 1978-91, chmn. bd., 1979-91; pres., chief exec. officer Nova Corp., Calgary, Alta., 1991—; bd. dirs. Alcan Aluminum Ltd., BCE Inc., Nova Corp., Molson Cos. Ltd., Pratt & Whitney Can. Inc., Royal Bank Can. Mem. exec. compensation in the pub. svc. Adv. Group to the Prime Min.; chmn. Bus. Coun. on Nat. Issues. Office: Nova Corp Alberta, 801 7th Ave SW, Calgary, AB Canada T2P 2N6

NEWBERG, DOROTHY BECK (MRS. WILLIAM C. NEWBERG), portrait artist; b. Detroit, May 30, 1919; d. Charles William and Mary (Labedz) Beck; student Detroit Conservatory Music, 1938; m. William C. Newberg, Nov. 3, 1939; children: Judith Bookwalter Bracken, Robert Charles, James William, William Charles. Trustee Detroit Adventure, 1967-71, originator A Drop in Bucket Program for artistically talented inner-city children. Cmty. outreach coord. Reno Police Dept.; bd. dirs. Bloomfield Art Assn., 1960-62, trustee 1965-67; bd. dirs. Your Heritage House, 1972-75, Franklin Wright Settlement, 1972-75, Meadowbrook Art Gallery, Oakland U., 1973-75; bd. dirs. Sierra Nevada Mus. Art, 1978-80; bd. dirs. Nat. Conf. Christians and Jews, Gang Alternatives Partnership. Recipient Heart of Gold award, 1969; Mich. vol. leadership award, 1969, Outstanding Vol. award City of Reno, 1989-90. Mem. Nevada Mus. Art, No. Nev. Black Cultural Awareness Soc. (bd. dirs.), Hispanic 500 C. of C. No. Nev., Sierra Art Found, Serra Club of Reno. Roman Catholic. Home: 2000 Dant Blvd Reno NV 89509-5193

NEWBERG, WILLIAM CHARLES, stock broker, real estate broker, automotive engineer; b. Seattle, Dec. 17, 1910; s. Charles John and Anna Elizabeth (Anderson) N.; B.S. in Mech. Engring., U. Wash., 1933; M. in Mech. Engring., Chrysler Inst. Engring., 1935; LL.B. (hon.), Parsons Coll., 1958; m. Dorothy Beck, Nov. 3, 1939; children—Judith N. Newberg Bookwalter, Robert Charles, James William, William Charles. Salesman, Am. Auto Co., Seattle, 1932-33; student engr. Chrysler Corp., Detroit, 1933-35, exptl. engr., 1935-42, chief engr. Chgo. plant, 1942-45, mem. subs. ops. staff, Detroit, 1945-47, pres. airtemp. div., Dayton, Ohio, 1947-50, v.p., dir. Dodge div., Detroit, 1950-51, pres. Dodge div., 1951-56, group v.p., Detroit, 1956-58, exec. v.p., 1958-60, pres., 1960; corp. dir. Detroit Bank & Trust, Detroit, 1955-60; corp. cons., Detroit, 1960-76; realtor Myers Realty, Inc., Reno, 1976-79; owner Bill Newberg Realty, 1979—; account exec. Allied Capital Corp., Reno, 1980—; chmn. Newberg Corp., 1982; treas. Perfect "10" Industries. Elder, St. John's Presbyterian Ch., Reno, 1976—; exec. bd. Detroit Area council Boy Scouts Am., 1955-74, Nev. Area council Boy Scouts Am., 1976—; Mich. state chmn. March of Dimes, 1967-68. Mem. Soc. Automotive Engrs., Am. Def. Preparedness Assn. (life), Automotive Orgn. Team (life), U. Wash. Alumni Assn. (life), Newcomen Soc., Franklin Inst., Alpha Tau Omega. Clubs: Prospectors, Harley Owners Group. Home: 2000 Dant Blvd Reno NV 89509-5193

NEWBERRY, CONRAD FLOYDE, aerospace engineering educator; b. Neodesha, Kans., Nov. 10, 1931; s. Ragan McGregor and Audra Anitia (Newmaster) N.; m. Sarah Louise Thonn, Jan. 26, 1958; children: Conrad Floyde Jr., Thomas Edwin, Susan Louise. AA, Independence Jr. Coll., 1951; BEME in Aero. Sequence, U. So. Calif., 1957; MSME, Calif. State U., Los Angeles, 1971, MA in Edn., 1974; D.Environ. Sci. and Engring., UCLA, 1985. Registered profl. engr., Calif., Kans., N.C., Tex. Mathematician L.A. divsn. N.Am. Aviation Inc., 1951-53, jr. engr., 1953-54, engr., 1954-57, sr. engr., 1957-64; asst. prof. aerospace engring. Calif. State Poly. U., Pomona, 1964-70, assoc. prof. aerospace engring., 1970-75, prof. aerospace engring., 1975-90, prof. emeritus, 1990—; staff engr. EPA, 1980-82; engring. specialist space transp. systems div. Rockwell Internat. Corp., 1984-90; prof. aeronautics and astronautics Naval Postgrad. Sch., Monterey, Calif., 1990—, acad. assoc. space systems engring., 1992-94. Recipient John Leland Atwood award as outstanding aerospace engring. educator AIAA/Am. Soc. Engring. Edn., 1986. Fellow AIAA (dep. dir. edn. region VI 1976-79, dep. dir. career enhancement 1982-91, chmn. L.A. sect. 1989-90, chmn. Point Lobos sect. 1990-91, dir. tech.-aircraft sys. 1990-93), Inst. Advancement Engring., Brit. Interplanetary Soc.; mem. IEEE, AAAS, ASME, NSPE, Royal Aero. Soc., Calif. Soc. Profl. Engrs., Am. Acad. Environ. Engrs. (cert. air pollution control engr.), Am. Soc. Engring. Edn. (profl. interest coun. chmn. aerospace divsn. 1979-80, divsn. exec. com. 1976-80, 89-94, exec. com. ocean and marine engring. divsn. 1982-85, 90—, program chmn., 1991-93), Am. Soc. Pub. Adminstrn., Am. Meteorol. Soc., U.S. Naval Inst., Am. Helicopter Soc., Soc. Naval Architects and Marine Engrs., Air and Waste Mgmt. Assn., Inst. Environ. Scis., Exptl. Aircraft Assn., Water Environ. Fedn., Soc. Automotive Engrs., Soc. Allied Weight Engrs., Assn. Unmanned Vehicle Sys., Calif. Water Pollution Control Assn., Nat. Assn. Environ. Profls., Am. Soc. Naval Engrs., Planetary Soc., Tau Beta Pi, Sigma Gamma Tau, Kappa Delta Pi. Democrat. Mem. Christian Ch. (Disciples of Christ). Home: 9463 Willow Oak Rd Salinas CA 93907-1037 Office: Naval Postgrad Sch Dept Aeronautics and Astronautics AA/NE 699 Dyer Rd Monterey CA 93943-5195

NEWBY, IDUS ATWELL, historian, educator; b. Hawkinsville, Ga., Oct. 3, 1931; s. Idus A. and Nomie Bell (Floyd) N. BS, Ga. So. U., 1951; MA, U. S.C., 1957; PhD, UCLA, 1962. Asst. prof. history Western Wash. U., Bellingham, 1962-63, Calif. State U., Fullerton, 1963-66; asst. prof. U. Hawaii, Honolulu, 1966-68, assoc. prof., 1968-70, prof., 1970—, grad. chmn. dept. history, 1993-94, dept. chmn., 1994—. Author: Jim Crow's Defense, 1965, Challenge to the Court, 1968, Black Carolinians, 1971, The South: A History, 1978, Plain Folk in the New South, 1989. Sgt. USAF, 1951-55. Mem. Am. Hist. Assn., Orgn. Am. Historians, So. Hist. Assn., Am. Studies Assn. Home: 2533 Ala Wai Blvd Honolulu HI 96815 Office: U Hawaii Dept History 2530 Dole St Honolulu HI 96822-2303

NEWELL, CASTLE SKIP, III, marketing executive, foundation administrator; b. Detroit, Aug. 10, 1940; s. Castle and Leona (Herrick) N.; m. Nancy Elizabeth Taylor, Aug. 7, 1964; children: Andrew Scott, Samantha Suzanne. AA, Orange Coast Coll., Costa Mesa, Calif., 1962. Sports announcer Sta. ABC-TV Wide World of Sports, N.Y.C., 1965-70; dir. pub. rels. Kawasaki Inc., Santa Ana, Calif., 1970-73; shovelman Mendocino County Dept. Pub. Works, Laytonville, Calif., 1973-74; dir. pub. rels. Harwood Products, Branscomb, Calif., 1974-80; v.p. mktg. pub. rels. Bailey's, Inc., Laytonville, 1980—; pres. Castle Newell & Assocs., Laytonville, 1993—; mem. ANSI B 175 com. Comsumer Products Safety Commn., Washington, 1985—. Fireman Laytonville Vol. Fire Dept., 1974—; reserve dep. Mendocino County Sheriff's Dept., 1983—; pres., founder Rural Visions Found., Laytonville, 1986—; mem. bd. govs. Mendocino-Lake Community Coll. Found. Recipient recognition as 237th "Daily Point of Light", U.S. Pres. George Bush, 1990, Community Svc. tribute U.S. Senate, 1990, Commendation award Calif. State Assembly, 1987, Congl. salute U.S. Congress, 1987; nominee Pres.'s Vol. Action award, 1987. Home: PO Box 717 Laytonville CA 95454-0717 Office: Rural Visions Found PO Box 1371 Laytonville CA 95454-1371 Office: Castle Newell and Assocs 116 S School St Ukiah CA 95482-4826

NEWELL, GREGORY JOHN, international business advisor; b. Geneseo, Ill., Aug. 30, 1949; s. Eugene Earl Sr. and Ima Delores (Stamper) Newell; m. Candilyn Jones, Oct. 2, 1978; children: David, Kendall, Catherine, Michael, Mattson, Thomas. BA in Internat. Rels. Polit. Sci., Brigham Young U., 1988. Staff asst. to the Pres. White House, Washington, 1974-77; adminstrv. staff Lang. Tng. Mission, Provo, Utah, 1977-78; polit. aide U.S. Senator Dole, Washington, 1978-79; dep. adminstr. Gov. of Pa., Harrisburg, 1979-81; spl. asst. to the Pres. White House, Washington, 1981-82; U.S. asst. sec. of state U.S. Dept. State, Washington, 1982-85; U.S. amb. U.S. Dept. State, Stockholm, 1985-89; pres. Dow, Lohnes & Albertson, Washington, 1989-91, Internat. Commerce Devel. Corp., Provo, 1993—; bd. dirs. Landmark Legal Found., Kansas City, Mo.; adj. fellow Ctr. for Strategic and Internat. Studies, Washington, 1989-90. Voluntary missionary LDS Ch., France, Belgium, Luxembourg, 1968-71; bd. mem. Bachauer-Internat. Piano Competition, Salt Lake City, 1991—. Named Hon. Consul Gen., Govt. Sweden, Hon. Chmn. Am. Scandinavian Assn., Washington, Swedish Am. Cultural Union, Washington. Mem. Coun. Am. Ambs., Internat. Soc. Mormon. Office: Internat Commerce Devel 2696 N University Ave Ste 130 Provo UT 84604-3863

NEWELL, L. JACKSON, education educator; b. Dayton, Ohio, Oct. 11, 1938; s. Leonard J. and Henrietta (Wahlenmaier) N.; m. Linda King, June 15, 1963; children: Christine, Jennifer, Eric, Heather. Student Deep Springs Coll., Calif., 1956-59; B.A. in History, Ohio State U., 1961, Ph.D. in Higher Edn., 1972; M.A. in History, Duke U., 1964. Instr. history Deep Springs Coll., Calif., 1965-67, bd. trustees, 1987-95, chair, 1994-95; asst. dean Coll. Liberal Arts, U. N.H., 1967-70; assoc. dir. Univ. Council for Ednl. Adminstrn., Columbus, Ohio, 1970-74; successively asst. prof., assoc. prof., prof. higher edn., then univ. prof. U. Utah, Salt Lake City, 1974—, Case prof., 1991-92, dean liberal edn., 1974-90; pres. Deep Springs Coll., Calif., 1995—. vis. prof. Anglican Mgmt. Ctr., Danbury, Essex, Eng., 1978, U. Victoria, B.C., Can., 1989-91, U. Auckland, New Zealand, 1993; World Bank cons. to Govt. Bahamas, 1990-91; cons. Budapest, Hungary, 1993; prin. investigator curricular devel. fund for improvement of post-secondary Nat. Inst. Edn., 1981-83; Co-author: A History of Thought and Practice in Educational Administration, 1987, Under Scrutiny, 1988, Creating Distinctiveness: Lessons From Uncommon Colleges, 1992, Conversations with Sterling M. McMurrin, 1995; editor Rev. of Higher Edn., 1986-91; co-editor: Dialogue: A Journal of Mormon Thought, 1982-87. Bd. dirs. Bennion Ctr. Community Svc., 1988—. Thomas Holy fellow Ohio State U., 1971, Hatch prize U. Utah, 1993, Joseph Katz award Nat. Assn. for Gen. and Liberal Studies, 1994, Presdl. Teaching scholar U. Utah, 1994—. Mem. Assn. Gen. and Liberal Studies (pres. 1988—), Am. Ednl. Rsch. Assn. (assoc. program chmn. 1986—), Assn. Study of Higher Edn. (program chair 1994), Assn. Am. Colls. (instl. rep. 1983—), Phi Beta Kappa, Phi Kappa Phi (chpt. pres. 1985), Phi Alpha Theta, Phi Delta Kappa. Home and Office: 1218 Harvard Ave Salt Lake City UT 84105-1906

NEWELL, MICHAEL STEPHEN, finance company executive, international finance, security-protection consultant; b. Denver, Dec. 22, 1949; s. Henry Michael and Marlene (McRae) N.; m. Linda Margaret Wolfe, Sept. 19, 1987; children: Katherine Margaret, Brittany Nicole; children from previous marriage: Troy, Angela, Michael, Jennifer. Grad., Denver Police Acad., 1972; CO Real Estate Lic., Real Estate Prep., 1977. Cert. peace officer, Colo. Police officer Denver Police Dept., 1972-79; prin. Michael Newell & Assocs., Denver, 1979-82; sr. account exec. Am. Protection Industries, Los Angeles, 1982-84; chief exec. officer Newco Fin., Huntington Beach, Calif., 1984—; chmn. The Newco Internat. Group/Newco Fin., Huntington Beach; founder, bd. dirs. EDEN Philanthropic Found., Fountain Valley, Calif., VALUES Self Improvement Program, Fountain Valley; cofounder, bd. dirs. Self-Love, Sexuality & Spirituality seminars, Fountain Valley; bd. dirs. Lifesong Self-Esteem workshops, Huntington Beach.; chmn. bd., bd. dirs. Steel Head Investment Group; proprietor Steel Head Inn, Michael's Supper Club. Founder, bd. dirs. Law Enforcement Support Assn., Denver, 1981. Served with U.S. Army, 1968-71, Viet Nam. Decorated Bronze Star, Viet Svc. medal with clusters; recipient numerous civilian/police awards Denver Police Dept. Republican. Mem. Religious Sci. Ch. Office: Internat Risk Cons PO Box 621091 Littleton CO 80162-1091

NEWHART, BOB, entertainer; b. Oak Park, Ill., Sept. 29, 1929; m. Virginia Quinn, Jan. 12, 1963; 4 children. BS, Loyola U., Chgo., 1952. Acct. U.S. Gypsum Co.; copywriter Fred Niles Film Co.; appeared on Jack Paar Show, 1960; TV performer numerous guest appearances, 1961—; star TV series Newhart, 1982-90. Rec. artist (album) Button Down Mind on TV; royal command performance, London, 1964, appeared in films Hot Millions, 1968, Catch 22, 1970, Cold Turkey, 1971, First Family, 1980, Little Miss Marker, 1982; TV films include Thursday's Game, 1978, Marathon, 1980. Grand marshall Tournament Roses Parade, 1991. Served with U.S. Army, 1952-54. Recipient Emmy award, 1961, Peabody award, 1961, Sword of Loyola award, 1976, Legend to Legend award, 1993; named to Acad. Hall of Fame, 1993.

NEWHOUSE, ERIC, newspaper editor; b. Madison, Wis., Mar. 4, 1945; s. John Newhouse and Frances (Herrick) Myers; m. Susie Newhouse; children: Erica, Sarah. BS, U. Wis., 1967; MA, U. Md., 1970; MS, Columbia U., 1972. Corr. AP, Chattanooga, 1976-78, Pierre, S.D., 1976-80, St. Louis, 1978-80; chief bur. AP, Charleston, W.Va., 1984-88; news editor Great Falls (Mont.) Tribune, 1988-91, editl. editor, 1991—. Internat. fellow Columbia U., N.Y.C., 1972. Office: Great Falls Tribune 205 River Dr S Great Falls MT 59405-1854

NEWHOUSE, IRVING RALPH, state legislator; b. Mabton, Wash., Oct. 16, 1920; s. John and Tina (Bos) N.; m. Ruth Martha Gardner, July 14, 1945; children: Joyce, James, Linda, Laura, Daniel, Dorothy. BS, Wash. State U., 1943. County agt. Egrl. Extension Svc., Ellensburg, Wash., 1946; farmer Mabton, 1947—; mem. Wash. Ho. of Reps., Olympia, 1964-80; mem. Wash. State Senate, Olympia, 1980—, Rep. floor leader. Lt. (j.g.) USNR, 1943-45, PTO. Republican. Mem. Christian Reformed Ch. Home: 1160 Murray Rd Mabton WA 98935-9714 Office: Wash State Sen 403 Legislative Bldg Olympia WA 98504

NEWKIRK, RAYMOND LESLIE, management consultant; b. Shreveport, La., July 13, 1944; s. Raymond Clay and Dorothy Emily (Parker) N.; m. Felicisima Guese Calma, Jan. 19, 1985. AA, Dayton Community Coll., 1973; BS in Behavioral Sci., N.Y. Inst. Tech., 1976; MS in Philosophy, Columbia Pacific U., 1980, PhD in Behavioral Sci., 1982; PhD in Human Sci., Saybrook Inst., 1992. Chief exec. officer, cons. Newkirk & Assocs., Ft. Lauderdale, Fla., 1980-84; head dept. ADP Royal Saudi Naval Forces, Jeddah, 1984-86; pres., cons. Internat. Assn. Info. Mgmt., Santa Clara, Calif., 1984; cert. quality analyst Quality Assurance Inst., Orlando, Fla., 1986—; prin. cons. Info. Impact Internat., Nashville, 1988—; exec. dir. Systems Mgmt. Inst., Pleasant Hill, Calif., 1987; pres., COO P.Q. Info. Group, Egmont ann Hoeff, The Netherlands, 1992-94; pres., CEO Systems Mgmt. Inst., 1994—. Author: Chronicles of the Making of A Philosopher, 1983; contbr. articles to profl. jours. Speaker, mem. Union for Concerned Scientists, San Francisco, 1988. Fellow Brit. Inst. Mgmt., Internat. Biog. Assn.; mem. Assn. Systems Mgmt., Assn. Profl. Cons., Planetary Soc., Columbia Pacific Alumni Assn. (pres. Mid-east chpt. 1985), Assn. Computing Machinery, IEEE Computer Soc., Phi Theta Kappa (outstanding scholar award 1973), Confedn. of Chivalry (knight). Roman Catholic. Home: 803 Treehaven Ct Pleasant Hill CA 94523-2473

NEWLAND, RUTH LAURA, small business owner; b. Ellensburg, Wash., June 4, 1949; d. George J. and Ruth Marjorie (Porter) N. BA, Cen. Wash. State Coll., 1970, MEd, 1972; EdS, Vanderbilt U., 1973; PhD, Columbia Pacific U., 1981. Tchr. Union Gap (Wash.) Sch., 1970-71; ptnr. Newland Ranch Gravel Co., Yakima, Wash., 1970—, Arnold Artificial Limb, Yakima, 1981-86; owner, pres. Arnold Artificial Limb, Yakima and Richland, Wash., 1986—; ptnr. Newland Ranch, Yakima, 1969—. Mem. Ctr. Marine Conservation, Public Citizen, We The People, Nat. Humane Edn. Soc.; contbg. mem. Dem. Nat. Com.; charter mem. Nat. Mus. Am. Indian. George Washington scholar Masons, Yakima, 1967. Mem. NAFE, NOW, Am. Orthotic and Prosthetic Assn., Internat. Platform Assn., Nat. Antivivisection Soc. (life), Vanderbilt U. Alumni Assn., George Peabody Coll. Alumni Assn., Columbia Pacific U. Alumni Assn., World Wildlife Fund, Nat. Audubon Soc., Greenpeace, Irish Nat. Caucus Found. (contbg.), Mus. Fine Arts, Humane soc. U.S., Wilderness Soc., Nature Conservancy, People for Ethical Treatment of Animals, Amnesty Internat., The Windstar Found., Rodale Inst., Sierra Club (life), Emily's List. Democrat. Home: 2004 Riverside Rd Yakima WA 98901-9560 Office: Arnold Artificial Limb 9 S 12th Ave Yakima WA 98902-3106

NEWLANDS, SHEILA ANN, consumer products company executive, controller; b. Worcester, Mass., Mar. 8, 1953; d. Joseph and Doris Edna (Bachand) N.; m. Domenic V. Testa Jr., Oct. 2, 1976 (div. 1983). BA summa cum laude, Worcester State Coll., 1975; cert. interior design, Bunkerhill Community Coll., 1976; MS, Simmons Coll., 1976; MBA, Suffolk U., 1983. Cert. real estate broker, Mass.; CPA, Wash. Dir. health scis. library Lynn Hosp., Mass., 1976-78, Mt. Auburn Hosp., Cambridge, 1978-81; assoc. fin. analyst Data Gen., Westboro, Mass., 1981-82, fin. analyst, 1982-84, sr. fin. analyst, 1984; fin. analyst Stimson Lane Wine and Spirits, Woodinville, Wash., 1985-86, dir. fin., 1986-91, v.p., contr., 1991—; guest lectr. Simmons Coll. Sch. Library Sci., Boston, 1980-81. Mem. Burlington (Mass.) Conservation Commn., 1978-84. Mem. Fin. Mgmt. Honor Soc., Phi Alpha Theta. Home: PO Box 514 Issaquah WA 98027-0514 Office: Stimson Lane Wine & Spirits One Stimson Ln Woodinville WA 98072

NEWLIN, DOUGLAS RANDAL, learning products engineer; b. Denver, Mar. 26, 1940; s. Loren Randall and Nola Berniece (Paris) N.; m. Sandra Temple, June 22, 1968; children: Jason Britt, Jeremy Owen. BS in Journalism, U. Colo., 1968. Advt. prodn. mgr. Am. Sheep Producers Council, Denver, 1968-70; promotion dir. Sta. KLZ-AM-FM, Denver, 1970-71; account mgr. Curran-Morton Advt., Denver, 1971-72; advt. and sales promotion specialist Gates Rubber Co., Denver, 1972-78; mktg. communications mgr. Hewlett Packard Co., Ft. Collins, Colo., 1978-90; learning products engr., 1990—; vis. lectr. U. Colo., Boulder, 1972-73, statis. quality control course George Washington U., Washington, 1984. Author hardware and software catalogs, 1984-90, UNIX Tech. Documentation, 1990—; contbr. articles to profl. jours. Pres. Lake Sherwood Homeowners Assn., Ft. Collins, 1982; treas. Lake Sherwood Lake Com., Ft. Collins, 1983-85. Served with US Army, 1959-61. Recipient Gold Key award Bus. and Profl. Advt. Assn., 1976. Republican. Home: 4112 Mt Vernon Ct Fort Collins CO 80525-3335 Office: Hewlett Packard Co 3404 E Harmony Rd Fort Collins CO 80525-9544

NEWMAN, CAROL L., lawyer; b. Yonkers, N.Y., Aug. 7, 1949; d. Richard J. and Pauline Frances (Stoll) N. AB/MA summa cum laude, Brown U., 1971; postgrad. Harvard U. Law Sch., 1972-73; JD cum laude, George Washington U., 1977. Bar: D.C., 1977, Calif., 1979. With antitrust div. U.S. Dept. Justice, Washington and L.A., 1977-80; assoc. Alschuler, Grossman & Pines, L.A., 1980-82, Costello & Walcher, L.A., 1982-85, Rosen, Wachtell & Gilbert, 1985-88, ptnr., 1988-90; ptnr. Keck, Mahin & Cate, 1990-94; pvt. practice, L.A., 1994—; adj. prof. Sch. Bus., Golden Gate U., spring 1982. Candidate for State Atty. Gen., 1986; L.A. city commr. L.A. Bd. Transp. Commrs., 1993—. Mem. ABA, State Bar Calif., L.A. County Bar Assn., L.A. Lawyers for Human Rights (co. pres. 1991-92), Log Cabin (bd. dirs. 1992—), Calif. Women Lawyers (bd. dirs., bd. govs. 1991-94), Order of Coif, Phi Beta Kappa.

NEWMAN, DARRELL FRANCIS, research and development manager, nuclear engineer; b. Ft. Knox, Ky., Mar. 22, 1940; s. Charles Carlisle Newman and Lillian Evelyn (Karmann) McDonald; m. Sue Carol Farley, June 18, 1966; 1 child, Donald Farley (dec.). BS in Nuclear Engring., Kans. State U., 1963; MS in Nuclear Engring., U. Wash., 1970. Registered profl. nuclear engr., Wash. Engr. Gen. Electric Co., Richland, Wash., 1963; ordnance lt. U.S. Army, Aberdeen Proving Grounds, Md., 1963-65; sr. research engr. Battelle Northwest Lab., Richland, 1966-80; tech. advisor U.S. Dept. of Energy, Washington, 1980-81; spent fuel program mgr. Battelle Pacific Northwest Lab., Richland, 1982-85, nuclear waste systems program mgr., 1985-86, mgr. tech. integration, 1987-88; project mgr. Supercondr. Techs., 1988-89; project mgr. Heavy Water Reactor Tech. Battelle Pacific Northwest Lab., Richland, 1989-94, internat. reactor safety, 1994—; cons. U.S. State Dept., Washington, 1983-84. Author: Glossary of Terms in Nuclear Science and Technology, 1986; co-author: Radioactive Waste Technology, 1985; patentee in the field. Served to 1st lt. U.S. Army, 1963-

65. Recipient Lab. Dir. award Pacific Northwest Lab., 1968, excellence in sci. and tech. award Battelle Meml. Inst., 1968. Mem. Nat. Soc. Profl. Engrs. (named engr. of the yr. 1978-79), Am. Nuclear Soc. (standard chmn. 1977-84), Wash. Soc. Profl. Engrs. (chmn. energy com. 1978-80), N.Y. Acad. Scis., AAAS, Sand and Sage Sports Car Club, Eastern Wash. Sports Car Council. Republican. Home: 1100 Mcmurray St Richland WA 99352-2120 Office: Battelle Pacific NW Labs PO Box 999 Richland WA 99352-0999

NEWMAN, DAVID E., physicist, consultant, inventor; b. Jan. 4, 1947. BS, MS, MIT, 1970; PhD, Princeton (N.J.) U., 1975. Rsch. scientist U. Mich., Ann Arbor, 1974-82; staff scientist Gen. Atomics, San Diego, 1982-89; pres. Physics Solutions, Encinitas, Calif., 1989—. Office: Physics Solutions 132 N El Camino Real # 244 Encinitas CA 92024-2801

NEWMAN, EDGAR LEON, historian, educator; b. New Orleans, Jan. 21, 1939; s. Isidore and Anna (Pfeifer) N.; children: Jonathan, Suzanne; m. Linda Loeb Clark, Apr. 21, 1989. BA, Yale U., 1962; PhD, U. Chgo., 1969. Asst. prof. N.Mex. State U., Las Cruces, 1969-75, assoc. prof. history, 1975—; lectr. U. Peking, 1985; bd. dirs. Am. Congress on Bicentennial of French Revolution of 1989. Fulbright fellow, 1965-66; Am. Philos. Soc. fellow, 1971; Nat. Endowment for Humanities fellow, 1975-76. Mem. Western Soc. for French History (pres. 1977-78, governing coun. 1990-92), Societe d'histoire de la Revolution de 1848 (comite directeur), Soc. Scis. History Assn., French Hist. Studies Assn., Am. Hist. Assn. (annotator for France bibliographical survey 1815-52). Editor: Historical Dictionary of France from the 1815 Restoration to the Second Empire; author: (with others) Dictionnaire de Biographique; contbr. Dictionnaire de Biographie Française, Dictionnaire du Movement Ouvrier Français. Office: NMex State U PO Box 3H Las Cruces NM 88004-0003

NEWMAN, FRANK NEIL, federal official; b. Quincy, Mass., Apr. 20, 1942; m. Lizabeth Newman. B.A. in Econs. magna cum laude, Harvard U., 1963. Exec. v.p., CFO Wells Fargo & Co. and Wells Fargo Bank, San Francisco, 1980-86; CFO, vice-chmn. bd. dirs. Bank Am. Corp, Bank of Am., San Francisco, 1986-93; under sec. domestic fin. Dept. Treasury, Washington, 1993-94, dep. sec., 1994—. Office: Dep Sec Dept Treasury 15th & Pennsylvania Ave NW Washington DC 20220

NEWMAN, GERARD KEVIN, software engineer; b. New Haven, Sept. 5, 1959; s. Eugene and Joan Barbara (Crosby) N.; m. Victoria Elisabeth Goehner, Jan. 11, 1992. BA in Computer Sci., U. Tenn., 1984. Software engr. Unique Software Devel., Knoxville, Tenn., 1980-83; software engr. II Digital Equipment Corp., Mallborough, Mass., 1983; sr. software engr. SAIC, Oak Ridge, Tenn., 1983-86; prin. scientist San Diego Super Computer Ctr., 1986-92; software engr. TGV, Inc., Santa Cruz, Calif., 1992—. Donor mem. Smithsonian Inst., Washington. Mem. (IEEE), Assn. for Computing Machinery, Internet Soc.

NEWMAN, J. ROBERT, psychologist, educator; b. Providence, Nov. 24, 1928; s. Edward Francis and Elinor Helene (Cronin) N.; 1 child, Danielle. BA in Psychology, U. Mass., 1950, MS in Psychology, 1952; PhD in Psychology, U. Ill., 1955. Lic. psychologist, Calif. Head, human factors Hughes Aircraft, Fullerton, Calif., 1955-62; sr. human factors scientist System Devel. Corp., Santa Monica, Calif., 1962-67; sr. rsch. assoc. Social Sci. Rsch. Inst. U. So. Calif., L.A., 1972-84; prof. psychology Calif. State U., Long Beach, Calif., 1967—; cons. psychologist, Redondo Beach, Calif., 1975—. Author: Evaluation Technology Multiattribute Evaluation, 1983; contbr. articles to profl. jours. Mem. Am. Psychol. Assn., Am. Psychol. Soc., Human Factors Soc., Psychometric Soc. Home: 173 Via Monte Doro Redondo Beach CA 90277-6522 Office: Calif State U Dept Psychology Long Beach CA 90840

NEWMAN, JAN HARLAN, marketing consulting firm executive; b. Dayton, Ohio, Feb. 25, 1950; d. Roy and Pearl (Fischer) Harlan; m. Robert L. Newman, Jan. 9, 1972. BSBA, NYU, 1972. Rsch. asst. J. Walter Thompson, Chgo., 1972-74; rsch. assoc. Booz Allen Hamilton, Chgo., 1974-76; pres. The Newman Group Ltd., Burlingame, Calif., 1977—.

NEWMAN, JULLIANA, marketing executive; b. Huntington, N.Y., June 5, 1957; d. Coleman and Lillian (Saboe) Newell; m. John Sherfy Newman, Nov. 7, 1988; children: Ana, Anders, Hayley. AA, Suffolk County Community, Selden, N.Y., 1978; BA, Queens (N.Y.) Coll., 1980; postgrad., CUNY, 1980-82. Prodn. editor Plenum Press, N.Y.C., 1982-83; mng. editor LeJacq Pub., N.Y.C., 1984-86; mng. editor/project dir. Audio Visual Med. Mktg., N.Y.C., 1986-88; editorial dir. Haymarket Doyma, N.Y.C., 1988-90; dir. healthcare communication Macmillan Healthcare Info., Florham Park, N.J., 1990-91; communications specialist PCS, Inc., Scottsdale, Ariz., 1991-93; v.p. mktg. Diagnostek, Inc., Albuquerque, N.Mex., 1993—; founder Jour. of Outcomes Mgmt., 1994; co-developer (software) Pro Tracker; editl. dir. Diagnostek Report, 1993—, PRN: Information As Needed, 1993—; cons. Nat. Asthma Edn. Program, Bethesda, Md., 1991, Asthma and Allergy Found., Washington, 1991, Pres.'s Coun. on Phys. Fitness and Sports, Washington, 1991. Cert. editor of Life Scis. Vol. Pres.'s Coun. on Phys. Fitness and Sports, Washington, 1991—. Ednl. grantee Connaught Labs., 1991, Allen & Hanburys, Research Triangle Park, N.C., 1991, 92. Mem. Coun. of Biology Editors, Am. Med. Writers Assn., NAFE, Am. Heart Assn., Arthritis Found., Nat. Council on Prescription Drug Programs. Democrat. Lutheran. Office: Diagnostek Inc 4500 Alexander Blvd NE Albuquerque NM 87107-6805

NEWMAN, KATHARINE DEALY, author, consultant; b. Phila., Aug. 17, 1911; d. Creswell Victor and Harriet Elizabeth (Hetherington) Dealy; m. Morton Newman, May 11, 1946 (div. 1968); children: Deborah Silverstein, Blaze. BS in Edn. summa cum laude, Temple U., 1933; MA in English, U. Pa., 1937, PhD in English, 1961. Cert. secondary and coll. English educator, Commonwealth of Pa. Tchr. Phila. High Schs., 1933-46, 49-50; asst. prof. U. Minn., Mpls., 1946-47, Temple U. C.C., Phila., 1959; assoc. prof. Moore Coll. Art, Phila., 1961-63; tchr. Abington (PA.) High Sch., 1963-67; prof. West Chester (Pa.) State U., 1967-77; cons. Inst. for Ethnic Studies, West Chester U., 1975-77; exch. prof. Cheyney State (Pa.) U., 1971, San Dieguito Adult Sch., 1993-94; cons. in field. Author: The Gentleman's Novelist: Robert Plumer Ward, 1765-1846, 1961, The American Equation: Literature in a Multi-Ethnic Culture, 1971, Ethnic American Short Stories, 1975, The Girl of the Golden West, 1978, Never Without a Song, 1995; contbr. articles to profl. jours. Named Outstanding Bd. Mem. Jr. League, 1987; Coordinating Coun. Literary Mags. Editor fellow, 1980. Mem. MLA (emeritus), Soc. for Study of Multi-Ethnic Lit. of U.S. (founder, officer 1973, editor newsletter 1973-77, editor MELUS jour. 1977-81, editor emeritus 1983—, Contbn. award 1982), Inst. for Ethnic Studies (founder, chmn. 1975-77), Episc. Svc. Alliance (co-founder 1978, bd. dirs. 1978-87, v.p. 1982, 86, pres. 1983-84, cert. appreciation 1987). Democrat. Episcopalian. Home: 910 Bonita Dr Encinitas CA 92024-3805

NEWMAN, LOIS MAE, marketing executive; b. Phoenix, Aug. 16, 1942; d. Harold Orville and Agnes Louise (Rindos) Little; children: Annette Horning, Tyler Katonak. BA, Hamilton Coll., Utica, N.Y., 1964; MA, Hamilton Coll., 1968; postgrad., U. Ariz., 1969, Ariz. State U., 1970. Office mgr. Dunes Hotel and Country Club, Phoenix, 1962-83; prin., treas. Sincere Press, Inc., Phoenix, 1982-90; pres., CEO Euneek, Phoenix, 1983—; staff Ridd Assocs., Inc., Phoenix, 1986-89; reg. mktg. exec. Golden Nugget, Phoenix, 1988-89; adminstr. James F. O'Toole Co., Inc., 1991-94; bd. dirs. Sincere Press, Inc., Internat. Wines & Spirits Ltd., Encino, Calif., Euneek, Inc. Bd. dirs. Sml. Bus. Coun., Phoenix, Congl. Action Com., Phoenix, Israel Bonds, Phoenix; active Better Bus. Bur., Arizonians for Jobs & Energy, Valley Leadership, others; chmn. Phoenix Childrens Hosp. Peregrinations; original founder, endorser Maimonides Day Sch.; chmn. Anti-Defamation League; adv. com. vice chmn. Nat. Coun. Christians and Jews; arrangements chmn. City of Hope. Mem. Phoenix Met. C. of C., Ariz. World Trade Assn. Home: 6808 N 26th St Phoenix AZ 85016-1208 Office: Euneek 3104 E Camelback Rd Phoenix AZ 85016-4502

NEWMAN, MARC ALAN, electrical engineer; b. Jasper, Ind., Nov. 21, 1955; s. Leonard Jay and P. Louise (Shainberg) N.; m. Shelley Jane Martin, Aug. 13, 1977; 1 child, Kelsey Renée. BSEE, Purdue U., 1977, MSEE, 1979. Sr. elec. engr. Sperry Corp. Flight Systems, Phoenix, 1979-85; staff engr. Motorola Inc., Tempe, Ariz., 1985-88, Quincy St. Corp., Phoenix, 1988-89; prin. staff scientist Motorola Inc., Chandler, Ariz., 1989-91, Scottsdale, Ariz., 1991—; Prolog and artificial intelligence expert Motorola Inc., Tempe, Chandler and Scottsdale, 1985—. Mem. IEEE, The Assn. for Logic Programming (London), Am. Assn. Artificial Intelligence, Ariz. Artificial Intelligence Assn. (founder), Internat. Platform Assn., Phi Sigma Kappa, Eta Kappa Nu. Home: 1539 N Hobson St Mesa AZ 85203-3653 Office: Motorola Inc 8201 E Mcdowell Rd Scottsdale AZ 85257-3812

NEWMAN, MARY ALICE, county official; b. Newark, Mar. 8, 1946; d. Stanley L. and Estelle C. (Forrest) Senk; m. Jack David Newman, Oct. 7, 1967; children: Jonathan Christopher, Alison Marie. AA, Newark State Coll., Union, N.J., 1967. Editor R.L. Polk, Portland, Oreg., 1969-71; clk. U.S. Forest Svc., Portland, 1971-74; sec. Def. Contract Adminstrn., Portland, 1974-76; vets. svcs. clk. VA, Portland, 1976-82; intake officer Clackamas County Community Corrections, Oregon City, Oreg., 1982-84; vets. svc. officer Clackamas County Vets. Svcs., Oregon City, 1984—. Co-author: The Horsekeeper, 1985; editor Union Label newsletter, 1980-82, VA Employee newsletter, 1980-82. Mem. Clackamas County Horse Adv., 1989—; judge Oreg. 4-H Horse Program, 1990—; chmn. dressage program Clackamas County 4-H Horse Program, 1989-94; chmn. Oreg. State 4-H Dressage Program, 1991—; dist. commr. Lake Oswego Pony Club, Oregon City, 1989-94; treas. Oreg. region U.S. Pony Clubs, Oregon City, 1988-92; leader 4-H Club, 1985—, Oreg. 4-H Horse Devel. Bd., 1993—. Recipient Minuteman Flag and Star award U.S. treas. Dept., 1980, Svc. award West Linn VFW Post, 1987,. 4-H Leader of Yr. award Clackamas County 4-H Ext., 1990, 92; named County Vets. Svc. Officer of Yr. Oreg. Dept. Vets. Affairs, 1993. Mem. Oreg. County Vets. Svc. Officers (exec. bd. 1988-90, v.p. 1990-91, pres. 1991-94, exec. bd. 1994—), Nat. Assn. Atomic Vets., Western Paraders Assn. (3d v.p. 1988-92, 2d v.p. 1993—). Home: 20500 S Ridge Rd Oregon City OR 97045-9645 Office: Clackamas County Vets Svcs 719 Main St Oregon City OR 97045-1814

NEWMAN, MICHAEL RODNEY, lawyer; b. N.Y.C., Oct. 2, 1945; s. Morris and Helen Gloria (Hendler) N.; m. Cheryl Jeanne Anker, June 11, 1967; children: Hillary Abra, Nicole Brooke. BA, U. Denver, 1967; JD, U. Chgo., 1970. Bar: Calif. 1971, U.S. Dist. Ct. (cen. dist.) Calif. 1972, U.S. Ct. Appeals (9th cir.) 1974, U.S. Dist. Ct. (no. dist.) Calif. 1975, U.S. Dist. Ct. (so. dist.) Calif. 1979, U.S. Dist. Ct. (ea. dist.) Calif. 1983, U.S. Tax Ct. 1979, U.S. Supreme Ct. 1978. Assoc. David Daar, 1971-76; ptnr. Daar & Newman, 1976-78, Miller & Daar, 1978-88, Miller, Daar & Newman, 1988-89, Daar & Newman, 1989—; judge pro tem L.A. Mcpl. Ct., 1982—, L.A. Superior Ct., 1988—. Lectr. Eastern Claims Conf., Eastern Life Claims Conf., Nat. Health Care Anti-Fraud Assn., AIA Conf. on Ins. Fraud; mem. L.A. Citizens Organizing Com. for Olympic Summer Games, 1984, mem. govtl. liaison adv. commn. 1984; mem. So. Calif. Com. for Olympic Summer Games, 1984; cert. ofcl. Athletics Congress of U.S., co-chmn. legal com. S.P.A-T.A.C, chief finish judge; trustee Massada lodge B'Nai Brith. Recipient NYU Bronze medal in Physics, 1962, TAC Disting. Svc. award, 1988, Maths. award USN Sci., 1963. Mem. ABA (multi-dist. litigation subcom., com. on class actions), L.A. County Bar Assn. (chmn. attys. errors and omissions prevention com.), Conf. of Ins. Counsel, So. Pacific Assn., TAC (bd. dirs.), Porter Valley Country Club. Office: 865 S Figueroa St Ste 2500 Los Angeles CA 90017-2567

NEWMAN, MURRAY ARTHUR, aquarium administrator; b. Chgo., Mar. 6, 1924; emigrated to Can., 1953, naturalized, 1970; s. Paul Jones and Virginia (Murray) N.; m. Katherine Greene Rose, Aug. 8, 1952; 1 child, Susan. B.Sc., U. Chgo., 1949; postgrad., U. Hawaii, 1950; M.A., U. Calif., Berkeley, 1951; Ph.D., U. B.C. (Can.), Vancouver, 1960. Curator fisheries UCLA, 1951-53, Ichthyology Museum, U. B.C., 1953-56; curator Vancouver Public Aquarium, 1956-66, dir., 1966-93; pres. Mana Aquarium Cons.; fgn. adv. Nat. Mus./Aquarium Project, Taiwan, Republic of China; past chmn. adv. com. Western Can. Univs. Marine Biol. Soc. Author: Life in a Fishbowl: Confessions of an Aquarium Director, 1994. Served with USN, 1943-46. Decorated Order of Can.; recipient Man of Yr. award City of Vancouver, 1964; Centennial award Govt. Can., 1967, cert. of merit, 1988; Harold J. Merilees award Vancouver Visitors Bur., 1976, 75 Achievers award, 1987, Silver Bravery medal Royal Soc. Canada, 1992, Canada 125 medal, 1992. Mem. Am. Assn. Zool. Parks and Aquariums, Internat. Union Dirs. Zool. Gardens, Can. Assn. Zool. Pks. and Aquariums (pres. 1978-79), Vancouver Club (bd. dirs.), Round Table Club. Office: Vancouver Pub Aquarium, PO Box 3232, Vancouver, BC Canada V6B 3X8

NEWMAN, NANCY MARILYN, ophthalmologist, educator, consultant, inventor, entrepreneur; b. San Francisco, Mar. 16, 1941. BA in Psychology magna cum laude, Stanford U., 1962, MD, 1967. Diplomate Am. Bd. Ophthalmology. NIH trainee neurophysiology Inst. Visual Scis., San Francisco, 1964-65; clin. clk. Nat. Hosp. for Nervous and Mental Disease, London, 1966-67; intern Mount Auburn Hosp., Cambridge, Mass., 1967-68; NIH trainee neuro-ophthalmology, from jr. asst. resident to sr. asst. resident to assoc. resident dept. ophthalmology sch. medicine Washington U., St. Louis, 1968-71; NIH spl. fellow in neuro-ophthalmology depts. ophthalmology and neurol. surgery sch. medicine U. Calif., San Francisco, 1971-72, clin. asst. prof. ophthalmology sch. medicine, 1972; asst. prof., chief divsn. neuro-ophthalmology Pacific Med. Ctr., San Francisco, 1972-73, assoc. prof., chief, 1973-88; physician, cons. dept. neurology sch. medicine U. Calif., VA Med. Ctr., Martinez, Calif., 1978—; prof. dept. spl. edn. Calif. State U., San Francisco, 1974-79; vis. prof. Centre Nat. D'Ophtalmologie des Quinze-Vingts, Paris, 1980; clin. assoc. prof. sch. optometry U. Calif., Berkeley, 1990—; bd. dirs., adv. bd. Frank B. Walsh Soc., 1974-91, Rose Resnick Ctr. for the Blind and Handicapped, 1988-92, Fifer St. Fitness, Larkspur, 1990-92; Internat. Soc. for Orbital Disorders, 1983—, North Calif. Soc. Prevention of Blindness, 1978-88, North African Ctr. for Sight, Tunis, Tunisia, 1988—; pres., CEO Minerva Medica; cons. in field. Author: Eye Movement Disorders; Neuro-ophthalmology: A Practical Text, 1992; mem. editoral bd. Jour. of Clin. Neuro-ophthalmology, Am. Jour. Opthalmology, 1980-92, Soc. Francaise d'Ophtalmogie, Ophthalmology Practice, 1993—; contbr. numerous articles to profl. jours. Recipient NSPI award Self Instrnl. Materials Ophthalmology, Merit award Internat. Eye Found., fellow 1971; Smith-Kettlewell Inst. Vis. Scis. fellow , 1971-72. Mem. AMA (leader Calif. del. continuing med. edn. 1982, 83), San Francisco Med. Soc., Calif. Med. Assn. (sub com. med. policy coms. 1984—, chair com. on accreditation continuing med. edn. 1981-88, chair quality care rev. commn. 1984), Assn. for Rsch. in Vision and Ophthalmology, Pan Am. Assn. of Ophthalmology, Soc. of Heed Fellows, Pacific Coast Oto-Ophthalmology Soc., Lane Medical Soc. (v.p. 1975-76), Internat. Soc. of Neuro-Ophthalmology (founder), Cordes Soc., Am. Soc. Ophthalmic Ultrasound (charter), Orbital Soc. (founder), West Bay Health Systems Agy., Oxford Opthalmology Soc., Pacific Physician Assocs., Soc. Francaise D'Ophtalmologie (mem. editorial bd. jour.). Home: 819 Spring Dr Mill Valley CA 94941-3924

NEWMAN, PAMELA ANN, secondary education educator; b. Cheyenne, Wyo., Apr. 15, 1945; d. Clark Leroy and Helen Roberta (Jamison) N. BS in Social Sci., Colo. State U., 1967, MA in Asian Studies, 1970; PhD in Curriculum and Leadership, U. Denver, 1989. Tchr., researcher Sch. Edn. U. Wis., Madison, 1991-93; developer social studies programs, chair social studies com. Adams County Five Star Sch. Dist., 1991—; staff devel. coord., chmn. profl. devel. com. Horizon High Sch., Adams County Five Star Sch. Dist., 1993—; mem. social studies ad hoc adv. com. Colo. Dept. Edn., 1993—; presenter in field; grad. rsch. asst. U. Denver, 1983-85. Author: A Guide for Traveling Abroad; contbg. author: Bringing the World into the Classroom, 1986, Teaching About Korea, 1987; author, photographer (videos) Land of the Morning Calm: Traditional Korea, 1985, Contrast in Harmony: Contemporary Korea, 1985; editor: Colorado Resources on Africa: A Directory for Eductors, 1986; contbg. author, editor (video) Egyptian Peaks: From the Rockies to the Pyramids, From the Pharoahs to the Presidents, From Inventions to Islam, 1988. Co-dir. Fulbright Group Projects Abroad, India, 1974, 76-77, Korea, 1982, Kenya, 1984-87, Egypt, 1987-88. Grantee Fulbright Found., 1982, Danforth Found., 1983, 84-88, NCSS/Japan Found., 1983, March of Dimes, 1984, NEH, 1986, 94, Social Sci. Edn. Consortium, 1991-92, Rocky Mountain Regional Japan Project, 1988-89. Mem. ASCD, NEA, Colo. Coun. for Social Studies (v.p. 1992-94), Nat. Coun. for Social Studies, UN Assn. (adv. bd. 1989-94), Fulbright Alumni Assn., Phi Kappa Phi.

NEWMAN, PETER CHARLES, journalist; b. Vienna, Austria, May 10, 1929; emigrated to Can., 1940, naturalized, 1945; s. Oscar C. and Wanda (Newman) N. Ed., Upper Can. Coll., 1948; M.A., U. Toronto, 1951; LL.D. (hon.), Brock U., 1974; D.Litt. (hon.), York U., 1975; LL.D. (hon.), Wilfrid Laurier U., 1983, Royal Mil. Coll., 1986, Queens U., 1986. Asst. editor The Financial Post, 1951-55; Ottawa editor Maclean's Mag., 1955-64; Ottawa editor Toronto Daily Star, 1964-69, editor-in-chief, 1969-71; editor Maclean's, Toronto, 1971-82, sr. contbg. editor, 1982; Dep. chmn. for Can. Internat. Press Inst., 1970-74; vis. assoc. prof. polit. sci. McMaster U., Hamilton, Ont., 1970—; adj. prof. Sask. Indian Federated Coll., 1985; prof. creative writing U. Victoria, 1986; vis. prof. York U., 1979; dir. Maclean Hunter Ltd., 1972-82, Key Radio Ltd., 1982. Author: Flame of Power, 1959, Renegade in Power, 1963, The Distemper of Our Times, 1968, Home Country, 1973, The Canadian Establishment, 1975, Bronfman Dynasty, 1978, The Acquisitors, 1981, The Establishment Man, 1982, True North: Not Strong and Free, 1983, The Debrett's Guide to the Canadian Establishment, 1983, Company of Adventurers, 1985, Caesars of the Wilderness, 1987, Sometimes a Great Nation, 1988, Empire of the Bay, 1989, Merchant Princes, 1992, Canada: 1892-Portrait of a Promised Land, 1994, The Canadian Revolution: From Deference to Defiance, 1995. Gov. Shaw Festival, 1984; bd. dirs. Can. Coun. Native Bus., 1985, Can. Coun. Econ. Edn., 1985; dir. St. Paul's Hosp. Capt. Royal Can. Navy Res. Decorated companion Order of Can., knight comdr. St. Lazarus; recipient Nat. Newspaper award for feature writing, 1966, Wilderness award CBC, 1967, Michener award for journalism, 1971, Pres.'s medal U. We. Ont., 1974, Quill award-Journalist of Yr., 1977, Best TV Program of Yr. award Assn. Can. TV and Radio Artists, 1981, Nat. Bus. Writing award for disting. svc., 1986; elected to News Hall of Fame, 1989. Home: 2324 W 1st Ave Ste 1205, Vancouver, BC Canada V6K 1G3 Office: Maclean Hunter Bldg, 777 Bay St, Toronto, ON Canada

NEWMAN, RICHARD, engineering executive. With Cahn Gengr Inc., L.A., 1960-77; pres. of subsidiary Daniel Mann Johnnson & Mendenhall, L.A., 1977-88; pres. Aecom Tech Corp., L.A., 1989—, now chmn. bd. dirs., pres., CEO. Office: Aecom Tech Corp 3250 Wilshire Blvd # 5 Los Angeles CA 90010-1502*

NEWMAN, RICHARD D., computer resources professional, software developer; b. Puyallup, Wash., Nov. 20, 1964; s. Rovaughn Drone and Beverly Joan (Vehrs) N.; m. Manuela Erickson, June 24, 1984 (div. 1986); m. Jodi Irene Kortman, July 27, 1991; 1 child, Alexander Rovaughn. Grad. high sch., Spanaway, Wash. cert. computer profl. Computer output control specialist Weyerhaeuser Co., Tacoma, Wash., 1983, records specialist, 1983-84, sr. records specialist, 1984-85; programmer/analyst IPC Pension Svcs. Co., Seattle, 1986-88, sr. programmer/analyst, 1988-89, adminstr., 1989-90, sr. adminstr., 1990-91, sr. adminstrv. programmer, 1991-93; programmer/analyst Idaho Lottery, 1994-95; cons. Meridian, Idaho, 1994-95; computer cons. ACLU, 1995. Advocate, counselor Seattle Rape Relief, 1987; campaign worker Dem. Ctrl. Com., Seattle, 1988.

NEWMAN, RICHARD STEPHEN, pathology educator; b. L.A., Oct. 13, 1951; s. Emanuel and Pauline Newman. BS with honors, Calif. Inst. Tech., 1973; MD, U. Calif., Irvine, 1980. Resident Coll. Medicine U. Calif., Irvine, 1980-81, fellow in bloodbanking Coll. Medicine, 1981-83, resident Coll. Medicine, 1983-84; asst. clin. prof. pathology U. Calif. Irvine, 1984-90, assoc. clin. prof. pathology, 1990—; assoc. dir. blood bank U. Calif. Irvine Med. Ctr., Orange, Calif., 1984—, dir. coagulation and histocompatibility labs., 1984—; cons. ARC Blood Svcs., L.A., Orange County, 1991-92. Contbr. chpts. to books and articles to profl. jours. Mem. Am. Assn. Blood Banks, Am. Soc. Histocompatibility and Immunogenetics, Am. Soc. Hematology, Calif. Blood Bank Sys. Office: Univ Calif Irvine Med Ctr 101 The City Dr S Orange CA 92668-3201

NEWMAN, RUTH TANTLINGER, artist; b. Hooker, Okla., May 28, 1910; d. Walter Warren and Jean Louise (Hayward) Tantlinger; m. John Vincent Newman; children: Peter Vincent, Michael John. Student, Pomona Coll; BFA, UCLA, 1932; postgrad., Instituto Allende, U. Guanajuato, Mex. Art tchr. Santa Ana (Calif.) Schs., 1933-34, Santa Ana Adult Edn., 1934-40; watercolor tchr. Ventura (Calif.) Recreation Ctr., 1941-50; pvt. tchr. watercolor Calif., 1950-85. One woman shows include Ventura County Mus. History & Art , 1993, Santa Barbara Art Assn., Ojai Art Ctr., Ventura Art Club, Oxnard (Calif.) Art Club, Art Club of Westlake Village, Thousand Oaks (Calif.) Art Club, others; commd. to paint 12 Calif. missions, 1958, watercolors at San Juan Bautista Retreat House, Calif., oils at Ch. of San Bernardino, Mallorca, Spain. Mem. Westlake Village Art Guild, Thousand Oaks Art Club, Buena Ventura Art Club (charter). Home: 32120 Oakshore Dr Westlake Village CA 91362

NEWMAN, STANLEY RAY, oil refining company executive; b. Milo, Idaho, Mar. 5, 1923; s. Franklin Hughes and Ethel Amelda (Crowley) N.; student Tex. A&M U, 1944-45; B.S., U. Utah, 1947, Ph.D., 1952. m. Rosa Klein, May 27, 1961 (div. Mar. 1980); children: Trudy Lynn, Susan Louise, Karen Elizabeth, Paul Daniel, Phillip John; m. Madelyn Wycherly, Jan. 10, 1991; children: Heidi, Heather, Amy. With Texaco Res. Ctr., Beacon, N.Y., 1951-82, technologist, 1973-77, sr. technologist research mfg.-fuels, 1977-82, profl. cons. on fuels and chems., 1983—. Chmn., Planning Bd., Village of Fishkill, N.Y., 1973- 77; village trustee, 1990-92; mem. Dutchess County Solid Waste Mgmt. Bd., 1974-76. With inf. Signal Corps U.S. Army, 1944-46. Mem. AAAS, N.Y. Acad. Sci., Dutchess County Geneal. Soc. (pres. 1981-87, exec. v.p. 1987-88), N.Y. Fruit Testing Assn., Sigma Xi (pres. Texaco Res. Ctr. br. 1980-81). Republican. Mormon. Patentee in field. Home: 285 Plantation Cir Idaho Falls ID 83404-7990

NEWMARK, MILTON MAXWELL, lawyer; b. Oakland, Calif., Feb. 24, 1916; s. Milton and Mary (Maxwell) N.; m. Marion Irene Johnson, July 31, 1941 (dec.); children—Mari Newmark Anderson, Lucy Newmark Sammons, Grace Newmark Lucini; m. Aylene Pruett Rosselli, June 21, 1991. A.B., U. Calif.-Berkeley, 1936, J.D., 1947. Bar: Calif. 1940, U.S. Supreme Ct. 1944. Ptnr. Milton Newmark, San Francisco, 1941-56; sole practice, 1956-62; sole practice, Lafayette, Calif., 1962-80, Walnut Creek, Calif., 1980—; lectr. bankruptcy State Bar of Calif. Continuing Edn. Program. Served with U.S. Army, 1942-46; to lt. col. USAR. Mem. Alameda County Rep. Cen. Com., 1940-41; pres. Alameda Rep. Assembly, 1950. Mem. Am. Legion, ABA, San Francisco Bar Assn., Contra Costa Bar Assn., Alameda County Bar Assn., Scabbard and Blade. Lodges: Masons, Shriners, Rotary. Home: 609 Terra California Dr Apt 6 Walnut Creek CA 94595-3344

NEWQUIST, DONALD STEWART, designer, technical director, consultant; b. Frankfort, Ky., May 25, 1953; s. Edward Wallace N. and Jeanne Gayle (Utterback) Caddy; m. Linda Susan Carter, Oct. 10, 1987. BA, Centre Coll. of Ky., Danville, 1975; MA, U. Nev., Las Vegas, 1979; postgrad., U. Nev., 1987—. Grad. fellow Ctr. Coll. of Ky., 1975-76; grad. teaching asst. U. Nev., Las Vegas, 1976-78; instr. tech. theater Clark County Community Coll., N. Las Vegas, Nev., 1978-80; tech. supr. City of Las Vegas, 1979-91; adminstr. Las Vegas Civic Ballet, 1988-90; engring. analyst City of Las Vegas Project Unit, 1991; lighting designer T.J. Krob Cons. Engrs., Las Vegas, 1991—; tech. dir. USAF Base Talent Show, Davis-Monthan AFB, Ariz., 1986, 87; tech. cons. USAF Recreation Ctr., Nellis AFB, Nev., 1982-85; resident designer Ecdysis Dance Theater, Las Vegas, 1980-84; mem. Lorenzi Park Amphitheater Task Force, Las Vegas, 1988. Designer: stage renovation, Reed Whipple Cultural Ctr., 1981; stage addition, Charleston Heights Arts Ctr., 1980. Lic. lay reader, Christ Episcopal Ch., Las Vegas, 1981—. Mem. U.S. Inst. for Theater Tech., Illuminating Engring. Soc. N.Am. (sect. treas. 1989-90, sect. pres. 1990-92, bi-regional conf. chmn., regional v.p. 1994—). Republican. Office: TJ Krob Cons Engrs 1919 S Jones Blvd Ste B Las Vegas NV 89102-1299

NEWSOME, EDWARD BALDWIN, real estate broker, retired insurance agent; b. Utica, Miss., Dec. 1, 1920; s. Baldwin Mims and Tommie Effie (Pickett) N.; m. Mary Janet Kirkwood, June 11, 944; children: Janet Therese, Kirk Edward. BS, Miss. State U., 1941. Cert. ins. agent, real estate agent; CPCU, GRI. Ins. agent Jim Newsome Ins., Moscow, Idaho, 1948-88; real estate broker, owner Jim Newsome Real Estate, Moscow, 1988—; adj. prof. ins. U. Idaho, Moscow, 1975-87, Wash. State U., 1989-90. Bd. mem. Moscow Cemetary Bd. Lt. USN, 1942-45. Mem. VFW, Am. Legion (dept. state commdr. 1967-68, local commdr.), Elks (bd. trustees chmn. 1948);

Moose, Moscow C. of C. (pres., bd. trustees). Republican. Office: Jim Newsome Real Estate 205 S Main St Moscow ID 83843-2807

NEWSOME, RANDALL JACKSON, judge; b. Dayton, Ohio, July 13, 1950; s. Harold I. and Sultana S. (Stony) N.; B.A. summa cum laude, Boston U., 1972; J.D., U. Cin., 1975. Bar: Ohio 1975, U.S. Dist. Ct. (so. dist.) Ohio 1977, U.S. Ct. Appeals (6th cir.) 1979, U.S. Supreme Ct. 1981. Law clk. to chief judge U.S. Dist. Ct., So. Dist. Ohio, 1975-77; assoc. Dinsmore & Shohl, Cin., 1978-82; judge U.S. Bankruptcy Ct., So. Dist. Ohio, Cin., 1982-88, No. Dist. Calif., Oakland, 1988—. Faculty mem. Fed. Jud. Ctr., ALI-ABA, 1987—; mem. Nat. Conf. of Bankruptcy Judges, 1983—, mem. bd. govs., 1987-88. Fellow Am. Coll. Bankruptcy; mem. Am. Bankruptcy Inst., Phi Beta Kappa. Democrat. Mem. United Ch. of Christ. Office: US Bankruptcy Ct PO Box 2070 Oakland CA 94604-2070

NEWSTEAD, ROBERT RICHARD, urologist; b. Detroit, Sept. 16, 1935; s. Oran Henry and Agnes Audery (Lewandowski) N.; m. Marie Carmela LiPuma, Aug. 5, 1961; children: Elizabeth Marie, Peter Joseph, Angela Agnes, Paul Michael. Student, Coll. Idaho, 1955-57, Quincy Coll., 1957-58; MD, Loyola U., Chgo., 1963. Intern Walter Reed Gen. Hosp., Washington, 1963-64; resident U. Iowa, Iowa City, 1967-71; urologist Urology Clinic Yakima, Wash., 1971-84, pres., 1984—; chief of staff Yakima Valley Meml. Hosp., 1995—; chief of surgery St. Elizabeth Med. Ctr., Yakima, 1980-81, Yakima Valley Hosp., 1978-79. Bd. dirs. St. Elizabeth Found., Yakima, 1983-93, The Capital Theater, 1987-93, Boy Scouts Am., Yakima, 1982-86. Capt. U.S. Army, 1962-67. Fellow Am. Cancer Soc., Iowa City, 1969-70, Am. Cancer Soc., 1961; named one of Outstanding Young Men Am., 1968. Fellow Am. Bd. Urology, ACS, Am. Urol. Assn., Wash. State Urol. Bd. (mem. at large exec. com.); mem. AMA, Rubin Flocks Soc. (pres. 1985-86), Yakima Surgical Soc. (pres. 1982-83), Yakima County Med. Soc. (pres. 1989-90), Rotary. Roman Catholic. Home: 814 Conestoga Blvd Yakima WA 98908-2419 Office: Urology Clinic Yakima 206 S 11th Ave Yakima WA 98902-3205

NEWTON, RICHARD EDWARD, filmmaker; b. Oakland, Calif., Feb. 29, 1948; s. Richard Edward and Eva (Marin) Wachtler; m. Michele Lamy; 1 child, Scarlett Rouge. MFA, U. Calif., Irvine, 1973. Artist L.A., 1967—; mfr. Too Soon To Know, Inc., L.A., 1979-88; pvt. practice filmmaker L.A., 1970—. Producer and director: (film) Small White House, 1990, and others; artist several books and shows. Democrat. Home and Office: 569 N Rossmore Ave Apt 406 Los Angeles CA 90004-2446

NEYKOV, GEORGE STRAHILOV, photographer; b. Sofia, Bulgaria, Oct. 18, 1954; came to U.S., 1990; s. Strahil D. and Vera G. (Stoimenova) N.; m. Zlatka Paneva-Neykova, May, 1981. Grad. Fine Art and Photography, Sofia U., 1974; M in Fine Arts, Fine Art Academy, 1976. Art dir. Bulgarian Photo Soc., 1982-86; head of photography dept. Nat. Art Gallery, Sofia, 1986-89; free-lance art photographer L.A., 1990—. Author: (photographs) 60 Years Literature in Japan, 1985, Nippon Camera. Japan, 1989, Prayers of the Multitude, Tokyo, 1990; contbr. articles to profl. jours. Art bd. mem. Foto Fest, Houston, 1993.

NG, ALBERT YOUNG, city manager; b. Kaiping, Kwangtung, China, Oct. 1, 1934; came to U.S., 1952; s. George Yuck Ng and May Tak-Ching Tan; m. Jean Lee; children: Nolan R., Ronald W., Linda J. BS, U. Calif., L.A., 1960. With City of Torrance, Calif., 1960—, asst. city mgr., 1986—; mem. adv. bd. Am. Internat. Bank, Torrance, 1990-92, Internat. Bank Calif., L.A., 1992—. Mem. fundraising campaign YMCA, Torrance, 1978-80; vol. 1985 Olympic Com., L.A.; bd. dirs. Vol. Ctr., Torrance, 1990-93, 95—. Mem. Am. Soc. Pub. Adminstrsn., Am. Heart Assn. (bd. dirs. 1992—), Internat. City Mgmt. Assn., Internat. Assn. Budget Officers (charter), Govt. Fin. Officers Assn., UCLA Asian-Pacific Alumni Assn. (bd. dirs. 1993—), Optimist Internat. (charter, life, past pres., sec.-treas., bd. dirs.). Democrat. Baptist. Home: 23329 Henry Ct Torrance CA 90505-3127 Office: City of Torrance 3031 Torrance Blvd Torrance CA 90503-5015

NG, ASSUNTA, newspaper publisher; b. Canton, China, Oct. 5, 1951; came to U.S., 1970; d. Eric and Hoi Sai (Wong) Woo; m. George Liu, July 6, 1974; children: Ho-Yin, Ho-Ghan. BA, U. Wash., 1974, MA, 1979. Tchr. Seattle Pub. Sch., 1974-79; pub. Seattle Chinese Post, 1982—, Northwest Asian Weekly, Seattle, 1983—; judging panelist Leadership Tomorrow, 1992; founding mem. Seattle Chinese Voice, KRAB Radio program; bd. dir. Stellar Connection; founding mem. Chinese Info. and Svc. Ctr. Newspaper columnist. Adv. bd. First Lady of Seattle; com. mem. Gov.-elect Mike Lowry's Transition Team; bd. dirs. YWCA Nominating Com., awards judge; organize, chair numerous fundraising campaigns for civic orgns. Recipient Small Bus. award Mayor Charles Royer, 1984, The Best of Men and Women Under 40 award Esquire mag., 1984, The Brightest Under 40 award Pacific Northwest mag., 1986, Mentor award Network Managerial and Profl. Women, 1989, Influential People Under 40 award Seattle Weekly, 1989, Matrix Table Women of Achievement award Women in Comm., 1990, Cmty. Svc. award Japanese Am. Citizens League, 1991, Cultural Diversity award Nordstrom's, 1991, Women of Enterprise awards Avon and Small Bus. Adminstrs., 1991, Influential People Under 40 award Eastside Week, 1991; named Western Wash. Woman Bus. Advocate of Yr., Small Bus. Adminstrs., 1992, Minority Bus. Advocate of Yr., 1992, Region X's Bus. Advocate of Yr., 1993; featured in Remarkable People of the Northwest, Sta. KCTS, Wash. Mem. Rotary Internat., Minority Pub. Assn. (pres. 1988—), Greater Seattle C. of C. (bd. trustees 1992—), Chinatown C. of C., Taiwan C. of C., Internat. Women's Forum (Women Making a Difference in Corp. World award 1992). Buddhist. Office: Seattle Chinese Post Inc 414 8th Ave S Seattle WA 98104-3002

NG, CHOOON MENG, design engineer, consultant; b. Kuala Lumpur, Malaysia, Nov. 27, 1961; came to U.S., 1975; s. Kok Toong and Choong Kam (Lau) N. BS, Poly. Inst. N.Y., 1985; MS, U. Cin., 1989. EIT, Ohio. Coop. engr. Johnson Space Ctr. NASA, Houston, 1982-84; nozzle engr., combustor design engr., aerospace propulsion controls engr. GE, Cin., 1985-89; design engr. space propulsion and space power systems Rocketdyne Rockwell Internat., Canoga Park, Calif., 1989—; computer cons. CMN Microsystems, Simi Valley, Calif., 1993—. Inventor, patentee convergent nozzle, coal combustor. Mem. AIAA (sr.), Sigma Gamma Tau, Tau Beta Pi. Home: 6542 Stoney View Ln Apt 3 Simi Valley CA 93063-6431 Office: Rocketdyne PO Box 7922 MS 306/LB03 Canoga Park CA 91309

NG, DOMINICK, bank executive; b. Hong Kong, Jan. 24, 1959; s. William N.; m. Ellen Wong. BBA in Acctg., U. Houston, 1980. CPA, Calif., Tex. Dir. Chinese bus. svcs. group, sr. mgr. audit group Deloitte & Touche, L.A., Houston, 1980-90; pres., CEO Seyin Investment, Inc., L.A., 1990-92, East-West Fed. Bank f.s.b., San Marino, Calif., 1992—. Dir. Kiang Su-Chiang Kiang Assn. So. Calif.; past chmn. adv. coun. Asian Pacific Family Ctr.; dir. Family Clinics; dir. adv. coun. San Gabriel chpt. Am. Red Cross; dir. Asian adv. coun. Loyola Marymount U.; active Jonathan Club. Mem. AICPA, Am. League Fin. Instns. (dir.), Nat. Assn. Chinese Am. Bankers (pres.). Office: East-West Fed Bank FSB 415 Huntington Dr San Marino CA 91108-2358

NG, LAWRENCE MING-LOY, pediatric cardiologist; b. Hong Kong, Mar. 21, 1940; came to U.S., 1967, naturalized, 1977; s. John Iu-cheung and Mary Wing (Wong) N.; m. Bella May Ha Kan, June 25, 1971; children: Jennifer Wing-mui, Jessica Wing-yee. B in Medicine, U. Hong Kong, 1965, B in Surgery, 1965. House physician Queen Elizabeth Hosp., Hong Kong, 1965-66, med. officer, 1966-67; resident physician Children's Hosp. of Los Angeles, 1967-68; resident physician Children's Hosp. Med. Center, Oakland, Calif., 1968-70, fellow in pediatric cardiology, 1970-72, now mem. teaching staff; practice medicine, specializing in pediatrics and pediatric cardiology, San Leandro, Calif., 1972—, Oakland, Calif., 1982—; mng. ptnr. Pediatric Assocs. of East Bay, 1990—; chief of pediatrics Oakland Hosp., 1974-77; chief of pediatrics Vesper Meml. Hosp., 1977-79, sec. staff, 1984, v.p. staff, 1985; chief pediatrics Meml. Hosp., San Leandro, 1986-88; founder Pediatric Assocs. of East Bay, 1990. Active Republican Party. Diplomate Am. Bd. Pediatrics. Fellow Am. Acad. Pediatrics; mem. AMA, Calif. Med. Assn., Am. Heart Assn., Alameda County Assn. Primary Care Practitioners (membership chmn. 1993—, sec. treas 1994—), Los Angeles Pediatric Soc., East Bay Pediatric Soc., Smithsonian Assocs., Nat. Geog. Soc., Orgn. Chinese Ams. (chpt. pres. 1984), Chinese-Am. Physicians Soc. (co-founder, sec. 1980, pres. 1983), Chinese-Am. Polit. Assn. (life), Oakland Mus. Assns., Oakland Chinatown C. of C. (bd. dirs. 1986-91), Hong Kong U. Alumni Assn. (sec. No. Calif. chpt. 1992—), Stanford U. Alumni Assn. (life), Commonwealth Club, Consumers' Union (life). Buddhist. Office: 345 9th St Ste 204 Oakland CA 94607-4206 also: 101 Callan Ave Ste 401 San Leandro CA 94577-4519

NG, WING CHIU, accountant, computer software consultant, educator, activist; b. Hong Kong, Hong Kong, Oct. 14, 1947; came to U.S., 1966; s. Bing Nuen and Oi Ying (Lee) Ng. BS, Yale U., 1969, MS, 1969; PhD, NYU, 1972. CPA, Hawaii. Rsch. assoc. SUNY, Stony Brook, 1972-74; asst. prof. U. Md., College Park, 1974-76; rsch. physicist U. Bonn, Fed. Republic of Germany, 1976-78; chartered acct. Richter, Usher & Vineberg, Montreal, Can., 1978-80; pvt. practice Honolulu, Hawaii, 1980—; pres. Bowen, Ng & Co., Honolulu, 1983-84, Asia-Am. Investment, Inc., Honolulu, 1983—, Mathematica Pacific, Inc., Honolulu, 1984—; part-time prof. U. Hawaii, Honolulu, 1982—; ptnr. Advance Realty Investment, Honolulu, 1980—; dir. S & L Internat., Inc., Honolulu, 1987—. Creator: (computer software) Time Billing, 1994, Dbase General Ledger, 1987, Dbase Payroll, 1987, Dbase Accounts Receivable, 1989; co-author: Draft Constitution of the Federal Republic of China, 1994. Dir. Orgn. of Chinese Ams., Honolulu, 1984-86, Fedn. for a Dem. China, Honolulu, 1990—, Hong Kong, 1991—. Included in Prominent People of Hawaii, Delta Pub. Co., 1988. Mem. AICPA, Hong Kong Soc. Accts., Hawaiian Trail & Mountain Club (auditor 1987—). Democrat. Buddhist. Office: 1149 Bethel St Ste 411 Honolulu HI 96813-2211

NGUYEN, ANN CAC KHUE, pharmaceutical and medicinal chemist; b. Sontay, Vietnam; came to U.S., 1975; naturalized citizen; d. Nguyen Van Soan and Luu Thi Hieu. BS, U. Saigon, 1973; MS, San Francisco State U., 1978; PhD, U. Calif., San Francisco, 1983. Teaching and research asst. U. Calif., San Francisco, 1978-83, postdoctoral fellow, 1983-86; research scientist U. Calif., 1987—. Contbr. articles to profl. jours. Recipient Nat. Research Service award, NIH, 1981-83; Regents fellow U. Calif., San Francisco, 1978-81. Mem. AAAS, Am. Chem. Soc., N.Y.Acad. Scis., Bay Area Enzyme Mechanism Group, Am. Assn. Pharm. Scientists, Am. Assn. Dental Rsch., Internat. Assn. Dental Rsch. Roman Catholic. Home: 1488 Portola Dr San Francisco CA 94127-1409 Office: U Calif Box 0989 San Francisco CA 94143

NGUYEN, EDWARD DUY, real estate developer; b. Saigon, Vietnam, May 26, 1963; came to U.S., 1975; BSEE summa cum laude, Calif. State U., L.A., 1982; MSEE, Calif. Inst. Tech., 1983; postgrad. in Elec. Engring., U. So. Calif., 1983-87; postgrad in Law, U. West L.A., 1990-91. Lic. real estate broker, Calif. Comm. systems engr. Hughes Aircraft Co., El Segundo, Calif., 1983-88; pres. Far East Devel. Co., Beverly Hills, Calif., 1988-91; mng. dir. Global Devel. Group, L.A., 1991—. Recipient Howard Hughes Doctoral fellowship, 1983-87, Am. Jurisprudence awards on Tort and Contracts, 1990-91; named to Dean's Honor list, 1990-91. Office: Global Devel Group Ste 1160 2029 Century Park E Los Angeles CA 90067

NGUYEN, HAN VAN, mechanical engineer; b. Danang, Vietnam, June 10, 1956; came to U.S., 1974; s. Tien Van and Dieuanh Khoa Nguyen; m. Thien-Tam Trang, Jan. 7, 1995. BSME with distinction, Iowa State U., 1979; MSME, Purdue U., 1981, PhD, 1986. Registered profl. engr., Calif. Grad. rsch. asst. Purdue U., West Lafayette, 1979-83; sr. engr. Westinghouse Electric Corp., Sunnyvale, Calif., 1983-87; engring. specialist Rockwell Internat., Downey, Calif., 1987—; lectr. Calif. State Poly. U., Pomona, 1995—. Contbr. articles to profl. jours. Recipient NASA award, Rockwell Internat. award; Iowa State U. scholar; Purdue U. fellow;. Mem. AIAA (sr.), Sigma Xi, Phi Kappa Phi, Tau Beta Pi, Pi Tau Sigma, Eta Kappa Nu, Pi Mu Epsilon, Phi Eta Sigma. Buddhist. Office: Rockwell Internat MS AE-70 12214 Lakewood Blvd # 70 Downey CA 90242-2655

NGUYEN, JOSEPH KIM QUY, foreign language educator; b. Nhatrang, Vietnam, Sept. 10, 1939; came to the U.S., 1985; BA in French Lit., U. Saigon, 1963; MA in Tchg., Portland State U., 1986; PhD in Romance Langs., U. Oreg., 1990. Tchr. Nhatrang (Vietnam) H.S., 1963-68; asst. prof. French U. Dalat, Vietnam, 1973-75; grad. tchg. fellow U. Oreg., Eugene, 1986-90; asst. prof. French Ea. Wash. U., Cheney, 1990-92; health info. specialist Multnomah County Health Dept., Portland, 1993—; vis. prof. French Portland (Oreg.) State U., summer 1988; participant MLA Convs., Washington and San Francisco, 1989, 91; spkr. in field. Recipient recognition award Portland (Oreg.) State U., 1986, recognition award Refugee Forum of Oreg. & Southwest Wash., 1994; Gilbert Chinard scholar Inst. Francais de WA, Chapel Hill, N.C., 1989; recipient grad. student award U. Oreg., 1989. Mem. Confedn. Oreg. Fgn. Lang. Tchrs., Soc. des Professeurs Francais et Francophones en Amerique, Phi Kappa Phi. Home: 2363 SE 45th Ave Portland OR 97215-3729

NGUYEN, KING XUAN, language educator; b. Hue, Vietnam, Dec. 20, 1930; came to U.S., 1975; s. Duong Xuan Nguyen and Thi Thi Ton-Nu. BA, U. Saigon, 1960, LLB, 1963; MEd, Boise State U., 1980. Tchr. Boise Sch. Dist., 1975—; lectr. S.E. Asian Studies Summer Inst./U. Wash., 1992-93, SEASSI, U. Wis., 1994—; spl. lectr. Boise State U., 1975-77. Col. Vietnamese Air Force to 1975. Recipient Red Apple Award for Outstanding Svc. to Edn., Boise, 1990. Mem. NEA, Idaho Edn. Assn., Boise Edn. Assn., Consortium Tchrs. Southeast Asian Langs., Assn. of TESOL. Home: 9674 W Pattie Ct Boise ID 83704-2824 Office: Boise Lang Acad 300 W Fort St Boise ID 83702-4529

NGUYEN, LAM DUC, business executive, consultant; b. Ninh Binh, Vietnam, July 20, 1945; came to the U.S., 1975; s. Phuong-Duc and Thien-Thi Nguyen; m. Trang Thu Nghiem, June 17, 1978; children: Katherine, Andrew, Alexander. BA, U. Saigon, 1968; diploma in TEFL, U. Sydney, Australia, 1973; postgrad., Furman U., 1977, San Jose State U., 1980; AS in Computer Sci., Condie Coll., 1981; postgrad., Nat. U., 1987-88, La Salle U., 1994—. Cert. Emergency Specialist Tchg. credential ESL grades K-12; Calif. C.C. tchg. credential for ltd. svcs. in basic edn.; Calif. C.C. instr. credential in computer scis. Materials/mfg. sys. analyst, project leader Shugart Corp., Sunnyvale, Calif., 1979-84; mgr. programming and sys. devel. Televideo Sys., Inc., San Jose, Calif., 1984-86; sales and mktg. sys. analyst, project leader Spectra-Physics, San Jose, 1986; project mgr. U.S. Wind Power, Livermore, Calif., 1986-87; asst. mgr. ops. Burger King Corp., San Jose, 1987-88; dir. programs, dep. exec. dir. IRCC Inc., San Jose, 1988-93; pres., founder WIN-Visions, San Jose, 1993—; asst. chief tng. team Comvined Document Exploration Ctr., 1965-68; lang. instr. Military Asst. Command Civil Ops. for Rural Devel. Strategies/USAID, Bien Hoa, Vietnam, 1968-69; tchr. ESL/EFL Vietnamese-Am. Assn., Saigon, 1970-75; lectr. med. English U. Saigon-Med. Coll., 1974-75; spl. asst. to dir. refugee liaison officer, chief interpreter staff Refugee Camp, Eglin AFB, Fla., 1975; refugee camp mgmt. counselor Indochinese Inter-Agy. Task Force, U.S. State Dept., Indiantown Gap Refugee Camp, Pa., 1975; statis. quality control Michelin Tire Corp., S.C., 1976-78, others; part-time ESL instr. Foothill-De Anza Coll., San Jose, Calif., 1979-80; bilingual elem. and ESL tchr. San Jose Unified Sch. Dist., 1979-80; spkr., panelist in field. Co-editor, reporter Tin Bien News; contbr. articles to profl. jours. Active Nat. Asian Pacific Islanders Am. Adv. Coun., Democratic Nat. Com., 1991—, San Jose City Mayor's Gang Prevention Policy Team, 1992—, Coalition of Asian Pacific-Ams., No. Calif., 1992—, Nat. Immigration Forum, 1994; nat. co-chair Nat. Vietnamese-Am. Voter's League, 1992—, Nat. League Indochinese Am. Voters, 1992—; pres. Vietnamese-Ams. Civic Action Com., 1992—; mem., contbr. World Affairs Coun., 1993—; mem. adv. com. on voter registration and Get Out To Vote, Santa Clara County, co-chair, 1993, 94; mem. Dem. Congl. Campaign Com., 1992—; charter mem. Senate Task Force, 1992—; mem. Dem. Nat. Com.; mem. Calif. State Adv. Coun. Refugee Assistance, 1992—, mem. various coms.; chair Vietnamese-Ams. Com. for Clinton/Gore, No. Calif., 1992; chair Tet Festival, 1988-91; leader Vietnamese Ams. Dukakis' Presdl. Campaign, 1988. Recipient Appreciation cert. Nat. ARC, 1975, Appreciation cert. and letter of commendation Refugee Liaison Office, USAF, 1975, Achievement cert. Dept. Army, 1975, Outstand Svc. to Refugee citation World YMCA, 1975, Peter Casey Asian Am. Leadership award, 1987, Letter of Commendation, Senator Art Torres, 1989, Letter Commendation, Santa Clara County Greater Ave. for Independence/Refugee Employment and Social Svcs. Adminstrn., 1990, Appreciation cert. State Calif. Dept. Social Svcs., 1990, Appreciation Cert. Calif. Dept. Health Svcs., Tobacco Control, 1991, Appreciation cert. U. Berkeley, Extended Foods and Nutrition Edn. Program, 1991, Merit award Coalition of Nationalist Vietnamese Orgns. of So. Calif., 1991, Leadership award No. Calif. Asian Pacific Americans, 1992, Cmty. Svc. award City of San Jose, 1993, Spirit of Democracy award State of Calif., 1994. Democrat. Buddhist. Home and Office: WIN-Visions 4864 Miramar Ave San Jose CA 95129-1004

NGUYEN, SONBINH, chemistry educator; b. Saigon, Vietnam, Dec. 6, 1968; came to U.S., 1984; s. Nhung The and Van Hong (Pham) N. BS in Physics, BS in Chemistry, Pa. State U., 1990; PhD in Chemistry, Calif. Inst. Tech., Pasadena, 1994. NSF post-doctoral fellow Scripps Rsch. Inst., La Jolla, Calif., 1994; asst. prof. chemistry Northwestern U., Evanston, Ill., 1994—. Contbr. articles to profl. jours. Patentee in field. Recipient duPont Achievement award E.I. duPont de Nemours & Co., 1989; DOD-NDSEG fellow, 1991, NSF pre-doctoral fellow, 1990; Pa. State U. scholar, 1986. Mem. Am. Chem. Soc., Nat. Coun. Tchrs. of Math., Soc. of Physics/Am. Inst. of Physics, Phi Beta Kappa, Phi Lambda Upsilon, Sigma Pi Sigma, Nat. Golden Key Honor Soc. Office: CalTech 127-72 Pasadena CA 91125

NGUYEN, TAI ANH, minister. Supt. Vietnamese Ministry Dist. of the Christian and Missionary Alliance. Office: 1681 W Broadway Anaheim CA 92802-1107

NGUYEN, TAM VAN, artist, photographer; b. Battambang, Cambodia, July 25, 1929; came to U.S., 1975; s. Giao and Ven Thi N.; children: Dung, Son, Sa, Lien. BA in Applied Art, Royal Applied Art Coll., Phnom Penh, 1942. Neo-Impressionist artist pvt. practice; sec. Art and Crafts Assn. of Vietnam, Saigon, 1961-75. Numerous landscapes, portraits, figures, and still-lifes, 1955-94. Home: 8781 Hazard Ave Westminster CA 92683-4681

NGUYEN, TAN DINH, pharmacist; b. Saigon, Vietnam, June 3, 1956; came to U.S. 1974; s. Soan Van and Hieu Thi (Luu) N. BA in Chemistry with honors, San Francisco State U., 1980, BS in Biochemistry with honors, 1980; PharmD, U. Calif., San Francisco, 1985. Lic. in pharmacy, Calif. Rsch. asst. San Francisco State U., 1979-80; pharmacy intern U. Calif., San Francisco, 1984-85; staff pharmacist Walgreens Drug Co., Oakland, Calif., 1986-90; pharmacy mgr. Walgreens Drug Co., San Francisco, 1990—; adj. prof. pharmacy practice U. of Pacific, Stockton, Calif., 1991—. Roman Catholic. Home: 1488 Portola Dr San Francisco CA 94127-1409

NGUYEN, THANG DINH (MANNY NGUYEN), chemist; b. Cantho, Vietnam, May 30, 1962; came to U.S., 1975; s. Tuan Dinh and Chan Le (Mong) N.; m. Rose (Hoa) Thi Nguyen, Dec. 2, 1989; 1 child, Alan Michael Nguyen. BA in Biochemistry, San Jose State U., 1987. Lab tech. Kaiser Aluminum, San Jose, 1987-88, I-Chem Rsch., Hayward, Calif., 1988; chemist Inchcape Testing Svcs., San Jose, 1988-92, lab supr., 1992—. Office: 1961 Concourse Dr Ste E San Jose CA 95131-1729

NGUYEN, THINH VAN, physician; b. Vietnam, Apr. 16, 1948; came to U.S., 1971; s. Thao Van and Phuong Thi (Tran) N.; m. Phi Thi Ho, Jan. 2, 1973; children: Anh-Quan, Andrew. BS, U. Saigon, 1970; MS, U. Mo., 1973; MD, U. Tex., 1982. Diplomate Am. Bd. Internal Medicine, Am. Acad. Pain Mgmt., Fed. Lic. Examination. Rsch. asst. U. Tex. Med. Sch., Dallas, 1974-78; intern U. Tex. Med. Br., Galveston, 1982-83, resident, 1983-85; internist Family Health Plan, Inc., Long Beach, Calif., 1985-88, internist, area chief, 1988-89; pvt. practice San Jose, Calif., 1990—; chmn. interdisciplinary com. Charter Cmty. Hosp., Hawaiian Gardens, Calif., 1988-89, San Jose Med. Ctr., 1993—. Mem. ACP, AMA, Am. Acad. Pain Mgmt., Calif. Assn. Med. Dirs. (bd. dirs. 1988-92). Office: 2470 Alvin Ave Ste 5 San Jose CA 95121-1664

NGUYEN, THOMAS, computer executive; b. 1958; came to U.S., 1983; Grad., U. Calif., Berkeley, 1987. With electronics and mech. field Vietnam, 1975-83; with IBM, San Jose, Calif., 1983-87, U. Calif., 1983-87, Olivetti, Cupertino, Calif., 1988, Advanced Integrated Rsch., 1989—. Office: Advanced Integrated Research 2188 Del Franco St San Jose CA 95131-1575*

NGUYEN, TIEN MANH, communications systems engineer; b. Saigon, Vietnam, Apr. 5, 1957; came to the U.S., 1975; s. Hung The and Bi Thi (Luu) N.; m. Thu Hang Thi, Dec. 28 1986. BS in Engring., Calif. State U., Fullerton, 1979, MS in Engring., 1980; MSEE, U. Calif., San Diego, 1982; PhD in Elec. Engring., Columbia Pacific U., 1986; MA in Math., Claremont Grad. Sch., 1993, PhD in Engring. Math., 1995. Cert. EMC engr., Mfg. tech. Teaching asst. U. Calif., San Diego, 1982-83; chief automated mfg. dept. ITT Ednl. Svcs., West Covina, Calif., 1983-85; mem. tech. staff Jet Propulsion Lab., Pasadena, Calif., 1985—; prin. tech. advisor Internat. Consultative Com. for Space Data Systems, Pasadena, 1985-90, 93—. Editor: Proceedings of CCSDS RF & Modulation, 1989, 94; contbr. more than 35 articles to profl. jours. Grad. rep. EECS dept. U. Calif., San Diego, 1982-83; NASA del. to internat. CCSDS, 1986—. San Deigo fellow, 1980-82, Long Beach Found. scholar Calif. State U.; recipient Bendix Mgmt. Club award, 1987, NASA Honor award, 1988, over 20 NASA monetary awards, 1989—, 2 NASA honor awards, 1993. Mem. IEEE (sr., vice chmn. 1987-94, session chmn. internat. symposium on EMC 1986, internat. conf. on telecomm. 1995, session organizer, award 1986, 95), AIAA (sr.), AAAS, Soc. Mfg. Engrs., Am. Math. Soc., Armed Forces Commn. and Electronics Assn., Vietnamese-Am. Sci. & Profl. Engring. Soc., N.Y. Acad. Scis., U.S. Naval Inst., Phi Kappa Phi, Sigma Xi. Republican. Buddhist. Home: 1501 W Maxzim Ave Fullerton CA 92633-4511 Office: Jet Propulsion Lab 4800 Oak Grove Dr Pasadena CA 91109-8001

NGUYEN, TOAN DINH, gastroenterologist; b. Hanoi, Vietnam, Aug. 19, 1953; came to U.S. 1971; s. Hoang Dinh and Viet-Kham (Ton-Nu) N.; m. Anh Tran, July 20, 1985; children: Eric, Grant. BA, U. Chgo., 1974, MD, 1978. Diplomate Am. Bd. Gastroenterology. Med. intern U. Chgo. Hosps. & Clinics, 1978-79, resident in medicine, 1979-81; gastroenterology fellow Stanford Med. Ctr., 1981-87, clin. instr., 1984-87; asst. prof. gastroenterology Duke U., Durham, N.C., 1987-93; staff physician Durham VA Med. Ctr., Durham, N.C., 1987-93; assoc. prof. medicine U. Wash., Seattle, 1994—; staff physician Seattle VA Med. Ctr., 1994—. Contbr. articles to profl. jours. including Biochemistry, Jour. Biol. Chemistry, Am. Jour. Physiology, Toxicology and Applied Pharmacology, Jour. Membrane Biology, Gastroenterology, Biochem. Pharmacology. Jour. Nutrition. NIH grantee, 1982-84, 84-87, 88-93. Fellow ACP; mem. AAAS, AFCR, ASBMB; mem. Am. Gastroenterology Assn., Gastroenterology Rsch. Group, Phi Beta Kappa. Office: Seattle VA Med Ctr 1660 S Columbian Way Seattle WA 98108-1532

NGUYEN TRUNG, B., plastic surgeon; b. Saigon, Vietnam, June 19, 1937; s. Buu and Thinh (Ngo) Nguyen; m. Hang B. Nguyen, June, 1966; children: Alison, Amy, Johnny, Andy. MD, Saigon Med. Sch., 1966. Chief resident plastic surgery N.Y. Cornell Hosp., N.Y.C., 1982-83; attending plastic surgeon Kaiser Bellflower (Calif.) Med. Ctr., 1983-85, chief plastic surgery dept., 1985-95. Capt. South Vietnamese Army, 1966-75. Decorated Valiant medal Vietnamese Army, 1968; recipient N.Y. Hosp. Corp. award, 1980. Mem. Am. Soc. Plastic and Reconstructive Surgery, L.A. Calif. Med. Assn. Office: Bellflower Kaiser Med Ctr 9600 Rosecran Bellflower CA 90706

NIBLEY, ROBERT RICKS, retired lawyer; b. Salt Lake City, Sept. 24, 1913; s. Joel and Teresa (Taylor) N.; m. Lee Allen, Jan. 31, 1945 (dec.); children—Jane, Annette. A.B., U. Utah, 1934; J.D., Loyola U., Los Angeles, 1942. Bar: Calif. bar 1943. Accountant Nat. Parks Airways, Salt Lake City, 1934-37, Western Air Lines, Los Angeles, 1937-40; asst. mgr. market research dept. Lockheed Aircraft Corp., Burbank, Calif., 1940-43; asso. firm Hill, Farrer and Burrill, Los Angeles, 1946-53; partner Hill, Farrer and Burrill, 1953-70, of counsel, 1971-78. Served from ensign to lt. comdr. USNR, 1943-46. Mem. ABA, L.A. Bar Assn., Calif. Club, Phi Delta Phi, Phi Kappa Phi, Phi Delta Theta. Home: 4860 Ambrose Ave Los Angeles CA 90027-1866

NICE, CARTER, conductor, music director; b. Jacksonville, Fla., Apr. 5, 1940; s. Clarence Carter and Elizabeth Jane (Hintermister) N.; m. Jennifer Charlotte Smith, Apr. 4, 1983; children: Danielle, Christian, Olivia. MusB, Eastman Sch. Music, 1962; MusM, Manhattan Sch. Music, 1964. Asst. condr., concert master New Orleans Philharm., 1967-79; condr., music dir.

Sacramento Symphony, 1979-92; music dir., conductor Bear Valley Music Fest., 1985—. Office: 200 P St Apt B36 Sacramento CA 95814-6231

NICE, JAMES WILLIAM, electronics educator; b. La Grande, Oreg., Apr. 10, 1948; s. Glenn Orvin and Jeana Mae (Sullivan) N.; m. Claudia Jo Salzer, Oct. 21, 1967; children: Laura Lee, Chandra Rae. AS in Bus. Mgmt., Mt. Hood Community Coll., Gresham, Oreg., 1979; student, Thomas A. Edison State Coll., 1988—; AS in Electronics Engring. Tech., ITT Tech. Inst., Portland, 1988-90; BS in Mgmt. & Comm., Concordia Coll., Portland, 1993. Enlisted USN, 1966, electronics technician, 1988-92, resigned, 1976; field service technician AM Corp., Portland, Oreg., 1976-78; sci. inst. technician State of Oreg., Portland, 1978-81; quality control mgr. Landa Inc., Portland, 1981-83; master electronics instr. ITT Tech. Inst., Portland, 1983—. Mem. Land Use Planning Bd., Gresham, 1977-78; chmn. budget com. Rockwood Water Dist., Gresham, 1982-86; capt. Portland Police Bur. Res. Mounted Patrol. Mem. IEEE (assoc.), Internat. Soc. Cert. Electronic Technicians, Nat. Assn. Radio and Telecommunications Engrs. Democrat. Mormon. Home: 940 NE Littlepage Rd Corbett OR 97019-9736 Office: ITT Tech Inst 6035 NE 78th Ct Portland OR 97218-2854

NICHOLAW, GEORGE, communications executive; b. Salinas, Calif., Nov. 17, 1927; s. Costas and Anna G. (Melissa) N.; m. Betty Baron. B in Fgn. Trade, Am. Grad. Sch Internat. Mgmt.; BS, U. Calif., Berkeley. Program dir. Sta. KDON, Salinas, 1953-55; asst. dir. promotion, publicity Sta. KNXT-TV, Los Angeles, 1955-63; dir. info. services and community relations Sta. WBBM-TV, Chgo., 1963-66; dir. community services Sta. WCBS-TV, N.Y.C., 1966-67; v.p. CBS radio div., gen. mgr. Sta. KNX, Los Angeles, 1967—. Commr. Los Angeles Energy Commn.; active Communications Task Force Greater Los Angeles Urban Coalition., Calif. Air Pollution Emergency Traffic Control Com. Served with U.S. Army. Recipient Abe Lincoln award, Peabody award, Ohio State award, Alfred I DuPont award, Columbia U. Mem. Nat. Assn. Broadcasters, Calif. Broadcasters Assn. (dir. Los Angeles chpt.), Hollywood Radio and TV Soc. (dir. Los Angeles chpt.), Arbitron Radio Adv. Council (past chmn.), Calif. Inst. Cancer Research (bd. dirs.), Permanent Charities Com. Entertainment Industries (bd. dirs.). Office: Sta KNX-AM 6121 W Sunset Blvd Los Angeles CA 90028-6455*

NICHOLS, ALAN HAMMOND, lawyer; b. Palo Alto, Calif., Feb. 14, 1940; s. John Ralph and Shirley Weston (Charles) N.; children: Alan Hammond, Sharon Elizabeth, Shan Darwin. BA, Stanford U., 1951, JD, 1955; DS (hon.), Calif. Coll. Podiatric Medicine, 1980. Bar: Calif. 1955, U.S. Dist. Ct. (no. dist.) Calif. 1955, U.S. Dist. Ct. (cen. dist.) Calif. 1969, U.S. Dist. Ct. (ea. dist.) Calif. 1978, U.S. Dist. Ct. Ariz. 1978, U.S. Supreme Ct. 1978, U.S. Dist. Ct. Minn. 1979, U.S. Dist. Ct. (so. dist.) Calif. 1980, U.S. Tax Ct. 1981. Assoc. Lillick, Geary, Wheat, Adams & Charles, San Francisco, 1955-61; pres. Nichols & Rogers, San Francisco, 1961-74; pres. Nichols Law Corp., San Francisco, 1974-83, 1992—; pres. Nichols, Doi, Rapaport & Chan, San Francisco, 1987-92; prof. forensic medicine Calif. Coll. Podiatric Medicine, 1975-77; bd. dirs. and sec. Assocs. of Stanford, Calif. Mem. San Francisco Library Commn., 1962-65; v.p. San Francisco Council Chs., 1965-68; pres. sch. bd. San Francisco Unified Sch. Dist., 1967-71; exec. com. Council Great City Schs. of U.S.; del. Calif. Sch. Bd. Assn. Assembly; mem. Civil Grand Jury, San Francisco, 1975-76; pres. Young Republicans San Francisco, 1957, Calif., 1959; mem. Rep. Central Com., San Francisco, 1961-93, pres., 1976; trustee City Coll. San Francisco, 1966-71, pres. bd. trustees, 1970-71; trustee Calif. Coll. Podiatric Medicine, 1973-85, Cathedral Sch., 1973-74, vice-chmn., 1983-90; bd. govs. Webb Sch., 1992—, Claremont, Calif., 1993—; past trustee Prescott Center Coll.; Rep. candidate Calif. 5th congl. dist. U.S. Congress. Served to lt. AUS, 1951-54. Decorated Commendation medal with 4 clusters; named Young Man of Yr. San Francisco newspapers, 1961. Mem. ABA (local govt. sect., real property probate and trust law sect., urban, state and local govt. sect., corp., banking and bus. law sect.), San Francisco Bar Assn., State Bar Assn. Calif. (estate planning, trust and probate law sect.), Am. Arbitration Assn. (arbitrator), Phi Beta Kappa, Phi Delta Phi, Sigma Nu, Bohemian Club. Author: (with Harold E. Rogers, Jr.) Water for California, 2 vols., 1967, To Climb a Sacred Mountain, 1979, (poetry) San Francisco Commuter, 1970; (play) Siddartha, 1977, A Gift from the Master, 1978, San Quentin-Inside the Walls, 1991, Journey-A Bicycle Odyssey Through Central Asia, 1992; contbr. articles to profl. jours. including Stanford Law Rev., UCLA Law Rev., Am. Bar Rev. Office: Nichols Profl Law Corp Atkinson-Nichols Landmark Bldg 35 Aladdin Ter San Francisco CA 94133-2603

NICHOLS, JOHN ROGER, county official; b. Des Moines, Dec. 11, 1949; s. John Woodrow and Mary Ann (West) N.; m. Terry Lynn Huffman (div. June 1985); children: Lauren Ashley, John Clarke; m. Terrie Lynne Jacobson, Apr. 17, 1989 (div. Nov. 1994); 1 child, Anthony. BS in Bus. Adminstrn., Drake U., 1974. Project supt. Weitz Corp., Des Moines, 1979-84; project mgr. maj. projects E.G. Bowen Co. Inc., L.A., 1987-92, Hussmann Corp., Sacramento, 1992-93; bldg. insp. comml. constrn. County of Sacramento, Calif., 1994—; bd. dirs. J-T Publs., Sacramento; trustee T's Calif. Trust, Sacramento, 1993—. Author: How to Inspect Homes, 1992; editor: Do it yourself inspections, 1992. Tchr. Cath. Sch., St. John the Evangelist Ch., Carmichael, Calif. Mem. Internat. Coun. Bldg. Ofcls. (profl. mem.), Carpenters Union 1147 (master carpenter), Masons. Republican. Home: 12801 Fair Oaks Blvd Apt 213 Citrus Heights CA 95610-5172

NICHOLS, JUDITH ELLEN, academic administrator; b. N.Y.C., Aug. 20, 1947; d. Harold and Rosalyn (Yanover) Nadler; children: Brian David, Stacey Lynne, Cassandra Beth. BA in English, CCNY, 1969; MBA, N.Y. Inst. Tech., 1983; PhD in Bus. Mgmt., Calif. Coast U., 1992. mem. fin. and devel com. Detroit Area Pre Coll. Engring. Program,1986-87. Pvt. cons. mktg. N.Y. and N.J., 1970-76; dir. mktg. YMCA's Greater N.Y.C., 1976-79; dir. devel. N.Y.C. Coll. Podiatric Medicine, 1979-81; exec. dir. alumni relation N.J. Inst. Tech., Newark, 1981-85; exec. dir. univ. devel. Wayne State U., 1985-87; v.p. for devel. Portland (Oreg.) State U., 1987-88; pvt. fundraising cons., 1988—. Author: By the Numbers: Using Demographics and Psychographics for Business Growth in the 90s, 1990, Changing Demographics: Fund Raising in the 1990s, 1990, Targeted Fund Raising: Defining and Refining Your Development Strategy, 1991, Pinpointing Affluence: Increasing Your Share of Major Down Dollars, 1994, Growing From Good to Great, 1995; editor Trends that Count. Mem. mktg. com. YMCA Greater Detroit, 1986-87, YMCA, Multnomah, Oreg., 1989—. Mem. Nat. Soc. Fund Raising Execs. (cert., long-range plan com. 1986—, bd. dirs. Oreg. chpt., chmn. Philanthropy Day 1988).

NICHOLS, MARK ALLAN, theatre administrator; b. Atlanta, Dec. 20, 1958; s. Allan Douglas Nichols and Gail Whitaker Long. BSBA, SUNY, 1979. Pres., owner Manna Theatrical Prodns. and Devel., N.Y.C., 1987-90; assoc. gen. mgr. Ctr. Theatre Group, L.A., 1990—; analyst First Boston Corp., N.Y.C., 1984-89. Active Gay and Lesbian Alliance Against Defamation. Mem. Theatre Comms. Group (charter), Theatre L.A., Nat. Gay and Lesbian Task Force, Nat. Trust for Hist. Preservation. Office: Center Theatre Group 135 N Grand Ave Los Angeles CA 90012-3013

NICHOLS, MARK EDWARD, engineer; b. Schenectady, N.Y., Sept. 3, 1950; s. John Burton and Betty Jane (Paulsen) N. BS in Engring. Physics, U. Calif., Berkeley, 1972; MS in Sci. and Engring. Mgmt., West Coast U., 1984; postgrad., Ind. Coll. Armed Forces, 1977. Cert. in nat. security mgmt. Inst. and mech. technician Wetzel-Moreau Engring. Co., Inglewood, Calif., 1970-71; sales engr., supr. United Tech. Industries/Turbocooler Divsn., Manhattan Beach, Calif., 1972-73; wind tunnel test engr. Space divsn. Rockwell Internat., Downey, Calif., 1973-76; flight and sys. engr. Space Sys. divsn. Rockwell Internat., Palmdale, Calif., 1976-78; aero. test engr. Space Systems div. Rockwell Internat., Downey, 1980-85, project engr. Payloads/Cargo Integration Aerospace divsn., 1985—; flight test entegration engr. Gen. Dynamics/Convair, San Diego, 1978-80; instr. Aerodynamics and Aeronautics Adv. Career Tng., Downey, 1986—; instrnl. aide, lectr. Discover-E, Downey, 1992—. Columnist, Long Beach Press-Telegram, 1987-90. With USN, 1968-69. With USN, 1968-69. Recipient Achievement award Bank of Am., 1968; Gov.'s scholar, 1968. Mem. ASME, AIAA, Nat. Mgmt. Assn., Am. Legion, Planetary Soc., Moose # 1739, Los Amigos Men's Club. Republican. Presbyterian. Home: 11682 Lakewood Blvd Downey CA 90241-5272 Office: Rockwell/Aerospace-Space Sys Divsn 12214 Lakewood Blvd Downey CA 90242-2655

NICHOLS, MIKE, stage and film director; b. Berlin, Nov. 6, 1931; s. Nicholaievitch and Brigitte (Landauer) Peschowsky; m. Patricia Scott, 1957 (div.); m. Margot Callas, 1974 (div.); m. Annabel (div.); m. Diane Sawyer, Apr. 29, 1988. Student, U. Chgo., 1950-53; student acting, Lee Strasberg. Ptnr. with Elaine May in comedy act; first appeared at Playwrights Theatre Club, Compass Theatre, Chgo.; N.Y. debut An Evening with Mike Nichols and Elaine May, 1960; acted in A Matter of Position, Phila., 1962; dir.: (plays) Barefoot in the Park, 1963 (Tony award), The Knack, 1964, Luv, 1964 (Tony award), The Odd Couple, 1965 (Tony award for best dir.), The Apple Tree, 1966, The Little Foxes, 1967, Plaza Suite, 1968 (Tony award), The Prisoner of 2d Avenue, 1971 (Tony award), Uncle Vanya (co-adapted), 1973, Streamers, 1976, Comedians, 1976, The Gin Game, 1977, Billy Bishop Goes to War, Lunch Hour, 1980, Fools, 1981, The Real Thing, 1984 (Tony award 1984,), Hurlyburly, 1984, Social Security, 1984, Elliot Loves, 1990, Death and the Maiden, 1992; (films) Who's Afraid of Virginia Woolf?, 1966, (Academy award nomination best director 1966), The Graduate, 1967 (Academy award best director 1967), Catch-22, 1970, Carnal Knowledge, 1971, The Day of the Dolphin, 1973, The Fortune, 1975, Gilda Live, 1980, Silkwood, 1983 (Academy award nomination best director 1983), Heartburn, 1986, Biloxi Blues, 1987, Working Girl, 1988 (Academy award nomination best director 1988), Postcards From the Edge, 1990, Regarding Henry, 1991, Wolf, 1994; producer: (musical) Annie, 1977; performed at N.Y. musical Pres. Johnson's Inaugural Gala, 1965; TV appearances include Today Show. Office: care Mike Ovitz CAA 9830 Wilshire Blvd Beverly Hills CA 90212-1804

NICHOLS, PATRICIA CAUSEY, linguist; b. Conway, S.C., Dec. 29, 1938; d. Lonnie Dornie and Mildred Louise (Mitchell) C.; m. Frank Howard Nichols Jr., Nov. 22, 1959; children: Keith Veric, Marnia. BA in English, Winthrop Coll., 1958; MA in English, U. Minn., 1966; MA in Linguistics, San Jose State U., 1972; PhD in Linguistics, Stanford U., 1976. Cert. tchr., Calif. Tchr. Hampton (Va.) City Schs., 1958-60; instr. Ohlone Coll., Fremont, Calif., 1969-70, West Valley Coll., Campbell, Calif., 1970-72; from asst. prof. to prof. San Jose (Calif.) State U., 1985—; vis. asst. prof. U. S.C., Columbia, 1980-81. Co-editor: San José Studies: By and About Chicanos y Chicanas, 1993; contbr. articles to profl. jours. Woodrow Wilson Dissertation fellow, 1974-75, Rockefeller fellow, 1992-93. Democrat. Home: 1430 Westmont Ave Campbell CA 95008-5905 Office: San Jose State Univ LLD Dept San Jose CA 95192-0093

NICHOLS, ROBERT E(DMUND), editor, writer, journalist; b. Daytona Beach, Fla., Feb. 14, 1925; s. Joe D. and Edna A. (Casper) N.; m. Diana R. Grosso; children by previous marriage: Craig S., Kim S., Robin K. Student, San Diego State Coll., 1942-43, St. John's Coll., 1944-45, George Washington U., 1948-49. Reporter San Diego Union, 1942-44; corr. Washington bur. N.Y. Herald Tribune, 1945-48, CBS, 1948-51, Time, Inc., 1951-61; contbg. editor Time, asst. edn. dir. Life mag., N.Y.C., 1951-52; corr. representing Time, Life, Fortune, Sports Illus. mags., San Diego area, 1952-61; Sunday editor San Diego Union, 1952-61; fin. editor Los Angeles Times, 1961-68, mem. editorial bd., 1965-68; spl. asst. to bd. govs. Fed. Res. System, 1968-70; v.p., dir. various editorial svcs. Bank of Am., 1970-85; prin. Robert E. Nichols Communications, San Francisco, 1985—. Writer, dir. film and radio documentaries. Mem. U.S. Antarctic Expedition, 1946-47. Recipient Loeb Newspaper Spl. Achievement award, 1963, Loeb award disting. fin. reporting, 1964. Fellow Royal Geog. Soc., Explorers Club; mem. Am. Polar Soc., Calif. Scholarship fedn. (hon., life), Soc. Am. Bus. Editors and Writers (hon., life, pres. 1967-68), South Polar Press Club. Home and Office: 38 Ord Ct San Francisco CA 94114-1417

NICHOLS, TOM A., nurse; b. Killeen, Tex., Dec. 2, 1954; s. Elton Allen and Norma Jean (Hawke) N.; 1 child, Andrea. ADN, Lorain County Community Coll., 1980-83. RN, Calif.; cert. mobile intensive care nurse. Staff nurse St. Alexis Hosp., Cleve., 1983-85, Valley Med. Ctr., Fresno, Calif., 1985—, Fresno Cmty. Hosp., 1987—; RNP Genentech, Inc.; RN preceptor Genentech. Mem. Nat. Ski Patrol Sierra Summit, Huntington, Calif. Mem. Emergency Nurses Assn., Am. Heart Assn., ARC, Christian Mens Fellowship, Internat. Assn. Forensic Nurses. Republican. Office: Valley Med Ctr Emergency 445 S Cedar Ave Fresno CA 93702-2907

NICHOLS, VICKI ANNE, financial consultant, librarian; b. Denver, June 10, 1949; d. Glenn Warner and Loretta Irene (Chalender) Adams; B.A., Colo. Coll., 1972; postgrad. U. Denver, 1976-77; m. Robert H. Nichols, Oct. 28, 1972 (div.); children—Christopher Travis, Lindsay Meredith. Treas., controller, dir. Polaris Resources, Inc., Denver, 1972-86; controller InterCap Devel. Corp, 1986-87; treas., controller, dir. Transnat. Cons., Ltd., 1986-91; mgr. collection svcs. Jefferson County (Colo.) Pub. Library, 1986—; dir., owner Nichols Bus. Services. Home: 4305 Brentwood St Wheat Ridge CO 80033-4412 Office: 10500 W 38th Ave Wheat Ridge CO 80033

NICHOLS, WILLIAM FORD, JR., foundation executive, business executive; b. Palo Alto, Calif., July 4, 1934; s. William Ford and Elizabeth (Woodyatt) N.; m. Rosemary Peterson, 1988; children: Deborah, John, Andrew. A.B., Stanford U., 1956, M.B.A., 1958. C.P.A., Calif. With Price Waterhouse, San Francisco, 1958-69, Price Waterhouse & Co., Sydney, Australia, 1966; asst. controller Saga Corp., Menlo Park, Calif., 1969-72; controller Saga Corp., 1972—, asst. treas., 1981-83; assoc. prof. San Jose State U., 1983-88; treas. William and Flora Hewlett Found., Menlo Park, 1985—; Mem. bd. trustees The Investment Fund for Founds., 1991—. Mem. AICPAs, Calif. Soc. CPAs, Inst. Mgmt. Accts. (nat. v.p. 1974-75, dir.), Fin. Execs. Inst. (pres. Santa Clara Valley chpt. 1979-80). Home: 330 August Cir Menlo Park CA 94025-5829

NICKEL, JAMES WESLEY, philosophy educator; b. Shafter, Calif., Mar. 12, 1943; s. W.H. and Elsie (Sawatsky) N.; m. Phyllis Dick, May 23, 1964 (div. 1982); children: Jonathan Aaron, Philip James; m. Regina Celi, Aug. 24, 1984. BA, Tabor Coll., 1964; PhD, U. Kans., 1968. Prof. Wichita (Kans.) State U., 1968-80; vis. prof. Sch. Law U. Calif., Berkeley, 1980-82; dir. Ctr. for Values and Social Policy U. Colo., Boulder, 1982-88; prof. philosophy U. Colo., 1982—, chair dept. philosophy, 1992—; vis. prof. U. Utah, Salt Lake City, 1988. Author: Making Sense of Human Rights, 1987; contbr. numerous articles to scholarly publs. Recipient fellowship, Nat. Endowment Humanities, 1973, Am. Coun. Learned Socs., 1976, Nat. Humanities Ctr., 1978, Rockefeller Found., 1981. Home: 3055 6th St Boulder CO 80304-2505 Office: U Colo Boulder Campus Box 232 Boulder CO 80309

NICKEL, ROSALIE JEAN, reading specialist; b. Hooker, Okla., Oct. 10, 1939; d. Edwin Charles and Esther Elizabeth (Wiens) Ollenburger; m. Ted W. Nickel, June 3, 1960; 1 child, Sandra Jean. BA, Tabor Coll., 1961; MA, Calif. State U., Fresno, 1970. Cert. tchr., Calif. Elem. tchr. Visalia (Calif.) Pub. Schs., 1961-62; overseas tchr. Kodaikanal Internat. Sch., Madras State, India, 1963-65; tchr. Mendota (Calif.) Jr. High Sch., 1966; elem. tchr. Fresno Pub. Schs., 1966-68, Inglewood (Calif.) Pub. Schs., 1968-73; spl. reading tchr. Tulsa Pub. Schs., 1974-81; salesperson, mgr. Compaq, Marion, Kans., 1981-85; gifted student tchr. Wichita (Kans.) Pub. Schs., 1986; reading specialist and resource tchr., 1987—, sch. technology coord., 1989—, dist. K-3 literacy task force, 1995—, dist. lang. arts adoption com. 1995——; evaluator State Textbook Com., Tulsa, 1976, 78; mem. quality rev. team Birney Elem. Sch., Fresno. Newsletter editor Marion County Arts Council, 1981-82. Co-dir. Am. Field Svc., Tulsa, 1980-81; v.p. Women's Federated Clubs Am., Marion, 1985-86; pres. Butler Mennonite Brethern Women's Fellowship, 1989-91. Mem. Internat. Reading Assn., Tulsa Reading Assn., Fresno Area Reading Council. Home: 2821 W Compton Ct Fresno CA 93711-1181 Office: Fresno Unified Schs Tulare And M St Fresno CA 93701

NICKERSON, JOHN HENRY, artist, sculptor, designer; b. Mpsl., May 15, 1939; s. John and Lucile Ruth (Jones) Scott; m. Margie Lynette Hay, Sept. 9, 1962 (div. June 1970); 1 child, Shae Mikell Nickerson Elliott. BA, Mont. State U., 1964; MFA, Alfred (N.Y.) U., 1969. Ceramic designer Pacific Stoneware, Inc., Portland, Oreg., 1964; indsl. design sculptor GM Styling Staff, Warren, Mich., 1965-66; staff designer Shuron-Continental, Div. Textron Corp., Rochester, N.Y., 1967; asst. prof. ceramics and design Colo. State U., Ft. Collins, 1969-70; designer in residence Blenko Glass Co., Inc., Milton, W.Va., 1970-74; assoc. master design, drawing, sculpture, ceramics and glass Georgian Coll. Art and Technol., Barrie, Ont., Can., 1976-77; artist in residence Kanawha County Continuing Edn. Program, Charleston, W.Va., 1976-77; artist Cleve. Inst. Art Summer Sessions, 1989—, pvt. practice, 1979—. Numerous exhbtns. include Corning (N.Y.) Mus., 1979, Woodson Mus. Art, Wausaw, Wis., 1984, C. Corcoran Gallery, Muskegan, Mich., 1988, 89, Cartons, Cans, and Other Containers, Salem (Oreg.) Art Assn., 1989, Glassworks I Joan Robery Gallery, Denver, 1989, Sculptural Glass, Grohe Glass Gallery, Hyannis, Mass., 1990; permanent collections include Corning Mus., Del. Art Mus., Wilmington, Denver Art Mus., Muskegan (Mich.) Mus. Art, Musée des Arts Décortifs, Lausanne, Switzerland. Nat. Endowment for the Arts craftsman's fellow, 1981, creative fellow, 1986; Colo. Gov.;s Awards Commn., 1986. Home: PO Box 457 Sedalia CO 80135-0457 Office: Nickerson Glassworks 7327 Reynolds Dr Sedalia CO 80135-8805

NICKERSON, MARK, food products executive; b. 1946. With Maggio-Tostado, Inc., Bakersfield, Calif., 1972-75, Sun World, Inc. (formerly Maggio-Tostado Inc.), Bakersfield, 1975-92; ptnr. Sun & Sands Enterprises, Coachella, Calif., 1986—. Office: Sun & Sands Enterprises 86705 Avenue 54 Ste A Coachella CA 92236-3811*

NICKSON, CHRISTOPHER HOWARD, music journalist; b. Leeds, Yorkshire, Eng., July 9, 1954; came to U.S., 1976; s. Raymond Ewart and Jocelyn Betty (Townend) N.; m. Julie Marlene Bedore, May 24, 1974 (div. Feb. 1984); m. Linda Robin Hornberg, Mar. 12, 1993. Student, St. Matthew's Sch., Eng., Roundhay Sch. Leeds C.B.C.E., Birmingham, Eng., 1959-73. Author: Mariah Carey-Her Story, 1995; contbr. articles to profl. jours. Home: 3700 25th Pl W Apt 102 Seattle WA 98199-2026

NICOL, NOREEN HEER, dermatology nurse practitioner, educator; b. Jamestown, N.D., July 16, 1955; d. Clifford Howard and Lois Ann (Smith) Heer; m. Robert Bruce Nicol, June 18, 1983; children: Brent Jeffrey, Erica Marie. BSN, U. No. Colo., 1977; MS in Nursing, U. Utah, 1981. RN, Colo., N.D., Utah; lic. nurse practitioner, Utah; cert. tchr., Colo. Sch. nurse, tchr. health Weld County Sch. Dist. 6, Greeley, Colo., 1977-78; nurse coord. emotionally disturbed summer camp program, charge nurse chem. dependency unit N.D. State Hosp., Jamestown, 1978-79; pediatric clin. specialist, charge nurse U. Utah Med. Ctr., Salt Lake City, 1979-81, dir. pediatric dialysis dept., nurse practitioner, adminstr., intermountain pediatric and adolescent renal disease program, 1981-84; instr. clin. nursing Loretto Heights Coll., Denver, 1984-86; dermatology clin. specialist, nurse practitioner Nat. Jewish Ctr. for Immunology and Respiratory Medicine, Denver, 1986—; clin. instr. Coll. Nursing, U. Utah, 1982-85, assoc. instr. dept. pediatrics Coll. Medicine, 1983-85; mem. adj. faculty Loretto Heights Coll., Denver, 1987-88; clin. sr. instr. U. Colo. Health Sci. Ctr. Sch. Nursing, Denver, 1989—; nurse clinician home intravenous therapy and nutrition Travenol Labs., Inc., Denver, 1984-86; speaker, presenter in field. Contbr. articles to profl. jours., chpts. to books. Mem. Weld County Drug and Alcohol Coun., 1977-78, health adv. com. Douglas County (Colo.) Schs., 1993—. Nursing scholar U. No. Colo., 1975-77. Mem. Nat. Fedn. for Splty. Nursing Orgns. (edn. com. 1991, health policy com. 1991-92, treas. 1992-93, pres. 1993-94), Colo. Nurses Assn. (Garnet Milhone scholar 1976-77), Dermatology Nurses Assn. (edn. com. 1987, liaison for Colo. 1987-88, nat. edn. vice chmn. 1988, chmn. nat. conv. 1988, nat. bd. dirs. western region dir. 1989-90, nat. bd. dirs. 1991—, nat. pres. elect, 1991, nat. pres. 1992—, edn. com. core curriculum chmn., 1993—), Am. Acad. Allergy and Innunology, Skin Photorauma Found., Sigma Theta Tau (hosp. liason 1991—). Office: Nat Jewish Ctr Immunology and Respiratory Medicine 1400 Jackson St Denver CO 80206-2761

NICOL, ROBERT DUNCAN, architect; b. La Jolla, Calif., Sept. 16, 1936; s. Duncan and Catherine (Muffly) N.; m. Susann Kay Larson; 1 child, Jennifer E. AA, Principia Coll., 1967; BArch, U. Calif., Berkeley, 1961. Registered arch., Ariz., Calif., Mont., Wash. Designer Kawneer Mfg. Co., Richmond, Calif., 1961-62, Claude Oakland, San Francisco, 1962-64; project arch. David T. Johnson, Oakland, Calif., 1964-68; pvt. practice Oakland, Calif., 1968—. Mem. bd. appeals City of Alameda, 1971-73, vice chair planning commn., 1973-77, founder, chair, vice chair design rev. bd., 1974-80, founder, chair, vice chair hist. adv. bd., 1976—, co-founder, chair, vice chair mayor's com. for handicapped, 1980-86;. Recipient Design award Am. Registered Archs., 1969, Harper Plz. Design award Calif. Bldg. Officials Assn., 1985. Fellow AIA; mem. Soc. Am. Registered Archs., Nat. Coun. Archtl. Registration Bds. (sr.), Alexander Graham Bell Assn. for Deaf (lectr.), Oral Hearing Impaired Sec., San Leandro Hist. Railway Soc. (founder, charter mem., chair, vice-chair), Alameda Jr. C. of C. (project dir. 1969), Alameda Victorian Preservation Soc. Republican. Office: 455 17th St Oakland CA 94612-2101

NICOLAI, EUGENE RALPH, public relations consultant, editor, writer; b. Renton, Wash., June 26, 1911; s. Eugene George and Josephine (Heidinger) N.; student U. Wash., 1929, Whitman Coll., 1929-30; B.A., U. Wash., 1934; postgrad. Am. U., 1942; M.A., George Washington U., 1965; m. Helen Margaret Manogue, June 5, 1935; 1 son, Paul Eugene. Editor, U. Wash. Daily, Seattle, 1934; asst. city editor, writer, nat. def. editor Seattle Times, 1934-41; writer Sta. KJR, Seattle, 1937-39; writer, editor, safety edn. officer Bur. Mines, Washington, 1941-45; news dir. Grand Coulee Dam and Columbia Basin Project, Washington, 1945-50; regional info. dir. Bur. Mines, Denver and Pitts., 1950-55, asst. chief mineral reports, Washington, 1955-61, news dir. office of oil and gas, 1956-57; sr. info. officer, later sr. public info. officer Office Sec. Interior, Washington, 1961-71, staff White House Nat. Conf. on Natural Beauty, spl. detail to White House, 1971, ret.; now public relations cons., tech. editor, writer. Formerly safety policy adviser Interior Dept.; com. mem. Internat. Cooperation Year, State Dept., 1971. With George Washington U. Alumni Found.; founder, mng. dir. Josephine Nature Preserve; pres. Media Assocs. Bd. dirs. Wash. State Council on Alcoholism; adviser Pierce Transit Authority, Pierce County Growth Mgmt., Pierce County Ethics Commn. Named Disting. Alumnus, recipient Penrose award, both Whitman Coll., 1979. Mem. Nature Conservancy, Wash. Environ. Council, Nat. Audubon Soc. (Am. Belgian Tervuren dist. rep.), Crook County (Oreg.) Hist. Soc., Washington State Hist. Soc., Emerald Shores Assn, Sigma Delta Chi, Pi Kappa Alpha. Presbyn. Clubs: George Washington U., Purdy (pres.). Lodge: Masons. Author: The Middle East Emergency Committee; editor: Fed. Conservation Yearbooks. Home: 9809 N Seminole Dr Spokane WA 99208-8608

NICOLAÏ, JUDITHE, international business trade executive; b. Lawrence, Mass., Dec. 15, 1945; d. Victor and Evelyn (Otash) Abisalih. Student in photography, L.A. City Coll., 1967, UCLA, 1971; AA in Fgn. Langs., Coll. of Marin, 1983; hon. degree, Culinary Inst., San Francisco, 1981. Photographer Scott Paper Co., N.Y.C., 1975; owner, operator restaurant The Raincheck Room, West Hollywood, Calif., 1976; prin., pres., chief exec. officer, photographer fashion Photographie sub. Nicolaï Internat. Svcs., Nice, France, 1977—; prin., pres., chief exec. officer, instr. catering and cooking Back to Basics sub. Nicolaï Internat. Svcs., San Francisco, 1980—; chief photographer exhibit and trade show, chief of staff food div. Agri-Bus. U.S.A., Moscow and Washington, 1983; head transp. U.S. Summer Olympics, L.A., 1984, interpreter for Spanish, French, Portuguese, and Italian, 1985; prin., pres., chief exec. officer, interpreter Intertrans subs. (Nicolaï Internat. Svcs.), San Francisco, 1985—; founder, pres. Nicolaï Internat. Svcs., San Francisco, 1985—; pres., CEO Cyprus Personal Care Products, 1994—. Contbr. column on food and nutrition to jour., 1983-84. Mem. Alpha Gamma Sigma. Office: Nicolai Internat Svcs 1686 Union St Ste 203 San Francisco CA 94123-4509 Mailing Address: 2269 Chestnut St Ste 237 San Francisco CA 94123-2607

NICOLAS, J. BERNARD, home video distribution executive; b. Port-au-Prince, Haiti, Nov. 7, 1950; came to U.S., 1962; s. Roger Gerard and Anna (Etheart) N. BA, UCLA, 1974, MFA, 1982. Film prodr. Zimbabwe Prodn. Svcs., Harare, 1982-83; gen. mgr. Internat. Home Cinema, L.A., 1984-85; asst. dir. creative affairs Motown Prodns., N.Y.C., 1987; founder, CEO Inter Image Video, L.A., 1991—.

NICOLAU, ALEXANDRU, educator; b. Bucharest, Romania, June 7, 1957; came to U.S., 1976; s. Frederick and Silvia (Pach) N.; m. Anca Arivei, Oct. 22, 1978; children: Danielle, Rebecca. BA, Brandeis U., 1980; MA, Yale U., 1982, PhD, 1984. Asst. prof. Cornell U., Ithaca, N.Y., 1984-88; assoc. prof. U. Calif., Irvine, 1988-92, prof., 1992—. Editor-in-chief Internat. Jour. Parallel Programming, 1993—; editor: Language and Compilers for Parallel

Computing, 1994, Advanced in Languages and Compilers, 1994; contbr. articles to profl. jours. Mem. IEEE, Assn. for Computing Machinery. Office: U Calif Irvine CA 94717

NICOLET, WILLIAM EDWARD, mechanical engineer; b. Bakersfield, Calif., Mar. 21, 1937; s. Edward Mark and Louanna (Buckley) N.; m. Vivian Irene Wik, Apr. 28, 1962; children: Bradley S., Lori D., Jill P. BS, U. Calif., Berkeley, 1958; MS, UCLA. Sr. scientist Lockheed Palo Alto (Calif.) Rsch. Lab., 1961-67; mgr. gas dynamics sect., aerothermochemistry, technology Acurex Corp., Mountain View, Calif., 1967-79; CEO Thermal Scis., Inc., Mountain View, 1979—. Contbr. articles to profl. jours.; author conf. procs. Mem. AIAA. Home: 955 Edgecliff Way Redwood City CA 94061-1160

NICOLETTI, WILLIAM WALTER, pharmaceutical company executive; b. Phila., Dec. 30, 1952; s. Louis Joseph and Jessie B. (Geddes) N.; m. Patricia Ellen Berry; 1 child, Jessica. BA in Sci., Temple U., 1974, BS in Pharmacy, 1977, MBA in Mktg., 1984. Registered pharmacist Pa., Nev. Dir. pharmacy St. Joseph's Villa, Flourtown, Pa., 1980-83, Booth Maternity Ctr., Salvation Army, Phila., 1980-83; nat sales mgr. Boiron Labs., Norwood, Pa., 1983-87; pres. DoLisos Homeopathy, Las Vegas, 1987—. Mem. Am. Assn. Homeopathic Pharmacists (treas. 1993), Am. Pharm. Assn., Nev. Pharm. Assn., Homeopathic Pharmacopeia of U.S. Office: DoLisos America 3014 Rigel Ave Las Vegas NV 89102-0709

NICOSIA, GERALD MARTIN, author, freelance writer; b. Berwyn, Ill., Nov. 18, 1949; s. Peter and Sylvia Anna (Fremer) N.; m. Marcia Selene Vincent, Oct. 16, 1989 (div. Jan. 15, 1992; m. Ellen Louise Wilson, July 5, 1992. BA, U. Ill., Chgo., 1971, MA, 1973. Cert. H.S. tchr., Ill. Tchr. Cook County high schs., Chgo., Ill., 1971-77; freelance writer, 1978—; prof. nonfiction writing U. Ill., Chgo., 1986-87; guest lectr. Naropa Inst., U.Wis., New Coll. Calif., U. Wash., Columbia Coll., others, 1983—; extension lectr. UCLA, 1991-92; advisor (movie) Kerouac, San Francisco, 1983-84; playwright in residence, advisor Am. Blues Theatre, Chgo., 1986-87; creator Vietnam Peach Archive, Santa Cruz, Calif., 1993; advisor, organizer Cafe Arts Week, San Francisco; organizer Jan Kerouac Benefits, San Francisco, 1995. Author: Memory Babe: A Critical Biography of Jack Kerouac (disting. young writer award Nat. Soc. Arts and Letters 1978), 1983, Bughouse Blues, 1977, Lunatics, Lovers, Poets, Vets and Bargirls, 1990; playwright: Jack in Ghost-town, 1986. Mem. PEN (bd. dirs. midwest 1986-88, west 1991—), Authors Guild. Home and Office: 11 Palm Ave Corte Madera CA 94925-1424

NIDEFFER, ROBERT FOSTER, artist, educator; b. Ventura, Calif., Feb. 3, 1964; s. Robert Morse Nideffer and Elvira (Daunhauer) Barthelemy. BA in Cultural Anthropology, U. Calif., Santa Barbara, 1988, MA in Sociology, 1990, PhD in Sociology, 1994, postgrad. Rsch. asst., tchg. asst. U. Calif., Santa Barbara, 1988-94, tchg. assoc., instr. sociology, 1991-95; cons. Social Sci. Computing Facility, U. Calif., Santa Barbara, 1992-95. Contbr. articles to profl. jours. Organizer, presider Siggraph 93, L.A., 1993, Virtual Incs., Villanova, Pa., 1995, Social Theory, Politics and the Arts, U. Calif., Santa Barbara, 1995. Grantee Regents of U. Calif., 1992—, 94, U. Calif., Santa Barbara, 1993, 94; Calif. State U. grad. fellow, 1993—, 94. Mem. Am. Sociol. Assn., Assn. for Computing Machinery, Pacific Sociol. Assn. Office: U Calif Art Studio Santa Barbara CA 93106-9430

NIEBUR, ERNST DIETRICH, computational neuroscientist; b. Lipperode, West Germany, Apr. 7, 1955; came to U.S., 1989; s. Ernst and Helene (Brand) N.; m. Dagmar Kryn, July 4, 1986. MS, U. Dortmund, Germany, 1982; PhD, U. Lausanne, Switzerland, 1988. Asst. diplomé U. Lausanne, 1983-88, premier asst., 1988-89; rsch. fellow Calif. Inst. Tech., Pasadena, 1989-92, sr. rsch. fellow, 1992—. With German Navy, 1974-76. Recipient Seymour Cray award Cray Rsch., Switzerland, 1989. Mem. AAAS, Soc. Neurosci., Internat. Neural Network Soc. Office: Calif Inst Tech Mail Stop 139-74 Pasadena CA 91125

NIEDERAUER, GEORGE H., bishop; b. Los Angeles, CA, June 14, 1936; s. George and Elaine N. B.A. Philosophy, St. John's Seminary, Camarillo, CA, 1959; B.A. Sacred Theology, Catholic U., Washington, DC, 1962; M.A. English Lit., Loyola U., Los Angeles, CA, 1962; Ph.D. English Lit., USC, 1966. ordained priest April 30, 1962; named prelate of honor (monsignor) 1984; named bishop of Diocese of Salt Lake City, Nov. 3, 1994. Asst. pastor Our Lady of the Assumption Parish, Claremont, CA, 1962-63; priest in residence Holy Name of Jesus Parish, Los Angeles, CA, 1963-65; instr. English Lit. St. John's Seminary Coll., Camarillo, CA, 1965-79; instr. of English Lit. Mt. St. Mary's Coll., Los Angeles, CA, 1967-74; English Dept. chmn. St. John's Seminary Coll., Camarillo, CA, 1968-77; spiritual dir. St. John's Seminary Coll., 1972-79; part-time instr. of Spiritual Theology St. John's Seminary Theologate, 1976-79, full-time instr. of Spiritual Theology, 1979-87; part-time instr. of English Lit. St. John's Seminary Coll., 1979-92; rector St. John's Seminary, 1987-92, spiritual dir., 1979—; co-dir. Cardinal Manning House of Prayer for Priests, Los Angeles, CA, 1992—; mem. Nat. Fedn. of Spiritual Dirs. (pres. 1975-77); mem. Alpha Sigma Nu (Jesuit Honor Soc. - LMU Chapter); pres. Western Assn. of Spiritual Dirs., 1973-75; mem. bd. of the Comm. of Priests' Retreat, Archdiocese of Los Angeles; mem. select comm. for the revision of the U.S. Catholic Conf. "Program for Priestly Formation" 3rd edition; mem. Vatican Visitation Team for Theologates; speaker World Vision Internat, Fuller Theological Seminary, Calif. Lutheran Coll.; mem. Camarillo Ministerial Assn. Office: Chancery Office 27 C St Salt Lake City UT 84103*

NIEDZIELSKI, HENRI ZYGMUNT, French and English language educator; b. Troyes, France, Mar. 30, 1931; came to U.S., 1956, naturalized, 1963; s. Zygmunt and Anna (Pelik) N.; children: Henri Zygmunt, Daniel Domenic, Robert Nicholas, Anna-Pia Irene. B.A., U. Conn., 1959, M.A., 1963, Ph.D., 1964. Instr. U. Mass., 1962-64, asst. prof., 1965-66; free-lance interpreter, 1960—; asst. prof. U. Laval, Quebec, Can., 1964-65; assoc. prof. U. Hawaii, 1966-72, prof., 1972-90, chmn. div. French, 1968-70, prof. emeritus; linguistic specialist NDEA, Edn. Profl. Devel. Act, 1963-69; Fulbright lectr. linguistics and TESL Krakow, Poland, 1972-74, Bujumbura, Burundi, 1980-81, Poznan, Poland, 1990-92; guest prof. Avignon, France, 1983-84, Bonn, Fed. Republic Germany, 1986-87; Disting. fellow Auckland U., New Zealand, 1989. Author: Le Roman de Helcanus, 1966, Basic French: A Programmed Course, 1968, Handbook of French Structure; A Systematic Review, 1968, Intermediate French: An Individualized Course, 1972, The Silent Language of France, 1975, French Sound Visuals, 1976; Films on Polish Body Language, 1989; editor: Language and Literature in Hawaii, 1968-72, Jean Misrahi Memorial Volume: Studies in Medieval Languages and Literature, 1977, Studies on the Seven Sages of Rome, 1978; assoc. editor: The Phonetician, 1994—. Pres. Family Counseling Center Hawaii, 1968-70; chmn. bd. Family Edn. Centers Hawaii, 1969-72. Served with French Armored Cav., 1951-53. Mem. MLA, Am. Translators Assn., Am. Assn. Tchrs. French (pres. Hawaii chpt. 1981-83), Am. Coun. Tchg. Fgn. Langs. (dir. 1970-72), Internat. Sociol. Assn., Hawaii Assn. Lang. Tchrs. (pres. 1968-69), Chopin Soc. Hawaii (dir. 1990—), Alliance Française Hawaii (pres. 1978-80), Hawaii Assn. Translators (founding pres.s 1982—), Hawaii Second Lang. Articulation Com. (chmn. 1986-89), Rotary, Elks, Phi Beta Kappa, Pi Delta Phi, Phi Kappa Phi, Sigma Delta Pi.

NIELSEN, DAVID EDWARD, history and physical education educator; b. Pasadena, Calif., Apr. 22, 1946; s. David Stjerne and Ruth (Norvell) N.; m. Faye Ann Brough, June 4, 1970; children: David, Kirsten, Kelli, Chris. BA, Brigham Young U., 1971; MA, Calif. State U., L.A., 1975. Cert. secondary, elem. edn., adminstrn. Tchr. secondary edn. Brigham Young U., Provo, Utah, 1970-72; tchr. history San Gabriel H.S., Alhambra, Calif., 1973; tchr. history and phys. edn. Repetto Sch., Monterey Park, Calif., 1973-84, Mark Keppel H.S., Alhambra, 1984—; athletic dir. LDS Ch., Arcadia, Calif., 1982-84; teen club. advisor Repetto Sch., Monterey Park, 1972-84, student govt. advisor, 1983-84; coach football, softball, basketball, cross country, track Mark Keppel H.S., Alhambra, 1984-95. Sports editor Banyan, 1969-71; author: (syllabus) I Step - BYU, 1971. 2nd v.p. PTA, Monterey Park, 1983-84; pres. Duarte Parks & Recreation Commn., 1989-95. Recipient Hon. Svc. award PTA, Monterey Park, 1976, 80, 82, Cmty. Svc. award Duarte Parks & Recreation Commn., 1993. Mem. NEA, Nat. Coaches Assn., Calif. Tchrs. Assn., Alhambra Tchrs. Assn., Calif. Commrs. Assn., Calif. Hist. Soc., Duarte Hist. Soc., U.S. Olympic Soc. Democrat. Mem. LDS Ch. Home: 87 Cedarwood Ave Duarte CA 91010-3604 Office: Mark Keppel HS 501 E Hellman Alhambra CA 91801

NIELSEN, DONALD RODNEY, soil and water science educator; b. Phoenix, Oct. 10, 1931; s. Irven Roy and Irma Evelyn (Chase) N.; m. Joanne Joyce Locke, Sept. 26, 1953; children: Cynthia, Pamela, Barbara, Wayne, David. BS, U. Ariz., 1953, MS, 1954; PhD, Iowa State U., 1958; DSc (hon.), Ghent (Belgium) State U., 1986. Asst. prof. soil and water sci. U. Calif., Davis, 1958-63, assoc. prof., 1963-68, prof., 1968-94, dir. Kearney Found. of Soil Sci., 1970-75, assoc. dean, 1970-80, dir. Food Protection and Toxicology Ctr., 1974-75, chmn. dept. land, air and water resources, 1975-77, exec. assoc. dean Coll. Agrl. Environ. Scis., 1986-89, chmn. dept. agronomy and range sci., 1989-91; cons. Davis, 1994—; cons. corps. and govtl. agys. Editor Nitrogen in the Environment; co-editor Water Resources Research, 1985-88; mem. editorial bd. Jour. Soil Sci., Soil Sci., Soil and Tillage Rsch.; contbr. articles to profl. jours. NSF fellow, 1965-66. Fellow Am. Geophys. Union (pres. hydrology sect. 1990-92), Soil Sci. Soc. Am. (pres. 1983-84), Am. Soc. Agronomy (pres. 1990-91); mem. Sigma Xi, Phi Kappa Phi, Gamma Sigma Delta, Phi Lambda Upsilon, Alpha Zeta. Democrat. Home and Office: 1004 Pine Ln Davis CA 95616-1728

NIELSEN, GLADE BENJAMIN, mayor, former state senator; b. Hyrum, Utah, Mar. 8, 1926; s. George Benjamin and Katie Ione (Jensen) N.; m. Alpha Fern Strempke, Oct. 15, 1955; children: Karen Lynn, Sharon Kay, Roger Glade, Laura Mae, Lance Eric. BS, Utah State U., 1949. Supt. various constrn. cos., Wyo., Nev., and Calif., 1949-55; pres. Glade Nielsen Builder, Roy, Utah, 1955-86; mem. Utah State Senate, Salt Lake City, 1987-92; may Roy City, 1994—. Pres. Weber Basin Homebuilders Assn., 1967-68, Home Builders Assn. Utah, 1972-73; v.p. Nat. Assn. Home Builders, Washington, 1974-75, mem. exec. com., 1976-79; exec. com. Weber Econ. Devel. Corp.; pres. Roy C. of C., 1980; bd. dirs. Utah Housing Fin. Agy., Salt Lake, 1975-83. With USN, 1944-46, PTO. Recipient Builder of Yr. award Home Builders Assn. Utah, 1988, Svc. award Utah State Com. Consumer Svcs., 1989, Recognition award Utah State Dept. Commerce, 1989, Hon. Commendation award Ogden Air Logistics Command, 1989, Roy City Outstanding Citizen award, 1993. Mem. VFW, Am. Legion, Thunderbird Motor Club Utah (pres.), Elks, Odgen/Weber C. of C. (dir.). Republican.

NIELSEN, WILLIAM FREMMING, federal judge; b. 1934. BA, U. Wash., 1956, LLB, 1963. Law clk. to Hon. Charles L. Powell U.S. Dist. Ct. (ea. dist.) Wash., 1963-64; mem. firm Paine, Hamblen, Coffin, Brooke & Miller, 1964-91; judge U.S. Dist. Ct. (ea. dist.) Wash., Spokane, 1991—. Lt. col. USAFR. Fellow Am. Coll. Trial Lawyers; mem. ABA, Wash. State Bar Assn., Spokane County Bar Assn. (pres. 1981-82), Fed. Bar Assn. (pres. 1988), Spokane County Legal Svcs. Corp. (past pres.), Lawyer Pilot Bar Assn., Assn. Trial Lawyers Am., Wash. State Trial Lawyers Assn., Assn. Def. Trial Attys., Am. Inns of Ct., Charles L. Powell Inn (pres. 1987), The Spokane Club, Rotary, Alpha Delta Phi, Phi Delta Phi. Office: US Dist Ct PO Box 2208 W920 W Riverside Ave Spokane WA 99201-1007*

NIELSON, THEO GILBERT, law enforcement official, university official; b. Roosevelt, Utah, June 29, 1938; s. John Gilbert and Mazie (Alexander) N.; m. Martha Perez, May 22, 1961; children: Lucille Marie, Sherry Lou, Mark Andrew, Rex Alexander, Theo Gilbert Jr., Cristal Ina, Gregory Angus, Mazie Leah, Rosanna Alma. Grad., FBI Nat. Acad., 1970; BA, Ariz. State U., 1975, MS, 1977. Officer Univ. Police, Ariz. State U., Tempe, 1963-67, sgt., 1967-70, lt., 1970-79; chief police Douglas (Ariz.) Police Dept., 1979-82; div. adminstr. Ariz. Criminal Intelligence Systems Agy., Tucson, 1982-84; dir. campus safety and security No. Ariz. U., Flagstaff, 1984-92; chief police Ariz. Dept. Adminstrn., 1993—. Mem. Am. Soc. for Indsl. Security (chmn. No. Ariz. chpt. 1987), Internat. Assn. Chiefs Police, Internat. Assn. Campus Law Enforcement Adminstrs., Ariz. Assn. Campus Law Enforcement (pres. 1989-90). Republican. Mormon. Home: 3335 E Hampton Ave Mesa AZ 85204-6410 Office: Ariz State Capitol Police 1700 W Washington Ave Ste B15 Phoenix AZ 85007

NIEMEIER, CYNTHIA LEE, critical care nurse; b. Phila., Feb. 13, 1952; d. David Baine and Norma June (Beucus) Johnston; m. Rodger Craig Niemeier, June 15, 1975; 1 child, Seth Christian. ADN with honors, Sinclair C.C., 1981. Cert. provider BLS; cert. instr. BCLS, cert. provider ACLS Am. Heart Assn. Staff nurse Miami Valley Hosp., Dayton, Ohio, 1982; staff nurse CCU St. Elizabeth Med. Ctr., Dayton, 1982-84; staff nurse med.-surg. ICU/CCU Humana Hosp., Lexington, Ky., 1984; staff nurse med. ICU VA Hosp., Lexington, 1984-85; staff nurse surg. ICU Good Samaritan Hosp., Lexington, 1985-88; staff nurse PACU Swedish Hosp., Seattle, 1988-90; staff nurse PACU Polyclinic Surgery Ctr., Seattle, 1990—, nurse polyclinic code team, 1994—; staff nurse ICU, CCU CIC Providence Med. Ctr., Seattle, 1992; mem. polyclinic code team, 1994—; instr. BCLS Am. Heart Assn., Ky., 1988-89, ARC, Dayton, 1983-84; ACLS provider Am. Heart Assn., Wash., 1991—. Mem. Caledonian and St. Andrews Soc., Phi Theta Kappa. Republican. Office: Polyclinic Surgery Ctr 1145 Broadway Seattle WA 98122-4201

NIEMI, JANICE, lawyer, former state legislator; b. Flint, Mich., Sept. 18, 1928; d. Richard Jesse and Norma (Bell) Bailey; m. Preston Niemi, Feb. 4, 1953 (divorced 1987); children—Ries, Patricia. BA, U. Wash., 1950, LL.B., 1967; postgrad. U. Mich., 1950-52; cert. Hague Acad. Internat. Law, Netherlands, 1954. Bar: Wash. 1968. Assoc. firm Powell, Livengood, Dunlap & Silverdale, Kirkland, Wash., 1968; staff atty. Legal Service Ctr., Seattle, 1968-70; judge Seattle Dist. Ct., 1971-72, King County Superior Ct., Seattle, 1973-78; acting gen. counsel, dep. gen. counsel SBA, Washington, 1979-81; mem. Wash. State Ho. of Reps., Olympia, 1983-87, chmn. com. on state govt., 1984; mem. Wash. State Senate, 1987-95; sole practice, Seattle, 1981—; mem. White House Fellows Regional Selection Panel, Seattle, 1974-77, chmn., 1976, 77; incorporator Sound Savs. & Loan, Seattle, 1975. Bd. dirs. Allied Arts, Seattle, 1971—, Ctr. Contemporary Art, Seattle, 1981-83, Women's Network, Seattle, 1981-84, Pub. Defender Assn., Seattle, 1982-84; bd. visitors dept. psychology U. Wash., Seattle, 1983-87, bd. visitors dept sociology, 1988— . Named Woman of Yr. in Law, Past Pres.'s Assn., Seattle, 1971; Woman of Yr., Matrix Table, Seattle, 1973, Capitol Hill Bus. and Profl. Women, 1975. Mem. Wash. State Bar Assn., Wash. Women Lawyers. Democrat. Home: PO Box 20516 Seattle WA 98102-1516

NIERENBERG, WILLIAM AARON, oceanography educator; b. N.Y.C., Feb. 13, 1919; s. Joseph and Minnie (Drucker) N.; m. Edith Meyerson, Nov. 21, 1941; children—Victoria Jean (Mrs. Tschinkel), Nicolas Clarke Eugene. Aaron Naumberg scholar, U. Paris, 1937-38; B.S., CCNY, 1939; M.A., Columbia U., 1942, Ph.D. (NRC predoctoral fellow), 1947. Tutor CCNY, 1939-42; sect. leader Manhattan Project, 1942-45; instr. physics Columbia U., 1946-48; asst. prof. physics U. Mich., 1948-50; assoc. prof. physics U. Calif. at Berkeley, 1950-53, prof., 1954-65; dir. Scripps Instn. Oceanography, 1965-86, dir. emeritus, 1986—; vice chancellor for marine scis. U. Calif. at San Diego, 1969-86; dir. Hudson Labs., Columbia, 1953-54; assoc. prof. U. Paris, 1960-62; asst. sec. gen. NATO for sci. affairs, 1960-62; spl. cons. Exec. Office Pres., 1958-60; sr. cons. White House Office Sci. and Tech. Policy, 1976-78. Contbr. papers to profl. jours. E.O. Lawrence lectr. Nat. Acad. Sci., 1958, Miller Found. fellow, 1957-59, Sloan Found. fellow, 1958, Fulbright fellow, 1960-61; mem. U.S. Nat. Commn. UNESCO, 1964-68, Calif. Adv. Com. on Marine and Coastal Resources, 1967-71; adviser-at-large U.S. Dept. State, 1968—; mem. Nat Sci. Bd., 1972-78, 82-88, cons., 1988-89; chmn. USNC/PSA, NRC, 1988—; mem. Nat. Adv. Com. on Oceans and Atmosphere, 1971-77, chmn., 1971-75; mem. sci. and tech. adv. Council Calif. Assembly; mem. adv. council NASA, 1978-83, chmn. adv. council, 1978-82. NATO Sr. Sci. fellow, 1969; Decorated officer Nat. Order of Merit France; recipient Golden Dolphin award Assn. Artistico Letteraria Internazionale, Disting. Pub. Service medal NASA, 1982, Delmer S. Fahrney medal The Franklin Inst., 1987, Compass award Marine Tech. Soc., 1975. Fellow Am. Phys. Soc. (coun., sec. Pacific Coast sect. 1955-64); mem. Am. Acad. Arts and Scis., NAE, NAS (coun. 1973—), Am. Philos. Soc., Sigma Xi (pres. 1981-82, Procter prize 1977). Home: PO Box 927269 San Diego CA 92192-7269 Office: U Calif Scripps Instn Oceanography 0221 La Jolla CA 92093

NIERMEYER, SUSAN, medical educator; b. Indpls., July 24, 1953; d. John H. and Elnora Lorraine (Eissler) N.; m. John Allen Brett, Apr. 25, 1987. BA in Zoology/Chemistry, Butler U., 1975; MD, Vanderbilt U., 1979. Diplomate Am. Bd. Pediatrics. Cert. sub-bd. Nat. Bd. Med. Examiners, Colo. State Bd. Med. Examiners. Neonatologist The Children's Hosp. Neonatal Group, Denver, 1984-85; neonatologist Neonatal Consultants, P.C., Denver, 1985-90; asst. prof. pediatrics, neonatology U. Colo. Sch. Medicine, Denver, 1990—; doctoral program grad. faculty, health and behavioral scis. U. Colo. Denver, 1994—; med. dir. Perinatal Outreach Edn. program, Denver, 1986-94, dir. Neonatal Edn., 1994—; steering com. Nat. Neonatal Resuscitation Program, editor NRP Instr. Update, 1995—. Contbr. book chpt., articles to profl. jours. Com. mem. Colo. Dept. Health Am. Stop Smoking Intervention Study, Denver, 1992—. Grantee WHO, Chiapas, Mexico, 1991-92, Am. Heart Assn., 1994-95, Kempe Rsch. Ctr., Denver, 1989-90. Fellow Am. Acad. Pediatrics (chair Colo. chpt. 1992—, internat. pediatrics com.); mem. Western Soc. for Pediatric Rsch., Am. Anthropol. Assn., Denver Med. Soc. Office: The Childrens Hosp 1056 E 19th Ave Denver CO 80218-1007

NIESLUCHOWSKI, WITOLD S., cardiovascular and thoracic surgeon; b. Warsaw, Poland, Mar. 2, 1944; came to U.S., 1975; s. Stanislaw Leon and Izabela Anna (Swierczynska) N.; m. Bonnie Jean Thomas, Apr. 15, 1978; children: Jason Brian, Christopher Thomas, Megan Jean, Jennifer Anne. MD, Warsaw Med. Sch., 1967. With Akademicki Zwiazek Sportowy, Warsaw, 1961-75; cardiovascular surgeon Oxnard (Calif.) Hosp., 1975—. Mem. Oxnard Humanitarians, 1987—; bd. dirs. Am. Heart Assn., Camarillo, Calif., 1988—. Fellow ACS, Am. Coll. Cardiologists; mem. Soc. for Thoracic Surgeons. Club: Cabrillo Tennis (Camarillo). Office: 1700 N Rose Ave # 420 Oxnard CA 93030

NIETO, JOHN WESLEY, artist; b. Denver, Aug. 6, 1936; s. Simon and Natalia (Venegas) N.; m. Renay Hagin, Nov. 15, 1974; children: John Arthur, Laura Elizabeth, Anaya, Quint. Student, Pan Am. U., 1955-56, So. Meth. U., 1957-59. Artist: work has been reproduced in numerous publications including The Indian Trader, Tucson Mag., Austin (Tex.) Mag., Scottsdale Mag., Ariz. Daily Star, Art in the West, 1988, Nat. Geographic, 1990, New Mex. Mag., Horizon Mag., The Art Experience; featured on radio and TV shows including Japan Nat. TV, 1989, ABC TV Network, 1984, Nat. Pub. Radio, Washington, 1982, Voice of Am., 1981. Mem. adv. bd. Wheelwright Mus., Santa Fe, New Mex., 1985-86, Am. Indian Coll. Fund in N.Y., 1989, Native Am. Prep. Sch., Pecos, New Mex., 1991—; trustee Meadow Sch. of Arts So. Meth. U., Dallas, 1993-94, So. Meth. U., 1993-94; vol. lectr. sponsored tour for Navajo children of Wheelwright Mus., 1988, gallery talk at Ventana for Mescalero Apache children, Tularose Elem. Sch., 1991, six classes for children of migrant workers Guadalupe Sch., Salt Lake City, 1993; contbr. works to numerous benefits. Recipient Gov.'s award, New Mex., 1994. Home and Studio: PO Box 910 Corrales NM 87048-0910

NIGAM, BISHAN PERKASH, physics educator; b. Delhi, India, July 14, 1928; came to U.S., 1952; s. Rajeshwar Nath and Durga (Vati) N.; m. Indira Bahadur, Nov. 14, 1956; children—Sanjay, Shobhna, Ajay. B.S., U. Delhi, 1946, M.S., 1948; Ph.D., U. Rochester, N.Y., 1955. Research fellow U. Delhi, 1948-50; lectr. in physics, 1950-52, 55-56; postdoctoral fellow Case Inst. Tech., Cleve., 1954-55; postdoctoral research fellow NRC, Ottawa, Can., 1956-59; research assoc. U. Rochester, 1959-60, asst. prof. physics, part-time 1960-61; prin. scientist Gen. Dynamics/Electronics, Rochester, N.Y., 1960-61; assoc. prof. physics SUNY, Buffalo, 1961-64; prof. physics Ariz. State U., Tempe, 1964—, U. Wis., Milw., 1966-67. Author: (with R.R. Roy) Nuclear Physics, 1967; also articles. Govt. of India scholar U. Rochester, 1952-54. Fellow Am. Phys. Soc. Office: Ariz State U Dept Physics Box 871504 Tempe AZ 85287-1504

NIIHARA, YUTAKA, physician, educator; b. Tokyo, Oct. 7, 1959; came to U.S., 1973; s. Harushi and Chiyoko (Kang) N.; m. Soomi Song; children: Albert, Hope. BA, Loma Linda U., 1982, MD, 1986. Intern, resident Kettering (Ohio) Med. Ctr., 1986-89; fellow in hematology and oncology Harbor UCLA Med. Ctr., Torrance, Calif., 1989-92; asst. clin. prof. UCLA Sch. Medicine, Torrance and L.A., 1992—. Mem. ACP, N.Y. Acad. Scis. Mem. Seventh Day Adventist Ch. Office: Harbor UCLA Med Ctr PO Box 2910 Torrance CA 90509-2910

NIJENHUIS, ALBERT, mathematician, educator; b. Eindhoven, Netherlands, Nov. 21, 1926; came to U.S., 1952, naturalized, 1959; s. Hendrik and Lijdia (Koornneef) N.; m. Marianne Dannhauser, Aug. 14, 1955; children: Erika, Karin, Sabien, Alaine. Candidaat, U. Amsterdam, Netherlands, 1947, Doctorandus, 1950, Doctor cum laude, 1952. Assoc. Math. Ctr., Amsterdam, Netherlands, 1951-52; asst. Inst. Advanced Study, Princeton, N.J., 1955; mem. Inst. Advanced Study, 1953-55, 61-62; instr., rsch. assoc. U. Chgo., 1955-56; faculty U. Wash., Seattle, 1956-63, prof., 1961-63, affiliate prof., 1988—; prof. math. U. Pa., Phila., 1963-87, prof. emeritus, 1987—; Fulbright lectr. U. Amsterdam, 1963-64; vis. prof. U. Geneva, Switzerland, 1967-68, Dartmouth Coll., 1977-78; researcher and author publs. on subjects including differential geometry, deformation theory in algebra, combinatorics, especially tensors, holonomy groups, graded lie algebras, algorithms. Co-author: Combinatorial Algorithms, 1975, 78; editor: Jour. Algorithms. Postdoctoral fellow Princeton, 1952-53; Fulbright grantee, 1952-53, 63-64; Guggenheim fellow, 1961-62. Mem. Am. Math. Soc., Math. Assn. Am., Netherlands Math. Soc., Assn. for Computing Machinery, AAUP, Royal Netherlands Acad. Scis. (corr.). Office: U Wash Dept Math Box 354350 Seattle WA 98195-4350

NIKIDES, BILL, military officer; b. N.Y.C., Dec. 16, 1954; s. Diomides and Martha N.; m. Cheryl Ocilla Meredith, May 21, 1977; children: Meredith Irene, Mary Elizabeth, Martha Leigh. BA in History, The Citadel, 1977; MA in European History, Webster U., 1986; postgrad., Fla. State U., 1990—, Samford U., 1994—. Ordained to ministry So. Baptist Ch., 1994. Commd. 2nd lt. USAF, 1977, advanced through grades to maj., 1988; chief target intelligence br. 23 Tactical Fighter Wing/HQ Rapid Deployment Air Force, Alexandria, La., Sumter, S.C., 1978-80, 80-83; intelligence instr. The NATO Sch., Oberammergau, Germany, 1983-85; master instr./supr. Air Intelligence Sch., Denver, 1985-87; chief spl. program/covert targeting HQ Tactical Air Command, Hampton, Va., 1987-90; chief of intelligence 325 Fighter Wing, Panama City, Fla., 1990-93, 4440 Composite Wing, Dhahran, Saudi Arabia, 1992; chief electronic combat targeting HQ Cen. Air Forces, Riyadh, Saudi Arabia, 1991; target intelligence flight comdr. 12th Air Force, Tucson, Ariz., 1993-94. Contbr. articles to jours. Counselor Spl. Olympics, Panama City, 1990-93; guest tchr. Panama City Pub. Schs., 1992. Decorated various mil. medals including Liberation of Kuwait medal, Humanitarian Svc. medal, others. Mem. Am. Hist. Assn., Am. Soc. Church Historians, Air Force Assn., Phi Alpha Theta. Republican. Baptist. Home: 148 E Glenwood Dr Birmingham AL 35209-3950 Office: 12th Air Force/AIF Tucson AZ 85707

NIKULA, KRISTEN JAN, veterinary and experimental pathologist; b. Fitchburg, Mass., May 15, 1954; d. Peter Eugene and Phyllis Beverly (Burger) N.; m. Tony Lynn Lantzer, Aug. 7, 1982. BS, U. Calif., Davis, 1977, DVM, 1979, PhD, 1986. Diplomate Am. Coll. of Vet. Pathologists; lic. vet. Calif., N.Mex. Vet. Jamul, Calif., 1979-82; postdoctoral fellow Nat. Cancer Inst./Univ. Calif., Davis, 1982-84; environmental pathology trainee Nat. Inst. Environ. Health Scis./U. Calif., Davis, 1984-85; postdoctoral fellow Am. Lung Assn./U. Calif., Davis, 1985-86; asst. prof. Coll. of Vet. Med. and Biomed. Scis./Colo. State U., Fort Collins, 1986-88; clin. assoc. prof. Coll. of Pharmacy/U. N.Mex., Albuquerque, 1992—; exptl. pathologist Inhalation Toxicology Rsch. Inst., Albuquerque, 1988—. Contbr. articles to profl. jours.; contbr. book chpts. to Biological Reactive Intermediate IV, 1990, Handbook of Toxicologic Pathology, 1991, Proceedings of 8th International Radiation Protection Association, 1992, Toxic and Carcinogenic Effects of Solid Particles in Respiratory Tract, 1994, Concepts in Inhalation Toxicology, 1995. Recipient Sch. Vet. Medicine medal, 1979; Regents scholar U. Calif., 1972. Mem. Am. Coll. Vet. Pathologists, Am. Vet. Med. Assn., Soc. Toxicol. Pathologists, Phi Zeta, Phi Kappa Phi, Alpha Zeta. Office: Inhalation Toxicology Rsch Inst PO Box 5890 Albuquerque NM 87185

NILLES, DARRELL F., artist, inventor, architectural consultant; b. Madison, Wis., Nov. 30, 1957; s. Fred and Agnes Nilles. BArch., U. Minn., 1981. Architect LKA Ptnrs., Colorado Springs, Colo., 1983-86; architect, designer Wolff Lang Christopher, Rancho Cucamonga, Calif., 1986-89, Hill Pinkert, Irvine, Calif., 1989, Wimberly Allison Tony Goo, Newport Beach,

Calif., 1989-91; owner, artist, inventor Nilles Studios, Orange, Calif., 1991—; architect/designer RTKL Internat., L.A., 1995—; student project juror U. Calif., Fullerton, 1993-94. Exhibited in shows at L.A. Art Assn., 1991, Fine Arts Inst., San Bernardino County Mus., Redlands, Calif., 1993, Irvine (Calif.) Fine Art Ctr., 1994, numerous others. Mem. Orange County Visual Artists.

NILLES, JOHN MATHIAS (JACK NILLES), entrepreneur; b. Evanston, Ill., Aug. 25, 1932; s. Elmer Edward and Hazel Evelyn (Wickum) N.; m. Laila Padorr, July 8, 1957. BA magna cum laude, Lawrence Coll., 1954; MS in Engring., U. Calif., Los Angeles, 1964. Sr. engr. Raytheon Mfg. Co., Santa Barbara, Calif., 1956-58; section head. Ramo-Woodridge Corp., L.A., 1958-59; project engr. Space Technology Lab., L.A., 1960; dir. The Aerospace Corp., L.A., 1961-67; sr. systems engr. TRW Systems, L.A., 1967-69; assoc. group dir. The Aerospace Corp., L.A., 1965-72; dir. interdisciplinary programs U. So. Calif., L.A., 1972-81, dir. info. technology program, 1981-89; pres. JALA Internat. Inc., L.A., 1980—; coord. EC Teleforum, Brussels, 1992—; dir. Telecommuting Adv. Coun., L.A., 1991—, pres., 1993-94; chmn. Telecommuting Rsch. Inst., Inc., L.A., 1990—. Author: The Telecommunications Transportation Tradeoff, 1976, Japanese edit., 1977, Exploring the World of the Personal Computer, 1982, French edit., 1985, Micros and Modems, 1983, French edit., 1986, Making Telecommuting Happen, 1994. Capt. USAF, 1954-56. Recipient Rod Rose award Soc. Rsch. Adminstrs., 1976, Environ. Pride award L.A. Mag., 1993, Environ. Achievement award Renew Am., 1994. Mem. IEEE, IEEE Computer Soc., AAAS, Assn. Computing Machinery, Inst. Mgmt. Scis., World Future Soc., Calif. Yacht Club. Office: JALA Internat Inc 971 Stonehill Ln Los Angeles CA 90049-1400

NING, CUN-ZHENG, physicist; b. Xianyang, Shaanxi, China, Oct. 21, 1958; arrived in Germany, 1988; s. Xi-Wu and Shu-Xian (Cheng) N.; m. Ya-E Zhang, Jan. 1, 1983; children: Feng-Tao, Anna. BS, Northwestern U., 1982, MS, 1985; D in Natural Sci., U. Stuttgart, Fed. Republic of Germany, 1991. Vis. scientist U. Stuttgart, 1986-87, rsch. scientist, 1988-93; lectr. Northwestern U., Xian, 1987-88; rsch. assoc. Ariz. Ctr. Math. Sci. U. Ariz., Tucson, 1994—. Co-editor: Lectures in Synergetics, 1987; contbr. numerous papers to profl. jours.; referee several internat. profl. jours. Mem. Am. Phys. Soc., Chinese Phys. Soc., German Phys. Soc., N.Y. Acad. Scis. Home: # 104 3814 E 4th St Apt 104 Tucson AZ 85716-5032 Office: U Ariz Ariz Ctr Math Sci Tucson AZ 85721

NING, XUE-HAN (HSUEH-HAN NING), physiologist, researcher; b. Peng-Lai, Shandong, People's Republic of China, Apr. 15, 1936; came to U.S., 1984; s. Yi-Xing and Liu Ning; m. Jian-Xin Fan, May 28, 1967; 1 child, Di Fan. MD, Shanghai 1st Med. Coll., People's Republic of China, 1960. Rsch. investigator Shanghai Inst. Physiology, 1960-72, leader cardiovasc. rsch. group, 1973-83, head, assoc. prof. cardiovasc. rsch. unit, 1984-87, leader cardiovascular rsch. group, 1979-83, head and assoc. prof. cardiovascular rsch., 1984-87, prof. and chair hypoxia dept., 1988-90, vice chairperson academic com., 1988-90; NIH internat. rsch. fellow U. Mich., Ann Arbor, 1984-87, vis. prof. and rsch. investigator, 1990-95, adj. prof. dept. surgery, 1991-95; prof. and dir. Hypoxia Physiology Lab. Academia Sinica, Shanghai, 1989—; acting leader High Alt. Physiology Group, Chinese mountaineering and sci. expdn. team to Mt. Everest, 1975, Dept. Metall. Industry of China and Ry. Engring. Corps, 1979; vis. prof. dept. physiology Mich. State U., East Lansing, 1989-90; vis. prof. dept. pediatrics U. Wash., Seattle, 1994—. Author: High Altitude Physiology and Medicine, 1981, Reports on Scientific Expedition to Mt. Qomolunyma, High Altitude Physiology, 1980, Environment and Ecology of Qinghai-Xizong (Tibet) Plateau, 1982; mem. editl. bd. Chinese Jour. Applied Physiology, 1984—, Acta Physiologica, 1988—; contbr. articles to profl. jours. Recipient Merit award Shanghai Sci. Congress, 1977, All-China Sci. Congress, Beijing, 1978, Super Class award Academia Sinica, Beijing, 1986, 1st Class award Nat. Natural Scis., Beijing, 1987. Mem. Am. Physiol. Soc., Internat. Soc. Heart Rsch., Royal Soc. Medicine, Shanghai Assn. Physiol. (com. applied physiology 1984—, com. blood, cardiovascular, respiratory and renal physiology 1988—), Chinese Soc. Medicine, Chinese Soc. Biomed. Engring. Home: 7033 43rd Ave NE Seattle WA 98115-6015 Office: U Washington Dept Pediatrics Box 356320 1959 NE Pacific St Seattle WA 98195

NINNEMAN, THOMAS GEORGE, broadcast executive; b. Chgo., Apr. 13, 1950; s. Milton Charles and Bernice Helen (Sharp) N.; m. Nancy Gail Rogers, Aug. 12, 1972; children: Stephanie Christine, Peter Christopher. BA, U. No. Colo., 1972. Dir. news. Sta. KGLN, Glenwood Springs, Colo., 1972-73; program mgr. Sta. KKEP, Estes Park, Colo., 1973-74; ops. mgr. Sta. WMST-AM-FM, Mt. Sterling, Ky., 1974-75; dir. news Sta. KPIK-AM-FM, Colorado Springs, Colo., 1975-77; news stringer AP, UPI, various stas., Colorado Springs, Colo., 1977-78; mgr. driver edn., safety dept. Am. Automobile Assn., Denver, 1978-81; pres. mkt. rschr. Rampart Range Broadcasting Inc., Castle Rock, Colo., 1981-83; news editor Sta. KDEN, Denver, 1983-84; dir. news Stas. KSGT and KMTN-FM, Jackson, Wyo., 1984-94; instr. TV/prodr. dist. TV programming Teton County Sch. Dist., Jackson, 1989—; panelist Yellowstone Fire Rev., Yellowstone Nat. Pk., 1989; contract spokesperson on fire safety Bridger-Teton Nat. Forest, Jackson, 1990—; mem. adv. commn. Wyo. Pub. Radio, 1991—. Asst. scoutmaster, then scoutmaster Boy Scouts Am., Castle Rock, Colo., 1979-84, mem. dist. com., 1984-93; vice chairperson Teton County Centennial Com., Jackson, 1989; co-founder, mgr. Jackson Hole Cmty. Band, 1989—; charter mem., mem. coun. Shepherd of the Mountains Luth. Ch.; active Jackson Hole Brass Quintet, 1985—; mem. local com. Christian Ministry in Nat. Pks., 1988—; comm. chairperson Jackson divsn. Am. Heart Assn., 1994—. Recipient Tony Bevinette Friend of Wyo. Tourism award Wyo. Travel Commn., 1993; co-recipient Wyo. News Station of Yr. award AP, 1990; named Broadcast Newsman of Yr. AP, 1976. Home: Jakcson Hole HS PO Box 568 Jackson WY 83001-0105 Office: Jackson Hole HS PO Box 568 Jackson WY 83001-0100

NINOS, NICHOLAS PETER, retired miliatry officer, physician; b. Chgo., May 11, 1936; s. Peter Spiros and Ann (Lesczynsky) N. BA in Art, Bradley U., 1958, BS in Chemistry, 1959; MD, U. Ill., Chgo., 1963. Diplomate Am. Bd. Internal Med., Am. Bd. Cardiology, Am. Bd. Critical Care Medicne. Intern Cook County Hosp., Chgo., 1963-64, resident in internal medicine, 1964-67, fellow in cardiology, 1967-68; commd. capt. U.S. Army, 1968, advanced through grades to col., 1979; chief dept. medicine U.S. Army Community Hosp. U.S. Army, Bremerhaven, Fed. Republic Germany, 1968-69, Wurzberg, Fed. Republic Germany, 1969-72; chief critical care Letterman Army Med. Ctr., San Francisco, 1976-91; dep. comdr. San Francisco med. command Letterman Army Med. Ctr./Naval Hosp. of Oakland, San Francisco and Oakland, Calif., 1988-90; ret., 1991; assoc. prof. medicine and surgery Uniformed Svcs., U. Health Scis., Bethesda, Md., 1981—; critical care medicine cons. to U.S. Army Surgeon Gen., 1981-91; lectr. in field. Author (jour.): Ethics, 1988; co-editor: Nutrition, 1988, Problems in Critical Care, Nutrition Support; mem. editorial bd. Jour. Critical Care Medicine, 1988-91; illustrator: Medical Decision Making, 1988. 2d v.p. Twin Springs Condominium Homeowners Assn., Palm Springs, Calif., 1993-94, sec., 1994—; ch. bd. councilman St. George Orthodox Ch. of the Desert, Palm Desert, Calif., 1993-95; active Palm Springs Comm., 1993—. Decorated Legion of Merit, Meritorious Svc. medal with oak leaf cluster. Fellow Am. Coll. Crit. Care Medicine; mem. AMA, Soc. Crit. Care Medicine (pres. uniformed svcs. sect. 1987-90, Shubin/Weil award 1988), Am. Coll. Crit. Care Medicine (bd. regents 1989-94, chmn. 1989-91), Soc. Med. Cons. to Armed Forces (assoc.), Inst. Crit. Care Medicine (exec. v.p. 1991-92), Toastmasters Internat. (sec.-treas. Palm Springs chpt. 1993-94, pres. 1994, area gov. dist. 12, div. D-3 1994-95, dist. 12, div. D gov. 1995—).

NISH, ALBERT RAYMOND, JR., retired newspaper editor; b. San Bernardino, Calif., Mar. 16, 1922; s. Albert Raymond and Mabel Claire (Shay) N.; m. Lois Maxine Ringgenberg, June 21, 1942; children: Steven Raymond, Richard Henry, Kathleen Lorie Jenner. Student San Bernardino Valley Jr. Coll., 1939-41, U. Calif., Berkeley, 1941-42, Wash. State Coll., 1943; Am. Press Inst., 1977. Pony wire editor AP, San Francisco, 1941-42; reporter Chico Record, Calif., 1945-46, Berkeley Daily Gazette, Calif., 1946-48; valley editor Modesto Bee, Calif., 1948-60, asst. mng. editor, 1960-62, mng. editor, 1962-85. Served as fighter pilot USAAC, 1942-45, PTO. Decorated DFC.

NISHIMURA, ROBERT NEAL, physician, medical educator, researcher; b. Spokane, Wash., Feb. 12, 1947; s. Roy Y. and Masako (Kamikido) N. BS, Wash. State U., 1968; MD, Johns Hopkins U., 1972. Diplomate Am. Bd. Neurology and Psychiatry. Intern in medicine U. Calif., San Diego, 1972-73; resident in neurology U. Calif., San Francisco, 1973-76; rsch. fellow NIH, Bethesda, Md., 1976-79; asst. prof. U. Oreg., Portland, 1979-81; asst. prof. UCLA, 1981-87, assoc. prof. neurology, 1987—; com. for protection of human subjects State of Calif., Sacramento, 1994—. Contbr. articles to profl. jours. Rsch. fellow United Cerebral Palsy Fedn., 1971, postdoctoral fellow Nat. Multiple Sclerosis Soc., 1976-78. Mem. Am. Acad. Neurology, Soc. for Neurosci., Am. Soc. for Neurochemistry, Royal Soc. Medicine. Office: VA Med Ctr 16111 Plummer St Sepulveda CA 91343-2036

NISHIOKA, TERUO (TED NISHIOKA), electrical engineer; b. Crystal City, Tex., Sept. 6, 1945; s. Kazuto Benjamin and Kofumi (Shinkawa) N.; m. Suzanne Nayeko Hayashi, June 24, 1978; 1 child, Stephanie. BSEE, Calif. State Poly. U., 1970. Engr. Salt River Project, Phoenix, 1970-72, Pacific Gas and Electric, San Francisco, 1972-74; power plant engr. Wismer and Becker, Sacramento, 1975-78; sr. elec. engr. Ariz. Pub. Svc., Phoenix, 1978—. Author: Underground Cable Thermal Backfill, 1981. Active Japanese-Am. Citizens League, Phoenix, 1978—, bd. dirs. 1991—; v.p. Ariz. Buddhist Ch., Phoenix, 1987-88, pres., 1989-91; mem. Matsuri steering com., 1992—. With U.S. Army, 1966-68. Mem. IEEE, Power Engring. Soc., Elec. Insulation Soc. Office: Ariz Pub Svc PO Box 53999 Phoenix AZ 85072-3999

NISHITANI, MARTHA, dancer; b. Seattle, Feb. 27, 1920; d. Denjiro and Jin (Auto) N. BA in Comparative Arts, U. Wash., 1958; studied with, Eleanor King, Mary Ann Wells, Perry Mansfield, Cornish Sch., Conn. Coll. Sch. Dance, Long Beach State U. Founder, dir. Martha Nishitani Modern Dance Sch. and Co., Seattle, 1950—; dance dir. Helen Bush Sch. and Central YWCA, 1951-54; choreographer U. Wash. Opera Theater, 1955-65, Intiman Theater, 1972—; dance instr. Elementary and Secondary Edn. Act Program, 1966; dance specialist spl. edn. program Shoreline Pub. Schs., 1970-72; condr. workshops and concerts King County Youth Correctional Instns., 1972-73; Dance adv. counsel Wash. Cultural Enrichment Program; dance adv. bd. Seattle Parks and Recreation. Dancer Eleanor King Co., Seattle, 1946-50, dance films, 1946-51, Channel 9, Ednl. TV, 1967-68; lectr. demonstrator numerous colls., festivals, convs., childrens theater.; author articles on dance; one of the subjects: A Celebration of 100 Years of Dance in Washington, 1989. Trustee Allied Arts Seattle, 1967. Recipient Theta Sigma Phi Matrix Table award, 1968, Asian Am. Living Treasure award Northwest Asian Am. Theater, 1984; listed Dance Archives, N.Y.C. Libr., 1991, N.Y.C. Lincoln Ctr. Dance Archives, 1991, U. Wash. Libr. Archives, 1993, exhibit of Japanese Am. Women of Achievement, Burke Mus., 1994, 40th Anniversary of Martha Nishitani Modern Dance Sch. Mem. Am. Dance Guild (exec. com. 1961-63), Com. Research in Dance, Seattle Art Mus., Internat. Dance Alliance (adv. council 1984), Smithsonian Assos., Progressive Animal Welfare Soc. Address: 4205 University Way NE PO Box 45264 Seattle WA 98145-0264

NISKANEN, PAUL MCCORD, travel company executive; b. Bend, Oreg., July 6, 1943; s. William Arthur and Nina Elizabeth (McCord) N.; m. Christine Campbell; 1 son, Tapio. Student U. Freiburg, Germany, 1963-64; BA, Stanford U., 1965; MBA, U. Chgo., 1966. Fin. analyst Kimberly-Clark Corp., Neenah, Wis., 1966-68; bus. mgr. Avent Inc. subs. Kimberley-Clark Corp., Tucson, 1968-70; v.p., gen. mgr. Pacific Trailways Bus. Line, Portland, Oreg., 1970-81; chmn. bd., owner Niskanen & Jones, Inc., Moab, Utah, 1982—, Perspectives, Inc., Portland; co-owner Cruise Holidays, Beaverton, Oreg., 1989—. Apptd. consul for Finland, 1980—; active Gov.'s Travel Adv. Com., Salem, Oreg., 1976-81; 1st pres. Oreg. Hospitality and Visitors Assn., Portland, 1977-78; bd. dirs. Suomi Coll., Hancock, Mich., 1981—; nat. co-chmn. Dole for Pres. Com., 1987; co-chmn. Vistory 88. Decorated knight 1st Class Order White Rose Republic of Finland. Mem. Travel Industry Assn. Am., Am. Assn. Travel Agts., Pacific Northwest Travel Assn. (chmn. 1978-79), Scandinavian Heritage Found. (bd. dirs. 1984). Republican. Home: 4366 SW Hewett Blvd Portland OR 97221-3107 Office: Cruise Holidays 2730 SW Cedar Hills Blvd Beaverton OR 97005-1356

NISSEL, MARTIN, radiologist, consultant; b. N.Y.C., July 29, 1921; s. Samuel David and Etta Rebecca (Ostrie) N.; m. Beatrice Goldberg, Dec. 26, 1943; children: Philippa Lyn, Jeremy Michael. BA, NYU, 1941; MD, N.Y. Med. Coll., 1944. Diplomate Am. Bd. Radiology. Intern Met. Hosp., N.Y.C., 1944-45, Lincoln Hosp., N.Y.C., 1947-48; resident in radiology Bronx Hosp., 1948-50, attending radiologist, 1952-54; resident in radiotherapy Montefiore Hosp., Bronx, 1950-51, attending radiotherapist, 1954-56; attending radiologist Buffalo (N.Y.) VA Hosp., 1951-52; attending radiotherapist Univ. Hosp. Boston City Hosp., 1965-69; asst. prof. radiology Boston U. Sch. of Medicine, 1965-69; chief radiotherapist,dir. radiation ctr. Brookside Hosp., San Pablo, Calif., 1969-77; group leader, radiopharm. drugs FDA, Rockville, Md., 1977-86; pvt. cons. radiopharm. drug devel., 1986—. Contbr. articles to profl. jours. Lectr. Am. Cancer Soc., Contra Costa County, Calif., 1973-76. Capt. MC AUS, 1945-47, Korea. Recipient Contra Costa County Speakers Bur. award Am. Cancer Soc., 1973, 76, Responsible Person for Radiol. Health Program for Radiopharm. Drugs award FDA, 1980-86. Mem. Am. Coll. Radiology, Radiol. Soc. N.Am. Office: PO Box 5537 Eugene OR 97405-0537

NISULA, LARRY WILLIAM, artist; b. Phoenix, Oct. 10, 1960; s. William Elmer and Mavis Marie (Ball) N. Student, Glendale C.C., 1979-81. Artist, 1985—; lectr. in field. One-man shows include Phoenix Coll. Art Gallery, 1985, Fagen-Peterson Fine Art, 1987-95, Glendale C.C., 1992; exhibited in group shows Mars Gallery, 1986, Hospice of Valley, 1986, Galleria Mesa, 1988; works represented in collections throughout U.S. and Europe. Mem. Phoenix Blues Soc., Mus. Modern Art N.Y. Home and Studio: 1506 W Fillmore St Phoenix AZ 85007-2213

NISWANDER, ADAM, bookstore owner, real estate broker, writer; b. Flushing, N.Y., Feb. 2, 1946; s. Francis Emerson and Olga (Serafin) N.; m. Philissa Jo Webber, Sept. 10, 1994. Trainee Ft. Lauderdale (Fla.) Symphony, 1964-65; actor, 1971-77; minister Macro Soc. Cmty. Ch., Phoenix, 1979—; majority owner Adam's Bookstore Owner, Phoenix, 1986—; real estate broker AMI Mgmt., Phoenix, 1991—. Author: The Charm, 1993, The Serpent Slayers, 1994, The Hound Hunters, 1994; editor: Antholog One, 1991, Minute of Silence, 1991, Antholog Two, 1994. With USN, 1966-71, Vietnam. Mem. Horror Writers Assn., Sci. Fiction and Fantasy Writers of Am., Ctrl. Ariz. Speculative Fiction Soc. (pres. 1988—), Fraternal Order of Eagles. Republican. Home: 1817 N 10th St Phoenix AZ 85006-2134

NITTA, EUGENE TADASHI, endangered species biologist; b. Lodi, Calif., Aug. 19, 1946; s. Kenji and Emiko (Taguchi) N.; m. Teresa Thelma Tanibe, Dec. 26, 1987; stepchildren: Sheri Y. Yokota, Tani-Lyn T. Tamamoto, Staci S. Yamamoto. BA, U. Calif., Santa Barbara, 1969. Observer Internat. Whaling Commn., Cambridge, England, 1972-75; marine mammal and endangered species program coord. NOAA Nat. Marine Fisheries Svcs. Southwest Region, Terminal Island, Calif., 1976-79; protected species program coord. NOAA Nat. Marine Fisheries Svcs. Southwest Region, Honolulu, 1980—; instr. coll. continuing edn. U. Hawaii, Honolulu, 1988-93. Mem. Soc. for Marine Mammalogy (charter mem.), Am. Soc. Mammalogists. Democrat. Episcopalian.

NITZ, FREDERIC WILLIAM, electronics company executive; b. St. Louis, June 22, 1943; s. Arthur Carl Paul and Dorothy Louise (Kahm) N.; m. Kathleen Sue Rapp, June 8, 1968; children: Frederic Theodore, Anna Louise. AS, Coll. Marin, 1970; BS in Electronics, Calif. Poly. State U., San Luis Obispo, 1972. Electronic engr. Sierra Electronics, Menlo Park, Calif., 1973-77, RCA, Somerville, N.J., 1977-79; engring. mgr. EGG-Geometrics, Sunnyvale, Calif., 1979-83; v.p. engring. Basic Measuring Insts., Foster City, Calif., 1983-91; exec. v.p. Reliable Power Meters, Los Gatos, Calif., 1991—; cons. in field, Boulder Creek, Calif., 1978—. Patentee in field. Bd. dirs. San Lorenzo Valley Water Dist., Boulder Creek, 1983—, Water Policy Task Force, Santa Cruz County, Calif., 1983-84. With U.S. Army, 1965-67. Democrat. Lutheran. Home: 12711 East St Boulder Creek CA 95006-9148 Office: Reliable Power Meters 400 Blossom Hill Rd Los Gatos CA 95032-4511

NITZ, GARY LEE, psychiatrist; b. Goodland, Kans., Mar. 3, 1936; s. Gilbert Benjamin and Marjorie (Wilcox) N.; m. Judith Hood, June 3, 1958; children: Brenda Nitz Vanderberry, Daren Hood. BA, U. Kans., 1958, MD, 1962. Postgrad. Strong Meml. Hosp./U. Rochester, 1962-65, Johns Hopkins Hosp., 1965-67; clin. psychiatrist U.S. Army, Tex. and Colo., 1967-69; pvt. practice psychiatrist Colorado Springs, Colo., 1969-81, Scottsdale, Ariz., 1981—. Fellow Am. Psychiat. Assn.; mem Rotary Internat. Home: 4818 E Roadrunner Rd Scottsdale AZ 85253 Office: 7432 E Camelback Rd Scottsdale AZ 85251

NIVEN, WILLIAM JOHN, historian, educator; b. Bklyn., Oct. 26, 1921; s. William John and Marion (Fredricks) N.; m. Elizabeth Thomson, Sept. 11, 1948; children: John Drake, Katherine Pope. BA, U. Conn., 1943; MA, Columbia U., 1947, PhD, 1954. Instr. Mitchell Coll., New London, Conn., 1949-51; supr. employee rels. Electric Boat divsn. Gen. Dynamics Corp., Groton, Conn., 1951-54; asst. to v.p. comm. Gen. Dynamics Corp., N.Y.C., 1954-55, asst. to CEO and pres., 1955-57, dir. pubs., 1955-60; assoc. prof., prof. Claremont (Calif.) Grad. Sch., 1965-90; prof. emeritus, 1990—; cons. in field. Asst. editor: Struggle for Survival, 1952, Dynamic America, 1960; author: Connecticut for the Union, 1965, Years of Turmoil: The Civil War and Reconstruction, 1969, Gideon Welles, Lincoln's Secretary of the Navy, 1973, Connecticut Hero: Israel Putnam, 1977, Martin Van Buren and the Romantic Era of American Politics, 1983, The American President Lines and Its Forebears, 1848-1984: From Paddle Wheelers to Container Ships, 1986, The Coming of the Civil War, 1989, John C. Calhoun and the Price of Union, 1987, Salmon P. Chase, A Study in Paradox, 1995; contbr. articles to profl. jours. Lt. USNR, 1942-46, WWII. Recipient Award of Merit, Nat. Assn. State and Local History, 1966, Jules and Frances Landry award; Commonwealth Club Calif. Silver medal, 1974; grantee Am. Philos. Soc., 1962, Am. Coun. Learned Socs., 1962. Fellow Smithsonian Inst. (sr. 1965-66), Soc. Am. Historians; mem. Am. Hist. Assn. (chmn. Avery Craven award com. 1985, Beveridge-Dunning award com. 1974, 75, chmn. 1976, Pacific Coast Br. award 1966), Orgn. Am. Historians, So. Hist. Assn. (Charles Sydnor prize com. 1983, 84), Zamorano Club, Coffee House. Home: 2275 Forbes Ave Claremont CA 91711 Office: Claremont Grad Sch 170 E 10th St Claremont CA 91711-5909

NIX, BARBARA LOIS, real estate broker; b. Yakima, Wash., Sept. 25, 1929; d. Martin Clayton and Norma (Gunter) Westfield; A.A., Sierra Coll., 1978; m. B.H. Nix, July 12, 1968; children—William Martin Dahl, Theresa Irene Dahl; step-children—Dennis Leon, Denise Lynn. Bookkeeper, office mgr. Lakeport (Calif.) Tire Service, 1966-69, Dr. K.J. Absher, Grass Valley, Calif., 1972-75; real estate sales and office mgr. Rough and Ready Land Co., Penn Valley, Calif., 1976-77, co-owner, v.p., sec., 1978—, also of Wildwood West Real Estate and Lake of the Pines Sales, Gateway Real Estate. Youth and welfare chmn. Yakima Federated Jr. Women's Club, 1957; den mother Cub Scouts, 1959-60; leader Girl Scouts, 1961-62; mem. Friends of Hospice; mem. Sierra, Nev. Meml. Hosp. Found.; adv. bd. dirs. Roots and Wings Ednl. Found. Recipient Pres.'s award Sierra Coll., 1973; others. Mem. Antique Soc. Penn Valley (founder, pres. 1978), Sierra Nevada Meml. Hosp. Aux. Democrat. Roman Catholic. Clubs: Job's Daus. (life). Home: 19365 Wildflower Dr Penn Valley CA 95946-9720 Office: PO Box 191 Rough and Ready CA 95975

NIX, NANCY JEAN, librarian, designer; b. Denver; d. James Frederik and Josephine (Britt) N. AB in History, U. So. Calif., L.A., 1959, MLS, 1960. Exhibited in group shows at the Iemoto Historical Flower Arrangement Exhibit, 1992. Mem. guiding com. Art Assn. Egg and the Eye Gallery and Restaurant, 1973—; participant Arts & Humanities Symposium, Palm Desert, Calif., 1974; patron cultural symposium L.A. Garden Club, 1975. Recipient Kakan Monpyo award Ikenobo Ikebana Soc. Floral Art, 1988. Mem. Ikebana Internat. (bd. dirs. L.A. chpt. 1978-82, mem. chmn. 1980-82), Japanese Am. Citizens League (historian, exec. bd. L.A. Downtown chpt. 1990—). Republican. Jewish.

NIXON, JOHN HARMON, economist; b. Mpls., Apr. 7, 1915; s. Justin Wroe and Ida Elisabeth (Wickenden) N. AB, Swarthmore Coll., 1935; AM, Harvard U., 1949, PhD, 1953. Analyst U.S. R.R. Retirement Bd., Washington, 1938-41; economist U.S. Office of Price Adminstrn., Washington, 1941-46; teaching fellow, sr. tutor Harvard Coll., Cambridge, Mass., 1947-50; asst. prof. econs. CCNY, 1953-56; dir. econ. devel. N.Y. State Dept. Commerce, Albany, 1956-59; dir. area devel. Com. for Econ. Devel., N.Y.C., 1959-65; dir. tech. assistance U.S. Econ. Devel. Adminstrn., Washington, 1966-67; urban economist U.S. AID, Saigon, Vietnam, 1967; economist Ralph M. Parsons Co., Washington, 1968-70; chief economist/systems Ralph M. Parsons Co., Pasadena, Calif., 1971-82; mem. adv. bd. U.S. Area Devel. Adminstrn., Washington, 1963-65. Co-author, editor: Community Economic Development Efforts, 1964, Living Without Water (Cairo), 1980. Vice chmn. Mayor's Com. on Econ. Devel., L.A., 1974-75; pres. Pasadena Devel. Corp., 1982-84. Mem. Nat. Economists Club, Nat. Assn. Bus. Economists, Harvard Club N.Y.C., Town Hall of Calif., Phi Beta Kappa. Democrat. Presbyterian. Office: PO Box 76267 Los Angeles CA 90076-0267

NIXON, NORA, educational director; b. Alexandria, Va., Sept. 19, 1956; d. Robert Tharp and Alice Mary (FitzGerald) Nixon; m. Alexander Paul Vertikoff, Dec. 24, 1984; 1 child, Cole Robert. BA in Spanish/Portuguese, U. N.Mex., 1981; MA in TESL/Applied Linguistics, UCLA, 1986. Lang. lab. asst. dept. modern and classical langs. U. N.Mex., 1981-82, English instr., 1981-82; ednl. aide II Venice High Sch., L.A. Unified Sch. Dist., 1981-82; teaching asst. intermediate ESL UCLA, 1984, teaching assoc. advanced composition ESL, 1985-86; fgn. expert/researcher Zhongshan U., People's Republic China, 1984-85; ESL instr. West L.A. C.C., 1986-87, UCLA Extension, 1983-87; asst. dir. English, asst. prof. English, EAP, ESP West Coast U., L.A., 1987-91; assoc. dir. acad. yr. programs Ednl. Resource Devel. Trust, Marina Del Rey, Calif., 1991—. Author: Advanced Writing in EST: A Coursebook for Graduate Students of Science and Technology, 1985; contbr. articles to profl. publs. Grantee Fulbright Found., 1988, USIA, 1991. Mem. TESOL, CATESOL. Office: Ednl Resource Devel Trust 475 Washington Blvd Ste 220 Marina Del Rey CA 90292

NIXON, ROBERT OBEY, SR., business educator; b. Pitts., Feb. 14, 1922; s. Frank Obey and Margurite (Van Buren) N.; m. Marilyn Cavanagh, Oct. 25, 1944 (dec. 1990); children: Nan Nixon Friend, Robert Obey, Jr., Dwight Cavanagh. BS in bus. adminstrn., U. Pitts., 1948; MS, Ohio State U., 1964; MBA, U. Phoenix, 1984. Commd. 2d lt. USAF, 1943, advanced through grades to col., 1970, master navigator WWII, Korea, Vietnam; sales, adminstrn. U.S. Rubber Corp., Pitts., 1940-41; asst. engr. Am. Bridge Corp., Pitts., 1941-42; underwriter, sales Penn Mutual Life Ins. Corp., Pitts., 1945-50; capt., nav. instr. USAF Reserves, 1945-50; ret. USAF Col., divsn. chief Joint Chiefs of Staff, 1973; educator, cons. U. Ariz., 1973-79; bus. dept. chmn., coord., founder weekend coll. Pima Community Coll., Tucson, 1979-90, prof. mgmt., coord. Weekend Coll. program, 1991—; founder, pres. Multiple Adv. Group ednl. cons., Tucson, 1978—. Contbr. articles to profl. jours. Mem. Soc. Logistics Engrs. (sr., charter mem.), Phi Delta Theta. Presbyterian. Home: 1824 S Regina Cleri Dr Tucson AZ 85710-8664

NIZZE, JUDITH ANNE, physician assistant; b. L.A., Nov. 1, 1942; d. Robert George and Charlotte Ann (Wise) Swan; m. Norbert Adolph Otto Paul Nizze, Dec. 31, 1966. BA, UCLA, 1966, postgrad., 1966-76; grad. physician asst. tng. program, Charles R. Drew Sch. Postgrad., L.A., 1979; BS, Calif. State U., Dominguez, 1980. Cert. physician asst., Calif. Staff rsch. assoc. I-II Wadsworth Vet. Hosp., L.A., 1965-71; staff rsch. assoc. III-IV John Wayne Clinic Jonsson Comprehensive Cancer Ctr., UCLA, 1971-78; clin. asst. Robert S. Ozeran, Gardena, Calif., 1978; physician asst. family practice Fred Chasan, Torrance, Calif., 1980-82; sr. physician asst. Donald L. Morton prof., chief surg. oncology Jonsson Comprehensive Cancer Ctr., UCLA, 1983-91; adminstrv. dir. clin. rsch. John Wayne Cancer Inst., Santa Monica, Calif., 1991—. Contbr. articles to profl. jours. Fellow Am. Acad. Physician Assts., Am. Assn. Surgeons Assts., Calif. Acad. Physician Assts.; mem. Assn. Physician Assts. in Oncology, Am. Sailing Assn. Republican. Presbyterian. Home: 13243 Fiji Way Unit J Marina Dl Rey CA 90292-7079 Office: John Wayne Cancer Inst St John's Hosp & Health Ctr 1328 22nd St Santa Monica CA 90404-2032

NOBE, KENNETH CHARLES, international agricultural and water resource economics consultant; b. Venedy, Ill., Oct. 26, 1930; s. Elmer F. and

Alvina (Froekhe) N.; m. Hazel Leona McCullough, Oct. 22, 1949; children—Sandra, Jeffrey, Michael. B.S., So. Ill. U., 1953; M.S., Cornell U., 1954, Ph.D., 1959. Mktg. agt. USDA, Ithaca, N.Y., 1954-55; instr. Cornell U., 1955-56; economist USDA, Washington, 1958-61, USPHS, Denver, 1961-63, U.S. Dept. Interior, Washington, 1963-64; econ. cons. Harza Engring. Co. Internat., Lahore, West Pakistan, 1964-65; assoc. prof. econs. Colo. State U., Ft. Collins, 1966-69; prof. econs., chmn. econs. dept. Colo. State U., 1969-83, prof. agrl. econs., chmn. dept. agr. and resource econs., 1984-87, emeritus prof., 1987—; exec. v.p. RAD Internat. Inc., Ft. Collins, 1987—; chmn. exec. council Environ. Resources Center, 1970-71; dir. Internat. Sch. Econ. Devel. Studies, 1980-83; exec. dir. Internat. Sch. Agr. and Resource Devel., 1983-85; econ. advisor to dir. West Pakistan Water and Power Devel. Authority, 1964-65; cons. U.S. Dept. State, AID, 1966, 76-92, Ford Found., India, 1980, World Bank, 1984-88, FAO, UN, 1988-90, Philippines Dept. Agriculture, 1977, U.N. Devel. Program, Viet Nam, 1993; chmn. Western Agrl. Econs. Coun., 1976-78. econs. advisor to dir. West Pakistan Water and Power Devel. Authority, 1964-65; cons. U.s. Dept. State, AID, 1966, 76-92, Ford Found., India, 1980, World Bank, 1984-88, 94, FAO, UN, 1988-90, Philippines Dept. Agriculutre, 1977, UN Devel. Program Viet Nam, 1993; chmn. Western Agr. Econs. Coun., 1976-78. Served with USAF, 1948-50. Recipient Ill. State Farmer award Future Farmers Am., 1947, Disting. Service award Colo. State U., 1979. Mem. Am. Econs. Assn., Am. Agrl. Econs. Assn., Western Argl. Econs. Assn., Omicron Delta Epsilon. Home: 3510 Terryridge Rd Fort Collins CO 80524-1661

NOBLE, DONALD CHARLES, geologist, educator; b. N.Y.C., Mar. 2, 1937; s. Oliver Donald and Ella DeCoursey (Kratz) N.; m. Bettie Eleanor Hardy, 1955 (div. 1971); children: Jean Elizabeth, William Hardy, Thomas Charles; m. Carol Jane Rasmussen, 1973. BS, Cornell U., 1958; MS, Stanford U., 1961, PhD, 1962. Geologist U.S. Geol. Survey, Denver, 1962-66; asst. prof. Harvard U., Cambridge, Mass., 1966-71; vis. prof., rsch. prof. U. Nev., Reno, 1972-75; geol. cons. Reno, also Peru, 1971-75; from assoc. prof. to prof. geology Mich. Technol. U., Houghton, 1975-80; prof. geology and econ. geology Mackay Sch. Mines, U. Nev., Reno, 1980—; cons. econ. geologist we. N.Am. and S.Am., 1980—. Contbr. more than 100 articles to Econ. Geology, Geology, Bull. of Geol. Soc. Am., Earth and Planetary Sci. Letters, Jour. Geophys. Rsch., Lithos, Am. Jour. Sci., others. 1st lt. USAR, 1958-59. Recipient numerous NSF grants, 1960s-1980s; Nev. Nuclear Waste Project Office grantee, numerous others. Fellow Soc. Econ. Geologists, Mineral. Soc. Am.; mem. Sociedad Geologica del Peru, Soc. Mining, Metallurgy and Exploration, Geol. Soc. Am., Geol. Soc. Nev. Home: 3450 Rolling Ridge Rd Reno NV 89506-9770 Office: Mackay Sch Mines MS 172 U Nev Reno Reno NV 89557

NOBLE, HELEN BONNER, artist; b. Northville, Mich., Mar. 27, 1922; d. George Coburn and Helen Josephine (McCambridge) Harper; m. Morton Noble, Jr., June 27, 1943; children: Martha, Kathryn, Elizabeth, John. Student, Wayne State U., We. Res. U., 1939-43, Santa Barbar Art Inst. One-woman shows include Gallery 932, Ventura, Calif., 1983, The Oaks Gallery, Ojai, Calif., 1988; group shows include Bradley Galleries, Santa Barbara, Calif., 1978, 79, Meredith Niles Gallery, Santa Barbara, 1980-83, Merida-Rapp Graphics, Louisville, 1986; other exhibits include 3rd Women in Art Exhbn., Springfield, Ill., 1983, 2nd Ann. Nat. Print Exhbn. of Springfield Art Assn., 1982, 24th Ann. Nat. Exhbn. of Prints & Drawings, Oklahoma City, 1982, others; represented in collections.

NOBLE, JOHN PARTRIDGE, English language educator; b. Mpls., Feb. 18, 1959; s. John Curtiss Noble and Estelle (Blunt) King; m. Meredith Ellen Schuster, Mar. 19, 1983; children: Arin Rachel, Luke Alexander, Asher Blunt. BA, Dartmouth Coll., 1981; PhD, U. Va., 1992. Head tutor Dartmouth Coll., Hanover, N.H., 1982-84; asst. prof. Calif. Bapt. Coll., Riverside, 1992—; dir. Northwestern Travel Svc., Mpls., 1977—. Mem. MLA, Am. Acad. Religion. Office: Calif Bapt Coll Dept English Box 1096 7250 Metro Blvd Minneapolis MN 55439-2138

NOBLE, RICHARD LLOYD, lawyer; b. Oklahoma City, Oct. 11, 1939; s. Samuel Lloyd and Eloise Joyce (Millard) N. AB with distinction, Stanford, 1961, LLB, 1964. Bar: Calif. 1964. Assoc. firm Cooper, White & Cooper, San Francisco, 1965-67; assoc., ptnr. firm Voegelin, Barton, Harris & Callister, Los Angeles, 1967-70; ptnr. Noble & Campbell, Los Angeles, San Francisco, 1970—; dir. Langdale Corp., L.A., Gt. Pacific Fin. Co., Sacramento; lectr. Tax Inst. U. So. Calif., 1970; mem. bd. law and bus. program Stanford Law Sch. Contbr. articles to legal jours. Bd. govs. St. Thomas Aquinas Coll. Recipient Hilmer Dehlman Jr. award Stanford Law Sch., 1962; Benjamin Harrison fellow Stanford U., 1967. Mem. ABA, State Bar Calif., L.A. Bar Assn., San Francisco Bar Assn., Commercial Club (San Francisco), Commonwealth Club (San Francisco), Petroleum Club (L.A.), Capitol Hill Club (Washington), Pi Sigma Alpha. Republican. Home: 2222 Avenue Of The Stars Los Angeles CA 90067-5655 Office: Noble & Campbell 333 N Grand Ave Los Angeles CA 90012-2622

NOBLE-PERRY, DEBORAH ASHLEY, school counselor, horse trainer; b. White Plains, N.Y., Aug. 3, 1956; d. Liston Jr. and Celia Peckham (Slade) Noble; m. Charles David Perry, June 11, 1983; 1 child, Sarah Ashley. BA, Pacific Luth. U., 1978; MA in Counseling, St. Martin's Coll., 1990, cert. in sch. counseling, 1990. Substitute tchr. Longview (Wash.) Kelso Schs., 1978-79; phys. edn. tchr. Evergreen Schs., Vancouver, Wash., 1979-81; phys. edn. and math. tchr. Bethel Sch. Dist., Spanaway, Wash., 1981-84, alternate sch. tchr., 1984-86, mem. spl. programs, 1986-92, counselor Spanaway Jr. H.S., 1992—, parenting skills tchr., 1992—; cons., rally judge U.S. Pony Club, Yelm, Wash., 1989—; equestrian cons. breeding analysis, Graham, Wash., 1994—. Coach Pony Club, Deaf Persons, and Sight Impaired, 1994—; volleyball and track athletics coach, 1981-84. Recipients award Horseshows Assn. Wash., 1978, Wash. State Hunter/Jumper Assn., 1978. Mem. NEA, Am. Horse Shows Assn., Wash. State Horsemen Assn. (High Point awards 1978), U.S. Combined Assn., U.S. Dresssage Fedn. (learner judge 1994—), Equestrians Inst. (Preliminary Championship award 1989), Bethel Edn. Assn., Internat. Assn. Marriage and Family Therapists, Wash. State Counselors Assn. Lutheran. Home: 31710 Webster Rd E Eatonville WA 98328-9656 Office: Spanaway Jr HS Sch 15701 B St E Tacoma WA 98445-1163

NOBLIT, BETTY JEAN, publishing technician; b. St. Elmo, Ill., June 12, 1948; d. Clyde W. and Lucille M. (Haggard) N. Grad. in restaurant and club food mgmt., LaSalle U., 1973; grad., Am. Sch. Travel, 1975. Teletype puncher Sarasota (Fla.) Herald-Tribune, 1968-70, Pueblo Chieftain, 1970—; unified composer; pagination operator Star Jour. Pub. Co., Pueblo, Colo.; personal corr. Prime Min. Indira Gandhi. Sec. Pueblo Chieftain and Star-Journal Credit Union. Mem. Nat. Geog. Soc., Colo. Hist. Soc., Pueblo Hist. Soc. Home: 1 Cambridge Ave Apt 4B Pueblo CO 81005-2024

NOCE, ROBERT HENRY, neuropsychiatrist, educator; b. Phila., Feb. 19, 1914; s. Rev. Sisto Julius and Madeleine (Saulino) N.; m. Carole Lee Landis, 1987. A.B., Kenyon Coll., 1935; M.D., U. Louisville, 1939; postgrad., U. Pa. Sch. Medicine, 1947, Langley-Porter Neuropsychiat. Inst., 1949, 52. Rotating intern Hamot Hosp., Erie, Pa., 1939-40; resident psychiatrist Warren (Pa.) State Hosp., 1940-41, staff psysician, 1946-48; staff physician Met. State Hosp., Norwalk, Calif., 1948-50; dir. clin. services Pacific State Hosp., Spadra, Calif., 1950-52; dir. clin. services Modesto (Calif.) State Hosp., 1952-58, asst. supt. psychiat. services, 1958-64; pvt. practice medicine specializing in neuropsychiatry, 1965-73; Mem. faculty postgrad. symposiums in psychiatry for physicians U. Calif., 1958, 66. Author: (film) Reserpine Treatment of Psychotic Patients; contbr. articles to profl. jours. Served from lt. (j.g.) to lt. comdr. M.C. USNR, 1941-46. Recipient Albert and Mary Lasker award for integration reserpine treatment mentally ill and mentally retarded, 1957; Wisdom award of honor, 1970. Life fellow Am. Psychiat. Assn. (sec. 1954, 55); fellow Royal Soc. Health; mem. Phi Beta Kappa, Delta Psi. Episcopalian. Home: 407 E Colgate Dr Tempe AZ 85283-1809

NOCE, WALTER WILLIAM, JR., hospital administrator; b. Neptune, N.J., Sept. 27, 1945; s. Walter William and Louise Marie (Jenkins) N.; m. Cinda Ann Miller, Apr. 15, 1967; children: Krista Suzanne, David Michael. B.A., LaSalle Coll., Phila., 1967; M.P.H., UCLA, 1969. Regional coordinator USPHS, Rockville, Md., 1969-71; v.p. Hollywood Presbyn. Hosp., Los Angeles, 1971-75; sr. v.p. Hollywood Presbyn. Med. ctr., 1975-77; v.p. administrn. Huntington Meml. Hosp, Pasadena, Calif., 1977-83; pres., chief exec. officer St. Joseph Hosp., Orange, Calif., 1983-90; pres. so. Calif. region St. Joseph Health System, 1987-90, exec. v.p., 1990-94; pres., CEO Children's Hosp., L.A., 1995—; preceptor UCLA Health Services Mgmt. Program, 1977—; chmn. bd. Health Plan of Am., 1985-91; chmn. Hosp. Coun. So. Calif., 1989. Exec. v.p. Mental Health Assn. in Los Angeles County, 1979-82; regional v.p. Calif. Mental Health Assn., 1982-83. W. Glenn Ebersole finalist Assn. Western Hosp., 1969; recipient USPHS letter commendation, 1971. Mem. Am. Coll. Hosp. Adminstrs., Am. Hosp. Assn. (ho. of dels. 1994—), Calif. Assn. Cath. Hosps. (chmn. 1990-91), Calif. Assn. Hosps. and Health Sys. (chmn. 1992), UCLA Hosp. Adminstrn. Alumni Assn. (pres. 1979-80), Pasadena C. of C. (v.p. 1980-82). Home: 20388 Via Marwah Yorba Linda CA 92686-4522 Office: Children's Hosp Los Angeles 4650 Sunset Blvd Los Angeles CA 90027

NODELMAN, JARED ROBERT, investment advisor; b. N.Y.C., May 24, 1937; s. George and Ray (Mayerson) N.; children: Seth, Ilisa. BA, Ohio State U., 1958. Registered investment advisor. Pres. Commonwealth Assocs. Inc., San Juan, P.R., 1964-74, Inversiones Metropolitanas, Inc., Santa Rosa, Calif., 1974—, Orinoco Capital Advisers Ltd., N.Y.C. Mem. cabinet Marin Gen. Hosp., Pres.' Coun. Meml. Sloan Kettering Cancer Ctr. Recipient Leadership award Meml. Sloan-Kettering Cancer Ctr., N.Y.C., 1989. Mem. World Trade Club, St. Francis Yacht Club, San Francisco Yacht Club, San Francisco Rotary, Villa Taverna, Olympic Club. Office: Orinco Capital Advisers Ltd Ste 903 1250 Jones St Apt 903 San Francisco CA 94109-4205

NOE, LEWIS JOHN, chemistry educator; b. Cleve., Oct. 26, 1941; s. Russell Harold and Estell (Holecek) N.; m. Nancy Lee Washburn, Nov. 22, 1968; children: Richard Christopher, Matthew Russell. AB, Western Res. U., 1963; PhD, Case Western Res. U., 1967. Asst. prof. of chemistry U. Wyo., Laramie, 1969-73, assoc. prof. chemistry, 1973-81, prof. chemistry, 1982—, head dept. chemistry, 1983-87. Mem. Am. Chem. Soc., Sigma Xi. Home: 1706 Arnold St Laramie WY 82070-5423 Office: Dept Chemistry U Wyo Phys Sci Bldg Laramie WY 82071

NOEL, MICHAEL LEE, utility executive; b. Rapid City, S.D., Apr. 5, 1941; s. Milton George and Merel Lyreen (Roth) N.; children—Christy Carole, Craig Arnold. B.S. in Finance cum laude, Calif. State U., Long Beach, 1964; M.B.A. summa cum laude, U. So. Calif., 1973. With So. Calif. Edison Co., Rosemead, 1964—, mgr. corp. planning, 1974-75, asst. treas., 1975-76, treas., 1976—, v.p., 1980—; guest lectr. U. So. Calif., Fullerton, Calif. State U., Long Beach; bd dirs. Current Income Shares, Inc., Hancock Savs. and Loan Assn., Software Toolworks Inc. Chmn., bd. dirs. Los Angeles Jr. C. of C. Mem. L.A. Soc. Fin. Analysts, Pacific Coast Elec. Assn., L.A. Treas., Seacliff Tennis Club. Club: Seacliff Racquet. Home: 353 Ultimo Ave Long Beach CA 90814-3200 Office: So Calif Edison Co 2244 Walnut Grove Ave Rosemead CA 91770-3714

NOETH, LOUISE ANN, journalist; b. Evergreen Park, Ill., Nov. 17, 1954; d. Cy John and Alice Rose (Bobrovich) N.; m. Michael T. Lanigan, Aug. 29, 1992. Editor Petersen Pub. Co., Inc., Calif., 1980; assoc. pub., editor Autoscene Mag., Westlake Village, Calif., 1981; investigative editor Four Wheeler Mag., Canoga Park, Calif., 1982—; owner, founder Landspeed Productions, 1985—; automotive writer, columnist Press-Courier Newspaper, Oxnard, Calif., 1992-94, Ventura County Newspapers, 1994-95, L.A. Times, 1995; Car Craft Mag., 1994—; with EG&G, Inc., 1992; auto writer, columnist Ventura County Newspapers, 1994-95; cons. Spirit Am. World Speed Record Team, Pontiac Motor Divsn., Land Rover of N.Am., others; mem. Green Mamba Racing Team, Reseda, Calif., 1978—, Spirit of Am. World Speed Racing Record; graphic art commns. for Wallenius Lines, Colony Harbortown Resort, GTE, Ferro Corp., Nikon Profl. Svcs., Kodak Profl. Network, Forbes mag., SEA Sailing. Author: Ventura County Destination Guide: Channel Islands Harbor Retrospect; editor: Hot Rod Performance and Custom, 1979; prodr.: Renewing Pride, Schoolroom in Paradise, Heritage Square; contbr. articles to numerous automotive mags.; photography exhibited at Ventura Village Art Gallery, 1994, Ventura County Mus. History and Art, 1991, Ventura County Nat. Bank, 1990, 92, Ventura County Fair, 1990 (Spl. Non-Competition award Profl. Category); represented in permanent collection Harbor Town Marina Resort Gallery. Mem. project R.A.F.T. Russians and Ams. for Teamwork, Buffalo Bill's West Show; mem. bd. dirs., pub. chair Carnegie Art Mus., 1995—. Recipient Moto award in investigative news category, Automotive Journalism Conference, 1983-84, 86. Mem. Tallship Californian Quarter deck Comm., Oxnard C. of C., Edn. Comm. Youth Edn. Motivation Program, Internat. Motor Press Assn. (sec. 1986—), Specialty Equipment Market Assn. (pub. relations com. 1983, suspension and tire com. 1984-85), Am. Auto Racing Writers and Broadcasters Assn.

NOGUCHI, THOMAS TSUNETOMI, author, forensic pathologist; b. Fukuoka, Japan, Jan. 4, 1927; came to U.S., 1952; s. Wataru and Tomika Narahashi N. D of Medicine, Nippon Med. Sch., Tokyo, 1951; LLD (hon.), U. Braz Cubas Fedn. Faculties Mogi Das Cruzes, Sao Paolo, Brazil, 1980; DSc (hon.), Worcester State Coll., 1985. Dep. med. examiner Los Angeles County Dept. Chief Med. Examiner, L.A., 1961-67, coroner, 1967-82; prof. forensic pathology U. So. Calif., L.A., 1982—. Author: Coroner, 1983 (N.Y. Times Bestseller 1984), Coroner At Large, 1985; (fiction) Unnatural Causes, 1988, Physical Evidence, 1990. Fellow Am. Acad. Forensic Sci. (chmn. sect. 1966); mem. Nat. Assn. Med. Examiners (pres. 1983), Calif. State Coroners Assn. (pres. 1974), World Assn. Med. Law (v.p.). Republican. Home: 1110 Avoca Ave Pasadena CA 91105-3405 Office: U So Calif Med Ctr 1200 N State St Rm 2520 Los Angeles CA 90033-4525

NOKES, JOHN RICHARD, retired newspaper editor, author; b. Portland, Oreg., Feb. 23, 1915; s. James Abraham and Bernice Alfaretta (Bailey) N.; m. Evelyn Junkin, Sept. 13, 1936; children: Richard Gregory, William G., Gail (Mrs. William M. Hulden), Douglas J., Kathy E. B.S., Linfield Coll., 1936, LHD (hon.), 1988. With The Oregonian, Portland, 1936-82, city editor, 1950-65, asst. mng. editor, 1965-71, mng. editor, 1971-75, editor, 1975-82; disting. vis. prof. journalism Linfield Coll., 1982-85; cons. editor The Hong Kong Standard, 1994. Author: American Form of Government, 1939, Columbia's River: The Voyages of Robert Gray 1787-1793, 1991; editor Oreg. Edn. Jour., 1944. Bd. dirs. Portland U.S.O., 1968-72, U.S. Coast Guard Acad. Found., 1972-74, Portland Opera Assn., 1976-78; trustee Linfield Coll., 1977-93; v.p. Oreg. UN Assn., 1983-85, chmn. Oreg. UN Day, 1983. Lt. (j.g.) USNR, 1944-46; comdr. Res. (ret.). Mem. Navy League U.S. (pres. Portland coun. 1969-71), Linfield Coll. Alumni Assn. (pres. 1940), World Affairs Coun. Oreg. (pres. 1973-74), AP Mng. Editors Assn. (dir. 1973-80), Am. Soc. Newspaper Editors, N.W. China Coun., Sigma Delta Chi (pres. Willamette Valley chpt. 1975-76). Republican. Methodist. Club: Multnomah Athletic (Portland). Home: 14650 SW 103rd Ave Tigard OR 97224-4740

NOLAN, JAMES MICHAEL, fire chief; b. Orlando, Fla., Sept. 30, 1943; s. James Douglas and Marjorie Kathleen (Rouse) N.; m. Patricia Ann Fenwick Nolan, Jan. 31, 1969; children: Michael Douglas, Teresa Kathleen. AA in Fire Sci., U. AK, 1977; exec. fire officer, Nat. Fire Acad., 1993. Hazardous Materials Incident Mgr. Fed. Emergency Mgmt. Agency. Computer technician KLM Office Machines, Anchorage, AK, 1969-73; firefighter Anchorage (AK) Fire Dept., 1973-76, fire apparatus engr., 1976-80, fire capt., 1980-84, sr. fire capt., 1984-86, battalion chief, tng., 1986-88, battalion chief, 1988, deputy chief, chief of ops., 1988-94, fire chief, 1994—; chmn. Anchorage Police & Fire Ret. Bd., 1982; mem. Anchorage Regional Fire Tng. Ctr. Bd., 1984-89; mem. State of AK Fire Svc. Tng. award Com., 1986-90; adj. instr. in Fire Sci. U. AK, Anchorage, 1982-85. Contbr. articles and photographs to book. Chmn. 457 Deferred Compensation Bd., Anchorage, AK, 1995—; mem . Local Chpt. Am. Red Cross, 1995—; mem. Emergency Planning Commn., 1995, Environ. Quality Control Com., 1994—. Mem. Nat. Fire Protection Assn., AK State Fire Chiefs Assn., Internat. Assn. of Fire Chiefs, Anchorage Area Interagnecoy Emergency Mgmt. Assn. (pres. 1994—). Office: Anchorage Fire Dept 1301 E 80th Ave Anchorage AK 99518

NOLAN, MARK GREGORY, advertising executive; b. San Francisco, July 3, 1958; m. Robyn Lynn Nolan, June 7, 1980. Mktg. mgr. Shelton-Turnbull, Eugene, Oreg., 1977-80; v.p. mktg. Shelton-Turnbull, Eugene, 1980-81; founder, chief exec. officer Mark Nolan & Assocs., Inc., Citrus Heights, Calif., 1981-87; v.p., ptnr. Nolan Mktg. Group Inc., Citrus Heights, 1987—; mktg. dir., ptnr. Fin. Mktg. Corp., Citrus Heights, 1989—; keynote speaker Marin Self-Pubs. Assn., Ross, Calif., 1986; featured speaker Community Entrepreneurs Assn., Sacramento, 1986, home-based bus. conf., 1991; treas. COSMEP, San Francisco, 1986-88; lectr. UCLA, 1987. Author: The Instant Marketing Plan, 1995; editor: Info. Mktg., 1985-87. Mem. Better Bus. Bur., Eagle Scouts. Mem. S.C. Publicists Assn., Community Entrepreneurs Assn., Internat. Assn. Self-Pubs. (treas. 1986-88), Com. of Small Mag. Editors and Pubs., C. of C., Turtles, Oregon Advt. Club, Entrepreneurs Am., Active 20-30 Club. Office: Nolan Mktg Group Inc PO Box 2570 Fair Oaks CA 95628-9570

NOLAND, CHARLES DONALD, lawyer, educator; b. Tulsa, July 31, 1946; s. Clyde Earl and Birdeen Elizabeth (White) N.; m. Elisabeth Hooper, June 27, 1987; 1 stepchild, Richard G. Reynolds. BA in Journalism, U. N.Mex., 1972, JD, 1978. Bar: N.Mex. 1978, U.S. Dist. Ct. N.Mex. 1979, U.S. Ct. Appeals (10th cir.) 1991, U.S. Supreme Ct. 1991. Reporter, copy editor New Mexican, Santa Fe, 1969; newsman AP, Des Moines, 1969-71, Albuquerque, 1973-74; editor programmed instrn. materials Systema Corp., Albuquerque, 1974-75; pvt. practice Albuquerque, 1978-79; asst. gen. counsel, then gen. counsel N.Mex. Dept. Edn., Santa Fe, 1979-83; asst. atty. gen. State of N.Mex., Santa Fe, 1984-85; pvt. practice Santa Fe, 1985—; adj. prof. U. N.Mex. Grad. Sch. Edn., 1981, 92, N.Mex. Highlands U. Grad. Sch. Edn., 1985, Coll. Santa Fe, 1984-89; of counsel, sole practioner, pvt. practice Simons, Cuddy & Friedman, Santa Fe, 1985—; cons. in field; hearing officer tchr. termination appeals N.Mex. Bd. Edn., 1980, 81; panelist pub. sch. reduction in force Nat. Sch. Bds. Assn. Conv., Dallas, 1981; mem. vol. lawyer multidisciplinary ednl. advocacy team parents pub. sch. spl. edn. students, Albuquerque, 1978-79; hearing officer for spl. edn. placement appeal Albuquerque Pub. Schs., 1979; vol. nursing home ombudsman N.Mex. Agy. on Aging, 1995—. Contbr. articles to profl. publs. Founding bd. dirs. Santa Fe Symphony Orch., 1984-85, corp. sec., 1985-88; community musician Santa Fe Concert Band, Santa Fe Brass Ensemble, 1983-89. With U.S. Army, 1971-72. Mem. N.Mex. Assn. Sch. Bd. Attys. (treas. 1980-83, pres. 1987-88, 90-93), Nat. Orgn. Legal Problems Edn., Coun. Sch. Attys., Nat. Sch. Bds. Assn., N.Am. Assn. Ednl. Negotiators, State Bar N.Mex. (employment and labor law sect., appellate practice sect., elder law sect., real property/probate/trust sect.). Home: 3 Pino Pl Santa Fe NM 87505-8750 Office: 1701 Old Pecos Trl Santa Fe NM 87505-4758

NOLEN-HOEKSEMA, RICHARD C., consulting geophysicist, researcher; b. Washington, Mar. 17, 1956; s. Renze Lyle and Olive Marjorie (Coombes) Hoeksema; m. Susan Kay Nolen, May 10, 1981; 1 child, Michael Richard. AB, Hope Coll., Holland, Mich., 1977; MS, Yale U., 1979, MPhil, 1980, PhD, 1983. Postdoctoral assoc. Yale U., New Haven, 1983-84; rsch. geologist Cities Svc. Oil & Gas Corp., Tulsa, 1984-85; rsch. geophysicist Chevron Oil Field Rsch. Co., La Habra, Calif., 1985-88; rsch. assoc. Stanford U., Palo Alto, Calif., 1988-92, cons. scientist, 1992—; cons. geophysicist, Menlo Park, Calif., 1992—; cons. Chevron Petroleum Tech. Co., La Habra, 1992—; manuscript reviewer for sci. orgns., 1977—; peer reviewer U.S. EPA Grad. Student Fellowships, 1995—. Contbr. articles to sci. jours. Mem. AAAS (environ. sci. and engring. fellow 1993), Geol. Soc. Am., Am. Geophys. Union, Soc. Petroleum Engrs. (tech. editor 1994—), Soc. Exploration Geophysicists, Internat. Soc. for Rock Mechanics, Soc. for Core Analysts. Office: 14 Homer Ln Menlo Park CA 94025-6320

NOLLE, RICHARD, writer, astrological consultant; b. Orlando, Fla., Mar. 13, 1950; s. Frank Richard and Jeannie (Gilham) N.; m. Maria Barbara Standish, Sept. 29, 1974; children: Dylan R., Jonah B. BA, U. Fla., 1971. Cert. profl. astrologer Am. Fedn. Astrologers. Urban planner Planning Office of Orange County, Orlando, 1971-73; free-lance astrolog. cons. Orlando, 1973-84; free-lance writer, columnist Dell Pub. Co. Horoscope Mag., N.Y.C., 1975-92; editor Am. Fedn. Astrol. Rsch. Jour., Tempe, Ariz., 1984-86, Star*Tech Mag., Tempe, 1987-89; feature writer, cons. numerous nat. periodicals, Tempe, 1984—. Author: Critical Astrology, 1981, Chiron, 1983, Interpreting Astrology, 1986; co-author: Astrology of the Macrocosm, 1990. Mem. Assn. for Astrol. Networking (chmn. legal com. 1989-90). Office: PO Box 26599 Tempe AZ 85285-6599

NOLTE, JOHN MICHAEL, lawyer, consultant; b. England, Mar. 20, 1941; s. Ernest H. Nolte and Katheryn A. (Reinhart) Robertson; m. S.K. Marren (div. 1979); children: Stephanie Ann, Jennifer Lee, Sarah Sookwang; m. Diane L. Staufenbeil, Apr. 1982. BS, Ariz. State U., Tempe, 1963; MBA in Fin., U. Calif., Berkeley, JD, 1966. Bar: Oreg. 1966, Calif. 1973. Assoc. Keane, Haessler, Bauman & Harper, Portland, Oreg., 1966-71; assoc. gen. counsel Boise Cascade Corp., Palo Alto, Calif., 1972-73, Larwin Group, L.A., 1973-74; mng. ptnr. Leahy, O'Dea & Givens, San Francisco, 1974-81; pvt. practice law and cons. Canterbury and Tunbridge Wells, Eng., 1981-88, Montecito, Calif., 1988—; assoc. mng. dir. Staufenbeil Co., A.G., Boppard, Germany; officer Larwin Co., Encino, Calif.; mem. adv. bd. dirs. ID, Inc., Savo Electronics Divsn., Corvallis, Oreg. Hon. mem. East Sussex Conservative Party, Buxted, Eng., 1986—; pres. Glen Oaks Comty. Assn., Montecito, 1990-92; bd. trustees Castaic Union Edn. Found. With USMC, 1960-66; lt. comdr. USNR, 1966-70. Mem. ABA, Calif. Bar Assn., Oreg. Bar Assn., L.A. Bar Assn., Am. Judicature Soc., Order of Coif, Phi Kappa Phi. Republican. Home: 1362 Plaza De Sonadores Montecito CA 93108-2824 Office: PO Box 5493 Santa Barbara CA 93150-5493

NOLTE, SCOTT LLOYD, artistic director, actor; b. Aberdeen, Wash., Oct. 13, 1954; s. Lloyd Lester and Jaquelyn Fern (Edwards) N.; m. Pamela Baldwin Bailey, Aug. 17, 1974; children: Peter, Lisa. BA in Dramatic Arts, Seattle Pacific U., 1976. Artistic dir. Taproot Theatre Co., Seattle, 1976—; adj. faculty Seattle Pacific U., 1980-82, comml. actor. Pres. Greenwood C. of C., Seattle, 1992. Recipient Alumni Medallion award Seattle Pacific U., 1979, Howard E. Cummings Meml. award Greenwood C. of C. Presbyterian. Office: Taproot Theatre Co 204 N 85th St Seattle WA 98103-3604

NOON, JOHN PATRICK, editor, publisher; b. Jersey City, N.J., Oct. 25, 1954; s. John and Margaret Noon; m. Ellen Mary Uphaus, Sept. 5, 1981; children: Patrick, Lisa, Jeffrey. With editorial and mktg. depts. Addison-Wesley Pub. Co., 1979-83; v.p. sales and mktg. Intellisance Corp., 1983-87; pres. PUBLIX Info. Products, Inc., Sunnyvale, Calif., 1987-94; pres., CEO Syllabus Press, Inc., Sunnyvale, 1994—; founder Syllabus Mag., Query Mag., Higher Edn. Products Mag., Computer Sci. Products, Syllabus-European Edition, Syllabus Japan. Office: Syllabus Press Inc 1307 S Mary Ave Ste 211 Sunnyvale CA 94087-3018

NOONAN, DEBORAH RAE, dietitian; b. Augsburg, Germany, Jan. 31, 1965; came to U.S., 1965; d. Donald Lester and Wanda Kay (Maxwell) M.; m. Matthew William Noonan, Nov. 20, 1993. BS, Oreg. State U., 1991; cert., Detroit Medical Ctr., 1992. Cert. dietetic intern Harper Hosp. Detroit Med. Ctr., 1992. Dietary aide Corvallis (Oreg.) Care Ctr., 1989-90; biochemistry teaching asst. Oreg. Inst. Tech., Klamath Falls, Oreg., 1990; cashier Payless Drug Store, Klamath Falls, Oreg., 1982-92; clinical dietitian Merle West Medical Ctr., Klamath Falls, 1992—. Mem. Am. Dietetic Assn., Oreg. Dietetic Assn., Oreg. State Dietetic Assn. Republican. Roman Catholic. Home: 9845 Springlake Rd Klamath Falls OR 97603-8615 Office: Merle West Medical Ctr 2865 Daggett Ave Klamath Falls OR 97601-1106

NOONAN, EDWARD JAMES, student activity director; b. Butte, Mont., Mar. 11, 1949; s. Edward J. and Sara L. (McCartan) N. BA in Speech, Lewis U., 1971; MA in Speech (Theatre), Ball State U., 1983. Tchr. Cantwell High Sch., Montebello, Calif., 1971-75, Brother Rice High Sch., Chgo., 1975-79; dir., performer After Church Players, Helena, Mont., 1979—, Last Chance Storytellers, Helena, Mont., 1979—; resident dir. Carroll Coll., Helena, Mont., 1986-90, student activity dir., 1990—, adj. theatre prof., 1986—; bd. dirs. Grandstreet Theatre, Helena. Author: (play) War of the Copper Kings, 1989, Warren Street House, 1992, Frontier Justice, 1994, Taking History, 1995. Chmn. Spring Meadow Resources, Helena, 1994—. Recipient award to publish (book of poetry) Fresh Recognition, 1994, (novel) Missing Pieces, 1994. Democrat. Roman Catholic. Home: 409 Dearborn Ave Helena MT 59601-6146 Office: Carroll Coll Box 102 Carroll Coll Helena MT 59625

NOONAN, JOHN T., JR., federal judge, legal educator; b. Boston, Oct. 24, 1926; s. John T. and Marie (Shea) N.; m. Mary Lee Bennett, Dec. 27, 1967; children: John Kenneth, Rebecca Lee, Susanna Bain. B.A., Harvard U.,

1946, LL.B., 1954; student, Cambridge U., 1946-47; M.A., Cath. U. Am., 1949, Ph.D., 1951, LHD, 1980; LL.D., U. Santa Clara, 1974, U. Notre Dame, 1976, Loyola U. South, 1978; LHD, Holy Cross Coll., 1980; LL.D., St. Louis U., 1981, U. San Francisco, 1985; student, Holy Cross Coll., 1980, Cath. U. Am., 1980, Gonzaga U., 1986, U. San Francisco, 1986. Bar: Mass. 1954, U.S. Supreme Ct. 1971. Mem. spl. staff Nat. Security Council, 1954-55; pvt. practice Herrick & Smith, Boston, 1955-60; prof. law U. Notre Dame, 1961-66; prof. law U. Calif., Berkeley, 1967-86, chmn. religious studies, 1970-73, chmn. medieval studies, 1978-79; judge U.S. Ct. Appeals (9th cir.), San Francisco, 1985—; Oliver Wendell Holmes, Jr. lectr. Harvard U. Law Sch., 1972, Pope John XXIII lectr. Cath. U. Law Sch., 1973, Cardinal Bellarmine lectr. St. Louis U. Div. Sch., 1973, Baum lectr. U. Ill., 1988, Strassberger lectr. U. Tex., 1989; chmn. bd. Games Rsch., Inc., 1961-76; overseer Harvard U., 1991—. Author: The Scholastic Analyst of Usury, 1957; Contraception: A History of Its Treatment by the Catholic Theologians and Canonists, 1965; Power to Dissolve, 1972; Persons and Masks of the Law, 1976; The Antelope, 1977; A Private Choice, 1979; Bribes, 1984; editor: Natural Law Forum, 1961-70, Am. Jour. Jurisprudence, 1970, The Morality of Abortion, 1970. Chmn. Brookline Redevel. Authority, Mass., 1958-62; cons. Papal Commn. on Family, 1965-66, Ford Found., Indonesian Legal Program, 1968; NIH, 1973, NIH, 1974; expert Presdl. Commn. on Population and Am. Future, 1971; cons. U.S. Cath. Conf., 1979-86; sec., treas. Inst. for Research in Medieval Canon Law, 1970-88; pres. Thomas More-Jacques Maritain Inst., 1977—; trustee Population Council, 1969-76, Phi Kappa Found., 1970-76, Grad. Theol. Union, 1970-73, U. San Francisco, 1971-75; mem. com. theol. edn. Yale U., 1972-77; exec. com. Cath. Commn. Intellectual and Cultural Affairs, 1972-75; bd. dirs. Ctr. for Human Values in the Health Scis., 1969-71, S.W. Intergroup Relations Council, 1970-72, Inst. for Study Ethical Issues, 1971-73. Recipient St. Thomas More award U. San Francisco, 1974, Christian Culture medal, 1975, Laetare medal U. Notre Dame, 1984, Campion medal Cath. Book Club, 1987; Guggenheim fellow, 1965-66, 79-80, Laetare medal U. Notre Dame, 1984, Campion medal, 1987, Alemany medal Western Dominican Province, 1988; Ctr. for advanced Studies in Behavioral Scis. fellow, 1973-74; Wilson Ctr. fellow, 1979-80. Fellow Am. Acad. Arts and Scis., Am. Soc. Legal Historians (hon.); mem. Am. Soc. Polit. and Legal Philosophy (v.p. 1964), Canon Law Soc. Am. (gov. 1970-72), Am. Law Inst., Phi Beta Kappa (senator United chpts. 1970-72, pres. Alpha of Calif. chpt. 1972-73). Office: US Ct Appeals 9th Cir PO Box 193939 San Francisco CA 94119-3939

NOONAN, WILLIAM MOSS, information systems executive, consultant; b. Plainfield, N.J., Nov. 8, 1942; s. Raymond Edgar and Edna Maida (Sanger) N.; m. Jo Ann Gardiner, July 3, 1966 (div. July 1984); m. Cynthia Gail Lynch, Aug. 22, 1985; children by previous marriages: Larissa, Leigh, Matthew, Duncan, Darby. BSBA, U. Richmond, 1964; MBA, Stanford U., 1966. Asst. acct. exec. Benton & Bowles, N.Y.C., 1966-67; sr. cons. Arthur Andersen & Co., San Francisco, 1969-71, mgr., 1971-79; ptnr. Arthur Andersen & Co., Rio de Janeiro, 1979-82, Houston, 1982-84; sr. cons. Arthur D. Little, San Francisco, 1984-86; sr. mgr. Price Waterhouse, San Francisco, 1986-88, ptnr., 1988—; spkr. info. tech. mgmt., change mgmt., bus. process reengineering. vol. U.S. Peace Corps, Colombia, 1967-69; asst. treas. Am. Sch. of Rio de Janeiro, 1980-82; dir. fundraising peninsula chpt. Amigos de las Americas, 1987; vice-chmn. fundraising bus. sch. Stanford U., 1983—; bd. dirs. Rio de Janeiro chpt. Am. C. of C., 1981-82. Mem. Assn. for Systems Mgmt. (sec. San Francisco chpt. 1989-90, program chmn. 1990-92, v.p. 1990-91, pres. 1991-92), Coun. Logistics Mgmt. Office: Price Waterhouse 555 California St San Francisco CA 94104-1502

NOORDA, RAYMOND J., computer software company executive; b. Ogden, Utah.. BSEE, Utah, 1949. CEO Novell Inc., 1982—. Office: MTI Technology Corp 4905 E La Palma Ave Anaheim CA 92807-1915

NOORZOY, MOHAMMAD SIDDIEQ, economist, educator; b. Kabul, Afghanistan, July 5, 1934; came to the U.S., 1954; s. Noor Ul and Bibi Aisha Haq; m. V. Elizabeth Haviside, Aug. 30, 1957 (div. 1984); children: Shah Hamid, Aisha Aryana, Zia Jamal; m. Farkhunda Fakhri, Mar. 30, 1990. BA, U. Calif., Berkeley, 1957, MA, 1960; PhD, U. Wash., 1965. Instr. U. Calif., U. Wash., Berkeley, 1959-63; mem. rsch. dept. Fed. Res. Bank San Francisco, 1963; asst. prof. Calif. State U., San Luis Obispo, 1963-64; asst. prof. U. Alberta, 1965-69, assoc. prof., 1971-80, prof., 1981-87, emeritus prof. econs., 1988—; rsch. assoc. inst. internat. studies U. Calif., Berkeley, 1986-90; vis. scholar Hoover Instn. Stanford U., 1984, 91; adj. prof. Naval Postgrad. Sch., Monterey, Calif., 1989-90; fellow Ctr. for Middle Eastern Studies U. Calif., Berkeley, 1992—. Contbr. articles to profl. jours. Pres. Afghanistan Assistance Coun. Grantee Earhart Found., 1986-87; recipient rsch. award in humanities and social scis. Can. Coun., 1969-70; scholar U. Wash., 1961-62. Mem. Am. Econ. Assn., Middle East Studies Assn., Western Econ. Assn. Home: 3070 Lopez Rd Pebble Beach CA 93953

NOPAR, ALAN SCOTT, lawyer; b. Chgo., Nov. 14, 1951; s. Myron E. and Evelyn R. (Millman) N. BS, U. Ill., 1976; JD, Stanford U., 1979. Bar: Ariz. 1979, U.S. Dist. Ct. Ariz. 1980, U.S. Ct. Appeals (9th cir.) 1980, U.S. Supreme Ct. 1982, Calif. 1989; CPA, Ill. Assoc. O'Connor, Cavanagh, Anderson, Westover, Killingsworth & Beshears P.A., Phoenix, 1979-85, ptnr., 1985-87; of counsel Tower, Byrne & Beaugureau, Phoenix, 1987-88; ptnr. Minutillo & Gorman, San Jose, Calif., 1989-91, Bosco, Blau, Ward & Nopar, San Jose, 1991—. Mem. Ariz. Rep. Caucus, Phoenix, 1984-88. Mem. AICPA, ABA (bus. law and law practice mgmt. sects., mem. forum com. on franchising), Ariz. Bar Assn. (bus. law sect.), Calif. State Bar Assn. (bus. law sect.). Office: Bosco Blau Ward & Nopar 2166 The Alameda San Jose CA 95126-1144

NORA, JAMES JACKSON, physician, author, educator; b. Chgo., June 26, 1928; s. Joseph James and May Henrietta (Jackson) N.; m. Barbara June Fluhrer, Sept. 7, 1949 (div. 1963); children: Wendy Alison, Penelope Welbon, Marianne Leslie; m. Audrey Faye Hart, Apr. 9, 1966; children: James Jackson Jr., Elizabeth Hart Nora. AB, Harvard U., 1950; MD, Yale U., 1954; MPH, U. Calif., Berkeley, 1978. Intern Detroit Receiving Hosp., 1954-55; resident in pediatrics U. Wis. Hosps., Madison, 1959-61, fellow in cardiology, 1962-64; fellow in genetics McGill U. Children's Hosp., Montreal, Can., 1964-65; assoc. prof. pediatrics Baylor Coll. Medicine, Houston, 1965-71; prof. genetics, preventive medicine and pediatrics U. Colo. Med. Sch., Denver, 1971—; dir. genetics Rose Med. Ctr., Denver, 1980—; dir. pediatric cardiology and cardiovascular tng. U. Colo. Sch. Medicine, 1971-78; mem. task force Nat. Heart and Lung Program, Bethesda, Md., 1973; cons. WHO, Geneva, 1983—; mem. U.S.-U.S.S.R. Exchange Program on Heart Disease, Moscow and Leningrad, 1975. Author: The Whole Heart Book, 1980, 2d rev. edit., 1989, (with F.C. Fraser) Medical Genetics, 4th rev. edit., 1994, Genetics of Man, 2d rev. edit., 1986, Cardiovascular Diseases: Genetics, Epidemiology and Prevention, 1991; (novels) The Upstart Spring, 1989, The Psi Delegation, 1989, Sabbatical, 1995. Com. mem. March of Dimes, Am. Heart Assn., Boy Scouts Am. Served to lt. USAAC, 1945-47. Grantee Nat. Heart, Lung and Blood Inst., Nat. Inst. Child Health and Human Devel., Am. Heart Assn., NIH; recipient Virginia Apgar Meml. award. Fellow Am. Coll. Cardiology, Am. Acad. Pediatrics, Am. Coll. Med. Genetics; mem. Am. Pediatric Soc., Soc. Pediatric Rsch., Am. Heart Assn., Teratology Soc., Transplantation Soc., Am. Soc. Human Genetics, Authors Guild, Authors League, Acad. Am. Poets, Mystery Writers Am., Rocky Mountain Harvard Club. Democrat. Presbyterian. Home: 3110 Fairweather Ct Olney MD 20832-3021 Office: Parklawn Bldg 5600 Fishers Ln Rm 18-05 Rockville MD 20857-0001

NORBERG, JARON B., public service company executive; b. 1937; married. JD, U. Utah, 1967; postgrad., Brigham Young U. Ptnr. Snell & Wilmer, 1967-73; gen. counsel Ariz. Pub. Svc. Co., Phoenix, 1972-82, sr. v.p., corp. counsel, from 1982, now exec. v.p., chief fin. officer, also bd. dirs. Office: Ariz Pub Svc Co PO Box 53999 Phoenix AZ 85072-3999

NORBY-LOUD, MARIE BARBARA, secondary education educator; b. Chgo., Sept. 14, 1947; d. Walter Carl and Emma Dell (Fowler) Norby; m. Robert Thiel, Mar. 17, 1967 (div. Dec. 1988); children: William, Steven, Christopher; m. Bennie Lee Loud, Mar. 20, 1992. BS, U. Minn., 1985; MA, U. No. Colo., 1991, postgrad., 1995. Cert. English and lang. arts, Minn.; cert. fgn. lang., Colo. English instr. Ea. Wyo. Coll., Douglas, 1986-89; tchg. asst. U. No. Colo., Greeley, 1989-91; exec. dir. Right to Read, Greeley, 1991-92; adj. faculty Aims C.C., Greeley, 1992-93; Spanish tchr. R.E. 5J Sch. Dist., Johnstown, Colo., 1993—; mem. student fees allocation com. U. No. Colo., Greeley, 1991-93. Mem., v.p. Wyo. Child Care Cert. Adv. Commn., Cheyenne, 1979-82; mem. Planning Commn., Douglas, 1980-82; unit commr. Boy Scouts Ctrl. Wyo. Coun., Casper, 1984-85. Colo. Grad. fellow U. No. Colo., Greeley, 1990. Mem. Phi Delta Kappa, Sigma Tau Delta. Home: 1610 7th Ave Greeley CO 80631-5802 Office: PO Box G Johnstown CO 80534

NORD, HAROLD EMIL, JR., small business owner, consultant; b. Manistee, Mich., Dec. 28, 1928; s. Harold Emil Nord and Anna Margaret (Simmons) Chase; m. Dolores Lillian Matistic, Apr. 26, 1952; children: Harold Emil III, Karen. BS in Hotel Adminstrn., Mich. State U., 1950; M Aero. Sci. Mgmt., Embry-Riddle Aero. U., 1993. Cert. air transport pilot. Capt. Eastern Airlines, Miami, Fla., 1957-88; owner, operator Golden Gate Cottages, Laconia, N.H., 1969-73, Seaplane Svcs., Inc., Laconia, 1969-73; pres. Aviation Mgmt. Advisors, Inc., West Palm Beach, Fla., 1978—; gen. ptnr. Airports Mgmt. Group, Tucson, 1993; bd. dirs. Tucson U.; nat. chmn. Aviators Legal Fund, Inc.; v.p. pub. rels. and govt. affairs Air Boston Airlines; sales and mktg. Alpine Air of Am., Blaine, Minn.; ptnr., dir. Jeriko Corp., Tucson. Mem. U.S. Rep. Senatorial Club, Washington, 1977—, Futures Group of Palm Beach, 1984, Pundits of Palm Beach, 1983, Safety, Health and Environ. Resource Ctr. Internat., Vets. of Safety, 1993; nat. chmn. com. Postal Commemorative Stamp for Capt. Edward V. Rickenbacker; sr. advisor CAP. Named Master Bush Pilot, Ladd Air Force Base, Fairbanks, Alaska, 1955; Paul Harris fellow Palm Beach Rotary Club, 1987—. Mem. Airline Pilots Assn., Internat. Fellowship Flying Rotarians, Mich. State U. Alumni Assn. (pres. Atlanta chpt. 1959-61, pres. N.H. chpt.), Ret. Ea. Pilots Assn., Eastern Airlines Retirees Assn., Early Birds Aviation, Nat. Eagle Scout Assn., Nat. Seaplane Pilots Assn., Nat. Aero. Assn., Exptl. Aricraft Assn., Dadaelians Assn., N.J. Rotary Club, Quiet Birdmen, Toastmasters, Silver Wings Club, Delta Upsilon. Home and Office: Aviation Mgmt Advisors Inc PO Box 425 Rye Beach NH 03871-0425 also: 5200 N Dixie Hwy Apt 2101 West Palm Beach FL 33407

NORD, THOMAS ALLISON, hospital administrator; b. Boise, Idaho, Dec. 29, 1934; s. Everett Oliver and Alice Susan (Sherry) N.; m. Kay Hahn, Apr. 19, 1958; children: Mark Allison, Matthew Brendan, Julia Christian Nord Jenkins, Christopher Thomas. BSBA, Denver U., 1957, MBA, 1971; postgrad., Cornell U., 1974. Office mgr. Mountain States Sprinkler Supply, Denver, 1957-61; owner, mgr. Desert Rain, Roswell, N.Mex., 1961-68; sheriff Chaves County, Roswell, 1966-71; adminstr. St. Vincent Gen. Hosp., Leadville, Colo., 1972-78, Grand River Hosp. Dist., Rifle, Colo., 1980-83; planner, coord. outreach St. Mary's Hosp. and Med. Ctr., Grand Junction, Colo., 1978-80, assoc. adminstr., 1980; pres., CEO, Ivinson Meml. Hosp., Laramie, Wyo., 1983—; Mem. Garfield County Human Svc. Commn., 1980-83, chmn., 1982-83; mem. governing bd. Westrn Colo. Health Sys. Agy., 1980; chmn. steering com. Southeastern Colo. Health Sys. Agy., 1975, chmn. governing bd., 1976-79; mem. liaison com. for U. Wyo. Sch. Nursing, 1984-85; mem. clin. faculty programs in health svcs. adminstrn. U. Minn. Sch. Pub. Health, 1984; bd. dirs. Blue Cross/Blue Shield Wyo., 1988—, mem. exec. com., 1993—; mem. Wyo. Healthcare Reform Commn., 1994; chmn. bd. VHA Mountain States. Active Boy Scouts Am., United Way. Fellow Am. Coll. Healthcare Execs. (Wyo. regent 1994); mem. Am. Hosp. Assn. (Colo. Hosp. Assn. del. 1980-83, mem. task force for input price adjustments 1988, del. regional policy bd. 1994), Wyo. Hosp. Assn. (bd. dirs. 1984—, chmn. 1986), Healthcare Forum (membership com. 1985, bd. dirs. 1986-89), Laramie C. of C., Rotary, Lions, Elks. Republican. Home: PO Box 155 Centennial WY 82055-0155 Office: Ivinson Memorial Hospital 255 N 30th St Laramie WY 82070-5140

NORDEL, PATRICIA A. OLMSTEAD, medical/surgical, critical care, and obstetrical nurse; b. New Britain, Conn., Jan. 19, 1965; d. Lester B. and Patricia (Tufts) Olmstead; m. David R. Nordel; 1 child, David M. BSN, U. Conn., 1987. Cert. med.-surg. nurse. Commd. 2d lt. USAF, 1987, advanced through grades to capt., 1991; staff nurse med.-surg. USAF, Scott AFB, Ill., Travis AFB, Calif.; charge nurse outpatient USAF, RAF Greenham Common, Eng.; staff nurse obstetrics USAF, RAF Upper Heyford, Eng., 1987-94; staff nurse Travel Nurse Broker Svc., Napa, Calif., 1994—.

NORDGREN, WILLIAM BENNETT, engineering executive; b. Salt Lake City, Mar. 5, 1960; s. Kent Widstoe and Eliza (Schmuhl) N.; m. Carolyn B. Erickson, June 26, 1981; 1 child, William Tyson. BS, Brigham Young U., 1986, MS, 1989. Engr. Boeing Airplanes Co., Seattle, 1986-88; pres. CIM Engring. Assocs., Orem, Utah, 1988-89; v.p. engring. Prodn. Modeling Corp., Orem, 1989-93; pres. F & H Simulations, Inc., Orem, 1993—. Developer, polar coordinant mill. Mem. Soc. Mfg. Engrs., Inst. Indsl. Engrs. Republican. Mormon. Office: PO Box 658 Orem UT 84059-0658

NORDLUND, JAMES ROBERT, state agency administrator; b. St. Paul, Minn., Dec. 23, 1952; s. Leonard Gustav and Catherine Ann (Lindow) N. BS, St. John U., 1975; MPA, U. Colo., 1982. Journeyman carpenter Carpenter's Locals Denver and Anchorage, 1981-85; housing rehab. specialist Anchorage Neighborhood Housing Svcs., 1983-86; legis. asst. Alaska State Legislature, Anchorage, Juneau, 1986-92, state legislator, 1993-95; dir. divsn. pub. assistance State of Alaska, Juneau, 1995—; pres., CEO Macuir Co. Inc., Anchorage, 1990—; comml. fisherman, Alaska, 1987—. Founding pres. Anchorage Waterways Coun., 1985. Democrat. Roman Catholic. Office: PO Box 110640 Juneau AK 99811-0640

NORDLUND, PATRICIA JEAN, school system administrator; b. Billings, Mont., June 29, 1952; d. C. Jerry and Mary Ellen (McKeever) Whittle; m. Ronald G. Nordlund, June 8, 1973; children: Eric M., Ryan C. AA in Bus., Mont. State U., 1972. Cert. fitness leader YMCA. Fitness/aerobics coord. Billings Family YMCA, 1982-86; dir. alumni rels. Billings Cath. Schs., 1989-92, dir. devel., 1992—. Mem. NAFE, Nat. Soc. Fund Raising Execs. (sec. 1994). Roman Catholic. Office: Billings Cath Sch System PO Box 31158 Billings MT 59107-1158

NORDMEYER, MARY BETSY, vocational educator; b. New Haven, May 19, 1939; d. George and Barbara Stedman (Thompson) N. ABPhil, Wheaton Coll., Norton, Mass., 1960; MA, San Jose State U., 1968; AS in Computer Sci., West Valley Coll., 1985. Cert. tchr. spl. edn., Calif.; cert. secondary tchr., Calif. Instr. English Santa Clara (Calif.) Unified Sch. Dist., 1965-77, vocat. specialist, 1977—, dir. project work ability, 1984—, also mem. community adv. com.; facilitator Project Work-Ability, Region 5, 1985-86, sec., 1988-90. Author poetry, 1960, Career and Vocat. Edn. for Students With Spl. Needs, 1986; author/designer Career English, 1974, Career Information, 1975. Recipient Outstanding Secondary Educator award, 1975, Award of Excellence, Nat. Assn. Vocat. Edn., 1984; named Tchr. of Yr. in Spl. Edn., Santa Clara Unified Sch. Dist., 1984-85. Mem. Calif. Assn. Work Experience Educators, Sierra Club, Epsilon Eta Sigma. Democrat. Home: 14920 Sobey Rd Saratoga CA 95070-6236 Office: Santa Clara Unified Sch Dist 1889 Lawrence Rd Santa Clara CA 95051-2108

NORDSTROM, BRUCE A., department store executive; b. 1933; married. BA, U. Wash., 1956. With Nordstrom, Inc., Seattle, 1956—, v.p., 1964-70, pres., 1970-75, chmn., 1975-77, co-chmn., 1977—, dir. Office: Nordstrom Inc 1501 5th Ave Seattle WA 98101-1603*

NORDSTROM, JAMES F., department store executive; b. 1940; married. BBA, U. Wash., 1962. Various positions Nordstrom, Inc., Seattle, 1960—, exec. v.p., 1975-78, pres., 1975-78, from 1978, co-chmn., also bd. dirs. Office: Nordstrom Inc 1501 5th Ave Seattle WA 98101-1603

NORDSTROM, JOHN N., department store executive; b. 1937; married. BA, U. Wash., 1958. With Nordstrom, Inc., Seattle, 1958—, v.p., 1965-70, exec. v.p., 1970-75, pres., 1975-77, co-chmn., 1977—, dir.; bd. dirs. Fed. Res. Bank San Francisco. Office: Nordstrom Inc 1501 5th Ave Seattle WA 98101-1603*

NORDYKE, ELEANOR COLE, population researcher, public health nurse; b. Los Angeles, June 15, 1927; d. Ralph G. and Louise Noble (Carter) Cole; m. Robert Allan Nordyke, June 18, 1950; children: Mary Ellen Nordyke-Grace, Carolyn Nordyke-Cozzette, Thomas A., Susan E., Gretchen Nordyke Worthington. BS, Stanford U., 1950; P.H.N. accreditation, U. Calif.-Berkeley, 1952; MPH, U. Hawaii, 1969. RN. Pub. health nurse San Francisco Dept. Health, 1950-52; nurse-tchr. Punahou Sch., Honolulu, 1966-67; clinic coordinator East-West Population Inst., East-West Ctr., Honolulu, 1969-75, population rschr., 1975-82, rsch. fellow, 1982-92; cons. Hawaii Commn. on Population, Honolulu, 1970-83; mem. Hawaii Policy Action Group for Family Planning, Honolulu, 1971-89, chmn., 1976-77. Author: The Peopling of Hawaii, 1977, 2d rev. edit., 1989, A Profile of Hawaii's Elderly Population, 1984, (with Robert Gardner) The Demographic Situation in Hawaii, 1974, mem. editorial bd. Hawaiian Jour. History, 1980—; contbr. articles to profl. jours. Bd. dirs. YMCA, Honolulu, 1970—, vice-chmn. 1978-79, chmn. YMCA Camp Erdman, 1989-92; bd. dirs. Hawaii Planned Parenthood, 1974-78, Friends of Libr. of Hawaii, 1985-87; trustee Hawaiian Hist. Soc., 1978-82, Arcadia Retirement Residence, Honolulu, 1978-87; bd. dirs. Hawaii Pacific U., 1988—, mem. liberal arts coun. Mem. Population Assn. Am., Population Reference Bur., Hawaii Pub. Health Assn., Am. Statis. Assn., Hawaii Econ. Assn., Hawaiian Hist. Soc., Friends of East-West Ctr., Friends of Univ. Hawaii Sch. Medicine, Stanford Nurses Alumni Assn., Stanford Alumni Assn. (bd. dirs. Hawaii chpt.), Friends of Iolani Palace, Gen. Fed. Women's History Club, Book Reading Club, Outrigger Canoe Club, Morning Music Club, Phi Beta Kappa. Democrat. Congregationalist. Home: 2013 Kakela Dr Honolulu HI 96822-2158

NORGAARD, RICHARD BRUCE, economist, educator, consultant; b. Washington, Aug. 18, 1943; s. John Trout and Marva Dawn (Andersen) N.; m. Marida Jane Fowle, June 19, 1965 (div.); children—Kari Marie, Marc Anders; m. Nancy A. Rader, June, 5, 1993. B.A. in Econs., U. Calif.-Berkeley, 1965; M.S. in Agrl. Econs. Oreg. State U., 1967; Ph.D. in Econs., U. Chgo., 1971. Instr. Oreg. Coll. Edn., 1967-68; asst. prof. agrl. and resource econs. U. Calif.-Berkeley, 1970-76, assoc. prof., 1976-77, 80-87, assoc. prof. energy and resources, 1987-92, prof. energy and resources, 1992—; project specialist Ford Found., Brazil, 1978-79; cons. Ford Found., Calif. Dept. Water Resources, Pub. Interest Econs., Ind. Petroleum Producers of Calif., Plan Sierra Dominican Republic, UN Food & Agrl. Orgn., UN Environment Program, USAID-Thailand, The World Bank; mem. sci. com. on problems of the environment U.S. Nat. Rsch. Coun. Author: Development Betrayed: The End of Progress and a Coevolutionary Revisioning of the Future, 1994; contbr. numerous articles to acad. jours. Active civil rights, environ, and peace orgns. Mem. AAAS, Assn. Pub. Policy and Mgmt., Latin Am. Studies Assn., Am. Econs. Assn., v.p. Internat. Soc. Ecol. Econs., Fedn. Am. Scientists, Assn. Environ. and Resource Econs. Home: 1198 Keith Ave Berkeley CA 94708-1607 Office: U Calif Energy & Resources Program Bldg T-4 Berkeley CA 94720

NORKIN, MARK MITCHELL, sales executive; b. Whittier, Calif., Nov. 19, 1955; s. Cleo Donald and Carol Ann (Stewart) Mathis. Grad., Gemmological Inst. Am., 1976. Gemmologist Slavicks Jewelers, Newport Beach, Calif., 1976-77; apprentice Troy Sheet Metal Works, Montebello, Calif., 1977-79, journeyman, 1979-80, foreman, 1980-82, project engr., 1982-85, v.p. sales and engring., 1985—; bd. dirs. Troy Sheet Metal. Republican. Office: 1026 S Vail Ave Montebello CA 90640

NORKOOL, DIANE MARIE, nursing administrator, medical/surgical nurse; b. Tacoma; d. Carl G.E. and Rosella Ann (Dotson) N. BSN, U. Wash., 1965, M in Nursing, 1976. RN, Wash. Med./surg. charge nurse Virginia Mason Hosp., Seattle, ICU/CCU/emergency rm. float nurse, staff nurse, nurse mgr. in hyperbaric dept.; clin. asst. prof. physiological nursing, U. Wash., Seattle, lectr. various nat./internat. med. nursing confs. Contbr. articles to profl. jours. Mem. Undersea and Hyperbaric Med. Soc. (v.p. No. Pacific chpt.), Baromed. Nurses Assn. Home: 10494 Dixon Dr S Seattle WA 98178-2713 Office: Virginia Mason Hosp Hyperbaric Dept 925 Seneca St Seattle WA 98101-2742

NORLING, JAMES A., electronics company executive. BSEE, U. Ill., 1964, MSEE, 1965. Engring. trainee Motorola Inc., Schaumburg, Ill., 1965-70, ops. mgr. spl. products, 1970-71, ops. mgr. bipolar digital integrated cir. businesses, timepiece electric ops. mgr., bipolar ops. planning mgr., power metal transistors ops. mgr., 1971-73, power products dir. ops., 1973-79, gen. mgr. power products div., 1979-83, sr. v.p., gen. mgr. internat. group semicondr., 1981-85, sr. v.p., asst. gen. mgr. semicondr. products sector, 1985-86, exec. v.p., gen. mgr. semicondr. products sector, 1986—. Office: Motorola Inc Semiconductor Products Sector 56th St & Thomas Ave Phoenix AZ 85008

NORMAN, ARNOLD MCCALLUM, JR., engineering executive; b. Little Rock, May 1, 1940; s. Arnold McCallum and Ann Carolyn (Gibson) N.; m. Sylvia Burton, July 1, 1962 (div. 1967); m. Marisha Irene Malin, June 7, 1969; children: Frank Lee, Paul James. BS in Physics, Ga. Inst. Tech., 1962. Test engr. Rocketdyne div. Rockwell Internat., Canoga Park, Calif., 1962-64, engr. in charge of various programs, 1964-75, engr. in charge, project engr. large chem. lasers, 1975-85, project engr. space sta. propulsion system, 1985-87, project engr. nat. launch system health mgmt. systems, 1987-92, project engr. kinetic energy weapons, 1993-94; project engr. advanced propulsion systems Rockwell Internat., Canoga Park, Calif., 1994-95, sr. engring. specialist, 1995—; mem. ops. com. health mgmt. ctr. U. Cin., 1988-94; mem. program com. Ann. Internat. Conf. on Engring. Applications of Artificial Intelligence, 1988-90; presenter in field. Mem. editorial bd. Jour. Applied Intelligence, 1990-94; author numerous papers in field. Fellow AIAA (assoc., sect. chair sr. adv. com. 1991-93, chmn. San Fernando Valley sect. 1989-90, sys. effectiveness and safety tech. com. 1995—), Inst. Advancement Engring.; mem. Tau Beta Pi. Home: 20238 Mobile St Canoga Park CA 91306-4241 Office: Rockwell Internat Rocketdyne divsn 6633 Canoga Ave Canoga Park CA 91303-2703

NORMAN, DANIEL WILEY, computer technician/programmer; b. High Point, N.C., June 20, 1961; s. Jerry William and Christine Eugenia (Steed) N.; m. Debra Kloss, June 23, 1984; 1 child, Thomas William. BS in Math., Mars Hill Coll., 1986. Data control lead Tymshare, Garden Grove, Calif., 1982-84; sys. technician GI Trucking Co., La Mirada, Calif., 1986-95; LAN adminstr. Union Pacific R.R., 1995—; scorekeeper/programmer NRA/Charlton Heston Celebrity Shoot, Irvine, Calif., 1993, 94; owner A.H.C. Computer Solutions, La Mirada, 1993—. Ind. instr. gun safety, Whittier, Calif., 1993—. Mem. IEEE, NRA (instr.), Gun Owner's Action Com. Republican. Baptist. Office: PO Box 10 La Mirada CA 90637-0010

NORMAN, DAVID A., business equipment company executive; b. St. Paul, Nov. 15, 1935; s. Robert Albin and Nellie (Williams) N.; m. M. Ruth Landrum, July 19, 1959; children: David, Susan. BS in Mech. Engring., U. Minn., 1963; MS in Indsl. Engring., Stanford U., 1966. Engr. Lockheed Missiles and Space Co., Sunnyvale, Calif., 1963-67; project leader Stanford Research Inst., Calif., 1967-69; v.p., dir. Creative Strategies, Inc., Palo Alto, Calif., 1969-71; pres., chief exec. officer Dataquest, Inc., San Jose, Calif., 1971-82; pres., chief exec. officer Businessland, Inc., San Jose, 1982—. Served with USN, 1955-60.

NORMAN, DONALD ARTHUR, cognitive scientist; b. N.Y.C., Dec. 25, 1935; s. Noah N. and Miriam F. N.; m. Martha Karpati (div.); children—Cynthia, Michael; m. Julie Jacobsen; 1 child, Eric. B.S.E.E., MIT, 1957; M.S.E.E., U. Pa., 1959, Ph.D. in Psychology, 1962; degree in Psychology (hon.), U. Padua, Italy, 1995. Lectr. Harvard U., 1962-66; Prof. dept. psychology U. Calif.-San Diego, La Jolla, 1966-92, prof. emeritus, 1992—, prof., chair dept. cognitive sci., 1988-92, chair dept.psychology, 1974-78, dir. cognitive sci. program, 1977-88, dir. Inst. for Cognitive Sci., 1981-89; Apple fellow Apple Computer Inc., Cupertino, Calif., 1993—; mem. sci. adv. bd. Naval Pers. Rsch. Ctr., San Diego, 1982-86; cons. to industry on human computer interaction and user-centered design. Author: Learning and Memory, 1982, Human Information Processing, 2d edit., 1977, User Centered System Design, 1986, The Psychology of Everyday Things, 1988, The Design of Everyday Things, 1989, Turn Signals Are the Facial Expressions of Automobiles, 1992, Things That Make Us Smart, 1993; editor: Perspectives on Cognitive Science, 1981, Exploration in Cognition, 1975, Cognitive Sci. Jour., 1981-85; series editor Cognitive Sci. Series Lawrence Earlbaum Assoc., 1979—. Recipient Excellence in Rsch. award U. Calif., 1984. Fellow Am. Psychol. Soc., Am. Acad. Arts and Scis.; mem. Am. Assn. Arts and Scis., Am. Assn. for Artificial Intelligence, Assn. for Computational Machinery, Cognitive Sci. Soc. (chmn. founding mem.). Office:

Apple Computer Inc MS 301-4UE 1 Infinite Loop Cupertino CA 95014-2083

NORMAN, E. GLADYS, business computer educator, consultant; b. Oklahoma City, June 13, 1933; d. Joseph Eldon and Mildred Lou (Truitt) Biggs; m. Joseph R.R. Radeck, Mar. 1, 1953 (div. Aug. 1962); children: Jody Matti, Ray Norman, Warren Norman (dec. May 1993), Dana Norman; m. Leslie P. Norman, Aug. 26, 1963 (dec. Feb. 1994); 1 child, Elayne Pearce. Student, Fresno (Calif.) State Coll., 1951-52, UCLA, 1956-59, Linfield Coll., 1986-95. Math. aid U.S. Naval Weapons Ctr., China Lake, Calif., 1952-56, computing systems specialist, 1957-68; systems programmer Oreg. Motor Vehicles Dept., Salem, 1968-69; instr. in data processing, dir. Computer Programming Ctr., Salem, 1969-72; instr. in data processing Merritt-Davis Bus. Coll., Salem, 1972-73; sr. programmer, analyst Teledyne Wah Chang, Albany, Oreg., 1973-79; sr. systems analyst Oreg. Dept. Vets. Affairs, Albany, 1979-80; instr. in bus. computers Linn-Benton Community Coll., Albany, 1980-95; ret., 1995; computer cons. for LBCC Ret. Sr. Vol. Program, 1995—; presenter computer software seminars State of Oreg., 1991-93, Oreg. Credit Assoc. Conf., 1991, Oreg. Regional Users Group Conf., 1992; computer cons. in field. Mem. Data Processing Mgmt. Assn. (bd. dirs. 1977-84, 89-95, sec. 1995, assoc. v.p. 1988, Diamond Individual Performance award 1985). Democrat.

NORMAN, JOHN BARSTOW, JR., designer, educator; b. Paloa, Kans., Feb. 5, 1940; s. John B. and Ruby Maxine (Johnson) N.; m. Roberta Jeanne Martin, June 6, 1967; children: John Barstow III, Elizabeth Jeanne. BFA, U. Kans., 1962, MFA, 1966. Designer and illustrator Advt. Design, Kansas City, Mo., 1962-64; asst. instr. U. Kans., Lawrence, 1964-66; art dir. Hallmark Cards, Inc., Kansas City, Mo., 1966-69; instr. dept. art U. Denver, 1969-73, asst. prof., 1973-78, assoc. prof., 1978—, Disting. prof., 1980; sr. designer Mo. Coun. Arts and Humanities, 1966-67; cons. designer Rocky Mountain Bank Note Corp., Denver, 1971—, Signage Identity System, U. Dever; bd. dirs. communications U. Denver; tech. cons. Denver Art Mus., 1974—, designed exhbns., 1974-75; adv., cons. Jefferson County (Colo.) Sch., System, 1976—; chmn. Design and Sculpture Exhbn., Colo. Celebration of the Arts, 1975-76. One man shows include: Gallery Cortina, Aspen, Colo., 1983; commd. works include: Jedda, Saudi Arabia, Synegistics Corp., Denver; represented in permanent collections Pasadena Ctr. for the Arts, N.Y. Art Dirs. Club, Calif. State U./Fiber Collection, Pasadena (Calif.) Ctr. for the Arts, 1984, N.Y. Art Dirs. Club, 1985 Midland Art Coun./Fiber Collection, 1985, Geologic Soc. Am.; represented in traveling exhbns. L.A. Art Dirs. Show and N.Y. Art Dirs. Show, U.S., Europe, Japan, 1985; feartured in Denver Post, 1984, Post Electric City Mag., 1984, Rocky Mt. News, 1984, Douglas County Press, 1984, Mile High Cable Vision, 1985, Sta. KWGN-TV, 1985, Les Krantz's Am. Artists, 1988, Illustrated Survey of Leading Contemporaries, 1988, U.S. Surface Design Jour., 1988; co-work represented in film collection Mus. Modern Art, N.Y.C.; selected fashion show designs displayed to Sister City dels., Denver, 1987. Co-recipient Silver Medal award N.Y. Internat. Film and Video Competition, 1976, Design awards Coun. Advancement and Support of Edn., 1969, 71, 73, 76, Honor Mention award L.A. Art Dirs. Club, 1984, Honor Mention award N.Y. Art Dirs. Club, 1984, Native Am. Wearable Art Competition, 1985, 5th pl. Nat. Wind Sail Am. Banners Competition, Midland, Mich., 1985, also awards for surface designs in Colo. Ctr. for the Arts Wearable Art Competition, 1984-85, Foothills Art Gallery Nat. Wearable Art Competition, 1984-85, Fashion Group of Denver Competition, 1984-85. Mem. Art Dirs. Club Denver (Gold medals 1974-82, Best of Show Gold medal 1983, Honor Mention award, 1984, 3 Gold medals 1989), Univ. Art Dirs. Assn. Home: PO Box 302 751 Willow Lake Dr Franktown CO 80116 Office: U Denver Sch Art 2121 E Asbury Ave Denver CO 80210-4303

NORMAN, JOHN EDWARD, petroleum landman; b. Denver, May 22, 1922; s. John Edward and Ella (Warren) N.; m. Hope Sabin, Sept. 5, 1946; children—J. Thomas, Gerould W., Nancy E., Susan G., Douglas E. BSBA, U. Denver, 1949, MBA, 1972. Clk., bookkeeper Capitol Life Ins. Co., Denver, 1940-42, 45-46; salesman Security Life and Accident Co., Denver, 1947; bookkeeper Central Bank and Trust Co., Denver, 1947-50; automobile salesman H.A. Hennies, Denver, 1950; petroleum landman Continental Oil Co. (name changed to Conoco Inc. 1979), Denver, 1950-85; ind. petroleum landman, 1985; ind. investor 1985—. Lectr. pub. lands Colo. Sch. Mines, 1968-85; lectr. mineral titles and landmen's role in oil industry Casper Coll., 1969-71. Mem. Casper Mcpl. Band Commn., 1965-71, mem. band, 1961-71, mgr., 1968-71; former musician, bd. dirs. Casper Civic Symphony; former bd. dirs. Jefferson Symphony, performing mem., 1972-75. Served with AUS, World War II. Mem. Am. Assn. Petroleum Landmen (dir. at large, chmn. publs. for regional dir.), Wyo. Assn. Petroleum Landmen (pres.), Denver Assn. Petroleum Landmen, Rocky Mountain Oil and Gas Assn. (pub. lands com. 1981-85), Rocky Mountain Petroleum Pioneers. Episcopalian (mem. choir, vestryman, past dir. acolytes). Club: Elks. Home and Office: 2710 S Jay St Denver CO 80227-3856

NORMAN, NITA VEGAMORA, librarian, storyteller; b. Sariaya, Philippines, Aug. 29; came to U.S., 1968; d. Romualdo and Leoncia (Cereza) Vegamora; m. Michael B. Norman, June 15, 1972. BS in Edn., U. Santo Tomas, 1965; Rosary Coll.MLS, 1975, 1975; student, Eastern Tenn. State U. Sch. tchr. Quiapo Parochial Sch., Manila, 1965-68; asst. libr. Cen. States Inst. of Addiction, Chgo., 1970-75; out-reach libr. Chgo. Pub. Libr., 1975-77, branch head, 1977-83; branch mgr. Phoenix Pub. Libr., 1983—. Speaker in field. Named Libr. of the Year., Friende of the Chgo. Pub. Libr., 1980; recipient Outstnading Pub. Svc. award City of Phoenix , 1985, Disting. Svc. award Murphy Elem. Sch., Phoenix, 1990; Contbn. to Literacy award Hamilton Sch., Phoenix, 1993-94. Mem. ALA (local program com. Chgo. 1978), Pub. Libr. Assn. (alternative edn. program com. 1985—, multilingual libr. svcs. com. 1985—), Reforma (libr. svcs. to Spanish speaking), Ariz. State Libr. Assn. (libr. svcs. to Spanish speaking round table 1983—), Asian Pacific Am. Library Assn. Democrat. Home: 1513 W Culver St Phoenix AZ 85007-1823 Office: Harmon Branch Libr 411 W Yavapai St Phoenix AZ 85003-2661

NORRIS, D. WAYNE, insurance and financial services company executive; b. Portland, Ind., Feb. 9, 1939; s. Leo D. and Mable L. (Miller) N.; m. Bonnie K. Smith, Mar. 6, 1965; children: Julia A., Elizabeth. Student, Ball State U., 1961-64. CLU. Gen. mgr. Am. Gen. Ins., Muncie, Inc., 1964-69; owner D. Wayne Norris CLU and Assocs., Muncie, 1969-73, Tucson, 1973—. Contbr. articles to profl. jours. Bd. dirs. Jr. Achievement Ariz., 1985—; life mem. Nat. Cowboy Hall of Fame, 1981—. Recipient nat. award Jr. Achievement, 1990. Mem. Nat. Assn. Life Underwriters (pres. Ind. chpt. 1971-72, Nat. Quality award 1965, Underwriter of Yr. award 1972), Am. Soc. CLU's (bd. dirs. Tucson 1975-79), Nat. Assn. Security Dealers, Tucson Metro C. of C. (chmn. Los Compadres 1986-88, Bus. Leader of Yr. award 1990), Pime Early Rising Execs. (founder, past pres. 1975—). Office: 5620 N Kolb Rd Ste 166 Tucson AZ 85715-1384

NORRIS, JAMES LEO, historian, editor, publisher; b. Salt Lake City, July 7, 1930; s. Leo H. and Erma B. (Davis) N.; m. Lynne Oldmen, Apr., 1951; children: Michael, John, Jean, Jane Suzanne. BS, U. So. Calif., L.A., 1952; MA, Calif. State U., L.A., 1960. Cert. Marriage Family Child Counselor. Tchr., counselor, coach El Segundo H.S., L.A., 1957-61, Palos Verdes H.S., L.A., 1961-64; prof. El Camino Coll., L.A., 1964-81; pub. Olive Press Publs., L.A. and Santa Barbara, Calif., 1981—; historian L.A. and Santa Barbara, 1981—; pres. El Comino Coll. Faculty Assn., L.A., 1975, Calif. C.C. Counseling Assn., 1972. Editor, pub.: Women of My Other Worlds, 1985, Mattei's Tavern, 1986, Urho Saari: Olympian, 1986, San Ramon Chapel Pioneers & Their California Heritage, 1990, It Don't Hurt To Laugh: Cowboy Poetry, 1993, Around the World in Sixty Years, 1993, Let Me Tell You, 1993, History of Zaca Lake, 1994, others; reader Huntington and Bancroft Librs.; contbr. numerous articles to hist. publs. Editor Santa Ynez (Calif.) Valley Hist. Soc., 1984-94; pres. Los Olivos Imporovement Assn., Los Olivos, 1981-83; chmn. Santa Barbara County Landmark Com., Santa Barbara, 1990-92. Lt. (j.g.) USN, 1952-55, PTO. Mem. Santa Barbara Corral Westeners (keeper of the chips 1983—), Los Californianos, Wet Noodle (pres. 1980). Home: 2980 San Marcos Ave Los Olivos CA 93441 Office: Olive Press Publs PO Box 99 Los Olivos CA 93441-0099

NORRIS, MARGOT CHRISTA, English language educator; b. Baden, Austria, Dec. 23, 1944; came to the U.S., 1954; d. Josef Hofstaetter and Helga (Hochberger) Barisits; m. m. Thomas Elfred Norris, Aug. 22, 1964 (div. Sept. 1967); 1 child, A. Josef; m. Rowland Hallowell Davis, June 5, 1994. BA, U. Fla., 1967; PhD, SUNY, Buffalo, 1972. Asst. prof. English U. Tulsa, Okla., 1972-76; asst. to full prof. English U. Mich., Ann Arbor, 1976-87; prof. English and comparative lit. U. Calif., Irvine, 1987—; vis. prof. English U. Basel, Switzerland, 1982-83; mem. adv. com. Publ. of the MLA, N.Y.C., 1990-94. Author: The Decentered Universe of Finnegans Wake, 1976, Beasts of the Modern Imagination, 1985, Joyce's Web, 1992. Fellow Am. Coun. Learned Socs., Heidelberg, Germany, 1977-78, Guggenheim Meml. fellow, 1988-89. Mem. MLA (chair divsn. for 20th century British lit. 1990-94). Democrat. Office: Dept English & Comparative Lit Univ Calif Irvine Irvine CA 92717

NORRIS, MARY BETH, flutist, educator; b. Great Bend, Kans., June 6, 1950; d. Clyde D. and Elizabeth M. (Penner) N.; m. Mark J. Fischer, Nov. 23, 1990. B Music Edn., Ft. Hays State U., 1972. Cert. Suzuki method flute tchr. Tchr. music Hays (Kans.)Pub. Schs., 1975-77; coord. music program Horizons for the Handicapped, Steamboat Springs, Colo., 1978-80; music instr. Colorado Mountain Coll., Steamboat Springs, 1982—; freelance flutist Steamboat Springs, 1981—, ind. flute instr., 1981—; founder, dir. Steamboat Internat. Flute Festival, Steamboat Springs, 1987—; founder, exec. dir. Steamboat Springs Cmty. Orch., 1991—. Flute soloist United Meth. Ch., Steamboat Springs. Mem. Nat. Flute Assn., Suzuki Assn. of the Ams., Music Tchrs. Nat. Assn., Sigma Alpha Iota. Home: 1190 Merritt St Steamboat Springs CO 80477

NORRIS, ROBERT MATHESON, geologist; b. Los Angeles, Apr. 24, 1921; s. Robert DeWitt and Jessie (Matheson) N.; m. Virginia Grace Oakley, Jan. 5, 1952; children—Donald Oakley, James Matheson, Elizabeth Anne. A.B., UCLA, 1943, M.A., 1949; Ph.D. Scripps Inst. Oceanography, U. Calif., San Diego, 1951. Teaching asst. UCLA, 1946-49; asso. marine geology Scripps Inst. Oceanography, 1951-52; mem. faculty U. Calif., Santa Barbara, 1952—; prof. geology U. Calif., 1968-86, prof. emeritus, 1986—; also dir. Channel Islands Field Sta., 1970-75. Contbr. articles profl. jours. Served with USNR, 1944-46. Fulbright scholar, 1961-62. Mem. Geol. Soc. Am., Geol. Soc. N.Z., Nat. Assn. Geology Tchrs. (pres. 1988-89), Am. Assn. Petroleum Geologists, Soc. Econ. Paleontologists and Mineralogists, Sigma Xi, Phi Kappa Sigma, Phi Delta Kappa. Congregationalist. Address: 4424 Nueces Dr Santa Barbara CA 93110-2006

NORRIS, WILLIAM ALBERT, federal judge; b. Turtle Creek, Pa., Aug. 30, 1927; s. George and Florence (Clive) N.; m. Merry Wright, Nov. 23, 1974; children: Barbara, Donald, Kim, Alison; m. Jane Jelenko. Student, U. Wis., 1945; B.A., Princeton U., 1951; J.D., Stanford U., 1954. Bar: Calif. and D.C. 1955. Assoc. firm Northcutt Ely, Washington, 1954-55; law clk. to Justice William O. Douglas U.S. Supreme Ct., Washington, 1955-56; sr. mem. firm Tuttle & Taylor, Inc., L.A., 1956-80; judge U.S. Ct. Appeals (9th cir.), L.A., 1980—; spl. counsel Pres.' Kennedy's Com. on Airlines Controversy, 1961; mem., v.p. Calif. State Bd. Edn., 1961-67. Trustee Calif. State Colls., 1967-72; pres. L.A. Bd. Police Commrs., 1973-74; Democratic nominee for atty. gen. State of Calif., 1974; founding pres. bd. trustees Mus. Contemporary Art, L.A., 1979—; trustee Craft and Folk Art Mus., 1979—. With USN, 1945-47. Home: 1473 Oriole Dr West Hollywood CA 90069-1155 Office: US Ct Appeals 9th Cir 312 N Spring St Los Angeles CA 90012-4701*

NORSBY, KIMBERLY LYN, tax specialist, consultant; b. Tacoma, Wash., Aug. 3, 1962; d. Donald F. and Nancy L. (Getty) Westcott; m. Jeffrey David Norsby, Nov. 29, 1980; 1 child, Kenneth Donald. Student, Tacoma C.C., 1986, Rancho Santiago Coll., Santa Ana, Calif., 1987-89, Calif. State U., Fullerton, 1989. Property mgr. Am. Republic Realty Corp., Dallas and Milw., 1981-84, Victor L. Lyon Realtors, Tacoma, 1985-86; acctg. mgr. Robotronics, Stanton, Calif., 1986-88; staff acct. Harold Dilbeck Accts., Inc., Tustin, Calif., 1988-93; co-owner Coast Mobile Wash, Garden Grove, Calif., 1987—; agt., owner Tax Tyme, Garden Grove, Calif., 1992—. del. White House Conf. Small Bus., 1995. Mem. Nat. Assn. Enrolled Agts., Orange County Soc. Enrolled Agts., Garden Grove C. of C. (pres. elect. 1995—, CFO 1994—). Republican. Home and Office: 11381 Jerry Ln Garden Grove CA 92640

NORSELL, PAUL ERNEST, service executive; b. Salt Lake City, Jan. 28, 1933; s. Alf Raae and Florence Emily (Freer) N.; m. Mary Elizabeth Rynd, Sept. 2, 1958; children: Stuart, Daryl, Paula. BSEE, Purdue U., 1954; MSE, UCLA, 1956. Program mgr. applications tech. satellite Hughes Aircraft Co., Culver City, Calif., 1954-64; v.p. engrng., ops. Litton Data Systems Div., Van Nuys, Calif., 1964-69; pres. Litton LITCOM Div., Melville, N.Y., 1969-73; v.p. Litton Indsl. Profl. Svcs. and Equipment Group, Beverly Hills, Calif., 1973; pres. EXECUDEX West L.A., Inc., 1974—. Contbr. articles to profl. jours. Mem. econ. devel. council Los Angeles Area C. of C., 1985, mem. transp. and pub. works council, 1985; mem. exec. com., chmn. exploring div. Boy Scouts Am., Suffolk County, N.Y, 1971-73; mem. exec. com., bd. mgrs. YMCA, Huntington, L.I., N.Y., 1972-73; bd. dirs. exec. com. L.I. Assn. Commerce and Industry, 1970-73. Hughes Masters Engring. fellow Hughes Aircraft Co., 1954-56; Purdue Alumni scholar Purdue Alumni Assn., 1952-54. Mem. IEEE, AAAS, Ctr. Entrepreneurial Mgmt., Nat. Assn. Accts., Chem. Engrng. Soc., Calif. Exec. Recruiters Assn., U.S. Yacht Racing Union, Eta Kappa Nu. Clubs: Long Beach Yacht (Long Beach, Calif.); Transpacific Yacht (Honolulu). Office: EXECUDEX West Los Angeles Inc PO Box 6686 Auburn CA 95604-6686

NORSWORTHY, DAVID RAY, sociology educator; b. Florien, La., Nov. 15, 1931; s. Henry Walcott and Annie Cordelia (Durrett) N.; m. Florence Claire Cameron, Aug. 25, 1957; children: Stephen Scott, Janet Ruth, Vance Wolcott. BS, La. State U., 1954; MA, U. N.C., 1959, PhD, 1961. Asst. prof. sociology Tulane U., New Orleans, 1961-64, U. Mich., Ann Arbor, 1964-65; assoc. prof. Colo. Woman's Coll., Denver, 1965-68; from assoc. to full prof. Whitman Coll., Walla Walla, Wash., 1968—; cons. Kirschner Assocs., Albuquerque, 1968-72. Author: (with others) Southern Baptists Observed, 1993. Chair Walla Walla Dem. Ctrl. Com., 1982-84, state committeeman, 1993—. Nat. Defense Edn. Act Fgn. Lang. Study grantee U.S. Govt., 1963. Home: 1049 Francis Ave Walla Walla WA 99362-2447 Office: Whitman Coll Dept Sociology Walla Walla WA 99362

NORTH, ANNE VIA, public relations administrator; b. Clifton Forge, Va., Mar. 15, 1939; d. Charles Ashland Via Jr. and Mary Constance (Scales) Tregenza; m. Richard Conrad Waldburger, Nov. 7, 1964 (div. Nov. 1980); children: Jennifer Radell, Erica Wells; m. Brian Royce North, Oct. 6, 1990. Student, Goucher Coll., 1957-59; cert., Katharine Gibbs Sch., N.Y.C., 1960. Asst. WNEW Radio, N.Y.C., 1960-64, Columbia Rec., N.Y.C., 1964-65; personal asst. Anne Morrow Lindbergh, Darien, Conn., 1978-81, Gerry Mulligan, Darien, 1980-81; asst. to news dir. & exec. producer Satellite News Channel, Stamford, Conn., 1981-83; mgr. bus. devel. & pub. rels. Chapman/Warwick Advt., San Diego, 1983-86; dir. nat. pub. rels. San Diego Conv. & Vis. Bur., 1986—. Mem. Pub. Rels. Soc. Am., Soc. Am. Travel Writers. Office: San Diego Conv & Visitors Bur 401 B St Ste 1400 San Diego CA 92101-4237

NORTHROP, STUART JOHNSTON, manufacturing company executive; b. New Haven, Oct. 22, 1925; s. Filmer Stuart Cuchow and Christine (Johnston) N.; divorced; children: Christine Daniell, Richard Rockwell Stafford. B.A. in Physics, Yale U., 1948. Indsl. engr. U.S. Rubber Co., Naugatuck, Conn., 1948-51; head indsl. engrng. dept. Am. Cyanamid Co., Wallingford, Conn., 1951-54; mfg. mgr. Linear, Inc., Phila., 1954-57; mgr. quality control and mfg. Westinghouse Electric Co., Pitts., 1957-58; mfg. supt. SKF Industries, Phila., 1958-61; v.p. mfg. Am. Meter Co., Phila., 1961-69; founder, v.p., gen. mgr. water resources div. Singer Co., Phila.; pres., dir. Buffalo Meter Co., Four Layne Cos.; dir. Gen. Filter Co., 1969-72; chmn., CEO Huffy Corp., Dayton, Ohio, 1972-85, chmn. exec. com., 1985-94; bd. dirs. Lukens, Inc., Coatesville, Pa., Union Corp., N.Y.C., Power Spectra, Sunnyvale, Calif., Wolverine Worldwide, Rockford, Mich., DSLT Inc., St. Clair, Mich., Elbit Sys. Am., Ft. Worth. County fin. chmn. George Bush Presdl. campaign, 1980; presdl. appointee Pres.'s Commn. on Ams. Outdoors, 1985-86; chmn. nat. hwy. safety adv. com. Dept. Transp., 1986—; founder, dir. emeritus Recreation Roundtable, Washington. Served with USAAF, 1944-45. Named Chief Exec. Officer of Yr. for leisure industry Wall Street Transcript, 1980. Mem. Del. Valley Investors (past pres.), Interlocutors, Elihu, Am. Bus. Conf. (founding), Fin. Commn. of Funds Am. Future, Boulders Club (Scottsdale), KOA Soc., Delta Kappa Epsilon. Home: 7474 E Boulders Pky Unit 4 Scottsdale AZ 85262-1247 Office: Huffy Corp 7701 Byers Rd Miamisburg OH 45342-3657

NORTON, DUNBAR SUTTON, economic developer; b. Hoquiam, Wash., Jan. 30, 1926; s. Percy Dunbar and Anna Fedelia (Sutton) N.; m. Kathleen Margaret Mullarky, Dec. 21, 1948 (dec. Apr. 1994); children: Priscilla K., Rebecca C., Jennifer A., Douglas S. Student, U. Oreg., 1946-48; diploma, U.S. Army Command & Gen. Staff, 1964. Commd. 2d lt. U.S. Army, 1948, advanced through grades to lt. col., ret., 1974; dir. econ. devel. dept. Yuma (Ariz.) County C. of C., 1974-83; exec. v.p. Lakin Enterprises, Yuma, 1983-87; owner Norton Cons., Yuma, 1987—; corp. mem. Yuma Econ. Devel. Corp., 1984—, vice chmn., 1993—. Mem. Yuma County Indsl. Devel. Authority, 1984-90, 92—, pres., 1992—; chmn. fundraising com. Yuma Cross Park Coun., 1984-88, sec., 1988-90, v.p., 1990-92, bd. dirs., 1982-95; chmn. devel. com. Yuma County Airport Authority, 1985-92, v.p., 1992—; vice chmn. Yuma Main St. Bd., 1988-90, Yuma County Geog. Info. Sys. Task Force, 1991—, Yuma Kids Voting, 1990-91; bd. dirs. Ariz. Partnership Air Transp., 1990—, v.p., 1993-95; bd. dirs. Yuma County Civic Trusteeship, 1993-95. Decorated Legion of merit with oak leaf cluster, Bronze Star. Mem. Ariz. Assn. for Econ. Devel. (bd. dirs. 1975-82, pres. 1982-83, Developer of Yr. 1977), Yuma Execs. Assn. (sec.-treas., exec. dir. 1987—). Republican. Episcopalian. Home: 12267 E Del Norte Yuma AZ 85367-7356 Office: 11411 S Fortuna Rd Ste 205 Yuma AZ 85367-7827

NORTON, GALE A., state attorney general; b. Wichita, Mar. 11, 1954; d. Dale Bentsen and Anna Jacqueline (Lansdowne) N.; m. John Goethe Hughes, Mar. 26, 1990. BA, U. Denver, 1975, JD, 1978. Bar: Colo. 1978, U.S. Supreme Ct. 1981. Jud. clk. Colo. Ct. of Appeals, Denver, 1978-79; sr. atty. Mountain States Legal Found., Denver, 1979-83; nat. fellow Hoover Instn. Stanford (Calif.) U., 1983-84; asst. to dep. sec. U.S. Dept. of Agr., Washington, 1984-85; assoc. solicitor U.S. Dept. of Interior, Washington, 1985-87; pvt. practice law Denver, 1987-90; atty. gen. State of Colo., Denver, 1991—; Murdock fellow Polit. Economy Rsch. Ctr., Bozeman, Mont., 1984; sr. fellow Ind. Inst., Golden, Colo., 1988-90; policy analyst Pres. Coun. on Environ. Quality, Washington, 1985-88; lectr. U. Denver Law Sch., 1989; transp. law program dir. U. Denver, 1978-79. Contbr. chpts. to books, articles to profl. jours. Participant Rep. Leadership Program, Colo., 1988, Colo. Leadership Forum, 1989; past chair Nat. Assn. Attys. Gen. Environ. Com.; co-chair Nat. Policy Forum Environment Coun. Named Young Career Woman Bus. and Profl. Wome, 1981, Young Lawyer of Yr., 1991. Mem. Federalist Soc., Colo. Women's Forum, Order of St. Ives. Republican. Methodist. Office: Colo Dept of Law 1525 Sherman St Fl 5 Denver CO 80203-1714

NORTON, GOLDY See GOLDSTEIN, NORTON MAURICE

NORTON, KAREN ANN, accountant; b. Paynesville, Minn., Nov. 1, 1950; d. Dale Francis and Ruby Grace (Gehlhar) N. BA, U. Minn., 1972; postgrad. U. Md., 1978; cert. acctg. U.S. Dept. Agr. Grad. Sch., 1978; MBA, Calif. State Poly. U.-Pomona, 1989. CPA, Md. Securities transactions analyst Bur. of Pub. Debt., Washington, 1972-79, internal auditor, 1979-81; internal auditor IRS, Washington, 1981; sr. acct. World Vision Internat., Monrovia, Calif., 1981-83, acctg. supr., 1983-87; sr. systems liaison supr., Home Savs. Am., 1987—; cons. (vol.) info. systems John M. Perkins Found., Pasadena, Calif., 1985-86. Author (poetry): Ode to Joyce, 1985 (Golden Poet award 1985). Second v.p. chpt. Nat. Treasury Employees Union, Washington, 1978, editor chpt. newsletter; mem. M-2 Prisoners Sponsorship Program, Chino, Calif., 1984-86. Recipient Spl. Achievement award Dept. Treasury, 1976, Superior Performance award, 1977-78; Charles and Ellora Alliss scholar, 1968. Mem. Angel Flight, Covenant Ch. Avocations: flying, chess, racquetball, whitewater rafting.

NORTON, RUTH ANN, education educator; b. Sioux City, Iowa, Mar. 7, 1947; d. Burton Ellwood and Mildred Ruth (Schneider) N.; m. Jack William Moskal, May 30, 1985. BA, U. No. Iowa, 1969; MS, Syracuse U., 1984, EdD, 1985. Cert. tchr., Iowa, Vt. Tchr. Cedar Falls (Iowa) Unified Sch. Dist., 1969-79; asst. didr. Area 7 Tchr. Ctr., Waterloo, Iowa, 1979-80; tchr. Moretown (Vt.) Elem. Sch., 1980-81; doctoral candidate Syracuse (N.Y.) U., 1981-85; prof. Calif. State U., San Bernardino, 1985—, dir. student teaching, 1989-95; cons. tech. tng. inst. Calif. State U., San Bernardino, Constl. Heritage Inst.; trainer supervision workshops Calif. State U., San Bernardino; cons. Lime St. Elem. Sch., Hesperia, Calif.; bd. dirs. Redlands Ednl. Partnership Found.; chairperson Reflections Com. for Redlands PTA Coun. Contbr. articles to profl. jours. Recipient Affirmative Action Faculty Devel. grant Calif. State U., 1986, Profl. Devel. Monetary grant Calif. State U., 1987, Meritorious Performance & Profl. Promise award Calif. State U., 1988. Mem. ASCD, Am. Ednl. Rsch. Assn., Assn. Tchr. Educators, Calif. Assn. for Supervision and Curriculum Devel., Calif. Coun. for Social Studies, Nat. Coun. for Social Studies, So. Calif. Assn. Tchr. Educators, Phi Delta Kappa. Office: Calif State U 5500 University Pky San Bernardino CA 92407-2318

NORTON, THOMAS EDMOND, state senator, engineer; b. Bremerton, Wash., July 31, 1940; s. Edmond Stanley and Violet Marian (Gustafson) N.; children by previous marriage: Konnie, Kent, Kim; m. Pamalyn Kay McEver, Dec. 23, 1976; children: Paige, Whitney. BS in Civil Engrng., Colo. State U., 1964, MS in Sanitary Engring., 1969. Profl. engr. V.p. engrng. svcs. Nelson, Haley, Patterson, Quirk, Greeley, Colo., 1963-76; v.p. Norton, Underwood and Lamb/KLH Engrng., Greeley, 1976—; rep. Colo Legis., Denver, 1986-88, senator, 1988—; pres. Colo. State Senate, Denver, 1993—; bd. dirs. First Nat. Bank, Greeley, Colo. Natural Gas Assistance Found., Denver. Recipient Annual Ralph Cole awrd Colo. Community Corrections Coalition, 1990, Spl. Recognition award Am. Inst. Architects, 1989; named Bus. Legislator of Yr. Colo. Pub. Affairs Coun., 1989. Republican. Methodist. Office: Office State Senate State Capital Denver CO 80203

NORVELLE, JOAN WILSON, forensic accountant, educator, consultant; b. Shreveport, La., May 14, 1939; d. Alexander Culberson and Ruby (Crouch) Wilson; m. Larry Cole Thompson (div.); 1 child, Cole; m. Michael E. Norvelle (div.). BS in Bus. Adminstrn., Centenary Coll. of La., 1966; MS in Bus. Adminstrn., Acctg., Va. Commonwealth U., 1968; PhD of Higher Edn. Adminstrn., U. Ariz., 1978. Instr. Smithdeal-Massey Bus. Coll., Richmond, Va., 1965-67; divsn. chmn. bus. scis. John Tyler C.C., Richmond, Va., 1967-70; asst. prof. dept. acctg. Va. State Coll., Petersburg, 1970-71; grad. teaching assoc. in acctg. U. Ariz., Tucson, 1971-73; rsch. assoc. dean's office, Coll. Bus. and Pub. Adminstrn. instr. acctg. U. Ariz., Tucson, 1973-75; lectr. dept. acctg. U. Ariz., Tucson, 1975-77; rsch. assoc., acctg. cons. Bur. Indian Affairs Contract, Office Lands and Studies, U. Ariz., Tucson, 1977-78; instr. dept. acctg. U. Ariz., Tucson, 1978-79, assoc. dept. head and lectr., 1979—; mem. adj. faculty Va. Commonwealth U., Richmond, 1967-70, So. Ariz. Law Enforcement Inst., Tucson, 1973-77, Pima Coll., Tucson, 1975-77; presenter on Fund Acctg. U. Ariz., CPA Rev. Course, 1981, 87, 89; fiscal officer Divsn. Indsl. Coop., U. Ariz. Found., 1981-87; mgmt. cons. several agrl. projects in Ariz., 1979-82; presenter workshops 1978—; tng. various tribes for Bur. Indian affairs, 1977-78; acad. decathelon judge State Ariz., 1984, 86; cons. to many law enforcement agys. nationwide; conducted numerous seminars fin. and fraud exposure. Author: Introduction to Fund Accounting, fifth edit., 1994; co-author: (with Richard A. Nossen) The Detection, Investigation and Prosecution of Financial Crimes, 2d edit., 1993, (with Larry C. Thompson) Writer's Guide to Educational Periodicals, 1973; contbr. articles to profl. jours. in legal prosecution and acctg. Mem. Assn. Cert. Fraud Examiners (cert. fraud examiner, rsch. com. 1992, bd. regents 1993). Home: PO Box 85151 Tucson AZ 85754-5151 Office: Univ Ariz Dept Acctg McClelland Hall 301 Tucson AZ 85721

NOSLER, PETER COLE, construction company executive; b. Portland, Oreg., May 7, 1940; s. Lyle and Elizabeth (Lewis) N.; m. Kay Hanson, Apr. 25, 1971; 1 child, Alexander. BS in Physics and Math., Walla Walla Coll., 1962; postgrad., U. Wash., 1962-63, U. Calif., Berkeley, 1965-70. Physicist GE, Richland, Wash., 1963-65; pvt. practice Portland, 1970-72; project mgr. Stolte Constrn., San Leandro, Calif., 1972-75; v.p. ops. Rudolph & Sletten, Foster City, Calif., 1975-90; pres. DPR Constrn. Inc., Redwood City, Calif., 1990—; lectr. Stanford U., Palo Alto, Calif., 1988—. Recipient Young Constrn. Profl. of Yr. award Jour. Bldg. Design and Constrn., 1978. Mem.

Soc. Model Exptl. Engring. Office: DPR Constrn Inc 555 Twin Dolphin Dr Ste 260 Redwood City CA 94065-2102

NOSLER, ROBERT AMOS, sports company executive; b. Ashland, Oreg., Apr. 21, 1946; s. John Amos and Louise (Booz) N.; m. Joan Kathleen Hilliard, July 15, 1967; children: Christie Lynn, Jill Ann, John Robert. Student, U. Oreg., 1965. V.p., gen. mgr. Nosler Bullets, Inc., Bend, Oreg., 1974-88; pres., chief exec. officer Nosler Bullets, Inc., 1988-90; pres., CEO Nosler, Inc., Bend, 1990—. Editor: Nosler Reloading Manual #1, 1976. Bd. dirs. Bend C. of C., 1984-88, treas., 1988; chmn. Central Oreg. Welcome Ctr. Steering Com., 1988. With USN, 1966-70; trustee Ctrl. Oreg. Community Coll. Found., 1992—. Recipient Pres.' award Bend C. of C., 1984, 87, 88. Mem. Nat. Reloading Mfrs. Assn. (bd. dirs. 1982-86, 90-93, pres. 1984-86), Oreg. Grad. Inst. Sci. & Tech. Chief Exec. Roundtable, Greater Bend Rotary (dir. 1989-91). Republican. Lutheran. Office: Nosler Inc 107 SW Columbia St Bend OR 97702-1014

NOSRATIAN, FARSHAD JOSEPH, internist, cardiologist; b. Tehran, Iran, Sept. 1, 1956; came to U.S., 1979; s. Yahoude Nosrat and Violet (Pousadeh) N.; m. Faranak Daravi, June 24, 1990; 1 child, Michelle. Student, U. Tehran, 1974-78; MD, Albert Einstein Coll. Medicine, Bronx, N.Y., 1983. Diplomate Am. Bd. Internal Medicine, Am. Bd. Cardiovascular Diseases. Resident in internal medicine Harbor-UCLA Med. Ctr., Torrance, 1983-86; fellow in cardiology U. Calif., Irvine, 1986-89, asst. clin. prof., 1989—; clin. staff cardiologist UCLA, 1990—, Centinela Hosp. Med. Ctr., Inglewood, Calif., 1989—, Daniel Freeman Meml. Hosp., Inglewood, 1989—, Little Company of Mary Hosp., Torrance, 1990—, Santa Monica (Calif.) Med. Ctr., 1990—; clin. staff cardiologist Kennedy Med. Ctr., Hawthorne, Calif., 1989—, chmn. critical care com., 1992—. Contbr. chpt. to book, articles to profl. jours. Fellow Am. Coll. Cardiology; mem. Los Angeles County Med. Assn., Alpha Omega Alpha. Office: 4477 W 118th St Ste 301 Hawthorne CA 90250-2258

NOTHMANN, RUDOLF S., legal researcher; b. Hamburg, Fed. Republic of Germany, Feb. 4, 1907; came to U.S., 1941, naturalized, 1943; s. Nathan and Henrietta G. (Heymann) N. Referendar, U. Hamburg, 1929, PhD in Law, 1932; postgrad. U. Liverpool Law Sch. (Eng.), 1931-32. Law clk. Hamburg Cts., 1929-31, 32-33; export, legal adviser, adviser ocean marine ins. various firms, Ger., Eng., Sweden, Calif., 1933-43, 46-47; instr. fgn. exchange, fgn. trade Extension div. UCLA, 1947-48, vis. assoc. prof. UCLA, 1951; asst. prof. econs. Whittier Coll., 1948-50, assoc. prof., 1950-51; contract work U.S. Air Force, U.S. Navy, 1953-59; contract negotiator space projects, space and missile systems orgn. USAF, L.A., 1959-77; pvt. researcher in internat. comml. law, Pacific Palisades, Calif., 1977—; pres. Hanseatic Devel. Corp., Pacific Palisades, Calif., 1989—. With U.S. Army, 1943-45; ETO. Recipient Gold Tape award Air Force Systems Command, 1970. Mem. Internat. Bar Assn. (vice chmn. internat. sales and related comml. trans. com. 1977-82), Am. Econ. Assn., Calif. Bar Assn. (internat. law sect.), Am. Soc. Internat. Law, Uebersee Club (Hamburg, Germany). Author: The Insurance Certificate in International Ocean Marine Insurance Law and Foreign Trade, 1932; The Oldest Corporation in the World: Six Hundred Years of Economic Evolution, 1949. Home: PO Box 32 Pacific Palisades CA 90272-0032

NOTKIN, DAVID, computer science educator; b. Syracuse, N.Y., Jan. 1, 1955; s. Herbert and Isabell (Schulman) N.; m. Catherine Vaughn Tuttle, July 3, 1988; 1 child, Emma Michael. ScB in computer sci., Brown U., 1977; PhD in computer sci., Carnegie-Mellon U., 1984. Prof. computer sci. and engring. U. Wash., Seattle, 1984—; vis. assoc. prof. Tokyo Inst. Tech., 1990, Osaka U., 1990-91; chair program com. assoc. computing machinery spl. interest group software engring., Symposium on Founds. of Software Engring., 1993; co-chair program com. 17th Internat. Conf. Software Engring. Assoc. editor: Assn. for Computing Machinery Transactions on Software Engring. and Methodology, 1990—; contbr. articles to profl. jours. Named NSF Presdl. Young Investigator, 1988, others. Mem. IEEE, Assn. Computing Machinery, Sigma Xi. Democrat. Jewish. Home: 4412 Corliss Ave N Seattle WA 98103-7657 Office: U Washington Dept Computer Sci & Engring Seattle WA 98195

NOTO, BLAISE JOHN, film marketing executive; b. Amityville, N.Y., Sept. 24, 1952; s. Salvatore Noto and Adrienne Marie Johnson. BA in Sociology, Wesleyan U., 1974; MA in Comm., U. Pa., 1985. Regional publicity rep. United Artists, N.Y.C., 1976-78; publicity coord. United Artists, Culver City, Calif., 1978-80; dir. West Coast publicity Warner Bros., Burbank, Calif., 1980-82; dir. nat. promotions Orion Pictures, L.A., 1982-85; v.p. publicity and promotion DeLaurentiis Entertainment Group, Beverly Hills, Calif., 1985-87; v.p. mktg. Vestron Pictures, L.A., 1987-89; v.p. nat. publicity Paramount Pictures, L.A., 1990-95, sr. v.p. nat. publicity, 1995—. N.W. Ayer Advt. scholar, 1975. Mem. IATSE. Home: 8455 Fountain Ave #529 West Hollywood CA 90069 Office: Paramount Pictures 5555 Melrose Ave Los Angeles CA 90038-3149

NOTTINGHAM, EDWARD WILLIS, JR., federal judge; b. Denver, Jan. 9, 1948; s. Edward Willis and Willie Newton (Gullett) N.; m. Cheryl Ann Card, June 6, 1970 (div. Feb. 1981); children: Amelia Charlene, Edward Willis III; m. Janis Ellen Chapman, Aug. 18, 1984; 1 child, Spencer Chapman. AB, Cornell U., 1969; JD, U. Colo., 1972. Bar: Colo. 1972, U.S. Dist. Ct. Colo. 1972, U.S. Ct. Appeals (10th cir.) 1973. Law clk. to presiding judge U.S. Dist. Ct. Colo., Denver, 1972-73; assoc. Sherman & Howard, Denver, 1973-76, 78-80, ptnr., 1980-87; ptnr. Beckner & Nottingham, Grand Junction, Colo., 1987-89; asst. U.S. atty. U.S. Dept. Justice, Denver, 1976-78; U.S. dist. judge Dist. of Colo., Denver, 1989—. Bd. dirs. Beaver Creek Met. Dist., Avon, Colo., 1980-88, Justice Info. Ctr., Denver, 1985-87, 21st Jud. Dist. Victim Compensation Fund, Grand Junction, Colo., 1987-89. Mem. ABA, Colo. Bar Assn. (chmn. criminal law sect. 1983-85, chmn. ethics com. 1988-89), Order of Coif, Denver Athletic Club, Delta Sigma Rho, Tau Kappa Alpha. Episcopalian. Office: US Dist Ct 1929 Stout St Denver CO 80294-2900

NOUBAN, BEHZAD, design engineer, researcher; b. Tehran, Iran, July 26, 1959; s. Nasser Malek and Tabandeh (Salour) N.; m. Soussan Teymouri, July 29, 1990. BSEE, U. Mich., 1980, MSEE, 1981. Sr. design engr. Nat. Semiconductor, Salt Lake City, 1982-86, AMD/MMI, San Jose, Calif., 1986-89; staff design engr. Altera Corp., San Jose, 1989—. Patentee (3) in field. Mem. IEEE, Am. Anthropological Assn., Am. Engring. Assn., Tau Beta Pi, Eta Kappa Nu, Pi Mu Epsilon. Office: Altera Corp 2610 Orchard Pky San Jose CA 95134

NOUR, MOHAMMAD, computer engineer; b. Tehran, Iran, Mar. 19, 1958; s. Hossein Nour and Kobra M.M. Tabib; m. Oresa Cuthbertson, Apr. 9, 1988; 1 child, Armand R. BS, So. Ill. U., Edwardsville, 1982; MSEE, Calif. State U., Long Beach, 1985. Cert. computer engr. Computer sys. engr. Ballanda Corp., L.A., 1984-86; sr. v.p. sys. engrs. A.C.E. Consulting Firm, Beverly Hills, Calif., 1986—. Creator sys. software programs. Mem. IEEE, ASChE, Am. Computer Assn., Am. Tng. Sou-Do Assn. (pres. 1982).

NOVAK, JULIE COWAN, nursing educator, researcher, clinician; b. Peoria, Ill., Oct. 2, 1950; m. Robert E. Novak, 1972; children: Andrew, Christopher, Nicholas. BS in Nursing, U. Iowa, 1972, MA in Nursing of Children, 1976; D.N.Sc., U. San Diego, 1989. RN, Va., Calif. Charge nurse surg. and med. ICU U. Iowa Hosp. and Clinics, 1972-73; instr. med. sur. nursing St. Luke's Sch. Nursing, Cedar Rapids, Iowa, 1973-74; instr. family and cmty. health U. Iowa Coll. of Nursing, 1974-75; perinatal nurse clinician U. Iowa Hosps., 1976-77; pediatric nurse practitioner Chicano Cmty. Health Ctr., 1978-80; lectr., asst. prof. child health nursing and physical assessment San Diego State U., 1977-79; child health nurse practitioner program coord. U. Calif., San Diego, 1978-82; pediatric nurse practitioner San Diego City Schs., 1980-82; coord. infant spl. care ctr. follow-up program U. Calif., San Diego, 1982-83, assoc. clin. prof. intercampus grad. studies, 1983-90, dir. health promotion divsn. cmty. and family medicine, 1985-90; assoc. clin. prof. dept. cmty. family medicine U. Calif. Divsn. Health Care Sci., San Diego, 1990-94; assoc. prof. San Diego State U. Sch. Nursing, 1990-94, Calif. Nursing Students Assn. faculty advisor, 1992-94; pediatric nurse practitioner Naval Hosp., 1990-92, Comp. Health Clinic, 1990-94; prof., dir. Master's in Primary Care/FNP, PNP, WHNP programs U. Va. Schs., Charlottesville, 1994—; cons. child health San Diego State U. Child Study Ctr.; mem. accident prevention com. Am. Acad. Pediatrics; lectr. in field. Contbr. numerous articles to profl. jours. and book chpts. to 7 texts; co-author: Ingall's & Salerno's Maternal Child Nursing, 1995, Mosby Year Book; mem. editl. bd. Jour. Perinatal and Neonatal Nursing, 1986-93, Children's Nurse, 1982-88, ; mem. editl. bd., reviewer Jour. Pediatric Health Care, 1987-93; speaker in field. Chair Ann. Refugee Clothing Drive, East San Diego, ESL Program, Car Seat Roundup U. Calif., San Diego, 1983-85; mem. telethon March of Dimes; mem. steering com. Healthy Mothers/ Healthy Babies Coalition; chair ways and means com. Benchley-Weinberger Elem. Sch. PTA, 1985-87, pres., 1988-90; v.p., pres. Friends Jamul Schs. Found.; co-chair teen outreach program Jr. League San Diego, 1987-88, chair, 1989-90, bd. dirs., 1990-92; educator presch. health San Carlos Meth. Ch.; mem. Head Start Policy Coun., 1992-94, San Diego County Dropout Prevention Roundtable, 1991-93, Western Albemarle H.S. Planning Team, 1994—. Recipient Svc. award Benchley-Weinberger Elem. Sch. PTA, 1988, Hon. Youth Svc. award Calif. Congress Parents and Tchrs., Loretta C. Ford Award for excellence as an nurse practitioner in edn. U. Colo., 1990, March of Dimes Svc. commendation, 1983, Project Hope Svc. commendation, 1983,Hon. Svc. award Calif. Congress of Parents, Tchrs. & Students, 1988, Doctoral Student fellowship U. San Diego, 1986, and numerous others. Mem. ANA, Nat. Assn. Pediatric Nurse Practitioners Assoc. (chpt. pres., program com., coord. legis. field, nat. cert. chair 1992—), Calif. Nurses Assn., Pi Lambda Theta, Sigma Theta Tau (mem. nominations com. 1990-91, pres.-elect Gamma Gamma chpt. 1993-94). Home: 2415 Harmony Dr Charlottesville VA 22901-8990

NOVAK, TERRY LEE, public adminstration educator; b. Chamberlain, S.D., Sept. 1, 1940; s. Warren F. and Elaine M. N.; m. Barbara Hosea, Aug. 29, 1981; 1 child, David. B.Sc., S.D. State U., 1962; postgrad. (Rotary fellow), U. Paris, 1962-63; M.P.A., Colo. U., 1965, Ph.D., 1970. Asst. city mgr. City of Anchorage, 1966-68; city mgr. City of Hopkins, Minn., 1968-74, City of Columbia, Mo., 1974-78, City of Spokane, Wash., 1978-91; v.p. bus. and fin. Ea. Wash. U., Cheney, 1991-92, prof. public adminstrn., 1992—, dir. grad. program pub. adminstrn., 1994—; exec. dir. Spokane Joint Ctr. for Higher Edn., 1995—; asst. adj. prof. U. Mo., Columbia, 1975, 77; adj. instr. Gonzaga U., Spokane, 1986-88; mem. nat. adv. coun. on environ. policy and tech. EPA. Author: Special Assessment Financing in American Cities, 1970; contbr. articles to profl. jours. Mem. Internat. City Mgrs. Assn. (Acad. Profl. Devel.), Am. Soc. Public Adminstrn. Episcopalian. Office: Ea Wash U Spokane Ctr 705 W 1st Ave Spokane WA 99204-0409

NOVAK-LYSSAND, RANDI RUTH, computer scientist; b. Chgo., July 10, 1954; d. Bernard Richard and Shirley Ann (Fiedorczyk) Novak; children: Rona Rachel, Bonnie Shaina; m. Knut Lyssand, Jan. 1, 1995. BS in Math., U. Calif., Santa Cruz, 1976, BA in Econs. with honors, 1976; postgrad., U. Rochester, 1976-78. Rsch. asst. U. Calif., Santa Cruz, 1974-76; Russian translator U. Chgo., 1977-78; intern economist Congl. Budget Office, Washington, 1977; engr. Lockheed MSC, Sunnyvale, Calif., 1978-82; software engr. contractor Silicon Valley Systems, Belmont, Calif., 1982, 83-84, Data Encore (subs. of Verbatim), Sunnyvale, 1982-83; systems programmer CompuPro/Viasyn Corp., Hayward, Calif., 1984-87; mem. tech. staff Network Equipment Techs., Redwood City, Calif., 1987-89; software engr. contractor Segue Setups, Burlingame, Calif., 1989-92, ptnr., 1992—; sr. mem. tech. staff NEC Am., San Jose, Calif., 1992-94; sr. systems engr. Hitachi Computer Products, Santa Clara, Calif., 1994—. Fellow Dept. Treasury, 1974-76, NSF, 1977-78, U. Rochester, Rush Rhees fellow. Mem. IEEE Computer Soc., Am. Math. Assn., Computer Profls. for Social Responsibility, Soc. for Computing and Info. Processing, Internat. Platform Assn., Calif. Scholarship Fedn. (life). Home: 4166 School St Pleasanton CA 94566

NOVATNE, LAUREN JEAN, environmental health specialist; b. Hackensack, N.J., June 7, 1955; d. Phillip Vincent and Lillian Jean Chase; m. Michael Anthony Graffigna, Dec. 27, 1973 (div. Aug. 1979); children: Michael Jeremy Graffigna, Daniel Josiah Graffigna. BS in Physics, Sonoma State U., 1989. Registered environ. mental health specialist. Test technician Hewlett-Packard Co., Santa Rosa, Calif., 1989-90; reliability engr. Microsource, Inc., Santa Rosa, 1990-91; asst. mgr. Taco Bell Corp., Santa Rosa, 1992-93; environ. health specialist Monterey (Calif.) County Health, 1993—; reliability cons. Versatron Inc., Healdsburg, Calif., 1991-92. Author: (poetry) Jeg Me Gana, 1991. Tchr. asst. elem. edn. Throughout Sons' Edn., 1978-86; tchr. Sacramento Revival Ctr., 1975-77; avicultural vol. Monterey Bay Aquarium, Monterey. Mem. Mensa. Office: Monterey County Health Dept 1200 Aguajito Rd Monterey CA 93940-4834

NOVICK, STUART ALLAN, publishing executive; b. Savannah, Ga., Aug. 21, 1944; s. Jehiel and Dorothy Ruth (Selicovitz) N.; m. Francesca Julita Lim, June 22, 1986 (div. Mar. 1993); 1 child, Casey Adam. Grad., Stanford U., 1967. Mgr. Chico-San, Inc., Seattle, 1969-72; bus. mgr. Seventh Inn, Boston, 1972-74; owner, mgr. Simulsense, Seattle, 1974-77, More Time! Good Time!, Honolulu, 1977-80; pres. Foodpower, Honolulu, 1980-83, Profitability Cons., Honolulu, 1983-88, Novick and Einstein Advt., Honolulu, 1988-93; pub. Hawaii Environ. Gazette, Honolulu, 1993—; cons. WorkHawaii, Honolulu, 1990, Am. Lung Assn., Honolulu, 1991. Pub. Hawaii Environ. Gazette, 1994—. Coord. Gov.'s Energy Awards Program, 1991; chmn. Hunger Project Found., Honolulu, 1977-80; coord. Pau Hunger Found., Honolulu, 1980-81; co-founder, coord. Partnership for the Environment, 1992—. Mem. Exch. Club (coord. Hilo 1990-91). Office: 1487 Hiikala Pl Unit 8 Honolulu HI 96816

NOWEL, DAVID JOHN, marketing professional; b. New Britain, Conn., Mar. 29, 1935; s. John Joseph and Sophie C. (Nowel) Bonkowski; m. July 20, 1961 (div. 1979); children: Lynn Marie, Bruce Edward. BA in Chemistry and Psychology, Hobart Coll., 1959; MA in Bus., Bklyn. Coll. of Pharmacy, 1964. Neurophysiology rsch. technician Inst. of Living Rsch. Lab., Hartford, 1955-57; sales rep. Sandoz Pharms., Bklyn., 1961-65, Becton Dickenson, Huntington Beach, Calif., 1965-71; sales mgr. Scott Labs., N. Hollywood, Calif., 1971-79; area mgr. Beckman Instruments, Fullerton, Calif., 1979-86; sales rep. Indsl. Tng. Corp.; sales mgr. Pacific Toxicology Lab., L.A., 1987-89, The Mark Group, Santa Ana, Calif., 1989-91; dir. of mktg. Remedial Mgmt. Corp., Newport Beach, Calif., 1991-92; bus. devel. mgr. Tech. Waste Inc., Placentia, Calif., 1993-94; sales engr. Nat. Tech. Sys., Calabasas, Calif., 1994—. Author: Space Station "ARK," 1987, 2nd edit., 1994. Chairperson energy Orange County C. of C., 1989, mem. air subcom., 1991; co-chairperson environment Irvine C. of C., 1989. With USN, 1959-61. Mem. Assn. of Hazardous Materials Profls. Republican. Unitarian. Home: 19585 Seagull Ln Huntington Beach CA 92648-3034 Office: Nat Tech Sys Environ Svcs 1536 E Valencia Dr Fullerton CA 92631-4734

NOWIK, DOROTHY ADAM, medical equipment company executive; b. Chgo., July 25, 1944; d. Adam Harry and Helen (Kichkaylo) Wanaski; m. Eugene Nicholas Nowik, Aug. 9, 1978; children: George Eugene, Helen Eugene. A.A., Columbia Coll., 1980. Cert. lactation counselor, lactation educator, lactation cons. Sec., adminstrv. asst. to pres. Zenco Engring Corp., Chgo., 1970-71; sales rep. Medizenco USA Ltd., Chgo., 1971-73; ptnr. Pacific Med. Systems, Inc., Bellevue, Wash., 1973-76, pres., 1976—. Mem. NAFE, Pacific Mothers Support, Inc. (pres. 1991). Mem. Orthodox Ch. Am. Home: 303 126th Ave NE Bellevue WA 98005-3217 Office: 1407 132nd Ave NE # 10 Bellevue WA 98005-2259

NOWLAN, DANIEL RALPH, engineering executive; b. Hammond, Ind., Feb. 23, 1947; s. Kenneth Edwin and Patricia Jane (Prendergast) N.; m. Sharon Louise Greichunos, Sept. 7, 1968; children: Daniel Ralph Jr., Kevin Anthony, Cynthia Ann. BSEE, Purdue U., 1969, MSEE, 1969. Engr./scientist McDonnell Douglas Astronautics Co, Santa Monica, Calif., 1969-75; engring. mgr. McDonnell Douglas Aerospace-West, Huntington Beach, Calif., 1975—; tax preparer Tax Corp. of Am., Montrose, Calif., 1975-76; cons. in field. Eucharistic minister to convalescent homes St. Vincent De Paul Soc., Huntington Beach, 1993—; youth soccer coach Am. Youth Soccer Orgn., Westminster and Huntington Beach, 1975-82; bldg. fund dr. capt. St. Vincent De Paul Cath. Ch., Huntington Beach, 1979, 82. Recipient Popular Sci. Achievement award L.A. and Orange County Engring. Coun., 1993, Space Frontier award, 1994, Engring. Project Achievement award, 1994. Mem. AIAA (sr.), IEEE, Phi Kappa Theta, Tau Beta Pi, Eta Kappa Nu, Phi Eta Sigma. Roman Catholic. Home: 15931 Diamond St Westminster CA 92683-7203 Office: McDonnell Douglas Aerospace 5301 Bolsa Ave Huntington Beach CA 92647-2048

NOWOSATKO, JEROME RAYMOND, software engineer; b. Detroit, Apr. 30, 1965; s. Raymond Peter and Sophie Helen (Pendzik) N. AA in Computer Sci., U. Md., Naples, Italy, 1989, BS in Info. Systems, 1989; MS in Software Engring., Colo. Tech., 1995. Cert. data processor, sys. profl., computing profl. Commd. E-4 U.S. Army, 1984; software engr. Compuware Corp., Detroit, 1990-91, Columbus, Ohio, 1991-92, Colorado Springs, 1992—. Mem. Data Processing Mgmt. Assn., Inst. for Certification of Computing Profls., Buckley Sch. Forensic Soc. Republican. Roman Catholic. Home: 7215 Big Valley Ct Colorado Springs CO 80919-1035 Office: Compuware Corp 5575 Tech Center Dr Ste 118 Colorado Springs CO 80919-2349

NOY, GARY DAVID, history educator, association executive; b. Grass Valley, Calif., June 12, 1951; s. Howard Elliston and Velma Loretta (Winkle) N. BA, U. Calif., Berkeley, 1973; MA, Calif. State U., Sacramento, 1986. Cert. secondary tchr., community coll. instr. and supr., Calif. Tchr. history and social sci. San Ramon Valley Unified Sch. Dist., Danville, Calif., 1977-84; exec. dir. Sierra Coll. Found., Rocklin, Calif, 1986-88, Paul's Place Assn., Loomis, Calif, 1986—; instr. history and social sci. Sierra Coll., Rocklin, 1987—; instr. history Sacramento City Coll., 1989—. COntbr. articles to profl. jours. Exec. dir., treas. Paul's Place Assn. Scholarship and Community Fund, 1986—. Calif. Alumni scholar, 1969. Mem. Nat. Wildlife Fedn. (life), Phi Alpha Theta. Home: 2410 Laurelwood Ct Rocklin CA 95677 Office: Paul's Place Assn 3739 Taylor Rd PO Box 1167 Loomis CA 95650

NOYES, RICHARD MACY, physical chemist, educator; b. Champaign, Ill., Apr. 6, 1919; s. William Albert and Katharine Haworth (Macy) N.; m. Winninette Arnold, July 12, 1946 (dec. Mar. 1972); m. Patricia Jean Harris, Jan. 26, 1973. A.B. summa cum laude, Harvard U., 1939; Ph.D., Calif. Inst. Tech., 1942. Research assoc. rocket propellants Calif. Inst. Tech., 1942-46; mem. faculty Columbia U., 1946-58, assoc. prof., 1954-58; Guggenheim fellow, vis. prof. U. Leeds, Eng., 1955-56; prof. chemistry U. Oreg., 1958—, head dept., 1963-68, 75-78, ret., 1984—. Editorial adv. com.: Chem. Revs, 1967-69; editorial adv. com.: Jour. Phys. Chemistry, 1973-80; assoc. editor: Internat. Jour. Chem. Kinetics, 1972-82, Jour. Phys. Chemistry, 1980-82; Contbr. to profl. jours. Fulbright fellow; Victoria U. Wellington, New Zealand, 1964; NSF sr. postdoctoral fellow Max Planck Inst. für Physikalische Chemie, Göttingen, Fed. Republic Germany, 1965; sr. Am. scientist awardee Alexander von Humboldt Found., 1978-79. Fellow Am. Phys. Soc.; mem. NAS, Am. Acad. Arts and Scis., Am. Chem. Soc. (chmn. div. phys. chemistry 1961-62, exec. com. div. 1960-75, mem. coun. 1960-75, chmn. Oreg. sect. 1967-68, com. on nominations and elections 1962-68, com. on publs. 1969-72), Chem. Soc. (London), Wilderness Soc., ACLU, Hungarian Acad. Scis. (hon.), Sierra Club (past chmn. Atlantic and Pacific N.W. chpts., N.W. regional v.p. 1973-74), Phi Beta Kappa, Sigma Xi. Home: 2014 Elk Ave Eugene OR 97403-1734 Office: U of Oregon Dept Chemistry Eugene OR 97403

NOYES, TOM ENDERBY, psychiatrist; b. Apr. 16, 1944. MD, Queen's U., Ont., Can., 1969. Diplomate Am. Bd. Psychiatry and Neurology. Intern Wellesley Hosp., Toronto, Can., 1969-70; resident in psychiatiry Mayo Clinic, Rochester, Minn., 1970-73; unit chief adolescent unit King's View Hosp., Fresno, Calif., 1976-77; med. staff St. Agnes Med. Ctr., Fresno, 1986-90, Valley Children's Hosp., Fresno, 1986-90; staff psychiatrist Fresno Community Hosp., 1975-90; staff psychiatrist King's View Ctr., Reedley, Calif., 1977-90, med. dir., CEO, 1977-90; med. dir. Capistrano by the Sea Hosp., Dana Point, Calif., 1990—; staff psychiatrist South Coast Hosp., Dana Point, Calif., 1990—, Mission Hosp., Mission Viejo, Calif., 1990—, Samaritan Hosp., San Clemente, Calif., 1990—; psychiat. cons. Hosp. for the Criminally Insane, St. Peter, Minn., 1972-73, Assoc. Ctr. for Therapy, Fresno, 1976-79; mem. numerous hosp. and med. coms. Fellow APA; mem. Can. Med. Assn., Ont. Med. Assn., Calif. Med. Assn., Fresno County Med. Soc., AMA, Cen. Neuropsychiat. Hosp. Assn., Nat. Assn. Pvt. Psychiat. Hosps., Nat. Assn. Psychiatric Health Systems, Calif. Behavioral Health Systems, Calif. Psychiat. Assn., Am. Assn. Psychiat. Adminstrs., Am. Hosp. Assn., Orange County Psychiat. Soc., Orange County Med. Assn. Office: Capistrano By the Sea Hosp 34000 Capistrano By The Sea Dana Point CA 92629-2959

NOZIGLIA, CARLA MILLER, forensic scientist; b. Erie, Pa., Oct. 11, 1941; d. Earnest Carl and Eileen (Murphy) Miller; m. Keith William Noziglia, Nov. 21, 1969; children: Pama Noziglia Cook, Kathryn Noziglia Volpi. BS, Villa Maria Coll., 1963; MS, Lindenwood Coll., 1984. Cert. med. technologist, Am. Soc. Clin. Pathologists. Med. technologist Monmouth (N.J.) Gen. Hosp., 1963-64; spl. chem. med. technologist Hamot Hosp. Med. Ctr., Erie, Pa., 1965-69; pathologist's assoc. Galion (Ohio) Comm. Hosp., 1969-75; dir. crime lab. Mansfield (Ohio) Police Dept., Richland County Crime Lab., 1978-81; crime lab. supr. St. Louis County Police, Clayton, Mo., 1981-84; dir. crime lab. Las Vegas (Nev.) Met. Police, 1984-88, dir. lab. svcs., 1988-93, dir., cons. forensic scis., 1993-95; lab. dir. Tulsa Police Dept., 1995—. Tech. abstracts editor Jour. Police Sci. and Adminstrn., 1983-91; editorial bd. Jour. Forensic Identification, 1988—; contbr. to (book) Journal of Police Science, 1989, Encyclopedia of Police Science, 1989. Mem. Gov.'s Com. on Testing for Intoxication, Las Vegas, 1984-93; mem. adv. bd. Nev. Bd. Pharmacy, 1988-93; recruiter United Blood Svcs., Las Vegas, 1986-93; bd. dirs., pres. Cmty. Action Against Rape, Las Vegas, 1987-94; co-founder So. Nev. Sexual Assault Protocol, 1986. Recipient award Ohio Ho. of Reps., 1981, Alumni of Yr. award Villa Maria Coll., 1981; named Outstanding Cath. Erie Diocese N.W. Pa., 1988, Woman of Achievement Las Vegas C. of C., 1989. Fellow Am. Acad. Forensic Sci. (bd. dirs. 1988-91, sec. Criminalistics sect. 1986, sect. chmn. 1987, Sect. award 1995); mem. Am. Soc. Crime Lab Dirs. (emeritus, bd. dirs. 1980-87, treas. 1981-82, 88-91, pres. 1986-87), Internat. Police Assn., Internat. Assn. for Identification (emeritus), S.W. Assn. Forensic Scientists, Am. Bus. Women's Assn. (Woman of Yr. 1988, one of Nat. Top Bus. Women 1993). Republican. Roman Catholic. Office: Tulsa Police Dept 600 Civic Ctr Tulsa OK 74103

NOZIK, ARTHUR JACK, research physical chemist; b. Springfield, Mass., Jan. 10, 1936; s. Morris and Lillian (Golden) N.; m. Rhoda Ann Fisher, Sept. 6, 1958; children: Eva Sue, Jane Marla. B Chem. Engring., Cornell U., 1958; MS, Yale U., 1962, PhD, 1967. Rsch. engr. McDonnell-Douglas Aircraft Co., Santa Monica, Calif., 1958-60; staff engr. Am. Cyanamid Co., Stamford, Conn., 1961-64, staff scientist, 1967-74; group leader Allied-Signal Corp., Morristown, N.J., 1974-78; sr. scientist Solar Energy Rsch. Inst., Golden, Colo., 1978-80, br. chief, 1980-85, sr. rsch. fellow, 1985—; lectr. over 125 univs. and sci. confs.; mem. sci. rev. coms. U.S. Dept. Energy and NSF; disting. lectr. Dept. Energy and Am. Western Univs., Salt Lake City, 1990. Co-author: Surface Electron Transfer Processes 1994; editor: Photoeffects at Semiconductor-Electrolyte Interfaces, 1981; sr. editor: Jour. Phys. Chemistry, 1993—; co-editor: Photoelectrochemistry, 1982-87; mem. editorial bd. Jour. Solar Energy Materials, 1982—; also over 100 articles: patentee in field. Recipient Outstanding Achievement award Solar Energy Rsch. Inst., 1984, H.M. Hubbard award, 1991, Van Morris award Midwest Rsch. Inst., 1985. Mem. Am. Phys. Soc., Am. Chem. Soc., Electrochem. Soc. (chmn. energy tech. group 1984-85), Materials Rsch. Soc., Sigma Xi. Office: Nat Renewable Energy Lab 1617 Cole Blvd Golden CO 80401

NUCE, MADONNA MARIE, military officer; b. Denver, Jan. 15, 1952; d. Donald William and Marie Dorothy (Ruscio) N.; m. Edward Ray Geron, Oct. 9, 1982; 1 child, Maria Louise. BA, U. No. Colo., 1974; grad., Command and Gen. Staff Coll., Ft. Leavenworth, 1993. Enlisted U.S. ANG, 1973; commd. 2d lt. U.S. Army, 1981, advanced through grades to lt. col., 1993; adminstrv. supply tech. Colo. Army Nat. Guard, Denver, 1974-79; supply technician Colo. Army Nat. Guard, Golden, Colo., 1979-81; tng. officer Colo. Army Nat. Guard, Aurora, Colo., 1981-84, adminstrv. officer, 1984-85; maintenance officer Colo. Army Nat. Guard, Golden, Colo., 1985-86, asst. supply officer, 1986-91, data processing chief, 1991-92, supply mgmt. officer, 1992-93, comptroller, 1993-94, dir. maintenance, 1994—; Mem. Colo. Nat. Guard Assn. (sec. 1981-83, bd. dirs. 1983-85), Assn. of the U.S. Army (treas. 1986-88), Colo. Artists Assn. Group leader 5th grade Archdiocese of Denver Jr. Great Books Program, St. Anne Sch., 1987-89, group leader 7th grade Holy Family, 1991-92; bd. dirs. 9 Health Fair, Denver, 1985-90. Decorated Meritorious Svc. medal, Army Commendation medal, Army Achievement medal. Mem. NAFE, AAUW, Colo. Nat Guard

Assn. (sec. 1981-83, bd. dirs. 1983-85), Assn. of U.S. Army (treas. 1986-88). Roman Catholic. Office: Colo Army Nat Guard 6848 S Revere Pky Englewood CO 80112-3904

NUCKOLLS, LEONARD ARNOLD, retired hospital administrator; b. Park City, Utah, Feb. 22, 1917; s. Harry Leonard and Mabel Hill (Ganson) N.; m. Rachel A. Beckner, Apr. 18, 1942; children: Rachel Nuckolls Conine, Peter Leonard. AB, Pueblo Jr. Coll., 1938; BA, U. Colo., 1940. Commd. U.S. Army, 1942, advanced through grades to lt. col., 1962; adj. gen. 2d Army Div., Ft. Hood, Tex., 1960-62; ret., 1962; acct. Colo. State Hosp., Pueblo, 1963-64; caseworker N.Mex. Dept. Pub. Welfare, Clovis, 1964-66; unit coord. N.Mex. Dept. Hosps. and Instns., Las Vegas State Hosp., 1966-69; hosp. adminstr. Las Vegas Med. Ctr., 1969-76; adminstr. Vista Sandia Hosp., Albuquerque, 1980-83. Vol. Internat. Exec. Svc. Corp. Mem. Ret. Officers Assn., Mensa, Rotary. Home: 810 Faldas De La Sierra Santa Fe NM 87501-1252

NUGENT, ROBERT J., JR., fast food company executive; b. 1942. BBA, U. Cin., 1964. loan officer Citizens Savs., 1964-67; asst. v.p. Gem City Savs., 1967-69; v.p. Ponderosa System Inc., 1969-78, Ky. Fried Chicken, 1978-79; v.p. Foodmaker Inc., San Diego, from 1979, exec. v.p. ops., mktg., 1985—. Office: Foodmaker Inc PO Box 783 San Diego CA 92112-4126

NULL, PAUL BRYAN, minister; b. Oakland, Calif., May 7, 1944; s. Carleton Elliot and Dorothy Irene (Bryan) N.; m. Renee Yvonne Howell, Aug. 23, 1969; children: Bryan Joseph, Kara Renee. BS, Western Bapt. Coll., 1973; MDiv, Western Conservative Bapt. Sem., 1979; DMin, Trinity Theol. Sem., 1994. Ordained to ministry Bapt. Ch., 1982. Asst. pastor Bethel Bapt. Ch., Aumsville, Oreg., 1972-74, sr. pastor, 1974-87; sr. pastor The Calvary Congregation, Stockton, Calif., 1987-94; pastor Sierra Comty. Ch., South Lake Tahoe, Calif., 1994—; trustee Conservative Bapt. Assn. of Oreg., 1982-85, mem. Ch. extension com., 1975-85. Radio show commentator Food for Thought, 1987. Panel mem. Presdl. Anti-Drug Campaign, 1984. Served with U.S. Army, 1965-67. Named Outstanding Young Man Am., 1979. Mem. Conservative Bapt. Assn. of Am., No. Calif. Conservative Bapt. Assn. (pres. 1992-93), Delta Epsilon Chi. Home: 1399 Iroquois Circle South Lake Tahoe CA 96150 Office: Sierra Comty Ch 1165 Sierra Blvd South Lake Tahoe CA 96150

NUNES, FRANK R., JR., food products executive; b. 1952. BA in English, Sacramento State U., 1975. Carpenter various gen. contractors, Lake Tahoe, Calif., 1975-79; pvt. practice as carpenter Lake Tahoe, Calif., 1979-82; with The Nunes Co., Inc., Salinas, Calif., 1982—; v.p. Nunes Vegetables, Inc., 1992—. Office: Nunes Vegetables Inc 757 Abbott St Salinas CA 93901-4314*

NUNES, THOMAS, marketing director; b. East Providence, R.I., Nov. 26, 1942; s. Manuel and Catherine Marie (McIntosh) N.; m. Pamela Antonia Monti, Nov. 28, 1964; children: Daniel A., Jennifer E., Christopher M. BS, USCG Acad., 1964; MPA, NYU, 1974. Commd. ensign USCG USCG, 1964; advanced through grades to comdr., 1979, ret., 1984; mktg. dir. Advanced Circuit Tech., Nashua, N.H., 1984-88; mgr. bus. unit Rogers Corp., Chandler, Ariz., 1988-90; mktg. and sales mgr. Semflex, Mesa, Ariz., 1990-92; cons., 1992-94; sales mgr. Kroy, Inc., Scottsdale, Ariz., 1994—. Mem. Am. Mktg. Assn., Lic. Execs. Soc. Roman Catholic. Office: Kroy Inc 14555 N Hayden Rd Scottsdale AZ 85260-3443

NUNES, THOMAS P., food products executive; b. 1951. BA, Calif. Polytech. Inst., 1973. With Nunes Farms, Salinas, Calif., 1973-74; owner Nunes Ranches, Salinas, Calif., 1975-78; pres. Nunes Vegetables Inc., Salinas, Calif., 1978—. *

NUNZ, GREGORY JOSEPH, program manager, aerospace engineer, educator; b. Batavia, N.Y., May 28, 1934; s. Sylvester Joseph and Elizabeth Marie (Loesell) N.; m. Georgia Monyea Costas, Mar. 30, 1958; children: Karen, John, Rebecca, Deirdre, Jaimie, Marta. BSChemE, Cooper Union, 1955; postgrad., U. So. Calif., Calif. State U.; MS in Applied Math., Columbia Pacific U., 1991, PhD in Mgmt. Sci., 1993. Adv. design staff, propulsion mgr. U.K. project Rocketdyne div. Rockwell, Canoga Park, Calif., 1955-65; mem. tech. staff Aerospace Corp., El Segundo, Calif., 1965-70; mem. tech. staff propulsion div. Jet Propulsion Lab., Pasadena, Calif., 1970-72; chief. monoprop. engring. Bell Aerospace Corp., Buffalo, N.Y., 1972-74; group supr. comb. devices Jet Propulsion Lab., Pasadena, 1974-76; asst. div. leader, program mgr. internat. HDR geothermal energy program, project mgr. space-related projects Los Alamos (N.Mex.) Nat. Lab., 1977—; assoc. prof. electronics L.A. Pierce Coll., Woodland Hills, Calif., 1961-72; instr. No. N.Mex. Community Coll., Los Alamos, 1978-80, div. head scis., 1980-92; adj. prof. math. U. N.Mex., Los Alamos, 1980—. Author: Electronics Lab Manual I, 1964, Electronics in our World, 1972; co-author: Electronics Mathematics, vol. I, II, 1967; contbg. author Prentice-Hall Textbook of Cosmetology, 1975, Alternative Energy Sources VII, 1987; contbr. articles to profl. jours.; inventor smallest catalytic liquid N2H4 rocket thrustor, co-inventor first monoprop/biprop bimodal rocket engine, tech. advisor internat. multi-prize winning documentary film One With the Earth. Mem. Aerial Phenomena Research Orgn., L.A., 1975. Fellow AIAA (assoc.); mem. Tech. Mktg. Soc. Am., Math. Assn. Am., ARISTA, Shrine Club, Masons, Ballut Abyad Temple. Office: Los Alamos Nat Lab PO Box 1663 MS D460 Los Alamos NM 87545

NUSE, DELAND LYNN, film director, writer, producer; b. Las Vegas, N.Mex., June 20, 1946; s. Herbert C. and Magdalena L. (Landrum) N.; m. Angela June Allaire, Jan. 22, 1994. BA in Psychology, Calif. State U., Stanislaw, 1969; postgrad., U. N.Mex., 1970-72; MA in Film, San Francisco State U., 1983. Lectr. in film San Francisco State U., 1980-82; cinematographer Hausberg Prodns., L.A., 1987-89; dir. Transbay Prodns., L.A., 1989-90; writer, dir. Screenplayers Co., L.A., 1991-93; prodr., dir. Matador Prodns., Palmdale, Calif., 1994—. Dir. photography (documentary) The Other Bridge, 1982 (Sci. Film award 1983); dir. photography (feature) War Birds, 1988; dir. films (short) City of Death, 1983, (feature) The Chilling, 1990; writer film (feature) M.M., 1992. Democrat. Home: 37211 Oak Hill St Palmdale CA 93552-4407

NUSSBAUM, JON KIMBAL, defense contractor executive; b. Muncie, Ind., Sept. 21, 1957; s. Alvin A. and Maxine E. (Meyer) N.; m. Lisa Ann Schwer, June 14, 1980; 1 child, J. Ethan. BS, U.S. Mil. Acad., 1980. Commd. 2d lt. U.S. Army, 1980, advanced through grades to capt., 1984, resigned, 1988; mgr. advanced programs Alcoa Def. Systems, Inc., San Diego, 1988-89; sr. mgr. bus. devel. McDonnell Douglas Techs., Inc., San Diego, 1989-92; dir., bus. devel. land systems, signature tech. div. Sci. Applications Internat. Corp., San Diego, 1992-94, divsn. mgr. signature tech. divsn., 1994—; self-employed def. cons., Temecula, Calif., 1990—. With USAR, 1988—. Mem. Am. Def. Preparedness Assn., U.S. Armor Assn., West. Point Assn. Grads., Res. Officers Assn., West Point Soc. of the Inland Empire (treas. 1991—). Republican. Office: Sci Applications Internat Corp 10260 Campus Point Dr San Diego CA 92121-1522

NUSSINOW, JILL ANNE, nutritionist; b. Bklyn., Apr. 13, 1955; d. Bernard L. and Mary Lou (Siegel) N.; m. Timothy J. Marchel, June 1, 1985 (div. Aug. 1991); m. Richard B. Cratty Jr., Oct. 1, 1992; 1 child, Shane Scott. BBA in Mktg., U. Miami, 1976; MS in Dietetics and Nutrition, Fla. Internat. U., 1981. Registered dietitian. Bd. dirs., purchasing coord. South Dade Food Coop, South Miami, Fla., 1978-80; dietitian Mercy Hosp., Miami, 1980-81; nutritionist trainee dept. pediatrics The Mailman Ctr. for Child Devel., U. Miami (Fla.) Med. Sch., 1981-82; dietitian in pvt. practice Calif., 1982—; nutrition cons. Control Data Corp., Westchester, Calif., Montecito Heights Health and Racquet Club, Santa Rosa, Calif., The Airport Club, Santa Rosa, Amy's Kitchen, Natural Frozen Food Mfr., Petaluma, Calif., others; instr. Calif. State U. Northridge, 1987-88, West L.A. Coll. Cmty. Svcs., Bay Cities Jewish Cmty. Ctr., Mont. Mercantile Cooking Sch.; nutritionist Maxicare, Inc., L.A., 1985-88, others; adj. faculty Santa Rosa Jr. Coll., 1989—; presenter in field. Author, editor: Vegetarian Cooking For Everyone, Vol. 1, 1993. Past. pres. Westside Consumers Edn. Found. Mem. Am. Dietetic Assn. (registered mem., vegetarian practice group), Soc. for Nutrition Edn., Dietitians in Bus. and Industry Practice Group, Sports and Cardiovascular Nutritionists Practice Group, Internat. Food, Wine and Travel Writers Assn., Internat. Assn. Culinary Profls., Sonoma County Culinary Guild (founder, past pres., pub. rels. chairperson). Home: 1988 Respite Pl Santa Rosa CA 95403-7947 Office: The Vegetarian Connection PO Box 218 Petaluma CA 94953-0218

NUSZ, PHYLLIS JANE, fundraising consultant, meeting planner; b. Lodi, Calif., Dec. 16, 1941; d. Fred Henry and Esther Emma (Enzminger) N. BA, U. Pacific, 1963, MA, 1965; EdD, Nova Southwestern U., 1987. Cert. fund raising exec. Prof. speech comm. Bakersfield (Calif.) Coll., 1965-86; from asst. dir. student activites to found. exec. dir. Bakersfield (Calif) Coll., 1965-86; mgmt. seminar dir. Delta Kappa Gamma Soc. Internat., Austin, Tex., 1983-86; loaned exec. United Way San Joaquin County, Stockton, Calif., 1990; fund raising cons. PJ Enterprises, Lodi, Calif., 1987—. Bd. dirs. U. Calif. Sch. Medicine Surg. Found., San Francisco, 1989—; mem. Heritage Circle and Chancellor's Assn., U. Calif. San Francisco, 1987—. Recipient archives award of merit Evang. Luth. Ch. in Am., 1988; fellow Calif. Luth. U., 1985—. Mem. Nat. Soc. Fund Raising Execs. (chmn. mentor program Calif. Capital chpt. 1991, bd. dirs. 1988-91, chmn. acad. fund raising 1991, chmn. mentor program Golden Gate chpt. 1991, founding, pres. San Joaquin chpt. 1992-93, Pres.'s award for Meritorious Svc., Golden Gate chpt. 1991), U. Pacific Alumni Assn. (bd. dirs. 1974-82), Calif. Tchrs. Assn., Nat. Assn. Parliamentarians, Rotary (North Stockton bd. dirs. 1993—, treas. 1994—, found. treas. 1994—), Delta Kappa Gamma (internat. scholar 1986). Republican. Lutheran. Office: PJ Enterprises 1300 W Lodi Ave Ste A11 Lodi CA 95242-3000

NUTTALL, MICHAEL LEE, engineer, educator; b. Salem, Mass.; s. Leonard John IV and Ethel (Pecukonis) N.; m. Susan Patricia Wade, July 12, 1988; children: Leonard John VI, Andrew Norman. BSChemE, Brigham Young U., 1987; MEE, U. Utah, 1994. Japanese linguist Utah Army N.G., Provo, 1984-87; math tutor Utah Valley C.C., Provo, 1987; engr. Micron Tech., Boise, Idaho, 1988-89, lead engr., 1989-91; instr. Salt Lake C.C., Salt Lake City, 1991-92; process devel. engr. Micron Tech., Boise, Idaho, 1994—. Home: 1469 N Deep Creek Way Meridian ID 83642-4215 Office: Micro Tech 8000 S Federal Way Boise ID 83707

NUTTALL, RICHARD NORRIS, state agency administrator; b. Hamilton, Ont., Can., Feb. 7, 1940; s. James William and Margaret Gay (Walsh) N.; m. Ethel Jane Pickering, July 9, 1977; children: Andrew Richard, John Patrick. BSA, U. Toronto, 1961; MPA, Harvard U., 1964; MB, BS, U. London, Eng., 1974. Cert. Coll. Family Physicians Can., Mgmt. Cons. Zone dir. Health and Welfare Can., Prime Rupert, B.C., 1977-79; regional dir. Health and Welfare Can., Edmonton, Alta., 1980-82; pres. Rutland Consulting Group, Ltd., Vancouver, B.C., 1982-87, Richmond Assocs. Internat., Vancouver, 1988-90; med. health officer Govt. N.W. Ters., Yellowknife, B.C., 1990-93, Regina (Can.) Health Dist., 1993—. Mem. Can. Pub. Health Assn. (bd. dirs. 1991-93), Rotary Club North Regina. Office: Regina Health Dist, 1910 McIntyre St, Regina, SK Canada S4P 2R3

NUTZLE, FUTZIE (BRUCE JOHN KLEINSMITH), artist, author, cartoonist; b. Lakewood, Ohio, Feb. 21, 1942; s. Adrian Ralph and Naomi Irene (Rupert) Kleinsmith; children: Adrian David, Arielle Justine and Tess Alexandra (twins). Represented by The Pope Gallery, Santa Cruz, Calif. Author: Modern Loafer, Thames and Hudson, 1981, (authobiography) Futzie Nutzle, 1983, Earthquake, 1989, Run the World: 50 Cents Chronicle Books, 1991; illustrator: The Armies Encamped Beyond Unfinished Avenues (Morton Marcus), 1977, Box of Nothing, 1982, The Duke of Chemical Birds (Howard McCord), 1989, Book of Solutions, 1990, Fact and Friction, 1990, Managing for the 90s, 1992, Soundbites for Success, 1994; feature cartoonist Rolling Stone, N.Y.C., 1975-80, The Japan Times, Tokyo and L.A., 1986—, The Prague Post, Czechoslovakia, 1991—; contbr. exhbns. include Inaugural, 1966, Cupola, 1967, Rolling Renaissance, San Francisco, 1968, 100 Acres, O.K. Harris 1971, N.Y.C., San Francisco Mus. Art, 1972, Indpls. and Cin. Mus. Art, 1975, Leica, L.A., 1978, Santa Barbara Mus. Annex, Calif., 1978, Swope, Santa Monica, West Beach Cafe, Venice, Calif., 1985, Les Oranges, Santa Monica, Correspondence Sch., 1970-78, 1st Ann. Art-A-Thon, N.Y.C., 1985, Am. Epiphany with Phillip Hefferton, 1986, Polit. Cartoon Show, Braunstein, San Francisco, Komsomolskaya Pravda, 1988, retrospective Eloise Packard Smith, 1990, exemplary contemporary, Cowell, U. Calif. Santa Cruz, 1991, Silicon Graphics Inc., Computer Graphics for NAB, Las Vegas, 1993, Prague Eco-Fair, 1991; represented in pvt. and pub. collections (complete archives) Spl. Collections, McHenry Libr., U. Calif., Santa Cruz, Mus. Modern Art, N.Y.C., San Francisco Mus. Modern Art, Oakland Mus., San Francisco Mus. Cartoon Art, Whitney Mus. Am. Art, N.Y.C. regular contbr. The Japan Times. Ltd., Tokyo. Address: PO Box 325 Aromas CA 95004-0325

NUWER, MARC ROMAN, neuroscientist, physician; b. Buffalo, July 8, 1948; s. Donald Charles and Arlene Ruth (Ebert) N.; m. Beverly Ann Jones, Oct. 12, 1978; children: Jamie Marie, Charles Marc, Stephen John, Catherine Ann. BA, Stanford U., 1970, MSEE, 1972, PhD, 1975, MD, 1975. Diplomate Am. Bd. Psychiatry and Neurology. Asst. prof. neurology UCLA, 1979-87, assoc. prof. neurology, 1987-93, prof. neurology, 1993—, chief evoked potential lab., 1979—, chief EEG lab., 1986—; dept. head for clin. neurophysiology UCLA Med Ctr.; chmn. UCLA Neurology Profl. Group, 1985-90. Author: Evoked Potential Monitoring in the Operating Room, 1986; mem. editorial bd. Electroencephalography and Clin. Neurophysiology, Brain Topography. Med. research grantee NIH, 1980—, FDA Adv. Panel, 1994—. Fellow Am. Acad. Neurology (mem. practice com. 1991—), Am. EEG Soc. (pres. 1993-94), Am. Epilepsy Soc., Am. Soc. Neurol. Investigation (pres. 1984-85), Am. Neurol. Assn., Internat. Fedn. Clin Neurophysiology (exec. bd. 1993—), Western EEG Soc. (pres. 1990-91). Office: UCLA Dept Neurology 710 Westwood Plz Los Angeles CA 90024-8300

NYARADY, STEFAN ALAN, analytical chemist; b. Ft. Ord, Calif., May 11, 1950; s. Stefan Albert and Wanda Helen (Heltman) N.; m. Barbara Jean Millage, June 2, 1973; 1 child, Claire Kathryn. BS in Chemistry, Stanford U., 1972; MS in Chemistry, Naval Postgrad. Sch., 1973; PhD in Chemistry, U. Colo., 1985. Analytical chemist Tenn. Eastman Co., Kingsport, 1978-81; grad. rsch. asst. U. Colo., Boulder, 1982-85; devel. scientist Pfizer Pharm. Co., Groton, Conn., 1985-88; sr. devel. chemist Coors Brewing Co., Golden, Colo., 1988—. Inventor in field; contbr. articles to profl. jours. Lt. USN, 1972-78. Mem. AAAS, Am. Chem. Soc. (analytical divsn.), Am. Soc. Brewing Chemists (tech. subcom. chair 1988-94), Sigma Xi. Office: Coors Brewing Co M/S BC 600 Golden CO 80401

NYBAKKEN, JAMES WILLARD, marine biology educator; b. Warren, Minn., Sept. 16, 1936; s. Clarence G. and Effie Pearl (Knutson) N.; m. Bette Halvorsen, Aug. 20, 1960; children: Kent Edward, Scott Jordan. B.A. summa cum laude, St. Olaf Coll., Northfield, Minn., 1958; M.S., U. Wis., 1961, Ph.D., 1965. Curator zool. museum U. Wis., 1961-62, 64-65; mem. faculty Calif. State U., Hayward, 1965—; prof. marine ecology and invertebrate zoology Calif. State U., 1972—; mem. staff Moss Landing (Calif.) Marine Lab., 1966—; environ. cons., 1972—. Author: Readings in Marine Ecology, 1971, 2d edit., 1986, Elements of Zoology, 4th edit, 1977, General Zoology, 6th edit, 1978, Guide to the Nudibranchs of California, 1980, Marine Biology: An Ecological Approach, 1982, 2d edit., 1987, 3d edit., 1992. Fellow Calif. Acad. Scis.; mem. AAAS, Am. Soc. Zoologists, Am. Malacological Union (pres. 1985-86), Ecol. Soc. Am., Malacological Soc. London, Western Soc. Malacologists (pres. 1974-75), Western Soc. Naturalists (pres.-elect 1985, pres, 1986), Sigma Xi. Office: PO Box 450 Moss Landing CA 95039-0450

NYBERG, WALTER LAWRENCE, psychology and religion educator emeritus; b. Mpls., Nov. 20, 1922; s. Knute Harold and Helga (Bergman) N.; m. Ruth Brewster Whitney, Dec. 15, 1944; children: Jane, James, Peter, Paul. BA, Macalester Coll., St. Paul, 1946; STB, Boston U., 1949, STM, 1953; PhD, NYU, 1964. Ordained to ministry Meth. Ch., 1949. Pastor Meth. chs. in Mass., Oreg., Kans., 1949-59; assoc. min. Community Ch., Great Neck, N.Y., 1959-61; prof. religious studies U. of the Pacific, Stockton, Calif., 1962-90, emeritus, 1990; therapist Human Achievement Counseling Ctr., Stockton, 1969-86. Dir. Wesley Found, 1951-59. Democrat. Home: 420 Bristol Ave Stockton CA 95204-4330

NYBORG, JENNIFER KAY, biochemistry educator; b. Loma Linda, Calif., Sept. 2, 1958; d. Alan Orson and Shelby Jean (Fletcher) N. BS, U. Calif., 1981, PhD, 1986. Postdoctoral fellow U. Colo., Boulder, 1986-90; asst. prof. Colo. State U., Ft. Collins, 1990—; cons. Somatogen, Boulder, 1992. Contbr. articles to profl. jours. Bd. dirs. Am. Cancer Soc., Larimer County, 1992. Rsch. grant NIH, 1991, Am. Cancer Soc., 1992. Mem. AAAS, Am. Soc. for Microbiology, ASBMB. Democrat. Office: Dept Biochemistry Colo State U Colorado State University CO 80523

NYBORG, LESTER PHIL, physician; b. Twin Groves, Idaho, May 4, 1925; s. Lester Thorsted and LaVernie Mildred (Hathaway) H.; m. LaWana Blanchard, Nov. 23, 1949; children: Jeffrey, Valeah, Vicki. BS, Utah State U., 1951; MD, Northwestern U., 1956; MPH, U. Calif., Berkeley, 1967. Diplomate Am. Bd. Preventive Medicine. Commd. med. officer, lt. USN, 1957, advanced through grades to lt. comdr., 1964; commd. major USAF, 1964, advanced through grades to col., 1970; intern LDS Hosp., Salt Lake City, 1957; resident USAF Sch. Aviation Medicine, 1968-69; chief profl. svcs. 9th Air Force, 1969-70; med. advisor Vietnamese USAF, Vietnam, 1970-71; ret. USAF, 1975; med. dir. Boise (Idaho) State U., 1976—. Decorated Bronze Star, Vietnamese Congressional medal Vietnamese Nat. Air Force, 1971. Mem. Ada County Med. Soc. Home: 660 Ballentine Ln Eagle ID 83616-4648 Office: Boise State U Boise ID 83725

NYE, ERIC WILLIAM, English language educator; b. Omaha, July 31, 1952; s. William Frank and Mary Roberta (Lueder) N.; m. Carol Denison Frost, Dec. 21, 1980; children: Charles William, Ellen Mary. BA, St. Olaf Coll., 1974; MA, U. Chgo., 1976, PhD, 1983; postgrad., Queens' Coll., Cambridge, England, 1979-82. Tutor in coll. writing com. U. Chgo., 1976-79, teaching intern, 1978; supr., tutor in Am. Lit. Cambridge U., England, 1979-82; asst. prof. English U. Wyo., Laramie, 1983-89; assoc. prof. English U. Wyo., Laramie, Wyo., 1989—; v.p., bd. dirs. Plainview Tel. Co., Nebr.; hon. vis. fellow U. Edinburgh (Scotland) Inst. for Advanced Studies in the Humanities, 1987; guest lectr. NEH summer Inst., Laramie, Wyo., 1985, Carlyle Soc. of Edinburgh, 1987, Wordsworth summer Conf., Grasmere, Eng., 1988, cons. NEH. Contbr. articles and reviews to profl. jours. Mem. Am. Friends of Cambridge U.; elected mem. Wyo. Coun. for Humanities, 1992—, exec. com., 1993-94; mem. adv. bd. Wyo. Ctr. for the Book, 1995—. Named Nat. Merit Scholar St. Olaf Coll., 1970-74; recipient Grad. Fellowship, Rotary Found., 1979-80, grant U. Wyo., 1984-85, Am. Coun. of Learned Socs., 1988, Disting. Alumnus award, Lincoln (Neb.) E. High Sch., 1986. Mem. MLA (del. assembly 1991-93), Assn. for Documentary Editing, Bibliographical Soc. London, Assn. for Computers and the Humanities, Assn. for Literary and Linguistic Computing, Coleridge Soc. (life), Friends of Dove Cottage (life), Charles Lamb Soc., Carlyle Soc., Rsch. Soc. for Victorian Periodicals, The Victorians Inst., The Tennyson Soc., Penn Club (London), Queens' Coll. Club (Cambridge), Phi Beta Kappa (pres., v.p., sec. Wyo. chpt. 1988—). Home: 1495 Apache Dr Laramie WY 82070-6966 Office: U Wyo Dept English PO Box 3353 Laramie WY 82071-3353

NYE, GENE WARREN, art educator; b. Sacramento, July 3, 1939; s. Charles Frederick and Dorthy Dell Nye; m. Alena Mae Nye, Sept. 20, 1974; children: Dirk, Ronni, Anthony, Timothy. AA, American River Coll., Sacramento, 1962; AB, Sacramento State U., 1964; student, U. Calif., Berkeley. Cert. secondary tchr., Calif. Printer Roseville (Calif.) Press Tribune, 1957-60; typographer Oakland (Calif.) Tribune, 1960-65; tchr. art Long Beach (Calif.) Unified Sch. Dist., 1965-67; tchr., chair art dept. Woodland (Calif.) Unified Sch. Dist., 1967—; freelance artist Wildcat Art, Sacramento, 1985—; cons. N.Mex. Ctrl. Coun. Student Activities, 1991; workshop presenter. Author: (workbook set and video) Posters Made EZ, 1990. Mem. task force Constn. Revision of CADA, L.A., 1988-89. Named to Calif. Assn. Dirs. of Activities Hall of Fame, 1992. Mem. NEA (life), Woodland Edn. Assn. (v.p. 1971-72), Calif. Art Edn. Assn., Nat. Art Edn. Assn., Calif. League of Mid. Schs., U. Calif. Alumni Assn. (life). Home: 2200 Eastern Ave Sacramento CA 95864-0805 Office: Lee Jr HS 520 West St Woodland CA 95695-3705

NYE, MARY JO, historian, humanities educator; b. Nashville, Dec. 5, 1944; d. Joe Allen and Mildred (Heath) Mann; m. Robert Allen Nye, Feb. 17, 1968; 1 child, Lesley Noel. Student, Vanderbilt U., 1962-64; BA, U. Wis., 1964-65, PhD, 1965-70. From asst. prof. to assoc. prof. then prof. U. Okla., 1970-94; prof. humanities and history Oreg. State U., Corvallis, 1994—; assoc. fellow ctr. for Hist. Study Rutgers U., New Brunswick, N.J., 1989-90; mem. sch. hist. studies Inst. Advanced Study, Princeton, N.J., 1981-82; vis. prof. Harvard U., Cambridge, Mass., 1988. Author: Molecular Reality, 1972, Science in the Provinces, 1986; editor: The Question of the Atom, 1984, From Chemical Philosophy to Theoretical Chemistry, 1993. Fellow AAAS; mem. Hist. Sci. Soc. (pres. 1988-89), Am. Hist. Assn., Internat. Union of History and Philosphy of Sci. (U.S. nat. com. 1986-89), Internat. Union of History and Philosophy of Sci. (2d v.p. divsn. history and sci. 1993—), Phi Beta Kappa.

NYE, W. MARCUS W., lawyer; b. N.Y.C., Aug. 3, 1945; s. Walter R. and Nora (McLaren) N.; m. Eva Johnson; children: Robbie, Stephanie, Philip, Jennifer. BA, Harvard U., 1967; JD, U. Idaho, 1974. Bar: Idaho 1974, U.S. Dist. Ct. Idaho 1974, U.S. Ct. Appeals (9th cir.) 1980. Ptnr. Racine, Olson, Nye, Cooper & Budge, Pocatello, Idaho, 1974—; vis. prof. law U. Idaho, Moscow, 1984; adj. prof. Coll. Engring. IDaho State U., 1993—. Recipient Alumni Svc. award U. Idaho, 1988. Fellow ABA (mem. ho. dels. 1988—, state chmn. ho. of dels. 1991—), Am. Bar Found. (stat. chmn. 1992—); mem. Am. Bd. Trial Advs., Am. Coll. Trial Lawyers, Idaho Bar Assn. (commr. 1985—, pres. bd. commrs. 1987-88), Idaho Def. Counsel Assn. (pres. 1982), Idaho State Centennial Found. (commr. 1985-90), 6th Dist. Bar Assn. (pres. 1982). Home: 173 S 15th Ave Pocatello ID 83201-4056 Office: Racine Olson Nye Cooper & Budge PO Box 1391 Pocatello ID 83204-1391

NYIRI, JOSEPH ANTON, sculptor, art educator; b. Racine, Wis., May 24, 1937; s. Joseph Anton Nyiri and Dorothy Marion (Larson) Zink; m. Laura Lee Primeau, Aug. 29, 1959 (dec. Mar. 1982); children: Krista, Nicole, Page; m. Melissa Trent, July 28, 1985. BA, U. Wis., 1959, MS, 1961. Tchr. art Madison (Wis.) Sch. Dist., 1959-62; art cons. San Diego Unified Schs., 1962-65, dist. resource tchr., 1965-73, regional tchr. occupational art, 1973-76, mentor tchr., 1985-95; sculptor San Diego, 1962—, fine arts cons., 1966—; head dept. art edn. Serra High Sch., San Diego, 1976—; instr. art U. Calif. at San Diego, La Jolla, 1967-80, San Diego State U. Extension, 1969—; fine art restorer, 1963—, lectr. art and art edn., 1963—; pvt. art tchr. San Diego City Zoo. Exhibited sculpture in numerous one-man, two-person, juried and invitational shows, 1960—, U. Mex.-Baja Calif., 1983; rev. Calif. Art Rev., 1989. Active Art Guild San Diego Mus. Art; bd. dirs. San Diego Art Inst. Sgt. Wis. N.G., 1955-61. Named One of 3 Tchrs. of Yr., San Diego County, 1983, One of Outstanding Art Tchrs. in U.S., RISD, 1984, Secondary Tchr. of Yr., San Diego City Schs., 1982; recipient creativity award Pacific Inst., 1969. Mem. Arts/Worth: Nat. Coun. Art (charter), Allied Craftsmen San Diego, Internat. Platform Assn., San Diego Art Inst. (bd. dirs.), San Diego Mus. Art (mem. Art Guild). Democrat. Mem. Christian Ch. Home: 3525 Albatross St San Diego CA 92103-4807 Office: Serra High Sch 5156 Santo Rd San Diego CA 92124-2037

NYMAN, DAVID HAROLD, nuclear engineer; b. Aberdeen, Wash., May 21, 1938; s. Carl Victor and Elsie Ingagord (Laaksonen) N. Assoc., Grays Harbor Coll., 1958; BSMetE, U. Wash., 1961, MSMetE, 1963. Engr. Gen. Electric Co., Richland, Wash., 1963-68; engring. specialist United Nuclear Corp., New Haven, 1968-73; mgr. Westinghouse Hanford subs. Westinghouse Corp., Richland, 1973—. Contbr. articles to profl jours. Mem. Robotics Internat. of Soc. Mfg. Engrs. (div. chmn. 1985-86, tech. v.p. 1986-88), Robots West Conf. (adv. com. 1984, vice-chmn. 1986, Pres.'s award 1989), Am. Nuclear Soc. (chmn. meetings, proceedings, and transactions com. 1992—), Am. Soc. Metals., Inst. Nuclear Materials Mgmt., Columbia Basin Dog Tng. Club (pres. 1982-84), Richland Kennel Club, West Highland White Terrier Club of Puget Sound, West Highland White Terrier Club Am. (obedience com. 1982-88), Am. Kennel Club (judge tracking dog excellent tests). Republican. Lutheran.

NYQUIST, MAURICE OTTO, government agency administrator and scientist; b. Fairmont, Minn., May 30, 1944; s. Carl Arther and Wilda Yvette (Freitag) N.; m. Mary Maud Magee, Aug. 8, 1977; children: Gretchen, Beth. BS in Biology, Hamline U., 1966; MA in Biology, Mankato State U., 1968; PhD in Zoology, Wash. State U., 1973. Asst. prof. zoology Wash. State U., Pullman, 1973-74; scientist Nat. Park Svc., Lakewood, Colo., 1974-

76, mgr., 1979-93; mgr., scientist Nat. Biol. Svc., Denver, 1993—; mem. peer rev. coms. for academia, govt. and pvt. industry; agy. rep. Fed. Geographic Data Com. Dir. prodn. interactive computer exhibit on remote sensing for Denver Mus. Nat. History; contbr. sci. articles to profl. jours. Bd. dirs. Nat. Park Service Equal Employment Opportunity Com., Denver, 1981, chmn., 1982. Recipient Mgrs. award Nat. Park Service, Lakewood, 1981, Performance Commendation award, 1988; research grantee Nat. Rifle Assn., 1972. Mem. Am. Soc. Potogrammetry and Remote Sensing (exec. com., bd. dirs. 1988-90, v.p. 1992, pres.-elect 1993, pres. 1994, asst. dir. remote sensing applications divsn. 1985-87, dir. 1988-90), Am. Congress on Surveying and Mapping (joint satellite mapping and remote sensing com.), The Wildlife Soc., GRASS Users Group (steering com. 1986—, treas. 1987—), ELAS Users Group (co-chmn. 1985-86, chmn. 1986-87), Sigma Xi. Office: Nat Biol Svc Tech Transfer Ctr PO Box 25387-TTC Denver CO 80225-0387

NYQUIST, MICHAEL S., civil engineer; b. Marquette, Mich., Oct. 22, 1949; s. George R. and Hazel (Moyle) N.; m. Valda M. Marais, July 31, 1982. BME, 1972; MPA, No. Ariz. U., 1983. With engrng. staff Gen. Motors, 1967-73; with Frederic R. Harris, Inc., Ft. Lauderdale, Fla., and Haiti, Trinidad, Lesotho, 1976-82; constrn. engr. Bur. of Indian Affairs, Phoenix and Keams Canyon, 1983-85, highway design sect. leader, 1985-87; highway design engr. Evans, Kuhn and Assocs., Phoenix, 1987-88; roads advisor, head of roads sect. Chemonics Internat., Cairo, Egypt, 1988-90; road/traffic engr. Burrow Binnie Ltd. (formerly John Burrow and Ptnrs.), Mbabane, Swaziland, 1990-92; civil engr. Louis Berger Internat., General Santos City, Philippines, 1990, 92-93; chief of party Mozambique, 1993—; mem. U.S. Peace Corps, Lesotho, Swaziland, 1973-76.

OAK, CLAIRE MORISSET, artist, educator; b. St. Georges, Quebec, Can., May 31, 1921; came to U.S., 1945; d. Louis and Bernadette (Coulombe) Morisset; m. Alan Ben Oak, July 2, 1947. Student, Ecole des Beaux Arts, 1938-42, Parsons Sch. Design, N.Y.C., 1945, Art Students League, N.Y.C., 1945-46. Staff artist Henry Morgan & R. Simpson, Montreal, 1942-45; artist illustrator W.B. Golovin Advt. Agy., N.Y.C., 1947-49; freelance illustrator Arnold Constable & Advt. Agy., N.Y.C., 1948-50, Le Jardin des Modes, Paris, 1950-51, May & Co., L.A., 1956, Katten & Marengo Advt., Stockton, Calif., 1962-84; pvt. practice illustrator, designer San Joaquin Valley, Calif., 1984-92; art instr. San Joaquin Delta Coll., Stockton, 1973—; owner Fashion Illustrator's Workshop, N.Y.C., 1953-54; instr. Bauder Coll., Sacramento, 1975-76; painting workshop leader Lodi Art Ctr., 1991—; watercolor workshop leader D'Pharr Painting Adventures, Virginia City, Nev., 1992; ongoing watercolor workshop Galerie Iona, Stockton, Calif., 1993—. Named S.B. Anthony Woman of Achievement in the Arts, U. Pacific, 1982. Mem. Stockton Art League, Lodi Art Ctr., Ctrl. Calif. Art League, The League of Carmichael Artists, Delta Watercolor Soc. (bd. mem. 1988—). Home: 2140 Waudman Ave Stockton CA 95209-1755

OAK, RONALD STUART, health and safety administrator; b. Fargo, N.D., Dec. 20, 1956; s. Duane Lowel and Beverly Alice (Anderson) O. BS in Environ. Health, Colo. State U., 1979. Cert. indsl. hygienist Am. Bd. Indsl. Hygiene, cert. hazardous materials mgr. Inst. Hazardous Materials Mgmt. Compliance officer Wyo. Occupational Health and Safety Dept., Cheyenne, 1980-82, OSHA consultation program cons., 1982-84; indsl. hygienist Hager Labs., Inc., Denver, 1984-86; from assoc. to sr. indsl. hygienist Ecology and Environment, Inc., Denver, 1987-91; sr. indsl. hygienist Harding Lawson Assocs., Inc., Santa Ana, Calif., 1991-92; health and safety mgr. IT Corp., San Jose, Calif., 1993—. Mem. adv. com. Wyo. Gov.'s Com. on Hazardous Materials Response, Cheyenne, 1983-84; nat. mem. Smithsonian Assocs., Washington, 1990—, contbg. mem., 1995—. Mem. AAAS, N.Y. Acad. Scis., Am. Indsl. Hygiene Assn. Office: IT Corp 2055 Junction Ave San Jose CA 95131-2105

OAKES, TERRY LOUIS, retail clothing store executive; b. Denver, June 12, 1953; s. Robert Walter and Stella Marie (Ray) O.; m. Cynthia Alison Bailey, Jan. 10, 1981; children: Madeleine Bailey, Robert Alan. BBA, So. Meth. U., 1975. Dept. mgr. Woolf Bros., Dallas, 1975-76; buyer I.K.O. Dry Goods, Denver, 1976-79, gen. sales mgr., 1979-81, exec. v.p., mdse. mgr., 1981-86; nat. sales mgr. Fresh Squeeze div. Bayly Corp., Denver, 1986-88; owner, pres. Bolderdash, Denver, 1988—; mem. adv. bd. fashion mdse. divsn. Colo. Inst. Art., Denver, 1991—. Democrat. Presbyterian. Home: 5332 S Geneva Way Englewood CO 80111-6219 Office: Bolderdash 2817 E 3rd Ave Denver CO 80206-4919

OAKLAND, NANCY NELL, geriatrics nurse; b. El Paso, Tex., Apr. 26, 1947; d. Clarence L. and Ruth Alice (King) North; div.; children: Heather Lynn, Joshua Glen. BSN, Tex. Christian U., 1969. RN, Ariz. Staff nurse Tex. Children's Hosp., Houston, 1969-72; office nurse Pediatric Assocs., Houston, 1972-74; staff nurse, charge nurse pediatric unit Good Samaritan Hosp., Phoenix, 1974-75; office nurse Pediatric Clinic, Phoenix, 1975-76; sch. nurse Mesa (Ariz.) Pub. Schs., 1986; staff nurse acute care unit Cosada Villa Nursing Ctr., Mesa, 1986-88; staff nurse Valley Luth. Hosp., Mesa, 1988-89, case mgmt. coord., 1989-93; case mgr. LHS Home and Cmty. Care, Chandler, Ariz., 1993-95; dir. clin. svc. LHS Home and Cmty. Care, Chandler, 1995—; preceptor BSN students U. Phoenix, 1991-93. Home: 5928 E Ingram St Mesa AZ 85205-3537

OAKLEY, CAROLYN LE, state legislator, small business owner; b. Portland, Oreg., June 28, 1942; d. George Thomas and Ruth Alveta Victoria (Engberg) Penketh; m. Donald Keith Oakley, June 27, 1965; children: Christine, Michelle. BS in Edn., Oreg. State U., 1965. Educator Linn County (Oreg.) Schs., 1965-76; owner Linn County Tractor, 1965-90; mem. Oreg. Legis. Assembly, Salem, 1989—, asst. majority leader, 1993—, majority whip, 1994; mem. exec. bd. Oreg. Retail Coun., 1987-90. Chmn. Linn County Rep. Ctrl. Com., 1982-84; chmn. bd. dirs. North Albany Svc. Dist., 1988-90; chair Salvation Army, Linn and Benton Counties, 1987—; vice chmn. bd. trustees Linn-Benton C.C. Found., 1987—; pres. Women for Agr., Linn and Benton Counties, 1984-86; mem. STRIDE Leadership Round Table, 1991—; state chair Am. Legis. Exch. Coun., 1991—, nat. bd. dirs., 1992—; mem. Edn. Commn. of the States, 1991—, com. policies and priorities, 1993—; hon. mem. Linn-Benton Compact Bd., 1993—; active Linn County Criminal Justice Coun., 1994—. Named Woman of Yr. Albany chpt. Beta Sigma Phi, 1970. Mem. Nat Conf. State Legislators (chmn. edn. com. 1992—), Albany C. of C. (bd. dirs. 1986-93), Linn County Rep. women (legis. chmn. 1982-91). Republican. Methodist. Home: 3197 NW Crest Loop Albany OR 97321-9627 Office: Oreg Legis Assembly State Capital Salem OR 97310

OAKS, DALLIN HARRIS, lawyer, church official; b. Provo, Utah, Aug. 12, 1932; s. Lloyd E. and Stella (Harris) O.; m. June Dixon, June 24, 1952; children: Sharmon, Cheri Lyn, Lloyd D., Dallin D., TruAnn, Jenny June. B.A. with high honors, Brigham Young U., 1954, LL.D. (hon.), 1980; J.D. cum laude, U. Chgo., 1957; LL.D. (hon.), Pepperdine U., 1982, So. Utah U., 1991. Bar: Ill. 1957, Utah 1971. Law clk. to Supreme Ct. chief justice Earl Warren, 1957-58; with firm Kirkland, Ellis, Hodson, Chaffetz & Masters, Chgo., 1958-61; mem. faculty U. Chgo. Law Sch., 1961-71, assoc. dean and acting dean, 1962, prof., 1964-71, mem. vis. com., 1971-74; pres. Brigham Young U., Provo, Utah, 1971-80; also prof. law J. Reuben Clark Law Sch., 1974-80; justice Utah Supreme Ct., 1981-84; mem. Coun. of Twelve Apostles Ch. Jesus Christ of Latter Day Sts., 1984—; legal counsel Bill of Rights com. Ill. Constl. Conv., 1970. Author: (with G.G. Bogert) Cases on Trusts, 1967, 78, (with W. Lehman) A Criminal Justice System and The Indigent, 1968, The Criminal Justice Act in the Federal District Courts, 1969, (with M. Hill) Carthage Conspiracy, 1975, Trust Doctrines in Church Controversies, 1984, Pure in Heart, 1988, The Lord's Way, 1991; editor: The Wall Between Church and State, 1963. Mem. Wilson coun. Woodrow Wilson Internat. Ctr. for Scholars, 1973-80; trustee Intermountain Health Care Inc., 1975-80; mem. adv. com. Nat. Inst. Law Enforcement and Criminal Justice, 1974-76; bd. dirs. Notre Dame Ctr. for Constl. Studies, 1977-80, Rockford Inst., 1980—; bd. dirs. Pub. Broadcasting Svc., 1977-85, chmn., 1980-85; bd. dirs. Polynesian Cultural Ctr., 1987—, chmn., 1988—. Fellow Am. Bar Found. (exec. dir. 1970-71); mem. Am. Assn. Pres. Ind. Colls. and Univs. (pres. 1975-78, dir. 1971-78), Order of Coif. Mem. Ch. of Jesus Christ of Latter-day Saints (regional rep. 1974-80; past 1st counselor Chgo. South Stake). Address: 47 E South Temple Salt Lake City UT 84150

OAKS, M(ARGARET) MARLENE, minister; b. Grove City, Pa., Mar. 30, 1940; d. Allen Roy and Alberta Bell (Pinner) Eakin; m. Lowell B. Chaney, July 30, 1963 (dec. Jan. 1977); children: Christopher Allen, Linda Michelle; m. Harold G. Younger, Aug. 1978 (div. 1986); m. Gilbert E. Oaks, Aug. 3, 1987. BA, Calif. State U., L.A., 1972; religious sci. studies with several instrs. Ordained to ministry Ch. Religious Sci., 1986. Tchr. Whittier (Calif.) Sch. Dists., 1972-74, Garden Grove (Calif.) Sch. Dist., 1974-78; instr. Fullerton Coll., 1974-75; founding min. Community Ch. of the Islands (now Ch. of Religious Sci.), Honolulu, 1978-80; min. Ch. of Divine Sci., Pueblo, Colo., 1980-83; founding min. Ch. Religious Sci., Palo Alto, Calif., 1983-86; min. First ch. Religious Sci., Fullerton, Calif., 1986-94, min. emeritus, 1994—; 2d v.p., chmn., corp. sec. VCC Internat., Anaheim, Calif., 1994—; founder, pres. LaVida Inst., Inc., 1994—; workshop leader Religious Sci. Dist. Conv., San Jose, Calif., 1985, Internat. New Thought Alliance Conf., Las Vegas, 1984, 92, Calgary, Alta., Can., 1985, Washington, 1988, Denver, 1989, Anaheim, Calif., 1990, Golden Valley Unity Women's Advance, Mpls., 1986, 87, Qume Corp., San Jose, 1985; presenter SANTI Conf., 1992-94; guest workshop leader Ctr. for Life Enrichment, 1990-92; speaker to cmty. of Tartarstan, 1993. Author: The Christmas in You, 1983, rev. edit., 1994, Ki Aikido the Inner Martial Art, 1984, Old Time Religion Is a Cult, 1985, 2d rev. edit., 1992, Service the Sure Path to Enlightenment, 1985, Stretch Marks on My Aura, 1987, rev. edit., 1995, Beyond Addiction, 1990, 10 Core Concepts of Science of Mind, 1991, Forgiveness and Beyond, 1992, rev. edit. Christmas for All Seasons, 1994, 21 Seeds, Miracle Grow For the Soul, 1995, Values Remembered, 1995; contbr. articles to profl. jours. Del. Soviet and Am. Citizens Summit Conf., 1988, 89; pres. Soviet-Am. New Thought Initiatives, 1991, chmn. conf. St. Petersburg, 1992, Moscow, 1992, weekly radio program Radio Moscow, The Philippines, 1992—; founder Operation K.I.D.S., La Vida Inst., 1994; founder, bd. dirs. Awakening Oaks Found., 1990; pres. SANTI, 1991-94, founder and pres. La Vida Inst., 1994. Named Outstanding Businesswoman, Am. Businesswomen's Assn., 1989. Mem. Fullerton Interfaith Ministerial Assn. (sec.-treas. 1987-89, pres. 1991-92), United Clergy of Religious Sci. (treas. 1991-92, sec. 1992-93, treas. So. Calif. chpt. 1991-92, v.p. 1993-94, pres. 1994-95), Internat. New Thought Alliance (O.C. chpt. pres. 1990), Soroptomists (chair com. internat. coop. and goodwill 1987-88), Kappa Delta Pi. Republican. Office: LaVida Inst Awakening Oaks Press 1775 E Lincoln Ave Ste 101 Anaheim CA 92805-4300

OAKS, ROBERT QUINCY, JR., geology educator, petroleum consultant; b. Houston, Aug. 29, 1938; s. Robert Quincy and Susie Elizabeth (Lawton) O.; children—Katherine Anne, John Robert Jordan. B.A. in Geology, Rice U., 1960; Ph.D. in Geology, Yale U., 1965. Field geologist Va. Div. Mineral Resources, Charlottesville, 1963; research geologist Exxon Prodn. Research Co., Houston, 1964-66; asst. prof. Utah State U., Logan, 1966-70, assoc. prof., 1970-79, prof. geology, 1979—; petroleum cons. Magellan Petroleum Australia Ltd., Brisbane, 1979-86 . Editor, author articles: Post-Miocene Stratigraphy, Central and Southern Atlantic Coastal Plain, 1972. Contbr. articles to jours. Mem. Geol. Soc. Am., Internat. Assn. Sedimentologists, Soc. Econ. Paleontologists and Mineralogists, Am. Assn. Petroleum Geologists, AAAS, Utah Geol. Assn. Office: Utah State Univ Dept Geology Logan UT 84322-4505

OARD, MICHAEL JOHN, meteorologist; b. Seattle, Sept. 23, 1945; s. John Lionel and Frances (Vawter) O.; m. Beverly Maureen Muoth, June 18, 1969; children: David, Tara, Amy, Nathan. BS, U. Wash., 1969; MS, U. Wash., 1973. Researcher U. Wash., Seattle, 1969-70; agrl. meteorologist Nat. Weather Svc., Bakersfield, Calif., 1975-77; aviation forecaster Nat. Weather Svc., Great Falls, Mont., 1977-80, lead forecaster, 1980—. Author: An Ice Age Caused by the Genesis Flood, 1990; co-author: Life in the Great Ice Age, 1993; contbr. articles to profl. jours. With USN, 1964-66. Mem. Am. Meteorol. Soc., Nat. Weather Assn., Creation Rsch. Soc., Bible-Sci. Assn. Republican. Home: 3600 7th Ave S Great Falls MT 59405-3409

OATES, BART STEVEN, professional football player; b. Mesa, Ariz., Dec. 16, 1958; m. Michelle Oats. BA in Acctg., Brigham Young U.; JD, Seton Hall U. Bar: N.J. 1990. With Phila. Stars, USFL, 1983-85, N.Y. Giants, 1985-94, San Francisco 49ers, 1994-94; assoc. Ribis, Graham & Curtin, Morristown, N.J.; Player Super Bowl XXI, 1986, XXV, 1990, XXVIV, 1994. Named USFL All-Star Team Ctr. by Sporting News, 1983.

OATNEY, CECILIA KAY, army officer; b. McCall, Idaho, May 18, 1956; d. Cecil Edward and Ruby Ilene (Wine) O.; m. Nelvin Eugene Tyler Jr., Dec. 24, 1991. BBA in Acctg., Idaho State U., 1978; MS in Econs. and Ops. Research, Colo. Sch. Mines, 1987. Commd. 2d lt. U.S. Army, 1978, advanced through grades to lt. col., 1995; platoon leader A, B and C Cos. 8th Signal Battalion U.S. Army, Bad Kreuznach, Fed. Republic of Germany, 1978-81, logistics officer, 1981; promoted to capt., 1982; div. radio officer 142d Signal Battalion U.S. Army, Ft. Hood, Tex., 1982-83, comdr. C Co. 142d Signal Battalion, 1983-85, asst. ops. officer, 1985; chief market analysis 6th Recruiting Brigade U.S. Army, Ft. Baker, Calif., 1987-89; with command and gen. staff coll. U.S. Army, Leavenworth, Kans., 1989-90; promoted to maj., 1990; chief strategic systems plans br. 5th Signal Command U.S. Army, Fed. Republic of Germany, 1990-91, chief plans & programs div., 1991; exec. officer 509th Signal Battalion U.S. Army, Italy, 1991-92; exec. officer office dep. chief staff, info. mgmt. U.S. Army, Germany, 1992-94; promoted to lt. col. U.S. Army, 1995; dep. brigade comdr. 2d Sig BDE, Germany, 1995—. Pres. 4-H Club, Valley County, Idaho, 1973-74. Mem. Armed Forces Communication-Electronics Assn., Assn. U.S. Army. Home: PO Box 92 Donnelly ID 83615-0092 Office: HHD 2D Sig BDE Unit 29919 Box 14 APO AE 09086

O'BANION, TERRY UNDERWOOD, academic administrator, consultant; b. La Belle, Fla., Aug. 19, 1936; s. Terry Hugh and Olney Cuthbert (Blount) O'Banion; m. Yolande Ringoot, June 27, 1980; children: Kerry, Erin. BA, U. Fla., 1958, MEd, 1961; PhD, Fla. State U., 1966. Dean of students Ctrl. Fla. Jr. Coll., Ocala, 1960-64; dean of students Santa Fe C.C., Gainesville, Fla., 1964-67; prof. higher edn. U. Ill., Urbana, 1967-75; exec. dir. League for Innovation in the C.C., L.A., 1975-80, League for Innovation, Mission Viejo, Calif., 1982—; vice chancellor Dallas C.C.s, 1980-82; cons. 500 c.c. and univs, 46 states, 1985—; vis. prof. U. Calif., Berkeley, Fla. State U., U. Hawaii; disting. vis. prof. U. Tex. Author: (11 books) including Teaching and Learning in the Community College, 1994, Innovation in the Community College, 1991; contbr. articles, book chpts. to profl. publs. Recipient Nat. Leadership award Am. Assn. C.C.s, 1994. Home: 26 Vienna Newport Beach CA 92660-6832 Office: League for Innovation 26522 La Alameda Ste 370 Mission Viejo CA 92691-6330

OBENHAUS, KATHY ANN, special education educator; b. Columbus, Ind., Dec. 1, 1954; d. Ivan Dale and Marcella Ruth (Krienke) Van Reenan; m. Fredericus Theodorus Hagenbeek, 1975; children: Matthew Van Hagenbeek, Cristian Van Hagenbeek; m. Ernest Derrell Obenhaus, Mar. 5, 1988; 1 child, Rachel M. BA summa cum laude, U. Guam, 1976; MS in Edn. Deaf, Idaho State U., 1993. Cert. elem. edn. tchr. K-12 aurally handicapped. Tchr. of deaf Guam Dept. Edn., 1976-78, Clark County Sch. Dist., Las Vegas, Nev., 1979—; chmn. Task Force on Deaf Edn., Las Vegas, 1990-92. Editor: Intermountain Deaf Education Advocates of Learning. Mem. sch. bd. First Good Shepherd Luth. Sch., 1992-95, ch. coun., 1993-95. Named Outstanding Spl. Educator Clark County Sch. Dist., 1991. Mem. Am. Soc. Deaf Children, Calif. Educators of Deaf, Independently Merging Parent Assns. Calif.-Together. Lutheran. Office: Clark County Sch Dist 1560 Cherokee Ln Las Vegas NV 89109-3106

OBERDORFER, JEFF, architect, firm executive; b. Bronx, N.Y., May 8, 1947. BArch, Kent State U., 1970. Lic. arch., Calif. Instr. spatial design, lighting, multi-media Mus. Fine Arts, Boston, 1972-76; prin. Jeff Oberdorfer & Assocs. Archs., Cambridge, Mass., 1973-76, Jeff Oberdorfer & Assocs., Inc., Santa Cruz, Calif., 1980—; instr. Goodard/Cambridge Grad. Sch. for Social Change, 1975-76; vis. instr. comty. design U. Calif., Santa Cruz, 1979-80. Prin. works include North Cambridge Cmty. Ctr. (Quality of Life Competition award City of Cambridge, Mass.), Agassiz Cmty. Planning Process, Cambridge (City Spirit award NEH, 1979), Boulder Creek Libr. (Nat. Excellence award in libr. design ALA/AIA, 1987), Felton Covered Bridge (Renaissance 87 Design awards Nat. Assn. Home Builders Remodelers Coun., 1987, Ann. Design award for outstanding achievement in design preservation projects Calif. Preservation Found., 1987, Nat. Hist. Preservation award Adv. Coun. Hist. Preservation, 1988), Felton Town Plan (Outstanding Planning award Am. Planning Assn., 1988), Soquel Village Plan (Outstanding Planning award Am. Planning Assn., 1991), Washington St. Cooperative Apts., 1991, others. Active Lighthouse Field Adv. Commn., 1978-84, City of Santa Cruz (Calif.) Zoning Bd., 1980-84, Environ. Coun. Bd. Dirs., 1989-92. Mem. AIA, Am. Planning Assn., Internat. Conf. Bldg. Officials, Environ. Design Rsch. Assn. Office: Jeff Oberdorfer & Assoc Inc 303 Potrero St # 306 Santa Cruz CA 95060-2741

OBERG, LARRY REYNOLD, librarian; b. Midvale, Idaho; s. Gustav Wilhelm and Esther Marie (Watkins) O.; m. Marilyn Ann Gow, Jan. 1, 1964 (div. 1985); 1 child, Marc Aurelien. AB in Anthropology, U. Calif., Berkeley, 1977, MLS, 1978. Reference librarian Stanford (Calif.) U., 1979-80, U. Calif., Berkeley, 1981-82; dir. library Lewis-Clark State Coll., Lewiston, Idaho, 1984-86, Albion (Mich.) Coll., 1986-92; univ. libr. Willamette U., Salem, Oreg., 1993—. Author: Human Services in Postrevolutionary Cuba, 1985 (named a Choice Outstanding Acad. Book, Choice Editors 1984-85); mem. editl. bd. College and Research Libraries; mem. adv. bd. Jour. Info. Ethics; contbr. articles to profl. jours. Mem. Am. Library Assn., Oreg. Library Assn., Phi Beta Kappa. Democrat. Office: Willamette U Mark O Hatfield Libr 900 State St Salem OR 97301

OBERG, MARY KATHLEEN, paramedic/nurse coordinator; d. Roy Edward and Kathleen Anne (Davis) Henson; m. Scott Douglas Oberg; 1 child, Kathleen Eleanor Belcher. AA in Nursing, Imperial Valley Coll., 1988; postgrad., SUNY; BSN, U. Phoenix, 1994. RN, Calif.; CEN; cert. ACLS provider and instr., trauma care nurse, pub. health nurse, BLS, mobile intensive care nurse, first aid instr., pediatric advanced life support instr. and provider. Nurse El Centro (Calif.) Regional Med. Ctr., 1987—, peer educator, 1988—, staff and charge nurse ICU, 1988-90, emergency dept. nurse, 1989—; patient educator, clin. instr. El Centro Regional Med. Ctr., 1991-92; acting assoc. dir. clin. svcs., dir. nurse-client edn. Kimberly Quality Care, El Centro, 1992—, paramedic, nurse coord., 1992—; paramedic, EMT instr. Imperial Valley Coll., 1992—. Vol. tchr. first aid Girl Scouts U.S.A.; tchr. BLS various cmty. groups; participant ARC Health Fair; nurse vol. S.W. med. teams for worldwide outreach of med.-nursing tng. and care. Mem. Emergency Nurses Assn., Am. Assn. Diabetic Educators. Home: 1790 W Olive Ave Apt 16 El Centro CA 92243-5401 Office: PO Box 52069 4615 E Elwood St Phoenix AZ 85040-1936

OBERLANDER, CORNELIA HAHN, landscape architect; b. Muelheim-Ruhr, Germany, June 20, 1924; arrived in U.S., 1939; d. Franz and Lotte Beate (Jastrow) H.; m. H. Peter Oberlander, Jan. 2, 1953; children: Judith A., Timothy A., Wendy E. BA, Smith Coll., 1944; B of Landscape Architecture, Harvard U., 1947; LLD (hon.), U. British Columbia, 1991. guest prof. U. B.C. Dept. Landscape Architecture, 1992; lectr. for guided tour Renaissance Gardens of No. Italy, Smith Coll. Alumni Assn., 1988; mem. adv. com. on design Nat. Capital Commn., 1975-82; mem. adv. panel, co-founder Children's Play Resource Centre, Vancouver, 1978—; lectr. in field. Prin. works include Cathedral Place, Vancouver, B.C., 1991-93, New Pub. Library, 1992—, Asian Inst., U. B.C., 1993—, Thunderbird Housing, U. B.C., 1992—, Chan Shun Performing Arts Centre, 1992—, Kwantlen Coll., 1991—, Cariboo Coll., 1991—, N.W. Territories Legis. Bldg., 1991—, UN Peacekeeping Meml., 1990—, Ritsumeikan U. B.C. Ho., 1990—, Ottawa City Hall, 1989—, Environ. Sci. Bd., Ward Environ. Garden, Trent U., 1989—, Canadian Chancery, Washington D.C., 1983-89. Recipient medal Smith Coll., 1982, Regional Honor award and Nat. Merit award Christopher Phillips Landcape Architects, Inc., 1992, Cathedral Place, 1983-88, Nat. Gallery of Can., Ottawa, Ontario, Can. Chancery Am. Assn. of Nurserymen, 1990, Grand award for L'Ambassade du Can., Landscape Contractors Assn., 1989, Can. Architect award of Excellence, Matsuzaki Wright Architects, Inc., 1989, Amenity award City of Vancouver for Robson Square, 1986, Citation award Can. Soc. of Architects for Chancery & Nat. Gallery, 1990. Fellow Am. Soc. Landscape Architects, Can. Soc. Landscape Architects (pres. 1986-87, pres. elect. 1985-86, chair environ. com. 1987-88, Internat. Citation award 1991, Nat. and Regional Citation award 1989); mem. Order of Can., Royal Can. Acad. Arts. Home: 1372 Acadia Rd, Vancouver, BC Canada V6T 1P6

OBERLINK, JAMES RICHARD, environmental association executive, lawyer; b. Vandalia, Ill., Feb. 20, 1953; s. James Wendell and Gladys Mae (Stine) O. AB, U. Ill., 1976; JD, U. Calif., Berkeley, 1980. Bar: Calif. 1981. Law clk. Sierra Club Legal Def. Fund, San Francisco, 1979; atty. Law Office of Robert Lane, Oakland, Calif., 1982-83, Law Office of Garrett Riegg, Oakland, 1989-92; exec. dir. Californians for Population Stabilization, Sacramento, 1992—; mem. Chancellor's Com. on Conservation and Environ. Quality, Berkeley, 1978-79; speaker in field. Served with U.S. Army, 1971-73, Germany. Mem. Sierra Club, East Bay Bicycle Coalition. Office: Californians for Population Stabilization 926 J St Ste 915 Sacramento CA 95814-2707

OBERSTEIN, MARYDALE, geriatric specialist; b. Red Wing, Minn., Dec. 30; d. Dale Robert and Jean Ebba-Marie (Holmquist) Johnson; children: Kirk Robert, Mark Paul, MaryJean. Student, U. Oreg., 1961-62, Portland State U., 1962-64, Long Beach State U., 1974-76. Cert. geriatric specialist, Calif. Florist, owner sunshine Flowers, Santa Ana, Calif., 1982—; pvt. duty nurse Aides in Action, Costa Mesa, Calif., 1985-87; owner, activity dir., adminstr. Lovelight Christian Home for the Elderly, Santa Ana, 1987—; activity dir. Bristol Care Nursing Home, Santa Ana, 1985-88; evangelist, speaker radio show Sta. KPRZ-FM, Anaheim, Calif., 1985-88; nursing home activist in reforming laws to eliminate bad homes, 1984-90; founder, tchr. hugging classes/laughter therapy terminally ill patients, 1987—; founder healing and touch therapy laughter Therapy, 1991-93; bd. dirs. Performing Arts Ctr.; speaker for enlightenment and healing. Author (rewrite) Title 22 Nursing Home Reform Law, Little Hoover Commn.; model, actress and voiceovers. Bd. dirs. Orange County Coun. on Aging, 1984—; chairperson Helping Hands, 1985—, Pat Robertson Com., 1988, George Bush Presdl. Campaign, Orange County, 1988; bd. dirs., v.p. Women Aglow Orange County, 1985—; evanglist, pub. spkr., v.p. Women Aglow Huntington Beach; active with laughter therapy and hugging classes for terminally ill. Recipient Carnation Silver Bowl, Carnation Svc. Co., 1984-85; named Woman of Yr., Kiwanis, 1985, ABI, 1990, Am. Biog. Soc.; honored AM L.A. TV Show, Lt. Gov. McCarthy, 1984. Mem. Calif. Assn. Residential Care Homes, Orange County Epilepsy Soc. (bd. dirs. 1986—), Calif. Assn. Long Term Facilities. Home: 2722 S Diamond St Santa Ana CA 92704-6013

OBERTI, SYLVIA MARÍE ANTOINETTE, rehabilitation counselor and administrator, career advisor, textile consultant; b. Fresno, Calif., Dec. 29, 1952. BA in Communicative Disorders, Calif. State U.-Fresno, 1976, MA in Rehab. Counseling, 1977. Cert. rehab. counselor Commn. Rehab. Counselors; cert. life tchr. community coll., nat. cert. counselor. Sr. rehab. cons. Crawford Rehab. Services, Inc., Emeryville, Calif., 1978-80; vocat. rehab. counselor Rehab. Assocs., Inc., San Leandro, Calif., 1980-81; owner, textile cons. Rugs and Carpets of the Orient, Oakland, Calif., 1979—; exec. dir. TheOberti Co., Oakland and San Jose, Calif., 1981—; cons. to industry, ins. cos., disabled, ADA; tchr. job seeking skills to the disabled; expert witness in the field. Bd. dirs., treas. Pacific Basin Sch. Textile Arts, 1982-86; active Calif. Assn. Physically Handicapped, Inc., 1976—; fundraising chairperson CARP, 1990; fund raiser Special Olympics, 1992-94. HEW grantee, 1976-77; first woman to solo and finish Mille Miglia, 1992; recipient Pacific Region Community Svc. Trophy Ferrari Club Am., 1992, Silver award Musical Watch Veteran Car Club Mille Miglia Organizers, 1992, 93, 3d of U.S.A., 1993. Mem. Am. Personnel and Guidance Assn., Am. Rehab. Counseling Assn., Calif. Assn. Rehab. Profls., Indsl. Claims Assn., Internat. Round Table Advancement of Counseling, Nat. Rehab. Assn., Nat. Rehab. Counseling Assn., Nat. Vocat. Guidance Assn., LWV. Office: 3629 Grand Ave Ste 101 Oakland CA 94610-2009

OBIORA, EMMANUEL CHUMA, accountant; b. Jos, Nigeria, Aug. 1, 1945; came to U.S., 1977; s. Charles N. and Christiana M. (Ogalue) O.; m. Dorothy N. Obiora, June 16, 1984; children: Nkemdium, Uchenna, Chung Jr., Chika. AA, Southwe. Coll., 1979; BS in Acctg., Calif. State U., L.A., 1981; MPA, Calif. State U., Carson, 1984. Acct. trainee L.A. Dept. Transp., 1983-87, acctg. officer, 1987-89, sr. acctg. specialist, 1989, sr. acctg. office supr., 1989—; bd. dirs. Chuma Fin. Svcs.; preparer taxes H&R Block, L.A., 1985-89. Capt. Nigerian Infantry, 1966-71. Fellow Am. Soc. Pub. Adminstrn. Home: 2511 W 85th St Inglewood CA 90305-1817 Office: LA Dept Transp 120 S Spring St Los Angeles CA 90012-3606

OBNAMIA, REYNALDO ZAIDE, quality assurance professional; b. Sampaloc, Quezon, Philippines, Apr. 7, 1959; came to U.S., 1986; s. Tong Talabong and Sixta Cada (Zaide) O.; m. Melinda Antiproda Garcia, Dec. 27, 1986. BSChemE, Mapua Inst. of Tech., Manila, Philippines, 1980; MBA, De La Salle U., Manila, Philippines, 1982-83. Registered chem. engr. Process control engr. Republic Glass Corp., Manila, 1981; quality control head San Miguel Corp., Manila, 1981-85, sr. assoc. plastics, 1985-86; process engr. Filam Nat. Plastics, Paramount, Calif., 1986-87; project/quality engr. Bryant Rubber, Harbor City, Calif., 1987-91, ops. mgr., 1992; bus. unit mgr. Bryant Rubber, Harbor City, 1992; quality assurance mgr. Hi-Tech Rubber, Anaheim, Calif., 1993—. Mem. Am. Soc. for Quality Control (sr.), Asian Pacific Exch., L.A. Rubber Group, Inc., Philippine Soc. for Quality Control. Republican. Roman Catholic. Home: 9141 Walnut St Bellflower CA 90706-5639 Office: Hi Tech Rubber Inc 1350 N Hundley St Anaheim CA 92806-1301

OBNINSKY, VICTOR PETER, lawyer; b. San Rafael, Calif., Oct. 12, 1944; s. Peter Victor and Anne Bartholdi (Donston) O.; m. Clara Alice Bechtel, June 8, 1969; children: Mari, Warren. BA, Columbia U., 1966; JD, U. Calif., Hastings, 1969. Bar: Calif. 1970. Sole practice, Novato, Calif., 1970—; arbitrator Marin County Superior Ct., San Rafael, 1979—; superior ct. judge pro tem, 1979—; lectr. real estate and partnership law. Author: The Russians in Early California, 1966. Bd. dirs. Calif. Young Reps., 1968-69, Richardson Bay San. Dist., 1974-75, Marin County Legal Aid Soc., 1976-78; baseball coach Little League, Babe Ruth League, 1970-84; mem. nat. panel consumer arbitrators Better Bus. Bur., 1974-88; leader Boy Scouts Am., 1970-84; permanent sec. Phillips Acad. Class of 1962, 1987—; mem. Phillips Acad. Alumni Council, 1991-95; bd. community advisors Buck Ctr. for Rsch. on Aging. Mem. AMA, State Bar Calif., Marin County Bar Assn. (bd. dirs. 1985-91, treas. 1987-88, pres.-elect 1989, pres. 1990), Phi Delta Phi, Phi Gamma Delta. Republican. Russian Orthodox. Office: 2 Commercial Blvd Apt 103 Novato CA 94949-6121

OBORN, KATHLEEN MARIE, college administrator, educator; b. L.A., July 20, 1954; d. Daniel Willis and Nan Sherwood (Wallace) O.; children: Kelly, Jadrienne, Brittany, Jacen, Kimber, Michael, McKenna. AA, L.A. Pierce Coll., Woodland Hills, Calif., 1981; BA, Calif. State U., Northridge, 1992, MS, 1994. Police officer L.A. Police Dept., 1983-88; educator, adminstr. L.A. Pierce Coll., 1989—; cons. Homestays USA, West Hills, Calif., 1993-94. Author: Handbook for International Students, 1994. Edmund Peckham scholar Calif. State U., Northridge, 1993-94; Patricia Roberts Harris fellow, 1993-94. Mem. Am. Coll. Counseling Assn., Am. Coll. Pers. Assn., Calif. Placement Assn., Assn. for Multicultural Counseling and Devel. Office: PO Box 4324 West Hills CA 91308-4324

OBRADOVIC, ZORAN, computer scientist, educator. PhD in Computer Sci., Pa. State U., 1991. Prof. elec. engring. and computer sci. Wash. State U., Pullman, 1991—. Contbr. articles to profl. jours. Mem. IEEE, Assn. Computing Machinery, Internat. Neural Network Soc. Office: Wash State U Dept Elec Engring Computer Pullman WA 99164-2752

O'BRAIN, NIALL P., wood products company executive. Formerly sr. v.p. Fraser Inc., Edmundston, N. B., Canada, pres., 1988—; sr. v.p. Noranda Forest Inc., Toronto, Ont., 1988—. Office: Fraser Inc, 27 RIce St, Edmonton, AB Canada E3V 1S9

O'BRIAN, BONNIE JEAN, library services supervisor; b. Great Bend, Kans., Oct. 19, 1940; d. Claude Marion and Mildred Geraldine (Schmaider) Baker; m. Patrick Gilbert Gibson (div.); 1 child, Debra Kathleen; m. John Robinson O'Brian, Nov. 2, 1968. BS, UCLA, 1961; MS, Calif. State U., Northridge, 1977; Credential in Libr. Media Svcs., Calif. State U., Long Beach, 1978. Libr. L.A. Unified Sch. Dist., Northridge, 1978-84; supr. chpt. 2 L.A. Unified Sch. Dist., L.A., 1984, coord. field libr., 1984-87, supr. libr. svcs., 1987—; asst. prof. libr. sci. Calif. State U., L.A.; condr. workshops in field. Recipient N.W. Valley Parent Tchr. Student award 1978, San Fernando Valley Reading Assn. Myrtle Shirley Reading Motivation award 1986. Mem. ALA, Am. Assn. Sch. Librs., Calif. Sch. Libr. Assn. (pres.), So. Calif. Coun. on Lit. for Children and Young People, White House Conf. on Libr. and Info. Svcs. Republican. Office: Los Angeles Unifed Sch Dist 1320 W 3rd St Los Angeles CA 90017-1410

O'BRIEN, DAVID KERAN, marine geologist, environmental scientist; b. Queens, N.Y., Oct. 2, 1962; s. Keran and Barbara Hope (Zwickel) O'B.; m. Irene Marie Russell, May 18, 1988; children: Thomas Matthew, Daniel Kenneth. BS Earth and Space Sci. magna cum laude, SUNY, Stony Brook, 1983; MS in Geology, U. Calif., Berkeley, 1985; PhD in Geology and Geophysics, U. Hawaii, Manoa, 1990. Teaching asst. U. Calif., Berkeley, 1983-84, rsch. asst., 1984-85; rsch. asst. U. Hawaii, Manoa, Honolulu, 1985-90; phys. properties specialist Ocean Drilling Program, College Station, Tex., 1988; marine geologist, environ. scientist EMCON Alaska, Inc., Anchorage, 1990—; adj. instr. U. Alaska, Anchorage, 1991, Alaska Pacific U., Anchorage, 1990, 92. Contbr. chpts. to books, articles to profl. jours. Mem. Alaska Geol. Soc., Am. Geophys. Union, Geol. Soc. Am., Am. Assn. Environ. Profls., Sigma Xi, Sigma Gamma Epsilon (chpt. pres. 1983). Home: 8651 Swiss Pl Anchorage AK 99507-3646 Office: EMCON Alaska Inc 201 E 56th Ave # 300 Anchorage AK 99518-1241

O'BRIEN, HAROLD ALOYSIUS, JR., nuclear chemist, physics researcher, consultant; b. Dallas, May 17, 1936; s. Harold Aloysius and Adelaide (Esser) O'B.; m. Ann Akard, Aug. 22, 1958; children: Walter, Sheri, Matthew. BA, U. Tex., 1959; MS, N.Mex. State U., 1961; PhD, U. Tenn., 1968. Hon. diplomate Am. Bd. Sci. in Nuclear Medicine. Rsch. scientist Oak Ridge (Tenn.) Nat. Lab., 1962-68; mem. rsch. staff Los Alamos Nat. Lab., 1968-74, 86-93, asssoc. group leader, 1974-80, group leader, 1980-85; sr. tech. mgr. Sci. Applications Internat. Corp., Los Alamos, 1994—; pres. O'Brien & Assocs., Los Alamos, 1994—; vis. scientist Lawrence Berkeley (Calif.) Lab., 1985-86, Lawrence Livermore (Calif.) Lab., 1985-86, U. Calif., Davis, 1985-86; bd. dirs. Am. Bd. Sci. in Nuclear Medicine, 1976-85, pres., 1983-85; bd. dirs. Rho Med, Inc., Albuquerque; mem. subcom. on nuclear and radio chemistry NAS-NRC, 1974-78; mem. spl. study sect. NIH, 1976. Contbr. numerous articles to profl. jours., chpts. to books; patentee in field. Chmn. N.Mex. Radiation Tech. Adv. Coun., Santa Fe, 1974-85, 90—. Mem. Am. Chem. Soc. (exec. com. 1981-84), AAAS, Soc. Nuclear Medicine (trustee 1975-76, bd. dirs. Edn. and Rsch. Found. 1985—). Home: 10 La Senda Rd Los Alamos NM 87544-3819 Office: O'Brien & Assocs 107 La Senda Rd Los Alamos NM 87544-3819

O'BRIEN, JACK GEORGE, artistic director; b. Saginaw, Mich., June 18, 1939; s. J. George and Evelyn (MacArthur Martens) O'B. A.B., U. Mich., 1961, M.A., 1962. Asst. dir. APA Repertory Theatre, N.Y.C., 1963-67; asso. dir. APA Repertory Theatre, 1967-69; worked with San Diego Nat. Shakespeare Festival, 1969-82, A.C.T., 1970-80, Loretto Hilton, 1975, Ahmanson, Los Angeles, 1978-80, San Francisco Opera, Houston Grand Opera, Washington Opera Soc., N.Y.C. Opera. Lyricist: Broadway prodn. The Selling of the President, 1972; dir.: on Broadway Porgy and Bess (Tony award nominee 1977), Most Happy Fella, Street Scene, Two Shakespearean Actors, 1993, Damn Yankees, 1994, Hapgood, 1994, others; artistic dir.: Old Globe Theatre, San Diego, 1981. Mem. Actors' Equity, Am. Soc. Composers and Performers, Soc. Stage Dirs. and Choreographers, Dirs. Guild Am. *

O'BRIEN, MARK DAVID, poet, journalist; b. Boston, July 31, 1949; s. Walter Francis and Helen Agnes (Kelly) O'B. BA in English, U. Calif., Berkeley, 1982. Author: Breathing, 1990; author poems; contbr. articles to popular mags. Ingram-Merril Found. grantee, N.Y.C., 1987. Democrat. Roman Catholic. Home: 2420 Dwight Way Apt 1 Berkeley CA 94704-2337

O'BRIEN, PATRICIA ANN, history educator; b. Cambridge, Mass., Dec. 29, 1945; d. Maurice Joseph and Elizabeth Mary (Sullivan) O'B. BA, Regis Coll., 1967; MA, Columbia U., 1968, PhD, 1973. Instr. Yale U., New Haven, 1971-73; asst. prof. Yale U., 1973-74, U. Calif., Irvine, 1974-80; assoc. prof. U. Calif., 1980-93, prof., 1993—; acting assoc. dean undergrad. studies U. Calif., Irvine, 1981, acting chair history dept., 1983-84, chair history dept., 1985-88, assoc. vice chancellor for rsch., 1990-94, acting vice chancellor for rsch., dean grad. studies, 1993; NSF, NEH referee. Author: The Promise of Punishment: Prisons in Nineteenth-Century France, 1982 (French translation, 1988); co-author: Civilization in the West, 1991, Unfinished Legacies, 1992, Societies and Cultures in World History, 1995; contbr. articles to profl. jours. Woodrow Wilson fellow, 1968, NEH fellow, 1973, Nat. Humanities Ctr. Rsch. fellow, 1988. Office: U Calif Humanities Rsch Inst Irvine CA 92717

O'BRIEN, PATRICIA NEVIN, computer scientist; b. Hanover, Pa., June 13, 1957; d. Malcolm Hugh and Lida Mae (Smith) Nevin; m. Thomas Gerard O'Brien, May 2, 1981; children: Thomas Joseph, Karen Louise. BS in Psychology, Towson State U., 1978, MA, 1980. Rsch. asst. Johns Hopkins U., Balt., 1980-82; programmer-analyst Johns Hopkins U., Towson, Md., 1982; ops. rsch. analyst U.S. Army, Aberdeen, Md., 1983-84, 86-87; officer BDM Corp., Albuquerque, 1984-85; pres. Maverick, Inc., Albuquerque, 1985-86; chief analysis div. Def. Test and Evaluation Support Agy., Albuquerque, 1987-89; ops. rsch. analyst Operational Test and Evaluation Ctr. USAF, Albuquerque, 1989—. Mem. Am. Soc. for Quality Control. Home: PO Box 1060 Tijeras NM 87059-1060 Office: HQ AFOTEC/SAN 8500 Gibson Blvd SE Kirtland AFB NM 87117

O'BRIEN, PHILIP MICHAEL, library administrator; b. Albion, Nebr., Jan. 5, 1940; s. Lawrence Joseph and Mary Helen (Ruplinger) O'B.; m. Ann Topjon, Mar. 10, 1990; children: Tara, Kristen. BA, Whittier Coll., 1961; MS in LS, U. So. Calif., 1962, PhD, 1974. Asst. libr. Whittier (Calif.) Coll., 1962-66; social scis. libr. Chico State Coll., 1966-67; spl. collections libr. Whittier Coll., 1970-74, libr. dir., 1974—; libr. U.S. Army, Fed. Republic of Germany, 1967-70. Author: T.E. Lawrence and Fine Printing, 1980, T.E. Lawrence A Bibliography, 1988 (Besterman medal 1989). Recipient Title II fellowship HEW, 1973-74; inducted into Whittier Coll. Athletic Hall of Fame, 1988. Mem. ALA, Assn. Coll. and Rsch. Librs., Calif. Pvt. Acad. Librs. (bd. dirs. 1984-87), Univ. Club Whittier (pres. 1984). Office: Whittier Coll Wardman Libr Whittier CA 90608

O'BRIEN, RAYMOND FRANCIS, transportation executive; b. Atchison, Kans., May 31, 1922; s. James C. and Anna M. (Wagner) O'B.; m. Mary Ann Baugher, Sept. 3, 1947; children: James B., William T., Kathleen A., Christopher R. B.S. in Bus. Adminstrn., U. Mo., 1948; grad., Advanced Mgmt. Program, Harvard, 1966. Accountant-auditor Peat, Marwick, Mitchell & Co., Kansas City, Mo., 1948-52; contr., treas. Riss & Co., Kansas City, Mo., 1952-58; regional contr. Consol. Freightways Corp. of Del., Indpls., also, Akron, Ohio, 1958-61; contr. Consol. Freightways, Inc., San Francisco, 1961—; v.p., treas. Consol. Freightways, Inc., 1962-63, bd. dirs., 1966, v.p. fin., 1967-69, exec. v.p., 1969-75, pres., 1975—, chief exec. officer, 1977-88, 90-91, chmn., 1988—; pres. CF Motor Freight subs. Consol. Freightways, Inc., 1973; dir. Transam. Corp., Watkins-Johnson, Inc.; past chmn. WesternHwy. Inst., Champion Road Machinery, Ltd. Former mem. bus. adv. bd. Northwestern U., U. Calif., Berkeley; bd. dirs., regent, former chmn. bd. trustees St. Mary's Coll.; bd. dirs., regent Charles Armstrong Sch., 1991—; mem. Pres.'s Adv. Herbert Hoover Boys and Girls Club; dir. Boy Scouts Am. Bay Area Coun.; adv. coun. Nat. Commn. Agaisnt Drunk Driving. Served to 1st lt. USAAF, 1942-45. Recipient Disting. Svc. Citation Automotive Hall Fame, 1991; named Outstanding Chief Exec. five times Financial World Mag. Mem. Am. Trucking Assn. (bd. dirs. Found., exec. com.), Pacific Union Club, World Trade Club, Commonwealth Club (San Francisco), Burning Tree Country Club, Menlo Country Club. Home: 26347 Esperanza Dr Los Altos CA 94022-2601 Office: Consol Freightways Inc 3000 Sand Hill Rd Menlo Park CA 94025-7116*

O'BRIEN, ROBERT S., state official; b. Seattle, Sept. 14, 1918; s. Edward R. and Maude (Ransom) O'B.; m. Kathryn E. Arvan, Oct. 18, 1941 (dec. June 1984). Student public schs. With Kaiser Co., 1938-46; restaurant owner, 1946-50; treas. Grant County, Wash., 1950-65, State of Wash., 1965-89; chmn. Wash. State Fin. Com., 1965-89, Wash. Public Deposit Protection Commn., 1969-89, Wash. Public Employees Retirement Bd., 1969-77, Law Enforcement Officers and Firefighters Retirement System, 1971-77, Wash. State Investment Bd., 1981-89; retired, 1989; mem. Wash. Data Processing Adv. Bd., 1967-73; Gov.'s Exec. Mgmt. and Fiscal Affairs Com., 1978-80, Gov.'s Cabinet Com. on Tax Alternatives, 1978-80; trustee Wash. Tchr.'s Retirement System, 1965-89; bd. dirs. Centennial Bank, Olympia, Wash. Recipient Leadership award Joint Council County and City Employees-Fedn. State Employees, 1970, Eagles Leadership award, 1967. Mem. Nat. Assn. State Auditors, Comptrollers and Treasurers (pres. 1977), Nat. Assn. Mcpl. Fin. Officers, Nat. Assn. State Treasurers, Western State Treasurers Assn. (pres. 1970), Wash. County Treas. Assn. (pres. 1955-56), Wash. Assn. Elected County Ofcls. (pres. 1955-58), Olympia Area C. of C., Soap Lake C. of C. (pres. 1948). Democrat. Clubs: Elks (hon. life); Moose, Eagles, Lions, Olympia Yacht, Olympia Country and Golf; Empire (Spokane); Wash. Athletic (Seattle). Address: 3613 Plummer St SE Olympia WA 98501-2126

O'BRIEN, THOMAS JOSEPH, bishop; b. Indpls., Nov. 29, 1935. Grad., St. Meinrad Coll. Sem. Ordained priest Roman Catholic Ch., 1961. Bishop of Phoenix, 1982—. Office: 400 E Monroe St Phoenix AZ 85004-2336*

O'BRYAN, MICHAEL GAVIN, lawyer; b. Detroit, Mar. 16, 1961; s. Robert Marnell and Mary Lee (McCarthy) O'B. BA with highest distinction, U. Mich., 1983; JD with honors, Harvard U., 1988. Bar: Calif. 1988, U.S. Dist. Ct. (cen. dist.) Calif. Law clk. Hashidate Law Office, Tokyo, 1985-87; atty. Morrison & Foerster, L.A., 1988—. Editor Harvard Internat. Law Jour., 1987-88. Mem. Calif. State Bar Assn. (intellectual property, bus. and internat. law sects.). Office: Morrison & Foerster 345 California St San Francisco CA 94104-2635

OBSTFELD, MAURICE, economics educator and consultant; b. N.Y.C., Mar. 19, 1952; s. George Eliakim and Selma Giselle O. BA, U. Pa., 1973; MA, Cambridge U. (Eng.), 1975; PhD, MIT, 1979. Asst. prof. Columbia U., N.Y.C., 1979-81, assoc prof. dept. econs., 1981-85, prof., 1985-86; prof. U. Pa., Phila., 1986—; class of 1958 prof., U. Calif., Berkeley, 1989—; prof. U. Calif., Berkeley, 1995—. vis. scholar Fed. Res., Washington, 1981, 94, MIT, Cambridge, 1982, Stockholm U., 1988, 93, IMF, 1989; vis. prof. Tel-Aviv U., Israel, 1984, Harvard U., 1989-90; mem. econs. adv. panel NSF, 1983-84. Author: (with others) International Economics: Theory and Policy, 1987, 2d edit. 1991, 3d edit., 1994; co-editor: Financial Policies and the World Capital Market, 1983; editl. bd. Jour. Monetary Econs., 1983—, Jour. Internat. Econs., 1985—, Internat. Econ. Rev., 1986—, Rev. Internat. Econs., 1992—; rsch. assoc. Nat. Bur. Econ. Rsch., Cambridge, Mass.; rsch. fellow Ctr. Econ. Policy Rsch., London; author articles. Danforth Found. grad. fellow, 1973; NSF research grantee, 1981, 84, 86, 88, 91, 94; Alfred P. Sloan Found. rsch. fellow, 1984. Mem. Am. Econ. Assn. (editorial bd. jour. 1987—), Econometric Soc. Office: Dept Econs U Calif Berkeley CA 94720

O'BYRNE, MICHAEL, equipment dealer executive; b. Butte, Mont., Dec. 26, 1938; s. Michael E. and Margaret F. (Turner) O'B.; m. Penny L. Graham, Nov. 14, 1964; children: Jennifer L. McLellan, Gregory M. O'Byrne, Andrew G. O'Byrne. BSME, U. Wash., 1961. Cert. engr., Wash. V.p. PACCAR, Inc., Bellevue, Wash., 1969-84; pres. Mobi-Dock, Inc., Mercer Island, Wash., 1985-86; ptnr. The Catalyst Group, Mercer Island, 1986-89; pres. Raimor Group, Bellevue, 1988-89, Pacific N. Equiptment Co., Kent, Wash., 1990—. Council mem. Hunts Point, Wash., 1908-94; mem. bd. dirs. Mcpl. League of King County, Seattle, 1994—; dist. chmn. Boy Scouts of Am., Seattle, 1994—. Lt. comdr. USN, 1961-69. Mem. Soc. Automotive Engrs., Assoc. Equipment Distributors (chpt. pres. 1994-95), Rotary Internat., Seattle Yacht Club. Republican. Home: 4224 Hunts Point Rd Bellevue WA 98004

O'BYRNE, PAUL J., bishop; b. Calgary, Alta., Can., Dec. 21, 1922. Ordained priest Roman Catholic Ch., 1948; bishop of Calgary, 1968—. Office: Cath Pastoral Care Ctr, 1916 2nd Ave SW Rm 205, Calgary, AB Canada T2S 1S3*

OCCHIATO, MICHAEL ANTHONY, city official; b. Pueblo, Colo.; s. Joseph Michael and Joan Occhiato; m. Peggy Ann Stefonowicz, June 27, 1964 (div. Sept. 1983); children: Michael, James, Jennifer; m. Patsy Gay Payne, June 2, 1984; children: Kim Carr, Jerry Don Webb. BBA, U. Denver, 1961; MBA, U. Colo., 1984; postgrad., U. So. Colo. Sales mgr. Tivoli Brewing co., Denver, 1965-67, acting brewmaster, prodn. control mgr., 1967-68, plant mgr., 1968-69; adminstrv. mgr. King Resources Co., Denver, 1969-70; ops. mgr. Canners Inc., Pepsi-Cola Bottling Co., Pueblo, 1970-76; pres. Pepsi-Cola Bottling Co., Pueblo, 1978-82; gen. mgr. Pepsi-Cola Bottling Group div. PepsiCo., Pueblo, 1982, area v.p., 1982-83; ind. cons. Pueblo, 1983—; pres. Ethnic Foods Internat. dba Taco Rancho, Pueblo, Colo.; chmn. Weifang (China) Sister City del., 1991—; bd. dirs. HMO So. Colo. Health Plan, 1988-93; rancher, 1976—. Mem. coun. City of Pueblo, 1978-93, pres., 1986, 87, 90, 91; mem. bd. health, 1978-80, regional planning commn., 1980-81, Pueblo Action Inc., 1978-80, Pueblo Planning and Zoning Commn., 1985; chmn. Pueblo Area Coun. Govts., 1980-82; mem. Pueblo Econ. Devel. Corp., 1983-91; chmn. fundraising Pueblo chpt. Am. Heart Assn., 1983—; bd. dirs. El Pueblo Boys Ranch, 1971-73; del. 1st World Conf. Local Elected Officials to 1st UN Internat. Coun. for Local Environ. Initiative; active Earth Wise Pueble, 1991. Lt. USN, 1961-65. Mem. So. Colo. Emergency Med. Technicians Assn. (pres. 1975), Am. Saler Assn., Am. Quarter Horse Assn., Colo. Cattle Assn., Pueblo C. of C., Pi Kappa Alpha (v.p. 1960), Rotary. Home and Office: 11 Harrogate Ter Pueblo CO 81001-1723

OCCHIPINTI, CARL JOSEPH, broadcasting executive; b. New Orleans, Feb. 11, 1931; s. Victor and Anne (Maenza) O.; m. Ila M. Fanning, Nov. 22, 1939; children—Vickie, Michael, Diane. B.S., U. Wyo., 1956. Bus. and advt. mgr. Laramie (Wyo.) Newspapers, Inc., 1957-63; gen. mgr. Sta. KTVS-TV, Sterling, Colo., 1963-75; gen. mgr., v.p. Wyneco Communications, Inc., including Stas. KYCU-TV, Cheyenne, Wyo., KSTF-TV, Scottsbluff, Nebr., KTVS-TV, Sterling, Colo., 1975-86; gen. mgr. Sta. KGWN TV Cheyenne, 1986—, Sta. KSTF TV, Scottsbluff, Nebr., 1986—, Sta. KTVS TV, Sterling, Colo., Sta. KGWC TV, Casper Wyo., 1986—, STa. KGWL TV., Lander-Riverton, Wyo., Sta. KGWR TV, Rock Springs, Wyo., 1986—. With USAF, 1950-53. Mem. Advt. Assn. Denver, Colo. Broadcasters Assn. (past v.p.), Am. Legion, Cheyenne C. of C. (past 1st v.p.). Roman Catholic. Clubs: Cheyenne Country, Sterling Country, Elks. Office: Sta KGWN-TV 2923 E Lincolnway Cheyenne WY 82001-6149

OCCHIPINTI, JOSEPH R., optometrist; b. Syracuse, N.Y., Dec. 23, 1960; s. Rosario and Carmela (Catanzaro) O. BS in Biol. Scis., U. Calif., Irvine, 1984, BA in Psychology, 1985; BS in Visual Sci., So. Calif. Coll. Optometry, 1987, OD, 1989. Lic. optometrist, Calif. Pvt. practice Anaheim, Calif., 1989—; mem. staff student health svcs. eye clinic U. Calif., Irvine, 1989—, instr., 1991—. Contbr. articles to profl. jours. Calif. grad. fellow, 1985-89; recipient Harold Kohn Meml. award, 1989. Mem. Am. Optometrists Assn. (polit. action com. 1987—, sports vision sect., contact lens sect. 1988—, del. Calif. chpt. 1991, 92, 93, 94), Omega Delta (historian 1987), Beta Sigma Kappa (rsch. grantee 1987, 88). Office: 10502 Katella Ave Anaheim CA 92804-6528

OCHITILL, HERBERT NOLAN, psychiatrist, educator; b. Phila., May 27, 1946; s. Samuel Joseph and Gertrude Ochitill; m. Sally Thresher, Apr. 20. 1974; children: Emily, Sarah. BS in Natural Sci., Muhlenberg Coll., 1968; MD, Jefferson Med. Coll., 1972. Diplomate Am. Bd. Neurology and Psychiatry (bd. examiner 1983—). Intern Med. Coll. Pa., Phila., 1972-73; resident in psychiatry Johns Hopkins Hosp., Balt., 1973-76; fellow in psychosocial medicine med. ctr. U. Rochester, N.Y., 1976-77; staff cons. San Francisco Gen. Hosp., 1977-81, chief consultation svc., 1981—, asst. med. chief med. staff devel. and quality assurance program of psychiatry svc., 1989—; assoc. clin. prof. dept. psychiatry sch. medicine U. Calif., San Francisco, 1992—; lectr. San Francisco chpt. Am. Heart Assn., 1980—; mem. com. physician hiring and compensation Dept. Pub. Health, 1990—; cons. Laguna Honda Hosp., 1990-92; mem. various univ. and hosp. coms.; presenter in field. Author: (with others) Treatment of Mental Disorders, 1982, Assaults within Psychiatric Facilities, 1983, Review of General Psychiatry, 1984, AIDS Knowledge Base, 1986, AIDS and the Nervous System, 1988, San Francisco AIDS Knowledgebase, 1988; ad hoc referee Psychosomatics, 1983—, Psychiatry in Medicine, 1985—, N.Y. State Jour. Medicine, 1989—. Reviewer behavioral sci. topics Burke Sch., 1985—. Mem. AAAS, Am. Psychosomatic Soc. (mem. membership com. 1992—), Acad. Psychosomatic Medicine. Office: San Francisco Gen Hosp 1001 Potrero Ave San Francisco CA 94110-3518

OCHOA, ARMANDO, bishop; b. Oxnard, Calif., Apr. 3, 1943. Grad., Ventura (Calif.) Coll., St. John's Coll., Camarillo, Calif. Ordained priest Roman Cath. Ch., 1970. Titular bishop of Sitifi Calif.; aux. bishop, vicar gen. L.A., 1987—. Office: San Fernando Rectory 15101 San Fernando Mission Blvd Mission Hills CA 91345-1109*

OCHOA, ENRIQUE LUIS-MARIA, pediatrician; b. Buenos Aires, Argentina, Nov. 23, 1941; s. Enrique Jose Ochoa and Esilda Livia Cobos; m. Maria-Etelvina Toretti; children: Maria-Genoveva, Maria-Cecilia, Inés-Maria. MD, U. Buenos Aires, Argentina, 1965, PhD summa cum laude, 1973. Internship and residency clin. medicine Inst. de Investigaciones Medicas, U. Buenos Aires, Argentina, 1965-67; clin. rsch. fellow Nat. Rsch. Coun., U. Buenos Aires, Argentina, 1967-70; sr. demonstrator in histology and cell biology U. Buenos Aires, Argentina, 1971-73; rsch. fellow CONICET Inst. Animal Physiology, Babraham, Cambridge, Eng., 1974-75; career investigator, assoc. rschr. CONICET Inst. Cell Biology, U. Buenos Aires, Argentina, 1975-80, career investigator, rschr. CONICET, 1980-87, assoc. prof. histology and cell biology, 1982-87; sabbatical dept. biochemistry and biophysics U. Calif., Davis, 1988-90, asst. rsch. biochemistry Step III Dept. Pediatrics, 1990-92, asst. rschr. biochemistry Step III Dept. Pediatrics, 1992—. Mem. editorial bd. Communicaciones Biológicas, Cellular and Molecular Neurobiology; contbr. articles to profl. jours. Recipient award for Continued Excellence in Rsch. and for Disting. Achievement in Argentinian Sci., 1987; grantee in field. Mem. Soc. Argentina de Investigación, Soc. Argentina de Farmacología Experimental, Soc. Argentina de Investigaciones Bioquímicas, Soc. Argentina de Biofísica, Internat. Brain Rsch. Orgn., Internat. Soc. for Neurochemistry, Soc. Argentina de Neuroquímica, Soc. for Neurosci. Office: U Calif at Davis Dept Pediatrics Tb # 193 Davis CA 95616

OCHOA, JOSE LUIS, neurologist; b. Santiago, Chile, July 28, 1936; m. Wendy Comstock, Dec. 31, 1983; children: Juanita Paz, Maria Pilar, Marcela Soledad, Pepita, Andrés Jorge, Elise Angela. BA, St. George's Coll., 1953; MD, U. London, 1961, PhD, 1970, DSc, 1983. Ho. physician Hosp. Naval Dept. Internal Medicine, Valparaiso, Chile, 1961-62; resident Hosp. Univ. Catolica and Hosp. Trudeau, Santiago, 1962-66; British Coun. scholar Inst. of Neurology, London, 1966-67, rsch. fellow, 1967-68, lectr. dept. neuropathology, 1968-69, lectr. dept. clin. neurology, 1969-71, sr. lectr., 1971-74; hon. registrar Nat. Hosp. for Nervous Diseases, London, 1968-71; hon. cons. in clin. neurophysiology Nat. Hosps. for Nervous Diseases, Queen Square, 1973-74; attending neurologist Dartmouth-Hitchcock Med. Ctr., Hanover, N.H., 1974-83; from asst. to assoc. prof. medicine Dartmouth Med. Sch., Hanover, 1974-81, prof., 1981-83; attending neurologist U. Wis. Hosp., Madison, 1983-86; prof. neurology U. Wis., Madison, 1983-86; neurologist Good Samaritan Hosp. and Med. Ctr., Portland, Oreg., 1986—, head neuromuscular divsn. neurol. scis. ctr., 1986—; prof. neurology Oreg. Health Scis. U., Portland, 1988—, prof. surgery, 1991—; vis. clin. scientist dept. neurophysiology Acad. Hosp., Uppsala, Sweden, 1980; mem. sci. com. dept. neuromuscular disorders Internat. Sch. Neurol. Scis., Venice, Italy, 1992—. Editl. bd. Jour. Muscle and Nerve, 1991; assoc. editor Schmerz, Pain, Douleur, 1991; dir. editl. panel Peripheral Nerve, Pain Jour., 1975-90; contbr. numerous articles to profl. jours. Swedish Med. Rsch. Coun. fellow, 1980; co-recipient Alvarengas Prize Swedish Soc. of Med. Sci., 1981; grantee NIH, 1982-90, 87-92, 90—. Mem. Am. Neurol. Assn., British Neuropathol. Soc., Internat. Assn. for the Study of Pain (rsch. com. 1990), Peripheral Nerve Study Group, Am. Assn. of Electromyography and Electrodiagnosis, Soc. for Neurosci. (program com. 1984-87). Office: Neurol Scis Ctr Good Samaritan Hosp 1040 NW 22nd Ave # 460 Portland OR 97210-3057

OCHOMOGO, MARÍA GARCÍA, manufacturing company executive; b. Holguin, Oriente, Cuba, Feb. 19, 1950; came to U.S., 1965; d. Ariel A. and Maria del C. (Fernandez) Garcia; m. Oscar Rene Ochomogo, May 29, 1971; children: Mary, Michelle, Oscar Jr. BS, La. State U., 1972, MS, 1974, PhD, 1978. Lab. mgr. Ralston Purina, Campinas, Brazil, 1974-76; rschr. La. State U., Baton Rouge, 1976-78; lab. mgr. Eggo Foods div. Kellogg's, Milpitas,

Calif., 1978-85; R&D mgr. Bunge Foods div. Bunge Corp., Atlanta, 1985-87; sr. rsch. chemist Chevron Corp., Richmond, Calif., 1987-92; project mgr. The Clorox Co., Pleasanton, Calif., 1992—. Inventor a low voc pest conc., process stability of Orthene, A new pest tech. Vol. Young Rep. Party, 1968-72; vol. community sci. sch. program Chevron, Richmond, 1991, Clorox, 1992; coord. United Way Chevron Chem., Richmond, 1991. Named First Woman Sanitarian for La. State of La., 1973; T.H. Harris scholarship, La. State U., 1968-72. Mem. Am. Soc. Testing Materials, Chem. Specialty Mfg. Assn., Woeman Engring. in Bus., Am. Chem. Soc., Inst. Food Technologist, Gamma Sigma Delta, Phi Tau Sigma.

OCHOTORENA, DOMINGO RAFAEL, military officer; b. Miami, Oct. 24, 1963; s. Jose Oriol Ochotorena and Marta Rosa Quintana; m. Heidi Dawn Wimmer, Nov. 24, 1993. BSME, U. Bridgeport, 1986; MSME, Boston U., 1991; grad., Test Pilot Sch., 1994. Commd. 2d lt. USAF, 1986, advanced through grades to capt., 1990; navigator USAF, Zweibrücken AFB, Germany, 1988-91, Cannon AFB, N.Mex., 1991-93; test pilot sch. student USAF, Edwards AFB, Calif., 1993-94; flight test navigator on B-2 program USAF. Decorated DFC, 1991, Air medal, 1991. Mem. ASME.

OCHS, HANS DIETER, pediatrics educator; b. Spaichingen, Germany, Sept. 29, 1936; came to U.S., 1968; s. Anton and Anna (Braun) O.; m. Ute Hanna Brintzinger, June 20, 1963; children: Oliver D., Ulrike I. BS, Gymnasium, 1956; MD, U. Freidburg, 1961, U. Wash., 1969. Intern Flower Hosp., Toledo, Ohio, 1963-64; resident Children's Hosp., Honolulu, 1964-65, Children's Hosp., U. Tuebingen, Germany, 1967-68, Children's Hosp., U. Wash., Seattle, 1968-69; asst. prof. pediatrics U. Wash., Seattle, 1972-75, assoc. prof., 1975-80, prof., 1980—, fellow immunology dept. pediatrics, 1969-72. Contbr. over 200 scientific articles to profl. jours. Howard Hughes Med. Inst. grantee, 1972-80. Mem. Am. Assn. Immunologists, Soc. Pediatric Rsch., Clin. Immunology Soc. Office: U Wash Sch Medicine Dept Pediatrics Box 356320 Seattle WA 98195-6320

OCKER, CHRISTOPHER MICHAEL, historian, educator; b. Queens, N.Y., Nov. 23, 1958; s. Ralph Franz and Christa Gertrud (Holder) O.; m. Varda Koch, Aug. 29, 1987; children: Gabriel, Tanya. MDiv, Fuller Theol. Sem., 1983; ThM, Princeton Theol. Sem., 1985, PhD, 1991. Rsch. fellow Institut für Europäische Geschichte, Mainz, Germany, 1988-91; asst. prof. history San Francisco Theol. Sem., San Anselmo, 1991—, Grad. Theol. Union, Berkeley, Calif., 1991—; assoc. dir. Ctr. for Hermeneutical Studies, Berkeley, 1991-94; vis. fellow Max-Planck-Inst. Geschichte, Göttingen, Germany, 1995. Author: Johannes Klenkok: A Friar's Life, 1993; editor: Protocol of the Colloguy of the Center for Hermeneutical Studies, 1992-94. Bd. dirs. San Anselmo Organ Festival, 1994. Recipient Theol. Scholarship and Rsch. award Assn. Theol. Schs., 1995, Rsch. award Deutscher Akademischer Austauschdienst, 1987; Alexander von Humboldt-Stiftung fellow, 1995. Mem. Am. Hist. Assn., Am. Soc. Ch. History, Medieval Acad. Am., Am. Acad. Religion. Presbyterian. Office: San Francisco Theol Sem 2 Kensington Rd San Anselmo CA 94960-2905

OCKEY, RONALD J., lawyer; b. Green River, Wyo., June 12, 1934; s. Theron G. and Ruby O. (Sackett) O.; m. Arline M. Hawkins, Nov. 27, 1957; children: Carolyn S. Ockey Baggett, Deborah K. Ockey Christiansen, David, Kathleen M. Ockey Hellewell, Valerie Ockey Sachs, Robert. B.A., U. Utah, 1959, postgrad. 1959-60; J.D. with honors, George Washington U., 1966. Bar: Colo. 1967, Utah 1968, U.S. Dist. Ct. Colo. 1967, U.S. Dist. Ct. Utah 1968, U.S. Ct. Appeals (10th cir.) 1969, U.S. Ct. Claims 1987. Missionary to France for Mormon Ch., 1954-57; law clk. to judge U.S. Dist. Ct. Colo., 1966-67; assoc. ptnr., shareholder, v.p., treas., dir. Jones, Waldo, Holbrook & McDonough, Salt Lake City, 1967-91, pres., IntelliTrans Internat. Corp., 1992-94; mem. Utah Ho. Reps., 1988-90, Utah State Senate, 1991-94; of counsel Mackey Price & Williams, Salt Lake City, 1995—; trustee SmartUTAH, Inc., 1995—; lectr. in securities, pub. fin. and bankruptcy law. State govtl. affairs chmn. Utah Jaycees, 1969; del. state Rep. Convs., 1972-74, 1976-78, 1980-82, 84-86, del. Salt Lake County Rep. Conv., 1978-80, 88; sec. Wright for Gov. campaign, 1980; legis. dist. chmn. Utah Rep. Party, 1983-87; trustee Food for Poland, 1981—, pres., trustee, Unity to Assist Humanity Alliance, 1992—; bd. dirs. Utah Opera Co., 1991-94; trustee, mem. exec. com. Utah Info. Tech. Assn., 1991-94; bd. dir., mem. exec. com. Smart Utah, Inc., 1995—. Lt. U.S. Army, 1960-66; to capt. Judge Adv. Gen. USAR, 1966-81. Mem. Utah State Bar Assn. (various coms.), , Nat. Assn. Bond Lawyers (chmn. com. on state legislation 1982-85), George Washington U. Law Alumni Assn. (bd. dirs. 1981-85), Order of Coif, Salt Lake Rotary, Phi Delta Phi. Contbr. articles on law to profl. jours.; mem. editorial bd. Utah Bar Jour., 1973-75; mem. staff and bd. editors George Washington Law Rev., 1964-66. Home: 4502 Crest Oak Cir Salt Lake City UT 84124-3825

O'CONNELL, GWYNETH PIETA, art educator, graphic artist; b. Portland, Oreg., Nov. 25, 1944; d. Ellis Hedrick and Helen Florence (Newland) Jones; m. Kenneth Robert O'Connell, June 21, 1969; children: Anneka Erin, Marlika Megan, Sean Daugherty. BS in Art Edn., U. Oreg., 1966, MFA in Graphic Arts, 1968, Generalist, 1993. Art instr. Tongue Point Job Corp, Astoria, Oreg., 1968-69, Treasure Valley C.C., Ontario, Oreg., 1969-71, 73-78, U. Oreg., Maude I. Kerns Lane C.C., Eugene, 1972-73, 78-84; art/computer instr. Eugene (Oreg.) Pub. Sch. Dist. 4J, 1984—. Co-author Sch. Arts mag., 1990-94. Bd. dirs. Western Rivers coun. Girl Scouts U.S.A., Eugene, 1984-90, leader, 1978-93, Troop Leader of Yr. 1981). HEW prospective tchrs. fellow, U. Oreg., 1966-68, Maude I. Kern's scholar, 1966. Mem. AAUW (bd. mem. 1978-80). Democrat. Home: 220 W 23rd Ave Eugene OR 97405 Office: School Zoo N Monroe 400 E 19th Ave Eugene OR 97403

O'CONNELL, HUGH MELLEN, JR., architect, retired; b. Oak Park, Ill., Nov. 29, 1929; s. Hugh M. and Helen Mae (Evans) O'C.; m. Frances Ann Small, Apr. 13, 1957; children—Patricia Lynn, Susan Marie, Jeanette Maureen. Designer, John Mackel. Student mech. engring., Purdue U., 1948-50; B.S. in Archtl. Engring, U. Ill., 1953. Registered architect, Ariz., Calif., La., Nev., Nat. Council Archtl. Registration Bds. Structural engr. Los Angeles, 1955-57; architect Harnish & Morgan & Causey, Ontario, Calif., 1957-63; self-employed architect Ventura, Calif., 1963-69; architect Andrews/O'Connell, Ventura, 1970-78; dir. engring. div. Naval Constrn. Bn. Center, Port Hueneme, Calif., 1978-91; supervisory architect Naval Constrn. Bn. Center, Port Hueneme, 1991-93; ret., 1993; mem. tech. adv. com. Ventura Coll., 1965-78; sec. Oxnard Citizens' Adv. Com., 1969-79, v.p., 1970-72, pres., 1972—; chmn. Oxnard Beautification Com., 1969, 74, Oxnard Cmty. Block Grant adv. com., 1975-76; mem. Oxnard Planning Commn., 1976-86, vice chmn., 1978-79, chmn., 1980-81. Mem. Oxnard Art-in-Pub. Places Commn., 1988—. Served with AUS, 1953-55. Mem. AIA (emeritus, pres. Ventura chpt. 1973), Am. Concrete Inst., Soc. Am. Registered Architects (Design award 1968, dir. 1970), Am. Legion, Soc. for Preservation and Encouragement of Barbershop Quartet Singing in Am. (chpt. pres. 1979, chpt. sec. 1980-83), Acad. Model Aeros. (#9190 1948—), Alpha Rho Chi. Presbyterian (elder 1963, deacon 1967). Lodges: Kiwanis (pres. 1969, div. sec. 1974-75), Elks. Home and Office: 520 Ivywood Dr Oxnard CA 93030-3527

O'CONNELL, KATHRYN A., small business owner; b. Great Falls, Mont., Oct. 9, 1955; d. Patrick M. and Patricia J. (Berek) O'C.; m. Gerald P. Foley, Nov. 1, 1980. Student, Carroll Coll., 1979. Owner Ballons Etc., Helena, Mont., 1986—. Guest dir. Grandstreet Theatre, Helena, 1986-94, bd. dirs., 1987-93, chmn. bd., 1990, chmn. fund dr., 1990-91. Mem. Nat. Assn. Balloon Artists (cert master balloon artist, 1st balloon delivery competition, Designer of Monty award 1993, cons. 1993), MOnt. Soc. Assn. Execs. Office: Balloons Etc 1429 11th Ave Helena MT 59601-4524

O'CONNELL, KATHY L., biochemist, research assistant; b. Saginaw, Mich., July 16, 1964; d. George A. and Jacqueline J. (Reeder) O'C. Student, Delta Coll., 1985; BA in Chemistry, Kalamazoo Coll., 1990. Technologist Dow Chem., Midland, Mich., 1984-86; lab. technician II Upjohn Co., Kalamazoo, Mich., 1986-91, biochemistry asst., 1991; rsch. asst. II Genentech, Inc., South San Francisco, 1991—. Contbr. articles to profl. jours. Kurt D. Kaufman Rsch. fellow Kalamazoo Coll., 1990. Mem. Am. Chem. Soc., Am. Soc. for Mass Spectrometry. Office: Genentech Inc 460 Point San Bruno Blvd South San Francisco CA 94080-4918

O'CONNELL, KENNETH ROBERT, artist, animator, educator; b. Ogden, Utah, Jan. 22, 1945; s. Daniel D. and Virginia N. (Kyle) O'C.; m. Gwyneth P. Jones, June 21, 1969; children: Anneka, Marlika, Sean. BS in Art Edn., U. Oreg., 1966, MFA in Graphic Design with honors, 1972. Mem. faculty Treasure Valley C.C., Ontario, Oreg., 1973-78, chair dept. art, 1975-78; adj. faculty (multi-image) Goddard Coll., Plainfield, Vt., 1980-81; asst. prof. fine and applied arts U. Oreg., Eugene, 1978-82, assoc. prof., head fine and applied arts, 1983-91, prof., head fine and applied arts, 1991—; vis. faculty in film, animation, photography Evergreen State Coll., Olympia, Wash., 1976; art gallery chair SIGGRAPH 95 Conf., 1994-95; cons., workshop facilitator, lectr., presenter in field. Exhibited works at Ann Arbor (Mich.) Film Festival, 1974, Coos Art Mus., Coos Bay, Oreg., 1977, 78, USA Film Festival, Dallas, 1980, Hong Kong Film Festival, 1981, Athens (Ohio) Internat. Film Festival, 1981, Internat. Animation Festival of Japan, Hiroshima, 1985, Zagreb (Yugoslavia) World Animation Festival, 1986, Portland Art Mus., 1987, Sapporo (Japan) Art Park, 1989, Chgo. Internat. Festival of Children's Films, 1991, Toyoma (Japan) Mus. Art, 1992, others; featured in mag. articles. Recipient award First N.W. Film and Video Festival, 1973, 3d prize USA Film FEstival, Dallas, 1980, Dirs. Choice award Sinking Creek Film Celebration, Nashville, 1986, others; Horseshoe grantee Grad. Sch. U. Oreg., 1982, 84,86, 89; Getty grantee, 1988, others; named to Outstanding Young Men of Am., 1977. Mem. Found. Art, Theory and Edn., Assn. for Computer Machinery/SIGGRAPH, Coll. ARt Assn., Nat. Coun. Art Adminstrs., Soc. for Animation Studies. Office: U Oreg Dept Fine and Applied Arts Eugene OR 97403

O'CONNELL, KEVIN, lawyer; b. Boston, Sept. 4, 1933; s. Michael Frederick and Kathryn Agnes (Kelley) O'C.; m. Mary Adams, July 14, 1990; children: Tiffany W., Elizabeth H., Dana A., Liesel E. A.B., Harvard, 1955, J.D., 1960. Bar: Calif. 1961. Assoc. firm O'Melveny & Myers, L.A., 1960-63; asst. U.S. atty. criminal div. Cen. Dist. Calif., L.A., 1963-65; staff counsel Gov. Calif. Commn. to Investigate Watts Riot, L.A., 1965-66; ptnr. Tuttle & Taylor, L.A., 1966-70, Coleman & O'Connell, L.A., 1971-75; pvt. practice law L.A., 1975-78; of counsel firm Simon & Sheridan, L.A., 1978-89; ptnr. Manatt, Phelps & Phillips, L.A., 1989—. Bd. editors: Harvard Law Rev, 1958-60. Mem. Los Angeles County (Calif.) Democratic Central Com., 1973-74. Served to lt. USMCR, 1955-57. Mem. Am. Law Inst. Home: 426 N Mccadden Pl Los Angeles CA 90004-1026 Office: Manatt Phelps & Phillips Trident Ctr E Tower 11355 W Olympic Blvd Los Angeles CA 90064-1614

O'CONNELL, MARY ANN, state senator, business owner; b. Albuquerque, Aug. 3, 1934; d. James Aubrey and Dorothy Nell (Batsel) Gray; m. Robert Emmett O'Connell, Feb. 21, 1977; children: Jeffery Crampton, Gray Crampton. Student, U. N.Mex., Internat. Coun. Shopping Ctrs. Exec. dir. Blvd. Shopping Ctr., Las Vegas, Nev., 1968-76, Citizen Pvt. Enterprise, Las Vegas, 1976; media supr. Southwest Advt., Las Vegas, 1977—; owner, operator Meadows Inn, Las Vegas, 1985—, 3 Christian bookstores, Las Vegas, 1985—; state senator Nev. Senate, 1985-93; chmn. gov. affairs; vice chmn. commerce and labor; mem. taxation com.; alt. Legis. Commn., 1985-86, mem., 1987-88, 91-93; commr. Edn. Commn. States; rep. Nat. Conf. State Legislators; past vice chair State Mental Hygiene & Mental Retardation Adv. Bd. Pres. explorer div. Boulder Dam Area coun. Boy Scouts Am., Las Vegas, 1979-80, former mem. exec. bd.; mem. adv. bd. Boy Scouts Am.; pres., bd. dirs. Citizens Pvt. Enterprise, Las Vegas, 1982-84, Secret Witness, Las Vegas, 1081-82; vice chmn. Gov.'s Mental Health-Mental Retardation, Nev., 1983—; past mem. community adv. bd. Care Unit Hosp., Las Vegas; past mem. adv. bd. Kidney Found., Milligan Coll., Charter Hosp.; tchr. Young Adult Sunday Sch. Recipient Commendation award Mayor O. Grayson, Las Vegas, 1975, Outstanding Citizenship award Bd. Realtors, 1975, Silver Beaver award Boy Scouts Am., 1980, Free Enterprise award Greater Las Vegas C. of C., Federated Employers Assn., Downtown Breakfast Exch., 1988, Award of Excellence for Women in Politics, 1989, Legislator of Yr. award Bldg. and Trades, 1991, Legislator of Yr. award Nat. ASA Trade Assn., 1991, 94, Guardian of Liberty award Nev. Coalition of Conservative Citizens, 1991, Internat. Maxi Awards Promotional Excellence; named Legislator of Yr., Nev. Retail Assn., 1992. Mem. Retail Mchts. Assn. (former pres., bd. dirs.), Taxpayers Assn. (bd. dirs.), Greater Las Vegas C. of C. (past pres., bd. dirs., Woman of Achievement Politics women's coun. 1988). Republican. Mem. Christian Ch. Home: 7225 Montecito Cir Las Vegas NV 89120-3118 Office: Nev Legislature Senate 401 S Carson St Carson City NV 89701-4747

O'CONNELL, MICHAEL ALEXANDER, social worker; b. Dayton, Ohio, May 28, 1948; s. William J. and Aida May (Duncan) O'Co. BS in econ., U. Pa., 1970; MSW, U. Wash., 1977. Cert. social worker, Wash. Dir. Second Chance Youth Alcoholism Program, Seattle, 1977-78; social worker Riverton Hosp., Burren, Wash., 1979-80; therapist Robinson William & Assocs., Seattle, 1981-82; therapist & cons. Alteran Assocs., Seattle, 1982-83, Everett, 1983—. Author: Working With Sex Offenders, 1990. Lt. USN., 1970-75. Mem. Acad. Cert. Social Workers, Assn. Treatment of Sexual Abusers, Am. Profl. Soc. on the Abuse of Children. Office: Michael A O'Connell & Assocs 8625 Evergreen Way # 203 Everett WA 98208

O'CONNELL, ROBERT HOUSTON, religious educator; b. Kitchener, Ont., Can., Dec. 4, 1955; s. Ronald J. O'Connell and Joan H. (Roberts) Molloy; m. Mina M. Fain, Aug. 14, 1982; children: Nathan H., Sean M. BA in music, U. Western Ont., 1978; ThM in old testament, Dallas Theological Sem., 1982, ThD in old testament, 1989; PhD in Divinity, U. Cambridge, Cambridge, Eng., 1993. Assoc. prof. old testament Colo. Christian U., Lakewood, Colo., 1991—. Author: Concentricity and Continuity: The Literary Structure of Isaiah, 1994, The Rhetoric of the Book of Judges, 1995. Shipley scholarship Fitzwilliam Coll., 1988-89, Crosse scholarship U. Cambridge, 1989-91, Overseas Rsch. Student award, London, Eng., 1988-91. Mem. Soc. Bibl. Lit., Nat. Assn. Profs. of Hebrew, Soc. for Old Testament Studies (U.K.). Home: 3250 S Lafayette St Englewood CO 80110-2924 Office: Colo Christian U 180 S Garrison St Lakewood CO 80226-1053

O'CONNELL, THEODORE XAVIER, surgical oncologist, educator; b. N.Y.C., Aug. 30, 1943; s. Theodore X. and Marie E. (McNulty) O'C.; m. Frances F. Coan, July 4, 1970; children: Theodore X., Brendan P., Daniel J. BA, UCLA, 1966, MD, 1969. Diplomate Am. Bd. Surgery. Assoc. prof. surg. oncology UCLA Med. Sch., L.A., 1978-79, assoc. clin. prof. surg. oncology, 1984—; chief surg. oncology Kaiser Permanente Med. Ctr., L.A., 1979—. Editor: Surgical Oncology: Controversies in Cancer, 1981; contbr. articles to med. jours. Lt. comdr. USN, 1976-78. Fellow ACS (program chmn. So. Calif. chpt. 1994); mem. Am. Soc. Clin. Oncology, Am. Cancer Soc. (mem. awards task force Calif. divsn. 1994), Soc. Surg. Oncology (mem. exam. com. 1993—), Pacific Coast Surg. Assn., Bay Surg. Soc., L.A. Surg. Soc. Democrat. Roman Catholic. Office: Kaiser Permanente Med Ctr 4747 W Sunset Blvd Los Angeles CA 90027-6021

O'CONNER, LORETTA RAE, former court reporter; b. Denver, Dec. 23, 1958; d. Ronald Lee and Norma Jareene (Warner) Barkdoll; m. George Ellis Bentley, Dec. 31, 1976 (div. 1979); m. Donald Hugh O'Conner, Feb. 3, 1987; children: Justin Lee, Brandon Craig. AS, Denver Acad. Ct. Reporting, 1983; BA summa cum laude, Regis U., 1992; postgrad., U. Colo., 1992—. Cert. registered profl. reporter. Ct. reporter Denver, 1983-87; dist. ct. reporter Judicial Dept., State of Colo., Pueblo, 1987-91; ct. reporter Pueblo, 1991-93. Chief justice Student Govt. Ct., U. So. Colo., Pueblo, 1992; trained facilitator Kettering Found., Pub. Policy, Dayton, Ohio, 1992; sec. So. Colo. Registered Interpretors for Deaf, Pueblo, 1991. President's scholar U. So. Colo., 1991-92, Alumni Assn. scholar, 1991-92; grantee Kettering Found., 1992; Colo. Legislature grantee and scholar Regis U., 1992; Colo. Legislature grantee U. Colo. Sch. Law, 1993-95, Dean's scholar and Dazzo Scholar U. Colo. Sch. Law, 1993-95. Mem. ATLA, ABA, Nat. Ct. Reporters Assn., Colo. Trial Lawyers Assn., Colo. Bar Assn., Colo. Womens Bar Assn., Colo. Ct. Reporters Assn., Boulder Bar Assn., Phi Delta Phi (clk. 1994-95). Home: 1330 19th St Boulder CO 80302-6503

O'CONNOR, BETTY LOU, service executive; b. Phoenix, Oct. 29, 1927; d. Georg Eliot and Tillie Edith (Miller) Miller; m. William Spoeri O'Connor, Oct. 10, 1948 (dec. Feb. 1994); children: Thomas W., William K., Kelli Anne. Student, U. So. Calif., 1946-48, Calif. State U., Los Angeles, 1949-50. V.p. O'Connor Food Svcs., Inc., Jack in the Box Restaurants, Granada Hills, Calif., 1983-93; pres. O'Connor Food Svcs., Inc., Granada Hills, Calif., 1994—, Western Restaurant Mgmt. Co., Granada Hills, 1986—; mem. adv. bd. Bank of Granada Hills. Recipient Frannie award Foodmaker, Inc., Northridge, Calif., 1984, First Rate award, 1992. Mem. Jack in the Box Franchisee Assn., Spurs Hon. (sec. U. So. Calif. 1947-48), Associated Women Students (sec. U. So. Calif. 1946-47), Gamma Alpha Chi (v.p. 1947-48), Chi Omega. Republican. Roman Catholic. Office: Western Restaurant Mgmt Co 17545 Chatsworth St Granada Hills CA 91344-5720

O'CONNOR, JOHN EDWARD, physician; b. Sidney, Nebr., Dec. 28, 1928; s. Daniel Edward and Lenore (Gilbert) O'C.; m. Beverly L. O'Connor, Jan. 31, 1956; children: Daniel L. John D., William E. BS, U. Nebr., 1951, DDS, 1954; MD, U. Nebr., Omaha, 1961. Diplomate Am. Bd. Plastic Surgery, Am. Bd. Otolaryngology. Pvt. practice. Lt. Commdr. USNR, 1951-63. Fellow ACS; mem. Am. Cleft Palate Assn., Am. Soc. Maxillofacial Surgeons. Office: 2519 13th Ave S Great Falls MT 59405-5155

O'CONNOR, KEVIN THOMAS, archdiocese development official; b. Dubuque, Iowa, Oct. 9, 1950; s. Francis John and Marion Helen (Rhomberg) O'C. BS, Regis Coll., Denver, 1973. Spl. agt. Northwestern Mut. Life, Denver, 1973-78; account exec. Blue Cross/Blue Shield of Colo., Denver, 1978-82; pres., owner O'Connor Ins. Cons., Denver, 1982-92; dir. devel. Archdiocese of Denver, 1992-95, mgr. Cath. appeal & planned giving, 1995—. Chmn. Ragis Coll. Telefund, Denver, 1987-88, 90-91; treas., 1st vice chmn. Serra Trust Fund for Vocations, 1988-93, chmn., 1993—; mem. fin. coun. St. James Parish, 1988-95, chmn. autumn bazaar, 1985, 87, mem. choir, 1993-95; sec. Mother Teresa Com., 1989. Recipient Share Serra Comm. award Serra Internat., 1989, Spl. Project award Dist. 6, 1986, 88, Spl. Recognition award, 1989, Alumni Svc. award Regis Coll., 1990, Disting. Alumnus award Wahlert H.S., 1994. Mem. Serra Club of Denver (sec. 1986-89, v.p. membership 1989-90, pres.-elect 1990-91, pres. 1991-92, trustee 1992-95, chmn. founders com. Colorado Springs chpt. 1994-95, dist. 6 gov. elect 1994-95, gov. 1995—, USACC for membership 1990—). Roman Catholic. Home: 7025 E Costilla Dr Englewood CO 80112-1105 Office: Archdiocese of Denver 200 Josephine St Denver CO 80206-4710

O'CONNOR, PATRICIA ERYL, telecommunications consultant; b. Kansas City, Mo., Oct. 16, 1945; d. Jesse Edwin O'Connor and Olive Mae (Geagan) Brooks; m. James Harrie Reed, Dec. 18, 1964 (div. July 1972); 1 child, Jana Diann Reed; m. John Robert Morgan, Sept. 27, 1985. AAS, Pima Community Coll., Tucson, 1982. Cert. Nat. Assn. Broadcast Engrs. Radio, radio-telephone lic. gen. class FCC. Communications technician AT&T, Kansas City, Mo., 1972-79, Tucson, 1979-85, San Francisco, 1985-91, Denver, 1991—; chief exec. officer, cons. Profl. Forum Mgmt./MacCircles, Pleasanton, Calif., 1990-92, Denver, 1992—; co-adminstr. Mac Symposium, Cupertino, Calif., 1987-93. Editor: (electronic mag.) Handshake, 1985-94. Election judge, Tucson, 1979-81; area v.p. CWA Local 8150, Ariz., N.Mex., 1984-84, exec. v.p., 1984-85. Home: 24949 Montane Dr W Golden CO 80401-9192

O'CONNOR, PATRICIA RANVILLE, secondary and special education educator; b. Flint, Mich., Feb. 24, 1951; d. Marcel L. and Ruth Ellen (Smith) Ranville. BS, Ea. Mich. U., 1973, MA, 1978; MS in Adminstrn., Pepperdine U., 1995. Cert. tchr. (life) Calif., severely handicapped and learning handicapped, multiple subject, resource specialist. Spl. edn. tchr. Genessee Intermediate Sch. Dist., Flint, 1974-78, Barstow (Calif.) Unified Sch. Dist., 1978-81, Westport Sch., L.A., 1981-83; resource specialist Culver City (Calif.) Unified Sch. Dist., 1983—, mentor tchr., chmn. dept. spl. edn., coord. sch. improvement program; coord. sch. improvement program; chair sch. site coun.; team leader dept. edn. program quality rev. State of Calif.; mem. C.A.R.E. Team; reader, scorer Calif. Assessment Program; coord. sch. wide goal setting esteem program Striving For My Personal Best. Recipient Hon. Svc. award PTA. Mem. NEA, Calif. Tchrs. Assn. Home: 5460 White Oak Ave Apt 210C Encino CA 91316-2401

O'CONNOR, PAULINE R., interior design consultant; b. L.A., Dec. 21, 1964; d. David Arthur and Lilia (Freire) O'C. Grad., Glendale Coll., 1986; BA, UCLA, 1990. Jr. interior designer Peller Interiors, Glendale, Calif., 1986-91; fabric, textile cons./salesperson J. Robert Scott Assocs., L.A., 1991-94; interior designer D&L Interiors, Glendale, 1987-94; interior design cons./salesperson Initials Showroom, L.A., 1994—. Mem. Am. Soc. Interior Designers (charter). Office: D&L Interiors 1147 E Broadway Ste 80 Glendale CA 91205-1315

O'CONNOR, WILLIAM CHARLES, automobile agency finance executive; b. Poplar Bluff, Mo., July 19, 1943; s. Thomas Francis and Luella Darlene (Davis) O'C.; m. Leigh Volkening, Dec. 21, 1975 (div. May 1992); children: Kelli, Megan, Katie. BA in English, Memphis State U., 1966. High rigger Boiler Makers Union, St. Louis, 1968-70; br. mgr. Pub. Fin. Corp., St. Louis, 1970-74; fin. specialist Pat Ryan & Assocs., Chgo., 1974-77; fin. mgr. Drew Ford, La Mesa, Calif., 1978-80; fin. dir. Honda of Pasadena, Calif., 1980-89, Goudy Honda, Alhambra, Calif., 1989-94, Scott Robinson Honda, Torrance, Calif., 1994—; cons. Am. Honda Fin. Corp., Torrance, 1987—. Contbr. articles to profl. jours. Mem. Fin. and Ins. Profls., KC, Jr. C. of C., Young Dems. Orgn. (pres. 1968-69). Home: 613 E Camellia Dr Covina CA 91723-3608 Office: 20340 Hawthorne Blvd Torrance CA 90503

ODA, TODD I., quality assurance professional; b. Inglewood, Calif., Feb. 15, 1963; s. Sam Chuck and Takeko Nitta O. BS in Mech. Engring., Calif. State U., Long Beach, 1987. Mfg. engr. Rollcut, Harbor City, Calif., 1987-89; tooling engr. DXL USA, Torrance, Calif., 1989-91, dir. quality, 1991—. Mem. ASME, Soc. Auto. Engrs., Am. Soc. Quality Control, Am. Soc. Mfg. Engrs. Home: 2603 W 178th St Torrance CA 90504-4114 Office: DXL USA 2540 W 237th St Torrance CA 90505-5217

ODA, YOSHIO, physician, internist; b. Papaaloa, Hawaii, Jan. 14, 1933; s. Hakuai and Usako (Yamamoto) O.; AB, Cornell U., 1955; MD, U. Chgo., 1959. Diplomate Am. Bd. Internal Medicine. Intern U. Chgo. Clinics, 1959-60; resident in pathology U. Chgo., 1960-62, Queen's Hosp., Hawaii, 1962-63, Long Beach (Calif.) VA Hosp., 1963-65; resident in allergy, immunology U. Colo. Med. Center, 1966-67; pvt. practice, L.A., 1965-66; pvt. practice internal medicine, allergy and immunology, Honolulu, 1970—; asst. clin. prof. medicine U. Hawaii, Honolulu, 1970—. Maj., AUS, 1968-70. Mem. ACP, Am. Acad. Allergy. Office: Piikoi Med Bldg 1024 Piikoi St Honolulu HI 96814-1925

ODEKIRK, BRUCE, physicist; b. Washington, Apr. 17, 1951; s. Max Dean Odekirk and Kathryn May (Cooper) Negri; m. Rose Marie Murray, Dec. 26, 1979; children: Brandy Danielle. BS in Physics, Sonoma State U., 1978; PhD in Applied Physics, Oreg. Grad. Inst. Sci. & Tech., 1982. Sr. scientist Tektronix, Beaverton, Oreg., 1983-86; prin. device engr. TriQuint Semiconductor, Beaverton, 1986-95, process engring. mgr., 1995—. Contbr. articles to profl. jours.; patentee in field. Staff sgt. USAF, 1969-73. Mem. IEEE. Democrat. Presbyterian. Home: 430 NE 18th Ave Hillsboro OR 97124-3506 Office: TriQuint Semiconductor 430 NE 18th Ave Hillsboro OR 97124-3506

ODELL, JOHN H., construction company executive; b. Toledo, Oct. 31, 1955; s. John H. and Doris Irene (Haskell) O.; m. Kathryn Lau, Oct. 1, 1988; children: Cezra, Heather. B of Environ. Design, U. Miami, Oxford, Ohio, 1977. Staff architect Richard Halford and Assocs., Santa Fe, 1978-79; ptnr. B.O.A. Constrn., Santa Fe, 1980-84; assoc. Stanley Design Works, Santa Fe, 1984-85; owner John H. Odell Constrn., Santa Fe, 1985—; v.p. Los Pintores Inc., Santa Fe, 1990—, Uncle Joey's Food Svcs. Inc., 1991—. Musician Santa Fe Community Orch., 1982, Huntington Community Orch., Huntington, W.Va., 1972-73. Mem. AIA (assoc. mem., treas., bd. dirs. Santa Fe chpt. yearly 1988-95, mem. liaison com. on design 1987—, Cmty. Svc. award 1993), Vine and Wine Soc. (N.Mex. No. Rio Grande chpt. pres., bd. dirs.). Home: PO Box 2967 Santa Fe NM 87504-2967 Office: John H Odell Assn 729 Dunlap Santa Fe NM 87501-3689

ODELL, WILLIAM DOUGLAS, physician, scientist, educator; b. Oakland, Calif., June 11, 1929; s. Ernest A. and Emma L. (Mayer) O.; m. Margaret F. Reilly, Aug. 19, 1950; children: Michael, Timothy, John D., Debbie, Charles. AB, U. Calif., Berkeley, 1952; MD, MS in Physiology, U. Chgo., 1956; PhD in Biochemistry and Physiology, George Washington U., 1965.

Intern, resident, chief resident in medicine U. Wash., 1956-60, postdoctoral fellow in endocrinology and metabolism, 1957-58; sr. investigator Nat. Cancer Inst., Bethesda, Md., 1960-65; chief endocrine service NICHD, 1965-66; chief endocrinology Harbor-UCLA Med. Center, Torrance, Calif., 1966-72; chmn. dept. medicine Harbor-UCLA Med. Center, 1972-79; vis. prof. medicine Auckland Sch. Medicine, New Zealand, 1979-80; prof. medicine and physiology, chmn. dept. medicine U. Utah Sch. Medicine, Salt Lake City, 1980—. Mem. editorial bds. med. jours.; author 6 books in field; contbr. over 300 artilces to med. jours. Served with USPHS, 1960-66. Recipient Disting. Svc. award U. Chgo., 1973, Pharmacia award for outstanding contbns. to clin. chemistry, 1977, Gov.'s award State of Utah Sci. and Tech., 1988, also rsch. awards, Mastership award ACP, 1987. Mem. Am. Soc. Clin. Investigation, Am. Physiol. Soc., Assn. Am. PHysicians, Am. Soc. Andrology (pres.), Endocrine Soc. (v.p. Robert Williams award 1991), Soc. Study of Reprodn. (bd. dirs.), Pacific Coast Fertility Soc. (pres.), Western Assn. Physicians (pres.), Western Soc. Clin. Rsch. (Mayo Soley award), Soc. Pediatric Rsch., Alpha Omega Alpha. Office: U of Utah Med Ctr 50 N Medical Dr Salt Lake City UT 84132-0001

ODEN, ROBERT RUDOLPH, surgeon; b. Chgo., Dec. 2, 1922; s. Rudolph J.E. and Olga H. (Wahlquist) O.; m. Nancy Clow. BS, U. Ill., 1943; MD, Northwestern U., 1947, MS in Anatomy, 1947. Intern Augustana Hosp., Chgo., 1947-48, resident in surgery, 1948-49; resident in orthopaedics Hines Vets. Hosp., Chgo., 1949-51; resident in children's orthopaedics Shriner's Hosp., 1953-54; pvt. practice Chgo., 1954-57, Aspen, Colo., 1957—; clin. assoc. prof. in orthopaedics U. Colo.; orthopaedic surgeon U.S. Olympic Com., 1960, 72, 76, 80. Assoc. editor: Clin. Orthopaedics and Related Rsch. Trustee U.S. Ski Ednl. Found., 1967-82, Aspen Valley Hosp., 1978-86; founder Aspen Orthopaedic and Sports Medicine Pub. Found., 1985, Aspen Inst. for Theol. Futures, 1978, Great Tchrs. and Preachers Series Christ Episc. Ch., 1989; mem. organizing com. Aspen World Cup, 1976-92; founder, trustee Pitkin County Bank, 1983—; founder Aspen Pitkin Employee Housing, 1975. Recipient Blegan award for most outstanding svc. to U.S. skiing, 1985, Halsted award U.S. Ski Assn., 1987. Mem. Am. Acad. Orthopaedic Surgeons, ACS, Internat. Coll. Surgeons, Western Orthopaedic Assn., SICOT, Am. Assn. Bone & Joint Surgeons, Rocky Mountain Traumatologic Soc., Canadian Orthopaedic Assn., Am. Orthopaedic Soc. for Sports Medicine, Internat. Ski Safety Soc., ACL Study Group, Internat. Soc. Knee, Internat. Knee Inst., Phi Beta Kappa. Home: PO Box 660 Aspen CO 81612-0660 Office: 100 E Main St Aspen CO 81611-1778

ODEN, WILLIAM ARTHUR, minister, artist; b. Dallas, Mar. 27, 1920; s. William Arthur and Mattie Lee (Griffin) O.; m. Dorothy Lee Robinson, Nov. 21, 1941; children: Anna Lee, William Arthur III, Virginia Christina Oden Martin, Nicholas Robinson, Samuel Garner. BA, U. Tex., El Paso, 1953, MA, 1959; BFA, U. N.Mex., 1987. Ordained to ministry, Anglican Cath. Ch., 1991. Clerical N.Am. Aviation Co., Grand Prairie, Tex., 1941-42; examiner, auditor U.S. VA, Dallas, 1948-51; air traffic control specialist CAA and FAA, El Paso, Tex. and Albuquerque, 1951-77; artist Placitas, N.Mex., 1977—; min. Anglican Cath. Ch., Albuquerque, 1991—; chmn. Air Traffic Control Assn., El Paso, 1959-61; catechist Anglican Cath. Ch., Albuquerque, 1987—. Pioneered air traffic control procedures USAF, 1942-46; supply priest Anglican Cath. Ch., 1993—; author, speaker Air Traffic Control Goes to Coll., 1959; author, editor Fisherman publ., 1990—. Bd. dirs. Ranchos De Placitas Water and Sanitation Dist., 1980-94. Sgt. USAF, 1942-46. Mem. Art in the Mountain, Sons of Am. Revolution, Md. Geneol. Soc., Sandoval County Hist. Soc., Vintage Thunderbird Club Internat. Democrat. Home: Star Rt Box 312 Placitas NM 87043 Office: Saint Peters Ch 8100 Hamilton St NE Albuquerque NM 87122-3002

ODER, BROECK NEWTON, school emergency management consultant; b. Highland Park, Ill., Apr. 20, 1953; s. Bruce Newton and Mary Louise (Roe) O.; m. Jolene Marie Peragine, June 28, 1975 (dec. June 1979). BA in History, U. San Diego, 1974, MA in History, 1975; postgrad., U. N.Mex., 1976-79. Life C.C. teaching credential, Calif. Rsch. asst. to pres. U. San Diego, 1975; grad. asst. U. N.Mex., Albuquerque, 1976-79; tchr. history, chmn. dept. Santa Catalina Sch., Monterey, Calif., 1979—, asst. dean students, 1981-83, dir. ind. study, 1981—, dean students, 1983-91, dir. emergency planning, 1986—, dean campus affairs, 1991-94; dir. security, 1994—; mem. disaster preparedness coun. Monterey County Office Edn., 1988—; chair Diocesan Sch. Emergency Preparedness Coun., 1991—. Mem. bd. of tchrs. The Concord Rev.; contbr. articles to profl. publs. Participant Jail and Bail, Am. Cancer Soc., Monterey, 1988, 89; reviewer sch. emergency plans, Monterey, 1989—. Recipient award of merit San Diego Hist. Soc., 1975, Outstanding Tchr. award U. Chgo., 1985, Outstanding Young Educator award Monterey Peninsula Jaycees, 1988, resolution of commendation Calif. Senate Rules Com., 1988, cert. of commendation Calif. Gov.'s Office Emergency Svcs., 1991, nat. cert. of achievement Fed. Emergency Mgmt. Agy., 1991. Mem. ACLU, Am. Hist. Assn., Orgn. Am. Historians, Nat. Coun. on History Edn., Soc. for History Edn., Second Amendment Found., Individual Rights Found., NRA (life), Phi Alpha Theta. Office: Santa Catalina Sch 1500 Mark Thomas Dr Monterey CA 93940-5238

ODERMATT, DIANA B., educational administrator, educational consultant; b. Hollywood, Calif., Nov. 25, 1938; d. Harold Jr. and Mary H. (Wilson) Birtwistle; m. Robert Allen Odermatt, June 9, 1960; children: Kristin Ann, Kyle David. BA, Mills Coll., 1960. Statis. asst. Inst. Human Devel., U. Calif., Berkeley, 1960-62; from admissions counselor to dean admissions and fin. aid Mills Coll., Oakland, Calif., 1978-86; asst. dir. devel. Head-Royce Sch., Oakland, 1986-87, dir. devel., 1987-92; regional dir. devel. U. Calif., Berkeley, 1993—; cons. Western Region Coll. Bd., 1986—. Contbr. articles to profl. publs. Mem. Council for the Advancement and Support of Edn. (commn. on enrollment), Jr. League-Oakland-East Bay. Home: 140 Camino Don Miguel Orinda CA 94563-1710

ODLAND, ROBERT OLIVER, land use consultant; b. Yankton, S.D., Aug. 27, 1939; s. Orlando Marion and Dorothy (Oliver) O.; m. Charlotte Kelly. BS in Engring., U.S. Mil. Acad., West Point, N.Y., 1963; JD, U. Calif., Berkeley, 1972, M in City Planning, 1973. Bar: Calif. 1974; cert. land use planner. Regional planner Assn. Bay Area Govts., Berkeley, 1973-74; legis. staff Calif. Legislature, Sacramento, Calif., 1974-75; assoc. planner Sedway/Cooke, Planning Cons., San francisco, 1975-78; br. chief Nat. Renewable Energy Lab., Golden, Colo., 1978-81; cons. Odland Assocs., Livermore, Calif., 1981-85; sr. assoc. Sedway Cooke Assocs. Planning Cons., San Francisco, 1985—; lectr. in field. Contbr. numerous articles to profl. jours. Mem. state task force to draft changes Calif. Environ. Quality Act. Capt. U.S. Army, 1963-69. Mem. ABA, AAAS, AICP, Am. Planning Assn. (chairú environ. natural resources and energy divsn.), Am. Solar Energy Soc., State Bar Calif., Assn. Environ. Profls., World Future Soc., Urban Ecology (bd. dirs.). Unitarian. Home: 7530 Terrace Dr El Cerrito CA 94530-3017

O'DONNELL, LESLIE ANN, newspaper editor; b. Worcester, Mass., July 19, 1947; d. Jack and Beverly (Silverman) Kadis; m. L. Michael O'Donnell, Feb. 14, 1988; children: Christopher J. Glode, Jeremy G. Glode. AB, Barnard Coll., 1969; MSW, W.Va. U., 1975. News corr. Statesman Jour., Salem, Oreg., 1981-83; reporter Polk County Itemizer-Observer, Dallas, Oreg., 1984-85; trend editor News-Times, Newport, Oreg., 1985-89; freelance writer Oreg. Coast Mag., Florence, Oreg., 1987-90; entertainment editor News-Times, Newport, 1989-90, assoc. editor, 1990, mng. editor, 1990—. Sch. bd. mem. Falls City (Oreg.) Sch. Dist., 1981-85. Recipient Best Editorial First Pl. award Nat. Fedn. Press Women, 1993, 1st Pl. Best Editorial award Oreg. Newspaper Pubs. Assn., 1993, 1st Pl. Best News Coverage, 1993, Seven 1st Pl. awards Oreg. Press Women, 1987, 89, 90, 91, 92, 94. Mem. Oreg. Press Women, Oreg. Coast Coun. for the Arts, U. OReg. Seminar for Profl. Journalists (Wendell Webb fellow, 1987, 90). Office: News-Times PO Box 965 Newport OR 97365-0075

O'DONNELL, VICTORIA J., communication educator; b. Greensburg, Pa., Feb. 12, 1938; d. Victor C. and Helen A. (Detar) O'D.; children from previous marriage: Christopher O'Donnell Stupp, Browning William Stupp; m. Paul M. Monaco, Apr. 9, 1993. BA, Pa. State U., 1959, MA, 1961, PhD, 1968. Asst. prof. comm. Midwestern State U., Wichita Falls, Tex., 1965-67; prof., dept. chair comms. U. No. Tex., Denton, 1967-89, Ore. State U., Corvallis, 1989-91; prof. comm., basic course dir. Mont. State U., Bozeman, 1991-93, prof. comm., dir. honors program, 1993—; prof. Am. Inst. Fgn. Studies, London, 1988; cons. Arco Oil & Gas, Dallas, 1983-86, Federal Emergency Mgrs. Agy., Salt Lake City, 1986; speechwriter Sen. Mae Yih, Salem, Ore., 1989-91; steering com. Ore. Alliance Film & TV Educators, 1990-91. Author: Introduction to Public Communication, 1992, 2d edit., 1993; co-author: Persuasion, 1982, Propaganda and Persuasion, 1986, 2d edit., 1992; producer: (video) Women, War and Work, 1994. Bd. dirs. Friends of the Family, Denton, 1987-89, Bozeman Film Festival, 1991—; del. Tex. Dem. Convention, Denton, 1976. Grantee Mont. Com. for the Humanities, 1993, Ore. Coun. for the Humanities, 1991. Mem. Nat. Collegiate Honors Coun., Speech Comm. Assn., Internat. Comm. Assn., Univ. Film & Video Assn. (conf. v.p. 1989-91, bd. dirs. 1978-80), Western States Comm. Assn. Home: 290 Low Bench Rd Gallatin Gateway MT 59730-9741 Office: Univ Honors Program Mont State U Bozeman MT 59717

O'DONNELL, WILLIAM THOMAS, management consultant; b. Latrobe, Pa., Feb. 22, 1939; s. William Regis and Kathryn Ann (Coneff) O'D.; m. Judith Koetke, Oct. 1, 1965; children: William Thomas, William Patrick, Allison Rose, Kevin Raymond. Student Ea. N.Mex. U., 1958-61; student in mktg. John Carroll U., 1961-65, Ill. Inst. Tech., 1965-66; BSBA, U. Phoenix, 1982, MBA with distinction, 1984. Various sales positions Hickok Elec. Instrument Co., Cleve., 1961-65, Fairchild Semicondr., Mpls., 1965-67; Transitron Semicondr., Mpls., 1967-69; regional sales mgr. Burroughs Corp., Plainfield, N.J., 1967-71; mktg. mgr. Owens-Ill. Co., 1972-73, v.p. mktg. Pantek Co., subs. Owens-Ill. Co., Lewistown, Pa., 1973-75, v.p. mktg., nat. sales mgr., Toledo, 1975-76; mktg. mgr. Govt. Electronics div. group Motorola Co., Scottsdale, Ariz., 1976-80, U.S. mktg. mgr. radar positioning systems Motorola Govt. Electronics Group, 1981—; gen. mgr. J.K. Internat., Scottsdale, 1980-81; mgmt. cons. Pres. Cambridge Group, 1987—; v.p. mktg. Pinnacle Surg. Products, 1989, v.p. marketing, Kroy, Inc., 1992-94; mgmt. cons., 1994—; v.p. mktg. and bus. devel. Kroy Inc., 1992; adj. prof. Union Grad. Sch.; guest lectr. U. Mich. Grad. Sch. Bus. Adminstrn.; instr., chair strategic mgmt. U. Phoenix, 1988, pres. faculty, 1989—; Scottsdale Community Coll., Paradise Valley Community Coll.; talk show host Sta. KFNN, 1992-93. Area chair-gen. mgmt. Union Grad. Sch. Maricopa Community Coll., U. Phoenix. Chmn., Rep. Precinct, Burnsville, Minn., 1968-70; city fin. chmn., Burnsville; dir. community devel. U.S. Jaycees, Mpls., 1968-69; mem. Scottsdale 2000 Com. With USAF, 1957-61. Recipient Outstanding Performance award Maricopa Community Coll. System, 1987, Faciliation award, Maricopa Community Coll., Citation for Faciliation Ability U. Phoenix, 1986, 90, 93; named Hon. Citizen, Donaldsville, La., 1978; others. Mem. Am. Mktg. Assn., Afro-Am. Small Bus. Assn. (bd. dirs.), Amateur Athletic Union (swimming ofcl. 1980-82), Phoenix Execs. Club, U. Phoenix Faculty Club (bd. dirs., pres. 1988-91, recipient Presdl. Designation award, officer), North Cape Yacht Club, Scottsdale Racquet Club, Toftnees Country Club. Roman Catholic. Home: 8650 E Via Del Arbor Scottsdale AZ 85258-3526

O'DONNELL, WILSON EDWARD, museum director; b. Sharon, Pa., Feb. 17, 1952; s. Charles John and Charolette Jane (Magargee) O'D.; m. Carol Ann Brodeen, July 25, 1987. BA in Anthropology, Pa. State U., 1974; MA in History Mus. Studies, SUNY, Oneonta, 1982. Intern William Penn Meml. Mus., Harrisburg, Pa., 1975, Hist. Soc. York County, York, Pa., 1975; cons. Perry County Hist. Soc., Newport, Pa., 1978-79; curator of collections Cumberland County Hist. Soc., Carlisle, Pa., 1976-80; dir. Monmouth County Hist. Assn., Freehold, N.J., 1982-86; chief curator and mus. dir. N.J. Hist. Soc., Newark, 1986-88, dir., 1988-92; exec. dir. Mus. History and Industry, Seattle, 1993—; adj. faculty Mus. Am. Folk Art, N.Y.C., 1987. Author: (exhibit catalogues) It's in the Cards, 1976, Thus United Free: New Jersey in the Age of the Constitution, 1976. Mem. Monmouth County Heritage Com., Freehold, N.J., 1982-87; active Mountains to Sound, Greenway Trust. Mem. Am. Assn. Mus., Am. Assn. for State and Local History, Rotary (Puget Sound chpt.), Phi Beta Kappa (bd. trustees Puget Sound chpt. 1994-95). Office: Mus of History & Industry 2700 24th Ave E Seattle WA 98112-2031

O'DOWD, DONALD DAVY, retired university administrator; b. Manchester, N.H., Jan. 23, 1927; s. Hugh Davy and Laura (Morin) O'D.; m. Janet Louise Fithian, Aug. 23, 1953; children: Daniel D., Diane K., James E., John M. BA summa cum laude, Dartmouth Coll., 1951; postgrad. (Fulbright fellow), U. Edinburgh, Scotland, 1951-52; MA, Harvard U., 1955, PhD, 1957. Instr., asst. prof. psychology, dean freshmen Wesleyan U., Middletown, Conn., 1955-60; assoc. prof., prof. of psychology, dean Univ. Oakland Univ., Rochester, Mich., 1960-65, provost, 1965-70; pres. Oakland U., Rochester, Mich., 1970-80; exec. vice chancellor SUNY, Albany, 1980-84; pres. U. of Alaska Statewide System, 1984-90. Chmn. U.S. Arctic Rsch. Commn.; sr. cons. Assn. Governing Bds. of Univs. and Colls. Carnegie Corp. fellow, 1965-66. Mem. Am. Psychol. Assn., AAAS, Phi Beta Kappa, Sigma Xi. Home and Office: 1550 La Vista Del Oceano Santa Barbara CA 93109-1739

O'DRISCOLL, MARILYN LUTZ, kindergarten educator; b. L.A.; d. Robert Thomas and Helen Mary (Cardamone) Lutz; m. John P. O'Driscoll Jr., Jan. 15, 1966 (dec. 1978); children: Kelley, John, Patrick. BS in Edn., U. So. Calif., 1961, cert. lang. devel. specialist, 1990. Cert. tchr., Calif. Tchr. kindergarten Montebello (Calif.) Sch. Dist., 1961-64, Garvey Sch. Dist., Rosemead, Calif., 1964—; program quality reviewer San Gabriel Consortium, 1988-94; mem. parent bd. Incarnation Sch., Glendale, Calif., 1990-92, chmn. sch. site coun., 1990-93; participant ednl. TV program, 1989—. Pres. Incarnation Parish Coun., 1993-95. Mem. ASCD, NEA, Garvey Edn. Assn., Calif. Tchrs. Assn., Wome of Troy (life), Spirit of Troy (life), Kappa Delta.

OECHEL, WALTER CLARENCE, ecologist; b. San Diego, Jan. 15, 1945; s. Walter C. Oechel and Gloria Dawn Gordon; m. Judith Lynne Oechel, 1967. BA, San Diego State U., 1966; PhD, U. Calif., Riverside, 1970. Asst. to assoc. prof. McGill U., Montreal, Que., Can., 1970-78; rsch. prof. San Diego State U., 1978-83, prof., 1983—; dir. systems ecology rsch. group San Diego State U., 1982-87, Global Change Rsch. Group, 1992—; cons. in field, 1970—. Editor: Dynamics and Management of Mediterranean Type Ecosystems, 1981, Being Alive on Land, 1984, Plant Response to Stress, 1985, The Role of Fire in Mediterranean Type Ecosystems, 1994; contbr. 120 articles to profl. jours.; mem. many editorial bds. Grantee NSF, 1972-85, 92—, Dept. of Energy, 1978—, Nat. Park Svc., 1990-94. Mem. AAAS, Ecol. Soc. Am. (chmn. physiol. ecology sect. 1978-79). Office: San Diego State U Dept Biology San Diego CA 92182

OEDEKOVEN, BYRON FRANK, protective services official; b. Gillette, Wyo., Feb. 15, 1955; s. Charles Robert and Rhyllis Rae (Richmond) O.; m. Marjorie Grace Orvalla, Feb. 1, 1985. Student, Black Hills State Coll., 1974; AS in Criminal Justice, Sheridan C.C., 1980. Animal control officer Gillette Police Dept., 1974-75, police officer I, 1975-77, police officer II, 1977-78, police sgt., 1978-83, police lt., 1983-86; sheriff Campbell County Sheriff's Dept., Gillette, 1987—. Mem. Wyo. Com. Employer Support of the Guard and Res. Named Outstanding Young Law Enforcement Officer, Gillette Jaycees, 1977, 80, Outstanding Young Men in Am., Nat. Jaycees, 1977; recipient Dale Carnegie Impromptu Speaking award, 1983, Dale Carnegie Human Rels. Achievement award, 1983, Svc. to the City award Mayor of Gillette, 1986, Friend of Edn. award Campbell County Sch. Dist., 1989. Mem. NRA (life), SAR, Wyo. Assn. Sheriffs and Chiefs (2d v.p.), Internat. Assn. Chiefs of Police, Nat. Sheriffs' Assn., FBI Nat. Acad. Assocs., Wyo. Peace Officers' Assn., Wyo. Sheriffs' Assn., Mont. Snowmobile Assn., S.D. Snowmobile Assn., Wyo. Snowmobile Assn., Am. Quarter Horse Assn., Mayflower Soc., Thomas Rogers Soc., Gillette Jaycees, Masons, Shriners, Order Ea. Star, Valley of Orient of Sheridan, Kalif Temple Sheridan. Republican. Office: Campbell County Sheriff 600 W Boxelder Rd Gillette WY 82718-5219

OEHLBERG, RICHARD N., technical management executive; b. Evanston, Ill., Nov. 7, 1942; s. Nicholas Mathias and Margaret (Hoyne) O.; m. Donna Klein, Dec. 21, 1968; children—Daniel Richard, Mark Richard, Lora Ann. B.S. in Physics and Math., Loyola U., 1965; M.S. in Physics, So. Ill. U., 1967; Ph.D., U. Notre Dame, 1972; M.P.A., U. So. Calif., 1976. Physicist, U.S. Naval Weapons Ctr., China Lake, Calif., 1972-74; program mgr. U.S. Nuclear Regulatory Commn., Washington, 1974-76; project mgr. Electric Power Research Inst., Palo Alto, Calif., 1976-85, technical asst. to v.p., 1985-87; sr. project mgr., 1987-94, tech. transfer exec., 1994—. Contbr. articles to profl. jours. Bd. dirs. Stanford Fed. Credit Union, 1979-82, pres., 1981-82. NDEA fellow, 1967-68; U. So. Ill. Fellow, 1966-67. Mem. Am. Phys. Soc., Am. Nuclear Soc., Am. Mgmt. Assn., Sigma Pi Sigma. Club: Decathelon. Office: Electric Power Research Inst 3412 Hillview Ave Palo Alto CA 94304-1395

OESTMANN, IRMA EMMA, minister, artist, educator; b. Auburn, Nebr., May 6, 1930; d. Martin Edward and Magdalene Augusta (Volkman) O.; m. Allister Roland Behrends, July 29, 1948 (div. 1968); children: John, Allan, Patricia, William, Michael, Russell, Kurt. BS in Edn., U. Nebr., 1972. Ordained min. Unity Ch., Unity Village, Mo., 1982. Dairy farm pvt. farmer Johnson, Nebr., 1948-68; art tchr. Burke High Sch., Omaha, 1972-73, L.A. (Calif.) Pub. Schs., 1974-77; mgr. U-Rent Furniture, Canoga Park, Calif., 1978-80; min. There Is A Way TV Ministry, Palm Springs, Calif., 1982-83, Unity Ch. of Truth, Pomona, Calif., 1983-85, Unity of Del Ray Beach, Fla., 1986-87, Unity of Jupiter, Fla., 1988-90, Unity Ch. of San Gabriel, Calif., 1991-94, United Fellowship of Grants Pass, Oreg., 1994—; cert. hypnotist, self-instr., therapist Encino, Calif., 1978-80; pvt. children's art tchr., Upland, Calif., 1986-87. Artist oil and watercolor paintings, 1968—; author, artist: (audio tapes) Self Help and Meditation, 1980—; producer, host: (tv panel series) The Truth Is, 1989; contbr. poems and articles to mags. Mem. San Gabriel (Calif.) Cmty. Coun., 1991-93. Home: 233 SW Rogue River Ave Ste 846 Grants Pass OR 97526-2935 Office: Unity Fellowship Grants Pass Grants Pass OR 97526

OESTREICH, PAUL CHRISTOPHER, electronics engineer; b. Salt Lake City, Dec. 14, 1963; s. Alfred H. and Carol Deane (Salmon) O.; m. Sheryl L. Dirksen, Aug. 20, 1989. BSEE, U. Utah, 1987; MS in Engring. Mgmt., U. Dayton, 1989; ME in Elec. Engring., U. Utah, 1994. Elec. engr. AFMC Ogden Air Logistics Ctr., Hill AFB, Utah, 1987, HQ Air Force Logistics Command, Wright Patterson AFB, Ohio, 1987-88; elec. engr. Indsl. Process Br. HQ Air Force Logistics Command, Wright Patterson AFB, 1989; elec. engr. Software Engring. div. Ogden Air Logistics Ctr., Hill AFB, Utah, 1989—. Mem. IEEE, U.S. Cycling Fedn. Home: 3548 Country Manor Rd Salt Lake City UT 84121-5566 Office: Ogden Air Logistics Ctr 7278 4th St Bldg 100 Hill Air Force Base UT 84056-5205

OFFENKRANTZ, WILLIAM CHARLES, psychiatrist; b. Sept. 2, 1924. BS in Biol. Sci., Rutgers U., 1945; MD, Columbia U., 1947; cert. in psychoanalysis, William Alanson White Inst., N.Y.C., 1957, Chgo. Inst. Psychoanalysis, 1966. Diplomate Am. Bd. Psychiatry and Neurology, Nat. Bd. Med. Examiners. Intern Jersey City Med. Ctr., 1947-48; resident in neuropsychiatry VA Hosp., Lyon, N.J., 1948-50; resident in psychiatry N.Y. State Psychiat. Inst.-Columbia-Presbyn. Med. Ctr., N.Y.C., 1950-51; pvt. practice N.Y.C., 1951-53; assoc. rsch. scientist in psychiatry Creedmoor Inst. for Psychobiologic Studies, Queens Village, N.Y., 1955-56; pvt. practice San Diego, 1956-57; chief cons. and liaison svc. psychiatry U. Chgo. Hosps. and Clinics, 1957-58; from asst. to assoc. prof. dept. psychiatry sch. medicine U. Chgo., 1957-71, prof., 1971-79, dir. residency tng. in psychiatry Sch. Medicine, 1958-69; prof. psychoanalysis and psychiatry dept. psychiatry and mental health scis., dir. divsn. psychoanalysis Med. Coll. Wis., Milw., 1979-87; pvt. practice Milw., 1979-87; dir. consultation and liaison svc. Milwaukee County Gen. Hosp., Milw., 1979-80; dir. out-patient svcs. Milwaukee County Mental Health Complex, Milw., 1980-81; dir. psychotherapy ctr. Columbia Hosp., Milw., 1981-87; pvt. practice Scottsdale, Ariz., 1987—; chief psychotherapy tng. Maricopa Med. Ctr., Phoenix, 1987—; asst. psychiatrist Vanderbilt Clinic Columbia-Presbyn. Med. Ctr., N.Y.C., 1950-51; cons. Family Svc. Assn., San Diego, 1956-57, TV series Sleep and Dreaming ABC-TV, Chgo., 1960, Peace Corps, Malaya Project, 1960, Youth Guidance Agy., Chgo., 1959-66, U. Chgo. Svc. at Ill. State Psychiat. Inst., 1959-70; mem. attending staff dept. psychiatry Maricopa Med. Ctr., 1988—; mem. consulting med. staff Camelback Hosps., Ariz., 1989—. Mem. editl. bd. Jour. Nervous and Mental Disease, 1965-71; reviewer Am. Jour. Psychiatry, 1965—, Archives of Gen. Psychiatry Vol. 30, 1974, Am. Handbook of Psychiatry, Vol. 5, 1975, Psychoanalytic Psychotherapy, Manual of Psychiatric Peer Rev., 1976, 3rd edit., 1980; (with John Crayton) The Pschiatric Formulation: A Handbook for Board Candidates, 1993. Capt. U.S. Army Med. Corps, 1953-55. Fellow Am. Psychiat. Assn. (life, therapy com. 1968-69, nat. adv. com. for CHAMPUS-APA peer rev. contract 1977-83, peer rev. com. 1980-86, com. on practice of psychotherapy 1986-90), Am. Psychoanalytic Assn. (life, co-chmn., peer rev. com. 1974-82, mem. 1982-86, chmn. joint DSM-III com. 1978-81, dir. Wis. psychoanalytic new tng. facility 1985-87), Chgo. Psychoanalytic Soc. (geographic rule tng. analyst Ariz. 1989—); mem. Internat. Psychoanalytic Assn., Group Advancement Psychiatry (mem. therapy com. 1962—, bd. dirs. 1981-83), Chgo. Inst. Psychoanalysis (mem. faculty 1966-87, mem. progression com. 1974-75, chmn. dream rsch. workshop 1964-79, tng. and supervising analyst 1978-87, geog. rule tng. analyst Wis. psychoanalytic new tng. facility 1979-87). Home: PO Box 6002 Carefree AZ 85377-6002 Office: 6619 N Scottsdale Rd Scottsdale AZ 85250-4421

O'FLAHERTY, TERRENCE, journalist; b. What Cheer, Iowa, July 15, 1917; s. Leo J. and Lelia (Thomas) O'F. B.A., U. Calif. at Berkeley, 1939. Hist. researcher Metro-Goldwyn-Mayer Studios, 1940-42; columnist San Francisco Chronicle, 1949-86; writer nationally syndicated TV column, 1960-86; mem. bd. Peabody Awards for Radio and TV, 1952-84. Host: TV program PM West, San Francisco, 1961-62; created The Terrence O'Flaherty TV Collection for UCLA TV Archives and Theater Arts Library, 1987; contbr. articles to McCalls, Reader's Digest, TV Guide. Served as lt. USNR, 1942-46. Recipient Gov.'s award (Emmy) NATAS, 1988. Mem. Beta Theta Pi. Home and Office: 4 Whiting St San Francisco CA 94133-2419

OFNER, WILLIAM BERNARD, lawyer; b. L.A., Aug. 24, 1929; s. Harry D. and Gertrude (Skoss) Offner; m. Florence Ila Maxwell, Apr. 13, 1953 (div. 1956). AA, L.A. City Coll., 1949; BA, Calif. State U., L.A., 1953; LLB, Loyola U., L.A., 1965; postgrad. Sorbonne, 1951, cert. de Langue Francaise, 1987; postgrad. U. So. Calif., 1966, Glendale Community Coll., 1986-92. Bar: Calif. 1966, U.S. Dist. Ct. Calif. 1966, U.S. Supreme Ct. 1972. Assoc. Thomas Moore and Assocs., L.A., 1967-69; pvt. practice, L.A., 1969-70, 74—; assoc. Peter Lam, L.A., 1981—, mgn. atty. 1993—; assoc. C.M. Coronel, 1986-87, Jack D. Janofsky, 1987-89, Mario P. Gonzalez, 1990-92; lectr. Van Norman U., 1975. With USNR, 1947-54. Mem. Inst. Gen. Semantics, Inst. for Antiquity and Christianity, Soc. Judgement, Soc. Etudes Juives, Soc. des Amis De l'Universite de Paris, Shakespeare Soc. (bd. dirs. 1987-91), L.A. Athletic Club, Toastmasters. Democrat. Avocations: painting, photography, linguistics. Office: 1102 N Brand Blvd # 24 Glendale CA 91202-2504

OFTE, DONALD, environmental executive, former management consultant; b. N.Y.C., Aug. 23, 1929; s. Sverre and Ingeborg Ofte; m. Margaret Mae McHenney, July 23, 1955; children: Marc Christian, Nancy Carolyn Ofte Appleby, Kirk Donald Jr. BA in Chemistry, Dana Coll., 1952; postgrad. study metall. engring., Ohio State U., 1958-60. Jr. chemist Inst. Atomic Research, Ames, Iowa, 1952-53; sr. research chemist Monsanto Research Corp., Miamisburg, Ohio, 1958-66; ops. engr. AEC, Miamisburg, 1966-69; br. chief, div. dir. ops. office AEC, Albuquerque, 1969-73; mgr. Pinellas area office AEC, Largo, Fla., 1973-79; mgr. Rocky Flats area office Dept. Energy, Golden, Colo., 1979-82; asst. mgr. devel. and prodn. Dept. Energy, Albuquerque, 1982-83, dep. mgr. ops. office, 1983-84; prin. dep. asst. sec. Dept. Energy Defense Programs, Washington, 1984-87; mgr. ops. office Dept. Energy, Idaho Falls, Idaho, 1987-89; mgmt. cons. Idaho Falls, 1989-92; v.p. govt. ops. United Engrs. and Constructors, Denver, 1992-93; v.p. Adv. Scis., Inc., Albuquerque, 1993-94; pres. FERMCO, Cin., 1994—; v.p. Fluor-Daniel, Inc., 1994—; affiliate prof. Idaho State U., 1990-92; bd. dirs. Denver Fed. Exec. Bd., 1979-82. Author: (with others) Plutonium 1960, 1965, Physiciochemical; contbr. articles to profl. jours. on metallurgy and ceramics. Campaign chmn. United Way Pinellas, St. Petersburg, Fla., 1978; bd. dirs. Bonneville County United Way, Idaho Rsch. Found.; mem. adv. bd. Teton Peaks Council Boy Scouts of Am., 1987-92, Eastern Idaho Tech. Coll.; chmn. Excellence in Edn. Fund Com., 1990-92; vice chmn., bd. dirs. Rio Grande Ch. ARC, Albuquerque, 1982-84. Served to lt. (j.g.) USN, 1953-57. Recipient citation AEC for Apollo 12 SNAP 27 Radioisotope Generator, 1969, High Quality Performance award AEC, 1968, Group Achievement award NASA, 1972; Meritorious Svc. award Dept. Energy, 1985, Disting. Career Svc. award, 1989. Mem. Am. Chem. Soc., Am. Nuclear Soc., Am. Soc. Metals, Nat. Contract Mgmt. Assn., Am. Soc. Pub. Adminstrs., Suncoast Archeol. Soc., Idaho Falls C. of C. (bd. dirs., cmty. svc. award 1990),

Rotary Internat. Home: 8820 Eagle Creek Ct West Chester OH 45069-6478 Office: Fermco PO Box 538704 Cincinnati OH 45253-8704

O'GARA, BARBARA ANN, soap company executive; b. Newark, Aug. 8, 1953; d. Frank Percy and Rose (Giordano) Stevens. AA, Keystone Jr. Coll., 1973; BS, U. Ariz., 1976. Media buyer Wells, Rich, Green/Townsend, Irvine, Calif., 1977-80; dist. sales mgr. Dial Corp., Phoenix, 1980-82; regional sales mgr. Guest Supply, Inc., North Brunswick, N.J., 1982-85; dir. hotel mktg. and sales Neutrogena Corp., L.A., 1985-92, v.p. hotel mktg. and sales, 1992—. Keystone Jr. Coll. scholar, 1972, Morris County scholar, 1971; recipient Outstanding Sales Accomplishment award Armour-Dial, 1981. Mem. Am. Mktg. Assn., Am. Mgmt. Assn., Am. Hotel and Motel Assn., Network Exec. Women in Hospitality. Republican. Roman Catholic. Avocations: tennis, aerobics, running, skiing, photography. Home: Penthouse A 2218 Main St Santa Monica CA 90405-2273 Office: Neutrogena Corp 5760 W 96th St Los Angeles CA 90045-5544

OGAWA, DENNIS MASAAKI, American studies educator; b. Manzanar, Calif., Sept. 7, 1943; s. Frank M. and Alice T. (Tanaka) O.; m. Amy Ranko, Jan. 1, 1973; children: Quin, Owen, Autumn. BA, UCLA, 1966, MA, 1967, PhD, 1969. Prof. Am. studies U. Hawaii at Manoa, Honolulu, 1969—; dir. Nippon Golden Network, Honolulu, 1982—. Author: Jan Ken Po, 1973, Kodomo No Tame Ni, 1978; co-author: Ellison Onizuka: Remembrance, 1986. Dir. Japanese Cultural Ctr., Hawaii, 1992—. Danforth Found. assoc., 1975; named Disting. Historian Hawaiian Hist. Soc., 1992; fellow Japan Soc. Promotion of Sci., 1978, East West Ctr., Honolulu, 1979. Mem. Assn. Asian-Am. Scholars. Democrat. Office: Univ Hawaii Am Studies Dept 1890 E West Rd Honolulu HI 96822-2318

OGDEN, DANIEL MILLER, JR., government official, educator; b. Clarksburg, W.Va., Apr. 28, 1922; s. Daniel Miller and Mary (Maphis) O.; m. Valeria Juan Munson, Dec. 28, 1946; children: Janeth Lee Martin, Patricia Jo Hunter, Daniel Munson. BA in Polit. Sci., Wash. State U., 1944; MA, U. Chgo., 1947, PhD, 1949. From instr. to assoc. prof. Wash. State U., Pullman, 1949-61; staff asst. resources program U.S. Dept. Interior, 1961-64; asst. dir. U.S. Bur. Outdoor Recreation, 1964-67; dir. budget U.S. Dept. Interior, Washington, 1967-68; dean Coll. Humanities and Social Scis. Colo. State U., Ft. Collins, 1968-76; disting. vis. prof. Lewis and Clark Coll. and Portland (Oreg.) State U., 1977-78; dir. Office of Power Mktg. Coordination U.S. Dept. Energy, 1978-84; mgr. Pub. Power Coun., Portland, Oreg., 1984-88, ret., 1988; mem. profl. staff com. interstate and fgn. commerce U.S. Senate, 1956-57; spll. asst. to chmn. Dem. Nat. Com., 1960-61; lectr. Mgmt. Devel. Ctrs., U.S. Office Pers. Mgmt., 1966—. Co-author: Electing the President, rev. edit., 1968, American National Government, 7th edit., 1970, American State and Local Government, 5th edit., 1972, Washington Politics, 1960, How National Policy Is Made, 2d edit., 1994, Committeeman Wash. Dem. Cen. Com., 1952-56; chmn. Whitman County Dem. Cen. Com., 1958-60; chmn. 49th Legis. Dist. Dem. Com., 1990-94; chmn. Clark County Dem. Cen. Com., 1994—. With U.S. Army, 1943-46. Committeeman Wash. Dem. Ctrl. Com., 1952-56; chmn. Whitman County Dem. Ctrl. Com., 1958-60; chmn. 49th Legis. Dist. Dem. Com., 1990-94; chmn. Clark County Dem. Ctrl. com., 1994—. With inf. U.S. Army, 1943-46. Mem. Phi Beta Kappa, Phi Kappa Phi, Pi Sigma Alpha, Sigma Delta Chi. Mem. Unitarian Ch. Home: 3118 NE Royal Oak Dr Vancouver WA 98662-7435

OGDEN, JEAN LUCILLE, sales executive; b. Chgo., Jan. 20, 1950; d. George William and Mary Elizabeth (MacKenzie) Anderson; m. Michael Jude Ogden, Aug. 27, 1977 (div. Dec. 1983). BA with honors, U. Calif., Santa Barbara, 1971. Sales rep. Am. Hosp. Supply Co., Irvine, Calif., 1975-77, Abbott Labs., HPD, L.A., 1977-78, Gillette Co., Albuquerque, 1978-79, Unitek Corp., Monrovia, Calif., 1979-86, Nat. Patent Dental Products, San Diego, 1986-87; area mgr. Branson Ultrasonics Corp., L.A., 1987—. Mem., co-chair Nat. Multiple Sclerosis Soc., San Diego, 1983—; mem. Am. Cancer Soc., San Diego, 1985—, Zool. Soc., San Diego, 1984-85. Named one of Outstanding Young Women in Am., 1984. Mem. AAUW, NAFE, Med. Mktg. Assn., Salesmasters Albuquerque, Soroptimist Internat. (officer Carlsbad and Oceanside, Calif. chpt. 1983-85), Alpha Phi (house corp. bd. Long Beach chpt. 1974-75, chpt. advisor 1975-76). Republican. Office: Branson Ultrasonics Corp 12955 E Perez Pl La Puente CA 91746-1414

OGDEN, VALERIA JUAN, management consultant, state representative; b. Okanogan, Wash., Feb. 11, 1924; d. Ivan Bodwell and Pearle (Wilson) Munson; m. Daniel Miller Ogden Jr., Dec. 28, 1946; children: Janeth Lee Ogden Martin, Patricia Jo Ogden Hunter, Daniel Munson Ogden. BA magna cum laude, Wash. State U., 1946. Exec. dir. Potomac Coun. Camp Fire, Washington, 1964-68, Ft. Collins (Colo.) United Way, 1969-73, Designing Tomorrow Today, Ft. Collins, 1973-74, Poudre Valley Community Edn. Assn., Ft. Collins, 1977-78; pres. Valeria M. Ogden, Inc., Kensington, Md., 1978-81; nat. field cons. Camp Fire, Inc., Kansas City, Mo., 1980-81; exec. dir. Nat. Capital Area YWCA, Washington, 1981-84, Clark County YWCA, Vancouver, Wash., 1985-89; pvt. practice mgmt. cons. Vancouver, 1989—; mem. Wash. Ho. of Reps., 1991—; lectr. in field; adj. faculty pub. adminstrn. program Lewis and Clark Coll., Portland (Oreg.) State U., 1979—; mem. Pvt. Industry Coun., Vancouver, 1986. Author: Camp Fire Membership, 1980. County V chair Larimer County Dems., Ft. Collins, 1974-75; mem. precinct com. Clark County Dems., Vancouver, 1986-88; mem. Wash. State Coun. Vol. Action, Olympia, 1986-90; treas. Mortar Bd. Nat. Found., Vancouver, 1987—; chair Clark County Coun. Homeless, Vancouver, 1989-94. Named Citizen of Yr. Ft. Collins Bd. of Realtors, 1975; recipient Gulick award Camp Fire Inc., 1956, Alumna Achievement award Wash. State U. Alumni Assn., 1988. Mem. Internat. Assn. Vol. Adminstrs. (pres. Boulder 1989-90), Nat. Assn. YWCA Exec. Dirs. Assn. (nat. bd. nominating com. 1988-90), Women in Action, Philanthropic and Ednl. Orgn., Phi Beta Kappa. Democrat. Home: 3118 NE Royal Oak Dr Vancouver WA 98662-7435 Office: John L O'Brien Bldg State Ave NE Rm 342 Olympia WA 98501-1134

OGG, WILSON REID, poet, lyricist, curator, publisher, lawyer, educator; b. Alhambra, Calif., Feb. 26, 1928; s. James Brooks and Mary (Wilson) O. Student Pasadena Jr. Coll., 1946; A.B., U. Calif. at Berkeley, 1949, J.D., 1952; Cultural D in Philosophy of Law, World Univ. Roundtable, 1983. Bar: Calif. Assoc. trust Dept. Wells Fargo Bank, San Francisco, 1954-55; pvt. practice law, Berkeley, 1955-78; adminstrv. law judge, 1974-93; real estate broker, cons., 1974-78; curator-in-residence Pinebrook, 1964—; owner Pinebrook Press, Berkeley, Calif., 1988—; rsch. atty., legal editor dept. of continuing edn. of bar U. Calif. Extension, 1958-63; psychology instr. 25th Sta. Hosp., Taegu, Korea, 1954; English instr. Taegu English Lang. Inst., Taegu, 1954. Trustee World U., 1976-80; dir. admissions Internat. Soc. for Phil. Enquiry, 1981-84; dep. dir. gen. Internat. Biographical Centre, Eng., 1986—; dep. gov. Am. Biographical Inst. Research Assn., 1986—. Served with AUS, 1952-54. Cert. community coll. instr. Mem. VFW, AAAS, ABA, State Bar Calif., San Francisco Bar Assn., Am. Arbitration Assn. (nat. panel arbitrators), World Univ. Round Table, World Future Soc. (profl. mem.), Calif. Soc. Psychical Study (pres., chmn. bd. 1963-65), Parapsychol. Assn. (assoc.), Internat. Soc. Unified Sci., Internat. Soc. Poets, (life), Internat. Platform Assn., Amnesty Internat., Am. Civil Liberties Union, Intertel, Internat. Soc. Individual Liberty, Mensa, Lawyers in Mensa, Triple Nine Soc., Wisdom Soc., Inst. Noetic Scis., Psychic Sci. Spl. Interest Group, Men's Inner Circle of Achievement, Truman Libr. Inst. (hon.), Am. Legion, Faculty Club (U. Calif.), City Commons Club (Berkeley), Commonwealth Club of Calif., Town Hall Club of Calif., Marines Meml. Club, Masons, Shriners, Elks. Unitarian. Contbr. numerous articles profl. jours; contbr. poetry to various mags. including American Poetry Anthology Vol. VI Number 5, Hearts on Fire: A Treasury of Poems on Love, Vol. IV, 1987, New Voices in American Poetry, 1987, The Best Poems of the 90's, Distinguished Poets of America, The Poetry of Life A Treasury of Moments Am. Poetry Anthology, Vol. VII, 1988, Nat. Libr. Poets, 1992, Disting. Poets Of Am., 1993, The Best Modern Writer of 1994, Parnassus of World Poets, 1994, 95, Best Poems of 1995. Home: Pinebrook 1104 Keith Ave Berkeley CA 94708-1607 Office: 8 Bret Harte Way Berkeley CA 94708-1611

OGIER, WALTER THOMAS, retired physics educator; b. Pasadena, Calif., June 18, 1925; s. Walter Williams and Aileen Vera (Polhamus) O.; m. Mayrene Miriam Gorton, June 27, 1954; children: Walter Charles, Margaret Miriam, Thomas Earl, Kathryn Aileen. B.S., Calif. Inst. Tech., 1947, Ph.D. in Physics, 1953. Research fellow Calif. Inst. Tech., 1953; instr. U. Calif. at Riverside, 1954-55, asst. prof. physics, 1955-60; asst. prof. physics Pomona Coll., Claremont, Calif., 1960-62, assoc. prof., 1962-67, prof. physics, 1967-89, prof. emeritus, 1989—, chmn. dept., 1972-89. Contbr. articles on metals, liquid helium, X-rays and proton produced X-rays to profl. jours. Served with USNR, 1944-46. NSF Sci. Faculty fellow, 1966-67. Mem. Am. Phys. Soc., Am. Assn. Physics Tchrs. (pres. So. Calif. sect. 1967-69), Tau Beta Pi. Home: 8555 San Gabriel Rd Atascadero CA 93422-4928

OGIMACHI, NAOMI NEIL, retired chemist; b. L.A., Oct. 20, 1925; s. Tamuro and Yasuko (Togashi) O.; m. Frances Imogene Bennett, July 27, 1956; children: David J., Catharine A., Shawn N., April J. BS, UCLA, 1950; PhD, U. Calif., Berkeley, 1956. Rsch. chemist E.I. DuPont de Nemours, Wilmington, Del., 1955-57, U.S. Naval Ordnance Test Sta., China Lake, Calif., 1957-59; sr. scientist Rocketdyne div. Rockwell Internat., Canoga Park, Calif., 1959-70; rsch. chemist Halocarbon Products Corp., Hackensack, N.J., 1970-75; mgr. chem. process devel. Teledyne McCormick, Hollister, Calif., 1975-89. Contbr. articles to profl. jours.; patentee in field. Sgt. U.S. Army, 1944-46, ETO. Fellow AAAS; mem. Royal Soc. Chemistry (assoc.), Am. Chem. Soc., Sigma Xi, Phi Kappa Phi. Democrat. Methodist. Home: 1218 Santa Clara St Eureka CA 95501-0935

OGLE, EDWARD PROCTOR, JR., investment counseling executive; b. Inglewood, Calif., Dec. 20, 1935; s. Edward Proctor and Allene Emma (Blumenthal) O.; m. Elizabeth Lovejoy Myers, Mar. 28, 1958; children: Kathryn Ogle Nava, Terry Ogle Nelson, Wendy Ogle Reeves. BA, U. So. Calif., 1964; MA, Claremont Grad. Sch., 1980. Cert. fin. planning practitioner. Zone mgr. Investors Diversified Svcs., Pasadena, Calif., 1964-66; asst. mgr. Merrill Lynch Pierce Fenner Smith, Pasadena, 1966-72; mgr. Clark Dodge & Co-Capital Place Dept., L.A., 1972-74; sr. v.p. Security Pacific Bank - Pacific Century Group, L.A., 1974-86; mgr., registered prin. Brown Bros. Harriman & Co., L.A., 1986—. Author: (booklet) Role of Bank Trust Department, 1981; editor (booklet) Parade Operations Manual, 1992, 93. Sec. Tournament of Roses Assn., Pasadena, 1976—; mem. Town Hall of Calif., L.A., 1977—; mem. Rep. Presdl Task Force, Orange County, Calif., 1984—; mem. L.A. World Affairs Coun., 1985—; elder Presbyn. Ch. Recipient Corp. Fund Raising Cert. United Way, L.A., 1978-80, Exec. Mgmt. Cert. Claremont Grad. Sch., 1979, Mgmt. and Exec. Cert. Security Pacific Bank, L.A., 1981. Mem. Internat. Assn. Fin. Planners, Drucker Ctr. Mgmt. Assn., Claremont Grad. Sch. Alumni Assn. (pres. 1984-86), Pasadena Bond Club, Bond Club L.A., Jonathan Club. Republican. Office: Brown Bros Harriman & Co 355 S Grand Ave Ste 3250 Los Angeles CA 90071-1592

OGLE, JACK TIMOTHY, army officer; b. Waukegan, Ill., Jan. 19, 1956; s. James Harrison Ogle and Addie (Prather) Gregory; m. Diane Christine Sherrill, Feb. 21, 1987; children: Sarah, Amanda, Andrew. AAS in Aviation Sci., Ctrl. Tex. Coll., 1982; BS in Aviation Mgmt./Gen. Bus., Am. Tech. U., 1983. Enlisted U.S. Army, 1975, advanced through grades to maj.; attack pilot U.S. Army/Tex. Nat. Guard, Austin, 1976-83; corp. pilot Chevron U.S.A., New Orleans, 1980-82; charter pilot Petroleum Helicopter, Lafayette, La., 1984-86; sect. leader, instr. pilot Western ARNG Aviation Tng. Site, Tucson, Ariz., 1986-89; airfield ops. officer Ariz. Army Nat. Guard, Tucson, 1989—. Mem. Nat. Guard Assn. U.S., Army Aviation Assn. Am. (sr. v.p. Tucson chpt.). Home: 521 E Mountain Sunrise Pl Tucson AZ 85704-7238 Office: Army Aviation Support Fclty Silver Bell AHP Marana AZ 85653

OGLE, JOSEPH WOMACK, composer, retired piano teacher; b. Guthrie, Okla., Oct. 25, 1902; s. James Taylor and Ella (Womack) O.; m. Inez Helen Klein, Aug. 9, 1929; 1 child, Dottie Ella. BA, MusB, Phillips U., 1925; postgrad., Columbia U., 1924-28; studied with various teachers. Chmn. piano dept. Lon Morris Coll., Jacksonville, Tex., 1928-29, 30, Milligan (Tenn.) Coll., 1929-32; pvt. studio tchr. Santa Ana, Calif., 1932-91; ret., 1991—. Musical compositions published by Boston Music, Schroeder and Gunther, Pro Art Publications, Summy-Birchard and Mills Music, and others; contbr. articles to profl. jours. Cpl. Nat. Guard, 1921-24. Rhodes scholar Oxford U., 1926. Mem. Music Tchrs. Assn. of Calif., Musical Arts Club of Orange County. Democrat. Studio: Joseph Ogle Piano Studio 1710 Greenleaf St Santa Ana CA 92706-3631

O'GRADY, BARBARA VINSON, community health nurse, nursing administrator; b. Alhambra, Calif., July 6, 1928; d. Weston Wright and Merdith Alida (Noble) Vinson; m. Joseph Putnam O'Grady, Oct. 24, 1952; children: Joseph Jr., Jeffrey, Kent, Kimberly, Kathryn. BS, UCLA, 1951; MS, U. Minn., 1972. Staff public health nurse San Diego Health Dept., 1952; staff nurse U. Minn. Hosp., 1954-56; staff public health nurse Family Nursing Svc., St. Paul, 1972; asst. prof. Gustavus Adolphus Coll., St. Peter, Minn., 1972-77; dir. Ramsey County Public Health Nursing Svc., St. Paul, 1977-88; health staff Senator Dave Durenberger, Mpls., 1988; cons. pvt. practice, Waterville, Minn., 1989—; mem. bd. govs. U. Minn. Hosp. and Clinic, Mpls., 1983-91, chair, 1985-87; clin. faculty Sch. Pub. Health, 1984-88. Author: (with others) Computer Applications in Medical Care, 1982, Nursing and Computers, 1989, NCNIP: Models for the Future of Nursing, 1989, Procs. of Impact of DRG's on Nursing Conf., 1988; mem. editl. bd. Jour. Cmty. Health Nursing, 1984-94. Mem. Mpls. Charter Commn., 1967-72; co-chair Minn. GOP Issues Devel., 1968, Minn. GOP Constrn. Com., 19660-70; chair Dick Erdall Campaign Com., 1965-71; bd. dirs. Presbyn. Homes of Minn., St. Paul, 1982-88; bd. dirs. Living at Home/Block Nurse Program, 1986—, chair future directions com., 1988—. Recipient Outstanding Contbn. Midwest Alliance in Nursing, 1984, Outstanding Achievement award Bd, of Ramsey County Commrs., 1987; Annie Yates scholar L.A. County General Hosp. Alumni Assn., 1948; Living At Home grantee The Commonwealth Fund, 1986. Fellow Am. Acad. of Nursing; mem. ANA, APHA, Nat. League for Nursing, Minn. Public Health Assn., Sigma Theta Tau. Republican. Presbyterian. Home and Office: 482 Calle Cadiz Apt A Laguna Hills CA 92653-3964

O'GRADY, JOHN PATRICK, American literature educator, writer; b. Newark, Mar. 3, 1958; s. Joseph Gabriel and Muriel Catherine (Cotter) O'G. BS in Forestry, U. Maine, 1980, MA in English, 1983; PhD in English, U. Calif., Davis, 1991. Acad. programmer U. Maine, Orono, 1983-85; instr. U. Calif., Davis, 1985-91, lectr., 1991-94; lectr. Guttenberg U., Mainz, Germany, 1987-88; asst. prof. English Boise (Idaho) State U., 1994—. Author: Pilgrims to the Wild, 1993. Mem. MLA, Assn. for Study of Literature and the Environment, Forest History Soc. Office: Boise State U Dept English 1910 University Dr Boise ID 83725-0001

OGREN, CARROLL WOODROW, retired hospital administrator; b. Mpls., Mar. 22, 1927; s. Peter L. and Mabel (Wohleen) O.; m. Patricia Ann Sweeney. B.A., U. Minn., 1952; M.Hosp. Adminstrn., Washington U., St. Louis, 1958. Asst. adminstr. Washoe Med. Center, Reno, 1958-64; adminstr. Washoe Med. Center, 1964-80, Jean Hannah Clark Rehab. Center, Las Vegas, Nev., 1980-92. Served with USNR, 1944-46, 50-54, PTO. Mem. Am. Coll. Hosp. Adminstrs., Am. Hosp. Assn. (nat. com. state hosp. assn. 1967—), Nev. Hosp. Assn. (pres. 1961-62, sec. 1961-66). Club: Gourmet Toastmasters (Reno) (pres. 1960). Home: 5860 Via Manigua Las Vegas NV 89120-2348

OGUNSOLA, OLAYINKA I., mineral, fuel and energy engineering educator; b. May 24, 1950; married; 3 children. Diploma in Engring./Tech., Filton Tech. Coll., Bristol, Eng., 1976; BSc in Fuel/Energy Engring. with honors, U. Leeds, Eng., 1979; PhD in Fuel Sci., Pa. State U., 1983. Rsch. asst. Pa. State U., University Park, 1979-83; rsch. scientist dept. chemistry George Washington U., Washington, 1983-84; cons. Uniport Konsult-U. of Pt. Harcourt, Nigeria, 1984-88; asst. prof. dept. petroleum engring. U. Pt. Harcourt, 1984-88, assoc. prof., 1988-92; vis. rsch. scientist CANMET Western Rsch. Ctr., Devon, Alta., Can., 1988-91; vis. asst. prof. coal tech. U. Alaska, Fairbanks, 1991-92, rsch. asst. prof. coal tech., 1992—. Contbr. numerous articles to profl. jours. Fellow Inst. Petroleum (London); mem. Am. Chem. Soc., Soc. Petroleum Engrs., Combustion Inst. Office: Univ Alaska Fairbanks Sch Mineral Engring PO Box 757240 Fairbanks AK 99775-7240

OH, SEHO, research engineer; b. Daejeon, Korea, Sept. 12, 1957; s. In-Sung and Un-Ok Oh; m. Suk-Yeon Chung, Apr. 21, 1985; children: Daniel Chun-Suk, David Hyung-Suk. BS, Seoul Nat. U., 1979; MS, KAIST, Seoul, 1981; PhD, U. Wash., 1989. Rsch. engr. Goldstar Co., Seoul, 1981-86; rsch. assoc. U. Wash., Seattle, 1990-93, affiliate asst. prof., 1993—; sr. rsch. engr. NeoPath Inc., Redmond, Wash., 1993—. Assoc. editor IEEE Trans. on Neural Networks, 1992-93. Christian. Office: NeoPath Inc 8271 154th Ave NE Redmond WA 98052

OH, TAI KEUN, business educator; b. Seoul, Korea, Mar. 25, 1934; s. Chin Young and Eui Kyung (Yun) O.; came to U.S., 1958, naturalized, 1969; B.A., Seijo U., 1957; M.A., No. Ill. U., 1961; M.L.S., U. Wis., 1965, Ph.D., 1970; m. Gretchen Brenneke, Dec. 26, 1964; children: Erica, Elizabeth, Emily. Asst. prof. mgmt. Roosevelt U., Chgo., 1969-73; assoc. prof. Calif. State U., Fullerton, 1973-76, prof. mgmt., 1976—; vis. prof. U. Hawaii, 1983-84, 86; advisor Pacific Asian Mgmt. Inst., U. Hawaii; internat. referee Asia-Pacific Jour. of Mgmt., 1990—; cons. Calty Design Research, Inc. subs. Toyota Motor Corp. The Employers Group; seminar leader and speaker. Named Outstanding Prof., Sch. Bus. Adminstrn. and Econs., Calif. State U., Fullerton, 1976, 78. NSF grantee, 1968-69, recipient Exceptional Merit Service award Calif. State U., 1984, Meritorious Performance and Profl. Promise award Calif. State U., 1987. Mem. Acad. Mgmt., Indsl. Relations Research Assn., Acad. Internat. Bus. Editorial bd. Acad. Mgmt. Rev., 1978-81; contbg. author: Ency. Profl. Mgmt., 1978, Handbook of Management 1985; contbr. articles to profl. jours. Home: 2044 E Eucalyptus Ln Brea CA 92621-5911 Office: Calif State U Fullerton CA 92634

O'HAGAN, WILLIAM GORDON, automotive repair shop owner; b. Allentown, N.J., Oct. 12, 1943; s. Forrest Allen and Voncile Arline (Linton) O'H.; m. Marcia Helen Beck, Aug. 12, 1947 (div. Oct. 1985). Grad. high sch., Azusa, Calif., 1962. Owner Richfield Oil Co., Baldwin Park, Calif., 1970-72; mgr. Am. Teaching Aids, Covina, Calif., 1972-88; owner Bill's Auto Repair Co., Covina, 1988—. Block commander Neighborhood Watch, Covina. Republican. Baptist. Home: 163 N Marcile Ave Glendora CA 91741-2453 Office: Bills Automotive 678 E San Bernardino Rd Covina CA 91723-1735

O'HALLORAN, THOMAS ALPHONSUS, JR., physicist, educator; b. Bklyn., Apr. 13, 1931; s. Thomas Alphonsus Sr. and Nora (Sheehan) O'H.; m. Barbara Joyce Hug, June 4, 1954; children: Theresa Joyce, Maureen Ann, Kevin Thomas, Patrick Joseph. Student, San Jose State U., 1948-50; BS in Physics & Math., Oreg. State U., 1953, MS in Physics, 1954; PhD, U. Calif., Berkeley, 1963. Rsch. asst. Lawrence Berkeley Lab., U. Calif., 1963-64; rsch. fellow Harvard U., Cambridge, Mass., 1964-66; asst. prof. physics U. Ill., Urbana, 1966-68, assoc. prof., 1968-70, prof., 1970-93, prof. emeritus, 1993—; vis. scholar U. Utah, Salt Lake City, 1990-93, rsch. prof. physics, 1993—; mem. program adv. com. Argonne Nat. Lab., Lemont, Ill., Fermi Lab., Batavia, Ill., Brookhaven Nat. Lab., Upton, L.I.; vis. scientist Lawrence Berkeley Lab., U. Calif., 1979-80. Contbr. numerous articles on elem. particle physics to profl. jours. Lt. USN, 1954-58. Guggenheim fellow, 1979-80. Fellow Am. Phys. Soc. Home: 4614 Ledgemont Dr Salt Lake City UT 84124-4735 Office: U Utah Physics Dept 201 Jfb Salt Lake City UT 84112

O'HANDLEY, DOUGLAS ALEXANDER, astronomer; b. Detroit, May 7, 1937; s. Malcolm Joseph and Georgie Roberta (MacPherson) O'H.; m. Christine Jeannette Stube, July 20, 1991; 1 child, Douglas Alexander, Jr. AB, U. Mich., 1960; MS, Yale U., 1964, PhD, 1967. Astronomer U.S. Naval Obs., Washington, 1960-67; scientist Jet Propulsion Lab., Pasadena, Calif., 1967-85; dir. space station Ames Rsch. Ctr., Moffett Field, Calif., 1985-86; mgr. TRW Space Tech. Group, Redondo Beach, Calif., 1986-88; dep. asst. adminstr. office exploration NASA, Washington, 1988-92; special asst. Center for Mars Exploration Ames Rsch. Ctr., Moffett Field, Calif.,1992—; chmn. com. for protection of human subjects in med. rsch., 1982-85; lectr. grad. sch. Georgetown U., Washington, 1964-67; speaker at med. soc. meetings. Contbr. articles to profl. jours. Bd. dirs. Cath. Big Bros.; extraordinary minister St. Bede's Roman Cath. Ch. Recipient NASA Group Achievement award Planetary Ephemeris Devel. Team, 1982. Fellow Royal Soc. Medicine, Internat. Astronomical Union, Internat. Acad. Astronautics, Aerospace Med. Assn. (fellow), AIAA (assoc.). Republican. Home: 1580 Grackle Way Sunnyvale CA 94087-4715 Office: Ctr Mars Exploration Ames Rsch Ctr Moffett Field CA 94035

O'HARA, KIRK BRANDT, management consultant; b. Michigan, N.D., June 13, 1955; s. Robert Keith and Bertha (Knudsen) O'H. BA, Ft. Hays State U., 1977, M in Psychology, 1979; D of Psychology, Ctrl. Mich. U., 1989. Cert. clin. psychologist, Ky. Staff psychologist Western Ky. Mental Health Bd. Inc., Murray, Ky., 1979-83; orgnl. specialist Dow Chem., Midland, Mich., 1983-85; mng. devel. cons. Taco Bell Corp., Irvine, Calif., 1987-89; rsch. scientist Human Interaction Rsch., L.A., 1987-89; v.p. Fuchs & Co., L.A., 1989—. Author: Organizational Change and Drug-free Workplaces: Templates for Success, 1991; contbr. chpts. to books, articles to profl. jours. Grad. scholar Ctrl. Mich. U., 1985, Disting. Grad. Rsch. award, 1987, 90. Mem. Am. Psychol. Assn. Home: 9814 Regent St Apt 1 Los Angeles CA 90034-5126 Office: Fuchs and Co 12424 Wilshire Blvd Ste 700 Los Angeles CA 90025-1041

O'HARA, MICHAEL J(AMES), physicist; b. Winthrop, Mass., Aug. 7, 1956; s. George J. and Gilda A. (Capone) O. BS in Physics, U. Lowell (Mass.), 1978; MS in Physics, U. Ill., 1980, MS in Computer Sci., 1984. Mem. tech. staff I Hughes Aircraft Co., El Segundo, Calif., 1984-86, mem. tech. staff II, 1986-87; tech. supr. Hughes Aircraft Co., 1987-89, sect. head, 1989-91, asst. dept. mgr., 1991—; software cons. Duosoft Corp., Urbana, 1982-83; bd. dirs. Ednl. Scis. Corp. Am., L.A., 1986—. Mem. N.Y. Acad. Sci., Planetary Soc., Soc. Photo-Optical Instrumentation Engrs., U. Ill. Alumni Club, Soc. Physics Students, Sigma Pi Sigma. Republican. Roman Catholic. Office: Hughes Aircraft Co Hughes Applied Info Systems 1616A McCormick Dr Cheverly MD 20785

O'HARA, PATRICK JOSEPH, biochemist, biotechnology company executive; b. Seattle, Aug. 13, 1953; s. Robert Patrick and Madeleine B. (Dent) O'H.; m. Caterina A. Randolph, Sept. 9, 1990. BA in Chemistry, BA in Biology, We. Wash. U., Bellingham, 1975; PhD in Biochemistry, U. Wash., 1980. Postdoctoral fellow U. Wash., Seattle, 1980-81, U. Calif., San Diego, 1981-84; sr. scientist ZymoGenetics, Seattle, 1984-87, rsch. mgr., 1987-90, dir. rsch., 1990-93, v.p. rsch., 1993—. Contbr. articles to profl. jours. Recipient Planetary Biology award NASA, 1980; Arthritis Found. fellow, 1981-84. Mem. AAAS, Planetary Soc.

O'HARE, SANDRA FERNANDEZ, secondary education educator; b. N.Y.C., Mar. 19, 1941; d. Ricardo Enrique and Rosario de Los Angeles (Arenas) Fernandez; m. S. James O'Hare, Oct. 12, 1963; children: James, Richard, Michael, Christopher. BA, Marymount Coll., 1962; MA, U. San Francisco, 1980. Cert. elem. and coll. tchr.; bilingual and lang. devel. specialist. Instr. adult edn. Guam, 1964-66, Spanish Speaking Ctr., Harrisburg, Pa., 1977-79; tchr. Colegio Salesiano, Rota, Spain, 1973, 84, Alisal Sch. Dist., Salinas, Calif., 1979-81, Liberty Sch., Petaluma, Calif., 1981-85, Cinnabar Sch., Petaluma, 1985—; instr. Chapman U., 1994—; also summer migrant edn. programs Cinnabar Sch., Petaluma, 1990, 91; instr. Santa Rosa (Calif.) Jr. Coll., 1982-83;mem. math. curriculum com. Sonoma County Office Edn., Santa Rosa, 1988; mem. Summer Sci. Connections Inst., Sonoma State U., 1994. Translator: Isabel la Catolica, 1962. Mem. Asian relief com. ARC, Harrisburg, 1975, Boy Scouts Am., Petaluma, 1983, Mechanicsburg, Pa., 1974, Monterey, Calif., 1971. Sarah D. Barder fellow Johns Hopkins U., 1990. Mem. NEA, AAUW (chair edn. founds. com. 1985-86), Calif. Assn. Bilingual Educators, Cinnabar Tchrs. Assn., Club Hispano-Americano Petaluma (pres. 1987-89). Roman Catholic. Home: 1289 Glenwood Dr Petaluma CA 94954-4326

OHARENKO, MARIA T., public relations official; b. Louvain, Belgium, Dec. 25, 1950; came to U.S., 1951; d. Vladimir and Lubomyra (Kotz) O. BS, Northwestern U., 1972, MS, 1973. Pub. info. officer U.S. AEC, ERDA, Dept. Energy, Argonne and Chgo., Ill., 1973-79; pub. info. and news media advance officer U.S. Dept. Energy, Washington, 1980-81; corp. pub. info. mgr. Northrop Corp., Los Angeles, 1981—. Mem. Aviation/Space Writers Assn., Women in Communications, Soc. Profl. Journalists. Ukrainian Catholic. Office: Northrop Corp 1840 Century Park E Los Angeles CA 90067-2101

O'HEARN, MICHAEL JOHN, lawyer; b. Akron, Ohio, Jan. 29, 1952; s. Leo Ambrose and Margaret Elizabeth (Clark) O'H. BA in Econs., UCLA, 1975; postgrad., U. San Diego, 1977; JD, San Fernando Valley Coll. Law, 1979. Bar: Calif. 1979, U.S. Dist. Ct. (cen. dist.) Calif. 1979. Document analyst Mellonics Info. Ctr., Litton Industries, Canoga Park, Calif., 1977-79; pvt. practice Encino, Calif., 1979-80; atty. VISTA/Grey Law Inc., L.A., 1980-81; assoc. Donald E. Chadwick & Assocs., Woodland Hills, Calif., 1981-84, Law Offices of Laurence Ring, Beverly Hills, Calif., 1984-85; atty., in-house counsel Coastal Ins. Co., Van Nuys, Calif., 1985-89; atty. Citrus Glen Apts., Ventura, Calif., 1989-92. Cert. of Appreciation, Agy. for Vol. Svc., 1981, San Fernando Valley Walk for Life, 1988. Mem. KC, Ventura County Bar Assn., Secular Franciscan Order. Republican. Roman Catholic. Home: 3730 Ketch Ave Apt 318 Oxnard CA 93035-3045 Office: 3650 Ketch Ave Oxnard CA 93035-3029

OHLSEN, GERALD G., real estate developer, lawyer; b. Eugene, Oreg., May 1, 1933; s. Glenn Randolph and Doris Louise (Perry) O.; m. Sally Slaughter, Sept. 1958 (div.); m. Linnea Delores Carlson McGehee, Mar. 1974. BA, U. Oreg., 1955; MS, Stanford U., 1957, PhD, 1960; JD, U. N.Mex., 1992. Bar: N.Mex. 1992; lic. real estate broker, N.Mex. Asst. prof. U. Tex., Austin, 1960-61; fellow Australian Nat. U., Canberra, 1961-65; mem. staff Los Alamos (N.Mex.) Nat. Lab., 1965-80; real estate developer Santa Fe, N.Mex., 1980—. Contbr. articles to profl. publs. Home and Office: 1169 E Alameda St Santa Fe NM 87501-2286

O'HOLLAREN, PAUL JOSEPH, former international fraternity administrator; b. Portland, Oreg., Dec. 24, 1927; s. Charles Edward and Helen Henrietta (McHugh) O'H.; m. Patricia Marie Foley, June 27, 1953; children: Mark T., Kevin J., Brian T., Patrick S., Kelly P. JD, Northwestern Coll. of Law, 1954. Bar: Oreg., 1954. Atty. Oreg. State Bar, 1954-83; mem. supreme coun. Moose Internat., Inc., Mooseheart, Ill., 1968-79; supreme gov. Loyal Order of Moose, Mooseheart, Ill., 1978-79, dir. gen., 1984-94, retired, 1994; chmn. exec. bd. Moose Internat., Inc., 1994—. Bd. dirs. Ill. Math. and Sci. Acad. Fund for the Advancement of Edn., Aurora, Ill., 1987—; chmn. Alliance for Drug Free Soc., Washington. With U.S. Army, 1945-46. Named Jr. First Citizen, U.S. Jr. C. of C., Portland, 1959; recipient Oreg. State Bar award of Merit, 1979. Mem. Multnomah Athletic Club, Loyal Order of Moose. Republican. Roman Catholic. Office: 680 Benjamin Franklin Plz 1 SW Columbia St Portland OR 97258-2002

OHTAKE, TAKESHI, meteorologist, educator; b. Abiko City, Japan, Jan. 22, 1926; came to U.S. 1964; s. Sakae and Sumiko (Ogawa) O.; m. Kumiko, Jan. 20, 1953; children: Tomoko, Atsuko J., Tadahiro. Diploma, Japan Meteorol. Coll., 1947; BS, Tohoku U., 1952, DSc, 1961. Rsch. asst. Meteorol. Rsch. Inst., Tokyo, 1947-49; rsch. assoc. Geophys. Inst., Tohoku U., Sendai, Japan, 1952-67; lectr. meteorology Coll. Art & Sci., Tohoku U., Sendai, 1961-64; assoc. prof. U. Alaska, Fairbanks, 1964-75, prof. geophysics, 1975-88, prof. emeritus, 1988—; vis. assoc. prof. Colo. State U., Ft. Collins, 1969-71; vis. prof. Nat. Inst. of Polar Rsch., Tokyo, 1979-80, Air Force Geophysics Lab., Bedford, Mass., 1985-87; disting. vis. prof. Nagoya U., 1990-91. Contbr. articles to profl. jours. Fellow Am. Meteorol. Soc., Royal Meteorol. Soc.; mem. Am. Geophys. Union, Meteorol. Soc. Japan, Sigma Xi. Home: 14250 W Warren Dr Lakewood CO 80228-5937

OIZUMI, JUN, pediatrician, geneticist; b. Tokyo, 1948; m. Ann Reid Cronin, May 28, 1994. MD, Tokyo-Jikei Med. Sch., 1973, PhD, 1982. Diplomate Am. Bd. Pediats., Am. Bd. Med. Genetics. Pediat. intern Children's Hosp., L.A., 1978, pediat. resident, 1979-80, fellow in genetics, 1980-81, asst. prof. med. staff, 1981-84; dir. Nat. Children's Med. Rsch. Ctr., Tokyo, 1985-93; dir. pediats. Orthop. Hosp., L.A., 1993—. Contbr. articles to profl. jours. Fellow Am. Coll. Med. Genetics (founding fellow), Am. Acad. Pediats.; mem. AMA, Calif. Med. Assn., L.A. County Med. Assn. Office: Orthop Hosp 2400 S Flower St Los Angeles CA 90007

O'JACK, HELEN MARGARET, clinical social worker; b. Denver, Jan. 31, 1951; d. Herbert Henry and Lillian Anna (Meyer) Thimm; m. William Allan Schmeling, Jr., July 24, 1982 (div. Dec. 1992); children: Dustin William, Alexander Thimm; m. Stanislav G. O'Jack, June 16, 1995. BA in Psychology, U. Colo., 1973; MSW, U. Denver, 1982. Lic. profl. social worker, Wyo. Peer counselor Met. Community Coll., Omaha, 1975-76; outreach worker South Omaha Crisis Ctr., 1976-77; child care worker Mt. St. Vincent's Youth Home, Denver, 1978-81; social work intern health scis. ctr. U. Colo., Denver, 1981-82; coord. crisis line Vol. Info. Referral Service, Rock Springs, Wyo., 1983-85; clin. social worker, coord. elderly svcs. S.W. Counseling Svc., Rock Springs, 1985-92; med. social worker Wyo. Home Health Care, Rock Springs, 1986—; pvt. practice, 1992—; facilitator Alzheimer's Family Support Group, Rock Springs, 1983-92; social work cons. Castle Rock Convalescent Ctr., Green River, Wyo., 1990, Sage View Care Ctr., 1992-95; sch. counselor Desert View Sch., 1992—. Mem. NEA, NASW (regional rep. on bd. dirs. Wyo. chpt. 1991-92). Democrat. Office: Desert View Elem Sweetwater Sch Dist # 1 PO Box 1089 Rock Springs WY 82902-1089

OKADA, TSUYOSHI, internist; b. Salinas, Calif., Aug. 3, 1930; s. Kanichi and Haruko (Yokohata) O.; m. Violet Sumiye Shimabukuro, Sept. 10, 1955; children: Cheryl Y., Douglas I., Joan M., Michael H. BA in Chemistry magna cum laude, U. Colo., 1952; MD, Northwestern U., Chgo., 1956. Diplomate Am. Bd. Internal Medicine, Am. Bd. Internal Medicine/Geriatric Medicine, Nat. Bd. Med. Examiners. Intern Chgo. Wesley Meml. Hosp., 1956-57; resident, internal medicine UCLA Harbor Gen. Hosp., Torrance, Calif., 1961-64; internist Gardena, Calif., 1964—. Contbr. articles to profl. jours. Capt. U.S. Army Med. Corps, 1957-61, Japan. Fellow ACP; mem. Calif. Med. Assn., Los Angeles County Med. Assn., Am. Geriatrics Soc., Phi Beta Kappa, Alpha Epsilon Delta. Democrat. Baptist. Office: 16020 S Western Ave Ste 204 Gardena CA 90247-3743

O'KEEFE, KATHLEEN MARY, state government official; b. Butte, Mont., Mar. 25, 1933; d. Hugh I. and Kathleen Mary (Harris) O'Keefe; B.A. in Communications, St. Mary Coll., Xavier, Kans., 1954; m. Nick B. Baker, Sept. 18, 1954 (div. 1970); children—Patrick, Susan, Michael, Cynthia, Hugh, Mardeen. Profl. singer, mem. Kathie Baker Quartet, 1962-72; research cons. Wash. Ho. of Reps., Olympia, 1972-73; info. officer Wash. Employment Security Commn., Seattle, 1973-81, dir. public affairs, 1981-90, video dir., 1990—; freelance writer, composer, producer, 1973—. Founder, pres. bd. Eden, Inc., visual and performing arts, 1975—; public relations chmn. Nat. Women's Democratic Conv., Seattle, 1979, Wash. Dem. Women, 1976-85; bd. dirs., public relations chmn. Eastside Mental Health Center, Bellevue, Wash., 1979-81; Dem. candidate Wash. State Senate, 1968. Recipient Black Community award for composition The Beaufort County Jail, Seattle, 1975, Silver medal Seattle Creative Awards Show for composing, directing and producing Rent A Kid, TV public service spot, 1979. Mem. Wash. Press Women. Democrat. Roman Catholic. Author: Job Finding In the Nineties, handbook on TV prodn., guide to coping with unemployment; composer numerous songs, also producer Job Service spots. Home: 4426 147th Pl NE # 12 Bellevue WA 98007-3162 Office: 212 Maple Park Ave SE Olympia WA 98501-2240

OKEN, RICHARD LESLIE, pediatrician; b. Balt., May 24, 1945; s. Louis E. and Rosa E. (Hudson) O.; m. Judith Carolyn Faulkner, July 15, 1967; children: Erik Richard, April Kelly. BS cum laude in Biology, Boston Coll., 1963-67; MD, U. Calif., San Francisco, 1967-71. Diplomate Am. Bd. Pediatrics. Pediatrician, mng. ptnr. East Bay Pediatric Med. Group, Berkeley, Calif., 1975—; clin. prof. Pediatrics U. Calif., San Francisco, 1991—; bd. dirs. Alta Bates Health Sys., Emeryville, Calif. Trustee The Coll. Prep. Sch., Oakland, Calif., 1991—; trustee, bd. dirs. Alta Bates Med. Ctr., Berkeley, 1987-90; mem. med. adv. bd. Found. for Osteoporosis Rsch. and Edn., Oakland, 1993—. Fellow Am. Acad. Pediatrics; mem. Calif. Med. Assn., Alameda Contra Costa Med. Assn. Home: 224 Pala Ave Piedmont CA 94611-3741 Office: East Bay Pediatric Med Group 2999 Regent St Ste 325 Berkeley CA 94705-2118

OKEZIE, NGOZI BABETTE, psychiatrist; b. N.Y.C., July 2, 1964; d. Okogbue and Nonyelum Ada (Obi) Okezie; m. Sean Patrick Curtis, June 6, 1992. BA, Bryn Mawr Coll., 1986; MD, Yale U., 1991. Diplomate Nat. Bd. Med. Examiners; lic. physician, Colo. Intern U. Colo. Health Sci. Ctr., Denver, 1991-92, resident in psychiatry, 1992-94; career resident in pub. psychiatry, attending psychiatry svc Colo. Mental Health Inst., Pueblo, 1994—. Mem. human rights com. Denver Options, 1993-94; vol. Columbus House Homeless Shelter, New Haven, 1986-88; mem. honor bd. Bryn Mawr Coll., 1985-86; tutor Kids Connection, Germantown, Pa., 1982-84; vol. pediatrics ward Queens Gen. Hosp., Jamaica, N.Y., 1982; vol. teaching asst. Dept. Social Svcs., New Haven, 1988-89. William T. Grant Behavioural Rsch. grantee, 1988, NSF grantee, summer 1985; Bryn Mawr Coll. Alumni Regional scholar, 1985-86. Mem. Am. Psychiat. Assn., Colo. Psychiat. Soc. (com. in cmty. affairs 1993-94).

OKI, BRIAN MASAO, software engineer; b. Inglewood, Calif., Oct. 17, 1958; s. Masao and Chiyoe (Yata) O. BS summa cum laude, U. Calif., Irvine, 1980; MS, MIT, 1983, PhD, 1988. Mem. rsch. staff Xerox Palo Alto (Calif.) Rsch. Ctr., 1988-92; sr. mem. tech. staff Teknekron Software Systems, Inc., Palo Alto, 1992-94; sr. tech. staff Oracle Corp., Redwood Shores, Calif., 1994—. Mem. IEEE, Assn. Computing Machinery, Phi Beta Kappa, Sigma Xi. Home: 493 Mill River Ln San Jose CA 95134-2420 Office: Oracle Corp Box 659414 500 Oracle Pkwy Redwood City CA 94065

OKO, ANDREW JAN, art gallery director, curator; b. London, Sept. 7, 1946; arrived in Can., 1948; s. Jan Kazimierz and Julia Helena (Suska) O.; m. Helen Marie Blanc, Dec. 21, 1972; children: Sonya Celeste, Michelle Kathleen. BA, U. Calgary, 1968; MA, U. Toronto, 1972. Preparator Glenbow Mus., Calgary, Alta., 1972-73, curatorial asst., 1973-74, asst. curator, 1974-77; curator Art Gallery of Hamilton, Ont., 1977-86; dir. MacKenzie Art Gallery, Regina, Sask., 1986—. Author: Country Pleasures: The Angling Art of Jack Cowin, 1984, (with others) Art Gallery Handbook 1982; author/curator: (exhbn. catalogue) The Frontier Art of R.B. Nevitt, 1974, T.R. MacDonald 1908-1978, 1980, The Society of Canadian Painter-Etchers and Engravers in Retrospect, 1981, The Prints of Carl Schaefer, 1983, Canada in the Nineteenth Century: The Bert and Barbara Stitt Family Collection, 1984, Jan Gerrit Wyers 1888-1973, 1989. Mem. Can. Mus. Assn., Can. Art Mus. Dirs.' Orgn., Sask. Arts Alliance (pres. 1991-93), Rotary. Office: MacKenzie Art Gallery, 3475 Albert St, Regina, SK Canada S4S 6X6

OKRASINSKI, RICHARD JOSEPH, meteorologist; b. Kingston, Pa., Dec. 24, 1951; s. Joseph and Catherine (Conway) O. BS in Meteorology, U. Utah, 1974, MS in Meteorology, 1977. Phys. scientist Phys. Sci. Lab., Las Cruces, N.Mex., 1977—. Mem. Am. Meteorol. Soc. Office: Phys Sci Lab PO Box 30002 Las Cruces NM 88003-8002

O'KUINGHTTONS, CAMILO OCTAVIO, mechanical engineer; b. San Felipe, Chile, May 4, 1935; came to U.S., 1974; s. Camilo Octavio and Lola Maria (Bunout) O'K.; m. Ingrid Gisela Kroneberg, Sept. 16, 1960 (div. July 1975); 1 child, Camilo Octavio; m. Andrea Jean Neuman, Aug. 31, 1978; 1 child, Ryan Lee. BSME, Chilean Mil. Sch., Santiago, 1954; MSME, Mil. Poly. Acad., Santiago, 1965. With Chilean Army, 1953-67; design engr. Famae, Santiago, 1965-67; pvt. practice Santiago, 1967-74; head metall. dept. U. Concepcion, Chile, 1969-74; prof. Cath. U., Santiago, 1969; head engring. dept. Intricast, Santa Rosa, Calif., 1974-79; sr. design engr. Fairchild Stratus, Manhattan Beach, Calif., 1979-81; head engring. dept. Chromalloy S.A., Mexicali, Mex., 1981-83; pres., CEO ECO-Energy Engring., Carson City, Nev., 1981—; advisor, registered contract cons. office project svcs. UN Devel. Programme; cons. Board City of Concepcion, 1970-74, cons. in field; part-time prof. Western Nerada C.C. Author: Physical Metallurgy, 1972. Founder first continuing edn. program for adults, Chile. Decorated Minerva medal, Malta Cross (Chile). Mem. ASHRAE, Am. Solar Assn., Solar Energy Internat., Nat. Bus. Assn., Found. Earth Resources Scis. and Tech. (v.p. 1994), Sierra Club, Audubon. Home and Office: Eco-Energy Engring 2239 Lake Shore Dr Carson City NV 89704-9215

OKUMA, ALBERT AKIRA, JR., architect; b. Cleve., Feb. 10, 1946; s. Albert Akira Sr. and Reiko (Suwa) O.; m. Janice Shirley Bono, July 17, 1971; children: Reiko Dawn, Benjamin Scott. BS in Archtl. Engring, Calif. Poly. State U., San Luis Obispo, 1970, BArch, 1975; ednl. facility planning cert., U. Calif., Riverside, 1990. Lic. architect, Calif., Mont., Ariz., Ill., Nev., N.Mex., Oreg., Maine; cert. Nat. Coun. Archtl. Bds. Architect USN, Point Mugu, Calif., 1975-76; designer Wilson Stroh Wilson Architects, Santa Paula, Calif., 1976-79; architect, project mgr. W.J. Kulwiec AIA & Assocs., Camarillo, Calif., 1979-83, Wilson & Conrad Architects, Ojai, Calif., 1983-84, Dziak, Immel & Lauterbach Services Inc., Oxnard, Calif., 1984-85; ptnr. Conrad & Okuma Architects, Oxnard, 1985—; commr. Calif. Bd. Archtl. Examiners, 1985—, City of San Buenaventura Hist. Preservation Commn., 1990-94, chmn., 1991-93, City of San Buenaventura Planning Commn., 1994—, City of San Buenaventura Design Rev. Com., 1994—, vice chair 1994—; peer reviewer Am. Cons. Engrs. Coun., 1987—; lectr. U. Calif. Ext., Riverside, 1991—. Prin. works include Hobson Bros. Bldg. (reconstrn. and preservation), Ventura, Calif., (Design for Excellence award 1991, Historic Bldg. of Yr. award 1992, Archtl. Rev. Design award 1993), Oxnard (Calif.) Main Post Office Renovation (Design for Excellence award 1994). Mem. Spiritual Assembly Baha'is of Venture, Calif., 1978—, treas., 1978-79, 84, 86-88, chmn., 1992-93; treas.'s rep. Nat. Spiritual Assembly Baha'is U.S., Wilmette, Ill., 1981-91, mem. dist. tchg. com., 1992-93; treas. Parents and Advs. for Gifted Edn., 1988-89; chmn. Ventura Unified Sch. Dist. Citizens Budget Adv. Com., 1990, 92; mem. City of San Buenaventura specific plan citizens com., 1990, 91, 92, 93, multicultural/cmty. heritage task force of the cultural arts plan com., 1991-92, strategic planning citizens adv. com., 1992-93. 1st lt. U.S. Army, 1971-73. Mem. AIA (chpt. bd. dirs. 1976-79, 81—, chpt. sec. 1981, v.p. 1982, pres. 1983, Intern Devel. Program Outstanding Firm award 1993), Am. Planning Assn., Internat. Conf. Bldg. Ofcls., Nat. Trust for Hist. Preservation, Calif. Preservation Found., Constrn. Specifications Inst., Design Methods Group, Coalition for Adequate Sch. Housing, Coun. Ednl. Facility Planners Internat., Structural Engrs. Assn. So. Calif. (affiliate), Ventura County Econ. Devel. Assn., Calif. Polytech. State U. Alumni Assn. (life), Toastmasters Internat. Office: Conrad & Okuma Architects 167 Lambert St Oxnard CA 93030-1044

OKUMURA, MITCHIO, chemical physics educator; b. Columbia, Mo., Sept. 1, 1957; s. Koji and Akiko O. BS, MS, Yale U., 1979; cert. postgrad. study, Cambridge (Eng.) U., 1980; PhD, U. Calif., Berkeley, 1986. Postdoctoral rsch. assoc. U. Chgo., 1987-88; asst. prof. chem. physics Calif. Inst. Tech., Pasadena, Calif., 1988-94, assoc. prof. chem. physics, 1994—. Recipient Churchill scholarship U.S. Winston Churchill Found., 1979-80, Newly Apptd. Faculty award Camille & Henry Dreyfus Found., 1981; named Presdl. Young investigator NSF, 1989-95. Mem. AAAS, Am. Phys. Soc., Am. Chem. Soc., Am. Geophys. Union. Office: Calif Inst Tech Chemistry Dept MC 127-72 Pasadena CA 91125

OLAH, GEORGE ANDREW, chemist, educator; b. Budapest, Hungary, May 22, 1927; came to U.S., 1964, naturalized, 1970; s. Julius and Magda (Rasznai) O.; m. Judith Agnes Lengyel, July 9, 1949; children: George John, Ronald Peter. PhD, Tech. U. Budapest, 1949, D honoris causa, 1989; DSc honoris causa, U. Durham, 1988, U. Munich, 1990, U. Crete, Greece, 1994, U. Szeged, Hungary, 1995, U. Vesprem, Hungary, 1995, Case Western Res. U., 1995; U. Veszprem, 1995. Mem. faculty Tech. U. Budapest, 1949-54; assoc. dir. Cen. Chem. Rsch. Inst., Hungarian Acad. Scis., 1954-56; rsch. scientist Dow Chem. Can. Ltd., 1957-64, Dow Chem. Co., Framingham, Mass., 1964-65; prof. chemistry Case-Western Res. U., Cleve., 1965-69, C.F. Mabery prof. rsch., 1969-77; Donald P. and Katherine B. Loker disting. prof. chemistry, dir. Hydrocarbon Rsch. Inst., U. So. Calif., L.A., 1977—; vis. prof. chemistry Ohio State U., 1963, U. Heidelberg, Germany, 1965, U. Colo., 1969, Swiss Fed. Inst. Tech., 1972, U. Munich, 1973, U. London, 1973-79, L. Pasteur U., Strasbourg, 1974, U. Paris, 1981; hon. vis. lectr. U. London, 1981; cons. to industry. Author: Friedel-Crafts Reactions, Vols. I-IV, 1963-64; (with P. Schleyer) Carbonium Ions, Vols. I-V, 1969-76, Friedel-Crafts Chemistry, 1973, Carbocations and Electrophilic Reactions, 1973, Halonium Ions, 1975; (with G.K.S. Prakash and J. Somer) Superacids, 1984; (with Prakash, R.E. Williams, L.D. Field and K. Wade) Hypercarbon Chemistry, 1987; (with R. Malthotra and S.C. Narang) Nitration, 1989, Cage Hydrocarbons, 1990; (with Wade and Williams) Electron Deficient Boron and Carbon Clusters, 1991; (with Chambers and Prakash) Synthetic Fluorine Chemistry, 1992; (with Molnar) Hydrocarbon Chemistry, 1995; also chpts. in books, numerous papers in field; patentee in field. Recipient Leo Hendrik Baekeland award N.J. sect. Am. Chem. Soc., 1966, Morley medal Cleve. sect., 1970, Alexander von Humboldt Sr. U.S. Scientist award, 1979, Pioneer of Chemistry award Am. Inst. Chemists, 1993, Mendeleev medal Russian Acad. Scis., 1992, Nobel Prize in Chemistry, 1994. Fellow AAAS, Chem. Inst. Can.; mem. NAS, Italian NAS, European Acad. Arts, Scis. and Humanities, Italy Chem. Soc. (hon.), Hungarian Acad. Sci. (hon.), Am. Chem. Soc. (award petroleum chemistry 1964, award Synthetic organic chemistry 1979, Roger Adams award in organic chemistry 1989), German Chem. Soc., Brit. Chem. Soc. (Centenary lectr. 1978), Swiss Chem. Soc., Sigma Xi. Home: 2252 Gloaming Way Beverly Hills CA 90210-1717 Office: U So Calif Labor Hydrocarbon Rsch Inst Los Angeles CA 90007

OLBRANTZ, PATRICIA, school counselor; b. Reno, Nev., June 13, 1958; d. Helio Gomez and Teresa (Garzon) Jackson; 1 child, Jessica Rose. BA in Psychology, U. Nev., 1980, BA in Music Edn., 1984, MA in Ednl. Psychology, 1989. Mental health therapist Children's Behavioral Svcs., Reno, 1979-91; elem. sch. counselor Washoe County Sch. Dist., Reno, 1991—. Recipient Educator of Yr. award Child Assault Prevention, Reno, 1994. Mem. Phi Kappa Phi. Home: 12700 Fellowship Way Reno NV 89511-8657 Office: Lois Allen Elementary 5155 Mcguffey Rd Sun Valley NV 89433-8125

OLDHAM, CHRISTOPHER RUSSELL, wine company executive; b. Basingstoke, U.K., Sept. 18, 1946; came to U.S., 1986; s. Henry Russell Oldham and Esme Grace (Craufurd) Anderson; m. Elizabeth Jacoba Graham, Jan. 9, 1971 (div. 1978); children: Justin, Mark; m. Janet Patricia Gough, Dec. 9, 1978; children: Carro, Nicholas. Student, Rugby Sch., U.K., 1965, Madrid U., 1967, London Bus. Sch., 1972. Mgmt. exec. Guthrie & Co. (U.K.) Ltd., London and Singapore, 1973-74; mktg. dir. Guthrie & Co. (U.K.) Ltd., London, 1974-75; mng. dir. William Armes & Son, Sudbury, U.K., 1975-76; chmn. Transmarine Air Holdings Ltd., Luton, U.K., 1976-80; pres., owner S.C.E.A. Du Chateau De Lacaze, Gabarret, France, 1980-87; corp. devel. dir. Chateaux Shippers Ltd., London, 1984—; pres. Wine Link Inc., San Diego, 1987—, 1990—; cons. Transmarine Holdings Ltd., London, 1980—. Author: Armagnac and Eaux-De-Vie, 1986; author, editor (bi-monthly pub.) Wine Line, 1990—; contbr. articles to profl. jours. Hist. rsch. Societe Borda, Pau, France, 1981-87; mem. Worshipful Co. of Glaziers, City of London, Liveryman. Capt. U.K. Cavalry, 1967-71. Recipient Freedom of City of London by Lord Mayor of London, 1975. Mem. British Inst. of Mgmt., Confrerie Cadets de Gascogne, Cavalry Club London, Fairbanks Ranch Country Club, Southwestern Yacht Club (San Diego). Office: Chateaux Shippers Group 12526 High Bluff Dr Ste 300 San Diego CA 92130-2067

OLDHAM, ELAINE DOROTHEA, retired educator; b. Coalinga, Calif., June 29, 1931; d. Claude Smith Oldham and Dorothy Elaine (Hill) Wilkins. AB in History, U. Calif., Berkeley, 1953; MS in Sch. Adminstrn., Calif. State U., Hayward, 1976; postgrad. U. Calif., Berkeley, Harvard U., Mills Coll. Tchr. Piedmont Unified Sch. Dist., Calif., 1956-94, ret., 1994. Pres., bd. dirs. Camron-Stanford House Preservation Assn., 1979-86, adminstrv. v.p., bd. dirs., 1976-79, 86—; mem. various civic and community support groups; bd. dirs. Anne Martin Children's Ctr., Lincoln Child Ctr., Acacia br. Children's Hosp. Med. Ctr., No. Light Sch. Aux., East Bay League II of San Francisco Symphony. Mem. Am. Assn. Museums, Am. Assn. Mus. Trustees, Internat. Council Museums, Inst. Internat. Edn., Am. Assn. State and Local History, Am. Decorative Arts Forum, Oakland Mus. Assn., DAR (Outstanding Tchr. Am. History award), Colonial Dames Am., Magna Charta Dames, Daus. of Confederacy (bd. dirs.), Hugeunot Soc. (bd. dirs.), Plantagenent Soc., Order of Washington, Colonial Order of Crown, Americans of Royal Descent, Order St. George and Descs. of Knights of Garter, U. Calif. Alumni Assn. (co-chmn. and chmn. of 10th and 25th yr. class reunion coms.), Internat. Churchill Soc., English Speaking Union, Pacific Mus. Soc., Prytanean Alumnae Assn. (bd. dirs.), Phi Delta Kappa, Delta Kappa Gamma. Republican. Episcopalian. Clubs: Harvard (San Francisco), Bellevue.

OLDHAM, MAXINE JERNIGAN, real estate broker; b. Whittier, Calif., Oct. 13, 1923; d. John K. and Lela Hessie (Mears) Jernigan; m. Laurance Montgomery Oldham, Oct. 28, 1941; 1 child, John Laurence. AA, San Diego City Coll., 1973; student Western State U. Law, San Diego, 1976-77, LaSalle U., 1977-78; grad. Realtors Inst., Sacramento, 1978. Mgr. Edin Harig Realty, LaMesa, Calif., 1966-70; tchr. Bd. Edn., San Diego, 1959-66; mgr. Julia Cave Real Estate, San Diego, 1970-73; salesman Computer Realty, San Diego, 1973-74; owner Shelter Island Realty, San Diego, 1974—. Author: Jernigan History, 1982, Mears Geneology, 1985, Fustons of Colonial America, 1988, Sissoms. Mem. Civil Svc. Commn., San Diego, 1957-58. Recipient Outstanding Speaker award Dale Carnegie. Mem. Nat. Assn. Realtors, Calif. Assn. Realtors, San Diego Bd. Realtors, San Diego Apt. Assn., Internationale des Professions Immobilieres (internat. platform speaker), DAR (vice regent Linares chpt.), Colonial Dames 17th Century, Internat. Fedn. Univ. Women. Republican. Roman Catholic. Avocations: music, theater, painting, geneology, continuing edn. Home: 3348 Lowell St San Diego CA 92106-1713 Office: Shelter Island Realty 2810 Lytton St San Diego CA 92110-4810

OLDSHUE, PAUL FREDERICK, financial executive; b. Chgo., Nov. 4, 1949; s. James Young and Betty Ann (Wiersema) O.; m. Mary Elizabeth Holl, July 12, 1975; children: Emily Jane, Andrew Armstrong. Abigail Anne. BA, Williams Coll., Williamstown, Mass., 1971; MBA, NYU, 1978. With Chem. Bank, N.Y.C., 1973-78, asst. sec., 1976-78; with Orbanco Fin. Svc. Corp., 1978-83, v.p., treas., 1980-83; exec. v.p. Oreg. Bank, Portland, 1984-88; v.p. syndications PacifiCorp Fin. Svcs., Inc., 1988-90; exec. v.p. U.S. Bancorp, Portland, 1991—. Mem. Fin. Execs. Inst., Multnomah Athletic Club (Portland). Republican.

O'LEARY, MICHAEL JOSEPH, surgeon, neurotologist; b. Denver, May 17, 1954; s. Denis J. O'Leary and Audrey M. Ryan; m. Leslie S. West, Jan. 5, 1985; children: Claire Michael, Dorian Marie, Graden Joseph. BA cum laude, U. Rochester, 1976; MD magna cum laude, Georgetown U., 1980. Diplomate Nat. Bd. Med. Examiners, Am. Bd. Otolaryngology. Commd. 2d lt. USN, 1976, advanced through grades to comdr., 1990; intern specialized medicine Balboa Naval Hosp., San Diego, 1980-81; med. officer USS Bainbridge, 1981-82; resident otolaryngology, head and neck surgery Balboa Naval Hosp., San Diego, 1982-86; chief otolaryngology, head and neck surgery Navy Hosp., Newport, R.I., 1986-89; neurotology clin. fellow skull base surgery House Ear Clinic, L.A., 1989-90; microvascular surgery fellow Washington U., St. Louis, 1990-91; asst. clin. prof. surgery Uniformed Svcs. U. Health Scis., Bethesda, Md., 1992—; chief neurotology and skull base surgery divsn. otolaryngology, head and neck surgery dept. Navy Hosp. Balboa, San Diego; chmn. med. records and utilization rev. com. Naval Hosp., Newport, 1987-88, ACLS affiliate faculty mem. mil. tng. network, 1988-89; ATLS instr. Naval Hosp. San Diego, 1992—; med. news reporter Archives of Otolaryngology, 1991—; book reviewer Mil. Medicine, Bethesda, 1989—; mem. computers com. Am. Acad. Otolaryngology, 1992—, mem. skull base surgery com., 1992; invited guest instr. St. Louis U. Med. Ctr., 1991, 92, 93; guest instr. House Ear Inst., L.A., 1991, 93; tchr. various courses Naval Hosp., Newport, 1987, So. Calif. Health Coalition, San Diego, 1992, NHSD, 1992, NAB Coronado, Calif., 1993, AAOA, San Francisco, Boston, 1988, AFIP, Washington, 1985, Johns Hopkins, Balt., 1987, NNMC, Bethesda, 1987, Washington U., St. Louis, 1991, Ear Inst., Nashville, 1988, Naval Hosp. Oak Knoll, Oakland, Calif., 1983, 88, Navy Hosp., San Diego, 1991—, Mt. Sinai Sch. Medicine, N.Y.C., 1991; presenter in field. Author: (with others) Insights in Otolaryngology, 1991, Facial Plastic and Reconstructive Surgery, 1992, Otolaryngology - Head and Neck Surgery, 1992, Proceedings of the 4th International Tinnitus Seminar, 1992; contbr. articles to med. jours. Decorated Navy Commendation medal, Navy Achievement medal; recipient 1st prize San Diego Assn. Otolaryngology/Head & Neck Surgery, 1984, 86, 1st prize Mil. Assn. Otolaryngology/Head & Neck Surgery, 1984, 86. Fellow Am. Acad. Otolaryngology/Head and Neck Surgery; mem. AMA, Am. Soc. Mil. Surgeons, Soc. Mil. Otolaryngologists (treas. 1991—, pres. 1993-94), Alpha Omega Alpha. Home: 1215 Cuchara Dr Del Mar CA 92014-2646 Office: Navy Hosp Balboa Otolaryngology/Head & Neck Surgery Dept San Diego CA 92134

O'LEARY, THOMAS HOWARD, resources executive; b. N.Y.C., Mar. 19, 1934; s. Arthur J. and Eleanor (Howard) O'L.; m. Cheryl L. Westrum; children: Mark, Timothy, Thomas, Denis, Daniel, Mary Frances. A.B., Holy Cross Coll., 1954; postgrad., U. Pa., 1959-61. Asst. cashier First Nat. City Bank, N.Y.C., 1961-65; asst. to chmn. finance com. Mo. Pacific R.R.

Co., 1966-70, v.p. finance, 1971-76, dir., 1972-82, chmn. finance com., 1976-82; treas. Mo. Pacific Corp., St. Louis, 1968-71; v.p. finance Mo. Pacific Corp., 1971-72, exec. v.p., 1972-74, dir., 1972-82, pres., 1974-82; chmn. bd., CEO Mississippi River Transmission Corp., 1974-82; vice chmn. Burlington No., Inc., Seattle, 1982-89; bd. dirs. BF Goodrich, Kroger Co. Served to capt. USMC, 1954-58. Mem. Blind Brook Club (N.Y.C.), Chgo. Club. Office: Burlington Resources Inc 999 3rd Ave Ste 2810 Seattle WA 98104-4001*

OLES, STUART GREGORY, lawyer; b. Seattle, Dec. 15, 1924; s. Floyd and Helen Louise (La Violette) O.; B.S. magna cum laude, U. Wash., 1947, J.D., 1948; m. Ilse Hanewald, Feb. 12, 1954; children: Douglas, Karl, Stephen. Admitted to Wash. bar, 1949, U.S. Supreme Ct. bar, 1960; dep. pros. atty. King County (Wash.), 1949, chief civil dept., 1949-50; gen. practice law, Seattle, 1950—; sr. partner firm Oles, Morrison & Rinker and predecessor, 1955-90, of counsel, 1991—. Author: A View From the Rock, 1994. Chmn. Seattle Community Concert Assn., 1955; pres. Friends Seattle Pub. Library, 1956; mem. Wash. Pub. Disclosure Commn., 1973-75; trustee Ch. Div. Sch. of Pacific, Berkeley, Calif., 1974-75; mem. bd. curators Wash. State Hist. Soc., 1983; former mem. Seattle Symphony Bd.; pres. King County Ct. House Rep. Club, 1950, U. Wash. Young Rep. Club, 1947; Wash. conv. floor leader Taft, 1952, Goldwater, 1964; Wash. chmn. Citizens for Goldwater, 1964; chmn. King County Rep. convs., 1966, 68, 76, 84, 86, 88, 90, 92, Wash. State Rep. Conv., 1980. Served with USMCR, 1943-45. Mem. ABA (past regional vice chmn. pub. contract law sect.), Wash. Bar Assn., Order of Coif, Scabbard and Blade, Am. Legion, Kapoho Beach Club (pres.), Am. Highland Cattle Assn. (v.p. and dir.), Phi Beta Kappa, Phi Alpha Delta. Episcopalian (vestryman, lay-reader), Rainier Club, Seattle Yacht Club. Home: 5051 50th Ave NE Apt 40 Seattle WA 98105-2869 Office: Oles Morrison & Rinker 701 5th Ave Ste 3300 Seattle WA 98104-7016

OLGUIN, VICTOR HUGO, school counselor, educator; b. Mexico City, July 28, 1941; came to U.S., 1967; s. Arnulfo and Columba (Rodriguez) O.; m. Vivian Karen Hogue, Apr. 21, 1967; 1 child, Nikolas Alejandro. Student, North Seattle C.C., 1970-72; BA in Psychology, U. Wash., 1974; MEd in Guidance and Counseling, City U., Bellevue, Wash., 1994. Cert. sch. counselor, Wash. Lang. instr. Berlitz Sch. Langs., Seattle, 1974-75; instr., interpreter, tech. translator Boeing Aircraft Co., Seattle, 1975; human rels. assoc., spl. edn./vocat. edn. tchr., advisor Seattle Sch. Dist., 1975—. Rep. evening students adv. bd. U. Wash., Seattle, 1978. Sgt. Mexican Army, 1960-61. Mem. ACA, APA, NEA, Wash. Edn. Assn., Seattle Edn. Assn., U. Wash. Alumni Assn., City U. Alumni Assn. Office: Seattle Sch Dist 815 4th Ave Seattle WA 98104-1603

OLIPHANT, CHARLES ROMIG, physician; b. Waukegan, Ill., Sept. 10, 1917; s. Charles L. and Mary (Goss) R.; student St. Louis U., 1936-40; m. Claire E. Canavan, Nov. 7, 1942; children: James R., Cathy Rose, Mary G., William D. Student, St. Louis U., 1936-40, MD, 1943; postgrad. Naval Med. Sch., 1946. Intern, Nat. Naval Med. Ctr., Bethesda, Md., 1943; pvt. practice medicine and surgery, San Diego, 1947—; pres., CEO Midway Med. Enterprises; former chief staff Balboa Hosp., Doctors Hosp., Cabrillo Med. Ctr.; chief staff emeritus Sharp Cabrillo Hosp.; mem. staff Mercy Hosp., Children's Hosp., Paradise Valley Hosp., Sharp Meml. Hosp.; sec. Sharp Sr. Health Care, S.D.; mem. exec. bd., program chmn. San Diego Power Squadron, 1985-93, 95. Charter mem. Am. Bd. Family Practice. Served with M.C., USN, 1943-47. Recipient Golden Staff award Sharp Cabrillo Hosp. Med. Staff, 1990. Fellow Am. Geriatrics Soc. (emeritus), Am. Acad. Family Practice, Am. Assn. Abdominal Surgeons; mem. AMA, Calif. Med. Assn., Am. Acad. Family Physicians (past pres. San Diego chpt., del. Calif. chpt.), San Diego Med. Soc., Public Health League, Navy League, San Diego Power Squadron (past comdr.), SAR. Clubs: San Diego Yacht, Cameron Highlanders. Home: 4310 Trias St San Diego CA 92103-1127

OLIPHANT, ELIZABETH KNOTT, food products executive; b. 1919. With Knott's Berry Farm, Buena Park, Calif., 1940—. Office: Knott's Berry Farm 8039 Beach Blvd Buena Park CA 90620-3225*

OLIVA, STEPHEN EDWARD, resource conservationist, lawyer; b. San Rafael, Calif., Jan. 31, 1946; s. George Verdelli Jr. and Dorothy Margaret (Austin) O.; m. Susan Rebecca Ellis, May 5, 1984; children: Stephanie, Mary. BA, U. Calif., Santa Barbara, 1972; JD, U. of the Pacific, 1992. Bar: Calif. 1993, U.S. Dist. Ct. (ea. dist.) Calif. 1993. Naturalist Calif. Dept. Transp., Sacramento, 1973-76; planner Calif. Energy Commn., Sacramento, 1976, Calif. Air Resources Bd., Sacramento, 1976-79; spl. asst. to sec. The Resources Agy., Sacramento, 1979-80; spl. asst. Calif. Dept. Conservation, Sacramento, 1980, mgr. land conservation unit, 1981-87; spl. asst. Calif. Dept. Forestry, Sacramento, 1980-81; chief Office Land Conservation Calif. Dept. Conservation, Sacramento, 1987-89, dep. chief Calif. div. of recycling, 1989-91, environ. coord., 1991-92, staff counsel, legal office, 1992—; mem. governing bd. Calif. Tahoe Regional Planning Agy., South Lake Tahoe, 1979-81; mem. policy adv. com. Sacramento County Local Agy. Formation Commn., 1988-89. Served with U.S. Army, 1966-68, Vietnam. Mem. ABA, Calif. State Bar, Sacramento County Bar Assn. Democrat. Office: Calif Dept Conservation 801 K St ms 24 #03 Sacramento CA 95814

OLIVER, DAN DAVID, banker; b. Walla Walla, Wash., Mar. 11, 1952; s. Harold Allen and Nydia Jane (Munns) O.; children: Ana Mary, Whitney Leigh. Univ. Coll., Cardiff, Wales, 1972-73; BA in Pre-Law, Wash. State U., 1974; MBA in Taxation, Golden Gate U., 1979; JD, Western State U., 1978; grad. with trust specialization, Pacific Coast Banking Sch., U. Wash., Seattle, 1987; grad. Banking Law Sch., George Mason U., Washington, 1993; grad., Nat. Compliance Sch., Norman, Okla., 1994. Tax acct. John F. Forbes & Co., San Francisco, 1979-81; cat skinner James Francis Munns Farms, Inc., Prescott, Wash., 1981-82; law clk. Sherwood, Tugman, Gose & Reser, Walla Walla, 1975-79; adminstrv. asst. Baker-Boyer Nat. Bank, Walla Walla, 1982-83, asst. trust officer, 1984, trust officer, 1985, asst. v.p., legal counsel, 1986, asst. v.p., legal/compliance officer, 1987, v.p. and legal/compliance officer, 1988—; vice chmn. bd. dirs. Elite Turf Farm, Inc., West Richland, Wash., sr. v.p., sec., legal counsel, 1988-92; commr. Walla Walla City Housing Authority, 1992—. Bd. dirs. Prescott (Wash.) Sch. Dist., 1983-87, vice chmn., 1985, chmn., 1986; vol. spirits religious edn. program St. Patrick's Cath. Ch., 1990—; mem. Walla Walla Park and Recreation Adv. Bd., 1991-92, vice chmn., 1992; chmn. Park Improvement Com. for Irrigation, 1992; chair Walla Walla Area Com. for Housing, 1991-94; linesman Youth Soccer League; mem. PTA, sch. vol. Prospect Point Elem. Sch.; mem. panel Govt. and Politics Seminar, Leadership Walla Walla, 1994. Mem. Am. Bankers Assn., Nat. Assn. of Housing and Redevelopment Officials, Wash. Bankers Assn. (compliance com. 1990—, vice chmn. 1994-95, cmty. reinvestment act panel, 1994), Walla Walla Valley Estate Planning Coun. (bd. dirs. 1986-87, treas. 1987-88, sec. 1988-89, v.p. 1989-90, pres. 1990-91), Nat. Arbor Day Found., Columbia Rural Elec. Assn., Walla Walla Men's Group (treas.), Walla Walla Exch. Club, Sigma Alpha Epsilon (recorder 1971-72), Nat. Assn. of Underwaters Instrs. (open water I cert. 1992, open water II cert. 1993, cert. CPR and oxygen provider 1994, mem. divers alert network 1993—, reef environ. edn. found. 1994—), Bergevin Family Reunion and Edn. Assn. (treas. 1993—), Frenchtown Found. (charter), Beta Sigma Phi. Office: Baker-Boyer Nat Bank Main And # 2D Sts Walla Walla WA 99362

OLIVER, JOHN EDWARD, bank training consultant; b. Bedford, Eng., Apr. 14, 1951; came to U.S., 1978; s. Fred K. and Marjorie F. (Brown) O.; m. Jacqueline L. Alcock, Oct. 7, 1972; 1 child, Sophie Rose. Student, Mander Coll., Bedford, 1968-71. Mgr.'s asst. Nat. Westminster Bank, Bedford, 1971-73; credit analyst Kleinwort Benson Ltd., London, 1973-76; mktg. coord. Amex Bank Ltd., London, 1976-78; v.p. Continental Ill. Energy Devel. Corp., Houston, 1978-85; pres. Laurel Mgmt. Systems Inc., San Francisco, 1986—; cons. various U.S. and internat. banks including Kansallis-Osake-Pankki, London, 1985—; bank edn. cons. Bank Am., San Francisco, 1986—; advisor Am. Inst. Banking, San Francisco, 1994—. Author bank tng. programs, utilizing computer simulations. Mem. ASTD, Assn. Bank Trainers and Cons. Office: Laurel Mgmt Systems Inc 235 Pine St Ste 1300 San Francisco CA 94104-2701

OLIVER, JOYCE ANNE, journalist, editorial consultant, columnist; b. Coral Gables, Fla., Sept. 19, 1958; d. John Joseph and Rosalie Cecile (Mack) O. BA in Communications, Calif. State U., Fullerton, 1980, MBA, 1990. Corp. editor Norris Industries Inc., Huntington Beach, Calif., 1979-82; pres. J.A. Oliver Assocs., La Habra Heights, Calif., 1982—; corp. editorial cons. Norris Industries, 1982, Better Methods Cons., Huntington Harbour, Calif., 1982-83, Summit Group, Orange, Calif., 1982-83, UDS, Encinitas, Calif., 1983-84, MacroMarketing, Costa Mesa, Calif., 1985-86, PM Software, Huntington Beach, Calif., 1985-86, CompuQuote, Canoga Park, Calif., 1985-86, Nat. Semicondr. Can. Ltd., Mississauga, Ont., Can., 1986, Maclean Hunter Ltd., Toronto, Ont., 1986-90; Frame Inc., Fullerton, Calif., 1987-88, The Johnson-Layton Co., L.A., 1988-89, Corp. Rsch. Inc., Chgo., 1988, Axon Group, Horsham, Pa., 1990-91, Am. Mktg. Assn., Chgo., 1990-92, Kenzaikai Co., Ltd., Tokyo, 1991, Penton Pub., Cleve., 1991, Bus. Computer Pub., Inc., Peterborough, N.H., 1991-92, Helmers Pub., Inc., Peterborough, 1992, Schnell Pub., Co., Inc., N.Y.C., 1992-93, Diversified Pub. Group, Carol Stream, Ill., 1993; mem. Rsch. Coun. of Scripps Clinic and Rsch. Found., 1987-92. Contbg. editor Computer Merchandising/ Resell, 1982-85, Computer Reselling, 1985, Reseller Mgmt., 1987-89; contbg. editor Can. Electronics Engring., 1986-90, west coast editor, 1990, Chem. Bus. mag., 1992-93; spl. feature editor Cleve. Inst. Electronics publ. The Electron, 1986-89; bus. columnist Mktg. News, 1990-92; contbr. articles to profl. jours. and mags. Bd. dirs. Action Comms., 1993—. Mem. IEEE, Internat. Platform Assn., Soc. Photo-optical Instrumentation Engrs., Inst. Mgmt. Scis., Nat. Writers Club (profl.), Internat. Mktg. Assn., Soc. Profl. Journalists, L.A. World Affairs Coun. Republican. Roman Catholic. Office: 2045 Fullerton Rd La Habra CA 90631-8213

OLIVER, MARVIN MAURICE, lawyer; b. Monroe, La., Oct. 6, 1947; s. Maurice and Fannie Lou (Reppond) O.; m. Frances Cristine Penn, July 21, 1984. AA, Grayson County Coll., 1973; BS, Western State U., 1986, JD, 1987. Profl. employment counselor Snelling & Snelling, Monroe, 1968; from dept. mgr. to sr. merchandising mgr. J.C. Penney Co., Alexandria, La., 1968-76; mfrs. rep. Maurice Oliver Sales, 1976-81; assoc. mgr. Gt. Am. Res. Ins. Co./J.C. Penney Fin. Svcs., Alexandria, 1979-84; ins. gen. agt. Oliver Ins. Svcs., Santa Ana, Calif., 1984-90; pvt. practice law Santa Ana, 1990—. Mem. ABA, Calif. Bar Assn., Western State Alumni Assn. (dir.), Orange County Barristers (past dir., continuing legal edn. chmn.). Office: 1551 N Tustin Ave Ste 550 Santa Ana CA 92701-3082

OLIVER, MARY ANNE MCPHERSON, religion educator; b. Montgomery, Ala., Nov. 21, 1935; d. James Curtis and Margaret Sinclair (Miller) McPherson; m. Raymond Davies Oliver, Aug. 28, 1959; children: Kathryn Sinclair, Nathan McPherson. BA, U. Ala., Tuscaloosa, 1956; cert., Sorbonne, Paris, 1958; MA, U. Wis., 1959; PhD, Grad. Theol. Union, Berkeley, Calif., 1972. Vol. tchr., preacher, counselor, 1972—; instr. U. Calif., Berkeley, St. Mary's Coll., Moraga, Calif., 1973; adj. faculty San Francisco Theol. Sem., San Anselmo, 1977-81; lectr. San Jose (Calif.) State U., 1980-81, San Francisco State U., 1985-86; adj. prof. dept. liberal arts John F. Kennedy U., Orinda, Calif., 1987—; vis. prof. Gen. Theol. Sem., N.Y.C., 1995. Author: History of Good Shepherd Episcopal Mission, 1978, Conjugal Spirituality: The Primacy of Mutual Love in Christian Tradition, 1994; contbr. articles to profl. jours. Rep. Ala. Coun. on Human Rels., Mobile, 1958; active deanery, conv. Good Shepherd Episc. Ch., Berkeley, Calif., 1970-75; rep. U. Calif. Fgn. Student Hospitality, Berkeley, 1965-70; vol. tchr. Berkeley pub. schs., 1965-73; bd. dirs. Canterbury Found., Berkeley, 1972-75; chmn. bd. dirs. West Berkeley Parish, Berkeley, 1976-78, adult edn. program St. Mark's Episc. Ch., 1992-93; mentor Edn. for Ministry, Univ. of the South, 1993—. Recipient award French Consulate, New Orleans, 1956; Fulbright grantee, 1956, grantee Mabelle McLeod Lewis Found., 1969. Mem. Am. Acad. Religion, Conf. on Christianity and Lit. Democrat. Home: 1632 Grant St Berkeley CA 94703-1356 Office: John F Kennedy U 12 Altarinda Rd Orinda CA 94563-2603

OLIVER, ROBERT WARNER, economics educator; b. L.A., Oct. 26, 1922; s. Ernest Warner and Elnore May (McConnell) O.; m. Darlene Hubbard, July 1, 1946 (dec. Mar. 1987); children: Lesley Joanne Oliver McClelland, Stewart Warner; m. Jean Tupman Smock, July 15, 1989. AB, U. So. Calif., 1943, AM, 1948; AM, Princeton U., 1950, PhD, 1958. Teaching asst. U. So. Calif., 1946-47; instr. Princeton U., 1947-50, Pomona Coll., L.A., Calif., 1950-52; asst. prof. U. So. Calif., Los Angeles, 1952-56; economist Stanford Research Inst., South Pasadena, Calif., 1956-59; mem. faculty dept. econs. Calif. Inst. Tech., 1959-88, prof. econs., 1973-88, prof. emeritus, 1988—; urban economist World Bank, Washington, 1970-71; cons. Brookings Instn., 1961, OECD, Paris, 1979; vis. prof. U. So. Calif., 1985; vis. scholar Pembrook Coll., Cambridge U., Eng., 1989-90. Author: An Economic Survey of Pasadena, 1959, International Economic Cooperation and the World Bank, 1975, Bretton Woods: A Retrospective Essay, 1985, Oral History Project: The World Bank, 1986; contbg. author: Ency. of Econs., 1981, 94, George Woods and the World Bank, 1995. Mem. Human Rels. Com. City of Pasadena, 1964-65, Planning Commn., 1972-75, 91—; bd. dirs. Pasadena City Coun., 1965-69; mem. Utilities Adv. Commn., 1984-88, Strategic Planning Com., 1985; pres. Pasadena Beautiful Found., 1972-74; bd. dirs. Pasadena Minority History Found., 1984—, Jackie Robinson Meml. Found., 1994—; trustee PAsadena Hist. Soc., 1992-94. Lt. (j.g.) USN, 1942-46. Social Sci. rsch. fellow London Sch. Econs., 1954-55; Rockefeller Found. fellow, 1974, 91; Danforth assoc., 1981; recipient Outstanding Teaching award, 1982, Master of the Student Houses, 1987; Hon. Alumnus, 1987—. Mem. Am. Econs. Assn., Royal Econs. Assn., Com. on Fgn. Rels., Phi Beta Kappa, Phi Kappa Phi, Delta Tau Delta. Democrat. Methodist. Club: Athenaeum. Home: 3197 San Pasqual St Pasadena CA 91107-5330 Office: 1201 E California Blvd Pasadena CA 91125-0001

OLIVER, STEPHEN RONALD, communications engineer, educator; b. Mountain Lake, Minn., Aug. 11, 1947; s. Stephen Thomas and Ella Hulda (Merry) O.; m. Joy Ella Parkinson, Oct. 16, 1976; children: Heather Joy, Shannon Thomas. BA in Math and Philosophy, Morningside Coll., 1970; MS in Computer Sci., U. Kans., 1975; PhD in Computer Sci., Colo. State U., 1988. Application programmer Dana F. Cole & Co., CPA's, Lincoln, Nebr., 1972-73; systems programmer U. Kans. Computation Ctr., Lawrence, 1973-76; custom products engr. Perkin Elmer Computer Systems, Arlington Heights, Ill., 1976-80; tech. staff MITRE, Colorado Springs, Colo., 1980-81; instr. U. Colo. Dept. Computer Sci., Colorado Springs, 1980-85; staff scientist Sci. Applications Internat. Corp., Colorado Springs, 1982-88; prof. Calif. Poly State U., San Luis Obispo, 1988—; dir., Calif. Polytech. Computer Systems Lab., 1989—. Outings chmn. Colo. Mountain Club, Colorado Springs, 1987-88; canvas dir. All Souls Unitarian Ch., Colorado Springs, 1988. NDEA fellow, 1970-72, Sci. Applications Internat. Corp. fellow, 1985-88. Mem. Assn. Computing Machinery (SIG Small/PC treas. 1979-83, chmn. 1983-85, SIG bd. fin. adv. 1984-88, chmn., 1988-90, v.p. 1990-92, Small/PC Oustanding Svc. award 1988, lectr. 1986-90). Office: Calif Poly State U Dept Computer Sci San Luis Obispo CA 93407

OLKEN, DEBORAH JEANNE, non-profit organization executive; b. Lynn, Mass., May 21, 1953; d. Harry G. and Ruth E. (Kaufman) Olken. AB, U. Pa., 1976; MBA, Babson Coll., Mass., 1983. Group ops. agt. Crimson Travel Service, Cambridge, Mass., 1977-79; research assoc. Inst. Cert. Travel Agts., Wellesley, Mass., 1979-80; sr. fin. analyst Bank of Am., San Francisco, 1984-85, fin. cons., 1985-86; cons. Info. Resources Inc., San Francisco, 1986-87; sr. fin. analyst Wells Fargo Bank, San Francisco, 1988-89, systems analyst, 1989-91; mgmt. cons., 1992-94; grants mgr. Jewish Cmty. Fedn., San Francisco, 1994—. Mem. World Affairs Coun. No. Calif., Commonwealth (San Francisco) Club, Sierra. Avocations: sailing, photography.

OLLANDER-KRANE, JASON ERIC, management consultant; b. New Haven, Apr. 14, 1955; s. Sherman Morton and June Carol (Pickus) Krane; m. Robert Ollander, May 4, 1980; 1 child, Craig Scott Ollander-Krane. BA, Rutgers Coll., 1978. Tng. exec. Macy's, N.Y.C., 1979-82; asst. to pres. Bus. Careers, N.Y.C., 1982-83; mgr. tng. devel. Young & Rubicam, N.Y.C., 1983-88; dir. human resources Wells Fargo Bank, San Francisco, 1988-89; v.p. tng. and staff devel. Adia Svcs. Inc., Menlo Park, Calif., 1989-90; owner, chief exec. Ollander-Krane/Johnson, San Francisco, 1990—. Author (book) Goodbye Willy Loman: Selling in the 90's, 1990. Mem. adv. com. Pres.'s Nat. Svc. Program, San Francisco, 1993; commr. Blue Ribbon Commn. for Nat. Svc., San Francisco, 1993—; chmn. Neil Johnson Meml. Fund, San Francisco, 1993—; cons. The Names Project/AIDS Meml. Quilt, San Francisco, 1993—. Eder Bros. Inc. scholar, 1973-78. Office: Ollander-Krane/Johnson 70 Zoe St San Francisco CA 94107-1733

OLLEY, ROBERT EDWARD, economist, educator; b. Vendun, Que., Can., Apr. 16, 1933; s. Edwin Henry and Elizabeth (Reed) O.; m. Shirley Ann Dahl, Jan. 19, 1957; children—Elizabeth Anne, George Steven, Susan Catherine, Maureen Carolyn. B.A., Carleton U., Can., 1960; M.A., Queen's U., Can., 1961, Ph.D. in Econs., 1969. Vis. asst. prof. Queen's U., Kingston, Ont., Can., 1967-68; asst. prof. econs. U. Sask., Saskatoon, Can., 1963-67, 68-69, assoc. prof., 1969-71, 73-75, prof., 1975-93, prof. emeritus, 1993—; pres. Gen. Econs. Ltd., 1993—; dir. rsch. Royal Commn. on Consumer Problems and Inflation, 1967-68; econ. advisor Bell Can., Montreal, Que., 1971-73, 78-79, Can. Telecom. Carriers Assn., 1978-85, Sask. Power Corp., 1980-83; econ. advisor AT&T, 1980-90, Waste Mgmt., Inc., 1990-92, SaskTel, 1989-93; chmn. adv. com. on consumer stds. Stds. Coun. Can., 1992-93; Can. rep. to ISO/COPOLCO, Geneva, 1992-93. Author, editor: Consumer Product Testing, 1979; Consumer Product Testing II, 1981; Consumer Credit in Canada, 1966; Economics of the Public Firm: Regulation, Rates, Costs, Productivity Analysis, 1983, Total Factor Productivity of Canadian Telecommunications, 1984; Consumer Reps. Conf. Procs., 1st-4th, 1982-91. Bd. dirs. Can. Found. for Econ. Edn., 1974-82, Can. Gen. Standards Bd., 1977-81. Recipient Her Magesty The Queen Silver Jubilee medal, 1977. Mem. Royal Econ. History Soc., Royal Econs. Assn., Econ. History Assn., Am. Econ. Assn., Can. Econ. Assn., Consumers Assn. Can. (v.p. 1967-75, chmn. 1975-77), Can. Stds. Assn. (dir., mem. exec. com. 1971-93, vice chmn. 1985-87, chmn. 1987-89, Award of Merit 1995), Consumer's Assn. Found. Can. (v.p. 1989-95), Can. Comms. Rsch. Ctr. (dir. 1992—), Internat. Telecom. Soc. (bd. dirs. 1986—), Shaw Guild. Home and office: PO Box 1040, 374 Queen St, Niagara on the Lake, ON Canada L0S 1J0

OLLMAN, ARTHUR LEE, museum director, photographer; b. Milw., Mar. 6, 1947; s. Benn and Shirley O. B.A., U. Wis., 1969; student, San Francisco Art Inst., 1974; M.F.A., Lone Mountain Coll., 1977. Instr. San Francisco Mus. Modern Art, 1976-78, Chabot Coll., 1977-83; mus. dir. Mus. Photog. Arts, San Diego. Founder, dir., producer Photo History Video Project; author: Samuel Bourne, Images of India, 1983, Arnold Newman, Five Decades, 1986, William Klein: An American in Paris, 1987, Revelaciones, The Art of Manuel Alvarez Bravo, 1990, Fata Morgana: The American Way of Life, 1992, Seduced by Life: The Art of Lou Stoumen, 1992; exhibited in one-man shows including Grapestake Gallery, San Francisco, 1979, Centre Georges Pompidou, Musee Nat. D'Art et De Culture, Paris, 1979, Inst. Contemporary Art, Boston, 1985, Night: Photograph Gallery, N.Y.C., 1981, Kodak Gallery, Tokyo, 1988; exhibited in group shows at Milw. Art Ctr., 1979, U. Hawaii, 1979-81, San Francisco Mus. Modern Art, 1980, Monas Heiroglyphicas, Milan, Italy, 1978, Mus. Modern Art, N.Y.C., 1978, Whitney Mus. Am. Art, N.Y.C., 1981, Detroit Inst. Arts, 1994, Mus. Contemporary Art, L.A., 1994; represented in permanent collections, including, Mus. Modern Art, N.Y.C, Centre Georges Pompidou, Bibliotheque Nationale, Paris, Tokyo Inst. Polytechnics, Met. Mus. Art, N.Y.C., Nat. Mus. Am. Art, Washington, Chase-Manhattan collection, N.Y.C. NEA fellow, 1979; Calif. Arts Council grantee, 1977-78, NEA grantee, 1978, exhbn. aid grantee, 1979-80. Mem. San Francisco CAMERAWORK (pres. bd. dirs. 1978-83), Am. Assn. Mus. Jewish. Address: 4310 Goldfinch St San Diego CA 92103-1315 also: Mus Photographic Arts Balboa Park San Diego CA 92101

OLMSTEAD, RICHARD GALE, JR., engineering manager; b. Cheyenne, Wyo., Sept. 13, 1950; s. Richard Gale and Dorothy Fern (Willis) O.; m. Patricia Ann Smith Olmstead Boultinghouse, July 21, 1974 (div. Sept. 1986); children: Melissa Michele, Richard Gale III; m. Cheryl Anne Reihel Sherman, June 25, 1993. BS in Gen. Bus., U. Wyo., 1973; MA in Human Resource Mgmr., Pepperdine U., 1978; postgrad., Woodbury U. Cert. profl. mgr. Engring. asst. Wyo. Hwy. Dept., Cheyenne, 1969-72; asst. mgr. Gen. Fin. Corp. of Wyo., 1980-81; office mgr. Cheyenne Country Club, 1981; owner, operator Sweet Tymes Ice Cream Parlour, Cheyenne, 1980-82; electronic systems engr. Lockheed Aeronautical Systems Co., Burbank, Calif., 1981-86; group engr. Lockheed Advanced Devel. Co., Palmdale, Calif., 1986—; supr. and mgmt. skills faciltator, Lockheed Mgmt. Assn., Palmdale, 1989—;. Lt. USN, 1967-80. Mem. Nat. Mgmt. Assn., Lockheed Mgmt. Assn. (dir. SMS tng. 1991-92, v.p. profl. devel. 1994-95), Inst. Cert. Profl. Mgrs., Naval Res. Assn., Kiwanis (club pres., div. sec.-treas., bd. dirs., leadership devel. trainer Burbank 1990—, Kiwanian of Yr. award 1982, 89, 91). Republican. Home: 3850 Paula Ln Lancaster CA 93535-5866 Office: Lockheed Advanced Devel Co 1011 Lockheed Way Palmdale CA 93599-0001

OLMSTED, RONALD DAVID, foundation executive, consultant; b. Portland, Oreg., June 27, 1937; s. Clifford Wolford and Ruth Emily (Driesner) O.; m. Susan Mary Spare, Dec. 27, 1961 (div. June 1972); 1 child, Craig William. Student, Lewis & Clark Coll., 1955-57, U. So. Calif., L.A., 1959-62. V.p., exec. dir. L.A. Ctr. for Internat. Visitors, 1961-67; assoc. dir. devel. U. Chgo., 1967-71; v.p. devel. and pub. affairs Northwestern Meml. Hosp., Chgo., 1971-79; dir. devel. Marimed Found., Honolulu, 1989-93; dir. devel., protection Advocacy Agy. of Hawaii, Honolulu, 1994—; cons. on health, edn. and human svc. orgns., Ill., Mich., Oreg., Hawaii, 1979—; mem. Honolulu Mayor's Com. on People with Disabilities, 1995—. Contbr. articles on African travels and African affair to profl. publs. Co-founder, treas. Civil Found. of Chelsea, Mich., 1982-83; treas. Chelsea Area C. of C., 1981-83; trustee Harris Sch., Chgo., 1972-73, Ogden Dunes (Ind.) Town Bd.; bd. dirs. United Way Porter County, Ind., 1969-71; mem. L.A. Com. on Fgn. Rels., 1965-69; bd. dirs. Am. Friends of Africa, 1965-68, Nat. Coun. for Cmty. Svcs. to Internat. Visitors, 1965-67; mem. exec. com. L.A. Mayor's Coun. for Internat. Visitors and Sister Cities, 1964-68; vice chmn. Greater L.A. Com. Internat. Student Svcs., 1966; mem. Honolulu Mayor's Com. on People with Disablities, 1995—. Recipient Koa Anvil award Pub. Rels. Soc. Am.-Honolulu, 1992, multiple awards Assn. Am. Colls., 1975-79, multiple MacEachern awards Am. Acad. Hosp. Pub. Rels., 1974-79, multiple awards Nat. Assn. for Hosp. Devel., 1975-79. Mem. Nat. Soc. Fund Raising Execs. Presbyterian. Home and Office: 469 Ena Rd Apt 1506 Honolulu HI 96815-1710

OLMSTED, SUZANNE M., photographer; b. Palo Alto, Calif., Apr. 15, 1956; d. Gerald W. and Frances M. (Barnett) O.; m. Edward A. Gillum, July 6, 1982; children: Gerald, James. BA, U. Calif., Santa Cruz, 1979; MFA, So. Ill. U., 1982. Lectr. in photography Ea. Mont. Coll., Billings, 1983-87; exec. dir. Artlink, Phoenix, 1991; artist-in-residence The City of Tempe, Ariz., 1990-92; photo editor The Current, Phoenix, 1993-94; gallery mgr., ass.t prof. art U. Nev., Reno, 1994—. Exhibits include Ea. N.Mex. U., Portales, 1993, Szabo Fine Arts Gallery, Phoenix, 1992, Tempe Art Ctr., 1992, So. Ill. U., Carbondale, 1991, Photo Art Gallery, Burbank, Calif., 1991, Gallery of Art, Rockford (Ill.) Coll., 1991, Red River Exhbn./Silver Anniversary, Plains Art Mus., Moorhead, Minn., 1990, John Michael Kohler Art Ctr., Sheboygan, Wis., 1990, numerous others; contbr. photographs to numerous publs. including Northern Lights, New Times, Quantum Metaphysics and more. Recipient Eben Demarest award Eben Demarest Trust, Pitts., 1987, Outstanding Young Women of Am. award, 1984. Home: 701 Ruby Ave Reno NV 89503-3429 Office: U Nev Dept Art/224 Reno NV 89557

OLPIN, ROBERT SPENCER, art history educator; b. Palo Alto, Calif., Aug. 30, 1940; s. Ralph Smith and Ethel Lucille (Harman) O.; m. Mary Florence Catharine Reynolds, Aug. 24, 1963; children: Mary Courtney, Cristin Lee, Catharine Elizabeth, Carrie Jean. BS, U. Utah, 1963; AM, Boston U., 1965, PhD, 1971. Lectr. art history Boston U., 1965-67; asst. prof. U. Utah, Salt Lake City, 1967-72, assoc. prof., 1972-76, prof., 1976—, chmn. dept., 1975-82, dir. art history program, 1968-76, 83-84, dean Coll. Fine Arts, 1987—; cons. curator Am. and English art Utah Mus. Fine Arts, 1973—. Grantee U. Utah, 1972, 85, Utah Mus. Fine Arts, 1975, Utah Bicentennial Commn., 1975, Ford Found., 1975, Utah Endowment for Humanities, 1984, 85, Quinney Found., 1986, U. Utah, 1987, State Utah, 1989, Christensen Found., 1993, Eccles Found, 1994, 95; trustee Pioneer State Theatre Found., 1988—; vice chair Utah Arts Coun., 1993-95, chair, 1995—, Utah Sci. Ctr. Authority, 1995—. Mem. NASULGC (commn. on the arts, 1989-93), Utah Arts Coun., Utah Sci. Authority, Archives Am. Art Smithsonian Instn., Coll. Art Assn. Am., Utah Acad. Scis. Arts Letters, Assn. Historians Am. Art, Internat. Coun. Fine Arts Deans, Phi Kappa Phi, Sigma Nu. Republican. Mormon. Author: Alexander Helwig Wyant, 1836-92, 1968, Mainstreams/Reflections-American/Utah Architecture, 1973, American Painting Around 1850, 1976, Art-Life of Utah, 1977, Dictionary of Utah Art, 1980, A Retrospective of Utah Art, 1981, Waldo Midgley: Birds,

Animals, People, Things, 1984, A Basket of Chips, 1985, The Works of Alexander Helwig Wyant, 1986, Salt Lake County Fine Arts Collection, 1987, Signs and Symbols...Utah Art, 1988, J.A.F. Everett, 1989, George Dibble, 1989, Utah Art, 1991; contbd. articles to profl. jours. including Utah, State of the Arts, 1993, Utah History Encyclopedia, 1994. Home: 887 Woodshire Ave Salt Lake City UT 84107-7639 Office: U Utah Coll Fine Arts 250 Art & Architecture Ctr Salt Lake City UT 84112

OLSBY, GREGORY SCOTT, financial executive; b. Seattle; s. Robert G. and M. JoAnn Olsby; m. Carol A. Murphy; children: Joshua, Julia, Jacob. BA, U. Wash., 1979; MBA, George Washington U., 1983. Budget analyst Tracor, Inc., Rockville, Md.; fin. mgr. Concurrent Computer, Rockville; mgr. govt. acctg. US West, Inc., Rockville and Bellevue, Wash., 1985-90; chief fin. officer, contr. MetriCor, Inc., Woodinville, Wash., 1990-92; v.p. finance Media Logic, Kent, Wash., 1992-94; prin. Wash. Bus. Consulting, Woodinville, 1992—; CFO Peopleware, Bellevue, Wash., 1994—. Mem. Am. Electronics Assn., Wash. Software Assn. Office: 18615 NE 194th St Woodinville WA 98072-8263

OLSCHWANG, ALAN PAUL, lawyer; b. Chgo., Jan. 30, 1942; s. Morton James and Ida (Ginsberg) O.; m. Barbara Claire Miller, Aug. 22, 1965; children: Elliot, Deborah, Jeffrey. B.S., U. Ill., 1963, J.D., 1966. Bar: Ill. 1966, N.Y. 1984, Calif. 1992. Law clk. Ill. Supreme Ct., Bloomington, 1966-67; assoc. Sidley & Austin, and predecessor, Chgo., 1967-73; with Montgomery Ward & Co., Inc., Chgo., 1973-81, assoc. gen. counsel, asst. sec., 1979-81; ptnr. Seki, Jarvis & Lynch, Chgo., 1981-84; exec. v.p., gen. counsel, sec. Mitsubishi Electric Am., Inc., N.Y.C., 1983-91, Cypress, Calif., 1991—. Mem. ABA, Am. Corp. Counsel Assn., Calif. Bar Assn., Ill. Bar Assn., Chgo. Bar Assn., N.Y. State Bar Assn., Bar Assn. of City of N.Y., Am. Arbitration Assn. (panel arbitrators). Office: Mitsubishi Electric Am 5665 Plaza Dr Cypress CA 90630-5023

OLSEN, CARL FRANKLIN, school superintendent; b. Conway, Ark., Dec. 5, 1950; s. Leo William and Norma G. (Patton) O.; m. Carol Jean Panter, Apr. 13, 1974; children: Amanda, Daniel. Student, Biola U., La Mirada, Calif., 1969-72; BA, Calif. State U., Fullerton, 1973; MA, Calif. State U., Bakersfield, 1979; EdD, U. So. Calif., L.A., 1984. Cert. in adminstrv. svcs., Calif. Tchr. jr. high sch. Wasco (Calif.) Union Sch. Dist., 1975-77, elem. tchr., 1977-79, spl. projects coord., 1979-81; prin. Fairfax Sch. Dist., Bakersfield, Calif., 1981-85; supr./prin. Maple Sch. Dist., Shaffer, Calif., 1985-87; supt. Fruitvale Sch. Dist., Bakersfield, 1987—; adj. prof. Calif. State U., Bakersfield, 1991—; exec. dir. Fruitvale Ednl. Found., Bakersfield, 1990—; bd. dirs. Kern County Spl. Edn. Consortium, Bakersfield, 1987—. Moderator First Congl. Ch., Wasco, 1987-92. Byram Meml. scholar, U. So. Calif., 1982. Mem. Assn. of Calif. Sch. Adminstrs., Am. Assn. Sch. Adminstrs., Phi Delta Kappa, Kappa Delta Pi. Office: Fruitvale Sch Dist 2114 Calloway Dr Bakersfield CA 93312-2706

OLSEN, CLIFFORD WAYNE, retired physical chemist; b. Placerville, Calif., Jan. 15, 1936; s. Christian William and Elsie May (Bishop) O.; m. Margaret Clara Gobel, June 16, 1962 (div. 1986); children: Anne Katherine Olsen Cordes, Charlotte Marie; m. Nancy Mayhew Kruger, July 21, 1990 (div. 1994). AA, Grant Tech. Coll., Sacramento, 1955; BA, U. Calif.-Davis, 1957, PhD, 1962. Physicist, project leader, program leader, task leader Lawrence Livermore Nat. Lab., Calif., 1962-93; ret., 1993; mem. Containment Evaluation Panel, U.S. Dept. Energy, 1984—, mem. Cadre for Joint Nuclear Verification Tests, 1988; organizer, editor procs. for 2nd through 7th Symposiums on Containment of Underground Nuclear Detonations, 1983-93. Contbr. articles to profl. jours. Mem. bd. convocators Calif. Luth. U., 1976-78; pres. Livermore Amateur Radio Klub, 1994—. Recipient Chevalier Degree, Order of DeMolay, 1953. Mem. AAAS, Am. Radio Relay League, Seismol. Soc. Am., Livermore Amateur Radio Klub (pres. 1994-95), Sigma Xi, Alpha Gamma Sigma, Gamma Alpha. Democrat. Lutheran.

OLSEN, DAVID MAGNOR, science educator; b. Deadwood, S.D., July 23, 1941; s. Russell Alvin and Dorothy M. Olson; m. Muriel Jean Bigler, Aug. 24, 1963; children: Merritt, Chad. BS, Luther Coll., 1963; MS in Nat. Sci., U. S.D., 1967. Instr. sci., math. Augustana Acad., Canton, S.D., 1963-66; instr. chemistry Iowa Lakes Community Coll., Estherville, Iowa, 1967-69; instr. chemistry Merced (Calif.) Coll., 1969—, instr. astronomy, 1975—, div. chmn., 1978-88, coord. environ. hazardous materials tech., 1989—. Trustee Merced Union High Sch. Dist., 1983—, pres., 1986-87. Mem. NEA, Am. Chem. Soc., Astron. Soc. of the Pacific, Calif. Tchrs. Assn., Planetary Soc., Calif. State Mining and Mineral Mus. Assn. (bd. dirs., sec. 1990-93), Nat. Space Soc., Merced Coll. Faculty Assn. (pres. 1975, 93, 94, treas. 1980-90, bd. dirs., sec. 1990-91), Castle Challenger Learning Ctr. Found. (bd. dirs.), Merced Track Club (exec. bd. 1981), M Star Lodge, Sons of Norway (v.p. 1983), Rotary Internat. Democrat. Lutheran. Home: 973 Idaho Dr Merced CA 95340-2513 Office: Merced Coll 3600 M St Merced CA 95348-2806

OLSEN, DEBORAH JEAN, journalist, writer; b. Mpls., Oct. 11, 1950; d. Leif Norman and Doris Marjorie (Hayhoe) Olsen; m. James William Johnson, June 29, 1973 (div. Oct. 1986); children: Jesse William Johnson, Lee Warner Johnson. BA in Journalism, English, U. N.Mex., 1975. Tchr. journalism, English Manzano H.S., Albuquerque, 1976-78, Overland H.S., Aurora, Colo., 1980-84; writer Steamboat Mag., Steamboat Springs, Colo., 1991—; reporter Steamboat Pilot and Today newspapers, Steamboat Springs, Colo., 1989—. Pub. rels. vol. Steamboat Springs Winter Sports Club, 1992—. Recipient Best Feature of Yr. award Colo. Press Assn., 1992, Best Letters-to-Editor Page award Nat. Newspaper Assn., 1992, Best Spot News Coverage award Colo. Press. Assn., 1993, Best Deadline News Reporting, 1994, Best News Photgraph, 1994. Home: PO Box 880891 Steamboat Springs CO 80488-0891 Office: Steamboat Pilot/Today 1041 Lincoln Ave Steamboat Springs CO 80487

OLSEN, HARRIS LELAND, real estate and international business executive, educator; b. Rochester, N.H., Dec. 8, 1947; s. Harries Edwin and Eva Alma (Turmelle) O.; m. Mimi Kwi Sun Yi, Mar. 15, 1953; children: Garin Lee, Gavin Yi, Sook Ja. AS, SUNY, Albany, 1983, BS, 1988; MA in Polit. Sci., U. Hawaii, 1990; PhD in Internat. Bus. Adminstrn., Kennedy Western U., Idaho, 1993. Enlisted USN, 1967, advanced through grades to; served in various nuclear power capacities USN, Conn., 1971-76, Hawaii, 1976-87; ret. USN, 1987; v.p. Waiono Land Corp., Honolulu, 1981-92, dir., 1993—; v.p. Asian Pacific Electricity, Honolulu, 1988-89, Kapano Land Assocs., Honolulu, 1988-92, 94—, MLY Networks, Inc., Honolulu, 1989—, THO Consultants Cor., 1991—, Clarix Internat. Corp., 1994; staff cons. Mariner-Icemakers, Honolulu, 1982-84, Transpacific Energy Corp., Honolulu, 1982-84; dir. Asian Pacific Devel. Bank, 1983; sr. cons. Western Rsch. Assocs., Honolulu, 1984-87, 94—; quality assurance cons. Asian Pacific, Inc., Honolulu, 1987-88; instr., lectr. Asian history and culture U. Chaminade in Honolulu, 1991; nuclear reactor plant specialist Pearl Harbor Emergency Recall Team, 1991-95; instr. nuclear reactor theory Pearl Harbor, Hawaii, 1992-95; v.p. Schwartz, Inc., 1992—; bd. dirs. Green Gold Corp., 1992-93; cons. Waiono/Kapano Devel. Co., 1993; bd. dirs., sec. Pacific Internat. Engring. Corp., 1994-95; Keiretsu sec. Global Ocean Cons., Inc. and Assocs., 1994-95; joint venture Premier Fisheries Pty. Ltd., Papua New Guinea, 1995—; cons. BFD Devel. Group, 1995—; co-drafter Nat. Tuna Industry Devel. Plan for Papua New Guinea, 1995; sec. bd devel Keiretsu group, 1995; quality analyst Pearl Harbor, Hawaii, 1995—. Inventor, alternate power supply system; contbr. articles to profl. publs. Active Nat. Democratic Com.; head coach USN Men's Softball, Honolulu, 1978-79; pres. Pearl Harbor (Hawaii) Welfare and Recreation Com., 1983-84; mem. Bishop Mus. Named Alumnus of Yr., Kennedy Western U., 1993. Mem. ASCD, AAAS, Internat. Fedn. Profl. and Tech. Engrs., Am. Polit. Sci. Assn., Semiotic Soc. Am., N.Y. Acad. Scis., Toronto Semiotics Cir., USCG Aux., Am. Legion, Fleet Res. Assn., Internat. Platform Assn., Navy League, U.S. Naval Inst., UN Assn., U.S. Submarine Vets., Honolulu Acad. Arts, U. Hawaii Founders Assn., U. Hawaii Coll. Arts and Sci. Found., Delta Epsilon Sigma. Democrat. Buddhist. Home: #56 94-1025 Anania Cir Apt 56 Mililani HI 96789-2045 Office: Schwartz Inc 1149 Bethel St Ste 314 Honolulu HI 96813-2210

OLSEN, MARK NORMAN, small business owner; b. Seattle, Mar. 3, 1947; s. Norman Henry and Agnes Carolyn (Hansen) O.; m. Antoinette Marie Korman, June 20, 1991. Student, U. Wash., Western Wash. U., 1965-67, BHM Tech. Coll., 1968. Cert. autobody journeyman, estimator, inter-industry conf. auto collision repair. Mgr. body shop Fraser Chevrolet, Bellingham, Wash., 1967-83; owner Olsen Auto Body, Bellingham, 1983—. Bd. dirs. Bellingham Tech. Coll. Mem. Auto Body Craftsman (treas.). Home: 1019 W Beachview Pl Bellingham WA 98226-9439 Office: Olsen Auto Body 1919 Humboldt St Bellingham WA 98225

OLSEN, PHILLIP BUCK, corporate pilot, retired educator; b. Duluth, Minn., Feb. 28, 1931; s. Henry Jomar Olsen and Hjordis (Buck) Henley; m. Frances Ann MacKay, May 22, 1961 (div. Dec. 1984); m. Minnie Eiko Komagome, Aug. 19, 1988 (div. Oct. 1994). AB, Wesleyan U., Middletown, Conn., 1953; MS in Journalism, UCLA, 1959. Cert. flight instr. FAA. Commd. 2d lt. USAF, 1953, advanced through grades to capt., 1961; pilot various locations, U.S. and Europe, 1953-73; vol. U.S. Peace Corps, Philippines, 1962-64; regional dir. Mindanao/Sulu, Philippines, 1964-66; desk officer Washington, 1966-67; dir., assoc. dean Coll. Arts and Scis. U. Hawaii/Manoa, Honolulu, 1967-86; capt., asst. chief pilot Alexander & Baldwin, Inc., Honolulu, 1986-94; pres., ptnr. Aviation Holding, Ltd., Honolulu, 1983—; v.p., bd. dirs. Honolulu Marathon Assn., 1976-80. adj. instr. Embry Riddle Aeronautical U., Hickam AFB, Hawaii, 1992. Editor jour. Western Airlines, 1959-60. Comdr. Aloha State Search and Rescue Squadron, Honolulu, 1972-79. Recipient Estella della Solidarieta, Republic of Italy, 1956. Mem. Asian Studies Assn., Aircraft Owners and Pilots Assn., Elks. Home: 2080 Mauna Pl Honolulu HI 96822-2502

OLSEN, ROBERT ARTHUR, finance educator; b. Pittsfield, Mass., June 30, 1943; s. Arthur Anton and Virginia O.; BBA, U. Mass., 1966, MBA, 1967; PhD, U. Oreg., 1974; m. Maureen . Joan Carmell, Aug. 21, 1965. Security analyst Am. Inst. Counselors, 1967-68; rsch. assoc. Center for Capital Market Rsch., U. Oreg., 1972-74; asst. prof. fin. U. Mass., 1974-75; prof. fin., chmn. dept. fin. & mktg. Calif. State U., Chico, 1975—; cons. bus. feasibility studies for Stinson, Isom Assocs. & Career Assocs., Calif. State U., Chico, Endowment Fund, U.S. Forest Svc. Stonier Banking fellow, 1971-72; Nat. Assn. Mut. Savs. Banks fellow, 1975-76; scholar Stanford U., 1986, rsch. fellow Decision Research, Inc., 1986, 95. Recipient Research award Calif. State U.-Chico, 1983, 86, Profl. Achievement award, 1985. Mem. Am. Fin. Assn., Fin. Execs. Inst., Western Fin. Assn. (Trefftzs award 1974), Southwestern Fin. Assn., Fin. Mgmt. Assn., Eastern Fin. Assn., Sierra Club. Contbr. articles to profl. jours. Office: Calif State U Sch Bus Chico CA 95929

OLSEN, ROBERT KENNETH, lawyer; b. Chgo., June 8, 1958; s. Robert Earl and Joyce (Dalicandro) O.; m. Lisa Ann Zeutzius, Apr. 8, 1989; children: Robert Glenn, Lauren Corinne. BA, U. Calif., Irvine, 1980; JD, UCLA, 1983. Bar: Calif. Law clk. U.S. Dist. Ct., L.A., 1983-84; assoc. Stroock & Stroock & Lavan, L.A., 1984-86, Morrison & Foerster, Irvine, 1986-91; sr. counsel Resolution Trust Corp., Newport Beach, Calif., 1991—. Roman Catholic. Office: Resolution Trust Corp PO Box 6210 Newport Beach CA 92658-6210

OLSEN, RODNEY WAYNE, business development manager, technical consultant; b. Provo, Utah, July 24, 1951; s. Wayne B. and Charleen (Chase) O.; m. Esther Lee Holmstead, Mar. 30, 1981 (div. Sept. 1993); children: Tiffanie Ann, Mathew Wayne. BSEE, U. Utah, 1981. Electronic technician Sperry Univac, Salt Lake City, 1978-79; electronic technician Evans & Sutherland, Salt Lake City, 1979-82, design engr., 1982-85, project engr., 1985-92, computer graphics bus. devel. mgr., 1992—. Home: 374 N 200 E Orem UT 84057-4707 Office: Evans & Sutherland 600 Komas Dr Salt Lake City UT 84108-1229

OLSHEN, ABRAHAM CHARLES, actuarial consultant; b. Portland, Oreg., Apr. 20, 1913; m. Dorothy Olds, June 21, 1934; children: Richard Allen, Beverly Ann Jacobs. AB, Reed Coll., 1933; MS, U. Iowa, 1935, PhD, 1937. Chief statistician City Planning Commn., Portland, Oreg., 1933-34; rsch. asst. math. dept. U. Iowa, 1934-37; biometrics asst. Med. Ctr., 1936-37; actuary, chief examiner Oreg. Ins. Dept., 1937-42, 45-46; actuary West Coast Life Ins. Co., San Francisco, 1946—, chief actuary, 1953-63, v.p., 1947—, 1st v.p., 1963-67, senior v.p., 1967-68, bd. dirs., 1955-68; cons. actuarial and ins. mgmt., pres. Olshen & Assocs., San Francisco, 1979—; bd. dirs. Home Federal Savs. & Loan Assn., San Francisco, 1972-85, vice-chmn. bd. 1979-85, bd. chmn. 1985-86; guest lectr. various univs. Contbg. writer Ency. Britannica, Underwriters' Report, The Nat. Underwriter, Life Underwriters Mag., Annals of Math. Stats., other publs. Mem. Calif. com. Health Ins. Coun., U. Calif. Med. Care Adminstrn. com., San Mateo County Retirement Bd. (1975-77). Rsch. assoc. Div. of War Rsch., 1942-44, Ops. Rsch. Gp., H/Q Comdr.-in-Chief, U.S. Fleet, 1944-45. Recipient U.S. Navy Ordnance Devel. award, 1945, Disting. Service award U.S. Office of Sci. Rsch. & Devel., 1945, Presdl. Cert. Merit, 1947. Fellow AAAS, Sigma Xi; mem. Health Ins. Assn. Am. (mem., past chmn. Blanks Com., actuarial & stat. com.), Actuarial Club of Pacific States (past pres.), Actuarial Club of San Francisco (past pres.), Am. Acad. of Actuaries (charter), Am. Math. Soc., Am. Risk and Ins. Assn., Calif. Math. Coun., Commonwealth Club (life), Fellow Conf. of Actuaries in Public Practice, Inst. Mgmt. Scis., Inst. Math. Stats., Internat. Actuarial Assn., Internat. Assn. Consulting Actuaries, Internat. Cong. Actuaries, Ops. Rsch. Soc. (charter), San Francisco Press Club (life). Office: Olshen & Assocs 760 Market St Ste 739 San Francisco CA 94102-2302

OLSHEN, RICHARD A., statistician, educator; b. Portland, Oreg., May 17, 1942; s. A.C. and Dorothy (Olds) O.; m. Susan Abroff, 1979. AB, U. Calif., Berkeley, 1963; PhD, Yale U., 1966. Rsch. staff statistician, lectr. Yale U., New Haven, 1966-67; asst. prof. of statistics Stanford (Calif.) U., 1967-72; assoc. prof. of statistics and math. U. Mich., Ann Arbor, 1972-75; assoc. prof. of math. U. Calif., San Diego, 1975-77, prof. of math., 1977-89, dir. lab. for math. and statistics, 1982-89; prof. of biostatistics Sch. Medicine Stanford U., 1989—, prof. by courtesy dept. statis., 1990—. Office: Stanford U Sch Medicine Hrp Bldg Stanford CA 94305

OLSON, BERNADETTE LUCIENNE, holographer; b. Bourg St. Andeol, France, Jan. 28, 1957; came to U.S., 1981; d. Gilbert Paul and Marie Adele (Chantepy) Grangaud; m. Ronald Burr Olson, Nov. 2, 1985. BSEE, U. New Mex., 1984. Engr. Advanced Micro Devices, Sunny Vale, Calif., 1985-92; holographer Positive Light Holographics, Felton, Calif., 1992—. Office: Laser Reflections 25 N Second St San Jose CA 95113

OLSON, BETTY HAAK, public health educator; b. Salt Lake City, Sept. 28, 1947; d. Howard Fredrick and Virginia Cecilia (Edholm) Haak; m. Harold G. Olson, Dec. 30, 1967; 1 child, Tristan Winston Godfrey. BS, U. Calif., Irvine, 1969; MS, U. Calif., Berkeley, 1971, PhD, 1974. Assoc. in pub. health Sch. Pub. Health, U. Calif., 1971-73; assoc. prof. U. Calif., Irvine, 1980-84, asst. vice chancellor, 1982-84, prof. sch. engring., prof. sch. medicine, 1984—, prof. environ. analysis and design, 1985—, chair environ. analysis and design, 1989-93; vis. asst. prof. U. Md., College Park, 1977; vis. sci. London U., 1980-81; counselor Soc. Environ. Geochemistry and Health, 1981-84; chair Microbiol. Problems Commn., 1982-86, Joint Task Group on Fecalstreptococci; mem. water resources com. NAS/NRC, 1986-91, chair, 1989-91, mem. water sci. and tech. bd., 1991-93; active Internat. Coun. Sci. Unions, 1988—. Contbr. articles to profl. jours. Named Woman of Yr., Women's Bus. and Profl. Assn., 1982. Fellow Am. Acad. Microbiology, Internat. Biotech. Inst.; mem. APHA (microbiol. coord.), Am. Soc. Microbiology (counselor 1984-86), Am. Water Works Assn. (chair 1982-86), Internat. Assn. Water Pollution (treas.). Office: Environ Microbiology and Genetics Lab Sch Social Ecology U Calif Irvine CA 92717

OLSON, BETTY-JEAN, elementary education educator; b. Camas, Wash., Apr. 26, 1934; d. Earl Raymond and Mabel Anna (Burden) Clemons; m. Arthur H. Geda, Dec. 31, 1957; children: Ann C. Geda-Wall, Scott A. Geda; m. Conrad A. Olson, June 14, 1980. AA, Clark Coll., 1954; BA in Edn., Cen. Wash. Coll. Edn., 1956; MEd, No. Monn. Coll., 1975. Cert. elem. tchr. class I, Mont., supr. K-9 class III. Supervising tchr., demo. teaching No. Mont. Coll.; kindergarten, 1st grade instr. Glasgow, Mont.; supervisor, head tchr. Reading Lab, Glasgow AFB, Mont.; 1st grade instr., kindergarten tchr., elem. adminstr. K-7 Medicine Lake (Mont.) Dist. 7; certification stds. and practices Adv. Coun. to the State Bd. Pub. Edn.; mem. bd. examiners Nat. Coun. for Accred. of Tchr. Edn., adv. com. Western Mont. Coll., U. Mont.; workshop leader and presenter in field. Mem. Sheridan County Community Protective Svcs. Com., Mid-Lake Scholarship Com. Mem. NEA, ASCD, Internat. Reading Assn., Nat. Coun. Social Studies, Nat. Elem. Prin. Assn., Medicine Lake Edn. Assn. (past pres.), Mont. Edn. Assn. (rev. bd., officerships), Mont. Elem. Prin., Delta Kappa Gamma (state pres., chpt. pres., exec. bd., committeeships, mem. internat. exec. bd.). Home: 108 E Antelope Rd Antelope MT 59211-9607

OLSON, CAROL LEE, public information officer; b. Akron, Ohio, Sept. 9, 1944; d. Elmer Mark and Elizabeth Virginia (Waterman) Haynes; m. John David Olson, Jan. 21, 1977; children: Marie Elizabeth, John Dean, Melanie Ann, Teresa Lynn, Jason David. Profl. Designation, U. Calif., Riverside, 1986, Cert. Non-Profit Mgmt., 1991. Comms. officer Am. Cancer Soc., Newport Beach, Calif., 1972-80; dir. comms. March of Dimes Birth Defects Found., San Bernardino, Calif., 1981-90; pub. info. officer Chaffey Coll., Rancho Cucamonga, Calif., 1990—; comms. officer Inland Empire Ednl. Found., San Bernardino, 1994; assoc. Career Inst., Rancho Cucamonga, Calif., 1995—. Editor periodical Revely, 1980-85, Dimemention, 1985-90. Mem. Citizens Commn. on Proposition 13, Santa Ana, Calif., 1985; bd. dirs. March of Dimes Birth Defects Found., 1993-94. Mem. Pub. Rels. Soc. Am. (accredited, v.p. bd. dirs. 1985-94), Nat. Coun. on Mktg. and Pub. Rels. (Polaris awards 1986, 88, 90, 95, medallion 1992, Pres.'s excellence award 1993, 95, Staff Devel. award 1994), Calif. C.C. Pub. Rels. Orgn., San Bernardino County Communicators Network. Baptist. Home: 522 Elk Grove Dr Mira Loma CA 91752-1514 Office: Chaffey Coll 5885 Haven Ave Rancho Cucamonga CA 91737-3002

OLSON, DAVID JOHN, political science educator; b. Brantford, N.D., May 18, 1941; s. Lloyd and Alice Ingrid (Black) O.; m. Sandra Jean Crabb, June 11, 1966; 1 dau., Maia Kari. B.A., Concordia Coll., Moorhead, Minn., 1963; Rockefeller fellow Union Theol. Sem, N.Y.C., 1963-64; M.A. (Brookings Instn. predoctoral research fellow 1968-69), U. Wis., Madison, 1966, Ph.D. (univ. fellow 1967), 1971. Community planner Madison Redvel. Authority, 1965-66; lectr. U. Wis., 1966-67; from lectr. to asso. prof. polit. sci. Ind. U., Bloomington, 1969-76; prof. polit. sci. U. Wash., Seattle, 1976—; chmn. dept. U. Wash., 1983-88, Harry Bridges endowed chairlabor studies, 1992-94; bd. dirs. Harry Bridges Inst.; dir.Ctr. Labor Studies U. Wash., 1992-94; Disting. lectr. in labor studies San Francisco State U., 1994; vis. prof. U. Bergen, 1987, Harvard U., 1988-89, U. Hawaii, 1989. Co-author: Governing the United States, 1978, Commission Politics, 1977, To Keep the Republic, 1975, Black Politics, 1971; co-editor: Theft of the City, 1974. Recipient Disting. Teaching award Ind. U., 1973, faculty fellow, 1973. Mem. Am. Polit. Sci. Assn., Western Polit. Sci. Assn. (v.p. 1984, pres. 1985), Midwest Polit. Sci. Assn., So. Polit. Sci. Assn. Democrat. Lutheran. Home: 6512 E Green Lake Way N Seattle WA 98103-5418 Office: Univ Wash Dept Polit Sci Seattle WA 98195

OLSON, DAVID MARK, college dean, physical education educator; b. St. Paul, Dec. 13, 1934; s. Vendel W. and Helme D. (Engman) O.; m. Arvis Joyce Garberg, Aug. 7, 1957; children: Jana, Mark, Julie, Michael. BA, Concordia Coll., Moorhead, Minn., 1956; MA, U. Minn., 1957; PhD, U. Iowa, 1966. Tchr. Nicolet High Sch., Milw., 1958-60, Wartburg Coll., Waverly, Iowa, 1960-66; tchr. Pacific Luth. U., Tacoma, 1968—, dean sch. phys. edn., dir. athletics; dir. N.W. regional clinic Pres.' Coun. on Phys. Fitness and Sports, 1979, 84; speaker in field. Lay pastor Emmanuel Luth. Ch., Yelm, Wash., 1988—; v.p. Trinity Luth. Ch., Parkland, Wash., 1972, pres., 1973; mem. adminstrv. team World Univ. Games, Sofia, Bulgaria, 1988, Poland, 1991, Japan, 1993, Spain, 1995; mem. steering com. U.S. Olympic Acad. XIII, Olympia, Wash., 1988-89; del. U.S. Olympic Com., L.A., 1986, 88. Mem. Am. Assn. Health, Phys. Edn., Recreation and Dance (pres. N.W. dist. 1981-82), Nat. Assn. Intercollegiate Athletics (dist. chmn. 1970-75, nat. exec. com. 1975-87, nat. pres. 1985-86, award of merit 1979, mem. Hall of Fame), Wash. Assn. Health, Phys. Edn., Recration and Dance (pres. 1975), Nat. Assn. Coll. Athletic Dirs., Rotary (local v.p. 1970-71, pres. 1971-72), Phi Delta Kappa, Phi Epsilon Kappa. Home: 15810 Lawrence Pl Yelm WA 98597-9103 Office: Sch of Phys Edn Pacific Luth U Tacoma WA 98597

OLSON, DONALD HAROLD, JR., marine engineer; b. San Mateo, Calif., Dec. 8, 1949; s. Donald H. Sr. and Betty Jean (Hemenway) D.; m. Susan Eugenia Youngblood, May 23, 1991. Degree in Geol. Engring., U. Nev., 1977; degree in Marine Engring., Calhoon MEBA Engring. Acad., 1984. Lic. marine engr. Various 1st asst. engring. positions Marine Engrs. Beneficial Assn., San Francisco, 1984—; cons. S.S. Potomic Restoration, San Francisco, 1985. Cons. State of Nev. Engring. Study Guide, 1984. With U.S. Army, 1970-72, Vietnam. Mem. ASME, Nat. Assn. Underwater Instrs. (advanced diver), Profl. Assn. Diving Instrs. (divemaster), Marine Engrs. Benefical Assn. Republican.

OLSON, EDWARD CHARLES, conservation foundation executive, writer, television producer; b. Jacksonville, Fla., July 6, 1956; s. Edward Charles and Marcine Era (Hall) O.; m. Krista Lynn Neuberger, Aug. 5, 1978; children: Laura Ellen, Edward Charles, Natalie Rose. BS, Miami U., Oxford, Ohio, 1978; MS, Wash. State U., 1980; PhD, Ohio State U., 1983. State dir. Nature Conservancy, Columbus, Ohio, 1983-86; pres. Florida Keys Land & Sea Trust, 1986-93, Catalina Island Conservancy, Avalon, Calif., 1993—; cons. non-profit orgns., 1987—. Editor: Guide to the Florida Keys, 1989. Bd. dirs. Catalina Community Pub. Radio, 1993—, Fla. Nat. Pks. and Monuments Assn., Homestead, 1988-93, Florida Keys Meml. Hosp., 1989-91, Florida Keys Guidance Clinic, Marathon, 1990-92. Recipient Leadership Fla. Grad. award Fla. C. of C., 1990, Outstanding Young Floridian, Fla. Jaycees, 1991; named Man of Yr., Marathon Jaycees, 1990. Office: Catalina Island Conservancy PO Box 2739 125 Claressa Avalon CA 90704

OLSON, FERRON ALLRED, metallurgist, educator; b. Tooele, Utah, July 2, 1921; s. John Ernest and Harriet Cynthia (Allred) O.; m. Donna Lee Jefferies, Feb. 1, 1944; children: Kandace, Randall, Paul, Jeffery, Richard. BS, U. Utah, 1953, PhD, 1956. Ordained bishop LDS Ch., 1962. Research chemist Shell Devel. Co., Emeryville, Calif., 1956-61; assoc. research prof. U. Utah, Salt Lake City, 1961-63, assoc. prof., 1963-68, chmn. dept mining, metall. and fuels engring., 1966-74, prof. dept. metallurgy and metall. engring., 1968—; cons. U.S. Bur. Mines, Salt Lake City, 1973-77, Ctr. for Investigation Mining and Metallurgy, Santiago, Chile, 1978; dir. U. Utah Minerals Inst., 1980-91. Author: Collection of Short Stories, 1985; contbr. articles to profl. jours. Del. State Rep. Conv., Salt Lake City, 1964; bishop, 1962-68, 76-82, missionary, 1988. With U.S. Army, 1943-46, PTO. Named Fulbright-Hayes lectr., Yugoslavia, 1974-75, Disting. prof. Fulbright-Hayes, Yugoslavia, 1980, Outstanding Metallurgy Instr., U. Utah, 1979-80, 88-89, Disting. Speaker U. Belgrade-Bor, Yugoslavia, 1974. Mem. Am. Inst. Mining, Metall. and Petroleum Engrs. (chmn. Utah chpt. 1978-79), Am. Soc. Engring. Edn. (chmn. Minerals div. 1972-73), Fulbright Alumni Assn., Am. Bd. Engring. and Tech. (bd. dirs. 1975-82). Republican. Home: 1862 Herbert Ave Salt Lake City UT 84108-1832 Office: U Utah Dept Metallurgy 412 Browning Building Bldg Salt Lake City UT 84112-1118

OLSON, GERALD THEODORE, educational consultant; b. Rockford, Ill., Mar. 10, 1928; s. Ernest Hjalmer and Irma Lena (Widgren) O.; B.S., U. San Francisco, 1953; M.A., San Francisco State U., 1960; M.Ed., U. So. Calif., 1964; Ph.D., U. Calif., Berkeley, 1974; m. Jean Vujovich, Aug. 28, 1949; children—Gerald Theodore, Kathleen Elaina Olson Groves, John Ernest, Carol Frances Olson Love. Counselor, tchr., dir. student activities Canyon High Sch., Castro Valley, Calif., 1964-70, also lectr. Calif. State U., Hayward, 1971-72 and instr. Chabot Coll., Hayward, 1964-73; cons. counseling and guidance Colo. Dept. Edn., Denver, 1973; cons. career, devel., ednl. services group L.A. County Office of Edn., 1973-92; adj. prof. edn. Nat. U., U. LaVerne; pvt. cons. and marriage, family, child counselor; mgr. Calif. Assn. Counseling and Devel. Discover Project. Served with USMC, 1946-49, with Army Res. and Calif. Army N.G., 1950-81. Cert. secondary sch. teaching, secondary sch. adminstrn., gen. pupil personnel services, community coll., marriage, family and child counseling, Calif. Contbr. articles to profl. jours. NDEA scholar, 1963-64; NIMH trainee, 1971-72; decorated Meritorious Service medal USAR, 1981. Mem. Am. Psychol. Assn., Calif. Career Edn. Assn. (pres. 1986-87), Calif. Assn. for Counseling and Devel. (editor Compass newsletter 1982-83, 86-87, pres. 1984-85), Calif. Assn. Measurement and Evaluation in Guidance (pres. 1981-82). Democrat. Home and Office: 3366 Tempe Dr Huntington Beach CA 92649-1921

OLSON, HENRY DEXTER, electrical engineer; b. San Mateo, Calif., Sept. 21, 1931; s. Oscar Henry and Bessie (Deyoung) O.; m. Jane Grace McKenzie; 1 child, Dana. BS, Stanford U., MS. Rsch. asst. Stanford (Calif.) U. Elecs. Rsch. Lab., 1956-58; sr. rsch. engr. Stanford Rsch. Inst., Menlo Park, Calif., 1958-87; consulting engr. pvt. practice, Menlo Park, Calif., 1987—; instr. Foothill Coll., Los Altos Hills, Calif., 1970-85; cons. in field. Contbr. articles to profl. jours. With U.S. Army, 1954-56. Mem. IEEE (sr.), Am. Radio Relay League, Ancient Wireless Assn. (life), Soc. Wireless Pioneers (life). Home and office: 1751 Croner Ave Menlo Park CA 94025-6062

OLSON, JAMES WILLIAM PARK, architect; b. St. Louis, Oct. 6, 1940; s. James William Park; s. Louis Garfield and Gladys Helen (Schuh) O.; m. Katherine Fovargue, June 11, 1971; children: Park, Reed. BArch, U. Wash., 1963. Registered architect, Wash., Oreg., Calif., Ill. Ptnr. Olson/Sundberg Architects, Seattle, 1985—; assoc. architect New Seattle Art Mus., 1991. Prin. works include Pike and Virginia Bldg. (AIA Honor award 1980), Seattle's Best Coffee Retail Locations (AIA Honor award 1984), Hauberg Residence Complex, 1992, Olympic Block Bldg. (Outstanding Merit award Wash. Trust Hist. Preservation 1986), numerous residences nationwide. Bd. dirs. On The Bds., Ctr. Contemporary Art, Seattle, 1982-86, Artist Trust, Seattle, 1986-90, U. Wash. Henry Art Gallery, Seattle, 1986-92; active Seattle Art Mus., Allied Arts. Recipient Best Architect award Seattle Mag., 1985. Fellow AIA; mem. IFRAA, NEA (juror). Office: Olson/Sundberg Architects 108 1st Ave S Fl 4 Seattle WA 98104-2502

OLSON, KENNETH HARVEY, computer company executive; b. Souris, N.D., May 7, 1927; s. Oscar L. and Clara (Haugen) O.; m. Darlene R. Gronseth, Aug. 19, 1950 (div. 1987); children: Kenneth David, Martha C., Marie K. BA, Concordia Coll., Moorhead, Minn., 1950; MS, U. N.D., 1953; postgrad., U. Minn., 1955. Instr. math. U. N.D., Grand Forks, 1952-54; programming supr. Convair, San Diego, 1955-59; mgr. software Control Data Corp., Mpls., 1959-61, product mgr., 1961-62; sales mgr. Control Data Corp., San Diego, 1962-70; v.p. Automated Med. Analysts, San Diego, 1970-90; pres., dir. Focus 010 Group, San Diego, 1975—; pres., dir. Health Care Svcs. Corp., San Diego, 1971-74, H.C.S. Corp., San Diego, 1972-75; v.p., trustee Calif. Prepaid Health Plan Coun., 1971-74; trustee HMO Assn. Am., 1974-75; bd. dirs. Touch Techs., Inc., San Diego. Editor: Approximations for the 1604 Computer, 1960; contbr. papers to Computer Applications, 1957-61. Pres. Lemon Grove (Calif.) Luth. Ch., 1957-59; treas. St. Luke's Luth. Ch., La Mesa, Calif., 1992-93; founder San Diego Nat. Bank, 1980, mem. bus. adv. com., 1981-85. Named Subcontractor of Yr., Small Bus. Assn. and SAI Corp., 1985; day proclaimed in his honor Mayor of San Diego, 1986; recipient Pres.'s award for disting. svc. Concordia Coll., 1991. Mem. Assn. for Computing Machinery, Sons of Norway. Republican.

OLSON, KENNETH PAUL, rehabilitation counselor; b. Providence, June 26, 1935; s. Gustave Frederick and Beatrice Evelyn (Backstrom) O.; m. Judith Luellan Hazard, Nov. 12, 1965; children: Glenn Edward Johnson. BA in Sociology, U. Denver, 1960; MA in Sociology, U. Colo., 1973. Cert. rehab. counselor, vocat. specialist; lic. profl. counselor, Colo. Exec. dir. Goodwill Industries, Colorado Springs, Co., 1960-65, San Francisco, 1965, Ft. Worth, 1966-70; counselor II Colo. Div. Rehab., Colorado Springs, 1972-83; pres. Olson Vocat. Svcs., Colorado Springs, 1983—; vocational expert Social Security Adminstn., Denver, 1984—; rehab counselor U.S. Dept. Labor, Denver, 1984-89. V.p. Bus. Arts Ctr., Manitou Springs, 1988-89; councilman Manitou Springs, 1975-78; mem. Econ. Devel. Com., Manitou Springs, 1984-86; chmn. Health Adv. Coun., Pikes Peak Region, 1979-80; commr. Commn. for Rehab. Counselor Cert., 1979-85, Bd. for Rehab. Cert., 1984-86; pres. Manitou Art Project, 1994-95. Fellow Nat. Rehab. Counseling Assn.; mem. Colo. Rehab. Counseling Assn. (pres. 1979, named Counselor of Yr. 1976), Great Plains Rehab. Assn. (pres. 1982-83), Colo. Rehab. Assn., Colo. Vocat. Evaluation Work Adjustment Assn., El Paso County Assn. Lic. Profl. Counselors (treas. 1994-96), Colorado Springs C. of C. (Small Bus. Person of Yr. award 1991), Manitou Springs C. of C. (pres. 1986). Home: PO Box 226 Manitou Springs CO 80829-0226 Office: Olson Vocat Svcs 701 S Cascade Ave Colorado Springs CO 80903-4003

OLSON, LENORA MARY, health facility administrator, epidemiologist; b. Hutchinson, Kans., Mar. 17, 1959; d. Harry Harper and Mary Agnes (Little) O.; m. James Michael Brandi, Oct. 21, 1989. BA in Anthropology, U. N.Mex., 1981, MA in Anthropology, 1988. Infection control practitioner Univ. Hosp., Albuquerque, 1989-90; program mgr. Emergency Dept. U. N.Mex., Albuquerque, 1990-94, dir. injury prevention, 1994—; mem. grant rev. panel Maternal Child Health, Rockville, Md., 1991—; mem. disability prevention adv coun. N.Mex. Dept. Health, Santa Fe, 1992—; mem. child abuse prevention com. N.Mex. Dept. Health, Santa Fe, 1991-93. Contbr. articles to profl. jours. Mem. APHA (com. chair injury control sect. 1991-93, challenge fund program grantee 1994), N.Mex. Health Assn. Office: U NMex-Sch Medicine Dept Emergency Medicine ACC 4 West Albuquerque NM 87131

OLSON, LUTE, university athletic coach; b. Mayville, N.D., Sept. 22, 1934; s. Albert E. and Alinda E. (Halvorson) O.; m. Roberta R. Russell, Nov. 27, 1953; children: Vicki, Jodi, Gregory, Christi, Steven. B.A., Augsburg Coll., Mpls., 1956; M.A., Chapman Coll., Orange, Calif., 1964. Cert. counselor. Head basketball coach Mahonomen High Sch., Minn., 1956-57, Two Harbors High Sch., Minn., 1957-61; dean of boys Baseline Jr. High Sch., Boulder, Colo., 1961-62; head basketball coach Loara High Sch., Anaheim, Calif., 1962-64, Marine High Sch., Huntington Beach, Calif., 1964-69, Long Beach City Coll., Calif., 1969-73, Long Beach State U., 1973-74, U. Iowa, Iowa City, 1974-83; head basketball coach U. Ariz. Wildcats, 1983—, head coach NCAA Divsn. 1A basketball, ranked #10, 1992, head coach NCAA Tournament winner West Region, semifinalist (overall), 1994. Author: Passing Game Offense, 1980, Multiple Zone Attack, 1981, Pressure Defense, 1981, Match-up Zone, 1983. Crusade chmn. Am. Cancer Soc., Iowa, 1982. Named Coach of Yr. Orange League, 1964; named Coach of Yr. Sunset League, 1968, Coach of Yr. Met. Conf. Calif., 1970-71, Coach of Yr. PCAA, 1974, Coach of Yr. Big Ten Conf., 1979, 80. Mem. Nat. Assn. Basketball Coaches (Coach of Yr. 1980). Lutheran. Office: U Ariz Mckale Ctr Tucson AZ 85721*

OLSON, MARIAN KATHERINE, emergency management executive, consultant, publisher, information broker; b. Tulsa, Oct. 15, 1933; d. Sherwood Joseph and Katherine M. (Miller) Lahman; m. Ronald Keith Olson, Oct 27, 1956, (dec. May 1991). BA in Polit. Sci., U. Colo., 1954, MA in Elem. Edn., 1962; EdD in Ednl. Adminstrn., U. Tulsa, 1969. Tchr. public schs., Wyo., Colo., Mont., 1958-67; teaching fellow, adj. instr. edn. U. Tulsa, 1968-69; asst. prof. edn. Eastern Mont. State Coll., 1970; program assoc. research adminstrn. Mont. State U., 1970-75; on leave with Energy Policy Office of White House, then with Fed. Energy Adminstrn., 1973-74; with Dept. Energy, and predecessor, 1975—, program analyst, 1975-79, chief planning and environ. compliance br., 1979-83; regional dir. Region VIII Fed. Emergency Mgmt. Agy., 1987-93; exec. dir., Search and Rescue Dogs of the U.S., 1993—; pres. Western Healthclaims, Inc., Golden, Co.; pres. Marian Olson Assocs., Bannack Pub. Co.; mem. Colo. Nat. Hazards Mitigation Coun., Colo. Urban Search and Rescue Task Force. Contbr. articles in field. Grantee Okla. Consortium Higher Edn., 1969, NIMH, 1974. Mem. Am. Soc. for Info. Sci., Am. Assn. Budget and Program Analysis, Internat. Assn. Ind. Pubs., Nat. Inst. Urban Search and Rescue (bd. dirs.), Nat. Assn. for Search and Rescue, Colo. Search and Rescue, Search and Rescue Dogs of U.S., Colo. Emergency Mgmt. Assn., Front Range Rescue Dogs, Colo. State Fire Chiefs Assn., Kappa Delta Pi, Phi Alpha Theta, Kappa Alpha Theta. Republican. Home: 203 Iowa Dr Golden CO 80403-1337 Office: Western Healthclaims Inc 203 Iowa Dr Ste B Golden CO 80403-1337

OLSON, PHILLIP DAVID LEROY, agriculturist, chemist; b. Anchorage, Feb. 3, 1940; s. Marvin Willard and Bernadette (McName) O.; m. Deborah Andreé Butler, Apr. 10, 1982; children from a previous marriage: Jamie Kay, Samuel Phillip, Jill Andre. BS, U. Idaho, 1963; MS, Oreg. State U., 1972. Technician U. Calif., Riverside, 1963-65; rsch. staff Oreg. State U., Corvallis, 1965-75; r & d mgr. Hoechst-Roussel Agri-Vet Co., Somerville, N.J., 1975-91; pres. Profl. Agrl. Cons., Hayden Lake, Idaho, 1991—; rsch. and devel, cons., investigator Atochem NA, Bryan, Tex., 1991—, Dupont, Wilmington, Del., 1991—, Ciba-Geigy, Greensboro, N.C., 1991—, BASF, Research Triangle Park, N.C., 1991, ISK-Bioscis., Fresno, Calif., 1992—, Rhône-Poulenc, Durham, N.C., 1992—, Sandoz Agro, Inc., Des Plaines, Ill., 1992—, Zeneca, Inc., Richmond, Calif., 1992—, Stewart AG, 1995—; cons. in field rsch. and devel. Mem. Soc. Quality Assurance, Pacific Regional Quality Assurance Soc., Elks. Office: Profl Agricultural Cons RR 3 Box 125 Hayden Lake ID 83835-8304

OLSON, RICHARD EARL, lawyer, state legislator; b. Elmhurst, Ill., Apr. 24, 1953; s. Earl Leroy and Helen Ellen (Wanamaker) O.; m. Patricia Michelle McKinney, May 16, 1976; children: Shelley, Rachel, Eric. BA, U. Miss., Oxford, 1975; Jd, So. Meth. U., 1978. Bar: N.Mex. 1978. Ptnr. Hinkle, Cox, Eaton, Coffield & Hensley, Roswell, N.Mex., 1978—; mem. N.Mex. Ho. of Reps., 1989-95, mem. various coms.; bd. trustees Eastern N.Mex. Med. Ctr., 1995—. Mem. Roswell City Coun., 1986-88, chmn. sts. and alleys com., mem. various other coms.; past chmn. pastor-parish rels. com. 1st United Meth. Ch., Roswell; bd. dirs. Roswell Econ. Forum, Roswell Mus. and Art Ctr. Found., city coun. liaison; bd. dirs. Assurance Home, 1980—, former v.p.; mem. N.Mex. 1st, former bd. dirs. Mem. ABA, Am. Legis. Exec. Coun. (civil justice task force), Def. Rsch. Inst., Noon Optimist Club, Order of Coif, Phi Kappa Phi. Republican. Home: 5003 Thunderbird Ln Roswell NM 88201-9386 Office: Hinkle Cox Eaton Coffield & Hensley PO Box 10 Roswell NM 88202-0010

OLSON, ROBERT HOWARD, lawyer; b. Indpls., July 6, 1944; s. Robert Howard and Jacquline (Wells) O.; m. Diane Carol Thorsen, Aug. 13, 1966; children: Jeffrey, Christopher. BA in Govt. summa cum laude, Ind. U., 1966; JD cum laude, Harvard U., 1969. Bar: Ohio 1969, Fla. 1980, U.S. Dist. Ct. (no. dist.) Ohio 1970, U.S. Dist. Ct. (no. Dist.) Ind. 1970, U.S. Dist. Ct. (so. Dist.) Ohio 1971, U.S. Supreme Ct. 1973, Ariz. 1985. Assoc. Squire, Sanders & Dempsey, Cleve., 1969, 70-71, 76-81, ptnr., 1981—, ptnr., Phoenix, 1985—; sr. law clk. U.S. Dist. Ct., No. Dist. Ind. 1969-70; chief civil rights div. Ohio Atty. Gen.'s Office, Columbus, 1971-73, chief consumer protection, 1973-75, chief counsel, 1975, 1st asst. (chief of staff), 1975-76; instr. Law Sch., Ohio State U., Columbus, 1974; mem. Cen. Phoenix com. to advise city council and mayor, 1987-89; bd. dirs., sec. Orpheum Theater Found., 1989-90, pres., 1990—; bd. dirs. The Ariz. Ctr. for Law in the Pub. Interest, 1988—, mem. exec. com., 1990—, treas. 1992-93, v.p., 1993-95; mem. Ariz. Ctr. for Disability Law, 1994—, treas. 1994-95; mem. Valley Leadership Class XIV. Author monograph on financing infrastructure, 1983; also law rev. articles on civil rights, consumer protection. Bd. dirs. 1st Unitarian Ch. Phoenix, v.p., 1987-89; bd. dirs. 1st Unitarian Ch. Found., 1987-93, pres., 1990-93. Mem. Am. Acad. Hosp. Attys., Ariz. State Bar Assn., Nat. Assn. of Healthcare Lawyers, Phi Beta Kappa. Democrat. Home: 5201 E Paradise Dr Scottsdale AZ 85254-4746 Office: Squire Sanders & Dempsey 40 N Central Ave Ste 2700 Phoenix AZ 85004-4424

OLSON, ROGER NORMAN, health service administrator; b. Spokane, July 3, 1936; s. Harry Leonard and Evelyn Helen (Pearson) O.; m. Joyce Marlene Markert, June 28, 1959; children: Leonard Mark, Brent Norman. BA, Pacific Luth. U., 1958; MDiv, Augustana Theol. Sem., 1962; MSW, U. Wash., 1970. Pastor Christ Luth. Ch., Des Moines, 1962-64; asst. pastor First Immanuel Luth. Ch., Portland, Oreg., 1964-68; planner Tri-County Community Coun., Portland, 1970-71; project coord. City-County Commn. on Aging, Portland, 1971-73; evaluation coord. Portland Bur. of Human Resources, 1973-74; asst. dir. Multnomah County Project Health Div., 1974-83; interim pastor Augustana Luth. Ch., 1984-85; dir. family support svcs. Met. Family Svc., 1985-91; dir. planning and rsch. Met. Family Svcs., 1992-94; dir. info. exch. Luth. Family Svc., 1994—. Rockefeller Bros. fellowship Rockefeller Fund for Theol. Edn., 1958-59, fellowship NIMH, 1968-69, Adminstn. on Aging, 1969-70. Democrat. Lutheran. Home: 3939 NE 21st Ave Portland OR 97212-1432 Office: Luth Family Svc 605 SE 39th Ave Portland OR 97214-3216

OLSON, RONALD BURR, holographer; b. Butte, Mont., May 20, 1950; s. Maurice Llewlyn and Hazel Marian (burr) O.; m. Bernadette Lucienne Grangaud, Nov. 2, 1985. AS in Optics, Electronics, Idaho State U., 1975-77; student English, U. Wash., 1969-71. Laser engr. Continuum, Inc., Santa Clara, Calif., 1977-90; v.p. sales and mktg. Positive Light, Inc., Los Gatos, Calif., 1990-93; holographer Positive Light Holograph, Felton, Calif., 1993—; chmn. bd. Positive Light, Inc., Los Gatos, 1991—. Office: Laser Reflections 25 N Second St San Jose CA 95113

OLSON, RONALD CHARLES, aerospace executive; b. Sioux Falls, S.D., Jan. 23, 1937; s. Arthur Helmer and Myrtle Esther (Gustafson) O.; m. Barbara Jean Newcomb, Apr. 7, 1957; children: Bradley Charles, Jodi Lynn. AA, North Idaho Coll., 1956; BS in EE, U. Idaho, 1958; grad. sr. exec. mgmt. program, MIT, 1988. Design engr. Boeing Aerospace, Seattle, 1958-72, engring. mgr., 1973-83; postgrad. in mgmt. MIT, Seattle, 1988; program mgr. Boeing Defense and Space Group, Seattle, 1985-95; v.p. Boeing Comml. Space Co., Seattle, 1995—; mem. engring. adv. bd. U. Idaho Coll. Engring., Moscow, 1988-95, chmn. bd., 1991-95. Recipient Gen. Ira C. Eaker, Air Force Assn., Vandenburg AFB, 1985. Mem. Boeing Mgmt. Assn. (sec. 1981-85), Big Band Dance Club (instr. 1980-85), Twin Lakes Golf & Country Club. Republican. Lutheran. Home: 1206 184th Avenue Ct E Sumner WA 98390-9419 Office: Boeing Defense Space Group PO Box 3999 Seattle WA 98124-2499

OLSON, STEVEN DOUGLAS, English language educator; b. Morris, Minn., Sept. 7, 1950; s. Warren Orlin and Eloise Lucille (Vig) O.; m. Ann Barrett Olson, Apr. 8, 1972; children: Carey Beth, Cavan John. BA, Moorhead State U., 1972; MA, U. Tex., El Paso, 1978; PhD, U. Ill., 1986. Asst. prof. English No. Mont. Coll., Havre, 1986-89; assoc. prof. English Ctrl. Wash. U., Ellensburg, 1989—. Author: The Prairie in 19th-Century American Poetry, 1994; contbr. articles, poem to profl. publs. With U.S. Army, 1972-75. Home: 113 E 9th Ave Ellensburg WA 98926-2904 Office: Ctrl Wash U Dept English Ellensburg WA 98926

OLSON, STEVEN STANLEY, social service executive; b. Longview, Wash., Aug. 5, 1950; s. Robert Martin and Martha Virginia (Duffin) O.; 1 child, Derek Thomas Dailey. BA, Wash. State U., 1972; MEd, Auburn U., 1977; postgrad., Seattle U., 1981-83. Cert. rehabilitation mgmt. Agrl. extensionist Action/Peace Corps, Popayan, Colombia, 1972-73; supr. Stonebelt Ctr. for the Mentally Retarded, Bloomington, Ind., 1974; adjustment counselor Exceptional Industries, Bowling Green, Ky., 1974-75; vocat. evaluator Exceptional Industries, 1975-76; alcohol counselor E. Ala. Mental Health, Opelika, 1976; intern Auburn Univ./Ptnrs. of the Americas, Guatemala City, Guatemala, 1976; planner, researcher Marion County Mental Health, Salem, Oreg., 1977-79; assoc. dir. Reliable Enterprises, Centralia, Wash., 1979-80; exec. dir. Reliable Enterprises, 1980—; v.p. govt. affairs Rehab. Enterprises Wash., Olympia, 1984-86, chmn. regional rep., 1986-89, pres. 1990-91; treas. Arc of Wash., Olympia, 1983-85, govt. affairs chmn., 1983-89, v.p., 1989-90, pres., 1994-95. Contbr. articles to Vocat. Evaluation and Work Adjustment Bull., 1976, Rehab. World, 1977. Treas. Communities United for Reponsible Energy, Lewis County, Wash., 1979—; vice chairperson Wash. Solar Coun., Olympia, Wash., 1980-83; co-chair Early Childhood Help Orgn., Olympia, 1988. Mem. Am. Assn. Mental Retardation, Assn. for Severely Handicapped, Wash. Assembly for Citizens with Disabilities, Alliance for Children, Youth, and Family. Home: 4333 Maytown Rd SW Olympia WA 98512-9239 Office: Reliable Enterprises 203 W Reynolds Ave Centralia WA 98531-3313

OLSON, SYLVESTER IRWIN, government official; b. Herman, Minn., Apr. 2, 1907; s. Jacob John and Theresia Mary (Kremer) O.; m. Virginia Varney Colbert, Aug. 19, 1948; children—Karen Therese, Eric Sylvester. Student, Marquette U., 1925-26; B.A., U. Minn., 1929, J.D., 1931. Bar: Minn. bar 1931, Wash. bar 1949, Republic of Korea bar 1954, D.C. bar 1962. Asso. Ewing & Lehmann, St. Paul, 1931-33, Harold E. Stassen, Elmer J. Ryan, Farmington, Minn., 1933-34; mem. firm Stassen, Olson, Kelly & LeVander, South St. Paul, Minn., 1935-39; asst. county atty. Dakota County, Minn., 1933-39; dep. chief counsel Dept. Rural Credit Minn., 1939-42; chief counsel div. adminstrv. mgmt. Minn., 1942-43, atty. and pub. relations counsel, 1944-48; mem. firm Brown, Olson & Clarke, Yakima, Wash.; asso. counsel Graves, Kizer & Graves, Spokane, 1949-54; legal cons. UN Econ. Coordinator, Korea, 1954; minister embassy, dir. U.S. Operations Mission to, Portugal, U.S. Operations Mission to (FOA), 1954-55; dep. dir. U.S. Operations Mission, ICA, also attache Am. Embassy, Tokyo, Japan, 1956-58; asst. dir. office Territories, Dept. Interior, 1959-61; practiced in Washington, 1962-66; program adviser Fed. Water Pollution Control Adminstrn., 1967-68; dir. enforcement div. EPA, 1969-76, spl. asst. dir. water enforcement, 1976-77; Pres. Wells Olson Co., Herman, 1946-78; dir. Pacific N.W., Trans-N.W. Gas, Inc., 1951-55. Chmn. Citation Crusade for Freedom, Central Wash., 1951. Mem. Yakima C. of C. (dir. 1951-53), Fed., Wash., Minn., D.C. bar assns., Tau Kappa Epsilon, Phi Alpha Delta. Home: Heatheridge 356 Pikes Peak Dr Grand Junction CO 81503-1740

OLSON, WAYNE ROGER, community college dean; b. South Gate, Calif., Sept. 17, 1945; s. Edgar Orlie and Mary Esther (Cantin) O.; m. Sharon Lee Sherman, June 11, 1966; 1 child, Wayne Edward. AS, L.A. Trade Tech. Coll., 1965; BA, Calif. State U., Long Beach, 1975, MA, 1981. Cert. community coll. instr., Calif., supr., Calif. Dir. tech. Rancho Santiago Coll., 1978-86, asst. dean, 1986-87, vocat. programs coord., 1987-88; assoc. dean El Camino Coll., 1988-92, acting dean, 1992; dean Golden West Coll., Huntington Beach, Calif., 1992—; instr. East L.A. Coll., 1976-77, Rancho Santiago Coll., 1975-86; fire equipment mechanic L.A. County Fire Dept., 1972-77, heavy duty equipment mechanic, 1968-72. Named Outstanding C.C. Educator State Dept. of Edn., 1987, Outstanding Coordination of Svcs. and Activities, 1988. Mem. Assn. of C.C. Adminstrs., Calif. C.C. Assn. for Occupational Edn., Nat. Coun. for Occupational Edn., Assn. for Instructional Adminstr., Calif. Automotive Tchrs. Assn. (v.p., pres., bd. dirs., exec. treas., Outstanding Svc. as Pres. award 1987, Outstanding Svc. to Statewide Automotive Edn. award, 1991, Outstanding Contbns. to Automotive Edn. award, 1994), N.Am. Coun. of Automotive Tchrs. (bd. dirs., newsletter editor 1977-94, Outstanding Svc. as Bd. Mem. and Newsletter Editor award, 1988), Calif. Automotive Svc. Couns. (bd. dirs. 1987-94), Nat. Automotive Tech. Edn. Found., Calif. Acad. and Vocat. Info. Exch. (forum operator, bd. dirs. 1992-94), Epsilon Pi. Home: 1741 W 154th St Gardena CA 90247-3205 Office: Golden West Coll 15744 Golden West St Huntington Beach CA 92647

OLSON, WILLIAM THOMAS, business executive, educator, consultant; b. Coeur d'Alene, Idaho, May 1, 1940; s. William Anthony and Julia Glenn (Hunter) O.; BA, U. N.Mex., 1968; postgrad. U. Va., 1968-72; m. Diana Jean Dodds, Aug. 22, 1962; children: Kristin Ann (dec.), Kira Lynn. Intelligence agt. U.S. Army, 1962-65; asso. editor Newspaper Printing Corp., Albuquerque, 1965-66; news and pub. affairs dir. Sta. KUNM-FM, U. N.M., 1966-68; news person KOAT-TV, Albuquerque, 1968; news dir. WCHV Radio, Charlottesville, Va., 1968-69; moderator, producer Radio-TV Center, U. Va., 1969-73; columnist The Jefferson Jour., Charlottesville, Va., 1972; instr. history U. Va., 1971-73; information specialist Wash. State U. Cooperative Ext. Service, Pullman, 1973-77, instr. Sch. Communications, 1976-77, asst. dir., Wash. Energy Ext. Service, 1977-79; founder, pres. Inland N.W. Soc. Consulting Profls., 1995—; dir. Spokane County Head Start, 1979-84; adminstr. Community Colls. of Spokane, 1984-89, dir. critical Thinking Project, 1988-89; pres. Effective Mgmt. Systems Corp., 1987-92, CEO, chmn., bd. dirs., 1992—. Dir. Connoisseur Concerts Assn., 1983-86, pres. 1985-86; dir. West Cen. Community Devel. Assn., pres., 1985-86; dir. Spokane Community Ctrs. Found., 1986—; mem. Mayor's budget com. City of Spokane, 1988-89. Served with AUS, 1962-65. Mem. Am. Soc. Quality Ctrl., advisory bd. Goal/QPC, Wash. Family Independence Program 1990-92, Inst. Mgmt. Conss. (mem. 1995—); founding pres., mem. Inland Northwest Soc. of Consulting Profls., 1995—; Author TV documentary (with Ken Fielding): The Golden Years?, 1973; film (with B. Dale Harrison and Lorraine Kingdon) New Directions Out of the Culture of Poverty, 1974. Home: 2018 E 14th Ave Spokane WA 99202-3562 Office: Stewart Bldg W-427 First Ave Spokane WA 99204

OLSSON, RONALD ARTHUR, computer science educator; b. Huntington, N.Y., Nov. 16, 1955; s. Ronald Alfred and Dorothy Gertrude (Hofmann) O. BA and MA, SUNY, 1977; MS, Cornell U., 1979; PhD, U. Ariz., 1986. Teaching asst. Cornell U., Ithaca, N.Y., 1977-79, rsch. asst., 1979; lectr. SUNY, Brockport, 1979-81; rsch. assoc. U. Ariz., Tucson, 1981-86; prof., vice chair Computer Sci. Dept. U. Calif., Davis, 1986—. Author (book) The SR Programming Language: Concurrency in Practice, 1993; contbr. articles to profl. jours. Grantee MICRO U. Calif., 1987, 92, NSF, 1988, Dept. Energy, 1988-92, Advanced Rsch. Projects Agy., 1993—. Mem. Assn. for Computing Machinery. Home: 2741 Brandywine Pl Davis CA 95616-2904 Office: U Calif Dept Computer Sci Davis CA 95616-8562

OLSTAD, ROGER GALE, science educator; b. Mpls., Jan. 16, 1934; s. Arnold William and Myra (Stroschein) O.; m. Constance Elizabeth Jackson, Aug. 20, 1955; children: Karen Louise, Kenneth Bradley. B.S., U. Minn., 1955, M.A., 1959, Ph.D., 1963. Instr., U. Minn., Mpls., 1956-63; asst. prof. U. Ill., Urbana, 1963-64; mem. faculty U. Wash., Seattle, 1964—; asso. prof. sci. edn. U. Wash., 1967-71, prof., 1971—, asso. dean grad. studies Coll. Edn., 1969-81. Fellow AAAS; mem. NSTA (bd. dirs.) Wash. Sci. Tchrs. Assn. (pres. 1973-74), Nat. Assn. Rsch. Sci. Teaching (pres. 1977-78, bd. dirs.), N.W. Sci. Assn. (chmn. 1966-68), Assn. Edn. Tchrs. in Sci. (regional pres. 1966-68, pres. 1991-92), Nat. Assn. Biology Tchrs., Biol. Scis. Curriculum Study (chmn., bd. dirs. 1989-94), U. Wash. Faculty Club, Phi Delta Kappa. Office: U Wash Coll Edn Seattle WA 98195

O'MAHONY, KIERAN T., writer; b. Cork, Ireland, Feb. 16, 1953; s. Michael John and Bridget (Horan) O'M.; m. Bernadette M. O'Leary, June 11, 1975; children: Darragh Shane, Ronan Daniel, Madelein Caoimhe Anne. BA, Nat. U. Ireland, Cork, 1973; Med, N.U.I., Cork, 1981. Tchr. high sch. Cork, 1973-82; pub. Glen Abbey Books, Seattle, 1984-89; writer Educare Press, Seattle, 1989—; cons. Microsoft, Redmond, Wash., 1992-94, Micro Media, Kirkland, Wash., 1994—. Author: Geography and Education, 1988, Geographical Literacy, 1992, Dictionary of Geographical Literacy, 1993. Founding mem. Irish Family Fund, Seattle, 1993—, N.W. Irish Cultural Ctr., Seattle, 1993—; coach Grace Sch. Soccer, Seattle, 1985-91. Fellow Royal Geog. Soc.; mem. Internat. Assn. Ind. Pubs. Office: Educare Press PO Box 66695 Scotts Valley CA 95067

O'MALLEY, PETER, professional baseball club executive; b. N.Y.C., Dec. 12, 1937; s. Walter F. and Kay (Hanson) O'M.; m. Annette Zacho, July 10, 1971; children: Katherine, Kevin, Brian. B.S. in Econs, U. Pa., 1960. Dir. Dodgertown, Vero Beach, Fla., 1962-64; pres., gen. mgr. Spokane Baseball Club, 1965-66; v.p. Los Angeles Dodgers Baseball Club, 1967-68, exec. v.p., from 1968; pres. Los Angeles Dodgers, Inc., 1970—, also bd. dirs.; bd. dirs. Tidings newspaper. Bd. dirs. L.A. Police Meml. Found., L.A. World Affairs Coun., Jackie Robinson Found., L.A.-Gungzhou (Republic of China) Sister City Assn., Amateur Athletic Found.; pres. Little League Found.; active L.A. County Bd. Govs., Music Ctr., So. Calif. Com. for the Olympic Games. Mem. Korean-Am. C. of C. of L.A. Office: LA Dodgers 1000 Elysian Park Ave Los Angeles CA 90012-1112

OMAN, RICHARD GEORGE, museum curator; b. Salt Lake City, Oct. 15, 1945; s. Dorse Miles and Margaret (Call) O.; m. Susan Staker, May 31, 1970 (div. 1983); children: Sarah Elizabeth, Nathan Bryan, Bevin Marie; m. Pamela Fillmore, Oct. 4, 1984; children: Emily Anne, Lisa Meleana. AA, Big Bend Community Coll., 1965; BA in History, Brigham Young U., 1970; BA in Art History, U. Wash., 1971, postgrad., 1971-75. Dir. audio-visual sect. Seattle Art Mus., 1973-75; mgr. mus. sect., hist. dept. Ch. of Jesus Christ of Latter-day Saints, Salt Lake City, 1975-86; curator acquisitions Mus. Ch. History and Art, Salt Lake City, 1986—; high priest missionary to Quebec and Ontario, 1965-67; v.p., Import Broker, Salt Lake City, 1984—; instr. Brigham Young U., Provo, 1979; cons., Utah State Hist. Soc., Salt Lake City, 1980—, Utah Endowment for Humanities, Salt Lake City, 1981; bd. dirs., Utah Children's Mus., Salt Lake City, 1981-83. Contbg. author: Arts and Inspiration, 1980, Utah Folk Art, 1980; contbr. articles to numerous publs. Asst. commr., Salt Lake City area Boy Scouts Am., 1979-82; chmn. Cen. City Parks Com., Salt Lake City, 1980-83; cons. L.D.S. Hosp. Found., Salt Lake City, 1984; cons., judge, Dixie Coll. Ann. Art Exhbn., St. George, Utah, 1987-89, Springville (Utah) Mus. Art; cons. art mus., Brigham Young U., 1984-87; mem. sesquicentennial com., Mormon Ch., Salt Lake City, 1980. Mem. Utah Mus. Assn. (pres. 1979-81), Am. Assn. State and Local History, Am. Assn. Mus., Mormon History Assn. Republican. Mormon. Home: 3266 Bonview Dr Salt Lake City UT 84109-3704 Office: Mus Ch History and Art 45 N West Temple Salt Lake City UT 84150

O'MEARA, SARA, foundation administrator; b. Knoxville, Tenn., Sept. 9; m. Robert O'Meara (dec.); children: John Hopkins, Charles Hopkins (dec.);

m. Robert Sigholtz, Nov. 1986; stepchildren: Taryn, Whitney. Chmn., CEO, co-founder Childhelp USA/Internat., Woodland Hills, Calif., 1960—; bd. dirs. Internat. Alliance of Child Abuse and Neglect, Children to Children, Inc. Past pres., sustaining mem. Spastic Children's League; past recording sec. Assistance League of Calif. Recipient Outstanding Achievement award YWCA, 1986, Internat. Collaboration to Prevent Child Abuse awarded by HRH Queen of England, 1989, Living Legacy award Women's Internat. Ctr., 1989, Kiwanis World Svc. medal, 1991, Family Circle award Family Circle Mag., 1992, Chancellor's Founders award U. Calif., 1993, Outstanding Woman from Tenn. award Nat. Mus. Women in Arts, 1993, Nat. Caring award Nat. Caring Inst., 1993, Hubert Humphrey award Touchdown Club, 1994 and numerous others. Mem. World Fund of Successful Women. Office: Childhelp USA Inc 6463 Independence Ave Woodland Hills CA 91370-0001

OMEL, HAROLD, protective services official; m. Patti, 1962; 2 children. A in Fire Sci., Long Beach City Coll. Joined Long Beach (Calif.) Fire Dept., 1964—, from firefighter to bn. chief, 1964-94, fire chief, 1994—; apptd. State Bd. Fire Svcs., 1986—, chmn. freeway sigh com. 1988, mem. hose thread com. 1988—; former chmn. joint apprenticeship com. Calif. State Marshal's Office Calif. Profl. Firefighters. Trustee Long Beach Police & Fire Meml. Trust Fund, 1979—. Recipient L.A. Cmty. Protectors award, 1985. Mem. Internat. Assn. Firefighters (chmn. grievance com. 1978-94, So. Calif. state rep. 1980-86), Long Beach Firefighter Union (pres. 1972-94, former bd. dirs., former treas.), Calif. State Firemen's Assn., Calif. State Fedn. Labor, L.A. County Fedn. Labor, Calif. Profl. Firefighters (1st dist. v.p. 1982-89, mem. legis. com. 1982-94, sec.-treas. 1989-94). Office: Long Beach Fire Dept 925 Harbor Plz Ste 100 Long Beach CA 90802*

OMENN, GILBERT STANLEY, university dean, physician; b. Chester, Pa., Aug. 30, 1941; s. Leonard and Leah (Miller) O.; m. Martha Darling; children: Rachel Andrea, Jason Montgomery, David Matthew. AB, Princeton U., 1961; MD, Harvard U., 1965; PhD in Genetics, U. Wash., 1972. Intern Mass. Gen. Hosp., Boston, 1965-66; asst. resident in medicine Mass. Gen. Hosp., 1966-67; research assoc. NIH, Bethesda, Md., 1967-69; fellow U. Wash., 1969-71, asst. prof. medicine, 1971-74, assoc. prof., 1974-79, investigator Howard Hughes Med. Inst., 1976-77, prof., 1979—, prof. environ. health, 1981—, chmn. dept., 1981-83, dean Sch. Pub. Health and Community Medicine, 1982—; bd. dirs. Rohm & Haas Co., Amgen, BioTechniques Labs. Inc., Immune Response Corp., Clean Sites, Inc., Population Svcs. Internat., Pacific N.W. Pollution Prevention Rsch. Ctr.; White House fellow/spl. asst. to chmn. AEC, 1973-74; assoc. dir. Office Sci. and Tech. Policy, The White House, 1977-80; assoc. dir. human resources Office Mgmt. and Budget, 1980-81; vis. sr. fellow Wilson Sch. Pub. and Internat. Affairs, Princeton U., 1981; sci. and pub. policy fellow Brookings Instn., Washington, 1981-82; cons. govt. agys., Lifetime Cable Network; mem. Nat. Com. on the Environment, environ. adv. com. Rohm & Haas, Rene Dubos Ctr. for Human Environments, AFL-CIO Workplace Health Fund., Electric Power Rsch. Inst., Carnegie Commn. Task Force on Sci. and Tech. in Jud. and Regulatory Decision Making, adv. com. to dir., Ctrs. Disease Control, 1992—, adv. com. Critical Technologies Inst., RAND; mem. Pres.'s Coun., U. Calif., 1992—. Co-author: Clearing the Air, Reforming the Clean Air Act, 1981. Editor: (with others) Genetics, Environment and Behavior: Implications for Educational Policy, 1972; Genetic Control of Environmental Pollutants, 1984; Genetic Variability in Responses to Chemical Exposure, 1984, Environmental Biotechnology: Reducing Risks from Environmental Chemicals through Biotechnology, 1988, Biotechnology in Biodegradation, 1990, Biotechnology and Human Genetic Predisposition to Disease, 1990, Annual Review of Public Health, 1991, 92, 93, 94, Clinics in Geriatric Medicine, 1992; assoc. editor Cancer Rsch., Cancer Epidemiology, Biomarkers and Prevention, Environ. Rsch., Am. Jour. Med. Genetics, Am. Jour. Preventive Medicine; contbr. articles on cancer prevention, human biochem. genetics, prenatal diagnosis of inherited disorders, susceptibility to environ. agts., clin. medicine and health policy to profl. publs. Mem. President's Council on Spinal Cord Injury; mem. Nat. Cancer Adv. Bd., Nat. Heart, Lung and Blood Adv. Council, Wash. State Gov.'s Commn. on Social and Health Services, Ctr. for Excellence in Govt.; chmn. awards panel Gen. Motors Cancer Research Found., 1985-86; chmn. bd. Environ. Studies and Toxicology, Nat. Rsch. Coun., 1988-91; mem. Bd. Health Promotion and Disease Prevention, Inst. Medicine; mem. adv. com. Woodrow Wilson Sch., Princeton U., 1978-84; bd. dirs. Inst. for Sci. in Society; trustee Pacific Sci. Ctr., Fred Hutchinson Cancer Research Ctr., Seattle Symphony Orch., Seattle Youth Symphony Orch., Seattle Chamber Music Festival, Santa Fe Chamber Music Festival; mem. Citizens for a Hunger-Free Washington; chmn. rules com. Democratic Conv., King County, Wash., 1972. Served with USPHS, 1967-69. Recipient Research Career Devel. award USPHS, 1972; White House fellow, 1973-74. Fellow ACP, AAAS, Nat. Acad. Social Ins., Western Assn. Physicians, Hastings Ctr., Collegium Ramazzini; mem. Inst. Medicine of NAS, White House Fellows Assn., Am. Soc. Human Genetics, Western Soc. Clin. Rsch. Jewish. Home: 5100 NE 55th St Seattle WA 98105-2821 Office: U Wash Dean Sch Pub Health Box 357230 Seattle WA 98195-7230

OMER, GEORGE ELBERT, JR., orthopaedic surgeon, hand surgeon, educator; b. Kansas City, Kans., Dec. 23, 1922; s. George Elbert and Edith May (Hines) O.; m. Wendie Vilven, Nov. 6, 1949; children: George Eric, Michael Lee. B.A., Ft. Hays State U., 1944; M.D., Kans. U., 1950; M.Sc. in Orthopaedic Surgery, Baylor U., 1955. Diplomate Am. Bd. Orthopaedic Surgery, 1959, re-cert. orthopaedics and hand surgery, 1983 (bd. dirs. 1983-92, pres. 1987-88), cert. surgery of the hand, 1989. Commd. 1st lt. U.S. Army, 1949; advanced through grades to col., 1967; ret. U.S. Army, 1970; rotating intern Bethany Hosp., Kansas City, 1950-51; resident in orthopaedic surgery Brooke Gen. Hosp., San Antonio, 1952-55, William Beaumont Gen. Hosp., El Paso, Tex., 1955-56; chief surgery Irwin Army Hosp., Ft. Riley, Kans., 1957-59; cons. in orthopaedic surgery 8th Army Korea, 1959-60; asst. chief orthopaedic surgery, chief hand surgeon Fitzsimons Army Med. Center, Denver, 1960-63; dir. orthopaedic residency tng. Armed Forces Inst. Pathology, Washington, 1963-65; chief orthopaedic surgery and chief Army Hand Surg. Center, Brooke Army Med. Center, 1965-70; cons. in orthopaedic and hand surgery Surgeon Gen. Army, 1967-70; prof. orthopaedics, surgery and anatomy, chmn. dept. orthopaedic surgery, chief div. hand surgery U. N.Mex., 1970-90, med. dir. phys. therapy, 1972-90, acting asst. dean grad. edn. Sch. Medicine, 1980-81; mem. active staff U. N.Mex. Hosp., Albuquerque, chief of med. staff, 1984-86; cons. staff other Albuquerque hosps.; cons. orthopaedic surgery USPHS, 1966-85, U.S. Army, 1970-92, USAF, 1970-78, VA, 1970—; cons. Carrier Tingley Hosp. for Crippled Children, 1970—, interim med. dir., 1970-72, 86-87, mem. bd. advisors, 1972—, chair, 1994-95. Mem. bd. editors Clin. Orthopaedics, 1973-90, Jour. AMA, 1973-74, Jour. Hand Surgery, 1976-81; trustee Jour. Bone and Joint Surgery, 1993—, sec., 1993—; contbr. more than 200 articles to profl. jours., numerous chpts. to books. Decorated Legion of Merit, Army Commendation medal with 2 oak leaf clusters; recipient Alumni Achievement award Ft. Hays State U., 1973, Recognition plaque Am. Soc. Surgery Hand, 1989, Recognition plaque N.Mex. Orthopaedic Assn., 1991. Fellow ACS, Am. Orthopaedic Assn. (pres. 1988-89, exec. dir. 1989-93), Am. Acad. Orthopaedic Surgeons, Assn. Orthopaedic Chmn., N.Mex. Orthopaedic Assn. (pres. 1979-81), La. Orthopaedic Assn. (hon.), Korean Orthopaedic Assn. (hon.), Peru Orthopaedic Soc. (hon.), Caribbean Hand Soc., Am. Soc. Surgery Hand (pres. 1978-79), Am. Assn. Surgery of Trauma, Assn. Bone and Joint Surgeons, Assn. Mil. Surgeons U.S., Riordan Hand Soc. (pres. 1967-68), Sunderland Soc. (pres. 1981-83), Soc. Mil. Orthopaedic Surgeons, Brazilian Hand Soc., S.Am. Hand Soc. (hon.), Groupe D'Etude de la Main, Brit. Hand Soc., Venezuela Hand Soc. (hon.), South African Hand Soc. (hon.), Western Orthopaedic Assn. (pres. 1981-82), AAAS, Russell A. Hibbs Soc. (pres. 1977-78), 38th Parallel Med. Soc. (Korea) (sec. 1959-60); mem. AMA, Phi Kappa Phi, Phi Sigma, Alpha Omega Alpha, Phi Beta Pi. Home: 316 Big Horn Ridge Rd NE Sandia Heights Albuquerque NM 87122 Office: U N Mex Dept Orthopaedic Surgery 2211 Lomas Blvd NE Albuquerque NM 87106-2745

OMORI, MORIO, lawyer; b. Maui, Hawaii, Oct. 15, 1921; m. Rachel T. Tanaka, June 29, 1946; children: Sharyn, Colleen. BE, U. Hawaii, 1942, 5th yr. cert., 1943; LLB, U. Colo., 1954. Bar: Hawaii 1955, U.S. Dist. Ct. Hawaii 1955, U.S. Supreme Ct. 1959. Law clk. to chief justice Supreme Ct. Hawaii, Honolulu, 1954-55, dep. atty. gen., 1955-56, spl. dep. atty. gen., 1956-68; pvt. practice law, 1957—; gen. counsel Pacific Savs. & Loan, Honolulu, 1968-76, chmn. bd., 1972-76; gen. counsel Halekulani Corp., Honolulu, 1985—, also bd. dirs. Campaign coord. for U.S. Senator Daniel Inouye, Hawaii, 1959, 62, state rep., 1959-70. With U.S. Army, 1944-46, ETO. Mem. ABA, Hawaii Bar Assn., 442d Vets. Club, Phi Delta Phi. Home: 1031 Waiiki St Honolulu HI 96821-1234

ONAK, THOMAS PHILIP, chemistry educator; b. Omaha, July 30, 1932; s. Louis Albert and Louise Marie (Penner) O.; m. Sharon Colleen Neal, June 18, 1954. B.A., Calif. State U., San Diego, 1954; Ph.D., U. Cal. at Berkeley, 1957. Research chemist Olin Mathieson Chem. Corp., Pasadena, Calif., 1957-59; asst. prof. Calif. State U., Los Angeles, 1959-63, assoc. prof., 1963-66, prof. chemistry, 1966—. Author: Organoborane Chemistry, 1975; Contbr. articles to profl. jours., chpts. to books. Recipient Rsch. Career award NIH, 1973-78, Nat. award Am. Chem. Soc., 1990; Fulbright rsch. fellow U. Cambridge, Eng., 1965-66, Outstanding Prof. award Calif. State U. System, 1993-94. Home: PO Box 1477 South Pasadena CA 91031-1477 Office: Calif State U Dept Chemistry 5151 State U Dr Los Angeles CA 90032

O'NEAL, DOROTHY DECKER, fabric sales company executive; b. Akron, Ohio, Dec. 8, 1923; d. Clyde Earl and Mary Iva (King) Decker; m. Robert Frank O'Neal, Dec. 4, 1943; 1 child, Aileen Adele. Purchasing agt. Firestone Tire and Rubber Co., Akron, 1941-43; free lance fashion model, Little Rock, 1944-46; freelance fashion cons., Akron, 1947-52; owner, mgr. Canal Shop, Peninsula, Ohio, 1953-60, Fashion With Fabrics, Sierra Vista, Ariz., 1979-89, The Fabric Connection, Sierra Vista. Editor: Bi-Centennial Cook Book, 1976; Yule in the Mules Cook Book, 1977. Chmn. Goldwater for Pres. Com., Battle Creek, Mich., 1963-64. Mem. Greater Fedn. Women's Clubs, Am. Assn. Hosp. Auxs. Republican. Unitarian. Club: The Internat. Fashion Group (N.Y.C.). Avocations: sewing, cooking, fashion shows, travel, career seminars. Home: 4391 E Plaza Oro Loma Sierra Vista AZ 85635-4351 Office: The Fabric Connection 4391 E Plaza Oro Loma Sierra Vista AZ 85635-4351

O'NEIL, WILLIAM J., aerospace engineer. Galileo project mgr. NASA. Recipient Laurels award-Space/Missiles Aviation Week & Space Tech., 1991. Home: 2081 Liliano Dr Sierra Madre CA 91024-1537*

O'NEILL, BEVERLY LEWIS, mayor, former college president; b. Long Beach, Calif., Sept. 8, 1930; d. Clarence John and Flossie Rachel (Nicholson) Lewis; m. William F. O'Neill, Dec. 21, 1952. AA, Long Beach City Coll., 1950; BA, Calif. State U., Long Beach, 1952, MA, 1956; EdD, U. So. Calif., 1977. Elem. tchr. Long Beach Unified Sch. Dist., 1952-57; instr., counsellor Compton (Calif.) Coll., 1957-60; curriculum supr. Little Lake Sch. Dist., Santa Fe Springs, Calif., 1960-62; women's advisor, campus dean Long Beach City Coll., 1962-71, dir. Continuing Edn. Ctr. for Women, 1969-75, dean student affairs, 1971-77, v.p. student svcs., 1977-88, supt.-pres., 1988—, exec. dir. Found., 1983—; mayor City of Long Beach, Calif. Advisor Jr. League, Long Beach, 1976—, Nat. Coun. on Alcoholism, Long Beach, 1979—, Assistance League, Long Beach, 1982—; bd. dirs. NCCJ, Long Beach, 1976—, Meml. Hosp. Found., Long Beach, 1984-92, Met. YMCA, Long Beach, 1986-92, United Way, Long Beach, 1986-92. Named Woman of Yr., Long Beach Human Rels. Commn., 1976, to Hall of Fame, Long Beach City Coll., 1977, Disting. Alumni of Yr., Calif. State U., Long Beach, 1985, Long Beach Woman of Yr. Rick Rackers, 1987, Assistance League Aux., 1987; recipient Hannah Solomon award Nat. Coun. Jewish Women, 1984, Outstanding Colleague award Long Beach City Coll., 1985, NCCJ Humanitarian award, 1991, Woman of Excellence award YWCA, 1990, Community Svc. award Community Svcs. Devel. Corp., 1991, Citizen of Yr. award Exch. Club, 1992, Pacific Regional CEO award Assn. Community Coll. Trustees, 1992. Mem. Assn. Calif. Community Coll. Adminstrs. (pres. 1988-90, Harry Buttimer award 1991), Calif. Community Colls. Chief Exec. Officers Assn., Rotary, Soroptimists (Women Helping Women award 1981, Hall of Fame award 1984). Democrat. Office: Office of the Mayor 333 W Ocean Blvd Long Beach CA 90802

O'NEILL, ELIZABETH STONE, writer; b. Wilmington, Del., Sept. 29, 1923; d. Paul David and Winona Adele (Lambert) Stone; m. John Carroll O'Neill, Aug. 26, 1942; children: Adele Nova, Claire Linnaea (dec.). Student, Goucher Coll., 1941-42, Stockton Coll., 1952-54; BA, U. of the Pacific, 1956, MA, 1968. Legal sec. Salisbury, Md., 1942-44; elem. tchr. Lincoln Unified Sch. Dist., Stockton, Calif., 1956-58; elem. tchr. Stockton (Calif.) Unified Sch. Dist., 1959-75, community rels. counselor, 1966-68; freelance writer Groveland, Calif., 1975—. Author: Meadow in the Sky-A History of Yosemite's Tuolumne Meadows Region, 1984, 3d edit., 1992, Mountain Sage-The Life Story of Carl Sharsmith, Yosemite's Famous Ranger/Naturalist, 1988; contbr. articles to profl. jours. and poems to mags. Mem. Sierra Club, Audubon Soc., Wilderness Soc.

O'NEILL, KIM LESLIE, microbiologist; b. Ballymoney, Northern Ireland, Oct. 12, 1958; came to the U.S., 1992; s. Desmond Rainey and Oonah (Bateman) O'N.; m. Allison Nesbitt, Mar. 9, 1966; children: Anu, Shannon. BS with honors, New U. Ulster, 1980; PhD, U. Ulster, 1986. Rsch. asst. U. Ulster, Coleraine, Ireland, 1983-86, rsch. officer, 1986-92; asst. prof. microbiology Brigham Young U., Provo, Utah, 1992—. Contbr. articles to profl. jours. Mem. U. Ulster Coleraine Genetical Soc. (founder, chairperson 1983-85, treas. 1985-86), Biomed. Scis. Soc., Am. Cancer Soc. (chmn. bd. Utah County 1992-93), Am. Assn. for Cancer Rsch. Office: Brigham Young U Dept Microbiology Provo UT 84602

O'NEILL, MARGARET E., psychological counselor; b. Youngstown, Ohio, Jan. 23, 1935; d. Julius and Anna (Zakel) Huegel; children: Paul McCann, Kathleen McCann, Kevin McCann; m. Thomas B. O'Neill, Oct. 21, 1971 (div. 1979). BSN, UCLA, 1961, MS in Nursing, 1963; MA in Counseling, Calif. Luth. Coll., Thousand Oaks, 1974; PhD in Psychology, U.S. Internat. U., San Diego, 1986. Cert. hypnotherapist, Calif. Instr. Ventura Coll., Calif., 1965-69, dept. chair, 1969-74, coordinator Women's Ctr., 1974-79, counselor, 1979-91; marriage, family and child psychologist, Ventura, 1981-92, Morro Bay and San Luis Obispo, 1992—; trainer, cons. County of Ventura, 1984-90, County of San Luis Obispo, 1991—. Mem. NAFE, San Luis Obispo Psychol. Assn., Rotary Morro Bay, New Comers Club San Luis Obispo. Democrat. Avocations: reading, dancing, hiking, walking, travel. Office: 895 Napa Ave Ste A4 Morro Bay CA 93442-1945

O'NEILL, MAUREEN ANNE, city administrator, arts administrator; b. Seattle, Nov. 11, 1948; d. Robert P. and Barbara F. (Pettinger) O. BA in Sociology cum laude, Wash. State U., 1971; MA, Bowling Green State U., 1972. Grad. asst. dept. coll. student personnel Bowling Green (Ohio) State U., 1971-72; asst. coordinator coll. activities SUNY-Geneseo, 1972-75, acting coordinator coll. activities, 1975-76; regional mgr. northeast Kazuko Hillyer Internat. Agy., N.Y.C., 1976-77; mgr. lectures and concerts Meany Theater U. Wash., Seattle, 1977-81; mgr. performing and visual arts Parks and Recreation, City of Seattle, 1981-83, recreation dist. mgr., 1983-92, recreation mgr. north divsn., 1992—; cons. Nat. Endowment for Arts: Site Evaluator, 1980; interarts panel 1981; multi-music panel 1988, 89, 90; workshop presenter Washington Parks and Recreation, 1989, Washington Recreation and Parks to Washington State Arts Commn., 1988, 89, 90, bd. dirs. liaison; mem. program and edn. com. Seattle Art Mus., 1981—; workshop presenter Nat. Recreation and Parks Assn. Regional Confs., 1985-86; mem. conf. com. Internat. NW Parks and Recreation Assn. Conf., 1986. Bd. dirs. Bumbershoot-Seattle Arts Festival, 1979, 80; bd. dirs. Northwest Folklife Inc., 1982—, treas., 1985, 86, pres. 1986-89, chmn. edn. com., 1991-94, chair ad hoc com. NEA Advancement Grant, 1994—; cantor Sacred Heart Ch., Seattle, 1982—; mem. Seattle Art Mus. Mem. Phi Beta Kappa, Mu Phi Epsilon, Alpha Delta Pi. Roman Catholic. Home: PO Box 19278 Seattle WA 98109-1278 Office: 100 Dexter Ave N Seattle WA 98109-5102

O'NEILL, MICHAEL FOY, business educator; b. Milw., Apr. 16, 1943; s. Edward James and Marcellian (Wesley) O'N.; m. Karen Lynn Shoots, June 13, 1968; children: Kristine, Brenna. BBA, Ohio State U., 1966; PhD in Bus. Adminstrn., U. Oreg., 1978. Cons. Robert E. Miller and Assocs., San Francisco, 1969-73; mem. faculty Calif. State U., Chico, 1971-73, 1980—, U. Oreg., Eugene, 1974-77, U. Ariz., Tucson, 1977-79; pres. Decision Sci. Inst., Atlanta, 1986-87, v.p., 1985-86. Contbr. articles to profl. jours. Served with U.S. Army, 1962-68. Recipient Dean's Research award Calif. State U., Chico, 1981. Home: 2819 North Ave Chico CA 95926-0916 Office: Calif State U Dept Fin and Mktg Chico CA 95926

O'NEILL, NORAH ELLEN, airline pilot; b. Seattle, Aug. 23, 1949; d. John Wilson and Bertha Ellen (Moore) O'N.; m. Scott Reynolds, Jan. 31, 1970 (div. Apr. 1973); m. Scott Edward Byerley, Jan. 29, 1983; children: Cameron, Bren Maxey. Student, U. Calif., Santa Barbara, 1967-68, San Diego State U., 1868-70; BS in Profl. Aeros., Embry-Riddle Aero. U. Lic. airline transport pilot (comml., instrument instr.). Flight instr. Reynolds Aviation, Anchorage, 1973; flight instr. Alaska Cen. Air, Fairbanks, 1973-74, mail, commuter, medivac pilot, 1974-76; DC-8 pilot Flying Tigers, L.A., Seattle, N.Y.C., 1976-80; 747 pilot Flying Tigers, Los Angeles, 1980—. Mem. Airline Pilots Assn., 747 Pilot Fed. Express, Women Airline Pilots Soc. (co-founder 1978, v.p. 1979-80), The 99's (hon.). Home: PO Box 1504 Walla Walla WA 99362-0027 Office: Fed Express PO Box 727 Memphis TN 38194-0001

O'NEILL, SALLIE BOYD, education educator, business owner, sculptor; b. Ft. Lauderdale, Fla., Feb. 17, 1926; d. Howard Prindle and Sarah Frances (Clark) Boyd; AA, Stephens Coll., 1945; m. Roger H. Noden, July 8, 1945; children: Stephanie Ann Ballard, Ross Hopkins Noden; m. Russell R. O'Neill, June 30, 1967. Course coord. UCLA Extension, 1960-72, specialist continuing edn. dept. human devel., acad. appointment, 1972-83; pres. Learning Adventures, Inc., 1985-86; v.p., CFO The Learning Network, Inc., 1985-86; ednl. cons., 1986—; sculptor, 1987—. Bd. dirs. Everywoman's Village, Sherman Oaks, Calif., 1988—, v.p. 1993-95. Mem. Women in Bus. (v.p., bd. dirs. 1976-77, 86-87), Golden State Sculpture Assn., UCLA Assn. Acad. Women. Democrat. Home and Studio: 15430 Longbow Dr Sherman Oaks CA 91403-4910

ONEK, DAVID ALEXANDER, social services organization researcher; b. Washington, Dec. 3, 1969; s. Joseph Nathan and Margot Deborah (Piore) O. BA, Brown U., 1991. Rsch. intern Peter Hart Rsch., Washington, 1991; counselor Walden House Adolescent Facility, San Francisco, 1991-92; rsch. assoc. Nat. Coun. on Crime and Delinquency, San Francisco, 1992—. Mentor Big Bros./Big Sisters, San Francisco, 1993—. Democrat. Home: 3549 23rd St San Francisco CA 94110-3010 Office: Nat Coun on Crime and Delinquency 685 Market St Ste 620 San Francisco CA 94105-4200

ONG, ERNEST GRANT, auditor, researcher, accountant; b. Phoenix, Ariz., Sept. 12, 1951; s. Samuel and Chack (Yee) O. AA, Solano C.C., 1977; BS, Ariz. State U., 1976; MPA, U. Ariz., 1981. Cert. C.C. instr. Math. aide Ames Rsch. Ctr., Moffett Field, Calif., 1979; program analyst EPA, San Francisco, 1982; auditor State of Calif.-Contr., Sacramento, 1983-92. Treas. Davis (Calif.) Chinese Christian Ch., 1988-92, Grad. Pub. Adminstrn. Community, L.A., 1993—; mem. Asian Pacific Planning Coun., L.A., 1993—. Staff sgt. USAF, 1974-77. Mem. ASPA.

ONIK, FRANK JOSEPH, JR., electronics engineer; b. Omaha, June 12, 1949; s. Frank Joseph and Irene Rose (Mruk) O.; m. Diane Marie Grace, July 14, 1984; 1 child, Stephanie Marie. BS in Electronics Engring. Tech., U. Nebr., Omaha, 1976. RF R & D engr. Reach Electronics, Lexington, Nebr., 1977-84, digital R & D engr., 1982-84; temperature compensated crystal oscillator and crystal filter product engr. Dale Electronics, Tempe, Ariz., 1985-86; oscillator design engr., quality assurance and engring. mgr. Standard Crystal Corp., El Monte, Calif., 1986—, applications engr., 1986—. Sgt. U.S. Army, 1969-72, Vietnam. Mem. VFW (life; all state post comdr. 1983-84), Am. Legion (post comdr. 1982-83), U. Nebr. Alumni Assn. (life), KC (4th degree, navigator 1992-93, grand knight 1987-89), Order of Alhambra (vice grand comdr. 1993-94). Democrat. Roman Catholic. Home: 4714 Arden Way El Monte CA 91731-1262 Office: Standard Crystal Corp 9940 Baldwin Pl El Monte CA 91731-2295

ONISHI, YASUO, environmental researcher; b. Osaka, Japan, Jan. 25, 1943; came to U.S., 1969; s. Osamu and Tokiko (Domukai) O.; m. Esther Anna Stronczek, Jan 22, 1972; children: Anna Tokiko and Lisa Michiyo. BS, U. Osaka Prefecture, 1967, MS, 1969; PhD, U. Iowa, 1972. Rsch. engr. U. Iowa, Iowa City, 1972-74; sr. rsch. engr. Battelle Meml. Inst., Richland, Wash., 1974-77, staff engr., 1977—, mgr. rsch. program office, 1984-92; adj. faculty Wash. State U., Tri-Cities, 1993—. Co-author: Principles of Health Risk Assessment, 1985, several other environ. books; contbr. articles to profl. jours.; featured in TV program NOVA. Recipient Best Platform Presentation award ASTM, 1979. Mem. ASCE (chmn. task com. 1986—), IAEA (advisor on environ. issues, U.S. coord. water and soil assessment bilateral joint work on Chernobyl nuclear accident), Nat. Coun. Radiation Protection and Measurements (adj., mem. task com. 1983—), Sigma Xi. Lutheran. Home: 144 Spengler Rd Richland WA 99352-1971 Office: Battelle Pacific NW Labs Batelle Blvd Richland WA 99352

ONOFRIO, JOE FREDERICK, III, piano company executive; b. Denver, Nov. 26, 1955; s. Joe Frederick Jr. and Vivien C. (Piogossi) O.; m. Paula Marie Vann, Dec. 23, 1963; children: Stephania, Olivia, Angelica, Sylvana Rosa. BS in Acctg., Bus. Adminstrn., Regis U., 1981. Outfitter, horse wrangler Colo., Ariz., Colo., Mont., Ariz., 1969-77; piano tech. Onofrio Piano Co., Denver, 1977-81; mfrs. rep. J&B Importers, Denver, 1981-91; pres. Onofrio Piano Co., Denver, 1991—. Sponsor Opera Colo., Denver, Colo. Ballet, Denver, 1993—, Ctrl. City (Colo.) Opera, 1993—. Recipient Joseph A. Ryan Excellence in Bus. Adminstrn. award Regis U., 1981. Mem. Alpha Sigma Nu. Republican. Roman Catholic. Office: Joe Onofrio Piano Co 1332 S Broadway Denver CO 80210-2205

ONOPA, ROBERT LAWRENCE, English language educator; b. Chgo., Jan. 5, 1943; s. Alexander and Anna (Gacioch) O.; m. Janet Kemble, Mar. 15, 1980; children: Ryder Kalani, Alexi Kaikaina. BA, U. Ill., 1964; MA, U. Conn., 1966; PhD, Northwestern U., 1974. Asst. prof. English U. Hawaii, Honolulu, 1974-80, assoc. prof., 1980—; Fulbright lectr. West Africa, 1970. Author: Pleasure Tube, 1979; co-editor: Triquar. Mag., 1979-80. Creative fellowship Nat. Endowment for the Arts, 1987. Home: 1040 Maunawili Loop Kailua HI 96734 Office: U Hawaii at Manoa Dept English Honolulu HI 96822

ONYEADOR, EMMANUEL OSITA, mathematics and computer educator; b. Okigwe, Imo, Nigeria, Mar. 4, 1957; came to U.S., 1985; s. Felix Anitche and Justina Mbokwo (Ezumah) O. BS in Physics with honors, U. Ife, Ile-Ife, Nigeria, 1982; BS in Computer Sci., San Francisco State U., 1991, MA in Edn., Computer Applications, 1993. Cert. tchr., Calif. Math. educator Oakland (Calif.) Unified Sch. Dist., 1987—, technology curriculum specialist, 1993—; exec. com. mem. Oakland Unified Sch. Dist./U. Calif. Partnership for Math., 1992-94; chmn. acad. achievement com. Comer process King Estates, Oakland, 1992—; rsch. assoc. Stanford Linear Accelerator Ctr., Palo Alto, Calif., 1992; advisor Leadership Inst. Chabot Observatory & Sci. Ctr., Oakland, 1994; physics/calculus educator Mills Coll., Oakland, 1991; curr. developer Oakland Unified Sch. Dist., 1991—; ednl. software developer King Estates, Oakland, 1991-94; curr. adviser KDOL-TV, Oakland, 1994—. Editor/developer: (curriculum) Math A, 1991, Math B, 1991; developer: (interactive software) Algebra Project Software, 1992, (activity software) Fractals Activity for Math., 1994. Mem. NEA, Am. Phys. Soc., Assn. Computing Machinery, Physic and Engring. Physic Assn., Calif. Tchrs. Assn. (Educators award 1991), Oakland Edn. Assn. (Super Tchr. 1992). Roman Catholic. Home: 1083 45th St Emeryville CA 94608-3329 Office: Oakland Unified Sch Dist 8251 Fontaine St Oakland CA 94605-4109

OOLIE, DARLENE, advertising executive; b. Rochester, N.Y., Nov. 14, 1961. BBA in Mktg. cum laude, Pace U., 1983. Coder, norms mgr., project dir. ASI Market Rsch., L.A., 1983-86; rsch. project mgr. Phillips-Ramsey Advt., San Diego, 1986—. Mem. Am. Mktg. Assn. Office: Phillips-Ramsey Advt 6863 Friars Rd San Diego CA 92108-1121

OPENSHAW, DALE KIM, educator, therapist; b. Salt Lake City, Mar. 10, 1950; s. Richard D. and Naoma Lillian (Tischner) O.; m. Anita B. Evans, Jan. 12, 1973; children: Damian, Cammarie, Derek, Jeffrey, Cody, Shandee, Joshua, Micah. BA, U. Utah, 1973, MSW, 1976; PhD, Brigham Young U., 1978. Cert. approved cons. in clin. hypnosis. Prof. human devel. U. Wis.-Stout, 1978-79; child devel. and family life specialist U. Wis.-Madison, 1979-81; prof., dir. marriage and family therapy Utah State U., Logan, 1981—; pvt. practice psychotherapist, Wis. and Utah, 1978—; adj. prof. adolescent devel. psychology. Active Optimist Internat. NIMH grantee U. Utah, 1974-76. Named Tchr. of Yr. Coll. Family Life, 1991-92, 92-93. Mem. Nat.

Coun. on Family Rels. (chair family therapy sect.), Soc. Rsch. Child Devel., Am. Assn. Marriage and Family Therapy, Nat. Marriage Consortium, Am. Soc. Clin. Hypnosis, Utah Soc. Clin. Hypnosis (pres. 1991-93), Omicron Nu, Phi Kappa Phi. Mem. Ch. of Jesus Christ of Latter-Day Saints. Presenter numerous workshops; contbr. articles to profl. jours. Home: 567 E 3700 S PO Box 424 Millville UT 84326-0424 Office: Utah State U Dept Family And Devel Logan UT 84322

OPFELL, JOHN BURTON, chemical engineer, educator; b. Cushing, Okla., July 24, 1924; s. Edward Uriah and Carrie Evelyn (Walker) O.; m. Olga Anna Strandvold, Sept. 10, 1954; children: Christopher Kaj, Thane Fredrick, Jon Guido. BS, U. Wis., 1945; MS, Calif. Inst. Tech., 1947, PhD, 1954; MBA, Stanford U., 1951. Registered profl. engr., Calif. Engr. Stanolind Oil and Gas Co., Tulsa, 1947-49, Cutter Labs., Berkeley, Calif., 1955-61, Dynamic Sci. Corp., South Pasadena, Calif., 1961-64, Philco-Ford Corp., Newport Beach, Calif., 1964-69; asst. mgr. corp. planning Sunkist Growers, Sherman Oaks, Calif., 1970-73; asst. to exec. v.p. Henningson, Durham and Richardson, Santa Barbara, Calif., 1980-83; engr. AiResearch Mfg. Co., Torrance, Calif., 1973-80, Allied-Signal Aerospace Co., Torrance, Calif., 1983-93; v.p. Ideation Internat., Santa Monica, Calif., 1993—; lectr. Calif. Inst. Tech., Pasadena, 1954, U. Calif., Santa Barbara, 1973, 82, Calif. State U., Northridge, 1986. Author: (with others) Momentum Transfer in Fluids, 1956, Equations of State for Hydrocarbons, 1959; contbr. articles to profl. jours. Lt. (j.g.) USN, 1944-54. Fellow AAAS, Royal Soc. Health (London); mem. AIChE, Ops. Rsch. Soc. Am., Masons, Sigma Xi. Democrat. Home: 1007 Park Circle Dr Torrance CA 90502-2817

OPFER, NEIL DAVID, educator, consultant; b. Spokane, Wash., June 3, 1954; s. Gus Chris and Alice Ann (Blom) O. BS in Bldg. Theory cum laude, Wash. State U., 1976, BA in Econs. cum laude, 1977, BA in Bus. cum laude, 1977; MS in Mgmt., Purdue U., 1982. Cert. cost engr., cert. project mgr. Estimator Standard Oil (Chevron), Richmond, Calif., 1975; gen. carpenter forman Opfer Constrn. Corp., Spokane, 1976; assoc. engr. Inland Steel Corp., East Chgo., Ind., 1977-78; millwright supr. Inland Steel Corp., 1978-79, field engr., 1979-82, project engr., 1982-84, sr. engr., 1984-87; asst. prof. Western Mich. U., Kalamazoo, 1987-89; asst. prof. U. Nev., Las Vegas, 1989-95, assoc. prof., 1995—. Contbr. articles to publs. Bd. dirs. Christmas in April, 1993—, Habitat for Humanity, 1991—. Mem. Am. Welding Soc. (dir. 1982-87), Am. Inst. Constructors, Am. Assn. Cost Engrs. (Order of Engr. award 1989, nat. dir. 1995—), Project Mgmt. Inst., Constrn. Mgmt. Assn. Am., Tau Beta Pi (life), Phi Kappa Phi (life). Methodist. Home: 1515 E Reno Ave Las Vegas NV 89119-2116 Office: Univ Nev 4505 S Maryland Pky Las Vegas NV 89154-9900

OPITZ, JOHN MARIUS, clinical geneticist, pediatrician; b. Hamburg, Germany, Aug. 15, 1935; came to U.S., 1950, naturalized, 1957; s. Friedrich and Erica Maria (Quadt) O.; m. Susan O. Lewin; children: Leigh, Teresa, John, Chrisanthi, Emma. BA, State U. Iowa, 1956, MD, 1959; DSc (hon.), Mont. State U., 1983; MD (hon.), U. Kiel, Fed. Republic of Germany, 1986. Diplomate Am. Bd. Pediatrics, Am. Bd. Med. Genetics. Intern, State U. Iowa Hosp., 1959-60, resident in pediatrics, 1960-61; resident and chief resident in pediatrics U. Wis. Hosp., Madison, 1961-62; fellow in pediatrics and med. genetics U. Wis., 1962-64, asst. prof. med. genetics and pediatrics, 1964-69, assoc. prof., 1969-72, prof., 1972-79; dir. Wis. Clin. Genetics Ctr., 1974-79; clin. prof. med. genetics and pediatrics U. Wash., Seattle, 1979—; adj. prof. medicine, biology, history and philosophy, vet. rsch. and vet. sci. Mont. State U., Bozeman, 1979-94, McKay lectr., 1992, Univ. prof. med. humanities MSU. Bozeman, 1994—; adj. prof. pediatrics, med. genetics U. Wis., Madison, 1979—, Class of 1947 Disting. prof., U. of Wis., 1992; coordinator Shodair Mont. Regional Genetic Svcs. Program, Helena, 1979-82; chmn. dept. med. genetics Shodair Children's Hosp., Helena, 1983-94; dir. Found. Devel. and Med. Genetics, Helena, Mont.; Farber lectr. Soc. Pediatric Pathology, 1987; Joseph Garfunkel lectr. So. Ill. U., Springfield, 1987, McKay lectr. Mont. State U., 1992; Warren Wheeler vis. prof. Columbus (Ohio) Children's Hospital, 1987. Editor, author 13 books; founder, editor in chief Am. Jour. Med. Genetics, 1977—; mng. editor European Jour. Pediatrics, 1977-85; contbr. numerous articles on clin. genetics. Chair Mont. Com. for Humanities, 1991. Recipient Pool of Bethesda award for excellence in mental retardation rsch. Bethesda Luth. Home, 1988, Med. Alumni Citation U. Wis., 1989, Col. Harlan Sanders Lifetime Achievement award for work in the field of genetic scis. March of Dimes. Fellow Am. Coll. Med. Genetics (founder); mem. German Acad. Scientists Leopoldina, Am. Soc. Human Genetics, Am. Pediatric Soc., Soc. Pediatric Rsch., Am. Bd. Med. Genetics, Birth Defects Clin. Genetic Soc., Am. Inst. Biol. Scis., Am. Soc. Zoologists, AAAS, Teratology Soc., Genetic Soc. Am., European Soc. Human Genetics, Soc. Study Social Biology, Am. Acad. Pediatrics, German Soc. Pediatrics (hon.), Western Soc. Pediatrics Rsch., Italian Soc. Med. Genetics, Israel Soc. Genetics (hon.), Russian Soc. Med. Genetics (hon.), So. Africa Soc. Med. Genetics (hon.), Japanese Soc. Human Genetics (hon.), Sigma Xi. Democrat. Roman Catholic. Home: 2180 Lime Kiln St Helena MT 59601-5871 Office: FRB 100 Neill Ave Ste 229 Helena MT 59601

OPPEDAHL, JOHN FREDRICK, newspaper editor; b. Duluth, Minn., Nov. 9, 1944; s. Walter H. and Lucille (Hole) O.; m. Alison Owen, 1975 (div. 1983); m. Gillian Coyro, Feb. 14, 1987; 1 child, Max. B.A., U. Calif., Berkeley, 1967; M.S., Columbia U., 1968. Reporter San Francisco Examiner, 1967; reporter, asst. city editor Detroit Free Press, 1968-75, city editor, 1975-80, exec. city editor, 1981, exec. news editor, 1981-82, asst. mng. editor, 1983; nat. editor Dallas Times Herald, 1983-85, asst. mng. editor, 1985-87; mng. editor/news L.A. Herald Examiner, 1987-89; mng. editor Ariz. Republic, Phoenix, 1989-93; exec. editor Phoenix Newspapers, 1993—. Mem. Am. Soc. Newspaper Editors, AP Mng. Editors. Office: Phoenix Newspapers Inc 120 E Van Buren St Phoenix AZ 85004-2227

OPPEDAHL, PHILLIP EDWARD, computer company executive; b. Renwick, Iowa, Sept. 17, 1935; s. Edward and Isadore Hannah (Gangstead) O.; B.S. in Naval Sci., Navy Postgrad. Sch., 1963, M.S. in Nuclear Physics, 1971; M.S. in Systems Mgmt., U. S.C., 1978; m. Sharon Elaine Ree, Aug. 3, 1957 (dec. Aug. 1989); children: Gary Lynn, Tamra Sue, Sue Ann, Lisa Kay. Commd. ensign U.S. Navy, 1956, advanced through grades to capt., 1977; with Airborne Early Warning Squadron, 1957-59, Anti-Submarine Squadron, 1959-65; asst. navigator USS Coral Sea, 1965-67; basic jet flight instr., 1967-69; student Armed Forces Staff Coll., 1971; test group dir. Def. Nuclear Agy., 1972-74; weapons officer USS Oriskany, 1974-76; program mgr. for armament Naval Air Systems Command, Washington, 1977-79; test dir. Def. Nuclear Agy., Kirtland AFB, N.Mex., 1979-82, dep. comdr. Def. Nuclear Agy., 1982-83; pres., chief exec. officer Am. Systems, Albuquerque, 1983—; dir., bd. dirs. BASIS Internat., 1991—. Pres., bd. dirs. Casa Esperanza, 1990-92. Decorated Disting. Service medal. Mem. Naval Inst., Am. Nuclear Soc., Aircraft Owners and Pilots Assn., Assn. Naval Aviation Navy League. Lutheran. Author: Energy Loss of High Energy Electrons in Beryllium, 1971; Understanding Contractor Motivation and Incentive Contracts, 1977. Home: 7916 Denrock Ave Los Angeles CA 90045-1113

OPPEDISANO, SUZANNE MARIE, marketing professional, dentist; b. Boston; d. Rocco Louis and Ruth Margaret (Webb) O. BS, Tufts U., 1976; DMD, U. Pa., 1980; MBA, Wharton, 1986. Adj. faculty U. Pa. Sch. Dental Medicine, Phila., 1984-86; nat. sales analyst E.R. Squibb & Sons, Princeton, N.J., 1986-87; cons. Prudential Life Ins. Co, Princeton, 1987-88; asst. product dir. Johnson & Johnson Dental Care Co., New Brunswick, N.J., 1988; asst. prof. U. of The Pacific, San Francisco, 1989—; Intern prodn. mgmt. Pharm. div. CIBA-Geigy, Summit, N.J., 1985; student cons. Albert Einstein Hosp., Phila., 1985. Capt. U.S. Army, 1980-84. Armed Forces Health Professions scholar U.S. Army Dental Corps. Mem. ADA, Wharton Alumni Assn.

OPPEL, ANDREW JOHN, apparel company executive; b. Kerrville, Tex., Dec. 22, 1952; s. Wallace Churchill and Anne Kathryn (Smith) O.; m. Laura Lee Partridge, Aug. 26, 1972; children: Keith Andrew, Luke Andrew. BA in Computer Sci., Transylvania U., 1974. Computer programmer Johns Hopkins U., Balt., 1974-77; data base programmer Equitable Trust Co., Balt., 1977-78; sr. programmer, analyst Md. Casualty Co., Balt., 1978-79; sr. programmer, analyst Levi Strauss & Co., San Francisco, 1979-82, sr. requirements mgr., 1982-84, tech. cons., 1984-91, tech. advisor, 1991-93, mgr. database mgmt. sys., 1994—; instr. U. Calif. Extension, Berkeley, 1983—. Ops. officer Alameda County Radio Amateur Civil Emergency Svc., San Leandro, Calif., 1980-92; cub master Boy Scouts Am., Alameda, Calif., 1991-92; referee U.S. Soccer Fedn., Alameda, 1988—. Democrat. Episcopalian. Home: 1308 Burbank St Alameda CA 94501-3946 Office: Levi Strauss & Co 1155 Battery St San Francisco CA 94111-1230

OPPELT, NORMAN THEODORE, park ranger, retired psychology educator; b. Chgo., Feb. 1, 1930; s. Norman Theodore Sr. and Jeannette (Willey) O.; m. Patricia Louise Bast, June 6, 1954; children: Eric Theodore, Karen Elizabeth. BS in Zoology, Colo. State U., 1954; MA in Psychology, U. No. Colo., 1955; PhD in Counseling Psychology, Mich. State U., 1962. Lic. psychologist, Colo. Dean of men U. No. Colo., Greeley, 1960-64, v.p. student affairs, 1964-70, prof. psychology, 1967-87, asst. to pres., 1970-72, chair dept. coll. student pers. adminstrn., 1972-83, prof. emeritus, 1987—; park ranger, rschr. Mesa Verde Nat. Park, Colo., 1987—. Author: Guide to Prehistoric Ruins, 1981, Southwestern Pottery, 1988, Tribal Indian Colleges, 1990, Earth, Water and Fire, 1991. Advisor Blue Key, 1960; v.p. Nat. Assn. Student Pers. Adminstrs., 1970-72; candidate City Coun., Greeley, 1973. Sgt. USMC, 1950-52, Korea. Mem. High Plains Archaeol. Soc. (pres. 1975-76), Colo. Psychol. Assn., Colo. Archaeol. Soc. (adv. com. 1964—), Phi Delta Kappa, Sigma Alpha Epsilon (regional v.p. 1964-68). Home: 2218 25th St Greeley CO 80631

OPPENHEIM, ANTONI KAZIMIERZ, mechanical engineer; b. Warsaw, Poland, Aug. 11, 1915; came to U.S., 1948, naturalized, 1954; s. Tadeusz and Zuzanna (Zuckerwar) O.; m. Lavinia Stephens, July 18, 1945; 1 dau., Terry Ann. Diploma in Engring., Warsaw Inst. Tech., London, 1943; PhD in Engring., U. London, 1945; diploma of Imperial Coll., 1945; DSc, U. London, 1976; Dr. Honoris Causa, U. Poitiers, France, 1981, Tech. U., Warsaw, 1989. Registered profl. engr., Calif. Research asst. City and Guilds Coll., 1942-48, lectr., 1946-48; asst. prof. mech. engring. Stanford U., 1948-50; faculty U. Calif. at Berkeley, 1950—, prof. mech. engring., 1958-86, Miller prof., 1961-62, prof. emeritus, 1986—; fellow Imperial Coll., London, 1995; vis. prof. Sorbonne, Paris, 1960-61, U. Poitiers, France, 1973, 80; staff cons. Shell Devel. Co., 1952-60. Editor-in-chief: Acta Astronautica, 1974-79; contbr. articles to profl. jours., also monographs. Chmn. Heat Transfer and Fluid Mechanics Inst., 1958; IAA Com. on Gasdynamics of Explosions, 1968—; organizer Internat. Colloquia on Gas Dynamics of Explosions and Reactive Systems, 1967, 69, 71, 73, 75, 77, 79, 81, 83; mem. NASA, adv. com. fluid mechanics, 1963-69. Fellow Imperial Coll., 1995; recipient Water Arbitration prize Inst. Mech. Engrs., 1948, Numa Manson medal Inst. for Dynamics of Explosions and Reactive Sys., 1981, Dionizy Smolenski medal Polish Acad. Scis., 1987, Alfred C. Egerton medal The Combustion Inst., 1988, citation U. Calif., Berkeley, 1988. Fellow Am. Rocket Soc. (nat. dir. 1959-62, founder, pres. No. Calif. sect. 1957), ASME (hon. mem.1989, chmn. profl. conf. 1958, program chmn. San Francisco 1959-60, hon. 1989), Am. Inst. Aeros. and Astronautics (Pendray award 1966); mem. AIAA, Soc. Automotive Engrs., Internat. Acad. Astronautics, Nat. Acad. Engring., Am. Phys. Soc., Sigma Xi, Psi Tau Sigma, Tau Beta Psi. Home: 54 Norwood Ave Kensington CA 94707-1119

OPPERMAN, HAL N., art historian; b. Kansas City, Mo., Oct. 18, 1938; s. Halbert Hoover and Anna Clara (Niedermeyer) O.; m. Isabelle Catherine Noiret, July 4, 1966 (div. Jan. 1985); children: Anne Elisabeth Opperman Reese, F. Lucien; m. JoLynn Edwards, Sept. 5, 1989. BA, Knox Coll., 1960; AM, U. Chgo., 1963, PhD, 1972. Asst. prof. art history U. Wash., Seattle, 1967-74, assoc. prof. art history, 1974-83, prof. art history, 1983-94, prof. emeritus, 1994—, chair comparative history of ideas, 1979-82; gen. editor fine arts Corbis Corp., Bellevue, Wash., 1991—; mem. Art Bull. Adv. Bd., 1990-94; mem. Gottschalk Prize Com., 1985, chair, 1986; mem. nat. screening com. Fulbright Grant Program, 1992-94; mem. editorial adv. bd. Eighteenth-Century Studies, 1993—. author: Jean-Baptiste Oudry, 1977 (Prix Cailleux), (exhbn. catalogue) Jean-Baptiste Oudry, 1982-83; contbr. numerous articles to profl. publs. Fulbright scholar, 1965-67, Nat. Merit scholar, 1956. Mem. Wash. Ornithol. Soc. (editor jour., bd. dirs. 1989—), Am. Soc. Eighteenth-Century Studies, Coll. Art Assn., Société de l'Histoire de l'Art Français. Home: PO Box 286 Medina WA 98039-0286 Office: Corbis Corp 15395 SE 30th Pl Ste 300 Bellevue WA 98007

ORBACH, RAYMOND LEE, physicist, educator; b. Los Angeles, July 12, 1934; s. Morris Albert and Mary Ruth (Miller) O.; m. Eva Hannah Spiegler, Aug. 26, 1956; children: David Miller, Deborah Hedwig, Thomas Randolph. BS, Calif. Inst. Tech., 1956; PhD, U. Calif., Berkeley, 1960. NSF postdoctoral fellow Oxford U., 1960-61; asst. prof. applied physics Harvard U., 1961-63; prof. physics UCLA, 1963-92, asst. vice chancellor acad. change and curriculum devel., 1970-72, chmn. acad. senate L.A. divsn., 1976-77, provost Coll. Letters and Sci., 1982-92; chancellor U. Calif., Riverside, 1992—; mem. physics adv. panel NSF, 1970-73; mem. vis. com. Brookhaven Nat. Lab., 1970-74; mem. materials rsch. lab. adv. panel NSF, 1974-77; mem. Nat. Comm. on Rsch., 1978-80; chmn. 16th Internat. Conf. on Low Temperature Physics, 1981; Joliot Curie prof. Ecole Superieure de la Physique et Chimie Industrielle de la Ville de Paris, 1982, chmn. Gordon Rsch. Conf. on Fractals, 1986; Lorentz prof. U. Leiden, Netherlands, 1987; Raymond and Beverly Sackler lectr. Tel Aviv U., 1989; faculty rsch. lectr. UCLA, 1990; Andrew Lawson lectr. U. Calif., Riverside, 1992; mem. external rev. com. Nat. High Magnetic Fields Lab., 1994—. Author: (with A.A. Manenkov) SpinLattice Relaxation in Ionic Solids, 1966; Div. assoc. editor Phys. Rev. Letters, 1980-83, Jour. Low Temperature Physics, 1980-90, Phys. Rev., 1983—; contbr. articles to profl. jours. Alfred P. Sloan Found. fellow, 1963-67; NSF sr. postdoctoral fellow Imperial Coll., 1967-68; Guggenheim fellow Tel Aviv U., 1973-74. Fellow Am. Phys. Soc. (chmn. nominations com. 1981-82, counselor-at-large 1987-91, chmn. divsn. condensed matter 1990-91); mem. AAAS (chairperson steering group physics sect.), NSF (mem. rsch. adv. com. divsn. materials 1992-93), Phys. Soc. (London), Univ. Rsch. Assn. (chair coun. pres. 1993), Sigma Xi, Phi Beta Kappa, Tau Beta Pi. Home: 4171 Watkins Dr Riverside CA 92507-4738 Office: U Calif Riverside Chancellor's Office Riverside CA 92521-0101

ORDINI, JOHN, JR., accountant; b. Passaic, N.J., Jan. 17, 1956; s. John and Mary (Cuoco) O. BSBA, Marquette U., 1978; MBA, Ariz. State U., 1994. CPA, Ariz. Bus. mgr. Milw. Stratton Coll., 1978-83; property adminstr. Ariz. State U., Tempe, 1983-85, asst. dir., 1985-94. Mem. AICPA, Ariz. Soc. CPAs, Am. Inst. Individual Investors, Phi Kappa Phi, Sigma Iota Epsilon, Beta Gamma Sigma. Home: 1618 N El Camino Dr Tempe AZ 85281-1457

ORDUNO, ROBERT DANIEL, artist, painter, sculptor; b. Ventura, Calif., Sept. 5, 1933; s. Octavio and Mary G.; children: Patrice Schulman, Nicole Franco. Pvt. practice Artist, Painter, Sculptor; pvt. and group tchg. Santa Fe, 1990—, Australia, 1993; guest lectr. Australian Coun. on Adult Edn., 1993. Exhibited in Great Falls Tribune, J.M. Swanson, 1985, Gazette, Cody Bur, Wyo., Tom Howard, 1987, Aurora, Great Falls, Mont., Shirley Edam Diaz, 1988, S.W. Art Mag., J.M. Swanson, 1990; featured artist Shaman's Drum, 1992, The Advocate, Tasmania, Australia, 1993, The New Mexican, Santa Fe, 1994, Wheelright Mus. Am. Indian, Santa Fe, 1995; featured artist and cover image Internat. Fine Art Collector, 1992, cover and featured artist Informart Mag., 1994. Recipient Best Oil, Denver Indian Mkt., Pine Ridge S.D., 1985, 86, 87, 1st and 2d graphics Red Cloud Indian Sch., Best Painting artists choice Great Falls Native Am. Exhibit, James Bama award Best of Show, Best Contemporary Painting Buffalo Bill Hist. Ctr., Cody, Wyo., 1987, Best Painting Artists Choice award Great Falls Native Am. Exhibit, 1989, Best Show award, 1993. Home: 153 Calle Don Jose Santa Fe NM 87501-2391

OREN, JOSEPH, pharmaceutical research company executive, physician; b. Albany, N.Y., Mar. 24, 1932; s. Abraham and Jennie (Zak) O.; m. Joan Weiner, Oct. 12, 1958 (div. July 1970); children: Leslie, Jonathan, Abraham, Tamara; m. Sonja Christine Barber, Nov. 23, 1979. BA, Cornell U., 1953, MD, 1956. Resident in pediatrics Rochester U. (N.Y.), 1958-59, 61-62; fellow in allergy Johns Hopkins U., Balt., 1962-63; fellow in immunology U. Colo., Denver, 1970-71; practice medicine, Honolulu, 1963-70; assoc. med. dir. Syntex Corp., Palo Alto, Calif., 1971-74, sect. head, 1974-77, 86-88, dept. head, 1977-79; v.p. clin. Schering Corp., Kenilworth, N.J., 1979-82; v.p. clin. rsch. Nelson Rsch. & Devel. Co., Irvine, Calif., 1982-86; v.p. clin. rsch. Praxis Biologics Corp., Rochester, N.Y., 1988-90; sr. dir. clin. affairs Fisons Corp., Rochester, 1990-92; founder, pres. Clinicom, Clin. Comm. and Rsch. Consultancy, Sonoma, Calif., 1992—; dir. med. affairs Arris Pharm., South San Francisco, 1993—. Bd. dirs. Addiction Rsch. Found., Palo Alto, 1977-79. Contbr. articles to profl. jours. Mem. steering com. Democrats for McCarthy, Hawaii, 1968. Served to lt. comdr. USPHS, 1959-61. Allergy Found. Am. fellow, 1970. Diplomate Am. Bd. Allergy and Immunology, Am. Bd. Pediatrics. Mem. AMA, Am. Acad. Pediatrics, Am. Acad. Allergy, Am. Thoracic Soc., Royal Soc. Medicine (United Kingdom), Phi Beta Kappa, Alpha Omega Alpha. Jewish. Home: 617 Barcelona Dr Sonoma CA 95476-4435 Office: Clinicom PO Box 2339 Napa CA 94558-0233

ORENSTEIN, (IAN) MICHAEL, philatelic dealer, columnist; b. Bklyn., Jan. 6, 1939; s. Harry and Myra (Klein) O.; m. Linda Turer, June 28, 1964; 1 child, Paul David. BS, Clemson U., 1960; postgrad., U. Calif., Berkeley, 1960-61. Career regional mgr. Minkus Stamp & Pub. Co., Calif., 1964-70; mgr. stamp div. Superior Stamp & Coin Co., Inc., Beverly Hills, Calif., 1970-90; dir. stamp divsn. Superior Galleries, Beverly Hills, Calif., 1991-94; dir. space memorabelia Superior Stamp and Coin. Co., Inc., Beverly Hills, Calif., 1992-94; dir. stamp and space divsn. Superior Stamp & Coin an A-Mark Co., Beverly Hills, 1994—; stamp columnist L.A. Times, 1965-93; bd. Adelphi U. N.Y. Inst. Philatelic and Numismatic Studies, 1978-81. Author: Stamp Collecting Is Fun, 1990; philatelic advisor/creator The Video Guide To Stamp Collecting, 1988. With AUS, 1962-64. Mem. Am. Stamp Dealers Assn., C.Z. Study Group, German Philatelic Soc., Confederate Stamp Alliance, Am. Philatelic Soc. (writers unit 1975-80, 89-93), Internat. Fedn. Stamp Dealers, Internat. Soc. Appraisers: Stamps, Space Memorabilia. Republican. Office: Superior Stamp & Coin An A-Mark Co 9478 W Olympic Blvd Beverly Hills CA 90212-4246

ORENSTEIN, PEGGY JO, writer, editor; b. Mpls., Nov. 22, 1961; d. Melvin Israyl and Beatrice (Dolf) O.; m. Steven Okazaki, June 4, 1992. BA, Oberlin Coll., 1983. Asst. editor Esquire mag., N.Y.C., 1983-86; assoc. editor, then sr. editor Manhattan, Inc. mag., N.Y.C., 1986-87; sr. editor 7 Days mag., N.Y.C., 1987-88; mng. editor Mother Jones mag., San Francisco, 1988-91. Author: Schoolgirls: Young Women, Self Esteem and the Confidence Gap, 1994; contbr. numerous articles to popular jours.

ORFIELD, ADRIENNE ADAMS, lawyer; b. Memphis, June 14, 1953; d. Vincent Orville and Darlene Jo (Johannes) Adams; m. Michael Bennett Orfield, Sept. 25, 1982; children: Sarah Catherine, Rebecca Forsyth. BA, Cal. State Coll., San Bernardino, 1975; JD, U. San Diego, 1979. Bar: Calif. 1979, U.S. Dist. Ct. 1979. Assoc. Shifflet & Sharp, San Diego, 1980-82, Ault, Deuprey, Jones, and Gorman, San Diego, 1982-87; ptnr. Ault, Deuprey, Jones & Gorman, San Diego, 1987—. Dir. Crime Victims Fund, San Diego, 1985-90. Mem. San Diego County Bar Assn. (treas. 1992, v.p. 1993, pres. 1994), San Diego Def. Lawyers (v.p. 1985), So. Calif. Def. Lawyers, Calif. Women Lawyers, Lawyers Club San Diego. Republican. Roman Catholic. Home: PO Box 9827 Rancho Santa Fe CA 92067-4827 Office: Ault Deuprey Jones & Gorman 402 W Broadway Ste 1600 San Diego CA 92101-8509

ORLAND, TED NORCROSS, artist; b. Berkeley, Calif., Apr. 21, 1941; s. William Hugh and Alice (Sweeny) Organ; m. Linda Ellen Dunne, June 23, 1963 (div. 1976); 1 child, Jon Dunne Orland; m. Frances Dolloff, Dec. 9, 1989. BS in Indsl. Design, U. So. Calif., 1963; MA in Interdiciplinary Creative Arts, San Francisco State U., 1972. Designer Charles Eames Design Office, Venice, Calif., 1965-71; photographic asst. Ansel Adams, Photographer, Carmel, Calif., 1971-75; owner Image Continuum Press, Santa Cruz, Calif., 1973—; instr. U. Calif. Extension, Santa Cruz, 1975—, Maine Photographic Workshops, Rockport, 1985-90; pres. Ctr. for Photographic Art, Carmel, 1992—. Author: Man and Yosemite, 1985, Scenes of Wonder and Curiosity, 1988; co-author: Art and Fear, 1993; co-editor: In a Quiet Voice, 1990. Recipient Cert. of Spl. Congrl. Recognition U.S. Congress, 1988, Roy Acuff Chair of Excellence Austin Peay State U., 1989; Polaroid Print Collection grant, Polaroid Corp., 1978-79, grantee Nat. Endowment for the Arts 1979.

ORLEBEKE, WILLIAM RONALD, lawyer; b. El Paso, Tex., Jan. 5, 1934; s. William Ronald and Frances Claire (Cook) O.; m. Barbara Raye Pike, Aug. 29, 1954 (div. 1988); children: Michelle, Julene, David; m. Kathie Waterson, 1989; 1 stepson, Jack D. Waterson. BA, Willamette U., 1956; MA, Kans. U., 1957; JD, Willamette U., 1966. Bar: Calif. 1966, U.S. Dist. Ct. (no. dist.) Calif. 1967, U.S. Ct. Appeals (9th cir.) 1967, U.S. Ct. Appeals (7th cir.) 1989, U.S. Dist. Ct. (no. dist.) Ill. 1989, U.S. Dist. Ct. (cen. dist.) Calif. 1989. Assoc. Eliassen & Postel, San Francisco, 1966-69; ptnr. Coll, Levy & Orlebeke, Concord, Calif., 1969-77, Orlebeke & Hutchings, Concord, 1977-86, Orlebeke, Hutchings & Pinkerton, 1986-88, Orlebeke & Hutchings, 1988-89; prin. Law Offices W. Ronald Orlebeke, 1989—; hearing officer Contra Costa County, Calif., 1981—; arbitrator Contra Costa County Superior Ct., 1977—, U.S. Dist. Ct. No. Calif., 1978—, Mt. Diablo Mcpl. Ct., 1987—; judge pro tem Mt. Diablo Mcpl. Ct., 1973-77. Alumni bd. dirs. Willamette U., 1978-81, trustee, 1980-81; scholarship chmn. Concord Elks, 1977-79; del. Joint U.S/China Internat. Trade Law Conf., Beijing, Peoples Republic of China, 1987. Served with USMCR, 1952-59. Sr. scholar, Willamette U., 1955-56; Woodrow Wilson fellow, Kans. U., 1956-57; U.S. Bur. Nat. Affairs fellow, 1966, others. Mem. SAR, Sons of Confederate Vets. (Award of Merit 1989), Sons of Union Veterans Civil War, U.S. Navy League, First Marine Divsn. Assn. Republican. Lodges: Order Ea. Star (worthy patron 1980), Masons, Shriners, Elks, Rotary (charter pres. Clayton Valley/Concord Sunrise club 1987-88, chmn. dist. 5160 Calif. membership devel. 1989-90, dist. govs. liaison dist. 5160 1990-92, dist. 5160 Rotarian of Yr. 1989-90, Paul Harris fellow 1988, 1992 dist. conf. chmn. benefactor 1990, award of merit 1990). Office: 3330 Clayton Rd Ste B Concord CA 94519-2836

ORLOFF, NEIL, lawyer; b. Chgo., May 9, 1943; s. Benjamin R. and Annette (Grabow) O.; m. Jan Krigbaum, Oct. 9, 1971 (div. 1979); m. Gudrun Mirin, Oct. 2, 1992. BS, MIT, 1964; MBA, Harvard U., 1966; JD, Columbia U., 1969. Bar: D.C. 1969, N.Y. 1975, Calif. 1989, Utah 1993. Ops. officer World Bank, Washington, 1969-71; dir. regional liaison staff EPA, Washington, 1971-73; legal counsel Pres.'s Council on Environ. Quality, Washington, 1973-75; prof. dept. environ. engring. Cornell U., Ithaca, N.Y., 1975-88, sch. law UCLA, 1992; dir. Ctr. for Environ. Research, 1984-87, Am. Ecology Corp., 1986-88; of counsel Morgan, Lewis & Bockius, N.Y.C., 1986-87; ptnr. Irell & Manella, Los Angeles, 1986-92, Parsons, Behle & Latimer, Salt Lake City, 1992—; vice chmn. bd. dirs. S.W. Research and Info. Ctr., Albuquerque, 1975-84; vice chmn. air quality commn. ABA, Chgo., 1983-92, co-chmn. intensive short course in environ. law ABA, 1994—. Author: The Environmental Impact Statement Process, 1978, The National Environmental Policy Act, 1980, Air Pollution-Cases and Materials, 1980, Community Right-to-Know Handbook, 1988; mem. editorial bd. Natural Resources and Environment, 1984-87. Adviser Internat. Joint Com. Can., 1979-81; governing bd. N.Y. Sea Grant Inst., 1984-87; vice chmn. City of Ithaca Environ. Commn., 1976-77; adviser N.Y. Dept. Environ. Conservation, 1984-87.

ORMAN, JOHN LEO, software engineer, writer; b. San Antonio, Mar. 19, 1949; s. Alton Woodlee and Isabel Joan (Paproski) O. BS in Physics, N.Mex. Inst. Mining & Tech., 1971, BS Math., MS Physics, 1974. Rsch. asst. N.Mex. Inst. Mining & Tech., Socorro, 1967-74; computer programmer State of N.Mex., Santa Fe, 1974-76; computer analyst Dikewood Corp., Albuquerque, 1976-83; nuclear engr. Sandia Nat. Labs., Albuquerque, 1983-88, software engr., 1988—. Author numerous poems. NSF fellow, 1971-74; recipient 2d place award N.Mex. State Postry Soc., 1987. Mem. IEEE Computer Soc., Am. Assn. Physics Tchrs., Assn. for Computing Machinery, Nat. Writer's Club (poetry award 1987), Southwest Writers Workshop (3d place award non-fiction 1987), N.Mex. Mountain Club. Home: 900 Solar Rd NW Albuquerque NM 87107-5750 Office: Sandia Nat Labs Orgn 9426 PO Box 5800 Albuquerque NM 87185

ORMASA, JOHN, retired utility executive, lawyer; b. Richmond, Calif., May 30, 1925; s. Juan Hormaza and Maria Inocencia Olondo; m. Dorothy Helen Trumble, Feb. 17, 1952; children: Newton Lee, John Trumble, Nancy Jean Davies. BA, U. Calif.-Berkeley, 1948; JD, Harvard U., 1951. Bar: Calif. 1952, U.S. Supreme Ct. 1959. Assoc. Clifford C. Anglim, 1951-52; assoc. Richmond, Carlson, Collins, Gordon & Bold, 1952-56, ptnr., 1956-59; with So. Calif. Gas Co., L.A., 1959-66, gen. atty., 1963-65, v.p., gen. counsel,

1965-66; v.p., sys. gen. counsel Pacific Lighting Service Co., Los Angeles, 1966-72; v.p., gen. counsel Pacific Lighting Corp., Los Angeles, 1973-75, v.p., sec., gen. counsel, 1975. Acting city atty., El Cerrito, Calif., 1952. Served with U.S. Navy, 1943-46. Mem. ABA, Calif. State Bar Assn., Richmond (Calif.) Bar Assn. (pres. 1959), Kiwanis (v.p. 1959). Republican. Roman Catholic.

ORMISTON, PATRICIA JANE, elementary education educator; b. Flint, Mich., Aug. 22, 1938; d. Elmer A. and Katheryn Lucille (Day) Knudson; m. Lester Murray Ormiston, June 13, 1964; 1 child, Brian Todd. BS, Minot State U., 1962; postgrad., U. Mont., 1963—, Mont. State U., 1963—, Western Mont. Coll., 1987. Elem. tchr. Lowell Sch., Gt. Falls, Mont., 1958, Webster Sch., Williston, N.D., 1958-59, Plaza (N.D.) Pub. Sch., 1959-61, Cen. Sch., Helena, Mont., 1962-63, Elrod Sch., Sch. Dist. 5, Kalispell, Mont., 1963—; core team Onward to Excellence, Sch. Dist. 5, Kalispell, 1989-92; participant Rocky Mountain Nat. Outcome-Based Edn. Conf., Greeley, Colo., 1990; presenter Kendall Hunt Lit. Reading Unit, Phi Delta Kappa, Kalispell, 1991, Mont. Assn. Gifted Talented Edn., 1991, Word Conf., Seattle, 1993; inst. presenter, symposium spkr. Utah Coun. Internat. Reading Assn. 28th Ann. State Reading Conf., Salt Lake City, 1994; univ. supr. student tchrs. Mont. State U., Bozeman, 1994—; mem. adv. bd. Kendall Hunt Pub. Co., Dubuque, Iowa, 1991—; symposium spkr., mem. reading coun., coun. tchrs. English S.D. State Conf., Mitchell, 1994; symposium spkr. Five Valleys Reading Conf. U. Mont., Missoula, 1994; insvc. presenter South Whidbey Intermediate Sch., Langley, Wash., 1994. Contbr. author lit. based reading units 2d grade level Kentall Hunt Pub. Co., Dubuque, Iowa, 1989—; author: PEGASUS Integrating Themes in Literature and Language Correlated to Gages Lake, Illinois State Goals for Learning Language Arts, Grades K-6, 1993, PEGASUS Integrating Themes in Literature and Language Correlated to State of Georgia Quality Core Curriculum for English and Language Arts, Grades K-6, 1994, PEGASUS Integrating Themes in Literature and Language Correlated to State of Indiana Essential Skills English/Language Arts, Grades K-6, 1994, PEGASUS Integrating Themes in Literature and Language Correlated to Dade County Public Schools Competency-Based Curriculum for Language Arts, Grades K-5, 1994. Vol. Conrad Mansion Restoration, Kalispell, 1976—; presenter 34th ann. conv. Lit. Base Reading Internat. Reading Assn., New Orleans, 1989. Named Tchr. of Yr., Kalispell Sch. Dist. 5, 1986; Chpt. 2 grantee, 1987-88; Gertrude Whipple Profl. Devel. grantee IRA, 1988. Mem. NEA, Internat. Reading Assn. (symposium speaker 38th ann. conv. San Antonio 1993), Nat. Coun. Tchrs. English, Kalispell Edn. Assn. (bldg. rep. 1987-88, chmn. profl. acknowledgement com. 1988-93), Nat. Hist. Preservation, Phi Delta Kappa, Delta Kappa Gamma. Home: PO Box 64 Kalispell MT 59903-0064 Office: Elrod Sch 3rd Ave W Kalispell MT 59901-4426

ORNDOFF, ELIZABETH CARLSON, retired reference librarian, educator; b. Spearville, Kans., Mar. 28, 1918; d. Carl Edward and Laura Rebecca (Pine) Carlson; m. John Delbert Orndoff, Dec. 26, 1942; children: Barbara Kay Orndoff Fazal, David Keith, Richard Lee. BA in Sociology, U. Colo., 1940, BEd, 1940; postgrad., U. So. Calif., 1941. Lic. pvt. pilot; cert. tchr. sociology. Head coll. librarian Trinidad (Colo.) State Jr. Coll., 1940-42, tchr. sociology, 1941-42; reference librarian Los Alamos (N.Mex.) Pub. Libr., 1963-73. Editor: (non-fiction book) All of These Things, 1974. Tchr. Sunday sch. Meth. Ch., Trinidad, 1940-41; den mother Boy Scouts Am., Los Alamos, 1953-55; leader Girl Scouts U.S.A., Los Alamos, 1955-56; charter mem. United Ch. Los Alamos, 1947—, historian, 1994, 95; active Friends Los Alamos Pub. Libr., 1989-90, 94—, Habitat for Humanity, 1994—; active Los Alamos Retirement Ctr., Inc., Blood Mobile, Meals on Wheels. Mem. AAUW (life), ALA, United Ostomy Assn., U. Colo. Alumni Assn., Sr. Citizens, Los Alamos Ski Club, Crohn's Colitis Found. Am., Am. Assn. Ret. Tchrs. Democrat. Home: 997-B 48th St Los Alamos NM 87544-1831

ORNELLAS, DONALD LOUIS, chemist researcher; b. San Leandro, Calif., July 7, 1932; s. Louis Donald and Anna (Gerro) O.; children: Timothy Donald, Kathryn Ann, Melinda Dawn. BS in chemistry, Santa Clara U., 1954. Chemist Kaiser Gypsum Co, Redwood City, Calif., 1954-55, Kaiser Aluminum & Chem. Co., Permanente, Calif., 1957-58, Lawrence Livermore (Calif.) Nat. Lab., 1958—; presenter at tech. meetings. Contbr. 17 articles to profl. jours. Capt. U.S. Army, 1955-57. Recipient Annual medal award, Am. Inst. Chemist, 1954. Mem. Parents Without Ptnrs. (chpt. 53 pres. 1971-73, chpt. 458 bd. dirs. 1982-91). Democrat. Roman Catholic. Home: 559 S N St Livermore CA 94550-4365 Office: Lawrence Livermore Nat Lab PO Box 808 L-325 Livermore CA 94550

ORNSTEIN, DONALD SAMUEL, mathematician, educator; b. N.Y.C., July 30, 1934; s. Harry and Rose (Wisner) O.; m. Shari Richman, Dec. 20, 1964; children—David, Kara, Ethan. Student, Swarthmore Coll., 1950-52; Ph.D., U. Chgo., 1957. Fellow Inst. for Advanced Study, Princeton, N.J., 1955-57; faculty U. Wis., Madison, 1958-60; faculty Stanford (Calif.) U., 1959—, prof. math., 1966—; faculty Hebrew U., Jerusalem, 1975-76. Author: Ergodic Theory Randomness and Dynamical Systems, 1974. Recipient Bocher prize Am. Math. Soc., 1974. Mem. NAS, Am. Acad. Arts and Sci. Jewish. Office: Dept Math Stanford U Stanford CA 94305

ORNSTEIN, RICK LEWIS, biophysical environmental researcher, educator; b. N.Y.C., Aug. 28, 1950; s. Joseph and Bella (Miller) O.; m. Cheryl Ann Levine, June 24, 1973; children: Bradley William, Michael Stewart, Jonathan Franklin. BA, Queens Coll. of CUNY, 1972; MS, Hunter Coll. of CUNY, 1974; PhD with honors, SUNY, Buffalo, 1979. NIH postdoctoral fellow Princeton (N.J.) U., 1979-81, rsch. staff, instr., 1982-85; rsch. scientist Eastman Kodak, Kingsport, Tenn., 1985-88; sr. rsch. scientist Battelle Pacific N.W. Lab., Richland, Wash., 1988—, tech. group leader, 1994—; grant rev. com. mem. NIH, 1986, 92; grant reviewer Dept. of Energy; adj. prof. chemistry Wash. State U., Pullman, 1990—, vis. prof. biophysics Roswell Park Cancer Ctr., Buffalo, 1992—. Contbr. articles to Chem.-Biol. Interactions, Biopolymers, Procs. NAS, Sci., Protein Progressive Clin. Biol. Rsch., Proteins, Protein Sci., Protein Engring., Jour. Computer Chemistry, Jour. Computer Aided Molecular Design, Biophysics Jour., Biochem. Biophys. Res. Comm., Science, J. Biol. Chemistry, Theoretical Chim. Acta, Molecular Structure, Jour. Biomolecular Structure and Dynamics, Internat. Jour. Quantum Chemistry; mem. editl. bd. Jour. Biomolecular Structure and Dynamics. NIH fellow Princeton U., 1979-81. Mem. Hazardous Materials Control Rsch. Inst., Am. Chem. Soc., The Protein Soc., Soc. Environ. Toxicology and Chemistry. Office: Molecular Sci Rsch Ctr Battelle-Pacific N W Labs Richland WA 99352

OROPALLO, DEBORAH, artist, educator; b. Hackensack, N.J., Nov. 29, 1954. BFA, Alfred (N.Y.) U., 1979; MA, U. Calif., Berkeley, 1982, MFA, 1983. Teaching asst. Alfred (N.Y.) U., 1979, U. Calif., Berkeley, 1982-83; instr. San Francisco Art Inst., 1984-85, San Francisco Art Acad. Coll., 1986, 87-92; vis. prof. San Francisco Art Inst., 1993; artist C. O. Stephen Wirtz Gallery, San Francisco, 1994—. One-woman shows include Media Gallery, N.Y., 1979, Stephen Wirtz Gallery, San Francisco, 1986, 88, 90, 93, Meml. Union Art Gallery, Davis, Calif., 1987, Raab Gallerie, Berlin, 1987, Inst. Contemporary Art, Boston, 1990, Artspace, San Francisco, 1990, Greenville County Mus. Art, Greenville, S.C., 1991, Germans van Eck Gallery, N.Y.C., 1991, Weatherspoon Gallery, Greensboro, N.C., 1992, Ann Jaffee Gallery, Bay Harbor Island, Fla., 1992, Kate Block Fine Arts, Boston, 1993, Stephen Wirtz Gallery, San Francisco, 1993, 95, San Jose Mus. Art, 1994; exhibited in group shows at Fosdick Nelson Gallery, Alfred, N.Y., 1979, Albright Knox Mus., Buffalo, 1980, Richmond (Calif.) Art Ctr., 1980, Civic Ctr., San Francisco, 1981, Calif. State Fair Art Exhbn., Sacramento, 1981, San Jose Inst. Contemporary Art, 1981, Worth Ryder Gallery, Berkeley, Calif., 1981, 1982, Annual Conf. of Mus. Assn. Am., 1983, Berkeley Art Mus., 1983, San Francisco Art Inst., 1984, San Francisco Arts Commn. Gallery, 1985, Acad. Art Gallery, San Francisco, 1986, Freson (Calif.) Art Ctr., 1987, Allport Gallery, San Francisco, 1988, Whitney Mus. Am. Art, N.Y.C., 1989, Stephen Wirtz Gallery, San Franscisco, 1989, 91, 95, Am. Acad. and Inst. Arts and Letters, N.Y.C., 1989, Cleve. Ctr. Contemporary Art, 1990, Milw. Art Mus., 1990, Okla. Mus. Art, Oklahoma City, 1990, Contemporary Art Mus., Houston, 1990, Oakland Mus., 1991, Molica Guidarte Gallery, N.Y.C., 1991, Susan Cummins Gallery, Mill Valley, Calif., 1992, Calif. Coll. Arts and Crafts, Oakland, 1992, Krakow Gallery, Boston, 1992, Kate Block Fine Art, Boston, 1992, Corcoran Gallery of Art, Washington, 1992, San Jose Mus., 1993, Galleria de Arte, Sao Paulo, Brazil, 1994, Palo Alto (Calif.), Cultural Ctr., 1994, Michael Kohler Arts Ctr., Sheboygan, Wis., 1994, Okeanos Press, Berkeley, Calif., 1994, CAPP Street Project, San Francisco, 1994, The Artists Contemporary Gallery, Hyatt Regency Plz., Sacramento, 1995, Gallery Concord, Concord, Calif., 1995, others. Recipient F.C.-J.C. Fine Art award Alfred U., 1977, Michael Cory Levins Sculpture award Alfred U., 1978, N.Y. Coll. Register Cert. of Recognition, 1977, Hon. mention Calif. State Fair Art Exhbn., 1981, Second Pl. award, 1981, Richmond (Calif.) Art Ctr. award, 1982, Ann Bremer award U. Calif., 1982, 22nd Ann. Art Exhibit Second Pl. award, 1983, Engelhard award Inst. Contemporary Art, Boston, 1987, Art Space Support grant, 1988, 90, NEA award, 1991, Fleishhacker award, 1993. Office: C O Stephen Wirtz Gallery 49 Geary 3rd Fl San Francisco CA 94108-5707

O'ROURKE, DENNIS HAROLD, anthropology educator; b. Mound City, Kans., Mar. 29, 1951; s. Harold William and Mary Florine (Holmes) O'R.; m. Tamia Jo Bloethe, Aug. 17, 1974; children: Jamie, Kelly, Darcy. BA in Anthropology with honors, U. Kans., 1973, MA in Anthropology, 1976, MPhil in Anthropology, 1977, PhD in Anthropology, 1980. Tchg. asst. U. Kans., Lawrence, 1973-74, rsch. asst., 1974-75, 75-77; post-doctoral trainee genetic epidemiology Washington U. Sch. Medicine, Dept. Psychiatry, St. Louis, 1980-81, post-doctoral rschr. genetic epidemiology psychopathology, 1982-84; instr., asst. prof. U. Utah, Dept. Anthropology, Salt Lake City, 1980-85, assoc. prof., 1985-94, prof., 1994—; assoc. dean rsch. and curricula Coll. Social and Behavioral Sci., U. Utah, 1989-90; chair dept. anthropology U. Utah, 1990—, chair internal grad. coun. rev. com. geography dept., 1993-94; adj. curator phys. anthropology Utah Mus. Natural History, 1990—; founding bd. dirs., nominations com. chair Am. Assn. Anthropol. Genetics, 1993-94; presenter in field. Editor: Genetics, Evolution and Disease, 1983; editorial bd.: Human Biology, 1993—; contbr. chpts. to books and articles to profl. jours. George Spiva Meml. scholar, 1969-70, James Otto Meml. scholar, 1971-72, James Davis scholar, 1972-73; U. Kans. Summer Rsch. fellow, 1976, U. Kans. Dissertation fellow, 1977-78; grantee U. Utah Rsch. Com., 1982, 93, Wenner-Gren Found. for Anthropol. Rsch., 1988, The Soros Found.-Soviet Union, 1990, NSF, 1990, 93, others. Fellow Am. Anthropol. Assn.; mem. AAAS, Am. Soc. Human Genetics, Am. Assn. Phys. Anthropologists (exec. com., chair student affairs com. 1994—), Soc. for Molecular Biology and Evolution, Soc. for the Study Evolution, Soc. for the Study Social Biology, Human Biology Coun. (com. mem. 1993—), Sigma Xi. Home: 7912 Deer Creek Rd Salt Lake City UT 84121-5753 Office: Dept Anthropology Univ Utah Salt Lake City UT 84112

O'ROURKE, J. TRACY, manufacturing company executive; b. Columbia, S.C., Mar. 14, 1935; s. James Tracy and Georgia Adella (Bridges) O'R.; m. Lou Ann Turner, Mar. 19. 1954; 1 son, James Tracy. BSME, Auburn U., 1956. Teflon specialist duPont Co., Wilmington, Del., 1957-62; pres., chief exec. officer LNP Corp., Malvern, Pa., 1962-72; v.p. Carborundum, Niagara Falls, N.Y., 1972-76; exec. v.p. Chemetron, Chgo., 1976-78; sr. v.p. Allen Bradley Co. subs. Rockwell Internat. Corp., Milw., 1978-81, pres., chief oper. officer, 1981-86, also chief exec. officer, dir., 1986-90; chmn., chief exec. officer Varian Assocs., Palo Alto, Calif., 1990—. Served as 1st lt. USAF, 1957-59. Office: Varian Assocs PO Box 10800 3050 Hansen Way Palo Alto CA 94304

O'ROURKE, MICHAEL, artistic director; b. Denver, July 31, 1949; s. Lee and Patricia (O'Rourke) Leberer; children: Toby Jarius, Morgan, Tansi Grant. AA, Casper Coll., 1969; BA, U. Wyo., 1971, MA, 1973. Founder, artistic dir. Casper (Wyo.) Coll. Amateur Dramatic Soc., 1967-69, Poor Yorick Players, Laramie, Wyo., 1970-73; dir., actor Oreg. Shakespeare Festival, Ashland, 1973-77; co-founder, artistic dir. Actors' Theatre, Ashland, Talent, Oreg., 1982—; actor Colo. Shakespeare Festival, Boulder, 1971; dir., producer Prodn. Co., Portland, Oreg., 1979; dir. Skid Road Theatre, Seattle, 1980; editor: In Passing, 1968-69; playwright: Pinocchio, Tom Sawyer, Fellowship of the Ring, Count of Monte Cristo, The Seven Dreams of Icarus, 1987-94; producer, dir. over 100 prodns., 1982-94. Named Best Dir. Sneak Preview News, 1990; recipient Outstanding Achievement award Arts Coun. So. Oreg., 1993. Office: Actors Theatre 101 Talent Ave Talent OR 97540

O'ROURKE, WILLIAM PATRICK, architect; b. Milw., Nov. 12, 1959; s. Donald A. and Patricia Ellenor (Grathwolh) O'R. BArch., Calif. State Poly. U., 1987. Project architect 30th St. Architects, Newport Beach, Calif., 1987-91; architect Weber Engring., Garden Grove, Calif., 1991-93, Sobin Harte Architects, Woodland Hills, Calif., 1993—. Home: 924 S Van Ness Ave Santa Ana CA 92701-5555 Office: Sobin Harte Archiects 22055 Clarendon St Ste 104 Woodland Hills CA 91367-6306

ORR, FRANKLIN MATTES, JR., petroleum engineering educator; b. Baytown, Tex., Dec. 27, 1946; s. Franklin Mattes and Selwyn Sage (Huddleston) O.; m. Susan Packard, Aug. 30, 1970; children: David, Katherine. BSChemE, Stanford U., 1969; PhDChemE, U. Minn., 1976. Asst. to dir. Office Fed. Activities EPA, Washington, 1970-72; research engr. Shell Devel. Co., Houston, 1976-78; sr. engr. N.Mex. Petroleum Recovery Research Ctr., Socorro, 1978-84; assoc. prof. petroleum engring. Stanford (Calif.) U., 1985-87, prof., 1987—, interim dean Sch. Earth Scis., 1994-95, dean Sch. Earth Scis., 1995—. Contbr. articles to profl. jours. Bd. dirs. Wolf Trap Found. for the Performing Arts, 1988-94, Monterey Bay Aquarium Rsch. Inst., 1987—; chair sci. adv. com. David and Lucile Packard Found. Fellowships for Sci. and Engring. With USPHS, 1970-72. Mem. Soc. Petroleum Engrs. (named Distin. Lectr. 1988-89, Disting. Achievement award for petroleum engring. faculty 1993), AIChE, AAAS, Soc. Indsl. and Applied Math. Home: 927 Cottrell Way Stanford CA 94305-1057

ORR, JOHN CHRISTOPHER, English language educator; b. Fruita, Colo., Dec. 4, 1949; s. E. Robert and Florence Marion (Ree) O.; m. Lynne Norma Jenkins, Oct. 6, 1979; children: Caitlin, Theresa, Lauren. BA magna cum laude, Amherst Coll., 1972; MA in English and Am. Lit., Claremont Grad. Sch., 1976; postgrad., U. Calif., Irvine, 1981, U. Rochester, 1983, Calif. Polytechnic U., 1984, 87, 92,, U. Edinburgh, Scotland, 1993. Instr. in English Walnut (Calif.) H.S., 1973-85; instr. in English Fullerton (Calif.) Coll., 1985, coord. proficiency exam. program, 1988—, coord. humanities divsn. vitality study, 1991-92; part-time English instr. Mt. San Antonio Coll., Walnut, 1980-85; lectr., presenter in field; mem. State Acad. Senate Com., 1990; reader Coll. Bd./Ednl. Testing Svc., Princeton, N.J., 1986—; chief writer Cleve. Project, Hoffman Custom Products, Duarte, Calif., 1989. Editor, proofreader The Legal Secretary, 3d edit., 1989. Judge creative writing scholarship competition Poets Reading Inc., 1989. NEH grantee, 1983; U. Calif.-Irvine fellow, 1981. Mem. NEA, Calif. Tchrs. Assn., Am. Studies Assn., Calif. Assn. Tchrs. English, English Coun. Calif. Two Yr. Colls. Democrat. Office: Fullerton Coll 321 E Chapman Ave Fullerton CA 92632-2011

ORR, ROY JOSEPH, hospital administrator; b. Bethany, Mo., Sept. 15, 1952; s. Jay Cedric and Carolyn Mae (Ellis) O.; m. Patrice Marie Kuta, Aug. 11, 1973; children: Sarah, Michaela, Kaitlyn, Hallie, Quentin. AA, Platte Coll., 1972; BS, U. Mo., 1974; MA, U. San Francisco, 1981. Occupational therapist Immanuel Med. Ctr., Omaha, 1974-79; administrative dir. Immanuel Rehab. Ctr., Omaha, 1979-80; dir. rehab. svcs. Bergan Mercy Hosp., Omaha, 1980-85, div. v.p., 1985-90; chief operating officer St. Elizabeth Hosp., Beaumont, Tex., 1990-92; pres., CEO McKenzie-Willamette Med. Svcs., Springfield, Oreg., 1992—. Bd. dirs. N.E. chpt. Arthritis Found., Omaha, 1978-86, pres. bd., 1980-81, chmn. bd., 1982, Nat. Svc. award 1986; mem. Leadership Beaumont, 1991-92; bd. dirs. So. Willamette Pvt. Industry Coun., Eugene, Oreg.; bd. dirs. Springfield C. of C., 1994—, United Way of Lane County, 1993—. Mem. Am. Coll. Healthcare Execs., Cardinal Club (v.p. 1991). Roman Catholic. Office: 1460 G St Springfield OR 97477-4112

ORSATTI, ALFRED KENDALL, organization executive; b. Los Angeles, Jan. 31, 1932; s. Alfredo and Margaret (Hayes) O.; m. Patricia Decker, Sept. 11, 1960; children: Scott, Christopher, Sean. B.S., U. So. Calif., 1956. Assoc. prodr., v.p. Sabre Prodns., L.A., 1957-58; assoc. prodr. Ror Vic Prodns., L.A., 1958-59; bus. rep. AFTRA, L.A., 1960-61; Hollywood exec., sec. SAG, L.A., 1961-81, nat. exec. dir., 1981—; trustee Pension Welfare Plan SAG, 1971—; del. Los Angeles County Fedn. Labor, Los Angeles, Hollywood Film Council, Los Angeles; v.p., mem. exec. Calif. Fedn. Labor; v.p. Calif. Theatrical Fedn.; chmn. arts, entertainment and media com. dept. profl. employees AFL-CIO. Mem. Mayor's Film Devel. Com., Los Angeles. Mem. Hollywood C. of C. (bd. dirs.), Actors and Artists Am. Assn. (1st v.p.). Office: SAG 5757 Wilshire Blvd Los Angeles CA 90036

ORTIZ, ANTONIO IGNACIO, public relations executive; b. Mexico City, Feb. 22, 1961; came to U.S., 1988; s. Antonio and Sylvia (Vega) O.; m. Socorro Chinolla, June 12, 1982. B in Bus., Universidad Autonoma de Baja Calif., Tijuana, 1984. With acctg. dept. Bank of the Atlantic, Tijuana, 1979-83; mgr. Aldaco, Tijuana, 1983-84; dir. pub. rels. Oh! Laser Club, Tijuana, 1984-88, Iguanas, Tijuana, 1988-90, Euebe, S.A., Tijuana, 1990—; cons. DDBSA Corp., Chula Vista, Calif., Calif. Alson Ltd., San Diego, Exim Trading Co., San Diego, R.P. Noble Enterprises, La Jolla, Ca.; dir. pub. rels. R. Noble Enterprises. Home: PO Box 431859 San Diego CA 92143-1859 Office: Exim Trading Corp PO Box 435108 San Diego CA 92143-5108

ORTIZ, DIANE, librarian, management analyst; b. Mpls., July 22, 1945; d. Edward Francis and Florence Eleanor (Thorman) O. BA in Polit. Sci., U. Nev., 1967; MA in Librarianship, San Jose (Calif.) State U., 1970; student, Am. U., 1973; MPA, U. Nev., 1977. Cert. secondary tcrh. and specialized libr., Caif., NCIC instr., Nev. Sub. tchr. Clark County (Nev.) Sch. Dist., Las Vegas, 1967; asst. law libr. Georgetown U. Law Ctr. Libr., Washington, 1970-71; head cataloger, cataloging supr. Xerox BiblioGraphics, Cheverly, Md., 1971-74; audiovidsual cataloger Xerox BiblioGraphics, Cheverly, 1974; project mgr. Automated Typographics, Inc., Arlington, Va., 1974; from mgmt. analyst trainee to mgmt. analyst I and II City of Las Vegas, 1978-88; bus. office mgr. Alt. Sentencing and Edn. divsn. Las Vegas Mcpl. Ct., 1988—. Mem. Clark County Dem. Cen. Com., Las Vegas. Mem. ALA, Am. Soc. Pub. Adminstrn., Am. Assn. Law Librs., Spl. Librs. Assn., Nev. Libr. Assn., Western Govtl. Rsch. Assn., Assn. of Records Mgrs. and Adminstrs., Alumni Assn. U. Nev. Las Vegas, Alumni Assn. San Jose State U., Beta Phi Mu, Pi Sigma Alpha. Democrat. Jewish/Unitarian. Office: Las Vegas Mcpl Ct Alt Sentencing & Edn Divsn Las Vegas NV 89101

ORTIZ, JAMES GEORGE, data information services company executive; b. Boston, June 6, 1961. BA suma cum laude, Monterey Inst. Internat. Studies, 1989, MA, 1990. Instr. lang. Blue Mountain C.C., Pendleton, Oreg., 1990—; pres., CEO, Data Info. Svc., Inc., Toppenish, Wash., 1991-93; founder JGO Internat., Hermiston, Oreg., 1992—. Regional dir. CASA of Oreg., Hermiston, 1990. Scholar Chevron Co., 1988-89. Republican. Adventist.

ORTIZ, JOSEPH VINCENT, chemistry educator; b. Bethpage, N.Y., Apr. 26, 1956; s. José Vicente and Mary Davies (Bryant) O.; m. Karen Fagin, Dec. 16, 1979. BS, U. Fla., 1976, PhD, 1981. Rsch. fellow Harvard U., Cambridge, Mass., 1981-82; postdoctoral fellow Cornell U., Ithaca, N.Y., 1982-83; asst. prof. U. of N.Mex., Albuquerque, 1983-89, assoc. prof., 1989-94, prof., 1994—; cons. Los Alamos (N.Mex.) Nat. Lab., 1986—; chemistry focus group coord. Mani High Performance Computing Ctr., 1994—; affiliate staff scientist Pacific N.W. Lab., 1995—. Editl. adv. bd. Internat. Jour. Quantum Chemistry, 1994—; contbr. articles to profl. jours. Am. Soc. Engring. Edn. sr. rsch. fellow, 1986, 87; Assoc. We. Univs. rsch. fellow, 1991; NSF grantee, 1985-91, 91-94, 94—; Petroleum Rsch. Fund grantee, 1984-86, 91-93, 95—; Sandia Rsch. Program grantee, 1983-85. Mem. Am. Chem. Soc., Am. Phys. Soc., Internat. Soc. for Theoretical Chem. Physics. Office: U NMex Chemistry Dept Clark Hall Albuquerque NM 87131

ORTNER, SHERRY B., anthropology educator; b. Bklyn., Sept. 19, 1941; d. Samuel and Gertrude (Panitch) Ortner; 1 child, Gwendolyn Ida Ortner Kelly; m. Timothy D. Taylor, July 25, 1994. AB, Bryn Mawr Coll., 1962; MA, U. Chgo., 1966, PhD, 1970. Lectr. Princeton (N.J.) U., 1969-70; asst. prof. Sarah Lawrence Coll., Bronxville, N.Y., 1971-77; assoc. prof. U. Mich., Ann Arbor, Mich., 1977-84, prof., 1984-94; prof. U. Calif., Berkeley, Calif., 1994—. Author: Sherpas Through Their Rituals, 1978, High Religion: A Cultural & Political History of Sherpa Buddhism, 1989; co-editor: Sexual Meanings: The Cultural Construction of Gender and Sexuality, 1981, Culture/Power/History: A Reader in Contemporary Social Theory, 1994; editorial bd. mem.: Social Analysis, 1986—, Comparative Studies in Soc. and History, 1987—. Guggenheim fellow, 1982-83, Mac Arthur fellow, 1990-95. Fellow Am. Anthropological Assn.; mem. AAAS, Nepal Studies Assn., Am. Ethnological Soc., Soc. Cultural Anthropology. Office: U Calif Dept Of Anthropology Berkeley CA 94720

ORTON, MARY C., nonprofit administrator; b. Prince George's County, Md., Oct. 28, 1954; d. Richard Earl and Shirley Mae (Johnson) O.; m. Michael David Paulson, Jan. 16, 1988. BA in Polit. Sci., Ariz. State U., 1993. Office mgr. Tex. Women's Polit. Caucus, Austin, 1976-77; coord. Austin (Tex.) Women's Ctr., 1977-78; organizer Assn. of Community Orgns. for Reform Now, Austin, Tex., Colorado Springs and Reno, Nev., 1979-81; voter registration coord. Maricopa County Dem. Party, 1982; asst. to congressman U.S. Rep. Morris K. Udall, Phoenix, 1982-84; field dir. Bill Schulz Gubernatorial Campaign, Phoenix, 1984-85; exec. dir. Cen. Ariz. Shelter Svcs., Inc., Phoenix, 1985—. Bd. dirs. Cen. Ariz. Shelter Svcs., Inc., 1984-85, Interfaith Coop. Ministries, 1987-88, Labor's Community Svc. Agy., 1987-93, Ariz. Coalition for Tomorrow, 1992—, pres.-elect 1993-94, pres. 1994-95; bd. dirs. Ariz. Town Hall, 1993—, Nucleus Club, 1992—, Mercy Housing, 1993—; mem. joint legis. com. to study the homeless, apptd. by Gov. Bruce Babbitt, 1986; mem. police protection subcom. City of Phoenix Citizens Bond Com., 1988, numerous others. Recipient Social Svcs. Citizen of Yr. award NASW Ariz. chpt. dist. 1, 1987. Mem. Am. Soc. Pub. Adminstrn. (Superior Svc. award 1990). Democrat. Home: 101 N 7th St Unit 259 Phoenix AZ 85034-1040 Office: Cen Ariz Shelter Svcs 1209 W Madison St Phoenix AZ 85007-3123

ORTON, WILLIAM H. (BILL ORTON), congressman, lawyer; b. North Ogden, Utah, Sept. 22, 1948. BS, Brigham Young U., 1973, JD, 1979. Adj. prof. Portland (Oreg.) State U./Portland C.C., 1974-76, Brigham Young. U., Provo, Utah, 1984-85; tax auditor IRS, 1976-77; atty., 1980-90; mem. 103rd-104th Congresses from 3rd Utah dist., 1990—; mem. budget com., mem. banking and fin. svcs. com. Democrat. Mormon. Office: US Ho of Reps 440 Cannon HOB Washington DC 20515-4403*

ORULLIAN, B. LARAE, bank executive; b. Salt Lake City, May 15, 1933; d. Alma and Bessie (Bacon) O.; cert. Am. Inst. Banking, 1961, 63, 67; grad. Nat. Real Estate Banking Sch., Ohio State U., 1969-71. With Tracy Collins Trust Co., Salt Lake City, 1951-54; sec. to exec. sec. Union Nat. Bank, Denver, 1954-57; exec. sec. Guaranty Bank, Denver, 1957-64, asst. cashier, 1964-67, asst. v.p., 1967-70, v.p., 1970-75, exec. v.p., 1975-77, also bd. dirs.; chair, CEO, dir. The Women's Bank N.A., Denver, 1989—, Equitable Bankshares of Colo., 1980—; vice chmn. Equitable Bank Littleton; chmn. bd., dir. Colo. Blue Cross/Blue Shield, lectr.; bd. dirs. Rocky Mountain Life Ins. Co., Frontier Airlines. Treas. Girl Scouts U.S.A., 1981-87, 1st. nat. v.p., chair exec. com., 1987-90, nat. pres., 1990—; bd. dirs., chair Rocky Mountain Health Care Corp.; bd. dirs. Ams. Clean Water Found., Denver Improvement Assn.; bd. dirs. Commn. Savings in Am. Recipient Woman Who Made a Difference award Internat. Women's Forum, 1994; named to Colo. Women Hall of Fame, 1988, Colo. Entrepreneur of Yr., Inc. Mag. and Arthur Young and Co., 1989, Woman of the Yr., YWCA, 1989, EMC Lion Club (citizen of the year, 1995). Mem. Bus. and Profl. Women Colo. (3d Century award 1977), Colo. State Ethics Bd., Denver C. of C., Am. Inst. Banking, Am. Bankers Assn. (adv. bd. edn. found.), Nat. Assn. Bank Women, Internat. Women's Forum (Woman Who Makes a Difference award 1994), Com. of 200. Republican. Mormon. Home: 10 S Ammons St Lakewood CO 80226-1331

ORWIG, EUGENE ROBERT, JR., petroleum geologist, consultant; b. L.A., May 29, 1919; s. Eugene Robert and Gladys Marie (Keppel) O.; m. Laurette Cecile LeComte, Aug. 23, 1943; children: Colette Doris, Russell Henry, Carey Bruce, Eugene Robert III. AB, UCLA, 1946, MA, 1947, PhD, 1957. Petroleum geologist Mobil Oil Corp., L.A., 1948-72, Denver, 1972-76, Dallas, 1976-82; fruit grower Temecula, Calif., 1982—; gen. mgr. DeLuz Ranchos Assn., Temecula, Calif., 1987—; cons. Corpoven, Venezuela, Caracas, 1979-81. Contbr. articles to profl. jours. Capt. USAF, 1942-45, ETO. Fellow Geol. Soc. Am.; mem. Am. Assn. Petroleum Geologists (pres. Pacific sect. 1965-66), Am. Inst. Profl. Geologists. Republican. Episcopalian. Home: 2389 Via Mariposa W Unit 2F Laguna Hills CA 92653-2040

OSADA, STAN, construction executive; b. 1936. With Dillingham Constrn. Pacific Ltd., 1966—, now sr. v.p. Office: Dillingham Cnstr Pcf Ltd 614 Kapahulu Ave Honolulu HI 96815-3846*

OSBORN, LUCIE P., library director; b. Cheshire, Conn., June 20, 1949; m. Harry L. Osborn II, Aug. 28, 1971. BA in Sociology, Wittenberg U., 1971; MA in Secondary Edn., Wright State U., 1978; MLS, Kent State U., 1979. Asst. county libr. Laramie County Libr. Sys., Cheyenne, Wyo., 1979-87, county libr., 1990—; libr. dir. Frederick C. Adams Pub. Libr., Kingston, Mass., 1988-90. Office: Laramie County Libr Sys 2800 Central Ave Cheyenne WY 82001-2799*

OSBORN, MARIJANE, language professional/educator, English; b. Cornwall-on-the-Hudson, N.Y., Nov. 18, 1934; d. D. Remington and Idella (Purnell) Stone; children: David, Desiree. BA, U. Calif., Berkeley, 1962; MA, Stanford U., 1965; postgrad., Oxford U., 1965-66; PhD, Stanford U., 1969. Vis. lectr, asst. prof., fellow various univs., 1968-81; asst. prof. U. Calif., Davis, 1981-83, assoc. prof., 1983-94, prof., 1994—; Fulbright scholar U. Iceland, Reykjavik, 1987; dir. medieval studies program U. Calif., Davis, 1991-92, 93-94. Translator: (book) Beowulf: A Verse Translation, 1983; co-author: (book) Landscape of Desire, 1994. Recorder for the blind Blindra Bokasafn, Reykjavik, 1993—. Named Fulbright prof. Fulbright Assn., Iceland, 1978, 79, 87. Mem. Phi Beta Kappa (pres. PBK-UC Davis 1993-94). Office: U Calif at Davis Dept of English Davis CA 95616

OSBORN, SUSAN TITUS, editor; b. Fresno, Calif., July 11, 1944; d. Clifford Leland Feldt and Jane (Taylor) Cousings; m. Richard G. Titus, Aug. 28, 1965 (div. Dec. 1990); children: Richard David, Michael Craig; m. Richard A. Osborn, Aug. 22, 1992. BA in Religious Studies, Calif. State U., Fullerton, 1988, MA in Comm., 1993. Svc. rep. Mountain Bell Tel., Colorado Springs, Colo., 1965-67; free-lance writer Fullerton, Calif., 1978—; assoc. dir. Biola U. Writers Inst., La Mirada, Calif., 1986-92; co-dir. Christian Communicators Conf. The Master's Coll., Santa Clarita, Calif., 1993—, adj. prof., 1993—; mem. adv. bd. Christian Writers Fellowship, Huntington Beach, Calif., 1987-93; mem. adv. bd. Christian Communicator, San Juan Capistrano, Calif., 1989-94, mng. editor, 1991-92, editor, 1992—; pub. cons. Ednl. Ministries, Brea, Calif., 1989-91; conf. spkr. numerous cities, 1987—; tchr. India Comm. Inst., Bombay; bd. dirs. Moscow Christian Sch. Psychology, 1992-95. Author: Parables for Young Teens, 1986, You Start With One, 1990, Meeting Jesus, 1990, Eyes Beyond the Horizon, 1991, Children Around the World Celebrate Christmas, 1993, The Complete Guide to Christian Writing and Speaking, 1994, Rest Stops for Single Mothers, 1995; editor The Christian Communicator. Bd. dirs. Jr. Ebell Club, Fullerton, 1969-75, Youth Sci. Ctr., Fullerton, 1970-75, YMCA Swim Club, Fullerton, 1976-82; pres. Troy Swim Boosters, Fullerton, 1982-88, Moscow Christian Sch. Psychology, 1992-95. Recipient Spl. Recognition award Troy Swim Boosters, 1986. Mem. Presbyn. Writers Guild., Spiritual Overseers Svc. Republican. Evangelical. Office: Master's Coll Dept Comm PO Box 221450 Santa Clarita CA 91322-1450

OSBORNE, JERRY PAUL, writer; b. Denver, Aug. 19, 1944; s. Philip and Margaret Osborne; m. Linda Ann Osborne. Student, L.A. City Coll., El Camino Coll. Radio/TV announcer numerous TV and radio stas., U.S., 1962-76; free-lance writer, 1975—, writer, syndicated columnist, 1984—; founder, pub. Record Digest, Music World, 1977-80, DISCoveries, 1987-92; producer To Elvis: Love Still Burning, 1978;. Author: Record Collector's Price Guide, 1976, 55 Years of Recorded Country & Western Music, 1976, The Complete Elvis, 1977, Popular and Rock Records, 1978, The Love of Elvis, 1979, Blues/Rhythm & Blues/Soul, 1979, The Elvis Cover-Up, 1980, Elvis: A 30-Year Chronicle, 1985, The Complete Library of American Phonograph Recordings -- 1959, 1987, The Official Price Guide to Memorabilia of Elvis Presley and the Beatles, 1988, numerous others; columnist weekly feature Mr. Music, 1986—. Home: PO Box 255 Port Townsend WA 98368-0255

OSBORNE, RICHARD HAZELET, anthropology and medical genetics educator; b. Kennecott, Alaska, June 18, 1920; s. Clarence Edward and Margaret Jerenne (Hazelet) O.; m. Barbara White, Oct. 14, 1944; children: Susan, Richard, David; m. Barbara Teachman, Sept. 1, 1970. Student, U. Alaska, 1939-41; BS, BA, U. Wash., 1949; postgrad., Harvard U., 1949-50; PhD (Viking Fund Pre-doctoral fellow, Spl. fellow Inst. for Study Human Variation), Columbia, 1956; hon. doctor odontology, U. Oulu, Finland, 1994. Research asso. Columbia U., 1953-58; asst. Sloan-Kettering Inst., N.Y.C., 1958-60; asso. Sloan-Kettering Inst., 1960-62, asso. mem., head sect. human genetics, 1962-64; prof. anthropology and med. genetics U. Wis., Madison, 1964-86, prof. emeritus, 1986—; asso. prof. preventive medicine Cornell Med. Coll., 1962-64; clin. geneticist Meml. Hosp. for Cancer, N.Y.C., 1963-65; vis. scientist Forsyth Dental Center, Boston, 1969-71; cons. human genetics Newington (Conn.) Childrens Hosp., 1971-73; Mem. com. on epidemiology and vets. follow-up studies NRC, 1969-73; mem. perinatal research com. Nat. Inst. Neurol. Diseases and Stroke, NIH, 1970-72; mem. cultural anthropology fellowship and rev. NIMH, 1969-73. Author: Genetic Basis of Morphological Variation, 1959, Biological and Social Meaning of Race, 1971; Editor: Social Biology, 1961-77, 81—; contbr. articles to profl. jours. Served to maj. USAAF, 1942-46. Decorated D.F.C., Air medal with 3 oak leaf clusters.; Named Health Research Council Career Scientist City N.Y., 1962-64. Fellow Explorers Club; Mem. Am. Assn. Phys. Anthropology (exec. com. 1965-67, v.p. 1968-70), Am. Soc. for Human Genetics (dir. 1960-61, 67-69), Behavior Genetics Assn. (pres. pro-tem 1970-71), Soc. for Study Social Biology (dir. 1981-83, 86—), Pioneers of Alaska (life), Sigma Xi. Office: PO Box 2349 Port Angeles WA 98362-0303

OSBORNE, THOMAS JOE, history educator; b. Long Beach, Calif., May 17, 1942; s. Thomas Jefferson and Dorothy Marie (Jacksie) O.; m. Ginger Tredway, June 28, 1975; children: Brooks Tredway Osborne, Todd Tredway Osborne. BA, Calif. State U., L.A., 1965; MA, Claremont Grad. Sch., 1968, PhD, 1979; negotiation cert., Harvard U., 1991. Instr. history Rancho Santiago Coll., Santa Ana, Calif., 1969—, dir. Oxford program, 1989-90, chmn. history dept., 1990-91, 92-93, coord. honors program, 1994—; asst. prof. Chapman U., Orange, Calif., 1970, U. Hawaii, Honolulu, 1981; cons. Libr. Congress, Washington, 1981-82. Co-author: Paths to the Present, 1973; author: Empire Can Wait, 1981; contbg. author: American National Biography; also articles. Mem. adv. bd. Orange County Educators for Social Responsibility, 1987—; bd. dirs. Beyond War Found., Palo Alto, Calif., 1989-91. Recipient Disting. Faculty Lectr. award Rancho Santiago Coll., 1987, Nat. Teaching Excellence award U. Tex., 1988; fellow Ford Found., 1975, NEH, 1981. Mem. Soc. for Historians Am. Fgn. Rels., Found. for Global Community, Am. Mensa, Sierra Club, Phi Alpha Theta. Democrat.

OSBOURN, GORDON CECIL, materials scientist; b. Kansas City, Mo., Aug. 13, 1954; 2 children. BS, U. Mo., 1974, MS, 1975; PhD in Physics, Calif. Inst. Tech., 1979. Tech. staff Sandia Nat. Labs., 1979-83, divsn. supr., 1983—. Recipient E.O. Lawrence award Dept. Energy, 1985; Internat. prize For New Materials Am. Physical Soc., 1993. Fellow Am. Physical Soc. Home: 5851 Lost Dutchman Ave NE Albuquerque NM 87111-5902 Office: Sandia Nat Labs MS 1423 Albuquerque NM 87185-1423

OSBURN, LISA MARIE, archives technician; b. Bellflower, Calif., Feb. 1, 1965; d. James Charles Osburn and Diane Marie (Austrum) Shannon. BA in Art History and Anthropology, U. Calif., Santa Barbara, 1989; postgrad., Calif. State U., Northridge. Archives tech. Pacific S.W. region Nat. Archives, Laguna Niguel, Calif., 1989-91, Ronald Reagan Presdl. Libr., Simi Valley, Calif., 1991—. Melba Barry Bennett scholar Plam Springs Hist. Soc., 1986-89, Pan Hellenic Soc. Coachella Valley scholar, 1985-88. Mem. Soc. Calif. Archivists. Office: Ronald Reagan Presdl Libr 40 Presidential Dr Simi Valley CA 93065-0666

OSBURN, MELVIN L., psychotherapist; b. Slaton, Tex., Nov. 6, 1938; s. James Leroy and Donnie Ovetra (Sanders) O.; m. Joyce Elaine Osburn, June 23, 1963; children: Julie Ann (dec.), Blaine Alan, Brenda Joyce. AA with honors, San Bernardino Valley Coll., 1975; BA with honors, Calif. State Coll., San Bernardino, 1977; MA, Chapman Coll., 1981. Lic. marriage, family and child counselor, Calif.; cert. hypnotherapist, Calif.; lic. marriage and family therapist, Nev. Therapist Knollwood Psychiatric Hosp., Riverside, Calif.; dir., therapist Merrill Community Svc., Fontana, Calif.; vol. therapist Parents United, San Bernardino; pvt. practice San Bernardino. Social worker PHP Healthcare, U.S. Army, Ft. Irwin, Calif. With U.S. Army, 1956-59. Mem. AACD, Psi Chi. Home: PO Box 621 Highland CA 92346-0621 Office: 971 W Main St Sp 43 Barstow CA 92311

O'SCANNLAIN, DIARMUID FIONNTAIN, federal judge; b. N.Y.C., Mar. 28, 1937; s. Sean Leo and Moira (Hegarty) O'S.; m. Maura Nolan, Sept. 7, 1963; children: Sean, Jane, Brendan, Kevin, Megan, Christopher, Anne, Kate. BA, St. John's U., 1957; JD, Harvard U., 1963; LLM, U. Va., 1992. Bar: Oreg. 1965, N.Y. 1964. Tax atty. Standard Oil Co. (N.J.), N.Y.C., 1963-65; assoc. Davies, Biggs, Strayer, Stoel & Boley, Portland, Oreg., 1965-69; dep. atty. gen. Oreg., 1969-71; public utility commr. of Oreg., 1971-73; dir. Oreg. Dept. Environ. Quality, 1973-74; sr. ptnr. Ragen, Roberts, O'Scannlain, Robertson & Neill, Portland, 1978-86; judge, U.S. Ct. Appeals (9th cir.), San Francisco, 1986—, mem. exec. com., 1988-89, 1993-94, mem. Jud. Coun. 9th Cir., 1991-93; mem. U.S. Judicial Conf. Com. on Automation and Tech., 1990—; cons. Office of Pres.-Elect and mem. Dept. Energy Transition Team (Reagan transition), Washington, 1980-81; chmn. com. adminstrv. law Oreg. State Bar, 1980-81. Mem. council of legal advisers Rep. Nat. Com., 1981-83; mem. Rep. Nat. Com., 1983-86, chmn. Oreg. Rep. Party, 1983-86; del. Rep. Nat. Convs., 1976, 80, chmn. Oreg. del., 1984; Rep. nominee U.S. Ho. of Reps., First Congl. Dist., 1974; team leader Energy Task Force, Pres.'s Pvt. Sector Survey on Cost Control, 1982-83, trustee Jesuit High Sch.; mem. bd. visitors U. Oreg. Law Sch., 1988—; mem. citizens adv. bd. Providence Hosp., 1986-92. Maj. USAR, 1955-78. Mem. Fed. Bar Assn., ABA (sec. Apellate Judges Conf. 1989-90, exec. com. 1990—, chmn.-elect 1994—), Arlington Club, Multnomah Club. Roman Catholic. Office: US Ct Appeals 313 Pioneer Courthouse 555 SW Yamhill St Portland OR 97204-1336*

OSCARSON, KATHLEEN DALE, writing assessment coordinator, educator; b. Hollywood, Calif., Sept. 16, 1928; d. Chauncey Dale and Hermine Marie Rulison; m. David Knowles Leslie, June 16, 1957 (div. Aug. 1970); m. William Randolph Oscarson, Apr. 27, 1974. AB, UCLA, 1950, MA, 1952; Cert. Advanced Study, Harvard U., 1965; Diplomé Elementaire, Le Cordon Bleu U. Paris, 1972. Gen. secondary life credential, Calif. Cons. Advanced Placement English Calif. Dept. Edn., Sacramento, 1968-70; reader Calif. Assessment Program, Sacramento, 1989—; instr. individual study U. Calif. Extension, Berkeley, 1979-92; reader, leader Ednl. Testing Svc., Princeton, N.J. and Emeryville, Calif., 1967—; reader San Jose (Calif.) State U., 1991—; tchr. English, counselor Palo Alto (Calif.) Unified Sch. Dist., 1954-90, H.S. writing assessment coord., 1987—; adj. lectr. English Santa Clara (Calif.) U., 1990-91; commr. Curriculum Study Commn., San Francisco Bay Area, 1978—; chair tchrs. English Spring Asilomar Conf., Pacific Grove, Calif., 1992, Asilomar 44, Pacific Grove, 1994. Mem. lang. arts assessment adv. com. Calif. State Dept. Edn., Sacramento, 1975-90; mem.-at-large exec. bd. Ctrl. Calif. Coun. Tchrs. English, Bay Area, 1969-71; mem. Medallion Soc. San Francisco Opera, 1984—. Mem. MLA, Nat. Coun. Tchrs. English (group leader conf. San Francisco), Calif. Assn. Tchrs. English, Internat. Diplomacy Coun. San Francisco, Harvard Club San Francisco, Christopher Marlowe Soc. Home: 230 Durazno Way Portola Valley CA 94028

OSEGUEDA, LAURA MARGARET, librarian; b. Oakland, Calif., Mar. 25, 1955; d. Eugene Walter and Elizabeth Victory (Mahan) O. BS in Biol. Scis., Calif. State U., 1979; MLS, U. Calif., Berkeley, 1980. Sci. libr. San Jose (Calif.) State U., 1981-84; agrl. and life scis. libr. N.C. State U., Raleigh, 1984-88; head Chemistry Libr. U. Calif., Berkeley, 1988—. Author: (with others) End Users in Libraries, 1988; contbr. articles to profl. jours. Pres. Friends of Melrose Libr., Oakland, 1994—. Mem. ALA (chmn. Assn. Rsch. Librs. sci. and tech. section 1989-90), Am. Chem. Soc., Nat. Audubon Soc. Office: U Calif 100 Hildebrand Berkeley CA 94720

OSGOOD, FRANK WILLIAM, urban and economic planner; b. Williamston, Mich., Sept. 3, 1931; s. Earle Victor and Blanche Mae (Eberly) O.; children: Ann Marie, Frank William Jr. BS, Mich. State U., 1953; M in City Planning, Ga. Inst. Tech., 1960. Prin. planner Tulsa Met. Area Plnning Commn., 1958-60; sr. assoc. Hammer & Co. Assocs., Washington, 1960-64; econ. cons. Marvin Springer & Assocs., Dallas, 1964-65; sr. assoc. Gladstone Assocs., Washington, 1965-67; prof. urban planning Iowa State U., Ames, 1967-73; pres. Frank Osgood Assoc./Osgood Urban Rsch., Dallas, 1973-84; dir. mktg. studies MPSI Americas Inc., Tulsa, 1984-85, Comarc Systems/Roulac & Co., San Francisco, 1985-86; pres. Osgood Urban Rsch., Millbrae, Calif., 1986-95; freelance writer Millbrae, Calif., 1984-85; VISTA vol. coord. Chrysalis, Santa Monica, Calif., 1985-86; adj. prof. U. Tulsa, 1974-76; lectr. U. Tex., Dallas, 1979, U. Tex., Arlington, 1983. Author: Control Land Uses Near Airports, 1960, Planning Small Business, 1967, Continuous Renewal Cities, 1970; contbr. articles to profl. jours. Chmn. awards Cub Scouts Am., Ames, 1971-73; deacon Calvary Presbyn. Ch., San Francisco, 1987-90. 1st lt. USAF, 1954-56. Recipient Community Leaders and Noteworthy Americans award 1976. Mem. Am. Planning Assn. (peninsula liaison 1987-89, dir. pro-tem 1990 No. Calif. sect., edn. coord. 1991-92, Calif., dir. N. Cen. Tex. sect., Tex. chpt. 1983), Am. Inst. Planners (v.p. Okla. chpt. 1975-77), Okla. Soc. Planning Cons. (sec., treas. 1976-79), Urban Land Inst., Le Club. Republican. Presbyterian. Home: Ter Trousdale 11400 National Blvd Los Angeles CA 90064

O'SHAUGHNESSY, ELLEN CASSELS, writer; b. Columbia, S.C., Oct. 1, 1937; d. Melvin O. and Grace Ellen (Cassels) Hemphill; m. John H. Sloan (dec.); children: John H., Anne H.; m. John F. O'Shaughnessy, Dec. 8, 1979 (div. Mar. 1990). BA, Internat. Coll., L.A., 1977; MA in Counseling Psychology, Fielding Inst., Santa Barbara, Calif., 1980. Tchr.'s aide, art instr. Monterey Peninsula (Calif.) Unified Sch. Dist., 1968-74; tchr. adult sch. Pacific Grove (Calif.) Unified Sch. Dist., 1974-82, spl. edn. cons., 1984-85; sustitute tchr. Monterey County Office Edn., Salinas, Calif., 1983-84; owner, writer, pub. Synthesis, Pacific Grove, Calif., 1984—. Author: Teaching Art to Children, 1974, Synthesis, 1981, You Love to Cook Book, 1983, I Could Ride on the Carousel Longer, 1989, Somebody Called Me A Retard Today...And My Heart Felt Sad, 1992. Episcopalian. Home: PO Box 51063 Pacific Grove CA 93950-6063

OSKOLKOFF, GRASSIM, Native American Indian tribal chief; b. Ninilchik, Alaska, Oct. 14, 1926; s. Michael and Zoya (Darien) O.; m. Marion Emma Encelewski, Oct. 30, 1952; children: Debra, Marla, Bruce, Gary, Becky. Student, Ninilchik Sch., Alaska. With Alaska R.R., Anchorage; comml. fisherman Ninilchik, Alaska; pres., dir. Ninilchik Native Assn., Inc., Alaska, 1971-82; chief, pres. Ninilchik Traditional Coun., Alaska, 1982—; former rep. Alaska Fedn. Natives, Anchorage; rep. Alaska Inter-Tribal Coun., Anchorage, Cook Inlet Treaty Tribes, Alaska; commr. Alaska Sea Otter Commn., Fairbanks. Bd. dirs. Russian Orthodox Ch., Ninilchik; environ. adv. Promotion of Peace Among People and Nations. With inf. AUS, WWII, PTO. Office: Ninilchik Traditional Coun PO Box 39070 Ninilchik AK 99639-0070

OSMAN, JACK WILLIAM, economics educator; b. N.Y.C., Nov. 30, 1938; s. Jacob Matias Osman (Asunmaa) and Tilda Maria (Wirtanen) Miller; m. Barbara Gail Lancaster, May 22, 1938; children: Richard William, Linda Ann. BS in Indsl. Engring., Rutgers U., 1961, MA in Econs., 1963, PhD in Econs., 1966. Teaching asst. dept. econs. Rutgers U., New Brunswick, N.J., 1962-64; instr. dept. econs. Rutgers U., Newark, 1964-66, asst. prof., 1966-67; asst. prof. dept. econs. San Francisco State U., 1967-69, assoc. prof., 1969-73, prof. econs., 1973—; vis. assoc. prof. U. Calif., Berkeley, 1970, U. Calif. Davis, 1979-80; vis. scholar U. Helsinki, Finland, 1990, U. Stockholm, 1990; bd. dirs. Franciscan Shops, San Francisco. Co-author (text) Basic Economic Problems, Principlss, Policy, 1972, rev. 2d edit. 1976; contbr. articles to profl. jours. Mem. Am. Econs. Assn., Western Econs. Assn. (local arrangemnts com.), Internat. Regional Sci. Assn., Western Regional Sci. Assn. Office: San Francisco State U Econs Dept 1600 Holloway Ave San Francisco CA 94132

OSMAN, MARVIN PHILLIP, psychiatrist and psychoanalyst; b. Mpls., Apr. 15, 1924; s. Samuel S. and Rose Marie (Bouis) O.; m. Patricia Diener, June 4, 1967; children: Suzanne G., Daniel S. BS, U. Minn., 1946, BA, 1947, MB, 1949, MD, 1950. Diplomate Am. Bd. Psychiatry and Neurology. Intern Los Angeles County Gen. Hosp., 1949-50; resident in psychiatry VA Hosp., Brentwood, Calif., 1950-51, 53-54; tng. in psychoanalysis So. Calif. Psychoanalytic Inst., 1951, 54-63; from instr. to assoc. clin. prof. psychiatry U. So. Calif. Med. Sch., L.A., 1957-84, clin. prof. psychiatry, 1984—; mem. faculty So. Calif. Psychoanalytic Inst., L.A., 1967—, tng. and supervising analyst, 1981—, pres., 1986-87, 92-94, dir advanced tng. program in psychodynamic psychotherapy, 1990—; pvt. practice psychiatry and psychoanalysis Beverly Hills, 1955—. Contbr. articles to profl. jours. Trustee L.A. Mental Health Assn., 1962-65, Resthaven Psychiat. Hosp., 1964-70. 1st lt. M.C., U.S. Army, 1951-53. Recipient Outstanding Tchr. award Clin. Assocs. of So. Calif. Psychoanalytic Inst., 1980. Fellow Am. Psychiat. Assn.; mem. Calif. Med. Assn., Los Angeles County Med. Assn., Am. Psychoanalytic Assn., Internat. Psychoanalytic Assn., So. Calif. Psychoanalytic Soc. and Inst. Office: 9735 Wilshire Blvd Beverly Hills CA 90212

OSMER, FRANK EDMOND, private investigator, consultant; b. Watsonville, Calif., Apr. 2, 1921; s. Herbert Harry and Lois Elizabeth (DeSpain) O.; m. Sept. 11, 1943 (dec. Oct. 1986); children: Lois B., Gerald M., Phillip T., Dennis H., Neil J. BS, U. Santa Clara, 1943. Chief police Watsonville Police Dept., 1947-62; sales mgr. produce Bud Antle Inc., Salinas, Calif., 1962-70; pvt. investigator Osmer & Ojeda Svc., Inc., Watsonville, 1970—; project mmgr., lobbyist Buena Vista Country Club, Santa Cruz, Calif., 1992—. Councilman City of Watsonville, 1979-87; city rep. Assoc. Monterey Bay Govts., Salinas, 1979-87; mem. Calif. Coastal Commn., 1986-87. Maj. U.S. Army, 1943-53, Korea. Decorated Purple Heart, Medal of Peace and Freedom (The Netherlands). Roman Catholic. Home: 34 Roosevelt St Watsonville CA 95076-3937

OSSERMAN, ROBERT, mathematician, educator; b. N.Y.C., Dec. 19, 1926; s. Herman Aaron and Charlotte (Adler) O.; m. Maria Anderson, June 15, 1952; 1 son, Paul; m. Janet Adelman, July 21, 1976; children—Brian, Stephen. B.A., NYU, 1946; postgrad., U. Zurich, U. Paris; M.A., Harvard U., 1948, Ph.D., 1955. Teaching fellow Harvard U., 1949-52, vis. lectr., research assoc., 1961-62; instr. U. Colo., 1952-53; mem. faculty Stanford U., 1955—, prof. math., 1966—, chmn. dept. math., 1973-79, Mellon Prof. Interdisciplinary Studies, 1987-90; dep. dir. Math. Scis. Rsch. Inst., Berkeley, Calif., 1990—; mem. NYU Inst. Math. Scis., 1957-58, Math. Scis. Rsch. Inst., Berkeley,., 1983-84, head math. br. Office Naval Rsch., 1960-61; researcher and author publs. on differential geometry, complex variables, differential equations, especially minimal surfaces, Laplace operator, isoperimetric inequalities, ergodic theory. Author: Two-Dimensional Calculus, 1968, A Survey of Minimal Surfaces, 1969, 2d edit., 1986, Poetry of the Universe, 1995. Fulbright lectr. U. Paris, 1965-66; Guggenheim fellow, 1976-77; vis. fellow U. Warwick, Imperial Coll., U. London. Fellow AAAS; mem. Am. Math. Soc., Math. Assn. Am. Office: Math Scis Rsch Inst Berkeley CA 94720

OSTBY, ALAN COLLIER, psychotherapist; b. Wolf Point, Mont., July 1, 1956; s. Riley Osborn and Louise Helen (Collier) O.; m. Margaret Rose Beeson, Nov. 14, 1991; 1 child, Julius Riley. BA in Polit. Sci. magna cum laude, Macalester Coll., 1977; MS in Polit. Sci., Yale U., 1980; MS in Mental Health Counseling, Mont. State U., 1994. State dir. Common Cause, Helena, Mont., 1980-81; pub. rels. specialist Common Cause, Washington, 1981-82; owner, dir. Ostley Artifacts, Point Arena, Calif., 1982-83; owner, operator Pope House Antiques, Helena, 1983-91, Ostby Auctions, Helena and Billings, 1989—; dir. Yellowstone Naturopathic Clinic, Billings, Mont., 1992-94; therapist, intern Mental Health Ctr., Billings, 1994; therapist Spring Creek Sch., Billings, 1994—; restorer Francis Pope House, Helena, 1985-91. Rep. Helena Citizen's Coun., 1989-90; activist, fundraiser Dem. Party, Helena and Billings, 1989—. Mem. Yellowstone Valley Citizens Coun., Nature Conservancy, Wilderness Soc., various book clubs, Phi Beta Kappa. Home: 328 Grand Ave Billings MT 59101-5923 Office: Mental Health Ctr 1245 N 29th St Billings MT 59101-0122

OSTENDORF, VIRGINIA ANGELITA, publishing executive, communications executive; b. Phoenix, Mar. 14, 1942; d. Joseph and Virginia (Carrillo) Gregori; m. Ronald C. Ostendorf, AUg. 9, 1980; children: from previous marriage: Gloria Frederici, Carleton Frederici. MusB, U. Iowa, 1964. Music tchr. various schs., Iowa, N.Y., 1964-78; dir. communications Iowa Dept. Social Svcs., Des Moines, 1979-82; dir. communications div. Kellogg Corp., Littleton, Colo., 1982-84; pres., chmn. Virgina A. Ostendorf, Inc., Littleton, 1984—; mem. adv. bd. Telecon Ann. Conf., 1986—. Author: Downlink Directory, Uplink Directory, Distance Learning Directory, At A Distance, What Every Principal, Teacher and School Board Member Should Know About Distance Education (Internat. Teleconferencing Assn. Best Book Gold award 1990), Teaching Through Interactive Television, (newsletter) Teletraining (spl. recognition 1989), (manual) Effective Telephone Meetings/Trusted Teletraining; pub. (with Susan Irwin) The Business Television Directory; contbr. numerous articles to profl. jours.; presenter numerous papers to confs., forums. Pres. Des Moines Symphony Guild; mem., bd. dirs. various non-profit orgns., 1969—. Recipient Gov.'s Letter of Recognition, Iowa Gov., 1982, Outstanding Achievement in Teletng. award Teleconf. Mag., 1983; named to Teleconf. Hall of Fame, Telecon X Conf., 1990; named one of Top 100 Satellite Execs., Via Satellite mag. Mem. Internat. Teleconferencing Assn. (charter bd. mem. 1984-86, v.p. 1985), Soc. Satellite Profls., Can. Assn. Distance Edn. Republican. Episcopalian. Office: PO Box 2896 Littleton CO 80161-2896

OSTER, CYNTHIA ANN, critical care nurse; b. Monmouth, Ill., Oct. 11, 1958; d. Paul Eugene and Carol Marlene (Isaacson) Hennenfent; m. Lewis Henry Oster, Jr., Mar. 14, 1981; children: Kristen, Jonathan. BSN, U. Iowa, 1980; MS in Nursing, U. Nebr., Omaha, 1985; postgrad. in nursing, U. Colo., 1995. RN, Colo.; cert. CCRN. Rsch. nurse U. Nebr. Med. Ctr. Coll. Nursing, 1985; clin. nurse specialist I, U. Iowa Hosps. and Clinics, Iowa City, 1987-88; critical care clin. specialist HealthONE Aurora Presbyn. Hosp., 1988—. Mem. ANA, AACN, Sigma Theta Tau. Office: HealthONE Aurora Presbyn Hosp 700 Potomac St Aurora CO 80011-6701

OSTER, PATRICK RALPH, journalist; b. Harvey, Ill., Oct. 9, 1944; m. Sally Anne Jacobsen. B.S. with honors, Loyola U., Chgo., 1966; student, Glasgow (Scotland) U. Soviet Inst., 1968-69; J.D., Cornell U., 1970. Asso. firm Price, Cushman, Keck, Mahin and Cate, Chgo., 1970-72; atty., investigator Better Govt. Assn., Chgo., 1972-73; reporter Chgo. Sun-Times, 1973-74, Washington corr., 1977-78, chief Washington bur., 1978-84; chief Mexico City Bur. Knight-Ridder Newspapers, 1984-87; corr. Business Week, Brussels, 1990—; asst. mng. editor The Bakersfield Californian; asso. editor U.S. News & World Report, Washington, 1974-77. Author: The Mexicans: Personal Portrait of a People, 1989. Recipient Silver Gavel award (3) ABA; InterAm. Press Club award, 1984; Worth Bingham award, 1982, Citation, Overseas Press Club, 1986; others.

OSTERHOFF, JAMES MARVIN, telecommunications company executive; b. Lafayette, Ind., May 18, 1936; s. Abel Lyman and Mildred Paulene (Post) O.; m. Marilyn Ann Morrison, Aug. 24, 1958; children—Anne Michelle Bitsie, Amy Louise Olmsted, Susan Marie. B.S.M.E., Purdue U., 1958; M.B.A., Stanford U., 1963. Staff asst. FMC Corp., San Jose, Calif., 1963-64; with Ford Motor Co., Dearborn, Mich., 1964-84; v.p. fin. Ford Motor Credit Co., Dearborn, 1973-75; controller car ops. N. Am. Automotive Ops., Ford Motor Co., Dearborn, 1975-76; asst. controller N. Am. Automotive Ops., Ford Motor Co., 1976-79; controller tractor ops. Ford Motor Co., Troy, Mich., 1979-84; v.p. fin., CFO Digital Equipment Corp., Maynard, Mass., 1985-91; exec. v.p., CFO U.S.West Inc., Englewood, Colo., 1991—; bd. dirs. GenCorp, Inc., FSA Holdings, Ltd., Pvt. Sector Coun.; mem. Conf. Bd. Fin. Coun. Served to lt. (j.g.) USN, 1958-61. Recipient Disting. Engring. Alumnus award Purdue U.; named Outstanding Mech. Engring. Alumnus, Purdue U. Mem. Fin. Execs. Inst. Office: US West Inc 7800 E Orchard Rd Englewood CO 80111-2533

OSTERMILLER, JOHN VICTOR, retired real estate company executive; b. Lincoln, Nebr., Nov. 4, 1910; s. John and Louise (Bernhardt) O.; m. Margaret Ellen Kerr, June 17, 1934; children: Karen Rea, John Kerr. Student, U. Nebr., 1927-28; BS, Colo. State U., 1932. Tchr. vocat. agr., pub. sch. Colo., 1934-42; agrl. fieldman Gt. Western Sugar Co., Brush, Colo., 1942-49; asst. mgr. Gt. Western Sugar Co., Brush and Ft. Morgan, 1949-57; mgr. Gt. Western Sugar Co., Longmont, Colo., 1957-63; agrl. mgr. Gt. Western Sugar Co., Ft. Morgan, 1963-70, N.E. Colo. asst. dist. agrl. mgr., 1970-73; v.p. Gt. Western Sugar Export Co., 1973-75; mgr. farm and ranch dept. Crown Realty Co., Denver, 1975-78, Carriage House Realtors, Ft. Morgan, 1978-83, Realty Assocs., Ft. Morgan, 1984-87, Accent Real

Estate, Ft. Morgan, 1987-93; bd. dirs. Lower South Platte Water Conservancy Dist. Contbr. articles to profl. jours. Instr. Adult Edn., Yuma, Colo., 1935-38, Brush, 1938-42. Rep. precinct committeeman, Morgan County, 1950-57, 64-74, Boulder County, 958-63; mem. St. Vrain Valley Sch. Bd., Longmont, 1961-63; bd. dirs. Brush Civic Club, 1944-50, Ft. Morgan Heritage Found., pres. 1969-75; bd. dirs., pres. Colo. State U. Found., 1973-86. Mem. Ft. Morgan C. of C. (dir. 1965-69, pres. 1968), Colo. State U. Alumni (dir. 1971-82, pres. 1975-76), Am. Sugar Beet Soc. Technologists, Masons, Lions, Alpha Tau Alpha, Lamda Gamma Delta, Sigma Phi Epsilon. Presbyterian. Home: 4 Yates Ter Fort Morgan CO 80701-9217

OSTLER, DAVID VAL, engineering executive; b. Cambridge, Mass., Jan. 22, 1957; s. David Sorenson and Sharon (Scott) O.; m. Cynthia Hale, Dec. 17, 1982; children: Andrew Hale, Sarah, Carly. BS in Computer Sci. cum laude, U. Utah, 1981, BS in Elec. Engring. cum laude, 1981, MS in Med. Biophysics and Computing, 1984. Summer intern R & D Hewlett Packard Corp., Corvallis, Oreg., 1981; applications programmer med. biophysics and computing U. Utah, Salt Lake City, 1978-81, rsch. asst. med. biophysics and computing, 1981-84; programmer, analyst Computer Sci. Rsch., Regenstrief Inst., Indpls., 1984-85; computer sys. engr. NASA/Johnson Space Ctr. Med. Ops. Br. Krug Internat., Houston, 1985-88; interface software engr. Motorola/EMTEK Health Care Sys., Phoenix, 1988, tech. mgr. interface devel., 1988-90, tech. mgr. product configuration, 1989-90, engring. mgr. integration and support, 1990, product mgr. integration products and platform, 1990-92, program mgr., engring. mgr., 1992-95, dir. computer tech., 1995—; presenter in field. Contbr. articles to profl. jours. Mem. IEEE, IEEE Computer Soc., IEEE Engring. in Medicine and Biology Soc. (stds. com. chmn. 1989-93), Am. Nat. Stds. Inst., Eta Kappa Nu. Home: 3627 E Summerhaven Dr Phoenix AZ 85044-4523 Office: EMTEK Health Care Systems #190 1501 W Fountainhead Pkwy Tempe AZ 85282

OSTLER, SCOTT, newspaper sports columnist. Sports columnist San Francisco Chronicle. Office: San Francisco Chronicle 901 Mission St San Francisco CA 94103-2905

OSTROM, CAROL MARIE, reporter; b. Seattle, June 27, 1947; d. Cameron Walthew and Eula Marie (Curry) O. BA in English Lit., U. Wash., 1970. Program asst. Sch. Medicine U. Wash., Seattle, 1970-73; asst. mgr. circulation Seattle Sun, 1974-75, reporter, asst. editor, 1974-77, editor, 1978-79; reporter, assoc. editor Willamette Week, Portland, Oreg., 1979-80; reporter features and news Seattle Times, 1980-83, reporter religion, 1983—. Recipient Excellence in Journalism awards Sigma Delta Chi, 1978-89; John S. Knight fellow Stanford U., 1984-85. Mem. Religion Newswriters Assn. (Supple award 1988). Office: Seattle Times Fairview Ave N & John St PO Box 70 Seattle WA 98111-0070

OSTROM, PHILIP GARDNER, computer company executive; b. New Haven, Aug. 8, 1942; s. David McKellar and Barbara (Kingsbury) O.; m. Toni Hammons, Dec. 21, 1965; n. Nancy Jean Kahl, Apr. 2, 1983; children: Eric Craig, Paige Lynne. BS, U. Ariz., 1965; postgrad., U. Calif., 1992-94. Cert. sr. examiner quality control, Calif. Sales mgr. Procter & Gamble Co., Louisville, 1968-70, Dun & Bradstreet, L.A., 1970-71; internat. sales mgr. Memorex Corp., Santa Clara, Calif., 1971-82; dir. ops. Memtek Products, Campbell, Calif., 1982-86, Victor Techs., Scotts Valley, Calif., 1986-88; ops. mgr. Apple Computer, Cupertino, Calif., 1988-93; pres./CEO Ostrom & Assocs., San Jose, Calif., 1993—; Malcolm Baldridge examiner, 1993—; ISO9000 lead assessor, 1992—; CCQS spl. examiner, State of Calif., 1994—. Capt. USMC, 1965-68, Vietnam. Home: 1099 Maraschino Dr San Jose CA 95129-3317 Office: Ostrom & Assocs 1099 Maraschino Dr San Jose CA 95129-3317

OSWALD, DELMONT RICHARD, humanities organization executive, writer; b. Idaho Falls, Idaho, Oct. 7, 1940; s. Philip Fredrick and Lucille (Andrus) O.; m. Jean Stringam, June 17, 1967 (div. Jan. 1979); children: Sarah Mary, Benjamin Philip. BA, Idaho State U., 1962; MA, Brigham Young U., 1967. Instr. history Brigham Young U., Provo, Utah, 1967-71, asst. to dean social sci., 1971-74; exec. dir. Utah Humanities Coun., Salt Lake City, 1974—; pres. elect Utah Acad. Sci., Arts, Letters, Salt Lake City, 1989-90, pres. 1991-93; nat. bd. dirs. Nat. Fedn. State Humanities Couns., Washington 1988-93, chmn. Nat. meeting, Portland, Oreg., 1990. Author: Autobiography of James Beckwourth, 1972 (U.S. Amb. Book 1972); mem. editorial bd. Dialogue Mag., 1992—. U.S. Senate Reauthorization N.E.H. testifier Fedn. State Humanities Coun., Washington, 1990, mem. gov.'s Martin Luther King Jr./Human Rights Commn.; mem. edn. com. Project 2000, 1989-90; bd. dirs. Utah Alliance for Arts and Humanities. Recipient N.E.H. Merit awards 1984, 86, 88, Exemplary award, 1990, 91; Dedicatory Address Jewitt Ctr. Humanities, Salt Lake City, 1989. Mem. Nat. Fedn. State Humanities Coun. (bd. dirs.), Utah Hist. Assn., Mormon Hist. Assn., Salt Lake City C. of C. (Honors in Arts 1990), Wasatch Westerners (Gov.'s award in the arts 1994, Cathedral of the Madeline award for arts and humanities 1995). Home: 209 4th Ave Salt Lake City UT 84103-2484 Office: Utah Humanities Coun 350 S 400 E Ste 110 Salt Lake City UT 84111-2946

OSWALD, DONALD JAMES, economics educator; b. Tacoma, Oct. 15, 1946; s. George Oswald and Arlene Patricia (Cowling) Wills; m. Christine Anna Lien, Sept. 9, 1967; children: Michael G., Brent A. BA in Econs., Wash. State U., 1968, MA in Econs., 1969, PhD in Econs., 1974; postgrad., Lincoln (Ill.) Christian Sem., 1979-81. Grad. rsch. asst. Wash. State U., Pullman, 1968-71; sr. cons. transp. program Ernst & Ernst, Washington, 1976-79; vis. lectr. econs. Lincoln Christian Coll. and Sem., 1979-81; asst. prof. econs. Calif. State U., Bakersfield, 1981-87, assoc. prof., 1987—, gen. studies fellow, 1981—, assoc. dir. Ctr. for Study Classical Econs., 1986-88; professorial lectr. Am. U., Washington, 1975; lectr. George Mason U., Fairfax, Va., 1976. Contbr. articles to profl. jours. Capt. USAF, 1971-76. Mem. Am. Econs. Assn., Western Econ. Assn. (conf. presenter, 1983, 92), Assn. Social Econs., Am. Scu. Affiliation. Home: 3800 Club Run Bakersfield CA 93309-7746

OSWALD, REGINA M., community health nurse; b. Altoona, Pa., May 8, 1947; d. Clayton O. and Bertha F. (Musselman) Edmiston; m. Dale G. Oswald, Apr. 18, 1970; children: Glen E., Kevin D. Diploma, Altoona Hosp. Sch. Nursing, 1968; BSN, George Mason U., 1981; MS, Tex. Woman's U., 1989; health svc. cert., Calif. State U., L.A., 1990. Cert. community health nurse; RN, Calif. Staff nurse Altoona (Pa.) Hosp.; primary nurse med./surgical Fairfax Hsop. & Assoc., Falls Church, Va., Charlton Meth. Hosp., Dallas; pub. health nurse City of Dallas; sch. nurse L.A. County Office Edn., Downey, San Bernardino County, Calif.; instr. nursing U. Phoenix, So. Calif. Mem. Nat. Assn. Sch. Nurses, Calif. Sch. Nurses Orgn., Calif. Nurses Assn.

O'TOOLE, ROBERT JOHN, II, telemarketing consultant; b. Binghamton, N.Y., Mar. 24, 1951; s. Robert John and Joan Ceclia (Martin) O'T.; m. Donna Sue Stevenson, Jan. 28, 1978 (div. 1984); children: Irene Grace, Erin Colleen, Robert John III; m. Karen Irene Cady, Dec. 21, 1994. Student, Corning (N.Y.) C.C., 1969-71, SUNY, Brockport, 1970-71; BA, Wake Forest U., 1973; MBA, Southwestern Coll., 1986. Asst. dir. devel. Duvall Home for Children, DeLand, Fla., 1978-81; gen. mgr. Royale Art Advt., Odessa, Tex., 1981-82; v.p. Barnes Assocs. Advt., Odessa, 1982-84, Tex. Assn. for Blind Athletes, Austin, 1985-86; sales mgr. Los Amables Pub., Albuquerque, 1987-88; dir. devel. Albuquerque (N.Mex.) Help for the Homeless, 1988-91; chmn., CEO Advantage Ventures, Inc. (formerly Advantage Mktg., Inc.), Albuquerque, 1991—; CEO LaCourt, Medina & Sterling, Albuquerque, 1993—; cons. Nat. Child Safety Coun., Austin, 1985, Assoc. Profl. Fire Fighters, Austin, 1985, Reynolds Aluminum, Austin, 1986, N.Mex. State Legis., 1990. Author: Telemarketing Tickets, 1988; founder, editor: (newspaper) Albuquerque Street News, 1990; publisher: (newspaper) The New Mexican, 1991; contbr. articles to jours. Founder Permian Basin Rehab. Ctr., Odessa, 1983, Albuquerque (N.Mex.) Help for the Homeless, Inc., 1988. Recipient Cert. of Merit, Small Bus. Adminstrn., Odessa, 1984. Mem. Direct Mktg. Assn., Amnesty Internat. Home: Historic Coke House 1023 2nd St SW Albuquerque NM 87102-4124 Office: Advantage Ventures Inc 201 Pacific Ave SW Albuquerque NM 87102-4176

OTOSHI, TOM YASUO, electrical engineer; b. Seattle, Sept. 4, 1931; s. Jitsuo and Shina Otoshi; m. Haruko Shirley Yumiba, Oct. 13, 1963; children: John, Kathryn. BSEE, U. Wash., 1954, MSEE, 1957. With Hughes Aircraft Co., Culver City, Calif., 1956-61; mem. tech. staff Jet Propulsion Lab., Calif. Inst. Tech., Pasadena, 1961—; cons. in field. Recipient NASA New Tech. awards, Exceptional Svc. medal NASA, 1994. Mem. Wagner Ensemble of Roger Wagner Choral Inst., L.A. Bach Festival Chorale. Fellow IEEE (life); mem. Sigma Xi, Tau Beta Pi. Contbr. articles to profl. jours; patentee in field. Home: 3551 Henrietta Ave La Crescenta CA 91214-1136 Office: Jet Propulsion Lab 4800 Oak Grove Dr Pasadena CA 91109-8001

OTREMBA, BERNARD OTTO, marketing executive; b. Munich, Feb. 3, 1944; came to U.S, 1985; s. Louis E. and Burgl (Koppel) O.; m. Roswitha J. Pietrzyk, Dec. 27, 1984; children: Gabriele Yvonne, Sonya Charlotte. MBA in Econs., Munich Coll., 1970; PhD in Bus. Adminstrn., Pacific Western U., 1987. Pres. Import Export Ltd., Tehran, Iran, 1976-81; dir. bus. devel. Intergraph Europe, Inc., London and Amsterdam, The Netherlands, 1981-84; exec. v.p., gen. mgr. SSI Schaefer Systems Internat. Inc., Eatontown, N.J., 1985-88; pres. Gardner Internat. Ops. Ltd., Tampa, Fla., 1989-93; CEO, chmn. PFT Am. Inc., Phoenix, 1993—. Author: Industrial Psychology and Physiology in Contemporary Management, 1970, Can Computers Draw? CAD in Architecture, 1984, The Interdependence in the Economic Relations Between Industrial and Developing Countries, 1987. Mem. Rotary Internat., World Trade Ctr., German-Am. C. of C.

OTT, DAVID MICHAEL, engineering company executive; b. Glendale, Calif., Feb. 24, 1952; s. Frank Michael and Roberta (Michie) O.; m. Cynthia Dianne Bunce. BSEE, U. Calif., Berkeley, 1974. Electronic engr. Teknekron Inc., Berkeley, 1974-79; chief engr. TCI, Berkeley, 1979-83; div. mgr. Integrated Automation Inc., Alameda, Calif., 1983-87, Litton Indsl. Automation, Alameda, 1987-92; founder, chmn. Picture Elements Inc., Berkeley, 1992—. Inventor method for verifying denomination of currency, method for processing digited images, automatic document image revision. Mem. IEEE, AAAS, Assn. Computing Machinery, Union of Concerned Scientists. Office: Picture Elements Inc 777 Panoramic Way Berkeley CA 94704-2538

OTT, ROBERT WILLIAM, publishing executive; b. Cleve., Feb. 13, 1945; s. R.W. Ott and Mary Jane (Evar) Sahle; 1 child, Noelle. Grad. high sch., Cleve., 1964; ind. studies Ea. and We. traditions, 1971-95. Mem. core staff Krishnamurti Found. Am., Ojai, Calif., 1975-79; v.p. Ojai Found., 1980-81; co-founder Sacred Arts, San Francisco, 1986; pres. The Terma Co., Santa Fe, Calif., 1990—; corp. trainer Living Systems, 1992—; bd. dirs. Ojai Found. Author: The Box: Remember the Gift, 1993. Bd. dirs. Concerned Citizens for Nuclear Safety, Santa Fe, 1991. Buddhist. Office: Terma PO Box 5495 Santa Fe NM 87502

OTT, WAYNE ROBERT, environmental engineer; b. San Mateo, Calif., Feb. 2, 1940; s. Florian Funstan and Evelyn Virginia (Smith) O.; m. Patricia Faustina Bertuzzi, June 28, 1967 (div. 1983). BA in Econs., Claremont McKenna Coll., 1962; BSEE, Stanford U., 1963, MS in Engring, 1965, MA in Comm., 1966, PhD in Environ. Engring., 1971. Commd. lt. USPHS, 1966, advanced to capt., 1986; chief lab. ops. br. U.S. EPA, Washington, 1971-73, sr. systems analyst, 1973-79, sr. rsch. engr., 1981-84, chief air toxics and radiation monitoring rsch. staff, 1984-90; vis. scientist dept. stats. Stanford (Calif.) U., 1979-81; vis. scholar Ctr. for Risk Analysis and dept. stats., civil engring., 1990-93; sr. environ. engr., EPA Atmospheric Rsch. and Exposure Assessment Lab, 1993-95; consulting prof. in civil engring. Stanford (Calif.) U., 1995—; dir. field studies Calif. Environ. Tobacco Smoke Study, 1993-95; cons. prof. civil engring. Stanford U., 1995—. Author: Environmental Indices: Theory and Practice, 1976, Environmental Statistics and Data Analysis, 1995; contbr. articles on indoor air pollution, total human exposure to chems., stochastic models of indoor exposure, motor vehicle exposures, personal monitoring instruments, and environ. tobacco smoke to profl. jours. Decorated Commendation medal USPHS, 1977; recipient Nat. Statistician award for outstanding contribution to environ. statistics EPA, 1995. Mem. Internat. Soc. Exposure Analysis (v.p. 1989-90, Jerome J. Weselowski Internat. award for career achievement in exposure assessmemt 1995), Am. Statis. Assn., Am. Soc. for Quality Control, Air and Waste Mgmt. Assn., Phi Beta Kappa, Sigma Xi, Tau Beta Pi, Kappa Mu Epsilon. Democrat. Clubs: Theater, Jazz, Sierra. Avocations: hiking, photography, model trains, jazz recording. Developer nationally uniform air pollution index, first total human exposure activity pattern models. Home: 1008 Cardiff Ln Redwood City CA 94061-3678 Office: Stanford U Dept Stats Sequoia Hall Stanford CA 94305

OTTEN, ARTHUR EDWARD, JR., lawyer, corporate executive; b. Buffalo, Oct. 11, 1930; s. Arthur Edward Sr. and Margaret (Ambrusko) O.; m. Mary Therese Torri, Oct. 1, 1960; children: Margaret, Michael, Maureen Staley, Suzanne, Jennifer. BA, Hamilton Coll., 1952; JD, Yale U., 1955. Bar: N.Y. 1955, Colo. 1959. Assoc. Hodges, Silverstein, Hodges & Harrington, Denver, 1959-64; ptnr. Hodges, Kerwin, Otten & Weeks (predecessor firms), Denver, 1964-73, Davis, Graham & Stubbs, Denver, 1973-86; pres., mem. Otten, Johnson, Robinson, Neff & Ragonetti, P.C., Denver, 1986—; rec. sec. Colo. Nat. Bankshares, Inc., Denver, 1983-93. Lt. USN, 1955-59. Mem. ABA, Colo. Bar Assn., Denver Bar Assn., Am. Arbitration Assn. (panel arbitrators, large complex case panel, mediator panel), Law Club, Univ. Club, Denver Mile High Rotary (pres. 1992-93), Phi Delta Phi. Republican. Roman Catholic. Home: 3774 S Niagara Way Denver CO 80237-1248 Office: Otten Johnson Robinson Neff & Ragonetti PC 1600 Colorado National Bldg Denver CO 80202-1056

OTTENSMEYER, DAVID JOSEPH, neurosurgeon, health care executive; b. Nashville, Tenn., Jan. 29, 1930; s. Raymond Stanley and Glenda Jessie (Helpingstein) O.; m. Mary Jean Langley, June 30, 1954; children: Kathryn Joan, Martha Langley. BA, Wis. State U., Superior, 1951; MD, U. Wis., Madison, 1959; MS in Health Svcs. Adminstrn., Coll. St. Francis, 1985. Diplomate Am. Bd. Neurological Surgery. Intern then resident in gen. surgery Univ. Hosps., Madison, Wis., 1959-61; resident in neurol. surgery Univ. Hosps., 1962-65; staff neurosurgeon Marshfield Clinic, Wis., 1965-76; from instr. of neurol. surgery to clin. asst. prof. U. Wis. Med. Sch., Madison, 1964-77; CEO Lovelace Med. Ctr., Albuquerque, 1976-86, chmn., 1986-91; clin. prof. community medicine U. N.Mex., Albuquerque, 1977-79, clin. prof. neurol. surgery, 1979—; exec. v.p., chief med. officer Equicor, 1986-90; v.p. Marshfield Clinic, 1970-71, pres., CEO, 1972-75; pres., CEO The Lovelace Insts., 1991—; sr. v.p., chief med. officer Travelers Ins. Co., 1990-91; served on numerous adv. and com. posts. Contbr. articles to profl. jours. Col. USAR, 1960-90. Fellow ACS, Am. Coll. Physician Execs. (pres. 1985-86); mem. Am. Group Practice Assn. (pres. 1983-84), Am. Bd. Med. Mgmt. (bd. dirs. 1989-95, chmn. 1995). Republican. Episcopalian. Home: 2815 Ridgecrest Dr SE Albuquerque NM 87108-5132*

OTTO, CATHERINE NAN, clinical laboratory scientist; b. Stockton, Calif., Dec. 17, 1953; d. Edward Joseph Otto and Arlene Maud (Holmes) Naylor. BS in Microbiology, Oreg. State U., 1976; BS in Med. Tech., Oreg. Health Scis. U., 1981; BA in French, Portland (Oreg.) State U., 1986, MBA, 1990. Cert. clin. lab. scienitst, clin. lab. dir., clin. lab. supr., clin. lab. specialist in hematology, med. technologist. Med. technologist night shift Ore. Health Scis. U., Portland, 1981-85; med. technologist night shift Bess Kaiser Med. Ctr., Portland, 1985, med. technologist hematology, 1985-86; lab. supr. div. med. office Kaiser Permanente, Portland, 1986-87, lab. supr. Vancouver Med. Office, 1987—. Bd. dirs. Friends of Ore. Pub. Broadcasting, Portland, 1985-88; mem. allied health subcom. Am. Cancer Soc., Portland, 1985-87. Mem. AAUW, NAFE, Assn. for Oreg. Med. Tech. (pres. 1986-87, bd. dirs. 1984-85, Mem. of Yr. 1989, 91), Portland Dist. Soc. Assn. for Oreg. Med. Tech. (pres. 1983-84), Am. Soc. Clin. Lab. Sci. (chair region IX immunology/immunohematology sci. assembly 1984-87, vice chmn. 1987-88, chair polit. action com. 1990-91, trustee polit. action com. 1987-91, commr. profl. and econ. affairs 1989-91, dir. at large 1991-92, sec./treas. 1992—), Am. Assn. Blood Banks, Am. Assn. Clin. Chemists, Clin. Lab. Mgmt. Assn., Beaverton Internat. Tng. in Communications (sec. 1985-86).

OTTO, CHARLES WILSON, anesthesiologist, educator; b. Omaha, Dec. 3, 1941; s. Claude W. and Mary A. (Adams) O.; m. Carol Elaine Todd, May 24, 1969; children: Christopher Wade, Deborah Anne. BA, Swarthmore Coll., 1963; MD, U. Mo., Columbia, 1968. Diplomate Am. Bd. Anesthesiology, Am. Bd. Internal Medicine. Intern, resident internal medicine U. Ky., Lexington, 1968-70; resident in anesthesiology and critical care Harvard U./Mass. Gen. Hosp., Boston, 1972-75; asst. prof. anesthesia and medicine U. Ariz. Coll. Medicine, Tucson, 1975-82, assoc. prof. anesthesia and medicine, 1982-88, prof. anesthesia, assoc. prof. medicine, 1988—; assoc. examiner Am. Bd. Anesthesiology, Hartford, Conn., 1986—; cons. FDA, Washington, 1986-88, NIH, Washington, 1991—. Assoc. editor Survey of Anesthesiology, Balt., 1984—; contbr. articles to profl. publs., chpts., to textbooks. Fellow Am. Coll. Critical Care Medicine; mem. AMA, Ariz. Med. Assn., Am. Soc. Anesthesiologists (alt. dir. 1989—), Ariz. Soc. Anesthesiologists (pres. 1984-85), Soc. Critical Care Medicine (dir. anesthesiology sect. 1991—), Assn. Univ. Anesthesiologists, Am. Soc. Critical Care Anesthesiologists. Office: U Ariz Dept Anesthesiology 1501 N Campbell Ave Tucson AZ 85724-0001

OTTO, JEAN HAMMOND, journalist; b. Kenosha, Wis., Aug. 27, 1925; d. Laurence Cyril and Beatrice Jane (Slater) Hammond; m. John A. Otto, Aug. 22, 1946; children: Jane L. Rahman, Mary Ellen Takayama, Peter J. Otto; m. Lee W. Baker, Nov. 23, 1973. Student, Ripon Coll., 1944-46. Women's editor Appleton (Wis.) Post-Crescent, 1960-68; reporter Milw. Jour., 1968-72, editorial writer, 1972-77, editor Op Ed page, 1977-83; editorial page editor Rocky Mountain News, Denver, 1983-89, assoc. editor, 1989-92, reader rep., 1992—; Endowed chair U. Denver, 1992—. Founder, chmn. bd. trustees First Amendment Congress, 1979-85, chmn. exec. com., 1985-88, 89-91, pres. 1991—, mem. bd. trustees, 1979—; founding mem. Wis. Freedom of Info. Council. Recipient Headliner award Wis. Women in Communications, 1974; Outstanding Woman in Journalism award YWCA, Milw., 1977; Knight of Golden Quill Milw. Presss Club, 1979; spl. citation in Journalism Ball State U., 1980; James Madison award Nat. Broadcast Editorial Assn., 1981; spl. citation for contbn. to journalism Nat. Press Photographers Assn., 1981; Ralph D. Casey award, 1984; U. Colo. Regents award, 1985; John Peter Zenger award U. Ariz., 1988; Paul Miller Medallion award Okla. State U., 1990; Colo. SPJ Lowell Thomas award, 1990, Disting. Alumna award Ripon Coll., 1992, Hugh M. Hefner First Amendment Lifetime Achievement award Playboy Found., 1994. Mem. Colo. Press Assn. (chmn. freedom of info. com. 1983-89), Assn. Edn. in Journalism and Mass Communications (Disting. Svc. award 1984), Am. Soc. Newspaper Editors (bd. dirs. 1987-92), Soc. Profl. Journalists (nat. treas. 1975, nat. sec. 1977, pres.-elect 1978, pres. 1979-80, First Amendment award 1981, Wells Key 1984, pres. Sigma Delta Chi Found. 1989-92, chair Found. 1992—), Milw. Press Club (mem. Hall of Fame 1993). Office: Rocky Mountain News 400 W Colfax Ave Denver CO 80204-2607

OTTO, JOSEPH CLAIR, information systems educator; b. Carroll, Iowa, Nov. 4, 1955; s. Clair Joseph and Lou Ann (Wolterman) O.; children: Tyler, Abigail, Hayley. BS, Iowa State U., 1978; MS, Ea. Ill. U., 1982; EdD, Memphis State U., 1987. Rsch. asst. Ea. Ill. U., Charleston, Ill., 1979-80; instr. Sparks Coll., Shelbyville, Ill., 1980-84, Memphis State U., 1984-86; prof. Calif. State U., L.A., 1986—; cons. Riverside C.C., Norco, Calif., 1992—, Glendale (Calif.) C.C., 1989—. Author: (textbooks) A Mastery Approach to Lotus 1-2-3, 2.3, 2.4, 1993, Spreadsheet Applications Job-Based Tasks, 1992, A Mastery Approach to Lotus 1-2-3, 2.2, 1991. Mem. Nat. Bus. Edn. Assn., Calif. Bus. Edn. Assn. (cert. of recognition 1994, Profl. Svc. award 1991; conf. com. 1986—, state legis. com., strategic planning com., past pres.), Delta Pi Epsilon (cert. of merit Nat. Coun. 1992, newsletter editor, treas. 1980—). Home: 12916 Saratoga Pl Chino Hills CA 91709-1103 Office: Calif State U 5151 State University Dr Los Angeles CA 90032-4221

OTTO, (BERTHA) MARIE, educational administrator, educational consulting company executive; b. Houston, July 11, 1930; d. Robert Lillard and Bertha Irene (Allen) Davis; m. Robert Lee Otto, Jan. 7, 1950; children: Lois Ann Otto Buschmann, Barbara Jeane Otto Hunt, Robert Lee Jr. Student, Tex. Christian U., 1947-49, Hardin-Simmons U., summers 1947, 49, 54; BA in Speech, Drama and Edn., Sul-Ross State U., 1954; postgrad., U. Wyo., 1961, U. Calif., Santa Barbara, 1962, Calif. State U., Northridge, 1964; MA, Calif. State U., Long Beach, 1969, postgrad., 1980-82. Lic. tchr., Tex., secondary tchr., Wyo., Calif.; lic. psychologist; lic. marriage and family counselor. Tchr. high schs., Tex., Wyo. and Calif., 1956-64; tchr., counselor Excelsior High Sch., Norwalk, Calif., 1964-66; counselor Neff High Sch., La Mirada, Calif., 1966-69; psychologist Huntington Beach (Calif.) Union High Sch. Dist., 1969-74, project mgr., dir. pupil pers., 1974-80, asst. supt., 1980-84, supt., 1984-88, supt. emeritus, 1988—; v.p. Poole-Young-Koehler Assocs., Inc., Long Beach, 1964-79; pvt. practice marriage and family counselor, Fountain Valley, Calif., 1970—; pres. Marie Otto Assocs., Fountain Valley, 1979—; supr. student tchrs. Chapman Univ. Orange, Calif., 1988—; sec.-treas., Ctr. for Teaching Thinking, Huntington Beach, 1991—. Mem. Fountain Valley Human Svcs. Com., Huntington Beach Human Resources Commn., state planning com. Girl Scouts U.S., Worland, Wyo., 1959-61; pres. Spl. Edn. Local Plan Orgn., 1983-84; bd. dirs. Humana Hosp. Huntington Beach, Golden West Coll. Found., Huntington Beach, Huntington Beach Community Clinic, Orange County chpt. ARC, Santa Ana, Calif, No on Drugs, 1988—; sec., treas. Ctr. for Teaching of Thinking, Huntington Beach, 1992—. Recipient numerous plaques, 1985—, including Fountain Valley Human Svcs. Com., 1979, City of Fountain Valley, 1975, 79, 88, City of Huntington Beach, 1988, Fountain Valley C. of C., 1988, City of Westminster, 1988, Orange Coast Coll., 1988, Golden West Coll., 1988, Ocean View Sch. Dist., 1988, Spl. Edn. Local Plan Orgn., 1984; named Woman of Yr., Soroptimist Club, Westminster, 1984, Disting. Alumnus, Grad. Sch. Edn. Calif. State U.-Long Beach, 1988. Home and Office: 16689 Mount Hoffman Cir Fountain Valley CA 92708

OTUS, SIMONE, public relations executive; b. Walnut Creek, Calif., Jan. 10, 1960; d. Mahmut and Alexa (Artemenko) O. BA, U. Calif., Berkeley, 1981. Account exec. Marx-David Advt., San Francisco, 1981-82; freelance writer Mpls. and San Francisco, 1982-83; account exec. D'Arcy, MacManus & Masius, San Francisco, 1983; account supr. Ralph Silver Assocs., San Francisco, 1984-85; ptnr., co-founder Blanc & Otus Pub. Relations, San Francisco, 1985—. Office: Blanc & Otus Pub Rels 100 Spear St Ste 425 San Francisco CA 94105-1524

OUSLEY, PAMELA DARLENE, legal assistant; b. Norman, Okla., June 26, 1956; d. Gary Lee and Edna Elmira (Horn) O. BA in Psychology, Phillips U., 1978; cert. paralegal, Denver Paralegal Inst., 1989. Office clk., sec. Marley Cooling Tower Co., Overland Park, Kans., 1980-81; acctg. clk. Colorado Springs (Colo.) Cablevision, 1981-84; check proofer-acctg. Current, Inc., Colorado Springs, 1985-86; accounts receivable clk. Garden of the Gods Club, Colorado Springs, 1986-89; paralegal intern Dist. Atty. 4th Jud. Dist., Colorado Springs, 1989; office clk. Western Temp. Svcs., Colorado Springs, 1989-90; legal researcher, writer Prestige Paralegal Svcs., Colorado Springs, 1990-91; office mgr. Queen & Co., Colorado Springs, 1990-91; legal asst. Wiley Hurst & Assocs., Yakima, Wash., 1991—. Author: Legal Dentistry = Toxic Free Dentistry, 1994, The Law and Mercury-Free Dentistry, 1994. Parliamentarian, v.p. Comet Club, Enid, Okla., 1975-78; v.p., pres. Circle K, Enid, 1976-78. Democrat.

OVERBY, PAUL, writer, political analyst; b. Hazelcrest, Ill., Nov. 27, 1942; m. Jane Leung Larson, June 21, 1980. BA, Reed Coll., Portland, Oreg., 1966. Founder Pub. Power Action Group, Portland, 1978-85. Author: Holy Blood: An Inside View of the Afghan War, 1993; contbr. articles to profl. jours.

OVERELL, WILLIAM LAWRENCE, finance executive; b. Bismarck, N.D., Dec. 30, 1947; s. Lawrence V. and M. Helen (Hynes) O.; m. Patricia Miskimen, June 7, 1969; children: Edward, Michael, Mary. BS, Purdue U., 1969; MBA, Stanford U., 1971. CPA, Calif. Cons. Arthur Andersen & Co., San Francisco, 1971-74; v.p., contr. Spectra Physics, San Jose, Calif., 1974-89; v.p. fin. and adminstrn., CFO Gamma Microwave, Santa Clara, Calif., 1989-90; cons. Los Altos, Calif., 1990-92; sr. v.p. fin., CFO Ins. Auto Auctions, North Hollywood, Calif., 1992—. Mem. Fin. Execs. Inst., AICPA, Assn. Computing Machinery. Roman Catholic. Home: 2120 Monterey Rd South Pasadena CA 91030-3939 Office: Ins Auto Auctions 7245 Laurel Canyon Blvd North Hollywood CA 91605-3709

OVERFELT, CLARENCE LAHUGH, lawyer; b. Big Timber, Mont., Apr. 15, 1935; s. Leo and Clara (Drivdahl) O.; m. Joyce Overfelt, Feb. 15, 1959 (div. 1977); children: Kent Leo, Reed Allen; m. Allyce Overfelt, Nov. 21, 1977. BA, U. Mont., 1958, JD, 1968. Bar: Mont. 1968, U.S. Dist. Ct. Mont. 1968. Ptnr. Randono Overfelt & Gianotti, Great Falls, Mont., 1968-73; pvt. practice Overfelt Law Firm, Great Falls, Mont., 1973-91, pres., sr. mem., 1980—; tchr. Cut Bank (Mont.) Pub. Schs., 1959-60, Helena (Mont.) Pub. Schs., 1960-65. Mem. Assn. Trial Lawyers Am., Mont. Trial Lawyers

Assn., Civil Justice Found., Meadowlark Country Club, Elks, Kiwanis. Democrat. Episcopalian. Home: 128 Lower River Rd Great Falls MT 59405-8203 Office: Overfelt Law Firm PC 121 4th St N Rm 2E Great Falls MT 59401-2552

OVERFELT, LEE, lawyer; b. Big Timber, Mont., Aug. 23, 1923; s. Leo and Clara (Drivdahl) O.; m. Dona Mae Skabo, June 11, 1947; children—Gary, Karen, Rika, Shelly, Brian. B.A., U. Mont., 1951, J.D., 1951. Bar: Mont. 1951, U.S. Dist. Ct. Mont. 1953, U.S. Ct. Appeals (9th cir.) Mont. 1955. Ptnr., Mouat & Overfelt, Billings, Mont., 1953-56; sole practice, Billings, 1956-79; ptnr. Overfelt Law Firm, Billings, 1981—; spl. prosecutor Custer County, Mont., 1971, Yellowstone County, Mont., 1973, Rosebud County, Mont., 1975. Served with USN, 1943-46. Mem. Am. Judicare, Assn. Trial Lawyers Am., Mont. Trial Lawyers, Yellowstone Valley Claimants Attys. (past pres.), Yellowstone County Bar Assn., VFW (past dist. comdr.), Mont. Wildlife Fedn. (past sec.), Phi Alpha Delta. Clubs: Billings Petroleum, Pryor Creek Golf, Elks, Mil. Order of Cooties. Office: Overfelt Law Firm 2812 1st Ave N Ste 410 Billings MT 59101-2312

OVERGAARD, WILLARD MICHELE, retired political scientist, jurisprudent; b. Montpelier, Idaho, Oct. 16, 1925; s. Elias Nielsen and Myrtle LaVerne (Humphrey) O.; m. Lucia Clare Cochrane, June 14, 1946; children: Eric Willard, Mark Fredrik, Alisa Claire. B.A., U. Oreg., 1949; Fulbright scholar, U. Oslo, 1949-50; M.A. (non-resident scholar 1954-55), U. Wis., Madison, 1955; Ph.D. in Polit. Sci. (adminstrv. fellow 1955-56, research fellow 1962-64), U. Minn., 1969. Instr., Soviet and internat. affairs Intelligence Sch., U.S. Army, Europe, 1956-62; dir. intelligence rsch. tng. program Intelligence Sch., U.S. Army, 1958-61; asst. prof. internat. affairs George Washington U., 1964-67; sr. staff polit. scientist Ops. Research Inst., U.S. Army Inst. Advanced Studies, Carlisle, Pa., 1967-70; assoc. prof. polit. sci., chmn. dept., dir. Internat. Studies Inst., Westminster Coll., New Wilmington, Pa., 1970-72; prof. polit. sci. and pub. law Boise (Idaho) State U., 1972-94, chmn. dept., 1972-87, acad. dir. M.P.A. degree program, personnel adminstr., mem. humanities council interdisciplinary studies in humanities, 1976-87, prof. of pub. law emeritus, 1994—, dir. Taft Inst. Seminars for Pub. Sch. Tchrs., 1985-87, coord. Legal Asst. Program, 1990—; mem. comml. panel Am. Arbitration Assn., 1974—; mem. Consortium for Idaho's Future, 1974-75; adv. com. Idaho Statewide Tng. Program Local Govt. Ofcls., 1974-78; adv. group Gov. Idaho Task Force Local Govt., 1977; co-dir. Idaho State Exec. Inst., Office of Gov., 1979-83; grievance hearing officer City of Boise, 1981-85; arbitrator U.S. Postal Svc., 1988-90; cons. in field. Author: The Schematic System of Soviet Totalitarianism, 3 vols, 1961, Legal Norms and Normative Bases for the Progressive Development of International Law as Defined in Soviet Treaty Relations, 1945-64, 1969; co-author: The Communist Bloc in Europe, 1959; editor: Continuity and Change in International Politics, 1972; chief editor: Idaho Jour. Politics, 1974-76. Served with USAAF, 1943-45; with AUS, 1951-54; ret. maj. USAR. Named Disting. Citizen of Idaho Idaho Statesman, 1979; named Outstanding Prof. of Sch. Social Scis. and Pub. Affairs, Boise State U., 1988. Mem. ABA (assoc.). Home: 2023 S Five Mile Rd Boise ID 83709-2316

OVERHOLT, MILES HARVARD, cable television consultant; b. Glendale, Calif., Sept. 30, 1921; s. Miles Harvard and Alma Overholt; A.B., Harvard Coll., 1943; m. Jessie Foster, Sept. 18, 1947; children: Miles Harvard, Keith Foster. Mktg. analyst Dun & Bradstreet, Phila., 1947-48; collection mgr. Standard Oil of Calif., L.A., 1948-53; br. mgr. RCA Svc. Co., Phila., 1953-63, ops. mgr. Classified Aerospace project RCA, Riverton, N.J., 1963; pres. CPS, Inc., Paoli, Pa., 1964-67; v.p. Gen. Time Corp.; mem. pres.'s exec. com. Gen. Time Corp., Mesa, Ariz., 1970-78; gen. mgr., dir. svc. Talley Industries, Mesa, 1967-78; v.p., gen. mgr. Northwest Entertainment Network, Inc., Seattle, 1979-81; v.p., dir. Cable Communication Cons., 1982—; mcpl. cable cons., 1981—; pub. The Mcpl. Cable Regulator. Served with USMCR, 1943-46. Decorated Bronze Star, Purple Heart (two). Mem. Nat. Assn. TV Officers and Advisors. Home: 8320 Frederick Pl Edmonds WA 98026-5033 Office: Cable Communication Cons 502 E Main St Auburn WA 98002-5502

OVERLY, FREDERICK DEAN, civilian military employee, entrepreneur; b. Miami, Fla., Jan. 2, 1953; s. Harry Robert and Beverly Beryl (Dengler) O.; m. Cheryl Diane Battle, June 23, 1975 (div. Aug. 1976); Joanne Elizabeth Smart, Dec. 28, 1979; children: Heidi Johanna, Melissa Elizabeth Emma. AA in Forestry, Fla. Jr. Coll., Jacksonville, 1975; BS in Ethology, So. Ill. U., 1980. Pers. officer First Interstate Bank, Anchorage, Alaska, 1985; pers. mgmt. Alaska NG, Anchorage, 1986-89, mgmt. analyst, 1989—; cons. Midnight Moon, Inc., Anchorage, 1989—. Participant Alaska Pacific rim issue, Commonwealth North, Anchorage, 1993. Maj. USAF, 1980-84; maj. Alaska Air N.G., 1984—. Mem. Res. Officers Assn., Air Force Assn. (past pres. chpt. 103), Found. N.Am. Wild Sheep, Alaska NG Officer Assn., Safari Club Internat., Roll-Royce Owners Club, Rotary Internat. Lutheran. Office: Alaskan NG 176 Group 5005 Raspberry Rd Anchorage AK 99502-1982

OVERMAN, LARRY EUGENE, chemistry educator; b. Chgo., Mar. 9, 1943; s. Lemoine Emerson and Dorothy Jane (Riggin) O.; m. Joanne Louise Dewey, June 5, 1966; children: Michael, Jackie. BA in Chemistry, Earlham Coll., 1965; PhD in Organic Chemistry, U. Wis., 1969. Asst. prof. chemistry U. Calif., Irvine, 1971-76, assoc. prof. chemistry, 1976-79, prof. chemistry, 1979—, chair dept. chemistry, 1990-93, disting. prof. chemistry, 1994—; bd. dirs. Organic Reactions, 1993—; mem. sci. adv. bd. Pharmacopeia, Inc., 1993—. Bd. editors Organic Reactions, 1984, Organic Synthesis, 1986-94; mem. editl. adv. bd. Ann. Reports in Hetero Chem., 1989—, Synlett, 1989—. NIH fellow, 1969-71, A.P. Sloan Found. fellow, 1975-77; Arthur C. Cope scholar, 1989; Guggenheim fellow, 1993-94; recipient Sr. Scientist award Alexander von Humboldt Found., 1985-87, Jacob Javits award Nat. Inst. Neurol. Sci., 1985-91. Mem. AAAS, Am. Chem. Soc. (exec. com. organic divsn., award for creative work in synthetic organic chemistry 1995), Japanese Chem. Soc., Swiss Chem. Soc., German Chem. Soc., Royal Soc. Chemistry. Office: U Calif Irvine Dept Chemistry Irvine CA 92717-2025

OVERMOEN, MARY ELLEN, dietitian; b. Mayville, N.D., Nov. 28, 1969; d. Lloyd Joseph and Denise Sharon (Ophus) O. BS, N.D. State U., 1992. Registered dietitian. Clin. dietitian S.D. Human Svcs. Ctr., Yankton, 1992-94; nutrition coord. Lewis County Sr. Svcs., Chehalis, Wash., 1994—. Mem. Am. Dietetic Assn. Office: Lewis County Sr Svcs 2545 N National Ave Chehalis WA 98532-2404

OVERTON, EDWIN DEAN, campus minister, educator; b. Beaver, Okla., Dec. 2, 1939; s. William Edward and Georgia Beryl (Fronk) O. BTh, Midwest Christian Coll., 1963; MA in Religion, Eastern N.Mex. U., 1969, EdS, 1978; postgrad. Fuller Theol. Sem., 1980. Ordained to ministry Christian Ch., 1978. Minister, Christian Ch., Englewood, Kans., 1962-63; youth minister First Christian Ch., Beaver, Okla., 1963-67; campus minister Central Christian Ch., Portales, N.Mex., 1967-68, Christian Campus House, Portales, N.Mex., 1968-70; tchr. religion, philosophy, counseling Eastern N.Mex. Univ., Portales, 1970—, campus minister, Christian Campus House, 1968—, dir., 1980—; farm and ranch partner, Beaver, Okla., 1963—. State dir. Beaver Jr. C. of C., 1964-65; pres. Beaver High Sch. Alumni Assn., 1964-65; elder Cen. Christian Ch., Portales, 1985-88, 1990-93; chmn. Beaver County March of Dimes, 1966; pres. Portales Tennis Assn., 1977-78. Mem. U.S. Tennis Assn., Am. Assn. Christian Counselors. Republican. Club: Lions. Home: 1129 Libra Dr Portales NM 88130-6123 Office: 223 S Avenue K Portales NM 88130-6643

OVERTON, JOHN FARRELL, electronic manufacturing executive, educator; b. San Francisco, Dec. 26, 1950; s. John J. and Lavaughn F. (Schaaf) O.; m. Merry Linda Reinke, Dec. 27, 1969; children: Shane Kelly, Todd Allan. BA, San Francisco State U., 1977; MBA, Golden Gate U., 1987. Electronics tchr. Buschser High Sch., Santa Clara, Calif., 1978; service station mgr. Chevron, Pacifica, Calif., 1978; supr. technicians Varian Assocs. EIMAC div., San Carlos, Calif., 1978-83; product assurance engr. Varian Assocs. EIMAC div., San Carlos, 1983-86, product assurance mgr., 1986-87, div. mfg. mgr., 1987-93; indsl. tech. instr. Bret Harte H.S., 1993—; adj. instr. Columbia Coll., 1993—. Served with USAF, 1969-76. Mem. Electronics Assn., Soc. Mfg. Engrs., Golden Gate Alumni Assn., Shriners, Masons, Eastern Star. Home: PO Box 968 Angels Camp CA 95222-0968 Office: Varian EIMAC Div PO Box 208 Altaville CA 95221-0208

OVIATT, KATY VALENTINE, editor, publisher; b. Orange, Calif.; d. Stanley Stephen and J. Margeurite Oviatt. Student, Golden West Coll., Huntington, Calif., 1 yr. Columnist Garden Grove (Calif.) Jour.; driver Yellow Cab, Orange County, Calif.; pub., editor Poor Katy's Almanac, Calif., 1994. Office: Poor Katys Almanac PO Box 913 Hayfork CA 96041-0913

OVIATT, LARRY ANDREW, educator; b. Boone, Iowa, Mar. 13, 1939; s. Eli Charles and T. Mae (Lathrop) O.; children: Julia, Vanessa, Dana. BA, Drake U., Des Moines, 1962; MS, San Diego State U., 1975. Tchr. art San Diego City Schs., 1969—, mentor tchr., 1992—; owner Perfect Travel of La Jolla, 1989—. San Diego dir. Anderson for Pres., 1976; dist. coord. Hedgecock for Mayor, San Diego, 1984; dir. Elder Help Corp., San Diego, 1988; v.p. African Am. Mus., 1989—; pres. Sushi Gallery, Inc., 1980—; bd. dirs. Mingei Internat. Mus., 1983-87; pres. Cmty. Svc. Assn., 1984-88; past pres. Diversionary Theatre, African Am. Mus.; dir. AIDS Walk for Life, 1988, 89; bd. dirs. AIDS Art Alive. Named 1986 Tchr. of Yr. Urban League, 1986, Sec. Art Tchr. of Yr. Calif. Art Tchrs. Assn., 1988, Art Tchr. of Yr. Calif. Art Tchrs. Assn., 1992, Vol. of Yr. San Diego City Schs., 1993. Mem. So. Calif. Art Tchrs. Assn. (pres. 1984-89), Calif. Art Edn. Assn. (dir. 1984-89, conf. adminstr., Art Edn. Tchr. of Yr. award 1992), Nat. Art Edn. Assn. (dir. 1987-93). Home: 1611 29th St San Diego CA 92102-1419 Office: San Diego City Schs 4100 Normal St San Diego CA 92103-2653

OW, DAVID WING, research geneticist; b. Hong Kong, Oct. 20, 1955; s. Polk Fay and Amy (Woo) O.; m. Yali Wang; children: Philip, Justin. AB, U. Calif., Berkeley, 1978; PhD, Harvard U., 1983. Postdoctoral fellow Mass. Gen. Hosp., Boston, 1983; vis. sci. Academia Sinica, Shanghai, China, 1983-84; NSF postdoctoral fellow U. Calif., La Jolla, 1984-86; sr. sci. Plant Gene Expression Ctr., USDA, Albany, 1986—. Monitoring editor Plant Physiology 1992—. Home: 127 Brenner Hercules CA 94547-3749 Office: USDA/ARS/PGEC 800 Buchanan St Berkeley CA 94710-1105

OWEN, CAROL THOMPSON, artist, educator; b. Pasadena, Calif., May 10, 1944; d. Sumner Comer and Cordelia (Whittemore) Thompson; m. James Eugene Owen, July 19, 1975; children: Kevin Christopher, Christine Celese. Student, Pasadena City Coll., 1963; BA with distinction, U. Redlands, 1966; MA, Calif. State U., L.A., 1967; MFA, Claremont Grad. Sch., 1969. Cert. community coll. instr., Calif. Head resident Pitzer Coll., Claremont, Calif., 1967-70; instr. art Mt. San Antonio Coll., Walnut, Calif., 1968—; dir. coll. art gallery Mt. San Antonio Coll., 1972-73. Group shows include Covina Pub. Libr., 1971, U. Redlands, 1964, 65, 66, 70, 78, 88, 92, Am. Ceramic Soc., 1969, Mt. San Antonio Coll., 1991, The Aesthetic Process, 1993, Separate Realities, 1995, others; ceramic mural commd. and installed U. Redlands, 1991. Mem. Calif. Scholarship Fedn., Faculty Assn. Mt. San Antonio Coll., Coll. Art Assn. Am., Calif. Tchrs. Assn., Friends of Huntington Library, L.A. County Mus. Art, Heard Mus. Assn., Sigma Tau Delta. Republican. Presbyterian. Home: 534 S Hepner Ave Covina CA 91723-2921 Office: Mt San Antonio Coll Grand Ave Walnut CA 91789

OWEN, CHARLES THEODORE, journalist, publisher; b. Beech Grove, Ind., June 14, 1941; s. James Robert and Helen Maurine (Sayre) O.; m. Kathleen Rose Dellaria, Apr. 29, 1967. AS in Journalism, Vincennes U., 1972; BA in Social Sci., Chapman Coll., 1976; MBA, Nat. U. San Diego, 1984. Enlisted U.S. Marine Corps, 1959-72, commd. 2d lt., 1973, advanced through grades to capt., 1979; combat journalist/photographer, Vietnam, 1967-68; dep. dir. Joint Pub. Affairs Office, Camp Pendleton, 1976-79; dir. Pub. Affairs Office, Marine Corps Recruit Depot, San Diego, 1980-81; dir. comm. and mil. affairs div. Greater San Diego C. of C., 1981-82, v.p. 1987—, bd. dirs., 1982-87; now pres., pub. San Diego Bus. Jour., 1987—; adj. prof. Nat. U., San Diego. Mem. San Diego County Cable TV Commn. Decorated Cross of Gallantry, medal of Honor 2d class (Vietnam); recipient Thomas Jefferson award, 1981. Mem. Marine Corps Combat Corrs. Assn., Pub. Rels. Soc. Am., Pub. Rels. Club San Diego (dir.), Press Club San Diego, Vietnam Vets. Leadership (dir.), Am. C. of C. Execs., Sigma Delta Chi. Republican. Pub. Newswriting Program Instruction, 1972. Office: 4909 Murphy Canyon Rd Ste 200 San Diego CA 92123-4300

OWEN, JOHN, retired newspaper editor; b. Helena, Mont., June 10, 1929; s. John Earl and Ella Jean (McMillian) O.; m. Alice Winnifred Kesler, June 9, 1951; children—David Scott, Kathy Lynn. B.A. in Journalism, U. Mont., 1951. Sports editor Bismarck (N.D.) Tribune, 1953-55; wire editor Yakima (Wash.) Herald, 1956; with Seattle Post-Intelligencer, 1956-94, sports editor, 1968-80, assoc. editor, 1980-94, columnist, 1968-94. Author: Intermediate Eater Cookbook, 1974, Gourmand Gutbusters Cookbook, 1980, Seattle Cookbook, 1983, Great Grub Hunt Cookbook, 1989, Press Pass, 1994; also short stories. Served with AUS, 1951-52. Named Top Sports Writer in Wash. Nat. Sportswriters Orgn., 1966, 68, 69, 71, 74, 85, 88. Home: 611 Bell St Apt 4 Edmonds WA 98020-3065

OWEN, PHILIP WALTER, mayor, business owner; b. Vancouver, B.C., Can., Mar. 11, 1933; s. Walter Stewart and Jean Margaret (Dowler) O.; m. Brita Johanne Busch, Dec. 6, 1957; children: Lise, Christian, Andrea. Store mgr. T. Eaton Co. Ltd., Vancouver, 1964-66; pres. Elysee Fabrics Ltd., N.Y.C., 1967-71, Elle Fabrics Ltd., Vancouver, 1972—, Manhasset Inv. Ltd., Vancouver, 1974—; v.p. L. Walker Industries Inc., Surrey, B.C., 1988—; commr. Bd. of Parks and Recreation, Vancouver, 1978-80; councillor City Coun., Vancouver, 1985-93; mayor City of Vancouver, 1993-96; chmn. Standing Com. on City Svcs. and Budgets; coun. rep. Downtown Parking Corp.; bd. dirs. Pacific Nat. Exhbn.; mem. Standing Com. on Planning and Environment, Vancouver Arts Initiative, Vancouver Liquor Licensing Commn. Mem. adv. com. B.C. Festival of the Arts; chmn. B.C. divsn. Nat. Fundraising Campaign, Can. Paraplegic Assn.; chmn. B.C. Paraplegic Found., B.C. Transit Pkwy. Com., The Bishop's Men; chmn. bd. variance Greater Vancouver Regional Dist.; chmn. transp. com. Independence '92, dir. Vancouver Art Gallery & the Endeavour Soc.; gov. St. George's Sch.; patron, dir. Rick Hansen Man in Motion World Tour; treas. Diocese New Westminster, pres. Downtown Vancouver Assn.; patron Internat. Found. of the Arts. Decorated Knights St. John, The Sovereign Order of St. John of Jerusalem-Knights Hospitaller, 1990. Mem. The Vancouver Club, The Arbutus Club. Anglican. Home: 3850 Marguerite St, Vancouver, BC Canada V6J 4E9 Office: City of Vancouver, 453 W 12th Ave, Vancouver, BC Canada V5Y 1V4

OWEN, WILLIAM FREDERICK, engineering and management consultant; b. Pontiac, Mich., July 27, 1947; s. Webster Jennings and Elizabeth (Hayes) W.; m. Delores T. Owen, Mar. 30, 1974 (div. Dec. 1978); m. Janice L. Pierce, July 29, 1983. BS, Mich. Tech. U., 1972; MS, U. Mich., 1973; PhD, Stanford U., 1978. Research engr. Neptune Microfloc, Corvallis, Oreg., 1973-75, process applications engr., 1975-76; process applications engr. Dr. Perry McCarty, Stanford, Calif., 1976-78; sr. engr. Culp/Wesner/Culp, Cameron Park, Calif., 1978-82; pres. Owen Engring. and Mgmt. Cos., Denver, 1982—. Author: Energy in Wastewater Treatment, 1982, Turbo Mainenance Manager. Del. People-to-People, People's Republic China, 1986. Served with USN, 1965-68. Recipient Local Govt. Innovations award Denver Regional Council Govt., 1983, Boettcher Innovations award Denver Regional Council Govt., 1984, Energy Innovations award Colo. Council Energy Ofcls., 1983. Club: Pinehurst Country (Denver). Home: 3829 S Chase St Denver CO 80235-2953 Office: Owen Engring and Mgmt Cons Inc 5353 W Dartmouth Ave Denver CO 80227

OWENS, A(RNOLD) DEAN, lawyer; b. Visalia, Calif., June 14, 1943; s. Clarence Cecil and Eula Mae (Boaz) O.; m. Marilyn Joyce Hatfield, Sept. 16, 1967; children: Eric, Rachel. BS, U. Calif., Berkeley, 1966; JD, U. Oreg., 1969. Bar: Oreg. 1969. Assoc. O'Reilly, Anderson, Richmonds & Adkins, Eugene, Oreg., 1969-71; ptnr. Anderson, Richmond & Owens, Eugene, 1971-74, Owens & Loomis, Eugene, 1975-79, Owens & Platt, Eugene, 1982-85; pvt. practice, Eugene, 1979-82, 85—; atty. City of Coburg, Oreg., 1971-79, City of Lowell, Oreg., 1973-79; hearings officer Lane County, Eugene, 1972—. Author: Advising Oregon Business Chpter 13, 1979; editor Lane County Bar News, 1980-87; also articles. Pres. Lane County Muscular Dystrophy Assn., Eugene, 1969-71; chmn. Eugene Human Rights Commn., 1969-71; bd. dirs. Asian Counseling Ctr., Eugene, 1991—; mem. exec. com. Lane County Rep. Party, Eugene, 1993—; mem. Eugene econ. devel. City of Eugene, 1989—; bd. dirs. Eugene-Springfield Met. Partnership, Inc., 1989-90; mem. exec. com. Eugene/Springfield Community Partnership, 1991—. Recipient cert. of appreciation Lane County Law Libr. Adv. Com., 1976-78, Bd. Lane County Legal Aid and Sr. Law Svcs., 1987, 90, spl. award and recognition of vol. svc. Eugene Sports Program, 1982. Mem. Eugene Area C. of C. (bd. dirs. 1986-90, pres. 1989, Disting. Svc. award 1986, 88), Emerald Exec. Assn. (pres. 1984), Eugene Swim and Tennis Club (pres. 1982), Eugene Country Club (chmn. tennis com. 1975-79), Downtown Athletic Club, Tri-Pass Water Ski Club, Eugene Active 20-30 Club (hon. life, editor newsletter 1969-72). Republican. Home: 2160 Oakmont Way Eugene OR 97401-2372 Office: 933 Pearl St Eugene OR 97401-2741

OWENS, GARY, broadcast personality, entrepreneur, author; b. Mitchell, S.D., May 10; s. Bernard and Vennetta O.; m. Arleta Lee Markell, June 26; children: Scott, Christopher. Student (speech and psychology scholar), Dakota Wesleyan U., Mitchell; student, Mpls. Art Inst. With Sta. KMPC, L.A., 1962-82; with Sta. KPRZ, L.A., 1982—, Sta KFI, L.A., 1986-90; pres. Foonman & Sons, Inc., 1987—; v.p., creative dir. GoldenWest Broadcasters, 1981-82; v.p., nat. creative dir. Gannett Broadcasting, 1984; TV performer, 1963—. writer Jay Ward Prodns., 1961-62; syndicated radio show The G.O. Spl. Report, from 1969; host: world-wide syndicated show Soundtrack of the 60's, 1981—, Biff Owens Sports Exclusive, 1981—; USA Today, Mut. Broadcasting System, 1982-83; radio host Gary Owens Music Weekend, Lorimar Telepictures, 1987—; performer, writer: world-wide syndicated show Sesame St, 1969—, Electric Co, 1969—, Dirkniblick (Mathnet) CTW, 1988; performer over 2500 animated cartoons including Dyno-Mutt, ABC-TV, 1975, Roger Ramjet, 1965, Space Ghost, 1968, Perils of Penelope Pitstop, 1970, Square One, 1987, Godzilla's Power Hour, 1979, Space Heroes, 1981, Mighty Orbots, 1984, World's Greatest Adventures, 1986, Garfield, Cops, Bobby's World, 1990, The 3 Musketeers, Return of Roger Ramjet, Alice in Wonderland, The Count of Monte Cristo, 20,000 Leagues Under the Sea, Godzilla, Mickey Mouse, Donald Duck, Goofy Chip N'Dale, Bill & Ted's Great Adventure, Tom & Jerry Jr., Eek the Cat, Swat Kats, Two Stupid Dogs, Ren & Stimpy, Bonkers, Dirk Niblick, numerous others, 1990; appeared: in films The Love Bug, 1968, Prisoner of Second Ave., 1975, Hysterical, 1982, Nat. Lampoon's European Vacation, 1985, I'm Gonna Get You Sucka, 1988, Kill Crazy, 1988, How I Got Into College, 1988, Say Bye Bye, 1989, Green Hornet, 1966 Regular on series; performer on camera more than 1000 nat. TV shows; performer: Rowan and Martin's Laugh-in, 1968-73; TV host: Gong Show, ABC-TV, 1976, Monty Pythons Flying Circus, 1975; regular performer: TV Games People Play, 1980-81, Breakaway, 1983; TV spls. include Bob Hope Spls., Like Hep, The Muppets Go Hollywood, Perry Como Visits Hollywood, The Gary Owens All-Nonsense News Network, Jonathan Winters & Friends, NBC's 50 Years, CBS's 50 Years, Battle of Beverly Hills, America's Choice. The American Comedy Awards, 1986—, Flip Wilson's Spls., Saturday Night at the Superbowl, Mickey Mouse's 50th Birthday; author: Elephants, Grapes and Pickles, 1963; 12 printings The Gary Owens What To Do While Your're Holding the Phone Book, revised edit., 1973, A Gary Owens Chrestomathy, 1980; host Encore Pay TV, 1992; author: (screenplay) Three Caraway Seeds and an Agent's Heart, 1979; columnist: Radio and Records newspaper, 1978—, Hollywood Citizen-News, 1965-67, Hollywood mag., 1983—, The Daily News, 1981—; rec. artist MGM, ABC, Epic, Warner Bros., RCA, Reprise, Decca; TV announcer NBC, 1968-80, ABC, 1980—; host many top video's in U.S. including Dinosaurs, More Dinosaurs, Son of Dinosaurs, TV's Greatest Bits; host: How to Collect Comic Books, Aliens, Dragons, Monsters and Me, Gone Fishing, 1993, The Gary Owens All-Nonsense News Network. Chmn. Multiple Sclerosis dr. L.A., 1972; chmn., grand marshall So. Calif. Diabetes Dr., 1974—; mayor City of Encino, Calif., 1972-74; bd. govs. Grammy Awards, 1968—, Emmy Awards, 1972; mem. adv. bd. Pasadena (Calif.) City Coll., 1969—, Sugar Ray Robinson Youth Found., 1971—; mem. nat. miracle com. Juvenile Diabetes Found., 1981—, nat. com. for Carousel Ball Children's Diabetes Found. Denver; radio adv. bd. U. So. Calif., 1980—; hon. chmn. Goodwill Industries Sporting Goods Dr., 1986, chmn., 1986; active telethons Cerebral Palsy, 1980, DARE program, 1985—, S.A.N.E. program, 1985—, comic relief to help U.S. Homeless, 1986. Named outstanding radio personality in U.S., 1965-79, top Radio Personality in World, Internat. Radio Forum, Toronto, 1977, Man of Yr. All-Cities Employees Assn., City of Los Angeles, 1968, Top RadAssn. Broadcasters, 1986, Radio Man of Yr. Nat. Assn. Broadcasters, 1986; recipient Distinguished Service award Hollywood Jaycees, 1966, David award, 1978, Hollywood Hall of Fame award, 1980, Am. award Cypress Coll., 1981, Carbon Mike award Pacific Broadcasters, 1987, 5 Grammy nominations, Emmy award for More Dinosaurs, 1986; Star on Hollywood Walk of Fame, 1981; honored by U.S. Dept. Treasury, 1985, Am. Diabetes Assn., 1990, Variety Clubs Internat., 1990; inducted into Nat. Broadcasters Hall of Fame, 1994, Radio Hall of Fame, 1994, Nat. Assn. Broadcasters Hall of Fame, 1995. Mem. Nat. Cartoonists Soc., So. Calif. Cartoonists Assn., Cartoonists and Artists Profl. Soc. Office: 2444 Wilshire Blvd Ste 506 Santa Monica CA 90403-5813

OWENS, HOWARD BENJAMIN, III, district director, writer; b. San Diego, Calif., June 19, 1961; s. Howard B. and Rosemary June (Stet)O.; m. Billie Sutherland, Aug. 21, 1993; stepchildren: Jacob, Charles. Student, U. Maine, 1980, Allen Hancocl Cmty. Coll., Santa Maria, Calif., 1982-84, Point Loma Nazarene Coll., San Diego, 1985-87. Law enforcement USAF, 1980-84; staff writer The Beacon, San Diego, 1987; co-owner, asst. editor The Beacon, 1987-88; reporter Carlsbad (Calif.) Journ., 1988-89; reporter, wire editor The Daily Californian, El Cajon, 1989-93; legislative aide Calif. Assembly, Lemon Grove, 1992-94; dist. dir., 1994—. Contbr. articles to profl. jours. Task force mem. Justice Fellowship, Sacramento, 1994; active San Diego Dem. Cen. Com., 1993—. Mem. Soc. Profl. Journalists (bd. dirs. San Diego chpt. 1990, treas. 1990-92), SDX Found. (bd. dirs. 1991-93), Calif. First Amendment Coalition, Am. Legion Post 282 (historian), AmVets Post 17. Office: Assemblyman Tom Connolly 3293 Olive St Lemon Grove CA 91945-1723

OWENS, ROBERT PATRICK, lawyer; b. Spokane, Wash., Feb. 17, 1954; s. Walter Patrick and Cecile (Phillippay) O.; m. Robin Miller, Aug. 12, 1978; children: Ryan Barry, Meghan Jane. BA, Wash. State U., 1976; JD, Gonzaga U., 1981; LLM in Admiralty Law, Tulane U., 1983. Bar: Wash. 1982, Alaska 1984, U.S. Dist. Ct. (ea. dist.) Wash. 1982, U.S. Dist. Ct. Alaska 1984, U.S. Ct. Appeals (5th cir.) 1983. Assoc. Groh, Eggers & Price, Anchorage, 1983-88; mng. atty. Taylor & Hintze, Anchorage, 1988-90; assoc. Copeland, Landye, Bennett and Wolf, Anchorage, 1990—. Coord. supplies Insight Seminars, Anchorage, 1985-86. Mem. ABA (dist. 27 rep. young lawyers div. 1988-90), Alaska Bar Assn., Wash. State Bar Assn., Anchorage Bar Assn. (pres. 1991-92, v.p. 1990-91, pres. young lawyers sect. 1986-88), Alaska Fly Fishers, Phi Alpha Delta. Roman Catholic. Office: Copeland Landye Bennett & Wolf 550 W 7th Ave Ste 1350 Anchorage AK 99501-3565

OWENS, ROBERT RAYMOND, minister; b. Janesville, Wis., June 18, 1949; s. William H. and Shirley May (Ross) O.; m. Maryellen Grady, Apr. 13, 1968 (div. Aug., 1976); m. Rosalie S. Owens, July 12, 1985; 1 child, Jefferson D. Teel. AA in Bible Studies, Internat. Sem., Orlando, Fla., 1980; B of Religious Edn., Trinity Bible Coll., Newburgh, Ind., 1982; M of Religious Edn., Trinity Theol. Sem., Newburgh, Ind., 1983; postgrad. studies, Northern Ariz. U., 1993—. Co-owner The Rust Shop Antiques, South Haven, Mich., 1972-76; owner, mgr. Rainbowsend Antiques, South Haven, 1976-79; owner St. Judes Christian Books, South Haven, 1977-84; owner, mgr. Owens Audio Art, Chgo., 1977-84; pastor The Full Gospel Redemption Ctr., Apache Junction, Ariz., 1984-92; pres., pastor Owens Family Ministries, Munds Park, Ariz., 1988—; pres. Hope Pregnancy Crisis Ctr., Apache Junction, 1992—. Author: Ephesians--a Pentecostal Survey, 1990, Backstreet Tales, 1994; co-inventor Uni-Directional Speakers, 1973. Mem. Rep. Nat. Com., Washington, 1980—. Mem. Arizona Clay Club, Golden Key, Mortar Bd., Phi Theta Kappa , Phi Alpha Theta. Pentecostal. Home: 17270 Navajo Pl Munds Park AZ 80017

OWENS, WARNER BARRY, physical therapist; b. Detroit, Apr. 29, 1939; s. Wendell Lee and Flora Lucille (Maddox) O.; m. Frances Hutton, June 11, 1960 (div. May 1973); children—Jeffrey, Karen; m. Sandra Irene Olstyn, Nov. 16, 1974. B.S., UCLA, 1962. Staff phys. therapist Valley Phys. Therapy Ctr., Van Nuys, Calif., 1962-63; chief phys. therapist St. Joseph Med. Ctr., Burbank, Calif., 1963-70, dir. rehab., 1970—, bd. dirs. Credit Union, 1974-76, 83-91, pres., 1986-91; pres. Therapeutic Assocs. Inc., Sherman Oaks, 1992—; dir. Tetrad and Assocs., Sherman Oaks, 1972—; chmn. bd. dirs. Nat. Physical Rehab. Network, Inc.; mem. admissions com. phys. therapy option Calif. State U.-Northridge, 1976—. Childrens Hosp. Sch. Phys. Therapy Kate Crutcher scholar, 1961; recipient Outstanding Contbn. to

Profession award Calif. State U.-Northridge, 1983. Mem. Am. Phys. Therapy Assn. (chmn. jud. com. 1981-82), Am. Coll. Sports Medicine, Phys. Therapy Dirs. Forum, Internat. Wine and Food Soc. (bd. dirs. San Fernando Valley 1979—, pres. 1980). Republican. Home: 4428 Gloria Ave Encino CA 91436-3451 Office: Therapeutic Assocs Inc 15060 Ventura Blvd Van Nuys CA 91403

OWINGS, DONALD HENRY, psychology educator; b. Atlanta, Dec. 7, 1943; s. Markley James and Loyce Erin (White) O.; m. Sharon Elizabeth Calhoun, Jan. 29, 1966; children: Ragon Matthew, Anna Rebekah. BA in Psychology, U. Tex., 1965; PhD, U. Wash., 1972. Asst. prof. psychology U. Calif., Davis, 1971-78, assoc. prof., 1978-83, prof., 1983—, chair dept., 1989-93. Contbr. articles to profl. jours., book chpts. NSF rsch. grantee, 1978-80, 82-84. Mem. Animal Behavior Soc., Internat. Soc. for Ecol. Psychology, Internat. Soc. for Behavioral Ecology, Internat. Soc. for Comparative Psychology. Democrat. Home: 815 Oeste Dr Davis CA 95616-1856 Office: U Calif Dept Psychology Davis CA 95616-8686

OWINGS, MARGARET WENTWORTH, conservationist, artist; b. Berkeley, Calif., Apr. 29, 1913; d. Frank W. and Jean (Pond) Wentworth; m. Malcolm Millard, 1937; 1 child, Wendy Millard Benjamin; m. Nathaniel Alexander Owings, Dec. 30, 1953. A.B., Mills Coll., 1934; postgrad., Radcliffe Coll., 1935; LHD, Mills Coll., 1993. One-woman shows include Santa Barbara (Calif.) Mus. Art, 1940, Stanford Art Gallery, 1951, stitchery exhbns. at M.H. De Young Mus., San Francisco, 1963, Internat. Folk Art Mus., Santa Fe, 1965. Commr. Calif. Parks, 1963-69, mem., Nat. Parks Found. Bd, 1968-69; bd. dirs. African Wildlife Leadership Found., 1968-80, Defenders of Wildlife, 1969-74; founder, pres. Friends of the Sea Otter, 1969-90; chair Calif. Mountain Lion Preservation Found., 1987; trustee Environmental Def. Fund, 1972-83; Regional trustee Mills Coll., 1962-68. Recipient Gold medal, Conservation Svc. award U.S. Dept. Interior, 1975, Conversation award Calif. Acad. Scis., 1979, Am. Motors Conservation award, 1980, Joseph Wood Krutch medal Humane Soc. U.S., Nat. Audubon Soc. medal, 1983, A. Starker Leopole award Calif. Nature Conservancy, 1986, Gold medal UN Environment Program, 1988, Conservation award DAR, 1990, Disting. Svc. award Sierra Club, 1991. Home: Grimes Point Big Sur CA 93920

OWINGS, SUZANN M., consultant, educator; b. L.A., Jan. 26, 1947; d. Theodore Raymond and Elizabeth Marie (Robb) O. BA, Calif. State U., L.A., 1969; MAT, Ind. U., 1971; PhD, U. N.Mex., 1978. Adminstr. Ind. U., Bloomington, 1970-71; tchr. Compton (Calif.) Sr. High Sch., 1971-75; cons. Owings, Albuquerque, 1975-78; assoc. dir. Energy Consumers of N.Mex., Albuquerque, 1978-79; statewide comprehensive planner CES, N.Mex. State U., Albuquerque, 1979; strategic planner Bechtel Inc., San Francisco, 1979-83; dean Golden Gate U., San Francisco, 1983-84; cons. Bitn Assocs., Corrales, N.Mex. and L.A., 1984—; instr. mgmt. Troy State U., U. Phoenix, Chapman U.. co-author, co-editor Southwest Images and Trends: Factors in Community Development, 1979 and numerous others. Co-founder Rio Rancho 2000, 1992-93; mem., chmn. Sandoval County Intergovtl./Bus. Adv. Coun., Bernalillo, N.Mex., 1993—; mem. Sandoval County Econ. Devel. Com., 1991—. Mem. ASTD (v.p., bd. dirs.), Am. Soc. for Pub. Adminstrn. (v.p. publs.), Optimist Club N.W. Albuquerque (bd. dirs., bull. editor). Home: PO Box 872 Placitas NM 87043-0872

OWNBEY, LENORE F. DALY, real estate investment specialist; b. Fremont, Nebr., Feb. 24; d. Joseph E. and Anna R. (Godel) Daly; m. Amos B. Ownbey, June 18, 1948; children: Kenton, Stephen. BBA, U. Nebr. Cert. comml. investment mem. Real estate and comml. investment specialist, 1976—; lectr. in field. Writer, speaker Investment, Business and Personal Skills, Motivational and Inspirational. Recipient Ptnrs. in Excellence Achievement award Colo. Chpt. Nat. Speakers Assn., 1988, Cert. of Proclamation Internat. Women of Yr., 1992-93. Mem. Nat. Assn. Realtors, Colo. Assn. Realtors, Denver Bd. Realtors (life mem.), Comml. Investment Real Estate Inst. (life mem., cert. comml. investment mem.).

OYER, SARAH ELIZABETH, lawyer; b. Elkhart, Ind., July 2, 1957; d. John Stanley and Carol Joyce (Schertz) O. Student, U. Vienna, Acad. of Music, 1978-79; BA in German and Music, Goshen Coll., 1980; MusM in Violin, Hartt Sch. Music, 1983; JD, Yale U., 1993. Bar: Wash. 1993. Libr. asst. Robinson & Cole, Hartford, Conn., 1983-85; instr. violin and viola Hartford Camerata Conservatory, 1985-90; assoc. Ctr. for Internat. Environ. Law, Washington, summer 1991, Preston, Thorgrimson, Shidler, Gates & Ellis, Seattle, summer 1992, Preston, Gates & Ellis, Seattle, 1993—. Sr. editor Yale Jour. Internat. Law. Violinist Hartford Symphony Orch., 1983-90, com. mem., 1985-89, musician's rep. to bd. of dirs., 1987-89, vice-chair negotiating com., 1988, chair orch. com., 1988-89. Conn. Bar Found. Pub. Interest fellow, 1991-93. Mem. Wash. Women Lawyers Assn., Sierra Club. Office: Preston Gates & Ellis 701 5th Ave Ste 5000 Seattle WA 98104-7016

OZANICH, CHARLES GEORGE, real estate broker; b. Fayette County, Pa. Aug. 11, 1933; s. Paul Anthony and Alma Bertha (Sablotne) O.; student Am. River Coll., Sierra Coll.; m. Betty Sue Carman, Feb. 20, 1955; children: Viki Lynn, Terri Sue, Charles Anthony, Nicole Lee. Owner, broker Terrace Realty, Basic Realty, Grass Valley, Calif., 1971—; compliance inspector Dept. Vets. Affairs. Mem. Grass Valley Vol. Fire Dept., 1965-93. Served with USAF, 1951-55; Korea. Decorated Bronze Star with three oak leaf clusters, Korean Presdl. citation, UN citation. Mem. Neveda County Bd. Realtors (dir. 1973-74). Lodges: Masons, Shriners. Nat. Champion award Truck Drivers Roadeo class 5 semi-trailer 18 wheeler div., 1954. Home: 15053 Chinook Ln Grass Valley CA 95945-8846 Office: 10113 Alta Sierra Dr Ste 100 Grass Valley CA 95949-6896

OZAWA, TERUTOMO, economics educator, consultant; b. Yokohama, Japan, Jan. 17, 1935; came to U.S., 1959, naturalized, 1973; s. Hanjiro and Tsuru (Teramura) O.; m. Hiroko Aoyama, Nov. 4, 1967; children: Edwin, Clare. BA, Tokyo U. of Fgn. Studies, 1958; MBA, Columbia U., 1962, PhD, 1966. Prof. econs. Colo. State U., Ft. Collins, 1974—; vis. rsch. assoc. Ctr. for Policy Alternatives, MIT, Cambridge, Mass., 1975-76; vis. scholar Cambridge (Eng.) U., 1982-83; vis. prof. U. Paris, Sorbonne, 1993; cons. to UN agys. and OECD. Author: Multinationalism, Japanese Style, 1979; Japan's General Trading Companies: Merchants of Economic Development, 1984, Recycling Japan's Surpluses for Developing Countries, 1989; also other books and articles. Mem. Am. Econ. Assn. Home: 648 Heather Ct Fort Collins CO 80525-2209 Office: Colo State U Dept Econs Fort Collins CO 80523

OZBIRN, KATHERINE MICHEALLE, English language educator and poet; b. Fullerton, Calif., June 22, 1957; d. James Allen Ozbirn and Donnie Maxine (Carawan) Dettle; 1 child, Alexander Ozbirn-Murray. BA in Speech, Calif. State U., Fullerton, 1979, MA in English, 1982. Cert. tchr. cmty. colls., tech. writing, Calif. Instructional writer Transamerica Fin. Svcs., L.A., 1982-83; asst. editor Rockwell Internat., Anaheim, Calif., 1983-85; editor Hughes Aircraft Co., Anaheim, 1985-88; prof. Chapman U., Orange, Calif., 1986—; adj. part-time prof. Mt. San Antonio Coll., Walnut, Calif., 1988—; cons. in bus. writing. Author: (poetry) Beyond Sand Crabs, 1982, The Screaming Machine, 1987; co-editor: Poetry Fullerton, Number 4, 1985; asst. editor: The Webs We Weave, 1986; editor Calif. Quar., 1993; author: Summarizing: The Art of Writing Abstracts and Executive Summaries, 1994. Mem. MLA, Acad. Am. Poets, Soc. Tech. Comm., Assn. for Bus. Communicators, Assn. for Study of Lit. and Environment. Republican. Roman Catholic. Office: Chapman Univ Dept English 333 N Glassell St Orange CA 92666-1011

OZBUTUN, CETIN, software engineer; b. Fatsa, Ordu, Turkey, Feb. 1, 1965; came to the U.S., 1987; s. Mahir and Meryem (Gunduz) O. BS in Computer Sci., Hacettepe U., 1986; MS in Computer Sci., Brown U., 1989. Sr. mem. tech. staff Oracle Corp., Redwood Shores, Calif., 1989—. Recipient High Achievement award Ihsan Dogramaci Found., Turkey, 1986. Mem. Assn. for Computing Machinery. Office: Oracle Corp 500 Oracle Pky Redwood City CA 94065-1600

ÖZKARAGÖZ, INCI ZÜHRA, linguist; b. Ankara, Turkey, Aug. 29, 1954; came to U.S., 1959; d. Ethem and Nihal (Aksoy) Ö. BA, U. Bosphorus, Istanbul, Turkey, 1976; MA, U. Calif., La Jolla, 1979, PhD, 1986. Tech. writer SoftCraft, Inc., San Diego, 1987-88; linguist Systran, La Jolla, 1988-89, Emerson & Stern Assocs., San Diego, 1989-90; tech. writer Sci. Applications Internat. Corp., San Diego, 1990-92; lectr. English, U Calif. San Diego Ext., La Jolla, 1992; asst. v.p. Chicks Franchising Ltd., San Diego, 1992-93; linguist Davidson, Torrance, Calif., 1994—. Contbr. articles to profl. jours. Mem. Linguistics Soc. Am., Assn. Computational Linguists.

OZMINKOWSKI, MARIUSZ, journalist, educator; b. Kowal, Poland, Mar. 26, 1956; came to the U.S., 1981; s. Jan and Jolanta Ozminkowski. BA in Philosophy, Warsaw U., 1981; MA in Comm., Calif. State U., L.A., 1990-92; postgrad., Claremont Grad. Sch., 1993—. Journalist various papers and radios, Poland, 1980-90; prof. Calif. State U., L.A., 1990-94; corr. in L.A. Gazeta Wyborcza, Warsaw, 1991—. Editor (underground jour. in Poland) Yes, But..., 1976-81. Activist in anti-communist student movement, 1976-81. Named Best of Show in the annual AA Competition, Oceanside/Carlsbad Art League, 1987. Office: 293 Ohio St # 11 Pasadena CA 91106

PAAP, CHRISTOPHER MARK, pharmacy educator and researcher. BS in Pharmacy, U. Colo., 1983; PharmD, U. Utah, 1988. Lic. pharmacist, Tex., Colo.; cert. pharmacotherapy specialist, 1992. Resident in clin. pharmacy U. Utah, Salt Lake City, 1988; rsch. fellow in pediat. pharmacokinetics/infectious disease Ohio State U. and Children's Hosp., Columbus, 1990; pharmacist intern Kohler's Bon Pharmacy, Colorado Springs, Colo., 1980-82, Mercy Med. Ctr., Denver, 1982-83; staff pharmacist U. Tex. Med. Br., Galveston, 1983-85, Humana Med. Ctr. Hosp., Dallas, 1985-86, VA Med. Ctr., Salt Lake City, 1986-88; clin. instr. Coll. Pharmacy U. Utah, Salt Lake City, 1987-88, Ohio State U., Columbus, 1988-90; asst. prof. Coll. Pharmacy U. Tex., Austin, 1990-94; asst. prof. Sch. Pharmacy, U. Colo., Denver, 1994—; clin. pharmacist Denver Children's Hosp., 1994—; poison info. pharmacist Intermountain Regional Poison Control Ctr., Salt Lake City, 1987-88; rsch. cons. Austin Diagnostic Clinic, 1991; pediatric clin. pharmacist, coord. Children's Hosp., Austin, 1990-94; referee Annals of Pharmacotherapy, Hosp. Formulary, Jour. Clin. Pharmacology and Therapeutics, Jour. Pharmacy Practice, Jour. Infectious Disease Pharmacotherapy, Pediat. Pharmacotherapy, 1990, Am. Soc. Hosp. Pharmacists Publs., 1992; mem. curriculum com. Coll. Pharmacy U. Utah, 1987-88; mem. postgrad. continuing edn. seminar com. Coll. Pharmacy U. Tex., Austin, 1991, PharmD admissions com., 1991-93, computer com., 1990, 92, joint PharmD com., 1990—, human rsch. departmental rev. com., 1992—, space utilization com., 1992—; mem. Ethical Bd. of Rev., Austin, 1991-94; Colo. Multi Instl. Review Bd., 1994—; presenter in field. Author: (with others) Pediatric Pharmacotherapy, 1990, 2d edit., 1992, The Clinical Use of Drugs, 1994; mem. editorial bd. Annals Pharmacotherapy; contbr. articles to profl. jours. Mem. adv. coun. task force on alcohol, drugs, and srs., Interagy. Coun. on Aging, Austin, 1993-94; mem. health occupations adv. com. Health Occupations Edn., Tex. Edn. Agy., Austin, 1992-93. Recipient NSF scholarship and enrichment award, 1977, scholarship U. Utah, 1987; grantee Upjohn Pharm. Co., 1993—, Tex. Soc. Hosp. Pharmacists Rsch. and Ednl. Found., 1991-92, U. Tex., 1990—, Austin Diagnostic Clinic, 1991—, Hoechst-Roussel Pharms., 1989-90, U. Utah, 1987, U. Colo., 1980, Nat. Inst. Drug Abuse, 1992; fellow Merck Co. Found., 1989. Mem. Am. Soc. Hosp. Pharmacists, Am. Coll. Clin. Pharmacy (rsch. affairs com. 1991-92), Am. Assn. Colls. Pharmacy (membership and resolution com. 1990-91), Tex. Soc. Hosp. Pharmacists (bd. dirs. 1992-94, Rsch. award 1991, Austin Area Soc. Hosp. Pharmacists (planning com. 1991-92, pres.-elect 1992-93, pres. 1993-94), Pediat. Pharmacy Advocacy Group, Internat. Assn. Therapeutic Drug Monitoring and Clin. Toxilogy (charter), Rho Chi. Office: Sch Pharmacy U Colo Box C238 4200 E 9th Ave Denver CO 80262

PAAUW, DOUGLAS STEPHEN, medical educator, primary care physician; b. Lake Forest, Ill., Nov. 16, 1958; s. Douglas Seymour and Helen Kaye (Horan) P.; m. Kathryn Ann Wells, Aug. 15, 1981; 1 child, Carly. BA, Macalaster Coll., St. Paul, 1980; MD, U. Mich., 1985. Diplomate Am. Bd. Internal Medicine. Assoc. prof. dept. medicine U. Wash. Sch. Medicine, Seattle, 1989—. Fellow ACP, Clerkship Dirs. in Internal Medicine; mem. Soc. Gen. Internal Medicine (regional coun. 1993-94). Home: 2617 185th Ave NE Redmond WA 98052-5922 Office: U Wash Med Ctr RG-20 Seattle WA 98195

PABISZ, MICHAEL JOSEPH, electrical engineer; b. Toppenish, Wa., Nov. 28, 1958; s. Max Joseph and Bonnie (Beezly) P.; m. Aida Luz Rivera, Apr. 1, 1989; children: Tania, Tasha. BS in forestry, Wash. State U., 1982, BSEE, 1988. Natural resource aide Wash. Dept. Natural Resources, Sultan, Wash., 1981-83, forest tech., 1983-84, forest worker, 1984; intern engr. Rockwell Hanford Ops., Richland, Wash., 1987; co-op engr. Westinghouse Hanford Co., Richland, Wash., 1987-88, plant elec. engr., 1988-89; flight controls engr. Boeing Comml. Airplane Group, Everett, Wash., 1989—; 777 Fly By Wire test team Boeing Comml. Airplanes, Seattle, 1991-92; ride quality engr., flight control systems, Everett, 1990—. Named to Wash. State U. Nat. Crew Team, 1981. Mem. Tau Beta Pi, Xi Sigma Pi. Republican. Roman Catholic. Home: 5428 Parkview Ln Everett WA 98203-3480 Office: Boeing Comml Airplane Group Seattle WA 98124

PACE, ELIZABETH KRISTIN, free lance researcher; b. Mpls., Jan. 31, 1956; d. Neal Frederick Johnson and Margaret (Brenneman) Laird. Student, Ohio State U., 1976, U. Minn., 1983-85. Compounding technician Pillsbury Co., Mpls., 1979-80; advt. prodn. mgr. Callan Publishing, Mpls., 1980-82; festival dir. New Front Programming Svcs., Mpls., 1984-85; comm. technician MBA Comm. Skills Program, Mpls., 1984-85; asst. to agt. William Morris Agy., Beverly Hills, Calif., 1985-87; asst. to producer Dreyfuss/James Prodns., L.A., 1987-89; office mgr. Van Zerneck, Seffner Prodns., Studio City, Calif., 1989-91; free lance, rschr., cons. L.A., 1991—; cons., rschr. BRC Imagination Arts, Ctr. for Fgn. Policy Options, Creative Artists Agy., Walt Disney Co., HBO, Steve White Prodns. Big sester Big Brothers, Big Sisters, Columbus, Ohio, 1974-75; precinct block capt. DFL Orgn., Mpls., 1983-84; co-chair LA Works In-kind Donations Com., project coord. Group Action; vol. Kathleen Brown for Gov. campaign, 1994. Recipient Catherine MacPherson scholarship U. Minn., 1982. Mem. Cinewomen (bd. dirs. 1990-93, newsletter columnist, 1993-94), Ind. Feature Project, West, Women in Non-Profits. Home and Office: 5044 Cahuenga Blvd Apt 10 North Hollywood CA 91601-4749

PACE, FELICE, environmentalist; b. Phila., Jan. 10, 1947; s. Frank Joseph and Kathryn Elizabeth (Lazzaro) P.; m. Diana Lynn Strickland, Apr. 8, 1987; children: Jacob Duncan, Miranda Rose. BA, Yale U., 1969; MA, Montclair State U., 1971. Life cert. tchr., Calif. Social studies tchr. Trenton (N.J.) High Sch., 1969-70; program specialist Project USE - Outdoor Edn., Princeton, N.J., 1970-73; assoc. trainer dept. psychiatry Yale U., New Haven, 1973-75; cmty. devel. specialist No. Calif. Indian Devel. Coun., Eureka, 1975-79; pvt. cons. to tribal govts. Peters & Assocs., Eureka, 1980-83; prevention coord. Siskiyou County Mental Health Svcs., Yreka, Calif., 1983-86; dir. social svcs. Karuk Tribe Calif., Happy Camp, Calif., 1986-88; program dir. Klamath Forest Alliance, Etna, Calif., 1989—; co-founder, bd. mem. Mable Mt. Audubon Soc., Ft. Jones, Calif., 1980—; chmn., exec. com. Calif. Ancient Forest Alliance, Davis; panelist Pres. Clinton's Forest Conf., Portland, Oreg., 1993; presenter Symposium on Ecosystem Mgmt./Libr. Congress, Washington, 1994. Author, contbr.: Clearcut: The Failure of Industrial Forestry, 1994, Landscape Linkages and Biodiversity, 1992; contbg. editor Siskiyon Jour., 1983-87; creator, reporter: (radio news feature) The Bioregional Report on KSOR Ashland, 1986-87. Treas. bd. dirs. Siskiyou Performing Arts Ctr., Siskiyou County, Calif., 1975-79; mem. ctrl. com. Dem. party, Siskiyou County, 1991—. Recipient Illilouette Fund award, San Francisco, 1993. Mem. Forest Mgmt. Roundtable. Office: Klamath Forest Alliance PO Box 820 508 N Hwy #3 Etna CA 96027

PACE, R(ALPH) WAYNE, organizational behavior educator; b. Wanship, Utah, May 15, 1931; s. Ralph W. and Elda (Fernelius) P.; m. Gae Tueller, Mar. 19, 1953; children: Michael, Rebecca, Lucinda, Gregory, Angela, Lavinia. BS, U. Utah, 1953; MS, Brigham Young U., 1957; PhD, Purdue U., 1960. Assoc. prof. Parsons Coll., Fairfield, Ia., 1960-62; vis. prof. Bowdoin Coll., Brunswick, Maine, 1961; asst. prof. Calif. State U., Fresno, 1962-66; prof., chmn. dept. speech communication U. Mont., 1966-72; lectr. Sch. Adminstrv. Leadership, 1968-72; prof., chmn. dept. speech communication U. N.Mex., 1972-78; prof. dept. communication, dir. Communication Research Ctr., coordinator human resource devel. program Brigham Young U., 1978-85, prof. orgnl. behavior Sch. Mgmt., 1986—; prof. human resource devel. Brigham Young U., Laie, Hawaii, 1987-88; sr. ptnr. Organizational Assocs., 1970—; cons. editor HRD series Prentice Hall Pub. Co., 1989—; disting. vis. prof. Boise State U., 1992; faculty rsch. fellow Sc. Cross U., Lismore, N.S.W., Australia, 1995. Author: (with R.R. Boren) The Human Transaction: Facets, Functions and Forms of Interpersonal Communication, 1973, (with Boren and B.D. Peterson) Communication Behavior: A Scientific Approach, 1975, Communication Experiments: A Manual for Conducting Experiments, 1975; co-editor: (with B.D. Peterson and T.R. Radcliffe) Communicating Interpersonally: A Reader, 1973, (with B.D. Peterson and G.M. Goldhaber) Communication Probes, 3d edit, 1982, (with B.D. Peterson and M.D. Burnett) Techniques for Effective Communication, 1979, Organizational Communication, 1983, (with G.E. Mills) Bibliography of Management Development Literature, 1987, Supplement, 1990, (with G.E. Mills and B.D. Peterson) Analysis in Human Resource Training and Organizaton Development, 1989, (with D.F. Faules) Organizational Communication, 1989, 2d edit., 1994, (with E. Stephan) The Perfect Leader, 1990, (with P.C. Smith and G.E. Mills) Human Resource Development, 1991, (with D. F. Faules) Organizational Communication, 3d edit., 1994, (with E. Stephan) Me Mum Sez, 1994. Served with AUS, 1953-55. Fellow AAAS, Acad. Human Resource Devel. (pres. 1993); mem. ASTD (Mgmt. Devel. award of Excellence 1987, Profs. Human Resource Devel. Disting. Scholar award 1992), Internat. Com. Assn. (pres. 1970-71, Divsn. IV Outstanding Mem. award 1986), Western States Comm. Assn. (pres. 1978), Internat. Soc. Gen. Semantics, Am. Bus. Comm. Assn., Speech Comm. Assn., Acad. Mgmt., Sons Utah Pioneers (nat. v.p. 1986-87, pres. Brigham Young chpt. 1986, Disting. Svc. award 1987). Republican. Mem. LDS Ch.

PACHECO, MANUEL TRINIDAD, university president; b. Rocky Ford, Colo., May 30, 1941; s. Manuel J. and Elizabeth (Lopez) P.; m. Karen M. King, Aug. 27, 1966; children: Daniel Mark, Andrew Charles, Sylvia Lois Elizabeth. BA, N.Mex. Highlands U., 1962; MA, Ohio State U., 1966, PhD, 1969. Prof. edn., univ. dean Tex. A&I U., Laredo, 1972-77, exec. dir. Bilingual Edn. Ctr., Kingsville, 1980-82; prof. multicultural edn., chmn. dept. San Diego State U., 1977-78; prof. Spanish and edn. Laredo State U., 1978-80, pres., 1984-88; assoc. dean Coll. Edn. U. Tex., El Paso, 1982-84, exec. dir. for planning, 1984; chief policy aide for edn. to gov. N.Mex., 1984; pres. U. Houston-Downtown, 1988-91, U. Ariz., Tucson, 1991—; cons. lang. div. Ency. Britannica, 1965-72; bd. dirs. Valley Nat. Bank Corp., Nat. Security Edn. Program.; mem. exec. com. Bus.-Higher Edn. Forum. Co-editor: Handbook for Planning and Managing Instruction in Basic Skills for Limited English Proficient Students, 1983; producer: (videotapes) Teacher Training, 1976. Treas. adv. com. U.S. Commn. on Civil Rights, L.A., 1987-91; trustee United Way of Houston, 1988-91; chmn. pub. rels. Buffalo Bayou Partnership, Houston, 1988-91; bd. dirs. Ctr. for Addiction and Substance Abuse, Greater Tucson Econ. Coun., Ariz. Econ. Coun., Ariz. Town Hall. Recipient Disting. Alumnus award Ohio State U., Columbus, 1984; named Most Prominent Am.-Hispancis Spanish Today mag., 1984, one of 100 Outstanding Hispanics Hispanic bus., 1988, Man of Yr. Hispanic Profl. Action Com., 1991; Fulbright fellow U. de Montepellier, France, 1962. Mem. Am. Assn. State Colls. and Univs., Nat. Acad. of Pub. Adminstrn., Hispanic Assn. Colls. and Univs., Tex. Assn. of Chicanos in Higher Edn., Rotary, Phi Delta Kappa. Office: U Ariz Office of Pres Tucson AZ 85721

PACHON, HARRY PETER, politics educator; b. Miami, Fla., June 4, 1945; s. Juan and Rebeca (Perez) P.; children: Marc, Melissa, Nicholas. BA, Calif. State U., Los Angeles, 1967, MA, 1968; PhD, Claremont (Calif.) Grad. Sch., 1973. Adminstrv. aide U.S. Ho. of Reps., Washington, 1977-81; assoc. prof. CUNY, 1981-86; Kenan prof. politics Pitzer Coll., Claremont, 1987—; pres. Tomas Rivera Ctr., 1993—; cons. Ford & Carnegie Founds., U.S. A.I.D. Co-author: Hispanics in the U.S., 1985, Americans by Choice, 1994; contbr. articles to profl. jours. NEH fellow, 1973-74, Nat. Assn. Schs. Pub. Affairs and Adminstrn. postdoctoral fellow, 1976-77. Mem. Am. Polit. Sci. Assn. (coun. fgn. rels.), Am. Soc. Pub. Adminstrs., Nat. Assn. Latino Elected and Appointed Ofcls. (chmn. ednl. found.). Democrat. Home: 404 Damien Ave La Verne CA 91750-4104 Office: Scripps Coll Steele Hall Toms River Ctr Claremont CA 91711

PACIFIC, JOSEPH NICHOLAS, JR., educator; b. Honolulu, Oct. 27, 1950; s. Joseph Nicholas Sr. and Christine Mary (Mondelli) P.; m. Paulette Kay Miller, July 7, 1975. BA in Math., BS in Biology, BSEE, Gonzaga U., 1974; MMSc in Clin. Microbiology, Emory U., 1978. Cert. tchr., Hawaii, Wash. Rsch. specialist Ctr. Disease Control, Atlanta, 1978-82; supr. Joe Pacific Shoe Repair, Honolulu, 1983; lab. technician Mont. State U., Bozeman, 1984; sci. tchr. Hawaii Preparatory Acad., Kamuela, 1985-87; unit mgr. Hawaii Med. Service Assn., Honolulu, 1987-88; tchr. biology St. Andrew's Priory Sch., Honolulu, 1988—. Mem. Nat. Registry Microbiologists, Sigma Xi, Pi Mu Epsilon, Phi Sigma, Kappa Delta Pi, Alpha sigma Nu. Home: 92-1221 Hunekai St Kapolei HI 96707-1514 Office: St Andrew's Priory Sch 224 Queen Emma Sq Honolulu HI 96813-2304

PACK, PHOEBE KATHERINE FINLEY, civic worker; b. Portland, Oreg., Feb. 2, 1907; d. William Lovell and Irene (Barnhart) Finley; student U. Calif., Berkeley, 1926-27; B.A., U. Oreg., 1930; m. Arthur Newton Pack, June 11, 1936; children: Charles Lathrop, Phoebe Irene. Layman referee Pima County Juvenile Ct., Tucson, 1958-71; mem. pres.'s council Menninger Found., Topeka; mem. Alcoholism Council So. Ariz., 1960—; bd. dirs. Kress Nursing Sch., Tucson, 1957-67, Pima County Assn. for Mental Health, 1958-—, Ariz. Assn. for Mental Health, Phoenix, 1963—, U. Ariz. Found., Casa de los Niños Crisis Nursery; co-founder Ariz.-Sonora Desert Mus., Tucson, 1975—, Ghost Ranch Found., N.Mex.; bd. dirs. Tucson Urban League, Tucson YMCA Youth Found. Mem. Mt. Vernon Ladies Assn. Union (state vice regent, 1962-84),Mt. Vernon One Hundred (founder), Nature Conservancy (life), Alpha Phi. Home: Villa Compana 6653 E Carondelet Dr Apt 415 Tucson AZ 85710-2153

PACK, RUSSELL T, theoretical chemist; b. Grace, Idaho, Nov. 20, 1937; s. John Terrell and Mardean (Izatt) P.; m. Marion Myrth Hassell, Aug. 21, 1962; children: John R., Nathan H., Allen H., Miriam, Elizabeth, Quinn R., Howard H. BS, Brigham Young U., 1962; PhD, U. Wis., 1967. Postdoctoral fellow U. Minn., Mpls., 1966-67; asst. prof. Brigham Young U., Provo, 1967-71; assoc. prof. Brigham Young U., 1971-75, adj. prof., 1975-88; staff scientist Los Alamos (N.Mex.) Nat. Lab., 1975-83, fellow, 1983—, assoc. grp. leader, 1979-81; vis. prof. Max Planck Institut, Gottingen, 1981; chmn. Gordon Rsch. Conf., 1982; lectr. in field. Contbr. articles to profl. jours. Named Sr. U.S. Scientist, Alexander Vol Humboldt Found., 1981. Fellow Am. Phys. Soc. (sec.-treas. div. Chem. Physics 1990-93); mem. Am. Chem. Soc., Sigma Xi. Mem. Ch. of Jesus Christ of Latter Day Saints. Home: 240 Kimberly Ln Los Alamos NM 87544-3526 Office: Los Alamos National Lab T-12 Ms # B268 Los Alamos NM 87545

PACK, WALTER FRANK, minister, religion educator emeritus; b. Memphis, Mar. 27, 1916; s. Joseph Walter and Mary Elizabeth (Gibson) P.; m. Della Carlton, June 22, 1947. A.A., David Lipscomb Coll., Nashville, 1935; B.A., U. Chattanooga, 1937; M.A., Vanderbilt U., 1939; Ph.D., U. So. Calif., 1948. Ordained to ministry Ch. of Christ, 1932. Minister various Chs. of Christ, 1932—; instr. David Lipscomb Coll., 1940-44; prof. religion Pepperdine U., Los Angeles, 1947-49, prof., chmn. dept. religion, 1963-76, disting. prof., 1978-86, disting. prof. emeritus, 1986—, dean Grad. Sch., 1967-78; chmn. div. religion Seaver Coll., 1980-83; prof. bible Abilene (Tex.) Christian U., 1949-63; Frank and Della Pack disting. prof. New Testament studies Abilene U., 1986. Staff writer: 20th Century Christian, Restoration Quarterly; Author: Great Preachers of Today, 1963, (with Prentice Meador) Preaching to Modern Man, 1969, Tongues and the Holy Spirit, 1973, The Living Word Commentary: Gospel according to St. John, 1975, The Book of Revelation, 1983; Editor: Our Bible, 1951. Mem. Soc. Bibl. Lit., Phi Beta Kappa, Phi Kappa Phi, Pi Gamma Mu, Alpha Chi. Home: 275 Garnet Way # 227 Upland CA 91786-5932 Office: 24255 Pacific Coast Hwy Malibu CA 90263-0001

PACKARD, DAVID, manufacturing company executive, electrical engineer; b. Pueblo, Colo., Sept. 7, 1912; s. Sperry Sidney and Ella Lorna (Graber) P.; m. Lucile Salter, Apr. 8, 1938 (dec., 1987); children: David Woodley, Nancy Ann Packard Burnett, Susan Packard Orr, Julie Elizabeth Stephens. B.A., Stanford U., 1934, EE, 1939; LLD (hon.), U. Calif., Santa Cruz, 1966, Catholic U., 1970, Pepperdine U., 1972; DSc (hon.), Colo. Coll., 1964; LittD (hon.), So. Colo. State Coll., 1973; D.Eng. (hon.), U. Notre Dame, 1974. With vacuum tube engring. dept. Gen. Electric Co., Schenectady, 1936-38; co-founder, ptnr. Hewlett-Packard Co., Palo Alto, Calif., 1939-47, pres., 1947-64, chief exec. officer, 1964-68, chmn. bd., 1964-68, 72-93, chmn. emeritus, 1993—; U.S. dep. sec. defense Washington, 1969-71; dir. Genetech, Inc., 1981-92; bd. dirs. Beckman Laser Inst. and Med. Clinic; chmn. Presdl. Commn. on Def. Mgmt., 1985-86; mem. White House Sci. Coun., 1982-88. Mem. President's Commn. Pers. Interchange, 1972-74, President's Coun. Advisors on Sci. and Tech., 1990-92, Trilateral Commn., 1973-81, Dirs. Coun. Exploratorium, 1987-90; pres. bd. regents Uniformed Svcs. U. of Health Scis., 1975-82; mem. U.S.-USSR Trade and Econ. Coun., 1975-82; mem. bd. overseers Hoover Instn., 1972—; bd. dirs. Nat. Merit Scholarship Corp., 1963-69, Found. for Study of Presdl. and Congl. Terms, 1978-86, Alliance to Save Energy, 1977-87, Atlantic Coun., 1972-83, vice chmn., 1972-80, Am. Enterprise Inst. for Public Policy Rsch., 1978—, Nat. Fish and Wildlife Found., 1985-87, Hitachi Found. Adv. Coun., 1986—; vice chmn. The Calif. Nature Conservancy, 1983-90; trustee Stanford U., 1954-69, pres., 1958-60, Hoover Instn., The Herbert Hoover Found., David and Lucile Packard Found., pres., chmn. 1964—, Herbert Hoover Found., 1974—, Monterey Bay Aquarium Found., chmn., 1978—, The Ronald Reagan Presdl. Found., 1986-91, Monterey Bay Aquarium Rsch. Inst., chmn., pres. 1987—. Decorated Grand Cross of Merit Fed. Republic of Germany, 1972, Medal Honor Electronic Industries, 1974; numerous other awards including Silver Helmet Def. award AMVETS, 1973, Washington award Western Soc. Engrs. 1975, Hoover medal ASME, 1975, Gold Medal award Nat. Football Found. and Hall of Fame, 1973, Good Scout award Boy Scouts Am., 1975, Vermilye medal Franklin Inst., 1976, Internat. Achievement award World Trade Club of San Francisco, 1976, Merit award Am. Cons. Engrs. Council Fellows, 1977, Achievement in Life award Ency. Britannica, 1977, Engring. Award of Distinction San Jose State U., 1980, Thomas D. White Nat. Def. award USAF Acad., 1981, Disting. Info. Scis. award Data Processing Mgmt. Assn., 1981, Sylvanus Thayer award U.S. Mil. Acad., 1982, Environ. Leadership award Natural Resources Def. Council, 1983, Dollar award Nat. Fgn. Trade Council, 1985, Gandhi Humanitarium Award, 1988, Roback Award Nat. Contract Mgmt. Assn., 1988, Pub. Welfare Medal NAS, 1989, Chevron Conservation Award, 1989, Doolittle Award Hudson Inst., 1989, Disting. Citizens Award Commonwealth Club San Francisco, 1989, William Wildback award, Nat. Conf. Standards Labs., Washington, 1990, Terrance Keenan Leadership award Grantmakers in Health, 1994, John Martin Excellence in Marine Scis. medal Stanford U., 1994, Nat. Disting. Svc. award Nat. Acads. Practice, 1994, Disting. Grantmakers award Coun. on Founds., 1994, Am. Philanthropy award Columbus Found., 1994, Lifetime Achievement award Lemelson-MIT, 1995; named to Silicon Valley Engring. Hall of Fame, Silicon Valley Engring. Coun., 1991, Pueblo (Colo.) Hall of Fame, 1991. Fellow IEEE (Founders medal 1973); mem. Nat. Acad. Engring. (Founders award 1979), Instrument Soc. Am. (hon. lifetime mem.), Wilson Council, The Bus. Roundtable, Bus. Council, Am. Ordnance Assn. (Crozier Gold medal 1970,) Henry M. Jackson award 1988, Nat. Medal Tech. 1988, Presdl. Medal of Freedom 1988, Sigma Xi, Phi Beta Kappa, Tau Beta Pi, Alpha Delta Phi (Disting. Alumnus of Yr. 1970). Office: Hewlett-Packard Co PO x 10301 Palo Alto CA 94304-1112 also: Monterey Bay Aquarium Rsch Inst 160 Central Ave Pacific Grove CA 93950-3067 also: David and Lucille Packard Found 300 2nd St Ste 200 Los Altos CA 94022-3621

PACKARD, NORMAN HARRY, research director; b. Billings, Mont., Mar. 26, 1954; s. Linzee Wells and Mary Nell (Brownlee) P.; m. Grazia Maria Peduzzi, June 3, 1989; children: Daniele, Chiara. BA, Reed Coll., 1977; PhD, U. Calif., Santa Cruz, 1982. NATO fellow Institut des Hautes Etudes Scientifiques, Paris, 1982-83; RCA fellow Inst. for Advanced Study, Princeton, N.J., 1983-86; assoc. prof. U. Ill., Urbana, 1986-92; dir. rsch. Prediction Co., Santa Fe, 1992—. Recipient Sloan fellowship, 1988-89. Office: Prediction Co 320 Aztec St Santa Fe NM 87501-2653

PACKARD, ROBERT GOODALE, III, planner; b. Denver, Apr. 12, 1951; s. Robert and Mary Ann (Woodward) P.; m. Jane Ann Collins, Aug. 25, 1973; children: Jessica Nelson, Robert Gregg. BA, Willamette U., 1973; M in Urban and Regional Planning/Community Devel., U. Colo., 1976. Project mgr. Environ. Disiciplines, Inc., Portland, Oreg., 1973-75; asst. dir. planning Portland Pub. Schs., 1976-78; dir. planning Bur. of Parks, Portland, 1978-79; dir. planning and urban design Zimmer Gunsul Frasca, Portland, 1979-81, dir. project devel., 1981-84, mng. ptnr., 1984—. Co-author: The Baker Neighborhood/Denver, 1976. Contbr. articles to profl. jours. Trustee Willamette U., 1994; mem. City of Portland Waterfront Commn., 1982-83; mem. Mayor's Task Force for Joint Use of Schs., Portland, 1979-80; mem. Washington Park Master Plan Steering com., Portland, 1980-81; bd. dirs. Washington Park Zoo, 1983-86, pres. Arts Celebration Inc./Artquake, 1986—, New Rose Theatre, 1981-83; dir., pres. Grant Park Neighborhood Assn., Portland, 1981-83; mem. Pioneer Sq. Bd., 1992, Archtl. Found. Oreg., 1992; mem. crafts bd. Oreg. Sch. Arts. Recipient Spl. Citation, Nat. Sch. Bds. Assn., 1978; Meritorious Planning Project award Am. Planning Assn., 1980, Nat. Am. Planning Assn., 1981; Meritorious Design award Am. Soc. Landscape Architects, 1981; Honor award Progressive Arch., 1983. Mem. AIA (Architecture Firm award 1991, assoc.), Am. Planning Assn., Young Pres. Assn., Racquet Club, Arlington Club, City Club, Racquet Club. Home: 3313 SW Fairmount Blvd Portland OR 97201-1478 Office: Zimmer Gunsul Frasca Ptnrship 320 SW Oak St Ste 500 Portland OR 97204-2735

PACKARD, RONALD, congressman; b. Meridian, Idaho, Jan. 19, 1931; m. Jean Sorenson, 1952; children: Chris, Debbie, Jeff, Vicki, Scott, Lisa, Theresa. Student, Brigham Young U., 1948-50, Portland State U., 1952-53; D.M.D., U. Oreg., Portland, 1953-57. Gen. practice dentistry Carlsbad, Calif., 1959-82; mem. 98th-104th Congresses from 43rd (now 48th) Dist. Calif., 1983—; chmn. appropriations legis. subcom., former mem. pub. works and transp. com., sci., space, tech. Mem. Carlsbad Sch. Dist. Bd., 1960-72; bd. dirs. Carlsbad C. of C., 1972-76; mem. Carlsbad Planning Commn., 1974-76, Carlsbad City Coun., 1976-78; Carlsbad chmn. Boy Scouts Am., 1977-79; mayor City of Carlsbad, 1978-82; mem. North County Armed Svcs. YMCA, North County Transit Dist., San Diego Assn. Govts., Coastal Policy Com., Transp. Policy Com.; pres. San Diego div. Calif. League of Cities. Served with Dental Corps USN, 1957-59. Republican. Mem. Ch. LDS. Office: US Ho of Reps 2162 Rayburn HOB Washington DC 20515*

PACKER, MARK BARRY, lawyer, financial consultant, foundation official; b. Phila., Sept. 18, 1944; s. Samuel and Eve (Devine) P.; m. Donna Elizabeth Ferguson (div. 1994); children: Daniel Joshua, Benjamin Dov, David Johannes; m. Helen Margaret (Jones) Klinedinst, July, 1995. AB magna cum laude, Harvard U., 1965, LLB, 1968. Bar: Wash. 1969, Mass. 1971. Assoc. Ziontz, Pirtle & Fulle, Seattle, 1968-70; pvt. practice, Bellingham, Wash., 1972—; bd. dirs., corp. sec. BMJ Holdings (formerly No. Sales Co., Inc.), 1977—; trustee No. Sales Profit Sharing Plan, 1977—; bd. dirs., corp. sec., gen. counsel Dr. Cookie, Inc., 1981-92. Mem. Bellingham Planning and Devel. Commn., 1975-84, chmn., 1977-81, mem. shoreline subcom., 1976-82; pres. Congregation Beth Israel, Bellingham, 1980-82; mem. Bellingham Mcpl. Arts Commn., 1986-91, landmark rev. bd., 1987-91; chmn. Bellingham campaign United Jewish Appeal, 1979-90; bd. dirs. Whatcom Community Coll. Found., 1989-92; lit. tutor Whatcom Lit. Coun., 1988-90; trustee, chmn. program com. Bellingham Pub. Sch. Found., 1991—; discussion leader, short story/novella reading group, 1988-92; active Heavy Culture classic lit. group, 1991—, Jewish studies group, 1993—; mng. trustee Bernard M. & Audrey Jaffe Found. Recipient Blood Donor award ARC, 1979, 8-Gallon Pin, 1988, Mayor's Arts award City of Bellingham, 1993. Mem. ABA (sec. real property probate and trust), Wash. State Bar Assn. (sec. environ. and land use law, com. law-related edn. 1990-92, sec. bus. law, sec. real property, probate and trust, com. law examiners 1992-94). Office: PO Box 1151 Bellingham WA 98227-1151

PACKMAN, VICKI SUE, assessment analyst; b. Piqua, Ohio, Dec. 8, 1948; d. Charles Richard Packman and Norma Gene (Zimpher) Westerveld. BA in Psychology, Calif. State U., Long Beach, 1977, MS in Indsl. Psychology, 1983. Ind. contractor, cons. L.A., Lafayette and Rosemead, Calif., 1981-83; sr. assessment analyst Salt River Project, Phoenix, 1983—. Pres. Tempe (Ariz.) Soroptimists, 1986. Mem. ACA, APA, Nat. Career Devel. Assn., Pers. Testing Coun. (co-founder, past pres., bd. dirs. 1989—), Ariz. Career Devel. Assn. (sec. 1993-94, v.p. edn. 1995), Soc. Indsl. and Orgnl. Psychology, Phi Kappa Phi. Home: 6333 E Carolina Dr Scottsdale AZ 85254-1933 Office: Salt River Project CRF 205 PO Box 52025 Phoenix AZ 85072-2025

PACKWOOD, BOB, senator; b. Portland, Oreg., Sept. 11, 1932; s. Frederick William and Gladys (Taft) P.; children: William Henderson, Shyla. BA, Willamette U., 1954; LLB, NYU, 1957; LLB (hon.), Yeshiva U., 1982, Gallaudet Coll., 1983. Bar: Oreg. Law clerk to Justice Harold J. Warner Oreg. Supreme Ct., 1957-58; pvt. atty., 1958-68; Chmn. Multnomah County Rep. Cen. Com., 1960-62; mem. Oreg. Legislature, 1963-69; U.S. senator from Oreg., 1969—, chmn. small bus. com., 1981-84, chmn. commerce com., 1981-85, chmn. fin. com., 1985-86, ranking min. mem. fin. com., 1987-94, chmn. fin. com., 1995—. Mem. Internat. Working Group of Parliamentarians on Population and Devel., 1977; mem. Pres.'s Commn. on Population Growth and the Am. Future, 1972; chmn. Nat. Rep. Senatorial Com., 1977-78, 81-82; bd. dirs. NYU, 1970; bd. overseers Lewis and Clark Coll., Portland, 1966. Named One of Three Outstanding Young Men of Oreg., 1967; Portland's Jr. 1st Citizen, 1966; Oreg. Speaker of Yr., 1968; recipient Arthur T. Vanderbilt award NYU Sch. Law, 1970; Anti-Defamation League Brotherhood award, 1971; Torch of Liberty award B'nai B'rith, 1971; Richard L. Neuberger award Oreg. Environ. Coun., 1972; Conservation award Omaha Woodmen Life Ins. Soc., 1974; Monongahela Forestry Leadership award, 1976; Solar Man of Yr., Solar Energy Industries Assn., 1980; Guardian of Small Bus. award Nat. Fedn. Ind. Bus., 1980; Forester of Yr., Western Forest Industries Assn., 1980; Am. Israel Friendship award B'nai Zion, 1982; Grover C. Cobb award Nat. Assn. Broadcasters, 1982; Religious Freedom award, Religious Coalition for Abortion Rights, 1983; 22d Ann. Conv. award, Oreg. State Bldg. and Constrn. Trade Council, 1983; United Cerebral Palsy Humanitarian award, 1984; Am. Heart Assn. Pub. Affairs award, 1985; Margaret Sanger award Planned Parenthood Assn., 1985; Worth his Wheat in Gold award for leadership on tax reform Gen. Mills., 1986; Am. Assn. Homes for the Aging for Outstanding Svc. in cause of elderly, 1987; NARAL award for congrl. leadership, 1987; James Madison award Nat. Broadcast Editorial Assn., 1987; Pub. Excellence award First Ann. Jacob K. Javits, 1987; Golden Bulldog award Watchdogs of Treasury, Inc., 1988, 90; Sound Dollar award, 1989; Golden Eagle award Nurse Anesthetists, 1990; John. F. Hogan Disting. Svc. award Radio-TV News Dirs. for def. of First Amendment, 1991; Nat. Conf. Soviet Jewry recognition, 1992, Space Shuttle Endeavor recognition, 1993, Spirit of Enterprise award U.S. C. of C., 1994, numerous others. Mem. Oreg. Bar Assn., D.C. Bar Assn., Beta Theta Pi. Office: US Senate 259 Russell Senate Bldg Washington DC 20510-3702

PADEREWSKI, CLARENCE JOSEPH, architect; b. Cleve., July 23, 1908. B.Arch., U. Calif., 1932. Chief draftsman Sam W. Hamill, 1939-44; with Heitschmidt-Matcham-Blanchard-Gill & Hamill (architects), 1943; then practiced as C.J. Paderewski, 1944-48; pres. Paderewski, Dean & Asso., Inc. (and predecessor), San Diego, 1948-78; instr. adult edn. San Diego city schs., 1939-44, U. Calif. extension div., 1945, 56; Lectr. in field. Prin. works include Charactron Labs, Gen. Dynamics Corp., Convair, S.D., 1954, South Bay Elem. Schs., S.D., 1948-74; additions to El Cortez Hotel; including first passenger glass elevator in the world and New Travolator Motor Hotel, S.D., 1959, Palomar Coll., San Marcos, 1951-80, San Diego County U. Gen. Hosp., San Diego Internat. Airport Terminal Bldgs., Fallbrook Elem. Schs., 1948-74, Silver Strand Elem. Sch., Coronado, Tourmaline Terrace Apt. Bldg., San Diego Salvation Army Office Bldg. Mem. adv. bd. Bayside Social Service Center, 1953-75, San Diego Polonia Newspaper, 1994—; mem. San Diego Urban Design Com.; mem. adv. bd. Camp Oliver, 1963—, pres., 1975-76; bd. dirs. San Diego Symphony Orch. Assn., 1954-62, San Diego chpt. ARC, 1971-74; bd. dirs., chmn. coms., pres. San Diego Downtown Assn., 1963—; bd. dirs. Nat. Council Archtl. Registration Bds., 1958-66, bd. dirs. other offices, 1961-64, pres., 1965-66, chmn. internat. relations com., 1967-68, Salvation Army, vice chmn., 1989, life mem. adv. bd., 1993—, Copernicus Found., 1994—; mem. Calif. Bd. Archtl. Examiners, 1949-61, past pres., commr., 1961—; mem. Nat. Panel Arbitrators, 1953—, Nat. Council on Schoolhouse Constrn.; bd. dirs. Salvation Army, vice chmn., 1989, mem. coms., life mem. adv. bd., 1993—; hon. chmn. Ignacy Jan Paderewski Meml. Com., 1991. Decorated Knight Order Polonia Restituta, Polish govt. in exile, 1982; recipient Award of Merit for San Diego County Gen. Hosp., San Diego chpt., AIA, 1961, Honor award for San Diego Internat. Airport Terminal, Honor award Portland Cement Co., Golden Trowel award Plastering Inst., 1958-60, 4 awards Masonry Inst., 1961, award Prestressed Concrete Inst., 1976, Outstanding Community Leadership award San Diego Downtown Assn., 1963, 64, 65, 80. Fellow AIA (pres. San Diego chpt. 1948, 49, bd. dirs. 1947-53, chmn. several coms., spl. award 1977, Calif. Coun. Spl. award 1979, Calif. Coun. Disting. Svc. award 1982); mem. San Diego C. of C. (bd. dirs. 1959-62, 64-67), Am. Arbitration Assn. (San Diego adv. coun. 1969—), Sister City Soc. (bd. dirs.), Lions (past pres. Hillcrest Club, Lion of Yr. 1990, fellow internat. found. 1991), Father Serra Club (charter, past pres.), Outboard Boating Club San Diego, Chi Alpha Kappa, Delta Sigma Chi.*. Home: 2837 Kalmia Pl San Diego CA 92104-5418

PADGET, JOHN E., insurance executive; b. L.A., Aug. 26, 1948; s. LeRoy and Gladys (Black) P. BA, U. Kans., 1969, postgrad., 1970. Instr. bridge Am. Contract Bridge League, 1971-77; owner Hectors, Kirkland, Wash., 1978-84; producer TV show Sta. 2, Oakland, 1985-88; regional mgr. Keithwood Agy.-Am. Health Care Adv., Pleasanton, Calif., 1991—; mgmt. cons. Performex, San Francisco, 1991—. Author: Winning Style, 1977. Mem. AAAS, Mensa, Internat. Platfrom Soc. Jewish. Office: Performex PO Box 271403 Concord CA 94527-1403

PADVE, MARTHA BERTONNEAU, urban planning and arts consultant, fundraiser; b. Scobey, Mont., Feb. 22; d. Henry Francis and Marie (Vaccaro) Bertonneau; m. Jacob Padve, May 9, 1954 (div. 1980). Student, Pasadena Jr. Coll., 1938-40; cert., S.W. U. Bus. Coll., L.A., 1940-41, Pasadena Inst. for Radio, 1946-47; student, Claremont Colls., 1972-74, U. So. Calif., 1983-84, Community Coll., Pasadena, 1987-88. Juvenile roles Pasadena (Calif.) Community Playhouse, 1935-37; ptnr., bus. mgr. restaurant devel. ventures, Pasadena, 1940-50; club dir. Red Cross, Nfld., Can., 1944-45; leading roles Penthouse Theatre, Altadena, Calif., 1946-48; club dir. armed forces spl. svcs. Red Cross, Austria, 1949-52; head dept. publs. Henry E. Huntington Libr., San Marino, Calif., 1953-57; cons. art planning Model Cities program, Omaha, 1975; founding instr. contemporary art collecting class, 1979-80; dir. devel. Bella Lewitzky Dance Found., L.A., 1980-81; instr. Art. Ctr. Coll. Design, Pasadena, 1981-82, assoc. dir. devel., 1981-83; instr. Coll. Continuing Edn. U. So. Calif., L.A., 1983-84; urban planning and arts cons. The Arroyo Group, Pasadena, 1979—; cons. in field, 1984—; developer edn. program Mus. Contemporary Art, L.A., 1984-86. Contbr. articles to newspapers; author (the arts segment) Pasadena Gen. Plan, 1980-83. Trustee, v.p. Pasadena Art Mus., 1967-74; co-chmn. bldg. fund Norton Simon Mus. Art, Pasadena 1968-70; chmn. Pasadena Planning Commn., 1973-81, Pasadena Street Tree Plan, 1975-76, Pasadena High Rise Task Force, 1979, San Gabriel Valley Planning Coun., 1977-78; mem. Pasadena Downtown Urban Design Plan, 1980-83; founding mem. Arts, Pks. & Recreation Task Force, 1978-80; vice-chmn. Pasadena Design Review Commn., 1974-78; founding chmn. So. Calif. Fellows of Contemporary Art, 1976-78; mem. adv. com. U. So. Calif. Art Galleries, 1976-82, UCLA oral history program contemporary art, 1983—; chmn. audit com. L.A. County Grand Jury, 1986-87; founder Pasadena Robinson Meml. Fund, Inc., 1990-92, bd. dirs. 1992-95; curator Vroman's Art on the Stairwell, 1992—; mem. exec. com. St. Andrew's Sch. Bd., 1993-94; co-chmn. restoration adv. com. St. Andrew's Ch., 1994; judge Pasadena Tournament of Roses, 1994. Named Woman of the Yr., Pasadena Women's Civic League, 1980; recipient Gold Crown award Tenth Muse, Pasadena Arts Coun., 1983, Commendation awards Pasadena City Dirs., 1975, 80, 82, 83, Commendation award L.A. County Bd. Suprs., 1987, Graphic Arts award Southern Calif. Fellows Contemporary Art, 1978. Republican. Roman Catholic. Home and Office: 350 Olympic View Ln Friday Harbor WA 98250-9662

PAGANI, ALBERT LOUIS, aerospace system engineer; b. Jersey City, Feb. 19, 1936; s. Alexander C. and Anne (Salvati) P.; m. Beverly Cameron, Feb. 23, 1971; children: Penelope, Deborah, Michael. BSEE, U.S. Naval Acad., 1957; MBA, So. Ill. U., 1971. Commd. 2d lt. USAF, 1957, advanced through grades to col., 1978; navigator USAF, Lake Charles, La., 1957-63; pilot USAF, McGuire AFB, N.J., 1963-65; command pilot USAF, Anchorage, Alaska, 1965-68; mgr. airlift USAF, Saigon, Socialist Republic of Vietnam, 1968-69; chief spl. missions USAF, Scott AFB, Ill., 1969-74; commd. tactical airlift group USAF Europe, Mildenhall, Eng., 1974-76; dep. comdr. Rhein Main Air Base USAF Europe, Frankfurt, Fed. Republic Germany, 1976-78; chief airlift mgmt. USAF Military Airlift Command, Scott AFB, Ill., 1978-81, dir. tech. plans and concepts, 1981, dir. command and control, 1982-85; ret., 1985; program mgr. Lockheed Missile and Space Co., Sunnyvale, Calif., 1985-94; dir. data applications, dir. adv. programs PAR Govt. Systems Corp., New Hartford, NY, 1994—. V.p. Cath. Ch. Council, Mildenhall, 1974, pres., 1975. Decorated Legion of Merit, Bronze Star, Air medal, Vietnam Cross of Gallantry. Mem. Nat. Def. Transp. Assn., Soc. Logistics Engrs., Air Force Assn., Armed Forces Communication and Electronics Assn., Air Lift Assn., Daedalions, Mensa. Home: 41090 Driscoll Ter Fremont CA 94539-3872 Office: PAR Govt Systems Victorville CA

PAGANI, BEVERLY DARLENE, retired government administrator; b. Compton, Calif., Aug. 29, 1937; d. Donald Marshell Cameron and Irene Von (Kirkendoll) Good; m. Albert Louis Pagani, Feb. 21, 1971; children: Penelope Collins, Deborah Anne, Michael Stuart. BS, So. Oreg. Coll., 1967; MBA, So. Ill. U., Edwardsville, 1972. Cert. cost estimator and analyst. Enlisted USAF, 1959, advanced through grades to capt., 1962, resigned, 1971; chief mgmt. analysis USAF, Mildenhall, Eng., 1974-76; personnel classifier USAF, Scott AFB, Ill., 1979-80; housing mgmt. analyst USAF, Scott AFB, 1980-81, cost analyst, 1981-85; chief manpower analyst USN, Moffett Field, Calif., 1985—; chief mgmt. support office Army Aviation Research and Tech. Activity, Moffett Field, Calif., 1986-88; project control mgr. NASA-AMES Rsch. Ctr., Moffett Field, Calif., 1988-94; retired, 1994. Mem. Soc. Logistic Engrs., Inst. Cost Analysts, Am. Soc. Mil. Comptrollers, Soc. Cost Estimating and Analysis. Republican. Roman Catholic.

PAGE, CATHERINE JO, chemistry educator; b. Portland, Oreg., Aug. 21, 1958; d. Urlin Scott and Barbara Ann (Williams) P.; m. David Charles Johnson, Aug. 22, 1981; children: Daniel Robert, Emily Page. BA in Chemisty cum laude, Oberlin Coll., 1980; PhD in Inorganic Chemistry, Cornell U., 1984. Researcher Rockwell Internat., Thousand Oaks, Calif., 1979; rsch. asst. Oberlin (Ohio) Coll., 1979-80, Cornell U., Ithaca, N.Y., 1981-84; rsch. chemist E.I. DuPont de Nemours & Co., Inc., Wilmington, Del., 1984-86; rsch. asst. prof. U. Oreg., Eugene, 1986-89, asst. prof., 1989—; mem. small bus. innovative rsch. rev. panel NSF, 1989, mem. materials synthesis and processing rev. panel, 1992; presenter papers Reed Coll., 1991, Portland State U., 1991, Lewis and Clark Coll., 1992, Fla. Advanced Materials Conf., 1992, Solid State Gordon Conf., 1992, Oreg. State U., 1992, Am. Crystallographic Assn., Albuquerque, 1993. Author: (with others) Better Ceramics Through Chemistry, 1992; contbr. articles to profl. jours.; patentee in field. Fellow NATO, 1982, 83, Oberlin Coll., 1979, 80. Mem. Am. Chem. Soc. (paper presenter 1992, 94), Materials Rsch. Soc. (paper presente 1992, 94), Sigma Xi, Iota Sigma Pi. Office: U Oreg Dept Chemistry Eugene OR 97403

PAGE, CURTIS MATTHEWSON, minister; b. Columbus, Ohio, Oct. 24, 1946; s. Charles N. and Alice Matthewson P.; m. Martha Poitevin, Feb. 12, 1977; children: Allison, Charles, Abigail. BS, Ariz. State U., 1968; MDiv, San Francisco Theol. Sem., 1971, D Ministry, 1985. Ordained to ministry Presbyn. Ch., 1971. Pastor Ketchum (Idaho) Presbyn. Ch., 1972-80, Kirk O'The Valley Presbyn. Ch., Reseda, Calif., 1980-90; campaign dir. Kids 1st Edn. Reform Partnership, L.A., 1990-91; sr. pastor Orangewood Presbyn. Ch., Phoenix, 1991-93, First Meridian Heights Presbyn. Ch., Indpls., 1993—; bd. dirs. Express Pub., Ketchum. Bd. dirs. Mary Magdalene Home, Reseda; moderator Kendall Presbytery, 1978; chmn. com. on preparation for the ministry, San Fernando, Calif., 1988-90; chmn. Ketchum City Zoning Commn., 1979-80; mem. Ketchum Master Planning Commn., 1974, Mayor's Citizen's Adv. Task Force on Ethics, 1990; co-chmn. Voice Community Orgn. in San Fernando Valley, 1988-90. Office: First Meridian Heights Pres 4701 Central Ave Indianapolis IN 46205-1828

PAGE, JAKE (JAMES K. PAGE, JR.), writer, editor; b. Boston, Jan. 24, 1936; s. James Keena Page and Ellen Van Dyke (Gibson) Kunath; m. Aida de Alva Bound, Nov. 28, 1959 (div. 1974); children: Dana de Alva Page, Lea Gibson Page Kuntz, Brooke Bound Page; m. Susanne Calista Stone, Mar. 10, 1974; stepchildren: Lindsey Truitt, Sally Truitt, Kendall Barrett. BA, Princeton U., 1958; MA, NYU, 1959. Asst. sales promotion mgr. Doubleday & Co., 1959-60; editor Doubleday Anchor Books, 1960-62, Natural History Press, Doubleday, N.Y.C., 1962-69; editorial dir. Natural History Mag., N.Y.C., 1966-69; editor-in-chief Walker & Co., N.Y.C., 1969-70; sci. editor Smithsonian Mag., Washington, 1970-76; founder, dir. Smithsonian Books, Washington, 1976-80; start-up editor Smithsonian Air & Space Mag., Washington, 1985; pvt. practice as writer Waterford, Va., Corrales, N.Mex., 1980—; mag. cons. Denver Mus. Nat. History, 1989-90; contract text editor Doubleday, 1992. Author: (with Richard Saltonstall Jr.) Brown Out & Slow Down, 1972, (with Larry R. Collins) Ling-Ling & Hsing Hsing: Year of the Panda, 1973, Shoot the Moon, 1979, (with Wilson Clark) Energy, Vulnerability and War: Alternatives for America, 1981, Blood: River of Life, 1981, (with Susanne Page) Hopi, 1982, Forest, 1983, Arid Lands, 1984, Pastorale: A Natural History of Sorts, 1985, Demon State, 1985, Navaho, 1995, (with Eugene S. Morton) Lords of the Air: The Smithsonian Book of Birds, 1989, Smithsonian's New Zoo, 1990, Zoo: The Modern Ark, 1990, Animal Talk: Science and the Voice of Nature, 1992, The Stolen Gods, 1993, Songs to Birds, 1993 (with Chalres B. Officer) Tales of the Earth, 1993, The Deadly Canyon, 1994 (with David Leeming) Goddess: Mythology of the Female Divine, 1994, The Knotted Strings, 1995, Smithsonian Guides to Natural America: Arizona and New Mexico, 1995, God: Mythology of the Male Divine; editor: (with Malcolm Baldwin) Law and the Environment, 1970; contbg. editorships Science Mag., 1980-86, Oceans Mag., 1987, Mother Earth News, 1990, National Geographic Traveler, 1990-93, TDC (now Destination Discovery), 1991—; contbg. author to numerous books and mags. Mem. nat. bd. advisors Futures for Children, Albuquerque, 1980—. Democrat. Home and Office: PO Box 78 345 Chimaja Rd Corrales NM 87048

PAGE, JOHN BOYD, physics educator; b. Columbus, Ohio, Sept. 4, 1938; s. John Boyd and Helen (Young) P.; m. Norma Kay Christensen, July 28, 1966; children: Rebecca, Elizabeth. BS, U. Utah, 1960, PhD, 1966. Rsch. assoc. Inst. for Theoretical Physics U. Frankfurt/Main, Fed. Republic of Germany, 1966-67; rsch. assoc. Cornell U., Ithaca, N.Y., 1968-69; asst. prof. physics Ariz. State U., 1969-75, assoc. prof., 1975-80, prof., 1980—; vis. prof. dept. physics Cornell U., 1989. Contbr. articles to profl. jours. Recipient Humboldt Rsch. award, 1991; NSF grantee, 1972-77, 77-80, 80-82, 82-86, 90-92, 91—. Fellow Am. Phys. Soc.; mem. Am. Assn. Physics Tchrs., Phi Beta Kappa, Sigma Xi, Phi Kappa Phi, Phi Eta Sigma. Office: Ariz State U Physics Dept Tempe AZ 85287-1504

PAGE, LESLIE ANDREW, disinfectant manufacturing company executive; b. Mpls., June 5, 1924; s. Henry R. and Amelia Kathryn (Steinmetz) P.; m. DeEtte Abernethy Griswold, July 6, 1952 (dec. Sept. 1975); children: Randolph, Michael, Kathryn, Caroline; m. Mary Ellen Decker, Nov. 26, 1976. BA, U. Minn., 1949; MA, U. Calif., Berkeley, 1953; PhD, U. Calif., 1956. Asst. microbiologist, lectr. U. Calif., Davis, 1956-61; cons. San Diego Zoological Soc. Zoo Hosp., 1957-60; microbiologist, research leader Nat. Animal Disease Ctr., USDA, Ames, Iowa, 1961-79; ret., 1979, specialist in Chlamydial nomenclature and disease; med. text cons. Bay St. Louis, Miss., 1979-85; founder, pres., chmn. bd. Steri-Derm Corp., Escondido, Calif., 1987—; specialist in Chlamydial nomenclature and disease; cons. McCormick Distilling Co., 1994—. Editor: Wildlife Diseases, 1976, Jour. Wildlife Diseases, 1965-68; contbr. chpts. to med. texts, more than 70 articles to profl. jours.; patentee Liquid Antiseptic Composition, 1989. Pres. Garden Island Community Assn., Bay St. Louis, 1980-81; chief commr. East Hancock Fire Protection Dist., Bay St. Louis, 1982-83; sec., treas. Woodridge Escondido Property Owners Assn., 1986-88. With AUS, 1943-46, ETO. Fellow Am. Acad. Microbiology (emeritus); mem. Wildlife Disease Assn. (pres. 1972-73, Disting. Svc. award 1980), Am. Soc. for Microbiology, Zool. Soc. San Diego, Sigma Xi, Phi Zeta (hon.). Home and Office: 1784 Deavers Dr San Marcos CA 92069

PAGE, RICHARD EDWARD, entertainment company executive, business owner; b. Providence, R.I., May 11, 1947; s. Clayton E. and Cherry C. (Ballard) P.; m. Joan L. Summers, Jan. 13, 1973. Student, Westmont Coll., 1967-69. Dir. Areopagus, Inc., Santa Barbara, Calif., 1970-74; founder, pres. R. Page Enterprises, Santa Barbara, Calif., 1974-81; dir. mktg. CBS Inc., Priority Records, Nashville, 1981; dir. artist devel. RCA Records, Nashville, 1981-85; founder, pres. Page Mgmt. Group, Malibu, Calif., 1985—; co-owner

Casa Malibu Inn on the Beach, Malibu, 1992—. Bd. dirs. Malibu C. of C., 1992—. Presbyterian. Office: Page Management Group 22752 Pacific Coast Hwy Malibu CA 90265-5039

PAGENKOPF, ANDREA LESUER, university official; b. Hamilton, Mont., July 28, 1942; d. Andrew and Martha Gail (Thompson) LeSuer; m. Gordon Kyle Pagenkopf, June 12, 1964 (dec. Feb. 1987); 1 child, Sarah Lynn. BA, U. Mont., 1964; PhD, Purdue U., 1968. Registered dietitian; lic. nutritionist. Asst. prof. Purdue U., West Lafayette, Ind., 1968, U. Ill., Champaign, 1968-69; asst. prof. Mont. State U., Bozeman, 1969-76, assoc. prof., 1976-86, prof. nutrition, 1986-91, dir. extension, 1991—, vice provost for outreach, 1993—. Author: (with others) Grow Healthy Kids, 1980. Worship commn. chair United Meth. Ch., Bozeman, 1989-90; cons. Gallatin Hospice, Bozeman, 1986-91. Recipient Excellence in Nutrition Edn. award Western Dairy Coun., 1987, Silver Buffalo award Mont. Extension, 1989, Mid-Career award Extension Hon., 1988; named Home Econs. Leader, Mont. Home Econs. Assn., 1990. Mem. Am. Dietetic Assn., Soc. Nutrition Edn. (interest group chair 1990-91), Am. Home Econs. Assn. Office: Mont State U Extension 211 N Montana Ave Bozeman MT 59715-3641

PAGET, JOHN ARTHUR, mechanical engineer; b. Ft. Frances, Ont., Can., Sept. 15, 1922; s. John and Ethel (Bishop) P.; B. in Applied Sci., Toronto, 1946; m. Vicenta Herrera Nunez, Dec. 16, 1963; children: Cynthia Ellen, Kevin Arthur, Keith William. Chief draftsman Gutta Percha & Rubber, Ltd., Toronto, Ont., 1946-49; chief draftsman Viceroy Mfg. Co., Toronto, 1949-52; supr., design engr. C.D. Howe Co. Ltd., Montreal, Que., Can., 1952-58, sr. design engr. Combustion Engring., Montreal, 1958-59; sr. staff engr. Gen. Atomic, Inc., La Jolla, 1959-81. Mem. ASME, Profl. Engrs. Ont., Soc. for History Tech., Inst. Mech. Engrs., Brit. Nuclear Energy Soc. Patentee in field. Home: 3183 Magellan St San Diego CA 92154-1515

PAGON, ROBERTA ANDERSON, pediatrics educator; b. Boston, Oct. 4, 1945; d. Donald Grigg and Erna Louise (Goettsch) Anderson; m. Garrett Dunn Pagon Jr., July 1, 1967; children: Katharine Blye, Garrett Dunn III, Alyssa Grigg, Alexander Goettsch. BA, Stanford U., 1967; MD, Harvard U., 1972. Diplomate Am. Bd. Pediatrics, Am. Bd. Med. Genetics. Pediatric intern U. Wash. Affiliated Hosp., Seattle, 1972-73, resident in pediatrics, 1973-75; fellow in med. genetics U. Wash. Sch. Medicine, Seattle, 1976-79, asst. prof. pediatrics, 1979-84, assoc. prof., 1984-92, prof., 1992—; supr. Helix: A Directory of DNA Diagnostic Labs., Seattle, 1992—. Sponsor N.W. region U.S. Pony Club, 1985-94. Mem. Am. Soc. Human Genetics, Phi Beta Kappa. Office: Children's Hosp Med Ctr Divsn Med Genetics CH 25 4800 Sand Point Way NE Seattle WA 98105-0371

PAIEMENT, GUY DARIUS, orthopedic surgeon, educator; b. St. Benoit, Que., Can., Sept. 1, 1953. BSc, U. Ottawa, Ont., Can., 1975; MD, U. Montreal (Que.), 1979. Diplomate Am. Bd. Orthopedic Surgeons. Intern, resident U. Montreal (Can.) Affiliated Hosp., 1979-84; asst. clin. prof. orthopedic surgery U. Montreal, 1987-92; assoc. prof. Orthopedic Surgery U. Calif., San Francisco, 1993—; chief Orthopedic Surgery San Francisco Gen. Hosp., San Francisco, 1993—. Rsch. fellow Harvard Med. Sch., 1984-87. Office: San Francisco Gen Hosp 1001 Potrero Ave # 3a36 San Francisco CA 94110-3518

PAIGE, ALFRED LEE, small business owner; b. Bklyn., Nov. 4, 1950; s. David B. and Myrtle (Chappel) P. Student, Seattle Ctrl. Community Coll., 1984-86; BA in Govt., Columbia Coll., 1992. Lic. refrigeration engr. Nursing asst. Portsmith (N.Mex.) Hosp., 1972-76; radar operator Pearl Harbor, Pearl City, Hawaii, 1978-84; boiler engr. City of Seattle, 1985-86; maintenance repair Mil. Sealift Command Pacific, Oakland, Calif., 1987-88; mgr., owner Small Engine Repair, Oakland, Calif., 1988—. Support mem. ARC, Seattle, 1984-92, CARE, N.Y.C., 1992, Planned Parenthood, 1992, Am. Legion, San Francisco, 1992. With USN, 1972-92. Recipient Sea Svc. Deployment ribbon, 1973-90, Navy Expeditionary medal, 1987-90, Humanitarian Svc. medal, 1982. Mem. U.S. Naval Inst., Navy League. Republican. Office: PO Box 2601 Oakland CA 94614-0601

PAIGE, WOODROW WILSON, columnist; b. Memphis, June 27, 1946; s. Woodrow Wilson and Billie (Montgomery) P.; m. Virginia Hunt, Oct. 28, 1973; 1 child, Shannon Hunt. Student, U. Tenn., 1964-68. Columnist/reporter Whitehaven Press, Memphis, 1963-64, Knoxville (Tenn.) Jour., 1966; columnist The Comml. Appeal, Memphis, 1968-74, The Rocky Mountain News, Denver, 1974-81, The Denver (Colo.) Post, 1981—; talk show host Variety Radio Sta., Denver, 1975-95; commentator KMGH-TV, Denver, 1989-90; tv talk show host KNBD-TV, Denver, 1993-94. Author: Orange Madness, 1978, Blitz, 1987, Sudden Death, 1995. Named Sportswriter of Yr., Nat. Assn. Sportswriters and Sportscasters, 1992, 93, 94, Best Column, Colo. Press Assn., 1979, 81, 84, 86, 88, 89, 91, 92, 93, 94.

PAINE, ROBERT TREAT, chemistry educator; b. Colorado Springs, Colo., Dec. 15, 1944; Robert T. and Marietta H. Paine; m. Bonnie Pauly Paine, Aug. 20, 1967; children: Andrew S., Matthew H., Joanna M. BS, U. Calif., Berkeley, 1966; PhD, U. Mich., 1970. Postdoctoral work Northwestern U., Evanston, Ill., 1970-72; postdoctoral work Los Alamos (N.Mex.) Nat. Lab., 1972-74, cons., 1974—; asst. prof. U. New Mex., Albuquerque, 1974-78, assoc. prof., 1978-82, prof., 1982—. Contbr. articles to profl. jours. Trainee NASA, 1966-69. Mem. AAAS, Am. Chem. Soc., Materials Research Soc. Office: U NMex Dept Chemistry Albuquerque NM 87131

PAINTER, MICHAEL ROBERT, landscape architect, urban designer; b. L.A., Jan. 27, 1935; s. John Guy and Lillias (Armour) P.; m. Susan Margaret Collins, Jan. 3, 1959; children: Melissa Ann, Joshua Michael. BS, U. Calif., Berkeley, 1956; M Landscape Architecture in Urban Design, Harvard U., 1966. Registered landscape architect, Calif., N.Y., Nev., Pa., Tex. Jr. designer Lawrence Halprin & Assoc., San Francisco, 1956-58; ptnr. John Carl Warnecke & Assoc., San Francisco, 1958-69; pres. Michael Painter & Assoc., San Francisco, 1969-87, MPA Design, San Francisco, 1987—. Maj. archtl. works include Kennedy Gravesite, Arlington, Va., 1968 (honor award Am. Soc. Landscape Architects 1970), Lafayette Pk., Washington, 1970 (merit award Am. Soc. Landscape Architects 1972), corp. campus PacBell Adminstrn. Ctr., San Ramon, Calif., 1988 (merit award Am. Soc. Landscape Architects 1989), waterfront restoration Gt. Hwy./Ocean Beach, San Francisco, 1989 (honor award Am. Soc. Landscape Architects 1989), Doyle Drive Scenic Pkwy. Plan (merit award Am. Soc. Landscape Architects, Cmty. Svc. award San Francisco chpt. AIA, 1993). Pres., bd. dirs. Friends of Recreation and Pks., San Francisco, 1969—; bd. dirs., advisor San Francisco Planning and Urban Rsch., 1972—; bd. dirs. Exploratorium, San Francisco, 1974—; coun. Grad. Sch. Design, Harvard U., 1983-86; chmn. Citizens Adv. Com., San Francisco. Fellow Am. Soc. Landscape Architecture (com. chair 1968-69, v.p. No. Calif. chpt. 1970-72, honor awards 1978, 82, merit awards 1981, 84); mem. Urban Land Inst. (assoc.), Calif. Coun. Landscape Architecture (design jury 1991), U. Calif. Coll. Environ. Design Alumni Assn. (bd. dirs. 1990—), Mill Valley Tennis Club, Lambda Alpha. Office: MPA Design 414 Mason St San Francisco CA 94102-1719

PAKVASA, SANDIP, physicist; b. Bombay, India, Dec. 24, 1935; came to U.S. 1961; s. Sirish V. and Sumitra (Surti) P.; m. Heide Miller, Nov. 19, 1978. BSc, M.S. U. Baroda, India, 1954; MSc, M.S. U. Baroda, 1957; PhD, Purdue U., 1966. Rsch. assoc. Syracuse (N.Y.) U., 1965-67; asst. prof. U. Hawaii, Honolulu, 1968-70, assoc. prof., 1970-73, prof. physics, 1974—; vis. prof. U. Wis., Madison, 1978, 81, Nat. High Energy Physics Lab., Japan, 1983, 89, U. Melbourne, Australia, 1986, TAta Inst. Fund Rsch., Bombay, 1983, 88; vis. assoc. CERN, Geneva, 1982. Contbr. articles to profl. jours., chpts. to books. Japan Soc. for Promotion of Sci. fellow, 1981, 85. Fellow Am. Phys. Soc. Office: Univ Hawaii 2505 Correa Rd Honolulu HI 96822-2219

PAL, PRATAPADITYA, museum curator; b. Bangladesh, Sept. 1, 1935; came to U.S., 1967; s. Gopesh Chandra and Bidyut Kana (Dam) P.; m. Chitralekha Bose, Apr. 20, 1968; children—Shalmali, Lopamudra. M.A., U. Calcutta, 1958, D.Phil., 1962; Ph.D. (U. K. Commonwealth Scholar), U. Cambridge, Eng., 1965. Research assoc. Am. Acad. of Benares, India, 1966-67; keeper Indian collections Mus. Fine Arts, Boston, 1967-69; sr. curator Indian and Southeast Asian art Los Angeles County Mus. Art, Los Angeles, 1970—, acting dir., 1979; adj. prof. fine arts U. So. Calif., 1971-89; vis. prof. U. Calif., Santa Barbara, 1980; William Cohn lectr. Oxford U., 1983; Catherine Mead Meml. lectr. U. Wis., 1985; Franklin Jasper Walls lectr. Pierpont Morgan Libr., N.Y., 1986; Ananda K. Coomaraswamy Meml. lectr. Prince of Wales Mus., Bombay, 1987; D.J. Sibley Pre-Historic Art lectr. U. Tex-Austin, 1989; mem. IRS Commr.'s Art Adv. Panel, Washington. Author: The Arts of Nepal, vol. 1, 1974, vol. 2, 1979, The Sensuous Immortals, 1977, The Ideal Image: Gupta Sculptures and its Influence, 1978, The Classical Tradition in Rajput Painting, 1978, Elephants and Ivories, 1981, A Buddhist Paradise: Murals of Alchi, 1982, Art of Tibet, 1983, Tibetan Painting, 1984, Art of Nepal, 1985, From Merchants to Emperors, 1986, Indian Sculpture, vol. 1, 1986, Icons of Piety, Images of Whimsey, 1987, Indian Sculpture, vol. 2, 1988, Buddhist Book Illuminations, 1988, Romance of The Taj Mahal, 1989, Art of the Himalayas, 1991, Pleasure Gardens of the Mind, 1993; Indian Painting, vol.1, 1993, The Peaceful Liberators: Jain Art from India, 1994. Bd. dirs. Music Circle, Pasadena, Calif. John D. Rockefeller III Fund fellow, 1964, 69; NEA fellow, 1974. Fellow Asia Soc. (hon., Bombay); mem. Asiatic Soc. (Calcutta). Office: Los Angeles County Mus Art 5905 Wilshire Blvd Los Angeles CA 90036-4523

PALACIO, THOMAS, secondary education educator, coach, sports official; b. Marysville, Calif., Feb. 8, 1954; s. Joe H. and Magdalena (Chavez) P.; divorced July 1994; 1 child, JoJo Palacio. AS, Yuba Coll., 1976; BS, Calif. State U., 1979; teaching cert., U. Calif., Berkeley, 1981. Tchr. Gridley (Calif.) H.S., 1979-80; Spanish lang. tchr. Live Oak (Calif.) H.S., 1982; tchr. Yuba Coll., Marysville, Calif., 1982, Butte Coll., Oroville, 1983-84, Sycamore Sch., Gridley, Calif., 1983-86, Delta H.S., Clarksburg, Calif., 1987—; dir. of sports Yuba Coll. Intramurals, Marysville, Calif., 1974-77; asst. coach Marysville (Calif.) H.S. 1976-79; head baseball coach Live Oak (Calif.) H.S., 1983—; head football coach Delta H.S., Clarksburg, Calif., 1987-90; head track coach, 1986-90; official football, baseball, basketball No. Calif. Officials Assn. Northern Calif., 1983-84; counselor, placement coord. Yuba City, Calif., 1978. Democrat. Roman Catholic. Home: PO Box 415 Marysville CA 95901 Office: Delta HS PO Box 100 Clarksburg CA 95612

PALACIOS, PEDRO PABLO, lawyer; b. Santo Tomas, N.Mex., June 29, 1953; s. Luis Flores and Refugio (Hernandez) P.; m. Kelle Haston, July 2, 1983; children: Pedro Pablo II, Charles Rey, Jose Luis. BA, Yale U., 1975; JD, U. N.Mex., 1979. Bar: N.Mex. 1979. Pvt. practice Las Cruces, N.Mex., 1983—. Mem. N.Mex. State Bar Assn. Democrat. Roman Catholic. Home: PO Box 16335 Las Cruces NM 88004-6335 Office: 1980 E Lohman Ave Ste D-3 Las Cruces NM 88001-3194

PALADE, GEORGE EMIL, biologist, educator; b. Jassy, Romania, Nov. 19, 1912; came to U.S., 1946, naturalized, 1952; s. Emil and Constanta (Cantemir) P.; m. Irina Malaxa, June 12, 1941 (dec. 1969); children—Georgia Teodora, Philip Theodore; m. Marilyn G. Farquhar, 1970. Bachelor, Hasdeu Lyceum, Buzau, Romania; M.D., U. Bucharest, Romania. Instr., asst. prof., then assoc. prof. anatomy Sch. Medicine, U. Bucharest, 1935-45; vis. investigator, asst. assoc., prof. cell biology Rockefeller U., 1946-73; prof. cell biology Yale U., New Haven, 1973-83; sr. research scientist Yale U., 1983-89; prof.-in-residence, dean sci. affairs Med. Sch., U. Calif., San Diego, 1990—. Author sci. papers. Recipient Albert Lasker Basic Research award, 1966, Gairdner Spl. award, 1967, Horwitz prize, 1970, Nobel prize in Physiology or Medicine, 1974, Nat. Medal Sci., 1986. Fellow Am. Acad. Arts and Scis.; mem. Nat. Acad. Sci., Pontifical Acad. Sci., Royal Soc. (London), Leopoldina Acad. (Halle), Romanian Acad., Royal Belgian Acad. Medicine.

PALANCA, TERILYN, information management consultant; b. Chicago Heights, Ill., Aug. 15, 1957; d. Raymond Anthony and Barbara Jean (Schweizer) P. BA, Coll. William and Mary, 1979; MBA, Rutgers U., 1983. Chief auditor, mgr. Williamsburg Hilton, Va., 1979-81; corp. auditor RCA Corp., Princeton, N.J., 1982-83; EDP cons. Price Waterhouse & Co., N.Y.C., 1983-84; data base adminstr. Chubb & Son, Inc., Warren, N.J., 1984-85; cons., tech. mgr. Applied Data Research, Inc., Princeton, N.J., 1985-88; bus. devel. and product mgr., Oracle Corp., Belmont, Calif., 1988-91; mgr. market analysis Sybase, Inc., Emeryville, Calif., 1991-92, dir. product mgmt., 1993—. Active San Francisco Symphony Chorus. Mem. NAFE, Assn. of Inst. for Cert. Computer Profls. (cert. in data processing), Am. Mgmt. Assn. Avocations: music, literature, outdoors activities, animal aid. Office: Sybase Inc 6475 Christie Ave Emeryville CA 94608-1010

PALANIAPPAN, NAT, financial executive; b. Pondicherry, India, Apr. 1, 1956; came to U.S., 1975; s. Srinivasan and Padmavathi Palaniappan; divorced; 1 child, Kabilan. BBA, U. Toledo, 1979; MS, Calif. State U., Long Beach, 1984; postgrad., Yale U., 1985. Sr. acct. St. Francis Meml. Ctr., Lynwood, Calif., 1980-83; asst. contr. Hosp. Corp. Am., Pasadena, Calif., 1983-84; contr. Hosp. Corp. Am., Long Beach, Calif., 1985-87; CFO Santaynez Valley, Santa Barbara, Calif., 1987-89; corp. contr. Vista Health Corp., El Segundo, Calif., 1989-90, pres., 1991-92; CFO Cmty. Health Mgmt. Svcs., Scottsdale, Ariz., 1992—. Home: PO Box 6333 Scottsdale AZ 85261-6333

PALERMO, NORMAN ANTHONY, lawyer; b. Whittier, Calif., Mar. 14, 1937; s. Anthony and Alice Lucille (Ingram) P.; m. Wynne Harrison Kieffer, Apr. 12, 1989; children by previous marriage: David I., Pamela B. BS in Geology, Tulane U., 1958; LLB, Georgetown U., 1966. Bar: Colo. 1966, U.S Dist. Ct. Colo. 1966, U.S. Ct. Appeals (10th cir.) 1966, U.S. Supreme Ct. 1971. Assoc., ptnr. Quigley Wilder & Palermo, Colorado Springs, Colo., 1966-75; v.p. Quigley & Palermo, P.C., Colorado Springs, 1975-85; pres. Norman A. Palermo, P.C., Colorado Springs, 1985—. Chmn. El Paso County Rep. Cen. Com., Colorado Springs, 1985-87; bd. dirs. Goodwill Industries, Colorado Springs, 1973—; mem. State Commn. on Jud. Performance, 1993—; bd. dirs. Colorado Springs Symphony, 1981-87. Comdr. USNR, 1958-66. Mem. ABA, Colo. Bar Assn., El Paso County Bar Assn., Colorado Springs C. of C. (bd. dirs. 1980-83, 93—, vice-chmn. bd. dirs.). Republican. Home: 74 Woodbridge Dr Colorado Springs CO 80906-4470 Office: 102 E Pikes Peak Ave Fl 5 Colorado Springs CO 80903-1823

PALIA, ASPY PHIROZE, marketing educator, researcher, consultant; b. Bombay, Nov. 27, 1944; came to U.S., 1973; s. Phiroze E. and Homai P. (Irani) P. BE in Mech. Engring., U. Bangalore, 1966; MBA, U. Hawaii at Manoa, 1976; DBA, Kent State U., 1985. Sales engr. Larsen & Toubro Ltd., 1966-72, export sales engr., 1972-73; teaching fellow Coll. Bus. Adminstrn. Kent State U., 1977-80, instr. Coll. Bus. Adminstrn., 1982-84; asst. prof. Coll. Bus. Adminstrn. U. Hawaii, Manoa, 1984-89, assoc. prof., 1990—; vis. prof. Coll. Mgmt. Nat. Sun Yat-sen U., Kaohsiung, Taiwan, 1992, Chulalongkorn U., Bangkok, Thailand, 1992, 93, Adminstrv. Staff Coll. India, Hyderabad, 1992; mem. U. Hawaii Manoa Ctr. for Teaching Excellence Faculty Adv. Group, 1991; mem. mktg. plan adv. com. U. Hawaii, Manoa, 1994, mem. honors and awards com., 1990-91; vis. scholar faculty bus. adminstrn. Nat. U. Singapore, 1991; affiliate faculty Japan Am. Inst. Mgmt. Sci., Honolulu, 1989-91; vis. prof. Grad. Sch. Internat. Mgmt., Internat. U. Japan, Uhrasa, Yamato-machi, 1991, U. Internat. Bus. and Econs., Beijing, 1991, U. Kebangsaan Malaysia, Bangi-Selangor, Kuala Lumpur, Malaysia, 1991, 92; lectr., cons., presenter in field. Editor: (with Dennis A. Rondinelli) Project Planning and Implementation in Developing Countries, 1976; contbr. conf. procs. and articles to profl. jours. and books, including Indsl. Mktg. Mgmt., Internat. Bus. Jour., Asia-Pacific Jour. Mgmt., Internat. Mktg. Rev., Fgn. Trade Rev., others; contbr. to numerous confs. and symposia in field; developer various mktg. decision support systems and decision-making tools for use in marketing simulations. Mem. various program rev. coms. Pacific and Asian Mgmt. Inst., Acad. Internat. Bus., Assn. Bus. Simulation and Exptl. Learning, others; bd. examiners Nat. U. Singapore Sch. Postgrad. Mgmt. Studies, 1991; mem. adv. bd. Soc. Coll. of Bus. Adminstrn. Alumni and Friends Exec. Com., 1991—; adv. bd. Salvation Army Resdl. Treatment Facilities for Children and Youth Adv. Coun., 1989—, vice chair, 1987-89; treas., bd. dirs. Kings Gate Homeowners assn., 1994;. Univ. fellow Kent State U., 1983; East-West Ctr. scholar East-West Ctr., 1973-75; Ednl. Improvement Fund grantee, 1989, Instrl. Travel and Devel. Fund grantee Office Faculty Devel. and Acad. Support, 1991, joint rsch. grants U. Kebangsaan Malaysia, Nat. U. Singapore, U. So. Queensland, Australia; recipient Internat. Agreements Fund award Office Internat. Programs and Svcs., 1990-91, 91-92, ORA travel award U. Rsch. Coun., 1986, 88, 89, 91, 92, 94. Mem. Am. Mktg. Assn. (academia editor Honolulu chpt. 1986-87), Acad. Internat. Bus., Pacific Asian Consortium for Internat. Bus. Edn. and Rsch., Assn. for Bus. Simulation and Exptl. Learning, Pan-Pacific Bus. Assn. (charter), Mortar Bd. (Outstanding Educator award 1993), East-West Ctr. Alumni Assn. U.S. (v.p. Hawaii chpt. 1987-89, ad campaign com. 1987-88), Beta Gamma Sigma (faculty advisor, sec.-treas. Alpha of Hawaii chpt. 1990—, Outstanding Svc. award 1992-93), Mu Kappa Tau, Pi Sigma Epsilon. Home: 2724 Kahaoloha Ln Apt 1605 Honolulu HI 96826-3337 Office: U Hawaii Manoa Dept Mktg 2404 Maile Way Honolulu HI 96822-2223

PALINKAS, LAWRENCE ALBERT, anthropologist, educator; b. Hamilton, Ont., Can., Jan. 10, 1953; came to U.S., 1964; s. Alexander Joseph and Elizabeth Margaret (Toth) P.; m. Terri Lee Stayner McLees, Oct. 26, 1984; children: Ashleigh, Jonathan. BA, U. Chgo., 1974, postgrad., 1975-76; MA, U. Calif., San Diego, 1975, PhD, 1981. Instr. U. Calif., San Diego, 1981-82; NRC postdoctoral rsch. assoc. U.S. Naval Health Rsch. Ctr., San Diego, 1982-84, dep. head environ. medicine, 1984-89; assoc. prof. U. Calif., San Diego, 1989—; grant proposal reviewer NSF, Naval Med. Rsch. and Devel. Command, Natural Scis. and Engring. Rsch. Coun. Can., Natural Environment Rsch. Coun. of Gt. Britain, Am. Acad. Family Physicians Found., Am. Acad. Family Physicians, Am. Inst. Biol. Scis.; editl. cons. Westview Press, Soc. Sci. and Medicine, Med. Anthropology Quar., Internat. Jour. Obesity, Human Orgn., Annals of Behavioral Medicine, Brit. Med. Jour., Life Support and Biosphere Sci.; book reviewer Am. Anthropologist; cons. U.S. Dept. Interior. 1985-87, 87-89, 88-89, San Diego Coun. Community Clinics, 1986, Wash. State Dept. Ecology, 1987-88, Calif. Dept. Health Svcs., 1988; presenter papers in field. Author: A Systems Approach to Social Impact Assessment, 1985, Rhetoric and Religious Experience, 1989; author: (with others) Women and the World of Work, 1982, The Many Faces of Psychohistory, 1984, Measurement Strategies in Health Psychology, 1985, Transformations of Christianity: An Anthropological Approach, 1988, Engineering, Construction, and Operations in Space, 1988, From Antarctica to Outer Space: Life in Isolation and Confinement, 1990; contbr. articles to profl. jours. Regents fellow U. Calif., 1974-75, dissertation rsch. fellow, 1980-81, NRC fellow, 1982-84; named Swift scholar U. Chgo., 1971-74; recipient AFL-CIO scholarship, 1970-71, Philips scholarship, U. Calif., 1976-77; dissertation rsch. grantee U. Calif., 1979-80; grantee Naval Med. Rsch. and Devel. Command, 1980-82, Dept. Interior, 1981, 82, 83-84, NRC/Naval Med. Rsch. and Devel. Command, 1982-84, 84-85, 84-86, 84-87, NSF, 1988—, Navy Sci. Adv. program, 1987-88, NIH, 1993-95. Fellow Am. Anthropol. Assn., Soc. for Applied Anthropology; mem. APHA, AAAS, N.Am. Primary Care Rsch. Group (bd. dirs. 1990—, Master's Presentation award 1991), Soc. for Med. Anthropology, Soc. for Psychol. Anthropology, Coastal Rsch. Group. Democrat. Office: U Calif-San Diego 9500 Gilman Dr La Jolla CA 92093

PALL, MARTIN LAWRENCE, science educator, researcher; b. Montreal, Que., Can., Jan. 20, 1942; came to U.S., 1947; s. Gordon and Eleanor (Dresdner) P.; m. Linda Blackwelder, May 30, 1970 (div. 1983); 1 child, Zachary Aaron. BA in Physics, Johns Hopkins U., 1962; PhD in Biochemistry and Genetics, Calif. Inst. Tech., 1967. Asst. prof. Reed Coll., Portland, Oreg., 1967-72; asst. prof. Wash. State U., Pullman, 1972-75, assoc. prof., 1975-83, prof. genetics, cell biology, biochemistry, 1983—; coord. scis. Wash. State U., Vancouver; adj. prof. U. Calif., San Francisco, 1985; vis. assoc. prof. Yale U., New Haven, 1979-80. Contbr. numerous articles to profl. jours. Research com. Am. Heart Assn. of Wash., Seattle, 1979-84. Arthur McCallum fellow, 1962-64; Nutrition Found. fellow, 1964-67. Mem. Am. Soc. Biol. Chemistry, Genetics Soc. Am., Sigma Xi, Phi Beta Kappa. Office: Wash State U Dept Genetics Cell Bio Pullman WA 99164

PALLASCH, THOMAS JOHN, periodontist, pharmacologist, educator; b. Milw., June 15, 1936; s. Joseph John and Stella (Zavis) P. D.D.S., Marquette U., 1960; M.S. in Pharmacology, certificate in periodontics, U. Wash., 1967; m. Christine Peterson, May 14, 1977; children: Brian, Jennifer, Robert. Rotating dental intern U.S. Navy, 1960-61; assoc. prof. pharmacology and periodontics, chmn. dept. pharmacology Sch. Dentistry, U. So. Calif., L.A., 1967—, dir. oral biology grad. program, 1968-77, dir. pain and anxiety control program, 1972-76, chmn. dept. periodontics, 1981-83, prof. pharmacology and periodontics, 1989—, sec. faculty senate, 1990—; pvt. practice periodontics Burbank, Calif., 1968—; expert witness on dental malpractice, 1970—; With USN, 1960-64. Named Disting. Practitioner Nat. Acads. of Practice, 1991. Fellow Am. Coll. Dentists, Pierre Fauchard Acad.; mem. Am. Dental Assn., Am. Coll. Dentists, AAAS, Delta Sigma Delta (dep. supreme grand master 1968-71), Omicron Kappa Epsilon. Author: Clinical Drug Therapy in Dental Practice, 1973, Synopsis of Pharmacology for Students in Dentistry, 1974, Pharmacology for Dental Students and Practitioners, 1980; editor, pub. Dental Drug Service Newsletter; contbg. editor Dentist's Med. Digest, 1986—. Home and Office: 1411 W Olive Ave Burbank CA 91506-2400

PALLOTTI, MARIANNE MARGUERITE, foundation administrator; b. Hartford, Conn., Apr. 23, 1937; d. Rocco D. and Marguerite (Long) P. BA, NYU, 1968, MA, 1972. Asst. to pres. Wilson, Haight & Welch, Hartford, 1964-65; exec. asst. Ford Found., N.Y.C., 1965-77; corp. sec. Hewlett Found., Menlo Park, Calif., 1977-84, v.p., 1985—; bd. dirs. Overseas Devel. Network. Bd. dirs. N.Y. Theatre Ballet, N.Y.C., 1986—, Consortium for Global Devel., 1992, Miramonte Mental Health Svcs., Palo Alto, Calif., 1989, Austin Montessori Sch., 1993. Mem. Women in Founds., No. Calif. Grantmakers, Peninsula Grantmakers. Home: 532 Marine World Pky # 6203 Redwood Shores CA 94065 Office: William & Flora Hewlett Found 525 Middlefield Rd Ste 200 Menlo Park CA 94025-3447

PALMATIER, MALCOLM ARTHUR, editor, consultant; b. Kalamazoo, Nov. 11, 1922; s. Karl Ernest and Cecile Caroline (Chase) P.; m. Mary Elizabeth Summerfield, June 16, 1948 (dec. Oct. 1982); children: Barnabus, Timothy K., Duncan M.; m. Marie-Anne Suzanne van Werveke, Jan. 12, 1985. BS in Math., Western Mich. U., 1945; MA in English, UCLA, 1947; MA in Econs., U. So. Calif., 1971. Instr. English Pomona Coll., Claremont, Calif., 1949-51; editor Naval Ordnance Test Sta., Pasadena, Calif., 1951-54; head editorial unit Rocketdyne, L.A., 1954-55; editor The RAND Corp., Santa Monica, Calif., 1955-87; cons. editor The RAND Corp., Santa Monica, 1987—; instr. English UCLA, L.A., summer 1950. Mng. editor, cons. editor Jour.: Studies in Comparative Communism, L.A., 1968-80; co-editor Perspectives in Economics, 1971; contbr. chpts. to book, book revs. and articles to profl. jours. Chmn. bd. New Start, West L.A., 1982-84. With USNR, 1943-45. Mem. Jonathan Club. Home: 516 Avondale Ave Los Angeles CA 90049-4804 Office: The RAND Corp 1700 Main St Santa Monica CA 90401-3208

PALMER, BEVERLY BLAZEY, psychologist, educator; b. Cleve., Nov. 22, 1945; d. Lawrence E. and Mildred M. Blazey; m. Richard C. Palmer, June 24, 1967; 1 child, Ryan Richard. PhD in Counseling Psychology, Ohio State U., 1972. Lic. clinical psychologist, Calif. Adminstrv. assoc. Ohio State U., Columbus, 1969-70; rsch. psychologist Health Svcs. Rsch. Ctr. UCLA, 1971-77; commr. pub. health L.A. County, 1978-81; pvt. practice clin. psychology Torrance, Calif., 1985—; prof. psychology Calif. State U., Dominguez Hills, 1973—. Reviewer manuscripts for numerous textbook pubs; contbr. numerous articles to profl. jours. Recipient Proclamation County of L.A., 1972, Proclamation County of L.A., 1981. Mem. Am. Psychol. Assn. Office: Calif State U Dominguez Hills Dept Psychology Carson CA 90747

PALMER, CHARLES RAY, graphics specialist and production controller; b. New Orleans, Oct. 17, 1940; s. Zack and Amy Cecilia Palmer; m. Jeanette Francis Smith, Oct. 24, 1964; 1 child, Bridgette Latrice. AA in Art, Southwest City Coll., 1975; BA in Art with honors, Calif. State U., Dominguez Hills, 1979. Binderyman System Devel. Corp., Santa Monica, Calif., 1964-66; duplicator operator System Devel. Corp., Santa Monica, 1966-73, Northrop Corp., Hawthorne, Calif., 1973-75; printing press operator Northrop Corp., Hawthorne, 1975-79, visual aid artist, 1979-83, graphics prodn. control specialist, 1983-87, graphic art service mgr., 1987-93; graphics specialist, 1994-95; ltd. partnership, Crenshaw Graphics, L.A., 1979-82. With USAF, 1960-64. Mem. Am. Legion. Democrat. Roman Catholic. Home: 7630 Cimarron St Los Angeles CA 90047-2319 Office: Northrop Corp One Northorne Ave Orgn Zone 1553 # 87 Hawthorne CA 90250

PALMER, CRAIG M., anesthesiologist, educator; b. Wilmington, Del., Feb. 17, 1956; s. Cutter D. Palmer; m. Cassa Coulter, Oct. 22, 1983; children: Aileen Coulter, Ian Prosper. BA with honors, with distinction in Econs., U.

Del., 1979; MD, Thomas Jefferson U., 1983. Diplomate Am. Bd. Medical Examiners, Am. Bd. Anesthesiology. Internship and residency in gen. surgery The Grad. Hosp., Phila., 1983-85; residency, dept anesthesiology Thomas Jefferson U. Hosp., Phila., 1987-88, rsch. and clin. fellowship, dept. anesthesiology, obstetric and cardiac anesthesia, 1987-88; asst. prof. clin. anesthesiology U. Ariz., Tucson, 1988—, dir., obstetric anesthesia, 1990—. Contbr. to profl. jours. Mem. Am. Soc. Anesthesiologists (com. on obstetrical anesthesia 1993-95), Internat. Anesthesia Rsch. Soc., Ariz. Soc. Anesthesiologists (rep. to Am. Soc. Anesthesiologists Conf. 1993), Soc. Obstetric Anesthesia and Perinatology (bd. dirs. 1993—), Childbirth Edn. Assn. of Tucson (cons.). Office: U Ariz Health Sci Ctr 1501 N Campbell Ave # 5319 Tucson AZ 85724-0001

PALMER, DANIEL LEE, data communication manufacturing company executive; b. Norman, Okla., July 6, 1958; s. James Daniel and Margret (Kupka) P.; m. Kathleen Marie Connolly, Aug. 31, 1985; children: Jonathan Daniel, Elizabeth Marie, Robert Edward. BSEE, U. Colo., 1980; MSEE, U. Santa Clara, 1985. Engr. GTE Lenkurt, San Carlos, Calif., 1980-82; div. mgr. Granger Assocs., Santa Clara, Calif., 1982-84; v.p. DSC Comm., Santa Clara, 1984-89; v.p. engring., corp. officer Digital Link, Sunnyvale, Calif., 1989-95, pres., COO, 1995—. Contbr. articles to profl. jours. Mem. IEEE, Eta Kappa Nu. Home: 36532 Montecito Dr Fremont CA 94536-2614 Office: Digital Link Corp 217 Humboldt Ct Sunnyvale CA 94089-1300

PALMER, HANS CHRISTIAN, economics educator; b. N.Y.C., Sept. 21, 1933; s. Hans P. and Dagny E. (Stockel) P.; m. Beverly Wilson, June 28, 1963; children: Margaret D., David E. B.A., U. Calif.-Berkeley, 1954, M.A., 1955, Ph.D., 1965. Instr. econs. Pomona Coll., Claremont, Calif., 1962-65, asst. prof., 1965-70, assoc. prof., 1970-77, prof. econs., 1977—. Co-author: Financial Barrier to Higher Education in California, 1965; co-author, co-editor: Long-Term Care: Perspectives from Research and Demonstrations, 1983. Served to 1st lt. U.S. Army, 1955-57. Grantee NSF, 1975-76. Mem. Am. Econs. Assn., Assn. Health Services Research, Econ. History Assn., Econ. History Soc. (U.K.), Gerontol. Soc., History of Econs. Soc., Assn. Comparative Econ. Studies. Office: Dept Econs Pomona Coll Claremont CA 91711

PALMER, JAMES DANIEL, inspector; b. Oklahoma City, Okla., Aug. 11, 1936; s. Athol Ford and Marjorie Lorraine (Ward) P.; m. Gail Dorothy Myers, June 1954 (div. Sept. 1956); 1 child, James Douglas; m. Gloria Jean West, Dec. 14, 1963; children: Diana Lorraine, Elana Louise, Sheri Francis. AB in Police Sci. with honors, San Jose (Calif.) State U., 1963, AB in Psychology, 1964; MPA, Golden Gate U., 1972. Cert. Calif. police officers standards and tng. Asst. foreman Hunts Foods, Inc., Hayward, Calif., 1959-64; spl. investigator Dept. A.B.C. State of Calif., Oakland, 1964-67; criminal inspector Contra Costa County Dist. Atty., Martinez, Calif., 1967-72, lt. of inspectors, 1972-92; ret., 1992; pres. Contra Costa County Peace Officers, Richmond, 1974-75; past v.p. Contra Costa County Dist. Atty's Inv. Assn., Martinez, 1971, tng. officer, 1990-92. Contbr. articles to profl. jours. Past pres. South Hayward (Calif.) Dem. Club, 1976, 77, San Leandro (Calif.) Dems., 1975; mem. Gov's Law Enforcement Adv. Commn., Sacramento, Calif., 1972-76, Calif. Dem. Coun., 1972-73; rev. Am. Fellowship Protestant Ch., 1990—, min., 1990—. With USAF, 1955-58. Home: 2788 Sydney Way Castro Valley CA 94546-2738

PALMER, MILES R., engineering scientist, consultant; b. Roby, Tex., Dec. 10, 1953; s. Jim H. and Sylva M. (Russell) P.; m. Mary K. Wallace June 21, 1975; 1 child, Oliver James. BSEE, MIT, 1976; PhD, U. Calif., San Diego, 1980. Sr. staff scientist Sci. Applications Internat., Albuquerque, 1986—. Contbr. articles to profl. jours. Pilot Civil Air Patrol, Albuquerque, 1992. Capt. USAF, 1981-86. Recipient NSF fellowship, 1977; named Astronaut nominee NASA, 1980, Astronaut selectee USAF, 1984. Mem. AIAA (tech. com. 1992—), IEEE (applications panel 1992—). Office: SAIC 2109 Airpark Rd SE Albuquerque NM 87106-3258

PALMER, PATRICIA ANN TEXTER, English language educator; b. Detroit, June 10, 1932; d. Elmer Clinton and Helen (Rotchford) Texter; m. David Jean Palmer, June 4, 1955. BA, U. Mich., 1953; MEd, Nat.-Louis U., 1958; MA, Calif. State U.-San Francisco, 1966; postgrad. Stanford U., 1968, Calif. State U.-Hayward, 1968-69. Chmn. speech dept. Grosse Pointe (Mich.) Univ. Sch., 1953-55; tchr. South Margerita Sch., Panama, 1955-56, Kipling Sch., Deerfield, Ill., 1955-56; grade level chmn. Rio San Gabriel Sch., Downey, Calif., 1957-59; tchr. newswriting and devel. reading Roosevelt High Sch., Honolulu, 1959-62; tchr. English, speech and newswriting El Camino High Sch., South San Francisco, 1962-68; chmn. ESL dept. South San Francisco Unified Sch. Dist., 1968-81; dir. ESL Inst., Millbrae, Calif., 1978—; adj. faculty New Coll. Calif., 1981—, Skyline Coll., 1990—; Calif. master tchr. ESL Calif. Coun. Adult Edn., 1979-82; cons. in field. Past chair Sister City Com. Millbrae. Recipient Concours de Francais Prix, 1947; Jeanette M. Liggett Meml. award for excellence in history, 1949. Mem. AAUW, NAFE, TESOL, ASCD, Am. Assn. of Intensive English Programs, Internat. Platform Assn., Calif. Assn. TESOL, Nat. Assn. for Fgn. Student Affairs, Computer Using Educators, Speech Commn. Assn., Faculty Assn. of Calif. C.C., U. Mich. Alumnae Assn., Nat.-Louis U. Alumnae Assn., Ninety Nines (chmn. Golden West chpt.), Cum Laude Soc., Soroptimist Internat. (Millbrae-San Bruno Women Helping Women award 1993), Peninsula Lioness Club (pres.), Rotary Club (Millbrae), Chi Omega, Zeta Phi Eta. Home: 2917 Franciscan Ct San Carlos CA 94070-4304 Office: 450 Chadbourne Ave Millbrae CA 94030-2401

PALMER, PHILIP EDWARD STEPHEN, radiologist; b. London, Apr. 26, 1921. Ed., Kelly Coll., Tavistock, Eng., 1938; M.B., B.S., U. London, 1944, D.M.R., 1946, D.M.R.T., 1947. Intern, then resident Westminster Hosp.; cons. radiologist West Cornwall (Eng.) Hosp. Group, 1947-54; sr. govt. radiologist Matabeleland, Rhodesia-Zimbabwe, 1954-64; prof. radiology U. Cape Town, South Africa, 1964-68; prof. U. Pa., 1968-70; prof. diagnostic radiology and vet. radiology U. Calif., Davis, 1970—; WHO cons. in field. Author: The Radiology of Tropical Diseases, 1980; contbr. articles to profl. publs. Recipient German Röentgen award, 1993. Fellow Calif. Radiol. Assn., Royal Coll. Physicians (Edinburgh), Royal Coll. Radiologists (Eng.), Romanian Soc. Radiol. and Nuclear Med.; mem. Brit. Inst. Radiology, Brit. Med. Assn., Calif. Med. Assn., Internat. Skeletal Soc., Assn. Univ. Radiologists, Radiol. Soc. N. Am., Kenya Radiol. Soc., South African Coll. Medicine, Egyptian Soc. Radiology and Nuclear Medicine, Yugoslav Assn. for Ultrasound, West African Assn. Radiologists. Address: 821 Miller Dr Davis CA 95616-3622

PALMER, ROBERT ARTHUR, private investigator; b. St. Augustine, Fla., May 20, 1948; m. Christine Lynn Creger, May 14, 1974. AA, Glendale C.C., 1975; BS, U. Phoenix, 1981; MA, Prescott Coll., 1993. Lic. pvt. investigator, Ariz. Dep. sheriff Maricopa County Sheriff's Office, Phoenix, 1971-79; owner Palmer Investigative Svcs., Prescott, Ariz., 1980-90; pres. The Magnum Corp., Prescott, 1990—. V.p. Mountain Club Homeowners, Prescott, 1986—. Mem. Internat. Assn. Chem. Testing, World Assn. Detectives, Nat. Assn. Legal Investigators, Nat. Assn. Profl. Process Servers, Ariz. Assn. Lic. Pvt. Investigators (pres. 1984), Ariz. Process Servers Assn. (pres. 1985-86), Prescott C. of C. (v.p. 1987-90). Office: Palmer Investigative Svcs PO Box 10760 Prescott AZ 86304-0760

PALMER, ROGER CAIN, information scientist; b. Corning, N.Y., Oct. 14, 1943; s. Wilbur Clarence and Eleanor Louise (Cain) P. AA, Corning (N.Y.) C.C., 1964; BA, Hartwick Coll., 1966; MLS, SUNY, Albany, 1972; PhD, U. Mich., 1978. Tchr. Penn Yan (N.Y.) Acad., 1966-68, 70-71; dep. head, grad. libr. SUNY, Buffalo, 1972-75; asst. prof. UCLA, 1978-83; sr. tech. writer Quotron Sys., Culver City, 1984; sr. sys. analyst Getty Art History Info., Santa Monica, Calif., 1984-90, mgr. tech. devel., 1990-93; mgr. internal cons. group The J. Paul Getty Trust, Santa Monica, 1993—; gen. ptnr. Liu-Palmer, L.A., 1989—. Author: Online Reference and Information Retrieval, 1987, dBase II and dBase III: An Introduction, 1984, Introduction to Computer Programming, 1983. With U.S. Army, 1968-70. Mem. IEEE Computer Soc., ALA, Am. Soc. for Info. Scis., Spl. Librs. Assn., Art Librs. Soc. of N.Am., Assn. for Computing Machinery, Pi Delta Epsilon, Beta Phi Mu. Home: 1045 N Kings Rd Ste 310 West Hollywood CA 90069 Office: The J Paul Getty Trust 401 Wilshire Blvd Ste 1100 Santa Monica CA 90401-1430

PALMER, VINCENT ALLAN, construction consultant; b. Wausa, Nebr., Feb. 18, 1913; s. Victor E. and Amy (Lindquist) P.; AA, Modesto Jr. Coll., 1933; BSCE, U. Calif., Berkeley, 1936; m. Louise V. Cramer, Mar. 12, 1938 (dec. June 1979); children: Margaret, Georgia, Vincent Allan; m. 2d, Hope Parker, Jan. 23, 1982. Constrn. engr. Kaiser Engrs., 1938-63, constrn. mgr., 1963-69, mgr. constrn., 1970-75, project mgr., 1975-76; project mgr. reef runway Universal Dredging Corp., Honolulu, 1975-76; pvt. practice constrn. cons., Walnut Creek, Calif., 1976—. Mem. ASCE (life), Project Mgmt. Inst. Home and Office: 1356 Corte Loma Walnut Creek CA 94598-2904

PALMER, WILLIAM EARL, private school educator; b. Oak Park, Ill., Oct. 11, 1961; s. Warren Everett and Leone Anne (Homan) P.; m. Jody Lynette Story, June 6, 1987; children: William Elijah, Jessy Katherine. BS in History, Coll. Great Falls, 1987. Dir. student life Mont. Wilderness Bible Coll., Augusta, Mont., 1983-84; social studies tchr., dept. head Tri-City Christian Sch., Vista, Calif., 1987—; art tchr., dept. head Tri-City Christian Sch., Vista, 1989—; guitar tchr., 1994—; art, music and drama ministry Ramona (Calif.) First Bapt. Ch., 1991-94; art tchr. Wasatch Acad., Mt. Pleasant, Utah, 1993; seminar leader on memory/study skills Tri-City Christian Sch. Home Sch., Vista, 1994. Econs. for Leaders scholar Found. for Tchg. Econs., Davis, Calif., 1994. Mem. Chess Club Suprs. Republican. Baptist. Office: Tri City Christian Sch 302 N Emerald Dr Vista CA 92083-6112

PALMER, WILLIAM JOSEPH, accountant; b. Lansing, Mich., Sept. 3, 1934; s. Joseph Flammin Lacchia and Henrietta (Yagerman) P.; m. Judith Pollock, Aug. 20, 1960 (div. Nov. 1980); children: William W., Kathryn E., Leslie A., Emily J.; m. Kathleen Francis Booth, June 30, 1990. BS, U. Calif., Berkeley, 1963; stepchildren: Blair T. Manwell, Lindsay A. Manwell. CPA. With Coopers and Lybrand, 1963-80, mng. ptnr., Sacramento, 1976-80; ptnr. Arthur Young & Co., San Francisco, 1980-89; ptnr. Ernst & Young, San Francisco, 1989-94; guest lectr. Stanford U. Engring. Sch., 1976; lectr. Golden Gate Coll., 1975; prof. U. Calif., Berkeley, 1994—. Author: (books) Businessman's Guide to Construction, 1981, Construction Management Book, 1984, Construction Accounting & Financial Management 5th Edition, 1994, Construction Litigation-Representing The Contractor, 1992, Construction Insurance, Bonding and Risk Management, 1995. Bd. dirs. Sacramento Met. YMCA, 1976-82, v.p., 1979-82; bd. dirs. Sacramento Symphony Found., 1977-80; asst. state fin. chmn. Calif. Reagan for Pres., 1980. Served to lt. USN, 1953-59. Mem. AICPA (vice chmn. com. constrn. industry, 1975-81), Nat. Assn. Accts. (pres. Oakland/East Bay chpt. 1972, Man of Yr. 1968), Calif. Soc. CPAs., Assn. Gen. Contractors Calif. (bd. dirs. 1971-74), World Trade Club, Commonwealth Club (San Francisco), Del Paso Country Club, Sutter Club, Comstock Club (Sacramento), Lambda Chi Alpha. Presbyterian. Avocations: antique boats, sailing, tennis, book collecting, pipe collecting. Home: 6 Heather Ln Orinda CA 94563-3508 Office: Ernst & Young 555 California St San Francisco CA 94104-1502

PALMIERI, RODNEY AUGUST, state agency administrator, pharmacist; b. Santa Rosa, Calif., July 12, 1944; s. August John and Olga (Giusti) P.; m. Phyllis Scott, Aug. 14, 1965; children: Christopher August, Joshua Scott. AA, Santa Rosa Jr. Coll., 1964; B of Pharmacy, U. Colo., 1968. Pvt. practice pharmacy, Santa Rosa, 1968-71; pharm. cons. State of Calif., San Jose, 1971-75; chief pharm. cons. State of Calif., Sacramento, 1975-80, sr. mgr., 1980-91; project dir. Vital Record Improvement Project, 1991—; gen. ptnr. Cold Springs Office Devel., Placerville, Calif., 1984—. Mem. El Dorado County Grand Jury, 1990; Weblos leader Boy Scouts Am., 1976-77, scoutmaster, 1977-82; referee, coach El Dorado (Calif.) Youth Soccer League, 1977-83; dir. El Dorado County Fair. Mem. Rho Chi (pres. 1967-68), Phi Delta Chi. Office: Cold Springs Cons 2900 Cold Springs Rd Placerville CA 95667-4220

PALOMBI, BARBARA JEAN, psychologist; b. Rockford, Ill., May 28, 1949; d. Frank and Vira Lavina (Gornet) P. BA, Luther Coll., Decorah, Iowa, 1971; MA, Pacific Lutheran U., Tacoma, Wash., 1974; PhD, Mich. State U., 1987. Career counselor Wright State U., Dayton, Ohio, 1974-77; asst. dean, dir. U. Calif., Irvine, 1977-80; grad. asst. Mich. State U., E. Lansing, 1980-83, clin. intern, 1983-84; clin. intern Colo. State U., Fort Collins, 1984-85; psychologist Ariz. State U., Tempe, 1985—, sr. psychologist, 1991—; cons. in field; dir. tng. Grand Valley State U., Allendale. Contbr. articles and papers to profl. jours. Mem. U.S. Wheelchair Olympic Team, 1976, U.S. Wheelchair Team to the Interna.t Stoke-Mandelville Games, 1979; alternative mem. U.S. Wheelchair Olympic Team, 1980; U.S. rep. Internat. Symposium on Sports, Physical Edn. and Recreation for the Handicapped, UNESCO, 1982. Grantee Nat. Sci. Found., U. Calif., 1977, 79; named Outstanding Handicapped Citizen Rock County 1982, Handicapped Profl. Woman of the Yr. Western Region, 1987. Mem. Am. Assn. Counseling and Devel. (Glen E. Hubele Nat. Grad. Student Research award 1988), Am. Coll. Personnel Assn. (bd. dirs. Div. VII-Counseling, mem. Div. VIII-Wellness, Burns B. Crookston Research award 1988, Commn. VII Grad. Student Research award 1988), Am. Psychology Assn. (rep. div. 17 handicapped task force). Democrat. Home: 4257 Stonebridge Dr SW Apt 3 Wyoming MI 49509-4163 Office: Ariz State U Counseling Consultation Tempe AZ 85287

PALOUNEK, ANDREA P.T., physicist; b. Prague, Czechoslovakia, Oct. 26, 1956; came to U.S, 1964; d. Lubos R. and Irene B.P. AB in Chemistry and Physics, Harvard U., 1978; MA in Physics, Duke U., 1980, PhD in Physics, 1984. Rschr. MIT Lab. for Nuclear Sci., Cambridge, Mass., 1984-87; physicist Stanford Linear Accelerator Ctr., Palo Alto, Calif., 1988; postdoctoral fellow Lawrence Berkeley Lab., Berkeley, Calif., 1988-91, Los Alamos (New Mex.) Nat. Lab., 1991—; lectr., cons. Gov.'s Sch. of N.C., 1974—, Gov.'s Sch. of Ark., 1993. Contbr. articles to profl. jours. Lectr. to elem., middle and high sch. students in N.C., Calif., New Mex., 1974—. Mem. AAAS, Am Phys. Soc., Sigma Xi. Office: Los Alamos Nat Lab MS D456 Los Alamos NM 87545

PALSMA, MARY J(ACOBSON), secondary education educator; b. Webster, S.D., Jan. 16, 1942; d. M. Sherman and Shirley Mae (Amsden) Jacobson; m. Wayne H. Palsma, Dec. 23, 1967; 1 child, Robert Wayne. BS, Northern State Coll., Aberdeen, S.D., MS, 1967. Cert. tchr., Community Coll., Ariz., Secondary High Schs., Ariz. & S.D. English tchr., libr. Northwestern High Sch., Northville, S.D., 1962; math. tchr. Milbank (S.D.) High Sch., 1962-64; math. and English tchr. Riggs High Sch., Pierre, S.D., 1964-68, Mitchell (S.D.) Jr. High Sch., 1969-70, Bourgade Catholic High Sch., Phoenix, 1975—; with Madeline Hunter's Essential Elements of Instrn., Phoenix, 1987-88. Pres. Inter-Club Coun. of Ariz., 1987-88. Mem. Am. Assn. of U. Women (several offices, 1965—, pres. 1977-79; fellowship grant, 1980), Nat. Catholic Edn. Assn. Republican. Lutheran.

PALUMBO, DENNIS JAMES, political scientist, educator; b. Chgo., Nov. 18, 1929; s. Richard Anthony and Nora (Griffin) P.; m. Sachiko Onishi, Apr. 15, 1954; children: Jean, Dennis, Linda. MA in Social Sci., U. Chgo., 1957, MA in Polit. Sci., 1958, PhD of Polit. Sci., 1960. Asst. prof. Mich. State U., East Lansing, 1960-62; asst. prof. dept. polit. sci., asst. rschr. U. Hawaii, Honolulu, 1962-63; asst. prof. polit. sci. U. Pa., Phila., 1963-66; assoc. prof., prof. polit. sci. CUNY, Bklyn. Coll., 1966-76; prof. Pub. and Environ. Affairs Ind. U., Bloomington, 1976-77; prof. polit. sci., exec. dir. Ctr. for Pub. Affairs U. Kans., Lawrence, 1977-83; prof. pub. affairs, dir. Morrison Inst. for Pub. Policy Ariz. State U., Tempe, 1983-86, prof. justice studies, 1986-88, Regents' prof. justice studies, 1988—; guest lectr. U. Ga., 1975, SUNY Stony Brook, 1975, U. Ala., 1976; cons. Ford Found. Evaluation of Minority Support Program, 1974, N.Y.C. Police Dept., 1975, Ctr. for Law and Poverty, Indpls., Hamilton-Pabinowitz, Inc., Pub. Mgmt. Svcs., Okla. Crime Commn., Shawnee County Kans. Comprehensive Plan for Cmty. Corrections, 1978-79; cons. Home Arrest in Ariz. Project Intervention, Gang Resistance Edn. and Tng., Project Care, Shock Incarceration; expert witness various law firms in discrimination cases.; presenter papers in field; panelist profl. meetings; participant workshops. Author: Workbook to Accompany Statistics in Political and Behavioral Science, 1969, Statistics in Political and Behavior Science, 1969, 2d edit., 1977, American Politics, 1973, American Politics Instructor's Manual, 1973, Public Policy In America: Government in Action, 1989, Workbook to Accompany Statistics in Political and Behavioral Science, 1969, (with J. Levine and M. Musheno) Criminal Justice A Public Policy Approach, 1980, Criminal Justice in America: Law in Action, 1986 (with Steven Maynard-Moody) Contemporary Public Administration, 1991; editor: The Politics of Program Evaluation, 1987, Optimizing, Implementing and Evaluating Public Policy, 1980, (with Mike Harder) Implementing Public Policy, 1981, (with Steve Fawcett and Paula Wright) Optimizing and Evaluating Public Policy, 1981, Implementation: What Have We Learned and Still Need to Know, 1987, (with Donald Calista) Implementation and the Policy Process: Opening up the Black Box, 1990; co-editor: Introduction to Social Sciences, 11 vols., 1962, (with George Taylor) Urban Policy, 1979; contbr. chpts. to books, numerous articles to profl. jours.; author monographs; founding editor, editor-in-chief Policy Studies Review, 1981-87, editor with Michael Musheno, 1987-90. Grantee Pub. Health Sys. Rsch. Project, 1965-67, Kans. Dept. Revenue, 1979-81, Nat. Inst. Justice, 1981-83, Nat. Highway Traffic and Safety Adminstrn., 1982-84, Ariz. Dept. Corrections, 1989-90. Mem. APHA (health programs evaluation com. 1971-73), Am. Polit. Sci. Assn., Am. Soc. Criminology, Am. Evaluation Assn., Assn. of Mgmt. in Pub. Health, Evaluation Rsch. Soc. (chair awards com. 1981), N.Y. State Polit. Sci. Assn. Office: Sch Justice Studies Ariz State Univ Tempe AZ 85287

PALUZZI, PETER RONALD, data processing professional; b. Little Falls, N.Y., Jan. 4, 1951; s. Victor and Lucille (Pepin) Paluzzi; m. Susan Laigner, July 10, 1982; 1 child, Claire. BS in Geology, SUNY, Albany, 1973; MS, U. So. Calif., 1979. Sr. scientist Jet Propulsion Lab. of Calif. Tech., Pasadena, 1973-81; sr. rsch. geophysicist Sohio Petroleum Co., Dallas, 1982-86; applications software mgr. Sterling Software, John von Neumann Nat. Supercomputer Ctr., Princeton, N.J., 1986-89; sr. staff mem. Sterling Software, Ames Divsn., NASA, Moffett Field, Calif., 1989—; orgnl. re-engring. com. NASA Ames Rsch. Ctr., Moffett Field, 1994; disting. lectr. U.S. Office of Naval Rsch. Lectr. Series, 1982. Registered Calif. disaster svc. worker, dep. chief radio officer Santa Clara County Office of Emergency Svcs., 1991—. Regents scholarship Univ. of the State of N.Y., 1969-73. Mem. Assn. of Computing Machinery, IEEE Geosci. and Remote Sensing Soc. (vice chairperson Santa Clara Valley chpt. 1991-92), Am. Soc. for Photgrammetry and Remote Sensing, Geol. Soc. of Am., Am. Geophys. Union. Home: PO Box 2244 Cupertino CA 95015-2244 Office: Sterling Software NASA Ames Divsn NASA Ames Rsch Ctr MS233-10 Moffett Field CA 94035-1000

PAMPLIN, ROBERT BOISSEAU, SR., textile manufacturing executive; b. Sutherland, Va., Nov. 25, 1911; s. John R. and Pauline (Beville) P.; m. Mary K. Reese, June 15, 1940; 1 child, Robert Boisseau Jr. BBA, Va. Poly. Inst. & State U., 1933; postgrad., Northwestern U., 1933-34; LLD (hon.), U. Portland (Oreg.), 1972; LHD (hon.), Warner Pacific Coll., 1976. With Ga.-Pacific Corp., Portland, 1934-76, sec., from 1936, adminstrv. v.p., 1952-55, exec. v.p., 1955-57, pres., 1957-67, chmn. bd., chief exec. officer, from 1967; ret., 1976; with R.B. Pamplin Corp., 1957—, chmn. bd., chief exec. officer; also chmn. bd., chief exec. officer Mt. Vernon Mills Inc. (subs. R.B. Pamplin Corp.), Greenville, S.C. Office: R B Pamplin Corp 900 SW 5th Ave Ste 1800 Portland OR 97204-1227 also: Mt Vernon Mills Inc PO Box 3478 1 Insignia Fin Plz Greenville SC 29602

PAN, WILLIAM JIAWEI, import/export company executive, consultant; b. Shanghai, People's Republic of China, July 24, 1935; came to U.S., 1985; s. You-Yuan Pan and Ruth Li Tien; m. Fengqiu Liu, Dec. 26, 1965; 1 child, Song. BS, Peking U., People's Republic of China, 1958. Cert. sr. engr., People's Republic of China. Engr. Beijing Radio Factory, 1958-78, Dong Feng TV Factory, Beijing, 1978-80; asst. gen. mgr. Beijing br. China Nat. Electronics Import/Export Corp., 1980-91; mgr. electronics dept. China Resource Products, N.Y.C., 1985-91; pres., chief exec. officer King Trading, Inc., San Francisco, 1987-91; pres., CEO Kings Internat., Inc., San Jose, Calif., 1991—. Office: Kings Internat Inc 467 Saratoga Ave Ste 150 San Jose CA 95129-1326

PANASCI, NANCY ERVIN, speech pathologist, cookbook writer, communications consultant; b. Fairborn, Ohio, Mar. 24, 1954; d. Lindsay James and Frances E. (Erickson) Ervin; m. Ernest James Panasci, Aug. 7, 1976; children: Caitlin Alba, Adele Frances, Carissa Anne. BS, Colo. State U., 1976; MA, Cath. U., Washington, 1979. Tchr. Montessori Sch., Rome, N.Y., 1971-72, Fairfax (Va.) Sch. Dist., 1976-77; speech pathologist Littleton (Colo.) Pub. Schs., 1979-92, pvt. practice, 1992—; communication cons. speech pathology Trial Attys., Denver, 1986—. Com. chairperson. Jr. League in Denver, 1982-91; com. chmn. Make-A-Wish Found. of Colo., 1991; com. chairperson. Denver Victims Svc. Ctr., Share Our Strength, Nat. Kidney Found. Named Best Cook in West, Rocky Mountain Newspaper, Denver, 1982. Mem. Am. Speech Hearing Lang. Assn. (cert. clin. competence 1980), Colo. Speech Hearing Assn. (com. chairperson 1982-86), Cherry Hills Country Club. Roman Catholic. Home: 5191 S Hanover St Englewood CO 80111-6244 Office: Littleton Public Schools Littleton CO 80120

PANDER, HENDRIK PIETER, artist; b. Haarlem, Netherlands, Nov. 21, 1937; came to the U.S., 1965; s. Jacob and Henderica (Smedes) P.; m. Marcia Lynch, 1964 (div.); children: Jacob, Arnold. Cert. completion, Rijksacademie van Beeldende, Amsterdam, 1961. co-founder, bd. mem. Storefront Theatre, Portland, 1970-87; founder, mem. selection com. Visual Chronicle Portland, 1985-91; commr. Met. Arts Commn., Portland, 1992-93, mem. pub. art adv. com., 1993—; presenter in field. One-person shows include Elizabeth Leach Gallery, Portland, 1993, 94, Davidson Galleries, Seattle, 1994, Index Gallery, Clark Coll., Vancouver, Wash., 1994; group shows include Seattle (Wash.) Art Fair, 1992, 93, 94, 95, U. Oreg. Mus. Art, Eugene, 1993, Tacoma (Wash.) Art Mus., 1993, Nordic Heritage Mus., Seattle, 1994, Artquake, Portland, 1994, Chgo. Art Fair; represented in permanent collections including City of Amsterdam, Netherlands, City of Portland, Oreg., Claremont Hotel, Berkeley, others. Recipient Prix de Rome, Dutch Govt., 1961, Talens prize Talens Art Supply Factory, 1961, Therese van Duyl Schwarze award, Amsterdam, 1964, Drammy award for best set Willamette Week Newspaper, Portland, 1992; Master fellow Oreg. Arts Commn., Salem, 1991. Mem. ARTNET, N.W. Figurative Art Alliance, Netherlands Bus. and Cultural Assn. Studio: 1801 NW Upshur St Portland OR 97209-1700

PANDEY, LAKSHMI NARAYAN, physicist, researcher; b. Varanasi, India, July 19, 1956; came to U.S., 1984; s. Ganapati Pandey and Phoolmati Devi; m. Nirmala Devi, June 11, 1973; children: Mata Prasad, Renu, Suman. BS, Banaras Hindu U., Varanasi, 1976, MS, 1978, PhD, 1984. Sr. fellow Banaras Hindu U., Varanasi, 1982-84; post-doctoral fellow SUNY, Buffalo, 1984-88, rsch. instr., 1988-91; scientist Wash. State U., Pullman, 1991—. Contbr. articles to Phys. Rev. Letters, Physics Letters A, Applied Physics Letters. Mem. Am. Phys. Soc., Material Rsch. Soc. Hindu. Home: 125 NW Larry St Apt 6 Pullman WA 99163-3537 Office: Wash State U Dept Physics Pullman WA 99164

PANDOL, JACK J., food products executive; b. 1952. With Pandol & Sons Inc., 1973—. Office: Pandol & Sons County Line Rd 192 Delano CA 93215*

PANDOL, MATT, food products executive; b. 1927. With Pandol & Sons, 1948—. Office: Pandol & Sons County Line Rd 192 Delano CA 93215*

PANEC, DONALD JOHN, marketing executive; b. Oak Park, Ill., Mar. 24, 1955; s. Donald Otto and Sherry (Heflin) P. BA, U. Calif., L.A., 1981; MBA, Harvard U., 1984. Profl. actor various children's theater and tv commls., 1975-78; adminstrv. dir. TNRC Prodns., Studio City, Calif., 1978-79; tv prodr. ednl. children's programming TNRC Prodns., Studio City, 1980-82; asst. mktg. mgr. He-Man (Masters of the Universe) Mattel Toys, Hawthorne, Calif., 1984-85; assoc. mktg. mgr. He-Man, BraveStarr Mattel Toys, Hawthorne, 1985-86, product mktg. mgr. Mad Scientist, BraveStarr, 1986-87; mgr. toy devel. and mktg. DIC, Burbank, 1987-88; mktg. mgr. video game hardware and software Epyx, Inc., Redwood City, 1988-89, Broderbund Software, San Rafael, 1989-90; from mktg. dir. to v.p. mktg. OddzOn Products, Campbell, 1990-92, 92—. Office: OddzOn Products 1696 Dell Ave Campbell CA 95008-6901

PANETTA, JOSEPH DANIEL, biotechnology executive; b. Syracuse, N.Y., Mar. 1, 1954; s. Salvatore and Josephine Mary (Sbardella) P.; m. Karin Ann

Hoffman, Oct. 21, 1978; children: Lauren Marie, Christopher Daniel. BS, LeMoyne Coll., 1976; MPH, U. Pitts., 1979. Environ. protection specialist U.S. EPA, Washington, 1979-82, sr. policy analyst, 1982-84; project leader Schering Corp./NorAm Chem Co., Wilmington, Del., 1984-85; mgr. regulatory affairs agrchems. divsn. Pennwalt Corp., Phila., 1985-88; mgr. corp. regulatory affairs Mycogen Corp., San Diego, 1988-90; dir. corp. regulatory affairs and quality assurance Mycogen Corp., 1990-92; dir. corp. regulatory, environ. affairs Mycogen Corp., San Diego, 1992—; chmn. agr. and environment subcom. Internat. Bioindustry Forum; chmn. maneb data task force Inter-industry, Washington, 1985-88; guest lectr. biotech. U. Calif., San Diego, and Calif. Western Law Sch. Contbr. articles to profl. jours. Mem. Rep. State Com. Del., 1987. Mem. Nat. Agrl. Chems. Assn. (mem. registrations com. 1986-89), Indsl. Biotech. Assn. (mem. food and agr. sect., chmn. bipesticides com., internat. affairs com.), Calif. Indsl. Biotech. Assn. (mem. agrl. affairs com.), Am. Chem. Soc. (mem. agrl. div.). Roman Catholic. Home: 4324 Corte Al Fresco San Diego CA 92130-2160 Office: Mycogen Corp 4980 Carroll Canyon Rd San Diego CA 92121-1736

PANG, HERBERT GEORGE, ophthalmologist; b. Honolulu, Dec. 23, 1922; s. See Hung and Hong Jim (Chuu) P.; student St. Louis Coll., 1941; BS, Northwestern U., 1944, MD, 1947; m. Dorothea Lopez, Dec. 27, 1953. Intern Queen's Hosp., Honolulu, 1947-48; postgraduate course ophthalmology N.Y.U., Med. Sch., 1948-49; resident ophthalmology Jersey City Med. Ctr., 1949-50, Manhattan Eye, Ear, & Throat Hosp., N.Y.C., 1950-52; practice medicine specializing in ophthalmology, Honolulu, 1952-54, 56—; mem. staffs Kuakini Hosp., Children's Hosp., Castle Meml. Hosp., Queen's Hosp., St. Francis Hosp.; asst. clin. prof. ophthalmology U. Hawaii Sch. Medicine, 1966-73, now asso. clin. prof. Cons. Bur. Crippled Children, 1952-73, Kapiolani Maternity Hosp., 1952-73, Leahi Tb. Hosp., 1952-62. Capt. M.C., AUS, 1954-56, Diplomate Am. Bd. Ophthalmology. Mem. AMA, Am. Acad. Ophthalmology and Otolaryngology, Assn. for Rsch. Ophthalmology, ACS, Hawaii Med. Soc. (gov. med. practice com. 1958-62, chmn. med. speakers com. 1957-58), Hawaii Eye, Ear, Nose and Throat Soc. (pres. 1960), Pacific Coast Oto-Ophthalmological Soc., Pan Am. Assn. Ophthalmology, Mason, Shriner, Eye Study Club (pres. 1972—). Home: 346 Lewers St Honolulu HI 96815-2345

PANG, LAURA JARNAGIN, political economy educator, consultant; b. El Paso, June 6, 1951; d. Ray Porter and Ruth (Peake) Jarnagin; m. Eul-Soo Pang, June 6, 1979. BA in Internat. Affairs, U. Colo., 1973; MA in Latin. Am. Studies, Vanderbilt U., 1977, PhD, 1981. Asst. prof. history U. Ala., Birmingham, 1981-82, Auburn U. at Montgomery, Ala., 1983-85; asst. rsch. prof. Colo. Sch. Mines, Golden, 1986-88, asst. prof. history and Latin Am. studies, 1988-91, assoc. prof., 1992—, dir. Latin Am. Ctr., 1992-94; sr. ptnr. Inter-Sierra Group, Inc., Evergreen, Colo., 1991—. Contbr. chpt. to book, articles to profl. jours. Mem. Gov.'s Task Force on Latin Am., State of Colo., Denver, 1987-88. Mem. Rocky Mountain Coun. on Latin Am. Studies, Inst. of the Americas. Presbyterian. Office: Colo Sch Mines 1500 Illinois St Golden CO 80401-1887

PANHUYZEN, RALPH PHILIP, trade relations promoter; b. The Hague, Netherlands, June 12, 1957; came to the U.S., 1992; s. Petrus Harry and Yvonne (Ornek) P. Doctorate in Hist. Scis., Leyden (Netherlands) U., 1985. Chief editor Grenzeloos Monthly Mag. on Internat. Affairs, Leyden, 1981-83; project mgr. Netherlands Study Ctr., Vlaardingen, Netherlands, 1985-89; mgr. internat. co-prodns. Expoconsult, Maarssen, Netherlands, 1989-92; mng. ptnr. ExpoForum, Irvine, Calif., 1992—; mem. European bd. Meeting Planners Internat., Brussels, 1990-92. Coord. U.S.-Netherlands polit. rels. Student Assn. for Internat. Affairs, Leyden, 1980-83. Mem. Internat. Assn. Exposition Mgmt. (So. Calif. chpt.), Internat. Assn. Exposition Mgrs., Netherlands-Am. Found. (rep. 1992—), Netherlands-Am. Bus. Assn., Long Beach (Calif.) C. of C. Office: ExpoForum A-208 C-102 15375 Barranca Pky # C-102 Irvine CA 92718-2217

PANICCIA, PATRICIA LYNN, television news reporter, lawyer; b. Glendale, Calif., Sept. 19, 1952; d. Valentino and Mary (Napoleon) P.; m. Jeffrey McDowell Mailes, Oct. 5, 1985; children: Alana Christine, Malia Noel. BA in Communication, U. Hawaii, Honolulu, 1977; JD, Pepperdine U., Malibu, Calif., 1981. Bar: Hawaii 1981, Calif. 1982, U.S. Dist. Ct. Hawaii 1981. Extern law clk. Hon. Samuel P. King U.S. Dist. Ct., Honolulu, 1980; reporter, anchor woman Sta. KEYT-TV, Santa Barbara, Calif., 1983-84; reporter Sta. KCOP-TV, Los Angeles, 1984-88; reporter CNN L.A., 1989-93; instr. communications law Pepperdine Sch. Law, 1987, 94—, adj. prof.; profl. surfer, 1977-81. Recipient Clarion award Women In Communication, Inc., 1988. Mem. ABA (chair of law and media com. young lawyers div., 1987-88, nat. conf. com. lawyers and reps. of media, 1987-91), Calif. State Bar (mem. com. on fair trial and free press 1983-84, pub. affairs com. 1985-87), Hawaii Bar Assn., Phi Delta Phi (historian 1980-81). Avocations: surfing, skiing, piano, guitar. Office: 1313 Foothill Blvd Ste 11 La Canada CA 91011

PANKOVE, JACQUES ISAAC, physicist; b. Chernigov, Russia, Nov. 23, 1922; came to U.S., 1942, naturalized, 1944; s. Evsey Leib and Miriam (Simkine) Pantchechnikoff; m. Ethel Wasserman, Nov. 24, 1950; children: Martin, Simon. B.S.E.E., U. Calif., Berkeley, 1944, M.S.E.E., 1948; Ph.D. in Physics, U. Paris, 1960. Mem. tech. staff RCA Labs., Princeton, N.J., 1948-70; physicist, fellow RCA Labs., 1970-85; prof. U. Colo., Boulder, 1985-93, prof. emeritus, 1993—, Hudson Moore Jr. Univ. prof., 1989-93, program mgr. materials and devices Ctr. for Optoelectronic Computing Systems, 1986-89; Disting. Rsch. fellow Nat. Renewal Energy Lab. (formerly Solar Energy Rsch. Inst.), 1985-93; v.p. for rsch. and tech. Astralux, Inc., 1993—; vis. McKay lectr. U. Calif., Berkeley, 1968-69; vis. prof. U. Campinas, Brazil, 1975; Disting. vis. prof. U. Mo. at Rolla, 1984; participant NAS sci. exch. program with: Romania, 1970, Hungary, 1972, Yugoslavia, 1976. Mem. hon. editorial bd. Solid State Electronics, 1970-94, Solar Energy Materials, 1984—, Optoelectronics, 1986—; regional editor Crystal Lattice Defects and Amorphous Materials, 1984-90; author: Optical Processes in Semiconductors, 1971, 75; editor: Electroluminescence, 1977, Display Devices, 1980, Hydrogenated Amorphous Silicon, 1984; co-editor: Hydrogen in Semiconductors, 1991, Wide Bandgap Semiconductors, 1992; author: (ednl. film) Energy Gap and Recombination Radiation, 1962; laser sculpture, Bklyn. Mus., 1968; contbr. articles to profl. jours.; organizer sci. confs.; patentee in field. Trustee Princeton Art Assn., 1970-82; mem. Experiment-in-Arts-and-Tech., Berkeley, 1968-69. Served with U.S. Army, 1944-46. Recipient RCA achievement awards, 1952, 53, 63; David Sarnoff scholar, 1956. Fellow IEEE (J. J. Ebers award 1975, assoc. editor Jour. Quantum Electronics 1968-77, mem-at-large IEEE awards bd. 1992-95), Am. Phys. Soc.; mem. AAAS, NAE (hon.), Materials Rsch. Soc., Internat. Soc. for Optical Engring., Sigma Xi. Home: 2386 Vassar Dr Boulder CO 80303-5763 Office: U Colo Dept Elec Engring Boulder CO 80309-0425

PANKRATZ, ROBERT LEE, psychologist; b. Hemet, Calif., Nov. 11, 1946; s. Otto J. and Emily (Frantz) P.; m. Karen Pankratz, July, 1971 (div. 1982); children: Aaron T., Loren D.; m. Saundra D. Morgan, Aug. 3, 1985; children: Brian P. Fleming, Jana N. Fleming. BA, Occidental Coll., 1968; MDiv, Am. Bapt. Seminary West, 1971; M in Counseling, Calif. State U., Fresno, 1982, postgrad., 1982-83. Lic. ednl. psychologist, Calif.; credentialed sch. psychologist, Calif. Youth and music pastor 1st Bapt. Ch., Bellflower, Calif., 1969-71, Stockton, Calif., 1971-74; sr. pastor East Princeton Bapt. Ch., Fresno, 1975-80; high sch. vocat. counselor Madera (Calif.) Unified Sch. Dist., 1981-83; sch. psychologist Los Banos (Calif.) Unified Sch. Dist., 1983-84, Fresno Unified Sch. Dist., 1984—. Min. of music Ch. of Brethren, Fresno, 1981-85. Mem. Calif. Assn. Sch. Psychologists, Nat. Assn. Sch. Psychologists, Am. Bapt. Mins. Assn. (pres. Ctrl. Valley chpt. 1978). Home: 1284 E Cromwell Ave Fresno CA 93720-2681

PANKS, GARY ALLEN, golf course architect; b. Flint, Mich., July 9, 1941; s. Allen T. and Lois (Dennis) P.; m. Judith Ann Panks, Oct. 9, 1972; children: Brian, Paul. BS in Landscape Arthitecture, Mich. State U., 1964. Registered landscape architect, Ariz. Landscape architect N.Y. State Dept. Pub. Works, N.Y.C., 1964-65, Maricopa County Parks and Recreation, Phoenix, 1965-67; architect, land planner City of Phoenix, 1967-71; golf course architect Gary Panks Assocs., Scottsdale, Ariz., 1971—, Graham & Panks Internat., Scottsdale, 1988—. Designer of courses include Grayhawk Course, Scottsdale, Ariz. Recipient Best New Pub. Course in U.S. award Golf Digest mag., 1986, Top Three New Resort Courses in U.S. award, 1989. Mem. Airz. Soc. Landscape Architects (Honor award), U.S. Golf Assn., Ariz. Golf Assn. (bd. dirs., mem. exec. com.). Office: Graham & Panks Internat 8777 E Via De Ventura Ste 315 Scottsdale AZ 85258-3345

PANNER, OWEN M., federal judge; b. 1924. Student, U. Okla., 1941-43, LL.B., 1949. Atty. Panner, Johnson, Marceau, Karnopp, Kennedy & Nash, 1950-80; judge, now sr. judge U.S. Dist. Ct. Oreg., Portland, 1980—. Office: US Dist Ct 335 US Courthouse 620 SW Main St Portland OR 97205-3037*

PANSKY, EMIL JOHN, entrepreneur; b. Manhattan, N.Y., June 1, 1921; s. Stanislaus and Anna (Jankovic) P.; m. Billie B. Byrne, May 27, 1955; 1 adopted child, Jimmy. BME, Cooper Union Coll., 1941; MBA, Harvard U., 1949; MADE, NYU, 1950. Registered profl. engr., Mich. Chief insp. flight line Republic Aviation, Farmingdale, L.I., 1941-45, salvage engr., 1946-47; product control supr. to product control mgr. Ford Motor, Detroit, 1949-51; asst. plant mgr. Anderson Brass, Birmingham, Ala., 1951-53; asst. v.p. to v.p. mfg. Cummins Engine, Columbus, Ind., 1953-54; pvt. practice Emil J. Pansky Assoc., San Leandro, Calif., 1954—; pres. Calif. Mfrs. Tech. Assn., San Francisco, 1978-80; cons. in field. Patentee die cast auto wheels, 1965. Pres. Menlo Circus Club, Menlo Park, Calif., 1974-81, Home Owners Assn., Kanuela, Hawaii, 1989-95; bd. dirs. No. Calif. Tennis Assn., San Francisco, 1984-87. Mem. ASME (life), Harvard Club San Francisco (bd. dirs. 1986-92), Harvard Bus. Sch. Club San Francisco (bd. dirs. 1970-73, cons. 1994-95). Democrat. Home: 901 Jackling Dr Hillsborough CA 94010-6127 Office: Emil J Pansky Assoc 1666 Timothy Dr San Leandro CA 94577-2312

PANTOS, WILLIAM PANTAZES, mechanical engineer, consultant; b. Ann Arbor, Mich., May 15, 1957; s. William Van and Lillian William (Skinner) P. BS in Mech. Engring., Northwestern U., Evanston, Ill., 1979; MS in Mech. Engring., San Diego State U., 1991. Registered profl. engr., Calif. Owner Signs & Symbols, Niles, Ill., 1975-80; engr. Hughes Aircraft, El Segundo, Calif., 1980-83, Gen. Dynamics, San Diego, 1983-85; staff engr. TRW, San Diego, 1985-90; pres. Tekton Industries, Carlsbad, Calif., 1990—. NROTC scholar USN, 1975. Mem. Am. Soc. Mech. Engrs., Nat. Soc. Profl. Engrs., Alpha Delta Phi. (pres. 1978). Greek Orthodox. Home: 6857 Seaspray Ln Carlsbad CA 92009-3738

PAPAMARCOS, MARK STANLEY, electronic design automation consultant; b. Elgin, Ill., Sept. 24, 1962; s. John and Barbara Ann (Johnson) P.; m. Barbara Joan Bauer. BS in Computer Engring., U. Ill., 1982, MS in Elec. Engring., 1984; MBA, U. Calif., Berkeley, 1993. Mem. tech. staff ESL, Sunnyvale, Calif., 1984-85; sr. engr. Valid Logic Systems, Inc., San Jose, Calif., 1985-87; dir. hardware devel. Modeling Systems, Inc., Milpitas, Calif., 1987-90; mgr. process integration Valid Logic Systems, Inc., San Jose, 1991; mgr. design methodology Cadence Design Systems, San Jose, 1991-93; owner, prin. EDA Assocs., San Jose, 1990-91, 93—. Patentee in field. Mem. IEEE (P896.2 standards com. 1984-87). Office: EDA Assocs 1738 Deer Creek Ct San Jose CA 95148-1402

PAPATHAKIS, PEGGY CALLAGHAN, registered dietitian; b. L.A., Sept. 29, 1955; d. Joseph Molnar and Jacqueline Ann (Gibney) Callaghan; m. John Anthony Papathakis, Apr. 12, 1980; children: Sean, Eric, Caitlin. BS in Dietetics, Calif. Poly. State U., 1977. Registered dietitian; cert. specialist in pediatric nutrition. Dietetic intern Alton Ochsner Med. Found., New Orleans, 1978-79; clin. nutritionist U. Calif. Davis Med. Ctr., Sacramento, 1979-81, pediatric nutritionist, 1981—; area dir. and instr. Shapers Nutrition Class, Kaiser, Sacramento and Roseville, Calif., 1985-88, 95—. Author articles; interviewed on TV, radio and in newspapers. Bd. dirs., fundraising chair, pub. rels. chair Cedar Springs Waldorf Sch., Placerville, Calif., 1992—. Mem. NOW, Am. Dietetic Assn. (Young Dietitian of Yr. 1984), Calif. Dietitian Assn. (media rels. liaison 1989—, legis. steering com. 1990—, dist. pres., sec. nominating com. 1983-90, Excellence in Clin. Practice award 1992, Jane Pirkey award 1992), Am. Soc. Parenteral and Enteral Nutrition. Office: U Calif Davis Med Ctr 2516 Stockton Blvd Sacramento CA 95817-2208

PAPE, ARNIS WESTON, minister; b. Portales, N.Mex., Dec. 24, 1950; s. Arnis Wilson and Lella Mae (Berry) P.; m. Lucena Ann Molzen, May 31, 1975; children: John Dayton, Jennifer Marie. BA in Psychology, U.N.Mex., 1974; MS in Biblical and Related Studies, Abilene Christian U., 1995. Ordained to ministry Church of Christ, 1972. Assoc. minister Ch. of Christ, Plainview, Tex., 1974-76; pulpit minister Ch. of Christ, Artesia, N.Mex., 1976-85, Ft. Collins, Colo., 1985—; tchr. Pepperdine U., Malibu, 1991, 93. Editor bull. Meadowlark Messenger, 1985—; contbr. articles to profl. jours.; author booklet: Happy Though Married, 1988, rev. edit., 1992. Co-founder Am. Children's Transplant Fund, Ft. Collins, 1987; mem. Parent Adv. Bd., Artesia, 1983-84; mem. pres.'s coun. Lubbock Christian U., 1985—. Recipient award for outstanding svc. Ch. of Christ, 1985. Home: 2212 Shawnee Ct Fort Collins CO 80525-1849 Office: Church of Christ 2810 Meadowlark Ave Fort Collins CO 80526-2838

PAPE, BARBARA KAREN, administrative assistant; b. Compton, Calif., Jan. 31, 1950; d. Louis and Theresa Carolyn (Gallup) Aprea; m. Jack William Pape, Dec. 31, 1969; children: Jack Lewis, Chad William. Diploma in med. assisting, Blair Coll. Med. and Dental; student, Orange Coast Coll., Saddleback Coll., U. Calif., Irvine. Lic. x-ray technician, Calif. Instrnl. aide remedial reading grades 7 and 8 Placentia (Calif.) Unified Sch. Dist., 1974-79; proficiency test coord. grades 9 to 12 Irvine (Calif.) Unified Sch. Dist., 1979-85; part time adminstrv. asst. Cirello Magnetos and Racing, Costa Mesa, Calif., 1972—; part time clerical specialist Fluor Daniel, Irvine, 1993—. Co-author, publisher: How to Begin a Successful Acting Career, 1993. Active Irvine (Calif.) Unified Sch. Dist. Adv. Com., 1983-84, 85; mem. citizens adv. com. Orange County Transit Dist., 1984-91; bd. mem., vol. Sutton Found., 1993—. Republican. Roman Catholic. Home: 11 Longstreet Irvine CA 92720-3368

PAPE, THOMAS EMIL, marketing professional, consultant; b. Redbud, Ill., Apr. 28, 1959; s. Gilbert Raymond and Delphine (Mehrtens) P. BA, So. Ill. U., 1981. Cert. energy auditor, Ill., residential conservation svc. trainer, Calif., master water auditor. Energy cons. VISTA, Carbondale, Ill., 1979-80; design cons. Applied Alternatives, Desoto, Ill., 1980-83; energy auditor DMC Energy Inc., Springfield, Ill., 1981-83, field cons., 1983-84; project supr. DMC Energy Inc., Santa Monica, Calif., 1984-85; mktg. rsch. cons. DMC Energy Inc., L.A., 1985-88; conservation specialist City of Pasadena, Calif., 1988-90; dir. Volt Delta Resources, Orange, Calif., 1990—; mem. solar speaker bur. Ill. Dept. Energy and Natural Resources, 1979-82. Mem. Assn. Profl. Energy Mgrs., Am. Water Works Assn. (chmn. water conservation com. on interior plumbing), Pacific Coast Electric Assn. (exec. dir.), Pacific Coast Gas Assn. (exec. dir.). Roman Catholic. Home: 1704 Elm St El Cerrito CA 94530-1909

PAPEN, FRANK O'BRIEN, banker, former state senator; b. Dec. 2, 1909; m. Julia Stevenson; 1 child, Michele Papen-Daniel. LLD (hon.), N.Mex. State U., 1988. Dir. First Nat. Bank Dona Ana County, Las Cruces, N.Mex., 1957-60, exec. v.p., 1957-60, pres., 1960-71, chmn. bd. dirs., chief exec. officer, 1971-82, 88—, pres., chmn. bd. dirs., 1982-87; mem. Ho. of reps. State of N.Mex., 1957-58, senator, 1969-84; vice-chmn. 12 regional adv. com. on banking practices and policies, 1965-66; mem. adv. com. on fed. legis., 1966; mem. N.Mex. State Investment Council, 1963-67; mem. N.Mex. Dept. Devel. Adv. Council, 1967-68; mem. steering com. Edn. Commn. States; mem. Albuquerque dist. adv. council SBA; pres. N.Mex. State U. Pres. Assocs. Mem. N.M. Ho. of Reps., 1957-58 (chmn. legis. fin. com. and legis. sch. study com.), N.M. State Senate, 1969-84. Recipient Citizen of Yr. award N.Mex. Assn. Realtors, 1966, Branding Iron award N.Mex. State U., 1977, The Pres.'s award for Service N.Mex. State U., 1983, Regent's medal N.Mex. State U., 1985, N.Mex. Sch. Banking Leadership award, 1987, Bob Haynsworth Sportsmanship award Sunland Park Race Track, 1987. Mem. Am. Bankers Assn. (savs. bond chmn. N.Mex. 1964-66), N.Mex. Bankers Assn. (pres., mem. exec. com. 1965-66), Las Cruces C. of C. (past pres.). Democrat. Lodges: Kiwanis, KC. Office: PO Box Fnb Las Cruces NM 88004-9536

PAPERNY, DAVID MARK N., pediatrician; b. L.A.; 1 child, Jerald. BS magna cum laude in Biochemistry, UCLA, 1973, MD, 1977. Diplomate Am. Bd. Pediatrics, Nat. Bd. Med. Examiners. Resident in pediat. Kapiolani-Children's Med. Ctr., Honolulu, 1977-80; fellow in adolescent medicine U. Wash., Seattle, 1980-81; from assoc. to asst. prof. pediat. and adolescent medicine U. Hawaii Sch. Medicine, Honolulu, 1981—; dir. Kaiser-Permanente Adolescent Svcs., 1981—, health promotion and preventive svcs. com., 1984—, project dir. pediat. patient edn. video, 1989, audio-visual task force/ednl. media task force, 1990, founder newborn drug abuse task force and drug intervention subcom. health promotion and preventive svcs. com., 1990, staff well-being com., 1989, ad hoc teen intervention adv. com., 1989; attending physician Hawaii Sex Abuse Treatment Ctr., 1979—; mem. adv. com. Hawaii State Dept. Commerce and Consumer Affairs, Regulated Industries Complaint Office, 1988—; mem. adv. coun. Cmty.-Based Teenage Health Clinic for Waikiki Health Ctr., Hawaii, 1990—. Dir. March of Dimes Teen Health Computer Project, 1984; med. affairs com. Hawaii Planned Parenthood, 1988—; mem. Hawaii Teen Parenting and Pregnancy Coun., 1980, Nat. Com. for Prevention Child Abuse, 1988. Recipient L.A. C. of C. Cmty. Svc. award, 1973. Fellow Am. Acad. Pediat. (chmn. com. on adolescence Hawaii chpt. 1986, Hawaii chpt. liaison to task force and provisional com. on substance abuse 1988, chpt. rep. to Hawaii family health svcs. divsn. task force drug edn. and prevention adv. com. 1987, exec. com. Sect. on Computer Tech. 1995); mem. Am. Soc. Clin. Hypnosis (cert. cons.), Soc. for Adolescent Medicine, Hawaii Acad. Hypnosis (founder), Phi Beta Kappa, Sigma Xi, Phi Eta Sigma. Office: Kaiser Permanente 1010 Pensacola St Honolulu HI 96814-2118

PAPILE, LUCILLE ANN, pediatrician, educator; b. Quincy, Mass., June 10, 1943; d. John Peter and Madeline Catherine (Jancaterino) P.; m. Stephen Francis Lawless, May 16, 1969 (div. Dec. 1987). BA in Chemistry, Albertus Magnus Coll., 1965; MD, Med. Coll. Pa., 1969. Diplomate Am. Bd. Neonatal/Perinatal Medicine. From instr. to assoc. prof. dept. pediatrics U. N.Mex., Albuquerque, 1972-89, from asst. prof. to assoc. prof. ob-gyn., 1974-89, prof. pediatrics and ob-gyn., 1989—; vis. scientist U. Calif., San Francisco, 1980-81; Congl. fellow U.S. Ho. of Reps., Washington, 1992; mem. sub-bd. com. Am. Bd. Pediatrics, 1988-94. Contbr. numerous articles to profl. jours. Grantee Thrasher Rsch. Found., 1980-83, U.S. Dept. Edn., 1988-91, 91-94, NIH, 1991-96. Mem. Am. Acad. Pediatrics (tech. com. bd. 1993—), Am. Pediatric Soc., Soc. for Pediatric Rsch. Office: U NMex ACC 3 West 8131 UNMH/BCMC Dept Pediatrics Albuquerque NM 87131

PAPIN, JERRY A., financial adviser, business owner; b. Monterey, Calif., July 1, 1966; m. Kris L. Papin, June 5, 1987; children: Sean, A.J. BS, SUNY, Albany, 1991. Owner Espresso Kitchen, Idaho Falls, 1994—, The Scholastic Edge, Idaho Falls, 1991—; fin. advisor, tng. mgr. Am. Express Fin. Advisors Inc. Columnist Money Matters, 1993—. With USN, 1985-91, 2d lt. Idaho NG, 1991. Mem. Civitan Internat. (pres. 1994, Civitan of Yr. 1993). Office: Am Express 1970 E 17th St Ste 203 Idaho Falls ID 83404-8014

PAPIN, NANCY SUE, educational computer coordinator; b. Long Beach, Calif., Apr. 5, 1951; d. Emil Richard and Marjorie (Wright) DeSmet; m. Robert N. Papin, Oct. 5, 1971; children: Karina L., Brianne M. Student, Apple Computer Co., 1987-91. Sec. Sebring Products, Inc., L.A., 1970-74, bus. owner, 1970—; bus. owner Sebring Internat. of Hollywood, Calif., 1971-74; computer coord. Centralia Sch. Dist., Buena Park, Calif., 1986—; Apple edn. advisor Apple Computer Co., 1993—; mem. edn. tech. com. Centralia Sch. Dist., Buena Park, 1991-95; mem. sch. site coun. Los Coyotes Sch., La Palma, Calif., 1986-92, San Marino Sch., Buena Park, 1991-94; mem. grant writing com. Kennedy H.S., La Palma, 1991; mem. Vision 21 coordinating counsel Centralia Sch. Dist.; mem. sch. site coun. Walker Jr. H.S., 1994—. Author: History/Social Science Frameworks Correlation, 1991. Republican. Roman Catholic. Office: San Marino Sch 6215 San Rolando Way Buena Park CA 90620-3635

PAPPAGIANIS, DEMOSTHENES, microbiology educator, physician; b. San Diego, Mar. 31, 1928; s. George John and Mary (Terzakis) P.; m. Alice Ertel, Jan. 28, 1956; children: Michele, Marika. A.B., U. Calif.-Berkeley, 1949, M.A., 1951, Ph.D., 1956; M.D., Stanford U., 1962. Diplomate Am. Bd. Microbiology. Rotating intern Walter Reed Gen. Hosp., Washington, 1962-63; asso. prof. Sch. Public Health, U. Calif., Berkeley, 1963-67; prof. med. microbiology Sch. Medicine, U. Calif., Davis, 1967—; chmn. dept. med. microbiology Sch. Medicine, U. Calif., 1968-85; asso. mem. Armed Forces Epidemiol. Bd. Contbr. to profl. jours. and books. Served from 1st lt. to capt. M.C. U.S. Army, 1962-63. Recipient Meridian award Med. Mycol. Soc. Ams., 1986, Calif. medal Am. Lung Assn. Calif., 1988, Rhoda Benham award Med. Mycol. Soc. Am., 1992, Charles E. Smith Meml. award, 1994. Fellow Infectious Disease Soc. Am.; mem. Am. Soc. Microbiology, Am. Thoracic Soc., Calif. Thoracic Soc., Internat. Soc. Human and Animal Mycology, Sigma Xi, Alpha Omega Alpha. Home: 1523 Orange Ln Davis CA 95616-0912 Office: U Calif Sch Medicine Dept Med Microbiology Davis CA 95616

PAPPAS, LEAH AGLAIA, civic worker, political consultant, educator; b. Ogden, Utah, Mar. 23, 1936; d. George Thomas and Maria (Harames) P. BA, Coll. St. Mary of the Wasatch, 1959. Tchr. Bishop Gorman High Sch., Las Vegas, Nev., 1959-64; with Dist. Atty.'s staff, Las Vegas, 1972-75; tchr. Weber State Coll., Las Vegas, 1985. Civic worker various orgns., including Opera Guild, Heart Fund, City of Hope, March of Dimes, also groups for prevention of blindness, sr. citizens' groups, others, Ogden and Las Vegas, 1955—; cons. numerous polit. campaigns, Ogden, Las Vegas and Boston, L.A., John F. Kennedy campaign, 1959; alt. del. Chgo. Nat. Conv.; vol. Senator Robert Kennedy Campaign, 1968; supr. Senator Edward M. Kennedy Campaign, Boston, 1970, 76, Presdl. Campaign, 1980; campaign worker Gov. Jerry Brown, L.A., 1978. Greek Orthodox. Home: 1323 Marilyn Dr Ogden UT 84403-0424

PAPPAS, NICHOLAS, psychiatrist; b. Bklyn., June 30, 1937; s. Michael George and Chrisanthy Anna (Nikolakakis) P.; m. Margaret Carol, Nov. 24, 1963; children: Katina Michelle, Christine Reneé. BA in Physiology and Anatomy, Ind. U., 1959; MD, Ind. U., Indpls., 1962. Diplomate Am. Bd. Psychiatry. Intern Detroit Receiving Hosp., 1962-63; resident Ind. U. Med. Ctr., 1963-65, Napa St. Hosp., Imola, Calif., 1968-70; staff psychiatrist Ctrl. State Hosp., Indpls., 1965-66, Napa State Hosp., Imola, 1970-73; pvt. practice Novato, Calif., 1971—; supr. Sonoma St. U. Nursing students, 1973—, Calif. Sch. Profl. Psychology interns, Berkeley, Calif., 1976—; staff sec. Novato Community Hosp., 1974; med. dir. Canyon Manor Hosp., Novato, Calif., 1974-75; med. cons. Erickson Inst., Santa Rosa, Calif., 1982—. Contbr. articles to profl. jours. With US Army, 1966-68. Mem. Calif. Biofeedback Soc. Republican. Greek Orthodox. Office: 1025 5th St Novato CA 94945-2413

PAQUETTE, RICHARD, airport executive; married; 2 children. V.p. airport devel. Calgary Airport, AB, Can. Mem. Calgary Conv. and Visitors Bureau, Alta. Aviation Coun. Mem. Am. Assn. Airport Execs., Calgary C. of C., Calgary Rotary Club. Office: Calgary International Airport, 2000 Airport Rd NE, Calgary, AB Canada T2E 6W5*

PARADY, JOHN EDWARD, information systems executive, consultant; b. Inglewood, Calif., Sept. 26, 1939; s. Raymond Oliver and Ella Louise (Timm) P.; m. Barbara Lyn Pettit, Aug. 13, 1966; children: John, Renee, Stacy. BS, Calif. State U., Los Angeles, 1966; MS, U. So. Calif., 1968. Cert. data processing. Dir. info. systems Weyerhauser Co., Tacoma, Wash., 1975-82; exec. dir. McKenna, Conner & Cuneo, Los Angeles, 1982-83; sr. v.p. Bank of Am., San Francisco, 1983-85; pvt. practice cons. L.A., 1986-88; exec. v.p. Pacific Stock Exchange, Los Angeles, 1988-93; chief info. officer Coldwell Banker Corp., Mission Viejo, 1994—; mem. The Rsch. Bd., N.Y.C., 1983-86; bd. dirs. The Ctr. for Info. Systems Rsch., Cambridge, Mass., 1977-85; bd. dirs. The Molding Corp., Am., Cal-Air, Inc. Served to 2d lt., U.S. Army, 1959-64. Served to 2d lt., U.S. Army, 1959-64. Republican. Mormon. Home: 1004 Vista Del Valley Rd La Canada Flintridge CA 91011-1805 Office: 27211 Las Ramblas Mission Viejo CA 92691

PARASRAMPURIA, JAGDISH, pharmacist; b. Rajasthan, Rajasthan, India, Apr. 5, 1958; came to U.S., 1983; s. Nathmal and Pana (Rungta) P.; m. Dolly Aggarwal, Dec. 22, 1987; children: Sonal, Kuhu. BS, Mysore U., Manipal, India, 1981; MS, Nagpur (India) U., 1983; Diploma in Bus. Mgmt., R.P. Inst. Communications and Mgmt., Nagpur, 1983; PhD, U. Houston, 1989. Cert. rsch. pharmacist. Intern scientist Biochem Labs., Bombay, 1980, Glaxo Labs., Bombay, 1981; teaching asst. U. Houston, 1985-87; intern scientist Boots Pharm., Shreveport, La., 1986; rsch. asst. U. Houston, 1987-89; sr. rsch. scientist Abbott Labs., Abbott Park, Ill., 1989-93; mgr. formulation Glycomed Inc., Alameda, Calif., 1993—; reviewer Jour. Pharm. Sics., vis. scientist Pharm. Mfrs. Assn., N.Y.C., 1991; chmn. program com. Chicagoland Pharm. Discussion Group, 1991-93. Contbr. over 25 rsch. articles in profl. jours. Recipient Outstanding Scholastic Achievement Indian Drug Mfrs.' Assn., 1981. Mem. Am. Assn. Coll. Pharmacy, Am. Assn. Pharm. Scientists (biotech. chmn. Midwest 1993-94), Royal Soc. Health (London), Sigma Xi (sec. 1993-94), Rho Chi. Office: Glycomed Inc PO Box 4018 Alameda CA 94501-0418

PARCELLS, DAYTON BALCOM, III, lawyer; b. Summit, N.J., Nov. 11, 1960; s. Dayton Balcom Jr. and Margie M. (Hall) P. BA in History and Psychology, U. Richmond, 1983; JD, Pepperdine U., 1986. Bar: Calif. 1987, U.S. Dist. Ct. (cen., so. and ea. dists.) Calif. 1987. Assoc. McCashin & Assocs., L.A., 1987—; instr. law Santa Monica (Calif.) Coll., 1987—. Mem. ABA, L.A. County Bar Assn, Assn. Trial Lawyers Am., Calif. Trial Lawyers Assn. Home: 227 11th St Manhattan Beach CA 90266-5420

PARDUE, A. MICHAEL, plastic and reconstructive surgeon; b. Nashville, June 23, 1931; s. Andrew Peyton and Ruby (Fly) P.; m. Jeanette Mabry, June, 1961 (div. Mar. 1964). BS, U. of the South, 1953; MD, U. Tenn., 1957. Resident in gen. surgery Pittsfield (Mass.) Affiliated Hosps., 1966; resident in plastic surgery N.Y. Hosp./Cornell Med. Ctr., 1968; plastic surgeon A. Michael Pardue, M.D., Thousand Oaks, Calif., 1968—. Lt. comdr. USN, 1956-62. Fellow ACS; mem. Am. Soc. Plastic and Reconstructive Surgeons, Am. Soc. Aesthetic Plastic Surgery, Calif. Soc. Plastic Surgeons. Episcopalian. Office: 327 S Moorpark Rd Thousand Oaks CA 91361-1008

PAREDES, BERT (NORBERT PAREDES), computer systems engineer; b. Frankfurt, Fed. Republic Germany, Dec. 27, 1947; s. George and Elfriede (Kleebach) P.; m. Linda L. Stubblefield, July 5, 1968 (div. 1986); m. Katherine Blacklock, Feb. 4, 1989. BS in Computer Sci., SUNY, Albany, 1970; postgrad., U. Colo., 1977-78. Enlisted U.S. Army, 1970, programmer/analyst, 1970-79, resigned, 1979; staff engr. Martin Marietta, Denver, 1979-81, sr. staff engr., 1984-92; regional analyst, mgr. Gould Computer Systems, Denver, 1981-84; mgr. tech. analysis and support Denelcor, Inc., Aurora, Colo., 1984; v.p. C-Quad Systems, Inc., Littleton, Colo., 1992-94, pres., 1994—; Pres., chief exec. officer A.C.T., Inc., Denver, 1982-84. Contbr. articles to profl. jours. Nat. Merit scholar, 1966. Mem. Assn. Computing Machinery, Armed Forces Communications and Electronics Assn., Am. Rose Soc., Mensa, Denver Bot. Gardens. Lutheran. Home: 6859 N Beaver Run Littleton CO 80125-9202 Office: C-Quad Systems Inc 26 W Dry Creek Cir Ste 600 Littleton CO 80120-4475

PAREKH, DILIP, surgeon, oncologist, educator; b. Johannesburg, South Africa, Oct. 2, 1955; came to U.S., 1988; MD, U. Witwatersrand, Johannesburg, South Africa, 1979. Diplomate Coll. Medicine South Africa. Intern Baragwanath Hosp., Johannesburg, 1980, med. officer ICU, 1981, resident, 1983-86, head surg. gastroenterology, 1991-92, prin. surgeon, 1991-92; resident in surgery Harare Hosp. and U. Zimbabwe, 1982; surgeon Baragwanath Hosp. and U. Witwatersrand, Johannesburg, 1986-88, sr. surgeon, 1988-91, head surgery unit 5, 1991-92; assoc. dir. surg. oncology Norris Cancer Hosp. and Rsch. Inst., 1992—; assoc. prof. surgery U. So. Calif., 1992—; gastrointestinal, endocrinology and surg. oncology rsch. fellow dept. surgery med. br. U. Tex., Galveston, 1988-90; sr. lectr. dept. surgery U. Witwatersrand; mem. surg. coun. U. So. Calif., surgery rep. med. faculty assembly; mem. attending staff L.A. County+USC Med. Ctr., 1992—, U. So. Calif. Univ. Hosp., 1992—, Kenneth Norris Jr. Cancer Hosp., 1992—; mem. profl. std. rev. cancer com. Kenneth Norris Jr. Cancer Ctr. and Hosp., 1993—, mem. med. records comm. com., 1993—, chmn. tumor, node, metastasis staging task force, 1993—, mem. clin. investigation com., 1993—; mem. cancer com. L.A. County+USC Med. Ctr., 1993—; presenter in field. Author: (with others) Modern Surgery in Southern Africa, 1988, Gastrointestinal Endocrinology, 1990; contbr. articles to profl. jours. Grantee NIH, 1994—, U. So. Calif., 1994—. Fellow ACS; mem. AAAS, Calif. Med. Assn., Am. Pancreatic Assn., Soc. of Am. Gastroent. Endoscopic Surgery, Soc. Surg. Oncology, Southwestern Surg. Assn., Surg. Rsch. Soc. South Africa, Assn. Surgeons South Africa, South African Gastroent. Assn., L.A. County Med. Assn., L.A. Surg. Soc., Internat. Soc. Surgery, Internat. Hepatopancreatobiliary Assn., Soc. Surgery for Alimentary Tract, Collegium Internationale Chirugiae Digestivae. Office: Dept Surgery 1510 San Pablo St Ste 438 Los Angeles CA 90033-4586

PARENT, EDWARD ALPHONSE, psychologist, consultant, publishing company executive; b. Vernal, Utah, Nov. 8, 1940; s. Joseph A. and Dorthea R. (Frost) P.; m. Sydney Minnette Brown, June 14, 1967; children: A. Roger, Sydney M., Ephraim E., Alexander A., Bethany A. BS in Physics, Math. and French, Brigham Young U., 1967, MBA in Bus., 1969, PhD in Counseling and Personnel Svcs., 1982. Lic. psychologist. Instr. in orgnl. behavior Brigham Young U., Provo, Utah, 1969-70; mktg. analyst Exxon Internat., Inc., N.Y.C., 1970-72; adminstr. Bonneville Med. Group, Salt Lake City, 1972-84; adminstr., counselor Dennis W. Remington, MD, Provo, 1984-88; pres. Vitality House Internat., Provo, 1982—; resident in psychology Utah Valley Regional Med. Ctr., Provo, 1988-90, staff psychologist, 1990—; cons. Green Valley Health Resort, St. George, Utah, 1987-90, Nat. Inst. of Consulting Svcs., Salt Lake City, 1992-94; mem. adv. bd. doctoral program com. ednl. psychology dept. Brigham Young U., Provo, 1993-94; chmn. staff psychologists Utah Valley Reg. Med. Ctr., Provo, Utah, 1995—. Co-author: How to Lower Your Fat Thermostat, 1982, Recipes for Kids to Lower their Fat Thermostat, 1994, (audio tape) The Neuropsychology of Weight Control, 1985, 12 Steps to Lower Your Fat Thermostat, 1993. Cub master pack 738 Boy Scouts Am., Provo, 1986-90, chmn. scout com., 1994. Mem. Utah Psychol. Assn. (membership com. 1990). Office: Vitality House Internat Inc 1675 N Freedom Blvd Ste 11C Provo UT 84604-2570

PARENTI, KATHY ANN, sales professional; b. Gary, Ind., Sept. 24, 1957; d. Lee Everett Huddleston and Barbara Elizabeth (Daves) Tilley; m. Michael A. Parenti, Mar. 31, 1979 (div. Sept. 1990). Student, Ind. U., Gary, 1977; cert., U. Nev., Las Vegas, 1978; diploma, Interior Design Inst., Las Vegas, 1984. Supr. Circus Circus Hotel, Las Vegas, 1980-87; owner Interior Views, Las Vegas, 1984-87; sales rep. Win-Glo Window Coverings, 1987-88; owner Dimension Design, 1988-90; sales rep. Sidney Goldberg & Assoc., Las Vegas, 1990—. Mem. NAFE, Am. Soc. Interior Designers, Internat. Interior Design Assn., Network of Exec. Women in Hospitality, Design Inst. Soc., Rep Network.

PARER, JULIAN THOMAS, obstetrics and gynecology educator; b. Melbourne, Australia, Sept. 2, 1934; m. Robin M.W. Fletcher, Apr. 23, 1962; 1 child, William John. B Agr. Sci., U. Melbourne, 1959; M Rural Sci. in Bioclimatology, U. New Eng., Australia, 1962; PhD, Oreg. State U., 1965; MD, U. Wash., 1971. Diplomate Am. Bd. Ob-Gyn, Am. Bd. Maternal and Fetal Medicine. Grad. fellow and asst., summer and rsch. fellow U. Oreg. Med. Ch., Portland, 1961-63; vis. scientist Oreg. Regional Primate Rsch. Ctr., Portland, 1964-66; instr. dept. ob-gyn U. Wash., Seattle, 1966-68, sr. fellow, mem. med. rsch. unit, mem. Anesthesia Rsch. Ctr., 1969-71; resident Los Angeles County-U. So. Calif. Sch. Medicine, L.A., 1971-74; asst. prof., assoc. prof. U. Calif., San Francisco, 1974-82, prof., 1982—, dir. obstetrics, 1980-87, dir. maternal-fetal medicine fellowship tng. program, 1983—, assoc. vice chmn dept., 1987—; rsch. affiliate Regional Primate Ctr., Seattle, 1969-71; assoc. staff Cardiovascular Rsch. Inst., U. Calif., 1976—; vis. scientist Nuffield Inst. for Med. Rsch., Oxford (Eng.) U., 1981-82; vis. scientist U. Chile, Santiago, 1985-93, Devel. Physiology Lab., U. Auckland, New Zealand, 1988-90. Author: Handbook of Fetal Heart Rate Monitoring, 1983; editor: (with P.W. Nathanielsz) Research in Perinatal Medicine, 1984; Antepartum and Intrapartum Management, 1989; contbr. numerous articles and abstracts to med. jours. Fellow Am. Coll. Obstetricians and Gynecologists; mem. Am. Physiol. Soc., Australian Perinatal Soc., Soc. for Gynecol. Investigation, Soc. Perinatal Obstetricians (bd. dirs. 1988-91), Soc. for Study Fetal Physiology, Chilean Soc. Ob-Gyn (fgn. corr.), Phi Kappa Phi, Phi Sigma. Office: U Calif 505 Parnassus Ave San Francisco CA 94122-2722

PAREZO, NANCY JEAN, anthropologist, curator; b. Buffalo, Jan. 8, 1951; d. Charles William and Georgia Leon (Pierce) P.; m. Richard V.N. Ahlstrom, Oct. 23, 1983. BA in Anthropology, Sociology cum laude, Miami U., 1973; MA, U. Ariz., 1976, PhD in Cultural Anthropology, 1981. Student registrar Elma Pratt Folk Art Collection Miami U., 1970-71, lab technician, teaching asst. dept anthropology, 1972-73; ceramic restorer Musee de l'Etat, Luxembourg, 1971-72; grad. rsch. asst. Bur. Ethnic Rsch. U. Ariz., 1974-75, grad. rsch. asst. dept. anthropology, v.p. rsch., 1975-78, from grad. teaching asst. to instr. dept. anthropology, 1979-81, instr. Elderhostel program divsn. continuing edn., 1982-83, rsch. prof. Am. Indian studies, anthropology, 1992—; instr. internship tng. program Nat. Mus. Natural History/Smithsonian Instn., 1981-82; ethnologist Ariz. State Mus., 1983-85, assoc. curator ethnology, 1985-90, curator ethnology, 1990—; instr. dept. landscape architecture U. Ariz., 1976, instr. divsn. continuing edn., 1979-81, dir. mus. studies program dept. anthropology, 1985-90, cons. agrl. ext., 1989, rsch. prof. Am. Indian Studies and Anthropology, 1992—, D'Arcy McNickle Indian fellow Newberry Libr., 1994-95; rschr. collections divsn. Ariz. State Mus., 1977; instr. Pima C.C., 1979-81; regents loaned exec. Ariz. Bd. Regents, 1990-91; assoc. program dir. anthropology NSF, 1987-88; field reviewer Inst. for Mus. Svcs., 1988-89; panel mem. NEH, 1986, 90; cons. and lectr. in field. Editor: Hidden Scholars. Women Anthropologists and the Native American Southwest, 1993; co-editor: Preserving the Anthropological Record, 1992; curator numerous exhibits in Anthropology and Native Am. studies; contbr. articles to profl. jours. Grantee Wenner-Gren Found., 1985-86, 89-91, 92-95, U. Ariz., 1977-80, 86-87, 92, NEH, 1985-86, 89, 92, Ednl. Commn. of States, 1990, Smithsonian Instn., 1986-90, Mus. No. Ariz., 1978, Ariz. Humanities Coun., Ind. Prodrs. Svcs., Haffenreffer Mus.; Undergrad. Rsch. fellow Miami U., 1971-72, Postdoctoral fellow Smithsonian Instn., 1981-82; Weatherhead Resident scholar Sch. Am. Rsch., 1978-79, Sigma Xi scholar, 1979, Grad. scholar U. Ariz., 1973-75, Alumni scholar Miami U., 1971-72, Nat. Purchasing Agts. scholar, 1971-72, N.Y. State regents scholar, 1969. Fellow AAAS, Am. Antrhop. Assn.; mem. AAUW, Am. Ethnological Assn., Soc. for Am. Archaeology, Soc. for Applied Anthropology, Soc. for Feminist Anthropology, Am. Assn. Mus. (accreditation com. 1989-90, MAP advisor and reviewer 1989-93), Coun. for Mus. Anthropology (bd. dirs. 1988-92, program chair 1992, treas. 1985-88), History Anthropology Network, Assn. for Women Faculty (sec. 1990-91, com. acad. profl. 1985-87), Southwestern Anthrop. Assn., Coun. for Preservation of Anthrop. Records (pres. 1994—), Phi Beta Kappa (bd. dirs. 1990-91), Alpha Kappa Delta. Democrat. Office: Univ Ariz Ariz State Mus Tucson AZ 85721

PARHAM, ROBERT BRUCE, archivist; b. Denver, June 4, 1948; s. James Monroe and Doris Demetral (Lands) P.; m. Meredith Howard, May 20, 1989; 1 stepchild, Gwendolyn. BA cum laude, Western State Coll., Gunnison, Colo., 1970; MA, U. Wis., 1974, U.Colo., 1981. Cert. archivist. Rsch. analyst Pub. Records Bd. Wis., Madison, 1974; manuscripts curator U. Ark., Fayetteville, 1974-77; film archivist Denver Mus. Natural History, 1979-80; archivist Boulder (Colo.) Hist. Soc., 1979-82; instr. history dept. Calif. State U.-Dominguez Hills, Carson, 1983-84, archivist, asst. prof. libr. sci., 1982-85; asst. prof. libr. sci., ast. archivist U. Alaska, Fairbanks, 1985-89; archivist Nat. Pers. Records Ctr., St. Louis, 1989-90; asst. dir. Nat. Archives-Alaska region, Anchorage, 1990—; cons. City of Valdez (Alaska) Mus., 1988, 92; sec.-treas. Alaska at War, Anchorage, 1992—; co-coord. Alaska History Day, Anchorage, 1994—. Author: (book rev.) Alaska History, 1994; contbr. articles to profl. jours. Mem. Soc. Am. Archivists, N.W. Archivists (Alaska rep. 1992—), Alaska Hist. Soc., Soc. Calif. Archivists, Midwest Archives Conf., Alaska Anthropol. Assn., Cook Inlet Hist. Soc. Democrat. Home: 4310 Seeley Ct Anchorage AK 99502-1957 Office: US Nat Archives & Records Adminstrn Alaska Region 654 W 3rd Ave Anchorage AK 99501-2145

PARIGIAN, MICHAEL JOHN, forensic scientist; b. Culver City, Calif., July 22, 1960; s. Abraham and Ann Louis Parigian; m. Trelene Tracey Fitzgerald, May 4, 1989; 1 child, Nichelle Ann. BS, U. Calif., Irvine, 1982; MS, Calif. State U., L.A., 1989. Chemist trainee Met. Water Dist., La Verne, Calif., 1980; chemist Day-Glo Color Corp./Pacific Dispersions, Cudahy, Calif., 1983-87; criminalist Ventura County (Calif.) Sheriff's Crime Lab, 1987—. Contbr. articles to profl. jours. Mem. Calif. Assn. Criminalists (resource and tng. com.), Calif. Homicide Investigators Assn., L.A. Soc. Coating Tech. Republican. LDS Ch. Office: Ventura County Sheriffs Lab 800 S Victoria Ave Ventura CA 93009-0001

PARIKH, ANJAN, electronics company executive; b. Devgadhbaria, Gujrat, India, Feb. 19, 1957; came to U.S., 1983; s. Rajnikant and Surbala (Modi) P.; m. Rita Mehta, Dec. 6, 1982; children: Pranay, Raxit. BSEE, S.P. Univ., India., 1979; MSEE, Santa Clara (Calif.) U., 1988. Sr. test engr. Hindustan Brown Boveri, Bombay, India, 1980-83, Signetics (Philips), Sunnyvale, Calif., 1983-88; mgr. test engr. Harris Semiconductor, Santa Clara, 1988-92, Siliconix, Santa Clara, 1992—. Home: 3809 Ashridge Ln San Jose CA 95121-1402 Office: Siliconix 2201 Laurelwood Rd Santa Clara CA 95054-1516

PARIS, EDWARD MARVIN, education administrator; b. Denver, Oct. 7, 1951; s. Marvin E. and Winifred A. (West) P.; m. Carol L. Powell, Aug. 2, 1975; 1 child, Julia. BA, U. Colo., Boulder, 1973, MPA, 1979; postgrad., U. Colo., Denver. Adminstrv. officer Colo. Dept. Revenue, Denver, 1979-80, Colo. Dept. Social Svc., Denver, 1980; budget analyst U. Colo., Boulder, 1980-84; instl. analyst U. Colo., Colorado Springs, 1984-89, dir. instl. rsch., 1989-94, interim dir. fin. svcs., 1991-94, assoc. vice chancellor adminstrn. and fin., 1994—; cons. in info. systems, Colorado Springs; instl. rep. Am. Coll. Testing prog. Mem. Assn. Instnl. Rsch. (mem. workshop selection com. for nat. conv. 1989), Pi Alpha Alpha. Home: 2614 Farragut Cir Colorado Springs CO 80907-6406 Office: U Colo PO Box 7150 Colorado Springs CO 80933-7150

PARIS, RICHARD WAYNE, forester; b. Corning, N.Y., July 22, 1956; s. Robert Lee and Ann (Seeley) P.; m. Alberta E. Blanchard, Mar. 21, 1992. BS in Forest Resource, Iowa State U., 1978; postgrad., Everett C.C., 1984. Forester Colville Tribal Forestry, Nespelem, Wash., 1979-81, U.S. Bur. Indian Affairs, Nespelem, 1986—; fire warden, forester State of Utah, Kamas, 1982; law enforcement park technician U.S. Nat. Park Svc., Coulee Dam N.R.A., Wash., 1983-85; park technician U.S. Corps Engrs., Somerset, Ky., 1985-86; instr. Inland Empire EMS Tng. Coun. EMT, ambulance dir. Grand Coulee (Wash.) Vol. Fire Dept., 1981—; first aid instr. ARC, Ephrata, Wash., 1980-94; instr.-trainer CPR, Am. Heart Assn., Grant Countym Wash., 1980—; mem. Wash. State EMS, Edn. Com.; vol. Boy Scouts Am., 1983-95. Recipient Outstanding Svc. award ARC, 1982. Mem. Soc. Am. Foresters, Am. Forestry Assn., Coulee Med. Found. (sec. 1987-88), Grant County EMS Coun. (pres. 1984-86, sec. 1987-95), North Ctrl. Wash. Regional EMS Coun. (pres. 1990—, EMS Adminstr. of Yr. 1989, 91). Baptist. Home: 417 W Grand Coulee Ave Grand Coulee WA 99133-9732 Office: US Bur Indian Affairs Colville Indian Agy Nespelem WA 99155

PARIS, VREDA, artist, educator; b. Manhattan, N.Y., Mar. 20, 1928; d. Jacob and Sarah (Meltzer) Alpert; m. Harold Persico Paris, Mar. 20, 1953 (div. May 1969); m. Vernon Clarence Zimmerman, Aug. 26, 1972. BA, Pratt Inst., 1949; MFA in Painting, Lone Mountain Coll., 1976. Assoc. prof. Calif. Coll. Arts and Crafts, Oakland, 1964-78; pvt. art tchr. Orange Cove, Calif., 1978-90; asst. prof. U. Calif., Santa Barbara, 1969; creative dir. Ad Fried Assocs., Oakland, 1965-69; art dir. Vernon Cash Assocs., Oakland, 1969-72; lectr. U. Sonora, Hermacillo, Mexico, 1970, U. Calif., Berkeley, 1971; artist-in-residence U. Nev., Las Vegas, 1972-73, Santa Rosa (Calif.) Jr. Coll., 1974-75; mktg. cons. Zico Mktg., San Francisco, 1973-75; pvt. practice art cons., 1977-79; presenter in field. One-person shows include Gumps Art Gallery, San Francisco, 1987, Merced (Calif.) Coll., 1988, Banco de Patricios, Buenos Aires, 1988, many others; group exhbns. include U.S. Embassy, Buenos Aires, 1989, U.S. Embassy, Santiago, Chile, 1989, Hilton Hotel Art Gallery, Buenos Aires, 1989, Ankrum Gallery, L.A., 1989, many others; represented in permanent collections including U. Tex., Austin, Phoenix (Ariz.) Art Mus., La Jolla (Calif.) Mus., Ft. Worth (Tex.) Mus. Modern Art, many others. Adminstr. for handicapped Moss Wood Park Sch., Oakland, 1967; creator graphic studio Walnut Creek (Calif.) Art Ctr., 1968. Mem. Coll. Art Assn. Am. Jewish. Home: 12293 Avenue 460 Orange Cove CA 93646-9502

PARK, DALE LEE, standup comedian, author; b. Pueblo, Colo., July 30, 1956; s. Robert Griffith and Eva Jean (Shackelford) P.; m. Katherine Le-Anne Waller, May 29, 1992; children: Joshua Scott Waller, Robyn Griffith. Acctg, diploma, Electronic Tech. Inst., 1986. Delivery and warehouse man Sturgeon Electric, Pueblo, 1973-76; chmn., rodman Hanten Surveying, Pueblo, 1977-78; salesman Am. Electric, Pueblo, 1979-81, C.E.D., Pueblo, 1981-82; outside salesman Nelectric Supply, Pueblo, 1981-82; clk., cashier Loaf N Jug, Pueblo, 1982-83, 7-11 Stores, Pueblo, 1983-84; with lighting, sound and videotaping dept. Comedy Corner, Colorado Springs, Colo., 1987-89; standup comedian, Pueblo, 1987—. Author: Humor on the Halfshell, 1992, Adlibs, Abstract Absurdities, 1993, The Celestial Brain Warp, 1994, Operation Funny Bone, 1994; country music singer, songwriter, TV and radio comml. writer. Speaker Keating Alternative Sch., Pueblo, 1993. Home and Office: 1825 Iroquois Rd Pueblo CO 81001-1640

PARK, EDWARD CAHILL, JR., physicist; b. Wollaston, Mass., Nov. 26, 1923; s. Edward Cahill and Fentress (Kerlin) P.; m. Helen Therese O'Boyle, July 28, 1951. AB, Harvard U., 1947; postgrad., Amherst Coll., 1947-49; PhD, U. Birmingham, Eng., 1956. Instr. Amherst (Mass.) Coll., 1954-55; mem. staff Lincoln Lab., Lexington, Mass., 1955-57, Arthur D. Little, Inc., Cambridge, Mass., 1957-60; group leader electronic systems Arthur D. Little, Inc., Santa Monica, Calif., 1960-64; sr. staff engr., head laser system sect. Hughes Aircraft Co., Culver City, Calif., 1964-68; sr. scientist Hughes Aircraft Co., El Segundo, Calif., 1986-88; mgr. electro optical systems sect. Litton Guidance and Control Systems, Woodland Hills, Calif., 1968-70; sr. phys. scientist The Rand Corp., Santa Monica, 1970-72; sr. scientist R&D Assocs., Marina Del Rey, Calif., 1972-1986, cons., 1986-89; sr. tech. specialist Rockwell Internat., N.Am. Aircraft, Seal Beach, Calif., 1988-94. Contbr. articles to profl. jours.; patentee in field. Served to 1st lt. USAAF, 1943-46. Grantee Dept. Indsl. and Sci. Research, 1953. Fellow Explorers Club (sec. So. Calif. chpt. 1978-79); mem. IEEE, Optical Soc. Am., N.Y. Acad. Scis., Armed Forces Communications and Electronics Assn., Assn. Old Crows, Sigma Xi. Democrat. Clubs: 20 Ghost (Eng.), Harvard (So. Calif.). Home: 932 Ocean Ave Frnt Santa Monica CA 90403-2406

PARK, JOSEPH CHUL HUI, computer scientist; b. Seoul, Korea, Aug. 6, 1937; s. Don Gil and Eui Kyung (Shin) P.; m. Young Ja Yoon, Aug. 17, 1968; children: Esther Y.J., Maria Y.S., David Y.W., Jonathan Y.S. BA, Coll of Wooster, Ohio, 1959; BS, MIT, 1959; MS, U. Ill., 1961, PhD, 1967. Mem. rsch. staff Stanford Linear Accelerator Ctr Stanford U., 1969-72, 73-75; assoc. prof., then prof. computer sci. Korea Advanced Inst. of Sci., Seoul, 1975-82; head Computer Sci. Rsch. Ctr. Korea Advanced Inst. Sci., Seoul, Korea, 1980-82; mem. tech. staff Braegen Corp., Milpitas, Calif., 1982-86, Hewlett-Packard Labs., Palo Alto, Calif., 1986-92; tech mgr. compiler Advanced Processor div. Intergraph Corp., Palo Alto, 1992-93; sr. staff engr. SPARC Labs., Sun Microsystems Compter Corp., Mountain View, Calif., 1993—; lectr. in computer engring. Santa Clara (Calif.) U., 1987—. Mem. IEEE, Assn. Computing Machinery. Baptist. Home: 14800 Masson Ct Saratoga CA 95070-9715

PARK, MARILYN MCKAY, mental health nurse; b. Grand Junction, Colo., Mar. 21, 1931; d. James Arthur and Mabel Frances (Ward) McKay; m. Ellas R. Park, Mar. 20, 1955; children: Robert Earl, Richard James. BSN, U. Colo., 1954; MS, U. Utah, 1967; grad. cert. in public admin., U. UTah, 1983, PhD, 1986. RN, Utah; lic. psychiat. mental health nurse, marriage and family therapist, Utah. Staff nurse Denver Gen. Hosp., 1954, VA Hosp., Salt Lake City, 1954-63; pub. health nurse Salt Lake County, 1963-65; mental health adminstr. Utah State Div. of Mental Health, Salt Lake City, 1967-87; authorization of psychiat. svcs. Utah State Dept. of Health, Salt Lake City, 1987-90; medicare surveyor Psychiat. Hosps. Health Care Financing Adminstrn., Balt., 1984—; rsch. investigator evaluation of Utah prepaid mental health plan U. Minn., Mpls., 1992-93; dir. QI CPC Olympus View Hosp., 1993-95. Contbr. Planned Parenthood Assn., Salt Lake City. Recipient scholarship U. Colo., 1949. Mem. ANA, Utah Nurses Assn. (advanced practice com. 1992, membership com. 1992, coun. specialists in mental health nursing 1975—, chmn. community liaison 1992, bd. dirs. nursing interest group 1990-92), Nat. Alliance for Mentally Ill, Mental Health Assn. Utah. Democrat. Presbyterian. Home: 1731 Imperial Park Ln Salt Lake City UT 84106-3379

PARK, RODERIC BRUCE, university chancellor; b. Cannes, France, Jan. 7, 1932; came to U.S., 1932; s. Malcolm Sewell and Dorothea (Turner) P.; m. Marijke DeJong, Aug. 29, 1953; children: Barbara, Marina, Malcolm. AB, Harvard U., 1953; PhD, Calif. Inst. Tech., 1958. Postdoctoral fellow Calif. Inst. Tech., 1958, Lawrence Radiation Lab., Berkeley, Calif., 1958-60; prof. botany U. Calif., Berkeley, 1960-89, prof. plant biology, 1989-93, prof. emeritus, 1993—; chmn. dept. instrn. in biology U. Calif., 1965-68; provost, dean U. Calif. (Coll. Letters and Sci.), 1972-80, vice chancellor, 1980-90; chancellor U. Colo., Boulder, 1994—; pres. Brickyard Cove Harbors, Inc., 1975-77; dir. William Kaufmann, Inc., 1976-86; mem. corp. Woods Hole Oceanographic Instn., 1974-80; mem. Harvard Vis. Com. on Biochemistry and Molecular Biology, 1990-93. Co-author: Cell Ultrastructure, 51967, Papers on Biological Membrane Structure, 1968; Biology editor, W.H. Freeman & Co., 1966-74; Contbr. articles to profl. jours. Trustee Athenian Sch., 1980—, U. Calif.-Berkeley Found., 1986-90; pres. Jepson Endowment, 1992—, pres., 1994—; bd. dirs. Assoc. Harvard Alumni, 1976-79; bd. overseers Harvard U., 1981-87; mem. exec. com. Coun. Acad. Affairs, 1986-90, chmn., 1988-89; mem. exec. com. Nat. Assn. State Univs. and Land Grant Colls., 1988-90; mem. vis. com. Arnold Arboretum, 1981-88, chmn., 1986-88; acting dir. Univ. and Jepson Herbaria, 1991-93. Recipient New York Bot. Gardens award, 1962. Fellow AAAS; mem. Am. Soc. Plant Physiologists, Am. Bot. Soc., Am. Soc. Photobiology, Danforth Assn. (pres. San Francisco chpt. 1972), Richmond Yacht Club (commodore 1972, dir. found. 1992—), Transpacific Yacht Club, Explorers Club. Home: Office 301 256 Cactus Ct Ofc 301 Boulder CO 80304-1001 Office: U Calif Regent Adminstr Ctr Univ Colo Boulder CO 80309-0017

PARK, SUEGIE JA, clinical pharmacist; b. Seoul, Korea, May 3, 1942; came to U.S., 1975; d. Ung s. and Jung K. (Lee) Chun; m. Nobok Park, Oct. 3, 1967; children: Sung H., Eun H. BS in Pharmacy, Duck Sung Womens Coll., Seoul, 1969, U. Colo., 1983; MTh, So. Calif. Theol. Sem., 1993; postgrad., Idaho State U., 1994—. Registered pharmacist; cert. pastoral counseling; cert. coronary pulmonary resuscitation; cert. acute coronary life support. Pharmacist self drug store, Seoul, 1969-75; pharmacy intern St. Luke's Hosp., Denver, 1980-81, Fitzsimons Army Med. Ctr., Aurora, Colo., 1980-83, VA Hosp., Denver, 1982, Presbyn. Denver Hosp., 1982-84; clin. pharmacist The Children's Hosp., Denver, 1987-90, Presbyn./St. Luke's Med. Ctr., Denver, 1984—; mem. Asian Edn. Adv. Coun. in Denver Pub. Sch., 1988—; mem. HIV/AIDS Resources and Planning Coun., Denver Mayor's Office, 1993—. Author: (brochure) Education and Prevention of HIV/AIDS, 1992. With U.S. Army, 1976-79. Recipient Svc. award Asian Edn. Adv. Coun., Denver Pub. Sch., 1992, Disting. Svc. award Korean Assn. Colo., 1995. Mem. ACA, Korean Scientists and Engrs. Am., Colo. Soc. Hosp. Pharmacists, Rocky Mountain Korea Lions Club (chmn. scholarship com., appreciation and recognition award 1993). Home: 2920 E Colorado Ave Denver CO 80210-3525 Office: Presbyn/St Luke's Med Ctr Pharmacy Dept 1719 E 19th Ave Denver CO 80218

PARK, TONG M., medical, physics and cybernetics researcher; b. San Francisco, Mar. 5, 1965; s. John K. and Duk Y (Lee) P. Student, U. Calif., Berkeley, 1982, Stanford U., 1986; BA, Oxbridge (Eng.) U., 1987; postgrad., Oxford (Eng.) U., 1989—. Elec. engr., computer scientist NASA Naval Sta., Moffett Field, Calif., 1983-86. Contbr. articles to profl. jours.; inventor in field. Jr. statesman Jr. Statesman of Am., San Francisco, 1980-82. Recipient Congrl. award congressman Mervyn Dymally, Washington, 1983, Sci. Talent award 1982; fellow NASA, Moffett Field, Calif., 1983-86. Mem. Oxford U. Union Soc. (life mem., debater 1989—, Grand Master Debater 1989), Oxford U. Law Soc. Republican. Home: 1088 Shell Blvd # B Foster City CA 94404-2902

PARKE, JANET DIANE, interior designer; b. Winnemucca, Nev., Aug. 20, 1930; d. Willard Virdell and Lois (Carlson) Booth; m. Jack Evan Parke, June 11, 1950; children—Deborah Diane Parke Smith, Cary Evan, James Robert. B.A., Brigham Young U., 1950. Interior designer Brunson Homes, Reno, Nev., 1972-74, Bakers Interiors, Reno, 1976-81, Tristan Parke Interiors, Reno, 1981-86. Designer showcase homes. Bd. dirs. Nev. Jr. Miss, 1969-79; hostes Miss Nev., Reno, 1974-77; com. mem. Congressman Jim Santini, Reno. Mem. AIA (assoc.), Nev. Home Builders Assn. (assoc.), Sigma Nu (pres. White Rose chpt. 1952-53). Democrat. Mormon. Lodges: Order Ea. Star, Daus. of Nile.

PARKER, ALAN DALE, financial development executive; b. Yonkers, N.Y., Mar. 2, 1935; s. Edward Frederick Charles and Olga Frieda (Turrian) P.; m. Hjördis Birgitta Maria Anderson, Sept. 14, 1963; children: Joakim Erik, Douglas Byron, Jenny Maria. BA, Stanford U., 1957; 2MA, UCLA, 1960; cert., U. Paris, 1962. V.p. devel. Sta. KCPB, pub. radio, Santa Barbara, Calif., 1978-82, Santa Barbara YMCA, 1982-85; dir. devel. Inst. of Ams., La Jolla, Calif., 1985-86, Army and Navy Acad., Carlsbad, Calif., 1986-90; cons. A.D. Parker Assocs., Carlsbad, 1990—; dir. devel. Santa Barbara Mus. Art, 1975-78; cons. Boojum Inst., Carlsbad, 1991—, 1991—, San Luis Rey Mission, Oceanside, Calif., 1992—. Contbr. numerous articles on European affairs to profl. publs. Pres. R.S.V.P., Santa Barbara, 1980-83, Santa Barbara chpt. UN Assn., 1982-84; dir. San Diego Internat. Children's Festival, 1987-89. Mem. San Diego Planned Giving Roundtable.

PARKER, BARRY RICHARD, physics educator; b. Penticton, B.C., Can., Apr. 13, 1935; came to U.S., 1960; s. Gladstone and Olive (Young) P.; m. Gloria Parker, 1960; 1 child, David. BA in Physics with honors, U. B.C., Vancouver, 1959, MSc, 1961; PhD, Utah State U., 1967. Asst. prof. physics Weber State Coll., Ogden, Utah, 1963-66, Idaho State U., Pocatello, Idaho, 1967—. Author: Einstein's Dream, 1986, Search for a Supertheory, 1987, Creation, 1988, Invisible Matter, 1989, Colliding Galaxies, 1990, Cosmic Time Travel, 1991, Vindication fo the Big Bang, 1993, Stairway to the Stars, 1994. Recipient Writing award U. Tex.-McDonald Obs. Home: 750 Fairway Dr Pocatello ID 83201-2014 Office: Idaho State Univ Dept Physics Pocatello ID 83209

PARKER, BRAD, public relations and advertising executive; b. Seattle, Feb. 11, 1957; s. I. J. and Judith Forsythe (Pearson) P. BA in Pub. Rels., U. So. Calif., L.A., 1979. Copy writer CBS News/Sta. KNX News Radio, Hollywood, Calif., 1977-78; account mgr. Morgan Comms., Beverly Hills, Calif., 1978-79; account exec. Joanne Ralston & Assocs., 1979-81; pub. rels. officer, editor 1st Interstate Bank of Ariz., 1981-82; sr. program mgr. Mullen Advt. & Pub. Rels., Phoenix, Ariz., 1982-84; pub. rels. dir. Owens & Assocs. Advt., Phoenix, 1984; media rep. Ariz. Pub. Svc. Co., Phoenix, 1984-85, sr. media rep., 1985-88; mgr. pub. rels. The Dial Corp, Phoenix, 1988-90, mgr. pub. rels. and advt., 1990-92, dir. pub. rels and advt., 1992—; mem. gov.'s media award judging com. Gov.'s Coun. Aging, 1986; guest lectr. Ariz. State U., 1987-88, U. Ariz., 1987-88; guest speaker Airport Operators Coun. Internat., Washington, 1990. Author: The Public Relations Survival Guide, 1987, Rape Escape, 1994. Bd. dirs. Jane Wayland Ctr. for Children, 1981, Ctrl. Ariz./Maricopa County Sheriff's Mountain Rescue Team, 1989—; instr. gang enforcement tng. unit, Maricopa County Sheriff's Office; chmn. comms. com. Ariz. Clean & Beautiful, 1988. Recipient Merit award Phoenix Advt. Club, 1994, Award of Excellence, L.A. Advt. Women, 1980; CBS/Sta. KNX Newsradio scholar, 1978. Mem. Pub. Rels. Soc. Am. (accredited, bd. dirs. Phoenix chpt. 1989-91, chmn. job bank com. Phoenix chpt. 1987-89), Internat. Assn. Bus. Communicators (bd. dirs. Phoenix chpt. 1983, Award of Merit 1981). Office: The Dial Corp 1850 N Central Ave Phoenix AZ 85077-0001

PARKER, BRIAN PRESCOTT, forensic scientist; b. Norfolk, Va., Aug. 31, 1929; s. Milton Ellsworth and Louise Randall (Smith) P.; BS in Quantitative Biology, M.I.T., 1953; JD, Northwestern U., 1957; M.Criminology, U. Calif., Berkeley, 1961, D.Criminology, 1967; m. Sonia Garcia Rosario, Dec. 23, 1960; children: Robin Marie, Augustin Keith. Research asst. U. P.R. Med. Sch., 1961; cons. P.R. Justice Dept., 1961-63; spl. asst. FDA, Washington, 1964; lectr., then asst. prof. criminology U. Calif., Berkeley, 1964-70; sr. criminalist, then sr. forensic scientist Stanford Research Inst., Menlo Park, Calif., 1971-73; prof. forensic sci. and criminal justice Calif. State U., Sacramento, 1973-92; prof. emeritus, 1988—; project dir. phys. evidence Dept. Justice, 1969-70; vis. fellow Nat. Police Research Unit, Australia, 1985; vis. prof. Elton Mayo Sch. Mgmt., South Australia Inst. Tech., 1985. Mem. Am. Chem. Soc. Co-author: Physical Evidence in the Administration of Criminal Justice, 1970, The Role of Criminalistics in the World of the Future, 1972; asso. editor Law, Medicine, Science—and Justice, 1964; contbr. to Ency. Crime and Justice, 1983. Home: 5117 Ridgegate Way Fair Oaks CA 95628-3603

PARKER, CATHERINE SUSANNE, psychotherapist; b. Norwood, Mass., Nov. 4, 1934; d. George Leonard and Hazel Olga (Remmer) P. BA, Bates Coll., 1956; MSW, U. Denver, 1961. Diplomate Acad. Cert. Social Workers; cert. social worker, Colo. Social worker Taunton (Mass.) State Hosp., 1956-59; social worker Ft. Logan Mental Health Ctr., Denver, 1961-66, clin. team leader, 1966-72; dir. adult services Western Inst. Human Resources, Denver, 1973-74; pvt. practice psychotherapy Denver, 1974—; instr. U. Denver, 1977-79; workshop facilitator Arapahoe Community Coll., 1986—. Mem. Nat. Assn. Social Workers, Internat. Transactional Analysis Assn. Home: 6453 S Downing St Littleton CO 80121-2517 Office: Denver Mental Health 165 Cook St Ste 100 Denver CO 80206-5308

PARKER, CHARLES EDWARD, lawyer; b. Santa Ana, Calif., Sept. 9, 1927; s. George Ainsworth and Dorothy P.; m. Marilyn Esther Perrin, June 23, 1956; children—Mary, Catherine, Helen, George. Student, Santa Ana Coll., U. So. Calif.; J.D., S.W. U.-La. Bar: Calif. 1958, U.S. Dist. Ct. (cen. dist.) Calif. 1958, U.S. Supreme Ct. 1969, D.C. 1971, U.S. Dist. Ct. (no. and so. dists.) Calif. 1981. Prof. law Western State U., Fullerton, Calif., 1973-83; spl. counsel Tidelands, First Am. Title Co., 1980-82; dir. First Am. Fin. Corp., 1981-82. Served to sgt. U.S. Army, 1951-53. Author: (book) Tidelands and The Public Trust, 1991. Mem. ABA (com. improvement land records, sect. real property, mem. com. on title ins. sect. real property), Orange County Bar Assn., Calif. Bar Assn., D.C. Bar Assn. Club: Santa Ana Kiwanis, Lodge: Elks (Santa Ana). Contbr. articles in field to profl. jours. Office: 18101 Charter Rd Orange CA 92667-2638

PARKER, GORDON RAE, natural resource company executive; b. Cape Town, South Africa, Dec. 2, 1935; came to U.S., 1981; s. David Rae and Gwen Elizabeth (Armstrong) P.; m. Pamela Margaret Pearce, Sept. 1, 1962; children: Gillian Rae, David Rae. BS, Mont. Coll. Mineral Sci. and Tech., 1958, MS, 1959; MBA, U. Cape Town, 1966. Mng. dir. Tsumeb Corp., Namibia, South Africa, 1975-81; mng. dir. O'okiep Copper Co., Cape, South Africa, 1975-81; v.p. Newmont Mining Corp., N.Y.C., 1981-84, pres., 1984-86, CEO, 1985-86, chmn., also bd. dirs., 1986—; bd. dirs. The Williams Cos., Inc., Newmont Gold Co., Newmont Australia Ltd., Peabody Holding Co. Inc.; past chmn. World Gold Council, 1986—, chmn. Western regional council, 1987—. Fellow Instn. Mining and Metallurgy (London), South African Inst. Mining and Metallurgy; mem. AIME, British North Am. Com. Clubs: Mining, Sky, Union League (N.Y.C.); Blind Brook (Purchase, N.Y.); Silver Spring Country (Ridgefield, Conn.), Mid Ocean, Hamilton, Bermuda. Home: 13 Sunset Dr Englewood CO 80110-4033

PARKER, JAMES AUBREY, federal judge; b. Houston, Jan. 8, 1937; s. Lewis Almeron and Emily Helen (Stuessy) P.; m. Florence Fisher, Aug. 26, 1960; children: Roger Alan, Pamela Elizabeth. BA, Rice U., 1959; LLB, U. Tex., 1962. Bar: Tex. 1962, N.Mex. 1963. With Modrall, Sperling, Roehl, Harris & Sisk, Albuquerque, 1962-87; judge U.S. Dist. Ct. N.Mex., Albuquerque, 1987—; mem. standing com. on rules of practice and procedures of U.S. cts., N.Mex. Commn. on Professionalism, 1986—. Articles editor Tex. Law Rev., 1961-62. Mem. ABA, Fed. Judges Assn., Am. Judicature Soc., Am. Bd. Trial Advocates, Tex. Bar Assn., N.Mex. Bar Assn., Albuquerque Bar Assn., Order of Coif, Chancellors, Phi Delta Phi. Office: US Dist Ct PO Box 566 Albuquerque NM 87103-0566

PARKER, JO ANN, nurse; b. Howell, Mich., Aug. 14, 1951; d. Peter Gordon and Catherine Alice (Davis) P. Student, Tacoma C.C., 1974-76; BSN cum laude, Pacific Luth. U., 1986; postgrad. in Nursing, U. Wash., 1995—. Nurses aide Meml. Hosp., Ft. Myers, Fla., 1969-70; psychiat. tech. Olive Med. Ctr., Pomona, Calif., 1970-71; nurses aide Meml. Hosp., Redding, Calif., 1971-72; ward clk. St. Joseph's Hosp., Tacoma, Wash., 1972-76, student nurse, 1976-78; charge/staff nurse Tacoma Gen. Hosp., 1978-81, critical care nurse, 1981-83; charge nurse geropsychiat. unit Western State Hosp., Steilacoom, Wash., 1983—. Mem. Wash. State Nurses Assn., Sigma Theta Tau. Episcopalian.

PARKER, JOHN BRIAN, broadcast executive; b. L.A., July 3, 1959; s. John Egar and Iris (Landry) P.; m. Dorothy Lynn McCorkle, Aug. 18, 1981; 1 child, Jennifer Lynn. BA in Econs., San Diego State U., 1982. V.p., gen. mgr. Parker Industries, San Diego, 1982—, v.p., 1986—, MIS dir., 1988—; asst. dir. Ctr. for Total Health, Solana Beach, Calif., 1982-83; v.p., CFO, chief info. officer Parker Broadcasting, San Diego, 1986-95; MIS dir. SFX Broadcasting, Inc. Foster parent San Diego Social Svcs., 1989—. Recipient Fredrick Lynn Ryan award San Diego State U., 1982. Mem. Nat. Assn. Broadcasting. Republican. Mem. Christian Ch. Home: 1330 Caminito Laura Encinitas CA 92024-7003 Office: Parker Industries 777 S Hwy 101 Solana Beach CA 92075

PARKER, JOHN MARCHBANK, consulting geologist; b. Manhattan, Kans., Sept. 13, 1920; s. John Huntington and Marjorie Elizabeth (Marchbank) P.; m. Agnes Elizabeth Potts, Mar. 17, 1978; m. Jan Goble, July 18, 1941 (div. 1968); children—Susan Kelly, Elizabeth Douglass, Deirdre Parker, John Eric; m. Nancy Booth, Jan. 24, 1970 (div. 1974). Student U. Minn., 1937, U. Wyo., 1938; B.S., Kans. State U., 1941. Cert. petroleum geologist Am. Inst. Profl. Geologists. Geologist, U.S. Pub. Roads Adminstrn., Alaska Hwy., Can., 1942-43; Field geologist Imperial Oil Ltd., Northwest Ter., Can., 1943-44; dist. geologist Stanolind Oil & Gas Co., Casper, Wyo., 1944-52; v.p. exploration Kirby Petroleum Co., Houston, 1952-74; v.p. exploration Northwest Exploration Co., Denver, 1974-75; cons. geologist Denver, 1975—. Contbr. articles to profl. jours. Recipient Disting. Service in Geology award Kans. State U., 1983. Fellow AAAS, Geol. Soc. Am.; mem. Am. Assn. Petroleum Geologists (pres. 1982-83, adv. council Tulsa 1983-84, Hon. Mem. award), Rocky Mountain Assn. Geologists (explorer of yr. 1979; pres. 1980-81). Home: 2615 Oak Dr No 32 Lakewood CO 80215 Office: PO Box 150187 Lakewood CO 80215-0187

PARKER, JOHN WILLIAM, pathology educator, investigator; b. Clifton, Ariz., Jan. 5, 1931; s. Vilas William and Helen E. Parker; m. Barbara A. Atkinson, June 8, 1957; children: Ann Elizabeth, Joy Noelle, John David, Heidi Susan. BS, U. Ariz., 1953; MD, Harvard U., 1957. Diplomate Am. Bd. Pathology. Clin. instr. pathology U. Calif. Sch. Medicine, San Francisco, 1962-64; asst. prof. U. So. Calif. Sch. Medicine, L.A., 1964-68, assoc. prof., 1968-75, prof., 1975—, dir. clin. labs., 1974-94, vice chmn. dept. pathology, 1985—, dir. pathology reference labs., 1991-94; assoc. dean sci. affairs U. So. Calif., 1987-89; co-chmn. 15th Internat. Leucocyte Culture Conf., Asilomar, Calif., 1982; chmn. 2d Internat. Lymphoma Conf., Athens, Greece, 1981; v.p. faculty senate U. So. Calif., 1991-92; bd. dirs. ann. meeting Clin. Applications of Cytometry, Charleston, S.C., 1988—. Founding editor (jour.) Hematological Oncology, 1982-93; assoc. editor Jour. Clin. Lab. Analysis, 1985—; co-editor: Intercellular Communication in Leucocyte Function, 1983; founding co-editor (jour.) Communications in Clin. Cytometry, 1994—; contbr. over 150 articles to profl. jours., chpts. to books. Named sr. oncology fellow Am. Cancer Soc., U. So. Calif. Sch. Medicine, 1964-69, Nat. Cancer Inst. vis. fellow Walter and Eliza Hall Inst. for Med. Research, Melbourne, Australia, 1972-73. Fellow Coll. Am. Pathologists, Am. Soc. Clin. Pathologists; mem. Am. Assn. Pathologists, Am. Soc. Hematology, Internat. Acad. Pathology, Clin. Cytometry Soc. (v.p., pres.-elect 1993-95, pres. 1995-97), Phi Beta Kappa, Phi Kappa Phi. Office: U So Calif Sch Medicine CSC 108 2250 Alcazar St Los Angeles CA 90033-4523

PARKER, JOYCE STEINFELD, social worker; b. Neptune, N.J., Dec. 11, 1946; d. Milton Donald and Lillian (Sonia) Steinfeld; m. Lawrence Neil Parker, Sept. 18, 1970 (div. Sept. 1990); children: Jill Monica, Gregory Robert. MEd, Boston U., 1969; MSW, UCLA, 1976; PhD, U.S.C., 1992. Lic. social worker. Tchr. spl. edn. Dearborn Sch., Boston, 1969-70, Christ Ch. Child Ctr., Bethesda, Md., 1970-71; tchr. 1st grade Hiroshima (Japan) Internat. Sch., 1971-72; clin. social worker Orange County Mental Health, Westminster, Calif., 1976-80; employee asst. affiliate Human Affairs Internat., L.A., 1987—; instr. U. So. Calif. Sch. Social Work, L.A., 1988-90; pvt. practice clin. social work Redondo Beach, Calif., 1981—; community speaker parenting, marriage, psychol. topics, So. Bay of La., 1983—. Fellow NASW, Soc. Clin. Social Work.

PARKER, KATHLEENE, writer, publishing executive; b. Medford, Oreg., Dec. 3, 1947; d. Theodore and Pearl (McDaniel) P.; m. Mel G. Burnett; 1 child, Kassidy Suzanne Burnett. BA, Ft. Lewis Coll., 1970. Editor Energy/Environ. Info., Denver, 1980-84; owner Thunder Mesa Publ., Inc., Los Alamos, N.Mex., 1990—; corres. The Santa Fe New Mexican. Author: The Only True People, 1991. Founder Taxpayers for the Animas River; active Four Corners Action Coalition. Home and Office: Thunder Mesa Publ Inc 208 Sherwood Blvd Los Alamos NM 87544-3467

PARKER, KENNETH DEAN, toxicologist, criminalist; b. Menan, Idaho, Feb. 27, 1935; s. Kenneth Lewis and Bernedene (Nichols) P.; m. Gay Hemmerling, June 16, 1961; 1 child, Dean Walter. BS, U. Calif., Berkeley, 1958, M Criminology, 1960. Diplomate Am. Bd. Forensic Toxicology. Rsch. asst. U. Calif., 1957-62; rsch. assoc. toxicologist Med. Ctr. U. Calif., San Francisco, 1969-70; toxicologist, criminalist, dir. Probe div. Hine Inc., San Francisco, 1973-81; owner, dir. Probe Sci., El Cerrito, Calif., 1981—; relief toxicologist to coroner City and County San Francisco, 1957-70; lab. inspector Coll. Am. Pathologists, Northfield, Ill., Am. Assn. Clin. Chemists; cons. in field. Fellow Am. Acad. Forensic Sci.; mem. AAAS, Am. Chem. Soc., Internat. Assn. Forensic Toxicologists, Western Pharmacology Soc., Calif. Assn. Toxicologists (chartered). Democrat. Home: 2109 Pinehurst Ct El Cerrito CA 94530-1879 Office: Probe Sci 2109 Pinehurst Ct El Cerrito CA 94530-1879

PARKER, KIMBERLY JANE, nonprofit association executive, paralegal; b. Ann Arbor, Mich., Sept. 24, 1958; d. John Richard and Jane Eleanor (Twichell) P. BA in Polit. Sci., U. Redlands, 1980; Cert. in Legal Assistantship, U. Calif. Irvine, 1983, Cert. in Non-Profit Exec. Mgmt., 1990; Cert. in Adminstrn. Non-Profit Programs, Calif. State U. Long Beach, 1991. Hostess Disneyland, Anaheim, Calif., 1976-80; legal sec., asst. John R. Parker Law Corp., Orange, Calif., 1976-81; legal asst. C.D. Daly Law Corp., Newport Beach, Calif., 1981-83; exec. dir. Christian Conciliation Svc., Anaheim, 1983—. Editor: Peacemaker's Handbook; contbr. articles to profl. jours. Bd. dirs. YWCA Ctrl. Orange, 1991—; mem. So. Calif. Head Injury Found., Downey, 1990—; chair women's forum Trinity United Presbyn. Ch., 1992-93; grad. Leadership Orange, 1993. Recipient Cert. of Appreciation, County of Orange, 1992; grantee Christian Conciliation, 1985. Mem. Calif. Assn. Marriage & Family Therapists, Christian Legal Soc., Christian Ministry Mgmt., So. Calif. Mediation Assn., County Assn. Dispute Resolution, Christian Conciliation Svc. (bd. dirs. 1983—), Assn. Christian Therapists, Christian Assn. Psychol. Studies, Vol. Ctr. of Orange County. Republican. Presbyterian. Office: Christian Conciliation Svc 18002 Irvine Blvd Ste 170 Tustin CA 92680-3301

PARKER, LARRY BENSON, lawyer; b. Harmony, N.C., July 29, 1947; s. Benson Thedford and Grace Agnes (Johnson) P.; m. Jayne Marie Miller, July 16, 1977; 2 children. AB in Econs., Pfeiffer Coll., Misenheimer, N.C., 1969; JD, U. N.C., 1973; LLM, U. Va., 1986. Bar: N.C. 1974, Calif. 1991, Wash. 1992. Law clk. N.C. Ct. Appeals, Raleigh, N.C., 1973-74; commd. 1st lt. USMC, 1974, advanced through grades to maj., jduge adv., 1979-92; litigation assoc. Copy Hatch & Blanchard, Inc., Lynnwood, Wash., 1992-93; dep. atty. gen. Atty. Gen. Calif., San Diego, 1993—. Author: Handbook for Summary Courts, 1979, Victim Witness Assistance Guide, 1992. Mem. ABA, San Diego County Bar Assn., Ret. Officers Assn., Am. Legion, Disabled Am. Vets. Democrat. Presbyterian. Home: 5219 Silver Bluff Dr Oceanside CA 92057-6334 Office: Office Atty Gen PO Box 85266 San Diego CA 92186-5266

PARKER, LAWRENCE NEIL, medical educator; b. N.Y.C., Nov. 8, 1943; s. Norman Samuel and Lee (Shapiro) P.; m. Joyce Parker, July 18, 1970 (div. 1988); children: Jill, Gregory. BA, Columbia Coll., 1964; MD, Stanford (Calif.) U., 1969. Diplomate Am. Bd. Internal Medicine: Internal Medicine, Endocrinology and Metabolism. Intern Boston City Hosp., 1969-70; resident in internal medicine U. Calif., San Diego, 1972-74; fellowship in endocrinology UCLA-Harbor Gen. Hosp., 1974-77; internist and endocrinologist Ross Loos Cigna Med. Group, Torrance, 1977; asst. chief of endocrinology VA Med. Ctr., Long Beach, Calif., 1977—; asst. prof. medicine Coll. of Medicine, U. Calif., Irvine, 1978-82, assoc. prof. medicine, 1982-88, prof. medicine, 1988—; edn. evaluation com. VA Med. Ctr., 1978-80, residency selection com., 1978, nutrition com., 1980—, med. libr. com., 1981-85, human studies com., 1981-84, med. svc. morbidity rev. com., 1983-89, clin. activity quality of care subcom., 1989—, quality assurance bd. of investigation, 1990, quality mgmt. team, 1992, chmn. drug usage evaluation subcom., 1991—; rsch. grant reviewer Dept. Vet. Affairs Merit Rev. Bd., Med. Rsch. Coun., Vancouver, Can.; lectr. in field; physician Marshall Islands Med. Program, 1994. Author: Adrenal Androgens in Clinical Medicine, 1989; jour. reviewer Jour. Clin. Endocrinology and Metabolism, Metabolism: Clin. and Exptl., Ob-Gyn., Acta Endocrinologica, Jour. Nat. Cancer Inst., Jour. Endocrinol. Investigation, Western Jour. Medicine, N.Y. State Jour. Medicine; guest editor Radioimmunoassay for Physicians; contbr. articles to profl. jours., chpts. to books. Lt. comdr. USPHS, 1970-72, Hiroshima. Grantee VA Rsch. Adv. Group, 1978-80, VA Merit Rev., 1980-82, 82-86, 86-88, 90-93. Fellow ACP; mem. Endocrine Soc., Am. Fedn. Clin. Rsch., Amnesty Internat., Union of Concerned Scientists. Office: VA Med Ctr 5901 E 7th St Long Beach CA 90822-5201

PARKER, LINDA SUSAN DENNIS, nonprofit organization executive; b. Chgo., Mar. 26, 1948; d. William Evert and Edwina Louise (Franke) Dennis; m. William Raymond Parker, Feb. 15, 1969; children: Anthony Wade, Kathleen Louise, Elizabeth Irene, Sarah Miriam. Student, Kenai Peninsula Coll., 1992—. Founder, dir. Kenai Peninsula Food Bank, Soldotna, Alaska, 1987—; co-chmn. Kenai Healthy Start, Soldotna, 1991—. Bd. dirs. Bishop's Attic, Soldotna, 1993—, Fed. Emergency Mgmt. Agy., Soldotna, 1992—; vol. Boy Scouts Am., Soldotna, 1980-93, Girl Scouts Am., Soldotna, 1980-87, Kenai Peninsula Sch. Dist., Soldotna, 1980—. Recipient Vol. of the Yr. award State of Alaska, 1986, Points of Light award Points of Light Found., 1992, Gold award United Way, Kenai, 1990, 91, 92, 93, Woman of Distinction award Soroptimist. Mem. NAFE, Am. Legion Aux., Phi Theta Kappa (treas.). Methodist. Office: Kenai Peninsula Food Bank PO Box 1267 Soldotna AK 99669-1267

PARKER, MARILYN ADELE, paralegal; b. San Diego, May 5, 1945; d. James Ralph and Hazel Adele (Scofield) Walton; div.; children: Adrianna Maria, Charles Edward, HEather Anne, Nicole Marie. AA, San Diego City Coll., 1968; JD, Nat. U., 1980; cert. real estate, Cuyamaca Coll., 1986. Tchr. Century Coll., San Diego, 1983-88; paralegal Defenders Inc., San Diego, 1980-84; rsch. libr. San Diego County Law Libr., San Diego, 1984-87; exec. dir. Pub. Paralegal Svs., El Cajon, Calif., 1987—. Mem. Better Bus. Bureau. Mem. Alliance of Paralegals. Office: Pub Paralegal Svcs 275 E Douglas Ave Ste 115 El Cajon CA 92020

PARKER, MARSHA L., nutrition services administrator; b. Mpls., Sept. 2, 1954; d. Gordon George and Sylvia Helene (Miller) Gartland; m. Anthony James Parker, Mar. 15, 1980; children: Elizabeth, Susan, Nancy. BS, U. Wis., Menomonie, 1976. Asst. dir. food svc. Walker Meth. Residence & Health Ctr., Mpls., 1979-80; pers. mgmt. dietitian St. Paul Ramsey Med. Ctr., 1980-84, food prodn. and svc. dietitian, 1984-85; clin. dietitian St. Mary-Corwin Regional Med. Ctr., Pueblo, Colo., 1985-89, chief clin. dietitian, 1990-91, dir. nutrition svcs., 1991—; cons. dietitian Villa Pueblo Towers, Pueblo, 1988-90, So. Colo. Clinic, Pueblo, 1989-90, So. Colo. Nephrology Assn., Pueblo, 1990. Sec. Belmont Elem. PTO, Pueblo, 1992; coach Odessey Mind, Pueblo, 1993-94, site coord. and coach, 1994—; co-facilitator site based decision team Belmont Elem., 1994—. Mem. Am. Dietetic Assn. (registered dietitian), Am. Soc. Hosp. Food Svc. Assn., Colo. Dietetic Assn. (mem. nominating com. 1992), Pueblo Dietetic Assn. (treas. 1991-93, pres. 1993-94). Home: 7 Briargate Ter Pueblo CO 81001-1707 Office: St Mary Corwin Regional Med Ctr 1008 Minnequa Ave Pueblo CO 81004-3733

PARKER, ROY ALFRED, transportation engineer, planner; b. Conway, Ark., Apr. 6, 1930; s. Walter Lane and Harriett Mae (Diffee) P.; m. Dixie Anna Dean, June 9, 1953; children: Walter Lane II, David Dean, Shauna Amyr. BS, U. Idaho, 1953; cert. in hwy. traffic, Yale U., 1958. Registered profl. traffic engr., Calif. Asst. planning programming engr. Bur. Pub. Roads (now Fed. Hwy. Adminstrn.), Sacramento, 1958-59; asst. city traffic engr. City of Phoenix, 1959-62; city traffic engr. Palo Alto, Calif., 1962-66; sr. transp. engr. Wilbur Smith & Assocs., London, 1966-68; project mgr. Wilbur Smith & Assocs., Sacramento, 1968; sr. transp. engr. F.R. Harris Engring. Corp., São Paulo, Brazil, 1968-69; prin. assoc. R.W. Crommelin & Assocs., Los Angeles, 1969-70; dep. transp. dir. City and County of Honolulu, 1970-75, dir. dept. transp. services, 1981-83; exec. dir. Oahu Met. Planning Orgn., Honolulu, 1975-79; sr. traffic engr. Lyon Assocs., Inc., Damascus, Syrian Arab Republic, 1979; pres. Roy A. Parker and Assocs., La Jolla, Calif., 1980; transp. engr. City of Concord, Calif., 1983-84, dep. pub. works dir., 1984-88; transp. adminstr. City San Leandro (Calif.), Calif., 1988-90, 91-93; acting dir. dept. engring. and transp. City San Leandro (Calif.), 1990-91; pres. Roy A. Parker and Assocs., Pismo Beach, Calif., 1994—; lectr. dept. civil engring. Coll. Engring., U. Hawaii, 1971-75; lectr. Inst. Transp. Studies, U. Calif., Berkeley, 1983-91. Served with USAF, 1953-57. Fellow Inst. Transp. Engrs. (pres. western dist. 1975-76, pres. San Francisco Bay Area sect. 1991-92); mem. Phi Eta Sigma, Sigma Tau. Democrat. Home and Office: 64 La Garza Pismo Beach CA 93449-2838

PARKER, SCOTT SMITH, hospital administrator; b. Salt Lake City, Mar. 3, 1935; married. BA, U. Utah, 1960; MA, U. Minn., 1962. Adminstrv. resident Northwestern Hosp., Mpls., 1961-62, asst. adminstr., 1962-67; adminstr. Southside Hosp., Mesa, Ariz., 1967-71; v.p. Good Samaritan Med. Ctr., Phoenix, 1971-73; adminstr. Hoag Meml. Hosp. Presbyn., Newport Beach, Calif., 1973-75; pres. Intermountain Health Care, Salt Lake City, 1975—. Mem. Am. Hosp. Assn. (bd. dirs. 1980-83, chmn. elect, 1985-86, chair 1986-87, past chmn. 1987), Internat. Hosp. Fed. (exec. com. 1991—, pres. elect 1993), Ariz. Hosp. Assn. (pres. 1972). Home: 1014 Woodmoor Dr Bountiful UT 84010-1952 Office: Intermountain Health Care Inc 36 S State St Fl 22 Salt Lake City UT 84111

PARKER, SUE TAYLOR, anthropologist, educator; b. Seattle, Jan. 1, 1938; d. Sidney Beverly Taylor and Kathryn Jane (Ivey) Plumb; m. Elbert W. Branscomb, Oct. 10, 1958 (div. 1970); 1 child, Aron. AB, U. Calif., Berkeley, 1966, MA, 1969, PhD, 1973. Asst. prof. Sonoma State U., Rohnert Park, Calif., 1971-78, assoc. prof., 1978-82, prof., 1982—, chair, 1992—. Reviewer numerous jours. including Current Anthropology, Internat. Jour. Primatology, Am. Jour. Primatology; author, co-editor: Language and Intelligence in Monkeys and Apes, 1990, Self-Awareness in Animals and Humans, 1994; co-editor: Naming Our Ancestors, 1994; contbr. articles to profl. jours. Commr. transp. City of Berkeley, Calif., 1993—. Fulbright rsch. scholar, 1986; grantee Sch. for Am. Rsch., 1995. Mem. Am. Primatological Soc., Internat. Soc. Primatologists, Calif. Acad. Scis., Jean Piaget Soc. (plenary speaker 1995). Office: Sonoma State U 1801 E Cotati Ave Rohnert Park CA 94928-3613

PARKER, THEODORE CLIFFORD, electronics engineer; b. Dallas, Oreg., Sept. 25, 1929; s. Theodore Clifford and Virginia Bernice (Rumsey) P.; B.S.E.E. magna cum laude, U. So. Calif., 1960; m. Jannet Ruby Barnes, Nov. 28, 1970; children: Sally Odette, Peggy Claudette. V.p. engring. Telemetrics, Inc., Gardena, Calif., 1963-65; chief info. systems Northrop-Nortronics, Anaheim, Calif., 1966-70; pres. AVTEL Corp., Covina, Calif., 1970-74, Aragon, Inc., Sunnyvale, Calif., 1975-78; v.p. Teledyne McCormick Selph, Hollister, Calif., 1978-82; sr. staff engr. FMC Corp., San Jose, Calif., 1982-85; pres. Power One Switching Products, Camarillo, Calif., 1985-86; pres. Condor D.C. Power Supplies, Inc., 1987-88, pres. Intelligence Power Tech. Inc., Camarillo, 1988—. Mem. IEEE (chmn. autotestcon '87), NRA (life), Am. Prodn. and Inventory Control Soc., Am. Def. Preparedness Assn., Armed Forces Communications and Electronics Assn., Tau Beta Pi, Eta Kappa Nu. Home: 1290 Saturn St Camarillo CA 93010-3520 Office: Intelligence Power Tech Inc PO Box 3158 Camarillo CA 93011-3158

PARKER, THOMAS GOOCH, retired surgeon; b. Dallas, Aug. 27, 1925; s. Buford M. Parker and Opal-Love Burckhalter; m. Martha Lea Reams, July 18, 1953; children: Melissa Parker Draper, Thomas R., Diana. Student, U. Tex., 1943-46; MD, Harvard U., 1949. Diplomate Am. Bd. Surgery, Am. Bd. Thoracic Surgery. From surg. intern to chief resident Mass. Meml. Hosp., Boston, 1949-56; mem. staff San Mateo (Calif.) Med. Clinic, 1958-71; pvt. practice gen. and thoracic surgery San Mateo, 1971-91; ret., 1991; mem. joint adv. commn. Korea, 1952; clin. nstr. Boston U. Sch. Medicine, 1956;

asst. in surgery Stanford Med. Sch., Calif., 1960—. 1st lt. USAF, USNR, 1943-53. Fellow Am. Coll. Surgeons, San Francisco Surg. Soc.; mem. Bohemian Club, Burlingame Country Club. Republican. Home: 531 Ravenscourt Rd Hillsborough CA 94010-6837

PARKER, WILLIAM ELBRIDGE, consulting civil engineer; b. Seattle, Mar. 18, 1913; s. Charles Elbridge and Florence E. (Plumb) P.; m. Dorris Laurie Freeman, June 15, 1935; children—Dorris Laurie, Jane Elizabeth. B.S., U.S. Naval Acad., 1935. Party chief King County Engrs., 1935-39; exec. sec., cons. engr. State Wash., 1946-49; city engr., chmn. Bd. Pub. Works, City of Seattle, 1953-57; cons. City of San Diego, 1957; ptnr. Parker-Fisher & Assocs., 1958-66; cons. engr. Minish & Webb Engrs., Seattle, 1966-70; city engr. City of Bremerton (Wash.), 1970-76; owner Parker & Assocs., Seattle, 1976—. Served to capt. C.E.C., USNR, 1939-45, 51-53. Named to Broadway Hall of Fame. Registered profl. engr., Wash. Mem. Am. Pub. Works Assn., U.S. Naval Inst., Pioneers of State Wash. (pres.), U.S. Naval Acad. Alumni Assn. (chpt. pres.), College Club (Seattle). Lodges: Masons, Shriners.

PARKER, WILMA JOAN, artist; b. Springfield, Mass., May 15, 1941; d. John Cuthbert and Wilhelmina P.; m. Peter de Pavloff, Feb. 22, 1989. BFA, R.I. Sch. Design, 1963; MFA, Sch. of the Art Inst., 1966. Solo exhibits include Commonwealth Club, San Francisco, 1994, 95, Hanlon Found., San Francisco, 1993, San Francisco, 1993, Nautilus Meml., Groton, Conn., 1993; Mus. of Fine Art, Springfield, Mass., 1992, Gumps, San Francisco, 1992, Lyman Allyn Art Mus., New London, 1992, Mus. of the Hudson Highlands, 1989, others; group shows includ U.S. Coast Guard, Governor's Island, N.Y.C. (COGAP prize '94), Mus. Naval Aviation, Pensacola, Fla., 1994, Columbia River Maritime Mus., Astoria, Oreg., 1994, others; works collected in various museums/corps. Mem. Salmagundi Club (recipient George Gray award '94 COGAP, N.Y.C.), Am. Soc. Marine Artists, Internat. Soc. of Marine Painters, Internat. Diplomacy Council, Commonwealth Club of San Francisco, Alliance Francaise.

PARKHURST, CHARLES LLOYD, electronics company executive; b. Nashville, Aug. 13, 1943; s. Charles Albert Parkhurst and Dorothy Elizabeth (Ballou) Parkhurst Crutchfield; m. Dolores Ann Oakley, June 6, 1970; children: Charles Thomas, Deborah Lynn, Jere Loy. Student, Hume-Fogg Tech. Coll., 1959-61; AA, Mesa Community Coll., 1973; student, Ariz. State U., 1973-76. Mem. design staff Tex. Instruments, Dallas, 1967-68; mgr. design Motorola, Inc., Phoenix, 1968-76; pres. LSI Cons., Inc., Tempe, Ariz., 1976-85, LSI Photomasks, Inc., Tempe, 1985-94, Charles Parkhurst Books, Inc., Prescott, Ariz., 1994—. Mem. Rep. Congl. Leadership Coun., Washington, 1988; life mem. Rep. Presdl. Task Force, 1990. Served as cpl. USMC, 1961-64. Mem. Bay Area Chrome Users Soc., Nat. Trust Hist. Preservation, Ariz. State U. Alumni Assn. (life), Antiquarian Booksellers Assn. Am. Baptist. Office: Charles Parkhurst Books Inc PO Box 10850 Prescott AZ 86304-0850

PARKHURST, GARY STEPHEN, publishing company executive; b. Berkeley, Calif., Feb. 16, 1951; s. Kenneth Leroy and Elaine Marie (Jones) P.; m. Carol Sue Bernier, Apr. 6, 1974; children: Stephen Jason, Elizabeth Anne. BS, Calif. State U., Chico, 1973; postgrad., Santa Clara U., 1975-76. Various positions Gen. Foods Corp., N.Y., L.A., San Francisco, 1974-79; product mgr. Gen. Foods Corp., N.Y.C., 1980-82; dist. mgr. Gen. Foods Corp., Memphis, 1982-83, N.Y.C., 1984; mktg. mgr. Majers, San Ramon, Calif., 1985, v.p., gen. mgr., 1986, v.p., dir. bus. devel., 1987-88, v.p., sr. nat. accounts, 1988-89; gen. mgr. Nielsen Mktg. Rsch., Fremont, Calif., 1989-91; div. v.p. Harmon Pub., Emeryville, Calif., 1991—. Mem. Nat. Ski Patrol, 1971-73; Little League Baseball coach, 1980; Webelos leader, 1987; Basketball coach Walnut Creek Youth Athletic League, 1991-92; registrar Rudgear Estates Swim Team, Walnut Creek, 1989-90, announcer/starter, 1990-94. Republican. Presbyterian. Home: 1837 Chaparro Ct Walnut Creek CA 94596-6100

PARKIN, SHARON KAYE, bookkeeper; b. Portland, Oreg., Nov. 21, 1940; d. Charles Edward and Beulah Elizabeth (Foraker) King; m. Russell Jerome Gartrell, Aug. 5, 1960 (div. Dec. 1971); children: Mark Russell, William Edward; m. Jack Edgar Parkin, Feb. 21, 1975 (div. July, 1994). Student, Portland State U., 1959-60. Timekeeper, Sears, Roebuck & Co., Redmond, Wash., 1971-77; bookkeeper, acct. Bristol Bay Area Health Corp., Dillingham, Alaska, Mental Health Corp., Bellingham, Wash., 1977-78, 82; bookkeeper Whatcom Counseling, 1978-80, Charlie's Marine, Juneau, Alaska, 1980-81, L & M Supplies, Dillingham, 1983—; owner, pres. Parkin Bookkeeping, Inc., 1984—; owner Hillbilly Ent.; notary pub. State of Alaska, 1983—; bookkeeper, acct. Bristol Baytimes & Mosquito Press, 1991—, McCormick, 1992—, JD's Fuel Co., Inc., 1994—. Democrat. Mem. Christian Ch. Avocations: boating, fishing, hunting, travel, crochet. Home: PO Box 685 Dillingham AK 99576-0685 Office: L & M Supplies PO Box 550 Dillingham AK 99576-0550

PARKINSON, HOWARD EVANS, insurance company executive; b. Logan, Utah, Nov. 3, 1936; s. Howard Maughan and Valeria Arlene (Evans) P.; m. Lucy Kay Bowen, Sept. 2, 1960; children: Blake, Gregory, Dwight, Lisa, David, Rebecca. BS, Brigham Young U., 1961; MBA, U. Utah, 1963. CLU. Chartered fin. cons. Mgmt. intern AEC, Richland, Wash., 1963-65; v.p. Belstar, Inc., Rexburg, Idaho, 1965-71, dir., 1966-76, pres., 1971-76; v.p., dir. Grand Targhee Resort, Inc., Rexburg, 1967-69; v.p. Fargo-Wilson-Wells Co., Pocatello, Idaho, 1974-76; equity qualified agt. Equitable Life Assurance So. U.S., Idaho Falls, 1977-80, mem. nat. coun. sales group, 1978; dist. mgr. Mass. Mut. Life Ins. Co., Idaho Falls, 1980—; fin. cons. small bus. Bd. dirs. Little League Baseball, 1974-75; coach Little League Basketball, 1975-76; high councilman Rexburg Stake, Ch. of Jesus Christ of Latter-day Saints, 1976-77, bishop, 1977—; mem. Pres.'s Coun., 1988. Recipient Bronze award Mass. Mut. Life Ins. Co., Gold award, 1984. Mem. Million Dollar Roundtable, Toastmasters (past pres.). Republican. Office: Mass Mut Life Ins Co 720 N Holmes Ave Idaho Falls ID 83401-2636

PARKINSON, THOMAS BRIAN, marketing executive; b. Lytham-St. Annes, Lancashire, Eng., Oct. 14, 1935; came to U.S., 1966; s. Alfred and Marjorie (Wright) P.; m. Margaret Moore, Oct. 12, 1957; children: Karen, Lynn, Stephen David. Cert. Mech. Engring., Harris Coll. Further Edn., Preston, Lancashire, Eng., 1962. Apprentice tool maker English Electric Co. Ltd., Preston, Lancashire, Eng., 1951-57; designer aircraft structure British Aircraft Corp., Warton, Lancashire, Eng., 1957-63, stress engr. aircraft, 1963-66; stress engr. aircraft Douglas Aircraft Co., Long Beach, Calif., 1966-76, sales engr. commercial mktg., 1976-78, project mgr. commercial mktg., 1978-85, sales mgr. comml. mktg. Pacific and Asia, 1985-89, exec. asst. comml. mktg. Pacific and Asia, 1989-91, sr. prin. specialist analyst mkt. devel., 1991-94; ret., 1994; cons. aircraft mktg. and performance field. Commr. Planning Commn., City of Huntington Beach (Calif.), 1975-77, Underground Utilities Commn., Huntington Beach, 1975-77; chmn. City Charter Revision Com., Huntington Beach, 1977; campaign mgr. Com. to Re-Elect Jerry Matney, Huntington Beach, 1973. With Royal Navy, 1953-55. Mem. Instn. Engring. Designers (assoc.), Pacific Area Travel Assn. (chmn. rsch. authority, bd. dirs. 1983-85, award of merit 1985). Episcopalian. Home: 944 Cattle Dr Roseburg OR 97470-9309

PARKISON, ROGER CLYDE, computer scientist; b. Oakland, Calif., May 19, 1949; s. Duane W. and Mary M. (Trotter) P.; m. Carole J. Suzuki, Aug. 7, 1971; children: Brian C., Diana L. BA, U. Calif., 1971; PhD, Stanford U., 1980. Rsch. asst. Stanford U., 1972-75; prin. programmer UCLA, 1975-84; sr. software engr. Isitec Corp., Sunnyvale, Calif., 1984-87; prin. software engr. Digital Equipment Corp., Cupertino, Calif., 1987-92; software designer Tandem Computers, Cupertino, Calif., 1992—. Contbr. articles to profl. jours. Mem. Assn. for Computing Machinery (spl. interest group on artificial intelligence), Am. Assn. for Artificial Intelligence (spl. interest group in mfg.), Assn. for Computational Linguistics. Home: PO Box 1179 Felton CA 95018-1179

PARKS, DONALD LEE, mechanical engineer, human factors engineer; b. Delphos, Kans., Feb. 23, 1931; s. George Delbert and Erma Josephine (Boucek) P.; student Kans. Wesleyan U., 1948-50; BSME, Kans. State U., 1957, BS in Bus. Adminstrn., 1957, MS in Psychology, 1959; cert. profl. Ergonomist; m. Bessie Lou Schur, Dec. 24, 1952; children: Elizabeth Parks Anderson, Patricia Parks-Holbrook, Donna, Charles, Sandra. Elem. tchr., 1950-51; with Kans. State U. Placement Svc., 1957-59; human factors engr., systems engr. Boeing Co., Seattle, 1959-90, sr. specialist engr., 1972-74, sr. engring. supr., 1974-90; pres. D-Square Assocs. Engring. Cons., 1990—; adj. lectr. UCLA Engring. Extension, 1989—; cons., lectr. in field; participant workshops on guidelines in profl. areas, NATO, NSF, Nat. Acad. Sci., NRC. Mem. Derby (Kans.) Planning Commn., 1961-62, chmn., 1962; del. King County (Wash.) Republican Conv., 1972. With AUS, 1952-54. Mem. Human Factors Soc. (Puget Sound Pres.'s award 1969), Assn. Aviation Psychologists, ASME, Am. Psychol. Assn., Midwestern Psychol. Assn., Elks. Presbyterian. Contbr. over 80 articles to publs., chpts. to 8 books. Home: 6232 127th Ave SE Bellevue WA 98006-3943

PARKS, GERALD THOMAS, JR., lawyer, business executive; b. Tacoma, Wash., Feb. 25, 1944; s. Gerald Thomas and Elizabeth (Bell) P.; m. Susan Simenstad, July 22, 1967; children: Julie, Christopher; m. Bonny Kay O'Connor, Jan. 15, 1979, children: Garrett, Ardrienne. BA in Polit. Sci., U. Wash., 1966; JD, U. Oreg., 1969. Bar: Wash. 1969. Assoc. Graham & Dunn, 1972-77, ptnr., 1977-82; sole practice, 1982—; sec., treas. Holaday-Parks Fabricators, Inc., 1972-78, v.p., gen. mgr. (named changed to Holaday-Parks, Inc.), 1978-84; pres., chief exec. officer, 1984—. Trustee The Bush Sch., 1992-95. Served to lt. with USN, 1969-72. Mem. Wash. State Bar Assn., Sheet Metal and Air Conditioning Contractors of Western Wash., Inc. (pres. 1989-91), Sheet Metal and Air Conditioning Contractors Nat. Assn. (dir. 1989-92, pres. 1994-95), Seattle Yacht Club, Broadmoor Golf Club, Seattle Tennis Club. Office: PO Box 69208 4600 S 134th Pl Seattle WA 98168

PARKS, HAROLD RAYMOND, mathematician, educator; b. Wilmington, Del., May 22, 1949; s. Lytle Raymond Jr. and Marjorie Ruth (Chambers) P.; m. Paula Sue Beaulieu, Aug. 21, 1971 (div. 1984); children: Paul Raymond, David Austin; m. Susan Irene Taylor, June 6, 1985; 1 stepchild, Kathryn McLaughlin. AB, Dartmouth Coll., 1971; PhD, Princeton U., 1974. Tamarkin instr. Brown U., Providence, 1974-77; asst. prof. Oreg. State U., Corvallis, 1977-82, assoc. prof., 1982-89, prof. math., 1989—; vis. assoc. prof. Ind. U., Bloomington, 1982-83. Author: Explicit Determination of Area Minimizing Hypersurfaces, vol. II, 1986, (with Steven G. Krantz) A Primer of Real Analytic Functions, 1992; contbr. articles to profl. publs. Cubmaster Oregon Trail Coun. Boy Scouts Am., 1990-92. NSF fellow, 1971-74. Mem. Am. Math. Soc., Math. Assn. Am., Soc. Indsl. and Applied Math., Phi Beta Kappa. Republican. Mem. Soc. of Friends. Home: 33194 Dorset Ln Philomath OR 97370-9555 Office: Oreg State U Dept Math Corvallis OR 97331-4605

PARKS, MICHAEL CHRISTOPHER, journalist; b. Detroit, Nov. 17, 1943; s. Robert James and Rosalind (Smith) P.; m. Linda Katherine Durocher, Dec. 26, 1964; children: Danielle Anne, Christopher, Matthew. AB, U. Windsor, Ont., Can., 1965. Reporter Detroit News, 1962-65; corr. Time-Life News Service, N.Y.C., 1965-66; asst. city editor Suffolk Sun, Long Island, N.Y., 1966-68; polit. reporter, foreign corr. The Balt. Sun, Saigon, Singapore, Moscow, Cairo, Hong Kong, Peking, 1968-80; fgn. corr. L.A. Times, L.A., Peking, Johannesburg, Moscow, Jerusalem, 1980-95, dpty. fgn. editor, 1995—. Recipient Pulitzer Prize, 1987. Mem. Royal Commonwealth Soc. London. Club: Foreign Corr. (Hong Kong). Office: L A Times Times Mirror Sq Los Angeles CA 90012

PARKS, MICHAEL JAMES, publisher, editor; b. Spokane, Wash., June 3, 1944; s. Floyd Lewis and C. Marie (McHugh) P.; m. Janet K. Holter, Aug. 12, 1967; children: Michael J., Gregory F., Sarah M. BA, Seattle U., 1966. Reporter The Seattle Times, 1966-74, fin. editor, 1974-77; pub., editor Marple's Bus. Newsletter, Seattle, 1977—. Bd. govs. Seattle U. Alumni Assn.; trustee Seattle Rotary Service Found. Fellow Am. Press Inst., N.Y.C., 1973. Roman Catholic. Lodge: Rotary. Office: Marples Bus Newsletter 117 W Mercer St Ste 200 Seattle WA 98119-3953

PARKS, RICHARD CAMERON, outdoor sports professional, small business owner; b. Cloquet, Minn., June 20, 1943; s. Merton James and Ellen Laura (Nightingale) P. BS, Mont. State U., 1966. Owner Parks Fly Shop, Gardiner, Mont., 1970—. Co-author: Tying and Fishing the West's Best Day Flies, 1978. Sec. No. Plains Resource Coun., Billings, 1988-90, vice chmn., 1990-91, chmn., 1991-93; chmn. Western Orgn. Resource Coun., 1994. Mem. Fishing Outfitters Assn. of Mont. (pres. 1986-90). Democrat. Unitarian.

PARKS, RICHARD KEITH, clinical social worker; b. Rock Springs, Wyo., Oct. 13, 1947; s. Keith Andrew and Mildred Ann (Matkovich) P.; m. Debra D. Thomas, Sept. 21, 1968 (div. Nov. 1971); m. Alberta Dea Henderson, Feb. 26, 1974; children: Heather, Richell. AA, Western Wyo. Coll., 1969; BSW, U. Wyo., 1985; MSW, Denver U., 1988. Lic. social worker. Owner, mgr. Rich's Britches, Rock Springs, 1974-77; asst. mgr. Wyo. Bearing, Rock Springs, 1976-82; residential counselor Southwest Wyo. Rehab. Ctr., Rock Springs, 1983-85; community care worker, therapist Southwest Counseling Svc., Rock Springs, 1985-89; sch. social worker Sch. Dist. #1, Rock Springs, 1989-90; mental health counselor State of Nev. Rural Clinics, Fernley, 1990-92; inpatient clin. social worker Nev. Mental Health Inst., Reno, 1992-93; social work cons. Pershing Gen. Hosp., Lovelock, Nev., 1991-93; clin. social worker Human Affaire Internat.-Aetna, Salt Lake City, 1993—; program mgr. Transitional Living Ctr., 1985-87; workshop presenter in field, 1986. Vol. counselor Sweetwater Crisis Intervention Ctr., Rock Springs, 1973-83, bd. dirs., 1979-83; v.p. Downtown Mchts. Assn., 1975. Mem. NASW, Alumni Assn. U. Wyo. Congregationalist.

PARKS, THOMAS NORVILLE, neurobiologist; b. Berkeley, Calif., May 27, 1950; s. Herbert Otho and Wilma Jean (Strong) P.; m. Patricia Legant, July 6, 1980; 1 child, Anna Legant. B.S., U. Calif., Irvine, 1972; Ph.D., Yale U., 1978. Lectr. psychology Yale U., New Haven, 1977; postdoctoral fellow U. Va., Charlottesville, 1977-78; asst. prof. anatomy U. Utah, Salt Lake City, 1978-83, assoc. prof., 1983-87, prof., 1987—, George and Lorna Winder prof. Neuroscience and chair, dept. Neurobiology and Anatomy, 1992—; bd. dirs. NPS Pharmaceuticals Inc., v.p., 1987-88. Mem. NIH (hearing rsch. study sect. 1986-90, Claude pepper award 1993—). Office: U Utah Sch Medicine Dept Neurobiology And Salt Lake City UT 84132

PARMA, FLORENCE VIRGINIA, magazine editor; b. Kenilworth, N.J., Aug. 30, 1940; d. Howard Frank and Mildred Faye (Lister) von Finkel; m. Wilson Henry Parma, June 15, 1973 (div. Aug. 1986). Studies with pvt. tutor, Chaumont, France, 1961-62; student, NYU, 1962-63. Copywriter Schless & Co., N.Y.C., 1963-65; editor, researcher Barchas Lab., Stanford, Calif., 1969-73; adminstrv. exec. Crater Inc., Honolulu, 1974-79; mgr., editor Off Duty mag., Honolulu, 1979—; v.p. Mapasa, Inc. (dba The Prides of New Zealand), 1992—. Editor: Welcome to Hawaii Guide, 1985—; co-editor: Serotonin and Behavior, 1972; freelance columnist. Republican. Episcopalian. Home and Office: Off Duty Hawaii 3771 Anuhea St Honolulu HI 96816-3849

PARMAN, SUSAN MORRISSETT, anthropologist, writer; b. Middletown, Conn., Aug. 17, 1945; d. Lee Ferguson and Edith Rosalie (Morrissett) Parman; m. Jacob Pandian, May 11, 1972; 1 child, Georgina Morrissett Pandian. BA, Antioch Coll., 1967; PhD, Rice U., 1972. Asst. prof. anthropology Calif. State U., Hayward, 1972-76; lectr. anthropology various colls. and univs., Calif., 1976-88; prof. anthropology Calif. State U., Fullerton, 1988—; cons. Holt, Rinehart & Winston, 1985—, Harcourt, Brace Jovanovich Pubs., 1985—. Author: Scottish Crofters, 1990, Dream and Culture, 1991; contbr. articles to Am. Anthropologist, Folklore, Ethnos. Founding mem., v.p. Placentia (Calif.) Pride Coun., 1992—. NEH rsch. fellow, Scotland, 1983, 92; Calif. State U. Found. grantee, 1991, 92, 93, 94, 95, NSF grantee, 1995. Fellow Soc. Antiquarians of Scotland; mem. Am. Anthrop. Assn., Soc. for the Anthropology of Europe (publs. chair 1992—), Pacific Coast Conf. on Brit. Studies. Democrat. Home: 4931 Hamer Dr Placentia CA 92670-3021 Office: Calif State U Fullerton Dept Anthropology Fullerton CA 92634

PARONI, GENEVIEVE MARIE SWICK, retired secondary education educator; b. Eureka, Nev., July 27, 1926; d. William Jackson and Myrtle Rose (Smith) S.; m. Walter Andrew Paroni, Dec. 26, 1954; 1 child, Andrea Marie. BA, U. Nev., Reno, 1948; MEd, U. Idaho, 1978; postgrad., MIT, Oreg. State U., U. Oreg., U. Wash., Ft. Wright Coll., U. Portland. Cert. elem. and secondary sect., Nev. Tchr., vice prin. Eureka County H.S., 1948-66; coast geodetic U.S. Govt., Eureka, 1950's; tchr. biol. and phys. scis., facilitator Pub. Schs. Dist. # 393, Wallace, Idaho, 1968-91; ret., 1991; regional dir. NSTA, Idaho, Panhandle, 1982-90; chmn. in svc. adv. State Dept. Edn., Boise, Idaho, 1980-83, mem. state sci. commn., 1981-82; mem. Idaho Sci. Curriculum Guide Com., 1987, Univ. Idaho Commn. on Math/Sci. Edn., 1988-89, Inland Empire Physics Alliance, 1989-90, Idaho Sci. Alliance Com., 1990. Contbr. history articles to profl. jours. Active Wallace City Coun., 1970-80; bd. dirs., Wallace Pub. Libr., 1983—, chmn. 1995—, Silver Valley Arts and Crafts Assn., 1991, Greater Wallace, 1980-93, Wallace Dist. Arts Coun., 1993—; mem. citizen's adv. bd. Idaho Nat. Engring. Lab., 1994—; facilitator Panhandle Area Ecolab., 1995—; Rep. precinct chairperson, Wallace, 1970-80; bishop's warden area Episc. Ch., 1990-94; mem. coun. Episc. Diocese Spokane, 1992—. Grantee Idaho Power, 1985; named Outstanding Tchr., Dist. #393. 1975; finalist Presdl. awards in High Sch. Sci. Teaching. Mem. NEA, AAUW (pres. 1970s), Wallace Edn. Assn. (sec. 1970s), Bus. and Profl. Women Assn. (v.p. Nev. chpt. 1953-55), Pythian Sisters (Grand Guard 1950), Order Ea. Star (matron Nev. chpt.), Delta Kappa Gamma (pres. 1980-82), Phi Delta Kappa. Home: PO Box 229 Wallace ID 83873-0229

PARQUETTE, JACK ROBERT, lawyer; b. Des Moines, July 2, 1934; s. Robert West and Helen (Cox) P.; m. Eva Miersch, Sept. 11, 1965; children: Jonathan R., Brian K. Student, U. Colo., 1959; LLB, Lincoln U., 1977. Bar: Calif. 1978, U.S. Ct. Appeals (9th cir.) 1978, U.S. Dist. Ct. (ea. dist.) Calif., 1978. Claims mgr. Unigard Ins. Calif., Sacramento, 1966-77; ptnr. Barker, Mikel & Parquette, Sacramento, 1979-81; pvt. practice, 1981—. Mem. Calif. State Bar Assn., No. Calif. Def. Assn. Home: 7748 Guenivere Way Citrus Heights CA 95610-8701

PARR, JOHN DAVID, not-for-profit executive; b. Lafayette, Ind., Feb. 7, 1948; s. Harlan and Dorothy (Widmer) P.; m. Robin Godfrey, May 1972 (div. Sept. 1976); m. Sandra Jean Widener, May 31, 1986; children: Chase Anna, Katherine Widener. BA in Polit. Sci., Purdue U., 1970; JD, U. Denver, 1976. Bar: Colo. 1977. Vol. coord., office mgr. Barnes for Congress, 1970; legis. coord., membership drive coord. Colo. Project/Common Cause, 1971, 73; coord. Campaign to Remove 1976 Winter Olympics from Colo. Citizens for Colorado's Future, 1971-72; dir. field orgn. Coloradans for Lamm, 1973-74; asst. to gov. Gov. Richard Lamm, 1974-77; campaign cons. Coloradans for Lamm, 1977; cons. ACTION, Washington, 1977-78; dir. Colo. Front Range Project Office of Gov., 1979-81; dir. Ctr. for Pub.-Pvt. Sector Coop. U. Colo., Denver, 1981-85; pres. Nat. Civic League, Denver, 1985—; Commr. Denver Urban Renewal Authority. Contbg. editor and author to profl. jours. Vol. Chinook Fund Fundraising Com., Denver Pub. Sch. Tutorial Program, U. Denver Fgn. Student Host Parent Program. Fellow Nat. Acad. for Pub. Adminstrn.; mem. Common Cause, Nature Conservancy, Vol. for Outdoor Colo., Friends of Denver Pub. Libr., Denver Natural History Mus., Nat. Pub. Radio Stas. KCFR and KUVO. Home: 720 Franklin St Denver CO 80218-3628 Office: Nat Civic League 1445 Market St Ste 300 Denver CO 80202-1728

PARRAGUIRRE, RONALD DAVID, judge; b. Reno, July 8, 1959; s. Paul Charles and Iris Mae (Bleick) P. BBA, San Diego State U., 1982; JD, U. San Diego, 1985. Bar: Pa. 1986, Nev. 1986, D.C. 1987. Legis. asst. U.S. Senator Paul Laxalt, Washington, 1985-86; counsel subcom. on criminal law, judiciary com. U.S. Senate, Washington, 1986-87; lawyer Parraguirre & Parraguirre, Las Vegas, Nev., 1987-91; mcpl. ct. judge Dept. 6 City of Las Vegas, 1991—. Mem. ABA, ATLA, Am. Judges Assn., Nev. Judges Assn., Clark County Bar Assn. (exec. bd. dirs.). Republican. Lutheran. Office: Las Vegas Mcpl Ct 400 Stewart Ave Las Vegas NV 89101-2942

PARRIS, ANNE WITMER, secondary education educator, writer; b. East Orange, N.J., Oct. 24, 1960; d. Paul Sutherland and Hannah Steele (Calkin) Parris; m. Andrew Patrick Murray, Aug. 14, 1982; m. Douglas K. Rogers, July 19, 1991. BA in English, U. Calif., Davis, 1983; postgrad., Mills Coll., 1990—. Cert. tchr., Calif. Tchr. English Castro Valley (Calif.) H.S., 1984—; mentor tchr. Castro Valley Unified Sch. Dist., 1989-91. Mem., faculty advisor Amnesty Internat., 1990—. NEH summer seminar study grantee, 1990, 93. Mem. Nat. Coun. Tchrs. English, Calif. Tchrs. Assn. (state coun. rep. 1990—), Delta Kappa Gamma. Office: Castro Valley HS 19400 Santa Maria Ave Castro Valley CA 94546-3400

PARRISH, PAMELA JO, counselor; b. Schenectady, N.Y., Sept. 20, 1953; d. Richard Owen and Joyce Elaine (Prichard) P.; m. James Headley Maish, May 25, 1991. BA, U. Ky., 1977; MA, U. Ariz., 1994. Reporter Georgetown (Ky.) News and Times, 1977-78; lifestyle/entertainment reporter The Lexington (Ky.) Leader, 1978-79; popular music writer Ariz. Daily Star, Tucson, 1979-81, asst. entertainment editor, 1981-86, children's reporter, 1986-88, entertainment editor, 1988-92; freelance music writer, 1986—; counselor Cath. Social Svc., Tucson, 1994—. Mem. Adlerian Soc. Ariz.

PARRISH, RICHARD B., manufacturing executive; b. Kalispell, Mont., June 4, 1938; s. Richard Wiley and Helen (Bancroft) P.; m. Susan Spring, Aug. 27, 1960; children: Julie Parrish Whalen, Mike. Grad., U. Wash., 1961; grad. exec. program, Stanford U., 1977. With Boise Cascade Corp., 1961—; acct. Boise Cascade Corp., Seattle, Portland, 1961-65; Timberlands mgr. Boise Cascade Corp., Salem, Oreg., 1965-67; asst. region mgr. Boise Cascade Corp., Medford, Oreg., 1967-70, region mgr., 1970-77; mgr. West Coast area Boise Cascade Corp., Portland, Oreg., 1977-80; v.p. ops. Boise Cascade Corp., Boise, Idaho, 1980-86; v.p., gen. mgr. Boise Cascade Corp., Boise, 1986-89, sr. v.p., gen. mgr., 1989—. Mem. Western Wood Products Assn. (chmn. 1986-88), Am. Lumber Standards (vice chmn. 1986—), Nat. Forest Products Assn. (bd. govs. 1987—, Mem. of Yr. 1991), Am. Plywood Assn. (trustee 1986—). Republican. Episcopalian. Office: Boise Cascade Corp 1 Jefferson Sq Boise ID 83728-0001

PARRO, DOUGLAS ARTHUR, nonprofit child care center administrator; b. Denver, Dec. 29, 1954; s. Russell James and Theresa Viola (Zapp) P.; m. Jamie Lou Sherberg, May 21, 1976. BA in Psychology and Sociology, U. Colo., 1978, MA in Clin. Psychology, 1987. Lic. profl. counselor. Delivery driver various cos., Denver, 1970-74; postal clk. U.S. Postal Svc., Denver, 1974-75; oil well roughneck Wildcat Driller, Nebr., 1975; liquor clk. Mayfair Liquors, Denver, 1980-82; counselor/asst. dir., 1977-80; exec. dir. Jefferson Hall, Arvada, Colo., 1983—; cons., trainer Community Learning Ctrs., Gemini Shelter, Shalom House, Adolescent Treatment Program, All My Children Homes, Denver, 1987—; grant writer, adminstr., Jefferson Hall, Arvada, 1983—; field instr. Colo. State U., 1987—, U. Denver, 1988—. Treas. Shadow Wood Homeowners Assn., Denver, 1986-93; assoc. mem. Denver Zool. Found., 1991—; commr. Placement Alternatives Commn., Jefferson County, Colo., 1983-89; mem. Colo. Juvenile Coun., Denver Youth Agy. Network. Mem. Phi Beta Kappa. Office: Jefferson Hall 7695 W 59th Ave Arvada CO 80004-5501

PARROTT, DENNIS BEECHER, sales executive; b. St. Louis, June 13, 1929; s. Maurice Ray and Mai Ledgerwood (Beecher) P.; m. Vivian Cleveland Miller, Mar. 24, 1952; children: Constance Beecher, Dennis Beecher, Anne Cleveland. BS in Econs., Fla. State U., Tallahassee, 1954; postgrad. Princeton U., 1964; MBA, Pepperdine U., 1982. With Prudential Ins. Co. Am., 1954-74, v.p. group mktg., L.A., 1971-74; sr. v.p. Frank B. Hall Cons. Co., L.A., 1974-83; v.p. Johnson & Higgins, L. A., 1983-95; exec. v.p. Arthur Gallagher & Co., L.A., 1995—; speaker in field. Chmn. Weekend with the Stars Telethon, 1976-80; chmn. bd. dirs. United Cerebral Palsy/Spastic Children's Found. Los Angeles County, 1979-82, chmn. bd. govs., 1982-83; bd. dirs. Nat. United Cerebral Palsy Assn., 1977-82, pres., 1977-79; bd. dirs. L.A. Emergency Task Force, 1992; mem. community adv. council Birmingham High Sch., Van Nuys, Calif., 1982-85; sect. chmn. United Way, Los Angeles, 1983-84; bd. dirs. The Betty Clooney Found. for Brain Injured, 1986-88; mem. com. to fund an endowed chair in cardiology at Cedars-Sinai Med. Ctr., 1986-88; adv. council Family Health Program Inc., 1986-88; bd. Deacons Bel Air Presbyn. Ch., 1990-92, chmn. 1991-92; elder Bel Air Presbyn. Ch. 1993—. Served to 1st lt. AUS, 1951-53. C.L.U. Mem. Am. Soc. C.L.U.s, Internat. Found. Employee Benefits, Merchants and Mfrs. Assns. 44th Annual Mgmt. Conf. (chmn. 1986), Employee Benefits Planning Assn. So. Calif. Republican. Presbyterian. Clubs: Los Angeles, Woodland

Hills Country, Jonathan (Los Angeles). Office: 5750 Wilshire Blvd Ste 560 Los Angeles CA 90036

PARRUCK, BIDYUT, electrical engineer; b. Calcutta, W. Bengal, India, Oct. 31, 1958; came to U.S., 1981; s. Birendra Singh and Jyotsna (Kothari) P. B in Tech., Indian Inst. Tech., Kharagpur, 1981; MS in Elec. Engring., Va. Poly. Inst., 1983. Mem. tech. staff ITT Advanced Tech. Ctr., Shelton, Conn., 1983-86; R & D engr. Contel Fin. Systems, Stamford, Conn., 1987-89; sr. design engr. TranSwitch Corp., Shelton, 1989-93; sect. head II Farinon divsn. Harris Corp., San carlos, Calif., 1993; prin. engr. Network Equipment Techs., Redwood City, Calif., 1993-94; dir. asynchronous transfer mode sonet Coreel MicroSystems, Fremont, Calif., 1994—, also bd. dirs.; founder, advisor Next Generation Systems, Matawan, N.J., 1986—; advisor, cons. OSS Corp., Shelton, Conn., 1988—. Contbr. articles to profl. jours.; patentee in field. Vol. Ourhouse-North, Daly City, Calif., 1993-94. Mem. IEEE. Home: 7331D Parkwood Cir Dublin CA 94568

PARRY, ATWELL J., JR., state senator, retailer; b. Ogden, Utah, June 14, 1925; s. John Atwell and Nina Virginia (McEntire) P.; m. Elaine Hughes, Feb. 6, 1946; children—Bonnie, Michael, Jay, Donald, David, Delbert, Kent. Student pub. schs., Nampa, Idaho. Salesman, King's Packing Co., Nampa, 1947-54, credit mgr., 1954-55; plant mgr. Stone Poultry Co., Nampa, 1955-56; salesman Nestle Chocolate Co., 1956-64; owner, mgr. Melba Foods, Idaho, 1964-82; mem. Idaho Senate, 1981—; bd. dirs. Western Idaho Tng. Ctr., 1987-90; chmn. Senate Finance Com. and co-chmn. Joint Fin. and Appropriations Com., 1987—; chmn. Idaho State Bd. for Nat. Ctr. for Constl. Studies, 1988-90. Bd dirs. Alcohol Treatment Ctr., Nampa, 1978-82; mem. adv. bd. Mercy Med. Ctr., Nampa, 1976-81; mem. Melba City Council, 1971-74. Recipient Silver Beaver award Boy Scouts Am., 1959, Service award Mercy Med. Ctr., Outstanding Rep. Legislator in Idaho State award, 1993. Republican. Mormon.

PARRY, BARBARA LOCKHART, psychiatry educator, researcher; b. Cheyenne, Wyo., Oct. 29, 1952; d. William Lockhart and June Shirley (Howorth) P. Student, Vassar Coll., 1973; BA, U. Rochester, 1974; MD, U. Okla., Oklahoma City, 1978. Diplomate Am. Bd. Psychiatry and Neurology. Intern in internal medicine UCLA-Wadsworth VA Hosp., 1978-79; resident in psychiatry UCLA Neuropsychiat. Inst., 1979-82; clin. rsch. fellow clin. psychobiology br. NIMH, Bethesda, Md., 1982-85; assoc. prof. psychiatry U. Calif. at San Diego, La Jolla, 1985—. Grantee NIMH, 1989-94. Mem. Rocky Mountain Trauma Soc., Sleep Rsch. Soc., Soc. Resch. Bio Rhythms, Psychiat. Rsch. Soc., Soc. Light Treatment Bio Rhythms, West Coast Coll. Bio Psychiatry. Office: U Calif San Diego 0804 9500 Gilman Dr La Jolla CA 92093-5003

PARRY, ELLWOOD COMLY, III, art history educator; b. Abington, Pa., Aug. 9, 1941; s. Ellwood Comly Jr. and Elizabeth (Graham) P.; m. Carol Jaqueline Newman, Feb. 1, 1964 (div. Nov. 1971); m. Pamela Gay Jeffcott, Nov. 20, 1971; children: Janna Jeffcott, Evan Graham, Taylor Jeffcott. BA cum laude, Harvard U., 1964; MA in Art History, UCLA, 1966; PhD in Art History, Yale U., 1970. Asst. prof. art history Columbia U., N.Y.C., 1969-75; fellow for ind. study and rsch. NEH, 1975-76; assoc. prof. U. Iowa, Iowa City, 1976-81; prof. U. Ariz., Tucson, 1981—. Author: Image of the Indian and the Black Man, 1974, (monograph) The Art of Thomas Cole, 1988. Home: 3775 N Bear Creek Cir Tucson AZ 85749-9454 Office: U Ariz Dept Art Tucson AZ 85721

PARRY, RICHARD GITTINGS, plastic and reconstructive surgeon, writer; b. Chgo., July 6, 1942; s. Norman Gittings and Lillian (Koudelka) P.; m. Katherine Sue Peck, June 12, 1965; children: David, Matthew. MD, U. Ill., Chgo., 1966. Intern in surgery, jr. resident Johns Hopkins U., Balt., 1966-68; surg. resident Boston City Hosp., 1968-72; plastic and reconstructive resident Harvard Med. Sch., Cambridge, Mass., 1974-76; plastic and reconstructive surgeon Lahey Clinic, Boston, 1976-78; pvt. practice Fairbanks, Alaska, 1978—. Author: (novels) Ice Warrior, 1991, Venom Victim, 1992; contbr. articles to profl. jours. Lt. comdr., surgeon USN, 1972-74. Mem. Alaska State Med. Assn. (pres. 1983-84), Fairbanks Med. Assn. (pres. 1982-83), Am. Cancer Soc. (pres. Alaska divsn. 1987-88), Phi Beta Pi, Alpha Omega Alpha. Home: 594 Ridgecrest Dr Fairbanks AK 99709 Office: 2111 Cowles Ste 3 Fairbanks AK 99701-5918

PARRY, ROBERT WALTER, chemistry educator; b. Ogden, Utah, Oct. 1, 1917; s. Walter and Jeanette (Petterson) P.; m. Marjorie J. Nelson, July 6, 1945; children: Robert Bryce, Mark Nelson. BS, Utah State Agr. Coll., 1940; MS, Cornell U., 1942; PhD, U. Ill., 1946; DSc (hon.), Utah State U., 1985. Research asst. NDRC Munitions Devel. Lab., U. Ill. at Urbana, 1943-45, teaching fellow 1945-46; mem. faculty U. Mich., 1946-69, prof. chemistry, 1958-69; Distinguished prof. chemistry U. Utah, 1969—; indsl. cons., 1952—; chmn. bd. trustees Gordon Rsch. Conf., 1967-68. Chmn. com. teaching chemistry Internat. Union Pure and Applied Chemistry 1968-74. Recipient Mfg. Chemists award for coll. teaching, 1972, Sr. U.S. Scientist award Alexander Von Humboldt-Stiftung (W. Ger.), 1980, First Govs. medal of Sci. State Utah, 1987. Mem. Am. Chem. Soc. (Utah award Utah Sect. 1978, past chmn. inorganic div. and div. chem. edn., award for distinguished service to inorganic chemistry 1965, for chem. edn., 1977, dir. 1973-83, bd. editors jour. 1969-80, pres.-elect 1981-82, pres. 1982-83, Priestly medal 1993), Internat. Union Pure and Applied Chemistry (chmn. U.S. nat. com.), AAAS, Sigma Xi. Founding editor Inorganic Chemistry, 1960-63. Research publs. on some structural problems of inorganic chemistry, and incorporation results into theoretical models; chemistry of phosphorus, boron and fluorine. Home: 5002 Fairbrook Ln Salt Lake City UT 84117-6205 Office: U Utah Dept Chemistry Henry Eyring Bldg Salt Lake City UT 84112-1194

PARSA, FEREYDOUN DON, plastic surgeon; b. Geneva, May 20, 1942; came to U.S., 1970; s. Issa and Zahra (Bismark) P.; m. Touri Akhlaghi, June 17, 1972; children: Natalie, Alan, Sean. MD, Lausanne U., Switzerland, 1969. Diplomate Am. Soc. Plastic Surgery. Chif of plastic surgery, prof. surgery U. Hawaii, Honolulu, 1981—. Contbr. articles to profl. jours. Mem. Am. Cancer Soc. (early detection and treatment com. 1993—). Office: U Hawaii Sch Med Surg 1356 Lusitana St Honolulu HI 96813-2421 Office: U Hawaii 1329 Lusitana St Honolulu HI 96813

PARSLEY, MARTIE, communications educator; b. Charleston, W.Va., June 13, 1953; d. George Martin and W. June (Maynor) P. BS, Andrews U., 1975; MS, W.Va. U., 1976. Prof. La Sierra U., Riverside, Calif., 1980—, dir. comm. studies, 1993—; pub. rels. cons. in pvt. practice, 1990—; dir., coord. pub. rels. internship Superior/Mcpl. Cts., San Bernardino County, Calif., 1993—. Mem. Pub. Rels. Soc. Am. (past. bd. dirs. Inland Empire chpt.). Seventh-Day Adventist. Office: La Sierra U 4700 Pierce St Riverside CA 92505-3331

PARSLEY, STEVEN DWAYNE, title company executive; b. Monrovia, Calif., Dec. 31, 1959. BBA magna cum laude, U. Albuquerque, 1985. Lic. agt. to issue title ins., N.Mex. Data processing asst. The Orion Corp., Albuquerque, 1978-79; title searcher N.Mex. Title, Albuquerque, 1979; sr. v.p., escrow officer Rio Grande Title Co., Albuquerque, 1979—, also bd. dirs. Recipient Presdl. scholarship U. N.Mex., Albuquerque, 1978. Mem. N.Mex. Land Title Assn. (v.p.), Albuquerque Bd. of Realtors (chmn. affiliate rels. com.). Home: 5417 Rayito Del Luna Ln NE Albuquerque NM 87111-1647 Office: Rio Grande Title Co 6400 Indian School Rd NE Albuquerque NM 87110-5305

PARSONS, C. LOWELL, surgery educator; b. Troy, N.Y., Sept. 21, 1944; s. H. Kenwood and Elsie (Herrick) P.; m. JoEllen Noonan, Mar. 28, 1967; 1 child, J. Kellogg Parsons. BS, Manhattan Coll., 1966; MD, Yale U., 1970. Intern Yale-New Haven Hosp., 1970-71; Resident in urology U. Pa., Phila., 1973-77; asst. prof. surgery U. Calif., San Diego, 1977-81, assoc. prof., 1981-88, prof., 1988—. Contbr. articles to profl. jours. Grantee USPHS-NIH, 1984-89, 89-94, 90-95. Fellow ACS, Am. Urol. Assn. Home: 6699 Avenida Andorra La Jolla CA 92037-6403 Office: UCSD Hosp 200 W Arbor Dr San Diego CA 92103-1911

PARSONS, CHRISTINA MARIE, science education consultant; b. San Diego, Oct. 16, 1953; d. Virgil and Margaret (Binau) P. BA in Biology, U. San Diego, 1975; MA in Edn., San Diego State U., 1983; postgrad., U. San Francisco. Field biologist, scuba diver Dept. Fish and Game State of Calif., San Diego, 1975-77; asst. edn. researcher Sea World, San Diego, 1978-80; educator Zool. Soc. San Diego Wild Animal Pk., 1982-84; edn. specialist Monterey (Calif.) Bay Aquarium, 1984-87; health promotion trainer Stanford U., Salinas, Calif., 1986-88; faculty Dept. of Mus. Studies J.F.K. U., Orinda, Calif., 1991-93; owner/mgr. Word Craft, Monterey, 1987—; bd. dirs., publs. chair Visitor Studies Assn., Jacksonville, Ala., 1993—. Author: Dangerous Marine Animals of Pacific, 1985, Monterey Bay Aquarium Coloring Book, 1988; contbr. articles to Ranger Rick mag., 1986, 90. Vol., 1988 grad. Leadership Monterey Peninsula; vol. Ventana Wilderness Sanctuary, Big Sur, Calif. Recipient Bronze award for Word Craft brochure Ad Club of Monterey Bay, 1990. Mem. Am. Assn. Museums, Assn. Sci-Tech. Ctrs., Am. Zoo and Aquarium Assn., Calif. Sci. Tchrs. Assn., Mus. Edn. Roundtable, Nat. Marine Educators Assn. Office: Word Craft 480 Calle Principal #2 PO Box 1271 Monterey CA 93942

PARSONS, DONALD D., bishop. Bishop of Alaska Evang. Luth. Ch. in Am., Anchorage. Office: Synod of Alaska 1847 W Northern Lights Blvd # 2 Anchorage AK 99517-3343

PARSONS, ELMER EARL, retired clergyman; b. Cloverland, Wash., Oct. 4, 1919; s. Claud Solomon and Bessie Lillian (Campbell) P.; m. Marjorie Emma Carlson, Aug. 29, 1942; children—Karl Elmer, James Myron, Helen Joy, Ann Elizabeth, Lois Marie, Louise Melba. B.A., Seattle Pacific U., 1942; S.T.B., N.Y. Theol. Sem., 1945; S.T.M., Asbury Theol. Sem., Wilmore, Ky., 1955; D.D. (hon.), Greenville (Ill.) Coll., 1958. Ordained to ministry Free Methodist Ch., 1944; acad. dean Wessington Springs (S.D.) Coll., 1945-47; missionary to China, 1947-49, missionary to Japan, 1949-54; supt. Japan Free Meth. Mission, 1950-54; pres. Central Coll., McPherson, Kans., 1955-64, Osaka (Japan) Christian Coll., 1964-74; Asia area sec., Free Meth. Ch., 1964-74; bishop Free Meth. Ch. N.Am., 1974-85. Author: Witness to the Resurrection, 1967. Chmn. Free Meth. Study Commn. on Doctrine. Named Alumnus of Year Seattle Pacific U., 1976. Mem. Wesleyan Theol. Soc.

PARSONS, J. A., paper and wood products company executive; b. 1935. BS, Portland State U., 1961. With Peat Marwick Mitchell & Co., 1961-66, sr. acct.; with Willamette Industries Inc., 1966—, contr., 1969-83, v.p., contr., from 1983, now exec. v.p., CFO. Office: Bohemia Inc 1300 SW 5th Ave Ste 3800 Portland OR 97201-5644

PARSONS, POLLY ELSBETH, internist; b. Bennington, Vt., Jan. 30, 1954; married; 1 child. AB in Biology magna cum laude, Harvard U., 1975; MD, U. Ariz., 1978. Diplomate Nat. Bd. Med. Examiners, Am. Bd. Internat. Medicine, Am. Bd. Pulmonary Medicine, Am. Bd. Critical Care Medicine. Intern, then resident in internal medicine U. Colo. Med. Ctr., 1978-81; rsch. fellow Nat. Jewish Hosp. and Rsch. Ctr., 1981-82; fellow in pulmonary medicine U. Colo. Health Scis. Ctr., 1982-85, instr. pulmonary medicine, 1985-86, asst. prof., 1986-92; staff physician Denver Gen. Hosp., 1985—, co-dir. med. ICU, 1991-93, dir. med. ICU, 1993—; assoc. prof. Sch. Medicine U. Colo., 1992—; mem. rsch. grant rev. com. Am. Lung Assn., 1991—; presenter nat. meetings NIH, 1987, 91, 92, mem. task force on rsch. in cardiopulmonary dysfunction, critical care medicine Nat. Heart, Blood and Lung Inst., 1993—; presenter various profl. confs., 1989-93. Co-editor: Critical Care Secrets, 1992; contbr. chpts. to several books, most recently: Seminars in Respiratory Medicine, Endotoxin and the Lung, The Adult Respiratory Distress Syndrome, Emergency Medicine Secrets, 1993; contbr. articles to profl. publs.; contbr. revs. to Critical Care Medicine, Chest, Alcoholism: Clin. and Exptl. Rsch., Jour. Lab. and Clin. Investigation, Jour. Clin. Investigation, Am. Rev. of Respiratory Disease. Mem. Am. Thoracic Soc. (mem. long-range planning com. 1993—), Western Soc. Clin. Medicine. Office: Denver Gen Hosp 777 Bannock St Denver CO 80204-4507

PARSONS, RODNEY HUNTER, lawyer; b. Pasadena, Calif., Feb. 4, 1947; s. Clarence Eugene and Agnes Prentice (Hunter) P.; m. Deneise Renee Trebotich, Aug. 2, 1980; children: Shannon, Justin, Ryan, Renee, Morgan. BA, UCLA, 1968, JD, 1975. Bar: Calif. 1975, U.S. Dist. Ct. (cen. dist.) Calif. 1980. Assoc. Law Offices Manley Freid, L.A., 1975-78, Robert P. Lawton Inc., Brea, Calif., 1978-79; ptnr. Lether & Parsons, Brea, Calif., 1979-84; owner, pres. Rodney H. Parsons Inc., Fullerton, Calif., 1984—; judge pro tem Superior Ct., 1989—. Bd. dirs. Brea C. of C., 1979-88, pres., 1980-82; bd. dirs. Brea Found., 1990. Mem. Orange County Bar Assn. (family law sect.), Rotary (bd. dirs. 1979-81). Office: 285 E Imperial Hwy Fullerton CA 92635-1048

PARSONS-PETERSEN, PAMELA ANNE, publishing executive. BA in Econs., UCLA, 1983. Sr. clk. L.A. Times, 1983-85; bus. mgr. The Chronicle, St. Helens, Oreg., 1985-91, pub., 1991—. Mem. St. Helens C. of C. (bd. dirs. 1994), Jaycees (pres. 1987). Office: The Chronicle PO Box 1153 Saint Helens OR 97051-8153

PARTIDA, GILBERT A., chamber of commerce executive; b. Nogales, Ariz., July 27, 1962; s. Enrique Gilberto and Mary Lou (Flores) P.; m. Soncee Ray Brown, July 30, 1992. BA with distinction, U. Ariz., 1984; JD cum laude, Pepperdine U., 1987; LLD (hon.), Calif. Western Sch Law, San Diego, 1993. V.p., bd. mem. Partida Brokerage, Inc., Nogales, 1983-91; law clk. Office of Ariz. Atty. Gen., Tucson, 1985; assoc. Gray, Cary, Ames & Frye, San Diego, 1986-89, sr. assoc., 1990-92; chmn. Mex. Practice Group Gray, Cary, Ames & Frye, 1992; pres. Greater San Diego C. of C., 1993—; corp. counsel San Diego Incubator Corp., 1990—. Contbr. articles to profl. jours. Mem. United Way Latino Future Scan Com., 1990; mentor Puente, 1991; leadership tng. mentor Chicano Fedn., 1992; dinner com. Young at Art, 1991; mem. Children's Initiative, 1993, Superbowl Task Force, 1993, San Diego Dialogue, 1993; hon. mem. Sister City, 1993, LEAD, 1993; hon. chair Easter Seals Telethon, 1994; vice chmn. Border Trade Alliance, 1989-91; mem. nat. gala com. HDI Ednl. Svcs., 1990; Calif. state del. U.S.-Mexico Border Govs.' Conf., 1990, 92; exec. com. San Diego Conv. Ctr./Vis. Bur. Mem. San Diego County Hispanic C. of C. (chmn. 1991, pres. 1990-91, v.p. 1989-90, internat. com. chair 1989-90, sec. 1989, founding bd. mem. 1988), Consejo Nacional de Maquiladoras, Calif. Hispanic C. of C. (state conv. joint venture com. 1991, spl. projects chair 1991), San Diego/Tijuana Sister Cities Soc. (adv. coun. 1993—), San Diego County Bar Assn. (U.S./Mexico liaison com.), ABA (U.S./Mexico bar liaison com.), Hispanic Alliance for Free Trade, Rotary Club San Diego. Office: Greater San Diego C of C 402 W Broadway Ste 1000 San Diego CA 92101-8507

PARTRIDGE, CATHLEEN FLANAGAN, library director; b. St. Paul, Apr. 21, 1945; d. John Theodore and Virginia Helen (McGuigan) Flanagan; m. Lyman Clark Partridge, Oct. 8, 1983; stepchildren: Elizabeth Partridge Rose, Erica Maren, Robert Edward. BA, U. Ill., 1967, MLS, 1969, PhD in Libr. Sci., 1976. Audio-visual libr. Marriott Libr. U. Utah, Salt Lake City, 1969-71, asst. prof. edn., 1976-82; supr. info. svcs. Hercules Aerospace, Magna, Utah, 1982-92; dir. learning resources Salt Lake C.C., 1992—. Author: Books and Other Printed Materials, 1980; editor: Utah Governors Conference on Libraries and Information Services, 1979; co-editor: American Folklore: A Bibliography, 1950-74. Mem. ALA, Utah Libr. Assn. (chair legis. com. 1994-95, pres. 1986-87, Disting. Svc. award 1994), Wasatch Mountain Club, Sierra Club, Phi Beta Kappa, Beta Phi Mu, Phi Kappa Phi, Pi Delta Phi, Phi Delta Kappa. Office: Salt Lake C C Markosian Lib PO Box 30808 4600 S Redwood Rd Salt Lake City UT 84130-0808

PARTRIDGE, L(LOYD) DONALD, science educator; b. Phila., May 10, 1945; s. Lloyd D. and Jean Marie (Rutledge) P.; m. Susan Patrick, May 25, 1984; children: Erika Morgan, Daniella Partridge, Rachel Conover. BS, MIT, 1967; PhD, U. Wash., 1973. Asst. prof. U. N.M., Albuquerque, 1976-84, assoc. prof., 1984-92, prof., 1992—; researcher Max-Planck Inst., Göttingen, Germany, 1991. Author: The Nervous System: Its Function and Its Interaction with the World, 1992; editor: Calcium Channels: Their Properties, Functions, Regulation and Clinical Relevance, 1991. Pres. Friends of Music, Albuquerque, 1988-92. 1st lt. U.S. Army Med. Svc. Corps, 1967-69. Welcome Rsch. fellow U. Bristol, Eng., 1973-74; NIH postdoctoral fellow U. Wash., 1974-76; Fulbright scholar Max-Planck Inst., Munich, Germany, 1985-86. Mem. Soc. for Neuroscience. Home: 3405 Mackland Ave NE Albuquerque NM 87106-1216 Office: Dept Physiology U NM Albuquerque NM 87131

PARTRIDGE, LOREN WAYNE, art historian, educator; b. Raton, N.Mex., Apr. 11, 1936; s. Don F. and Ruth (Isaacson) P.; widowed; children: Wendy, Amy. BA in English Lit., Yale U., 1958; cert. in L.Am. lit., U. Buenos Aires, 1959; diploma in Russian, U.S. Army Lang. Sch., Monterey, Calif., 1961; MA in Fine Arts, Harvard U., 1965, PhD in Fine Arts, 1969. Tchg. fellow Harvard U., Cambridge, Mass., 1964-66; lectr. U. Calif., Berkeley, 1968, acting asst. prof., 1969-70, asst. prof., 1970-76, assoc. prof., 1976-80, prof., 1980—, chmn. dept. history of art, 1978-87, 90-93; resident in art history Am. Acad. in Rome, 1985; reviewer Art Bull, 1972, 78, 80, 83, Renaissance Quar., 1984, 87, 90, Design Book Rev., 1987, Master Drawings, 1987, Am. Hist. Rev., 1993. Author: John Galen Howard and the Berkeley Campus: Beaux-Arts Architecture in the Athens of the West, 1978, Caprarola, Palazzo Farnese, 1988, (with Randolph Starn) A Renaissance Likeness: Art and Culture in Raphael's Julius II, 1980, Arts of Power: Three Halls of State in Italy 1300-1600, 1992; contbr. author: Ency. of Italian Renaissance, 1981, Internat. Dictionary Art and Artists, 1990, Dictionary of Art, 1994; contbr. articles to profl. jours. With U.S. Army, 1960-63. Scholar Yale U., 1955-58, Harvard U., 1964-66; Fulbright fellow, 1958-59, 75, Am. Acad. in Rome fellow, 1966-68, Kress fellow Inst. for Advanced Studies, 1974-75, U. Calif., 1971-71, 88-89, Guggenheim fellow, 1981-92; grantee Kress Found., 1968-69, 71-72, Getty. sr. rsch. grantee, 1988-89. Office: U Calif Dept History of Art 6020 405 Doe Libr Berkeley CA 94720-6020

PASCAL, C(ECIL) BENNETT, classics educator; b. Chgo., May 4, 1926; s. Jack and Goldie (Zeff) P.; m. Ilene Joy Shulman, Feb. 1, 1959; 1 child, Keith Irwin. BA, UCLA, 1949, MA, 1950; MA, Harvard U., 1953, PhD, 1956. Instr. U. Ill., Champaign, 1955-56, Cornell U., Ithaca, N.Y., 1957-60; asst. prof. U. Oreg., Eugene, 1960-75, prof. classics, 1975—, head dept., various years - 1965-85. Author: Cults of Cisalpine Gaul, 1964; contbr. articles to profl. jours. Mem. Eugene Bicycle Com., 1971-83. Served with USN, 1944-46. Traveling fellow, Italy, Harvard U., 1956-57, Fulbright-Hays fellow, Rome, 1967-68. Mem. Am. Philol. Assn., Classical Assn. Pacific N.W. (pres. 1965-66), AAUP, Archeol. Inst. of Am. (past pres., sec. Eugene Soc.). Democrat. Jewish. Home: 330 Fulvue Dr Eugene OR 97405-2788 Office: U of Oreg Dept Classics Eugene OR 97403

PASCOE, PATRICIA HILL, state senator, writer; b. Sparta, Wis., June 1, 1935; d. Fred Kirk and Edith (Kilpatrick) H.; m. D. Monte Pascoe, Aug. 3, 1957; children: Sarah, Ted, Will. BA, U. Colo., 1957; MA, U. Denver, 1968, PhD, 1982. Tchr. Sequoia Union High Sch. Dist., Redwood City, Calif. and Hayward (Calif.) Union High Sch. Dist., 1957-60; instr. Met. State Coll., Denver, 1969-75; instr. Denver U., 1975-77, 81, research asst. bur. ednl. research, 1981-82; tchr. Kent Denver Country Day, Englewood, Colo., 1982-84; freelance writer Denver, 1985—; mem. Colo. Senate, Denver, 1989-92, 95—; commr. Edn. Commn. of the States, Denver, 1975-82. Contbr. articles to numerous publs. and jours. Bd. dirs. Samaritan House, 1990-94, Cystic Fibrosis Found., 1989-93; pres. East High Sch. Parent, Tchr. and Student Assn., Denver, 1984-85; mem. Moore Budget Adv. Com., Denver, 1966-72; legis. chmn. alumni bd. U. Colo., Boulder, 1987-89; del. Dem. Nat. Conv., San Francisco, 1984, N.Y.C., 1992. Mem. Soc. Profl. Journalists, Common Cause (bd. dirs. Denver chpt. 1986-88), Phi Beta Kappa. Presbyterian.

PASCOTTO, ALVARO, lawyer; b. Rome, Mar. 8, 1949; came to U.S., 1984; s. Antonio and Anna Ludovica (Habig) P.; m. Linda Haldan, July 20, 1985. JD, U. Rome, 1973. Bar: Italy 1976, Calif. 1987, U.S. Dist. Ct. (cen. dist.) Calif. 1987, U.S. Ct. Appeals (9th cir.) 1987. Ptnr. Studio Legale Pascotto, Rome, 1976-86, Pascotto, Gallavotti & Gardner, L.A. and Rome, 1986-90, Pascotto & Gallavotti, L.A., 1990—; of counsel Irell & Manella, L.A.; counsel, cons. Quantum Inc., Reno, Nev., 1980-87, Execucorp Mgmt. Cons., Miami, Fla., 1980-85; official counsel Consulate Gen. Italy, L.A., 1987—. Mem. ABA, Calif. Bar Assn., Italian-Am. Bar Assn., Am. Mgmt. Assn., Consiglio dell'Ordine Degli Avvocati e Procuratori di Roma. Clubs: Circolo del Golf (Rome); Malibu (Calif.) Racquet Club, Regency Club (L.A.). Home: 6116 Merritt Dr Malibu CA 90265-3847 Office: Pascotto & Gallavotti 1800 Avenue Of The Stars Los Angeles CA 90067-4208*

PASE, MARILYN NELSEN, nurse, educator; b. Brigham City, Utah, Feb. 13, 1943; d. Daniel Clarence Nelsen and Aldine (Anderson) Nelsen Johns. BSN with high honors, U. Ala., Huntsville, 1974, BS in Biology with high honors, 1984; MSN, Vanderbilt U., 1975. RN, Ala., Utah, N.Mex. Staff nurse Med. Ctr. Hosp., Huntsville, 1974-77, LDS Hosp., Salt Lake City, 1977 summer; clin. preceptor for grad. students U. Ala., Birmingham, 1978; instr. nursing, then asst. prof. U. Ala., Huntsville, 1975-83; mem. nursing faculty Oakwood Coll., Huntsville, 1985-86; infection control nurse, employee health nurse Crestwood Hosp., Huntsville, 1984-86; staff nurse Meml. Med. Ctr., Las Cruces, N.Mex., 1987-91; asst. prof. dept. nursing N.Mex. State U., Las Cruces, 1988—. Cons., reviewer; contbr. articles to profl. jours. Mem. ANA, AACN (chpt. pres. 1991-92), N.Mex. Nurses Assn. (exec. bd. Dist. 14 1994, dist. pres. 1990-93, Nurse Researcher award 1994), Sigma Theta Tau, Delta Kappa. Mem. LDS Ch. Office: Dept Nursing N Mex State U Las Cruces NM 88003

PASQUA, THOMAS MARIO, JR., journalism educator; b. L.A., Aug. 13, 1938; s. Thomas Mario and Ann Ione (Anderson) P.; m. Sandra Mae Liddell; children: Bruce Burks, Julie Burks, Geoffrey, Alexis. BA, Whittier (Calif.) Coll., 1960; MA, UCLA, 1961; PhD, U. Tex., 1973. Cert. secondary tchr. Reporter, photographer Whittier Daily News, 1954-65; tchr. LaSerna High Sch., Whittier, 1961-63, 64-65; lectr. Calif. State U., Fullerton, 1973-75, Mesa Coll., San Diego, 1978-83, U. San Diego, 1979-80, San Diego State U., 1985; prof. Southwestern Coll., Chula Vista, Calif., 1965—. Co-author: Excellence in College Journalism, 1983, Mass Media in the Information Age, 1990, Historical Perspectives in Popular Music, 1993; editor C.C. Journalist, 1983—; bibliographer Journalism Quar., 1974-92; contbr. articles to profl. jours. Mem. ch. coun. St. Andrew Luth. Ch., Whittier, 1965; mem. Chula Vista Bd. of Ethics, 1978-86; mem. Chula Vista Charter Rev. Com., 1969; mem. adv. bd. Bay Gen. Hosp., Chula Vista, 1985-87; mem. ch. coun. Victory Luth. Ch., Chula Vista, 1989-90; adv. com. Otay Valley Regional Park Citizen Con., 1990—. Wall St. Jour. Newspaper Fund fellow U. Wash., 1962; recipient Nat. Teaching award Poynter Inst. Media Studies, 1987. Mem. C.C. Journalism Assn. (archivist 1989—, charter inductee Hall of Fame, 1994), Journalism Assn. C.C.'s (exec. sec. 1975-81), Assn. for Edn. in Journalism and Mass Comm. (Markham prize 1974), Internat. Comm. Assn., Coll. Media Advisers, Am. Fedn. Tchrs. (pres. Southwestern Coll. 1977-78, 81-87), Phi Kappa Phi, Kappa Tau Alpha, Pi Sigma Alpha. Democrat. Home: 760 Monterey Ave Chula Vista CA 91910-6318 Office: Southwestern Coll 900 Otay Lakes Rd Chula Vista CA 91910-7223

PASQUALE, JOSEPH, computer scientist, educator; b. Weehawken, N.J., Feb. 12, 1958; s. Carlo and Maria Pasquale; m. Barbara Katherine Bittel. BSEE, MSEE, MIT, 1982; PhD in Computer Sci., U. Calif., Berkeley, 1988. Computer systems cons. La Jolla, Calif., 1980—; asst. prof. U. Calif., San Diego, 1987-93, assoc. prof., 1993—; dir. Sequoia 2000 Project, 1994—; chmn. NASA Sci. User Network Working Group, 1993—; sr. fellow San Diego Supercomputer Ctr., La Jolla, 1990—. Contbr. articles to profl. jours. Recipient Presdl. Young Investigator award NSF, 1989, IBM Faculty Devel. award, 1991; named Outstanding Teaching Asst. of Yr. Eta Kappa Nu, 1983. Mem. Assn. Computing Machinery, IEEE. Office: U Calif San Diego Dept Computer Sci Engring La Jolla CA 92093-0114

PASQUINELLI, GARY, agricultural products executive; b. 1944. BA, Notre Dame U., 1966. With Pasquinelli Produce Co., 1966—, now pres. Office: Pasquinelli Produce Co 350 W 16th St Ste 400 Yuma AZ 85364*

PASSMAN, STEPHEN LEE, theoretical mechanics scientist; b. Suffolk, Va., Sept. 3, 1942; s. Milton Lawrence and Jean (Lehrman) P.; m. Anita Joy Greenwald, June 12, 1965; children: Michael, Rebecca, Sara, Rachel. BSEM, Ga. Inst. Tech., 1964, MSEM, 1966, PhD, 1968. Instr. U.S Naval Acad., Annapolis, Md., 1968-70; postdoctoral fellow Johns Hopkins U., Balt., 1970-71; from asst. to assoc. prof. Ga. Inst. Tech., Atlanta, 1971-78; sr. mem. tech. staff Sandia Nat. Labs., Albuquerque, 1978—; lectr. George Wasington U., Washington, 1969-70; vis. mem. Math. Rsch. Ctr., U. Wis., Madison, 1972, Inst. Math. and Its Applications, U. Minn., Mpls., 1984, 89, Math. Sci. Inst., Cornell U., 1987-90; cons. Bell Labs., Norcross, Ga., 1975-78; vis. scientist Pitts. Energy Tech. Ctr., 1988-90, cons., 1990—; vis. scholar Carnegie Mellon U., 1988-90; adj. prof. engring. U. Pitts.,

1990—; U.S. Rep. multiphase flow com., Internat. Energy Agy., 1992—. Contbr. articles to profl. jours. Served to capt. U.S. Army, 1968-70. Recipient Monie A. Ferst Rsch. award, 1968; scholar Johns Hopkins U., 1990. Mem. ASME (elasticity com. 1987—, multiphase flow com. 1990—), Soc. Natural Philosophy (treas. 1977-78, dir. 1978—, chmn. bd. dirs. 1985-86), Soc. Engring. Sci. (bd. dirs. 1986—, treas. 1987—), Am. Acad. Mechanics, Am. Phys. Soc., Soc. Rheology, Sigma Xi. Home: 6005 Concordia Rd NE Albuquerque NM 87111-1328 Office: Sandia Nat Labs MS 1393 Box 5800 Albuquerque NM 87185

PASTEGA, RICHARD LOUIS, retail specialist; b. Klamath Falls, Oreg., Mar. 25, 1936; s. Louie and Jennie (Borgialli) P. BS, So. Oreg. State Coll., 1960; MS, Mont. State U., Bozeman, 1961. Tchr. social studies Henley High Sch., Klamath Falls, Oreg., 1962-63, Juneau (Alaska) Douglas High Sch., 1964-67, Thessaloniki (Greece) Internat. High Sch., 1967-69; editor, pub. Breakdown Newspaper, Klamath Falls, Oreg., 1971-73; mgr. Pastega's Market, Klamath Falls, 1975—. Del. dem. Nat. Conv., N.Y.C., 1976, Oreg. Dem. Platform conv., Eugene, Beaverton and Ashland, 1978-80, 82; councilor City of Klamath Falls, 1986-88; bd. dirs. Basin Transit Svc., Klamath Falls, 1981-87; chair Klamath County Dem. Ctrl. Com., 1983-86, sec. 1992-94. Mem. Sons of Italy. Democrat. Home: 428 S 9th St Klamath Falls OR 97601-6126

PASTIN, MARK JOSEPH, executive consultant, society administrator; b. Ellwood City, Pa., July 16, 1949; s. Joseph and Patricia Jean (Camenite) P.; m. Joanne Marie Reagle, May 30, 1970 (div. Mar. 1983); m. Carrie Patricia Class, Dec. 22, 1984 (div. June 1990); m. Christina M. Brecto, June 15, 1991. BA summa cum laude, U. Pitts., 1970; MA, Harvard U., 1972, PhD, 1973. Asst. prof. Ind. U., Bloomington, 1973-78, assoc. prof., 1978-80; prof. mgmt., dir. Ariz. State U., Tempe, 1988-92; founder, bd. CTG, Inc., Tempe, 1983—; chmn., CEO, pres. Coun. of Ethical Orgns., Inc., Alexandria, Va., 1986—; sr. v.p. Strategic Mgmt. Sys., Alexandria, Va., 1994-95; chair Health Ethics Trust Found., 1995—; mem. adv. bd. Aberdeen Holdings, San Diego, 1988-90; dir. Sandpiper Group, Inc., N.Y.C., 1987—, S.W. Projects, Inc., San Diego, 1988-90, Learned, Nicholson, Ltd., 1990-91; chmn. bd. Japan Am. Soc. Phoenix, Found. for Ethical Orgns.; cons. GTE, Southwestern Bell, St. Louis, 1987-89, Tex. Instruments, MicroAge Computers, Med-Tronic, Blood Sys., Inc., Opus Corp., GTE, NyNex, Am. Express Bank, Kaiko Bussan Co., Japan, Arex Co., Japan, Century Audit Co., Japan, Scottsdale Meml. Hosp., Consanti Found., Lincoln Electric Co.; vis. faculty Harvard U., 1980; invited presenter Australian Inst. Mgmt., Nippon Tel. & Tel., Hong Kong Commn. Against Corruption, 1984, Young Pres.'s Orgn. Internat. U., 1990, Nat. Assn. Indsl. & Office Parks, 1990, ABA, 1991, Govt. of Brazil, 1991. Author: Hard Problems of Management, 1986 (Book of Yr. award Armed Forces Mil. Comptrs. 1986, Japanese edit., 1994, Power By Association, 1991, The State of Ethics in Arizona, 1991, Planning Forum, 1992; editor: Public-Private Sector Ethics, 1979; columnist Bus. Jour.; contbr. articles to jours. Founding bd. mem. Tempe Leadership, 1985-89; bd. mem. Ctr. for Behavioral Health, Phoenix, 1986-89, Tempe YMCA, 1986—, Valley Leadership Alumni Assn., 1989—; mem. Clean Air Com., Phoenix, 1987-90. Nat. Sci. Found. fellow, Cambridge, Mass., 1971-73; Nat. Endowment for the Humanities fellow, 1975; Exxon Edn. Found. grant, 1982-83. Mem. Strategic Mgmt. Soc. (invited presenter 1985), Am. Soc. Assn. Execs. (invited presenter 1987-95), Bus. Ethics Soc. (founding bd. mem. 1983), Found. Ethical Orgns. (chmn. 1988, pres.), Pres.'s Assn., Am. Mgmt. Assn., Ariz. Club, Golden Key Nat. Hon. Club, Harvard Club, Ariz. Club, Phi Beta Kappa. Home: 7206 Park Terrace Dr Alexandria VA 22307-2035 Office: 112 S West St Alexandria VA 22314-2825

PASTOR, ED, congressman; b. June 28, 1943. Mem. Maricopa County Bd. Suprs., Phoenix, Ariz., 1976-91; mem. 102nd-104th Congresses from Ariz. 2nd dist., 1991—. Office: House of Representatives Washington DC 20515

PASTORE, MICHAEL ANTHONY, college administrator; b. Fresno, Calif., Aug. 31, 1932; s. Michele Constantino and Rosa Maria (Damiani) P.; m. Elizabeth Anne York, Dec. 23, 1955; children: Michael Anthony, Christi Anna, Maria Delisa. AA, Coll. of Sequoias, Visalia, Calif., 1952; BS, U. San Francisco, 1954; MA, Fresno State Coll., 1969; PhD, U. Wash., 1976. Agt., M.A. Pastore Ins. Co., Fresno, 1963-69; instr., coordinator, div. chmn. Edmonds Community Coll., Lynwood, Wash., 1969-73; founder, pres. City Univ. Seattle, 1973—. Served with U.S. Army, 1956-57. Roman Catholic. Clubs: Wash. Athletic, Rainier (Seattle); Glendale Country (Bellevue, Wash.). Home: 618 175th Pl NE Bellevue WA 98008-4242 Office: 335 116th Ave SE Bellevue WA 98004-6407

PASTORE, THOMAS MICHAEL, telecommunications sales executive; b. Bronx, N.Y., Jan. 25, 1959; s. Philip J. and Olga E. (DeGenito) P.; m. Kimberly A. Coppersmith, Dec. 13, 1986; children: Gabriela Maria, Thomas John. BA in Bus., Western State Coll., 1981. Sales rep. Victor Technologies Inc., Denver, 1981-84; account mgr. No. Telecom Inc., Denver, 1984-87, v.p. sales coun., 1985—, sales engr., 1987-92, dist. sales mgr., 1992—. Mem. Better Air Campaign, 1990—; sec. Warren Sq. Homeowners Assn., Denver, 1987-92; player, contbr. Dale Tooley Tennis Tournament, 1991-92; fundraiser Am. Cancer Soc., Denver, 1991—; mem. Denver Art Mus., 1991-92. Republican. Roman Catholic. Home and Office: No Telecom Inc 16095 Quarry Hill Dr Parker CO 80134-9553

PASTREICH, PETER, orchestra executive director; b. Bklyn., Sept. 13, 1938; s. Ben and Hortense (Davis) P.; m. Jamie Garrard Whittington; children by previous marriages: Anna, Milena, Emanuel, Michael. A.B. magna cum laude, Yale Coll., 1959; postgrad., N.Y. U. Sch. Medicine, 1959-60; studied trumpet, with Robert Nagle at Yale U., with Raymond Sabarich, Paris. Asst. mgr. Denver Symphony, Balt. Symphony; mgr. Greenwich Village Symphony, N.Y.C., 1960-63; gen. mgr. Nashville Symphony, 1963-65, Kansas City Philharmonic, 1965-66; asst. mgr., mgr. St. Louis Symphony, 1966-78, exec. dir., 1966-78; exec. dir. San Francisco Symphony, 1978—; instr. orch. mgmt. Am. Symphony Orch. League; bd. dirs. Nat. Com. for Symphony Orch. Support; founder San Francisco Youth Orch.; rep. planning and constrn. Davies Symphony Hall, San Francisco Symphony, 1980. Author: TV comml., 1969 (CLIO award); contbr. articles to various newspapers. Mem. recommendation bd. of the Avery Fisher Artist Program, Yale U. Council com. on music; past mem. adv. panel Nat. Endowment for the Arts, co-chmn. music panel, 1985; founding mem. bd. dirs. St. Louis Conservatory, mem. policy com. Maj. Orch. Mgrs. Conf., chmn., 1980; bd. dirs. Laumeier Sculpture Park, St. Louis, Stern Grove Festival, San Francisco Conv. and Visitors Bur.; chmn. fund campaign French-Am. Internat. Sch., San Francisco. Served with U.S. Army, 1960. Recipient First Disting. Alumnus award Yale U. Band, 1977, cert. Merit Yale Sch. Music, 1984. Mem. Am. Symphony Orch. League (dir., chmn., former chmn. task force on mgmt. tng.; mem. exec. and long-range planning com., chmn. standing com. on adminstrv. policy), Assn. Calif. Symphony Orchs. (dir.), Bankers Club of San Francisco. Club: Yale (N.Y.C.). Office: San Francisco Symphony Davies Symphony Hall San Francisco CA 94102*

PATANO, PATRICIA ANN, health and fitness professional, marketing and public relations specialist; b. Chgo., June 14, 1950; d. Thomas Vincent and Gladys Estelle (Olejniczak) P. Student, Los Angeles Pierce Coll., 1968-70, UCLA, 1974-84. Pub. relations mgr. Motel 6, Inc., Century City, Calif., 1974-77; mgr. corp. communications 1st Travel Corp., Van Nuys, Calif., 1977-79; mktg. pub. relations mgr. Unitours, Inc., Los Angeles, 1979-81; asst. v.p. pub. relations Los Angeles Olympic Com., 1981-84; pres., co-owner PaVage Fitness Innovations, Playa del Rey, Calif., 1984-88; dir. spl. projects J.D. Power and Assocs., Agoura Hills, Calif., 1988—; trustee Nat. Injury Prevention Found., San Diego, 1983—; cons. Dick Clark Productions, Burbank, Calif., 1985, Reebok USA Ltd., Boston, 1983—. Co-author: MuscleAerobics, 1985; contbr. articles to profl. jours. Vol. Motion Picture Hosp., Woodland Hills, Calif., 1968-70; bd. dirs. Los Angeles Boys and Girls Club, 1984—; mem. council San Fernando Natural History Mus., 1987-89; big sister Pride House, Van Nuys, 1987-89; active juvenile delinquent program Pride House. Recipient Corp. award Pres.'s Council Phys. Fitness, 1983; fellow Alfred North Whitehead Leaderships Soc.-U. Redlands, 1995. Mem. L.A. Advt. Club, Nat. Injury Prevention Found. (trustee 1984-87), Child Shelter Homes: A Rescue Effort (bd. dirs.), Mid Valley Athletic Club (Reseda, Calif.), Marina City (Marina del Rey, Calif.). Republican. Presbyterian. Clubs: Mid Valley Athletic (Reseda, Calif.); Marina City (Marina del Rey, Calif.). Office: JD Power & Assocs 30401 Agoura Rd Agoura Hills CA 91301-2084

PATE, SUSAN LEE HARGRAVE, theatre arts educator, choreographer; b. Ithaca, N.Y., Mar. 5, 1950; d. Haas M. and Margaret Jean (Gladstone) Hargrave; m. Ronald D. Pate, Aug. 24, 1985; 1 child, Cameron D. BA in Theatre Arts, Cornell U., 1972; MA in Theatre, SUNY, Binghamton, 1974; PhD in Dance/Theatre History, Cornell U., 1980. Grad. teaching asst. SUNY, Binghamton, 1972-74; fine arts coord., theatre instr. SUNY, Brockport, 1974-76; grad. teaching asst. theatre arts Cornell U., Ithaca, N.Y., 1976-79; assoc. prof. theatre arts San Jose (Calif.) State U., 1979-84; prof. performance in theatre arts Calif. State U., Chico, 1986—; guest artist, tchr. of mime Fairbanks (Alaska) Summer Arts Festival, 1987-90, Pribilof Sch. Dist., Alaska, 1994; guest artist, choreographer, tchr. Fairbanks Summer Arts Camp, 1988, 89; instr. dance gymnastics camp Houston Bapt. U., 1980. Co-author: The Beginning Actor's Companion, 1989; dir. 41 plays and musicals, 1969—; choreographer more than 50 dances and musicals, 1979—; mime choreographer, 1979—. Home missionary So. Bapt. Conv., Chico, 1991-94; music team singer, soloist New Life Christian Fellowship and Esplanade Baptist, Chico, 1986—; group leader eating disorder recovery groups, Chico, 1992-93. Affirmative Action grantee Calif. State U., Chico, 1989; Cornell U. Grad. Sch. summer fellow, 1977, 78. Mem. Calif. Edn. Theatre Assn., Theater Comms. Group. Republican. Christian. Office: Calif State U Chico Theatre Arts Dept PAC 217 Chico CA 95929-8100

PATEL, CHANDRA KUMAR NARANBHAI, communications company executive, educator, researcher; b. Baramati, India, July 2, 1938; came to U.S., 1958, naturalized, 1970; s. Naranbhai Chaturbhai and Maniben P.; m. Shela Dixit, Aug. 20, 1961; children: Neela, Meena. B.Engring., Poona U., 1958; M.S., Stanford U., 1959, Ph.D., 1961. Mem. tech. staff Bell Telephone Labs., Murray Hill, N.J., 1961-93, head infrared physics and electronics rsch. dept., 1967-70, dir. electronics rsch. dept., 1970-76, dir. phys. rsch. lab., 1976-81, exec. dir. rsch. physics and acad. affairs div., 1981-87, exec. dir. rsch., materials sci., engring. and acad. affairs div., 1987-93; trustee Aerospace Corp., L.A., 1979-88; vice chancellor rsch. UCLA, 1993—; mem. governing bd. NRC, 1990-91; bd. dirs. Newport Corp., Fountain Valley, Calif., Cal Micro Devices Corp., Milpitas, Calif., Accuware Corp., Santa Monica, Calif. Contbr. articles to tech. jours. Chmn. Calif. Biomed. Found., 1994—; mem. exec. bd. Calif. Healthcare Inst., 1995—. Recipient Ballantine medal Franklin Inst., 1968, Coblentz award Am. Chem. Soc., 1974, Honor award Assn. Indians in Am., 1975, Founders prize Tex. Instruments Found., 1978, award N.Y. sect. Soc. Applied Spectroscopy, 1982, Schawlow medal Laser Inst. Am., 1984, Thomas Alva Edison Sci. award N.J. Gov., 1987. Fellow AAAS, IEEE (Lamme medal 1976, medal of honor 1989), Am. Acad. Arts and Scis., Am. Phys. Soc. (coun. 1987-91, exec. com. 1987-90, George E. Pake prize 1988, pres. 1995—), Optical Soc. Am. (Adolph Lomb medal 1966, Townes medal 1982, Ives medal 1989), Indian Nat. Sci. Acad. (fng.); mem. NAS (coun. 1988-91, exec. com. 1989-91), NAE (Zworykin award 1976), Gynecol. Laser Surgery Soc. (hon.), Am. Soc. for Laser Medicine and Surgery (hon.), Third World Acad. Scis. (assoc.), Calif. Biomed. Found. (pres. 1994—), Calif. Healthcare Inst. (exec. com. 1995—), Sigma Xi (pres. 1994—). Home: 1171 Roberto Ln Los Angeles CA 90077-2302 Office: UCLA Vice Chancellor Research 405 Hilgard Ave Los Angeles CA 90024-1301

PATEL, MARILYN HALL, federal judge; b. Amsterdam, N.Y., Sept. 2, 1938; d. Lloyd Manning and Nina J. (Thorpe) Hall; m. Magan C. Patel, Sept. 2, 1966; children: Brian, Gian. B.A., Wheaton Coll., 1959; J.D., Fordham U., 1963. Bar: N.Y. 1963, Calif. 1970. Mng. atty. Benson & Morris, Esq., N.Y.C., 1962-64; sole practice N.Y.C., 1964-67; atty. U.S. Immigration and Naturalization Svc., San Francisco, 1967-71; sole practice San Francisco, 1971-76; judge Alameda County Mcpl. Ct., Oakland, Calif., 1976-80, U.S. Dist. Ct. (no. dist.) Calif., San Francisco, 1980—; adj. prof. law Hastings Coll. of Law, San Francisco, 1974-76. Author: Immigration and Nationality Law, 1974; also numerous articles. Mem. bd. of visitors Fordham U. Sch. of Law. Mem. ABA (litigation sect., jud. adminstrn. sect.), ACLU (former bd. dirs.), NOW (former bd. dirs.), Am. Law Inst., Am. Judicature Soc. (bd. dirs.), Calif. Conf. Judges, Nat. Assn. Women Judges (founding mem.), Internat. Inst. (bd. dirs.), Advs. for Women (co-founder). Democrat. Office: US Dist Ct PO Box 36060 450 Golden Gate Ave San Francisco CA 94102*

PATEL, NAVIN J., electronics engineer, consultant; b. Chitravad, Gujarat, India, Sept. 4, 1949; came to U.S., 1970; s. Jamnadas R. and Diwali (Ghetiya) P.; m. Lalita Dadhania, Nov. 13, 1980; children: Nimish, Mitul. BSc in Physics, Math., Gujarat (India) U., 1969; BSEE, Pacific States U., L.A., 1973. Engr. Data Products Corp., Woodland Hills, Calif., 1973-81; cons. Internat. Svcs., Newburry Park, Calif., 1981-84; sr. engr. Librascope Corp., Glendale, Calif., 1984—; Cons. engr. Amtech Internat., Agoura Hills, Calif., 1987—. Democrat. Hindu. Home: 21333 Lassen St Chatsworth CA 91311-4203 Office: Librascope Corp 833 Sonora Ave Glendale CA 91201-2433

PATEL, SUKESH JANUBHAI, software engineer; b. Bombay, India, Oct. 5, 1957; came to U.S., 1983; s. Janubhai C. and Chandrika J. Patel; m. Rupam D. Patel, Apr. 17, 1987. BEE, Sardar Patel U., Nagar, Gujarat, India, 1982; MS in Computer Engring., U. Southwestern La., 1987, PhD in Computer Engring., 1990. Grad. asst. U. Southwestern La., Lafayette, 1984-86, user support svcs., 1986-87, rsch./teaching asst., 1987-90; assoc. rsch. scientist Lockheed Palo Alto (Calif.) Rsch. Labs., 1990, prin. investigator, 1990-92, group engr., 1992—, mem. tech. adv. group, 1992; ops. mgr. Lockheed Invision, Palo Alto, 1992-94. Mem. IEEE, Reuse Interoperability Group. Home: 2101 California St Apt 301 Mountain View CA 94040-1684

PATELLA, LAWRENCE M., city official; b. Danbury, Conn., Aug. 10, 1929; s. Frank Peter and Benevanuti (Negri) P.; m. Nancy Blackford, Dec. 13, 1953 (dec.); children: Richard, Terri Patella McHenry, DEbra Patella Holton, Susan Patella Planz, Michael; m. Nancy Lee Blakey, Apr. 22, 1978. AA, Mesa Coll., San Diego, 1976. Enlisted USN, 1947, commd. ensign, 1958, advanced through grades to lt. comdr.; asst. force ops. officer Amphibious Force Pacific Fleet, 1967-70; comdr. USS Wood County, 1970-74; dir. ship to shore dept. US Naval Amphibious Sch., Little Creek, Va., 1974-76; exec. officer USS Duluth, 1974-76; commanding officer USS Mount Vernon, 1976-78; mgr. navigation divsn. Port of Portland, Oreg., 1978—; exec. dir. Western Dredging Assn., Vancouver, Wash., 1992—. Decorated Bronze Star with Comba V, Navy Commendation medals (4). Mem. Ret. Officers Assn. (Columbia River chpt. pres. 1990-93), Navy League (1st v.p. 1994-95). Republican. Episcopalian. Home: 2714 NE 42nd Cir Vancouver WA 98663-3719 Office: Western Dredging Assn PO Box 5797 Vancouver WA 98668-5797

PATINO, ISIDRO FRANK, law enforcement educator; b. San Antonio, Mar. 10, 1943; s. Isidro F. and Maria (Narro) P.; children: Michael, Rebecca, Karleen. BS, Calif. State U., L.A., 1973; MBA, U. Redlands, 1995. Records comdr. Placentia (Calif.) Police Dept., 1980-85; asst. dean Criminal Justice Tng. Ctr. Golden West Coll., Huntington Beach, Calif., 1986-89, assoc. dean instrn., 1989-92; divsn. dean dept. pub. svc. Rio Hondo Coll., Whittier, Calif., 1992—; pres., mem. State Chancellors Adv. Com. Pub. Safety Edn., 1991—; chmn. So. Calif. Pub. Safety Tng. Consortium, 1994—, active, 1993—. Mem. Calif. Law Enforcement Assn. of Records Suprs. (pres. so. chpt. 1985-87, state pres. 1986-87), Calif. Acad. Dirs. Assn. (vice-chmn. 1987-88, chmn. 1988-89), Acad. Criminal Justice Scis., Western and Pacific Assn. Criminal Justice Educators, Calif. Assn. Adminstrn. of Justice Educators, Calif. Peace Officers Standards and Tng. Basic Course Consortium (chmn. instrn. com. 1987-88), World Future Soc. (pres. Orange County/Long Beach chpt. 1988-92), Nat. Assn. Field Tng. Officers (nat. pres. 1992-93), Nat. Assn. Chiefs of Police, Am. Soc. Law Enforcement Trainers. Roman Catholic.

PATKAU, JOHN, architect; b. Winnipeg, Man., Can., Aug. 18, 1947; s. Abe John and Bertha (Klassen) P.; m. Patricia Frances Gargett, Aug. 10, 1974. BA, U. Manitoba, 1969, BA in Environ. Studies, 1969, MArch, 1972. Registered architect, B.C., Ont. Designer Erickson/Massey Architects, Can., 1971; pvt. practice Winnipeg, Can., 1972-73; design architect Zeidler Partnership Architects, Toronto, Can., 1974-75; project architect Bittorf Holland Christianson Architects, Toronto, Can., 1975-77; prin. John Patkau Architect Ltd., Edmonton, Can., 1977-83; ptnr. Patkau Archs. Inc., Vancouver, B.C., Can., 1984—; chmn. edn. com. Alta. Assn. Architects, 1981; vis. critic U. Calgary, 1981, 92, U. Waterloo, 1987, 89, U. Pa., 1987, Tech. U. N.S., 1987, U. B.C., 1988, 89, UCLA, 1989; design critic U. B.C., 1985-86; urban design panel Vancouver, 1990-92; vis. prof. William Lyon Somerville Lectureship U. Calgary, 1994; Eliot Noyes vis. design critic Harvard U., 1995. U. Man. Alumni scholar, Alsip, Black Tile and Lumber Co. scholar, Isbister scholar U. Man.; Ctrl. Mortgage and Housing fellow; recipient Man. Assn. Architects prize, Progressive Architecture citation, 1981, Progressive Architecture award, 1993, 95, Can. Architects award, 1983, 86, 87, 89, 90, 92, 94, Wood Coun. First award, 1984, Gov. Gen. medal, 1986, 90, 92, 94, Gov. Gen. award, 1990, Lt. Gov. Archtl. medal, 1992, Honor award, 1992. Fellow Royal Archtl. Inst. Can. (chmn. design com. 1987); mem. Archtl. Inst. B.C., Royal Can. Coll. Art, Ont. Assn. Architects. Office: Patkau Archs, 560 Beatty St Ste L110, Vancouver, BC Canada V6B 2L3

PATKAU, PATRICIA, architect, architecture educator; b. Winnipeg, Manitoba, Can., Feb. 25, 1950; d. John Frederick and Aileen Constance (Emmett) Gargett; m. John Robert Patkau, Aug. 10, 1974. BA in Interior Design, U. Manitoba, 1973; MA in Architecture, Yale, New Haven, Conn., 1978. Arch. John Patkau Archs., Edmonton, Ont., Can., 1979-83; ptnr. Patkau Archs., Vancouver, B.C., Can., 1983—; asst. prof. Sch. Architecture UCLA, U.S.A., 1988-90; assoc. prof. Sch. Architecture U. B.C., Can., 1992—; vis. critic U. Calgary, 1981, 87, U. Waterloo, 1987, U. Pa., U.S.A., 1987, U. Toronto, 1988, Southern Calif. Inst. Architecture, U.S.A., 1990, UCLA, 1991, U. Oreg., U.S.A., 1992, MIT, U.S.A., 1993, Yale U., 1993; design critic U. B.C., 1984-87; vis. prof. Harvard U., U.S.A., 1993, U. Calgary, 1994. Recipient Nat. Soc. Interior Designers award, 1972, Mary Levy prize, 1973, IDIM Silver medal, 1973, U. Manitoba Gold medal, 1973, Central Mortgage and Housing fellow, 1977, 78, Progressive Architecture citation, 1981, 93, Can. Architect Excellence award, 1983, 86, 87, 89, 90, 92, 94, Can. Wood Coun. First award, 1984, Honor award, 1992, Gov. Gen. Architecture medal 1986, 90, 92, 94, Gov. Gen. Architecture award, 1990, Lt. Gov. Architecture medal, 1992, Can. Wood Coun. award, 1991,. Fellow Royal Archtl. Inst. Can.; mem. Archtl. Inst. B.C. (Honor award 1988). Office: Patkau Archs, 560 Beatty St Ste L110, Vancouver, BC Canada V6B 2L3

PATNAIK, OBADIAH, principal; b. Calcutta, India, Jan. 9, 1941; came to U.S., 1969; s. John and Bhagyabati (Das) P.; m. Raquel Ladines Layos. BA, Tribuvan U., Khatmandu, Nepal, 1968; B of Tchg., Calcutta U., 1969; MEd, Hardin-Simmons U., 1973; MA in Christian Edn., Golden Gate Theol. Sem., 1991. Adminstr., prin. Internat. Christian Sch., San Francisco, 1974-90; prin. Vista Christian Sch., 1991—. Bd. mgrs. Am. Bapt. Chs. of the West, 1988-92, 94, gen. bd. mem. Am. Bapt. Chs., 1994—; exec. com. Asian Am. Bapt. Caucus, U.S.A., 1986—, treas. 1992—; chmn. Internat. Christian Sch. com., San Francisco, 1993—. Baptist. Home: 96 Wavecrest Dr Daly City CA 94015

PATNAUDE, WILLIAM E., architect; b. Sanger, Calif., Sept. 24, 1937; s. Eugene Joseph Patnaude and Vera Mae (Giles) Patnaude Fagan; m. Mary Esther Simerly, Aug. 22, 1971 (div. 1987); children—Nathaniel, Matthew. B.Arch., U. Calif., Berkeley, 1961; postgrad., Calif. State U.-Fresno, 1968-72. Registered architect, Calif., Oreg., Wash., Idaho, Nev., N.Mex., Colo., Utah. Draftsman, architect Robert Stevens Assoc., Santa Cruz, Calif., 1963-66; architect Llewelyn Davies, Weeks & Ptnrs., London, 1966; architect Allen Y. Lew, Fresno, Calif., 1967-69, assoc., 1969-74; v.p., architect Lew & Patnaude, Inc., Fresno, Calif., 1978-84; pres. Lew & Patnaude, Inc., 1985—; instr. Calif. State U., Fresno, 1968-81. Constn. arbitrator Am. Arbitration Assn., 1976—; chair central area plan citizen's adv. com. City of Fresno, 1991-93, chair gen. plan update com., 1994-95; bd. dirs. Fresno Arts Ctr., 1971-74, Fresno County Alliance for the Arts, 1986-88, 91-94. With USNR, 1961-63. Recipient Award of Merit, Calif. Hist. Preservation Conf., Orange County, 1983; Award of Excellence Woodwork Inst. Calif., 1982. Fellow AIA (nat. dir. 1983-85, pres. Calif. coun. 1982, San Joaquin chpt. 1978, Awards of Excellence, 1972-83); mem. Constrn. Specifications Inst. (pres. Fresno chpt. 1977), Owls Club, Rotary. Democrat. Home: 4190 N Van Ness Blvd Fresno CA 93704-4213 Office: Lew & Patnaude Inc 1050 S St Fresno CA 93721-1407

PATRICK, KEVIN DANNYE, computer programmer; b. Oakland, Calif., Aug. 10, 1963; s. Clayton Patrick and Dorothy Mae (Green) Oakley; m. Carla Yvette Matthews, Aug. 12, 1989; children: Asha, Sydney, Patrick. BS, Grambling State U., 1987. Summer pre-profl. IBM, San Jose, Calif., 1985; media rschr. Michael Diamond Advt. Agy., Oakland, Calif., 1986; sales rep. Gallo Sales Co., San Francisco, 1987-88; field engr. CAE-Link Tactical Simulation, Moffett Field, Calif., 1988-89; computer programmer IBM, Boulder, Colo., 1989-94; quality assurance Evolving Systems, Inc., Englewood, Colo., 1994—. Tutor Anchor of Hope Ch., Denver, 1991, Colo. Assn. Profl. Black Engrs., Denver, 1992. Mem. Nat. Soc. Black Engrs. (bus. entrepreneural network), Kappa Alpha Psi. Home: 1516 S Paris Ct Aurora CO 80012-5203

PATRICK, LESLIE DAYLE, hydrologist; b. Grand Island, Nebr., Nov. 20, 1951; d. Robert Norman and Charlotte Ruth (Thomas) Mayfield; m. Jeffrey Rogan Patrick, July 1, 1972. BA in Geology, U. Alaska, Anchorage, 1975, MS in Mgmt., 1991. Data base mgr. U.S. Geol. Survey, Anchorage, 1975-78, with digital modeling, 1980-85, with water use studies, 1978-91, chief computer sect., systems analyst, 1985-91, asst. dist. chief mgmt. ops., 1991—. Mem. NAFE, Am. Mgmt. Assn., Am. Soc. Quality Control, Alaska Groundwater Assn. (sec., treas. 1980). Office: US Geol Survey Water Resources Div 4230 University Dr Ste 201 Anchorage AK 99508-4626

PATRICK, LUCILLE NICHOLS, artist, rancher; b. Oak Park, Ill., Apr. 23, 1924; d. James Calvin and Mary Lucille (Sullivan) Nichols; children: Patricia Lucille Patrick Williams, James Nichols, John Michael, Barbara Jo Patrick Knight. U. Minn., U. Ariz., U. Wyo. Author: Best Little Town By a Dam Site, 1968, The Candy Kid J.C. Nichols, 1969, Carolina Lockhart, 1984. Pres., sec. Park County Hist. Soc., Cody, Wyo, 1950-70, Cody (Wyo.) Country Art League, 1960-80. Republican. Episcopalian. Home: 2117 Southfork Rd Cody WY 82414-8006

PATRICK, ROBERT H., economist, educator. BA magna cum laude, Blackburn Coll., 1978; PhD in Econs., U. N.Mex., 1985. Mgr. Burroughs Corp., Fairbanks, Alaska, 1978-80; rsch. assoc. Purdue U., West Lafayette, Ind., 1985-87; asst. prof. Colo. Sch. Mines, Golden, 1987-91, assoc. prof., 1991-93; mgr. Electric Power Rsch. Inst., Palo Alto, Calif., 1992—; vis. scholar Stanford (Calif.) U., 1992—; assoc. prof. Rutgers U., Newark, 1994—; reviewer U.S. EPA, U.S. Dept. Energy, Calif. Energy Commn; mem. emission allowance adv. com. N.Y. Mercantile Exch., 1992—. Contbr. articles to profl. jours. and chpts. to books.; mem. editorial bd. Jour. Regulatory Econs., Jour. Environ. Econs. and Mgmt. Grantee Gas Rsch. Inst., 1991-92, 90-91, U.S. EPA, 1989-92, USDA, 1987, 85-87. Mem. Am. Econ. Assn., Assn. Environ. and Resource Econs., Econometric Soc., Internat. Assn. for Energy Econs. (v.p. Rocky Mountain chpt. 1992, bd. dirs. 1990-91), Mineral Econs. and Mgmt. Soc. (bd. dirs. 1992). Home: 150 Bar Harbor Ct Aptos CA 95003-5801 Office: Electric Power Rsch Inst 3412 Hillview Ave Palo Alto CA 94304-1395

PATRIE, PETER HUGO, gaming control board investigator; b. Dayton, Ohio, Dec. 19, 1946; s. C. Hugo and Margaret (Penny) P.; m. Janis Lee Yates, Feb. 5, 1968; children: Peter Todd, Brent, Ryan. BSBA, Miami U., Oxford, Ohio, 1968; postgrad., U. Fla., 1968-69. Mgr. credit dept. Atlantic Nat. Bank, Jacksonville, Fla., 1970-72; regional credit mgr. Kaiser Cement & Gypsum, Long Beach, Calif., 1972-73; dist. mgr. ITT Consumer Fin., Denver, 1973-80; sr. v.p. Nev. First Bank, Reno, 1981-89, Bank of Am. Nev., Reno, 1989-90; gen. mgr. Silver State Thrift & Loan, Reno, 1990-94; investigator State of Nev. Gaming Control Bd., Carson City, 1995—; grad. asst. U. Fla. Grad. Sch., Gainesville, 1968; prof. Reno Bus. Coll., 1991. Mem. Western Indsl. Nev., Reno, 1989-91; tchr. Jr. Achievement-Bus. Alliance, Reno, 1990. Recipient Grad. Fellowship U. Fla. Grad. Sch., Gainesville, 1969. Mem. Sparks C. of C., Greenbrae Lions. Republican. Office: 1150 E William Carson City NV 89710-9999

PATRIZIO, PASQUALE, reproductive endocrinologist, andrologist; b. Torre Annunziata, Napoli, Italy, Jan. 31, 1959; came to U.S., 1988; s.

Vincent and Assunta Patrizio; m. Teri Susan Ord, Aug. 27, 1993. MD summa cum laude, U. Naples, Italy, 1983. Diplomate of residency in ob-gyn., Italy; lic. physician, Calif., U.K., Italy; cert. Edn. Coun. for Fgn. Med. Grads. Intern in medicine and surgery U. Naples, 1983-84, resident in ob-gyn., 1983-87; postgrad. fellow in andrology U. Pisa, Italy, 1987-90; rsch. fellow in reproductive endocrinology and infertility U. Calif.-Irvine, Orange, 1988-90, resident in ob-gyn., 1989-93, clin. instr. in reproductive endocrinology and infertility dept. ob-gyn., 1993-94, asst. prof., 1994—; sr. house officer ob-gyn. Victoria Hosp. and Forth Park Hosp., Kirkcaldy, Fife, Scotland, 1986; sr. house officer ob-gyn. Royal Gwent Hosp., Newport, South Wales, 1987; clin. asst. in vitro fertilization and gametes intrafallopian transfer unit Dept. Reproductive Health, Bologna, Italy, 1987; pressenter in field. Contbr. chpts. to books, articles to med. jours. Recipient Wyeth-Ayerst Labs. prize for best rsch. paper 40th ann. meeting Pacific Coast Fertility Soc., 1992; co-recipient Practicing Physician award 37th ann. meeting Pacific Coast Fertility Soc., 1989, TAP Poster award 40th ann. meeting, 1992; ACOG/Mead Johnson clin. fellow, 1992-93; Meml. Health Svcs. grantee, 1994-95. Fellow ACOG (jr.); mem. AMA, Am. Fertility Soc. (co-winner poster presentation 45th ann. meeting 1989), Am. Soc. Andrology, European Soc. Human Reprodn., Italian Soc. Fertility and Sterility (hon.), Italian Soc. Obstetricians & Gynecologists, Italian Soc. Andrology, Royal Coll. Obstetricians & Gynecologists (Eng.), Soc. for Study of Reprodn. Office: U Calif-Irvine Reproductive Health Pav II 101 The City Dr S Orange CA 92668-3201

PATRON, SUSAN HALL, librarian, writer; b. San Gabriel, Calif., Mar. 18, 1948; d. George Thomas and Rubye Denver (Brewer) H.; m. René Albert Patron, July 27, 1969. BA, Pitzer Coll., 1969; MLS, Immaculate Heart Coll., 1972. Children's libr. LA Pub. Libr., 1972-79, sr. children's libr., 1980—; reviewer Sch. Libr. Jour., 1980—, Pubs. Weekly, 1986-91, The Five Owls, 1987—; mem. award com. Friends of Children and Lit. Award, 1984. Author: Burgoo Stew, 1991, Five Bad Boys, Billy Que, and the Dustdobbin, 1992, Maybe Yes, Maybe No, Maybe Maybe, 1993 (ALA Notable Book 1994), Bobbin Dustdobbin, 1993, Dark Cloud Strong Breeze, 1994, (with Christopher Weiman) Marbled Papers, 1979. Mem. ALA (Caldecott award com. 1988), Calif. Libr. Assn. (Patricia Beatty award com. 1987-89, 91-92), Internat. Bd. on Books for Young Children, Soc. of Children's Book Writers and Illustrators, So. Calif. Coun. on Lit. for Children and Young People (awards com. 1985), Authors Guild. Office: LA Pub Libr Childrens Svcs 630 W 5th St Los Angeles CA 90071-2002

PATTEN, BEBE HARRISON, minister; b. Waverly, Tenn., Sept. 3, 1913; d. Newton Felix and Mattie Priscilla (Whitson) Harrison; m. Carl Thomas Patten, Oct. 23, 1935; children: Priscilla Carla and Bebe Rebecca (twins), Carl Thomas. D.D., McKinley-Roosevelt Coll., 1941; D.Litt., Temple Hall Coll. and Sem., 1943. Ordained to ministry Ministerial Assn. of Evangelism, 1935; evangelist in various cities of U.S., 1933-50; founder, pres. Christian Evang. Chs. Am., Inc., Oakland, Calif., 1944—, Patten Acad. Christian Edn., Oakland, 1944—, Patten Bible Coll., Oakland, 1944-83; chancellor Patten Coll., Oakland, 1983—; founder, pastor Christian Cathedral of Oakland, 1950—; held pvt. interviews with David Ben-Gurion, 1972, Menachim Begin, 1977, Yitzhak Shamir, 1991; condr. Sta. KUSW world-wide radio ministry, 70 countries around the world, 1989-90, Stas. WHRI and WWCR world coverage short wave, 1990—. Founder, condr.: radio program The Shepherd Hour, 1934—; daily TV, 1976—, nationwide telecast, 1979—; Author: Give Me Back My Soul, 1973; Editor: Trumpet Call, 1953—; composer 20 gospel and religious songs, 1945—. Mem. exec. bd. Bar-Ilan U. Assn., Israel, 1983; mem. global bd. trustees Bar-Ilan U., 1991. Recipient numerous awards including medallion Ministry of Religious Affairs, Israel, 1969; medal Govt. Press Office, Jerusalem, 1971; Christian honoree of yr. Jewish Nat. Fund of No. Calif., 1975; Hidden Heroine award San Francisco Bay coun. Girl Scouts U.S.A., 1976, Golden State award Who's Who Hist. Soc., 1988; Ben-Gurion medallion Ben-Gurion Rsch. Inst., 1977; Resolutions of Commendation, Calif. Senate Rules Com., 1978, 94; hon. fellow Bar-Ilan U., Israel, 1981; Dr. Bebe Patten Social Action chair established Bar-Ilan U., 1982. Mem. Am. Assn. for Higher Edn., Religious Edn. Assn., Am. Acad. Religion and Soc. Bibl. Lit., Zionist Orgn. Am., Am. Assn. Pres. of Ind. Colls. and Univs., Am. Jewish Hist. Soc., Am.-Isreal Pub. Affairs Com. Address: 2433 Coolidge Ave Oakland CA 94601-2630

PATTEN, CAROLYN S., public relations professional; b. Glendale, Calif., Nov. 16, 1946; d. Charels and Estelle Patten; 1 child, Jasmine. BJ, U. Mo., 1968; MA, U. Denver, 1979. Sunday Mag. spl. supplements editor Santa Fe New Mexican, 1973-76; exec. dir. Met. Lawyer Referral Svc., Denver, 1978-82, Cabletime Mag., Telecomms., Inc., Denver, 1982-83; spl. projects dir. Commtek Pub., Inc., Hailey, Idaho, 1983-84; publ. dir. Video Pub., Inc., Palm Springs, Calif., 1984-85; mng. editor Palm Springs Life Mag., 1985-86; pub. rels. cons. Palm Springs, 1986-87; dir. pub. rels. The Ritz-Carlton, Rancho Mirage, Calif., 1987-89; tourism pub. rels. dir. City of Palm Springs Tourism Div., 1989—. Mem. exec. com. Agua Caliente Cultural Mus. Mem. Pub. Rels. Soc. Am., Soc. Am. Travel Writers. Office: Palm Springs Tourism 401 S Pavilion Way Palm Springs CA 92262-7947

PATTEN, RICHARD E., personnel company owner; b. Seattle, May 17, 1953; s. Donald Wesley and Lorraine Louise (Kienholz) P.; m. Monica Rose Bourg, Mar. 20, 1976; children: Richard Douglas, Wesley Bourg, Melinda Rose. BA, U. Wash., 1976. Exec. v.p. Microfilm Svc. Co., Seattle, 1976-84, gen. mgr., 1985-87, chmn. bd., 1988-90; pres. Express Svcs. Temporary and Permanent Pers., Seattle, 1990—. Candidate for U.S. Ho. of Reps., 1982; deacon Bethany Bapt. Ch., Seattle, 1983-86; co-chmn. fin. com. Wash. State Billy Graham Crusade, 1990-91. Mem. Nat. Micrographics Assn. (pres. N.W. chpt. 1979-80, bd. dirs. 1978-79), Assn. Image and Info. Mgmt. (chmn. svc. co. 1987), Assn. Records Mgrs. and Adminstrs., Wash. Athletic Club, Rotary. Republican. Baptist. Home: 7012 NE 161st St Bothell WA 98011-4265 Office: Express Pers Svcs Ste 101 1201 4th Ave Seattle WA 98134-1531 also: Express Pers Svcs 11005 Main St Bellevue WA 98004

PATTERSON, ANNE MARGARET, nutritionist; b. Syracuse, N.Y., July 25, 1951; d. John Homer Carpenter and Jean Armeda Newberry Balajty; m. Robert Stephen Patterson, July 12, 1975; children: Sarah Lynn, Kelly Anne. BS, U. Calif., Berkeley, 1975, MPH, 1977. Migrant health nutritionist U. Colo. Med. Sch., Denver, 1977; state nutrition cons. Colo. Dept. Health, Denver, 1977-82; pub. health nutritionist Santa Barbara County (Calif.) Health Care Svcs., 1983-89, supervising pub. health nutritionist, 1989—. Mem. Healthy Mothers, Healthy Babies, Santa Barbara, 1986—; mem. health adv. com. March of Dimes, Santa Barbara, 1990—; mem. com. Am. Heart Assn., Santa Barbara, 1988—; active PTA, 1987—. HEW scholar, 1976. Mem. Am. Dietetic Assn. (registered), Calif. WIC Assn. (bd. dirs., regional rep. 1993—). Office: Santa Barbara County Health 315 Camino Del Remedio Santa Barbara CA 93110-1332

PATTERSON, BEVERLEY PAMELA GRACE, accountant; b. London, Feb. 6, 1956; came to U.S., 1975; d. Ernest Charles and Barbara (Wiseman) Patterson; children: Tamara, Russell, Stuart. AAS with honors, Tacoma C.C., 1978; BBA with honors, U. Puget Sound, 1980. CPA, Wash. Accounts payable clk. Hillhaven Corp., Tacoma, 1975-76, staff acct., 1980-83, acquisition analyst, 1984-86; contr., chief fin. officer Tacoma Luth. Home and Retirement Community, 1987—; cons. in field, 1984—. Bd. dirs., treas. YWCA, 1992-94; bd. dirs. Tacoma Farmers Market, 1995. Mem. AICPA, Wash. Soc. CPAs (healthcare com. 1993-95), Am. Soc. Women Accts. (chmn. bd. dirs. Tacoma chpt., mem. edtl. bd. The Woman CPA mag. 1989-92, pres. 1991-92), Healthcare Fin. Mgmt. Assn., City Club. Home: PO Box 1507 Gig Harbor WA 98335-3507 Office: Tacoma Luth Home & Retirement Community 1301 N Highland Pky Tacoma WA 98406-2116

PATTERSON, DANIEL WILLIAM, dentist; b. Minot, N.D., Aug. 12, 1948; s. Girdell William and Fern Lemay (Sullivan) P. DDS, Northwestern U., 1972; Alumnus degree (hon.), U. Colo., 1977; BS in Biology, U.N.Y., 1993; M in Healthcare Systems, U. Denver, 1994. Cert. health industry orgn., ops. U. Denver, 1993. Dentist Dan L. Hansen, DDS, P.C., Lakewood, Colo., 1974-75; pvt. practice dentistry Littleton, Colo., 1975-88; clin. instr. dept. applied dentistry U. Colo., Denver, 1981-83, lectr., 1983, clin. asst. prof. depts. restorative and applied dentistry, 1989-91, dir. advanced dentistry program, 1989-90, asst. prof. clin. track dept. restorative dentistry, 1991—. Mem. editorial adv. panel Dental Econs. Jour., 1981; also articles. Active Chatfield Jaycees, Littleton, 1976-81; vocal soloist, mem. Denver Concert Chorale, 1978-82. Lt. USN, 1968-74. Fellow Acad. Gen. Dentistry (bd. eligible certifying bd. gen. dentistry); mem. ADA, Met. Denver Dental Soc., Colo. Dental Assn. (Pres.'s Honor Roll 1982-84), Mensa, Sedalia Wild Game Club. Lutheran. Home: 6984 N Fargo Trl Littleton CO 80125-9270 Office: U Colo Health Scis Ctr Sch Dentistry 4200 E 9th Ave Denver CO 80220-3706

PATTERSON, DAVID, geneticist, biologist, educator; b. Medford, Mass., Aug. 24, 1944; s. David and Mildred (Hughes) P.; m. Norma Jean Riggs, June 3, 1967; children: Matthew, Jennifer. B.S., MIT, 1966; Ph.D., Brandeis U., 1971. Assoc. dir. Eleanor Roosevelt Inst. Cancer Rsch., Denver, 1978—, v.p. sci. affairs, 1980-84, pres., 1984—; prof. dept. biochemistry U. Colo. Health Scis. Ctr., Denver, 1983—, prof. dept. medicine, 1984—; mem. adv. com. M.D. Anderson Hosp., Houston ; mem. editorial Somatic Cell and Molecular Genetics, 1983—; contbr. numerous articles and abstracts to profl. jours. Bd. dirs. Community Outreach Therapeutic Day Care, Denver, 1981-83; mem. biotech. subcom. Colo. Commn. Higher Edn., Denver, 1982. Grantee study chromosome 21, NIH, 1979-94, aging process NIH, 1974-94, cell biology NIH, 1983-88; Damon Runyon-Walter Winchell fellow, 1971-74; recipient Theodore T. Jossem Rsch. award Nat. Down Syndrome Congress, 1989, Sci. award for sci. Bonfils-Stanton Found., 1992. Mem. Am. Soc. Cell Biology, Am. Soc. Human Genetics, AAAS, Gerontol. Soc., Nat. Down Syndrome Soc. (scientific adv. bd.), Sigma Xi. Office: E Roosevelt Inst for Cancer Rsch 1899 Gaylord St Denver CO 80206-1210

PATTERSON, DAWN MARIE, dean, consultant, writer; b. Gloversville, N.Y., July 30; d. Robert Morris and Dora Margaret (Perham) P.; m. Robert Henry Hollenbeck, Aug. 3, 1958 (div. 1976); children: Adrienne Lyn, Nathaniel Conrad. BS in Edn., SUNY, Geneseo, 1962; MA, Mich. State U., 1973, PhD, 1977; postgrad., U. So. Calif. and Inst. Ednl. Leadership. Librarian Brighton (N.Y.) Cen. Schs., 1962-67; asst. to regional dir. Mich. State U. Ctr., Bloomfield Hills, 1973-74; grad. asst. Mich. State U., East Lansing, 1975-77; cons. Mich. Efficiency Task Force, 1977; asst. dean Coll. Continuing Edn., U. So. Calif., Los Angeles, 1978-84; dean, assoc. prof. continuing edn. Calif. State U., Los Angeles, 1985—; CEO Acclaims Enterprises Internat.; pres. Co-Pro Assocs. Mem. Air Univ. Bd. Visitors, 1986-90, Commn. on Extended Edn. Calif. State U. Calif., 1988-91; Hist. Soc., Los Angeles Town Hall, Los Angeles World Affairs Council. Dora Louden scholar, 1958-61; Langworthy fellow, 1961-62; Edn. Professions Devel. fellow, 1974-75; Ednl. Leadership Policy fellow, 1982-83; Leadership Calif., 1992, Leadership Am., 1994. Mem. AAUW (pres. Pasadena br. 1985-86), Am. Assn. Adult and Continuing Edn. (charter), Nat. Univ. Continuing Edn. Assn., Internat. Assn. Continuing Edn. and Tng. (bd. dirs. 1990—), Calif. Coll. and Mil. Educators Assn. (pres.), Los Angeles Airport Area Edn. Industry Assn. (pres. 1984), Rotary Club of Alhambra (bd. dirs.), Fine Arts (Pasadena), Zonta (pres. 1994—), Kappa Delta Pi, Phi Delta Kappa, Phi Beta Delta, Phi Kappa Phi. Republican. Unitarian. Office: 5151 State University Dr Los Angeles CA 90032-4221

PATTERSON, DONALD SCOTT, psychiatrist; b. Detroit, Jan. 4, 1916; s. Glenn Scott and Leola Catherine (Atkinson) P.; m. Jane Carrard Rodman Ketron, July 23, 1950. AB, U. Mich. Lit. Sci. & Arts Coll, 1937; MD, U. Mich., 1940. Diplomate Am. Bd. Psychiatry, Am. Bd. Forensic Psychiatry; qualified med. evaluator for State of Calif. Intern Kings County Hosp., Bklyn., 1940-41; resident Neuropsychiatric Inst., Ann Arbor, Mich., 1945-46, VA, Palo Alto, Calif., 1946-48; psychiatrist pvt. practice, Santa Barbara, Calif., 1948—; hon. staff mem. St. Francis Hosp., Santa Barbara, Santa Barbara Cottage Hosp., dept. chair, 1948-88; attending psychiatrist VA Regional Office, Santa Barbara, 1948-49; cons. Calif. Youth Authority Ventura Sch. for Girls, 1948-50, cons. adminstrv. law judge Office of Hearings and Appleas, Santa Barabra, 1984—; mem. med. panel-ct. psychiatrists Cos. of Santa Barbara Venture, 1949—; clin. dir. Santa Barbara Gen. Hosp., 1949-78. Lt. col. U.S. Army Med. Corps, 1941-46. Mem. Am. Psychiat. Assn. (life), So. Calif. Psychiatris Assn. (life), Am. Acad. Psychiatry & Law, Alpha Omega Alpha, Phi Kappa Phi. Home and office: 835 San Ysidro Ln Santa Barbara CA 93108-1324

PATTERSON, FRANCINE G. P., foundation administrator; b. Chgo., Feb. 13, 1947; d. Cecil H. and Frances L. (Spano) P. AB in Psychology, U. Ill., 1970; PhD in Devel. Psychology, Stanford U., 1979. Rsch. asst. U. Ill. Children's Rsch. Ctr., Urbana, 1969-70; pres., rsch. dir. The Gorilla Found., Woodside, Calif., 1976—; adj. rsch. assoc. dept. anthropology and ctr. anthrop. rsch. San Jose (Calif.) State U., 1982—; adj. assoc. prof. dept. psychology U. Santa Clara (Calif.), 1984—; bd. consultants Ctr. for Cross-Cultural Communications, Washington. Author: Koko's Kitten, 1985 (Tex. Bluebonnet award 1987), Koko's Story, 1987 (N.J. Libr. Assn. award 1990); co-author: The Education of Koko, 1981. Grantee for gorilla lang. rsch. Nat. Geog. Soc., 1976-83, 85; recipient Rolex award for enterprise Rolex, Geneva, 1978, Award for Outstanding Profl. Svc., Preservation of the Animal World Soc., 1986. Mem. Am. Soc. Primatologists, Am. Ednl. Rsch. Assn. Am. Assn. Zool. Parks and Aquariums, Am. Assn. Zookeepers, Animal Behavior Soc., Phi Beta Kappa. Office: The Gorilla Found PO Box 620530 Redwood City CA 94062-0530

PATTERSON, JAMEE JORDAN, lawyer; b. L.A., Sept. 28, 1955; d. James Joseph Jr. and Marie Antanette (Kunz) Jordan; m. Timothy Raymond, Aug. 6, 1983; 1 child, Joseph Thomas. BA, UCLA, 1977; JD, Loyola U., L.A., 1981. Bar: Calif. 1981, U.S. Dist. Ct. (ctrl. dist.) Calif. 1981, U.S. Dist. Ct. (so. dist.) Calif. 1982, U.S. Supreme Ct. 1986, U.S. Ct. Appeals (9th cir.) 1991. Dep. atty. gen. Atty. Gen.'s Office, L.A., 1981-83, San Diego, 1983—. Co-chair Women Employees Adv. Com., San Diego, 1986-87. Regents scholar UCLA, 1973-77, regents fellow, 1977-78. Mem. Assn. Deps. Atty. Gen. (pres. 1987, 94), San Diego County Bar, Lawyers Club San Diego (co-chair reproductive rights com. 1990). Office: Calif Atty Gen PO Box 85266 110 W A St Ste 1100 San Diego CA 92186-5266

PATTERSON, JAMES, mayor; b. San Mateo, Calif., Feb. 18, 1948; m. Sharon LeTourneau, 1968; children: B.J., Jason, Lindsay. BA in Polit. Sci. summa cum laude, Calif. State U., Fresno, 1992. Radio broadcasting exec. Sta. KIRV-AM, Fresno, Calif., 1968—; mayor City of Fresno, 1993—. Chmn. NO on Measure H Com., 1989, Criminal Justice and Law Enforcement Commn., 1990-91; vice chmn. YES on Measure E Com., 1988; mem. Human Rels. Commn., City of Fresno, 1987-91; bd. dirs. Leadership Fresno Alumni Assn., 1989-91, Fresno County YFC/Campus Life, 1984-88. Mem. Fresno City and County C. of C. (chmn. local govt. affairs com. 1990-91, bd. dirs. FRESPAC 1990-91, city budget rev. com. 1989-91, privatization task force 1988-89, charter sect. 809 rev. task force 1987-88). Office: Office of the Mayor/City Coun City Hall 2600 Fresno St Fresno CA 93721-3620

PATTERSON, JOSEPH CROMWELL, financial company executive; b. Detroit, Nov. 21, 1928; s. Walter Rodney and Mildred Lona (Cromwell) P.; student Ohio State U., 1953; B.A., Ohio Wesleyan U., 1954; m. Anne Elizabeth Ferrall, Jan. 19, 1952; children—J. Sean, Kevin B., Michael B., Mary A., Kathleen M., Julia M., Susan E., Margaret A., Patrick D., Jane M. Pres., Med. Mgmt. Inc., Dayton, Ohio, 1954-60; exec. staff Research Inst. Am., N.Y.C., 1960-62, 62-64; cons. E.F. MacDonald Co., Dayton, 6 mos.; pres. Fin. Mgmt. Inst., Dayton, 1964-72, Fiscal Concepts Inc., Newport Beach, Calif., 1972-90; pres., chief exec. officer Tessa Fin. Group, Inc., Costa Mesa, Calif., 1991—; cons. in field. Served with USAAF, 1946-49, 51-52. Mem. Am. Mgmt. Assn., Am. Soc. Mgmt. Cons., Am. Profl. Practice Assn. (editor ofcl. jour. 1966-68), Internat. Assn. Fin. Planners. Republican. Roman Catholic. Editorial adviser Med. Econs. mag., 1956-60. Office: Tessa Fin Group Inc 2910 Red Hill Ave Costa Mesa CA 92626-5993

PATTERSON, LLOYD CLIFFORD, psychiatrist; b. Toronto, Ont., Can., Jan. 16, 1917; came to U.S., 1942; s. William Henry and Florence May (Sonley) P.; m. Gloria May Patterson, Nov. 12, 1943; children: Diane Meisenheimer, Pamela DeBarr. MD, U. Western Ont., London, 1942. Diplomate Am. Bd. Psychiatry; cert. Am. Psychoanalytic Assn. Intern Hollywood Presybn. Hosp., L.A., 1942-43; fellow in intern medicine U. Calif. Hosp., San Francisco, 1943-44; resident in psychiatry Langley Porter Neuropsychiat. Inst., San Francisco, 1944-48; cons. psychiatrist student health U. Calif., Berkeley, 1960-70; assoc. clin. prof. U. Calif. Med. Sch., San Francisco, 1972—; dir. med. edn. Alta Bates Med. Ctr., Berkeley, 1988—; program chair Western Divisional Psychoanalytic meetings, San Francisco, 1966. Mem. East Bay Psychiat. Assn. (pres. 1962), No. Calif. Psychiat. Assn. (pres. 1968-69), San Francisco Psychoanalytic Soc. (pres. 1972-73), Am. Psychiat. Soc., Am. Psychoanalytic Soc., Calif. Med. Assn. (hosp. surveyor, mem. continuing med. edn. com. 1985-91, cons. CME com. 1992), Alameda Contra Costa Med. Assn. Home: 409 Cola Ballena Alameda CA 94501-3608 Office: 3021 Telegraph Ave Berkeley CA 94705-2013

PATTERSON, MARK JEROME, computer software designer; b. Inglewood, Calif., July 23, 1960; s. Jerry Lee Patterson and Robin Helen McCracken Steely. Programmer Green & Assocs., L.A., 1985-87; systems analyst The Software Works, Glendale, Calif., 1987-90; programmer Snow Software, Clearwater, Fla., 1990; pres. Atomic Software, Altadena, Calif., 1990-94; tech. mgr. KPMG Peat Marwick LLP, Palo Alto, Calif., 1994—; design cons. Prestige Station, Inc., 1990-93, Petro-Can., Inc., Calgary, Alta., 1988-90. Author computer prolgrams: Set of Dataflex Macros, 1990, Ultimate File Viewer, 1992, Data Communications and Client/Server Systems, 1993-95. Libertarian. Scientologist. Home: 1945 Washington St Santa Clara CA 95050

PATTERSON, MELISSA, elementary education educator; b. Grand Island, Nebr., Nov. 24, 1956; d. John Abbott and Mabel Edith (Schimmer) P. BA, So. Calif. Coll., Costa Mesa, 1979; postgrad., San Diego State U., Imperial (Calif.) Valley Coll. Cert. multiple subject tchr., learned handicapped specialist, Calif., life sci. tchr. Dir., tchr. It's a Small World Presch., Imperial, Calif., 1980-82; prin., tchr. Faith Acad. Christian Sch., Imperial, 1982-87; tchr. 2d grade Imperial Unified Sch. Dist., 1988-90, secondary tchr. biology and chemistry, elem. reading specialist, 1990-91, reading, resource specialist, 1991—. Mem. NEA, Coun. for Exceptional Children, Nat. Assn. Biology Tchrs., Calif. Sci. Tchrs. Assn., Calif. Edn. Assn., Southwest Marine Educators Assn. Home: 514 S F St Imperial CA 92251-1530 Office: Ben Hulse Elem Sch 303 S D St Imperial CA 92251-1433

PATTERSON, NADINE WARNER, communications manager. BA in English, Colo. State U., 1962; MA in Edn., San Jose State U., 1969; MS in Bus. Adminstrn.-Mgmt., U. No. Colo., 1986; postgrad., U. Denver. Asst. mgr. bus. sales Mountain Bell, 1978-82, telemarketing cons. bus. sales, 1983-85, customer svc. mgr., 1985-87; comms. mgr. U.S. West Comms., Denver, 1987—. Mem., past bd. dirs. Assistance League of Denver. Mem. Pub. Rels. Soc. Am. (profl. cert.), Internat. Assn. Bus. Communicators, U.S. WEST Women, Rocky Mountain Telemarketing Assn. (charter, past bd. dirs.). Office: 1801 California St # 1250 Denver CO 80202-2658

PATTIE, STEVEN NORRIS, advertising executive, artist, author; b. Alexandria, Va., Aug. 26, 1952; s. Frank Norris and Mary Jane (Shunk) P.; m. Sage Lenhart, Jan. 13, 1980; children: Nathan Norris, Lucas Ohio. Student, Stanford U.; BA, Westmont Coll., 1974; MDiv, Fuller Theol. Sem., 1978. Adminstr., teaching fellow Carmen Deo Ctr. Christian Study, Santa Barbara, Calif., 1978-80; area dir. Fuller Extended Edn., Santa Barbara, 1978-83; author, visual artist Poppyfields Studio, Pleasanton, Calif., 1980—; supr. cultural arts divsn. City of San Buenaventura Parks and Recreation, Ventura, Calif., 1982-83; asst. to pres. Fuller Theol. Sem., Pasadena, Calif., 1983-87; sr. acct. exec. Russ Reid Co., Pasadena, 1987-93, 94—; pres. New Coll. Berkeley, Calif., 1993-94. Author: For Fathers of Sons, 1995; mem. editl. bd. La Paz Mag., 1990—; contbg. articles, essays, poems and mags.; exhbns. include Arlington Gallery, Santa Barbara, Nanny Goat Hill Gallery, San Francisco, Faulkner Gallery, Santa Barbara, Springville (Utah) Mus. Art, Canton (China) Inst. Art, Santa Barbara Arts Festival, Good Earth Restaurants, Santa Barbara, Santa Cruz Art League, Arroyo Arts Collective, L.A., Gallery 52, Pasadena, Casillas, Compean and Williams, Inc., L.A., Bade Mus., Berkeley, Kerrwood Gallery, Santa Barbara, Melrose Village Gallery, West Hollywood, Peconic Gallery, N.Y.C., Weingart Galleries, L.A., Boise (Idaho) State Univ. Galleries, City of L.A. Cultural Affairs Dept., Santa Barbara Mus. Nat. History, Dirs. Guild Am., L.A., Hole in the Wall Gallery, West Hollywood, San Diego Art Inst., First St. Gallery, Danville, Calif. Recipient Fine Arts award Bank Am., 1970, Program of Yr. award Calif. Dept. Parks & Recreation, 1983, Gold Medal Echo award Direct Mktg. Assn., 1992, 1st Place award Santa Barbara Art Assn., 1983, 1 st Place award Pleasanton Art Assn., 1994. Mem. L.A. Art Assn., Christians in the Visual Arts, Arroyo ArtsCollective, Omicron Delta Kappa. Democrat. Office: Russ Reid Co 2 N Lake Ave Ste 600 Pasadena CA 91101-1868

PATTISON, JOHN CURTIS, business owner, researcher; b. Cin., Mar. 1, 1951; s. Paul Joseph and Eunice Evelyn (Curtis) P.; m. Kathleen Robinson, 1980 (div. 1986); 1 child, Brent Curtis; m. Erin Prell, Apr. 12, 1992 (div. Nov. 1993). Student, Calif. Polytech., 1973-74. Tchr. various sch. dists., 1973-78; bus. owner Lefthanded Leather, Monrovia, Calif., 1973-77, Pasadena, Calif., 1977-80, Burbank, Calif., 1981-83; rsch. for film bus. Ellis Mercantile, L.A., 1984-89; property master various film cos., 1989—; rsch. for film and leather work Pattison Props & Studio Leather, Simi Valley, Calif., 1993—; pres. Leathercraft Guild, Rosemead, Calif., 1975-76. Crafted leather items used in over 100 films; contbr. articles to profl. jours. Mem. Gene Autry Western Heritage Mus. (charter), Smithsonian Am. Indian Mus. Office: Pattison Props & Studio Leather PO Box 556 Lake Hughes CA 93532 address: 575 Country Club Dr #234 Simi Valley CA 93065-7694

PATTON, ANNE JEWELL, elementary school counselor; b. New Haven, Nov. 22, 1941; d. Dominic A. and Immaculata M. (Lucarelli) Messina; m. John Beacham Patton, Aug. 24, 1966; children: John Alan, Michele Anne, Elisabeth Ellen. BS in Edn., So. Conn. State U., 1964; MA in Edn., No. Ariz. U., 1967; M. Counseling Edn., Idaho State U., 1994; postgrad., U. Ariz., 1966-69. Lic. profl. counselor, Idaho; nat. cert. counselor. Tchr. grade 3 Branford (Conn.) Sch. Dist., 1964-65; tchr. grades 3-6 Amphitheater Pub. Schs., Tucson, 1966-69; tchr. grade 6 Sierra Sands Sch. Dist., Ridgecrest, Calif., 1979-80; tchr. grade 1 Holy Rosary Sch., Idaho Falls, Idaho, 1982-94; counselor Blackfoot (Idaho) Sch. Dist., 1994—; asst. prin. Holy Rosary Sch., Idaho Falls, 1988-89, dept. chair, 1989-94. Vol. Girl Scouts Am., Idaho Falls, 1980—, Boy Scouts Am., Idaho Falls, 1980—, Civil Air Patrol, Idaho Falls, 1988—. Mem. Assn. for Play Therapy, Am. Counseling Assn., Am. Sch. Counselor Assn., Idaho Sch. Counselor Assn., Idaho Counseling Assn., Idaho Soc. Individual Psychology. Office: Blackfoot Sch Dist 55 270 Bridge St Blackfoot ID 83221

PATTON, CARL ELLIOTT, physics educator; b. San Antonio, Sept. 14, 1941; s. Carl Elliott and Geraldine Barnett (Perry) P. BS, MIT, 1963; MS, Calif. Inst. Tech., 1964, PhD, 1967. Sr. scientist Raytheon Co., Waltham, Mass., 1967-71; assoc. prof. physics Colo. State U., Ft. Collins, 1971-75, prof., 1975—; IEEE Magnetics Soc. Disting. lectr., 1993. editor-in-chief IEEE Transactions on Magnetics, 1987-91. Fellow IEEE, Am. Phys. Soc. Office: Colo State Univ Dept Physics Fort Collins CO 80523

PATTON, CHARLIE C., biologist; b. Detroit, Dec. 14, 1962; s. Roy B. and Hazel (Pederson) P. BA in Biology, Lewis & Clark Coll., Portland, Oreg., 1985; postgrad., U. Mont., 1993—. Cert. EMT, Oreg., Mont. Trip coord. Lewis & Clark Coll., 1981-85; instr., sr. instr. Pacific Crest Outward Bound, Portland, 1984-87; site supr. Mt. Hood C.C., Gresham, Oreg., 1988; human resources technician U.S. Forest Svc., Greshman, 1988, forestry technician, 1989; wildlife biologist U.S. Forest Svc., Hood River, Oreg., 1990-93; dir. snow safety/ski patrol Mt. Hood (Oreg.) Meadows, 1988-91; grad. rsch. asst. U. Mont., Missoula, 1993—. Firefighter, EMT Parkdale (Oreg.) Rural Fire Protection Dist., 1989-92. Mem. Nat. Ski Patrol, Crag Rats Search and Rescue, Wildlife Soc. Home: 333 E Kent Ave Missoula MT 59801-6023 Office: Sch Forestry U Mont Missoula MT 59801

PATTON, STUART, biochemist, educator; b. Ebenezer, N.Y., Nov. 2, 1920; s. George and Ina (Neher) P.; m. Colleen Cecelia Lavelle, May 17, 1945; children—John, Richard, Gail, Thomas, Mary Catherine, Patricia, Joseph. B.S., Pa. State U., 1943; M.S., Ohio State U., 1947, Ph.D., 1948. Chemist Borden Co., 1943-44; research fellow Ohio State U., Columbus, 1946-48; mem. faculty Pa. State U., University Park, 1949-80, prof., 1959-80; Evan Pugh rsch. prof. agr. Pa. State U., 1966-80; adj. prof. neurosci. Sch. Medicine U. Calif., San Diego, 1981—; vis. scientist Scripps Instn. Oceanography; cons. in field, 1950—. Author: (with Robert Jenness) Principles of Dairy Chemistry, 1959, (with Robert G. Jensen) Biomedical Aspects of Lactation, 1975. Served to lt. (j.g.) USNR, 1944-46. Recipient Borden award chemistry milk Am. Chem. Soc., 1957, Agrl. and Food Chemistry award, 1975; Alexander von Humboldt sr. scientist award, 1981. Mem. Am.

Dairy Sci. Assn. (bd. dirs. 1963-66), Am. Soc. Biochemistry and Molecular Biology, Am. Soc. Cell Biology. Home: 6208 Avenida Cresta La Jolla CA 92037-6510 Office: U Calif San Diego Ctr Molecular Genetics 0634-J La Jolla CA 92093

PATTY, LING CRUZ, dietitian, health program administrator; b. Agana, Guam; d. Jose P. Cruz and Isabel Duenas Leon Guerrero; m. Richard M. Patty, Apr. 19, 1968; children: Mishelle C., Melinda C. BS, Coll. of St. Scholastica, Duluth, Minn., 1965; student, U. So. Calif., 1979; postgrad., Ariz. State U., Tempe, 1980. Registered dietitian; cert. pub. mgr. Cons. Naval Regional Med. Ctr., Agana, 1967-69; therapeutic dietitian Temple U. Hosp., Phila., 1969-71; cons. Freeport (Ill.) Nursing Home, 1970-71; instr. Freeport Sch. Nursing, 1970-71; cons. Office on Aging Dept. Pub. Health and Social Svcs., Agana, 1972-76; chief adminstrv. dietitian Guam Meml. Hosp., Tamuning, 1971-76; WIC adminstr. Maricopa County Dept. Health, Phoenix, 1976-78; nutrition cons. Ariz. Dept. Health Svcs., Phoenix, 1978-87, helth program mgr., 1987—. Author: (activity book) Parents and Children, Staff Resource Book: Nutrition, Well Being, Fitness, 1993. Vol., interviewer St. Vincent de Paul Soc., Phoenix, 1993—. Recipient Meritorious award Sun Valley Gleaners Assn., 1981-83, 91; named to Outstanding Young Women of Am., 1968. Mem. Am. Dietetic Assn. (chair continuing edn. com. 1980-81, treas. 1978-80), Ariz. Dietetic Assn. (chair cmty. dietetics 1979-81, chair cmty. nutrition 1984-85, pres. 1989-90), Ariz. Pub. Health Assn., Ctrl. Ariz. Dist. Dietetic Assn., Assn. State and Terr. Nutrition Dirs., Ariz. Soc. Cert. Pub. Mgrs. Republican. Roman Catholic. Office: Ariz Dept Health Svcs 1740 W Adams St Phoenix AZ 85007-2602

PAUL, BENJAMIN DAVID, anthropologist, educator; b. N.Y.C., Jan. 25, 1911; s. Phillip and Esther (Kranz) P.; m. Lois Fleischman, Jan. 4, 1936; children: Robert Allen, Janice Carol. Student, U. Wis., 1928-29; AB, U. Chgo., 1938, PhD in Anthropology, 1942. Lectr., rsch. dir. Yale U., 1942-44; community orgn. expert Inter-Am. Ednl. Found., 1946; from lectr. to assoc. prof. anthropology Harvard U., 1946-62, dir. social sci. program Sch. Pub. Health, 1951-62; prof. anthropology Stanford (Calif.) U., 1963—, chmn. dept., 1967-71, dir. program in medicine and behavioral sci., 1963-70; cons. NIH, 1957—. Editor: Health, Culture and Community: Case Studies of Public Reactions to Health Programs, 1955, Changing Marriage Patterns in a Highland Guatemalan Community, 1963, The Maya Midwife as Sacred Professional, 1975, Mayan Migrants in Guatemala City, 1981, The Operation of a Death Squad in San Pedro la Laguna, 1988. 2d lt. AUS, 1944-46. Travelling fellow Social Sci. Rsch. Coun., 1940-41, Ctr. Advanced Study Behavioral Scis. fellow, 1962-63. Fellow Am. Anthrop. Assn.; me. Phi Beta Kappa, Sigma Xi. Home: 622 Salvatierra St Palo Alto CA 94305-8538 Office: Stanford U Dept Anthropology Stanford CA 94305

PAUL, CHARLA JO, home health director, chemical abuse counselor; b. Salem, Ill., Oct. 12, 1955; d. Charles Ross and Marietta (Garrett) P.; m. Albert G. Mueller, Dec. 24, 1976; children: Aimee Marie, David Ross, Marita Jo. LPN, Clark County Community Coll., 1981; BS, 1987; AAS in Nursing, Clark County Community Coll., 1989. Cert. substance abuse counselor, Nev. Drug and alcohol cons. CareUnit Hosp., Las Vegas, 1987-90; charge nurse South Lyon Med. Ctr., Yerington, Nev., 1990-91; dir. Mt. Grant Home Health, Hawthorne, Nev., 1991-93; dir. prof. svcs. Las Vegas Nursing Bur., 1994—; dir. C.J. Paul and Assocs., Hawthorne, 1992-94; field rep. RSVP-Mineral County, Hawthorne, 1991-94; adv. chmn. Am. Cancer Soc.-Mineral County, Hawthorne, 1992-94, I Can Cope facilitator, 1991—. Crisis counselor Hawthorne (Nev.) Vol. Fire Dept., 1991—; in-svc. instr. domesti violence, Hawthorne, 1992—; mem ladies guild Our Lady of Perpetual Help Cath. Ch., 1990—. Mem. Rebekahs Internat. Order of Rebekahs and Oddfellows. Democrat. Home: 3016 Fern Hollow Ct Las Vegas NV 89108 Office: Las Vegas Nursing Bur 3300 E Flamingo Ste 21 Las Vegas NV 89121

PAUL, COURTLAND PRICE, landscape architect, planner; b. Pasadena, Calif., Mar. 11, 1927; s. Charles Price and Ethyle Louisa (Stanyer) P.; m. Kathryn Nadine Knauss, July 5, 1947; children: Pamela Kathryn, Courtland Scott, Kimberly Carol, Robyn Annette, Sanford Elliott. AA, John Muir Coll., 1948; student, Calif. Poly. U., 1948-49. Lic. landscape architect Ariz., Nebr., Nev., Calif. Founder, sr. prin., landscape architect Peridian Group, P.C., Pasadena, 1951—; examiner oral test Calif. Bd. Landscape Archs., 1987—, pres., 1964; lectr. Calif. Poly. U., Pomona, Tex. A&M U., UCLA, Orange Coast Coll. Bd. dirs. Landscape Architecture Found., 1981-85 (pres. 1983). Served with USN, 1944-46. Recipient Achievement award Calif. Landscape Contractors Assn., 1963, citation award Pasadena Beautiful Found., 1969, Landscape Architecture award of merit Calif. Garden Clubs, 1970, commendation resolution Calif. State Senate Rules Com.,1 986, Profl. of Yr. Life Mem. award, 1986, 1st outstanding svc. to industry and environ. award Long Beach/O.C., Meridian award Landscape Contractors Assn., Max Tipton Meml. award, 1993; named Man of Yr. Landscape and Irrigation mag., 1987. Fellow Am. Soc. Landscape Archs. (at-large coun. fellows); mem. Calif. Coun. Landscape Archs. (pres. 1958, Outstanding Svc. citation 1984). Office: Peridian Internat Inc 28th St Marina 2600 Newport Blvd Ste 130 Newport Beach CA 92663

PAUL, DAVID JACOB, nuclear energy industry executive; b. Wilmington, Del., Sept. 19, 1932; s. Benjamin Paul and Betty (Weinburg) Katz; m. Rachel Mercia Ibbetson, Oct. 8, 1967; children: Benjamin, Sara. B in Chem. Engring., U. Del., 1956; MS in Nuclear Engring., U. Va., 1960. Lic. profl. mech. and profl. nuclear engr., Calif. Rsch. engr. United Aircraft Rsch. Labs., East Hartford, Conn., 1961-64; sr. scientist NUMEC, Apollo, Pa., 1964-65; sr. engr. Westinghouse Electric, Pitts., 1965-69; safety project mgr., breeder reactor Atomics Internat., Canoga Park, Calif., 1969-70; group supr. General Atomics, LaJolla, Calif., 1970-75; systems integration project mgr. GE, San Jose, Calif., 1975-77; fusion project mgr. Electric Power Rsch. Inst., Palo Alto, Calif., 1977-80; v.p. ENTOR Corp., Campbell, Calif., 1980—; also bd. dirs. ENTOR Corp., Campbell; bd. dirs. Utility Computernet Corp., Campbell, 1986—. Author: (paper for European Nuclear conf.) HTGR Safety Characteristics, 1975; editor, project mgr. several rsch. reports. Mem. Am. Israeli Pub. Affairs Com., San Francisco, 1989—, Jewish Fedn. Greater San Jose, 1989—. Engring. fellow U. Va., 1959. Mem. AAAS, Am. Nuclear Soc. (chpt. v.p. 1959-60), Bibl. Archeol. Soc. Jewish. Office: ENTOR Corp 62 S San Tomas Aquino Rd Campbell CA 95008-2562

PAUL, DWAYNE GLENN, information systems company executive; b. Beaumont, Tex., Aug. 1, 1962; s. James Madison and Mildred Eula (Tatum) P. BA in phil., U. Chgo., 1985. Project mgr. Daystar Computer Systems, Chgo., 1986-88; application devel. cons. Altos Computer Systems, San Jose, Calif., 1988-89; project mgr. cons. Sequent Computer Systems, Santa Clara, Calif., 1989-93; exec. dir. info. systems UniHealth Am., Burbank, Calif., 1993—. Founding mem. Progressive Coalition of Cen. Ky., Lexington, 1980. Mem. Healthcare Info. and Mgmt. Systems Soc., Am. Civil Liberties Union. Democrat. Office: UniHealth 3400 Riverside Dr Burbank CA 91505-4346

PAUL, PAULA GRIFFITH, writer; b. Lubbock County, Tex., July 31, 1938; d. George Franklin and Sarah Julia (Bailey) Griffith; m. W. Kenneth Paul, May 31, 1959; children: Timothy Shain, Kristen Sarah. BA in Journalism, Ea. N.Mex. U., 1960. Reporter Morton (Tex.) Tribune, 1957-58, Portales (N.Mex.) News Tribune, 1960-61, Albuquerque Tribune, 1961-63, 80-87; substitute tchr. Albuquerque pub. schs. Author: Inn of the Clowns, 1976, The Wail of La Llorona, 1977, Geronimo Chino, 1980, You Can Hear A Magpie Smile, 1980, Dance With Me, Gods, 1982, Sarah, Sissy Weed, And The Ships of the Desert, 1985, Silent Partner, 1986, Last Summer I Got In Trouble, 1987, Night Of The Jaguar, 1987, Lady Of The Shadows, 1992, The Mistress At Blackwater, 1993, Sweet Ivy's Gold, 1993, A Bad Girl's Money, 1993; numerous free-lance mag. articles on bus., health, family interest, environment, religion and people. Recipient Most Outstanding Alumni award Ea. N.Mex. U., 1988, N.Mex. Zia award for fiction, 1984, 87, Tex. Inst. of Letters award for children's lit., 1987, Nat. Edn. Writers First Place award, 1985, N.Mex. Med. Soc. award for excellence in med. journalism, 1984, AP/Mng. Editors' award for feature writing, 1984, N.Mex. Press Assn. Cmty. Svc. award for investigative reporting, 1981, others. Mem. Nat. Authors Guild, S.W. Writers Workshop, N.Mex. Assn. Press Women (awards for feature writing and news writing 1981-87), Na.t Assn. Press Women (Award for Book-length fiction 1982). Democrat. Presbyterian.

PAUL, THOMAS FRANK, lawyer; b. Aberdeen, Wash., Sept. 23, 1925; s. Thomas and Loretta (Ounstead) P.; m. Dolores Marion Zaugg, Apr. 1, 1950; chilren: Pamela, Peggy, Thomas Frank. BS in Psychology, Wash. State U., 1951; JD, U. Wash., 1957. Bar: Wash. 1958, U.S. Dist. Ct. (no. and so. dists.) Wash. 1958, U.S. Ct. Appeals (9th cir.) 1958, U.S. Supreme Ct. 1970. Ptnr., shareholder, dir. LeGros, Buchanan & Paul, Seattle, 1958—; lectr. on admiralty and maritime law. Mem. ABA (chmn. com. on admiralty and maritime litigation 1982-86), Wash. State Bar Assn., Maritime Law Assn. U.S.A. (com. on nav. and C.G. matters 1981-82, com. on U.S. Mcht. Marine program 1981-82, com. on practice and procedure 1982-86, com. on limitation of liability 1982-86, com. on maritime legislation 1982—), Asia Pacific Lawyers Assn., Rainier Club, Columbia Tower Club. Republican. Home: 1323 Willard Ave W Seattle WA 98119-3460 Office: LeGros Buchanan & Paul 701 5th Ave Seattle WA 98104-7016

PAULE, LAWRENCE DAVID, chiropractor; b. Chgo., Sept. 29, 1960; s. Herbert Isidore and Joyce (Friedman) P. BA, U. Ariz., 1983; BS, L.A. Coll. Chiropractic, Whittier, Calif., 1987, D of Chiropractic, 1987. Diplomate Nat. Bd. Chiropractic Examiners. Chaplain Boy Scouts Am., Payson, Ariz., 1982-84; assoc. dr. Neurological Orthopaedic Assocs., Panorama City, Calif., 1989-93; clinic dir. Panda Rehab., Phoenix, 1993—. Recipient Jewish Community Svc. award Hillel, 1983. Mem. Young Demo., City of Hope, Kiwanis, Toastmasters.

PAULES, PAUL MICHAEL, city administrator; b. Oakland, Calif., June 22, 1956; m. Elena Angela De Jesus, Oct., 1980; children: Gregory David, Kathleen Diane. BA in Polit. Sci., Calif. State U., Fullerton, 1978; MPA, U. So. Calif., 1980. Adminstrv. intern City of Anaheim, Calif., 1977; adminstrv. aide City of La Mirada, Calif., 1978; asst. to city mgr. City of Stanton, Calif., 1978-81; asst. city mgr. Alhambra, Calif., 1991-92; city adminstr. City of San Gabriel, Calif., 1992—. Bd. dirs. Wysong Pla. Sr. Citizen Housing Complex; corp. sponsorship chmn. Musical Theatre So. Calif.; regional campaign coord. United Way; active in Am. Youth Soccer, Immaculate Conception Ch. and Sch. Mem. Internat. City/County Mgmt. Assn. (internat. affairs com. 1990-93, U.S. rep. to 1990 mgmt. exchange with Australia; scholarship Pacific Rim Symposium, Fletcher Bowron award), San Gabriel Valley City Mgrs. Assn., Asn. Cities Transp. Com., Mcpl. Mgmt. Assts. of So. Calif. (past chmn.) West Snn Gabriel Valley Planning Coun. Office: City of San Gabriel 532 W Mission Dr San Gabriel CA 91776-1202

PAULEY, RICHARD HEIM, real estate counselor; b. Cleve., Dec. 14, 1932; s. Kenneth H. and Romaine (Heim) P.; m. Jan E. Minnick, Oct. 26, 1957; children: Tyler Kent, Elysa Pauley Del Guercio. BA in Polit. Sci., Stanford U., 1954; postgrad. U. So. Calif., 1956-57. Sr. cons. Coldwell Banker & Co., Newport Beach, Calif., 1963-77; owner Richard H. Pauley Co., Investment Realtors, Newport Beach, and Tustin, Calif., 1977—; sr. mktg. exec. The Seeley Co., Irvine, Calif., 1986-89. Bd. dirs. Orange Coast YMCA, 1973-78. Capt. USAFR, 1965. Recipient Cert. of Appreciation City of Newport Beach, 1975-76; Disting. Svc. award Rehab. Inst. Orange County, 1973. Mem. Am. Soc. Real Estate Counselors (chmn. internat. activities com.), Internat. Real Estate Fedn., Calif. Assn. Realtors, Nat. Assn. Realtors, SAR, The Ctr. Club (bd. govs., Costa Mesa, Calif.), Stanford Club Orange County (past pres.), Lambda Alpha Internat. Hon. Real Estate Soc., Beta Theta Pi, Phi Delta Phi. Republican. Home: 22 Morning Sun Irvine CA 92715-3715 Office: 100 Pauley Bldg 17371 Irvine Blvd Tustin CA 92680-3045

PAULIN, MICHAEL VINCENT, resort development executive; b. Los Angeles, July 10, 1941; s. Clarence Harold and Barbara Louisa (Gerardi) P.; m. Rosemarie Kathe Anne Haase, Dec. 15, 1972; 1 child by previous marriage: Derek Michael; children by present marriage: Annemarie, Maya. BS, U. So. Calif., 1963. Pres. Worldwide Living, Inc., Los Angeles, 1964-68; v.p. sales Colony Hotels, Los Angeles, 1968-71; regional v.p. for Pacific Colony Hotels, Honolulu, 1971-78; sr. v.p. Aston Hotels & Resorts, Honolulu, 1978-87; pres. Paulin Pacific Group, Ltd., Honolulu, 1987—; bd. dirs. Pacific Asia Travel Assocs., San Francisco, 1987—, chmn. 1995—. Pres. Festival of Pacific, Honolulu, 1983-86; bd. dirs. Hawaii Visitors Bur., Honolulu, 1977-78. Mem. Pacific Asia Travel Assocs., Hawaii Hotel Assn. (chmn. 1995-96), Kappa Alpha (pres. 1962-63, 67-68). Republican. Lutheran. Club: Outrigger Canoe. Office: Paulin Pacific Group Ltd 2155 Kalakaua Ave 7th Fl Honolulu HI 96815-2355

PAULLIN, JOANN MARIE, accountant, educator; b. Spokane, Wash., July 25, 1946; d. Carl Victor and Gladyls Marie (Soderstrom) Koford; m. William Charles Paullin, Oct. 14, 1967 (div. Jan. 1986); children: Kimberly Rae, Angela Rae. BS in Bus., Mont. State U., 1968. Tchr. bus. various locations, 1968-83; office mgr. Century 21/Jim Bennetts Realty, Kalispell, 1981, Flathead Land Cons., Kalispell, 1981-83; acctg. mgr. Semltool, Inc., Kalispell, 1983-84; office mgr. Ureco Inc., Columbia Falls, Mont., 1984-86; controller Glacier View Hosp., Kalispell, 1986; acct. Kalispell Regional Hosp., 1987-91, Serac Inc., Spokane, 1991-92, Pentzer Devel. Corp., Spokane, 1992—. Mem. fin. com. Epworth United Meth. Ch., Kalispell, 1986-91, mem. loan and grant com., 1986-88; chairperson CORE team Region XII Assn. of Div., Separated and Widowed Caths., Kalispell, 1988-90. Mem. AAUW (chmn. edn. com. 1990-91), Hosp. Fin. Mgrs. Assn., Kalispell C. of C. (ambassador, community edn. com.), Exec. Women Internat. Democrat.

PAULSEN, VIVIAN, magazine editor; b. Salt Lake City, May 10, 1942; d. Paul Herman and Martha Oline (Blattman) P. B.A., Brigham Young U., 1964, postgrad., 1965; postgrad., U. Grenoble, France, 1966. Cert. tchr., Utah. Tchr. French Granite Sch. Dist., Salt Lake City, 1966-67; assoc. editor New Era mag., Salt Lake City, 1970-82; mng. editor Friend mag., Salt Lake City, 1982—. Am. Field Service scholar, 1959; grad. fellow Brigham Young U., 1964-66. Mem. Soc. Children's Book Writers. Republican. Mem. Ch. of Jesus Christ of Latter-day Saints. Office: The Friend 50 E North Temple Salt Lake City UT 84150-0002*

PAULSON, DENNIS ROY, museum director, biology educator, curator; b. Chgo., 1937. BS in Zoology, U. Miami, 1958, PhD in Zoology, 1966. Asst. curator vertebrate rsch. collection U. Miami, Fla., 1954-64; instr. zoology U. N.C., Chapel Hill, 1964-65, USPHS fellow, 1966; rsch. assoc. dept. zoology U. Wash., Seattle, 1966-69, 74-76, asst. prof., 1969-74, affiliate curator vertebrates Burke Mus., 1976-82, acting curator zoology, 1982-83, affiliate curator birds, 1983—; dir. Slater Mus. Natural History, instr. biology dept. U. Puget Sound, Tacoma, 1990—; instr. Orgn. for Tropical Studies, U. Costa Rica, 1967, 69, 70, 75; vis. instr. Evergreen State Coll., 1976-77; resource assoc. Jones & Jones, archs., landscape archs., planners, Seattle, 1976-80, Inst. for Field Ornithology, U. Maine, Machias, 1988, Resource Inst., Seattle, 1984-90, Seattle Audubon Soc., 1991—, Nat. Audubon Soc. Camp, Maine, 1993, also others; field experience in U.S., so. Can., C.Am., Mex., Asia, Kenya, S.Am., W.I., Europe, Mid. East. Author: Exotic Birds, 1989, Shorebirds of the Pacific Northwest, 1993, (with others) A Guide to Bird Finding in Washington, 1991; editor Wash. Birds, 1988—; mem. editl. bd. Western Birds and Odonatologica; contbr. articles to sci. jours., also popular publs. Rsch. grantee NSF, 1970, 72-74, Burke Mus. Modern Verteebrates Fund, 1989. Mem. Am. Ortnithologists Union, Cooper Ornithol. Soc., Wilson Ornithol. Soc., Assn. Field Ornithologists, Western Field Ornithologists, Wash. Ornithol. Soc. (bd. dirs.), Oreg. Field Ornithologists, Am. Birding Assn., Soc. Internat. Odonatologica. Home: 1724 NE 98th St Seattle WA 98115-2327 Office: U Puget Sound Slater Mus Natural His Tacoma WA 98416

PAULSON, DONALD ROBERT, chemistry educator; b. Oak Park, Ill., Sept. 6, 1943; s. Robert Smith and Florence Teresa (Beese) P.; m. Elizabeth Anne Goodwin, Aug. 20, 1966; children: Matthew, Andrew. BA, Monmouth Coll., 1965; PhD, Ind. U., 1968. Asst. prof. chemistry Calif. State U., Los Angeles, 1970-74, assoc. prof., 1974-78, prof., 1979—, chmn. dept., 1982-90; vis. prof. U. B.C., Vancouver, Can., 1977-78, U. Sussex, Brighton, Eng., 1984-85. Author: Alicyclic Chemistry, 1976; contbr. articles to profl. jours. Named Outstanding Prof., Calif. State U., Los Angeles, 1978. Mem. Am. Chem. Soc., Chem. Soc. (London), InterAm. Photochem. Soc., Nat. Assn. Sci. Tchrs., Sigma Xi. Democrat. Episcopalian. Home: 1627 Laurel St South Pasadena CA 91030-4710 Office: Calif State U Dept Chemistry 5151 State University Dr Los Angeles CA 90032-4221

PAULSON, RICHARD JOHN, obstetrician/gynecologist, educator; b. Prague, Czech Republic, Feb. 2, 1955; came to U.S., 1966, naturalized citizen, 1972.; m. Lorraine M. Cummings, Oct. 11, 1987; children: Jessica, Jennifer, Philip, Erika, Josef. BS in Physics magna cum laude, UCLA, 1976, MD, 1980; postdoctoral study Sch. Medicine, U. So. Calif., 1992—. Diplomate Am. Bd. Ob-Gyn. Rotating intern Harbor-UCLA Med. Ctr., Torrance, 1980-81, resident in ob-gyn., 1981-84; clin. rsch. fellow dept. ob-gyn. Los Angeles County/U. So. Calif. Med. Ctr., L.A., 1984-86, mem. staff, 1984—; clin. instr. ob-gyn. Sch. Medicine U. So. Calif., L.A., 1984-86, asst. prof., 1986-91, assoc. prof., 1991—; mem. cons. staff Kaiser Permanente, Harbor City, Calif., 1981—; affiliate staff mem. Good Samaritan Hosp., L.A., 1986—, Calif. Med. Ctr., L.A., 1986—; dir. in vitro fertilization program Sch. Medicine U. So. Calif., 1986—, active various univ. coms.; vis. prof. in vitro fertilization lecture series Clinica Kennedy, Guayaquil, Ecuador, 1989; presenter numerous profl. confs., symposia and grand rounds, recently including U. Chgo., 1993, Med. Edn. Collaborative, Banff, Alta., Can., 1994, Keystone, Colo., 1994. Contbr. chpt. to: Management of Common Problems in Obstetrics and Gynecology, 2nd. edit., 1988, 3rd edit., 1994, Infertility, Contraception and Reproductive Endocrinology, 1991; co-author 2 book chpts.; contbr. or co-contbr. over 75 articles to sci. jours.; mem. editl. bd. Jour. of Assisted Reprodn. and Genetics, Jour. Soc. for Gynecologic Investigation; mem. ad hoc editl. bd. Fertility and Sterility, Am. Jour. Ob-Gyn., Jour. of AMA, Contraception, Am. Jour Reproductive Immunology, others. Co-recipient Wyeth award 1985, recipient, 1989; co-recipient Serono award, 1991, 92, 93, Poster award 1994; rsch. grantee Ortho Pharm. Corp., 1986-87, Tap Pharmas., 1989-91, Irvine Sci., 1990-91, Syntex, 1990-92, Serono, 1992-93. Fellow ACOG (mem. PROLOG task force for reproductive endocrinology 1993), L.A. Obsetrical and Gynecologic Soc.; mem. Pacific Coast Fertility Soc. (bd. dirs. 1992—), Am. Fertility Soc., Soc. Reproductive Surgeons, Soc. for Assisted Reproductive Tech., Soc. Reproductive Endocrinologists, Endocrine Soc. Office: Womens Hosp 1240 N Mission Rd Rm L-1022 Los Angeles CA 90033-1078

PAULSON-EHRHARDT, PATRICIA HELEN, laboratory administrator; b. Moses Lake, Wash., June 10, 1956; d. Luther Roanoke and Helen Jane (Baird) Paulson; m. Terry Lee Ehrhardt, Mar. 12, 1983. Student, Pacific Luth. U., 1974-76; BS in Med. Tech., U. Wash., 1976; BS in Biology, MS in Biology, Eastern Wash. U., 1982. Med. technologist Samaritan Hosp., Moses Lake, 1979-81; lab. supr. Moses Lake Clinic, Kalispell Regional Hosp., Mont., 1987-88; with Kalispell (Mont.) Regional Hosp., 1987; account exec. Pathology Assocs. Med. Lab., Spokane, Wash., 1988—; mem. med. lab. tech. adv. com. Wenatchee (Wash.) Valley Coll., 1984-85, chmn., 1985-86. Mem. Flathead Valley Community Band, 1987-90. Mem. Am. Soc. Clin. Lab. Scientists, Clin. Lab. Mgmt. Assn. (pres. Inland N.W. chpt. 1993-94, bd. dirs. 1994-95), Am. Soc. Clin. Pathologists (cert.), Pan Players Flute Soc., Flathead Tennis Assn., Sigma Xi, Kappa Delta (pledge class pres. 1976). Republican. Lutheran. Home: 2901 Kendall Rd Walla Walla WA 99362

PAULUS, NORMA JEAN PETERSEN, lawyer, state school system administrator; b. Belgrade, Nebr., Mar. 13, 1933; d. Paul Emil and Ella Marie (Hellbusch) Petersen; LL.B., Willamette Law Sch., 1962; LL.D., Linfield Coll., 1985; m. William G. Paulus, Aug. 16, 1958; children: Elizabeth, William Frederick. Sec. to Harney County Dist. Atty., 1950-53; legal sec., Salem, Oreg., 1953-55; sec. to chief justice Oreg. Supreme Ct., 1955-61; admitted to Oreg. bar, 1962; of counsel Paulus and Callaghan, Salem, mem. Oreg. Ho. of Reps., 1971-77; sec. state State of Oreg., Salem, 1977-85; of counsel firm Paulus, Rhoten & Lien, 1985-86; supt. pub. instrn. State of Oreg., 1990—; Oreg. exec. bd. US West, 1985—; adj. prof. Willamette U. Grad. Sch, 1985; mem. N.W. Power Planning Com., 1986-89. Fellow Eagleton Inst. Politics, 1971; mem. Pacific NW Power Planning Council, 1987-89; adv. com. Defense Adv. Com. for Women in the Service, 1986, Nat. Trust for Hist. Preservation, 1988—; trustee Willamette U., 1978—; bd. dirs. Benedictine Found. of Oreg., 1980—, Oreg. Grade. Instn. Sci. and Tech., 1985—, Mid Willamette Valley council Camp Fire Girls, 1985-87; overseer Whitman Coll., 1985—; bd. cons. Goodwill Industries of Oreg.; mem. Salem Human Relations Commn., 1967-70, Marion-Polk Boundary Commn., 1970-71; mem. Presdl. Commn. to Monitor Philippines Election, 1986. Recipient Distinguished Service award City of Salem, 1971; Path Breaker award Oreg. Women's Polit. Caucus, 1976; named One of 10 Women of Future, Ladies Home Jour., 1979. Woman of Yr., Oreg. Inst Managerial and Profl. Women, 1982, Oreg. Women Lawyers, 1982, Woman Who Made a Difference award Nat. Women's Forum, 1985. Mem. Oreg. State Bar, Nat. Order Women Legislators, Women Execs. in State Govt., Women's Polit. Caucus Bus. and Profl. Women's Club (Golden Torch award 1971), Zonta Internat., Delta Kappa Gamma.

PAUP, MARTIN ARNOLD, real estate and securities investor; b. Seattle, Aug. 30, 1930; s. Clarence Jacob and Emaline Ethel (Lodestein) P.; m. Mary Jean Iske, Apr. 4, 1959; children: Barbara Ann Paup Soriano, Jennifer Marie, Elizabeth Paup Gail. BS, U. Wash., 1952. Indsl. engr. Boeing Airplane Co., Seattle, 1954-60; owner Coopers Unfinished Furniture, Seattle, 1960-63; claims rep. Unigard Ins., Seattle, 1963-66; asst. benefits mgr. Equitable Life Assurance, Seattle, 1966-85; owner Paup Ventures, Seattle, 1974--, Paup Investment Co., Seattle, 1963--, Ella Paup Properties, Seattle, 1963--. Bd. dirs. Denny Regrade Property Owners' Assn., Seattle, Denny Regrade Bus. Assn., Seattle, First Ave. Assn., Seattle. Seattle Dept. Community Devel. grantee, 1980. Mem. Greenwood C. of C., Seattle Opera Guild. Democrat. Roman Catholic. Home: 2021 1st Ave Ste 4G Seattle WA 98121-2135 Office: Paup Co 2021 1st Ave # 4G Seattle WA 98121-2135

PAUPP, TERRENCE EDWARD, legal research associate, educator; b. Joliet, Ill., Aug. 10, 1952; s. Edward Theodore and Mary Alice (Combs) P. BA in Social Scis., San Diego State U., 1974; ThM, Luth. Sch. Theology, 1978; JD, U. San Diego, 1990. Instr. philosophy San Diego City Coll., 1983-86, Southwestern Coll., Chula Vista, Calif., 1980-83; law clerk Sch. Law U. San Diego, 1987-88; law clerk Office of Atty. Gen., San Diego, 1988-89; rsch. assoc. Frank & Milchen, San Diego, 1989, Dougherty & Hildre, San Diego, 1990-95; cons. Cmty. Reinvestment Act, San Diego, 1993-95; sr. rsch. assoc. Inst. Ctrl. and Ea. European Studies San Diego State U., 1994-95. Contbr. articles to law jours. Cons. Neighborhood House 5th Ave., 1994-95, Bethel Baptist Ch., 1994-95, PBS Frontline documentary The Nicotine Wars, 1994. Mem. ATLA, N.Y. Acad. Scis. Democrat. Lutheran. Home: 4430 North Ave #9 San Diego CA 92116

PAURA, CATHERINE, marketing professional. With Louis Harris Orgn., N.Y.C., 1973-77; with Nat. Rsch. Group Inc., 1977—, now pres. Office: Nat Research Group Inc 5900 Wilshire Blvd Los Angeles CA 90036-5013*

PAUSTENBACH, DENNIS JAMES, environmental toxicologist; b. Pitts., Oct. 29, 1952; s. Albert Paustenbach and Patricia Jean (Iseman) Murray; m. Louise Dunning, Feb. 23, 1985; children: Mark Douglas, Anna Louise. B-SChemE, Rose-Hulman Inst. Tech., 1974; MS in Indsl. Hygiene, U. Mich., 1977; MS in Indsl. Psychology, Ind. State U., 1978; PhD in Environ. Toxicology, Purdue U., 1982. Diplomate Am. Bd. Toxicology, Am. Bd. Indsl. Hygiene, Bd. Cert. Safety Profls.; cert. indsl. hygienist, safety profl., environ. assessor. Chem. process engr. Eli Lilly & Co., Clinton, Ind., 1974-76; indsl. hygiene engr. Eli Lilly & Co., Lafayette, Ind., 1977-80; prof. toxicology and indsl. hygiene Purdue U., West Lafayette, Ind., 1979-82; risk assessment scientist Stauffer Chem. Co., Westport, Conn., 1982-84; mgr. indsl. and environ. toxicology Syntex Corp., Palo Alto, Calif., 1984-87; v.p. McLaren/Hart Environ. Engring., Alameda, Calif., 1987-91, chief tech. officer, 1991—; cons. IBM, Kodak, Hercules, Exxon, GE, Ft. Wayne, Ind., 1980-82, Weyerhauser, 1980-82, 95, Maxus Energy Corp., 1980-82, 87-95, Hewlett-Packard, San Diego, 1984-86, Semicondr. Indsl. Assn., San Jose, Calif., 1984-86, Hughes Aircraft, L.A., 1987-92; com. mem. nat. coun. on radiol. protection and sci. adv. bd. U.S. EPA. Contbr. over 130 articles to profl. jours., 10 chpts. to books; author coll. textbook on environ. risk assessment. Recipient Kusnetz award in Indsl. Hygiene. Fellow Am. Acad. Toxicological Scis.; mem. AICE, Am. Indsl. Hygiene Assn., Soc. Toxicology, Soc. Risk Analysis, Soc. Environ. Toxicology and Chemistry, Soc. Exposure Assessment, Am. Conf. Govtl. Indsl. Hygienists, N.Y. Acad. Scis., Sigma Xi. Roman Catholic. Home: 65 Roan Pl Woodside CA 94062-4229 Office: McLaren/Hart Environ Engrng 1135 Atlantic Ave Alameda CA 94501-1145

PAVA, ESTHER SHUB, artist, educator; b. Hartford, Conn., June 29, 1921; d. Jacob H. and Rose (Rietkop) Shub; m. Jacob Pava, June 16, 1946; children: David Lauren, Jonathan Michael, Daniel Seth, Nathaniel Alexander. BFA, R.I. Sch. of Design, 1944; MA, San Francisco State U., 1971. Artist New Eng. Roto Engraving Co., Holyoke, Mass., 1944-46, Wyckoff Advt. Agy., San Francisco, 1963-66; tchr. San Francisco Unified Sch. Dist., 1963-66, Laguna Salada Sch. Dist., Pacifica, Calif., 1966-83; artist, educator Belmont, Calif., 1983—. Recipient numerous awards for artwork. Mem. Burlingame Art Soc. (prs. 1983-84), Thirty and One Artists (pres. 1992-93), Peninsula Art Assn., Soc. Western Artists (signature mem., exhibited in many juried shows), Belmont Art Assn., others. Home: 2318 Hastings Dr Belmont CA 94002-3318

PAVITT, WILLIAM HESSER, JR., lawyer; b. Bklyn., Dec. 9, 1916; s. William Hesser an Elsie (Haring) P.; m. Mary Oden, June 19, 1937; children: William, Howard, Gale, Bruce. A.B., Columbia U., 1937, J.D., 1939. Bar: N.Y. 1939, Philippines 1945, Md. 1946, D.C. 1947, Ohio 1955, Calif. 1958. Law clk. to judge N.Y. Ct. Appeals, 1939-40; assoc. Spence, Windels, Walser, Hotchkiss & Angell, N.Y.C., 1940-44; ptnr. Whiting & Pavitt, Washington, 1948-54; assoc. Toulmin & Toulmin, Dayton, Ohio, 1954-57, Smyth & Roston, Los Angeles, 1957-59; ptnr. Smyth, Roston & Pavitt, Los Angeles, 1960-76, Smyth, Pavitt & Siegemund & Martella, Los Angeles, 1976-82, Beehler, Pavitt, Siegemund, Jagger & Martella, Los Angeles, 1982-89, Beehler & Pavitt, 1990—. Contbr. articles on patent law to profl. jours. Elder, Pacific Palisades Presbyn. Ch., 1963-65. Lt. USN, 1944-46, with Res. 1946-51. Mem. ABA, Los Angeles Intellectual Property Law Assn. (pres. 1969-70), State Bar Patent Conf. (chmn. 1970-71), Fed. Bar Assn. Republican. Office: 100 Corporate Pointe Ste 330 Culver City CA 90230-7632

PAVLATH, ATTILA ENDRE, research chemist; b. Budapest, Hungary, Mar. 11, 1930; came to U.S., 1958; s. Eugene Rudolph and Yolanda Elizabeth (Hortobagyi) P.; m. Katalin Wappel, July 27, 1951; children: George, Grace. Diploma in chem. engring., Tech. U., Budapest, 1952; D in Chemistry, Hungarian Acad. of Sci., Budapest, 1955. Asst. prof. Tech. U., Budapest, 1952-56; group leader Cen. Chem. Rsch. Inst., Budapest, 1954-56; rsch. fellow McGill U., Montreal, Can., 1957-58; sr. group leader Stauffer Chem. Co., Richmond, Calif., 1958-67; project leader Western regional rsch. ctr. USDA, Albany, Calif., 1967-78, rsch. leader Western regional rsch. ctr., 1979—. Author three books; contbr. articles to profl. jours; patentee in field. Fellow Am. Inst. Chemists (councilor 1985—, dir. 1993—); mem. Am. Chem. Soc. (councilor 1973-90, dir. 1991—), Royal Chem. Soc. Great Britain, N.Am. Thermonalysis Soc., Internat. Union of Pure and Applied Chemistry. Office: USDA Western Regional Rsch Ctr 800 Buchanan St Berkeley CA 94710-1100

PAVLIK, NANCY, convention services executive; b. Hamtramck, Mich., July 18, 1935; d. Frank and Helen (Vorobojoff) Phillips; m. G. Edward Pavlik, June 30, 1956; children: Kathleen, Christine, Laureen, Michael, Bonnie Jean. Student, U. Ariz., 1956-80. Exec. sec. Mich. Bell, Detroit, 1951-56, RCA, Camden, N.J., 1956-58; owner, pres. Southwest Events Etc., Scottsdale, Ariz., 1969—. Chmn. hospitality industry com. Scottsdale City Coun., 1989—; bd. dirs. Scottsdale Curatorial Bd., 1987-89. Mem. Soc. Incentive Travel Execs., Meeting Planners Internat., Am. Soc. Assn. Execs., Indian Arts and Crafts Assn., Scottsdale C. of C. (bd. dirs., tourism steering com. 1984-88), Contemporary Watercolorists Club. Democrat. Roman Catholic. Home: 7500 E Mccormick Pky # 33 Scottsdale AZ 85258-3454 Office: SW Events Etc 8233 E Paseo Del Norte A-600 Scottsdale AZ 85258

PAWLAK, MICHELLE EVANTHE, dietitian, nutrition educator, consultant; b. Milw., Oct. 14, 1964; d. Oraian and Joan Pawlak. BS in Dietetics, Mount Mary Coll., Milw., 1987. Registered dietition. Outpatient dietitian Family Health Plan - Health Maint. Orgn., Milw., 1987-90; instr. nutrition L.A. Coll. Chiropractic, Whittier, Calif., 1992—; pvt. practice nutrition cons. Newport Beach (Calif.) Nutritional Svcs., 1991—. Contbr. articles to regional mag. Mem. Am. Dietetic Assn., Calif. Dietetic Assn.

PAWULA, KENNETH JOHN, artist, educator; b. Chgo., Feb. 4, 1935; s. John and Clara (Brzezinski) P.; student Northwestern U., 1956, Art Inst. Chgo., 1956; B.F.A., U. Ill., 1959; M.A. in Painting, U. Calif., Berkeley, 1962. Graphic designer Motorola, Inc., Chgo., 1959-60; grad. asst. printmaking U. Calif., Berkeley, 1961-62, asso. in art, 1962-63; archaeol. delineator for Islamic excavation Am. Research Center, Egypt, 1964-65; instr. Sch. of Art, U. Wash., Seattle, 1965-67, asst. prof., 1967-73, asso. prof., 1974—; participant artist-in-residence program of Ecole Superieure Des Beaux-Arts D'Athenes at Rhodos Art Center, Greece, 1978; cons. to Wydawnictwo Interpress, Warsaw, Poland, 1978; mem. art jury ann. painting, drawing and sculpture show Art Mus. of Greater Victoria, Can., 1971, Unitarian Art Gallery, Seattle, 1968, Cellar Gallery, Kirkland, Wash., 1968, Lakewood Artist's Outdoor Exhibit, Tacoma, Wash., 1968; participant Painting Symposium, Janow Podlaski, Poland, 1977. One-man shows of paintings include: Univ. Unitarian Fine Arts Gallery, Seattle, 1970, Polly Friedlander Gallery, Seattle, 1970, Lynn Kottler Galleries, N.Y.C., 1971, U. Minn. Art Gallery, Mpls., 1971, Art Mus. of Greater Victoria, Can., 1972, Second Story Gallery, Seattle, 1972, Yuuhigaoka Gallery Osaka, Japan, Universidade Federal Fluminense Niteroi, Rio de Janiero, Brazil, 1990, Pyramid Gallery, N.Y.C., 1991; group shows include: Worth Ryder Gallery, U. Calif., Berkeley, 1962, Seattle Art Mus., 1964, 70, 65, 66, Frye Art Mus., Seattle, 1966, San Francisco Art Ins., 1966, Henry Gallery, U. Wash., Seattle, 1966, 67, 70, State Capitol Mus., Olympia, Wash., 1967, Attica Gallery, Seattle, 1967, 69, Sec. of State's Office, Olympia, 1968, Eastern Mich. U., Ypsilanti, 1968, Rogue Gallery, Medford, Oreg., 1968, Marylhurst Coll., Oreg., 1968, Spokane Art Mus., 1968, Cheney Cowles Mus., Spokane, 1969, Jade Gallery, Richland, Wash., 1969, Alaska U., 1970, Polly Friedlander Gallery, Mpls., 1971, Anchorage Art Mus., 1972, U. Nev. Art Gallery, 1972, Juneau (Alaska) Art Mus., 1972, Springfield (Mo.) Art Mus., 1973, U. N.D., Grand Forks, 1974, Washington and Jefferson Coll., Washington, Pa., 1975, MacMurray Coll., Jacksonville, Ill., 1976, Gallery of Fine Arts, Eastern Mont. Coll., 1976, Inst. of Culture, Janow Podlaski, Poland, 1977, Seattle Arts Commn., 1978, Polish Cultural Center, Buffalo, 1979, Cabo Frio Internat. Print Biennial, Brazil, 1983, Sunderland (Eng.) Poly. U. Faculty Exchange Exhbn., 1984, Internat Art Biennial Mus. Hosio Capranica-Viterbo, Italy, 1985; represented in permanent collections: San Francisco Art Mus., Seattle Art Mus., Henry Gallery, U. Wash., Seattle, Highline Coll., Midway, Wash., Marylhurst Coll., Art Mus., Janow Podlaski, Poland, Tacoma Nat. Bank, Fine Arts Gallery of San Diego. Mem. Coll. Art Assn., AAUP. Home: 2242 NE 177th St Seattle WA 98155-5241 Office: U Wash Coll Arts & Scis Sch Art Dm # 10 Seattle WA 98195

PAXMAN, DAVID BROCKBANK, English literature educator; b. Salt Lake City, Dec. 31, 1946; s. Monroe Junior and Shirley (Brockbank) P.; m. Susan Wear, Apr. 1, 1970 (div. Dec. 1989); children: Isaac, Jonathan, Jane, Judith. BA, Brigham Young U., 1971; MA, U. Chgo., 1972, PhD, 1982. Asst. prof. Brigham Young U.-Hawaii campus, Laie, 1976-82; assoc. prof. Brigham Young U., Provo, Utah, 1982-88. Author: A Newcomer's Guide to Hawaii, 1993; contbr. articles to profl. jours. Mem. Am. Soc. for Eighteenth-Century Studies. Mem. LDS Ch. Office: English Dept Brigham Young Univ Provo UT 84602

PAYEA, NORMAN PHILIP, II, plastic surgeon; b. Detroit, May 11, 1949; s. Norman Philip and Helen (Kucera) P.; 1 child, Heather Marie. BS in Biology, Mich. State U., 1970, MD, 1974; JD, U. Denver, 1991, MBA, 1992. Diplomate Am. Bd. Plastic Surgery; cert. hand surgeon. Intern, gen. surgery Loyola U. Med. Ctr., Chgo., 1974-75, resident, gen. surgery, 1975-77; resident, plastic/reconstructive and hand surgery McGill U. Teaching Hosps., Montreal, Que., Can., 1977-79; plastic surgeon East Tawas, Mich., 1979-81, Wheat Ridge, Colo., 1981-82, Lakewood, Colo., 1983—; aviation med. examiner Fed. Aviation Agy.; lectr. in field. Contbr. articles to profl. jours. Active numerous civic orgns. and founds. including Denver Art Mus., Denver Botanical Gardens, Denver Art Mus., Denver Mus. of Natural History, Denver Zool. Found., Internat. Soc. for Athletic Plastic Surgery, others. Fellow Royal Coll. Physicians and Surgeons of Can., Am. Coll. of Surgeons, Internat. Coll. of Surgeons, Coll. of Legal Medicine; mem. ABA, AMA, Flying Physicians Assn., Am. Coll. Legal Medicine, Assn. Trial Lawyers Am., Colo. Bar Assn., Colo. Trial Lawyers Assn., Colo. State Soc. Plastic and Reconstructive Surgeons (various offices), Clear Creek Valley Med. Soc. (various offices), Colo. Med. Soc., Am. Soc. Plastic and Reconstructive Surgeons, Am. Burn Assn., Rocky Mountain Hand Surgery Soc., Am. Assn. for Hand Surgery. Home: 3470 Ward Rd Wheat Ridge CO 80033-5225 Office: Lakewood Med Ctr 8805 W 14th Ave Denver CO 80215-4848

PAYNE, ANCIL HORACE, retired broadcasting executive; b. Mitchell, Oreg., Sept. 5, 1921; s. Leslie L. and Pearl A. (Brown) P.; m. Valerie Dorrance Davies, Apr. 6, 1959; children: Anne Sparrow, Alison Louise, Lucinda Catherine. Student, Willamette U., 1939-41, U. Oreg., 1941, U. Notre Dame, Ohio State U., 1943; B.A., U. Wash., 1947; postgrad., Am. U., 1950-51; hon. PhD, Willamette Univ., 1991. Adminstrv. asst. to congressman, Washington, 1949-52; gen. mgr. Martin Van Lines, Anchorage, 1952-56; mgr. Frontiers-Oreg. Ltd., Portland, Oreg., 1956-59; asst. v.p. bus. div. King Broadcasting Co., Seattle, 1959-63, v.p., 1963-70, exec. v.p., 1970-71, pres., 1971-87; chmn. bd. affiliates NBC, 1975-79; bd. dirs. Airborne Freight Co., 1977-94. Mem. Oreg. Bd. Higher Edn., 1966-70; bd. dirs. Centrum Found., Cobalt Inc., U. Wash. Press. Lt. (j.g.) USNR, 1942-45, PTO. Mem. Monday Club, Rainier Club, Phi Beta Kappa Assoc., Alpha Delta Sigma. Episcopalian.

PAYNE, ARLIE JEAN, parent education administrator; b. Priest River, Idaho, Oct. 9, 1920; d. Charles Ross and Novella (Person) Randall; m. Edgar E. Payne, July 18, 1942; children: Randy, Nancy, Kathleen, Charles, Stacy. BA, East Washington U., 1942, MEd, 1968. Tchr. Rainier (Wash.) Pub. Schs., 1941-42; tchr. phys. edn. George Dewey Jr. High Sch., Bremerton, Wash., 1946; coll. dir. nursery sch. Farragut, Idaho, 1946-47; tchr. kindergarten West Valley Pub. Schs., Dishman, Washington, 1951-52; tchr. kindergarten Mercer Island, Washington, 1952-53, active devel. and op. pvt. child care ctr., 1957-63; tchr. pvt. nursery sch. Community Colls. of Spokane, Mercer Island, Washington, 1964-65; developer 1st program for presch. age handicapped children Lake Washington Spl. Edn. Ctr., Kirkland, Washington, 1965-67; cons. parent edn. Lake Wash. Sch. Dist., Kirkland, Washington, 1967-68; legis. chairperson A.H.E., 1970-72; coord. family life Shoreline Community Coll., Seattle, 1968-72; dir. parent cooperative program Community Colls. of Spokane, 1973-85; mem. Gov.'s Commn. for Child Care, 1985; owner Whimisical Jean's Books. Author: Kids Crazy, 1993; editor, publisher Lake Spokane News Forum. Recipient Crystal Apple award for Support for Edn. Wash. State Pub. Rels. Assn., 1995. Home: 16094 N Saddlebrook Rd Nine Mile Falls WA 99026-9352

PAYNE, CLAIRE MARGARET, molecular and cellular biologist; b. N.Y.C., Mar. 2, 1943; d. Frederick John Luscher and Florence Muriel (Seiler) Nothdurft; m. Thomas Bennett Payne, Apr. 19, 1969. BS, SUNY, Stony Brook, 1963; MS, Adelphi U., 1965; PhD, SUNY, Stony Brook, 1971. Biology tchr. North Babylon (N.Y.) High Sch., 1970-72; rsch. asst. Dept. Pathology U. Ariz., Tucson, 1972-73, lectr. Dept. Pathology, 1973-86, rsch. assoc. prof. Pathology, 1986-89, rsch. prof. Pathology, 1989-93; rsch. prof. Ariz. Rsch. Labs. and Dept. Microbiology & Immunology, Tucson, 1993—; supr. Clin. Electron Microscopy Lab., U. Ariz., Tucson, 1973-86, adminstrv. chief, 1986-93. Vol. Am. Cancer Soc., 1988—. Ariz. Disease Control Rsch. Commn. grantee, 1990-93, 95-98, Mathers Found. grantee, 1992-95. Mem. AAAS, Soc. for Diagnostic Ultrastructural Pathology (sec.-treas. 1991—), Ariz. Soc. for Electron Microscopy and Microbeam Analysis (pres. 1983-84), Ariz. Imaging and Microanalysis Soc. (pres.-elect 1994-95, pres. 1995-96), Ariz. Soc. Pathologists, Tucson Soc. Pathologists, Am. Soc. Cell Biology, European Soc. Cutaneous Ultrastructure Rsch., Biomed. Diagnostics and Rsch. (pres.). Office: Dept Microbiology & Immunology 1501 N Campbell Ave Tucson AZ 85724-0001

PAYNE, DARRELL LEE, small business owner; b. Houston, Oct. 21, 1948; s. Alvis Lee and Freddie Jean (Harmeier) P.; m. Carol Jo Quesenbury, Dec. 15, 1967 (div. 1973); children: Patricia Ann, Alan Chandler; m. Karen Nadine Brown, Feb. 29, 1980; children: Kari Ann, Sara Jean. Grad. high sch., Houston. Customer engr. Control Data Corp., Houston, 1969-73; asst. mgr. City Wide TV, Houston, 1972-74; prodn. mgr. JRW Electronics, Sunnyvale, Calif., 1975-77; test engr. Compression Labs., Inc., San Jose, 1977, Apple Computer Inc., Cupertino, Calif., 1977-82; test engring. cons. San Martin, Calif., 1982-85; test mfg. engring. mgr. Headland Tech., Fremont, Calif., 1985-88; gen. ptnr. Digital Image Duplication, San Martin, 1988—. Mem. So. County Alano Club (v.p. 1988-89). Home and Office: Digital Image Duplication 240 Hindiyeh Ln San Martin CA 95046-9509

PAYNE, LISA MOSSMAN, middle school educator; b. Chula Vista, Calif., May 9, 1966; d. William George Jr. and Lynne (Burke) Mossman; m. Charles Alan Payne, June 2, 1990; children: Molly Alexandra, Max Emerson. BA in English, U. Calif., Irvine, 1988; MA in English, Chapman U., 1990. Cert. jr. coll. tchr., Calif. Tchr. Chapman U., Orange, Calif., 1989-90, Orange Coast Coll., Costa Mesa, Calif., 1990, Riverside (Calif.) C.C., 1990; tchr. English, head dept. St. John's Sch., Rancho Santa Margarita, Calif., 1990-94, dir. middle sch. summer program, 1993; leader Jr. Great Books Found., Chgo., 1992—; mem. Middle Sch. Restructuring Team, 1993; Library Accreditation Team, 1993-94. Author curriculua in field; writer children's books. Mem. Soc. Children's Bookwriters and Illustrators. Home: 183 Cornell Irvine CA 92715-2687

PAYNTER, HOWARD LAGER, mechanical engineer, educator, consultant; b. West Allis, Wis., Jan. 3, 1931; s. Raymond Grey and Helen Emilie (Lager) P.; m. Janet Alice Trushinski, Apr. 9, 1949; children: Pamela Dawn Wright, Howard Jon, David Ray. BS in Mech. Engring., U. Wis., 1955; postgrad., UCLA, San Diego, 1956-60; MS in Mech. Engring., U. Denver, 1965. Reg. profl. engr., Colo. Jr. engr. York (Pa.) Corp., 1954; sr. thermodynamics engr. Convair Divsn. Gen. Dynamics, San Diego, 1955-60; rsch. chief theormodynamics and fluid mechanics sect. Martin Marietta Corp., Denver, 1960-74; assoc. prof. mech. engr. tech. Met. State Coll. Denver, 1974-82, prof., 1982—, dept. chair, 1977-80, prog. coord., 1990-93, prog. dir., 1994—; pres. H. Lager Engring., Littleton, Colo., 1975—; invited lectr. U. Stuttgart, Germany, 1973, Sperry Rand, Ltd., Bracknell, Eng.; advisor engring. and engring. tech. bd. No. Ariz. U., Flagstaff, 1991-93; invited faculty mem. Chinese Assn. Sci. and Tech., Beijing., 1989. Co-author: Rocket Propellant and Pressurization Systems, 1964; patentee in field. Precinct leader Republican party, Littleton, Colo., 1975-86. NASA/Am. Soc. Engring. Edn. Summer Faculty fellow, 1977, 79, 84. Mem. Am. Soc. Mech. Engrs. (v.p. Rocky Mountain region), Nat. Soc. Profl. Engrs., Am. Soc. Engring. Edn., Colo. Symphony Assn., Planetary Soc. Home: 3 Meadowbrook Rd Littleton CO 80120

PAYTON, DANIEL NELSON, III, physicist; b. Lamar, Mo., July 2, 1940; s. Daniel Nelson Jr. and L. Gay (Evilsizer) P.; m. H. Jane Whitting, July 30, 1960; 1 child, Janna Nicole Morter. PhD, U. Mo., Rolla, 1966. Staff mem. Los Alamos (N.Mex.) Nat. Lab., 1963-67; tech. dir. Air Force Weapons Lab., Albuquerque, N.Mex., 1967-84; v.p., systems engr. Eos Techs., Inc., Albuquerque, 1984-92; v.p., N.Mex. ops. Sci. Applications Internat., Albuquerque, 1992—; mem. adv. bd. AAMPEC Industry, Albuquerque, 1992—. Contbr. articles to profl. jours. Active Econ. Forum, Albuquerque, 1993—; pres. N.Mex. Zool. Soc., Albuquerque, 1980-88. Recipient Civilian Disting. Svc. award USAF, 1982. Mem. Am. Phys. Soc., AIAA, Greater Albuquerque C. of C., Hispano C. of C. Office: Sci Applications Internat 2109 Airpark Rd SE Albuquerque NM 87106-3258

PEACOCK, HARRY RICHARD, city manager; b. Portsmouth, Va., July 16, 1941; s. Harry Peacock and Hazel Ward (Hunning) Hansen; m. Barbara Elias, June 13, 1964; 1 child, Rebecca Jean. AB, UCLA, 1964; MPA, U. So. Calif., 1969, DPA, 1993. Adminstrv. asst. City of West Covina, Calif., 1966-69; asst. adminstrv. officer, adminstrv. officer City of Gardena, Calif., 1969-72; city mgr. City of Rolling Hills Estates, Calif., 1973-85, City of Saratoga, Calif., 1985-95. Contbr. articles to profl. jours. Lt. USN, 1964-66. Named City Mgr. of Yr. Mcpl. Mgmt. Assts., 1985. Mem. Internat. City Mgmt. Assn., Am. Soc. Pub. Adminstrn. (Outstanding Govt. Program award 1986), Rotary Internat., UCLA Alumni Assn., Alpha Phi Alpha. Republican. Presbyterian. Office: City of Saratoga 13777 Fruitvale Ave Saratoga CA 95070-5151

PEALE, STANTON JERROLD, physics educator; b. Indpls., Jan. 23, 1937; s. Robert Frederick and Edith May (Murphy) P.; m. Priscilla Laing Cobb; June 25, 1960; children: Robert Edwin, Douglas Andrew. BSE, Purdue U., 1959; MS in Engring. Physics, Cornell U., 1962, PhD in Engring. Physics, 1965. Research asst. Cornell U., Ithaca, N.Y., 1962-64, research assoc., 1964-65; asst. research geophysicist, asst. prof. astronomy UCLA, 1965-68; asst. prof. physics U. Calif., Santa Barbara, 1968-70, assoc. prof., 1970-76, prof., 1976-94, prof. emeritus, rsch. prof., 1994—; mem. com. lunar and planetary exploration NAS-NRC, Washington, 1980-84, lunar and planetary geosci. rev. panel, 1979-80, 86-89, 94—, Planetary Sys. Sci. Working Group, 1988-93, Lunar and Planetary Sci. Coun., 1984-87; lunar sci. adv. group NASA-JPL, Pasadena, Calif., 1970-72. Assoc. editor: Jour. Geophys. Research, 1987; contbr. articles to profl. jours. Recipient Exceptional Scientific Achievement medal NASA, 1980, James Craig Watson award Nat. Acad. Scis., 1982; vis. fellowships U. Colo., Boulder, 1972-73, 1979-80. Fellow AAAS (Newcomb Cleveland prize 1979), Am. Geophys. Union; mem. Am. Astron. Soc. (divsns. planet sci. and dynamic astronomy, Dirk Brouwer award 1992), Internat. Astron. Union. Office: U Calif Santa Barbara Dept Physics Santa Barbara CA 93106

PEARCE, DRUE, state legislator; b. Fairfield, Ill., Apr. 2, 1951; d. H. Phil and Julia Detroy (Bannister) P.; m. Michael F.G. Williams; 1 child, Tate Hanna. AB, Ind. U., 1973; MPA, Harvard U., 1984. Sch. tchr. Clark County, Ind., 1973-74; curator of edn. Louisville Zoo, 1974-77; dir. Summerscene, Louisville, 1974-77; asst. v.p. Alaska Nat. Bank of the North, 1977-82; legis. aide to Alaska State Rep. John Ringstad, 1983; mem. Alaska Ho. of Reps., 1984-88; state senator Alaska Senate, 1988—, pres. senate, 1995—. Mem. Alaska Resource Devel. Coun., Alaska Women's Polit. Caucus. Mem. DAR, Alaska C. of C. Republican. Home: 716 W 4th Ave Ste 500 Anchorage AK 99501 Office: Office of the State Senate State Capitol Juneau AK 99801

PEARCE, HUGH MORRIS, engineering executive; b. Tillsonburg, Ont., Can., Jan. 12, 1943; came to U.S., 1965; s. Harold Wilfred and Catherine Ada (Broad) P.; m. Julie Ann Jackson, Aug. 26, 1967; children: David Andrew, Brian Scott. BSc in Engring. Physics, Queen's U., Kingston, Ont., 1965; MS in Elec. Engring., MIT, 1966, EE in Elec. Engring., 1967; PhD in Elec. Engring., U. Mich., 1970. Rsch. engr. Calspan Corp., Buffalo, N.Y., 1971-73; v.p. Sys. Control Inc., Palo Alto, Calif., 1973-81; exec. v.p. Sys. Control Tech., Palo Alto, 1981-84; divsn. mgr. Tech. Svc. Corp., Los Gatos, Calif., 1984-88; pres. Advanced Def. Techs., Mountain View, Calif., 1988-90; v.p., gen. mgr. Radar/Digital Sys., Auburn, Calif., 1990; cons. Los Altos Hills, Calif., 1991-93; pres., CEO Wireless Transactions Corp., Sunnyvale, Calif., 1993—. Pres. Los Altos Edn. Found., 1984-85. Mem. IEEE, AIAA. Office: Wireless Transactions Corp 1183 Bordeaux Dr Ste 22 Sunnyvale CA 94089-1201

PEARCE, JEANNIE, writer, insurance administrator; b. Casa Grande, Ariz., Sept. 24, 1948; d. Johnnie E. and Barbara (Dismukes) Pearce; m. Bryce Hallice Storseth, Aug. 15, 1981; 1 child, Michael Scott. B.S., U. Ariz., 1979. Mktg. rep. Group Health Coop., Seattle, 1981-83; dist. mgr. Health Plus/Blue Cross, Seattle, 1983-84; mktg. dir. Personal Health, Seattle, 1984-85; sales dir. Cigna Health Plan, Seattle, 1985-88; real estate agent John L. Scott Real Estate, Seattle, 1988-92; freelance writer, 1992—; prin. Bus. Writers Northwest, Seattle, 1994—. Avocations: oil painting, writing. Office: Bus Writers Northwest PO Box 66003 Seattle WA 98166-0003

PEARCE, JOAN DELAP, research company executive; b. Oakland, Calif., June 13, 1930; d. Robert Jerome and Wilhelmina (Reaume) DeLap; m. Gerald Allan Pearce, June 18, 1953; 1 child, Scott Ford. Student, U. Oreg., 1948-55. Rsch. assoc. deForest Rsch., L.A., 1966-78, assoc. dir., 1978-92; dir. rsch. Walt Disney Prodns., Burbank, Calif., 1978; pres., bd. dirs. Joan Pearce Rsch. Assocs., 1992—; lighting dir. Wilcoxen Players, Beverly Hills, Calif., 1955-60, Theatre 40, L.A., 1960-66. Bd. advisors Living History Ctr., Marin County, Calif., 1982-89, bd. dirs., 1989—. Mem. Am. Film Inst. Democrat. Avocations: photography; travel; theater; swimming. Home: 2621 Rutherford Dr Los Angeles CA 90068-3042 Office: Joan Pearce Rsch Assocs 8111 Beverly Blvd Ste 308 Los Angeles CA 90048-4525

PEARCE-PERCY, HENRY THOMAS, physicist, electronics executive; b. Melbourne, Victoria, Australia, Sept. 7, 1947; came to U.S., 1970; s. Thomas Walker Pearce-Percy and Valda Marion (Mills) Woinarski; m. Virginia Kathleen Shattuck, Apr. 18, 1975; children: Patrick Walker, Nicole Kathleen. BS, U. Melbourne, 1968, MS, 1970; PhD, Ariz. State U., 1975. Guest sci. Inst. für Elektronenmikroskopie, Max-Planck-Gesellschaft, Berlin, 1974-76; mem. tech. staff Tex. Instruments, Inc., Dallas, 1977-84; mgr. KLA Instruments, Inc., Santa Clara, Calif., 1984-86; pvt. practice cons., Los Gatos, Calif., 1986-88; prin. engr. Etec Systems, Inc. (formerly Perkin-Elmer Corp.), Hayward, Calif., 1988—. Author numerous research articles. Pres. Richardson Noon Toastmasters, Tex., 1983. Mem. Am. Phys. Soc., Microscopy Soc. Am., Am. Vacuum Soc., Toastmasters Club. Office: Etec Systems Inc 26460 Corporate Ave Hayward CA 94545-3914

PEARL, GEORGE CLAYTON, architect; b. London, Tex., Nov. 4, 1923; s. George William and Virgie Adlaid (Ford) P. BArch, U. Tex., 1950. Dir. design Stevens, Mallory, Pearl & Campbell, Albuquerque, 1953-89, dir. emeritus, 1989—. One man shows include St. Johns Coll., Santa Fe, 1987. Chmn. Albuquerque Landmarkers and Urban Conservation Commn., 1980-85; bd. advisors Nat. Trust for Hist. Preservation, Washington, 1976-86; bd. dirs. N.Mex. Archtl. Found., Santa Fe, 1988—, Hispanic Cultural Found., Albuquerque, 1985-90; active Commn. for Preservation Hist. N.Mex. Chs.; mem. Capitol Arts Found., 1990—, Guadaupe Hist. Found., 1991—; pres. N.Mex. Archtl. Found., 1991—. Recipient Bunting award Albuquerque Conservation Assn., 1988, Life Achievement award Historic Preservation State N.M.. 1993, Lifetime Achievement award Design and Historic Preservation Albuquerque Community Found. Fellow AIA (Silver medal western mountain region 1987). Democrat. Roman Catholic. Home: 215 12th St NW Albuquerque NM 87102-1815

PEARLMAN, NANCY SUE, environmental broadcaster; b. Huntington, W.Va., Apr. 17, 1948. BA in Anthropology cum laude, UCLA, 1971; MA in Urban Studies and Planning, Antioch U., 1979; postgrad., U. So. Calif., 1979. Cert. secondary, C.C. and adult edn. tchr. Former secondary social studies tchr. pub. and pvt. schs.; pres. Multi-City Svcs.; host, exec. producer, dir. Environ. Directions and Environ. Viewpoints radio series; exec. producer, host ECONEWS TV Series, Ednl. Communications, 1972—; lectr., speaker, talk show guest; instr. San Diego State U., 1989, Calif. State U., Fullerton, 1990, L.A. C.C., 1977—; adminstr., cons. Calif. League Conservation Voters, 1973-75, Calif. Citizen Action Group, 1975, Zero Population Growth, L.A., 1973-75, others. Dir., producer, writer, host for numerous video and TV prodns. including Using the Apple IIe, Santa Susana: Where the Past in Present, The Great East Mojave, Gem in the Heart of the City, Wind: Energy for the 90's and Beyond, Population Crisis, USA; narrator, host, producer radio prodns. including Environ. Viewpoints, KXLU, 1988-94; editor The Compendium Newsletter; contbr. articles to newspapers and mags. Founder Ecology Ctr. of So. Calif.; mem. career network program UCLA; citizen diplomat Internat. Visitors Coun. L.A.; founding co-coord. Earth Day 1970; adv. bd. Carry Capacity Network, 1990—, Ballona Lagoon Marine Preserve, 1992-93, Let's Live, 1990—, L.A. Earth Day, 1990, Earth Summit Fast, 1992; past bd. dirs. Calif. State U. Network for Environ. Sci. Tng., Task Force on Calif. Recycling, Calif. Wilderness Coalition, Calif. Desert Alliance, Citizens for Mojave Nat. Park, numerous other civic and environ. orgns.; judge Chevron Conservation Awards, 1989—, Acad. TV Arts and Scis. EMMY awards, 1986—, Nat. Acad. Cable Programming Nat. ACE Awards, 1986-93. Recipient numerous awards, including Commendation Resolutions, City of West Hollywood, 1986, County of L.A., 1986, City of L.A., 1986, State of Calif., 1986, Best of the West Spl. Merit award Western Ednl. Soc. for Telecomms., 1987, ACE nomination Nat. Acad. Cable Programming, 1987, Diamond award So. Calif. Cable Assn., 1989, Emmy award nomination, 1987, 88, 93, Buccaneer award for Excellence in Pub. Svc., Pub. Interest Radio and TV Ednl. Soc., 1988, 89, 91, Earth Harmony Achievement award 1st Ann. Earth Harmony Expo, 1991, others; laureate Global 500 Roll of Honour, UN Environment Programme, 1989. Mem. Acad. TV Arts and Scis., Calif. Wilderness Coalition (bd. dirs., adv. coun.), Universal Pantheist Soc. (bd. dirs., adv. coun.). Office: Ednl Comms PO Box 351419 Los Angeles CA 90035-9119

PEARSALL, THOMAS PERINE, physics and electronics educator; b. Richmond, Va., Nov. 2, 1945. BEng, Dartmouth Coll., 1968; MSc in Solid-

State Physics, U. London, 1970; PhD in Applied Physics, Cornell U., 1973. With Bell Labs., Holmdel, N.J., 1973-76, Laboratoire Central de Recherches, Thomson/CSF, Orsay, France, 1976-80; program mgr. optical electronics systems Bell Labs., Murray Hill, N.J., 1980—, mgr. European mktg. for optical communications, 1986-88, mgr. internat. bus. devel. Far East, 1988-89; Boeing chair semiconductor electronics U. Wash., Seattle, 1989—; dir. Ctr. for Compound Semicondr. Tech. Wash. Tech. Ctr., Seattle. Patentee GaInAsP long wave LED, 1976; long-wavelength GaInAs photodiode, 1978; noise-free, high temperature photodetector, 1980; developer long distance optical fiber telecommunications. Recipient Design News award; NSF Fellow to India, 1983-87; James B. Reynolds fellow. Office: U Wash Dept Elec Engring Seattle WA 98195

PEARSON, BELINDA KEMP, economist, consultant; b. Kansas City, Mo., Apr. 14, 1931; d. William Ewing and Margaret Norton (Johnson) Kemp; m. Carl Erik Pearson, Sept. 15, 1953; children: Erik, Frederick, Margaret. BA, Wellesley Coll., 1952; MA, Tufts U., 1954, PhD, 1958. Rsch. asst. Harvard U., Cambridge, Mass., 1954-55; instr. econs. Suffolk U., Boston, 1956-59; lectr. econs., Wellesley Coll., Mass., 1964-65; econ. analyst, asst. econs. Seafirst Bank, Seattle, 1966-79, v.p., 1974-85; chief economist, 1979-85; dir. Lektor, Inc., Issaquah, Wash., 1984—, pres., 1987—; mem. Wash. Gov's. Coun. Econ. Advisors, Olympia, 1979—; dir. Pacific N.W. Regional Econ. Conf., 1979—, chair, Seattle Conf., 1987; mem. Western Blue Chip Econ. Forecast Panel, 1988—; mem. King County, Wash., Land Capacity Task Force, 1995; mem. bd. regents Wash. State U., Pullman, 1985-90, v.p., 1988-90, Regents Found. Investment Com. of Wash. State U., 1987-91; mem. Wash. State Libr. Commn., Olympia, 1976-84. Fulbright scholar London Sch. Econs., 1952-53. Mem. Am. Econ. Assn., Nat. Assn. Bus. Economists (chmn. arrangements 1982 ann. meeting), Seattle Economists Club (pres. 1973-74), Mcpl. League, City Club (Seattle) (chmn. reports com. 1986-88), pres. LWV, Lake Wash. East, 1993-95. Office: Lektor Inc 4227 Providence Point Fr SE Issaquah WA 98029

PEARSON, CLAUDE MEREDITH, legal consultant; b. Hudson, Wyo., Dec. 20, 1921; s. Claude Meredith and Golda May (King) P.; m. Helen Lucille Adams, Feb. 1, 1947; children: Susan Mae Pearson-Davis, Marcia Kay Pearson Vaughan. BA, Jamestown Coll., 1943; JD, U. Mich., 1948. Bar: Wash. 1949, U.S. Dist. Ct. (we. dist.) Wash., 1950. Ptnr. Pearson & Anderson, Tacoma, 1946-52, Pearson Anderson & Pearson, Tacoma, 1953-60, Davies Pearson & Anderson, Tacoma, 1960-72; shareholder Davies Pearson P.C., Tacoma, 1972-91, legal cons., 1991—; chair bus. sect. Wash. State Bar, Seattle, 1972, chair specialization bd., 1985-87, chair alt. dispute resolution sect., 1990; bd. dirs. Law Fund, 1993; adj. instr. McChord campus Chapman U., 1992-93. Pres. United Good Neighbor Fund, Tacoma, 1964. With USNR, 1942-73, capt. 1966. Mem. Mich. Alumni Assn. (past dir.-at-large, 1st v.p., citation 1984), Vashon Golf and Country Club. Home: 3419 N 24th St Tacoma WA 98406-5805 Office: Davies Pearson PC 920 S Fawcett Ave Tacoma WA 98402-5606

PEARSON, JOHN, mechanical engineer; b. Leyburn, Yorkshire, U.K., Apr. 24, 1923; came to U.S., 1930, naturalized, 1944; s. William and Nellie Pearson; m. Ruth Ann Billhardt, July 10, 1944 (wid. Nov. 1984); children: John, Armin, Roger; m. Sharoll L. Chisolm, Sept. 8, 1993. B.S.M.E., Northwestern U., 1949, M.S., 1951. Registered profl. engr., Calif. Rsch. engr. Naval Ordnance Test Sta., China Lake, Calif., 1951-55, head warhead rsch. br., 1955-58, head solid dynamics br., 1958-59, head detonation physics group, 1959-67; head detonation physics div. Naval Weapons Ctr., China Lake, Calif., 1967-83, sr. rsch. scientist, 1983—; cons., lectr. in field; founding mem. adv. bd. Ctr. for High Energy Forming, U. Denver; mem. bd. examiners Sambalpur U., India, 1982-83. Author: Explosive Working of Metals, 1963; Behavior of Metals Under Impulsive Loads, 1954; contbr. articles to profl. publs; patentee impulsive loading, explosives applications. Charter mem. Sr. Exec. Svc. U.S., 1979. With C.E., U.S. Army, 1943-46, ETO. Recipient L.T.E. Thompson medal, 1965, William B. McLean medal, 1979, Superior Civilian Svc. medal USN, 1984, Haskell G. Wilson award, 1985, cert. of recognition Sec. Navy, 1975, merit award Dept. Navy, 1979, cert. of commendation Sec. Navy, 1981, Career Svcs. award Sec. Navy, 1988, John A. Ulrich award Am. Def. Preparedness Assn., 1991; 1st disting. fellow award Naval Weapons Ctr., 1989. Fellow ASME; mem. Am. Soc. Metals, Am. Phys. Soc., AIME, Fed. Exec. League, Sigma Xi, Tau Beta Pi, Pi Tau Sigma, Triangle. Home and Office: PO Box 1390 858 N Primavera St Ridgecrest CA 93555-7907

PEARSON, KEITH LAURENCE, retired environmental scientist; b. Chgo., Apr. 1, 1929; s. Victor R. and Ingeborg E. (Olson) P.; m. Ellen M. O'Dell, May 28, 1955; 1 child, Brian V. BA, Augustana Coll., 1951; MA, U. Ariz., 1965, PhD, 1969. Asst. prof. U. Wis., Superior, 1967-68; assoc. prof. No. Ariz. U., Flagstaff, 1968-76; environ. analyst Bur. Land Mgmt., Washington, 1976-78; environ. planner Bur. Land Mgmt., Phoenix, 1979-95, ret., 1995. Author: The Indian in American History, 1973; contbg. author: A Slice of Life, 1975; contbr. articles to profl. jours. Fellow Am. Anthropol. Assn.; mem. Soc. for Applied Anthropology. Democrat. Episcopalian. Home: 12634 N Rosewood Ave Phoenix AZ 85029-2125

PEARSON, LARRY LESTER, journalism educator, communication consultant; b. Sioux Falls, S.D., Sept. 27, 1942; s. Lester Loren and Lois Ursula (Cochran) P.; m. Alice Marie Simons, Sept. 15, 1979; children: Gregory Eric, Hillary Yvette, Andrew Todd. BA cum laude, U. Minn., 1964, PhD, 1990; MA, U. Wis., 1969. Newsman UPI, Mpls., 1962-63; newsman Daily American, Rome, Italy, 1964-65; instr. Journalism Sch., U. Wis., 1965-67; with Mpls. Tribune, 1967-85, wire editor, 1970-72, news editor, 1972-82; news editor Mpls. Star & Tribune, 1982; asst. prof. U. Alaska, Anchorage, 1985-92, assoc. prof., 1992—, dir. Ctr. for Info. Tech., 1990-92; spl. cons. to Alaska Ho. Com. on Telecomm., 1985-90. Mem. Internat. Communication Assn., Am. Soc. Newspaper Design, Assn. Edn. in Journalism and Mass Communication. Lutheran. Home: 2410 E 16th Ave Anchorage AK 99508-2906 Office: U Alaska Anchorage AK 99508

PEARSON, RICHARD JOSEPH, archaeologist, educator; b. Kitchener, Ont., Can., May 2, 1938; s. John Cecil and Henrietta Anne (Wallwin) P.; m. Kazue Miyazaki, Dec. 12, 1964; 1 child, Sarina Riye. B.A. in Anthropology with honours, U. Toronto, 1960; Ph.D., Yale U., 1966. Asst. prof., then assoc. prof. archaeology U. Hawaii, 1966-71; mem. faculty U. B.C., Vancouver, 1971—; now prof. archaeology U. B.C. Author: The Archaeology of the Ryukyu Islands, 1969, Higashi Ajia no Kodai Shakai to Kokogaku, 1984, Windows on the Japanese Past, Studies in Archaeology and Prehistory, 1986, Ancient Japan, 1992; contbr. articles to profl. jours. Guggenheim fellow. Mem. Am. Anthrop. Assn., Soc. Am. Archaeology, Indo-Pacific Prehistory Assn., Assn. Asian Studies. Office: Dept Anthropology/Sociology, U BC, Vancouver, BC Canada V6T 1Z1

PEARSON, ROBERT ALLEN, optometrist; b. Scottsbluff, Nebr., Dec. 8, 1946; s. William Franklin and Hope Jacqueline (Williams) P.; m. Sue Ione Parmelee, Sept. 6, 1969. BS, BA, U. Wyo., 1970; OD, So. Calif. Coll. Optometry, 1986. Microbiologist State of Nev., Las Vegas, 1970-82; optometrist S.W. Vision, Las Vegas, 1986—. Mem. LIGA Internat. Inc., Santa Ana, Calif., 1992, Vision U.S.A., St. Louis, 1992, VOSH-Calif. Mem. APHA, Nev. Pub. Health Assn., Am. Optometric Assn., Nev. Optometric Assn. (Optometrist of Yr. 1988), Nev. State Bd. Optometry. Home: 3404 El Cortez Ave Las Vegas NV 89102-3925 Office: SW Vision PO Box 15645 Las Vegas NV 89114-5645

PEARSON, SCOTT ROBERTS, economics educator; b. Madison, Wis., Mar. 13, 1938; s. Carlyle Roberts and Edith Hope (Smith) P.; m. Sandra Carol Anderson, Sept. 12, 1962; children—Sarah Roberts, Elizabeth Hovden. BS, U. Wis.-Madison, 1961; MA, Johns Hopkins U., 1965; PhD, Harvard U., 1969. Asst. prof. Stanford U., Calif., 1968-74, assoc. prof., 1974-80, assoc. dir. Food Research Inst., 1977-84, dir., 1992—, prof. food econs., 1980—. Cons. AID, World Bank, Washington, 1965—; staff economist Commn. Internat. Trade, Washington, 1970-71. Author: Petroleum and the Nigerian Economy, 1970; (with others) Commodity Exports and African Economic Development, 1974, (with others) Rice in West Africa, Policy and Economics, 1981, (with others) Food Policy Analysis, 1983, (with others) The Cassava Economy of Java, 1984, (with others) Portuguese Agriculture in Transition, 1987, (with Eric Monke) The Policy Analysis Matrix, 1989, (with others) Rice Policy in Indonesia, 1991, (with others) Structural Change and Small-Farm Agriculture in Northwest Portugal, 1993. Mem. Am. Agrl. Econs. Assn., Am. Econ. Assn. Home: 691 Mirada Ave Palo Alto CA 94305-8477 Office: Stanford U Food Rsch Institute Stanford CA 94305

PEARSON, THOMAS CARLETON, management consultant; b. Somerville, Mass., Sept. 11, 1941; s. Thomas and Dorothy Gertrude (White) P.; m. Carol Louise Baird, June 15, 1962; children: Thomas David, Deborah Anne, Sheri Lynn. BSBA, Calif. State Poly. U., Pomona, 1964; MBA, Calif. State U., Long Beach, 1971; MA in Mgmt., Claremont (Calif.) Grad. Sch., 1983, PhD in Exec. Mgmt., 1986. Ops. analyst Douglas Oil Divsn. Conoco, L.A., 1968-72; mgr. spl. projects Douglas Oil Divsn. Conoco, Costa Mesa, Calif., 1979-84; dist. mgr. bus. devel. Am. Appraisal Co., L.A., 1972-76; mgr. ops. analysis Amtrak, Washington, 1976-79; dir. supplies bus. CalComp, Inc., Anaheim, 1984-89, dir. team 90 product devel., 1989-90; dir. product devel. Harman/JBL, Northridge, Calif., 1991-93; pres. Competitive Improvement Cons., Laguna Hills, Calif., 1993—. Lt. USN, 1964-68. Mem. Train Collector's Assn., Assn. Naval Aviation. Home and Office: 10 Autumn Hill Ln Laguna Hills CA 92653-6016

PEARSON, VELVET D., English and composition educator; b. Bakersfield, Calif., Mar. 13, 1964; d. Timothy Tilden and Nelda S. (Collins) P.; m. Hiroshi Sasaki, May 26, 1995. BA in English, U. Calif., Santa Barbara, 1987; MA in English, San Diego State U., 1989; postgrad., U. So. Calif., L.A. Reporter, editorials writer The Daily Nexus, Santa Barbara, 1986-87; grad. tchg. asst. San Diego State U., 1987-89; vis. lectr. Universite de Provence, Aix-En-Provence, France, 1989-90; adj. lectr. Bakersfield C.C., 1991; asst. lectr. U. So. Calif., L.A., 1991—; instrnl. coord. U. So. Calif., L.A., 1993-95. Mem. editl. bd. The Writing Instructor, 1991-95, asst. mng. editor, 1995—, editor (issue), 1992, 93, 94; contbr. articles to popular mags. and newspapers. Active NOW, L.A., 1992—, Greenpeace, L.A., 1992—, Amnesty Internat., L.A., 1989—. Mem. MLA, AAUW, 16th Century Conf., Nat. Coun. Tchrs. English, Assn. English Grad. Students. Democrat.

PEARSON, WALTER HOWARD, marine biologist, researcher; b. Troy, N.Y., Mar. 25, 1946; s. Howard Stevenson and Mazel Mott (Brownhill) P.; m.. Cynthia-Ruth Egan, June 16, 1972 (div. Oct. 1989); children: Kristin Turnbull, Jeffrey Mott; m. Terri L. Sumner, Nov. 28, 1992. BS in Biology, Bates Coll., 1967; MS in Biology, U. Alaska, 1970; PhD in Oceanography, Oreg. State U., 1977. Fishery biologist, rschr. Nat. Marine Fisheries Svc., Sandy Hook Lab., Highlands, N.J., 1975-78; sr. rsch. scientist Battelle Marine Rsch. Lab., Sequim, Wash., 1978-88, tech. group leader marine scis. lab., 1988-91, mgr. tech. devel. program, 1991-93, sr. rsch. scientist, 1993-95, staff rsch. scientist, 1995—; program dir. environ. studies program Western Wash. U., Port Angeles Ctr., 1993—; tech. leader large multidisciplinary studies of oil spill effect. Contbr. articles on behavior of marine organisms and effects of pollution and human activity to jours. Sgt. U.S. Army, 1969-71. NSF grantee, 1967-69. Mem. Assn. Chemoreception Scis. (charter), AAAS, N.Y. Acad. Sci., Animal Behavior Soc., Crustacean Soc., Western Soc. Naturalists. Episcopalian. Home: PO Box 1858 Sequim WA 98382-1858 Office: Battelle Marine Scis Lab 1529 W Sequim Bay Rd Sequim WA 98382-9000

PEARSON, WARREN THOMAS, surgeon; b. Burlington, Iowa, Dec. 8, 1929; s. George John and Elma Ann (Pollock) P.; m. Margaret Louise Kofoed, Sept. 5, 1965; children: George Maxwell, Ralph Warren. MD, U. Iowa, 1955. Diplomate Am. Bd. Surgery, Am. Bd. Thoracic Surgery. Intern Grasslands Hosp., Valhalla, N.Y., 1955-56; resident in gen. surgery Bronx (N.Y.) VA Hosp., 1956-60; resident in thoracic and cardiovascular surgery Walter Reed Army Hosp., Washington, 1963-65; fellow dept. cardiovascular surgery Upstate Med. Ctr., Syracuse, N.Y., 1960-61; instr. surgery NYU, N.Y.C., 1968-79; pvt. practice N.Y.C., 1968-79; asst. clin. prof. Mt. Sinai Coll. Medicine, CUNY, 1974-79; pvt. practice Encino, Calif., 1979-86; pvt. practice, Santa Monica, Calif., 1986—; clin. instr. cardiothoracic surgery UCLA, 1989—. Contbr. articles to med. jours. Maj. M.C., U.S. Army, 1961-67. Fellow ACS, Am. Coll. Chest Physicians, Am. Coll. Cardiology; mem. AMA, Soc. Thoracic Surgeons, N.Am. Soc. for Pacing and Electrophysiology, Internat. Soc. for Study Lung Cancer, Am. Thoracic Soc., Am. Heart Assn. (coun. on cardiovascular surgery), Pan-Am. Med. Assn., Calif. Med. Assn., N.Y. Acad. Medicine, N.Y. Acad. Scis., Los Angeles County Med. Assn., L.A. Trudeau Soc. Republican. Episcopalian. Home: 1701 Midvale Ave Los Angeles CA 90024 Office: 2021 Santa Monica Blvd Santa Monica CA 90404-2208

PEASE, ROBERT ALLEN, electrical engineer; b. Rockville, Conn., Aug. 22, 1940; s. Mahlon Harold and Beulah May (Kammer) P.; m. Nancy Jean Baker, Aug. 12, 1961; children: Benjamin, Jonathan. BSEE, MIT, 1961. Chief engr. Teledyne PhilBrick, Dedham, Mass., 1961-75; staff scientist Nat. Semiconductor Corp., Santa Clara, Calif., 1976—; cons. editor EDN CAHNERS, Newton, Mass., 1978—. Contbr. 56 articles to profl. jours.; monthly columnist "Pease Porridge" Electronic Design, 1990—; 8 U.S. patents. Mem. IEEE, Com. Concerned Elec. Engrs. Episcopalian. Home: 682 Miramar Ave San Francisco CA 94112-1232 Office: Nat Semiconductor MS-D 2597A 2900 Semiconductor Dr Santa Clara CA 95051-0606

PEASLAND, BRUCE RANDALL, financial executive; b. Buffalo, N.Y., Mar. 24, 1945; s. Kenneth Arthur and Edith Grace (Bristow) P.; m. Debra Myers Peasland, June 13, 1981; children: Michael John, Timothy Scott, Amanda Jean. BS, U. So. Calif., 1971, MBA in Fin., 1978; JD, Western St. U., 1983. Price and cost analyst McDonnell Douglas Corp., Long Beach, Calif., 1966-70; cost mgr. The Gillette Co., Santa Monica, Calif., 1971-78; controller Lear Siegler Inc., Santa Ana, Calif., 1978-85, British Petroleum, Hitco, Newport Beach, Calif., 1986-87; v.p. fin., dir. Control Components Inc., Rancho Santa Margarita, Calif., 1987-90; chief fin. officer MacGillivray Freeman Films, Laguna Beach, Calif., 1990-91; exec. v.p., chief fin. officer Intervest Industries Inc, Carlsbad, Calif., 1992—. Youth advisor YMCA, Dana Point, Calif., 1985—. With USMC, 1963-69. Recipient of Mgr. of Yr. award Nat. Mgmt. Assn., 1984. Fellow U. So. Calif. MBA Assn.; mem. Nat. Assn. of Accts., Nat. Mgmt. Assn. (dir. 1978-85), U. So. Calif. Trojan Club, U. So. Calif. Alumni Club. Republican. Episcopalian. Home: 25211 Yacht Dr Dana Point CA 92629-1439 Office: Intervest Industries Inc 7720B El Camino Real Ste 201 Carlsbad CA 92009-8506

PEAVEY, CHARLES CARMAN, engineering executive; b. Westfield, Mass., Apr. 10, 1955; s. John Forrest and Ann Gordon (Carman) P.; m. Pockhui Kara Kim, Nov. 16, 1979; children: Russell Kim, Sarah Kim. BSE, Princeton U., 1977; MS, Stanford U., 1978. Sr. engr./scientist aerodynamics Douglas Aircraft Co., Long Beach, Calif., 1978-85; engr. specialist aerodynamics Northrop Advanced Sys. Divsn., Pico Rivera, Calif., 1985-88; mgr. CFD devel. B-2 divsn. Northrop Grumman Corp., Pico Rivera, 1988—. Stanford Engring. Grad. fellow, 1977. Mem. AIAA (sr. mem., fluid dynamics tech. com. 1988-91). Republican. Home: 4795 Via Corona Yorba Linda CA 92687-1823 Office: Northrop Grumman Corp 8900 Washington Blvd Pico Rivera CA 90660-3765

PEAVY, FRANK, management consultant; b. Columbus, Ga., Oct. 16, 1957. BA, U. Wash., 1979; MBA, U. So. Calif., L.A., 1984. Sr. cons. Deloitte Haskins & Sells, San Francisco; mgr. GE Cons. Svcs., San Francisco; dir. corp. info. svcs. Visa Internat., San Mateo, Calif.; prin. I.T.M. Group, Foster City, Calif. Author: Client Server Technology: Management Essentials, 1994. Mem. Japan Soc. No. Calif., Commonwealth Club.

PECHMANN, CORNELIA ANN RACHEL, marketing professional; b. Binghamton, N.Y., May 22, 1959; d. Karl and Helen (Guley) P. BA, Bucknell U., 1981; MS, Vanderbilt U., 1985, MBA, 1985, PhD in Mgmt., 1988. Asst. prof. mktg. Calif. State U., Fullerton, 1986-88, U. Calif., Irvine, 1988—; rsch. asst. Vanderbilt Diabetes Rsch. & Tng. Ctr., Nashville, 1982-83, Neighborhood Housing Svcs., Nashville, 1982-83, Nashville Cons. Group, 1984-86. Contbr. articles to profl. jours. Recipient Alden G. Clayton Doctoral Dissertation award Mktg. Sci. Inst., 1987; grantee Tobacco Related Disease Rsch. Program. Mem. Assn. for Consumer Rsch., Am. Mktg. Assn., Am. Acad. of Advt., Soc. for Consumer Psychol., Phi Beta Kappa, Beta Gamma Sigma. Democrat. Office: U Calif Grad Sch Mgmt Irvine CA 92717

PECK, DONALD HARVEY, chiropractor; b. Oak Park, Ill., July 18, 1945; s. Donald Ray and Dorothy Sylvia (LaFlamme) P.; m. Mary Evelyn Lamb, June 15, 1964 (div. 1971); children: Donald Lee, Nancy Ellen; m. Cheryl Jean Cox, July 7, 1973; children: Richard Krom Watkins Jr., Bradley Alan, Steven Edward. AA, Mt. San Antonio Coll., 1966; DC, Palmer Coll. of Chiropractic, 1970. Diplomate Nat. Bd. Chiropractic Examiners. Engring. technician Besteel Corp., Industry, Calif., 1965-66, City of Ontario, Calif., 1966-67; supr. Mercy Hosp., Davenport, Iowa, 1967-70; pvt. practice chiropractor San Bernardino and Redlands, Calif., 1971-81; pvt. practice Cottonwood, Ariz., 1981—; instr. Yavapai Coll. Clarkdale, Ariz., 1982-88. Scoutmaster Calif. Inland Empire coun. Boy Scouts Am., 1974-81, Grand Canyon coun. Boy Scouts Am., 1981—; active Am. Youth Soccer Orgn., Cottonwood, 1977-92, regional commr., 1984-88; instr. trainer, chief instr. Ariz. Game and Fish Dept., Cottonwood, 1983—. Recipient Award of Merit Boy Scouts Am., 1980, Silver Beaver award, 1988; named Vol. of Yr. Verde Valley C. of C., 1987. Mem. Kiwanis (bd. dirs. 1985-87), Order of Arrow (chpt. adviser, vigil honor mem., Cert. Merit Boy Scout Am. Nat. Ct. of Honor 1990). Republican. Office: 703 S Main St Cottonwood AZ 86326-4615

PECK, ELLIE ENRIQUEZ, retired state administrator; b. Sacramento, Oct. 21, 1934; d. Rafael Enriquez and Eloisa Garcia Rivera; m. Raymond Charles Peck, Sept. 5, 1957; children: Reginaldo, Enrico, Francisca Guerrero, Teresa, Linda, Margaret, Raymond Charles, Christina. Student polit. sci. Sacramento State U., 1974. Tng. services coord. Calif. Div. Hwys., Sacramento, 1963-67; tech. and mgmt. cons., Sacramento, 1968-78; expert examiner Calif. Pers. Bd., 1976-78; tng. cons. Calif. Pers. Devel. Ctr., Sacramento, 1978; spl. cons. Calif. Commn. on Fair Employment and Housing, 1978, community svcs. rep. U.S. Bur. of Census, No. Calif. counties, 1978-80; spl. cons. Calif. Dept. Consumer Affairs, Sacramento, 1980-83, project dir. Golden State Sr. Discount Program, 1980-83; dir. spl. programs for Calif. Lt Gov., 1983-90, ret., 1990; pvt. cons., 1990—; cons., project dir. nat. sr. health issues summit Congress Calif. Srs. Edn. and Rsch. Fund, 1995; project dir. SSI/QMB Outreach Project, 1993-94. Author Calif. Dept. Consumer Affairs publ., 1981, U.S. Office Consumer Edn. publ., 1982. Bd. dirs Sacramento/Sierra Am. Diabetes Assn., 1989-90. Author: Diabetes and Ethnic Minorities: A Community at Risk. Trustee, Stanford Settlement, Inc., Sacramento, 1975-79; bd. dirs. Sacramento Emergency Housing Ctr., 1974-77, Sacramento Community Svcs. Planning Coun., 1987-90; v.p. Calif. Advs. for Nursing Home Reform, 1990—; v.p. bd. dirs. Calif. Advocates; campaign workshop dir. Chicano/Latino Youth Leadership Conf., 1982-95; v.p. Comision Femenil Nacional, Inc., 1987-90; del. Dem. Nat. Conv., 1976; mem. exec. bd. Calif. Dem. Cen. Com., 1977-89; chairperson ethnic minority task force Am. Diabetes Assn., 1988-90; steering com. Calif. Self-Esteem Minority Task Force, 1990-93. Recipient numerous awards including Outstanding Community Svc. award Comuicaciones Unidos de Norte Atzlan, 1975, 77, Outstanding Svc. award, Chicano/Hispanic Dem. Caucus, 1979, Vol. Svc. award Calif. Human Devel. Corp., 1981, Dem. of Yr. award Sacramento County Dem. Com., 1987, Outstanding Advocate award Calif. Sr. Legis., 1988, 89, Calif. Assn. of Homes for Aging, Advocacy award, 1989, Resolution of Advocacy award, League Latin-Ams. Citizens, 1989, Meritorious Svc. to Hispanic Community award Comite Patriotico, 1989, Meritorious Svc. Resolution award Lt. Gov. of Calif., 1989, Cert. Recognition award Sacramento County Human Rights Commn., 1991, Tish Sommers award Older Women's League/Joint Resolution Calif. Legislature, 1993, Latino Eagle award in govt. Tomas Lopez Meml. Found., 1994. Mem. Hispanic C. of C., CongressCalif. Srs., Sacramento Gray Panthers, Latino Dem. Club Sacramento County (v.p. 1982-83). Home and Office: 2667 Coleman Way Sacramento CA 95818-4459

PECK, GAILLARD RAY, JR., aerospace and business consultant, business owner; b. San Antonio, Oct. 31, 1940; s. Gaillard Ray and Lois (Manning) P.; m. Jean Adair Hilger, Dec. 23, 19662 (div. Oct. 1969); children: Scott Gaillard III, Katherine Adair; m. Peggy Ann Lundt, July 3, 1975; children: Jennifer Caroline, Elizabeth Ann. BS, Air Force Acad., 1962; MA, Cen. Mich. U., 1976; MBA, U. Nev. Las Vegas, 1990. Lic. comml. pilot, flight instr. Commd. 2d lt. USAF, 1962, advanced through grades to col., 1983, ret., 1988, air force instr. pilot, fighter pilot, 1963-72; instr. Fighter Weapons Sch. USAF, Nellis AFB, 1972-75; fighter tactics officer Pentagon, Washington, 1975-78; aggressor pilot, comdr. 4477th Test & Evaluation Squadron, Nellis AFB, Nev., 1978-80; mil. advisor Royal Saudi Air Force, Saudi Arabia, 1980-82; student Nat. War Coll., Washington, 1982-83; dir. ops., vice comdr. Kadena Air Base, Japan, 1983-85; wing comdr. Zweibrucken Air Base, Germany, 1985-87; dep. dir. Aerospace Safety directorate USAF, Norton AFB, Calif., 1987-88; rsch. asst. U. Nev., Las Vegas, 1988-90; mktg. cons. Ctr. for Bus. & Econ. Rsch. U. Nev., Las Vegas, 1990; adminstr. Lung Ctr. of Nev., Las Vegas, 1991-93; bus. owner, cons. Las Vegas, 1993—; owner Great Western Aircraft Parts, LLC. Author: The Enemy, 1973, As Best I Recall, 1994. Recipient Silver Star, Legion of Merit (2), DFC (3), Air Medal (11). Mem. Phi Kappa Phi Nat. Honor Soc., Order of Daedalians, Red River Fighter Pilots Assn., Air Force Assn., Ky. Col., U. Nev. Las Vegas and Air Force Acad. Alumni Assn., The Ret. Officers Assn. Home: 1775 Sheree Cir Las Vegas NV 89119-2716

PECK, GEORGE HOLMES, public relations executive; b. Altoona, Pa., May 11, 1946; s. George Heckler and Regina (Jackson) P.; m. Barbara Ann Izydorczak, Feb. 21, 1970; children: Mark David, Heather Anne. BA, U. Montana, 1968; MA, Ball State U., 1978. Staff announcer KDRG Radio, Deer Lodge, Mont., 1963-66; staff announcer, producer KUFM Radio-TV, Missoula, Mont., 1965-68; commd. 2d lt. USAF, 1968; info. officer 4621st Air Base Group, Niagara Falls, N.Y., 1968-70; film writer, editor Aerospace Def. Command, Colorado Springs, 1970-72; chief info. Incirlik Common Def. Inst., Adana, Turkey, 1973-75; sr. pub. affairs rep. Camp New Amsterdam, Soesterberg, The Netherlands, 1975-78; dir. pub. affairs Wurtsmith AFB, Oscoda, Mich., 1978-80; spl. asst. pub. affairs Strategic Sys./B-1B Sys. Program, Dayton, Ohio, 1980-84; asst. to vice cmdr. HQ Air Force Sys. Command, Washington, 1984-88; dir. pub. affairs Aeronautical Sys. Divsn., Dayton, Ohio, 1986-88; chief media and civil affairs Hqrs. Strategic Air Command, Omaha, 1988-91; dep. pub. affairs officer UN Command, Seoul, South Korea, 1991-92; dir. pub. affairs Lowry Tng. Ctr., Denver, 1992-94; dir. pub. rels. Lowry Redevel. Authority, Denver, 1994—. Author: Understanding the Media, 1991. Bd. dirs. Aurora (Colo.) Edn. Found., 1991—, Leadership Aurora, 1991—; bd. mgrs. Aurora YMCA, 1992—. Mem. Pub. Rels. Soc. Am. (accredited), Air Force Assn., Soc. Strategic Air Command, Aviation & Space Writers Assn., Aurora Rotary, Aurora C. of C. Roman Catholic. Home: 13250 E Center Ave Aurora CO 80012-3514 Office: Lowry Redevel Authority 8000 6th Ave Pky Denver CO 80220

PECK, PAUL LACHLAN, minister; b. Glens Falls, N.Y., Sept. 11, 1928; s. Paul Lee and Caroline Jeannette (Stanton) P.; children: Paul Barrett, Kathryn Elizabeth Peck Kadick. BS, U. Conn., 1952; ThD, Bernadean U., 1976; MEd, Westfield State Coll., 1983. Ordained to ministry Truth Ctr., 1972. With Proctor and Gamble Co., Watertown, N.Y., 1956-60; dir. deferred giving programs Syracuse (N.Y.) U., 1960-68, v.p., 1968-70; v.p. Fairleigh-Dickinson U., N.J., 1970-71, Manhattan Coll., Bronx, N.Y., 1971-75; founder, pastor Arete' Truth Ctr., San Diego, 1975—. Author: Footsteps Along the Path, 1978, Inherit the Kingdom, 1978, Milestones of the Way, 1978, Freeway to Health, 1980, Freeway to Work and Wealth, 1981, Freeway to Human Love, 1982, Freeway to Personal Growth, 1982, Your Dreams Count, 1990, Heroic Love Poems, 1990. Bd. dirs. Girl Scouts U.S.A., Syracuse, 1967-70; trustee, bd. dirs. Erickson Ednl. Found., 1970-75; vol. chaplain Auburn (N.Y.) State Prison, 1967-68; mem. chaplains' coun. Syracuse U., 1960-70; co-founder suicide and drug abuse prevention program Syracuse U., 1968-71, Fairleigh-Dickinson U., 1970-71, Manhattan Coll., 1971-75. Staff sgt. USNG, 1947-50. Mem. Internat. New Thought Alliance, SAR, Rotary, Knights of Malta (svc. award 1973), Masons, Shriners, Spiritual Frontiers Fellowship. Home and Office: 6996 Camino Revueltos San Diego CA 92111-7642

PECK, RAYMOND CHARLES, SR., driver and traffic safety research specialist; b. Sacramento, Nov. 18, 1937; s. Emory Earl and Margaret Helen (Fiebiger) P.; m. Ellie Ruth Enriquez, Sept. 5, 1957; children: Teresa M. Peck Montijo, Linda M. Peck Heisler, Margaret H. Peck Henley, Raymond C., Christina M. Peck Reich. BA in Exptl. Psychology, Calif. State U., Sacramento, 1961, MA in Exptl. Psychology, 1968. Rsch. analyst Calif. Dept. Motor Vehicles, Sacramento, 1962-71, sr. rsch. analyst, program mgr., 1971-80, rsch. program specialist II, 1980, acting, chief rsch., 1980-81, rsch.

program specialist II, 1981-84, chief of rsch., 1984—; statis. cons. to pvt. and pub. orgns., 1970—. Chmn. com. on operator regulation Transportation Rsch. Bd., Nat. Acad. Scis., 1976-82; past mem. editorial adv. bd. Traffic Safety Evaluation Rsch. Review; mem. editorial bd. Jour Safety Research, Alcohol, Drugs and Driving, Accident Analysis and Prevention; contbr. articles to profl. jours. Recipient Met. Life award of Hon., Nat. Safety Council, 1970, Met. Life Cert. of Commendation, 1972, A.R. Lauer award Human Factor Soc., 1981, award of Hon., award of Merit Traffic Safety Evaluation Rsch. Rev., 1983. Mem. APHA, Am. Statis. Assn., Assn. Automotive Medicine, Internat. Coun. Alcohol, Drugs and Traffic Safety, Human Factors Soc.. Democrat. Home: 2667 Coleman Way Sacramento CA 95818-4459 Office: Calif Dept Motor Vehicles 2415 First Ave Sacramento CA 95818

PECK, ROBERT DAVID, educational foundation administrator; b. Devil's Lake, N.D., June 1, 1929; s. Lester David and Bernice Marie (Peterson) P.; m. Lylia June Smith, Sept. 6, 1953; children: David Allan, Kathleen Marie. BA, Whitworth Coll., 1951; MDiv, Berkeley (Calif.) Bapt. Div. Sch., 1958; ThD, Pacific Sch. Religion, 1964; postgrad., U. Calif., Berkeley, 1959-60, 62-63, Wadham Coll., Oxford U., Eng., 1963. Music tchr. pub. schs. Bridgeport, Wash., 1954-55; prof., registrar Linfield Coll., McMinnville, Oreg., 1963-69; asst. dir. Ednl. Coordinating Coun., Salem, Oreg., 1969-75; assoc. prof. Pacific Luth. U., Tacoma, 1976-79, U. Puget Sound, Tacoma, 1977; v.p. John Minter Assocs., Boulder, Colo., 1979-81, Coun. Ind. Colls., Washington, 1981-84; adminstrv. v.p. Alaska Pacific U., Anchorage, 1984-88; pres. Phillips U., Enid, Okla., 1988-94, chancellor, 1994-95; chmn. The Pres. Found. for Support of Higher Edn., Washington, 1995—; pres. Phillips U. Ednl. Enterprises Inc., 1994-95; cons. Higher Edn. Exec. Assocs., Denver, 1984—; owner Tyee Marina, Tacoma, 1975-77; yacht broker Seattle, 1977-79. Author: Future Focusing: An Alternative to Strategic Planning, 1983, also articles. Dem. county chmn., McMinnville, 1968, Dem. candidate for state Ho. of Reps., McMinnville, 1969; pres. McMinnville Kiwanis, 1965-69. Cpl. Signal Corps, U.S. Army, 1952-54. Carnegie Corp. grantee, 1982, 84. Mem. Okla. Ind. Coll. Assn. (sec. 1989—). Mem. Christian Ch. Office: Pres Found for Support Higher Edn 1919 Pennsylvania Ave NW Washington DC 20006-3404

PECKOL, JAMES KENNETH, consulting engineer; b. Cleve., Oct. 24, 1944; s. William John and Elinor Elizabeth (Bustard) P.; children: Erin, Robyn. BS Engring., Case Inst. Tech., 1966; MSEE, U. Wash., 1975, PhDEE, 1985. Cons. GE, Raytheon, Ling Temco Vought, RCA, Boeing Co., 1966-72; sr. staff engr. indsl. products bus. unit John Fluke Mfg. Co., Seattle, 1972-83, sr. staff engr. automated systems bus. unit, 1983-86, sr. staff engr. MR&D Bus. unit, 1986-93; cons. Oxford Cons., Ltd., Edmonds, Wash., 1993—; affiliate asst. prof. dept. elec. engring. U. Wash., Seattle, 1984-87, 1995—; sr. lectr., assoc. prof. dept. elec. engring. U. Aberdeen, Scotland, 1987; lectr. dept. computer sci. Seattle U., 1989; lectr. dept. math and sci. Shorline C.C., Seattle, 1989—; lectr. dept. computer sci. Edmonds (Wash.) C.C., 1992—; assoc. prof. dept. engring./computer sci. U. Nantes, France, 1993; mem. computer sci. and elec. engring. curriculum adv. bd. Wash. State U., 1990—; lectr. various confs. and univs. Contbr. articles to profl. jours.; patentee in field. Mem. IEEE, Am. Assn. Artificial Intelligence, Assn. Computing Machinery, Tau Beta Pi. Home and Office: Oxford Cons Ltd 859 14th St SW Edmonds WA 98020-6611

PECORA, ROBERT, chemistry educator; b. Bklyn., Aug. 6, 1938; s. Alfonso Edward and Helen (Buscavage) P. A.B., Columbia U., 1959, A.M., 1960, Ph.D., 1962. Asst. prof. chemistry Stanford U., 1964-71, assoc. prof., 1971-78, prof., 1978—; chmn. chemistry, 1992—; vis. prof. U. Manchester, (Eng.), 1970-71, U. Nice, (France), 1978; cons. chemistry to maj. corps. Co-author: Dynamic Light Scattering, 1976; contbr. articles to profl. jours. Recipient Sr. Scientist award Alexander von Humboldt Found., 1985; NSF fellow, 1960-62, Am. Acad. Scis. postdoctoral fellow U. libre de Bruxelles, Belgium, 1963. Fellow AAAS, Am. Phys. Soc.; mem. Am. Chem. Soc. Home: 707 Continental Cir Mountain View CA 94040-3366 Office: Stanford U Dept Chemistry Stanford CA 94305

PECSOK, ROBERT LOUIS, chemist, educator; b. Cleve., Dec. 18, 1918; s. Michael C. and Katherine (Richter) P.; m. Mary Bodell, Oct. 12, 1940; children: Helen Pecsok Wong, Katherine, Jean Pecsok Nagle, Michael, Ruth Pecsok Hughes, Alice, Sara Pecsok Lima. S.B. summa cum laude, Harvard, 1940, Ph.D., 1948. Prodn. foreman Procter & Gamble Co., Balt., 1940-43; instr. chemistry Harvard, 1948; asst. prof. chemistry U. Calif. at Los Angeles, 1948-55, asso. prof., 1955-61, prof., 1961-71, vice chmn. dept., 1965-70; prof., chmn. dept. U. Hawaii, Honolulu, 1971-80; dean natural scis. U. Hawaii, 1981-89; sci. adviser FDA, 1966-69. Author: Principles and Practice of Gas Chromatography, 1959, Analytical Methods of Organic and Biochemistry, 1966, Modern Methods of Chemical Analysis, 1968, 2d edit., 1976, Modern Chemical Technology, 1970, rev. edit. 1989, Physicochemical Applications of Gas Chromatography, 1978. Served as lt. USNR, 1943-46. Recipient Tolman medal, 1971; Guggenheim fellow, 1956-57; Petroleum Research Fund Internat. fellow, 1963-64. Mem. Am. Chem. Soc., Am. Inst. Chemists, Phi Beta Kappa, Alpha Chi Sigma, Phi Lambda Upsilon. Home: 13855 Riverhead Ct San Diego CA 92129-3222

PEDDY, JULIE ANN, federal agent; b. Chicago Heights, Ill., Apr. 2, 1959; d. Ronald Ryno and Myra Jean (Clark) P. MPA, Ind. U., Gary, 1984. Benefit authorizer trainee U.S. HHS, Chgo., 1979-80; investigator U.S. Office of Personnel Mgmt., Chgo., 1980-81, Def. Investigative Svc., Chgo., 1981-83; investigator, sr. resident agt. Def. Investigative Svc., Hammond, Ind., 1983-84; supervisory investigator, team chief Def. Investigative Svc., Chgo., 1984-89; spl. agt. in charge Def. Investigative Svc., Seattle, 1989—; mem. Seattle Fed. Exec. Bd., 1990—. Bd. dirs. Lynwood (Ill.) Terr. Condominium Assn., 1989. Mem. ASPA, Ind. U. Alumni Assn. (life), Pi Alpha Alpha. Methodist. Office: Def Investigative Svc PO Box 33520 Seattle WA 98133-0520

PEDEN, LYNN ELLEN, marketing executive; b. L.A., Mar. 1, 1946; d. Orlan Sidney and Erna Lou (Harris) Friedman; m. Ernest Peden, Aug. 1994. Student UCLA, 1963-65, 71-72, Willis Bus. Coll., 1965-66, Fin. Schs. Am., 1982, Viewpoints Inst., 1970-71. Office mgr. Harleigh Sandler Co., L.A., 1965-67; customer svc. Investors Diversified Svcs., West L.A., Calif., 1968-76; exec. sec. McCulloch Oil Corp., West L.A., 1976; mgr. publs. Security 1st Group, Century City, Calif., 1976-80; office mgr. Morehead & Co., Century City, 1980-81; dir. mktg., mgr. customer svc. Ins. Mktg. Services, Santa Monica, Calif., 1981-82; v.p. Decatur Petroleum Corp., Santa Monica, 1982-83; asst. v.p., broker svcs., dir. Angeles Corp., L.A., 1984-87; asst. to pres. Pacific Ventures, Santa Monica, 1988-90; La Grange Group, West L.A., 1990—. Mem. Migi Car Am. Club (sec., newsletter editor). Fin. and ins. writer; contbr. poetry to UCLA Literary Mag., 1964. Home: 4365 Mclaughlin Ave Apt 12 Los Angeles CA 90066-5957

PEDERSEN, GAYLEN, organization executive, marketing consultant; b. Salt Lake City, Mar. 4, 1934; s. Oliver Cowdery and Phoebe Gold (Gedge) P.; m. Mary Ann Hunter, Sept. 13, 1957; children: Mark Alan, Gordon Hunter, Gay Lynn, Eric David, Scott Douglas, Julie Ann, Dale Ryan. BS in Physics, Brigham Young U., 1959. Missionary Ch. of Jesus Christ of Latter-day Saints, New England states, 1954-56; instr. math. Cen. Utah Vocat. Sch., Provo, Utah, 1958-59; assoc., design engr. Boeing Co., Seattle, Washington, 1959-62; gen. mgr. Ogden Air Logistics Ctr., Hill Air Force Base (Utah), 1962-87; sr. instr. Shipley Assocs., Bountiful, Utah, 1987-89; pres., CEO Pedersen Pub., Bountiful, 1987-89; pres., chmn. bd. Gaylen Pedersen Family Orgn., Bountiful, 1976—; dir. mktg. Redcon-Resource Data Consultants, Bountiful, 1989-90; USAF sr. mgmt. staff Ogden Air Logistics Ctr., Hill Air Force Base, 1983-87, USAF mid. mgr., 1976-83; pvt. cons., 1990—. Author: System Level, Post Production Support: Tendencies, Conditions and Principles, 1988; editor: Nutritional Herbology, Vol. I, 1987, Vol. II, 1988. Instl. rep. Boy Scouts Am., Bountiful, 1965-67, basketball coach Explorer Scouts, 1980-87; bishop Ch. Jesus Christ Latter-day Saints, 1969-73. With U.S. Army, 1956-58. Republican. Office: Gaylen Pedersen Family Orgn 1311 Indian Trail Cir Bountiful UT 84010-1461

PEDERSEN, KIM AASBERG, newsletter publisher, video producer; b. Bakersfield, Calif., Feb. 11, 1952; s. Gill Aasberg Pedersen and Gerda Lykke (Petersen) Bishop; m. Carol Ellen Stephens, May 31, 1981; children: Kory Carl, Skyler Drew. AA, Cañada Coll., Redwood City, Calif., 1972. Cook Spaghettory, Redwood City, 1972; car washer Genie Car Wash, San Diego, 1973-75; aerospace artist Foster City, Calif., 1976-78; accounts receivable clk. Beechcraft West, Hayward, Calif., 1978-85; fin. asst. II City of Fremont, Calif., 1985-94; pres., editor, owner The Monorail Soc., Calif., 1989—. Editor Monorail Newsletter, 1989—; prodr. (video) Roller Coaster Films of Kim Pedersen, 1989, Monorails of Japan, 1992.

PEDERSEN, MARTIN ALBERT, consulting engineer, surveyor; b. Rawlins, Wyo., Dec. 2, 1946; s. Rasmus and Ella (Rasmussen) P.; m. Karen Louise Bond, Aug. 26, 1967 (div. 1978); children: David Frank, Jennifer Louise; m. Patricia Ann Smith, Mar. 1, 1980; 1 child, Hans Rasmus. Student, U. Wyo., 1965. Registered land surveyor, Wyo., Mont., Idaho, Nev., Ariz., N.Mex., N.D., S.D., Colo., Calif., U.S. mineral surveyor. Surveyor Robert Jack Smith & Assocs., Rawlins, 1966-75, prin., 1975—. Scoutmaster Boy Scouts Am., Rawlins, 1969-75, dist. chmn., 1975-81; active Rawlins Search and Rescue Dive Team; mem. Christ Luth. Ch., Rotary. Mem. Wyo. Assn. Cons. Engrs. and Surveyors (pres. 1978), Wyo. State Bd. for Registration for Profl. Engrs. & Profl. Land Surveyors, Profl. Land Surveyors Wyo. (pres. 1980-81), Am. Congress Surveying and Mapping, Wyo. Engring. Soc. (sec.-treas. 1988—), Ducks Unltd., Elks. Home: 207 E Heath St Rawlins WY 82301-4307 Office: Robert Jack Smith Assocs Inc PO Box 1104 1015 Harshman St Rawlins WY 82301-1104

PEDERSON, CLAY LEONARD, nonprofit organization administrator; b. Winner, S.D., Mar. 29, 1961; s. Albert and Vernice Marie (Blomstrom) P.; m. Rita Ann Bloom, July 25, 1987; children: Joseph Fransen, Ruth Pederson, Hannah Pederson. Student, U. S.D., 1979-80, Brown Inst., 1980, Moorhead (Minn.) State U., 1985-88. News dir. Sta. KGFX Radio, Pierre, S.D., 1981-85; farm dir. Am. Agrl. Network, Fargo, N.D., 1985-88; comm. dir. Nat. Farmers Union, Denver, 1988-92, v.p. edn. and pub. rels., 1992—. Mem. Clinton Transition Team, Washington, 1992-93. Named Farm Reporter of Yr. S.D. Farmers Union, 1985, Prime Promoter S.D. Beef Industry Coun., 1985. Mem. PRSA (Colo. chpt.), Nat. Assn. of Farm Broadcasters. Democrat. Lutheran. Office: Nat Farmers Union 10065 E Harvard Ave Denver CO 80231-5968

PEDERSON, HOLLY LYNN, critical care administrator; b. Mason City, Iowa, May 27, 1956; d. Herbert Gene and Marlys Madelyn (Tibbits) P.; m. Howard Glen Yeoman; 1 child, Zachary Pederson-Yeoman. Diploma, Lutheran Hosp., 1977; BS in Health Sci., Coll. St. Francis, 1987; MAin Adminstrn Svcs., No. Michigan U., 1990, BSN, 1991. RN., Colo., Iowa, Mich.; cert. ACLS, BCLS instr. Staff nurse Des Moines (Iowa) Gen. Hosp., 1976-78; staff, charge nurse N. Colo. Med. Ctr., Greeley, Colo., 1978-82; flight nurse coord. N. Colo. Med. Ctr., Greeley, 1982-88; staff nurse on call Marquette (Mich.) Gen Hosp., 1989-91; dir. emergency svcs. Avista Hosp., Louisville, Colo., 1991-94, Bouler (Colo.) Cmty. Hosp., 1994—. Mem. Emergency Nurse Assn., Sigma Theta Tau. Home: 9839 W 99th Ave Broomfield CO 80021-4253 Office: Boulder Cmty Hosp PO Box 9019 Boulder CO 80301-9019

PEDERSON, SANFORD LLOYD, psychologist; b. Lynwood, Calif., July 13, 1952; s. Alan Fay and Maryalice (Faulkner) P.; m. Lisa Ellen Collins, Sept. 7, 1975; children: Clifford Collins, Craig Alan. BA in Psychology, U. CAlif., Riverside, 1974; postgrad., Calif. State U., San Bernardino, 1975-78; PhD in Psychology, U. Maine, 1984. Lic. psychologist, Ill., Wis. Instr. Unity (Maine) Coll., 1982-83; psychologist VA Med Ctr., Togus, Maine, 1983-85, VA Med. Ctr., North Chicago, Ill., 1985-91; coop. asst. prof. dept. psychology U. Maine, Orono, 1985; clin. asst. prof. dept. psychology Chgo. Med. Sch., North Chicago, Ill., 1986-91; pvt. practice clin. psychology Arlington Heights, Ill., 1987-91; chief psychologist VA Med. Ctr., Livermore, Calif., 1991-95; assoc. prof. psychology Wright State U., Dayton, Ohio, 1995—; presenter in field. Contbr. articles to profl. publs. NIMH fellow, 1978-81. Mem. Am. Psychol. Assn., Nat. Orgn. VA Psychologists (trustee 1988-91, chair tng. and edn. com. 1988-95, cert. of recognition 1989), Internat. Neuropsychol. Soc., Midwestern Psychol. Assn., Assn. Psychology Internship Ctrs. (assoc. editor newsletter 1988-92, editor 1992-95, bd. dirs. 1991-95), Assn. VA Chief Psychologists (sec., treas. 1993-95, chair 1995—), Psi Chi. Office: Wright State U Sch Profl Psychology Dayton OH 45434

PEDESKY, GERALDINE GOLICK, school administrator; b. Hayward, Calif., Oct. 27, 1935; d. Charles Anthony and Dolores Irene (Lemon) Golick; m. Charles Francis Pedesky, Nov. 10, 1960. BA, San Jose State Coll., 1957. Flight attendant Trans Continental Airlines, Burbank, Calif., 1958-62; office mgr. The Hertz Corp., L.A., 1964-77; v.p. adminstr. Vitousek Real Estate Sch., Honolulu, 1977—; mem., sec. Hawaii Assn. Real Estate Schs., Honolulu, 1977—. Trustee Bernice Pauahi Bishop Mus., Honolulu, 1988-94, mem. exec. com., 1994; mem. Bishop Mus. Assn., Honolulu, 1983-87 (past pres.), Bishop Mus. Svc. League, Honolulu, 1977-83 (pres. 1982); bd. dirs. Outrigger Duke Kahanamoku Found., Honollulu, 1986-94 (pres.1989). Mem. Outrigger Canoe Club (bd. dirs., sec.-treas., v.p. ops.), Honolulu Acad. Arts, Contemporary Mus. Art, Nature Conservancy. Office: Vitousek Real Estate Sch 91-1039 Laaulu St Apt F Ewa Beach HI 96706-3895

PEDITTO, CHRISTOPHER NATALE, humanities, English and communications educator; b. Riverside, N.J., Dec. 3, 1943; s. Christopher Natale and Constance (LaFreda) P.; m. Cathleen Hughes, May 1978 (div. 1982). BA, Rutgers U., 1966; MA, Calif. State U., Northridge, 1990. Instr., coord. Graterford prison writing program Montgomery County C.C., Norristown, Pa., 1984-85; instr. cmty. outreach writing program La Salle U., Phila., 1985; instr. Bus. Comm. Adelphi Bus. Coll., Van Nuys, Calif., 1985-87; instr. Bus. English and Comm., Proofreading Barclay Coll., L.A., 1987-90; adj. instr. civic outreach program L.A. Trade-Tech Coll., L.A., 1990—; instr. Columbia Coll., Hollywood, Calif., 1990-91; asst. prof. Charles R. Drew U. of Medicine & Sci., L.A., 1990—; lectr. pub. speaking/interpersonal comm. Loyola Marymont U., L.A., 1990-91. Contbg. editor: Home Planet News, 1985—; publ., gen. editor: Heat Press, 1993—; artistic dir.: (theatrical) Gray Pony Prodns., 1990—; dir. (poetry series) Open Mouth Poetry, 1982-85. NEH fellow, 1993, 94. Mem. Speech Comm. Assn., Nat. Coun. Tchrs. English, Conf. Coll. Composition and Comm., Am.-Italian Hist. Assn., Arba Sicula. Home: 1919 Scott Ave Los Angeles CA 90026-2539

PEEBLES, CAROL LYNN, immunology researcher; b. Wellington, Kans., Jan. 20, 1941; d. Harry Alexander and Phyllis Dorothy (Pyle) P. BA, Kans. State Coll. of Pittsburg, 1962, MS, 1964; cert. med. technology, St. Francis Hosp., Wichita, Kans., 1965. Med. technologist St. Francis Hosp., Wichita, 1965-74; lab. supr. allergy and immunology Scripps Clinic and Rsch. Found., La Jolla, Calif., 1974-77; sr. rsch. asst. autoimmune disease ctr. Scripps Clinic and Rsch. Found., La Jolla, 1982—; lab. supr. rheumatology lab. U. Colo. Health Scis. Ctr., Denver, 1977-82. Author workshop manual; contbr. articles to sci. publs. Mem. Am. Coll. Rheumatology, AAAS, Am. Soc. Microbiology, Am. Soc. Med. Tech., Am. Soc. Clin. Pathology. Office: Scripps Rsch Inst Rm SBR6 10666 N Torrey Pines Rd La Jolla CA 92037-1027

PEELER, STUART THORNE, petroleum industry executive and independent oil operator; b. Los Angeles, Oct. 28, 1929; s. Joseph David and Elizabeth Fiske (Boggess) P.; m. Sylvia Frances Townley, Nov. 5, 1985. B.A., Stanford U., 1950, J.D., 1953. Bar: Calif. 1953. Ptnr. Musick, Peeler & Garrett, Los Angeles, 1958-73; with Santa Fe Internat. Corp., Orange, Calif., 1973-81; v.p., sec., assoc. gen. counsel Santa Fe Internat. Corp., 1973-74, sr. v.p., gen. counsel, dir., 1975-81; vice-chmn. bd., chmn. exec. com. Supron Energy Corp., 1978-82; chmn. bd., chief exec. officer Statex Petroleum, Inc., 1982-89; chmn., pres. and chief exec. officer Putumayo Prodn. Co., 1989—; bd. dirs. Cal Mat Co., Homestake Mining Co., Homestake Gold of Australia Ltd., Chieftain Internat. Inc. Trustee J. Paul Getty Trust; mem. U.S. Tuna Team, 1957-67, capt., 1966. Served with U.S. Army, 1953-55. Decorated Army Commendation medal. Mem. State Bar Calif., Am. Judicature Soc., AIME, Theta Chi, Phi Delta Phi, Tucson Country Club. Republican. Congregationalist. Office: PO Box 35852 Tucson AZ 85740-5852

PEETE, RUSSELL FITCH, JR., aircraft appraiser; b. Memphis, June 15, 1920; s. Russell Fitch and Louise Gift (Edmondson) P.; m. Esther Eletha Mosley, Feb. 7, 1942 (dec. Jan. 1987); children: Miriam, Russell III, William; m. Margery May George, Sept. 2, 1988. BS in Aerospace Engring., Miss. State U., 1942. Dredge hand U.S. Corp. Engrs., West Memphis, Ark., 1937; rodman U.S. Corp. Engrs., Mobile, Ala., 1939; rsch. engr. Chicago & Southern Airlines, Memphis, 1941-51; tech. sales rep. Lockheed Corp., Burbank, Calif., 1951-82; ops. analyst Flying Tiger Line, L.A., 1982; dir. sales engring. Cammacorp, El Segundo, Calif., 1982-85, Anacorp, Marina Del Rey, Calif., 1987-89; aviation cons. Avcons, Sedona, Ariz., 1985—; aircraft appraiser Nat. Aircraft Appraiser Assn., Tucson, 1993—; cons. Avcons, Camarillo, Calif., 1985-86. Sec. Conejo Y's Mens Clubs, Thousand Oaks, Calif., 1960-63. With U.S. Army, 1944-46. Mem. Soc. Automotive Engrs., Exptl. Aircraft Assn., Aircraft Owners and Pilots Assn., Confederate Air Force, Internat. Aerobatic Club, Nat. Aircraft Appraisers Assn. Republican. Lutheran. Office: 63652 E Squash Blossom Ln Tucson AZ 85737-1263

PEEVER, ROBERT LEROY, electronic engineer; b. Eau Claire, Mich., Sept. 27, 1933; s. Royal Wilber and Beaulah Marion (Kendal) P.; m. Shirley Bell, 1959 (div. 1973). Student, Mich. State U., 1956-59. Test equip. stds. tech. to design engr. The Heath Co., St. Joseph, Mich., 1967-76; sr. design engr. Memcor divsn., E-Systems, Inc., Huntington, Ind., 1977-78, Fisher Engring., Huntington, Ind., 1978-83; project engr. Inex, Inc., Broomfield, Colo., 1983-84; contracting elec. engr. ARF Products, Boulder, Colo., 1984-85, Centrilist, Tulsa, 1985-88; sr. prodn. engr. Digital Storage Sys., Inc., Longmont, 1986-88; engring. mgr. ETTA Industries, Boulder, 1991; prodn. engr. Interpreter, Inc., Wheat Ridge, 1991-92. With U.S. Army, 1954-56. Republican. Home: 1708 Collyer St Longmont CO 80501-2008

PEI, YAZHONG, chemist; b. Yushu, Jilin, China, July 26, 1962; came to the U.S., 1985; s. Guanghui and Runxian (Fu) P.; m. Min Teng, July 7, 1988. BS in Chemistry, Jilin U., ChangChun, China, 1984; PhD in Chemistry, SUNY, Stony Brook, 1990. Post-doctoral fellow Parke-Davis/Warner-Lambert Co., Ann Arbor, Mich., 1990-92; scientist Chiron Corp., Emeryville, Calif., 1992-94; sr. scientist Cortex Pharmaceuticals, Inc., Irvine, Calif., 1994—. Patentee in field. Chemistry Grad. Program fellow Ministry of Edn., China, 1985. Mem. Am. Chem. Soc. Office: Cortex Pharmaceuticals Inc 15241 Barranca Pky Irvine CA 92718-2201

PEIRANO, LAWRENCE EDWARD, civil engineer; b. Stockton, Calif., May 13, 1929; s. Frank Lloyd and Esther Marie (Carigiet) P.; m. Mary Ellen Alabaster, July 26, 1952; children: Thomas Lawrence, Ellen Marie. BSCE, U. Calif., Berkeley, 1951, MSCE, 1952. Registered profl. engr., Calif., Nev.; diplomate Am. Acad. Environ. Engrs. Assoc. civil engr. Calif. Div. Water Resources, 1952-53; with Kennedy Engrs., Inc., San Francisco, 1955-94, project mgr., 1960-79, v.p., chief environ. engr., 1974-79; dir. ops. Kennedy/Jenks Engrs., Inc., San Francisco, 1979-86; sr. v.p., regional mgr. Kennedy/Jenks/Chilton, Inc., San Francisco, 1986-90; exec. v.p., chief tech. officer Kennedy/Jenks Cons., Inc. (formerly Kennedy Engrs., Inc.), San Francisco, 1990-94, also bd. dirs., chmn. bd., 1972-94; ret., 1994; spl. lectr. san. engring. U. Calif., Berkeley, 1976. Served with U.S. Army, 1953-55, Korea. James Monroe McDonald scholar, 1950-51. Fellow ASCE (life); mem. Water Environ. Fedn., Internat. Assn. on Water Quality, U. Calif. Alumni Assn., U.S. Ski Assn., Sierra Club, Chi Epsilon. Republican. Roman Catholic. Home: 3435 Blackhawk Rd Lafayette CA 94549-2326

PEIRSON, GEORGE EWELL, art director, educator; b. L.A., May 16, 1957; s. Malcolm Alan and Beth (Wanlass) P. BFA, Art Ctr. Coll. of Design, Pasadena, Calif., 1986. Photographer Griffith Park Observatory, L.A., 1981-84; owner, art dir. Peirson to Peirson Studio, West Hills, Calif., 1983—; instr. Art Workshops, L.A., 1988-89, Learning Tree U., Chatsworth, Calif., 1990-93. Art dir., films include Valentine's Day, 1986, Private Demons, 1986, The Courtyard, 1987, Hope of the Future, Escape from Lethargia, 1988, Time Scrambler, 1988, Star Quest, 1988, Star Runner, 1989, The World of Early Bird, 1989, Dominic's Castle, 1991, The Deadly Avenger, 1991, Hell Comes to Frogtown II, 1991, The Minister's Wife, 1991, Endangered, 1991, Hell Comes to Frogtown III, 1992, Eye of the Stranger, 1992, Showtime, 1992, Star Runners, 1992, Monty, 1992, Guyver, Dark Hero, 1993, Lone Tiger, 1994, Dragon Fury, 1994, Arizona Werewolf, 1994, Drifting School, 1994; prodr.: Jurassic Women, 1995, Wolves Carnival, 1995, King of Hearts, 1995, Wheel Zone Rangers, 1995. Mem. Assn. for Astron. Arts (bd. mem., v.p. 1987-89), Costumers Guild West, Assn. of Sci. Fiction and Fantasy Artists. Republican. Office: Peirson to Peirson Studio 23409 Gilmore St Canoga Park CA 91307-3314

PEISER, RICHARD BONDY, real estate developer, educator; b. Houston, Aug. 12, 1948; s. Maurice Bondy and Patricia (Levy) P.; m. Beverly Siegal, May 26, 1981; children: Allison, Michael. BA, Yale U., 1970; MBA, Harvard U., 1973; PhD, Cambridge U., 1980. Planner N.Y.C. Planning Commn., 1970-71, Gerald D. Hines Interests, Houston, 1974-75; ptnr. Peiser Bldg. Co./Doyle Stuckey Homes, Houston, 1975-77; asst. prof. So. Meth. U., Dallas, 1978-85; dir. Lusk Ctr. for Real Estate Devel. U. So. Calif., L.A., 1986—; vis. prof. Stanford U., 1981; owner Peiser Corp., Dallas and L.A., 1984—. Author: Professional Real Estte Development: The ULI Guide to the Business; editor: The Lusk Development of Real Estate and Urban Transformation. Bd. dirs. South Coast Botanical Garden, L.A., 1988—, Bus. Policy Coun., L.A., 1988—, YMCA Camp Grady Spruce, Dallas, 1986—. Fellow Urban Land Inst.; mem. Yale Club L.A. (bd. dirs. 1988—). Office: U So Calif Sch Urban and Regional 351 Von Kleinsmid Ctr Los Angeles CA 90089-0042

PEKAR, PETER, JR., business professional; b. Chgo., June 15, 1942; s. Peter Paul and Mildred (Samec) P.; m. Michele McFaull; children: Michele, Erik, William, Patrick. MA in Math., U. Ill., 1969; PhD in Bus. and Econs., Ill. Inst. Tech., 1974. V.p. Michael Allen Co., Conn., 1980-83; head bus. devel. Dun & Bradstreet, N.Y.C., 1983-87; pres. U.S.A. Bührmann-Tetterode N.V., Greenwich, Conn., 1987-91; sr. advisor Booz Allen & Hamilton, L.A., 1992—; pres., mng. dir. Claremont (Calif.) Alliance Group, 1991. Author: Planning for Non-Planners, 1980 (Top 5 Book award Am. Mgmt. Assn. 1980); contbg. editor Planning Rev., 1983-86; contbr. articles to profl. jours. Active Chgo. United Way, Am. Cancer Soc., Chgo. Mem. Am. Mgmt. Assn., The Planning Forum, Univ. Club, N.Y.C., Chgo. Home: 2272 Indian Hill Blvd Claremont CA 91711 Office: Booz Allen & Hamilton 5220 Pacific Con Dr 390 Los Angeles CA 90045

PELKEY, TEENA FERRIS, elementary education educator, consultant; b. San Rafael, Calif., Dec. 3, 1949; d. Ernest Herbert and Fern Cleone (Wyman) Simmons; children: April F., Allison M. AA, Solano Coll., 1970; BA, Calif. State U., 1987. Credential multiple subject profl. clear, Calif. Lectr. to high sch. civics classes Vallejo, Calif., 1986; substitute tchr. Vallejo (Calif.) Unified Sch. Dist., 1987, instr. jr. high level, 1988; 1st grade instr. St. Apollinaris Sch., Napa, Calif., 1988-90; substitute Del Norte Unified Sch. Dist., Crescent City, Calif., 1991-92; substitute tchr. Vallejo Unified Sch. Dist., 1992—; del. to Napa/Solano PTA Coun., Vallejo, 1986-87; bd. dirs. Interagy. Commn., Vallejo, 1987-90; gen. mgr. Teena Ferris Pelkey Prodns., TFP Enterprises-Polit. Coords.; long-term substitute tchr. 3rd grade Notre Dame Sch., Vacaville, Calif., Highland Elem. Sch., Vallejo; 2nd grade instr., lang. arts instr. Al-Noor Elem. Sch., Vallejo. Author: Policy Manual Affirmative Action, 1989, 90. Bd. dirs. Greater Vallejo Recreation Dist., 1987-90, vice chair, 1990; bd. dirs. North Bay Opera Assn., Sister City Assn. of Vallejo, 1989-90, 92, v.p. fund raising, 1993; coord. United Dem. Campaign, Lower Solano County, Calif., 1992; Solano County coord. spl. election campaign for Senator Mike Thompson, Solano County, 1993; Dem. del. 7th Assembly Caucus; pres. Vallejo Sister City Assn., 1995—; apptd. bd. dirs. Vallejo Alcohol Policy Coalition; assembly dit. del. Calif. State Party Conv. Recipient award for svc., 1990, Challenge the Future award, 1989, Dare 2 B Different award, Cert. of Appreciation, Assembly Dems. of Calif., 1992, Cert. of Gratitude Akashi, Japan (sister city to Vallejo), Plaque of Gratitude Greater Vallejo Recreation Dist. Mem. Internat. Reading Assn., Solano County League of Women Voters, Vallejo Sister City Assn., United Dems. of Vallejo, Women In the Arts. Democrat. Roman Catholic. Home: 216 Sandy Neck Way Vallejo CA 94591-7850

PELLA, JEROME JACOB, statistician; b. Pierz, Minn., Mar. 13, 1939; s. Joseph Pella and Louisa Petronella (Schommer) Thrasher; m. Judith Suzanne Annable, Dec. 8, 1979; children: John Knull, Kathleen Knull, Daniel Knull. BS, U. Minn., 1961; MS, U. Wash., 1964, PhD, 1967. Statistician Inter-American Tropical Tuna Commn., La Jolla, Calif., 1965-69, Nat. Marine Fisheries Svc., Auke Bay, Alaska, 1969—; cons. Pacific Salmon Commn., Vancouver, B.C., Can., 1982—. Author: (with others) Stock Mixtures, 1987. Mem. Am. Inst. Fishery Biologists, Sigma Xi. Office: Nat Marine Fisheries Svc 11305 Glacier Hwy Juneau AK 99801-8626

PELLEGRINI, CARLOS ALBERTO, surgeon, educator; b. Freye, Argentina, June 23, 1946; m. Vivien Imperial; children: Michael David, John Edward. MD, U. Rosario Med. Sch., 1971. Intern in surgery Rosario U. Hosp., Argentina, 1970-71; resident in gen. surgery Rosario U. Hosp., 1971-75; fellow in surgery U. Chgo., 1975-76, resident in surgery, 1976-79; asst. prof. U. Calif., San Francisco, 1979-84; assoc. prof. U. Calif., 1984-89, prof., 1989-92; prof., chmn. dept. surgery U. Wash., Seattle, 1993—; staff physician VA Med. Ctr., San Francisco, 1979-92, chief surgical outpatient clinics, 1979-89, chief exptl. surgery, 1980-89; attending physician U. Calif., San Francisco, 1979-92, chief blue surgery svc., 1987-92, asst. chief surgery faculty practice, 1988-92, dir. ctr. for study of gastrointestinal motility and secretions, 1989-92; attending surgeon, U. Wash., 1993—; surgery physician VA Med. Ctr., Seattle, 1993—; attending surgeon Harborview Med. Ctr., Seattle, 1993—. Fellow ACS (internat. rels. com. 1983—, subcom. on guest scholars 1985-88, chmn. 1988-89, liaison and rep. to Latin Am. Congress of Fellows 1989-92, com. on motion pictures 1988—, exec. com. mem. 1991, chmn. 1993, chmn. gen. surgery program com. No. Calif. chpt. 1980-83, councilor San Francisco 1984-86, sec.-treas. 1986-89, pres.-elect 1989-90, pres. 1990, chmn. No. Calif. dist. #1 com. on applicants 1987-92); mem. AAAS, AMA (cons. diagnostic & therapeutic tech. assessment 1992), Am. Assn. Study of Liver Disease, Am. Motility Soc., Am. Gastroenterological Assn., Am. Surg. Assn., Am. Bd. Surgery (guest examiner 1985, 88), ACGME (residency review com., rep.), Soc. Surgery of Alimentary Tract (mem. membership com. 1985-89), Collegium Internationale Chirurgiae Digestivae (U.S.A. sect., pres. 1992-94, chmn. edn. com., 1995—), Pan Pacific Surg. Assn. (v.p. 1993), Assn. Acad. Surgery, H.C. Naffziger Surg. Soc., San Francisco Med. Soc., Assn. Argentina de Cirugia, Soc. Univ. Surgeons, Western Surg. Assn., Pacific Coast Surg. Assn., Soc. Am. Gastrointestinal Endoscopy Surgeons, Soc. Argentina de Cirugia Digestiva (hon.), Internat. Hepato-Biliary-Pancreatic Assn., Soc. Internat. de Chirugie, Soc. Clin. Surgery, Southwestern Clin. Congress, Soc. Colombiana de Cirugia, Calif. Acad. Medicine, North Pacific Surg. Assn., Soc. Surg. Chmn., Surg. Biology Club, Esophageal Surg. Club, The Pancreas Club (chmn. local arrangements com. 1986, 92). Home: 11755 NE 36th Pl Bellevue WA 98005-1234 Office: U Wash Dept Surgery 1959 NE Pacific St Seattle WA 98195-0004

PELLEGRINI, CRISTIAN ANDRES, insurance company executive, consultant; b. Buenos Aires, Argentina, Sept. 10, 1966; came to U.S., Feb. 2, 1986; s. Vicente Francisco Andres P. and Maria Cristina Savioli Schultz; m. Gabriela Rossi, June 1986 (div. Dec. 1987); m. Viviana Laura Bierschuvall Pellegrini, May 15, 1994. Student, Calif. State U., Northridge, 1995—. Programmer Varig Airlines, L.A., 1986-88, David Grant Consulting, Encino, Calif., 1988-89; principal Software Evolution, Sherman Oaks, Calif., 1989-93; MIS dir. Centerstone, Woodland Hills, Calif., 1993—. Office: Centerstone Ins 20750 Ventura Blvd #350 Woodland Hills CA 91364

PELLETIER, KENNETH R., behavioral physician, educator, author; b. Nashua, N.H., Apr. 27, 1946; s. Roger Norman and Lucy Barbara (Leonetti) P.; m. Elizabeth Anne Berryhill, Oct. 28, 1980. BA in Psychology, U. Calif., Berkeley, 1969, PhD in Clin. Psychology, 1974; MD, Ministry of Health, 1985. Lic. clin. psychologist, Calif. Assoc. clin. prof., dept. medicine and dept. psychiatry Univ. Calif., Sch. of Medicine, San Francisco, 1974-90; clin. assoc. prof. Stanford Ctr. for Disease Prevention Stanford U. Sch. Medicine, Calif., 1990—, dir. Stanford Corp. health program, 1990—; v.p. Healthtrac, Inc., Menlo Park, Calif., 1995—; sr. clin. assoc. Johnson & Johnson Health Mgmt. Inc., New Brunswick, N.J., Santa Monica, Calif., 1985-95; advisor U.S. Dept. Health and Human Svcs.; bd. Nat. Resource Ctr. on Worksite Health Promotion, Blue Shield, The Can. Ministry of Health, World Health Orgn.; bd. dirs. Health Sys. Internat., Am. Inst. of Stress, Conservation Internat., Calif. Wellness Found., Nat. Health Mgmt. Found., Am. Holistic Med. Assn. Co-author: Consciousness: East and West, 1976; author: Mind as Healer, Mind as Slayer, 1977, rev. edit., 1992, Toward a Science of Consciousness, 1978, Holistic Medicine: From Stress to Optimum Health, 1979, Longevity: Fulfilling our Biological Potential, 1981, rev. edit., 1991, Health People in Unhealthy Places: Stress and Fitness at Work, 1984, Sound Mind, Sound Body, 1994; mem. editorial bd. Medical Self-Care Mag., Am. Jour. Health Promotion, Longevity, Am. Health; contbr. over 250 articles to jours. Named Woodrow Wilson fellow Woodrow Wilson Found., 1970, USPHS Svc. fellow, 1973-74. Mem. AAAS, Am. Psychol. Assn., Washington Bus. Group on Health, Soc. Behavioral Medicine, Am. Heart Assoc. Office: Stanford Univ Sch Medicine 1000 Welch Rd Palo Alto CA 94304-1811

PELLETT, HOWARD ARTHUR, tax investigator; b. Monterey Park, Calif., May 27, 1939; s. Howard Holland and Dorothy Lois (Judson) P.; m. Carol Lynn Underhill, Feb. 19, 1960; children: William, Michael, Stephen, Douglas, Matthew. AA, E. L.A. Coll., 1959; BS, L.A. State Coll., 1961. Agt. IRS, L.A., Bellingham, Wash., 1961-67, Anchorage, Juneau, Alaska, 1968-71; asst. dist. dir., group mgr. IRS, Anchorage, 1971-74; returns program mgr. IRS, Seattle, 1974-78; group mgr. IRS, Everett, Wash., 1978-80; agt. IRS, Seattle, 1980—. Sec.-treas. Friends of Skagit County, Mount Vernon, Wash., 1993—; pres. Guemes Island (Wash.) Property Owners Assn., 1991—. Mem. Beta Alpha Psi. Democrat. Home: 421A Guemes Island Rd Anacortes WA 98221 Office: IRS 915 2nd Ave Ste 2290 Seattle WA 98174-1001

PELOSI, NANCY, congresswoman; b. Balt., Mar. 26, 1941; d. Thomas J. D'Alesandro Jr.; m. Paul Pelosi; children: Nancy Corinne, Christine, Jacqueline, Paul, Alexandra. Grad., Trinity Coll. Former chmn. Calif. State Dem. Com., 1981; committeewoman Dem. Nat. Com., 1976, 80, 84; fin. chmn. Dem. Senatorial Campaign Com., 1987; mem. 99th-102d Congresses from 5th Calif. dist., 1987-1992, 103rd Congress from 8th Calif. dist., 1993—; mem. appropriations com., subcoms. labor, HHD & edn., fgn. ops., D.C.; intelligence (select) com., standard official conduct com. Office: US House of Rep 2457 Rayburn Washington DC 20515-0508*

PELOTTE, DONALD EDMOND, bishop; b. Waterville, Maine, Apr. 13, 1945; s. Norris Albert and Margaret Yvonne (LaBrie) P. AA, Eymard Sem. and Jr. Coll., Hyde Park, N.Y., 1965; BA, John Carroll U., 1969; MA, Fordham U., 1971, PhD, 1975. Ordained priest Roman Cath. Ch., 1972. Provincial superior Blessed Sacrament, Cleve., from 1978; ordained coadjutor bishop Diocese of Gallup, N.Mex., 1986-90, bishop, 1990—; nat. bd. dirs. Maj. Superiors of Men, Silver Spring, Md., 1981-86, Tekakwitha Conf., Great Falls, Mont., 1981—. Author: John Courtney Murray: Theologian in Conflict, 1976. 1st native Am. bishop. Mem. Cath. Theol. Soc. Am., Am. Cath. Hist. Soc. *

PELTASON, JACK WALTER, university president; b. St. Louis, Aug. 29, 1923; s. Walter B. and Emma (Hartman) P.; m. Suzanne Toll, Dec. 21,1946; children: Nancy Hartman, Timothy Walter H., Jill K. BA, U. Mo., 1943, MA, 1944, LLD (hon.), 1978; AM, Princeton U., 1946, PhD, 1947; LLD (hon.), U. Md., 1979, Ill. Coll., 1979, Gannon U., 1980, U. Maine, 1980, Union Coll., 1981, Moorehead (N.D.) State U., 1980; LHD (hon.), 1980, Ohio State U., 1980, Mont. Coll. Mineral Scis. and Tech., 1982, Buena Vista Coll., 1982, Assumption Coll., 1983, Chapman Coll., 1986, U. Ill., 1989. Asst. prof. Smith Coll., Mass., 1947-51; asst. prof. polit. sci. U. Ill., Urbana, 1951-52, assoc. prof., 1953-59, dean Coll. Liberal Arts and Scis., 1960-64, chancellor, 1967-77; vice chancellor acad. affairs U. Calif., Irvine, 1964-67, chancellor, 1984-92; pres. U. Calif. System, Oakland, 1992—, Am. Coun. Edn., Washington, 1977-84; Cons. Mass. Little Hoover Commn., 1950. Author: The Missouri Plan for the Selection of Judges, 1947, Federal Courts and the Political Process, 1957, Fifty-eight Lonely Men, 1961, Understanding the Constitution, 13th edit., 1994, orig. edition, 1949, (with James M. Burns) Government By the People, 16th edit., 1995, orig. edit., 1952; contbr. articles and revs. to profl. jours. Recipient James Madison medal Princeton U., 1982. Fellow Am. Acad. Arts and Scis.; mem. Am. Polit. Sci. Assn. (council 1952-54), Phi Beta Kappa, Phi Kappa Phi, Omicron Delta Kappa, Alpha Phi Omega, Beta Gamma Sigma. Home: 18 Whistler Ct Irvine CA 92715-4069 also: 70 Rincon Rd Kensington CA 94707-1047 Office: U Calif Office of Pres 300 Lakeside Dr Oakland CA 94612-3550

PELTON, HAROLD MARCEL, mortgage broker; b. Montreal, Que., Can., Jan. 24, 1922; s. Grover Cleveland and Denise (Pigeon) P.; m. Frances Farley, June 1947 (div. 1968); children: Mary Virginia Joyner, Diane Jean Slagowski; m. Virginia L. King, July 11, 1970. Student, L.A. City Coll., 1948-49, Anthony Schs., Van Nuys, Calif., 1966. Lic. real estate real broker, Calif. Stockbroker, agt. Mitchum, Jones, Templeton Assurance Co., L.A., 1957-60; owner Assurance Investment Co., Van Nuys, Calif., 1960-65; sales syndicator TSI Investment Co., L.A., 1965-69; pres., owner Univest Co., Beverly Hills, Calif., 1970-72, Am. Oil Recovery, L.A., 1973-79; v.p. Newport Pacific Funding Co., Newport Beach, Calif., 1979-81; chmn. bd. dirs. TD Publs., El Toro, Calif., 1981-83; pres., broker HP Fin., Inc., Laguna Hills, Calif., 1983-. Contbg. editor Am. Oil Recovery newspaper, 1973-79; editor Trust Deed Jour., 1981-83. Served with U.S. Army, 1942-46, PTO. Mem. L. A. Mus. Art, Laguna Hills C. of C., Kiwanis, Toastmasters. Republican. Office: HP Fin Inc 24942 Georgia Sue Laguna Hills CA 92653-4323

PELTON, VIRGINIA LUE, small business owner; b. Utica, Kans., Apr. 15, 1928; d. Forrest Selby and Nellie (Simmons) Meier; m. Theodore Trower King Jr., Oct. 27, 1956 (div.); m. Harold Marcel Pelton, July 11, 1970; children: Mary Virginia Joyner, Diana Jean. Student, Kans. State U., 1946-47, Ft. Hays U., 1947-48, Washington U., St. Louis, 1950-51. Instr. Patricia Stevens Modeling Sch., Kansas City, Mo., 1948-50; model various cos., Calif. and N.Y., 1951-53; fashion cons. Giorgio, Beverly Hills, Calif., 1967-68, Charles Gallay, Beverly Hills, 1975-77, Dorso's, Beverly Hills, 1977-79; buyer, mgr. giftware Slavick's, Laguna Hills, Calif., 1980-83; owner P.J. Secretarial Svcs., Laguna Hills, 1980—; v.p. HP Fin. Inc., Laguna Hills, 1983—. Editor Profl. Network newsletter, 1980—. Sec. Leukemia Soc. Am., Santa Ana, 1985—; mem. Laguna Beach Art Mus., 1986—. Mem. Profl. Network Assn. (sec. 1986—), Market Plus The Consumer Network, Saddleback C. of C., Laguna Hills Club, Kappa Delta. Republican. Methodist. Home: 24942 Georgia Sue Laguna Beach CA 92653-4323

PELZL, BEVERLY RUTH, perioperative nurse; b. Springer, N.Mex., Sept. 11, 1943; d. Earnest W. and Pauline F. Weir; m. Robert M. Pelzl, Dec. 18, 1965; 1 child, Virginia. Diploma, Regina Sch. Nursing, 1964. RN, N.Mex.; cert. oper. rm. nurse, RN first asst. Clin. nurse specialist III gen. surgery, gynecology, laparoscopy and urology St. Joseph Hosp., Albuquerque. Mem. Assn. Operating Room Nurses.

PEMBERTON, MATTHEW ANTHONY, insurance agent; b. Vallejo, Calif., Apr. 2, 1947; s. Matthew I. and Mildred (Commottor) Cotabish; m. Mary Lafollette, Nov. 24, 1972 (div. 1978); 1 child, Sally Elizabeth; m. Suzan Leigh Kutchins, June 5, 1982; children: Alexandra, Vanessa. BA in Econs. with honors, U. Calif., Berkeley, 1969; MA in Econs., Northwestern U., Ill., 1971. CLU; Chartered Fin. Cons. Instr. econs. U. Ky. & U. Louisville, Ft. Knox, 1971-73; spl. agt. NML Ins. Co., San Francsico, 1974—; investment officer Robert W. Baird & Co., Inc., San Francisco, 1984—. 1st lt. U.S. Army, 1971-73. Office: Northwestern/Baird 1 Sansome St Ste 1700 San Francisco CA 94104-4448

PEMBERTON, RANDALL GRANT, industrial engineer; b. Sacramento, Jan. 29, 1953; s. Rodney Olson and Diana Joyce (Button) Kohrs; m. Vivian Lee Koirtyohann, May 29, 1976; children: Grant Austin, Travis Andrew. Student, Purdue U., 1971-73; BS in Indsl. Engring., U. Mo., 1976; MSE in Indsl. Engring., Ariz. State U., 1992. Indsl. engr. B F Goodrich, Akron, Ohio, 1976-78; aero systems engr. Gen. Dynamics, Ft. Worth, 1978-79; sr. indsl. engr. Am. Airlines, Ft. Worth, 1979-83, mgr. fleet planning, 1983-87; sr. rsch. analyst United Airlines, Chgo., 1987-89; cons. Integrated Systems Solutions, Phoenix, 1989-92; cons. supr. Univ. Tech. Assistance Program, Bozeman, Mont., 1993—. Coach Gilbert (Ariz.) Youth Soccer Assn., 1993-94; vol. musician Morning Sounds, Bozeman, 1994. U. Mo. Honors scholar, 1975. Mem. Inst. Indsl. Engrs. (chpt. pres. 1973—, award of Excellence 1983), Soc. Mfg. Engrs., Tau Beta Pi, Alpha Pi Mu. Democrat. Home: 1208 E Campbell Ave Gilbert AZ 85234-4865

PEÑA, FEDERICO FABIAN, federal official; b. Laredo, Tex., Mar. 15, 1947; s. Gustavo J. and Lucille P.; m. Ellen Hart, May 1988. BA, U. Tex., Austin, 1969, JD, 1972. Bar: Colo. 1973. Ptnr. Pena & Pena, Denver, 1973-83; mayor City and County of Denver, 1983-91; pres. Peña Investment Advisors, Inc., Denver, 1991-93; sec. U.S. Dept. of Transp., Washington, 1993—; assoc. Harvard U. Ctr. for Law and Edn., Cambridge, Mass.; mem. Colo. Bd. Law Examiners. Mem. Colo. Ho. of Reps., 1979-83, Dem. leader, 1981. Named Outstanding House Dem. Legislator, Colo. Gen. Assembly, 1981. Roman Catholic. Home: 3517 Sterling Ave Alexandria VA 22304-1834 Office: Dept of Transportation Office Sec 400 7th St SW Washington DC 20590-0001*

PEÑA, HEATHER MARIA, internist; b. North Hampton, Mass., Sept. 30, 1955; d. Cesareo Dennis and Eloise Verna (Morrison) P.; m. Christopher Searl. BS summa cum laude, Tufts U., 1977; MD, Harvard U., 1981. Intern, resident in internal medicine UCLA Hosp. and Clinics, 1981-84; staff physician Santa Monica (Calif) Hosp., St. John's Hosp., 1992—, Oceanview Med. Group at Pritikin Long Ctr., Santa Monica, Calif., 1984—. Mem. Am. Heart Assn. Epidemiology Council. Mem. Am. Coll. Physicians (assoc.), Harvard Med. Hamilton-Hunt Soc., Phi Beta Kappa. Democrat.

PENA, JUAN JOSE, interpreter; b. Hagerman, N.Mex., Dec. 13, 1945; s. Rosa Pena; m. Petra Cervantes, Dec. 22, 1974 (div. 1982); children: Federico Ezequiel, Margarita María Blea. BA, N.Mex. Highlands U., 1968, MA, 1972, postgrad. With Albert Garcia Gen. Contr., Las Vegas, N.Mex., 1955-67; teaching asst. N.Mex. Highlands U., Las Vegas, 1971-72, prof. Spanish, Chicano studies, 1972--78; teaching asst. U. N.Mex., Albuquerque, 1978-79; attendant N.Mex. State Mental Hosp., Las Vegas, 1982-83; staff and supervisory interpreter U.S. Dist. Ct. N.Mex., Albqeurque, 1983—; head Raza Unida del to PLO in Lebanon, 1981, head negotiator with Iranians for release of 2 Chicanos and 1 Indian; supr ct. interpreters and reporters sect. U.S. Dist. Ct. N.Mex. Author collection of poetry: Angustias y Remembranzas; contbr. articles to profl. jours.; author play: Canto a La Raza, 1978. Pres. Dads Against Discrimination, Albuquerque, 1993—; chmn. bd. trustees No. N.Mex. Legal Svcs., Las Vegas, 1972-81; mem. exec. com. Ind. Socialist Parties of Latin Am. With U.S. Army, 1969-70. Decorated Bronze Star medal. Mem. N.Mex. Translator and Interpreters Assn. (pres. 1984-86), Nat. Assn. Judiciary Interpreters (sec. 1986-88), Nat. Partido Raza Unida (pres. 1976-81), N.Mex. Partido Raza Unida (pres. 1972-75, 77-78), Vietnam Vets. Am. (vice chmn. chpt. 318 1993—), Vietnam Vets. N.Mex., Am. GI Forum (Alubquerque Chpt. 1, comdr. 1993-94), Nat. Assn. Chicano Studies (founding mem.), N.Mex. Chicano Studies Assn. (pres. 1972-78), Phi Sigma Iota. Democrat. Roman Catholic. Home: 1115 9th St SW Albuquerque NM 87102-4027 Office: US Dist Ct Dist of NM 421 Gold Ave SW Rm 108 Albuquerque NM 87102-3254

PENDERGHAST, THOMAS FREDERICK, business educator; b. Cin., Apr. 23, 1936; s. Elmer T. and Dolores C. (Huber) P.; BS, Marquette U., 1958; MBA, Calif. State U., Long Beach, 1967; D in Bus. Adminstrn. Nova U., 1987; m. Marjorie Craig, Aug. 12, 1983; children: Brian, Shawna, Steven, Dean, Maria. Sci. programmer Autonetics, Inc., Anaheim, Calif., 1960-64; bus. programmer Douglas Missile & Space Ctr., Huntington Beach, Calif., 1964-66; computer specialist N.Am. Rockwell Co., 1966-69; asst. prof. Calif. State U., Long Beach, 1969-72; prof. Sch. Bus. and Mgmt., Pepperdine U., Los Angeles, 1972—; spl. adviser Commn. on Engring. Edn., 1968; v.p. Visual Computing Co., 1969-71; founder, pres. Scoreboard Animation Systems, 1971-77; exec. v.p. Microfilm Identification Systems, 1977-79; pres. Data Processing Auditors, Inc., 1981—; data processing cons. designing computer system for fin. health and mfg. orgns., 1972—. Mem. Orange County Blue Ribbon Com. on Data Processing, 1973; mem. Orange County TEC Policy Bd., 1982-87; mgmt. and organization devel. cons. Assn. Psychological Type, 1993—. Served to lt. USNR, 1958-60. Cert. in data processing. Mem. Users of Automatic Info. Display Equipment (pres. 1966). Author: Entrepreneurial Simulation Program, 1988. Home: 17867 Bay St Fountain Valley CA 92708-4443

PENDLETON, ALAN R., conservation agency executive; b. Riverside, Calif., May 26, 1940; s. Roy Clayton and Carolyn (Parker) P.; m. Joyce Ellen Edwards, Aug. 22, 1964; 1 child, David. AB, U. Calif., Berkeley, 1961; JD, U. Calif., San Francisco, 1969. Bar: Calif. Tchr. Anderson Valley Sch. Dist., Boonville, Calif., 1970; atty. San Francisco Bay Conservation and Devel. Commn., 1971-76, chief regulatory functions, 1976-81, dep. dir., 1981-83, exec. dir., 1983—; bd. dirs. East Brothers Light Station, Richmond, Calif., Flowerlane, Inc., Oakland, Calif.; mem. environ. com. 9th Dist. Ct. Calif., 1985—. Contbr. articles to profl. jours. Mem. Save San Francisco Bay Assn., Berkeley. Lt. USAF, 1962-67. Mem. Bay Area Planning Dirs. Assn. (bd. dirs. 1987—), Calif. Bar Assn., Sierra Club. Office: San Francisco Bay Conservation & Devel Commn 30 Van Ness Ave Ste 2011 San Francisco CA 94102-6026

PENDLETON, JOAN MARIE, microprocessor designer; b. Cleve., July 7, 1954; d. Alvin Dial and Alta Beatrice (Brown) P. BS in Physics, Elec. Engring., MIT, 1976; MSEE, Stanford U., 1978; PhDEE, U. Calif., Berkeley, 1985. Sr. design engr. Fairchild Semiconductor, Palo Alto, Calif., 1978-82; staff engr. Sun Microsystems, Mountain View, Calif., 1986-87; CEO Harvest VLSI Design Ctr. Inc., Palo Alto, 1988—; dir. engring. Silicon Engring. Inc., Scotts Valley, Calif., 1994—; cons., designer computer sci. dept. U. Calif., Berkeley, 1988-90. Contbr. articles to profl. jours.; inventor, patnetee serpentine charge transfer device. Recipient several 1st, 2d and 3d place awards U.S. Rowing Assn., Fairchild Tech. Achievement award, 1982, 1st place A award Fed. Internat. Soc Aviron, 1991. Mem. IEEE, Assn. for Computing Machinery, Lake Merritt Rowing Club, Stanford Rowing Club, U.S. Rowing Assn. Home: 1950 Montecito Ave Apt 22 Mountain View CA 94043-4334

PENDLETON, OTHNIEL ALSOP, fundraiser, clergyman; b. Washington, Aug. 22, 1911; s. Othniel Alsop and Ingeborg (Berg) P.; m. Flordora Mellquist, May 16, 1935; children: John, James (dec.), Thomas, Ann, Susan. AB, Union Coll., Schenectady, N.Y., 1933; BD, Eastern Bapt. Theol. Sem., 1936; MA, U. Pa., 1936, PhD, 1945; postgrad., Columbia U., 1937-38. Ordained to ministry Bapt. Ch., 1936. Pastor chs. Jersey City, 1935-39, Phila., 1939-43; dean Sioux Falls Coll., S.D., 1943-45; fund raiser Am. Bapt. Ch., N.Y.C., 1945-47; fund-raiser Mass. Bapt. Ch., Boston, 1947-54; fund-raiser Seattle, Chgo., Boston, Washington, N.Y.C. and Paris, France, 1955-64, Westwood, Mass., 1971-84; staff mem. Marts & Lundy, Inc., N.Y.C., 1964-71; lectr. Andover-Newton (Mass.) Sem., 1958, Boston U. Sch. Theology, 1958, Harvard U., Cambridge, Mass., 1977-84; cons. Grant MacEwan Coll., Edmonton, Alta., Can. Author: New Techniques for Church Fund Raising, 1955, Fund Raising: A Guide to Non-Profit Organizations, 1981; contbr. articles in field to profl. jours. Address: 529 Berkeley Ave Claremont CA 91711-4227

PENDLETON, VERNE H., JR., geologist; b. Medford, Oreg., Sept. 17, 1945; s. Verne H. and Ilene Clara Koepsell) P.; m. Paula Jean Obenshain, June 22, 1968. BS in Geology, Oreg. State U., 1973. Geologist/engring. inspector/tech. Soils Testing Lab., Inc., Medford, 1976-81; rsch. tech. Dept. Civil Engring., U. Idaho, Moscow, 1982-84; constrn. geologist, lab. mgr. Soils Testing Lab., Inc., Medford, 1984-88; quality control insp. LTM Inc., Medford, 1988-91; sr. materials specialist/coord. Hwy. div. Oreg. Dept. Transp., Bend, 1991-92; ATE region materials inspector hwy. div. Oreg. Dept. Transp., Roseburg, 1992—. With U.S. Army, 1966-69. Republican. Ch. of the Nazarene. Home: 1834 NE Todd St Roseburg OR 97470-5601

PENG, ZHONG, electrical engineer; b. Tianjin, China, May 20, 1946; came to U.S, 1981; s. Shichang and Rungeng (Bu) P. BSEE, Tianjin U., 1968; MSEE, Purdue U., 1982; MS in Computer Engring., U. So. Calif., 1984. Registered profl. engr., Calif. Elec. engr. Henan Power Adminstrn., Anyang, China, 1968-78; rsch. assoc. Electric Power Rsch. Inst., Beijing, 1980-81; lectr. Calif. State U., L.A., 1985; power system analyst CAE Electronics, Montreal, Que., Can., 1987-89; power system engr. Pacific Gas & Electric, San Francisco, 1985-87, elec. engr., 1989-94; utility engr. Nev. Pub. Svc. Commn., Las Vegas, 1994—. Contbr. articles to profl. jours. Coord. alumni svcs. Grad. Sch. Chinese Acad. Scis., 1991—. Mem. IEEE (sr., prize paper award 1987, 88). Office: Pub Svc Commn State of Nev 555 E Washington 4600 Las Vegas NV 89101

PENISTON, LORRAINE CAROL, special education educator, therapeutic recreation specialist; b. East Orange, N.J., July 12, 1959; d. Leonard and Carol Elaine (Harris) P. BA, Kean Coll. N.J., 1981, MA, 1983; PhD, U. N.Mex., 1990. Activity therapist Newark Extended Care, 1981-82; activity therapy program asst. Green Brook (N.J.) Regional Ctr., 1982-83; vocat. counselor Occupational Ctr. Essex County, Orange, N.J., 1983-84; latch key coord. YMCA Mountainside, Albuquerque, 1984-85; asst. supr. therapeutic site City of Albuquerque, 1985; dir. recreation therapy Manor Care Heights, Albuquerque, 1985-88; coord. therapeutic recreation svcs. Care Unit Hosp., Albuquerque, 1988-89; therapeutic recreation specialist Lovelace Hosp., Albuquerque, 1988-94; learning disabilities specialist U. N.Mex. Ctr. for Acad. Program Support, Albuquerque, 1989—. Editor Learning Disability Newsbriefs, 1991-94; reviewer Therapeutic Recreation Jour., 1990-94; assoc. editor Therapeutic Recreation Jour., 1996—. Bicycling bd. dirs. City of Albuquerque, 1987; ombudsman for elderly State of N.Mex., Albuquerque, 1986. Mem. Nat. Parks and Recreation Assn., Nat. Therapeutic Recreation Assn., N.Mex. Coll. Reading and Learning Assn., N.Mex. Coun. on Learning Disabilities, N.Mex. Parks and Recreation Assn. (br. pres. 1988), Coll. Reading and Learning Assn. (chair learning disabilities Spl. Interest Group 1991-94), Phi Epsilon. Office: Univ NMex CAPS 3d Fl Zimmerman Library Albuquerque NM 87131

PENKAVA, RICHARD ANTON, secondary school administrator; b. N.Y.C., July 12, 1925; s. Antonin and Josephine (Skudera) P.; m. Paula Elizabeth Schwarzenberg, July 22, 1950; children: Paula Cathy, Richard, Barbara Mila. BS in Social Scis., CCNY, 1949; MA, UCLA, 1950; diploma, U.S. Army War Coll., 1971; EdD, U. So. Calif., 1974. Cert. secondary sch. adminstr., counselor, pupil personnel svcs., Calif. Tchr. adult evening schs. L.A., 1951-56; tchr.-counselor L.A. City Schs., 1950-58, tchr.-coord., 1958-61; tchr.-coord. U.S. DOD Dependents Schs., Wuerzburg, Germany, 1961-62; asst. prin. U.S. DOD Dependents Schs., Frankfurt, Germany, 1962-65; secondary sch. prin. U.S. DOD Dependents Schs., Zweibruecken, Germany, 1965-90; edn. cons. Laguna Hills, Calif., 1991—. 1st lt. U.S. Army, 1943-46. Decorated Legion of Merit. Mem. Mil. Order of World Wars (chpt. comdr. 1991-93, dept. comdr. 1993-94), ASCD (assoc.), Res. Officers Assn. (pres. 1976-78), Phi Delta Kappa. Republican. Home and Office: 3191 Via Buena Vis Laguna Hills CA 92653-3027

PENN, ARTHUR HILLER, film and theatre producer; b. Phila., Sept. 27, 1922; s. Harvy and Sonia (Greenberg) P.; m. Peggy Maurer, Jan. 27, 1955; children: Matthew, Molly. Student, Joshua Logan's Stage Co., Black Mountain Coll., Asheville, N.C., U. Perugia, Florence, Italy, Actors Studio, Los Angeles; studied with Michael Chekhov. Joined Army Theatre Co. during World War II; worked in TV, 1951-53; producer plays for Broadway theatre including The Miracle Worker (Tony award 1960), All The Way Home, Toys in the Attic, Two for the Seesaw, In the Council House, Wait Until Dark, Sly Fox, Monday After the Miracle; films include The Left-Handed Gun, 1957, The Miracle Worker, 1962, Mickey One, 1964, The Chase, 1965, Bonnie and Clyde, 1967, Alice's Restaurant, 1969, Little Big Man, 1971, Night Moves, 1975, The Missouri Breaks, 1976, Four Friends, 1981, Target, 1985, Dead of Winter, 1987; co-dir. film Visions of Eight, 1973; dir. theatre: Golden Boy, Hunting Cockroaches. Office: care Sam Cohn Internat Creative Mgmt 40 W 57th St New York NY 10019-4001 also: William Morris Agy 151 S El Camino Dr Beverly Hills CA 90212-2704

PENN, MEADE LOVE THOMAS, social sciences researcher, library assistant; b. New Roads, La., Nov. 18, 1967; d. Windsor Pipes Jr. and Alice (Brasfield) Thomas; m. Douglas Robert Penn, Apr. 22, 1995. BS in Psychology and Polit. Sci., U. of the South, 1989; MA in Internat. Studies, U. Denver, 1992, postgrad., 1992—. Intern Brit. Consulate, Boston, 1988; asst. mgr. Japanese macaque rsch. facility U. Colo. Health Sci. Ctr., Denver, 1989-92; rsch. asst. Sierra Club Legal Def. Fund, Denver, 1990; mgr. rsch. fellowship program Wildlife Conservation Internat., Bronx, N.Y., 1992; rsch. asst. policy agendas project U. Denver, 1993, asst. pub. svc. desk Penrose Libr., 1989—, asst. to reference dept. Penrose Libr., 1993—; facilitator Environ. Policy Clinics, Grad. Sch. Internat. Studies, U. Denver, 1991—. Editor: (conf. procs.) Conservation and Environment in Papua New Guinea, 1991. Student rep. Sewanee (Tenn.) Women's Coun., 1988-89; spkr. internat. environ. issues UN Modelling Group, Cherry Creek H.S., Denver, 1993.

Mem. AAAS, Soc. Conservation Biology. Office: Penrose Libr Reference Dept 2150 E Evans Ave Denver CO 80210-4704

PENNAK, ROBERT WILLIAM, biologist, educator; b. Milw., June 13, 1912; s. William Henry and Ella Sophia (Clemeson) P.; m. Alberta Vivian Pope, Sept. 7, 1935; children: Richard Dean, Cathy Ann. BS, U. Wis., 1934, MS, 1935, PhD, 1938. Instr. biology U. Colo., Boulder, 1938-40, prof. biology, 1941-74, prof. emeritus, 1974—; cons. numerous nat. and internat. corps. Author: Fresh-water Invertebrates of the U.S., 1953, Collegiate Dictionary of Zoology, 1964; contbr. over 120 articles to profl. jours. Rsch. grantee various orgns. Mem. Am. Microscopical Soc., Am. Benthological Soc. (Excellence in Benthic Sci. award 1991), Am. Soc. Limnology and Oceanography, Am. Soc. Zoologists, Internat. Assn. Meiobenthologists. Home: 14215 E Marina Dr Aurora CO 80014-3761

PENNER-SEKERA, CYNTHIA DAWN, elementary education educator; b. Stockton, Calif., Mar. 23, 1959; d. Donald Dean and Frances Lee (Cox) Penner; m. Carl Joseph Sekera, June 21, 1981; children: Matthew Carl, Samantha Dawn. BA, Calif. State U., 1981, postgrad., 1983, MA in Edn., 1984, postgrad., 1991. Cert. tchr., Calif. Tchr. KinderCare Schs., Santa Ana, Calif., 1981-84, Long Beach (Calif.) Sch. Dist., 1984-87, Tracy (Calif.) Adult/Elem. Dist., 1987—; tech. tchr. Tracy High Sch. Dist., 1995—; mem. Tracy Dist. Tech. Steering Com., 1991—; tech. mentor tchr. Tracy Elem. Dist., 1992-95; pub. C.U.E. (Computer Using Educators) Newsletter, 1994-95. Contbr. articles to profl. jours. Tchr. McHenry House for the Homeless, Tracy, 1990-93. Mem. AAUW (vol. coord. 1988—, v.p. 1990-91). Office: Merrill F West High Sch 1775 W Lowell Ave Tracy CA 95376

PENNEY, BRYAN LE ROY HUMPHREY, lay pastor, nursing assistant; b. Port Hueneme, Calif., Mar. 8, 1954; s. Chester Ulysses Jr. and Carlene (Fisher) Humphrey; m. Judith Deanna Klann, Apr. 14, 1990. Lay preacher, pulpit supply First So. Bapt. Ch., Red Bluff, Calif., 1986-88; lay pastor Fairvale Bapt. Ch., Fair Oaks, Calif., 1988-89; security officer Carrow's Restaurant, Citrus Heights, Calif., 1990-91, Kaiser Permanente Med. Ctr., Rancho Cordova, Calif., 1991-92; nursing asst. Stat Nurses Svc., Sacramento, Calif., 1992-93, Sutter Oaks Nursing Ctr., Carmichael, Calif., 1992—, Sutter Sr. Care, Sacramento, 1994; guest clown (Bubbles the Clown) Bentley Bros. Circus, Carson & Barnes Circus, 1982; cowboy, Murphy, Idaho, 1984, Baker, Oreg., 1985; mem. staff Costa Rica Children;s Home, Golfito, 1986. Author: (poems) Heartfelt Reflections, 1988, God...My Father, My Inspiration, 1990. Dir. Santa Clarita Valley Jaycees, Canyon Country, Calif., 1980-81. Sgt. USAF, 1973-76. Named Patriot of Christian Liberty, 1989, Poet of Merit, Am. Poetry Assn., 1989, Golden Poet, World of Poetry Press, 1985, 90, Silver Poet, 1986; recipient Presdl. Medal of Merit, Presdl. Task Force, 1989. Home and Office: 34 Goodwin Cir Sacramento CA 95823-5141

PENNEY, ROGER LEE, artist; b. Boston, Nov. 19, 1939; s. Frank E. and Ann (Lee) P.; m. Gale Ensie, May 19, 1968 (div. May 1974); m. Elizabeth Swegle, June 12, 1978; 1 child, Spencer Swegle Penney. Artist murals Circle's Cup Coffee House, San Diego, 1961-62; artist painting and talk Madmen & Fools, San Francisco, L.A.., 1963-66; artist portraits Madmen & Fools, L.A., San Diego, 1966-75; artist shipyard signs Madmen & Fools, San Diego, 1975-86, artist painting and books, 1975—; artist Unindurable Pleasure Infinitly Prolonged, San Diego, 1966—. Prin. works include Homotopic Soviet Surrealism, 1963-68, An Unknown Magic, 1968-69, Human Dominiums, 1970—. Pvt. 1st class U.S. Army, 1958-60. Home: 8089 Hillandale Dr San Diego CA 92120-1512 Office: Unindurable Pleasure Infinitly Prolonged 8089 Hillandale Dr San Diego CA 92120

PENNINGTON, JOSEPH RUSSELL, financial services professional; b. Panama City, Fla., Mar. 1, 1945; s. Joseph Russell Sr. and Nellie Blanch (Rumley) P.; m. Margaret Rose Sutherland, Jan. 15, 1977. BS, Memphis State U., 1968; MPA, Ga. State U., 1976. Cert. fin. planner. Chief adminstrv. officer City of Tullahoma, Tenn., 1973-74; grad. asst. Ga. State U., Atlanta, 1974-76; town mgr. Town of Clifton, Ariz., 1976-78; city mgr. City of Holbrook, Ariz., 1978-81; exec. dir. Holy Cross Hosp., Taos, N.Mex., 1981-82; owner Omni Ltd., Taos, 1982-84; pres. Fin. Planning Cons., Tuscon, 1984-85, Harris Trust Bank Ariz., Tucson, 1993-94; pres., chmn. Personal Fin. Advisors, Inc., Tuscon, 1985—. Treas. Tuscon Boys Choir, 1989-91; chmn. bd. dirs. Lighthouse YMCA, Tuscon, 1989-91; active Mcpl. Tax Code Commn. Ariz. Dept. Revenue, Phoenix, 1991-94. Named Hon. Citizen, City of Huntsville, Ala., 1973. Mem. Internat. Assn. Fin. Planning (nat. pres., Leader of Yr.), Inst. Fin. Planners (pres. Tucson Soc. 1990), Phoenix Soc. Fin. Analysts, Tucson Met. C. of C. (sec., bd. dirs. 1990-92). Republican. Home: 4565 N Flecha Dr Tucson AZ 85718-6748 Office: Personal Fin Advisors Inc PO Box 65300 Tucson AZ 85728-5300

PENNOCK, CECIL ALAN, electronic engineer; b. Siloam Springs, Ark., Mar. 20, 1946; s. Cecil Floyd and Wanda (Perkins) P.; m. Melody Pennock (div. Feb. 1983); 1 child, Joseph Alan; m. Linda Gowan. AS in Engring. Tech., Grantham Coll., 1978, BS in Electronics Engring., 1981; AA in Math., Butte Coll., 1981. Broadcast engr. Sta. KHSL-TV, Chico, Calif., 1969—. Sgt. USAF, 1966-69. Mem. Soc. Broadcast Engrs. (cert. chmn.). Home: 701 E Lassen Ave Unit 174 Chico CA 95926-0700

PENNY, LAURA JEAN, librarian; b. Union City, Tenn., June 25, 1956; d. Glen Jones and Harriet Smith (Gould) P. BS in Econs., Lambuth Coll., 1978; MLS, U. Ariz., 1980. Asst. librarian local history and genealogy Pikes Peak Library Dist., Colorado Springs, Colo., 1981-84; info. officer Inmos Corp., Colorado Springs, 1984-86; dir. library Colo. State Hosp., Pueblo, 1987—. Author: A Tempstuous Voyage, 1987, Abstracts of Strafford County, 1987, Abstracts of Washington County, 1988. Pres. El Paso County Democratic Women's Club, Colorado Springs, 1986-87; chmn. El Paso County Democratic Com., 1987—. Mem. Colo. Council Library Devel., Pikes Peak Genealogical Soc. (editor 1985-87). Methodist. Office: Colo State Hosp 1600 W 24th St Pueblo CO 81003-1411

PENNY, ROBERT, pediatrician, educator, researcher; b. Cin., June 6, 1935; s. Ralph and Marie (Cottrell) P.; m. Joselyn Baily, May 21, 1971; 1 child, Angline. BS, U. Cin., 1959; MD, Ohio State U., 1963. Diplomate Am. Bd. Pediatrics, Am. Bd. Pediatric Subspecialty in Pediatric Endocrinology. Intern Children's Hosp., Columbus, Ohio, 1963-64; resident in pediatrics Children's Hosp., Cin., 1964-66; instr. pediatrics Loma Linda (Calif.) U., 1967-68; fellow pediatric endocrinology John Hopkins Hosp., Balt., 1968-71; asst. prof. pediatrics U. So. Calif., L.A., 1971-75, assoc. prof. pediatrics, 1975-81, prof. pediatrics, 1981—, prof. rsch. medicine, 1991—; sabbatical molecular biology U. Calif., Riverside, 1990-91. Mem. editorial bd. Am. Jour. Disease of Childhood, 1988-93, Archives of Pediatrics and Adolescent Medicine, 1993—; contbr. over 103 articles to profl. jours. V.p. Rancho Palos Verdes (Calif.) Coun. Homeowners Assn., 1994—; oral examiner Am. Bd. Pediatrics, 1987, mem. com. programs for renewal of certification in pediatrcis, 1989-91. Capt. USAF, 1966-68. Fellow Am. Acad. Pediatrics; mem. Am. Fedn. Clin. Rsch., Am. Pediatric Soc., Endocrine Soc., Soc. Pediatric Rsch., Lawson Wilkins Pediatric Endocrine Soc. Home: PO Box 427 904 Silver Spur Rd Rolling Hills CA 90274 Office: U Soc Calif Med Ctr 2025 Zonal Ave Unit I Los Angeles CA 90033-4526

PENSO, PIERPAOLO, ship repair company executive; b. Venice, Italy, Aug. 3, 1942; came to U.S., 1968; s. Silvano and Margherita (Maestri) P. BS in Marine Engring., Nautical U., Camogli, Italy, 1961. Cadet engr. F.LLI Cosulich, Genoa, Italy, 1961-62; 3d engr. Filli Cosulich, Genoa, Italy, 1962-63, 2d engr., 1963-64, 1st engr., 1964-67, chief engr., 1967-78; tech. dir. Panteknik SRL, Milan, 1978-80; pres. Internat. Wine Imports, Jacksonville, Fla., 1980-88; gen. mgr. Marine and Indsl. Repairs, Long Beach, Calif., 1988—; cons. various fleet operators, 1988—. Mem. L.A./Long Beach Port Engrs. Roman Catholic. Home: 312 1/2 33rd St Newport Beach CA 92663-3132

PENWELL, DONNA CAROL, museum director; b. Waltham, Mass., Oct. 22, 1954. BA in Am. History and Art History, U. N.C., 1976; MA in Mus. Adminstrn., SUNY, 1977. Curator art Mus. Collection Mgmt. Unit Calif. Dept. Parks and Recreation, Sacramento, 1977-78, chief curator, 1978-79; historic cons. Pine Lodge, Ehrman Manson, Lake Tahoe, Tahoma, Calif., 1979-80; exhibit designer State Capitol Restoration Project, Sacramento, 1980-82; exhibit designer mus. devel. unit Calif. Dept. Parks and Recreation, Sacramento, 1982-84; mus. dir., cultural arts mgr. Colton Hall Mus. of City of Monterey, Calif., 1984-90; mus. dir. Maritime Mus. Monterey, 1990—. Bd. mem. Monterey County Hospitality Assn., 1993—, Monterey County Cultural History Assn., 1994—. Nat. Mus. Art scholar, 1977. Mem. Am. Assn. Museums, Calif. Assn. Museums, Coun. Maritime Museums. Office: Maritime Mus Monterey 5 Custom House Plz Monterey CA 93940-2430

PENWELL, JONES CLARK, real estate appraiser, consultant; b. Crisp, Tex., Dec. 19, 1921; s. Clark Moses and Sarah Lucille (Jones) P.; B.S., Colo. State U., 1949; m. A. Jerry Jones, July 1, 1967; children—Dale Maria, Alan Lee, John Steven, Laurel Anne, Tracy Lynn. Farm mgmt. supr. Farmers Home Adminstrn., Dept. Agr., 1949-58; rancher 1958-61; real estate appraiser/realty officer Dept. Interior, Tex., Calif., Ariz., Colo., Washington, 1961-78, chief appraiser Bur. Reclamation, Lakewood, Colo., 1978-80; ind. fee appraiser, cons., 1980—. Served with USN, 1940-46. Accredited rural appraiser; cert. review appraiser, gen. appraiser; recipient Outstanding Performance awards U.S. Bur. Reclamation, 1964, 75, 80. Mem. Am. Soc. Farm Mgrs. and Rural Appraisers, Internat. Right-of-Way Assn., Nat. Assn. Rev. Appraisers (regional v.p. 1978-79), Jefferson County Bd. Realtors. Democrat. Presbyterian. Clubs: Elks, Rotary, Mt. Vernon Country. Author: Reviewing Condemnation Appraisal Reports, 1980; The Valuation of Easements, 1980. Home and office: 10100 W 21st Pl Lakewood CO 80215-1406

PEOPLES, CHRISTOPHER JAMES, physics educator; b. Whittier, Calif., Nov. 23, 1963; s. William Nicholas and Karen Elizabeth (Halvorson) P. BS in Geophysics, U. Calif., Riverside, 1986; MS in Geophysics, Tex. A&M U., 1993. Scientist, engr. IT Corp., Irvine, Calif., 1986-87; rsch. asst. Chevron Oil Field Rsch. Co., La Habra, Calif., 1987-89; geophys. intern Chevron Exploration & Prodn. Svcs. Co., New Orleans, 1990, Houston, 1991; physics instr. Irvine (Calif.) Valley Coll., 1993-94, Cypress (Calif.) Coll., 1994—. Inventor vertical component seismograph for use in class room demonstrations. Grad. fellowship AMOCO Found., 1991. Mem. Am. Geophys. Union, Soc. Exploration Geophysicists. Episcopalian. Home: 16552 Wanderer Ln Huntington Beach CA 92649-2144

PEOPLES, DONALD R., research scientist; b. 1939. Athletic dir. Butte (Mont.) Ctrl. High Sch., 1967-69; dir. info. and evaluation Butte Model Cities Program, 1969-70; dir. pub. works, model cities and cmty. devel. Butte, 1970-77; dir. pub. works dept. Butte-Silver Bow City-County Govt., 1977-79, CEO, 1979-89; with Mont. Tech. Cos., Butte, 1989—, now pres., CEO. Office: Montana Tech Companies 220 N Alaska St Butte MT 59701-9212*

PEPPER, DAVID M., physicist, educator, author, inventor; b. L.A., Mar. 9, 1949; s. Harold and Edith (Kleinplatz) P.; m. Denise Danyelle Koster, Mar. 19, 1992. BS in Physics summa cum laude, UCLA, 1971; MS in Applied Physics, Calif. Inst. Tech., 1974, PhD in Applied Physics, 1980. Mem. tech. staff Hughes Rsch. Labs., Malibu, Calif., 1973-87, sr. staff physicist, 1987-91, head nonlinear and electro-optic devices sect., 1989-91, sr. scientist, 1991—; adj. prof. math. and physics Pepperdine U., Malibu, 1981—. co-author: Optical Phase Conjugation, 1983, Laser Handbook, Vol. 4, 1985, Optical Phase Conjugation, 1995, Spatial Light Modulator Technology, 1995, CRC Handbook of Laser Science and Technology, 1995; tech. referee profl. jours.; contbr. articles to tech. jours. including Sci. Am.; holder 15 patents. Mem. Sons and Daughters of 1939 Club, 2d Generation of Martyrs Meml., Mus. Holocaust. Recipient Rudolf Kingslake award Soc. Photo-Optical Instrumentation Engrs., 1982, Publ. of Yr. award Hughes Rsch. Lab., 1986; NSF trainee Calif. Inst. Tech., 1971; Howard Hughes fellow Hughes Aircraft Co., 1973-80. Fellow Optical Soc. Am.; mem. AAAS, IEEE (guest editor, assoc. editor), SPIE (guest editor), N.Y. Acad. Scis., Am. Phys. Soc., Internat. Coun. Sci. Unions (com. on sci. and tech. in developing countries), Sigma Xi (v.p. 1986-87, chpt. pres. 1987-88, 90-91, 91-92), Sigma Pi Sigma. Jewish. Office: Hughes Rsch Labs RL 65 3011 Malibu Canyon Rd Malibu CA 90265-4737

PEPPER, JOHN ROY, oil and gas executive; b. Denver, Feb. 24, 1937; s. Wesley Wayne and Lucille (Stith) P.; m. Sallie K. Force, Dec. 13, 1958 (div. July 1970); m. Judithea Lawrence Douglas, Sept. 24, 1977; stepchildren: Sarah Douglas-Broten, Kenneth R. Douglas. BBA, U. Denver, 1961; postgrad., UCLA, 1962, U. Denver, 1965. Analyst Texaco, Inc., L.A., 1962-63; landman Texaco, Inc., Bakersfield, Calif., 1963-65; prin. John Pepper, Landman, Denver, 1965-75; owner, operator John R. Pepper Oil & Gas Co., Denver, 1975—; bd. dirs. Trans-Telecom, Miami, Fla.; cons. Organizer Friends of Bob Crider campaign, Denver, 1985. Mem. Ind. Petroleum Assn. Mountain States, Ind. Petroleum Assn. of Ams. (pub. lands com. 1968-74). Republican. Lutheran. Home: 2499 S Colorado Blvd Apt 608 Denver CO 80222-5926 Office: John R Pepper Oil & Gas Co 1800 Glenarm Pl Ste 200 Denver CO 80202-3829

PERADOTTO, NICOLE ANNE, journalist; b. Buffalo; d. John and Noreen (Doran) P. Student classical ballet, 1975-91, L'Univ. Grenoble, N.Y.C., summer 1983, 84; student, Joffrey Sch. Ballet; BA with honors, SUNY, Binghamton, 1985; student, L'Univ. Grenoble, 1987-88; postgrad., U. N.C., 1991. Instr. French U. N.C., Chapel Hill, 1989-91; reporter SUNY, Buffalo, 1990; gen. assignment reporter The Buffalo News, 1991, feature writer, film, theater, rock reviewer, summer 1992; stringer DuPage (Ill.) Daily Herald, 1991-92; Washington corr. Waterloo (Iowa) Courier, 1992; editorial intern Washingtonian, 1993; arts and entertainment, gen. assignment reporter Lewiston (Idaho) Morning Tribune, 1993-95; features reporter Buffalo News, 1995—. Recipient first place, Rookie of Yr., Idaho Press Club, 1994, 3rd place First Amendment Reporting, Soc. Profl. Journalists, Inland Northwest Chpt., 1st place award arts reporting Idaho Press Club, Assocd. Press Pacific NW chpt. Mem. Kappa Tau Alpha. Office: Buffalo News 1 News Plz Buffalo NY 14240

PERALTA, RICHARD CARL, groundwater engineer; b. Enid, Okla., Nov. 8, 1949; s. John Francis and Christina Margareta (Reinl) P.; m. Ann Wilson Blanchard, Mar. 27, 1972; children: Dia, Samantha, Nancy, Hugh. BS, U. S.C., 1971; MS, Utah State U., 1977; PhD, Okla. State U., 1979. Registered profl. engr., Ark. Grad. research assoc. Oklahoma State U., Stillwater, 1977-79; from asst. prof. to assoc. prof. agrl. engring. U. Ark., Fayetteville, 1980-88; assoc. prof. dept. biol. & irrigation engring. Utah State U., Logan, 1988-91, prof., 1991—; cons. hydrologist U.S. Geol. Survey, Fayetteville, 1985-87; cons. engr. Mid-Am. Internat. Agrl. Consortium, Lima, Peru, 1986-87; cons. engr. ARD, FAO, 1989—. Contbr. articles to sci. jours. Co-dir. Citizens for Responsible Legis., Stillwater, 1979; elders quorum, pres., exec. sec., fin. asst. clk., activities com. chmn. LDS Ch., 1979—, elders quorum, counsellor, 1992-94; scoutmaster Boy Scouts Am., 1988-89, cubmaster, 1989-91, 94-95. from 2d lt. to 1st lt. USAF, 1971-75, lt. col. USAFR. Mem. ASCE, Am. Soc. of Agrl. Engrs., Am. Water Resources Assn., Gamma Sigma Delta, Sigma Xi. Home: PO Box 412 Millville UT 84326-0412 Office: Utah State U Dept Biol & Irrigation Engring Logan UT 84322

PEREL, MICHAEL JOSEPH, dermatologist; b. Memphis, Oct. 29, 1947; s. Philip Alexander and Dorothy Louise (Dansby) P.; m. Georgia Chris Roberts, Nov. 20, 1973; 1 child, Eric. BS, Tulane U., 1969; MD, U. Tenn., Memphis, 1972. Diplomate Am. Bd. Dermatology. Pvt. practice dermatology Oxnard, Calif., 1977-89; dermatologist Riverside (Calif.) Med. Clinic, 1989—. Inventor electronic med. record, 1993. Mem. Inland Counties Dermatologic Soc., Calif. Med. Soc. Libertarian. Home: 2328 Caserta Ct Henderson NV 89014-5316

PERELMAN, RONALD OWEN, diversified holding company executive; b. Greensboro, N.C., 1943; s. Raymond and Ruth (Caplan) P.; m. Claudia Cohen; 4 children. BA, U. Pa., 1964; MBA, Wharton Sch. Fin., 1966. With Belmont Industries Inc., 1966-78; chmn., chief exec. officer, dir. MacAndrews & Forbes Holdings Inc., Wilmington, Del., 1983—; chmn., chief exec. officer MacAndrews & Forbes Group Inc. (subs.), N.Y.C., 1978—; chmn., chief exec. officer, dir. Revlon Group Inc. (subs. MacAndrews & Forbes Group Inc.), N.Y.C., 1985—, Revlon Inc. (subs.), N.Y.C., 1985—; also chmn. Nat. Health Labs. Inc., La Jolla, Calif., 1985—, Andrews Group Inc., N.Y.C., 1985—. Jewish. Office: Revlon Group Inc 21 E 63rd St New York NY 10021-7226 also: MacAndrews & Forbes Group Inc 36 E 63rd St New York NY 10021-8005 Office: National Health Labs Inc 7590 Fay Ave La Jolla CA 92037-4849

PERENCHIO, ANDREW JERROLD, film and television executive; b. Fresno, Calif., Dec. 20, 1930; s. Andrew Joseph and Dorothea (Harvey) P.; m. Robin Green, July 16, 1954 (div.); children: Candace L., Catherine M., John Gardner; m. Jacquelyn Claire, Nov. 14, 1969. BS, UCLA, 1954. V.p. Music Corp. Am., 1958-62, Gen. Artists Corp., 1962-64; pres., owner theatrical agy. Chartwell Artists, Ltd., L.A., from 1964; chmn. bd. Tandem Prodns., Inc. and TAT Communications Co., L.A., 1973-83; pres., CEO Embassy Pictures, L.A., from 1983; now pres. Chartwell Partnerships Group, L.A. Promoter Muhammad Ali-Joe Frazier heavyweight fight, 1971, Bobby Riggs-Billie Jean King tennis match, 1973. Served to 1st lt. USAF, 1954-57. Clubs: Bel-Air Country (Los Angeles); Westchester (N.Y.) Country; Friars (N.Y.C.). Office: Chartwell Partnerships Group 1901 Avenue Of The Stars Los Angeles CA 90067-6008

PERER, MARVIN A., gastroenterologist; b. Pitts., Dec. 18, 1939; s. William A. and Ethel R. (Green) P.; m. Irene S. Waldman; Sept. 13, 1972; children: Elise, Michael. BA, Washington & Jefferson Coll., 1961; MD, Northwestern U., 1965. Intern U. Mich., Ann Arbor, 1965-66, resident in internal medicine, 1966-69; gastroenterology fellow U. Wis., Madison, 1971-73; gastroenterologist Fallon Clinic, Inc., Worcester, Mass., 1973-82; pvt. practice Las Vegas, Nev., 1982—. Pres. Jewish Fedn. Las Vegas, 1990-92. Maj. M.C., U.S. Army, 1969-71, Vietnam. Mem. ACP, Am. Coll. Gastroenterology, Am. Gastroent. Assn., Am. Soc. for Gastrointestinal Endoscopy. Office: PO Box 81560 Las Vegas NV 89180-1560

PERERA, VICTOR HAIM, journalism educator, writer; b. Guatemala City, Guatemala, Apr. 12, 1934; came to U.S., 1946; s. Salomon and Tamar (Nisim) P.; m. Padma Hejmadi, Aug. 8, 1960 (div. 1974). BA, Bklyn. Coll., 1956; MA, U. Mich., 1958. Fact editor, reporter The New Yorker, N.Y.C., 1963-66; lectr. English dept. Vassar Coll., Poughkeepsie, N.Y., 1968-70; freelance reporter The N.Y. Times Mag., N.Y.C., 1971-75; program specialist, lit. Nat. Endowment for the Arts, Washington, 1983-84; lectr. lit. & creative writing U. Calif., Santa Cruz, 1972-88; lectr. grad. sch. journalism U. Calif., Berkeley, 1992—; peer panelist NEA, Washington, 1983-94; mem. edit. bd. Tikkun Mag., N.Y.C., 1989—. Author: Rites: A Guatemalan Boyhood, 1986, Unfinished Conquest: The Guatemalan Tragedy, 1993, The Cross and the Pear Tree: A Sephardic Journey, 1995; co-author: Last Lords of Palenque: The Lacandon Mayas of the Mexican Rain Forest, 1982. Recipient Lila Wallace Readers Digest Fund Writing award, 1992-94, Creative Writing award NEA, 1980, Major Essay award Avery Hopwood U. Mich., 1961. Mem. PEN Am. Ctr. Jewish. Office: Watkins-Loomis Agy 133 E 35th St New York NY 10036

PEREY, RON, lawyer; b. Cleve., Feb. 2, 1943; s. John Perecinsky and Anne (Nagy) Disman; 1 child, Page Suzanne. BA in Polit. Sci., Miami U., Oxford, Ohio, 1965; JD cum laude, Ohio State U., 1968. Bar: Wash. 1968, U.S. Dist. Ct. (we. dist.) Wash. 1968, U.S. Ct. Appeals (9th cir.) 1973, U.S. Supreme Ct. 1985. Assoc. Reed McClure, Seattle, 1968-71, ptnr., 1971-82; ptnr. Perey & Smith, Seattle, 1982-86, Perey Langley, Seattle, 1986-92; owner Law Offices of Ron Perey, Seattle, 1992—; speaker in field. Contbr. articles to profl jours. Mem. ABA (litigation sect.), Seattle-King County Bar Assn., Assn. Trial Lawyers Am., Wash. State Trial Lawyers Assn. (mem. bd. govs. 1983-85), Am. Bd. Trial Advs., Wash. State Bar Assn. (mem. bd. govs. 1994-97), Damage Attys. Round Table.

PEREYRA-SUAREZ, CHARLES ALBERT, lawyer; b. Paysandu, Uruguay, Sept. 7, 1947; came to U.S., 1954, naturalized, 1962; s. Hector and Esther (Enriquez-Sarano) P.-S.; m. Susan H. Cross, Dec. 30, 1983. BA in History magna cum laude, Pacific Union Coll., 1970; postgrad., UCLA, 1970-71; JD, U. Calif., Berkeley, 1975. Bar: Calif. 1975, D.C. 1980. Staff atty. Western Ctr. Law and Poverty, Inc., Los Angeles, 1976; trial atty. civil rights div. U.S. Dept. Justice, Washington, 1976-79; asst. U.S. atty., criminal div. U.S. Dept. Justice, Los Angeles, 1979-82; sr. litigation assoc. Gibson, Dunn & Crutcher, Los Angeles, 1982-84; sole practice Los Angeles, 1984-86; ptnr. McKenna & Cuneo, Los Angeles, 1986-95, Davis Wright Tremane, L.A., 1995—. Democrat.

PEREZ, MARK, food products executive; b. 1953. With Perez Parking Inc., Firebaugh, Calif., 1974—. Office: Perez Parking Inc 5879 N Washoe Ave Firebaugh CA 93622-9509*

PEREZ, OSCAR ALFREDO, architect; b. Santiago de Cuba, Cuba, June 1, 1956; s. Oscar and Lucila de las Mercedes (Domingo) P. B Design, U. Fla., 1978, MArch., 1980. Registered architect Mass., Calif., Fla., D.C.; lic. gen. contractor, Mass. Job capt. Sumner Schein Architects, Boston, 1981-84; project architect Ecodesign, Boston, 1984-88; sr. constrn. mgr. Andrew Chartwell & Co., Washington, 1988-90, DMJM/TRI, San Francisco, 1991-94; prin. Alfred Hawkmoon & Co., San Francisco, 1992-93, Oscar A. Perez, San Francisco, 1986—. Author: (book) Sex in Architecture, 1980. Exec. dir. Symphony Area Renaissance, Inc., Boston, 1987-88, pres. 1986-87, bd. dirs. 1982-86. Mem. AIA, Bay Area Video Coalition, Am. Film Inst., Frameline. Democrat. Home: 170 Guerrero St # E San Francisco CA 94103-1013

PÉREZ, RAUL ANTONIO, family practitioner; b. Bklyn., Jan. 11, 1955; s. Raul and Angela (Maldonado) P.; m. Wendy Dawn Reed, May 26, 1991; 1 child, Rorey. BS, Fordham U., 1977; MD, Hahnemann U., 1984. Diplomate Am. Bd. Family Medicine. Resident Temple U., Phila., 1984-87; staff physician Monroe Health Ctr., Union, W.Va., 1987-90, med. dir., 1990-91; med. dir. Andrew S. Rowan Meml. Home, Sweet Springs, W.Va., 1990-91, Springfield Comprehensive Care Ctr., Lindside, W.Va., 1990-91; staff physician Linden St. Family Practice, Bethlehem, Pa., 1991-93, Kaweah Sierra Med. Ctr., Visalia, Calif., 1993-94, Visalia (Calif.) Med. Clinic, 1994—. Mem. AMA (Physician Recognition award 1992), Am. Acad. Family Practice, Calif. Med. Assn., Tulare County Med. Soc. Republican. Roman Catholic. Home: 3245 W Victor Ct Visalia CA 93277-7118 Office: Visalia Med Clinic 5400 W Hillsdale Ave Visalia CA 93291-8222

PEREZ, REINALDO JOSEPH, electrical engineer; b. Palm River, Cuba, July 25, 1957; came to U.S., 1975; s. Reinaldo I. and Palminia Ulloa (Rodriguez) P.; m. Madeline Kelly Reilly, Mar. 11, 1989; children: Alexander, Laura-Marie, Richard Kelly. BSc in Physics, U. Fla., 1979, MSc in Physics, 1981; MScEE, Fla. Atlantic U., 1983, PhD, 1989. Communications engr. Kennedy Space Ctr., NASA, Cape Canaveral, Fla., 1983-84; chief reliability engr. jet propulsion lab. JPL JPL, Calif. Inst. Tech., Pasadena, 1988—; instr. engring. UCLA, 1990—. Contbr. articles to profl. publs. Mem. AAAS, IEEE (book rev. editor 1990—), NSPE, Electromagnetic Compatibility Soc. (assoc. editor jour.), Am. Soc. Physics Tchrs., N.Y. Acad. Scis., Applied Computational Electromagnetic Soc. (assoc. editor jour., chief editor newsletter), Phi Kappa Phi. Republican. Baptist. Office: JPL Calif Inst Tech 4800 Oak Grove Dr MS: 301-460 Pasadena CA 91109

PEREZ, RICHARD LEE, lawyer; b. L.A., Nov. 17, 1946; s. Salvador Navarro and Shirley Mae (Selbrede) P.; children: Kristina, Kevin, Ryan. BA, UCLA, 1968; JD, U. Calif., Berkeley, 1971. Bar: U.S. Dist. Ct. (no. dist.) Calif. 1974, U.S. Ct. Appeals (9th cir.) 1974, U.S. Dist. Ct. (ea. dist.) Calif. 1982, U.S. Dist. Ct. (no. dist.) Tex. 1984, U.S. Dist. Ct. (so. dist.) Calif. 1991. Assoc. McCutchen, Doyle, Brown & Enersen, San Francisco, 1972-74, John R. Hetland, Orinda, Calif., 1974-75; ptnr. Lempres & Wulsfberg, Oakland, Calif., 1975-82, Perez & McNabb, Orinda, 1982—; speaker real estate brokerage and computer groups and seminars; mem. adv. bd. Computer Litigation Reporter, Washington, 1982-85, Boalt Hall High Tech. Law Jour., 1984-90. Assoc. editor U. Calif. Law Rev., 1970-71. Served to capt. U.S. Army, 1968-79. Mem. ABA, Alameda County Bar Assn., Contra Costa County Bar Assn. Office: Perez & McNabb 140 Brookwood Rd Orinda CA 94563

PEREZ, THOMAS, food products executive; b. 1925. Officer Perez Ranches, Inc., Crows Landing, Calif., 1946—; with Perez Packing, Inc., 1972—. With U.S. Army, 1945-46. Office: Perez Packing Inc 6879 N Washoe Ave Firebaugh CA 93622-9502*

PEREZ, TIMOTHY ALLEN, software company administrator; b. Carmel, Calif., Apr. 30, 1961; s. Robert L. and Karen G. (Stanfield) P.; m. Cynthia Lorraine Whipple, June 1, 1984; children: Dansell, Robert, Steven, Joshua. BS, Brigham Young U., 1987. Instructional trainer Missionary

Tng. Ctr., Provo, Utah, 1983-86, MIS tng. supr., 1986-87; mktg. rep. IBM Corp., Denver, 1987-92; sr. account mgr. Interactaive Software Systems, Inc., Denver, 1992-94; sr. sales rep. Compuware/Uniface Corp., Denver, 1994—; fin. industry specialist IBM Corp., Denver, 1988-89, law enforcement cons., 1990-92. Missionary, Ch. of Jesus Christ of Latter-Day Saints, Fla., 1980-82; dir. youth job hunt Colo. Alliance of Bus., 1988. Recipient Duty to God award Ch. of Jesus Christ of Latter-Day Saints, 1978. Republican. Home: 4938 S Cathay Ct Aurora CO 80015-4943 Office: Compuware/Uniface Corp Systems Inc 7900 E Union Ave Ste 1100 Denver CO 80237-2746

PEREZ-CASTRO, ANA VERONICA, developmental biology researcher; b. Lima, Peru, Jan. 27, 1962; came to U.S., 1986; d. Cesar Antonio and Ines Gladys (Marquina) P.; m. Alonso Castro, June 11, 1988. BS, Cayetano Heredia U., Lima, 1984, licentiate in chemistry and biology, 1985; MA, Columbia U., 1988, MPhil, 1990, PhD in Microbiology, 1992. Jr. prof. dept. chemistry Cayetano Heredia U., 1985-86; teaching asst. dept. microbiology U. Ga., Athens, 1987, Columbia U., N.Y.C., 1989; postdoctoral fellow life scis. div. Los Alamos (N.Mex.) Nat. Lab., 1992—; speaker Fedn. Am. Socs. for Exptl. Biology, 1992, Baylor Coll. Medicine, Houston, 1992, Mexican Soc. Genetics, Guanajuato, 1993, Mexico City 1994. Contbr. articles to sci. jours. Recipient young scientist award Fedn. Am Socs. for Exptl. Biology, 1992; Nat. Coun. Sci. and Tech. grad. fellow Cayetano Heredia U., 1985-86; Fieger predoctoral scholar Norris Comprehensive Cancer Ctr., U. So. Calif., 1991-92. Mem. AAAS, Am. Soc. Microbiology. Home: 505 Oppenheimer Dr Apt 605 Los Alamos NM 87544-2393 Office: Los Alamos Nat Lab MS-M880 Life Scis Divsn LS-2 Los Alamos NM 87545

PEREZ-MENDEZ, VICTOR, physics educator; b. Guatemala, Aug. 8, 1923; came to U.S., 1946; m. 1949; 2 children. MS, Hebrew U., Israel, 1947; PhD, Columbia U., 1951. Rsch. assoc. Columbia U., N.Y.C., 1951-53, staff physicist, 1953-61; sr. scientist Lawrence Berkeley Lab., U. Calif., Berkeley, 1960—; vis. lectr. Hebrew U., 1959—; prof. physics dept. radiology U. Calif., San Francisco, 1968—. Fellow IEEE, AAAS, Am. Phys. Soc., N.Y. Acad. Sci.; mem. Soc. Photo Instrumentation Engrs. Office: U Calif Lawrence Berkeley Lab Berkeley CA 94720

PERFETTI, ROBERT NICKOLAS, career education coordinator, educator; b. Staples, Minn., Jan. 8, 1937; s. Nickolas Albert and Lila Bertha (Beurge) P. BS, St. Cloud State U., 1960; postgrad., Bemidji State U., 1961-62, Calif. State U., L.A., 1964-68, Pepperdine U., 1967-68; MA, La Verne U., 1970; postgrad., U. So. Calif., 1972-73, Point Loma U., Pasadena, Calif., 1974-75; EdD, Pacific States U., 1975. Cert. adminstr., counselor, secondary, community coll., jr. high sch., adult, and elem. edn. Calif. Prin. Richmond (Minn.) Pub. Schs., 1960-62; elem. tchr. Sebeka (Minn.) Sch. Dist., 1962-63; team leader lang. arts, social sci. and summer sch. Rowland Unified Sch. Dist., Rowland Heights, Calif., 1965-76, coord. math. lab., 1976-79, secondary counselor, 1979-81, coord. work experience edn., career edn. and career ctr., 1981—, home ind. study coord., 1992—; coord. Gender Equity, 1980—, Job Tng. Partnership Act, 1980—; advisor Nat. Vocat. Tech. Honor Soc., 1991—. Editor: (profl. newspaper) Reaction. Officer parish coun. Our Lady of the Assumption Ch., Claremont, Calif., chmn. edn. com.; chmn. PTA, Rowland Heights; rep. fed. project, Rowland Heights; scoutmaster, chmn. troop com. Boy Scouts Am. Recipient Svc. Commendation Rowland Unified Sch. Dist., 1978; named. L.A. County Tchr. of Yr. Calif. State Dept. Edn., 1975, Outstanding Secondary Educator of Am., 1974, Giano Tchr. of Yr. Giano Intermediate Sch., 1973, Tchr. of Yr. Rowland Unified Sch. Dist., 1974. Mem. NEA (life), Calif. Tchrs. Assn., Assn. Rowland Educators (v.p.), Calif. Assn. Work Experience Educators (Alpha chpt. v.p.), Alpha Phi Omega (pres.), Pi Delta Epsilon (pres.), KC (3d degree). Roman CAtholic. Home: 3137 Robin Way Pomona CA 91767-1070 Office: Rowland High Sch 2000 Otterbein Ave Rowland Heights CA 91748

PERI, WINNIE LEE BRANCH, educational director; b. Dallas; d. Floyd Hamilton and Eula Dee (Richardson) Branch; m. Fred Ronald Peri; children: Kenneth Michael, Michael Anthony, Desiree Denise. BA in Psychology, Calif. State U., Long Beach, 1978, English teaching credential, 1988; social sci. teaching credential, Calif. State U., Northridge, 1979. Republic of South Africa tchr. Internat. Sch. Svcs., Princeton, N.J., 1980-82; tchr. English, St. Jeanne de Lestonnac Sch., Tustin, Calif., 1988-91; dir. edn. Sylvan Learning Ctr., Mission Viejo, Calif., 1993-94; self-employed as tutor, 1994—; facilitator Rainbows for All God's Children, 1989; mem. team experience sch. evaluation com. WASC/WCEA. Mem. adv. bd. Thomas Paine Sch. PTA; dep. sheriff Los Angeles County. Mem. Psi Chi.

PERILLOUX, BRUCE EDGAR, optical engineer; b. New Orleans, Mar. 24, 1961; s. Louis Francis and Edna Eloise P.; m. Anne Mary Jeansonne, Jan. 29, 1985; 1 child, Katherine. BSEE, U. New Orleans, 1983, MS in Engring., 1984. Grad. teaching asst. U. New Orleans, 1983-84, grad. rsch. asst., 1984-85; thin film engr. I Coherent, Inc., Auburn, Calif., 1985-86, thin film engr. II, 1986-87, sr. thin film engr., 1988, product line mgr., 1989-93, staff thin film engr., 1994—; 5 optical engring. patents. Mem. Optical Soc. Am. (editing referee 1984—), Sigma Xi, Phi Kappa Phi. Office: Coherent Inc 2301 Lindberg St Auburn CA 95602-9562

PERITORE, LAURA, law librarian; b. San Francisco, Nov. 28, 1945; d. Attilio and Anita (Firenzi) Marcenaro; children: Victor Anthony, Phillip Michael. BA, U. Calif., Santa Barbara, 1967, MA, 1970; MLS, U. Mo., 1986—. Asst. libr. Mo. Hist. Soc., Columbia, 1971-74, 77-79; asst. libr. Hastings Law Libr., San Francisco, 1980-86, assoc. libr., 1986—; part-time tchr. legal rsch. City Coll., San Francisco, 1990-91. Author: Guide to California County Probate and Vital Records; contbr. articles and monographs to profl. jours. Mem. Am. Assn. Law Librs., No. Calif. Assn. Law Librs. (asst. editor newsletter 1984-86, workshop com. 1988, advt. editor 1990-91, sec. 1993-94, grantee 1984). Office: Hastings Law Libr 200 Mcallister St San Francisco CA 94102-4707

PERKINS, DALE WARREN, library director; b. Wichita, Kans., Feb. 27, 1933; s. Lawrence Waldo and Georgia (Powell) P.; m. Linda Ann Perkins, Aug. 14, 1960 (div. Feb. 1974); 1 child, Kerry; m. Barbara Lee Miller, Apr. 12, 1976. BA, Ball State U., 1958; MLS, Kansas State U., 1960. Libr. Mid-Columbia Regional Libr., Kennewick, Wash., 1960-62; dir. Baker (Oreg.) City Libr., 1962-65; field libr. Idaho State Libr., Boise, 1965-66; coord. Mountain Valley Libr. System, Sacramento, Calif., 1967-70; dir. San Luis Obispo (Calif.) City-County Libr., 1970—. Contbr. articles to profl. jours. With USAF, 1954-55. Mem. ALA, Calif. Library Assn., Calif. Inst. Libraries (past pres.). Democrat. Home: 741 Stratford St Pismo Beach CA 93449-2444 Office: San Luis Obispo Libr 3220 S Higuera St San Luis Obispo CA 93401-6959

PERKINS, DOROTHY A., marketing professional; b. Weiser, Idaho, Aug. 13, 1926; d. Ross William and Josephine Stanford (Gwilliam) Anderson; m. Leonard Taylor Perkins, Nov. 16, 1948; children: Larry Taylor, Michael A., Drew A., Nancy. Grad. high sch., Boise, Idaho. Sec. Meadow Gold Dairies, Boise, 1944-46; sec. to supt. Idaho State Police, Boise, 1946-48, Idaho State Dept. Edn., Boise, 1952-56; sec. to maintenance engr. Idaho State Dept. Hwys., Boise, 1956-58; adminstrv. sec., asst. mgr. Casper (Wyo.) C. of C., 1962-72, exec. v.p., 1972-91; mktg. rep. World Wide Travel, Casper, 1991—. Mem. Wyo. Ho. of Reps., 1982—, chmn. house labor, health and social svcs. com., 1990—; found. bd. dirs., pres. Nat. Hist. Ctr., 1995. Mem. Wyo. C. of C. Execs. (sec.-treas. 1978-91, past pres.), Mountain States Assn. (bd. dirs. 1979-91, past pres.), Wyo. Hwy. Users Fedn. (bd. dirs. 1978—, pres. 1993—). Republican. Home: 1014 Surrey Ct Casper WY 82609-3270 Office: World Wide Travel PO Box 9370 Casper WY 82609-0370

PERKINS, FLOYD JERRY, theology educator; b. Bertha, Minn., May 9, 1924; s. Ray Lester and Nancy Emily (Kelley) P.; m. Mary Elizabeth Owen, Sept. 21, 1947 (dec. June 1982); children: Douglas Jerry, David Floyd, Sheryl Pauline; m. Phyllis Genevra Hartley, July 14, 1984. AB, BTh, N.W. Nazarene Coll., 1949; MA, U. Mo., 1952; MDiv, Nazarene Theol. Sem., 1952; ThM, Burton Sem., 1964; PhD, U. Witwatersrand, Johannesburg, South Africa, 1974; ThD, Internat. Sem., 1994. Ordained to Christian ministry, 1951. Pres. South African Nazarene Theol. Sem., Florida Transvaal, Africa, 1955-67; pres. Nazarene Bible Sem., Lourenzo Marques, Mozambique, 1967-73, Campinas, Brazil, 1974-76; prof. missions N.W. Nazarene Coll., Nampa, Idaho, 1976; prof. theology Nazarene Bible Coll., Colorado Springs, Colo., 1976—; chmn., founder com. higher theol. edn. Ch. of Nazarene in Africa, 1967-74; sec. All African Nazarene Mission Exec., 1967-74; ofcl. Christian Council Mozambique, 1952-74. Author: A History of the Christian Church in Swaziland, 1974. Served with USN, 1944-46. Mem. Soc. Christian Philosophers, Evang. Theol. Soc., Am. Schs. Orientan Rsch., Am. Soc. Missiology, Assn. Evang. Missions Profs. Republican. Home: 1529 Lyle Dr Colorado Springs CO 80915-2009 Office: Nazarene Bible Coll 1111 Chapman Dr Colorado Springs CO 80916-1901

PERKINS, GARY MICHAEL, writer, political consultant; b. Omak, Wash., May 28, 1960; s. Lynn Andrew Perkins and Shirley Marie Woods Valentine; life ptnr. Henry Lee Stockbridge, Feb. 24, 1991. AA, Spokane Falls C.C., 1983; BA, Evergreen State Coll., Oympia, Wash., 1986; M in Journalism, U. Mont., 1987. Dep. comms. dir. Ed Garvey for U.S. Senate, Milw., 1986; ea. Wash. coord. Don Bonker for U.S. Senate, Spokane, 1988; adminstrv. asst. Rep. Shirley Rector, Olympia, Wash., 1988-91; campaign mgr. Com. to Re-Elect George Oll, Spokane, 1992; editor Office of the Gov., Olympia, 1993—. Chair Gay, Lesbian and Bisexual Caucus, Young Dems. of Am., 1994—. Named to Outstanding Young Men of Am., 1985. Home: 2178 Lakemoor Dr SW Olympia WA 98512-5564

PERKINS, GLADYS PATRICIA, retired aerospace engineer; b. Crenshaw, Miss., Oct. 30, 1921; d. Douglas and Zula Francis (Crenshaw) Franklin; m. Benjamin Franklin Walker, Sept. 26, 1952 (dec.); m. William Silas Perkins, Sept. 16, 1956 (dec.). BS in Math., Le Moyne Coll., 1943; postgrad., U. Mich., 1949, U. Calif., L.A., 1955-62. Mathematician Nat. Adv. Com. for Aeronautics (now NASA), Hampton, Va., 1944-49, Nat. Bur. of Standards, L.A., 1950-53, Aberdeen Bombing Mission, L.A., 1953-55; assoc. engr. Lockheed Missiles Systems Div., Van Nuys, Calif., 1955-57; staff engr. Hughes Aircraft Co., El Segundo, Calif., 1957-80; engring. specialist Rockwell Internat., Downey, Calif., 1980-87, ret., 1987. Contbr. articles to profl. publs. Named Alumnus of Yr. Le Moyne-Owen Coll., 1952; recipient Nat. Assn. for Equal Opportunity in Higher Edn. award Le Moyne-Owen Coll. Mem. Soc. of Women Engrs., Assn. of Computing Machinery, Le Moyne-Owen Alumni Assn. (pres. 1984), U. Mich. Alumni Club, Alpha Kappa Alpha. Democrat. Congregationalist. Home: 4001 W 22nd Pl Los Angeles CA 90018-1029

PERKINS, JOSEPH JOHN, JR., lawyer; b. Pitts., Feb. 22, 1954; s. Joseph John Sr. and Joan Elizabeth (Challingsworth) P.; m. Rebecca Ellen Graham, Apr. 7, 1984; children: Benjamin Joseph, Nathaniel Graham. BS in Geol. Engring. magna cum laude, Princeton U., 1976; JD, U. Denver, 1979. Bar: Alaska 1979, U.S. Dist. Ct. Alaska 1979, U.S. Ct. Appeals (9th cir.) 1983, U.S. Supreme Ct. 1986. Assoc. Guess & Rudd, Anchorage, 1979-84, shareholder, 1984—. Trustee Rocky Mountain Mineral Law Found., Denver, 1988—. Mem. ABA (vice chmn. hard mineral com., sect. on natural resources and environ. law 1992-93), Alaska Bar Assn. (chmn. natural resources law sect. 1984-88), Sigma Xi, Tau Beta Pi. Republican. Episcopalian. Home: 7202 Hunter Cir Anchorage AK 99502-4185 Office: Guess & Rudd 510 L St Ste 700 Anchorage AK 99501-1959

PERKINS, ROY FRANK, internist, former university official; b. Rock Island, Ill., Aug. 31, 1918; s. Frank and Jennie (Baker) P.; m. Marion Karen Mazursky, Mar. 13, 1942; children: Marc, Nancy, Franklin, John, James. BS, U. Ill., Urbana, 1939; MD, U. Ill., Chgo., 1941; MS, U. Minn., 1949. Diplomate Am. Bd. Internal Medicine. Intern LA County Hosp, 1941-42; fellow Mayo Clinic, Rochester, Minn., 1942-48, staff physician, 1948-49; pvt. practice, Alhambra, Calif., 1949-79; staff physician Scripps Clinic and Rsch. Found., La Jolla, Calif., 1979-87; v.p. for med. affairs Baylor U. Med. Ctr., Dallas, 1988-92; ret., 1992; dir. health care svcs. AMA, Chgo., 1966-67; sr. mgmt. counsel Booz, Allen & Hamilton, Chgo., 1967-90; clin. prof. medicine U. So. Calif., L.A., 1968-92. Contbg. author: The New Health Care Market, 1985; also articles. Capt. M.C., U.S. Army, 1944-46. Mem. Am. Coll. Physician Execs., Am. Diabetes Assn. (bd. govs. So. Calif. 1955-57), L.A. Diabetes Assn. (pres. 1955, San Gabriel br. 1960-61). Home: 6427 Caminito Aronimink La Jolla CA 92037-5801

PERKINS, THOMAS JAMES, venture capital company executive; b. Oak Park, Ill., Jan. 7, 1932; s. Harry H. and Elizabeth P.; m. Gerd Thune-Ellefsen, Dec. 9, 1961; children: Tor Kristian, Elizabeth Siri. B.S.E.E., M.I.T., 1953; M.B.A., Harvard U., 1957. Gen. mgr. computer div. Hewlett Packard Co., Cupertino, Calif., 1965-70, dir. corp. devel., 1970-72; gen. partner Kleiner & Perkins, San Francisco, 1972-80; sr. ptnr. Kleiner Perkins Caufield & Byers, San Francisco, from 1980; chmn. bd. Tandem Computers, Inc., Cupertino, Calif.; chmn. bd. Tandem Computers, Genentech; dir. Spectra Physics., Corning Glass Works, Collagen Corp., LSI Logic Corp., Hybritech Inc., Econics Corp., Vitalink Communications Corp. Author: Classic Supercharged Sports Cars, 1984. Trustee San Francisco Ballet, 1980—. Mem. Nat. Venture Capital Assn. (chmn. 1981-82, pres. 1980-81). Clubs: N.Y. Yacht, Links, Am. Bugatti (pres. 1983—). Office: Tandem Computers Inc 10435 Tantau Ave Cupertino CA 95014-3548 also: Genentech Inc 460 Point San Bruno Blvd South San Francisco CA 94080-4918*

PERKINS, WENDY FRANCES, author, speaker; b. Chgo., May 9, 1953; d. Francis Joseph and Elaine (Birmingham) P. BA, Bradley u., 1975; M in Internat. Mgmt., Am. Grad. Sch., 1978. Cert. stockbroker. Temporary worker different agys., L.A., 1987-90; lectr., speaker Permanently Collectible, L.A. and Phoneix, 1990—; stockbroker and bond trader, Beverly Hills, Calif., 1983-86. Author, pub.: Temporarily Yours, 1989; contbr. articles to profl. jours. Temporary worker adv. OWN, 1990-94; testified to U.S. Senate Labor Com., Washington, 1993. Mem. Cosmep, Calif. Book Publicists, Mu Epsilon Pi. Democrat. Office: Permanently Collectible PO Box 897 Scottsdale AZ 85252-0897

PERKINS, WILLIAM CLINTON, company executive; b. Decatur, Ill., Mar. 7, 1920; s. Glen Rupert and Frances Lola (Clinton) P.; m. Eunice Cagle, Sept. 7, 1939 (div. 1954); stepchildren: William Rea Cagle, Howard Christy Cagle; 1 child, Clinton Colcord; m. Lillian Wuollet, Sept. 7, 1955 (div. 1965); m. Shirley Thomas, Oct. 24, 1969. BS Mil. Sci. and Meteorology, U. Md., 1954; MS in Bus. and Pub. Adminstrn., Sussex Coll., Eng., 1975. Commd. USAF, 1943-73, advanced through grades to col.; with Ship Systems div. Litton Ind., Culver City, Calif., 1973-75; dir. material Hughes Aircraft Co., Tehran, Iran, 1974-78; mgr. internat. s/c Northrop Corp., Dahran, Saudi Arabia, 1978-81; dir. materiel CRS, Riyadh, Saudi Arabia, 1981-83; head major subcontracts Lear Ziegler Corp., Santa Monica, Calif., 1984-88; pres., CEO Ice Village Ctrs., Inc., L.A., 1988—; bd. dirs. Ice Village Ctrs., Inc., L.A., Forefront Industries, Maywood, Calif. Bd. dirs. World Children's Transplant Fund, L.A., 1987—; mem. Mayor's Space Adv. Com., L.A., 1970-74; mem. aerospace hist. com. Mus. Sci. and Industry, L.A., 1988—. Mem. AIAA (sect. chmn. 1970), Ret. Officers Assn. (pres. 1992—), Soc. for Non-destructive Testing (program chmn. 1973), Am. Soc. Quality Control, Am. Meteorol. Soc., Sigma Alpha Epsilon (alumni chpt. pres. 1974-76). Home: 8027 Hollywood Blvd Los Angeles CA 90046-2510

PERKO, WALTER KIM, computer consultant, systems analyst; b. Mpls., Dec. 8, 1950; s. Eero Nestor and Lorene (Hansen) P. AS in Computer Sci./Aeronautics, U. Minn., 1975. Contract computer analyst/cons. Dept. Def., Dept. Justice, NASA and pvt. industry; systems operator The Home Multi Media Hobbyst BBS, San Francisco, 1987—. Author: EarthCom, 1993, 10,000 Sounds & Songs of the Digital Data Archives, 1993, MegaMODMadNess, 1994. With USN, 1968-72, Korea and Vietnam. Mem. Soc. Automotive Engring. Lutheran. Office: MIDI & MultiMedia Exch Home MultiMedia Hobbyist PO Box 640608 San Francisco CA 94164-0608

PERKOWSKI, MAREK ANDRZEJ, electrical engineering educator; b. Warszawa, Poland, Oct. 6, 1946; came to U.S., 1981; s. Adam Perkowski and Hanna (Zielinska) Mystkowska; m. Ewa Kaja Wilkowska, Oct. 26, 1974; 1 child, Mateusz Jan. MS in Electronics with distinction, T.U. of Warsaw, 1970, PhD in Automatics with distinction, 1980. Sr. asst. Inst. of Automatics, T.U. of Warsaw, 1973-80, asst. prof., 1980-81; vis. asst. prof. Dept. Elec. Engring., U. Minn., Mpls., 1981-83; assoc. prof. Portland State U., 1983-94, prof., 1994—. Co-author: Theory of Automata, 3d edit., 1976, Problems in Theory of Logic Circuits, 4th edit., 1986, Theory of Logic Circuits-Selected Problems, 3d edit., 1984; contbr. 134 articles to profl. jours., 11 chpts. to books. Mem. Solidarity, Warsaw, 1980-81. Recipient Design Automation award SIGDA/ACM/DATC IEEE, 1986-91; rsch. grantee NSF, 1991, 94, Commn. for Families Roman Cath. Ch., Vatican, 1981, Air Force Office Sci. Rsch., 1995. Mem. IEEE (Computer Soc.), Polish Nat. Alliance, Assn. for Computing Machinery, Am. Soc. for Engring. Edn. Roman Catholic. Home: 15720 NW Perimeter Dr Beaverton OR 97006-5391 Office: Portland State U Dept Elec Engring PO Box 751 Portland OR 97207-0751

PERLMAN, DAVID, science editor, journalist; b. Balt., Dec. 30, 1918; s. Jess and Sara P.; m. Anne Salz, Oct. 15, 1941; children: Katherine, Eric, Thomas. A.B., Columbia U., 1939, M.S., 1940. Reporter Bismarck (N.D.) Capital, 1940; reporter San Francisco Chronicle, 1940-41, reporter, sci. editor, 1952-77, city editor, 1977-79, assoc. editor, sci. editor, 1979—; reporter New York Herald Tribune, Paris, N.Y.C., 1945-49; European corr. Colliers mag. and New York Post, 1949-51; Regents prof. human biology U. Calif., San Francisco 1974; vis. lectr. China Assn. Sci. and Tech., Beijing, Chengdu and Shanghai, 1983; sci. writer-in-residence U. Wis., 1989. Contbr. articles to major mags. Founding dir. Squaw Valley (Calif.) Community of Writers; dir. Alan Guttmacher Inst., 1985—; trustee Scientists Inst. for Pub. Info., 1986-94. Served with inf. USAAF, 1941-45. Recipient Atomic Indsl. Forum award, 1975, Westinghouse Sci. Writing award, 1976, Ralph Coates Roe medal ASME, 1978, Margaret Sanger Community Svc. award, 1981, Fellows' medal Calif. Acad. Scis., 1984, Career Achievement award Soc. Profl. Journalists, 1989, Glenn T. Seaborg award Internat. Platform Assn., 1993; Poynter fellow Yale U., 1984, Carnegie fellow Stanford U., 1987. Fellow Calif. Acad. Scis.; mem. AAAS (adv. bd. Science-81-86 mag., com. Pub. Understanding of Sci. 1985-90), Coun. for Advancement Sci. Writing (pres. 1976-80), Nat. Assn. Sci. Writers (pres. 1970-71, Disting. Sci. Journalism award 1994), Astron. Soc. Pacific (dir. 1976-78), Sigma Xi. Office: Chronicle Pub Co 901 Mission St San Francisco CA 94103-2905

PERLMAN, JANET, indexer, editor, writer; b. Bklyn.; m. Gerald M. Perlman, Jan. 21, 1962; children: Eric S., Joshua N. BS in Chemistry, CUNY, 1961; MA in Mgmt., U. Phoenix, 1990. Editorial asst. Crowell Collier Pub., N.Y.C., 1961-62; editorial supr. John Wiley & Sons, N.Y.C., 1962-65; pvt. practice N.Y.C., 1965-77; adminstrv. asst. Jewish Community Ctr., Phoenix, 1978-80, Jewish Fedn. Greater Phoenix, 1980-83, City of Phoenix Parks Dept., 1983-94; free-lance indexer, owner Southwest Editorial, Phoenix, 1991—. Mem. AAUW, Am. Soc. Indexers, Am. Med. Writers Assn., Ariz. Ctr. for the Book, Women's Am. ORT (pres. Phoenix region 1992-94). Home: 2114 E Escuda Rd Phoenix AZ 85024-1250

PERLMAN, SETH JOSEPH, political risk analyst; b. Newark, Dec. 4, 1960; s. Preston Leonard and Evelyn Ann (Binder) P.; m. Lisette Antonia Quinones, 1990 (div. May 1992); 1 child, Rachel Aleeza; m. Alexandria Melissa Molyneaux, Apr. 2, 1993; children: Grant, Rachel. BA in Internat. Rels., George Washington U., 1985; MA in Internat. Rels., Am. U., 1988; PhD in Internat. Security Policies, U. Md., 1990. Cert. Spanish lang. translator U.S. Dept. of State. Rsch. analyst mid.-east program U.S. Dept. State, Washington, 1984-86; legis. asst. fgn. affairs U.S. Rep. Edward F. Feighan, Washington, 1986-88; sr. writer Def. & Fgn. Affairs mag. Internat. Media, Inc., Alexandria, Va., 1988-90; S.W. editor Pacific Shipper Mag., Long Beach, Calif., 1990-91; mng. dir. Polecon Resources, Inc., Huntington Beach, Calif., 1991—; contbr. Knight-Ridder, Inc., El Segundo, Calif., 1990-91, Reuter's News Svc., L.A., 1990-91. Contbr. articles to profl. jours., periodicals, mags. Congl. Rsch. Svc. Def. and Fgn. Affairs rsch. grantee Libr. of Congress, 1988; Ctr. for Rsch. and Documentation of European Community grantee, 1989. Mem. Am. U. Alumni Assn. (v.p. 1989-90). Office: Polecon Resources Inc 19744 Beach Blvd Ste 433 Huntington Beach CA 92648

PERLMAN, SUSAN GAIL, organization executive; b. N.Y.C., Dec. 29, 1950; d. Philip and Pearl Perlman; ed. Hunter Coll., N.Y.C., 1967-71. Copywriter, Blaine Thompson Advt., N.Y.C., 1968-71; copywriter J.C. Penney Co., N.Y.C., 1971-72; assoc. exec. dir. Jews for Jesus, San Francisco, 1972—, bd. dirs., also editor Issues mag.; speaker, cons. in field; steering com. mem. Lausanne Consultation on Jewish Evangelism, Copenhagen, Denmark; del. Bapt. Gen. Conf.; mem. Lausanne Com. for World Evangelization, Oxford, Eng. Mem. editorial bd. Evang. Missions Quar. Mem. Am. Jewish Congress, Interdenominational Fgn. Missions Assn. (mem. exec. com.). Democrat. Baptist. Office: 60 Haight St San Francisco CA 94102-5802

PERLOFF, JEFFREY MARK, agricultural and resource economics educator; b. Chgo., Jan. 28, 1950; s. Harvey S. and Miriam (Seligman) P.; m. Jaqueline B. Persons, Aug. 15, 1976; 1 child, Lisa. BA, U. Chgo., 1972; PhD, MIT, 1976. Asst. prof. U. Pa., Phila., 1976-80; asst. prof. U. Calif., Berkeley, 1980-82, assoc. prof., 1982-89, prof., 1989—. Author: (with Dennis Carlton) Modern Industrial Organization, 1990, 2d edit., 1994; contbr. numerous articles to profl. jours. Office: U Calif Dept Agrl Econs 207 Giannini Hall Berkeley CA 94720

PEROOMIAN, RUBINA, literature and history educator; b. Tabriz, Iran; came to the U.S., 1978; d. Bagdasar and Parik (Sarkissian) Minassian; m. Neshan Peroomian, June 16, 1963; children: Vahé, Oshin. BS in Civil Engring., U. Tehran, 1960; diplome d'Etude Française, Sorbonne U., Iran, 1963; MA in Middle Eastern Language and Culture, U. Calif., L.A., 1982, PhD in Middle Eastern Language and Culture, 1989. Site engr. and office engr. Lausanne Construction Co., Tehran, Iran, 1960-72; ptnr. and office mgr. SPILAT Construction Co., Tehran, 1972-78; tchr. Modern Armenian History Ferahian H.S., Encino, Calif., 1985-86; teaching asst., teaching fellow UCLA, 1986-89; instr. Armenian Lit. Armenian Relief Soc., Amherst, Mass., 1987; lectr. Armenian Lang. Glendale C.C., Calif., 1989-90; lectr. Armenian Lit. U. Laverne, Calif., 1991-92; guest lectr. Armenian Hist. Dept. History UCLA, 1991-92, lectr. Armenian Studies, 1989—; mem. com. preparing handbooks for tchrs. on minority students Calif. State Dept. Edn., 1982-84; mem. writing/adv. com. Assembly Bill 1273 Human Rights Genocide Model Curriculum for K-12 Social Sci. and History courses, Calif. State Dept. Edn., 1985-87; mem. com. to prepare curriculum and program for teaching the Armenian Question (recent Armenian history) in Armenian Schs., 1986; chair rsch. and info. projects Armenian Nat. Com., 1986-88; mem. com. in charge of developing sets of examinations for minority langs. to certify bilingual tchrs. in Calif. Commn. on Tchr. Credentialing, 1992—; mem. editorial bd. Haykakan Spiurk Encyclopedia; mem. cen. bd. govs. Armenian Prelacy Schs., 1976-78; chair Com. for Armenian Schs. Extra-Curricular Activities, Tehran, Iran, 1976-78; mem. bd. dirs. Armenian Nat. Com., 1981-82, 87-89; chair Cen. Exec. Armenian Youth Fedn., 1982-84; mem. ednl. coun. Western Prelacy Exec. Coun., 1994—; mem. Com. for Armenian Students in Pub. Schs., 1994—; lectr. in field. Author: Hay Tad-11 and Hay Tad-12 (The Armenian Question), 1990-94, Literary Responses to Catastrophe, A Comparison of the Armenian and the Jewish Experience, 1993; contbr. articles to profl. jours. Recipient scholar NDEA, Karekin Der Avedissian scholar; rsch. fellow G.E. Von Grunebaum, Near Eastern Langs. Mem. MLA, Am. Fedn. Tchrs., Nat. Assn. Armenian Studies, Middle Eastern Studies Assn., Soc. Armenian Studies.

PERRAULT, CHARLES RAYMOND, computer scientist; b. Arvida, Que., Can., Mar. 7, 1949; came to U.S., 1983; s. Charles H. and Lucette (Benington) P.; m. Elizabeth J. Trueman, Mar. 12, 1983; 1 child, Andrew. BSc, McGill U., Montreal, Can., 1969; MA, U. Mich., 1971, PhD, 1975. Asst. to assoc. to full prof. U. Toronto, Ont., Can., 1974-83; sr. computer scientist SRI Intenrat., Menlo Park, Calif., 1983-85, dir. natural lang. program, 1985-88, dir. artificial intelligence ctr., 1988—; cons. prof. Stanford U., 1983—. Fellow Am. Assn. for Artificial Intelligence; mem. AAAS, Assn. Computing Machinery, Internat. Joint Confs. on Artificial Intelligence (chair of trustees), Assn. for Computational Linguistics, Sigma Xi. Office: SRI Internat 333 Ravenswood Ave Menlo Park CA 94025-3453

PERRELLA, ANTHONY JOSEPH, electronics engineer; b. Boulder, Colo., Sept. 16, 1942; s. Anthony Vincent and Mary Domenica (Forte) P.; B.S., U. Wyo., 1964, postgrad., 1965; postgrad. U. Calif. at San Diego, 1966-67, U. Calif. at Irvine, 1968-70; m. Pamela Smith, July 19, 1980; 1 child, Kathleen. Flight engr. U.S. Naval Tng. Devices Center, San Diego, 1965-67; rsch. engr. Collins div. Rockwell Internat. (formerly Collins Radio Co.), Newport Beach, Calif., 1967-69, electromagnetic interference and TEMPEST group head, 1969-74, supr., 1974-75, mgr., 1975-77, mgr. systems integration, 1977, mgr. space communication systems, 1977-78; sr. mem. tech. staff ARGOSystems Inc., Sunnyvale, Calif., 1978—, program mgr., 1978-81, dep.

dept. mgr. EW Systems, 1980-83, div. EW staff engr., 1983-84, dept. mgr., 1984-87, Sun Microsystems Inc., Mountain View, 1987-89; prin. A.J. Perrella-Cons., Cupertino, Calif., 1989—; v.p. rsch. and devel. Things Unlimited, Inc., Laramie, Wyo., 1965-72, pres., 1972-75; bd. dirs., v.p. Columbian Credit Union. Bd. dirs. Bay Area Found. Mentally Retarded Children, 1994—. Mem. IEEE, AAAS, Am. Mgmt. Assn., N.Y. Acad. Scis., Assn. Old Crows (v.p. San Jose chpt., dep. dist. 21), KC, Tau Kappa Epsilon. Roman Catholic. Home: 931 Brookgrove Ln Cupertino CA 95014-4667 Office: 2550 Garcia Ave Mountain View CA 94043-1109

PERRILL, FREDERICK EUGENE, information systems executive; b. Charlotte, N.C., Sept. 11, 1939; s. Frederick Eugene and Dorothy (Miller) P.; m. Kathryne Sims, June 1, 1963. BS in Engring., U.S. Naval Acad., 1962; MS in Bus., Naval Postgrad. Sch., 1969; postgrad., NAval War Coll., 1972-73. USCG Masters lic. Commd. ensign USN, 1962, advanced through grades to capt., 1982; supply officer USS Biddle DDG-5, 1962-63, USS Hermitage LSD-34, 1963-64; comptr. Amphibious Staff, 1964-68; dir. MIS systems, acctg., transp. Naval Supply Depot, Yokouka, Japan, 1969-72; project mgr. fin. systems design Asst. Sec. of Navy, 1973-76; dir. logistics USS Concord, 1976-78; project mgr. Fin. Systems, Washington, 1978-81; commanding officer Fin. and Acctg. Ctr., San Diego, 1981-83; dir. ops. Naval Supply Ctr., Oakland, 1984-85; asst. chief of staff MIS, COMMS. Naval Airforce Pacific, Coronado, Calif., 1985-86; ret. Naval Airforce Pacific, Coronado, 1986; sr. group mgr. Planning Rsch. Corp., San Diego, 1986-87; v.p. OPS/COO R.D. Ram Corp., San Diego, 1987-88; dir. Fourth Generation Tech., LaJolla, Calif., 1988-90; pres. Perrill Info. Systems, San Diego, 1990—; cons. Titan Corp. LaJolla, 1991—, Monger Industries, San Diego, 1988—, Delfin Corp., San Jose, 1990-91, Dobbs Ho., Memphis, 1986; farmer owner Pine Tree (property mgmt. co.), 1965—; owner, pres. Ancient Mariner Boat Svcs., 1990—. Contbr. articles to profl. jours. Asst. scout master Boy Scouts Am., Yokosuka, Japan, 1969-72; Protestant lay leader USS Concord AFS-5, Norfolk, Va., 1976-78. Mem. VFW, Naval Sailing Assn., Am. Legion, Humane Soc. of U.S., Disabled Am. Vets. Presbyterian. Home: 4785 Seda Dr San Diego CA 92124-2457

PERRIN, KENNETH LYNN, university chancellor; b. L.A., July 29, 1937; s. Freeman Whitaker and Lois Eileen (Bowen) P.; m. Shirley Anne Cupp, Apr. 2, 1960; children: Steven, Lynne. BA, Occidental Coll., 1959; MA, Calif. State U., Long Beach, 1964; PhD, Stanford U., 1969. Lic. in speech pathology, Calif. Chmn. dept. communicative disorders U. Pacific, Stockton, Calif., 1969-77; dir. edn. and sci. programs Am. Speech-Lang.-Hearing Assn., Rockville, Md., 1977-80; dean Faculty Profl. Studies West Chester U., Pa., 1980-82; acting acad. v.p. West Chester U., 1982, pres., 1983-91; pres. Coun. on Postsecondary Edn., Washington, 1991-93; chancellor, system sr. v.p. U. Hawaii, Hilo and West Oahu, 1993—; cons. in field, 1969-76; pres. north region Calif. Speech Hearing Assn., 1975-76. Co-author: monograph Prevalence of Communicative Disorders, 1981; contbr. articles to profl. jours.; editor: Guide to Graduate Education Speech Pathology and Audiology, 1980. Chmn. Southeastern chpt. Greater Brandywine Br. ARC; trainee Vocat. Rehab. Adminstrn., 1965-69. Named Disting. Alumnus Sch. Humanities Calif. State U., Long Beach, 1988. Fellow Am. Speech-Lang.-Hearing Assn. (vice chmn. edn. tng. bd. 1975-77 cert. clin. competence in speech pathology); mem. West Chester C. of C. (pres. 1988). Home: 543 Kaanini St Hilo HI 96720 Office: 200 W Kawili St Hilo HI 96720-4075*

PERROT, PAUL NORMAN, museum director; b. Paris, France, July 28, 1926; came to U.S., 1946, naturalized, 1954; s. Paul and K. Norman (Derr) P.; m. Joanne Stovall, Oct. 23, 1954; children—Paul Latham, Chantal Marie Claire, Jeannine, Robert. Student, Ecole du Louvre, 1945-46, N.Y. U. Inst. Fine Arts, 1946-52. Asst. The Cloisters, Met. Mus. Art, 1948-52; asst. to dir. Corning (N.Y.) Mus. Glass, 1952-54, asst. dir. mus., 1954-60, dir., 1960-72; editor Jour. Glass Studies, 1959-72; asst. sec. for mus. programs Smithsonian Instn., Washington, 1972-84; dir. Va. Mus. Fine Arts, 1984-91; dir. Santa Barbara Mus. Art, 1991-94, cons., 1994—; lectr. glass history, aesthetics, museology; past v.p. Internat. Coun. Mus. Found.; past pres. N.E. Conf. Mus.; past pres. Internat. Centre for Study of Preservation and Restoration of Cultural Property, Rome, mem. coun., 1974-88. Author: Three Great Centuries of Venetian Glass, 1958, also numerous articles on various hist. and archael. subjects. Former trustee Winterthur Mus.; former trustee, treas. Mus. Computer NEtwork; mem. Internat. Cons. Com. for the Preservation of Moenjodaro; chmn. adv. com. World Monuments Fund; mem. vis. com. Getty Conservation Inst. Mem. Am. Assn. Mus. (past v.p., coun. 1967-78), N.Y. State Assn. Mus. (past pres.), Internat. Assn. History Glass (past v.p.) Corning Friends of Library (past pres.), So. Tier Library System (past pres.).

PERRY, DALE LYNN, chemist; b. Greenville, Tex., May 12, 1947; s. Francis Leon and Violet (Inabinette) P. BS, Midwestern U., 1969; MS, Lamar U., 1972; PhD, U. Houston, 1974. NSF fellow dept. chemistry Rice U., Houston, 1976-77; Miller Research fellow dept. chemistry U. Calif.-Berkeley, 1977-79; prin. investigator solid state chemistry and spectroscopy Lawrence Berkeley Lab. U. Calif., 1979—, sr. scientist, 1987—; lectr. Ana G. Mendez Ednl. Found., 1988. Author, editor: Instrumental Surface Analysis of Geologic Materials, 1990, Applications of Analytical Techniques to the Characterization of Materials, 1992, Applications of Synchrotron Radiation Techniques to Materials Science, 1993, Applications of Synchrotron Radiation Techniques to Materials Science II, 1995; contbr. articles to profl. jours. Recipient Sigma Xi Nat. Research award U. Houston, 1974. Fellow Royal Soc. Chemistry (London); mem. Am. Chem. Soc. (chmn. materials chemistry and engring. subdiv., indsl. and engring. chemistry div. 1992—), Soc. Applied Spectroscopy, Coblentz Soc., Materials Rsch. Soc. (corp. participation com. 1991—), Sigma Xi. Office: U Calif Lawrence Berkeley Lab Mail Stop 70A-1150 Berkeley CA 94720

PERRY, DAVID NILES, public relations executive; b. Utica, N.Y., Mar. 7, 1940; s. Francis N. and Marion H. P.; B.S., Utica Coll. Syracuse U., 1962; m. Jacqueline J. Adams, Dec. 21, 1962. Pub. affairs rep. Allstate Ins. Co., Pasadena, Calif., 1966-67; dir. press rels. L.A. C. of C., 1968; rep. pub. rels. Lockheed Propulsion Co., Redlands, Calif., 1968-70; mgr. pub. rels. Bozell & Jacobs Inc., L.A., 1970-73, Phoenix, 1974; pres. David Perry Pub. Rels. Inc., Scottsdale, Ariz.; exec. dir. Ariz. Water Quality Assn., Cert. Collision Repair Assn. Mem. Ariz. Commn. Ariz. Environment, 1972—. Served with USNR, 1962-65. Mem. Pub. Rels. Soc. Am. (accredited, dir. Phoenix chpt. 1975-82, pres. 1978). Office: 6819 E Diamond St Scottsdale AZ 85257-3233

PERRY, DONALD LESTER, II, venture capitalist; b. Culver City, Calif., Jan. 21, 1958; s. Donald Lester Sr. and Joyce Estella (Kirklin) P.; m. Michael Albert Behn, July 24, 1982. BA in Econs. and Polit. Sci., Williams Coll., 1979; MBA in Strategic Mgmt., Claremont (Calif.) Grad. Sch., 1990. Fgn. exch. trader Morgan Guaranty Trust Co., N.Y.C., 1979-80; exec. recruiter Benson-McBride & Assoc., Beverly Hills, Calif., 1980-82; asst. v.p. money markets divsn. Nat. Australia Bank, L.A., 1982-86; v.p., eurodollar trader Sanwa Bank of Calif., L.A., 1986-88; v.p. comml. loans Union Bank, L.A., 1989-90; mng. ptnr. Pine Cobble Ptnrs., L.A., 1990—; speaker Pacific Coast Regional SBDC, L.A., 1989—, Nat. Assn. Black MBAs, L.A., 1990—, So. Calif. Edison/Joint Coun., L.A., 1990—. Contbr. articles to mags. Mem. Town Hall of Calif., L.A., 1990. Recipient Outstanding Entrepreneur of Yr., Peter F. Drucker Ctr. at Claremont Grad. Sch., 1995; named Positive Black Role Model, Assn. Black Women Entrepreneurs, 1993. Mem. L.A. Venture Assn., L.A. Urban Bankers, Pacific Coast Regional Small Bus. Devel. Corp. (mem. loan com. 1990-94), L.A. World Affairs Coun. Republican. Office: 811 W 7th St Ste 1000 Los Angeles CA 90017

PERRY, JAMES GREGORY, sales and marketing executive; b. Missoula, Mont., Oct. 4, 1952; s. Joseph Tarsisus and Mary Cathrine (Schneider) P.; m. Diana Sue Coen, May 24, 1974; 1 child, Natalie Shureé. Student, Yuba Coll., Marysville, Calif., 1970-72. Credit supr. CBS Mus. Instruments, Fullerton, Calif., 1975-76, mktg. rep., 1976-80, sales rep., 1980-82; mktg. rep. Paiste Am., Inc., Brea, Calif., 1982-85, nat. sales mgr., 1985-91; field sales mgr. Am. Med. Sales, 1991-93; dir. sales and mktg., 1993—; caption chief percussion So. Calif. Judges Assn., 1983—; percussion judge So. Calif. Sch. Band Orch. Assn., 1985-93. With USN, 1972-75. Mem. Mu Sigma Kappa (pres. 1972), Jaycees (pres. Castleton, Ind. chpt. 1981), Am. Drum Line Assn. (v.p. 1994—). Office: Am Med Sales Inc 4928 W Rosecrans Ave Hawthorne CA 90250-6616

PERRY, JAMES R., construction company executive; b. 1936. With Great Lakes Dredge & Dock & Co., Ohio, 1958-67; various positions to exec. v.p. Hawaiian Dredging Constrn. Co., Honolulu, 1967-89; pres. Dillingham Constrn. Pacific Ltd., Honolulu, 1989-93; pres., COO Dillingham Constrn. Pacific Ltd., Pleasanton, Calif., 1993—. Office: Dillingham Constrn Corp 5960 Inglewood Dr Pleasanton CA 94588-8535*

PERRY, JOHN C., retired officer, non-profit development executive; b. Danville, Ill., Nov. 13, 1932; s. Frank and Ellen (Blew) P.; children: Jon C., LuAnne. BA, U. Ill., 1955; MBA, So. Ill. U., 1972. Commd. 2d lt. USAF, 1956, advanced through grades to lt. col., 1973, navigator, bombadier, 1956-76, ret., 1976; campaign assoc. United Way Pierce County, Tacoma, Wash., 1976-80, sr. campaign mgr., 1980-86, dir. planned giving, 1986-92, dir. ctr. for nonprofit devel., 1992—. Mem. Soc. Fundraising Execs., N.W. Devel. Officers Assn., Ret. Officers Assn., Air Force Assn. Republican. Baptist. Office: United Way Pierce County 734 Broadway Tacoma WA 98402-3710

PERRY, JOSEPH MARTIN, fire chief; b. Oakland, Calif., Oct. 25, 1950; s. Joseph Martin and Doris Elizabeth (Wagner) P.; m. Cynthia Marie John Perry, Jan. 10, 1970; children: Marsha, David. AA in Fire Sci., Chabot C.C., 1978; BA in Pub. Affairs and Adminstrn., Calif. State U., Hayward, 1995. Firefighter Newark (Calif.) Fire Dept., 1971-76; fire capt. Union City (Calif.) Fire Dept., 1976-82, fire divsn. capt., 1983-91; fire chief Napa (Calif.) Fire Dept., 1991—. Mem. Nat. Fire Protection Assn., Calif. Fire Chief's Assn. (2d v.p. 1995, Fire Prevention Liaison, 1992-95), Internat. Fire Chief's Assn., Internat. Fire Code Inst. Office: Napa Fire Dept PO Box 660 Napa CA 94559-0660

PERRY, JOYCE FITZWILLIAM, secondary school educator; b. San Francisco, Aug. 12, 1946; d. Leo Matthew and Mildred E. (McBain) Fitzwilliam; m. Robert James Perry, June 21, 1969 (div. Apr. 1980); children: Dominic Matthew, Alex Michael. BA, Gonzaga U., 1968; M in Counseling, U. Phoenix, 1995. Cert. tchr., counselor, Ariz. Middle sch. lang. arts and social studies tchr. Frank Odle Jr. High, Bellevue, Wash., 1969-72, Greenway Middle Sch., Phoenix, 1979-82, Sunrise Middle Sch., Scottsdale, Ariz., 1982—; mem. evaluation team North Ctrl. Schs. Accreditation, Ariz., 1988-90. Author: Seasons of the Heart, 1982. Named Middle Level Educator of Yr., Ctrl. Ariz. Middle Level Assn., 1994. Mem. ACA, Phi Delta Kappa.

PERRY, MICHAEL DEAN, professional football player; b. Aiken, S.C., Aug. 27, 1965. Student, Clemson. Defensive tackle Cleveland Browns, 1988-94, Denver Broncos, 1994—. Voted to Pro Bowl, 1989-91, 93; named defensive tackle The Sporting News All-Pro team, 1989-93. Office: Denver Broncos 13655 Broncos Pkwy Englewood CO 80112

PERRY, WILLIAM JOSEPH, food processing company executive; b. Sacramento, Calif., Nov. 4, 1930; s. Joseph Nasciemeto and Jennie (Nunez) P.; m. Beverly Ann Styles, Dec. 9, 1956 (div. May 1981); children: Katherine, Bill Jr., Kathleen, Barbara; m. Leslie Z. Blumberg, June 30, 1986. BS, U. Calif., Berkeley, 1953; MBA, U. So. Calif., 1995. Quality control supr. Stokely Van Camp, Oakland, Calif., 1953-54; plant mgr. Safeway Stores, Brookside div., Grandview, Wash., 1954-61, Gallo Winery, Modesto, Calif., 1961-62; gen. mgr. Bocca Bella Olive Assoc., Wallace, Calif., 1962-65; v.p. Early Calif. Ind., L.A., 1965-74, Fairmont Foods, Santa Ana, Calif., 1974-75; pres. Cal Agra Ind., Stockton, Calif., 1975-76; exec. v.p. Food Brokers Internat., L.A., 1976—; pres., co-owner G.F.F., Inc., L.A., 1981—; dir. G.F.F., Inc., L.A., 1981—, Food Brokers, Inc., L.A., 1976—, Cozad & Assoc. Ad Agy., Encino, Calif., 1985-87. Wrestling com., dir. protocol, L.A. Olympic Com., 1981-84. Mem. Nat. Food Brokers Assn., Assn. of Dressings and Sauces, Nat. Juice Processing Assn., Nat. Single Service Assn., Am. Chem. Soc., Westlake Tennis & Swim Club. Republican. Roman Catholic. Home: 3700 Brigantine Cir Westlake Vlg CA 91361-3816 Office: GFF Inc 5443 E Washington Blvd Los Angeles CA 90040-2105

PERSCHBACHER, DEBRA BASSETT, lawyer; b. Pleasanton, Calif., Oct. 28, 1956; d. James Arthur and Shirley Ann (Russell) Bassett; m. Rex Robert Perschbacher, June 4, 1989. BA, U. Vt., 1977; MS, San Diego State U., 1982; JD, U. Calif., Davis, 1987. Bar: Calif. 1987, D.C. 1990, U.S. Dist Ct. (no. and ea. dists.) Calif. 1988, U.S. Ct. Appeals (9th cir.), 1988, U.S. Supreme Ct., 1991. Guidance counselor Addison Cen. Supr. Union, Middlebury, Vt., 1982-83, Milton (Vt.) Elem. Sch., 1983-84; assoc. Morrison & Foerster, San Francisco, 1986; jud. clk. U.S. Ct. Appeals (9th cir.), Phoenix, 1987-88; assoc. Morrison & Foerster, Walnut Creek, Calif., 1988-92; sr. atty. Calif. Ct. Appeal (3d appellate dist.), Sacramento, 1992—; tutor civil procedure, rsch. asst. U. Calif., Davis, 1985-87. Sr. articles editor U. Calif. Law Rev., Davis, 1986-87; editor, 1985-86. Bd. dirs. Samaritan Counseling Ctr., 1994—. Mem. AAUW, ABA (vice chmn. ethics com. young lawyers divsn. 1989-91, exec. com. labor and employment law com. 1989-90), Sacramento County Bar Assn., Women Lawyers of Sacramento. Democrat. Home: 1438 41st St Sacramento CA 95819-4041 Office: Ct Appeal 914 Capitol Mall Sacramento CA 95814-4811

PERSE, ARIA LEON, international business marketing professional; b. L.A., Dec. 30, 1962; s. Constante A. and Marianne (Cobetti) P. BS, State U. Long Beach, 1982; MS, UCLA, 1987, PhD, 1989. Chmn., CEO Advanced Tech. USA, Inc., Wilmington, Del., 1991—; cons. Kaempen U.S.A. Inc. Mem. exec. campaign bd. Republican Party, L.A., 1992. Home: 17311 Castellammare Dr Pacific Palisades CA 90272-4139

PERSON, DONALD AMES, SR., pediatrician, rheumatologist; b. Fargo, N.D., July 17, 1938; s. Ingwald Haldor and Elma Wilhelmenia (Karlstrom) P.; m. Blanche Durand, Apr. 28, 1962; children: Donald Ames Jr., David Wesley. Student, Gustavus Adolphus Coll., 1956-58, U. Minn., 1958-59; BS, U. N.D., 1961; MD, U. Minn., 1963. Intern Mpls.-Hennepin County Gen. Hosp., 1963-64; resident neurol. surgery Mayo Clinic and Mayo Grad. Sch. Medicine, Rochester, Minn., 1967, fellow in microbiology, 1968-70; rsch. assoc. Baylor Coll. Medicine, Houston, 1971, Arthritis Found. fellow, 1972-74, mem. faculty, asst. prof. internal medicine, 1971-78, asst. prof. pediatrics, 1980-87, resident in pediatrics, 1978-80; asst. attending pediatrics Harris County Hosp. Dist., 1980-88; rheumatologist Tex. Children's Hosp., 1980-88, attending pediatrician, 1982-88; cons. Kelsey Seybold Clinic, 1980-88, Houston Shriner's Crippled Children's Hosp., 1983-88 , Houston Meth. Hosp., 1983-88, St. Luke's Episcopal Hosp., 1983-88, Honolulu Shriner's Crippled Children's Hosp., 1988—; prof. clin. pediatrics U. Hawaii Sch. Medicine, Honolulu, 1991—; prof. clin. pediatrics Uniformed Svcs. U. Health Scis., Bethesda, Md., 1993—, chief gen. pediatric svc., 1991-94; chief ambulatory pediatrics, Tripler Army Med. Ctr., Tripler AMC, Hawaii, 1988-94, asst. chief dept. pediatrics, 1988-94, chief dept. pediatrics, 1994—; "A" proficiency designator in pediatrics from Surgeon Gen. of the Army, 1990. Contbr. articles to profl. jours. With AUS, 1964-66, col., 1987—. Arthritis Found. sr. investigator, 1975-77. Fellow Am. Acad. Pediatrics (v.p. chpt. west uniformed svcs. sect. 1994-95, mem. exec. com. uniformed svcs. sect., 1995—, adv. mem. exec. com. Hawaii chpt. 1994—); mem. AAAS, Am. Fedn. Clin. Rsch., AMA, Am. Coll. Rheumatology, Am. Soc. Microbiology, Soc. Pediatric Rsch., Am. Soc. Tropical Medicine and Hygiene, Arthritis Found. (dir., med. adv. bd.), Assn. Mil. Surgeons U.S. (Philip Hench award 1990), Harris County Med. Soc., Houston Acad. Medicine, Houston Pediatric Soc., Internat. Orgn. Mycoplasmologists, N.Y. Acad. Sci., N.D. Acad. Sci., Soc. Exptl. Biology and Medicine, So. Soc. Pediatric Rsch., S.W. Sci. Forum, Tex. Med. Assn., Tex. Pediatric Soc., Tex. Rheumatism Assn., Tissue Culture Assn., Honolulu Pediatric Soc., U.S. Fedn. Culture Collections. Mem. Evang. Luth. Ch. in Am., deacon, 1991-94. Home: 1321 Parks Rd Honolulu HI 96819-2131 Office: Tripler Army Med Ctr Honolulu HI 96859

PERSON, TOM (STANLEY THOMAS PERSON), publisher, editor; b. Seattle, Oct. 7, 1952; s. Stanley Nicholas and Lenore Margarite (Hansen) P.; m. Frances Louise Schroeder, Feb. 17, 1990 (div. Mar. 1995). BA in Edn., Western Wash. U., 1974. Faculty advisor Shoreline C.C., Seattle, 1976-78; logistics support specialist Martin Marietta Astronautics, Denver, 1983-90; ops. mgr. Quantum CM, Inc., Wheat Ridge, Colo., 1993—; pub., editor Laughing Bear Press, Denver, 1976—. Columnist: (periodical) New Pages, 1990-91, Small Press, 1995; editor: (periodical) Laughing Bear, 1976-78, (newsletter) Laughing Bear Newsletter, 1976— (Small Press Newsletter award 1992), The Newsletter Cons., 1994—. Mem. COSMEP. Home: 65 Clarkson St Apt 608 Denver CO 80218-3747 Office: Laughing Bear Press PO Box 36159 Denver CO 80236-0159

PERTHOU, ALISON CHANDLER, interior designer; b. Bremerton, Wash., July 22, 1945; d. Benson and Elizabeth (Holdsworth) Chandler; m. A.V. Perthou III, Sept. 9, 1967 (div. Dec. 1977); children: Peter T.R., Stewart A.C. BFA, Cornish Coll. Arts, 1972. Pres. Alison Perthou Interior Design, Seattle, 1972—, Optima Design, Inc., Seattle, 1986-89; treas. Framejoist Corp., Bellevue, Wash., 1973-90; pres. Classics: Interiors & Antiques, Inc., 1988—; cons. bldg. and interiors com. Children's Hosp., Seattle, 1976—; guest lectr. U. Wash., Seattle, 1980-81. Mem. bd. trustees Cornish Coll. Arts, Seattle, 1973-80, sec. exec. com., 1975-77; mem. procurement com. Patrons of N.W. Cultural and Charitable Orgn., 1985—, mem. antiques com., 1991—. Mem. Am. Soc. Interior Design, Seattle Tennis Club (mem. house and grounds com. 1974-75), City Club. Office: 4216 E Madison St Seattle WA 98112-3237

PESIC, PETER DRAGAN, liberal arts educator; b. San Francisco, May 11, 1948; s. Paul Sviatoslavovic and Milena Ljubomirovna (Bojovic) Pesic; m. Ssu Isabel Weng, June 2, 1984; children: Andrei Petrovic, Alexei Petrovic. AB, Harvard U., 1969; MS, Stanford U., 1970, PhD, 1975. Lectr. Stanford (Calif.) U., 1976-80; tutor St. John's Coll., Santa Fe, 1980—, musician-in-residence, 1984—. Contbr. articles to profl. jours. Danforth fellow Danforth Found., 1969-75. Democrat. Orthodox. Office: Saint John's Coll 1160 Camino de la Cruz Blanca Santa Fe NM 87501

PESTANA-NASCIMENTO, JUAN M., civil, geotechnical and geoenvironmental engineer, consultant; b. Caracas, Venezuela, June 24, 1963; came to U.S., 1986; s. Domingos Pestana and Maria Cisaltina Nascimento; m. Sandra Mattar, Oct. 29, 1988; 1 child, Maria Teresa Pestana. BS summa cum laude, U. Catolica Andres Bello, Caracas, 1985; MS, MIT, 1988, ScD, 1994. Registered civil engr., Venezuela. Teaching asst. U. Catolica Andres Bello, Caracas, 1982-85, instr., lectr., 1986; cons. engr. GEODEC, Geotech. Cons., Caracas, 1986-92; civil engr. CALTEC, Hydraulic Cons., Caracas, 1983-86, asst. engr., 1983-85; asst. engr. T.W. Lambe, Inc., Cambridge, Mass., 1990; cons. Portfolio Mgmt., Cambridge, 1990-92; rsch. asst. MIT, Cambridge, Mass., 1992-94; asst. prof. U. Calif., Berkeley, 1994—. Contbr. articles to profl. jours. Gran Mariscal de Ayacucho scholar, 1986-88, INTEVEP scholar, 1989-92. Mem. ASCE, ASTM, Can. Soc. Geotech. Engrs., Internat. Soc. Soil Mechanics and Found. Engring., Sigma Xi. Home: 10 San Antonio Ct Walnut Creek CA 94598 Office: U Calif Dept Civil Engring 440 Davis Hall Berkeley CA 94720-1710

PETER, ARNOLD PHILIMON, lawyer; b. Karachi, Pakistan, Apr. 3, 1957; came to U.S., 1968; s. Kundan Lal and Irene Primrose (Mall) P. BS, Calif. State U., Long Beach, 1981; JD, Loyola U., L.A., 1984; MS, Calif. State U., Fresno, 1991. Bar: Calif. 1985, U.S. Dist. Ct. (ea., so., no. and cen. dists.) Calif. 1986, U.S. Ct. Appeals (9th cir.) 1989, U.S. Ct. Appeals (11th cir.) 1990. Law clk. appellate dept. Superior Ct., L.A., 1984-85, U.S. Dist. Ct. (ea. dist.) Calif., Fresno, 1986-88; assoc. Pepper, Hamilton & Scheetz, L.A., 1988-89, McDermott, Will & Emery, P.A., L.A., 1989-90, Cadwalader, Wickersham & Taft, L.A., 1990-91; labor and employment counsel City of Fresno, Calif., 1991-94; dir. labor rels. Universal Studios, Hollywood, Calif.; adj. prof. law San Joaquin (Calif.) Sch. Law, 1993—, Calif. State U., Fresno, 1993—, acad. inquiry officer, 1993—, Calif. State U., Fresno. Contbr. articles to profl. jours. Mem. ABA, L.A. County Bar Assn. (mem. conf. of dels., com. on fed. cts.), Calif. State Bar Assn. (chmn. com. on fed. cts., exec. com. labor and employment law sect.), L.A. Athletic Club. Office: Universal Studios Bldg #SC79 100 Universal City Pl Universal City CA 91608

PETERLIN, BORIS MATIJA, physician; b. Ljubljana, Slovenia, July 4, 1947; came to U.S., 1961; s. Anton and Leopoldina (Leskovic) P.; m. Anne Scheel-Larsen, July 21, 1984; children: Anton Alexander, Sebastian Bogomir. BS, Duke U., 1968; MD, Harvard U., 1973. Diplomate Am. Bd. Internal Medicine, Am. Bd. Rheumatology. Intern, resident Stanford (Calif.) Univ. Hosp., 1973-75, sr. resident, 1977-78; fellow in rheumatology, immunology Stanford (Calif.) U. Hosp., 1978-81; asst. prof. U. Calif., San Francisco, 1981-88, assoc. prof., 1988-94, prof., 1994—; asst. investigator HHMI, Bethesda, Md., 1984-89, assoc. investigator, 1989-95, investigator, 1995—. Contbr. articles to Nature, Cell, Genes and Development, others. Lt. commdr. USPHS, 1975-77. Rosalind Russell Arthritis scholar U. Calif.; recipient Alexander von Humboldt prize, 1995. Fellow Am. Soc. for Clin. Investigation; mem. Am. Assn. Immunology, Am. Fedn. Clin. Rsch., Am. Soc. for Microbiology, Am. Coll. Rheumatology, Phi Beta Kappa, Phi Lambda Upsilon. Democrat. Roman Catholic. Home: 14 Hill Point Ave San Francisco CA 94117-3603 Office: U Calif San Francisco-HHMI 3d and Parnassus San Francisco CA 94143-0724

PETERLIN, CAROL MARIE, mental health nurse; b. Medina, N.Y., Nov. 9, 1944; d. Charles William and Sophia (Polick) Roesel; m. Stanley Morgan Peterlin, Aug. 27, 1967; children: Paul Stanley, Marcus Morgan. BSN, Loma Linda U., 1966; MS, U. Alaska, Juneau, 1987; PhD, U. San Jose, 1994. RN, Calif.; cert. pub. health nurse, reality therapist, basic practicum instr. Pub. health nurse Santa Cruz County Pub. Health Dept., Watsonville, Calif., 1967, 69-71; lab. asst. LaMel Lab., L.A., 1968-69; instr. nursing L.A. Coll. Vocat. Nursing, 1968-69; dir. nurses Capitola (Calif.) Extended Care Hosp., 1974-75; nurse, counselor Am. Weight Control Clinic, Santa Cruz, Calif., 1975; staff nurse Community Hosp. Santa Cruz, 1975-76; quality assurance nurse coord. Monterey Bay Area PSRO, Salinas, Calif., 1976-78; substitute tchr. various sch. dists., 1975-82, pvt. youth counselor, 1980-87; dep. dir., clin. supr., quality assurance coord. San Benito County Mental Health Svcs., Hollister, Calif., 1989—; dep. dir., youth counselor Pathfinders, Alhambra, Calif., 1967-69, Monument Valley, Utah, 1980, Glendale, Ariz., 1980-82; mem. Alcohol, Mental Health and Social Svcs. Bd., City and Borough of Juneau, 1986-87. Sec.-treas. Little League Baseball, Petersburg and Juneau, 1982-83, head scorekeeper, 1983-87; mem. Petersburg Parks and Recreation Bd., 1983-84; head scorekeeper varsity baseball team San Benito H.S., Hollister, 1988, 89, mem. parents' graduation com., 1988, 89; mem. San Benito County Maternal, Child, Adolescent Health Bd. Mem. Inst. for Ctrl. Theory Reality Therapy & Quality Mgmt., Adult Sys. of Care Com. in Bay Area, Children's Sys. of Care Com. in Bay Area, Calif. Children's Coords., Calif. 3632 Coords., Bay Area Psychiat. Emergency Svcs. Dirs., Calif. Quality Assurance Coords., No. Calif. Quality Assurance Coords., Phi Delta Kappa. Office: San Benito County Mntl Hlth Svcs 1111 San Felipe Rd Ste 104 Hollister CA 95023-2814

PETERS, ANN M., linguistics educator; b. Pasadena, Calif., July 31, 1938; d. J. Harold and Virginia Jane Wayland; m. Michael W. Peters, June 3, 1959 (div. 1972); 1 child, Ted. AB, Bryn Mawr Coll., 1959; MA, U. Wis., 1961, PhD, 1966. From asst. researcher to assoc. prof. U. Hawaii, Honolulu, 1966-85, prof. linguistics, 1985—. Author: The Units of Language Acquisition, 1983; editorial bd. Jour. of Child Language, 1986—; contbr. articles to profl. jours. NSF grantee, 1984-85. Mem. Linguistic Soc. Am.

PETERS, BARBARA HUMBIRD, writer, editor; b. Santa Monica, Calif., Sept. 26, 1948; d. Philip Rising and Caroline Jean (Dickason) P. AA, Santa Monica Coll., 1971; BS, San Diego State U., 1976; postgrad. UCLA, 1981-82, 84. Ptnr. Signet Properties, L.A., 1971-85; tech. editor C. Brewer & Co., Hilo, Hawaii, 1975; editor The Aztec Engineer mag., San Diego, 1976-77; regional publicist YWCA, San Diego, 1977-78; campaign cons. Rep. Congl. and Assembly Candidates San Diego; pollster L.A. Times, 1983; pres., dir. Humbird Hopkins Inc., San Clemente, Calif., 1978-91; pub. rels. cons. ASCE, San Diego, 1975-76, Am. Soc. Mag. Photographers, San Diego, 1980. Author: The Layman's Guide to Raising Cane: A Guide to the Hawaiian Sugar Industry, 1975, The Students' Survival Guide, 1976, 2d edit. 1977. Mem. Mayor's Coun. on Librs., L.A., 1969; mem. Wilshire Blvd. Property Owners Assn., Santa Monica, 1972-78; docent Mus. Sci. and Industry, L.A., 1970; founding mem. Comml. and Indsl. Properties Assn., Santa Monica, 1982-89. Recipient Acting award Santa Monica Coll., 1970. Mem. NAFE, Internat. Assn. Bus. Communicators, Sales and Mktg. Execs. Assn. Avocations: travel, opera, puns.

PETERS, BARBARA M. STRATTON, career counselor, administrator; b. Pocatello, Idaho, Apr. 18, 1949; d. Richard Wendell and Margaret Mae (Harris) Stratton; m. Thomas Henry Peters, Aug. 7, 1984. BA in Polit. Sci., Idaho State U., 1967, MEdn in Student Personnel Work, 1976. Asst. dir.

career planning and placement Idaho State U., Pocatello, 1972-77; assoc. dir. Career Devel. Ctr., Humboldt State U., Arcata, Calif., 1977-90, career counselor, 1990—, mem. academic senate, 1984-87, 1992—, cooperative edn. adv. bd., 1980—, student retention com., 1984—, adv. com. on services to disabled students, 1980—. Campaign worker Bosco for Congress Campaign, Arcata, 1982; mem. Redwoods Occupational Edn. Council, Eureka, 1977—, pres., 1985-86. Mem. Am. Assn. Counseling and Devel., Am. Coll. Personnel Assn., Western Assn. Student Employment Adminstrs., Idaho Personnel and Guidance Assn., AAUW (Mitchell-Loux scholarship 1967-68), Phi Kappa Phi. Democrat. Roman Catholic. Avocations: singing, camping, baseball. Home: 221 Dollison St Eureka CA 95501-4307 Office: Humboldt State U Career Devel Ctr Arcata CA 95521

PETERS, CAL ANTHONY, engineer; b. Lebannon, Oreg., Oct. 28, 1957; s. Cecil Laverne and Shirley Ann (Swem) P.; m. Laurel Ann Hubert, Aug. 11, 1988. Cert. mechanic, small engine repair. Gen. machine operator South Bay Cable, Idyllwild, Calif., 1974-77, asst. engr., 1977-84, chief engr., 1984—. Mem. Marine Tech. Soc. Office: South Bay Cable PO Box 67 54125 Maranatha Dr Idyllwild CA 92549

PETERS, CLAIRE LEILA, public relations, advertising executive; b. Tulsa, Okla., July 12, 1948; d. Elmer Ernest and Eleanor Claire (Wyvell) Hogg.; m. Glen Allen Bluemel, July 29, 1969 (div. Apr. 1977); m. William Robert Peters, Dec. 2, 1977. BA in Journalism, Advt. Sequence, Tex. Tech. U., 1970. Account exec. Wm. Golden Avt., Stockton, Calif., 1973-77; asst. dir. mktg. Stockton (Calif.) Savings & Loan Assn., 1977-78; account exec. Press Courier Newspaper, Oxnard, Calif., 1979-81; asst. v.p. mktg., pub. and mem. rels. Farm Credit Banks of Sacramento (Calif.) and Tex,, 1981-86; mgr. pub. rels. Sunkist Growers, Inc., Sherman Oaks, Calif., 1986—. mem. Internat. Assn. Bus. Comms. (v.p. membership 1991—), Pub. Rels. Soc. Am., Nat. Coun. Farmer Coops. (pub. rels. com.), Agrl. Coun. Am. (pub. rels. com.), Nat. Agri-mktg. Assn. (pres. So. Calif. chpt.). Office: Sunkist Growers Inc 14130 Riverside Dr Sherman Oaks CA 91423-2313

PETERS, DOUGLAS CAMERON, mining engineer, geologist; b. Pitts., June 19, 1955; s. Donald Cameron and Twila (Bingel) P. BS in Earth and Planetary Sci., U. Pitts., 1977; MS in Geology, Colo. Sch. Mines, 1981, MS in Mining Engring., 1983. Technician, inspector Engring. Mechanics Inc., Pitts., 1973-77. Research asst. Potential Gas Agy., Golden, Colo., 1977-78; geologist U.S. Geol. Survey, Denver, 1978-80; cons. Climax Molybdenum Co., Golden, 1981-82; cons., Golden, 1982-84; mining engr., prin. investigator U.S. Bur. Mines, Denver, 1984—; bur. rep. to Geosat Com., 1984—; program chmn. GeoTech Conf., Denver, 1984-88, mem. long. range planning subcom., 1989-92, gen. chmn., 1991; engr. in tng. #11800, Colo., Wyo., profl. geologist #367. Author: Physical Modeling of Draw of Broken Rock in Caving, 1984, Bur. Mines Articles and Reports; editor COGS Computer Contbns., 1986—, Geology in Coal Resource Utilization, 1988-91; assoc. editor Computers & Geosciences, 1989—; contbr. articles to profl. jours.; guest editor various jours. Am. Inst. Profl. Geologists, 1984, 85, 86, Appreciation award, 87, Spl. award Denver Geotech Com., 1988, Appreciation award, 1989. Mem. Computer Oriented Geol. Soc. (charter, com. chmn. 1983—, pres. 1985, dir. 1986, contbg. editor newsletter 1985—), Geol. Soc. Am., Rocky Mountain Assn. Geologists, Am. Inst. Profl. Geologists (cert. profl. geologist #8274), Soc. Mining Metallurgy and Exploration, Am. Assn. Petroleum Geologists (astrogeology com., 1984—, remote sensing com. Energy Mineral div. v.p. 1990-91, pres. 1991-92, Cert. of Merit award 1992, 93, Pres.'s award 1993, Disting. Svc. award 1995), Am. Soc. Photogrammetry and Remote Sensing, Nat. Space Soc., Colo. Mining Assn., Pitts. Geol. Soc., Planetary Soc., Space Studies Inst. Republican. Office: US Bur Mines Denver Fed Ctr PO Box 25086 Denver CO 80225-0086

PETERS, JOHN U., English language educator; b. Snohomish, Wash., June 20, 1945; s. John and Virginia Jean (Eagle) Ursulescu. BA, UCLA, 1967; MA, Johns Hopkins U., 1970; PhD, U. Wis., 1973. Lectr. in English L.A. C.C. Dist., 1972—, Calif. State U., Northridge, 1977—; textbook cons., 1984—. Author: The Elements of Critical Reading, 1991; contbr. articles, revs. to profl. jours. Mem. MLA. Home: PO Box 416 Sunland CA 91041-0416 Office: Calif State U Dept English Northridge CA 91330

PETERS, KENNETH DARRYL, SR., contracts administrator; b. Englewood, N.J., Jan. 27, 1949; s. John Conna Jr. and Lena Ponease (Jones) P.; m. Katie M. Coleman, Nov. 27, 1976; children: Kenneth Jr., Kevin. BA, Fisk U., 1971; MSW, U. Kans., 1973; postgrad., U. Calif., Berkeley, 1974, U. Calif., Davis, 1979. Sch. cons. Cath. Social Svcs., Stockton, Calif., 1973-78; placement coord. Dept. Devel. Disabilities, Stockton, Calif., 1978-80; program cons. Dept. Social Svcs., Sacramento, Calif., 1980-84; program analyst Dept. Devel. Disabilities, Sacramento, Calif., 1984-87; contracts adminstr. Dept. Transp., Stockton, 1987-95; health program advisor Dept. Health Svcs., Sacramento, 1995—; mem. Mental Health Adv. Bd., Stockton, 1978-90, Child Health & Disability Prevention, Stockton, 1979-90, Nat. Conf. Social Welfare, San Francisco, 1983. Lt. col. USAR, 1980—. Recipient Comendation Calif. State Senate, 1983, Calif. State Assembly, 1983. Mem. NAACP, Nat. Assn. Black Social Workers (bd. dirs.), Orgn. Black Calif. Voters (bd. dirs.), Calif. Bd. Respiratory Care (subcom. chmn. 1990—), Alpha Phi Alpha (sec. 1992—). Democrat. Baptist. Home: 2663 Fallenleaf Dr Stockton CA 95209-1169 Office: Dept Health Svcs 830 S St Sacramento CA 95814

PETERS, KEVIN CASEY, university library worker; b. L.A., Nov. 14, 1952; s. Edwin Dale Peters and Marylee (Loftus) Green. AA in Speech, L.A. City Coll., 1975; BA in Govt. and Social Rels., Immaculate Heart Coll., 1980; MA in Film and TV, UCLA, 1992. Nat. sec. People's Party, Washington, 1976-79; office mgr., statewide campaign hdqrs. Californians for a Bilateral Nuclear Weapons Freeze, 1982; studio transp. driver Teamsters # 399, L.A., 1979-89; libr. gifts coord. UCLA Univ. Rsch. Libr., 1989—. Author: C-SPAN: Congress on Television, 1992, (poems) Atoms for Peace, 1984. Mem. state exec. com. Peace and Freedom Party, Calif., 1980—; mem. exec. com. AFSCME local 3235, UCLA, 1990—; campaign treas. Gerald Horne for U.S. Senate, Calif., 1992; candidate for trustee L.A. C.C., 1993; apptd. Libr. Com. for Diversity, UCLA, 1990-93. Mem. ACLU, Union for Dem. Comms., Ctr. for Voting and Democracy. Home: 446 S Van Ness Ave Los Angeles CA 90020-4615

PETERS, LOIS ANN, healthcare manager, nutritionist; b. St. Louis, Sept. 30, 1954; d. John and Frances Mary (Justice) P. BS in human nutrition, food mgmt., U. Mo., 1977. Registered dietitian. Clinical interventionist St. Louis Heart Assn., St. Louis, Mo., 1977-79; clinical dietitian St. Charles Med. Ctr., Bend, Oreg., 1979-86; pvt. practice Bend, Oreg., 1979-86; edn. mgr. St. Charles Med. Ctr., 1986-93, adminstrn. and human resources cluster mgr., 1993—. Commn. Bend Urban Area Planning Comm., 1992-95; bd. liaison Bend Devel. Bd., 1992-94; bd. dirs. Child Care Coun., Bend, 1979-81, Women, Infants and Children adv. bd., Bend, 1979-81; bd. dirs., exec. com. Am. Heart Assn., 1986-89, Area Health Edn. Ctr., 1991—. Recipient Cert. of Appreciation Oreg. Health Svcs., 1990. Mem. Am. Coll. Healthcare Execs., Am. Soc. Healthcare, Edn. and Traning, Am. Soc. Human Resources Adminstrn., Bend Rotary Club (com. chair 1988—), Bend C. of C. (com. chair. 1987—, Pres. award 1988). Roman Catholic. Office: St Charles Med Ctr 2500 NE Neff Rd Bend OR 97701-6015

PETERS, RAYMOND EUGENE, computer systems company executive; b. New Haven, Aug. 24, 1933; s. Raymond and Doris Winthrop (Smith) P.; m. Millie Mather, July 14, 1978 (div. Nov. 1983). Student, San Diego City Coll., 1956-61; cert., Lumbleau Real Estate Sch., 1973, Southwestern Coll., Chula Vista, Calif., 1980. Cert. quality assurance engr. Founder, pub. Silhouette Pub. Co., San Diego, 1960-75; co-founder, news dir. Sta. XEGM, San Diego, 1964-68; news dir. Sta. XERB, Tijuana, Mex., 1973-74; founder, chief exec. officer New World Airways, Inc., San Diego, 1974-75; co-founder, exec. vice chmn. bd. San Cal Rail, Inc.-San Diego Trolley, San Diego, 1974-77; founder, pres. Ansonia Sta., micro systems, San Diego, 1986—; co-founder, dir. S.E. Community Theatre, San Diego, 1960-68; commr. New World Aviation Acad., Otay Mesa, Calif., 1971-77; co-founder New World Internat. Trade & Commerce Commn., Inc., 1991—. Author: Black Americans in Aviation, 197l, Profiles in Black American History, 1974, Eagles Don't Cry, 1988; founder, pub., editor Oceanside Lighthouse, 1958-60, San Diego Herald Dispatch, 1959-60. Co-founder, bd. dirs. San Diego County Econ. Opportunity Commn., 1964-67; co-founder Edn. Cultural Complex, San Diego, 1966-75; co-founder, exec. dir. S.E. Anti-Poverty Planning Coun., Inc., 1964-67; mem. U.S. Rep. Sectarian Inner Circle Com., Washington, 1990; mem. United Ch. Crist. With U.S. Army, 1950-53, Korea. Mem. Am. Soc. Quality Control, Nat. City C. of C., Internat. Biog. Soc., Afro-Am. Micro Systems Soc. (exec. dir. 1987—), Negro Airmen Internat. (Calif. pres. 1970-75, nat. v.p. 1975-77), Internat. Masonic Supreme Coun. (Belgium), Internat. Platform Assn., U.S. C. of C., Greater San Diego Minority C. of C. (bd. dirs. 1974—, past chmn. bd.), Masons (Most Worshipful Grand Master), Shriners (Disting. Community Svc. award 1975), Imperial Grand Potentate, Nubian Order. Republican. Home: Meadowbrook Estates # 245 8301 Mission Gorge Rd Santee CA 92071-3500

PETERS, RICHARD, lawyer; b. Bklyn., June 6, 1945; s. Edmund Richard and Louise (Parks) P. BA, Tulane U., 1967; MA, Fla. State U., 1968, PhD, 1985; JD, Calif. Western, 1988. Bar: Calif. 1989. Instr. English U. San Diego, 1991, San Diego City Coll., 1989—, San Diego Mesa Coll., 1989—; panel atty. Appellate Defenders, Inc., San Diego, 1989—. Author: (poetry) On Aging, 1991. Mem. ABA, San Diego County Bar Assn. Office: Richard Peters Atty 304 W Ivy St Apt 204 San Diego CA 92101-1837

PETERS, RITA, university administrator; b. Riverhead, N.Y., Sept. 1, 1953; d. Herbert E. and Loni S. Peters. BA, Lycoming Coll., Williamsport, Pa., 1974; MS, U. Calif., Davis, 1990. Cert. fund raising exec. Cons. The Winning Edge, Stockton, Calif., 1984-92; dir. grants and founds. U. of the Pacific, Stockton, 1992—. Lilly Endowment Rsch. awardee, 1991. Mem. Nat. Soc. Fund Raising Execs., Sister City Assn. of Stockton, Rotary. Home: PO Box 9020 Stockton CA 95208-1020 Office: Univ of Pacific 2d Floor Burns Tower 3601 Pacific Cir Stockton CA 95211-0110

PETERS, ROBERT WAYNE, direct mail and catalog sales specialist; b. LaPorte, Ind., Jan. 2, 1950; s. Harry Carl and Dorothy May (Fischer) P.; m. Frances Kay Cooley, Aug. 21, 1971; children: Carolyn Marie, Angela Lynn. BA, Purdue U., 1972. CLU. Mgr. pension adminstrn. Gen. Life Ins. Corp., Milw., 1973-75; dir. qualified plan devel. Cen. Life Assurance Co., Des Moines, 1976-84; v.p. individual ops. First Farwest Ins. Co., Portland, Oreg., 1984-90; pres. CAF Enterprises, Inc., Portland, 1990—; lectr. various govt. agys. Contbr. articles to profl. jours. Mem. N.W. Vintage Thunderbird (v.p. 1988, pres. 1989-90, exec. bd. 1991, sec. 1992-93, treas. 1995), Optimists (treas. West Des Moines chpt. Iowa Club 1983-84). Office: CAF Enterprises Inc 9997 SW Avery St Tualatin OR 97062-9517

PETERS, ROBERT WOOLSEY, architect; b. Mpls., Mar. 24, 1935; s. John Eugene and Adelaide Elizabeth (Woolsey) P. BArch., U. Minn., 1958; MArch., Yale U., 1961. Registered architect, N.Mex., Ariz. Dir. design Schaefer & Assocs., Wichita, Kans., 1975-76; participating assoc. Skidmore Owings & Merrill, Chgo., 1961-74; ptnr. Addy & Peters, Albuquerque, 1979-82; owner Robert W. Peters AIA Architect, Albuquerque, 1982—. Exhibited work Centre Georges Pompidou, Paris, 1980; Univ. Art Mus., Albuquerque, 1982, 92, Albuquerque Mus., 1988. Bd. dirs. Contemporary Art Soc. N.Mex. Contbr. articles to Century Mag., Progressive Architecture, House & Garden, House Beautiful, also others. Recipient honor awards N.Mex. Soc. Architects, 1980-83, 86, 87, 92; honor award HUD, 1980, 5th Nat. Passive Solar Conf., Amherst, Mass., 1981. Fellow AIA. Democrat. Roman Catholic. Club: Yale of N.Mex.

PETERS, ROXANNE LEIGH, nurse practitioner, consultant; b. Gillette, Wyo., Sept. 11, 1954; d. Leonard Andrew and Margaret Rose (DeGering) McCullough; m. Michael James Thiry, Dec. 27, 1975 (div. Aug. 1978); m. John Peters, Oct. 28, 1978; 1 child, Mandi. BA in Nursing, Augustana Coll., Sioux Falls, S.D., 1976; BS in Bus. Adminstrn., Black Hills State U., 1995. RN, Wyo.; cert. nurse practitioner, physicians asst. Nurse Crook County Meml. Hosp., Sundance, Wyo., 1976-77; nurse practitioner So. Nev. Meml. Hosp., Las Vegas, 1978, Advanced Health Systems, Sundance, 1978-82; v.p. Med. Emergency Rescue Cons., Sundance, 1981—; bus. mgr., patient edn. coordinator N.W. Wyo. Med. Ctr., Sundance, 1986-88; assoc. prof. Eastern Wyo. Coll. Outreach Program, 1994—; cons. Parachute Med. Ruscue Service, Kalamazoo, Mich., 1981, Refugee Relief Internat., Boulder, Colo., 1983—. Treas., trustee Crook County Sch. Dist., Sundance, 1982-85; chmn. Crook County unit Am. Cancer Soc., Cheyenne, Wyo., 1983-88; trustee Bd. Coop. Ednl. Services, Gillette, 1982-85, vice chmn., 1984-85; bd. dirs. Crook County Family Violence and Sexual Assault Services, 1985-92, also vice chmn., vol. trainer; commr. Wyo. Commn. for Women, 1983-89; speaker Adolescent Drug/Alcohol Community Group, 1987-94; co-presenter Bush Faculty Devel. Conf.; presenter Midcontinent Inst. Undergrad. Rsch. Conf.; rechr., author Local Bank Rsch. project. Kellogg Found. grantee, 1977; S.D. Small Bus. Inst. Project winner, 1992. Fellow Wyo. Assn. Physician Assts. (bd. dirs. 1978); mem. Am. Acad. Physicians Assts. Republican. Home: PO Box 1070 Sundance WY 82729-1070 Office: 18 Valley Rd Sundance WY 82729

PETERS, SAMUEL ANTHONY, lawyer; b. N.Y.C., Oct. 25, 1934; s. Clyde and Amy (Matterson) P.; m. Ruby M. Mitchell, Apr. 28, 1962; children: Robert, Samuel, Bernard. BA, N.Y.U.; LLB, Fordham U. Bar: N.Y. 1961, Calif. 1973, U.S. Supreme Ct. 1967. Trial atty. Dept. Justice, 1961-68; staff atty. Lawyer's Com. for Civil Rights Under Law, 1968-69; atty. legal dept. Atlantic Richfield Co., L.A., 1970, litigation counsel, price and wage control counsel, 1970-73, labor counsel, 1972-79, sr. counsel pub. affairs, 1980-85; coord., instr. paralegal edn. Rio Hondo Coll.; bd. dirs. Weingart Ctr. Assn., Women's Transitional Living Ctr. With U.S. Army, 1955-58. Mem. ABA, Langston Bar Assn., L.A. County Bar Assn., Toastmasters Internat. (pres. chpt. 1391), Alpha Phi Alpha. Home: 11471 Kensington Rd Los Alamitos CA 90720-3803

PETERS, SHIRLEY ANN, pediatrics nurse; b. Burbank, Calif., July 25, 1948; d. Frank F. and Marion Belle (Thorn) P. Diploma, Kaiser Found. Sch. Nursing, 1970; BS in Health Sci., Chapman Coll., 1978, MS in Health Sci., 1981. RN, Calif.; cert. pediatric nurse practitioner. Pediatric nurse practitioner Kaiser-Permanente Med. Ctr., Panorama City, Calif., 1974-87; rsch. nurse practitioner Pharmacology Rsch. Inst., Van Nuys, Calif., 1987-88; pediatric nurse practitioner, infection control practitioner Granada Hills (Calif.) Community Hosp., 1988-89; pediatric nurse practitioner Med. Ctr. of North Hollywood, Calif., 1989-90, CIGNA Health Plans of Calif., North Hollywood, 1990-92; patient care coord., quality improvement/utilization rev. Alternative Health Care, Chatsworth, Calif., 1992-94; pediatric nruse practitioner Childrens Hosp. of L.A., L.A., 1994—. Mem. United Nurse's Assn. Calif. (clinic co-chair, parliamentarian, negotiator, NAPNAP, Assn. Infection Control Practitioners.

PETERS, WILLIAM FRANK, art educator; b. Oakland, Calif., Nov. 8, 1934; s. Clifford Leslie and Gladys Fay (Parrish) P.; m. Patricia Ann Redgwick, June 3, 1956 (div. 1973); 1 child, David William. B. Art Edn. with honors, Calif. Coll. Arts & Crafts, 1961; postgrad., various schools, various locations. Cert. spl. secondary art edn. life, gen. jr. high life. Summer campus art dir., instr. Richmond (Calif.) Unified Sch. Dist., 1961-66, Sch. of Fine Arts, Mt. Diablo Unified Sch. Dist., Concord, Calif., 1967-74; instr. Liberty Union H.S. Dist., Brentwood, Calif., 1961—, chmn. arts & crafts dept., 1976-91; dist. rep. Pacific Art Assn., East Contra Costa County, Calif., 1967-70, Calif. Art Assn., East Contra Costa County, 1970-74; accreditation team mem. Western Assn. Schs. and Colls., Albany, Calif., 1981; film evaluator Contra Costa County Schs., 1965-84. Exhibited in group shows at Contra Costa County Fair (oil painting Best of Show 1968, watercolor Best of Show 1990, 1st pl. photography 1987-95), Delta Art Show, Antioch, Calif. (1st pl. jewelry 1979), Festival of Color, Concord, Calif. (1st pl. ceramic 1963);. Fundraiser United Crusade, Brentwood, Calif., 1980-83; publicity vol. East Contra Costa County Soroptimist Club, East County Rape/Crisis Ctr., Kappa Beta, John Marsh Meml. Assn., Knightsen 4-H, Delta Rotary Club, Delta Recreation Dept., Oakley Women's Club, Town of Byron, others. Named Contra Costa County Tchr. of Yr. AAUW, 1981; postgrad scholar Calif. Coll. of Arts and Crafts, 1962-63. Mem. NEA, Calif. Tchrs. Assn., Liberty Edn. Assn. (chmn. salary com., past v.p., chmn. evaluation com., chmn. pers. policies com., chmn. scholarship com.), Delta Art Assn. (past bd. dirs.), Brentwood C. of C. (dir. Brentwood Christmas decorations 1968-94). Democrat. Office: Liberty Union HS Dist 104 Oak St Brentwood CA 94513-1132

PETERSEN, AIMEE BERNICE, interior designer, artist, landscape designer; b. North Vancouver, B.C., Can., Apr. 13, 1939; d. Samuel Nathaniel and Aimee Selena (Topping) Hadley; m. Gary Andrew Petersen, May 1, 1959; children: Todd William, Troy Andrew. Student, U. Wash., 1957-59, Edmonds (Wash.) C.C., 1967-74. Owner, designer The Designing Woman, Edmonds, 1979—. Pres. Ballinger Elem. PTA, 1969-71, Madrona Jr. H.S., 1973, 74; deaconess United Presbyn. Ch., Edmonds, 1967-75. Recipient Golden Acorn award Ballinger Sch. PTA, 1972; named Woman of Yr., Jr. Women Federated Women's, 1967. Mem. Nat. Fedn. Ind. Bus. People, Better Bus. Bur., Bus. and Profl. Women, Women Investing Now (founder 1991), Edmonds C. of C., Sons of Norway (Lodge 130 social chmn. 1987—). Presbyterian. Home: 5528 173rd Pl SW Lynnwood WA 98037-3034 Office: The Designing Woman 9691 Firdale Ave Edmonds WA 98020-6519

PETERSEN, ANN NEVIN, computer systems administrator, consultant; b. Mexico City, Aug. 7, 1937; parents Am. citizens; d. Thomas Marshall and Gerry (Cox) Nevin; m. Norman William Petersen, Aug. 24, 1956; children: Richard, Robert, Thomas, Anita, David. AS in Electronics, Monterey Peninsula Coll., Monterey, Calif., 1962; student, U. N.Mex., 1956, Las Positas Coll., Livermore, Calif., 1992. Cert. computer profl. CAD mgr. Naval Air Rework Facility, Alameda, Calif., 1979-80; computer systems analyst Space and Naval Warfare System Command, Washington, 1980-84, Facilities Computer Systems Office, Port Hueneme, Calif., 1984-86; systems mgr. Lawrence Livermore Nat. Lab., Livermore, 1986-89; data base mgr. Clayton Environ. Cons., Pleasanton, Calif., 1989-90; computer systems mgr. Waltrip & Assocs., Sacramento, 1990-94; dir. computer systems, CFO Innovative Techs. Inc., Pleasanton, 1992—. Author databases. Bd. dirs. Am. Field Svc., Port Hueneme, 1976-78; mem. various adv. bds. U.S. Navy, 1957-86; mem. adv. bd. Calif. Deaf/Blind Regional Ctr., Sacramento, 1976-80; bd. dirs. ARC Alameda County, Hayward, Calif., 1992—. Recipient Superior Performance award U.S. Navy, 1980, Speaker of Month award Toastmasters, 1985. Mem. Data Processing Mgmt. Assn., bd. dirs., sec.), Assn. for Computing Machinery, Tri Valley MacIntosh Users Group, Inst. for Cert. of Computer Profls. Office: Innovative Techs Inc 5238 Riverdale Ct Pleasanton CA 94588-3759

PETERSEN, ARNE JOAQUIN, chemist; b. L.A., Jan. 27, 1932; s. Hans Marie Theodore and Astrid Marie (Pedersen) P.; m. Sandra Joyce Sharp, Aug. 12, 1961; children: Christina Lynn, Kurt Arne. AA, Compton Coll., 1957; BS, Calif. State U., Long Beach, 1959; BA, U. Calif., Irvine, 1975. Comml. pilots lic. Chemist/scientist Beckman Instruments, Inc., Fullerton, Calif., 1959-62, engr., scientist, 1962-65, project, sr. project engr., 1965-74; project/program mgr. Beckman Clin. Ops., Fullerton/Brea, Calif., 1974-80; ops. mgr. Graphic Controls Corp., Irvine, 1980-82; engr./rsch. and devel. mgr. Carle Instruments, Anaheim, Calif., 1982-84; ops. mgr. Magnaflux/X-Ray Devel., L.A., 1984-85; rsch. and devel. dir., new products Am. Chem. Systems, Irvine, Calif., 1985-86; rsch. assoc. U. Calif., Irvine, 1987-88; ind. cons., contractor, sales real estate investment, 1989—. Author scientific papers in field; patentee in field. Vol. F.I.S.H., Costa Mesa and Newport Beach, Calif.; basketball coach Boys-Girls, Newport Beach, 1975-78, baseball coach Newport Beach Parks, 1975-78; adv. com. Newport/Costa Mesa Sch. Bd., 1974-75. Sgt. USAF, 1951-55. Mem. AAAS, Am. Chem. Soc., Biomed. Engring. Soc., Am. Mgmt. Assn., Internat. Exec. Svc. Corp., U. Calif. Irvine Club (bd. dirs.), Kappa Sigma.

PETERSEN, CHRISTOPHER ALLEN, child and adolescent psychiatrist; b. Washington, July 20, 1947. BA, BS, Carnegie-Mellon U., 1971; MD, Med. Coll. Ga., 1976. Diplomate in psychiatry and child psychiatry Am. Bd. Psychiatry and Neurology, Nat. Bd. Med. Examiners; lic. physician, Nev., Calif., N.C. Resident in gen. psychiatry U. Mich. Med. Ctr./Univ. Hosp., Ann Arbor, 1976-80; fellow in child psychiatry U. Mich. Med. Ctr./ Children's Psychiat. Hosp., 1979-81; pvt. practice child and adolescent psychiatry Charlotte, N.C., 1981-92, Reno, 1992—; psychiat. cons. Children's Behavioral Svcs., Reno, 1992—; clin. faculty U. Nev. Sch. Medicine, Reno, 1992—. Contbr. articles to profl. jours.; presenter in field. Fellow Am. Acad. Child and Adolescent Psychiatry, Am Psychiat. Assn.; mem. No. Nev. Assn. Psychiat. Physicians. Office: PO Box 6810 Reno NV 89513-6810

PETERSEN, DONALD FELIX, consultant; b. Centralia, Wash., Nov. 16, 1928; s. Otto Anders and Martha Hilda (Peck) P.; m. Norma Ingeborg Wise, Jan. 17, 1954; children: Marilyn, Ronald, Kenneth. BBA, U. Wash., 1950. Transp. rate analyst Pub. Utility Commr., Salem, Oreg., 1953-57; mgmt. effectiveness analyst Dept. of Fin. and Adminstrn., Salem, 1958, mgmt. analyst, 1958-61, supr., fiscal analyst, 1962-67; prin. fiscal analyst Legis. Budget Com., Olympia, Wash., 1967-79, legis. auditor, 1980-85; program analysis mgr. Dept. Social and Health Svcs., Olympia, 1986-91; mem. state career exec. program dept. pers. State of Wash., Olympia, 1986-89; team mem. Price-Waterhouse, Olympia, 1987. Freeholder Thurston County Bd. Freeholders, 1978-79; chmn. Tanglewilde Park and Recreation Dist., Lacey, 1987, 89-90, vice-chmn., 1988; active Dem. Party, Thurston County, 1987—; vol. RSVP, 1988-92; 3rd congl. dist. coord. vote program Am. Assn. Ret. Persons, 1990-94, state legis. com. Wash. 1994—. With U.S. Army, 1951-52. Cert. of Appreciation, North Thurston Kiwanis, 1988, State of Wash., 1988, Dept. Social and Health Svcs., 1989, ACTION, 1990. Mem. AARP (3d congl. dist. coord. Vote Program 1990-94, mem. state legis. com.), Masons, Kiwanis (pres. 1973-74, sec. 1970-71). Democrat. Home and Office: 423 Ranger Dr SE Olympia WA 98503-6728

PETERSEN, FINN BO, oncologist, educator; b. Copenhagen, Mar. 26, 1951; came to U.S., 1983; s. Jorgen and Ebba Gjeding (Jorgensen) P.; m. Merete Secher Lund, Mar. 7, 1979; children: Lars Secher, Thomas Secher, Andreas Secher. BA, Niels Steensen, Copenhagen, 1971; MD, U. Copenhagen, 1978. Intern in internal medicine Copenhagen, 1978-79, resident in hematology, 1980-83; fellow oncology Fred Hutchinson Cancer Rsch. Ctr. U. Wash., Seattle, 1983-85, assoc. researcher oncology, 1985-87, asst. mem. in clin. rsch., 1987-91, asst. prof., 1988-91, prof. medicine, 1992—; clin. dir. bone marrow transplant program U. Utah Sch. Medicine, 1992—. Author: Hematology, 1977; contbr. articles to profl. jours. Mem. AMA, AAAS, ISEH, ASCO, Am. Soc. Hematology, Assn. Gnotobiology. Office: U Uath Bone Marrow Transplant Program Div of Hematology and Oncology Salt Lake City UT 84132

PETERSEN, GERALD MICHAEL, city official; b. Cheltenham, Eng., Sept. 25, 1953; (parents Am. citizens); s. Iner Leroy and Ann Estelle Peterson; m. Valerie Jacobson, July 22, 1978; children: Julia Rose, Andrea, Estelle. Student, Mont. State U., 1975-78, Missoula Vocat.-Tech. Sch., 1979-81. Desk clk. Palace Hotel, Missoula, Mont., 1979-81; bench technician Dana Corp., Bozeman, Mont., 1981-82; wastewater treatment operator City of Bozeman, 1982-91, operator water plant, 1991—. 3d class petty officer USN, 1971-75. Mem. Beall Park Art Ctr., Folklore Soc. Bozeman, Big Sky Wind Drinkers. Home: 201 N Western Dr Bozeman MT 59715-2667 Office: City of Bozeman Water Treatment Plant 7022 Sourdough Canyon Rd Bozeman MT 59715-8020

PETERSEN, GLADYS, accounting clerk, writer; b. Guayaquil, Ecuador, June 3, 1941; d. Ezio and Rebeca (Ratti) Bellettini; m. Ronald Petersen, July 4, 1965. Grad. in med. secretarial, Nat. Sch, L.A., 1987; student, Los Angeles Valley Coll., 1992. With accounts receivable/accounts payable So. Calif. Wholesales Co., L.A.; acctg. clk. Prudential Ins. Co., L.A. Mem. World of Poets (3 awards). Home: 330 N Cordova St Burbank CA 91505-3412

PETERSEN, JAMES NIELS, chemical engineering educator; b. Great Falls, Mont., July 26, 1954; s. Theodore Peter and Mary Elenor (Murphy) P.; m. Renee Karla Barnes, June 9, 1975; children: Matthew, Jonathan, Johanna, Michaela. BSChemE, Mont. State U., 1976; PhD in Chem. Engring., Iowa State U., 1979. Vis. prof. Weyerhaeuser Co., Tacoma, 1980, Chevron Rsch. Co., Richmond, Calif., 1981; asst. prof. Wash. State U., Pullman, 1979-85; vis. rsch. assoc. Oak Ridge (Tenn.) Nat. Lab., 1989-90; faculty rsch. assoc. Battelle Pacific Northwest Labs., Richland, Wash., 1992—, affiliate staff scientist, 1994—; assoc. prof. Wash. State U., Pullman, 1985-94, prof., 1994—; cons. Chevron, U.S.A., San Francisco, 1982, Martin Marietta Energy System, Oak Ridge, 1993. Patentee continuous fluidited bed contactor; author: (book chpt.) Immobilized Biosorbents for Dissolved

Metals, 1991. Grantee Battelle PNL, 1990-95, Martin Marietta Energy Systems, 1990-95, NSF, 1993-95, Nat. Supercomputer Ctr. for Energy and the Environment, 1993. Mem. AICE, Am. Soc. Engring. Edn. (Outstanding Young Faculty mem. 1985), Sigma Xi. Office: Wash State U Chem Engring Dept Pullman WA 99164-2710

PETERSEN, MARGARET SARA, civil engineering consultant, retired civil engineering educator; b. Moline, Ill., Apr. 28, 1920; d. Charles and Alvena Catherine (Fischer) P. BS in Civil Engring., U. Iowa, 1947, MS in Mechanics and Hydraulics, 1953. Registered civil engr., Iowa. Hydraulic engr. Waterways Experiment Sta. C.E., U.S. Army, Jackson, Miss., 1947-52; hydraulic engr. Mo. River Divsn. C.E., U.S. Army, Omaha, 1953-55; hydraulic engr. Little Rock Dist. C.E., U.S. Army, 1955-64; hydraulic engr. Waterways Experiment Sta. C.E., U.S. Army, Vicksburg, Miss., 1964; hydraulic engr. Sacramento Dist. C.E., U.S. Army, 1964-77; assoc. prof. dept. civil engring. U. Ariz., Tucson, 1981-91, assoc. prof. emerita, 1991—; mem. adjudication commn. Ariz. Navigable Streams, Phoenix, 1992-94; cons. Vicksburg Dist. Corps of Engrs., 1985-89; lectr. U. Witwatersrand, Johannesburg, South Africa, 1988, 93, Morocco, China; mem. U.S. com. Internat. Commn. Large Dams. Author: Water Resources Planning and Development, 1984, River Engineering, 1986; co-author: Water Resources Development in Developing Countries, 1991; contbr. chpts. to books, articles to profl. jours. Recipient Disting. Alumni award U. Iowa, 1987. Mem. (hon.) ASCE (sec. com. on metrication 1978-94, mem. water resources engring. rsch. and edn. com. 1993—, mgmt. group D 1978-80, hydraulics divsn. exec. com. 1972-76), Permanent Internat. Assn. of Navigation Congresses, Internat. Assn. for Hydraulic Rsch., Internat. Water Resources Assn., Assn. Arid Lands, Sigma Xi, Chi Epsilon. Office: Dept Civil Engring U Ariz Tucson AZ 85721

PETERSEN, MARK L., public relations executive; b. Ogden, Utah, Jan. 3, 1959; s. Ronald L. and Charlene Mary (Moore) P.; m. Becky Lyn Stott, Mar. 12, 1981; children: Melissa, Julie, Derek, Adam, Kalynn, Nathan. BS in Theatre Arts/Comm., Weber State U., 1985. Asst. bus./pub. rels. mgr. Weber State Theatre, Odgen, 1980-82, bus./pub. rels. mgr., 1982-84; dir. mktg., pub. rels. Coll. of Arts and Human, Weber State U., Odgen, 1984-86; mktg. coord. Area Tech. Ctr., Odgen, 1986-87; dir. pub. rels. Dixie Coll., St. George, Utah, 1987—; cons. KIWI Pub., St. George, 1993—; biographer, family histories, St. George, 1989—. Contbr. articles to profl. jours. Bd. dirs. Utah's Dixie Internat. Folkfest, St. George, 1991—, Washington County Children's Safety Coun., St. George, 1993—; pres-elect Chamber Pub. Rels. Group, St. George, 1995—; mem. Spirit of Dixie Com., St. George, 1987-90. Recipient Community Svc. award City of St. George, 1990. Mem. Nat. Coun. for Mktg. and Pub. Rels., Nat. Sch. Pub. Rels. Assn. (Merit award 1991), Nat. Assn. of Vocat. Tech. Edn. Communicators (3rd Pl. 1987), Dixie Coll. Staff Assn. (pres. 1995), St. George C. of C. Home: 975 S 770 E Saint George UT 84770-5616 Office: Dixie Coll 225 S 700 East Saint George UT 84770

PETERSEN, MARTA JEAN, dermatologist, educator; b. Spokane, Wash., Feb. 13, 1953; d. William Harry and Patricia Ann (Gramling) P.; m. Harold Hume Sears, Oct. 9, 1982; 1 child, Madeleine Rose Helen. BA, U. Minn., 1975; MD, U. Utah, 1979. Diplomate Am. Bd. Dermatology, Am. Bd. Internal Medicine. Intern in internal medicine Strong Meml. Hosp., U. Rochester, N.Y., 1979-80; resident U. Utah Hosps., Salt Lake City, 1980-82; rsch. fellow in dermatology U. Utah, Salt Lake City, 1982-84; resident in dermatology Sch. Medicine U. N.C., Chapel Hill, 1984-87, asst. prof., 1987-89; asst. prof. U. Utah, Salt Lake City, 1989—; sec.-treas. Sulzberger Inst. for Dermatologic Edn., Schaumburg, Ill., 1994—. Contbr. articles to profl. jours. Fellow Am. Acad. Dermatology; mem. Soc. Investigative Dermatology, Dermatology Found., Am. Soc. Cell Biology, Alpha Omega Alpha. Office: U Utah Sch Medicine 50 N Medical Dr Salt Lake City UT 84132-0001

PETERSEN, MARTIN EUGENE, museum curator; b. Grafton, Iowa, Apr. 21, 1931; s. Martin S. and Martha Dorothea (Paulsen) P. B.A., State U. Iowa, 1951, M.A., 1957; postgrad., The Hague (Netherlands), 1964. Curator San Diego Mus. Art, 1957—; extension instr. U. Calif., 1958, lectr., 1960. Author art catalogues, articles in field. Served with AUS, 1952-54. Mem. So. Calif. Art Historians. Home: 4571 Narragansett Ave San Diego CA 92107-2915 Office: San Diego Mus Art PO Box 2107 San Diego CA 92112-2107

PETERSEN, MICHAEL JON, utility company executive; b. Longview, Wash., Feb. 26, 1945; s. Norman Clair and Ferne Opel (Christenson) P.; m. Priscilla Louise Johnson, July 24, 1971; children: Jon Matthew, Timothy Scott, Kristen Marie. BA, U. Puget Sound, 1969. CPA, Wash. Cost acct. Weyerhaeuser Co., Longview, Wash., 1970-74; controller, treas. Cowlitz Pub. Utility Dist. No.1, Longview, 1974—. V.p., treas. Cowlitz Valley chpt. Assn. for Retarded Citizens, Longview, 1971-74; area rep. Cowlitz Little League, Kelso, Wash., 1985—. Served to sgt. U.S. Army, 1967-69, Vietnam. Home: 2465 Archwood Dr Longview WA 98632-5782 Office: Cowlitz Pub Utility Dist #1 960 Commerce Ave Longview WA 98632-2512

PETERSEN, NORMAN WILLIAM, naval officer, engineering facility administrator; b. Highland Park, Ill., Aug. 26, 1933; s. Jens Edlef and Marie (Wenderling) P.; m. Ann Nevin, Aug. 24, 1956; children: Richard Nevin, Robert William, Thomas Marshall, Anita, David Arthur. BEE, U. N.Mex., 1956; MEE with distinction, Naval Postgrad. Sch., Monterey, Calif., 1962; postgrad., Harvard Bus. Sch., 1982. Registered profl. engr., Mass., Calif. Shops engr. Naval Station, Key West, Fla., 1956-59; personnel dir. Bur. Yards and Docks, Washington, 1959-60; pub. works officer Fleet Anti-Air Warfare Ctr., Dam Neck, Va., 1962-64; engring. coord. Southwest div. Naval Facilities Engring. Command, San Diego, 1964-66; exec. officer Amphibious Constrn. Battalion 1, San Diego, 1966-67; force civil engr. Comdr. Naval Air Force Pacific, San Diego, 1967-70; pub. works officer Naval Air Sta. Miramar, San Diego, 1970-73; exec. officer Pub. Works Ctr., Great Lakes, Ill., 1973-75; comdg. officer Navy Civil Engring. Rsch. Lab., Port Hueneme, Calif., 1975-78, Pub. Works Ctr. San Francisco Bay Area, Oakland, Calif., 1978-80; comptroller, programs dir. Naval Facilities Engring. Command, Washington, 1980-84; pub. works officer Pacific Missile Test Ctr., Point Mugu, Calif., 1984-86; deputy assoc. dir. for plant engring. Lawrence Livermore (Calif.) Nat. Lab., 1986-91, sr. facilities advisor, 1991-94; v.p. Innovative Techs., Inc., Pleasanton, Calif., 1994—. Contbr. articles to profl. jours. Bd. dirs. CBC Fed. Credit Union, Port Hueneme, 1984-86, Ventura County Untied Way, Oxnard, Calif., 1976-78, strategic planning com., Camarillo, Calif., 1984-86; guest mem. Ventura County Assn. Govts., 1984-86; pres. Garnet Austin chpt. ARC, 1992-94, v.p. Alameda County chpt. Decorated (twice) Legion of Merit; Gallantry Cross (Republic Vietnam). Mem. Am. Soc. Mil. Comptrollers, Soc. Am. Mil. Engrs., Assn. Phys. Plant Adminstrs. (affiliate), Navy League, Oxnard Gem and Mineral Soc. (2d v.p.), Sigma Xi, Lambda Chi Alpha. Office: Innovative Techs Inc 5238 Riverdale Ct Pleasanton CA 94588-3759

PETERSEN, PHIL BRENT, psychiatrist, educator; b. Tempe, Ariz., Oct. 13, 1945; mm. Carol Jean Gold, June 2, 1972; children: Ryan C., Amy, Barr J., Camie. BA in Zoology, San Diego State U., 1968; MD, U. Utah, 1972. Diplomate Am. Bd. Psychiatry and Neurology. Resident in gen. psychiatry U. Utah, Salt Lake City, 1972-74; fellow in child psychiatry U. Utah Coll. Medicine-Primary Children's Med. Ctr., Salt Lake City, 1974-76; clin. instr. in med. hypnosis U. Utah, Salt Lake City, 1972-73, instr. psychiatry, 1976-80, clin. instr., 1981-90, clin. assoc. prof., 1990—; child psychiatrist Salt Lake Cmty. Mental Health Ctr., 1976—; child psychiatrist Primary Children's Mental Ctr., 1976-80, acting. clin. dir. outpatient Children's Psychiat. Ctr., 1977-78, clin. dir. outpatient dept. child psychiatry, 1978-80; pvt. practice Salt Lake City, 1981—; assoc. dir. children's specialty svcs. Salt Lake Valley Mental Health Ctr., 1982-93; psychiat. cons. Odyssey House, 1973-75; med. cons. Salt Lake Drug/Alchol Detoxification Ctr., 1975-82; dir. children's svcs. Salt Lake Cmty. Mental Helath Ctr., 1976-81, clin. dir. children's behavior therapy unit, 1976—, chmn. children's com., 1976-81; asst. clin. dir. inpatient unit Children's Psychiat. Ctr. of Primary Children's Med. Ctr., 1976-78; mem. ad hoc com. State Divsn. to Mental Health, 1976-78; mem. Utah State Mental Adv. Coun., 1977-79; assoc. clin. prof. psychiatry U. Utah, 1990; presenter in field. Contbr. articles to profl. jours. Fellow Am. Psychiat. Assn.; mem. Utah State Med. Assn. (com. on psychiat. emergencies 1976-78), Utah Sco. for Autistic Children (mem. adv. bd. 1979—), Salt Lake County Med. Soc. (del. ho. dels.), Utah Psychiatry Assn., Am. Acad. of Child Psychiatry (alt. del.), Intermountain Acad. Child Psychiatry (sec. 1976-78, pres. 1978-80). Office: 1414 E 4500 S Salt Lake City UT 84117-4208

PETERSEN, ROLAND, artist, printmaker; b. Endelave, Horsens, Denmark, 1926; came to U.S., 1928; m. Sharane Havlina, Aug. 12, 1950; children—Dana Mark, Maura Brooke, Julien Conrad, Karena Caia. B.A., U. Calif.-Berkeley, 1949, M.A., 1950; postgrad., Han Hofmann's Sch. Fine Arts, summers 1950-51, S.W. Hayter's Atelier 17, Paris, 1950, 63, 70, Islington Studio, London, 1976, The Print Workshop, London, 1980. Tchr. State Coll. Wash., Pullman, 1952-56; mem. faculty U. Calif., Davis, 1956-91, prof. art, 1991; ret., 1991. Exhibited one-man shows: Gump's Gallery, San Francisco, 1962, Staempfli Gallery, N.Y.C., 1963, 65, 67, Adele Bednarz Gallery, Los Angeles, 1966, 69, 70, 72, 73, 75, 76, Crocker Art Gallery, Sacramento, 1965, de Young Mus., San Francisco, 1968, La Jolla Mus., 1971, Phoenix Mus., 1972, Santa Barbara Mus., 1973, USIS sponsored touring one-man exhbn., Turkey, U. Reading, Eng., 1977, 80, U. Calif., Davis, 1978, 92, Brubaker Gallery, Sarasota, Fla., 1979, Rorick Gallery, San Francisco, 1981, 82, 83, 84, 85, Himovitz-Salomon Gallery, Sacramento, 1987-88, 91, Vanderwoude Tananbaum Gallery, N.Y.C., 1987-89, Harcourts Gallery, San Francisco, 1989, 91, 93, U. Calif., Davis, 1992, Maxwell Galleries, San Francisco, 1995; group shows include Calif. Palace Legion of Honor, San Francisco Art Inst., 1962, Mus. Art, Carnegie Inst., Pitts., 1964, Obelisk Gallery, Washington, John Herron Art Inst., Indpls., 1964, Pa. Acad. Fine Arts, Phila., Crocker Art Gallery, Sacramento, 1965, 81, Art Inst. Chgo., 1965, Va. Mus. Fine Arts, Richmond, 1966, U. Ariz. Art Gallery, Tucson, 1967, Am. Cultural Center, Paris, 1971, Nat. Gallery, Washington, 1972, Otis Art Inst. Gallery, Los Angeles, 1974, Auerbach Fine Art Gallery, London, 1977, U. Wis., Madison, 1977, Bklyn. Mus., 1978, U. Ill., 1978, U. Nev., Las Vegas, 1980, Brubaker Gallery, Sarasota, Fla., 1983, U.S.A. World Print Council, San Francisco, Nat. Mus., Singapore, Nat. Gallery, Bangkok, Thailand, Amerika Haus, Berlin, Malmo Konsthall, Sweden, Museo Carrillo Gil, Mexico City, all 1984-86, Crocker Art Mus., 1991, Fresno Met. Mus., 1992, Hall of Pictures, Uman, Russia, 1992, Calif. State U., L.A., 1992, San Bernardino, 1993 Pence Gallery, Davis, Calif., 1993, Artists Contemporary Gallery, Sacramento, 1994, Andre Milan Gallery, Sao Paulo, Brazil, 1995; represented in permanent collections: de Young Mus., San Francisco, San Francisco Mus. Modern Art, Va. Mus. Fine Arts, Richmond, Mus. Modern Art, N.Y.C., Phila. Mus. Art, Whitney Mus. Am. Art, Phoenix Mus., Santa Barbara Mus., Musée Municipal, Brest, France, Smithsonian Instn. Nat. Collection Fine Arts & Archives of Am. Art, others. Served with USN, 1944-46, PTO. Recipient numerous prizes and awards, 1950—; Guggenheim fellow, 1963; U. Calif. creative arts fellow, 1967, 70, 77; Fulbright grantee, 1970. Mem. AAUP, San Francisco Art Assn., Calif. Soc. Printmakers. Home: 6 Lanai Way PO Box 1 Dillon Beach CA 94929-0001

PETERSEN, VERNON LEROY, communications and engineering corporation executive; b. Mason, Nev., Nov. 3, 1926; s. Vernon and Lenora Eloise (Dickson) P.; children: Anne C., Ruth F. Cert. naval architecture, U. Calif., 1944, cert. in plant engring., adminstrn. and supervision UCLA, 1977; cert. in real estate exchanging Orange Coast Coll., 1978. Philippines Real Estate Office, U.S. C.E., 1950-55; pres., gen. mgr. Mason Merc. Co., 1956-62; pres., gen. mgr. Mason Water Co., 1956-62; pres. Petersen Enterprises, Cons. Engrs., Nev. and Calif., Downey, 1962-79, Vernon L. Peterson, Inc., 1980—; pres., chief exec. officer Castle Communications Co. Inc., 1985—; Sta. KCCD-TV, 1985-89; installation mgr. Pacific Architects & Engrs., L.A. and South Vietnam, 1969-72, facilities engr., ops. supr., acting contract mgr. L.A. and Saudi Arabia, 1979-82; bldg. engr. Purex Co., Inc., Lakewood, Calif., 1975-79; lectr. plant engring., various colls. in Calif., 1975—. Candidate for U.S. Congress, 1956, del. Rep. State Conv., 1960-64; candidate for U.S. Presidency, 1980. With AUS, 1944-47. Inducted into the Order of the Engrs. Fellow Soc. Am. Mil. Engrs. (life mem., named Orange County Post's Engr. of Year 1977, founder Da Nang Post 1969, Orange County Post 1977, pres. 1978-79, Red Sea Post, Jeddah, Saudi Arabia 1980), Internat. Platform Assn., Orange County Engr. Coun. (pres. 1978-79), Am. Inst. Plant Engrs. (chpt. 38 Engring. Merit award 1977-78), Soc. Women Engrs. (assoc.), AIAA. Mormon. Office: Castle Communications PO Box 787 Temecula CA 92593-0787

PETERSON, BARBARA ANN BENNETT, history educator, television personality; b. Portland, Oreg., Sept. 6, 1942; d. George Wright and Hope (Chatfield) Bennett; m. Frank Lynn Peterson, July 1, 1967. BA, BS, Oreg. State U., 1964; MA, Stanford U., 1965; PhD, U. Hawaii, 1978; PhD (hon.), London Inst. Applied Rsch., 1991. Prof. history U. Hawaii, Honolulu, 1967—, chmn. social scis. dept., 1971-73, 75-76, asst. dean, 1973-74; prof. Asian history and European colonial history and world problems Chapman Coll. World Campus Afloat, 1974; prof. European overseas exploration, expansion, and colonialism U. Colo., Boulder, 1978; assoc. prof. U. Hawaii-Manoa Coll. Continuing Edn., 1981; Fulbright prof. history Wuhan (China) U., 1988-89; Fulbright rsch. prof. Sophia U., Japan, 1967; lectr. Capital Speakers, Washington, 1987—; prof. Hawaii State Edn. Channel, 1993—. Co-author: Women's Place is in the History Books, Her Story, 1962-1980: A Curriculum Guide for American History Teachers, 1980; author: America in British Eyes, 1988; editor: Notable Women of Hawaii, 1984, (with W. Solheim) The Pacific Region, 1990, 91, American History: 17th, 18th, and 19th Centuries, 1993, America: 19th and 20th Centuries, 1993; assoc. editor Am. Nat. Biography; contbr. articles to profl. publs. Participant People-to-People Program, Eng., 1964, Expt. in Internat. Living Program, Nigeria, 1966; chmn. 1st Nat. Women's History Week, Hawaii, 1982; pres. Bishop Mus. Coun., 1993-94; active Hawaii Commn. on Status of Women. Recipient state proclamations Gov. of Hawaii, 1982, City of Honolulu, 1982, Outstanding Tchr. of yr. award Wuhan (China) U., 1988, Medallion of Excellence award Am. Biog. Assn., 1989, Woman of Yr. award, 1991; Fulbright scholar, Japan, 1967, China, 1988-89; NEH-Woodrow Wilson fellow Princeton U., 1980. Fellow World Literacy Acad. (Eng.), Internat. Biog. Assn. (Cambridge, Eng. chpt.); mem. AAUW, Am. Hist. Assn., Am. Studies Assn., Am. Studies Assn. (pres. 1984-85), Fulbright Alumni Assn. (founding pres. Hawaii chpt. 1984-88, mem. nat. steering com. chairwomen Fulbright Assn. ann. conf. 1990), Am. Hist. Assn. (mem. numerous coms.), Am. Coun. on Edn., Maison Internat. des Intellectuals, France, Hawaii Found. History and Humanities (mem. editl. bd. 1972-73), Hawaii Found. Women's History, Hawaii Hist. Assn., Nat. League Am. Pen Women (contest chaprperson 1986), Women in Acad. Adminstrn., Pi Beta Phi, Phi Kappa Phi.

PETERSON, CHASE N., university president; b. Logan, Utah, Dec. 27, 1929; s. E.G. and Phebe (Nebeker) P.; m. Grethe Ballif, 1956; children: Erika Elizabeth, Stuart Ballif, Edward Chase. A.B., Harvard U., 1952, M.D., 1956. Diplomate: Am. Bd. Internal Medicine. Asst. prof. medicine U. Utah Med. Sch., 1965-67; assoc. Salt Lake Clinic; dean admissions and fin. aids to students Harvard U., 1967-72, v.p. univ., 1972-78; v.p. health scis. U. Utah, Salt Lake City, 1978-83, prof. medicine, 1983—, pres., 1983-91, clin. prof. medicine, 1991—; pres. emeritus U. Utah, Salt Lake City, 1992—; bd. dirs. First Security Corp., Utah Power & Light Co., D.C. Tanner Co., OEC Med. Systems. Mem. Nat. Assn. State Univs. and Land-Grant Colls. (chmn. 1988-89, chair U.S. Ofc. Tech. Assessment adv. bd. 1990-92). Home: 66 Thaynes Canyon Dr Park City UT 84060-6711 Office: U Utah 1C26 Sch Medicine Salt Lake City UT 84112

PETERSON, DANA LYNN, human anatomy and physiology educator; b. San Diego, June 30, 1958; d. Brock Armor and Kathryn Anne (Williams) P. BA in Biol. Sci., U. Mo., 1982; MEd in Secondary Adminstrn., U. Okla., 1990. Cert. secondary sci. tchr., Mo., Okla., Fla., Calif. H.s. anatomy tchr. Hollywood (Fla.) Hills H.S., 1983-84; vice prin. San Diego Outdoor Ednl. Program, 1984-88; curriculum, textbook author U.S. Space Found., Colorado Springs, Colo., 1990-92; anatomy and physiology instr. C.C. of Denver, 1992—. Vol. athletics coach Spl. Olympics of Denver, Metro Area, 1992-94. Mem. AAAS. Nat. Sci. Tchrs. Assn., Nat. Assn. Biology Tchrs., Mensa. Office: CC of Denver PO Box 173363 Campus Box 800 Denver CO 80217-3363

PETERSON, DONALD CURTIS, life care executive, consultant; b. Seattle, Feb. 27, 1931; s. Arthur O. and Agnes V. (Erickson) P.; m. Marilyn Jane, June 21, 1952; children: Bruce D., Mark A., Daryl R., Debra L., Joseph J. AA, North Park Coll., 1950; cert. in mgmt., Am. Mgmt. Assn., 1965. With fgn. ops. staff Internat. Harvester Co., Chgo., 1950-54; mktg. exec. UARCO, Inc., Barrington, Ill., 1954-67; group v.p. Victor Comptometer, Lincoln, Nebr., 1967-68; pres. Nationwide Data, Wheeling, Ill., 1968-71, Nationwide Bus. Forms, Wheeling, 1968-71, Ins. Producers Bulletin, Wheeling, 1968-71, Alpha Internat., Sawyer, Mich., 1971-83; exec. dir. Freedom Sq. U.S.A., Seminole, Fla., 1983-92; adminstr., CEO Mount Miguel Covenant Village, Spring Valley, Calif., 1992—; mktg. cons. Balt. Bus. Forms., Hunt Valley, Md., 1974-76. Supr., chmn. water bd., sanitary bd. Chikaming Twp., Lakeside, Mich., 1972-76. Served with U.S. Army, 1952-57. Republican. Baptist. Home: 10405 Pine Grove St Spring Valley CA 91978-1505

PETERSON, DONNA RAE, marketing professional; b. Wichita, Kans., Aug. 29, 1948; d. Raymond Houston and Edna Brooks (Waddell) Hobbs; m. William E. Peterson, Nov. 7, 1993; 1 child, Shauna Layne Reed. Student, Wichita State U., 1966-68, N.W. Christian Coll., 1994. Adminstrv. asst. postgrad. edn. Med. Sch. U. Kans., Wichita, 1974-80; activity coord. continuing med. edn. Wesley Med. Ctr., Wichita, 1980-84; mgr. support svcs. 9th dist. Farm Credit Svcs., Wichita, 1984-88; sales and mktg. mgr. Amb. Travel, Eugene, 1988-93; acct. exec. Sta. KPNW, 1993; mktg. dir. Peterson Design Devel., Eugene, Oreg., 1993—; cons. Jr. League Wichita, 1983, Plancon, Inc., Martinsville, N.J., 1987-88. Mem. Wichita Conv. and Visitors Bur., 1987; mem. events com. Wichita Festivals, Inc., 1987; mem. Eugene Conv. and Visitors Bur., 1988—; mem. Eugene Airport Commn., 1991—, chmn., 1992-93; bd. dirs. Campus Life, chmn., 1993-94; mem. steering com. Eugene Celebration, 1991-94. Mem. Am. Mktg. Assn. (pres. S.W. chpt. 1991—, pres. 1992-94, bd. dirs.), Soc. Travel Agts. in Govt., Adminstrv. Mgmt. Soc., Forum for Exec. Bus. Women, Gt. Plains Bus. Adminstrn. Group, Assn. Travel Execs., Eugene C. of C. (bus. devel. com. 1990-91), Eugene High Ground Assocs. (chmn.), Delta Gamma Alumni Assn. Republican. Home: 1460 Olive St Apt 32 Eugene OR 97401-3991 Office: Peterson Design 8 Coburg Rd Ste 3 Eugene OR 97401-2448

PETERSON, DOUGLAS SHURTLEFF, state legislator, packaging company official; b. Ogden, Utah, Dec. 9, 1966; s. Lowell Skeen and Kathleen (Shurtleff) P. BS in Polit. Sci. and English, Weber State U., 1994. With UPS, Ogden, 1989—; rep. Utah Ho. of Reps., Salt Lake City, 1993—; cons. Rep. Gov.'s Assn. Pres. Assn. Students Weber State U., Ogden, 1990-91; trustee Weber State U., 1990-91; regent Utah Bd. Regents of Higher Edn., Salt Lake City, 1991-92. Republican. Mem. LDS Ch. Home: 4538 S 1725 W Roy UT 84067-3026

PETERSON, EDWIN J., retired supreme court justice, law educator; b. Gilmanton, Wis., Mar. 30, 1930; s. Edwin A. and Leora Grace (Kitelinger) P.; m. Anna Chadwick, Feb. 7, 1971; children: Patricia, Andrew, Sherry. B.S., U. Oreg., 1951, LL.B., 1957. Bar: Oreg. 1957. Assoc. firm Tooze, Kerr, Peterson, Marshall & Shenker, Portland, 1957-61; mem. firm Tooze, Kerr, Peterson, Marshall & Shenker, 1961-79; assoc. justice Supreme Ct. Oreg., Salem, 1979-83, chief justice, 1983-91; ret., 1993; adj. instr. Willamette Coll. of Law, Salem, Oreg., 1994—; chmn. Supreme Ct. Task Force on Racial Issues, 1992-94; mem. standing com. on fed. rules of practice and procedure, 1987-93; bd. dirs. Conf. Chief Justices, 1985-87, 88-91. Chmn. Portland Citizens Sch. Com., 1968-70; vice chmn. Young Republican Fedn. Orgn., 1951; bd. visitors U. Oreg. Law Sch., 1978-83, 87-93, chmn. bd. visitors, 1981-83. Served to 1st lt. USAF, 1952-54. Mem. ABA, Am. Judicature Soc., Oreg. State Bar (bd. examiners 1963-66, gov. 1973-76, vice chmn. profl. liability fund 1977-78), Multnomah County Bar Assn. (pres. 1972-73), Phi Alpha Delta, Lambda Chi Alpha. Episcopalian. Home: 3365 Sunridge Dr S Salem OR 97302-5950 Office: Willamette Univ Coll Law 250 Winter St SE Salem OR 97301-3900

PETERSON, ERLE VIDAILLET, retired metallurgical engineer; b. Idaho Falls, Idaho, Apr. 29, 1915; s. Vier P. and Marie (Vidaillet) P.; m. Rosemary Sherwood, June 3, 1955; children: Kent Sherwood, Pamela Jo. BS in Mining Engring., U. Idaho, 1940; MS in Mining Engring., U. Utah, 1941. Tech. advisor Remington Arms Co., Salt Lake City, 1941-43; constrn. engr. plutonium plant duPont, Hanford, Wash., 1943-44; R & D engr. exptl. sta. duPont, Wilmington, Del., 1944-51; plant metallurgist heavy water plant duPont, Newport, Ind., 1951-57; rsch. metallurgist metals program duPont, Balt., 1957-62, prin. project engr. USAF contracts, 1962-68; devel. engr. duPont, Wilmington, 1969-80; ret., 1980. Patentee in field; contbr. articles to profl. jours. Candidate for State Senate-Am. Party, Wilmington, 1974; com. chmn. Boy Scouts Am., Wilmington, 1975-78; treas. Local Civic Assn., Wilmington, 1977-79. Rsch. fellow U. Utah, 1940. Mem. Am. Soc. Metallurgists Internat., Del. Assn. Profl. Engrs. Republican. Home: PO Box 74 Rigby ID 83442-0074

PETERSON, GLENN VIGGO, industrial arts educator; b. Gothenburg, Nebr., Oct. 16, 1928; s. Peter and Nellie D. (Young) P.; m. Dorothy Bernice Pollat, June 4, 1948; children: Connie Anne, Kent Leon, Sandra Kay. BA, Kearney State Coll., 1952; MA, U. No. Colo., 1956-61. Cert. secondary tchr. Tchr. indsl. arts Kearney, Nebr., 1956-62, Colorado Springs, Colo., 1962-89. Mem. Colorado Springs Coin Club (pres. 1990-92), Colorado Springs Numismatic Soc., Rob Morris #46 (3d degree 1962-92), Phi Delta Kappa. Republican. Presbyterian. Home: 7504 Gillen Rd Colorado Springs CO 80919-2602

PETERSON, HOWARD COOPER, lawyer, accountant; b. Decatur, Ill., Oct. 12, 1939; s. Howard and Lorraine (Cooper) P.; BEE, U. Ill., 1963; MEE, San Diego State Coll., 1967; MBA, Columbia U., 1969; JD, Calif. Western Sch. Law, 1983; LLM in Taxation NYU, 1985. Bar: Calif.; cert. fin. planner.; CPA, Tex.; registered profl. Engr., Calif.; cert. neuro-linguistic profl. Elec. engr. Convair div. Gen. Dynamics Corp., San Diego, 1963-67, sr. electronics engr., 1967-68; gen. ptnr. Costumes Characters & Classics Co., San Diego, 1979-86; v.p., dir. Equity Programs Corp., San Diego, 1973-83; pres., dir. Coastal Properties Trust, San Diego, 1979-89, Juno Securities, Inc., 1983—, Juno Real Estate INc., 1974—, Scripps Mortgage Corp., 1987-90, Juno Transport Inc., 1988—; chief fin. officer and dir. Imperial Screens of San Diego, 1977—, Heritage Transp. Mgmt. Inc., 1989-91, A.S.A.P. Ins. Svcs. Inc., 1983-85. Mem. ABA, Interamerican Bar Assn., Nat. Soc. Public Accts., Internat. Assn. Fin. Planning, Assn. Enrolled Agts.

PETERSON, JAMES ALGERT, geologist, educator; b. Baroda, Mich., Apr. 17, 1915; s. Djalma Hardaman and Mary Avis (McAnally) P.; m. Gladys Marie Pearson, Aug. 18, 1944; children—James D., Wendy A., Brian H. Student, Northwestern U., 1941-43, U. Wis., 1943; B.S. magna cum laude, St. Louis U., 1948; M.S. (Shell fellow), U. Minn., 1950, Ph.D., 1951. Mem. staff U.S. Geol. Survey, Spokane, Wash., 1949-51; instr. geology Wash. State U., Pullman, 1951; geologist Shell Oil Co., 1952-65; geologist div. stratigrapher, 1958-63, sr. geologist, 1963-65; instr. geology N. Mex. State U., San Juan, (P.R.), br., 1959-65; prof. geology U. Mont., Missoula, 1965—; cons. U.S. Geol. Survey, 1976-82, rsch. geologist, 1982—. Editor: Geology of East Central Utah, 1956, Geometry of Sandstone Bodies, 1960, Rocky Mountain Sedimentary Basins, 1965, (with others) Pacific Geology, Paleotectonics and Sedimentation, 1986; Contbr. (with others) articles to profl. jours. Served to 1st lt. USAAF, 1943-46. Recipient Alumni Merit award St. Louis U., 1960, Outstanding Achievement award U. Minn., 1995. Fellow AAAS, Geol. Soc. Am.; mem. Am. Assn. Petroleum Geologists (pres. Rocky Mountain sect. 1964, Pres.'s award 1988, Disting. Svc. award 1992), Rocky Mountain Assn. Geologists (Outstanding Scientist award 1987), Four Corners Geol. Soc. (hon., pres. 1962), Am. Inst. Profl. Geologists (pres. Mont. sect. 1971), Soc. Econ. Paleontologists and Mineralogists (hon. 1985, sec.-treas. 1969-71, editor 1976-78, Disting. Pioneer Geologist award 1988), Mont. Geol. Soc. (hon. 1987), Utah Geol. Soc. Club: Explorers. Home: 301 Pattee Canyon Dr Missoula MT 59803-1624

PETERSON, KEVIN BRUCE, newspaper editor, publishing executive; b. Kitchener, Ont., Can., Feb. 11, 1948; s. Bruce Russell and Marguerite Elizabeth (Hammond) P.; m. Constance Maureen Bailey, Feb. 11, 1975 (dec. May 1975); m. Sheila Helen O'Brien, Jan. 9, 1981. B.A., U. Calgary, Alta., Can., 1968. Chief bur. Calgary Herald, 1972-75, city editor, 1976-77, news editor, 1977-78, bus. editor, 1978, mng. editor, 1978-86, editor, asst. pub., 1986-87, gen. mgr., 1987-88, pub., 1989—; pres. Canadian Univ. Press, Ottawa, Ont., Can., 1968-69; dir. New Directions for News. Harry Brittain Meml. fellow Commonwealth Press Union, London, 1979. Mem. Can. Mng. Editors (bd. dirs. 1983-87), Am. Soc. Newspaper Editors, Horsemen's Benevolent and Protective Assn., Alta. Legis. Press Gallery Assn. (v.p. 1971-

76), Can. Daily Newspaper Assn. (bd. dirs. 1990—, vice chmn., treas. 1992, chmn. 1993), Calgary Petroleum Club, Ranchmen's Club, 100-to-1 Club (Arcadia, Calif.). Clubs: Calgary Petroleum, Ranchmen's, 100-to-1 (Arcadia, Calif.). Office: Calgary Herald, 215 16th St Se, Calgary, AB Canada T2P 0W8

PETERSON, LAURENCE ROBERT, pathologist; b. Mpls., July 30, 1947; s. Robert E. and Beverly J. (Robinson) P.; m. Carol Ann Seeburger, June 20, 1970; children: Nathaniel Dow, Alexander Jorgan. BA, Carleton Coll., 1969; MD, U. Chgo., 1973. Diplomate Am. Bd. Pathology. Residency pathology U. Wash., Seattle, 1973-77; pathologist, owner Skagit Pathology Labs. Inc., Mount Vernon, Wash., 1977—. Fellow Coll. of Am. Pathologists, Am. Soc. Clin. Pathologists; mem. AMA, Pacifi N.W. Soc. Pathologists. Office: Skagit Valley Labs Inc 1310 E Division St Mount Vernon WA 98273-4133

PETERSON, LEROY, retired secondary education educator; b. Fairfield, Ala., Feb. 15, 1930; s. Leroy and Ludie Pearl (Henderson) P.; m. Theresa Petite, Apr. 6, 1968 (div. Oct. 1984); children: Leroy III, Monica Teresa; m. Ruby Willodine Hopkins, July 21, 1985 (div. Apr. 1995). Cert. in piano, Bavarian State Acad., Wuerzburg, Fed. Republic Germany, 1954; BS in Music Edn., Miami U., Oxford, Ohio, 1957. Life credential music tchr., Calif. Tchr. music Cleve. Pub. Schs., 1957-62, L.A. Unified Schs., 1963-94; retired, 1994. Song composer. With U.S. Army, 1952-54. Mem. Alpha Phi Alpha, Phi Mu Alpha Sinfonia. Republican. Home: 2646 Lime St Riverside CA 92501

PETERSON, LEVI SAVAGE, English language educator; b. Snowflake, Ariz., Dec. 13, 1933; s. Joseph and Lydia Jane (Savage) P.; m. Althea Grace Sand, Aug. 31, 1958; 1 child, Karrin. BA, Brigham Young U., 1958, MA, 1960; PhD, U. Utah, 1965. Asst. prof. Weber State U., Ogden, Utah, 1965-68, assoc. prof., 1968-72, prof., 1972—; dir. honors program Weber State U., 1973-82. Author: Canyons of Grace, 1982, The Backslider, 1986, Juanita Brooks, 1988 (Evans award 1988), Night Soil, 1990; editor: Greening Wheat, 1983. Trustee Weber County Libr., Ogden, 1988—. Mem. Assn. for Mormon Letters (bd. dirs., pres. 1980, 90), Rocky Mountain Modern Lang. Assn., Utah Acad. of Scis., Arts and Letters (editor Encyclia 1976-81, Disting. Coll. Svc. award 1984), Western Lit. Assn. Democrat. Home: 1561 25th St Ogden UT 84401-2923 Office: Weber State U Dept English Ogden UT 84408

PETERSON, LOWELL, cinematographer; b. L.A., Feb. 1, 1950; s. Lowell Stanley and Catherine Linda (Hess) P.; m. Deanna Rae Terry, Aug. 2, 1981. Student, Yale U., 1968; BA in Theater Arts, UCLA, 1973. Asst. cinematographer, Hollywood, Calif., 1973-83; camera operator Hollywood, 1983-92, dir. photography, 1992—. Asst. cinematographer various prodns. including Blind Ambition, 1979, Hawaii Five-O, 1979-80, White Shadow, 1980-81, Lou Grant, 1981-82, Two of a Kind, 1982, Remington Steele, 1982-83, Something About Amelia, 1983; camera operator various prodns. including Tourist Trap, 1979, Newhart, 1983, Scarecrow and Mrs. King, 1983-85, Children in the Crossfire, 1984, Stranded, 1986, Knots Landing, 1986-87, 89-92, Like Father Like Son, 1987, Star Trek: The Next Generation, 1987-89, Coupe de Ville, 1990, Show of Force, 1990, Postcards from the Edge, 1990, Guilty by Suspicion, 1991, The Mambo Kings, 1992, Dracula, 1992; dir. photography Knots Landing, 1992-93, Second Chances, 1993-94 (Am. Soc. Cinematographers award nomination), Galaxy Beat, 1994, Hotel Malibu, 1994; contbr. articles to Film Comment, 1974, Internat. Photographer, 1984—, Lois and Clark, 1995, The Client, 1995—. Mem. Soc. Motion Picture and TV Engrs., Internat. Photographers Guild, L.A. Music Ctr. Opera League, Friends of UCLA Film Archive, Am. Cinematheque, U.S. Chess Fedn., Acad. TV Arts & Scis. Home and Office: 3815 Ventura Canyon Ave Sherman Oaks CA 91423-4710

PETERSON, MARTIN LYNN, public administrator; b. Lewiston, Idaho, Apr. 22, 1943; s. Conrad E. and Charlotte K. (Hoffman) P.; m. Barbara Ann Dodson, May 31, 1975; children: Julia Beata, Emily Ann. AAS, Columbia Basin Coll., 1964; BA, U. Idaho, 1968. Asst. to Senator Frank Church U.S. Senate, Washington, 1968-71; dir. manpower planning State of Idaho, Boise, 1971-74; dir. govt. rels. Assn. Idaho Cities, Boise, 1975-78, exec. dir., 1978-83; budget dir. State of Idaho, Boise, 1983-88; pres. Idaho Centennial Found., Boise, 1988-91; cons. Boise, 1991-92; asst. to pres. U. Idaho, Boise, 1992—. Author: Celebrating Idaho, 1991. Founding incorporator Idaho Heritage Trust, Boise, 1989-92; assoc. lay leader 1st United Meth. Ch., Boise; trustee Idaho Bicentennial Trust Fund; mem. Boise Art Mus.; mem. Hemingway Soc.; v.p. Silver City Homeowners Assn. Recipient Cert. of Appreciation Gov. of Idaho, 1979, 82, Boyd A. Martin award Assn. Idaho Cities, 1989. Mem. North Idaho C. of C., Boise C. of C. Home: 743 Hearthstone Dr Boise ID 83702-1823 Office: U Idaho/Boise Ctr 800 Park Blvd Boise ID 83712-7742

PETERSON, MILLIE M., state legislator; b. Merced, Calif., June 11, 1944. BS, U. Utah, 1979, MSW, 1984. Mem. Utah State Senate from 12th dist., 1991—. Mem. Assn. Am. Med. Colls. Democrat. Address: 7131 W 3800 S West Valley City UT 84120-3416 Office: Senate House State Capitol Salt Lake City UT 84114

PETERSON, RALPH R., engineering executive; b. 1944. BS in Civil Engring., Oreg. State U., 1969; MS in Environ. Engring., Stanford U., 1970. Engring. aide Johnson, Underkofler & Briggs, Boise, 1962-63; surveyor Smith, Keyes & Blakely, Caldwell, Idaho, 1963-64; with Chrome & Assocs., Boise, 1964-65; with CH2M Hill Cos., Ltd., 1978—, sr. v.p., dir. tech., 1988, pres., CEO, 1990. Office: CH2M Hill Cos Ltd 4565 SW Research Way Corvallis OR 97333-1063*

PETERSON, RICHARD ALLAN, pediatrician; b. Oak Park, Ill., Aug. 10, 1934; s. Otto Stewart and Catherine Helen (Esin) P.; m. Sue Anne Schaefer, Sept. 15, 1956 (div. Sept. 1972); children: Ben, Andrew, Jennifer, Dan. AB, Grinnell Coll., 1956; BS, MD, U. Ill., 1960. Diplomate Am. Bd. Pediatrics. Intern Ind. U. Med. Ctr., Indpls., 1960-61; resident in pediatrics Mayo Clinic, Rochester, Minn., 1961-64; pediatrician Anchorage Pediatric Group, 1967-71, The Children's Clinic, Anchorage, 1971-76; pediatric neurology fellow UCLA, 1976-77; pvt. practice Templeton, Calif., 1977—; bd. dirs. Affiliated Health Providers North County, Templeton. Chmn. health educator curriculum com. Anchorage Borough Sch. Dist., 1968-70; bd. dirs. Mozart Festival, San Luis Obispo, Calif., 1988-91. Capt. USAF, 1964-67. Fellow Am. Acad. Pediatrics (Alaska state chmn. 1972-73); mem. AMA, North Pacific Pediatric Soc., Calif. Med. Assn., San Luis Obispo County Med. Soc., L.A. Pediatric Soc. Home: 35 15th St Paso Robles CA 93446-2059 Office: 1050 Las Tablas Rd Templeton CA 93465-9729

PETERSON, RICHARD HERMANN, history educator; b. Berkeley, Calif., Jan. 16, 1942; s. William Martin and Dorothy Jean (Heyne) P.; m. Nora Ann Lorenzo, June 21, 1970; 1 child, Nina Elizabeth. AB, U. Calif., Berkeley, 1963; MA, San Francisco State U., 1966; PhD, U. Calif., Davis, 1971. Calif. community coll. teaching credential. Asst. prof. history Ind. U., Kokomo, 1971-76; instr. social studies Coll. of the Redwoods, Ft. Bragg, Calif., 1976-78; assoc. prof. history San Diego State U., 1978-82, prof. history, 1982—. Author: Manifest Destiny in the Mines, 1975, The Bonanza Kings, 1977, 91, Bonanza Rich, 1991; book rev. editor Jour. of San Diego History, 1978-82, editorial cons., 1980-82; contbr. articles to profl. jours. Judge for papers Internat. History Fair, San Diego, Tijuana, Mex., 1983-88. Faculty Summer fellow Ind. U., 1975, 76, San Diego State U., 1980; rsch. grantee Sourisseau Acad., 1977, Am. Assn. State/Local History, 1988; named Golden Poet of Yr., World of Poetry, 1987-89. Mem. Calif. Hist. Soc., Hist. Soc. of So. Calif., Western History Assn., Calif. Studies Assn. Home: 7956 Lake Adlon Dr San Diego CA 92119-3117 Office: San Diego State U History Dept 5500 Campanile Dr San Diego CA 92182-0001

PETERSON, ROLAND OSCAR, retired electronics company executive; b. Bklyn., Jan. 18, 1932; s. Oscar Gustaf and Klara Ingegerd (Lindau) P.; m. Agnes Frances Walsh, Sept. 12, 1953; children: Joan, Lauren, Paul, Michael. BEE, Poly. Inst. N.Y., 1953, MEE, 1954. Registered profl. engr., N.Y. Research fellow Microwave Research Inst., Bklyn., 1953-54; sr. engr. Sperry Gyroscope Co., Great Neck, N.Y., 1956-60; with Litton Industries, Inc., Woodland Hills, Calif., 1961—; v.p. advanced systems engring. Guidance and Control Systems div., Litton Industries, Inc., Woodland Hills, Calif., 1973-76; v.p. bus. devel. Guidance and Control Systems div., Litton Industries Inc., Woodland Hills, Calif., 1976-77, pres., 1977-83; v.p. Litton Industries, Inc., 1979-83; sr. v.p., group exec. Litton Industries, Inc., Beverly Hills, Calif., 1983-88, pres., chief operating officer, 1988-90, sr. v.p., group exec., chief scientist, 1990-92; retired, 1992. Regional chmn. Los Angeles United Way campaign , 1985-86. Served to 1st lt. U.S. Army, 1954-56. Recipient Disting. Alumni award Poly. Inst. N.Y., 1986. Mem. Am. Electronics Assn., Inst. Navigation (western regional v.p. 1975-76, Hays award 1982). Roman Catholic.

PETERSON, RONALD ARTHUR, business law educator; b. Valley, Nebr., June 21, 1920; s. Arthur Lawrence and Hazel McClellan (Foster) P.; m. Patricia Marguerite North, Aug. 29, 1942; children: Ronald, Kathleen, Patrick, James, John, Thomas, Mary, Joseph. B.A. in Poly. Sci., U. Omaha, 1943; J.D. in Law, Creighton U., 1948; postgrad. U. Wash., 1963-64. Bar: Nebr. 1948, Wash. 1949. Asst. prof. Seattle U., 1963-76, dir. legal studies, 1973-83, assoc. prof., 1976-84, prof. emeritus dept. bus. law, 1984—. Author: The Old English Year Books. Dir. high sch.-coll. and alumni rels. Seattle U., 1950-58, dir. admissions, 1958-73; founding mem. Wash. State Coun. on High Sch.-Coll. Rels., 1953-73, chmn., 1962-63; founding mem. Seattle Archdiocese Sch. Bd., Western Wash., 1969; mem. Spl. Task Force on Legis. for Wash. System of Pub. Librs., 1971-73; assoc. dir. Wash. Criminal Justice Edn. and Tng. Ctr., 1973; mem. editorial bd. Introduction to Law and the Legal Process, 1980, mem. Oreg.-Wash. Commn. on the Pub. of Mapping Your Education; vol. chaplain juvenile ct. King County Dept. Youth Svcs., 1991; bd. dirs. Cath. Community Svcs. Legal Action Ctr., 1994—. Lt. USNR, 1943-46. Recipient Exemplary Tchr. award Alpha Kappa Psi, 1964. Mem. Am. Bus. Law Assn. (del. 1980), Pacific Northwest Bus. Law Assn. (pres. 1984-85), Seattle U. Alumni Assn. (Campus Svc. award 1989), Beta Gamma Sigma. Roman Catholic. Home: 1625 Mcgilvra Blvd E Seattle WA 98112-3119

PETERSON, SPENCER ALAN, ecologist; b. Sioux Falls, S.D., Jan. 6, 1940; s. Earl Harold and Josephine Henrietta (Giebink) P.; m. Shirley Ann White, Sept. 16, 1961; children: Scott Joseph, Sheila Marie. BS, Sioux Falls Coll., 1965; MS, U. N.D., 1967, PhD, 1971. Project leader Mich. Dept. Natural Resources, Lansing, 1971-72; rsch. biologist U.S. EPA, Corvallis, Oreg., 1972-74, team leader, 1974-77, program leader, 1977-81, br. chief, 1981-89; regional scientist U.S. EPA, Seattle, 1989-90; program leader U.S. EPA, Corvallis, Oreg., 1990—; adj. assoc. prof. Fish and Wildlife Dept. Oreg. State U. Co-author: Role of Water Urban Ecology, 1979, Restoration of Lakes and Reservoirs, 1986, 93. Chair bd. trustees 1st United Meth. Ch., Corvallis, 1971-72. Staff sgt. U.S. Army, 1961-62. Nat. Def. Grad. fellow U.S. Dept. HEW, 1966-69, fellow NSF, 1969, Nat. Wildlife Fedn., 1970. Mem. N.Am. Lake Mgmt. Soc. (bd. dirs. 1970, Tech. Excellence award 1990), Oreg. Lakes Assn., Sigma Xi. Office: US EPA 200 SW 35th St Corvallis OR 97333-4902

PETERSON, STANLEY LEE, artist; b. Viborg, S.D., Mar. 26, 1949; s. Norman and Neva Jean (Harns) P.; m. Katherine Anne Burnett. BFA, U. S.D., 1971. Artist W.H. Over Museum, Vermillion, S.D., 1971-72; graphic artist S.D. Pub. TV, Brookings, 1972-76; free lance artist San Francisco, 1976-77; engring. technician City of Tracy, Calif., 1977-85; artist Stanley Peterson Graphics, Los Banos, Calif., 1985—; contract engring. technician, system mgr. City of Tracy, 1985-89, system mgr., 1989-90; engring. technician IV County of Sacramento, 1991, prin. engring. technician, 1991—; cons. in field. Artist/designer Nat. History Diorama, W.H. Over Museum, 1972. Democrat. Home: 427 N Santa Monica St Los Banos CA 93635-3223

PETERSON, VANCE TULLIN, academic administrator, educator; b. Santa Monica, Calif., Nov. 4, 1944; s. William Tullin and Chanuth Joy (Griggs) P.; m. Anne Rose Breck, Apr. 7, 1968; children: Sara Rose, Theresa Pauline. BA, Occidental Coll., 1966; MS, George Washington U., 1971; PhD, Stanford (Calif.) U., 1976. Instr. Stanford U., 1972-73; researcher Carnegie Commn. on Higher Edn., Berkeley, Calif., 1973-74; asst. prof. U. Toledo, 1974-77; exec. dir. univ. rels. U. So. Calif., L.A., 1977-83; assoc. provost UCLA, 1983-89; v.p. Occidental Coll., L.A., 1989—. Editor: The Law & Higher Education, 1976; contbr. articles to profl. jours. Trustee CASE Dist. VII, 1980-83, chair campaign reporting adv. com., 1990-94; trustee Arcadia Ednl. Found., 1989-93; mem. Pasadena (Calif.) 2000 Commn., 1988. Capt. USNR (ret.). World ranked track 400m IH, 1965-66. Mem. Nat. Soc. Fundraising Execs., Coun. for Advancement and Support of Edn., Jonathan Club, Rotary, Alpha Tau Omega. Republican. Episcopalian. Office: Occidental Coll 1600 Campus Rd Los Angeles CA 90041-3384

PETERSON, VICTOR LOWELL, aerospace engineer, management consultant; b. Saskatoon, Sask., Can., June 11, 1934; came to U.S., 1937; s. Edwin Galladet and Ruth Mildred (McKeeby) P.; m. Jacqueline Dianne Hubbard, Dec. 21, 1955; children: Linda Kay Peterson Landrith, Janet Gale, Victor Craig. BS in Aero. Engring., Oreg. State U., 1956; MS in Aerospace Engring., Stanford U., 1964; MS in Mgmt., MIT, 1973. Rsch. scientist NASA-Ames Rsch. Ctr., Moffett Field, Calif., 1956-68, asst. chief hypersonic aerodyns., 1968-71, chief aerodyns. br., 1971-74, chief thermo and gas dynamics div., 1974-84, dir. aerophysics, 1984-90, dep. dir., 1990-94; pvt. mgmt. cons., 1994—; mem. nat. adv. bd. U. Tenn. Space Inst., Tullahoma, 1984-94. Contbr. numerous articles to profl. jours. Treas. Woodland Acres Homeowners Assn., Los Altos, Calif., 1978—. Capt. USAF, 1957-60. Recipient medal for outstanding leadership NASA, 1982; Alfred P. Sloan fellow MIT, 1972-73. Fellow AIAA. Republican. Methodist. Home: 484 Aspen Way Los Altos CA 94024-7126

PETERSON, WAYNE TURNER, composer, pianist; b. Albert Sea, Minn., Sept. 3, 1927; s. Leslie Jules and Irma Thelma (Turner) P.; m. Harriet Christiansen, 1948 (div. 1978); children: Alan, Craig, Drew, Grant. BA, U. Minn., 1951, MA, 1953; postgrad., Royal Acad. Music, London, 1953-54. Instr. music U. Minn., 1955-59; asst. prof. music Chico (Calif.) State U., 1959-60; prof. music San Francisco State U., 1960—; vis. prof. composition U. Ind., Bloomington, 1992; artist in residence Briarcombe Found., Bolinas, Calif., 1983; vis. artist Am. Acad. in Rome, 1990. Composer: Allegro for String Quartet, 1952, Introduction and Allegro, 1953, Free Variations for Orch., 1954-58, Can Death Be Sleep, 1955, Earth, Sweet Earth, 1956, (cappella chorus) Cape Ann, 1957, Three Songs for Soprano and Piano, 1957, (cappella chorus) Psalm 56, 1959, Exaltation, Dithyramb and Caprice, 1959-60, (cappella chorus) An e e Cummings Triptych, 1962, Tangents for flute, clarinet, horn and violin, 1963, An e e Cummings Cantata, 1964, Fantasy Concertante for violin and piano, 1965, Reflections, 1965, Metamorphosis for Wind Quintet, 1967, Phantasmagoria for flute, clarinet, double bass, 1968, Cataclysms, 1968, Clusters and Fragments for string orch., 1969, Ceremony After a Fire Raid, 1969, Sinfonia and Canticle for baritone voice and organ, 1969, Capriccio for Flute and Piano, 1973, Transformations for String Quartet, 1974, Trialogue for violin, cello and piano, 1975, Diatribe for violin and piano, 1975, Encounters, 1976, Rhapsody for Cello and Piano, 1976, An Interrupted Serenade for flute, harp and cello, 1978, Dark Reflections (cycle of four songs for high voice, violin and piano), 1980, Mallets Aforethought (symphony for percussion ensemble), 1981, Sextet for flute, clarinet, percussion, harp, violin and cello, 1982, Doubles for 2 flutes and 2 clarinets, 1982, Debussy Song Cycle, 1983, String Quartet, 1983-84, Ariadne's Thread for harp, flute, clarinet, horn, percussion and violin, 1985, Transformations for chamber orch., 1986, Duo for viola and cello, 1986-87, Trilogy for Orch., 1987, Labyrinth for flute, clarinet, violin and piano, 1987, The Widening Gyre for full orch., 1991, The Face of the Night, the Heart of the Dark for full orch., 1991 (Pulitzer prize for music 1992), Mallets Aforthought, 1991, String Quartet # 2, 1992, Diptych, 1992, Janus, 1993, Duo for Violin and Piano, 1993, And the Winds Shall Blow, a fantasy for saxophone quartet, symphony winds, brass and percussion, 1994; recs. with Mercury Records, Desto Records, Arch Records, Grenadilla Records, Koch Internat.; Recordings commd. Am. Music Ctr., 1959, Virtuosi of San Francisco, 1968, Unitarian Ch., 1969, Paul Mason, Inc., 1974, 87, NEA Consortium Commn., 1982, Charles Wuorinen and San Francisco Symphony, 1985, Am. Composers Symphony, Inc., 1987, San Francisco Symphony, 1991, Gerbode Found., 1990, Koussevitzky Found., 1990, Fromm Music Found., 1992, Philharmonic Orch. of Freiburg in Breisgau, Germany, 1993. Recipient 11th Ann. Norman Fromm Composer's award, 1982, Meritorious Svc. award Calif. State U. System, 1984, Top award Am. Harp Soc., 1985, Composer's award Am. Acad. and Inst. Arts and Letters, 1986, Pulitzer Prize for music, 1992; Fulbright scholar, Royal Acad. Music, 1953-54; NEA grantee, 1976; Guggenheim fellow, 1989-90, Djerassi Found. fellow, 1989-91. Home: 140 S Lake Merced Hls San Francisco CA 94132-2935

PETICOLAS, WARNER LELAND, physical chemistry educator; b. Lubbock, Tex., July 29, 1929; s. Warner Marion and Beulah Francis (Lowe) P.; m. Virginia Marie Wolf, June 30, 1969; children—Laura M., Alicia B.; children by previous marriage—Cynthia M., Nina P., Phillip W. B.S., Tex. Technol. Coll., 1950; Ph.D., Northwestern U., 1954. Research asso. DuPont Co., Wilmington, Del., 1954-60; research div. IBM, San Jose, Calif., 1960-67; cons. IBM, 1967-69, mgr. chem. physics group, 1965-67; prof. phys. chemistry U. Oreg., 1967—; vis. prof. U. Paris-Pierre and Marie Curie, 1980-81; cons. in field. Committeeman Democratic party, Eugene, Oreg., 1967-70. Served with USPHS, 1955-57. Recipient Alexander von Humboldt award, W. Ger., 1984-85. Guggenheim fellow Max von Laue-Paul Langevin Inst., Grenoble, France, 1973-74. Fellow Am. Phys. Soc.; mem. Am. Chem. Soc., Am. Phys. Soc., Sigma Xi, Alpha Chi Sigma, Tau Beta Pi. Episcopalian. Home: 2829 Arline Way Eugene OR 97403-2527 Office: U Oregon Dept Of Chemistry Eugene OR 97403

PETILLON, LEE RITCHEY, lawyer; b. Gary, Ind., May 6, 1929; s. Charles Ernest and Blanche Lurene (Mackay) P.; m. Mary Anne Keeton, Feb. 20, 1960; children: Andrew G., Joseph R. BBA, U. Minn., 1952; LLB, U. Calif., Berkeley, 1959. Bar: Calif. 1960, U.S. Dist. Ct. (so. dist.) Calif. 1960. V.p. Creative Investment Capital, Inc., L.A., 1969-70; corp. counsel Harvest Industries, L.A., 1970-71; v.p., gen. counsel, dir. Tech. Svcs. Corp., Santa Monica, Calif., 1971-78; ptnr. Petillon & Davidoff, L.A., 1978-92, Gipson Hoffman & Pancione, 1992-93; pvt. practice, Torrance, Calif., 1993-94; ptnr. Petillon & Hansen, Torrance, Calif., 1994—; Co-author: R&D Partnerships, 2d edit., 1985, Representing Start-Up Companies, 1992, 3d edit., 1995. Co-author: R&D Partnerships, 2d edit., 1985, Representing Start-Up Companies, 1992, 3d edit., 1995. Chmn. Neighborhood Justice Ctr. Com., 1983-85, Middle Income Com., 1983-85; active Calif. Senate Commn. on Corp. Governance, State Bar Calif. Task Force on Alternative Dispute Resolution, 1984-85. 1st lt. USAF, 1952-54. Recipient Cert. of Appreciation L.A. City Demonstration Agy., 1975, United Indian Devel. Assn., 1981, City of L.A. for Outstanding Vol. Svcs., 1984. Mem. ABA, Calif. State Bar Assn. (pres., Pro Bono Svcs. award 1983), L.A. County Bar Found. (bd. dirs. 1986-89), L.A. County Bar Assn. (chmn. law tech. sect., alt. dispute resolution sect. 1992-94, trustee 1984-85, Griffin Bell Vol. Svc. award 1993). Home: 1636 Via Machado Palos Verdes Estates CA 90274-1930 Office: Petillon & Hansen PC 21515 Hawthorne Blvd # 1260 Torrance CA 90503

PETOW, JOAN CLAUDIA, orthopedic nurse; b. Spokane, Wash., Mar. 5, 1946; d. August and Ella (McHargue) P. Diploma summa cum laude, Deaconess Hosp. Sch. Nursing, Spokane, 1967; BSN cum laude, Pacific Luth. U., 1969. RN, Wash.; cert. orthopedic nurse. Staff nurse orthopedic unit Deaconess Med. Ctr., Spokane, 1969-70, nurse ICU, 1970-72, asst. head nurse adult surg. unit, 1972-73, head nurse orthopedics unit, 1973-83; orthopedic staff nurse Valley Hosp. and Med. Ctr., Spokane, 1984—; nurse N.W. Orthopedic and Fracture Clinic, Spokane, 1995—; orthopedic quality assurance rep. Valley Hosp. and Med. Ctr., Spokane, 1988-90. Chmn. Spokane Coun. Christian Bus. and Profl. Women, 1976-77. Mem. Nat. Assn. Orthopedic Nurses (cert.), Sigma Theta Tau.

PETRAKIS, JULIA WARD, small business owner; b. Englewood, N.J., Apr. 24, 1936; d. William Davis and Elizabeth (Shaw) Ticknor; children by previous marriage: Elizabeth Anne Kinnunen Stam, Allan Conrad III; m. Peter L. Petrakis, Jan. 2, 1988. BA in Biochemistry, Radcliffe Coll., 1958. Ct. reporter Miller Reporting, Washington, 1979-81; sec. Whittaker Corp., Arlington, Va., 1981-82; adminstrv. asst. Entre Computers, Tysons Corner, Va., 1982-84; bus. owner Facts on Line, Camano Island, Wash., 1984—; U.S. agent MITEK Info. Svcs., Moscow; cons., researcher, book indexer, writer, and instr. in field. Interviewer Harvard-Radcliff Colls., Cambridge, Mass., 1984-85; vol. Cancer Drive, Heart Drive, Annapolis, 1986-899; dir. Cape St. Claire Security Fund, Annapolis, Md., 1988-89; treas. Camano Laguna Vista Community, 1992-94. Home and Office: 812 W Vista Dr Camano Island WA 98292-8688

PETRASICH, JOHN MORIS, lawyer; b. Long Beach, Calif., Oct. 13, 1945; s. Louis A. and Margaret A. (Moris) P.; m. Kathleen D. Krenek, July 4, 1969; children: Jason, Jacquelyn. BA, U. So. Calif., 1967, JD, 1970. Bar: Calif. 1971, U.S. Dist. Ct. (cen. dist.) 1971, U.S. Ct. Appeals (9th cir.) 1973, U.S. Dist. Ct. (no. dist.) Calif. 1974, U.S. Ct. Appeals (ea. dist.) Calif. 1976. Assoc. Fulop, Rolson, Burns & McKittrick, Beverly Hills and Newport Beach, Calif., 1971-74, ptnr., 1975-82; ptnr., head litigation McKittrick, Jackson, DeMarco & Peckenpaugh, Newport Beach, 1983-93; shareholder, head litigation Jackson, DeMarco & Peckenpaugh, Newport Beach, 1993—; also bd. dirs. McKittrick, Jackson, DeMarco & Peckenpaugh, Newport Beach. Mem. editorial staff U. So. Calif. Law Rev., 1969-70. Mem. ABA, Beverly Hills Bar Assn., L.A. Bar Assn., Assn. Trial Lawyers Am., Orange County Bar Assn., Lawyers Club L.A., Order of Coif. Office: Jackson DeMarco Peckenpaugh PO Box 19704 Irvine CA 92713-9704

PETRON, DONALD ROBERT, magazine editor; b. South Bend, Ind., Sept. 21, 1946; s. Robert Henry and Margaret Henrietta (Ostrowski) P.; m. Carmen Gloria Rodriguez, Feb. 15, 1969 (div. Nov. 1982); children: Gloria Louise, Margaret Evelyn; m. Yong Brandon, 1992. AA, Am. River Coll., 1974; BA, Calif. State U., Sacramento, 1991. Enlisted USAF, 1966, advanced through grades to master sgt., 1986; electronic technician USAF Air Weather Svc., Southwestern U.S., 1966-71, Western U.S., 1972-74; technician, instr. USAF Royal Thai Air Base, Ubon, Thailand, 1971-72; instr. electronics Chanute Tech. Tng. Ctr., Rantoul, Ill., 1974-78; mgr. installations USAF Comm. Command, Pacific area, 1978-84; dir. pub. rels. 1849th Electronic Installation Squadron USAF, Sacramento, 1984-86; ret. USAF, 1986; writer, photographer Country Music Forum mag., Sacramento, 1986-87, editor, 1987-88; elec. tech. Sacramento Army Depot, 1988-94, McClellan AFB, 1994—. Contbr. articles to profl. jours. Mem. Air Force Assn., Golden Key. Republican. Roman Catholic.

PETRUCCI, VINCENT EMILIO, retired viticulture educator, consultant; b. Crockett, Calif., July 13, 1925; s. Vincent C. and Assunta (Spero) P.; m. Josephine San Julian, July 12, 1948; children: Julianne, Kristene, Stephanie, Vincent P., Teresa. BS in Biology, U. Calif., Davis, 1948, MS in Pomology, 1951; DSc (hon.), U. Calif., Fresno, 1994. Tchr. agr., asst. football and basketball coach Esparto (Calif.) H.S., 1947-48; prof. viticulture Calif. State U., Fresno, 1948-93, prof. emeritus, 1993—, dir. Viticulture Rsch. Ctr., 1977-85, dir. Viticulture and Enology Rsch. Ctr., 1985-93; mem., cons. Calif. Raisin Adv. Bd.; advisor Am. Vineyard Found.; mem. wine grape quality com. Wine Inst.; co-chmn. Calif. Grape Growers Coalition; presenter in field; cons. to numerous vineyards, univs., colls., profl. orgns., including Almaden Vineyards, Brazil, Chateau Lafite, Pouliat, France, Viticulture and Enology Expt. Sta., Montpellier, France, 1986, U. Llerido, Spain, Orgn. Internat. Orgn. Viticulturists, Rome, 1987; U.S. rep. USA Exhibit, Moldavia; participant numerous seminars, confs., meetings in field. Contbr. numerous articles to sci. jours. Mem. bd. rev. com. Boy Scouts Am.; past pres. St. Anthony's Men's Club, Young Men's Inst.; wine and juice judge Fla. State Fair, Tampa, 1990. With AC Svc., USN, 1944-45. Recipient Disting. Svc. award Calif. Assn. Future Farms, 1966, Cath. Man of Yr. award, 1968; Outstanding Tchr. award Calif. State U., 1971, Salgo-Noren Excellence in Tchg. in Agr., 1974; Man of Yr. award Wines and Vines, 1981, Disting. Svc. award Fresno County Farm Bur., 1983, award of appreciation U.S. Bur. Alcohol, Tobacco and Firearms, 1984, Lifetime Achievement award Calif. Restaurant Assn., 1990, award of appreciation Am. Soc. Farm Mgrs. and Rural Appraisers, 1990, Davis Disting. Alumni Achievement award U. Calif., Davis, 1995; also others. Mem. Am. Soc. Hort. Sci., Am. Soc. Enologists (bd. dirs. 1976), Calif. Fertilization Assn. (former mem. soil improvement com.), Ft. Washington Golf and Country Club, Phi Kappa Phi. Home: 5604 N Flora Ave Fresno CA 93710-6327

PETRUZZI, CHRISTOPHER ROBERT, business educator, consultant; b. Peoria, Ill., July 28, 1951; s. Benjamin Robert and Mary Katherine (Urban) P.; m. Therese Michele Vaughan, Aug. 21, 1982 (div.1987); m. Georgina Sailer, June 20, 1992. BA, Wabash Coll., 1972; MBA, U. Chgo., 1974; PhD, U. Southern Calif., 1983. Lectr. bus. U. Wis., Milw., 1975-77; cons. H.C. Wainwright, Boston, 1978-79; lectr. U. So. Calif., 1978-81; prof. bus. U. Pa.,

Phila., 1981-84; prof. acctg. NYU, 1984-89, Calif. State U., Fullerton, 1989—; pres. ECON, N.Y.C., L.A., 1987—. Earhart fellow, 1972-73; U. Chgo. fellow, 1974-76. Libertarian. Home: 1527 Via Tulipan San Clemente CA 92673-3717

PETRZILKA, HENRY See FILIP, HENRY

PETTERSEN, THOMAS MORGAN, accountant, computer company executive; b. Poughkeepsie, N.Y., Nov. 9, 1950; s. Olsen Thomas and Reva Frances (Palmer) P. BS, U. Albany, 1973. CPA, N.Y. Sr. acct. Arthur Andersen and Co., N.Y.C., 1973-76; sr. ops. auditor Gulf and Western Inc., N.Y.C., 1977, fin. analyst, 1978; adminstr. auditing NBC, N.Y.C., 1979; mgr. auditing NBC, Burbank, Calif., 1980, dir. auditing, 1981-88, dir. acctg. systems and ops. analysis, 1988-90; v.p. fin. and adminstrn. Data Dimensions, Inc., Culver City, Calif., 1991-92; cons. Westwood One, Inc., Culver City, 1992-93; CFO Computer Image Sys., Inc., Torrance, Calif., 1993—. Mem. AICPA, Fin. Execs. Inst. Republican. Roman Catholic. Home: 217 1st Pl Manhattan Beach CA 90266-6503 Office: Computer Image Sys Inc 20030 Normandie Ave Torrance CA 90502-1210

PETTIGREW, STEVEN LEE, healthcare management company executive, consultant; b. Colorado Springs, May 8, 1949; s. Wesley N. and Mary Ellen (Howard) P.; m. Elise Woodcock, Dec. 12, 1987. BS in Mech. Engring., Colo. State U., 1972. Regional dir. Mgmt. Engring. Svcs. Assn. Program, Inc., Phoenix, 1972-76; v.p. Ariz. Hosp. Assn., Phoenix, 1976-79; corp. exec. dir. Samaritan Health Svc., Phoenix, 1976-78, 93-94; lectr. Ariz. State U., Tempe, 1976-78, 93-94. Contbr. articles to tech. publs. Bd. dirs. Hospice of Valley, Phoenix, 1981-88, pres., 1986-88, trustee endowmentfund, 1983—; Valley Leadership Class X11, 1990-91. NSF rsch. grantee, 1971-72. Fellow Healthcare Info. and Mgmt. Sys. Soc. (bd. dirs. 1980-81); mem. Healthcare Fin. Mgmt. Assn. (sr.), Instn. Indsl. Engrs. (sr.), Sigma Tau, Kiwanis (bd. dirs. Phoenix chpt. 1985-86, 94-95, treas. 1994-95, Spl. Svc. award 1986, 92, 93, 94). Methodist. Office: Phoenix Samaritan Health Sys 1441 N 12th St Phoenix AZ 85006-2887

PETTIGREW WELCH, DANA MARY, musician, insurance agent; b. Oklahoma City, Jan. 15, 1951; d. Richard Clester and Alice Butler (Sargent) Pettigrew; m. Douglas A. Welch, Aug. 4, 1994; children: Marilyn Yvonne Pettigrew, Lonnie Dean Pettigrew Jr. Student, Oklahoma City U., 1966-68. Cert. profl. ins. agt. Cert. Profl. Ins. Assn. Profl. performance musician Oklahoma City, 1965—, Seattle, 1989—; ind. agt. Pettigrew Ins. Agy., Oklahoma City, 1974-89, Protection Designs, Seattle, 1989—; owner Protection Designs Ins. Agy. Ch. organist Pa. Ave Christian Ch., 1979-89. Life Underwriter Tng. Council fellow, 1984. Mem. NAFE, Oklahoma City Health Underwriters Assn. (bd. dirs., sec. 1986—, v.p. 1987, pres. 1989), Oklahoma City Life Underwriters Assn. (bd. dirs. 1984-85), Seattle Musicians Assn., Renton-Auburn Musicians Assn., Okla. Country Music Assn., Ind. Ins. Agts. Assn., Profl. Ins. Agts. Assn., Cascade Assn. Life Underwriters, Renton C. of C., Kiwanis (sec. Renton chpt. 1988, 89, pianist 1987—). Republican. Mem. Christian Ch. Home and Office: 3511 NE 11th Pl Renton WA 98056-3442

PETTIS, RONALD EUGENE, lawyer; b. Williston, N.D., Sept. 5, 1939; s. Elmer Roy and Hildur Ann (Olson) P.; m. T. Mary Whitehead, June 12, 1961; children: Anna T. Scott, Phillip A. BA, U. Idaho, 1961; JD, U. Calif., Berkeley, 1969. Bar: Calif. 1970, U.S. Dist. Ct. (cen. dist.) Calif. 1974, U.S. Supreme Ct. 1978. Assoc. Hennigan, Butterwick & Clepper, Riverside, Calif., 1971-74, ptnr., shareholder, 1974-79; ptnr., shareholder Butterwick, Bright, Pettis & Cunnison, Inc., Riverside, 1979-82; ptnr. Gray Cary Ware & Freidenrich, San Diego, 1982—; bd. dirs. Western Maquidadora Trade Assn. Mem. bd. dirs., chmn., environ com. Border Trade Alliance. Served to capt. USMC, 1961-66. Mem. ABA, Internat. Bar Assn., Border Trade Alliance, U.S.-Mex. C. of C. (bd. dirs., pres. Pacific chpt.), Masons. Office: Gray Cary Ware & Friedenrich 1700 1st Interstate Plz 401 B St San Diego CA 92101-4223

PETTIS-ROBERSON, SHIRLEY MCCUMBER, former congresswoman; b. Mountain View, Calif.; d. Harold Oliver and Dorothy Susan (O'Neil) McCumber; m. John J. McNulty (dec.); m. Jerry L. Pettis (dec. Feb. 1975); m. Ben Roberson, Feb. 6, 1988; children: Peter Dwight Pettis, Deborah Neil Pettis Moyer. Student, Andrews U., U. Calif., Berkeley. Mgr. Audio-Digest Found., L.A., Glendale; sec.-treas. Pettis, Inc., Hollywood, 1958-68; mem. 94th-95th Congresses from 37th Calif. Dist., mem. coms. on interior, internat. rels., edn. and labor; pres. Women's Rsch. and Edn. Inst., 1979-80; bd. dirs. Kemper Nat. Ins. Cos., 1979—. Mem. Pres.'s Commn. on Arms Control and Disarmament, 1980-83, Commn. on Presdl. Scholars, 1990-92; trustee U. Redlands, Calif., 1980-83, Loma Linda (Calif.) U. and Med. Ctr., 1990—; chair Loma Linda U. Children's Hosp. Found.; bd. dirs. Former Mems. Congress, Capitol Hill Club, Washington. Mem. Morningside Country Club (Rancho Mirage, Calif.).

PETTIT, GEORGE ROBERT, chemistry educator, cancer researcher; b. Long Branch, N.J., June 8, 1929; s. George Robert and Florence Elizabeth (Seymour) P.; m. Margaret Jean Benger, June 20, 1953; children: William Edward, Margaret Sharon, Robin Kathleen, Lynn Benger, George Robert III. B.S., Wash. State U., 1952; M.S. Wayne State U., 1954, Ph.D., 1956. Teaching asst. Wash. State U., 1950-52, lecture demonstrator, 1952; rsch. chemist E.I. duPont de Nemours and Co., 1953; grad. teaching asst. Wayne State U., 1952-53, rsch. fellow, 1954-56; sr. rsch. chemist Norwich Eaton Pharms., Inc., 1956-57; asst. prof. chemistry U. Maine, 1957-61, assoc. prof. chemistry, 1961-65, prof. chemistry, 1965; vis. prof. chemistry Stanford U., 1965; chmn. organic div. Ariz. State U., 1966-68, prof. chemistry, 1965—; vis. prof. So. African, Univs., 1978; dir. Cancer Rsch. Lab., 1974-75, Cancer Rsch. Inst., 1975—; lectr. various colls. and univs.; cons. in field. Contbr. articles to profl. jours. Mem. adv. bd. Wash. State U. Found., 1981-85. Served with USAFR, 1951-54. Recipient Disting. Rsch. Professorship award Ariz. State U., 1978-79, Alumni Achievement award Wash. State U., 1984; named Dalton Prof. Medicinal Chemistry and Cancer Rsch., 1986—, Regents Prof. Chemistry, 1990—. Fellow Am. Inst. Chemists (Pioneer award 1989, Ariz. Gov.'s Excellence award 1993); mem. Am. Chem. Soc. (awards com. 1968-71, 78-81), Chem. Soc. (London), Pharmacognosy Soc., Am. Assn. Cancer Rsch., Sigma Xi, Phi Lambda Upsilon. Office: Ariz State U Cancer Rsch Inst Tempe AZ 85287

PETTIT, GHERY DEWITT, retired veterinary medicine educator; b. Oakland, Calif., Sept. 6, 1926; s. Hermon DeWitt Pettit and Marion Esther (St. John) Menzies; m. Frances Marie Seitz, July 5, 1948; children: Ghery St. John, Paul Michael. BS in Animal Sci., U. Calif., Davis, 1948, BS in Vet. Sci., 1951, DVM, 1953. Diplomate Am. Coll. Vet. Surgeons (recorder 1970-77, pres., chmn. bd. dirs. 1978-80). Asst. prof. vet. surgery U. Calif., Davis, 1953-61; prof. vet. surgery Wash. State U., Pullman, 1961-91, prof. emeritus, 1991—; mem. Wash. State Vet. Bd. Govs., 1981-88, chmn., 1987; vis. fellow Sydney (Australia) U., 1977. Author/editor: Intervertebral Disc Protrusion in the Dog, 1966; cons. editoral bd. Jour. Small Animal Practice, Eng., 1970-88; mem. editoral bd. Compendium on C.E., Lawrenceville, N.J., 1983-86, editoral rev. bd. Jour. Vet. Surgery, Phila., 1984-86, editor 1987-92; contbr. articles to profl. jours., chpts. to books. Elder Presbyn. Ch., Pullman, 1967—. Served with USN, 1944-46. Recipient Norden Disting. Tchr. award Wash. State U. Class 1971, Faculty of Yr. award Wash. State U. Student Com., 1985. Mem. Am. Vet. Med. Assn., Sigma Xi, Phi Zeta, Phi Kappa Sigma (chpt. advisor 1981-93, 2d v.p. 1993-95). Republican.

PETTIT, JOHN W., hospital administrator; b. Detroit, Mar. 6, 1942; s. John W. and Clara (Schartz) P.; m. Kathleen Endres, Aug. 8, 1970; children: Julie, Andrew, Michael. BBA, U. Notre Dame, 1964; MBA, Mich. State U., 1974. CPA, Mich. Acct. Ernst & Ernst, Detroit, 1964-67; chief acct. Detroit Inst. Tech., Detroit, 1967-69; controller, dir. adminstrn. & fin. Mich. Cancer Found., Detroit, 1969-80; chief adminstrv. officer Dana-Farber Cancer Inst., Boston, 1980-94; exec. v.p., chief oper. officer John Wayne Cancer Inst., Santa Monica, Calif., 1995—; grant reviewer Nat. Cancer Inst., Bethesda, Md., 1979—. Pres. advanced mgmt. program Mich. State U., 1978-79. Mem. Am. Inst. CPA's. Office: John Wayne Cancer Inst 2200 Santa Monica Blvd Santa Monica CA 90404-2301

PETTIT, MARGARET ESTA, broadcasting executive; b. Provo, Utah, July 22, 1926; d. Howard Hammil and Edith Susan (Cummins) Cain; student public schs.; m. Claud Martin Pettit, July 30, 1948; children—Ruth Elaine, Paul Martin. Co-owner, office supr. Sta. KEOS, Flagstaff, Ariz., 1960-61; co-owner, bookkeeper Sta. KWIV, Douglas, Wyo., 1965-74; co-owner, bookkeeper, program dir., office supr. Sta. KCMP, Brush Colo., 1976-82; dir. Custom Broadcasting Co., Denver; sec.-treas., dir. Ranchland Broadcasting Co.; dir., v.p. Better Day, Inc., Arvada, Colo. Bd. dirs. Jefferson Park Community Activity Assn., Denver, 1981-84, North Fed. Recreation, Denver, 1984-93; dir., treas. Better Life Ministries, Arvada, Colo., 1993—. Mem. Model T Ford Club. Baptist. Home and Office: 8320 W 66th Ave Arvada CO 80004-3327

PETTITE, WILLIAM CLINTON, public affairs consultant; b. Reno, Nev.; s. Sidney Clinton and Wilma (Stibal) P.; m. Charlotte Denise Fryer; children: Patrick Keane, William Ellis, Joseph Clinton. Owner, Market Lake Citizen & Clark County Enterprise Newspapers, Roberts, Idaho, 1959-70, pub., 1959-61; publicity dir. Golden Days World Boxing Champs, Reno, 1970; pub. Virginia City (Nev.) Legend newspaper, 1970; public affairs cons., Fair Oaks, Calif., 1966—, owner PT Cattle Co., Firth, Idaho; cons. in Ireland, Wales, Korea, Japan, France, Czech Republic, Alberta, British Columbia, New Brunswick, Prince Edward Island, Nova Scotia, Can., Channel Islands, Costa Rica 1984—. County probate judge, Idaho, 1959-61; acting County coroner, 1960-61; sec., trustee Fair Oaks Cemetery Dist., 1963-72; bd. dir. Fair Oaks Water Dist., 1964-72, v.p., 1967-68, pres., 1968-70; dir., v.p. San Juan Cmty. Svcs. Dist., 1962-66, 68-72; exec. sec. Calif. Bd. Landscape Archs., 1976-78, Calif. Assn. Collectors, 1966-68. Cons. Senate-Assembly Joint Audit Com. Calif. Legislature, 1971-73; exec. officer Occupational Safety and Health Appeals Bd., 1981-83; mem. regulatory rev. commn. Calif. FabricCare Bd., 1981-82; mem. Sacramento County Grand Jury, 1981-82, cons. bd. supvs. Sacramento County, 1985-86; chmn. bus. adv. bd. East Lawn Corp, 1991—. Election campaign coord. for E.S. Wright, majority leader Idaho Senate, 1968, Henry Dworshak, U.S. Senator, 1960, Hamer Budge, U.S. Rep., 1960, Charles C. Gossett, former Gov. Idaho, 1959-74; asst. sgt. at arms Rep. Nat. Conv., 1956; chmn. Rep. County Cen. Com., 1959-61; del. Rep. State Conv., 1960. Chmn. Idaho County Centennial Commn., 1959-61. Recipient Idaho Centennial award, 1968, 69. Mem. Assn. Sacramento County Water Dists. (bd. dir. 1967-72, pres. 1970-72), No. Calif. Peace Officers Assn., Nat. Coun. Juvenile Ct. Judges (com. 1959-61). Club. Author: Memories of Market Lake, Vol. I, 1965; A History of Southeastern Idaho, Vol. II, 1977, Vol. III, 1983, Vol. IV, 1990; contbr. articles to newspapers, profl. jours. Home: PO Box 2127 Fair Oaks CA 95628-2127 Office: 2631 K St Sacramento CA 95816-5103

PETTY, KEITH, lawyer; b. Swan Lake, Idaho, June 13, 1920; s. William Dorris and Emma Louise (Johnson) P.; m. Gail Wells, Jan. 11, 1943; children—Kaye Wells Paugh, Jane Wells Taylor, Richard Keith, Scott Robert. B.S., U. Idaho, 1942; J.D., Stanford U., 1948; postgrad. Harvard U., 1943. Bar: Calif., 1949, Idaho, 1948. Tax acct. Pacific Telephone Co., San Francisco, 1948-50; acct. John F. Forbes & Co., San Francisco, 1950-54; partner Petty, Andrews, Tufts & Jackson and predecessor firms, San Francisco, San Jose and Palo Alto, Calif., 1954-86; sole practice Palo Alto, 1986—; lectr. in field. Served to lt. USNR, 1942-46. Mem. Calif. Soc. C.P.A.s, San Francisco Bar Assn. Mormon. Clubs: Commonwealth, Univ., Bankers. Home: 1420 Pitman Ave Palo Alto CA 94301-3055 Office: 1755 Embarcadero Rd Ste 110 Palo Alto CA 94303-3304

PETTY, LEONORA KATHLEEN, psychiatrist. BA, Mt. Holyoke Coll., 1970; MD, U. Pa., 1973. Diplomate Am. Bd. Psychiatry and Neurology, Am. Bd. Quality Assurance and Utilization Review Physicians. Psychiatry residency U. Pa. Hosp., 1973-75; assoc. medical dir. intramural program Phila. Child Guidance Clinic, 1977, acting medical dir. intramural program, 1977-78; child psychiatrist, unit dir. neuropsychiatric inst. U. Calif., L.A., 1978-91; asst. prof. in resident in psychiatry & bio-behavioral scis. Neuropsychiatric Inst. U. Calif., L.A., 1978-82, adj. asst. prof., 1982-87; clinical asst. prof. psychiatry U. Calif., L.A., 1987-91; medical dir. Preferred Health Care, LTD, Irvine, Calif., 1987-88, Life Link Inc, Pasadena, Calif., 1988-91; medical dir. adolescent unit Spartanburg (S.C.) Regional Medical Ctr., 1991; clin. dir. children's unit Montevista Hosp., Las Vegas, 1992; pvt. practice Las Vegas, 1992—; consulting psychiatrist Behavioral Health Care Options, Las Vegas, 1992—; physician adv. Southern Calif. Edison, 1988-91, Boys Republic, Chino, Calif., 1987-91, Southern Nev. Child and Adolescent Mental Health Svcs., 1987-91; cons. to adolescent program Montevista Hosp., Las Vegas, 1987, Charter Hosp., Las Vegas, 1986-87. Contbr. articles to profl. jours. Appointed to chair APA com. in psychiatric svcs. in military, 1986, 87-88, com. psychiatric svcs. in the military, 1984-90. Recipient Nat. Sci. Found. fellowship, 1970, CIBA-Geigy, 1970, Falk fellowship Am. Psychiatry Assn., 1975-77. Mem. Am. Psychiatric Assn. (task force Changing Family Patterns, 1980), Southern Calif. Psychiatric Soc., Sigma Xi. Office: 2235 E Flamingo Rd Ste 404 Las Vegas NV 89119-5197

PEYTON, MARY JOHANNA, secondary educator; b. Salt Lake City, Apr. 15, 1946; d. John Edward and Ellen Bernice (Michaud) P. B in Music, U. Mont., 1968, M in Music Edn., 1970. Cert. secondary tchr., Calif. Elem. instr. music Ceres (Calif.) Unified Sch. Dist., 1969-71, instr. jr. high music, 1971-75, instr. jr. high English, 1975-84, instr. jr. high econs., 1984-86, coordinator career edn., 1984—, instr. ind. study, 1986—; cons. various edn. orgns., 1984—; trainer career edn. Nat. Diffusion Network, U.S. Dept. Edn., Washington, 1985—. Producer, writer film Project Ceres, 1985; speaker in field. Mem. NEA, Calif. Tchrs. Assn., Calif. Career Edn. Assn., Ceres Unified Tchrs. Assn. (faculty rep. 1969—, negotiations team 1979—, 2nd v.p. 1980, negotiations chair 1984—), Phi Delta Kappa. Republican. Roman Catholic. Home: 3128 Scenic Dr Modesto CA 95355-4771

PEZESHKI, KAMBIZ A., metallurgical engineer; b. Tabriz, Iran, Sept. 30, 1949; came to U.S., 1970, naturalized; s. Amir Aziz and Azam (Mazi) P.; m. Shiron Cashmir Wisenbaker, Apr. 7, 1976; children: Shahene A., Shahla J. BS in Metall. Engring., U. Utah, 1977; MBA in Mktg. and Human Rels., U. Phoenix, 1983. Cert. tchr., Ariz. Process metallurgist Amax, Inc., Golden, Colo., 1977-79; process, rsch. engr. Cities Svcs. Co./Oxidental, Miami, Ariz., 1979-84; tech. svcs. engr. Am. Cyanamid, Wayne, N.J., 1984-87; mgr. western mining Rhone-Poulenc, Inc., Salt Lake City, 1987-93; nat. sales engr. Hychem, Inc., Salt Lake City, 1993—; polymerization cons. RTZ/Kennecott Copper, Salt Lake City, 1989—. Fund raiser Jake Garn for Senate, Salt Lake City, 1976; fund raiser, motivator Barry Goldwater for Senate re-election, 1980-81; vol. Ted Wilson for Gov., Salt Lake City, 1988. Mem. Am. Mining Engrs. Soc. Republican. Presbyterian.

PFAELZER, MARIANA R., federal judge; b. L.A., Feb. 4, 1926. AB, U. Calif., 1947; LLB, UCLA, 1957. Bar: Calif. 1958. Assoc. Wyman, Bautzer, Rothman & Kuchel, 1957-69, ptnr., 1969-78; judge U.S. Dist. Ct. (ctrl. dist.) Calif., 1978—. pres., v.p., dir. Bd. Police Commrs. City of L.A., 1974-78; bd. vis. Loyola Law Sch. Named Alumna of Yr. by UCLA Law Sch., 1980. Mem. ABA, Calif. Bar Assn. (local adminstrv. com., spl. com. study rules procedure 1972, joint subcom. profl. ethics and computers and the law coms. 1972, profl. ethics com. 1972-74, spl. com. juvenile justice, women's rights subcom. human rights sect.), L.A. County Bar Assn. (spl. com. study rules procedure state bar 1974). Office: US Dist Ct 312 N Spring St Los Angeles CA 90012-4701*

PFEIFFER, GERALD G., human resources consultant; b. Bowling Green, Ohio, Oct. 23, 1939; s. Harry A. and Velma C. (Morrow) P.; m. Jill S. Kimber, Apr. 20, 1980. BS, George Washington U., 1962; MBA, Wayne State U., Detroit, 1970. CLU. With FBI, Washington, Detroit, 1960-63, Am. Std. Corp., Detroit, 1963-70; labor rels. supr. to dir. personnel ITT Corp., various cities, 1970-76; labor rels. and safety advisor to sr. e.r. cons. various cities Mobil Oil Corp., 1976-85; exec. v.p., gen. mgr. HAP Ent., Inc., San Diego, 1985-90; human resources cons. Merit Resource Group, San Francisco, 1991-93; v.p. human resources Nat. Refractories and Minerals Corp., Livermore, Calif., 1993—. Contbr. articles to profl. jours. Advisor Jr. Achievement, 1967-84; human resources cons. Joan Kroc Homeless Ctr., San Diego, 1989-92, United Way, San Diego, 1989-92. Capt. USAF, 1962. W.I.N. grantee, 1968. Mem. Rotary. Home: 2199 Prestwick Dr Discovery Bay CA 94514

PFEIFFER, JOHN WILLIAM, publisher, management consultant; b. Wallace, Idaho, July 10, 1937; s. John William and Mary Loretta (Schmidt) P.; children: Heidi Erika, Charles Wilson. BA, U. Md., 1962; PhD (fellow), U. Iowa, 1968; JD, Western State U., 1982; DABS (hon.), Calif. Am. U., Escondido, 1980. Instr. U. Md., 1965-67; dir. adult edn. Kirkwood (Iowa) Community Coll., 1967-69; dir. ednl. resources Ind. Higher Edn. Telecommunications Systems, Indpls., 1969-72; pres. Univ. Assocs., San Diego, 1972-90, Pfeiffer & Co., San Diego, 1991—; adj. tchr. Ind. U., 1969-72, Purdue U., 1971-72. Author: Instrumentation in Human Relations Training, 1973, 2d edit. 1976, Reference Guide to Handbooks and Annuals, 1975, 2d edit. 1977, 3d. edit. 1981, (With Goodstein and Nolan) Applied Strategic Planning, 1986, 2d edit. 1988, (with Judith A. Pfeiffer) LBP, 1990; editor: A Handbook of Structured Experiences for Human Relations Training, 10 vols., 1969-85, The Annual Handbook for Facilitators, 10 vols. 1972-81, Group and Orgns. Studies Internat. Jour. for Group Facilitators, 1976-79, The Annual for Facilitators, Trainers and Consultants, 1982-91, Strategic Planning: Selected Readings, 1986, The Instrumentation Kit, 1988, Shaping Strategic Planning, 1988, Training Technology, 7 vols., 1988, Theories and Models, 4 vols., 1992, Plan or Die, 1993, Pfeiffer Library, 28 vols., 1993. Served with U.S. Army, 1958-62. Office: Pfeiffer & Co 8517 Production Ave San Diego CA 92121-2204

PFEIFFER, ROBERT JOHN, transportation executive; b. Suva, Fiji Islands, Mar. 7, 1920; came to U.S., 1921, naturalized, 1927; s. William Albert and Nina (MacDonald) P.; m. Mary Elizabeth Worts, Nov. 29, 1945; children—Elizabeth Pfeiffer Tumbas, Margaret Pfeiffer Hughes, George, Kathleen. Grad. high sch., Honolulu, 1937; DSc (hon.), Maine Maritime Acad.; HHD (hon.), U. Hawaii; DHL (hon.), Hawaii Loa Coll. With Inter-Island Steam Navigation Co., Ltd., Honolulu, (re-organized to Overseas Terminal Ltd. 1950); with (merged into Oahu Ry. & Land Co. 1954), 1937-55, v.p., gen. mgr., 1950-54, mgr. ship agy. dept., 1954-55; v.p., gen. mgr. Pacific Cut Stone & Granite Co., Inc., Alhambra, Calif., 1955-56, Matcinal Corp., Alameda, Calif., 1956-58; mgr. div. Pacific Far East Line, Inc., San Francisco, 1958-60; with Matson Nav. Co., San Francisco, 1960—, v.p., 1966-70, sr. v.p., 1970-71, exec. v.p., 1971-73, pres., 1973-79, 84-85, 89-90, CEO, 1979-92, chmn. bd., bd.dirs., 1979-95, chmn. emeritus, 1995—, 1995—; v.p. The Matson Co., San Francisco, 1968-70; pres. The Matson Co., 1970-82; v.p., gen. mgr. Matson Terminals, Inc., San Francisco, 1960-62; pres. Matson Terminals, Inc., 1962-70, chmn. bd., 1970-79; chmn. bd. Matson Svcs. Co., 1973-79, Matson Agys., Inc., 1973-78; sr. v.p. Alexander & Baldwin, Inc., Honolulu, 1973-77; exec. v.p. Alexander & Baldwin, Inc., 1977-79, chmn. bd., 1980-95; chmn. emeritus Alexander & Baldwin, Inc., Honolulu, 1995—; CEO Alexander & Baldwin, Inc., 1980-92, pres., 1979-84, 89-91; chmn. bd., pres., dir. A&B-Hawaii, Inc., 1988-89, chmn. bd., 1989-95; chmn. emeritus A&B Hawaii, Honolulu, 1995—; former mem. Gov.'s commn. on exec. salaries State of Hawaii, com. on jud. salaries. Past chmn. maritime transp. rsch. bd. Nat. Acad. Sci.; former mem. select com. for Am. Mcht. Marine Seamanship Trophy Award, commn. sociotech. systems NRC.; mem. adv. com. Joint Maritime Congress; trustee Pacific Tropical Bot. Garden, Pacific Aerospace Mus., also bd. dirs.; mem. Japan-Hawaii Econ. Coun., Army Civilian Adv. Group; vice-chmn. Hawaii Maritime Ctr.; former chmn. A Commitee on Excellence (ACE), Hawaii; mem. adv. coun. Girl Scouts U.S.A. coun. of the Pacific; mem. exec. com. Rsch. Round Table Alameda County chpt. Am. Heart Assn.; bd. govs. Japanese Cultural Ctr. Hawaii; mem. bd. nominators Am. Inst. for Pub. Svc.; life mem. Vets. Fgn. Wars U.S.; hon. co-chmn. McKinley High Sch. Found.; mem. adv. bd. Hawaii Bldg. and Constrn. Trades Coun., AFL-CIO Ednl. and Charitable Found. Lt. USNR, World War II; comdr. Res. ret. Mem. Nat. Assn. Stevedores (past pres.), Internat. Cargo Handling Coord. Assn. (past pres. U.S. com.), Propeller Club U.S. (past pres. Honolulu), Nat. Def. Transp. Assn., Conf. Bd., Containerization & Intermodal Inst. (hon. bd. advisors), 200 Club, Maui C. of C., Aircraft Owners and Pilots Assn., Pacific Club, Outrigger Club, Oahu Country Club, Maui Country Club, Pacific Union Club, Bohemian Club, World Trade Club (San Francisco), Masons, Shriners. Republican. Home: 535 Miner Rd Orinda CA 94563-1429 Office: Alexander & Baldwin Inc 822 Bishop St Honolulu HI 96813-3924

PFEUFFER, JOSEPH JOHN, electrical engineer, director; b. N.Y.C., Nov. 18, 1944; s. Joseph and Florence (Gucwa) P.; m. Geraldine Rodi, Oct. 30, 1971; children: Evan Joseph, Marc Stewart, Carey Paul. B of Engring., Stevens Inst. of Technology, 1967; MBA, E. Wash. State U., Cheney, 1993. Engr. Potter Instrument Co., Plainview, N.Y., 1967-72; mgr. Qantex, Plainview, 1973-79, Documation, Melbourne, Fla., 1979-82; dir. Medicomp, Palm Bay, Fla., 1982-84, Centronics, Hudson, N.H., 1984-85, Storage Tech., Melbourne, Fla., 1985-88, Megascan, Gibsonia, Pa., 1988-89, Bruning, Martinez, Calif., 1989-90, Output Tech., Spokane, Wash., 1990—; dir. Indian River Rsch., Melbourne, Fla., 1981—, Gonzaga U. Engring. Ctr., Spokane, Wash., 1992—. Inventor magnetic record, 1970, voice recognition, 1982, laser printing, 1990. Fellow IEEE; mem. Am. Radio Relay League. Republican. Roman Catholic. Home: 4838 S Bella Vista Dr Veradale WA 99037-9148 Office: Output Tech Corp 2310 N Fancher Rd Spokane WA 99212-1329

PFLUEGER, JOHN MILTON, architect; b. San Francisco, Aug. 23, 1937; s. Milton Theodore and Genevive (Wendgard) P.; BS, Stanford, 1959, BArch, 1960; m. Lynne Williams, Jan. 23, 1963; children: Peter, John Thomas, Christopher Timothy. Pres., chief exec. officer Pflueger Architects, Inc., San Francisco, 1976; lectr. Urban Life Inst., U. San Francisco, U. Colo., 1978; campus architect U. San Francisco, Coll. of Holy Names, City Coll. San Francisco. Mem. planning com. San Francisco Downtown Assn., 1971-83. Lic. architect, Calif., Nev., Hawaii. Mem. AIA (pub. edn. com. No. Calif. chpt. 1970-79), NCARB, Constrn. Specifications Inst., Soc. Coll. and Univ. Planning, San Francisco Planning and Urban Renewal, Sierra Club, U.S. C. of C., Calif. Acad. Scis., Soc. Am. Mil. Engrs., Delta Tau Delta. Clubs: Olympic (bldg. com. 1973-78, properties commn. 1979-81), Family (San Francisco). Major works include: Cowell Hall, Calif. Acad. Scis. (Prestress Concrete Inst. award 1969), Creative Arts Extension, City Coll. San Francisco (AIA design excellence award 1974), Fish Roundabout, Calif. Acad. Scis., 1976, Natural Energy Office Bldg., 1977 (Honor award State of Calif.), Batmale Hall, City Coll. San Francisco, 1978, Calif. Farm Bur. Fedn., Sacramento, 1980 (Owens Corning, Dept. Energy and ASHRAE awards), San Jose State U. Library, 1982, Nev. Nat. Bank Hdqrs., Reno, 1982 (ASHRAE award), Performing Arts Ctr. and Fine Arts Mus., Sierra Arts Found., Reno; 8 major bldgs. at Stanford U., including Environ. Safety Facility, 1986; Co-Generation facility and Health and Recreation Ctr., U. San Francisco, 1987; rehabilitation Santa Rosa Ferry Boat, James Licks Bathhouse, 1981, Warfield Office Bldg. and Theater, 1985; major hosps. include Shriners Hosp. for Crippled Children, Walter Reed Army Med. Ctr. (Pre-Stressed Concrete Inst., Dept. Def. design awards 1980). Office: John M Pflueger Architect 165 Lark Ln Mill Valley CA 94941-3570

PFLUG, EDUARD, contractor; b. Belgrade, Serbia, Apr. 25, 1938; came to U.S., 1961; s. Rudolf and Mary (Kovacevic) P.; m. Rose Marie Amato, Jan. 21, 1973. AAS, DeVry Inst., 1963; BA in Bus. Adminstrn. and Mgmt., Ind. Inst. Tech., 1992. Field tech. rep. East Coast and Midwest area Siemens Am., Inc., N.Y.C., 1963-67; dist. svc. mgr. Midwest area Philips Electronic Instruments, 1967-88; regional svc. mgr. West Coast area Hitachi Instruments, Inc.; ind. contractor Pflug's Enterprises, 1992—. Mem. Assn. for Field Svc. Mgrs. Internat. (officer local chpt. 1982—), Nat. Orgn. for Self-Employed (enroller 1994—), Alpha Chi (Ind. Lambda chpt.). Republican. Seventh Day Adventist. Home and Office: 1032 Edgewater Blvd Foster City CA 94404-3710

PFORZHEIMER, HARRY, JR., oil consultant; b. Manila, Nov. 19, 1915; s. Harry and Mary Ann (Horan) P.; BS in Chem. Engring., Purdue U., 1938; postgrad. Case Inst. Tech., Law Sch., George Washington U., Case Western Res. U.; m. Jean Lois Barnard, June 2, 1945; children: Harry, Thomas. with Standard Oil Co. (Ohio), various locations, 1938-80, pres. White River Shale Oil Corp., 1974-76, v.p. Sohio Natural Resources Co., 1971-80, program dir. Paraho oil shale demonstration, Grand Junction, 1974-80; pres., chmn. bd., chief exec. officer Paraho Devel. Corp., 1980-82, sr. mgmt. advisor and dir., 1982-85, cons., 1985—; pres. Harry Pforzheimer Jr. and Assocs., 1983—, Ind. Colo. West Fin., Inc.; dir. IntraWest Bank Grand Junction; adj. prof. chem. engring. Cleve. State U. Contbr. articles to tech. and trade jours. Mem. planning adv. bd. St. Mary's Hosp. and Med. Ctr.; long-range planning com. Immaculate Heart of Mary Ch.; bd. dirs. Colo. Sch. Mines Research Inst.; mem. Petroleum Adminstrn. for War, Washington, 1942-45,

Purdue U. Pres.'s Coun.; chmn. Wayne N. Aspinall Found.; mem. long range planning com. Immaculate Heart Mary Ch. Mem. Am. Inst. Chem. Engrs. (chmn. Cleve. 1955, gen. chmn. internat. meeting, Cleve. 1961), Am. Petroleum Inst., Am. Mining Congress, Colo. Mining Assn., Rocky Mountain Oil and Gas Assn., Denver Petroleum Club, Purdue Alumni Assn., Sigma Alpha Epsilon. Clubs: Army and Navy (Washington), Bookcliff Country, Rio Verde Country. Lodge: Kiwanis. Home: 2700 G Rd # 1-c Grand Junction CO 81506-1408 Office: 743 Horizon Ct Grand Junction CO 81506-8714

PFUND, EDWARD THEODORE, JR., electronics company executive; b. Methuen, Mass., Dec. 10, 1923; s. Edward Theodore and Mary Elizabeth (Banning) P.; BS magna cum laude, Tufts Coll., 1950; postgrad U. So. Calif., 1950, Columbia U., 1953, U. Calif., L.A., 1956, 58; m. Marga Emmi Andre, Nov. 10, 1954 (div. 1978); children: Angela M., Gloria I., Edward Theodore III; m. Ann Lorenne Dille, Jan. 10, 1988 (div. 1990). Radio engr., WLAW, Lawrence-Boston, 1942-50; fgn. svc. staff officer Voice of Am., Tangier, Munich, 1950-54; project. engr. Crusade for Freedom, Munich, Ger., 1955; project mgr., materials specialist United Electrodynamics Inc., Pasadena, Calif., 1956-59; cons. H.I. Thompson Fiber Glass Co., L.A., Andrew Corp., Chgo., 1959, Satellite Broadcast Assocs., Encino, Calif., 1982; teaching staff Pasadena City Coll. (Calif.), 1959; dir. engring., chief engr. Electronics Specialty Co., L.A. and Thomaston, Conn., 1959-61; with Hughes Aircraft Co., various locations, 1955, 61-69, mgr. Middle East programs, also Far East, Latin Am. and African market devel., L.A., 1971-89, dir. internat. programs devel., Hughes Comm. Internat., 1985-89; mng. dir. E.T. Satellite Assocs. Internat., Rolling Hills Estates, Calif., 1989—; dir. programs devel. Asia-Pacific TRW Space and Tech. Group, Redondo Beach, Calif., 1990-93, Pacific Telecom. Coun., Honolulu, 1993—. With AUS, 1942-46. Mem. AIAA, Phi Beta Kappa, Sigma Pi Sigma. Contbr. articles to profl. jours. Home: 25 Silver Saddle Ln Palos Verdes Peninsula CA 90274-2437

PFUNTNER, ALLAN ROBERT, entomologist; b. Buffalo, May 19, 1946; s. Robert James and Verna May (Colton) P.; m. Sri Hartini Hartono, Aug. 23, 1970; children: Nicolis Dean, Erin Tristina. BA in Biology, San Jose State U., 1969, MA in Biology, 1977. Cert. entomologist. Sanitarian Monterey County Health Dept., Salinas, Calif., 1972-73; vector control asst. Santa Clara County Health Dept., San Jose, Calif., 1973-75; entomologist Northwest Mosquito Abatement Dist., Riverside, Calif., 1975-84; asst. mgr. West Valley Vector Control Dist., Chino, Calif., 1984-89, mgr., 1989—. Contbr. articles to jours. Served with U.S. Army, 1969-72. Mem. Entomol. Soc. Am., Am. Mosquito Control Assn., Soc. for Vector Ecology. Office: West Valley Vector Control Dist 13355 Elliot Ave Chino CA 91710-5255

PHAM, KINH DINH, electrical engineer, educator, administrator; b. Saigon, Republic of Vietnam, Oct. 6, 1956; came to U.S., 1974; s. Nhuong D. and Phuong T. (Tran) P.; m. Ngan-Lien T. Nguyen, May 27, 1985; children: Larissa, Galen. BS with honors, Portland State U., 1979; MSEE, U. Portland, 1982; postgrad., Portland State U., 1988—. Registered profl. engr., Oreg., Calif., Ariz., Fla., Wash. Elec. engr. Irvington-Moore, Tigard, Oreg., 1979-80; elec. engr. Elcon Assocs., Inc., Beaverton, Oreg., 1980-87, sr. elec. engr., assoc. ptnr., 1987—; adj. prof. Portland (Oreg.) Community Coll., 1982—; mem. adv. bd. Mass Transit System Compatibility, 1994. Contbr. articles to profl. jours. Recipient Cert. Appreciation Am. Pub. Transit Assn. and Transit Industry, 1987. Mem. IEEE, Mass Transit Sys. Compatibility Adv. Bd, Eta Kappa Nu. Buddhist. Office: Elcon Assocs Inc 12670 NW Barnes Rd Portland OR 97229-6016

PHANES, MARGARET ASTRID, trainer, visual designer; b. San Francisco, May 11, 1949; d. John Hollister Hilton and Eleanor Elizabeth (Roe) Seymour. BA, Calif. State Coll., Sonoma, 1971; MA, Lone Mountain Coll., 1972; postgrad., Humanistic Psychology Inst., 1973-74, Calif. Inst. Integral Studies, 1980-81. Lic. marriage, family and child counselor. Image editing and graphic software trainer Santa Cruz (Calif.) Adult Edn., 1991-95; trainer U. Calif. Extension, Santa Cruz, 1994-95; counselor Solano C.C., Suisun, Calif., 1973-80; trainer U. Calif., Davis, 1975. Prin. works include Grace, Making Women Artists Visible Galeria Tonantzin. Mem. IEEE, NAFE, Women's Caucus for Art, Union Concerned Scientists, Artists Using Sci. and Tech., U. Calif. Santa Cruz Alumni Assn. Office: 1112 Mission St Apt F Santa Cruz CA 95060-3501

PHEIFER, TERRENCE ALBERT, obstetrician/gynecologist; b. Platte, S.D., June 22, 1945; s. Kars and Anna (Bultsma) P.; m. Beatrice Joann Lieuwer, May 31, 1968; children: Todd, Teressa, Tracy. BA, U. S.D., Vermillian, 1967, BS, 1968; MD, Washington U., St. Louis, 1970. Intern Harborview Med. Ctr., Seattle, 1970-71; resident in ob-gyn. U. Wash., Seattle, 1971-74, fellow in infectious disease, 1974-76; pvt. practice ob-gyn. Kirkland, Wash., 1976—. Fellow Am. Coll. Ob-gyn.; mem. Wash. State Med. Assn., Wash. State Obstet. Assn., Seattle Gynecol. Soc. Office: Evergreen Women's Care 12303 NE 130th Ln Kirkland WA 98034-3041

PHELAN, JEFFREY PATRICK, obstetrician/gynecologist; b. Boston, Apr. 7, 1946; m. Marilyn Marcy, May 3, 1969; children: Kelly Elizabeth, Shane Patrick, Shannon Leigh. MD, U. Miami, 1973; JD, Loyola Law Sch., 1988. Diplomate Am. Bd. Ob-Gyn. Intern, resident Naval Regional Med. Ctr., Portsmouth, Va., 1973-77; obstet. cons. Pregnant Cardiac Clinic U. So. Calif.-L.A. County Med. Ctr., 1981-83, dir. Normal Birth Ctr., 1981-88, dir. External Cephalic Version Clinic, 1982-85, obstet. cons. Post Date Clinic, 1984-86, assoc. dir. Women's ICU, 1984-88, dir. antepartum fetal surveillance, 1984-88; dir. maternal-fetal medicine Queen of the Valley Hosp., West Covina, Calif., 1987-91; co-dir. maternal-fetal medicine Pomona (Calif.) Valley Hosp. Med. Ctr., 1987—; dir. maternal-fetal medicine San Antonio Hosp., Upland, Calif., 1991—; co-dir. maternal-fetal medicine Garfield Med. Ctr., 1995—. Editor: Critical Care Obstetrics, 1987, Cesarean Delivery, 1988, Prevention in Prematurity, 1992; editor jour. Ob-Gyn. and the Law, 1989; perinatal editor Jour Perinatology, 1993; editor in chief OBG Mgmt., 1994. Named Best Doctor in Am., 1994. Fellow Am. Coll. Ob-Gyn. (1st award for sci. presentation 1989), Am. Coll. Legal Medicine; mem. ABA, Calif. Bar Assn., Soc. Perinatal Obstetricians (Soc. award 1989). Office: 1030 S Arroyo Pky # 200 Pasadena CA 91105

PHELPS, BARTON CHASE, architect, educator; b. Bklyn., June 27, 1946; s. Julian Orville and Elizabeth Willis (Faulk) P.; m. Karen Joy Simonson; 1 child, Charlotte Simonson Phelps. BA in Art with honors, Williams Coll., 1968; MArch, Yale U., 1973. Registered architect, Calif. With Colin St. John Wilson & Ptnrs., London, 1972-73, Frank O. Gehry and Assocs., Inc., Santa Monica, Calif., 1973-76; project architect Charles Moore/Urban Innovations Group, L.A., 1976-78; dir. architecture Urban Innovations Group, L.A., 1980-84; prin. Barton Phelps & Assocs., L.A., 1984—; asst. prof. architecture Rice U. Sch. of Architecture, Houston, 1977-79; asst. dean Grad. Sch. Architecture and Urban Planning, UCLA, 1980-83; prof. architecture Sch. Arts and Architecture UCLA; faculty mem. Nat. Endowment Arts, Mayor's Inst. for City Design, 1990, 92. Author, editor: Architecture California, 1988-92. Fellow Gramham Found. for Advanced Studies in Fine Art, 1989, Nat. Endowment for the Arts, 1988. Mem. AIA (Coll. of Fellows, chair com. on design, recipient design awards for Arrovo House, Kranz House, North Range Clark Libr. UCLA, D.W.P. Ctrl. Dist. Hdqrs., No. Hollywood Pump Sta., East Bldg. Seeds U. Elem. Sch., UCLA, Inst. Honor for Collaborative Design, Games XXIII Olympiad L.A. 1985). Democrat. Home: 10256 Lelia Ln Los Angeles CA 90077-3144 Office: Barton Phelps & Assocs 5514 Wilshire Blvd Los Angeles CA 90036-3829

PHELPS, GAIL LANITA, medical/surgical and oncology nurse; b. Guymon, Okla., June 13, 1952; d. Lawrence Mearl and Ulah Mae (Fox) Blackwelder; m. James D. Phelps, Jan. 9, 1976; children: Chandra, Kelly, Codie, Calab, Sean. ADN, Garden City C.C., Kans., 1991. RN, Oreg.; nat. cert. oncology nurse, Nat. Oncological Soc. Nurses aid Tex. County Hosp., Guymon, 1968-70, Edmond (Okla.) Meml. Hosp., 1972-75, St. Catherine Hosp., Garden City, 1980-82, 90-91; staff nurse Rogue Valley Med. Ctr., Medford, Oreg., 1991-95; relief nursing coord. Meml. Hosp. Tex. County, Geymon, Okla., 1995—; mem. hazardous waste com. Rogue Valley Med. Ctr., 1991-92, mem. quality assurance rev. bd., 1991-92, staff mix com., 1993—, action com., 1993—, controlled quality ins. com. emergency rm. units, 1993—; mem. Inter-Dept. Quality Assurance Task Force, 1994—. Team mom Medford Little League Assn., 1992; guard leader Approved Workmen Are Not Ashamed, Medford, 1991-92. Mem. ANA, Nat. Oncology Soc., Oreg. Nurses Assn. Democrat. Baptist. Home: P O Box 884 Hooker OK 73945 Office: Rogue Valley Med Ctr 2825 E Barnett Rd Medford OR 97504-8332

PHELPS, KATHRYN ANNETTE, mental health counseling executive; b. Creswell, Oreg., Aug. 1, 1940; d. Henry Wilbur and Lake Ilene (Wall) M.; children: David Bryan (dec.), Derek Alan, Darla Ailene. BS in edn., Western Oreg. State Coll., 1962; MSW, Columbia State U., 1992, PhD, 1993. Tchr. Germany, Thailand, U.S., 1962-88; acct. exec. ins. industry; weight-loss counselor, alchohol/drug abuse prevention/intervention counselor teens, 1990-93; counselor Eugene, 1989-94; sr. exec. v.p., edn. dir. Light Streams, Inc., Eugene, 1993—; sr. exec. v.p., therapist The Focus Inst., Inc., Eugene, 1994—; mental health counselor in pvt. practice; cons. consumer edn. Author: Easy Does It, books 1 & 2; hosted weekly TV cooking segment, Portland and U.S. Guardian Jobs Daughters, 1980-82; bd. dirs., den mother Cub Scouts, Boy Scouts, Kansas, Oreg., 1974-82; coach girls volleyball, 1974-80; vol. in orphanages, elderly nursing homes, Thailand, Germany, U.S., 1954-95; sunday sch. tchr., 1956-90; sponsored exchange student, 1984-88. Mem. Eastern Star, Nat. Assn. Social Workers, Am. Counseling Assn., Columbia State U. Alumni Assn., Women's Internat. Bowling Conf. Home: 3838 Kendra St Eugene OR 97404 Office: The Focus Inst Inc 400 E 2d St Ste 103 Eugene OR 97401

PHELPS, MICHAEL EVERETT JOSEPH, energy company executive; b. Montreal, Que., Can., June 27, 1947; s. Arthur A. and Hendrina (Von De Roer) P.; m. Joy Elimmon, Aug. 8, 1970; children: Erica, Julia, Lindsay. BA, U. Manitoba, 1967, LLB, 1970; LLM, London Sch. Econs., 1971. Crown atty. Province of Man., Winnipeg, 1971-73; ptnr. Christie, Degraves, Winnipeg, 1973-76; counsel Dept. Justice, Ottawa, Ont., 1976-78; exec. asst. Minister of Justice, Ottawa, 1978-79, Minister of Energy, Mines & Resources, Ottawa, 1980-82; sr. advisor to pres. & chief exec. officer Westcoast Transmission Co. Ltd., Vancouver, B.C., 1982-83; v.p. strategic planning Westcoast Transmission Co. Ltd., Vancouver, 1983-87, sr. v.p., 1987, exec. v.p., chief fin. officer, 1987-88; pres., chief exec. officer Westcoast Energy, Inc. (formerly Westcoast Transmission Co Ltd.), Vancouver, 1988—, also bd. dirs.; bd. dirs. Saratoga Processing Co. Ltd.; chmn. bd. Westcoast Petroleum Co. Ltd., chmn. bd. dirs. Can. Roxy Petroleum Ltd., vice-chmn., bd. dirs. Foothills Pipe Lines (Yukon) Ltd. Mem. Interstate Natural Gas Assn. Am. (bd. dirs.), Can. Petroleum Assn. (bd. dirs.), Bus. coun. British Columbia, The Vancouver, Hollyburn Country, Terminal City (Vancouver), Vancouver Club, Hollyburn Golf & Country Club, Terminal City Ckub. Office: Westcoast Energy Inc, 1333 W Georgia St, Vancouver, BC Canada V6E 3K9

PHELPS, WILLARD, Canadian government official. Min. Edn., Health and Social Svcs., Can., 1993—. Office: Govt Yukon, PO Box 2703, Whitehorse, YK Canada Y1A 2C6

PHIBBS, HARRY ALBERT, interior designer, professional speaker, lecturer; b. Denver, Jan. 9, 1933; s. Harry Andrew and Mary May (Perriam) P.; m. Alice Conners Glynn, Oct. 23, 1957 (div. Jan. 1988); children: Kathleen Ann, Paul Robert, Mary Alice, Michael John, Peter James, Daniel Edward; m. Nevelle Haley Jones, Feb. 1988. B.A., U. Colo., 1954, B.F.A., 1957. Interior designer Howard Lorton, Inc., Denver, 1957-68; interior designer, v.p. Ronald Ansay Inc., Wheatridge, Colo., 1969-71; interior designer, pres. Phibbs Design Assos., Inc., Denver, 1972-78; interior designer, mgr. Howard Lorton, Inc., Colorado Springs, Colo., 1979-93; prin. Phibbs Design, Colorado Springs, 1993—; pres. Interior Designers Housing Devel. Corp., 1969-72. V.p. Arvada (Colo.) Hist. Soc., 1973; bd. dirs. Colo. Opera Festival, also pres., 1986; bd. dirs. Downtown Colorado Springs, Inc., also pres., 1984; chmn. bd. trustees Interior Design Inst. Denver, 1991-94. With U.S. Army, 1954-56. Fellow Am. Soc. Interior Designers (nat. pres. 1977); mem. Am. Arbitration Assn., Theta Xi (pres. Denver Area alumni club 1958-64). Democrat. Roman Catholic. Home: 91 W Boulder St Colorado Springs CO 80903-3371 Office: 10 Boulder Crescent St Colorado Springs CO 80903-3344

PHILBRICK, DOUGLAS ROBERT, principal, librarian, mental health professional; b. St. Louis, Mar. 17, 1942; s. Robert Gilbert and Alice Hazel (LaRoche) P.; m. Lynda J. Harmon; children: Alma Robert, Amber, David, Mark, Holly, Amos, June. B of Pub. Address, Brigham Young U., 1969, MLS, 1972; MA in Secondary Adminstrn., No. State Coll., 1977; EdS, U. S.D., 1991. Cert. EMT, N.Mex.; cert. supt. specialty, edn. specialist U. S.D. Libr. dir. Inst. of Am. Indian Arts, Santa Fe, N.Mex., 1973, D.Q. Univ., Davis, Calif., 1973-74; tchr., libr. Lower Brule (S.D.) High Sch., 1974-75; prin. Crow Creek Sioux Tribe, Fort Thompson, S.D., 1975; prin. Bur. Indian Affairs, Lower Brule, 1975-76, Kinlichee, Ariz., 1977-79; edn. supt. Bur. Indian Affairs, Stewart, Nev., 1979-80, Sells, Ariz., 1980, Fort Thompson, S.D., 1981-85; edn. specialist Bur. Indian Affairs, Phoenix, Ariz., 1985-91; prin. Bur. Indian Affairs, Keam Canyon, Ariz., 1992-94; mental health technician Indian Health Svc., Sacaton, Ariz., 1994-95; farmer/rancher, Chamberlain, S.D., 1956-61; chmn. curriculum com. Inst. Am. Indian Arts, Santa Fe, 1973; fed. intern Washington, 1971. Author adapted Libr. of Congress classification system for Indians, 1973, Bibliography of Indian Newspapers and Periodicals, 1974. Leader 4-H, Crow Creek Indian Reservation, 1956-61; scout master Boy Scouts Am., Chamberlain, 1984. With USAF, 1961-64. Recipient scholarship Libr. Adminstrn. Devel. Program, U. Md., 1972. Republican. Mormon. Home: 1014 E 8th Pl Mesa AZ 85203-5610

PHILIP, THOMAS PETER, mining executive; b. Bellville, Cape, Republic South Africa, Feb. 5, 1933; came to U.S., 1984; s. David Henderson and Nora (VanWyk) P.; m. Adriana van Schalkwyk, Dec. 3, 1954 (div. 1982); children: Wayne, Lorinda, Lynette, Debra. BSMetE, U. Ariz., 1958. Asst. gen. mgr. Tsumeb Corp., Namibia, 1970-74; gen. mgr. O'okiep Copper Co., Nababeep, Republic South Africa, 1975-84; chief exec. officer O'okiep Copper Co., Nababeep, 1981-84, also bd. dirs.; exec. v.p., gen. mgr. Carlin (Nev.) Gold Mining Co., 1984-85; pres. Newmont Gold Co., Carlin, 1985—, also bd. dirs.; sr. v.p. Newmont Mining Corp., N.Y.C., 1986—; bd. dirs. Newmont Autstralia, Ltd., Melbourne. Fellow South Africa Inst. Mining and Metallurgy; mem. Soc. Mining Engring., Denver Club, Namutoni Club (master 1971). Home: 5403 S Fulton Cir Englewood CO 80111-3660 Office: Newmont Mining Corp 1700 Lincoln St Denver CO 80203-4501

PHILIPPI, ERVIN WILLIAM, mortician; b. Lodi, Calif., June 4, 1922; s. William and Rebecca (Steinert) P.; m. Emma Grace Mosely, May 8, 1958 (div. Mar. 1979); m. Helen Jo Hunt, June 3, 1979. Grad., Calif. Coll. Motuary Sci., 1948. Embalmer, mortician, mgr. Salas Bros. Chapel, Modesto, Calif., 1946-92; dep. coroner Stanislaus County, Calif., 1955-75. With U.S. Army, 1942-46.

PHILIPS, PETER MAURY, magazine advertising executive; b. Seattle, Mar. 14, 1962; s. Richard H. and Suzanne (Maury) P. BA, Whitman Coll., 1984. Assoc. pub. Pacific Maritime mag., Seattle, 1985—. Tutor Cen. Area Youth Assn., Seattle, 1986-88; com. mem. Seattle Benefit Gang, 1988—. Fellow Cityclub, Propeller Club U.S.A. Home: 3023 1st Ave #601 Seattle WA 98121 Office: Pacific Maritime Mag 1818 Westlake Ave N Ste 430 Seattle WA 98109-2707

PHILIPSBORN, JOHN TIMOTHY, lawyer, author; b. Paris, Oct. 19, 1949; s. John David and Helen (Worth) P. AB, Bowdoin Coll., 1971; MEd, Antioch Coll., 1975; JD, U. Calif., Davis, 1978. Bar: Calif. 1978, U.S. Dist. Ct. (no. and ea. dists.) Calif. 1978, U.S. Ct. Appeals (9th cir.) 1985, U.S. Supreme Ct. 1985; cert-specialist in criminal law State of Calif., 1985. VISTA vol. Office of Gov. State of Mont., Helena, 1972-73; cons. U.S. Govt., Denver, 1974; lectr. Antioch New Eng. Grad. Sch., Keene, N.H., 1973-75, U. N.H., Durham, 1973-75; ptnr. Philipsborn & Cohn, San Jose, Calif., 1978-80; atty., supr. Defenders Inc., San Diego, 1980-83; assoc. Garry, Dreyfus & McTernan, San Francisco, 1983-87; pvt. practice, San Diego and San Francisco, 1987—; cons. Nicaraguan ct. evaluation projects, 1987—; coord. Internat. Conf. Adversarial System, Lisbon, Portugal, 1990; mem. adj. faculty New Coll. Law, San Francisco, 1991—; legal asst. project refugee camps S.E. Asia, 1992—. Author: California Criminal Law and Procedures, 1994; co-author, cons. CBE, 1994; bd. editors Champion, Forum; contbr. articles to profl. jours. Founder trial program San Francisco Schs., 1986; bd. dirs. Calif. Indian Legal Svcs., 1990—. Fulbright scholar, Portugal, 1989. Mem. Nat. Assn. Criminal Def. Lawyers (assoc., co-chmn. death penalty impact litigation group 1989, co-chmn. govtl. misconduct com. 1990-92, vice chmn. task force on emerging democracies 1990-91), Calif. State Bar (evaluation panel criminal law specialists 1986—, com. on continuing edn. of bar 1991-94, criminal law subcom. state bd. legal specialists 1995—), Calif. Attys. for Criminal Justice (bd. govs. 1989-94, assoc. editor jour. 1987—, chmn. Amicus Curiae com. 1992—, co-chmn. govtl. misconduct com. 1989-92), World Affairs Coun. Office: 1231 Market St San Francisco CA 94103-1411

PHILIPSBORN, RANDALL H., disaster preparedness consultant; b. Chgo., Nov. 14, 1952; s. Herbert F. and Margery (Lederer) P.; m. Mary E. Brooks, July 5, 1986. Student, Boston U., 1971-73; BA, Northwestern U., 1975; MA, U. Colo., 1978. Rsch. asst. U. Colo., Boulder, 1976-78; planner Disaster Preparedness Office, V.I., 1979; hazard mitigation specialist Fed. Emergency Mgmt. Agy., Denver, 1978-87; pres. Mitigation Assistance Corp., Boulder, 1987—, Hazard Mitigation Tech. Assistance Partnership, Inc., Boulder, Colo., 1994—; presenter workshops, symposia; lectr. in field. Author articles on emergency mgmt. to various publs., conf. procs. Recipient Gov.'s Cert. Appreciation, Utah, 1986, Wyo., 1989, 90, Legislature Citation of Honor, Alaska, 1990, Citation award Applied Geography Group, 1984. Mem. Assn. State Floodplain Mgrs. (assoc. del. 1986-89, bd. dirs. 1989, chair mitigation com. 1991-94), Internat. Disaster and Emergency Specialists, Colo. Assn. Stormwater and Floodplain Mgrs., Colo. Emergency Mgmt. Assn., Colo. Soc. Natural Hazard Rsch., Wyo. Emergency Mgmt. Assn. Office: Mitigation Assistance Corp PO Box 19645 Boulder CO 80308-2645

PHILL, DANIEL STOUFFER, artist; b. Tacoma, Oct. 1, 1955; s. Philip George and Martha Marie (Stouffer) P. Student, Wash. State U., 1974-77; BFA, San Francisco Art Inst., 1978; MFA, Stanford U., 1983. Tchg. asst. Stanford (Calif.) U., 1981-83, lectr. undergrad. studies, 1982; photographer, technician IBM Sci. Ctr., Palo Alto, Calif., 1981-84. One man shows Dana Reich Gallery, San Francisco, 984, Wade Gallery, 1989, John Pence Gallery, San Francisco, 1994; group exhbn. San Diego Mus. Art, 1993; permanent collections include Jossey-Bass Inc., San Francisco, Kimberly Clark Inc., Dallas, KMS Corp., Seattle, Koret Found., San Francisco, Nordstrom, San Francisco and Skokie, Ill., Societe Generale Bank, Atlanta, SAP Am. Inc., Foster City, Calif., Sterling Software, Dallas, Tucson Mus. Art, Yuma (Ariz.) Art Ctr. Fellow Stanford U., 1981-83. Office: Daniel Phill Studio 1086 Folsom St San Francisco CA 94103-4022

PHILLIPS, ADRAN ABNER (ABE PHILLIPS), geologist, oil and gas exploration consultant; b. Sugden, Okla., Feb. 6, 1924; s. James M. and Jennie Elizabeth (Norman) P.; m. Carmel Darlene Pesterfield, Aug. 20, 1949 (div.); 1 son, John David. B.S. in Geology, U. Okla., 1949. With Exxon Corp. and affiliates, 1949-79, dist. geologist, Chico, Calif., 1959-64, ops. geologist, Sydney, Australia, 1964-67, exploration coordinator North Slope Alaska, Houston, 1968-70, div. geologist, Denver, 1970-71, exploration mgr. P.T. Inc., Stanvac, Jakarta, Indonesia, 1971-73, exploration mgr. ESSO exploration, Singapore, 1973-76; div. mgr. Exxon U.S.A., Denver, 1976-79; v.p. Coors Energy div., Golden, Colo., 1979-80, pres., 1980-92; oil and gas exploration cons., 1992—. Bd. dirs. Mountain States Legal Found., 1991—. Mem. Am. Assn. Petroleum Geologists, Ind. Petroleum Assn. Mountain States (past pres.), Ind. Petroleum Assn. Am. (dir.), Nat. Coal Council. Home and Office: 2194 S Augusta Dr Evergreen CO 80439-8923

PHILLIPS, ANNA, publisher, editor-in-chief newspaper; b. Oakalla, Tex., Nov. 19, 1936; d. Edward C. and Barbara W. (Roberts) Spinks; 1 child, Kenny E. Phillips. Asst. sales mgr. Am. Legion Newspaper, San Antonio, 1961-68; sales profl. Sta. KLRN-TV Ednl. Broadcasting, San Antonio, 1969-73; sales mgr. Victor Bloom Advt. Agy., L.A., 1973-77, Non-Commd. Officers Assn., Oceanside, Calif., 1977-80; asst. sales mgr. Marshals Assn., San Diego, 1978-81; editor-in-chief, founder World of Entertainment, 1981-90; founder, pub. Associated News of So. Calif., San Bernardino, 1985-93; news editor, publ. films, Hollywood and Las Vegas, Nev., 1980-94. Editorial columnist City Police and Sheriffs of San Bernardino, 1987-93. Mgr. pub. rels. dept. Student Coun., Trinity U., San Antonio, Funds for Nat. Celebrity Jazz Concerts; news and pub. rels. coord. for Native Am. Indians; fundraiser scholarships for American Indian students, 1989-94. Recipient Nat. Pub. award Nat. Fedn. of Fed. Employees, 1967. Office: Associated News PO Box 3104 San Bernardino CA 92413-3104

PHILLIPS, BETTY LOU (ELIZABETH LOUISE PHILLIPS), author, interior designer; b. Cleve.; d. Michael N. and Elizabeth D. (Materna) Suvak; m. John S. Phillips, Jan. 27, 1963 (div. Jan. 1981); children: Bruce, Bryce, Brian; m. John D.C. Roach, Aug. 28, 1982. BS, Syracuse U., 1960; postgrad. in English, Case Western Res. U., 1963-64. Cert. elem. and spl. edn. tchr., N.Y. Tchr. pub. schs. Shaker Heights, Ohio, 1960-66; sportswriter Cleve. Press, 1976-77; spl. features editor Pro Quarterback Mag., N.Y.C., 1976-79; freelance writer specializing in books for young people, 1976—; interior designer residential and comml.; bd. dirs. Cast Specialties Inc., Cleve. Author: Chris Evert: First Lady of Tennis, 1977; Picture Story of Dorothy Hamill (ALA Booklist selection), 1978; American Quarter Horse, 1979; Earl Campbell: Houston Oiler Superstar, 1979; Picture Story of Nancy Lopez, (ALA Notable book), 1980; Go! Fight! Win! The NCA Guide for Cheerleaders (ALA Booklist), 1981; Something for Nothing, 1981; Brush Up on Your Hair (ALA Booklist), 1981; Texas ... The Lone Star State, 1989, Who Needs Friends? We All Do!, 1989; also contbr. articles to young adult and sports mags. Bd. dirs. The Children's Mus., Denver; mem. Friends of Fine Arts Found., Denver Art Mus., Cen. City Opera Guild, Alameda County Cancer League. Mem. Soc. Children's Book Writers, Internat. Interior Design Assn. (profl. mem.), Am. Soc. Interior Designers (profl. mem., cert.),. Delta Delta Delta. Republican. Roman Catholic. Home: 125 Guilford Rd Piedmont CA 94611-3804

PHILLIPS, BILLY SAXTON, artist, designer, painter; b. Louisville, Nebr., June 20, 1915; d. Charles William and Georgia Hazel (de le Zene) Tremblay; m. John Henry Phillips, Sept. 3, 1937; 1 dau., Terry. Grad., Art Ctr. Coll. of Design, 1950. Free-lance artist L.A., 1951—; package designer Wilson Paper-Disneyland, Anaheim, Calif., 1952-56; inventor Vernon (Calif.) Container Corp., 1952-56; instr. Clatsop Community Coll., Astoria, Oreg., 1990-92; painter Reva-Reva Gallery, Papeete, French Polynesia, 1972-92, Royal Gallery, Lahaina, Maui, Hawaii, 1993-94; artist P.M. Prodns., L.A., 1951-90; instr., motivator Maoridom, New Zealand, 1980—; instr. Art Ctr. Coll. Design, 1952-53. Designer, patentee Ukili, 1967, packages, 1960 (Zipper openings on cardboard containers); designer Disneyland's Tinkerbell; group shows include Royal Art Gallery, Met. Gallery, Lahanina, Maui, Hawaii, 1994, Kona, Hawaii, 1995. Developer Cultural Exchange Program First Ams.-Maori, S.W. Am. Indians and New Zealand Maoris, 1986. Mem. Art Ctr. Alumni (charter, life), Trail's End Art Assn., Lady Elk, Inventors and Scientists Am.

PHILLIPS, DANA WAYNE, lawyer; b. Corpus Christi, Tex., Oct. 5, 1951; s. David Wayne and Mildred (Elliott) P.; m. Dene' Elaine Batelaan, July 21, 1973 (div. 1981); m. Susan Jeanne Predmore, Mar. 23, 1985; 1 child Tristan Reid Phillips, step daughter: Lindsey Ann Midgley. Student, So. Meth. U., Dallas, 1969-70; BA, U. Calif., Santa Barbara, 1973; JD, U. San Diego, 1976. Bar: Calif. 1976, U.S. Dist. Ct. (ctrl. dist.) Calif. 1977. Atty. Pell & Phillips, Ventura, Calif., 1976-80, Drucker & Steinschriber, Sherman Oaks, Calif., 1980-82; gen. counsel Pension Vest, Inc., Montrose, Calif., 1982-85; atty. Drucker & Steinschriber, Sherman Oaks, Calif., 1985-86; gen. counsel Sacramento Housing & Redevelopment Agy., Sacramento, 1986—; bd. mem. Nat. Assn. Pvt. Pracement Syndicators, L.A., 1984-85; v.p., bd. dirs. Calif. Housing Authority Risk Mgmt. Agy., Oakland. Mem. ABA, Sacrmento Mother Lode Govt. Atty. Assn. Office: Sacramento Housing & Redevelopment Agy 630 I St Sacramento CA 95814-2404

PHILLIPS, DARRELL, retail executive; b. Hamilton, Ohio, Oct. 7, 1956; s. Bill L. and Lois J. (Marcum) P. Student, Western State Coll., Gunnison, Colo., 1974-77; BSBA, U. No. Colo., Greeley, 1979. Sales rep. Econ. Lab., White Plains, N.Y., 1979, Color Tile, Inc., Denver, 1980-81; store mgr. Color Tile, Inc., Lake Charles, La., 1981-82; v.p. Phillips Stationers, Inc., Denver, 1982-87; pres. Pro-Dispatch Office Supply, Denver, 1988—; pres., CEO BDLS & Assocs., Inc., 1994—. Mem. Nat. Office Products Assn. Republican.

PHILLIPS, DAVID PARKER, legal foundation executive, lawyer; b. Buffalo, Apr. 7, 1934; s. David Harvey and Mary Louise (Parker) P.; m. Elizabeth Ann Edwards, Mar. 30, 1964; children: Elizabeth P., David Page, Sara Ann. BS in Engring. with honors, Princeton U., 1956; MA, U. Wyo., 1958; JD, U. Colo., 1966. Bar: Colo. 1966. Geologist Exxon U.S.A., Inc., Mont., Colo., Tex., 1958-63; atty. Indsl. Resources, Inc., Golden, Colo., 1966-70; exec. dir. Rocky Mountain Mineral Law Found., Denver, 1971—. Bd. dirs. Natural Resources Law Ctr., U. Colo., 1981—; bd. dirs. Denver chpt. Amigos de Ams., 1985-92, pres., 1988-90. Mem. Denver Petroleum Club, Sigma Xi. Office: Rocky Mountain Mineral Law Found 7039 E 18th Ave Denver CO 80220-1826

PHILLIPS, DAVID SPENCER, statistician, educator; b. Marion, Ind., Oct. 10, 1936; s. Harold F. and Catherine Ann (Spenser) P.; m. Sally Gregory, Aug. 16, 1958; children: Michael, Daniel, Beth. AB, Wabash Coll., 1958; MS, Purdue U., 1960, PhD, 1962. Asst. prof. stats. Oreg. Health Scis. U., Portland, 1965-67, assoc. prof., 1967-78, prof., chief biostats. sect., 1978—. Author: Basic Statistics for Health Science Students, 1978; contbr. over 40 articles to profl. jours. NIMH postdoctoral fellow, 1963-65. Mem. APHA, APS, AAAS, Am. Statis. Assn., Psychonomic Soc., Sigma Xi. Home: 3155 SW Grace Ln Portland OR 97225-3354 Office: Oreg Health Scis Univ CB669 3181 SW Sam Jackson Park Rd Portland OR 97201

PHILLIPS, DONNA ROSE, production artist, writer; b. Cheyenne, Wyo., June 16, 1961; d. Leyson Kirk and Leona Anna (Rasmussen) P.; m. Steven Gary Steinsapir, May 17, 1992; 1 child, Andrew Trevor Steinsapir. Student, Mt. San Antonio Coll., Walnut, Calif., 1982-83, Citrus Coll., Azusa, Calif., 1988. Prodn. artist Treasure Chest Advt., Pomona, Calif., 1986-89, Rutland Tool & Supply Co. Inc., Industry, Calif., 1989-92; pvt. practice Baldwin Park, Calif., 1992—. Author, editor: Book of Days, 1989; contbr. articles to mags. Recipient award for art Bank of Am., Covina, Calif., 1979. Mem. Sons of the Desert. Republican. Lutheran. Home: 3700 Baldwin Park Blvd Unit D Baldwin Park CA 91706-4101

PHILLIPS, FRANK SIGMUND, business executive; b. Anchorage, June 17, 1952; s. Charles W. and Kirsten H. (Alsos) P. BA, U. Calif., San Diego, 1973; JD, NYU, 1976; postgrad., U. Mo., 1977. Bar: Calif. 1977. Atty. Nat. Labor Rels. Bd., Washington, 1976-77; ptnr. Phillips and Phillips, San Diego, 1978-83; sr. atty. Namco of Am., Inc., Sunnyvale, Calif., 1983-85; v.p., gen. counsel Hang Ten Internat., San Diego, 1985-89; ptnr. Scenic Visuals Publs., San Diego, 1988—; exec. v.p. Licensing Enterprises, Inc., San Clemente, Calif., 1990-93; sr. cons. J. Bergman and Assocs., Inc., 1993—; instr. U. San Diego, 1979-83; gen. counsel San Diego Booksellers Assn., 1986—; bd. dirs. Green Found. for Earth Scis., La Jolla, Calif., 1986—. Bd. regents U. Calif., 1981-83; mem. chancellors assocs. U. Calif. San Diego, La Jolla, 1982—. Root-Tilden scholar NYU, 1973-76. Mem. Calif. State Bar, San Diego County Bar Assn., U. Calif. San Diego Alumni Assn. (pres. 1981-83). Democrat. Home: PO Box 633090 San Diego CA 92163-3090

PHILLIPS, GAIL, state legislator; b. Juneau, Alaska; m. Walt Phillips; children: Robin, Kim. BA in Bus. Edn., U. Alaska. Mem. Homer (Alaska) City Coun., 1981-84, Kenai Peninsula Borough Assembly, 1986-87; chmn. legis. com. Alaska Mcpl. League; mem. Alaska Ho. of Reps., 1990, 92, 94, house majority leader, 1993-94, speaker, 1995—; high sch. bus. tchr., Fairbanks, Nome, Alaska; airline agt., exec. sec. and sta. mgr. Alaska Airlines, Western Airlines, Wien Air; owner, mgr. Quiet Sporting Goods; ptnr. Lindphil Mining Co.; pub. rels. cons.; legis. aide to Senate pres. Active Homer United Meth. Ch., Rep. Ctrl. Com. Alaska, Kenai Peninsula Coll. Coun.; past bd. dirs. Homer Soc. Natural History; past mem. com. bd. and race coord. Iditarod Trail Dog Sled Race. Mem. Western States Legis. Coun. (exec. com.), Am. Legis. Exch. Coun. (state chmn.), Resource Devel. Coun. Alaska, U. Alaska Coll. Fellows, Homer Emblem Club, Homer, Seldovia, Anchor Point, Soldotna and Kenai C. of C., Peninsula Coun. Chambers, Kachemak Bay Visitors Assn. Home: PO Box 3304 Homer AK 99603-3304 Office: 126 W Pioneer Ave Homer AK 99603-7564 also: Alaska House of Reps State Capitol Juneau AK 99811

PHILLIPS, GENEVA FICKER, editor; b. Staunton, Ill., Aug. 1, 1920; d. Arthur Edwin and Lillian Agnes (Woods) Ficker; m. James Emerson Phillips, Jr., June 6, 1955 (dec. 1979). B.S. in Journalism, U. Ill., 1942; M.A. in English Lit., UCLA, 1953. Copy desk Chgo. Jour. Commerce, 1942-43; editorial asst. patents Radio Research Lab., Harvard U., Cambridge, Mass., 1943-45; asst. editor adminstrv. publs. U. Ill., Urbana, 1946-47; editorial asst. Quar. of Film, Radio and TV, UCLA, 1952-53; mng. editor The Works of John Dryden, Dept. English, UCLA, 1964—. Bd. dirs. Univ. Religious Conf., Los Angeles, 1979—. UCLA teaching fellow, 1950-53, grad. fellow 1954-55. Mem. Assn. Acad. Women UCLA, Dean's Coun., Coll. Letters and Scis. UCLA, Friends of Huntington Library, Friends of UCLA Library, Friends of Ctr. for Medieval and Renaissance Studies, Samuel Johnson Soc. of So. Calif., Assocs. of U. Calif. Press., Conf. Christianity and Lit., Soc. Mayflower Descs. Lutheran. Home: 213 1st Anita Dr Los Angeles CA 90049-3815 Office: UCLA Dept English 2225 Rolfe Hall Los Angeles CA 90024

PHILLIPS, GERTRUDE MARILYNN, fine artist, educator, transformational psychologist; b. Niagara Falls, N.Y., Feb. 22, 1931; d. James Dickens and Gertrude Myrtle (Anderson) Phillips; m. Thomas Conant Davis, June 3, 1953 (div. Nov. 1961); children: Christian Conant Davis, Cary Phillips Davis; m. Gordon Archer Wood (div. 1975); 1 child, Gordon Anderson Wood. AB, BSc, Hood Coll., Frederick, Md., 1953; postgrad., Syracuse U., 1966-68, U. Pitts., 1962; MA, U. Wash., 1974. Cert. tchr., Wash. Fine artist, cons. Orcas Island, Wash., 1984—; edn. cons. in pvt. practice Orcas Island, 1989—; rschr. in child growth and devel., 1968-84, in expansion of IQ and creativity, 1962—. Artist, including ltd. edit. of prints, 1990. Mem. Establishment of Presbyn. Mission, Orcas Island, 1989-90; chair Bellevue (Wash.) Art Commn., 1974-81; founder art fairs B.C. Arts League, Ottawa, Ont., 1964, West Coast Jazz Festivals, 1974-81. Recipient award Nat. Gallery of Art, Ottawa, 1983. Mem. AAUW (v.p. Orcas Island br. 1990-92, program chair 1990-92), N.Y. Acad. Sci., Jung Soc. Office: PO Box 772 Eastsound WA 98245-0772

PHILLIPS, JAMES ROBERT, counselor, educator; b. Wichita, Kans., Apr. 21, 1950; s. Earnest Delmar Phillips; m. Patti Jo Marie Marsh, Nov. 9, 1974; children: Jason Todd, Jill Elizabeth. BA, San Diego State U., 1972; MA, Pepperdine U., 1973; PhD, U. Idaho, 1994. Lic. psychologist, profl. counselor, Idaho; nat. cert. counselor. Asst. dir. psycho-ednl. program for emotionally disturbed children Harbor Area Retarded Children's Found., San Pedro, Calif., 1972-73, dir., 1973-74; continuing edn. instr. Boise (Idaho) State U., 1976-77; psychologist II Idaho State Sch. and Hosp., Nampa, 1975-77; psychologist III, program coord. Region II Mental Health Svcs., Grangeville, Idaho, 1977-80; community rehab. mgr. dept. health and welfare Region II State of Idaho, Lewiston, 1980-81; regional program mgr. dept. health and welfare Region II Mental Health Svcs., State of Idaho, Lewiston, 1981-89, psychologist specialist, 1989-92; adj. faculty Lewis-Clark State Coll., Lewiston, 1980—; pvt. practice Lewiston, 1989—. Mem. Rotary. Office: 504 Main St Ste 460 Lewiston ID 83501-1869

PHILLIPS, JEFFREY RICHARD, magazine writer; b. San Francisco, Mar. 9, 1947; s. Robert Maxim and Dorothy Phillips; m. Rosalind Jill Phillips, Aug.4, 1973; children: Scott, Katherine. AA, Coll. San Mateo, 1967; BA, Calif. State U., San Francisco, 1969; Pub. Program, Stanford U., 1981. Sr. writer Sunset Mag., Menlo Park, Calif., 1969—; Pub. speaker Maui Writers Conf., 1994; writer various mags.; cons. films-pub. TV. Coach Am. Youth Soccer, Palo Alto, 1985-91, Little League, Palo Alto, 1984-87; Calif. del. White House Conf. on Travel and Tourism, 1995. Recipient Maggie award Western Publs. Assn. Calif., 1991. Mem. Soc. Am. Travel Writers (Lowell Thomas award 1985, 89, 92), Soc. Profl. Journalists, Sierra Club, Audubon Soc., Calif. Trout (Disting. Svc. award 1987), Sierra Nev. Alliance. Office: Sunset Mag 80 Willow Rd Menlo Park CA 94025-3661

PHILLIPS, JILL META, novelist, critic, astrologer; b. Detroit, Oct. 22, 1952; d. Leyson Kirk and Leona Anna (Rasmussen) P. Student pub. schs., Calif. Lit. counselor Book Builders, Charter Oak, Calif., 1966-77; pres. Moon Dance Astro Graphics, Covina, Calif., 1994—. Author: (with Leona Phillips) A Directory of American Film Scholars, 1975, The Good Morning Cookbook, 1976, G.B. Shaw: A Review of the Literature, 1976, T.E. Lawrence: Portrait of the Artist as Hero, 1977, The Archaeology of the Collective East, 1977, The Occult, 1977, D.H. Lawrence: A Review of the Literature and Biographies, 1978, Film Appreciation: A College Guide Book, 1979, Annus Mirabilis: Europe in the Dark and Middle Centuries, 1979, (with Leona Rasmussen Phillips) The Dark Frame: Occult Cinema, 1979, Misfit: The Films of Montgomery Clift, 1979, Butterflies in the Mind: A Précis of Dreams and Dreamers, 1980; The Rain Maiden: A Novel of History, 1987, Walford's Oak: A Novel, 1990, The Fate Weaver: A Novel in Two Centuries, 1991, Saturn Falls: A Novel of the Apocalypse, 1993; contbr. book revs. to New Guard mag., 1974-76; contbr. numerous articles to profl. jours. Mem. Young Ams. for Freedom, Am. Conservative Union, Elmer Bernstein's Film Music Collection, Ghost Club London, Count Dracula Soc., Dracula Soc. London, Richard III Soc. Republican. Home: 851 N Garsden Ave Covina CA 91724-2636 Office: Moon Dancer Astro Graphics 1037 N Grand Ave Ste 202 Covina CA 91724-2048

PHILLIPS, JOHN GARDNER, educator, astrophysicist; b. New Haven, Jan. 9, 1917; s. Ray Edmund and Dora (Larson) P.; m. Margaret Ann Butler, June 11, 1944; children: Mary Jane, Cynthia Ann Hart, Gail Elizabeth. B.A., Carleton Coll., 1939; M.A., U. Ariz., 1942; Ph.D., U. Chgo., 1948. Instr. Yerkes Obs., U. Chgo., 1948-50; faculty U. Calif. at Berkeley, 1950—, prof. astrophysics, 1960-87, prof. emeritus, 1987—, chmn. dept. astronomy, 1964-67, 71-75; dir. Leuschner Obs., 1964-67, 71-75; Cons. NASA, Ames Lab. Author: (with S.P. Davis) The Red System of the CN Molecule, 1963, The Swam System of the C2 Molecule, The Spectrum of the HgH Molecule, (with Alter and Cleminshaw) Pictorial Astronomy, 1963, rev., 1969, 75, 82; assoc. editor: Ann. Revs. Astronomy and Astrophysics, 1966-89. Guggenheim fellow, 1956. Mem. AAAS, Am. Astron. Soc., Internat. Astron. Union (pres. commn. 14, 1979-82), Astron. Soc. Pacific (sec.-treas. 1968-88). Home: 1234 Lawrence St El Cerrito CA 94530-2437 Office: Dept Astronomy U Calif Berkeley CA 94720

PHILLIPS, JOHN RICHARD, engineering educator; b. Albany, Calif., Jan. 30, 1934; s. Eric Lester and Adele Catherine (Rengel) P.; m. Joan Elizabeth Soyster, Mar. 23, 1957; children: Elizabeth Huntley, Sarah Rengel, Catherine Hale. BS, U. Calif., Berkeley, 1956; M in Engring., Yale U., 1958, PhD in Engring., 1960. Registered profl. engr., Calif. Chem. engr. Stanford Rsch. Inst., Menlo Park, Calif., 1960; rsch. engr. Chevron Rsch. Co., Richmond, Calif., 1962-66; mem. faculty Harvey Mudd Coll., Claremont, Calif., 1966—, prof. engring., 1974—, James Howard Kindleberger prof. engring., 1991—, dir. engring. clinic, 1977-93, chmn. engring. dept., 1993—; vis. prof. U. Edinburgh, Scotland, 1975, Cambridge (Eng.) U., 1981, ESIEE, France, 1981, Naval Postgrad. Sch., 1984-85, Calif. Poly. U., San Luis Obispo, 1992; vis. scientist So. Calif. Edison Co., 1980; founder Claremont Engring., 1973; cons. in field. Contbr. articles to profl. jours. 1st lt. AUS, 1960-62. Mem. Am. Inst. Chem. Engrs., Sigma Xi, Alpha Delta Phi, Tau Beta Pi. Home: 911 W Maryhurst Dr Claremont CA 91711-3320

PHILLIPS, KATHRYN ANN, health services researcher; b. Austin, Tex., Nov. 22, 1957; d. Beeman Noal and Sarah Ann (Haworth) P.; m. Abram B. Rosenblatt, May 19, 1991. BA in Psychology, U. Tex., 1978; MPA in Policy Analysis, Harvard U., 1986; PhD in Health Svcs. Rsch., U. Calif., Berkeley, 1991. Rsch. agt., counselor Med. Rsch. Assn., San Antonio, 1979-80; pers. specialist Kelly AFB, San Antonio, 1980-83; asst. to pers. dir., analyst Office of Naval Rsch., Arlington, Va., 1983-86; strategic planner FAA, Washington, 1987; instr. U. Calif., Berkeley, 1987-90, rsch. asst., 1987-90; postdoctoral fellow U. Calif., San Francisco, 1991-93, asst. prof., 1993—. Reviewer Jour. of AMA, 1989—, Agy. for Health Care Policy and Rsch., 1993; contbr. articles to profl. jours. Grantee Am. Cancer Soc., 1989-90, Agy. for Health Care Policy and Rsch., 1990-91, NIAID, 1993—, CDC, 1994—. Mem. APHA, Am. Econs. Assn., Assn. Health Svcs. Rsch., Assn. Pub. Policy Analysis and Mgmt., Soc. Med. Decision Making, Soc. Advancement Socio-Econs. Office: U Calif 74 New Montgomery St Ste 600 San Francisco CA 94105-3444

PHILLIPS, KAY RANDELLE, association executive; b. St. Louis, Nov. 13, 1947; d. Clyde Randol and Esther (Moore) P.; m. Murvel D. Pretorius, Aug. 17, 1968; 1 dau., Jennifer Marie; m. 2d, A. Fred Timmerman, Apr. 1, 1980. Student Knox Coll., 1966-68; B.A. in Sociology, U. Ill., 1971; M.A. in Pub. Adminstrn., Sangamon State U., 1978. Juvenile probation officer, program coordinator DRI-Roads Program, Peoria County (Ill.), 1971-76; sales rep. Xerox Corp., Peoria, 1976; personnel coordinator, staff devel. and tng. mgr. Methodist Med. Ctr., Peoria, 1977; adminstrv. asst. Lutheran Med. Ctr., Wheat Ridge, Colo., 1978; assoc. dir. planning Swedish Med. Ctr., Englewood, Colo., 1979; v.p. planning, mktg. and pub. affairs Colo. Hosp. Assn., Denver, 1980—; cons. in field. Bd. dirs. Parent Tchr. League, University Hills Luth. Sch., 1982-83; fund raiser United Way; Mem. Am. Coll. Hosp. Adminstrs., Colo. Code of Cooperation (sec.), Pub. Relations Soc. Am., Am. Soc. Hosp. Pub. Relations, Colo. Soc. Hosp. Pub. Relations, Soc. for Hosp. Planning. Republican. Presbyterian. Office: Spaldin Rehab Hosp 4500 E Iliff Ave Denver CO 80222-6021

PHILLIPS, KEITH WENDALL, minister; b. Portland, Oreg., Oct. 21, 1946; s. Frank Clark and Velma Georgina (Black) P.; m. Mary Katherine Garland, July 16, 1973; children: Joshua, Paul, David. BA, UCLA, 1968; MDiv, Fuller Theology Sem., 1971, D. of Ministries, 1972; LHD (hon.), John Brown U., 1990. Dir. Youth For Christ Clubs, L.A., 1965-71; pres. World Impact, L.A., 1971—; mem. urban ministries resources svcs. editorial adv. bd. Zondervan Pub. House; commencement speaker Tabor Coll., 1969, 91, John Brown U., 1990. Author: Everybody's Afraid in the Ghetto, 1973, They Dare to Love the Ghetto, 1975, The Making of a Disciple, 1981, No Quick Fix, 1985. Chmn. L.A. Mayor's Prayer Breakfast Com., 1985—. Named Disting. Staley lectr., 1969. Mem. Evangelistic Com. of Newark (pres. 1976—), World Impact of Can. (pres. 1978—), The Oaks (pres. 1985—), Faith Works (pres. 1987—). Baptist. Office: World Impact 2001 S Vermont Ave Los Angeles CA 90007-1256

PHILLIPS, OWEN RICHARD, economics educator, antitrust consultant; b. Gt. Falls, Mont., Aug. 23, 1953; s. Owen Albert Phillips and Dorothy June (Austin) West; m. Lori Jo Yerger, Aug. 24, 1974; children: Jillian Kate, Jonathan Lloyd. BA in Econs., Stanford U., 1974, PhD, 1980. Asst. prof. econs. Tex. A&M U., College Station, 1979-85; asst. prof. econs. U. Wyo., Laramie, 1985-88, assoc. prof., 1988-95; prof., 1995—; chmn. dept. econs. and fin. U. Wyo., Laramie, 1993—; econ. cons. antitrust div. U.S. Dept. Justice, Washington, 1988-91. Author: Economic Analysis, 1992; also articles. Rsch. grantee NSF, 1984, 89. Office: U Wyo Dept Econs Laramie WY 82071-3985

PHILLIPS, RICHARD RANDOLPH, physicist; b. N.Y.C., Aug. 7, 1960; s. Randolph Godfrey and Lily Renee (Wilheim) P.; m. Allison Annette Low, June 12, 1993. BS in Applied Physics, Calif. Inst. Tech., 1984; postgrad., U. So. Calif., 1985-86. Mem. tech. staff TRW, Redondo Beach, Calif., 1982-85; project mgr. Hughes Aircraft Co., El Segundo, Calif., 1985—. Patentee bidirectional superconducting counter. Mem. L.A. World Affairs Coun., 1986-88. USAF ROTC scholar, 1978. Mem. IEEE. Office: Hughes Aircraft Co PO Box 902 El Segundo CA 90245-0902

PHILLIPS, ROGER, steel company executive; b. Ottawa, Ont., Can., Dec. 17, 1939; s. Norman William Frederick and Elizabeth (Marshall) P.; m. Katherine Ann Wilson, June 9, 1962; 1 child, Andrée Claire. B.Sc., McGill U., Montreal, 1960. Vice pres. mill products Alcan Can. Products Ltd., Toronto, Ont., Can., 1969-70, exec. v.p., 1971-75; pres. Alcan Smelters and Chems. Ltd., Montreal, Que., Can., 1976-79; v.p. tech. Alcan Aluminium Ltd., Montreal, Que., Can., 1980-81; pres. Alcan Internat. Ltd., Montreal, Que., Can., 1980-81; pres., chief exec. officer IPSCO Inc., Regina, Sask., Can., 1982—; sr. mem. Conf. Bd. Inc., N.Y., 1987—; bd. dirs. Toronto Dominion Bank. Dir. Coun. for Can. Unity, Montreal, 1987—; bd. dirs. Conf. Bd. of Can., 1984-87, Inst. for Polit. Involvement, Toronto, 1982-88. Mem. Can. Assn. Physicists, Bus. Coun. on Nat. Issues, Am. Iron and Steel Inst. (bd. dirs. 1984—), Saskatchewan C. of C. (bd. dirs. 1984—), Que. C. of C. (pres. 1981), Inst. for Saskatchewan Enterprise (hon. chmn.), Pub. Policy Forum (bd. dirs.), Assiniboia Club (Regina), St. Denis Club, Univ. Club (Montreal). Home: 3220 Albert St, Regina, SK Canada S4S 3N9 Office: IPSCO Inc, Armour Rd, Regina, SK Canada S4P 3C7

PHILLIPS, RONALD EDWARD, artist, sales executive; b. Clovis, N.Mex., Apr. 10, 1937; s. Rodney Vernon and Ethel Edna (Huff) P.; m. May Frances Willingham, Aug. 27, 1957; children: Rhonda Louise, Russell Kent, Teresa Gail; m. Janet Irene Johnsonbaugh Smith, July 4, 1938; stepchildren: Steven, Gregg, Laura. Student, Ea. N.Mex. U., 1955-56, U. N.Mex., 1957, Famous Artist Schs., 1963-64, North Light Art Sch., 1989-90. Group merchandiser women's fashions J.C. Penney Inc., Albuquerque, 1957-64; chem. salesman Take Over Products, Clovis, N.Mex., 1964-65; with International Auto Leasing, Albuquerque, 1965; salesman Pennsalt Chems., N.Mex. div., Albuquerque, 1965-67; N.Mex. sales rep. W.W. Grainger Inc., Chgo., 1967-72; founder Pueblo Arts, Inc., Albuquerque, 1972—; mgr. Dairy Queen, Santa Rosa and Lovington, N.Mex., 1982-85; owner, mgr. Western Pit n Grill & Food Gallery, Lovington, 1985-88; owner Pueblo Arts Inc./Trailwest Gallery, Albuquerque, 1988—; tchr. quick draw, continuous line drawing, 1990; artist, guide Pueblo Arts Inc. Trailwest Paintouts, Guide for Artists, 1990-92; ind. sales cons. SWEPCO Bldg. Projects, 1993—. Artist, author sketchbooks Traveling Man's Old Town Sketchbook, 1990, The Shooting of Wyatt Earp, 1994, also others; movie extra Whitesands, 1991, Next Fire on Earth, 1992, Wyatt Earp, 1993, Desperate Trails, 1993, Buffalo Girls, 1995, East Meets West. Pres. Albuquerque Wildlife and Conservation, 1963-64; active Albuquerque Conf. & Vis. Bur., 1988—, Albuquerque Arts Alliance, 1994-95, Tourism Assoc. of N.Mex., Albuquerque Film Commn. With N.Mex. Air Nat. Guard, 1955-61. Mem. N.Mex. Art League (hon. life, pres. 1964-65), Indian Arts and Crafts Assn. (mem. ethics com. 1973-74), Albuquerque Arts Alliance, Guild of Albuquerque Artist Models (advisor, bd. dirs. 1994-95). Republican. Office: Pueblo Arts Inc 5555 Zuni Rd SE # 154 Albuquerque NM 87108-2935

PHILLIPS, RONALD FRANK, legal educator, university vice chancellor; b. Houston, Nov. 25, 1934; s. Franklin Jackson and Maudie Ethel (Merrill) P.; m. Jamie Jo Bottoms, Apr. 5, 1957; children: Barbara Celeste Phillips Oliveira, Joel Jackson, Phil Edward. B.S., Abilene Christian U., 1955; J.D., U. Tex., 1965. Bar: Tex. 1965, Calif. 1972. Bldg. contractor Phillips Homes, Abilene, Tex., 1955-56; br. mgr. Phillips Weatherstripping Co., Midland and Austin, Tex., 1957-65; corp. staff atty. McWood Corp., Abilene, 1965-67; sole practice law Abilene, 1967-70; mem. adj. faculty Abilene Christian U., 1967-70; prof. law Pepperdine U. Sch. Law, Malibu, Calif., 1970—; dean Pepperdine U. Sch. Law, 1970—, vice chancellor, 1995—; bd. dirs. PNB Fin. Group. Deacon North A and Tenn. Ch. of Christ, Midland, 1959-62; deacon Highland Ch. of Christ, Abilene, 1965-70; elder Malibu Ch. of Christ, 1978-95; mgr., coach Little League Baseball, Abilene, Huntington Beach and Malibu, 1966-78, 90—; coach Youth Soccer, Huntington Beach, Westlake Village and Malibu, 1972-80, 85-86, 91. Recipient Alumni citation Abilene Christian U., 1974. Fellow Am. Bar Found.; mem. ABA, State Bar Tex., State Bar Calif. (com. on law sch. edn. 1970—), Christian Legal Soc., L.A. Bar Assn., Assn. Am. Law Schs. (chmn. sect. on adminstrn. law schs. 1982, com. on cts. 1985-87), Am. Law Inst., Nat. Conf. Commrs. on Uniform State Laws. Republican. Office: Pepperdine U Sch Law 24255 Pacific Coast Hwy Malibu CA 90263-0001

PHILLIPS, RONDALL VAN, city manager; b. Beech Grove, Ind., June 24, 1945; s. Gene Edwin and Inez Pearl (Perry) P.; m. Karen Louise Nichols, Aug. 18, 1966; children: Kristen, Jarrod, Allison, Scott, Monica. BS, So. Nazarene U., 1967; M of Regional and City Planning, U. Okla., 1970. Fed. aid coord. City of Aurora, Colo., 1970-71; planning dir., exec. dir. San Luis Valley Coun. of Govts., Alamosa, Colo., 1971-79; v.p., gen. mgr. Wespro, Inc., Oklahoma City, 1979-82; mgr., govt. rels. Wilson Foods Corp., Oklahoma City, 1982-84, dir., foodservice mktg., bus. devel., 1982-84; town mgr. Town of Vail, Colo., 1984-93; pres. Phillips Cons. Group, Ft. Collins, Colo., 1993—; dir. transp. svcs. City of Ft. Collins, 1994—; bd. dirs. Colo. Mcpl. League, Denver, Colo., former sec.-treas., Nuclear Materials Transp. Com., Denver; planning dir. City of Ft. Collins, 1994. Past sec.-tres. Colo. Assn. Ski Towns; active World Alpine Ski Championships Orgn. Com., Vail, 1985-89, Colo. Tourism Bd. Adv. Coun., Denver, 1989-93, Vail Br. Latter-Day Sts. Ch. (pres. 1985-93). Named one of Outstanding Young Men of Am., 1976. Mem. Internat. City Mgmt. Assn., Okla. City Internat. Trade Assn. (pres. 1980-83). Republican.

PHILLIPS, SCOTT DAVID, toxicologist; b. Colville, Wash., Nov. 23, 1955; s. Kenneth Wade Phillips; m. Cyrel Joann Wiener, July 20, 1986; children: David, Daniel. BS, Gonzaga U., 1978; MD, Am. U. of Caribbean, 1984. Resident in internal medicine Framingham (Mass.) Union Hosp., 1984-87, chief resident, internal medicine, 1987-88; attending physician Landmark Med. Ctr., Woonsocket, R.I., 1988-90; fellow Rocky Mt. Poison Ctr., Denver, 1990-92; ptnr. Toxicology Assocs., Denver, 1993—; dir. environ. toxicology U. Colo. Health Sci. Ctr., Denver, 1993—; mem. site specific adv. bd. Rocky Mt. Arsenal, Denver, 1994—. Contbr. book chpts., scientific papers to profl. jours. Fellow ACP; mem. Am. Acad. Clin. Toxicology, Internat. Soc. Toxinology, Undusea and Hyperbolic Med. Soc. Office: Toxicology Assocs 8547 E Arapaho Rd #J268 Greenwood Village CO 80112

PHILLIPS, TED RAY, advertising agency executive; b. American Falls, Idaho, Oct. 27, 1948; s. Virn E. and Jessie N. (Aldous) P.; m. Dianne Jacqulynne Walker, May 28, 1971; children: Scott, Russell, Stephen, Michael. BA, Brigham Young U., 1972, MA, 1975. Account exec. David W. Evans, Inc., Salt Lake City, 1972-75; dir. advt. Div. Continuing Edn., U. Utah, Salt Lake City, 1975-78; sr. v.p. Evans/Lowe & Stevens, Inc., Atlanta, 1978, exec. v.p., 1979; pres., chief exec. officer David W. Evans/Atlanta, Inc., 1979-80; dir. advt. O.C. Tanner Co., Salt Lake City, 1980-82; pres. Thomas/Phillips/Clawson Advt., Inc., Salt Lake City, 1982-86; pres. Hurst & Phillips, Salt Lake City, 1986-94; pres., CEO Phillips Radley Advt., Inc., Salt Lake City, 1994—; advt. instr. div. continuing edn. Brigham Young U., 1983-85. Dir. publicity, promotion Western States Republican Con., 1976. Recipient Silver Beaver award Boy Scouts Am., 1994, Spurgeon award, 1995. Mem. Am. Advt. Fedn. (8 Best-in-West awards, 2 nat. Addy awards, Clio finalist 1984, Telly award 1991, 92), Utah Advt. Fedn. (bd. dirs. 1976-78, 80-87, pres. 1984-85). Mormon. Home: 1792 Cornwall Ct Sandy UT 84092-5436 Office: Phillips Radley Advt Inc 428 E 6400 S Salt Lake City UT 84107-7500

PHILLIPS, WADE, former professional football team coach; b. Orange, Tex., June 21, 1947; s. Bum Phillips; m. Laurie Phillips; children: Tracey, Wesley. Student, U. Houston. Asst. football coach U. Houston, 1969; football coach Orange (Tex.) High Sch., 1970-72, Okla. State U., 1973-74, U. Kans., 1975; linebacker coach Houston Oilers, 1976, defensive line coach, 1977-80; defensive coord. New Orleans Saints, 1981-85, Phila. Eagles, 1986-88; defensive coord. Denver Broncos, 1989-93, head coach, 1993-94. Office: Denver Broncos 13655 Broncos Pky Englewood CO 80112-4150*

PHILLIPS, WANDA CHARITY, secondary education educator, writer; b. Gettysburg, Pa., Apr. 1, 1947; d. Roy Homer and Frances Marie (White) Kuykendall; m. James E. Phillips; children: Jenny, Peter, Micah. BS in Secondary Edn., Shippensburg U., 1968; elem. edn. cert., Grand Canyon Coll., 1973; MA in Adminstrn., No. Ariz. U., 1993. Tchr. Littlestown (Pa.) H.S., 1969, Phoenix (Ariz.) Indian Sch., 1971-72, Peoria (Ariz.) Sch. Dist., 1973—; author ISHA Enterprises, Inc., Scottsdale, Ariz., 1985—; ednl. seminar presenter ISHA Enterprises, Scottsdale, 1986—. Assn. Christian Schs. Internat., Calif., 1988—. Author: Easy Grammar, 1986, Daily Grams: Guided Review Aiding Mastery Skills, 1986, Daily Grams: Guided Review Aiding Mastery Skills for Grades 4-5, 1987, Grades 3-4, 1988, Grades 5-6, 1993, Easy Writing, 1991, Daily Grams: Guided Teaching and Review for Grades 2 and 3, 1992, Easy Grammar, Level 1, 1994 (children's book) My Mother Doesn't Like to Cook, 1993. Active Concerned Women of Am., 1993—. Mem. Nat. Trust for Hist. Preservation, Paradise Valley Women's Club, Phi Delta Kappa. Office: PO Box 12520 Scottsdale AZ 85267

PHILLIPS, WILLIAM GRANT, health physicist, nuclear emergency consultant; b. Boulder City, Nev., July 7, 1949; s. William Lewis and Shirley Jean (Bakerink) P.; m. Janice Kaye Lanuti, Dec. 24, 1987. BS in Physics, U. Nev., Las Vegas, 1971, MS in Nuclear Physics, 1973; MS in Radiol. Scis., U. Wash., 1990. Cert. radiation health physcist Am. Bd. Health Physics; diplomate Health Physics Soc. Physicist USPHS, Las Vegas, 1976-76; physicist/pilot U.S. EPA, Las Vegas, 1976-81; corp. pilot West Coast Holdings Inc., Las Vegas, 1981-82; physicist U.S. EPA, Las Vegas, 1982-88, health physicist, 1988-93; pvt. cons. Profl. Analysts Inc./U.S. Dept. Energy,

Las Vegas, 1993—; cons., bd. dirs. Sci. and Aviation Cons. Inc., Las Vegas, 1981—; cons. JANAL Corp./Lockheed, Las Vegas, 1989—; corp. officer Brentwood Fin. Group Inc., Las Vegas, 1992-94, BID Investment and Devel. Inc., Las Vegas, 1992-94; internat. lectr. nuc. physics Nev. Tech. Assocs., 1993—. Author: (poem) A Tourist of the Earth, 1978; contbr. articles to physics publs. and other mags. Mem. U.S. Ultralight Assn., Soaring Soc. Am., Am. Nuclear Soc. Home and Office: 4755 N Grand Canyon Dr Las Vegas NV 89129

PHILLIPS, WILLIAM REVELL, retired geology educator; b. Salt Lake City, Jan. 9, 1929; s. William L. and Della (Weight) P.; m. LaRue Vail, July 21, 1950; children: Lee Revell, Lyle Vail, Lane William, Kathryn Ann. BS, U. Utah, 1950, MS, 1951, PhD, 1954. Petrographer Kennecott Copper Corp., Salt Lake City, 1954-56; asst. prof. La. Poly. Inst., Ruston, 1956-57; prof. geology Brigham Young U., Provo, 1957, chmn. dept., 1972-75; asst. dir. archaeol. expdn. Brigham Young U., Fayum, Egypt, 1981-92; pres. faculty acad. Brigham Young U., 1988-89, prof., 1991—; sr. seasonal ranger U.S. Park Svc., Mammoth, Wyo., 1956-66; cons. geologist U.S. Forest Svc., Provo, 1969-71; Fulbright prof. U. Sind, Hyderabad, Pakistan, 1963-64, Mid. East Tech. U., Ankara, Turkey, 1966-67; vis. prof. Waterloo U., Ont. Can., 1971-72; vis. rsch. prof. Haceteppe U., Ankara, Turkey, 1975-76. Author: Mineral Optics, 1971, Optical Mineralogy, 1981; also articles. Dir. hosting Ramses II Exhbn., Provo, 1985-86. Recipient Karl G. Maeser teaching award Brigham Young U., 1986. Fellow Geol. Soc. Am.; mem. Am. Mineral. Soc., Utah Geol. Soc. (asst. editor), Sigma Xi (pres. Brigham Young U. 1978-79). Mem. LDS Ch. Home: 1839 N 1500 E Provo UT 84604-5749 Office: Brigham Young U Dept Geology Provo UT 84602-4646

PHILLIPS-GARCIA, GARY LEE, equal employment specialist; b. Moline, Ill., Aug. 6, 1948; s. Ivan L. Phillips and Florence Garcia; m. Susan M. McKellar, Dec. 18, 1971 (div. Feb. 1987); children: Christopher, Jennifer; m. Bernadette F. Johnson, May 25, 1987. BA, Wichita State U., 1974; MPA, Ariz. State U., 1991. Dir. office veterans affairs Wichita (Kans.) State U., 1974-76; asst. pers. dir. Sedgwick County, Wichita, 1976-78; mgr. corp. compensation Gates Lear Jet, Wichita, 1979; from asst. pers. dir. to pers. dir. City of Peoria, Ill., 1980-84; mgr. project Honeywell, Inc., Phoenix, 1984-85; equal employment opportunity specialist City of Phoenix, 1985—; cons. in field. Sgt. USAF, 1966-70. Mem. Am. Soc. Pub. Adminstrn., Am. Compensation Assn. (cert.), Nat. Assn. Human Rights Workers, Phoenix Pers. Mgmt. Assn. (bd. dirs. 1988, conf. chair 1989), Internat. Pers. Mgmt. Assn. (human rights com. 1989-91), Soc. Human Resource Mgmt. Mem. Assembly of God Ch. Office: City of Phoenix 251 W Washington St Phoenix AZ 85003-2201

PHILON, JAMES LEON, retired hotel executive; b. La Porte, Ind., June 10, 1928; s. Leon John and Leontine (Pol) P.; m. Margareet Metoyer, July 1, 1960; children: Christi, Anthony, Bryan. PhB, U. Chgo., 1948. Various operating positions Stevens/Conrad Hilton Hotel unit Hilton Hotels Corp., Chgo., 1951-60; asst. to v.p. Hilton Hotels Corp., Beverly Hills, Calif., 1960-65, asst. v.p., 1965-72, v.p. real estate and devel., 1972-80, sr. v.p. real estate and devel. and real estate and constrn., 1980-91, sr. v.p. real estate, 1991-94; ret., 1994. Mem. Urban Land Inst. (coun. 1980-94), Internat. Assn. Assessing Officers. Republican. Office: Hilton Hotels Corp 9336 Civic Center Dr Beverly Hills CA 90210-3604

PHILPOTT, LARRY LA FAYETTE, horn player; b. Alma, Ark., Apr. 5, 1937; s. Lester and Rena (Owens) P.; m. Elise Robichaud, Nov. 24, 1962 (div. June 1975); children: Daniel, Stacy; m. Anne Sokol, Feb. 14, 1984. B.S., Ga. So. Coll., 1962; Mus.M., Butler U., 1972. Instr. in horn Butler U., De Pauw U.; dir. music Cedarcrest Sch., Marysville, Wash., 1991—. Mem., N.C. Symphony, 1960, Savannah (Ga.) Symphony, L'Orchestre Symphonique de Quebec, Que., Can., 1962-64, prin. horn player, Indpls. Symphony Orch., 1964-89, Flagstaff Summer Festival, 1968—; artist in-residence Ind.-Purdue Indpls.; appeared with, Am. Shakespeare Theatre, summer 1965, Charlottetown Festival, summers 1967-68, Flagstaff Summer Festival, 1968-85, Marrowstone Music Festival, 1985—. Served with USN, 1956-60. Mem. Music Educators Nat. Conf., Am. Fedn. Musicians, Internat. Conf. Symphony and Opera Musicians, Internat. Horn Soc., Coll. Music Soc., Phi Mu Alpha Sinfonia. Home: 14925 63rd Ave SE Snohomish WA 98290-5277 Office: Cedarcrest Sch 6400 88th St NE Marysville WA 98270-2800

PHILPOTT, LINDSEY, civil engineer, researcher, educator; b. Bridestowe, Devonshire, Eng., Aug. 2, 1948; came to U.S., 1983; s. George Anthony and Joyce Thirza (Teeling) P.; m. Christine May Pembury, Aug. 20, 1974 (div.); children: David, Elizabeth; m. Kathleen Linda Matson, Feb. 17, 1982 (div.); children: Nicholas, Benjamin; m. Kim Elaine Moore, Nov. 24, 1991. Higher Nat. Cert. in Civil Engring., Bristol (Eng.) Poly., 1973; BSCE, U. Ariz., 1986, MSCE, 1987. Registered profl. engr., Calif. Area structural engr. Dept. Environment (Property Svcs. Agy.), Bristol, 1971-73; civil engr. Webco Civil Engring., Exeter, Eng., 1973-75; tech. mgr. Devon & Cornwall Housing Assn., Plymouth, Eng., 1975-79; prin., architect S.W. Design, Plymouth, 1979-81; archtl. engr. United Bldg. Factories, Bahrain, 1981-83; jr. engr. Cheyne Owen, Tucson, 1983-87; civil engr. Engring. Sci. Inc., Pasadena, Calif., 1987-89; project engr. Black & Veatch, Santa Ana, Calif., 1989-90; sr. engr. Brown & Caldwell, Irvine, Calif., 1990-91; environ. engr. Met. Water Dist. So. Calif., San Dimas, 1991—; adj. prof. hydraulics and instrumentation, San Antonio Coll., Walnut, Calif., 1995—. Foster parent Foster Parents Plan, Tucson, 1985-87; vol. reader tech. books Recording for the Blind, Hollywood, Calif., 1988-89, South Bay, Calif., 1990-91, Pomona, Calif., 1991—; vol. sailor/tchr. L.A. Maritime Inst. Topsail Youth Program, 1994—; vice commodore, South Bay Yacht Racing Club, Marina del Rey, Calif., 1995. Mem. ASCE, Am. Water Works Assn., Am. Water Resources Assn. (water quality com. 1990—), Internat. Ozone Assn., Water Pollution Control Fedn., Mensa, Engrs. Soc. (pres. 1985-96), South Bay Yacht Racing Club (Marina del Rey, Calif., vice commodore 1995). Office: Met Water Dist Environ Compliance Divsn PO Box 699 San Dimas CA 91773

PHIPPS, CLAUDE RAYMOND, research scientist; b. Ponca City, Okla., Mar. 15, 1940; s. Claude Raymond Louis and Deva Pauline (DeWitt) P.; m. Lynn Malarney, Dec. 1, 1962 (div. Feb. 1989); 1 child, David Andrew; life ptnr. Shanti E. Bannwart. BS, MIT, 1961, MS, 1963; PhD, Stanford U., 1972. Rsch. staff Lawrence Livermore (Calif.) Nat. Lab., 1972-74; rsch. staff Los Alamos (N.Mex.) Nat. Lab., 1974-95, project leader engine support sys. tech. program, 1993; assoc. dir. Alliance for Photonic Tech., Albuquerque, 1992-95; CEO Photonic Assocs., Santa Fe, 1995—; co-instr. (with Shanti E. Bannwart) "Pairs" Relationship Tng., Santa Fe, N.Mex., 1990—; dir. Santa Fe Investment Conf., 1987; mem. program com. MIT Workshop on High Temperature Superconductors, Cambridge, 1988; mem. Instl. R & D Com., Los Alamos Nat. Lab., 1990-92, project leader laser effects, 1982-87, mem. internat. rsch. tour, Australia, Japan, Scotland, 1988-89; invited discussion leader Gordon Conf. on Laser Particle Interactions, N.H., 1992. Co-author: Laser Ionization Mass Analysis, 1993; author internat. lecture series on laser surface interactions, Berlin, Antwerp, Marseilles, Xiamen, Cape Town, Durban, 1987—; contbr. articles to profl. jours. Lt. USN, 1963-65. Grad. fellow W. Alton Jones Found., N.Y.C., 1962-63. Home and Office: Photonic Assocs 1621 Calle Torreon Santa Fe NM 87501

PI, EDMOND HSIN-TUNG, psychiatry educator; b. China, June 1, 1948. MD, Cath. U. Coll. Medicine, 1972. Cert. Am. Bd. Psychiatry and Neurology. Chief resident U. Ky. Med. Ctr., Lexington, 1977-78; instr. psychiatry U. So. Calif. Sch. Medicine, L.A., 1978-80, asst. prof., 1980-83; assoc. prof. Med. Coll. Pa., Phila., 1983-85; assoc. prof. U. So. Calif. Sch. Medicine, 1985-88, prof. clin. psychiatry, 1988—; asst. dir. psychopharmacology U. So. Calif. Sch. Medicine, 1978-80; asst. dir. adult psychiat. clinic L.A. County & U. So. Calif. Med. Ctr., 1980-83; dir. adult psychiat. clinic Med. Coll. Pa., Phila., 1983-85; dir. Adult Psychiat. Inpatient Svcs., L.A. County & U. So. Calif. Med. Ctr., 1985-91; dir. transcultural psychaitry U. So. Calif. Sch. Medicine, 1991—. Author: Reactions to Psychotropic Medications, 1987, (book chpts.) Clinical Psychopharmacology, 1985—; contbr. articles to profl. jours. Bd. dirs. Chinese Bus. Assn., L.A., 1990-92, Com. of 100, N.Y.C., 1993—, Gov.'s Com. Employment of Disabled Persons, Sacramento, 1993—, mem. exec. com. Vis. scholar China U.S. Nat. Acad. Scis., Washington, 1987-88; Treval fellow Am. Coll. Neuropsychopharmacology, 1982. Fellow Am. Psychiat. Assn., Am. Soc. Social Psychiatry, Pacific Rim Coll. Psychiatry (treas. 1991—); mem. Am. Coll. Psychiatrists, Soc. Study Psychiatry and Culture, Pacific Rim Assn. Clin. Pharmogenetics, Assn. Chinese Am. Psychiatrists (pres. 1995—). Office: U So Calif Sch Medicine Dept Psychiatry 1934 Hosp Pl Los Angeles CA 90033

PI, WEN-YI SHIH, aircraft company engineer, researcher; b. Peiping, People's Republic of China, Feb. 28, 1935; came to U.S., 1959; d. Chih-Chuan and Hsiu-Yun (Yang) Shih; m. William Shu-Jong Pi, July 2, 1961; 1 child, Wilfred. BS, Nat. Taiwan U., Taipei, Republic of China, 1956; MS, Stanford U., 1961, PhD, 1963. Research assoc. Stanford (Calif.) U., 1963-64; engring. specialist Northrop-Grumman, Hawthorne, Calif., 1965-83; sr. tech. specialist Northrop Corp., Hawthorne, Calif., 1983—. Contbr. articles to profl. jours. Recipient Silver Achievement award Los Angeles YWCA, 1983; Amelia Earhart Scholar Zonta Internat., 1961-62. Fellow: AIAA (assoc.); mem. Sigma Xi. Office: Northrop Grumman Corp Mil Aircraft Divsn One Northrop Ave 3852/63 Hawthorne CA 90250-3277

PIANETTI, CATHERINE NATALIE, occupational therapist; b. Rock Spring, Wyo., June 4, 1909; d. Anthony and Anna Mary (Picco) P.; diploma Seattle Pacific Coll., 1932; B.A. in Edn., Central Wash. U., 1938; postgrad. U. Wash., 1940; cert. of proficiency in occupational therapy Mills Coll., 1945. Tchr., Wash. Public Schs., 1936-45; chief occupational therapist Marion (Ind.) VA Hosp., 1948-50, 54-69; head occupational therapist NP sect. Walter Reed Army Hosp., 1950, Valley Forge Army Hsop., 1952-53; chief occupational therapist Downey (Ill.) VA Hosp., 1953-54; ret., 1969; lectr. Ball State U., Purdue U., Marion and Anderson colls. Bd. dirs., sec., v.p. Family Service Orgn.; bd. dirs., treas., v.p. Grant County Mental Health Assn.; bd. dirs. Blind Assn., Retarded Children Assn. Served from 1st lt. to capt., Womens Med. Specialists Corps., U.S. Army, 1950-53. Recipient Excellence in Communications with Pub. award, 1969, Mgrs. commendation on retirement, 1969. Mem. Am., Ind. occupational therapy assns., Am. Legion Aux. (1st and 2d vice comdr. Rainier Valley Post 139, 1971-72, comdr. 1976, comdr. Service Girls Post 1977, comdr. 1st Seattle Dist. 1978-79), 20 and 4, 8 and 40 (pres. 1976, chmn. 1979—), Pioneers of Columbia, Nat. Assn. Fed. Employees. Roman Catholic. Clubs: Seattle Womens Century (publicity chmn. rec. sec. Past Pres.'s Assembly 1974-75, treas. 1975-77, v.p. 1976-78, pres. 1979-81), DAV, Gen. Fedn. Womens' Clubs. Contbr. articles to profl. jours. Home: 4221 47th Ave S Seattle WA 98118-1408

PIAZZA, DUANE EUGENE, biomedical researcher; b. San Jose, Calif., June 5, 1954; s. Salvador Richard and Mary Bernice (Mirassou) P.; m. Sandra Patrignani, Sept. 19, 1992. BS in Biology, U. San Francisco, 1976; MA in Biology, San Francisco State U., 1986. Staff rsch. assoc. I U. Calif., San Francisco, 1975-81; sr. rsch. technician XOMA Corp., San Francisco, 1981-82; biologist II Syntex USA Inc., Palo Alto, Calif., 1982-85; pres., cons. Ryte For You, Oakland, Calif., 1985—; rsch. assoc. I Cetus Corp., Emeryville, Calif., 1986-90; rsch. assoc. II John Muir Cancer and Aging Rsch. Inst., Walnut Creek, Calif., 1991-92; rsch. assoc. Pharmagenesis, Palo Alto, Calif., 1993—. CPR & first aid instr. ARC, 1980-92, vol. 1st aid sta. instr., Santa Cruz, 1985-86, vol. 1st aid sta. disaster action team, Oakland, 1986—, br. chmn. disaster action team, 1987-88; treas. Reganti Homeowner Assn., 1990-92. Mem. AAAS, Am. Soc. Microbiology, N.Y. Acad. Scis., Astron. Soc. Pacific, Planetary Soc., Mt. Diablo Astronomy Soc. Republican. Roman Catholic. Home: 1055 Rebecca Dr Boulder Creek CA 95006-9442

PIAZZA, MICHAEL JOSEPH, professional baseball player; b. Norristown, Pa., Sept. 4, 1968. Student, Miami (Fla.)-Dade C.C. Player L.A. Dodgers, 1988—; mem. Nat. League All-Star Team, 1994. Named Nat. League Rookie Player of Yr., Sporting News, 1993, Catcher on the Sporting News N.L. All-Star Team, 1993-94, N.L. Silver Slugger Team, 1993-94, named to Nat. League Slugger Team, 1993; named Nat. League Rookie of Yr., Baseball Writers Assn., 1993. Office: LA Dodgers Dodger Stadium 100 Elysian Park Ave Los Angeles CA 90012*

PICARD, ROBERT REAL, oil company executive; b. Montreal, Que., Can., Aug. 24, 1932; s. Jerry and Irene (Charbonneau) P.; m. Lise Lariviere, June 14, 1958; children: Robert R. Jr., Johanne Picard Thomson. ME, McGill U., Montreal, 1958. Jr. engr. Montreal East Refinery, Shell Can. Ltd., 1958-65, dept. mgr., 1965-68, refinery supt. Montreal East Refinery, 1972-74, refinery mgr., 1974-79; plant mgr. Waterton Gas Plant, Shell Can. Ltd., Pincher Creek, Alta., 1968-70; mgr. planning Head office Shell Can. Ltd., Toronto, Ont., 1970-72, gen. mgr. rsch., 1979-84; v.p. rsch. Shell Can. Ltd., Calgary, Alta., 1984-86, v.p. human resources, 1986-90, sr. v.p. tech., safety and environ., 1990—. Mem. adv. coun. Ecole Hautes Etudes Commerciales, Montreal, 1988—; bd. dirs. Tech. Svc. Coun., Toronto, 1991—, Alta. Rsch. Coun., Calgary, 1991—, Calgary R & D Authority, 1991—, Can. Inst. for Advanced Rsch., Toronto, 1991—. Office: Shell Can Ltd, 400 4th Ave SW Box 100, Calgary, AB Canada T2P 2H5

PICCARD-KRONE, KAREN ALIOTTE, public relations executive, political consultant; b. La Jolla, Calif., Aug. 10, 1959; d. Peter Elliot and Connie (Anaya) Piccard; m. F. William Krone III, Aug., 1980. BA in History, Portland (Oreg.) State U., 1981; degree in law, U. West Los Angeles, 1985; grad. in polit. mgmt., U. Calif., Davis, 1992-94. Radio talk show host So. Calif. KPZE-AM, Anaheim, Calif., 1986-87; pres. Krones and Assocs., Inc., Portland, 1988—; mem. adv. bd. Pacific N.W. Grantmakers/Grantseekers Conf., 1990-92. Contbr. articles to profl. jours. Com. chmn., mem. adjustment com. Portland Planning Bur., 1991—; chmn. auction com. Oreg. Mus. Sci. and Industry, 1991, PSU "Ultimate Tailgate" Auction, 1994; chmn. steering com. Scanfair, Portland, 1989-90; mem. variance com., Portland, 1989-91; campaign mgr. numerous ballot measures, polit. candidates, 1990-94; exec. dir. Oreg. Non-Profits Assn., 1991—; dir. devel. Oreg. LWV, 1992—; dir. Columbia Symphony Orch., 1993—; chmn. vol. coun. Portland Art Mus., 1995—; dir. Loaves and Fishes, 1994—; pres. Friends of Mystery, 1995—. Charles S. Linderman scholar, 1992; recipient Pub. Svc. award Portland City Coun., 1991. Mem. Soc. Fund Raising Execs. (advocate, nonprofit lobbyist, mem. exec. bd.), Portlandia Club, Inc. (bd. dirs., Woman of Yr. 1990), Oreg. Art Inst., Oreg. Nordic Coun. (pres. 1992—), Sherlock Holmes Soc. Portland, Scandinavian Heritage Found., Rotary, Optimist Club (pres. 1991-92), City Club Portland (com. mem.). Office: 333 S State St Ste 166 Lake Oswego OR 97034-3959

PICHAL, HENRI THOMAS, electronics engineer, physicist, consultant; b. London, Feb. 14, 1923; came to the U.S., 1957; s. Henri and Mary (Conway) P.; m. Vida Eloise Collum Jones, Mar. 7, 1966; children: Chris C., Henri T. III, Thomas William Billingsley. MSc in Engring., U. London, 1953, PhD in Physics, 1955. Registered profl. engr., Wash., Fla. Product engr. John Fluke Mfg. Corp., Everett, Wash., 1970-73; engring. specialist Harris Corp., Melbourne, Fla., 1973-75; pres., prin. Profl. Engring. Co., Inc., Kissimmee, Fla., 1975-91. Contbr. articles to Electronics, Microwaves, and others. Named one of Two Thousand Men Achievement, 1972. Mem. Inst. Physics, Am. Phys. Soc., Fla. Engring. Soc. (sr.), Inst. Environ. Scis. (sr.), IEEE (past chmn. microwave theory and techniques communications systems), Aerospace/Navigational Electronics, Space Electronics and Telemetry, Mil. Electronics. Republican. Home: PO Box 969 Kingston WA 98346-0969

PICK, JAMES BLOCK, management and sociology educator; b. Chgo., July 29, 1943; s. Grant Julius and Helen (Block) P. BA, Northwestern U., 1966; MS in Edn., No. Ill. U., 1969; PhD, U. Calif., Irvine, 1974. Cert. computer profl. Asst. rsch. statistician, lectr. Grad. Sch. Mgmt. U. Calif., Riverside, 1975-91, dir. computing, 1984-91; co-dir. U.S.-Mex. Database Project, 1988-91; assoc. prof. mgmt. and bus., dir. info. mgmt. program U. Redlands, Calif., 1991-95, prof. mgmt. and bus., dept. chair 1995—, chair dept. mgmt. and bus., 1995—; cons. U.S. Census Bur. Internat. Div., 1978; mem. Univ. Commons Bd., 1982-86; mem. bd. govs. PCCLAS, Assn. Borderlands Studies, 1989-92. Trustee Newport Harbor Art Mus., 1981-87, 88—, chmn. permanent collection com., 1987-91, v.p., 1991—. Recipient Thunderbird award Bus. Assn. Latin Am. Studies, 1993. Mem. AAAS, Assn. Computing Machinery, Assn. Systems Mgmt. (pres. Orange County chpt. 1978-79), Am. Statis. Assn., Population Assn. Am., Internat. Union for Sci. Study of Population, Soc. Info. Mgmt. Club, Standard (Chgo.). Author: Geothermal Energy Development, 1982, Computer Systems in Business, 1986, Atlas of Mexico, 1989, The Mexico Handbook, 1994; condr. research in info. systems, population, environ. studies; contbr. sci. articles to publs. in fields.

PICKARD, DEAN, philosophy and humanities educator; b. Geneva, N.Y., Mar. 12, 1947; s. William Otis and Frances (Dean) P.; m. Wendy Eileen Blank, Nov. 23, 1966; chidlren: Justin Matthew, Christopher Dean. BA cum laude, U. Calif., Riverside, 1973; MA, Calif. State U., Long Beach, 1976-77; PhD, Claremont (Calif.) Grad. Sch., 1992. Instr. phys. edn. Pomona Coll., Claremont, 1975-82; instr. philosophy, humanities, and phys. edn. Moorpark (Calif.) Coll., 1978-82; assoc. prof. philosophy, humanities, and phys. edn. Mission Coll., Sylmar, Calif., 1979-83; instr. philosophy Calif. State U., Northridge, 1988-94; prof. philosophy and humanities Pierce Coll., Woodland Hills, Calif., 1983—. Author: Nietzsche, Transformation and Postmodernism; contbr. articles to profl. jours. Marious De Brabent & Henry Carter scholar, 1973; fellow Claremont Grad. Sch., 1988-89. Mem. Am. Philos. Assn., Am. Fedn. Tchrs., N.Am. Nietzsche Soc., L.A. Area Nietzsche Soc. (bd. dirs. 1994-95). Office: Pierce Coll 6201 Winnetka Ave Woodland Hills CA 91371-0001

PICKEL, FREDERICK HUGH, energy company executive; b. Seattle, June 12, 1952; s. Hugh E. Jr. and Dorothy J. (Miller) P.; m. Carol Chilk, Jan. 15, 1983. BS in Engring. and Econs., Harvey Mudd Coll., Claremont, Calif., 1974; MS in Ops. Rsch., MIT, 1978, MCE, 1978, PhD in Engring. Econs., 1982. Gen. engr. FPC, Washington, 1974-75; mgmt. cons. SRI Internat. Decision Analysis Group, Menlo Park, Calif., 1976-77; adminstr. spl. energy projects New Eng. Electric, Westboro, Mass., 1981-84; dir. bus. devel. and energy sales Pacific Enterprises/Pacific Energy, L.A., 1984-86; mgr. strategy and devel. Pacific Enterprises, L.A., 1986-89; mgr. gas acquisition policy Pacific Enterprises/So. Calif. Gas Co., L.A., 1989-93; pres. Virtual Energy, L.A., 1993-94; sr. mgr. Venture Assocs./Arthur Andersen, L.A., 1994—; cons. New Eng. Electric, others, Cambridge, Mass., 1978-81. Contbr. articles to profl. jours. Trustee Harvey Mudd Coll., 1989-92, campaign cabinet, 1991-94; mem. La Brea Hancock Homeowners Assn., L.A., 1990—; mem. Gov.'s Commn. on Cogeneration, Boston, 1977-78. NSF scholar, 1975-76. Mem. L.A. Athletic Club, Internat. Assn. Energy Econs. (pres. L.A. chpt. 1989, Boston chpt. 1984), Am. Econs. Assn., Harvey Mudd Coll. Alumni Assn. (gov. 1986—, treas. 1988-89). Home: 618 S Mansfield Ave Los Angeles CA 90036-3514 Office: Venture Assocs 12121 Wilshire Blvd Ste 1325 Los Angeles CA 90025-1123

PICKENS, ALEXANDER LEGRAND, education educator; b. Waco, Tex., Aug. 31, 1921; s. Alex LeGrand and Elma L. (Johnson) P.; m. Frances M. Jenkins, Aug. 20, 1955. B.A., So. Methodist U., 1950; M.A., North Tex. State U., Denton, 1952; Ed.D., Columbia U., 1959. Tchr. art public schs. Dallas, 1950-53, Elizabeth, N.J., 1953-54; instr. Coll. Architecture and Design U. Mich., 1954-59; assoc. prof. dept. art U. Ga., Athens, 1959-62; assoc. prof. Coll. Edn. U. Hawaii, Honolulu, 1962—, prof. edn., 1968—; U. Hawaii; chmn. doctoral studies curriculum instrn. Coll. Edn. U. Hawaii, Honolulu, 1984-89, asst. to dean for coll. devel., 1989—; dir. children's classes Ft. Worth Children's Museum, 1951-53; head art Nat. Music Camp, Interlochen, Mich., summers 1957-58, U. Oreg., Portland, summers 1959-60, 62; cons. youth art activities Foremost Dairies, 1964-74; cons. art films United World Films, 1970-75; art edn. cons. Honolulu Paper Co., 1970-76, Kamehameha Sch., Bishop Estate, 1978—. Exhibited ceramics, Wichita Internat. Exhbn., Syracuse (N.Y.) Nat. Exhbn., St. Louis Mus., Dallas Mus., San Antonio Mus., Detroit Art Inst., Hawaii Craftsmen, also others; editorial bd.: Arts and Activities mag, 1955-82; editor: U. Hawaii Ednl. Perspectives, 1964—; contbr. articles to profl. jours. Memm. adult com. Dallas County chpt. Jr. ARC, 1951-53; exec. com. Dallas Crafts Guild, 1950-53; v.p., publicity chmn. U. Ga. Community Concert Assn., 1960-62, mem., program chmn. Gov.'s Commn. Observing 150 Yrs. Pub. Edn. in Hawaii, 1990-91. Served with USAAF. Recipient award merit, Tex. State Fair, 1957, All-Am. award, Ednl. Press Assn. Am., 1968, 70, 72, 75, 79, Regents' medal for excellence in teaching, U. Hawaii, 1989, Gov.'s Commn. Observance of 150 Yrs. Pub. Edn., 1990-91. Mem. AAUP, NEA, Internat. Soc. Edn., Nat. Art Edn. Assn., Coun. for Advancement and Support of Edn., Nat. Soc. Fundraising Execs., Hawaii Planned Giving Coun., Phi Delta Kappa, Kappa Delta Pi. Address: 1471 Kalaepohaku St Honolulu HI 96816

PICKERING, AVAJANE, specialized education facility executive; b. New Castle, Ind., Nov. 5, 1951; d. George Willard and Elsie Jean (Wicker) P. BA, Purdue U., 1974; MS in Spl. Edn., U. Utah, 1983, PhD, 1991. Cert. spl. edn. Co-dir. presch. for gifted students, 1970-74; tchr. Granite Community Edn., Salt Lake City, 1974-79; tchr. coordinator Salt Lake City Schs., 1975-85; adminstrv. dir., owner Specialized Ednl. Programming Svc., Inc., Salt Lake City, 1976—; mem. Utah Profl. Adv. Bd.; adj. instr. U. Utah, Salt Lake City, 1985—; instr. Brigham Young U., 1993—. Rep. del. Utah State Conv., also county conv.; vol. tour guide, hostess Temple Square, Ch. Jesus Christ of Latter-Day Saints, 1983-88. Mem. Coun. for Exceptional Children, Coun. for Learning Disabilities, Learning Disability Assn., Ednl. Therapy Assn. Profl., Learning Disabilities Assn. Utah (profl. adv. bd.), Attention Deficit Coalition Utah (treas.), Hadassah, Delta Kappa Gamma, Phi Kappa Phi. Home: 1595 S 2100 E Salt Lake City UT 84108-2750 Office: Specialized Ednl Programming Svcs 1760 S 1100 E Salt Lake City UT 84105-3430

PICKERING, MARY BARBARA, history educator, writer; b. San Francisco, June 22, 1954; d. Robert Alexander and Helen Veronica (Blasko) P.; m. Francis Edward Lauricella, Sept. 2, 1979; children: Nicolas Pickering, Natalia Pickering, Michael Pickering. AB in History magna cum laude, Harvard U., 1975, AM in History, 1976; Diplôme d'Etudes Approfondies, Inst. d'Etudes Politiques, 1984; PhD in History, Harvard U., 1988. Teaching asst., teaching fellow Harvard U., Cambridge, Mass., 1977-79; adj. asst. prof. history Manhattan Coll., N.Y.C., 1988; adj. asst. prof. history Pace U., N.Y.C., 1988-89, lectr., 1989-90, asst. prof. history, 1990-94; asst. prof. European history San Jose (Calif.) State U., 1994—. Author: Auguste Comte: An Intellectual Biography vol. 1, 1993; contbr. articles to profl. jours. Gilbert Chinard scholar Inst. Français de Washington, 1983; French Govt. fellow, 1983-84; Exch. scholar Harvard U., Inst. d'Etudes Politiques, 1983-84; NEH fellow, 1991-92. Fellow The Pierpont Morgan Libr.; mem. AAUW, Am. Hist. Assn., N.Y. State Assn. European Historians, Berkshire Conf. Women Historians, Soc. French Hist. Studies, Southeastern Nineteenth-Century Studies Assn., Coord. Com. Women in the Hist. Profession-N.Y. Met. Region (chair program com. 1991-93, pres. 1993-94), Phi Beta Kappa. Democrat. Home: 2360 Vallejo St San Francisco CA 94123-4712 Office: San Jose State U History Dept San Jose CA 95192-0117

PICKETT, DAVID FRANKLIN, JR., aerospace company executive; b. Littlefield, Tex., May 3, 1936; s. David Franklin and Dottie Ardell (Britton) P.; m. B. Christine Klop, Aug. 21, 1971. AA, Del Mar Coll., Corpus Christi, 1960; BS in Chem., U. Tex., 1962, MA, 1965, PhD, 1970. Rsch. chemist Am. Magnesium Co., Snyder, Tex., 1969-70; chemist, chem. engr. Air Force Aero Propulsion Lab., Dayton, Ohio, 1970-78; sect. head Hughes Aircraft Co., El Segundo, Calif., 1978-84; asst. dept. mgr. Hughes Aircraft Co., El Segundo, 1984-86, dept. mgr., 1986-89, prodn. line mgr., 1990-91, program mgr., 1991—; ECS coordinator ann. battery conf. Calif. State U., Long Beach, 1987-89. Author: Nickel Electrode and NiCd Cell Technology, 1984-88; inventor in field. With USN, 1955-57. Mem. Southern Calif./Nev. Electrochem. Soc. (sec. 1980-81, vice chmn. 1981-82, chmn. 1982-83), Am. Chem. Soc., Am. Inst. Aeronautics and Astronautics, Phi Lambda Upsilon. Baptist. Home: 4 Hilltop Cir Palos Verdes Peninsula CA 90275-3432 Office: Hughes Indsl Electronics Co Electron Dynamics Divsn 3100 Lomita Blvd Torrance CA 90505-5104

PICKETT, MICHAEL D., computer hardware and software distributor; b. 1947. BSBA, U. So. Calif. With Deloitte Haskins & Sells, 1969-83; v.p. fin., chief fin. officer Merisel Internat. (formerly Softsel Computer Products), 1983-86, pres., chief oper. officer, 1986-88, now vice chmn., CEO. Office: Merisel Internat 200 Continental Blvd El Segundo CA 90245-4526*

PICKETT, NANCY ELIZABETH, vocational rehabilitation consultant, government council executive; b. Barksdale AFB, La., Nov. 7, 1948; d. Richard Dewey and Evelyn (Weis) P.; m. Wendell Alfred Smith III, May 31, 1968 (div. 1976); children: Melinira Lynne, Wendell Alfred, IV. BA, Nicholls State U., 1970, MEd, 1972. Tchr. Cert. Vocat. expert; qualified mental retardation profl.; lic. profl. counselor, rehab. counselor. St. Charles Sch. Bd., Luling, La., 1970-71; counselor, coordinator River Parishes Council Govt., Convent, La., 1973-74, exec. dir., Boutte, La., 1974-86; exec. asst. Centec Corp., New Orleans, 1986-87; vocat. rehab. cons. Crawford Health and Rehab., Metairie, La., 1987-89; mgr., Alexandria, 1989-92, vocat. counselor/

supr., Las Vegas, 1993-94; vocat. counselor MED/VOC, Inc., Las Vegas, 1994—; pres. pvt. industry council, LaPlace, La., 1981-83; pvt. practice trainer, cons., Boutte, La., 1979-87; mem. bd. examiners La. Licensed Vocat. Rehab. Counselors, 1992; mem. adv. bd. La. Family Planning Program, New Orleans, 1976-90. Editor: Directory Community Resources, 1977. Del. White House Conf. Families, Mpls., 1978, La. Gov.'s Conf. Libraries, Baton Rouge, 1978; founding bd. dirs. St. Charles Community Theatre, Luling, La., 1979-84; bd. dirs., v.p. S.E. La. Girl Scout Coun., New Orleans, 1978-83. Nat. Merit scholar, 1966. Mem. Am. Soc. for Tng. and Devel. (bd. dirs., treas. 1984, chmn. position referral 1983), Service Delivery Area Dirs. Assn., La. Assn. Rehab. Profls. Pvt. Sector (bd. dirs. 1992). Office: MED/VOC Inc 4550 W Oakey Blvd Ste 111 Las Vegas NV 98102

PICKLE, JOSEPH WESLEY, JR., religion educator; b. Denver, Apr. 8, 1935; s. Joseph Wesley and Wilhelmina (Blacketor) P.; m. Judith Ann Siebert, June 28, 1958; children: David E., Kathryn E., Steven J. BA, Carleton Coll., 1957; B.D., Chgo. Theol. Sem., 1961; MA, U. Chgo., 1962, PhD, 1969. Ordained to ministry Am. Bapt. Conv., 1962. Asst. pastor Judson Meml. Ch., N.Y.C., 1959-60; acting dean summer session Colo. Coll., Colorado Springs, 1969-70, from asst. prof. to prof. religion, 1964—; vis. prof. theology Iliff Sch. Theology, Denver, 1984; vis. prof. religious studies U. Zimbabwe, Harare, 1989; cons. Colo. Humanities Program, Denver, 1975-89; coord. Sheffer Meml. Fund, Colo. Coll., Colorado Springs, 1983—. Co-editor Papers of the 19th Century Theology Group, 1978, 88, 93. Pres. bd. dirs. Pikes Peak Mental Health Ctr., Colorado Springs, 1975; chmn. Colo. Health Facilities Rev. Coun., Denver, 1979-84; mem. Colo. Health Facilities Rev. Coun., Denver, 1976-84, Colo. Bd. Health, Denver, 1986-91. Am. Bapt. Conv. scholar, 1953-59; Fulbright Hays Grad. fellow U. Tübingen, Fed. Republic Germany, 1963-64, Danforth fellow, 1957-63, Joseph Malone fellow, 1987. Fellow Soc. for Values in Higher Edn.; mem. Am. Theol. Soc., Am. Acad. Religion (regional pres. 1983-84, 92-93), Cath. Theol. Soc. Am., Fulbright Assn., Phi Beta Kappa. Democrat. Home: 20 W Caramillo St Colorado Springs CO 80907-7314 Office: Colo Coll 14 E Cache La Poudre St Colorado Springs CO 80903-3243

PICKMAN, PHILLIP, management consultant; b. Mpls., May 6, 1938; s. Sam and Rose G. (Chiat) P.; m. 1962; children: Michael, Kara, Todd. BS, U. Minn., 1960, MSME, 1962. Supr. oper. systems Bell Telephone Labs., Whippany, N.J., 1962-68; mgr. systems planning Dayton Hudson Corp., Mpls., 1968-73; dir. info. svcs. Red Owl Stores, Inc., Mpls., 1973-74; dir. systems and mgmt. info Cook United, Cleve., 1974-77; regional v.p. May Dept. Stores, L.A., 1977-79; sr. assoc., exec. recruiter Westlake Group, Westlake Village, Calif., 1980-81; pres. and founder Info. Resources Group, Westlake Village, Calif., 1981-87; dir. product mgmt. Cap Gemini Am., Canoga Park, Calif., 1987-93; account mgr. mgmt. devel. consulting and tng. Leadership Mgmt. Assocs. Calif., Agoura Hills, 1994—. Treas. Foxmoor Hills Homeowners Assn., Westlake Village, 1989-91, pres., 1991-92, 92-93; treas. Morris County (N.J.) Dem. County Com., 1965-68; vice chmn. Parsippany-Troy Hills (N.J.) Planning Bd., 1967-68; mem. adv. bd. B'nai Brith Hillel Found., U. Minn., 1972-73. Mem. Tau Beta Pi, Pi Tau Sigma. Jewish. Home: 1815 Stonesgate St Westlake Vlg CA 91361-1612 Office: Leadership Mgmt Assocs 6053 Lake Nadine Pl Agoura Hills CA 91301-1420

PICKRELL, THOMAS RICHARD, retired oil company executive; b. Jermyn, Tex., Dec. 30, 1926; s. Mont Bolt and Martha Alice (Dodson) P.; m. M. Earline Bowen, Sept. 9, 1950; children—Thomas Wayne, Michael Bowen, Kent Richard, Paul Keith. B.S., North Tex. State U., 1951, M.B.A., 1952; postgrad., Ohio State U., 1954-55; advanced mgmt. program, Harvard U., 1979. CPA, Tex. Auditor, acct. Conoco, Inc., Ponca City, Okla., 1955-62; mgr. acctg. Conoco, Inc., Houston, 1965-67; asst. controller Conoco, Inc., Ponca City, 1967-81; v.p., controller Conoco, Inc., Stamford, Conn., 1982-83, Wilmington, Del., 1983-85; asst. prof. Okla. State U., Stillwater, Okla., 1962-63; controller Douglas Oil Co., Los Angeles, 1963-65; mem. adv. bd. dept. acctg. North Tex. State U., Denton, 1978-85; mem. adv. bd. Coll. Bus., Kansas State U., Manhattan, 1979-81. Bd. dirs. YMCA, Ponca City, 1976-78, Kay Guidance Clinic, Ponca City, 1971-74, United Way, Ponca City, 1979-81; chmn. Charter Rev. Com., Ponca City, 1971-72. Served to sgt. U.S. Army, 1944-46; ETO. Mem. AICPA, Fin. Execs. Inst. (pres. Okla. chpt. 1972), Am. Petroleum Inst. (acctg. com., gen. com.), Ponca City Country Club (pres. 1980-81), Rotary (pres. Ponca City club 1973-74), Beta Gamma Sigma, Beta Alpha Psi. Republican. Presbyterian. Home: 10 San Juan Ranch Rd Santa Fe NM 87501-9804

PICRAUX, SAMUEL THOMAS, physics researcher; b. St. Charles, Mo., Mar. 3, 1943; s. Samuel F. and Jeannette D.; m. Danice R. Kent, July 12, 1970; children: Jeanine, Laura, Daryl. BS in Elec. Engring., U. Mo., 1965; postgrad. Cambridge U., Eng., 1965-66; MS in Engring. Sci., Calif. Inst. Tech., 1967, PhD in Engring. Scis. and Physics, 1969. Mem. tech. staff Sandia Nat. Labs., Albuquerque, 1969-72, div. supr., 1972-86, dept. mgr., 1986—; vis. scientist dept. physics Aarhus U., Denmark, 1975; NATO lectr., 1979, 81, 83, 86,; NSF lectr. 1976, 81. Author: Materials Analysis by Ion Channeling, 1982; editor: Applications of Ion Beams to Metals, 1974, Metastable Materials Formation by Ion Implantation, 1982, Nuclear Instruments and Methods International jour., 1983-91, Surface Alloying by Ion Electon and Laser Beams, 1986, Beam-Solid Interactions and Transient Processes, 1987; contbr. numerous articles to profl. jours. Fulbright fellow, 1965-66. Recipient Ernest Orlando Lawrence Meml. award, U.S. Dept. Energy, 1990, 3 basic Energy Scis. Outstanding Rsch. awards, U.S. Dept. Energy. 1985, 92, 94. Fellow Am. Physical Soc. (chmn. materials physics divsn., 1990); mem. Am. Vacuum Soc., Materials Rsch. Soc. (pres. 1993), IEEE, Am. Vacuum Soc. Office: Sandia Nat Labs POB 5800 Albuquerque NM 87185-1415

PIEPER, DAROLD D., lawyer; b. Vallejo, Calif., Dec. 30, 1944; s. Walter A. H. and Vera Mae (Ellis) P.; m. Barbara Gillis, Dec. 20, 1969; 1 child, Christopher Radcliffe. AB, UCLA, 1967; JD, USC, 1970. Bar: Calif. 1971. Ops. rsch. analyst Naval Weapons Ctr., China Lake, Calif., 1966-69; assoc. Richards, Watson & Gershon, L.A., 1970-76, ptnr., 1976—; spl. counsel L.A. County Transp. Commn., 1984-93, L.A. County Met. Transp. Authority, 1993-94; commr. L.A. County Delinquency and Crime Commn., 1983—, pres., 1987—; chmn. L.A. County Delinquency Prevention Planning Coun., 1987-90. Contbr. articles to profl. jours. Peace officer Pasadena (Calif.) Police Res. Unit, 1972-87, dep. comdr., 1979-81, comdr., 1982-84; chmn. pub. safety commn. City of La Canada Flintridge, Calif., 1977-82, commr. 1977-88; bd. dirs. La Canada Flintridge Coordinating Council, 1975-82, pres. 1977-78; exec. dir. Cityhood Action Com., 1975-76; active Calif. Rep. Party, Appellate Circle of Legion Lex U. So. Calif.; chmn. Youth Opportunities United, Inc., 1990—, vice-chmn. 1988-89, bd. dirs. 1988—; mem. L.A. County Justice Systems Adv. Group, 1987-92; trustee Lanterman Hist. Mus. Found., 1989-94, Calif. City Mgmt. Found., 1992—. Recipient commendation for Community Service, L.A. County Bd. Suprs., 1978. Mem. La Canada Flintridge C. of C. and Cmty. Assn. (pres. 1981, bd. dirs. 1976-83), Navy League U.S., Pacific Legal Found., Peace Officers Assn., L.A. County, UCLA Alumni Assn. (life), U. So. Calif. Alumni Assn. (life), L.A. County Bar Assn., Calif. Bar Assn., ABA, U. So. Calif. Law Alumni Assn. Office: Richards Watson & Gershon 333 S Hope St Fl 38 Los Angeles CA 90071-1406

PIEPER, REX DELANE, range ecologist, educator; b. Idaho Falls, Idaho, Jan. 18, 1934; s. Gustave H. and Maud E. (Beam) P.; m. Susan J. Twyeffort, June 11, 1965; children: Julie, Loren, Tracy. BS, U. Idaho, 1956; MS, Utah State U., 1958; PhD, U. Calif., Berkeley, 1963. Asst. prof. animal and range sci. N.Mex. State U., Las Cruces, 1963-69, assoc. prof., 1969-75, prof., 1975—. Contbr. numerous articles to profl. jours. Recipient Disting. Tchr. award N.Mex. State U. Coll. Agr., 1972, Disting. Research award N.Mex. U. Coll. Agr., 1979. Fellow AAAS, Soc. Range Mgmt.; mem. S.W. Assn. Nature, Am. Soc. Animal Sci. Home: 4825 Senita Dr Las Cruces NM 88011-7628 Office: New Mex State U Dept Animal and Range Scis PO Box 3I Las Cruces NM 88003-0003

PIERCE, DEBORAH MARY, educational administrator; b. Charleston, W. Va.; d. Edward Ernest and Elizabeth Anne (Trent) P.; m. Henry M. Armetta, Sept. 1, 1967 (div. 1981); children: Rosse Matthew Armetta, Stacey Elizabeth Pierce. Student, U. Tenn., 1956-59, Broward Jr. Coll., 1968-69; BA, San Francisco State U., 1977. Cert. elem. tchr., Calif. Pub. relations assoc. San Francisco Internat. Film Festival, 1965-66; account exec. Stover & Assocs., San Francisco, 1966-67; tchr. San Francisco Archdiocese Office of Cath. Schs., 1980-87; with The Calif. Study, Inc. (formerly Tchr's. Registry), Tiburon, Calif., 1988—; pvt. practice as paralegal San Francisco, 1989—; tchr. Jefferson Sch. Dist., Daly City, Calif., 1989-91. Author: (with Frances Spatz Leighton) I Prayed Myself Slim, 1960. Pres. Mothers Alone Working, San Francisco, 1966, PTA, San Francisco, 1979, Parent Teacher Student Assn., San Francisco, 1984; apptd. Calif. State Bd. Welfare Community Rels., Com., 1964-66; active feminist movement. Named Model of the Yr. Modeling Assn. Am., 1962. Mem. People Med. Soc., Assn. for Rsch. and Enlightenment, A Course in Miracles, Commonwealth Club Calif, Angel Club San Francisco. Democrat. Mem. Unity Christ Ch. Home: 1479 48th Ave Apt 2 San Francisco CA 94122-2832

PIERCE, GEORGE ADAMS, university administrator, educator; b. Carlsbad, N.Mex., May 21, 1943; s. Jack Colwell and Shirley (Adams) P.; m. Margaret Mary Brakel, Feb. 10, 1980; children: Christopher, Catherine Rose. BA in Polit. Sci., Fairleigh Dickinson U., 1969; MA in Polit. Sci., New Sch. Social Rsch., 1971; PhD in Higher Edn., Claremont Grad. Sch., 1976. Asst. dir. promotion Afco, N.Y.C., 1969-71; dir. spl. programs U. Calif., Riverside, 1971-73; asst. to pres. Claremont (Calif.) Grad. Sch., 1973-75; asst. to pres. Seattle U., 1975-78, dir. planning, 1978-83, v.p. adminstrn., 1983-87, v.p. planning, 1987-89; v.p. bus. and fin. affairs Western Wash. U., Bellingham, 1989—; chmn. regional rev. panel Truman Scholarship Found., 1977-90. Chmn. Seattle Ctr. Adv. Commn., 1977-83; bd. dirs. N.W. Kidney Found., Seattle, 1986—, YMCA, Bellingham, 1990—; chmn. pack 41 Boy Scouts Am., Bellingham, 1992-94. With USAF, 1963-65. Recipient Cert. Merit Riverside County Comprehensive Health Planning, 1972, Cert. Appreciation Office Mayor City of Seattle, 1983, Nat. Truman Scholarship Found., 1986. Mem. Am. Assn. Higher Edn., Assn. Instnl. Rsch. (regional pres. 1977), Nat. Assn. Coll. and Univ. Bus. Officers (chmn. pers. and benefits com. 1992-94), Rotary. Democrat. Roman Catholic. Home: 421 Morey Ave Bellingham WA 98225-6344 Office: Western Wash U Old Main 300 Bellingham WA 98225

PIERCE, GRETCHEN NATALIE, investment company executive; b. Eugene, Oreg., July 7, 1945; d. Nils Bernard and Jewel (Bauman) Hult; m. Howard Walter Pierce, Dec. 26, 1970; children: Eric Nils, Hailey Lynn, . BA, U. Oreg., 1966. Rsch. analyst Boise (Idaho) Cascade Corp., 1966-68, mgr. divs., 1968-84, dir. info. adminstrn., 1984-86; pres., gen. mgr. Hult & Assocs., Eugene, 1986—; bd. dirs. Siuslaw Valley Bank, Florence, Oreg. Trustee U. Oreg., Sacred Heart Hosp., 1987-91; bd. dirs. City Club of Eugene, 1990-91; pres. Eugene Area C. of C., 1992; mem. Oreg. Econ. Devel. Commn., 1993—. Mem. Oreg. Women's Forum, U. Oreg. Alumni (Disting. Alumni award 1984). Republican. Lutheran. Lodge: Rotary. Office: Hult & Assocs 401 E 10th Ave Ste 500 Eugene OR 97401-3367

PIERCE, HILDA (HILDA HERTA HARMEL), painter; b. Vienna, Austria; came to U.S., 1940; 1 child, Diana Rubin Daly. Student, Art Inst. of Chgo.; studied with Oskar Kokoschka, Salzburg, Austria. Art tchr. Highland Park (Ill.) Art Ctr., Sandburg Village Art Workshop, Chgo., Old Town Art Center, Chgo.; owner, operator Hilda Pierce Art Gallery, Laguna Beach, Calif., 1981-85; guest lectr. major art mus. and Art Tours in France, Switzerland, Austria, Italy; guest lectr. Russian river cruise and major art mus. St. Petersburg and Moscow, 1994. One-woman shows include Fairweather Hardin Gallery, Chgo., Sherman Art Gallery, Chgo., Marshall Field Gallery , Chgo.; exhibited in group shows at Old Orchard Art Festival, Skokie, Ill., Union League Club (awards), North Shore Art League (awards), ARS Gallery of Art Inst. of Chgo.; represented in numerous private and corporate collections; commissioned for all art work including monoprints, oils, and murals for Carnival Cruise Lines megaliner M.S. Fantasy, 1990, 17 murals for megaliner M.S. Imagination, 1995, 49 paintings for megaliner M.S. Imagination, 1995; contbr. articles to Chgo. Tribune Mag., American Artist Mag., Southwest Art Mag., SRA publs., others. Recipient Outstanding Achievement award in Field of Art for Citizen Foreign Birth Chgo. Immigrant's Svc. League. Mem. Arts Club of Chgo. Studio: PO Box 7390 Laguna Niguel CA 92607-7390

PIERCE, LESTER LAURIN, aviation consultant; b. Merlin, Oreg., Sept. 26, 1907; s. Frank Arthur and Charlotte (Allen) P.; m. Helen Ramona Thomas, Mar. 22, 1937; children: Adrienne C. Freeman, Nancy E. Johnson. Grad. high sch., 1925. Theatre mgr. Redwood Theatres, Inc., Fortuna and Eureka, Calif., 1927-28; salesman, bookkeeper Thomas Furniture House, Eureka, 1930-39; pilot, mgr. Pierce Bros. Flying Svc., Eureka, 1934-41; aerial photographer Pierce Flying Svc., Eureka, 1934-75; chief flight instr. Govt. Approved Flight Sch., Eureka, 1947-60; aerial seeder, mgr., pres., salesman Pierce Flying Svc., Inc., Eureka, 1946-68; flight examiner FAA, Eureka, 1948-68, aircraft maintenance insp., 1950-68; mapping pilot Stand Aerial Surveys, Newark, 1948. Lt., flight tng., safety officer USNR, 1942, comdr., 1950. Mem. Soc. Aircraft Safety Investigators and Aviation Cons., OX-5 Club, Elks. Home and Office: 3428 Jacoby Creek Rd Bayside CA 95524-9304

PIERCE, PAUL ROBERT, software engineer; b. Madison, Wis., July 2, 1954; s. Richard Leaver and Nelda (Henrickson) P.; m. Joanne Fuller, Aug. 22, 1992. BSEE, U. Wis., 1976, MS in Computer Sci., 1979. Software engr. Intel, Hillsboro, Oreg., 1979-83, Multisoft, Beaverton, Oreg., 1983-85; cons. in pvt. practice, Beaverton, 1985-86; software engr. Intel, Beaverton, 1986—. Patentee in field. Mem. IEEE, The Computer Mus., City Club of Portland. Office: Intel 15201 NW Greenbrier Pky Beaverton OR 97006-5771

PIERCE, ROBERT LORNE, petrochemical, oil and gas company executive. Chmn. and chief exec. officer Foothills Pipe Lines Ltd., Calgary, Alta., Can.; bd. dirs. NOVA Corp. of Alta., Bank of N.S. Mem. Internstate Natural Gas Assn. Am. (bd. dirs.). Office: Foothills Pipe Lines Ltd, 3100 707 8th Ave SW, Calgary, AB Canada T2P 3W8

PIERCE, WILLIAM RODGERS, retired educator; b. Topeka, Aug. 13, 1915; s. Robert Stevens and Esther (Rodgers) P.; m. Joann Geddes Randall, Sept. 19, 1942; children: Patricia Martha, John Randall. BSF, U. Wash., 1940, PhD, 1958; MF, Yale U., 1947. Inspector Dept. of Justice-Border Patrol, El Paso, Tex., 1940-42, Vaughn, N.Mex., 1940-42, Missoula, Mont., 1940-42; dist. ranger Dept. Agrl. Forest Svc. Region One, Mont. and Idaho, 1946-55; prof. forestry U. Mont., Missoula, 1955-81, ret., 1981; expert witness Quinault Indians, Tahola, Wash., 1971-87; computer programmer State of Mont., Missoula, 1981-85. chmn. Gig Harbor Penninsula Adv. Commn., Gig Harbor, 1986—. Lt. USNR, 1943-45. Mem. AAAS, Soc. of Am. Foresters (club and chpt. chmn., Golden Mem. 1991), Gig Harbor Lions, Nature Conservancy, Sigma Xi. Home: 5801 28th Ave NW Gig Harbor WA 98335-1303

PIERCY, GORDON CLAYTON, bank executive; b. Takoma Park, Md., Nov. 23, 1944; s. Gordon Clayton and Dorothy Florence (Brummer) P.; m. Roberta Margaret Walton, 1985; children: Elizabeth Anne, Kenneth Charles, Virginia Walton, Zachary Taylor Walton. BS, Syracuse U., 1966; MBA, Pace U., 1973. Mgmt. trainee Suburban Bank, Bethesda, Md., 1962-66; mktg. planning assoc. Chem. Bank, N.Y.C., 1966-70; sr. market devel. officer Seattle-First Nat. Bank, 1970-74; product expansion adminstr., mktg. planning mgr. VISA, Inc., San Francisco, 1974-76; v.p., dir. mktg. Wash. Mut. Savs. Bank, Seattle, 1976-82; v.p., mktg. dir. First Interstate Bank of Wash. N.A., 1983-86; sr. v.p. mktg., dir. Puget Sound Nat. Bank, Tacoma, 1986-92; sr. v.p., dir. mktg. and sales Key Bank, 1993-94, dir. corp. sales, 1994-95; dir. mktg., sales InterWest Bancorp, Oak Harbor, Wash., 1995—; Bd. dirs. Seattle BBB, Seattle Aquarium Soc., Concerts on the Cove. Mem. Am. Mktg. Assn. (bd. dirs.), Bank Mktg. Assn., Mktg. Communications Execs. Internat., Seattle Advt. Fedn., Sigma Nu, Alpha Kappa Psi, Delta Mu Delta. Episcopalian. Home: 750 Snowberry Ln Coupeville WA 98239 Office: PO Box 1649 Oak Harbor WA 98277

PIERIK, MARILYN ANNE, librarian; b. Bellingham, Wash., Nov. 12, 1939; d. Estell Leslie and Anna Margarethe (Onigkeit) Bowers; m. Robert Vincent Pierik, July 25, 1964; children: David Vincent, Donald Lesley. AA, Chaffey Jr. Coll., Ontario, Calif., 1959; BA, Upland (Calif.) Coll., 1962; cert. in teaching, Claremont (Calif.) Coll., 1963; MSLS, U. So. Calif., L.A., 1973. Tchr. elem. Christ Episcopal Day Sch., Ontario, 1959-60; tchr. Bonita High Sch., La Verne, Calif., 1962-63; tchr., libr. Kettle Valley Sch. Dist. 14, Greenwood, Can., 1963-64; libr. asst. Monrovia (Calif.) Pub. Libr., 1964-67; with Mt. Hood C.C., Gresham, Oreg., 1972—, reference libr., 1983—, chair faculty scholarship com., 1987—; campus archivist Mt. Hood C.C., Gresham, 1994—; mem. site selection com. Multnomah County (Oreg.) Libr., New Gresham br., 1987, adv. com. Multnomah County Libr., Portland, Oreg., 1988-89; bd. dirs. Oreg. Episcopal Conf. of Deaf, 1985-92. Bd. dirs. East County Arts Alliance, Gresham, 1987-91; vestry person, jr. warden St. Luke's Episc. Ch., 1989-92; founding pres. Mt. Hood Pops, 1983-88, orch. mgr., 1983-91, 93—, bd. dirs., 1983-88, 91—. Recipient Jeanette Parkhill Meml. award Chaffey Jr. Coll., 1959, Svc. award St. Luke's Episcopal Ch., 1983, 87, Edn. Svc. award Soroptimists, 1989. Mem. AAUW, NEA, Oreg. Edn. Assn., Oreg. Libr. Assn., ALA, Gresham Hist. Soc. Office: Mt Hood CC Libr 26000 SE Stark St Gresham OR 97030-3300

PIERONI, LEONARD J., engineering and construction company executive; b. 1939. BSChemE, Notre Dame U., 1960; MSChemE, Northwestern U., 1961. With M.W. Kellogg Co., N.Y.C., 1961-70, Rust Engring., N.Y.C., 1970-72; with Parsons, Pasadena, Calif., 1972-77, 78—, exec. v.p., 1987-90, chmn., chief exec. officer, 1990—, also dir.; pres. SIP Engring. Inc., 1983-84; mng. dir. Ralph M. Parsons Co. Ltd., London, 1984-85; pres., gen. mgr. Charles T. Main Inc., 1985-87; v.p. sales KTI Corp., 1977-78. Office: Parsons Corp 100 W Walnut St Pasadena CA 91124-0001

PIERRE, JOSEPH HORACE, JR., commercial artist; b. Salem, Oreg., Oct. 3, 1929; s. Joseph Horace and Miriam Elisabeth (Holder) P.; m. June Anne Rice, Dec. 20, 1952; children: Joseph Horace III, Thomas E., Laurie E., Mark R., Ruth A. Grad., Advt. Art Sch., Portland, Oreg., 1954, Inst. Comml. Art, 1951-52. Lithographic printer Your Town Press, Inc., Salem, Oreg., 1955-58; correctional officer Oreg. State Correctional Instn., 1958-60; owner Illustrators Workshop, Inc., Salem, 1960-61; advt. mgr. North Pacific Lumber Co., Portland, 1961-63; vocat. instr. graphic arts Oreg. Correctional Instn., 1963-70; lithographic printer Lloyd's Printing, Monterey, Calif., 1971-72; illustrator McGraw Hill, 1972-73; owner Publishers Art Svc., Monterey, 1972-81; correctional officer Oreg. State Penitentiary, 1982-90; ret. Editor/publisher: The Pro Cartoonist & Gagwriter; author: The Road to Damascus, 1981, The Descendants of Thomas Pier, 1992, The Origin and History of the Callaway and Holder Families, 1992; author numerous OpEd cols. in Salem, Oreg. Statesman Jour., others; pub. cartoons nat. mags.; mural Mardi Gras Restaurant, Salem; cartoon strip Fabu, Oreg. Agr. mo. Mem. Rep. Nat. Com., Citizens Com. for Right to Keep and Bear Arms. Served with USN, 1946-51. Decorated Victory medal, China Svc. medal, Korea medal. Mem. U.S. Power Squadron, Nat. Rifle Assn., Acad. of Model Aeronautics, Oreg. Correctional Officers Assn. (co-founder, hon. mem.), Four Corners Rod and Gun Club. Republican. Home: 4822 Oak Park Dr NE Salem OR 97305-2931

PIERRE, PHIL, food products executive; b. 1944. With Ventura (Calif.) Coastal Corp., 1968-82; exec. v.p. S & J Ranch Inc., Madera, Calif., 1982—. Office: S & J Ranch Inc 29639 Ave 10 Madera CA 93639*

PIERSON, PETER O'MALLEY, history educator; b. Indpls., Oct. 4, 1932; s. Russell Frazier and Mary Emily (Bingham) P. Student, Denison U., 1950-52; BA in Polit. Sci., UCLA, 1954, MA in History, 1963, PhD, 1966. From asst. prof. to assoc. prof. dept. history Santa Clara (Calif.) U., 1966-89, prof., 1989—, chmn. history dept., 1988-92, Lee and Seymour Graff prof., 1993—; mem. adv. bd. Humanities West, San Francisco, 1982—. Author: Philip II of Spain, 1975, Commander of the Armada, 1989; contbr. articles to various pubs. Lt. j.g. USNR, 1954-58. Recipient Fulbright grant, Spain, 1964-66; named NEH fellow, Europe, 1974. Mem. Am. Hist. Assn., Soc. Spanish & Portugese Hist. Studies (exec. com. 1977-81), Bohemian Club (San Francisco), Phi Gamma Delta. Roman Catholic. Office: Santa Clara U History Dept Santa Clara CA 95053

PIERSON, WAYNE GEORGE, trust company executive; b. L.A., Nov. 5, 1950; s. Norman Einar and Annabelle Florence (McLay) P.; m. Margaret Aileen Boyle, Mar. 18, 1972; children: Heather, Dawn, Mark, Michael. BS in Bus. Adminstrn. with honors, Calif. State U., Northridge, 1973. CPA, Oreg., Calif. Audit supr. Ernst & Whinney (now Ernst & Young), L.A. and Portland, Oreg., 1973-80; treas. Gregory Affiliates, Beaverton, Oreg., 1980-82, Meyer Meml. Trust, Portland, 1982—; mem. adv. com. New Enterprise Assocs. Investment com. Columbia Cascade Scout Coun. Mem. AICPA, Inst. Chartered Fin. Analysts Fedn., Assn. for Investment Mgmt. and Rsch., Oreg. Soc. CPAs, Portland Soc. Fin. Analysts, Found. Fin. Officers Group (steering com.). Office: Meyer Meml Trust 1515 SW 5th Ave Ste 500 Portland OR 97201-5450

PIERSON-STEIN, MARJORIE MAXINE GORDON, property management and investment administrator; b. Boston, Feb. 22, 1925; d. David A. and Fannie (Klevansky) Gordon; m. Melvin Pierson, Nov. 10, 1946 (dec. Jan. 1981); children: Frederick, Eric, Jon; m. Daniel Stein, Dec. 4, 1982. AB in Edn., UCLA, 1945. Dir. The Mel Piersons Rec. Club, L.A., Malibu, Calif., 1953-70; adminstr. Property Mgmt. & Investments, San Diego, Malibu, Mexico, Hawaii, 1970—. Clk., judge precinct voting, Studio City, 1980-91, 94—; bd. dirs. Big Bros. L.A.; v.p. membership Valley Cmty. Philharm. Assn., 1994—. Mem. AAUW, Valley U. Women (v.p. 1994-95, pres. 1992-94), UCLA Women's Sports (bd. dirs.), Bruin Boosters Women's Sports, Jewish Big Bros., Jewish Fedn. Coun. Democrat.

PIERZCHALA, EDMUND, electronics engineer; b. Warsaw, Jan. 15, 1958; came to the U.S., 1989; s. Henryk and Wieslawa P.; m. Sarah Kirk Williams, May 1, 1993. MSEE, Warsaw (Poland) U. Tech., 1982. Rsch. asst. Inst. Biocybernetics & Biomed. Engring., Polish Acad. Scis., Warsaw, 1982-84; rsch. asst., sr. rsch. asst. Inst. Atomic Energy, Swierk, Poland, 1984-89; cons. software engring. Cypress Semiconductor, Beaverton, Oreg., 1990; tester Analogy, Inc., Beaverton, 1991-92; v.p. product devel., founder Analogix Corp., Portland, Oreg., 1993—; tchg. asst., adj. instr. Portland (Oreg.) State U., 1989—. Inventor in field. Officer grad. students in elec. engring. Portland (Oreg.) State U., 1991-94, pres., 1992-93. Co-recipient award Design Automation Conf., San Francisco, 1991. Mem. IEEE (student mem.), Assn. Computing Machinery (student mem.), Polish Nat. Alliance, Eta Kappa Nu. Roman Catholic. Office: Portland State U Dept Elec Engring PO Box 751 Portland OR 97207-0751

PIES, RONALD E., city official; b. Rochester, N.Y., Mar. 21, 1940; s. Herman S. and Sylvia P.; m. Bernita Orloff, Aug. 27, 1964; children: Cara Jean, David Paul. BS, Ariz. State U., 1963. Recreation leader City of Phoenix, Ariz., 1962-64; head recreation div. City of Scottsdale (Ariz.) Parks and Recreation Dept., 1964-69; dir. parks and recreation, City of Tempe, Ariz., 1969-84, community services dir., 1984—; guest lectr. Ariz. State U. Mem., pres. Kyrene Sch. Dist. Governing Bd., 1979-82. Chmn., bd. regents Pacific Revenue Sources Mgmt. Sch. NRPA; gen. chmn. Fiesta Bowl Soccer Classic, 1982—; founding mem. Tempe YMCA bd. mgrs.; apptd. mem. Ariz. State Parks Bd., 1987-93, chair, 1991. Named Outstanding Young Man, Jaycees; recipient Superior Svc. Mgmt. award ASPA, Ariz. chpt., 1988. Mem. Tempe C. of C., Ariz. Parks and Recreation Assn. (bd. dirs. 1986—, pres. adminstrs., Disting. Fellow award 1983), Nat. Recreation and Parks Assn. (Outstanding Profl. 1991), Cactus League Baseball Assn. (pres. 1993-94, appointed mem. of Ariz. baseball commn. by Gov. Symington, 1994—), Sigma Alpha Epsilon. Club: Tempe Diablos. Office: Box 3500 Rural Road Tempe AZ 85282-5482

PIGOTT, CHARLES MCGEE, transportation equipment manufacturing executive; b. Seattle, Apr. 21, 1929; s. Paul and Theiline (McGee) P.; m. Yvonne Flood, Apr. 18, 1953. B.S., Stanford U., 1951. With PACCAR Inc, Seattle, 1959—, exec. v.p., 1962-65, pres., 1965-86, chmn., pres., 1986-87, chmn., chief exec. officer, 1987—, also bd. dirs.; dir. The Seattle Times, Chevron Corp., The Boeing Co. Pres. Nat. Boy Scouts Am., 1986-88, mem. exec. bd. Mem. Bus. Council. Office: Paccar Inc 777 106th Ave NE Bellevue WA 98004-5001*

PIHL, JAMES MELVIN, electrical engineer; b. Seattle, May 29, 1943; s. Melvin Charles and Carrie Josephine (Cummings) P.; divorced; 1 child, Christopher James. AASEE, Seattle, 1971; postgrad., City Univ., Bellevue, Wash., 1982—. 1st class operators lic., FCC; lic. in real estate sales. Journeyman machinist Svc. Exch. Corp., Seattle, 1964-67; design engr. P.M. Electronics, Seattle, 1970-73, Physio Control Corp., Redmond, Wash., 1973-

79; project engr. SeaMed Corp., Redmond, 1979-83; sr. design engr. Internat. Submarine Tech., Redmond, 1983-85; engring. mgr. First Med. Devices, Bellevue, Wash., 1985-89; rsch. engr. Pentco Products, Bothell, Wash., 1989—. Inventor, patentee protection system for preventing defibrillation with incorrect or improperly connected electrodes, impedance measurement circuit. With U.S. Army,, 1961-64. Mem. N.Y. Acad. Scis. Home: 14303 82nd Ave NE Bothell WA 98011-5016 Office: Pentco Products PO Box 403 Seattle WA 98111-0403

PIHLAJA, MAXINE MURIEL MEAD, orchestra executive; b. Windom, Minn., July 19, 1935; d. Julian Wright and Mildred Eleanor (Ray) Mead; m. Donald Francis Pihlaja, Jan. 4, 1963; children: Geoffrey Blake, Kirsten Louise, Jocelyn Erika. BA, Hamline U., 1957; postgrad., Columbia U., 1957-58. Group worker Fedn. of Chs., L.A., 1956; case worker St. John's Guild Floating Hosp. Ship, N.Y.C., 1957-59; Y-Teen program dir. YWCA, Elizabeth, N.J., 1957-60, Boulder, Colo., 1964-65; spl. svcs. program and club dir. U.S. Army, Ingrandes and Nancy, France, 1960-62; music buyer, salesperson Guinn's Music, Billings, Mont., 1977-78, N.W. Music, Billings, 1978-79; office adminstr. Am. Luth. Ch., Billings, 1979-84; gen. mgr. Billings Symphony Orchestra, 1984—; substitute tchr. Community Day Care and Enrichment Ctr., Billings, 1971-76. Dir. Handbell choir 1st Presybn. Ch., Billings, 1972—, Am. Luth. Ch., 1981-84, 1st English Luth. Ch., 1982—; mem. Billings Symphony Chorale, 1965-91, Bellissimo!, 1983-93. Mem. Nat. Soc. Fund Raising Execs. (sec. Mont. 1988), Mont. Assn. Female Execs., Am. Guild English Handbell Ringers (state chmn., 1988-89, treas. Area X bd. dirs. 1990-94, membership chmn. 1994—), Mont Assn. Symphony Orchs. (treas, 1987-92). Lutheran. Office: Billings Symphony Orch Box 7055 401 N 31st St Ste 530 Billings MT 59103

PIIRTO, DOUGLAS DONALD, forester, educator; b. Reno, Nev., Sept. 25, 1948; s. Rueben Arvid and Martha Hilma (Giebel) P.; BS, U. Nev., 1970; MS, Colo. State U., 1971; PhD, U. Calif., Berkeley, 1977; m. Mary Louise Cruz, Oct. 28, 1978. Rsch. asst. Colo. State U., 1970-71, U. Calif., Berkeley, 1972-77; forester, silviculturist U.S. Dept. Agr., Forest Svc., Sierra Nat. Forest, Trimmer and Shaver Lake, Calif., 1977-85; assoc. prof. natural resources mgmt. dept. Calif. Poly. State U., San Luis Obispo, 1985-90, prof. 1990—; researcher in field; instr. part-time Kings River Community Coll., Reedley, Calif.; forestry cons., expert witness. Registered profl. forester, Calif.; cert. silviculturist USDA Forest Svc. Recipient Meritorious Performance and Profl. Promise award CalPoly, 1989, CalPoly Coll. Agr. Outstanding Tchg. award Dale Food Co., 1995. Mem. Soc. Am. Foresters, Am. Forestry Assn., Forest Products Rsch. Soc., Soc. Wood Sci. and Tech., Alpha Zeta, Xi Sigma Pi, Sigma Xi, Beta Beta Beta, Phi Sigma Kappa. Lutheran. Contbr. articles to sci. and forestry jours. Home: 7605 El Retiro Ave Atascadero CA 93422-3722 Office: Calif Poly State U Dept Natural Resources Mgmt San Luis Obispo CA 93710

PIKE, RICHARD JOSEPH, JR., geologist; b. Nantucket, Mass., June 28, 1937; s. Richard Joseph and Idolize Evelyn (Roderick) P.; m. Jane Ellen Nielson, Sept. 2, 1967 (div. 1982); children: Benjamin R., Owen S.; m. Linda Hutchinson Grossman, May 4, 1986. BS, Tufts Coll., 1959; MA, Clark U., 1963; PhD, U. Mich., 1968. Geographer U.S. Army, Natick, Mass., 1962-63; ops. analyst Cornell Aero Labs., Buffalo, 1964; geologist astrogeology br. U.S. Geol. Survey, Flagstaff, Ariz. and Menlo Park, Calif., 1968-86; geologist br. of regional geology U.S. Geol. Survey, Menlo Park, 1987—; mem. various NASA panels, Ariz., Calif., and Tex., 1968-70, 74-78; vis. prof. Instituto di Ricerce per la Protezione Idrogeologica nell Italia centrale del Consiglio Nazionale delle Ricerche, Perugia, Italy, 1988-89. Author: (with others) Impact Craters on Mercury, 1988, (with G.P. Thelin) Digital Shaded-Relief Map of the U.S., 1991 (in map exhibit Cooper-Hewitt Mus., N.Y.C., 1992-93 and Smithsonian Inst., Washington, 1993-94); contbr. articles to profl. jours. Recipient Apollo medallion NASA Hdqrs., 1971. Mem. AAAS, Am. Geophys. Union, Geol. Soc. Am., 356 Registry (essayist, editor 1978-93), Sigma Xi. Office: US Geol Survey M/S 975 345 Middlefield Rd Menlo Park CA 94025-3561

PIKE, STEVEN, occupational health physician. BS magna cum laude in Chemistry, Coll. Santa Fe, 1973, BS magna cum laude in Math., 1973; MD, U. N.Mex., 1979; MS in Toxicology, U. Ariz., 1990. Diplomate Am. Bd. Emergency Medicine, Am. Bd. Preventive Medicine/Occupational Medicine, Am. Bd. Med. Toxicology, Nat. Bd. Med. Examiners. Intern Tucson Med. Ctr., 1979-80; resident Ariz. Ctr. for Occupational Safety & Health, Tucson, 1980-81; dir. emergency svcs. Miami (Ariz.) Inspiration Hosp., 1981-86; pres. EnviroMD, Tuscon, 1986—; program chmn. 37th ann. Western Occupational Health Conf., 1993; cons. Ariz. Poison Control Ctr., 1981—; emergency physician Tucson Med. Ctr., 1981—; med. dir., pres. Cobre Valley Emergency Physicians, 1981-82, Anasazi Emergency Physicians, 1982-87; v.p. Tabershaw & Pike, Inc., Tucson, 1983-86; emergency physician El Dorado Med. Ctr., Tuscon, 1986-87, St. Joseph's Hosp., Tucson, 1987—; pres. TEManalytics, Inc., 1989—; cons. Kingdom of Lesotho, Africa, 1992. Chmn. Ariz. Comparative Environ. Risk Project, 1993-94; mem. Ariz. Corp. Commn. externalities prioritization working group, 1993-94; steering com. Tucson/Almaty (Kazakhstan) Health Care Coalition, 1992—; multi-profl. com. Pima County Bd. Health, 1991; chair occupational and environ. health com. Ariz.-Mex. Commn. pub. health com. Fellow Am. Coll. Emergency Physicians (bd. dirs. Ariz. chpt. 1990—, editor 1990-92), Am. Coll. Occupational and Environ. Medicine, Western Occupational and Environ. Med. Assn. (bd. dirs. 1992-94, newsletter editor 1994); mem. Am. Acad. Clin. Toxicologists, Am. Coll. Presventive Medicine, Internat. Assn. Occupational Health, Am. Acad. Cons. Toxicologists. Office: EnvironMD Ste 300 4400 E Broadway Blvd Tucson AZ 85711-3517

PILE, JAMES WILLIAM, artist educator; b. Pueblo, Colo., Nov. 7, 1943; s. William H. and Annabelle (Bryan) P.; m. Marcia E. Bell, Apr. 22, 1943; children: Larissa, Taylor James. BFA in Edn., U. Nebr., 1965, MFA, 1971. Instr. art Ariz. State U., Tempe, 1971-74, asst. prof. art, 1974-78, assoc. prof. art, 1978-88, prof. art, 1988—. Represented in pub./corp. collections West Pub. Co., St. Paul, Ariz. State U. Art Mus., Tempe, Medley Distilling, Louisville, Federated Dept. Stores, Fla., IBM Collection, Tucson, Sioux City Art Ctr., U. S.D. Art Collection, Vermillion, Kalicow Corp., N.Y.C., Krasdale Foods Inc., Bronx, N.Y.; represented in numerous pvt. collections in N.Y.C., Scottsdale, Ariz., Beverly Hills, Calif., N.J., Houston, Huntingdon Valley, Pa., L.A., Nashville, Greenwich, Conn., Old Westbury, N.Y., Phila., Dallas. Recipient Purchase award First Ann. Upper Midwest Art Festival, 1970, Purchase award 32nd Ann. Fall Show Sioux City Art Ctr., 1970, Woods fellowship, 1971, Hon. diploma Univ. de Sonora, 1972, First prize New West Invitational '81, 1981, NEA Visual Artist fellowship, 1987. Office: Ariz State U Sch of Art Tempe AZ 85287-1505

PILLAR, CHARLES LITTLEFIELD, retired mining consultant; b. Denver, May 25, 1911; s. Charles and Alice May (Littlefield) P.; m. Elizabeth Reed Broadhead, Sept. 10, 1932 (div. May 1939); m. Gwendola Elizabeth Lotz, Sept. 16, 1939; children: Ann, Catherine, Pamela. Engr. mines, Colo. Sch. Mines, 1935. Registered profl. engr., B.C., Ariz. Various positions in field, 1935-75; mine cons. Pillar, Lowell & Assocs., Tucson, Ariz., 1976-83; cons. Bechtel Corp., San Francisco, 1976-79, Fluor Corp., Redwood City, Calif., 1979-83; mem. Colo. Sch. Mines Rsch. Inst., Golden, 1975-83, pvt. practice Tucson, 1985-89; bd. dir. Internat. Geosystems Corp., Vancouver, B.C. Contbr. articles to profl. jours. Mem. Nat. Rep. Senatorial com.; rep. Presdl. Task Force. Capt. USAF, 1942-45; maj. USAF Res. 1946-54. Recipient Achievement in the Mining Field award Colo. Sch. Mines, 1995. Mem. AIME (William Saunders Gold Medal award, Disting. mem. award), Can. Inst. Mining and Metallurgy, Profl. Engrs. B.C., Heritage Found., Smithsonian Assocs., Mining Found. S.W., Nat. Exch. Club, U.S. Senatorial Club (presdl. task force), Vancouver Club, Tucson Nat. Country Club. Republican. Episcopalian.

PILLAY, GAUTAM, chemical engineer, electrochemist; b. Buffalo, Jan. 28, 1967; s. Sivasankara K.K. and Revathi (Krishnamurthy) P. BS, N.Mex. State U., Las Cruces, 1988; PhD, Tex. A&M U., 1993. Grad. rschr., staff mem. Los Alamos Nat. Lab., 1984-87; grad. rschr. Tex. A&M U., College Station, 1988-92; rsch. engr. Pacific N.W. Lab., Richland, Wash., 1992-95; sr. rsch. engr. Pacific N.W. Lab., Richland, 1995—; adj. faculty Wash. State U., Richland, 1993—. Contbr. articles to profl. jours. NSF grad. rsch. [illegible] 1988-91. Mem. AIChE (symposium chair), The Electrochem. Soc. [illegible] com. 1994—, pres. Pacific N.W. sect. 1995—), Am. Chem. Soc., Am. Nuclear Soc., Am. Electroplaters and Surface Finishers Soc., Tau Beta Pi, Omega Chi Epsilon, Alpha Chi, Phi Kappa Phi. Office: Pacific NW Lab PO Box 999 Richland WA 99352-0999

PILLAY, MICHAEL, botanist, researcher; b. Durban, Natal, South Africa, June 27, 1950; came to U.S., 1984; s. Dorasamy and Muniamma Pillay; m. Grace Veronica Michael, Oct. 10, 1981; children: Delicia, Anton, Alban. BSc, U. Durban Westville, 1973; BEd, U. South Africa, Pretoria, 1977, BA, 1980; MS, La. State U., 1986; PhD, Va. Tech., 1991. Tchr. sci. Durban, 1974-84; rsch. asst. Wash. State U., Prosser, 1991—. Scholar South African Edn. Program, 1984-86. Mem. Internat. Soc. Plant Molecular Biologists, Soc. for Systematic Biolgists, Crop Sci. Soc. Am. Baptist. Home: # A 1212 S Kinney Way Apt A Prosser WA 99350-1064 Office: Wash State U RR 2 Box 2953-a Prosser WA 99350-9678

PILLERS, DE-ANN MARGARET, neonatologist; b. San Pedro, Calif., Aug. 1, 1957; d. Lauritz and June Pillers; m. Robert Nourse, July 25, 1981. BS in Chem. Engring., AB, Washington U., St. Louis, 1979; MD, Oreg. Health Sci. U., 1984, PhD, 1986. Resident pediatrics Oreg. Health Scis. U., Portland, 1986-89, chief resident pediatrics, 1988-89, fellow neonatal medicine, 1989-91, asst. prof. pediatrics, 1991—, asst. prof. molecular and med. genetics, 1991—. Contbr. articles to profl. jours. Recipient David Smith Pediatric Resident Rsch. award We. Soc. Pediatric Rsch., Carmel, Calif., 1991. Fellow Am. Acad. Pediatrics; mem. AMA, Am. Soc. Human Genetics, Am. Inst. Chem. Engrs. Office: Oreg Health Scis U 3181 SW Sam Jackson Park Rd Portland OR 97201-3011

PILTZ, JOSEPHINE AMANTI, English language educator, writing consultant; b. N.Y.C., May 22, 1938; d. Jerome Joseph and Margaret Elizabeth (Galey) Amanti; m. Guy Hiwa Piltz, June 16, 1960; children: Linda, Kristin, Jennifer. AB, Mt. Holyoke Coll., 1960; MEd, U. Hawaii, Manoa, 1983. Tchr. Le Jardin d'Enfants, Kailua, Hawaii, 1965-66, Hawaii Prep. Acad., Kamuela, 1975—; mem. steering com. Conf. on Lit. and Hawaii's Children, Honolulu, 1986-92. Mem. Kona Hist. Soc., 1988—. Mem. Nat. Coun. Tchrs. English, Kappa Kappa Phi. Democrat. Episcopalian. Home: PO Box 1973 Kamuela HI 96743-1973

PINCUS, HOWARD JONAH, geologist, engineer, educator; b. N.Y.C., June 24, 1922; s. Otto Max and Gertrude (Jankowsky) P.; m. Maud Lydia Roback, Sept. 6, 1953; children: Glenn David, Philip E. BS, CCNY, 1942; PhD, Columbia U., 1949. Mem. faculty Ohio State U., 1949-67, successively instr., asst. prof., assoc. prof., 1949-59, prof., 1959-67, chmn. dept. geology, 1960-65; rsch. geologist U. S. Bur. Mines, summers 1963-67; geologist, rsch. supr. U.S. Bur. Mines, 1967-68; prof. geol. sci. and civil engring. U. Wis., Milw., 1968-87, prof. emeritus, 1987—, dean Coll. Letters and Sci., 1969-72; rsch. assoc. Lamont Geol. Obs., Columbia, 1949, 50, 51; geologist Ohio Dept. Natural Resources, summers 1950-61; cons. geology and rock mechanics, 1954-67, 68—; mem. U.S. nat. com. on tunnelling tech. NAE, 1972-74, mem. U.S. nat. com. on rock mechanics NAS/NAE, 1975-78, 80-89, chmn., 1985-87; mem. U.S. com. Internat. Assn. Engring. Geology/NAS, chmn., 1987-90; sr. postdoctoral fellow NSF, 1962. Tech. editor: Geotech. Testing Jour., 1992-95. Served to 1st lt. C.E. AUS, 1942-46. Recipient award for teaching excellence U. Wis.-Milw. Alumni Assn., 1978. Fellow ASTM (Reinhart award 1987, Award of Merit 1989), AAAS, Geol. Soc. Am.; mem. NSPE, AAUP (pres. Ohio State U. chpt. 1955-56, mem. coun. 1965-67, pres. U. Wis.-Milw. chpt. 1976-77), Am. Geophys. Union, Geol. Soc. Am. (chmn. engring. geology divsn. 1973-74), Soc. Mining Engrs., Internat. Assn. Engring. Geology, Internat. Soc. Rock Mechanics, Assn. Engring. Geologists, Am. Inst. Profl. Geologists (pres. Ohio sect. 1965-66), Computer Oriented Geol. Soc., Phi Beta Kappa (pres. Ohio State U. chpt. 1959-60, pres. U. Wis.-Milw. chpt. 1976-77), Sigma Xi. Home: 17523 Plaza Marlena San Diego CA 92128-1807 Office: PO Box 27598 San Diego CA 92198-1598

PINCUS, LAURIE JANE, artist; b. N.Y.C., Dec. 14, 1951; d. Irving Lewis and Louise Violet (Cropper) P.; m. Roderick Justin Carroll, Oct. 5, 1980 (div. Dec. 1990); m. Mark Samuel Whitney, Sept. 11, 1994; 1 child, Kate Pincus-Whitney. BA, Sarah Lawrence Coll., 1975; MA, Pacifica Grad. Inst., Carpenteria, Calif., 1994. Founder Imagination Work, Pacific Palisades, Calif., 1994—. One-woman shows include Loyola Marymount U., L.A., Jan Baum Gallery, L.A., Dobrick Gallery, Chgo., Galleria Grafica Tokio, Tokyo, Laguna Art Mus., Laguna Beach, Calif., Internat. Airport, San Francisco, Pima C.C., Tucson, Allrich Gallery, San Francisco; group shows include Occidental Coll., L.A., Sonrisa, L.A., Brea (Calif.) Civic and Cultural Ctr. Gallery, La Foret Mus., Tokyo, Valerie Miller Gallery, Palm Desert, Calif., Hebrew Union Coll., L.A., L.A. Mcpt. Art Gallery, Barnsdall Park, Gallery at the Plaza, Security Pacific Bank, L.A., Monique Knowlton Gallery, N.Y.C., U. So. Calif. Atelier Gallery, Santa Monica, Irvine (Calif.) Fine Arts Gallery; featured in numerous articles, represented in collections. Bd. dirs. Westside Arts Ctr., Santa Monica, Calif., 1988-93, Friends of the Jr. Arts Ctr., L.A., 1985—. Mem. Daus. of Darjeeling (co-founder).

PINE, LOIS ANN HASENKAMP, nurse; b. Cheyenne, Wyo., Feb. 21, 1950; d. Clifford Norbert and Julie Adda (Younglund) Hasenkamp; m. Julius William Pine Jr., Feb. 16, 1974; children: Margaret Ann, Julius William III, Lawrence Michael. BS, U. Wyo., 1976, MS in Parent-Child Nursing, 1989. RN. From staff nurse to charge nurse Ivinson Meml. Hosp., Laramie, Wyo., 1976-86; maternal-child nurse cons. Perinatal and Prevention Program, Wyo. Dept. Health, Cheyenne, 1988—. Mem. St. Lawrence Coun. of Cath. Women, Laramie, 1980—, St. Cecilia's Group, Laramie, 1980—, Albany County PTA, Laramie, 1985-91; mem. health profl. adv. com. March of Dimes Wyo. Chpt., 1988—. Mem. ANA, NAACOG (sect. vice chmn. 1980-86), Wyo. Nurses Assn., Am. Acad. Pediat. (perinatal pediat. dist. VIII sect.), Nat. Assn. Neonatal Nurses (charter), Sigma Theta Tau (Alpha Pi chpt. treas. 1990-94, corr. sec. 1983-84, sec. 1994—). Democrat. Home: 1062 Empinado St Laramie WY 82070-5019

PINEDA, JAIME ARMANDO, science educator; b. Comayagua, Honduras, June 13, 1953; came to U.S., 1964; s. Jaime Pineda Rodriguez and Marietta (Bardales) Pineda; m. Elizabeth Mary Meinholz, June 18, 1977. BS, Univ. Coll., College Park, Md., 1978; MA, Fla. Atlantic U., 1982; PhD, U. Calif., San Diego, 1987. Sys. analyst Metro Dade County, Miami, Fla., 1978-80; asst. prof. dept. cognitive sci. U. Calif.-San Diego, La Jolla, 1989—. Contbr. articles to sci. jours. Active Big Bros. Orgn., San Diego, 1985-86. Sgt. USAF, 1973-78. Mem. AAAS, Soc. for Neurosci., Soc. for Psychophysiol. Rsch., Cognitive Neurosci. Soc. Zen Buddhist. Home: 6938 Kensley Way San Diego CA 92126-5903 Office: U Calif-San Diego Dept Cognitive Sci 0515 La Jolla CA 92093

PINES, ALEXANDER, chemistry educator, researcher; b. Tel Aviv, June 22, 1945; came to U.S., 1968.; s. Michael and Neima (Ratner) P.; m. Ayala Malach, Aug. 31, 1967 (div. 1983); children: Itai, Shani; m. Ditsa Kafry, May 5, 1983; children: Noami, Jonathan, Talia. BS, Hebrew U., Jerusalem, 1967; PhD, MIT, 1972. Asst. prof. chemistry U. Calif., Berkeley, 1972-75, assoc. prof., 1975-80, prof., 1980—, Pres.'s chair, 1993; faculty sr. scientist materials scis. div. Lawrence Berkeley Lab., 1975—; cons. Mobil Oil Co., Princeton, N.J., 1980-84, Shell Oil Co., Houston, 1981—; chmn. Bytel Corp., Berkeley, Calif., 1981-85; vis. prof. Weizmann Inst. Sci., 1982; adv. prof. East China Normal U., Shanghai, People's Rep. of China, 1985; sci. dir. Nalorac, Martinez, Calif., 1986—; Joliot-Curie prof. Ecole Superieure de Physique et Chemie, Paris, 1987; Walter J. Chute Disting. lectr. Dalhousie U., 1989, Charles A. McDowell lectr. U. B.C., 1989, E. Leon Watkins lectr. Wichita State U., 1990; Hinshelwood lectr., U. Oxford, 1990, A.R. Gordon Disting. lectr. U. Toronto, 1990, Venable lectr. U. N.C., 1990, Max Born lectr. Hebrew U. of Jerusalem, 1990; William Draper Harkins lectr. U. Chgo., 1991, Kolthoff lectr. U. Minn., 1991; Md.-Grace lectr. U. Md., 1992; mem. adv bd. Nat. High Magnetic Field Lab., Inst. Theoretical Physics, U. Calif. Santa Barbara; mem. adv. panel chem. Nat. Sci. Found.; Randolph T. Major Disting. Lectr. U. Conn., 1992; Peter Smith lectr. Duke U., 1993, Arthur William Davidson lect. U. Kansas, 1992, Arthur Birch lect. Australian Nat. U., 1993, Richard C. Lord Meml. lectr. MIT, 1993, Steacie lectr. Nat. Rsch. Coun. Can., 1993, Centenary lectr. Royal Soc. Chemistry, 1994, Morris Loeb lectr. Harvard U., 1994, Jesse Boot Found. Lectr., U. Nottingham, 1994. Editor Molecular Physics, 1987-91; mem. bd. editors Chem. Physics, Chem. Physics Letters, Nmr: Basic Principles and Progress, Advances in Magnetic Resonance; adv. editor Oxford U. Press; contbr. articles to profl. jours.; patentee in field. Recipient Strait award North Calif. Spectroscopy Soc., Outstanding Achievement award U.S. Dept. of Energy, 1983, 87, 89, R & D 100 awards, 1987, 89, Disting. Teaching award U. Calif., E.O. Lawrence award, 1988, Pitts. Spectroscopy award, 1989, Wolf Prize for chemistry, 1991, Donald Noyce Undergrad. Teaching award U. Calif., 1992, Robert Foster Cherry award for Great Tchrs. Baylor U., Pres.'s Chair for undergrad. edn. U. Calif., 1993; Guggenheim fellow, 1988, Christensen fellow St. Catherine's Coll., Oxford, 1990. Fellow Am. Phys. Soc. (chmn. divsn. chem. physics), Inst. Physics; mem. NAS, Am. Chem. soc. (mem. exec. com. divsn. phys. chemistry, Signature award, Baekeland medal, Harrison Howe award 1991), Royal soc. Chemistry (Bourke lectr.), Internat. Soc. Magnetic Resonance (v.p., pres.). Office: U Calif Chemistry Dept D 64 Hildebrand Hall Berkeley CA 94720

PINGS, ANTHONY CLAUDE, architect; b. Fresno, Calif., Dec. 16, 1951; s. Clarence Hubert and Mary (Murray) P.; m. Carole Clements, June 25, 1983; children, Adam Reed, Rebecca Mary. AA, Fresno City Coll., 1972; BArch, Calif. Poly. State U., San Luis Obispo, 1976. Lic. architect, Calif.; cert. Nat. Council Archtl. Registration Bds. Architect Aubrey Moore Jr., Fresno, 1976-81; architect, prin. Pings & Assocs., Fresno, 1981-83, 86—, Pings-Taylor Assocs., Fresno, 1983-85. Prin. works include Gollaher Profl. Office (Masonry Merit award 1985, Best Office Bldg. award 1986), Fresno Imaging Ctr. (Best Instnl. Project award 1986, Nat. Healthcare award Modern Health Care mag. 1986), Orthopedic Facility (award of honor Masonry Inst. 1987, award of merit San Joaquin chpt. AIA 1987), Modesto Imaging Ctr. (award of merit San Joaquin chpt. AIA 1991). Mem. Calif. Indsl. Tech. Edn. Consortium Calif. State Dept. Edn., 1983, 84. Mem. AIA (bd. dirs. Calif. chpt. 1983-84, v.p. San Joaquin chpt. 1982, pres. 1983, Calif. Coun. evaluation team 1983, team leader Coalinga Emergency Design Assistance team), Fresno Arts (bd. dirs., counsel 1989—, pres. 1990-93). Republican. Home: 4350 N Safford Ave Fresno CA 93704-3509 Office: 1640 W Shaw Ave Ste 107 Fresno CA 93711-3506

PINIELLA, LOUIS VICTOR, professional baseball team manager; b. Tampa, Fla., Aug. 28, 1943; m. Anita Garcia, Apr. 12, 1967; children: Lou, Kristi, Derrick. Student, U. Tampa. Baseball player various minor-league teams, 1962-68, Cleve. Indians, 1968, Kansas City Royals, 1969-73; baseball player N.Y. Yankees, 1974-84, coach, 1984-85, mgr., 1985-87, 1988, gen. mgr., 1987-88, spl. advisor, TV announcer, 1989; mgr. Cin. Reds, 1990-92, Seattle Mariners, 1992—. Named to Am. League All-Star Team, 1972; recipient Ellis Island Medal of Honor, 1990. Office: Seattle Mariners PO Box 4100 83 S King St Seattle WA 98104-2875*

PINK, ERNEST EDWIN, insurance agency executive; b. Rochester, N.Y., Apr. 1, 1942; s. Ernest Hugh and Bertha (Frachel) P.; m. Sharon K. German, Dec. 27, 1961 (div. July 1978); children: Ernest R., Stacy L. BSBA, Tri-State U., Angola, Ind., 1964; M Fin. Svcs., Am. Coll., Bryn Mawr, Pa., 1991. CLU; chartered fin. cons., ins. counselor. Claim investigator Lincoln Nat. Life Ins. Co., Ft. Wayne, Ind., 1964-70; ins. salesman Lincoln Nat. Sales Corp., Missoula, Mont., 1970-76, sr. v.p., sales mgr., 1976-80; ptnr. Toole & Easter Agy., Missoula, 1984-86; owner, mgr., life underwriter Pink Ins. Agy., Inc., Missoula, 1980-84, 87—; bd. dirs. Mont. Ins. Edn. Found., Helena, 1981-90, pres., 1989-90. Chmn. Ducks Unltd., Missoula, 1978—; commr. Missoula Housing Authority, 1985—, chmn. 1993. Mem. NRA (life), Nat. Assn. Life Underwriters (nat. quality awards), Mont. Assn. Life Underwriters (sec.-treas. 1976-77), Western Mont. Assn. Life Underwriters (pres. 1975-76), Am. Soc. CLUs and Chartered Fin. Cons., Western Mont. Estate Planning Coun., Ind. Ins. Agts. (adj. mem. strategic planning com. 1988-90), Nat. Skeet Shooting Assn. (life), Missoula Trap and Skeet Club, Rotary. Office: PO Box 9139 127 E Front St Ste 302 Missoula MT 59802-4448

PINKAVA, DONALD JOHN, botany educator, researcher; b. Cleve., Aug. 29, 1933; s. Yaroslav Joseph and Agnes (Stovicek) P.; m. Mary Jane Klements, May 14, 1976; 1 child, Michelle Marie. BS, Ohio State U., 1955, MS, 1961, PhD, 1964. Tchr. sci. Solon (Ohio) High Sch., 1955-60; instr. Ohio State U., Lakewood, 1963; asst. prof., assoc. prof. botany Ariz. State U., Tempe, 1964-78, prof., 1978—, dir. herbarium, 1964—; team leader Ariz. recovery team for endangered and threatened plants U.S. Fish and Wildlife Svc. Region II, Albuquerque, 1983—. Author: (with E. Lehto) A Vegetative Key to Cultivated Woody Plants of Salt River Valley, Arizona, 1970; editor (with H.S. Gentry): Symposium on Agaves, Desert Bot. Garden, Phoenix, 1985; mem. editorial bd. Vascular Plants of Ariz. Manual; contbr. articles to sci. jours. Trustee Desert Bot. Garden, 1978-85. Fellow NSF, 1961-63, DuPont fellow Ohio State U., 1957, Systematic Inst. at Smithsonian Instn., 1968. Fellow AAAS, Ariz.-Nev. Acad. Sci. (co-editor jour. 1992—), Cactus & Succulent Soc. Am.; mem. Sigma Xi (pres., sec. Ariz. State U. chpt. 1975-80). Home: 2704 S Estrella Cir Mesa AZ 85202-7203 Office: Ariz State U Dept Botany Tempe AZ 85287-1601

PINKERT, TED CHARLES, pathologist, nuclear medicine physician; b. Ames, IA, Oct. 4, 1947; s. Paul August and Elinor Caroline (Schultz) P.; m. Joan Marie Sliger, Dec. 12, 1972 (div. Apr. 1989); m. Susan Delle Rooney, June 22, 1989; children: Emery, Vincent. BA, U. Minn., Mpls., 1970, MD, 1974. Am. Bd. of Pathology. Resident pathologist St. Mary's Hosp., Duluth, Minn., 1974-75, Providence Med. Ctr., Portland, Oreg., 1975-78; fellow in nuclear medicine Oreg. Health Sci. U., Portland, Oreg., 1978-79; pathologist Tuality Community Hosp., Hillsboro, Oreg., 1979—, nuclear medicine physician, 1979—. Mem. Oreg. Pathologists Assn., Oreg. Med. Assn., Coll. of Am. Pathologists. Home: 11801 SW Langley Dr Gaston OR 97119-8565 Office: Tuality Community Hosp 335 SE 8th Ave Hillsboro OR 97123-4246

PINKERTON, ALBERT DUANE, II, lawyer; b. Portland, Oreg., Aug. 28, 1942; s. Albert Duane and Barbara Jean (Payne) P.; 1 child, Albert Duane III; m. Mary-Clare Bittle, 1993. BA, Willamette U., 1964, JD, 1966. Bar: Oreg. 1966, U.S. Dist. Ct. Oreg. 1966, U.S. Ct. Appeals (9th cir.) 1966, Alaska 1985, Calif. 1986, U.S. Dist. Ct. Calif. 1987. Gen. practice Springfield, Oreg., 1966-69, Burns, Oreg., 1969-86, Concord, Calif., 1986-88; assoc. Sellar Hazard Snyder Kelly & Fitzgerald, Walnut Creek, Calif., 1988—;. Chmn. diocesen council Episcopal Diocese Eastern Oreg., 1978-83; mem. exec. com. Eastern Oreg. Comprehensive Mental Health Ctr., 1983-86. Mem. Oreg. State Bar (com. Uniform Jury Instrns. sec. 1972-73, 82-83, chmn. 1973-74, 83-84; com. Procedure and Practice sec. 1985-86, chmn. 1986-87), Am. Judicature Soc., Masons (master 1980-81), Grand Lodge of Oreg. (dist. dep. 1983-86). Home: PO Box 21347 Concord CA 94521-0347 Office: 1111 Civic Dr Ste 300 Walnut Creek CA 94596-3831

PINKERTON, GUY CALVIN, savings and loan executive; b. Seattle, Aug. 1, 1934; s. John L. and Dorothy V. (Kock) P.; children: Deborah, Lisa. BA, U. Wash., 1959. CPA, Wash. Supr. Touche Ross & Co., Seattle, 1959-65; pres., CEO Wash. Fed. Savs., Seattle, 1965—. With USN, 1956-58. Mem. Fin. Mgrs. Soc. (dist. gov.), Fin. Execs. Inst. (sec.). Republican. Presbyterian. Office: Wash Fed Savs 425 Pike St Seattle WA 98101-2334*

PINNEY, EDMUND, educator, mathematician; b. Seattle, Aug. 19, 1917; s. Henry Lewis and Alice (Joy) P.; m. Eleanor Russell, Mar. 10, 1945; children—Henry Russell, Gail Shiela. B.S., Calif. Inst. Tech., 1939, Ph.D., 1942. Research asso. Radiation Lab., Mass. Inst. Tech., 1942-43; research analyst Consol.-Vultee Aircraft Corp., 1943-45; instr. Ore. State Coll., 1945-46; mem. faculty U. Calif., Berkeley, 1946—, prof. math., 1959—; cons. in field. Author: Ordinary Difference-Differential Equations, 1958. Fellow AAAS; mem. Am. Math. Soc., Am. Phys. Soc. Home: 66 Scenic Dr Orinda CA 94563-3412 Office: Univ Calif 839 Evans Hall Berkeley CA 94720

PINOLI, BURT ARTHUR, airline executive; b. Santa Rosa, Calif., Nov. 23, 1954; s. Norris L. and Grace G. (Williams) P.; m. So Yen, May 9, 1987; 1 child, Lucas. BS in Agri-Bus., Calif. State U., Fresno, 1979; M. Internat. Mgmt., Am. Grad. Sch. Internat. Mgmt., Glendale, Ariz., 1988. Loan officer, mgmt. trainee Lloyds Bank Calif., Sanger, 1979-81; mgr. sales/bus. devel. Transamerica Airlines, Oakland, Calif., 1981-86; credit analyst, comml. loan officer Farm Credit Bank System, Ukiah, Calif., 1986-87; city mgr. Northwest Airlines, Beijing, 1988-90, Shanghai, People's Rep. of China, 1991-94; gen. mgr. sales and mktg. Northwest Airlines, Beijing, People's Rep. of China, 1994—. Del. to India, Internat. Youth Exch. Mem. Blue

Key, Alpha Gamma Rho, Alpha Zeta. Home: 1551 Boonville Rd Ukiah CA 95482-8806 Office: Northwest Airlines, Beijing Office, Beijing China

PINSKY, CHARLOTTE LEE (CHERIE PINSKY), academic administrator; b. Hartford, Conn., Aug. 12, 1946; d. David and Charlotte (Abrams) P. BFA, R.I. Sch. Design, 1968. Nutritionist, developer U.S. Peace Corps., Narino, Colombia, 1971-74; adminstr. dept. radiology U. Calif., San Francisco, 1987—. Mem. de Young Meml. Mus. (docent). Mem. de Young Meml. Mus. (artist, docent). Home: 1925 Leavenworth St # 12 San Francisco CA 94133-2503

PINTER, JOSEPH KALMAN, mathematician; b. Janoshalma, Hungary, Jan. 12, 1953; arrived in Can., 1981; s. József and Teréz (Hoványi) P.; m. Mary Tan, Oct. 12, 1985; children: Kálmán Bonaventure, Elizabeth Anne. MS in Elec. Engring., Tech. U. Budapest, Hungary, 1976, PhD in Elec. Engring., 1979; MS in Math., U. Calgary, Can., 1986; postgrad., U. Calgary, 1992—. Researcher Sefel Geophys., Calgary, Alta., Can., 1981-82; applied geophysicist Sci. and Exploration Computer Applications, Dome Pete Ltd., Calgary, Alta., Can., 1982-87, sr. applied geophysicist, 1987-88; researcher Amoco Can., Ltd., Calgary, Alta., 1988-92. Author: Propositions on the Geophysical Applications of the Radon Integral, 1990; inventor fully automated interpreter for refraction data, direct and inverse scattering in the Radon domain. Mem. Am. Math. Soc., Soc. for Indsl. and Applied Math., Assn. of Profl. Engrs. Geologists and Geophysicists of Alta. Roman Catholic. Home: # 864 Lake Lucerne Dr SE, Calgary, AB Canada T2J 3H4

PINTOZZI, CHESTALENE, librarian; b. Macomb, Okla., Apr. 4, 1947; d. Otis William and Edith Marie (Jordan) Bowerman; m. Nicola Francis Xavier Pintozzi, Aug. 2, 1967. Student, U. Okla., 1965-67; BA in English, No. Ill. U., 1969; MLS, U. Tex., 1981. Geology libr. U. Tex., Austin, 1982-84; environ. libr., Ann Marbut Environ. Libr. Sarasota (Fla.) County Pub. Libr. Sys., 1985-87; temporary reference libr. Sci.-Engring. Libr. U. Ariz., Tuscon, 1989-90, reference libr. Sci.-Engring. Libr., 1990—. Mem. ALA (chair Reference and Adult Svcs. Divsn. codes liaison with users group 1994—, Whitney-Carnegie award 1993), Ariz. State Libr. Assn., Arix. Online Users Group, N.Am. Serials Interest Group, Beta Phi Mu, Phi Kappa Phi. Democrat. Office: U Ariz Bldg 54 Rm 216 Tucson AZ 85720

PIPAL, GEORGE HENRY, journalist; b. Lafayette, Ind., Oct. 14, 1916; s. Francis John and Belle (Kadavy) P.; m. Caroline Dunsmore, Aug. 17, 1946; children—John, Susan, Philip, Frank. B.A., U. Nebr., 1937; M.S., Columbia, 1939. Corr. various bureaus UPI, 1937-41; bur. mgr. UPI, Prague, 1946; mgr. for UPI, Eastern Europe, 1947, Germany, 1948; dir. European Services, 1949-51; gen. bus. mgr. Europe, Middle East, Africa, 1952-65; gen. sales exec. computer svcs. N.Y.C., 1966-68; gen. mgr. internat. features div., 1968-78; mng. dir. UPI (U.K.), Ltd., 1964-65; v.p. United Feature Syndicate, 1978-84, United Media Enterprises, 1985—. Served as lt. USNR, 1942-46. Office: United Media 1 Snoopy Pl Santa Rosa CA 95403-2665

PIRAINO, ANN MAE, seminar trainer, leader, vocational counselor; b. Vancouver, Wash.; d. Elsworth Wallace Schmoeckel and Alice Marie (Blankenbickler) Avalos; m. Michael Salvatore, Nov. 19, 1983. BA in Edn., Seattle U., 1972; MA in Appl. Behavioral Sci., City U. Leadership Inst of Sea, 1987. Cert. rehab. counselor. Sec. to supt. Pasco (Wash.) Sch. Dist. No. 1, 1972-74; adminstrv. asst. Burns and Roe, Inc., Richland, Wash., 1974-81; exec. sec. UNC Nuclear Industries, Inc., Richland, Wash., 1981-83, Fairchild Semiconductor, Inc., Puyallup, Wash., 1984-87; instr. Eton Tech. Inst. (ETI), Federal Way, Wash., 1987-89; trainer, cons. Piraino Prodns., Wash., 1985—; seminar leader and cons. Profl. Sec. Internat., Wash., Alaska and Oreg. state chpts., 1985—; cons. Fed. Way Women's Network and Career Devel. Network, Wash., 1985-88; employment coord. Bus. Computer Tng. Inst., Tacoma, 1989-90; adj. faculty Office Automation Griffin Coll., Tacoma, 1990; vocat. rehab. counselor Total Care Svcs., 1990-92, 94—, Favorite Cons., 1990-94. Editor: (newsletter) The Circuit Writer, 1985-87, (pub. assn. newsletters) Hear Ye, Hear Ye, 1986-88, Training Wheels, 1987-90, Speak Up!, 1991-92, Reflections, 1991-94; role expert: (competency study) ASTD Competency and Standards Project, 1988. Co. rep. United Way/Fairchild Semiconductor, Wash., 1986; team co-leader March of Dimes/Fairchild Semiconductor, Wash., 1986; team leader March of Dimes/Town Criers Toastmasters, Wash., 1989, 90. Recipient Xi Alpha Epsilon and Beta Sigma Phi Woman of Yr. award, 1979-81; named Sec. of Yr. Pas-Ric-Ken/Sea Tac Chpts., Profl. Secs. Internat., Richland/Fed. Way, Wash., 1979, 90; Sec. of Yr. Wash.-Alaska Div. Profl. Secs. Internat., Spokane, 1980. Mem. NAFE, ASTD (chpt. v.p. 1988-89, pres. 1990), Profl. Secs. Internat. (chpt. pres. 1985-86, 91-92, pres.-elect Wash./Alaska divsn. 1986-87, pres. 1987-88), Internat. Platform Soc., Toastmasters (area gov. 1991-92, dean Leadership Inst. dist. 32 1992-94), Nat. Assn. Rehab. Profls. in Pvt. Sector, Wash. Women in Worker's Compensation. Home: 38807 134th Pl SE Auburn WA 98092-8583

PIRCHER, LEO JOSEPH, lawyer; b. Berkeley, Calif., Jan. 4, 1933; s. Leo Charles and Christine (Moore) P.; m. Phyllis McConnell, Aug. 4, 1956 (div. April 1981); children: Christopher, David, Eric; m. Nina Silverman, June 14, 1987; B.S., U. Calif.-Berkeley, 1954, J.D., 1957. Bar: Calif. 1958, N.Y. 1985; cert. specialist taxation law Calif. Bd. Legal Specialization. Assoc. Lawler, Felix & Hall, L.A., 1957-62, ptnr., 1962-65, sr. ptnr., 1965-83; sr. ptnr. Pircher, Nichols & Meeks, L.A., 1983—; adj. prof. Loyola U. Law Sch., L.A., 1959-61; corp. sec. Am. Metal Bearing Co., Gardena, Calif., 1975—, dir. Varco Internat. Inc., Orange, Calif.; speaker various law schs. and bar assns. edn. programs. Author: (with others) Definition and Utility of Leases, 1968. Chmn. pub. fin. and taxation sect. Calif. Town Hall, Los Angeles, 1970-71. Mem. Calif. State Bar, N.Y. State Bar, Los Angeles County Bar Assn. (exec. com. comml. law secton), ABA, Nat. Assn. Real Estate Investment Trusts Inc. (cert. specialist taxation law). Republican. Club: Regency (L.A.). Office: Pircher Nichols & Meeks 1999 Avenue Of The Stars Los Angeles CA 90067-6022

PIROFSKY, HARVEY, psychiatrist; b. N.Y.C., Nov. 13, 1920; s. Samuel and Esther (Wolpin) P.; m. Florence Pirofski, Mar. 30, 1950; children: Liise Anne, Kira. BS, CCNY; MD, U. Geneva. Diplomate Am. Bd. Psychiatry and Neurology. Intern Kings County Med. Ctr., Bklyn., 1955, resident in psychiatry, 1956-59; sr. psychiatrist Agnew (Calif.) State Hosp.; pvt. practice Calif. Mental Rsch., Palo Alto, 1961-94; assoc. clin. prof. Stanford (Calif.) Med. Ctr., 1964-94, assoc. prof. emeritus, 1994—. With USN, 1944-46. Fellow APA (life). Office: Mental Rsch Inst 555 Middlefield Rd Palo Alto CA 94301-2124

PIRONTI, LAVONNE DE LAERE, association executive; b. L.A., Jan. 11, 1946; d. Emil Joseph and Pearl Mary (Vilmur) De Laere; m. Aldo Pironti, May 21, 1977. BA in Internat. Rels., U. So. Calif., L.A., 1967. Commd. ensign USN, 1968-91, advanced through grades to comdr., 1979; pers. officer Lemoore (Calif.) Naval Air Sta., 1972-74; human rels. mgmt. specialist Human Resource Mgmt. Detachment, Naples, Italy, 1975-78; comms. staff officer Supreme Hdqrs. Allied Powers Europe, Shape, Belgium, 1979-83; dir. Navy Family Svc. Ctr. Sigonella Naval Air Sta., Sicily, 1983-85; exec. officer Naval Sta. Guam, Apra Harbor, 1985-87; comms. staff officer NATO Comm. and Info. Sys. Agy., Brussels, Belgium, 1987-89; polit. officer for Guam, trust Territories Pacific Islands Comdr. Naval Forces Marianas, Agana, Guam, 1989-91; store mgr. Sandal Tree, Lihue, Hawaii, 1991-92; CEO, exec. dir. YWCA of Kauai County, Lihue, 1992—. Vice pres. Kauai Sex. Abuse Core Group, Lihue, 1993—; co-chair Kauai Human Svcs. Coun., Lihue; bd. dirs. Hawaii Health & Human Svcs. Alliance, Lihue, 1993—; adv. bd. Hauai County Family Self-Sufficiency Program, Lihue, 1993—. Decorated Navy Commendation medal, Meritorious Svc. Medal with 1 star, Def. Meritorious Svc. Medal with 2 stars, others; named Fed. Woman of the Yr. Comdr. Naval Forces Marianas, 1986-87. Roman Catholic. Office: YWCA Kauai County 3094 Elua St Lihue HI 96766-1209

PIROOZMANDI, FARID, mechanical engineer; b. Abadan, Iran, Mar. 27, 1958; came to U.S., 1979; s. Ruhollah Pirooz and Ghodsi (Roshana'i) P.; m. Neda Sayyah, Aug. 2, 1991. BSME, U. Tex., 1981; MSME, Portland State U., 1985. Rsch. asst. U. Tex., Austin, 1979-81; engring. asst. Tex. Nuclear Div., Austin, 1981; rsch. engr. Portland (Oreg.) State U., 1983-83; prodn. mgr. Hy-Tek Industries, Beaverton, Oreg., 1983-84; gen. mgr. Electro Mech. Tech. Inc., West Linn, Oreg., 1984-91; mgr. transducer design project Kistler-Morse Corp., Redmond, Wash., 1991—. Author: Carbide Insert Crusher, 1981, Control System Computer Aided Design, 1983, Transient Flow Inverse Study Calculation of Unsaturated Permeability of Wood, 1985; patentee load cell for weighting contents of storage vessels. Chmn. local spiritual assembly Baha'i Faith, Bothell, Wash., 1993-94. Mem. Tau Beta Pi, Pi Tau Sigma. Home: 9005 NE 151st Pl Bothell WA 98011-4590

PISCIOTTA, SAMUEL JAMES, small business owner; b. Pueblo, Colo., Dec. 10, 1938; s. Sam Jr. and Eva May (Padula) P.; m. Cynthia Diane Garrett, Aug. 8, 1961; children: Samuel, Pamela, Richard, Michael. BA, Western State Coll., 1967. Pres., mgr. Pueblo (Colo.) Bus. Men's Club, Inc., DBA Capt. Sam's Family Athletic Club, Inc., 1961—. Composer symphonic music. Co-founder, v.p. Pueblo Performing Arts Guild, 1986—; founder, co-organizer Pueblo Office So. Colo. Better Bus. Bur., 1985—, chmn. bd. 1987-88). Recipient Order of Arrow, Boy Scouts Am., 1972; named Small Bus. Man of Yr., Colo. C. of C., 1988. Mem. Nat. Swim and Recreation Assn. (pres. 1976-77), Greater Pueblo Sports Assn. and Hall of Fame (co-founder 1972), Pueblo Jaycees (state bd. dirs. 1973-75), Pueblo Bus. Exch. (co-founder 1982, pres. 1984), Kiwanis (bd. dirs. 1986), Elks, Masons, Knight Templar, Jesters, Shriners (potentate 1992), Dante Alighieri Soc., Royal Order Scotland, Order of Quetzalcoatl (charter camaxtli 1992), Tau Kappa Epsilon. Republican. Home: 27 Pedregal Ln Pueblo CO 81005-2917 Office: Capt Sam's Family Athletic Club Inc 1500 W 4th St Pueblo CO 81004-1207

PISKOTI, JAMES, artist, educator; b. Logan, W.Va., July 5, 1944; s. Charles and Mary (Bokkon) P.; m. Carol Lee, June 16, 1984. BS in Design, U. Mich., 1967; MFA, Yale U., 1969. Prof. art Calif. State Coll. Stanislaus, Turlock, Calif., 1969—; one man shows include Djurovich Gallery, Sacramento, 1986, Slusser Gallery, U. Mich., Ann Arbor, 1985; exhibited group shows including Flint (Mich.) Annual, 1964, 65, 67, Detroit Inst. Arts, 1965, 66, 70, Grand Rapids Art Mus., 1967, SUNY, New Paltz, 1968, Flint Jr. Coll., 1968, Concert Gallery, Flint, 1968, Alpha Gallery, Boston, 1969, Otis Art Inst. of Los Angeles County, 1969, Calif. State Coll. Stanislaus Gallery, 1970, San Francisco Mus. Art, 1971, Yale Sch. Art and Arch., 1972, Haggin Mus., 1972, Olive Hyde Art Ctr., 1972, John Bolles Gallery, 1973, Palo Alto Art Ctr., 1974, Appalachian State U., 1975, Oakland Mus. Art, Santa Barbara Mus., 1975, E. B. Crocker Art Gallery, 1976, U. Pacific, 1976, Calif. State Fair Art Exhbn., 1977, Provincetown Art Assn. Competition, 1977, Calif. State U., 1978, Tex. Tech U., 1978, Univ. Art Gallery, N.Mex. State U., 1979, Dulin Gallery Art, Knoxville, 1979, Calif. Poly. Inst., 1979, Decordova Mus., 1979-80, Art Space Gallery, 1982, Cerritos Coll. Gallery, 1982, Brand Library Art Galleries, 1983, San Jose Inst. Contemporary Art, 1983, Calif. State Fair, 1983, Richmond (Calif.) Art Ctr., 1983, Pinnacle Gallery, Rochester, N.Y., 1984, Manhattan (Kans.) Nat. Print, 1985, Haggin Mus., Stockton, Calif., 1985, Univ. City Arts League, Phila., 1985, Thomas Center Gallery, Gainsville, Fla., 1987, others. Recipient 1st place Cash award Calif. State Fair, 1983, 3d place Cash award No. Calif. Regional Print Competition, Palo Alto, 1984, Jurors award U. Mich. Sch. Art, Ann Arbor, 1984, Purchase award Minot State Coll., N.D., 1985; Calif. State Coll. grantee 1973, 74, 75, 77, 78, and others. Mem. Calif. Soc. Printmakers, Los Angeles Printmaking Soc. Address: Calif State U Stanislaus Art Dept 801 Monte Vista Ave Turlock CA 95382

PISTER, KARL STARK, engineering educator; b. Stockton, Calif., June 27, 1925; s. Edwin LeRoy and Mary Kimball (Smith) P.; m. Rita Olsen, Nov. 18, 1950; children: Francis, Therese, Anita, Jacinta, Claire, Kristofer. BS with honors, U. Calif., Berkeley, 1945, MS, 1948; PhD, U. Ill., 1952. Instr. theoretical and applied mechanics U. Ill., 1949-52; mem. faculty U. Calif., Berkeley, 1952-91, prof. engring. scis., 1962—, Roy W. Carlson prof. engring., 1985-90, dean Coll. Engring., 1980-90; chancellor U. Calif., Santa Cruz, 1991—, now pres., chancellor; Richard Merton guest prof. U. Stuttgart, W. Ger., 1978; cons. to govt. and industry; bd. dirs. Monterey Bay Aquarium Rsch. Inst.; bd. trustees Monterey Inst. Internat. Studies; chmn. bd. Calif. Coun. Sci. and Tech. Author research papers in field; assoc. editor: Computer Methods in Applied Mechanics and Engring, 1972, Jour. Optimization Theory and Applications, 1982; editorial adv. bd. Encyclopedia Phys. Sci. and Tech. Served with USNR, World War II. Recipient Wason rsch. medal Am. Concrete Inst., 1960, Vincent Bendix Minorities in Engring. award Am. Soc. for Engring. Edn., 1988, Lamme medal, 1993, Alumni Honor award U. Ill. Coll. Engring., Disting. Engring. Alumnus award U. Calif. Coll. Engring. Fellow ASME, AAAS, Am. Acad. Mechanics, Am. Acad. Arts and Scis., Calif. Acad. Scis. (hon.); mem. NAE, ASCE, Soc. Engring. Sci. Office: U Calif Santa Cruz Office of Chancellor 1156 High St Santa Cruz CA 95064-1077

PITCHER, HELEN IONE, healthcare services administrator; b. Colorado Springs, Colo., Aug. 6, 1931; d. William Forest Medlock and Frankie La Vone (Hamilton) Tweed; m. Richard Edwin Pitcher, Sept. 16, 1949; children: Dushka Myers, Suzanne, Marc. Student, U. Colo., 1962-64, Ariz. State U., 1966, Maricopa Tech. Coll., 1967, Scottsdale C.C., 1979-81. Design draftsman Sundstrand Aviation, Denver, 1962-65; tech. illustrator Sperry, Phoenix, 1966-68; art dir. Integrated Circuit Engring., Scottsdale, Ariz., 1968-71, dir. advt., 1981-92; advt. artist Motorola Inc., Phoenix, 1971-74; pres. Pitcher Tech. Pubs., Scottsdale, 1974-81; nursing cons. Nursing Cons. Connection, Fountain Hills, Ariz., 1993—. Profl. advisor Paradise Valley Sch. Dist., Phoenix, 1984—; mem. bd. advisors graphic arts dept. Ariz. State U., Tempe. mem. Nat. Audio Visual Assn., Bus. Profl. Advt. Assn. (treas. 1982-86), Direct Mktg. Club. Democrat. Mem. Ch. Christ. Home: 13681 N Pima Rd Scottsdale AZ 85260-4105

PITERNICK, ANNE BREARLEY, librarian, educator; b. Blackburn, Eng.; emigrated to Can., 1956, naturalized, 1965; d. Walter and Ellen (Harris) Clayton; m. George Piternick, May 6, 1971. B.A., U. Manchester (Eng.), 1948, F.L.A., 1983. Mem. library staff U. B.C., Vancouver, Can., 1956-66; head sci. div. U. B.C., 1960-61, head social scis. div., 1965-66, prof. Sch. Library, Archival and Info. Studies, 1966-91, prof. emerita, 1991—, assoc. dean Faculty of Arts, 1985-90; mem. Nat. Com. Bibliog. Svcs. Can., 1975-80, chmn. com. on bibliography and info. services for social scis. and humanities, 1981-84; mem. adv. acad. panel Social Scis. and Humanities Research Council, 1981-84; mem. adv. bd. Nat. Libr. Can., 1978-84; mem. Nat. Adv. Com. Culture Stats., 1985-90; organizer Confs. on Can. Bibliography, 1974, 81; pres. Can. Assn. Spl. Librs. Info. Svcs., 1969-70, Can. Libr. Assn., 1976-77. Author articles on electronic info. svcs. and scholarly communication. Recipient Queen's Silver Jubilee medal, 1977, award for Spl. Librarianship Can. Assn. Spl. Librs. and Info. Svcs., 1987, 75th Anniversary medal U.B.C., 1990, Can. 125 medal, 1993. Fellow Council on Library Resources (1980). Home: 1849 W 63rd Ave, Vancouver, BC Canada V6P 2H9

PITNEY, JOHN JOSEPH, JR., political science educator; b. Saratoga Springs, N.Y., June 18, 1955; s. John Joseph and Mary Katherine (Furey) P.; m. Lisa Michelle Minshew, May 27, 1989. BA, Union Coll., Schenectady, N.Y., 1977; MA, Yale U., 1978, MPhil, 1981, PhD, 1985. Legis. asst. N.Y. State Senate, Albany, 1978-80; Congl. fellow Am. Polit. Sci. Assn., Washington, 1983-84; sr. domestic policy analyst Ho. Rep. Rsch., Washington, 1984-86; dep. rsch. dir. Rep. Nat. Com., Washington, 1989-91; asst. prof. Claremont McKenna Coll., Claremont, Calif., 1986-94; assoc. prof. Claremont McKenna Coll., Claremont, 1994—. Co-author: Congress' Permanent Minority?, 1994; contbr. articles to profl. jours. Dep. editor Rep. Nat. Conv. platform, Houston, 1992; rsch. advisor George Bush for Pres., Washington, 1988. Recipient rsch. grant Gould Humanities Ctr., Claremont, 1992, grad. fellowship Nat. Sci. Found., 1977, Danforth Found., St. Louis, 1977. Mem. Am. Polit. Sci. Assn. (rsch. grant 1987), Western Polit. Sci. Assn., Nat. Assn. Scholars, Phi Beta Kappa (chpt. sec. 1993-95), Pi Sigma Alpha. Republican. Office: Govt Dept Claremont McKenna Coll 850 Columbia Ave Claremont CA 91711

PITT, CHARLES HORACE, metallurgy educator, consultant; b. Fremont, Wis., Aug. 9, 1929; s. Horace B. and Nelda Ruby (Sommer) P.; m. Margaret Louise Park, June 8, 1956; children—Roland, William, Jennifer, Rosanne, Barbara. B.S., U. Wis., 1951; Ph.D., U. Utah, 1959. Registered prof. engr., Wash., Utah. Engr. Gen. Electric Co., Richland, Wash., 1951-53; asst. prof. metallurgy dept U. Utah, Salt Lake City, 1959-65, assoc. prof., 1965-71, prof., 1971—. Served with U.S. Army, 1954-56. Mem. Nat. Assn. Corrosion Engrs., Am. Soc. Metals (chmn. Utah chpt. 1967-68), AIME, Phi Kappa Phi (pres. Utah chpt. 1980-81). Mem. Ch. of Jesus Christ of Latter-day Saints. Home: 3082 S 400 W Bountiful UT 84010-7813 Office: U Utah Metallurgy Dept 412 Wbb Salt Lake City UT 84112-1113

PITT, WILLIAM ALEXANDER, cardiologist; b. Vancouver, B.C., Can., July 17, 1942; came to U.S., 1970; s. Reginald William and Una Sylvia (Alexander) P.; m. Judith Mae Wilson, May 21, 1965; children: William Matthew, Joanne Katharine. MD, U. B.C., Vancouver, 1967. Diplomate Royal Coll. Physicians Can. Intern, Mercy Hosp., San Diego, 1967-68, resident, 1970-71; resident Vancouver Gen. Hosp., 1968-70, U. Calif., San Diego, 1971-72; assoc. dir. cardiology Mercy Hosp., San Diego, 1972-92; with So. Calif. Cardiology Med. Group, San Diego, 1984—; pvt. practice Clin. Cons. Cardiology. bd. trustees San Diego Found. for Med. Care, 1983-89, pres., chmn. bd. trustees, 1986-88, med. dir., 1991—; bd. dirs. Mut. Assn. for Profl. Services, Phila., 1984-92; pres. Alternet Med. Svcs., Inc., 1992—. Fellow Royal Coll. Physicians Can., Am. Coll. Cardiology (assoc.); mem. AMA, Am. Heart Assn., Calif. Med. Assn., San Diego County Med. Soc., San Diego County Heart Assn. (bd. dirs. 1982-88). Episcopalian. Office: So Calif Cardiology Med Group 6386 Alvarado Ct Ste 101 San Diego CA 92120-4906

PITTS, BARBARA TOWLE, accountant; b. St. Paul, Minn., Nov. 8, 1944; d. James Francis and Helen (Gorman) Towle; m. E.R. Pitts, Oct. 19, 1965; 1 child, Paris Tucker Pitts. BSBA, U. Ala., 1980. CPA, Wash., Tenn. Prin. Barbara M. Pitts Assocs., Fayetteville, Tenn., 1982-90, Barbara M. Pitts CPA, Seattle, 1990—. Bd. dirs. United Way Lincoln County, Fayetteville, 1989, Lincoln County Bd. Edn., Fayetteville, 1988-90; mem. planning com. Tenn. Hist. Soc., Nashville, 1989. Recipient Cert. of Recognition Tenn. Main St. Program, 1989; named Woman of Yr. Fayetteville Bus. and Profl. Women, 1988. Mem. AICPA, Wash. Soc. CPA, Northwest Watercolor Soc. (treas.). Home: 3515 E Marion St Seattle WA 98122-5258

PITTS, TERENCE RANDOLPH, curator, museum director; b. St. Louis, Feb. 5, 1950; s. Benjamin Randolph and Barbara Avalon (Gilliam) P.; m. Judith Ellen Brown, Oct. 21, 1979; children: Jacob Richard, Rebecca Suzanne. BA, U. Ill., 1972, MLS, 1974, MA in Art History U. Ariz., 1986. Registrar Ctr. for Creative Photography, Tucson, 1976-77, curator, 1978-88, dir., 1989—; cons. Art and Architecture Thesaurus, Getty Mus., 1984—. Author: (with others) George Fiske: Yosemite Photographer, 1981, Edward Weston: Color Photography; book reviews Picturescope Mag., 1983-86; author: exhibition catalogs: Four Spanish Photographers, 100 Years of Photography in the American West, Photography in the American Grain; contbr. reviews to mags. NEA fellow, 1983; travel grantee Nat. Mus. Act, 1979, rsch. grantee U. Ariz., 1983.

PITTS, WILLIAM CLARENCE, physicist; b. Seattle, Apr. 19, 1929; s. Clarence H. and Emily B. (Kepp) P.; m. Joanne R. Lawson, May 18, 1952 (dec. Jan. 1978); children: Starr R., Nancy H.; m. Patricia A. Kirkland, May 1, 1981. BS in Physics, U. Wash., 1951; postgrad., Stanford U., 1951-58. Rsch. scientist NACA/NASA, Moffett Field, Calif., 1951-86, Eloret Inst., Moffett Field, 1986—. Contbr. numerous articles to profl. publs.; inventor two-force measuring balance for earth orbit application. Office: NASA Ames Rsch Ctr N 234-1 Moffett Field CA 94035

PITZAK, AVERY NORMAN, advertising and marketing consultant; b. Highland Park, Mich., Oct. 23, 1946; s. Irving and Mollie (Portner) P.; m. Susan Starr, June 24, 1969; 1 child, Sandra Beth. BSc in Geology, Wayne State U., Detroit, 1968, MSc in Geology, 1976. Geologist Exxon Co., U.S.A., Harvey, La., 1977-78; offshore geologist Exxon Co., U.S.A., New Orleans, 1978-79; prodn. geologist Husky Oil Co., Denver, 1979-82; devel. geologist Northwest Exploration Co., Denver, 1982-84; geol. and mktg. cons. M.A.R. Cons. Co., Aurora, Colo., 1984-88, pres., owner, 1988—; mem. adv. bd. Warren Technical, 1990-92. Author: Make Your Business Card Incredibly Effective!, 1992; contbr. articles to profl. jours. and newspapers. Sgt. USAF, 1968-72. Mem. Internat. Platform Assn. (invitee), Am. Bus. Card Club (pres. 1990—). Office: The Business Card PO Box 460297 Aurora CO 80046-0297

PITZER, KENNETH SANBORN, chemist, educator; b. Pomona, Calif., Jan. 6, 1914; s. Russell K. and Flora (Sanborn) P.; m. Jean Mosher, July 1935; children—Ann, Russell, John. B.S., Calif. Inst. Tech., 1935; Ph.D., U. Calif., 1937; D.Sc., Wesleyan U., 1962; LL.D., U. Calif. at Berkeley, 1963, Mills Coll., 1969. Instr. chemistry U. Calif., 1937-39, asst. prof., 1939-42, asso. prof., 1942-45, prof., 1945-61, asst. dean letters and sci., 1947-48, dean coll. chemistry, 1951-60; pres., prof. chemistry Rice U., Houston, 1961-68, Stanford, Calif., 1968-70; prof. chemistry U. Calif. at Berkeley, 1971—; tech. dir. Md. Rsch. Lab. for OSRD, 1943-44; dir. research U.S. AEC, 1949-51, mem. gen. adv. com., 1958-65, chmn., 1960-62; Centenary lectr. Chem. Soc. Gt. Britain, 1978; mem. adv. bd. U.S. Naval Ordnance Test Sta., 1956-59, chmn., 1958-59; mem. commn. chem. thermo-dynamics Internat. Union Pure and Applied Chemistry, 1953-61; mem. Pres.'s Sci. Adv. Com., 1965-68; dir. Owens-Ill., Inc., 1967-86. Author: (with others) Selected Values of Properties of Hydrocarbons, 1947, Quantum Chemistry, 1953, (with L. Brewer) Thermodynamics, 2d edit., 1961, Activity Coefficients in Electrolyte Solutions, 2d edit., 1992, Molecular Structure and Statistical Thermodynamics, 1993, 3d edit., 1995; editor: Prentice-Hall Chemistry series, 1955-61; contbr. articles to profl. jours. Trustee Pitzer Coll., 1966—; Mem. program com. for phys. scis. Sloan Found., 1955-60. Recipient Precision Sci. Co. award in petroleum chemistry, 1950, Clayton prize Instn. Mech. Engrs., London, 1958, Priestley medal Am. Chem. Soc., 1969, Nat. medal for sci., 1975, Robert A. Welch award, 1984, Clark Kerr award U. Calif., Berkeley, 1991; named to Outstanding Young Men, U.S. Jaycees, 1950; named to Hall of Fame of Alpha Chi Sigma, 1994; Guggenheim fellow, 1951. Fellow Am. Nuclear Soc., Am. Inst. Chemists (Gold Medal award 1976), Am. Acad. Arts and Scis., Am. Phys. Soc.; mem. AAAS, NAS (councilor 1964-67, 73-76), Am. Chem. Soc. (award pure chemistry 1943, Gilbert N. Lewis medal 1965, Williard Gibbs medal 1976), Faraday Soc., Geochem. Soc., Am. Philos. Soc., Chem. Soc. (London), Am. Coun. Edn., Chemists Club (hon.), Bohemian Club, Cosmos Club of Washington. Clubs: Chemists (hon.), Bohemian; Cosmos (Washington). Home: 12 Eagle Hl Kensington CA 94707-1408 Office: U Calif Dept Chemistry Berkeley CA 94720

PIVNICKA, BARBARA MILLIKEN, marketing executive; b. Fremont, Nebr., Apr. 24, 1953; d. James Dale and Jane (Little) Milliken; m. Richard J. Pivnicka, Sept. 24, 1977. BA in English and Art History magna cum laude, U. San Francisco, 1975. Dir. pub. rels. Schwabacher/Frey Inc., San Francisco, 1977-79; dir. mktg. and pub. rels. Beier and Gunderson, Oakland, Calif., 1979-83; dir. pub. rels. Servamatic Systems Inc., San Ramon, Calif., 1983-86; mgr. investor rels. Deloitte & Touche, San Francisco, 1986—. Editor Servamatic Jour., 1983. Dir. Sanctuary for the Homeless, San Francisco, 1986—; mem. Arthritis Found., San Francisco, 1986— ; co-chair Commonwealth Club Arts Sect., chmn. 1994; chmn. Transitional Housing Fund. Mem. Internat. Assn. Bus. Communicators, Am. Mgmt. Soc., Sales and Mktg. Execs. Assn. Republican. Roman Catholic. Home: 2220 Stockbridge Ave Woodside CA 94062 Office: Deloitte & Touche 50 Fremont St San Francisco CA 94105-2230

PIZZORNO, JOSEPH EGIDIO, JR., college president; b. San Gabriel, Calif., Dec. 7, 1947; s. Joseph Egidio Sr. and Mary (Carmela) P.; m. Mavis Bonnar (div. Oct. 1983); 1 child, Raven Muir; m. Lara Elise Udell, Sept. 28, 1985; 1 child, Galen Udell. BS with Distinction, Harvey Mudd Coll., Claremont, Calif., 1969; Naturopathic Doctor with honors, Nat. Coll. Naturopathic Medicine, Portland, Oreg., 1975. Rsch. asst. Lockheed Aircraft, Ontario, Calif., 1968; rsch. technologist U. Wash., Seattle, 1970-75; practice naturopathic medicine Seattle, 1975-80, practice midwifery, 1978-82; pres., researcher Bastyr U., Seattle, 1978—; pres. Coun. on Naturopathic Med. Edn., Portland, Oreg., 1985-87; apptd. adv. panel safety and efficacy of dietary supplements U.S. Office of Tech. Assessment, 1993-95; sr. med. advisor Alternative and Complementary Therapies, 1995—. Co-author: A Textbook of Natural Medicine, 1985, Encyclopedia of Natural Medicine, 1990; contbg. editor Let's Live mag., Los Angeles, 1987—; contbr. articles to profl. jours. Mem. Am. Assn. Naturopathic Physicians (bd. dirs. 1984—), Wash. Assn. Naturopathic Physicians (edn. dir. 1976), Seattle Midwifery Sch. (edn. com. 1978-91), Northwest Sci. Fiction Soc. Libertarian. Home: 13502 42nd St NE Seattle WA 98125 Office: Bastyr Coll 144 NE 54th St Seattle WA 98105-3753

PLAMBECK, TOM, mechanical engineer; b. Covina, Calif., Aug. 14, 1935; s. Charles L. and Iola B. (Wilson) P.; m. Madeline Catherine Kilian, Dec. 16, 1956 (div. 1972); children: Teri Plambeck Brown, Kevin; m. Winifred R. Breakey White, Aug. 25, 1985. BS in Physics, Calif. Inst. Tech., 1956, MS in Mech. Engring., 1957. Mem. tech. staff Hughes Aircraft Co., Culver City, Calif., 1956-58; mech. engr. Raytheon Co., Goleta, Calif., 1958-62; mem. tech. staff Def. Rsch. Corp., Santa Barbara, Calif., 1962-74; dept. dir. Geodynamics Corp., Santa Barbara, Calif., 1974-78; staff scientist Gen. Rsch. Corp., Santa Barbara, Calif., 1978-92; sr. staff analyst Toyon Rsch. Corp., Goleta, 1992—; computer cons. Plambeck Consulting, Santa Barbara, 1989-92. Chmn. Mediation Task Force, Santa Barbara, 1980s.

PLAMONDON, MAYNARD ALFRED, civil engineer; b. Hanover, N.H., Dec. 29, 1940; s. Maynard Albert and Lucille Norma (McNamara) P.; m. Mona Clare Peck, June 17, 1961; children: Michael A., Steven D. BS, U. N.H., 1962; MS, U. Ill., 1964, PhD, 1966. Registered profl. engr., N.Mex. Tech. advisor civil engring. AFWL, Kirtland AFB, N.Mex., 1966-87; v.p. engring. tech. BDM Internat., Albuquerque, 1987-88; prin. engr. Applied Rsch. Assn., Inc., Albuquerque, 1988—. Fellow ASCE. Home: 3705 Tewa Dr NE Albuquerque NM 87111-4317 Office: Applied Rsch Assoc PO Box 3588 Albuquerque NM 87190-3588

PLANE, FREDRICK ALAN, county official; b. Eugene, Oreg., Dec. 25, 1955; s. Richard Alan Plane and Dorothy Elizabeth (Morris) Touchstone; m. Karen Maureen Dirksen Bryant, Aug. 1, 1976 (div. Sept. 1987); children: Alison Michelle, Breanna Renee; m. Sheila Kay Brown, Oct. 18, 1992. BS in Bus., Calif. State U., Bakersfield, 1978, MPA, 1994. Bus. mgr. Niles Med. Group, Bakersfield, 1978-80; sr. buyer County Kern, Bakersfield, 1980-87, dep. adminstrv. officer, 1988—. Sec., treas. So. Valley Toastmasters, Bakersfield, 1989, pres., 1990, v.p., 1991, 92; bd. dirs. Kern County Econ. Opportunity Corp., Bakersfield, 1992—. Mem. Am. Soc. Pub. Adminstrn. (sec. 1991, pres. 1992, 93, past pres. 1994). Democrat. Home: 11901 April Ann Ave Bakersfield CA 93312-4601 Office: Kern County Adminstrv Office 5th Fl 1115 Truxtun Ave Bakersfield CA 93301

PLANN, SUSAN JOAN, linguist, foreign language educator; b. Hollywood, Calif., Aug. 3, 1946; d. Paul I. and Paula Mae (Witaschek) P.; m. Gonzalo Navajas, Nov. 8, 1975 (div. May 1988); 1 child, Paul Navajas-Plann. BA in Spanish, UCLA, 1968, MA in Spanish, 1970, PhD in Romance Linguistics, 1975. Prof. Spanish and Portuguese UCLA, 1975—; cons. Projecto Educativo Comunitario, L.A. Author: Relative Clauses in Spanish, 1980; reviewer jours. Hispanic Linguistics, Issues in Applied Linguistics, Linguistic Inquiry; contbr. articles to profl. jours. Del Amo Faculty fellow UCLA, 1985; Com. Internat. Exch. of Scholars grantee Fulbright, 1987; named Powrie Doctor Chair Deaf Studies Gallaudet U., 1994. Mem. Linguistic Soc. Am., Deaf History Internat. Office: UCLA Dept Spanish & Portuguese 405 Hilgard Ave Los Angeles CA 90024-1301

PLAT, RICHARD VERTIN, corporate finance executive; b. San Jose, Calif., July 14, 1929; s. Gaston and Frances (Vertin) P.; children from previous marriage: Julie, Carl, Marsha; m. Janet Toll Davidson, Dec. 19, 1992. BEE, U. Santa Clara, 1951; MBA, Washington U., St. Louis, 1957. Sr. ind. econ. Stanford Rsch. Inst., Menlo Park, Calif., 1959-65; dir. planning Litton Industries, Inc., Beverly Hills, Calif., 1965-70; v.p. Waltham Industries, N.Y.C., 1970-71, Computer Machinery Corp., L.A., 1971-77; exec. v.p. Pacific Scientific Co., Newport Beach, Calif., 1978—; bd. dirs. Powertec Indsl. Corp., Rock Hill, S.C., Automation Intelligence, Inc., Duluth, Ga., High Yield Tech., Inc., Sunnyvale, Calif., Helisys, Inc., Torrance, Calif., Pacific Sci. Ltd., Royce Thompson Ltd., Eng., Pacific Sci. S.A.R.L., France, Pacific Sci. GmbH, Eduard Bautz GmbH, Fed. Republic of Germany, Pacific Sci. Internat., Inc., U.S., V.I. 1st lt. U.S. Army, 1951-54. Mem. Fin. Execs. Inst. (bd. dirs., v.p. 1984—). Republican. Club: Jonathan (L.A.), Balboa Bay (Newport Beach, Calif.). Home: 2027 Bayside Dr Corona Del Mar CA 92625-1847 Office: Pacific Scientific Co 620 Newport Center Dr Newport Beach CA 92660-6420

PLATT, JAMES ROBERT, business executive; b. Batavia, N.Y., Oct. 23, 1948; s. Robert John and Mildred J. (Foote) P.; m. Shelly A. Tunis, May 24, 1980; children: Shane Christopher, Tristan Robert. BS, SUNY, Brockport, 1970; MA, Ariz. State U., 1982. Cert. tchr., N.Y. Inside sales supr. Mallco Distbrs., Phoenix, 1972-77; grad. teaching asst. Ariz. State U., Tempe, 1978-79; sales rep. Wisco Equipment Co., Inc., Phoenix, 1979-82, sales mgr., 1984-88; sales rep. Clyde Hardware Co., Tucson, 1982-84; v.p. Wistech Controls, Phoenix, 1988—. Mem. Ariz. Coun. Excellence. Regents scholar SUNY, 1966-70. Mem. Instrument Soc. Am., Young Execs.-Fluid Power Distbrs. Assn., Am. Soc. Environ. History, Soc. Mfg. Engrs., Phi Alpha Theta. Office: Wistech Controls 4810 S 36th St Phoenix AZ 85040-2905

PLATT, JOSEPH BEAVEN, former college president; b. Portland, Oreg., Aug. 12, 1915; s. William Bradbury and Mary (Beaven) P.; m. Jean Ferguson Rusk, Feb. 9, 1946; children: Ann Ferguson Walker, Elizabeth Beaven Garrow. BA, U. Rochester, 1937; PhD, Cornell U., 1942; LLD, U. So. Calif., 1969, Claremont McKenna Coll., 1982; DSc, Harvey Mudd Coll., 1981. Instr. physics U. Rochester, N.Y., 1941-43, from asst. prof. to prof., 1946-56, assoc. chmn. dept. physics, 1954-56; staff mem. radiation lab. MIT, Cambridge, 1943-46; pres. Harvey Mudd Coll., Claremont, Calif., 1956-76, now part-time sr. prof. physics; pres. Claremont U. Ctr., 1976-81; trustee Aerospace Corp., 1972-85, Consortium for Advancement of Pvt. Higher Edn., 1985-92; chief physics br. AEC, 1949-51; cons. U.S. Office Ordnance Rsch., NSF, 1953-56; mem. com. on sci. in UNESCO, Nat. Acad. Scis.-NRC, 1960-62, mem. com. on internat. orgns. and programs, 1962-64; sci. advisor U.S. Del., UNESCO Gen. Conf., Paris, 1960, alt. del., 1962; mem. panel on internat. sci. Pres.'s Sci. Adv. Com., 1961; chmn. Subcom. on Sino-Am. Sci. Cooperation, 1965-79; trustee Analytic Svcs., Inc., 1958-89, chmn., 1961-89; mem. adv. com. on sci. edn. NSF, 1965-70, 72-76, chmn., 1969-70, 73-74, 74-75; bd. dirs. Lincoln Found., 1979-85, Bell & Howell Corp., 1978-88, Am. Mut. Fund, 1981-88, DeVry, Inc., 1984-87, Sigma Rsch., 1983-87, Jacobs Engring. Co., 1978-86. Author: Harvey Mudd College: The First Twenty YEars, 1994. Trustee China Found. for Promotion of Edn. and Culture, 1966—, Carnegie Found. for Advancement Tchg., 1970-78; chmn. select com. Master Plan for Higher Edn. Calif., 1971-73; mem. Carnegie Coun. for Policy Studies in Higher Edn., 1975-80. Fellow Am. Phys. Soc.; mem. IEEE, Automobile Club So. Calif. (bd. dirs. 1973-90, chmn. bd. dirs. 1986-87), Calif. Club, Sunset Club, Twilight Club, Cosmos Club, Bohemian Club, Phi Beta Kappa, Sigma Xi, Phi Kappa Phi. Home: 452 W 11th St Claremont CA 91711-3833

PLATT, LEWIS EMMETT, electronics company executive; b. Johnson City, N.Y., Apr. 11, 1941; s. Norval Lewis and Margaret Dora (Williams) P.; m. Joan Ellen Redmund, Jan. 15, 1983; children: Caryn, Laura, Amanda, Hillary. BME, Cornell U., 1964; MBA, U. Pa., 1966. With Hewlett Packard, Waltham, Mass., 1966-71, engring. mgr., 1971-74, ops. mgr., 1976-77, div. gen. mgr., 1974-80, group gen. mgr., Palo Alto, Calif., 1980-84, v.p., 1983-85, exec. v.p., 1987-92, pres., CEO, chmn., 1993—; dir. Molex Inc., Lisle, Ill.; trustee Pacific Telesis. Trustee Waltham Hosp., 1978-80, Wharton Sch. Bd. Overseers, 1993; mem. Mid-Penisula YMCA, 1980-86; mem. Mid-Peninsula YMCA, 1980—, Cornell U. Coun., 1992, Computer Sys. Policy Project, 1993, Calif. Bus. Roundtable, 1993, Bus. Coun., 1993, Bay Area Coun., 1993, Bus. Roundtable, 1993; vice chmn. Y Coun., 1989. Recipient Red Triangle award Min-Peninsula YMCA, 1992, Internat. Citizens award World Forum Silicon Valley, San Jose, Calif., 1994. Mem. IEEE, Sci. Apparatus Mfg. Assn. (dir. 1978-80). Office: Hewlett Packard Co 3000 Hanover St Palo Alto CA 94304-1112

PLATTNER, RICHARD SERBER, lawyer; b. N.Y.C., Aug. 10, 1952; s. Milton and Sallee Sarah (Serber) P.; m. Susan M. Madden, June 4, 1976 (div. June 1979); m. Susan K. Morris, Mar. 30, 1983; children: Samuel Morris, Katherine Elise. BA cum laude, Mich. State U., 1973; JD, Ariz. State U., 1977. Bar: Ariz. 1977, U.S. Dist. Ct. Ariz. 1977, U.S. Ct. Appeals (9th cir.) 1987; cert. specialist personal injury and wrongful death. Assoc. Wolfe & Harris, Pa., 1977-79, Monbleau, Vermeire & Turley, Phoenix, 1979-81, Phillips & Lyon, Phoenix, 1981; sole practice Phoenix, 1982-91; ptnr. Plattner Verderame, P.C., 1991—. Editor: Trial Judges of Maricopa County, 1985; co-editor Jury Verdict Research newsletter, 1982-83. Posse comdr. Maricopa County Sheriff Adj. Posse, 1986—; judge pro tem Maricopa County Superior Ct., 1986—, Ariz. Ct. Appeals, 1993—. Mem. Assn. Trial Lawyers Am. (sustaining mem.), Ariz. Trial Lawyers Assn. (sustaining mem., editor Ariz. Appellate Highlights, 1985—, bd. dirs., 1987—, pres. 1991), Ariz. Bar Assn. (mem. civil practice and procedure com. 1988-91, 92—, civil jury instrn. com. 1991), Maricopa County Bar Assn., Phoenix Trial Lawyers Assn. (bd. dirs. 1983—, pres. 1986-87), Ariz. Bus. and Profl. Assn. (pres. 1984-86). Office: 333 E Osborn Rd Ste 315 Phoenix AZ 85012-2365

PLAZAK, DEAN JAMES, physician, psychiatrist; b. Wisconsin Rapids, Wis., June 1, 1927; s. James Joseph and Amelia Elizabeth (Liska) Plzak; m. Carole Jane Marshall, Feb. 21, 1964; children: David, Deanna, Nancy, Elisabeth. BS in Med. Sci., U. Wis., 1949, MD, 1951. Diplomate Am. Bd. Psychiatry and Neurology, Am. Bd. Forensic Psychiatry. Intern Abington Meml. Hosp., 1951-52; resident U. Colo. Med. Ctr., 1952-53, Nat. Naval Med. Corps, 1954-56; pvt. practice forensic psychiatry, gen. psychiatry Boulder, Colo., 1957—; Nat. Naval Med. Ctr.; forensic psychiatry cons. to state and fed. cts., Colo. and others, 1957—; nat. examiner Am. Bd. Psychiatry and Neurology, 1974—. Contbr. articles to profl. jours. Co-founder devel. disabilities program and various offices Boulder County Devel. Disabilities Ctr., 1968-91. Lt. M.C. USN, 1950-57. Fellow Am. Acad. Forensic Scis.; mem. Am. Psychiat. Assn. (life), Am. Acad. Psychiatry and The Law. Office: Dean J Plazak MD 2260 Baseline Rd Ste 105 Boulder CO 80302-7737

PLEDGER, LELAND JAMES (LEE PLEDGER), publisher, travel writer; b. Black River Falls, Wis., June 14, 1943; s. Lyle James and Verna L. (Nelson) P.; m. Sharon Dell Mathews, Dec. 30, 1964; children: Troy Edward, Shawnna Patrice. Student, Kans. State U., 1961-63; BA, U. Alaska, 1966; grad., Columbia Sch. Broadcasting, 1971. Sales rep. Xerox Corp., Torrance, Calif., 1968-70, adminstrv. mgr., 1970-72; mgr., owner Marshall (Wis.) Lumber Co., Inc., Calif., 1972-77; radio broadcaster Sta. WTTN, Watertown, Wis., 1975-76; pub. Freighter Travel News, Roy, Wash., 1977—, tour leader, 1977—; piano tuner, Alaska, Wis., Oreg., Wash., 1964—; guide Pacific Trailways and Evergreen Stage Lines, Salem, Oreg., 1972-77. Contbr. numerous articles on travel and automotives to mags., newspapers, and periodicals; inventor air purification and fuel enhancement devices. Alderman Village of Marshall, 1973-75; bd. pres. Unity of Salem (Oreg.) Ch., 1985-86. 1st lt. U.S. Army, 1966-68. Named One of Outstanding Young Men in Am. 1975, Village of Marshall, Wis. and Farmers & Merchants Bank, Marshall. Fellow Am. Assn. Travel Editors, World Ship Soc. Home: 3524 Harts Lake Rd Roy WA 98580 Office: Freighter Travel Club Am 3524 Harts Lake Loop Rd S Roy WA 98580-9195

PLESSNER, GERALD MAURICE, business executive; b. St. Louis, Oct. 10, 1934; s. Herman and Rose (Goldstein) P.; m. Carole Renee Spirtas, May 25, 1959; children: Mitchell Scott, Janice Aurelia, Ellen Beth Bartell. BA, Missouri Valley Coll., Marshall, Mo., 1957. Cert. fund-raising exec. Exec. dir. Boy Scouts Am., various locations, 1957-75; mng. editor Consumer Newsletter, L.A., 1975-76; pres. Fundraiser, Inc., Arcadia, Calif., 1976—, Non-Profit Network, Arcadia, 1986-90, Am. Breathing Machines, Inc., Arcadia, 1992—; adj. faculty U. So. Calif., L.A., 1985-92, UCLA, 1992-94. Author: Ency. of Fundraising, 1980-90; pub. video tapes: Internat. Certification in Fund Raising, 1987. Mem. Nat. Soc. Fund Raising Exec. (vice chmn., treas. 1988-91, greater L.A. chpt. pres. 1984-86, Outstanding Profl. 1983). Office: American Breathing Machines PO Box 661148 Arcadia CA 91066-1148

PLETCHER, PEGGY JO, program director; b. Wheeler, Tex., Apr. 2, 1932; d. Robert Lee and Carrie Leola (McClain) Rodgers; m. Bernard A. Pletcher, Nov. 10, 1955 (div. 1989); children: Robert A., George F., David J. BS, Baylor U., 1953; MEd in Counseling, Coll. Idaho, 1974; PhD, U. Idaho, 1979. Cert. home economist, secondary tchr., counselor. Tchr. Perryton (Tex.) High Sch., 1953-55; home economist S.W. Pub. Svc., Lubbock, Tex., 1955-56; extension home economist U. Idaho, Boise, 1968-80; dir. Dist. I Coll. Agr. U. Idaho, Moscow, 1980-89, head communications Coll. Agr., 1983-84, dir. Sch. Home Econ., 1986-92; dir. Dist. II Coll. Agriculture U. Idaho, Boise, 1992—; cons. Postharvest Inst. Perishables U. Idaho, Moscow, 1983-84. Author: Implementation of Technology in Rural Areas, 1983, Influencing Legislation, 1979, Electronic Mail, 1983. Dir. U. Idaho Credit Union, Moscow, 1984-89; pres. Soroptimists Internat., Boise, Idaho, 1980; mem. Toastmasters Internat., Moscow, Idaho, 1989-92, Boise, 1992—. Nat. Assn. Extension Home Economists fellow, 1974; recipient Superior Svc. award USDA, 1973, provost's fellow Bryn Mawr Summer Inst. for Women in Higher Edn. Adminstrn., 1992. Mem. AAUW, Am. Home Econs. Assn. (leader award 1993), Nat. Assn. Home Econ. Adminstrs., Idaho Home Econs. Assn. (Disting. Svc. award 1987), Epsilon Sigma Phi, Gamma Sigma Delta, Phi Delta Kappa. Office: Univ Idaho Boise Ctr 800 Park Blvd Boise ID 83712-7742

PLETCHER, ROBERT ANTHONY, lawyer; b. Lubbock, Tex., Aug. 31, 1956; s. Bernard Anthony and Peggy Jo (Rogers) P.; m. Mikele Lynn Hamre, Aug. 22, 1987; children: Brittany Jordan, Brandon David. BS in Civil Engring., BS in Bus., U. Colo., 1979; JD, Western State U., 1992. Registered profl. engr., Colo., Calif.; lic. real estate broker, Tex., Colo., Calif. Mgr. constrn. Gilbane Bldg. Co., Providence, 1979-80; design engr. Bovay Engrs., Houston, 1980-81; project engr. Canfield, Kraettli and Porter, Steamboat Springs, Colo., 1981-82, Zeiler and Pennock, Denver, 1982-83, Holland West Inc., Denver, 1983-87; with Rick Engring. Co., San Diego, 1987-92; atty. Dicaro, Highman, D'Anthony, Dillard, Fuller & Gregory, San Diego, 1993—. Mem. ASCE, Am. Pub. Works Assn., San Diego County Bar Assn. Republican. Roman Catholic. Office: Dicaro Highman D'Anthony Dillard Gregor & Fuller 4350 La Jolla Village Dr Ste 900 San Diego CA 92122-1247

PLETSCH, MARIE ELEANOR, plastic surgeon; b. Walkerton, Ont., Can., May 3, 1938; came to U.S. 1962; d. Ernest John and Olive Wilhemina (Hossfeld) P.; m. Ludwig Philip Breiling, Aug. 25, 1967; children: John, Michael, Anne. Dr. Med., U. Toronto, 1962. Diplomate Am. Bd. Plastic Surgery. Intern Cook County Hosp., Chgo., 1962-63, resident, gen. surgery, 1963-64; resident, gen. surgery St. Mary's Hosp., San Francisco, 1964-66; resident in plastic surgery St. Francis Hosp., San Francisco, 1966-69; practice med. specializing in plastic surgery Santa Cruz, Calif., 1969—; adminstr. Plasticenter, Inc., Santa Cruz, 1976-88, med. dir., 1987-88. Mem. AMA, Am. Soc. Plastic and Reconstructive Surgeons, Calif. Soc. Plastic Surgeons (mem. coun. 1986—, sec. 1989-93, v.p. 1994-95), Calif. Med. Assn., Assn. Calif. Surgery Ctrs. (pres. 1988-92), Santa Cruz County Med. Soc. (bd. govs. 1983-88, 1992-94), Santa Cruz Surgery Ctr. (bd. dirs. 1988-93). Roman Catholic. Office: Santa Cruz Can-Am Med Group 1669 Dominican Way Santa Cruz CA 95065-1523

PLEWS, LARRY DALE, aerospace engineer; b. Spokane, Wash., Oct. 1, 1941; s. Albert Dale and Mable Lillian (Day) P.; m. Ellen Marie Child, Dec. 19, 1969. BSME, Gonzaga U., Spokane, 1963. Aerospace engr. NASA Lewis Rsch. Ctr., Cleve., 1963-66, Pacific Missile Ctr., Point Mugu, Calif., 1966-67, Air Force Flight Test Ctr., Edwards AFB, Calif., 1967—. Chmn. Airport Commn., City of Tehachapi, Calif., 1991—; mem. High Tech. Coun., L.A., 1994. Fellow AIAA (assoc.; sect. chmn. 1972); mem. Soc. Automotive Engrs., Coast Guard Aux., Tehachapi Soc. Pilots (pres. 1988-92). Office: 412 TW/TSIDM 25 N Wolfe Ave Edwards CA 93524

PLOMGREN, RONALD ARTHUR, retail executive; b. Oakland, Calif., Apr. 1, 1934; s. Arthur Ivar and Augusta W. (Nelson) P.; m. Sharon Jensen, May 15, 1959; children: David, Susan, Karen. B.S., U. Calif.-Berkeley, 1956. Clk. Longs Drug Stores, Walnut Creek, Calif., 1948-56; clk. to store mgr. Long Drug Stores, Walnut Creek, Calif., 1957-68; property supr., constrn. mgr. Longs Drug Stores, Walnut Creek, Calif., 1968-74, v.p., 1974-76, sr. v.p., 1976—, dir.; dir. APS, Oakland. Vice chmn. Orinda Parks and Recreation Dist., Calif., 1974-78; vice chmn. Orinda Found., 1978-83; chmn. Orinda Planning Commn.; co-chmn. U. Calif.-Berkeley Engring. Fund. Mem. Nat. Assn. Corp. Real Estate Execs. (sec. No. Calif. chpt.). Office: Longs Drug Stores Inc 141 N Civic Dr Walnut Creek CA 94596-3815

PLOMP, TEUNIS (TONY PLOMP), minister; b. Rotterdam, The Netherlands, Jan. 28, 1938; arrived in Can., 1951; s. Teunis and Cornelia (Pietersma) P.; m. Margaret Louise Bone, July 21, 1962; children: Jennifer Anne, Deborah Adele. BA, U. B.C. (Can.), Vancouver, 1960; BD, Knox Coll., Toronto, Ont., Can., 1963, DD (hon.), 1988. Ordained to ministry Presbyn. Ch., 1963. Minister Goforth Meml. Presbyn. Ch., Saskatoon, Sask., Can., 1963-68, Richmond (B.C.) Presbyn. Ch., 1968—; clerk Presbytery of Westminster, Vancouver, 1969—; moderator 113th Gen. Assembly Presbyn. Ch. Can., 1987-88, dep. clk., 1987—; chaplain New Haven Correctional Centre, Burnaby, B.C. Contbr. mag. column You Were Asking, 1982-89. Office: Richmond Presbyn Ch, 7111 #2 Rd, Richmond, BC Canada V7C 3L7

PLOPPER, CHARLES GEORGE, anatomist, cell biologist; b. Oakland, Calif., June 16, 1944; s. George Eli and Josephine Viola (Gates) P.; m. Suzanne May, Nov. 9, 1969. AB, U. Calif., Davis, 1967, PhD, 1972. Chief. electron microscopy br. U.S. Army Med. Research Nutrition Lab., Denver, 1972-73; vis. scientist Calif. Primate Research Ctr., Davis, 1974-75; chief. electron microscopy div. Letterman Army Inst. Research, San Francisco, 1974-75; asst. prof. U. Hawaii Sch. Medicine, Honolulu, 1975-77; assoc. prof. Kuwait U. Sch. Medicine, 1977-78; sr. staff fellow Nat. Inst. Environ. Health Sci. Research, Triangle Park, N.C., 1978-79; from asst. to assoc. prof. U. Calif. Sch. Vet. Medicine, Davis, 1979-86, dept. chmn., 1984-88; prof. anatomy, physiology and cell biology, Sch. Vet. Medicine U. Calif., Davis, 1986—; mem. study sect. NIH div. Research Grants, Bethesda, Md., 1986-90; Paley vis. prof. Boston U. Sch. Medicine, 1985; vis. pulmonary scholar Duke U., U. N.C., N.C. State U., 1991. Served to capt. U.S. Army, 1972-75. Mem. Am. Soc. Cell Biology, Am. Thoracic Soc., Am. Assn. Antomists, Am. Assn. Pathologists, Anat. Soc. Great Britain and Ireland, Davis Aquatic Masters (bd. dirs.). Democrat. Club: Davis Aquatic Masters. Home: 511 Hubble St Davis CA 95616-2720 Office: Univ Calif Sch Vet Medicine Dept Anatomy Physiol Cell Biology Davis CA 95616

PLOUGH, CHARLES TOBIAS, JR., electronic research and development executive; b. Oakland, Calif., Sept. 7, 1926; s. Charles Tobias Sr. and Miriam Lucille (Miller) P.; m. Jean Elizabeth Rose, June 13, 1950 (div. May 1969); children: Charles III, Cathleen, Mark, Barbara; m. Janet Mary Ansell Lumley, July 5, 1969; children: Mark Ansell Lumley, Simon John Lumley. AB with honors, Amherst Coll., 1950; BSEE with honors, U. Calif., Berkeley, 1953. Mgr. tech. devel. Fairchild Semiconductor, Palo Alto, Calif., 1958-71; v.p. Multi-State Devices, Montreal, Can., 1971-78; mgr. research and devel. Dale Electronics, Norfolk, Nebr., 1978-89, ret., 1989. Patentee in field. Mem. Lions (sec. Norfolk 1982-86). Home: 2030 Quail Run Dr NE Albuquerque NM 87122-1100

PLOUTZ, LLOYD GENE, management executive, marketing professional, historian; b. El Centro, Calif., June 26, 1942; s. Dennis Author and Betty Jean (Clark) P.; m. Susan Lucille Brown, July 14, 1964 (div. Mar. 1977); children: Corey Earl, Kerri Jean; m. Denice Margaret Sabers, Jan. 14, 1989; stepchildren: Allen, Stephany. AA, Modesto Jr. Coll., 1968. Lic. real estate broker, Calif.; lic. bldg. contr., Calif. Salesman Modesto (Calif.) Tobacco and Candy, 1963-65; mgmt. trainee Sears Roebuck and Co., Modesto, 1965-69; mng. agt. Lincoln Nat. Life Ins., Modesto, 1969-74; v.p. Mines Engring. and Equip., Hickman, Calif., 1974-80; exec. v.p. Belt Printing and Litho Co., Modesto, 1980-85; chief funding officer 1st Deposit Savs. Bank, San Francisco, 1985-87; pres. Mariposa Land and Devel. Co., Modesto, 1987—, Lloyd Ploutz Enterprises, Modesto, 1964—, Quail Mining Corp., Incline Village, Nev., 1993—, Q.M. Excel, Incline Village, 1994—; state dir. Calif. Assn. Realtors, Modesto, 1975-78, Toastmasters Internat., Modesto, 1975-79, dist. gov.; v.p. Modesto Bd. Realtors, 1978. Author: Hugag History, 1988, E Clampus Vitus 40 Years, 1994. Chmn. Stanislaus Ctrl. Rep. Com., Modesto, 1977-79, Stanislaus Housing Resources Com., Modesto, 1975-77; founding dir., life mem. Great Valley Mus., 1974-78; founding dir., pres., life mem. La Grange Mus. and Hist., 1992—; pres. La Grange Improvement Assn., 1995. With U.S. Army, 1960-63. Mem. E Clampus Vitus (pres. 1969—, dir. grand coun. 1994—, Noble Grand Humbug), Toastmasters, Masons, Shriners, Elks. Mem. LDS Ch. Home: 1833 Woodview Ct Ceres CA 95307-3580 Office: PO Box 4217 928 12th St Ste 401 Modesto CA 95354

PLUM, RICHARD EUGENE, retired flight engineer; b. Alliance, Ohio, Feb. 24, 1928; s. Vernon and Mida Lucile (Halverstadt) P.; m. Bea Hernandez; children: Pamela Sue Lachman, Patricia Ann Quaranto, Peggy Lynn, Richard John. Grad., Calif. Flyers Sch. Aeronautics. Cert. master aircraft mechanic, flight engr. Flight engr. Am. Airlines, Inc., Dallas, Ft. Worth, 1951-90, ret., 1990; check airman Am. Airlines, Chgo., 1968-70. Editor Pub Newsletter, 1964-68. Served with USN, 1945-47. Recipient Top Gun award Western Fast Draw Assn., 1969. Mem. NRA, Calif. Rifle and Pistol Assn., World Fast Draw Assn. (chmn. 1984-89, editor-pub. newsletter 1984-89, Top Gun award 1988), Mid-Western Fast Draw Assn. (chmn. 1964-68, Mid-Am. champion 1967, Chgo. conf. champion 1968), Old Frontier Thumbers Conf., Ohio Fast Draw Assn., Ariz. Fast Draw Assn., Kans. Fast Draw Assn., Restless Guns Fast Draw Club, Bordertown Fast Draw Club. Republican. Home: 83 E Cargil Dr Sierra Vista AZ 85635-1139

PLUM, THOMAS SCHUNIOR, software company executive; b. Washington, Sept. 8, 1943; s. George E. and Ruby (Pritchett) S.; m. Joan Hall, Sept. 18, 1975 (dec. Aug. 1989); m. Lana Lee Eastman Plum, Oct. 1, 1990. BS, Rice U., 1965; PhD, U. Mich., 1972. Asst. prof. SUNY, Binghamton, 1972-76; instr. Yourdon Inc., N.Y.C., 1976-78; mgr. AGS Computers, Piscataway, N.J., 1978-79; chmn. Plum Hall, Inc., Cardiff, N.J., 1979-89; pres. Plum Hall, Inc., Kamuela, Hawaii, 1990—; vice-chair X3J11, Washington, 1984-94; internat. rep. X3J16, Washington, 1991-94. Author: Learning to Program in C, 1982, C Programming Guidelines, 1983, Reliable Data Structures in C, 1985; co-author: C Programming Guidelines, 1991 (Jolt award 1992). Mem. Rotary Club North Hawaii (club svc.). Office: Plum Hall Inc PO Box 44610 Kamuela HI 96743-4610

PLUMLEE, KENNETH B., health products executive; b. 1983. BA in Journalism, Pacific Union Coll., 1983. Product mgmt. and mktg. dir. Hanford Cmty. Hosp., Hartford, Calif., 1983-86; with Adventist Health Sys./West Referral Sys. Group, 1986-88; co-founder, pres. Access Health Mktg. Inc., 1988—. Office: Accrss Health Marketing Inc 11020 White Rock Rd Rancho Cordova CA 95670-6010*

PLUMLEY, S. PATRIC, retail executive; b. West Hamlin, W.Va., Jan. 2, 1949; s. Caudle and Nellie Brook (Honaker) P.; m. Rose M. McBee, Jan. 16, 1970. BA in Acctg. cum laude, U. South Fla., 1980, M Accountancy, 1986. CPA, Fla., Calif. Mem. acctg. staff Lucky Stores, Inc., Tampa, Fla., 1973-82, acctg. mgr., 1982-84, contr., 1984-86; v.p., contr. Lucky Stores, Inc., Buena Park, Calif., 1986-90; sr. v.p. adminstrn. Lucky Stores, Inc., Dublin, Calif., 1990-94; with Am. Stores, Inc., Salt Lake City, 1994—. Vice chmn. bd. dirs. Olive Crest, homes for abused children, Anaheim, Calif., 1988-90; bd. dirs. Jr. Achievement of Bay Area, 1992-94. With USN, 1967-71. Mem. AICPA, Inst. Mgmt. Accts. (cert.). Baptist. Office: Am Stores Inc 709 E South Temple Salt Lake City UT 84102-1205

PLUMMER, CHARLES MCDONALD, retired community college administrator; b. Garibaldi, Oreg., Mar. 21, 1934; s. Earl Carlos and Florence Elta (Lamb) P.; m. Diane Hansen, July 7, 1957; children: Jeffrey Earl, Susan Lynn Plummer Johnson. BS in Edn., So. Oreg. State Coll., 1957; MEd, U. Oreg., 1967. Tchr. Canyonville (Oreg.) High Sch., 1957-59, Glendale (Oreg.) High Sch., 1959-60; tchr. Roseburg (Oreg.) High Sch., 1960-66, dir. student activities, pub. info., 1963-66; registrar Umpqua C.C., Roseburg, 1966-68, dean admissions and records, 1968-74, dean instrn., 1974-86, v.p. instructional svcs., 1986-94; ret., 1994; exec. bd. N.W. Student Success Conf., Portland, 1989-92; co-founder, staff Pacific NW Great Tchrs. Seminar, Portland, 1979-94. Pres. Greater Douglas United Way, 1989, bd. dirs. 1983-94; pres. Roseburg Concert Chorale, 1982-94; bd. dirs. Roseburg Community Concert Assn., 1989—. Mem. Kiwanis Club (pres. 1979, bd. dirs. 1973-79), Oreg. Coun. of Instrnl. Adminstrs. (chair 1990), Roseburg Area C. of C. (bd. dirs. 1982-85, Roseburg First Citizen 1991), Phi Delta Kappa. Presbyterian. Home: 567 NE Winchester St Roseburg OR 97470-3259

PLUMMER, STEVEN TSOSIE, bishop; b. Coalmine, N. Mex., Aug. 14, 1944; m. Catherine B. Tso; children: Brian Tso, Byron Tso, Steven, Jr., Cathlena. Student, San Juan Community Coll., Farmington, N. Mex., Phoenix (Ariz.) Jr. Coll., Ch. Divinity Sch. of the Pacific, San Francisco. Ordained deacon, The Episc. Ch., 1975, priest, 1976. Deacon, priest Good Shepherd Mission, Fort Defiance, Ariz., 1976-77; vicar St. John the Baptizer, Montezuma Creek, Utah, 1977-83; regional vicar for Utah Bluff, Utah, from 1983; consecrated bishop Episc. Ch. in Navajoland, Farmington, N. Mex.,

1990; mem. Episc. Council of Indian Ministries. Office: The Episcopal Ch Navajoland Area Mission PO Box 720 Farmington NM 87499-0720*

PLUNKETT, MARVIN WAYNE, data processing company executive; b. Roseburg, Oreg., Mar. 16, 1952; s. Kenneth V. and Minnie E. (Bible) P. Student, Umpqua C.C., 1978-79. Founder, owner Profit Systems Software, Roseburg, 1979—. Mem. Roseburg Optimist Club (bd. dirs. 1993—). Office: Profit Systems Software 1641 NW Rutter Ln Roseburg OR 97470-1949

PLUNKETT, MICHAEL C., psychotherapist; b. Nyack, N.Y., Feb. 23, 1953; s. Stephen J. Jr. and Naomi M. (Davies) P.; m. Barbara E. Sellers, Sept. 2, 1983; 1 child, Joshua E. BSBA, St. Thomas Aquinas Coll., 1975; MA in Psychology, U. No. Colo., 1986. Lic. profl. counselor, Colo.; cert. addiction counselor, Colo., instr. in prevention of HIV disease among substance abusers, Nat. Inst. Drug Abuse, instr. in outreach and retention of methadone clients. Diagnostic coord. El Paso County Dept. Health and Environ./McMaster Ctr., Colorado Springs, 1987—; instr. psychology Pikes Peak C.C., Colorado Springs, 1988-94;, 1988—. Bd. dirs. So. Colo. AIDS Project, 1989—; mem. ad hoc com. HIV Prevention Community Planning Com., 1994; bd. dirs. Pikes Peak Region Nat. Coun. Alcoholism and Drug Dependency, 1988-91, vice-chmn., 1990. Office: El Paso County Health/Envrn 301 S Union Blvd Colorado Springs CO 80910-3123

POCKLINGTON, PETER H., business executive; b. Regina, Sask., Can., Nov. 18, 1941; s. Basil B. and Eileen (Dempsey) P.; m. Eva d. Jack McAvoy, June 2, 1974; 4 children. Pres. Westown Ford, Tilbury, Ont., Can., 1967-69; pres. Chatham, Ont., 1969-71, Edmonton, Alta., Can., 1971-82; chmn. Pocklington Fin. Corp., Edmonton, 1982—; owner, gov. Edmonton Oiler Hockey Club, 1976—; owner Edmonton Trapper Triple A Baseball Club, 1981—; formed Hartford Properties, Inc., 1985, Edmonton, Club Fit Inc., 1990; purchased Superior Furniture Systems Mfg., Inc., 1987, Canbra Foods Ltd., 1988, Green Acre Farms, Sabastool, Miss., 1988, Green Acre Foods Inc., Nacadoches, Tex., 1988. Mem. Mayfair Golf and Country Club, Edmonton Golf and Country Club, Vintage Golf Club, Indian Wells, Calif. Office: Pocklington Fin Corp Ltd, 2500 Sun Life Pl 10123-99 St, Edmonton, AB Canada T5J 3H1 also: Edmonton Oilers, Edmonton, AB Canada T5B 4M9

POCRASS, RICHARD DALE, management consultant; b. Meadville, Pa., Mar. 7, 1940; s. Irving F. and Roslyn (Sperber) P.; m. Rena Levy, Feb. 3, 1968; children: Michael B., S. Douglas. BS in Math., U. Pitts., 1962; MBA in Fin., 1964. EDP sales mgr. NCR Corp., Pitts., 1962-67, retail mktg. mgr., Los Angeles, 1972-74; v.p., dir. Nanoseconds Systems, Fairfield, Conn., 1967-69, dir. 1968-72; v.p. gen. mgr. Hart Jewelry Co., Warren, Ohio, 1969-71, dir. 1981-84; mktg. mgr. Data Source Corps subs. Hercules, Inc., El Segundo, 1974-75; pres. Webster-Pocrass & O'Neil (name changed to Pocrass Assocs. 1981), Los Angeles, 1976—, Health Tech. Inc. Pub.; chief exec. officer, chmn. bd. dirs. Chocolates a la Carte, Sylmar, Calif. Author: The Recruitment Letter; author (with Maronde) Drug Abuse Study for Hoffman LaRoche, 1980. Bd. dirs. West Valley Little League. Mem. Am. Mktg. Assn. L.A. Speakers Bur., Soc. for Human Resource Mgmt., Woodland Hills C. of C., Bank Mktg. Assn., Retail Controllers Assn., Calif. Exec. Recruiters Assn., Pers. and Indsl. Rels. Assn., Internat. Platform Assn., Rotary. Republican. Jewish. Home: 18815 Paseo Nuevo Dr Tarzana CA 91356-5136 Office: 13190 Telfair Ave Sylmar CA 91342-3573

PODBER, JAKE, broadcasting educator; b. July 3, 1954. BA in Theatre, U. Fla., 1976; MFA in Film, Columbia U., 1982. Stage mgr. Manhattan Yellow Pages Theatre, Atlanta, 1976-77; prodn. asst., 1982-85; producer Relax Video, N.Y.C., 1985-91; cameraman, prodn. coord. Churchill Films, Santa Monica, Calif., 1992; mem. adj. faculty Orange Coast Coll., Costa Mesa, Calif., 1993—. Home: PO Box 461038 Los Angeles CA 90046-9038

PODBOY, JOHN WATTS, clinical, forensic psychologist; b. York, Pa., Sept. 27, 1943; s. August John and Harriett Virginia (Watts) P.; 1 son, Matthew John. B.A., Dickinson Coll., 1966; M.S., San Diego State Coll., 1971; Ph.D., U. Ariz., 1973. Dir., Vets. Counseling Center, U. Ariz., Tucson, 1972-73; project dir. San Mateo County (Calif.) Human Relations Dept., Redwood City, 1974; staff psychologist Sonoma State Hosp., Eldridge, Calif., 1975-81; cons. clin. psychologist Comprehensive Care Corp., Newport Beach, Calif., 1974-75, Sonoma County (Calif.) Probation Dept., 1976-88; pvt. practice, Kenwood, Calif., 1982—; cons. to No. Calif. Superior Cts., 1983-85; asst. prof. Sonoma State U., 1977-81; dir. Sonoma Diagnostic and Remedial Center, 1979-82. Chmn. San Mateo County Diabetes Assn., 1975. Served to lt. USNR, 1966-69. Fellow Am. Coll. Forensic Psychology, Am. Bd. Med. Psychotherapists (fellow); mem. APA, Western Psychol. Assn., Redwood Psychol. Assn. (pres. 1983), Nat. Council Alcoholism, Nat. Rehab. Assn. Home: PO Box 488 Kenwood CA 95452-0488

PODD, MARSHA DIANNE, small business owner, nurse; b. Washington, Apr. 14, 1951; d. John Francis and Gretchen (Green) P. BS in Child Devel., U. Calif., Davis, 1973; AA in Nursing, De Anza Coll., 1978. RN, Calif., cert. Lactation Educator. Nurse Palo Alto (Calif.) Med. Clinic, 1973-78, St. Joseph Hosp., Orange, Calif., 1979-80, Diet Ctr., Petaluma, Calif., 1982-89; maternal/child home care nurse specialist, 1991—; nurse Pealuma Valley Hosp., 1980-86; cons. Diet Ctr., Rexburg, Idaho, 1984-85; co-founder Health in Motion Prodns., 1987-91, maternal/child nurse specialist, 1991—. Nurse Vietnam Refugee Placement, Hamilton AFB, 1980; earthquake relief vol. ARC, San Francisco, 1989-90. Recipient award for one of top ten fastest growing Diet Ctrs. in U.S. and Can., 1987. Mem. Bay Area Diet Ctr. Assn. (pres. 1984, treas. 1987-88), U. Calif. Aggie Alumni Assn. Republican. Home: 1108 Susan Way Novato CA 94947-6919

POE, LENORA MADISON, psychotherapist and author; b. New Bern, Ala., Jan. 3, 1934; d. Tommy and Carrie (Norfleet) Madison; m. Levi Mathis Poe, June 21, 1957; children: Michael DeWayne, Michaelle DaNita Burke. BS, Stillman Coll., Tuscaloosa, Ala., 1956; MA, Calif. State U., Hayward, 1972, MS, 1980; PhD, Ctr. for Psychol. Studies, Albany, Calif., 1991. Lic. marriage, family and child therapist. Classroom tchr. Perry County Schs., Uniontown, Ala., 1956-59, Richmond (Calif.) Unified Schs., 1962-69; guidance counselor Berkeley (Calif.) Unified Schs., 1969-79; psychotherapist in pvt. practice Berkeley, 1982—, West Coast Children's Ctr., El Cerrito, Calif., 1982—; lectr. Grandparents as Parents, 1992—; part-time prof. J.F.K. U., Orinda, Calif., 1993; del. White House Conf. on Aging, Washington, 1995; cons. in field; staff cons. Cmty. Adult Day Health Svcs., Highland Gen. Hosp., Oakland. Author: Black Grandparents as Parents, 1992. Pres. nat. bd. dirs. Stillman Coll., 1992—; mentor cons. Black Women Organized for Ednl. Devel., Oakland, Calif., 1994—; mem. adv. bd. Nat. Black Aging Network, Oakland, 1992—; founding mem., advisor Realmindcas Civic Club, Richmond, 1976—; mem. Families United Against Crack Cocaine, Oakland; bd. dirs. Ctr. for Elders for Independence, Oakland; trustee Ctr. for Psychol. Studies, Albany; chairperson Grandparents Caregivers Advocacy Task Force, Oakland, Calif.; mem. bd. edn. Ministry of Ch. by Side of Road, Berkeley; also others. Recipient cert. of Appreciation African Am. Hist. and Cultural Soc., San Francisco, 1992, President's citation for Excellence Nat. Assn. for Equal Opportunity in Higher Edn., 1993, award Excellence in Edn. Nat. Coun. Negro Women, 1993, S award Stillman Coll., Appreciation award for Excellence Nystrom Elem. Sch., Richmond, 1994, Outstanding Alumna of the Yr. award Ctr. for Psychological Studies, 1995. Mem. Nat. Coalition Grandparents as Parents (adv. com. 1992—), No. Coalition Grandparents as Parents (co-chmn. 1991-93), Stillman Coll. Nat. Alumni Assn. (pres.). Home: 940 Arlington Ave Berkeley CA 94707-1929 Office: 2034 Blake St Ste 1 Berkeley CA 94704-2604

POEDTKE, CARL HENRY GEORGE, JR., management consultant; b. Chgo., Jan. 12, 1938; s. Carl H. Sr. and Irene F. (Eskilson) P.; m. Marie-Paule M. Thiriet, Mar. 10, 1962 (dec.); children: Gislaine Canavan, Carl Henry George III; m. Janice M. Barron, Aug. 26, 1991. BS, MIT, 1959. Mgr. value engring. Chgo. Rawhide Mfg. Co., Chgo., 1962-66; ptnr. Price Waterhouse, Chgo., Paris, N.Y.C., 1966-91; ret. Price Waterhouse, Chgo., 1991. Author: Managing and Accounting for Inventories, 1980; contbr. articles to profl. jours. Bd. dir. Guild Bd. Lyric Opera, Chgo., 1984-92; mem. vis. adv. com. sch. acctg. De Paul U., Chgo., 1986-91. 1st lt. U.S. Army, 1959-62. Fellow Am. Prodn. and Inventory Control Soc.; mem. AIIE (sr., cert.) Inst. Mgmt. Cons. (bd. dirs. 1987-90, life mem.), Coun. Cons. Orgns. (bd. dirs. 1989-90), Union League Club, Masons. Home: PO Box 677 Tesuque NM 87574-0677

POERTNER, LEE ANNE, English language educator; b. Salt Lake City, Nov. 4, 1936; d. Robert Gail Beckstrand and Norma Ruth (Tobias) Beckstrand Bueche; m. Jerry Vance Horner, July 8, 1954 (div. 1968); children: Jeri Lynn Horner, Alan Dale Horner; m. Kenneth Wayne Poertner, Dec. 26, 1979. BA, U. St. Thomas, Houston, 1963; MA, Ind. U., 1965. Tchr. McTigue Sch., Toledo, 1964-65, dean of girls, 1965-67; cellist Long Beach (Calif.) Symphony Orch., 1970-74; English prof. Long Beach City Coll., 1967—. cellist Long Beach Community Orchestra, 1992—. Mem. Aquinas Honor Soc., U. St. Thomas, 1960-63. Mem. NEA, Calif. Tchrs. Assn. Republican. Mormon. Office: Long Beach City Coll 4901 E Carson St Long Beach CA 90808-1706

POHL, JOHN HENNING, chemical engineer, consultant; b. Ft. Riley, Kans., May 29, 1944; s. Herbert Otto and Ellen Irene (Henning) P.; m. Judith Lynn Sykes, Aug. 10, 1968; children: J. Otto, Clint. AA, Sacramento City Coll., 1964; BS, U. Calif., Berkeley, 1966; MS, MIT, 1973, DSc, 1976. Inspector constrn. C.O. Henning Cons. Engrs., Sacramento, 1965; engr. E.I. du Pont Nemours, Wilmington, Del., 1966-70; rsch. asst. MIT, Cambridge, 1971-75, lectr., 1975-76; mem. tech. staff Sandia Nat. Labs., Livermore, Calif., 1976-81; dir. fossil fuels Energy and Environ. Rsch., Irvine, Calif., 1981-86; dir. R & D Energy Systems Assocs., Tustin, Calif., 1986-89; sr. scientist energy W.J. Schafer Assocs., Irvine, 1989-91; pres. Energy Internat., Laguna Hills, Calif., 1988—; sr. cons. ESA Engring., Laguna Hills, 1989—; v.p. Advanced Combustion Tech. Co., Hsinchu, Taiwan, 1993-95; v.p. tech. Energeo, Inc., San Mateo, Calif., 1995—. Contbr. articles to profl. jours.; patentee in field. Treas. Headstart, Cambridge, 1975-76. Recipient Sci. and Tech. Achievement award U.S. EPA, 1987, Best Energy Projects award Energy Commn., Taiwan, coal evaluation, 1989, Low NOx Burner, 1992. Mem. ASME (advisor corrosion and deposits com. 1989—, rsch. project subcom. 1994—), AIChE (combustion advisor 1988-92), Am. Flame Rsch. Com., Am. Chem. Soc., Combustion Inst. Western States (mem. exec. com. 1988—), Combustion Inst. (mem. program subcom. 1976—), Engring. Found. (mem. steering com. on ash deposits 1989—). Home: 26632 Cortina Dr Mission Viejo CA 92691-5429

POHLMAN, DAVID LAWRENCE, training systems consultant; b. Detroit, May 17, 1944; s. Lawrence Luther and Lois Betty (Huffcut) P.; m. Diane Lee Ewing, Dec. 27, 1967 (div. 1980); children: Scott David, Anne Kiersten; m. Katherine Margaret Wattigney, Dec. 11, 1981; children: Ann Margaret Williams, David Joseph Williams. BS in Edn., Ohio U., 1967; MA in Psychology, U. No. Colo., 1977. Commd. officer USAF, 1967, advanced through grades to lt. col.; instr. pilot USAF, Chandler, Ariz., 1975-78, rsch. pilot., 1978-82; div. chief USAF, San Antonio, 1982-87; ret., 1987; tng. div. mgr. Gallegos Rsch. Group, Wheatridge, Colo., 1987-88; mgr. fed. systems div. Andersen Consulting, Denver, 1988-90; pres. Dave Pohlman Assocs., Aurora, 1990—; com. chmn. Dept. Def., Washington, 1982-87, subcom. chmn. industry panel, 1988-92; subcom. mem. intersvc.-Industry Tng. Sys., Orlando, Fla., 1987; industry co-chmn. Computer-Aided Acquisition and Logistics Human Systems Components com., 1987-92; vice-chair Aurora Vets. Affairs Commn., 1993-95; mem. 6th Congrl. Dist. Vets. Adv. Coun., 1993. Contbr. articles to profl. publs. Mem. Am. Ednl. Rsch. Assn., Am. Def. Preparedness Assn., Nat. Security Indsl. Assn., Air Force Assn. Roman Catholic. Home: 2557 S Evanston St Aurora CO 80014-2519 Office: 15200 E Girard Ave Ste 4400 Aurora CO 80014-5040

POIGNANT, GARY DONALD, newspaper editor; b. Quesnel, B.C., Can., Mar. 12, 1957; s. Ernie Donald and Rose Marie (Zack) P.; m. Karen Patricia Morcom, Apr. 11, 1992; 1 child, Sean Luther. Diploma, Cariboo Coll., Kamloops, B.C. Reporter, photographer Fraser Valley Record, Mission, B.C., 1976, Maple Ridge (B.C.) Gazette, 1977-79; reporter Kamloops News, 1980, 81; asst. sports editor Kamloops Daily Sentinel, 1981; sr. reporter Edmonton Sun, Alta., Can., 1981-86, asst. city editor, 1986-88, city editor, 1988-92, asst. news editor, 1992—. Recipient Spl. Citation, Dunlop Awards, 1991. Home: 2020 89 St, Edmonton, AB Canada T6K 2A2 Office: The Edmonton Sun, 250, 4990-92 Ave, Edmonton, AB Canada T6K 2A2

POIMIROO, JOHN ROBERT, state agency administrator; b. San Mateo, Calif., Nov. 7, 1946; s. Maurice John and Irene Frances (Ducasse) P.; m. Joan Kathryn Gabler. AA, Coll. San Mateo, 1967; BA in Pub. Rels., San Jose State U., 1969; MA in Journalism, U. Colo., 1973. Grad. teaching asst. U. Colo., Boulder, 1972-73; dir. pub. rels. Lake Eldora Ski Area, Nederland, Calif., 1973-74; dir. mktg. Squaw Valley USA, Olympic Valley, Calif., 1974-75; gen. sales mgr. Marriott's Great Am., Santa Clara, Calif., 1975-81; v.p. Hoefer Amidei, San Francisco, 1981-82; group v.p. Ketchum Pub. Rels., San Francisco, 1982-85; v.p. mktg., pub. rels. Roaring Camp Inc., Felton, 1985-86; v.p. communications Yosemite (Calif.) Park & Curry Co., MCA Inc., 1986-92; dep. sec. tourism Calif. Trade and Commerce Agy. Divsn. Tourism, Sacramento, 1992—; photographer, travel writer. Capt. USN, 1969-72, USNR, 1965-95. Mem. Calif. Travel Industry Assn. (2nd v.p. 1987-88, v.p. 1988-89, pres. 1989—), Soc. Am. Travel Writers, Pub. Rels. Soc. Am., U.S. Ski Writers Assn. Roman Catholic.

POIROT, FRANCK JACQUES, software engineer; b. Thionville, France, Oct. 18, 1961; s. Gilles and Josette (Delmond) P. Degree in engring., Ecole Superieure d'Ingenieurs, 1986; PhD in Microelectronics, Poly. Inst., Grenoble, France, 1990. Software engr. VLSI Tech., San Jose, Calif., 1988-91; from software engring. mgr. to sr. software engr. Compass Design Automation, San Jose, 1991-94; staff software engr. Compass Design Automation, 1994—. Patentee in field. Mem. IEEE. Home: 1865 Lundy Ave San Jose CA 95131-1834

PŌKĀ LAENUI See BURGESS, HAYDEN FERN

POLAKOFF, KEITH IAN, historian, university administrator; b. N.Y.C., Dec. 12, 1941; s. Irwin L. and Edna (Sopkin) P.; m. Carol J. Gershuny, June 21, 1964; children: Amy Ellen, Adam Matthew. BA magna cum laude, Clark U., 1963; MA, Northwestern U., Evanston, Ill., 1966, PhD, 1968. Lectr. Herbert H. Lehman Coll., CUNY, 1967-69; asst. prof. history Calif. State U., Long Beach, 1969-73, assoc. prof. 1973-78, prof., 1978—, assoc. dean instrnl. support Sch. Social and Behavioral Scis., 1980-81, assoc. dean ednl. policy, 1981-84, dean, 1985-86; dean Sch. Fine Arts, 1984-85, asst. v.p. acad. affairs, dean grad. studies, 1986-90, assoc. v.p. acad. affairs, dean grad. studies, 1991—; co-chair Calif. Minority Grad. Edn. Forum, 1990—; mem. coun. Big West Conf. (formerly Pacific Coast Athletic Assn.), 1982-90, Western Collegiate Athletic Assn., 1982-85. Author: The Politics of Inertia, 1973, (with others) Generations of Americans, 1976, Political Parties in American History, 1981; contbg. author: The Presidents: A Reference History, 1984; editor: The History Tchr., 1972-77, prodn. mgr., 1977-80. Mem., clk. bd. trustees Los Alamitos Sch. Dist., 1980-81; mem. Los Alamitos Unified Sch. Dist. Bd. Edn., 1990-94, pres. 1992-93; chmn. adv. com. on facilities, Los Alamitos Sch. Dist., 1989, chair steering com. for measure K for kids, 1990; bd. dirs. Long Beach Opera Assn., 1981-89, pres. 1982-83, treas., 1987-88; bd. dirs. Los Alamitos Jr. Baseball, 1988-90, Los Alamitos Basball, 1990-92. Avocations: travel, photography. Home: 2971 Druid Ln Los Alamitos CA 90720-4948 Office: Calif State U 1250 N Bellflower Blvd Long Beach CA 90840-0006

POLAN, DAVID JAY, lawyer; b. Chgo., Feb. 16, 1951; s. Julius and Jeanne Warsaw (Fox) P.; m. Terri Susan Lapin, Aug. 3, 1980; children: Adam Michael, Daniel Jacob, Jennifer Leigh. BA, U. Ill., 1972; JD, John Marshall Law Sch., Chgo., 1975. Bar: Ill. 1975, Ariz. 1990, U.S. Dist. Ct. (no. dist.) Ill. 1975, U.S. Dist. Ct. Ariz. 1990, U.S. Ct. Appeals (7th cir.) 1977. Atty., Pritzker & Glass, Ltd., Chgo., 1975-78, Barnett, Ettinger, Glass, Berkson & Braverman, Chgo., 1978-79; gen. mgr. Y.P. Aurora, Ltd., Ill., 1979-83; counsel, corp. sec. JP Communications Co., Tucson, 1981-90; sta. mgr. KPOL-TV, Tucson, 1983-86, gen. mgr., 1986-90; gen. counsel Northtown Bus Svc., Ltd., Lincolnwood, Ill., 1975-88; gen. ptnr. THC Ptnrs., Chgo., 1980—; co-owner LV Pictures, Las Vegas, 1984-86. Active Orchard Village Assn. for Handicapped, Skokie, Ill., 1981-87, co-owner Rockford Lightning Continental Basketball Assn., 1986-91; mem. Soviet Jewry commn., Jewish Fedn. So. Ariz., Tucson, 1984, leadership devel. program, 1984-87, chmn., 1985-87, bd. dirs., 1985-91, active various coms.; bd. dirs. Congregation Bet Shalom, 1984, Congregation Anshei, Israel, 1993—; assoc. mem. Hadassah, Tucson, 1984; mem. nat. com. for leadership devel. Coun. Jewish Fedn., 1986-91, chmn. western area 1988-91; bd. dirs. Jewish Family and Children's Svcs., 1986-92, also sec. 1988-89, v.p. 1989-92; bd. dirs. Jewish Community Found., 1987-91, Tucsonans Say No to Drugs, 1986-87; bd. dirs., vice chmn. Ping-Welch's Championship LPGA Tournament, 1992. Recipient Community Svc. Award Jewish Fedn. So. Ariz., 1987, Meritorious Svc. award, 1988, Gary I. Sarver Young Man of Yr. award, 1989. Mem. Ariz. State Bar, Pima County Bar Assn., Tucson Pks. Found. (bd. dirs.), Volk Jewish Community Ctr. Club, Diehard Cubs Fan Club, Ventana Canyon Golf and Racquet Club. Office: 1200 E Ajo Way Ste 105 Tucson AZ 85713-5056

POLAN, MORRIS, librarian; b. St. Louis, Jan. 24, 1924; s. Jacob and Fannie (Poe) P.; m. Cecelia Hassan, Nov. 16, 1947 (div. 1974); children: Miriam, Ruth. Student, So. Ill. U., 1941-42; B.A., UCLA, 1949; postgrad., 1949-50; M.S. in L.S, U. So. Calif., 1951. Libr. Mcpl. Reference Libr., L.A., 1951-52; serials and reference libr. Hancock Libr. of Biology and Oceanography, U. So. Calif., L.A., 1952-55; periodicals libr. Calif. State U., L.A., 1955, supervising reference libr., 1956-57, chief reader svcs., 1958-64, acting coll. libr., 1965, univ. libr., 1966-89, univ. libr. emeritus, 1989—; libr. and media resources cons., 1990—; publs. coord. Edmund G. "Pat" Brown Inst. Pub. Affairs, 1992-94, pub. rels. assoc., 1995—; univ. adminstr. Ctr. Pub. Resources Calif. State U., 1980-86, mem. chancellor's library adv. com., 1984; lectr. library sci. U. So. Calif., 1967; mem. chancellor's library personnel study com. Calif. State Univs. and Colls., 1969, mem. adv. com. library devel., 1974; chmn. Council Calif. State Univ. and Colls. Library Dirs., 1967-68, 70, 74; Mem. adv. bd. U. So. Calif. Library Sch., 1966-69, Productivity Council of Southwest, 1981-84; mem. library edn. adv. com. U. Calif. System, 1966-70; mem. U. Calif.-Calif. State Univ. and Colls. Task Force on Library Co-op., 1974-76; co-founder Los Angeles Coop. Library Consortium, 1983. Editor: California Librarian, 1971-74. Mem. Com. to Advise Gov. on State Librarian, 1972; mem. planning com. Calif. Library Authority for Systems and Services, 1973-75, adv. council, 1977-80, long range planning group, 1979-81, pres. congress of mems., 1979; mem. adv. bd. Arnold Schoenberg Ins., U. So. Calif., 1974-86, 89-92, Edmund G. (Pat) Brown Inst. Pub. Affairs, 1987-89; exec. com. Roy Harris Archive, 1978-86; mem. Mayor's Blue Ribbon Com. on L.A. Pub. Libr., 1976-77; mem. bd. scholars El Pueblo State Hist. Park, 1978-91; chmn. Calif. del. White House Conf. on Libraries and Info. Services, 1979; bd. dirs. ETHIKON: Inst. Study Ethical Diversity, 1981-88; Calif. state coord. Ctr. for the Book in Library of Congress, 1986-89; mem. adv. com. Ctr. for Study of Media and Values, 1988-90; treas. Frank Casado Meml. Scholarship Fund, 1992-95. With USAF, 1943-46. Mem. ALA, Calif. Library Assn. (pres. 1975, chmn. govt. relations com. 1977). Office: Calif State U 5151 State University Dr Los Angeles CA 90032-4221

POLISAR, JOSEPH MICHAEL, protective services official; b. Bklyn., June 25, 1952; s. Ira Allen and Rose (Gimpelman) P.; m. Shirley Elizabeth Chavez, Nov. 1, 1986; children: Brooklyn Joseph, Savannah Janelle. BA in Mgmt., U. Phoenix, 1993; grad., FBI Acad., 1993; postgrad., FBI Nat. Exec. Inst., 1995. Officer, detective Albuquerque Police Dept., 1977-81, sgt., 1981-85, lt., 1985-92, capt., 1992-94, chief of police, 1994—; staff instr. Northwestern U., Evanston, Ill., 1989—. Fund raiser Am. Cancer Soc., Muscular Dystrophy, Juvenile Diabetes, Crimestoppers, Cystic Fibrosis. Recipient 1995 Albuquerque Human Rights award. Mem. Internat. Police Assn., FOP, Internat. Assn. Chiefs of Police, FBI Nat. Acad. Assn., Kiwanis. Office: Albuquerque Police Dept 400 Roma NW Albuquerque NM 87102

POLITES, DEMETRI JOHN, psychiatrist; b. New Orleans, Sept. 6, 1934. MD, La. State U., 1959. Diplomate Am. Bd. Psychiatry and Neurology. Intern S. Pacific Meml. Hosp., San Francisco, 1959-60; resident U. Va. Hosp., 1960-63; pvt. practice San Francisco, 1966—; mem. staff Calif. Pacific Med. Ctr., San Francisco, 1966—.

POLITTE, RICHARD ANDREW, social services administrator; b. St. Louis, Oct. 9, 1958; s. John A. and Theresa R. (Heilich) P.; m. Ruth C. Politte, Oct. 4, 1986. BS in Recreation, So. Ill. U., Edwardsville, 1981. Sr. program dir. South County YMCA, St. Louis, 1982-89; dir. health and phys. edn. West County YMCA, Chesterfield, Mo., 1989-91; assoc. exec. dir. Mid County YMCA, Brentwood, Mo., 1992-93; exec. dir. Lompoc Family YMCA, Calif., 1993—. Com. mem. Arnold (Mo.) City Libr., 1987-89; bd. dirs. Aquatic Safety Com. ARC; mem. Am. Heart Assn. Bd., Santa Barbara Fdn. steering com. Mem. Lompoc C. of C. (ambassador 1994—). Home: 204 S Rose St Lompoc CA 93436-6420 Office: Lompoc Family YMCA 201 W College Ave Lompoc CA 93436-4415

POLK, WILLIAM MERRILL, architect; b. Cleburne, Tex., July 26, 1935; s. William Merrill and Lucille (Ray) P.; m. Karla Leopold, July 26, 1958; children: Lucy Jennifer, Elizabeth Helene, Andrew James. B.A. in Architecture, Cornell U., Ithaca, N.Y., 1958. Registered architect, Wash., Hawaii, Idaho, Oreg., Mont., Calif., Nev., Wyo., Ariz., Ky., Tex., Utah. Architect NBBJ Group, Seattle, 1962-64; exec. v.p., ptnr. Waldron, Pomeroy, Polk & Smith, Seattle, 1964-81; ptnr., chief operating officer John Graham and Co., Seattle, 1981-85; prin. William Polk Assocs., Seattle; treas. Cornish Coll. Arts, Seattle, 1986-92. Author: (with others) The Architect's Handbook of Professional Practice, 1988. Mem. Wash. State Ho. of Reps., 1971-82, Speaker of house, 1981-83, Wash. State Redistricting Commn., 1991; trustee Hist. Soc. Seattle and King County, 1986-88; vice chmn. Washington Inst. for Policy Studies; bd. dirs. Met. Bd.-YMCA, Seattle, 1972-76, Ryther Child Ctr., 1977-90, Am. Legis. Exchange Council, Washington, 1977-83; bd. govs. Council on Nat. Policy, Washington, 1981-86; bd. dirs. Providence Hosp. Found., Seattle, 1984—, vice chmn., 1986, 87, chmn., 1988-90. Served to 1st lt. U.S. Army, 1958-60, to capt. Wash. N.G. Named Citizen of Yr. Wash. State Young Republicans, 1981. Fellow AIA (mem. govt. affairs adv. bd. 1982), Seattle C. of C. (1982). Mem. Evangelical Covenant Ch. Am. Clubs: Rainier, Bellevue Athletic. Lodge: Rotary. Home: 7220 92nd Ave SE Mercer Island WA 98040-5813 Office: William Polk Assocs 1120 Post Ave Seattle WA 98101-2915

POLL, MAX HENRY, hospital administrator; b. Fremont, Mich., Sept. 10, 1946; s. Henry and Margaret Poll; m. Judith Poll; children: Melanie, Amy. BA, Western Mich. U., 1964; M of Hosp. Adminstrn., U. Minn., 1972. Adminstrv. resident St. Luke's Hosp., Kansas City, Mo., 1973-74, asst. dir., 1974-77; adminstr., chief exec. officer Boone Hosp. Ctr., Columbia, Mo., 1977-82; exec. v.p. Barnes Hosp., St. Louis, 1982-86, pres., chief exec. officer, 1986—; founding pres. First Tier Healthcare, Inc.; exec. com., founder, chmn. Vol. Hosps. Am.-Mid-America, Inc.; mem. Health Insights, Inc.; clin. faculty, preceptor Washington U. Sch. Medicine Health Adminstrn. and Planning Program, St. Louis, U. Minn. Hosp. and Health Care Adminstrn., U. Mo. Health Services Mgmt. Studies Program, Columbia, St. Louis U. Dept. Hosp. and Health Care Adminstrn. Bd. dirs., exec. com. Washington U. Med. Ctr., St. Louis; mem. Joint Senate-Ho. Reps. Interim Com. on Mo. Health Care Systems, 1987; sponsor-rep. St. Louis Sr. Olympics. With M.C., U.S. Army, 1968-70, Vietnam. Mem. Am. Hosp. Assn. (governing council for Assembly Hosps. Schs. Nursing), Mo. Hosp. Assn. (trustee 1985-87, 88—), Assn. Am. Med. Colls. (rep. 1987—), Am. Coll. Healthcare Execs. Office: Scottsdale Mem Health Systems 3621 N Wells Fargo Ave Scottsdale AZ 85251-5607

POLLACK, ALAN MYRON, physician; b. N.Y.C., Feb. 16, 1958; s. Samuel and Jean Anna (Friedman) P. BS in Biochemistry, UCLA, 1979; MD, U. Tex., 1983. Diplomate Am. Bd. Internal Medicine. Intern Cedars Sinai Med. Ctr., L.A., 1983-84, resident, 1984-86; physician internal medicine Kaiser Permanente, Panorama City, Calif., 1986—. Mem. Phi Beta Kappa, Alpha Omega Alpha. Home: 6227 Morse Ave Apt 302 North Hollywood CA 91606-2902 Office: Kaiser Permanente 13652 Cantara St Panorama City CA 91402-5423

POLLACK, JEFFREY LEE, restaurateur; b. San Francisco, May 1, 1945; s. Albert and Loretta (Popper) P.; m. Patricia Bowdle Connell, Feb. 20, 1983; children: Lizabeth Ann, Hilary Margaret, Nicholas Albert. BA, San Jose State U. Owner, surety underwriter North Beach Bonding Co., San Francisco, 1968-75; proprietor Old Waldorf, San Francisco, 1974-80, Punchline, 1978-80, Julius' Castle, San Francisco, 1980—, New Joe's, San Francisco, 1984—, Shadows, San Francisco, 1985—, Iron Horse, 1986-92, Pollack Group, San Francisco, 1985—, Nick's Lighthouse Restaurant, San

Francisco, 1991—, Original Joe's # 2, 1992—, O'Counell's, 1994—. Mem. Downtown Assn. (bd. dirs. 1987—, v.p. 1992), Union Sq. Assn., North Beach C. of C. (bd. dirs. 1989, v.p. 1992), Port Tenants Assn., Fisherman Wharf Assn., Commonwealth Club. Democrat. Home: 302 Greenwich St San Francisco CA 94133-3210 Office: Pollack Group Ltd 347 Geary St San Francisco CA 94102-1801

POLLAK, NORMAN L., retired accountant; b. Chgo., Aug. 16, 1931; s. Emery and Helen P.; m. Barbara Zeff, Aug. 21, 1955 (div. 1980); m. Jean Lambert, Sept. 21, 1986 (div. 1991); children: Martin Joel, Elise Susan McNeal, Rhonda Louise Wilder. BS, Northwestern U., 1955. CPA, Calif.; lic. real estate agt. Calif. Sr. acct., staff acct., 1952-58, pvt. practice acctg., 1958-86; ret. acct., fin. and mgmt. cons., pres. Norman L. Pollak Accountancy Corp., Westlake Village, 1958-86, prin., 1986—; expert witness on domestic dissolution, 1984-86; lectr. profl. orgns.; bus. mgr. for Steven Martin, Nitty Gritty Dirt Band, 1967-77; acct. for Gregg and Howard Allman, 1967, Marion Ross. Former pres. Ventura County Estate Planning Coun., 1975-78, 78-79); founder San Fernando Valley Estate Planning Coun., 1962, chpt. pres., 1964-65; founder Ventura Co. Estate Planning Coun.; chmn. Comm. Contest for Hearing Impaired, emegency com. Disaster Preparedness, Oak Forest Mobile Estates Assn.; compiled disaster preparedness plan; coach Braile Olympics for Blind; active Conejo Future Found.; bd. dirs. Oak Forest Homeowners Assn., Honokowai Palms Homeowners Assn.; bd. trustees Westlake Cultural Found.; sponsor Code 3 for Homeless Children, 1993. Mem. AICPA, Planning Coun. Fin. Planners, Calif. Soc. CPAs (former chmn. San Fernando tech. discussion group 1960-61), Nat. Assn. Accts., Westlake Village C. of C., Conejo C. of C., Northwestern U. Alumni Club, Optimists, Delta Mu Delta. Home and Office: 143 Sherwood Dr Westlake Village CA 91361-4814

POLLARD, KENNETH MICHAEL, molecular immunologist, researcher; b. Dubbo, Australia, June 11, 1952; came to U.S., 1982; s. Jack and Norma M. (Bourke) P. BS with honors, Australian Nat. U., Canberra, 1975; PhD, U. Sydney, Australia, 1983. Scientific officer Sutton Rheumatism Rsch. Lab. Royal North Shore Hosp., St. Leonards, NSW, Australia, 1975-78; rsch. assoc. Scripps Clinic and Rsch. Found., La Jolla, Calif., 1982-85, sr. rsch. assoc., 1987-91; rsch. officer Sutton Rheumatism Rsch. Lab. Royal North Shore Hosp., St. Leonards, NSW, Australia, 1985-87; asst. mem. Scripps Rsch. Inst., La Jolla, 1992—. Contbr. articles to profl. jours. Named Eleanor Sophia travelling fellow U. Sydney, Australia Scripps Clinic and Rsch. Found., 1982-83, fellow Terri Gotthelf Lupus Rsch. Inst., 1988-91. Mem. Am. Coll. Rheumatology, Am. Soc. Microbiology. Office: Scripps Rsch Inst 10666 N Torrey Pines Rd La Jolla CA 92037-1027

POLLEY, HARVEY LEE, retired missionary and educator; b. Wapato, Wash., Aug. 14, 1924; s. Edward Prestley and Alda June Polley; m. Corinne Weber; children: Catherine, David, Corinne, Robert. BA, Whitworth Coll., Spokane, Wash., 1951; postgrad., East Wash. Coll., 1953, Berkeley Bapt. Div. Sch., 1958-59; MEd, Cen. Wash. Coll., 1958; postgrad., Ecole d'Adminstrn. des Affaires Africaines, Brussels, 1959-60. Tchr. Quincy (Wash.) Pub. Schs., 1953-57, N.W. Christian Schs., Spokane, 1958; missionary Am. Bapt. Fgn. Missionary Soc., Zaire, 1958-89; tchr. Evang. Pedagogical Inst., Kimpese, Zaire, 1961-69, asst. legal rep., dir., prin., supt., 1969-72; dir. BIM Hostel, Kinshasa, Zaire, 1972-73; mem. staff Ctr. for Agrl. Devel. Lusekele, Zaire, 1975-85, dir., 1976-79, 83-85; dir. Plateau Bateke Devel. Program, Kinshasa, 1985-89; ret., 1989. Author: Rural Development Guide, 1989. Mem. Coun. Elders, Kimpese, 1969-72; pres. bd. adminstrn. Vanga (Zaire) Hosp., 1981-83; mem. exec. com. Nat. Human Nutrition Planning Coun. Govt. Zaire-USAID, Kikwit, 1983-85. Home: W2405 W Johansen Rd Spokane WA 99208-9616

POLLEY, TERRY LEE, lawyer; b. Long Beach, Calif., June 2, 1947; s. Frederick F. and Geraldine E. (Davis) P.; m. Patricia Yamanoha, Aug. 4, 1973; children: Todd, Matthew. AB, UCLA, 1970; JD, Coll. William and Mary, 1973. Bar: Calif. 1973, U.S. Tax Ct. 1974, U.S. Supreme Ct. 1987. Assoc. Loeb & Loeb, L.A., 1973-78; ptnr. Ajalat, Polley & Ayoob, L.A., 1978—; lectr. taxation law U. So.Calif., 1978-94. Author (with Charles R. Ajalat) California's Water's Edge Legislation, 1987; contbr. articles to profl. jours, legal jours.; editorial bd. William and Mary Law Rev. Chmn. bd. dirs. Greater Long Beach Christian Schs., 1988-92, sec., 1994—; elder Grace Brethren Ch., Long Beach, 1988—. Mem. ABA (state and local tax com. 1973-92), Calif. Bar Assn. (chmn. taxation sect. 1990-91, exec. com. 1987-92, state and local tax com. 1975—, taxation sect., recipient V. Judson Klein award, 1993), L.A. County Bar Assn. (exec. com. 1980-87, chmn. exec. com. 1985-86, taxation sect.), Omicron Delta Epsilon. Republican. Office: Ajalat Polley & Ayoob 643 S Olive St Bldg 200 Los Angeles CA 90014-1685

POLLOCK, JOHN PHLEGER, lawyer; b. Sacramento, Apr. 28, 1920; s. George Gordon and Irma (Phleger) P.; m. Juanita Irene Gossman, Oct. 26, 1945; children: Linda Pollock Harrison, Madeline Pollock Chiotti, John, Gordon. A.B., Stanford U., 1942; J.D., Harvard U., 1948. Bar: Calif. 1949, U.S. Supreme Ct. 1954. Ptnr. Musick, Peeler & Garrett, L.A., 1953-60, Pollock, Williams & Berwanger, L.A., 1960-80; ptnr. Rodi, Pollock, Pettker, Galbraith & Phillips, L.A., 1980-89, of counsel, 1989—. Contbr. articles to profl. publs. Active Boy Scouts Am.; former trustee Pitser Coll., Claremont, Calif., 1968-76, Pacific Legal Found., 1981-91; trustee Fletcher Jones Found., Good Hope Med. Found. With AUS, 1942-45. Fellow Am. Coll. Trial Lawyers; mem. ABA, L.A. County Bar Assn. (trustee 1964-66). Home: 30602 Paseo Del Valle Laguna Niguel CA 92677-2317 Office: 801 S Grand Ave Los Angeles CA 90017-4613

POLLOCK, RICHARD EDWIN, former county administrator; b. Phila., Aug. 27, 1928; s. Ernest Edwin and Evelyn Marie (Scarlett) P. Student Armstrong Coll., 1947, U. Calif., Berkeley, 1949-51, 55; BA in Recreation, San Jose State U., 1961; postgrad. San Fernando Valley State U., 1969-70, U. Calif., Davis, 1963-77, UCLA, 1964, U. Calif., Santa Barbara, 1970, U. Redlands, 1979; m. Yvonne May Graves, Oct. 11, 1952 (div. Aug. 1989); children: Colleen May, Karen Marie, Richard Irvin, Annette Yvonne, Mary Ann. Swim pool mgr. and instr. Berkley Tennis Club, 1955-56; police officer City of Berkeley, 1956; recreation and aquatic supr. Pleasant Hill (Calif.) Recreation and Park Dist., 1956-62; gen. mgr. Pleasant Valley Recreation and Park Dist., Camarillo, Calif., 1962-68; bldg. insp. Ventura County (Calif.), 1969-71; adminstr. Sacramento County-Carmichael Recreation and Park Dist., 1971-73; dir. parks and recreation Imperial County (Calif.), 1973-81; ret.; mem. faculty Imperial Valley Jr. Coll., 1974-94, aquatic cons., 1957—; real estate investor, 1984—; chmn. San Francisco Bay Area Conf. for Cooperation in Aquatics, 1958-59. Adviser/scoutmaster Desert Trails council Boy Scouts Am.; bd. dirs., instr. ARC; work with devel. disabled and handicapped children and adults; res. dep. Sheriff, 1981— Served from pvt. to lt. U.S. Army, 1951-55; Korea. Recipient recognition for 52 years vol. service ARC, 1989; registered recreator and park mgr.; cert. elem., secondary and community coll. tchr., Calif.; reg. hypnotherapist. Mem. Nat. Recreation and Park Assn., AAHPER, Calif. Park and Recreation Soc., Calif. County Dirs. Parks and Recreation Assn., Calif. Boating Safety Officers Assn., Aircraft Owners and Pilots Assn., Nat. Assn. Emergency Med. Technicians. Democrat. Mormon. Author: Bibliography: A Pool of Aquatic Sources, 1960. Home: PO Box 3011 El Centro CA 92244-3011

POLON, LINDA BETH, elementary school educator, writer, illustrator; b. Balt., Oct. 7, 1943; d. Harold Bernard and Edith Judith Wolff; m. Marty I. Polon, Dec. 18, 1966 (div. Aug. 1983). BA in History, UCLA, 1966. Elem. tchr. L.A. Bd. Edn., 1967—; writer-illustrator Scott Foresman Pub. Co., Glenview, Ill., 1979—, Frank Schaffer Pub. Co., Torrance, Calif., 1981-82, Learning Works, Santa Barbara, Calif., 1981-82, Harper Row Co.; editorial reviewer Prentice Hall Pub. Co., Santa Monica, Calif., 1982-83. Author: (juvenile books) Creative Teaching Games, 1974, Teaching Games for Fun, 1976, Making Kids Click, 1979, Write up a Storm, 1979, Stir Up a Story, 1981, Paragraph Production, 1981, Using Words Correctly, 3d-4th grades, 1981, 5th-6th grades, 1981, Whole Earth Holiday Book, 1983, Writing Whirlwind, 1986, Magic Story Starters, 1987, (teacher's resource guides) Just Good Books, 1991, Kid's Choice/Libraries, 1991. Mem. Soc. Children's Book Writers. Democrat. Home: 11640 Kiowa Ave Apt 205 Los Angeles CA 90049-6244 Office: L A Bd of Edn 980 S Hobart Blvd Los Angeles CA 90006-1220

POLSON, DONALD ALLAN, surgeon; b. Gallup, N.Mex., May 12, 1911; s. Thomas Cress and Carrie Fern (Cantrall) P.; m. Cecily, Lady Avebury, Nov. 9, 1946; 1 child, Carolyn Kathleen. Student Stanford U.; MD, Northwestern U., 1936, MSc, 1947. Diplomate Am. Bd. Surgery. Intern, then resident in surgery St. Luke's Hosp., Chgo., 1936-38; practice medicine specializing in gen. surgery, Phoenix, 1947-83; formerly chmn. Drs. Polson, Berens & Petelin, Ltd.; chief staff Maricopa County Hosp., 1952-53, St. Joseph's Hosp., 1961; bd. dirs. Ariz. Blue Shield, 1950-55, pres., 1956. Served to col. M.C., AUS, World War II. Mem. AMA, ACS, Ariz. Med. Assn. (dir. 1955-60), Maricopa County Med. Soc. (pres. 1954), Phoenix Surg. Soc. (pres. 1959), White Mountain Country Club, Alpha Omega Alpha, Nu Sigma Nu. Republican. Episcopalian. Home: 7619 N Tatum Blvd Paradise Valley AZ 85253-3378

POLSTER, ARNIM HENRY, computer scientist consultant; b. Meridian, Miss., Oct. 31, 1959; s. Arnim Henry and Jan (Swoboda) P. BA in Math., U. Calif., Berkeley, 1982, MA in German, 1984, PhD in German, 1994. Instr. U. Calif., Berkeley, 1983-91; cons. Alta Bates Med. Ctr., Berkeley, 1992—. Editor: Rethinking Germanistik, 1991. Fulbright travel grant, 1988-89, Germanistic Soc. Am. rsch. grantee, 1988-89. Mem. MLA, Phi Beta Kappa. Office: Alta Bates Med Ctr/IRM 2850 Telegraph Ave Berkeley CA 94705-1132

POLSTER, LEONARD H., investment company executive; b. Columbus, Ohio, June 24, 1921; s. Max and Henrietta Polster; m. Constance L. Buderus, Mar. 20, 1948 (dec. Aug. 1967); children: Leonard M., Lance E., Lewis E.; m. Edith Motridge, Nov. 19, 1968. BA, Ohio State U., 1942. Pres. Polster, Inc., 1952-68; pres. real estate and investments co. Polster, Inc., Rancho Santa Fe, 1968—; sr. v.p. PaineWebber Inc., L.A. and Rancho Santa Fe, Calif., 1971-91. Author: Pearls Before Swine, 1994. Pres. Polster Found., Rancho Santa Fe, 1988—; fin. officer, bd. dirs. San Dieguito Boys Club, Solana Beach, Calif., 1991—; bd. dirs. Fairbanks Ranch Cmty. Svcs. Dist., Rancho Santa Fe, 1987-92; pres. Fairbanks Ranch Assn., Rancho Santa Fe, 1985-86, bd. dirs., 1984-86. With USAF, 1942-46. Recipient Commitment to Youth award San Dieguito Boys and Girls Club, 1989. Mem. Fairbanks Ranch Country Club, Phi Alpha Theta. Republican. Presbyterian. Home and Office: PO Box 8291 Rancho Santa Fe CA 92067-8291

POMBO, RICHARD, congressman, rancher, farmer; b. Tracy, Calif., 1961; m. Annette, 1983; children: Richard Jr., Rena. Student, Calif. State U., Pomona, 1981-83. Councilman City of Tracy, 1991-92; mayor pro-tem Tracy City Coun., 1992; mem. 103rd-104th Congresses from 11th Calif. dist., 1993—; mem. Agrl. Com., Resources Com. Co-founder San Joaquin County Citizen's Land Alliance, Calif., 1986—; active San Joaquin County Econ. Devel. Assn., Tracy Bus. Improvement Dist., City Coun. (vice chmn. Cmty. Devel. Agy., Cmty. Parks Com., and Waste Mgmt. Com.), San Joaquin County Rep. Ctrl. Com. Mem. Rotary Club. Roman Catholic. Office: US Ho of Reps 1519 Longworth HOB Washington DC 20515-0511

POMERANZ, YESHAJAHU, research chemist, technologist; b. Tlumacz, Poland, Nov. 28, 1922; came to U.S., 1959, naturalized, 1967; s. David and Rysia (Bildner) P.; m. Ada Waisberg, Oct. 27, 1948; children: Shlomo, David. B.S., Israeli Inst. Tech., Haifa, 1946; Chem. Engr., Israeli Inst. Tech., 1947; student, U. London, 1954-55; Ph.D., Kans. State U., 1959-62. Dir. Central Food Testing Lab., Haifa, 1948-59; research chemist Agrl. Research Service, U.S. Dept. Agr., Manhattan, Kans., 1962-69; dir. Barley and Malt Lab. Agrl. Research Service, U.S. Dept. Agr., Madison, Wis., 1969-73; dir. U.S. Grain Mktg. Research Ctr. Agrl. Research Service, U.S. Dept. Agr., Manhattan, 1973-86; research prof. dept. food sci. Wash. State U., Pullman, 1986—; vis. prof. U.S. and abroad. Sci. editor, Am. Assn. Cereal Chemists; author, co-author, editor numerous book, symposia procs. in cereal sci., tech., food sci. tech. analysis; patentee high protein bread lipid syntheses and uses. Von Humboldt awardee, 1981; recipient Wiley award, 1980, Osborne award, 1981, W.F. Geddes medal, 1982, Disting. Svc. award U.S. Dept. Agr., 1983, Nat. Assn. Wheat Growers, 1990. Fellow AAAS, Inst. Food Technologists, Assn. Cereal Chemists; mem. Am. Chem. Soc. (Food Agr. award 1984), Assn. Ofcl. Analytical Chemists, Sigma Xi, Gamma Sigma Delta. Home: 1405 SW Wadleigh Dr Pullman WA 99163-2048 Office: Wash State Univ Dept Food Sci & Human Nutrition Pullman WA 99164-6376

POMEROY, KENT LYTLE, physical medicine and rehabilitation physician; b. Phoenix, Apr. 21, 1935; s. Benjamin Kent and LaVerne (Hamblin) P.; m. Karen Jodelle Thomas (dec. Dec. 1962); 1 child, Charlotte Ann; m. Margo Delilah Tuttle, Mar. 27, 1964 (div. Jan. 1990); children: Benjamin Kent II, Janel Elise, Jonathan Barrett, Kimberly Eve; m. Brenda Pauline North, Sept. 1, 1990. BS in Phys. Sci., Ariz. State U., 1960; MD, U. Utah, 1963. Diplomate Am. Bd. Phys. Medicine and Rehab., Am. Bd. Pain Medicine. Rotating intern Good Samaritan Hosp., Phoenix, 1963-64; resident in phys. medicine and rehab. Good Samaritan Hosp., 1966-69, asst. tng. dir. Inst. Rehab. Medicine, 1970-74, dir. residency tng., 1974-76, asst. med. dir., 1973-76; dir. Phoenix Phys. Medicine Ctr., 1980-85, Ariz. Found. on Study Pain, Phoenix, 1980-85; pvt. practice, Scottsdale, Ariz., 1988—; lectr. in field. Contbr. articles to med. jours. Leader Theodore Roosevelt coun. Boy Scouts Am.; mem. exec. posse Maricopa County Sheriff's Office, Phoenix, 1981—, posse comdr., 1992-94, qualified armed posseman; mem. med. adv. bd. Grand Canyon-Saguaro chpt. Nat. Found. March of Dimes, 1970-78. Recipient Scouter's Tng. award Theodore Roosevelt coun. Boy Scouts Am., 1984, Scouter's Woodbadge, 1985. Mem. AMA, Am. Acad. Phys. Medicine and Rehab., Internat. Rehab. Medicine Assn., Am. Assn. Orthopaedic Medicine (co-founder, sec.-treas. 1982-88, pres. 1988-90), Pan Am. Med. Assn. (diplomate), Prolotherapy Assn. (pres. 1981-83), Am. Pain Soc., Western Pain Soc., Am. Assn. for Study Headache, Am. Thermographic Soc. (charter), Am. Soc. Addiction Medicine (sec. Ariz. chpt.), Am. Acad. Pain Medicine, Nat. Eagle Scout Assn., Acad. Clin. Neurophysiology, Ariz. Soc. Phys. Medicine (pres. 1977-78), Ariz. Med. Assn., Maricopa County Med. Soc., others, Nat. Sheriff's Assn., Law Enforcement Alliance of Am. Mem. LDS Ch. Office: Royal Orthopedic & Pain Rehab Assocs 9755 N 90th St Ste A-205 Scottsdale AZ 85258-5046 also: 2536 N 3rd St Ste 3 Phoenix AZ 85004-1308

POMEROY, MARY BARNAS, artist, illustrator, writer; b. Frankfurt, Hessen, Germany, Mar. 3, 1921; came to U.S., 1946; d. Carl Franz Joseph and Elizabeth Jacoba Gertruida (Van Holk) Barnas; m. Frederick George Pomeroy, Dec. 20, 1953; children: Anne Lilian Pomeroy Hess, Flora Jane Pomeroy. Student, coll., Quito, Ecuador, 1936-38; studied with father/German-Ecuadorean, artist Carl Barnas, Quito, 1938-46; student, Pa. Acad. Fine Arts, Phila., 1946-48; studied with Daniel Garber, Roy Nuse,, Franklin Watkins and Henry, Pitz. Illustrator geology dept. U. Cen., Quito, 1939-42; illustrator paleontology dept. Internat. Petroleum Co., Guayaquil, Ecuador, 1943-44; scientific illustrator botany dept. U. Calif., Berkeley, 1948-53; freelance artist, 1953—. Artwork pub. in numerous publs. including Américas mag., Mus. of Calif. mag., 1993, poster for Asilomar Operating Corp. and Calif. Dept. Parks and Recreation, Pacific Grove, 1990, cover of Fremontia mag./Native Plant Soc., 1988, others; exbhns. include Pacific Grove Art Ctr., 1992, Sangre de Cristo Art and Conf. Ctr., Pueblo, Colo., 1989, Marjorie Evans Gallery, Sunset Ctr., Carmel, Calif., 1986, Mus. of Art, Monterey, Calif., 1985, City Hall, Seaside, Calif., 1983, Hunt Inst. Botanical Documentation, Pitts., others; work in various pvt. collections; contbr. 300 botanical illustrations to textbook.

POMRANING, GERALD CARLTON, engineering educator; b. Oshkosh, Wis., Feb. 23, 1936; s. Carlton Chester and Lorraine Helen (Volkman) P.; m. Gayle Ann Burkitt, May 27, 1961 (div. 1983); children: Linda Marie, Sandra Lee. BS, U. Wis., 1957; cert., Technische Hogeschool, Delft, Holland, 1958; Ph.D. (NSF fellow), MIT, 1962. Mgr. GE, Pleasanton, Calif., 1962-64; group leader Gen. Atomic Co., La Jolla, Calif., 1964-69; v.p. Sci. Applications, La Jolla, 1969-76; prof. engring. UCLA, 1976—; cons. to govt. and industry. Author: Radiation Hydrodynamics, 1973, Transport in Stochastic Mixtures, 1991; editor: Reactor Physics, 1966; contbr. articles to profl. jours. Fulbright fellow, 1957-58. Fellow AAAS, Am. Nuclear Soc. (Mark Mills award 1963), Am. Phys. Soc.; mem. Math. Assn. Am., Soc. Indsl. Applied Math., Am. Math. Soc., Sigma Xi, Alpha Xi Sigma, Phi Eta Sigma, Phi Kappa Phi, Tau Beta Pi, Phi Lambda Upsilon.

PON-BROWN, KAY MIGYOKU, technical marketing engineer; b. Ft. Lewis, Wash., Mar. 15, 1956; d. Gin Ung and Toyo (China) Pon; m. John Joseph Brown, July 28, 1979; 1 child, J. Jason. BS in Chemistry, U. Idaho, 1978, BA in Zoology, 1978; BS in Math., Boise State U., 1984. Chemist Century Labs., Inc., Boise, Idaho, 1982-84; from customer support specialist to tech. support specialist Learned-Mahn, Inc., Boise, 1984-87; from computer programmer to coord. Idaho Power, Boise, 1987-90, customer solution rep., 1990-92; tech. specialist Hewlett-Packard Co., Boise, 1992-95, tech. mktg. engr., 1995—; cons. Eclipse, Inc., Boise, 1991—, bd. dirs. 1991—, pres., 1992—, Discovery Ctr. Idaho, Boise, 1992-95. Bd. dirs. Idaho Zool. Soc., Boise, 1986-95, Ada County Divsn. Am. Heart Assn., Boise, 1992-94, divsn. sec., 1992-93; mem. Jr. League Boise, 1989—; vol. Am. Cancer Soc., 1990—; vol. newsletter editor Idaho Soc. Profl. Engrs., 1992-94. 1st Place husband & wife team Royal Victoria Marathon, 1992. Mem. Data Processing Mgmt. Assn. (bd. dirs. 1993-94, newsletter editor 1993-94), Meridian Toastmasters (pres. 1986, dist. 15. best newsletter 1986), Idaho PC Users Group, Greater Boise Rd. Runners Club (bd. dirs. 1993—, charter pres. 1993, newsletter editor 1994—). Home: 1350 Nova Ln Meridian ID 83642-6483 Office: Hewlett-Packard Co 11311 Chinden Blvd Boise ID 83714-1021

PONICHTERA, BRENDA JOYCE, dietitian, cookbook author; b. Acushnet, Mass., Mar. 6, 1947; d. Walter Martin and Mary E. (Moinheiro) Niemic; m. Kenneth Carl Ponichtera, Aug. 3, 1968; children: Kevin Carl, Kyle Steven. BS in Edn., Framingham (Mass.) State Coll., 1968; postgrad., U. Mont., 1969-70. Lic. dietitian, Oreg.; cert. diabetes educator; cert. tchr., Mass., Mont. Tchr. home econs. Sentinel High Sch., Missoula, Mont., 1968-70; cons. nutritionist Nutrition Clinic and Cons. Svc., Eugene, Oreg., 1972-73; clin. and adminstrv. dietitian McKenzie Willamette Meml. Hosp., Springfield, Oreg., 1972-73; W.I.C. Program nutritionist Wasco and Sherman Counties, Oreg., 1975-76; pvt. practice in nutrition counseling and diabetes edn. The Dalles and Hood River, Oreg., 1976-93; pub., author ScaleDown Pub., The Dalles, 1991—; dietary cons. for nursing homes and hosps. Dietitian Cons. Svcs., Portland, 1974-76; prenatal and infant nutrition instr. March of Dimes Prenatal Classes, The Dalles, 1975-81; coord. and instr. Mid-Columbia Diabetes Edn. Program, 1983-89; nutrition cons. Mid-Columbia Surg. Assocs., 1984-88, Wasco Habilitation Group, 1987-90, Mid-Columbia Head Start, 1985-88. Author: Quick and Healthy Recipes and Ideas, vol. II, 1995; author, pub.: Scale Down Publishing. Bd. dirs. Wasco County chpt. Oreg. Heart Assn., 1987-89. Recipient Mid-Columbia Home Econs. Assn. Cert. of Award for radio program participation, 1982, Disting. Leadership award March of Dimes, 1979; named Recognized Young Dietitian of the Yr., State of Oreg., 1975. Mem. Am. Dietetic Assn. (registered, media rep. for Mid-Columbia area), Oreg. Dietetic Assn., Am. Diabetes Assn. (Oreg. affiliate), Diabetes Educators Group Oreg., N.W. Assn. Book Pubs., Pubs. Mktg. Assn. Office: Scale Down 1519 Hermits Way The Dalles OR 97058-3808

PONTSLER, DONALD N., electrical engineer; b. Wenatchee, Wash., Jan. 18, 1943; s. Clement M. and Exer LaVern (Preston) P.; m. Kathy J. Johnson, June 12, 1965; children: Jon D., Steven W. BSEE, Washington StateU., 1966; M in Pub. Adminstrn., U. Puget Sound, 1981. registered profl. engr., Wash. Electrical engr. Tacoma (Wash.) Pub. Utilities, 1966, profl. electrical engr., 1972, prin. profl. electrical engr., 1975—. Mem. IEEE. Presbyterian. Home: 6806 86th St E Puyallup WA 98371 Office: Tacoma Pub Utilities 3628 S 35th Rear Tacoma WA 98409

PONZETTO, ENNIO, research and development executive; b. 1951. Pres. Olivetti Advanced Tech. Ctr., 1993—. Office: Olivetti Advanced Tech Ctr 20300 Stevens Creek Blvd Cupertino CA 95014-2240*

POOLE, ARNETTA MARIE, neonatal intensive care nurse; b. Cleve., July 17, 1966; d. Sylvester and Sylvia (Poole) Blue. BSN, Loma Linda U., 1990. Cert. BLS. Relief charge nurse Loma Linda Community Hosp., 1989-91; staff nurse Pomona Valley (Calif.) Med. Ctr., 1990—. Recipient We Care award Loma Linda Community Hosp., 1989-90. Mem. Nat. Assn. Neonatal Nurses, Orgn. for Obstetric, Gynecologic and Neonatal Nurses, Nat. League for Nurses, Sigma Theta Tau. Office: 12480 Iroquois Rd Apple Valley CA 92308-6848

POOLE, CECIL F., federal judge; b. Birmingham, Ala.; children: Gayle, Patricia. LL.B., U. Mich.; LL.M., Harvard U., 1939. Practice of law San Francisco, former asst. dist. atty., 1951-58; clemency sec. to Gov. Brown of Calif., 1958-61; U.S. atty. No. Dist. Calif., 1961-70; Regents prof. Law U. Calif., Berkeley, 1970; counsel firm Jacobs, Sills & Coblentz, San Francisco, 1970-76; judge U.S. Dist. Ct., No. Dist. Calif., 1976-79, U.S. Ct. of Appeals for 9th Circuit, 1979—; adj. prof. Golden Gate U. Sch. Law, 1953-58; mem. adv. com. Nat. Commn. for Reform Fed. Criminal Laws, 1968-70. Served to 2d lt. AUS, World War II. Mem. ABA (chmn. sect. individual rights 1971-72, ho. of dels. 1972-74), San Francisco Bar Assn. (dir. 1975-76). Office: US Ct Appeals 9th Cir PO Box 193939 San Francisco CA 94119-3939

POOLE, HARRY WENDELL, county group probation counselor; b. Paces, Va., Jan. 29, 1953; s. Charlie Washington and Minnie Beatrice (Oliver) P. AA, Riverside Community Coll., 1981; BS, U. Redlands, 1983; MS, Calif. State U., Dominuez Hills, Calif., 1985. With payroll Kaiser Steel Corp., Fontana, Calif., 1975-83; group counselor I Riverside County Probation, Riverside, Calif., 1983-86; group counselor II Riverside County Probation, 1986—; youth counselor Calif. Youth Authority, Chino, 1978. Democrat. Baptist. Office: Riverside County Probation 3933 Harrison St Riverside CA 92503-3523

POOLE, HENRY JOE, JR., business executive; b. Rocky Point, N.C., July 5, 1957; s. Henry Joe Sr. and Marjorie (Morse) P.; m. Loretta Lynn Scott, Sept. 12, 1981; children: Robert Howard, Amanda Lynn. AA, Cypress Coll., 1977; student, San Diego State U., 1978, Calif. State U., Fullerton, 1978-79. Pres. Poole Ventura Inc., Ventura, Calif., 1979-92; gen. mgr. W.I.C. PVI systems divsn., Ventura, Calif., 1992-94; pres. PVI, Oxnard, Calif., 1995—. Inventor in field. Mem. ASME, Soc. Mfg. Engrs., Am. Vacuum Soc., Am. Welding Soc., Soc. Vacuum Coaters. Office: PVI PO Box 5023 Oxnard CA 93031

POOLE, MONTE LARUE, sports columnist, consultant; b. Oakland, Calif., Nov. 30, 1955. AA, Chabot Coll., 1983; BA, San Jose State U., 1985. Dist. mgr. Mervyn's, Hayward, Calif., 1979-81; sports writer Oakland Tribune, 1982-91, Oakland Tribune/Alameda Newspaper Group, Oakland, 1991—; host talk show Sta. KSFO, San Francisco, 1992; instr. New Coll. Calif., 1994. Mem. com. U. Calif. Hall of Fame, Berkeley, 1993—. Mem. Nat. Assn. Black Journalists, Baseball Writers' Assn. Am. Office: Oakland Tribune PO Box 28884 66 Jack London Sq Oakland CA 94607

POOLE, ROBERT ANTHONY, journalist; b. St. Austell, Cornwall, Eng., Dec. 17, 1944; arrived in Can., 1977; m. Valerie Avril Taggart, Apr. 14, 1973; children—Claire Lucy, Emma Louise. Irish editor Press Assn., Belfast, Northern Ireland, 1970-77; gen. reporter Calgary Herald, Alta., Can., 1977-79; city editor Calgary Albertan, 1979-80; city editor Calgary Sun, 1980-81, mng. editor, 1981-84, editor-in-chief, 1984—. Office: Calgary Sun, 2615 12th St NE, Calgary, AB Canada T2E 7W9

POON, PETER TIN-YAU, engineer; b. Hengyang, Hunan, China, May 31, 1944; came to U.S., 1967; s. Sam. Chak-Kwong and Lai (Yiu) P.; m. Mable Tsang, Apr. 13, 1974; children: Amy Wei-Ling, Brian Wing-Yan. BS, U. Hong Kong, 1965; MA, Calif. State U., Long Beach, 1969; PhD, U. So. Calif., L.A., 1974. Mem. tech. staff, group leader, sr. engr., telemetry sys. mgr. Jet Propulsion Lab./Calif. Inst. Tech., Pasadena, 1974-88, tech. mgr., 1988-94; telecomm. and mission svcs. mgr. Cassini mission to Saturn, 1993—; USA chmn., program com. 2nd Internat. Software Engring. Standards Symposium, Montreal, Can., 1994-95; program com. session chair Software Engring. Stds. Symposium, Brighton, Eng., 1992-93. Author numerous profl. publs. Recipient numerous group awards in field, NASA, 1977-93. Mem. IEEE Software Engring. Stds. (co-author long range plans 1993, mem. exec. com.), Arcadia Music Club (pres. 1994-95, 1st v.p. 1993-94), AIDA (program com. mem. 1990-91).

POONJA, MOHAMED, business reorganization, financial and management consultant; b. Mombasa, Kenya, Nov. 8, 1948; came to U.S., 1984; s.

Abdulrasul and Maleksultan (Dharsee) P.; m. Zaitun Virji, Feb. 24, 1979; children: Jamil Husayn, Karim Ali. Student, Inst. Chartered Accts., Eng., Wales; MS in Mgmt. and Organizational Behavior, U.S. Internat. U. CPA. Audit supr. Ernst & Young (formerly Ernst & Whinney), Dublin, Ireland, 1966-72, Coopers & Lybrand, Dublin, 1973-76; group controller Diamond Trust of Kenya, Nairobi, 1976-78; chief operating officer Kenya Uniforms, Ltd., Nairobi, 1978-81; sr. mgr. Coopers & Lybrand, Calgary, Alta., Can., 1981-84; ptnr. Coopers & Lybrand, San Jose, Calif., 1984-92; chpt. 7 panel bankruptcy trustee No. Dist. Calif., San Jose, Calif., 1991—; with Poonja & Co., 1992—; ptnr. Manzanita Capital Ptnrs. Ltd., 1993—; former pres. Bay Area Bankruptcy Forum; bd. dirs. Calif. Bankruptcy Forum. Mem. ABA, Am. Bankruptcy Inst., Assn. Insolvency Accts., Inst. Bus. Appraisers, Cert. Fraud Examiners, Rotary. Home: 630 Milverton Rd Los Altos CA 94022-3930 Office: Poonja & Co 167 S San Antonio Rd Ste 17 Los Altos CA 94022-3049

POOR, CLARENCE ALEXANDER, physician; b. Ashland, Oreg., Oct. 29, 1911; s. Lester Clarence and Matilda Ellen (Doty) P.; AB, Willamette U., 1932; MD, U. Oreg., 1936. Diplomate Am. Bd. Internal Medicine. Intern U. Wis., Madison, 1936-37, resident in internal medicine, 1937-40, instr. dept. pathology Med. Sch., 1940-41, clin. instr., clin. asst. dept. internal medicine, 1942-44; pvt. practice medicine specializing in internal medicine, Oakland, Calif., 1944—; mem. emeritus staff Highland Alameda County Hosp., Oakland, 1949—; mem. staff Providence Hosp., Oakland, 1947—, pres. staff, 1968-69; staff mem. Samuel Meritt Hosp., Oakland, 1958—; staff mem. Summit Med. Ctr. (merger Providence Hosp. and Samuel Merritt Hosp.), 1991—. Mem. Nat. Coun. on Alcoholism, 1974—, bd. dirs. Bay Area, 1977—. Mem. Am., Calif., Alameda-Contra Costa med. assns., Alameda County Heart Assn. (trustee 1955-62, 72-82, pres. 1960-61), Calif. Heart Assn. (dir. 1962-72), Soc. for Clin. and Exptl. Hypnosis, Am. Soc. Clin. Hypnosis, San Francisco Acad. Hypnosis (dir. 1966—, pres. 1973). Home: 1241 Westview Dr Berkeley CA 94705-1650 Office: 400 29th St Ste 201 Oakland CA 94609-3547

POORE, JAMES ALBERT, III, lawyer; b. Butte, Mont., June 28, 1943; s. James A. Jr. and Jesse (Wild) P.; m. Shelley A. Borgstede, Feb. 12, 1989; children: James IV, Jeffrey. AB, Stanford U., 1965; JD with honors, U. Mont., 1968. Bar: Mont. 1968, U.S. Dist. Ct. Mont. 1968, U.S. Ct. Appeals (9th cir.) 1972, U.S. Supreme Ct. 1973. Assoc. Poore, Poore, McKenzie & Roth, Butte, 1968-74; prin., v.p. Poore, Roth & Robinson, P.C., Butte, 1974—; speaker in field. Assoc. editor U. Mont. Law Rev., 1967-68; contbg. editor Product Liability Desk Reference, 1995; contbr. articles to profl. publs. Dist. dir. Boy Scouts Am., S.W. Mont., 1969; dir. YMCA, Butte, 1981-83; founding bd. dirs. Hospice of Butte, 1982-85, Butte Community Theater, 1977-80; pres. Butte Uptown Assn., 1974; dir. Butte Silverbow Am. Cancer Soc. Bd., 1992—. Fellow Am. Bar Found.; mem. ABA, State Bar Mont., Am. Judicature Soc., Silver Bow Bar Assn., Phi Delta Phi. Home: 6 Cedar Lake Dr Butte MT 59701-4338 Office: Poore Roth & Robinson PC 1341 Harrison Ave Butte MT 59701-4801

POPE, EDWARD JOHN ANDREW, corporate executive, consultant; b. N.Y.C., July 18, 1962; s. Thomas Andrew and Barbara (McInnes) P. BS, U. Calif., L.A., 1983, MS, 1985, PhD, 1989. Engring. asst. U. Calif., 1979-83, rsch. asst., 1984-89; pres. MATECH, Westlake Village, Calif., 1989—; cons. Orion Labs., Inc., Camarillo, Calif., 1988-89, Refractory Composites, Inc., Whittier, Calif., 1989-90, ENSCI, Inc., Woodland Hills, Calif., 1990—; bd. dirs. Ventura County World Affairs Coun. Contbr. numerous articles to profl. jours. Mem. State Ctrl. Com. of Rep. Party, Calif., 1981-83; pres. UCLA Bruin Reps., L.A., 1981-82; active UCLA Chem. Adv. Coun., 1993; apptd. Ventura County Coun. on Econ. Vitality, 1993. Regent's scholar U. Calif., 1979, Chancellor's scholar, 1979; IBM Corp. fellow Watson Rsch. Ctr., 1988. Mem. Am. Ceramic Soc. (chair edn. com. 1990—), Nat. Inst. Ceramic Engrs., Materials Rsch. Soc. (acad. affairs com. 1987-89), UCLA chpt. Materials Rsch. Soc. (pres. 1982-89). Office: MATECH 31304 Via Colinas Ste 102 Thousand Oaks CA 91362-3901

POPE, MARK L., information scientist; b. St. Louis, Apr. 23, 1952; s. Isom Lavern Pope and Ethyle R. (Ray) Harget. AB, U. Mo., 1973, MEd, 1974; student, Northwestern U., 1977-78; EdD, U. San Francisco, 1988. Nat. cert. counselor; nat. cert. career counselor; lic. psychol. asst. Drug abuse counselor Brotherhood Clinic Ill. Drug Abuse Program, Chgo., 1974-75; mental health worker, career counselor adolescent unit Northwestern Inst. Psychiatry, Chgo., 1975-76; career counselor, psychol. test cons. Meth. Youth Svcs., Chgo., 1976-77; rsch. interviewer, drug abuse counselor Cook County Treatment Alternatives to Street Crimes, Chgo., 1977-78; cons., pres. Data Psych Systems, N.Y.C. and San Francisco, 1978-90; computer ops. mgr. Pacific Am. Group, San Francisco, 1981-83; supr. info. systems Bechtel Engring. & Constrn. Cos., San Francisco, 1983-87; software devel. editor Cons. Psychologists Press, Palo Alto, Calif., 1987-89; pres. Career Decisions, San Francisco, 1989—; pres., pub. Cognito Press, San Francisco, 1995—; dir., founder Horizons Gay and Lesbian Profl. and Peer Counseling Svcs., Chgo., 1975-77; lectr. Cen. YMCA Community Coll. Dept. Psychology, Chgo., 1977-78, Northwestern U. Indsl. Engring. and Orgn. Devel. Dept., 1977-78, John F. Kennedy U. Career Devel. and Planning, Orinda, Calif., 1987—; adj. prof. Golden Gate U. Grad. Sch. Mgmt. Human Resource Mgmt., San Francisco, 1984—, U. San Francisco Info. Systems Mgmt., 1986—, counseling and edn. psychology, 1988—; counseling San Francisco State U., 1990—; clin. supr. counseling and health psychology Stanford U., 1990—; career devel. cons. Pacific Bell, San Francisco, 1988-93; human resources cons. Alpha Computer Svcs., San Rafael, Calif., 1988-91; founder West Coast Counselors With Computers Conf., 1989; program chair Calif. Career Conf., 1989, 95; psychologist Am. Indian AIDS Inst., 1990-94, Native Am. AIDS Project, 1994—. Contbr. articles to profl. jours. and chpts. to books. Mem. collaborative planning com. U. San Francisco Sch. Edn., 1987-88, Mo. Gen. Assembly drug abuse adv. com., 1972; bd. dirs. Ill. Civil Liberties Union, Chgo., 1976-78; appointee Mo. Gov.'s Reorganization Commn., 1973. Mem. ACA (mem. couseling software rev. bd. 1987-89, chmn. task force on exhibits 1990-92, mem. com. on gay, lesbian bisexual issues, 1991-92, human rights com. 1995—), AAAS, APA (mem. divs. 5, 8, 17, 21, 44, 45), Assn. for Computing Machinery, Assn. for Counselor Edn. and Supervision (co-chair internat. network 1988-90, chair subcom. on internat. counselor edn. database 1986-88, mem. counseling and tech. network 1985—, counseling in bus. and industry network 1985—), Assn. for Assessment in Counseling (chmn. interorgnl. affairs com. 1989-90), Bay Area Career Devel. Assn. (co-chair 1987-91), Nat. Mus. Am. Indian (charter), Calif. Assn. for Counseling and Devel. (chair subcom. human rights com. 1986-88, exec. com. 1989-91, chair gay, lesbian, bisexual caucus 1991, conv. program com. 1989-90, chmn. convention program com. 1991-92, mem. exec. com. 1989-91), Calif. Assn. Measurement and Evaluation in Counseling and Devel. (sec., treas. 1988-89, pres. elect 1989-90, pres. 1990-91), Calif. Assn. Multi-Cultural Counseling, Calif. Career Devel. Assn. (profl. devel. chair 1988-91, no. Calif. regional coord. 1991-93, chair task force to devel. registered career counselor exam. 1991-92, pres.-elect 1993-94, pres. 1994-95, past pres. 1995—), N.Y. Acad. Scis., Computers in Psychology, Human Factors Soc., Nat. Career Devel. Assn. (nat. sec. 1992-94, chmn. pub. rels. com. 1991-92, nat. treas. 1994—, site coord. nat. conf. 1994—, bd. dirs. exec. com. 1994—), No. Calif. Assn. for Counseling and Devel., Nat. Coun. on Measurement in Edn., Phi Delta Kappa. Office: Career Decisions Ste 962 760 Market St San Francisco CA 94114-1408

POPE, ROBERT S., agricultural products executive; b. 1939. With Anderson Clayton Corp., 1963—, v.p.-treas., 1987—, sr. v.p.-sec.-treas. Office: Anderson Clayton Corp 615 S 51st Ave Phoenix AZ 85043-4706*

POPPA, RYAL ROBERT, manufacturing company executive; b. Wahpeton, N.D., Nov. 7, 1933; s. Ray Edward and Annabelle (Phillips) P.; m. Ruth Ann Curry, June 21, 1952; children: Sheryl Lynn, Kimberly Marie. BBA, Claremont Men's Coll., 1957. Sales trainee IBM, L.A., 1957-59, sales rep., 1959-62, product mktg. rep., 1963, sales mgr., 1964-66; v.p., gen. mgr. Comml. Computers Inc., L.A., 1966-67; v.p. Greyhound Computer Corp., Chgo., 1967-68, pres., chief exec. officer, bd. dirs., 1969-70; pres., chief exec. officer, bd. dirs., mem. exec. com. Data Processing Fin. & Gen., Hartsdale, N.Y., 1970-72; exec. v.p., chief fin. officer, bd. dirs., mem. exec. com. Mohawk Data Sci. Corp., Utica, N.Y., 1972-73; chmn., pres., chief exec. officer Pertec Computer Corp., L.A., 1973-81, BMC Industries, Inc., St. Paul, 1982-85; pres., chmn., chief exec. officer Storage Tech. Corp., Louisville, Colo., 1985—; founder Charles Babbage Inst. Trustee Claremont Men's Coll.; mem. Chmn.'s Circle Colo. Reps.; past mem. Pres. Com. Nat. Medal of Sci. Recipient Exec. of Yr. award U. Colo. MBA Alum Assn., 1986, Community Svc. award Inst. Human Rels. Am. Jewish Com., 1980, Colo. Bus. Leader of Yr. award CACI, 1991. Mem. Computer and Comm. Industry Assn. (chmn., past bd. dirs., mem. exec. com., vice chmn.), Am. Electronics Assn. (past bd. dirs., mem. exec. com. Colo. chpt.), Electronic Mfrs. Club, Boulder Country Club. Office: Storage Tech Corp 2270 S 88th St Louisville CO 80028-0001*

POPPE, DONNA, music educator; b. Newton, Kans., Feb. 25, 1953; d. Louis Gustav and Dorothy Elizabeth (VanDenBrand) P. Student, Hastings Coll., 1970-72; BA in Music Edn., U. North Colo., 1974; cert. Orff-Schulwerk, U. Denver, 1977; MEd in Curriculum, Seattle Pacific U., 1990, MA in Integrated Arts, 1990. Band, music, orch. tchr. Weld County Sch. Dist., Greeley, Colo., 1974-79; spl. edn. tchr. Franklin Pierce Sch. Dist., Tacoma, Wash., 1979-84; music tchr. Sumner (Wash.) Sch. Dist., 1984—; cons. Seattle Pacific U., 1982; cons., prof. Fla. State U., Tallahassee, 1985-89, U. Ga., Athens, 1988-89; mem. adj. faculty Pacific Luth. U., Tacoma, 1995—; clinician/presenter U. Nebr., Lincoln, 1991; clinician N.W. Orff Conf., 1994, Orff 100 Conf., Melbourne, Australia, 1995. Contbr. articles to profl. jours. Mem. Tacoma Symphony, 1983-85; coord. team Wash. State Tchrs. Strike, 1991; chair dist. Valuing Diversity, 1993-95; drama clinician N.W. Orff Conf., 1994. Am. Orff-Schulwerk Assn. grantee, 1991. Mem. NEA, Nat. Audubon Soc. (newsletter editor 1974-79, field trip leader Seattle 1992), Am. Orff-Schulwerk Assn. (nat. bd. trustees 1987-90, editorial bd. 1984-87, clinician and presenter Cleve. 1983, Denver, 1990), Music Educators Nat. Conf. (rep. 1983-85, rsch. session Olympia, Wash. 1990), Drum Corps Internat. Democrat. Home: 11609 Marine View Dr SW Seattle WA 98146-1825 Office: Sumner Sch Dist 230 Wood Ave Sumner WA 98390-1279

POPPOFF, ILIA GEORGE, science writer, consultant; b. San Diego, Apr. 9, 1924; s. George Ilia and Stamatka P.; m. Betty Ann Sieh, Oct. 19, 1944; children: Mark David, Robin Marie, Christine Lea. Student, San Diego State U., 1942-43; BA, Whittier (Calif.) Coll., 1947; postgrad., U. Calif., Berkeley, 1947-48, Stanford U., 1954-55. Radiol. physicist U.S. Naval Radiol. Def. Lab., San Francisco, 1948-53; chmn. atmospheric scis., sr. physicist Stanford Rsch. Inst., Menlo Park, Calif., 1953-67; chief stratospheric projects NASA/Ames Rsch. Ctr., Mt. View, Calif., 1967-79; freelance sci. writer Carnelian Bay, 1980-90, Pebble Beach, Calif., 1990—; organizer, editor of proceedings, chmn. Mountain Watershed Symposium, Crystal Bay, Nev., 1988. Co-author: (monograph) Physics of the Lower Ionosphere; (textbook) Fundamentals of Aeronomy; editor proceedings Internat. Mountain Watershed Symposium, 1990; contbr. articles to profl. jours. Commr. Tahoe Regional Planning Agy. Adv. Planning Commn., Zephyr Cove, Nev., 1983—; bd. mem. Calif. Regional Water Quality Control Bd., South Lake Tahoe, Calif., 1984—; bd. dirs., pres. Tahoe Resource Conservation Dist., South Lake Tahoe, 1982-88. Mem. AAAS, Am. Geophys. Union, Am. Cetacean Soc.

PORAD, LAURIE JO, jewelry company official; b. Seattle, Dec. 19, 1951; d. Bernard L. and Francine J. (Harvitz) P. BA, U. Wash., 1974; postgrad., Seattle Pacific U., summers 1975-76. Cert. standard tchr., Wash. Substitute tchr. Issaquah (Wash.) Sch. Dist., 1974-77; with data processing dept. Ben Bridge Jeweler, Seattle, 1977-83, auditing mgr., 1983-87, systems mgr., 1987-92, MIS special project mgr., 1992—; mem. adv. bd. computer sci. dept. Highline Community Coll., Midway, Wash., 1985—, mem. tech. prep. leadership com. 1993—. Tchr. religion sch. Temple de Hirsch Sinai, Seattle, 1972-76, 84—, coord. computerized Hebrew learning ctr., 1987-88, coord. of religion sch. city facility, 1988-93, coord. mentor tchr. program, 1993—; tutor Children's Home Soc. Wash., Seattle, 1976-77. Mem. Assn. for Women in Computing (life mem., chmn. chpt. workshop 1985-88, nat. chpts. v.p. 1985-88, nat. pres. 1988-90, nat. chpt. v.p. 1992-93, rep. ind. mems. 1993—), Wash. Women United. Home: 14616 NE 44th St Apt M-2 Bellevue WA 98007-3196 Office: Ben Bridge Jeweler PO Box 1908 Seattle WA 98111-1908

PORCARO, MICHAEL FRANCIS, advertising agency executive; b. N.Y.C., Apr. 3, 1948; s. Girolamo M. and Marianna (DePasquale) P.; m. Bonnie Kerr, Apr. 7, 1972; children: Sabrina, Jon. BA in English, Rockford (Ill.) Coll., 1969. Broadcaster Sta. KFQD, Anchorage, 1970-71, Sta. KENI, Anchorage, 1972-73; v.p. ops. Cook Inlet Broadcasters, Anchorage, 1973-74; owner Audio Enterprises, Anchorage, 1974-75; asst. Alaska Pub. Broadcasting Commn., Anchorage, 1975-76; exec. dir. Alaska Pub. Broadcasting Commn., 1976-81; chief exec. officer, ptnr. Porcaro Blankenship Advt. Corp., Anchorage, 1981—; cons. Arco Alaska TV sta., Anchorage, 1981; expert witness U.S. Sen. Subcom. on Telecommunications, Washington, 1978; mem. citizens adv. com. U. Alaska Dept. Journalism. Chmn. Municipality of Anchorage Urban Design Commn., 1990-93; mem. mayor's transition team Municipality of Anchorage, 1987-88; bd. dirs. Anchorage Glacier Polits Baseball Club, 1987-88, Anchorage Mus. History and Art, Anchorage C. of C., Anchorage Symphony Orch.; chmn. bd. dirs. Bro. Francis Shelter for the Homeless, Anchorage; mem. mktg. com. gov.'s transition team, 1995. Recipient Silver Mike award Billboard mag., 1974, Bronze award N.Y. Film Critics, 1981, Best of North award Ad. Fedn. Alaska, 1982—, Addy award, 1985, 91, Grand Addy award 1990, Cable TV Mktg. award 1986; Paul Harris fellow. Mem. Advt. Fedn. Alaska, Anchorage C. of C. (bd. dirs.). Republican. Roman Catholic. Office: Porcaro Blankenship Advt 433 W 9th Ave Anchorage AK 99501-3519

POROSKY, MICHAEL HANNY, real estate and investment company executive; b. Detroit, Mar. 28, 1930; s. Walter Michael and Ruth (Hanny) P.; m. Paula Lea Dickinson; children: Michael Winston, Patrick Dickens, Wendy Christine. BA in Journalism, U. Wash., 1953. Agt. Phoenix Mut. Life Ins. Co., Seattle, 1957-66; pres. Profl. Cons. Cos., Seattle, 1967—. V.p. N.W. region Pacific N.W. Lawn Tennis Assn., 1974-78. Lt. commdr. USN, 1952-57; USNR, '57-68. Mem. Seattle Tennis Club. Republican.

PORRAS, JORGE ENRIQUE, educator; b. Floresta (Boyacá), Colombia, S.Am., Oct. 4, 1942; came to U.S., 1980; s. Uldarico and Rebeca P.; m. Doris Jaímes. BA, U. Pedagogica Tech., Colombia, 1965; MA, Ohio State U., 1973; PhD, U. Tex., Austin, 1984. Prof. of Spanish U. Pedagogica y Tecnologica de Colombia, Tunja, 1973-80; instr. of Spanish Ohio State U., Columbus, 1984-87; asst. prof. Spanish U. Nebr., Lincoln, 1987-90; assoc. prof. Spanish Sonoma State U., Rohnert Park, Calif., 1990—; Spanish coord. U. Nebr., 1988-90, Sonoma State U., Rohnert Park, 1994—; prin. investigator Calif. Fgn. Lang. Project, Redwood Area, 1992—. Mem. MLA, Am. Assn. of Tchrs. of Spanish and Portuguese, Sigma Delta Pi (advisor). Democrat. Roman Catholic. Office: Sonoma State U 1801 E Cotati Ave Rohnert Park CA 94928-3613

PORRECA, BETTY LOU, education educator; b. Cin., Aug. 8, 1927; d. James Long and Hallie Marie (Jacobs) Hackathorn; m. Charles C. Porreca, Aug. 26, 1949 (widowed 1966); 1 child, Zana Sue Porreca Easley. BA, U. Ariz., 1970, MEd, 1973; PhD, Pacific Western U., 1990. Faculty Cochise Coll., Douglas, Ariz., 1973-83, Pima Community Coll., Tucson, 1983—. Author: (poetry) Selected Poems, 1975; contbr. articles to profl. jours. Chairperson Adult Continuing Christian Edn. Catalina Meth. Ch., Tucson, 1990—; vol. Crisis Pregnancy ctr., Tucson, 1989-91. Mem. Modern Lang. Assn., Nat. Coun. Tchrs. English, Pi Lambda Theta. Democrat. Methodist. Office: Pima Community College 1255 N Stone Ave Tucson AZ 85709-3002

PORRERO, HENRY, JR., construction company executive; b. Upland, Calif., Aug. 16, 1945. AA, Chaffey Coll., 1970; BS, Calpoly Pomona U., 1973. Bus. mgr. Guy F. Atkinson Co., South San Francisco, 1973-83; controller Laird Constrn. Co., Inc., R. Cucamonga, Calif., 1983-85; pres., founder PLT Computer Systems, Inc., Upland, Calif., 1986-93; founder, mgr. Porrero Constrn. Co., Chino, Calif., 1993—; fin. cons. Parrott & Wright Constrn., Corona, Calif., 1987-93. With USN, 1966-69. Mem. Am. Legion, Friends Upland Library, Calif. Sheriffs Assn. Republican. Home: 854 Carson St Upland CA 91784-1828 Office: 13930 Oaks Ave Chino CA 91710-7010

PORTER, A. DUANE, mathematics educator; b. Detroit, Dec. 31, 1936; s. Alphonse Walter and Nelda (Hoffman) P.; m. Carol Burt, Aug. 12, 1960; children: Lisa Luane, Joshua Duane. BS, Mich. State U., 1960, MS, 1961; PhD, U. Colo., 1964. Statistician Gen. Motors, Flint, Mich., 1960; asst. prof. U. Wyo., Laramie, 1964-67, assoc. prof., 1967-69, prof., 1969—, acting head math. dept., 1976-79; vis. prof. Clemson (S.C.) U., 1977, Humboldt State U., Arcata, Calif., 1978; dir. Sci. & Math. Teaching Ctr., Laramie, 1979-83, RMMC Summer Sch., Laramie, 1982—, NSF Faculty Enhancement, Laramie, 1988—. Contbr. articles to profl. jours. Grantee NSF. Mem. Am. Math. Soc., Math. Assn. Am. (gov. 1978-81), Nat. Coun. Tchrs. Math., N.Y. Acad. Scis. Office: U Wyo Math Dept Laramie WY 82071

PORTER, ALBERT WRIGHT, author, artist, educator; b. Bklyn., Nov. 25, 1923; s. Arthur and Gertrude (Wright) P.; m. Shirley Alberta Owens, Feb. 2, 1946; children: Kim Kronfeld, Todd. AA, Compton Jr. Coll., 1942; BA, UCLA, 1950; MA, Calif. State U., L.A., 1957. Tchr. L.A. Pub. Schs., 1950-58, art supr., 1958-71; freelance artist, lectr. L.A., 1958—, author, 1974—; prof. art Calif. State U., Fullerton, 1971-89, prof. emeritus, 1989—. Author: (textbooks) Shape and Form, 1974, Pattern, 1975, Art of Sketching, 1977, Expressive Watercolor Techniques, 1982; co-author: Exploring Visual Design, 1987. Capt. USAF, 1944-45, ETO. Recipient 1st pl. award Palos Verdes Art Festival, 1977. Mem. Nat. Watercolor Soc. (v.p. 1977-78, award 1972), Watercolor West, Art Educators L.A. (Outstanding Achievement award 1988). Home: 8554 Day St Sunland CA 91040-1812

PORTER, BRIAN STANLEY, police chief; b. Seattle, May 2, 1938; s. Jack D. and Margaret I. (Tuter) P.; grad. U. Alaska, 1970, Northwestern U. Traffic Inst., 1970-71, FBI Nat. Exec. Inst., 1981; m. Bette K. Schakohl, Apr. 26, 1958; children—Kelle, Kerry, Kory. With Anchorage Police Dept., 1960—, chief of police, 1980—; chmn. Alaska Police Standards Council, 1978-80. Served with U.S. Army, 1957-58. Office: House of Reps 3430 Fordham Dr Anchorage AK 99508-4556

PORTER, DIXIE LEE, insurance executive, consultant; b. Bountiful, Utah, June 7, 1931; d. John Lloyd and Ida May (Robinson) Mathis. B.S., U. Calif. at Berkeley, 1956, M.B.A., 1957. Personnel aide City of Berkeley (Calif.), 1957-59; employment supr. Kaiser Health Found., Los Angeles, 1959-60; personnel analyst U. Calif. at Los Angeles, 1961-63; personnel mgr. Reuben H. Donnelley, Santa Monica, Calif., 1963-64; personnel officer Good Samaritan Hosp., San Jose, Calif., 1965-67; fgn. service officer AID, Saigon, Vietnam, 1967-71; gen. agt. Charter Life Ins. Co., Los Angeles, 1972-77, Kennesaw Life Ins. Co., Atlanta, from 1978, Phila. Life Ins. Co., San Francisco, from 1978; now pres. Women's Ins. Enterprises, Ltd.; cons. in field. Co-chairperson Comprehensive Health Planning Commn. Santa Clara County, Calif., 1973-76; bd. dirs. Family Care, 1978-80, Aegis Health Corp., 1977-92, U. Calif. Sch. Bus. Adminstrn., Berkeley, 1974-76; mem. task force on equal access to econ. power U.S. Nat. Women's Agenda, 1977—. Served with USMC, 1950-52. C.L.U. Mem. C.L.U. Soc., U. Calif. Alumni Assn., U. Calif. Sch. Bus. Adminstrn. Alumni Assn., AAUW, Bus. and Profl. Women, Prytanean Alumni, The Animal Soc. Los Gatos/Saratoga (pres. 1987-90), Beta Gamma Sigma, Phi Chi Theta. Republican. Episcopalian.

PORTER, DONNA J., genealogist; b. Monte Vista, Colo., Aug. 20, 1931; d. Earl Edwin Carmack, Nov. 15, 1949 (div. 1955); m. Paul W. Porter, June 4, 1955; children: LeiLonia Virginia, Paul Benjamin, Rebecca Ann. Registered profl. genealogist. Genealogist Denver, 1969—; owner Stagecoach Libr. for Geneal. Rsch., Denver; instr., lectr. in field. Co-author: Welding Lind, An Introduction to Genealogy, 1968; editor Colo. Genealogist mag., 1970-75; contbr. articles to profl. jours. and mags. Asst. libr. Family History Ctr. Libr., LDS Ch., Denver, 1966-76, mem. acquisition com., instr. spl. geneal. instrn. com.; v.p. Colo. chpt. Palatines to Am., Denver, 1985-86, pres., 1986-87, exhibitor's chair Nat. Conf., 1988. Mem. West Palm Beach Geneal. Soc. (founder, pres. 1964-66), Colo. Geneal. Soc. (corr. sec. 1968-69, pres. 1969-70, 2d v.p., program chair 1971-73, seminar chair 1974, chair, judge Black Sheep contest 1988), Foothills Geneal. Soc. (genealogist 1983-88, ednl. dir. 1992—, staff genealogist The Foothills Inquirer mag. 1983—, Genie of Yr. award 1992), Colo. Coun. Geneal. Socs. (v.p. 1986-87, pres. 1987-90, chair Colo. State Archives Ednl. Gift Fund 1991—), Nat. Soc. DAR (Peach Pipe chpt. state lineage chair 1970-73, registrar, 1971-77), Ind. Hist. Soc., Ind. Geneal. Soc., Nat. Geneal. Soc., Internat. Soc. for British Genealogy and Family History, Ohio Geneal. Soc. (life, Colo. chpt., Champaign County chpt., Madison County chpt., Ross County chpt., Monroe County chpt.), Mo. Geneal. Soc. (life), Maryland Geneal. Soc. (life), Md. Geneal Soc (life), St. Andrew Soc. (life), Inst. of Heraldic and Geneal. Studies, Assn., of Profl. Genealogist, Assn. for Gravestone Studies, Palatines to Am. (Colo. chpt.), Lower Delmarza Geneal. Socl, Balt. County Geneal. Soc., Shockey Family Meml. Fellowship. Home: 1840 S Wolcott Ct Denver CO 80219-4309

PORTER, JAMES B., hieroglyphics specialist; b. Berkeley, Calif., June 11, 1954; s. Neil Robert and Mary Newcomb (Edwards) P. BA History of Sci., Antioch U., 1979; MA in Anthropology, U. Calif., Berkeley, 1983, PhD in Anthropology, 1989. Cert. adult tchr. Staff artist U. Calif. Berkeley Abaj Takalik Project, Guatemala, 1978-80; illustrator U Calif. Berkeley Archaeol. Rsch. Facility, 1980-88; tchng. asst. anthropology U. Calif., Berkeley, 1984, rsch. asst., 1988-89, instr. anthropology univ. ext. classes, 1989-95; tour lectr. Calif. Alumni Assn. Tours, Berkeley, 1988; instr. calligraphy Oakland (Calif.) Art Supply, 1992; instr. humanities Rose St. Sch., Berkeley, 1993; instr. anthropology Piedmont (Calif.) Adult Sch., 1993-95; instr. anthropology and archaeology Laney Coll., Oakland, Calif., 1995—; presenter, lectr. in field. Exhbns. include Escultura monumental de la costa sur; Nat. Mus., Guatemala, 1979, Berkeley Community Arts Ctr., 1989, Pro-Arts Gallery, Oakland, 1993; contbr. articles to numerous profl. jours. and publs. Recipient scholarship Studio Study Ctr., Yakima, Wash., 1972-73; Tinker Travel Fund grantee, Ctr. for Latin Am. Studies, U. Calif., Berkeley, 1983-84, Robert H. Lowie Fund grantee, 1985, Olsen scholar, 1986-89; recipient scholarship Mesoamerican Art Rsch. Inst., San Francisco, 1989. Manichaean.

PORTER, JAMES NEIL, marketing executive; b. Sacramento, Oct. 3, 1931; s. Neil Lendell and Alice Elizabeth (Hummell) P.; m. Susan Elizabeth Moore, Apr. 16, 1955 (div. Feb. 1990); children: David James, Mary Katherine, Anne Elizabeth. BA, San Jose State U., 1953. Mgr. product mgmt. Memorex Corp., Santa Clara, Calif., 1968-71; dir. mktg. planning Cartridge TV, Inc., San Jose, Calif., 1971-73; dir. mktg. CMX Systems, joint venture CBS and Memorex, Sunnyvale, Calif., 1973-74; product mgr. Unicom Systems subs. Rockwell Internat., Sunnyvale, 1974-75; mgmt. cons. Mountain View, Calif., 1975-77; pres. Disk/Trend, Inc., Mountain View, 1977—. Prin. contbr. (annual market study) Disk/Trend Report, 1977—. With U.S. Army, 1953-55. Mem. IEEE, Internat. Data Storage Equipment and Materials Assn. (bd. dirs. 1986—, exec. com. 1988—). Office: Disk/Trend Inc 1925 Landings Dr Mountain View CA 94043-0808

PORTER, L(AWRENCE) B(ENJAMIN), artist; b. Friona, Tex., Mar. 3, 1929; s. Carter Clayton and Lilly Katherine (Patching) P.; m. Helen Duffy Burchell, Mar. 13, 1950 (div. 1986); children: Carter Burchell, Katherine Unity; m. Marcia Joan Orcutt, May 12, 1993. BS in Agriculture, N.Mex. Coll. Agriculture, 1955; MA, N.Mex. State U., 1959; HHD, London Inst. Applied Rsch., 1972. Tchr. Clovis & Las Cruces (N.Mex.) Pub. Schs., 1955-57; field man Western Cotton Oil Co., El Paso, 1957-60; visual info. specialist White Sands (N.Mex.) Missile Range, 1960-64; artist Anthony, N.Mex., 1964—. Author: Some Famous New Mexico Ranches, 1957. Staff sgt. USAF, 1948-53. Home: PO Box 2300 Anthony NM 88021-2300

PORTER, MICHAEL PELL, lawyer; b. Indpls., Mar. 31, 1940; s. Harold Troxel and Mildred Maxine (Pell) P.; m. Alliene Laura Jenkins, Sept. 23, 1967 (div.); children: Genevieve Natalie, Porter Eason; m. Janet Kay Smith Hayes, Feb. 13, 1983 (div.). Student, DePauw U., 1957-58; BA, Tulane U., 1961, LLB, 1963. Bar: La. 1963, U.S. Ct. Mil. Appeals 1964, N.Y. 1969, Hawaii 1971. Clk. U.S. Ct. Appeals (5th cir.), New Orleans, 1963; assoc. Sullivan & Cromwell, N.Y.C., 1968-71, Cades Schutte Fleming & Wright, Honolulu, 1971-74, ptnr., 1975-94; mem. faculty Addis Ababa (Ethiopia) U. Sch Law, 1995—; mem. deans coun. Law Sch. Tulane U., 1981-88; dep. vice chancellor Episcopal Diocese Hawaii, 1980-88, chancellor, 1988-94; chancellor Episcopal Ch., Micronesia, 1988-95. Author: Hawaii Corporation Law & Practice, 1989, Nat. Corp. Law Series, 1989; Hawaii reporter: State Limited Partnership Laws, 1992-94. Bd. dirs. Jr. Achievement Hawaii, Inc., 1974-84, Inst. Human Svcs., Inc., 1980-88; donor Michael P. Porter Dean's Scholastic award U. Hawaii Law Sch., 1977—; lectorship named in his honor, Addis Abba, Etheopia, 1994—; established Michael P. Porter Prizes on Ethnic Harmony and Religious Tolerance in a Dem. Soc. at Addis Ababa U., 1995. With JAGC, U.S. Army, 1963-66, Vietnam. Tulane U. fellow, 1981. Mem. ABA, Assn. of Bar of City of N.Y., Hawaii State Bar Assn. Republican.

PORTER, PETER, food products executive; b. 1945. Mgr. William Porter Tile Co., L.A., 1968-71; with Hoson Produce Inc., 1971—, now pres.-CEO. Office: Hoson Produce Inc 400 W Claremont St Pasadena CA 91103-2414*

PORTER, RICHARD ERNEST, speech educator, author; b. Long Beach, Calif., Dec. 7, 1933; s. Ernest Long and Arlene Mary (Dietz) P.; m. Rosemary Jean Macias, June 18, 1957; children: Tamre Lynn Cardozo, Gregory Richard. BA, Calif. State U., Long Beach, 1956; MA, San Diego State U., 1968; PhD, U. So. Calif., L.A., 1974. Commd. ensign USN, 1956, advanced through grades to lt. comdr., 1965, resigned, 1967; prof. Calif. State U., 1970—. Author: Understanding Intercultural Communication, 1981, Communication Between Cultures, 1990-95; editor: Intercultural Communication: A Reader, 1972-93 (Best Book awrd 1986). Mem. Speech Communication Assn., Western Speech Communication Assn., Long Beach Yacht Club. Office: Calif State U Dept Speech Communication Long Beach CA 90840

PORTER, RICHARD KANE, audio engineer, consultant; b. Pitts., Apr. 26, 1953; s. James Albert and Dorothy Louise (Kane) P.; m. Pamela Jean Mongeon, July 6, 1990. Student, U. Pitts., 1971-74; BA, Muskingum Coll., 1977. Field engr. customer svc. divsn. Singer Bus. Machine/TRW, 1979-81; field specialist data comm. Internat. Computers Ltd., 1981-85; applications engr. Burr-Brown Corp., Tucson, 1985-88; sr. rsch. assoc. II optical scis. ctr., lunar & planetary lab. U. Ariz., Tucson, 1988-89; systems design engr. Math. Systems Design, L.A., 1989-90; field engr. Siemens Audio Inc., Hollywood, Calif., 1991-94; chief engr. Waves Sound Recorders, Hollywood, 1993—; composer, performer RavenWolf Music, Marina Del Rey, Calif., 1991—. Contbr. articles to profl. publs. Mem. Soc. Composers and Lyricists.

PORTER, ROBERTA ANN, counselor, educator, school system administrator; b. Oregon City, Oreg., May 28, 1949; d. Charles Paul and Verle Maxine (Zimmerman) Zacur; m. Vernon Louis Porter, Dec. 27, 1975. B in Bus. Edn., So. Oreg. Coll., 1971, M in Bus. Edn., 1977; cert. in counseling, Western Oreg. Coll., 1986; cert. adminstrn., Lewis and Clark Coll., 1995. Cert. in leadership Nat. Seminars, 1991. Tchr. Klamath Union High Sch., Klamath Falls, Oreg., 1971-73, Mazama Mid. High Sch., Klamath Falls, 1973-83; instr. Oreg. Inst. Tech., Klamath Falls, 1975-92; counselor Mazama H.S., Klamath Falls, 1983-93, mem. site based mgmt. steering com., 1991-95; vice prin. Bonanza (Oreg.) Schs., 1993-95; counselor Klamath County Sch. Dist., Oreg., 1995—; presenter Oreg. and Nat. Assn. Student Coun., 1989-92, Oreg. Sch. Bds. Assn., Sch. Counselor Assn., 1995, state mini workshops counselors/adminstrs.; mem. task force for ednl. reform in Oreg., 1993-94; trainer asst. Leadership Devel. Am. Sch. Counselor Assn. Trainer U.S. Army and Marines Recruiters, Portland and Medford, Oreg., 1988-89; master trainer Armed Svcs. Vocat. Aptitude Battery/Career Exploration Program, 1992—; candidate Klamath County Sch. Bd., Klamath Falls. Recipient Promising, Innovative Practices award Oreg. Sch. Counselors, 1990. Mem. NEA, ACA, COSA, ASCD, Oreg. Sch. Counseling Assn. (presenter, v.p. h.s. 1988-91, membership com. 1991-93, pres. 1992-95), Oreg. Edn. Assn., Oreg. Counseling Assn., Oreg. Assn. Student Couns. (bd. dirs. activity advisors 1989-91, parliamentarian 1994-95, area 8 rep. 1995—), Nat. Assn. Student Couns., Klamath Falls Edn. Assn. (bldg. rep. 1990-93, sec. 1991-92, negotiations team 1992-93), Delta Kappa Gamma (exec. bd. Alpha chpt. 1985-94, pres. 1990-92, state conv. chmn. 1992, state legis. com. 1991-93, chmn. 1993-95, state expansion com.). Home: 3131 Derby St Klamath Falls OR 97603-7313

PORTER, VERNA LOUISE, lawyer; b. L.A., May 31, 1941. B.A., Calif. State U., 1963; JD, Southwestern U., 1977. Bar: Calif. 1977, U.S. Dist. Ct. (cen. dist.) Calif. 1978, U.S. Ct. Appeals (9th cir.) 1978. Ptnr. Eisler & Porter, L.A., 1978-79, mng. ptnr., 1979-86, pvt. practice law, 1986—; judge pro-tempore L.A. Mcpl. Ct., 1983—, L.A. Superior Ct., 1989—, Beverly Hills Mcpl. Ct., 1992—; mem. state of Calif. subcom. on landlord tenant law, panelist conv., mem. real property law sect. Calif. State Bar, 1983; speaker on landlord-tenant law to real estate profls., including San Fernando Bd. Realtors; vol. atty. L.A. County Bar Dispute Resolution, mem. client rels. panel, fee arbitrator. Mem. adv. coun. Freddie Mac Vendor, 1995—. Editl. asst., contbr. Apt. Owner Builder; contbr. to Apt. Bus. Outlook, Real Property News, Apt. Age; mem. World Affairs Coun. Fre Mem. ABA, L.A. County Bar Assn. (client-rels. vol. dispute resolution and fee arbitration, 1981—), L.A. Trial Lawyers Assn., Wilshire Bar Assn., Women Lawyer's Assn., Landlord Trial Lawyers Assn. (founding mem., pres.), Freddie Mac Vendor Adv. Coun., da Camera Soc. Republican. Office: 2500 Wilshire Blvd Fl 1226 Los Angeles CA 90057-4317

PORTER, WILLIAM EMME, state legislator, small business owner; b. Lucknow, India, Mar. 29, 1925; (parents Am. citizens); s. Ruben Boring and Lenore Carolyn (Emme) P.; m. E. Caryl Wilbur, June 3, 1947; children: Elisabeth, Katherine, Kristin. Student, Doane Coll., 1945-47; AB, Albion Coll., 1949; MS, Kans. State U., 1950. Tchr. Garden City (Kans.) Pub. Schs., 1951-53; prin. pub. schs. Wilson, Kans., 1953-55; tchr., head sci. dept.pub. schs. Las Cruces, N.Mex., 1955-84, farmer-mgr., 1975—; mem. N.Mex. Ho. Reps., Santa Fe, 1990—; Mem. agriculture and water com., N.Mex. State Ho. Reps., 1990—, tax and revenue com., 1990—, tax equalization com., 1990—, border devel. com., 1992—, internat. spaceport com., 1992—, agriculture and forestry com. Nat. Conf. State Legis., 1993-95, vice chair capital outlay com. Contbr. articles to newspapers; patentee Porter Bermuda Grass. Founder Friends of Fort Selden, N.Mex., 1988. With U.S. Army, 1943-45, ETO. Mem. N.Mex. Acad. Sci. (pres. 1960-61), Beta Beta Beta. Democrat. Home and Office: 5200 N Highway 85 Las Cruces NM 88005-6847

PORTNEY, JOSEPH NATHANIEL, aerospace executive; b. L.A., Aug. 15, 1927; s. Marcus and Sarah (Pilson) P.; m. Ina Mae Leibson, June 20, 1959; children: Philip, Jeffrey. BS, U.S. Naval Acad., 1952. Commd. 2d lt. USAF, 1952, advanced through grades to capt., 1956, resigned, 1960; with Litton Systems, Inc., Woodland Hills, Calif., 1960—; project engr. Litton Aero Products Litton Aero Products, 1967-68; program mgr. Litton Aero Products Litton Systems, Inc., Woodland Hills, 1968-72, advanced program mgr. Guidance and Control Sys., 1972-85, mgr. advanced programs Guidance and Control Sys., 1985—; navigator engr. on 3 historic inertial crossings of the North Pole. Creator solar compass, pilot and navigator calendar. Mem. Inst. of Navigation (v.p. 1988-89, pres. 1989-90), U.S. Naval Acad. Alumni Assn. (trustee 1980-83). Jewish. Home: 4981 Amigo Ave Tarzana CA 91356-4505 Office: Litton Systems Inc 5500 Canoga Ave Woodland Hills CA 91367-6621

PORTWAY, PATRICK STEPHEN, telecommunications consulting company executive, telecommunications educator; b. June 18, 1939; s. Christopher Leo and Ceciala (King) P.; m. Malle M. Portway; children by previous marriage—Shawn, Pam, Vicki. BA, U. Cin., 1963; MA, U. Md., 1973; postgrad., Columbia U. Regional ADP coordinator GSA, Washington, 1963-68; mgr. strategic mkt. planning Xerox Corp., 1969-74; mgr. plans and programs System Devel. Corp., 1974-78; fin. indsl. mktg. exec. Satellite Bus. Systems, 1978-80; western regional mgr. Am. Satellite Co., 1980-81; pres. Applied Bus. Telecomm., San Ramon, Calif., 1981—; prof., lectr. Golden Gate U. Grad. Sch., San Francisco, 1983—; pub. mag. Teleconference, 1981—. Author: (with others) Teleconferencing and Distance Learning, 1992, 2d edit. 1994. Presdl. elector Electoral Coll., Va., 1976; candidate Va. State Legislature from 19th Dist., 1971; chmn. Discovery Bay Mcpl. Adv. Coun., 1992—; mem adv. coun. Discovery Bay Mcpl., 1992—, chmn. 1992. Served to 1st lt. U.S. Army, 1963-65. Mem. Internat. Teleconferencing Assn. (founder, bd. dirs. 1983-88), Nat. Univ. Teleconferencing Networdk (mem. adv. bd., bd. dirs. 1986-89), U.S. Distance Learning Assn. (founder, exec. dir. 1987—) Electronic Funds Transfer Assn. (founder, bd. dirs. 1980), Satellite Profls., Jaycees charter pres. Chantilly, VA., Disting. Service award Dale City, VA. Club: Commonwealth. Office: Applied Bus Telecomm 2600 Kitty Hawk Rd Ste 110 Livermore CA 94550-9625

POSERT, HARVEY PERES, public relations professional; b. Memphis, May 29, 1930; s. Hardwig Peres and Natlee Alice (Isenberg) P.; m. Myra Gail Gainsboro, June 28, 1958 (div. Apr. 1982); children: Harvey Peres III, Robert L., Peter D. BA, Yale U., 1951. Diplomate Acad. Wine Comm. Reporter Comml. Appeal, Memphis, 1944-54; account exec. Edelman Pub. Rels., Inc., Chgo., N.Y.C., and San Francisco, 1956-75; owner Harvey Posert & Assocs., Memphis, 1960-62; pub. rels. dir. Wine Inst., San Francisco, 1975-80; v.p. comm. Robert Mondavi Winery, Napa Valley, Calif., 1980—; lectr. pub. rels. various profl. and ednl. instns. Author: Public Relations for Wineries, 1976; editor Alcohol in Moderation, 1992—. Sgt. CIC, U.S. Army, 1951-54, Germany. Recipient Consumer Program award Pub. Rels. News, N.Y.C., 1970, Golden Corkscrew award Order of Knights of the Vine, Sacramento, 1976. Mem. Am. Wine Alliance (bd. dirs. 1990—). Democrat. Jewish. Office: Robert Mondavi Winery 7801 Saint Helena Way Oakville CA 94562

POSEY, JAMES MADISON, oil company executive; b. Beaumont, Tex., June 14, 1946; s. Herbert Miles and Albertha (Howard) P.; m. Cassandra Delois Holt, Nov. 20, 1976; children: Elizabeth, Cathryn, Joseph, David, Patricia. BA, Wichita State U., 1972; JD, U. Kans., 1975. Landman Atlantic Richfield Co., Dallas and Denver, 1975-77; sr. landman Atlantic Richfield Co., Anchorage, Alaska, 1979-82; oil and gas atty. Worldwide Energy Co., Denver, 1977-79; dist. landman Arco Alaska Inc., Denver, 1982-84, land mgr., 1984-85, issues advocacy mgr., 1985-91, mgr. fed. govt. rels., 1991—. Pres. Bayshore/Klatt Cmty. Coun., Anchorage, 1987-94; treas. Alaska Dem. Party, 1990-94; bd. dirs. Jr. Achievement of Alaska, Anchorage, 1986-92. Mem. ABA, Am. Assn. Blacks in Energy (bd. dirs. 1994-95), Rotary. Baptist. Office: Arco Alaska Inc 700 G St Anchorage AK 99501-3439

POSIN, DANIEL Q., physics educator, television lecturer; b. Turkestan, Aug. 13, 1909; came to U.S., 1918, naturalized, 1927; s. Abram and Anna (Izritz) P.; m. Frances Schweitzer, 1934; children: Dan, Kathryn. A.B., U. Cal., 1932, A.M., 1934, Ph.D., 1935. Instr. U. Cal., 1932-37; prof. U. Panama, 1937-41; dean natural scis. U. Mont., prof., 1941-44, chmn. dept. physics and math., 1942-44; staff Mass. Inst. Tech., 1944-46; prof. physics, chmn. dept. N.D. State Coll., Fargo, 1946-55; prof. dept. physics DePaul U., 1956-67; prof. phys. sci. dept. Calif. State U., San Francisco, 1967—; chmn. dept. interdisciplinary scis. Calif. State U., 1969—; dir. Schwab Sci. Lecture Series, Atoms for Peace exhibit Mus. Sci. and Industry, Chgo.; Chief cons. Borg Warner Sci. Hall and Allied Chem. Sci. Hall, Times Square; scientific cons. CBS-TV. (Recipient 6 Emmy awards for best educator on TV in Chgo., and best ednl. TV programs). Author: Trigonometria, 1937-41, Fisica Experimental, Fisica, 1937-41, Mendeleyev—The Story of a Great Scientist, 1948, I Have Been to the Village, with Introduction by Einstein, 1948, rev. edit., 1974, Out of This World, 1959, What is a Star, 1961, What is Chemistry, 1961, What is a Dinosaur, 1961, The Marvels of Physics, 1961, Find Out, 1961, Chemistry for the Space Age, 1961, Experiments and Exercises in Chemistry, 1961, What is Matter, 1962, What is Electronic Communication, 1962, What is Energy, Dr. Posin's Giants, 1962, Life Beyond our Planet, 1962, Man and the Sea, 1962, Man and the Earth, 1962, Man and the Jungle, 1962, Man and the Desert, 1962, Science in the Age of Space, 1965, Rockets and Satellites, Our Solar System, The Next Billion Years, 1973; contbr. to: Today's Health; sci. cons.: Compton's Yearbook; contbr. to: feature articles Chgo. Tribune, (book) After Einstein-Remembering Einstein, 1981; co-contbr. to book The Courage to Grow Old, 1989; appearances, CBS Radio-TV, WTTW-WGN-TV, 1956-67, NET; ABC TV series Dr. Posin's Universe. Chmn. edn. com. Chgo. Heart Assn., 1963-67; Trustee Leukemia Soc. James T. Grady award Am. Chem. Soc., 1972. Fellow Am. Phys. Soc.; mem. A.A.A.S., Phi Beta Kappa, Sigma Xi. Office: Calif State Univ San Francisco CA 94132

POSKANZER, ARTHUR M., nuclear physicist and chemist; b. N.Y.C., June 28, 1931; s. Samual I. and Adele (Kerman) P.; m. Lucille Block, June 12, 1954; children: Deborah, Jeffrey, Harold. AB, Harvard U., 1953; MA, Columbia U., 1954; PhD, MIT, 1957. Chemist Brookhaven Nat. Lab., Upton, N.Y., 1957-66; sr. scientist Lawrence Berkeley Lab., Berkeley, Calif., 1966—, Bevalac sci. dir., 1978-79; head Relatiristic Nuclear Collisions Program, 1990—; chmn. nuclear chemistry Gordon Conf., 1970; sci. assoc. European Ctr. for Particle Physics, Geneva, 1979-80; mem. panel on future nuclear sci. Nat. Acad. Sci., 1976; organizer Quark Matter Conf., 1995. Fellow Guggenheim Found., 1970-71; recipient NATO sr. fellowship, 1975, Von Humboldt Sr. U.S. Scientist award, 1986. Fellow AAAS, Am. Phys. Soc.; mem. Am. chem. Soc. (chmn. div. nuclear chemistry and tech. 1977, nuclear chemistry award 1980). Discovered isotopes of light elements at the limits of stability; co-discovered collective flow of nuclear matter.

POSNANSKY, MERRICK, history and archaeology educator; b. Bolton, Lancashire, Eng., Mar. 8, 1931; came to U.S., 1977; s. Simon and Dora (Cohen) P.; m. Eunice Sarah Lubega, Feb. 10, 1962; children: Sheba, Tessa, Helen. B.A., U. Nottingham, Eng., 1952, Ph.D., 1956; Dip. Arch., Peterhouse, Cambridge U., Eng., 1953. Warden of prehist. sites Royal Nat. Parks, Nairobi, Kenya, 1956-58; curator Uganda Museum, Kampala, 1958-62; asst. dir. Brit. Inst. in Eastern Africa, Kampala, 1962-64; dir. African studies Makerere U. Coll., Kampala, 1964-67; prof. archaeology U. Ghana, Legon, 1967-76; prof. history and anthropology UCLA, 1976—, chmn. archaeology program, 1979-81, chmn. adv. com. James S. Coleman African Studies Ctr., 1983-88, dir. Inst. Archaeology, 1984-87, dir. African Studies Ctr., 1988-92; chmn. Hist. Monuments Commn. Uganda, 1964-67. Editor: Nile Quest, 1962, Prelude to East African History, 1966; joint editor: The Archaeological and Linguistic Reconstruction of African History, 1982; guest editor: Jour. New World Archaeology, 1982, 86. Grantee UNESCO, Brit. Acad., Leverhulme Trust, L.S.B. Leakey Found., Valco Found., Wenner-Gren Found., Nat. Geog. Soc., Fulbright Program, Rotary Found.; hon. fellow Brit. Inst. in Eastern Africa, 1964; vis. fellow Clare Hall, Cambridge U., 1974. Fellow Soc. Antiquaries of London; mem. Uganda Soc. (editor jour. 1962-67, pres. 1964), Soc. Hist. Archeology, African Studies Assn., UCLA Friends of Archaeology, Mus. Assn. Middle Africa (founding pres. 1959-61), Soc. African Archaeology (pres. 1990-92). Home: 5107 Rubio Ave Encino CA 91436-1124

POST, JONATHAN VOS, publishing company executive, aerospace computer consultant; b. N.Y.C., Sept. 3, 1951; s. Samuel H. and Patricia Francis (Vos) P.; m. Christine M. Carmichael, Feb. 14, 1986; 1 child, Andrew Carmichael. BS in Math., BS in Poetry, Calif. Inst. Tech., 1973; MS in Computer and Info. Sci., U. Mass., 1975, postgrad., 1975-77. Freelance computer author, cons. N.Y., N.J., Mass., 1967-79; with computer systems design and analysis Boeing Aerospace Co., Seattle, 1979-83; software engr. Jet Propulsion Lab. of NASA, Pasadena, Calif., 1983-85, Voyager mission planning engr., 1984-85; aerospace computer cons. FAA, Fullerton, Calif., 1985-86; CEO Computer Futures Inc., Los Angeles, 1984-87, Sherlock Holmes Resume Svc., 1993—; mem. sr. mgmt. and tech. staff Rockwell Internat., Downey, Calif., 1987-91; cons., pub. Computer Futures Inc., Pasadena, 1986—; exec. v.p. Palo/Hacklar Multimedia, 1994-95, Magic Dragon Multimedia, 1994—; chief exec. officer Emerald City Pub., Seattle, 1979—; speaker in field. Sci. editor: Quantum Rev.; co-pub. Space and Time mag., 1993—; contbr. numerous articles to profl. jours. Advisor Euterpe Opera Co.; mem. Town Meeting, City of Amherst, Mass., 1977; mem. Town Coun., City of Altadena, Calif., 1993-94. Recipient Rhysling Best Sci. Fiction Poem award, 1987. Fellow Brit. Interplanetary Soc.; mem. Orgn. Advancement Space Industrialization and Settlement (bd. dirs. So. Calif. nat. space soc.), World Sci. Fiction (sci. dir.), Nat. Writers Union (steering com. 1989—), Beverly Hills Mgmt. Assn. (sec. 1974—), Sci. Fiction Writers Am., Mystery Writers Am., Assn. for Computing Machinery, Poets and Writers Inc., Internat. Platform Assn., Altadena C. of C., Pasadena C. of C., U.S. C. of C. Home: 3225 Marengo Ave Altadena CA 91001-4403 Office: Computer Futures Inc 1575 N Lake Ave Ste 202 Pasadena CA 91104-2340

POSTEN, THOMAS ALLEN, emergency nurse; b. Ky., Apr. 19, 1947; s. Donald T. and Rebecca (Clements) P. AA in Nursing, Manatee Community Coll., 1974; AS in Mortuary Sci., San Francisco Coll., 1985. RN, Nev., Calif., Fla., Ala.; RNC; CEN; TNCC; ACLS; cert. funeral svc. practitioner. RN critical care, emergency room Meml. Hosp., Sarasota, Fla., 1974-81; RN jail med. svc. City and County of San Francisco, 1982-87; clin. RN VA Med. Ctr., Reno, 1987—; RN per diem Sparks (Nev.) Family Hosp., 1987-93; nurse Northern Nev. Med. Ctr., Sparks, 1993—; nursing svc. documentation com. VA Med. Ctr., Reno, 1989-93. Assoc. group facilitator San Francisco AIDS Foundation Bereavement Support Groups, 1991—. Mem. Am. Correctional Health Svcs. Assn., Emergency Nurses Assn., Mu Sigma Alpha. Office: No Nev Med Ctr Emergency Ward Sparks NV 89434

POSTER, VANESSA IRENE, development administrator; b. L.A., Nov. 12, 1963; d. David and Mary Grace P.; m. K.D. Worth, Mar. 29, 1988. BA in Humanities with honors and distinction, Stanford U., 1985, MA in Modern Thought and Lit., 1986. Event coord. Nat. Women's Polit. Caucus, Washington, 1986-88; assoc. media dir. Ctr. for Population Options, Studio City, Calif., 1989-92; dir. of devel. South Bay Free Clinic, Manhattan Beach, Calif., 1992—. Chair Redondo Beach (Calif.) Youth Commn., 1993—; coord. Women's Coalition South Bay, Redondo Beach, 1989—; mem. Redondo Beach Safer City Coun., 1994—. Mem. Stanford Profl. Women (bd. dirs. 1993—), Phi Beta Kappa. Democrat. Office: South Bay Free Clinic 1807 Manhattan Beach Blvd Manhattan Beach CA 90266-6221

POSTLETHWAIT, JOHN HARVEY, biology educator; b. Kittery, Maine, July 15, 1944; s. Samuel Noel and Sara Madeline (Cover) P. B.A., Purdue U., 1966; Ph.D., Case Western Res. U., 1970; postdoctoral student Harvard U., 1971. Asst. prof. biology U. Oreg., Eugene, 1971-77, assoc. prof., 1977-81, prof., 1981—; vis. scientist Austrian Acad., Saltzburg, 1978, Nat. Ctr. Sci. Research, Strasbourg, France, 1983, Imperial Cancer Rsch. Fund, Oxford, Eng., 1990. Fellow AAAS, Genetics Soc. Am., Soc. for Devel. Biology. Office: Dept Biology Univ Oreg Eugene OR 97403

POSTMA, JAMES LEE, computer software engineer, consultant; b. Chgo., Aug. 9, 1934; s. John Jr. and Grace E. (Lee) P.; m. Yukiko Honda, Dec. 21, 1960 (div. Feb. 1980); children: Monica Lee, Cindy Jane, Joy Marie; m. Frances Ann Speers, July 26, 1980. BSME, Purdue U., 1956; postgrad., Alexander Hamilton Inst., 1962. Registered profl. engr., Calif; cert. flight instr., FAA. Sr. engr. North Am. Aviation, Canoga Park, Calif., 1960-67; mgr. CELESCO, Costa Mesa, Calif., 1967-72, Calif. Computer Corp., Anaheim, 1972-73; pvt. practice investment adviser Anaheim, 1973-78, pvt. practice computer software engineering cons., 1978-80; pvt. practice computer software engineering cons. Steilacoom, Wash., 1980—; pres. Brainware Corp., Anaheim, 1967-77; dir. 2003 Corp., Steilacoom, 1992; CEO Western Air Lines, Steilacoom, 1995. 1st lt. USAF, 1957-60, Japan. Recipient Sci. award Bausch & Lomb, 1952. Mem. ASME (pres. student chpt. 1955), Theta Xi. Republican. Lutheran.

POSTMA, STEVEN J., owner distribution business; b. Logan, Utah, Dec. 17, 1947; s. S.J. and Stella (Carlson) P.; m. Kathy Blair, Aug. 26, 1970; children: Tamara, Blair, Trish, Lisa, Mandy. BSME, Utah State U., 1972; postgrad, Ariz. State, 1973-74; MBA, U. Utah, 1978. Cert. profl. engr., Utah, nat. fluid power specialist, fluid power engr. Design engr. Caterpillar Tractor, Peoria, Ill., 1970-71, Garrett Airesearch, Phoenix, 1972-75; aerospace engr. E. System, Salt Lake City, 1975-76; product mgr. Elmco PEC, Salt Lake City, 1976-80; owner Interstate Hyrdaulics Inc., Salt Lake City, 1980 --; cons. Postma and Assocs., Salt Lake City, 1986 --. Inventor: Compressor CNG, 1985, Wire Line Winch Control, 1982. Com. mem. Sandy City Dist. Coun., 1984-86; delegate Utah Rep. Convention, 1988; pres. LDS Stake, Sandy, 1985-90. Mem. Fluid Power Distbrs. Assn., Reroth Nat. Distbr. Coun. (Disting. Svc. award), Ad Hoc Distbr. Coun. (nad. chmn. 1989, 93), Parker/Ross Distbr. Coun., Phi Kappa Phi, Sigma Tau. Office: Interstate Hydraulics Inc 4123 S 500 W Salt Lake City UT 84123-1399

POTASH, STEPHEN JON, international public relations practitioner; b. Houston, Feb. 25, 1945; s. Melvin L. and Petrice (Edelstein) P.; m. Jeremy Warner, Oct. 19, 1969; 1 son, Aaron Warner. BA in Internat. Rels., Pomona Coll., 1967. Account exec. Charles von Loewenfeldt, Inc., San Francisco, 1969-74, v.p., 1974-80; founder, pres. Potash & Co., Pub. Rels., Oakland, Calif., 1980-87; cons. Am. Pres. Lines and Am. Pres. Cos., 1979-87; exec. dir. Calif. Coun. Internat. Trade, 1970-87; v.p. corp. communications Am. Pres. Cos., Oakland, 1987-90; chmn. Potash & Co., Oakland, 1990—. Bd. dirs. Calif. Coun. Internat. Trade, 1987-94, Calif.-Southeast Asia Bus. Coun., 1992—, Temple Sinai, Oakland, 1979-81. Mem. Pub. Rels. Soc. Am., Commonwealth Club of Calif., World Trade Club San Francisco. Office: Potash & Co 1946 Embarcadero Oakland CA 94606-5213

POTOCKI, JOSEPH EDMUND, marketing company executive; b. Jersey City, Jan. 31, 1936; s. Joseph and Estelle (Bielski) P.; m. Margaret Mary Shine, May 21, 1960; children: Joseph, Meg, David. BS, Seton Hall U., 1957. Asst. regional sales mgr. Gen. Mills Inc., Valley Stream, N.Y., 1960-67; group mgr. merchandising Warner Lambert Co., Morris Plains, N.J., 1967-74; dir. merchandising svcs. Beatrice Hunt/Wesson, Fullerton, Calif., 1974-81; pres., chief exec. officer Joseph Potocki & Assocs., Irvine, Calif., 1981-92; pres. Mktg. Fulfillment Svcs., Tustin, Calif., 1985-87; chmn. Clarke Hooper Am., 1987-92; sr. exec. Gage Mktg, Newport Beach, 1992—; instr. nat. bus. seminars. Bd. dirs. L.A. Parent Inst. Quality Edn., 1994—. Recipient Mktg. Motivator award L.A. Mktg. Exhbn., 1981, Mktg. Gold medal Am. Mktg. Assn. 1957. Mem. Promotion Mktg. Assn. (chmn. bd. dirs. 1977-79, v.p West sect. 1980-87, bd. dirs. 1990, chmn. edn. com., Reggie award 1984, 85, 87), Promotion Mktg. Assn. Am. (bd. dirs. exec. com. 1978-87, Chmn.'s Bowl 1979, Named to Chmn.'s Cir. 1986, chmn. basics and advanced edn.), Nat. Premium Sales Execs. (sec. 1985-86, Pres. award 1985, Cert. Incentive Profl. Republican. Roman Catholic. Home: Monarch Pointe 22772 Azure Sea Laguna Niguel CA 92677-5439 Office: Gage Mktg Group 3620 Birch St Newport Beach CA 92660-2619

POTROVITZA, NICHOLAS POMPEI, mechanical engineer, solar energy researcher; b. Oradea, Romania, July 7, 1952; came to U.S., 1989; s. Valentin and Aurelia (Pop) P.; m. Victoria Cornelia Caproiu Potrovitza, July 9, 1974; children: Jessica, Tanissa. BA in Mech. Engring., Mech. Faculty Poly. Inst., Romania, 1977. Cert. quality engr., welding inspector, quality assurance mgmt. Mech. engr. Vulcan Boiler Mfg. Co., Bucharest, Romania, 1977-79, Crane Factory, Timishoara, Romania, 1979-81; researcher Dept. Tech. Mech. Faculty, Timishoara, Romania, 1981-86; solar power plant designer Luz Industries Ltd., Jerusalem, Israel, 1986-89, Borom, Calif., 1989-91; sr. mech. engr. KJC Oper. Co., Borom, Calif., 1991—. Contbr. articles to profl. jours. Mem. Am. Welding Soc., Am. Soc. Quality Control, Soc. Mfg. Engrs. Office: KJC Operating Co 41100 Us Highway 395 Boron CA 93516-2109

POTTER, DAVID ERIC, computer executive, organizational consultant and trainer; b. San Jose, Calif., Sept. 12, 1949; s. Charles Devere and Ada (Ranelli) P.; m. Lauren Fins, Sept. 22, 1974; 1 child, Tracy Brianne. BA, U. Calif., 1971, MA, 1974, postgrad., 1978. Tng. instr. Intel Corp., Santa Clara, Calif., 1978-79; sales devel. mgr. Intel Corp., Santa Clara, 1979-80; pres., chief exec. officer Concurrent Sciences, Inc., Moscow, Idaho, 1980—. Contbr. articles to profl. jours. Mem. Assn. Computing Machinery, Internat. RMX User's Group (v.p. 1985-87). Home: 1191 Tolo Trl Moscow ID 83843-8707 Office: Concurrent Scis PO Box 9666 530 S Asbury St Moscow ID 83843-2228

POTTER, J(EFFREY) STEWART, property manager; b. Ft. Worth, July 8, 1943; s. Gerald Robert Potter and Marion June (Mustain) Tombler; m. Dianne Eileen Roberb, Dec. 31, 1970 (div. Aug. 1983); 1 child, Christopher Stewart; m. Deborah Ann Blevins, Oct. 20, 1991. AA, San Diego Mesa Coll., 1967. Cert. apartment mgr., apartment property supr., housing adminstr. Sales mgr. Sta. KJLM, La Jolla, Calif., 1964-67; mgr. inflight catering Host Internat., San Diego, 1967-69; lead aircraft refueler Lockheed Co., San Diego, 1969-70; property mgr. Internat. Devel. and Fin Corp., La Jolla, 1970-72; mgr. bus. property BWY Constn. Co., San Diego, 1972-73; mgr. residents Coldwell Banker, San Diego, 1973-74; mgr. Grove Investments, Carlsbad, Calif., 1974-76, Villa Granada, Villa Seville Properties Ltd., Don Cohn, Chula Vista, Calif., 1976-83; gen. mgr. AFL-CIO Bldg. Trades Corp., National City, Calif., 1983—; instr., Cert. Apt. Mgmt. San Diego Apt. Assn. Bd. dirs. San Diego County Apt. Assn., 1995—. Fellow Internat. Platform Assn., Nat. City C. of C., Toastmasters, Founding Families San Diego Hist. Soc., Am. Assn. Retired Persons, San Diego County Apt. Assn. (bd. dirs.), La Jolla Monday Night Club (treas. 1984-89). Roman Catholic. Home: 4616 Granger St San Diego CA 92107-4012 Office: AFL-CIO Bldg Trades Corp 2323 D Ave National City CA 91950-6730

POTTER, ROBERT ALONZO, dramatic art educator; b. N.Y.C., Dec. 28, 1934; s. Henry Codman and Lucilla Annie (Wylie) P.; m. Sally Alabaster (div.); m. Nancy Elizabeth Collinge (div.); m. Pamela Howard (div.); children: Lucilla Callander Potter Hoshor, Daniel Latimer, Jane Wylie, Maria Theresa, Bryn Ann. BA, Pomona Coll., 1956; MA, Claremont Grad. Sch., 1963, PhD, 1965. Lectr. in humanities Harvey Mudd Coll., Claremont, Calif., 1964-65; asst. prof. English U. Calif., Santa Barbara, 1965-72, lectr. in dramatic art, 1972-75, assoc. prof. of dramatic art, 1975-81, prof. dramatic art, 1981—; vis. prof. theatre studies U. Kent, Canterbury, Eng., 1984-85. Author: The English Morality Play, 1975 (plays) Where is Sicily, 1969, In A Pig's Eye, 1975, Fifteen Signs of the Apocalypse, 1978, Just Across the Border, 1980, The Vision of Children, 1980, The Sea Lion, 1983, The Wind Dancers, 1987, The Lady in the Labyrinth, 1987, (with Ellen Anderson) A Fine and Private Place, 1991, Bedtime Story, 1992, Saint Barbara in the Flesh, 1995. Mem. County Dem. Ctrl. Com., Santa Barbara, 1968-74. Cpl. U.S. Army, 1957. Fulbright scholar U. Bristol, Eng., 1963-64. Home: 1070 Miramonte Dr Apt 7 Santa Barbara CA 93109-1367 Office: U Calif Dept Dramatic Art Santa Barbara CA 93106

POTTER, STEPHEN ARNOLD, production designer; b. Glendale, Calif., July 11, 1937; s. Lorne Arnold and Mary Elizabeth (Bilheimer) P.; m. Cathleen Burt, July 11, 1957 (dec. 1987); m. Fumiko Morio, Oct. 8, 1992. Spl. studies, Am. Acad., Rome, 1957, Bishop Mus. Acad., Honolulu; AA, UCLA. Producer, dir. Gloria Swanson Film Festival, Orlando, Fla., 1980; prodn. designer, set decorator Zoetrope/Francis Ford Coppola, 20th Century Fox, Hollywood, Calif., 1990; prodn. designer Landmark Entertainment, North Hollywood, Calif., 1990-91, Concorde Pictures, West L.A., Calif., 1991-93; founder S.W. Props, Phoenix, 1978—; pres. Jupiter Prodns., Beverly Hills, Calif., 1968—. Author: The Nile Triangle, 1979, Dragonsong, 1980. Active Rep. Presdl. Task Force, Washington, 1986—; dir. S.E. campaign Youth Movement for Reagan, Orlando, 1986. Recipient Bronze Halo of Special Merit So. Calif. Motion Picture Coun., 1983. Mem. Acad. Motion Picture Arts and Scis. (fgn. film com. 1990—, Nichols scholar 1991—), Set Decorators Soc. Am. (v.p. 1993-94), SAR (v.p. 1964-68), Sons of Confederacy, Barons of Runnymede, Order of Crown. Office: PO Box 11416 Beverly Hills CA 90213-4416

POTTERAT, JOHN JAMES, public health officer, researcher; b. Geneva, Switzerland, July 5, 1942; came to U.S., 1956; s. Lucien Charles and Liliane Johanna (Jacot) P.; m. Susan Louise Block, Oct. 3, 1969; children: Nico Christopher, Anna Louise. BA, UCLA, 1965. Pub. health officer L.A. County Health Dept., 1968-72; dir. STD/HIV control El Paso County Health Dept., Colorado Springs, Colo., 1972—; cons. WHO, 1990, El Paso County Med. Soc., 1986—; presenter in field. Author: (with others) Strategies for Management of Sexual Partners, 1984, rev. edit., 1990, Prostitution, Intravenous Drug Use and HIV-1 in the U.S., 1990; contbr. numerous articles to profl. jours. With U.S. Army, 1965-67, Vietnam. Recipient Dr. Nathan Davis award AMA, Chgo., 1993, Dr. Cleere award Colo. Pub. Health Assn., Denver, 1992, P.W. Jacoe award, 1979; named Soldier of Month U.S. Army, 1966. Mem. Internat. AIDS Soc., Colo. Pub. Health Assn. Home: 2901 Country Club Dr Colorado Springs CO 80909-1020 Office: El Paso County Health Dept 301 S Union Blvd Colorado Springs CO 80910-3123

POTTIER, GERALD J., JR., management consultant; b. Springfield, Mass., July 10, 1946; s. Gerald J. and Florence Lee (Flagg) P.; m. Sharon Lee Weatherby; children—Gerald J., Kelley Scott, Erica. Student Holyoke Community Coll. Mgmt. trainee Friendly's Ice Cream, Wilbraham, Mass., 1969-71; owner restaurant, Cromwell, Conn., 1971-76; state dir. Leisure Life, Inc., Erie, Pa., 1976-80; gen. mgr. Mgmt. Recruiters, Springfield, 1980-83; pres. Consignment Resources, Springfield, 1983—; pres. Gerald J. Pottier Jr. Mgmt. Cons., Pearce, Ariz., 1991—. Served with USMC, 1964-68, Vietnam. Mem. Am. Defense Prepardness Assn., Nat. Security Intelligence Assn., U.S. Defense Com., Old Crows. Mem. Christian Ch. Avocations: bridge; remodeling.

POTTRUCK, DAVID STEVEN, brokerage house executive; b. 1948. BA, U. Pa., 1970, MBA, 1972. Now pres., CEO U.S. Govt., 1972-74; with Arthur Young & Co., 1974-76, sr. cons.; with Citibank N.Am., 1976-81, v.p.; with Shearson/Am. Express, 1981-84, sr. v.p. consumer mktg. and advt.; with Charles Schwab & Co., San Francisco, 1984—; exec. v.p. mktg., br. adminstr. Charles Schwab and Co., Inc.; pres., CEO The Charles Corp., Charles Schwab & Co.; pres., COO The Charles Schwab Corp. Office: Charles Schwab & Co Inc 101 Montgomery St San Francisco CA 94104-4122

POTTS, CHARLES AARON, management executive, writer; b. Idaho Falls, Idaho, Aug. 28, 1943; s. Verl S. and Sarah (Gray) P.; m. Judith Samimi, 1977 (div. 1986); 1 child, Emily Karen; m. Ann Weatherill, June 19, 1988; 1 child, Natalie Larise. BA in English, Idaho State U., 1965. Lic. real estate broker, Wash. Owner Palouse Mgmt., Inc., Walla Walla, Wash.; founder, dir. Litmus Inc., 1967-77; founding editor COSMEP, Berkeley, Calif., 1968; host poetry radio program Oasis, NPR-KUER, Salt Lake City, 1976-77; N.W. rep. Chinese Computer Communications, Inc., Lansing, Mich., 1988. Author: Little Lord Shiva, 1969, Rocky Mountain Man, 1978, A Rite to the Body, 1989, The Dictatorship of the Environment, 1991, Loading Las Vegas, 1991, How the South Finally Won the Civil War, 1994. Rep. to exec. com. 5th Congl. Dist., Wash. State Dem. Party, 1993. Recipient First Place Novel award Manuscript's Internat., 1991, Disting. Profl. Achievement award Idaho State U., 1994. Mem. Italian Heritage Assn. (ice cream chair 1990, award 1993), Walla Walla Area C. of C., Downtown W2 Found., Blue Mountain Arts Alliance. Office: Palouse Mgmt 34 S Colville St Walla Walla WA 99362-1920

POTTS, DENNIS WALKER, lawyer; b. Santa Monica, Calif., Dec. 17, 1945; s. James Longworth and Donna (Neely) P.; m. Chung Wan; children: Brandon Earl Woodward, Trevor Shipley. B.A., U. Calif.-Santa Barbara, 1967; J.D., U. Calif.-San Francisco, 1970. Bar: Hawaii 1971, Calif. 1971, U.S. Dist. Ct. Hawaii 1971, U.S. Dist. Ct. (cen. dist.) Calif. 1983, U.S. Ct. Appeals (9th cir.) 1973, U.S. Supreme Ct. 1978. Assoc. Chuck Mau, Honolulu, 1971-74; sole practice, Honolulu, 1974—; mem. litigation com. ACLU Hawaii, 1977-82. Recipient cert. Coll. of Advocacy Hastings Coll. Law-Loyola U. Sch. Law, San Francisco, 1973. Mem. Assn. Trial Lawyers Am. (sustaining), ACLU of Hawaii (Disting. Svc. cert. 1974), Hawaii Trial Lawyers Assn., Honolulu Club, Kailua Racquet Club.

POTTS, SANDRA D., elementary education educator; b. Lakeview, Oreg., Aug. 17, 1937; d. George A. and Maxine E. (Withers) Campbell; children: Alexander B. Potts, Casey C. Potts. BA, Chico (Calif.) State U., 1959; postgrad., San Jose State U., Santa Clara U. Elem. tchr. Cupertino Union Sch. Dist., 1959—; tchr. parent edn. classes Smart Start and Megaskills, 1994—. Recipient hon. svc. award PTA; named Tchr. of Yr., Santa Clara County, 1991-92. Mem. NEA, ASCD, Calif. Tchrs. Assn., Cupertino Edn. Assn.

POULOS, CLARA JEAN, nutritionist; b. L.A., Jan. 1, 1941; d. James P. and Clara Georgie (Creighton) Hill; PhD in Biology, Fla. State Christian U., 1974; PhD in Nutrition, Lafayette U., 1984; D in Nutritional Medicine, Hearts of Jesus and Mary Coll., 1986; Cert. in Diabetes Edn.; m. Themis Poulos, Jan. 31, 1960. Registered nutritionist; cert. hypnotherapist. Dir. rsch. Leapou Lab., Aptos, Calif., 1973-76, Monterey Bay Rsch. Inst., Santa Cruz, Calif., 1976—; nutrition specialist, Santa Cruz, 1975—; dir. nutritional svcs., health enhancement, lifestyle planning, Santa Cruz, 1983—; instr. Santa Cruz Extention U. Calif. and Stoddard Assocs. Seminars; cons. Biol-Med. Lab., Chgo., Nutra-Med Rsch. Corp., N.Y., Akorn-Miller Pharmacal, Chgo., Monterey Bay Aquaculture Farms, Threshhold Lab., Calif., Resurrection Lab., Calif. Recipient Najulander Internat. Rsch. award, 1971, Wainwright Found. award., 1979, various state and local awards. Fellow Internat. Coll. Applied Nutrition, Am. Nutritionist Assn., Internat. Acad. Nutritional Consultants; mem. Am. Diabetes Assn. (profl., pres. Santa Cruz chpt., editor newsletter The Daily Balance Santa Cruz chpt., sec. No. Calif. chpt.), AAAS, Internat. Platform Soc., Am. Heart Assn. (pres. Santa Cruz br. 1990-91), Am. Public Health Assn. Calif. Acad. Sci., Internat. Fishery Assn. (health asct.), Am. Women's Bowling Assn., MUSE- Computer Users Group. Clubs: Toastmistress, Quota. Author: Alcoholism - Stress - Hypoglycemia, 1976; The Relationship of Stress to Alcoholism and Hypoglycemia, 1979; assoc. editor Internat. Jour. Bio-social Research, Health Promotion Features; editor Nutrition and Dietary Consultant Jour.; columnist The New Newspaper, Santa Cruz; contbr. articles to profl. jours. Office: 1595 Soquel Dr Ste 330 Santa Cruz CA 95065-1717

POULSEN, DENNIS ROBERT, environmentalist; b. Boston, Jan. 17, 1946; s. Stephen Dudley and Dorothy Hope (Davis) P.; m. Bonnie Lou Reed; children: David, Zachery, Patrick. AS in Forestry, U. Mass., Stockbridge-Amherst, 1965; AS in Indsl. Supervision, Chaffey Coll., Alta Loma, Calif., 1977; BS in Bus. Adminstrn., U. Redlands (Calif.), 1979; postgrad., U. Calif., Riverside, 1986, U. Calif., Davis, 1991-93; cert. program, U. Calif., Davis, 1991-94. Cert. environ. profl., registered environ. profl., registered environ. assessor, Calif., cert. hazardous materials mgr., cert. lab. technolgoist; diplomate Inst. Hazardous Materials Mgmt. Water control technician Weyerhaeuser Co. Chem. Lab., Fitchburg, Mass., 1965-69; environ. rsch. technician Kaiser Steel Corp., Fontana, Calif., 1969-78, environ. rsch. engr., 1978-83, asst. environ. dir., 1983-87; mgr. environ. svcs. Calif. Steel Industries Inc., Fontana, 1987—; mem. adv. group Calif. EPA (CAL EPA), 1993—; originator AISE Nat. Environ. Com., Pitts., papers chmn., 1993, com. vice chmn., 1994, chmn., 1995; mem. adv. group Calif. Environ. Protection Agy., 1993—; mem. com. on the environment Am. Iron and Steel Inst., Washington, 1995—; mem. White House Environ. Task Force, 1993; editor-in-chief NAEP News, Washington, 1993—; mem. editl. adv. bd. Indsl. Wastewater Mag., 1993—; mem. adv. bd. Occupl. Health and Safety Mag., 1993—; mem. U.S. EPA Common Sense Initiative Subcom., Washington, 1994—. Editorial adv. bd. Indsl. Wastewater Mag., 1993—; contbr. articles and papers on environmental issues to profl. publs. Del. U.S. Environ. Delegation, Soviet Union, 1990; mem. U.S. Citizens Network of the UN Conf. on Environment and Devel.; del. U.N. Conf. on agenda 21 ethical implications; trustee Acad. Bd. Cert. Environ. Profls.; mem. Hazmat/West Adv. Coun., 1995. Mem. Nat. Assn. Environ. Profls. (cert. rev. bd., mem. internat. com. 1992—, mem. bd. dirs. 1993—), Air and Water Mgmt. Assn., Nat. Environ. Health Assn., Environ. Info. Assn., Hazardous Materials Control Rsch. Inst., Water Environment Fedn. (groundwater com.), World Safety Orgn. (cert. hazardous materials supr.), Assn. Energy Engrs. (environ. engr.s mgrs. inst., environ. project of yr. award 1992), Chino Basin Water Dist. Watermaster Adv. Coun., Calif. Water Pollution Control Assn., Inst. Hazardous Materials Mgmt., People to People Internat., U. Redlands Alumni Assn. (bd. mem., recipient Gordon Adkins award for profl. achievement 1994). Home: 5005 Hedrick Ave Riverside CA 92505-1425 Office: Calif Steel Industries Inc 14000 San Bernardino Ave Fontana CA 92335-5258

POULSON, LYNN HANSEN, home and family studies educator, writer; b. Roosevelt, Utah, Jan. 11, 1949; s. Kermit and Gertrude Ilean (Hansen) P.; m. Julie Karen Gividen, Nov. 2, 1972; children: Kermit Ty, Cory, Nickolas, Kimilyn, Kareena. AA, Snow Coll., Ephraim, Utah, 1972; BA, Utah State U., 1974; MEd, Brigham Young U., 1975. Counselor Snow Coll., 1975-80, assoc. prof. home and family studies, 1980—, chmn. div. social and behavioral scis., 1991-93. Author: Uncommon Common Sense: A Guide for Engaged and Married Couples, 1993. Sec., Sanpete Cmty. Theater, Ephraim, 1977, pres., 1978; asst. chmn. Scandinavian Festival, Ephraim, 1989-90. Named Tchr. of Yr., Snow Coll., 1991. Mem. Nat. Coun. on Family Rels. Republican. Mem. LDS Ch. Home: 110 N 460 E # 86 1 Ephraim UT 84627-1215 Office: Snow Coll 150 College Ave Ephraim UT 84627

POWELL, HERBERT J., architect; b. Chgo., Jan. 30, 1898; s. Benjamin F. and Hattie (Turner) P.; m. Alice Jewel Morse, 1926; children: James M., Robert F., Maybelle E. AB, U. Redlands, 1920, LHD (hon.), 1961; AM, Harvard U., 1924. Registered architect, Calif. Draftsman McKinn, Mead & White, N.Y.C., 1925; instr. archtl. design U. So. Calif., 1927-28; prin., designer Marsh, Smith & Powell, L.A., from 1928; sr. ptnr. Powell, Morgridge, Richards and Coghlan, from 1964; mem. Calif. State Bd. Archtl. Examiners, 1944-52, pres., 1946; mem. panel Am. Arbitration Assn., L.A. Past editor coll. newspaper U. Redlands, Rotarian newsletter, L.A.; designer Oneonta Congl. Ch., Pasadena, Calif., 1950. Moderator 1st Congl. Ch., Santa Barbara, Calif., 1974-75; mem. Citizens Task Force, Santa Barbara, 1979, City Housing Authority, Santa Barbara, 1980-89. With U.S. Army. Sheldon travelling fellow, 1924. Fellow AIA (pres. So. Calif. chpt. 1944). Home: 900 Calle De Los Amigos E105 Santa Barbara CA 93105

POWELL, JAMES LAWRENCE, museum president; b. Berea, Ky., July 17, 1936; s. Robert Lain and Lizena (Davis) P.; m. Joan Hartmann; children: Marla, Dirk, Joanna. AB, Berea Coll., 1958; PhD, MIT, 1962; DSc (hon.), Oberlin Coll., 1983; LHD (hon.), Tohoku Gakuin U., 1986; DSc (hon.), Beaver Coll., 1992. Mem. faculty Oberlin Coll., Ohio, 1962-83, also prof. geology, asso. dean, 1973-75, v.p., provost, 1976-83; pres. Franklin and Marshall Coll., Lancaster, Pa., 1983-88, Reed Coll., Portland, Oreg., 1988-91; pres., chief exec. officer The Franklin Inst., Phila., 1991-94; pres., dir. Los Angeles County Mus. Natural History, L.A., 1994—; mem. Nat. Sci. Bd., 1986—. Author: Strontium Isotope Geology, 1972, Pathways to Leadership: Achieving and Sustaining Success: A Guide for Nonprofit Executives, 1995. Fellow Geol. Soc. Am. Home: 150 S Muirfield Rd Los Angeles CA 90004-3729 Office: LA County Mus Natural Histo 900 Exposition Blvd Los Angeles CA 90007-4057

POWELL, JOSEPH EDWARD, English language educator; b. Ellensburg, Wash., Jan. 22, 1952; s. Arthur G. and Dorothy J. (Davis) P.; m. Judith A. Kleck, July 14, 1988; 1 child, Evan Ellis. BA, U. Wash., 1975; MA, Ctrl. Wash. U., 1978, BA, 1982; MFA, U. Ariz., 1981. Classroom tchr. Sequim (Wash.) H.S., 1982-83; instr. Ctrl. Wash. U., Ellensburg, 1983-88, asst. prof. English, 1989-90, assoc. prof. English, 1991—. Author: Counting the Change, 1986, Winter Insomnia, 1993; contbr. poems and essays to publs. V.p. Ellensburg (Wash.) Arts Commn., 1988-90, 91-92, pres., 1989-90, 92-93. Mem. Associated Writing Programs, Alpine Lakes Protection Soc. Home: 221 Cross Creek Dr Ellensburg WA 98926 Office: Dept English Ctrl Wash Univ Ellensburg WA 98926-7558

POWELL, JULIA GERTRUDE, volunteer; b. Fenton, Mich., Jan. 25, 1907; d. Thomas James and Leila May (Bishop) Selman; m. Ronald Douglas Powell, June 25, 1924 (div. May 4, 1961); 1 child, Delva Dorothea (dec.). BA in Edn., Colo. Coll., 1949, MA in Edn., 1949; M in Adminstrn., UCLA, 1950; postgrad., Chapman Coll. Tchr. kindergarten Garden Grove (Calif.) Elem. Sch., Garden Grove Unified Sch. Dist., 1950-71. Pres. Garden Grove Tchrs. Assn., Calif., 1961, Ebell of Laguna Hills, Leisure World, 1983, Beethoven chpt. Guild, Orange County, 1984; Worthy Matron Hermosa chpt. Eastern Star, Santa Ana, Calif., 1972; Worthy High Priestess White Shrine of Jerusalem, 1976; Queen Merret Temple Daus. of Nile, Anaheim, Calif., 1988-89. Mem. NEA-Am. Assn. Ret. Persons, AAUW, Calif. Ret. Tchrs. Assn. Republican. Presbyterian.

POWELL, LANE ALAN, editor; b. Alamogordo, N.Mex., Mar. 8, 1955; s. Cecil Lane Holmes and Janet Marie (LeRoux) Powell; m. Mari Catherine Priemesberger, July 15, 1989; children: Lane Cody, Sarah Blais. BS in Journalism, U. Fla., 1984. Info. specialist Engring. Coll. U. Fla., Gainesville, 1983-85; editor Windsor Publs., L.A., 1985-89; coord. publs. East Bay Regional Park Dist., Oakland, Calif., 1989—. Editor: Jacksonville and Florida's First Coast, 1989. Named Outstanding Hard Cover Pub. of Yr. Am. Chambers of Commerce Execs., 1989; recipient Best Spl. Facility Brochure in Calif. Calif. Park and Recreation Soc., 1990, Best Brochure Calif. Park and Recreation Soc., 1995. Home: 1882 N 5th St Concord CA 94519-2628 Office: East Bay Regional Park Dist 2950 Peralta Oaks Ct Oakland CA 94605-5320

POWELL, MEL, composer; b. N.Y.C., Feb. 12, 1923. Studied piano from age 4; studied composition with Ernst Toch, L.A., 1946-48; with Paul Hindemith, Yale U., from 1948, MusB, 1952. Mem., chmn. faculty composition Yale U., 1957-69; mem. staff, head faculty composition, formerly dean Calif. Inst. Arts, Valencia, provost, 1972-76, now Inst. fellow, Roy E. Disney chair in mus. composition. Albums include Six Recent Works, 1982-88; composer: Duplicates: A Concerto for Two Pianos and Orchestra (premier L.A. Philharm. 1990, Pulitzer prize for music 1990), Modules for chamber orch. (recorded L.A. Philharm. 1991), Woodwind Quintet (recorded 1991), Setting for Two Pianos (recorded 1992), Settings for Small Orch., 1992 (commissioned by chamber orchs. of St. Paul, L.A., N.J.), Settings for Guitar (recorded 1993), numerous other compositions; subject of profile in New Yorker mag. Recipient Creative Arts medal Brandeis U., 1989; Pulitzer Prize for music, 1990; Guggenheim fellow; Nat. Inst. Arts and Letters grantee. Mem. Arnold Schoenburg Inst. (hon. life). Office: Calif Arts Inst Dept Composition 24700 Mcbean Pky Santa Clarita CA 91355-2340

POWELL, STEPHANIE, visual effects director; b. Dayton, Ohio, Sept. 27, 1946; d. Harley Franklin and Evelyn Luella (Reed) Pence. Pres., CEO Video Assist Systems, Inc., North Hollywood, Calif., 1979—, Out of the Blue Visual Effects, 1989; Blue Screen Effects supr. Jurassic Park, Flintstones; Visual Effects supr. MGM's Blown Away, CBS My Brothers Keeper. Supr. visual effects: (motion pictures) Jurassic Park, 1993, Flintstones, 1994, Blown Away, 1994, (TV) Quantum Leap, My Brother's Keeper, 1994, Powder, 1995, various commls.; developer using 3/4-inch videotape for broadcast; co-developer color videotape for motion picture work. Mem. Acad. TV Arts and Scis., Acad. Magical Arts and Scis. Office: Video Assist Systems Inc 11030 Weddington St North Hollywood CA 91601-3212

POWELL, TED FERRELL, micrographics specialist; b. Rexburg, Idaho, Feb. 2, 1935; s. Edward Lewis and Thelma Mae (Arnold) P.; m. Nedra Scoresby, Jan. 15, 1954; children: Janeal, Julia, Greg F., Megan, Kara, N. Elizabeth. BS in Acctg., U. Utah, 1962; MBA, U. Phoenix, 1987. Supr. geneal. libr. LDS Ch., Salt Lake City, 1967-70; supr. granite mountain records vault Ch. Jesus Christ Latter Day Sts., Salt Lake City, 1970-71, dir. microfilming field ops., 1971-85, ops. analyst geneal. dept., 1985—; chmn. East Canyon Resort, Inc., 1988—; chmn., chief exec. officer Bus. Edn. and Cons. Inst., 1991; mem. com. on preservation of hist. records NRC, Washington, 1984—. Co-author: A Guide to Micrographics, 1984; also articles. Mem. Assn. Info. and Image Mgmt. (chpt. pres. 1976-77, bd. dirs. 1977-80, Disting. award 1978), Inst. Internal Auditors (cert.), Internat. Council Archives (com. reprography 1976—). Republican. Home: 3144 S 160 W Bountiful UT 84010-6501 Office: Ch Jesus Christ Latter-Day Saints 50 E North Temple Salt Lake City UT 84150-0002

POWELL-ENZMANN, DIANA TERESA, speech pathologist, administrator; b. San Francisco, Mar. 26, 1960; d. Donald J. Powell and Rosa (Sanchez) Agnost. AA, City Coll. of San Francisco, 1979; BA, San Diego State U., 1981; MA, U. San Francisco, 1983. Clin. fellowship year Santa Clara Valley Med. Ctr., San Jose, Calif., 1983-84; clin. speech pathologist Santa Clara Valley Med. Ctr., 1985-87; speech pathologist N. Coast Rehab. Ctr., Santa Rosa, Calif., 1987-88, Western Med. Ctr., Santa Ana, Calif., 1988-89, U. Calif., San Francisco, 1989-90; dir. speech pathology Stanford (Calif.) U., 1990—. Mem. Am. Speech Lang. Hearing Assn.(Polit. Action Com.), Calif. Am. Speech Hearing Assn., Dir's. Forum No. Calif., Soc. Hosp. Dirs. (communicative disorders programs). Home: 462 Sand Hill Cir Menlo Park CA 94025

POWER, DENNIS MICHAEL, museum director; b. Pasadena, Calif., Feb. 18, 1941; s. John Dennis Power and Ruth Augusta (Mott) Zwicky; m. Kristine Moneva Fisher, Feb. 14, 1965 (div. Aug. 1984); children: Michael Lawrence, Matthew David; m. Leslie Gabrielle Baldwin, July 6, 1985; 1 stepchild, Katherine G. Petrosky. B.A., Occidental Coll., 1962, M.A., 1964; Ph.D. (NSF fellow), U. Kans., 1967. Asst. curator ornithology Royal Ont. Mus.; also asst. prof. zoology U. Toronto, 1967-71; asso. curator Royal Ont. Mus., Toronto, 1971-72; exec. dir. Santa Barbara (Calif.) Mus. Natural History, 1972-94, Oakland Mus. of Calif., 1994—; biol. researcher; cons. ecology. Editor: The California Islands: Proceedings of a Multidisciplinary Symposium, 1980, Current Ornithology, vol. 6, 1989, vol. 7, 1990, vol. 8, 1991, vol. 9, 1992, vol. 10, 1993, vol. 11, 1993, vol. 12, 1995; contbr. articles to sci. jours. Bd. dirs. Univ. Club Santa Barbara, 1989-92, v.p., 1991-92; bd. dirs. Santa Barbara Chamber Orch., 1990-94, v.p., 1991-94; mem. adv. coun. Santa Cruz Island Found., 1989—; mem. discipline adv. com. for museology Coun. fo rInternat. Exch. of Scholars, 1991-95. Grantee NRC Can., 1968-72, 1974-78. Fellow Am. Ornithologists Union (life, sec. 1981-83, v.p. 1988-89), Am. Assn. Mus. (coun. 1980-83); mem. AAAS, Cooper Ornithol. Soc. (dir. 1976-79, pres. 1978-81, hon. mem. 1993), Calif. Assn. Mus. (dir. 1990-91, chmn. 1987-89), Western Mus. Conf. (dir. 1977-83, pres. 1981-83), Am. Soc. Naturalists, Assn. Sci. Mus. Dirs., Ecol. Soc., Am. Soc. Study of Evolution, Soc. Systematic Zoology, Bohemian Club, Sigma Xi. Office: Oakland Mus of California 1000 Oak St Oakland CA 94607-4820

POWER, JOHN BRUCE, lawyer; b. Glendale, Calif., Nov. 11, 1936; m. Ann Power, June 17, 1961 (div. 1980); children: Grant, Mark, Boyd. AB magna cum laude, Occidental Coll., 1958; JD, NYU, 1961; postdoctoral, Columbia U., 1972. Bar: Calif. 1962. Assoc. O'Melveny & Myers, Los Angeles, 1961-69, ptnr., 1969—; resident ptnr. O'Melveny & Myers, Paris, 1973-75; mem. Social Svcs. Commn., City of L.A., 1993, pres., 1993; lectr. in field. Contbr. articles to jours. Dir. Met. L.A. YMCA, 1988—; mem. bd. mgrs. Stuart Ketchum Downtown YMCA, 1985-92, pres., 1989-90; mem. Los Angeles County Rep. Ctrl. Com., 1962-63; trustee Occidental Coll., 1992—. Root Tilden scholar. Mem. ABA (vice chmn. internat. fin. subcom. 1984-91, comml. fin. svcs. com., com. 3rd party legal opinions, bus. law sect.), Am. Bar Found. (life), Calif. Bar Assn. (chmn. partnerships and unincorp. assns. com. 1982-83, chmn. uniform commn. code com. 1984-85, exec. com. 1987-91, treas. bus. law sect. 1988-89, vice chmn. 1989-90, chmn. 1990-91, chmn. coun. sect. chairs 1992-93, liaison to state bar commn. on the future of the legal profession and the state bar), L.A. County Bar Assn. (exec. com. comml. law and bankruptcy sect. 1970-73, 86-89), Internat. Bar Assn., Fin. Lawyers Conf. (bd. govs., pres. 1984-85), Exec. Svc. Corps. (sec. 1985—), Occidental Coll. Alumni Assn. (pres. 1967-68, pres. circle, exec. com. 1979-82, 91—, vice chair 1992-93, chair 1993-94), Phi Beta Kappa (pres. 1988-90 So. Calif.). Club: California. Office: O'Melveny & Myers 400 S Hope St Los Angeles CA 90071-2801

POWERS, ALAN DALE, geologist, retired federal government executive; b. Eugene, Oreg., June 10, 1929; s. Thomas Richard and Gwenn Beryl Stivers P.; m. Lelah Phena Hall, Mar. 23, 1951; children: Sandra L., Thomas R., Janice M. Powers Yankus, Karen A. Powers Jones. BS in Geology, U. Oreg., 1951. Geologist Dept. Interior Bur. Reclamation, Stockton and Sacramento, Calif., 1952-60; water resource project planner Dept. Interior Bur. Reclamation, Sacramento, 1960-63; recreation resource planner Dept. Interior Bur. Outdoor Recreation, Washington, 1963-65; budget analyst Bur. Budget, Office of Mgmt. and Budget, Washington, 1966-75; dir. office of outer continental shelf program coordination Dept. Interior, Washington, 1976-82; deputy assoc. dir. offshore leasing Dept. of Interior Minerals Mgmt. Svc., Washington, 1982; regional dir. Minerals Mgmt. Svc., Anchorage, 1983-94. Recipient Disting. Svc. award Sec. of Interior, 1985. Mem. Sr. Exec. Svc. (Meritorious Exec. 1982, Disting. Exec. 1987, Presdl. awards). Home: PO Box 210116 Anchorage AK 99521-0116

POWERS, EDWIN MALVIN, consulting engineer; b. Denver, July 20, 1915; s. Emmett and Bertha Malvina (Guido) P.; m. Dorothy Lavane Debler, Jan. 18, 1941; children: Dennis M., Kenneth E., James M., Steven R. BS in Chem. Engring., U. Denver, 1939, MS, 1940. Registered profl. engr., N.J., Colo., Fall Out Analysts Engr., U.S. Fed. Emergency Mgmt. Agency, 1975-87. Prodn. supr. Nat. Aniline Div., Buffalo, 1940-45; engr., project supr. Merck & Co., Rahway, N.J., 1945-67, chief project coordinator, 1967-72, purchasing engr., 1972-82; ret., 1982; cons. engr., Conifer, Colo., 1982—. Capt. Air Raid Wardens, River dist., Buffalo, 1942-45. Mem., del. Conifer Home Owners Assns. Protect Our Single Homes, 1984-86, Regional Environ. Assn. Concerned Home Owners, 1985-86, task force area devel. Hwy. 285/ Conifer Area County Planning Bd. Community, 1986-88. Mem. NSPE, Am. Chem. Soc. (emeritus), Am. Inst. Chem. Engrs. (emeritus, treas. N.J. 1960, exec. com. 1961-63), Nat. Soc. Profl. Engrs. Home and Office: 26106 Amy Cir Conifer CO 80433-6102

POWERS, JAMES EARL, public relations executive; b. Oak Park, Ill., July 11, 1957; s. Warren Earl and Virginia Marie (Wenzel) P. children: Judith Powers Peelo, William, Janis Powers Benzuly, Christopher. BS in Mass Comms., Ill. State U., 1979; postgrad., Grand Canyon U., 1992—. Sports editor Des Plaines (Ill.) Publishing, 1979-84, Pioneer Press, Wilmette, Ill., 1984-89; comms. specialist U-Haul Internat., Phoenix, 1989-92; account exec. Walker Agy., Scottsdale, Ariz., 1992—. Mem. Pub. Rels. Soc. Am. (job bank editor Valley of Sun chpt. 1992-94), Soc. Profl. Journalists. Home: 639 W Hazelwood St Phoenix AZ 85013-2726 Office: Walker Agy 15855 N Greenway Hayden Loop Scottsdale AZ 85260-1726

POWERS, JEFFREY, business executive, speaker; b. Milw., Nov. 25; s. Averill and Rose Powers. BA in Psychology, U. Wis., 1971. Pres. Powers

Travel Svc. Inc., Milw., 1973-86; CEO Checkpoint World Team, Westlake Village, Calif., 1988—, Twin Vision, Westlake Village, 1989—, Psychic Inst., Westlake Village, 1992—, Health Watch, Westlake Village, 1993—, Invisible Empire, Westlake Village, 1993—. Creator, pioneer Live, Interactive Pay-Per-Call Tech. for Bus. Applications, 1989. Recipient Phi Eta Sigma Nat. Scholastic Honors award U. Wis., 1968. Office: Checkpoint World Team 31220 La Baya Dr Ste 110 Westlake Village CA 91362

POWERS, JUDITH KAY, educational administrator, English educator; b. Eau Claire, Wis., Sept. 23, 1942; d. Clifford Lyle and Marcille Leone (Bunce) P.; m. Rex Earl Gantenbein, May 13, 1983. BA in English, U. Wis., 1964; MA in English, U. Wyo., 1965; PhD in English, Rice U., 1971. Asst. prof. Iowa State U., Ames, 1973-79; test specialist Am. Coll. Testing, Iowa City, 1979-85; lectr., acad. profl. U. Wyo., Laramie, 1985-94; program asst. Wyo. Coun. for the Humanities, Laramie, 1994—; writer, rschr. Wyo. Territorial Prison, 1989-91. Assoc. editor: Iowa Woman mag., 1983-85; contbr. articles to profl. jours. Mem. Com. for Campus Access for the Disabled, Laramie, 1986—. Wyo. Coun. for the Humanities scholar, 1991-94; grantee Ctr. for Tchg. Excellence, Laramie, 1991, 92, 93, 94. Mem. MLA, TESOL, Conf. Coll. Composition and Comm., Nat. Coun. Tchrs. English. Democrat. Home: 1358 Indian Hills Dr Laramie WY 82070-6946 Office: Wyoming Coun Humanities PO Box 3643 Laramie WY 82071-3643

POWERS, LINDA SUE, biophysicist, educator; b. Pitts., Feb. 8, 1948; d. Luther Thurston and Helen Grace (Currence) Powers. BS in Physics and Chemistry, Va. Poly. Inst. and State U., 1970; MA in Physics, Harvard U., 1972, PhD in Biophysics, 1976. Mem. tech. staff AT&T Bell Labs., Murray Hill, N.J., 1976-88; dir. bio-catalysis sci. ctr., prof. chemistry & biochemistry Utah State U., Logan, 1988-91, prof. elec. engring., biol. & irrigation engring., 1991—; dir. Nat. Ctr. for the Design of Molecular Function, Logan, 1991—; adj. prof. U. Pa. Med. Sch., Phila., 1978—, organizer VII Internat. Biophysics Congress, 1981. Mem. editl. corr. Comments Molecular Cellular Biophysics, 1980-89; editl. bd. Biophysics Jour., 1989—, Am. Inst. of Physics Internat. Basic and Applied Biol. Physics, 1993—; contbr. articles to profl. jours. and books. Recipient 1st U.S. Bioenergetics award, 1982, State of Utah Gov.'s medal for sci. and tech., 1994. Fellow Am. Phys. Soc. (exec. bd. 1977-83, chmn. 1984-85, vice chmn. 1985-86), Am. Inst. Chemists; mem. IEEE, AAAS, Biophys. Soc., Protein Soc., Soc. Applied Spectroscopy, Sigma Pi Sigma, Phi Lambda Upsilon. Office: Utah State U Nat Ctr for Design of Molecular Function 101 Animal Sci Bldg Logan UT 84322-4630

POWERS, PHILIP HEMSLEY, lawyer, consultant; b. Washington, Aug. 24, 1937; s. Bennet Gordon and Lillian Dorothea (Hemsley) P.; m. Judith Florence Piersante, June 6, 1959 (div. May 1969); children: Bret Monsarrat, Jeffrey Douglas; m. Jeanne Marie Heckendorn, May 31, 1969 (div. Dec. 1982); 1 child, Kristal Liliana; m. Valfridur Jensdottir, Aug. 9, 1987. BS, U.S. Naval Acad., 1959; MS in Systems Mgmt., U. So. Calif., 1981; JD, George Mason U., 1987. Bar: Va. 1987. Commd. ensign USN, 1959, advanced through grades to lt. comdr., 1968, nuclear propulsion qualified officer, 1962-75, submarine qualified officer, 1966-79, with naval intelligence, 1973-79, ret., 1979; research staff, cons. System Planning Corp., Arlington, Va., 1979-93; with Powers and Assocs., Honolulu, 1993—. Mem. ABA, Va. Bar, U.S. Naval Acad. Alumni Assn. Republican. Home: 1350 Ala Moana Blvd Apt 1909 Honolulu HI 96814-4213

POWERS, RICHARD FREDERICK, management consultant; b. Tulsa, Oct. 4, 1936; s. Richard Kenneth and Jewel Mae Powers; B.A., Rice U., 1958; M.B.A., Mich. State U., 1965; Ph.D., U. Minn., 1971; m. Janet Sue Clerico, June 7, 1958; children—Laurie Diann, Richard Bradley. Commd. ensign U.S. Navy, 1958, advanced through grades to comdr., 1971; dir. control div. Royal Can. Navy Depot, Victoria, B.C., 1963-64; dir. computer tng. Navy Supply Corps Sch., 1965-68; advisor to sec. of def. manpower resources div., 1971-75; dir. modeling and analysis material distbn. study Dept. Def., 1975-78; ret., 1978; pres. Insight, Inc., Alexandria, Va., 1978—; mem. faculty George Mason U., Central Mich. U. Vice pres. Kings Park Civic Assn., 1973, Kings Park PTA, 1974; mem. Fairfax County Citizens Planning Task Force, 1973. Decorated Def. Superior Service medal, Legion of Merit. Mem. Inst. Mgmt. Sci., Council Logistics Mgmt. (exec. com., pres. 1990), Mgmt. Sci. Roundtable, Coll. Practice of Mgmt. Sci., Phi Kappa Phi, Beta Gamma Sigma. Contbr. articles to profl. jours. Home: PO Box 1503 Bend OR 97709-1503 Office: Insight Inc PO Box 1609 Bend OR 97709-1609

POWERS, STEPHEN, educational researcher, consultant; b. Bakersfield, Calif., June 10, 1936; s. Robert Boyd and Mildred (Irwin) P.; m. Gail Marguerite Allen, Dec. 28, 1968; children: Rick, Joseph, Rebecca. BS in Edn., No. Ariz. U., 1959; MA, U. Ariz., Tucson, 1970, MEd, 1972, PhD, 1978. Cert. tchr., Calif.; cert. tchr., adminstr., jr. coll. tchr., Ariz. Policeman, City of Bakersfield, 1967-69; tchr. Marana (Ariz.) Pub. Schs., 1969-72; dir. Am. Sch. Belo Horizonte, Brazil, 1972-73; tchr. Nogales (Ariz.) Pub. Schs., 1973-75; rsch. specialist Tucson Unified Sch. Dist., 1975-94; prof. Walden U., U. Ariz., 1981, U. Phoenix, 1990; founder Creative Rsch. Assocs., 1991—, now pres.; bd. dirs. Manchester Coll., Oxford U.; internat. evaluator USAID, 1991. Contbr. articles to profl. jours. Nat. Inst. Edn. grantee, 1980. Mem. Am. Ednl. Rsch. Assn., Royal Statis. Soc. (U.K. chpt.), Am. Statis. Assn. Bahai. Office: 2030 E Broadway Ste 9 Tucson AZ 85719-5813

POWLEY, LINDA GALT, dietitian; b. Palo Alto, Calif., Nov. 1, 1953; d. William Craig and Betty Lou (Branch) Galt; m. John Stephan Powley, Oct. 7, 1984; children: Lauren, John. BS, Calif. Poly. State U., San Luis Obispo, 1974; MS, San Diego State U., 1980. Registered dietitian; cert. diabetic educator. Grad. asst. Food Sci. and Human Nutrition dept. San Diego State U., 1979-80; food svc. dir. Hale Makua, Kahului, Hawaii, 1980-87; cons. dietitian Hale Makua, Kahului, Hawaii, 1987-91; clin. nutritionist/neighbor island health edn. coord. Kaiser Permanente Health Plan, Inc., Wailuku, Hawaii, 1991—; cons. dietitian Kula (Hawaii) Hosp., 1989-91, Aloha House Drug Rehab., Makawao, Hawaii, 1987-89, Teen Challenge Drug Rehab., Lahaina, Hawaii, 1987-89. Bd. dirs. Am. Heart Assn., Wailuku, 1987; adv. com. YMCA Cardiac Therapy Program, Kahului, 1991—; vol. Am. Cancer Soc., Hale Makua, Valley Isle Road Runners, promotional sec., 1985-86. San Diego State U. grantee, 1979. Mem. Am. Dietetics Assn., Am. Diabetes Assn. Office: Kaiser Permanente 80 Mahalani St Wailuku HI 96793-2531

POWLISON, HOWARD WHITFIELD, religious organization administrator; b. Torracari, Charcas, Bolivia, Oct. 12, 1919; came to U.S., 1932; s. Kenneth Whitfield and Pansy Arvada (Fitch) P.; m. Doris Ruth Waggoner, Sept. 5, 1942; children: Kenneth, Gordon, Douglas, Robert, Cynthia, Steven, Kathleen, Warren, Roland, John, Timothy, Dale, Donald. BA in Biblical Edn., Columbia Bible Coll., 1942; cert., Buffalo Bible Coll., 1943. Ordained minister Bapt. Ch., 1942. Pastor Springbrook (N.Y.) Cmty. Ch., 1942-49, 1st Bapt. Ch., Marilla, N.Y., 1947-52, New Testament Bapt. Ch., Alden, N.Y., 1952-62; precision grinder Consol. Electrodynamics, East Pasadena, Calif., 1962-66; gen. dynamics optical polisher stainless steel mirrors Red Eye Missiles, 1966-68; dir. Christian teens Christian Rsch., Portland, Oreg., 1969-72; assoc. pastor Country Ch., Colton, Oreg., 1973-75; elder, treas. Bethel Ch. - East Portland, 1975-77; sec./treas. Christian Rsch., Inc., Portland, 1977—; chaplain Am. Family Enterprises, 1995—; asst. prin. Bethel Christian Acad., Portland, 1975-77; pastor Canby (Oreg.) Cmty. Ch., 1979-88; mgr., sec. Mineral Rsch. Corp., Portland, 1993-94. Bd. dirs. Love in Action, Portland, 1991-93; mem. com. Concerned Citizens, Portland, 1988; precinct worker Rep., Portland, 1989; foster care vol. Children Svcs., Molalla, Oreg., and Portland, 1975-80. Home: 2345 11th St Baker City OR 97814-2535 Office: Berg Christian Enterprises 4525 SE 63rd Ave Portland OR 97206-4617

POY, GLENN DERRICK, corporate executive; b. Johannesburg, South Africa, Apr. 23, 1957; arrived in Can., 1966; BCommerce/Fin. and Acctg., McMaster U., 1980. Staff acct. Touche Ross & Co., Toronto, Ont., 1979-82; sports cons. Peter Burwash Internat., Houston, 1983-85; dir., fin. Magna Internat., Inc., Toronto, 1985-88; mng. dir. Designworks/USA (A Magna Co.), Newbury Park, Calif., 1988-92, Inside Leadership, Agoura Hills, Calif., 1992—. Editor: Open Forum, 1990—; contbr. articles to profl. jours. Mem. Soc. Mgmt. Accts. of Ont. (bd. dirs. 1986-88), So. Calif. Planning Forum (co-chmn., mark of excellence com. 1990, v.p. communications 1990—), Calif. Luth. U. (Pres.'s Coun. of Advisors 1990—), ASTD (leadership devel. com. 1992). Office: Inside Leadership Inc 4240 Lost Hills Rd Apt 1108 Agoura CA 91301-5348

POYNTER, DANIEL FRANK, publisher; b. N.Y.C., Sept. 17, 1938; s. William Frank and Josephine E. (Thompson) P. BA, Calif. State U., Chico, 1960; postgrad., San Francisco Law Sch., 1961-63. federally lic. master parachute rigger; lic. pilot. Pub., prin. Para Pub., Santa Barbara, Calif., 1969—; listed as expert witness Nat. Forensic Ctr., Tech. Adv. Service for Attys., Consultants and Consulting Organizations Directory, Lawyer's Guide to Legal Consultants, Expert Witnesses, Services, Books and Products. Author: The Parachute Manual, Parachuting, The Skydiver's Handbook, Parachuting Manual with Log, Hang Gliding, Manned Kiting, The Self-Publishing Manual, How to Write, Print & Sell You Own Book, Publishing Short Run Books, Business Letters For Publishers, Computer Selection Guide, Word Processing and Information Processing, Publishing Forms, Parachuting Manual for Square/Piggyback Equipment, Frisbee Players' Handbook, Toobee Players' Handbook, some translated in fgn. languages; past editor news mag. Spotter; monthly columnist Parachute mag., 1963—; contbr. over 500 tech. and popular articles and photographs to mags; patentee parachute pack, POP TOP. Recipient numerous certs. of appreciation for directing parachuting competitions. Mem. U.S. Parachute Assn. (life, chmn. bd., exec. com. 12 yrs., nat. and internat. del., achievement award, 1981, cert. 25 yr. mem., awarded Gold Parachute Wings, 1972), Parachute Industry Assn. (pres. 1985, 86), AIAA, Soc. Automotive Engrs., Nat. Aeronautic Assn., Aviation Space Writers Assn. (internat. conf. mem. 1978,79, 82), Calistoga Skydivers (past sec.), No. Calif. Parachute Council (past sec.), U.S. Hang Gliding Assn. (life, past dir., del.), Internat. Assn. Ind. Pubs. (past bd. dirs., pres. Santa Barbara chpt. 1979-82), Assn. Am. Pubs., Pub. Mktg. Assn. (bd. dirs.), Book Pubs. So. Calif., Am. Booksellers Assn., Commn. Internat de Vol Libre of Fedn. Aero. Internat. in Paris (U.S. del., past pres., lifetime Pres. d'Honneur award 1979, recipient Paul Tissander Diploma, 1984). Home: RR 1 Santa Barbara CA 93117-1047 Office: Para Publishing PO Box 8206 Santa Barbara CA 93118-8206

PRACKO, BERNARD FRANCIS, II, artist, business owner; b. Ada, Okla., Jan. 17, 1945; m. Patricia Fairmont Butterfield Stone, 1967 (div. 1971); 1 child, Genevieve Suydam Stone Davis; m. Elaine Jean Nisky, 1980 (div. 1981); m. Renee Ericson Whitman, 1982 (div. 1986). AA, N.Mex. Mil. Inst., 1965; BA, U. Colo., 1970; postgrad., Ariz. State U., 1991. Owner, pres. Sunrise, Ltd., Boulder, Colo., 1971-74, Benchmark Findings, Albuquerque, 1974-78; pres. Fayber Assocs., Inc., Phoenix, 1974—, N.Mex., Ariz., Colo., 1974—; owner, pres. BCB Mfg. Inc., Albuquerque, 1975-77, Travel Concepts Inc., Aspen, Colo., 1980-81, Series Ins. Ltd., Hamilton, Bermuda, 1981-82; with Cypress Investments Inc., Scottsdale, Ariz., 1987—; educational researcher Tomatis Ctr., Phoenix, 1991—. One-man shows include Grand Champions, Aspen, 1992, Scottsdale Culinary Inst., 1992; exhibited in group shows at Sena Galleries, Santa Fe, 1991, Sacred Spaces, L.I., N.Y., 1991, Cultural Exch. Gallery, Scottsdale, 1992, Nelson Fine Art Mus., Tempe, Ariz., 1992, Aspen Art Mus., 1992, Sun Cities Art Mus., Sun City, ARiz., 1992, San Diego Art Inst., 1993; represented in permanent collections Scottsdale Culinary Inst., Am. West Airlines, Tempe, U. Colo., Boulder, Ariz. State U., Tempe, Sun Cities Art Mus., Sun City, Amnesty Internat., Washington. Peace awareness trainer Egypt, Israel, South Africa, Kenya, Nigeria, 1986; vol., artist coord. Amnesty Internat., U.S.A. calendar, 1990. Office: Fayber Assocs Inc PO Box 20007 Boulder CO 80308-3007

PRADA, GLORIA INES, mathematics and Spanish language educator; b. San Vicente de Chucuri, Colombia, Dec. 2, 1954; came to U.S., 1985; d. Roberto Gomez and Maria Celina (Serrano) Duran; m. Luis Eduardo Prada, June 19, 1975; children: Luis Ricardo, Nicholas. BS in Math., U. Indsl., Santander, Colombia, 1978. Tchr. h.s. math. Santander Sch. Dist., Bucaramanga, 1973-84; tchr. mid. sch. math. Hayward (Calif.) Unified Sch. Dist., 1989—; pres. Bilingual Adv. Com., Hayward, 1986-89; mem. Gate Task Force, Hayward, 1990-93. Author: Prada's Spanish Course, 1992, Family Math, 1992, Stations on Probabilities, 1994, (math. replacement unit) Success, 1994. Office: Hayward Unified Sch Dist Winton Intermediate Sch 119 Winton Ave Hayward CA 94544-1413

PRADIER, JEROME MARTIN, air force officer, educator, administrator, pilot, businessman; b. Baton Rouge; s. Francois and Effie Catherine (Martin) P.; 1 child, Jennifer Melissa. BA in Philosophy, Cath. U. Am., 1970; MS in Mgmt., Troy State U., Brindisi, Italy, 1979; MA in Philosophy, SUNY, Albany, 1981. Commd. 2d lt. USAF, 1973, advanced through grades to lt. col., 1990; pilot Blytheville (Ark.) AFB, 1974-75, human rels. officer, 1975-77; chief social actions San Vito dei Normanni Air Sta., Brindisi, 1977-79; asst. prof. philosophy USAF Acad., Colorado Springs, Colo., 1981-86, dir. honor edn., 1984-86; dean acad. Def. Lang. Inst., English Lang. Ctr., San Antonio, 1986-89; chief teaching skills div. Acad. Instr. Sch., Maxwell AFB, Ala., 1989-92, chief curriculum and plans div., 1992; owner, mgr. Buyer Svcs. Internat., Montgomery, Ala., 1989—; chief teaching skills div. Air Force Acad. Instr. Sch., Montgomery, Ala., 1990-91; chief of programs Air Force Acad. Instr. Sch., Maxwell AFB, Ala., 1992-93; assoc. dean program evaluation rsch. and testing Def. Lang. Inst., Fgn. Lang. Ctr., Monterey, Calif., 1993—, dir. evaluation divsn., 1993—. Translator Freeing the Spirit mag., 1978. Pres. HOPE Coun., Brindisi, 1978-80; long-range planning bd. Leadership Monterey Peninsula; mem. Child Abuse Prevention Coun. Monterey Peninsula; bd. dirs. Mozart Soc. Calif., Internat. Lang. and Cultural Found. Mem. Air Force Assn., Officer Tng. Sch. Alumni Assn. (nat. pres. 1988-89), Jr. Officer's Coun. and Assn. (v.p. Brindisi chpt. 1978), Internat. Bus. Club (v.p. Brindisi chpt. 1979), Leadership San Antonio, Leadership Montgomery, Leadership Monterey Peninsula Alumni Assn. (bd. dirs.), Lions, Kappa Delta Pi, Phi Delta Kappa. Roman Catholic. Home: PO Box 5714 Monterey CA 93944-0714 Office: DLIFLC ATFL-ES-AD Presidio Of Monterey Monterey CA 93944

PRAGER, SUSAN WESTERBERG, dean, law educator; b. Sacramento, Dec. 14, 1942; d. Percy Foster Westerberg and Aileen M. (McKinley) P.; m. James Martin Prager, Dec. 14, 1973; children: McKinley Ann, Case Mahone. AB, Stanford U., 1964, MA, 1967; JD, UCLA, 1971. Bar: N.C. 1971, Calif. 1972. Atty. Powe, Porter & Alphin, Durham, N.C., 1971-72; acting prof. law UCLA, 1972-77, prof. Sch. Law, 1977—, Arjay and Frances Fearing Miller prof. of law, 1992—, assoc. dean Sch. Law, 1979-82, dean, 1982—; bd. dirs. Pacific Mut. Life Ins. Co., Newport Beach, Calif. Editor-in-chief, UCLA Law Rev., 1970-71. Trustee Stanford U., 1976-80, 87—. Mem. ABA (council of sect. on legal edn. and admissions to the bar 1983-85), Assn. Am. Law Schs. (pres. 1986), Order of Coif. Office: UCLA Sch Law 405 Hilgard Ave Los Angeles CA 90024-1301

PRAKAPAS, EUGENE JOSEPH, art gallery director; b. Lowell, Mass., July 29, 1932; s. Joseph S. Prakapas and Viola Schensnol; m. Dorothy A. Seitner, Dec. 1, 1971. BA, Yale U., 1953; MA, Oxford U., Balliol, 1959. Vice-pres., editor-in-chief Trident Press and Pocket Books div. Simon & Schuster, Inc., N.Y.C., 1960-70; co-dir. Carus Gallery, N.Y.C., 1973-75; dir. Prakapas Gallery, N.Y.C., 1976—; vis. curator San Francisco Mus. Modern Art, 1986. Author: Bauhaus Photography, 1985. Lt. (s.g.) USNR, 1953-57. Fulbright fellow, 1957-59; Yale U. scholar, 1949-53. Mem. Art Dealers Assn. Am., Assn. Internat. Photography Art Dealers.

PRASAD, JAYASIMHA SWAMY, electrical engineer; b. Pavagada, India, Oct. 18, 1948; came to U.S. 1978.; BE, Indian Inst. Sci., Bangalore, 1971; MTech, Indian Inst. Tech., Madras, 1973; MS, Oreg. State U., 1980, PhD, 1985. Sr. engr. Hindustan Aeronautics Ltd., Hyderabad, India, 1973-74; asst. prof. Indian Inst. Tech., Madras, 1974-78; sr. engr. Nat. Semiconductor Corp., Santa Clara, Calif., 1980-82; tech. fellow Tektronix Inc., Beaverton, Oreg., 1985—; cons. Internat. Microelectronic Products, San Jose, 1982-83, Textronix, 1983-85; adj. prof. Oreg. State U., 1985—. Contbr. articles to profl. jours.; inventor in field. Chevron scholar, 1983-84. Mem. IEEE (sr.). Home: 11265 SW Morgen Ct Portland OR 97223-3967

PRATT, GEORGE JANES, JR., psychologist, author; b. Mpls., May 3, 1948; s. George Janes and Sally Elvina (Hanson) P.; BA cum laude, U. Minn., 1970, MA, 1973; PhD with spl. commendation for overall excellence, Calif. Sch. Profl. Psychology, San Diego, 1976; married; 1 dau., Whitney Beth. Psychology trainee Ctr. for Behavior Modification, Mpls., 1971-72, U. Minn. Student Counseling Bur., 1972-73; predoctoral clin. psychology intern San Bernardino County (Calif.) Mental Health Svcs., 1973-74, San Diego County Mental Health Services, 1974-76; affiliate staff San Luis Rey Hosp., 1977-78; postdoctoral clin. psychology intern Mesa Vista Hosp., San Diego, Calif., 1976; clin. psychologist, dir. Psychology and Cons. Assocs. of San Diego, 1976—; chmn. Psychology and Cons. Assocs. Press, 1977—; bd. dirs. Optimax, Inc., 1985—; pres. George Pratt Ph.D., Psychol. Corp., 1979—; chmn. Pratt, Korn & Assocs., Inc., 1984—; mem. staff Scripps Meml. Hosp., La Jolla, Calif., 1986—, chmn. psychology, 1993—; founder La Jolla Profl. Workshops, 1977; clin. psychologist El Camino Psychology Ctr., San Clemente, Calif., 1977-78; grad. teaching asst. U. Minn. Psychology and Family Studies div., 1971; teaching assoc. U. Minn. Psychology and Family Studies div., Mpls., 1972-73; instr. U. Minn. Extension div., Mpls., 1971-73; faculty Calif. Sch. Profl. Psychology, 1974-83, San Diego Evening Coll., 1975-77, Nat. U., 1978-79, Chapman Coll., 1978, San Diego State U., 1979-80; vis. prof. Pepperdine U., L.A., 1976-80; cons. U. Calif. at San Diego Med. Sch., 1976—, also instr. univ., 1978—; psychology chmn. Workshops in Clin. Hypnosis, 1980-84; cons. Calif. Health Dept., 1974, Naval Regional Med. Ctr., 1978-82, ABC-TV; also speaker. Mem. South Bay Youth Svcs. Com., San Diego, 1976-80. With USAR, 1970-76. Licensed and cert. psychologist, Calif. Fellow Am. Soc. Clin. Hypnosis; mem. Am. Psychol. Assn., Calif. Psychol. Assn., Internat. Soc. Hypnosis, San Diego Psychology Law Soc. (exec. com.), Am. Assn. Sex Educators, Counselors and Therapists (cert.), San Diego Soc. Sex Therapy and Edn. (past pres.), San Diego Soc. Clin. Hypnosis (past pres.), Acad. San Diego Psychologists, Soc. Clin. and Exptl. Hypnosis., U. Minn. Alumni Assn., Nat. Speakers Assn., Beta Theta Pi. Author: Rx for Stress, 1994, HyperPerformance, 1987, A Clinical Hypnosis Primer, 1984, 88, Release Your Business Potential, 1988, Sensory/Progressive Relaxation, 1979, Effective Stress Management, 1979, Clinical Hypnosis: Techniques and Applications, 1985; contbr. chpts. to various books. Office: Scripps Hosp Med Bldg 9834 Genesee Ave Ste 321 La Jolla CA 92037-1216

PRATT, RONALD FRANKLIN, public relations executive; b. Savannah, Ga., July 15, 1948; s. Frank Tecumseh and Lila Elizabeth (Lee) P. BA, Washington U., St. Louis, 1972. Reporter Savannah News-Press, 1972; news dir. WSOK Radio, Savannah, 1973; editor Hilton Head News, Hilton Head Island, S.C., 1974-77; account exec. Russom & Leeper, San Francisco, 1978-80; sr. account exec. Russom & Leeper, 1981-83, v.p., 1983-85; sr. v.p., prin. The Leeper Grp., San Francisco, 1985-86; pres. Ronald Pratt Pub. Rels., San Francisco, 1987-90; sr. v.p., mgmt. supr. Porter/Novelli, L.A., 1990-92, sr. v.p., group exec., 1993-94, exec. v.p., gen. mgr., 1995—; cons. Coro Found., San Francisco, 1989-90. Bd. dirs. Hilton Head Jazz Festival, 1976-77; pres. Hilton Head Inst. for the Arts, 1976-77; dir., v.p. San Francisco Coun. on Entertainment, 1985-87. Recipient Enterprise award, AP, Ga., 1973. Mem. Internat. Assn. Bus. Communicators (Gold Quill 1983), Internat. Foodsvc. Editl. Coun., Agrl. Rels. Coun., Am. Inst. Wine and Food. Office: 1160 Battery St Ste 200 San Francisco CA 94111

PRATT, ROSALIE REBOLLO, harpist, educator; b. N.Y.C., Dec. 4, 1933; d. Antonio Ernesto and Eleanor Gertrude (Gibney) Rebollo; Mus.B., Manhattanville Coll., 1954; Mus.M., Pius XII Inst. Fine Arts, Florence, Italy, 1955; Ed.D., Columbia U., 1976; m. George H. Mortimer, Esquire, Apr. 22, 1987; children: Francesca Christina Rebollo-Sborgi, Alessandra Maria Pratt Jones. Prin. harpist N.J. Symphony Orch., 1963-65; soloist Mozart Haydn Festival, Avery Fisher Hall, N.Y.C., 1968; tchr. music public schs., Bloomfield and Montclair, N.J., 1962-73; mem. faculty Montclair State Coll., 1973-79; prof. Brigham Young U., Provo, Utah, 1984—, coord. grad. studies dept. music, 1985-87.; biofeedback and neurofeedback rsch. specialist, 1993—. U.S. chair 1st internat. arts medicine leadership conf., Tokyo Med. Coll., 1993. Co-author: Elementary Music for All Learners, 1980; editor Internat. Jour. Arts Medicine, 1991—, (proceedings) 2d, 3d, 4th Internat. Symposia Music Edn. for Handicapped; contbr. articles to Am. Harp Jour., Music Educators Jour., others. Fulbright grantee, 1979; Myron Taylor scholar, 1954. Mem. Am. Harp Soc. (Outstanding Service award 1973), AAUP (co-chmn. legis. rels. com. N.J. 1978-79), Internat. Soc. Music Edn. (chair commn. music in spl. edn., music therapy, and medicine 1985—), Internat. Soc. Music in Medicine (v.p. 1993—), Internat. Assn. of Music for the Handicapped (co-founder, exec. dir., jour. editor), Coll. Music Soc., Music Educators Nat. Conf., Brigham Young U. Grad. Coun., Phi Kappa Phi, Sigma Alpha Iota. Office: Brigham Young U Harris Fine Arts Ctr Provo UT 84602

PRATT, WALDEN PENFIELD, research geologist; b. Columbus, Ohio, Mar. 22, 1928; s. Julius William and Louisa Gabriella (Williamson) P.; m. Janice May Eddy, Dec. 21, 1957; children: Julius William II, Susan Elizabeth, David Milton. AB, U. Rochester, 1948; postgrad. Yale U., 1948-49; MS, Stanford U., 1956, PhD, 1964. Geologist, U.S. Geol. Survey, Iron River, Mich., 1949-51, Claremont, Calif., 1953-55, research geologist, Lakewood, Colo., 1956-89, scientist emeritus, 1989—; geologist Pacific Coast Borax Co., Salta, Argentina, 1955. Co-editor: United States Mineral Resources, 1973 (U.S. Geol Survey monetary award), Proceedings, Internat. Conf. on Miss. Valley-type lead-zinc deposits, 1984; editor Soc. Econ. Geologists Newsletter, 1986-91; contbr. articles to U.S. Geol. Survey publs. Served with U.S. Army, 1951-53. Recipient Meritorious Service award Dept. Interior, 1983. Fellow Geol. Soc. Am., Soc. Econ. Geologists (hon., Marsden award 1994); mem. Am. Assn. Petroleum Geologists, Rocky Mountain Assn. Geologists, Colo. Sci. Soc. Republican. Presbyterian. Office: U S Geol Survey MS 905 PO Box 25046 Denver CO 80225-0046

PRAUS, ROBERT WAYNE, II, research and development services company executive, software engineer; b. San Antonio, Aug. 9, 1962; s. Robert Wayne and Phyllis Kathryn (Estes) P.; m. Cindy Jean Thompson Praus, Apr. 26, 1981; children: Kristina, Shawn, Stephen, Robert III. BS in Applied Math., U. Colo., Colorado Springs, 1990. Computer programmer Phillips Lab., Albuquerque, 1980-84; asst. through assoc. staff mem. BOM Corp., Albuquerque, 1984-87; programmer, analyst R & D Assocs., Colorado Springs, Colo., 1987-89; software mgr. Nat. Test Facility Martin Marietta, Colorado Springs, 1989-91; pres., software engr. MZA Assocs. Corp., Albuquerque, 1991—; cons. Phillips Lab., 1991-92. Author: The Cray Advanced Users Guide, 1985. Sgt. USAF, 1980-84. Mem. Assn. Computing Machinery. Republican. Home and Office: MZA Assocs Corp 10616 Royal Troon NE Albuquerque NM 87111-6577

PRAUSNITZ, JOHN MICHAEL, chemical engineer, educator; b. Berlin, Jan. 7, 1928; came to U.S., 1937, naturalized, 1944; s. Paul Georg and Susi Prausnitz; m. Susan Prausnitz, June 10, 1956; children: Stephanie, Mark Robert. B Chem. Engring., Cornell U., 1950; MS, U. Rochester, 1951; Ph.D., Princeton, 1955; Dr. Ing., U. L'Aquila, 1983, Tech. U. Berlin, 1989; DSc, Princeton U., 1995. Mem. faculty U. Calif., Berkeley, 1955—, prof. chem. engring., 1963—; cons. to cryogenic, polymer, petroleum and petrochem. industries. Author: (with others) Computer Calculations for Multicomponent Vapor-Liquid Equilibria, 1967, (with P.L. Chueh) Computer Calculations for High-Pressure Vapor-Liquid Equilibria, 1968, Molecular Thermodynamics of Fluid-Phase Equilibria, 1969, 2d edit., 1986, (with others) Regular and Related Solutions, 1970, Properties of Gases and Liquids, 3d edit., 1977, 4th edit., 1987, Computer Calculations for Multicomponent Vapor-Liquid and Liquid-Liquid Equilibria, 1980; contbr. to profl. jours. Recipient Alexander von Humboldt Sr. Scientist award, 1976, Carl von Linde Gold Meml. medal German Inst. for Cryogenics, 1987, Solvay prize Solvay Found. for Chem. Scis., 1990, Corcoran award Am. Soc. for Engring. Edn., 1991, D.L. Katz award Gas Processors Assn., 1992; named W.K. Lewis lectr. MIT, 1993; Guggenheim fellow, 1962, 73, fellow Inst. Advanced Study, Berlin, 1985; Miller rsch. prof., 1966, 78; Chistensen fellow St. Catherine's Coll. Oxford U., 1994. Mem. AIChE (Colburn award 1962, Walker award 1967, Inst. Lectr. award 1994), Am. Chem. Soc. (E.V. Murphree award 1979, Petroleum Chemistry Rsch. award 1995), NAE, NAS, Am. Acad. Arts and Scis. Office: U Calif 308 Gilman Hall Berkeley CA 94720

PRAY, RALPH EMERSON, metallurgical engineer; b. Troy, N.Y., May 12, 1926; s. George Emerson and Jansje Cornelius (Owejan) P.; student N.Mex. Inst. of Mining and Tech., 1953-56, U. N.Mex., 1956; BSMetE, U. Alaska, 1961; DScMetE. (Ideal Cement fellowship, Rsch. grant), Colo. Sch. of Mines, 1966; m. Beverley Margaret Ramsey, May 10, 1959; children: Maxwell, Ross, Leslie, Marlene. Engr.-in-charge Dept. Mines and Minerals, Ketchikan, Alaska, 1957-61; asst. mgr. mfg. rsch. Universal Atlas Cement div. U.S. Steel Corp., Gary, Ind., 1965-66; rsch. metallurgist Inland Steel Co., Hammond, Ind., 1966-67; owner, dir. Mineral Rsch. Lab., Monrovia, Calif., 1968—; pres., Keystone Canyon Mining Co., Inc., Pasadena, Calif., 1972-79, U.S. Western Mines, 1973—, Silveroil Rsch. Inc., 1980-85; v.p. Mineral Drill Inc., 1981-90; pres., CEO Copper de Mex. S.A. de C.V.; prime contractor def. logistics agy. U.S. Dept. Def., 1989-92; owner Precision Plastics, 1973-82; bd. dirs. Bagdad-Chase Inc., 1972-75; ptnr. Mineral R&D Co., 1981-86; lectr., Purdue U., Hammond, Ind., 1966-67, Nat. Mining Seminar, Barstow (Calif.) Coll., 1969-70; guest lectr. Calif. State Poly U., 1977-81, Western Placer Mining Conf., Reno, Nev., 1983, Dredging and Placer Mining Conf., Reno, 1985, others; v.p., dir. Wilbur Foote Plastics, Pasadena, 1968-72; strategic minerals del. People to People, Republic of South Africa, 1983; vol. Monrovia Police Dept.; city coord. Neighborhood Watch, 1990—. With U.S. Army, 1950-52. Fellow Geol. Mining and Metall. Soc. India (life), Am. Inst. Chemists, South African Inst. Mining and Metallurgy; mem. Soc. Mining Engrs., Am. Chem. Soc., Am. Inst. Mining, Metall. and Petroleum Engrs., NSPE, Can. Inst. Mining and Metallurgy, Geol. Soc. South Africa, Sigma Xi, Sigma Mu. Achievements include research on recovery of metals from refractory ores, benefication plant design, construction and operation, underground and surface mine development and operation, mine and process plant management; syndication of natural resource assets with finance sources; contbr. articles to sci. jours.; guest editor Calif. Mining Jour., 1978—; patentee chem. processing and steel manufacture. Office: 805 S Shamrock Ave Monrovia CA 91016-3651

PREBLE, LOU-ANN M., state legislator; m. Bill Preble. Grad., Tuomey Hosp. Sch. Nursing, 1950, Prima C.C., 1978. RN S.C., 1951-77; physical evaluator Medi-Quik, Tucson, 1978-82; co-owner, mgr. retail apparel store, 1972-75, ret.; mem. Ariz. Ho. of Reps., mem. assignments com. former precinct committeeman, dep. registr.; state committeeman, 1974-92; rep. at large State Exec. Com., 1991-92. Republican. Roman Catholic. Office: House of Representatives 1700 W Washington St Phoenix AZ 85007-2812

PREBLE, PATRICIA JOAN, visual artist, writer; b. Great Lakes, Ill., Oct. 29, 1951. Cert. in broadcast announcing, Brown Inst., Mpls., 1972; BA in Philosophy and Art cum laude, U. Minn., 1978. asst. to dir. Real Art Ways, Hartford, Conn., 1982-83. Contbr. articles to profl. jours.; represented in permanent collections in pvt., corp. and mus., N.Y., Chgo., Miami, Houston, Mpls.-St. Paul, San Francisco, Boston, Oklahoma City, Hartford, Conn.; exhibited in group shows at U. Minn., 1978, Quinlan Art Ctr., Gainesville, Ga., 1979, Image South Gallery, Atlanta, 1980-84, Minnetonka (Minn.) Art Ctr., 1980, Studio 203 Fine Arts, Mpls., 1981, Gallery Bwana, Denver, 1985, Circle Works Visions Gallery, 1986, Artistic Visions: San Francisco, Haight Asbury Cmty. Cultural Ctr., 1987, Fall Group Showing: Weir Gallery, Berkeley, Calif., 1990, Earth Art: Art Resources, Internat. Mill Valley, 1990; solo exhibits include Earth & Sky: L.E. Ross Fine Art, Mpls., 1979, Journey to the Light U. Storrs, Conn., 1984, Summer Colors M.S. Gallery, Hartford, Conn., 1984, Seven Colors: N.Y. Open Ctr., 1986, Drawings: Cornelia Street Cafe, West Village, N.Y., 1986, Mus. of the Nat. Arts Found., Oklahoma City, 1986, Colorado Skies N.Y. Open Ctr., 1987, Open Studio San Francisco Open Studio Program, 1988, Five Yr. Perspective: Studio 141, San Francisco, 1990, Biblical Themes in Modern Dress, San Francisco, 1995, Angels, Archangels and the Clear Light, San Francisco, 1995. Chmn., bd. dirs. Mus. of Nat. Arts Found., Denver, 1985-86. Recipient Marathon Traveler award Ctr. for Rsch. and Enlightenment, 1984. Biddhism and comparative religion. Office: Preble Studios PO Box 22682 San Francisco CA 94122-0682

PREECE, NORMA, executive secretary; b. Kaysville, Utah, May 19, 1922; d. Walter and Wilma (Witt) Buhler; m. Joseph Franklin Preece, July 26, 1946 (dec. 1991); children: Terry Joe, Shannette Preece Keeler. Grad. high sch., Kaysville, 1940. Telephone operator Mountain States Telephone & Telegraph Co., Kaysville, 1940-43; clk. Civil Svc., Ogden, Utah, 1943-50; newspaper corr. Davis County Clipper, North Davis County, Utah, 1954-85; pub. communication dir. Latter-day Saints Ch., Kaysville, 1988-89; exec. sec. Kaysville Area C. of C., Kaysville, 1985-90; stake missionary Latter-Day Saints Ch., Kaysville, 1991—. Publicity chmn. Boy Scouts Am., Kaysville, 1965-69, Am. Cancer Dr., Davis County, 1967, Kaysville Civic Assn., 1960-80; mem. Utah Press Women Assn., Salt Lake City, 1973-75; active publicity Utah Congress PTA, Salt Lake City, 1977—; judge FFA, Davis County, 1968; campaign com. mem. Rep. Party, Davis County, 1990; ordinance worker LDS Temple, Ogden, Utah, 1992-94, Bountiful, Utah, 1995—; co-chmn. Kaysville City Centennial, 1950. Recipient award for outstanding contbn. Davis High Sch., Kaysville, 1979, Total Citizen award Utah C. of C., 1988, Disting. Svc. award Kaysville Arts Coun., 1981; Outstanding Svc. award Kaysville Jaycees, 1972, Disting. Svc. award, 1985, Cmty. Unsung Hero award City of Kaysville, 1994; named Citizen of Yr., City of Kaysville, 1985. Mem. Lit. Club (Athena chpt., sec. 1984, 87, v.p. 1989, pres. 1990), Fine Arts Club (pres. 1964, sec. 1994). Mem. LDS Ch. Home: 347 E 200 N Kaysville UT 84037-2039 Office: Kaysville Area C of C 44 E 100 N Kaysville UT 84037-1910

PREGERSON, HARRY, federal judge; b. L.A., Oct. 13, 1923; s. Abraham and Bessie (Rubin) P.; m. Bernardine Seyma Chapkis, June 28, 1947; children: Dean Douglas, Kathryn Ann. B.A., UCLA, 1947; LL.B., U. Calif.-Berkeley, 1950. Bar: Calif. 1951. Pvt. practice Los Angeles, 1951-52; Assoc. Morris D. Coppersmith, 1952; ptnr. Pregerson & Costley, Van Nuys, 1953-65; judge Los Angeles Mcpl. Ct., 1965-66, Los Angeles Superior Ct., 1966-67, U.S. Dist. Ct. Central Dist. Calif., 1967-79, U.S. Ct. Appeals for 9th Circuit, Los Angeles, 1979—; faculty mem., seminar for newly appointed distr. Judges Fed. Jud. Center, Washington, 1970-72; mem. faculty Am. Soc. Pub. Adminstrn., Inst. for Ct. Mgmt., Denver, 1973—; panelist Fed. Bar Assn., L.A. chpt., 1989, Calif. Continuing Edn. of Bar, 9th Ann. Fed. Practice Inst., San Francisco, 1986, Internat. Acad. Trial Lawyers, L.A., 1983; lect. seminars for newly-appointed Fed. judges, 1970-71. Author over 450 published legal opinions. Mem. Community Rels. Com., Jewish Fedn. Coun., 1984—, Temple Judea, Encino, 1955—; bd. dirs. Marine Corps Res. Toys for Tots Program, 1965—, Greater Los Angeles Partnership for the Homeless, 1988—; bd. trustees Devil Pups Inc., 1988—; adv. bd. Internat. Orphans Inc., 1966—, Jewish Big Brothers Assn., 1970—, Salvation Army, Los Angeles Met. area, 1988—; worked with U.S. Govt. Gen. Svcs. to establish the Bell Shelter for the homeless, the Child Day Care Ctr., the Food Partnership and Westwood Transitional Village, 1988. 1st lt. USMCR, 1944-46. Decorated Purple Heart, Medal of Valor Apache Tribe, 1989; recipient Promotion of Justice Civic award, City of San Fernando, 1965, award San Fernando Valley Jewish Fedn. Coun., 1966, Profl. Achievement award Los Angeles Athletic Club, 1980, Profl. Achievement award UCLA Alumni Assn., 1985, Louis D. Brandeis award Am. Friends of Hebrew U., 1987, award of merit Inner City Law Ctr., 1987, Appreciation award Navajo Nation and USMC for Toys for Tots program, 1987, Humanitarian award Los Angeles Fed. Exec. Bd., 1987-88, Grateful Acknowledgement award Bet Tzedek Legal Svcs., 1988, Commendation award Bd. Suprs. Los Angeles County, 1988, Others award Salvation Army, 1988, numerous others. Mem. ABA (vice-chmn., com. on fed. rules of criminal procedure and evidence sect. of criminal 1972—, panelist Advocacy Inst., Phoenix, 1988), L.A. County Bar Assn., San Fernando Valley Bar Assn. (program chmn. 1964-65), State Bar Calif., Marines Corps Res. Officers Assn. (pres. San Fernando Valley 1966—), DAV (Birmingham chpt.), Am. Legion (Van Nuys Post),. Office: US Ct Appeals 9th Cir 21800 Oxnard St Ste 1140 Woodland Hills CA 91367-3657*

PRELL, JOEL JAMES, medical group administrator; b. L.A., Aug. 16, 1944; s. Samuel and Mary Devorah (Schwartz) P.; children: Vanessa S., Matthew. BA, U. So. Calif., L.A., 1967; cert. fin. mgmt., Ohio State U., 1979; M. Pub. Health, UCLA, 1981. Various positions, 1967-72; chief adminstrv. office sr. adminstrv. analyst L.A. County, 1972-73; dep. regional dir. for planning and community rels. L.A. County Dept. Health Svcs. Region, 1973-75; adminstr. ambulatory care L.A. County Harbro Gen. Hosp., 1975-76; assoc. dir. hosp. and clinics ambulatory care svcs. U. Calif.-Irvine Med. Ctr., 1976-78; asst. to the dir. rsch. and analysis unit U. Calif., Davis, 1978-80; v.p. profl. svcs. San Pedro Peninsula Hosp., 1981-84; sr. v.p. South Coast Med. Ctr., 1984-87; pres., CEO Harbor Health Systems, Inc., 1987-90; CEO Santa Monica (Calif.) Plz. Med. Group, Inc., 1990-93; administrator Pathology Cons. Med. Group, Torrance, Calif., 1993—; spl. asst. to the contr. UCLA Hosp. and Clinics, 1980-81, adminstr. emergency medicine ctr., 1981. Mem. Hosp. Coun .So. Calif. (polit. action steering com., chmn. legis. affairs com.), Calif. Hosp. Polit. Action Com. (bd. dirs.), Health Care Execs. So. Calif., UCLA Health Svcs. Adminstrs. Alumni Assn. (pres.), Med. Group Mgmt. Assn., Am. Coll. Health Care Adminstrs., Friends of Castle Heights. Office: Pathology Cons Med Group 20221 Hamilton Ave Torrance CA 90502-1321

PRELLBERG, JOANNE MARIE, office manager; b. Rockford, Ill., Aug. 27, 1960; d. Frederick Charles II and Dolores Yvonne (Ronk) P.; m. Daniel A. Clay. BS, Boston U., 1983; JD, U. Mo., 1990. Intern Boston (Mass.) Univ. Med. Ctr., 1981-82; pub. rels. specialist Houston (Tex.) NW Med. Ctr., 1982-83; mgr. Bennigans Restaurant, Houston, 1982-84; copy editor HEI Pub., Houston, 1984-85; mgr. Function Junction, Kansas City, Mo., 1985-87; waitress, bartender Houston's Restaurants, Kansas City, 1987-89; law clk. Holbrook, Ellis & Heaven, Merriam, Kans., 1989-91; office mgr. Squaw Peak Animal Hosp., Phoenix, 1991-93; bus. mgr. Coady Enterprises, Inc., 1993-94; office mgr. Tatum Point Animal Hosp., Phoenix, 1994—; v.p. Boston Univ.-Pub. Rels. Student Soc. Am., 1981-83; pres. The Law Coun., Kansas City, 1988-89. Mem. Heartland Bernese Mt. Dog Club (v.p. 1990), Bernese Mt. Dog Club Am. (nat. specialty coord. 1993—), Grand Canyon State Bernese Mt. Dog Club (pres. 1994), Phoenix Field and Obedience Club. Sunflower Kennel Club. Office: Tatum Point Animal Hosp 4601 E Bell Rd Ste 5 Phoenix AZ 85032-9338

PREMARATNE, SHYAMAL, physician, clinical surgery educator; b. Colombo, Sri Lanka, July 28, 1957; came to U.S., 1989; s. Aluthwala Domingo and Margaret (Silva) P.; m. Manuri Janika Peiris, Oct. 14, 1988; children: Inesha Noelani, Ishani Dakshika. Bachelors degree with honors, U. Liverpool, Eng., 1980, Masters degree, 1981; MD, North Colombo Med. Sch., Ragama, Sri Lanka, 1992; PhD, U. Hawaii, 1992. Med. rschr. U. Hawaii, Honolulu, 1992—; R & D officer Queen's Med. Ctr., Honolulu, 1992—; clin. asst. prof. U. Hawaii, 1994; presenter Sch. Medicine U. Hawaii, 1994. Mem. editorial bd. Coronary Artery Disease, 1994—, Biotechniques, 1994—; contbr. articles to profl. jours.; inventor in field. Recipient Pan Pacific Surg. Assn. award, 1994, Davis and Geck award, 1994. Mem. AAAS, Hawaii Thoracic Soc., Internat. Assn. Advancement Genetic Engring. and Biotechnology, Med. Coun. Sri Lanka. Office: Queen's Med Ctr Dept of Surgery 1356 Lusitana St Honolulu HI 96813-2421

PREMINGER, ERIK LEE, writer, television producer; b. N.Y.C., Dec. 11, 1944; s. Otto Preminger and Gypsy Rose Lee; 1 child, Christopher Lee. Student, Columbia U., 1962. Assoc. producer Sigma Prodns., N.Y.C., 1967-72; producer Palomar Pictures, N.Y.C., 1972; producer/writer Help Prodn., Inc., N.Y.C. and L.A., 1972-79; writer San Francisco, 1979-89; producer Sta. KGO-TV, San Francisco, 1989-92; producer, writer, dir. Preminger Prodns., Concord, Calif., 1992—. Author: Gypsy and Me: At Home and on the Road with Gypsy Rose Lee, 1984. Sgt. U.S. Army, 1963-67, Germany. Recipient Emmy, No. Calif. Arts, San Francisco, 1989-90, nomination for Best Pub. Affairs Show, 1990-91.

PRENDERGAST, THOMAS JOHN, JR., physician, epidemiologist; b. St. Louis, June 17, 1940; s. Thomas John Sr. and Virginia (Hyatt) P.; m. Mary Lou Fairfield, Mar. 7, 1965 (div. Apr. 1981); children: Thomas John III, Allen David, Brian Lee; m. Carolyn Swatzel, Apr. 28, 1990; children: Paul Swatzel, David Swatzel. BA, Washington U., St. Louis, 1962, MD, 1966; MPH, U. N.C., 1972. Lic. physician, Mo., N.C., Calif.; Diplomate Am. Bd. Preventive Medicine. Intern St. Luke's Hosp., St. Louis, 1966-67, resident, 1967; assoc. Duke U. Med. Ctr., Durham, N.C., 1971-72; asst. prof. U. Mo., Columbia, 1972-77; dir. epidemiology and disease control Health Care Agy., Orange County, Calif., 1977-90; dep. dir. Dept. Pub. Health, San Bernardino County, Calif., 1990-93, health officer, dir., 1993—; assoc. clin. prof. U. Calif. Med. Ctr., Irvine, 1977-90, pub. health/preventive medicine Loma Linda U., 1990—; cons. Disease Control Com. Calif. Conf. Local Health Officials, Sacramento, 1977-93, chair, 1994—; lectr. in field. Contbr. articles to profl. jours. Served to maj. USAF, 1968-71. Recipient Community Service award Vietnamese Cultural Soc., Orange County, 1980, Disting. Service award, AIDS Response Program, Orange County, 1986, Vol. Service Recognition award, Am. Cancer Soc., 1981. Mem. Am. Pub. Health Assn., Soc. Tchrs. Preventive Medicine, Assn. Practitioners in Infection Control, So. Calif. Pub. Health Assn. (chmn. epidemiology sect. 1979—, Best Section 1982, pres. 1983-84), Sigma Xi, Delta Omega, Pi Tau Epsilon Pi. Home: Box 4939 950 Jungfrau Dr Crestline CA 92325 Office: San Bernardino Dept Pub Health 351 N Mountain View Ave San Bernardino CA 92401-1609

PRENDERGAST, WILLIAM JOHN, ophthalmologist; b. Portland, Oreg., June 12, 1942; s. William John and Marjorie (Scott) P.; m. Carolyn Grace Perkins, Aug. 17, 1963 (div. 1990); children: William John, Scott; m. Sherryl Irene Guenther, Aug. 25, 1991. BS, U. Oreg., Eugene, 1964; MD, U. Oreg., Portland, 1967. Diplomate Am. Bd. Ophthalmology. Resident in ophthalmology U. Oreg., Portland, 1970-73; pvt. practice specializing in ophthalmology Portland, 1973-82; physician, founder, ptnr. Oreg. Med. Eye Clinic, Portland, 1983—; founder, pres. (Focus Group) Inc. Ophthalmic Clinic Networking Venture, Portland, 1992—; clin. asst. prof. ophthalmology Oreg. Health Sci. U., 1985—; pres. Focus Group. Vol. surgeon N.W. Med. Teams, Oaxaca, Mexico, 1989, 90. With USPHS, 1968-70. Fellow Am. Acad. Ophthalmology; mem. Met. Bus. Assn., Multnomah Athletic Club, Mazamas Mountaineering Club, Portland Yacht Club, Phi Beta Kappa, Alpha Omega Alpha. Office: Oregon Med Eye Clinic 1955 NW Northrup St Portland OR 97209-1614

PRENNER, BRUCE MICHAEL, physician; b. Bklyn., Feb. 19, 1945; s. Joseph and Mollie (Rosenberg) P.; m. Harriet Nancy, June 30, 1968; children: Wendy Dale, Amy Elizabeth, Laura Susanne. BS, Bklyn. Coll., 1966; MD, SUNY, Buffalo, 1970. Intern pediatrics Babies Hosp., N.Y.C., 1970-71; resident in pediatrics U. Calif.-San Diego/Univ. Hosp., 1973-74; fellow dept. pediatrics divsn. pediatric immunology and allergy U. Calif.-San Siego, La Jolla, 1974-76; pres. Allergy Assocs. Med. Group, Inc., San Diego, 1986—. Lt. comdr. USPHS, 1971-73. Fellow Am. Coll. Allergy and Immunology. Mem. Am. Acad. Allergy and Immunology.

PRENSNER, STEVEN R., nonprofit organization executive; b. Houston, Oct. 19, 1949; s. Steven and Selma I. (Berger) P.; m. Melanie Porter, July 23, 1977; children: David S., Jonathan D., Benjamin A., Matthew J. BA in Bus. and Math., Howard Payne Coll., 1972; MBA in Fin. and Mgmt., So. Ill. U., 1974. V.p. bus. affairs Trinity Coll., Chgo., 1974-79; v.p. adminstrn. The Navigators, Colo. Springs, 1979—; prin. Mgmt. Devel. Network, Colorado Springs, 1984-88. Office: The Navigators 2830 N 30th St Colorado Springs CO 80934

PREOVOLOS, PENELOPE ATHENE, lawyer; b. San Francisco, Sept. 16, 1955; d. James Peter and Lorraine Lucille (Tiscornia) P.; m. Richard Gonzalo Katerndahl, Mar. 24, 1984. AB, U. Calif., Berkeley, 1976; JD, Harvard U., 1979. Bar: Calif. 1979, U.S. Dist. Ct. (no. dist.) Calif. 1979, U.S. Ct. Appeals (9th cir.) 1979. Law clk. to Hon. Charles M. Merrill U.S. Ct. Appeals (9th cir.), San Francisco, 1979-80; assoc. Morrison & Foerster, San Francisco, 1980-85; ptnr. Morrison & Foerster, San Franciso, 1985—; mng. ptnr. San Francisco office Morrison & Foerster, San Francisco, 1995—. Contbr. articles to profl. jours. Bd. dirs. San Francisco Neighborhood Legal Assistance Found., 1990—. Mem. ABA (antitrust sect.), State Bar of Calif. (chair antitrust and trade regulation law sect. 1994-95). Democrat. Roman Catholic. Home: 225 Evergreen Dr Kentfield CA 94904-2707 Office: Morrison & Foerster 345 California St San Francisco CA 94104-2635

PRESCOTT, GERALD LEROY, history educator; b. Mpls., Mar. 23, 1933; s. Gerald Roscoe and Elsie Mae (Fussell) P.; m. Shirley Margaret Steinhilpert, Dec. 14, 1935; children: Pamela, Cynthia, Thomas. BS, U. Minn., 1959, MA, 1962; PhD, U. Wis., 1968. History tchr. Janesville (Wis.) H.S., 1960-63; instr. U. Wis., Madison, 1963-68; asst. prof. Calif. State U., Northridge, 1968-72, assoc. prof., 1972-78, prof., 1978—; coord. off-campus instrn. Calif. State U., 1975-89, spl. major program, 1975-89, coord. dept. program revs., 1980; mem. ednl. policies com., 1971-74, liberal studies program com., 1973-75, ad hoc adv. com. on the learning resource ctr., 1974, chair urban archives rev. com., urban archives adv. bd., 1984-93, univ. planning coun., 1985-86, faculty senate, 1985-87, others. Contbr. articles to profl. jours. Bd. dirs. Hist. Soc. of So. Calif., L.A., 1993—. With USMC, 1954-57. Mem. Western History Assn., Grange Studies Group. Office: Calif State Univ Northridge CA 91330

PRESCOTT, LAWRENCE MALCOLM, medical and health writer; b. Boston, July 31, 1934; s. Benjamin and Lillian (Stein) P. BA, Harvard U., 1957; MSc, George Washington U., 1959, PhD, 1966; m. Ellen Gay Kober, Feb. 19, 1961 (dec. Sept. 1981); children: Jennifer Maya, Adam Barrett; m. Sharon Lynn Kirshen, May 16, 1982; children: Gary Leon Kirshen, Marc Paul Kirshen. Nat. Acad. Scis. postdoctoral fellow U.S. Army Rsch., Ft. Detrick, Md., 1965-66; microbiologist/scientist WHO, India, 1967-70, Indonesia, 1970-72, Thailand, 1972-78; with pub. rels. Ted Klein & Co., Hill & Knowlton, Interscience, , Smith, Kline, Beecham, others, 1984—; cons. health to internat. orgns., San Diego, 1978—; author manuals; contbr. articles in diarrheal diseases and lab. scis. to profl. jours., numerous articles, stories, poems to mags., newspapers, including Living in Thailand, Jack and Jill, Strawberry, Bangkok Times, Sprint, 1977-81; mng. editor Caduceus, 1981-82; pub., editor: Teenage Scene, 1982-83; pres. Prescott Pub. Co., 1982-83; med. writer numerous jours. including Modern Medicine, Dermatology Times, Internal Medicine World Report, Drugtherapy, P&T, Clinical Cancer Letter, Hospital Formulary, Female Patient, Australian Doctor, Inpharma Weekly, American Family Physician, Ophthalmology Times, Group Practice News, Newspaper of Cardiology, Paacnotes, Genetic Engineering News, Medical Week, Medical World News, Urology Times, Gastroenterology and Endoscopy News; author: Curry Every Sunday, 1984. Home and Office: 18264 Verano Dr San Diego CA 92128-1262

PRESECAN, NICHOLAS LEE, civil, environmental engineer, consultant; b. Indpls., Sept. 4, 1940; s. Nicholas Eli and Dorothy Lee (Moore) P.; m. Joan Westin, Nov. 11, 1940; children: Julie Marie, Mary Lee, Anne Westin. BSCE, Purdue U., 1963; MS in Engring., U. Calif., Berkeley, 1967. Cert. profl. engr., 31 states. Project engr. San Bernardino County (Calif.) Flood Control, 1963, Engring. Sci. Inc., Arcadia, Calif., 1968-70; office mgr. Engring. Sci. Inc., Cleve., 1970-72, v.p., chief engr., 1972-81; v.p. internat. divsn. Engring. Sci. Inc., Arcadia, 1981-84, group v.p., 1984-87; sr. v.p. Engring. Sci. Inc., Pasadena, Calif., 1987—; mem. industry adv. bd. Sch. Engring. and Tech. Calif. State U., L.A., 1986—. Contbr. articles to profl. jours. Commr. Archtl. Commn., Claremont, Calif., 1980-86; councilman Claremont City Coun., 1986-94; mayor City of Claremont, 1989-92; mem. Pasadena Tournament of Roses Assn., 1980—, L.A. 2000 Environ. Com., 1987-88. With USMC, 1963-67. Recipient Disting. Engring. Achievement award Inst. for Advancement of Engring., 1993. Fellow ASCE (mem. internat. adv. com. 1987-90); mem. NSPE, Am. Acad. Environ. Engrs., Am. Water Works Assn. (life), Water Environ. Fedn., Soc. Am. Value Engrs., Rotary. Republican. Home: 727 E Alamosa Dr Claremont CA 91711-2008 Office: Parsons Engring Sci Inc 100 W Walnut St Pasadena CA 91124-0001

PRESSEL, ESTHER JOAN, anthropologist; b. Loysburg, Pa., Jan. 15, 1937; d. J. William and Rachel Pressel. PhD, Ohio State U., 1971. Assoc. prof. anthropology Colo. State U., Fort Collins, 1968—. Fellow Am. Anthropol. Assn.; mem. Soc. for Psychol. Anthropology, Soc. for Med. Anthropology, Sigma Xi. Home: 829 Juniper Ln Fort Collins CO 80526-1975 Office: Colo State U Dept Anthropology Fort Collins CO 80523

PRESSLEY, JAMES RAY, electrical engineer; b. Ft. Worth, July 14, 1946; s. Loy Dale and Dorothy Helen (Foust) P.; m. Barbara Kay McMillin, Oct. 9, 1968 (div. 1981); children: James Foust Pressley, Kreg Milam Pressley; m. Susan Marie Straw, Apr. 27, 1985 (div.); children: Shaye Eugene Straw, Rebecca Alycen Straw, Rachel Leilani Straw. BSEE, U. Tex., Arlington, 1970. Registered profl. engr., Alaska, Hawaii, Oreg., Wash. Designer/draftsman Romine & Slaughter, Ft. Worth, 1967-71; engr. Crews MacInnes & Hoffman, Anchorage, 1971-73, O'Kelly & Schoenlank, Anchorage, 1973-75, Theodore G. Creedon, Anchorage, 1975-77; v.p. Fryer, Pressley Elliott, Anchorage, 1977-80, Fryer/Pressley Engring., 1980-91, FPE/Roen Engrs., Inc., 1991—, also chmn. bd., 1991—; mem. elec. constrn. and maintenance industry evaluation panel, 1982—. Mem. IEEE, Illuminating Engring. Soc. (sustaining), Internat. Assn. Elec. Inspectors, Nat. Assn. Corrosion Engrs., Am. Soc. Quality Control. Office: FPE/Roen Engrs Inc 560 E 34th Ave Ste 300 Anchorage AK 99503-4161

PRESTON, ASTRID DEBORAH, artist; b. Stockholm, Sept. 29, 1945; came to U.S., 1952; d. Stanley and Milda E. Borbals; m. Howard J. Preston, Sept. 1, 1943; 1 child, Max. BA, UCLA, 1967. One-woman shows include L.A. Inst. of Contemporary Art, 1982, Newspace, L.A., 1983, 84, 85, Patty Aande Gallery, San Diego, 1986, Krygier/Landau Contemporary Art, L.A., 1987, Laguna Art Mus., Laguna Beach., Calif., 1987, Jan Turner Gallery, L.A., 1989, 91, Peter Blake Gallery, Laguna Beach, 1994. Bd. dirs. L.A. Contemporary Exhibits, 1984-89, Beyond Baroque, Venice, Calif., 1994—. Grantee Nat. Endowment of the Arts, 1987.

PRESTON, ROBERT ARTHUR, astronomer; b. N.Y.C., June 29, 1944; s. Arthur Lloyd and Dorothy Elizabeth (Smith) P.; m. Ann Lee Archer, July 18, 1970; 1 child, Karen Ann. BS, Cornell U., 1966, MS, 1967; PhD, MIT, 1972. Rsch. scientist Lockheed Rsch. Lab., Palo Alto, Calif., 1972-73; astronomer Jet Propulsion Lab., Calif. Inst. Tech., Pasadena, 1973—, supr. astronomical measurements group, 1975—, mgr. astrophysics rsch. program, 1983-92, project scientist Space VLBI project, 1991—; leader U.S. Sci. teams for Vega Venus Balloon and Phobos Lander Missions, 1982-90. Recipient Exceptional Svc. award NASA, 1986; rsch. grantee NASA, 1975—, Nat. Park Svc., 1980—. Mem. Am. Astron. Soc., Internat. Astron. Union. Home: 24618 Golfview Dr Santa Clarita CA 91355-2301 Office: Calif Inst Tech Jet Propulsion Lab 4800 Oak Grove Dr Pasadena CA 91109-8001

PREUSS, PAUL FREDERICK, writer; b. Albany, Ga., Mar. 7, 1942; s. Paul Theodore and Mona Elizabeth (McDonald) P.; m. Marsha Pettit, Mar. 10, 1963 (div. Nov. 1968); 1 child, Mona Helen; m. Karen Reiser, Mar. 3, 1973 (div. Oct. 1989); m. Debra Turner, June 1993. BA, Yale U., 1966. Writer mktg. projects BBDO Advt., N.Y.C., 1966-67; floor dir. King TV, Seattle, 1967-68; creative dir. King Screen Prodns., Seattle, 1968-72; staff cons., author, producer Biol. Scis. Curriculum Study, Boulder, Colo., 1972-74, San Francisco, 1974—. Author: Broken Symmetries, 1983, Human Error, 1985, Venus Prime #1: Breaking Strain, 1987, Starfire, 1988, Venus Prime #2: Maelstrom, 1988, Venus Prime #3: Hide and Seek, 1988, Venus Prime #4: The Medusa Encounter, 1990, Venus Prime #5: The Diamond Moon, 1990, Venus Prime #6: The Shining Ones, 1990, Core, 1993; contbr. to profl. publs. Recipient Gold Medal Spl. award N.Y. Film & TV Festival, 1972. Mem. AAAS, Authors Guild, No. Calif. Sci. Writers Assn., Bay Area Book Reviewers Assn. Democrat. Home and Office: PO Box 590773 San Francisco CA 94159-0773

PREUSSER, FRANK DIETRICH, cultural heritage preservation consultant; b. Wiesbaden, Germany, Feb. 1, 1944; came to U.S., 1983; s. Camillo Clemens and Irma Kaethe (Voland) P.; m. Margarete Weininger, May 13, 1977; 1 child, Bernhard F.L. BS in Chemistry, Tech. U. Munich, 1967, MS in Chemistry, 1969, PhD in Phys. Chemistry & Chem. Tech., 1973. Curator, head of rsch. lab. Doerner Inst., Munich, 1973-76, sr. curator, head of rsch. lab., 1976-83; conservation scientist, head of lab. J. Paul Getty Mus., Calif., 1983-84, sr. conservation scientist, head of lab., 1984-85; program dir. sci. rsch. Getty Conservation Inst., Calif., 1985-90, acting co-dir., 1990, head of publs., 1990-92, acting program dir. sci. rsch., 1991-92, assoc. dir. programs, 1990-93; pres. Frank Preusser & Assocs., Inc., West Hills, Calif., 1993—; vis. lectr. Doerner Inst., 1974-77, Ludwig-Maximilians U., Munich, 1974-82, Tech. Acad. Esslingen, Germany, 1976-82, Tech. Acad. Wuppertal, Germany, 1977-82, Funación Mexicana para los Monumentos del Mundo, Puebla, Mexico, 1991; numerous coms. for various orgns. Contbr. over 60 articles to profl. jours.; also abstracts, book revs. Mem. Am. Chem. Soc., Internat. Inst. for Conservation, Am. Inst. for Conservations, German Chem. Soc., German Soc. Conservators, Internat. Coun. on Monuments and Sites (U.S. com.), Internat. Coun. Museums, Nat. Parks and Conservation Assn., Nat. Trust for Historic Preservation, Sci.-Tech. Assn. for Conservation of Bldgs. and Monuments, Western Assn. Art Conservators. Office: Frank Preusser & Assocs Inc 6434 Pat Ave West Hills CA 91307-2740

PREVITE, RICHARD, computer company executive; b. Boston, 1935. BS, San Jose State U., 1956, MA. Contr. Sierra Elec. Corp., Menlo Park, Calif., 1961-69; with Advanced Micro Devices, Inc., Sunnyvale, Calif., 1969—, sr. v.p., treas., chief adminstrv. officer, pres., COO, bd. dirs.; bd. dirs. Robinson Nugent, Inc. Office: Advanced Micro Devices Inc PO Box 3453 Sunnyvale CA 94088-3453*

PREVO, RANDALL MURRAY, personnel administrator; b. Casper, Wyo., Oct. 15, 1921; s. William Henry and Florence Jane (Moses) P.; m. Irene Marie Thouvenin, July 14, 1945; children: Martine Jane, Odile L., Ann-Marie, Bernadette Phyllis Kidd. AA, S.J. Jr. Coll., Stockton, Calif., 1949; AB, Coll. of Pacific, Stockton, Calif., 1951; Cert. in Pub. Adminstrn., U.

Calif., Alameda, 1963. Registered lobbyist, 1988. Pers. adminstr. City of Stockton, 1952-56; pers. dir. San Joaquin County, Stockton, 1956-68; gen. mgr. Marin County Employees Assn., San Rafael, Calif., 1968-70; pers. officer, dep. adminstr. Napa County, Calif., 1970-71; gen. mgr. Calif. Pub. Employees Fedn., Sacramento, 1971-73, Kern County Employees Assn. Local 700, Bakersfield, Calif., 1973-74, Alameda Employee Assn. Local 616, Oakland, Calif., 1974-76; gen. mgr., rep. San Diego Pub. Employees Assn., 1976-88. Contbr. articles to profl. jours. Trustee exec. com. Coun. 2 of S.E.I.U., San Francisco, 1974-76; bd. dirs. Indsl. Rels. Coun., U. Calif., Alameda, 1974-76; pres. IKE for Pres. Club, Stockton, 1952. With U.S. Army, 1940-45; ETO. Decorated Bronze Star medal; named Sertoman of the Yr., Sertoma Club, 1987-88. Mem. Am. Legion, VFW, K.C. (3d degree), Elks, Pi Gamma Mu, Phi Kappa Phi. Republican. Roman Catholic. Home: 1925 W Benjamin Holt Dr Stockton CA 95207-3426

PREWOZNIK, JEROME FRANK, lawyer; b. Detroit, July 15, 1934; s. Frank Joseph and Loretta Ann (Parzych) P.; m. Marilyn Johnson, 1970; 1 son, Frank Joseph II. AB cum laude, U. Detroit, 1955; JD with distinction, U. Mich., 1958. Bar: Calif. 1959. Pvt. practice, Calif., 1960-91. Served in U.S. Army, 1958-60. Mem. ABA (bus. law sect., law and acctg. com., chmn. auditing standards subcom. 1981-86), State Bar Calif. (bus. law sect., exec. com., vice chmn., 1985-86), Order of Coif. Republican. Home and Office: 431 Georgina Ave Santa Monica CA 90402-1909

PRICE, BETTY JEANNE, choirchime soloist, writer; b. Long Beach, Calif., June 12, 1942; d. Grant E. and Miriam A. (Francis) Sickles; m. Harvey H. price, Aug. 6, 1975; 1 child, Thomas Neil Gering. Degree in Acctg., Northland Pioneer Coll., Show Low, Ariz., 1977. Typographer Joel H. Weldon & Assocs., Scottsdale, Ariz., 1980-89; coord. music and worship College Ave. Bapt. Ch., San Diego, 1994—; ChoirChime soloist, 1986—. Author: 101 Ways to Fix Broccoli, 1994. Home: PO Box 151115 San Diego CA 92175-1115

PRICE, BONNIE BURNS, political science educator; b. San Diego, June 26, 1940; d. Jack and June (Chandonia) Burns, stepdau. Lois (Maus) Burns; m. John Paul Price, Sept. 2, 1961; 1 child, Jacqueline. Student, Am. U., 1961; BA in Polit. Sci., Albright Coll., 1962; MA in Polit. Sci., U. Pa., 1966; PhD in Polit. Sci., Temple U., 1979. Secondary tchr. Daniel Boone Sch. Dist., Athol, Pa., 1962-63, Muhlenberg Sch. Dist., Laureldale, Pa., 1963-66; instr. polit. sci. Albright Coll., Reading, Pa., 1966-67, adj. instr. history, 1969; asst. prof. history Kutztown (Pa.) U., 1970; prof. polit. sci. Reading Area Community Coll., 1971-87, 89-92, acting v.p. acad. affairs, 1987-88; v.p. adminstrn. Prof. Sch. Psychol. Studies, San Diego, 1991; founder, pres. Western Am. U., San Diego, 1992—; chief cons. Orgnl. Techs., Inc., Reading, 1980-87. Bd. dirs. Muhlenberg Sch. Dist., 1975-87, Planned Parenthood N.E. Pa., Trexlertown, 1987-90; mem. steering com. Pa. Choice Coalition, 1989-91. Lilly fellow U. Pa., Phila., 1983-85; grantee Pa. Pub. Commn. for Humanities, 1980, NSF grantee U. Pa., 1989-90. Mem. Am. Soc. Pub. Adminstrn., Pa. Polit. Sci. Assn., Am. Fedn. Tchrs., AAAS, ACLU (bd. dirs. Berks chpt. 1979-87). Democrat. Home: 2750 Wheatstone St Spc 160 San Diego CA 92111-5446 Office: Western Am U 3517 Camino Del Rio S Ste 215 San Diego CA 92108-4028

PRICE, CHARLES STEVEN, lawyer; b. Inglewood, Calif., June 10, 1955; s. Frank Dean Price and Ann (Rounds) Bolling; m. Sandra Helen Laney, Feb. 26, 1983; children: Katherine Laney, Courtney Ann, Diana Emily. BA, U. Calif., Santa Barbara, 1976; JD, U. Chgo., 1979. Bar: Ariz. 1980, U.S. Dist. Ariz. 1980, U.S. Ct. Appeals (9th cir.) 1982. Assoc. Brown & Bain P.A., Phoenix, Ariz., 1979-85, ptnr., 1985—. Office: Brown & Bain PA 2901 N Central Ave Phoenix AZ 85012

PRICE, CLIFFORD WARREN, retired metallurgist, researcher; b. Denver, Apr. 22, 1935; s. Warren Wilson and Vivian Fredricka (Cady) P.; m. Carole Joyce Waterman, June 14, 1969; children: Carla Beth, Krista Lynn Kilton. MetE, Colo. Sch. Mines, 1957; MS, Ohio State U., 1970, PhD, 1975. Design engr. Sundstrand Aviation-Denver, 1957-60; materials specialist Denver Rsch. Inst., 1960-63; sr. metallurgist Rocky Flats div. Dow Chem. Co., Golden, Colo., 1963-66; staff metallurgist Battelle Columbus (Ohio) Labs., 1966-75; sr. scientist Owens-Corning Fiberglas, Granville, Ohio, 1975-80; metallurgist Lawrence Livermore (Calif.) Nat. Lab., 1980-93; retired, 1993. Contbr. articles to profl. jours. Battelle Columbus Labs. fellow, 1974-75. Mem. Metall. Soc. AIME, Microscopy Soc. Am. (treas. Denver 1961-62), Am. Soc. for Metals. Republican.

PRICE, DAROLD WAYNE, real estate investor; b. Salina, Kans., July 12, 1933; s. Irvin Merrill and Bertha Olive (Molander) P.; m. Beverly Joan Vevang Price, Jan. 1, 1967; 1 child, Christine Anne Price. BS in Bus. Adminstrn., Kans. State U., 1955. Cert. gen. contractor, Wash.; lic. fed. pilot. Student Kans. State U., 1951-55; U.S. Naval aviator USN, Pensacola, Fla., 1955-56, Corpus Christi, Tex., 1956-57, Guantanamo Bay, Cuba, 1957-59; indsl. sales engr. Alcoa, Oklahoma City, 1960-62, Wichita, Kans., 1962-65; mgr. spl. products Alcoa, Seattle, 1965-70; mgr. Alcoa Constrn. Sys., Seattle, 1970-73; pres., owner Western House, Issaquah, Wash., 1973—; pres., bd. dirs. Kihei (Hi.) Surfside Home Owner Assn., 1981,83, 89-91. Mem. Concord Coalition, Seattle, 1993—. Mem. Kiwanis Club of Issaquah (pres. 1987-88), Issaquah C. of C. Republican. Lutheran. Home and Office: 22405 SE 20th St Issaquah WA 98027-9566

PRICE, DAVID, recreational facilities executive; b. 1933. With Am. Golf Corp., Santa Monica, Calif., 1972—, now chief exec. officer; chmn. Nat. Golf Properties, Santa Monica, Calif., 1993—. Office: Am Golf Corp 1633 26th St Santa Monica CA 90404-4023

PRICE, EDWARD DEAN, federal judge; b. Sanger, Calif., Feb. 12, 1919; s. Earl Trousdale and Daisy Shaw (Biggs) P.; m. Katherine S. Merritt, July 18, 1943; children: Katherine Price O'Brien, Edward M., Jane E. B.A., U. Calif., Berkeley, 1947, LL.B., 1949. Bar: Calif. 1949. Assoc. Cleary & Zeff, Modesto, Calif., 1949-51; assoc. Zeff & Halley, Modesto, Calif., 1951-54; ptnr. Zeff, Halley & Price, Modesto, Calif., 1954-63, Zeff & Price, Modesto, Calif., 1963-65, Price & Martin, Modesto, Calif., 1965-69, Price, Martin & Crabtree, Modesto, Calif., 1969-79; judge U.S. Dist. Ct., Fresno, Calif., 1980-90, sr. judge, 1990—; mem. adv. bd. governing com. Continuing Edn. of Bar, San Francisco, 1963-71, governing bd. Calif. State Bar, 1973-76; v.p. Jud. Council, Calif., 1978-79. Contbr. articles to profl. jours. Served with U.S. Army, 1943-46. Mem. ABA, Am. Coll. Trial Lawyers, Am. Bd. Trial Advocates. Democrat. Methodist. Home: 1012 Wellesley Ave Modesto CA 95350-5042 Office: US Dist Ct 5554 US Courthouse 1130 O St Fresno CA 93721-2201

PRICE, GAYL BAADER, residential construction company administrator; b. Gothenburg, Sweden, Mar. 1, 1949; came to U.S., 1951; d. Harold Edgar Anderson and Jeanette Helen (Hallberg) Akeson; m. Daniel J. Baader, Nov. 27, 1971 (div. Sept. 1980); m. Leigh C. Price, Feb. 28, 1983; foster children: Heidi, Heather. BA in Fgn. Lang., U. Ill., 1971. Asst. buyer The Denver, 1971-73, buyer, 1973-75; escrow sec. Transam. Title, Evergreen, Colo., 1975-76, escrow officer, 1976-78, sr. escrow officer, 1978-79, br. mgr., 1979-84; sr. account mgr. Transam. Title, Denver, 1984-87, sales mgr., 1987-91, v.p., 1989-94; cmty. mgr. Village Homes of Colo., Littleton, Colo., 1994—. Vol. Safehouse for Battered Women, Denver, 1986—, Spl. Olympics, 1986—, Adult Learning Svcs., 1993—, Kids Cure for Cancer, 1994—. Mem. Home Builders Assn. Met. Denver (bd. dirs. 1989—, exec. com. 1992, assoc. mem. coun. chair 1991, Arthur Gaeth Assoc. of Yr. 1989), Sales and Mktg. Coun. Met. Denver (chair, Most Profl. award 1989), Douglas County Econ. Devel., Zonta Club (Denver II, pres. 1990, Zontian of Yr. 1988), Colo. Assn. of Homebuilders (Assoc. of Yr. 1992). Home: 1975 Linda Ln Evergreen CO 80439 Office: Village Homes 6 W Dry Creek Cir Ste 200 Littleton CO 80120-8031

PRICE, HUMPHREY WALLACE, aerospace engineer; b. San Antonio, Sept. 25, 1954; s. Humphrey Rodes and Ruth (Wallace) P. BS in Engring., U. Tex., 1976, MS in Engring., 1978. Rsch. asst. nuclear reactor lab. U. Tex., Austin, 1976; nuclear engr. EDS Nuclear, Inc., San Francisco, 1977-78; engr. Jet Propulsion Lab., Pasadena, Calif., 1978-82; rsch. engr. SW Rsch. Inst., San Antonio, 1982-84; tech. group leader Jet Propulsion Lab., Pasadena, Calif., 1984-89; configuration engr. Cassini spacecraft NASA, 1989-93, sys. engr. Pluto spacecraft, 1994—; system engr. Pluto Spacecraft, 1994—; cons. Am. Rocket Co., Camarillo, Calif., 1986-87; tech. staff World Space Found., Pasadena, 1980—. Patentee in field; contbr. to tech. papers in field. Mem. AIAA (sr.), Brit. Interplanetary Soc. Office: HW Price Cons PO Box 454 La Canada Flintridge CA 91012-0454

PRICE, JEANNINE ALLEENICA, clinical psychologist; b. Cleve., Oct. 29, 1949; d. Q. Q. and Lisa Denise (Wilson) Ewing; m. T. R. Price, Sept. 2, 1976. BS, Western Res. U., 1969; MS, Vanderbilt U., 1974; MBA, Stanford U., 1985. Cert. alcoholism counselor, Calif. Health Service coordinator Am. Profile, Nashville, 1970-72; exec. dir. Awareness Concept, San Jose, Calif., 1977-80, counselor, 1989—, exec. dir., 1989-90, v.p. Image Makers (formerly Awareness Concepts), 1991—; mgr. employee assistance program Nat. Semiconductor, Santa Clara, Calif., 1980-81; mgmt. cons. employee assistant programs. Mem. Gov.'s Adv. Council Child Devel. Programs. Mem. Am. Bus. Women's Assn., NAFE, AAUW, Coalition Labor Women, Calif. Assn. Alcohol counselors, Almaca. Author: Smile a Little, Cry a Lot, Gifts of Love, Reflection in the Mirror, The Light at the Top of the Mountain, The Dreamer, The Girl I Never Knew, An Act of Love, Walk Toward the Light.

PRICE, JOE (ALLEN), artist, former educator; b. Ferriday, La., Feb. 6, 1935; s. Edward Neill and Margaret (Hester) P. BS, Northwestern U., 1957; postgrad., Art Ctr. Coll., L.A., 1967-68; MA, Stanford U., 1970. Free-lance actor, artist N.Y.C., 1957-60; freelance illustrator, actor, L.A., 1960-68; free-lance comml. artist, San Carlos, Calif., 1968-69; package designer Container Corp. Am., Santa Clara, Calif., 1969; prof. studio art and filmmaking, chmn. dept. art Coll. San Mateo, Calif., 1970-94. One-man shows include Richard Sumner Gallery, Palo Alto, Calif., 1975, San Mateo County Cultural Ctr., 1976, 82, Tahir Galleries, New Orleans, 1977, 82, Kerwin Galleries, Burlingame, Calif., 1977, Edits. Gallery, Melbourne, Australia, 1977, Ankrum Gallery, Los Angeles, 1978, 84, Edits. Ltd. West Gallery, San Francisco, 1981, Miriam Perlman Gallery, Chgo., 1982, San Mateo County Arts Council Gallery, 1982, Candy Stick Gallery, Ferndale, Calif., 1984, Assoc. Am. Artists, N.Y.C. and Phila., 1984, Gallery 30, Burlingame, 1991, San Mateo, 1984, Triton Mus. Art, Santa Clara, Calif., 1986, Huntsville (Ala.) Mus. Art, 1987, Gallery 30, San Mateo, 1988-91, Concept Art Gallery, Pitts., 1991, Eleonore Austerer Gallery, San Francisco, 1995; exhibited in groups shows at Berkeley Art Ctr., Calif., 1976, Burlingame Civic Art Gallery, 1976, Syntex Gallery, Palo Alto, Calif., 1977, Gump's Gallery, San Francisco, 1976, 77, Nat. Gallery of Australia, 1978, Sonoma County Gallery, 1979, Gov. Dummer Acad. Art, Byfield, Mass., 1979, Miss. Mus. Art, 1982, C.A.A. Galleries, Chautauqua, N.Y., 1982, Huntsville Mus. Art, 1983, Tahir Gallery, New Orleans, 1983, Hunterdon Art Ctr., N.J., 1984, Editions Galleries, Melbourne, Australia, 1988, Van Stratten Gallery, Chgo., 1988, 6th Internat. Exhbn., Carnegie-Mellon U., Pa., 1988, Forum Gallery, Jamestown, N.Y., 1988, 5th Internat. Biennale Petite Format de Papier, Belgium, 1989, 4th Internat. Biennial Print Exhibit, Taipei Fine Arts Mus., People's Republic China, 1990, Interprint, Lviv '90, USSR, 1990, New Orleans Mus. Art, 1990, Internat. Print Triennale, Cracow, Poland, 1991, 15th Ann. Nat. Invitational Drawing Exhbn. Emporia State U., Kans., 1991, Haggar U. Gallery, U. Dallas, 1991, Directions in Bay Area Printmaking: Three Decades Palo Alto Cultural Ctr., 1992, Am. Prints: Last Half 20th Century, Jane Haslem Gallery, Washington, 1992, Wenniger Graphics, Boston, 1993, Eleonore Austerer Gallery, San Francisco, 1994, Triton Mus. Art, Santa Clara, 1994, Mobile Mus. Art, 1995; represented in permanent collections San Francisco Mus. Modern Art, Achenbach Found. Graphic Arts, San Francisco, Phila. Mus. Art, New Orleans Mus. Art, Portland Mus. Art, Maine, The Libr. of Congress, Washington. Huntsville Mus. Art, Midwest Mus. Am. Art, Ind., Cracow Nat. Mus., Poland, Cabo Frio Mus., Brazil, Nat. Mus. Am. Art, Smithsonian Inst., Washington. Recipient Kempshall Clark award Peoria Art Guild, 1981, Paul Lindsay Sample Meml. award 25th Chautauqua Nat. Exhbn. of Am. Art, 1982, 1st Ann. Creative Achievement award Calif. State Legislature/Arts Coun. San Mateo County, 1989. Mem. Am. Color Print Soc., Audubon Artists (Louis Lozowick Meml. award 1978, Silver medal of honor award 1991), Boston Printmakers (Ture Bengtz Meml. award 1987), Calif. Soc. Printmakers (mem. council 1979-81), Los Angeles Printmaking Soc., Phila. Print Club (Lessing J. Rosenwald prize 1979), Arts Council of San Mateo Count, Theta Chi. Democrat. Studio and Office: PO Box 3305 Sonora CA 95370-3305

PRICE, KATHLEEN MCCORMICK, book editor, writer; b. Topeka, Kans., Dec. 25, 1932; d. Raymond Chesley and Kathleen (Shoffner) McCormick; m. William Faulkner Black, Aug. 25, 1956 (div. 1961); 1 child, Kathleen Serena; m. William Hillard Price, Aug. 13, 1976. BA, U. Colo., Denver, 1971. Book reviewer Denver Post, 1971-78; book editor San Diego Mag., 1978-92; cons. editor St. John's Cathedral, Denver, 1985-95. Author: There's a Dactyl Under My Foot, 1986, The Lady and the Unicorn, 1994. Historian, Altar Guild, St. John's Cathedral, Denver. Mem. PEN Internat., Denver Women's Press Club, Denver Country Club, La Garita Club, Phi Beta Kappa. Episcopalian. Home: 27 Crestmoor Dr Denver CO 80220-5853

PRICE, KEITH GLENN, accountant; b. Ft. Morgan, Colo., Nov. 24, 1941; s. George Felt and Irene Lois (Gibbs) P.; m. Norma Helen Witt, Feb. 28, 1970; children: Diana, Michael, Troy, Aaron, Christopher. BS, BA, Colo. State U., 1968. CPA. Auditor IRS, Casper, Wyo., 1968-75; ptnr. Hines, Price and Co., Cheyenne, Wyo., 1975-76, Fisher, Hines and Price, Cheyenne, Wyo., 1976-80; sole practice Cheyenne, Wyo., 1980—; co-founder, pres. High Plains Mortgage Co., 1990-91; chmn. bd. dirs. Goodwill Industries of Wyo., 1980-87. Treas. North Christian Ch., 1986—, Salesman with a Purpose, 1980; mem. Heels, 1975—; founder Cheyenne Typing Svc. Served to sgt. USMCR, 1963-71. Mem. AICPA, Wyo. Soc. CPAs, Nat. Soc. Pub. Accts., Nat. Fedn. Ind. Bus., U.S. C. of C., Cheyenne C. of C., Nat. Soc. Tax Profls. Republican. Mem. Ind. Ch. of Christ. Home: 5333 Frederick Dr Cheyenne WY 82009 Office: 721 E 16th St Cheyenne WY 82001-4703

PRICE, LEIGH CHARLES, petroleum geologist and geochemist; b. Whittier, Calif., Feb. 27, 1944; s. Charles Stewart and Barbara Mary (Moyle) P.; m. Martha Sue Allen, Sept. 18, 1970 (div. June 1979); m. Gayl Anderson Baader, Feb. 28, 1983. BS in Chemistry, U. Calif., Riverside, 1966, BS in Geology, 1968, MS in Geology, 1970, PhD in Geology/Geochemistry, 1973. Rsch. scientist Exxon Prodn. Rsch., Houston, 1972-73, U.S. Geol. Survey, Denver, 1974—; lectr. in field. Editor Jour. Petroleum Geology, 1992—; reviewer Geochemica Cosmochimica Acta, Nature, Energy & Fuels, others; contbr. articles and abstracts to profl. jours. Active various civic orgns. NDEA fellow, 1968-72. Mem. Am. Assn. Petroleum Geologists (Matson award 1973, 75, Disting. lectr. 1974, 75), Assn. Petroleum Geochem. Explorations, Geochem. Soc. (Paper of Yr. 1993, best paper com. 1993—). Home: 1075 S Linda Ln Evergreen CO 80439-9528 Office: US Geol Survey Denver Fed Ctr MS 940 Denver CO 80225

PRICE, MARGARET RUTH, financial services company executive; b. Phoenix, Sept. 12, 1956; d. James John and Mavis Marie (Anderson) Knopp; m. Michael Reid Price, Sept. 15, 1979. BS in Instl. Food Svc. and Mgmt., Mont. State U., 1978. CFP. Dir. nutrition programs Human Resource Devel. Coun., Bozeman, Mont., 1979-82; investment cons. Shearson Lehman Bros., Anchorage, 1982-85; v.p., investment cons. Boettcher & Co.-Kemper Fin. Svcs., Anchorage, 1985-88; sr. v.p. investment cons., fin. planner Kemper Securities, Inc.-Kemper Fin. Svcs., Anchorage, 1988—; nutrition cons., Bozeman, 1979-82; presenter radio talk show Sta. KENI, Anchorage, 1987; mem. qualified plan adv. bd. Kemper Securities, mem. Chmns. Circle of Excellence. Chairperson Anchorage Employee Retirement Income Security Act, 1987—, Anchorage Estate Planning Coun., 1991—. Mem. Amnesty Internat., Anchorage Nordic Ski Club. Home: 831 Harbor Cir Anchorage AK 99515-3641 Office: Kemper Securities Inc 550 W 7th Ave Ste 1980 Anchorage AK 99501-3571

PRICE, PATRICIA ANNE, artist; b. Tulsa, Feb. 4, 1950; d. Max Edward and Katharine (Jordan) P. BA, Oral Roberts U., 1974. Pvt. practice oil and gas lease broker Burleson County, Tex., 1978-84; rsch. and sale clk. The Kiva Indian Arts, Santa Fe, 1984-90; owner, mgr. Singing Coyote-Southwestern Art, Santa Fe, 1992—. Exhibited in Romanian Libr., N.Y.C., 1975, Boston (Mass.) Coll., 1975, S.W. Tex. State, San Marcos, 1977, Ohio State U., Columbus, 1977. East European scholar, S.W. Tex. State U., 1977, Romania Ministry of Tourism scholar, 1976. Mem. Women's Divsn. Aux. C. of C. Santa Fe, The Cherokee Nation (tribal mem.), VFW Women's Aux., Am. Legion Women's Aux. Home and Office: 142 Verano Loop Santa Fe NM 87505-8350

PRICE, PAUL BUFORD, physicist, educator; b. Memphis, Nov. 8, 1932; s. Paul Buford and Eva (Dupuy) P.; m. JoAnn Margaret Baum, June 28, 1958; children—Paul Buford III, Heather Alynn, Pamela Margaret, Alison Gaynor. BS summa cum laude, Davidson Coll., 1954, DSc, 1973; MS, U. Va., 1956, PhD, 1958. Fulbright scholar U. (Eng.) Bristol, 1958-59; NSF postdoctoral fellow Cambridge (Eng.) U., 1959-60; physicist R&D Ctr. GE, Schenectady, 1960-69; vis. prof. Tata Inst. Fundamental Rsch., Bombay, India, 1965-66; adj. prof. physics Rensselaer Poly. Inst., 1967-68; prof. physics U. Calif., Berkeley, 1969—, chmn. dept. physics, 1987-91, McAdams prof. physics, 1990-92, dean phys. scis., 1992—, dir. Space Scis. Lab., 1979-85; bd. dirs. Terradex Corp., Walnut Creek, Calif.; vis. com. Bartol Rsch. Inst., 1991-94; adv. bd. Indian Inst. Astrophysics, Bangalore, 1993—; cons. to lunar sample analysis planning team NASA; space sci. bd. Nat. Acad. Scis.; vis. prof. U. Rome, 1983, 92; sci. assoc. Ctr. d'Etude Rsch. Nuclear, 1984; Miller rsch. prof. U. Calif., Berkeley, 1972-73; researcher in space and astrophycs, nuclear physics. Author: (with others) Nuclear Tracks in Solids; Contbr. (with others) articles to profl. jours. Recipient Disting. Svc. award Am. Nuclear Soc., 1964, Indsl. Rsch. awards, 1964, 65, E.O. Lawrence Meml. award AEC, 1971, medal for exceptional sci. achievement NASA, 1973; John Simon Guggenheim fellow, 1976-77. Fellow Am. Phys. Soc., Am. Geophys. Union; mem. Nat. Acad. Scis. (chmn. geophysics sect. 1981-84, sec. class phys.-math. scis. 1985-88, chmn. 1988-91).

PRICE, RICHARD TAFT, JR., manufacturing company executive; b. San Diego, June 7, 1954; s. Richard Taft and Murial Martha (Weinhold) T. Student, Brigham Young U., 1972-76; BS, Ariz. State U., 1978. Sales mgr. Imperial Metals, L.A., 1978-83; pres. Alumatone, Inc., No. Hollywood, Calif., 1983-88; acquisitions mgr. Calif. Custom Shapes Inc., L.A., 1988-90, pres., 1990—; bd. dirs. IMCOA, Inc., L.A., Calif. Window Corp., Walnut; pres., bd. dirs. Taft Holdings, Inc., Anaheim, Calif., 1995—. Republican. Office: Calif. Custom Shapes Inc 1800 E Talbot Way Anaheim CA 92805-6727

PRICE, ROBERT WILLIAM, school superintendent, consultant; b. Ogden, Utah, May 13, 1950; s. William Robert and Eileen Louise (Rabe) P.; m. Sally Sandman, Sept. 20, 1975; children: Geoffrey Thomas, Caitlin Elizabeth. BS in Child Devel., Calif. State U., Hayward, 1973, MS in Sch. Adminstrn., 1986; postgrad., U. Pacific, 1988—. Cert. elem. tchr., Calif. Tchr. Turlock (Calif.) Sch. Dist., 1974-81; asst. prin. Monte Vista Mid. Sch., Tracy, Calif., 1981-82, prin., 1982-87; asst. supt. instrn. Tracy Pub. Schs., 1987-90, 91-93, interim supt., 1990-91; supt. Empire Union Sch. Dist., Modesto, Calif., 1993—. Cons. Campfire, Tracy, 1983; founding mem. Tracy Exch. Club, 1985; co-founder Project Bus. & Edn. Together, Tracy, 1985; bd. dirs. Boys and Girls Club of Tracy, 1987-93. Recipient Adminstrv. Leadership award Calif. Media & Libr. Educators Assn., 1994. Mem. Assn. Calif. Sch. Adminstrs. (planning com. supts. symposium 1995—, v.p. programs Region 7 1994—), Calif. League Mid. Schs. (adv. panel Region 6 1993—, chair legis. action 1994-95, Region 6 Educator of Yr. 1991). Democrat. Office: Empire Union Sch Dist 116 N McClure Rd Modesto CA 95357

PRICE, SUSAN KAY LIND, employment training organization administrator; b. Burley Cassia, Idaho, Apr. 27, 1958; d. Ray Elden and Melba Jean (Koyle) Lind; m. Randy Sam Price, July 18, 1986; 1 child, Jordan Richard. Student, Brigham Young U., 1976-79, U. Utah, 1983-84; BS magna cum laude, Utah State U., 1988, postgrad., 1991-92. Cert. assertive comm. trainer, Utah State Office Edn.; cert. hypnotist, Am. Coun. Hypnotist Examiners; cert. advanced rapid eye tech. with self discovery processing; cert. core belief therapy. Project coord. single parent/displaced homemaker program Bridgerland Applied Tech. Ctr., Logan; aide, exec. sec., job developer, employment counselor Bear River Assn. of Govt., Logan, Utah; mem. adv. bd. Cmty.-Falmily Partnership; mem. social work community adv. com., supr. social work practicum, supr. family and human devel. practicum Utah State U. Named Outstanding Job Developer, 1987; recipient Master Tchr. award, 1983. Mem. NAFE, Nat. Displaced Homemaker's Network (Utah rep. 1989-93), Box Elder County Self-Sufficiency Coun., Cache County Interagency Coun., Utah Assn. Adult Cmty. and Continuing Edn. (state bd. 1989-92), Bear River Refugee Coun. (sec. 1986-90), Logan Bus. and Profl. Women (Young Careerist 1991), Soroptimist Internat. Home: 376 E 700 S Logan UT 84321-5532

PRICE, THOMAS FREDERICK, theatre educator; b. Salt Lake City, June 19, 1937; s. Thomas William P. and Caryl Susan Brown; children: Devin, Jennifer. BA in Drama, Pomona Coll., 1960; MA in Theatre, San Francisco State U., 1962; PhD in Drama, Stanford U., 1968. Asst. prof. English U. of the Pacific, Stockton, Calif., 1968-70; asst. prof. drama U.S. Internat. U., Sch. Performing Arts, San Diego, 1970-74; archivist, curator The Philibrick Libr., Los Altos Hills, Calif., 1975-85; prof. English Tianjin (China) Normal U., 1985-87; adj. prof. theatre So. Oreg. State Coll., Ashland, 1991—; assoc. prof. English Tamkang U., Taipei, Taiwan, 1993—; ednl. broadcaster KPFA-FM, L.A., 1960-62, KSRO-FM, Ashland, Oreg. Author: Dramatic Structure and Meaning, 1992; contbr. articles to profl. jours. Mem. Calif. Scholarship Fedn. (hon. life), Assn. for Theatre in Higher Edn., Nat. Trust for Historic Preservation.

PRICE, THOMAS MUNRO, computer consultant; b. Madison, Wis., Oct. 2, 1937; s. John Edward and Georgia Winifred (Day) P.; m. Judith Ann Holm, Aug. 8, 1959; children: Scott Michael, Andrea Lynn. BS, Carroll Coll., Waukesha, Wis., 1959; MS, U. Wis., 1961, PhD, 1964. Prof. math. U. Iowa, 1964-77, U. Wyo., Laramie, 1978-79; computer user cons. U. Wyo., 1979-85, MIS prof., 1985-89; computer cons. Laramie, 1989-93; home rebuilder Pecos, N.Mex., 1994—. Contbr. articles to profl. jours. Home: HC 70 Box 235 Pecos NM 87552-9728

PRICE, WESTCOTT WILKIN, III, health care company executive; b. Glendale, Calif., May 6, 1939; s. Westcott Wilkin Jr. and Edna Johnson P.; m. Hillary Clark Haney, Apr. 12, 1941; children: Christopher, Gretchen, Wendy. BS in Bus., U. Colo., 1961; MBA, U. So. Calif., 1967. V.p., chief operating officer Calif. Med. Ctrs., Los Angeles, 1970-73; pres., chief exec. officer Wm. Flaggs Inc., Commerce, Calif., 1973-80; pres., vice chmn. FHP Inc., Fountain Valley, Calif., 1981—. Bd. dirs. FHP Found., Long Beach, Calif., 1985—; bd. govs. U. So. Calif. Sch. Pub. Adminstrn., Los Angeles, 1987—. Served to lt. (j.g.) USN, 1961-63. Republican. Episcopalian. Club: Calif. (Los Angeles). Office: FHP Internat Corp 9900 Talbert Ave Fountain Valley CA 92708*

PRICE, WILLIS JOSEPH, retired oil company executive; b. Louisville, Sept. 23, 1931; s. Zinn O'Hara and Geraldine Susan Violette P.; m. Gloria Rick, Sept. 5, 1970; children by previous marriage—Deborah, Barbara, Natalie. B.A. in English, Fla. State U., 1953. With Standard Oil Co. Ky., 1953-65, pres., 1970-77; with Standard Oil Co. of Calif., San Francisco, 1965-67; pres. Chevron Oil Co. East, 1967-70; sr. v.p. mfg., supply and mktg. Chevron U.S.A., San Francisco, 1977-87, pres., 1987—; v.p. Chevron Corp., San Francisco;, 1987-91, retired, 1991. Bd. dirs. San Francisco Opera, Met. br. YMCA, San Francisco, United Way of Bay Area.; bd. advisers NCCJ, San Francisco; mem. bd. councillors Am. Cancer Soc., Bay Area Sci. Fair, Inc. Mem. NAM (bd. dirs.), Am. Petroleum Inst., Nat. Assn. Mfrs., Western States Petroleum Assn., Calif. C. of C., BIPAC. Republican. Office: Chevron USA Inc 225 Bush St PO Box 7137 San Francisco CA 94104

PRICER, JAMIE LEE, magazine editor; b. Pomona, Calif., Oct. 22, 1948; d. James Mevin Parker and Delcie Erma (Hobson) Vuncannon; m. Leslie Stuart Pricer, June 18, 1988; children: Adam, Blake, Morgan. AA in Social Scis., Col. of Desert, Palm Springs, Calif., 1978; BS in Bus. Adminstrn., Bloomsburg U., 1987. Writer Hi-Desert Pub. Co., 29 Palms, Calif., 1974-77; asst. editor Hi-Desert Pub. Co., Yucca Valley, Calif., 1977-78; copy editor Lubbock (Tex.) Evening Jour., 1981-83; copy editor, writer Press-Enterprise, Bloomsburg, Pa., 1983-87; writer, editor Underwater USA, Bloomsburg, 1984-87; copy editor, writer N.E. Pa. Bus. Jour., Bloomsburg, 1985-87; exec. editor Post Newspapers, Palm Desert, Calif., 1987-89; editor Palm Springs (Calif.) Life Mag., 1989—; pub. speaker numerous civic orgns., Palm Springs, 1989—; workshop leader ednl. insts., So. Calif., 1989—. Editor: History of Indian Wells, 1990. Mem. San Bernardino County Econ. Devel. Commn., San Bernardino, Calif., 1979-80. Named Best Feature section Calif. Newspaper Publishers Assn., Sacramento, 1975; Maggie finalist We. Publishers Assn., Sherman Oaks, Calif., 1990, 91. Office: Palm Springs Life 303 N Indian Canyon Dr Palm Springs CA 92262-6015

PRICKETT, DAVID CLINTON, physician; b. Fairmont, W.Va., Nov. 26, 1918; s. Clinton Evert and Mary Anna (Gottschalk) P.; m. Mary Ellen Holt, June 29, 1940; children: David C., Rebecca Ellen, William Radcliffe, Mary Anne, James Thomas, Sara Elizabeth; m. Pamela S. Blackstone, Nov. 17, 1991. AB, W.Va. U., 1944; MD, U. Louisville, 1946; MPH, U. Pitts., 1955. Lab. asst., instr. in chemistry, W.Va. U., 1943; intern, Louisville Gen. Hosp., 1947; surg. resident St. Joseph's Hosp., Parkersburg, W.Va., 1948-49; gen. practice, 1949-50, 55-61; physician USAF, N.Mex., 1961-62, U.S. Army, Calif., 1963-64, San Luis Obispo County Hosp., 1965-66, So. Calif. Edison Co., 1981-84; assoc. physician indsl. and gen. practice Los Angeles County, Calif., 1967—; med. dir. S. Gate plant GM, 1969-71; physician staff City of L.A., 1971-76; relief med. practice Applachia summer seasons, 1977, 1986, 1988-95. Med. Officer USPHS, Navajo Indian Reservation, Tohatchi (N.Mex.) Health Ctr., 1953-55, surgeon, res. officer, 1957-59; pres. W.Va. Pub. Health Assn., 1951-52, health officer, 1951-53, sec. indsl. and pub. health sect. W.Va. Med. Assn., 1956. Author: The Newer Epidemiology, 1962, rev., 1990, Public Health, A Science Resolvable by Mathematics, 1965. Served to 2d lt. AUS, 1943-46. Dr. Thomas Parran fellow U. Pitts. Sch. Pub. Health, 1955; named to Hon. Order Ky. Cols. Mem. Am. Occupational Med. Assn., Western Occupational Med. Assn., Am. Med. Assn., Calif. Med. Assn., L.A. County Med. Assn., Am. Acad. Family Physicians, Phi Chi. Address: PO Box 4032 Whittier CA 90607-4032

PRICKETT, ROBERT, transit executive. AS Tech., Lane Coll.; BSBA cum laude, U. San Francisco; Calif. tchr. credentials bus., UCLA; mgmt. cert., San Mateo Coll. Mgr. Trans World Airlines; mgr. maintenance and engring. BART; dir. light rail, dep. dir. Santa Clara County Transit; cons., dir. transit systems Am. Transit Cons. (Bechtel), Taipei; ind. cons. Morrison-Knudsen, Pitts., project supt., 1994—. Home: 625 N Madison St Stockton CA 95202-1918

PRIEBE, NORMAN FRANK, electronics engineer; b. Marshall, Minn., Oct. 27, 1934; s. Frank Albert and Hildegard Emma (Schert) P.; m. Jeanette Mae Raedeke, Apr. 26, 1958; children: Brian, Michael, Suzanne, Steven. BSEE, S.D. State U., 1956. Logic designer Sperry Univac, St. Paul, 1957-66, prin. sys. engr., 1966-71; staff sys. engr. Sperry Univac, Salt Lake City, 1971-85; sr. staff sys. engr. Unisys Comm. Sys. Divsn., Salt Lake City, 1985—; mem. Am. Standards Com. X3S3, Washington, 1968-89, Am. Standards Com. T1D1.T1S1, Washington, 1985-89, Am. Standards Com. Subcom. X3S3.4, Washington, 1969-85, Electronics Industry Assn. TR-30, 1965-86. Patentee in field. Active Def. Conversion Task Force, Salt Lake City, 1990. Mem. Great No. Rlwy. Hist. Soc. (dir. 1990—). Office: Unisys Corp 640 N 2200 W Salt Lake City UT 84116-2925

PRIGGE, LIZ MAYNARD, publishing executive; b. L.A., Jan. 5, 1952; d. Robert Graham and Emily Jeannette (Prouty) Maynard; m. Paul J. Prigge, May 1, 1982; children: Amanda Elizabeth, Alexandra Jeannette. BS in Tech. Mgmt., Regis Coll., 1990. Prodn. asst. ABC-Clio, Inc., Santa Barbara, Calif., 1971-75; sales asst. R.R. Donnelley & Sons, Palo Alto, Calif., 1975-76; asst. mfg. mgr. Addison-Wesley Pub. Co., Menlo Park, Calif., 1976-77; prodn. editor Information Handling Svs., Englewood, Colo., 1977-80, mng. editor, 1980-88, sr. mgr., corp. rels., 1988-92; editor-in-chief IHS Pub. Group, Libertyville, Ill., 1992-93; dir. internat. mktg. Info. Handling Svcs., Englewood, Colo., 1993—; cons. Jefferson County Schs., Colo., 1981—. Liaison Gov.'s Conf. on Libr. and Info. Systems, Denver, White House Conf. on Libr. and Info. Systems, Washington. Mem. Am. Mktg. Assn. (asst. v.p. 1990—), Pub. Rels. Soc. Am., Info. Industry Assn. (mem. proprietary rights com. 1990—). Democrat.

PRIMACK, MARVIN HERBERT, anesthesiologist; b. Detroit, Mar. 20, 1931; s. Abraham and Florence (Zeman) P.; m. Bune Fay Rothbart, Sept. 4, 1955; children: Todd, Teri, Daren, Heidi. BS, Wayne State U., 1953; MD, U. Mich., 1957. Diplomate Am. Bd. Anesthesiology. Intern Sinai Hosp., Detroit, 1957-58; resident Harper Hosp., Detroit, 1958-60; ptnr. Associated Anesthesiologists Detroit, 1960-66; v.p., chief exec. officer Stockton Anesthesia Med. Group Inc., Stockton, Calif., 1966-79; pres. Marvin H. Primack M.D. Inc., Stockton, 1979-88; chief of staff St. Joseph's Med. Ctr., Stockton, 1975-76; v.p., chief exec. officer Stockton Anesthesia Med. Group Inc., 1989—; med. dir. Lodi Outpatient Surgery Ctr., 1994—. Bd. trustees Found. for Med. Care San Joaquin, Stockton, 1970-85, chmn. bd. trustees, 1980-83. Fellow Am. Coll. Anesthesiologists; mem. AMA, Am. Soc. Anesthesiologists, Calif. Soc. Anesthesiologists, Calif. Med. Soc., San Joaquin Med. Soc. Office: Stockton Anesthesia Med Group Inc 2626 N California St Ste G Stockton CA 95204-5527

PRINCE, PATRICIA, lawyer; b. Redwood City, Calif., May 16, 1959; d. Frederick Seaton Jr. and Anne (Armstrong) P. BA, Stanford U., 1981; JD, U. San Francisco, 1991. Bar: Calif. 1991; U.S. Dist. Ct. (no. dist.) Calif., 1991; U.S. Ct. Appeals (9th cir.), 1992. Dir. sales and mktg. Stein Eriksen Lodge, Park City, Utah, 1982-84; v.p. mktg. Tower Mgmt. Co., Park City, 1984-86; cons. Laventhol & Horwath, San Francisco, 1986-87; mktg. mgr. Innkeeper Assocs., San Francisco, 1987; assoc. Feldman, Waldman & Kline, San Francisco, 1991-93, Cohen, Nelson & Makoff, Triburon, San Francisco, 1993—. Active Queen's Bench and Reproductive Rights Com., San Francisco, 1992—. Recipient Am. Jurisprudence award Lawyers Coop. Pub. Co. and Bancroft-Whitney Co., 1988. Mem. State Bar of Calif., Bar Assn. San Francisco, Marin County Women Lawyers. Democrat. Home: 31 Wordsworth Ct Mill Valley CA 94941-4637 Office: Cohen Nelson & Makoff 625 Market St Ste 1100 San Francisco CA 94105-3313

PRINCIPE, HELEN MARY, medical case manager; b. Santa Monica, Calif., May 18, 1953; d. William John and Bessie Sylvia (Amsden) McGonagle; 1 child, Francis Edward. AS, Northeastern U., 1978; BSN cum laude, Worcester (Mass.) State Coll., 1981. RN, Mass., Calif. Critical care nurse Mt. Auburn Hosp., Cambridge, Mass.; adminstrv. nurse, critical care nurse, instr. Alta Bates Hosp., Berkeley, Calif.; clin. instr. med.-surg. staff devel., critical care nurse Valley Hosp., Las Vegas, Nev.; med. case mgr., supr. Intracorp, Oakland, Calif.; spl. case cons. Lincoln Nat., Pleasanton, Calif.; with Conservco, Walnut Creek, Calif.; assoc. mgr. PruCare of No. Calif., San Mateo, Calif.; mem. quality assessment and improvement com. Stat Nursing Adv. Bd. Utilization Rev., 1994. Mem. AAUW, Rehab. Ins. Nurses Group, Case Mgmt. Soc. Am. (founding pres. No. Calif. chpt., nat. bd. dirs., chmn. membership com.), Individual Case Mgmt. Assn.

PRINDLE, ROBERT WILLIAM, geotechnical engineer; b. L.A., Nov. 19, 1950; s. Robert Edward and Margaret Elizabeth (Johnson) P.; m. Nancy K. Hayden, Apr. 5, 1986; children: William Robert, Amy Elizabeth. Student St. John's Coll., Camarillo, Calif., 1968-70; BSCE summa cum laude, Loyola U., L.A., 1974; MS, Calif. Inst. Tech., 1975; 40-hours hazardous waste ops. and emergency response tng.; 8-hours hazardous waste ops. supr./mgr. tng. Lic. geotechnical engr., Calif.; registered profl. civil engr., Ariz., Calif., Colo., N. Mex. Engring. aide L.A. County Sanitation Dists., 1973-74; student engr. L.A. Dept. Water and Power, 1974, 75; staff engr. Fugro, Inc., Long Beach, Calif., 1976-78; sr. staff engr. Woodward-Clyde Consultants, Orange, Calif., 1978-79; mem. tech. staff Sandia Nat. Labs., Albuquerque, 1980-89; v.p. engring. Deuel & Assocs, Inc., Albuquerque, 1989-90, pres., 1990-94; pres. Prindle-Hinds Environ., Inc., 1990—. Contbr. articles to profl. jours. Mem. N. Mex. Symphony Orch. Chorus, 1981-84. Calif. State Grad. fellow, 1974-75, Calif. Inst. Tech. Inst. fellow, 1974-75. Mem. ASCE, NSPE, Internat. Soc. for Soil Mechanics and Found. Engring., Soc. Mining, Metallurgy and Exploration, Assn. Ground Water Scis. and Engrs., N.Mex. Hazardous Waste Mgmt. Soc., Tau Beta Pi. Republican. Roman Catholic. Office: Prindle-Hinds Environ Inc 7208 Jefferson St NE Albuquerque NM 87109-4309

PRINE, STEPHEN BRENT, publisher; b. Alton, Ill., Feb. 21, 1952; s. Virgil Earl and Isabelle (Antoinette) P.; m. Bonnie Lynn White; children: Stephen, Evan, Nicole, Jacqueline. AA with honors, Am. River Coll., Sacramento, Calif., 1971; BA, Washington U., 1973. Owner Vitrino's Pizza, St. Louis, 1972-73, S.B. Prine & Assocs., St. Louis, 1973-75, PM Petroleum, La Jolla, Calif., 1975-76, Pacific Western Imports, San Francisco, 1976-78, Prine & Assocs. Real Estate and Land Devel., Sacramento, Calif., 1978-83, Brent Oil & Gas, Houston, 1983-88, Ctrs. West Investments, Sacramento, 1987-88; pub. U.S. Realty Report, Sacramento, 1988-90, S.P. Publications, Sacramento, 1990—. Chmn. Big Hearts Internat., Sacramento, Calif. 1990—; founder, exec. dir. Missing Children Report, 1992—. Author: Foreign Investment in U.S. Real Estate, 1990. Roman Catholic.

PRINGLE, BRUCE D., federal magistrate; b. Denver, June 17, 1944; s. Edward E. and Pauline (Judd) P.; children: Jeffrey, Jennifer; m. Gail G. Pringle, Jan. 5, 1992. Student, Northwestern U., 1962-63; BA, U. Colo., 1966, JD, 1969. Bar: U.S. Ct. Appeals (10th cir.), Colo. Supreme Ct. Law clk. to Hon. William Doyle U.S. Dist. Ct. (Colo. dist.), Denver, 1969-70; assoc. Winner, Berge, Martin & Clark, Denver, 1970-75; ptnr. Clark, Martin & Pringle, Denver, 1975-81, Baker & Hostetler, Denver, 1981-91; U.S. Magistrate Judge U.S. Dist. Ct., Denver, 1991—; instr. law, lectr. U. Denver Law Sch., Fed. Bar Assn., Aurora C.C., Met. State Coll. Author of treatise Colo. Law Annotated (7 vols.), 1984-88, (2 vols.), 91. Mem. com. conduct of U.S. Dist. Ct., 1981-84; mem. Colo. Supreme Ct. com. on Colo. Rules of Civil Procedure; former mem. Litigation Subcom. for Freedom of Info. Coun. Mem. ABA, Am. Judicature Soc., U.S. Magistrates Assn., Colo. Bar Assn., Aurora Bar Assn., Order of Coif. Office: US Dist Ct C-338 1929 Stout St Denver CO 80294-2900

PRINGLE, EDWARD E., legal educator, former state supreme court chief justice; b. Chgo., Apr. 12, 1914; s. Abraham J. and Lena (Oher) P.; m. Pauline Judd, Aug. 17, 1941; children: Bruce, Eric. LL.B., U. Colo., 1936, LL.D., 1976; LL.D., U. Denver, 1979. Bar: Colo. Practiced in Denver, 1936-42, 47-57; with fed. govt. service Washington, 1943-47; dist. judge Colo. Dist. Ct., Denver, 1957-61; justice Supreme Ct. Colo., Denver, 1961-79; chief justice Supreme Ct. Colo., 1970-78; dir. research and writing program U. Denver Coll. Law, 1979-90, prof. emeritus, 1990—. Contbr. articles to profl. jours. Bd. dirs. Am. Med. Center, Denver; mem. Nat. Commn. for Establishment of Nat. Inst. Justice. Served with USAAF, 1942. Recipient William Lee Knous award U. Colo. Law Sch., 1975. Mem. Am., Colo., Denver bar assns., Conf. Chief Justices (chmn. 1973-74), Am. Judicature Soc. (Herbert Lincoln Harley award 1973, chmn. bd. 1974-76), Nat. Center State Cts. (pres. 1977-79). Jewish. Club: Masons (33 deg.). Office: U Denver Coll Law 1900 Olive St Denver CO 80220-1857

PRINGLE, WESTON STEWART, JR., traffic engineer; b. Santa Cruz, Calif., Apr. 25, 1937; s. Weston Stewart and Marjory Jean (Pierce) P.; m. Ludena Fern Cobb, Dec. 14, 1963; children: Weston Stewart, Amanda Le. BS in Engring., Calif. State U.-Fresno, 1960. Registered profl. engr., Calif. Civil engring., traffic engring. asst. City of West Covina, Calif., 1960-62; traffic engr. City of Downey, Calif., 1962-66; prin. engr. Wilbur Smith & Assocs., Los Angeles, 1966-69; v.p. Lampman & Assocs., Pomona, Calif., 1969-73; v.p. Crommelin-Pringle, Placentia, Calif., 1973-76; prin. Weston Pringle & Assocs., Fullerton, Calif., 1976—. Editor, Tech. Notes Quar., 1977-81. Recipient award for street lighting design Illuminating Engring. Soc., 1973. Fellow Inst. for Advancement of Engring., Inst. Transp. Engrs. (dist. pres. 1978-79, internat. dir. 1987-90); mem. ASCE, Inst. Transp. Engrs. Cons. (dir.). Office: Weston Pringle and Assocs 680 N Langsdorf Dr Ste 222 Fullerton CA 92631-3702

PRINS, DAVID, speech pathologist, educator; b. Herkimer, N.Y., Oct. 4, 1930; s. Tunis W. and Harriet Z. (Baker) P.; m. Gloria B. Fleming, June 4, 1955; children: Leslie, Steven, Douglas, Michael. B.A., Central Coll. Iowa, 1952; M.A., U. Mich., 1957, Ph.D., 1961. Tchr., Denison (Iowa) High Sch., 1954-55; instr. U. Mich., 1960-63, asst. prof., 1963-66, assoc. prof., 1966-69; asst. dir. U. Mich. Speech and Hearing Camp, 1960-64, dir., 1964-69; dir. program in speech and hearing scis. U. Wash., 1974-75, assoc. prof., 1969-72, prof., 1973-92, chmn. dept. speech and hearing scis., 1975-79, assoc. dean Coll. Arts & Scis., 1979-88, prof. emeritus, 1992—; vis. prof. U. Va. Contbr. articles in field of stuttering and articulation disorders to profl. jours. Served with U.S. Army, 1952-54. Mem. AAAS, Am. Speech and Hearing Assn., Wash. Speech and Hearing Assn., Mich. Speech and Hearing Assn. (past pres.), Phi Beta Kappa, Phi Kappa Phi. Office: U Wash Dept Speech And Scis Seattle WA 98195

PRISBREY, REX PRINCE, insurance agent, underwriter, financial consultant; b. Washington, Utah, Mar. 18, 1922; s. Hyrum William and Susan (Prince) P.; m. Pinka Julieta Lucero, Nov. 16, 1943; children: Karol Sue Prisbey Lewallen, Pamela Blanche Prisbrey Ebert, Michael Rex. BA in Acctg., Denver U., 1949. CLU. Ptnr. Allen Stamm & Assocs., home builders, Farmington, N.Mex., 1949-52; acct. Linder Burke & Stevenson, Santa Fe, N.Mex., 1949-52; agt. State Farm Ins. Cos., Farmington, 1952-56; mgr. State Farm Ins. Cos., Phoenix, 1956-60; contractor, agt. State Farm Ins. Cos., Scottsdale, Ariz., 1960—; v.p., treas. Original Curio Store Inc., Santa Fe. Pres. Farmington Jr. C. of C., 1952; v.p. N.Mex. Jr. C. of C., 1953. 1st lt. USAAF, 1941-46, CBI. Decorated DFC, Air medal with oak leaf cluster; recipient Disting. Life Underwriter award Cen. Ariz. Mgrs. Assn., 1979. Mem. Am. Soc. CLU's, Scottsdale Assn. Life Underwriters (pres. 1980-81), Airplane Owners and Pilots Assn., Hump Pilots Assn. (life, speaker at meml. of Hump Flyers, Kunming, China 1993), Pinewood Country Club (bd. dirs., treas., v.p. 1985—), Civitans (pres. Scottsdale 1962-63). Home: 4011 N 65th St Scottsdale AZ 85251-4235 Office: State Farm Ins Cos 6730 E Mcdowell Rd Scottsdale AZ 85257-3141

PRITCHARD, JOAN TREHY, retired aerospace company executive; b. N.Y.C., Jan. 28, 1942; d. William Ignatius T. and Winifred Ann (Dodge) Campbell; m. Gene Banning Pritchard, Dec. 28, 1991. BS, SUNY, Oneonta, 1963; postgrad., Chapman U., Orange, Calif., 1987—. Tchr. third grade Elwood Sch. Dist., Huntington, N.Y., 1963-64; asst. to exec. v.p. Conover-Mast Div., Cahners Publ., N.Y.C., 1964-71; prodn. coordinator The Dreyfus Corp., N.Y.C., 1971-75; sales supr. Gorsuch Ltd., Vail, Colo, 1976-77; asst. sec. Vail Nat. Bank, 1977; subcontract adminstr. Ford Aerospace Corp., Newport Beach, Calif., 1978-83, sr. subcontract adminstr., 1983-92; v.p. The Pritchard Group, Inc., Newport Beach, Calif., 1992—. Active Serving People In Need Ministry to feed the homeless, Our Lady Queen of Angels Ch., Newport Beach, 1987—. Mem. Nat. Contract Mgmt. Assn., Nat. Assn. Purchasing Mgmt., Nat. Mgmt. Assn. Republican. Roman Catholic. Toastmasters (Newport Beach) (treas. 1985-86, sec. 86-87). Home: 102 Stanford Ct Irvine CA 92715-1631 Office: The Pritchard Group Inc Box 9305 Newport Beach CA 92658

PRITCHARD, JOEL, state lieutenant governor; b. Seattle, May 5, 1925; children: Peggy, Frank, Anne, Jeanie. Student, Marietta Coll.; PhD (Hon.), Seattle U. Pres. Griffin Envelope Co., Seattle; mem. Wash. Ho. of Reps., Olympia, 1958-66, Wash. State Senate, 1966-70, U.S. Ho. of Reps., Washington, 1972-84; dir. govt. rels. Bogle & Gates, 1985-88; lt. gov. State of Wash., Olympia, 1989—; mem. Merchant Marine and Fisheries Com. U.S. Ho. of Reps., subcom. on Asia and the Pacific Fgn. Rels. Com., Panama Canal Consultative Commn., 1987-88; U.S. del. to UN Gen. Assembly, 1983. With U.S. Army, PTO, WWII. Office: Lt Gov's Office PO Box 40482 304 Legislative Bldg Olympia WA 98504-0482

PRITCHETT, B(RUCE) MICHAEL, SR., economics educator, consultant; b. American Fork, Utah, Nov. 3, 1940; s. Melrose Jed and Lois (Watson) P.; m. Patricia Louise Sunderland, June 19, 1964; children: Bruce Michael Jr., Laura, Steven Louis. BS, Brigham Young U., 1965; MS, Purdue U., 1967, PhD, 1970. Bd. dirs. Pritchett Constrn. Co. Inc., Provo, Utah, 1954—; grad. instr. in econs. Purdue U., West Lafayette, Ind., 1967-68; asst. prof. econs. Brigham Young U., Provo, 1969-76, assoc. prof. econs., 1977-90, prof. managerial econs., 1990—; cons. in field. Author: A Study of Capital Mobilization..., 1977, Financing Growth..., 1985, Applications of the GB2 Distribution in Modeling Insurance Loss Processes, 1990. NDEA fellow Purdue U., 1966-68, Krannert fellow Purdue U., 1968-69. Mem. Am. Econ. Assn., Western Econ. Assn., Nat. Assn. Bus. Economists. Office: Brigham Young U 614 Tanner Bldg Provo UT 84602

PRITCHETT, JAMES W., orthopaedic surgeon, educator; b. Seattle, Aug. 8, 1953; s. James W. Pritchett Jr. BS, U. Wash., 1974, MD, 1979. Resident, surgery Phoenix VA Med. Ctr., 1979-80, resident, orthopaedic surgery, 1983-84; resident, surgery Phoenix Indian Med. Ctr., 1980-81; resident, orthopaedic surgery Maricopa County Hosp., Phoenix, 1981-82, Ariz. Children's Hosp., Tempe, Ariz., 1982-83; instr., orthopaedic surgery U. Wash. Med. Ctr., Seattle, 1985-88, asst. clin. prof. orthopaedic surgery, 1988-93, assoc. clin. prof., 1993—; chief, orthopaedic surgery Pacific Med. Ctr., Seattle, 1984—, Providence Med. Ctr., Seattle, 1993—. Author: Practical Bone Growth, 1993; contbr. articles to profl. jours. Inventor hip, shoulder, spine implants. Med. dir. Bone Reconstrn. Assn., Seattle, 1983—. Recipient Meyerding award for fracture rsch. Am. Fracture Assn., 1985. Fellow Am. Acad. Orthopaedic Surgeons, Am. Acad. Pediatrics (exec. com. 1990-93); mem. ACS, Assn. Bone and Joint Surgeons (membership com. 1992-95), North Pacific Orthopaedic Soc. Office: 226 2nd Ave W Seattle WA 98119-4204

PRITZ, MICHAEL BURTON, neurological surgeon; b. New Brunswick, N.J., Oct. 8, 1947; s. John Ernest and Helen Violet (Rockoff) P.; m. Edmay Marie Gregorcy, Feb. 18, 1973; children: Edmond Louis, Benjamin David. BS, U. Ill., 1969; PhD, Case Western Res. U., 1973, MD, 1975. Diplomate Am. Bd. Neurol. Surgery. Asst. prof. neurol. surgery U. Calif. Irvine Med. Ctr., Orange, 1981-85, assoc. prof., 1985-93; prof., 1993, U. Calif. Irvine Med. Ctr., Orange, 1993—; prof. sect. neurol. surgery Ind. U. Sch. Medicine, Indpls., 1993—, prof. neurol. surgery, 1993—. Contbr. articles to profl. jours. Recipient Herbert S. Steuer award Case Western Res. U., Cleve., 1975; NSF fellow, 1968; Edmund J. James scholar U. Ill., Champaign, 1968-69. Mem. Soc. Neurosci., Am. Assn. Anatomists, Am. Assn. Neurol. Surgeons, Congress Neurol. Surgeons, Soc. Neurol. Surgeons of Orange County (pres. 1985-86, sec.-treas. 1984-85).

PRITZLAFF, JOHN CHARLES, JR., former state senator; b. Milw., May 10, 1925; s. John C. and Elinor (Gallun) P.; m. Mary Dell Olin, Feb. 10, 1951; children: Ann, John, Barbara, Richard. B.A., Princeton U., 1949. Pres., John Pritzlaff Hardware Co., Milw., 1957-59; v.p. Arrow Valve Co., Phoenix, 1959-60; exec. v.p. Oxford Life Ins. Co., Scottsdale, Ariz., 1960-63; v.p. Republic Properties, Scottsdale, 1961-67; chmn. bd. Republic Properties, 1963-67; pres. Rockmount Mgmt. Corp., 1967-86; treas. Seamair Farm Inc.; dir. Marshall & Ilsey Trust Co. Ariz.; U.S. ambassador to Malta, 1969-72; mem. Ariz. senate, 1975-82, minority whip, 1977-78, chmn. appropriations com., 1979-83; mem. Ariz. Ho. of Reps., 1963-69, chmn. appropriations com., 1966-69. Mem. Republican Nat. Fin. Com., 1968-69; bd. dirs. Santa Barbara Botanic Gardens, Ariz. nat. chpts. Nature Conservancy. Served with AUS, 1943-45. Home: PO Box 202 Scottsdale AZ 85252-0202 Office: 4419 N Scottsdale Rd Scottsdale AZ 85251-3334

PRIVAT, JEANNETTE MARY, bank librarian; b. Seattle, May 2, 1938; d. Glenn McKenzie and Katherine (VanDerveer) P. BA in Bus. Adminstrn., U. Wash., 1960, MLS, 1969. Asst. libr. United Control Corp., Redmond, Wash., 1960-64, libr., 1964-68; libr. Seattle-First National Bank, Seattle, 1968-75, asst. v.p. and mgr., 1975-93; exec. dir. King County Libr. System Found., Seattle, 1993—; mem. vis. com. U. Wash. Grad. Sch. Libr. and Info. Sci., 1981—, chmn., 1991—; mem. adv. bd. extension libr. mgmt. program U. Washington, 1989—. Bd. trustees Northwest Chamber Orch., Seattle, 1986—, pres. 1987-92, exec. com., 1992—. Named disting. alumnus Wash. Grad. Sch. Libr. and Info. Sci. Fellow Spl. Librs. Assn. (nat. bd. dirs. 1977-79, various offices 1966-89). Office: King County Libr Sys Found 300 8th Ave N Seattle WA 98109-5116

PRIZIO, BETTY J., property manager, civic worker; b. L.A., Jan. 23, 1928; d. Harry W. and Irene L. (Connell) Campbell; divorced; children: David P., John W., Robert H., James R. AA in Social Sci., L.A. City Coll., 1949. Owner, mgr. indsl. bldgs. and condominiums indsl. bldgs. and condominiums, Tustin, Calif., 1976—; owner Baskets and Bows by Jean, Tustin, 1994—; ind. mktg. exec., Melaleuca. Bd. dirs. Founders Chpt. Aux., Providence Speech and Hearing Ctr., 1986-88, aux. pres., 1986-89; vol. Western Med. Ctr. Aux., 1985-89, chmn. gift shop com., 1987-88, 2d v.p., 1992, jr. vol. adv., mem. bd. dirs. fund raising group; mem. adv. coun. Chapman Coll., Orange, Calif., 1986-87, bd. mem. Pres. Assocs., 1985-86; bd. dirs. Chapman Music Assocs., 1986—, Tustin Hist. Soc., 1988—, Santa Ana YWCA, 1976-77; mem. adv. coun. Orange County chpt. Freedoms Found. at Valley Forge, 1985—; mem. Orange County chpt. Charter 100, 1985-87; active United Meth. Ch.; others. Mem. Tustin Hist. Soc. (bd. dirs. 1988-90). Republican. Home: 17342 Village Dr Tustin CA 92680-2546

PRO, PHILIP MARTIN, federal judge, lawyer; b. Richmond, Calif., Dec. 12, 1946; s. Leo Martin and Mildred Louise (Beck) P.; m. Dori Sue Hallas, Nov. 13, 1982; 1 child, Brenda Kay. BA, San Francisco State U., 1968; JD Golden Gate U., 1972. Bar: Calif. 1972, Nev. 1973, U.S. Ct. Appeals (9th cir.) 1973, U.S. Dist. Ct. Nev. 1973, U.S. Supreme Ct. 1976. Pub. defender, Las Vegas, 1973-75; asst. U.S. atty., Dist. Nev., Las Vegas, 1975-78; ptnr. Semenza, Murphy & Pro, Reno, 1978-79; dep. atty. gen. State of Nev., Carson City, 1979-80; U.S. magistrate U.S. Dist. Ct. Nev., Las Vegas, 1980-87; U.S. dist. judge, 1987—; instr. Atty. Gen.'s Advocacy Inst., Nat. Inst. Trial Advocacy, 1992; chmn. com. adminstrn. of magistrate judge system Jud. Conf. U.S., 1993—. Bd. dirs. NCCJ, Las Vegas, 1982—, mem. program com. and issues in justice com. Mem. ABA, Fed. Judges Assn. (bd. dirs. 1992—), Nev. State Bar Assn., Calif. State Bar Assn., Nev. Judges Assn. (instr.), Assn. Trial Lawyers Am., Nev. Am. Inn Ct. (pres. 1989—), Ninth Cir. Jury (instructions com.), Nat. Conf. U.S. Magistrates (sec.), Nev. Am. Inn of Ct. (pres. 1989-91). Republican. Episcopalian. Office: US Dist Ct 341 Fed Bldg 300 Las Vegas Bldv S Las Vegas NV 89101

PROBASCO, CALVIN HENRY CHARLES, clergyman, college administrator; b. Petaluma, Calif., Apr. 5, 1926; s. Calvin Warren and Ruth Charlene (Winans) P.; m. Nixie June Farnsworth, Feb. 14, 1947; children—Calvin, Carol, David, Ruth. B.A. cum laude, Biola Bible Coll., La Mirada, Calif., 1953; D.D. (hon.), Talbot Theol. Sem., La Mirada, 1983. Ordained to ministry, 1950. Pastor Sharon Baptist Ch., El Monte, Calif., 1951-58, Carmichael Bible Ch., Calif., 1958—; pres. Sacramento Bible Inst., Carmichael, 1968—. Mem. Ind. Fundamental Chs. Am. (rec. sec. 1978-81, pres. 1981-84, 1st v.p. 1987-88), Delta Epsilon Chi. Republican. Office: Carmichael Bible Ch 7100 Fair Oaks Blvd Carmichael CA 95608-6452

PROBASCO, DALE RICHARD, management consultant; b. Ogden, Utah, July 23, 1946; s. Robert Vere and Dorleen E. (Oppliger) P.; m. Joan Michele Takacs, Dec. 20, 1969; children: Todd Aaron, Brad Dillon. BS, Utah State U., 1975; MS, U. Phoenix, 1988. Inventory asst. Moore Bus. Form, Logan, Utah, 1973-75; systems engr. Electronic Data Systems, Dallas, 1975-76; start-up engr. Bechtel Corp., San Francisco, 1976-78; supr. project scheduling Toledo Edison Co., 1978-80; mgr. project controls Utah Power and Light Co., Salt Lake City, 1980-87, mgr. mktg. strategy, 1987-89; pres. Probasco Cons., Inc., West Jordan, Utah, 1989-90; mgr. Metzler & Assocs., Deerfield, Ill., 1990—. Contbr. articles to profl. publs. Pres. Emery County Little League, Castledale, Utah, 1981-84; coach Little League Baseball, West Jordan, Utah, 1985-86. With USN, 1965-72. Mem. Am. Econ. Devel. Conf., Nuclear Info. and Records Mgmt. Assn., Assn. for Info. and Image Mgmt. Lutheran.

PROCCI, WARREN R., psychiatrist; b. S.I., N.Y., Jan. 19, 1947; s. Waddie R. and Anita M. (Veen) P.; m. Linda L. Kautza, June 4, 1972. BS, Wagner Coll., 1968; MD, U. Wis., 1972; PhD, So. Calif. Psychoanalytic Inst., 1984. Diplomate Am. Bd. Psychiatry and Neurology. Intern Univ. Hosps., Madison, Wis., 1972-73; resident Univ. Hosps., Madison, 1971-74; asst. prof., then assoc. prof. psychiatry Sch. Medicine U. So. Calif., L.A., 1975-82; assoc. prof., dir. residency edn. in psychiatry Harbor-UCLA Med. Ctr., Torrance, 1982-88, assoc. clin. prof., 1988—. Mem. So. Calif. Psychoanalytic Inst. (pres. 1994-96, tng./supervising psychoanalyst 1991—). Office: 181 N Oak Knoll Ave Ste 1 Pasadena CA 91101-1817

PROCTOR, BETTINA REA, fish and wildlife organization administrator; b. Columbia, Mo., Oct. 29, 1946; d. Charles Johnson and Mary Elizabeth (Rea) P.; m. Dennis Stockdale Grogan, Apr. 21, 1973; children: Kelley Grogan, Tyler Grogan, Dylan Grogan. BA in Biology, U. Colo., 1968; MS in Wildlife Biology, Colo. State U., 1975. Ops. mgr. Boulder (Colo.) County Pks. and Open Space Dept., 1976-79; rsch. scientist Sci. Applications, Inc., Boulder, 1980-81; rsch. assoc. Resource Assocs., Denver, 1983-85; asst. dir. Colo. Natural Areas Program, Denver, 1985; pub. affairs dir. Planned Parenthood, Denver, 1985-92; partnerships coord. U.S. Fish and Wildlife Svc., Denver, 1992—; sec. nongame adv. coun. Colo. Div. Wildlife, Denver, 1979-80; v.p. Check-off for Wildlife, Lincoln, Nebr., 1981. Editor: (handbooks) Practices for Protecting and Enhancing, Fish and Wildlife in Coal Surface, Mined Land, 1983. Bd. dirs. Colo. Nat. Abortion Rights

Action League, Denver, 1987, Colo. Open Space Coun., Denver, 1983-84, Colo. Wildlife Fedn. (treas. 1995); pres. Boulder Audubon Soc., 1975-76. Office: US Fish and Wildlife Svc PO Box 25486 Denver Federal Ctr Denver CO 80207

PROCUNIER, RICHARD WERNER, environmental scientist, administrator; b. Dallas, Tex., Oct. 27, 1936; s. Werner Richard and Dorothy (Koch) P.; m. Janet Mesing, Sept. 5, 1958 (div. Aug. 28, 1984); children: Nancy, Carol, Ellen; m. Carolyn Harris, June 25, 1988. BSEE, MIT, 1958; PhD, Univ. Coll. London, 1966. Prof. U. London, 1966-68; rsch. scientist Lockheed, Palo Alto, Calif., 1968-72; mgr. Hewlett Packard, Santa Clara, Calif., 1972-74; chief of noise control U.S. EPA, San Francisco, 1974-82, sci. advisor, 1982-83, environ. scientist, 1990—; prof. U. Calif., Davis, 1984-85; adminstr. County Health Svcs., Martinez, Calif., 1986-89; mem. Nat. Edn. Com., Nat. Environ. Health Assn., Denver, 1980-87; enforcement coord., U.S. EPA, San Francisco, 1990. Contbr. many articles to profl. jours. Proponent to incorporate Orinda, Calif., 1984. Recipient Presidential citation, Nat. Environmental Health Assn., 1981. Fellow Royal Soc. London; mem. World Affairs Coun., Commonwealth Club, Kappa Sigma (Leadership award 1958).

PRODAN, RICHARD STEPHEN, electrical engineer; b. Yonkers, N.Y., Oct. 26, 1952; s. Victor L. and Stella (Erbe) P.; m. Judith Mirabella, June 17, 1978; children: Adam L., Michael D. BEE, CCNY, 1976, MEE, 1979; PhD, Columbia U., 1981. Sr. mem. rsch. staff Philips Labs., Briarcliff Manor, N.Y., 1976-88; sr. engr. StellaCom, Inc., Arlington, Va., 1988-90; v.p. CableLabs, Inc., Louisville, Colo., 1990—. Mem. Eta Kappa Nu, Sigma Xi. Office: CableLabs Inc 400 Centennial Pky Louisville CO 80027-1266

PROEBSTING, EDWARD LOUIS, JR., retired research horticulturist; b. Woodland, Calif., Mar. 2, 1926; s. Edward Louis and Dorothy (Critzer) P.; m. Patricia Jean Connolly, June 28, 1947; children: William Martin, Patricia Louise, Thomas Alan (dec.). BS, U. Calif., Davis, 1948; PhD, Mich. State U., 1951. Asst. horticulturist Wash. State U., Prosser, 1951-57, assoc. horticulturist, 1957-63, horticulturist, 1963-93, supt. Irrigated Agrl. Rsch. and Ext. Ctr., 1990-93; ret., 1993; vis. prof. Cornell U., Ithaca, N.Y., 1966; vis. scientist Hokkaido U., Sapporo, Japan, 1978, Victoria Dept. Agr., Tatura, Australia, 1986—. Contbr. numerous articles to profl. jours. Scoutmaster Boy Scouts Am., Prosser, 1963-76, dist. chmn., 1976-78. Served to lt. USNR, 1943-46, 52-54. Recipient Silver Beaver award Boy Scouts Am.; fellow Japan Soc. Promotion Sci., Sapporo, 1978, Res. Bank. Australia, 1986. Fellow AAAS, Am. Soc. Hort. Sci. (pres. 1983-84, sci. editor jour. 1993—). Methodist. Home: 1929 Miller Ave Prosser WA 99350-1532 Office: Wash State U Irrigated Agrl Rsch Ctr and Ext RR 2 Box 2953A Prosser WA 99350-9678

PROFFITT, LAWRENCE ALAN, secondary school educator; b. Encino, Calif., July 1, 1959; s. George Leslie and Cleah (James) Proffitt; m. Melissa Sue. BS, U. Utah, 1982; MA, U. Calif., Riverside, 1988. Cert. tchr., adminstr., Calif. Sterilization technician Deseret Med., Inc., Sandy, Utah, 1977-82; tchr. Jordan Sch. Dist., Sandy, 1982-85, Yucaipa-Calimesa Joint Unified Sch. Dist., Yucaipa, Calif., 1985—; pres. Citrus Belt Uniserv, Rialto, Calif., 1991-94. Named to Outstanding Young Men of Am., 1989. Mem. Calif. Tchrs. Assn. (task force on extremist attacks on edn. 1990—, mem. congl. contact team 1993—), Yucaipa-Calimesa Educators Assn. (fin. dir. 1987, v.p. 1988, pres. 1988—), Yucaipa-Calimesa C. of C. Democrat. Home: 620 Golden West Dr Redlands CA 92373-6416

PRONKO, LEONARD CABELL, theater educator; b. Cebu, The Philippines, Oct. 3, 1927; s. Stephen Michael and Alice Lee Ludwell (Beal) P. BA, Drury Coll., 1947; MA, Washington U., St. Louis, 1951; PhD, Tulane U., 1957. Asst. prof. langs. Lake Erie Coll., Painesville, Ohio, 1955-56; from asst. prof. to prof. romance langs. Pomona Coll., Claremont, Calif., 1957-84, prof. to theater, 1985—, chair theater dept., 1985-91; dir. kabuki Mixed Blood Theatre, Mpls., 1984. Author: The World of Jean Anouilh, 1961, Avante-Garde, 1962, Eugene Ionesco, 1965, Theatre East and West, 1967, Guide to Japanese Drama, 1973, George Feydeau, 1975, Eugene Labiche and Georges Feydeau, 1982; contbr. articles to profl. publs. Fellow Guggenheim Soc., 1963-64, Japan Found., 1976; recipient award L.A. Drama Critics Circle, 1972, award of excellence Am. Coll. Theatre Festival, 1974, Order of Sacred Treasure, Govt. of Japan, 1986. Democrat. Home: 1543 N Bates Pl Claremont CA 91711-3107 Office: Pomona Coll Theater Dept 300 E Bonita 333 N College Way Claremont CA 91711-4429

PRONZINI, BILL JOHN (WILLIAM PRONZINI), author; b. Petaluma, Calif., Apr. 13, 1943; s. Joseph and Helene (Guder) P. Coll. student, 2 years. Author: 50 novels (including under pseudonyms), 4 books of nonfiction, 6 collections of short stories, 1971—; first novel, The Stalker, 1971; editor 80 anthologies; contbr. numerous short stories to publs. Recipient Scroll award, Best First Novel, Mystery Writers Am., 1972, Life Achievement award Pvt. Eye Writers Am., 1987. Democrat. Office: PO Box 2536 Petaluma CA 94953-2536

PROUD, EILEEN MARIEL, financial planner; b. Sendaii, Japan, Apr. 7, 1954; d. Stewart William Petersen and Toshie (Miyomoto) McMannama; m. Neville A. Proud, July 7, 1991; stepchildren: Kathleen, Natalie. Registered investment advisor, SEC. Pres. Fortune Fin. Inc., Seattle, 1981-94; registered rep. Sentra Securities Corp., San Diego, 1986—; agt. Prin. Fin. Group, Tucson, 1986—; sec., treas. Nicole Miller Ariz., Inc., Tucson, 1991—; owner Proud Fin Adv., Tucson, 1994—. Chmn. region art group experience Assoc. Guild Seattle Art Mus., 1977-79; chmn. Lakeside Villa Homeowners Assn., Chelan, Wash., 1989-91. Mem. Inst. CFP (cert.), Internat. Assn. Fin. Planning. Republican.

PROUDFIT, DONNA MAE, executive search consultant; b. Washington, Iowa, Nov. 28, 1951; d. Donald Eugene and Virginia Ruth (Warden) P. BS in Journalism, Iowa State U., 1974. Asst. dir. pub. rels. St. Luke's Hosp., Cedar Rapids, Iowa, 1974-78; from adminstrv. asst. to v.p. LaCrosse (Wis.) Luth. Hosp., 1978-85; v.p. mktg. Franciscan Health Svcs. of Wash., Tacoma, 1985-89; exec. search cons. Almond & Rogers, Tacoma, 1989-91; dir. nat. rehab. employment The Hillhaven Corp., Tacoma, 1991-95, nat. dir. mgmt. recruitment, 1995—. Named among outstanding young women in Am., 1984; recipient Advt. Excellence award Employment Mgmt. Assn., 1994, Human Resources Exec. Mag. Advt. award, 1994. Mem. Am. Mktg. Assn. (Distbn. award 1986), Soc. Human Resources Mgmt. Republican. Methodist. Office: The Hillhaven Corp 1148 Broadway Tacoma WA 98402-3513

PROUDFOOT, JAMES MICHAEL, research and development executive; b. Oakland, Md., Feb. 12, 1955; s. James Milton and Mary Rose (Gallagher) P.; m. Cynthia Louise Ross, Nov. 7, 1987. BA in Polit. Sci., Internat. Rels. summa cum laude, Am. U., 1976. Sytems analyst, engr. Sci. Applications, Inc., Norfolk, Va., 1978-81; sr. program mgr. Sci. Applications Internat. Corp., Torrance, Calif., 1981-91, v.p. for bus. devel., 1991—. Mem. AIAA, Am. Astronautical Soc., Am. Assn. Ind. Investors, Assn. Computing Machinery, Internat. Interactive Comm. Soc., CATO Inst. Mem. LDS Ch.

PROUGH, STEPHEN W., savings and loan executive; b. 1945. COO Westcorp, Irvine, Calif., 1983—, bd. dirs. Office: Downey Savs Loan Assn 3501 Jamboree Rd Newport Beach CA 92660-2939*

PROUT, CARL WESLEY, history educator; b. Bakersfield, Calif., Apr. 19, 1941; s. George Hecla and Ruth (King) P. BA, U. Calif., Santa Barbara, 1964, MA, 1965; postgrad., U. Tenn., Knoxville, 1968-71, Am. U., Cairo, 1974, U. So. Calif., 1981, Ain Shams U., Cairo, 1981. Instr. history Santa Barbara Coll., 1965-66, U. Tenn., Knoxville, 1968-71; instr. Orange Coast Coll., Costa Mesa, 1966-68, asst. prof., 1971-73, assoc. prof., 1973-75, prof., 1975—; treas. Willmore Corp., 1980-81, sec., 1984-85, v.p., 1985-86, pres., chmn., 1988-89, also bd. dirs.; group facilitator Coastview Meml. Hosp., Long Beach, 1986-89. Research and publs. in field. Pres., chmn. bd. Alamitos Heights Improvement Assn., 1979-80, bd. dirs., 1980-82; mem. East Long Beach Joint Council, 1979-80, Local Coastal Planning Adv. Com., 1979-80 mem. preservation bd. Palm Springs Historic Site, 1994—. Recipient Salgo Outstanding Tchr. award, 1974-76. Mem. Am. Hist. Assn., Meml. West Alumni Club, Sigma Nu. Office: Orange Coast Coll 2701 Fairview Rd Costa Mesa CA 92626-5563

PROUT, RALPH EUGENE, physician; b. Los Angeles, Feb. 27, 1933; s. Ralph Byron and Fern (Taylor) P.; m. Joanne Morris, Sept. 17, 1980; children: Michael, Michelle. BA, La Sierra Coll., 1953; MD, Loma Linda U., 1957; D of Nutri-Medicine (hon.), John F. Kennedy Coll., 1987. Diplomate: Nat. Bd. Med. Examiners. Intern Los Angeles County Hosp., 1957-58; resident internal medicine White Meml. Hosp., Los Angeles, 1958-60; resident psychiatry Harding Hosp., Worthington, Ohio, 1960-61; practice medicine specializing in internal medicine Napa, Calif., 1961-63; staff internist Calif. Med. Facility, Vacaville, 1963-68, chief med. officer, 1968-84; chief med. cons. Calif. Dept. Corrections, 1977-86, chief med. services, 1983; med. cons. Wellness Cons., Placerville, Calif., 1986—; pres. Addiction Medicine treatment Ctr., Placerville, Calif., 1991-95; instr. Sch. Medicine, Loma Linda U., 1965-66; clin. assoc. U. Calif.-Davis Sch. Medicine, 1978-84; med. cons. Substance Abuse Pine Grove Camp, 1985-90. Treas. Vacaville Republican Assembly, 1972-75; del. Republican Central Com. Solano County, 1975-78; Bd. dirs. Napa-Solano County United Crusade, Vallejo, Calif., 1969-71, v.p., 1970-71; bd. dirs. Project Clinic, Vacaville, 1974-77, Home Health Com. Inter-Community Hosp., Fairfield, 1978-80; pres. MotherLode Citizens for Drug-Free Youth, Amador County, 1985—. Named One of Outstanding Young Men of Am., 1968. Mem. AMA, Internat. Acad. Nutrition and Preventive Medicine, Calif. Soc. Internal Medicine, Am. Soc. Internal Medicine, Am. Assn. Sr. Physicians, Internat. Assn. New Sci., Union Concerned Scis., Mother Lode Citizens for Drug-Free Youth, Native Sons of Golden West, Alpha Omega Alpha. Republican. Home and Office: 24405 Shake Ridge Rd Volcano CA 95689-9728

PROUTY, ALAN LESLIE, environmental engineer; b. Weiser, Idaho, Dec. 3, 1960; s. Alton L. and Carole Jean Prouty; m. Shelley Joe Eyrand, June 7, 1986. BSc in Chemistry, Idaho State U., 1983; MSc in Forest Products, U. Idaho, 1987. Process analyst City of Pullman, Wash., 1986-87; assoc. chemist James River Corp., Camas, Wash., 1987-89, sr. environ. engr., 1989-93, mgr. air quality engring., 1993—. Mem. TAPPI, Air and Waste Mgmt. Assn., Pacific Coast TAPPI (Shibley award 1992). Office: James River Corp 4th And Adams Camas WA 98607

PROVENZANO, MAUREEN LYNN, secondary educator; b. Anaheim, Calif., Nov. 25, 1963; d. Andrew Eugene and Maura Ann (McGivern) P. BA in English, Loyola Marymount U., L.A., 1986; teaching credential, Calif. State U., Fullerton, 1991; MA in Teaching English to Speakers of Other Langs., Calif. State U., L.A., 1993. Cert. Language Devel. Specialist, Calif.; English teaching credential, Calif.; lic. real estate saleswoman, Calif. Tchr. English, Temple City (Calif.) High Sch., 1991—, supr. Saturday sch., 1991-92; tchr. English lit., intermediate level ESL Temple City Adult Sch., 1994; mem. adv. bd. Peer Listeners, 1991-92; mem. intercultural com. Temple City Unified Sch. Dist., 1994, sr. class advisor, 1994, co-advisor Students Against Drunk Driving, 1993-94. Mem. NEA, Nat. Coun. Tchrs. English, Calif. Assn. Tchrs. English, Southland Coun. Tchrs. English, Calif. Tchrs. Assn., Calif. Tchrs. English to Speakers of Other Languages, Club Europa. Republican. Roman Catholic. Home: 8821 3/4 E Fairview Ave San Gabriel CA 91775-1209

PROVINCE, SHARON G., research and development executive; b. 1948. Staff counsel Madaf, Tex., 1972-73; staff atty. Fed. Power Commn., Washington, 1973-74; various positions Analytical Tech. Inc., San Diego, 1974—, now sr. v.p., sec. Office: Analytical Tech Inc 5550 Morehouse Dr San Diego CA 92121*

PROYECT, MARTIN H., investment banker; b. N.Y.C., Oct. 24, 1932; s. Max and Fay (Madison) P.; children—Christopher T., Michele F. B.A., Columbia U., 1954, L.D., 1956. Bar: N.Y. bar 1956. Assoc. Reavis & McGrath, N.Y.C., 1956-59; exec. v.p. Calvin Bullock Ltd., N.Y.C., 1959-79; chmn. Selected/Venture Advisers, L.P., Santa Fe, 1968—; chmn., pres. N.Y. Venture Fund, Inc., 1968—, Venture Income Plus, Inc., 1980—, Venture Muni Plus, Inc., 1984—, Retirement Planning Funds Am., Inc., 1984—; pres. Selected Am. Shares, Selected Special Shares; bd. govs. Investment Co. Inst. Author: Investors Guide to the Economic Recovery Tax Act of 1981; editor: How to Succeed in Spite of Yourself. Home: 4963 Crooked Stick Way Las Vegas NV 89113-0110 Office: 124 E Marcy St Santa Fe NM 87501-2019

PRUDHOMME, RONALD EDWARD, food processing executive; b. San Jose, Calif., June 3, 1941; s. Edward L. and Julie M. Prudhomme; m. Paula L. Pimentel, Nov. 1, 1987. BS, U. Calif., Davis, 1964, MS, 1966; MBA, Pepperdine U., 1977. Asst. head micro div. Nat. Food Processing Assn., Berkeley, Calif., 1966-72; quality control mgr. Gentry Internat. Inc., Gilroy, Calif., 1972-74; new product devel. staff Tri Valley Growers, Modesto, Calif., 1974-76, asst. prodn. mgr., 1976-83; plant mgr. Ingomar Packing Co., Los Banos, Calif., 1983-89, gen. mgr., 1989—. Mem. Calif. League of Food Processors (bd. dirs. 1989—), Am. Inst. Plant Engrs., Sportsmen of Stanislaus. Office: Ingomar Packing Co PO Box 1448 Los Banos CA 93635-1448

PRUNES-CARRILLO, FERNANDO, plastic surgeon, educator; b. Chihuahua, Mex., Sept. 24, 1944; m. Linda R. Underwood; children: Alexander, Ariadne, Anthony. MD, U. Chihuahua, Mex., 1968. Chief divsn. plastic surgery Kern Med. Ctr., Bakersfield, Calif., 1983—; asst. clin. prof. surgery U. Calif., San Diego, 1983—. Mem. Am. Soc. Plastic and Reconstructive Surgeons, Mayo Alumni Assn. Office: Kern Med Ctr 1830 Flower St Bakersfield CA 93305-5838

PRUSA, JAMES GRAHAM, association executive; b. Cleve., Dec. 1, 1948; s. James Leonard and Mary LaVerne (Graham) P.; m. Patricia Ann Thwaits, June 20, 1971 (dec. 1975); m. Karen Beth Adamo, Nov. 30, 1980; children: Nathasha Clare, Shamus Graham. BS, Calif. State Poly. U., 1975; postgrad., U. Santa Clara, 1977-79, Stanford U., 1984. Golf course supt. China Lake NWC Golf Course, China Lake, Calif., 1975-77; golf course mgr. Pasatiempo, Inc., Santa Cruz, Calif., 1977-82; assoc. exec. dir. Golf Course Supt. Assn. Am., Lawrence, Kans., 1982-87; adminstr., chief staff exec. Nat. Office Machine Dealers Assn., Kansas City, Mo., 1987-90; gen. mgr., COO Ridgemark Golf and Country Club Resort, Hollister, Calif., 1990-93; exec. dir. Diving Equipment & Market Assn., Laguna Hills, Calif., 1993—. Contbr. articles to profl. jours.; tech. editor Golf Course Mgmt.; pubr. Spokesman mag. With USN, 1967-71, Calif. N.G. 1971-72. Decorated Air medal. Named Alumnus of the Yr., Calif. Poly. Hort. Dept., 1984. Mem. Am. Soc. Assn. Execs., Golf Writers Assn. Am., U.S. Golf Assn., Club Mgrs. Assn. of Am., Rotary Internat. Republican. Roman Catholic. Office: Diving Equipment & Market Assn 27071 Cabot Rd Ste 103 Laguna Hills CA 92653

PRUSAN, LILIAN, fundraising executive; b. Brookline, Mass., May 26; d. Jack and Esther Brown; m. Nathan Prusan, Nov. 30, 1952; children: Paul, Jody. Student, Lee Coll., 1983-85; BA in Psychology, UCLA. Adminstr. China Health Inst., 1983-85; field rep., asst. dir. B'nai B'rith Women Pacific S.W. Regions, 1985-87; devel. dir., fundraiser Hebrew U., Beverly Hills, Calif., 1987-89; exec. dir. Friends of Tel Hashomer, L.A., 1989-91; devel. dir. shelter for battered women Havan House, Inc., L.A., 1992—. Pres. John Douglas French Found. for Alzheimer's Disease, 1985-86, Beverly Hills Hadassah, 1980-83; v.p. So. Calif. Opera Guild, 1980—; v.p. bd. dirs. CTGV and Music Ctr. Club 100, 1982—; co-dir. L.A. Dist. Met. Opera Auditions, 1978-80; fundraiser Assn. Breast Cancer Rsch., St. John's Hosp., 1991-94. Meml. Nat. Soc. Fund Raising Execs. Home: 2587 Hutton Dr Beverly Hills CA 90210-1211

PRUSINER, STANLEY BEN, neurology and biochemistry educator, researcher; b. Des Moines, May 28, 1942; s. Lawrence Albert and Miriam (Spigel) P.; m. Sandra Lee Turk, Oct. 18, 1970; children: Helen Chloe, Leah Anne. AB cum laude, U. Pa., 1964, MD, 1968; PhD (hon.), Hebrew U., Jerusalem, 1995. Diplomate Am. Bd. Neurology. Intern in medicine U. Calif., San Francisco, 1968-69, resident in neurology, 1972-74, asst. prof. neurology, 1974-80, assoc. prof., 1980-84, prof., 1984—, prof. biochemistry, 1988—, acad. senate faculty rsch. lectr., 1989-90; prof. virology U. Calif., Berkeley, 1984—; mem. neurology rev. com. Nat. Inst. Neurol. Disease and Strokes, NIH, Bethesda, Md., 1982-86, 90-92; mem. sci. adv. bd. French Fedn., L.A., 1985—; mem. sci. rev. com. Alzheimer's Disease Diagnostic Ctr. & Rsch. Grant Program, State of Calif., 1985-89; chmn. sci. adv. bd. Am. Health Assistance Found., Rockville, Md., 1986—. Editor: The Enzymes of Glutamine Metabolism, 1973, Slow Transmissible Diseases of the Nervous System, 2 vols., 1979, Prions - Novel Infectious Pathogens Causing Scrapie and CJD, 1987, Prion Diseases of Humans and Animals, 1992, Molecular and Genetic Basis of Neurologic Disease, 1993; contbr. over 200 rsch. articles to profl. jours. Mem. adv. bd. Family Survival Project for Adults with Chronic Brain Disorders, San Francisco, 1982—, San Francisco chpt. Alzheimer's Disease and Related Disorder Assn., 1985—. Lt. comdr. USPHS, 1969-72. Alfred P. Sloan Rsch. fellow U. Calif., 1976-78; Med. Investigator grantee Howard Hughes Med. Inst., 1976-81; grantee for excellence in neurosci. Senator Jacob Javits Ctr., NIH, 1985-1990; recipient Leadership and Excellence for Alzheimer's Disease award NIH, 1990—, Potamkin prize for Alzheimer's Disease Rsch., 1991, Presdl. award, 1993, Med. Rsch. award Met. Life Found., 1992, Christopher Columbus Discovery award NIH and Med. Soc. Genoa, Italy, 1992, Charles A. Dana award for pioneering achievements in health, 1992, Dickson prize for outstanding contbns. to medicine U. Pitts., 1992, Max Planck Rsch. award Alexander von Humboldt Found. and Max Planck Soc., 1992, Gairdner Found. Internat. award, 1993, Disting. Achievement in Neuroscience Rsch. award Bristol-Myers Squibb, 1994, Albert Lasker award for Basic Med. Rsch., 1994, Caledonian Rsch. Found. prize Royal Soc. Edinburgh, 1995, Paul Ehrlich and Ludwig Darmstaedter award Germany, 1995, Paul Hoch award Am. Psychopathological Assn., 1995. Mem. NAS (Inst. Medicine, Richard Lounsbery award for extraordinary achievements in biology and medicine 1993), Am. Acad. Arts and Scis., Am. Acad. Neurology (George Cotzias award for outstanding rsch. 1987, Presdl. award 1993), Am. Assn. Physicians, Am. Soc. Microbiology, Am. Soc. Neurochemistry, Internat. Soc. Neurochemistry, Am. Soc. Virology, Am. Neurol. Assn., Am. Soc. Clin. Investigation, Am. Soc. Cellular Biology, Am. Soc. Molecular Biol. Biochemistry, Protein Soc., Concordia Argonaut Clu.

PRYOR, CAROLYN ANN, church musician, educator; b. Auburn, Ind., Aug. 13, 1934; d. Leland Alvin and Ruth Alberta (Norton) P.; children: Maria Vanessa, Anthony Hugh. BA in Music, Occidental Coll., 1957. Organist, dir. Goodsell Meth. Ch., Bklyn., 1959-63; organist Boro Park Prog. Synagogue, Bklyn., 1959-63; kindergarten tchr. L.A. City Schs., 1966-67; tchr., adminstr. St. Michael's Ch., N.Y.C., 1967-69, various schs., N.Y.C., 1969-77; organist, dir. United Meth. Ch., Seacliff, N.Y., 1970-78; sr. sec. to rsch. doctors Columbia U., N.Y.C., 1978-79; dir. music ministries 1st United Meth. Ch., Campbell, Calif., 1979—. Contbr. articles to profl. jours. Mem. Am. Guild Organists, Choral Condrs. Guild, Choristers Guild.

PRYOR, KAREN WYLIE, biologist, writer; b. N.Y.C., May 14, 1932; d. Philip Gordon Wylie and Sally Ondeck; m. Taylor A. Pryor, June 25, 1954 (div. 1973); children: Tedmund, Michael, Gale; m. Jon M. Lindbergh, May 14, 1983. BA in English, Cornell U., 1954; postgrad., U. Hawaii, 1957-59, NYU, 1977-79, Rutgers U., 1979-82. Founder, curator Sea Life Park Oceanarium, Honolulu, 1960-71; copywriter Fawcett-McDermott, Honolulu, 1973-76; drama critic Honolulu Advertiser, 1971-75; free lance writer, 1963—, marine mammal cons., 1970—; sci. advisor U.S. Tuna Found., Washington, 1976-82; cons. NSF, NASA, Nat. Geographic Soc., 1976—; commr. Marine Mammal Commn., Washington, 1984-87; pres. Sunshine Books, Inc., 1992—; pub. and video prodr. Author: Nursing Your Baby, 1963, rev. edit., 1973, Lads Before the Wind: Adventures in Porpoise Training, 1975, Don't Shoot the Dog! The New Art of Teaching and Training, 1984 (Excellence in Media award APA 1984), How to Teach Your Dog to Play Frisbee, 1985, (with K.S. Norris) Dolphin Societies: Discoveries and Puzzles, 1991; editor: Crunch and Des: Classic Stories of Salt Water Fishing by Philip Wylie, 1991, (with Gale Pryor) Nursing Your Baby, 1991, On Behavior, 1995; contbr. articles to profl. jours. Mem. Internat. Marine Amimal Trainers Assn., Authors Guild, Marine Mammal Soc. (charter mem.), Soc. Women Geographers, Cosmopolitan Club. Home: 44811 SE 166th St North Bend WA 98045-9007

PRYSTUPA, ESTER ANA, accountant; b. Buenos Aires, Argentina, Nov. 19, 1956; came to U.S., 1989; d. Wladimiro and Nina (Iwanczuk) P. Grad. Bus. Adminstrn., UADE Argentina. CPA, UADE Argentina. Acct., tax cons. Mazza S.A., Di Pablo S.A., Fabi, S.A., Buenos Aires, 1981-89, The Homeowners Fin. Ctr., San Gabriel, Calif., 1989-91; bookeeper Dearden's Furniture, L.A., 1991—. Mem. Consejo Profl. de Ccias. Econs. de Capital Fed. Argentina. Home: 10926 Hortense St Apt 18 Toluca Lake CA 91602-1756

PRZEKURAT, CAROLYN BJORKMAN, dietitian; b. Salt Lake City, Mar. 4, 1940; d. Arthur Edmund and Eveline Jone (Brough) Bjorkman; m. Emil Henry Przekurat, June 14, 1969; 1 child, Susan. BS, U. Utah, 1962; MS, U. Wis., Stevens Point, 1973. Lic. dietitian, N.Mex. Dir. dietetic programs St. Michaels Hosp., Stevens Point, 1968-74; chief dietitian, capt. USPHS, Shiprock, N.Mex., 1976-78; dietetic tng. officer USPHS, Santa Fe, 1978-80; chief dietitian USPHS, Albuquerque, 1980-86, dir. dietetic programs, 1986—; chief profl. officer dietetic category Office Surgeon Gen. USPHS, Rockville, Md., 1993—; adv. com. culinary arts program N.Mex. Tech. Vocat. Inst., Albuquerque, 1985-90; adv. com. Southwestern Indian Poly. Inst., Albuquerque, 1987-92, U. N.Mex. Approved Preprofl. Practice Program, Albuquerque, 1988-94. Maj. U.S. Army, 1963-68, 74-76. Mem. Am. Dietetic Assn. (registered dietitian), N.Mex. Dietetic Assn. (pres. 1993-94, sec. 1976, Outstanding Dietitian of Yr. 1991), Soc. for Nutrition Edn. Mormon. Home: 5333 Jessie Dr NE Albuquerque NM 87111-1930 Office: USPHS 505 Marquette Ave NW Albuquerque NM 87102-2158

PTACEK, WILLIAM H., library director. BA in English and Psychology, U. Ill., 1972; MLS, SUNY, Geneseo, 1974; cert. of advanced study, U. Ill., Chgo., 1979. Reference libr. South Br. Chgo. Pub. Libr., 1974-75, head libr. Mt. Greenwood br., 1975-76, head system-wide circulation, 1976-77, asst. dir. personnel, 1977-78, chief Northeast Dist., 1978-79; dir. Idaho Falls Pub. Libr., 1979-83, Louisville Free Pub. Libr., 1984-89, King County Libr. System, Seattle, 1989—. Co-author: (with Peggy Sullivan) Public Libraries: Smart Practices in Personnel, 1982; contbr. articles to profl. jours. Office: King County Libr System 300 8th Ave N Seattle WA 98109-5116

PTASYNSKI, HARRY, geologist, oil producer; b. Milw., May 26, 1926; s. Stanley S. and Frances V. (Stawicki) P.; m. Nola G. Whitestine, Sept. 15, 1951; children: Ross F., Lisa Joy. BS, Stanford U., 1950. Cert. profl. geologist; cert. petroleum geologist. Dist. geologist Pure Oil Co., Amarillo, Tex., 1951-55, Casper, Wyo., 1955-58; ind. geologist, Casper, 1958—. With USN, 1944-46, PTO. Mem. Am. Assn. Petroleum Geologists, Am. Inst. Profl. Geologists, Ind. Petroleum Assn. Am. (v.p., bd. dirs. 1976—), Ind. Petroleum Assn. Mountain States (v.p., bd. dirs. 1976-80, Rocky Mountain Oil and Gas Assn. (bd. dirs., exec. com. 1980—). Republican. Episcopalian. Home: 1515 Brookview Dr Casper WY 82604-4895 Office: 123 W 1st St Ste 560 Casper WY 82601-2483

PUCKETT, PAUL DAVID, electronics company executive; b. Atlanta, July 31, 1941; s. Jonas Levi and Ovella (Juhan) P.; m. Margaret Ann Straetz, June 29, 1974, (div. Jan. 1984); m. Catherine Marie Ryan, Apr. 5, 1984; children: Shawn Michael, Glen David. BS in Edn., Nyack Coll., 1963; MBA in Mgmt., Pace U., 1988. Mgr. quality Rockland Systems Corp., Blauvelt, N.Y., 1971-75, Electronics for Medicine, Inc., White Plains, N.Y., 1975-77; mgr. ops. Tele-Resources, Inc., Armonk, N.Y., 1977-79; mgr. quality Materials Rsch. Corp., Orangeberg, N.Y., 1979-83; mgr. quality plasma systems div. Perkin-Elmer, Wilton, Conn., 1983-84, dir. ops. plasma systems div., 1984-86, mgr. spl. studies semiconductor group, 1986-87; mgr. quality programs instrument group Perkin-Elmer, Norwalk, Conn., 1987-90; dir. ops. applied sci. div. Perkin-Elmer (sold applied sci. div. to Orbital Scis. Corp.), Pomona, Calif., 1990-93; dir. ops. Pomona (Calif.) ops. Orbital Scis. Corp., 1993—; examiner Malcolm Baldrige Nat. Quality award, Gathersberg, Md., 1989-90, Conn. State Quality award, Stamford, 1988-90, cons., trainer, 1990. Contbr. articles to profl. jours. Mem. Young Reps., New City, N.Y., 1975-76; vol. police officer Rockland County Sheriff's Dept., New City, 1974-83; coach Am. Youth Soccer Orgn., Bethel, Conn., 1984-85. Recipient Conn. State Quality award, 1989. Mem. N.Y. Acad. Sci., Am. Soc. Quality Control, Assn. for Quality and Participation, Am. Electronics Assn. Republican. Episcopalian. Home: 1500 Mansfield Ct Upland CA 91784-

7963 Office: Orbital Scis Corp Pomona Ops 2771 N Garey Ave Pomona CA 91767-1809

PUCKETT, RICHARD EDWARD, artist, consultant, retired recreation executive; b. Klamath Falls, Oreg., Sept. 9, 1932; s. Vernon Elijah and Leona Belle (Clevenger) P.; m. Velma Faye Hamrick, Apr. 14, 1957 (dec. 1985); children: Katherine Michelle Briggs, Deborah Alison Bolinger, Susan Lin Rowland, Gregory Richard. Student So. Oreg. Coll. Edn., 1951-56, Lake Forest Coll., 1957-58; Hartnell Jr. Coll., 1960-70; B.A., U. San Francisco, 1978. Asst. arts and crafts dir., Fort Leonard Wood, Mo., 1956-57; arts and crafts dir., asst. spl. services officer, mus. dir., Fort Sheridan, Ill., 1957-59; arts and crafts dir., Fort Irwin, Calif., 1959-60, Fort Ord, Calif., 1960-86; dir. arts and crafts br. Art Gallery, Arts and Crafts Center Materials Sales Store, 1960; opening dir. Presidio of Monterey Army Mus., 1968; dir. Model Army Arts and Crafts Program. Recipient First Place, Dept. Army and U.S. Army Forces Command awards for programming and publicity, 1979-81, 83-85, 1st and 3d place sculpture awards Monterey County Fair Fine Arts Exhibit, 1979, Comdrs. medal for civilian svcs., 1986, numerous other awards, Golden Acad. award, Internat. Man of Yr. award, 1991-92. Mem. Am. Craftsman Assn. (former), Glass Arts Soc., Monterey Peninsula Art Assn., Salinas Fine Arts Assn., Am. Park and Recreation Soc. One-man shows: Seaside City Hall, 1975, Fort Ord Arts and Crafts Center Gallery, 1967, 73, 79, 81, 84, 86, Presidio of Monterey Art Gallery, 1979, Rogue Valley Art Assn.; Glass on Holiday, 1981, 82; also pvt. collections; designed and opened first Ft. Sheridan Army Mus., Presidio of Monterey Mus. Home: 110 Ashland Ave Medford OR 97504-7523

PUCKLE, DONNE ERVING, priest; b. London, June 17, 1940; came to U.S., 1946; s. Raymond Donne Aufrere and Elizabeth (Price) P.; m. Lola Rose Avery, June 24, 1972; children: Donne Edward Christopher, Elizabeth Berry Rose. AA, Phoenix Coll., 1960; BA, Ariz. State U., 1962; MDiv, Bexley Hall, Rochester, N.Y., 1966; M in Counseling, U. Phoenix, 1994. Priest, rector St. John's Ch., Bisbee, Ariz., 1967-73; priest, vicar Grace Episcopal Ch., Lake Havasu City, Ariz., 1973-76; asst. priest Christ Episcopal Ch., Lacrosse, Wis., 1976-78; priest, rector Trinity Episcopal Ch., Mattoon, Ill., 1979-81, Christ Episcopal Ch., Chippewa Falls, Wis., 1981-90; priest St. John's Episcopal Ch., Bisbee, 1993—; asst. chaplain L.E. Phillips Treatment Ctr., Chippewa Falls, 1981-90; acad. dean, instr. Episcopal Sch. Ch. Studies, Eau Claire, Wis., 1987-90; counselor U.S. Salvation Army, Tucson, 1993-94; cons. Standing Liturgical Commn., N.Y.C., 1976-79; mem. Pub. Health Adv. Bd., Chippewa Falls, 1986-89, Diocesan Exec. coun., Eau Claire, 1982-90, Anglican/Roman Catholic Dialogue, Springfield, Ill., 1979-81. Author: Winter Sunday in Norway, Maine, 1990 (award 1992), Ceremonial Guide for Lent and Holy Week, 1980; editor: Prayers for Advent, Christmas and Epiphany, 1972. Coord. food pantry Chippewa Falls, 1984-90; mem. dist. com. Boy Scouts Am., Chippewa Falls, 1986-88; chmn. Red Cross County Bd., Chippewa Falls, 1985-90. Recipient award Am. Bible Soc., 1966. Mem. ACA, Nat. Assn. Alcohol and Drug Abuse Counselors, Soc. of Holy Cross, Mensa, Delta Psi Omega, Phi Theta Kappa. Democrat. Home: 125 Kayetan Dr NE Sierra Vista AZ 85635-1117

PUDNEY, GARY LAURENCE, television executive; b. Mpls., July 20, 1934; s. Lawrence D. and Agnes (Hansen) P. BA, UCLA, 1956. V.p. ABC, Inc., N.Y.C., 1968—; v.p., sr. exec. in charge of spls. and talent ABC Entertainment, 1979-89; pres. The Gary L. Pudney Co., Beverly Hills, Calif., 1988—; chief oper. officer Paradigm Entertainment, Beverly Hills, 1989-92; exec. producer World Music Awards, ABC-TV, 1993—, World's Greatest Magic, NBC-TV, 1994—, Grand Illusions, 1994, Caesar's World Entertainment, 1994-95, Lance Burton and Houdini, NBC-TV, 1995. Exec. producer for United Cerebral Palsy Aspen and Lake Tahoe Pro-Celebrity Tennis Festivals, 4 yrs., AIDS Project L.A. Dinner, 1985, The 25th Anniversary of the L.A. Music Ctr. Bd. dirs. nat. Cerebral Palsy Found., Ctr. Theatre Group Ahmanson Theatre, L.A., Ctr. Theatre Group of L.A. Music Ctr.; mem. bd. La Quinta Arts Found., 1991—. Recipient Helena T. Deveraux Meml. award, 1985, Humanitarian award Nat. Jewish Ctr. for Immunology and Respiratory Medicine, 1986, Gift of Love award Nat. Ctr. Hyperactive Children, 1988, Winner award Excellence The L.A. Film Adv. Bd. Mem. Hollywood Radio and TV Soc. (bd. dirs.), Acad. TV Arts and Scis. (exec. com.), Met. Mus. Art, Mus. Modern Art. Democrat. Lutheran.

PUENTE, JOSE GARZA, safety engineer; b. Cuero, Tex., Mar. 19, 1949; s. Roque Leos and Juanita Vela (Garza) P.; m. Francisca Rodriguez Estrada, Sept. 7, 1969; 1 son, Anthony Burk. B.A., W. Tex. State U., Canyon, 1972; postgrad. U. Ariz.-Tucson, 1980; grad. U.S. Army transp. courses, 1972, 78, grad. Command & Gen. Staff Coll., 1989; grad. U.S. Army Command and Gen. Staff Coll. Cert. U.S. Council Accreditation in Occupational Hearing; cert. Audiometric Technicians of Am. Indsl. Hygiene Assn. Asst. gen. mgr. Am. Transit Corp., Tucson, 1972-75; pub. transp. supt. City of Tucson, 1975-77; asst. safety coord., Tucson, 1977-81; safety coord. Mesa, Ariz., 1981-88; corp. safety dir. Am. Fence Corp., Phoenix, 1988-89; safety adminstr. Ariz.-ADOT, Phoenix, 1989—; owner La Paz Gospel Supplies & Gift shop, Tucson, 1979-80. Mem. Tucson Child Care Assn., 1973-74; mem. Citizen Task Force, Sunnyside sch. bd., 1977; mem. minority selection for Hispanic seatbelt program vendor Govs. Office of Hwy. Safety, 1989—; mem. Mayors Task Force on seatbelt awareness City of Mesa, 1988-89. Lt. col. USAR, 1971—. Fellow Advanced Mgmt. Seminar Urban Mass Transp. Adminstrn., Northeastern U., Boston, 1976-77; recipient Excellence award Ariz-Safety Assn., 1984. Mem. Am. Soc. Safety Engrs. (pres. elect Ariz. chpt. 1989-90, pres., 1990-91, Safety Profl. of Yr. 1984), Mexican-Am. Govtl. Employees (charter Tucson chpt.), Res. Officers Assn., Ariz. Safety Engrs., Ariz. Mcpl. Safety Assn. (Profl. of Yr. 1986), Internat. Platform Assn. Democrat. Baptist. Clubs: Internat. Order DeMolay (charter), Lions, Mesa Bowling League, Toastmasters. Home: PO Box 90 Mesa AZ 85211-0090 Office: 206 S 17th Ave Phoenix AZ 85007-3213

PUENTE, TITO ANTHONY, orchestra leader, composer, arranger; b. N.Y.C., Apr. 20, 1923; s. Ernest Anthony and Ercilia (Ortiz) P.; m. Margaret Asencio, Oct. 19, 1963; children: Ronald, Audrey, Tito Anthony. Student, Julliard Conservatory Music, N.Y. Sch. Music, Schillinger System; MusD (hon.), SUNY, Albany, 1987. Orch. leader appearing in numerous night clubs and ballrooms, throughout U.S., 1949—; appeared in Woody Allen's Radio Days, John Candy's Armed & Dangerous, 1986-87; recorded 96 albums; appeared in concert Red Sea Jazz Festival, Israel, all major jazz festivals, including Montreaux, Monterey, Munich, North Sea, others, Tribute in P.R., 1986, Los Angeles Ford Theatre Tribute, 1987; composer Para Los Rumberos, 1960, Oye Como Va, 1962, numerous other works recorded with Dizzy Gillespie, Lionel Hampton, George Shearing, Woody Herman, other major jazz artists; sold out performance Radio City Music Hall & Apollo Theatre, 1986; appeared Madison Square Garden, N.Y.C., 1986, Los Angeles Amphitheatre, 1986, on Bill Cosby Show, 1987, Regis Philbin, Bill Boggs shows, 1987; guest artist with Bklyn. Philharmonic Symphony Orch., N.Y. and Phila., 1987. Founder T. Puente Scholarship fund, 1980. Served with USN, 1942-45. Recipient Bronze medallion City of N.Y., 1969, Key to City Los Angeles, 1976, Key to City of Chgo., 1985, Key to City of Miami, 1986; named Musician of Month on several occasions by Downbeat, Metronome, Playboy and trade mags., 1950's; named King of Latin Music, La Prensa newspaper, 1955; his band named Best Latin Am. Orch. New York Daily News, 1977; recipient 6 Grammy nominations, Grammy award, 1978, 83, 85, 90; N.Y. Music award, 1986. Office: Thomas Cassidy Inc 366 Horseshoe Dr Basalt CO 81621

PUETZ, PAMELA ANN, human resources executive; b. Lawrence, Mass., Aug. 17, 1949; d. Gregory and Eleanor Christine (Stull) Bedrosian; m. Tracy Barnum Braun, Jan. 26, 1974 (div. 1985); 1 child, Susannah Barnum; m. Dan Lee Puetz, May 31, 1986. AS, Fisher Jr. Coll., Boston, 1969; BS in Mgmt. with high distinction, Babson Coll., Wellesley, Mass., 1973. Br. mgr. First Security Bank of Utah, N.A., Salt Lake City, 1974-76; bus. mgr. U.S. Ski Team, Inc., Park City, Utah, 1976-77; banking specialist Tracy Collins Bank, Salt Lake City, 1980-83; instr. Fitness Inst., LDS Hosp., Salt Lake City, 1983-85; owner/operator Grapevine Svcs., Redondo Beach, Calif., 1987-88; human resources adminstr. PacifiCare Health Systems, Inc., Cypress, Calif., 1988-89, human resources analyst, 1989-91, human resources project mgr., 1991—, human resources info. systems mgr., 1992—; assoc. DLP Constrn. & Devel., Garden Grove, Calif., 1992-94; sr. mgr. human resources systems Mattel, Inc., El Segundo, Calif., 1994—. Mem. Personnel and Indsl. Rels. Assn., Assn. Human Resource Systems Profls.

PUFFER, RUTH RICE, statistician, epidemiologist; b. Berlin, Mass., Aug. 31, 1907; d. J. Adams and Emily Hope (Rice) P. BA, Smith Coll., 1929, ScD (hon.), 1970; posgrad., Johns Hopkins U., 1937-38; DPH, Harvard U., 1943. Dir. statis. svcs. Tenn. Dept. Pub. Health, Nashville, 1933-53; chief dept. health stats. Pan Am. Health Orgn., regional office WHO, Washington, 1953-70, cons., 1970—; cons. U.S. Dept. State, New Delhi, India, 1981, 85, Jakarta, Indonesia, 1983. Author: Familial Susceptibility to Tuberculosis, 1944, Practical Statistics for Health and Medical Workers, 1950, Patterns of Urban Mortality, 1967, Caracteristicas de Mortalidad Urbana, 1968, Patterns of Mortality in Childhood, 1973, Caracteristicas de la Mortalidada en la Ninez, 1973, Patterns of Birthweights, 1987, Caracteristicas del Peso al Nacer, 1988; author numerous papers. Recipient Centennial award Tenn. Dept. Pub. Health, 1977, Abraham Horwitz award for Internat. Health Pan-Am. Orgn., 1978. Fellow Am. Pub. Health Assn. (v.p. 1950), Am. Statis. Assn.; mem. Delta Omega. Unitarian.

PUFFER, SHARON KAYE, residential loan officer; b. Portland, Oreg., June 23, 1944; d. Henry and Linda Katherine (Olsen) Clearwater; m. Arleigh Rocco Puffer, Feb. 5, 1965; children: Michele Lynn, Heidi Leigh. Student, Portland State U., 1962-64. Lic. real estate salesperson. Real estate sales agt. Valley Realty, Dublin, Calif., 1979-82; with real estate sales The Ryness Co., Danville, Calif., 1982-83; sales coord. spl. projects Coldwell Banker, San Ramon, Calif., 1983-86; residential loan officer Coldwell Banker Mortgage, Danville, 1986-87, Glenfed Mortgage, San Ramon, 1987-89; sr. real estate loan officer Bank of America Residential Loan Ctr., Walnut Creek, Calif., 1989—. Membership chmn. Livermore (Calif.) Jr. Women affiliate Nat. Fedn. of Women, 1974-75, pres., 1975-76. Mem. Contra Costa Bd. Realtors. Republican. Home: 330 Mccloud Pl Danville CA 94526-5017

PUGAY, JEFFREY IBANEZ, mechanical engineer; b. San Francisco, June 26, 1958; s. Herminio Salazar and Petronila (Ibanez) P. BSME, U. Calif., Berkeley, 1981, MSME, 1982; MBA, Pepperdine U., 1986, MS in Tech. Mgmt., 1991. Registered profl. engr., Calif. Engring. asst. Lawrence Berkeley Nat. Lab., 1978-80; assoc. tech. staff Aerospace Corp., L.A., 1981; mem. tech. staff Hughes Space & Comm. Co., El Segundo, Calif., 1982-85, project engr., 1985-88, tech. head, 1988-89, sr. staff engr., 1989-90, mgr. tech. ops. and strategic systems, 1991-92, ops. leader, info. tech., 1992-94, project mgr., 1994-95; mgr. mktg. Hughes Comm., Inc.-Spaceway, L.A., 1994—. Active ARC Emergency Svcs. White House Fellow regional finalist, 1991, 92. Mem. ASME, Soc. Competitor Intelligence Profls., Am. Mgmt. Assn., L.A. World Affairs Coun., Make A Wish Found., Pi Tau Sigma, Delta Mu Delta. Republican. Roman Catholic. Home: 8180 Manitoba St Apt 120 Playa Del Rey CA 90293-8651 Office: Hughes Space & Comm Co PO Box 92919 Los Angeles CA 90009-2919

PUGH, JAMIE KATHLEEN, statistician, researcher; b. Redlands, Calif., Oct. 30, 1946; d. James Richard and Martha Grace (Lewis) Caudle; m. William Marshell Pugh, June 24, 1967; children: Kimberly Ann, Alice Louise. BS in Physics, San Diego State U., 1969, MS in Stats., 1983. Mem. tech. staff Computer Scis. Corp., San Diego, 1977-80; scientist Rsch., Devel., Test and Evaluation div. Naval Command Control and Ocean Surveillance Ctr., San Diego, 1980—; lect. San Diego State U., 1985-86. Mem. AAAS, Am. Soc. Quality Control, Soc. Indsl. and Applied Math., Am. Statis. Assn.

PUGH, KYLE MITCHELL, JR., musician, music educator; b. Spokane, Wash., Jan. 6, 1937; s. Kyle Mitchel, Sr. and Lenore Fae (Johnson) P.; m. Susan Deane Waite, July 16, 1961; children: Jeffray, Kari. BA in Edu., East Wash. U., 1975. Cert. tchr., Wash. Tuba player Spokane Symphony Orch., 1958-63; rec. assoc. Century Records, Spokane, 1965-73; tuba player World's Fair Expo '74, Spokane, 1974; bass player Russ Carlyle Orch., Las Vegas, 1976, Many Sounds of Nine Orch., northwest area, 1969-81; band tchr. Garry Jr. High School, Spokane, 1976-79, Elementary Band Program, Spokane, 1979—; bass player Doug Scott Cabaret Band, Spokane, 1982-91; dept. head Elem. Band Dept., Spokane, 1984-89. Editor (newsletter) The Repeater, 1987 (Amateur Radio News Svc. award 1987); extra in movie Always, 1989. Active in communications Lilac Bloomsday Assn., Spokane, 1977. Served to E-5 USNR, 1955-63. Recipient Disting. Service award Wash. State Commn., 1974, Nev. Hollerin' Champ Carl Hayden Scribe, 1979. Mem. Am. Fedn. Musicians (life), Spokane Edn. Assn. (rec. sec. 1987), Music Educator's Nat. Conf., Am. Radio Relay League (asst. dir. 1987), Ea. Wash. Music Educator's Assn. (pres. 1978-79), Dial Twisters Club (pres. 1979-80), VHF Radio Amateurs (dir. 1980-83), Elks, Moose. Home: 5006 W Houston Ave Spokane WA 99208-3728 Office: Elem Mus Office 503 W 4th Ave Spokane WA 99204-2603

PUGH, MICHAEL DUANE, healthcare executive; b. Aberdeen, Md., May 9, 1953; s. Duane Wood and Martha Marie (Barnes) P.; m. Drucilla Nance Crabtree, Dec. 30, 1976; children: Allyson Hunter, Emily Kirkpatrick. BS, Tulane U., 1975, MPH, 1978. Asst. adminstr. Hosp. Affiliate, Internat., Austin, Tex., 1978-79; adminstr., CEO United Gen. Hosp., Sedro Woolley, Wash., 1979-84; pres., CEO Parkview Health Sys., Pueblo, Colo., 1984—. Pres. United Way of Pueblo County, 1987. Mem. Pueblo Ch. of C. (Bus. Leader of Yr. 1993), Am. Hosp. Assn. (trustee 1993—), Colo. Hosp. Assn. (chmn. 1991). Home: 700 W 17th St Pueblo CO 81003-2113 Office: Parkview Health Sys 400 W 16th St Pueblo CO 81003-2745

PUGLIESE, JOHN DAVID, mechanical engineer, consultant, programmer; b. San Jose, Calif., Apr. 5, 1966; s. Joseph Anthony and Linda Jeanette (Hodgkins) P. BSME, Calif. Poly. State U., San Luis Obispo, 1990. Registered engr.-in-tng., Calif. Engring. aide NASA Ames Rsch. Ctr., Moffett Field, Calif., 1987-88, Treese & Assocs., Santa Barbara, Calif., 1990; field application engr. Minarik Electric Co., Portland, Oreg., 1990-92; engr., trainer, instr. Berkeley Process Control, Richmond, Calif., 1992—; cons. Computer Reporting Svc., San Jose, Calif., 1992—; instr. seminars on motion control topics, 1992. Mem. Order of Omega. Home: 705 Springwood Dr San Jose CA 95129-2152 Office: Berkeley Process Control 705 Springwood Dr San Jose CA 95129-2152

PUGLIESE, VINCENT JOSEPH ALFRED, manufacturing executive; b. Washington, Apr. 9, 1962; s. Vincent Augustus and Judith Ann (Excog) P.; m. Nancy Lynne Baker Pugliese, Jan. 9, 1987; children: Amanda Lynne, Andrea Gail. BS in Adminstrn., Mgmt. Sci., Carnegie Mellon U., Pitts., 1984; BS in Applied Math., Carnegie Mellon U., 1984; MBA, U. Balt., 1989. Indsl. engr. Westinghouse Electric Corp., Balt., 1984-87, mfg. engr., 1987-88, sr. mfg. engr., 1988-89, mfg. ops. program mgr., 1989-92; ops. mgr. Edge Emitter Tech., Inc., Fremont, Calif., 1992-94; project mgr. Hewlett Packard, Fremont, 1994—. Office: Hewlett Packard 49001 Lakeview Blvd Fremont CA 94538

PUGSLEY, ROBERT ADRIAN, legal educator; b. Mineola, N.Y., Dec. 27, 1946; s. Irvin Harold and Mary Catherine (Brusselars) P. BA, SUNY-Stony Brook, 1968; JD, NYU, 1975, LLM in Criminal Justice, 1977. Instr. sociology The New Sch. Social Rsch., N.Y.C., 1969-71; coordinator Peace Edn. programs The Christophers, N.Y.C., 1971-78; assoc. prof. law Southwestern U., L.A., 1978-81, prof., 1981—; adj. asst. prof. criminology and criminal justice Southampton Coll.-Long Island U., 1975-76; acting dep. dir. Criminal Law Edn. and Rsch. Ctr., NYU, 1983-86; bd. advisors Ctr. Legal Edn. CCNY-CUNY, 1978, Sta. KPFK-FM, 1985-86; founder, coordinator The Wednesday Evening Soc., L.A., 1979—; vis. prof. Jacob D. Fuchsberg Law Ctr. Touro Coll., L.I., N.Y., summers 1988, 89; lectr. in criminal law and procedure Legal Edn. Conf. Ctr., L.A., 1982—; legal analyst/commentator for print and electronic media, 1992—. Creative advisor Christopher Closeup (nationally syndicated pub. svc. TV program), 1975-83; host Earth Alert, Cable TV, 1983-87; producer, moderator (pub. affairs discussion program) Inside L.A., Sta. KPFK-FM, 1979-86, Open Jour. program, Sta. KPFK-FM, 1991-94; contbr. articles to legal jours. Founding mem. Southwestern U. Pub. Interest Law com., 1992—; mem. L.A. County Bar Assn. Adv. Com. on Alcohol & Drug Abuse, 1991-95, co-chair, 1993-95; mem. exec. com. non-govtl. orgns. UN Office of Pub. Info., 1977; mem. issues task force L.A. Conservancy, 1980-81, seminar for law tchrs. NEH UCLA, 1979; co-convener So. Calif. Coalition Against Death Penalty, 1981-83, convener, 1983-84; mem. death penalty com. Lawyer's Support Group, Amnesty Internat. U.S.A.; founding mem. Ch.-State Coun., L.A., 1984-88. Robert Marshall fellow Criminal Law Edn. and Rsch. Ctr., NYU Sch. Law, 1976-78; bd. dirs. Equal Rights Sentencing Found., 1983-85, Earth Alert Inc., 1984-87; mem. adv. bd. First Amendment Info. Resources Ctr., Grad. Sch. of Libr. and Info. Sci., UCLA, 1990—; mem. coun. Friends UCLA Libr., 1993—. Mem. Am. Legal Studies Assn., Am. Soc. Polit. and Legal Philosophy, Assn. Am. Law Schs., Inst. Soc. Ethics and Life Scis., Soc. Am. Law Tchrs., The Scribes. Democrat. Roman Catholic. Office: Southwestern U Sch Law 675 S Westmoreland Ave Rm 410 Los Angeles CA 90005-3905 Address: PO Box 440 East Hampton NY 11937

PULCRANO, DAN MICHAEL, newspaper executive; b. New Brunswick, N.J., Oct. 1, 1958; s. Charles A. and Edith (Tanner) P. BA in Journalism and Newspaper Mgmt., U. Calif., Santa Cruz, 1980. Reporter Santa Barbara (Calif.) News & Rev., 1978; asst. to pub. L.A. Weekly, 1978, 79; editor, pub. Santa Cruz (Calif.) Weekly, 1981, Los Gatos (Calif.) Weekly, 1982-84; editor Metro, San Jose, Calif., 1985-93; exec. editor Metro Newspapers, San Jose, 1990—; pres., CEO Metro Pub., Inc., San Jose, 1992—, Virtual Valley, Inc., San Jose, 1993—. Founding pres., bd. mem. San Jose Downtown Assn., 1986—. Recipient Disting. Svc. award Oakes Coll., 1980; named Dist. Honoree City of San Jose, Dist. 3, 1989. Mem. Calif. Free Press Assn. (pres. 1991-92), Assn. Alternative Newspapers (v.p. 1993-94, bd. dirs.s 1993-95), Rotary. Home: PO Box 7 San Jose CA 95103-0007 Office: Metro Newspapers 550 S 1st St San Jose CA 95113-2806

PULLEN, KENT EDWARD, state legislator, chemist; b. El Paso, Tex., May 4, 1942; s. Eugene Hoyt and Maris Morie (Glover) P.; m. Fay Lynnette Endres, June 13, 1964; children: Katherine Ann, Walter David. BS, U. N.Mex., 1963; PhD, U. Wash., 1967. Asst. prof. chemistry U. Idaho, Moscow, 1967-68; engr. Boeing Co., Seattle, 1968-90; mem. Wash. Ho. Reps., Olympia, 1973-75, Wash. Senate, 1975-90; chmn. Senate Law and Justice com., 1988-89; mem. King County Coun., 1990—, chmn., 1994—. Bd. dirs. Citizen Taxpayers Assn., Kent, Wash., 1979-85; chmn. Citizens Against Crime, 1975; co-chmn. Com. for Honest Elections, Kent, 1977. Mem. Mountaineers Club. Wash. State Chess Champion, 1985. Office: King County Coun King County Courthouse Seattle WA 98104

PULLEN, MARGARET I., genetic physicist; b. Nebr., Sept. 13, 1950; d. Robert and Martha (Holtort) P. AA, Stephens Coll., 1971; BA in Internat. Rels., Econs., Bus. & Trade, U. Colo., 1975; BS in Physics, Northeastern U., 1983; MS in Physics, Tufts U., 1984; postgrad., U. Calif., 1984-86. Mathematician lawrence Livermore Lab., Calif., 1987; cons. Porterfield Enterprise, 1988; entrepreneur Evergreen Applied Rsch. Inc., 1988--; mem. Biotechnolgy Roundtable, Denver, 1987--. Vol. Nat. Sports Ctr. for the Physically Disabled, Winter Park, Colo., 1988-92. Tufts U. grantee, U. Colo. grantee; Nat. Sci. fellow; Stephens scholar, Perry Mansfield Ctr. for the Preforming Arts scholar. Mem. Am. Phys. Soc. Office: Evergreen Applied Rsch Inc PO Box 2870 Evergreen CO 80439-2870

PULLIAM, EUGENE SMITH, newspaper publisher; b. Atchison, Kans., Sept. 7, 1914; s. Eugene Collins and Myrta (Smith) P.; m. Jane Bleecker, May 29, 1943; children: Myrta, Russell, Deborah. A.B., DePauw U., 1935, LL.D., 1973. Reporter, UP, Chgo., Detroit, Buffalo, 1935-36; news editor Radio Sta. WIRE, Indpls., 1937-41; city editor Indpls. Star, 1947-48; mng. editor Indpls. News, 1948-62; asst. publisher Indpls. Star and News, 1962-76; pres. Phoenix Newspapers, 1979—; exec. v.p. Central Newspapers, Indpls., 1979—. Mem. Am. Soc. Newspaper Editors, Am. Newspaper Pubs. Assn. Found. (past pres.), Soc. Profl. Journalists, Delta Kappa Epsilon. Club: Crooked Stick Golf. Office: Indpls Star Indpls Newspapers Inc 307 N Pennsylvania St Indianapolis IN 46204-1811 also: Phoenix Newspapers Inc 120 E Van Buren St Phoenix AZ 85004-2227

PULLIAM, FRANCINE SARNO, real estate broker and developer; b. San Francisco, Sept. 14, 1937; d. Ralph C. Stevens and Frances I. (Wilson) Sarno; m. John Donald Pulliam, Aug. 14, 1957 (div. Mar. 1965); 1 child, Wendy; m. Terry Kent Graves, Dec. 14, 1974. Student, U. Ariz., 1955-56, U. Nev., Las Vegas, 1957. Airline stewardess Bonanza Airlines, Las Vegas, 1957; real estate agt. The Pulliam Co., Las Vegas, 1958-68, Levy Realty, Las Vegas, 1976-76; real estate broker, owner Prestige Properties, Las Vegas, 1976—; importer, exporter Exports Internat., Las Vegas, 1984—; bd. dirs. Citicorp Bank of Nev.; mem. adv. bd. to Amb. to Bahamas Chic Hect. Bd. dirs. Las Vegas Bd. Realtors, Fedn. Internat. Realtors, Nat. Kidney Found., Assistance League, Cancer Soc., Easter Seals, Econ. Rsch. Bd., Children's Discovery Mus., New Horizons Ctr. for Children with Learning Disabilities, Girl Scouts, Home of the Good Shepard, St. Jude's Ranch for Homeless Children; pres., bd. dirs. Better Bus. Bur.; chmn. Las Vegas Taxi Cab Authority; pres. Citizens for Pvt. Enterprises. Mem. Las Vegas C. of C. (bd. dirs., developer). Republican. Roman Catholic. Office: 2340 Paseo Del Prado Ste D202 Las Vegas NV 89102-4360

PUNNETT, AUDREY FRANCES, clinical psychologist, educator; b. Bremerton, Wash., Oct. 25, 1947; d. Louis and Marjorie Velma (Gibson) P.; m. Harlan E. Ratmeyer, July 30, 1988. AA, Victor Valley Coll., Victorville, Calif., 1967; BS, U. Utah, 1971, MS, 1975; PhD, Calif. Sch. Profl. Psychology, 1981. Diplomate Am. Bd. Med. Psychotherapists; cert. play therapist Assn. for Play Therapy. Psychometrist Washington U., St. Louis, Mo., 1974-75; sch. psychologist St. Louis County Sch. Dist., St. Louis, Mo., 1976-78; psychologist Valley Med. Ctr., Fresno, Calif., 1984-85; coord. pediatric rehab. psychology Fresno (Calif.) Community Hosp., 1981-85; pvt. practice, Fresno, 1981—; clin. psychologist II med. edn. program U. Calif.-San Francisco, Fresno, 1983-84, asst. clin. prof., 1986—; instr. West Hills Coll., Lemoore, Calif., 1983-84; pediat. psychologist Valley Children's Hosp., Fresno, 1985—; cons. Calif. State U., Fresno, 1988, Exceptional Parents Unlimited, Fresno, 1987-88, Dept. Rehab. Counseling, Fresno, 1988-89. Contrb. articles to profl. jours. Bd. dirs. Ctrl. Calif. Lung Assn., Fresno, 1989—, treas., 1990-91, pres.-elect, 1991, pres., 1992-94. Mem. APA, Soc. Pediatric Psychology (western regional conf. chair 1988-90), Calif. Psychol. Assn., San Joaquin Psychol. Assn. (chair 1983), Jr. League Fresno, Leadership Fresno (co-chair class project). Episcopalian. Office: 5151 N Palm Ave Ste 605 Fresno CA 93704-2208

PURAT, JACEK, library director; b. Poznan, Poland, Nov. 8, 1957; came to U.S., 1981; s. Czeskaw and Boleskawa (Wizta) P.; m. Katie Mangotich, May 1, 1986; children: Nemo, Felix, Jan. BA, U. Poznan, 1981. Animal keeper Poznan Zoo, 1980, U. Calif. Amphibian Lab., Berkeley, 1985; exec. dir. Green Libr., Berkeley, 1986—; chmn. of bd. Ecol. Libr., Poznan, 1988—, Green Libr., Inc., Berkeley, 1988—; spl. advisor to minister of environment Min. Environ. Protection, Warsaw, Polan d, 1992; researcher dept. geography Ocean Initiative, U. Calif., Berkeley, 1993. Founder, publisher: Green Libr. Jour., 1991. Pres. N. Calif. div. Polish Am. Congress, San Francisco, 1991-92, chmn. Environ. Commn., Chgo., 1991-92. Recipient scholarship Kosciuszko Found.; named Honorary Citizen Poznan, 1990. Mem. Nature Protection League. Home: 1929 Fairview St Berkeley CA 94703-2718 Office: Green Libr PO Box 11284 Berkeley CA 94701

PURCELL, ALEXANDER HOLMES, entomologist, educator; b. Summit, Miss., Oct. 12, 1942; s. Alexander H. and Dorothy (Adams) P.; m. Rita Hall, Oct. 14, 1946. BS, USAF Acad., 1964; PhD, U. Calif., Davis, 1974. Commd. capt. USAF, 1964, officer, pilot, 1964-70, resigned, 1970; grad. rsch. asst. U. Calif., Davis, 1971-74; prof. entomology U. Calif., Berkeley, 1974—, dept. chair, 1993, head div. entomology and plant and soil microbiology, 1994, head divsn. environ. biology dept. environ. sci., policy and mgmt.; cons. FAO (UN), 1981. Contbr. articles to profl. jours. Mem. AAAS, Entomological Soc. Am., Am. Phytopath. Soc., Soc. Invertebrate Pathology. Office: U Calif Dept Environ Sci and Policy and Mgmt 201 Wellman Hall Berkeley CA 94720-3112

PURCELL, CHARLES KIPPS, lawyer; b. Bellefonte, Pa., Mar. 15, 1959; s. Geoffrey and Alice (Kipps) P. BA, U. Va., 1981; JD, Harvard U., 1984. Bar: N.Mex. 1986, U.S. Dist. Ct. N.Mex. 1986, U.S. Ct. Appeals (D.C. and 10th cirs.) 1986, U.S. Supreme Ct. 1991. Law clk. to Hon. Ruth Bader Ginsburg U.S. Ct. Appeals (D.C.) Cir., Washington, 1984-85; lawyer Rodey, Dickason, Sloan, Akin & Robb, Albuquerque, 1986—. Bd. dirs. Quintessence-Choral Artists of the S.W., Albuquerque, 1990. Home: 1820 Calle Del Vis NW Albuquerque NM 87105-1014 Office: Rodey Dickason et al PO Box 1888 Albuquerque NM 87103-1888

PURCELL, PATRICK B., motion picture company executive; b. Dublin, Ireland, Mar. 16, 1943; s. James P. and Rita (Donohoe) P.; m. Simone Gros-Long, Feb. 1, 1968; children: Alexander J., Christopher P., Benjamin J. Student, Staffordshire Coll. Commerce, 1964-66; M.B.A., Fordham U., 1973. CPA, Calif. Various positions in pub. and pvt. acctg. Eng. and U.S., 1960-70; with Paramount Pictures Corp., N.Y.C., Los Angeles, 1970—, v.p. fin., 1980—83, exec. v.p. fin. and adminstrn., 1983-89, exec. v.p., chief fin. and adminstrv. officer, 1989—. Fellow AICPA, Calif. Soc. CPAs, Chartered Assn. Cert. Accts.; mem. Fin. Execs. Inst., Inst. Taxation. Roman Catholic. Club: Jonathan. Home: 1449 Capri Dr Pacific Palisades CA 90272-2706 Office: Paramount Pictures 5555 Melrose Ave Hollywood CA 90038

PURCELL, ROY EVERETT, artist; b. L.A., June 25, 1936; s. Clifford Loren and Alice Elladean (Mace) P.; m. Florence Kinsey Bunker, Feb. 12, 1959 (div. 1983); children; Cyntea, Rischelle, Ramiel, Loren, Taana, Saronna, Kasyn; m. Beverly Woodruff, Sept. 12, 1992. BA, Utah State U., 1965, postgrad. Dir. Mohave Mus. History and Arts, Kingman, Ariz., 1967-70, So. Nev. Mus., Henderson, 1970-74; artist Las Vegas, 1974—. Prin. works of etchings, watercolors and acrylics, including murals; represented in numerous pvt. and corp. collections including Standard Oil, Dow Chem., many others. Studio: 3433 Losee Rd # 3 North Las Vegas NV 89030-3322

PURCELL, STUART MCLEOD, III, financial planner; b. Santa Monica, Calif., Feb. 16, 1944; s. Stuart McLeod Jr. and Carol (Howe) P. AA, Santa Monica City Coll., 1964; BS, Calif. State U., Northridge, 1967; grad., CPA Advanced Personal Fin. Planning Curriculum, San Francisco, 1985. CPA, Calif.; CFP. Sr. acct. Pannell Kerr Forster, San Francisco, 1970-73; fin. cons. Purcell Fin. Services, San Francisco, 1973-74, San Rafael, Calif., 1980-81; controller Decimus Corp., San Francisco, 1974-76, Grubb & Ellis Co., Oakland, Calif., 1976-78, Marwais Steel Co., Richmond, Calif., 1979-80; owner, fin. counselor Purcell Wealth Mgmt., San Rafael, 1981—; guest lectr. Golden Gate U., San Francisco, 1985—; leader ednl. workshops, Larkspur, Calif., 1984; speaker Commonwealth Club Calif., 1989, 91. Contbr. articles to newspapers and profl. jours. Treas. Salvation Army, San Rafael-San Anselmo-Fairfax, Calif., 1987—; chmn. fin. planners div. United Way Marin County, Calif., 1984; mem. fundraising com. Marin County March of Dimes, 1987—, Marin County Arthritis Found., 1988—; mem. Marin Estate Planning Council. Served to lt. (j.g.) USNR, 1968-76. Named Eagle Scout, 1959, Best Fin. Advisor Marin County Independent-Jour. newspaper, 1987, Top Producer Unimarc, 1986; recipient Outstanding Achievement award United Way, 1984; named to The Registry of Fin. Planning Practitioners, 1987. Mem. AICPA, Calif. Soc. CPAs, Nat. Speakers Assn., Internat. Assn. for Fin. Planners (exec. dir. North Bay chpt., San Francisco 1984), Internat. Soc. Pre-Retired Planners, Soc. CPA-Fin. Planners (dist. membership chmn. San Francisco 1986), Registry Fin. Planning Practitioners, Sigma Alpha Epsilon. Presbyterian. Home: 45 Vineyard Dr San Rafael CA 94901-1228 Office: Purcell Wealth Mgmt 1811 Grand Ave Ste B San Rafael CA 94901-1925

PURDIE, ROBIN STANFORD, retired air force officer; b. Cambridge, Eng., Feb. 14, 1940; came to U.S., 1943; s. Donald and Mary Carol (Brown) P.; m. Marian Zola Abbott, June 24, 1959; children: Scott, Michael, Jeffrey. BA, San Diego State U., 1961; MS, Auburn U., 1973. Commd. 2nd lt. USAF, 1961, advanced through grades to col., retired, 1991; pilot tng. USAF, Williams AFB, 1962; pilot instr., examiner USAF, Travis AFB, Calif., 1962-69, Altus AFB, Okla., 1969-72; pilot EC-47 USAF, Nakhan Phanom, Thailand, 1973-74; from C-5 squadron commdr. to dep. commdr. ops. USAF, Dover AFB, Del., 1979-85; chief pilot military airlift command USAF, Scott AFB, Ill., 1985-89; dep. chief of staff, ops. 22nd Air Force, Travis AFB, Calif., 1989-91. Editor: (textbook) Tongue and Quill, 1976; contbr. articles to profl. jours. Decorated with Legion of Merit with 1 oak leaf cluster, Air medal with 3 oak leaf clusters. Mem. AARP, Air Force Assn., Order of Daedalians (vice flight capt.), Retired Officers' Assn., Airlift Assn.

PURDY, JOSEPH DONALD, small business owner; b. Oklahoma City, May 28, 1942; s. Allen B. and Ruth (Sanders) P.; m. Annelie S. Purdy, Sept. 7, 1969; 1 child, Kimberly. BA, Calif. State U., Berkeley, 1960; MA, Chapman Coll., Orange, Calif., 1965; PhD, U. Okla., 1968. Asst. prof. U. Miss., Oxford, 1969-71; assoc. prof., head dept. Okla. State U., Morman, 1971-75; assoc. supt. Santa Barbara County (Calif.) Schs., 1975-81; chief exec. officer, owner Purdy Enterprises, Santa Maria, Calif., 1981—. Author: Selling, 1990; contbr. articles to profl. jours. Pres. bd. dirs. Santa Maria Symphony Orch., 1986-87. With U.S. Army, 1955-57. Mem. Internat. Reading Assn., Santa Maria Valley Developers (chmn. membership com. 1987-89), Lake Maria Valley Club (pres. 1984-86). Office: PO Box 2802 Santa Maria CA 93457-2802

PURDY, TEDDY GEORGE, JR., programmer, analyst, researcher, consultant; b. Leadville, Colo., May 11, 1954; s. Teddy George and Geneva Ruth P.; m. Karen Ann Puleo, May 28, 1977 (div. Dec. 19, 1983); children: Christopher, Sarah. Student, Colo. U., 1972-75. Free-lance programmer/analyst Boulder, Colo., 1975-84; pres., treas. IBEX Bus. Systems, Leadville, 1984—; Cons. Carlson Promotions, Mpls., 1987-91, Unidata, Inc., Denver, 1992, Household Fin., Chesapeake, Va., 1992—.

PURSEL, HAROLD MAX, SR., mining engineer, civil engineer, architectural engineer.; b. Fruita, Colo., Sept. 15, 1921; s. Harold Maurice and Viola Pearl (Wagner) P.; m. Virginia Anna Brady, May 6, 1950; children: Harold Max, Leo William, Dawn Allen, Helen Virginia, Viola Ruth. BS in Civil Engring., U. Wyo., 1950. Asst. univ. architect U. Wyo., 1948-50; with Sharrock & Pursel, Contractors, 1951-55; owner Max Pursel, Earthwork Constrn., 1955-59; project engr. Farson (Wyo.) Irrigation Project, 1960-61; owner Wyo. Builders Service, Casper, 1962-66; head dept. home improvement Gamble Stores, Rawlins, Wyo., 1967; resident work instr. Casper (Wyo.) Job Corps Conservation Center, 1968; P.M. coordinator Lucky Mc Uranium Mine, Riverton, Wyo., 1969-80; constrn. insp. U.S. Bur. Reclamation, 1983—; cons. freelance heavy and light constrn., 1984—. Served with U.S. Army, 1942-45. Mem. Nat. Rifle Assn., Internat. Platform Assn., Mensa. Lodges: Eagles, Masons, Shriners. Exptl. research with log, timber and frame constrn. in conjunction with residential applications.; expanded experimental research to develop methods to up-date and modernize early area residences while retaining period styles, materials and general construction methods. Home: PO Box 572 Riverton WY 82501-0572

PURSELL, PAUL DENNIS, rehabilitation director; b. Altadena, Calif., Jan. 26, 1950; s. Robert Ralph and Thelma (Winifred) P. BS, Calif. State U., 1972. Registered phys. therapist. Asst. athletic trainer Orange County Ramblers Football, Inc., Anaheim, Calif., 1968, Calif. State U., Long Beach, 1968-71; athletic trainer U.S. Olympic Track & Field Tng. Camp, San Diego, 1971; phys. therapy aide Fountain Valley (Calif.) Community Hosp., 1971-72; chief phys. therapy Tustin (Calif.) Community Hosp., 1972-78; disaster planning coord. St. Joseph Hosp., Orange, Calif., 1984-90, dir. human devel., 1987-91, dir. phys. rehab. svcs., 1978—; instr. Calif. State U., Long Beach, 1989—; pres. Calif. Phys. Therapy Fund, Inc., Sacramento, 1983-84; chmn. bd. Orange County/Long Beach Health Edn. Ctr., 1984-85, Health Assocs. Fed. Credit Union, 1985-86. Chmn. Calif. Allied Health Coalition, Sacramento, 1983-84; speaker of assembly Orange County (Calif.) Health Planning Coun., 1986-87; trustee Gail Pattison Youth Leadership Trust, Orange, 1990-91; mem. mgmt. audit com., City of Orange, 1991—, ad hoc fin. com., 1993; chmn. bd. Leadership Orange, 1992-94; mem. Orange Citizen of Yr. Selection Com., 1988-89; pres. adv. coun. phys. therapy Calif. State U., Long Beach, chmn. 1987—. Recipient Commendation for Volutneerism, Carnation Found., 1984. Mem. Am. Coll. Sports Medicine, Am. Phys. Therapy Assn. (pres. Calif. chpt. 1983-84, Outstanding Svc. award 1980, 84), Nat. Fire Protection Assn., Orange County/Long Beach Health Consortium (chmn. bd. 1984-85), Orange C. of C. (pres. 1990-91),. Democrat. Roman Catholic. Office: St Joseph Hosp 1310 W Stewart Dr Ste 203 Orange CA 92667

PURSGLOVE, BETTY MERLE, small business owner, technical writer; b. Pitts., Sept. 15, 1923; d. Earle E. and Merle A. (Smith) Baer; m. Larry A. Pursglove, June 30, 1944; children: Diana, Kathleen, Merry, Tanya, Yvonne. BS in Physics, U. Pitts., 1944; postgrad., Carnegie-Mellon U., 1947-49, W. Va. U., 1949-51, Mich. State U., 1968-69. Micro-pilot plant operator Minn. Mining and Mfg., St. Paul, 1944-46; cons. rsch. chemist Food Mach Co., Pitts., 1947-49; computer coder Dow Chem. Co., Midland, Minn., 1954; asst. entomologist pvt. collections, Midland, 1955-56; instr. chemistry Cen. Mich. U., Midland, 1958; head chem. dept. Midland Hosp., 1958-64; tchr. chemistry and physics parochial schs., Bay City, Mich., 1964; prin., chief exec. officer Crypticlear, Inc., Applegate, Oreg., 1965—. Leader Midland troup Girl Scout U.S., 1953-63. Mem. Sigma Xi, Sigma Pi Sigma. Home and Office: PO Box 3125 Applegate OR 97530-3125

PURVIS, JOHN ANDERSON, lawyer; b. Greeley, Colo., Aug. 31, 1942; s. Virgil J. and Emma Lou (Anderson) P.; m. Charlotte Johnson, Apr. 3, 1976; 1 child, Whitney; children by previous marriage: Jennifer, Matt. B.A. cum laude, Harvard U., 1965; J.D., U. Colo., 1968. Bar: Colo. 1968, U.S. Dist. Ct. Colo. 1968, U.S. Ct. Appeals (10th cir.) 1978, U.S. Ct. Claims, 1980. Dep. dist. atty. Boulder, Colo., 1968-69; asst. dir. and dir. legal aid U. Colo. Sch. Law, 1969; assoc. Williams, Taussig & Trine, Boulder, 1969; head Boulder office Colo. Pub. Defender System, 1970-72; assoc. and ptnr. Hutchinson, Black, Hill, Buchanan & Cook, Boulder, 1972-85; ptnr. Purvis, Gray, Schuetze and Gordon, 1985—; acting Colo. State Pub. Defender, 1978; adj. prof. law U. Colo., 1981, 84-88, 94, others; lectr. in field. Chmn., Colo. Pub. Defender Commn., 1979-89; mem. nominating commn. Colo. Supreme Ct., 1984-90; mem. com. on conduct U.S. Dist. Ct., 1993—; chmn. Boulder County Criminal Justice Com., 1975-81, Boulder County Manpower Coun., 1977-78. Recipient Ames award Harvard U., 1964; Outstanding Young Lawyer award Colo. Bar Assn., 1978. Mem. Internat. Soc. Barristers, Am. Coll. of Trial Lawyers, Colo. Bar Assn. (chair litigation sect. 1994-95), Boulder County Bar Assn., Colo. Trial Lawyers Assn., Am. Trial Lawyers Assn., Trial Lawyers for Pub. Justice. Democrat. Address: 1050 Walnut St Ste 501 Boulder CO 80302-5144

PURVIS, RANDALL W. B., lawyer; b. Summit, N.J., Mar. 2, 1957; s. Merton B. and Marjory L. (Baker) P.; m. Robin Head Intemann Purvis; children: Zachary, Timothy, Andrew. BS, Ohio State U., 1979; JD, Georgetown U., 1982. Bar: Colo. 1983, U.S. Dist. Ct. Colo. 1983, U.S. Ct. Appeals (10th cir.) 1983. Pvt. practice Colorado Springs, Colo., 1983—; bd. dirs. Nova Resources Corp., Dallas, 1985-88. Councilman Colorado Springs City Coun., 1987—, re-elected 1991, 95; mem. steering com. Nat. League of Cities, Washington; elder 1st Presbyn. Ch., Colorado Springs, 1987-91; bd. trustees Meml. Hosp. Colorado Springs, 1991—. Mem. Colo. Bar Assn., El Paso County Bar Assn. (com. chmn. 1986), Colorado Springs C. of C. (com. chmn. 1986), Colorado Springs Bridge Club, Phi Beta Kappa. Republican. Office: 13 S Tejon Ste 201 Colorado Springs CO 80903-1520

PUTMAN, ROBERT DEAN, golf course architect; b. Wallace, Idaho, Dec. 18, 1924; m. Sally Harmon, 1945; 3 children. Grad., Fresno State Coll. Art dir. Sta. KJEO-TV, Fresno, Calif. Prin. works include Arvin Mcpl. Golf Course, Wasco, Calif., Madera (Calif.) Mcpl. Golf Course, Rancho Canada Golf Course, Carmel Valley, Calif., La Manga Golf Couse, Costa Blanca, Spain, Monterey (Calif.) Country Club Shore Course, San Joaquin Country Club, Fresno, Visalia (Calif.) Mcpl. Golf Course, River Island Golf Course, Poterville, Calif., Kings River Country Club, Kingsburg, Calif. Office: Robert Dean Putman GCA 5644 N Briarwood Ave Fresno CA 93711-2501

PUTNAM, J. O., construction executive; b. 1951. MBA, U. Alta., Can., 1975. With PCL Constrn. Group Inc., Edmonton, Alta., Can., 1975-86; v.p. PCL Constrn. Svcs., Denver, 1986—. Office: PCL Construction Svcs 2000 S Cook St Ste 400 Denver CO 80210*

PUTNAM, TODD HOFF, consumer activist; b. Sioux Falls, S.D., Apr. 15, 1963; s. Charles De Grange and Alethea Nadine (Hoff) P. Founder, pres. Nat. Boycott News, Seattle, 1984—, Inst. for Consumer Responsibility, Seattle, 1989—; leading boycott expert, 1987—. Home: 3618 Wallingford Ave N Seattle WA 98103-8242 Office: Inst Consumer Responsibility 6506 28th Ave NE Seattle WA 98115

PUTNEY, MARY ENGLER, federal auditor; b. Overland, Mo., May 1, 1933; d. Bernard J. and Marie (Kunkler) Engler; children: Glennon (dec.), Pat Michael, Michelle. Student Fontbonne Coll., 1951-52; AA, Sacramento City Coll., 1975; BS in Bus., Calif. State U., 1981; CPA, Calif. From asst. to acct. Mo. Rsch. Labs., Inc., St. Louis, 1953-55, adminstrv. asst., 1955-60; sec. western region fin. office Gen. Electric Co., St. Louis, 1960-62; sec. Crocker Nat. Bank, Sacramento, 1962-72 ; student tchr. Sacramento County Dept. Edn., 1979-81; acctg. technician East Yolo Community Services Dist., 1983; mgmt. specialist USAF Logistics Command, 1984; staff auditor Office Insp. Gen., U.S. Dept. Transp., 1984-92; staff auditor Adminstrn. for Children and Families U.S. Dept Health and Human Svcs., 1992—. Mem. Sacramento Community Commn. for Women, 1978-81, bd. dirs., 1980—; mem. planning bd. Golden Empire Health Systems Agy. Mem. AARP (tax counselor for the elderly), AAUW (fin. officer 1983—), AICPA, Nat. Assn. Accts. (dir., newsletter editor), Fontbonne Coll. Alumni Assn., Calif. State Alumni Assn., Assn. Govt. Accts. (chpt. officer), Calif. Soc. CPAs, German Geneological Soc. (bd. dirs. 1990—, publicity dir. 1994—), Rio Del Oro Racquet Club, Beta Gamma Sigma, Beta Alpha Psi. Roman Catholic. Home: 2616 Point Reyes Way Sacramento CA 95826-2416 Office: US Dept Health & Human Svcs ACF/OCSE Div of Audits 2989 Fulton Ave Sacramento CA 95821-4909

PUTTERMAN, WILLIAM ZEV, foundation executive, television producer; b. Bronx, N.Y., Nov. 6, 1928; s. David Joseph and Amy Belle (Racoosin) P.; m. Anita Ruth Woien, Mar. 3, 1964 (div. 1971); children: Rachel Amy, Naomi Leah; m. Mary Elizabeth Kudlacik, Nov. 18, 1984. Student Colgate U., 1946-47; BA with honors in Philosophy, Syracuse U., 1949. Stage mgr. on Broadway, 1958; dir. Off-Broadway, 1960-61; with Synnanon found., 1962-64; prodr. Sta. KGO-TV, ABC, San Francisco, 1964-66; exec. prodr. Sta. KTTV, Metromedia, 1967-68; program cons. Sta. KABC-TV, ABC, L.A., 1969; dir. program devel. Metromedia TV, Inc., L.A., 1969-70; dir. nat. programs Sta. KQED, PBS, San Francisco, 1970-79; dir. comm. Werner Erhard and Assocs., San Francisco, 1980-83; v.p. program devel. Furia/Oringer Prodns., Inc., Sherman Oaks, Calif., 1984-86; supervising prodr. The Landsburg Co., L.A., 1986-88; pres. Zev Putterman Prodns., Tucson, 1989—; exec. dir. Amity Found., Tucson, 1991—; prodr. Alan Landsburg Prodns., L.A., 1972; vis. lectr. Calif. State U., Northridge, 1966; instr. U. Calif. Ext., Berkeley, 1972; lectr. Berkeley Film Inst., 1977, 79; mem. Norman Corwin student documentary program adv. bd. U. So. Calif., 1989—; U.S. del. Internat. Pub. TV Screening Conf., Milan, 1978. Prodr. On Location, Am. Broadcasting System, 1972, The Boarding House, PBS, 1975, Leukemia Soc.'s Televent '90, Nat. Leukemia Broadcast Coun., L.A., 1990; supervising prodr. Photoplay, 1986, 87; exec. prodr. Internat. Animation Festival, 1976, World Press, 1975-77, Music from Aspen/MoreMusic from Aspen spls., 1977, People vs. Inez Garcia, 1977, Turnabout, 1978, Transport of Delight, 1978, Black Filmmakers Hall of Fame spls., 1977, 78, Inside the Cuckoo's Nest, 1978; numerous others. Bd. dirs. Found. for Mideast Comm., 1985—, The Holiday Project, 1983-88, Am. Jewish Congress, 1985—, Marin Cmty. Workshop, 1977-78; mem. adv. coun. New Israel Fund, 1986—; bd. dirs. Chabad of No. Calif., 1975-84, chmn., 1984. Recipient Golden Eagle award for Vasectomy, Coun. for Internat. Non-Theatrical Events, 1973, for Private Lives of Americans, 1974, The Place for No Story, 1975, 13 Emmy awards, DuPont-Columbia award for 1985, 1970. Mem. NATAS, Nat. Assn. TV Program Execs., Nat. Assn. Fund Raising Execs., Internat. Documentary Assn., Theta Beta Phi. Democrat. Jewish. Office: Amity Inc 10621 E Northern Crest Dr Tucson AZ 85748

PYBRUM, STEVEN MARK, tax specialist, accountant; b. Santa Cruz, Calif., Mar. 12, 1951; m. Belinda J. Pybrum, Sept. 18, 1987. BS, Calif. Poly. U., 1973; MBA, Golden Gate U., 1988. CPA, Calif. Cost acct. William Wrigley Co., Santa Cruz, 1973-75; tax acct. Ackerman Stranuhal and Co. CPAs, Santa Cruz, 1975-77; prin., mgmt. cons. Pybrum and Co., Santa Barbara, Calif., 1979—. Nat. speaker Tax Tips radio program, 1980; contbr. articles to mags., newspapers. Mem. Calif. Soc. CPAs, Elks, C. of C. Office: Pybrum and Co PO Box 23209 Santa Barbara CA 93121-3209

PYE, DAVID THOMAS, computer technology company executive; b. Darby, Pa., June 12, 1942; s. David and Grace Marie (Dale) P. BS, Widener U., 1964. CPA, Pa., Calif. Tax cons. Price Waterhouse & Co., Phila., 1964-70; dir. taxes Am. Instl. Devel., Inc., Phila., 1970-75; dir. tax adminstrn. Syntex Corp., Palo Alto, Calif., 1975-93; group tax mgr. Logitech Inc., Fremont, Calif., 1995—. Mem. AICPAs, Calif. CPA Soc., Pa. Inst. CPAs, Tax Execs. Inst. Home: 201 S 4th St Ste 704 San Jose CA 95112 Office: Logitech Inc 6505 Kalser Dr Fremont CA 94555

PYLE, WALTER ROBERT, mechanical engineer, consultant; b. Orange, Calif., Sept. 10, 1944; s. Larry Thomas and Muriel Dorothy (Korb) P. BSME and Elec. Engring., Calif. Polytech. Inst., 1966. Rsch. engr. Chevron Rsch. Co., Richmond, Calif., 1966-86, sr. rsch. engr., 1986-88, engring. assoc., 1988-90, sr. engring. assoc., 1990-92; staff engr. Chevron Chem. Co., Richmond, Calif., 1992—; cons. Shadowbox Constrn. Co., Richmond, Calif., 1979—, Ebonex Techs., Inc., Emeryville, Calif., 1986-89, Electrochlor Co., San Anselmo, Calif., 1984-86; Nat. Renewable Energy Lab., 1994—; bd. dirs. H-Ion Solar Co., Richmond. Inventor gasoline nozzles, photoseparatory nozzle, 1983. Supporter Calif. Polytech. Alumni Found., San Luis Obispo, 1966—; trustee UHF Engring. Soc., San Pablo, Calif., 1976—. Mem. Am. Ceramic Soc., Am. Solar Energy Soc., Nat. Hydrogen Energy Assn., Am. Hydrogen Assn., Soc. Automotive Engrs., Internat. Hydrogen Energy Assn. Mormon and Buddhist. Office: Chevron Chem Co OTG 100 Chevron Way Richmond CA 94801-2016

PYPER, JAMES WILLIAM, chemist; b. Wells, Nev., Sept. 5, 1934; s. William Jones and Wilma (Bjelke) P.; m. Phyllis Diane Henry, Aug. 30, 1957; children: Scott, Mark, Gregory, Heather, Melanie, Tara, Tammy, Wendy, Michael, Tanya, David. BS, Brigham Young U., 1958, MS, 1960; PhD, Cornell U., 1964. Ordained bishop Ch. Jesus Christ of Latter-day Saints, 1973. Research chemist Lawrence Livermore (Calif.) Nat. Lab., 1963-84, mass spectrometry group leader, 1973-75, tritium tech. group leader, 1977-78, applied phys. chemistry group leader, 1979-80, sect. leader for analytical chemistry, 1980-83, dep. sect. leader for analytical chemistry, 1983-87, assoc. div. leader condensed matter and analytical scis. div., 1987-89, quality assurance mgr., 1989-90, ret., 1990. Contbr. articles to sci. jours. Presided over local congrs., 1973-75, 87-91, 91-93; mem. stake high coun., 1976-87; missionary Ch. of Jesus Christ of Latter Saints, Thessaloniki, Greece, 1991-93, Scotland and Eng., 1994—. Republican.

PYUN, MATTHEW SUNG KWAN, lawyer; b. Honolulu, Mar. 21, 1937; s. Matthew S.K. and Elsie S.O. (Chee) P.; m. Mary Ann Kagawa, Feb. 26, 1959; children: Leslie S.H. Anne K. BBA, U. Hawaii, 1959; LLB, Drake U., 1963. Bar: Hawaii 1964, U.S. Ct. Appeals (9th cir.) 1964. Law clk., bailiff U.S. Dist. Ct. Hawaii, 1964; dep. corp. counsel City and County of Honolulu, 1965; atty. Legal Aid Soc. Hawaii, 1965-68; sole practice, Honolulu, 1968—; judge Hon. Dist. Ct. Ct. 1st Cir., 1981-84; mem. Rep. Nat. Com. With USAF, 1960-61. Mem. ABA, Assn. Trial Lawyers Am., Am. Judicature Soc., Honolulu Club, Phi Alpha Delta, Phi Kappa Pi. Episcopalian. Office: 615 Piikoi St Ste 1601 Honolulu HI 96814-3142

QIN, YULIN, cognitive neuropsychologist; b. Zhenjian, Jiansu, China, Jan. 19, 1947; came to U.S., 1985; s. Heng-Wan Qin and Jin-Yu Cai; m. Jie Wang, Jan. 20, 1979; 1 child, Julia. BE, Nanjing (China) Aero. Inst., 1968; ME, Bejing U. Aero. & Astro., 1982; MS, Carnegie Mellon U., 1990, PhD, 1992. Aircraft designer Chensdu Aircraft Mfg. Co., Sichuan, China, 1968-73; quality control engr. China Aviation Inst. Standardization, Beijing, 1974-79; lectr. Beijing U. Aero. & Astro., 1982-85; computer software engr. Syscorp Internal Co., Austin, Tex., 1986-87; teaching asst. Carnegie Mellon U., Pitts., 1990; postdoctoral rsch. assoc. U. Ariz., Tucson, 1992—. Author: Statistical Pattern Recognition, 1983; co-author: The Foundation of Total Quality Control, 1981. Carnegie Mellon U. scholar and fellow, 1987-92. Mem. AAAS, APS, Soc. Neurosci., Cognitive Sci. Soc. Home: 3660 E 3d St # D20 Tucson AZ 85716 Office: U Ariz 384 Life Scis N Bldg Tucson AZ 95724

QUACKENBUSH, JUSTIN LOWE, chief federal judge; b. Spokane, Wash., Oct. 3, 1929; s. Carl Clifford and Marian Huldah (Lowe) Q.; m. Marie McAtee; children: Karl Justin, Kathleen Marie, Robert Craig. BA, U. Idaho, 1951; LLB, Gonzaga U., Spokane, 1957. Bar: Wash. 1957. Dep. pros. atty. Spokane County, 1957-59; ptnr. Quackenbush, Dean, Bailey & Henderson, Spokane, 1959-80; dist. judge U.S. Dist. Ct. (ea. dist.) Wash., Spokane, 1980—, now chief judge; part-time instr. Gonzaga U. Law Sch., 1960-67. Chmn. Spokane County Planning Commn., 1969-73. Served with USN, 1951-54. Mem. ABA, Wash. Bar Assn., Spokane County Bar Assn. (trustee 1976-78), Internat. Footprint Assn. (nat. pres. 1967), Spokane C. of C. (trustee, exec. com. 1978-79). Episcopalian. Club: Spokane Country. Lodge: Shriners. Office: US Dist Ct PO Box 1432 Spokane WA 99210-1432

QUALLEY, CHARLES ALBERT, fine arts educator; b. Creston, Iowa, Mar. 19, 1930; s. Albert Olaf and Cleora (Dietrick) Q.; m. Betty Jean Griffith, Nov. 26, 1954; children: Janet Lynn, John Stuart. B.F.A., Drake U., 1952; M.A., U. Iowa, 1956, M.F.A., 1958; Ed.D., Ill. State U., 1967. Art tchr. Des Moines Pub. Schs., 1952,, 54-55; critic art tchr. U. Iowa, 1955-57; prof. fine arts U. Colo., Boulder, 1958-90, prof. emeritus, 1990—; chmn. dept. fine arts U. Colo., 1968-71, assoc. chmn., 1981-82; vis. prof. Inst. for Shipboard Edn., semester at sea, 1979, Ill. State U., 1985. Author: Safety in the Art Room, 1986; contbg. editor Sch. Arts, 1978-85, mem. editorial adv. bd., 1985-87; author column Safetypoint, 1981-85. Served with AUS, 1952-54, Korea. Mem. Nat. Art Edn. Assn. (v.p. 1980-82, pres. 1987-89, dir. conv. svcs. 1990—, fellow 1990—, art educator of yr. 1993), Nat. Art Edn. Found. (trustee 1987—), Colo. Art Edn. Assn. (editor 1965-67, 75, pres. 1976-78), Delta Phi Delta, Omicron Delta Kappa, Pi Kappa Delta. Home: 409 Fillmore Ct Louisville CO 80027-2273

QUALLS, CORETHIA, archaeologist; b. Sparta, Tenn., Jan. 17, 1948; d. Malcolm Talmadge and Lucille (Jackson) Qualls. BA, Marlboro Coll., 1970; MPhil, Columbia U., 1980, PhD, 1981. Exec. curator Mus. of Archaeology of Staten Island, 1981; asst. prof. St. John's U., S.I., 1981-82; cons. curator Queens Mus., N.Y., 1982-83; cons. curator Kuwait Nat. Mus., 1984-86; curatorial advisor for archaeology, Bahrain Nat. Mus., 1987-90; assoc. chief archaeologist Mt. Carmel Project, 1990-92; instr. Diocese of Salt Lake City, 1994—, Editor-in-chief Datum Point Books, 1995—; archaeologist Columbia U., 1970-74, NYU Inst. Fine Arts, 1972-73, 84, Johns Hopkins U., 1974, Fulbright prof. archaeology, 1985-86. Dir. excavations Hamad Town, Bahrain, 1985-86. Editor: Seals of the Marcopoli Collection, vol. 1, 1984; contbr. articles to profl. jours. Columbia U. fellow, 1970-74; Am. Schs. Oriental Rsch. fellow, 1973-74. Mem. Am. Inst. Archaeology, Am. Oriental Soc., Am. Schs. Oriental Rsch., Inst. Nautical Archaeology, Brit. Sch. Archaeol. in Iraq, Oriental Club of N.Y.C., Egypt Exploration Soc., Am. Soc. Profl. and Exec. Women, Nat. Assn. Bus. and Profl. Women, NAFE. Roman Catholic.

QUERSHEY, SAFI U., computer company executive; b. 1951. BS in Engring., U. Tex., 1975. Test specialist A M Internat., 1975-77; engr. Computer Automation Corp., Irvine, Calif., 1977-78, Telefile Computer Corp., Irvine, 1978-79; chmn bd., CEO AST Research%, 1979—. Office: AST Research Inc 16215 Alton Pkwy Irvine CA 92718

QUESNEL, GREGORY L., transportation company executive; b. Woodburn, Oreg., May 24, 1948. Sr. v.p., CFO Consol. Freightways, Inc., Palo Alto, Calif., 1991—.

QUEVEDO, SYLVESTRE GRADO, nephrologist; b. L.A., Jan. 4, 1949; married; 3 children. AB in Biology with honors, U. Calif., Berkeley, 1971; MD, Harvard U., 1975, MPH, 1975. Diplomate Am. Bd. Internal Medicine, Nat. Bd. Med. Examiners; lic. MD, Calif. Intern in family and cmty. medicine U. Ariz. Sch. of Medicine and Affiliated Hosps., Tucson, 1975-76; med. dir., staff physician Pueblo (Colo.) Neighborhood Health Ctrs., Inc., 1976-80; pvt. cons. Health Svcs. Devel., 1980-83; asst. resident physician dept. medicine Santa Clara Valley Med. Ctr., San Jose, Calif., 1983-85, attending physician dept. medicine, 1989—; fellow divsn. nephrology Stanford (Calif.) U. Med. Ctr., 1985-88, clin. asst. prof. medicine divsn. nephrology, 1989—, consulting nephrologist, 1989—; med. dir. Artificial Kidney Ctr. Santa Clara Valley Med. Ctr., San Jose, 1991-94; bd. trustees Am. Kidney Fund; bd. dirs. Transpacific Renal Network; instr. dept. polit. sci. U. Colo., Denver, 1976-77; clin. instr. dept. preventive medicine U. Colo., 1976-80; mem. med. staff Parkview Hosp., Pueblo, 1979-80, St. Mary Corwin Hosp., Pueblo, 1979-80; assoc. mem. med. staff San Jose (Calif.) Hosp. and Health Ctr., 1981-84; staff physician med. clinics Santa Clara Valley Med. Ctr., 1985-87; attending nephrologist Santa Teresa Hosp. and

Med. Ctr., San Jose, 1988-89. Contbr. chpt. to Handbook of Difficult Diagnosis, 1990 and articles to Am. Kidney Fund Nephrology Letter, Nephrology News and Issues and others. Mem. adv. and admissions com. Harvard U. Health Careers Summer Program, Cambridge, Mass., 1971-74; participant Nat. Conf. on Health Manpower, Howard U., Washington, 1973; mem. com. of admissions Harvard Med. Sch., Boston, 1974-75; physician Clinic of the Traditional Indian Alliance, Tucson, 1975-76; mem. bd. dirs. Calif. Dialysis Coun., Sacramento, 1992; mem. med. rev. bd. Transpacific Renal Network, Sausalito, Calif., 1992. Mem. AAAS, ACP (chmn. health and pub. policy com., mem. membership and awards com.), Coun. on Kidney in Cardiovascular Disease, Am. Pub. Health Assn., Soc. for Gen. Internal Medicine (task force on social responsibility), N.Y. Acad. Sci. Home: Sylvestre Grado Quevedo MD 330 Quinnhill Ave Los Altos CA 94024 Office: 751 S Bascom Ave San Jose CA 95128-2604

QUICK, JOHN ANTONY, film and video producer; b. Avonwick, Devon, U.K., Jan. 28, 1941; came to U.S., 1962; s. Ken and Mary Stephanie (Weeks) Q.; m. Barbara Tritel, Aug. 1, 1988; 1 child, Julian Antony. BA in Motion Pictures with honors, UCLA, 1966. Freelance cameraman and editor, 1966—; prodr., dir., photographer and editor U. Calif., Berkeley, 1967—; film cameraman and editor KQED TV, San Francisco, 1970-72. Prodr. films including: Don't Tell Me, I'll Find Out! (CINE Golden Eagle award), What Would Happen If...? (CINE Golden Eagle award), Discover: The LHS Approach (CINE Golden Eagle award), Natural Rubber Bearings for Earthquake Protection (Creative Excellence award U.S. Indsl. Film Festival); co-photographer and editor: Let's Speak English! (Gold Award for Excellence in Promotions, Nat. U. Continuing Edn. Assn.). Office: PO Box 2416 Berkeley CA 94702-0416

QUICK, WILLIAM THOMAS, author, consultant; b. Muncie, Ind., May 30, 1946; s. Clifford Willett and Della May (Ellis) Q. Student, Ind. U., 1964-66. Pres. Iceberg Prodns., San Francisco, 1986—. Author: Dreams of Flesh and Sand, 1988, Dreams of Gods and Men, 1989, Yesterday's Pawn, 1989, Systems, 1989, Singularities, 1990; (as Quentin Thomas) Chains of Light, 1992; (as Margaret Allan) The Mammoth Stone, 1993, Keeper of the Stone, 1994, The Last Mammoth, 1995. Mem. Sci. Fiction and Fantasy Writers Am., The Authors Guild. Home and Office: 1558 Leavenworth St San Francisco CA 94109-3220

QUIGLEY, JOHN MICHAEL, economist, educator; b. N.Y.C., Feb. 12, 1942. B.S. with distinction, U.S. Air Force Acad., 1964; M.Sc. with honors, U. Stockholm, Sweden, 1965; A.M., Harvard U., 1971, Ph.D., 1972. Commd. 2d lt. USAF, 1964, advanced through grades to capt., 1968; asst. prof. econs. Yale U., 1972-74, assoc. prof., 1974-81; prof. pub. policy U. Calif., Berkeley, 1979—, prof. econs., 1981—, chmn, dept. econs., 1992—; vis. prof. econs. and stats. U. Gothenberg, 1978; cons. numerous govt. agys. and pvt. firms; econometrician Hdqrs. U.S. Air Force, Pentagon, 1965-68; research assoc. Nat. Bur. Econ. Research, N.Y.C., 1968-78; mem. com. on nat. urban policy Nat. Acad. Sci., 1985—. Author, editor, contbr. articles to profl. jours.; editor in chief Reg. Sci. and Urban Econs., 1987—; mem. editorial bd. Land Econs., 1974-81, Jour. Urban Econs., 1978—, Coun. on Pub. Policy and Mgmt., 1979—, AREUEA Jour., 1985—, Property Tax Jour., 1990—, Jour. Housing Econs., 1990—. Fulbright scholar, 1964-65; fellow NSF, 1968-69, Woodrow Wilson, 1968-71, Harvard IBM, 1969-71, NDEA, 1969-71, Thord-Gray Am. Scandinavian Found. 1971-72, Social Sci. Research Council, 1971-72. Mem. Am. Econ. Assn., Econometric Soc., Regional Sci. Assn. (bd. dirs. 1986—), Nat. Tax Assn., Assn. for Pub. Policy and Mgmt. (bd. dirs. 1986-89, v.p. 1987-89), AREUEA (bd. dirs. 1987—, v.p. 1995—). Home: 875 Hilldale Ave Berkeley CA 94708-1319 Office: U Calif 2607 Hearst Ave Berkeley CA 94709-1005

QUIGLEY, PHILIP J., telecommunications industry executive; b. 1943. With Advanced Mobile Phone Svc. Inc., 1982-84, v.p., gen. mgr., Pacific region; with Pac Tel Mobile Access, 1984-86, pres., chief exec. officer; with Pac Tel Personal Communications, 1986-87, pres., chief exec. officer; exec. v.p., chief oper. officer Pac Tel Corp., 1987; with Pacific Bell, San Francisco, 1987—; now chmn., pres., chief exec. officer Pacific Bell Group, Pacific Telesis, San Francisco. Office: Pacific Bell 140 New Montgomery St San Francisco CA 94105-3705*

QUIGLEY, RICHARD LAWRENCE, artist, educator; b. Spokane, Wash., June 13, 1951; s. Richard Eldrid and Barbara June (Frisk) Q.; m. Sandra Lee White, Aug. 26, 1972; children: Shasta Dawn, Sean Richard. AA, Lower Columbia Coll., 1970-72; BA, Western Washington Coll., 1974; BFA, Cornish Art Inst., 1976. Instr. oil and watercolor painting Dept. Parks and Recreation, City of Eugene, Oreg., 1976-77; instr. oil and acrylic painting, watercolor, multimedia, drawing, life drawing and graphics Lane C.C., Eugene, 1976—; instr. oil painting and drawing Maude I. Kerns Art Ctr., Eugene, 1977, dept. head painting and drawing, instr. oil, acrylic, watercolor and life drawing, 1978-79; juror and lectr. in field, art inst., lectr. One-person shows include Maude I. Kearns Art Ctr., Eugene, 1977, Lane C.C., Eugene, 1979, High Street Cafe Gallery, Eugene, 1980, U. Oreg., Eugene, 1986, Argus Fine Arts Gallery, Eugene, 1988, Hanson Howard Gallery, Ashland, Oreg., 1988, Jacobs Gallery, Eugene, 1990, Excelsior Gallery, Eugene, 1991, Maryhill Mus. Art, Goldendale, Wash., 1992, Artworks Gallery, Florence, Oreg., 1993, Alder Gallery, Eugene, 1994, others; selected group shows include Emily Thorpe Gallery, Sisters, Oreg., 1984, Oceanside Gallery, Lincoln City, Oreg., 1985, Green Earth Gallery, Eugene, 1986, Argus Gallery, Eugene, 1987-90, Vistra Gallery, Eugene, 1987, Whitebird Gallery, Cannon Beach, Oreg., 1988-89, Graystone Gallery, Portland, Oreg., 1989, Alder Gallery, 1991, 93, Augen Gallery, 1992, Artworks Gallery, Bandon, Oreg., 1994, Mindpower Gallery, Reedsport, Oreg., 1995, others; numerous juried shows; permanent collection Maryhill Mus., Goldendale, Wash. Mem. Watercolor Soc. Oreg., Colorpencil Soc. Am.

QUIGLEY, RUTH HELEN, entrepreneur; b. Hutchinson, Kans., Feb. 4, 1935; d. John Baird and Zelda (Marks) Q. BA, Smith Coll., 1953; MBA, Stanford U., 1956. Investment analyst Wells Fargo Bank, San Francisco, 1956-59, De Vegh & Co., N.Y.C., 1960-62, Ralph E. Samuels & Co., N.Y.C., 1962-64; v.p. Mitchell, Hutchins, San Francisco, 1964-67, Irving Lundborg & Co., San Francisco, 1967-70; pres. Quigley, Friedlander & Co., San Francisco, 1983-86, Joan Quigley Astrology Products (formerly Joan Quigley Enterprises), San Francisco, 1988—; Bd. dirs. GT Global Growth Funds, San Francisco. Mem. San Francisco Rep. Finance Com., 1974—; bd. dirs. ARCS Found., Inc., No. Calif. Chpt., 1976—. Mem. San Francisco Security Analysts Soc. Home: 1055 California St San Francisco CA 94108-2214

QUILLEN, EDWARD KENNETH, III, freelance writer, columnist; b. Greeley, Colo., Nov. 12, 1950; s. Edward Kenneth II and Dorothy May (Wollen) Q.; m. Martha Alice Patterson, June 26, 1969; children: Columbine Kay, Abigail Cynara. Student, U. No. Colo., 1968-74. Reporter Longmont (Colo.) Scene, 1972; editor Middle Park Times, Kremmling, Colo., 1974-77, Summit County Jour., Breckenridge, Colo., 1977-78; mng. editor Mountain Mail, Salida, Colo., 1978-83; freelance writer, Salida, 1983—; columnist Denver Post, 1986—. Author: The White Stuff, 1985, 11 westerns under pseudonym; editor Colo. Cen. Mag., 1994—; contbr. numerous articles to mags. Recipient award for best personal column Colo. Press Assn., 1983, 88. Democrat. Office: PO Box 548 Salida CO 81201-0548

QUINLAN, JAMES JOSEPH, mining geologist, consultant; b. Wallace, Idaho, Oct. 16, 1924; s. James Ernest and Clara (Carson) Q.; m. Patricia Luann Ziegler, Nov. 29, 1952; children: James P., Claudia, Timothy, Daniel, Michael, Bradley, Robert, Sean. BS in Mining, U. Wash., 1945, postgrad., 1946-47. Mine geologist Sunshine Mining Co., Kellogg, Idaho, 1947-51; geologist U.S. Geol. Survey, Spokane, 1951-57; exploration geologist Hecla Mining Co., Spokane, Tucson and Salt Lake City, 1957-69; chief geologist, chief mine engr. Lakeshore Project Hecla Mining Co., Casa Grande, Ariz., 1969-74; project mgr. Red Mountain Project Kerr-McGee Corp., Patagonia, Ariz., 1974-78; sr. staff geologist Kerr-McGee Corp., Oklahoma City, 1978-86; cons. geologist J.J. Quinlan and Sons, Norman, Okla. and Tucson, 1986—; co-chair ad hoc task force for Red Mountain Continental Sci. Drilling Com., Oklahoma City, 1984-85. Contbr. articles to profl. jours. Docent Arizona-Sonora Desert Museum. Lt. (j.g.) USNR, 1943-46. Mem. AIME (sr. mem.; chmn. Columbia sect. 1964, chmn. geology br. Ariz. sect. 1975), Ariz. Geol. Soc. Republican. Roman Catholic. Home and Office: 5626 E Holmes St Tucson AZ 85711

QUINN, FRANCIS A., bishop; b. L.A., Sept. 11, 1921. Ed., St. Joseph's Coll., Mountain View, Calif., St. Patrick's Sem., Menlo Park, Calif., Cath. U., Washington, U. Calif., Berkeley. Ordained priest Roman Cath. Ch., 1946; ordained titular bishop of Numana and aux. bishop of San Francisco, 1978; bishop Diocese of Sacramento, 1979-94, bishop emeritus, 1994—. Office: 2110 Broadway Sacramento CA 95818-2518

QUINN, HARRY JOHN, government administrator, real estate consultant; b. San Francisco, Nov. 20, 1943; s. Harry Joseph and Adiline (Kansora) Q.; m. Rita Marie Pedranzini, July 2, 1966; children: Patrick, Michelle. BA, U. San Francisco, 1965, MPA, 1979. Exec. adminstrv. asst. Calif. Dept. Transp., San Francisco, 1966-84; asst. dir. property City and County of San Francisco, 1984—; bd. dirs. San Francisco City Employees Credit Union. Grand jury foreman San Mateo County, Calif., 1987, mem., 1986. Served with U.S. Army, 1966-67. Mem. San Mateo Grand Jury Assn., Olympic Club (properties com. 1994). Office: City & County of San Francisco 25 Van Ness Ave # 400 San Francisco CA 94102

QUINN, JOHN R., archbishop; b. Riverside, Calif., Mar. 28, 1929; s. Ralph J. and Elizabeth (Carroll) Q. Student, St. Francis Sem., Immaculate Heart Sem., San Diego, 1947-48; Ph.B., Gregorian U., Rome, 1950, Licentiate in Sacred Theology, 1954, S.T.L., 1954. Ordained priest Roman Cath. Ch., 1953, as bishop, 1967. Assoc. pastor St. George Ch., Ontario, Calif., 1954-55; prof. theology Immaculate Heart Sem., San Diego, 1955-62, vice rector, 1960-62; pres. St. Francis Coll. Sem., El Cajon, Calif., 1962-64; rector Immaculate Heart Sem., 1964-68; aux. bishop, vicar gen. San Diego, 1967-72; bishop Oklahoma City, 1972-73, archbishop, 1973-77; archbishop San Francisco, 1977—; provost U. San Diego, 1968-72; pastor St. Therese Parish, San Diego, 1969; apptd. consultor to Sacred Congregation for the Clergy in Rome, 1971; pres. Nat. Conf. Cath. Bishops, 1977-80, chmn. Com. of Liturgy; chmn. com. on Family Life U.S. Cath. Conf.; chmn. Bishops' Com. on Pastoral Rsch. and Practices, Bishops' Com. on Doctrine; mem. Bishops' Com. on Sems., Pontifical Commn., Seattle, 1987-88, Bishops' Com. for Pro-Life Activies, 1989—; apptd. pontifical del. for religious in U.S., 1983; pres. Calif. Cath. Conf., 1985; mem. Synod of Bishops, Rome, 1994; chmn. Nat. Conf. Cath. Bishops Com. on Doctrine, 1994—. Trustee U. San Diego, 1991-93. Mem. Cath. Theol. Soc. Am., Canon Law Soc. Am., Am. Cath. Hist. Soc. Address: 445 Church St San Francisco CA 94114-1720

QUINN, PAT (JOHN BRIAN PATRICK QUINN), professional sports team manager; b. Hamilton, Ont., Can., Jan. 29, 1943; s. John Ernest and Jean (Ireland) Q.; m. Sandra Georgia Baker, May 1, 1963; children: Valerie, Kathleen. BA in Econs., York U., 1972; JD, Del. Law Sch., 1987. Player Toronto Maple Leafs, Ont., 1968-70, Vancouver Canucks, B.C., Can., 1970-72, Atlanta Flames, 1972-77; coach Phila. Flyers, 1977-82, L.A. Kings, 1984-86; head coach Team Canada, 1986; pres., gen. mgr. Vancouver Canucks, 1987—, head coach, 1990—; player rep. NHL, Atlanta, 1973-77, bd. govs., 1987—. Named Def. Man of Yr., Vancouver Canucks, 1971, Coach of Yr. NHL, 1979-80, Coach of Yr., Sporting News, 1980, 92, Coach of the Yr. Hockey News, 1980, 92, Coach of the Yr. Acad. Awards of Sports, named to the Longest Unbeaten Record in Profl. Sports of 35 Games, 1979-80, named to the Best Record in the History of the Canucks Franchise, 1991-92; recipient Jake Milford award, 1994, Jack Diamond award, 1994. Roman Catholic. Office: care Vancouver Canucks, Pacific Coliseum, 100 N Renfrew St, Vancouver, BC Canada V5K 3N7

QUINT, BERT, journalist; b. N.Y.C., Sept. 22, 1930; s. George and Sadye (Slonim) Q.; m. Diane Frances Schwab, Apr. 10, 1975; children: Lara Gabrielle, Amy Frances. BS, NYU, 1952. Reporter Worcester (Mass.) Telegram, 1953-54, AP, 1953-54, N.Y. Herald Tribune, 1956-58; mag. editor, free lance corr. Mexico City, 1958-65; corr. CBS News, 1965-93; adj. prof. broadcast journalism U. Colo., Boulder, 1993—; freelance journalist, 1993—. Anchor-writer documentary for Cable TV, 1993; contbr. articles to mags. Recipient Radio Reporting award Overseas Press Club, 1971. Mem. Soc. Profl. Journalists, Fgn. Corr. Assn. Mex. (pres.). Home and Office: 539 Bari Ct Boulder CO 80303-4312

QUINTANA, LEROY V., English language educator; b. Albuquerque, June 10, 1944; m. Yolanda Holguin, Nov. 1, 1969; children: Sandra, Elisa, Jose. BA in English, U. N.Mex., Albuquerque, 1971; MA in English, U. N.Mex., Las Cruces, 1974; MA in Counseling, Western N.Mex. U., 1984. Lic. marriage, family and child counselor, Calif. Prof. English El Paso (Tex.) C.C., 1975-80; reporter The Albuquerque Tribune, 1981-82; therapist Border Area Mental Health, Silver City, N.Mex., 1982-84; therapist, mgr. Nat. City Mental Health, San Diego, 1984-87; prof. English Mesa Coll., San Diego, 1987—. Author: Hijo del Pueblo, 1978, Sangre, 1984 (Am. Book award), The History of Home, 1993 (Am. Book award 1993), Interrogations, 1993, Paper Dance: 55 Latino Poets, Persea Books, 1995. With U.S. Army, 1967-69. Nat. Endowment for the Arts creative writing fellow, 1978; named runner-up Paterson Poetry prize Paterson Poetry Ctr., 1994. Mem. MLA, PEN. Democrat. Roman Catholic. Home: 9230 Lake Murray Blvd Apt C San Diego CA 92119-1471 Office: Mesa Coll 7250 Mesa College Dr San Diego CA 92111-4902

QUINTERO, BERNHILD ELSE, health care executive; b. Schwagstorf, Germany, Sept. 21, 1943; d. Paul Fritz and Hildegard W. (Linsen) Binkert; m. Michael Keith Terry, June 4, 1965 (div. 1971); children: David Carl, Michelle Lee; m. Robert Quintero, June 12, 1976. AA, Pasadena City Coll., 1974; BA, U. So. Calif., 1976, MA, 1979. Writer Beverly Hosp., Montebello, Calif., 1976-78; dir. Encino (Calif.) Hosp., 1978-79, U. So. Calif. Hosp., L.A., 1979-80; v.p. Queen of Angels Hosp., L.A., 1980-85; dir., v.p. Health West/Unihealth, Northridge, Calif., 1985-88; v.p. Managed Health Network, Culver City, Calif., 1988-91, MCC Behavioral Care of Calif., Glendale, 1991-95. Office: MCC Behavioral Care Calif 801 N Brand # 1150 Glendale CA 91001

QUINTON, PAUL MARQUIS, physiology educator, researcher; b. Houston, Tex., Sept. 17, 1944; s. Curtis Lincoln and Mercedes Genale (Danley) Q.; m. Liesbet Joris, Dec. 31, 1992; 1 child, Marquis. B.A., Univ. Tex., 1967; Ph.D., Rice U., 1971. Asst. prof. physiology and medicine UCLA Med. Sch., 1975-79; asst. prof. biomed. scis. U. Calif., Riverside, 1979-81, assoc. prof., 1981-84, prof., 1984—; assoc. prof. physiology UCLA, 1981-91. Assoc. ed. Am. Journal Physiology: Cell Biology (Bethesda), assoc. ed. Experimental Physiology (Cambridge). Recipient Paul di Sant'Agnese Disting. Sci. Achievement award Nat. Cystic Fibrosis Found., 1991, Joseph Levy Meml. award Internat. Cystic Fibrosis (Mucovisidosis) Assn., 1994. Office: U Calif Biomed Scis Weber Hall W Riverside CA 92521

QUIROS, CARLOS FRANCISCO, plant genetics educator; b. Lima, Peru, Mar. 17, 1946; came to U.S., 1970; s. Carlos A. and Hilda (Raffo) Q.; m. Ana Raquel Velando, Mar. 15, 1970; children: Carlos M., Cesar S. BSc, Agrarian U., Lima, 1967, AE, 1968; MSc, U. N.H., 1972; PhD, U. Calif., Davis, 1975. Researcher Nat. Inst. Agr., Celaya, Mex., 1976-77; postdoctoral researcher U. Sherbrooke, Que., Can., 1976-77; rsch. assoc. U. Alta., Edmonton, Can., 1977-81; assoc. scientist Internat. Plant Rsch. Inst., San Carlos, Calif., 1981-83; asst. prof. vegetable crops U. Calif., 1983-87, assoc. prof., 1987-91, prof., 1991—. Contbr. articles to sci. jours., chpts. to books. Grantee Calif. Celery Rsch. Bd., 1983—, USDA, 1984—, AID, 1987-90, NSF, 1990; Fulbright fellow, France, 1990-91. Mem. AAAS, Am. Assn. Hort. Sci., Am. Potato Assn., Econ. Bot. Soc. Roman Catholic. Office: U Calif Dept Vegetable Crops Davis CA 95616

QUIRÓZ, ALFRED JAMES, art educator, artist, lecturer; b. Tucson, May 9, 1944; s. Nicolas J. Segura and Hilda F. (Quiróz) Alvarado; m. Marcia Denis Duff, Sept. 15, 1977; children: Demian A., James A. BFA in Painting, San Francisco Art Inst., 1971; MAT in Art Edn., RISD, 1974; MFA in Studio Arts, U. Ariz., 1984. Visual arts and film specialist R.I. State Coun. on Arts, Providence, 1974-77; art coord. Sch. One, Providence, 1975-77; project dir. ESAA Spl. Arts, Central Falls, R.I., 1978-79; freelance artist Lisa Frank Inc., Tucson, 1981-84; instr. art Tucson Dept. Parks and Recreation, 1981-86; artist in residence Ariz. Commn. on Arts, Phoenix, 1985-89; asst. prof. U. Ariz., Tucson, 1989-93, assoc. prof., 1993—; adj. lectr. U. Ariz., Tucson, 1988; bd. dirs. Tucson Pima Arts Coun., Western States Arts Fedn., Santa Fe, visual arts com., 1993—; advisor Ariz. Arts Edn. Planning Partnership, Phoenix, 1993—. One-man shows include Scottsdale (Ariz.) Ctr. for Arts, 1994; exhibited in group shows at Walker Art Ctr., Minn., 1992, San Francisco Ctr. for Art, 1993, San Diego Mus. Contemporary Art, 1993. Cmty. mem. Tucson Vis. Artist's Consortium, 1989—; mem. Pub. Art Com., Tucson, 1989-93; juror at large WESTAF, Arts Midwest, others, 1993—; panelist Nat. Endowment of Arts, 1994, 95. With USN, 1963-67. Recipient Visual Arts fellowship Ariz. Commn. on Arts, Phoenix, 1989, 95, Ariz. Arts award Tucson Cmty. Found., 1989; New Forms Regional grantee Diverseworks, Houston, 1991; commd. work for San Francisco Ctr. for the Arts, 1993. Mem. AAUP, Nat. Arts and Arts Orgns., Coll. Art Assn., Am. Coun. for Arts. Office: Univ of Arizona Art Dept Tucson AZ 85721

QUISENBERRY, ROBERT MAX, architect, industrial designer; b. Eugene, Oreg., Nov. 18, 1956; s. Clifford Hale and Annemaria Gertrude (Frank) Q.; m. Dawnese Elaine Tarr, Sept. 18, 1982. BArch, U. Oreg., 1982. Registered architect, Wash. Intern R. Merriman Assocs., Tacoma, 1978-81; owner Solar Design Assocs., Tacoma, 1981-83; job capt. Robert Jones, AIA, Tacoma, 1983; project architect Merritt & Pardini, Tacoma, 1984-87; project mgr. Lorimer-Case, San Diego, 1987-89; project design architect The Austin Hansen Group, San Diego, 1989-91; prin. Studio Q Architecture, Chula Vista, Calif., 1991-93; design dir. Exponents, Inc., San Diego, 1993-94, Powerhouse Exhibits, San Diego, 1995—. Recipient Washington State Passive Solar Design and Building award Western Solar Utilization Network, 1981. Mem. AIA, Earthquake Engrng. Rsch. Inst. Republican. Home: 644 Hartford St Chula Vista CA 91913-2456

QUITALES, RAMON JUN BONTO, import/export company executive, consultant; b. Tabaco, Albay, The Philippines, Oct. 27, 1952; came to U.S., 1992; s. Ramon Vela and Salome Castilla (Bonto) Q.; m. Li Chin Chong, Mar. 18, 1993. BS in Commerce, Aquinas U., 1976. Gen. mgr. Palican Constrn Pty. Ltd., Papua New Guinea, 1990—; mng. dir. Newick Pty. Ltd., Papua New Guinea, 1990—, Filipino-Papuan Twin Towers Pty. Ltd., Papua New Guinea, 1990—, HOI-HOI Co. No. 96 Pty. Ltd., Papua New Guinea, 1990—, Pan Asia Mgmt. Cons., The Phillipines, U.S.A., 1990—, Texon Investment Group, U.S.A., 1990—, Herea Dae Co. No. 3 Pty. Ltd., L.A., Papua New Guinea, 1990—, Backson Logfred Fin., Papua New Guinea and U.S.A., 1990—, Eaglebanque Fin. Svcs., U.S.A., 1994—. Author: Quitales Directory & Trade Manual, 1994. Bd. dirs. Chambers Corp. Secs., The Philippines, 1978-83. Mem. Internat. Soc. Financiers, Am. Mgmt. Assn., Melanesian C. of C. ((Businessman of Yr. 1992), Port Moresby C. of C., Oxford Club, Small Bus. Club, Lions Club (The Philippines)(Outstanding Man of Yr. 1979). Office: Herea Dae Co No 3 Pty Ltd 819 S Flower St # 102 Los Angeles CA 90017-4607

QURESHEY, SAFI U., electronics manufacturing company executive; b. Karachi, Pakistan, Feb. 15, 1951; s. Razi and Ishrat (Temuri) Q.; m. Anita Sue Savory, Sept. 19, 1976; children: Uns, Zeshan, Anisa. BS in Physics, U. Karachi, 1971; BSEE, U. Tex., 1975. Test specialist Documentor div. A.M. Internat., Santa Ana, Calif., 1975-77; test engr. Computer Automation, Irvine, Calif., 1977-78; design engr. Telefile Computer Products, Irvine, 1978-80; founder, pres. AST Research, Inc., Irvine, 1980—; CEO AST Research Inc., 1988—. Mem. So. Calif. Tech. Execs. Network (bd. dirs.). Islamic. Office: AST Rsch Inc PO Box 19658 Irvine CA 92713-9658*

RAAS, DANIEL ALAN, lawyer; b. Portland, Oreg., July 6, 1947; s. Alan Charles and Mitzi (Cooper) R.; m. Deborah Ann Becker, Aug. 5, 1973; children: Amanda Beth, Adam Louis. BA, Reed Coll., 1969; JD, NYU, 1972. Bar: Wash. 1973, Calif. 1973, U.S. Dist. Ct. (we. dist.) Wash. 1973, U.S. Ct. Appeals (9th cir.) 1975, U.S. Supreme Ct. 1977, U.S. Tax Ct. 1983, U.S. Ct. Claims 1984. Atty. Seattle Legal Svcs, VISTA, 1972-73; reservation atty. Quinault Indian Nation, Taholah, Wash., 1973-76, Lummi Indian Nation, Bellingham, Wash., 1976—; mem. Raas, Johnsen & Stuen, P.S., Bellingham, 1982—; cons. Falmouth Inst., Fairfax, Va., 1992—, Nat. Am. and Ct. Judges Assn., McLean, Va., 1976-80. Rules chmn. Watcom County Den. Conv., Bellingham, 1988, 92; bd. dirs. Congregation Beth Israel, Bellingham, pres. 1990-92; mem. adv. com. legal asst. program Bellingham Vocat. Tech. Inst., 1985-91; trustee Watcom County Law Libr., 1978—; pres. Vol. Lawyer Program, 1990-93, bd. dirs., 1988-94; pres. Cliffside Cmty. Assn., 1978-80, bd. dirs. 1977-89; bd. dirs. Friends Maritime Heritage Ctr., 1983-86, Samish Camp Fire Coun., 1988-94, pres. 1991-94, v.p. 1989-91, regional v.p. Union Am. Hebrew Congregations, 1986-93, nat. trustee, exec. com., 1995—, sec. Pacific N.W. region, 1993-95, pres. 1995—. John Ben Snow scholar, NYU, 1969-70, Root-Tilden scholar, NYU, 1970-72. Mem. Wash. State Bar Assn. (trustee Ind. law sect. 1989—, Pro Bono award 1991), Whatcom County Bar Assn. (v.p. 1981, pres. 1982), Grays Harbor Bar Assn. (v.p. 1976). Home: 1929 Lake Crest Dr Bellingham WA 98226-4510 Office: Raas Johnsen & Stuen PS 1503 E St Bellingham WA 98225-3007

RABANAL, LISA LOUISE, youth counselor; b. Seward, Nebr., June 8, 1968; d. Daniel Norman and Sandra Louise (Rhode) Seim; m. Albert Lucas Rabanal, July 30, 1994. BS in Elem. Edn., Concordia Coll., 1989; postgrad., Chaminade U., 1991—. Substitute tchr. elem. sch. Trinity Luth. Sch., Wahiawa, Hawaii, 1985-90; summer program children's leader City and County of Honolulu, Wahiawa, 1986, swimming instr., 1988-92; kindergarten tchr. Emmanuel Luth. Sch., Kahului, Hawaii, 1990; outreach counselor Hale Kipa, Inc., Honolulu, 1991-93; outreach svcs. supr. Ctrl. Oahu Youth Svcs., Wahiawa, 1993—; supervisory bd. Ctrl. Oahu Youth Svcs., Wahiawa, 1993—. Recipient Presdl. scholarship USA Coll. Bd., 1985, Luth. Missionary scholarship Luth. Ch. Hawaii, 1985-89, Alumni scholarship Concordia Alumni Assn., 1987-89. Mem. Am. Counseling Assn. Home: 58 Kalie St # A Wahiawa HI 96786-2501

RABE, STEVEN GLEN, town manager, consultant; b. Mpls., Jan. 27, 1961; s. William Herman and Mary Lou (Toensing) R.; m. Catharine Marie Weirich, May 24, 1986. BS in Pub. Adminstrn., Kennedy-Western U., 1994. Maintenance man Town of Meeker, Colo., 1978-80; chief plant operator, lab. tech. Meeker (Colo.) Sanitation Dist., 1980-83; town mgr. Town of Eads, Colo., 1984—; water cons. Town of Haswell, Colo., 1993—; wastewater cons. Wiley (Colo.) Sanitation Dist., 1994—, City of Las Animas, Colo., 1994—; chair S.E. and Ctrl. Recycling Assn., 1995—. Recipient Internat. Safety Triangle award Nat. Assn. Chiefs of Police, 1987. Mem. Am. Water Works Assn. (Distbn. Sys. Operator award 1992), Water Environment Fedn., Colo. Community Revitalization Assn. Home: 508 W 15th St Eads CO 81036-9691 Office: Town of Eads 110 W 13th St Eads CO 81036

RABINOWITZ, HOWARD NEIL, history educator; b. Bklyn., June 19, 1942; s. Abe and Gertrude (Finkelman) R.; m. Anita Joyce Blau, Aug. 28, 1966 (div. Mar. 1981); children: Lori Karen, Deborah Michelle; m. Marsha Diane Wood, July 6, 1991. BA magna cum laude, Swarthmore Coll., 1964; MA, U. Chgo., 1967, PhD, 1973. Vis. instr. in history Grinnell (Iowa) Coll., 1970-71; instr. in history U. New Mex., Albuquerque, 1971-73, asst. prof. of history, 1973-77, assoc. prof. history, 1977-85, prof., 1985—; cons. Ednl. Testing Svc., Princeton, N.J., 1971, 77-88, Albuquerque Mus., 1981, NEH, Washington, 1983—, Valentine Mus., Richmond, Va., 1988—. Author: Race Relations in the Urban South 1865-1890, 1978, 80 (Pulitzer prize nominee 1978), The First New South, 1865-1920, 1992, Race, Ethnicity and Urbanization: Selected Essays, 1994; editor and contbr. Southern Black Leaders of the Reconstruction Era, 1982; contbr. numerous articles to hist. jours., anthologies and golf jours. Vice chmn. Albuquerque Landmark and Urban Conservation Commission, 1978-82, chmn. 1982-84; bd. dirs. Albuquerque Conservation Assn., 1986-89; mem. Good Government Com., Albuquerque, 1989—. NEH fellow, 1978; Newberry Libr. fellow, 1978; Ctr. for Advanced Study in Behavioral Scis., Stanford, 1989-90; Am. Assn. State and Local History grantee, 1985. Mem. Am. Hist. Assn., Urban Hist. Assn. (bd. dirs. 1993-95), Orgn. Am. Historians (Frederick Jackson Turner prize com. 1989), So. Hist. Assn. (bd. editors Jour. So. History 1980-84, chmn. program com. 1992, exec. coun. 1995-98). Democrat. Jewish. Office: Univ New Mex Dept History Mesa Vista Hall Albuquerque NM 87131

RABINOWITZ, JAY ANDREW, state supreme court justice; b. Phila., Feb. 25, 1927; s. Milton and Rose (Rittenberg) R.; m. Anne Marie Nesbit, June 14, 1957; children: Judith, Mara, Max, Sara. B.A., Syracuse U., 1949; LL.B., Harvard, 1952. Bar: N.Y. 1952, Alaska 1958. Pvt. practice law N.Y.C., 1952-57; law clk. to presiding judge U.S. Dist. Ct., Fairbanks, Alaska, 1957-58; asst. U.S. atty. Fairbanks, 1958-59; dep. atty. gen., chief civil div. State of Alaska, 1959-60; judge Superior Ct. Alaska, 1960-65; justice Alaska Supreme Ct., 1965—; chief justice Alaska Supreme Ct.,

Juneau, 1972-75, 78-81, 1984-87, 90-92. Served with AUS, 1945-46. Mem. N.Y. Bar Assn., Alaska Bar Assn. (commr. on uniform laws 1971—). Office: Alaska Supreme Ct 303 K St Anchorage AK 99501-2013*

RABINOWITZ, MARIO, physicist; b. Mexico City, Mex., Oct. 24, 1936; came to U.S., 1939; s. Laib and Rachel (Loschak) R.; m. Laverne Marcotte; children: Daniel L., Benjamin M., Lisa B. BS in Physics, U. Wash., 1959, MS in Physics, 1960; PhD in Physics, Washington State U., 1963. Electronics engr. Collins Radio Co., Burbank, Calif., 1957; rsch. engr. Boeing Co., Seattle, 1958-61; rsch. asst. Physics dept. Wash. State U., Pullman, 1961-63; sr. physicist Westinghouse Rsch. Ctr., Pitts., 1963-66; mgr. gas discharges and vacuum physics Varian Assocs., Palo Alto, Calif., 1966-67; rsch. physicist Stanford (Calif.) Linear Accelerator Ctr., 1967-74; sr. scientist and mgr. Electric Power Rsch. Inst., Palo Alto, 1974—; adj. prof. Ga. Inst. Tech., Atlanta, 1987—, U. Houston, 1990—, Va. Commonwealth U., Richmond, 1990—, Case Western Res. U., Cleve., 1975-77, Boston U., 1975-77. Contbr. numerous articles to profl. jours.; patentee in field. Del., counselor Boys State, Ellensburg, Wash., 1953-55. Scholarship Baker Found., 1955-58; recipient Alumni Achievement award Wash. State U., 1992. Home: 715 Lakemead Way Redwood City CA 94062-3922

RABOVSKY, JEAN, toxicologist; b. Balt., Aug. 18, 1937. BS in Chemistry, U. Md., 1959; PhD in Biochemistry, Brandeis U., 1964. Asst. rsch. biologist U. Calif., Irvine, 1972-76; postdoctoral assoc. U. Fla., Gainesville, 1976-78, rsch. chemist Nat. Inst. Occupational Safety & Health, Morgantown, W.Va., 1978-89; staff toxicologist Calif. EPA, Sacramento, 1989—. Contbr. sci. lit., prepare risk assessments and other govtl. documents. Mem. AAAS, Am. Chem. Soc., N.Y. Acad. Scis., Soc. Toxicology, Sigma Xi. Office: Office Environ Health Hazard Assessment 2151 Berkeley Way # 11 Berkeley CA 94704-1011

RABY, WILLIAM LOUIS, author; b. Chgo., July 16, 1927; s. Gustave E. and Helen (Burgess) R.; m. Norma Claire Schreiner, Sept. 8, 1956; children: Burgess, Marianne, Marlene. BSBA, Northwestern U., 1949; MBA, U. Ariz., 1961, PhD, 1971. Ptnr. VAR CPA Firms, 1950-76, Touche Ross & Co., N.Y.C., 1977-87; pres. Ariz. State Bd. Accountancy, 1993-94; mem. Ariz. State Bd. Tax Appeals, 1994—; prof. acctg. emeritus Ariz. State U., 1994—; columnist Tax Notes mag., Arlington, Va., 1990—. Author: The Income Tax and Business Decisions, 1964, Building and Maintaining a Successful Tax Practice, 1964, The Reluctant Taxpayer, 1970, Tax Practice Management, 1974, Introduction to Federal Taxation, annually, 1980-91, Tax Practice Management: Client Servicing, 1986; editor: Raby Report on Tax Practice, 1986—, PPC Guide To Successful Tax Practice, 1991; mem. editorial adv. bd. Taxation for Accountants, The Tax Adviser; contbr. articles to profl. jours. Served with USN, 1942-45. Mem. AICPA (chmn. fed. tax divsn. 1980-83, v.p. 1983-84, coun. 1983-90), Tax Ct. Bar, Ariz. State U. Club, Beta Gamma Sigma (past pres. Ariz. alumni chpt.), Delta Mu Delta, Beta Alpha Psi, Alpha Kappa Psi. Presbyterian (elder, chmn. adv. coun. on ch. and soc. 1979-81). Office: PO Box 26846 Tempe AZ 85285-6846

RACHELEFSKY, GARY S., medical educator; b. N.Y.C., 1942. Intern Bellevue Hosp. Ctr., N.Y.C., 1967-68; resident in pediatrics Johns Hopkins Hosp., 1968-70, Ctr. Disease Control, 1970-72; fellow UCLA Med. Ctr., 1972-74; clin. prof., assoc. dir. A/I Tng. Program UCLA. Mem. Am. Acad. Allergy, Asthma and Immunology (bd. dirs., sec., treas.). Office: 11620 Wilshire Blvd Ste 200 Los Angeles CA 90025-1767*

RACHMELER, MARTIN, university administrator; b. Bklyn., Nov. 21, 1928; s. Jack and Sophie (Rosenbloom) R.; m. Elizabeth Karkalis, June 9, 1956; children: Susan, Ann, Helen. AB, Ind. U., 1950; PhD, Case Western Res. U., 1960. USPHS postdoctoral researcher U. Calif., Berkeley, 1959-61, asst. rsch. geneticist, 1961-62; asst. prof. Northwestern U. Med. Sch., Chgo., 1962-67, assoc. prof., 1967-89; dir. rsch. svcs. adminstrn. Northwestern U., Evanston, Ill., 1977-89; dir. tech. transfer U. Calif., San Diego, 1989—. Author: Lectures in Medical Genetics, 1966; contbr. article to profl. jours. With U.S. Army, 1952-54. Recipient USPHS Rsch. Career Devel. award, 1968-72. Mem. Assn. Univ. Tech. Mgrs. (v.p. 1983-85, trustee 1986-88, pres.-elect 1990, pres. 1991), Licensing Exec. Soc., Am. Soc. for Microbiology, Nat. Coun. Univ. Rsch. Adminstrs. (regional chair 1988), Sigma Xi (sec.-treas. 1982-86, chpt. pres. 1988). Office: U Calif Mail Code 0093 9500 Gilman Dr La Jolla CA 92093-5003

RACICOT, MARC F., governor; b. Thompson Falls, Mont., July 24, 1948; s. William E. and Patricia E. (Bentley) R.; m. Theresa J. Barber, July 25, 1970; children: Ann, Timothy, Mary Catherine, Theresa, Joseph. BA, Carroll Coll., Helena, Mont., 1970; JD, U. Mont., 1973; postgrad., U. Va., 1973, Cornell U., 1977. Bar: Mont. 1973. With U.S. Army, 1973-76; advanced through grades to capt., 1973; legal assistance officer U.S. Army, Ft. Lewis, Wash., 1973; chief trial counsel U.S. Army, Kaiserslautern, Fed. Republic of Germany, 1975-76; resigned, 1976; dep. county atty. Missoula (Mont.) County, 1976-77; bur. chief County Prosecutor Svcs. Bur., Helena, Mont., 1977-89; asst. atty. gen. State of Mont., Helena, 1977-89; spl. prosecutor for the Atty. Gen.'s Office State of Mont., atty. gen., 1989-93, gov., 1993—. Founder Missoula Drug Treatment Program, 1977; active United Way, Helena; bd. visitors U. Mont. Sch. Law. Inducted into Basketball Hall of Fame Carroll Coll., 1982. Mem. Mont. Bar Assn., Carroll Coll. Century Club. Republican. Roman Catholic. Office: State Capitol RM 204 Helena MT 59620

RACINA, THOM (THOMAS FRANK RAUCINA), television writer, editor; b. Kenosha, Wis., June 4, 1946; s. Frank G. and Esther May (Benko) Raucina. B.F.A., Goodman Sch. Drama, Art Inst. Chgo., 1970, M.F.A. in Theatre Arts and Directing with honors, 1971. TV writer Hanna-Barbera Co., Hollywood, Calif., 1973-74, MTM Enterprises, Inc., Hollywood, 1974-76; head writer General Hospital ABC-TV, Hollywood, 1981-84; head writer Days of Our Lives NBC-TV, 1984-86, head writer Another World, 1986-88, co-head writer Generations daytime series, 1988-91, head writer syndicated Dangerous Women night-time TV series, 1991-92; assoc. head writer daytime TV series Santa Barbara, 1992-93. Author: Lifeguard, 1976, The Great Los Angeles Blizzard, 1977, Quincy, M.E., 2 vols., 1977, Kodak in San Francisco, 1977, F.M., 1978, Sweet Revenge, 1978, The Gannon Girls, 1979, Nine to Five, 1980, Tomcat, 1981, Secret Sex: Male Erotic Fantasies (as Tom Anicar), 1976, Magda (as Lisa Wells), 1981, Snow Angel, 1995; ghost writer: non-fiction The Happy Hustler (Grant Tracy Saxon), 1976, Marilyn Chambers: My Story (Marilyn Chambers), 1976, Xaviera Meets Marilyn (Xaviera Hollander and Marilyn Chambers), 1977; musical plays A Midsummer Night's Dream, music and lyrics, 1968, Allison Wonderland, music and lyrics, 1970, The Marvelous Misadventure of Sherlock Holmes, book, music and lyrics, 1971; TV scripts Sleeping Over segment of Family, ABC, 1978, Russian Pianist segment, ABC, 1979, 1 Child of the Owl, NBC After-Sch. Spl., 1979; contbr. articles to Playboy, Cosmopolitan, Penhouse, Oui, Los Angeles, Gentleman's Quar., Westways; West Coast editor: Grosset & Dunlap, Inc., N.Y.C., 1978—; lead writer for TV: Family Passions, 1993-94, Life's A Bitch!, 1994, Friends & Lovers, 1994; theatre dir., pianist, organist, composer. Recipient Emmy award nomination 1982, 83, 84, 85, 87; U.S. Nat. Student Assn. grantee, 1965. Mem. Authors Guild Am., Writers Guild Am. West. Democrat. Roman Catholic. Home: 3449 Waverly Dr Los Angeles CA 90027-2526

RACITI, CHERIE, artist; b. Chgo., June 17, 1942; d. Russell J. and Jacque (Crimmins) R. Student, Memphis Coll. Art, 1963-65; B.A. in Art, San Francisco State U., 1968; M.F.A., Mills Coll., 1979. Assoc. prof. art San Francisco State U., 1984-89, prof., 1989—; lectr. Calif. State U., Hayward, 1974, San Francisco Art Inst., 1978; mem. artist com. San Francisco Art Inst., 1974-85, sec., 1980-81. One woman show U. Calif., Berkeley, 1972, Nicholas Wilder Gallery, Los Angeles, 1975, San Francisco Art Inst., 1977, Marianne Deson Gallery, Chgo., 1980, Site 375, San Francisco, 1989, Reese Bullen Gallery, Humboldt State U., Arcata, Calif., 1990; group shows include Whitney Mus. Art, 1975, San Francisco Sci. Fiction, The Clocktower, N.Y.C., Otis-Parsons Gallery, Los Angeles, 1984-85, San Francisco Art Inst., 1985, Artists Space, N.Y.C., 1988, Angles Gallery, Santa Monica, 1987, Terrain Gallery, San Francisco, 1992, Ctr. for the Arts, San Francisco, 1993. Bd. dirs. New Langton Arts, 1988-92. Recipient Adaline Kent award San Francisco Art Inst., 1976; Eureka fellow Fleishhacker Found., San Francisco, 1988; Djerassi resident, 1994. Office: San Francisco State U Art Dept 1600 Holloway Ave San Francisco CA 94132-1722

RACOWSKY, CATHERINE, reproductive physiologist, researcher; b. Oxford, Eng., May 30, 1951; came to U.S., 1976; d. Derek Gerald and Joan (Elsey) Wyatt; m. Marshall Lewis Racowsky, June 13, 1982; triplets: Adam, Lauren, Daniel. BA, U. Oxford, 1974; PhD, U. Cambridge, Eng., 1978. Postdoctoral fellow in ob-gyn. Harvard Med. Sch., Boston, 1976-78, Lalor fellow in reproduction, 1978-79; rsch. assoc. Ariz. State U., Tempe, 1979-83, rsch. asst. prof., 1983-89, rsch. assoc. prof., 1989-91; assoc. prof. ob-gyn. U. Ariz., Tucson, 1991—; in vitro fertilization cons. S.W. Fertility Ctr., Phoenix, 1989-91; dir. rsch. ob-gyn. U. Ariz., Tucson, 1991—, dir. In-Vitro Fertilization Lab., 1991—; interviewed for TV and mag. Guest editor: Jour. Microscopy Rsch. Tech., 1994; contbr. chpt. to book, articles to profl. jours. Lectr. Valley Presbyn. Ch., Green Valley, Ariz., 1994. NIH grantee, 1982-85, 85-89; recipient Career Advancement award NSF, 1992, Internat. Basic Sci. award Soc. Assisted Reproduction Tech. and Andrology, 1992. Mem. Soc. Study of Reproduction (mem. editorial bd. 1990-94), Am. Fertility Soc. Office: Univ of Ariz Coll Medicine Dept Ob-Gyn Tucson AZ 85724

RADA, ALEXANDER, university official; b. Kvasy, Czechoslovakia, Mar. 28, 1923; s. Frantisek and Anna (Tonnkova) R.; came to U.S., 1954, naturalized, 1959; M.S., U. Tech. Coll. of Prague, 1948; postgrad. Va. Poly. Inst., 1956-59, St. Clara U., 1966-67; Ed.D., U. Pacific, 1975; m. Ingeborg Solveig Blakstad, Aug. 8, 1953; children: Alexander Sverre, Frank Thore, David Harald. Head prodn. planning dept. Mine & Iron Corp., Kolin, Czechoslovakia, 1941-42; mgr. experimenting and testing dept. Avia Aircraft, Prague, 1943-45; sec.-gen. Central Bldg. Office, Prague, 1948; head metal courses dept. Internat. Tech. Sch. of UN, Grafenaschau, W.Ger., 1949-50; works mgr. Igref A/S, Oslo, 1950-51; cons. engr., chief sect. machines Steel Products Ltd., Oslo, 1951-54; chief engr., plant supr. Nelson J. Pepin & Co., Lowell, Mass., 1954-55; sr. project engr., mfg. supt. Celanese Corp. Am., Narrows, Va., 1955-60; mgr. mfg., facilities and maint. FMC Corp., San Jose, Calif., 1960-62; mgr. adminstrn. Sylvania Electronic Systems, Santa Cruz, Calif., 1962-72; asst. to pres., devel. officer Napa (Calif.) Coll., 1972-88; chief exec. officer NAVCO Pacific Devel. Corp., Napa, 1984-91; pres. NAVCO Calif. Co., 1991—; prof. indsl. mgmt. Cabrillo Coll., Aptos, Calif., 1963-72; mgmt. and engring. cons., 1972—. Pres. ARC, Santa Cruz, 1965-72, bd. dirs., pres., Napa, 1977-88; mem. Nat. Def. Exec. Res., U.S. Dept. Commerce, Washington, 1966—, chmn. No. Calif. region 9, 1981-88; mem. President's Export Council-DEC, San Francisco, 1982—. Recipient Meritorious Service citation ARC, 1972, Etoile Civique l'Ordre de l'Etoile Civique, French Acad., 1985; registered profl. engr., Calif. Mem. NSPE, Calif. Soc. Profl. Engrs., Am. Def. Preparedness Assn., Assn. Calif. Community Coll. Adminstrs., Nat. Assn. Corp. Dirs., World Affairs Council No. Calif., Phi Delta Kappa. Editor-in-chief Our Youth, 1945-48; co-editor (with P. Boulden) Innovative Management Concepts, 1967. Home and Office: 1019 Ross Cir Napa CA 94558-2118

RADANOVICH, GEORGE P., congressman. BS in Agr. Bus. Mgmt., Calif. State Polytechnic U. Radanovich Wine, Mariposa, Calif., 1982—; County supr.; chair County Planning Comm.; mem. U.S. Ho. of Reps., 104th Congress, Washington, 1995—; mem. Budget Com., Resources Com., subcoms. Water & Power Resources, Nat. Parks, Forests & Lands. U.S. Ho. of Reps., 104th Congress, also mem. Resources Com. Task Force dealing with Endangered Species Act. Mem. Calif. Agrl. Leadership Program Class XXI, Rotary (Paul Harris Fellowship). Office: US House Reps Office House Mem Washington DC 20515*

RADCLIFFE, NANCY JEAN DYMOND, communications analyst; b. Utica, N.Y., Sept. 21, 1946; d. Thomas Edgar and Ruth Jane (Blanchard) Dymond; m. Robert Dean Radcliffe, June 4, 1972. BA, Vassar Coll., 1968. Registrar Adirondack Mus., Blue Mountain Lake, N.Y., 1968-70; curator of collections Jacksonville (Oreg.) Mus., 1970-71; sub. tchr. Riddle, Days Cir., Douglas County, Oreg., 1972-74; receptionist Roseburg (Oreg.) Forest Products, 1974-87, office svc. supr., 1987-88, communications analyst, 1988-94. Riding instr. for neighborhood kids, 1987-94; co-chair, mem. Direct Dialogue U.S. West. Adv. Bd., Portland, 1989-94. Mem. Telecomms. Assn., Umpqua Valley Combined Tng. (v.p. 1993), Oreg. Dressage Soc. (membership chair 1992), Oreg. Equestrian Trails, Oreg. Horse Coun., Am. Quarter Horse Assn. Democrat. Home: 8794 Upper Olalla Rd Winston OR 97496-9626 Office: Roseburg Forest Products PO Box 1088 Roseburg OR 97470-0252

RADER, PAUL ALEXANDER, minister, administrator; b. N.Y.C., Mar. 4, 1934; s. Lyell M. and Gladys Mina (Damon) R.; m. Kay Fuller, May 29, 1956; children: Edith Jeanne, James Paul, Jennifer Kay. BA, Asbury Coll., Wilmore, Ky., 1956; BD, Asbury Theol. Sem., 1959; LLD (hon.), Asbury Coll., Wilmore, Ky., 1984; ThM, So. Bapt. Theol. Sem., Louisville, 1961; D Missiology, Fuller Theol. Sem., 1973. Ordained to ministry Salvation Army, 1961. Tng. prin. The Salvation Army, Seoul, 1973-74, edn. sec., 1974-77, chief sec., 1979-83; tng. prin. The Salvation Army, Suffern, N.Y., 1983-86; divisional comdr. for Ea. Pa. and Del. The Salvation Army, Phila., 1986-88; chief sec. ea. ter. The Salvation Army, N.Y.C., 1988; territorial comdr. U.S.A. western ter. The Salvation Army, Rancho Palos Verdes, Calif., 1989—; adj. prof. Seoul Theol. Sem., 1980-82; trustee Asian Ctr. for Theol. Studies and Mission, 1980-83, Asbury Coll., 1988—; pres. The Salvation Army Calif. Corp., Rancho Palos Verdes, 1989—. Recipient Alumnus A award Asbury Coll., 1982, Disting. Alumni award Asbury Theol. Sem., 1989; Paul Harris fellow Rotary Internat., 1989. Mem. Am. Soc. Missiology, Internat. Assn. Mission Studies. Office: The Salvation Army 639 Sabrina Way Vista CA 92084-6264

RADFORD-MCGRADY, STEPHANIE JILL, speech communications educator; b. Enid, Okla., May 25, 1950; d. James Monroe and Evelyn Fern (Pursell) Payne; m. Charles Radford, May 10, 1969 (div. 1976); children: Stacy, Steven; m. Ron L. McGrady, Nov. 28, 1992. BA, No. Okla. State U., 1978; MA, Okla. State U., 1979; postgrad., UCLA, Ctrl. State U., Okla. State U., U. LaVerne, U. Calif. Riverside. Lic. tchr., Okla., Calif.; C.C. credential, Calif. Tchr. English, drama, speech, music Crescent (Okla.) Pub. Schs., 1980-86; tchr. English and drama Palmdale (Calif.) High Sch., 1986-89, Desert Winds High Sch., Lancaster, Calif., 1988-91; tchr. English Highland High Sch., Palmdale, 1991-92; instr. speech comm. Antelope Valley Coll., Lancaster, Calif., 1988—; edn. program advisor, Antelope Valley Acad. Ctr. Chapman Univ., Palmdale, Calif.; tchr. power cons. Antelope Valley Union High Sch., Palmdale, 1987-88, reader's theatre cons., Lancaster and Palmdale, 1987-92, mentor tchr., Lancaster, 1991-92, curriculum writer, Lancaster, 1989-92; mem. adv. bd. Cedar St. Theatre, Lancaster, 1988-89; owner, mgr. Golden Goose, Palmdale, Calif.; tchr. ceramics, porcelain dolls. Author: (screenplays) Color Blind, 1988, Forever Yours, 1992; performed stage, TV, movies; directed more than 25 prodns. Dir. Cedar St. Theatre, Lancaster, 1987-89, Palmdale Repertory Theatre, 1992, mem. adv. bd., 1994—. Mem. SAG, Am. Fedn. TV Actors. Republican.

RADHA, SIVANANDA (URSULA SYLVIA HELLMAN), religious association executive; b. Berlin, Mar. 20, 1911; came to Can., 1952. Photography diploma Berlin Sch. Photography, 1942; grad. Berlin Sch. Advt., 1940. Initiated into Sanyas, Saraswati Order of Sanyas, 1956. Dir. Divine Life Soc., Burnaby, B.C., Can., 1957-63; dir. Yasodhara Ashram Soc., Kootenay Bay, B.C., 1963—; adj. faculty Antioch Coll., Seattle, L.A., 1979-80, 82-84; mem. faculty C.I.T.P., Menlo Park, Calif., 1975-82; founder Assn. for Devel. Human Potential, Idaho, 1970—; founder 11 Radha Houses, 1982—. Author: Kundalini Yoga for the West, 1978; Mantras Words of Power, 1980, Seeds of Light, 1980, Radha: Diary of a Woman's Search, 1981, Hatha Yoga: The Hidden Language, 1987, Divine Light Invocation, 1990, In the Company of the Wise, 1991, From the Mating Dance to the Cosmic Dance, 1992, Realities of the Dreaming Mind, 1994. Mem. Assn. for Humanistic Psychology, Assn. for Transpersonal Psychology, Divine Life Soc., Internat. Transpersonal Assn., Am. Soc. for Psychical Rsch. Home: 2328 W Pacific Ave Spokane WA 99204-1064 Office: Assn Devel Human Potential PO Box 3543 Spokane WA 99220-3543

RADKE, LINDA FOSTER, publishing consultant; b. Gary, Ind., July 14, 1952; d. Marvin Bremmy and Ann (Weiss) Foster; m. Lowell Radke, Mar. 10, 1983; 1 child, Gradey Benjamin. BA, Ariz. state U., 1978. Cert. elem. spl. edn., edn. mentally handicapped and learning disabilities tchr. Instr. Ariz. State U., Tempe; instrnl. aid Coronado High Sch., Scottsdale, Ariz.; learning resource specialist Saguaro High Sch., Scottsdale; tchr. 6th grade Griffith Elem. Sch. Balsz Sch. Dist., Phoenix, 1981-83; owner, mgr. Domestic Cons. Inc., Scottsdale, 1983-88; publ., cons. Five Star Publs., Chandler, Ariz., 1988—. Author: (book directory) The Options Directory of Child and Senior Care, 1987, 89, (book) Nannies Maids and More, 1989, That Hungarian's in My Kitchen, 1990, 94, Household Careers, 1993 (Citation 1994, Citation for Excellence 1994, 1st Pl. non-fiction book award Ariz. Pres Women, Inc. 1994, Citation for Career Edn. Initiatives, Am. Assn. Career Edn. Initiatives 1994); pub. Shakespeare for Children, 1989 (Named Best Toys Under $10 Ladies Home Jour. 1993), The Sixty-Minute Shakespeare, 1990, Shakespeare: To Teach or Not to Teach, 1992, 94. Mem. Ariz. Book Publ. Assn. (founding mem.), Ariz. Authors' Assn., Ariz. Prss Women Inc., Pub. Rels. Soc. Am., Internat. Assn. Ind. Pubs., Pubs. Mktg. Assn. Democrat.

RADLEY, GREGORY NORMAN, custom furniture maker, educator; b. Santa Monica, Calif., May 30, 1956; s. Norman Carlyle and Donna May (Ludlow) R.; m. Debra Kay Policky; children: Scott, Melissa, Matthew. BS in Endsl. Tech. Edn., Brigham Young U., 1989. Custom cabinet/furniture maker Radley Woodworks, Ventura, Calif., 1983-89; indsl. arts tchr. Buena High Sch., Ventura, 1990-91, Moorpark (Calif.) H.S., 1991-92; craftsman, owner Greg Radley Cabinetmaker, Ventura, 1992—; speaker at woodworking shows, 1992-93. Contbr. chpt. to book. Recipient 1st place nat. cabinetmaking competition Vocat. Indsl. Clubs Am., 1989, 2d place traditional furniture award Design in Wood, 1994, 3d place furniture award Art of Calif. mag., 1993, Best Craftsman-Traditional Furniture award Early Am. Life mag., 1994. Mem. San Diego Fine Woodworkers. Office: Radley Fine Furniture 2745 Sherwin Ave # 12 Ventura CA 93003

RADOVSKY, FRANK JAY, zoologist, museum administrator; b. Fall River, Mass., Jan. 5, 1929; s. David Reuben and Minnie Esther (Simon) R. AB, U. Colo., 1951; MS, U. Calif., Berkeley, 1959, PhD, 1964. Asst. rsch. parasitologist U. Calif., San Francisco, 1963-69; acarologist Bishop Mus., Honolulu, 1969-85, chmn. dept. entomology, 1972-85, asst. dir., 1977-85, disting. chair of zoology, 1984-86; rsch. assoc. Calif. Acad. Scis., San Francisco, 1986; vis. prof. entomology Oreg. State U., Corvallis, 1987; dir. rsch. and collections N.C. State Mus. Natural Scis., Raleigh, 1987-91; editor Annual Review of Entomology, Raleigh, 1991—; prof. Oreg. State U., 1994—; faculty affiliate U. Hawaii, Honolulu, 1971-85, U. Okla., 1991; rsch. assoc. Bishop Mus., 1986—. Author: (book) Mites Parasitic on Bats, 1967, Pacific Tropical Biogeography, 1984; (with others) Life Histories and Reproductive Patterns of Mites, 1993; editor Ann. Rev. Entomology, 1978—, Jour. of Med. Entomology, 1969-85, 87; contbr. over 70 articles to profl. jours. Mem. Animal Species Adv. Commn., Hawaii, 1972-80. Lt. USNR, 1951-55. Fellow NIH, USPHS, 1959-62; grantee NIH, 1964-76, NSF, 1970-85. Mem. AAAS, Entomol. Soc. Am., Internat. Congress Acarology (exec. sec. 1971-78), Soc. Vector Ecologists, Am. Soc. Tropical Medicine and Hygiene, Assn. Systematics Collections (bd. dirs. 1982-85), Acarological Soc. Am. (bd. dirs. 1988-90), Sigma Xi. Democrat. Jewish. Office: Cordley Hall 2046 Dept Entomology Oreg State U Corvallis OR 97331-2907

RADTKE, CLAYTON WALTER, structural engineer, engineering administrator; b. Fond du Lac, Wis., Oct. 5, 1933; s. Edwin Henry and Hulda Matilda (Hagenau) R.; m. Sherill Ann Lensch, Sept. 14, 1958; children: Karen Radtke Veers, Gretchen Radtke Stroud, John, Sharon Radtke Ragner. BS in Civil Engring., Valparaiso U., 1955; cert. in bus. mgmt., U. Calif., Irvine, 1974. Structural test engr. Douglas Aircraft Co., Santa Monica, Calif., 1955-61; test engr. RocketDyne, Canoga Park, Calif., 1961-66; staff mgr. McDonnell Douglas Energy Systems, Orange, Calif., 1985-86; structures design engr. McDonnell Douglas Aerospace, Huntington Beach, Calif., 1966-85; structures design mgr. McDonnell Douglas Aerospace, Huntington Beach, 1986-89; prin. engr. program engring. McDonnell Douglas Aerospace Co., Huntington Beach, 1989—; cons. in solar energy, Westminster, Calif., 1986—. Pres., bd. elders, trustee King of Kings Luth. Ch., Garden Grove, Calif., 1966—. Republican. Office: McDonnell Douglas Aerospace 5301 Bolsa Ave Huntington Beach CA 92647-2048

RADTKE, RICHARD LYNN, oceanic biology educator; b. North Judson, Ind., July 9, 1952; s. Clarence C. and Eunice M. (Weidner) R. BA, Wabash Coll., Crawfordsville, Ind., 1974; PhD in Marine Sci., U. S.C., 1978. Rsch. and teaching asst. U. S.C., Columbia, 1974-77, instr. marine sci., 1977-78; staff mem. Jean-Michel Cousteau Inst., Hilton Head, S.C., 1978; postdoctoral researcher in fisheries and oceans Can. Vis. Fellowship, St. John's, Nfld., 1978-80; rsch. scientist Pacific Gamefish Found., 1981-82; asst. rsch. prof. Belle W. Baruch Inst. U. S.C., Columbia, 1981-82; rsch. prof oceanic biology U. Hawaii, Honolulu, 1982—; presenter sci. meetings, 1985—. Contbr. numerous articles and abstraccts to sci. jours. Bd. dirs. Multiple Sclerosis Soc., Honolulu, 1986-91. Recipient U.S. Presdl. commendation, 1984, Acad. award for handicapped, nat. achievement award Nat. Multiple Sclerosis Soc., 1986, Disabled Person of Yr. award Commn. on Persons with Disabilities, 1990; recipient numerous grants, including U. S.C., S.C. Sea Grant, Fisheries and Oceans Can., Nat. Marine Fisheries Svc., Hawaii Sea Grant, U.S. Fish and Wildlife Sc., NATO, Hawaii and Calif. Sea Grant, NSF, Nat. Geog. Soc., NIH, NOAA. Mem. Am. Soc. Ichthyologists and Herpetologists, Am. Soc. Zoologists, Honolulu Jaycees (One of 3 Outstanding Young Persons award 1990), Sigma Xi. Home: 45-106 Pookela Pl Kaneohe HI 96744-5706 Office: U Hawaii Hawaii Inst Geophysics Honolulu HI 96813

RADY, ERNEST S., thrift and loan association executive; b. 1938. Chmn. bd. Western Thrift & Loan, Orange, Calif., 1973—; chmn. bd., CEO Westcorp, Irvine, Calif., 1975—. Office: Westcorp 23 Pasteur Irvine CA 92718-3816*

RAE, MATTHEW SANDERSON, JR., lawyer; b. Pitts., Sept. 12, 1922; s. Matthew Sanderson and Olive (Waite) R.; m. Janet Hettman, May 2, 1953; children: Mary-Anna, Margaret Rae Mallory, Janet S. Rae Dupree. AB, Duke, 1946, LLB, 1947; postgrad., Stanford U., 1951. Bar: Md. 1948, Calif. 1951. Asst. to dean Duke Sch. Law, Durham, N.C., 1947-48; assoc. Karl F. Steinmann, Balt., 1948-49, Guthrie, Darling & Shattuck, L.A., 1953-54; nat. field rep. Phi Alpha Delta Law Frat., L.A., 1949-51; research atty. Calif. Supreme Ct., San Francisco, 1951-52; ptnr. Darling, Hall & Rae (and predecessor firms), L.A., 1955—; mem. Calif. Commn. Uniform State Laws, 1985—, chmn., 1993-94; chmn. drafting com. for revision Uniform Prin. and Income Act of Nat. Conf., 1991—. V.p. L.A. County Rep. Cen. Com., 1960-64, 77-90, exec. com., 1977-90; vice chmn. 17th Congl. Dist., 1960-62, 28th Congl. Dist., 1962-64; chmn. 46th Assy. Dist., 1962-64, 27th Senatorial Dist., 1977-85, 29th Senatorial Dist., 1985-90; mem. Calif. Rep. State Cen. Com., 1966—, exec. com., 1966-67; trustee Rep. Assocs., 1979-94, pres., 1983-85, chmn. bd. dirs., 1985-87. 2d lt. USAAF, WWII. Fellow Am. Coll. Trust and Estate Counsel; academician Internat. Acad. Estate and Trust Law (exec. coun. 1974-78); mem. ABA, Los Angeles County Bar Assn. (chmn. probate and trust law com. 1964-66, Arthur K. Marshall award probate and trust law sect. 1984, chmn. legislation com. 1980-86, chmn. program com. 1981-82, chmn. membership retention com. 1982-83, trustee 1983-85, Shattuck-Price Meml. award 1990, dir. Bar Found. 1987-93), South Bay Bar Assn., State Bar Calif. (chmn. state bar jour. com. 1970-71, chmn. probate com. 1974-75, exec. com. estate planning trust and probate law sect. 1977-83, chmn. legislation com. 1977-89, co-chmn. 1991-92, probate law cons. group Calif. Bd. Legal Specialization 1977-88, chmn. conf. dels. resolutions com. 1987, exec. com. conf. dels. 1987-90), Lawyers Club of Los Angeles (bd. govs. 1981-87, 1st v.p. 1982-83), Am. Legion (comdr. Allied post 1969-70), Legion Lex (dir. 1964—, pres. 1969-71), Air Force Assn., Aircraft Owners and Pilots Assn., Town Hall (gov. 1970-78, pres. 1975), World Affairs Coun., Internat. Platform Assn., Los Angeles Com. on Fgn. Rels., Breakfast Club (law, pres. 1989-90), Commonwealth Club, Chancery Club (v.p. 1995—), Rotary, Phi Beta Kappa (councilor Alpha Assn. 1983—, v.p. 1984-86, 1994—), Omicron Delta Kappa, Phi Alpha Delta (supreme justice 1972-74, elected to Disting. Service chpt. 1978), Sigma Nu. Presbyterian. Home: 600 John St Manhattan Beach CA 90266-5837 Office: Darling Hall & Rae 777 S Figueroa St Fl 37 Los Angeles CA 90017-5800

RAEBER, JOHN ARTHUR, architect, construction specifier consultant; b. St. Louis, Nov. 24, 1947; s. Arthur William and Marie (Laux) R.; m. Sandi Hartupee, Aug. 16, 1969. AA, Jefferson Coll., 1968; AB, Washington U., 1970, MArch, 1973. Registered architect, Calif., Mo.; cert. constrn. specifier; cert. Nat. Coun. Artcht. Registration Bds. Specification writer Hellmuth,

Obata & Kassabaum, St. Louis, 1973-78, constrn. administr., 1978-79; mgr. of specifications Gensler & Assocs., San Francisco, 1979-82; ind. constrn. specifier San Francisco, 1982—; adj. prof. architecture Calif. Coll. Arts and Crafts, San Francisco, 1986—; access code advisor Constrn. Industry & Owners, 1982—; spkr., instr. seminars orgns., univs., 1982—; mem. Calif. State Bldg. Standards Commn. Accessibility Adv. Panel, Sacramento, 1981, Calif. Subcom. Rights of Disabled Adv. Panel, Sacramento, 1993. Author: CAL/ABL: Interpretative Manual to California's Access Barriers Laws, 1982; co-author: (with Peter S. Hopf) Access for the Handicapped, 1984; columnist Constrn. Specifier Mag., 1988-95. Vol. Calif. Office Emergency Svcs. Safety Assessment, Sacramento, 1991—. Fellow AIA (San Francisco chpt. codes com., Calif. coun. codes and standards com., nat. masterspec rev. com. 1982-84, nat. codes com. corr.), Contrns. Specifications Inst. (cert., columnist newsletter San Francisco chpt. 1984—, Ben John Small award for Outstanding Stature as practicing specifications writer 1994, pres. St. Louis chpt. 1978-79, pres. San Francisco chpt. 1993-94, tech. com., edn. com., publs. com., Specifications Proficiency award San Francisco chpt. 1989, Tech. Commendation award 1987); mem. Specifications Cons. in Ind. Practice (nat. pres. 1990-92, nat. sec./treas. 1988-90), Am. Soc. Testing and Materials, Internat. Conf. Bldg. Officials, Phi Theta Kappa. Home and Office: 519 Teresita Blvd San Francisco CA 94127-1830

RAEBURN, ANDREW HARVEY, performing arts association executive, record producer; b. London, July 22, 1933; arrived in U.S., 1964, Can., 1993; s. Walter Augustus Leopold and Dora Adelaide Harvey (Williams) R. M.A. in History, King's Coll., Cambridge (Eng.) U., 1959. Mus. dir. Argo Record Co., London, 1959-64; asst. to music dir., program editor Boston Symphony Orch., 1964-73; dir. artists and repertory New World Records, N.Y.C., 1975-79; artistic adminstr. Detroit Symphony Orch., 1979-82; exec. dir. Van Cliburn Found. Inc., Ft. Worth, 1982-85; performing arts cons., 1985-93; exec. v.p. The Peter Pan Children's Fund, 1990-91; exec. dir. Esther Honens Internat. Piano Competition Found., 1993-95, pres., 1995—; cons. music; radio and TV commentator; mem. faculty Boston U., 1966-67; condr. New World String Orch., 1978. Author record liner notes, Argo, RCA, Time-Life records, 1960-79, program notes, Boston Symphony Orch., 1968-73. Served with Royal Arty. Brit. Army, 1952-55. Home: Apt 406, 929 18th Ave SW, Calgary AB, AB Canada T2T 0H2 Office: 116 8th Ave SE 3rd Fl, Calgary, AB Canada T2G OK6

RAEDEKE, LINDA DISMORE, geologist; b. Great Falls, Mont., Aug. 20, 1950; d. Albert Browning and Madge (Hogan) Dismore; m. Kenneth John Raedeke, Dec. 26, 1971 (div. 1982); m. Charles Moore Swift, Jr., Mar. 14, 1992. BA in History, U. Wash., 1971, MS in Geology, 1979, PhD, 1982. Geomorphologist, park planner Corporacion Nacional Forestal and U.S. Peace Corps, Punta Arenas, Chile, 1972-74; glacial geologist Empresa Nacional del Petroleo, Punta Arenas, 1972-75; geologist FAO, UN, Punta Arenas, 1974; geologist Lamont-Doherty Geol. Obs., Columbia U., Tierra del Fuego, Chile, 1974-75; Wetlands evaluation project coord. Wash. Dept. Agr., U. Wash., Seattle, 1975-76; curator Remote Sensing Applications Lab., U. Wash., 1976-77; geol. rsch. asst. U. Wash., Seattle, 1977-81; exploration geologist Chevron Resources Co., Denver, 1981-84; rsch. geologist Chevron Oil Field Rsch. Co., La Habra, Calif., 1984-89; sr. compensation analyst Chevron Corp., San Francisco, 1989-90; staff geologist Chevron Overseas Petroleum, Inc., San Ramon, Calif. 1990-91, project leader, 1991-95, new ventures coord. for the far east, 1995—. Contbr. articles to profl. jours. Recipient Cert. of Achievement YWCA, 1988. Mem. Am. Geophys. Union, Geol. Soc. Am., Am. Assn. Petroleum Geologists (poster chmn. 1987). Office: Chevron Overseas Petroleum Inc PO Box 5046 San Ramon CA 94583-0946

RAEL, HENRY SYLVESTER, health administrator; b. Pueblo, Colo., Oct. 2, 1928; s. Daniel and Grace (Abyeta) R.; m. Helen Warner Loring Brace, June 30, 1956 (dec. Aug. 1980); children: Henry Sylvester, Loring Victoria. AB, U. So. Colo., 1955; BA in Bus Adminstrn., U. Denver, 1957, MBA, 1958. Sr. boys counselor Denver Juvenile Hall, 1955-58; adminstrv. asst. to pres. Stanley Aviation Corp., Denver, 1958-61; Titan III budget and fin. control supr. Martin Marietta Corp., Denver, 1961-65; mgmt. adv. services officer U. Colo. Med. Center, Denver, 1965-72; v.p. fin., treas. Loretto Heights Coll., Denver, 1972-73; dir. fin. and adminstrn. Colo. Found. for Med. Care, 1973-86, Tri-County Health Dept., Denver, 1986—; instr. fin. mgmt., mem. fin. com. Am. Assn. Profl. Standards Rev. Orgn., 1980-85; speaker systems devel., design assns., univs., 1967-71. Mem. budget lay adv. com. Park Hill Elem. Sch., Denver, 1967-68, chmn., 1968-69; vol. worker Boy and Girl Scouts, 1967-73; bd. dirs. Community Arts Symphony, 1981-83, 85-87; controller St. John's Episcopal Cathedral, 1982-83; charter mem. Pueblo (Colo.) Coll. Young Democrats, 1954-55; block worker Republican party, Denver, 1965-68, precinct committeeman, 1978-84; trustee Van Nattan Scholarship Fund, 1974—; bd. dirs. Vis. Nurse Assn., 1977-84, treas., 1982-84. Served with USAF, 1947-53; res. 1954-61. Recipient Disting. Service award Denver Astron. Soc., 1968, Citation Chamberlin Obs., 1985; Stanley Aviation masters scholar, 1957; Ballard scholar, 1956. Mem. Assn. Systems Mgmt. (pres. 1971-72), Hosp. Systems Mgmt. Soc., Budget Execs Inst. (v.p. chpt. 1964-65, sec. 1963-64), Colo. Pub. Employees Retirement Assn. (bd. dirs. 1993), Denver Astron. Soc. (pres. 1965-66, bd. dirs. 1982-94), Am. Assn. Founds. for Med. Care (fin. com. 1981-82), Nat. Astronomers Assn. (exec. bd. 1965—). Epsilon Xi, Delta Psi Omega. Episcopalian. Home: 70 S Albion St Denver CO 80222-1002

RAESE, JOHN THOMAS, physiologist; b. West Chester, Pa., Apr. 3, 1930; s. John Crutis and Alice Nelson (McKelvey) R.; m. Joan Marie Keeney, Sept. 12, 1953; children: John Craig, David Senna, Carolyn Kendall, Mary Ann. BS in Agr., W.Va. U., 1952, MS in Agronomy, 1959; PhD in Agronomy, U. Md., 1963. Soil tester for state W.Va. U., Morgantown, 1956-59, instr., 1958-59; rsch. asst. U. Md., College Park, 1959-62; tchr. biology Wheaton (Md.) High Sch., 1962-63; rsch. plant physiologist USDA Agrl. Rsch. Svc., Bogalusa, La., 1963-68; plant physiologist USDA Agrl. Rsch. Svc., Monticello, Fla., 1968-71; rsch. plant physiologist USDA Agrl. Rsch. Svc., Wenatchee, Wash., 1971-89, collaborator, 1990—; rschr. Wash. State U., Wenatchee, 1990—; hon. prof. Wenatchee Valley Coll., 1994—; speaker and cons. in field. Author: (with others) Horticultural; Reviews, 1989; editor: Pear Production-Pacific Northwest, 1990; contbr. 150 articles to profl. jours. Scoutmaster Boy Scouts Am., Bogalusa, 1967-=68, chmn. bd. com., Tallahassee, Fla., 1969-71, com. mem., Wenatchee, 1972-73; coach girls softball Little League, Wenatchee, 1973-75; co-organizer pear meeting Internat. Horticulture, Corvallis, Oreg., 1981. With USN, 1952-56. Recipient Pear Growers award Wash. Pear Growers, 1990; grantee Wash. State Horticulture, 1965-89, Comml. Cos., 1990—. Mem. Am. Soc. Horticulture Sci., Am. Soc. Agronomy, Internat. Soc. Horticulture Sci., Wash. Horticulture Assn., Fla. Horticulture Soc., Soc. for Cryobiology, Sigma Xi, Phi Epsilon Phi. Republican. Presbyterian. Office: US Tree Fruit Rsch Lab 1104 N Western Ave Wenatchee WA 98801-1230

RAFAEL, RUTH KELSON, archivist, librarian, consultant; b. Wilmington, N.C., Oct. 28, 1929; d. Benjamin and Jeanette (Spicer) Kelson; m. Richard Vernon Rafael, Aug. 26, 1951; children: Barbara Martinez Yates, Brenda Elaine. BA, San Francisco State U., 1953, MA, 1954; MLS, U. Calif.-Berkeley, 1968. Cert. archivist, 1989; life credential. Libr. Tchr. San Francisco Unified Sch. Dist., 1956-57; libr. Congregation Beth Sholom, San Francisco, 1965-83; archivist Western Jewish History Ctr. of Judah L. Magnes Mus., Berkeley, Calif., 1968, head archivist, libr., curator of exhibits, 1969-94; cons. NEH, Washington, NHPRC, Congregation Sherith Israel, San Francisco, Mount Zion Hosp., San Francisco, Benjamin Swig archives project, San Francisco, Koret Found., Camp Swig, Saratoga, Calif.; project dir. Ethnicity in Calif. Agriculture, 1989, San Francisco Jews of European Origin, 1880-1940, an oral history project, 1976, curator exhibits Western U.S. Jewry. Author: Continuum, San Francisco Jews of Eastern European Origin, 1880-1940, 1976, rev. edit., 1977; (with Davies and Woogmaster) poetry book Relatively Speaking, 1981; Western Jewish History Center: Archival and Oral History Collections, Judah L. Magnes Meml. Mus., 1987; contbg. editor Western States Jewish History, 1979—. Mem. exec. bd. Bay Area Library Info. Network, 1986-88. Bur. Jewish Edn. scholar, San Francisco, 1983; NEH grantee, 1985. Mem. Calif. Libr. Assn., Soc. Am. Archivists, Soc. Calif. Archivists, No. Calif. Assn. Jewish Librarians (pres. 1975-76), Jewish Arts Council of the Bay (bd. dirs. 1981-83),

RAFEEDIE, EDWARD, federal judge; b. Orange, N.J., Jan. 6, 1929; s. Fred and Nabeeha (Hishmeh) R.; m. Ruth Alice Horton, Oct. 8, 1961; children: Fredrick Alexander, Jennifer Ann. BS in Law, U. So. Calif., 1957, JD, 1959; LLD (hon.), Pepperdine U., 1978. Bar: Calif. 1960. Pvt. practice law Santa Monica, Calif., 1960-69; mcpl. ct. judge Santa Monica Jud. Dist., Santa Monica, 1969-71; judge Superior Ct. State of Calif., Los Angeles, 1971-82; dist. judge U.S. Dist. Court for (cen. dist.) Calif., Los Angeles, 1982—. Trustee Santa Monica Hosp. Med. Ctr., 1979—; bd. dirs. UniHealth, L.A., 1985. With U.S. Army, 1950-52, Korea. Office: US Dist Ct 312 N Spring St Los Angeles CA 90012-4701

RAFFERTY, KEVIN ALFRED, behavioral studies educator; b. Albany, N.Y., Aug. 21, 1953; s. Edward Michael and Marie Teresa (Walsh) R.; m. Rhonda Olivia Salkin, Aug. 10, 1975; children: Jessica Alison, Melissa Ann, Matthew Kevin. BA in Liberal Arts, Eisenhower Coll., 1975; MA in Anthropology, SUNY, Stony Brook, 1978, PhD in Archaeology, 1982. Field archaeologist Ariz. State U., Tempe, 1977-80; resource area archaeologist Bur. of Land Mgmt., Las Vegas, 1980-83; dir. archaeology Div. of Anthropol. Studies, U. Nev., Las Vegas, 1983-89; prof. ethnology C.C. So. Nev., North Las Vegas, 1989-91, chmn. dept. behavioral scis., 1991—; owner, prin., investigator Archaeol. Rsch. of So. Nev., 1990—; chmn. Nev. Coun. of Profl. Archaeologists, North Las Vegas, 1988—; vice-chmn. Adv. Coun. for Historic Preservation, Carson City, Nev., 1988—. Contbr. articles to profl. publs. Eucharistic min. Christ the King Cath. Community, Las Vegas, 1982-86, lector, 1989-92, mem. pro-life com., 1989—. Grad. fellowship SUNY, 1975-78. Mem. Soc. for Am. Archaeology, Southwestern Anthropol. Assn., Nev. Coun. of Profl. Archaeologists, Nev. ARchaeol. Assn., Ariz.-Nev. Acad. of Sci., Great Basin Anthropol. Conf. Democrat. Roman Catholic. Home: 1600 Camarillo Dr North Las Vegas NV 89031-1022 Office: CC So Nev 3200 E Cheyenne Ave North Las Vegas NV 89030-4228

RAFKIN, ALAN, television and film director; b. N.Y.C., July 23, 1928; s. Victor and Til (Bernstein) R.; children—Dru, Leigh Ann. B.S., Syracuse U., 1950. guest lectr. Bowling Green State U., 1975. Actor Robert Q. Lewis TV Show, 1955, daytime shows, CBS-TV; dir. Verdict is Yours, 1960, Mary Tyler Moore Show, 1970-71, Sanford and Son, 1972, Bob Newhart Show, 1972-73, Rhoda, 1973, Let's Switch, 1975, MASH, 1976-77, Love, American Style, 1970-71, Laverne & Shirley, 1977-83; TV movie: One Day at a Time: Barbara's Crisis, 1981-82; films include Ski Party, 1965, The Ghost and Mr. Chicken, 1966, The Ride to Hangman's Tree, 1967, Nobody's Perfect, 1968, The Shakiest Gun in the West, 1968, Angel in my Pocket, 1969, How to Frame a Figg, 1971. Served with U.S. Army, 1950-52. Democrat. Jewish. Office: care Catherine Byrne Gelford Rennert & Feldman 1800 Century Park E Ste 900 Los Angeles CA 90067-1512 also: The Brillstein Co 9200 W Sunset Blvd Los Angeles CA 90069-3502

RAFTERY, MIRIAM GENSER, writer, columnist; b. San Diego, Apr. 22, 1957; d. Philip and Mary Evelyn (Vick) Genser; m. Mark Raymond Raftery, July 21, 1979; children: Jason Michael, Kathleen Shannon. BA in Environ. Studies, U. Calif., Santa Barbara, 1979. Intern Planning & Conservation League, Sacramento, 1979; legis. aide Senator Bob Wilson, Sacramento, 1979-80, Assemblyman Elihu Harris, Sacramento, 1981-82; newsroom copy asst. Idaho Statesman, Boise, 1983-84; regional mktg. mgr. Con Am, San Diego, 1984-86; freelance writer La Mesa, Calif., 1986—; columnist San Diego Union-Tribune, 1992—; contracted feature writer San Diego Decorating Mag., 1994—; instr. The Writing Ctr., San Diego, 1994. Contbr. articles to popular mags. Mem. Nat. Fedn. Press Women, Nat. Assn. Real Estate Editors, Romance Writers Am. (workshop co-chair San Diego chpt. 1993-94), Calif. Press Women (pres. so. dist. 1993-95, v.p. membership 1993, Sweepstakes award 1992), Internat. Interior Designers Assn. (press mem.), San Diego Press Club, Phi Beta Kappa. Home and Office: 4438 Hideaway Pl La Mesa CA 91941-6800

RAGAN, SUSAN SWARTZ, art educator; b. Ft. Scott, Kans., Dec. 14, 1947; d. Daniel V. and Jean (Berry) Swartz; m. James Burton Ragan; children: Alison, John, Jennifer. BS in Edn., Mo. U., 1969; MEd, Colo. State U., Ft. Collins, 1974. Cert. tchr., Colo., Mo. Tchr. Colorado Springs (Colo.) Schs., 1970-72, Ft. Collins Schs., 1973-74; counselor St. Vrain Schs., Longmont, Colo., 1979-80; counselor, tchr. Sch. Dist. R32J, Salida, Colo., 1980—. Freelance artist for local and area agys., Salida, 1980—. Bd. dirs. Developmental Tng. Svcs., Salida, 1983-85; bd. trustees Salida Libr., 1992—. Recipient Excellence in Quilting award That Patchwork Pl., Bothell, Wash., 1991. Mem. NEA, PEO, Salida Edn. Assn., Colo. Quilt Coun. (Quilt Colo. 1st Pl. 1994), Delta Kappa Gamma. Democrat. Office: Salida Schs PO Box 70 Salida CO 81201

RAGEN, BROOKS GEER, investment banker; b. Portland, July 6, 1933; s. Louis Brooks and Florence (Grayden) R.; m. Suzanne Ljuba Munk, June 17, 1958; children: Matthew Brooks, Lisa Suzanne, Cameron Brooks. BA, Yale U., 1955; JD, Stanford U., 1958; MBA, NYU, 1966. Bar: Oreg. 1958. V.p. Dominick & Dominick, N.Y.C. and Seattle, 1964-72; 1st v.p. Blyth Eastman Dillon, Seattle, 1972-80; mng. dir. Blyth Eastman Paine Webber, Seattle, 1980-82; mng. pntr. Cable, Howse & Ragen, Seattle, 1982-87; pres. Cable, Howse & Ragen. Seattle, 1987-88; chmn., chief exec. officer Ragen MacKenzie, Inc., 1988—; mem. regional firms adv. com. N.Y. Stock Exchange, 1983-86; dir. Cascade Natural Gas Corp., Seattle. Past pres., bd. dirs. Bush Sch., Cardio-Pulmonary Rsch. Inst., Contemporary Theatre, The U. Washington Med. Ctr., Seattle Found.; now chmn. bd. Seattle Found., Seattle Art Mus., The U. Washington Med. Ctr. Mem. Seattle Bond Club (pres., bd. dir. 1979-80), Seattle Tennis Club, Rainier Club, Broadmoor Country Club. Avocations: Pacific northwest history. Office: Ragen MacKenzie Inc 999 3rd Ave Ste 4300 Seattle WA 98104-4001

RAGETH, DAVID ALLEN, telecommunications executive, network engineer; b. Hamburg, Iowa, June 12, 1962; s. Max Elburn and Cheryl Anne (Ninas) R.; m. Brenda Mae Buckman, Oct. 29, 1983; children: Michael, Gregory, Amanda. BS in Math., Mont. Tech. Coll., 1984, BS in Computer Sci., 1984; MEngring. in Computer Sci., U. Colo., 1991. Student programmer Mont. Power, Butte, 1981-84; assoc. programmer IBM, San Jose, Calif., 1984-85; software engr. No. Telecom, Inc., Denver, 1985-87; software engr. Martin Marietta, Denver, 1987, network engr., 1987—. Coach, YMCA, Littleton, Colo., 1991—. Mem. Assn. for Computing Machinery. Presbyterian. Home: 9868 Fairwood St Littleton CO 80125-8804

RAGHAVAN, VIJAYA NADIPURAM, engineering manager; b. India, May 1, 1939; came to U.S., 1963; s. Venkatanarashimachar and Ramamma (Achar) Nadipuram; m. Latha S. Purushothamy, July 11, 1971; children: Kartk, Sharat. MS, U. Bombay, 1963; PhD, U. R.I., 1969. Rsch. assoc. Stanford (Calif.) U., 1971-73; rsch. & devel. mgr. Am. Microsystems, Santa Clara, Calif., 1973-79; engring. mgr. Hewlett Packard, Santa Clara, Calif., 1979—. Mem. SPIE, Sigma Xi. Office: Hewlett Packard 5301 Stevens Creek Blvd Santa Clara CA 95051-7201

RAGLAND, SAMUEL CONNELLY, industrial engineer; b. Nashville, July 12, 1946; s. Julian Potter and Stella (Thompson) R.; m. Marilyn Margaret Oppelt, July 15, 1967; children: Sherry Anne, David Michael. BSBA, Ariz. State U., 1974; MBA U. Phoenix, 1991. Indsl. engr. First Interstate Bank, Phoenix, 1966-76, Beckman Instruments, Scottsdale, Ariz., 1976-78; mgmt. analyst Ariz. Legislative Budget Com., Phoenix, 1978; indsl. engr. mgmt. systems ITT Courier Terminal Systems, Tempe, Ariz., 1978-81; project control adminstr. Gen. Host Corp., Phoenix, 1981; sr. cons. Arthur Young & Co., Phoenix, 1981-82; ops. analyst City of Phoenix, 1982-84; project leader Garrett Engine div. Allied-Signal Corp. (formerly Garrett Turbine Engine Co.), Phoenix, 1984-92, cons., program mgr., TRW, Mesa, 1992-93; prin., owner Ragland Assocs., 1994—; dir. Mary Moppets of Highland Inc., 1977-81. Mem. Inst. Indsl. Engrs. (sr. mem. cen. Ariz. chpt., dir. community rels. 1983-85, dir. chpt. devel. 1985-86, v.p., pres.-elect 1986-87, pres. 1987-88), Inst. Indsl. Engrs. (nat. chpt. devel. com. 1988-91, chmn.), Assn. Systems Mgmt. (div. dir. 1989-92, pres. 1992-93), Phoenix Philatelic Assn. Contbr. articles to profl. publs. Address: 11319 E Jenan Dr Scottsdale AZ 85259-3121

RAGSDALE, CHRISTINA ANN, public relations executive, consultant; b. Long Beach, Calif., July 27, 1956; d. David Neal and Mary Lou (Kaiser) Webber; m. Joel Gordon Ragsdale, Mar. 14, 1987. BA in Creative Writing, Lone Mountain Coll., 1978; MA in Communication Studies, Calif. State U., Sacramento, 1983. Instr. communication studies Calif. State U., Sacramento, 1981-84; prodn. mgr. Videomedia, Inc., Sunnyvale, Calif., 1984-85; comm. specialist Mercy Gen. Hosp., Sacramento, 1985-88, community rels. mgr., 1988; owner Ragsdale Comm., Sacramento, 1988-93; water quality info. mgr. County of Sacramento, 1993—; cons. Cablevision of Sacramento, 1982; presenter Calif. Water Pollution Control Assn. conv., 1994, Ideas Unltd. workshop Soc. Healthcare Pub. Rels. and Mktg., 1985. Mem. exec. com. Harry S. Truman Dem. Club, Sacramento, 1990—; active comm. com. Am. Lung Assn., Sacramento, 1988—, chair Clean Air Week, 1993, 94, bd. dirs. Mem. Sacramento Pub. Rels. Assn. (bd. dirs. and sec. 1989-91, numerous awards), Natomas Optimist (charter), Nat. Assn. Profl. Environ. Communicators. Home: 14887 Trinidad Dr Rancho Murieta CA 95683

RAHE, RICHARD HENRY, psychiatrist, educator; b. Seattle, May 28, 1936; s. Henry Joseph and Delora Lee (Laube) R.; m. Laurie Ann Davies, Nov. 24, 1960 (div. Dec. 1990); children: Richard Bradley, Annika Lee. Student, Princeton U., 1954-57; MD, U. Wash., 1961. Diplomate Am. Bd. Psychiatry and Neurology. Chief resident in psychiatry U. Wash. Sch. Medicine, Seattle, 1965; rsch. psychiatrist USN, San Diego, 1965-75; commdg. officer Naval Health Rsch. Ctr., San Diego, 1976-80; exec. officer Long Beach (Calif.) Naval Hosp., 1980-82; commdg. officer Guam Naval Hosp., Agana, 1982-84; prof. psychiatry U.S. Univ. Health Scis. Mil. Med. Sch., Bethesda, Md., 1984-86, U. Nev. Sch. Medicine, Reno, 1986—; dir. Mil. Stress Studies Ctr., Bethesda, 1984-86, Nev. Stress Ctr., Reno, 1986—. Contbr. numerous articles to sci. jours., chpts. to books; photographer prints and video. Med. dir. Nev. Mental Health Inst., Sparks, 1991-94. Capt. USN, 1965-86. Recipient Humanitarian award Vietnamese Refugee Com., 1974, Dept. of State award for treatment of Am. hostages held in Iran, 1981. Fellow Am. Psychiat. Assn.; mem. Am. Psychosomatic Soc. (past pres.), World Psychiat. Assn. (past. pres. mil. sect.). Home: 638 Saint Lawrence Ave Reno NV 89509-1440 Office: VA Med Ctr Code 151-C 1000 Locust St Reno NV 89520-0102

RAIBLE, PETER SPILMAN, minister; b. Peterborough, N.H., Nov. 22, 1929; s. Robert Jules and Mildred (Galt) R.; m. Dee Dee Rainbow, June 18, 1950 (div. 1968); children: Stephen M., Robin S., Robert R., Deborah R.; m. Marcia McClellan Barton, June 5, 1987. PhB, U. Chgo., 1949; BA, U. Calif., Berkeley, 1952; MDiv, Starr King Sch. Ministry, 1953, D in Sacred Theology (hon.), 1974. Ordained to ministry Unitarian Ch. Asst. minister First Unitarian Ch., Providence, 1953-55; minister Unitarian Ch., Lincoln, Nebr., 1955-61, Univ. Unitarian Ch., Seattle, 1961—; bd. pres. Starr King Sch., Berkeley, 1967-68; mem. exec. com. Coun. Chs., Seattle, 1982-88; adj. prof. Meadville Lombard, 1987-88, N.W. Theol. Union, 1989. Author: How to Case a Church, 1982, Manual for Ordination Installation Services, 1994; book editor: Jour. Liberal Ministry, 1965-71; editor: UU Policy Manual, 1992. Bd. dirs. Council Planning Affiliates, Seattle, 1969-73, Wash. State chpt. ACLU, Seattle, 1963-67; chmn. ministerial adv. com. Planned Parenthood Ctr., Seattle, 1963-68; pres. United Nations Assn., Lincoln, 1959-61. Served as cpl. USAF, 1948-49. Merrill fellow Harvard U., Cambridge, Mass., 1972. Mem. Unitarian Universalist Ministers Assn. (pres. 1973-75), Pacific N.W. dist. Unitarian Universalist Assn. (exec. 1962-64, pres. 1985-87, mem. commn. on appraisal 1977-81). Office: U Unitarian Ch 6556 35th Ave NE Seattle WA 98115-7332

RAIKLEN, HAROLD, aerospace engineering consultant; b. Boston, June 7, 1920; s. Michael Isaac and Jennie Zelda (Jaffee) R.; m. Shirley Gesetz, Nov. 24, 1954; children: David R., Margery Claire. B, MIT, 1947, M, 1949. Dir. electronics and electrics Rockwell, El Segundo, Calif.; v.p. program mgr. Saturn II Rockwell, Downey and Seal Beach, Calif., 1965-70; v.p. rsch. and engrng. Rockwell, Downey, Calif., 1970-72; v.p. B-1 bomber engring. Rockwell, El Segundo, Calif., 1972-80, v.p. strategic aircraft, 1980-82; amateur anthropoligist, Long Beach, Calif., 1982—. Contbr. articles to profl. jours.; co-patentee in anti-skid sys. Recipient Collier trophy NASA, 1976, Pub. Svc. award, 1969. Fellow AIAA (Aircraft Design award 1979); mem. IEEE (life), Old Crows Assn., Pi Tau Sigma, Tau Beta Pi, Phi Kappa Phi. Home and Office: 4300 Cerritos Ave Long Beach CA 90807-2462

RAIN, RHONDA L., counselor, educator; b. Grinnell, Iowa, Feb. 28, 1952; d. Henry Garrett and Anne Lucille (Roberts) Rook; m. Daniel Charles Fuller, Aug. 25, 1984 (div. Sept. 1994). B in Univ. Studies, U. N.Mex., 1984, MA in Counseling, 1993. Lic. profl. counselor, N.Mex. Tchr., counselor Rough Rock (Ariz.) Demo. Sch., 1973; acad. support staff U. N.Mex. Med. Sch., Albuquerque, 1974-84, U. N.Mex. Main Campus, Albuquerque, 1988-91; intern counselor Manzanita Ctr. U. N.Mex., Albuquerque, 1993; intern counselor Career Ctr., Albuquerque, 1993, career counselor, 1993—; acad. advisor and counselor, coord. advisement and testing U. N.Mex.-Valencia, Los Lunas, 1994—; vocat. adv. com. New Futures H.S., Albuquerque, 1988-93; peer counselor U. N.Mex. Main Campus, Albuquerque, 1988-93; grad. asst. counseling dept. U. N.Mex., Albuquerque, 1991-92; vol. counselor Youth Diagnostic and Detention Ctr., Albuquerque, 1992. Neighborhood Watch capt. Crime Prevention Program, N.Mex., 1986-94; sec.-treas. Grad. Students in Counseling, U. N.Mex., Albuquerque, 1991-92. Recipient Fine Arts award Bank of Am., Huntington Beach, Calif., 1970. Mem. Am. Counseling Assn., Nat. Acad. Advising Assn., N.Mex. Mental Health Counselors Assn., S.W. Psychol. Assn., Nat. Bd. Cert. Counselors (nat. cert. counselor), Pi Lambda Theta, Golden Key Internat. Honor Soc. Home: 1611 Jack Nicklaus Dr Belen NM 87002 Office: Univ NMex Valencia 280 La Entrada Rd Los Lunas NM 87031-7633

RAINEY, BARBARA ANN, sensory evaluation consultant; b. Fond du Lac, Wis., Nov. 11, 1949; d. Warren and Helen Eileen (Ginther) Bradley; m. Phillip Michael Rainey, Sept. 5, 1970; 1 child, Nicolette. BS, Kans. State U., 1975. Group leader Armour & Co. R&D Ctr., Scottsdale, Ariz., 1976-80; owner Barbara A. Rainey Cons., Manteca, Calif., 1980—. Contbr. articles to profl. jours. Kans. State Alumni fellow Kans. State U. Alumni Assn., 1990. Mem. ASTM, Inst. Food Tehcnologists (sec. 1980-82, prof. sensory divsn. chmn. 1984-85, Ctrl. Valley subsect. chmn. 1992-93, chmn.-elect/sec. 1991-92, treas. 1989-91, short course spkr. 1979-81, 50th Anniversary Sensory Evaluation divsn. chmn. 1989), Phi Kappa Phi, Beta Sigma Phi, Delta Zeta Iota (sec. 1989-90, 94-95, treas. 1984-85, named for Best Program 1989, 90, 92, 93, 94, chmn. 1993-94). Office: PO Box 622 Manteca CA 95336-0622

RAISBECK, JAMES DAVID, aircraft design executive; b. Milw., Sept. 29, 1936; s. Clifford Clinton and Minnie (Hommersand) R.; BS in Aero. Engring., Purdue U., 1961; m. Sherry Bylund; 1 child, Jennifer Lee Raisbeck Hunter. Aero. rsch. engr. Boeing Co., Seattle, 1961-69, rsch. aerodynamist, 1961-64, commercial aircraft preliminary design, 1965-66; liaison to U.S. Air Force, 1966-68, program mgr. comml. STOL programs, 1968-69; chmn., CEO Robertson Aircraft Corp., Renton, Wash., 1969-73; v.p. tech. Am. Jet Industries, L.A., 1973-74; founder, chmn. bd., CEO Raisbeck Engring., Inc., 1974—; cons. Served with SAC, USAF, 1955-58. Recipient Disting. Engring. Alumnus in Aeronautics, Purdue U. Fellow AIAA (assoc. fellow); mem. Soc. Automotive Engrs., Tau Beta Pi, Sigma Gamma Tau, Phi Eta Sigma. Patentee in field of wing design, propellors and aircraft systems; achievements include designing and building aerodynamic improvement systems for airline business and corp. turbine-powered airplanes. Address: 7536 Seward Park Ave S Seattle WA 98118-4247

RAISIAN, JOHN, public policy institute executive, economist; b. Conneaut, Ohio, July 30, 1949; s. Ernest James and Ruby Lee (Owens) R.; m. Joyce Ann Klak, Aug. 17, 1984; children: Alison Kathleen, Sarah Elizabeth. BA, Ohio U., 1971; PhD, UCLA, 1978. Rsch. assoc. Human Resources Rsch. Ctr., U. So. Calif., L.A., 1972-73; cons. Rand Corp., Santa Monica, Calif., 1974-75, 76; vis. asst. prof. econs. U. Wash., Seattle, 1975-76; asst. prof. econs. U. Houston, 1976-80; sr. economist Office Rsch. and Evaluation, U.S. Bur. Labor Stats., Washington, 1980-81; spl. asst. for econ. policy Office Asst. Sc. for Policy, U.S. Dept. Labor, Washington, 1981-83, dir. rsch. and tech. support, 1981-84; pres. Unicon Rsch. Corp., L.A., 1984-86; sr. fellow Hoover Instn., Stanford, Calif., 1986—, assoc. dir., dep. dir., 1986-90, dir., 1990—; exec. dir. Presdl. Task Force on Food Assistance, Washington, 1983-84. Mem. editorial bd. Jour. Labor Rsch., 1983—; contbr. articles to profl. jours. Advisor Nat. Coun. on Handicapped, Washington, 1985-86, Nat. Commn. on Employment Policy, Washington, 1987-88; chmn. minimum wage bd. Calif. Indsl. Welfare Commn., 1987; mem. nat. adv.com. Student Fin. Assistance, Washington, 1987-89; corp. mem. Blue Shield Calif.

Recipient Best Publ. of Yr. award Econ. Inquiry, Western Econ. Assn., 1979, Disting. Teaching award U. Houston Coll. Social Scis., 1980, Disting. Svc. award U.S. Dept. Labor, 1983; predoctoral fellow Rand Corp., 1976. Mem. Am. Econs. Assn., Western Econ. Assn. (chmn. nominating com. 1992), Commonwealth Club of Calif., World Affairs Coun., Mont Pelerin Soc., Coun. on Fgn. Rels., Nat. Assn. Scholars, Phi Beta Kappa. Republican. Office: Stanford U Hoover Hoover Inst War-Revolution Stanford CA 94305-6010

RAJABI-ASL, ALI, information systems specialist, consultant; b. Abadan, Iran, June 13, 1963; came to U.S., 1979; s. Saleh and Mary R.-A. Student, L.A. Pierce Coll., 1982-83; BS, U. So. Calif., L.A., 1986. Part-time software and system cons. Falcon United Industries, Van Nuys, Calif., 1986-89, DejBan Structural Engring. Firm, Encino, Calif., 1986-88, Accu-Link Corp., Northridge, Calif., 1988-89; software engr. Orion Info. Systems, Sylmar, Calif., 1987-88, Am. Benefit Plan Adminstrs., L.A., 1988-89; sr. info. systems officer Security Pacific Automation Co., L.A., 1989-93; ind. cons. D.P. Specialists and Microsoft Consulting Svcs., 1993—. Mem. Assn. for Computing Machinery, Digital Equipment Computer Users Soc. Office: 705 Westmount Dr Apt 202 West Hollywood CA 90069-5131

RAJAGOPALAN, MALINI, molecular and cellular biologist; b. Madras, India, Oct. 24, 1960; came to U.S., 1987; d. Pulaveri Srinivasa and Madhavi (Rajagopalachari) R.; m. Mysore Padmanabha Ramprasad, Dec. 12, 1988. BS, Mt. Carmel Coll., Bangalore, India, 1979; MS, Delhi U., New Delhi, India, 1981; PhD, Indian Inst. Sci., Bangalore, India, 1987. Postdoctoral fellow dept. Biochemistry U. Ala., Birmingham, 1987-90, rsch. assoc. divsn. Endocrinology dept. Medicine, 1991-94; fellow in dept. medicine U. Calif., San Diego, 1994—. Author: Bacterial Chromosome, 1990, Procedure of UCLA Symposium, 1990. Indian Coun. Med. Rsch. fellow, Delhi, 1982-84, Dept. Atomic Energy fellow, Bombay, India, 1985-87. Mem. Am. Soc. Cell Biology.

RAJALA, KAREN RAE, economic and community development administrator; b. Richland, Wash., July 30, 1950; d. Raymond Edward and Georgia Marie (Dickson) Burns; m. Jacob August Rajala, Sept. 2, 1972; children: Matthew August, Andrew George. BA in Sociology with distinction, Wash. State U., 1972, BA in Polit. Sci. cum laude, 1974, MA in Polit. Sci., 1978. Adminstrv. asst. Whitman County Epton Soc., Pullman, Wash., 1973-78; cons., grantwriter, planner Ely, Nev., 1981-83; coord. White Pine County Econ. Diversification Program, Ely, 1983—, White Pine Power Project, Ely, 1988—; alt. Block Grant Adv. Bd., Carson City, Nev., 1994, adv. bd. 1995—; vol. cons. Little People's Hedstart, Ely, 1981-83; cons. White Pine C. of C., Ely, 1982-83; mem. Nev. State Comty. Devel., 1992. Project leader, mem. 4-H Parents and Leaders Coun., Ely, 1988—; active No. Nev. Comty. Coll. Adv. Bd., Ely, 1984—, White Pine Pub. Mus., Ely, 1992—, PEO Sisterhood, 1970—, v.p., 1981, pres., 1986. Recipient Meritorious Svc. award White Pine Dist. 4-H, 1993, Rural Nevadans Who Dare to Care award U. Nev. Med. Sch., 1994. Mem. Am. Soc. Pub. Adminstrn., Nev. Econ. Devel. Assn., Pi Sigma Alpha. Democrat. Methodist. Office: White Pine County Econ Div 457 5th St Ely NV 89301-1973

RAKOWSKI, JOHN MICHAEL, geologist; b. Southampton, N.Y., June 25, 1946; s. John J. and Gertrude (Kuroski) R.; m. Alice D. Reiber, Dec. 20, 1968; children: Janet L., David A. BS in Geology, Fla. State U., 1968. Geologist Amoco Prodn. Co., New Orleans, 1968-73, 75-79, Denver, 1979-81; geologist Amoco Internat. Oil Co., Chgo., 1973-74; geologist Tesoro Petroleum, Jakarta, Indonesia, 1974-75, La Paz, Bolivia, 1975; v.p. exploration Striker Petroleum Corp., Denver, 1981-84; geol. cons. Rak-Energy, Lakewood, Colo., 1984—. Counselor, asst. cub scout troop Boy Scouts Am., Lakewood, Colo., 1983-86. Mem. Am. Assn. Petroleum Geologists (cert.), New Orleans Geol. Soc., Rocky Mountain Assn. Geologists, Soc. Ind. Profl. Earth Scientists (bd. dirs. 1993-95), Houston Geol. Soc., Nat. Fedn. Ind. Bus., Denver Gem and Mineral Guild (pres. 1995). Republican. Office: Rak-Energy 2357 S Devinney St Lakewood CO 80228-4807

RAKOWSKY, RONALD JOHN, lawyer; b. Cleve., Sept. 24, 1944; s. John and Rose Frances (Hoffman) R.; m. Margaret Follin Hughes, Aug. 13, 1966; children: Catherine, Robert. BA, Denison U., Granville, Ohio, 1966; JD, Case Western Res. U., 1969. Bar: Ohio 1970, Fla. 1971, U.S. Ct. Mil. Appeals 1971, U.S. Supreme Ct. 1973, Colo. 1993. Staff atty. Law Medicine Ctr. Case Western Res. U., Cleve., 1970; staff atty. MacDill AFB, Tampa, Fla., 1970-74; from commd. to col. USAF, 1966-; staff atty. Clark Air Base, Philippines, 1974-75, Mil. Personnel Ctr., Universal City, Tex., 1975-79; staff judge advocate March Air Force Base, Riverside, Calif., 1979-83; chief personnel law HQ USAF, Washington, D.C., 1983, chief legis. div., 1987, chief preventive law, 1988; staff judge advocate Air Res. Personnel Ctr., Denver, 1988-94; bd. dirs. Space Age Fed. Credit Union, chmn. 1991-94, dir. CU Leasing Corp., Arvada, Co. Mem. Judge Advocates Assn. (pres. 1986-87), Army Navy Club, Alpha Tau Omega. Office: HQ ARPC/JA 4950 West 60th Ave Arvada CO 80003

RALEIGH, CECIL BARING, geophysicist; b. Little Rock, Aug. 11, 1934; s. Cecil Baring and Lucile Nell (Stewart) R.; m. Diane Lauster, July 17, 1982; children: Alison, Marianne, Lawrence, David. B.A., Pomona (Calif.) Coll., 1956; M.A., Claremont (Calif.) Grad. Sch., 1958; Ph.D., UCLA, 1963. Fellow Research Sch. Phys. Sci., Australian Nat. U., Canberra, 1963-66; geophysicist U.S. Geol. Survey, Menlo Park, Calif., 1966-80; program mgr. for earthquake prediction research program U.S. Geol. Survey, 1980-81; dir. Lamont-Doherty Geol. Obs. and prof. geol. scis. Columbia U., Palisades, N.Y., 1981-89; dean Sch. Ocean and Earth Sci. and Tech. U. Hawaii, Honolulu, 1989—; chmn. bd. dirs. DOSECC, Inc., 1985-88; mem. NAS/NRC Ocean Studies Bd.; bd. dirs. JOI, Inc.; bd. dirs. Nat. Energy Lab. Hawaii Authority; chmn. NAS/NRC Yucca Mountain Panel. Author papers control earthquakes, rheology of the mantle, mechanics of faulting, crystal plasticity. Recipient Interdisciplinary award U.S. Nat. Com. Rock Mechanics, 1969, 74; Meritorious Service award Dept. Interior, 1974; Barrows Dist. Alumnus award Pomona Coll. Fellow Am. Geophys. Union, Geol. Soc. Am. Democrat. Office: U Hawaii Sch Ocean Earth Sci & Tech Honolulu HI 96822

RALEY, WILLIAM GREENE, systems analyst; b. Pensacola, Fla., July 8, 1958; s. Nathaniel Greene and Virginia Phillips (Glass) R. BS magna cum laude, U. Ala., 1979, MA, 1980. FLMI; cert. in gen. ins. Programmer Shell Oil, Houston, 1981-82; staff cons. Am. Gen., Houston, 1982-85; host computer tech. specialist Avco Aerostructures, Nashville, Tenn., 1985-86; sr. programmer/analyst Auto Club So. Calif., Costa Mesa, 1986—. Editor, pub. After Hours mag., 1989—; copy editor Huntington Beach News, 1991. Active Mus. Neon Art, L.A., 1988—, Ctr. for Sci. in Pub. Interest, Washington, 1992—. Mem. Horror Writers Assn., Mensa, Phi Beta Kappa, Delta Phi Alpha, Pi Mu Epsilon. Home: PO Box 538 Sunset Beach CA 90742-0538

RALLISON, MARVIN L., pediatrician, educator; b. Coalville, Utah, Feb. 8, 1929; s. Robert Leo and Lucile (Peterson) R.; m. Beth West, June 21, 1957; children: Scott W., Mark W., Todd W., Lisa. BS in Chemistry, Utah State U., 1954; MD, U. Utah, 1957. Diplomate Am. Bd. Pediatrics, Am. Bd. Endocrinology. Intern Mpls. Gen. Hosp., 1957-58; resident in pediatrics U. Minn. Hosp., 1958-61; instr. U. Minn., Mpls., 1960-61; pediatrician Salt Lake Clinic, Salt Lake City, 1961-63; fellow in endocrinology U. Utah, Salt Lake City, 1963-65, asst. prof., 1968-73, assoc. prof. pediatrics, 1973-79, prof. pediatrics, 1979—. Author: Growth Problems in Children, 1986; contbr. numerous articles to profl. jours. Med. dir. Camp Utada for diabetic youth, Salt Lake City area, 1963-93. Maj. Med. Corps U.S. Army, 1957-68. Mem. Am. Thyroid Assn. (pub. health com.), Am. Diabetes Assn. (bd. dirs. 1987-89, chmn. com. on edn. 1981-83, mem. youth com. 1984-89, Outstanding Contbr. to Camping and Am. Diabetes Assn. award 1993), Lawson Wilkins Pediatric Endocrine Soc., Western Soc. Pediatric Rsch. Home: 1706 Oakridge Dr Salt Lake City UT 84106-3253 Office: U Utah Med Ctr Salt Lake City UT 84132

RALSTON, GILBERT ALEXANDER, writer, educator; b. L.A., Jan. 5, 1912; s. Alexander Gilbert and Jeanette (Johnston) R.; grad. Pasadena Coll., 1929-32; grad. Am. Acad. Dramatic Arts, 1935; B.C.A., Sierra Nev. Coll., 1972; D in Psychology, Fielding Inst., 1983, PhD in Health Sci., 1987, Columbia Pacific U., 1986; m. Mary K. Hart, Dec. 20, 1938; children—Michael, David. Actor, stage mgr. theatre prodns. N.Y.C., 1931-35; writer, dir. radio shows NBC, N.Y.C., 1936-38; prodn. supr. Compton Advt., Inc., N.Y.C., West Coast, 1939-42; organizer, mgr. radio dept. Proctor & Gamble, Cin., 1943-47, exec. producer inc. TV div., 1947-50; free lance producer TV films, 1950-55; exec. producer in charge TV drama CBS, 1955, dir. network programs originating in N.Y.C., 1956; producer High Adventure documentaries with Lowell Thomas, 1957; chmn. sch. communication arts Tahoe (Cal.) Paradise Coll., 1968; dean sch. communicative arts Sierra Nevada Coll., Incline Village, Nev., 1960-73, pres., 1973-83, pres. emeritus, 1983—; pres. Ralston Sch. Communicative Arts, Genoa, Nev., 1971—, Ralston Sch. Massage; v.p. Rule of Three Prodns., Los Angeles, 1973—; lectr. Fordham U., City Coll. City U. N.Y., Loyola U. of Los Angeles, St. Mary's Coll. of Calif. Mem. Authors Guild, ASCAP, Western Writers Am., Writers Guild Am., Am. Massage and Therapy Assn. Author: Ben, 1972; (with Richard Newhafer) The Frightful Sin of Cisco Newman, 1972; Dakota Warpath, 1973; Dakota: Red Revenge, 1973; Dakota Cat Trap, 1974; Dakota Murder's Money, 1974; Dakota: Chain Reaction, The Deadly Art, 1975, The Third Circle, 1976, The Tao of Touch, 1983, Gods Fist, 1989, Hamelin House, 1989, Hunter Fentress, 1990, Fattura Della Morte, 1990, others. Author screenplays: No Strings Attached, 1962; A Gallery of Six, 1963; A Feast of Jackals, 1963; Cockatrice, 1965; Kona Coast, 1967; Night of the Locust, 1969; Ben, 1971, Third Circle, 1975, Sure, 1975. Author screen adaptations: Willard (by Stephen Gilbert), 1970; Bluebonnet (by Boris Sobelman and Jack H. Robinson), 1971; Dakota Red, 1987. Author scripts for TV under sometime pseudonym Gil Alexander: High Adventure, Naked City, Route 66, Follow the Sun, Bus Stop, The Untouchables, Alcoa Theatre, Ben Casey, Richard Boone Show, 12 O'Clock High, The Name of the Game, Daktari, Laredo, Combat, Big Valley, Gunsmoke, Amos Burke, Slattery's People, Alfred Hitchcock, Star Trek, It Takes a Thief, O'Hara, Cannon, numerous others. Address: PO Box 490 Sullivans Island SC 29482-0490

RALSTON, JOANNE SMOOT, public relations counseling firm executive; b. Phoenix, May 13, 1939; d. A. Glen and Virginia (Lee) Smoot; m. W. Hamilton Weigelt, Aug. 15, 1991. B.A. in Journalism, Ariz. State U., 1960. Reporter, The Ariz. Republic, Phoenix, 1960-62; co-owner, pub. relations dir. The Patton Agy., Phoenix, 1962-71; founder, pres., owner Joanne Ralston & Assocs., Inc., Phoenix, 1971-87, 92—; pres. Nelson Ralston Robb Comm., Phoenix, 1987-91; pres. Joanne Ralston & Assoc., Inc., Scottsdale, Ariz., 1992—. Contbr. articles to profl. jours. Bd. dirs. Ariz. Parklands Found., 1984-86, Gov.'s Council on Health, Phys. Fitness and Sports, 1984-86; task force mem. Water and Natural Resources Council, Phoenix, 1984-86; mem. Ariz. Republican Caucus, 1984—, others. Recipient Lulu' awards (36) Los Angeles Advt. Women, 1964—, Gold Quill (2) Internat. Assn. Bus. Communicators, Excellence awards Fin. World mag., 1982-93, others; named to Walter Cronkite Sch. Journalism Hall of Fame, Coll. Pub. Programs Ariz. State U., 1987; name one of 25 Most Influential Arizonians, Phoenix Mag., 1991. Mem. Pub. Relations Soc. Am. (counselor sect.), Internat. Assn. Bus. Communicators, Phoenix Press Club (pres. bd.), Investor Rels. Inst., Phoenix Met. C. of C. (bd. dirs. 1977-84, 85-91), Phoenix Country Club. Republican. Avocations: horses, skiing.

RALSTON, LENORE DALE, academic policy and program analyst; b. Oakland, Calif., Feb. 21, 1949; d. Leonard Earnest and Emily Allison (Hudnut) R. BA in Anthropology, U. Calif., Berkeley, 1971, MPH in Behavioral Sci., 1981; MA in Anthropology, Bryn Mawr Coll., 1973, PhD in Anthropology, 1980. Asst. researcher anthropology inst. internat. studies U. Calif., Berkeley, 1979-82, rsch. assoc. Latin Am. Study Ctr., 1982-83, acad. asst. to dean Sch. of Optometry, 1990-95; mem. Chancellor's Office, Planning and Analysis Latin Am. Study Ctr., 1995—; assoc. scientist, rsch. adminstr. Med. Rsch. Inst., San Francisco, 1982-85; cons. health sci. Berkeley, 1986-90; mem. fin. bd. Med. Rsch. Inst., 1983-84; speaker in field. Co-author: Voluntary Effects in Decentralized Management, 1983; contbr. articles to profl. jours. Commr. Cmty. Health Adv. Com., Berkeley, 1988-90; vice chair, commr. Cmty. Health Commn., Berkeley, 1990-93; mem. bd. safety com. Miles, Inc., Berkeley, 1992—. Grantee Nat. Rsch. Svc. Award, WHO, NIMH, NSF. Fellow Applied Anthropology Assn.; mem. Am. Pub. Health Assn., Am. Anthropology Assn., Sigma Xi. Home: 1232 Carlotta Ave Berkeley CA 94707-2707

RALSTON, RACHEL WALTERS, developmental psychologist; b. Max, N.D., June 13, 1915; d. Lewis David and Wilhelmina May Bertha (Freitag) Walters; m. William Clifton Hollowell, May 22, 1944 (div. May 1962); m. John Elvin Ralston, June 24, 1964. AA, Foothill Jr. Coll., 1964; BA, San Francisco State U., 1969; postgrad., Can. Coll., 1975-81. Chair North Fair Oaks Adv. Coun., Redwood City, Calif., 1975-77; initiator Community Concern for Sr. Citizens, Menlo Park and San Mateo County, Calif., 1975-80; organizer, pres. Concerned Srs., Inc., San Mateo County, 1980-86; chair exec. bd. Concerned Srs., Inc., Redwood City, 1987—; peer counselor for the elders Mental Health div. Health Dept., San Mateo County, 1986-94; Mem. Older Adults Com., Mental Health Adv. Bd., 1985—; mem. adv. bd. Emeritus Inst. Coll. of San Mateo, 1987—. Mem. Com. on Aging San Mateo County, 1978-90; del. State House Conf. on Aging, Sacramento, 1980. Recipient Commendation Pvt. Sector Initiative, Washington, D. C., 1986; named Citizen of The Day Sta. KABL, San Francisco, 1985. Mem. AAUW, Am. Soc. on Aging, Am. Assn. Ret. Persons. Republican. Home: 610 17th Ave Menlo Park CA 94025-2039

RALSTON, ROY B., petroleum consultant; b. Monmouth, Ill., June 7, 1917; s. Roy Crews and Helen Ruth (Boggs) R.; m. Catherine Elizabeth Thompson, Aug. 6, 1940; 1 child, John Richard. BA, Cornell Coll., 1939; student, Iowa U., 1938; postgrad., U. Ill., 1940-41. Petroleum cons. Colorado Springs, Colo., 1977—; dist. mgr. exploration Skelly Oil Co., Evansville, Ind., 1941-46; div. mgr. exploration and prodn. Ashland Oil Co., Henderson, Ky., 1946-50; mgr. exploration and prodn. Ashland Oil Co., Ashland, Ky., 1950-54; div. mgr. exploration Phillips Petroleum Co., Evansville, 1955-58, Amarillo, Tex., 1958-65, Oklahoma City, 1965-69; v.p. exploration and prodn. Phillips Petroleum Can. Ltd., Calgary, Alta., Can., 1969-73; exploraton mgr. North Am. Phillips Petroleum Co., Bartlesville, Okla., 1973-75; regional mgr. exploration and prodn. Phillips Petroleum Co., Denver, 1975-77; petroleum con. 1st Nat. Bank, Amarillo, Tex., 1977-93, Valley Nat. Bank, Phoenix, 1977-93, 1st Interstate Bank, Phoenix, 1977-86. Youth career dir. Oklahoma City C. of C., 1966-68. Recipient Disting. Svc. award Okla. Petroleum Coun., 1968, Svc. award Land Mgmt. Sch. Okla. U., 1978. Mem. Am. Assn. Petroleum Geologists (publicity dir. nat. conv. Oklahoma City 1968, cert. petroleum geologist), Am. Assn. Petroleum Landmen, Soc. Petroleum Engrs. AIME, Ariz. Geol. Soc., N.Mex. Geol. Soc., Rotary. Republican. Presbyterian.

RAM, TRACY SCHAEFER, ballet company manager; b. San Francisco, June 4, 1960; d. Donald Worth and Leslie Lorraine Wells Schaefer; m. Michael Francis Ram, May 29, 1987. BA in Polit. Sci. and Mass Communications, U. Calif., Berkeley, 1982. Legal asst. Morrison & Foerster, San Francisco, 1982-84; asst. to gen. mgr. San Francisco Ballet, 1984-86, mgr. co., 1986—. Democrat. Home: 761 Noe St San Francisco CA 94114-2941 Office: San Francisco Ballet 455 Franklin St San Francisco CA 94102-4438

RAMALEY, JUDITH AITKEN, university president, endocrinologist; b. Vincennes, Ind., Jan. 11, 1941; d. Robert Henry and Mary Krebs (McCullough) Aitken; m. Robert Folk Ramaley, Mar. 1966 (div. 1976); children: Alan Aitken, Andrew Folk. BA, Swarthmore Coll., 1963; PhD, UCLA, 1966; postgrad., Ind. U., 1967-69. Rsch. assoc., lectr. Ind. U., Bloomington, 1967-68, asst. prof. dept. anatomy and physiology, 1969-72; asst. prof. dept. physiology and biophysics U. Nebr. Med. Ctr., Omaha, 1972-74, assoc. prof., 1974-78, prof., 1978-82, assoc. dean for rsch. and devel., 1979-81; asst. v.p. for acad. affairs U. Nebr., Lincoln, 1980-82; prof. biol. scis. SUNY, Albany, N.Y., 1982-87, v.p. for acad. affairs, 1982-85, acting pres., 1984, exec. v.p. for acad. affairs, 1985-87; exec. vice chancellor U. Kans., Lawrence, 1987-90; pres. Portland (Oreg.) State U., Oreg., 1990—; bd. dirs. Bank of Am.; mem. endocrinology study sect. NIH, 1981-84; cons.-evaluator North Cen. Accreditation, 1978-82, 89-90; mem. regulatory panel NSF, 1979-82; mem. Ill. Commn. Scholars, 1980—. Co-author: Progesterone Function: Molecular and Biochemical Aspects, 1972; Essentials of Histology, 8th edit., 1979; editor: Covert Discrimination, Women in the Sciences, 1978; contbr. articles to profl. jours. Bd. dirs. Family Svc. of Omaha, 1979-82, Albany Symphony Orch., 1984-87, mem. exec. com., 1986-87, Urban League Albany, 1984-87, 2d v.p., mem. exec. com., 1986-87, Upper Hudson Planned Parenthood, 1984-87, Capital Repertory Co., 1986-89, Assn. Portland Progress, 1990—, City Club of Portland, 1991-92, Metro Family Svcs., 1993—, Campbell Inst. for Children, Portland Met. Sports Authority, 1994; bd. dirs. NCAA Pres. Commn., 1991, chair divsn. II subcom., 1994, mem. joint policy bd., 1994; chmn. bd. dirs. Albany Water Fin. Authority, 1987; mem. exec. com. United Way Douglas County, 1989-90; mem. adv. bd. Emily Taylor Women's Resource Ctr., U. Kans., 1988-90; mem. Silicon Prarie Tech. Assn., 1989-90, Portland Opera Bd., 1991-92, Portland Leaders Roundtable, 1991—; mem. bd. devel. com. United Way of Columbia-Williamette, 1991—; active Oreg. Women's Forum, 1991—, Portland Met. Sports Authority; progress bd. Portland-Multinomah County, 1993—. NSF grantee, 1969-71, 71-77, 75-82, 77-80, 80-83. Fellow AAAS; mem. Nat. Assn. State Univs. and Land Grant Colls. (exec. com., mem. senate 1986-88, vice chair comn. urban agenda 1992—), Assn. Am. Colls. and Univs. (bd. dirs. 1995), Endocrine Soc. (chmn. edn. com. 1980-85), Soc. Study Reprodn. (treas. 1983-85), Soc. for Neuroscis., Am. Physiol. Soc., Am. Coun. on Edn. (chmn. commn. on women in higher edn. 1987-88), Assn. Portland Progress (bd. dirs.), Portland C. of C. (bd. dirs. 1995), Western Assn. of Schs. and Colls. (commr. 1994). Office: Portland State U Office of the President PO Box 751 Portland OR 97207-0751

RAMASWAMY, PADMANABHAN, materials scientist; b. Ambattur, India, Mar. 5, 1953; came to U.S., 1977; s. Ramaswamy Iyer and Bhagavathy (Narayanan) Padmanabhan. BSc in Physics, Loyola Coll., Madras, India, 1972; B of Engring. in Metallurgy, Indian Inst. Sci., Bangalore, 1975; PhD in Materials Sci., Oreg. Grad. Ctr., 1982. Research and devel. engr. Bharat Electronics, Ltd., Bangalore, 1975-77; research scientist Oreg. Grad. Ctr., Beaverton, 1982-83; sr. staff engr. Motorola, Inc., Phoenix, 1984-86, prin. staff scientist, 1987-91, mem. tech. staff, mgr. materials and characterization lab., adv. pkg. deve. ctr., 1991—. Contbr. articles to profl. jours. Mem. Electron Microscopy Soc. Am., Electrochem. Soc., Materials Rsch. Soc. Home: 1325 E Grandview St Mesa AZ 85203-4427 Office: Motorola Inc B-136 5005 E Mcdowell Phoenix AZ 85026

RAMBO, A. TERRY, anthropologist, research program director; b. San Francisco, Apr. 3, 1940; s. Arthur Ira Rambo and Dorothy V. (Miller) Schlee; m. Dawn Jean Bowman, Jan. 24, 1971 (dec. July 1987); children: Charmaine Malia, Claire Norani. AB in Anthropology with distinction, U. Mich., 1963; MA in Anthropology, Am. U., 1969; PhD in Anthropology, U. Hawaii, 1972. Rsch. scientist Human Scis. Rsch., Inc., McLean, Va., 1964-69; acting asst. prof. anthropology U. Hawaii, 1971-72; asst. prof. anthropology Wash. State U., 1972-73; vis. prof. social sci. Grad. Sch. Politics and Econs., Dalat U., Saigon, Vietnam, 1973-75; lectr. dept. anthropology and sociology U. Malaya, 1975-80; sr. fellow, coord. program on renewable resources mgmt. East-West Ctr. Environ. and Policy Inst., Honolulu, 1980-92; dir. program on environ., coord. Indochina initiative East-West Ctr., Honolulu, 1992—; bd. dirs. S.E. Asian Univs. Agroecosystem Network; cons. in field. Author: Primitive Polluters, 1985, Comparison of Peasant Social Systems of Northern and Southern Viet-nam, 1973; editor: Profiles in Cultural Evolution, 1991; mem. editorial bd. Biodiversity Letters; assoc. Current Anthropology; co-editor: An Introduction to Human Ecology Research on Agricultural Systems in Southeast Asia, 1984, also reports, papers, monographs, procs. in field; contbr. articles and revs. to profl. publs., chpts. to books. Grantee Asia Soc./SEADAG, 1969-70, U. Malaya, 1976-79, Ford Found., 1978-79, 84, 85-87, 87-89, 91-93, 95—, U. Hawaii/East-West Ctr., 1981-82, 84-85, Rockefeller Bros. Fund, 1988-89, 90-92, 94-95, MacArthur Found., 1990-91, 91-93, 93—; Nat. Def. Fgn. Lang. fellow, 1970-71, Ford Found. S.E. Asia rsch. fellow, 1972, 73-74, 75-76. Office: East-West Ctr Program on Environment 1777 East-West Rd Honolulu HI 96848

RAMBO, ELIZABETH LOUISE, English literature educator; b. Phila., July 27, 1954; d. Victor Birch and Margaret (Gordon) R.; m. James Worth Pence III, May 20, 1989. BA in English, St. Andrews Presbyn. Coll., 1976; MA in English and Creative Writing, U. Mo., 1978; PhD in English, U. N.C., 1990. Asst. prof. English Biola U., La Mirada, Calif., 1990—, chair dept. English, 1993—. Author: Colonial Ireland in Medieval English Literature, 1994. Mem. MLA, Nat. Coun. Tchrs. of English, Medieval Acad. Am., Conf. on Christianity and Lit., Medieval Assn. of Pacific. Presbyterian. Office: Biola U English Dept 13800 Biola Ave La Mirada CA 90639-0002

RAMER, BRUCE M., lawyer; b. Teaneck, N.J., Aug. 2, 1933; s. Sidney and Anne S. (Strassman) R.; m. Ann Greenberg Ramer, Feb. 15, 1965; children: Gregg B., Marc K., Neal I. BA, Princeton U., 1955; LLB, Harvard U., 1958. Bar: Calif. 1963, N.J. 1958. Assoc., Morrison, Lloyd & Griggs, Hackensack, N.J., 1959-60; ptnr. Gang, Tyre, Ramer & Brown, Inc., L.A., 1963—. Exec. dir. Entertainment Law Inst., Law Ctr. of U. So. Calif.; bd. of councilors Law Ctr. U. So. Calif.; past pres. L.A. chpt.; bd. govs., chmn. nat. exec. coun. Am. Jewish Com. (nat. v.p. 1982-88, pres. L.A. chpt. 1980-83, chair Western region 1984-86, community svc. award, 1987); chmn. Pacific Rim Inst.; trustee Loyola Marymount U. (mem. exec. com.); vice chair United Way, 1991-93, corp. bd. dirs., 1981-93, chair coun. pres. 1989-90, mem. community issues coun., 1989-90, chair discretionary fund distbn. com., 1987-89; bd. dirs. L.A. Urban League, 1987—, Jewish Fedn. Coun. of greater L.A. (mem. Community Rels. com.), Jewish TV Network, Sta. KCET-TV; mem., bd. dirs. Rebuild L.A.; vice chmn., bd. govs. Calif. Community Found.; recipient Ann. Brotherhood award Nat. Conf. of Christians and Jews, 1990; mem. Fellows of Am. Bar Found. Pvt. U.S. Army, 1958-59, 2d lt., 1961-62. Mem. ABA, L.A. County Bar Assn., Calif. Bar Assn., Beverly Hills Bar Assn. (exec. dirs. award 1988), L.A. Copyright Soc. (pres. 1974-75), Calif. Copyright Conf. (pres. 1973-74), Princeton Club (pres. 1975-78). Office: Gang Tyre Ramer & Brown Inc 132 S Rodeo Dr Beverly Hills CA 90212

RAMESH, KALAHASTI SUBRAHMANYAM, materials scientist; b. Tiruchi, Madras, India, Mar. 22, 1949; s. Subrahmanyam Veeraragaviah and Kuntala (Chinnaswami) Kalahasti; m. Atsumi Yoshida Ramesh, Jan. 30, 1990; 1 child, Siva. MS in Ceramic Engring., Benaras Hindu U., India, 1973; D in Engring., Tokyo Inst. Tech., 1986. Asst. rsch. mgr. Steel Authority India Ltd., Ranchi, Bihar, 1979-80; lectr. dept. ceramic engring. Benaras U., Varanasi, India, 1980-82; tech. mgr. ceramics div. TYK Corp., Tokyo, 1986-89; mgr. rsch. and devel. Mer Corp., Tuscon, Ariz., 1989; prin. scientist Battelle meml. Inst., Columbus, Ohio, 1989-93; sr. sci. Pacific N.W. Lab., Richland, Wash., 1993—; adv. Internat. Bus. Svc., Tokyo, 1988-89; cons. HTP Inc., Sharon, Pa., 1989—; mem. U.S. Dept. Energy Ceramics Adv. Com., Washington, 1991—; tech. dir. XTALONIX, Inc., Columbus, Ohio, 1993—. Panel mem. NSF on Materials and Mechanics, 1995. Mombusho Rsch. fellow Min. Edn. Japan, 1982-85. Fellow Indian Inst. Ceramics, Inst. Ceramics U.K.; mem. Japan India Assn., Found. for Indsl. Rsch. (expert), Max Planck Soc., N.Y. Acad. Scis. Hindu. Home: 100 Hillview Dr Richland WA 99352-9668 Office: Pacific Northwest Labs PO Box 999 Richland WA 99352-0999

RAMESH, UTPALA, biochemist; b. Delhi, India, Oct. 12, 1956; came to U.S., 1982; d. Gopal Krishna and Prema Kamath; m. S.K. Ramesh, Jan. 21, 1987; 1 child, Arvind. BSc, Bombay U., 1976, MSc, 1978; PhD, So. Ill. U., 1987. Postdoctoral fellow U. Calif., Davis, 1987-90; scientist Baxter MicroScan, West Sacramento, Calif., 1990—; sr. scientist, supr. Dade Internat., West Sacramento, Calif., 1994—. Dakshina fellow Bombay U., 1976-78. Fellow Biophys. Soc.; mem. AAAS, Am. Chem. Soc., Am. Soc. Microbiologists. Office: Dade Internat 2040 Enterprise Blvd West Sacramento CA 95691-3427

RAMEY, FELICENNE HOUSTON, dean academic affairs, educator; b. Phila.; m. Melvin R. Ramey, Sept. 5, 1964; 2 children. BS, Pa. State U., University Park, 1961; MS, Duquesne U., 1967; JD, U. Calif., Davis, 1972; MA, Calif. State U., Sacramento, 1978. Bar: Calif. Microbiologist Pa. Dept. of Labs., Phila., Walter Reed Army Med. Ctr., Washington; chemist Calgon Corp., Pitts.; instr. Carnegie-Mellon U., Pitts.; dep. atty. gen. Calif. Dept. of Justice, Sacramento; clk. U.S. Dist. Ct. Calif., Sacramento; asst. prof. Calif. State U., Sacramento, assoc. prof., chair dept. behavior and environment, assoc. dean Sch. Bus.; exec. officer U. Calif., Davis; dir. litigation Human Rights Commn., Sacramento; bd. dirs. Legal Aid Soc., Sacramento mag.; vis. scholar Ga. Inst. Tech., 1981, Boston Coll., 1988. Mem. edn. com. Blacks for Effective Community Action, 1978—. ACE fellow U. Calif., Santa Cruz, 1992—. Mem. Calif. Agrl. Alumni Assn. (bd. dirs.), Western Bus. Law

Assn. (pres., pres. elect, v.p., exec. sec. Calif. and Nev. chpts. 1983-89), Nat. Assn. Women Deans and Adminstrs., Sacramento Black C. of C. (edn. com. 1990—, bd. dirs. 1989—). Home: 612 Cleveland St Davis CA 95616-3128 Office: Univ Calif Offices Chancellor/Provost 519 Mrak Hall Davis CA 95616-8558

RAMIREZ, JANICE L., assistant school superintendent; b. Dodge City, Kans., July 16, 1947; d. Chris William and Lois (Moore) Langvardt; 1 child, Jessica. BS, Emporia State U., 1969, MA, 1970; PhD, Kans. State U., 1982. Div. prin. Highland Park High Sch./Topeka (Kans.) pub. schs.; prin. Topeka pub. schs.; prin. Mesa (Ariz.) pub. schs., asst. supt.; mem. mid. level task force Ariz. Dept. Edn. Contbr. articles to profl. jours. Recipient Kamelot award. Mem. Am. Assn. Sch. Pers. Adminstrs., Ariz. Sch. Pers. Adminstrs. Assn., Nat. Assn. Ednl. Negotiators, Kans. Assn. for Middle Level Edn., Nat. Mid. Sch. Assn., Ariz. Hispanic Sch. Adminstrs. Assn., Pi Gamma Mu, Phi Delta Phi, Delta Kappa Gamma, Phi Delta Kappa. Office: 546 N Stapley Dr Mesa AZ 85203-7204

RAMIREZ, JOEL TITO, artist; b. Albuquerque, June 3, 1923; s. Fortunato and Juliana Armijo Ramirez; m. Carmen M. Varela, Dec. 7, 1946; children: Joel Robert, Eugene Peter, Jo Anne. Student, U. N.Mex. Illustrator (coloring book) Juan Diego and the Virgin of Guadalupe, 1975, St. Vincent de Paul, 1978; contbg. artist Across America, 1986, Art Studies, 1989; art dir. Quijotes de Am. Bibliography Jacinto Quiarte. Commissions include Ford Motor Co., 1973, Kennecott Copper Corp., 1974, Keep N.Mex. Beautiful Campaign, Tex. Internat. Airlines, Paramount Pictures, Universal Studios, Arthritis Found., Greek Cath. Melekite Ch., Albuquerque, Mrs. Mary Olin Harrell, Albuquerque; exhibited in group shows at Mus. N.Mex., Santa Fe, Galerie de Paris, 1965, Mus. Iberiano, Madrid, 1985—. With USAF, 1942-45. Winning artist for portrayal of discovery of Am. quincentenial competition Bur. Land Mgmt., 1992; recipient Insignia for 98th Bombardment Group, Freedom Force, 1988-94. Mem. China-Burma-India-Albuquerque Basher, VFW. Roman Catholic. Home: 10305 Santa Paula Ave NE Albuquerque NM 87111-3654 Office: Ramirez Art Signs 701 Aspen NW Albuquerque NM 87102

RAMIREZ, JORGE ALBERTO, civil engineering educator; b. Manizales, Caldas, Colombia, Apr. 4, 1954; s. Alberto and Amparo (Rodriguez) R.; m. Gloria Vallejo, Jan. 24, 1980; children: Felipe A., Alejandro, Sebastian. Ingeniero Civil, Nat. U. Colombia, Medellín, 1981; MSc in Hydrology and Water Resources, MIT, 1982, PhD in Hydrometeorology, 1988. Teaching asst. Facultad Nat. de Minas, Medellín, 1976; engring. asst. soils and dams dept. Sedic Ltda., Medellín, 1978; design engr. spl. studies divsn. hydraulic works dept. Integral Ltda., Medellín, 1979-80, 82-84; teaching asst. Ralph M. Parsons Lab. Water Resources MIT, Cambridge, 1982, rsch. asst., 1980-82, 84-87, postdoctoral rsch. assoc., 1987-88; internat. expert Interam. Devel. Bank/Colombian Inst. Higher Edn., 1989; assoc. prof. Postgrado en Recursos Hidráulicos Facultad Nat. de Minas, Medellín, 1989; rsch. assoc. Earth Sci. and Applications Divsn. Univs. Space Rsch. Assn., NASA Marshall Space Flight Ctr., Huntsville, Ala., 1989-90; asst. prof. civil engring. hydrologic sci. and engring. Colo. State U., Ft. Collins, 1990—; hydrology cons. Univs. Space Rsch. Assn., NASA Marshall Space Flight Ctr./Earth Sci. and Applications Divsn., Huntsville, 1991, 92; expert Rocky Mountain U. Consortium, 1992-93, Facultad Nat. de Minas, Medellín, Public Utility Co. Medellín, 1993; hydrometeorology cons. UN Devel. Programme Nat. Inst. Hydrology, Roorkee, India, 1993-94; phys. climate and hydrology panel NASA Earth Observing System, 1991—; mem. sci. adv. com. Terrestrial Ecosystems Regional Rsch. and Analysis Lab., 1992—. Reviewer Am. Geophys. Union Water Resources Rsch., Jour. Geophys. Rsch.-Atmospheres, ASCE Water Resources Planning and Mgmt. Divsn. Jour., ASCE Hydraulics Divsn. Jour.; contbr. articles to profl. jours. Den leader Pack 91 Webelos Scouts, Longs Peak Coun., 1992—; team capt., judge trainer Odyssey of the Mind, Poudre R-1 Sch. Dist., 1993. Arthur T. Ippen fellow MIT, 1986, 88; Orgn. Am. States scholar MIT, 1984-86. mem. Am. Geophys. Union (mem. precipitation com. hydrology sect. 1993—, mem. surface runoff com. 1993—, chmn. elect. exec. com. Front Range 1993—), Am. Meteorol. Soc., Soc. Antigueña de Ingenieros, Sigma Xi. Office: Colo State U Hydrologic Sci & Engring Civil Engring Dept Fort Collins CO 80523

RAMIREZ, RALPH ROY, management consultant; b. L.A., Nov. 9, 1937; s. Jorge Williams and Eleanor (Reyes) R.; m. Margot Joyce Cote, Aug. 17, 1959; children: Aaron, Alvina, Belinda, Felicia. AA, East L.A. Coll., 1962; CLU degree, Am. Coll., 1970; tchg. cert., Pasadena City Coll., 1980; BA, Sierra U., 1987. Cert. community coll. tchr., Calif. Safety engr. spl. agt. mgmt. trainee Ins. Co. N.Am., L.A., 1961-64; owner Ramirez Fin. Svcs., San Gabriel, Calif., 1964—; field underwriter Mutual Life Ins. Co. N.Y., Pasadena, Calif., 1964-69; dist. mgr. Franklin Life Ins. Co., Pasadena, 1969-86; mgmt. cons. Ramirez Mgmt. Svcs., San Gabriel, 1985—; guest lectr. Whittier (Calif.) Coll., 1980-86, East L.A. Coll., Calif. Poly. U., Calif. State U., L.A., Northridge; adminstrv. dir. State Calif. Divsn. Indsl. Accidents, San Francisco, 1983-85; instr. ins. Pasadena City Coll., 1981-83; ins. broker Ramirez Ins. Svcs., Alhambra, Calif., 1964-80. contbr articles to profl. jours. Chmn. san Gabriel Valley March of Dimes, Calif. Coun. Calif. Mil. Mus., 1994—; past co-chmn. Covenant House of Calif.; bd. dirs. Calif. Consortium for Prevention Child Abuse, San Gabriel Valley Med. Ctr. Found.; probation monitor State Bar Ct. Calif.; mem. productivity/Quality Mgmt. Forum Indsl. Rels. Ctr. Calif. Inst. Tech., Soc. of Industrial Medicine and Surgery; spkr. Rep. Nat. Conv., New Orleans, 1988, Calif. Mfg. Assn., Calif. Self Ins. Assn., Calif. Assn. Rehab. Profls., Calif. Applicant Attys. Assn., Calif. Applicant Hearing Reps. Assn.; congrl. candidate, 1982, 88; voting mem. Calif. Rep. Ctrl. Com., 1968-90. Res. petty officer USN, 1955-61; maj. Calif. Army Nat. Guard Res. Recipient Civitan of Yr. Civitan Internat., Gold Medallion award Boy Scouts Am., Cmty. Svc. award L.A. County Bd. Suprs., Hispanic Alumni of Yr. Whittier Coll. Mem. Nat. Assn. Life Underwriters (past pres. San Gabriel Valley chpt.), Latin Bus. Assn. (founder), Hispanic Leaders Coalition (founder, past pres.), Monterey Park Boys and Girls Club (founder, past pres.), Christian Svcs. for Blind Internat. (v.p.), L.A. Ctrs. for Prevention of Alcohol and Drug Abuse (v.p., past pres.), So. Calif. coun. Self Insurers (past pres.), L.A. County Pvt. Industry Coun. (chmn. fin. and budget com.). Office: 219 Segovia Ave San Gabriel CA 91775-2945

RAMIREZ, RICARDO, bishop; b. Bay City, Tex., Sept. 12, 1936; s. Natividad and Maria (Espinosa) R. B.A., U. St. Thomas, Houston, 1959; M.A., U. Detroit, 1968; Diploma in Pastoral Studies, East Asian Pastoral Inst., Manila, 1973-74. Ordained priest Roman Catholic Ch., 1966; missionary Basilian Fathers, Mex., 1968-76; exec. v.p. Mexican Am. Cultural Ctr., San Antonio, 1976-81; aux. bishop Archdiocese of San Antonio, 1981-82; bishop Diocese of Las Cruces, N.M., 1982—; cons. U.S. Bishop's Com. on Liturgy, from 1981; advisor U.S. Bishop's Com. on Hispanic Affairs, from 1981. Author: Fiesta, Worship and Family, 1981. Mem. N.Am. Acad. on Liturgy, Hispanic Liturgical Inst., Padres Asociada Derechos Religiosos Educativos y Sociales. Lodges: K.C; Holy Order Knights of Holy Sepulcher. Office: Diocese of Las Cruces 1280 Med Park Dr Las Cruces NM 88005-3239*

RAMIREZ, STEVEN ADRIAN, SR., city official; b. San Diego, Apr. 19, 1961; s. Ponciano Jr. and Josephine (Campos) R.; m. Dora Ann Perez, Feb. 20, 1993; 1 child, Steven Adrian Jr. AA in Psychology, San Diego Mesa Coll., 1984; BA in Indsl. Psychology, San Diego State U., 1985, MA in Indsl. Psychology, 1989. Orgn. devel. specialist City of San Diego, 1987—, cultural diversity trainer, 1992-93; chmn. city mgrs. multi-lingual task force City of San Deigo, 1992—; soccer coach, counselor Samuel F.B. Morse High Sch., San Diego, 1981-91. Vol. Logan Hts. Family Health Ctr., San Diego, 1985—, Alba 80 Soc./Alba Ednl. Found., San Diego, 1984—, charter pres., bd. dirs.; mem., chmn. Orgn. Devel. Network, 1992-93. Named Vol. of Yr., Logan Hts. Family Health Ctr., 1990; recipient Mayor's commendation for Leadership, 1992. Mem. Latino City Employees Assn. (charter pres. 1991). Office: City of San Diego 4950 Murphy Canyon Rd San Diego CA 92123-4325

RAMLER, SIEGFRIED, school administrator; b. Vienna, Austria, Oct. 30, 1924; s. Lazar and Eugenia Ramler; m. Piilani Andrietta Ahuna, Jan. 27, 1948; children: David K., Dita L., Laurence K., Malia R. Diplôme supérieur, U. Paris, 1958; MA, U. Hawaii, 1961. Interpreter Internat. Mil. Tribunal, Nuremberg, Germany, 1945-46, chief interpreting br., 1946-49; chair fgn. lang. dept. Punahou Sch., Honolulu, 1951-71, dir. instnl. svcs., 1971-91, dir. Wo Internat. Ctr., 1990—; exec. dir. Found. for Study in Hawaii and Abroad, Honolulu, 1969-90. Contbr. articles to profl. publs. Sec., bd. dirs. crown Prince Akihito Scholarship Found., 1989—. Decorated medal Freedom Found., 1958, Order of the Palmes Académiques, French Govt., 1964, Order of the Sacred Treasure, Japanese Govt., 1992, Ordre National du Mérite, French Govt., 1993. Mem. ASCD, Internat./Global Edn. Com. (chair nat. adv. com. 1987-93), Japan-Am. Soc. Hawaii (pres. 1986-87, program chmn. 1975—, Alliance Française of Hawaii (pres. 1961, bd. dirs. 1992—). Home: 921 Maunawili Cir Kailua HI 96734-4620 Office: Wo Internat Ctr Punahou Sch 1601 Punahou St Honolulu HI 96822-3336

RAMO, SIMON, engineering executive; b. Salt Lake City, May 7, 1913; s. Benjamin and Clara (Trestman) R.; m. Virginia Smith, July 25, 1937; children: James Brian, Alan Martin. BS, U. Utah, 1933, DSc (hon.), 1961; PhD, Calif. Inst. Tech., 1936; DEng (hon.), Case Western Res. U., 1960, U. Mich., 1966, Poly. Inst. N.Y., 1971; DSc (hon.), Union Coll., 1963, Worcester Polytechnic Inst., 1968, U. Akron, 1969, Cleve. State U., 1976; LLD (hon.), Carnegie-Mellon U., 1970, U. So. Calif., 1972, Gonzaga U., 1983, Occidental Coll., 1984, Claremont U., 1985. With Gen. Electric Co., 1936-46; v.p. ops. Hughes Aircraft Co., 1946-53; with Ramo-Woolridge Corp., 1953-58, Ramo-Wooldridge Corp., 1954-58; dir. TRW Inc., 1954-85, exec. v.p., 1958-61, vice chmn. bd., 1961-78, chmn. exec. com., 1969-78, cons., 1978—; pres. The Bunker-Ramo Corp., 1964-66; chmn. bd. TRW-Fujitsu Co., 1980-83; bd. dirs. Arco Power Techs.; vis. prof. mgmt. sci. Calif. Inst. Tech., 1978—; Regents lectr. UCLA, 1981-82, U. Calif. at Santa Cruz, 1978-79; chmn. Center for Study Am. Experience, U. So. Calif., 1978-80; Faculty fellow John F. Kennedy Sch. Govt., Harvard U., 1980-84; mem. White House Energy Research and Devel. Adv. Council, 1973-75; mem. adv. com. on sci. and fgn. affairs U.S. State Dept., 1973-75; chmn. Pres.'s Com. on Sci. and Tech., 1976-77; mem. adv. council to Sec. Commerce, 1976-77, Gen. Atomics Corp., 1988—, Aurora Capital Ptnrs., 1991—, Chartwell Investments, 1992—; co-chmn. Transition Task Force on Sci. and Tech. for Pres.-elect Reagan; mem. roster consultants to adminstr. ERDA, 1976-77; bd. advisors for sci. and tech. Republic of China, 1981-84; chmn. bd. Aetna, Jacobs & Ramo Venture Capital, 1987-90, Allenwood Ventures Inc., 1987—. Author: The Business of Science, 1988, other sci., engring. and mgmt. books. Bd. dirs. L.A. World Affairs Coun. 1973-85, Mus. Ctr. Found., L.A., L.A. Philharm. Assn., 1981-84; life trustee Calif. Inst. Tech., Nat. Symphony Orch. Assn., 1973-83; trustee emeritus Calif. State Univs.; bd. visitors UCLA Sch. Medicine, 1980—; bd. dirs. W.M. Keck Found., 1983—; bd. govs. Performing Arts Coun. Mus. Ctr. L.A., pres., 1976-77. Recipient award IAS, 1956; award Am. Inst. Elec. Engrs., 1959; award Arnold Air Soc., 1960; Am. Acad. Achievement award, 1964; award Am. Iron and Steel Inst., 1968; Disting. Svc. medal Armed Forces Communication and Electronics Assn., 1970; medal of achievement WEMA, 1970; awards U. So. Calif., 1971, 79; Kayan medal Columbia U., 1972; award Am. Cons. Engrs. Coun., 1974; medal Franklin Inst., 1978; award Harvard Bus. Sch. Assn., 1979; award Nat. Medal Sci., 1979; Disting. Alumnus award U. Utah, 1981; UCLA medal, 1982; Presdl. Medal of Freedom, 1983; named to Bus. Hall of Fame, 1984; recipient Aesculapian award UCLA, 1984, Durand medal AAIA, 1984, John Fritz medal, 1986, Henry Townley Heald award Ill. Inst. Tech., 1988, Nat. Engring. award Am. Assn. Engring. Socs., 1988, Franklin-Jefferson medal, 1988, Howard Hughes Meml. award, 1989. Fellow IEEE (Electronic Achievement award 1953, Golden Omega award 1975, Founders medal 1980, Centennial medal 1984), Am. Acad. Arts and Scis.; mem. NAE (founder, coun. mem. Bueche award), NAS, Internat. Acad. Astronautics, Am. Phys. Soc., Am. Philos. Soc., Inst. Advancement Engring., Coun. Fgn. Rels., Pacific Coun. on Internat. Policy, N.Y. Acad. Sci., Eta Kappa Nu (eminent mem. award 1966), Theta Tau (Hall of Fame laureate). Office: 9200 W Sunset Blvd Ste 801 Los Angeles CA 90069-3603

RAMO, VIRGINIA M. SMITH, civic worker; b. Yonkers, N.Y.; d. Abraham Harold and Freda (Kasnetz) Smith; B.S. in Edn., U. So. Calif., DHL (hon.), 1978; m. Simon Ramo; children—James Brian, Alan Martin. Nat. co-chmn. ann. giving U. So. Calif., 1968-70, vice chmn., trustee, 1971—, co-chmn. bd. councilors Sch. Performing Arts, 1975-76, co-chmn. bd. councillors Schs. Med. and Engring.; vice-chmn. bd. overseers Hebrew Union Coll., 1972-75; bd. dirs. The Muses of Calif. Mus. Sci. and industry, UCLA Affiliates, Estelle Doheny Eye Found., U. So. Calif. Sch. Medicine; adv. council Los Angeles County Heart Assn., chmn. com. to endow Chair in cardiology at U. So. Calif.; vice-chmn., bd. dirs. Friends of Library U. So. Calif.; bd. dirs., nat. pres. Achievement Rewards for Coll. Scientists Found., 1975-77; bd. dirs. Les Dames Los Angeles, Community TV So. Calif.; bd. dirs., v.p. Founders Los Angeles Music Center; v.p. Los Angeles Music Center Opera Assn.; v.p. corp. bd. United Way; v.p. Blue Ribbon-400 Performing Arts Council; chmn. com. to endow chair in gerontology U. So. Calif.; vice chmn. campaign Doheny Eye Inst., 1986. Recipient Service award Friends of Libraries, 1974, Nat. Community Service award Alpha Epsilon Phi, 1975, Disting. Service award Am. Heart Assn. 1978, Service award U. So. Calif., Spl. award U. So. Calif. Music Alumni Assn., 1979, Life Achievement award Mannequins of Los Angeles Assistance League, 1979, Woman of Yr. award PanHellenic Assn., 1981, Disting. Service award U. So. Calif. Sch. Medicine, 1981, U. So. Calif. Town and Gown Recognition award, 1986, Asa V. Call Achievement award U. So. Calif., 1986, Phi Kappa Phi scholarship award U. So. Calif., 1986, Vision award Luminaires of Doheny Eye Inst., 1994. Mem. UCLA Med. Aux., U. So. Calif. Pres.'s Circle, Commerce Assos. U. So. Calif., Cedars of Lebanon Hosp. Women's Guild (dir. 1967-68), Blue Key, Skull and Dagger.

RAMOS, ALBERT A., electrical engineer; b. L.A., Feb. 28, 1927; s. Jesus D. and Carmen F. (Fontes) R.; B.S. in Elec. Engring., U. So. Calif., 1950, M.S. in Systems Mgmt., 1972; Ph.D., U.S. Internat. U., 1975; m. Joan C. Pailing, Sept. 23, 1950; children—Albert A., Richard R., James J., Katherine. With guided missile test group Hughes Aircraft Co., 1950-60; with TRW DSG, 1960-91, sr. staff engr. Norton AFB, San Bernardino, Calif., 1969-91, ret., 1991. Served with USNR, 1945-46. Registered profl. engr., Calif. Mem. IEEE, NSPE, Air Force Assn., Mexican-Am. Engring. Soc., Mexican-Am. Profl. Mgmt. Assn. (mem. administering commn. dept. community svcs.), Sigma Phi Delta, Eta Kappa Nu, Tau Beta Pi. Home: 8937 Napoli Dr Las Vegas NV 89117-1182

RAMOS, CHRISTINA SIERRA, natural resource specialist; b. El Paso, Tex., Aug. 26, 1961; d. Albert Garcia and Emma Sierra Ramos; m. David L. Walker, June 11, 1988. BS in Range Sci., N.Mex. State U., 1984; MBA, U. Phoenix, 1991. Range conservationist Bur. Land Mgmt., U.S. Dept. Interior, Phoenix and Kingman, Ariz., 1981-92; range conservationist Bur. Land Mgmt., U.S. Dept. Interior, Phoenix, 1993—, ops. mgr. interagy. assignment Ariz. Conservation Corps., 1992-93. Am. Field Svc. scholar, 1979. Mem. Am. Bus. Women's Assn. (pres. 1992-93), Soc. for Range Mgmt., Image. Office: US Dept Interior Bur Land Mgmt 3707 N 7th St Phoenix AZ 85014-5059

RAMOS, LINDA MARIE, endoscopy technician; b. San Jose, Calif., July 8, 1961; d. Albert Sequeira and Catherine Marie (Souza) Vieira; m. John Bettencourt Ramos, June 12, 1982 (div. July 1993). AA, De Anza Coll., 1986; BA, St. Mary's Coll. Calif., Moraga, 1988. Cert. gastrointestinal clinician, aerobic instr. Endoscopy technician O'Connor Hosp., San Jose, 1979-94, Good Samaritan Health Sys., Los Gatos, Calif., 1994—; aerobic instr. Mountain View (Calif.) Athletic club, 1984-95, Decathlon Club, Santa Clara, 1991—, Golds Gym, Mountain View, 1994—. Contbr. articles to profl. jours. Vol. O'Connor Hosp., 1975-79; active campaign Santa Clara City Council, 1980-81. Fellow Irmandade Da Festa Do Espirito Santo (sec. 1974-82, queen 1975-76), Soc. Gastrointestinal Assts., No. Soc. Gastrointestinal Assts., Soc. Espirito Santo of Santa Clara, Luso Am. Fraternal Fedn. (state youth pres. 1979-80, youth leader local coun. Santa Clara Mountain View 1979-87, scholar, 1979, founder, organizer Mountain View-Santa Clara chpt. 1980, pres. local region 1980-84, state 20-30 pres. 1984-85, state dir. youth programs 1988-94, state dir. 1994); mem. Aerobics and Fitness Assn. Am. Republican. Roman Catholic. Home: 1618 Roll St Santa Clara CA 95050-4024 Office: Good Samaritan Health Sys 15066 Los Gatos Almaden Rd Los Gatos CA 95032-3909

RAMOS, NELSON HERBERT, healthcare executive; b. Bklyn., Oct. 14, 1950; s. Herbert and Asia (Perez) R.; m. Penny Helene Williams, Sept. 4, 1982; children: Katalyn, Kelsey. BS in Econs., BS in Engring., Renseelaer Poly. Inst., Troy, N.Y., 1972; M in Engring., Rensselaer Polytechnic Inst., Troy, N.Y., 1973. Engring. supr. Air Force Systems Command, Edwards AFB, Calif., 1973-76; mgmt. engr. Sharp Meml. Hosp., San Diego, 1976-79; supr. mgmt. engring. Kaiser Found. Hosp., San Diego, 1977-80; dir. mgmt. engring. Meml. Hosps. Assn., Modesto, Calif., 1980-83; ptnr. MMC Healthcare, Modesto, 1983-86; dir. mgmt. svcs. Mercy Gen. Hosp., Sacramento, Calif., 1986-89; v.p. mgmt. systems Meml. Hosps. Assn., Modesto, 1989—; pres. Am. Inst. Indsl. Engr., San Diego, 1978-79. Mem. Calif. Hosps. Polit. Action Com., Sacramento, 1992. Lt. USAF, 1973-76. Mem. Am. Hosp. Assn., Hosp. Fin. Mgmt. Assn., Ctrl. Calif. Hosp. Mgmt. Sys. Soc. (pres.-elect 1993, pres. 1994—), Rensselaer Polytech. Alumni Assn. (class pres. 1972-77), Modesto Performing Arts, Modesto C. of C., Alpha Phi Omega. Office: Meml Hosps Assn 1700 Coffee Rd Modesto CA 95355-2803

RAMSAY, ERIC GUY, surgeon; b. Accrington, England, Sept. 22, 1927; came to U.S., 1954; s. Robert Guy and Gertrude Elizabeth (Osborne) R.; m. Lois Clark, July 25, 1953; children: Michael, Timothy, Jennifer, Peter. M.B.Ch.B., U. Glasgow (Scotland), 1950. Diplomate Am. Bd. Surgery. Intern Falkirk Royal Infirmary, Glasgow Western Infirmary, Scotland, 1950-51; resident surgery Mo. Pacific Hosp., St. Louis, 1954-58; pvt. practice surgeon Tucson, 1959—; chief surgery Kino Community Hosp., Tucson, 1966—; dir. med. edn. St. Mary's Hosp., Tucson, 1963-65, Tuscon Hosps. Med. Edn. Program, 1966—; clin. prof. surgery U. Ariz. Coll. Medicine, 1972—. Flight lt. RCAF, 1951-54. Mem. Am. Coll. Surgeons, AMA, Assn. for Hosp. Med. Edn., Southwestern Surg. Congress, Ariz. Med. Assn., Pima County Med. Soc., Tucson Surg. Soc. Home: 5476 E River Rd Tucson AZ 85718-7246 Office: Tucson Hosps Med Edn Program PO Box 42195 Tucson AZ 85733-2195

RAMSAY, JANICE SUSAN, computer programmer, analyst; b. Nashville, Ark., Aug. 20, 1952; d. Reginald Carlyle and Jesse Evelyn (Hill) R. BA in English, Ariz. State U., 1977. With data ops. Maricopa County Govt., Phoenix, 1973-82, programmer analyst I, 1982-84, programmer analyst II, 1984-86; sr. programmer analyst Peralta Community Colls., Oakland, Calif., 1986-90; applications programmer analyst East Bay Mcp. Utilities Dist., Oakland, 1990—. Author: Recovery Techniques, 1984, User-Friendly FAMS, 1985. Active Sierra Club, World Wildlife. Mem. Assn. for Women in Computing, No. Calif. Profls., Assn. Systems Mgmt. Home: # 404 909 Marina Village Pky # 404 Alameda CA 94501-1048 Office: East Bay Mcpl Utilities Dist PO Box 24055 Oakland CA 94623-1055

RAMSAY, JOHN BARADA, research chemist, educator; b. Phoenix, Dec. 28, 1929; s. John A. and Helen G. Ramsay; m. Barbara Ann Hilsenhoff, Apr. 18, 1953; children: Bryan J., Kathleen L., Carol A., David A. BS in Chemistry, Tex. Western U., 1950; PhD in Analytical Chemistry, U. Wis., 1954. Mem. staff Los Alamos Nat. Lab., 1954-70, 73-93; assoc. prof. Coll. Petroleum and Minerals, Dhahran, Saudi Arabia, 1970-73; cons. U.S. Navy, USAF, 1980—; adj. prof. U. N.Mex., Los Alamos, 1980-85. Author sci. articles. Recipient award of excellence U.S. Dept. Energy, 1984, 92. Mem. N.Mex. Acad. Sci. (pres. 1988), Am. Archeol. Soc. (chpt. pres. 1979), Nat. Ski Patrol (appt. 7651), Westerners Internat. (chpt. pres. 1988-90), Sigma Xi. Democrat. Home: 6 Erie Ln Los Alamos NM 87544-3810

RAMSAY, MACKAY, food executive; b. 1953. Student, Calif. Polytechnic State U.; MBA, Calif. State U., Fullerton, 1984. With Sunkist Growers, L.A., 1976-78, Topco Assocs., Skokie, Ill., 1978-80; exec. v.p., gen. mgr. Calberti Inc., Santa Ana, Calif., 1981—. Office: Calberti Inc 3605 W Pendleton Ave Santa Ana CA 92704*

RAMSAY, ROBERT HENRY, investment manager; b. Atchison, Kans., June 18, 1925; s. Ronald and Dorcas (Carlisle) R.; m. Margaret Packard, Aug. 16, 1952 (dec. Dec. 1989); children: Margaret R. Gray, William P., David C.; m. Carolyn McKillop, Dec. 8, 1991. BS in Aeronautical Engring., U. Kans., 1945; M in Retailing, U. Pitts., 1948. Br. mgr. Boettcher & Co., Grand Junction, Colo., 1956-65, Colorado Springs, Colo., 1965-71; pres. Robert H. Ramsay Fin. Svcs., Colorado Springs, 1971-74, Ramsay & Ellsworth, Inc., Colorado Springs, 1974-87, Ramsay Investment Counsel Inc., Colorado Springs, 1987—; bd. dirs. Norwest Bank of Colorado Springs. Bd. dirs. Colorado Springs Sch. Mem. Rotary Club of Colorado Springs. Office: Ramsay Investment Counsel Inc 810 Holly Sugar Bldg Colorado Springs CO 80903

RAMSBY, MARK DELIVAN, lighting designer and consultant; b. Portland, Oreg., Nov. 20, 1947; s. Marshall Delivan and Verna Pansy (Culver) R.; divorced; children: Aaron Delivan, Venessa Mercedes. Student, Portland (Oreg.) State U., 1966-67. With C.E.D., Portland, 1970-75; minority ptnr. The Light Source, Portland, 1975-78, pres., 1978-87; prin. Illume Lighting Design, Portland, 1987-90; ptnr. Ramsby, Dupuy & Seats, Inc., Portland, 1990-91; dir. lighting design PAE Cons. Engrs., Inc., Portland, 1991—; pvt. practice cons. Portland, 1979—. Recipient Top 10 Outstanding Achievement award Metalux Lighting, 1981-85, 100% award, 1985, Edwin F. Guth award of merit, 1990, Edison award of excellence, 1990, Edwin F. Guth award of excellence, 1993, 94. Mem. Illuminating Engring. Soc. Am. (sec.-treas. Oreg. sect. 1978-79, Oreg. Section and Regional and Internat. awards 1989, 90, 93, 94, Lighting Design awards), Internat. Assn. Lighting Designers. Republican. Lutheran. Office: PAE Cons Engrs 808 SW 3rd Ave Ste 300 Portland OR 97204-2426

RAMSCHER, ELIZABETH ANN, physics educator, researcher; b. Berkeley, Calif., Mar. 18, 1943; d. Philip Jakins and Claire Elsa (Soderblom) Webster; m. Warren Carleton Ramscher, Oct. 5, 1962 (div. June 1965); 1 child, Brent Allan; m. William Lloyd Van Bise, Mar. 1, 1985. BS in Chemistry and Physics, U. Calif., Berkeley, 1962, MS in Nuclear Engring., 1964, PhD in Nuclear Sci., 1979. Staff rschr. Lawrence Berkeley Lab. U. Calif., 1963-79; staff rschr. LLNL, Livermore, Calif., 1966-69; prof., instr. U. Calif., 1971-74; instr., rschr. SLAC, Stanford, Calif., 1971-72; rschr. SRI Internat., Menlo Park, Calif., 1974-76; dir. Tecnic Rsch. Labs., San Leandro, Calif., 1979—; v.p. Magtek Labs, Inc., Reno, 1988—; prof. physics U. Nev., Stanford, 1990—; cons. McDonnell-Douglass, L.A., 1978, 80, Learned Soc. Can., Montreal, 1981, USN, Silver Spring, Md., 1983, NASA, Martin-Marietta, New Orleans, 1988-89; adviser Engring. Inst., Provo, Utah, 1979. Patentee in field. Del. UN, N.Y.C., 1979, mem. UN com., 1989; adviser Congress OTA, Washington, 1979-81; adviser, cons. City Coun., Reno, 1993. Recipient Outstanding Contbn. award Am. Astron. Soc., 1978, Honor award Rosebridge Grad. Sch., 1988; grantee USN, 1970-74, PF Found., 1978, 79, 81. Mem. IEEE, Am. Phys. Soc. (chair), Am. Chem. Soc. (v.p.), LBL Fundamental Physics (chair, pres.), PRG San Francisco (bd. dirs., pres.). Office: Tecnic Rsch Labs 7685 Hughes Dr Reno NV 89506

RAMSEY, JERRY VIRGIL, radio broadcaster, educator, financial planner; b. Tacoma, July 24, 1940; s. Virgil Emory and Winifred Victoria (Carothers) R.; m. Elaine Sigrid Perdue, June 24, 1967; 1 child, Jason Perdue. BA in Elem. Edn., U. Puget Sound, 1967; MEd in Tchr. Tng. and Curriculum Devel., U. Wash., 1971; PhD in Econ. Geography, Columbia Pacific U., 1995. Tchr. Tacoma Pub. Schs., 1967-95; fin. planner Primerica Corp., Tacoma, 1986-90, Gig Harbor Fin. Svcs., 1986—, Waddell & Reed, Inc., Tacoma, 1990-93; N.Am. Mgmt., 1993—; real estate investor, CEO Ramsey Properties, Gig Harbor, Wash., 1970—; radio broadcaster KGHP/KJUN, The Country Gold Network/KMAS, 1990—; lectr. Pacific Luth. U., Tacoma, 1972-86. Precinct committeeman Pierce County Rep. Com., Tacoma, 1968-78; mem. steering com. Peninsula Neighborhood Assn., Gig Harbor, Wash., 1991-92. With USAF, 1959-62. Recipient Golden Acorn award PTA, 1975, Meritorious Teaching award Nat. Coun. Geog. Edn., 1978, achievement award Rep. Nat. Com., 1985; grantee U.S. Office Edn., 1971. Mem. NEA (life), Knife and Fork Club (pres. 1983), Kiwanis (pres. Tacoma 1976), Phi Delta Kappa. Methodist. Office: Ramsey Properties Gig Harbor Fin Svcs PO Box 1311 Gig Harbor WA 98335-3311

RAMSEY, ROBERT JOHN, merchant marine; b. Jacksonville, Fla., Jan. 6, 1954; s. George Ervin Ramsey and Mary Susan (Sanna) Reeves; m. Lynn Casey Ramsey, Mar. 6, 1982 (div. Apr. 1987); m. Karen Sue Ketteman, July 21, 1992; 1 child, Thomas Anthony. BS of Marine Transp., U.S. Merchant Marine Acad., 1977. Lic. master unltd. tonnage/any oceans; 1st class pilot. Ships navigator USN/USS Portland, Little Creek, Va., 1977-80; third/second mate Sea-Land Svcs. SS, Tacoma, Wash., 1980-84, chief mate/relief capt., 1984-87, chiefmate, 1987—; maritime cons., Tacoma, 1984-94; shipyard set-trial capt., Seattle, 1987-94. Lt. comdr. USNR. Mem. Am. Legion. Roman Catholic.

RAN, XIAONONG, research and development engineer; b. Chengdu, Sichuan, China, Jan. 25, 1958; s. Yinhua and Minzhen (Wang) R.; m. Minmin Qin, Mar. 13, 1985; children: Mengchen, Chungchen. BSEE, Chongqing (China) U., 1982, MSEE, 1984; PhD, U. Md., 1992. Scientific rschr., lectr. Chongqing U., 1984-86; sr. engr. Nat. Semiconductor Corp., Santa Clara, Calif., 1992—. Contbr. articles to profl. jours. Scholarship The L.I. Found., 1986, SRC fellowship Sys. Rsch. Ctr. U. Md., 1987, Grad. Sch. Dissertation fellowship U. Md., 1991. Mem. IEEE. Home: 10980 Barranca Dr Cupertino CA 95014-0102 Office: Nat Semiconductor Corp M/S D3-969 2900 Semiconductor Dr Santa Clara CA 95051-0606

RANAHAN, MICHAEL PATRICK, obstetrician/gynecologist; b. Palo Alto, Calif., May 28, 1944; s. John Joseph and Rosemary Therese (Schleppenbach) R.; m. Demerris Colette Moon, Aug. 26, 1967; children: Patrick, Megan, Marisa, Kerry. BA, U. Santa Clara, 1966; MD, Loyola U., 1970. Diplomate Am. Bd. Ob-Gyn. Intern Mayo Grad. Sch. of Medicine, Rochester, Minn., 1970-71; obstetrician/gynecologist Valley Meml. Hosp., Livermore, Calif., 1977—, Valley Care Med. Ctr., Pleasanton, Calif., 1991—; chief of staff Valley Meml. Hosp., Livermore, 1981-83, bd. dirs., 1983; bd. dirs. Pacific Health Care, Pleasanton, 1985, 90, 91, 92, 93, East Bay Med. Network, Emoryville, Calif., 1993—; mng. gen. ptnr. Pleasanton Physician Affiliates, 1987-94; med. dir. Tri Valley Surgery Ctr., Pleasanton, 1993—. Del. Alameda, Contra-Costa Med. Assn., Oakland, Calif., 1993—, Calif. Med. Assn., San Francisco, 1994, alt. del., 1990, 92. Lt. comdr. USN, 1971-77. Mem. Am. Assn. Gynecologic Laparascopists, Am. Fertility Soc.

RANCE, QUENTIN E., interior designer; b. St. Albans, Eng., Mar. 22, 1935; came to U.S., 1981.; s. Herbert Leonard and Irene Ann (Haynes) R.; m. India Adams, May 17, 1974. Grad., Eastbourne (Eng.) Sch. Art, 1960. Soft furnishings buyer Dickeson & French Ltd., Eastbourne, 1960-61, outside sales mgr., 1961-62; design dir. Laszlo Hoenig, Ltd., London, 1962-73; mng. dir. Quentin Rance Interiors Ltd., London, 1973-81; pres. Quentin Rance Enterprises, Inc., Encino, Calif., 1981—. Works featured in Designers West, 1983, Design House Rev., 1983, Profiles mag., 1987, Nat. Assn. Mirror Mfrs. Jour., 1988, Designer Specifier, 1990. Mem. Founders for Diabetic Research/City of Hope. Served with RAF, 1953-55. Recipient Hon. Mention award Nat. Assn. Mirror Mfrs., 1987, 1st Pl. Nat. Pub. Svc. award, Designer Specifier, 1990. Fellow Chartered Soc. Designers (Eng.); mem. Am. Soc. Interior Designers (profl., chpt. bd. dirs. 1983-87, 89-91, chmn. Avanti 1983-85, admissions chmn. 1985—, Presdl. citations 1984-87, 91), Knights of Vine. Home and Office: 18005 Rancho St Encino CA 91316-4214

RANCK, JOHN STEVENS, human resources executive, consultant; b. Warren, Ohio, Sept. 14, 1945; s. Charles Thomas and Helen Marie (Weir) R.; m. Bibbie-Ann Rose Robertson, Dec. 25, 1975; children: James L., Edward L. BS, USAF Acad., 1971; MS in Human Resources, Gonzaga U., 1979, MBA, 1984. Cert. adminstrv. mgr.; sr. profl. in human resources mgmt. Salesman Neal's Family Shoes, Warren, 1964-65; prodn. staff Packard Elec. div. GMC, Warren, 1965-66; personnel mgr. United Paint Mfg., Inc., Greenacres, Wash., 1981-82; personnel dir. Sheraton-Spokane Hotel, 1982-83; personnel mgr. Students Book Corp., Pullman, Wash., 1984-87; personnel analyst Spokane Co., 1988-90; pres. Top Ranck Mgmt., Spokane and Loon Lake, Wash., 1990—; v.p., sec.-treas. TONGA Coffee, Co., 1993; pres. ArabiCafe, Inc., 1993-94. Active Stevens County Rep. Com. Capt. USAF, 1966-80. Mem. Am. Compensation Assn., Internat. Pers. Mgmt. Assn., N.W. Human Resource Mgmt. Assn. (exec. bd. 1989-93, treas. 1993, legis. liaison 1991-92, v.p. programs 1990, coll. rels. com. 1989), Soc. Human Resource Mgmt., Masons (Kinght York Grand Cross of Honor, Order of Purple Cross, Knight Comdr. Ct. of Honor), K.T. (grand comdr. 1987-88), Red Cross Constantine, Royal Order Scotland, Shriners, Grotto. Lutheran. Home: 40151 Morgan Rd PO Box 297 Loon Lake WA 99148-0297 Office: Top Ranck Mgmt PO Box 501 Loon Lake WA 99148-0501

RAND, DUNCAN D., librarian; b. Biggar, Sask., Can., Oct. 28, 1940; s. Dawson Ellis and Elizabeth Edna (Gabie) R.; m. Nancy Jean Daugherty, Sept. 7, 1963; children: Jacqueline Nancy, Duncan Dawson, Thomas Nelson, John David. B.A., U. Sask., 1963; B.L.S., McGill U., 1964. Young adult librarian Regina Pub. Library, Sask., 1964-65; coordinator library services Regina Separate Sch. Bd., 1965-68; asst. chief librarian Regina Pub. Library, 1968-71; dep. dir. London Pub. Library and Art Mus., 1971-73, acting dir., 1973-74; chief librarian Lethbridge Pub. Library, Alta., 1974—; dir. So. Alta. Art Gallery. Editor: Sask. Geneal. Soc. Bull, 1968-71. Vice pres. Alta. council Boy Scouts. Mem. Libr. Assn. Atlanta (dir., pres. 1986-87), Can. Libr. Assn. (dir.), Sask. Geneal. Soc. (pres.), Assn. Profl. Librs. of Lethbridge (chmn. 1982-84), Samaritans (bd. dirs. 1993—), Allied Arts Coun. (bd. dirs. 1993—), Rotary Internat., Ippallosh (archivist, sec. 1980-94). Office: 810 5th Ave S, Lethbridge, AB Canada T1J 4C4

RAND, KATHLEEN SUZETTE, buyer; b. Reno, Apr. 7, 1962; d. Paul William and Nancy Lavinnia (Grabel) Rand-Ajazzi; 1 child, Chanda Victoria Rand. AAS in Adminstrn. of Justice, Truckee Meadows C.C., Reno, 1982; BA in Criminal Justice, U. Nev., Reno, 1984. Editor Sparks (Nev.) H.S., 1976-80; columnist Sparks (Nev.) Tribune, 1979-80; buyer City of Sparks, Nev., 1984—; founder, dir. No. Nev. Women's Network, Inc., Reno, 1993—; trustee Truckee Meadows Fair Housing Inc., Reno, 1993—. Mem. City of Sparks Cmty, Support Funding Com., Nev., 1990—. Mem. NAFE, Nat. Assn. Purchasing Mgrs.; fellow Internat. Biographical Assn. Office: City of Sparks 431 Prater Way Sparks NV 89431-4598

RAND, RUTH A., science and computer educator; b. Phila., Mar. 31, 1935; m. Dr. Wilfred Kolman, 1957, (dec. 1980); children: Marc, Ross, Rachel. AB, Swarthmore Coll., 1956; MS, U. Pa., 1964. Tchr. N.C. Sch. Sci. and Maths., 1981-82, Phila. Community Coll., 1983-84, Abington (Pa.) Friends Sch., Latin Sch. Chgo., 1984-92, Albuquerque Acad., 1992—; rsch. asst. Dept. Physiology, Sch. of Medicine U. N.C., 1977-82; policy rsch. assoc. Eagleton Inst. Ruters U., 1972-73; sr. chemist Bur. Rsch. in Neurology and Psychiatry, Princeton, 1967-70; sci. cons. Video Dialog, 1989; participant Chem. Scis. in Modern World conf. Beckman Ctr. History of Chemistry U. Pa., 1990; facilitator Project 2061; founder Sigma Pi. Author: Understanding and Designing the Microcomputer Based Lab. 1987, Getting Started in Organic and Biochemistry, 1985, revised, 1987; contbg. editor: Modern Chemistry, 1989—; contbr. articles to profl. jours. Recipient Dreyfus Master Tchr. award Woodrow Wilson Nat. Fellowship Found., 1983, 93, Master Tchr. Leader award, 1989, Presdl. Edn. award State of Ill., 1986, Nat. award, 1987, State award IMPACT II: Creative Teaching Ideas, 1990, CBE award 1993, N. Mex. ACS Outstanding High Sch. Chem. award, 1995. Mem. Nat. Sci. Tchrs. Assn., Pa. Sci. Tchrs. Assn., Ill. Sci. Tchrs. Assn., Am. Chem. Soc., Ind. Sch. Assn. Greater Chgo., Ind. Sch. Assn. Cen. States, Achievement Test Com.-ETS, Assn. Presdl. Awardees in Teaching (exec. bd. 1988), Tchrs. Acad. for Math. and Sci. (bd. dirs.). Home: 869 Tramway Ln NE # D Albuquerque NM 87122-1408 Office: Albuquerque Acad 6400 Wyoming Blvd Albuquerque NM 87109

RANDALL, CRAIG, financial management consultant, accountant, computer specialist; b. Santa Monica, Calif., Oct. 29, 1957; s. Les Shepard and Marian Hand; m. Jeanne Runsvold, July 14, 1984. Student, Pierce Coll., 1975-76, Calif. State U.-Northridge, 1977-79. Asst. controller Becker CPA Rev., Encino, Calif., 1979-81; staff acct. Kress and Goldstein, CPAs, Sherman Oaks, Calif., 1981-84; pres., chief exec. officer Bus. Computers Network, Inc., Woodland Hills, 1984—, Randall Accountancy Corp., Woodland Hills, 1984—. Office: Randall Accountancy Corp 5525 Oakdale Ave Ste 250 Woodland Hills CA 91364-2614

RANDALL, EARL VANCE, educational leadership educator, consultant; b. Monticello, Utah, June 14, 1951; s. Earl Larson and Dorothy Rae (Frost) R.; m. Vickie Heaton, Oct. 10, 1974; children: Melissa, Curtis, Matthew, Marilee, April, Jonathan. BS, Brigham Young U., 1975, M of Ednl. Adminstrn., 1978; PhD, Cornell U., 1989. Cert. secondary tchr. Asst. prof. ednl. leadership Brigham Young U., Provo, Utah, 1992—. Author: Private Schools and Public Power, 1994; contbr. articles to profl. jours. Instr., prin. ch. ednl. system LDS Ch., Phoenix, 1975-79, Farmington, Minn., 1979-82, Ithaca, N.Y., 1982-92; sec., pres. adv. com. Dryden (N.Y.) Sch. Dist., 1985-86; v.p. Cornell United Religious Work, Ithaca, N.Y., 1987-88. Recipient Marvin Glock award Cornell U., 1990. Mem. Am. Ednl. Fin. Assn., Assocs. for Rsch. on Pvt. Edn., Am. Ednl. Rsch. Assn. Office: Brigham Young Univ 310C Mckb Provo UT 84602-1038

RANDALL, ROGER PAUL, religious organization consultant; b. Cottage Grove, Oreg., Nov. 3, 1946; s. Vinal Truman and Janet Louise (Peterson) R.; m. Sara Holt Clemmons, Sept. 26, 1968; 1 child, Allison L. BS, Oreg. State U., 1968; postgrad., Internat. Grad. Sch. Theology, San Bernardino, Calif., 1968, 71, Regis U., 1991—. Campus dir. Auburn U. Campus Crusade for Christ, Auburn, Ala., 1969-72; Tex. area dir. Campus Crusade for Christ, Dallas, 1972-73; so. regional dir. Campus Crusade for Christ, San Bernardino, 1973-75, univ. ministry nat. dir., 1980-85; dir. internat. univ. resources Campus Crusade for Christ, Boulder, Colo., 1988—; nat. dir. Student Venture, San Bernardino, 1975-80; Africa univ. ministry coord. Life Ministry, Nairobi, Kenya, 1985-88; founder, dir. Nat. Network of Youth Ministries, San Diego, 1977-79; co-founder, dir. World-wide Student Network, Orlando, Fla., 1986—; cons. Internat. Leadership Devel. Task Force, Laguna Niguel, Calif., 1991—. Editor: Make Your Mark, 1981, International University Resource Manual, 1986; contbr. articles to profl. jours. Long range planning cons. Platt Jr. High Sch., Boulder, 1989; resource person U.S. Dept. HHS, Washington, 1980-88; commn. mem. UN Internat. Youth Yr. Commn., N.Y.C., 1983. Home: 1302 S Gibson Ct Superior CO 80027-8019

RANDAU, KAREN LYNETTE, public relations executive; b. Grand Junction, Colo., Feb. 13, 1953; d. George Irvin Gray and Phyllis Joanita (Knaak) Helton; m. James V. Arp, 1979 (div. 1988); 1 child, Joanna; m. Eric E. Randau, Jan. 21, 1989; 1 child, Nathan. BA in Journalism, U. Tex., 1979. Merchandising mgr. Tex. Instruments, Austin, Tex., 1979-82; mktg. comms. mgr. Intel, Chandler, Ariz., 1982-86; self-employed writer Chandler, Ariz., 1986-87; mktg.dir. Charter Hosp., Chandler, Ariz., 1987-88, Hope Comty., Scottsdale, Ariz., 1988-90; dir. pub. rels. Food for the Hungry, Scottsdale, 1990—. Author: (books) Conquering Fear, 1990, Life Doesn't Have to Hurt, 1991; (booklet) Anxiety Attacks, 1991. Mem. Pub. Rels. Soc. Am. (accredited pub. rels. profl.), Christian Bus. Women (newsletter editor Phoenix 1992-93). Office: Food for the Hungry Inc 7729 E Greenway Rd Scottsdale AZ 85260-1705

RANDEL, WILLIAM JOHN, physicist; b. Cleve., May 13, 1956; s. Marvin William and Virginia Mary (Pettit) R.; m. Sharon Lea Gutche, Aug. 20, 1983; children: Matthew William, Katherine Grace. BS in Physics, U. Cin., 1978; PhD, Iowa State U., 1984. Postdoctoral rsch. fellow Nat. Ctr. for Atmospheric Rsch., Boulder, Colo., 1986-87, rsch. scientist, 1988—; mem. ozone trends panel UN Environ. Program World Meterol. Orgn., Geneva, 1993-94. Contbr. articles to profl. jours. and chpts. to books. Pres. Mt. Hope Luth. Ch., Boulder, 1994—. Rsch. grantee NASA, 1990-94; fellow Nat. Ctr. for Atmospheric Rsch., 1985-87. Mem. Am. Meterol. Soc. (com. chair 1994—), Am. Geophys. Union, Sigma Pi Sigma. Home: 4458 Wellington Rd Boulder CO 80301-3144 Office: Nat Ctr Atmospheric Rsch PO Box 3000 Boulder CO 80307

RANDHAWA, BIKKAR SINGH, psychologist, educator; b. Jullundur, India, June 14, 1933; came to Can., 1961, naturalized, 1966; s. Pritam S. and Sawaran K. (Basakhi) R.; m. Leona Emily Bujnowski, Oct. 8, 1966; children—Jason, Lisa. B.A. in Math., Panjab U., 1954, B.T. in Edn., 1955, M.A. in History, 1959; B.Ed., U. Alta., Can., 1963; M.Ed. in Measurement and Evaluation, U. Toronto, Ont., Can., 1967, Ph.D., 1969. Registered psychologist. Tchr. secondary sch. math. Panjab, 1955-61; asst. headmaster, then headmaster, 1955-61; tchr. high sch. math. and sci. Beaver County, Riley, Alta., 1964-65, Camrose County, Alta., 1961-64; tchr. high sch. math. and sci. Edmonton (Alta.) Public Schs., 1965-67; tutor in math. for social sci. Ont. Inst. Studies in Edn., Toronto, 1968-69; mem. faculty U. Sask., Saskatoon, 1969-76, 77—; prof. ednl. psychology U. Sask., 1977—, asst. dean research and field services, 1982-87; prof., coord. Visual Scholars' Program, U. Iowa, 1976-77; cons. in field. Contbr. articles profl. jours. Fellow Am. Psychol. Assn., Am. Psychol. Soc. (charter), Can. Psychol. Assn., mem. Am. Ednl. Research Assn., Can. Soc. Study Edn., Nat. Coun. Measurement in Edn., Sask. Psychol. Assn., Phi Delta Kappa (pres. Saskatoon chpt. 1971, 85). Home: 510 Forsyth Crescent, Saskatoon, SK Canada S7N 4H8 Office: U Sask, 3117 Edn Bldg, Saskatoon, SK Canada S7N 0W0

RANDISH, JOAN MARIE, dentist; b. Seattle, Oct. 2, 1954; d. Matthew John and Margaret Cecelia (Waham) R. DDS, U. Wash., 1981. Dentist S.E. Dental Clinic, Seattle, 1981-82, Indian Health Bd., Seattle, 1982-84, Joe Whiting Dental Clinic, Seattle, 1984-85, Georgetown Dental Clinic, Seattle, 1981-88, King County Pub. Health, Seattle, 1987—; pvt. practice dentist Bellevue, Wash., 1981—. Recipient Women of Yr. award Bellevue Bus. and Profl. Women, Seattle, 1987. Mem. ADA, Seattle King County Dental Soc., Soroptimist Club of Bellevue (del. 1983-91). Office: 25 102nd Ave NE Bellevue WA 98004-5622

RANDISI, ELAINE MARIE, law corporation executive, educator; b. Racine, Wis., Dec 19, 1926; d. John Dewey and Alveta Irene (Raffety) Fehd; AA, Pasadena Jr. Coll., 1946; BS cum laude (Giannini scholar), Golden Gate U., 1978; m. John Paul Randisi, Oct. 12, 1946 (div. July 1972); children: Jeanine Randisi Manson, Martha Randisi Chaney (dec.), Joseph, Paula, Catherine Randisi Carvalho, George, Anthony (dec.); m. John R. Woodfin, June 18, 1994. With Raymond Kaiser Engrs., Inc., Oakland, Calif., 1969-75, 77-86, corp. acct., 1978-79, sr. corp. acct., 1979-82, sr. payroll acct., 1983-86, acctg. mgr., Lilli Ann Corp., San Francisco, 1986-89, Crosby, Heafey, Roach & May, Oakland, Calif., 1990—; corp. buyer Kaiser Industries Corp., Oakland, 1975-77; lectr. on astrology Theosophical Soc., San Francisco, 1979—; mem. faculty Am. Fedn. Astrologers Internat. Conv., Chgo., 1982, 84. Mem. Speakers Bur., Calif. Assn. for Neurologically Handicapped Children, 1964-70, v.p. 1969; bd. dirs. Ravenwood Homeowners Assn., 1979-82, v.p., 1979-80, sec., 1980-81; mem. organizing com. Minority Bus. Fair, San Francisco, 1976; pres., bd. dirs. Lakewood Condominium Assn., 1984-87; mem., trustee Ch. of Religious Sci., 1992—; treas. First Ch. Religious Sci., 1994—. Mem. Am. Fedn. Astrologers, Nat. Assn. Female Execs., Calif. Scholarship Fedn. (life), Alpha Gamma Sigma (life). Mem. Ch. of Religious Science (lic. practioner pres. 1990-91, sec. 1989-90). Initiated Minority Vendor Purchasing Program for Kaiser Engrs., Inc., 1975-76. Home: 742 Wesley Way Apt 1C Oakland CA 94610-2339 Office: Crosby Heafey Roach & May 1999 Harrison St Oakland CA 94612-3517

RANDLE, ELLEN EUGENIA FOSTER, opera and classical singer, educator; b. New Haven, Conn., Oct. 2, 1948; d. Richard A.G. and Thelma Lousie (Brooks) Foster; m. Ira James William, 1967 (div. 1972); m. John Willis Randle. Student, Calif. State Coll., Sonoma, 1970; studied with Boris Goldovsky, 1970; student, Grad. Sch. Fine Arts, Florence, Italy, 1974; studied with Tito Gobbi, Florence, 1974; student, U. Calif., Berkeley, 1977; BA in World History, Lone Mountain Coll., 1976, MA in Performing Arts, 1978; studied with Madam Eleanor Steber, Graz, Austria, 1979; studied with Patricia Goehl, Munich, Fed. Republic Germany, 1979; MA in Counseling and Psychology, U. San Francisco, 1990, MA in Marital Family Therapy, 1994. Exec. mgr., psychotherapist Just 4 People, Inc., Richmond, Calif.; instr. East Bay Performing Art Ctr., Richmond, Calif., 1986, Chapman Coll., 1986. Singer opera prodns. Porgy & Bess, Oakland, Calif., 1980-81, La-Traviata, Oakland, Calif., 1981-82, Aida, Oakland, 1981-82, Madame Butterfly, Oakland, 1982-83, The Magic Flute, Oakland, 1984, numerous others; performances include TV specials, religous concerts, musicals; music dir. Natural Man, Berkeley, 1986; asst. artistic dir. Opera Piccola, Oakland, Calif., 1990—. Art commr. City of Richmond, Calif. Recipient Bk. Am. Achievement award. Mem. Music Tchrs. Assn., Internat. Black Writers and Artists Inc. (life mem., local #5), Nat. Coun. Negro Women, Nat. Assn. Negro Musicians, Calif. Arts Fedn., Calif. Assn. for Counseling and Devel. (mem. black caucus), Nat. Black Child Devel. Inst., The Calif.-Nebraskan Orgn., Inc., Calif. Marital & Family Therapist Assn. (San Francisco chpt.), Black Psychotherpist of San Francisco and East Bay Area, San Francisco Commonwealth Club, Gamma Phi Delta. Democrat. Mem. A.M.E. Zion Ch. Home: 5314 Boyd Ave Oakland CA 94618-1112

RANDLE, KATHE MCGEHEE, publisher, writer; b. Helena, Mont., June 12, 1946; d. Lorry M. and Helen T. (Schatz) McG.; m. Paul S. Willis, Oct. 1, 1981 (div. 1984); m. Daye-Llyn D. Randle, Sept. 17, 1988. BA in Sociology, Journalism, U. Mont., 1969; MA in Family Counseling, Coll. Gt. Falls, 1989, MS in Profl. Counseling, 1993. Lic. clin. profl. counselor. Info. specialist State of Mont., Helena, 1971-78; editor, v.p. Art West Mag., Kalispell, Mont., 1978-81; owner Vixen Enterprises, Kalispell, 1982-86; dir. Lake County Chem. Dependency Program, Polson, Mont., 1991—; mental health counselor in pvt. practice Polson, Mont., 1993—; instr. Flathead Valley Community Coll., 1980-83; cons. Media Ranking Service, 1978-84; dir. investigative authors' league, Big Fork, Mont., 1980-84. Author: Publish For Profit, 1989, Private Family Counselor, 1989; contbr. interviews to various mags., 1980—. Role cons. Big Brothers-Big Sisters, 1971-75; founder Handicap Aquatics Program, 1981; tchr. Gifted Talented Program, 1982-83; bd. dirs. United Way, Kalispell, 1981-83. Mem. Mensa. Roman Catholic. Home: Bay Links View PO Box 1743 Polson MT 59860-9999

RANDOLPH, KEVIN H., marketing executive; b. Seattle, July 6, 1949; s. Howard Amos and Betty Elaine (Leahy) R.; m. Deborah Lou Newell, Sept. 18, 1976; children: Heather, Lyndsay. BA, Wash. State U., 1972. Mgr. Computers for Mktg., L.A., 1972-74; data processing mgr. Parker Rsch., Pasadena, Calif., 1974-77; prin. Randolph & Assocs., L.A., 1977-79; v.p. Bank Am. Corp., San Francisco, 1979-87, Interactive Network, Mountain View, Calif., 1987-91; sr. v.p. ICTV, Santa Clara, Calif., 1991-93; pres. Interactive Enterprises, San Ramon, Calif., 1993—; v.p. U.S. West Mrg., Inc., Benicia, Calif., 1993-94; exec. v.p., COO Interactive Video Enterprises, Inc., San Ramon, 1994—; cons. Randolph Home Ctr., Ephrata, Wash., 1972—. Mem. Am. Mktg. Assn., Am. Mgmt. Assn. Home: 170 Edinburgh Cir Danville CA 94526

RANDOLPH, LINDA MARIE, geneticist; b. Bakersfield, Calif., Nov. 12, 1953; d. Clinton Elwood and Dorothy Jane (Swanson) R.; m. Jonathan Bole Eddison, Nov. 30, 1985; children: Marie Randolph, Elizabeth Jane. BS, U. Redlands, 1975; MA, U. Calif., Irvine, 1980; MD, George Washington U., 1982. Diplomate Am. Bd. Pediatrics, Am. Bd. Med. Genetics. Pediatric resident Children's Nat. Med. Ctr., Washington, 1982-85; clin. and rsch. fellow Harbor-UCLA Med. Ctr., L.A., 1985-88; rsch. scientist Cedars Sinai Med. Ctr., L.A., 1988-89; clin. geneticist, cytogeneticist Alfigen/The Genetics Inst., Pasadena, Calif., 1989-92, med. dir. prenatal genetics, 1993—; assoc. med. dir. Integrated Genetics, Long Beach, Calif., 1992-93. Rsch. fellowship Blinder Found., 1988, Nat. Found. for Iletis and Colitis, 1988. Mem. AMA, Am. Acad. Pediat., Am. Soc. Human Genetics, Alpha Omega Alpha. Office: Alfigen/The Genetics Inst 11 W Del Mar Blvd Pasadena CA 91105-2505

RANDOLPH, PAUL G., history educator, minister; b. Henderson, Tenn., Oct. 10, 1927; s. Paul Dorris and Clara Cathleen (Titsworth) R.; m. Virginia Seal, June 8, 1952; children: Paul Kevin, Mark Edward, Lisa Virginia. BA with highest honors, U. Ill., 1950, MA, 1951; PhD, U. Mich., 1972. Instr. Freed-Hardeman U., Henderson, 1951-53; min. Redford Ch. of Christ, Detroit, 1953-55, Hayes Ave. Ch. of Christ, Detroit, 1956-58; asst. prof. Pepperdine U., L.A., 1958-70; prof. Pepperdine U., Malibu, 1978—; from assoc. prof. to prof. Morehead (Ky.) State U., 1970-78. Faculty sponsor Pepperdine U. Young Dems., 1980—; mem. Woodland Hills Ch. of Christ, 1984—. With U.S. Army, 1946-47. Mem. Phi Beta Kappa, Phi Alpha Theta, Pi Gamma Mu. Home: 43 Pinewood Ave Agoura CA 91301-1223 Office: Pepperdine U Humanities Divsn Malibu CA 91301

RANDOLPH, STEVEN, insurance and estate planning agent; b. Nebr., Oct. 14, 1946; m. Sherri Hamrick, 1980 (div. 1989); children: David, John, Michelle; m. Kathleen Riley, 1991. BS, U. Nebr., 1971. Registered rep., SEC; variable annuities license; ins. and disabilities license. Rep. Real Estate Consulting Svcs., Inc., Newport Beach, Calif., 1971-86; fin. svcs. advisor Prudential Fin. Group, Laguna Hills, Calif., 1986—. With USMC, 1964-68, Vietnam. Mem. Nat. Assn. Securities Dealers, Nat. Assn. Life Underwriters (Nat. Sales Achievement award, Nat. Quality award), Million Dollar Round Table Club, Pres.'s Club (awards). Home and Office: PO Box 9612 Newport Beach CA 92658-9612

RANDS, JEFFREY RAYMOND, government consultant; b. Inglewood, Calif., June 19, 1963; s. Gary Monroe and Marilyn LaFay (Robinson) R.; m. Lynnett Diane Reynolds, Oct. 9, 1993. BA in Internat. Rels., Brigham Young U., 1987; MBA cum laude, U. Chgo., 1992. Rsch. asst. ICF-LEWIN, Fairfax, Va., 1988; congrl. liaison U.S. Dept. HUD, Washington, 1989-90; analyst Ssongyong Investment and Securities, Seoul, 1991; cons., policy analyst Change Mgmt. Svcs., Andersen Cons., 1993—. Author, pub.: Seattle Style Guide, 1993. Polit. campaign worker, Seattle, 1992. Mormon. Home: 62 Boylston St Apt 920 Boston MA 02116-4786

RANFTL, ROBERT MATTHEW, management consulting company executive; b. Milw., May 31, 1925; s. Joseph Sebastian and Leona Elaine (Goetz) R.; m. Marion Smith Goodman, Oct. 12, 1946. BSEE, U. Mich., 1946; postgrad. UCLA, 1953-55. Product engr. Russell Electric Co., Chgo., 1946-47; head engring. dept. Radio Inst. Chgo., 1947-50; sr. project engr. Webster Chgo. Corp., 1950-51, product design engr., 1951-53, head equipment design group, 1953-54, head electronic equipment sect., 1954-55, mgr. product engring. dept., 1955-58, mgr. reliability and quality control, 1958-59, mgr. adminstrn. 1959-61, mgr. product effectiveness lab., 1961-74; corp. dir. engring./design mgmt., 1974-84, corp. dir. managerial productivity Hughes Aircraft Co., Los Angeles, 1984-86; pres. Ranftl Enterprises Inc., Mgmt. Cons., Los Angeles, 1981—; guest lectr. Calif. Inst. Tech., Cornell U., U. Calif.; mem. White House Conf. on Productivity, 1983; mem. human resources productivity task force Dept. of Def., 1985-86. Author: R&D Productivity, 1974, 78; (with others) Productivity: Prospects for Growth, 1981; contbr. articles to profl. jours. Mem. AAAS, AIAA, Am. Soc. Engring. Edn., Am. Soc. Tng. and Devel., IEEE, Inst. Mgmt. Scis., Acad. Mgmt., N.Y. Acad. Scis., U. Mich. Alumni Assn., UCLA Alumni Assn. Office: Ranftl Enterprises Inc PO Box 49892 Los Angeles CA 90049-0892

RANGILA, NANCY ARNEVNA KUSALA, investment consultant; b. Petrozavodsk, Russia, Mar. 23, 1936; came to U.S., 1937; d. Henry Hjalmar and Myrtle Marie (Jacobson) R. BA in Am. History, U. South Carolina, 1958, MA in Am. History, 1964; MBA in Fin., U. So. Calif., 1973. Chartered fin. analyst; cert. employee benefit specialist, cert. fin. planner, chartered investment counselor. Fin. analyst Capital Rsch. Co., L.A., 1964-73; v.p., portfolio mgr., fin. analyst Capital Cons., Inc., Portland, Oreg., 1973-82; sr. v.p., Franklin Fin. Svcs. (subs. Bank of Am. Fed. Savs. Bank), Portland, 1982-91; v.p. rsch., exec. asst. to chair Cutler & Co., Medford, Oreg., 1992-94; fin. cons. Prime Cons., Portland, 1994—; lectr. investments, retirement plans. Chmn. City of Portland Hosp. Facilities Authority. Mem. Portland Soc. Fin. Analysts, Assn. Investment Mgmt. and Rsch., L.A. Soc. Fin. Analysts, Oreg. Women's Forum, City Club, Multnomah Athletic Club (Portland). Republican. Home: 2221 SW 1st Ave Apt 1625 Portland OR 97201-5019 Office: Prime Cons PO Box 518 Portland OR 97207-0518

RANISH, DONALD ROSEMAN, political science educator, political consultant; b. Newburgh, N.Y., Nov. 19, 1943; s. Harry and Sylvia (Roseman) R.; m. Leslee Ann Guttman, Aug. 29, 1970. BA, Calif. State U., Fullerton, 1970; MA, U. Calif., Santa Barbara, 1972, PhD, 1975. Prof. polit. sci. Alma (Mich.) U., 1975-76, Calif. State U., San Bernardino, 1976-77; prof. polit. sci. and law Antelope Valley Coll., Lancaster, Calif., 1977—, Kyung Hee U., Seoul, 1987—; Fulbright lectr., Republic of Korea, 1987. Author: American Political Process, 1982, 5th edit., 1993, Rhetoric of a Rebel, 1975; contbr. articles and papers to profl. publs. Bd. dirs. United Way Antelope Valley, Lancaster, 1986-88; mem. Lancaster Edn. Found., 1994—. U.S. Sea grantee, 1974-75; U.Calif. Regents grantee, 1975. Mem. Am. Polit. Sci. Assn., Acad. Criminal Justice Scis., Fulbright Alumni Assn., Phi Kappa Phi, Pi Sigma Alpha. Democrat. Home: 42953 Cherbourg Ln Lancaster CA 93536-4827

RANKEN, ANTHONY L., lawyer; b. Phila., Oct. 2, 1956; s. Howard B. and Nani (Lengyel) R. AB, Indiana U., 1979; JD, U. Calif., Berkeley, 1992. Assoc. atty. Lowenthal & August, Wailuku, Hawaii, 1983-89; prin. Anthony L. Ranken, Atty. at Law, Wailuku, Hawaii, 1989—. Author: Workouts with Weights, 1993; editor in chief Ecology Law Quarterly, Berkeley, 1981-82. Co-dir. Maui Tomorrow, Hawaii, 1989-94, pres. 1994—. Office: 222 N Church St Wailuku HI 96793

RANKIN, HELEN CROSS, cattle rancher, guest ranch executive; b. Mojave, Calif; d. John Whisman and Cleo Rebecca (Tilley) Cross; m. Leroy

Rankin, Jan. 4, 1936 (dec. 1954); children—Julia Jane King Sharr, Patricia Helen Denvir, William John. A.B., Calif. State U.-Fresno, 1935. Owner, operator Rankin Cattle Ranch, Caliente, Calif., 1954—; founder, pres. Rankin Ranch, Inc., Guest Ranch, 1965—; mem. sect. 15, U.S. Bur. Land Mgmt.; mem. U.S. Food and Agrl. Leaders Tour China, 1983, Australia and N.Z., 1985; dir. U.S. Bur. Land Mgmt. sect. 15. Pres., Children's Home Soc. Calif., 1945; mem. adv. bd. Camp Ronald McDonald. Recipient award Calif. Hist. Soc., 1983, Kern River Valley Hist. Soc., 1983. Mem. Am. Nat. Cattlemen's Assn., Calif. Cattlemen's Assn., Kern County Cattlemen's Assn., Kern County Cowbelles (pres. 1949, Cattlewoman of Yr. 1988), Calif. Cowbelles, Nat. Cowbelles, Bakersfield Country Club, Bakersfield Raquet Club. Republican. Baptist. Office: Rankin Ranch Caliente CA 93518

RANKIN, WILLIAM PARKMAN, educator, former publishing company executive; b. Boston, Feb. 6, 1917; s. George William and Bertha W. (Clowe) R.; m. Ruth E. Gerard, Sept. 12, 1942; children: Douglas W., Joan W. BS, Syracuse U., 1941; MBA, NYU, 1949, PhD, 1979. Sales exec. Redbook mag., N.Y.C., 1945-49; sales exec. This Week mag., N.Y.C., 1949-55, adminstrv. exec., 1955-60, v.p., 1957-60, v.p., dir. advt. sales, sales devel. dir., 1960-63, exec. v.p., 1963-69; gen. exec. newspaper div. Time Inc., N.Y.C., 1969-70; gen. mgr. feature svc. Newsweek, Inc., N.Y.C., 1970-74, fin. and ins. advt. mgr., 1974-81; prof., asst. to the dir. Walter Cronkite Sch. Journalism and Telecommunication, Ariz. State U., Tempe, 1981—; lectr. Syracuse U., NYU, Berkeley Sch. Author: Selling Retail Advertising, 1944; The Technique of Selling Magazine Advertising, 1949; Business Management of Consumer Magazines, 1980, 2 ed. 1984, The Practice of Newspaper Management, 1986. Mem. Dutch Treat Club. Home: 1220 E Krista Way Tempe AZ 85284-1545 also: Bridge Rd Bomoseen VT 05732 Office: Ariz State U Walter Cronkite Sch Journalism/Telecom Tempe AZ 85287-1305

RANSDELL, TOD ELLIOT, pharmaceutical, parenteral and in vitro diagnostics validation specialist; b. Imperial, Nebr., May 17, 1953; s. Merrill Guy and Rosalie E. (Nissen) R. BS in Botany, Mont. State U., Bozeman, 1977. Police officer Dillon (Mont.) Police Dept., 1979-80; dept. mgr. Woolco, Bozeman, Mont., 1980-83; lab. coord. Skyland Sci. Svcs., Inc., Bozeman, Mont., 1983-86; sales assoc. S&P Office Supply, Bozeman, Mont., 1986-87; validation specialist Skyland Sci. Svcs., Inc., Bozeman, Mont., 1987-92, sr. validation specialist, 1992; sr. validation specialist Genetic Systems Corp., Redmond, Wash., 1992—; cons. Skyland Sci. Svcs., Inc., Bozeman, Mont., 1987-92. Order of Arrow, brotherhood, chpt. chief Boy Scouts Am. (life rank), 1973; pres. Bozeman (Mont.) Jaycees, 1983, 85, Crime Stoppers, 1982; mem. Benevolent and Prtective Order of the Elks, Bozeman, Mont. 1989-94. Mem. Union of Concerned Scientists, Parenteral Drug Assn., Bozeman Jr. C. of C., Internat. Soc. Pharm. Engring., Nat. Rifle Assn., Nature Conservency, Greenpeace, Nat. Pks. and Conservation Assn., Seattle Mountaineers. Office: Genetic Systems Corp Sanofi Diagnostics Pasteur 6565 185th Ave NE Redmond WA 98052-5039

RANSMEIER, DENIS SIRERA, university administrator; b. Hanover, N.H., Sept. 23, 1947; s. Joseph Sirera and Margaret (Mitchel) R.; m. Deborah Carter (div. 1988); m. Ethel Atkins, Apr. 2, 1989. BA, Amherst (Mass.) Coll., 1970; MEd, Boston Coll., 1973; MBA, Columbia U., 1975. Staff acct. Price Waterhouse & Co., Washington, 1975-78; asst. dean for adminstrn. Law Ctr. Georgetown U., Washington, 1978-87; v.p. fin. and adminstrn., treas. Seattle U., 1987—. Mem. Assn. Jesuit Coll. and Univs. (exec. com. 1988—), Nat. Assn. Coll. and Univ. Bus. Officers, N.W. Ind. Colls. Bus. Officers. Office: Seattle U Seattle WA 98122

RANSOM, MICHAEL R., economics educator; b. Salt Lake City, Oct. 21, 1952; s. Wendell Bybee and Beth (Kirby) R.; m. Laurie Noel Wilson, Aug. 17, 1976; children: James, Melissa, Todd, Tyler, Jessica. BA, Brigham Young U., 1977; MA in Econs., Princeton U., 1980, PhD in Econs., 1983. Asst. prof. econs. U. Ariz., Tucson, 1982-88; assoc. prof. econs. Brigham Young U., Provo, Utah, 1988—; vis. asst. prof. Princeton (N.J.) U., 1985. Contbr. articles to profl. jours. Mem. Am. Econ. Assn., Econometric Soc. Mormon. Office: Brigham Young U Dept Econs Provo UT 84602

RANSOM, RICHARD EDWARD, state supreme court justice; b. Hampton, Iowa, Dec. 9, 1932. BA, U. N.Mex., 1954; LLB, Georgetown U., 1959. Bar: N.Mex. 1959, D.C. 1959. Trial lawyer Albuquerque, 1959-86; justice N.Mex. Supreme Ct., Santa Fe, 1987—; chief justice N. Mex. Supreme Ct., 1992-94. 1st lt. USMC, 1954-56. Fellow Am. Coll. Trial Lawyers, Internat. Soc. Barristers, Internat. Acad. Trial Lawyers. Office: N Mex Supreme Ct PO Box 848 237 Don Gaspar Ave Santa Fe NM 87504-0848*

RAO, TADIMETI SEETAPATI, pharmacologist; b. Munjuluru, Amdhra Pra, India, Apr. 15, 1959; came to U.S., 1987; s. Sastry and Sarojini Devi Tadimeti; m. Krishna Kumari Meduri, Oct. 9, 1992. B.Pharm., Andhra U., India, 1979, M.Pharm., 1982; PhD, U. Alta., Edmonton, Can., 1986. Postdoctoral vis. scientist Ciba-Geigy Corp., Summit, N.J., 1987-88; rsch. investigator G.D. Searle-Monsanto, St. Louis, 1988-90, sr. rsch. investigator, 1990-91, rsch. scientist, 1991-93; sr. rsch. scientist Salt Inst. Biotech. Industries Assoc., LaJolla, Calif., 1993—. Author chpts. in books: Biology of Trace Amines, 1988, Mass Spectrometry of Biologic Materials, 1989. U. Alta. Alma Mater Travel grantee, 1986; Western Pharmacol. Soc. Travel grantee. Fellow Can. Coll. Neuropsycho Pharmacology; mem. Soc. for Neurosci., Internat. Soc. for Neurochemistry, Inflammation Rsch. Assn., Internat. Brain Rsch. Orgn. Home: 8889 Cmuto Pl Centro #7406 San Diego CA 92122 Office: SIBIA 505 Coast Blvd S Ste 300 La Jolla CA 92037-4616

RAPHAEL, MARTIN GEORGE, research wildlife biologist; b. Denver, Oct. 5, 1946; s. Jerome Maurice and Alys (Salmonson) R.; m. Susan Williams, August 4, 1967; 1 child, Samantha Marie. BA, Sacramento State U., 1968; BS, U. Calif., Berkeley, 1972, MS, 1976, PhD, 1980. Staff research assoc. U. Calif., Berkeley, 1974-80, assoc. specialist, 1980-84; project leader USDA Forest Svc., Laramie, 1984-89, Olympia, Wash., 1989—; adj. prof. U. Wyo., Laramie, 1986-89; cons. ecologist Pacific Gas and Electric Co., San Ramon, Calif., 1981-84. Contbr. articles to sci. jours. Mem. Ecol. Soc. Am. (editl. bd. Ecol. Applications), Soc. for Conservation Biology, Am. Ornithologists' Union, Cooper Ornithol. Soc. (chmn. membership com. 1985-90, asst. sec. 1986—, bd. dirs. 1989-92), The Wildlife Soc. (local pres. publs. com. 1983-84, assoc. editor Wildlife Soc. Bull. 1987-90), Phi Beta Kappa, Sigma Xi, Xi Sigma Pi. Home: 3224 Biscay Ct NW Olympia WA 98502-3558 Office: Pacific NW Rsch Sta 3625 93rd Ave SW Olympia WA 98512-9145

RAPHAEL, TAMAR AMITA, development director; b. L.A., Mar. 14, 1962; d. Eli and Judith Raphael. BA, Smith Coll., 1983; student, Inst. Polit. & Econ. Studies, Eng. Legis. aide Sen. John Garamendi Calif. State Legis., Sacramento, 1984-86; nat. press asst. NOW, Washington, 1986-87; nat. comms. dir. Feminist Majority, Washington, 1987-91; devel. dir. Feminist Majority, San Rafael, Calif., 1991—. Editor Feminist Majority Report, 1988-91. Bd. dirs. Family Law Ctr., San Rafael, 1993-95, Marin Abuse Women's Svcs., San Rafael, 1994—. Office: Feminist Majority PO Box 6412 San Rafael CA 94903-0412

RAPIER, PASCAL MORAN, chemical engineer, physicist; b. Atlanta, Jan. 11, 1914; s. Paul Edward and Mary Claire (Moran) R.; m. Martha Elizabeth Doyle, May 19, 1945; children: Caroline Elizabeth, Paul Doyle, Mollie Claire, John Lawrence, James Andrew. BSChemE, Ga. Inst. Tech., 1939; MS in Theoretical Physics, U. Nev., 1959; postgrad., U. Calif., Berkeley, 1961. Registered profl. engr., Calif., N.J. Plant engr. Archer-Daniels-Midland, Pensacola, Fla., 1940-42; group supr. Dicalite div. Grefco, Los Angeles, 1943-54; process engr. Celatom div. Eagle Picher, Reno, Nev., 1955-57; project mgr., assoc. research engr. U. Calif. Field Sta., Richmond, 1959-62; project mgr. sea water conversion Bechtel Corp., San Francisco, 1962-66; sr. supervising chem. engr. Burns & Roe, Oradell, N.J., 1966-74; cons. engr. Kenite Corp., Scarsdale, N.Y., Rees Blowpipe, Berkeley, 1960-66; sr. cons. engr. Sanderson & Porter, N.Y.C., 1975-77; staff scientist III Lawrence Berkeley Lab., 1977-84; bd. dirs. Newtonian Sci. Found.; v.p. Calif. Rep. Assembly, 1964-65; discoverer phenomena faster than light, origin of cosmic rays and galactic red shifts. Contbr. articles to profl jours.; patentee agts. to render non-polar solvents electrically conductive, direct-contact geothermal energy recovery devices. Mem. Am. Inst. Chem. Engrs., Gideons Internat., Lions Internat., Corvallis, Sigma Pi Sigma. Home and Office: 8015 NW Ridgewood Dr Corvallis OR 97330-3026

RAPIER, STEPHEN MICHAEL, marketing executive; b. Inglewood, Calif., Apr. 8, 1957; s. Oliver C. III and Helen (Bilsn) R. BSBA, Calif. State U., Long Beach, 1981. Sales rep. Dieterich-Post Co., Monterey Park, Calif., 1981-82; pres. S.M. Rapier Corp./Sebring Hard Disc Sys., Carson, Calif., 1982-87; v.p. J.B. Schultz & Assocs., L.A., 1987-88; v.p., pres. Concept Data Corp./Quality Rsch. Inst., L.A., 1988-95; dir. mktg. Power Lift SCMH, Pico Rivera, Calif., 1995—; guest lectr. U. So. Calif., 1984, Calif. State U., Long Beach, 1985, Calif. State U., L.A., 1990. Mem. Am. Mktg. Assn. (So. Calif.) chpt.). Republican. Roman Catholic. Office: 8314 E Slauson Ave Pico Rivera CA 90660

RAPOPORT, RONALD JON, journalist; b. Detroit, Aug. 14, 1940; s. Daniel B. and Shirley G.; m. Joan Zucker, Sept. 2, 1968; children—Rebecca, Julie. B.A., Stanford U., 1962; M.S., Columbia U., 1963. Reporter Mpls. Star, 1963-65; asso. editor Sport mag., 1965-66; sports reporter AP, N.Y.C., San Francisco, 1966-70, Los Angeles Times, 1970-77; sports columnist Chgo. Sun-Times, 1977-88, Los Angeles Daily News, 1988—; sports commentatorWeekend Edit. Nat. Pub. Radio, 1986—. Author: (with Chip Oliver) High for the Game, 1971, (with Stan Love) Love in the NBA, 1975, (with Jim McGregor) Called for Travelling, 1979; editor: A Kind of Grace: A Treasury of Sportswriting by Women, 1994. Served with U.S. Army Res., 1963. Office: Los Angeles Daily News 21221 Oxnard St Woodland Hills CA 91367-5015

RAPOZA, GLENN ROBERTS, vocational rehabilitation counselor, teacher; b. Honolulu, May 16, 1948; s. Frank Gordon and Geralding Evelyn (Souza) R.; m. Cathy Louise Bristow Iriarte, SEpt. 6, 1980 (div. Oct. 1982); 1 child, Heather. BS suma cum laude, Calif. State U., Fresno, 1973, MA, 1975. Cert. C.C. tchr. adult edn., cert. C.C. counselor, Calif. Group counselor I Solano County Juvenile Hall, Fairfield, Calif., 1975-76; vocat. specialist for handicapped Office Solano County Supt. Schs., Fairfield, Calif., 1976-79; case mgr., program coord. Westcom Rehab Ctr., Richmond, Calif., 1979-81; mgr. rehab. svcs. Westcom Rehab Ctr., El Ceritto, Calif., 1981-86; employment svc. specialist SETA, Sacramento, Calif., 1989-94; vocat. rehab. counselor Dept. of Vet. Affairs, Sacramento, 1994; mem. adv. bd. North Bay Regional Ctr., Napa, Calif., 1976-77; bd. dirs. Solano Workshop Svcs., 1977-78; guidance counselor Youth for Christ, Sacramento, 1989-91; group co-facilitator Kaiser Alcohol & Drug Program, Sacramento, 1989-91. Vol. Com. to Elect Dr. Dan Muller, Vallejo, Calif., 1977-78; local bd. dirs., Am Fedn. State-County Mcpl. Employees, Sacramento, 1994. Democrat. Roman Catholic. Home: 2649 River Plaza Dr # 243 B Sacramento CA 95833 Office: Dept VA 1825 Bell St Ste 202 Sacramento CA 95825-1020

RAPP, NINA BEATRICE, financial company executive; b. Copenhagen, Denmark, Sept. 3, 1958; came to the U.S., 1984; d. Sven Ove Lars Larsen and Kirsten Rung Jorgensen Mechik; m. Steven Douglas Rapp, July 14, 1984; 1 child, Stephanie Beatrice. BA in Econs. and Polit. Sci., Danish Royal Mil. Acad., 1982; MBA in Fin., Harvard U., 1992. Cert. explosives expert; lic. ins. and securites rep. Cons. Mei & Assocs., Waltham, Mass., 1987-88; leasing mgr. Wright Runstad & Co., Seattle, 1990-92; regional v.p. Primerica Fin. Svcs., Seattle, 1992—; ptnr. R & R Assocs., Seattle, 1990-93. Author: International Terrorism, 1982. Capt. Danish Army, 1977-82, lt., 1982-84. Mem. NAFE. Home: 6516 163rd St SW Lynnwood WA 98037-2717 Office: Primerica Fin Svcs 12811 8th Ave W # B205 Everett WA 98204-6300

RAPPAPORT, IRVING, immunologist, researcher; b. N.Y.C., Sept. 4, 1923; s. Hyman and Sarah (Frock) R.; m. Helen Magid, June 27, 1948 (dec. Apr., 1973); children: Glenn, Jeffrey, Paul; m. Louise Cohen, Mar. 23, 1975; children: Ellen, Lawrence. AB, Cornell U., 1948; PhD, Calif. Inst. Tech., 1953. Rsch. botanist UCLA, L.A., 1953-61; asst. prof. U. Chgo., 1961-64; prof. N.Y. Med. Coll., Valhalla, N.Y., 1964—. Contbr. numerous articles to profl. jours.; assoc. editor Virology, 1969. 1st. lt. U.S. Air Force, 1942-46. Fellow AAAS, N.Y. Acad. Med.; mem. Am. Assn. Immunologists, Genetics Soc. Am., Am. Soc. Microbiologists, Am. Inst. Biol. Sci. Home: PO Box 721 North Bennington VT 05257-0721 Office: 9833 Brentwood Dr Santa Ana CA 92705-1534

RAPPAPORT, MICHAEL DAVID, college dean, labor arbitrator; b. Chgo., Aug. 21, 1943; s. Harold and Ida (Snitoff) R.; m. Susan Joy Ketay, June 16, 1968; children: Rachel, Isaac. BS, U. Wis., 1965, JD, 1968. Bar: Wis. 1968, Trust Ter. Pacific 1968. Asst. dean UCLA Law Sch., 1970—; labor arbitrator, L.A., 1972—; chmn. Bet Tzedek Legal Svcs., L.A., 1972-74, bd. dirs., 1970-82. Contbr. articles to profl. jours. Mem. Nat. Acad. Arbitrators, Am. Arbitration Assn. (program cons., lectr.). Jewish. Office: UCLA Law Sch 405 Hilgard Ave Los Angeles CA 90024-1301

RAPSON, RICHARD L., history educator; b. N.Y.C., Mar. 8, 1937; s. Louis and Grace Lillian (Levenkind) R.; m. Susan Burns, Feb. 22, 1975 (div. June 1981); m. Elaine Catherine Hatfield, June 15, 1982; 1 child, Kim Elizabeth. BA, Amherst Coll., 1958; PhD, Columbia U., 1966. Asst. prof. Amherst (Mass.) Coll., 1960-61, Stanford (Calif.) U., 1961-65; from assoc. prof. to prof. history U. Hawaii, Honolulu, 1965—, founder, dir. New Coll., 1968-73; bd. dirs. Semester at Sea, U. Pittsburgh, 1979—; psychotherapist, Honolulu, 1982—. Author: Individualism and Conformity in the American Character, 1967, Britons View America, 1971, The Cult of Youth, 1972, Major Interpretations of the American Past, 1978, Denials of Doubt, 1980, Cultural Pluralism in Hawaii, 1981, American Yearnings, 1989; co-author: (with Elaine Hatfield) Love, Sex and Intimacy: Their Psychology, Biology and History, 1993, Emotional Contagion, 1994, A World of Passion: Cross-Cultural Perspectives on Love and Sex, 1995; mem. editorial bd. Univ. Press Am., 1981—. Woodrow Wilson fellow, Wilson Found., Princeton, 1960; Edward Perkins scholar, Columbia U., 1961; Danforth tchr., Danforth Found., St. Louis, 1965; recipient E. Harris Harbison for Gifted Teaching award, Danforth Found., 1973, Outstanding Tchr. award Stanford U. 25th Reunion Class, 1992. Mem. Am. Hist. Assn., Orgn. Am. Hist., Nat. Womens Hist. Project, Phi Beta Kappa, Outrigger Canoe Club, Honolulu Club. Office: U Hawaii Dept History 2530 Dole St Honolulu HI 96822-2303

RASCO, BARBARA A., food chemistry educator. BS in Engring & Chem. Engring., U. Pa., 1979; PhD in Food Sci. & Nutrition, U. Mass., 1983; JD, Seattle U., 1995. Biochem. engr. Cargill, Inc., Mpls., 1982-83; quality control mgmt. Cargill, Inc., Memphis, 1983-84; asst. prof. U. Wash., Seattle, 1984-89, assoc. prof., 1989—; advisor Northwest Food Safety Coun., 1992—. Contbr. chpts. to books and articles to profl. jours.; inventor in field. Mem. ABA, Am. Chem. Soc., Inst. Food Technologists. Office: Univ Washington Inst Food Sci & Tech Box 355680 Seattle WA 98195

RASGON, BARRY MITCHELL, otolaryngologist; b. L.A., Dec. 18, 1958; s. Irving and Ethel R. BA magna cum laude, U. Calif., Riverside, 1981; MD, U. So. Calif., 1985. Diplomate Am. Bd. Otolaryngology. Intern Kaiser Permanente, 1986, resident in gen. surgery, 1987-90, resident in head and neck surgery, 1990; staff otolarygologist, head and neck surgeon Oakland Kaiser Head and Neck Surgery Residency Tng. Program, 1990—; mem. East Bay Head and Neck Pretreatment Tumor Bd., 1990—. Contbr. articles to profl. jours. Recipient Golden Adam's Apple award, 1993; grantee in field. Mem. Pacific Coast Oto-Ophthalmic Soc. (coun. 1994—), Phi Beta Kappa.

RASH, DAVID ALLEN, construction executive; b. Galveston, Tex., May 20, 1953; s. Edker Leroy and Bobbie Jeanette (Hastings) R. BS in Archtl. Studies, Wash. State U., 1977, BArch, 1978; postgrad., Cornell U., 1979-81. Estimator Pacific Rainier Roofing, Inc., Seattle, 1973-75, project mgr., 1976, 77, 81—; undergrad. tchg. asst. Wash. State U., Pullman, 1977-78; archtl. designer Mandeville and Berge, Seattle, 1978-79; libr. supr. Cornell U., Ithaca, N.Y., 1979-81; curator exhbn. The Changing Face of Carpenter Hall, 1992. Author, co-editor: Shaping Seattle Architecture, 1994. Mem. downtown com. Allied Arts of Seattle, Wash., 1982-87; mem. viewpoints com. Seattle (Wash.) Archtl. Found., 1990—. Mem. Soc. Archtl. Historians, Nat. Trust for Historic Preservation, Tau Beta Pi, Phi Kappa Phi. Baptist. Home: #001 10750 Greenwood Ave N Apt 001 Seattle WA 98133-8700

RASHEED, SURAIYA, pathology educator, cancer and AIDS researcher; b. Hyderabad, India, Sept. 2, 1936; d. Yasin and Mehrunnisan Begum Alvi; m. Nasir Rasheed, Jan. 4, 1958; children: Samrina, Saquib. BS with honors, Osmania U., Hyderabad, 1953, MS with honors, 1955, PhD, 1958; PhD, London U., 1964. Rsch. assoc. dept. cancer rsch. Mt. Vernon Hosp., Northwood, Middlesex, Eng., 1964-70; from instr. to asst. prof. to assoc. prof. pathology U. So. Calif. Sch. Medicine, L.A., 1970-82, dir. viral-chem. carcinogenesis, viral oncology program, prof. pathology, 1982—, dir. Lab. Viral Oncology and AIDS Rsch.; mem. site-oriented investigative team comprehensive cancer ctr. U. So. Calif., 1980-84, mem. health sci. caucus faculty senate, 1984-87, 89-91, mem. rsch. com. faculty senate, 1988—, pathology dept. rep. faculty senate, 1989-91, mem. sci. coun., 1990—, mem. com. faculty rights and responsibilities faculty senate, 1992, mem. exec. bd. acad. senate 1993-95, pres. med. faculty assembly 1994-95; ; cons., mem. internat. organizing com. human retroviruses and oncogenes Inst. Microbiology, Genoa, Italy, 1983; dir. ctrl. ref. labs. for human retrovirus-related rsch. programs med. ctr. U. So. Calif. and Kenneth Norris Cancer Inst., 1985—; expert scientist manpower divsn. Govt. Pakistan, 1986—; guest scientist Dept. Med. Microbiology, Solvegatan Lund, Sweden; mem. virology core com. AIDS clin. trials group NIAID, NIH, 1986—, chair protocol virologists com., 1989-92, mem. quantitative virology working group, 1989—, mem. virology tech. adv. com., 1991—; mem. Ariz. Disease Control Rsch. Commn., Ariz. Dept. Health Svcs., 1987—; mem. Internat. Adv. Bd. Future Trends Chemotherapy, Italy, 1987, Switzerland, 1990—; mem. various coms. Nat. Cancer Inst., NIH; mem. Biol. Safety Com., 1988—; mem. AIDS and Related Rsch. Rev. Small Grants Program, 1990; judge sci. project of yr. com. Calif. State Sci. Fair, 1991, chair microbiology judges com. sr. divsn., 1992, mem. judging policy adv. com., 1992—; mem. AIDS adv. bd. Hoffman-LaRoche, 1992; mem. tech. rev. panel Nebr. Cancer Adv. Com., 1992; mem. adv. bd. Internat. Working Group Tropical Virology, 1992; cons. in field. Mem. editl. bd. Internat. Jour. Anticancer Rsch., Internat. Jour. In Vivo Rsch., Internat. Jour. Immunotherapy; reviewer: Jour. Virology, Jour. Clin. Immunology, Jour. Inferential and Deductive Biology, Am. Jour. Human Genetics, also procs.; contbr. chpts. to books, articles to med. jours. Recipient Disting. Speaker award Eisenhower Med. Ctr. Annenberg Ctr. for Health Svcs., 1987, Hon. award Pakistan-U.S. Lab. for Seroepidemiology, 1989, Outstanding Svc. award Armed Forces Inst. of Pathology Rawalpindi, 1989, Cert. of Appreciation, NIH, 1990, Cert. of Appreciation, AIDS Clin. Trials Nat. Inst. Allergy and Infectious Diseases, Achievement award ICSC L.A., 1992, Gold medal BioMerieux Behring Progressive Meds. Ltd., plaque Pakistan Assn. Pathologists, 1992, Internat. award Future Trends in Chemotherapy, 1994; named hon. prof. 1st Med. U. Shanghai, China, 1988-89, Zhejiang Med. U., Hangzhou, China, 1988-92, Inst. Basic Med. Scis., Beijing, 1988-92; Postdoctoral Commonwealth scholar London U., 1961-93. Fellow Royal Coll. Pathologists Eng.; mem. AAAS, AAUP, Internat. Assn. for Comparative Rsch. in Leukemia and Related Diseases, Am. Soc. Virologists, Am. Soc. Microbiology, Internat. AIDS Soc., U. So. Calif. Med. Faculty Women's Assn. (mem. exec. com. 1982—, mem. profl. devel. com. 1982—, co-chair 1992-93, mem. by-laws com. 1987-89, chair 1989-90, mem. sci. rev. com. 1988-89, mem. scholarships com. 1988-89, chair program com. 1990-91, chair nominating com. 1992-93, pres. elect 1992-93, pres. 1993-94, Outstanding Accomplishment and Leadership award 1994). Office: U So Calif Sch Medicine Dept Pathology Rm 103 1840 N Soto St Los Angeles CA 90032-3626

RASHER, GEORGE JOSEPH, sales executive; b. Northridge, Calif., Apr. 18, 1956; s. Clarence Emerson and Berta (Sturm) R.; m. Kim Eileen Abel, Mar. 27, 1978. BA in Radio, TV & Film with highest honors, Calif. State U., Northridge, 1978; MBA magna cum laude, Pepperdine U., 1981. Account exec. various advt. agys., L.A., 1978-81; product mgr. Mattel Electronics, Hawthorne, Calif., 1981-83; dir. product mktg. Epson Am., Torrance, Calif., 1983-90; v.p. sales and mktg. Parana Supplies Corp., Torrance, 1990-93; founder Shoestring Mktg., Santa Barbara, Calif., 1993—. Mem. Am. Motor Cyclist Assn., Nat. Office Products Assn., Nat. Office Machine Dealers Assn., A Better Computer Dealer Channel, Torrance C. of C., L.A. C. of C., Apple Multimedia Program. Office: Shoestring Mktg 610 Anacapa St Santa Barbara CA 93101

RASHKIN, ESTHER J., language and literature educator; b. N.Y.C., Feb. 14, 1951; d. Milton P. and Linda (Mandel) R. BA, CUNY, 1973; MA, Yale U., 1974, PhD, 1979. Instr. French lit. Dartmouth Coll., Hanover, N.H., 1979-80, asst. prof. French and comparative lit., 1980-86, assoc. prof. French and comparative lit., adj. profl. film, 1986-89; assoc. prof. French and comparative lit. U. Utah, Salt Lake City, 1989—; mem. exec. com. Western Humanities Conf., 1983—; reader Princeton U. Press, 1992—. Author: Family Secrets and the Psychoanalysis of Narrative, 1992; contbr. articles to profl. jours. Fellow U. Utah Humanities Ctr., 1992-93, NEH, 1984. Mem. MLA (exec. com. 1990-94, reader jour. 1991—), Soc. for Study of Narrative Lit., Phi Beta Kappa. Office: U Utah Dept Langs and Lit Salt Lake City UT 84112

RASMUSON, BRENT (JACOBSEN), photographer, graphic artist; b. Logan, Utah, Nov. 28, 1950; s. Eleroy West and Fae (Jacobsen) R.; m. Tess Bullen, Sept. 30, 1981; children: John, Mark, Lisa. Grad. auto repair and painting sch., Utah State U. Pre-press supr. Herald Printing Co., Logan, 1969-79; profl. drummer, 1971-75; owner Valley Automotive Specialties, 1971-76; exec. sec. Herald Printing Co., 1979-89; owner Brent Rasmuson Photography, Smithfield, Utah, 1986—. Author photo prints of LDS temples: Logan, 1987, Manti, 1989, Jordan River, 1989, Provo, 1990, Mesa, Ariz., 1990, Boise, Idaho, 1990, Salt Lake LDS Temple, 1990, Idaho Falls, 1991, St. George, 1991, Portland, Oreg., 1991, L.A., 1991, Las Vegas, Nev., 1991, Seattle, Wash., 1992, Oakland, Calif., 1993; author photo print: Statue of Angel Moroni, 1994; author photos used to make mens' neck-ties of LDS temples: Salt Lake, Manti, Logan, L.A., Oakland, Seattle, Las Vegas, Mesa, Portland, St. George, Jordan River, scenic tie Mammoth Hot Springs in Yellowstone Park, 1995; landscape scenic photographs featured in Best of Photography Ann., 1987, 88, 89, also in calendars and book covers. Mem. Internat. Platform Assn., Assoc. Photographers Internat., Internat. Freelance Photographers Orgn. Republican. Mem. LDS Ch. Home and Office: 40 N 200 E Smithfield UT 84335-1543

RASMUSON, ELMER EDWIN, banker, former mayor; b. Yakutat, Alaska, Feb. 15, 1909; s. Edward Anton and Jenny (Olson) R.; m. Lile Vivian Bernard, Oct. 27, 1939 (dec. 1960); children: Edward Bernard, Lile Muchmore (Mrs. John Gibbons, Jr.), Judy Ann; m. Col. Mary Louise Milligan, Nov. 4, 1961. BS magna cum laude, Harvard U., 1930, AM, 1935; student, U. Grenoble, 1930; LLD, U. Alaska, 1970, Alaska Pacific U., 1993. C.P.A., N.Y., Tex., Alaska. Chief accountant Nat. Investors Corp., N.Y.C., 1933-35; prin. Arthur Andersen & Co., N.Y.C., 1935-43; pres. Nat. Bank of Alaska, 1943-65, chmn. bd., 1966-74, chmn. exec. com., 1975-82, now chmn. emeritus; mayor City of Anchorage, 1964-67, dir., emeritus and cons., 1989; civilian aide from Alaska to sec. army, 1959-67; Swedish consul Alaska, 1955-77; Chmn. Rasmuson Found.; Rep. nominee U.S. Senate from Alaska, 1968; U.S. commr. Internat. N. Pacific Fisheries Commn., 1969-84; mem. Nat. Marine Fisheries Adv. Com., 1974-77, North Pacific Fishery Mgmt. Council, 1976-77, U.S. Arctic Research Commn., 1984-92. Mem. City Coun. Anchorage, 1945, chmn. city planning commn., 1950-53; pres. Alaska coun. Boy Scouts Am., 1953; regent U. Alaska, 1950-69; trustee King's Lake Camp, Inc., 1944—, Alaska Permanent Fund Corp., 1980-82; bd. dirs. Nat. Mus. Natural History Smithsonian Inst. 1994—. Decorated knight first class Order of Vasa, comdr. Sweden; recipient silver Antelope award Boy Scouts Am., Japanese citation Order of the Sacred Treasure, Gold and Silver Star, 1988; outstanding civilian service medal U.S. Army; Alaskan of Year award, 1976. Mem. Pioneers Alaska, Alaska Bankers Assn. (past pres.), Defense Orientation Conf. Assn., NAACP, Alaska Native Brotherhood, Explorers Club, Phi Beta Kappa. Republican. Presbyn. Clubs: Masons, Elks, Anchorage Rotary (past pres.); Harvard (N.Y.C.; Boston); Wash. Athletic (Seattle), Seattle Yacht (Seattle), Rainier (Seattle); Thunderbird Country (Palm Desert, Calif.); Bohemian (San Francisco); Eldorado Country (Indian Wells, Calif.); Boone & Crockett. Home: PO Box 100600 Anchorage AK 99510-0600

RASMUSSEN, GAIL MAUREEN, critical care nurse; b. Can., Feb. 22, 1941; d. Thomas Alfred and Bernice Hilda (Sayler) Salisbury; m. Byron Karl Rasmussen, June 28, 1964; children: Stephen, Carla, Wade, Gregory. AS, Riverside City Coll., 1961; BSN, U. Phoenix, 1987; MS in Health Professions Edn., Osteo. Coll. the Pacific, 1991. RN, Calif.; CCRN. Staff nurse Meml.

Med. Ctr., Long Beach, Calif., 1961-63, UCLA Med. Ctr., 1963-64; clin. nurse critical care unit Intercommunity Med. Ctr., Covina, Calif., 1964-71, 78-95; instr. ACLS, Los Angeles County, 1991—. Mem. AACN.

RASMUSSEN, HARRY PAUL, horticulture and landscape educator; b. Tremonton, Utah, July 18, 1939; s. Peter Y. and Lorna (Nielsen) R.; m. Mary Jane Dalley, Sept. 4, 1959; children—Randy Paul, Lorianne, Trent Dalley, Rachelle. A.S., Coll. of So. Utah, 1959; B.S., Utah State U., 1961; M.S., Mich. State U., 1962, Ph.D., 1965. Research scientist Conn. Agr. Expt. Sta., New Haven, 1965-66; researcher, instr. Mich. State U., East Lansing, 1966-81; chmn. dept. horticulture and landscape architecture Wash. State U., Pullman, 1981-88; dir. Utah Agrl. Expt. Sta., Utah State U., 1988—; assoc. v.p. Utah State U., Logan, 1992—. Contbr. articles to profl. jours., chpts. to books. Mem. bd. control YMCA, Lansing, Mich., 1976; mem. council Boy Scouts Am., Lansing, 1980; stake pres. Ch. of Jesus Christ of Latter-day Saints, Lansing, 1973-81. NDEA fellow, 1961-65. Fellow Am. Soc. Horticulture Sci.; mem. AAAS, Scanning Electron Microscopy (chmn. plant sect. 1976-83). Home: 1949 N 950 E Logan UT 84341-1813 Office: Utah State U 235 Agr Sci Bldg Logan UT 84322

RASMUSSEN, MIKE JOSEPH, college financial aid administrator; b. Avalon, Calif., Aug. 1, 1947; s. Herman Joseph and Nina (Walker) R.; m. Jo Anne Eckhardt; children: Dawn Michelle, Stephen Michael. AA, West Valley Coll., 1967; AA (two), Butte Coll., 1980, 83; BA, San Jose State Coll., 1969; MA, San Jose State Univ., 1976. Cert. community coll. counselor, instr., chief adminstrv. officer, super., Calif. Vets. counselor San Jose (Calif.) State Univ., Office of Vets. Affairs, 1976-77; vets. counselor, program coord. Butte Coll., Office of Vets. Affairs, Oroville, Calif., 1977-80; dir. fin. aid and vets. affairs Butte Coll., Oroville, 1980-92, dir. spl. programs and svcs., 1992-94, interim asst. dean of student svcs., 1994-95; asst. dean of EOPS and spl. programs and svcs., 1995—; bd. dirs. Chico (Calif.) Community Hosp. Found. With USN, 1970-74, Vietnam. Recipient Cert. Appreciation Butte-Glenn County Vets. Employment Com., 1979, Boy Scouts Am. Troop 770, Paradise, Calif., 1985, Paradise (Calif.) Lioness Club, 1986, Pub. Svc. award State of Calif. Oroville Employment Devel. Dept., 1980. Mem. Calif. Community Coll. Student Fin. Aid Adminstrs. Assn. (treas. 1984-86, coord. region I, 1985-87, bd. dirs. No. Calif. 1986-87, pres.-elect 1988-89, pres. 1989-90, immediate past pres. 1990-91, Outstanding Svc. award 1985, 87, cert. of appreciation 1985, 86, 89, 90). Home: 2209 Mariposa Ave Chico CA 95926-1539 Office: Butte Coll 3536 Butte Campus Dr Oroville CA 95965-8303

RASMUSSEN, NEIL WOODLAND, insurance agent; b. Portland, Oreg., Sept. 14, 1926; s. Ernest Roy and Lulu Mildred (Woodland) R.; m. Mary Ann Cannon, Aug. 10, 1957; children: Kirk, Sally, P. Cannon, Eric (dec.). BA, Stanford U., 1949. Registered mut. funds rep. Warehouseman Consol. Supply Co., Portland, Oreg., 1949-50, sales rep., 1955-56; sales rep. Consol. Supply Co., Eugene, Oreg., 1950-52; sales rep. Consol. Supply Co., Salem, Oreg., 1956-64, br. mgr., 1964-82; agt. life and health ins. N.Y. Life Ins. Co., Salem, 1982—. Lt. Cmdr. USN, 1952-55, Res. ret. Recipient Nat. Quality award Nat. Assn. Life Underwriters, 1986-88. Mem. Salem Assn. Life Underwriters, Res. Officers Assn. (bd. dirs. 1988-91, v.p. 1988-91), Rotary (bd. dirs. East Salem 1980-83, sr. active mem. 1990-92, Paul Harris fellow). Republican. Episcopalian. Office: NY Life Ins Co 530 Center St NE Salem OR 97301-3744

RASMUSSEN, R. KENT, writer; b. Albany, Calif., Oct. 11, 1943; s. Clyde L. and Marian (Bambrough) R.; m. Nancy Carpenter, July 2, 1966 (div. Mar. 1985); children: Christopher, Erik; m. Kathleen Nancy Patrick, June 18, 1988; stepchildren: Erin Heenan Moreno, Noelle Heenan, Heather Heenan. BA in Econs., U. Calif., Berkeley, 1966; MA in History, UCLA, 1969, PhD, 1975. Mng. editor FourWay Comms., L.A., 1983-86; assoc. editor Marcus Garvey Papers Project UCLA, 1986-91; editl. assoc. Ctr. Civic Edn., Calabasas, Calif., 1992-93; editor Salem Press, Pasadena, Calif., 1994—. Author: Mzilikazi of the Ndebele, 1977, Migrant Kingdom: Mzilikazi's Ndebele in South Africa, 1978, Historical Dictionary of Rhodesia/Zimbabwe, 1979, On This Day in History, 1991, 92, 93, 94, Mark Twain A to Z, 1995; co-author: Dictionary of African Historical Biography, 1978, revised and expanded edit., 1986, Historical Dictionary of Zimbabwe 2d edit., 1990; editor: Tournament of Roses, 1988, Mark Twain's Book for Bad Boys and Girls, 1995; co-editor: Black Empire, 1991; contbg. editor: Africa for the Africans: The Marcus Garvey and Universal Negro Improvement Association Papers, 1995; contbr. articles to profl. jours. Office: Salem Press 131 N El Molino #350 Pasadena CA 91101

RASMUSSEN, RENEE M., secondary education educator; b. Williston, N.D., June 27, 1955; d. Wayne C. and Janice E. (Harmon) Knudsen; m. Rick D. Thorness, July 17, 1977 (divorced); children: Gabriel Thorness, Taylor Thorness, Andrew Thorness; m. Roger K. Rasmussen, Dec. 26, 1992. BA in English and Psychology, Sioux Falls Coll., 1977. Cert. secondary educator. Tchr. English, dept. head Chester (Mont.) Pub. Schs., 1991—; mem. lang. arts master com. Golden Triangle Co-operative, Shelby, Mont., 1991—. Mem. Nat. Coun. Tchrs. English. Office: Chester Pub Schs Box 550 School and Main Chester MT 59522

RASMUSSEN, THOMAS VAL, JR., lawyer, small business owner; b. Salt Lake City, Aug. 11, 1954; s. Thomas Val and Georgia (Smedley) R.; m. Donita Gubler, Aug. 15, 1978; children: James, Katherine, Kristin. BA magna cum laude, U. Utah, 1978, JD, 1981. Bar: Utah 1981, U.S. Dist. Ct. Utah 1981, U.S. Supreme Ct. 1985. Atty. Salt Lake Legal Defender Assn., Salt Lake City, 1981-83, Utah Power and Light Co., Salt Lake City, 1983-89, Hatch, Morton & Skeen, Salt Lake City, 1989-90; ptnr. Morton, Skeen & Rasmussen, Salt Lake City, 1991-94, Skeen & Rasmussen, Salt Lake City, 1994—; co-owner, developer Handi Self-Storage, Kaysville, Utah, 1984-93; instr. bus. law Brigham Young U., Salt Lake City, 1988-90. Adminstrv. editor Jour. Contemporary Law, 1980-81, Jour. Energy Law and Policy, 1980-81. Missionary Ch. of Jesus Christ of Latter-Day Sts., Brazil, 1973-75. Mem. Utah, Salt Lake County Bar Assn., Intermountain Miniature Horse Club (pres. 1989, 2d v.p. 1990), Phi Eta Sigma, Phi Kappa Phi, Beta Gamma Sigma. Home: 3094 Whitewater Dr Salt Lake City UT 84121-1561 Office: Skeen & Rasmussen 4659 Highland Dr Salt Lake City UT 84117-5137

RATCLIFF, BRUCE EPHLIN, hoist company executive; b. Canton, Ill., Oct. 3, 1941; s. Ralph A. and Margaret H. (Buck) R.; student Coll. San Mateo, 1960-62, U. Ariz., 1962, U. Calif. at Santa Barbara, 1965; B.A. in Econs., San Francisco State U., 1967. Vice pres. sales Ratcliff Hoist Co., Belmont, Calif., 1967-69, exec. v.p., 1969-75, pres., COO, 1975—, also dir.; pres., CEO Ratcliff Co., 1977—. Home: 1308 Sunnyslope Ave Belmont CA 94002-3728 Office: 1655 Old County Rd San Carlos CA 94070-5205

RATH, ALAN T., sculptor; b. Cin., Nov. 25, 1959; s. George and Carolyn R. BSEE, MIT, 1982. One-man exhbns. include San Jose (Calif.) Art Mus., 1990, Dorothy Goldeen Gallery, Santa Monica, Calif., 1990, 92, Walker Art Ctr., Mpls., 1991, Mus. Contemporary Art, Chgo., 1991, Carl Solway Gallery, Cin., 1991, Inst. Contemporary Art, Phila., 1992, The Contemporary Mus., Honolulu, 1992, Ctr. Fine Art, Miami, Fla., 1992, Galerie Hans Mayer, Dusseldorf, Germany, 1992, Hiroshima (Japan) City Mus. Contemporary Art, 1994, Worcester (Mass.) Art Mus., 1994, John Weber Gallery, N.Y.C., 1994, Haines Gallery, San Francisco, 1995; group exhbns. include Visiona, Zurich, 1989, Ars Electronica, Linz, Austria, 1989, L.A. Contemporary Exhbns., 1989, Mus. Folkwang, Essen, Germany, 1989, Cite des Arts et des Nouvelles Technologies, Montreal, 1990, Stadtmuseum Siegburg, Siegburg, Germany, 1990, San Francisco Mus. Modern Art, 1990, Denver Art Mus., 1991, Whitney Mus. Am. Art, N.Y.C., 1991, Alvar Alto Mus., Jyvaskyla, Finland, 1992, Internat. Ctr. Photography, N.Y.C., 1992, Padiglione d'Arte Contemporanea, Ferrara, Italy, 1992, John Weber Gallery, N.Y.C., 1993, Spiral Art Ctr., Tokyo, 1994, Aldrich Mus. Contemporary Art, Rudgefield, Conn., 1995. Grantee NEA, 1988; Guggenheim fellow, 1994. Office: IKON 830 E 15th St Oakland CA 94606-3631

RATHBUN, LARRY PETER, education consultant; b. Modesto, Calif., July 15, 1941; s. Carl A. and Nellie M. (Fenno) R.; m. Patricia A. Shirk, Oct. 4, 1958 (div. July 1974); children: Peter, Mark, Joyce, Cathie, Chris, Alan; m. Elaine E. Fuller, Oct. 7, 1982; children: Stephanie, Monica, Angela. BS in Poultry, Calif. Poly. State U., 1964, MA in Agrl. Edn., 1967; PhD in Vocat. Edn., Ohio State U., 1974. Cert. secondary sch. tchr. and adminstr., Calif. Tchr. Rio Vista (Calif.) High Sch., 1965-67, Los Banos (Calif.) High Sch., 1967-70; from asst. to assoc. prof. Calif. Poly. State U., San Luis Obispo, 1970-76, prof., dept. head, 1976-82, prof. emeritus, 1992, assoc. dean, 1982-88, 90-92; chief of party Escuela de Agricultura de la Region Tropical Humeda, San Jose, Costa Rica, 1988-90; edn. cons. Rathbun Assocs., San Luis Obispo, 1992—. Pub. mem. Local Agy. Formation Commn., 1992—. Mem. Calif. Agr. Tchrs. Assn. (Founder's award 1987), Rotary, Phi Delta Kappa. Home and Office: 5275 Edna Rd San Luis Obispo CA 93401-7986

RATHE, KAREN MARIE, editor; b. Eugene, Oreg., May 18, 1954; d. Hjalmar Jacob and Janet Roberta (Johnson) R.; m. Kevin Smith Donnelly, June 28, 1992; stepchildren: Amanda Moon Donnelly, Sara Logan Donnelly. B in Interior Arch., U. Oreg., 1979, MS in Journalism, 1986. Reporter, editor, photographer The Headlight-Herald, Tillamook, Oreg., 1981-84; news desk copy editor The Oregonian, Portland, 1985; news desk copy editor The Seattle Times, 1987, letters editor, columnist, 1987-91, news features copy editor, layout editor, 1991—. Co-founder, v.p. bd. Tillamook Crisis and Resource Ctr., 1982-84; bd. dirs. Columbia County Women's Resource Ctr., St. Helens, Oreg., 1980-81. Recipient 1st pl. award Wash. Press Assn., 1994, and other awards; grad. teaching fellow U. Oreg., 1984-86; Poynter Inst. fellow, 1986. mem. Soc. Profl. Journalists (sec. Western Wash. chpt. 1989-90, pres. 1990-91), Kappa Tau Alpha. Democrat. Presbyterian. Office: The Seattle Times PO Box 70 Seattle WA 98111-0070

RATHLESBERGER, JAMES HOWARD, medical board executive; b. Pitts., May 2, 1948; s. Howard Erwin and Jean Edna (Heiden) R.; m. M. Elizabeth Ware, Jan. 2, 1988. BA, U. Calif., Berkeley, 1971; MPA, NYU, 1986. Staff dir. environ. study conf. U.S. Congress, Washington, 1974-75; v.p. Nat. Limestone Inst., Washington, 1975-76; mem. Carter-Mondale Transition Team, Atlanta and Washington, 1976-77; spl. asst. to the asst. sec. U.S. Dept. of the Interior, Washington, 1977-81; spl. asst. to dean of the faculty of arts and scis. NYU, 1981-85; asst. exec. v.p. Nat. Health Coun., N.Y.C., 1985-89; exec. officer Bd. of Podiatric Medicine, Sacramento, Calif., 1989—. Editor: Nixon and the Environment, 1972; contbr. articles to profl. jours. Vol. VISTA, Charleston, W.Va., 1968-69. Named Hon. Citizen Paola, Kans., 1968. Home: 2757 11th Ave Sacramento CA 95818-4420 Office: Bd of Podiatric Medicine 1420 Howe Ave Ste 8 Sacramento CA 95825-3219

RATICAN, PETER JAY, health maintenance organization executive; b. L.A., Dec. 10, 1943; m. Diane Berman, Aug. 1967; children: Kimberly, Eric, Michael. BS in Acctg., UCLA, 1966. Sr. audit mgr. Price Waterhouse, L.A.; asst. contr., dir. internal audit MCA, Inc., 1978-87; v.p. fin. MCA TV Group, 1986-87; pres., chief fin. officer De Laurentiis Entertainment Group, 1987-88; now chmn., pres., chief exec. officer Maxicare Health Plans Inc., 1988—, also bd. dirs. Office: Maxicare Health Plans Inc 1149 S Broadway Los Angeles CA 90015-2213

RATLIFF, JAMES CONWAY, hotel executive; b. Evanston, Ill., Mar. 28, 1940; s. Harold Sugart and Marjorie (Elmore) R. BA, Mich. State U., 1967. Dir. food & beverage ops. Detroit Hilton, 1970-71; dir. food & beverage purchasing Hilton Hotels Corp., N.Y.C., 1972-77; corp. dir. procurement Hilton Hotels Corp., Beverly Hills, Calif., 1977—; bd. dirs. Am. Inst. Food Distbn., Fair Lawn, N.J., 1984-88, treas., 1989-90, vice-chmn., 1991—, chmn., 1993-95; instr. Calif. State Poly. U., Pomona, 1987, 88. With U.S. Army, 1963-65. Mem. Food Svc. Purchasing Assn. Can. (hon.), Produce Mktg. Assn. (bd. dirs. 1986-88, v.p. 1989-90, sec.-treas. 1991—, chmn. elect 1992, chmn. 1993, chmn. exec. com. 1994), Product Mktg. Assn. (chmn. foodsvc. divsn. 1989-90, bd. dirs. foodsvc. divsn. 1985-88), Nat. Restaurant Assn. Foodsvc. Purchasing Mgrs. (bd. dirs. 1977-81, chmn. 1981-83), Pacific Corinthian Yacht Club. Republican. Methodist. Office: Hilton Hotels Corp 9336 Civic Center Dr Beverly Hills CA 90210-3604

RATLIFF, LEIGH ANN, pharmacist; b. Long Beach, Calif., May 20, 1961; d. Harry Warren and Verna Lee (Zwink) R. D in Pharmacy, U. Pacific, 1984. Registered pharmacist, Calif., Nev. Pharmacist intern Green Bros. Inc., Stockton, Calif., 1982-84, staff pharmacist Thrifty Corp., Long Beach, Calif., 1984-85, head pharmacist, 1986-87, pharm. buyer, 1987-92; pharmacy. mgr. Kmart Pharmacy, Long Beach, Calif., 1992—; mem. joint mktg. com. Calif. Pharmicist's Assn. Mem. Pacific Alumni Assocs., Nat. Trust for Hist. Preservation, Friends of Rancho Los Cerritos; treas. Bixby Knolls Ter. Homeowners Assn., 1988-92, pres. 1992—; vol. Docent Rancho Los Cerritos Hist. Site, 1988—; vol. preceptor U. So. Calif. Sch. Pharmacy; vol. Fairfield YMCA, Long Beach. Mem. Am. Pharm. Assn., Am. Inst. History Pharmacy, Calif. Pharmacist Assn., Lambda Kappa Sigma. Republican. Methodist. Avocations: creative writing, raising aquarium fish, house plants, collecting Lladro pieces. Home: 3913 N Virginia Rd Apt 301 Long Beach CA 90807-2670 Office: Kmart Pharmacy 5450 Cherry Ave Long Beach CA 90805-5502

RATLIFF, WILLIAM ELMORE, curator, researcher; b. Evanston, Ill., Feb. 11, 1937; s. Harold Shugart and Marjorie (Elmore) R.; m. Lynn Louise Robbins, June 1959; children: Sharon, Paul, Susan, David, John. BA, Oberlin Coll., 1959; MA, U. Wash., 1968, PhD, 1974. Rsch. fellow Hoover Instn., Stanford, Calif., 1968-79; cons., dir. rsch. Rsch. Internat., San Francisco, 1976-82; critic, chief editorial writer Times Tribune, Palo Alto, Calif., 1979-86; sr. rsch. fellow Hoover Instn., Stanford, 1986—; music stringer L.A. Times, 1975—, Opera News, 1978-93; cons., lectr. U.S. Info. Agy., Washington, 1986, 88, 89, 90; lectr. U.S. Dept. Def. confs./seminars, Washington, 1984—. Author: Castroism in Latin America, 1978; author, editor: Media and Cuban Revolution, 1987; co-author: Capitalist Revolution in Argentina, 1990, The Civil War in Nicaragua, 1992, Argentina's Capitalist Revolution Revisited, 1993, Inside the Cuban Interior Ministry, 1994; co-editor: Juan Peron Cartas del exilio, 1991; area editor: Yearbook on Internat. Communist Affairs, 1968-91; contbr. articles to profl. jours.; book rev. editor: Jour. of Interam. Studies. Office: Hoover Inst Stanford U Stanford CA 94305

RATZLAFF, VERNON PAUL, elementary education educator, consultant; b. Mt. Lake, Minn., May 16, 1925; s. Peter Benjamin and Helen (Dick) R.; m. Bonnie Lou Sommers, Dec. 17, 1955; children: Paul, Gwen, Jay, Peter. BA in Elem. Edn., German, Goshen Coll., 1954; MA, U. N.D., 1971; student, U. Minn., 1956-57, U. Oreg., 1965, U. No. Ariz., 1968. Cert. tchr. Elem. tchr. Richfield (Minn.) Pub. Schs., 1954-74; tchr. Tuba City (Ariz.) Pub. Sch., 1975—; resource person to tchrs., Grand Forks, N.C., 1970-72, resource person to upper elem. tchrs. and children, Richfield, 1967-70; adminstr. of Christian Sch. Hopi Mission, Oraibi, Ariz., 1971-75; math tchr. Nortland Pioneer Coll.; established "Look Folks-No Fail" classrooms. Author: Side by Side " Up from the Pit to Become a Shining Star" (Where Students Take Responsibility for Learning), 1990; contbr. articles to numerous jours. Mem. NEA, Ariz. Edn. Assn., Am. Assn. Retired People. Republican. Home: 440 Circle View Dr Flagstaff AZ 86001-4812

RAUCINA, THOMAS FRANK See RACINA, THOM

RAUGH, MICHAEL RANDOLPH, mathematician; b. Altoona, Pa., Sept. 26, 1938. BS, UCLA, 1962; MS, Stanford U., 1978, PhD, 1979. Programmer Lawrence Berkeley (Calif.) Lab., 1967-71, Inst. for Math Studies in Social Scis./Stanford U., Stanford, Calif., 1971-74; mathematician, computer sci. profl. U.S. Geol. Survey, Menlo Park, Calif., 1978-82; mem. tech. staff Hewlett-Packard Labs., Palo Alto, Calif., 1982-85; chief scientist, sr. scientist Rsch. Inst. for Advanced Computer Sci., Mountain View, Calif., 1985-94; co-founder, v.p. Interconnect Tech. Corp., Mountain View, Calif., 1993—; adj. prof. dept. mech. engring. and engring. sci., U. N.C., 1992-95. Inventor, patentee of X-Y stage calibration of mathematically rigourous techniques for lithographic imaging equipment. Recipient certs. of appreciation for creation of innovative rsch. programs NASA, Ames Rsch. Ctr., Mountain View; NSF fellow; Fulbright-Hayes fellow in math. at Manchester U., 1963-64; internship at design studio of Charles and Ray Eames, Venice, Calif. Mem. Geol. Soc. Am., Am. Geophys. Union, Calif. Botanical Soc., Soc. Indsl. and Applied Math., Calif. Native Plant Soc., Sigma Xi. Office: Interconnect Tech Corp PO Box 4158 Mountain View CA 94040-0158

RAUGHTON, JIMMIE LEONARD, educational foundation administrator, urban planner; b. Knoxville, Tenn., Oct. 9, 1943; s. George L. and Ann (Simotes) R. BA in Urban and Regional Planning, U. No. Colo., 1974, MA, 1976, PhD, U. Colo., 1993. Mgr., Flexitran div. Gathers, De Vilbliss Architects and Planners, 1966-68; asst. dir. planning City of Aurora, Colo., 1970-71; planner City of Lakewood, Colo., 1971-73; planner City of Boulder, Colo., 1973-74; instr. urban planning C.C. of Denver, 1974-76, div. dir. human resources and svcs., 1976-81, div. dir. sci. and tech., 1981-85; v.p. State of Colo. C.Cs., 1985-93; exec. dir. Edn. Found. Colo., 1989—; coord. devel. Rocky Mountain Energy and Environ. Tech. Center, 1980. cons. Denver Regional Council of Govts. for Model Sign Code, 1973, City of Boulder Transp. Dept., 1975—; chmn. profl. advisory com. to Colo. Gov.'s Land Use Adviser, 1973; also public speaker. Mem. exec. bd. Civic Center Assn., Denver, 1973-75; supervisory com. Colo. State Employees Credit Union, 1986—;mem. bd. Support Systems Consol., 1984, Bridge Industry, 1984-85; candidate Denver City Council, 1975; bd. dirs. Plan Metro Denver, 1975-76, Four Corner Art Collection, 1973—. Recipient Citizen Award of Honor, Assn. of Beautiful Colo. Roads, 1972. Mem. Am. Inst. of Planners (mem. exec. bd. Colo. 1970-75, treas. 1972-73), Colo. City Mgrs. Assn., Am. Soc. Planning Ofcls., Am. Vocat. Assn., Am. Soc. for Tng. and Devel., Pi Alpha Alpha. Methodist. Contbr. articles to local newspapers. Home: 2501 High St Denver CO 80205-5565 Office: State of Colo CCs 1391 Speer Blvd Denver CO 80204-2552

RAUH, J. RANDALL, physician; b. Hardtner, Kans., June 30, 1947; s. John Harry and Dorothy Mae (Dimmick) R.; m. Janice Yvonne Weigand, July 1, 1967 (div. Jan. 1989); children: HEather Elaine, Sarah Elaine, Travis Randall, Joshua Blaine. BS in Chemistry and Biology, Northwestern Okla. State U., 1969; MD, U. Okla., 1973. Diplomate Am. Bd. Ob-Gyn. Resident Tulsa Med. Coll. U. Okla., 1973-76; pvt. practice Okmulgee, Okla., 1976-80; pvt. group practice Stillwater Women's Clinic, Okla., 1980; pvt. practice Miles City, Mont., 1981--; clin. instr. Tulsa Med. Coll., 1977—, U. N.D. Sch. Medicine; chief of staff Holy Rosary Hosp., Miles City, 1981-82, 88-89, trustee, 1983-89; mem. Ethics Com. Presentation Health System, Aberdeen, S.D., 1986-90. Contbr. articles to profl. jours. Pres. Little League Com. Miles City Youth Baseball Assn., 1988-90. Recipient Excellence in Clin. Tchg. award Am. Acad. Fam. Practice, 1977. Fellow ACOG, ACS, mem. AMA, Nat. Rural Health Assn., Am. Fertility Soc., Mont. Med. Assn., U. Okla. Coll. Med. Alumni Assn. (life mem.), Miles City Area C. of C. Republican. Lutheran. Office: 219 N Merriam Ave Miles City MT 59301-2735

RAUMER, RONALD JAY, management consultant; b. Albany, Calif., June 23, 1947; s. Raymond and Alvera (Oberlander) R.; m. Sheila L. Boynton, May 20, 1982. BA, San Francisco State U., 1970; MBA, U. San Francisco, 1975. Mgr. info. tech. Chevron U.S.A., San Francisco, 1969-78, Chevron Oil Europe, London, 1978-82; mgmt. cons. Peat Marwick, San Francisco, 1982-84, Deloitte & Touche, San Francisco, 1984-90; dir. info. tech. Wedge Innovations, San Jose, Calif., 1990-92; mgmt. cons. Raumer & Assocs., Walnut Creek, Calif., 1992—. Bd. dirs. Friends of Shanta Bhawan health Care Clinic, Walnut Creek, 1989—; bd. dirs., cmty. advisor Univ. Rsch. Expedition Program, Berkeley, Calif., 1992—. Mem. Am. Prodn. and Inventory Control Soc. Home and Office: 130 Bando Ct Walnut Creek CA 94595-2701

RAUSCH, PAUL MATTHEW, financial executive; b. Lafayette, Ind., Dec. 14, 1953; s. Richard Leo and Vernice Ruth (Rhoades) R. Student, Purdue U., 1976. County supr. Farmers Home Adminstrn., Richmond and Falmouth, Ky., 1979-87; loan officer spl. accounts team Farm Credit Svcs., LaPorte, Ind., 1987; br. mgr. Nat. Mortgage Corp., Merrillville, Ind., 1987-89; collection mgr. Greentree Acceptance, Lexington, Ky., 1989; county supv. Farmers Home Adminstrn., Springfield & Alamosa, Colo., 1990—; v.p. Internat. Children's Soc., Hooper, Colo., 1993-94. Pres. rural devel. Madison County, Richmond, 1980-85; bd. dirs. Mosca-Hooper Soil Conservation Dist., 1993-94, San Luis Valley Rural Devel. Coun., Alamosa, 1993-94. Recipient Dedication to Cmty. award Madison County, Richmond, 1983; named Ky. Col., Richmond, 1985. Mem. Nat. Parks and Conservation Assn., Am. Soc. Farm Mgrs. and Rural Appraisers, Nature Conservancy, Wilderness Soc., Sierra Club (agr. com. 1987-94), Kiwanis (bd. dirs. 1980-85). Home: 9531 Ln 9N Mosca CO 81146 Office: US Govt 422 E 1st St Trinidad CO 81082-3044

RAUTENBERG, ROBERT FRANK, consulting statistician; b. Milw., Sept. 14, 1943; s. Raymond Clarence and Anna Josephine (Winter) R.; m. Meredith Taylor, June 2, 1965 (div. Feb. 1975); 1 child, Matthew Carl. PhD in Bus. Adminstrn., Pacific Western U., 1983; post doctorate rsch., Sorbonne U., Paris. Pvt. practice acctg. Kansas City, Mo., 1975-76; pres. Seven Diamond Enterprises, San Francisco, 1976-78; chief exec. officer Assurance Systems, San Francisco, 1984—. Author: The Analytical Management Handbook, 1985, Supplement to the Analytical Management Handbook, 1991; contbr. articles to profl. jours. and conf. proceedings. Fellow Royal Statis. Soc.; mem. Internat. Soc. Bayesian Analysis (charter). Episcopalian. Home: 711 Leavenworth St San Francisco CA 94109-6084 Office: Assurance Systems 588 Sutter St Ste 434 San Francisco CA 94102-1102

RAVELING, GEORGE, former university athletic coach. Head coach U. So. Calif. Trojans, 1992-94. Named college basketball Coach of the Year by Kodak, Basketball Weekly, 1992, twice named PAC-10 Coach of the Year. Office: care U Southern California Athletic Dept Univ Park Los Angeles CA 90089

RAVELY, VICTORIA ALLINE, postal clerk; b. Seattle, Nov. 22, 1946; d. Ganam Emery and Wilma Edith (Bressie) Dodson; m. William L. Rose, 1963 (div. 1967); m. Norman W. Ravely, 1967; children: Romy Roseann, Caryn Alice, John-William Harold. AA in Liberal Arts, Columbia Basin Coll., 1979, AS in Legal Secretarial, 1979; BA in Law magna cum laude, Cen. Wash. U., 1981. Clk. U.S. Postal Svc., Costa Mesa, Calif., 1965-68, Pasco, Wash., 1968-75; legal sec. Port of Posco, 1979-80; gen. office clk. U.S. Post Office, Richland, Wash., 1980—; union counselor Office of Workers Compensation, U.S. Dept. Labor, 1980—. Guardian ad litem Benton Franklin Counties Juvenile Ct. System, Kennewick, Wash., 1983—; tutor with literacy coun. ESL; mem. Grace Gospel fellowship, Westside Presbyn. Ch. Named Outstanding Wash. State Vol. as guardian ad litem, 1987. Mem. Am. Postal Workers Union, Concerned Women Am., Eagle Forum, Berean Bible Soc., Human Life. Republican. Office: PO Box 135 Richland WA 99352-0135

RAVEN, BERTRAM H(ERBERT), psychology educator; b. Youngstown, Ohio, Sept. 26, 1926; s. Morris and Lillian (Greenfeld) R.; m. Celia Cutler, Jan. 21, 1961; children: Michelle G., Jonathan H. BA, Ohio State U., 1948, MA, 1949; PhD, U. Mich., 1953. Research assoc. Research Ctr. for Group Dynamics, Ann Arbor, Mich., 1952-54; lectr. psychology U. Mich., Ann Arbor, 1953-54; vis. prof. U. Nijmegen, U. Utrecht, Netherlands, 1954-55; psychologist RAND Corp., Santa Monica, Calif., 1955-56; prof. UCLA, 1956—, chair dept. psychology, 1983-88; vis. prof. Hebrew U., Jerusalem, 1962-63, U. Wash., Seattle, U. Hawaii, Honolulu, 1968, London Sch. Econs. and Polit. Sci., London, 1969-70; external examiner U. of the W.I., Trinidad and Jamaica, 1980—, rsch. assoc. Psychol. Rsch. Ctr., 1993—; participant Internat. Expert Conf. on Health Psychology, Tilburg, The Netherlands, 1986; cons., expert witness in field, 1979—. co-dir. Tng. Program in Health Psychology, UCLA, 1979-88; cons. World Health Orgn., Manila, 1985-86; cons., expert witness various Calif. cts., 1978—. Author: (with others) People in Groups, 1976, Discovering Psychology, 1977, Social Psychology, 1983, Social Psychology: People in Groups (Chinese edition), 1994; editor: (with others) Contemporary Health Services, 1982, Policy Studies Rev. Ann., 1980; editor: Jour. Social Issues, 1969-74; contbr. articles to profl. jours. Guggenheim fellow, Israel, 1962-63; Fulbright scholar The Netherlands, 1954-55, Israel, 1962-63, Britain, 1969-70; Citation from Los Angeles City Council, 1966, Rsch. on Soc. power by Calif. Sch. of profl. psychology, L.A., 1991; NATO sr. fellow, Italy, 1989. Fellow Am. Psychol. Assn. (chair bd. social and ethical responsibility 1978-82), Am. Psychol. Soc., Soc. for Psychol. Study of Social Issues (pres. 1973-74); mem. AAAS, Am. Sociol. Assn., Internat. Assn. Applied Psychology, Soc. Exptl. Social Psychology, Assn. Advancement of Psychology (founding, bd. dirs. 1974-81), Internat. Soc. Polit. Psychology, Interam. Psychol. Soc., Am. Psychology-Law Soc. Home: 2212 Camden Ave Los Angeles CA 90064-1906 Office: UCLA Dept Psychology Los Angeles CA 90095-1563

RAVEY, DONALD LEE, business educator; b. San Diego, July 22, 1929; s. Robert Lee and Marian Adelaide (Hyams) R. BS, San Diego State U., 1950; MS, MIT, 1961. Mfg. facilities engr. Convair, a Div. Gen. Dynamics, San Diego, 1955-59; unit chief procurement planning/control Boeing, Seattle and New Orleans, 1961-63; tchr. Sacramento Bus. Coll., 1964-65; sr. systems analyst Matson Navigation Co., San Francisco, 1965-67; mgr. systems and data svcs. Ampex Corp., Redwood City, Calif., 1967-72; adminstrv. svcs. mgr. Sunland Mktg., Inc., Menlo Park, Calif., 1972-73; mgmt. analyst Tri-Valley Growers, Inc., San Francisco, 1973-76; mgr. engring. systems Unisys Peripherals Div., Santa Clara, Calif., 1976-89; adj. prof. San Mateo County Community Coll. Dist., 1990—. Patentee on sequence switching circuit with latching alarm, 1978. Lt. USNR, 1951-55. Mem. Commonwealth Club of Calif., MIT Club of No. Calif. Home: 127 Chukker Ct San Mateo CA 94403-1306

RAVICCHIO, GRACE VENETA, home health nurse; b. Spokane, Wash., Jan. 30, 1967; d. Russell Dean and Claudia Sue (Cook) Beaver; m. Steven Richard Ravicchio, Sept. 19, 1987; 1 child, Stephanie Lynn. BSN, U. Ariz., 1989. RN, Ariz.; cert. instr. BLS and pediat. BLS, ARC. Nurse extern Tucson Med. Ctr., 1989; staff nurse St. Mary's Hosp., Tucson, 1990-91; field nurse Kimberly Quality Care, Tucson, 1991-93; Medicare case mgr. Nursefinders, Tucson, 1992-94, clin. dir. pvt. svcs., 1994—.

RAWLINGS, JAMES SCOTT, neonatologist; b. Ft. Oglethorpe, Ga., Feb. 17, 1943; s. James Garland and Mary Katherine (Coffey) R.; m. Virginia Buess, June 14, 1969; children: Mary Margaret Anderson, Scott Kirkpatrick. BS in Engring., Va. Polytech Inst., 1965; MD, Vanderbilt U., 1973. Commd. 2d lt. U.S. Army, 1965, advanced through grades to col., 1993; assoc. prof. F. edward Herbert Sch. Medicine, Uniformed Svcs. of Health Scis., Bethesda, Md., 1980—. Contbr. rsch. papers to profl. jours. Mem. March of Dimes Task Force on Infant Mortality, Pierce County, Wash., 1987-89. Neonatal-Perinatal Medicine fellow, Honolulu, 1980-86. Fellow Am. Acad. Pediatrics (Andrew M. Margileth award, 1985, 88, 91, 94); mem. AMA, Western Soc. Pediatric Rsch., So. Soc. PEdiatric Rsch. Episcopalian. Home: 1107 Sequalish St Steilacoom WA 98388-2412 Office: Madigan Army Med Ctr Dept Pediatrics Tacoma WA 98431

RAWLINGS, ROBERT HOAG, newspaper publisher; b. Pueblo, Colo., Aug. 3, 1924; s. John W. and Dorothy (Hoag) R. Student Colo. U., 1943-44; BA, Colo. Coll., 1947; m. Mary Alexandra Graham, Oct. 18, 1947; children: Jane Louise, John Graham, Carolyn Anne, Robert Hoag II. Reporter Pueblo Chieftain and Pueblo Star-Jour., 1947-51, advt. rep. 1951-62, gen. mgr., 1962-79, pub. and editor, 1980—; sec. Star-Jour. Pub. Corp., 1962-84, pres., 1984—; Chmn. bd. dir. Colo. Nat. Bank-Pueblo; bd. dir. U.S. Air Force Acad. Found., U. So. Colo. Found., Colo. Water Edn. Found.; pres. Robert Hoag Rawlings Found. Served with USNR, 1942-46. Named Colo. Newspaper Person of the Year, 1989, Disting. Univ. Fellow Pres. Club U. So. Colo., 1993, Outstanding Citizen of Yr. Pueblo C. of C., 1994, Colo. Bus. Leader of the Yr. Colo. Assn. of Commerce and Industry, 1994; recipient Outstanding Svc. to Univ. award U. So. Colo. Alumni Assn., 1993, Colo. Corp. Philanthropy award Nat. Philanthropy Assoc., 1993. Mem. Colo. Press Assn., (dir. 1963-66, 76-78, pres. 1985, chmn. bd. dirs. 1986), Rocky Mountain Ad Mgrs. (past pres.), Colo. AP (past pres.), Elks, Rotary. Presbyterian. Home: 3100 Country Club Dr Pueblo CO 81008-1301 Office: Star-Jour Pub Corp PO Box 4040 Pueblo CO 81003-0040

RAWLS, JAMES JABUS, history educator; b. Washington, Nov. 10, 1945; s. Jabus W. and Jane Kathleen (Brumfield) R.; m. Linda Joyce Higdon, Dec. 29, 1967; children: Benjamin Jabus, Elizabeth Jane Kathleen. BA with honors in History, Stanford U., 1967; MA, U. Calif., Berkeley, 1969, PhD, 1975. Instr. history San Francisco State U., 1971-75, Diablo Valley Coll., Pleasant Hill, Calif., 1975—; vis. lectr. U. Calif., 1977-81, vis. assoc. prof., 1989; scholar-in-residence Calif. State U., Sacramento, 1987; moderator Chautauqua progrma NEH, Calif., Oreg., 1992; radio pseronality Dr. History, Sta. KNBR, San Francisco, 1990-94. Co-author: Land of Liberty: A United States History, 1985, California: An Interpretive History, 1993; author: Indians of California, 1986, Dr. History's Whizz-Bang, 1992, Dame Shirley and the Gold Rush, 1993, Never Turn Back: Father Serra's Mission, 1993, Dr. History's Sampler, 1994, California Dreaming, 1995; editor: Dan De Quille of the Big Bonanza, 1980, New Directions in California History, 1989; co-editor: California: A Place, A People, A Dream, 1986; contbr. Worldmark Ency. of the States, 1981; World Book Ency., 1993, Ency. of the Am. West, 1995, Am. NAt. Biography, 1995, Dictionary of Am. History, 1995. Recipient faculty lectr. award Diablo Valley Coll., 1988, Nat. Teaching Excellence award U. Tex., 1989. Fellow Calif. Hist. Soc. (book rev. editor Calif. History 1983—); mem. Am. Hist. Assn. Democrat. Office: Diablo Valley Coll Dept History Pleasant Hill CA 94523

RAY, DAVID CHRISTIAN, aerospace engineer; b. Northridge, Calif., July 31, 1961; s. Don Brandon and Laurel Irene (Epstein) R. BA in Phys. Sci., U. Calif., Berkeley, 1984. Aerospace engr. Space Scis. Lab. U. Calif., Berkeley, 1984—, cons. high voltage, high vacuum systems, contamination control, 1987—. Contbr. articles to profl. jours. and mags.; presenter rsch. studies to profl. soc. Office: U Calif Space Sci Lab Centennial At Grizzly Blvd Berkeley CA 94720

RAY, DAVID L., financial planning executive, consultant; b. 1957. Grad., Tex. A&M U., 1983. With Peat Marwick, San Antonio, 1983-84, Dee Howard Co., San Antonio, 1985, United Svc. Advisors, San Antonio, 1986-89; treas. Founders Asset Mgmt., Denver, 1990—. Office: Founders Asset Management 2930 E 3rd Ave Denver CO 80206-5002*

RAY, HAROLD BYRD, utilities executive; b. Lynwood, Calif., Aug. 30, 1940; s. Chester Bennett and Essie (Byrd) R.; m. Penny Lee Headding, Mar. 30, 1963; children: Claire, Jill. BS in Engring. with honors, UCLA, 1963; MS in Engring, Calif. Inst. Tech., 1970; MA in Mgmt., Claremont Grad Sch., 1979. Registered profl. nuclear and mech. engr., Calif. Systems engr. AEC, Washington, 1964-69; supervising engr. So. Calif. Edison Co., Rosemead, 1970-75, quality assurance mgr., 1975-79, San Onofre project mgr., 1979-81, San Onofre sta. mgr., 1981-83, v.p., 1983—. Served to lt. USN, 1963-69. Oak Ridge fellow, 1969. Mem. ASME, Sigma Xi. Republican. Presbyterian. Office: So Calif Edison Co 2244 Walnut Grove Ave Rosemead CA 91770-3714

RAY, JEFFEREY WAYNE, military officer; b. Lawrenceburg, Tenn., Apr. 22, 1958; s. Lonnie Mack Ray and Ruby Marie (Clayton) Davis; m. Carey Suzanne Tolsma, June 9, 1984; children: Peyton Amanda, Margaret Roxanne, James Spencer. BS, Mich. State U., 1980; MA, Tex. Christian U., 1987. Commd. 2d lt. USAF, 1980, advanced through grades to maj., 1993; student pilot USAF, Laughlin AFB, Tex., 1981-82; co-pilot USAF, Carswell AFB, Tex., 1982-85, aircraft comdr., 1985-87; instr. air staff tng. program USAF, Pentagon, Va., 1987-88; instr. pilot USAF, Griffiss AFB, N.Y., 1988-93; regional planner USAF, Hickam AFB, Hawaii, 1993—. Mem. Triangle Fraternity. Lutheran. Home: 603 Julian Ave Honolulu HI 96818-4917 Office: HQ PACAF/XPXX 25 E St Ste F212 Hickam AFB HI 96853-5417

RAY, LEO ELDON, fish breeding and marketing company executive; b. Logan County, Okla., Dec. 9, 1937; s. Wilbur Houston and Florence Ivy (Doggett) R.; B.S. in Zoology, U. Okla., 1963; m. Judith Kay Croddy, Aug. 29, 1959; children—Tana Kim, Tod Kent, Kacy Kay. Research asst. U. Okla., 1961-63; tchr. public schs., Dumas, Tex., 1963-64, Grants, N.Mex., 1964-65, Anaheim, Calif., 1965-69; co-owner Fish Breeders, Niland, Calif., 1969-87; owner, pres. Fish Breeders of Idaho, Inc., Buhl, 1971—, Fish Processors, Inc., 1971—. Served with U.S. Army, 1957-60. Mem. Calif. Catfish Farmers Am. (past pres.), Catfish Farmers Am. (past pres., dir.), U.S. Trout Farmers Assn. (past pres., dir.). Address: 4647 River Rd # D Buhl ID 83316-5104

RAY, MARIANNE YURASKO, social services administrator; b. Mpls., Sept. 25, 1934; d. Andrew George and Ann (Rusinko) Yurasko; m. Raymond Robert Ray, Nov. 22, 1962 (div. July 1980); children: Joel Christopher, Angela Christine. BA, U. Utah, 1956; student, U. Wash., 1975; MA, Pacific Lutheran U., 1978. Case worker, vol. agy. liaison State of Wash. Dept. Social and Health Services, Tacoma, Wash., 1963-65, 1971-79, 1983; child placement project dir. State of Wash. Dept. Social and Health Services, Olympia, Wash., 1979-80; casework supr. Child Protective Service State of Wash. Dept. Social and Health Services, Tacoma, Wash., 1980-81, foster home recruiter and licenser, 1981-83; owner, cons. Myray Focuses, Seattle, 1983—; pres. Delta Dynamics Inc., Seattle, 1984-86; mental health therapist Children's Indsl. Home, Tacoma, 1985-86, Good Samaritan Mental Health, Puyallup, Wash., 1986-87; part-time faculty Cen. Wash. U., Ellensburg, 1985—, Highline Community Coll., Midway, Wash., 1985-87, Renton (Wash.) Vocational Tech. Inst., 1985—, Lake Washington Vocational Tech. Inst., Kirkland, Wash., 1985—; dir. child abuse treatment Cath. Community Services, Seattle, 1987—; cons. Tacoma Sch. Dist., 1985-86; presenter nat. conferences and workshops. Creator workshops: Humor Techniques for Stress Management in the Classroom, 1985, Humor in Stress Management: Applications in Helping Professions, 1987, Kicking the Holiday Blues, 1986, Humor for the Health of It, 1987, Laughing Matters--It Really Does!, 1984—, Relocation: What it means for the Employee and Family, 1984—, Humor in the Workplace for Higher Productivity and Team Building, 1984—, Laughter and Liberation in the Classroom to Promote Learning, 1987—, Creative Imagery in Relaxation Techniques, 1987—. Mem. Am. Psychol. Assn. (assoc.), Pacific Northwest Orgn. Devel. Network, Pacific Northwest Speakers Assn. Office: Myray Focuses Counseling/Consulting PO Box 98570 Seattle WA 98198-0570 also: Cath Cmty Svcs 100 23d Ave S Seattle WA 98144-2302

RAY, MARY-ANN, architect, educator; b. Seattle, July 19, 1958; d. Norman Gene and Barbara Ann (Wechsler) R. BFA, U. Wash., 1981; MArch, Princeton U., 1987. Designer Michael Graves, Architect, Princeton, N.J., 1984, Richard Meier and Ptnrs., L.A. and N.Y.C., 1987-88; prin., designer Studio Works, L.A., 1985—; grad. faculty So. Calif. Inst. Architecture, L.A., 1988—; mem. adv. bd. L.A. Mcpl. Art Gallery, 1992—. Prin. works include (master plans) Progressive Architecture, 1990-91 (Urban Design award 1992), Inland Architect, 1990-91, Lotus Internat., 1990-91. Recipient Lili Auchincloss fellowship Am. Acad. Rome, 1987-88, Norton prize Princeton U., 1987, Max Beckmann Meml. fellowship Bklyn. Mus., 1981-82, Ford Found. grant in fine arts U. Wash. and Ford Found., 1978, 80, 81. Home and Office: Studio Works Bldg # 3 6775 S Centinela Ave Culver City CA 90230-6303

RAY, RICHARD STANLEY, accountant; b. Miami, Ariz., June 12, 1937; s. Milton Sevier and Anne Elizabeth (Mickelson) R.; m. Laura Ann Young, Apr. 11, 1963; children: Denise, Mark, Melanie, Laura, Jordon. AA, Ea. Ariz. Jr. Coll., 1957; BS in Acctg., Ariz. State U., 1962, MS in Acctg., 1964. CPA, Ariz. Staff acct. Deloitte, Haskins & Sells, Phoenix, 1963-65; controller AMECO, Phoenix, 1965-70, U-Haul Co., Phoenix, 1970-76; dir. audit svcs. Ariz. Pub. Service Co., Phoenix, 1976—; advisor to bd. Credit Data of Ariz., Phoenix, 1981—, chmn. bd., 1980-81; dir. Arcoa Internat., Phoenix, 1973-76. Treas., bd. mem. Big Sisters of Ariz., Phoenix, 1972-78; dist. coun. Boy Scouts Am., Phoenix, 1982-84; stake pres. Mormon Ch., Tempe, Ariz. 1987—. Grad. rsch. fellowship, Ariz. Bankers Assn., Phoenix, 1962. Mem. Am. Inst. CPA's, Ariz. Soc. CPA's (Acctg. Achievement award 1962), Ariz. State Bd. Accountancy (continuing profl. edn. com. 1986—), Edison Electric Inst. (com. mem. 1976—), Rotary. Republican.

RAY, ROBERT DONALD, artist; b. Denver, Oct. 2, 1924; s. Carl James and Irene (Wilt) R. B.F.A. cum laude, U. So. Calif., 1950; M.A. magna cum laude, Mex. City Coll., 1952. Represented in permanent collections Denver Art Mus., Balt. Mus. Art, Joslyn Art Mus., Omaha, Roswell Mus., N.Mex., Columbia Mus. Art, S.C., Colorado Springs Fine Arts Ctr, Aspen Inst. Exec. Ctr., Utah State U., U. Tex., Austin, U. N.Mex., Albuquerque, Bklyn. Mus., Mus. N.Mex., Santa Fe, Sheldon Mus, U. Nebr., others. Pres., adv. bd. Harwood Found. U. N.Mex., Taos, 1983; bd. dirs. Taos Sch. Music, 1980—, 1st v.p., 1980-83. Served with USNR, 1943-46; PTO. Home: HC 68 Box 4B Taos NM 87571-9408

RAY, SUSAN STROM, chiropractor; b. Portland, Oreg., Feb. 23, 1947; d. Gordon Rodlun and Ruth LaVerne (Lindstrom) Strom; m. Stephen George Ray, July 31, 1976; children: Savanna Diane, Katherine Olivia. BA in Psychology, Columbia U., 1968; postgrad., Portland State U., 1971-74; D Chiropractic, Western States Chiropractic, Portland, 1978; grad. cert. gerontology, Portland State U., 1995. Lic. chiropractor, Oreg., Hawaii. Rsch. asst. psychology dept. Barnard Coll., N.Y.C., summer 1965; rsch. asst. sleep rsch. Shands Teaching Hosp., U. Fla., Gainesville, 1968-69; program asst. Good Samaritan Hosp., Portland, 1971-73; clin. scis. instr. Western States Chiropractic Coll., Portland, 1979; chiropractic physician Newport (Oreg.) Chiropractic Assocs., 1979-91, South Maui Chiropractic Group, Kihei, Hawaii, 1992—; bd. mem., chair Oreg. State Bd. Chiropractic Examiners, Salem, 1981-87; reviewer written clin. competency exam Nat. Bd. Chiropractic Examiners, Denver, 1987; grant reviewer HHS, Bethesda, Md., 1990; Oreg. del. Fedn. Chiropractic Licensing Bds., 1982-87. Dem. candidate Oreg. State Senate, Dist. 2, Newport, 1988; mem., chair Oreg. State Commn. on Judicial Fitness and Disability, Salem, 1989-92; chair Home Rule Com., Lincoln County, Oreg., 1989; commr. Children & Youth Svcs. Commn., Lincoln County, 1989-91. Recipient Disting. Svc. award Chiropractic Soc. Oreg., 1986; named Alumna of Yr. Western States Chiropractic Coll., Portland, 1988. Mem. Am. Chiropractic Assn. (Hawaii del sr. citizens subcom. 1992—), Hawaii State Chiropractic Assn. (island dir. 1993-95). Democrat. Home: 2180 Haukai Pl Kihei HI 96753-8527 Office: S Maui Chiropractic Group 535 Lipoa Pky Kihei HI 96753

RAYMOND, C. ELIZABETH, history educator; b. Kansas City, Mo., Feb. 9, 1953; m. James R. Pagliarini. AB cum laude, Princeton (N.J.) U., 1974; MA, U. Pa., 1975, PhD, 1979. Rsch. assoc. Nev. Hist. Soc., Reno, 1981-84; asst. prof. history U. Nev., Reno, 1984-91, assoc. prof. history, 1991—; acting asst. dean Coll. of Arts and Scis., U. Nev., 1994, faculty senate chair, 1991-92. Author: George Wingfield: Owner and Operator of Nevada, 1992 (Shepperson Humanities award 1993), (with others) Shopping Time: A Rephotographic Survey of Lake Tahoe, 1992; contbr. articles to profl. jours. Rsch. grantee Nev. Humanities Com., 1993, Newberry Libr. Fellowship, 1993. Mem. Am. Studies Assn., Orgn. of Am. Historians, Western History Assn.

RAYMOND, EUGENE THOMAS, technical writer, consultant, retired aircraft engineer; b. Seattle, Apr. 17, 1923; s. Evan James and Katheryn Dorothy (Kranick) R.; m. Bette Mae Bergeson, Mar. 1, 1948; children: Joan Kay Hibbs, Patricia Lynn Adams, Robin Louise Flashman. BSME, U. Wash., 1944; postgrad., 1953-55; registered profl. engr., Tex. Rsch. engr. The Boeing Co., Seattle, 1946-59, sr. group engr., 1959-63, 66-71, sr. specialist engr., 1971-81, prin. engr. flight control tech., 1982-88; project design engr. Gen. Dynamics, Ft. Worth, 1963-66. Lt., USNR, 1943-46, 49-52; PTO. Author (book) Aircraft Flight Control Actuation System Design, 1993. Recipient prize Hydraulics and Pneumatics mag., 1958. Mem. Soc. Automotive Engrs. (cert. of appreciation, chmn. adv. bd. com. A-6 nat. com. for aerospace fluid power and control tech. 1983-88, vice-chmn. com. 1986-88, cons.), Fluid Power Soc. (dir. northwest region 1973-74), Puget Sound Fluid Power Assn., AIAA, Beta Theta Pi, Meridian Valley Country Club, Masons, Shriners. Lutheran. Aircraft editorial adv. bd. Hydraulics and Pneumatics mag., 1960-70; achievements include 5 patents in Fluid Sealing Arrangements, Quasi-Open-Loop Hydraulic Ram Incremental Actuator with Power Conserving Properties, Rotary Digital Electrohydraulic Actuator, Two-Fluid Nonflammable Hydraulic System and Load-Adaptive Hydraulic Actuator System and Method for Actuating Control Surfaces; designed and developed mechanical systems for the XB-47 and B-52 jet bombers, 707 airliner and many other aircraft, including the X-20 Dyna-Soar hypersonic space plane, the American SST, the rewinged Navy A-6 attack plane the B-2 Stealth Bomber and the Chinese XAC Y-7 commuter; contbr. over 20 technical papers and articles to profl. jours. Home and Office: 25301 144th Ave SE Kent WA 98042-3401

RAYMOND, GREGORY ALAN, political science educator; b. Irvington, N.J., Jan. 5, 1947; s. Andrew and Irene (Skalicky) R.; m. Christine Lawton, June 12, 1971. BA, Park Coll., 1968; MA, U. S.C., 1973, PhD, 1975. Asst. prof. Boise (Idaho) State U., 1975-79, assoc. prof., 1979-83, prof. polit. sci., 1983—; cons. State Exec. Inst., Idaho, 1985, Human Rights Commn., Idaho, 1988, Office of the Gov., Idaho, 1988; bd. dirs. Univ. Survey Rsch. Ctr., Boise, 1986-89, chair dept. polit. sci., 1990—. Author: Conflict Resolution and the Structures of the State System, 1980, The Other Western Europe, 1983, When Trust Breaks Down, 1990, A Multipolar Peace?, 1994. Mem. State Higher Edn. Resource Coun., Idaho, 1988—. With U.S. Army, 1969-71. Recipient Outstanding Tchg. award Boise State U. Alumni Assn., 1985, Outstanding Rsch. award, 1994; named Idaho Prof. of Yr., Carnegie Found. for Advancement of Tchg., 1994. Mem. Internat. Studies Assn., Internat. Polit. Sci. Assn. Office: Boise State U 1910 University Dr Boise ID 83725-0001

RAYMOND, SUSAN GRANT, sculptor; b. Denver, May 23, 1943; d. Edwin Hendrie and Marybelle (McIntyre) G; m. Macpherson Raymond Jr., Aug. 18, 1967 (div. Mar. 1987); children: Lance Ramsay (dec.), Mariah McIntyre. BA in English, Cornell U., 1965; MA in Anthropology, U. Colo., 1968. Curator of anthropology Denver Mus. of Nat. History, 1968-71, contract artist, 1976-77, 79, 81, 83; instr. in anthropology U.S. Internat. U., Steamboat Springs, Colo., 1971-73. Sculpted monumental bronze sculpture for Littleton Colo., 1987, Vail, Colo., 1986, inspirational sculpture Childrens Hosp., 1977, diorama figures for Denver Mus. of Nat. History, 1971, 76, 77, 79, 81, 83, sculptures Routt Meml. Hosp, 1977, U. Denver, 1982, Craig Hosp. 1984, 94, Lakewood Westernaires, 1984, Stonegate swimming hole, Scottsdale, 1989, 10th Mtn. div. Monument, Ft. Drum, N.Y., Ketring Park, Littleton, Colo., 1994, Denver Zoo, 1993, Tulsa Zoo, 1994, Ritchie Assocs., Wichita, Kans., 1993-94; exhibited at Western Heritage Art Fair, Littleton, 1991, Sculpture in the Park, Loveland, Co., 1993, 94, Nat. Western Stock Show Art Exhib., 1994, 95. Mem. Nat. Ski Patrol, 1965-75; bd. dirs. Tread of Pioneers Mus., Steamboat Springs, 1971-87. Recipient Maurice Hexter award Nat. Sculpture Soc., 1984, Art Castings award N. Am. Sculpture Exhibition, 1982, Summerart award Steamboat Springs Arts and Humanities, 1984; winner 10th Mountain Div. Monumental Sculpture at Ft. Drum, Watertown, N.Y., 1990: named hon. mem. 10th Mountain Division at work's completion, 1992.

RAYMUS, TONI MARIE, real estate executive, newspaper publisher; b. Stockton, Calif., Feb. 11, 1957; d. Antone Edward and Marie Fatima (Medeiros) R.; m. Andrew Sephos, Oct. 1, 1989. BA, U. Pacific, 1979; postgrad., Richmond Coll., London, 1980. Gen. asst. Manteca (Calif.) News, 1977-79, asst. to pub., 1980-82, entertainment editor, 1980-82; pub. Ripon (Calif.) Record, 1982—; v.p. fin. Raymus Devel. & Sales, Inc., Manteca, 1984—. Chmn. Jr. Miss. Scholarship Program, Manteca, 1980—; mem. Stockton Juvenile Justice Commn., 1981-82; bd. dirs. Manteca Boys and Girls Club, 1981-91, pres., 1988—. Mem. Manteca Builders Assn., Builder's Industry Assn. of Delta (bd. dirs. 1987—, sec., 1990, treas. 1991, v.p. 1992), Calif. Pubs. Assn., Ripon C. of C, Venture Club (v.p. 1981-82). Republican. Roman Catholic. Office: Raymus Devel & Sales 544 E Yosemite Ave Manteca CA 95336-5807

RAYNER, STEVEN ROBERT, management consultant; b. Portland, Dec. 8, 1959. Student, U. Birmingham, Eng., 1980; BA with distinction of honors, Lewis and Clark Coll., 1982; MS in Orgn. Devel. with honors, Pepperdine U., 1986. Historian Tektronix Corp., Forest Grove, Oreg., 1982-83; orgn. devel. specialist Tektronix Corp., Vancouver, Wash., 1983-85, sr. orgn. devel. cons., 1985-89; mgr. thin film fabrication Tektronix Corp., Beaverton, Oreg., 1988; co-founder, co-chmn. Belgard Fisher Rayner, Inc., Beaverton and Freeland, Wash., 1989—; founder Rayner & Assocs., Inc., Freeland, 1994—; presenter in field. Author: New Excellence: The Forest Grove Project, 1984, Re-Creating the Workplace: The Pathway to High Performance Work Systems, 1993; co-author: (with K. Kimball Fisher and William Belgard) Tips for Teams: A Ready Reference for Solving Common Team Problems Packed with 100s of Solutions, 1994; author essays and guides in field.

RAYNER, WILLIAM ALEXANDER, retired newspaper editor; b. Winnipeg, Man., Can., Nov. 7, 1929; s. William and Annie Mitchell (McDonald) R.; divorced; 1 child, Robert William. Student Can. schs. Sports editor Trail Times, B.C., 1954-55; sportswriter Victoria (B.C.) Times, 1955-57, Vancouver (B.C.) Herald, 1957; copy editor, reporter Montreal (Que.) Star, 1957-58; asst. sports editor Vancouver Sun, 1958-62, copy editor, then slotman, 1962-74, news editor, 1974-83, systems mgr., 1983-88, ret., 1988; copy editor Toronto Globe & Mail, 1962. Author: Vancouver Sun Style Guide, 1976. Dir. Vancouver Press Club Found. With Can. Navy, 1947-52, Korea. Mem. Vancouver Press Club.

RAYNOLDS, DAVID ROBERT, buffalo breeder, author; b. N.Y., Feb. 15, 1928; s. Robert Frederick and Marguerite Evelyn (Gerdau) R.; m. May (Kean) Raynolds, May 12, 1951; children: Robert, Linda, Martha, Laura, David A.F. AB, Dartmouth Coll., 1949; MA, Wesleyan U., Middletown, Conn., 1955; predoctoral, Johns Hopkins Sch. Advanced Internat. Studies, Washington, 1956; grad., Nat. War Coll., Washington, 1973. Account exec. R.H. Morris Assoc., Newtown, Conn., 1949-50; fgn. svc. officer Dept. of State, Washington, 1956-76; pres. Ranch Rangers, Inc., Lander, Wyo., 1976—; pres. Nat. Buffalo Assn., Ft. Pierre, S.D., 1987-88. Author: Rapid Development in Small Economies (Praeger); contbr. articles to profl. jours. Mem. mgmt. com. Wyo. Heritage Soc.; bd. dirs. Liberty Hall Found., Wyo. Community Found. With U.S. Army, 1950-53. Recipient Meritorious Svc. Award, Dept. of State, Washington, 1966. Mem. The Explorers Club, Fremont County Farm Bur., Fgn. Svc. Assn., Am. Legion, Rotary, Elks. Republican. Episcopalian. Office: Table Mountain Group PO Box 1310 Lander WY 82520-1310

RAY-SIMS, DEBORAH, marketing analyst; b. Detroit, May 5, 1953; d. June Louis and Irma Waldine (Prentice) Ray; m. Dexter Sims, June 27, 1987; 1 child, Aishah Nicole. BA in TV, Radio and Film, Mich. State U., 1975; postgrad. in telecom. mgmt., NYU, 1984-85, Golden Gate U., 1993—. TV producer WTVS, Detroit, 1978-83; tng. instr. Jacaranda Internat., Lagos, Nigeria, 1983-84; account exec. US Sprint Comm., Sacto., 1986-88; mktg. rep. Employment Devel. Dept. State of Calif., Sacto., 1989-93; mktg. programs analyst Dept. Gen. Svcs. State of Calif., Sacramento, 1993—; mem. adv. bd. Sacramento Valley Black United Fund; pres. Diasporic Comms., Sacramento, 1989—. Summit scholar, Golden Gate U., 1993, Minority Bus. scholar, 1993; recipient Mayor's award of merit, City of Detroit, 1983. Mem. Internat. TV Assn., Internat. Teleconferencing Assn. (Merit award 1994), Sacramento Black Journalists Assn., NAFE, Assn. Black Women Entrepreneurs. Home: 7975 Caceres Way Sacramento CA 95823-5060

RAYSON, GARY DONN, chemistry educator; b. Oklahoma City, Okla., Apr. 27, 1957; s. Ralph LeRoy and Muriel (Frank) R.; m. Jenny Ruth Moorer, June 18, 1988. BS, Baker U., 1979; PhD, U. Tex., Austin, 1983. Teaching asst. U. Tex., Austin, 1979-80, rsch. asst., 1980-83; rsch. assoc. Ind. U., Bloomington, 1983-86; asst. prof. N.Mex. State U., Las Cruces, 1986-93, assoc. prof., 1993—. Inventor in field. Mem. Am. Chem. Soc., Soc. Applied Spectroscopy, Optical Soc. Am. Republican. Methodist. Office: NM State U PO Box 30001 # 3C Las Cruces NM 88003-8001

RAZOUK, RASHAD ELIAS, retired chemistry educator; b. Dumiat, Egypt, Aug. 22, 1911; came to U.S., 1968; s. Elias A. and Martha A. (Israfil) R.; m. Emily S. Habib, Aug. 24, 1946 (dec. Dec. 1988); children: Reda R., Rami R.; m. Henrietta Doche, July 8, 1990. BSc with honors, Cairo U., 1933, MSc, 1936, PhD, 1939. Asst. prof. Cairo U., 1939-46, assoc. prof., 1946-50; prof. chemistry, chmn. dept. Ain Shams U., Cairo, 1950-66; prof. Am. U. Cairo, 1966-68; prof. Calif. State U., L.A., 1968-78, emeritus prof., 1978—; vice dean Faculty Sci. Ain Shams U., Cairo, 1954-60; acting dir. div. surface and coll. chem. Nat. Rsch. Ctr., Cairo, 1954-68; cons. Lockheed Aircraft Co., L.A., 1971-73. Contbr. articles on adsorption, active solids, wetting and wettability, solid reactions, surface tension, and contact angles to profl. jours. Fellow Am. Inst. Chemists (emeritus); mem. Am. Chem. Soc. (emeritus), Royal Soc. Chemistry (life). Democrat. Roman Catholic. Home: 1140 Keats St Manhattan Beach CA 90266-6810

REA, AMADEO MICHAEL, ethnobiologist, ornithologist; b. Oakland, Calif., Oct. 15, 1939. BA, San Luis Rey Coll., 1963; MS, Ariz. State U., 1969; PhD, U. Ariz., 1977. Curator birds and mammals San Diego Natural History Mus., 1977-91, rsch. assoc., 1991—. Author: Once a River, Bird Life and Habitat Changes on the Middle Gila, 1983. Mem. Soc. Ethnobiology (pres. 1987-89). Democrat. Roman Catholic. Home: 1455 49th St San Diego CA 92102-2625

REA, WILLIAM J., district judge; b. 1950; BA, Loyola U., 1942, LLB, U. Colo., 1949. With U.S. Census Bur., Denver, 1949-50; adjuster Farmers Ins. Group, L.A., 1950; pvt. practice law, L.A., 1950-64, Santa Ana, Calif., 1964-68; judge Superior Ct., L.A., 1968-84; judge U.S. Dist. Ct. (cen. dist.) Calif., L.A., 1984—. Past pres. L.A. chpt. Nat. Exec. Com.; chmn. Constn. and By-Laws Com. With USN, WWII. Mem. L.A. County Bar Assn. (Outstanding Jurist award 1985), So. Calif. Def. Counsel Assn. Disting. Svc. award 1982), Internat. Acad. Trial Lawyers (Trial Judge of Yr. 1982), L.A. Trial Lawyers Assn., Am. Bd. Trial Advs. (nat. pres.). Office: US Dist Ct 312 N Spring St Los Angeles CA 90012-4701*

READ, CHARLES RAYMOND, SR., business executive; b. Clovis, N.Mex., Apr. 21, 1915; s. Charles Edward and Mary Ellen (Elder) R.; m. Elenore Littlefield, Oct. 10, 1936 (dec. July 1985); children: Charles Raymond Jr., Nancy Ann Walsh; m. Debra Rae Stutzman, Mar. 30, 1989. Baker, candymaker Peter-Paul's Candy, Clovis, 1932-34; baker Holsum Bakery, Boise, Idaho, 1934-35, Elsner's Bakery, Everett, Wash., 1935-37; head baker United Bakery, Ellensburg, Wash., 1937-40; owner, baker Read's Royal Bakery, Ellensburg, 1940-42; mgr., baker Clark's Bakery, Seattle, 1945-57; owner, baker Read's Bakery, Seattle, 1957-62; pres. Read Products, Inc., Seattle, 1962—; ptnr. Peasley-Read, Seattle, 1968—; guest TV programs KING-5, Seattle, 1950-62; distbr. Richlite, 1962—. With USN, 1942-45. Scattle Pacific U. fellow; recipient trophies, plaques for cake decorating Pacific N.W. Clinary Arts Exhibit, 1950-62. Mem. United Comml. Travelers, Smithsonian Inst., Masons (3d degree). Office: Read Products Inc 3615 15th Ave W Seattle WA 98119-1303

READ, DAVID THOMAS, physicist; b. Seattle, Sept. 17, 1947; s. John Paul and Louise Marie (Smyth) R.; m. Susan Marie Voss, Aug. 19, 1972; children—Michael, Philip, Elizabeth, Angela. B.S. in Physics, U. Santa Clara (Calif.), 1969; M.S. in Physics, U. Ill., 1971, Ph.D. in Physics, 1974. Postdoctoral physicist Nat. Bur. Standards, Boulder, Colo., 1975-76, physicist, 1977—, group leader, 1983-87. Contbr. articles to tech. jours., chpt. to book. Mem. Am. Phys. Soc., ASTM. Home: 3320 Longwood Ave Boulder CO 80303-7204 Office: Nat Inst Standards and Tech 325 Broadway St # 853 Boulder CO 80303-3337

READ, FRANK THOMPSON, law educator; b. Ogden, Utah, July 16, 1938; s. Frank Archie and Fay Melrose (Thompson) R.; m. Lenet Hadley; 5 children. BS with high honors, Brigham Young U., 1960; JD, Duke U., 1963. Bar: Minn. 1963, Mo. 1966, N.Y. 1968, Okla. 1975. Pvt. practice Mpls., St. Paul, 1963-65; atty. AT&T, Kansas City, Mo., and N.Y.C., 1965-68; asst. prof. law, asst. dean Law Sch., Duke U., 1968-70, assoc. prof., asst. dean, 1970-72, prof., assoc. dean, 1972-73, prof., 1973-74; dean, prof. law U. Tulsa Coll. Law, 1974-79, Ind. U. Sch Law., Indpls., 1979-81, U. Fla. Coll. Law, 1981-88; dean, chief exec. officer Hastings Coll. Law, U. Calif., San Francisco, 1988-93; dep. cons. sect. on legal edn. ABA, Indpls., 1993-95; pres., dean S. Tex. Coll. Law, 1995—; trustee Law Sch. Admission Coun., 1976-88, pres., 1984-85; chmn. Okla. Jud. Coun., 1976-78, pres., 1984-85; vis. prof. U. N.C., So. Meth. U., Brigham Young U. Author: Let Them Be Jugged: The Judicial Integration of the Deep South, 1978, The Oklahoma Evidence Handbook, 1979, Read's Florida Evidence, 2 vols., 1987; contbr. articles to profl. jours. Mem. ABA (sect. legal edn.), Am. Law Inst., Assn. Am. Law Schs., Order of Coif, Phi Kappa Phi. Home: 281 Arbor Dr Carmel IN 46032-5824

READE, JAMES GARRETSON, artist, illustrator; b. Phoenix, Oct. 21, 1952; s. David Franklin and Velma Royce (Underwood) R.; m. Amy Fate Andrews, Apr. 10, 1980 (div. Aug. 1984); m. Jeanne Anne Howard, Aug. 4, 1994; 2 stepchildren. Grad. high sch., Phoenix. Self-employed artist Phoenix, 1979—; artist/muralist Castles n' Coasters Amusement Parks, 1992-94; musician, guitarist 1895 House, Phoenix, 1992—; art dir. Printed in the Dark, Phoenix, 1987—; condr. airbrush workshop Std. Brands, 1990-91; prodr., distbr. comic books Capital City Distbrs., 1984. Producer wall murals and soft sculpture Gatsby's night club, 1985-86; fabric designer T-Shirts Etc., Tucson, Ariz., 1987, Tee-Tops, Phoenix, 1988; artist protraits, comic strips, anaimation, wall murals, window displays, sign work, custon designs for motor vehicles, bus. logos, camera ready art for silkscreening, airbrush art for T-chirts, lithography, theater prodn., costume design, original art; one-man shows include House Gallery and Mus., 1989; group shows include Yellow House Gallery, 1984. Recipient 3rd pl. film makers competition Ariz. State U., Phoenix, 1972. Home: 1814 E Waltann Ln Phoenix AZ 85022-3336

READMOND, RONALD WARREN, investment banking firm executive; b. Balt., Jan. 17, 1943; s. George Melvin and Dorothy Louise (Phillips) R.; m. Beth Blades, June 6, 1965 (div.); children: Robert, David; m. Janet Marie Adams, Dec. 20, 1974; children: Jefferson, Lorin, Carey. BA, Western Md. Coll., 1965. Mng. dir. Alexander Brown & Sons, Inc., Balt., 1970—, also bd. dirs.; bd. dirs. Nat. Securities Clearance Corp., N.Y.C., Govt. Securities Clearance Corp., N.Y.C.; trustee Securities Industry Inst., 1986—; adv. com. New York Stock Exchange Ops., 1987—. Capt. U.S. Army, 1965-70, Vietnam. Mem. Fin. Industry Securities Council (co-chair 1984-86). Republican. Roman Catholic. Home: 1501 Phoenix Rd W Phoenix MD 21131-1021 Office: Schwab & Co 101 Montgomery St San Francisco CA 94104-4122

REAGAN, GARY DON, state legislator, lawyer; b. Amarillo, Tex., Aug. 23, 1941; s. Hester and Lois Irene (Marcum) R.; m. Nedra Ann Nash, Sept. 12, 1964; children: Marc, Kristi, Kari, Brent. AB, Stanford U., 1963, JD, 1965. Bar: N.Mex. 1965, U.S. Dist. Ct. N.Mex., 1965, U.S. Supreme Ct. 1986. Assoc. Smith & Ransom, Albuquerque, 1965-67; ptnr. Smith, Ransom, Deaton & Reagan, Albuquerque, 1967-68, Williams, Johnson, Houston, Reagan & Porter, Hobbs, N.Mex., 1968-77, Williams, Johnson, Reagan, Porter & Love, Hobbs, 1977-82; sole practice, Hobbs, 1982—; city atty. City of Hobbs, 1978-80; City of Eunice, N.M., 1980—; mem. N.Mex. State Senate, 1993—; instr. N.Mex. Jr. Coll. and Coll. of S.W., Hobbs, 1978-84; N.Mex. commr. Nat. Conf. Commrs. Uniform State Laws, 1993—; mem. adv. mem. N.Mex. Constl. Revision Commn., 1993—. Mayor, City of Hobbs, 1972-73, 76-77, city commr., 1970-78; pres., dir. Jr. Achievement of Hobbs, 1974-85; pres., trustee Landsun Homes, Inc., Carlsbad, N.Mex., 1972-84; trustee Lydia Patterson Inst., El Paso, Tex., 1972-84, N.Mex. Conf. United Meth. Ch., 1988—, Coll. of S.W., Hobbs, 1989—; chmn. County Democratic Com., 1983-85. Mem. ABA, State Bar N.Mex. (coms. 1989—, v.p. 1992-93, pres. 1994—), Lea County Bar Assn. (pres. 1976-77), Hobbs C. of C. (pres. 1989-90), Rotary (pres. Hobbs 1985-86), Hobbs Tennis (pres. 1974-75). Home: 200 E Eagle Dr Hobbs NM 88240-5323 Office: 501 N Linam St Hobbs NM 88240-5715

REAGAN, JAMES DALE, writer, editor; b. L.A., June 30, 1948; s. Bennie Cedric and Blanche Emily (Lieb) R.; m. Wanda Ann Barber, 1975 (div. 1980); m. DeeAnne Kirby DePue, July 12, 1990. BA, Sonoma State U., Rohnert Park, Calif., 1980. Writer, editor The New Press, N.Y.C., 1992—. Author: (novel) Castle King-Four, 1990, (short stories) The Scene, 1994. Served with U.S. Army, 1969-71, Germany. Home: 14537 Longworth Ave Norwalk CA 90650-4724

REAGAN, JANET THOMPSON, psychologist, educator; b. Monticello, Ken., Sept. 15, 1945; d. Virgil Joe and Carrie Mae (Alexander) Thompson; m. Robert Barry Reagan, Jr., Aug. 7, 1977; children: Natalia Alexandria, Robert Barry. B.A. in Psychology, Berea Coll., 1967; Ph.D. in Psychology, Vanderbilt U., 1972. Mgr. research and eval. Nashville Mental Health Center, 1971-72; mgr. eval. Family Health Found., New Orleans, 1973-74; asst. prof. dept. health systems mgmt. Tulane U., New Orleans, 1974-77; dir. eval. Project Heavy West, Los Angeles, 1977-78; asst. prof. health adminstrn. Calif. State U.-Northridge, 1978-83, assoc. prof., director health adminstrn., 1983-87, prof., dir. health adminstrn., 1987—; cons. in field. Mem. Am. Pub. Health Assn., Am. Coll. Health Care Adminstrn., Assn. Health Svcs. Rsch., Am. Coll. Health Care Execs. (com. on higher edn. 1987, chmn. 1991), Assn. Univ. Programs in Health Adminstrn. (task force on undergrad. edn. 1985-90, chmn. 1988-90, mem. bd. dirs. 1995), Psi Chi, Phi Kappa Phi. Mem. editorial adv. bd. Jour. of Long Term Care Adminstrn.; contbr. to books, articles to profl. jours., papers to profl. assns. Home: 9354 Encino Ave Northridge CA 91325-2414 Office: Calif State U Dept Health Sci Northridge CA 91330

REAGAN, JOSEPH BERNARD, aerospace executive; b. Somerville, Mass., Nov. 26, 1934; s. Joseph B. and Helen Lowry R.; m. Dorothy Hughes; children: Patrick, Michael, Kevin, Kathleen, Brian, John, Maureen. BS in Physics, Boston Coll., 1956, MS in Physics, 1959; PhD in Space Sci., Stanford U., 1975; postgrad. exec. mgmt., Pa. State U., State College, 1981. Staff scientist, rsch. scientist, sr. scientist, scientist Lockheed Rsch. & Devel. Div., Palo Alto, Calif., 1959-75, mgr., 1975-84, dir., 1984-86, dep. gen. mgr., 1986-88, v.p., asst. gen. mgr., 1988-90; v.p. gen. mgr., 1991—; bd. dirs. Southwall Technologies Inc., Palo Alto. Contbr. articles to profl. jours. Bd. dirs. Tech. Mus., San Jose. Capt. U.S. Army, 1956-64. Recipient Career Achievement in Sci. award Boston Coll. Alumni Assn., 1993. Fellow AIAA (outstanding engr. San Francisco chpt. 1988); mem. Am. Geophys. Union. Republican. Roman Catholic. Home: 13554 Mandarin Way Saratoga CA 95070-4847 Office: Lockheed Martin Rsch & Devel Orgn 90-01 3251 Hanover St Palo Alto CA 94304-1121

REAGAN, NANCY DAVIS (ANNE FRANCIS ROBBINS), volunteer, wife of former President of United States; b. N.Y.C., July 6, 1923; d. Kenneth and Edith (Luckett) Robbins; step dau. Loyal Davis; m. Ronald Reagan, Mar. 4, 1952; children: Patricia Ann, Ronald Prescott; stepchildren: Maureen, Michael. BA, Smith Coll.; LLD (hon.), Pepperdine U., 1983; LHD (hon.), Georgetown U., 1987. Contract actress, MGM, 1949-56; films include The Next Voice You Hear, 1950, Donovan's Brain, 1953, Hellcats of the Navy, 1957; Author: Nancy, 1980; formerly author syndicated column on prisoner-of-war and missing-in-action soldiers and their families; author: (with Jane Wilkie) To Love a Child, (with William Novak) My Turn: The Memoirs of Nancy Reagan, 1989. Civic worker, visited wounded Viet Nam vets., sr. citizens, hosps. and schs. for physically and emotionally handicapped children, active in furthering foster grandparents for handicapped children program; hon. nat. chmn. Aid to Adoption of Spl. Kids, 1977; spl. interest in fighting alcohol and drug abuse among youth: hosted first ladies from around the world for 2d Internat. Drug Conf., 1985; hon. chmn. Just Say No Found., Nat. Fedn. of Parents for Drug-Free Youth, Nat. Child Watch Campaign, President's Com. on the Arts and Humanities, Wolf Trap Found. bd. of trustees, Nat. Trust for Historic Preservation, Cystic Fibrosis Found., Nat. Republican Women's Club; hon. pres. Girl Scouts of Am. Named one of Ten Most Admired Am. Women, Good Housekeeping mag., ranking #1 in poll, 1984, 85, 86; Woman of Yr. Los Angeles Times, 1977; permanent mem. Hall of Fame of Ten Best Dressed Women in U.S.; recipient humanitarian awards from Am. Camping Assn., Nat. Council on Alcoholism, United Cerebral Palsy Assn., Internat. Ctr. for Disabled; Boys Town Father Flanagan award; 1986 Kiwanis World Service medal; Variety Clubs Internat. Lifeline award; numerous awards for her role in fight against drug abuse. *

REAGAN, RONALD WILSON, former President of United States; b. Tampico, Ill., Feb. 6, 1911; s. John Edward and Nelle (Wilson) R.; m. Jane Wyman, Jan. 25, 1940 (div. 1948); children: Maureen E., Michael E.; m. Nancy Davis, Mar. 4, 1952; children: Patricia, Ronald. AB, Eureka Coll., 1932. Gov. State of Calif., 1967-74; businessman, rancher, commentator on public policy, 1975-80, Pres. of U.S., 1981-89. Sports announcer, motion picture and TV actor, 1932-66. Author: Where's The Rest of Me?, Speaking My Mind: Selected Speeches, 1989, An American Life: The Autobiography, 1990. Served as capt. USAAF, 1942-45. Mem. Screen Actors Guild (pres. 1947-52, 59), Tau Kappa Epsilon. Republican. Address: Fox Plaza 2121 Avenue Of The Stars Fl 34 Los Angeles CA 90067-5010*

REAL, MANUEL LAWRENCE, federal judge; b. San Pedro, Calif., Jan. 27, 1924; s. Francisco Jose and Maria (Mansano) R.; m. Stella Emilia Michalik, Oct. 15, 1955; children: Michael, Melanie Marie, Timothy, John Robert. B.S., U. So. Calif., 1944, student fgn. trade, 1946-48, LL.B., Loyola Sch. Law, Los Angeles, 1951. Bar: Calif. 1952. Asst. U.S. Atty.'s Office, Los Angeles, 1952-55; pvt. practice law San Pedro, Calif., 1955-64; U.S. atty. So. Dist. Calif., 1964-66; judge U.S. Dist. Ct. (cen. dist.) Calif., L.A., 1966—. Served to ensign USNR, 1943-46. Mem. Am., Fed., Los Angeles County bar assns., State Bar Calif., Am. Judicature Soc., Chief Spl. Agts. Assn., Phi Delta Phi, Sigma Chi. Roman Catholic. Club: Anchor (Los Angeles). Office: US Dist Ct 312 N Spring St Los Angeles CA 90012-4701*

REAM, JAMES TERRILL, architect, sculptor; b. Summit, N.J., Sept. 8, 1929; s. Merrill Jay and Catherine Ada (Terrill) R.; m. Joyce Kimball Johnson, June 9, 1953 (div. Dec. 1976); children—Claudia, Sarah, Benjamin, m. Nancy Ann Buford, Jan. 1, 1980; stepchildren—Kathleen, Ann Maguire. BArch, Cornell U., 1953; postgrad., Pratt Inst., 1953-54, U. Rome, 1956-57. Registered architect. Assoc. W. C. Muchow Assocs., Denver, 1959-62; prin. Ream, Quinn & Assocs., Denver, 1962-66; v.p. design John Carl Warnecke & Assocs., San Francisco, 1966-69; prin., pres. James Ream & Assocs., Inc., San Francisco, 1969-78, Robbins and Ream Inc., San Francisco, 1978-83; prin. James Ream Architect, San Francisco, 1983—. Prin. archtl. works include Denver Convention Ctr., Currigan Hall, Pasadena Conf. Ctr., Stapleton Plaza Hotel, Vail Transp. Ctr. Bd. dirs. San Francisco Planning and Urban Rsch. Assn., 1977—; chmn. bd. dirs. San Francisco Heritage, 1984-91, pres., 1983-84. Served to 1st lt. USAF, 1954-56. Recipient citation for design in steel Am. Iron and Steel Inst., 1975; Honor award Am. Concrete Inst., 1975; Nat. Design award Prestressed Concrete Inst., 1983; Honor award for design in steel Am. Inst. Steel Constrn., 1970. Fellow AIA (honor award western region 1969, fellowship in design 1979, honor award for design excellence 1983, design cons. San Jose Arena). Democrat. Office: James Ream/Architect 1 Market Plz # 400 San Francisco CA 94105

REAM, LLOYD WALTER, JR., molecular biology educator; b. Chester, Pa., Mar. 20, 1953; s. Lloyd Walter Sr. and Mary Elizabeth (Alexander) R.; m. Nancy Jane Smith, May 17, 1975. BA in Molecular Biology cum laude, Vanderbilt U., 1975; PhD in Molecular Biology, U. Calif., Berkeley, 1980. Am. Cancer Soc. sr. rsch. fellow dept. microbiology U. Wash., Seattle, 1980-83; asst. prof. biology Ind. U., Bloomington, 1983-88; assoc. prof. dept. agrl. chemistry Oreg. State U., Corvallis, 1988—, co-dir. genetics program, 1994—; sci. advisor Midwest Plant Biotechnology Consortium, West Lafayette, Ind., 1989—; sci. adv. panel mem. Am. Cancer Soc., Atlanta, 1989—. Editor Plant Molecular Biology/Kluwer, Dordrecht, Netherlands, 1984-94; contbr. chpt. to book and articles to profl. jours. Active Calvin Presbyn. Ch.; classroom instr. curriculum devel. Scientist/Educator Partnerships, Corvallis, 1993—. Recipient Jr. Faculty Rsch. award Am. Cancer Soc., 1987, Rsch. Career Devel. award NIH, 1987-92; Regents fellow U. Calif., Berkeley, 1977-78; rsch. grantee USDA, 1993—. Mem. AAAS, Am. Soc. for Microbiology, Genetics Soc. Am., NRA, Albany Rifle and Pistol Club (small bore rifle team, marksman award 1994), Delta Kappa Epsilon. Republican. Home: 6005 NW Vineyard Dr Corvallis OR 97330-9737 Office: Oreg State Univ Dept Agrl Chemistry Corvallis OR 97331

REARDEN, CAROLE ANN, clinical pathologist, educator; b. Belleville, Ont., Can., June 11, 1946; d. Joseph Brady and Honora Patricia (O'Halloran) R. BSc, McGill U., 1969, MSc, MDCM, 1971. Diplomate Am. Bd. Pathology, Am. Bd. Immunohematology and Blood Banking. Resident and fellow Children's Meml. Hosp., Chgo., 1971-73; resident in pediatrics U. Calif., San Diego, 1974, resident then fellow, 1975-79, dir. histocompatability and immunogenetics lab., asst. prof. pathology, 1979-86, assoc. prof., 1986-92, prof., 1992—, head div. lab. medicine, 1989-94; dir. med. ctr. U. Calif. Thorton Hosp. Clin. Labs., San Diego, 1993—; prin. investigator devel. monoclonal antibodies to erythroid antigens, recombinant autoantigens; dir. lab. exam. com. Am. Bd. Histocompatibility and Immunogenetics. Contbr. articles to profl. jours. Mem. Mayor's Task Force on AIDS, San Diego, 1983. Recipient Young Investigator Rsch. award NIH, 1979; grantee U. Calif. Cancer Rsch. Coordinating Com., 1982, NIH, 1983. Mem. Am. Soc. Investigative Pathology, Acad. Clin. Lab. Physicians and Scientists, Am. Soc. Hematology, Am. Assn. Blood Banks (com. organ transplantation and tissue typing 1982-87), Am. Soc. Histocompatibility and Immunogenetics. Office: U Calif San Diego Dept Pathology 0612 9500 Gilman Dr La Jolla CA 92093-5003

REARDON, MARK WILLIAM, lawyer; b. Englewood, N.J., June 7, 1956; s. Matthew Francis and Rose Mary (Snyder) R.; m. Patricia Louise Powers, Apr. 19, 1985. BA, Knox Coll., 1977; JD, Seton Hall U., 1980. Bar: N.J. 1980, U.S. Dist. Ct. N.J. 1980, U.S. Ct. Mil. Appeals 1981, Wash. 1987, U.S. Supreme Ct. 1987, U.S. Ct. Appeals (fed. cir.) 1988. Atty. The Boeing Co., Seattle, 1986—. Served to capt. JAGC, U.S. Army, 1981-86. Mem. ABA, Wash. Bar Assn., Computer Law Assn. Republican. Roman Catholic. Office: Boeing Computer Svcs PO Box 3707 MS 13-08 Seattle WA 98124-2207

REAVILL, DAVID WILLIAM, financial investment company executive; b. L.A., Sept. 18, 1948; s. William Arthur and Marian Elizabeth (Stocks) R.; m. Karen Anne McDonnell, Mar. 6, 1993. BA, Westmont Coll., 1971; MA, U. Calif., Santa Barbara, 1978, Calif. State U., L.A., 1988. Registered fin. and ops. prin., gen. securities prin., mcpl. securities prin. Assoc. prof. U. Calif., Santa Barbara, 1975-78; pres. 1st L.A. Securities, 1979-86; cons. Wedbush Securities, L.A., 1986-87; regional dir. Fidelity Investments, L.A., 1988-94; regional dir., v.p. Reich & Tang, Westlake Village, Calif., 1994—. TV broadcaster KWHY-TV, 1980-85, KSCI-TV, 1981-83; commentator Am. Radio Network, 1985-86; editor-in-chief Univ. Times newspaper, 1987. Mem. County Art Mus., Los Angeles, 1979-88. Mem. Nat. Assn. Securities Dealers, Securities Industry Assn., Fin. Mgrs. Assn., Greater L.A. Zoo Assn., Sunset Hills Country Club (Thousand Oaks, Calif.). Office: Reich & Tang 920-A14 Hampshire Rd Westlake Village CA 91361

REBAGAY, TEOFILA VELASCO, chemist, chemical engineer; b. Pangasinan, Philippines, Feb. 5, 1928; came to U.S., 1965; d. Dionisio Opiniano and Antonia (Flora) Velasco; m. Guillermo Rabadam Rebagay, Apr. 4, 1956; children: Guillermo V., Teofilo V. BS in Chemistry, U. Philippines, Quezon City, 1951; BS in Chem. Engring., Nat. U., Manila, 1954; PhD in Chemistry, U. Ky., 1969. Postdoctoral fellow U. Ky., Lexington, 1969-71, U. Va., Charlottesville, 1971-72; rsch. assoc. U. Ky., Lexington, 1973-76; sr. chemist Ky. Ctr. Energy Rsch., Lexington, 1976-78; radiochemist Allied-Gen. Nuclear Svcs., Barnwell, S.C., 1978-83; sr. chemist Rockwell Hanford Ops., Richland, Wash., 1983-87; prin. scientist Westinghouse Hanford Co., Richland, 1987—. Contbr. articles to profl. publs. IAEA fellow UN, Tokyo, 1963; grantee Rockefeller Found., 1965. Mem. ASTM, Soc. Applied Spectroscopy. Office: Westinghouse Hanford Co Richland WA 99352

REBER, JOSEPH E., lawyer; b. Butte, Mont., Aug. 9, 1940; s. Joseph Bryant and Marie Terry (Tauriainen) R. BA in Hist., U. Mont., 1962, JD, 1965; LLM in Tax, NYU, 1982. Bar: Mont. 1965, U.S. Supreme Ct. 1970, N.Y. 1980, D.C. 1982, Calif. 1989. Law clk. Mont. Supreme Ct., Helena, 1965; ptnr. Heron & Reber, Helena, 1965-70; pvt. practice Helena, 1970-80; assoc. various law firms, N.Y.C., 1980-84; v.p. Pension & Actuarial Co., Colorado Springs, Colo., 1984-89; gen. counsel Great Am. Life Ins., L.A., 1989-90; pvt. practice Marina Del Rey, Calif., 1990—; presenter in field. Author: Trust and Tax Estate Planning, 1993; editor law rev. U. Mont., 1964-65; contbr. articles to Fin. Planning Mag., 1987-89. State chmn. Robert F. Kennedy for Pres., Mont., 1968, Senator Frank Church for Pres., 1976; del. platform com. Dem. Nat. Conv., 1976-80; active endowment steering com. L.A. Philharmonic, 1992—. Capt. USMC, 1966-72. Mem. Nat. Acad. Elder Law Attys., Calif. Bar Assn. (trust com. 1992—), Mont. State Hist. Soc. (v.p. 1979-80), Marina-Culver City Bar Assn. (pres. 1994), Marina del Rey C. of C. (lawyers group 1994), L.A. County Bar Assn.

REBER, WILLIAM FRANCIS, music educator, conductor; b. Oakland, Calif., Dec. 3, 1940; s. Otto Francis and Garna (Wiman) R.; m. Donna Lee Knight, Oct. 18, 1965 (div.); children: Arianna Lynnette, William Daniel; m. Margaret Susan Moffatt, June 24, 1986. MusB magna cum laude, U. Utah, 1964, MusM, 1966; D of Mus. Arts, U. Tex., 1977; student, Wesley Balk Opera/Mus. Theatre Inst., 1976. Condr., vocal coach Minn. Opera Co., St. Paul, 1976-77; asst. prof., lectr. music U. Tex., Austin, 1978-90; condr. Corpus Christi (Tex.) Ballet, 1986—; assoc. prof. Calif. State U., Fullerton, 1990-91; assoc. prof. Ariz. State U., Tempe, 1991—, dir., prin. condr. lyric opera theatre, 1991—; mem. music staff Minn. Dance Theatre; condr. U. Tex., 1978-90, founder, mus. dir. chamber orch., condr. opera theatre, assoc. condr. symphony, music dir. mus. theatre; coach, condr. Am. Inst. Mus. Studies, Graz, Austria, 1985, 86, 93—; guest condr. Corpus Christi Symphony, 1986-91; music dir. symphony, condr. opera theatre Calif. State U., 1990-91; music advisor Staatsoperette Dresden, Germany, 1993; condr., vocal coach Altenburger Musiktheater Akademie, Altenburg, Germany; jury chair Corpus Christi Young Artists' Competition, Kingsville Internat. Young Performers' Competition, flute/piano recital Odrid Internat. Festival, Skopje Summer Festival, 1994; accompanist various instrumental and vocal recitals. Author: Operas of Ralph Vaughan Williams, 1977; translator: Das Christelflein, 1977. Selection panelist Ariz. Commn. Arts, Phoenix, 1993. Capt. USAF, 1966-72. Recipient B. Iden Payne award Austin Circle Theatres, 1990; Cultural travel grantee U.S. Info. Svc., 1992, 95. Mem. Opera Am., Nat. Opera Assn., Am. Symphony Orch. League, Condrs.' Guild, Coll. Music Soc. Office: Ariz State U Lyric Opera Theatre Box 870405 Tempe AZ 85287-0405

REBERT, CHARLES SIDNEY, research neuroscientist, educator; b. Detroit, Feb. 8, 1938; s. Ivan R. and Gertrude C. (Murdoch) R.; m. Lana L. Jolley, Jan. 6, 1962 (div. Aug. 1989); children: Alison L., Andrea L. BA, San Diego State Coll., 1962, MA, 1964; PhD, U. Iowa, 1968. Cert. jr. coll. tchr.; lic. psychologist, Calif. Assoc. dir. dept. neurosci. SRI Internat., Menlo Park, Calif., 1968—; prof. Calif. Sch. Profl. Psychology, San Francisco, 1975-76; vis. scholar Hoover Inst., Stanford (Calif.) U., 1994; vis. prof. Inst. for Psychology, U. Vienna, Austria, 1990; mem. animal care ad hoc com. SRI Internat., 1992-94, mktg. com., 1994. Contbr. sci. articles to profl. jours.; mem. editl. bd. Internat. Jour. Psychophysiology, 1991—. Rsch. grantee NIH, EPA, Nat. Bur. Standards, Jet Propulsion Lab., Nat. Inst. on Drug Abuse, Air Force Office of Sci. Rsch., Styrene Info. and Rsch. Ctr., Advanced Rsch. Projects Adminstrn., 1969-93. Mem. Internat. Orgn. Psychophysiology (bd. dirs. 1987—), Internat. Neurotoxicology Assn. Libertarian. Home: 3015-127 E Bayshore Rd Redwood City CA 94063 Office: SRI Internat 333 Ravenswood Ave Menlo Park CA 94025-3453

RECHARD, OTTIS WILLIAM, mathematics and computer science educator; b. Laramie, Wyo., Nov. 13, 1924; s. Ottis H. and Mary (Bird) R.; m. Dorothy Lee Duble, Nov. 19, 1943; children—Katherine L. (Mrs. Larry V. Baxter), Carol G. (Mrs. David P. Reiter), Nancy L. (Mrs. William Moore), Elizabeth A. B.A., U. Wyo., 1943; postgrad., U. Calif., Los Angeles, 1943; M.A., U. Wis., 1946, Ph.D., 1948. Instr. U. Wis., 1948; instr., asst. prof. Ohio State U., 1948-51; staff mem. Los Alamos (N.Mex.) Nat. Lab., 1951-56; prof., dir. computing ctr. Wash. State U., Pullman, 1956-68; prof., chmn. dept. computer sci. Wash. State U., 1963-76, prof., dir. systems and computing, 1968-70; prof. math. and computer scis. U. Denver, 1976—, dir. computing services, 1976-79; vis. prof., chmn. dept. computer sci. U. Wyo., 1986-87; cons. NSF, Idaho Nuclear Corp., Los Alamos Nat. Lab.; program dir. computer sci. program NSF, 1964-65, chmn. adv. panel on instl. computing facilities, 1969-70. Mem. Los Alamos Sch. Bd., 1954-56; mem. Pullman Sch. Bd., 1967-74; Trustee, past pres. Westminster Found., Synod Wash.-Alaska. Served to 1st lt. USAAF, 1943-45. Decorated Order of Leopold II Belgium). Fellow AAAS; mem. Assn. for Computing Machinery, Am. Math. Soc., Math. Assn. Am., IEEE Computer Soc., Soc. Indsl. and Applied Math., AAUP, Phi Beta Kappa, Sigma Xi, Phi Kappa Phi. Presbyn. (elder). Club: Rotarian. Home: RR 3 Box 369 Calder ID 83808 also: 6980 E Girard Ave Apt 405 Denver CO 80224-2915

RECHHOLTZ, ROBERT AUGUST, brewing company executive; b. N.Y.C., Mar. 29, 1937; s. Agust Bruno and Frances Maude (Wirth) R.; m. Caroline Morton Osborne, May 2, 1959; children—Laurie Virginia, Jennifer Paige, Kristen Caroline. B.S. in Bus., U. N.C., 1958. Asst. copy supr. Proctor & Gamble, Cin., 1958-60; v.p. mktg. R.J. Reynolds Co., Winston-Salem, N.C., 1961-72, Gallo, Modesto, Calif., 1973; sr. v.p. sales and mktg. Liggett Group, Durham, N.C., 1974-77; sr. v.p. sales and mktg Joseph Schlitz Brewing Co., Milw., 1977-81; exec. v.p. sales and mktg. Adolph Coors, Golden, Colo., 1981—. Served with USAR, 1958, 62. Mem. Assn. Nat. Advertisers (dir. 1983-86), Advt. Council (bd. dirs. 1986-89), Winston-Salem Jr. C. of C. Republican. Episcopalian. Club: Rolling Hills Country. Home: 1375 Southridge Ct Golden CO 80401-9108 Office: Coors Distributing Co 1819 Denver West Dr # 425 Golden CO 80401-3118

REDA, MARK ANTHONY, television producer; b. Alliance, Ohio, Mar. 6, 1958; s. Gene Joseph and Elizabeth Ada (Dawson) R.; m. Sheryl Lynn Dotson, July 25, 1987; children: Anthony Joseph Jackson, Brianna Elizabeth. BA in English, UCLA, 1979. Producer TCS/Metrosports, Pitts., 1983-85, Prime Ticket TV, L.A., 1986-88; graphics producer Minn.

Timberwolves TV, Mpls., 1989-93; graphics producer L.A. Dodgers KTTV-TV, L.A., 1985-92; producer Oakland A's KRON-TV, San Francisco, 1993; graphics producer L.A. Clippers KLOP-TV, L.A., 1994—; producer Colorado Rockies TV, Denver, 1994—; v.p. Graphics Plus, Inc., L.A., 1984-92. Creator, cons. graphic design/style Prime Ticket, 1985, L.A. Dodgers Baseball, 1986, Oakland A's Baseball, 1993, Charlotte Hornets, San Antonio Sprus, Denver Nuggets, Utah Jazz, 1994. Recipient local Emmy, 1986, 88, 89, 95, nat. Emmy, 1990.

REDDAN, JOHN GORDON, III, computer scientist; b. Joliet, Ill., July 9, 1955; s. John Gordon and Dorothy Ollana (Jordan) R.; m. Stacy Layne Wilson, June 12, 1976; children: Patricia Lynette, Jerel Evan. BS in Math., U. Redlands, 1976; MS in Computer Sci., West Coast U., 1981. Software analyst Cubic Corp., 1977-78, Johnson Controls, Inc., 1978-81, Bolt, Beranek, and Newman, 1981; software devel. mgr. SYSCON Corp., San Diego, 1981—. Contbr. articles to profl. jours. Mem. IEEE, IEEE Computer Soc., Assn. for Computing Machinery. Home: 4328 Del Monte Ave San Diego CA 92107-3646

REDDEN, JAMES ANTHONY, federal judge; b. Springfield, Mass., Mar. 13, 1929; s. James A. and Alma (Cheek) R.; m. Joan Ida Johnson, July 13, 1950; children: James A., William F. Student, Boston U., 1951; LL.B., Boston Coll., 1954. Bar: Mass., 1954, Oreg., 1955. Pvt. practice Mass., 1954-55; title examiner Title & Trust Ins. Co., Oreg., 1955; claims adjuster Allstate Ins. Co., 1956; mem. firm Collins, Redden, Ferris & Velure, Medford, Oreg., 1957-73; treas. State of Oreg., 1973-77; atty. gen., 1977-80; U.S. dist. judge, now sr. judge U.S. Dist. Ct. Oreg., Portland, 1980—. Chmn. Oreg. Pub. Employee Relations Bd.; mem. Oreg. Ho. of Reps., 1963-69, minority leader, 1967-69. With AUS, 1946-48. Mem. ABA, Mass. Bar Assn., Oreg. State Bar. Office: US Dist Ct 612 US Courthouse 620 SW Main St Portland OR 97205-3037

REDDIEN, CHARLES HENRY, II, lawyer, corporate executive, consultant; b. San Diego, Aug. 27, 1944; s. Charles Henry and Betty Jane (McCormick) R.; m. Paula Gayle, June 16, 1974; 1 child, Tyler Charles. BSEE, U. Colo., Boulder, 1966; MSEE, U. So. Calif., 1968; JD, Loyola U., L.A., 1972. Bar: Calif. 1972, Colo. 1981, U.S. Dist. Ct. 1981. Mgr., Hughes Aircraft Co., 1966-81; pvt. practice, 1972—; pres., broker R&D Realty Ltd., 1978-91; mem. spl. staff, co-dir. tax advantage group OTC Net Inc., 1981-82; pres., chmn. Heritage Group Inc., investment banking holding co., 1982-84, Plans and Assistance Inc., mgmt. cons., 1982-83, Orchard Group Ltd., investment banking holding co., 1982-84, J.W. Gant & Assocs., Inc., investment bankers, 1983-84; mng. ptnr., CEO J.W. Gant & Assocs., Ltd., 1984-85; chmn. bd. Kalamath Group Ltd., 1985-87, Heritage group Ltd. Investment Bankers, 1985-87; dir. Virtusonics Corp., 1985-92; v.p., dir. Heritage Fin. Planners Inc., 1982-83; pres., chmn. PDN Inc., 1987-89; pub., exec. v.p., dir. World News Digest Inc., 1987-90, LeisureNet Entertainment, Inc., 1989-90; chief exec. officer, Somerset Group Ltd., 1988-93, Inland Pacific Corp., 1989-91, World Info. Network, Inc., 1990-92, pres., CEO, chmn., Europa Cruises Corp., 1992-94; CEO, chmn. Casino World Inc., 1993—, Miss. Gaming Corp., 1993—. Recipient Teaching Internship award, 1964. Mem. Calif. Bar Assn., Nat. Assn. Securities Dealers, IEEE (chmn. U. Colo. chpt. 1965), Am. Inst. Aero. and Astronautical Engrs., Phi Alpha Delta, Tau Beta Pi, Eta Kappa Nu. Contbr. articles to profl. jours. Office: 2305 E Arapahoe Rd Ste 200 Littleton CO 80122-1538

REDDING-STEWART, DEBORAH LYNN, psychologist; b. Miami, Fla., Feb. 16, 1953; d. Sidney Douglas and Lois May (Tily) R.; m. John Thomas Stewart, Aug. 19, 1978; children: Garrett Lorne, Tyler Douglas, Kelly Lynn. BA in Psychology, San Diego State U., 1975; MA in Psychology, U. Calif., Santa Barbara, 1980. Instr. Allan Hancock Coll., Lompoc, Calif., 1980-86; adminstr., dir. clin. svcs. Mary Lou Stewart Learning Ctr., Lompoc, Calif., 1982—. Author: The Soft Voice of the Rain, 1993. State Coun. Devel. Disabilities PDF grantee, 1990, Instructional Deve. grantee U. Calif., 1979. Mem. Nat. Physique Com. (promoter 1992). Home: 1019 Onstott Rd Lompoc CA 93436-2342

REDDY, A. S. N., plant molecular biology educator; b. India, July 8, 1956; came to U.S., 1985; s. Anireddy Kantha and Julakanti (Kanthamma) R.; m. Katt Padma Latha, May 29, 1987; children: A. Rashmi, A. Sudhira. MS in Botany, Kakatiya U., India, 1979; PhD in Plant Molecular Biology, Jawaharlal Nehru U., New Delhi, 1984. Rsch. assoc. molecular biology unit Jawaharlal Nehru U. Sch. Life Scis., 1980-84, postdoctoral rsch. assoc., 1984-85; postdoctoral rsch. assoc. Lab. Plant Molecular Biology Wash. State U., Pullman, 1985-89, staff scientist, 1989-92; asst. prof. dept. biology Colo. State U., Ft. Collins, 1992—; rsch. presenter profl. confs., lectr. in field; reviewer grant proposals U.S.-Israel Binat. Agrl. R & D Fund, Australian Rsch. Coun., USDA. Contbr. numerous articles and abstracts to profl. jours. Jr. rsch. fellow Coun. Sci. and Indsl. Rsch., 1980-82, sr. rsch. fellow, 1982-84; computer analysis tng. fellow Molecular Biology Computer Resource Ctr., Dana Farber Cancer Inst., Harvard Sch. Pub. Health, Harvard Med. Sch., 1990; scholar Cold Spring Harbor Lab., 1991; rsch. grantee Colo. State U., 1992-94, San Luis Valley Rsch. Ctr., 1993-95, Colo. RNA Ctr., 1993-94, USDA, 1994-96, NASA, 1995. Mem. AAAS, Am. Soc. Plant Physiologists, Colo.-Wyo. Acad. Sci., Soc. Plant Biochemistry and Biotech. (life), Sigma Xi. Office: Colo State U Dept Biology Fort Collins CO 80523

REDDY, NAGENDRANATH K., biochemist, researcher; b. Bangalore, India, Nov. 18, 1937; came to U.S., 1968; s. K. Rami and K. (Gnanamma) R.; m. Saraswati K., May 11, 1967; children: Kalpana, Sandip. BS, SRI Venkateswara U., Andhra, India, 1957; MS, U. Saugor, Madhya Pradesh, India, 1959; PhD, Indian Inst. Sci., Bangalore, 1971. Jr. research asst. Nat. Dairy Research Inst., Bangalore, 1959-60; sr. research asst. Indian Inst. Sci., Bangalore, 1965-68; research assoc. Roswell Park Meml. Inst., Buffalo, 1968-73; asst. prof. U. Cin., 1975-80; asst. prof. research biochemistry U. So. Calif., L.A., 1980-90; biochemist Sci. Svcs. Bur., L.A., 1990—. Editor: Fibrinolysis, 1980; patentee fibrinolytic enzyme from snake venom; contbr. articles to profl. jours. Recipient Research Career Devel. award NIH, 1978. Mem. AAAS, Am. Soc. Biol. Chemists. Home: 3402 S Punta Del Este Dr La Puente CA 91745-6634

REDENBACH, SANDRA IRENE, educational consultant; b. Boston, Nov. 18, 1940; d. David and Celia (Wish) Goldstein; m. Gunter L. Redenbach, Mar. 16, 1963 (div. 1980); 1 child, Cori-Lin; m. Kenneth L. Gelatt, June 25, 1989. BA, U. Calif., Davis, 1972; postgrad. in Ednl. Leadership, St. Mary's Coll., Moraga, Calif., 1988, 93-95. Cert. tchr., Calif. Tchr. Solano County Juvenile Hall, Fairfield, Calif., 1968-70, St. Basil's Sch., Vallejo, Calif., 1970-73, St. Philomenes Sch., Sacramento, 1973; tchr., assoc. dean Vet.'s Spl. Edn. Program, U. Calif., Davis, 1973-75, Woodland (Calif.) Jr. High Sch., 1973-76, Lee Jr. High Sch., Woodland, 1976-79, Woodland High Sch., 1979-89; founder, coord., tchr. Ind. Learning Ctr., Woodland, 1989-94; dir. curriculum and instrn. Dixon (Calif.) Unified Sch. Dist., 1994—; teaching asst., lectr. U. Calif., Davis, 1985-86; pres., cons. Esteem Seminar Programs and Pubs., Davis, 1983—; cons., leader workshop. Author: Self-Esteem: The Necessary Ingredient for Success, 1991; author tng. manual: Self-Esteem: A Training Manual, 1990-91, Innovative Discipline: Managing Your Own Flight Plan, 1994. Active Dem. Club of Davis, 1976-79; human rights chair Capitol Svc. Ctr., Sacramento, 1987-92. Martin Luther King scholar, 1986; Nat. Found. for Improvement of Edn. grantee, 1987-88. Mem. Assn. Calif. Sch. Adminstrs., Woodland Edn. Assn. (pres. 1980-83, Outstanding Educator 1992, 93), Phi Delta Kappa (pres. 1992-93). Jewish. Home: 313 Del Oro Ave Davis CA 95616-0416 Office: Esteem Seminar Programs & Publs 313 Del Oro Ave Davis CA 95616-0416

REDFIELD, JOHN DUNCAN, computer programmer; b. Hackensack, N.J., Sept. 27, 1947; s. Daniel Smith and Shirley Carolyn (Gray) R. AA, San Bernardino Valley Jr. Coll., Colton, Calif., 1971, Westark C.C., Ft. Smith, Ark., 1984. Free-lance programmer Phoenix, 1975-78, San Bernardino, 1978-80, Ft. Smith, Ark., 1980-90, Las Vegas, Nev., 1990—. With USN, 1966-70, Vietnam. Mem. DAV (life), Mobile Riverine Forces Assn. Moravian/Presbyterian.

REDHEFFER, RAYMOND MOOS, mathematician, educator; b. Chgo., Apr. 17, 1921; s. Raymond L. and Elizabeth (Moos) R.; m. Heddy Gross Stiefel, Aug. 25, 1951; 1 son, Peter Bernard. S.B., MIT, 1943, S.M., 1946, Ph.D., 1948; DSc (hon.), U. Karlruhe, 1991. Rsch. assoc. MIT Radiation Lab., 1942-45, Rsch. Lab. of Electronics, 1946-48; instr. Harvard U., Radcliffe Coll., 1948-50; mem. faculty UCLA, 1950—, prof. math., 1960—; guest prof. Tech. U. Berlin, 1962, Inst. for Angewandte Math., Hamburg, 1966, Math. Inst. U. Karlsruhe, 1971-72, 81, 88, 91, 95; U.S. sr. scientist Alexander von Humboldt Found., Karlsruhe, 1976, 85. Author: (with Ivan Sokolnikoff) Mathematics of Physics and Modern Engineering, 1958, (with Charles Eames) Men of Modern Mathematics, 1966, (with Norman Levinson) Complex Variables, 1970, Differential Equations, Theory and Applications, 1991, Introduction to Differential Equations, 1992; film author, animator, 1972-74; contbr. articles to profl. jours. Pierce fellow Harvard U., 1948-50; sr. postdoctoral fellow NSF, Göttingen, Germany, 1956; Fulbright rsch. scholar Vienna, 1957, Hamburg, 1961-62; recipient Disting. Teaching award UCLA Alumni Assn., 1969. Mem. Deutsche Akademie der Naturforscher (Leopoldina), Sigma Xi. Home: 176 N Kenter Ave Los Angeles CA 90049-2730 Office: UCLA Dept Mathematics 6224 Math Sci Bldg Los Angeles CA 90024

REDIESS, HERMAN ARTHUR, engineering executive; b. Pinneo, Colo., Apr. 2, 1936; s. Herman Henry and Ethel Velma (Andrews) R.; m. Sharon Purcell, June 7, 1958; children: Sharilyn, Nicholas Arthur. BSME, U. Calif., Berkeley, 1959; MS in Aerospace Engring., U. So. Calif., 1964; PhD in Aerospace and Astro. Engring., MIT, 1969. Rsch. engr. NASA Flight Rsch. Ctr., Edwards, Calif., 1959-60, br. chief, 1960-64, dep. divsn. chief, 1969-75; dir. rsch. NASA Dryden Flight Rsch. Ctr., Edwards, 1975-78; mgr. electronics and human factors NASA Hdqrs., Washington, 1978-82; v.p. sys. engring. HR Textron, Irvine, Calif., 1982-85; divsn. mgr. Sparta, Inc., Laguna Hills, Calif., 1985-90, v.p., ops. mgr., 1990-94, v.p., dir. strategic planning, 1994-95; pres. and cons. H.A.R. Assocs., Laguna Niguel, Calif., 1995—; pres. Paradigm 2000, 1995—. Sculptured commd. by NASA, 1992; contbr. articles to profl. publs. Mem. IEEE, AIAA, SAE (chmn. control and guidance sys. com. 1978-86). Home and Office: 23822 Brant Ln Laguna Niguel CA 92677

REDMOND, PAUL ANTHONY, utility executive; b. Lakeview, Oreg., 1937. BSEE, Gonzaga U., 1965. Asst. elec. engr. Wash. Water Power Co., Spokane, 1965-67, maintenance engr., 1967-69, supt. contract constrn., 1969-73, constrn. and maintenance supt., 1973-75, mgr. constrn. and maintenance, 1975-77, asst. to pres., 1977-78, v.p., asst. to pres., 1978-79, sr. v.p. ops., 1979-80, exec. v.p., 1980-82, pres., 1982-88, chief oper. officer, 1982-84, chief exec. officer, 1984—, chmn. bd., 1985—, also bd. dirs.; former pres. Wash. Irrigation & Devel. subs. Wash. Water Power Co., Spokane, now chmn., pres., chief exec. officer, 1985—; bd. dirs. Security Pacific Bank Washington, Spokane Indsl. Park Inc., Limestone Co. Inc., Devel. Assocs. Inc., Pentzer Corp., Water Power Improvement Co., Wash. Irrigation and Devel. Co., Itron Inc. Lt. col. USNG. Office: Wash Water Power Co PO Box 3727 Spokane WA 99220-3727

REDO, DAVID LUCIEN, investment company executive; b. Lakewood, Ohio, Sept. 1, 1937; s. Joseph L. and Florence M. (Morse) R.; m. Judy L. Ijams, Aug. 4, 1962; children: Jenny, Mark. BSEE, U. Calif., Berkeley, 1961; MBA, U. Santa Clara, 1967. Registered investment advisor. Asst. engring. mgr. AT&T, N.Y.C., 1968-71; pension fund mgr. Pacific Telephone, San Francisco, 1971-77; mng. dir. The Fremont Group (formerly Bechtel Investments Inc.), San Francisco, 1977—; pres., CEO Fremont Investment Advisors, Inc., San Francisco, 1986—; bd. dirs. The Fremont Group (formerly Bechtel Investments, Inc.) San Francisco, J.P. Morgan Securities Asia, Singapore, Sequoia Ventures Inc., San Francisco, Fremont Investment Advisors, Sit/Kim Internat. Investments. Bd. trustees U. Calif., Berkeley, 1988—; chmn. investment com. U. Calif. Found., 1988—. Mem. Sentinel Pension Inst. (bd. advisors), Fin. Execs. Inst., Treas. Club of San Francisco, Internat. Assn. of Fin. Planners. Office: Fremont Investment Advisors 50 Beale St Ste 100 San Francisco CA 94105-1813

REECE, DAVID BRYSON, health facility administrator, research administrator, nurse consultant, nurse educator; b. Phoenix, Aug. 5, 1953; s. Frank Williams and Margaret Leonora (Bryson) W.; div.; children: Ashley Cambridge, Christopher David. ADN, Phoenix C.C., 1974; Baccalaurette Sci. Wholistic Nursing, Westbrook U., 1991, Master Sci. Wholistic Nursing, 1992, PhD, 1993. V.p. Young Nursing Svc., Kingman, Ariz., 1987-89; CEO No. Ariz. Cons., Phoenix, 1987-92, Butterfield Health Systems, Phoenix, 1990—; v.p. United Submersible Sys., Phoenix, 1990-94; dean of nursing, cofounder Sch. Wholistic Nursing Westbrook U., Aztec, N.Mex., 1991—; v.p. R&D, grant procurement and various rsch. projects Am. Minority Bus. for Engring. and Rsch., Chadler, Ariz., 1993—; bd. dirs., sec., treas., v.p., R&D Grant Procurement, dir. sterolithography, dir. HIV vaccine lab; alternative health nurse practitioner. Rsch. includes homeopathic proving aspartame, stereolithography, advance dark field micro; cofactor for HIV and Ebola. Mem. Ariz. Assn. Healthcare Agys. (bd. dirs. 1988-90). Office: AMBER Inc PO Box 3323 Chandler AZ 85224-3323

REECE, MONTE MEREDITH, lawyer, judge; b. Jackson, Tenn., May 29, 1945; s. Jerrel Rexford Sr. and Marjorie (Ricks) R.; m. Melanie Fleshman; children: Hugh, Bryan, Andrew, Jerrel, Rebecca. Student, La. State U., 1963-64, 66, La. Coll., 1964-65; LLB, Western State U., 1974. Atty. English & Marotta A.P.C., Downey, Calif., 1974-78; pvt. practice, 1978—; magistrate judge U.S. Dist. Ct. (ea. dist.) Calif., South Lake Tahoe, 1983—; judge pro tem El Dorado County Mcpl. Ct., South Lake Tahoe, 1983—; cons. assembly judiciary com., Sacramento, 1993. Advisor Tahoe Human Svcs., South Lake Tahoe, 1986—; pres. Sudden Infant Death syndrome, South Lake Tahoe, 1988—. With USNR, 1968-70, Vietnam. Mem. Fed. Magistrate Judges Assn., El Dorado County Search and Rescue (pres. 1989—), Lions (pres. 1985—, Lion of Yr. 1988-89). Office: US Dist Ct PO Box 20000 3330 Lake Tahoe Blvd Ste 10 South Lake Tahoe CA 96150-7911

REECE MYRON, MONIQUE ELIZABETH, marketing, advertising and sales consultant; b. Eldora, Iowa, Jan. 12, 1960; d. Barry Lynne and Vera Marie (Powell) R.; m. Gordon Duane Myron, Mar. 14, 1992; 1 child, Morgan Reece. BSBA, Regis U., 1991. Mgr. regional advt. Silo, Inc., Denver, 1979-86; dir. mktg. LaserLand Corp., U.S.A., Denver, 1986-87; advt. mgr. King Soopers, Denver, 1987-90; supr. brand devel. Garrison-Lontine Advt., Denver, 1991; pres. Monique Myron and Assocs., Denver and La Jolla, Calif., 1991-94, MarketSmarter, Denver and San Diego, 1994—; chmn. bus. partnership com. Colo. Mktg. Tech. Advt. Com., Denver, 1987-91. Mem. publ. rels. com. Make-A-Wish Found., Denver, 1989. Recipient 1st Place Advt. award Nat. Frozen Food Assn., 1988, 89, 90, award Retail Advt. Coun., 1990. Mem. NAFE, Am. Soc. Tng. Devel., Nat. Assn. Women Bus. Owners, Nat. Assn. Profl. Saleswomen, Colo. Women's C. of C., Toastmasters, La Jolla C. of C. (bus., profl. com. 1992-93), Denver Metro. C. of C. Home: 430 S Garfield St Denver CO 80209-3505 Office: MarketSmarter 430 S Garfield St Denver CO 80209-3505

REED, ALAN BARRY, university executive, consultant, investor; b. Leavenworth, Kans., June 28, 1940; s. Warren Lillard and Violet Florence (Seichepine) R.; m. Shari Laine Waetzig, Oct. 5, 1962; 1 child, Selena Eden. PhD, U. Tex., 1971. Dir. U. N.Mex., Santa Fe, 1989—; sr. assoc. N.Mex. Engring. Rsch. Inst., Albuquerque, 1988—; advisor Navajo Nation, Window Rock, Ariz., 1988—; dir. Western Infrastructure Leadership Inst., Albuquerque, 1993. Contbr. articles to profl. jours. Councilman City of Albuquerque, 1975-79; chmn. Vols. for the Outdoors, N.Mex., 1982-83. Grantee Kellogg Found., 1992, U.S. Dept. Energy, 1994. Office: New Mexico Engr Rsch Inst 1001 University Blvd SE Ste 101 Albuquerque NM 87106-4342

REED, CAROL LOUISE, designer; b. Pontiac, Ill., Apr. 16, 1938; d. Rollin Kenneth and Lucille Hortence (Myer) Snethen; m. Richard Willis Reed, Feb. 13, 1960; children: Rena Louise Davis, Ronda Lee Howle. BBA in Mktg. and Advt., Tex. Tech. U., 1959. Office mgr. Sappington Devel., Inc., Rociada, N.Mex., 1990-91; owner Designs by Carol, Rociada, 1988—. Elected state officer Tierra y Montes Soil and Water Conservation Dist., Las Vegas, 1990—; mem. Mora-San Miguel Water Planning Bd., 1991—; treas. First Meth. Ch., Las Vegas, 1989-90; sec. Calvary Bapt. Ch., Las Vegas, 1991-92. Recipient award of merit Goodyear Tire and Rubber Co., 1991; named Outstanding Supr. of Tierra y Montes Soil and Conservation Dist., 1992, 95. Mem. N.Mex. Assn. Soil and Water Conservation Dists. (chair region IV 1994—), Phi Kappa Phi. Republican. Home: PO Box 853 Rociada NM 87742-0853 Office: Designs by Carol PO Box 853 Rociada NM 87742-0853

REED, DALE DEVON, engineering executive; b. Veedersburg, Ind., July 22, 1931; s. Clyde and Aline (Jones) R.; m Donna Ellen Bartley, Apr. 16, 1955; children, Katherine, Richard, Ann. BS in Engring., Purdue U., 1953. Engr. John Deere, Waterloo, Iowa, 1953-54; lt. U.S. Army Engrs., 1954-56; field engr. LeTourneau Westinghouse, Peoria, Ill., 1956-62; pres. Blakemore Equipment, Oakland, Calif., 1962-66, Buran Equipment Co., San Leandro, Calif., 1966-84; chmn., CEO Buram and Reed Inc., San Leandro, 1984—; bd. dirs. Civic Bank Corp., Oakland. Planning commr. City of San Leandro, 1984—; trustee San Leandro Hosp., 1986—; dir., vice-chmn. Goodwill of East Bay, Oakland, 1988—; pres. San Leandro Scholarship Fund, 1990—. Mem. San Leandro C. of C. (officer 1986-87). Republican. Home: 1560 Daily Ct San Leandro CA 94577-6815 Office: Buran and Reed Inc 1801 Adams Ave San Leandro CA 94577-1003

REED, DALLAS JOHN, criminal justice educator; b. Missoula, Mont., May 23, 1929; s. Dallas J. and Bess (Rocek) R.; m. Joyce E. Clark, June 22, 1962; children: Steven P., Pamela J., Allison E. BA, U. Mont., 1951, MA, 1955; PhD, U. Minn., 1968; postgrad., Rutgers, 1973. Instr. sociology U. Mont., Missoula, 1959-61; instr. to assoc. prof. sociology Idaho State U., Pocatello, 1961-70; exec. dir. West Area Alcohol Edn. and Tng. Program Inc., NIAAA, Reno, Nev., 1975-77; assoc. prof. sociology U. Nev., Las Vegas, 1970-75, assoc. prof. criminal justice, 1977-90; vis. prof. Jacksonville (Ala.) State U., 1990-91. Treas. bd. dirs. Community Action Against Rape, Las Vegas, Nev., 1984-90; chmn.bd. dir. Nevada State Advisory on Alcohol and Drug Abuse, 1976-77; capt. U.S. Army, 1951-53. Nevada Div. Alcoholism fellow, 1973. Mem. Am. Sociol. Assn., Acad. Criminal Justice Scis., Am. Correctional Assn., Am. Soc. Criminology, Nev. Arbitration Assn. (charter mem.), Phi Kappa Phi, Phi Lambda Alpha, Alpha Kappa Delta, Pi Gamma Mu.

REED, DAVID ANDREW, foundation executive; b. Butler, Pa., Feb. 24, 1933; s. Sherman W. and Caroline (Janner) R.; m. Virginia Rogers, Dec. 1, 1956; children: Kristine Lynn, Katherine Louise, Elizabeth Anne, Amy Janner. A.B., Allegheny Coll., 1955; M.S., U. Pitts., 1961. Diplomate: Sch. Pub. Health, Columbia U. Adminstrv. resident Titusville (Pa.) Hosp., 1959, Cin. Gen. Hosp., 1960-61; asst. adminstr. Warren (Pa.) Gen. Hosp., 1961-62, Western Pa. Gen. Hosp., Pitts., 1962-63; with Cin. Gen. Hosp., 1963-69, adminstr., 1964-69; asso. prof. hosp. adminstrn. U. Cin. Coll. Medicine, 1966-69; preceptor program med. and hosp. adminstrn. U. Pitts. Grad. Sch. Pub. Health, 1966-69; pres. Lenox Hill Hosp., N.Y.C., 1969-78; v.p., chief exec. officer Good Samaritan Hosp., Phoenix, 1978-82; pres. SamCor/Samaritan Health Service, Phoenix, 1982-89; pres., chief exec. officer The Samaritan Found., Phoenix, 1989, St. Joseph Health System, Orange, Calif., 1990—; instr.; past pres. Greater Cin. Hosp. Council, Phoenix Regional Hosp. Council; bd. govs. Greater N.Y. Hosp. Assn.; chmn. Am. Hosp. Assn., also trustee; cons. Hosp. Devel. and Research Inst. Contbr. articles to profl. jours. Bd. dirs. Urban League Cin. Served with AUS, 1955-57. Fellow Am. Coll. Hosp. Adminstrs.; mem. Hosp. Adminstrs. Club N.Y.C. (pres.), Hosp. Assn. N.Y., Phi Gamma Delta. Presbyterian. Clubs: Paradise Valley Country, Pacific Golf, Marbella Country, Center. Office: St Joseph Health System 440 S Batavia St Orange CA 92668-3907

REED, DAVID GEORGE, entrepreneur; b. Alameda, Calif., July 19, 1945; s. David Francis and Anna Amelia Vangeline (Paulson) R.; m. Marianne Louise Watson, Apr. 7, 1971 (div. June 1975); m. Michele Ann Hock, June 28, 1989; 1 child, Casey Christine Michele. AA in Bus. Adminstrn., Diablo Valley Coll., Pleasant Hill, Calif., 1965; BA in Design and Industry, San Francisco State U., 1967, MBA in Mktg., 1969; cert. res. police officer, Los Medanos Coll., Pittsburg, Calif., 1977. Owner Western Furs, Ltd., Walnut Creek, Calif., 1963-72; mgmt. cons. Controlled Interval Scheduling, Rolling Hills Estates, Calif., 1972-73; owner Dave Reed's Texaco, Concord, Calif., 1973-76; mgmt. cons. Mgmt. Scheduling Systems, Houston, 1974-76, Thomas-Ross Assocs., Mercer Island, Wash., 1972-82; plant mgr. Bonner Packing, Morgan Hill, Calif., 1981; mfg. engr. Systron Donner, Concord, 1982-84, Beckman Instruments, San Ramon, Calif., 1984-90; owner Dave Reed & Co. Water Ski Sch., White Water Rafting, Chiloquin, Oreg., 1987—, Dave Reed & Co., design, market, mfg. Contender boats, Chiloquin, Oreg., 1976—; lectr. wildlife mgmt. Dave Reed & Co., Chiloquin, 1965—, lectr. mgmt. seminars, 1982—; coach Japanese Water Ski Team, Bluff Water Ski Club, Tokyo, 1984; fin. mgr. Japanese investors Dave Reed & Co., Chiloquin, 1986—, design and supply solar electric power sys., 1994—. Res. dep. sheriff Contra Costa County Sheriff's Dept., Martinez, Calif., 1977-80. With U.S. Army, 1969-71, Vietnam. Recipient Gold medal internat. freestyle wrestling Sr. Olympics, Fullerton, Calif., 1983. Mem. Am. Water Ski Assn. (Calif. state water ski champion 1977, 86, western region water ski champion 1977, silver medal nat. water ski championships 1977), Bay Area Tournament Assn. (chmn. 1968—), Diablo Water Ski Club (bd. dirs. 1968—). Republican. Home: PO Box 336 Chiloquin OR 97624-0336

REED, DAVID PATRICK, infosystems specialist; b. Portsmouth, Va., Jan. 31, 1952; s. Sherman Clark and Bernice Lois (Maul) R.; m. Lynn Susan Schwartz, June 10, 1973 (div. Mar. 1979); 1 child, Colin Alexander; m. Jessica Amy Kenn, Sept. 4, 1983; children: Katherine Anne, Carly Diana. BS, MIT, 1973, SM, 1975, degree in elec. engring., 1976, PhD, 1978. Asst. prof. computer sci. and engring. MIT, Cambridge, 1978-84, lectr., 1984-86; chief scientist Software Arts, Wellesley, Mass., 1983-84, v.p. research and devel., 1984-85; v.p. rsch. and devel., chief scientist Lotus Devel., Cambridge, 1985-92; sr. scientist Interval Rsch. Corp., 1992—. Contbr. articles to profl. jours. Recipient Teaching award MIT Elec. Engring. Dept., 1975. Mem. IEEE, Assn. Computing Machinery, Computer Soc., Sigma Xi. Democrat. Office: 1801 Page Mill Rd Bldg C Palo Alto CA 94304-1216

REED, EDWARD CORNELIUS, JR., federal judge; b. Mason, Nev., July 8, 1924; s. Edward Cornelius Sr. and Evelyn (Walker) R.; m. Sally Torrance, July 14, 1952; children: Edward T., William W., John A., Mary E. BA, U. Nev., 1949; JD, Harvard U., 1952. Bar: Nev. 1952, U.S. Dist Ct. Nev. 1957, U.S. Supreme Ct. 1974. Atty. Arthur Andersen & Co., 1952-53; spl. dep. atty. gen. State of Nev., 1967-69; judge U.S. Dist. Ct. Nev., Reno, 1979—, chief judge, now sr. judge. Former vol. atty. Girl Scouts Am., Sierra Nevada Council, U. Nev., Nev. Agrl. Found., Nev. State Sch. Adminstrs. Assn., Nev. Congress of Parents and Teachers; mem. Washoe County Sch. Bd., 1956-72, pres. 1959, 63, 69; chmn. Gov.'s Sch. Survey Com., 1958-61; mem. Washoe County Bd. Tax Equalization, 1957-58, Washoe County Annexation Commn., 1968-72, Washoe County Personnel Com., 1973-77, chmn. 1973; mem. citizens adv. com. Washoe County Sch. Bond Issue, 1977-78, Sun Valley, Nev., Swimming Pool Com., 1978, Washoe County Blue Ribbon Task Force Com. on Growth, Nev. PTA (life); chmn. profl. div. United Way, 1978; bd. dirs. Reno Siver Sox, 1962-65. Served as staff sgt. U.S. Army, 1943-46, ETO, PTO. Mem. ABA (jud. adminstrn. sect.), Nev. State Bar Assn. (adminstrv. com. dist. 5, 1967-79, lien law com. 1965-78, chmn. 1965-72, probate law com. 1963-66, tax law com. 1962-65), Am. Judicature Soc. Democrat. Baptist. Office: US Dist Ct 5147 US Courthouse 300 Booth St Reno NV 89509-1316*

REED, ENID, neuropsychologist; b. N.Y.C., June 10, 1939; d. Edward and Laura (Gale) Janssen; m. Benjamin Halper, 1946 (dec. Nov. 1962); m. Lewis Reed, Dec. 24, 1963 (dec. Feb. 1970). Grad., UCLA, 1960, PhD in Comm., 1973; PhD in Psychology, U.S. Internat. U., San Diego, 1976. Buyer Sears, Roebuck, L.A., 1958-62; psychologist L.A. City Schs., 1962-73; psychologist Psychologics, Inc., Beverly Hills, Calif., 1976—, neuropsychologist, 1978—. Fellow Am. Psychol. Soc.; mem. AAAS, APA, Nat. Acad. Neuropsychologists (diplomate). Home: Box 1060 Beverly Hills CA 90213 Office: 337 S Beverly Dr Beverly Hills CA 90212

REED, EVA SILVER STAR, chieftain; b. Vinita, Okla., Nov. 29, 1929; d. Robert Elbert Jones and Anna Mae (Campfield) Reed; m. Johnnie Silver Eagle Reed, June 10, 1946 (dec. Sept. 1982); children: Patty Deeanne, Lorrie Ann, Billy John. Sec. United Lumbee Nation of N.C. and Am., Fall River Mills, Calif., 1979-82; nat. head chieftain United Lumbee Nation of N.C. and Am., Fall River Mills, 1982—, also bd. dirs.; bd. dirs., sec. Chapel of Our Lord Jesus, Exeter, Calif., 1974—, Native Am. Wolf Clan, Calif., 1977—;

tchr. Indian beading and crafts, Calif., 1977—. Author, compiler: Over the Cooking Fires, 1982, Lumbee Indian Ceremonies, 1982, United Lumbee Deer Clan Cook Book, 1988; editor: (newspaper) United Lumbee Nation Times, 1981—. Mem. parent com. Title IV & Johnson O'Malley Indian Edn. Program, Tulare/Kings County, 1976-80, Shasta County, Calif., 1982-84. Recipient United Lumbee Nation of N.C. and Am.'s Silver Eagle award, 1991, also various awards for beadwork Intermountain Fair, Shasta County, 1982-93. Office: United Lumbee Nation of NC & Am PO Box 512 Fall River Mills CA 96028

REED, FRANK FREMONT, II, retired lawyer; b. Chgo., June 15, 1928; s. Allen Martin and Frances (Faurot) R.; m. Jaquelin Silverthorne Cox, Apr. 27, 1963; children: Elizabeth Matthiessen Mason, Laurie Matthiessen Stern, Mark Matthiessen, Jeffrey, Nancy, Sarah. Student Chgo. Latin Sch.; grad. St. Paul's Sch., 1946; A.B., U. Mich., 1952, J.D., 1957. Bar: Ill., 1958. Assoc. Byron, Hume, Groen & Clement, 1958-61, Marks & Clerk, 1961-63; pvt. practice law, Chgo., 1963-78; dir. Western Acadia (Western Felt Works), 1960-75, chmn. exec. com., 1969-71. Rep. precinct capt. 1972-78; candidate for 43d ward alderman, 1975; bd. dirs., sec. Chgo. Found. Theater Arts, 1959-64; vestryman St. Chrysostom's Ch., 1975-79, mem. ushers guild, 1964-79, chmn., 1976-78; bd. dirs. North State, Astor, Lake Shore Dr. Assn., 1975-78, pres. 1977-78; bd. dirs. Community Arts Music Assn. of Santa Barbara, 1984-93, treas. 1988-93; bd. dirs. Santa Barbara Arts Coun., 1987-89. Cpl. AUS, 1952-54. Mem. ABA, Ill. Bar Assn., Phi Alpha Delta, Racquet Club, Wausaukee Club (sec., dir. 1968-71, 92-) (Chgo.); Birnam Wood Golf Club (Santa Barbara, Calif.). Episcopalian. Author: History of the Silverthorn Family, 4 vols., 1982, Allen Family of Allen's Grove, 1983, Goddard and Ware Ancestors, 1987, Faurot Family, 1988. Contbr. articles to The Am. Genealogist, 1972-73, 76-77. Home: 1944 E Valley Rd Santa Barbara CA 93108-1428

REED, FRANK METCALF, bank executive; b. Seattle, Dec. 22, 1912; s. Frank Ivan and Pauline B. (Hovey) R.; student U. Alaska, 1931-32; BA, U. Wash., 1937; m. Maxine Vivian McGary, June 11, 1937; children: Pauline Reed Mackay, Frank Metcalf. V.p. Anchorage Light & Power Co., 1937-42; pres. Alaska Electric & Equipment Co., Anchorage, 1946-50; sec., mgr. Turnagain, Inc., Anchorage, 1950-56; mgr. Gen. Credit Corp., Anchorage, 1957; br. mgr. Alaska SBA, Anchorage, 1958-60; sr. v.p. First Interstate Bank of Alaska, Anchorage, 1960-87, also dir., corp. sec.; dir. First Interstate Corp. of Alaska, pres., dir. Anchorage Broadcasters, Inc.; past pres., chmn. Microfast Software Corp.; ptnr. R.M.R. Co.; dir. Anchorage Light & Power Co., Turnagain, Inc., Alaska Fish and Farm, Inc., Life Ins. Co. Alaska, Alaska Hotel Properties, Spa Inc. Pres., Anchorage Federated Charities, Inc., 1953-54; mem. advisory bd. Salvation Army, 1948-58; mem. Alaska adv. bd. Hugh O'Brian Youth Found., 1987-91; trustee Anchor Age Endowment Fund, 1988—, chmn., 1991; mem. City of Anchorage Planning Commn., 1956; mem. City of Anchorage Coun., 1956-57; police commr. Ter. of Alaska, 1957-58; chmn. City Charter Commn., 1958; mem. exec. com. Greater Anchorage, Inc., 1955-65; pres. Sch. Bd., 1961-64; mem. Gov.'s Investment adv. com., 1970-72; mem. Alaska State Bd. Edn.; mem. citizens adv. com. Alaska Meth. U.; chmn. Anchorage Charter Commn., 1975; apptd. by Mayor as co-chmn. charter rev. commn. Municipality of Anchorage, 1990; chmn. bldg. fund dr. Community YMCA, 1976—; bd. dirs., mem. exec. com. Arts Alaska, 1976-78; sec.-treas. Breakthrough, 1976-78; bd. dirs. Anchorage Civic Opera, 1978, Rural Venture Alaska, Inc.; bd. dirs Alaska Treatment Ctr., 1980-87, pres. 1985-86; trustee Marston Found., Inc., 1978, exec. dir. 1988; pres. Sunset Balloon Flights, Inc., Del Mar, Calif., 1990. Served as lt. USNR, 1942-46. Elected to Hall Fame, Alaska Press Club, 1969; named Outstanding Alaskan of Year Alaska C. of C., 1976, Alaskan of Yr., 1990, Outstanding Vol. in Philanthropy Alaska chpt. Nat. Soc. Fundraising Execs, 1991; recipient Community Svc. award YMCA, 1975-78. Mem. Am. Inst. Banking, Am. (exec. council 1971-72) Alaska (pres. 1970-71) bankers assns., Nat. Assn. State Bds. Edn. (sec.-treas. 1969-70), C. of C. U.S. (Western region legislative com.), Anchorage C. of C. (pres. 1966-67, dir.), Pioneers of Alaska, Navy League (pres. Anchorage council 1961-62). Clubs: Tower (life), San Francisco Tennis. Lodges: Lions (sec. Anchorage, 1953-54, dir. 1988, pres., 1962-63), Elks. Home: 1361 W 12th Ave Anchorage AK 99501-4252

REED, GEORGE FORD, JR., investment executive; b. Hollywood, Calif., Dec. 26, 1946; s. George Ford and Mary Anita Reed; B.A. in Econs. with honors, U. So. Calif., 1969, M.A., 1971; m. Kathryn Nixon, 1981. Analyst planning and research Larwin Group, Beverly Hills, Calif., 1971-72; with Automobile Club So. Calif., Los Angeles, 1972-76, supr. mgmt. info., research and devel., 1973-74, mgr. fin. and market analysis, 1975-81, group mgr. fin. analysis and forecasting, 1981-86; pres. Reed Asset Mgmt. Co., Inc., Los Angeles, 1986—; instr. bus. and econs. Los Angeles Community Coll. Mem. population task force Los Angeles C. of C., 1974; mem. Gov. Calif. Statewide Econ. Summit Conf., 1974. Served with U.S. Army, 1969. Mem. Assn. Corp. Real Estate Execs., Fin. Execs. Inst., Nat. Assn. Bus. Economists, Western Regional Sci. Assn., Am. Mgmt. Assn., Am. Fin. Assn., So. Calif. Planners Assn., Rotary Internat., Omicron Delta Epsilon. Home: 1001 S Westgate Ave Los Angeles CA 90049-5905 Office: 10940 Wilshire Blvd Ste 1530 Los Angeles CA 90024-3915

REED, GERARD ALEXANDER, theology educator, history educator; b. Colorado Springs, Colo., Jan. 19, 1941; s. Paul Alexander and Lula (Taylor) R.; m. Roberta Kay Steininger, May 26, 1963. BA, So. Nazarene U., 1963; MA, Okla. U., 1964, PhD, 1967. Ordained to ministry Nazarene Ch., 1977. Asst. prof. So. Nazarene U., Bethany, Okla., 1966-68; prof. MidAm. Nazarene Coll., Olathe, Kans., 1968-82; prof., chaplain Point Loma Nazarene Coll., San Diego, 1982—. Contbr. articles to profl. publs. Parriott Found. fellow, 1964; summer seminar grantee NIH, 1979. Mem. Am. Maritain Assn., Conf. Faith and History, Wesleyan Theol. Soc., Western History Assn. Office: Point Loma Nazarene Coll 3900 Lomaland Dr San Diego CA 92106-2810

REED, HAROLD ERVIN, artist, educator; b. Frederick, Okla., Feb. 22, 1921; s. Perry and Eva (Ervin) R.; m. Gladys Lorraine Oulman, Dec. 7, 1968. Founder, CEO Art Video Prodns., Inc., Woodland Hills, Calif., 1987—. Prin. works include Ofcl. Bicentennial medals USN and USMC, 1975, Statue of Liberty coin medal, 1986, Am. Cup Race coin medal, 1986, U.S. Constn. Bicentennial medal, 1987, Walking Liberty coin, 1987, Uriah Levi medal, 1988, Summer Olympics coin, 1988, 10 Olympic coins, 1988, 45 coins Desert Storm, 1993, 45 coins World War II, 1993. With U.S. Army. Decorated Bronze star, 5 Battle stars, Unit citation, Battlefield commn. Home: 6225 Shoup Ave Apt 106 Woodland Hills CA 91367-1828

REED, HELEN BERNICE, artist; b. Watsonville, Calif., Dec. 22, 1917; d. Harry James and Loretta Elizabeth (Morgan) Aguirre; m. Clarence Varnick Reed, Sept. 8, 1944 (dec. Aug. 1988). Grad. high sch., Watsonville. Demonstrator Long Beach (Calif.) Art Assn., 1984; lectr., demonstrator Muckenthaler Cultural Ctr., Fullerton, Calif., 1984; juror Nat. Date Festival, Indio, Calif., 1987, Lakewood (Calif.) Art Guild, 1984; demonstrator San Bernardino (Calif.) Art Assn., 1984, Whittier (Calif.) Art Assn., 1984; art instr. Fullerton, 1967—. Exhibited in group shows at The Nat. Watercolor Soc., Stockholm, 1972, Farmington, N.Mex., Grants Pass, Oreg., Spokane, 1985, Am. Watercolor Soc., N.Y.C., 1979, Springville (Utah) Mus., 1983; art represented in books, 1986, 88, 93, 94. Recipient Strathmore Paper award Okla. Watercolor Soc., 1984, Arches Paper Cash award Watercolor West, 1984, Purchase award Tex. Fine Arts Assn., 1974. Mem. Watercolor West Transparent Watercolor Soc. (bd. dirs. 1979-84), Nat. Watercolor Soc. Republican.

REED, JAMES ANTHONY, hotel industry executive, consultant; b. Marion, Ohio, June 12, 1939; s. James E. and Sue (McCurdy) R. Student, Fla. State U., 1956-59, U. N.H., 1978. Food and beverage mgr. Caneel Bay Plantation, St. John, Virgin Islands, 1960-64; mgr. Mauna Kea Beach Hotel, Kamuela, Hawaii, 1964-72; v.p. C. Brewer & Co., Ltd., Honolulu, 1972-77, Dunfey Hotel Corp., Hampton, N.H., 1977-80, Marriott Hotels & Resorts, Calif., Hawaii and Asia, 1980-89; pres. The Reed Group, Irvine, Calif., 1989; gen. mgr. La Posada de Santa Fe, 1990-91, Hotel Santa Fe, 1991-93; pres. Reed Group, Santa Fe, 1993—; pres. Kilauea Volcano House Inc., Mackensie Hawaii Ltd., Augustine's Decor Spain; vice-chmn., bd. dirs. Picuris Pueblo Enterprises, cons. to Native Am. Tribes. Named Outstanding Young Men of Am., 1969. Mem. Calif. Thoroughbred Breeders Assn., Calif. Hotel Assn., Sch. Am. Rsch., Community Leaders of Am., Appaloosa Horse Club. Home and Office: 8111 Camino Del Oro La Jolla CA 92037-3104

REED, JAMES EARL, fire department commander; b. San Francisco, Mar. 21, 1957; s. Arlen Earl and Louise (Gibbs) R.; m. Jody Lynn Bales, Feb. 14, 1976 (div. Aug. 1978); 1 child, Darci Lynn; m. Donna Kaye Lewis, June 25, 1994. A in fire sci., Casper Coll., 1995. State cert. fire fighter I, II, III, state cert. fire svc. instr. I, state cert. fire prevention officer I. Shop worker, shop foreman, salesman Becker Fire Equipment, Casper, Wyo., 1975-78; safety equipment maintance Bell H2S Safety and Oilind Safety Engring., Casper, 1978-80; tchr. outreach program Casper Coll., 1988-90; owner operator J.R.'s Custom Hand Planted Signs, 1980-93; capt. Casper (Wyo.) Fire Dept., 1978-93, comdr., 1993—; artist Images Studio, Casper, 1991—; instr. CPR courses Am. Heart Soc., ARC, 1980—; instr. SCBA courses, 1983-85. Active fund raisers City/County Fire Fighters Burn Fund, 1982, 84—, fund raisers Muscular Dystrophy Assn., 1981, 82, 85-89, fund raisers March of Dimes, 1984, 85, 87, fund raisers Casper Mountain Racers Youth Olympics, 1985-87, Casper Event Ctr.'s "Spl. Christmas for Spl. Kids," 1984-87. Named Firefighter of Yr. Casper Fire Dept., Casper Ladies Auxiliary, Am. Legion Regional and Post 2, 1984, Man in Blue, Casper Fire Dept., 1994. Mem. Casper Fire Fighters Assn. (entertainment com. 1980—, exec. com. 1988-90), City County Fire Fighters Burn Fund (trustee 1985-86, treas. 1986-89, sec. 1989-91, pres. 1992—). Republican. Seventh-day Adventist. Home: 1847 Jim Bridger Ave Casper WY 82604-3118

REED, JOEL LESTON, diversified manufacturing company executive; b. Enid, Okla., Jan. 21, 1951; s. Arrel Leston and Velma Jo (Kesner) R.; m. Alicia Kay Biller, Nov. 28, 1970 (dec.); m. Ann Denise Timmersman, June 6, 1981; children: Benjamin Joel, Elizabeth Ann, Peter David. BS in Acctg., Okla. State U., 1972, MS in Acctg., 1973. CPA, Okla, Colo. Successively staff acct., sr. acct., mgr. Deloitte Haskins & Sells, Denver, 1973-81; contr., treas. Ensource Inc., Englewood, Colo., 1981-82, v.p., CFO, 1983-84; CFP Wagner & Brown, Midland, Tex., 1984-89, pres., CEO, 1993-94; ptnr. Batchelder & Ptnrs., Inc., La Jolla, Calif., 1994—; pres., CEO Insilco Corp., 1989-93. Contbr. articles to profl. jours. Mem. AICPA (oil and gas com., Elijah Watt Sells award 1973), Colo. Soc. CPAs, Am. Petroleum Inst., Ind. Petroleum Assn. Am., Porsche Car Club Am., Beta Alpha Psi. Home: 1608 Stanolind Ave Midland TX 79705-8651

REED, JOHN HOWARD, school administrator; b. Bloomfield, Mo., July 14, 1934; s. Floyd John and Lena Joyce (Howard) R.; m. Weymuth Heuiser; children: Cathy, David. BS cum laude, SE Mo. State U., 1956, M., U. Mo., 1959; edn. specialist, SE Mo. State U., 1977; PhD, So. Ill. U., 1983. Cert. supt., prin., tchr. Tchr., coach Scott County R-6 Schs., Sikeston, Mo., 1956-63; supr. student tchr. SE Mo. State U., Cape Girardeau, 1963-75; prin. Scott County R-3 Schs., Oran, Mo., 1975-76; supt. schs. Scott County R-2 Schs., Chaffee, Mo., 1976-79; bus. mgr. SE Mo. State U., Cape Girardeau, 1980-83; dean, pres. Sikeston C.C., 1983-86; supt. Marion County Sch. Dist. 1, Centralia, Ill., 1986-88; head New Life Montessori Sch., Shreveport, La., 1989-90, Belleview Schs., Westminster, Colo., 1990—. Editor: History of Missouri National Guard, 1963. Bd. dirs., sec. Scott County Bd. Edn., Benton, Mo., 1970-79. Lt. col. U.S. Army, 1960-63. Mem. Rotary (sec. 1976-78), Phi Alpha Theta (pres. 1976-78). Baptist. Home: 8175 Green Ct Westminster CO 80030-4101 Office: Belleview Schs 3455 W 83rd Ave Westminster CO 80030-4005

REED, KRISTEN KING, broadcast sales manager; b. Evanston, Ill., Mar. 24, 1962; d. Robert Bruce and Diane (Buchholz) King; m. Edward Cloy Reed, Oct. 30, 1987; children: Taylor Cloy, Zachary Edward. BA in Communications, U. Ariz., 1984. Sales asst. Avery Knodel TV, Chgo., 1984-85, account exec., 1985; account exec. WPWR-TV, Chgo., 1986-87, WZRC-FM, Chgo., 1987, KQIL-AM/KQIX-FM, Grand Junction, Colo., 1987-88; account exec. KJCT-TV, Grand Junction, 1988-91, sales mgr., 1991—. Co-chmn. leadership div. Mesa County Econ. Devel. Coun., Grand Junction, 1994. Mem. Rotary. Office: KJCT-TV 8 Foresight Cir Grand Junction CO 81505-1014

REED, LYNDA BERNAL, video producer, writer; b. Detroit, July 9, 1959; d. Bernard and Joyce Lydia (Gunnett) Harris; m. Ronald Daniel Bernal, June 21, 1980 (div. Oct. 1985); m. Jack Milton Reed, Nov. 4, 1993. BS in Health Sci., Ariz. State U., 1982. Audiovisual coord. Salt River Project, Phoenix, 1985-93; ind. writer/prodr. Phoenix, 1993—. Writer, dir.: (videotape) Montezuma Castle: Home of the Prehistoric Sinagua, 1994 (Southwest Book award 1995), Lake Powell: Heart of the Grand Circle, 1986 (Rocky Mountain Emmy award 1987, ITVA award 1986), The Wolf: A Howling in America's Parks, 1989 (CINDY award 1989), 1993 Page Promo (TELLY award 1994). Media cons. YWCA of Maricopa County, Phoenix, 1986-90. Mem. Nat. Acad. TV Arts and Scis. Office: 16423 N 54th Ave Glendale AZ 85306-1911

REED, MARY LOU, state legislator; m. Scott Reed; children: Tara, Bruce. BA, Mills Coll. Mem. Idaho State Senate, 1985—; Senate Minority Leader; coord. Com. for Fair Rates. Democrat. Office: 10 Giesa Rd Coeur D Alene ID 83814-9489

REED, MICHAEL RAYBREN, utilities executive, journalist; b. Reno, June 21, 1947; s. Jack Raybren and Mary Elizabeth (Williams) R.; m. Betty Joan Banta, July 29, 1967; children: Alicia L., Brian R., Kipp T. BA in Journalism, U. Nev., 1972; MA in Human Resources Mgmt., Troy State U., 1992; student, USAF Air War Coll., 1991-92. Printer Nev. Bell Tel. Co., Reno, 1966-67, 69-72; reporter Reno Evening Gazette, 1973-75; supr., mgr. corp. comm. Sierra Pacific Power Co., Reno, 1975-90, mgr. govtl. affairs, 1992-93, dir. govtl. affairs, 1993—. Lt. col. USAF, 1968-69, 90-92; state plans officer Nev. Air NG, 1972—. Named Outstanding Young Journalist Nev. State Press Assn., 1974. Mem. Pub. Rels. Soc. Am. (treas. 1989-90, Silver Spike award 1989), Greater Reno-Sparks C. of C., Soc. Profl. Journalists, Air Force Assn., Sparks Rotary Club, Reno South Kiwanis Club (pres. 1979-80, 84-85). Roman Catholic. Office: Sierra Pacific Power Co 6100 Neil Rd Reno NV 89511-1132

REED, NANCY ELLEN, educator; b. Mpls., Aug. 11, 1955; d. Jacob Alen and Mary Emeline (Howser) Lundgren; m. Todd Randall Reed, June 18, 1977. BS in Biology, U. Minn., 1977, MS in Computer and Info. Scis., 1988, PhD in Computer and Info. Scis., 1995. Teaching asst. U. Minn., 1985-86; lectr. Computer and Info. Sci. Dept. Sonoma State U., Rohnert Park, Calif., 1993-94, Computer Sci. Dept. U. Calif., Davis, 1994—; rsch. laboratory technician Gastroenterology Rsch. Unit Mayo Clinic, Rochester, Minn., 1978-81; physical sci. technician U.S. Environmental Hygiene Agency, Fitzsimons Army Med. Ctr., Aurora, Colo, 1982-83; profl. rsch. asst. Molecular, Cellular and Developmental Biology Dept. U. Colo., Boulder, 1983-84; computer programmer Control Data Corp., Arden Hills, Minn., 1986; rsch. asst. U. Minn. 1985-88; asst. Artificial Intelligence Laboratory Swiss Fed. Inst. of Technol., Lausanne, Switzerland, 1989-91. Contbr. articles to profl. jours.; speaker in field. Am. Electronics Assn. Fellowship, 1985-89, Microelectronic and Info. Scis. Fellowship, 1984-85. Mem. Am. Assn. for Artificial Intelligence (scholarship for travel nat. conf. on artificial intelligence 1992, 94), Assn. for Computing Machinery, IEEE, Swiss Group for Artificial Intelligence and Cognitive Sci. Office: U Calif Computer Sci Dept Davis CA 95616

REED, PATRICIA COLLEEN, adult education educator; b. Aurora, Mo., Oct. 27, 1939; d. Melvin Emerson and Maxine Lois (Coffer) Johnson; m. Kenneth Charles Reed, Oct. 7, 1961; children: Nathan Kenneth, Morgan Patrick. BA in Math., Pepperdine U., 1961; MA in Govt., Claremont Grad. Sch., 1978; postgrad., U. Calif., Riverside, 1970-76. Cert. tchr. designated subjects, pupil pers. svcs., and adminstrn., Calif. Computer programmer System Devel. Corp., Santa Monica, Calif., 1961-62; tchr. Yucaipa (Calif.) Adult Sch., 1971-74, counselor-tchr., 1974-76, 78-83, counselor, 1976-78, 83-86, prin., 1986—; sr. assoc. Calif. Sch. Leadership Acad., 1991. Pres. Yucaipa Literacy Coalition, 1991—; mem. Gen. Plan Adv. Com., Yucaipa, 1991—; centurion Calif. Coun. Adult Edn., sec. pres., 1974-75, pres., 1987-88. Fellow Robert Taft Inst., 1972. Mem. AAUW (Redlands br.), Assn. Calif. Sch. Adminstrs., Calif. Adult and Continuing Edn. Counselors Assn. (pres. 1983), Yucaipa Mgmt. Team (legislation chair 1989-90), Yucaipa C. of C., Calif. Coun. for Adult Edn. (Calif. coun. award 1978, Merit award 1988). Republican. Mem. Ch. of Christ. Home: 12941 Douglas St Yucaipa CA 92399-4856 Office: Yucaipa Adult Sch 12787 3rd St Yucaipa CA 92399-4544

REED, RAY PAUL, engineering mechanics measurement consultant; b. Abilene, Tex., May 26, 1927; s. Raymond Roseman and Gladys Daisy (Reddell) R.; m. Mary Antoinette Wied, Oct. 7, 1950; children: Mary Kathryn, Patricia Lynn. BSME, Tex. A&M U., 1950; MS in Engring. Mechanics, U. Tex., 1958, PhD, 1966. Registered profl. engr., N.Mex., Tex. Rsch. engr. S.W. Rsch. Inst., San Antonio, 1950-54; rsch. scientist U. Tex., Austin, 1954-56; mem. tech. staff Sandia Nat. Labs., Albuquerque, 1956-61, rsch. fellow, 1961-66, disting. mem. tech. staff, 1966-94. Author: manual on the use of thermocouples; contbr. numerous reports and articles on shock measurement and thermometry to profl. jours. With USNR, 1945-46, PTO. NIH grantee U. Tex., 1962-66. Mem. ASTM (chmn. com. 1985—), ASME, Instrument Soc. Am., Am. Physics Soc., Sigma Xi. Home and Office: Proteun Svcs 6640 Casa Loma NE Albuquerque NM 87109-3962

REED, ROBERT WILLIAM, city planner, educator; b. Cambridge, Mass., June 10, 1946; m. Diane C. Drigot, June 23, 1977 (div. Dec. 1989). BS in Econs., Cornell U., 1969; MS in Urban Planning, Wayne State U., 1973; PhD in Econs./Planning, U. Mich., 1979. Rsch. assoc. Johns Hopkins U., 1972-73; regional dir. Nat. Water Assessment, Washington, 1974-77; city planner City/County Honolulu, 1978-94; prof. econs. Hawaii Pacific U., Honolulu, 1994—; adj. prof. econs. Chaminade U., Honolulu, 1984—; adj. prof. bus. U. Hawaii, Manoa, 1986—; pres. R. W. Reed & Assocs., Honolulu, 1984—; cons. editor Irwin Pubs., Burr Ridge, Ill., 1991; advisor Internat. Joint Commn., Toronto, Can., 1974-77; cons. economist World Bank, Hong Kong, 1994. McVoy scholar Cornell U., 1966, Knickerbocker scholar, 1967. Mem. Sierra Club (exec. com. 1990-92), English Speaking Union, Honolulu Arts Acad., Honolulu Club, Hawaii Yacht Club, Waikiki Yacht Club. Republican. Home: 101 Ohana St Kailua HI 96734-2351

REEDER, RUSSELL ROBERT, automotive company executive, engineer; b. Laurel, Miss., June 28, 1952; s. Robert Roland and Laura Nonnie (Jordan) R.; m. Diane B. Burkes, Aug. 31, 1972; children: Richard, Russell. BS in Electronics Engring., Miss. State U., 1974; MBA in Mktg. and Fin., U. Wyo., 1977. Product engr., planning analyst Ford Motor Co., Dearborn, Mich., 1978-81; sr. sales engr. GTE/Sylvania, Dearborn, Mich., 1981-82; nat. sales mgr. Gen. Industries Co., Elyria, Ohio, 1982-84; chief import and joint venture programs Chrysler Corp., Auburn Hills, Mich., 1984-91; dir. product and strategic planning Hyundai Motor Am., Fountain Valley, Calif., 1991-93; pres., owner Am. Export Products, Irvine, Calif., 1994—; gen. mgr. Cardinal Automotive, L.A. Team capt. Nat. Multiple Sclerosis Soc., Irvine, 1992-93, Canning Hunger, Orange County chpt., Yorba Linda, Calif., 1993; mem. fin. com. Bethel Temple Ch., Parma, Ohio, 1983-84; chmn. sch. bd. Fairlane Christian Schs., Dearborn Heights, Mich., 1979-80. Capt. USAF, 1974-78. Mem. IEEE, Soc. Automotive Engrs., Soc. Audio Engrs., Toastmasters (pres. Hyundai chpt. 1992-93). Republican. Home: 1 Baristo Irvine CA 92715-2963

REEDER, SAMUEL KENNETH, analytical laboratory executive; b. Vinita, Okla., July 25, 1938; s. Dwight Cecil and Melba Mae (Mattox) R.; m. Camille Augusta Goepfert, Aug. 17, 1959; children: Jerold, Jeanne, Jodi. BA, La Sierra Coll., Riverside, Calif., 1960; PhD, Mont. State U., 1971. Tchr. Seventh-day Adventist Schs., San Diego and Springfield, Org., 1961-66; chief scientist R&D Sunkist Growers, Inc., Ontario, Calif., 1971-79; lab. mgr. R&D Beatrice/Hunt-Wesson, Inc., Fullerton, Calif., 1979-90; v.p. tech. svcs. C.L. Tech., Inc., Corona, Calif., 1990-94; lab. dir. C.L. tech. divsn. Microbac Analytic Svcs., Inc., Corona, Calif., 1994—. Contbr. sci. papers to profl. jours. Trustee Ontario City Libr., 1976-80, pres. bd. trustees, 1978-80. Recipient Bank of Am. award, 1956. Mem. Am. Chem. Soc., Inst. Food Technologists, Assn. Ofcl. Analytical Chemists (assoc.). Seventh-day Adventist. Home: 3253 Crystal Ridge Cir Corona CA 91720-7943 Office: C L Tech Inc 280 N Smith Ave Corona CA 91720-1740

REED-GRAHAM, LOIS L., administrator, secondary education educator; b. Muscogee, Okla., Jan. 19, 1933; d. Louis G. and Bonnie (Hill) Reed; children: Harold Gibson, Kathryn Ann Graham. RN, San Diego County Hosp., 1957; BA, Calif. State U., Sacramento, 1972, MPA, 1978; postgrad., Calif. State U., Sacremento; EdD, U. Laverne. Tchr., adminstr., job developer CETA, Sacramento, 1972-78; bus. instr. Los Rios Community Coll., Sacramento, 1978-84; tchr. grade 6 Mark Hopkins Sch., Sacramento, 1984-89; acting adminstr. Fern Bacon Sch., Sacramento; adminstr. Sacramento City Schs.; tchr. grades 7,8, mentor tchr. Fern Bacon Sch., Sacramento; asst. prin. secondary edn. Sacramento City Schs., 1989-93; elem. sch. prin. Theodore Judah Elem. Sch., Sacramento, 1993—; cons. Prentice Hall Pub. Co. Contbr. articles to profl. publs. Mem. Calif. State Fair Employment and Housing Commn. Mem. AAUW (bd. dirs., pres. Sacramento chpt. 1990), Nat. Assn. Univ. Women (pres.). Home: 7408 Toulon Ln Sacramento CA 95828-4641

REEL, JAMES, music critic, writer; b. Yuma, Ariz., May 2, 1958; s. Robert James Burton and Shirley Ray (Brown) Burton Hightower. BA, U. Ariz., 1979, MLS, 1980. Announcer arts producer KUAT Radio, Tucson, 1976-83, music dir., arts producer, 1983-88; classical music critic, feature writer Ariz. Daily Star, Tucson, 1988—. Author: The Timid Soul's Guide to Classical Music, 1992; program annotator: Ensemble 21, 1990-92; columnist, contbr. FanFare, 1991—. Recipient Project Reporting award Ariz. Press Club, 1991. Democrat. Office: Arizona Daily Star P O Box 26807 Tucson AZ 85726

REENSTJERNA, FREDERICK ROBERTS, librarian, writer; b. Lexington, S.C., Sept. 30, 1948; s. Otto Frederick and Miriam Swann (Roberts) R.; m. Hope Shields, June 3, 1971; 1 child, Elisabeth Shields. BA in Am. History, Coll. of Charleston, 1969; MLS, U. Md., 1971; M Adminstrn. in Human Resources, Lynchburg Coll., 1981; EdD, W.Va. U., 1991. Reference specialist congl. rsch. svc. Libr. of Congress, Washington, 1972-75; dir. Franklin County Libr., Rocky Mount, Va., 1975-77; br. libr. Hollins Br. Libr. Roanoke County (Va.) Pub. Libr., 1977-82, head reference main libr., 1982-84; bus. mgr. autism tng. ctr. Marshall U., Huntington, W.Va., 1984-86, asst. mgr. housing, 1986-88, head pub. svcs. Morrow Libr., 1989, asst. prof. instrnl. tech. Coll. Edn., 1989-90; freelance writer, Roseburg, Oreg., 1990-91; rsch. libr. Douglas County Mus., Roseburg, 1991—. Author: Library Survival Skills: A Guide to the Resources of the James Morrow Library, 1990, (with Jena Mitchell) Life in Douglas County, Oregon: The Western Experience, 1993; contbr. articles to various publs. Mem. needs task force Douglas County United Way, 1994. Mem. Am. Hist. Assn. Home: 964 SE Terrace Dr Roseburg OR 97470-4330 Office: Douglas County Mus PO Box 1550 1299 SW Medford Roseburg OR 97470

REES, NORMA S., university president, educator; b. N.Y.C., Dec. 27, 1929; d. Benjamin and Lottie (Schwartz) D.; m. Raymond R. Rees, Mar. 19, 1960; children—Evan Lloyd, Raymond Arthur. B.A., Queens Coll., 1952; M.A., Bklyn. Coll., 1954; Ph.D., NYU, 1959. Cert. speech-language pathology, audiology. Prof. communicative disorders Hunter Coll., N.Y.C., 1967-72; exec. officer, speech and hearing scis. grad. sch. CUNY, N.Y.C., 1972-74, assoc. dean for grad. studies, 1974-76, dean grad. studies, 1976-82; vice chancellor for acad. affairs U. Wis., Milw., 1982-85, from 1986, acting chancellor, 1985-86; vice chancellor for acad. policy and planning Mass. Bd. Regent for Higher Edn., Boston, 1987-90; pres. Calif. State U., Hayward, 1990—; bd. dirs. Coun. of Postsecondary Accreditation, Washington, 1985-94; chmn. Comm. Recognition of Postsecondary Accreditation, 1994—. Contbr. articles to profl. jours. Trustee Citizens Govtl. Rsch. Bur., Milw., 1985-87; active Task Force on Wis. World Trade Ctr., 1985-87; bd. dirs. Greater Boston YWCA, 1987-90; mem. Mayor's Cabinet Ednl. Excellence, Oakland, Calif.; mem. steering com. Econ. Devel. Adv. Bd. Alameda County, 1995—. Fellow Am. Speech-Lang-Hearing Assn. (honors); mem. Am. Coun. Edn. (com. internat. edn. 1991-93), Am. Assn. Colls. and Univs. (chair task force on quality assessment 1991-92, mem. steering com. of coun. of urban met. colls. & univs. 1992—), Nat. Assn. State Univs. and Land Grant Colls. (exec. com. divsn. urban affairs 1985-87, com. accreditation 1987-90). Office: Calif State Univ 25800 Carlos Bee Blvd Hayward CA 94542-3001

REES, RAYMOND F., military officer; b. Pendleton, Oreg., Sept. 29, 1944; s. Raymond Emmett and Lorna Doone (Gemmell) R.; m. Karen Kristine

Young, Nov. 1966 (div. Mar. 1974); children: Raymond Gordon, Christian Frederick; m. Mary Len Middleton, Dec. 30, 1977; 1 child, Carrie Evelyn. BS, U.S. Mil. Acad., 1966; JD, U. Oreg., 1976. Commd. 2d lt. U.S. Army, 1966; platoon leader, troop exec. officer, co. comdr. 2d Armored Cavalry Regiment, Bamberg, Fed. Republic Germany; resigned U.S. Army, 1973; with Oreg. Army Nat. Guard, 1973—, advanced through grades to maj. gen., 1990; asst. ops. officer Infantry Brigade; co. comdr. 2d Battalion, 162d Infantry, Corvallis, Oreg.; with 116th Armored Calvary Regiment, 1976-87; adjutant gen. Oreg. Army Nat. Guard, 1987-91; dir. Army N.G., 1991-92; vice chief N.G. Bur., Washington, 1992-94; adjutant gen. Oreg. N.G., 1994—. Decorated Bronze Star. Mem. Adjutant Gen. Assn. U.S., Nat. Guart Assn. U.S., Assn. of U.S. Army, Oreg. Nat. Guard Assn., U.S. Armor Assn., Oreg. Bar Assn., Am. Legion, Mil. Order World Wars, West Point Soc. Oreg., 101st Airborne Div. Assn., 116th Armored Cavalry Assn., 41st Infantry Div. Assn., Elks. Office: The Adjutant General P O Box 14350 1776 Militia Way Salem OR 97309-5047

REES, WILLIAM JAMES, dermatologist, consultant; b. Kansas City, Mo., July 13, 1922; s. John Archibald and Blanche Evelyn (Watson) R.; m. Marybeth Smith, Jan. 31, 1950; children: Virginia Lee, Diane Elizabeth, Carolyn Marie, Karen Jean, Mary Noel. BA, Rockhurst Coll., 1942; MD, St. Louis U., 1946; M in Pub. Health, U. Minn., 1950. Assoc. Am. Bd. Dermatology. Med. admimistrator Dept. of Army and Upjohn, Germany, Austria, U.S., 1952-61; clin. investigator Abbott Labs., North Chgo., Ill., 1961-63; resident in dermatology U. Calif. Med. Ctr., San Francisco, 1963-65; chmn. biomed. rsch. Stanford Rsch. Inst., Menlo Park, Calif., 1965-69; dir. life scis. Stanford Rsch. Inst., Zurich, Switzerland, 1969-71; asst. dir. Stanford Rsch. Inst., Washington, 1971-72; dir. internat. clin. rsch. G.D. Searle & Co., Chgo., 1972-83; dir. clin. rsch. Chemex Pharms., Denver, 1983-86; pres., mng. dir. Rhys Internat. Assocs., Edmonds, Wash., 1988—; cons. State of Calif. Div. Occupational Health, Berkeley, 1963-68; clin. instr. dermatology U. Calif. Med. Ctr., San Francisco, 1965-68, asst. prof., 1969-71. Col. U.S. Army, 1942-87, res. Mem. Am. Acad Dermatology (life, assoc.), Am. Acad. Med. Dirs., Am. Soc. Tropical Medicine and Hygiene, Am. Med. Soc. Vienna, Am. Pub. Health Assn., Assn. Mil. Dermatologists, Assn. of Mil. Surgeons U.S.; (charter) Am. Acad. Clin. Toxicology. Home: 550 Seamont Ln Edmonds WA 98020-4031 Office: Rhys Internat Assocs 9792 Edmonds Way Ste 248 Edmonds WA 98020-5940

REESE, DONNA LOUISE, speech language pathologist; b. Inglewood, Calif., Mar. 26, 1948; d. John George and Marjorie Louise (Churchill) P.; m. James Lynn Reese, June 14, 1970; children: Jonathan Matthew, Todd Ryan. BS in Speech-Hearing Disorders, Loma Linda U., 1970; MA in Speech-Pathology-Audiology, Calif. State U., Fullerton, 1971. Pathologist Hear Found., San Bernardino, 1969-70; sch. speech pathologist Riverside Unified Sch. Dist., 1970; outpatient and home visit specialist Riverside Community Hosp., 1972; spl. edn. tchr. San Bernardino (Calif.) County Schs., 1971-74; dir. speech rehab. Easter Seal Soc., San Bernardino, 1974; hosp. speech pathologist White Meml. Med. Ctr., L.A., 1976-78, Sonora (Calif.) Community Hosp., 1983; substitute spl. edn. tchr. Calavaras Office of Edn., Sonora, 1984-85; dir. profl. rels. Sonora Community Hosp., 1986-90; speech pathologist The Speech Path, Modesto, Turlock, Calif., 1993—; speech pathologist W.A.T.C.H. Adult Devel. Disabled Sheltered Workshop, Sonora, 1990-93, Tuolumne Gen. Hosp., Sonora, 1994—, 1st Am. Home Health, Sonora, 1994—. Campaigner/contbr. Rep. Presdl. Legion of Merit, 1992-94; vol. pilot Airlifeline, Sacramento, 1990—; neighbor vol. tchr., Sonora, 1982; contbr., cons. Rep. Adv. Com., Washington, 1992-94. Home: 18280 Avenida Bonita Sonora CA 95370-8740

REESE, DUDLEY, food products executive; b. 1958. Atty. Phila.; with Suma Fruit Internat. USA, Sanger, Calif. Office: Suma Fruit Internat USA 1810 Academy Ave Sanger CA 93657-3739*

REESE, JOHN ROBERT, lawyer; b. Salt Lake City, Nov. 3, 1939; s. Robert McCann and Glade (Stauffer) R.; m. Francesca Marroquin Gardner, Sept. 5, 1964 (div.); children—Jennifer Marie Gardner, Justine Francesca; m. Robin Ann Gunsul, June 18, 1988. AB cum laude, Harvard U., 1962; LLB, Stanford U., 1965. Bar: Calif. 1966, U.S. Dist. Ct. (no. dist.) Calif. 1966, U.S. Ct. Appeals (9th cir.) 1966, U.S. Dist. Ct. (cen. dist.) Calif. 1974, U.S. Supreme Ct. 1976, U.S. Dist. Ct. (ea. dist.) Calif. 1977, U.S. Ct. Appeals (6th cir.) 1982, U.S. Ct. Appeals (8th cir.) 1985, U.S. Ct. Appeals (10th cir.) 1992, U.S. Ct. Appeals (Fed. cir.) 1994. Assoc. McCutchen, Doyle, Brown & Enersen, San Francisco, 1965-74, ptnr., 1974—; adj. asst. prof. law Hastings Coll. of Law, 1991; lectr. U. Calif., Berkeley, 1987, 92. Mem. editorial, adv. bds. Antitrust Bull., Jour. Reprints for Antitrust Law and Econs. Bd. dirs. Friends of San Francisco Pub. Libr., 1981-87; bd. vis. Stanford U., 1983-86. Capt. U.S. Army, 1966-68. Decorated Bronze Star. Mem. ABA, State Bar Calif., San Francisco Bar Assn., U.S. Supreme Ct. Hist. Soc., Ninth Jud. Cir. Hist. Soc., Calif. Acad. Appellate Lawyers, Order of the Coif. Home: 9 Morning Sun Dr Petaluma CA 94952-4780 Office: McCutchen Doyle Brown & Enersen 3 Embarcadero Ctr San Francisco CA 94111-4003

REESE, MONTE NELSON, agricultural association executive; b. Mooreland, Okla., Mar. 31, 1947; s. James Nelson and Ruby Edith (Bond) R.; m. Treisa Lou Bartow, May 25, 1968; children: Bartow Allan, Monica Lynnelle. BS in Agrl. Econs., Okla. State U., 1969. Staff asst. Wilson Cert. Foods, Oklahoma City, 1969-71; assoc. farm dir. Sta. WKY Radio and TV, Oklahoma City, 1971-73; radio-TV specialist Tex. A&M U., College Station, 1973; dir. agrl. devel. Oklahoma City C. of C., 1973-76; asst. exec. dir. Am. Morgan Horse Assn., Westmoreland, N.Y., 1976-77; v.p. pub. affairs Farm Credit Banks of Wichita, Kans., 1977-87; exec. dir. Coffey County Econ. Devel., Burlington, Kans., 1987-88; farm dir. Mid-Am. Ag Network, Wichita, 1988-89; CEO Cattlemen's Beef Promotion and Rsch. Bd., Englewood, Colo., 1989—. Lt. comdr. USAR, 1969—. Home: 982 S Dearborn Way Apt 2 Aurora CO 80012-3878 Office: Cattlemen's Beef Promotion and Rsch Bd PO Box 3316 Englewood CO 80155*

REEVES, BILLY DEAN, obstetrics/gynecology educator emeritus; b. Franklin Park, Ill., Jan. 17, 1927; s. Barney William and Martha Dorcus (Benbrook) R.; m. Phyllis Joan Faber, Aug. 25, 1951; children: Philip, Pamela, Tina, Brian, Timothy. BA, Elmhurst (Ill.) Coll., 1953; BS, U. Ill., Chgo., 1958, MD, 1960; post grad., UCLA, N.Mex. State U., 1953-54, 75-76. Diplomate Am. Bd. Ob-Gyn. Intern Evanston (Ill.) Hosp., 1960-61, resident ob-gyn., 1961-64; NIH fellow in reproductive endocrinology Karolinska Hosp. and Inst., Stockholm, 1968-69; pvt. practice Evanston, 1964-71, Las Cruces, N.Mex., 1972-77; from instr. to asst. prof. Dept. Ob-gyn. Northwestern U. Med. Sch., 1964-71; assoc. prof. Dept. Ob-gyn. Rush Med. Coll., Chgo., 1971-72; clin. assoc. in ob-gyn. U. N.Mex. Med. Sch., Albuquerque, 1972-77; clin. assoc. U. Ariz. Sch. Medicine, Tucson, 1975-78; from clin. prof. to prof. emeritus Tex. Tech. Med. Sch., El Paso, 1976-91. Contbr. 70 articles and chpts. to med., profl. jours., 1958-93. Adv. bd. Associated Home Health Svcs., Inc., Las Cruces; adv. com. N.Mex. State U. Nursing Sch.; community adv. com. Meml. Gen. Hosp., Las Cruces; tech. advisor on health edn. N.Mex. Health Systems Agy.; mem. N.Mex. State U. Task Force 88; bd. dirs. Meml. Med. Ctr, Los Cruces, 1989-91, Parenthood Edn. Assn. of El Paso, Inc., Planned Parenthood of South Ctrl. N.Mex. (chmn. med. adv. com.). With USNR, 1945-46, 82-88, U.S. Army, 1946-47. Recipient Elmhurst Coll. Alumni Merit award, 1990, William W. Fry award for profl. excellence Tex. Tech. U. Sch. Medicine, 1979. Mem. AMA, ACS, AAAS, ACOG, Am. Coll. Physician Execs., Am. Assn. Advancement Humanities, Am. Fertility Soc., Assn. Profs. Ob-Gyn., North Am. Ob-Gyn. Soc., Ctrl. Assn. Ob-Gyn., Chgo. Gyn. Soc., Com. for Philosophy in Medicine, Dona Ana County Med. Soc. (assoc.), El Paso County Med. Soc., El Paso Surg. Soc., Endocrine Soc., Inst. Medicine in Chgo., Hasting Ctr., N.Mex. Med. Soc. (assoc.), N.Mex. Ob-Gyn. Soc., Soc. for Health and Human Values, Tex. Med. Assn., Tex. Assn. Ob-Gyn., U.S.-Mexico Border Health Assn. Home: 1620 Altura Ave Las Cruces NM 88001-1532

REEVES, BRUCE, social worker; b. Centerville, Utah, Jan. 8, 1955; s. Leon W. and Maxine (Hodson) R. BA, U. Utah, 1979, MSW, 1983. Mental health caseworker Traveler's Aid Soc. Salt Lake, Salt Lake City, 1983-86; socialwork cons. Home Health of Utah, Bountiful, 1985-86; victim svcs. counselor Salt Lake County Atty's. Office, Salt Lake City, 1986-87; dir., mgr., cons. AIDS assistance program Aetna and Human Affairs Internat., Salt Lake City, 1987—; presenter in field. Bd. dirs. Walk-ons, Inc., Salt Lake City, 1989—; mem. appropriations com. United Way Greater Salt Lake, Salt Lake City, 1990—, bd. assocs. Ririe-Woodbury Dance Co., Salt Lake City, 1991—, human svcs. com. Utah Stonewall Ctr., Salt Lake City, 1992—. Mem. NASW, APHA. Democrat. Office: Aetna/HAI 488 E 6400 S # 300 Salt Lake City UT 84107

REEVES, CAROL SWOPE, marriage and family counselor; b. Lexington, Ky., June 26, 1927; d. Roger Hunt and Wanda Lee (Wible) Swope; m. John Thomas Reeves, Oct. 20, 1956; children: Charlotte Reeves Clark, Catherine Reeves Anderson, Beth Davidson. BS in Med. Tech., U. Ky., 1949; MA in Guidance and Counseling, U. Colo., 1986. Lic. profl. counselor, Colo. Counselor Faith Presbyn. Ch., Denver, 1986-88, Care & Counsel, London, 1988-89, Inner City Health Ctr., Denver, 1990—, Hope Communities, Denver, 1993—; workshop facilitator Christian Impact, London, 1988-89, Myers-Briggs Type Indicator Community Bldg. Conflict Resolution, Faith Presbyn. Ch., Denver, 1986-88, Cherry Creek Presbyn., Denver, 1989-90, Bros. Redevel., Denver, 1993. Exhibited paintings in various one-woman and group shows. Docent Denver Art Mus., 1975—; fundraiser Hope Communities, Denver, 1989-90. Recipient various awards for paintings. Mem. ACA, 1993-94.

REEVES, DANIEL MORTON, shotgun shooting coach, writer; b. South Gate, Calif., Oct. 16, 1948; s. Norman Ives Reeves and Amy Elsie (Whitlock) Hopper; m. Merlyn Irene Latham, Fed. 10, 1968; 1 child, Spencer Latham. Grad. high sch., Manhattan Beach, Calif. Profl. shotgun shooting competitor, 1971—; shotgun shooting instr. Torrance, Calif., 1974—; shotgun shooting exhib. performer Torrance, 1976—, shotgun shooting coach world and olympic levels, 1984—; owner HIP SHOT! PRODNS., Torrance, 1986—; exclusive rep. ball trap events in the U.S., Fedn. Française de tir Profl., Paris, 1991—; coach, team photographer U.S. Team Internat. Skeet, 1991; mem. test staff Bob Allen Sportswear, 1986—, spokesperson, keynote speaker, 1990; capt. team remington Remington Firearms, 1987-88; designer, cons. sporting clay layouts world wide; spokesperson, keynote speaker ACTIV Industries, Inc., 1990, N.Am. Game Breeder's Assn., 1988, Du Pont Fish and Game club, 1988; cons. shotgun configuration and fabrication, Perazzi Gun Mfg., Italy, 1989—; cons. nat. and internat. ammunition mfrs., 1988—; instr. Beginning Anti-aircraft Shooting Marine Corps, Camp Pendleton, CAlif., 1981, instr. advanced shotgun tactics Gadena Calif. Police Dept. and L.A. Sheriff's Dept., 1981; cons. shotgun shooting tng. program U.S. Secret Svc., 1990—. Contributing editor: Shotgun Sports mag., 1988—, Guns & Ammo mag., 1989—; editor, featured instr. (video) Introduction to Sporting Clays, 1988; performer numerous shooting exhbns. including command performances for royalty and governments, Eng., France, Switzerland, 1987-91, Barron Hilton's Flying M Ranch, 1989, James River Corp.'s Upper Brandon Plantation, Va., 1989, Hil 'n Dale Club, Medina, Ohio, 1989, West Midlands Shooting Grounds, Eng., 1988, SKAT Upland Game Preserve, N.H., 1987, Game Hill Hunting Preserve, Mo., 1987, Shooting and Hunting Sports Fair, Phoenix, Ariz., 1987, Minn. Horse and Hunt Club, 1987, North Iowa Sporting Clays, St. Ansgar, Iowa, 1987, Migdale Pvt. Shooting Club, Millbrokk, N.Y., 1987; perfomer numerous radio and TV shows including Ted Dawson's Sports Show, 1985, Bob Uecker's Wacky World of Sports, 1986, Japan's Encyclopedia of the Fantastic, 1987, German TV Sports Show, Swedish TV Sports Show, 1988, That's Incredible, 1984, 88, StarShot, 1987-91; contbr. articles to profl. jours. Performer, pub. speaker Paralyzed Vets. Assn., performer Annual Muscular Dystrophy Benefit, Chino, Calif., 1987; pub. speaker Kiwanis, Rotary. Recipient Bronze medal Open de France, 1990, First Place Colo. State Sporting Clays Championship, 1987, Bronze medal Across the Seas Brit. Open Sporting Clays Championship, 987, First Place Pennsport Shooting Grounds, 1987, Team U.S.A. Gold medals Ball Trap Pro Flash Cup French Fedn. Profl. Shooters, 1991, 90, Bronze Team medal Beretta World Sporting Clays Championships, 1988. Mem. NRA (life), Calif. Rifle and Pistol Assn. (life), Nat. Skeet Shooting Assn. (life), U.S. Sporting Clays Assn. (life, chief shooting instr. 1987-90), Nat. Sporting Clays Assn., Ducks Unltd., Quail Unltd. Office: Hip Shot! Prodns 4017 Emerald St Torrance CA 90503-3103

REEVIS, MAUREEN PATRICIA, academic adminstrator; b. Missoula, Mont., Nov. 13, 1946; d. James Edward Sullivan and Theresa Marie (Martin) Woolery; widowed; children: Cynthia Diane, Brenna Colleen, William Patrick; m. Roger D. Reevis. BA in English, Ea. Wash. U., 1983, postgrad.; postgrad., Mont. State U., 1985-86, 94—, U. Okla., Mankato State U., 1990-91. Organizer Welfare Rights Orgn., Spokane, Wash., 1970-75; worker Spokane Falls Community Coll., 1973-75; tutor Ft. Wright Coll. Holy Names, Spokane, 1975-77; Title IV programmer Spokane Sch. Dist., 1979-81; substitute tchr. Loyola-Sacred Heart High Sch., Missoula, 1984-85; instr. reading Blackfeet Community Coll., Browning, Mont., 1985-86, grants writer, 1986, program dir., mem. devel. com., 1986; pres., founder, ednl./bus. cons., ptnr. Bus./Ednl. Cons., Ink, Spokane, Wash., 1989—; founder SunEagle, alt. edn. program, Mead, Wash., 1989—; supervising trainer Laubach Literacy Internat., Browning, 1985—, bd. dirs., 1985-86; tutor Blackfeet Literacy Program, Browning, 1985—, lead trainer, 1986—, pres., 1985-86; cons. Spokane Alliance for the Mentally Ill, Conf. for Ethnic Mental Health Svcs., Spokane Commn. Mental Health Ctr. Cons. Blackfeet C.C. libr., 1994—; mem. steering and substance coms., task force Greater Spokane Abuse Coun., 1989—; founder Sun Eagle, 1990—; bd. dirs., co-founder N.W. Intertribal Ctr., 1992—; mem. adv. bd. for mental health Protection & Advocacy Intervention for the Mentally Ill, Mont., 1993—. Grantee Quill Found., 1989-90. Mem. NAFE, Internat. Reading Assn., Nat. Indian Edn. Assn., Mont. Indian Edn. Assn., Minn. Indian Edn. Assn. Democrat. Bahai. Home: 115 N Charlo Box 121 Charlo MT 59824 Office: SunEagle 112 31st Ave S Seattle WA 98144-2512

REFF, MITCHELL ELLIOT, pharmaceutical company administrator; b. Queens, N.Y., May 16, 1951; s. Victor Hugo and Miriam (Atlas) R.; m. Miyo Ellen Tanaka, Oct. 1, 1977; children: Brian, Jeremy. BS in Chemistry, MIT, 1973; PhD in Med. Microbiology, Stanford U., 1976. Postdoctoral rsch. fellow Harvard Med. Sch., Boston, 1976-79; staff scientist Davis Inst. on Aging, Denver, 1979-80; asst. prof. U. Colo. Health Scis. Ctr., Denver, 1979-81; spl. asst. to assoc. dir. BCRM, Nat. Inst. on Aging/NIH, Bethesda, Md., 1980-81; sr. staff fellow Nat. Cancer Inst., Bethesda, 1981-82; sr. investigator SmithKline & French Labs., Phila., 1982-85, asst. dir., 1985-90; dir. gene expression IDEC Pharms. Corp., San Diego, 1990-94, sr. dir. gene expression, 1994—; adj. asst. prof. Temple U. Sch. Medicine, Phila., 1983-90. Contbr. articles to profl. jours. USPHS trainee, 1974-76. Jewish. Home: 4166 Combe Way San Diego CA 92122-2511 Office: IDEC Pharms Corp 11011 Torreyana Rd San Diego CA 92121-1104

REFVEM, ROBERT LOREN, sculptor; b. Frankfort, S.D., Dec. 25, 1933; s. Loren Elwood Refvem and Lois Alma (Phillips) Stoen; divorced; 1 child, Robert Loren. Recipient Isenburg Sculpture award Salmagundi Club, 1986, Joel Metsner award Salmagundi Club, 1987, Philip Isenberg award Allied Artists Am., 1988, Stanziani award Allied Artists Am., 1991, Best of Show-Bird Sculpture award N.Am. Wildlife Art Show, 1991, 92, 94, Leonard J. Meiselman prize Nat. Sculpture Soc., 1994. Mem. Allied Artists of Am., Am. Artists Profl. League, Soc. Animal Artists. Republican. Home and Office: 5113 Greenview Ct Fort Collins CO 80525

REGENSBURGER, LINDA SUSAN, public relations consultant, writer; b. Bklyn., Mar. 24, 1953; d. Robert Homer and Lorraine Bremers (Jarrett) Garrison; m. Keith A. Regensburger, Aug. 5, 1978; children: Drew Evan, Devin Rachel. BA, Met. State Coll., 1982. Journalist Sentinel Pub. Co., Denver, 1979-82; pub. relations coordinator Fuller Theol. Sem., Pasadena, Calif., 1982-84; pub. affairs mgr. Calif. State U., L.A., 1984-86; communications analyst So. Calif. Automobile Club, L.A., 1986-88; prin. Linda S. Regensburger Pub. Rels., Denver, 1988—. Writer Pasadena Jour. Bus., 1982-88; contbr. articles to mags. Vol. Am. Cancer Soc., Pasadena, 1985-88, Pasadena Centennial Com., 1986, Nat. Marrow Donor Program, 1991. Recipient Cert. of Achievement, Nat. Marrow Donor Program, 1991. Mem. Pub. Rels. Soc. Am. (accredited, Award of Merit 1991, Prism award 1993). Democrat. Episcopalian.

REGET, IONE HOZENDORF, business services company executive, enrolled agent; b. Jackson, Miss., Sept. 19, 1937; d. Glenn Frederick and Ione Belle (Lowry) Hozendorf; m. Francis John Reget, Jan. 17, 1967 (div. 1986); m. Charles Drago Misetich, May 28, 1993; children: Diane Michele, Philip Francis, Michael Trahern. B.A. cum laude, U. Minn., 1959. CFP. Pres., Ea. Sierra Bus. Svcs., Inc., Bishop, Calif., 1980—; sec.-treas. Meyer Cookie Co., Inc. Soprano, Bishop Cmty. Chorus, 1974-78; treas. Calvary Bapt. Ch., Bishop, 1975—, choir dir., 1980—; chmn. Civic Arts Commn., City of Bishop, 1984-87; bd. dirs. Inyo Council for the Arts, 1987-90; pres. Bishop Com. Concert Assn., 1989—. Mem. Nat. Assn. Enrolled Agts., Calif. Soc. Enrolled Agts., Calif. Assn. Ind. Accts., Internat. Assn. Fin. Planners, Inst. CFP, Aircraft Owners and Pilots Assn., DAR, Mensa, Playhouse 395, Bishop Toastmasters Club, Bishop Rotary Club. Republican. Home: 146 North St RR 1 Bishop CA 93514-0728 Office: 130 Short St Bishop CA 93514-3538 Address: PO Box 728 Bishop CA 93515-0728

REGINATO, ROBERT JOSEPH, soil scientist; b. Palo Alto, Calif., Apr. 13, 1935; s. Guiseppe Primo and Carolina Theresa (Boccignone) R.; m. Donna Marie LeStum, Aug. 26, 1956; children: Richard Lynn, David Lewis, Christopher Michael, Michael Jeffrey. B.S., U. Calif., Davis, 1957; M.S., U. Ill., 1959; Ph.D., U. Calif., Riverside, 1973. Rsch. asst. U. Calif., Davis, 1956-57, U. Ill., Urbana, 1957-59; soil scientist U.S. Water Conservation Lab., USDA-Agrl. Rsch. Svc., Phoenix, 1959-89 , rsch. leader, 1980-89; assoc. dir. Pacific W. Area USDA Agrl. Rsch. Svc., Albany, Calif., 1989-91, dir., 1991—; vis. scientist U. Calif., Davis, 1977-78; USDA collaborator U. Ariz., Tucson, 1959-89. Contbr. over 180 articles to tech. jours. Active Roosevelt coun. Boy Scouts Am., 1960-76. Fellow Am. Soc. Agronomy, Soil Sci. Soc. Am.; mem. Am. Geophys. Union, Internat. Soil Sci. Soc., Western Soil Sci. Soc., Sigma Xi, Alpha Zeta, Kappa Sigma. Roman Catholic. Home: 1494 London Cir Benicia CA 94510-1353 Office: Pacific West Area 800 Buchanan St Berkeley CA 94710-1105

REHG, KENNETH LEE, linguistics educator; b. East St. Louis, Ill., Nov. 21, 1939; s. Theophil Albert and Kathryn Louise (George) R.; 1 child, Laura Le'olani. BA, U. Ill., 1962; MA, So. Ill. U., 1965; PhD, U. Hawaii, 1986. Tng. officer Internat. Ctr. for Lang. Studies, Washington, 1966-67; lang. officer U.S. Peace Corp, Saipan, Micronesia, 1967-70; asst. rschr. social sci. rsch. inst. U. Hawaii, Honolulu, 1974-83, asst. prof., 1984—; cons. Micronesian govt., 1973-76, Samoa Dept. Edn., Pago Pago, 1978, U.S. Geol. Survey, Menlo Park, Calif., 1979-81, Japan Nat. Mus. Ethnology, Osaka, 1986; participant Fulbright-Hays Study Group, Ea. Indonesia, 1991. Author: Ponapean Reference Grammar, 1981; co-author: Kitail Lokaiahn Pohnpei, 1969, Ponapean-English Dictionary, 1979; mng. editor Oceanic Linguistics; contbr. articles to profl. jours. Rsch. fellow U. Hawaii, 1981-82; recipient Excellence in Teaching award Hawaii Tchrs. ESL, 1984, Mortar Bd., 1990. Mem. Linguistic Soc. Am., Linguistic Soc. Hawaii. Office: U Hawaii Dept Linguistics Moore Hall 569 1890 E West Rd Honolulu HI 96822-2318

REHM, MAURICE PATE, drama and classics educator, actor, director; b. Sept. 9, 1949; s. Maurice Pate and June Adams Rehm. BA in Creative Writing and Classics summa cum laude, Princeton U., 1973; MA in Classical Studies, Melbourne U., 1975; PhD in Drama and Humanities, Stanford U., 1985. Asst. prof. drama and classics Emory U., Atlanta, 1985-89; asst. prof. drama, asst. prof. classics Stanford U., 1990-95, assoc. prof., 1995—; presenter at confs. Dir. plays including Electra, The Oresteia, The Homecoming, Emperor Jones, Brand, Curse of the Starving Class, A Joy Forever, The Iliad, Persians, Macbeth, The Odyssey, The Suppliant Women; acted in plays including Twelfth Night, Tales from Vienna Woods, King Lear, The Alchemist, The Miracle of Greece; author: The Oresteia Trilogy, 1978, Greek Tragic Theatre, 1994, Marriage to Death, 1994; actor Pygmalion, 1972, The Rainmaker, 1972, Twelfth Night, 1972, Othello, 1975, Yankee Doodle Show, 1976, Measure for Measure, 1977, Tales from Vienna Woods, 1980, King Lear, 1982, The Good Soul of Setzuan, 1982, Singapore Sling, 1983, The Changeling, 1985, St. Joan of the Stockyards, 1986, Brand, 1986, Waiting for Godot, 1989, The Miracle of Greece, 1992; contbr. articles to profl. jours. Nat. Merit scholar, 1968-72; Fulbright-Hays fellow, 1973-75; Felix Meyer scholar, 1978-79; Whiting fellow, 1984-85; NEH summer stipend, 1986; ACLS grantee, 1987-88; Lila Wallace-Readers Digest Arts Ptnrs. grantee, 1993, others. Mem. Am. Philol. Assn., Phi Beta Kappa, others. Home: 835 Lakeview Way Redwood City CA 94062 Office: Dept Drama Stanford CA 94305-5010

REHORN, LOIS MARIE SMITH, nursing administrator; b. Larned, Kans., Apr. 15, 1919; d. Charles and Ethel L. (Canaday) Williamson; m. C. Howard Smith, Feb. 15, 1946 (dec. Aug. 1980); 1 child, Cynthia A. Huddleston; m. Harlan W. Rehorn, Aug. 25, 1981. RN, Bethany Hosp. Sch. Nursing, Kansas City, Kans., 1943; BS, Ft. Hays Kans. State U., Hays, 1968, MS, 1970. RN, N.Mex. Office nurse, surg. asst. Dr. John H. Luke, Kansas City, Kans., 1943-47; supr. nursing unit Larned (Kans.) State Hosp., 1949-68, dir. nursing edn., 1968-71, dir. nursing, 1972-81, ret., 1981. Named Nurse of Yr. DNA-4, 1986. Mem. Am. Nurses Assn., Kans. Nurses Assn. (dist. treas.), N.Mex. Nurses Assn. (dist. pres. 1982-86, dist. bd. dirs. 1992-94). Home: 1436 Brentwood Dr Clovis NM 88101-4602

REHR, JOHN J., physicist, educator; b. Carlisle, Pa., May 6, 1945; s. John J. and Florence M. (Ruhl) R.; m. Sherry A. Shopp, April 27, 1966; children: Jesse, Amanda. BSE, U. Mich., 1967; PhD, Cornell U., 1972. Prof. physics U. Washington, Seattle, 1975—; cons. prof. Stanford Synchrotron Radiation Lab., Calif., 1993—. Editor: XAFS V: Proceedings of the 5th Internat. Conf., 1989; contb. to profl. jours. Office: U Washington Physics FM 15 Seattle WA 98195

REIBER, GREGORY DUANE, forensic pathologist; b. Loma Linda, Calif., May 25, 1955; s. Clifford D. and Anna M. (Field) R.; m. Faustina Mae Davis, Feb. 10, 1980; children: Jenessa Anne, Zachary Duane. BS magna cum laude, Andrews U., Berrien Springs, Mich., 1977; MD, Loma Linda (Calif.) U., 1981. Diplomate Am. Bd. Pathology. Resident in pathology Loma Linda U. Med. Ctr., 1981-85; fellow in forensic pathology Root Pathology Lab., San Bernardino, Calif., 1985-86; assoc. pathologist Root Pathology Lab., 1986-90, No. Calif. Forensic Pathology, Sacramento, 1990—; asst. clin. prof. pathology Loma Linda U. Sch. Medicine, 1987-90, U. Calif., Davis, 1990—; apptd. Calif. SIDS Autopsy Protocol Com. Contbr. articles to profl. jours. Fellow Am. Soc. Clin. Pathologists; mem. Am. Bd. Forensic Examiners, AMA, Internat. Wound Ballistics Assn., Nat. Assn. Med. Examiners, Am. Acad. Forensic Scis., N.Y. Acad. Sci., Calif. Med. Assn., Sacramento-El Dorado Med. Soc., Alpha Omega Alpha. Republican. Seventh-day Adventist. Office: No Calif Forensic Pathology 2443 Fair Oaks Blvd Ste 311 Sacramento CA 95825-7684

REICH, SIMEON, mathematics researcher, educator; b. Cracow, Poland, Aug. 12, 1948; came to U.S., 1975; s. Moshe and Amalia (Alter) R.; m. Hayuta Cohen, Mar. 26, 1974; children: Uri, Daphna, Shelley. BSc summa cum laude, Israel Inst. Tech., Haifa, 1970, DSc, 1973. Lectr. Tel Aviv (Israel) U., 1973-75; L. E. Dickson instr. U. Chgo., 1975-77; asst. prof. U. So. Calif., L.A., 1977-79, assoc. prof., 1979-84, prof., 1984--; vis. scientist Argonne (Ill.) Nat. Lab., 1978; vis. assoc. prof. U. Calif., Berkeley, 1981; acting chmn. dept. of math. U. So. Calif., L.A., 1983-84; prof. Israel Inst. Tech., Haifa, 1987-90, 92—. Co-author: Uniform Convexity, Hyperbolic Geometry and Nonexpansive Mappings, 1984; co-editor: Optimization and Nonlinear Analysis, 1992; author 160 rsch. papers. NSF rsch. grantee, 1976-84, U. So. Calif. faculty rsch. grantee, 1983-84, 1993—, grantee San Diego SuperComputer Ctr., 1987-91. Mem. Am. Math. Soc., Math. Assn. Am., Soc. for Indsl. and Applied Math. Office: Univ So Calif Dept Math Los Angeles CA 90089

REICHARD, GARY WARREN, university administrator, history educator; b. Phila., Nov. 23, 1943; s. David Carl and Gabrielle Rosalind (Doane) R.; m. Marcia Ann King, Aug. 7, 1965 (div. 1978); children: Jennifer D., James J. BA, Coll. of Wooster (Ohio), 1965; MA, Vanderbilt U., Nashville, 1966; postgrad., Ohio U., 1966-67; PhD, Cornell U., 1971. Instr. history Coll. of Wooster, 1967-69; asst. prof. to assoc. prof. history, chmn. dept. Ohio State U., Columbus, 1971-82; assoc. prof. history and dir. univ. honors program U. Del., Newark, 1983-85; assoc. vice chancellor for acad. affairs, assoc. prof. hist. U. Md., College Park, 1985-89; prof. history and dean undergrad. studies Fla. Atlantic U., Boca Raton, Fla., 1989-92; chmn. dept. history Fla. Atlantic U., Boca Raton, 1992-94; assoc. vice pres. acad. affairs, prof. history Calif. State U., Long Beach, 1994—. Assoc. editor Ency. of Am. Legislative System; reviewer numerous comml. and univ. presses; author: The Reaffirmation of Republicanism, 1975, Politics as Usual, 1988; co-author; America: Changing Times, 1979, 2d edit., 1982; co-editor: Reshaping America, 1982, American Choices, 1986, American Issues, 1988, 2d edit., 1994; contbr.

articles to profl. jours. Moody rsch. grantee Lyndon B. Johnson found., 1977, Harry S. Truman Libr. Inst. rsch. grantee, 1979, Congl. Leadership rsch. grantee, 1981, Carl Albert Congl. rsch. grantee, 1993, Minn. Hist. Soc. grantee, 1993. Mem. Am. Assn. Higher Edn., Am. Hist. Assn., Orgn. Am. Historians, Immigration Hist. Soc., Phi Beta Kappa, Phi Kappa Phi. Office: Calif State U Long Beach Divsn Acad Affairs 1250 N Bellflower Blvd Long Beach CA 90840-0006

REICHARTZ, W. DAN, hotel executive; b. 1946. Exec. Hilton Hotels Corp., N.Y.C., 1965-76, 85-86; pres., treas. Va. Hot Springs Inc., Hot Springs Telephone Co. & Devel. Co., 1976-85; pres., CEO Caesars Palace, Las Vegas, 1987—. Office: Caesars Palace 3570 Las Vegas Blvd S Las Vegas NV 89109-8924

REICHBACH, NAOMI ESTELLE, social service administrator; b. N.Y.C., Apr. 19, 1934; d. Nathaniel S. and Sara (Hirsch) R. BS in Edn., SUNY, New Paltz, 1955; MS in Spl. Edn., CCNY, 1969. Tchr. Shield Inst., Bronx, N.Y., 1956-58; tchr., parent educator Shield Inst., 1961-63; head tchr., program developer Oakland (Calif.) Unified Sch. Dist., 1959-60; edn. dir. N.Y.C. Assn. Retarded Children, 1963-67, 1967-69; co-founder, exec. dir. Burt Children Ctr., Psychiatric Residential Treatment Ctr. and Sch., San Francisco, 1969—. Fellow Am. Orthopsychiat. Assn., Royal Soc. Health; mem. Calif. Svcs. for Children. Office: Burt Ctr 940 Grove St San Francisco CA 94117-1714

REICHEK, JESSE, artist; b. Bklyn., Aug. 16, 1916; s. Morris and Celia (Bernstein) R.; m. Laure Guyot, May 16, 1950; children—Jonathan, Joshua. Student, Inst. Design, Chgo., 1941-42; diploma, Academie Julian, Paris, 1951. Instr. dept. architecture U. Mich., Ann Arbor, 1946-47; prof. Inst. Design Ill. Inst. Tech., Chgo., 1951-53; prof. dept. architecture U. Calif., Berkeley, 1953-87, prof. emeritus, 1987—; cons. Nat. Design Inst. Ford Found. project, Ahmedabad, India, 1963, San Francisco Redevel. Agy. Embarcadero Center, 1966—; lectr. Nat. Inst. Architects, Rome, 1960, U. Florence, 1960, U. Naples, 1960, Israel Inst. Tech., 1960, Greek Architects Soc., Athens, 1960, U. Belgrade, 1960, MIT, 1965, U. N.Mex., 1964, Am. Cultural Center, Paris, 1960, 64, Gujarat Inst. Engrs. and Architects, 1963, U. Colo., 1961, Harvard, 1962, U. Minn., 1962, U. Coll. London, 1967, Inst. Contemporary Arts, London, 1967, Ecole Nationale des Beaux-Ats, 1967; artist in residence Tamarind Lithography Workshop, 1966, Am. Acad. in Rome, 1971-72; research prof. Creative Arts Inst. U. Calif., 1966-67; artist in residence IBM Los Angeles Sci. Center, 1970-71. Exhibited one man shows at, Galerie Cahiers d'Art Paris, 1951, 59, 68, U. Calif. at Berkeley, 1954, Betty Parsons Gallery, N.Y.C., 1958, 59, 63, 65, 67, 69, 70, Molton Gallery, London, 1962, Am. Culture Center, Florence, Italy, 1962, Bennington Coll., 1963, U. N.Mex., 1966, U. So. Calif., 1967, Axiom Gallery, London, 1968, Yoseido Gallery, Tokyo, 1968, Los Angeles County Mus. Art, 1971; exhibited in group shows, Bklyn. Mus., 1959, Mus. Modern Art, N.Y.C., 1962, 65, 69, Knox-Albright Art Gallery, 1962, Art Inst. Chgo., 1963, Cin. Art Mus., 1966, Balt. Art Mus., 1966, Yale Art Gallery, 1967, Grand Palais, Paris, 1970, Nat. Mus. Art, Santiago, Chile, 1970, art and tech. exhibit, Los Angeles County Mus. Art, 1971, Maeght Found., St. Paul de Vence, France, 1971, Mus. Modern Art, Paris, 1971; represented in permanent collections, Mus. Modern Art, Art Inst. Chgo., Bibliotheque Nationale, Paris, Victoria & Albert Mus., London, Los Angeles County Art Mus., Grunwald Graphic Arts Found., U. Calif. at Los Angeles, San Diego Mus. Art, Amon Carter Mus., Fort Worth; Author: Jesse Reichek-Dessins, 1960, La Monte de la Nuit, 1961, Fontis, 1961, Etcetera, 1965, Le Bulletin Des Baux, 1972; e.g., 1976. Served to capt. C.E. AUS, 1942-46. Home: 5925 Red Hill Rd Petaluma CA 94952-9437

REICHEL, JOHN KENTO, medical care organization official, writer; b. Oakland, Calif., Dec. 28, 1959; s. David and Hisae (Kawashima) R. BA, U. Calif., Berkeley, 1982. Lab. asst. Kaiser Permanente Med. Care Program, Berkeley, 1978-84; editor Kaiser Permanente Med. Care Program, Oakland, Calif., 1984-91; standards analyst, contbr. to corp. mag. Kaiser Permanente Med. Care Program, Walnut Creek, Calif., 1991—; advisor to editor Teen Assn. Model Railroaders, Oakland, 1990—. Contbr. music revs. and articles to various publs. Named Pivot Pin, Teen Assn. Model Railroaders. Democrat. Home: 1800 E 38th St Oakland CA 94602-1720

REICHEL, PHILIP LEE, sociology educator; b. Bakersfield, Calif., Oct. 8, 1946; s. Joseph J. and Virginia (Spry) R.; m. Paula Jean Hauschild, June 1969 (div. 1980); children: Scott Andrew, Matthew Jason; m. Eva Maria Jewell, Dec. 15, 1983. BS, Nebr. Wesleyan U., 1969; MA, Kans. State U., 1972, PhD, 1979. Classification officer Nebr. Penal and Correctional Complex, Lincoln, 1970-71; assoc. prof. Augusta (Ga.) Coll., 1972-83, U. No. Colo., Greeley, 1983-91; full prof. U. No. Colo., 1991—; dir. criminal justice studies U. No. Colo., Greeley, 1983-93. Author: Comparative Criminal Justice Systems: A Topical Approach, 1994; contbr. articles to profl. jours. Advisor United Way Greeley, 1989, 93; bd. dirs. Planned Parenthood, Augusta, 1982, Legal Aid Soc., Greeley, 1993—. Named Favorite Prof., Mortar Bd., U. No. Colo., 1990, 94. Mem. Acad. Criminal Justice Scis. (program com. mem. 1995). Democrat. Home: 2506 57th Ave Greeley CO 80634-4506 Office: U No Colo Sociology Dept Greeley CO 80639

REICHMAN, HENRY FREDERICK, history educator; b. N.Y.C., Feb. 10, 1947; s. Charles and Vera (Stein) R.; m. Susan Alyne Hutcher, June 27, 1976; children: Daniel, Alice. AB, Columbia Coll., 1969; PhD, U. Calif., Berkeley, 1977. Instr. U. Calif., Berkeley, 1975-76; lectr. history U. Calif., San Diego, 1978; asst. prof. history Northwestern U., Evanston, Ill., 1979-80; asst. dir. office for intellectual freedom Am. Libr. Assn., Chgo., 1980-81; asst. prof. history Memphis State U., 1983-89; asst. prof. history Calif. State U., Hayward, 1989-91, assoc. prof. history, 1991—; vis. asst. prof. history U. Calif., Davis, 1989; chair dept. history Calif. State U., 1994—; assoc. editor newsletter on intellectual freedom Am. Libr. Assn., 1982—. Author: Railwaymen and Revolution: Russia, 1905, 1987, Censorship and Selection, 1988, rev. edit., 1993; contbr. articles to profl. jours. Mem. Am. Hist. Assn., Am. Assn. for Advancement of Slavic Studies, Freedom to Read Found., Phi Beta Kappa. Democrat. Jewish. Office: Calif State U Dept History Hayward CA 94542

REICHMAN, RONALD PETER, medical educator; b. Chgo., Jan. 18, 1951; s. Heinz Charles and Margot Reichman; m. Carolyn Elizabeth Kean, May 27, 1984. BA in Psychology, UCLA, 1973, MD, 1977. Diplomate Nat. Bd. Med. Examiners, Am. Bd. Internal Medicine, Am. Bd. Rheumatology. Lab. asst., technician dept. biochemistry UCLA, 1971-73, teaching asst. dept. psychology, 1972-73, rsch. asst. dept. psychology, 1973, lab. technician hemodialysis unit med. ctr., 1973-74, med. curriculum evaluation com., 1973-75, lab. technician cardiopulmonary procedure rm. med. ctr., 1974-75; jr. resident Cedars-Sinai Med. Ctr., Fresno, 1978-79; sr. resident internal medicine Cedars-Sinai Med. Ctr., 1979-80; fellow in Rheumatology Cedars Sinai Med. Ctr./ UCLA, 1981-82, sr. fellow in Rheumatology, 1982-83, asst. clin. prof. Medicine, 1983—; housestaff liaison nursing recruitment and retainment com. Valley Med. Ctr. Fresno, Calif., 1977-78, intern in internal medicine, 1977-78, jr. resident in internal medicine, 1978; cons. Calif. State Office Emergency Svcs., 1980—; pvt. cons., med. tech. advisor TV and motion pictures, 1980—; guest speaker Am. Medicine Writers Assn. Conv., 1982; med. advisor Antelope Valley chpt. Am. Lupus Soc., 1983—; pres. San Vicente Rehab., Inc., 1985-89; med. adv. bd. Ankylosing Spondylitis Assn., 1985—; media contact physician Am. Coll. Rheumatology, 1992—; qualified med. evaluator Indsl. Med. Coun., State of Calif., 1992—. Author: (with others) Progress in Clinical Rheumatology, 1984; contbr. articles to profl. jours. Bd. dirs. Good Beginnings Charitable Found., 1985—. Fellow Am. Rheumatism Assn.; mem. AMA (physician adv. panel to TV, motion pictures and radio 1980—), Am. Coll. Physicians, Calif. Med. Assn., So. Calif. Rheumatism Assn., L.A. County Med. Assn., Medicus Assn., Phi Beta Kappa, Pi Gamma Mu, Phi Eta Sigma, Pi Lambda Phi, Phi Delta Epsilon.

REID, BELMONT MERVYN, brokerage house executive; b. San Jose, Calif., May 17, 1927; s. C. Belmont and Mary Irene (Kilfoyl) R. BS in Engring., San Jose State U., 1950, postgrad.; m. Evangeline Joan Rogers, June 1, 1952. Pres., Lifetime Realty Corp., San Jose, 1969-77, Lifetime Fin. Planning Corp., San Jose, 1967-77; founder, chmn. bd. Belmont Reid & Co., Inc., San Jose, 1960-77; pres., registered investment advisor JOBEL Fin. Inc., Carson City, Nev., 1980—; pres., chmn. bd. Data-West Systems, Inc., 1984-85. County chmn. 1982-85, Carson City Rep. Cen. Com., treas., 1979-81; chmn. Carson City Gen. Obligation Bond Commn., 1986—; rural county chmn. Nev. Rep. Cen. Com., 1984-88; mem. Carson City Charter Rev. Com., 1986-91, chmn., 1988-91. With USN, 1945-46, 51-55. Decorated Air medals. Mem. Nat. Assn. Securities Dealers, Mcpl. Securities Rulemaking Bd., Carson City C. of C. (pres. 1986-87, bd. dir. 1982-88), Capital Club of Carson City, Rotary (chpt. sec. 1983-84, 86-87, pres. 1988-89, Paul Harris fellow). Home: 610 Bonanza Dr Carson City NV 89706-0201 Office: 711 E Washington St Carson City NV 89701-4063

REID, CHARLES PHILLIP PATRICK, academic administrator, researcher, professor; b. Columbia, Mo., Jan. 8, 1940; s. Charles Henry and Fern Elnora (Chorlton) R.; m. Miriam Davis, July 17, 1961; children: Clayton Patrick, Miriam. BSF, U. Mo., 1961; MF, Duke U., 1966, PhD, 1968. Asst. prof. dept. forest and wood scis. Colo. State U., Ft. Collins, 1969-73, assoc. prof. dept. forest and wood scis., 1973-77, prof. dept. forest and wood scis., 1977-86; prof., chmn. dept. forestry U. Fla., Gainesville, 1986-92, interim dir. Sch. Forest Resources and Conservation, 1991-92; prof., dir. Sch. Renewable Natural Resources U. Ariz., Tucson, 1992—; vis. faculty mem. dept. botany Sheffield (Eng.) U., fall 1973; vis. scientist div. of soils Commonwealth Sci. and Indsl. Rsch. Orgn., Glen Osmond, South Australia, 1976-77; sr. Fulbright fellow dept. microbiology U. Innsbruck, Austria, 1985-86; chmn. working group on root physiology and symbiosis Internat. Union Forestry Rsch. Orgns., 1984-88. Contbr. articles to profl. jours. Co-pres. Barton Elem. Parent Tchr. Orgn., Ft. Collins, 1979-80; bd. dirs. Vol. Clearing House, Ft. Collins, 1974-76, Fla. 4-H Found., Gainesville, 1988-89. Lt. (j.g.) USNR, 1961-64, comdr. USNR, ret. Mem. AAAS, Ecol. Soc. Am., Soc. Am. Foresters, Nat. Assn. Profl. Forestry Schs. and Colls. (exec. com. 1994-95), Sertoma (treas., bd. dirs. Ft. Collins chpt. 1972-75), Rotary. Republican. Episcopalian. Office: U Ariz Sch Renewable Natural Resources Bioscience East Tucson AZ 85721

REID, FRANCES EVELYN KROLL, cinematographer, director, film company executive; b. Oakland, Calif., Mar. 25, 1944; d. William Farnham and Marion Storm (Teller) Kroll. BA, U. Oreg., 1966. Tchr. secondary sch., Los Angeles, 1968-69; sound recordist Churchill Films, Los Angeles, 1971; freelance sound recordist Los Angeles, 1972-75, freelance producer, dir., 1975-78; freelance cinematographer Berkeley, Calif., 1978—; pres. Iris Films, Berkeley, 1977—; vol. Peace Corps, Malawi, Africa, 1969-70. Dir. (film) In The Best Interests of the Children, 1977 (Blue Ribbon Am. Film Festival 1978), The Changer: A Record of the Times, 1991, Skin Deep, 1995, Talking About Race, 1994, Straight from the Heart, 1994 (Acad. award nominee 1995); cinematographer: (film) The Times of Harvey Milk, 1984 (Oscar 1985), Living with AIDS, 1986 (Student Acad. award 1987), Common Threads: Stories from the Quilt, 1989 (Oscar award 1990). Mem. Film Arts Found., Assn. Ind. Video and Filmmakers, No. Calif. Women in Film and TV. Office: Iris Films PO Box 5353 Berkeley CA 94705-0353

REID, HARRY, senator; b. Searchlight, Nev., Dec. 2, 1939; s. Harry and Inez Reid; m. Landra Joy Gould; children—Lana, Rory, Leif, Josh, Key. AS, Southern Utah State U., 1959; LLD (hon.), U. So. Utah, 1984; BA, Utah State U., 1961; JD, George Washington U., 1964.

REID, JOSEPH LEE, physical oceanographer, educator; b. Franklin, Tex., Feb. 7, 1923; s. Joseph Lee and Ruby (Cranford) R.; m. Freda Mary Hunt, Apr. 7, 1953; children: Ian Joseph, Julian Richard. BA in Math., U. Tex., 1942; MS, Scripps Instn. Oceanography, 1950. Rsch. staff Scripps Instn. Oceanography, La Jolla, Calif., 1957-74; prof. oceanography Scripps Instn. Oceanography, La Jolla, 1974-91, ret., 1991; dir. Marine Life Rsch. Group, 1974-87; assoc. dir. Inst. Marine Resources, 1975-82; cons. Sandia Nat. Labs., Albuquerque, 1980-86. Author: On the Total Geostrophic Circulation of the South Pacific Ocean: Flow Patterns, Tracers and Transports, 1986, On the Total Geostrophic Circulation of the South Atlantic Ocean: Flow Patterns, Tracers and Transports, 1989; contbr. articles to profl. jours. Lt. USNR, 1942-46, ETO, PTO. Recipient award Nat. Oceanographic Data Ctr., Washington, 1984, Albatross award Am. Miscellaneous Soc., 1988, Alexander Agassiz medal NAS, 1992. Fellow AAAS, Am. Geophys. Union (pres. Ocean Scis. sect. 1972-74, 84-86); mem. Am. Meteorol. Soc., Oceanography Soc. Home: 1105 Cuchara Dr Del Mar CA 92014-2623*

REID, RALPH RALSTON, JR., electronics executive, engineer; b. Topeka, Nov. 19, 1934; s. Ralph Ralston Sr. and Else May (Whitebread) R.; m. Gloria Ann Cook, Feb. 3, 1957; children: Terri L., Jeffrey S. BS in Physics, Washburn U., 1956. Sr. v.p. engring. div. Loral Def. Systems Ariz., Litchfield, Ariz., 1963-96; dir. Tech. Loral Corp., N.Y.C., Ariz., 1996—. Capt. USAF, 1957-60. Mem. Am. Electronics Assn., Am. Def. Preparedness Assn., Assn. U.S. Army. Republican. Home: 2527 E Vogel Ave Phoenix AZ 85028-4729 Office: Loral Def Systems Ariz PO Box 85 Litchfield Park AZ 85340-0085

REID, ROBERT TILDEN, medical association administrator, internist; b. Dallas, Feb. 20, 1931; s. Robert Tilden and Gldays Tressy (King) R.; divorced; children: Robert Tilden, Richard Thomas, Annette Marie, Randolph Young. BS, So. Meth. U., Dallas, 1957; MD, U. Tex.-Southwestern, Dallas, 1959. Diplomate Am. Bd. Internal Medicine, Am. Bd. Rheumatology, Am. Bd. Allergy and Immunology. With Scripps Clinic and Rsch., La Jollla, Calif., 1963-70; pvt. practice La Jollla, Calif., 1970—; chief staff Scripps Meml. Hosp., La Jollla, Calif., 1976-78; scientific dir. Erik and Ese Banck Clinical Rsch. Ctr., San Diego, 1994—. Mem. San Diego County Med. Soc. (pres. 1991), Calif. Med. Assn. (trustee 1992-95). Office: 9850 Genesse Ave Ste 860 La Jolla CA 92037 also: Erik & Ese Banck Clinical Rsch 12395 El Camino Real #117 San Diego CA 92130

REID, WALLACE LEO, manufacturing executive; b. Indpls., Dec. 30, 1924; s. Norman Oscar and Margaret (Quinn) R.; m. Jean Marie Berry, May 21, 1942; children: Kelly, Tim, Denise. Furrier Fur Wardrobe, 1978, Holiday Furs, 1969, Hall Reid Fur Co., 1949, Furrier Ind. Fur Co., 1949. Designer: Luster Life Cleaning Process, 1949, TVRC Garment Weather Vane, 1959. Served with USMC, 1941-45. Roman Catholic. Home: 11238 Bos St Cerritos CA 90703-6506

REIDER, CARROLL ANN, nutritionist, consultant; b. Phoenix, Feb. 28, 1960; d. John Jerome and Patricia Elaine (Heath) Reider. BS in Nutrition, Calif. State U., Long Beach, 1983; Advanced MS in Nutrition, Inst. Health Professions, Mass. Gen. Hosp., Boston, 1989. Registered dietitian, cert. nutrition support dietitian. Clin. dietetic technician Hoag Hosp., Newport Beach, Calif., 1982-84; dietetic intern U. Calif., San Francisco, 1984-85; chief clin. dietitian, nutrition support specialist St. Mary's Med. Ctr., San Francisco, 1986-88; nutrition support team dietitian, surg. rsch. dietitian Mass. Gen. Hosp., Brigham & Women's Hosp., Harvard U., Boston, 1988-89; critical care nutritionist UCLA Med. Ctr., 1989-92, associated faculty, instr., 1989-94; corp. mgr. nutritional support svcs. Salick Health Care/ INFUSX, Inc., Beverly Hills, 1992—; cons., lectr., 1986—; home care nutrition cons. Am. Dietetic Assn., Chgo., 1993—. Contbr. articles to profl. jours. Mem. Am. Dietetic Assn. (excellence/leadership award 1993, cert. of recognition 1992, cabinet mem. dietitians in nutrition support practice group), Am. Soc. Parenteral and Enteral Nutrition.

REIDY, RICHARD ROBERT, publishing company executive; b. Patchogue, N.Y., May 9, 1947; s. Joseph Robert and Irene (Jennings) R.; m. Carolyn Alyce Armstrong, Mar. 21, 1970; children: Dawn Patricia, Shawn Patrick, Christopher Keith. Student, Suffolk County Community Coll., 1966-68, L.I. Tech. Sch., 1969-70, Scottsdale Community Coll., 1983-84, 85-86. Lic. real estate agt., Ariz. Restaurant owner Reidy's, Patchogue, 1973-77; design draftsman Sverdrop & Parcel, Tempe, Ariz., 1978-79, Sullivan & Masson, Phoenix, 1979-81; pres. Success Pub. Co., Scottsdale, Ariz., 1983—; with U.S. Postal Dept., 1980—. Editor, owner, pub.: Who's Who in Arizona, 1984-85, 89-90. Chief Scottsdale YMCA, 1983-84; eucharistic minister St. Daniel the Prophet Cath. Ch., Scottsdale, 1985—; mem. World Wide Marriage Encounter, 1986—; pres. Coronado High Sch. Band Boosters, 1988-89. Mem. Scottsdale C. of C., Phoenix Better Bus. Bur. Office: Success Pub Co PO Box 3431 Scottsdale AZ 85271-3431

REIERSON, LAWRENCE EDWARD, organizational development consultant, executive; b. Astoria, Oreg., Feb. 27, 1934; s. Lawrence Engvold and Edith Fay (Raymond) R.; m. Gail Lorene Gronnel, Apr. 23, 1954 (div. June 1967); children: Careen Jump, Lorrie; m. Star Ellis Van Valkenburgh, Dec. 13,1969; stepchildren: Candalee Olstedt, Lonnie Foster. Student, Portland State U., 1957-59; MS in Orgn. Devel., Pepperdine U., 1977. With Tektronix, Inc., Beaverton, Oreg., 1959-79, mgr. mgmt. devel., 1974-77, mgr. employee devel., 1977-79; dir. mgmt. devel. Weyerhaeuser Co., Tacoma, 1979-82; mgr. adminstrn. Pro-Log Cos., Monterey, Calif., 1982-85; chmn., CEO, bd. dirs. Saltwater Inst., Monterey, 1986—; cons. U. Oreg. Med. Sch., Portland, 1967-70, Oreg. State System Higher Edn., Portland, 1966-70; sr. faculty mem. Mahler Assocs. Advanced Mgmt. Skills Program, Fair Lawn, N.J., 1986—. Contbr. articles to profl. publs. Mem. Oreg. Sci. Edn. Coun., Portland, 1966-72. Mem. Monterey C. of C. (bd. dirs. 1986). Office: Saltwater Inst 80 Garden Ct Ste 150 Monterey CA 93940-5340

REIF, (FRANK) DAVID, artist, educator; b. Cin., Dec. 14, 1941; s. Carl A. and Rachel L. (Clifton) R.; m. Ilona Jekabsons, July 30, 1966; 1 child, Megan Elizabeth. BFA, Art Inst. Chgo., 1968; MFA, Yale U., 1970. Asst. prof. art U. Wyo., Laramie, 1970-74, assoc. prof., 1974-81, prof., 1981—; assoc. prof. U. Mich., Ann Arbor, 1980-81; acting head dept. art U. Wyo., Laramie, 1986-87; selection cons. Ucross Found. Residency Program, Wyo., 1983—; exhibit juror Artwest Nat., Jackson, Wyo., 1986; panelist Colo. State U., Ft. Collins, 1981; lectr. U. Mich., 1980; apptd. Wyo. Arts Coun., 1993—. One-man shows include U. Wyo. Art Mus., 1993, Dorsky Galleries, N.Y.C., 1980, No. Ariz. U., 1977, 87, U. Mich., 1980, 81, One West Ctr. Contemporary Art, Ft. Collins, 1991; exhibited in group shows at First, Second and Third Who. Biennial Tour, 1984-86, U.S. Olympics Art Exhbn., L.A., 1984, Miss. Mus. Art and NEA Tour, 1981-83, L.A. Invitational Sculpture Tour Exhbn., 1991-92, Nicolaysen Art Mus., Casper, Wyo., 1994. With USAR, 1963-69. Recipient F.D. Pardee award Yale U., 1970; Best Sculpture award Joslyn Art Mus. Omaha, 1978; Nat. Endowment Arts grantee, 1978-79, Wyo. Basic Rsch. grantee, 1983-84, 86-87. Mem. Coll. Art Assn., Internat. Sculpture Ctr., Wyo. Arts Coun. (apptd. 1993, chair 1995—). Democrat. Home: 3340 Aspen Ln Laramie WY 82070-5702 Office: U Wyo Dept Art PO Box 3138 Laramie WY 82071-3138

REIFF, THEODORE CURTIS, investment banker; b. Cleve., Aug. 6, 1942; s. William Fred and Dorothy Louise (Knauer) R.; m. Janis Lynn Brunk, May 6, 1966 (div. Aug. 1980); m. Theresa Dolores Baranello, Oct. 30, 1982 (div. Dec. 1992). BS, Ohio State U., 1969. Lic. real estate broker. Dir. adminstrv. svcs. Mgmt. Horizons, Inc., Columbus, Ohio, 1969-73; v.p. Danco Mgmt. Co., Lancaster, Ohio, 1973-74; sr. v.p. Anchor Lighting Corp., Columbus, 1974-75; ptnr. Curtis-Lee & Assocs., Delaware, Ohio, 1974-77; pres. Cartunes Corp., San Diego, Calif., 1977-91; also bd. dirs. Cartunes Corp., San Diego; facilities coord. Raytheon Co., Burlington, Mass., 1979-82; ptnr. Greenstone & Reiff, San Diego, 1982-86; ptnr. Creative Bus. Strategies, Inc., San Diego, 1986-91, pres., bd. dirs.; pres. Bus. Pubs. Inc., San Diego, 1989-91, also bd. dirs.; mng. dir. PM Co., Tijuana, B.C., Mex., 1991-94; co-founder, pres. Bldg. Materials Distbrs., San Diego, 1994—, also bd. trustees; co-founder, treas. Materiales de Construccion de Baja California, Tijuana, Mex., 1995—, also bd. dirs.; bd. dirs. Integrated Ceramic Tech., San Marcos, Calif., 1986-88, Pacific Rim Interface Mems. Enterprises Inc., 1988-90, Distributed Communications Corp., San Diego, 1986-91, Paradox Devel. Corp., San Diego, 1990-91, Phoenix Systems & Techs., Chula Vista, Calif., 1990-91; instr. Miramar Coll., San Diego, 1984-90. Mem. Friends of San Diego Zoo, 1980—; chmn. bus. adv. com. San Diego State U. Coll. of Bus., 1979-82; mem. adv. com. Coll. Bus. Calif. State U., 1992-94. With Ohio N.G., 1966-72. Named Outstanding Businessman City of Columbus, Ohio, 1974; recipient Recognition award San Diego State U. Coll. of Bus., 1983, Appreciation award Am. Mktg. Assn., 1984, IEEE, 1986. Mem. Am. Electronics Assn. (chmn. small bus. com. 1988-89, chmn. fin. com. 1989-91), San Diego World Trade Assn., High Tech. Found. Home: 1514 7th Ave Apt 305 San Diego CA 92101-3236

REIHEL, RONALD ERNEST, pilot; b. Berwyn, Ill., Aug. 16, 1941; s. Elmer and Ella Reihel; m. Mary Kathleen Pellicer, June 30, 1963; children: Ronald E. Jr., Margaret Jennifer. BS in Math., U.S. Naval Acad., 1963; MS in Indsl. Engring., Stanford (Calif.) U., 1964. Pilot Ea. Airlines, Miami, Fla., 1970-89; B747 pilot, instr. pilot United Airlines, Denver, 1992—; master coord. Shaklee Corp., San Francisco, 1972—. Airport Commn. mem. Ocean Reef Club, Key Largo, Fla., 1981-86. Col. USAF, 1963-71, USAFR, 1971-93. Selected Outstanding Dep. Comdr. for Resource Mgmt., USAFR, 1989, IMA Chief of Programs, 1990-93. Mem. U.S. Naval Acad. Alumni Assn., U.S. Naval Acad. Athletic Assn. (baseball most valuable player 1963), Ocean Reef Club.

REILLEY, KATHLEEN PATRICIA, lawyer; b. Pitts., Oct. 31, 1948; d. Edward Michael and Mary Elizabeth (Davidson) R. BA, U. Calif., Berkeley, 1976; JD, Golden Gate U., 1979. Bar: Calif. Staff atty. Fresno County Legal Svcs., Calif., 1979-85, Santa Monica (Calif.) Rent Control Bd., 1985-89; asst. city atty. City of Berkeley, 1990-91; atty. Linda DeBene Inc., Danville, Calif., 1991-94. Co-founder Calif. Housing Action & Info. Network, 1976. Mem. Calif. State Bar Assn. (real property sect.), Contra Costa County Bar Assn., Alameda County Bar Assn. Democrat. Episcopalian. Office: 1563 Solano Ave # 528 Berkeley CA 94707-2116

REILLY, ROBERT JOSEPH, counselor; b. Spokane, Wash., Mar. 7, 1936; s. John Francis and Vivian Helen (White) R.; m. Joan Steiner, June 20, 1960; children: Sean Michael, Patrick Joseph, Bridget Colleen. BA in Psychology, Seattle U., 1985; postgrad., Infantry Officer Candidate Sch, Ft. Benning, 1960, EOAC, Ft. Belvoir, 1968, Leadership Inst. Seattle/City U., 1991-92. Ordained Congl. Ch. Practical Theology. Enlisted U.S. Army, 1953, advanced through grades to maj., 1981, ret., 1981; with U.S. Army, Korea, 1961-62, Vietnam, 1966-67, 68-69; counselor Schick Shadel Hosp., Seattle, 1984-89; dir. Canyon Counseling, Puyallup, Wash., 1987-92; counselor Wash. State Employee Adv. Svc., Olympia, 1992—; mem. Nat. Bd. for Hypnotherapy and Hypnotic Anaesthesiology, v.p. 1991—, pres. Wash Chpt., 1991-94; exec. v.p. Coll. Therapeutic Hypnosis, Puyallup, 1989-94; mem. adj. faculty Pierce Coll., Tacoma, 1991-92. Pres. Irich Cultural Club, Tacoma, 1983-85, 93-94; sec. Tacoma chpt. Ret. Officers Assn., 1983-87, pres., 1993-95. Decorated Vietnamese Cross of Gallentry with silver star, Bronze Star with oak leaf cluster, Meritorious Svc. medal, Army Commendation medal with 2 oak leaf clusters; named Prof. of Yr. Chem. Dependency Profls. Wash., 1994. Mem. Nat. Bd. Hypnotherapy and Hypnotic Anesthesiology (v.p. 1991—, Mem. of Yr. 1994, pres. Wash. chpt. 1991-94), Internat. Med. and Dental Hypnotherapy Assn., Nat. Assn. Alcohol and Drug Abuse Counselors, Am. Congress Hypnotist Examiners, Army Engr. Assn., Nat. 4th Inf. Divsn. Assn. (sec.-treas. N.W. chpt. 1993—), Employee Assistance Profls. Assn. Office: Wash State Employee Adv Svc PO Box 47540 Olympia WA 98504-7540

REILLY, WILLIAM KANE, former government official, educator, lawyer, conservationist; b. Decatur, Ill., Jan. 26, 1940; s. George P. and Margaret (Kane) R.; m. Elizabeth Buxton; children: Katherine, Megan. B.A. in History, Yale U., 1962; J.D., Harvard U., 1965; M.S. in Urban Planning, Columbia U., 1971. Bar: Ill., Mass. 1965. Atty. firm Ross & Hardies, Chgo., 1965; assoc. dir. Urban Policy Center, Urban Am., Inc., also Nat. Urban Coalition, Washington, 1969-70; sr. staff mem. Pres.'s Council Environ. Quality, 1970-72; exec. dir. Task Force Land Use and Urban Growth, 1972-73; pres. Conservation Found., Washington, 1973-89, World Wildlife Fund, Washington, 1985-89; adminstr. U.S. EPA, Washington, 1989-93; chmn. Natural Resources Coun. Am., 1982-83; head U.S. del. Earth Summit, 1992; head U.S. del. to negotiate Amendments to Montreal Protocol on the Ozone Layer, 1990, 92; Payne vis. prof. Stanford U., 1993—; assoc. Tex. Pacific Group, San Francisco, 1994—; chmn. bd. dirs. Clean Sites, Inc.; bd. dirs. Am. Farmland Trust, E.I. DuPont de Nemours and Co., Evergreen Holdings, Inc., Nat. Geog. Soc., Ptnrs. for Livable Communities, World Wildlife Fund, Yale U.; mem. sci. adv. bd. The Nature Conservancy. Editor: The Use of Land, 1973, Environment Strategy America, 1994; author articles in field, chpts. in books. Served to capt., CIC U.S. Army, 1966-67. Clubs: University (Washington), Univ. (N.Y.C.). Office: c/o World Wildlife Fund 1250 24th St NW Washington DC 20037-1175

REIM, RUTHANN, career and personal counselor, corporate trainer; b. Fresno, Calif., Oct. 4, 1943; d. F. Wayne and Charlene Marie (Young) Howd; m. Terry D., Nov. 29, 1963; children: Tracey, Brandon. BA in Sociology, San Jose State U., 1966; MA Guidance & Counseling, Pacific

Luth. U., 1984. Cert. counselor, nat. Tchr., elem. sch. Dupont Sch. Dist., Tacoma, 1966-67, Prince Georges Sch. Dist., Lanham, Md., 1967-68, Franklin Pierce sch. Dist., Tacoma, 1968-70; owner Rainbow Glassworks, Tacoma, 1973-76, Creative Womanlife, Tacoma, 1976-78; dir., counselor Individual Devel. Ctr., Tacoma, 1984-88; pres. Career Mgmt. Inst., Tacoma, 1989—; adj. faculty mem. dept. edn. Pacific Luth. U., 1980-84. Author: (career booklet) Career Change Made Easy, 1990; artist 5' round stained glass window "Dogwood", 1980. Trainer Jr. League Tacoma, 1977-79. Mem. Rotary (1st woman pres. 1991-92, bd. dirs. 1988—), Phi Kappa Phi. Office: Career Mgmt Inst 8404 27th St W Tacoma WA 98466-2723

REIMANN, BERNHARD ERWIN FERDINAND, biologist; b. Berlin, Germany, May 30, 1922; s. Philip Bernhard Ferdinand and Margarete (Kutzleb) R.; m. Beate Eleonore Hedwig, Sept. 1, 1949; 1 child, Joachim Oscar Ferdinand. Grad., Paulsen Oberschule, 1941; Lic. Med. Tech., Berlin, 1949; D in Botany, Zoology, Geology, Freie U., Berlin, 1959. Supr. electo microscopy facility Scripps Inst. Oceanography, La Jolla, Calif., 1961-67; chief electron microscopy dept. pathology and area lab. svcs. William Beaumont Army Med. Ctr., El Paso, Tex., 1967-87; ret.; assoc. grad. faculty U. Tex. El Paso, 1968-69, assoc. prof. biology dept. N.Mex. State U., Las Cruces, 1967-87; assoc. clin. prof. dept. patholgy Tex. Tech. U., El Paso, 1980-87. Contbr. articles to profl. jours. Vol. environ. adviser liquid waste disposal problems Village of Capitan N.Mex. and Lincoln County, 1988—. With German Air Force, 1941-47. Named Civil Servant of Yr., Fed. Bus. Assn., 1981; recipient Comdrs. Civilian Svc. award William Beaumont Army Med. Ctr., 1987, Recognition for Outstanding Svc. award 41 Legis., 2d Session, State of N.Mex., 1994. Fellow AAAS; mem. Microscopy Soc. Am. (emeritus). Democrat. Home: 115 E Lobo Rd Capitan NM 88316

REIMER, JAN, mayor; b. Edmonton, Alta., Can.; married; 2 children. BA, U. Alta. Councillor for Ward 2 City Coun. of Edmonton, 1980-89, chair various standing coms.; mayor City of Edmonton, 1989—; former chair City of Edmonton Task Force Econ. Devel., Inter-Mcpl. Task Force Out-of-Sch. Care, River Valley Steering Com., Mayor's Task Force Safer Cities; chair Safer Cities Initiatives Com., No. Alta. Mayors' Caucus; mem. Bd. Edmonton Power; Edmonton rep. Big City Mayors' Caucus, Can.; mem. Winter Cities Secretariat; organizer Edmonton Region Mayors and Reeves Caucus. Co-author: N.U.T.S. & B.O.L.T.S.: A Self-Help Guide for Community Groups. Pres. Mcpl. Non-Profit Housing Corp.; organizer Toxic Round-Up, Blue Box, various other environ. programs; mem. Bd. Edmonton Pub. Libr., Edmonton Met. Regional Planning Commn., Mayor's Task Force Citizen Participation, Inter-Mcpl. Task Force Waste Mgmt.; citizen coord. Calder Action Com., Edmonton; mem. bd. govs. Royal Alexandra Hosp.; bd. dirs. Edmonton Social Planning Coun., Econ. Devel. Edmonton. Office: City Hall, 1 Sir Winston Churchill Sq, Edmonton, AB Canada T5J 2R7

REINDERS, JAMES W., petroleum consultant; b. Alliance, Nebr., Sept. 20, 1927; s. Herman I. and Catherine L. (Tickner) R.; m. Violet A. Strong, Nov. 13, 1948; children: James M., Janice K., Jody M. BSEE, U. Nebr., 1950. Registered profl. engr. Mktg. mgr. Schlumberger, New Orleans, 1965-69; div. mgr. Schlumberger, Shreveport, La., 1969-71; tech. mgr. Schlumberger, Houston, 1971-73; mgr. Schlumberger, Tehran, Iran, 1973-75; tech. mgr. Schlumberger, London, 1975-81; pres. Geo Vann, Inc., Houston, 1982-84; petroleum cons. Houston, 1984-91, Albuquerque, 1991—. Sculpture entitled Carhenge, 1987. With USNR, 1944-46. Mem. Soc. of Petroleum Engrs., Nat. Forensic Ctr., Toastmasters, Pi Mu Epsilon. Republican. Home: 13215 Circulo Largo NE Albuquerque NM 87112-3771

REINER, JAMES ANTHONY, marketing executive; b. Orange, Calif., Sept. 12, 1958; s. Earl Arthur and Mary Ann (Cuff) R. BBA in Acctg., U. Mo., 1983, MBA in Mktg., 1984. Mktg. intern The Seven-UP Co., St. Louis, 1984-85; mktg. analyst Rawlings Sporting Goods, St. Louis, 1992-94; mktg. mgr. Rawlings Sporting Goods Co., St. Louis, 1986-88; product mgr. Con Agra Consumer Frozen Food Co., St. Louis, 1988-89, sr. product mgr., 1989-90, group product mgr., 1990-91, dir. mktg., 1991-92; exec. v.p. mktg. Luigiho's Inc., Duluth, Minn., 1992; dir. diversification Samsonite Corp., Denver, 1992—; pres. Global Voyager Corp., Denver, 1994—. Mem. Am. Mktg. Assn., Alpha Mu Alpha (hon.). Republican.

REINER, THOMAS KARL, manufacturing company executive; b. Budapest, Hungary, Dec. 29, 1931; came to U.S., 1959; s. Pál and Jozefa (Keller) R.; children from previous marriage: Paul A., Reneé K. Hedsand; m. Eleanor Ruth Aldridge (div.). Diploma optics trade sch., Budapest, 1952; MS, Tech. U., Budapest, 1955; postgrad., London Coll., 1958, U. Pitts. Engr. Cen. Power Generating Sta., Hungary, 1954-56; cons. engr., test engr. Blaw-Knox Co., London, 1956-57; sr. engr. Eubank & Ptnrs., London, 1957-59; rsch. engr. Pitts. Plate Glass Co., 1959-60, product mgr. Copes-Vulcan divsn., 1960-62; chief engr. J.W. Fecker divsn. Am. Optical Co., 1962-66; product mgr. Carco Electronics, Menlo Park, Calif., 1966-68; chief engr. Fairchild Camera, El Segundo, Calif., 1968-70; dir. engring. Templeton, Kenly & Co., L.A. and Chgo., 1970-72; gen. mgr. Foremark Corp., Gardena, 1972-74; pres. Kinetron, Inc., Long Beach, Calif., 1974-76, GRW, Inc., Hawthorne, Calif., 1977—; adj. prof. Tech. U., Budapest, 1951-54. Patentee in post tension device for concrete, spherical air bearing and gimballed slave connector, synchronization of hydraulic jacking sys., bending of automotive side windows; inventor tug/barge latching sys., membrane type loadcell, ultra low profile platform and truckscales. Bd. pres. Peacock Ridge Homeowners Assn., Palos Verdes, Calif. Lt. Hungarian Army, 1951-57. Mem. Internat. Soc. Weighing and Measurements. Office: GRW Inc 12600 Chadron Ave Hawthorne CA 90250-4810

REINERS, WILLIAM ARNOLD, botany educator; b. Chgo., June 10, 1937; s. Bernard Martin and Catharine Louise (Amidon) R.; m. Norma Marilyn Miller, Apr. 21, 1962; children: Peter William, Derek Seth. BA, Knox Coll., 1959; MS, Rutgers U., 1962, PhD, 1964. From instr. to asst. prof. U. Minn., Mpls., 1964-67; from asst. prof. to prof. Dartmouth Coll., Hanover, N.H., 1967-83; dept. chmn. Dartmouth Coll., Hanover, 1982-83; prof. U. Wyo., Laramie, 1983—, dept. head, 1983-89; program dir. NSF, Washington, 1976-77; fellow Wissenschaftskolleg zu Berlin, Germany, 1989-90. Contbr. articles to profl. jours. 2d lt. U.S. Army, 1959-60. Named H. J. Oosting lectr. Dept. Botany, Duke U., Dirham, N.C., 1981; recipient U. Wyo. Presdl. Award for scholarly work. Mem. AAAS, Am. Inst. Biol. Scis., Am. Geophys. Union, Ecol. Soc. Am. (treas. 1981-84). Unitarian-Universalist. Office: Univ Wyo Dept Botany PO Box 3165 Laramie WY 82071

REINES, FREDERICK, physicist, educator; b. Paterson, N.J., Mar. 16, 1918; s. Israel and Gussie (Cohen) R.; m. Sylvia Samuels, Aug. 30, 1940; children: Robert G., Alisa K. M.E., Stevens Inst. Tech., 1939, M.S., 1941; Ph.D., NYU, 1944; D.Sc. (hon.), U. Witwatersrand, 1966; D. Engring. (hon.), Stevens Inst. Tech., 1984. Mem. staff Los Alamos Sci. Lab., 1944-59; group leader Los Alamos Sci. Lab. (Theoretical div.), 1945-59; dir. (AEC expts. on Eniwetok Atoll), 1951; prof. physics, head dept. Case Inst. Tech., 1959-66; prof. physics U. Calif., Irvine, 1966-88, dean phys. scis., 1966-74, Disting. prof. physics, 1987-88, prof. emeritus, 1988—; Centennial lectr. U. Md., 1956; Disting. Faculty lectr. U. Calif., Irvine, 1979; L.I. Schiff Meml. lectr. Stanford U., 1988; Albert Einstein Meml. lectr. Israel Acad. Scis. and Humanities, Jerusalem, 1988; Goudschmidt Meml. lectr., 1990; co-discoverer elementary nuclear particles, free antineutrino, 1956. Contbr. numerous articles to profl. jours.; contbg. author: Effects of Atomic Weapons, 1950. Mem. Cleve. Symphony Chorus, 1959-62. Recipient J. Robert Oppenheimer Meml. prize, 1981, Nat. Medal Sci., 1983, medal U. Calif., Irvine, 1987, Michelson Morley award, 1990; co-recipient Rossi prize Am. Astron. Soc., 1990; Guggenheim fellow, 1958-59, Sloan fellow, 1959-63, Franklin medal Franklin Inst., 1992. Fellow Am. Phys. Soc. (W.K.H. Panofsky prize 1992), AAAS; mem. NAS, Am. Assn. Physics Tchrs., Argonne U. Assn. (trustee 1965-66), Am. Acad. Arts and Scis., Russian Acad. Sci. (fgn. mem.), Phi Beta Kappa, Sigma Xi, Tau Beta Pi. Office: U Calif Dept Physics Campus Dr Irvine CA 92717

REINFELDS, JURIS, computer science educator; b. Riga, Latvia, Apr. 1, 1936; came to U.S., 1989; s. Nikolais Janis and Irma (Kaulins) R.; m. Lauma Petersons, Sept. 15, 1962; children: Peteris Maris, Ivars Valdis, Martins Nikolais. BSc, U. Adelaide, Australia, 1959; PhD, U. Adelaide, 1963; postdoctoral work, ICI. Postdoctoral fellow U. Edinburgh, Scotland, 1961-64; postdoctoral rsch. fellow U. Adelaide, Australia, 1964-65; NSF postdoctoral rsch. assoc. NASA, Huntsville, Ala., 1965-66; asst. prof. computer sci. U. Ga., Athens, 1966-72; vis. scientist CERN, Geneva, 1972-75; found. prof. computer sci. U. Wollongong NSW, Australia, 1975-89; prof. computer sci. N.Mex. State U., Las Cruces, 1989—; cons. Australian Internat. Devel. Program, Hat Yai, Thailand, 1983-91, Los Banos, Philippines, 1983-90. Mem. IEEE Computer Soc., Assn. for Computer Machinery, Australian Computer Soc., Las Cruces Rotary Club. Office: N Mex State U Computer Sci Dept PO Box 30001 Las Cruces NM 88003-8001

REINHARDT, RICHARD WARREN, writer; b. Oakland, Calif., Mar. 25, 1927; s. Emil Charles Henry and Eloise (Rathbone) R.; m. Joan Maxwell, Dec. 15, 1951; children: Kurt, Paul, Andrew. BA, Stanford U., 1949; MS, Columbia U., 1950; postgrad., Princeton U., 1958. Reporter San Francisco (Calif.) Chronicle, 1951-57; campaign mgr. various local, state and nat. campaigns, 1960-67; lectr. Grad. Sch. Journalism, U. Calif., Berkeley, 1971-93. Author: The Ashes of Smyrna, 1971, Treasure Island, 1973, San Francisco's Chinatown, 1982; prin. author: California 2000: The Next Frontier, 1982; assoc. editor San Francisco Mag., 1964-67; contbg. editor Am. West Mag., 1965-75, World's Fair, 1981—. Trustee Calif. Hist. Soc., 1978-85; bd. dirs. Calif. Tomorrow, 1984-94; bd. mem., chair, pres. San Francisco Archtl. Heritage, 1980—. Ensign USNR, 1945-46. Pulitzer Traveling scholar Columbia U., N.Y.C., 1951; Near East Studies fellow Ford Found., 1957-60. Mem. Squaw Valley Cmty. Writers (adv. com., non-fiction dir. 1982—), Author's Guild, Delta Tau Delta. Office: 712 Lake St San Francisco CA 94118-1227

REINHARDT, STEPHEN ROY, federal judge; b. N.Y.C., Mar. 27, 1931; s. Gottfried and Silvia (Hanlon) R.; children: Mark, Justin, Dana. B.A. cum laude, Pomona Coll., 1951; LL.B., Yale, 1954. Bar: Calif. 1958. Law clk. to U.S. Dist. Judge Luther W. Youngdahl, Washington, 1956-57; atty. O'Melveny & Myers, L.A., 1957-59; partner Fogel Julber Reinhardt Rothschild & Feldman (L.C.), L.A., 1959-80; judge U.S. Ct. Appeals (9th cir.), L.A., 1980—; Mem. exec. com. Dem. Nat. Com., 1969-72, nat. Dem. committeeman for Calif., 1976-80; pres. L.A. Recreation an dParks Commn., 1974-75; mem. Coliseum Commn., 1974-75; mem. L.A. Police Commn., 1974-78, pres., 1978-80; sec., mem. exec. com. L.A. Olympic Organizing com., 1980-84; bd. dirs. Amateur Athletic Found. of L.A., 1984-92; adj. prof. Loyola Law Sch., L.A., 1988-90. Served to 1st lt. USAF, 1954-56. Mem. ABA (labor law coun. 1975-77). •

REINHARDT, WILLIAM PARKER, chemical physicist, educator; b. San Francisco, May 22, 1942; s. William Oscar and Elizabeth Ellen (Parker) R.; m. Katrina Hawley Currens, Mar. 14, 1979; children: James William, Alexander Hawley. BS in Basic Chemistry, U. Calif., Berkeley, 1964; AM in Chemistry, Harvard U., 1966, PhD in Chem. Physics, 1968; MA (hon.), U. Pa., 1985. Instr. chemistry Harvard U., 1967-69, asst. prof. chemistry, 1969-72, assoc. prof., 1972-74; prof. U. Colo., Boulder, 1974-84, chmn. dept. chemistry, 1977-80; prof. chemistry U. Pa., Phila., 1984-91, chmn. dept., 1985-88, D. Michael Crow prof., 1987-91; prof. chemistry U.Wash., Seattle, 1991—, assoc. chmn. undergrad. program, 1993—; vis. fellow Joint Inst. for Lab. Astrophysics of Nat. Bur. Stds. and U. Colo., 1972, 74, fellow, 1974-84; dir. Telluride Summer Rsch. Ctr., 1986-89, treas., 1989—; mem. com. on atomic, molecular and optical scis. NRC, 1988-90; vis. scientist Nat. Inst. Stds. and Tech., summers 1993, 94. Editorial bd. Phys. Rev. A., 1979-81, Chem. Physics, 1985—, Jour. Chem. Physics, 1987-89, Jour. Physics B. (U.K.), 1992—, Internat. Jour. Quantum Chemistry, 1994—; researcher theoretical chem. physics, theoretical atomic and molecular physics for numerous pubs. Recipient Camille and Henry Dreyfus Tchr. Scholar award, 1972; Alfred P. Sloan fellow, 1972; J.S. Guggenheim Meml. fellow, 1978; Coun. on Rsch. and Creative Work faculty fellow, 1978. Fellow AAAS, Am. Phys. Soc.; mem. Am. Chem. Soc., Phi Beta Kappa, Sigma Xi (nat. lectr. 1980-82), Phi Lambda Upsilon (Fresenius award 1977). Office: U Wash Dept Chemistry Box 1700 Seattle WA 98195

REINHART, MARIA RINNA, secondary education educator; b. Frosinone, Italy, Sept. 10, 1951; came to U.S., 1954; d. Pasquale and Anna Giovanna (Conti) R.; m. Christopher Newell, June 3, 1981 (div. Aug., 1986); children: Annalisa Rinna Newell, Hillary Robin Newell; m. William Edward Reinhart, Mar. 5, 1990. BA in Edn., Mich. State U., 1969-73; student of Spanish, Universidad del Valle, Guatemala, 1973; postgrad., Calif. State U., San Bernardino, 1992—. Purser Pan American World Airlines, L.A., 1978-90; kindergarten tchr. Palo Verde Sch. Dist., Blythe, Calif., 1990-92; H.S. tchr. Dept. Corrections, Blythe, Calif., 1993—. Mem. Eagle Mountain Sch. Site Coun. Mem. Correctional Edn. Assn., Indep. Union of Flight Attendants (N.Y. 1978-90). Home: 44983 Shadow Way Desert Center CA 92239 Office: Calif Dept Corrections Well's Wiley Way Desert Center CA 92239

REINHART, STEVEN ANTHONY, lawyer; b. Wichita Falls, Tex., Oct. 15, 1965; s. Richard Arthur and Linda Sue (Tuckey) R.; m. Kristina Suzanne Greene Reinhart, May 19, 1989; 1 child, Ryan Arthur. BA in Pub. Rels., Tex. Tech. U., 1988, JD, 1992. Bar: N.Mex. Assoc. atty. Hatch, Allen & Shepherd, PA, Albuquerque, 1992—. mem. adminstrv. bd. Cen. United Meth. Ch., Albuquerque, 1993—. Republican. Methodist. Office: 6501 Americas Pkwy NE Albuquerque NM 87190

REINHOLD, ALLEN KURT, graphic design educator; b. Salt Lake City, Feb. 21, 1936; s. Eric Kurt and Lillian (Hansen) R.; m. Irene Laura Rawlings, May 4, 1962; children: Cindy Anne, David, Alyce, Bryce, Eugene Patrick. BA, Brigham Young U., 1961, MA, 1962. Cert. secondary and post secondary tech. and indsl., Utah, color cons. Freelance artist Allen Reinhold Art & Design Studio, American Fork, Utah, 1962—; tchr. art Emery County High Sch., Castle Dale, Utah, 1962-63; graphic artist Brigham Young U., 1954-56, 63-66; prodn. artist Evans Advt. Agy., Salt Lake City, 1968; dir. ednl. media Olympus High Sch., Salt Lake City, 1966-68; art dir. Telelecture Utah div. Family Svcs., Salt Lake City, 1968-69; art instr. Utah Tech. Coll., Salt Lake City, 1969-85; prof. graphic design Salt Lake Community Coll., 1985—; advisor, coach Vocat. Indsl. Clubs of Am., Salt Lake City, 1978-91. Illustrator: Book of Mormon Stories, 5 vols., 1971-76; exhibited in group shows at Salt Lake Art Festival, 1982, Pageant of the Arts, Am. Fork, 1980-89. Active Boy Scouts Am., American Fork, 1975-90; bd. dirs. art Am. Fork City, 1976-80; team mem. Utah State Bd. for Vocat. Edn. Accreditation, Salt Lake city, 1990. With USAR, 1953-62. Fellow Delta Phi Kappa (historian 1961-62), Salt Lake Community Coll. Faculty Senate, Utah Watercolor Soc. Republican. Mem. LDS Ch. Home: 590 N 200 E American Fork UT 84003-1711 Office: Salt Lake Community Coll PO Box 31808 Salt Lake City UT 84131-0808

REINISCH, NANCY RAE, therapist, consultant; b. Chgo., Mar. 31, 1953; d. Charles Richard and Marianne (Gross) R.; m. Paul A. Salmen, June 14, 1980; children: Chas, Marcus. BA in Sociology cum laude, Colo. Coll., 1975; cert. drug and alcohol counseling, U. Minn., 1980; MSW, U. Denver, 1982. Cert. relationship therapist; lic. clin. social worker. Counselor Rampart Boys' Home, Colorado Springs, Colo., 1975; advocate bilinqual community Migrants in Action, St. Paul, 1976; therapist Chrysalis Ctr. for Women, Mpls., 1979; team leader and prevention specialist Project Charlie, Edina, Minn., 1977-80, also trainer, cons., 1985—; mental health worker Bethesda Mental Health Ctr. and Hosp., Denver, 1980-83; therapist Gateway Alcohol Recovery Ctr., Aurora, Colo., 1983-84; pvt. practice therapy, also dir. Family Practice Counseling Service, Glenwood Springs, Colo., 1984—; co-dir. Valley Sexual Abuse Ctr.; bd. dirs. Adv./Safehouse Project, Glenwood Springs; mem. Valley View Hosp. Ethics com., Glenwood Springs, 1986—. Mem. sch. accountability com. Glenwood Springs, Human Svcs. Commn., Garfield County. Recipient Countywide Humanitarian Svc. award Glenwood Post and Garfield County Human Svcs. Commn., 1995. Mem. Nat. Assn. Social Workers, NOW, Nat. Abortion Rights Action League, ACLU, Colo. Pub. Interest Research Group. Democrat. Office: Family Practice Counseling Svc 1905 Blake Ave Glenwood Springs CO 81601-4250

REINISCH, RONALD FABIAN, materials engineer; b. N.Y.C., Mar. 21, 1931; s. Leo Robert and Florence (Fried) R.; m. Shelley G. Begun; children: Marc C., Florence. BS in Chemistry, U. Mich., 1953; MA, Harvard U., 1955; PhD, Tulane U., 1959. Group leader NASA-Ames Rsch. Ctr., Mountain View, Calif., 1963-77; engr. Solar Energy Rsch. Inst., Golden, Colo., 1977-78; founder, pres. Solorado Inc., Denver, 1978-82; mgr. Control Data Corp., Mpls., 1982-85; prin. engr. Micropolis Corp., Chatsworth, 1985-88; sr. engr. Seagate Tech., Scotts Valley, 1988—. Editor, author: Photochemistry of Macromolecules, 1975; patentee disc drive gasket. Fulbright fellow, 1958-59. Mem. Am. Soc. Materials. Home: 3022 Baronian Ct Soquel CA 95073-2959 Office: Seagate Tech 920 Disc Dr Scotts Valley CA 95066-4544

REINKE, STEFAN MICHAEL, lawyer; b. Concord, Calif., May 7, 1958; s. Albert Richard and Patricia Eleanor (Stefan) R. AA, Bakersfield Coll., 1978; AB, U. So. Calif., 1981; JD, U. Calif., Davis, 1984. Bar: Hawaii 1984, U.S. Dist. Ct. Hawaii 1984, U.S. Ct. Appeals (9th and Fed. cirs.) 1985. Assoc. Carlsmith, Wichman, Case, Mukai & Ichiki, Honolulu, 1984-86; dir. Lyons, Brandt, Cook & Hiramatsu, Honolulu, 1986—; lectr. Windword C.C. Bd. dirs. Hawaii Ctrs. for Ind. Living, Honolulu, 1985-91. Mem. ABA, Fed. Bar Assn. (pres. 1994—), Hawaii Bar Assn., Am. Arbitration Assn. (arbitrator and mediator), Def. Rsch. Inst., Nat. Employment Law Assn., Phi Beta Kappa, Phi Alpha Delta. Office: Lyons Brandt Cook & Hiramatsu 841 Bishop St Ste 1800 Honolulu HI 96813-3918

REINKOESTER, ROBERT WILLIAM, JR., critical care nurse; b. Port Clinton, Ohio, Feb. 27, 1951; s. Robert W. and Betty C. (Wightman) R.; m. Pamela C. Ertel, Mar. 16, 1973; children: Andrew, Erin. BA cum laude, U. Utah, 1978, BSN cum laude, 1985. RN, Utah; cert. critical care nurse. With McKesson Drug Co., 1973-82; staff nurse, charge nurse intermountain burn ctr. U. Utah Med. Ctr., 1985-88, asst. head nurse, 1988-89; cardiac catheterization lab. nurse U. Utah Health Sci. Ctr., 1989-91, supr. catheterization lab., nurse cardiac catheterization lab., 1991—, co-coord. catheterization lab., 1993—; instr. advanced cardiac life support, advanced burn life support, basic cardiac life support; counselor HIV testing program; community lectr. intermountain burn unit U. Utah, 1986-89, tutorial staff, 1984-85. Michael Found. scholar, 1983, Clara Hansen Jensen scholar, 1985. Mem. Am. Assn. Critical Care Nurses, Intercollegiate Knights (life), Delta Tau Delta. Home: 2241 E Laney Ave H Holloday UT 84117

REINMUTH, JAMES E., college dean. Dean Coll. Bus. Adminstrn. U Oreg., Eugene. Office: Dean Business Administration U Oregon Eugene OR 97403

REINMUTH, OSCAR MACNAUGHTON, physician, educator; b. Lincoln, Nebr., Oct. 23, 1927; s. Oscar William and Catharine Anne (MacNaughton) R.; m. Patricia Dixon, June 19, 1951 (div. Jan. 1977); children—David Dixon, Diane MacNaughton, Douglas Stewart; m. Audrey Longridge Holland, June 26, 1980. B.S., U. Tex., Austin, 1948; M.D. (F.B. Hanes research fellow 1950-51), Duke U., 1952. Intern Duke Hosp., 1952-53; asst. resident in medicine Yale U. Med. Ctr., 1953-54, NIH research trainee, 1954-55; asst. resident in neurology Boston City Hosp., 1955-56, chief resident, teaching fellow in neurology Harvard U. Neurol. unit, 1956-57; NIH spl. trainee, clin. asst. Nat. Hosp., London, 1957-58; from asst. prof. to prof. neurology U. Miami (Fla.) Med. Sch., 1958-77; prof. neurology and behavioral neuroscience, chmn. dept. U. Pitts. Med. Sch., 1977-93, prof. emeritus, 1994—; prof. neurology U. Ariz. Med. Sch., Tucson, 1993—; mem. research tng. com. A and C NIH, 1966-73. Served with AUS, 1946-47. Recipient Mosby award, 1952. Fellow ACP, Am. Acad. Neurology (1st v.p. 1973-76), Am. Neurol. Assn. (1st v.p. 1977-78, 2d v.p. 1976-77), Am. Heart Assn. (fellow stroke coun., vice chmn. 1978-79, chmn. 1980-82, editor publs. 1975-78, editor-in-chief Stroke jour. 1987-91, Award of Merit 1992). Home: 5545 N Entrada Quince Tucson AZ 85718-4709 Office: U Med Ctr Dept Neurology 1501 N Campbell Ave Tucson AZ 85724-0001

REINSCH, HARRY ORVILLE, power company executive; b. Los Angeles, Feb. 12, 1922; s. Harry Orville and Olive Gladys (Cooper) R.; m. Helen Marsh, Oct. 19, 1942; children: E. James, John H.(dec.), Richard M., Linda Reinsch Marshall. Student engring., U. Calif.-Davis, 1940-42. Asst. supt. Bechtel Power Corp., San Francisco, 1950-55; gen. supt. to mgr. bus. devel. Bechtel Power Corp., San Francisco and Washington, 1955-68; v.p. Bechtel Power Corp., San Francisco, 1968-72, v.p., dir., 1972-73, exec. v.p., dir., 1973-75, pres., 1975-86, vice chmn., 1986-87, dir., 1973-87; dir. Wells Fargo & Co., Wells Fargo Bank; hon. chmn. Korean-Am. Bus. Inst. Dir. No. Calif. Soc. to Prevent Blindness, 1983; dir. That Man May See, 1982; com. Republic of China Econ. Council, U.S.; trustee U. Mont. Found., 1981-85; pres. Korean-Am. Ch. of Calif., 1982-83; dir. Calif. Council Environ. and Econ. Balance. Mem. ASCE, ASME, Council for Energy Awareness (fellow, vice chmn., exec. com.). Clubs: World Trade, Bankers, Pacific Union (San Francisco). Home: 1940 Broadway Apt 10 San Francisco CA 94109-2216 Office: Bechtel Energy Corp 50 Beale St San Francisco CA 94105-1813

REISBERG, LEON ELTON, education educator; b. Dallas, Sept. 1, 1949; s. Morris Abraham and Gertrude (Turner) R.; m. Iris Fudell, July 3, 1973 (div. 1986); children: Joshua Fudell, Leah Fudell; m. Donna Brodigan, July 11, 1993. BS in Edn., U. Tex., Austin, 1971; MEd, U. Ark., Fayetteville, 1972; EdD, U. Kans., Lawrence, 1981. Tchr. Oklahoma City Sch. Dist., 1972-75, Putnam City Sch. Dist., Oklahoma City, 1975-78, U. Kans. Med. Ctr., Kansas City, 1978-79; asst. prof. Pacific Luth. U., Tacoma, 1981-88; tchr. Tacoma (Wash.) Sch. Dist., 1989-90; assoc. prof. edn. Pacific Luth. U., 1988-94; chmn. dept. spl. edn. Pacific Luth. U., Tacoma, 1986-93, chmn. profl. edn. adv. bd., 1992-94, assoc. dean sch. edn., 1993—, prof., 1995—; project dir., Consulting Spl. Edn. Personnel Tng. Project, Tacoma, 1983-86; chmn. Profl. Edn. Adv. Bd. Cons. editor Learning Disability Quar., 1981-89, Acad. Therapy, 1988-90, Intervention, 1990—; contbr. articles to profl. pubIs. Mem. Coun. Exceptional Children, Coun. Learning Disabilities (Pacific Rim region rep.), Assn. Trainer Spl. Edn. Pers., Phi Kappa Phi. Democrat. Jewish. Office: Pacific Luth U Sch Edn Tacoma WA 98447

REISCH, MICHAEL STEWART, social work educator; b. N.Y.C., Mar. 4, 1948; s. Joseph and Charlotte (Rosenberg) R.; m. Amy Jane Lewis, May 21, 1972; children: Jennifer, Nikki. BA in History with highest honors, NYU, 1968; PhD in History, SUNY, Binghamton, 1975; MSW, CUNY, 1979. Youth worker Washington-Heights-Inwood YM-YWHA, N.Y.C., 1965-66; editor, columnist Heights Daily News, Bronx, N.Y., 1966-68; rsch./teaching asst. SUNY, Binghamton, 1970-72; unit dir., program cons. Child Study Assn.-Wel Met, Inc., N.Y.C., 1970-72; asst. dir. youth div. Mosholu-Montefiore Community Ctr., Bronx, 1972-73; project dir. Silberman Found./N.Y. Assn. Deans, N.Y.C., 1973-74; asst. dean Sch. Social Welfare, asst. prof. SUNY, Stony Brook, 1974-79; asst. prof., then assoc. prof. Sch. Social Work U. Md., Balt., 1979-86; dir. Sch. Social Work, prof. social work/pub. adminstrn. San Francisco State U., 1986-95; prof. social welfare U. Pa., Phila., 1995—; cons. and spkr. in field. Co-author: From Charity to Enterprise, 1989 (Social Sci. Book of Month); editor, author various books in field; contbr. articles to profl. publs., chpts. to books. Cons. to numerous local, state, and fed. polit. campaigns, 1971—; mem. Gov.'s Adv. Coun. Human Resources, Md., 1983-86; pres. Welfare Advs., Md., 1983-86; campaign mgr. Rep. Barbara Mikulski, Balt., 1982; bd. dirs. Coleman Advs. for Children and Youth, 1987-95, San Francisco Internat. Program, 1987-95, Calif. Social Work Edn. Ctr., 1991-95, Ctr. for S.E. Asian Refugee Resettlement, 1992-95, Am. Jewish Congress, N. Calif., 1994-95, Coun. Internat. Programs, 1995—; chair Children's Budget Task Force City of San Francisco, 1989-92; mem. Mayor's Adv. Coun. on Drug Abuse, San Francisco, 1988-91; mem. steering com. Poverty Action Alliance, 1993-95. Woodrow Wilson Found. fellow, 1972-73. Mem. NASW (del. 1990-92, 94-96, chair peace and justice com. 1992—), Coun. on Social Work Edn. (com. on status of women 1989-92, bd. dirs. 1993—, chair commn. on ednl. policy 1994—), Am. Hist. Assn., Nat. Assn. Deans/Dirs. of Schs. and Social Work (sec. 1993-95), Calif. Assn. Deans/Dirs. of Schs. of Social Work (pres. 1992-94).

REISINGER, GEORGE LAMBERT, management consultant; b. Pitts., Aug. 28, 1930; s. Eugene Merle and Pauline Jane (Lambert) R.; m. Judith Ann Brush, Nov. 24, 1967; children—Douglas Lambert, Christine Elizabeth. B.S. in Bus. Adminstrn., Central Coll., 1953; postgrad., Cleveland-Marshall Law Sch., 1962-67. Asst. personnel mgr. Continental Can Co., Houston, 1958-60; mgr. labor relations The Glidden Co., Cleve., 1960-67; dir. employee relations Mobil Oil Corp., N.Y.C., Caracas, Dallas, Denver, 1967-78; sr. v.p. Minton & Assocs., Denver, 1978-82; v.p., ptnr. Korn-Ferry Internat., Denver, 1982-86; pres. The Sigma Group, Inc., Denver, 1986—. Bd. dirs. Ponderosa Hills Civic Assn., 1977-80, Arapahoe County Youth League, Parker Action Team for Drug Free Colo.; pres. Douglas County Youth League; bd. dirs., steering com. Rocky Mountain Lions Eye Inst. With USAF, 1953-58. Mem. Am. Soc. Pers. Adminstrs.,

N.Y. Pers. Mgmt. Soc., Colo. Soc. Pers. Adminstrn., Am. Soc. Profl. Cons., Rocky Mountain Inst. Fgn. Trade and Fin., Employment Mgmt. Assn. Republican. Methodist. Clubs: Denver Petroleum, Pinery Country, Republican 1200. Home: 7924 Deertrail Dr Parker CO 80134-8262 Office: Sigma Group Internat 6551 S Revere Pky Ste 125 Englewood CO 80111

REISMAN, RICHARD S., publisher; b. Spring Valley, N.Y., Nov. 6, 1953; s. Herbert and Phyllis Sharon (Hendler) R.; children: Marisa, Kimberly. BA, SUNY, Binghamton, 1975; JD, George Washington U., 1978; MBA, UCLA, 1985. Assoc. McCandless & Barrett, Washington, 1978-80, Donahue, Gallagher, Thomas & Woods, Oakland, Calif., 1980-83; mgr. corp. strategy Times Mirror, L.A., 1985-87; dir. mktg. L.A. Times/Orange County Edit., Costa Mesa, Calif., 1987-90; pub. Orange County Bus. Jour., Newport Beach, Calif., 1990—; bd. dirs. Linc Housing Corp., L.A. Adv. bd. Orange County Com. for the Arts, 1993—; sr. adv. bd. Chapman U. Bus. Sch., 1993; bd. dirs. Orange County Bus. Coun., 1995—. R.C. Baker Found. fellow UCLA Sch. Mgmt., 1984. Mem. Jr. Achievement Assn. (bd. govs. 1992—), World Trade Ctr. Assn. (bd. dirs. 1992—), Partnership 2010 (bd. dirs. 1992—). Office: Orange County Bus Jour 4590 Macarthur Blvd Ste 100 Newport Beach CA 92660-2024

REITAN, HAROLD THEODORE, management consultant; b. Max, N.D., Nov. 3, 1928; s. Walter Rudolph and Anna Helga (Glesne) R.; m. Margaret Lucille Bonsac, Dec. 29, 1954 (div.); children: Eric, Karen, Chris, Jon. BA, St. Olaf Coll., 1950; MA in Social Psychology, U. Fla., 1962, PhD, 1967. Commd. officer U.S. Air Force, 1951, advanced through grades to col.; comdr., U.S. Air Force Spl. Treatment Ctr., Lackland, Tex., 1971-74, U.S. Air Force Corrections and Rehab. Group, Lowry, Colo., 1974-76, Tech. Tng. Wing, 1976-78, ret., 1978; mgr. health svcs. Coors Industries, Golden, Colo., 1978-84, mgr. tng. and organizational devel., 1984-89, cons. mgmt. asseessment, tng. and devel., 1989—. Decorated Legion of Merit with oak leaf cluster, D.F.C. with oak leaf cluster, Bronze Star, Meritorious Svc. medal, Air medal with five oak leaf clusters. Mem. Am. Psychol. Assn., Phi Kappa Phi. Republican. Lutheran. Contbr. articles to profl. jours. Office: 116 S Nome St Aurora CO 80012-1242

REITER, MICHAEL JAY, cardiologist educator; b. N.Y.C., May 28, 1942; s. Arthur and Sally (Schneider) R.; m. Catherine Morton, Feb. 6, 1983. BS, Rensselaer Polytech. Inst., 1964; PhD, U. Rochester, 1969; MD, SUNY, Stony Brook, 1975. Diplomate Am. Bd. Internal Medicine, Nat. Bd. Med. Examiners; lic. MD, Colo., N.C., Tex., Calif. Intern and resident Parkland Meml. Hosp., Dallas, 1975-78; dir. Physicians Assoc. Sch. Duke U., Durham, N.C., 1979-82; asst. prof. U. Colo. Health Scis. Ctr., Denver, 1982-88, assoc. prof., 1988—. Editl. reviewer Am. Jour. Cardiology, 1983—, Archives Internal Medicine, 1984—, Jour. Am. Coll. Cardiology, 1984—, Jour. Electrophysiology, 1987—, Chest, 1985—, Jour. Electrocardiology, 1988—, Circulation, 1989—, Am. Jour. Physiology, 1990; contbr. numerous articles to profl. jours. Rsch. fellow NIMH, 1969-71, Duke U., 1978-82, Mark C. Lidwill, 1991-92; staff physician VA Hosp., Denver, 1987—, Fitzsimons Army Med. Ctr., Denver, 1987—, Univ. Hosp., Denver, 1982—. Mem. Fellow Am. Coll. Cardiology (gov., pres. Colo. chpt. 1992-95, bd. govs. ad hoc task force for tort reform 1993—); mem. Am. Heart Assn. (Clin. Cardiology Coun.), Am. Fedn. Clin. Rsch. (sr.), N.Am. Soc. Pacing and Electrophysiology, Cardiac Electrophysiology Soc., Colo. Soc. Cardiovascular Medicine. Home: 8101 E Dartmouth Ave Apt 77 Denver CO 80231-4260 Office: Univ Colo Health Scis Ctr 4200 E 9th Ave Box B-130 Denver CO 80262

REITZ, BRUCE ARNOLD, cardiac surgeon, educator; b. Seattle, Sept. 14, 1944; s. Arnold B. and Ruth (Stillings) R.; m. Nan N. Norton, Oct. 3, 1970, children: Megan, Jay. B.S., Stanford U., 1966; M.D., Yale U., 1970. Diplomate: Am. Bd. Surgery, Am. Bd. Thoracic Surgery. Intern Johns Hopkins Hosp., Balt., 1970-71, cardiac surgeon-in-charge, 1982-92; resident Stanford U. Hosp., (Calif.), 1971-72, 74-78; clin. assoc. Nat. Heart Lung Blood Inst., NIH, Bethesda, Md., 1972-74; asst. prof. Stanford U. Sch. Medicine, 1977-81, assoc. prof., 1981-82; prof. surgery Johns Hopkins U. Sch. Medicine, Balt., 1982-92; prof., chmn. Sch Medicine Stanford (Calif.) U., 1992—. Developer heart-lung transplant technique, 1981. Office: Stanford U Sch Medicine Dept Cardiothoracic Surgery Stanford CA 94305

REITZ, RONALD CHARLES, biochemist, educator; b. Dallas, Feb. 27, 1939; s. Percy Allison and Hazel Alberta (Thomison) R.; m. Jeanne, Jan. 23, 1965; children: Erica, Brett. BS in Chemistry, Tex. A&M U., 1961; PhD in Biochemistry, Tulane U., 1966. Lab. instr., rsch. asst. Tulane U., New Orleans, 1962-66; rsch. assoc., NIH postdoc. fellow U. Mich., Ann Arbor, 1966-69; asst. prof. biochemistry U. N.C., Chapel Hill, 1969-75; assoc. prof. U. Nev., Reno, 1978-80, prof., 1980—, interim chmn. biochemistry, 1988-90; vis. scientist Unilever Rsch. Lab. The Frythe, Welwyn Herts., England, 1968, E.I. DuPont de Nemours, 1984; vis. prof. Nagoya City (Japan) U., 1990, Max-Planck Inst. fur Biophys. Chemie, Gottingen, Germany, 1990-91; vis. scientist lectr. idaho State U., Pocatello, 1987. Contbr. numerous papers and articles to profl. jours. Mem. AAAS, Am. Soc. Biol. Chemists, Am. Soc. Pharmacology and Exptl. Therapeutics, Am. Oil Chemists' Soc., Western Pharm. Soc., Rsch. Soc. Alcoholism, Entol. Soc. Am., Sigma Xi. Republican. Methodist. Office: U Nev Sch of Medicine Dept Biochemistry Reno NV 89557

REJMAN, DIANE LOUISE, systems analyst, aerospace; b. Hartford, Conn., Jan. 14, 1956; d. Louis P. and Genevieve (Walukevich) R. BS in Aviation Adminstrn., Embry Riddle Aero. U., 1980; M in Internat. Mgmt., Am. Grad. Sch. Internat. Mgmt., 1991; cert. in cross cultural negotiation, Western Internat. Univ., 1994. Indsl. engr./planner Hamilton Aviation, Tucson, 1980-82; indsl. engr. assoc. Gates Learjet, Tucson, 1984; tech. writer, FAA coord. Dee Howard Co., San Antonio, 1984-86; indsl. engr. McDonnell Douglas Helicopter Systems, Mesa, Ariz., 1986-88; systems analyst McDonnell Douglas Helicopter Co., Mesa, Ariz., 1988-95; sr. industry analyst Frost and Sullivan, Mountain View, Calif., 1995—; bd. dirs. McDonnell Douglas Helicopter Co. Employee Community Fund., adminstr. 1992-95. With U.S. Army, 1977-80. Home: 562 Kendall Ave #42 Palo Alto CA 94306

RELIGA, JAMES PAUL, software engineer; b. Berwyn, Ill., Sept. 11, 1953; s. John James and Stella Gertrude (Pavlis) R.; m. Peggy Lee Partlow, Mar. 15, 1982. BA in Physics, U. Calif., Irvine, 1975. Sci. programming specialist Lockheed Missiles and Space Co., Sunnyvale, Calif., 1983, sr. rsch. engr., 1983-85, rsch. specialist, 1985-94; software cons., 1994—.

RELMAN, DAVID ARNOLD, physician, educator; b. Boston, Sept. 28, 1955; s. Arnold Seymour and Harriet Morse (Vitkin) R. SB, MIT, 1973; MD, Harvard U., 1982. Diplomate Am. Bd. Internal Medicine, sub-bd. Infectious Diseases. Resident in medicine Mass. Gen. Hosp., Boston, 1982-85, fellow in infectious diseases, 1985-86; fellow in infectious diseases Stanford (Calif.) U., 1986-92, asst.prof. medicine and microbiology and immunology, 1992—. Contbg. author: Scientific American Medicine, 1987—. Vol. physician, adv. bd. Rock Medicine, Haight-Ashbury Free Med. Clinics, San Francisco, 1987—. Recipient Upjohn award, 1994; Markey Biomed. scholar Lucille P. Markey Charitable Trust, 1990—. Mem. Am. Soc. for Microbiology, Am. Fedn. for Clin. Rsch. Office: Palo Alto VA Med Ctr 3801 Miranda Ave # 154T Palo Alto CA 94304-1207

RELYEA, ROBERT GORDON, management consultant; b. Bloomington, N.Y., Nov. 10, 1917; s. Aaron Dewitt and Margaret (Smedes) R.; m. Eleanor Florence Caminiti, June 2, 1938 (dec. Feb. 1984); children: Robert Paul, Peter Douglas, Paula Florence Relyea Holsinger; m. Ann P. Delmonico, June 23, 1985. BGS, Rollins Coll., 1966; MS, Fla. State U., 1969; PhD, Clayton U., 1987. Mgr. UTC div. United Aircraft, Inc., Cape Canaveral, Fla., 1964-69; pres. Better Mgmt. Assocs. Inc., Satellite Beach, Fla., 1969-71, Sun Lakes, Ariz., 1973—; mgr. quality and svc. United Mobile Homes, Inc., Chandler, Ariz., 1971-73; instr. Maricopa Community Colls., PHoenix, 1974—; quality mgr. IMC Magnetics, Inc., Tempe, Ariz., 1979-80; asst. to pres. Ecotronics Labs., Inc., Scottsdale, Ariz., 1980-81; quality mgr. Parker-Hannifin Co., Goodyear, Ariz., 1981-83; sr. quality auditor Govt. Electronics Group/Radar Systems Div. Motorola, Inc., Tempe, 1983-88; bd. dirs. SanTan Adobe, Inc., Sun Lakes. Contbr. articles to profl. publs. Scoutmaster Boy Scouts Am., Ridgewood, N.J., 1946-57; bd. dirs. Sun Lakes Home Owners Assn., 1974-78, Adult Action, Inc., Mesa, 1975-91, Cactus-Pine coun. Girls Scouts U.S.A., Phoenix, 1980-83. Mem. Nat. Contract Mgmt. Assn., Am. Soc. for Quality Control (del. to USSR, Bulgaria and Hungary 1988), Missile, Space and Range Pioneers (life), Order of Arrow, Masons, Shriners, Pi Lambda Theta. Home and Office: Better Mgmt Assocs Inc 9003 N Citrus Ln Sun Lakes AZ 85248

REMEN, JOHN FREDRICK, aerospace engineer; b. Neurnberg, Germany, Feb. 4, 1964; parents Am. citizens; s. Donald Joseph and Ursula (Garweg) R. BS in Aerospace Engring., U. Kans., 1987; MS in Sys. Mgmt., U. So. Calif., 1995. Aerospace engr. Phillips Lab. USAF, Edwards AFB, Calif., 1989—. Mem. City of Lancaster (Calif.) Ptnrs: Citizens and Govt. Working for Tomorrow Program, 1992. Mem. AIAA (Solid Rocket Tech. Com. Recognition award 1991). Republican.

REMER, DONALD SHERWOOD, chemical engineer, engineering economist, educator, administrator; b. Detroit, Mich., Feb. 16, 1943; s. Nathan and Harriet R.; m. Louise Collen, Dec. 21, 1969; children: Tanya, Candace, Miles. B.S., U. Mich., 1965; M.S., Calif. Inst. Tech., 1966, Ph.D., 1970. Registered profl. engr., Calif., Mich., La. Tech. service engr., chem. raw materials div. coordinator, sr. running plan coordinator, task team mgr. Exxon, Baton Rouge, 1970-75; assoc. prof. engring. Harvey Mudd Coll., Claremont, Calif., 1975-79, prof., 1980—, Oliver C. Field prof. engring., dir. Energy Inst., 1981-83; cons., mem. tech. staff, mgr. planning analysis Jet Propulsion Lab., Calif. Inst. Tech., 1976—; co-founder, ptnr. Claremont Cons. Group, 1979—; mem. adv. council Nat. Energy Found., N.Y.C., 1981-85; mem. Inst. Mgmt. Cons., 1988-89. Case study editor Am. Soc. Engring. Edn., Inst. Indsl. Engrs., Engring. Economist, 1977-89; mem. editorial bd. Jour. Engring. Costs and Prodn. Econs., 1985-91, Internat. Jour. Prodn. Econs., 1992—; contbr. articles to profl. jours. Shelter mgr. ARC, Baton Rouge, 1965-70. Recipient Outstanding Chem. Engr. award U. Mich., 1965, First Place Pub. Relations award Am. Inst. Chem. Engring., 1975, Outstanding Alumni Fund Achievement award Calif. Inst. Tech., 1976, Outstanding Young Man of Am. award, 1976, NASA award, 1983, Best Paper of the Year in Jour. Parametrics, Internat. Soc. Parametric Analysts, 1991-92, Centennial award certificate Am. Soc. Engring. Edn., 1993; named Outstanding Research Seminar Speaker Occidental Research Corp., 1976. Mem. Am. Soc. Engring. Mgmt. (bd. dirs. 1981-83), Toastmasters Club (pres. Claremont-Pomona chpt. 1978).

REN, XIN, criminology educator; b. Beijing, China, Feb. 25, 1956; came to U.S., 1985; d. Futian and Zhilin (Zhang) Ren; m. Sijin (Brad) Li, Apr. 20, 1983; 1 child, Valerie Christina Li. BA, People's U. China, Beijing, 1981; MA, U. Ottawa, 1986; PhD, U. Pa., 1992. Rsch. intern Phila. Elder Abuse Task Force, 1987-88; rsch. asst. Office of Pub. Defender, State of N.J., Trenton, 1987-89, Nat. Acad. Sci., Washington, 1989-90; teaching asst. dept. criminology U. Ottawa, Ont., Can., 1983-85; lectr. dept. sociology Villanova (Pa.) U., 1988-89; instr. Sellin Ctr. Studies in Criminology and Criminal Law U. Pa., Phila., 1987-90; lectr. div. criminal justice Calif. State U., Sacramento, 1990-92, asst. prof. div. criminal justice, 1992—; guest lectr. Ctr. for Asian and Pacific Studies, Calif. State U., Sacramento, 1991. Contbr. chpts. to books. Third World scholar U. Ottawa, 1983-85; P.E.O. Internat. Peace scholar, 1984-85. Mem. Chinese Soc. Juvenile Delinquency Studies, Chinese Soc. Criminology (mem. adv. bd. 1994—), Am. Soc. Criminology, Internat. Soc. Victimology.

RENARD, RONALD LEE, allergist; b. Chgo., July 31, 1949; s. Robert James and Dorothy Mae (Fruik) R.; m. Maureen Ann Gilmore, Aug. 5, 1972 (div. Mar. 1992); children: Jeffrey, Steven, Justin, Leigh Ellen; m. Catherine L. Walker, Apr. 1, 1992; children: Morgan, Michal, Luke. 1 & 2 Degre de la Langue, U. de Montepellier, France, 1970; BS in French, U. San Francisco, 1971; MD, Creighton U., 1976. Dir. med. ICU, lt. U.S. Army Hosp., Ft. Leonard Wood, Md., 1980-81; dir. respiratory therapy, asst. chief allergy svc. Walter Reed Med. Ctr., Washington, 1981-84; staff allergist Chico (Calif.) Med. Group, 1984-86; allergist pvt. practice Redding, Calif., 1986—; dir. ACLS program Enloe Hosp., Chico, 1988-91; bd. dirs. Am. Lung Assn. Calif., 1989-91, med. dir. asthma camp, Chico, Redding, 1986-95; asst. prof. medicine USPHS, Bethesda, Md., 1982-84; asst. prof. family medicine U. Calif. Davis Med. Sch.. Redding, 1990-94; Shasta County Planning Commr., 1994-95. Contbr. articles to profl. jours. Fellow Am. Acad. Allergy & Immunology, Am. Coll. Allergists; mem. Alpha Omega Alpha Nat. Honor Med. Soc., Assn. Mil. Allergists, Calif. Thoracic Soc. Republican. Roman Catholic. Office: 1950 Rosaline Ave Ste A Redding CA 96001-2543

RENDALL, STEVEN FINLAY, language educator, editor, translator, critic; b. Geneva, Ill., May 2, 1939; s. Harvard John and Jessie Evangeline (Galbraith) R.; children from previous marriage: Matthew, Ruby Larisch; m. Lisa Dow Neal, May, 1992; 1 child, Josephine Dow Neal. BA summa cum laude in Philosophy, U. Colo., 1961; postgrad., Université de Lille, 1961-62, Johns Hopkins U., 1962-67; PhD, Johns Hopkins U., 1967. From asst. prof. romance langs. to assoc. prof. romance langs. U. Oreg., Eugene, 1967-79, prof. romance langs., 1979—; guest prof. Universität Konstanz, 1981; leader NEH summer seminar, 1987. Author: Distinguo: Reading Montaigne Differently, 1992; editor: Montaigne, 1984, Of History, 1994; translator: The Practice of Everyday Life, 1984, History and Memory, 1992, Astrea, 1995; co-editor: Comparative Literature, 1990—, assoc. editor 1978—, asst. editor, 1972-78, acting editor, 1980, 85-86; mem. editl. bd., adv. com. Montaigne Studies, 1989—; contbr. 35 articles to profl. jours., 37 book revs. NEH fellow Ctr. Rsch. on Translation SUNY, Binghamton, 1993, Camargo Found. fellow, 1988, Alexander von Humboldt-Stiftung Rsch. fellow, 1980-82, 94, NEH fellow, 1977, Danforth fellow, 1962-67, Gilman fellow, 1964-67, Woodrow Wilson fellow, 1962-63; Fulbright scholar, 1961-62. Mem. Modern Lang. Assn., Phi Beta Kappa. Home: 3217 N 25th St Tacoma WA 98406-6115 Office: U Oregon 223 Friendly Hall Eugene OR 97403

RENDON, LEONARD, interior designer. Interior designer Bobi Leonard, Inc., Santa Monica, Calif. Mem. Am. Soc. Interior Designer. Address: 1613 Chelsea Rd # 208 San Marino CA 91108-2419

RENECKER, LYLE ALFRED, animal science educator; b. Stratford, Ont., Can., July 6, 1952; came to the U.S., 1990; s. Alfred John and Ella Florence (Wickie) R.; m. Donna May Ashick, Aug. 28, 1976 (div. Oct. 1993); m. Teresa Ann Tomany, June 11, 1994. BSc, Wilfred Laurier U., 1974; honours Sc, Laurentian U., 1975, MSc, 1983; PhD, U. Alta., 1987. Grad. rsch. asst. dept. animal sci. U. Alta., Edmonton, 1980-87, rsch. assoc., post-doctoral fellow dept. animal sci., 1986-87, 88-90; asst. prof. in animal sci., reindeer and game farming U. Alaska, Fairbanks, 1990-93, assoc. prof. in animal sci., 1993—; rsch. cons. Ulapalakua Ranch, Maui, Hawaii, 1988, Cedar Falls Elk Ranch, Rockwood, Ont., 1988-89, Elk Island Nat. Pk., Alta., 1988, 88-90, Agrofair Can., Ltd., Ottawa, 1989, Daniel Munroe and Indsl. Rsch., Inc., St. John's, Newfoundland, 1991, Que. Securities Commn., Montreal, 1991, others; chmn. internat. steering com. Internat. Wildlife Ranching Symposium, 1990-92, 1992—; mem. Game Farm Rsch. and Devel. Adv. Coun., No. Lights Coll., Dawson Breek, B.C., 1991—; spkr. in field; others. Editor: The Game Grower, 1986-87; co-editor: Wildlife Production: Conservation and Sustainable Development, 1991; contbr. chpts. to books and numerous articles to profl. jours. Grantee U. Alaska at Fairbanks Equipment Grants Fund, 1991, Alaska Sci. and Tech. Found., 1991-93, U. Alaska at Fairbanks Reindeer Rsch. Program Support Fund, 1991—, Nat. Pk. Svc., 1991—, 92—, 93—, USDA-Bur. of Land Mgmt./USDA-Soil Conservation Svc./U. Alaska Fairbanks, 1992-93, N.W. Territories Govt., 1992-93, U.S. Fish & Wildlife Svc., 1993—, Alta. Venison Coun., 1993—, Internat. Rsch. Partnership, others. Mem. Reindeer Owners and Breeders' Assn., N.Am. Elk Breeders' Assn. (meat quality com. 1994), Soc. for Range Mgmt., Brit. Deer Farmers' Assn., Wildlife Diseases Assn., Alta. Venison Coun., Can. Venison Coun., Am. Bison Assn., Can. Bison Assn., Can. Wildlife Fedn., New Zealand Deer Farmers' Assn., The Wildlife Soc. Lutheran. Office: U Alaska Fairbanks Afes PO Box 757200 Fairbanks AK 99775

RENEKER, MAXINE HOHMAN, librarian; b. Chgo., Dec. 2, 1942; d. Roy Max and Helen Anna Christina (Anacker) Hohman; m. David Lee Reneker, June 20, 1964 (dec. Dec. 1979); children: Sarah Roeder, Amy Johannah, Benjamin Congdon. BA, Carleton Coll., 1964; MA, U. Chgo., 1970; DLS, Columbia U., 1992. Asst. reference libr. U. Chgo. Libraries, 1965-66; classics libr. U. Chgo. Libr., 1967-70, asst. head acquisitions, 1970-71, personnel libr., 1971-73; personnel/bus. libr. U. Colo. Libr., Boulder, 1978-80; asst. dir. sci. and engring. div. Columbia U., N.Y.C., 1981-85; assoc. dean of univ. librs. for pub. svcs. Ariz. State U. Libr., Tempe, 1985-89; dir. instrnl. and rsch. svcs. Stanford (Calif.) Univ. Librs., 1989-90; dir. info. svcs., dir. Dudley Knox Libr. Naval Postgrad. Sch., Monterey, Calif., 1993—; acad. libr. mgmt. intern Coun. on Libr. Resources, 1980-81; chmn. univ. librs. sect. Assn. Coll. and Rsch. Librs., 1989-90. Contbr. articles to profl. jours. Rsch. grantee Coun. on Library Resources, Columbia U., 1970-71, fellow, 1990-92. Mem. ALA, Am. Soc. Info. Sci., Sherlockian Scion Soc., Phi Beta Kappa, Beta Phi Mu. Home: 437 College Ave Palo Alto CA 94306-1525 Office: Naval Postgrad Sch Dudley Knox Libr 411 Dyer Rd Monterey CA 93943-5198

RENETZKY, ALVIN, publisher; b. Bklyn., Aug. 2, 1940; s. Sam and Anna (Preiser) R.; m. Phyllis Ann (div.); 1 child, Davida; m. Cheryl Linden. PhD, U. Southern Calif., 1966. Publisher Academic Media, Los Angeles, 1967-70, Ready Reference Press, Santa Monica, Calif., 1974—. Editor: Directory of Career Resources for Women, 1980, Directory of Career Resources for Minorities, 1981, Career Employment Opportunities Directory, 1985, Directory of Internships; exec. prodr.: (video series) Guidance Club for Kids, 1992, Guidance Club for Teens, 1993, 94, Guidance Club for Women, 1994, Guidance Club for Parents, 1994, Career Club, 1994. Office: Ready Reference Press PO Box 5879 Santa Monica CA 90409-5879

RENFORD, EDWARD J., hospital administrator; b. July 16, 1943; married. AA, L.A. City Coll., 1969; BA, Calif. State U., 1971; MA, Pepperdine U., 1983. Asst. fiscal officer Martin Luther King Jr., Drew Med. Ctr., L.A., 1974-75, assoc. adminstr. fin. svcs., 1984-86, hosp. adminstr., 1990—; dir. fiscal svcs. LAC Harbor UCLA Med. Ctr., Torrance, Calif., 1975-77, asst. adminstr. fin., 1977-79, assoc. adminstr., 1979-82; asst. adminstr. Centinela Hosp. Med. Ctr., Inglewood, Calif., 1982-84; assoc. exec. dir. LAC Rancho Los Amigos Med. Ctr., Downey, Calif., 1986-89; chief staff Hosp. Adminstrn./ Dept. Health Svcs., L.A., 1989-90. Recipient numerous awards. Home: PO Box 54221 Atlanta GA 30308-0221 Office: LAC-King-Drew Med Ctr 12021 Wilmington Ave Los Angeles CA 90059-3019

RENFRO, DONALD WILLIAM, architect; b. Bakersfield, Calif., Nov. 13, 1931; s. Donald Francis and Lennie Lorraine (Despain) R.; student Bakersfield Coll., 1949-51; cert. energy auditor, Calif.; registered, cert. Nat. Council Archtl. Registration Bds.; m. Nancy M. Henry, Aug. 6, 1982; children—Dayna, Trisha, Donna. Staff designer Whitney Biggar, Architect, 1955-61; asso. Eddy & Paynter Assos., Bakersfield, Calif., 1961-70; prin. Eddy Paynter Renfro & Assos., Bakersfield, 1970-78; pres. Donald Renfro & Assocs., Bakersfield, 1978-84; pres. Renfro-Russell & Assocs., Inc., 1984-90; pres. Renfro & Assocs, Bakersfield, Calif., 1990—. pres., dir. Design Research Assos., Inc.; past commr. Calif. Bd. Archtl. Examiners. Mem. Bakersfield Coll. Archtl. Adv. Com.; mem. Bakersfield Design Rev. Bd. Served with U.S. Army, 1952-54. Mem. AIA (past pres. Golden Empire chpt.) past dir. So. Calif. chpt.). Republican. Lodge: Kiwanis (past dir.). Office: 2200 Truxtun Ave Bakersfield CA 93301

RENFRO, LEONARD EARL, II, protective services professional; b. Ventura, Calif., July 18, 1937; s. Leonard Earl and Mary Frances (Gillette) R.; m. Mavis Helen Whitten, Jan. 27, 1956; children: Marjorie Lynne, Teresa Lea, Julie Eileen, Karen Jean. AA, Ventura Coll., 1957; BS, Calif. Luth. U., 1975. Advanced cert. law enforcement, Calif. Farm laborer Valley Ranch Assocs., Oxnard, Calif., 1955-57; roustabout oil field Texaco, Inc., Santa Paula, Calif., 1957-60; dep. sheriff Ventura (Calif.) County Sheriff's Dept., 1960-87; field rep. Calif. Bd. Corrections, Sacramento, 1987-95. Cpl. USMC, 1954-62. Mem. Calif. State Sheriff's Assn., Ventura County Dep. Sheriff's Assn. (pres. 1968-69), Al Malakiah Shrine, York Rite (Ventura Valley), Scottish Rite (Ventura Valley), Masons (master 1980-81). Republican. Baptist. Home: 102 Rawlings Ct Folsom CA 95630-4846 Office: State Bd Corrections 600 Bercut Dr Sacramento CA 95814-0131

RENGARAJAN, SEMBIAM RAJAGOPAL, electrical engineering educator, researcher, consultant; b. Mannargudi, Tamil Nadu, India, Dec. 12, 1948; came to U.S., 1980; s. Srinivasan and Rajalakshmi (Renganathan) Rajagopalan; m. Kalyani Srinivasan, June 24, 1982; children: Michelle, Sophie. BE with honors, U. Madras, India, 1971; MTech, Indian Inst. Tech., Kharagpur, 1974; PhD in Elec. Engring., U. N.B., Fredericton, Can., 1980. Mem. tech. staff Jet Propulsion Lab., Pasadena, Calif., 1983-84; asst. prof. elec. engring. Calif. State U., Northridge, 1980-83, assoc. prof., 1984-87, prof., 1987—; vis. prof. UCLA, 1987-88, vis. rschr., 1984-93; cons. Hughes Aircraft Co., Canoga Park, Calif., 1982-87, NASA-Jet Propulsion Lab., Pasadena, 1987-90, 92-94, Ericsson Radar Electronics, Sweden, 1990-92, Martin Mariette, 1995; guest rsch. Chalmers U. Sweden, 1990, UN Devel. Program, 1993. Contbr. sci. papers to profl. publs. recipient Outstanding Faculty award Calif. State U., Northridge, 1985, Disting. Engring. Educator or Yr. award Engrs. Coun., L.A., 1995, Meritorious Performance and profl. Promise award, 1986, 88, Merit award San Fernando Valley Engrs., Coun., 1989, cert. of recognition NASA, 1991, 92; Nat. Merit scholar Govt. India, 1965-71. Fellow Inst. Advancement Engrs., IEEE (L.A. chpt. sec., treas. antennas and propagation soc. 1981-82, vice chmn. 1982-83, chmn. 1983-84), Internat. Union Radio Sci. (U.S. nat. com.), The Electromagnetics Acad. Office: Calif State U 18111 Nordhoff St Northridge CA 91330-0001

RENIERS, ROBERT, food products executive; b. 1946. With Ernst & Ernst, Denver, 1972-75; sec.-treas. Exeter (Calif.) Packers Inc., Consolidated Growers Inc., 1975—; ptnr. 7th Std. Ranch Co., Bakersfield, Calif., 1986—. With U.S. Mil., 1968-72. Office: 7th Std Ranch Co 33374 Lerdo Hwy Bakersfield CA 93308*

RENNE, JANICE LYNN, interior designer; b. Los Angeles, July 16, 1952; d. George Joseph and Dolly Minni (Neubauer) R.; m. William Lee Kile, Dec. 6, 1975 (div. Sept. 1983). BA, Sweet Briar Coll., 1974; AA, Interior Designers Inst., 1985. Lic. gen. contractor, Calif.; cert. interior designer, Calif. Coun. for Interior Design Certification. Exec. trainee Bullock's, Santa Ana, Calif., 1974, Pub. Fin., Inc., Huntington Beach, Calif., 1975; bookkeeper William L. Kile DDS, Inc., Santa Barbara, Calif., 1979-81, Nelson & Hamilton, Inc., Santa Barbara, 1981-82; interior designer Ultimate Designs, Irvine, Calif., 1984-85, sr. designer, 1985-86; draftsperson JBI Inc., Long Beach, Calif., 1984-85; prin. designer Janice Renne Interior Designs, Newport Beach, Calif., 1986—; space planner Design Pak II, Newport Beach, 1987-88; State of Calif. rep. task force for developing self-cert. process for Calif. interior designers, Internat. Soc. Interior Design, 1991. Created utility room design for Easter Seals Design House, 1985; weekly radio show host on restaurant design, 1986; work published in Orange County mag. and L.A. Times., 1988. Recipient scholarship Calif. Inst. Applied Design, Newport Beach, 1984. Mem. Internat. Soc. Interior Designers (grad. assoc. designer butler's pantry, assoc. designer Design House powder rm. 1988, Orange County chpt. 1988-89, asst. editor Orange County chpt. 1988-89, asst. editor Orange County chpt. Quar. Newsletter, Orange County chpt. gen. bd. 1991-92, chair licensing com. 1991-92, bd. dirs. 1991-92), Color Assn. of U.S., Constrn. Specifier Inst., Nat. Exec. Women in Hospitality, Calif. Legis. Conf. in Interior Design (gen. bd. 1991-92, v.p. comm. 1992-93), Orange County and Newport Beach, Letip Internat. (sec. 1987, 89, 90, treas. 1991, pres. 1993), Internat. Interior Design Assn., Tall Club Orange County (Miss Congeniality 1994, exec. v.p. 1995, co-editor High Life 1994-95, editor 1995). Republican. Lutheran.

RENNER, JEANNETTE IRENE (JAY RENNER), publishing executive; b. Omaha, Feb. 28, 1930; d. Arthur Thomas and Agnes Irene (Miller) R.; m. Edward Francis Witucki, June 11, 1949 (div. June 1967); children: Lynn Witucki Rolston, Daniel Oren. BA in Anthropology summa cum laude, UCLA, 1960, PhD in Anthropology, 1966. Instr. anthropology Calif. State U., L.A., 1967-69, asst. prof., 1970-75, assoc. prof., 1976-82, prof., 1983-86, prof. emeritus, 1986—; owner, pub. Condor Book Co., Auburn, Calif., 1983—. Author: (textbooks) Introducing Linguistic Analysis: The Comprehensive Course, 1984, Introducing Linguistic Analysis: Phonemics, 1984, Introducing Linguistic Analysis: Morphology and Syntax, 1984; contbr. articles and rev. to profl. publs. Mem. Am. Anthropol. Assn. (presenter, past mem. panel on future cultures), West Coast Assn. Women Historians (presenter), Sigma Xi (field work grantee 1971), Phi Beta Kappa. Office: Condor Book Co 3037 Grass Valley Hwy Auburn CA 95602-2501

RENSE, PAIGE, editor, publishing company executive; b. Iowa, May 4, 1929; m. Kenneth Noland, Apr. 10, 1994. Student, Calif. State U., Los Angeles. Editor-in-chief Architectural Digest, Los Angeles, 1970—; sr. v.p., also bd. dirs. Knapp Communications Corp. Recipient Nat. Headliner Women in Communications award, 1983, Pacifica award So. Calif. Resources Coun., 1978, Editorial award Dallas Mkt. Ctr., 1978, Golden award Chgo. Design Resources Svc., 1982, Agora award, 1982, Outstanding Profls. in Communications award, 1982, Trailblazers award, 1983, ; named Woman of Yr. Los Angeles Times, 1976, Woman of Yr. Muses, 1986; named to Interior Design Hall of Fame. Office: Architectural Digest 6300 Wilshire Blvd Fl 11 Los Angeles CA 90048-5202

RENSON, JEAN FELIX, psychiatry educator; b. Liège, Belgium, Nov. 9, 1930; came to U.S., 1960; s. Louis and Laurence (Crahai) R.; m. Gisèle Bouillenne, Sept. 8, 1956; children: Marc, Dominique, Jean-Luc. MD, U. Liège, 1959; PhD in Biochemistry, George Washington U., 1971. Diplomate Am. Bd. Psychiatry. Asst. prof. U. Liège, 1957-60; rsch. fellow U. Liege, 1966-72; clin. assoc. prof. dept. psychiatry U. Calif., San Francisco, 1978—; vis. asst. prof. Stanford U., Palo Alto, Calif., 1972-77. Assoc. editor: Fundamentals of Biochemical Pharmacology, 1971. NIH fellow, 1960-66. Democrat.

RENWICK, EDWARD S., lawyer; b. L.A., May 10, 1934. AB, Stanford U., 1956, LLB, 1958. Bar: Calif. 1959, U.S. Dist. Ct. (cen. dist.) Calif. 1959, U.S. Ct. Appeals (9th cir.) 1963, U.S. Dist. Ct. (so. dist.) Calif. 1973, U.S. Dist. Ct. (no. dist.) Calif. 1977, U.S. Dist. Ct. (ea. dist.) Calif. 1981, U.S. Supreme Ct. 1985. Ptnr. Hanna and Morton, L.A.; mem., bd. vis. Stanford Law Sch., 1967-69; mem. environ. and natural resources adv. bd. Stanford Law Sch. Bd. dirs. Calif. Supreme Ct. Hist. Soc. Fellow Am. Coll. Trial Lawyers, Am. Bar Found.; mem. ABA (mem. sect. on litigation, antitrust law, bus. law, chmn. sect. of nat. resources, energy and environ. law 1987-88, mem. at large coord. group energy law 1989-92, sect. rep. coord. group energy law 1995—, Calif. del. legal com., interstate oil compact com.), Calif. Arboretum Assn. (trustee 1986-92), L.A. County Bar Assn. (chmn. natural resources law sect. 1974-75), The State Bar of Calif., Assn. Atty.- Mediators, Chancery Club (pres. 1992-93), Phi Delta Phi. Office: Hanna and Morton 600 Wilshire Blvd Fl 17 Los Angeles CA 90017-3212

RENZ, JEFFREY THOMAS, lawyer; b. Plainfield, N.J., June 23, 1949; s. Charles Joseph Jr. and Beatrice Elizabeth (Kellogg) R.; m. Heidi Christine Hyde, Sept. 15, 1970 (div. June 1973); m. Diane Benjamin, June 26, 1982; children: Linnaea, Wynne. BA, U. Mont., 1971, JD, 1979. Bar: Mont. 1979, Ill. 1979, U.S. Dist. Ct. Mont. 1979, U.S. Ct. Appeals (9th cir.) 1982, U.S. Supreme Ct. 1988. Assoc. Karaganis & Gail Ltd., Chgo., 1979-80; ptnr. Patten & Renz, Billings, Mont., 1980-85; pvt. practice law Billings, 1985-93; asst. prof. law U. Mont., Missoula, 1993—. Contbr. article to profl. jours. Mem. adv. com. Morrison fo Gov., Helena, Mont., 1987—; legal dir. ACLU Mont., Billings, 1983-92, bd. dirs. Affiliate Legal Dirs. ACLU,N.Y.C., 1985-92, lectr. Legal Dirs. Conf., 1987. Capt. U.S. Army, 1971-75. Mem. Mont. Bar Assn., Yellowstone County Bar Assn., Am. Judicature Soc., Assn. Trial Lawyers Am., Mont. Trial Lawyers Assn., Yellowstone Trial Lawyers Assn. (pres. 1989-90), Silent Sentinal Soc., Alpha Tau Omega. Democrat. Roman Catholic. Office: U Mont Sch of Law Missoula MT 59812

RESARE, CRAIG, food executive; b. 1952. BS, Calif. State U., Hayward, 1975. Account mgr. Sunshine Biscuits, Inc., Oakland, Calif., 1976-89; controller Sunland Products Calif., Pleasanton, 1989—. Office: Sun-Land Products of Calif 5568 Gibraltar Dr Pleasanton CA 94588-8544*

RESCH, CHARLOTTE SUSANNA, plastic surgeon; b. Charlottesville, Va., Sept. 24, 1957; d. Johann Heinrich and Eleonore Susanne (Stenzel) R.; m. John Arthur Niero, Jan. 31, 1990. Student, Dalhousie U., Halifax, Nova Scotia, Can., 1974-76; MD with distinction, Dalhousie U. Med. Sch., Halifax, Nova Scotia, Can., 1980. Diplomate Dalhousie U., Am. Bd. Plastic Surgery; licentiate Med. Coun. Can.; cert. Bd. Med. Quality Assurance Calif. Intern Ottawa Gen. Hosp., Ont., Can., 1980-81; gen. surgery resident Dalhousie U., Halifax, Nova Scotia, Can., 1981-85; plastic surgery resident Wayne State U., Detroit, 1985-87; pvt. practice San Francisco, 1988-89; pre-ptnr. Southern Calif. Permanente Physicians Group, Fontana, 1989-92, ptnr., 1992—. Contbr. articles to profl. jours. Fellow ACS; mem. Am. Soc. Plastic and Reconstructive Surgeons, Calif. Med. Soc., San Bernardino Med. Soc., Alpha Omega Alpha. Office: Kaiser Found Hosp Dept Plastic Surgery 9985 Sierra Ave Fontana CA 92335-6720

RESCIGNO, THOMAS NICOLA, theoretical physicist; b. N.Y.C., Sept. 10, 1947; s. Joseph Aiello and Leona Rees (Llewellyn) R.; m. Erie Ann Mills, May 24, 1986. BA, Columbia U., 1969; MA, Harvard U., 1971, PhD, 1973. Rsch. fellow Calif. Inst. Tech., Pasadena, 1973; staff scientist Lawrence Livermore Lab., Livermore, Calif., 1975-79, group leader, 1979-86, sr. scientist, 1986—; lectr. atomic and molecular physics U. N.Mex., Albuquerque, summers 1993, 94. Editor 2 sci. monographs; contbr. more than 100 articles to profl. jours., chpts. to books. Recipient Am. Inst. Chemists medal, 1969; Nat. Energy fellow NSF, 1975. Fellow Am. Phys. Soc. (local chair 1990). Office: Lawrence Livermore Nat Lab PO Box 808 Livermore CA 94551-0808

RESER, DANIEL M., trust banker; b. West Lafayette, Ind., Oct. 25, 1955; s. Edward A. and Sue M. Reser; m. Paula F. Reser, Aug. 4, 1979; children: Jared E., William W. BA, So. Meth. U., 1977, JD, 1980. Cert. corp. trust specialist. Trust officer Bank of the S.W., Houston, 1980-84; asst. v.p. Interfirst Bank, Houston, 1984-87; v.p. Security Pacific, L.A., 1987-92, Dai-Ichi Kangyo Bank, L.A., 1992—. Dir. Valley Cultural Arts Found., L.A., 1992—. Mem. Govt. Fin. Officers Assn., Corp. Trust Assocs., Western Pension and Benefits Conf. Home: 16380 Meadowridge Rd Encino CA 91436-3607

RESKO, JOHN ALLEN, physiology educator; b. Patton, Pa., Oct. 28, 1932; s. Eli Joseph and Mary Veronica (Haluska) R.; m. Magdalen Ester Redmond, June 23, 1962; children: Rebecca E., John T. PhB, St. Charles Sem., 1956; MS in Zoology, Marquette U., 1960; PhD in Animal Sci., U. Ill., 1963. Postdoctoral fellow U. Utah, Salt Lake City, 1963-64; asst. scientist Oreg. Regional Primary Research Ctr., Beaverton, 1964-67, assoc. scientist, 1967-71, scientist, 1971-81; prof., chmn. dept. physiology Oreg. Health Sci. U., Portland, 1981—; mem. reproductive biology study sect. NIH, Bethesda, Md., 1981-85. Recipient Wyeth award West Coast Fertility Soc., 1972. Mem. AAAS, Soc. Study Reproduction (pres. 1988-89, bd. dirs. 1981-84), Soc. Exptl. Biol. Medicine (mem. coun. 1981-84), Am. Physiol. Soc., Endocrine Soc. Democrat. Roman Catholic. Home: 1787 SE Brookwood Ave Hillsboro OR 97123-8042 Office: Oreg Health Sci U Dept Physiology 3181 SW Sam Jackson Park Rd Portland OR 97201-3011

RESNICK, JEFFREY I., plastic surgeon; b. Jersey City, Mar. 2, 1954; s. Victor and Regina (Bistritz) R.; m. Michele Gail Zinger, July 12, 1981; children: Andrew Gregory, Daniel Zachary. BS, Yale U., 1975; MD, U. Pa., 1980. Diplomate Am. Bd. Surgery, Am. Bd. Plastic Surgery. Resident in surgery Mass. Gen. Hosp., Boston, 1980-85, resident in plastic surgery, 1985-87; fellow in craniofacial surgery UCLA, 1987-88; pvt. practice plastic surgery Santa Monica, Calif., 1989—; asst. clin. prof. plastic surgery UCLA, 1987—. Contbr. articles to profl. jours. Surgeon Indochina Surg. Ednl. Exch., Vietnam, 1992. Mem. Am. Soc. Plastic and Reconstructive Surgeons, Am. Soc. Maxillofacial Surgeons, Am. Cleft Palate-Craniofacial Assn., Plastic Surgery Ednl. Found., Sigma Xi, Alpha Omega Alpha. Office: 1301 20th St Ste 470 Santa Monica CA 90404-2050

RESS, DAVID BRUCE, physicist, electrical engineer; b. Camden, N.J., Nov. 17, 1958; s. Thomas Ignaz and Edith (Heyer) R.; m. Lucille Mitrovich, Jan. 22, 1985. Student, U. Calif., Irvine, 1975-78; BSEE, U. Calif., Davis, 1980; MSEE, Stanford U., 1984, PhD in Elec. Engring., 1988. Tutor U. Calif., Davis, 1979-80; electronics engr. Pacific Measurements Inc., 1980-82; rsch. asst. Stanford U., Calif., 1982-84; exptl. physicist Lawrence Livermore (Calif.) Nat. Lab., 1984, physicist, 1985—. Inventor laser fusion diagnostic techniques, 1989; contbr. numerous articles to profl. jours. Mem. Am. Phys. Soc., IEEE, Sierra Club, Commonwealth Club, Tau Beta Pi. Office: Lawrence Livermore Nat Lab 7000 East Ave L-473 Livermore CA 94551-5508

RETALLACK, GREGORY JOHN, geologist, educator; b. Hobart, Australia, Nov. 8, 1951; came to U.S., 1977; s. Kenneth John Retallack and Moira Wynn (Dean) Gollan; m. Diane Alice Johnson, May 21, 1981; children: Nicholas John, Jeremy Douglas. B.A., Macquarie U., Sydney, 1973; B.Sc. with honors, U. New Eng., 1974, Ph.D., 1978. Vis. asst. prof. Northern Ill. U., Dekalb, 1977-78; vis. scholar Ind. U., Bloomington, 1978-81; asst. prof. U. Oreg., Eugene, 1981-86, assoc. prof., 1986-92, prof., 1992—. Author: Geological Excursion Guide to the Sea Cliffs North of Sydney, 1978, Late Eocene and Oligocene Paleosols from Badlands National Park, South Dakota, 1983, Soils of the Past, 1990, Miocene Paleosols and Ape Habitats in Pakistan and Kenya, 1991; contbr. numerous articles in field to profl. jours. Grantee NSF, 1979—, Wenner-Gren Found., 1983. Mem. Geol. Soc. Am., Geol. Soc. Australia, Bot. Soc. Am., Paleontol. Soc. (pres. Pacific sect. 1986), Oreg. Acad. Sci. (pres. 1986), Soc. Econ. Paleontologists and Mineralogists, Sigma Xi (pres. U. Oreg. chpt. 1983-84). Home: 2715 Elinor St Eugene OR 97403-2513

RETHERFORD, ROBERT DENNIS, demographer; b. N.Y.C., July 17, 1941; s. Robert Curtis and Ruth (Shere) R.; m. Ursula Cadalbert, Jan. 30, 1965; children: Tania, My-Hanh, Leah. BA in Phys. Sci., U. Calif., Berkeley, 1964, MA in Sociology, 1966, PhD of Sociology, 1970. Sr. fellow program on population East-West Ctr., Honolulu, 1970—; lectr. dept. demography U. Calif., Berkeley, 1970; grad. faculty dept. sociology U. Hawaii, Honolulu, 1973—; asst. specialist Internat. Population and Urban Rsch. Ctr. U. Calif., Berkeley, 1969-70; cons. UN Econ. Commn. for Asia and Far East, 1971-72, UN Fund for Population Activities, 1980, Nat. Inst. Child Health and Human Devel., 1984, UN Econ. and Social Commn. for Asia and Pacific, 1984. Author: Statistical Models for Causal Analysis, 1993; editor: Asian and Pacific Population Forum, 1980-85, assoc. editor 1985-91; contbr. articles to profl. jours. Grantee Commn. on Population and the Hawaiian Future, 1982, Nat. Inst. Child Health and Human Devel., 1983, 84-85, 85-86, 86-88, Ford Found., Pioneer Fund, Inc., 1984-85, U.S. Agy. for Internat. Devel., 1989-93. Mem. AAAS, Internat. Union of Sci. Study of Population, Population Assn. Am., Soc. for Study of Social Biology (pres. 1991-93, bd. dirs.). Office: Program on Population East-West Center Honolulu HI 96848

RETTIE, ALLAN EDWARD, medical educator; b. Inverness, Scotland, Feb. 25, 1957; came to U.S., 1984; s. Edward and Frances (Paterson) R.; m. Annette Plowman, Feb. 20, 1981; children: Alexander John Edward, Stephen Allan. BSc in Pharmacy with honors, Heriot-Watt U., Edinburgh, Scotland, 1979; PhD in Pharmacol. Scis., U. Newcastle-upon-Tyne, England, 1983. Sr. rsch. fellow dept. pharmacology U. Wash., Seattle, 1984-85, postdoctoral rsch. assoc. dept. medicinal chemistry, 1985-87, rsch. asst. prof. dept. medicinal chemistry, 1987-88, asst. prof., 1989-94, assoc. prof., 1994—; session chmn. Gordon Conf. on Drug Metabolism, Holderness Ch., N.H., 1992; invited speaker Fifth N.Am. ISSX Mtg., Tucson, Ariz., 1993; mem. U. Recombinant DNA Com., 1993—. Author: (with others) Principles of Drug and Chemical Action in Pregnancy, 1986, Pharmacology and the Skin, Vol. I, Skin Pharmacokinetics, 1987; contbr. articles to profl. jours.; reviewer jours. Recipient Partnership award Med. Rsch. Coun., 1980-83, FIRST award NIH, 1989-94; grantee NIH, 1993-98, 94-98. Mem. Internat. Soc. Study Xenobiotics, Royal Pharm. Soc. Great Britain. Office: Univ Wash Dept Medicinal Chemist Seattle WA 98195

REUS, VICTOR I., psychiatry educator, hospital administrator; b. Bordeaux, France, Oct. 18, 1947; came to U.S., 1949; BA, Cornell U., 1969; MD, U. Md., Balt., 1973; postgrad., U. Wis., 1973-76. Diplomate Nat. Bd. Med. Examiners, Am. Bd. Psychiatry and Neurology (examiner 1978—), Am. Bd. Geriatric Psychiatry. Clin. assoc. Inst. Psychiatry Maudsley Hosp., London, 1973; consulting physician Mendota Mental Health Inst., Madison, Wis., 1974-76; fellow in adminstrv. psychiatry, psychiatry edn. br., divsn. manpower tng. NIMH, Rockville, Md., 1975; clin. assoc., ward adminstr. sect. psychobiology, biol. psychiatry br. NIMH, Bethesda, Md., 1976-78; chief resident adult inpatient svc. U. Wis. Hosp., Madison, 1976; instr. George Washington Sch. Medicine, Washington, 1976-78; instr. sch. medicine Georgetown U., Washington, 1977-78; dir. behavioral neuroscience svc. Langley Porter Neuropsychiatric Hosp., U. Calif., San Francisco, 1978-87, med. dir., 1986—; from asst. prof. to assoc. prof. dept. psychiatry sch. medicine U. Calif., San Francisco, 1978-89, prof., 1989—; mem. various coms. sch. medicine U. Calif., 1978—; grant reviewer, site visitor NIMH, 1977, 1984—, mem. initial rev. group, small grant rev. com., biol. and neurosciences subcom., 1989-91, mem. initial rev. group, individual faculty scholar award, 1990, mem. initial rev. group, biol. psychopathology rev. com., 1991-93, mem. reviewers res., 1993—, reviewer behavioral sci. track award for rapid transition, 1994; mem. ad hoc com. on psychotropic drugs City of San Francisco Mental Health Adv. Coun., 1979-80; grant reviewer, site visitor Nat. Inst. Drug Abuse, 1979, 87, Nat. Inst. Aging, 1985, 92; cons., examining psychiatrist Superior Ct., City and County of San Francisco, 1979—, U.S. Dist. Ct. (no. dist.) Calif., 1980—, Juvenile Ct., Dept. Social Svcs., City and County of San Francisco, 1987-90; cons. Pfizer Pharms., 1984-85, Abbott Diagnostic Labs., 1987-88, Abbott Pharms. Product Devel., 1993; cons. to subcom. mental health Calif. State Legislature, Sacramento, 1984; grant reviewer NSF, 1985, others; mem. Scientist's Inst. Pub. Info., N.Y.C., 1985—; mem. grant rev. com. Dept. Mental Health, State of Calif., 1986; mem. San Francisco Peer Rev. Com., Pacific Peer Rev., 1986-89; mem. profl. adv. bd. No. Calif. chpt. Epilepsy Found. Am., 1989—; presenter in field. Mem. editl. bd. Western Jour. Medicine, 1991-93; editl. reviewer Internat. Jour. of Psychiatry in Medicine, Western Jour. Medicine, Archives of Gen. Psychiatry, Am. Jour. Physiology, Gordon and Breach, Sci. Pubs., Inc., others; contbr. chpts. to books and articles and book revs. to profl. jours. Lt. comdr. USPHS, 1976-78. Rsch. award Stanley Found., 1993-95; co-investigator Nat. Inst. Drug Abuse, 1980-94, NIMH, 1991—, Scottish Rite Schizophrenia Rsch. Program, 1993-95, Upjohn Pharms., 1993—. Fellow Am. Psychiat. Assn. (cons. consultation svc., rsch. program devel. 1991—), West Coast Coll. Biol. Psychiatry (charter, mem. edn. and tng. com. 1983-87, mem. and chmn. credentials com. 1983-87, pres. 1989); mem. AAAS, Am. Soc. Clin. Psychopharmacology (mem. membership com. 1994—), Am. Coll. Psychiatrists, No. Calif. Psychiat. Soc. (mem. and chmn. pub. info. com. 1978-82, chmn. psychobiology com. 1982-84, mem. hosp. com. 1987-91, councilor 1993—), Calif. Acad. Medicine, Calif. Psychiat. Assn. (mem. ann. meeting planning com. 1995), Soc. Biol. Psychiatry (sec. program com. 1982-83, 83-84, mem. and chair Ziskind-Somerfeld rsch. award com. 1991-94), Psychiat. Rsch. Soc., Internat. Soc. Psychoneuroendocrinology, Academia, Medicinae & Psychiatriae Found., Inc., Collegium Internationale Neuro-Psychopharmacologicum, Psi Chi. Office: U Calif Box F-0984 401 Parnassus Ave San Francisco CA 94143-0984

REVER, BARBARA L., medical educator, consultant, researcher; b. Bklyn., Dec. 18, 1947. B.A., Barnard Coll., 1969; M.P.H., U. Calif.-Berkeley, 1970; M.D., N.Y. Med. Coll., 1974. Diplomate Am. Bd. Internal Medicine, Splty. Nephrology. Intern, Los Angeles County Hosp., U. So. Calif., 1974-75; resident in internal medicine, Los Angeles County Hosp., 1975-76, Kaiser Found. Hosps., Los Angeles, 1976-77; fellow in nephrology U. Calif., L.A. Sch. Medicine, 1978-80, founder and specialist in Nephrology, Salinas Valley Dialysis Services, Inc., 1982—, also chmn. bd.; spl. cons. Calif. State Dept. Pub. Health, summer 1970; research assoc. Dept. Community and Preventive Medicine, N.Y. Hosp. Coll., summer 1971; instr. biology and physiology Community Health Medic Tng. Program, Indian Health Service Hosp., N. Mex., summer 1972; asst. prof. medicine, asst. dir. renal transplantation div. nephrology UCLA, 1980-81; founder Salinas Valley Dialysis Svcs., Inc., 1983; pvt. practice nephrology, 1981—. Office: 951 Blanco Cir # D Salinas CA 93901-4451

REVERAND, CEDRIC DWIGHT, II, English language educator; b. Bklyn., Dec. 3, 1941; s. Cedric Dwight and Muriel (Cestare) R.; m. Jane Myers, July 24, 1965. BA, Yale U., 1963; MA, Columbia U., 1964; PhD, Cornell U., 1972. Prof. English, dir. cultural programs U. Wyo., Laramie, 1983—. Author: Dryden's Final Poetic Mode, 1988; editor: 18th-Century English Literature: A Current Bibliography; contbr. articles to profl. jours. Recipient Ellbogen Outstanding Teaching award U. Wyo., 1987; hon. Cambridge fellow, Clare Hall, 1993—; named Ford Found. fellow Cornell U., 1967-72, Mellon fellow UCLA and Yale U., 1978, 85. Mem. MLA, Am. Soc. for 18th-Century Studies, Western Alliance Arts Adminstrs., Phi Beta Kappa. Home: 412 Garfield St Laramie WY 82070-3739 Office: U Wyo Dept English PO Box 3353 Laramie WY 82071-3353

REVIER, CHARLES FRANKLIN, academic administrator, economics educator; b. Lubbock, Tex., Sept. 1, 1944; s. Frank Fancher and Dorothy Charlene (Lawson) R.; m. Susan Ann Nethaway, Aug. 7, 1971; children: Emily Ann, Lauren Ann. BA in Physics, U. Colo., 1966, MA in Econs., 1968; PhD in Econs., MIT, 1978. Teaching asst. U. Colo., Boulder, 1968; rsch. asst. MIT, Cambridge, Mass., summer 1969; intern Coun. of Econ. Advisors, Washington, summer 1970; cons. intern Adv. Commn. on Intergovernmental Rels., Washington, 1971-72; teaching asst. MIT, Cambridge, Mass., 1972-73; rsch. asst. Nat. Bur. Econ. Rsch., Cambridge, Mass., 1973; instr. Colo. State U., Ft. Collins, 1974-78, asst. prof., 1978-87, assoc. prof., 1987-88, chair, assoc. prof., 1988—. Contbr. articles to profl. jours. NSF fellow, 1968-71, Charles Abrams fellow MIT, 1973-74. Mem. Am. Econ. Assn. Democrat. Methodist. Office: Colo State U Dept Econs Fort Collins CO 80523

REWERS, MARIAN JERZY, pediatrician, epidemiologist; b. Poznan, Poland, July 11, 1956; came to U.S., 1986; s. Stefan and Mieczyslawa (Sikora) R.; m. Arleta B. Klosiak, Jan. 16, 1982; children: Amanda, Marek. MD, Acad. Medicine, Poznan, 1981, PhD, 1986; MPH, U. Pitts., 1988. Lic. physician, Colo.; specialist in pediatric diabetes. Intern dept. pediatrics Sch. Medicine, Poznan, Poland, 1981-82; resident in pediatrics Acad. Medicine, Poland, 1982-87, Sch. Medicine, Poznan, 1982-84; instr. pediatrics Acad. Medicine, Poznan, 1982-85, asst. prof., 1985-90; asst. prof. U. Colo., Denver, 1990-94, assoc. prof. preventive medicine, 1994, assoc. prof. pediatrics, 1994—, head epidemiology and cmty. health, 1994—; mem. steering com. WHO, Diamond, Geneva, 1989—; mem. study sect. NIH, Bethesda, Md., 1992; mem. program com. Juvenile Diabetes Fedn. Internat., San Francisco, 1994; mem. program com. Internat. Diabetes Epidemiology Group, Himeji, Japan, 1994; mem. senate rules com. U. Colo. Sch. Medicine, Denver, 1992—; mem. teaching faculty WHO, Geneva, 1992. Contbr. articles to profl. jours., chpts. to books. Mem. Rocky Mountain chpt. Kosciuszko Found., Denver, 1993—. Tng. fellow U. Lund, Malmo, Sweden, 1984, rsch. and tng. fellow Am. Diabetes Assn., Alexandria, Va., 1986. Mem. Am. Diabetes Assn., European Assn. for Study of Diabetes, European Diabetes Epidemiology Study Group. Office: U Colo Dept Preventive Medicine & Biometrics HSC 4200 E 9th Ave Denver CO 80262

REWERTS, MILAN ALVIN, university administrator; b. Princeton, Ill., Sept. 10, 1942; s. Elmer Earl and Norma Ardis (Gleason) R.; m. Carol Ann Demaree, June 20, 1964; children: Michael Allen, Michelle Ann. BS in Agrl. Sci., U. Ill., 1964; MEd in Ednl. Adminstrn., Colo. State U., 1974, postgrad., 1975-92. Extension agt. Garfield county Colo. State U. Coop Extension, Glenwood Springs, 1966-68; area extension agt. Tri River area Colo. State U. Coop Extension, Grand Junction, Colo., 1968-73; extension agt., Weld county Colo. State U. Coop Extension, Greeley, Colo., 1974-80; dist. dir., south ctrl. Colo. State U. Coop Extension, Ft. Collins, Colo., 1980-88, pers. dir., field rep., 1988-90, interim state dir., 1990—; Colo. state univ. rep. Colo. Rural Devel. Coun., Ft. Collins, 1993—; mem. faculty improvement com. Colo. State U. 1st lt. U.S. Army, 1964-66, USAR, 1966-93. Contbr. articles to profl. jours. Advisor Colo. State 4-H Senate, Ft. Collins, 1977-89. Mem. Am. Mgmt. Assn., Res. Officers Assn., Nat. Assn. of County Agrl. Agts., Nat. Assn. of Extension 4-H Agts. (state pres. 1975-76, Disting. Svc. award 1976), Nat. Western Stock Show Assn., Nat. Assn. of State Univs. and Land Grant Coll. (chair nat. pers. and orgn. devel. com. 1993-94), Epsilon Sigma Phi, Gamma Sigma Delta. Office: Colo State Univ Coop Ext 1 Adminstration Bldg Fort Collins CO 80523

REYNA, TROY MICHAEL, surgeon; b. Ft. Hood, Tex., July 10, 1950; s. Trinidad and Brigitte (Stuber) R. BS in Chemistry, U.S. Mil. Acad., 1972; MD, Georgetown U., 1977. Diplomate Am. Bd. Surgery, Am. Bd. Pediatric Surgery. Commd. 2d lt. U.S. Army, 1972, advanced through grades to col., 1992; intern Walter Reed Army Med. Ctr., Washington, 1977-78; resident in surgery Tripler Army Med. Ctr., Honolulu, 1978-82; staff surgeon 5th Gen. Hosp., Stuttgart, Fed. Republic Germany, 1982-84, chief surgery, 1984-85; chief trauma services William Beaumont Army Med. Ctr., El Paso, Tex., 1985-88; fellow pediatric surgery Columbus (Ohio) Children's Hosp., 1987-89; chief pediatric surgery svc. William Beaumont Army Med. Ctr., El Paso, 1989-93; ret., 1993; clin. instr. surgery Uniformed Svcs. U. of Health Scis., Bethesda, Md., 1982-85; asst. prof. Tex. Tech. U., El Paso, 1985—; cons. Emergency Med. Svcs., Office of the Mayor of El Paso, 1986-87. Contbr. numerous articles to profl. jours. Lectr. on medicine Explorer Scouts, El Paso, 1986—; mem. exec. com. ARC, El Paso; mem. Las Vegas Suspected Child Abuse & Neglect, 1994—; bd. dirs. Greater Las Vegas Ronald McDonald House, 1994—. Fellow Am. Acad. Pediatrics; mem. AMA, ACS, Assn. Mil. Surgeons, Hawaiian Surg. Assn., Tex. Med. Assn., El Paso Med. Soc., Acad. Surgery, Soc. Am. Gastrointestinal Endoscopic Surgeons, Clark County Med. Soc., Clark County Pediatric Soc. Roman Catholic. Home: 1968 Troon Dr Henderson NV 89014-1039

REYNOLDS, ANGUS STUART, JR., instructional technologist; b. Bainbridge, N.Y., Mar. 11, 1936; s. Angus Stuart and Charlotte R. (Plankenhorn) R.; m. Emiko Anne Teruya, Oct. 4, 1967; children: Elizabeth, Mari Ellen, Thomas Charles. BS, Springfield (Mass.) Coll., 1957; BA, U. Md., 1962; MS, Canisius Coll., 1965; MPA, U. Okla., 1979; EdD, George Washington U., 1986. Various managerial positions U.S. Govt., various locations, 1957-77; pres. Reynolds Internat., Reston, Va., 1977-78; sr. cons. Control Data Edn. Co., Washington, 1978-83; chief cons. Control Data Corp., Rockville, Md., 1983-87; dir. grad. program N.Y. Inst. Tech., Old Westbury, 1987-88, assoc. dean, 1988-93; instrnl. technologist EG & G Energy Measurements, Albuquerque, 1993-94; prin. instrnl. technologist AlliedSignal Aerospace, Albuquerque, 1994—; cons. N.Y.C. Bd. Edn., 1989-90; bd. dirs. Ctr. for Gulf Studies, Washington, 1991-93; sr. assoc. The World Group, N.Y., 1991—; tech. dir. ARCON, 1991—. Author: The Trainer's Dictionary, 1993; co-author: (with Ronald Anderson) Selecting and Developing Media for Instruction, 1992, (with Len Nadler) Globalization: The International HRD Consultant's and Practitioner's Handbook, 1993, (with Michael Marquardt) The Global Learning Organization, 1994, (with Roberto Araya) Bulding Multimedia PSS, 1994, (with Thomas Iwinski) Developing Multimedia Training; editor: Technology Transfer, 1984, Instructional Technology News, 1988—; series editor Computer-Based Training, 1991-94; mem. editl. bd. Tng. and Devel. Bd. dirs. United Black Fund Mgmt. Svcs. Corp. United Way, 1986. Recipient Nat. Silver medal Polish Falcons of Am., 1963, Key to the City Govt. of Lackawanna, N.Y., 1963. Fellow Acad. Human Resources Devel.; mem. ASTD (bd. dirs. internat. divsn. 1985-86, bd. dirs. instrnl. tech. divsn. 1988—, mem. computer learning group 1983-85, Nat. Torch award 1989, Internat. Tng. Leadership award 1992, Instrnl. Tech. Leadership award 1993), Washington Soc. Tng. and Devel. (pres. 1984, Outstanding Mem. award 1985, Outstanding Internat. Trainer of Yr. award 1986), Soc. Applied Learning Tech. (sr.). Home: 11804 Apache NE Albuquerque NM 87112-3471

REYNOLDS, BRIAN ARTHUR, library director; b. Visalia, Calif., June 28, 1950; s. William Arthur and Marilyn (Hart) R.; m. Diane Leigh MacVeagh, June 20, 1977; children: Nathaniel Arthur, Matthew Wayne. BA, U. Calif., Berkeley, 1972; MLS, U. Calif., L.A., 1974; MPA, Calif. State U., Chico, 1984. Asst. libr. dir. Universidad Centroamericana, Managua, Nicaragua, 1975; pub. svcs. libr. Bensenville (Ill.) Pub. Libr., 1976; ref. libr. Shasta County Pub. Libr., Redding, Calif., 1977-82; libr. dir. Siskiyou County Pub. Libr., Yreka, Calif., 1982-93, San Luis Obispo (Calif.) City County Libr., 1993—. Producer (adult literacy radio series) READ Radio Series I, II, 1988-89. Mem. ALA, Calif. Libr. Assn., Calif. Soc. Librs. (pres. 1991), Rotary (San Luis Obispo). Democrat. Office: San Luis Obispo City Co Lib PO Box 8107 995 Palm St San Luis Obispo CA 93403-8107

REYNOLDS, CHARLES PATRICK, pediatric oncologist, researcher; b. El Paso, Tex., Aug. 8, 1952; s. Charles Albert and Lallah Elizabeth (Munro) R.; m. Debra Dawn Adams, Feb. 3, 1979; children: Amy Elizabeth, Jennifer Ann. BA in Biology, U. Tex., 1974; MD, U. Tex. Southwestern Med. Sch., Dallas, 1979; PhD, U. Tex., 1979. Lic. Tex., Calif. Postdoctoral fellow U. Tex. Southwestern Med. Sch., Dallas, 1979-80; pediatric intern Nat. Naval Med. Ctr., Bethesda, Md., 1980-81; battalion surg. Third Marine Div., Okinawa, Japan, 1981-82; rsch. med. officer Naval Med. Rsch. Inst.,

Bethesda, 1982-87; asst. prof. UCLA, 1987-89; assoc. prof. U. So. Calif., L.A., 1989—; head devel. therapeutics sect. Children's Hosp., L.A., 1993—; dir. Neuroblastoma Marrow Purging Lab. Childrens Cancer Group, L.A., 1988—; team physician U.S. Shooting Team, 1991—. Patentee in field; contbr. articles to profl. jours. Mem. 1992 USA Olympic Shooting Team, Barcelona, Spain. Grantee Nat. Cancer Inst., Am. Inst. Cancer Rsch. Mem. NRA, Am. Soc. Clin. Oncology, Am. Assn. Cancer Rsch., Soc. Analytical Cytology. Roman Catholic. Office: Childrens Hosp LA Div Hematology Oncology PO Box 54700 Los Angeles CA 90054-0700

REYNOLDS, CLARK ANDRE, management consultant; b. San Diego, Apr. 17, 1951. BS, U.S. Mil. Acad., 1974. Commd. 2d lt. U.S. Army, 1974, advanced through grades to capt., 1978; resigned, 1979; natural gas engr. Conoco, Inc., Houston, 1979-80; exec. search cons. The Exec. Suite, Houston, 1980, Egan Assocs., Inc., Houston, 1981-83; v.p. adminstrn., plans and ops. Vivigen, Inc., Santa Fe, 1988-93; exec. search cons. Clark Reynolds & Co., Los Alamos, N.Mex., 1983-88; mgmt. cons. Clark Reynolds & Co., Las Cruces, N.Mex., 1983—. Treas., bd. dirs. Los Alamos Econ. Devel. Corp., 1986-89. Maj. USAR, 1974-94. Home and Office: 2169 Sage Crest Las Cruces NM 88011

REYNOLDS, DAVID KENT, writer, educator; b. Dayton, Ohio, Sept. 28, 1940; s. Charles K. and Frances M. (Worrell) R.; m. Lynn Sanae Tamashiro, May 6, 1978. BA, UCLA, 1964, MA, 1965, PhD, 1969. Asst. prof. Sch. Pub. Health, Divsn. Behavioral Scis. UCLA, 1970-71; asst. prof. Sch. Medicine, Dept. Psychiatry U. So. Calif., 1974-79; assoc. prof. anthropology U. Houston, 1979-80; dir. ToDo Inst., L.A., 1980-89, Constructive Living Ctr., Coos Bay, Oreg., 1989—; temporary adviser WHO, People's Rep. of China; papers presented at Am. Anthropol. Assn., Am. Acad. Psychoanalysis, Am. Psychiat. Assn., VI World Congress of Psychiatry, Internat. Assn. for Suicide Prevention, Am. Assn. of Suicidology, Western Psychol. Assn., Western Gerontol. Soc., Soc. for Applied Anthropology, and others in the U.S. and Japan. Author: (in English and Japanese) Suicide: Inside and Out, 1976, Constructive Living, 1984, The Heart of the Japanese People, 1980, Morita Psychotherapy, 1976, (in English) Reflections on the Tao te Ching, 1993, Plunging Through the Clouds, 1993, Naikan Psychotherapy, 1991, The Quiet Therapies, 1980; author: (with others) Current Psychiatric Therapies, 1973, Suicide in Different Cultures, 1975, Emergency and Disaster Management, 1976, Modern Morita Therapy, 1977, Handbook of Innovative Psychotherapies, 1981, Living and Dying with Cancer, 1981, Coping with Aging, 1982, Encyclopedia of Japan, 1987, Encyclopedia of Psychology, 1987, Health, Illness, and Medical Care in Japan, 1987; contbr. to profl. jours. Mem. adv. bd. Okamoto Found., Japan, 1990—, Hakkenkai Orgn., 1978—. Fulbright-Hays scholar 1973, 78; grantee Tokyo Met. Inst. of Gerontology, 1979, NIMH, 1972, 73, 75-78, Japanese NIMH 1967, 68, NDEA, 1967, NSF, 1967, and others. Mem. Am. Anthropol. Assn., Japan Assn. Morita Therapy (Kora prize 1992). Office: Constructive Living PO Box 85 Coos Bay OR 97420-0007

REYNOLDS, DONALD DEAN, retired civil engineering technician; b. Bristol, Colo., Sept. 1, 1921; s. Charles Lloyd and Clara Lillian (Whitehead) R.; m. Jo Ann Vernon, Oct. 14, 1951; children: Paul Lloyd, Deana Jean Reynolds Mounts. BA, Northwestern State Coll., Okla., 1947. Jr. high tchr., coach Bonner Springs (Kans.) Bd. Edn., 1948-49; surveyor Kans. Dept. Hwys., Topeka, 1948; civil engr. technician U.S. Bur. Reclamation, Ephrata, Wash., 1950-54, Ephrata & Othello, Wash., 1964-84; civil engr. technician, conservationist U.S. Dept. Agr., Othello, 1954-57; lab. inspector Harza Engring., Ephrata, 1957-61; developer, owner Columbia Basin Farm, Wash., 1954-84; civil engr. tech. Cortez Co., 1984-86; retired Cortez Co., 1986. With USAF, 1943-45. Home: 349 5th Ave SE Ephrata WA 98823-2247

REYNOLDS, EDWARD BRUCE, history educator; b. Kansas City, Mo., May 29, 1947; s. Virgil Edward and Sibyl (Lane) R.; m. Pilaiwan Wongsarojana, May 9, 1982. BS in Speech, Ctrl. Mo. State U., 1969, MA in History, 1977; PhD in History, U. Hawaii, 1988. Announcer Sta. KOKO-AM, Warrensburg, Mo., 1973-77; reporter/editor Daily Star Jour., Warrensburg, 1977-79; lectr. Chulalongkorn U., Bangkok, Thailand, 1979-82; asst. prof. San Jose (Calif.) State U., 1988-92, assoc. prof., 1992—, chair, history dept., 1994—; dir. East Asian Regional Materials and Resources Ctr., San Jose, 1991—. Author: Thailand and Japan's Southern Advance, 1940-45, 1994; co-editor: Thai-Japanese Relations in Historical Perspective, 1988. Staff sgt. USAF, 1969-73. Recipient Fulbright fellowship U.S.-Japan Ednl. Commn., Tokyo, 1986-87, U.S. Dept. Edn., Bangkok, 1987-88, Crown Prince Akihito scholarship, Tokyo, 1985-86. Mem. Asian Studies on the Pacific Coast (bd. dirs. 1992-94), Assn. for Asian Studies, Am. Hist. Assn., Soc. of Historians of Am. Fgn. Rels., World History Assn., World War II Studies Assn. Office: History Dept San Jose State U 1 Washington Sq San Jose CA 95112-3613

REYNOLDS, GLENDA CAROL, elementary school educator; b. Cheyenne, Wyo., Dec. 7, 1947; d. Charlie Clyde and Mary Payton (Clatterbuck) Kidd; m. James Francis Reynolds, June 6, 1970; children: Todd, Craig. BA, U. Wyo., 1970. 2d grade tchr. San Felipe Sch. Dist., Del Rio, Tex., 1970-71; elem. tchr. Laramie County Sch. Dist., Cheyenne, 1971—; computer facilitator Laramie County Sch. Dist., 1986—, math. mentor tchr., 1990—; math. mentor tchr. U. Wyo., Laramie. Cub scout leader Boy Scouts Am., Cheyenne, 1988-92; vacation Bible sch. dir. Meadowbrooke Bapt. Ch., Cheyenne, 1987—; trainer, Family Math. Wyoming, 1990—. Recipient Presdl. award for Excellence Elem. Math. Teaching, NSF, 1991. Mem. NEA, Wyo. Edn. Assn., Cheyenne Tchrs. Edn. Assn., Wyo. Coun. Tchrs. Math. (state finalist 1991), Delta Kappa Gamma (state pres. 1991-93, grad. leadership/mgnt. seminar U. Tex., 1991). Democrat. Home: 5149 Mccue Dr Cheyenne WY 82009-4814

REYNOLDS, JAMES FRANCIS, JR., physician; b. St. Albans, Vt., June 20, 1947; s. James F. Sr. and Eleanor (Paquette) R.; married; 1 child, Matthew. BS, U.S. Mil. Acad., West Point, N.Y., 1969; MD, U. Louisville, 1978. Diplomate Am. Bd. Pediatrics, Am. Bd. Med. Genetics. Commd. U.S. Army, 1969, advanced through grades to capt., resigned, 1974; pediatrics resident U. Va., Charlottesville, 1978-81, genetics fellow, 1981-83; dir. med. div. dept. med. genetics Shodair Hosp., Helena, Mont., 1983—. Assoc. editor Am. Jour. Med. Genetics, 1983-95; editor various books on med. genetics; contbr. articles to profl. jours. Chmn. health profl. adv. com. Mont. March of Dimes, 1987—; v.p. Mont. Council for Maternal and Child Health, 1987—. Col. U.S. Army Res. Fellow Am. Acad. Pediatrics, Am. Coll. Med. Genetics; mem. Am. Soc. Human Genetics. Office: Shodair Hosp PO Box 5539 Helena MT 59604-5539

REYNOLDS, JO-ANNE ELAINE, banker; b. Kingston, Jamaica, July 1, 1956; d. Arthur Eugene Brooks and Barbara Fay Arscott Williams; m. Randolph Paul Reynolds, Aug. 11, 1977 (div. 1990); 1 child, Jason Dominic. BSc in Quantitative Decision Analysis, U. Redlands, 1977. Lic. real estate salesperson, Calif. Fgn. exch. trader Mercury Internat., Toronto, Ont., Can., 1977-82; fgn. exch. trader Bank of Am. Can., Toronto, Ont., 1982-83, ops. mgr., 1983-85; ops. mgr. Fgn. Currency Svcs., Bank of Am., L.A., 1985-89, v.p., mgr., 1989—; cons. Vincent Bugliosi, Author, L.A., 1989-91. Pres. Home Owners Assn. of Winnetka, Calif., 1987-88, treas., 1986-87; fundraiser United Way, L.A., 1990-91. Mem. Nat. Assn. Realtors. Office: Bank of America 525 S Flower St Los Angeles CA 90071-2202

REYNOLDS, JOHN CURBY, sales representative; b. San Jose, Calif., Aug. 15, 1948; s. Ivan Randolph and Lillie Murrel (McBrown) R.; m. Sharon Taylor, June 12, 1982; children: Brian James, Chris John. AA, Cabrillo Jr. Coll., Aptos, Calif., 1969; student, Calif. Polytechnic U., 1969-71. Sales rep. Equitable of Iowa Ins. Co., Sacramento, 1973-79, Grand Auto Inc., Sacramento, 1979-82, Princess House, Sacramento, 1982-84; sales telemktg. Montgomery Ward, Sacramento, 1984-85; sales rep. Sanitary Supply Co., Tucson, 1986—; mem. SVEA Bus. Group, Sierra Vista, Ariz., 1986—. Mem. First So. Bapt. Ch., Sierra Vista, 1989—. Mem. Sierra Vista C. of C. (mil. affairs com.). Republican. Office: Sanitary Supply Co Inc 360 S 7th St Sierra Vista AZ 85635-2506

REYNOLDS, KATHLEEN DIANE FOY (K.D.F. REYNOLDS), transportation executive; b. Chgo., Dec. 9, 1946; d. David Chancy Foy and Vivian Anne (Schwartz) R. Student, San Francisco State U., 1964-68. Studio coord. KTVU-TV, Oakland, Calif., 1968-70; assoc. prodr. KPIX-TV, San Francisco, 1970-72; music publicist Oakland, 1966-78; writer PLEXUS, West Coast Women's Press, Oakland, 1974-82, gen. mgr., 1984-86; screen writer Oakland, 1970—; gen. ptnr. Designated Driver Group, Oakland, 1990—; coun. mem. West Coast Women's Press, Oakland, 1975-86; founding assoc. Women's Inst. for Freedom of the Press, Washington, 1977—. Author of periodical news, reviews, features, 1974-82; author of six documentaries for comml. and PBS-TV, 1968-73. Mem. Soc. Mayflower Descendants, Casper, Wyo., 1967—. Mem. Profl. Businesswomen's Conf., Ind. Feature Project, San Francisco Film Soc. Home: PO Box 2742 Oakland CA 94602-0042

REYNOLDS, RAY THOMAS, planetary scientist; b. Lexington, Ky., Sept. 2, 1933; s. Oscar Ray and Margaret Louise (Gudgel) R.; m. Yolanda Maria de la Luz Gallegos, Oct. 15, 1962; children: Mark Andrew, Daniel Alan. BS in Chemistry, U. Ky., 1954, MS in Physics, 1960. Rsch. scientist Am. Geog. Soc., Thule, Greenland, 1960-61, U. Calif., Los Alamos, N.Mex., 1961; chief theoretical studies br. NASA Ames Rsch. Ctr., Moffett Field, Calif., 1969-78, rsch. scientist, 1962-69, 78-88, Ames assoc., 1988—. Recipient Exceptional Sci. Achievement award NASA, 1980. Fellow Am. Geophys. Union, Meteoritical Soc.; mem. Am. Astron. Soc., AAAS (Newcombe prize 1979), AIAA. Contbr. over 170 sci. reports on planetary formation structure and evolution, articles to profl. publs. Home: 1650 Shasta Ave San Jose CA 95128 Office: NASA Ames Rsch Ctr Moffett Field CA 94035

REYNOLDS, ROBERT HARRISON, retired export company executive; b. Mpls., Sept. 6, 1913; s. Clarence H. and Helen (Doyle) R.; m. Gladys Marie Gaster, Apr. 7, 1934; 1 child, Shirley Anne (Mrs. Frank S. Potestio); m. Viola E. Shimel, June 26, 1982. Export sales mgr., rolled products sales mgr. Colo. Fuel & Iron Corp., Denver, 1938-46; pres. Rocky Mountain Export Co., Inc., Denver, 1941-93. Mem. Denver Club (life). Home: 13850 E Marina Dr Aurora CO 80014-5509 Office: 12331 E Cornell Ave Aurora CO 80014-3323

REYNOLDS, ROGER LEE, composer; b. Detroit, July 18, 1934; s. George Arthur and Katherine Adelaide (Butler) R.; m. Karen Jeanne Hill, Apr. 11, 1964; children: Erika Lynn, Wendy Claire. BSE in Physics, U. Mich., 1957, MusB, 1960, MusM, 1961. Assoc. prof. U. Calif. San Diego, La Jolla, 1969-73, prof., 1973—, founding dir. Ctr. Music Expt. and Related Rsch., 1972-77; George Miller Prof. Amherst (Mass.) Coll., 1988; vis. prof. Yale U., New Haven, 1981; Rothschild composer in residence Peabody Conservatory of Music, 1992-93; sr. rsch. fellow ISAM, Bklyn. Coll., 1985. Author: MIND MODELS: New Forms of Musical Experience, 1975, A Searcher's Path: A Composer's Ways, 1987, A Jostled Silence: Contemporary Japanese Musical Thought, 1992-93; contbr. numerous articles and revs. to profl. jours. Bd. dirs. Am. Music. Ctr., Meet the Composer, Fromm Found. Harvard U.; mem. bd. govs. Inst. Current World Affairs. Recipient citation Nat. Inst. Arts and Letters, 1971, NEA awards, 1975, 78, 79, 86, Pulitzer prize for music, 1989; sr. fellow Inst. Studies in Am. Music, 1985, fellow Rockefeller Found., Guggenheim Found.; Fulbright scholar. Office: U Calif San Dieg Dept Music 0326 La Jolla CA 92093

REYNOLDS, STUART ARNOLD, surgeon; b. Berkeley, Calif., Oct. 16, 1936; s. Zen Vestal and Gladys Buellah (Rook) R.; m. Virginia A. Sterm-Reynolds; children: Karen E. Hanson, Julia E. Reynolds. BS in Med. Sci., Stanford U., 1959, MD, 1962. Cert. am. bd. surgery, 1970, 80, 91. Pvt. practice Havre, Mont., 1969—. Recipient Physicians Recognition award AMA, 1986, Trauma Achievement award, Am. Coll. Surgeons, 1986, 89, 92, Outstanding Svc. award Emergency Med. Svcs., 1988, Meritorious Svc. award Advanced trauma Life Support, 1991. Fellow ACS, AMA, Southwest Surgical Congress, Mont. Med. Assn. Office: No Mont Surg Assocs 120 13th St Havre MT 59501-5223

REYNOSA, BRENDA IVERSON, dietitian; b. Salt Lake City, Apr. 22, 1957; d. Reed Francis and Ann Frances (Kink) Iverson; m. David Edmond Montoya, 1976; m. Andrew Reynosa III, 1978; children: Andrew Reed IV, Brianne Marie. BS, U. Utah, 1980; MBA, Calif. State U., San Bernardino, 1983. Food svc. supr., diet tech. Barstow (Calif.) Cmty. Hosp., 1980-83; prodn. supr. Mercy Hosp. and Med. Ctr., San Diego, 1983-86; asst. dir. food and nutrition svc. Grossmont Hosp., La Mesa, Calif., 1986-92; dir. food svcs. Continental Rehab. Hosp., San Diego, 1992-93; menu sys. devel. dietitian San Diego (Calif.) City Schs., 1993—. Co-author Barstow Community Hospital Diet Manual, 1980. Com. chair Boy Scouts Am., San Diego, 1990-94. Recipient Heritage Dist. Leaders award Boy Scouts Am., 1994. Mem. Am. Soc. for Hosp. Food Svc. Adminstrs. (food membership chair 1991-92), Am. Sch. Food Svc. Assn., Am. Dietetic Assn. (registered dietitian), Calif. Dietetic Assn., San Diego Dietetic Assn.

REZA, JACQUELYN VALERIE, counselor, consultant; b. San Francisco, Sept. 12, 1953; d. Armando Rosalio Reza and Jacquelyn Joan Jordan; 1 child, Antonio Vincent Reza-James. BS in Zoology with honors, Ahmadu Bello U., Zaria, Nigeria, 1978; BA, San Francisco State U., 1979, MS in Rehab. Counseling, 1981; EdD in Internat. and Multicultural Edn., U. San Francisco, 1995. Lic. marriage family child counselor, nat. cert. counselor, cert. hypnotherapist. Counselor San Francisco State U., 1980-82, Calif. State U. Stanislaus, Turlock, 1982-84; marriage family child counselor pvt. practice therapist, workshop cons. San Francisco, Sacramento and San Jose, Calif., 1982—; counselor Gavilan C.C., Gilroy, Calif., 1984-85, De Anza C.C., Cupertino, Calif., 1985—; cons. Driver Performance Inst., San Francisco, 1984-91, Extended Opportunities and Svcs. Program Student Leadership Inst., Calif., 1987—; cons., examiner Bd. Behavioral Scis., Sacramento, 1986-92; pres. faculty senate De Anza C.C., 1989-90. Editor: (booklet) A Guide for I.D. and Referral of Students in Stress, 1985; contbr. articles to newsletters. Recipient Women Leaders in Edn. of Santa Clara County award, 1990, Golden Torch award San Francisco State U. Alumni, 1993; honoree Chicana Found. No. Calif., 1994; Title 7 fellow Office Bilingual & Minority Affairs, 1993-94, 94-95. Mem. Am. Assn. Women Community & Jr. Colls., Am. Counselor Assn., Am. Minority Counseling Assn., Latina Leadership Network Calif. C.C. (v.p. 1991-93, pres. 1993-94), Acad. Senate Calif. C.C. (mem. exec. bd. 1990-92), Minority Staff Assn., Third World Counselors Assn., De Anza Faculty Assn. (mem. exec. bd. 1987-89). Home: 6262 Thomas Ave Newark CA 94560-4042 Office: De Anza Coll 21250 Stevens Creek Blvd Cupertino CA 95014-5702

REZLER, JULIUS, labor arbitrator; b. Miskolc, Hungary, May 31, 1911; came to U.S., 1952; s. Gyula and Ilona (Kozma) R.; m. Agnes Graig, Aug. 16, 1954. PhD summa cum laude, U. Szeged, 1938; Dr.pol.sc. cum laude, U. Pecs, 1941, docent, 1948. Rapporteur, econ. rsch. sec. Hungarian Prime Ministry, 1938-41; dir. Hungarian Inst. Labor Studies, Budapest, 1943-45; econ. policy advisor to Min. of Reconstruction, Budapest, 1945-48; assoc. prof. econs. St. Francis Coll., Bklyn., 1954-57; prof. indsl. rels. Loyola U., Chgo., 1957-76, dir. inst. indsl. rels., 1965-69; labor arbitrator pvt. practice, Albuquerque, 1976—. Author: Automation and Industrial Labor, 1969, Arbitration and Health Care, 1981; contbr. articles to profl. jours. Recipient Cross of Distinction Hungarian Govt., 1993. Mem. Nat. Acad. Arbitrators, Indsl. Rels. Rsch. Assn. Home and Office: 2321 Ada Pl NE Albuquerque NM 87106-2501

RHAMY, JENNIFER FRANCES, marketing professional; b. Swindon, Eng., Nov. 14, 1954; d. Robert Keith and Evelyn Imel Rhamy. BS in Med. Tech., U. Ariz., 1977; postgrad., Vanderbilt U., 1979, U. Tex., Galveston, 1985; MBA, Colo. State U., 1994. Registered med. technologist. Med. technologist blood bank Vanderbilt U. Hosp., Nashville, 1979-84; tech. dir. United Blood Svcs., Tucson, 1985-87; supr. blood bank Park Plaza Hosp., Houston, 1987-88; mgr. transfusion svc. St. Luke's Episcopal Hosp., Houston, 1988-90; clin. application specialist blood component tech. COBE BCT, Inc., Lakewood, Colo., 1990—; presenter in field; rotation faculty blood bank U. Ariz., 1986-87; faculty, adminstr., specialist in blood banking program St. Luke's Episcopal Hosp., 1988-90. Scholar Gulf Coast Regional Blood Ctr., Houston, 1985. Mem. Am. Soc. Clin. Pathology, South Cen. Assn. Blood Banks, Am. Assn. Blood Banks, Am. Soc. for Apheresis. Democrat. Office: COBE BCT Inc 1201 Oak St Lakewood CO 80215-4409

RHEIN, TIMOTHY J., transportation company executive; b. 1941. BS, U. Santa Clara, 1962. Mil. contract and revenue analyst Am. Pres. Lines Ltd., Oakland, Calif., 1967-71, sr. analyst, 1971-72, mgr. mktg. planning, 1972-73, dir. traffic systems and adminstrn., 1973-75, dir. mktg. adminstrn., 1975-76, dir. worldwide sales, 1976-78, v.p. N.Am., 1978-80, v.p. traffic, 1980-84, sr. v.p., 1984-87, pres., also chief oper. officer, 1987-90; pres., chief exec. officer Am. Pres. Domestic Co. Ltd., Oakland, Calif., 1990—. With U.S. Army, 1962-67. Office: Am Pres Domestic Co Ltd 111 Broadway Fl 25 Oakland CA 94607-3730

RHEINISH, ROBERT KENT, university administrator; b. Mt. Vernon, N.Y., Oct. 27, 1934; s. Walter Washington and Doris Elizabeth (Standard) R.; m. Dorothy Ellen Steadman, May 3, 1957 (div. 1976); children: Robert Scott, Joel Nelson; m. Shirley Marie Suter, Aug. 1, 1976. BA, U. South Fla., 1963; MS, Ind. U., 1971, EdD, 1973. Staff engr. Armed Forces Radio & TV Svc., Anchorage, 1960-61; trainee Nat. Park Svc. Tng. Ctr., Grand Canyon, Ariz., 1965; historian Home of F.D.R., Nat. Historic Site, Hyde Park, N.Y., 1964-65, Sagamore Hill Nat. Hist. Site, Oyster Bay, N.Y., 1965-66; asst. coord. nat. environ. edn. devel. program Dept. of Interior, Washington, 1968; supervisory historian Lincoln Boyhood Nat. Meml., Lincoln City, Ind., 1966-68; dir. learning resources ctr. Whittier (Calif.) Coll., 1971-73; dir. media and learning resources Calif. State U., Long Beach, 1973-88; chmn. media dirs. The Calif. State Univs., Long Beach, 1975-76; radio announcer Sta. WTCX-FM, St. Petersburg, Fla., 1961-63; co-host with David Horowitz (2 broadcasts) On Campus, Sta. KNBC-TV, L.A., 1972-73; guest lectr. 6th Army Intelligence Sch., Los Alamitos Armed Forces Res. Ctr., 1987. Coord. multi-media program: In Search of Yourself, 1975 (Silver award Internat. Film and TV Festival of N.Y.), The House that Memory Built, 1981 (Cindy award Info. Film Producers of Am.), The Indochinese and Their Cultures, 1985 (Silver award Internat. Film & TV Festival of N.Y.). With RCAF, 1954-55, USAF, 1957-61. U.S. Office of Edn. grad. fellow, 1971-73; recipient Learning Resources Ctr. Fund Devel. award Pepsico, Sears, Prentice-Hall, et al, 1973; Nat. Def. Edn. Act grantee, 1974-76. Mem. Am. Legion, Lake Havasu Yacht Club. Republican. Home: 1975 Gold Dust Dr Lake Havasu City AZ 86404-1011

RHETTS, PAUL FISHER, public relations executive; b. Washington, Mar. 26, 1946; s. Charles Edward and Ruth (Fisher) R.; m. JoAnn Rhodes, Aug. 26, 1968 (div. Dec. 1979); children: Joanna Katherine, Alexandra Copeland; m. Barbe J. Awalt, Mar. 13, 1982. BA, Bucknell U., 1968; student Pub. Adminstrn. MS program, U. So. Calif., 1975-77. Pub. affairs producer Sta. WMAL-TV, Washington, 1969-70, Md. Pub. TV, Owings Mills, 1970-73; asst. supt. Balt. City Pub. Schs., 1973-74; publs. cons. Community Coll. Balt., 1975-78; pub. info. officer Howard County Schs., Ellicott City, Md., 1976-86; pres. Laser Pub. and Design, Md. and N.Mex., 1986—; trainer Pagemaker Desktop Pub. Software, 1986—; mem. adj. faculty Loyola Coll., Balt., 1978-80; bd. dirs. UNM Cancer Ctr., Maxwell Mus. of Anthropology. Author: Finding Out How People Feel, 1984, Charlie Carrillo: Tradition or Soul, 1994. Mem. exec. bd. Family Life Ctr., Columbia, Md., 1980-86, Humanities Inst., Columbia, 1978-82, Columbia Archives, 1984-86. Recipient award San Francisco Internat. Film Festival, 1971, Broadcasting award Ohio State U., 1972, Community Svc. Merit award So. Ednl. Communications Assn., 1973, Nat. Community Svc. award Corp. for Pub. Broadcasting, 1973, Publ. award of Excellence, 1986. Mem. Nat. Sch. Pub. Rels. Assn. (state coord. 1978-83, pres. Chesapeake chpt. 1981-82, 86-87, exec. bd., 1976-90, chmn. nat. conv. planning com., treas. N.Mex. chpt. 1991-92, Blue Ribbon award 1982, 87, Gold Medallion award 1985-92, Mariner award 1990, Pres. award 1991), Pub. Rels. Soc. Am. (treas. N.Mex. soc. 1991-92, Conquistado award 1991, 93, 94, 95, pres. elect 1993, pres. 1994, Nat. Pres.'s Citation for Leadership 1994), Am. Profl. Graphic Artists Assn., N.Mex. Book Assn., Columbia Bus. Exch., Ednl. Press Assn., Desktop Pub. Assn., C. of C. (bd. dirs.). Democrat. Episcopalian. Office: 925 Salamanca St NW Albuquerque NM 87107-5647

RHINE, MARK WOODFORDE, psychiatrist, psychoanalyst; b. Wellfleet, Mass., Nov. 10, 1934; s. Raymond Otto and Margaret Dorothy Mount (Woodforde) R.; m. Clare Williams, June 18, 1961; children: Kate, Michael, Maria. BA, Harvard U., 1957, MD, 1961; postgrad., Denver Psychoanalytic Inst., 1972-77. Diplomate Am. Bd. Psychiatry and Neurology; qualifications in addiction psychiatry. Inst. U. Colo. Med. Sch., Denver, 1968-74, asst. clin. prof., 1974—; pvt. practice Denver, 1974—; clin. dir. adult svcs. Columbine Psychiat. Ctr., Denver, 1990—. Lt. comdr. USPHS, 1962-64. Fellow Am. Psychiat. Assn.; mem. Denver Psychoanalytic Soc., Colo. Psychiat. Soc., Am. Assn. Psychiatrists in Alcohol and Addictions, Am. Geriatric Psychiat. Assn. Office: 3545 S Tamarac Dr Ste 370 Denver CO 80237-1432

RHO, EDWARD, information systems professional; b. Naples, Italy, Nov. 10, 1941; s. Pasquale and Rosa (Esposito) Rho; m. Lorraine Therese Craveira. BS equivalency, U. Naples, Taranto, Italy, 1964; postgrad., various schs., 1986-90. Programmer, analyst Cross & Brown, N.Y.C., 1967-69; project leader, sr. programmer, analyst Honfed Bank, 1970-81; d.p. cons., project mgr., sr. programmer, analyst Fin. Banking, Ins. and other orgns., Honolulu, 1981-83; cons., project mgr. MTL, Inc., Honolulu, 1983-84; data base analyst, chief analyst, project mgr. Universo Assicurazioni, Bologna, Italy, 1984-86; sr. programmer, analyst, project leader Allied Forces So. Europe/NATO, Naples, Italy, 1986-88; data base analyst, sr. systems analyst, acting task mgr. Planning Rsch. Corp./Hickam AFB, Aiea, Hawaii, 1989; sr. systems analyst, project leader, quality assurance rep. U.S. Dept. Def., Am. Express Bank, Ltd., Merchants Nat. Bank, Honolulu, 1989-90; data processing systems analyst V, project mgr. State of Hawaii/Exec. Br. Budget and Fin. Dept., 1990-91, data processing systems analyst VI, project mgr./sect. chief, 1991—. Developer computer software. Mem. Hist. Hawaii Found., Friends of Italy Soc. of Hawaii. Home: 47-409 Lulani St Kaneohe HI 96744-4718 Office: State of Hawaii Dept Budget and Fin 567 S King St Honolulu HI 96813-3036

RHOADES, JACQUELINE JO, education educator, consultant, writer; b. Chgo., Mar. 8, 1941; d. James Paul and Geraldine (Maxwell) R.; children: Cynthia Lyn Kreeger, Michael Todd Kreeger. BS in Sociology, Calif. State U., Long Beach, 1969; MS in Edn., Mt. Saint Mary's Coll., 1973. Cert. tchr., Calif. Resource specialist L.A. Unified Sch. Dist., 1970-76; reading coord., resource specialist Willits (Calif.) Unified Sch. Dist., 1976-81; edn. specialist Calif. State Dept. Edn., Ukiah, 1981-84; program specialist Mendocino County Schs., Ukiah, 1983-85; program specialist, tchr. Fontana (Calif.) Unified Sch. Dist., 1987—; adj. prof. Dominican Coll., San Rafael, 1982-87, Sonoma State U., Rohnert Park, Calif., 1981—; cons., writer Internat. Tng. Assn., Sacramento, 1983-94, Rhoades & Assocs., Alta Loma, Calif., 1994—. Author: Simple Cooperation in the Classroom, 1985, How to Say What You Mean, 1985, Cooperative Meeting Management, 1986, The Nurturing Classroom, 1988, Social and Academic Activities for the Cooperative Classroom, 1992, Outcome-Based Learning: A Teacher's Guide to Restructuring the Classroom, 1992, Lessons from Cherry Creek: A Handbook for Cooperative Learning, 1992, Language Arts & Simple Cooperation: Ideas for Writing Across the Curriculum, 1992, Staff Meetings That Work, 1994; author chpts. to books; editor mags.; contbr. articles to profl. jours. Mem. ASCD, Calif. Assn. for Resource Specialist, Calif. Math. Coun., Coun. for Exceptional Children, Learning Disabilities Assn., World Future Soc. Office: Rhoades & Assocs 8780 19th St Ste 194 Alta Loma CA 91701-4608

RHOADS, RICK, writer, editor; b. N.Y.C., Jan. 19, 1944; s. Lester and Doris (Geldzahler) R.; m. Margaret Cooke, June 6, 1979; children: Linden, Bonita, Maya. BA, CCNY, 1970. Writer, editor Expert Connections, N.Y.C., 1980-85; sr. editor Rick Rhoads & Assocs., L.A., 1985—. Pres. Westside Dem. Club, L.A., 1992-94. Mem. Assn. for Bus. Comm., L.A. MacIntosh Group. Home and Office: 3637 Glendon Ave Apt 201 Los Angeles CA 90034-6250

RHODE, EDWARD ALBERT, veterinary medicine educator, veterinary cardiologist; b. Amsterdam, N.Y., July 25, 1926; s. Edward A. and Katherine (Webb) R.; m. Dolores Bangert, 1955; children: David E., Peter R., Paul W., Robert M., Catherine E. DVM, Cornell U., 1947. Diplomate Am. Coll. Veterinary Internal Medicine. Prof. emeritus vet. medicine U. Calif., Davis, 1964—, chmn. dept. vet. medicine, 1968-71, assoc. dean instrn. Sch. Vet. Medicine, 1971-77, 78-81, dean sch. Vet. Medicine, 1982-91. Mem. AAAS, Nat. Acad. Practices, Am. Coll. Vet. Internal Medicine, Am. Vet. Medicine Assn., Basic Sci. Coun., Am. Heart Assn., Am. Acad. Vet. Cardiology, Am. Physiol. Soc., Calif. Vet. Medicine Assn. Office: U Calif Sch Vet Medicine Davis CA 95616

RHODES, DALLAS D., geologist and educator; b. El Dorado, Kans., Aug. 8, 1947; s. Earl and Peggy Lee (White) R.; m. Lisa Ann Rossbacher. BS with honors, U. Mo., 1969; MA, PhD, Syracuse U., 1973. Instr. Syracuse (N.Y.) U., 1972-73; asst. prof. geology U. Vt., Burlington, 1973-77; cons. geologist N.Y. State Geol. Survey, Albany, summers 1975-77; vis. rschr. U. Uppsala, Sweden, 1983-84; cons. geologist Jet Propulsion Lab., Pasadena, Calif., 1980-85; prof. geology Whittier (Calif.) Coll., 1977—, dir. Fairchild Aerial Photography Collection, 1981—; dir. W.M. Kech Found. Image Processing Lab. W.M. Keck Found. Image Processing Lab., 1990—. Editor: Adjustments of the Fluvial System, 1979. NASA Summer Faculty fellow, 1980, 81. Mem. Am. Geophys. Union, Geol. Soc. Am., Nat. Assn. Geology Tchrs., Sigma Xi. Democrat. Office: Whittier College Dept Geology Whittier CA 90608

RHODES, GERALD LEE, writer; b. Redding, Calif., June 18, 1954; s. Howard Gordon and Rosalie (Lowell) R.; m. Sue Ann Williams, April 28, 1990; 1 child, Erin Nicole Fossum. BA in Journalism and Native Am. Ethnic Studies, Calif. State U., Sacramento, 1976; MS in Interdisciplinary Studies, U. Oregon, 1984. Reporter The Springfield (Oreg.) News, 1984-90; writer bus. and sci. The Columbian, Vancouver, Wash., 1990-93; freelance writer, 1993—; fire fighter U.S. Forest Svc., Redding, 1971-73, U.S. Bur. Land Mgmt., Anchorage, 1975-78; fire mgmt. tng. instr., adminstr. U.S. Bur. Land Mgmt., Alaska Fire Svc., Fairbanks, 1979-84; freelance writer Comm. Works, Springfield, 1989-90; ind. rep. Excel Telecomm., 1993—; v.p. Lane Press Club, Eugene, 1990. Reporter, photographer: (newspaper series) Future Forests, 1987 (Bus. Reporting Award for Non-Daily Newspapers, Associated Oregon Industries, 1988). Vol. Evergreen chpt. Habitat for Humanity, Vancouver, 1992. Fellow Sci. Writers Workshop, Am. Chem. Soc., Washington, 1991; New Horizons fellow, Coun. for the Advancement of Sci. Writing, 1992; recipient 1st Gen. Column Writing award Soc. Profl. Journalists, Oreg., 1988, 1st Sci. and Environ. Reporting award, Pacific N.W., 1993. Mem. Nat. Assn. Sci. Writers. Lutheran.

RHODES, JAMES LAMAR, JR. (GRIZZLY BEAR RHODES), educator, research historian; b. Montgomery, Ala., May 3, 1948; s. James Lamar Rhodes and Mae Ellen (Childers) Holley; divorced; 1 child, Sharon Michelle Rhodes Carswell; m. Saturnina Alvarado Avina, Feb. 14, 1977; children: James Lamar III, Aaron Abraham, David Isaiah. AA in English Lit., Coll. of Marin, 1972; BS in Criminal Justice Adminstrn., Calif. State U., San Jose, 1977; AA in Law Enforcement, Canada Coll., Redwood City, Calif., 1978; MA in Bus. Mgmt., Webster U., St. Louis, 1988. Cert. peace officer, Calif.; cert. detention and corrections officer, Ariz. Communications technician Pacific Telephone Co., Calif., 1970-83; detention officer Yuma County, Yuma, Ariz., 1984-86; correctional svc. officer State of Ariz., Yuma, 1986-88; tchr. Immaculate Conception Sch., Yuma, 1988-91; writer Yuma, 1991—; 1st Am. tchr. with students touring Socialist Republic of Vietnam, 1990; rschr. agent orange/herbicidal poisoning, Saigon, summer 1992; conductor seminars field. Author detention and correctional handbooks; author: (with others) Where Dreams Begin, 1993; co-editor: Legacy of the American Indian: Lessons for the Classroom, 1989; Yuma security cons. (film) The Getaway, 1993; extra (film) Star Gate, 1994. Mem. Milpitas (Calif.) San. Dist. Bd., 1978-80; bd. dirs. Ctr. for Employment and Tng., Yuma, 1986—; founder no-fee counseling svcs. for Vietnam vets., Yuma; mem. Agt. Orange Adv. Com.; union organizer Communication Workers Am., Calif., 1972-80. Sgt. USAF, 1967-69, Vietnam. Recipient Citizen of Honor award Vietnamese Community, Santa Clara County, Calif., 1983, appreciation award Cath. Social Svc., Santa Clara County, 1983, Luth. Soc. Svc., Santa Clara County, 1983, Am. Legion, Indpls., 1983, AMVETS, Yuma, 1986. Mem. DAV, AFSCME, AMVETS (state judge advocate Ariz. chpt. 1986), Vietnam Combat Vets. (nat. chmn. 1981—), Justice for Vet. Victims of VA (v.p. 1988—), U.S. Chess Fedn., Tribal Coun. Southeastern Cherokee Confederacy (elected mem.), World Federalist Assn., Vietnam Helicopter Crew Mems. Assn., Ariz. Indian Vietnam Vets. Assn., Am. Legion (post comdr. 1983). Mem. Baha'i Faith. Home: 1740 W 24th Ln Yuma AZ 85364-7017

RHODES, JESS LYNN, counselor; b. Houston, Apr. 18, 1942; s. Jess Lynn and Eunice Pauline (Moser) R.; m. Martha Camille McNeill; children: Robert Lynn, Rhonda Cheri. BA, BS, Harding U., 1964; postgrad., Tex. Tech. U., 1964-66; MA, U. No. Colo., 1992. Lic. profl. counselor. Instr. Lubbock (Tex.) Christian Coll., 1964-65; min. Church of Christ, Abernathy, Tex., 1965-68, Tulia, Tex., 1969-73, Wichita Falls, Tex., 1973-82, Greeley, Colo., 1983-92; profl. counselor Luth. Family Svcs., Greeley, 1992-93, Pathways, Greeley, 1993—. Author: Sermons for the Seventies, 1973; contbr. articles to profl. jours.; mem. editorial bd. (jour.) Power for Today, 1967-94; guest editor (jour.) 20th Century Christian, 1966, 67. Mem. bd. devel. Lubbock Christian U., 1970-80; trustee Texhoma Christian Care Ctr., Wichita Falls, 1980-82, Christian Camp of the Rockies, Greeley, 1988-91, Wichita Christian Sch., Wichita Falls, 1975-82; mem. adv. bd. Tulia Satellite Sch. for Retarded, 1970-73. Mem. ACA, Internat. Assn. Marriage & Family Counselors. Home: 1964 28th Ave Greeley CO 80631-5719

RIACH, DOUGLAS ALEXANDER, marketing and sales executive, retired military officer; b. Victoria, B.C., Can., Oct. 8, 1919; s. Alex and Gladys (Provis) R.; came to U.S., 1925, naturalized, 1942; BA, UCLA, 1948; postgrad. in mktg. Fenn Coll., 1959, Grad. Sch. Sales Mgmt. and Mktg., 1960, U.S. Army Command and Gen. Staff Coll., 1966, Armed Forces Staff Coll., 1968, Indsl. Coll. of the Armed Forces, 1970-71; m. Eleanor Montague, Mar. 28, 1942; 1 child, Sandra Jean. With Gen. Foods Corp., 1948-80, terr. sales mgr., San Francisco, 1962-80; with Food Brokers, San Francisco Bay area, 1980-90; exec. v.p. Visual Market Plans Inc., Novato, Calif., 1984-87; ter. mgr. Ibbotson, Berri, DeNola Brokerage, Inc., Emeryville, Calif., 1990—. Served to capt. inf. AUS, 1941-46, ETO; to col. inf. USAR, 1946-79, from comdr. 2d inf. brigade Calif. State mil. res., 1984-87 to brigadier gen. (ret.) 1990. Decorated Legion of Merit, Bronze Star with V device and oak leaf cluster, Purple Heart, Combat Infantry Badge, Croix de Guerre avec Palme (France and Belgium), Fouragerre (Belgium), Combattant Cross-Voluntaire (France), Combattant Cross-Soldier (France), Medaille-Commemorative de la Liberee (France), Medaille-Commemorative Francais (France), Medaille-War Wounded (France), Medaille-Commemorative Belgique (Belgium), Medaille-de la Reconnaissance (Belgium), Medaille du Voluntaire (Belgium), Cross of Freedom (Poland), Royal Commemorative War Cross (Yugoslavia); named knight Order of the Compassionate Heart (internat.), knight commdr. Sovereign Mil. Order, Temple of Jerusalem (knights templar), CDR Commandery of Calif. (knights templar 1992-94); knight commdr. sovereign Order of St. John of Jerusalem (knights hospitaller), knight commdr. Polonia Restituta; named to U.S. Army Inf. Hall of Fame, 1982; recipient Calif. Medal of Merit and cluster, Commendation medal. Mem. Long Beach Food Sales Assn. (pres. 1950), Assn. Grocers Mfrs. Reps. (dir. 1955), Am. Security Coun. (nat. adv. bd. 1975—), Res. Officers Assn. (San Francisco Presidio pres. 1974-76, v.p. 1977-82, v.p. dept. Calif. 1979, exec. v.p. 1980, pres. 1981, nat. councilman 1981-82), Nat. Assn. Uniformed Svcs., Exchange Club (v.p. Long Beach 1955), St. Andrews Soc. Queens Club San Francisco, Combat Infantry Assn., Assn. U.S. Army, Am. Legion, Assn. Former Intelligence Officers, Presidio Soc., Navy League, Ret. Officers Assn., Mil. Order Purple Heart, DAV, Psychol. Ops. Assn., Nat. Guard Assn. Calif., State Def. Force Assn. Calif., Merchandising Execs. San Francisco (dir. 1970-75, sec. 1976-77, v.p. 1978-79, pres. 1980, bd. dirs. 1981-89), Commonwealth of Club Calif. (nat. def. sect. vice chmn. 1964-66, chmn. 1967-72), Elks, Masons (master, lodge 400, Shrine, Islam Temple, 32d degree Scottish Rite, sojouner chpt. #277). Republican. Presbyterian. Home: 2609 Trousdale Dr Burlingame CA 94010-5706

RIANDA, DAVID NOEL, medical foundation administrator; b. Salinas, Calif., Dec. 25, 1938; s. Lee F. and Dorothy M. L. (Hoertkorn) R.; m. Janice Evelyn Kautto, Sept. 7, 1963; children: Christopher Paul, Jill Noelle. BA, U. Oreg., 1960, MA, 1965. Program dir. U. Mont., Missoula, 1960-62; asst. dir. edn. activities Portland (Oreg.) State U., 1962-63; dir. union publicity U. Wis., Milw., 1965-68; dir. pub. affairs Reed Coll., Portland, 1968-73; dir. fund devel. Providence Med. Ctr., Portland, 1974-76; pres. Providence Child Ctr. Found., Portland, 1976-86; exec. dir. N.W. Osteo. Med. Found., Portland, 1986—; fund raising cons. to numerous non-profit orgns., 1974—; journalism arts adv. bd. Mt. Hood C.C., 1970-76, chmn. 1973-74; mem. Gov.'s Commn. on Youth, 1978-81; advancement coun. U. Oreg. Sch. Journalism and Comm., 1993—. Bd. dirs. Firehouse Theater, 1984-87, pres., 1984-86; mem. cmty. adv. bd. Providence Child Ctr., 1995—; bd. dirs. Women's Intercmty. AIDS Resource, 1995—. Named Man of the Yr., Assn. Retarded Citizens, Multnomah County, Oreg., 1986; recipient Award of Excellence, Pacific Indsl. Communicators Assn., 1970. Mem. Nat. Assn. Osteo. Founds. (pres. 1991), Grantmakers of Oreg. and S.W. Wash. (steering com. 1991-95, sec. 1991), Willamette Valley Devel. Officers (pres. 1987, Award of Merit 1993), Assn. Healthcare Philanthropy (cert. 1977, accredited 1981, v.p. Region 12, nat. bd. dirs. 1979-81), Oregon Internat. Assn. Bus. Communicators (pres. 1972-73, Awards of Merit/Excellence 1970, 71, 72, 74, 76, 79, Presdl. Citation for Outstanding Svc. 1974, Rodney Adair Meml. award 1975), U. Oreg. Friars, Phi Kappa Signa. Home: 4140 NE Alameda St Portland OR 97212-2909

RIBERA, ANTHONY D., protective services official. Police chief San Francisco Police Dept. Office: San Francisco Police Commn Hall of Justice Rm 505 850 Bryant St San Francisco CA 94103-4603*

RIBERO, MICHAEL ANTONIO, marketing executive; b. Miami, Fla., May 16, 1956; s. Miguel and Zoe (Prio) R.; m. Brenda Starr, Sept. 8, 1979; children: Michael, Kristen. BS in Ops. Research, U. Fla., 1979. Analyst mktg., mgr. through brand mgr. The Procter & Gamble Co., Cin., 1979-85; from dir. to v.p. Eastern Airlines, Miami, 1985-88; sr. v.p. mktg. Hilton Hotels Corp., Beverly Hills, Calif., 1988—; bd. dirs. Compass Comuter Corp., Hilton Svc. Corp. Bd. dirs. Miami Project to Cure Paralysis, 1987. Republican. Roman Catholic. Office: Hilton Hotels Corp 9336 Civic Center Dr Beverly Hills CA 90210-3604

RICARDO-CAMPBELL, RITA, economist, educator; b. Boston, Mar. 16, 1920; d. David and Elizabeth (Jones) Ricardo; m. Wesley Glenn Campbell, Sept. 15, 1946; children: Barbara Lee, Diane Rita, Nancy Elizabeth. BS, Simmons Coll., 1941; MA, Harvard U., 1945, PhD, 1946. Instr. Harvard U., Cambridge, Mass., 1946-48; asst. prof. Tufts U., Medford, Mass., 1948-51; labor economist U.S. Wage Stabilization Bd., 1951-53; economist Ways and Means Com. U.S. Ho. of Reps., 1953; cons. economist, 1957-60; vis. prof. San Jose State Coll., 1960-61; sr. fellow Hoover Instn. on War, Revolution, and Peace, Stanford, Calif., 1968—; lectr. health svc. adminstrn. Stanford U. Med. Sch., 1973-78; bd. dirs. Watkins-Johnson Co., Palo Alto, Calif., Gillette Co., Boston; mgmt. bd. Samaritan Med. Ctr., San Jose, Calif. Author: Voluntary Health Insurance in the U.S., 1960, Economics of Health and Public Policy, 1971, Food Safety Regulation: Use and Limitations of Cost-Benefit Analysis, 1974, Drug Lag: Federal Government Decision Making, 1976, Social Security: Promise and Reality, 1977, The Economics and Politics of Health, 1982, 2d edit., 1985; co-editor: Below-Replacement Fertility in Industrial Societies, 1987, Issues in Contemporary Retirement, 1988; contbr. articles to profl. jours. Commr. Western Interstate Commn. for Higher Edn. Calif., 1967-75, chmn., 1970-71; mem. Pres. Nixon's Adv. Coun. on Status Women, 1969-76; mem. task force on taxation Pres.'s Coun. on Environ. Quality, 1970-72; mem. Pres.'s Com. Health Services Industry, 1971-73, FDA Nat. Adv. Drug Com., 1972-75; mem. Econ. Policy Adv. Bd., 1981-90, Pres. Reagan's Nat. Coun. on Humanities, 1982-89, Pres. Nat. Medal of Sci. com., 1988-94; bd. dirs. Ind. Colls. No. Calif., 1971-87; mem. com. assessment of safety, benefits, risks Citizens Commn. Sci., Law and Food Supply, Rockefeller U., 1973-75; mem. adv. com. Ctr. Health Policy Rsch., Am. Enterprise Inst. Pub. Policy Rsch., Washington, 1974-80; mem. adv. coun. on social security Social Security Adminstrn., 1974-75; bd. dirs. Simmons Coll. Corp., Boston, 1975-80; mem. adv. coun. bd. assocs. Stanford Libr., 1975-78; mem. coun. SRI Internat., Menlo Park, Calif., 1977-90. Mem. Am. Econ. Assn., Mont Pelerin Soc. (bd. dirs. 1988-92, v.p. 1992-94), Harvard Grad. Soc. (coun. 1991), Phi Beta Kappa. Home: 26915 Alejandro Dr Los Altos Hills CA 94022 Office: Stanford U Hoover Instn Stanford CA 94305-6010

RICCARDI, VINCENT MICHAEL, pediatrician, researcher, educator; b. Bklyn., Oct. 14, 1940; s. Gabriel John and Frances Mary (Novak) R.; m. Susan Leona Bogda, July 27, 1967; children: Angela M., Ursula M., Mikah F. AB, UCLA, 1962; MD, Georgetown U., 1966; MBA, U. LaVerne, 1993. Intern, resident in medicine U. Pitts., 1966-68; fellow in genetics Harvard Med. Sch., Boston, 1968-70, 72; asst. prof. medicine U. Colo. Med. Ctr., Denver, 1973-75; assoc. prof. medicine, pediatrics Med. Coll. Wis., Milw., 1975-77; prof. medicine, pediatrics Baylor Coll. Medicine, Houston, 1977-90; med. dir. The Genetics Inst., Pasadena, Calif., 1990-92; clin. prof. pediatrics UCLA, 1991—; founder, CEO Am. Med. Consumers, La Crescenta, 1992; dir. The Neurofibromatosis Inst., La Crescenta, Calif., 1985—. Author: Genetic Approach to Human Disease, 1977, Communication and Counseling in Health Care, 1983, Neurofibromatosis, 1986, rev. edit., 1992. Maj. U.S. Army, 1970-71. Fellow ACP, AAAS, Am. Coll. Med. Genetics; mem. Am. Soc. Human Genetics, Am. Coll. Physician Execs. Home: 5415 Briggs Ave La Crescenta CA 91214-2205 Office: The Neurofibromatosis Inst 5415 Briggs Ave La Crescenta CA 91214-2205

RICCHIUTI, FRANCES, food executive; b. 1921. V.p. P.R. Farms Inc., Clovis, Calif. Office: P R Farms Inc 2917 E Shepherd Ave Clovis CA 93611*

RICCI, CAROLYNE YOUNGBLOOD, print shop owner; b. Westville, Okla., Jan. 11, 1951; d. Gifford Dewitt and Beatrice Louise (Owens) Youngblood; m. John James Ricci Jr., May 1, 1980 (div. June 1983); 1 child, Jared James. Student, Ea. N.Mex. U., 1969-70. File clk. Scott & White Hosp., Temple, Tex., 1971; office mgr. Dr. Gifford Youngblood, Clovis, N.Mex., 1972-75; owner Red Door Women's Wear, Clovis, 1975-77; apprentice contractor Gentry Real Estate, Clovis, 1977; office mgr. Rendering Plant, Clovis, 1980-81; ops. mgr. Sta. KMCC-TV, Clovis, 1981-83; salesperson Desert Beauty Supply, Tuscon, 1984-85; owner Pronto Printing, Tucson, 1985—. Mem. Jr. League of Tucson, 1987—; mem. State Pub. Affairs Com., Tucson Bus. Com. for the Arts, 1987—, sponsor Women's Expo, 1989-90, 91, chmn. Arts Smart Conf.; mem. Friends of the Ballet, Nat. Safety Coun., So. Ariz. Adv. Bd.; chmn. parish events St. Philips Episcopal Ch.; adv. bd. Open Inn; mem. Tucson Visitor and Conf. Bur.; mem. budget rev. com. City of Tucson, 1989—, co-chmn. Mem. NAFE, Quick Printer in Tucson (mem. steering com. 1987), Rincon Exch. Club, Resources for Women, Alpha Delta Pi Alumnae (past pres.) Key Group, Tucson Bus. Women, Pima Early Rising Execs. Republican. Office: Pronto Printing 122 S Kolb Rd Tucson AZ 85710-3604

RICCIARDELLI-DAILEY, MARY LYNDE, health services company executive and author; b. Colorado Springs, Colo., Dec. 9, 1948; d. Alexander J. and Vyrna G. (Nichols) Pavlica; m. Robert A. Dailey; children: Robert, Lisa, Vyrna Alexis. Student, Aims C.C., Ft. Lupton, Colo., 1990, Laramie County C.C., Cheyenne, Wyo., 1991. Author: Divorce and Kids It's OK, 1991, Different but the Same It's OK, 1992, Uncle Joe and Me, 1990. Mem. security com. Cheyenne Frontier Days, 1979—, ticket com., 1990—; election judge Dem. Party, Cheyenne, 1991—; exec. sec. Cmty. Action, 1986-88. Mem. Am. Legion Aux. Greek Orthodox. Home: Box 51 228 Wyoming Ave Burns WY 82053

RICCIO, THOMAS PATRICK, theater director; b. Cleve., Mar. 1, 1955; s. Anthony James and Filomena (Palmieri) R.; m. Lolita Lesheim, June 17, 1983 (div. Mar. 1990). BA, Cleve. State U., 1978; MFA, Boston U., 1982. Asst. lit. dir. Am. Repertory Theater, Cambridge, Mass., 1980-82; dramaturg Cleve. Play House, 1985-86; artistic dir. Organic Theater Co., Chgo., 1985-88; assoc. prof. theater U. Alaska, Fairbanks, 1988—; dir. Tuma Theatre, Fairbanks, Alaska. Dir. (plays) Titus Andronicus, 1987, Conduct and Life, 1988, Little Caesar, 1988, Qayaq: The Magical Man, 1991, Emandulo, 1992, Child from the Sea, 1992, Utetmun, 1992, Eagle's Gift, 1993, Makanda Mahlanu, 1993, Imiprolti, 1994; playwright The Box, 1984, La Mulata, 1984, Il Ronzo Del Mosche, 1984, End of the World, 1985 (Cleve. Critics award 1985), Rubber City, 1985, Betawulf, 1986, Christmas on Mars, 1986, Bosoms and Neglect, 1986; guest dir. Natal Performing Arts Coun., South Africa, 1992, 93, Sakha Nat. Theatre (Siberia), 1993, Ctr. for the Arts, Lusaka, Zambia, 1994; workshop dir.; contbr. articles to profl. jours. Alaska Native Studies travel grantee, 1989, NEH, 1990. Goethe Inst. grantee, 1987, Mellon Travel grantee, 1991, 92, 93. Mem. Soc. Stage Dirs., Am. Theater in Higher Edn., Found. Shamantic Studies. Office: U Alaska Theater Dept PO Box 755700 Fairbanks AK 99709

RICCO, RAYMOND JOSEPH, JR., computer systems engineer; b. Tullahoma, Tenn., Aug. 7, 1948; s. Raymond Joseph and Betty Jean (Collins) R.; m. Susan Rae Frey, Mar. 30, 1985. BS, Mid. Tenn. State U., 1971; MS, U. Tenn., Tullahoma, 1976. Rsch. asst. U. Tenn. Space Inst., Tullahoma, 1972-76; prin. analyst Teledyne Brown Engring., Huntsville, Ala., 1976-78; sr. analyst Sci. Applications Internat., Huntsville, 1978-82; sr. mem. tech. staff Mitre Corp., Colorado Springs, Colo., 1982-83; sr. engr. analyst Sci. Applications Internat., Huntsville, 1983-84; project mgr. Systems Devel. Corp., Dayton, Ohio, 1984-85; bus. assoc. Booz Allen & Hamilton Inc., Dayton, 1985-87; project dir. Bell Tech. Ops., Sierra Vista, Ariz., 1987-90; ptnr. Ricco-Thompson Cons. Engrs., Sierra Vista, 1990-92, Gazelle Affiliates, Sierra Vista, 1992—; sr. engr., scientist SAIC, Sierra Vista, 1992—; mem. adv. bd. Am. Security Coun., Arlington, Va., 1981—. Contbr. articles to profl. jours. Mem. NRA, IEEE, IEEE Computer Soc., Am. Def. Preparedness Assn., Armed Forces Comm. and Electronics Assn., Air Force Assn., Optimists Internat. Home: PO Box 3672 Sierra Vista AZ 85636-3672 Office: SAIC 333 W Wilcox Dr Ste 200 Sierra Vista AZ 85635-1756 also: Gazelle Affiliates 3323 E Willow Dr Sierra Vista AZ 85635-4273

RICE, BARBARA POLLAK, advertising and marketing executive; b. Ft. Scott, Kans., Nov. 11, 1937; d. Olin N. and Jeanette E. (Essen) Brigman; m. Stanley Rice, Apr. 28, 1978; 1 child, Beverly Johnson. Student N. Central Coll., 1955, Elmhurst Coll., 1956; BA in Communications, Calif. State U., Fullerton, 1982. Art dir. Gonterman & Assos., St. Louis, 1968-71; advt. mgr. Passpoint Corp., St. Louis, 1971-73; advt., pub. relations mgr. Permaneer Corp., St. Louis, 1973-74; advt. cons., advt. mgr. Hydro-Air Engring., Inc., St. Louis, 1974-76; mgr. mktg. services Hollytex Carpet Mills subs. U.S. Gypsum Co., City of Industry, Calif., 1976-79; pres. B.P. Rice & Co., Inc., Cerittos, Calif., 1979—; press affiliate Inst. Bus. Designers. Recipient Designer Best Exhibit award Nat. Farm Builders Trade Show, Creative Challenge Mead Top 60 award L.A. Bus. Profl. Advt. Assn. Mem. Am. Advt. Fedn. (past nat. bd. dirs., region chmn., Silver medal), L.A. Advt. Women (pres., dir., LULU award), Bus. Profl. Advt. Assn., Calif. State U.-Fullerton Sch. Comm. Alumni Assn., Beta Sigma Phi (past pres., outstanding mem.). Author: Truss Construction Manual, 1975. Office: 16330 Marquardt Ave Cerritos CA 90703-2350

RICE, DALE HOWARD, physician, educator; b. Pensacola, Fla., June 23, 1943; s. Charles Hefner and Earline (Moore) R.; 1 child, Alexander. MD, U. Mich., 1968. Diplomate Am. Bd. Otolaryngology. Assoc. prof., vice chmn. head and neck surgery UCLA, 1976-83; prof., chmn. dept. otolaryngology-head and neck surgery U. So. Calif., L.A., 1983—. Contbr. articles to profl. jours. Bd. dirs. YMCA, Pacific Palisades, Calif., 1979-83. Major USAF, 1970-72. Mem. ACS (adv. coun. 1987—, bd. govs. 1988—), Am. Soc. Head and Neck Surgery (treas. 1990—), Soc. U. Otolaryngologists (sec.-treas. 1990-93, pres. 1993-94), Am. Acad. Otolaryngology. Office: U So Calif Sch Medicine 1200 N State St Los Angeles CA 90033-4525

RICE, DONALD BLESSING, former secretary of air force, corporate executive; b. Frederick, Md., June 4, 1939; s. Donald Blessing and Mary Celia (Santangelo) R.; m. Susan Fitzgerald, Aug. 25, 1962; children: Donald Blessing III, Joseph John, Matthew Fitzgerald. BSChemE, U. Notre Dame, 1961, DEng (hon.), 1975; MS in Indsl. Adminstrn., Purdue U., 1962, PhD in Mgmt. and Econs., 1965, D. Mgmt. (hon.), 1985; LLD (hon.), Pepperdine U., 1989; LHD (hon.), West Coast U., 1993. Dir. cost analysis Office Sec. Def., Washington, 1967-69, dep. asst. sec. def. resource analysis, 1969-70; asst. dir. Office Mgmt. and Budget, Exec. Office Pres., 1970-72; pres., CEO The Rand Corp., Calif., 1972-89; sec. USAF, 1989-93; pres., COO Teledyne, Inc., L.A., 1993—; bd. dirs. Teledyne, Inc., Vulcan Materials Co., Wells Fargo Bank, Wells Fargo & Co.; mem. Nat. Sci. Bd., 1974-86; chmn. Nat. Commn. Supplies and Shortages, 1975-77; mem. Nat. Commn. on U.S.-China Relations; mem. nat. adv. com. oceans and atmosphere Dept. Commerce, 1972-75; mem. adv. panel Office Tech. Assessment, 1976-79; adv. council Coll. Engring., U. Notre Dame, 1974-88; mem. Def. Sci. Bd., 1977-83, sr. cons., 1984-88; U.S. mem. Trilateral Commn.; dir. for sec. def. and Pres. Def. Resource Mgmt. Study, 1977-79. Author articles. Served to capt. AUS, 1965-67. Recipient Sec. Def. Meritorious Civilian Service medal, 1970, Def. Exceptional Civilian Svc. medal, 1993, Forrestal award, 1992; Ford Found. fellow, 1962-65. Fellow AAAS; mem. Council Fgn. Relations, Inst. Mgmt. Scis. (past pres.), Tau Beta Pi. Office: Teledyne Inc 2049 Century Park E 15th Fl Los Angeles CA 90067

RICE, DOROTHY PECHMAN (MRS. JOHN DONALD RICE), medical economist; b. Bklyn., June 11, 1922; d. Gershon and Lena (Schiff) Pechman; m. John Donald Rice, Apr. 3, 1943; children: Kenneth D., Donald B., Thomas H. Student, Bklyn. Coll., 1938-39; BA, U. Wis., 1941; DSc (hon.), Coll. Medicine and Dentistry N.J., 1979. With hosp. and med. facilities USPHS, Washington, 1960-61; med. econs. studies Social Security Adminstrn., 1962-63; health econs. br. Community Health Svc., USPHS, 1964-65; chief health ins. rsch. br. Social Security Adminstrn., 1966-72, dep. asst. commr. for rsch. and statistics, 1972-75; dir. Nat. Ctr. for Health Stats., Rockville, Md., 1976-82; prof. Inst. Health & Aging U. Calif., San Francisco, 1982-94, prof. emeritus, 1994—; developer, mgr. nationwide health info. svcs.; expert on aging, health care costs, disability, and cost-of-illness. Contbr. articles to profl. jours. Recipient Social Security Adminstrn. citation, 1968, Disting. Service medal HEW, 1974, Jack C. Massey Found. award, 1978. Fellow Am. Public Health Assn. (domestic award for excellence 1978, Sedgwick Meml. medal, 1988), Am. Statis. Assn.; mem. Inst. Medicine, Assn. Health Svcs. Rsch. (President's award 1988), Am. Econ. Assn., Population Assn. Am., LWV. Home: 13895 Campus Dr Oakland CA 94605-3831 Office: U Calif Sch Nursing Calif # N631 San Francisco CA 94143-0612

RICE, DOUGLAS ALAN, foreign language professor; b. Concord, N.H., Oct. 17, 1949; s. Donald Neal and Mildred Evans (Thomas) R. BA, Bates Coll., 1971; BSEd, U. Idaho, 1975; MA, So. Ill. U., 1989. Asst. prof. English Universidad Nacional de Ancash, Huaraz, Peru, 1982-86; instr. Spanish and English Highland C.C., Freeport, Ill., 1989-91; asst. prof. Spanish and English Pikeville (Ky.) Coll., 1991-93; instr. fgn. lang. Blue Mountain C.C., Pendleton, Oreg., 1993—. Mem. Am. Coun. of Tchrs. of Fgn. Langs., Am. Assn. Tchrs. of Spanish and Portuguese. Office: Blue Mountain Comm Coll Pendleton OR 97801

RICE, JERRY LEE, professional football player; b. Starkville, Miss., Oct. 13, 1962; m. Jackie Rice; 1 child, Jaqui. Student, Miss. State Valley U. Football player San Francisco 49ers, 1985—. Named MVP, Super Bowl XXIII, 1989, Sporting News NFL Player of Yr., 1987, 90; named to Sporting News Coll. All-Am. team, 1984, Sporting News All-Pro team, 1986-92, Pro Bowl team, 1986-93. Office: care San Francisco 49ers 4949 Centennial Blvd Santa Clara CA 95054-1229*

RICE, JONATHAN C., educational television executive; b. St. Louis, Feb. 19, 1916; s. Charles M. and May R. (Goldman) R.; m. Kathleen Feiblman, Aug. 6, 1946 (dec. June 1964); children: Jefferson Charles, Kit (dec.), May Nanette. AB, Stanford U., 1938. War photographer, reporter Acme Newspix/NEA Svc., PTO of WWII, 1941-43; picture book editor Look Mag., N.Y.C., 1947-48; news/spl. events dir. Sta. KTLA-TV, L.A., 1948-53; program mgr. Sta. KQED-TV, San Francisco, 1953-67, dir. program ops., 1967-78, asst. to pres., 1978-90, bd. dirs., 1990—; cons. NET, PBS, Corp. for Pub. Broadcasting, Ford Found., TV Lima Peru, Sta. WGBH-TV, Boston, Sta. WNET-TV, N.Y.C., French TV, Europe Eastern Edn. TV, Dept. Justice, 1955-90; lectr. Stanford U., 1958-77. Editor: Look at America, The South, Official Picture Story of the FBI, 1947. Bd. dirs. NATAS, San Francisco, Planned Parenthood, San Francisco and Marin County, Calif. Maj. USMC, 1943-47, PTO. Recipient George Foster Peabody award, 1956, Thomas Alva Edison award for best station, N.Y.C., 1960, Gov.'s award NATAS, 1972-73, Ralph Lowell award Corp. for Pub. Broadcasting, 1972; Jonathan Rice Studio named in his honor, 1986. Home: 1 Russian Hill Pl San Francisco CA 94133-3605

RICE, JULIAN CASAVANT, lawyer; b. Miami, Fla., Dec. 31, 1923; s. Sylvan J. and Maybelle (Casavant) R.; m. Dorothy Mae Haynes, Feb. 14, 1958; children—Scott B., Craig M. (dec.), Julianne C., Linda D., Janette M. Student, U. San Francisco, 1941-43; JD cum laude, Gonzaga U., 1950. Bar: Wash. 1950, Alaska 1959, U.S. Tax Ct. 1988. Pvt. practice law Spokane, 1950-56, Fairbanks, Alaska, 1959—; prin. Law Office Julian C. Rice (and predecessor firms), Fairbanks, 1959; bd. dirs. Key Bank of Alaska, Anchorage; founder, gen. counsel Mt. McKinley Mut. Savs. Bank, Fairbanks, 1965—, chmn. bd., 1979-80; v.p., bd. dirs., gen. counsel Skimmers, Inc., Anchorage, 1966-67; gen. counsel Alaska Carriers Assn.,

Anchorage, 1960-71, Alaska Transp. Conf., 1960-67. Mayor City of Fairbanks, 1970-72. Served to maj. USNG and USAR, 1943-58. Decorated Bronze Star, Combat Infantryman's Badge. Fellow Am. Bar Found. (life); mem. ABA, Wash. Bar Assn., Alaska Bar Assn., Transp. Lawyers Assn., Spokane Exchange Club (pres. 1956). Office: 1008 16th Ave Ste 102 Fairbanks AK 99701-6038 Office: PO Box 70516 Fairbanks AK 99707-0516

RICE, KIMBERELY ANNE FURGASON, U.S. Army officer; b. Milw., Aug. 30, 1958; d. Richard Leo Furgason and Gwendolyn Dorothy (Dick) Wedor; m. Dennis E. Rice, Nov. 11, 1989. Student U. Nev.-Reno, 1976-78; BS, U. Pacific, 1980. Commd. 2d lt., U.S. Army, 1980, advanced through grades to capt., 1984; installation club officer U.S. Army, Ft. Ritchie, Md., 1984-85, asst. area club mgr., Kaiserslautern, Fed. Republic Germany, 1980-84, chief advt. br. 1st ROTC Region, Ft. Bragg, N.C., 1986-88, chief pers. mgmt. 1st corps support command, 1988-89; comdr. pers. svcs. co. USA John F. Kennedy Spl. Warfare Ctr. and Sch., 1989-91, chief pers. adminstrn. div., 1991-92; chief pers. actions bd. U.S. Army Pacific, Hawaii, 1992-93, equal opportunity advisor U.S. Army Pacific, 1993—. Mem. NAFE., Internat. Order of Rainbow. Presbyterian. Avocations: cross-stitch, gourmet cooking and baking, sailing. Home: 94 Mary Ln Apt 202 Glen Burnie MD 21061-4268

RICE, MICHAEL LEWIS, business educator; b. Ann Arbor, Mich., Jan. 7, 1943; s. Edwin Stevens and Elaine (Ivey) R.; m. Eileen Lynn Barnard, July 7, 1961. BS, Fla. State U., 1971, MBA, 1972; PhD, U. N.C., 1975. Asst. prof. U. N.C., Chapel Hill, 1974-80; assoc. prof. Wake Forest U., Winston-Salem, N.C., 1980-83; prof., dean U. Alaska, Fairbanks, 1983-91, vice chancellor adminstrv. svcs., 1991—. Contbr. numerous articles on fin. topics. Pres. United Way of Tanana Valley, Fairbanks, 1986-91. Mem. Am. Mgmt. Assn., Am. Mktg. Assn., Am. Econs. Assn., Am. Assembly Collegiate Schs. Bus., Western Assn. Collegiate Schs. Bus. (sec.-treas.), Rotary (bd. officer Fairbanks 1986-92, pres. 1992-93). Office: U Alaska Vice Chancellor Adminstrv Svcs Fairbanks AK 99775-7900

RICE, NORMAN B., mayor; b. 1943. With govt. City of Seattle, 1978—, city councilman, 1978-89, mayor, 1990—. Office: Office of the Mayor Municipal Bldg 12th Fl 600 4th Ave Seattle WA 98104-1826*

RICE, RICHARD EUGENE, science educator; b. Leominster, Mass., June 13, 1943. BS, U. N.H., 1965; MS, U. Mich., 1967; MFA, U. Mont., 1974; PhD, Mich. State U., 1982. Rsch. asst. St. Vincent Hosp., Worcester, Mass., 1968-72; rsch. assoc. U.S. Army Chem. R&D Ctr., Aberdeen Proving Ground, Md., 1983-84; rsch. scientist Holcomb Rsch. Inst., Indpls., 1984-88; visiting asst. prof. Ind. U. N.W., Gary, 1988-90; asst. prof. multidisciplinary studies N.C. State U., Raleigh, 1990-92; vis. asst. prof. chemistry U. Mont., Missoula, 1992-95, vis. assoc. prof. liberal studies, 1995—. Author short stories; contbr. articles to profl. jours. Recipient Profl. Devel. award, NSF, 1989-91; lectureship program grant, GTE Found., 1986-87; rsch. associateship, NRC, 1983-84; Mass Media Sci. fellowship, AAAS, 1981, grad. student fellowship, Internat. Rsch. & Exchanges Bd., Kiev, USSR, 1979-80. Mem. AAAS, Am. Chem. Soc. (program chair history of chemistry divsn. 1995—), Am. Geophysical Union (translations bd. 1986-90), History of Sci. Soc., Soc. Coll. Sci. Tchrs., Internat. History, Philosophy and Sci. Tchg. Group. Office: U Mont Liberal Studies Program Missoula MT 59812

RICE, RICHARD LEE, JR., minister, office manager; b. Hillsboro, Oreg., Mar. 29, 1967; s. Richard Lee Rice and Nanci Carol (Losli) Skriiko. AA in Biblical Studies, Multnomah Sch. of the Bible, Portland, 1988; LittD, Abilene (Kans.) Bible Coll. and Seminary, 1988. Youth dir. Rock Creek Foursquare Ch., Portland, 1984-86; assoc. pastor Valley Full Gospel Ch., Hillsboro, 1986-88; min. Congl. Bible Chs., Inc., Hillsboro, 1988—, bishop, 1988-90; office mgr. Alliance Properties, Inc., Aloha, Oreg., 1990—; founder, pres. Pentecostal-Fire Evangelical Assn., Hillsboro, 1986—; chmn. Gen. Presbytery, Congl. Bible Chs., Inc., 1988-90; bible tchr. Portland Foursquare Ch., 1993—. Author: A Study in Acts, 1986, Systematic Theology, 1988, A Study in the Word: Ephesians, 1993, A Study in the Word: Minor Prophets of the Old Testament, 1994, A Study in the Word: Matthew, 1994; editor (newsletter) Pentecostal Fire Crusader. Committeeperson Rep. Cen. Com., Hillsboro, 1992—; mem. Oreg. Right to Life Com., Hillsboro, 1990—, Portland City Club, 1993—. Mem. NRA, Nat. Rep. Senatorial Com., Rep. Nat. Com., Rep. Presdl. Task Force, Nat. Congl. Club, Federalist Soc.

RICE, ROBERT ARNOT, school administrator; b. San Francisco, Apr. 4, 1911; s. Abraham Lincoln and Mary Eugenia (Arnot) R.; m. Frances Von Dorsten, Aug. 15, 1936 (dec. sept. 1986); m. Esther Pauline Railton, July 11, 1989. BA, U. Calif., Berkeley, 1934, MA, 1947; postgrad., Columbia U., 1948. Various ednl. positions, 1935-61; supr. sci. and math. Berkeley Unified Sch. Dist., 1961-64; adminstr. NSF Summer Insts. for Sci. Tchr., U. Calif., Berkeley, 1957-65; dir. On Target Sch., Berkeley Unified Sch. Dist., 1971-73; coord. pub. programs Lawrence Hall of Sci., 1964-70; work experience edn. coord. Berkeley Unified Sch. Dist., 1973-75; exec. dir. Calif. Sci. Tchr. Assn., 1964-90; dir. No. Calif.-Western Nev. Jr. Sci. and Humanities Symposium, 1962-93; cons. Berkley Unified Sch. Dist., 1964-70; bd. dirs. San Francisco Bay Area Sci. Fair, 1960—; mem. steering com. Chem. Study, 1960-75; coord. Industry Initiatives for Sci. and Math. Edn. Program, 1985-86; dir. Industry Initiatives for Sci. and Math. Edn. Acad., 1987; mem. Internat. Sci. and Engrng. Fair Coun., Sci. Svc., Inc., 1959-68; dir. 18th Internat. Sci. and Engrng. Fair, San Francisco, 1967; exec. dir. San Francisco Bay Area Sci. Fair, 1954-59; resource cons. Calif. Farm Bur. Fedn.-Youth Power Conf., Asilomar, 1966; judging chair Nat. Jr. Sci. and Humanities Symposium, 1993—. Contbr. articles to profl. publs. Bd. dirs. Calif. Heart Assn., 1966-71, Alameda County Heart Assn., 1966-71; mem. Cen. Calif. Sci. Com., 1965-70; mem. rsch. com. Alameda County TB and Health Assn., 1965-69, mem. adv. com., 1965-69. Recipient Benjamin Ide Wheeler medal, 1985, San Francisco Bay Area Sci. Fair award of honor Calif. Acad. Sci., 1970, Armed Forces Chem. Assn. award for outstanding chemistry tchr. in San Francisco Bay Area, 1965; named to Berkeley H.S. Hall of Fame, 1994. Mem. NEA, Nat. Sci. Tchrs. Assn. (region VIII dir. 1955-57, Calif. state dir. 1949-56, mem. chemistry com. 1956-60, pres. 1960-61, Disting. Svc. to Sci. Edn. award 1986), No. Calif. Com. on Problem Solving in Sci., Calif. Sci. Tchrs. Assn. (pres. no. sect. 1949-50, Disting. Svc. to Sci. Teaching award 1981), Calif. Tchrs. Assn., Bay Area Curriculum Coords. (N.C. Sci. Specialists), Berkeley Kiwanis Club, Phi Delta Kappa (pres. Lambda chpt. 1942-43). Office: U Calif Berkeley Lawrence Hall of Sci Berkeley CA 94720-5200

RICE, SHARON MARGARET, clinical psychologist; b. Detroit, Sept. 4, 1943; d. William Christopher and Sylvia Lucille (Lawecki) R.; m. John Robert Speer, Aug. 14, 1977. AB, Oberlin Coll., 1965; MA, Boston U., 1968, PhD, 1977. Clin. psychologist Los Angeles County Juvenile Probation, L.A., 1969-75, Las Vegas (Nev.) Mental Health Ctr., 1976-81, Foothills Psychol. Assn., Upland, Calif., 1981—; pvt. cons., Claremont, Calif., 1984—. NIMH grantee, 1967-69; recipient Good Apple award Las Vegas Tchrs. Ctr., 1978-80. Mem. APA, Calif. Psychol. Assn., Internat. Soc. for Study of Dissociation, Inst. Noetic Scis., Sigma Xi. Office: Foothills Psychol Assn 715 N Mountain Ave # G Upland CA 91786-4364

RICE, STEVEN DALE, electronics educator; b. Valparaiso, Ind., Aug. 11, 1947; s. Lloyd Dale and Mary Helen (Breen) R.; m. Reyanna Danti, Mar. 4, 1972; children: Joshua, Breanna. AAS, Valparaiso Tech. Inst., 1969; BS Health Sci., Ball State U., 1973; BSEE, Valparaiso Tech. Inst., 1973; MS in Vocat. Edn., No. Mont. Coll., 1991. Electronics technician Heavy Mil. Electronic Systems GE, Syracuse, N.Y., 1969-70; electronics technician Ball State U., Muncie, Ind., 1974-75; with electronic sales Tandy Corp., Valparaiso, 1976-77; electronics technician Missoula (Mont.) Community Hosp., 1977-84; instr. electronics Missoula Coll. Tech. U. Montana-Missoula, 1984-88; chmn. dept. electronics Coll. of Tech. U. Mont., Missoula, 1988—. Book reviewer Merrill Pub., 1988—, Delmar, McGraw Hill. Bd. dirs. Victor (Mont.) Sch. Bd., 1989—, chmn. bd., 1992—. Mem. IEEE, Instrument Soc. Am., Mont. Fedn. Tchrs. Office: Coll Tech U Montana Missoula 909 South Ave W Missoula MT 59801-7910

RICE, V(IRGIL) THOMAS, lawyer, consultant; b. La Harpe, Ill., June 29, 1920; s. Vilas E. and Jane N. (Robertson) R.; m. Phyllis Ann Carpenter, Feb. 14, 1969; children: Lesley Jean Rice Luke, Sharon Leilani Rice Routt. BA, U. Ill., 1941, JD, 1948. Bar: Ill. Supreme Ct. 1948, U.S. Dist. Ct. Hawaii 1948, Hawaii Supreme Ct. 1949, U.S. Ct. Mil. Appeals 1960, U.S. Ct. Appeals (9th cir.) 1962, U.S. Customs Ct. 1963, U.S. Supreme Ct. 1971. Assoc. Blaisdell & Moore and predecessor firm, 1948-61; ptnr. Moore, Torkildson & Rice, 1961-64, Rice, Lee & Wong, and predecessor firms, Honolulu, 1964-86; of counsel Lee, Henderson & Wong, Honolulu, 1986-90; prin. V. Thomas Rice, Maunaloa, Molokai, Hawaii, 1990—. Mem. Hawaii Homes Commn., 1960; chmn., sec. Hawaii State Transp. Commn., 1961-63; life mem., bd. dirs. Child and Family Svc., 1960-66, 78-79, treas., 1963, pres. 1964-65; bd. dirs. Health and Community Svcs. Coun. Hawaii, 1967-77, treas. 1968-71, v.p., 1972-74, pres., 1975-77; bd. dirs., chmn. Hawaii Spl. Olympics, 1972-76; mem. State Hawaii Legis. Reapportionment Commn., 1972; hearing officer spl. needs br. Office Instructional Svcs., State Hawaii Dept. Edn., 1979-81; del. Hawaii Rep. State Conv., 1953-85, chmn. platform com., 1964, 78, party rules com., 1965, mem. Hawaii State Rep. Cen. Com., 1955, 69-73, chmn. Rep. Party Hawaii, 1969-71, chmn. State Rep. Dist. Com., 1955-61, mem. Rep. Nat. Com., 1969-71, del., mem. resolutions com. Nat. Convs., 1972, 76. Served to flying officer RCAF, 1941-43, to capt. USAAF, 1943-45, to maj. JAGC, USAF, 1950-52; lt. col. Res. ret. Decorated D.F.C., Air medal with 3 oak leaf clusters. Mem. ABA, Hawaii Bar Assn. (chmn. family law com. 1973-85), Judge Advs. Assn., Pacific Club, Phi Sigma Kappa, Phi Delta Phi. Home: PO Box 97 Maunaloa HI 96770-0097 Office: PO Box 97 Maunaloa HI 96770-0097

RICE, WALLACE WILLIAM, secondary education educator; b. Basin, Wyo., May 3, 1936; s. William Peace Jr. and Emma Anne (Wahl) R.; m. Rozella Peterson, June 23, 1962; children: Steven C., Kevin E. BS in Geology, U. Wyo., 1959, MS in Natural Sci., 1967. Oil well logger Anders Well Logging, Fort Collins, Colo., 1959-61; office mgr. Wyo. Hwy Dept., Cheyenne, Wyo., 1962; adminstrv. asst. Sch. Dist. #1, Cheyenne, 1962-63; sci. tchr. Johnson High Sch., Cheyenne, 1963-65; earth sci. tchr. Ctrl. H.S., Cheyenne, 1966—; athletic ticket mgr. Ctrl. H.S., Cheyenne, 1968—, asst. wrestling coach, 1962, 63, 67—. Sec., treas. Laramie County Rheumatic Fever Prevention Soc., Cheyenne, 1962—; leader Boy Scouts Am.; v.p. Trinity Luth. Ch., 1978, 79, King of Glory Luth. Ch., 1989, 90, 91. With USNG, 1954-62. Recipient Silver Beaver award Boy Scouts Am., 1985, Commr. award, 1988, Dist. award of Merit, 1994. Mem. Nat. Sci. Tchr. Assn. (regional meeting dir. 1972), Wyo. Math. Sci. Assn., Am. Fedn. Tchrs. (pres. 1978, 79, 82, sec. 1982—). Home: 222 E 2nd Ave Cheyenne WY 82001-1406 Office: Cen High Sch 5500 Education Dr Cheyenne WY 82009-4008

RICH, BEN ARTHUR, lawyer, university official; b. Springfield, Ill., Mar. 27, 1947; s. Ben Morris and Betty Lorraine (Ingalls) R.; m. Caroline Rose Castle, Oct. 4, 1984 (div. Nov. 1988). Student, U. St. Andrews, Scotland, 1967-68; BA, DePauw U., 1969; JD, Washington U., 1973; postgrad., U. Colo. Bar: Ill. 1973, N.C. 1975, Colo. 1984. Rsch. assoc. U. Ill. Coll. Law, Urbana, 1973-74; staff atty. Nat. Assn. Attys. Gen., Raleigh, N.C., 1974-76; prin. Hollowell, Silverstein, Rich & Brady, Raleigh, 1976-80; dep. commr. N.C. Indsl. Commn., Raleigh, 1980-81; counsel N.C. Meml. Hosp., Chapel Hill, 1981-84; assoc. univ. counsel U. Colo. Health Scis. Ctr., Denver, 1984-86; gen. counsel U. Colo., Boulder, 1986-89, spl. counsel to the regents, 1989-90; asst. prof. attendent U. Colo. Sch. Med., 1986-91, asst. clin. prof. 1992—, adj. instr. Sch. Law, 1988—, vis. assoc. prof., 1990-91, lectr. U. Denver Coll. Law. Contbr. articles to jours., chpt. to book. Mem. Am. Coll. Legal Medicine (assoc.-in-law 1987—), Am. Soc. Law, Am. Philos. Assn., Soc. for Health and Human Values, Medicine and Ethics (health law tchrs. sect.), Toastmaster Internat. (pres. Raleigh chpt. 1978). Unitarian. Home: 222 S Elm St Denver CO 80222-1133 Office: U Colo Dept Philosophy Box 232 Boulder CO 80309

RICH, DAVID BARRY, city official, auditor, accountant, entertainer; b. Bronx, N.Y., July 3, 1952; s. Steven and Gizella (Kornfeld) R.; 1 child, Suzanne Stephanie. BS in Health Adminstrn., Ithaca Coll., 1976; postgrad. in acctg., Bryant and Stratton Coll., Buffalo, 1977. Office mgr. Rubin Gorewitz, CPA, N.Y.C., 1977-78; auditor State of Ariz., Phoenix, 1979-83; internal auditor City of Phoenix, 1983-84; sales use tax auditor City of Mesa (Ariz.), 1984—; pres. Clovis Acctg. Inc., Mesa, 1980-94; rep. H.D. Vest Investment Inc., Irving, Tex., 1984-94; owner D.B. Rich Enterprises Import/Export, Mesa, 1992—; stage name Barry Rich, Stand-up Comedy, 1994—. Treas., bd. dirs. Missing Mutts Inc., Tempe, Ariz., 1986-88. With USAF, 1971-76. Fellow Nat. Assn. Tax Preparers; mem. Toastmasters (treas. Mesa 1986-87), Phi Beta Kappa.

RICH, ELIZABETH MARIE, nursing educator; b. Bklyn., Nov. 20, 1949; d. Oren Edward and Catherine (Raffaele) R. ADN, Grossmont Coll., El Cajon, Calif., 1983; BSN, U. Phoenix, 1988; MS, Nat. U., San Diego, 1991. Cert. pub. health nurse, gerontol. nurse. ICU-CCU staff nurse Villa View, San Diego, 1983-85, AMI Valley Hosp., El Cajon, 1985-86; nurse Nursing Registries, 1986-87; charge nurse, supr. nights Beverly Manor Convalescent Home, Escondido, Calif., 1987-88; dir. staff devel. Beverly Manor Convalescent Home, Escondido, 1988-90; DON, nurse educator cons. Vista Del Mar Care Ctr., San Diego, 1990; instr. vocat. nursing Maric Coll. Med. Careers, Vista, Calif., 1991-94, curriculum coord., placement coord., 1994—. Mem. Calif. Vocat. Nurse Educators. Home: 872 Venice Gln Escondido CA 92026-3165

RICH, GARETH EDWARD, financial planner; b. Gainesville, Fla., Feb. 28, 1961. Assoc. in Bus. Adminstrn., Gainesville Coll., 1981; BBA, U. Ga., 1983; postgrad., Coll. for Fin. Planning, Denver, 1986-88. Cert. fin. planner; registered prin., LASRO. Acct. exec. Gallo Wine Co., L.A., 1983-84; ins. and investment broker Fin. Design Group, Inc., Woodland Hills, Calif., 1984-92; ins. and investment broker, dir. equities and investments Calif. Fin. Advisors, Inc. and Lincoln Nat. Life/LNC Equities, Sherman Oaks, Calif., 1992—. Vol. City of Hope, L.A.; referee Am. Youth Soccer Orgn., Conejo Valley, Calif.; umpire Little League Baseball, Conejo Valley. Mem. San Fernando Valley Underwriters Assn., Internat. Assn. Fin. Planning, Gen. Agents and Mgrs. Assn. Republican. Home: 5626 Fairview Pl Agoura Hills CA 91301-2228 Office: 15260 Ventura Blvd Ste 200 Sherman Oaks CA 91403-5325

RICH, ROBERT STEPHEN, lawyer; b. N.Y.C., Apr. 30, 1938; s. Maurice H. and Natalie (Priess) R.; m. Myra N. Lakoff, May 31, 1964; children: David, Rebecca, Sarah. AB, Cornell U., 1959; JD, Yale U., 1963. Bar: N.Y. 1964, Colo. 1973, U.S. Tax Ct. 1966, U.S. Supreme Ct. 1967, U.S. Ct. Claims 1968, U.S. Dist. Ct. (so. dist.) N.Y. 1965, U.S. Dist. Ct. (ea. dist.) N.Y. 1965, U.S. Dist. Ct. Colo. 1980, U.S. Ct. Appeals (2d cir.) 1964, U.S. Ct. Appeals (10th cir.) 1978; conseil juridique, Paris, 1968. Assoc. Shearman & Sterling, N.Y.C., Paris, London, 1963-72; ptnr. Davis, Graham & Stubbs, Denver, 1973—; adj. faculty U. Denver Law Sch., 1977—; adv. bd. U. Denver Ann. Tax Inst., 1985—; adv. bd. global bus. and culture divsn. U. Denver, 1992—, Denver World Affairs Coun., 1993—; bd. dirs. Clos du Val Wine Co. Ltd., Danskin Cattle Co., Areti Wines, Ltd., Taltarni Vineyards, Christy Sports, Copper Valley Assn., pres.; bd. dirs. several other corps.; mem. Colo. Internat. Trade Adv. Coun., 1985—, tax adv. com. U.S. Senator Hank Brown; mem. Rocky Mountain Dist. Export Coun. U.S. Dept. Commerce, 1993—. Author treatises on internat. taxation; contbr. articles to profl. jours. Bd. dirs. Denver Internat. Film Festival, 1978-79, Alliance Française, 1977—; actor, musician N.Y. Shakespeare Festival, 1960; sponsor Am. Tax Policy inst., 1991—; trustee, sec. Denver Art Mus., 1982—; mem. adv. bd. Denver World Affairs Coun., 1993—. Capt., AUS, 1959-60. Fellow Am. Coll. Tax Counsel (bd. regents 10th cir. 1992—); mem. ABA, Internat. Bar Assn., Colo. Bar Assn., N.Y. State Bar Assn., Assn. of Bar of City of N.Y., Asia-Pacific Lawyers Assn., Union Internationale des Avocats, Internat. Fiscal Assn. (pres. Rocky Mt. br. 1992—, U.S. regional v.p. 1988—), Japan-Am. Soc. Colo. (bd. dirs., 1989—, pres. 1991-93), Confrerie des Chevaliers du Tastevin, Meadowood Club, Denver Club, Cactus Club Denver, Yale Club, Denver Tennis Club. Office: Cherry Creek Sta PO Box 61429 Denver CO 80206-8429

RICH, SUSAN ABBY, efficiency consultant; b. Bklyn., Apr. 11, 1946; d. Milton and Jeanette (Merns) Rich. BA, Bklyn. Coll., 1967, MA, 1976, advanced cert. in adminstrn. and supervision, 1977; cert. indsl. rels. UCLA, 1981. Tchr. speech, theater N.Y.C. Bd. Edn., 1967-77; employee rels. supr. Crocker Nat. Bank, 1977-81; plant personnel mgr. Boise Cascade Corp., 1981-82; speaker, cons. office, writer efficiency and productivity Get Organized, Get Rich, Playa del Rey, Calif. Bd. dirs. Barlow Respiratory Hosp.; bd. trustees South Bay Master Chorale. Mem. Women's Referral Svc. (Mem. of Year award 1985), Nat. Speakers Assn. (Greater L.A. chpt., Bronze award 1987). Office: Get Organized Get Rich 7777 W 91st St Unit 1154B Playa Del Rey CA 90293-8352

RICHARD, MARTY, fire chief; b. N.Y.C., Oct. 15, 1940; s. Jerry and Esther Richard; m. Liz F. Little, July 21, 1963; children: Victoria, Mervyn, Charles. AA in Fire Sci., Western Nev. C.C., Reno, 1974, AA in Law Enforcement, 1975. Cert. exec. fire officer Nat. Fire Acad. Firefighter Reno Fire Dept., 1964-73, fire inspector, 1973-74, capt. investigations, 1974-78, fire marshal, 1978-90, fire chief, 1990—. Mem. Washoe County Child Care Adv. Bd., Reno, 1978—, past pres.; mem. State Emergency Response Commn., Carson City, Nev., 1992; pres. Kerak Temple Band, 1980-81. Airman 1st class USAF, 1959-63. Recipient Firefighter of Yr. award Am. Legion, 1976. Mem. Nat. Fire Protection Assn., Internat. Fire Chiefs Assn., Reno Rodeo Assn. (assoc.), Fire Marshals N.Am. (pres. 1986). Home: 915 Maple Creek Ct Reno NV 89511-1063 Office: Reno Fire Dept 200 Evans Ave Reno NV 89501-1513*

RICHARD, ROBERT CARTER, psychologist; b. Waterloo, Iowa, Apr. 4, 1938; s. Quentin Leroy and Adeline Pauline (Halverson) R.; student Pomona Coll., 1956-57, Westmont Coll., 1957; BA, Wheaton (Ill.) Coll., 1960; BD, Fuller Theol. Sem., 1963, PhD, 1973; STM, Andover Newton Theol. Sch., 1964; m. Shirley Ruth Jones, Aug. 25, 1962; children: David, John. Ordained to ministry Am. Bapt. Conv., 1963; pastor Peninsula Bapt. Ch., Gig Harbor, Wash., 1965-68; marriage and family counselor Glendale (Calif.) Family Service, 1970-71; psychol. asst., Oakland and Pleasant Hill, Calif., 1972-74; clin. psychologist Rafa Counseling Assos., Pleasant Hill, 1974—; mem. faculty John F. Kennedy U., Orinda, Calif., 1975-78; adj. faculty mem. New Coll., Berkeley, Calif., 1986. Co-founder, bd. dirs. New Directions Counseling Center, 1974-81. Recipient Integration of Psychology and Theology award, 1973; lic. psychologist, marriage, family and child counselor, Calif. Mem. Am., Calif., Contra Costa (past pres.) psychol. assns., Christian Assn. Psychol. Studies. Republican. Am. Baptist. Author: (with Deacon Anderson) The Way Back: A Christian's Journey to Mental Wholeness, 1989; contbr. articles to profl. publs. Researcher assertiveness tng., long-term marriage, lay counselor tng., psychotherapy and religious experience, treatment of adults abused as children. Office: Rafa Counseling Assocs 101 Gregory Ln Ste 33 Pleasant Hill CA 94523-4915

RICHARD, ROBERT JOHN, library director; b. Oakland, Calif., Sept. 20, 1947; s. John Argyle and Vern Elizabeth (Bauer) R.; m. Anne Elizabeth Terrell, June 8, 1968 (div. 1982); children: Jennifer Lynn, Laura Ellen, Constance Anne, Andrea Lee. Student, Fullerton Coll., 1965-67; B.A. in Biology, Chapman Coll., Orange (Calif.), 1972; M.S.L.S., Calif. State U.-Fullerton, 1973. Cert. county librarian, Calif. Audiovisual specialist Fullerton Pub. Libr., 1969-72, asst. to city librarian, 1972-73, librarian, 1973-76; br. librarian Orange County Pub. Libr., Orange, 1976-78; regional adminstr. Orange County Pub. Libr., 1979-80; assoc. dir. Long Beach Pub. Libr., Calif., 1980-81; dir. Sacramento Pub. Libr., 1981-86, Santa Ana (Calif.) Pub. Libr., 1986—. Mem. ALA, Pub. Library Execs. Assn So. Calif., Calif. Library Assn., Library Adminstrn. and Mgmt. Assn., Library Info. and Tech. Assn., Pub. Library Assn. Office: Santa Ana Pub Libr 26 Civic Center Plz Santa Ana CA 92701-4010*

RICHARDS, EVELYN JEAN, journalist; b. Lake Forest, Ill., Mar. 2, 1952; d. Richard K. and Erika (Nord) R.; m. Greg L. Pickrell, 1982. BS in Journalism, Northwestern U., 1974, MS in Journalism, 1975. City hall reporter Elyria (Ohio) Chronicle-Telegram, 1975-76; reporter Palo Alto (Calif.) Times, 1976-79; bus. editor Peninsula Times Tribune, Palo Alto, 1979-81; tech. reporter San Jose (Calif.) Mercury News, 1981-84, tech. editor, 1984-88; staff writer The Washington Post, Washington, 1988-91; reporter, editor Waterman & Assocs., San Francisco, 1992; contbg. editor The Nikkei Weekly, Tokyo, 1993—; freelance writer Tokyo, 1993—. Recipient Davenport fellowship in Bus. & Econ. Reporting, U. Mo., 1980, Interant. Press Inst. fellowship Japan, 1983, John S. Knight fellowship for Profl. Journalists, Stanford U., 1986-87, First Pl. Reporting award World Affairs Coun. of No. Calif., 1986, Overseas Press Club 1st Pl. Reporting award, 1987. Mem. Soc. for Profl. Journalists, Investigative Reporters and Editors, Coll. Women Assn. Home: PO Box 4179 Mountain View CA 94040-0179

RICHARDS, GERALD THOMAS, lawyer, consultant; b. Monrovia, Calif., Mar. 17, 1933; s. Louis Jacquelyn Richards and Inez Vivian (Richardson) Hall; children: Patricia M. Richards Grauf, Laura J., Dag Hammarskjold; m. Mary Lou Richards, Dec. 27, 1986. BS magna cum laude, Lafayette Coll., 1957; MS, Purdue U., 1963; JD, Golden Gate U., 1976. Bar: Calif. 1976, U.S. Dist. Ct. (no. dist.) Calif. 1977, U.S. Patent Office 1981, U.S. Ct. Appeals (9th cir.) 1984, U.S. Supreme Ct. 1984. Computational physicist Lawrence Livermore (Calif.) Nat. Lab., 1967-73, planning staff lawyer, 1979, mgr. tech. transfer office, 1980-83, asst. lab. counsel, 1984-93; sole practice, Livermore, 1976-78, Oceanside, Calif., 1994—; mem. exec. com., policy advisor Fed. Lab. Consortium for Tech. Transfer, 1980-88; panelist, del. White House Conf. on Productivity, Washington, 1983; del. Nat. Conf. on Tech. and Aging, Wingspread, Wis., 1981. Commr. Housing Authority, City of Livermore, 1977, vice chairperson, 1978, chairperson, 1979; pres. Housing Choices, Inc., Livermore, 1980-84; bd. dirs. Valley Vol. Ctr., Pleasanton, Calif., 1983, pres., 1984-86. Recipient Engrng. award Gen. Electric Co., 1956. Maj. U.S. Army, 1959-67. Mem. ABA, Calif. State Bar (conv. alt. del. 1990-92), Alameda County Bar Assn., Eastern Alameda County Bar Assn. (sec. 1978, bd. dirs. 1991-92, chair lawyers referral com. 1992-93), Santa Barbara County Bar Assn., San Diego County Bar Assn., Bar Assn. of Northern San Diego County, Phi Beta Kappa, Tau Beta Pi, Sigma Pi Sigma. Home: 3747 Vista Campana S Apt 59 Oceanside CA 92057-8228

RICHARDS, HERBERT EAST, minister emeritus, commentator; b. Hazleton, Pa., Dec. 30, 1919; s. Herbert E. and Mabel (Vannaucker) R.; m. Lois Marcey, Jan. 1, 1942; children: Herbert Charles, Marcey Lynn, Robyn Lois, Fredrick East, Mark Allen. AB, Dickinson Coll., 1941; BD, Drew U., 1944; MA, Columbia, 1944; DD, Coll. of Idaho, 1953; postgrad., Union Theol. Sem., 1941-48, Bucknell U., 1943-44. Accredited news reporter Nat. Assn. Broadcasters. Ordained to ministry Methodist Ch., 1944; pastor in Boiling Springs, Pa., 1937-40, West Chester, Pa., 1940-41, Basking Ridge, N.J., 1941-47; mem. faculty Drew U. and Theol. Sem., 1944-51, assoc. prof. homiletics and Christian criticism, chmn. dept., asst. dean, 1947-51; spl. lectr. religion Howard U., 1947; minister 1st Meth. Cathedral, Boise, Idaho, 1951-69, 1st United Meth. Ch., Eugene, Oreg., 1969-78; minister Tabor Heights United Meth. Ch., Portland, Oreg., 1978-86, minister emeritus, 1986—; weekly radio broadcaster Sta. KBOI, Sta. KIDO, 1941—; weekly TV broadcaster CBS, 1945—, ABC, 1969—, NBC, 1973; pres. Inspiration, Inc., TV Found., 1965—, TV Ecology, 1973; producer Life TV series ABC, 1974-85, also BBC, Eng., Suise Romande, Geneva; chmn. Idaho bd. ministerial tng. Meth. Conf., 1954-60, TV, Radio and Film Commn., 1954-62, Oreg. Coun. Public Broadcasting, 1973; del. Idaho Conf. Meth. Gen. Conf., 1956, Jurisdictional Conf., 1956, World Meth. Coun., 1957, 81, World Meth. Conf., 1981, mem. Gen. Conf., 1956-60, Jurisdictional Conf., 1956, 60; meml. chaplain Idaho Supreme Ct., 1960; chaplain Idaho Senate, 1960-68; mem. Task Force on TV and Ch., 1983. Author: In Time of Need, 1986; contbr. articles to religious publs.; composer: oratorios Prophet Unwilling, 1966, Meet Martin Luther, 1968, Dear Jesus Boy, 1973. Mem. Commn. on Centennial Celebration for Idaho, 1962-63; committeeman Boy Scouts Am.; bd. dirs. Eugene chpt. ARC, 1954-73; trustee Willamette U., Cascade Manor Homes; adv. bd. Medic-Alert Found. Recipient Alumni citation in religious edn. Dickinson Coll., 1948, Golden Plate award Am. Acad. Achievement, 1965, Jason Lee Mass Media TV award, 1983; named Clergyman of Yr., Religious Heritage Am., 1964. Mem. AAUP, CAP (chaplain Idaho wing, lt. col.), Am. Acad. Achievement (bd. govs. 1967—), Am. Found. Religion and Psychiatry (charter gov.), Greater Boise Ministerial Assn. (pres.), Eugene Ministerial Assn. (pres. 1978), Masons (33 degree, editor Pike's Peak Albert That Is), Shriners, Elks, Rotary (editor Key and Cog, pres. dist. 510 Pioneer Club), Kappa Sigma (Grand Master of Beta Pi). Home: 10172 SE 99th Dr Portland OR 97266-7227 Office: Tabor Heights United Meth Ch 6161 SE Stark St Portland OR 97215-1935

RICHARDS, JAMES WILLIAM, electromechanical engineer; b. Portland, Oreg., Oct. 24, 1921; s. Jarvis William and Thelma Helen (Eoff) R.; m. Violet Victor Ray, Oct. 9, 1946; children: Betty, Sandra, Diane, William. Student, Nat. Tech. Sch., 1942, Nat. Radio Inst., 1948, Internat. Corr. Sch., 1955;

AA, Pierce Coll., 1968. Mgr. Western Design, Santa Barbara, Calif., 1948-55; sr. engr. Bendix Corp., North Hollywood, Calif., 1955-66; v.p. Talley Corp., Newbury Park, Calif., 1966-75, dir. engring., 1982-87; pvt. practice electromech. engr., Eugene, Oreg., 1975-82, 87-89; pres. Western Design, Eugene, Oreg., 1990—. Mem. Masons. Republican. Baptist. Home: PO Box 5498 Eugene OR 97405-0498 Office: Western Design 28983 Fox Hollow Rd PO Box 5549 Eugene OR 97405

RICHARDS, JOE MCCALL, chemical company executive; b. Eugene, Oreg., May 3, 1937; s. Joseph Albert and Bertha (McCall) R.; m. Katherine Mary Enright, June 30, 1961 (div. 1966); m. Ann F. Potter, Jan. 2, 1981; children: Dean A., Ann L. BSChE, Oreg. State U., 1959. Tech. asst. pulp mgr. Pubs. Paper Co., Oregon City, 1960-66; chem. engr. Boise Cascade, Vancouver, Wash., 1966-68; area mgr. Nalco Chem. Co., Milwaukie, Oreg., 1968-82; mgr. RPS, Milwaukie, 1982-86; Western regional mgr. Eka Nobel Paper Chems., Clackamas, Oreg., 1986—. With USAF, 1960-64. AIChE scholar, 1958. Mem. Am. Mgmt. Assn., Tech. Assn. Pulp and Paper Industry (v.p. 1982). Republican. Episcopalian. Home: 12027 SE 115th Ave Clackamas OR 97015-9605 Office: Eka Nobel Paper Chems Divsn 2211 New Market Pky Marietta GA 30067-9310

RICHARDS, JOHN M., wood and paper products company executive; b. 1937. BA, Stanford U., 1959; MBA, Harvard U., 1961. With Fernwood Tie Co., 1962-64, v.p.; with St. Maries Plywood Co., 1964-69, v.p., gen. mgr.; with Potlatch Corp., San Francisco, 1969—, sales mgr., wood products group mktg. div., 1970-72, v.p., wood products group western div., 1972-76, sr. v.p. fin., 1976-83, sr. v.p. fin. adminstrn., 1983-87, exec. v.p. fin. adminstrn., 1987-89, pres., chief oper. officer, 1989—. Office: Potlatch Corp PO Box 3591 1 Maritime Plz San Francisco CA 94111-3404*

RICHARDS, KENNETH EDWIN, management consultant; b. N.J., Oct. 9, 1917; s. Kenneth G. and Laura (Benson) R.; m. Evelyn Henderson, Dec. 12, 1942 (div. June 1963); children: Kenneth A., Grant B., Kyle E., Diane L. Parmley, Kathleen E. Hilton, Kim E. Richards-Davis, Cynthia G. Burger, Cheri O. Figuerora, Steven E. Benedict; m. Sylvia Marie Benedict, Nov. 1979. BA, Wesleyan U., 1939. Asst. buyer J.C. Penney Co., 1945-48, buyer, 1948-55, dept. head women's & girl's sportswear apparel, 1955-58; from v.p., mdse. mgr. to dir. S.H. Kress Co., 1958-60; v.p. mdse. and sales Firth Carpet Co., 1960-62, dir., 1961-62; spl. cons. to pres. Mohasco Industries Inc., 1962-63; v.p., dir. Yorkshire Terrace Motel Corp., 1963-66; ptnr. Roxbury Hollow Farm, Claverack, N.Y., 1955-66; sr. ptnr. Mgmt. Assocs., 1963-67; pres. Western Dept. Stores, L.A., 1968-70; v.p. merchandising Rapid Merchandising, Costa Mesa, Calif., 1970-72; exec. v.p., gen. mgr. Skor-Mor Products, Santa Barbara, Calif., 1972-75; pres., CEO Resort to Life, Inc., Calabasas, Calif., 1980-84; exec. dir. Retirement Jobs of Idaho, Boise, 1985-87; pres. Seniors, Inc., Boise, 1987-94; CEO Compunet, Boise, 1995—; chmn. bd. CompuNet, Inc., 1995—. Mem. adv. editorial bd. Surgeon Gen. U.S. Army, 1948-55; co-developer no-iron cotton; developer women's wear "skort"; pioneer use of mix and match sportswear. Lt. col. AUS, 1940-45. Decorated for action against enemy in Normandy, France, 1944. Mem. Chi Psi. Methodist. Office: PO Box 4304 Boise ID 83704

RICHARDS, KENT HAROLD, religion educator; b. Midland, Tex., July 6, 1939; s. Eva E. Richards; children: Lisken Lynn, Lisanne Elizabeth. BA, Calif. State U., 1961; MTh., Claremont Sch. Theology, 1964; PhD, Claremont Grad. Sch., 1969. Rsch. assoc. Inst. for Antiquities & Christianity, Claremont, Calif., 1967-68; asst. prof. Old Testament U. Dayton (Ohio), 1968-72; prof. Old Testament Iliff Sch. Theology, Denver, 1972—; vis. prof. Sch. of Theology/Grad. Sch., Claremont, 1969; mem. bd. of ordained ministry UMC, Rocky Mt. Conf., Denver, 1976-82, bd. of diaconal ministry, 1976-78. Editor: Biblical Scholarship in North America, 16 vols., 1981—, Writings in the Ancient World, (with David Peterson) Interpreting Hebrew Poetry, 1992, (with Tamara C. Eskenazi) Second Temple Studies 2, Temple Community in the Persian Period, 1994. Chmn. Colo. Gov.'s award in Edn. Com., Denver, 1989-91, Vision 2020: A Study of the Colo. Cts.; jud. adv. coun. Colo. Supreme Ct., 1993—; bd. dirs. Colo. Jud. Inst., 1991—. Rsch. grantee NEH, 1985-91, Lilly Found., 1985-86. Mem. Internat. Meeting Program (chair 1973-92), Cath. Bibl. Assn. (program com. 1976-80), Soc. Bibl. Lit. (exec. sec. 1981-87), Am. Coun. Learned Socs. (coun. sec. 1981-87), Profl. Ski Instrs. Am. Office: Iliff Sch of Theology 2201 S University Blvd Denver CO 80210-4707

RICHARDS, KYUNGNYUN KIM, Korean language educator; b. Seoul, Nov. 12, 1940; came to U.S., 1967; d. Johyun and Pongsoon (Ohm) Kim; m. Steffen Francis Richards, June 19, 1971; children: James, Kathleen. BA in French, Ewha Womans U., 1963, MA in French, 1966; MA in Linguistics, U. Calif., Berkeley, 1978. Instr. San Francisco C.C., 1974-80; edn. coord. The Korean Ctr., Inc., San Francisco, 1978-80; lectr. U. Calif., Berkeley, 1980—; cons. Calif. Dept. of Edn., Sacramento, 1990-91, City Coll. of San Francisco, 1990-91, San Francisco Unified Sch. Dist., 1994-95. Author: College Korean, 1992, Handbook for Teaching Korean-American Students, 1992; contbr. articles to profl. publs. Bd. dirs. Asian Community Mental Health, Oakland, 1990—. Mem. Internat. Circle of Linguistics, Internat. Assn. of Korean Lang. Educators, Am. Assn. of Tchrs. of Korean (bd. dirs.). Office: U Calif Dept of East Asian Lang Berkeley CA 94720-2230

RICHARDS, LYNN, company training executive, consultant; b. Kansas City, Mo., Sept. 2, 1949; d. Robert A. and Betty (Arnold) Nelson. BS in Edn., U. Kans., 1971; MA in Edn., San Diego State U., 1979. Prin. staff ORI, Inc., Silver Spring, Md., 1980-81; sr. corp. trainer Amerada Hess Corp., Woodbridge, N.J., 1981-83; tng. and devel. mgr. Kimberly-Clark Corp., Beech Island, S.C., 1983-85; orgn. devel. mgr. M&M Mars, Hackettstown, N.J., 1985-89; corp. tng. and devel. mgr. Rohr, Inc., Chula Vista, Calif., 1989-93; customer edn. mgr. ComputerVision, Corp., San Diego, 1993-95; leadership devel. cons. Children's Hosp., San Diego, 1995—; pvt. cons., San Diego, 1990—. Contbr. articles to profl. mags. Mem. NSPI (chmn. awards com. 1988, presdl. citations, achievement awards).

RICHARDS, MORRIS DICK, social work administrator, environmental analyst, educator; b. Los Angeles, Aug. 20, 1939; s. Morris Dick Richards and Annette (Fox) Briggs; m. Leslie Sondra Lefkowitz, Mar. 22, 1975. BA cum laude, Claremont Men's Coll., 1962; MA, U. Chgo., 1964; M in Pub. Adminstrn., U. So. Calif., 1965; LLB, La Salle Ext. U., 1971; MS in Hygiene, PhD in Social Work, U. Pitts., 1973; MBA, Chapman Coll., 1987. Diplomate Acad. Cert. Social Workers. Asst. dep. dir. children and youth services Orange County (Calif.) Dept. Mental Health, 1973-77; gen. mgr., indsl. therapist Paragon West, Anaheim, Calif., 1977-83; acting dir. alcohol and drug program Horizon Health Corp., Newport Beach, Calif., 1983-84; editor, pub. relations rep., sr. social worker Orange County Social Services Agy., 1983-85; staff analyst Environ. Mgmt. Agy., Orange County, 1985-90; exec. asst. to dir. planning Orange County, 1990-92; staff analyst Orange County Social Svc. Agy., 1992-95; ret., 1995; adj. clin. prof. Chapman Coll., Orange, Calif., 1974-85; instr. Calif. Grad. Inst., 1988-93; instr. U. Phoenix, 1992-95; program analyst, head child welfare worker L.A. County Pub. Social Svcs., 1967-71; psychiat. clin. specialist Jewish Big Bros., L.A. County, 1964-67; med. social work cons. Whittier (Calif.) Presbyn. Hosp., 1973-76; pvt. practice psychotherapy, Tustin, Calif., 1975-77. Editor newsletter Orange County Adv., 1984-85, Planning Perspective, 1990-91, Broadmoor Community News, 1992—; contbr. articles to profl. jours. Past bd. dirs. Orange County chpt. Am. Jewish Com., 1982-88, Broadmore Community Assn., Anaheim Hills, Calif., 1981-83, sec., 1990-94; mem. Orange County Mental Health Adv. Bd., 1981-88, sec., bd. dirs.; mem. bd. dirs. Orange County Mental Health Assn., 1988-91; mem. Juvenile Diversion Task Force of Orange County, 1977. Served with USAR, 1958-64. Fellow U. Chgo., 1962, NIMH, 1962, 72; Haynes scholar U. So. Calif. Sch. Pub. Adminstrn., 1964; grantee Faulk Program in Urban Mental Health, U. Pitts., 1973. Mem. ACLU (Orange County chpt.), Nat. Assn. Social Workers (mental health liaison, v.p. local chpt. 1975-88, Social Worker of Yr. award Orange County chpt. 1987), Acad. Cert. Social Workers (lic. clin. social worker and marriage, family, child counselor), Registry Clin. Social Workers (diplomate in clin. social work), Orange County Mental Health Assn. (past sec.). Home: 6506 E Via Estrada Anaheim CA 92807-4227

RICHARDS, PAUL A., lawyer; b. Oakland, Calif., May 27, 1927; s. Donnell C. and Theresa (Pasquale) R.; m. Ann Morgans, May 20, 1948 (dec. 1984); 1 child, Paul M. BA, U. Pacific, 1950; JD, U. San Francisco, 1953. Bar: Nev. 1953, U.S. Dist. Ct. Nev. 1953, U.S. Supreme Ct. 1964, U.S. Ct. Claims 1976, U.S. Ct. Appeals (9th cir.) 1982. Pvt. practice, Reno, 1953—, prin. Paul A. Richards, Ltd.; prof. environ. law Sierra Nevada Coll., 1970-80. Mem. Washoe Dem. Central Com., 1959-74, chmn., 1964-66, vice chmn., 1966-68; trustee Sierra Nevada Coll., 1970-82, Ducks Unltd., 1964-72; trustee emeritus, 1974—; mem. Fed. Land Law Commn., Nev., 1973-80; bd. dirs. Reno Rodeo Assn., 1963, pres., 1979. Served with U.S. Navy, 1945-46. Recipient Pres.'s Buckle and award Reno Rodeo Assn., 1979. Mem. Nev. Bar Assn., Washoe County Bar Assn., Am. Legion. Democrat. Roman Catholic. Club: Press. Lodge: Elks, Masons. Office: 248 S Sierra St Reno NV 89501-1908

RICHARDS, PAUL LINFORD, physics educator, researcher; b. Ithaca, N.Y., June 4, 1934; s. Lorenzo Adolph and Zilla (Linford) R.; m. Audrey Jarratt , Aug. 24, 1965; children: Elizabeth Anne, Mary-Ann. AB, Harvard U., 1956; PhD, U. Calif., Berkeley, 1960. Postdoctoral fellow U. Cambridge (Eng.), 1959-60; mem. tech. staff Bell Telephone Labs., Murray Hill, N.J., 1960-66; prof. physics U. Calif., Berkeley, 1966—; faculty sr. scientist Lawrence Berkeley Lab., 1966—; advisor NASA, 1975-92, Conductus Inc., Mountain View, Calif., 1988—; hon. prof. Miller Inst. Rsch. in Phys. Scis., Berkeley, 1969-70, 87-88; vis. prof. Ecole Normale Superieure, Paris, 1984, 92; vis. astronomer Paris Obs., 1984. Contbr. over 300 articles to profl. jours. Guggenheim Meml. Found. fellow, Cambridge, Eng., 1973-74; named Calif. Scientist of Yr. Mus. Sci., L.A., 1981; recipient sr. scientist award alexander von Humboldt Found., Stuttgart, Fed. Republic Germany, 1982; Berkeley Faculty Rsch. lectr. 1991. Fellow NAS, Am. Phys. Soc., Am. Acad. Arts and Scis.

RICHARDS, ROBERT CHARLES, management consultant; b. Portland, Oreg., Jan. 18, 1939; s. Charles Robert and Mildred Marie (Merrill) R.; m. Marilyn Cornelia Poole, Sept. 1, 1961 (div.); children: Kristin Elizabeth, Jeffrey Robert. BA, Lewis and Clark Coll., 1961. Tng. officer, mgr. edn. dept. U.S. Bancorp, Portland, Oreg., 1965-74; mgr. orgn. devel. Coors Container Co., Golden, Colo., 1974-77; mgmt. cons., mgr. western office Cons. Assocs. Internat., Inc., Lakewood, Colo., 1977-84; mgmt cons., pres. Cons. Network, Lakewood, 1985—; pres., CEO Epoch Prodns., 1986—; exec. v.p., sec.-treas. A Pretty Woman, Inc., Lakewood, Colo., 1994—; instr. Portland State U., 1972-73, U. Oreg., Portland Extension, 1973-74, Portland C.C., 1971-74; adj. faculty Bryant Coll. Ctr. for Mgmt. Devel., Smithfield, R.I., 1979—; mgmt. cons.; seminar leader; devel. cons. Martin Marietta Space Systems Co., 1989-91, Martin Marrietta Astronautics Group, 1991-92, Inst. Integrated Product/Process Design and Devel., 1993—, founder, chmn.; bd. dir., sec. Sr. Mgmt. Programs, Inc., 1971-73, pres., 1973-74. Author tng. materials; contbr. articles to profl. publs. Mem. adv. com. C.C. of Denver, scholarship and employment com. Portland State U. Found.; adj. faculty USMC Svc. Support Schs., Camp Lejeune, N.C. With USMCR, 1961-64; col. Res., 1966-92, Persian Gulf, 1990-91. Mem. Am. Soc. Tng. and Devel. (bd. dirs. chpt. 1976, v.p. 1977, bd. dirs. Oreg. chpt. 1972, pres. 1971, bd. dirs. Western region 1971-72), World Futures Soc., Planning Execs. Inst., Rocky Mountain Orgn. Devel. Network, Marine Corps Res. Officers Assn. (pres. Mile High chpt.), Marine Corps Meml. Assn. (sec.). Home and Office: 13362 W Montana Ave Lakewood CO 80228-3726

RICHARDS, VINCENT PHILIP HASLEWOOD, librarian; b. Sutton Bonington, Nottinghamshire, Eng., Aug. 1, 1933; emigrated to Can., 1956, naturalized, 1961; s. Philip Haslewood and Alice Hilda (Moore) R.; m. Ann Beardshall, Apr. 3, 1961; children: Mark, Christopher, Erika. A.L.A., Ealing Coll., London, 1954; B.L.S. with distinction, U. Okla., 1966. Cert. profl. librarian, B.C. Joined Third Order Mt. Carmel, Roman Catholic Ch., 1976; with Brentford and Chiswick Pub. Libraries, London, 1949-56; asst. librarian B.C. (Can.) Pub. Library Commn., Dawson Creek, 1956-57; asst. dir. Fraser Valley Regional Library, Abbotsford, B.C., 1957-67; chief librarian Red Deer (Alta., Can.) Coll., 1967-77; dir. libraries Edmonton (Alta.) Pub. Library, 1977-89; libr. and book industry cons. Ganges, Can., 1990—; pres. Faculty Assn. Red Deer Coll., 1971-72, bd. govs., 1972-73. Contbr. articles to profl. jours., 1954—. Vice pres. Jeunesses Musicales, Red Deer, 1969-70; bd. dirs. Red Deer TV Authority, 1975-76, Alta. Found. Lit. Arts, 1984-86; mem. Reform Party Can. Served with Royal Army Ednl. Corps, 1951-53.

RICHARDSON, A(RTHUR) LESLIE, former medical group consultant; b. Ramsgate, Kent, Eng., Feb. 21, 1910; s. John William and Emily Lilian (Wilkins) R.; came to U.S., 1930, naturalized, 1937; student spl. courses U. So. Calif., 1933-35; m. B. Kathleen Sargent, Oct. 15, 1937. Mgr., Tower Theater, Los Angeles, 1931-33; accountant Felix-Krueper Co., Los Angeles, 1933-35; indsl. engr. Pettengill, Inc., Los Angeles, 1935-37; purchasing agt. Gen. Petroleum Corp. Los Angeles, 1937-46; adminstr. Beaver Med. Clinic, Redlands, Calif., 1946-72, exec. cons. 1972-75; sec.-treas. Fern Properties, Inc., Redlands, 1955-75, Redelco, Inc., Redlands, 1960-67; pres. Buinco, Inc., Redlands, 1956-65; vice chmn. Redlands adv. bd. Bank of Am., 1973-80; exec. cons. Med. Adminstrs. Calif., 1975-83. Pres., Redlands Area Community Chest, 1953; volunteer exec. Internat. Exec. Service Corps; mem. San Bernardino County (Calif.) Grand Jury, 1952-53. Bd. dirs. Beaver Med. Clinic Found., Redlands, 1961—, sec.-treas., 1961-74, pres., 1974-75, chmn. bd. dirs. 1992—. Served to lt. Med. Adminstrv. Corps., AUS, 1942-45. Recipient Redlands Civic award Elks, 1953. Fellow Am. Coll. Med Group Adminstrs. (life, disting. fellow 1980, pres. 1965-66, dir.); mem. Med. Group Mgmt. Assn. (hon. life; mem. nat. long range planning com. 1963-68, pres. western sect. 1960), Kiwanis (pres. 1951), Masons. Episcopalian. Home: 1 Verlie Dr Redlands CA 92373-6943

RICHARDSON, ARTHUR WILHELM, lawyer; b. Glendale, Calif., Apr. 3, 1963; s. Douglas Fielding and Leni (Tempelaar-Lietz) R. AB, Occidental Coll., 1985; student, London Sch. Econs., 1983; JD, Harvard U., 1988. Bar: Calif. 1989. Assoc. Morgan, Lewis and Bockius, L.A., 1988-90; staff lawyer U.S. SEC, L.A., 1990-92, br. chief, 1992—. Contbr. Harvard Civil Rights/Civil Liberties Law Rev. Mem. ABA, Calif. Bar Assn., Harvard/Radcliffe Club So. Calif., Town Hall Calif., L.A. World Affairs Coun., Sierra Club, Phi Beta Kappa. Presbyterian. Home: 2615 Canada Blvd Apt 208 Glendale CA 91208-2077 Office: US SEC 11th Fl 5670 Wilshire Blvd Los Angeles CA 90036-3648

RICHARDSON, CAROLYN JANE, social worker; b. Dayton, Ohio, Nov. 23, 1943; d. John Robert and Elizabeth (Kuhns) Eck; m. Robert Allen Richardson, Dec. 9, 1967. BA, Denison U., Granville, Ohio, 1965; MS in Social Work, Case Western Res. U., 1967. Lic. ind. social worker, Ohio. Group worker and coord. vols. West Side Community House, Cleve., 1967-70; social worker family care prog. Univ. Hosps. of Cleve./Case Western Res. U. Sch. Medicine, 1970-80, social work coord. family care program, 1980-89; social worker Hospic Maui, Wailuku, Hawaii, 1991—. Sec. Mental Health Assn., Maui, Hawaii, 1989-92, v.p., 1993, pres., 1994; sec. bd. Alpha House, 1994; v.p. Art Maui, 1994-95; mem. bd. Maui Philharmonic Soc. Mem. Nat. Assn. Social Workers, Assn. Cert. Social Workers, Registry of Clin. Social Workers.

RICHARDSON, DENNIS MICHAEL, lawyer, educator; b. Los Angeles, July 30, 1949; s. Ralph Lee and Eva Catherine (McGuire) R.; 1 child from previous marriage, Scott Randol; m. Catherine Jean Coyl, July 27, 1973; children: Jennifer Eve, Valerie Jean, Rachel Catherine, Nicole Marie, Mary Rose, Marie Christina, Laura Michelle, Alyssa Rose. BA, Brigham Young U., 1976, JD, 1979. Bar: Oreg. 1979. Ptnr. Richardson and Andersen, P.C., Central Point, Oreg., 1979—; guest lectr. in field; contbr. articles to profl. jours.; bd. dirs. Oreg. Lung Assn., 1980, Oreg. Shakespearean Festival, Ashland, 1981, Jackson County Legal Services, 1982. Served as helicopter pilot U.S. Army, 1969-71, Vietnam. Decorated Vietnamese Cross Gallantry. Republican. Office: Richardson & Andersen PC 55 S 5th St Central Point OR 97502-2474

RICHARDSON, DONN CHARLES, marketing educator; b. Indpls., Mar. 3, 1940; s. George Covey and Edythe Francis (Chesterfield) R.; m. Carolyn Jean Hassan, Nov. 8, 1969; children: Bradley George, Jason Arthur, Christopher Charles. BA in Journalism and Polit. Sci., Butler U., 1962; MA in Mass Comm., Ohio State U., 1969. Staff editor Cin. Bell Mag. Cin. (Ohio) Bell, 1969-73; mgmt. newsletter editor, spl. projects mgr. US West Comms., Denver, 1973-76; Colo. pub. rels. and outreach dir. US West Comms., Boulder, 1976-84, Colo. employee comm. mgr., 1984-85, market mgr. market planning, 1986-88; fed. govt. market mgr. US West Comms., Englewood, Colo., 1989-94; pres. Richardson Info. Resources, Boulder, Colo., 1994—; cons. Northglenn (Colo.) Recreation Ctr., 1962; presenter in field. Contbr. articles to profl. jours. Pres. Shannon Estates Homeowners Assn., Boulder, 1978-80; pub. rels. dir. Boulder (Colo.) Mental Health Ctr. Benefit, 1980; publicity dir. FC Boulder (Colo.) Soccer Club, 1991-94. Capt. USAF, 1963-69. Mem. Internat. Assn. Bus. Communicators (dist. profl. devel. chair 1982-84, chpt. v.p. 1985, internat. pub. rels. chair 1985-86, accredited bus. communicator), Pub. Rels. Soc. Am. (accredition judge 1989, accredited pub. rels. profl.). Home: 1212 Cavan St Boulder CO 80303-1602

RICHARDSON, DOUGLAS FIELDING, lawyer; b. Glendale, Calif., Mar. 17, 1929; s. James D. and Dorothy (Huskins) R.; m. Leni Tempelaar-Lietz, June 26, 1959; children—Arthur Wilhelm, John Douglas. A.B., UCLA, 1950; J.D., Harvard U., 1953. Bar: Calif. 1953. Assoc. O'Melveny & Myers, Los Angeles, 1953-68, ptnr., 1968-86, of counsel, 1986—. Author: (with others) Drafting Agreements for the Sale of Businesses, 1971, Term Loan Handbook, 1983. bd. govs. Town Hall of Calif., L.A., 1974-87, sec., 1977, v.p., 1978-79, pres., 1984, mem. adv. coun., 1987—, chmn. sect. on legis. and adminstrn. of justice, 1968-70, pres. Town Hall West, 1975, mem. exec. bd. 1973-93; bd. dirs. Hist. Soc. Soc. Calif., 1976-82, pres., 1980-81; bd. dirs. Alliance Francaise de Pasadena, treas., 1993—. Mem. ABA (com. on devels. in bus. financing, com. state regulation of securities, com. corp. law and acctg., com. employee benefits and exec. compensation of sect corp. banking and bus. law.), Calif. Bar Assn., Los Angeles County Bar Assn. (chmn. com. Law Day 1968, exec. com. comml. law sect. 1974-78, exec. com. corp. law sect. 1975-86), Kiwanis, Phi Beta Kappa. Republican. Presbyterian (elder). Clubs: California, Harvard So. Calif. Home: 1637 Valley View Rd Glendale CA 91202-1340 Office: O'Melveny & Myers 400 S Hope St Los Angeles CA 90071-2801

RICHARDSON, ELSIE HELEN, retired elementary educator; b. Vancouver, Wash., Feb. 1, 1918; d. Anthony William and Marie Julia (Dusek) Podhora-Clark; m. Clyde Stanley Richardson, Oct. 16, 1944 (dec. 1989). BA, Cen. Washington Coll. Edn., 1939. Cert. jr. high sch. prin.; cert. life elem. tchr., Calif., life spl. secondary to teach mentally retarded; cert. psychometrist, Calif. Tchr. 2d and 3d grades Randle (Wash.) Sch. Dist., 1939-40; remedial tchr. Randle, 1940-41; 2d grade tchr. Seattle Sch. Dist., 1941-44; remedial tchr. Vancouver, Wash.; tchr. 3nd grade Lancaster (Calif.) Sch. Dist., 1946-48; tchr. spl. edn. Bakersfield (Calif.) Sch. Dist., 1948-49; tchr. 2d grade Norco (Calif.) Sch. Dist., 1950-51; tchr. 4th grade Chino (Calif.) Sch. Dist., 1951-55, tchr. spl. edn., 1955-79, ret., 1979. Leader Girl Res., Camp Rimrock, Wash., summer 1939; leader Bluebird Club, 1939. Recipient Cert. of Appreciaiton, State Assembly of Calif., 1979. Mem. NEA, AAUW, Am. Assn. Ret. Persons, Calif. Tchrs. Assn. (rep.), Calif. Ret. Tchrs. Assn., Vancouver Edn. Assn., Chino Tchrs. Assn. (past v.p., sec.), Wash. State Tchrs. Assn. (rep.), PTA (life), Fun After Fifty Club, Delta Kappa Gamma.

RICHARDSON, ERNEST RAY (ROCKY RICHARDSON), housing program supervisor; b. Dermott, Ark., Sept. 5, 1932; s. Louis and Leila Mae (Purdom) R.; m. Deloris Cobb, Mar. 25, 1955 (div. Apr. 1964); children: Victor Ray, Rodney Lynn, Regenia Ann; m. Doretha Tolbert, Apr. 1964 (div. June 1978); m. Shirley Ann Johnson, June 8, 1978; 1 child, Kimberly Ann; stepchildren: Janet, Kay, and Jerome Pate. BA in Bus. Adminstrn., Franklin U., 1975; AA of Real Estate, Parkland Coll., 1980; postgrad., Lewis U., 1980-83. Cert. real estate broker, Ill. Dir. edn. & tng. Champaign County Opportunities Industrialization Ctr., Champaign, Ill., 1968-70, exec. dir., pers. dir., 1970-73; fin. specialist City of Urbana, Ill., 1975-79; fin. specialist City of Joliet, Ill., 1979-82, dir. neighborhood svcs., 1982-87; exec. pers. dir. Aurora (Ill.) Housing Authority, 1987-89; housing program supr. City of Modesto, Calif., 1979—; mem. adv. com. Ctrl. Valley Opportunities Ctr., Inc. Modesto, 1992-94; vice chmn. mgmt. devel. com. City of Modesto, 1993-94; mem. funds allocation com. Nat. Opportunities Industrialization Ctr. Sgt. USAF, 1951-67. Mem. Nat. Assn. Real Estate Appraisers (pres.-elect Ill. chpt. 1984-85, pres. Ill. chpt. 1985-86, Ill. chpt. Mem. of the Yr., 1988). Home: 309 Yuba Ridge Ln Modesto CA 95354-3369 Office: City of Modesto Ofc Housing/Neighborhoods 940 11th St Modesto CA 95354-2319

RICHARDSON, JAMES TROY, sociology educator, consultant; b. Charleston, S.C., Aug. 25, 1941; s. Lylse Vega and Vera Veda (King) R.; m. Sept. 2, 1966; 1 child, Tamatha Lea. BA in Sociology, Tex. Tech U., 1964, MA in Sociology, 1965; PhD in Sociology, Wash. State U., Pullman, 1968; JD, Old Coll. Law Sch., 1986. Bar: Nev. 1986. Instr. Tex. Tech U., Lubbock, 1965-66; NIMH fellow Wash. State U., 1966-68; asst. prof. sociology U. Nev., Reno, 1968-71, assoc. prof. sociology, 1971-76, prof. sociology, 1976-88, prof. sociology and jud. studies, 1988—, dir. Master of Jud. Studies Degree Program, 1988—, dir. Ctr. Justice Studies, 1992-95; pres. Litigation Techs., Reno, 1986—; prof. U. Nev.-Reno Found., 1989; visitor London Sch. Econs., 1974-75. Author: Conversions Careers, 1978, Organized Miracles, 1979, The Brainwashing/Deprogramming Controversy, 1983, Money and Power in the New Religion, 1988, The Satanism Scare, 1991; contbr. numerous articles to profl. jours. Chair Washoe County Dems., 1976-78, State Group Ins. Com., Nev., 1984-90. Fulbright fellow The Netherlands, 1981. Mem. ABA, Nev. Bar Assn., Assn. for Sociology of Religion (pres. 1985-86), Am. Sociol. Assn., Soc. for Sci. Study of Religion, Internat. Soc. for Sociology of Religion (coun. mem. 1989—). Home: 2075 Marlette Ave Reno NV 89503-1441 Office: U Nev Dept Of Sociology Reno NV 89557

RICHARDSON, JEAN MCGLENN, retired civil engineer; b. Everett, Wash., Nov. 15, 1927; d. Clayton Charles and Marie Elizabeth (Mellish) McGlenn; BSCE, Oreg. State U., 1949; registered profl. engr., Ala., Oreg.; m. William York Richardson, II, June 11, 1949; children: William York III, Paul Kress II, Clayton McGlenn. Engr., Walter Schoel Engring. Co., Birmingham, Ala., 1950-54; office engr. G.C. McKinney Engring. Co., San Jose, Calif., 1972-74; civil design leader Harland Bartholomew & Assocs., Birmingham, 1974-78, Rust Engring. Co., Birmingham, 1978-82; owner, prin. Jean Richardson and Assocs. Inc., 1983-88; cons. engr. Rust Internat. Corp., 1988-90, Fed. Emergency Mgmt. Agy., 1986-90; sr. engr. City of Portland, Oreg., 1991-94; ret., 1994; women's engring. del. to China and USSR, 1984; counselor to female students on engring. as a career; state chmn. Mathcounts, Ala., 1986-88, Oreg., 1991—; math. vol. pub. schs. Fellow Soc. Women Engrs.; mem. NSPE, Soc. Women Engrs. (sr. sect. rep. to nat. bd.), Ala. Soc. Profl. Engrs. (pres. Birmingham chpt., state dir., state chmn. Mathcounts, Oreg. 1991), Women's Golf Assn. Club, Sunriver Golf Club, Alpha Phi. Republican. Episcopalian.

RICHARDSON, JOHN EDMON, marketing educator; b. Whittier, Calif., Oct. 22, 1942; s. John Edmon and Mildred Alice (Miller) R.; m. Dianne Elaine Ewald, July 15, 1967; 1 child, Sara Beth. BS, Calif. State U., Long Beach, 1964; MBA, U. So. Calif., 1966; MDiv, Fuller Theol. Sem., 1969, D of Ministry, 1981. Assoc. prof. mgmt. Sch. Bus. and Mgmt. Pepperdine U., Malibu, Calif., 1969—. Author: (leader's guides) Caring Enough to Confront, 1984, The Measure of a Man, 1985; editor: Ann. Editions: Marketing, 1987—, Bus. Ethics, 1990—. Lay counselor La Canada (Calif.) Presbyn. Ch., 1978-84, mem. lay counseling task force, 1982-84. Mem. Am. Mgmt. Assn., Soc. Bus. Ethics, Christian Writers Guild, Fuller Sem. Alumni Cabinet (pres. 1982-85), Am. Mktg. Assn., Beta Gamma Sigma. Office: Pepperdine U Sch Bus and Mgmt 400 Corporate Pt Culver City CA 90230-7615

RICHARDSON, JUDY MCEWEN, educational consultant, cartoonist; b. Appleton, Wis., June 3, 1947; d. John Mitchell and Isabel Annette (Ruble) McEwen; m. Larry Leroy Richardson, Mar. 19, 1972 (div. Oct. 1983). BA in English, Stanford U., 1968, MA in Edn., 1969; PhD in Higher Edn., U. Wash., 1975. Dir. ednl. rsch. St. Olaf Coll., Northfield, Minn., 1975-79; evaluation specialist Northwest Regional Ednl. Laboratory, Portland, 1980-82; legis. rsch. analyst Ariz. State Sen., Phoenix, 1982-87; dir. sch. fin. Ariz. Dept. Edn., Phoenix, 1987-92, assoc. superintendent, 1992-94; pvt. practice. Cartoonist for the Ariz. Capitol Times, 1995.

RICHARDSON, KATHLEEN, microbiologist, educator; b. Balt., Aug. 24, 1950; d. Wilbur Andeen and Elouise (Bidwell) R. BA, UCLA, 1972, PhD, 1981; MS, Calif. State U., San Diego, 1976. Teaching asst. dept. microbiology Calif. State U., 1973-76; predoctoral fellowship UCLA, 1976-81;

postdoctoral fellowship dept. microbiology/immunology U. Mo., Columbia, 1981-83; postdoctoral fellow Ctr. for Vaccine Devel. U. Md., Balt., 1983-85; asst. prof. dept. microbiology and immunology Oreg. Health Scis. U., Portland, 1985-93; staff scientist Gen. Atomics, San Diego, Calif., 1993—. Author rsch. publs. in bacterial pathogenesis of Vibrio cholerae. Rsch. grantee Oreg. Med. Rsch. Found., 1985-86, 89-90, NIH-NIAID, 1986-89, 91-96. Mem. Am. Soc. Microbiology, AAAS, Iota Sigma Pi. Office: Gen Atomics Bioscis 3550 General Atomics Ct San Diego CA 92121-1122

RICHARDSON, KENNETH T., JR., psychotherapist, consultant, educator, author; b. Santa Monica, Calif., Sept. 16, 1948; s. Kenneth T. Richardson and Florence (Wheeler) Neal; m. Mary L. Nutter, Dec. 31, 1983; children: Kenneth T. III, Russell A., Shad Martin, Cheralyn Martin. BA, Prescott (Ariz.) Coll., 1985; postgrad., Antioch (Ohio) Coll., 1987-88. Cert. addictions counselor, Ariz.; nat. cert. NCRC/ADOA. Program dir. Calvary Rehab. Ctr., Phoenix, 1979-82; clin. dir. Friendship House Comprehensive Recovery Ctr., San Francisco, 1982-84; dir. treatment The Meadows, Wickenburg, Ariz., 1984-87; co-founder, dir. The Orion Found., Phoenix, 1989—; owner, dir. Phoenix Cons. and Counseling Assocs., 1987—; cons. Addictions Svcs., The Hopi Tribe, Kykotsmoni, Ariz., 1989—, Baywood Hosp., Houston, 1988-89; advisor Nat. Coun. on Co-Dependence, Phoenix, 1990—, Recourse Found., Phoenix, 1989-93; faculty instr. Rio Salado C.C., Phoenix, 1987-90, The Recovery Source, Houston, 1989-90; co-chair Nat. Conv. of Men., Relationships and Recovery, Phoenix, 1990, 91. Creator, presenter audiotape series: Codependence and the Development of Addictions, 1991, Your Spiritual Self: The Child Within, 1991, Relationship Recovery, 1992, Men's Sexuality and Relationships, 1993, Body Mind and Spirit, 1994; creator edn. and support materials related to addictions, relationships and family sys., 1987—. Mem. Nat. Assn. Alcoholism and Drug Counselors, Am. Counseling Assn., Am. Mental Health Counselors Assn., Nat. Certification Reciprocity Consortium, Nat. Platform Assn. Office: Phoenix Cons and Counseling 5333 N 7th St Ste A202 Phoenix AZ 85014

RICHARDSON, MARY WELD, company executive; b. Port Washington, N.Y., Dec. 8, 1946; d. Weld and Florence (McBeth) R. BA, Columbia U., 1970; MA in Psychology, Sonoma State U., Calif., 1992. Ops. dir. restaurant divsn. Newhall Land & Farming Co., Valencia, Calif., 1976-80; regional tng. specialist World Savs. and Loan Assn., Oakland, Calif., 1982-89; tng. specialist San Francisco Fed. Savs. and Loan, 1989-92; sr. ptnr. WorkLife Resources, Kenwood, Calif., 1990—; tng., orgn. effectiveness sole official WorkLife Resources, Petaluma, Calif.; tng. cons. Redwood Conflict Resolution Svc., Santa Rosa, Calif., 1993—, SSU Cons. Group, Santa Rosa, 1990-93. Author: Client Centered Learning, 1993. Mediator RECOURSE, Santa Rosa, 1990—; family group facilitator Choices for Change, Santa Rosa, 1992—; facilitator Amer.Corps-The Sonona Project, 1993-95, Sonoma County AIDS Found., 1994. Mem. Nat. Soc. Performance and Instruction (pres. 1993-94). Office: WorkLife Resources PO Box 886 842 Warm Springs Rd Kenwood CA 95452-0886

RICHARDSON, MELVIN MARK, state legislator, broadcast executive; b. Salt Lake City, Apr. 29, 1928; s. Mark and Mary (Lundquist) R.; m. Dixie Joyce Gordon, 1952; children: Pamela, Mark, Lance, Todd, Kristi. Grad., Radio Operational Engring. Sch., Burbank, Calif., 1951. Radio announcer, program dir. Sta. KBUH, Brigham City, Utah, 1951-54; mgr. Sta. KLGN, Logan, Utah, 1954-58; announcer, sports dir. Sta. KID Radio/TV, Idaho Falls, Idaho, 1958-86; mgr., program dir. Sta. KID-FM/AM, Idaho Falls, 1986; mem. Idaho Ho. of Reps., 1988-92, Idaho Senate, 1992—; cons., dir. INEL Scholastic Tournament, Idaho Nat. Engring. Lab.; speaker in field. Host: Mel's Sports Scene, Thirty Minutes, Channel Three Reports, Probes. Dir. Assn. Idaho Cities, Ricks Coll. Booster Club, Bonneville County Crime Stoppers, Idaho Falls Child Devel. Ctr.; active Idaho Centennial Commn., Anti-Lottery Com., Gov.'s Conf. on Children; commr. Bonneville County Parks and Recreation Commn.; mayor City of Ammon, Idaho, 1966-72; candidate from Idaho Dist. # 2 for U.S. Congress. Sgt. USAR, 1951-57. Named Man of Yr., Ricks Coll., 1980. Mem. Idaho Broadcasters Assn. (bd. dirs.). Republican. Mem. LDS Ch. Home and Office: 3725 Brookfield Ln Idaho Falls ID 83406-6803

RICHARDSON, RAND MICHAEL, public relations executive; b. Detroit, May 9, 1949. BA in Distributive Edn., Wayne State U., 1970, BS in Mktg., 1971. Dir. mktg. adminstrn. Playboy, Inc., 1972-75; exec. v.p. Ritter/Geller Commns., 1975-86, Smith Mktg., 1987-89; exec. v.p., gen. mgr. Rowland Co./West, L.A., 1989-92, pres., COO, 1992—. Mem. Pub. Rels. Soc. Am.

RICHARDSON, RICHARD COLBY, JR., leadership and policy studies educator, researcher; b. Burlington, Vt., Sept. 10, 1933; s. Richard Colby and Florence May (Barlow) R.; m. Patricia Ann Barnhart, Dec. 21, 1954; children—Richard Colby III, Michael Donald, Christopher Robin. BS, Castleton State Coll., 1954; MA, Mich. State U., 1958; PhD, U. Tex., 1963; Litt.D. (hon.), Lafayette Coll., 1973. Instr., counselor Vt. Coll., Montpelier, 1958-61; dean instrn. Forest Park Community Coll., St. Louis, 1963-67; pres. Northampton County Area Community Coll., Bethelehem, Pa., 1967-77; chmn. dept. higher edn. and adult edn. Ariz. State U., Tempe, 1977-84, prof. edn. leadership and policy studies, 1984—. Jr. author: The Two Year College: A Social Synthesis, 1965; sr. author: Governance for the Two-Year College, 1972, Functional Literacy in the College Setting, 1981, Literacy in the Open Access College, 1983, Fostering Minority Access and Achievement in Higher Education, 1987, Achieving Quality and Diversity, 1991. Bd. dirs. Easton Hosp., 1973-77, v.p., 1975-77; exec. council Minsi Trails council Boy Scouts Am., Bethelehem, 1973-77. Named Disting. Grad., Coll. Edn., U. Tex., Austin, 1982; recipient Outstanding Research Publ. award Council Univ. and Colls.-Am. Assn. Community and Jr. Colls., 1983, Disting. Service award, 1984. Mem. Am. Assn. Higher Edn. (charter life, dir. 1970-73), AAUP, Assn. for Study of Higher Edn. (bd. dirs. 1984), Am. Assn. Community and Jr. Colls. (dir. 1980-83). Democrat. Home: 5654 E Wilshire Dr Scottsdale AZ 85257-1950 Office: Ariz State U Tempe AZ 85287

RICHARDSON, WALTER JOHN, architect; b. Long Beach, Calif., Nov. 14, 1926; s. Walter Francis and Ava Elizabeth (Brown) R.; m. Marilyn Joyce Brown, June 26, 1949 (div. 1982); children: Mark Steven, Glenn Stewart; m. Mary Sue Sutton, Dec. 4, 1982. Student, UCLA, 1944-45, Long Beach City Coll., 1946; BA, U. Calif., Berkeley, 1950. Registered architect, Ala., Ariz., Calif., Colo., Fla., Hawaii, Ill., Kans., Md., Mass., Nev., N.J., N.Y., Okla., Oreg., Tex., Utah, Vt., Va., Wash. Draftsman Wurster, Bernardi, Emmons, San Francisco, 1950-51, Skidmore, Owings & Merrill, San Francisco, 1951; designer Hugh Gibbs Architect, Long Beach, 1952-58; ptnr. Thomas & Richardson Architects, Long Beach, Costa Mesa, 1958-70; pres. Walter Richardson Assocs. Architects, Newport Beach, Calif., 1970-74; chmn. bd. Richardson, Nagy, Martin Architects and Planners, Newport Beach, 1974—. Co-author: The Architect and the Shelter Industry, 1975. Chmn. Planning Commn., City of Orange, Calif., 1967-68. With USAF, 1945. Recipient over 200 Gold Nugget Design awards Pacific Coast Builders Conf., San Francisco, 1969-94, 12 Builders Choice Design awards Builder Mag.; named Architect of Yr. Profl. Builder mag., 1986. Fellow AIA (pres. Orange County chpt. 1970, chmn. nat. housing com. 1976, 7 design awards); mem. Nat. Assn. Home Builders, Nat. Coun. Archtl. Registration Bds., Alpha Tau Omega. Republican. Office: Richardson Nagy Martin 4611 Teller Ave Ste 100 Newport Beach CA 92660-2104

RICHARDSON, WILLIAM BLAINE, congressman; b. Pasadena, Calif., Nov. 15, 1947; m. Barbara Flavin, 1972. BA, Tufts U., Medford, Mass., 1970; MA, Fletcher Sch. Law and Diplomacy, 1971. Mem. staff U.S. Ho. of Reps., 1971-72, Dept. State, 1973-75; mem. staff fgn. relations com. U.S. Senate, 1975-78; exec. dir. N. Mex. State Democratic Com., 1978, Bernalillo County Democratic Com., 1978; businessman Santa Fe, N. Mex., 1978-82; mem. 98th-103rd Congresses from 3rd N.Mex. dist., Washington, 1982—; democratic chief dep. majority whip 103d Congress; ranking minority mem. Resources Com. on Nat. Pks., Forests and Lands; mem. Select Com. on intelligence, Helsinki Commn. Vice chair Dem. Nat. Com.; active Big Bros.-Big Sisters, Santa Fe. Mem. Santa Fe Hispanic C. of C., Santa Fe C. of C., Council Fgn. Relations, NATO 2000 Bd., Congl. Hispanic Caucus, Am. G.I. Forum. Office: 2209 Rayburn House Office Bldg Washington DC 20515-0001*

RICHENS, MURIEL WHITTAKER, therapist, counselor, educator; b. Prineville, Oreg.; d. John Reginald and Victoria Cecilia (Pascale) Whittaker; children: Karen, John, Candice, Stephanie, Rebecca. BS, Oreg. State U.; MA, San Francisco State U., 1962; postgrad., U. Calif., Berkeley, 1967-69, U. Birmingham, Eng., 1973, U. Soria, Spain, 1981. Lic. sch. adminstr., tchr. 7-12, pupil personnel specialist, Calif., marriage, child and family counselor, Calif. Instr. Springfield (Oreg.) High Sch., San Francisco State U.; instr., counselor Coll. San Mateo, Calif., San Mateo High Sch. Dist., 1963-86; therapist AIDS Health Project U. Calif., San Francisco, 1988—; pvt. practice MFCC San Mateo; guest West German-European Acad. seminar, Berlin, 1975. Lifeguard, ARC. postgrad. student Ctr. for Human Communications, Los Gatos, Calif., 1974, U. P.R., 1977, U. Guadalajara (Mex.), 1978, U. Durango (Mex.), 1980, U. Guanajuato (Mex.) 1982. Mem. U. Calif. Berkeley Alumni Assn., Am. Contract Bridge League (Diamond Life Master, cert. instr., tournament dir.), Women in Comm., Computer-Using Educators, Commonwealth Club, Pi Lambda Theta, Delta Pi Epsilon. Republican. Roman Catholic. Home and Office: 847 N Humboldt St Apt 309 San Mateo CA 94401-1451

RICHES, KENNETH WILLIAM, nuclear regulatory engineer; b. Long Beach, Calif., Oct. 23, 1962; s. William Murray Riches and Carlene Katherine (Simmons) Anderson; m. Susan Ruth Flagg, Aug. 11, 1990; children: Benjamin William Bancroft Riches, Jennifer Ella Noel Riches. BSEE, U. Ill., 1984; MS in Engring. Mgmt., Santa Clara U., 1989. Registered profl. engr., Calif. Engr. Detroit Edison Co., Monroe, Mich.; engr. Pacific Gas & Electric Co., San Luis Obispo, Calif., 1984-95, elec. engr., 1988—; prin. K.W. Riches & Assocs., Arroyo Grande, Calif., 1988—; owner The Peaberry Coffee Pub, Arroyo Grande, Calif., 1991-92. Mem. Rep. Nat. Com., 1986—; active Corp. Action in Pub. Schs., San Francisco, 1987, 88, World Wildlife Fund. Univs. Rsch. Assn. scholar, 1980. Mem. NSPE, IEEE (chpt. chmn. 1986-87, sect. dir. 1988-90), Power Engring. Soc. of IEEE (mem. nat. chpts. coun. 1988-92), Pacific Coast Engring. Assn., Nature Conservancy, Order of DeMolay (master counselor Paul Revere chpt. 1979). Methodist. Home: 760 Washington St Monroe MI 48161 Office: PG&E Diablo Canyon Power Plant PO Box 117-M/S 104/5/21A Avila Beach CA 93424 Office: M/S 240-AIB 6400 N Dixie Hwy Newport MI 48166

RICHEY, EVERETT ELDON, religion educator; b. Claremont, Ill., Nov. 1, 1923; s. Hugh Arthur and Elosia Emma (Longnecker) R.; m. Mary Elizabeth Reynolds, Apr. 9, 1944; children: Eldon Arthur, Clive Everett, Loretta Arlene, Charles Estel. ThB, Anderson U., 1946; MDiv, Sch. Theology, Anderson, Ind., 1956; ThD, Iliff Sch. of Theology, Denver, 1960. Pastor Ch. of God, Bremen, Ind., 1946-47, Laurel, Miss., 1947-48; pastor First Ch. of God, Fordyce, Ark., 1948-52; prof. Arlington Coll., Long Beach, Calif., 1961-68; pastor Cherry Ave. Ch. of God, Long Beach, 1964-68; prof. Azusa (Calif.) Pacific U., 1968-93; mem. Christian Ministries Tng. Assn., 1968; mem., chmn. Commn. on Christian Higher Edn./Ch. of God, 1982-93; pres. Ch. Growth Investors, Inc., 1981—. Author: ednl. manual Church Periodical--Curriculum, 1971-83. Mem. Assn. Profs. and Rschrs. Religious Edn., Christian Ministries Tng. Assn. Republican. Home and Office: 413 N Valencia St Glendora CA 91741-2418

RICHMAN, ANTHONY E., textile rental company executive; b. Los Angeles, Dec. 13, 1941; s. Irving M. and Helen V. (Muchnic) R.; m. Judy Harriet Richman, Dec. 19, 1964; children: Lisa Michele, Jennifer Beth. BS, U. So. Calif., 1964. With Reliable Textile Rental Svcs., L.A., 1964—, svc. mgr., 1969, sales and svc. mgr., 1970-73, plant mgr., 1973-75, gen. mgr., bd. dirs., 1975-78, v.p., sec.-treas., 1975-82, exec. v.p., CEO, 1982-84, pres., CEO, 1984—. Bd. dirs. Guild for Children, 1979—, Valley Guild for Cystic Fibrosis, 1974—, Cystic Fibrosis Found. of L.A. and Orange Counties, 1989—; pres. Textile Rental/Svc. Assoc. Am., 1993-95. Office: Reliable Textile Rental Svcs 3200 N Figueroa St Los Angeles CA 90065-1526

RICHMAN, DAVID BRUCE, entomologist, educator; b. Dunkirk, N.Y., Nov. 6, 1942; s. Melvin Stanley and Florence Irene (Nottis) R.; m. Olive Lynda Goin, June 18, 1977; children: Julia Anne, Rebecca Leonna. AA, Ariz. Western Coll., 1968; BS, U. Ariz., 1970, MS, 1973; PhD, U. Fla., 1977. Grad. asst., then asst. curator U. Ariz., Tucson, 1970-73; grad. asst., then rsch. assoc. U. Fla., Gainesville, 1973-78, 81-82; rsch. assoc./asst. prof. N.Mex. State U., Las Cruces, 1978-81, rsch. assoc., 1983-85, coll. asst. prof., 1985-90, sci. specialist dept. entomology-plant pathology-weed sci., 1990—; rsch. assoc. Fla. State Collection Arthropods, Gainesville, 1978—. Contbr. articles to sci. jours. Mem. Am. Arachological Soc., Brit. Arachological Soc., Entomol. Soc. Am. (chmn. resolutions com. southwestern br. 1990-91), Assn. Systematic Collections, Ctr. Internat. Documentation Arachologique, Cambridge Entomol. Club, Entomol. Collections Network, Southwestern Entomol. Soc., Sigma Xi. Democrat. Mem. Soc. of Friends. Office: N Mex State U Dept Entomology Plant Las Cruces NM 88003

RICHMAN, DAVID WILLIAM, aerospace executive; b. LaPorte, Ind., Aug. 3, 1940; s. Milfred William and Ethelyn Belle (Morton) R.; m. Carolyn Jean Nicholson Bloom, Oct. 24, 1964 (div. Aug. 1971); children: Keith William, Michael David; m. Jean Shutts Dunn, June 2, 1990. BSME, Purdue U., 1962; MSME, U. Mo., 1968, MS in Engring. Mgmt., 1974. Thermodynamicist Gemini McDonnell Aircraft, St. Louis, 1962-65; thermodynamicist Skylab McDonnell Douglas Corp., St. Louis, 1965-69, subcontract mgr. Skylab, 1968-70, advanced designer Shuttle, 1970-71, aerodynamicist missiles, 1971-75, mgr. space commercialization, 1975-78; chief engr. electrophoresis McDonnell Douglas Corp., Huntington Beach, Calif., 1978-87, dir. integration, 1987-92, certrifuge program mgr., 1992—; mem. adv. bd. Univ. Space Rsch. Assn., Washington, 1984; cons. Ctr. for Cell Rsch., State College, Pa., 1990-94. Patentee electrophoresis chamber, sys. for hydrodynamic compensation, electrophoresis apparatus, continuous flow electrophoresis. Mem. AIAA (adv. bd. space processing com. 1982-84, tech. achievement award 1982), Am. Soc. Engring. Mgmt., Electrophoresis Soc., Am. Soc. Gravitational and Space Biology. Home: 20802 Hunter Ln Huntington Beach CA 92646-6414 Office: McDonnell Douglas Aerospace 5301 Bolsa Ave Huntington Beach CA 92647-2048

RICHMAN, MARVIN JORDAN, real estate developer, investor, educator; b. N.Y.C., July 13, 1939; s. Morris and Minnie (Graubart) R.; m. Amy Paula Rubin, July 31, 1966; children: Mark Jason, Keith Hayden, Susanne Elizabeth, Jessica Paige. BArch, MIT, 1962; M Urban Planning, NYU, 1966, postgrad., 1967-69; MBA, U. Chgo., 1977; U.S. Dept. State fellow U. Chile, 1960. Architect, planner Skidmore, Owings & Merrill, N.Y.C., 1964, Conklin & Rossant, N.Y.C., 1965-67; ptnr. Vizbaras & Ptnrs., N.Y.C., 1968-69; v.p. Urban Investment & Devel. Co., Chgo., 1969-79, sr. v.p., 1979; pres. bd. dirs. First City Devels. Corp., Beverly Hills, Calif., 1979-80; pres. Olympia & York (U.S.) Devel. (West), 1987-89, Olympia & York Calif. Equities Corp., L.A., 1981-87, Olympia & York Calif. Devel. Corp., 1981-87, Olympia & York Hope St. Mgmt. Corp., 1982-87, Olympia & York Homes Corp., 1983-89, Olympia & York Calif. Constrn. Corp., 1986-89, The Richman Co., L.A., 1989—, pres. Richman Real Estate Group, Salt Lake City, 1995—; dean Sch. Bus. and Mgmt. Woodbury U., Burbank, Calif., 1993—; lectr. NYU, 1967-69, UCLA, 1989-90, Nat. Humanities Inst., other univs. Adv. NEA. Bd. advisors UCLA Ctr. Fin. and Real Estate. With USAF, 1963-64. Registered architect; lic. real estate broker. Mem. AIA, Am Planning Assn., Internat. Coun. Shopping Ctrs., L.A. World Affairs Coun., Urban Land Inst., Nat. Assn. Office and Indsl. Parks, Chief Exec.'s Round Table, Air Force Assn., Lambda Alpha.

RICHMOND, HUGH MACRAE, English language educator; b. Burton-upon-Trent, Eng., Mar. 20, 1932; came to U.S., 1957; s. Ronald Jackson and Isabella (MacRae) R.; m. Velma Elizabeth Bourgeois, Aug. 9, 1958; children: Elizabeth Merle, Claire Isabel. Diploma, U. Florence, Italy, 1952, U. Munich, 1956; BA in English with honors, Cambridge (Eng.) U., 1954; DPhil in English, Oxford (Eng.) U., 1957. Asst. d'Anglais Lycée Jean Perrin, Lyon, France, 1954-55; prof. English U. Calif., Berkeley, 1957—, dir. Shakespeare Program, 1974—, dir. Shakespeare Forum, 1981—. Author: The School of Love, 1964, Shakespeare's Political Plays, 1967, Shakespeare's Sexual Comedy, 1971; prodr. video Shakespeare and the Globe, 1985; dir., prodr. stage and videos for NEH, 1984—. Bd. dirs. Calif. Shakespeare Festival, Berkeley, 1980-90; chair adv. coun. Internat. Globe Ctr., 1988—. 2d lt. Royal Arty., U.K., 1950-51. Fellow Am. Coun. Learned Socs., 1964-65, NEH, 1977, 88; NEH grantee, 1984-86. Mem. MLA, Shakespeare Assn. Am. Roman Catholic. Office: U Calif English Dept Berkeley CA 94720

RICHMOND, ROCSAN, television/video producer, publicist, inventor, interior designer; b. Chgo., Jan. 30; d. Alphonso and Annie Lou (Combest) R.; divorced; 1 child, Tina S. Student, Wilson Jr. Coll., 1963, 2d City Theatre, Chgo., 1969, Alice Liddel Theatre, Chgo., 1970. Lic. 3d class radio/tel. operator FCC. Vegetarian editor Aware mag., Chgo., 1977-78; investigative reporter, film critic Chgo. Metro News, 1975-81; producer, talk show host Sta. WSSD Radio, Chgo., 1980-81; dir. pub. rels. IRMCO Corp., Chgo., 1981-82; pub. rels. agt., newsletter editor Hollywood (Calif.) Reporter newspaper, 1985-86; exec. producer Donald Descendent's Prodns., Hollywood, 1983—, (TV show) Future News, 1983-86; pres. Richmond Estates. Inventor invisible drapery tieback. Jehovah's Witness. Office: PO Box 665 Los Angeles CA 90078-0665

RICHMOND, RONALD LEROY, aerospace engineer; b. L.A., Aug. 16, 1931; s. William Paul and Martha Emelia (Anderson) R.; m. Mary Louise Gates, Jan. 2, 1955; children: Pandora Deanne Richmond Perry, Steven Lee. BSME, U. Calif., Berkeley, 1952; MS in Aero. Engring., Calif. Inst. Tech., 1953, PhD in Aero. Engring., 1957. Aerodynamicist Lockheed Aircraft Co., Burbank, Calif., 1952-54; teaching/rsch. asst. Calif. Inst. Tech., Pasadena, 1952-57; asst. group leader aero. performance Douglas Aircraft Co., Long Beach, Calif., 1957-59; chief engr. adv. devel. Ford Aerospace, Newport Beach, Calif., 1959-87; adj. assoc. prof. Sch. Engring., U. Calif., Irvine, 1987-88; dir. engring. Brunswick Def., Costa Mesa, Calif., 1988-94; aerodynamics cons. Douglas Aircraft, 1956-57, Shelby-Am. (Ford) Auto., L.A., 1960-62; subgroup leader NATO Indsl. Adv. Group #16, Brussels, Belgium, 1984-86. Res. dep. Orange County Sheriff's Dept., 1976—. Calif. Inst. Tech. Rsch. assistantship, 1953, 54, 55, 56, 57, teaching asst., 1955, 56, 57, grantee, 1955, 56, 57. Assoc. fellow AIAA (Orange County sect. chmn. 1989-90); mem. Western States Assn. Sheriff's Air squadrons (comdr. 1987-88), Skylarks of So. Calif. (pres., chmn. bd. 1987-88). Republican. Home: 1307 Seacrest Dr Corona Del Mar CA 92625-1227

RICHMOND, THOMAS G., chemistry educator; b. Buffalo, Jan. 4, 1957; s. George E. and Joan S. (Steinmiller) R.; m. Cynthia Squire, Aug. 31, 1989. ScB, Brown U., 1979; MS, Northwestern U., 1980, PhD, 1984. Bantrell fellow Calif. Inst. Tech., Pasadena, 1983-85; asst. prof. chemistry U. Utah, Salt Lake City, 1985-91, assoc. prof., 1991—; presdl. young investigator NSF, 1989—. Contbr. articles to profl. publs. NSF fellow, 1980-83, Alfred P. Sloan Rsch. fellow, 1991—; Camille and Henry Dreyfus Found. grantee, 1985. Mem. Am. Chem. Soc. Office: U Utah Dept Chemistry Salt Lake City UT 84112

RICHTER, BURTON, physicist, educator; b. N.Y.C., Mar. 22, 1931; s. Abraham and Fanny (Pollack) R.; m. Laurose Becker, July 1, 1960; children: Elizabeth, Matthew. B.S., MIT, 1952, Ph.D., 1956. Research assoc. Stanford U., 1956-60, asst. prof. physics, 1960-63, assoc. prof., 1963-67, prof., 1967—, Paul Pigott prof. phys. sci., 1980—, tech. dir. Linear Accelerator Ctr., 1982-84, dir. Linear Accelerator Ctr., 1984—; cons. NSF, Dept. Energy; bd. dirs. Varian Corp., Litel Instruments; Loeb lectr. Harvard U., 1974; DeShalit lectr. Weizmann Inst., 1975. Contbr. over 300 articles to profl. publs. Recipient E.O. Lawrence medal Dept. Energy, 1975; Nobel prize in physics, 1976. Fellow Am. Phys. Soc. (pres. 1994), AAAS; mem. NAS, Am. Acad. Arts and Scis. Office: Stanford Linear Accel Ctr PO Box 4349 Palo Alto CA 94309-4349

RICKE, P. SCOTT, obstetrician/gynecologist; b. Indpls., June 28, 1948; s. Joseph and Betty (Rae) R.; divorced; 1 child. BA, Ind. U., 1970; MD, Ind. U. Sch. of Medicine, 1974. Bd. cert. ob-gyn., 1981. Intern St. Lukes Hosp., Denver, 1975; resident U. Calif. at Irvine, Orange, 1977-79; pvt. practice Ob-Gyn Tucson, 1981—; Pres., founder The Advocacy Group. Inventor (med. instrument) Vaginal Retractor, 1989. Bd. dirs. City of Hope, Tucson, 1981-85, Am. Cancer Soc., Tucson, 1981-83. Fellow Am. Bd. Ob-Gyn. Home: 3755 N Tanuri Dr Tucson AZ 85715-1939 Office: 3972 N Campbell Tucson AZ 85719

RICKELS, LAURENCE ARTHUR, foreign language educator; b. Cherokee, Iowa, Dec. 2, 1954; s. Karl and Christa (Loessin) R. BA in English Lit., U. Pa., 1975; Hauptseminaraufnahmeprufung, Freie U. Berlin, Germany, 1975; MA, PhD in German Lit., Princeton U., 1978, 80; MA in Clin. Psychology, Antioch U., Santa Barbara, Calif., 1994. Lectr. U. Dusseldorf, Germany, 1980-81; asst. prof. U. Calif., Santa Barbara, 1981-86, assoc. prof., 1986-90, prof., 1990—, chair dept. Germanic, Slavic and semitic studies, 1989-95; cons. Psychiat. Rsch. Group, 1982—; mem. Film Studies Adv. Bd., U. Calif. Santa Barbara, 1987—; regular contbr. Artforum Internat., 1992—. Author: Aberrations of Mourning, 1988, Der Unbetrauerbare Tod, 1989, The Case of California, 1991; editor: Looking After Nietzsche, 1990. Recipient Rsch. Assistance awards Ctr. for German and European Studies, Berkeley, 1991, 93, 94; rsch. fellow Alexander Von Humboldt-Stiftung, Berlin, 1985-86, 88, 89. Mem. MLA (del. assembly mem. 1988-90), Internat. Initiative on Tech. and the Unconscious-U. Calif. Humanities Rsch. Inst. (founding). Home: 959 Medio Rd Santa Barbara CA 93103-2445 Office: Dept Germanic Slavic & Semitic Studies Univ Calif Santa Barbara CA 93106

RICKER, JEFFREY PAUL, investment strategist, researcher, consultant; b. Ft. Lauderdale, Fla., Sept. 12, 1957; s. Harold Herbert and Joanne (DiBello) R. BA, Vanderbilt U., 1979; MBA, U. Chgo., 1981. CFA. Investment researcher Wells Fargo/Nikko Investment Advisors, San Francisco, 1981-84; cons. in pvt. practice San Francisco, 1984—; chmn. audit com. Security Analysts of San Francisco, 1984—; adv. bd. Alphanumeric Capital Ptnrs. Mem. Assn. for Invesment Mgmt. and Rsch., U. Chgo. Grad. Sch. Bus. Bay Area Alumni Assn. (chair 1991—). Office: 1730 Filbert St # 105 San Francisco CA 94123-3644

RICKEY, JEFFREY BARTON, academic administrator, consultant; b. McMinnville, Oreg., July 26, 1954; s. Barton Gilbert and Iva Clarice (Rockhill) R.; m. Deborah Lynn Leshana, Sept. 19, 1975; children: Jonathan Barton, Ailson Rebecca, David James. BS, George Fox Coll., 1976. Group benefits mgr. Harmon & Assocs., Seattle, 1976-78; program dir. Goodwill Industries of Oreg., Portland, 1979-82; vocat. rehab. counselor Ingram & Assocs., Portland, 1982-86; enrollment cons. D.H. Dagley Assocs., Inc., Atlanta, 1986-93; dean of admissions George Fox Coll., Newberg, Oreg., 1986—. Contbr. articles to profl. jours. Co-advisor Coll. Reps., George Fox Coll., 1993—, mem. Pres.'s Coun. Leadership Cir., 1987—, fundraiser, 1992-93; mem. Pres.'s Assocs., Western Evang. Sem., 1993—. Mem. Nat. Assn. Christian Coll. Admissions Pers. (dir. 1987-90), Oreg. Rehab. Assn. (pres. 1981-82), Am. Assn. Collegiate Registrars and Admissions Officers. Republican. Mem. Soc. of Friends. Office: George Fox Coll 414 N Meridian St Newberg OR 97132-2625

RICKEY, JUNE EVELYN MILLION, retired educator; b. Joliet, Ill., Oct. 15, 1923; d. Lawrence Ernest and Ethel Alden (Ringler) Million; m. Paul Rickey, June 29, 1944; children: William, Mary Ann, John, James. BS in Edn., Ill. State U., 1946; MA in Journalism, Adams State Coll., 1970. Cert. tchr., Colo. Tchr. English Ottawa (Ill.) Twp. High Sch., 1946-47, Alamosa (Colo.) High Sch., 1953-55, 59-77, Evans Jr. High Sch., Alamosa, 1956-59; tchr. drama McAllen (Tex.) High Sch., 1955-56. Publicity chmn. Women's Citizenship Club, Alamosa, 1978, Am. Cancer Soc., bd. dirs., 1986—; editorial staff San Luis Valley Hist. Soc., Alamosa, 1985—, Ethnic heritage Project, 1977-78; trustee Creede (Colo.) Repertory Theatre, 1987, sec.-treas., 1987-90. Wall St. Jour. grantee, 1964. Mem. AAUW (sec. 1983-87), Adams State Coll. Alumni Assn. (bd. dirs.), PEO Sisterhood, DAR. Democrat. Presbyterian. Home: 77 El Rio Dr Alamosa CO 81101

RICKLEY, DAVID ARTHUR, communications systems manager; b. Lawrence, Mass., Jan. 11, 1956; s. Arthur Anthony and Shirley Ann (Ryan) R. Student, Rio Hondo Coll., 1976, L.A. Trade Tech. Coll. Photomech. engr. L.A. Times, 1974-82, lead color operator, 1982-86, color lab. supr., 1986-89, prepress graphics supt., 1989-91, tech. systems mgr., 1991-92, prodn. editor, 1992—. Office: Los Angeles Times Times Mirror Sq Los Angeles CA 90012

RICKS, DAVID ARTEL, business educator, editor; b. Washington, July 21, 1942; s. Artel and Focha (Black) R. BS, Brigham Young U., 1966; MBA, Ind. U., 1968, PhD, 1970. Asst. prof. Ohio State U., 1970-75, assoc. prof.,

1975-81; prof. internat. bus. U. S.C., Columbia, 1981-92; v.p. acad. affairs Thunderbird-the Am. Grad. Sch. Internat. Mgmt., 1992-94, disting. prof., 1992—; editor Kent Pub. Co., Boston, 1978—. Author books, articles in field, including Directory of Foreign Manufactures in the U.S. (Best Reference Book 1974 ALA, 1975); editor-in-chief Jour. of Internat. Business Studies, 1984-92, Jour. Internat. Mgmt., 1994—. Mem. Acad. Internat. Bus. (treas. 1981-82), Acad. Mgmt. (chmn. internat. divsn. 1988-89). Home: 14815 N 15th Ave Phoenix AZ 85023-5174 Office: 15249 N 59th Ave Glendale AZ 85306-3236

RICKS, MARK G., state senator; b. Rexburg, Idaho, July 4, 1924; s. Peter J. and Emily E. (Arnold) R.; m. Evelyn Tonks, Aug. 9, 1944; children: Michael T., Gary M., Alan D., Adele Ricks Nielsen, Glen L., Kathie Ricks Tensmeyer, Grant H., Merle K., Douglas T. AS in Agr., Ricks Coll. Mem. Idaho Senate, 1979—, majority leader, 1983-88, chmn. reapportionment com., 1982, chmn. senate commerce and labor commn., 1981-82, vice chmn. senate fin. com., 1989—, state affairs com., chmn., 1989—, chmn. revenue and projection com., 1989—, chmn. reapportionment com., 1990—. Mem. exec. and adv. bd. council Boy Scouts Am. Named to Eastern Idaho Agrl. Hall of Fame, 1989, named One of Ten Outstanding Legislators Nat. Rep. Legislators Assn., 1987; recipient Community Svc. Prodn. and Example award Rexburg C. of C., 1976, Outstanding Svc. award Madison Sch. Dist., 1987, Distinguished Alumni award Ricks Coll., 1988. Mem. Nat. Conf. State Legis. (exec. com. 1985-87, chmn. nominating com. 1988, mem. rsch. and grants com., vice chmn. fed. taxation com., vice chmn. trade and econ. devel. com., mem. budget and rules com., co-chmn. reapportionment com. 1989, vice chmn. state fed. assembly 1988), Coun. State Govts. (exec. com., budget com. 1989-90, chmn. western legislative conf. 1988-89, chmn. ann. meeting com. 1989-90), Idaho Wheat Growers, Nat. Fedn. Ind. Bus., Rexburg C. of C. (maj. gifts com. Ricks Coll.). Republican. Mormon. Home: 3348 S 1400 W Rexburg ID 83440-4131 Office: Idaho State Legis Senate Capital Bldg Boise ID 83720

RICKS, MARY FRANCES, university administrator, anthropologist; b. Portland, Oreg., July 6, 1939; d. Leo and Frances Helen (Corcoran) Samuel; m. Robert Stanley Ricks, Jan. 7, 1961; children: Michael Stanley, Allen Gilbert. BA, Whitman Coll., 1961; MA, Portland State U., 1977, MPA, 1981, PhD, 1995. Asst. to dir. auxiliary services Portland State U., 1975-79, instnl. researcher, 1979-85, dir. instnl. research and planning, 1985—, rsch. assoc. prof., 1994—. Contbr. articles and presentations to profl. socs. Vol. archeologist BLM-USDI, Lakeview, Oreg., 1983—. Fellow Soc. Applied Anthropology; mem. Soc. Am. Archaeology, Soc. Coll. and U. Planning, Pacific N.W. Assn. Instnl. Rsch. and Planning (pres. 1990-91), Assn. Oreg. Archaeologists (v.p. 1988-90), Assn. Instl. Rsch., City Club of Portland, Sigma Xi. Home: 5466 SW Dover Loop Portland OR 97225-1033 Office: Portland State U Office Instnl Rsch/Planning PO Box 751 Portland OR 97207-0751

RIDDER, DANIEL HICKEY, newspaper publisher; b. N.Y.C., May 3, 1922; s. Bernard Herman and Nell (Hickey) R.; m. Frani Cooper Ackerman, Oct. 13, 1971; children by previous marriage: Daniel Hickey, Randy Helen, Richard J. AB, Princeton U., 1943. Reporter N.Y. Jour. Commerce, Grand Forks (N.D.) Herald; pub. St. Paul Dispatch and Pioneer-Press, 1952-58; co-pub. Long Beach (Calif.) Ind. Press-Telegram, 1958-69, pub., 1969-88; chmn. Long Beach (Calif.) Ind. Press-Telegram, Long Beach, Calif., 1988-90; mem. operating com. Knight-Ridder, Inc., Long Beach, Calif., 1989-94; bd. dirs. AP, 1975-84; v.p. Knight-Ridder, Inc., 1975-89. Chmn. bd. St. Mary Med. Ctr., 1987-92; past bd. dirs. Sta. KCET, L.A. United Way, Newspaper Advt. Bur., L.A. County Mus. Art, Calif., 1974-84; past chmn. bd. trustees Calif. State U. and Colls.; trustee Long Beach Mus. Art; vice chmn. bd. govs. Calif. Community Found. Lt. (j.g.) USN, 1942-46, ETO, PTO. Clubs: Virginia Country (Long Beach, Calif.); El Dorado Country (Palm Springs, C(life); L.A. Country; Cypress Point (Pebble Beach, Calif.). Home: 5531 Bryant Dr E Long Beach CA 90815-4111 Office: Knight-Ridder Inc 604 Pine Ave Long Beach CA 90844-0003

RIDDLE, MATTHEW C(ASEY), physician, educator; b. Portland, Oreg., Dec. 9, 1938; s. Matthew Casey and Katharine Hope (Kerr) R.; children from previous marriage: Matthew Casey III, Ann E., James K., Sarah A. BA in English magna cum laude, Yale U., 1960; MD, Harvard U., 1964. Diplomate Am. Bd. Internal Medicine. Resident in medicine Rush-Presbyn. St. Luke Hosp., Chgo., 1968-69, fellow endocrinology, 1969-70; fellow endocrinology U. Wash., Seattle, 1971-73; asst. prof. medicine Oreg. Health Scis. U., Portland, 1973-82, assoc. prof. medicine, 1982—, head diabetes sect., 1975—. Contbr. articles to profl. jours. Capt. U.S. Army, 1966-68, Vietnam. Mem. Am. Diabetes Assn. (bd. dirs., pres., chmn. bd. Oreg. affiliate), Am. Fedn. Clin. Rsch., Endocrine Soc., Am. Assn. Clin. Endocrinologists. Office: Oreg Health Scis U L-345 3181 SW Sam Jackson Park Rd Portland OR 97201-3011

RIDDLESWORTH, JUDITH HIMES, elementary education educator; b. Hammond, Ind., Feb. 2, 1954; d. James Bernerd and Jane (Hall) Himes; m. Kim A. Riddlesworth, July 30, 1977; children: Sara, Becky. BS, Ill. State U., Normal, 1976; MA, No. Ariz. U., 1981. Cert. elem., spl. edn. tchr., Ariz. With Safford (Ariz.) Sch. Dist., 1976—, tchr. middle sch., 1987—, grade level chmn., 1989-93; mem. bldg. team Safford Sch. Dist. Mem. AAUW, Delta Kappa gamma. Office: Safford Unified Sch Dist 734 W 11th St Safford AZ 85546-2967

RIDDOCH, HILDA JOHNSON, accountant; b. Salt Lake City, July 25, 1923; d. John and Ivy Alma (Wallis) Johnson; m. Leland Asa Riddoch, Nov. 22, 1942; children: Ivy Lee, Leland Mark. Vocal student, Ben Henry Smith, Seattle; student, Art Instrn. Schs. Sales clk, marking room and dist. office Sears, Roebuck & Co., Seattle, 1940-42; with billing dept., receptionist C.M. Lovsted & Co., Inc., Seattle, 1942-51; acct., exec. sec. Viking Equipment Co., Inc., Seattle, 1951-54; acct., office mgr. Charles Waynor Collection Agy., Seattle, 1955-57; pvt. practice, 1957—; acct., office mgr. Argus Mag., Seattle, 1962-67; acct. Law Offices Krutch, Lindell, Donnelly, Dempsey & Lageschulte, Seattle, 1967-72, Law Offices Sindell, Haley, Estep, et al, Seattle, 1972-77; co-founder, acct. Bus. Svc., Inc. and Diversified Design & Mktg., Fed. Way, Auburn & Orting, Wash., 1975—; co-founder L & H Advt. and Distbg. Co., Orting, Wash., 1992—; sec.-treas., dir. Jim Evans Realty, Inc., Seattle, 1973-87; agt. Wise Island Water Co., P.U.D., Victoria, B.C., 1973-88, Estate Executrix, Seattle, 1987—. Author: Ticking Time on a Metronome, 1989-90; writer, dir. hist. play Presidents of Relief Society Thru Ages; writer epic poetry; writer, dir. teenager activation video, 1984; pub., editor Extended Family Newsletter, 1983—. Dir. speech and drama LDS Ch., 1938-88, ward pres. young women's orgn., mem. ward and stake choirs, 1963-85, stake genealogy libr., Federal Way, 1983-85, ward and stake newsletter editors various areas, West Seattle, Seattle, Renton, Auburn, 1950-90, 1st counselor in presidency, tchr. various courses Ladies' Relief Soc. Orgn., 1965—; co-dir., organizer 1st Silver Saints Group, 1990-92; interviewer LDS Ch. Emplyment Svcs., 1992-93; founder WE CARE, 1993; co-resident mgr. Mountain View Estates, Orting. Recipient Letter of Recognition Howard W. Hunter, Pres. LDS Ch. Fellow Am. Biographical Assn. (life). Home: PO Box 1300 Orting WA 98360-1300

RIDEOUT, BRUCE WILLIAM, military officer, process and maintenance engineer; b. Dec. 25, 1958; s. Joseph Merrill III and Doris (Nelson) R.; m. Peggy Jane Musselwhite; 1 child, Kelsey. BSME cum laude, U. Fla., 1981; MPA, Valdosta State Coll., 1988; student, Amphibious Warfare Sch., 1988-89. Cert. engring. intern, Fla. Commd. 2d lt. USMC, advanced through grades to capt., team officer 2d Anglico, 1983-86, commdg. officer ship's detachment, 1986-88, logistics officer, 1989-90, ops. officer, artillery commdg. officer, 1990-91, tng. officer, 1992-93; maintenance engr., 1993-94, process engr., 1994-95, prodn. supt., 1995—; commr. Planning and Zoning Commn., Green River, Wyo., 1994—; teaching asst. U. Fla. 1979-81; mem. credit com. Wyochem Credit Union. Author: (manual) Jumpmaster Procedures, 1985. Svc. com. chmn. Rotoract, St. Marys, Ga., 1986. Mem. VFW, Tau Beta Pi, Pi Tau Sigma (v.p.), Kiwanis Club of Kings Bay (charter).

RIDEOUT, PHYLLIS MCCAIN, university official, educator; b. Macon, Ga., Sept. 15, 1938; d. Wayne Eugene and Lois Stone (Rollins) McC.; m. William Milford Rideout, Jr., Mar. 10, 1961; children: Christina Lynn, William Milford III, Julie Linda. AB in Modern European Lit., Stanford U., 1961; MA in English, Fla. State U., 1973, PhD in Humanities, 1981. Cert. community coll. life teaching credential, Calif. Teaching asst. Fla. State U., Tallahassee, 1974-75; program coord. humanities U. So. Calif., L.A., 1981-82, program adminstr. Norris Comprehensive Cancer Ctr., 1983-86, adminstrv. dir. Norris Comprehensive Cancer Ctr., 1986-89, assoc. dir. for adminstrn. and edn. Norris Comprehensive Cancer Ctr., 1989—, clin. instr. preventive medicine Sch. Medicine, Norris Comprehensive Cancer Ctr., 1989—. Leader, trainer Girl Scouts U.S.a., Tallahassee and Los Alamitos, Calif., 1975-81; bd. dirs. jr. and sr. high schs. PTA's, Los Alamitos, 1977-81; bd. dirs. Cancer Coalition Calif., 1986-91; bd. dirs., vice chair AIDS Healthcare Found., 1992—; treas. So. Calif. Cancer Pain Initiative. Mem. Nat. Assn. Women in Edn., Cancer Ctr. Adminstrs. Forum (exec. com. 1987-91), U. So. Calif. Women in Mgmt. (bd. dirs. 1986-89, 90—, pres. 1993-95), Stanford U. Alumni Assn. (life), Stanford Profl. Women (pres., bd. dirs. 1982-85), Stanford Club Los Angeles County (bd. dirs. 1985-88). Office: U So Calif Norris Comprehensive Cancer Ctr 1441 Eastlake Ave Los Angeles CA 90033-1048

RIDER, FREDERICK TIMOTHY, computer systems analyst; b. Boulder, Colo., June 17, 1947; s. Paul Aubert and Ruth P. (Peterson) R.; m. Jean H. Palmer, Apr. 24, 1971; children: Jason E., Timothy J. A in Applied Tech., C.C. of Air Force, Maxwell AFB, Ala., 1980; BS in Computer Sci., Chapman U., Orange, Calif., 1990. Enlisted U.S. Air Force, 1967; advanced through grades to cmsgt., 1988; supt. maintenance ops. 10th Tactical Reconanaissance Wing, RAF Alconbury, Eng., 1985-86; wing weapons mgr. 49th Tactical Fighter Wing, Holloman AFB, N.Mex., 1986-88; ret. USAF, 1988; aircraft armament supr. Holloman Support div. Dyncorp, Holloman AFB, 1988-91, computer system analyst, 1991—. Vol. United Way, Holloman AFB, 1990-91; ch. vestry mem. St. John's Ch., Alamogordo, N.Mex., 1987-89; coach Babe Ruth League/Little League, 1979-88; active Boy Scouts Am., 1980-85. Decorated DFC, Meritorious Svc. medal (2), Air medal (9), Air Force commendation medal. Mem. IEEE Computer Soc., Air Force Sgts. Assn. Episcopalian. Home: 3106 Thunder Rd Alamogordo NM 88310-4025

RIDER, JANE LOUISE, artist, educator; b. Brownfield, Tex., Sept. 11, 1919; d. Oscar Thomas and Florence Myrtle (Bliss) Halley; m. Rolla Wilson Rider Jr., Mar. 26, 1944 (dec. July 1992); 1 child, Dorothy Jo Neil. BA, UCLA, Westwood, 1943, tchg. diploma in secondary art; postgrad., Chgo. Art Inst., 1945, Chouinards, L.A., U. Oreg., Scripps, Claremont, Calif. Art supr., elem. and jr. high art tchr. Tulare (Calif.) City Schs. Dist., 1943-44, 44-45; art tchr. Beverly Hills (Calif.) High Sch., 1946-47; art tchr. jr. high gen. art and ceramics Santa Barbara City Schs., Goleta, Calif., 1964-66; head art dept., tchr. Morro Bay (Calif.) Jr.-Sr. High Sch. Dist., 1967-70; pvt. practice studio potter Cambria, Calif., 1961-85; artist, Santa Rosa, Calif., 1985—; founder, dir., tech. La Canada (Calif.) Youth House Art Program, 1953-60; dir. Pinedorado Art Show, Allied Arts Assn., Cambria, 1970-80. Exhibited in group shows Wine Country Artist's Spring Show, 1991, 92, 93, 94, 95, Gualala Art in Redwoods, 1986, 87, 88, Rodney Strong Vineyards Art Guild, 1994; revolving exhibits Berger Ctr. and Chalais-Oakmont, Santa Rosa, 1985-95, statewide art show Spring Palettes Mumm Cuvee Winery, Napa, Calif. 1994), Santa Rosa Art Guild show, 1986-94. Mem. Nat. League Am. Pen Woman, Inc. (artist 1994, 95), Santa Rosa Art Guild (rec. sec. 1989), Ctrl. Coast Watercolor Soc. (charter 1977). Republican. Home: 7019 Overlook Dr Santa Rosa CA 95409-6376

RIDGE, MARTIN, historian, educator; b. Chgo., May 7, 1923; s. John and Ann (Lew) R.; m. Marcella Jane VerHoef, Mar. 17, 1948; children: John Andrew, Judith Lee, Curtis Cordell, Wallace Karsten. AB, Chgo. State U., 1943; AM, Northwestern U., 1949, PhD, 1951. Asst. prof. history Westminster Coll., New Wilmington, Pa., 1951-55; from asst. prof. to prof. San Diego State Coll., 1955-66; prof. history Ind. U., Bloomington, 1966-79, Calif. Inst. Tech., 1980-95; vis. prof. UCLA, summer 1963, Northwestern U., summer 1959; editor Jour. Am. History, 1966-77; sr. research assoc. Huntington Library, 1977—; bd. dirs. Calif. Hist. Landmarks Commn., 1954-64; cons. in field; Tanner lectr. Mormon Hist. Assn., 1991; Whitsett Meml. lectr., Calif. State U., 1992. Author: Ignatius Donnelly: Portrait of a Politician, 1962, 91, The New Bilingualism: An American Dilemma, 1981, Frederick Jackson Turner: Wisconsin's Historian of the Frontier, 1986, Atlas of American Frontiers, 1992, My Life East and West, 1994; co-author: California Work and Workers, 1963, The American Adventure, 1964, America's Frontier Story, 1969, Liberty and Union, 1973, American History after 1865, 1981, Westward Expansion, 1982; editor: Children of Ol'Man River, 1988, Westward Journeys, 1989, History, Frontier and Section, 1993. Served with U.S. Maritime Service, 1943-45. William Randolph Hearst fellow, 1950; fellow Social Sci. Research Council, 1952; fellow Guggenheim Found., 1965; fellow Am. Council Learned Socs., 1960; Newberry fellow, 1964; Huntington fellow, 1974; Annenberg scholar U. So. Calif., 1979-80; recipient Best Book award Phi Alpha Theta, 1963, Gilberto Espinos prize N.Mex. Historical Review, 1989, Ray Allan Billington prize Western History Assn., 1991. Mem. Am. Hist. Assn. (Best Book award Pacific Coast br. 1963), Orgn. Am. Historians, Western History Assn. (v.p. 1985-86, pres. 1986-87), So. History Assn., Agrl. History Soc., Social Sci. History Soc., Hist. Soc. So. Calif. (pres. 1994—), Am. Hist. Assn. (v.p. Pacific coast br. 1994, pres. 1995—). Democrat. Address: Huntington Library San Marino CA 91108

RIDGWAY, DAVID WENZEL, educational film producer, director; b. Los Angeles, Dec. 12, 1904; s. David Nelson and Marie (Wenzel) R.; AB UCLA, 1926; MBA, Harvard U., 1928; m. Rochelle Devine, June 22, 1955. With RKO Studios, Hollywood, Calif., 1930-42; motion picture specialist WPB, Washington, 1942-43; prodn. mgr., producer Ency. Brit. Films, Wilmette, Ill., 1946-60; dir. film activities, exec. dir. Chem. Edn. Material Study, U. Calif. at Berkeley, 1960-90, dir., 1990—; producer, on-screen interviewer Am. Chem. Soc. TV series Eminent Chemists, 1981; advisor TV project Mech. Universe, Calif. Inst. Tech., 1985 also Am. Inst. Biol. Scis.; introduced CHEM study films to People's Republic of China, 1983. Lt. comdr. USNR, 1943-46. Recipient Chris award for prodn. CHEM Study Ednl. Films in Chemistry, Film Coun. Greater Columbus, 1962-63; Bronze medal, Padua, Italy, 1963; CINE Golden Eagle awards, 1962-64, 73; Gold Camera award for film Wondering About Things, U.S. Indsl. Film Festival, 1971; diploma of honour Internat. Sci. Film Assn. Festival, Cairo, 1st prize Am. Biol. Photog. Assn. for film MARS: Chemistry Looks for Life, 1978. Mem. Soc. Motion Pictures and TV Engrs. (chmn. San Francisco sect. 1970-72), Am. Chem. Soc., Am. Sci. Film Assn. (trustee 1974-81), Delta Upsilon, Alpha Kappa Psi. Clubs: Faculty (U. Calif.), Bohemian (San Francisco), Harvard (San Francisco). Author: (with Richard J. Merrill) The CHEM Study Story, 1969; also articles in ednl. jours. Home: 1735 Highland Pl Berkeley CA 94709-1074 Office: U Calif Lawrence Hall of Sci Berkeley CA 94720-5200

RIDGWAY, VIRGINIA FINNESTAD (GINGER RIDGWAY), archaeologist, physical anthropologist; b. Seattle, Sept. 2, 1939; d. Chester Ernest and Margaret Liberty (Bissell) Finnestad; m. Ronald A. Ridgway, 1960 (div. 1974); children: Derek, Paul, Cory. BA in Anthropology, Calif. State U., 1990. Owner, interior designer Quintessence Interior Design, San Diego, 1983-93; owner Moonridge Studios, San Diego, 1993—; physical anthropologist San Diego Mus, of Man, 1989—; instr. interior design Palomar Coll., San Marcos, Calif., 1986—. Mem. Am. Assn. Phys. Anthropologists, Southwestern Anthropology Assn., Soc. Calif. Archaeology, San Diego County Archaeology Soc. (membership chair 1985—), Paleopathology Assn. Office: Moonridge Studios 1010 Univ Ave Box 220 San Diego CA 92103

RIEBE, NORMAN JOHN, contractor; b. Michigan City, Ind., Mar. 9, 1903; s. William J. and Hattie (Fink) R.; m. Gwendolyn Ester Main (dec. 1924); children: Norman W., Harriet M. Kirchner; m. Eddie Lou Growden, 1978. PhD in Constrn., DSc (hon.). Registered profl. engr., Ind., Ark. Ariz. Draftsman, die designer Haskel and Barker Car Co.; with Steel Fabricating Corp., 1924-26; chief engr. Stefco Steel Co., 1926-36; pvt. practice Michigan City, Ind., 1936-40; v.p. R.E. McKee, Gen. Contractor, Los Alamos, N.Mex., 1947-52; v.p., gen. mgr. C.H. Leavell & Co., El Paso, 1952-61. Contbr. articles to profl. jours. Active Yuma County Bd. Adjustment; past vestryman Episc. Ch. Col. U.S. Army, 1932-62. Decorated Legion of Merit. Mem. Soc. Am. Mil. Engrs. (life), Ret. Officers Assn. (life), Associated Gen. Contractors (past pres. El Paso chpt. 1960), Am. Arbitration Assn., Am. Ordnance Assn. (past pres.), Masons, Shriners, Knights Templar. Republican. Home and Office: 14141 S Avenue 4 E Yuma AZ 85365-9339

RIECKE, HANS HEINRICH, architect; b. Münster, Westfalia, Germany, Mar. 30, 1929; came to U.S., 1955; s. Hans Joachim and Hildegard (Schwarze) R.; m. Elvira Maria Magdalena Kaatz, Nov. 30, 1954; children: Christine, Annette, Monica, Ralph, Heidi. Student architecture, Technische Hochschule, Hannover, Fed. Republic. Germany, 1953; BA in Architecture, U. Calif., Berkeley, 1957. Registered architect, Calif., Hawaii. Draftsman Orinoco Mining Co., Puerto Ordaz, Venezuela, 1954-55, H.K. Ferguson Co., San Francisco, 1956-57; architect, ptnr. Hammarberg and Herman, Oakland, Calif., 1957-74; prin. Hans Riecke, Architect Inc., Kahului, Maui, Hawaii, 1974-78, Riecke Sunnland Kono Architects Ltd, Kahului, Maui, Hawaii, 1978—. Bd. dirs. Kihei Community Assn., Maui, Hawaii, 1975-77, Seabury Hall, Makawao, Maui, 1980-82; chmn. Mayor's Com. on Housing, County of Maui, 1984. Recipient Merit award Pacific Coast Builders Con., Kahului, Hawaii, 1990. Fellow AIA (pres. Maui chpt. 1990); mem. Am. Arbitration Assn. (panel of arbitrators 1980). Office: Riecke Sunnland Kono Architect PO Box 1627 Kahului HI 96732-7627

RIECKMANN, JENS, German educator; b. Lüneburg, Germany, Sept. 29, 1944; came to U.S., 1971; s. Johannes and Gertrud (Krause) R. Staatsexamen, Göttingen (Germany) U., 1971; PhD, Harvard U., 1975. Asst. prof. U. Va., Charlottesville, 1975-80; Mellon faculty fellow Harvard U., Cambridge, Mass., 1980-81; prof. German, U. Wash., Seattle, 1981-93, U. Calif., Irvine, 1993—. Author: Thomas Mann's Magic Mountain, 1977, Aufbruch in die Moderne, 1985; contbr. articles to profl. jours. Fellow Am. Coun. Learned Socs., 1983-84, Guggenheim fellow, 1988-89. Mem. MLA, Am. Assn. Tchrs. German, Philol. Assn. Pacific Coast, German Studies Assn. Office: U Calif Dept German Irvine CA 92717

RIEDER, RONALD FREDERICK, public relations executive; b. Oshawa, Ont., Can., Nov. 10, 1932; s. Joseph Samuel and Minnie (Collis) R.; m. Pauline Feldman, Sept. 22, 1957; children: Mitchell, Stephen, Robert. BA, Sir George Williams U. (now Concordia U.), Montreal, 1955; BJ, Carleton U., Ottawa, 1956. Reporter Montreal Star, 1956-57; night city editor Valley News, Van Nuys, Calif., 1957-66; v.p. Hal Phillips & Assocs., Beverly Hills, Calif., 1966-71; dir. communications Daylin Inc., Beverly Hills, 1971-76; ptnr. The Phillips Group, Beverly Hills, 1976-87; dir. pub. affairs Jewish Fedn. Coun. Greater L.A., 1987-92; pres., prin. Ron Rieder and Assocs., Sherman Oaks, Calif., 1992—. Mem. Soc. Profl. Journalists, Pub. Rels. Soc. Am. Jewish. Home and Office: Ron Rieder and Assocs Ste 322 5420 Sylmar Ave Sherman Oaks CA 91401-5145

RIEDLSPERGER, MAX ERNST, history educator; b. San Luis Obispo, Calif., July 7, 1937; s. Helmuth Georg and Jean (Bennett) R.; m. Deanna Beckmann, Feb. 12, 1966; 1 child, Gretchen. AB, Wabash Coll., 1959; MA, U. Mich., 1961; PhD, U. Colo., 1969. Tchr. Eastern High Sch., Detroit, 1961-63, Day de Noc Community Coll., Escanaba, Mich., 1963-66; teaching assoc. U. Colo., Denver, 1966-67; instr. Colo. Women's Coll., Denver, 1967-68; asst. prof. Calif. Poly. State U., San Luis Obispo, 1969-72, assoc. prof., 1977-82, prof., 1983—, chmn. history dept., 1985-91; dir. internat. programs Calif. State U., Heidelberg, Fed. Republic Germany, 1983-84. Author: Lingering Shadow of Nazism, 1978; contbr. articles to profl. publs., chpts. to books. Bd. dirs. San Luis Obispo Mozart Festival, 1979-83, 84-85, v.p., 1985-86. Austrian Ministry of Edn. fellow, 1968-69; grantee Am. Coun. Learned Socs., 1972, NEH, 1976, U.S. Dept. Edn., 1986-88. Mem. Am. Hist. Assn., German Studies Assn. Democrat. Office: Calif Poly State U Dept History San Luis Obispo CA 93407

RIEGEL, BARBARA J., educator, clinical researcher, editor; b. St. Louis, Apr. 3, 1950; d. Lawrence Virgil and Shirley Jean (Weil) R.; m. m. Thomas A. Gillespie, May 23, 1978. Diploma, Jewish Hosp. Sch. Nursing, 1974; B in Nursing, San Diego State U., 1981; M in Nursing, UCLA, 1983; DNSc in Nursing, 1991. Staff nurse intensive care/coronary care unit Mo. Baptist Hosp., St. Louis, 1974-75; staff nurse coronary care unit Barnes Hosp., St. Louis, 1975-76; U.S. Army Community Health Orgn., Frankfurt, Fed. Republic of Germany, 1977-78; cardiovascular nurse specialist collaborative practice, San Diego, 1983-84, Scripps Clinic, La Jolla, Calif., 1984-85; faculty San Diego State U., 1984-87, assoc. prof., 1995—; adv. coun. San Diego State U. Sch. Nursing, 1983-85, Strategic Planning Comm., 1995—; clin. rschr. Sharp HealthCare, San Diego, 1990—; assoc. prof. San Diego State U., 1995—. Editor: Dreifus' Pacemaker Therapy: An Interprofessional Approach, 1986, Psychol. Aspects of Critical Care Nursing, 1989; editor Jour. Cardiovascular Nursing, 1986—; mem. editl. rev. bd. Heart and Lung, 1985—, Critical Care Nursing Quar., 1986—, Jour. of Advanced Med.-Surg. Nursing, 1988-89, Am. Jour. Critical Care, 1992—; contbr. articles to profl. jours. Fellow Am. Acad. Nursing; mem. ANA (cert.), AACN (mem. task force ethics in critical care rsch. 1983-84, rsch. com. 1990-92), Am. Heart Assn. (coun. on cardiovascular nursing, So. Calif. rep. 1993-95, automatic external defibrillator task force, co-chair rsch. sub task force 1994—, Am. Coll. Cardiology/Am. Heart Assn. acute myocardial infarction guideline com.), Sigma Theta Tau (chpt. pres. Gamma Gamma 1992-93). Republican. Home: 15578 Raptor Rd Poway CA 92064-6906 Office: Sharp Health Care Health Svcs R&D Dept 3131 Berger Ave San Diego CA 92123-2701

RIEGEL, BYRON WILLIAM, ophthalmologist; b. Evanston, Ill., Jan. 19, 1938; s. Byron and Belle Mae (Huot) R.; BS, Stanford U., 1960; MD, Cornell U., 1964; m. Marilyn Hills, May 18, 1968; children—Marc William, Ryan Marie, Andrea Elizabeth. Intern, King County Hosp., Seattle, 1964-65; asst. resident in surgery U. Wash., Seattle, 1965; resident in ophthalmology U. Fla., 1968-71; pvt. practice medicine specializing in ophthalmology, Sierra Eye Med. Group, Inc., Visalia, Calif., 1972—; mem. staff Kaweah Delta Dist. Hosp., chief of staff, 1978-79; mem. staff Visalia Community Hosp. Bd. dirs., asst. sec. Kaweah Delta Dist. Hosp., 1983-90. Served as flight surgeon USN, 1966-68. Co-recipient Fight-for-Sight citation for research in retinal dystrophy, 1970. Diplomate Am. Bd. Ophthalmology, Nat. Bd. Med. Examiners. Fellow ACS, Am. Acad. Ophthalmology; mem. AMA, Calif. Med. Assn. (del. 1978-79), Tulare County Med. Assns., Calif. Assn. Ophthalmology (v.p. 3d party liaison 1994—), Am. Soc. Cataract and Refractive Surgery, Internat. Phacoemulsification and Cataract Methodology Soc. Roman Catholic. Club: Rotary (Visalia). Home: 3027 W Keogh Ct Visalia CA 93291-4228 Office: 2830 W Main St Visalia CA 93291-4331

RIEGER, ELAINE JUNE, nursing consultant; b. Lebanon, Pa., June 7, 1937; d. Frank and Florence (Hitz) Plasterer; m. Jere LeFever Longenecker, Sept. 13, 1958 (div. 1968); children: Julie Lynn Porto, Jere Lee Longenecker; m. Bernhard Rieger, Oct. 12, 1971. Nursing diploma, Coatesville (Pa.) Hosp. Sch. of Nursing, 1958; BA, U. Redlands, 1976; MS in Healthcare Mgmt., Calif. State U., L.A., 1984. Cert. nursing adminstr., gerontol. nurse. From staff nurse to clin. supr. to dir. of nurses St. Johns Regional Med. Ctr., Oxnard, Calif., 1966-86; dir. of nurses Motion Picture and TV Hosp., Woodland Hills, Calif., 1987-89; with Care West, Nothridge-Reseda, Calif., 1989-90; dist. nurse mgr. Hillhaven Corp., Newbury Park, Calif., 1990-91; quality mgmt. nursing cons. Beverly Enterprises, Rancho Cordova, Calif., 1991-95, Memphis, 1995—. Home: 1817 Shady Brook Dr Thousand Oaks CA 91362-1335 Office: Beverly Enterprises 5350 Poplar Ave #406 Memphis TN 38119

RIENDL, PAUL ALEX, electrical engineer; b. Anchorage, Sept. 2, 1968; s. Paul and Eleanor (Braun) R.; m. Robin W. Brown. BS in Elec. Engring., U. Alaska, Fairbanks, 1991. Elec. engr. Raytheon TSSC, Anchorage, 1991-94; sys. engr. Fluor Daniel, Anchorage, 1994—. Mem. IEEE (awards chmn. 1994—). Home: PO Box 231276 Anchorage AK 99523-1276 Office: 801 B Street Ste 301 Anchorage AK 99501

RIENZI, THOMAS MATTHEW MICHAEL, retired army officer; b. Phila., Feb. 5, 1919; s. Luigi and Ethel (Johnston) R.; m. Claire M. Moore, Aug. 11, 1945; children: Thomas Matthew, Claire Mary. Student mech. engring., Lehigh U., 1937-38; BS in Mil. Sci., U.S. Mil. Acad., 1942; MEE, U. Ill., 1948; cert. in mgmt., U. Pitts., 1965; MA in Internat. Affairs, George Washington U., 1966. Commd. 2d lt. U.S. Army, 1942, advanced through grades to lt. gen., 1965; chief supply and maintenance div. signal sect. U.S. Army Pacific Hawaii, 1961; signal officer XVIII Airgorne Corps Ft. Bragg, N.C., 1961-63; exec. officer to chief signal officer, chief communications-electronics Washington, 1963-65, chief Combat Surveillance Office, Material Command, 1965-66; comdg. gen., comdt. Signal Center and Sch. Ft. Monmouth, N.J., 1966-68; comdg. gen., dep. comdg. gen 1st Signal Brigade S.E. Asia, Vietnam/Thailand/Laos, 1968-70; also dep. chief staff communications-electronics U.S. Army, Vietnam; comdg. gen Strategic Communications Command Pacific; also dep. chief of staff communications-electronics U.S. Army Pacific, 1970-72; dir. telecommunications and command and control Dept. Army, Washington, 1972-77; dep. dir. gen. NATO Integrated Communications System Mgmt. Agy., Brussels, 1977-79. Author: History of Communications-Electronics in Vietnam War, 1972; also articles. Permanent deacon Roman Catholic Ch., 1979—. Decorated D.S.M. with oak leaf cluster, Legion of Merit with oak leaf cluster, Bronze Star with oak leaf cluster, Air medal with 5 oak leaf clusters U.S.; Breast Order of Yun Hui Ribbon Nationalist China; Chung Mu Order of Merit Korea; Nat. Order Vietnam Knight Vietnam; recipient Papal award, 1970. Mem. Assn. U.S. Army (ann. mem.), Armed Forces Communications-Electronics Assn. (nat. officer 1972-77), Assn. Grads. U.S. Mil. Acad. (life), U. Lehigh Alumni Assn., U. Ill. Alumni Assn., George Washington U. Alumni Assn., Rotary (mem. Pearl Harbor chpt.). Home: 676 Elepaio St Honolulu HI 96816-4779

RIEPE, DALE MAURICE, philosopher, writer, illustrator, educator, Asian art dealer; b. Tacoma, June 22, 1918; s. Rol and Martha (Johnson) R.; m. Charleine Williams, 1948; children: Kathrine Leigh Riepe Herschlag, Dorothy Lorraine. B.A., U. Wash., 1944; M.A., U. Mich., 1946, Ph.D., 1954; postgrad. (Rockefeller-Watamull-McInerny fellow), U. Hawaii, Banaras and Madras, India, Tokyo and Waseda, Japan, 1949. Instr. philosophy Carleton Coll., 1948-51; asst. prof. U. S.D., 1952-54; asso. prof. U. N.D., 1954-59, prof., 1959-62, chmn. dept., 1954-62; prof., chmn. C.W. Post Coll., 1962-63; prof. philosophy SUNY, Buffalo, 1963—; chmn. dept. social scis., assoc. dean SUNY (Grad. Sch.), 1964—; exchange lectr. U. Man., 1955; vis. lectr. Western Wash. U., 1961; instr. marine electricity Naval Tng. Program, Seattle, 1943-45; mem. nat. screening bd. South Asia, Fulbright Selection, 1968-70, Asia, 1970-72; chmn. Fulbright Selection Com. for Asia, 1972, 82; vis. Fulbright lectr. Tokyo U., 1957-58, vis. lectr. Delhi U., 1967; exchange lectr. Moscow State U., 1979, Beijing Higher Edn. Inst., 1984; docent Albright-Knox Art Gallery; cons. Ctr. for Sci., Tech. and Devel., Council of Sci. adn Indsl. Rsch., Govt. India, 1978—, Inst. Fang Studies, 1987—; del. Cuban-N.Am. Philosophy Conf., Cuban Inst. Social Sci., 1982, Fang Centennial, Taiwan Nat. U., Taipeh, 1987, Hungarian-Am. Philos. Conf., Budapest, 1988; sports columnist The Town Crier. Author: The Naturalistic Tradition in Indian Thought, 1961, The Philosophy of India and its Impact on American Thought, 1970, Indian Philosophy Since Independence, 1979, The Owl Flies by Day, 1979, Asian Philosophy Today, 1981, Objectivity and Subjectivism in the Philosophy of Science, 1985, Philosophy and Revolutionary Theory, 1986, also articles in field.; editor: Phenomenology and Natural Existence, 1973, Philosophy and Political Economy; co-editor: The Structure of Philosophy, 1966, Contributions of American Sankritists in the Spread of Indian Philosophy in the United States, 1967, Radical Currents in Contemporary Philosophy, 1970, Reflections on Revolution, 1971, Philosophy at the Barricade, 1971, Contemporary East European Philosophy, 1971, Essays in East-West Dialogue, 1973, Explorations in Philosophy and Society, 1978; illustrator The Quick and the Dead, 1948; editorial com. Chinese Studies in History, 1970—, Chinese Studies in Philosophy, 1970—; publs. bd. Conf. for Asian Affairs; Editor various series.; editl. bd. Philos. Currents and Revolutionary World, 1972-86, Soviet Studies in Philosophy, 1979-87, Marxist Dimensions, 1987—,. Mem. com. overseers Chung-an U., Korea; bd. dirs. Evergreen Coll. Cmty. Orgn., 1988—; bd. dirs. Friends of Evergreen Coll. Libr., 1992—; active Henry Gallery, Frye Gallery; mem. Capital Mus. and Art Soc., Wash. State Hist. Soc., Seattle Art Mus. Fulbright scholar India, 1951-52; Fulbright lectr. U. Tokyo, 1957-58; U. Mich. fellow, 1945-48, Carnegie Corp. fellow Asian Studies, 1960-61; Am. Inst. Indian Studies research fellow, 1966-67; grantee 4th East-West Philosophers Conf., 1964; Penrose fund Am. Philos. Soc., 1963; SUNY Research Found., 1965, 66, 67, 69, 72, 73, Bulgarian Acad. Sci., 1975, London Sch. Oriental and African Studies grantee, 1971. Fellow Royal Asiatic Soc., Far Eastern Inst. (Tokyo); mem. AAAS, ACLU, Conf. Asian Affairs (sec. 1955), Am. Oriental Soc., Am. Philos. Soc., Indian Inst. Psychology, Philosophy and Psychical Research (hon. adviser), Soc. for Am. Philosophy (chmn. 1960), Am. Inst. Indian Studies (trustee 1965-66), Soc. for Creative Ethics (sec.), Am. Archaeol. Soc., Am. Assn. Asian Studies, Am. Math. Soc., Am. Aesthetics Soc., Internat. Soc. for Aesthetics, Am. Soc. Comparative and Asian Philosophy, Asiatic Soc. (Calcutta), Soc. for Philos. Study Dialectical Materialism (founding sec.-treas. 1962—), Soc. for Philos. Study Marxism (publs. sec. 1973-86), Union Am. and Japanese Profls. against Nuclear Omnicide (treas. U.S. sect. 1978—), Internat. House of Japan, t. Philosophers for Prevention Nuclear Omnicide, United Univ. Profs of SUNY-Buffalo (v.p.), Johnson Soc., Kokusai Bunka Shinkokai, Palm Springs Desert Mus., Seattle Art Mus., Tumwater Valley Golf Club, Alpha Pi Zeta. Office: SUNY 605 Baldy Hall Buffalo NY 14261

RIES, BARBARA ELLEN, alcohol and drug abuse services professional; b. Chgo., Oct. 27, 1952; d. Laurence B. and Genieveve (Wasiek) R. AAS in Human Svcs., Coll. of DuPage, Glen Ellyn, Ill., 1973; BA in Social Work, Sangamon State U., Springfield, Ill., 1978; postgrad., U. Mo., 1987-88, U. Tex., Arlington, 1991—. Cert. social therapist; nat. cert. alcohol and drug counselor; qualified chem. dependency counselor. Counselor Ray Graham Assn. for Handicapped, Addison, Ill., 1975-76; child abuse counselor Ill. Dept. Children and Family Svcs., Springfield, 1977-78; alcoholism counselor non-med. detoxification program S.H.A.R.E., Villa Park, Ill., 1978-80; outpatient therapist Ingalls Meml. Hosp., Harvey, Ill., 1980-83; dir. aftercare Lifeline Program, Chgo., 1984-85; case mgr. Lifecenter Program, Kansas City, Mo., 1985-87; counselor, acting clin. coord. Lakeside Hosp., Kansas City, 1988-89; program mgr., dir. chem. recovery programs Two Rivers Psychiat. Hosp., Kansas City, 1989-90; dir. day program and chem. dependency program SW Hosp./Citadel, Dallas, 1990—; dir. Flexcare program Dallas Meml. Hosp., 1990-91; pvt. practice Spokane, Wash., 1991—; program coord. Advanced Clin. Svcs., Federal Way, 1992-94. Recipient commendation Ingalls Hosp., 1983. Mem. Nat. Assn. Drug and Alcohol Counselors (cert.), Nat. Assn. for Relapse Prevention Counselors, Learning Disabilities Assn. Wash., Wash. Assocs. Alcoholism & Addictions Programs, Wash. Advs. Mentally Ill, Employee Assistance Profls. Am., Coalition Drug and Alcohol Leaders, Wash. Assn. Alcoholism and Drug Abuse Counselors, Nat. Assn. of Alcoholism and Drug Counselors (NCAC II), Am. Mktg. Assn., Dual Diagnosis Com.

RIES, RICHARD KIRKLAND, psychiatrist; b. Seattle, Dec. 6, 1947; s. Lincoln and Lorna (Kirkland) R.; m. Sarah Bledsoe, Aug. 6, 1977; 1 child, Stephanie. BA, Stanford U., 1970; MD, Northwestern U., 1975; postgrad. in Psychiatry, U. Wash., 1978. Diplomate Am. Bd. Psychiatry and Neurology. Asst. prof. psychiatry U. Wash. Med. Sch., Seattle, 1978-84, assoc. prof. psychiatry, 1984—; dir. in-patient psychiatry Harborview Med. Ctr., Seattle, 1978-92, dir. out-patient psychiatry, 1992—, dir. Harborview Mental Health Ctr., 1992—; dir. addictions edn. U. Wash. Med. Ctr., 1983—. Editor: Treatment Improvement Protocal Dual Diagnosis, 1994; contbr. articles to profl. jours. Bd. dirs. Wash. Physician Health Program, Seattle, 1990—. Fellow Am. Psychiat. Assn. (Teach of Psychiatry award 1992); mem. Am. Acad. Psychiats. Alcoholism and Addictions, Assn. Med. Educators Rsch. in Substance Abuse, Am. Soc. Addiction Medicine. Office: Harborview Med Ctr Dept Psychiatry Seattle WA 98104

RIESE, ARTHUR CARL, environmental engineering company executive, consultant; b. St. Albans, N.Y., Jan. 2, 1955; s. Walter Herman and Katherine Ellen (Moore) R. BS in Geology, N.Mex. Inst. Mining and Tech., 1976, MS in Chemistry, 1978; PhD in Geochemistry, Colo. Sch. Mines, 1982. Lic. geologist, N.C.; registered profl. geologist, N.C., S.C., Ark., Fla., Tenn., Wyo. Asst. petroleum geologist N.Mex. Bur. Mines and Mineral Resources, Socorro, 1973-76; geologist Nord Resources, Inc., Albuquerque, 1975; rsch. asst. N.Mex. Inst. Mining and Tech., Socorro, 1976-78; vis. faculty Colo. Sch. Mines, 1978-81; rsch. geochemist Gulf R & D Co., Houston, 1982-84; sr. planning analyst/mgr. tech. planning Atlantic Richfield Co., L.A., 1984-87; sr. v.p. Harding Assocs. and Harding Lawson Assocs., Denver, 1987—; mem. affiliate faculty U. Tex., Austin, 1983—; speaker, conf. chmn. in field. Numerous patents in field. Panel participant N.Mex. First, Gallup, 1990. Category winner Engring. Excellence award Conducting Engrs. Coun. Colo., 1991, 95. Mem. Am. Inst. Hydrology (cert. profl. hydrogeologist 1988), Am. Inst. Profl. Geologists (cert. geol. scientist 1988). Office: Harding Lawson Assocs 2400 Arco Tower 707 17th St Denver CO 80202-3404

RIESEN, AUSTIN HERBERT, psychologist, researcher; b. Newton, Kans., July 1, 1913; s. Emil Richert and Rachel (Penner) R.; m. Helen Haglin, July 20, 1939; children: Carol, Kent. AB, U. Ariz., 1935; PhD, Yale, 1939; DSc (hon.), U. Ariz., 1981. Rsch. assoc. Yale U., New Haven, Conn., 1939; asst. prof. psychobiology Yerkes Labs. Primate Biology, Orange Park, Fla., 1939-49; assoc. prof. U. Chgo., 1949-56, prof. psychology, 1956-62; prof. psychology U. Calif., Riverside, 1962-80, also chmn., 1962-68, prof. emeritus psychology, 1980-95, ann. faculty rsch. lectr., 1974; vis. rsch. prof. U. Rochester, 1951-53; researcher in psychiatry NIMH Found., Bethesda, Md., 1964-69; mem. vision rsch. com. NIH, 1959-63; rsch. lectr. Sigma Xi, U. Ariz., 1961, U. Calif., Riverside, 1975. Author: Development of Infant Chimpanzees, 1952; author, editor: Developmental Neuropsychology of Sensory Deprivation, 1975; editor: Advances in Psychobiology, 1972-76; contbr. numerous articles on visual development. Capt. USAF, 1943-46. Recipient emeritus faculty award U. Calif., 1992. Mem. NAS, APA (pres. divsn. 6 1965-67), Phi Beta Kappa, Sigma Xi, Phi Kappa Phi. Congregationalist. Office: Univ Calif Dept Psychology Riverside CA 92521

RIFE, MARY LOU, school counselor; b. Denver, Sept. 28, 1939; d. Paul Darlington and Marion Ambrose; m. David Bruce Rife, Sept. 1, 1961; children: Robin Lee, Renee Lou. BS, U. Colo., 1962; MA, U. No. Colo., 1965. Tchr. Brighton (Colo.) H.S., 1962, Bishop (Calif.) Union H.S., 1962-64; counselor Pioneer Elem. Sch., Quincy, Calif., 1965-66; counselor for disabled Plumas County, Calif., 1977-84; counselor/tchr. Portola (Calif.) Schs., 1984—; child custody investigator Plumas County Probation, 1994; home health social worker Ea. Plumas Dist. Hosp., Portola, 1994; pvt. counselor, Portola, 1993-94; juvenile justice commn. Plumas County, 1993—; chairperson impact team Portola Schs., 1985—. Mem. Beta Sigma Phi (citizen of yr. 1980).

RIFFENBURGH, RALPH SIDNEY, ophthalmologist; b. Washington, Feb. 27, 1923; s. Harry Buchholz and Ada Ernestine (Swallow) R.; m. Angelyn Faith Kelley, July 13, 1946; children: Roger R., Stephen K., Bruce A. Student, Calif. Inst. Tech., 1941-42; BS, Va. Polytech. Inst., 1943; MD, Med. Coll. of Va., 1947; MA, U. So. Calif., 1966. Diplomate Am. Bd. Ophthalmology; lic. med. bd. Calif. Instr. Washington U. Med. Sch., St. Louis, 1952-54; pvt. practice specializing in ophthalmology Pasadena, Calif., 1954—; from instr. to prof. U. So. Calif. Med. Sch., L.A., 1954—; eye pathologist, Doheny Eye Found., L.A., 1954—; mem. med. adv. bd. Planned Parenthood, Pasadena, 1984—, Young and Healthy, Pasadena, 1990—. Contbr. numerous articles to profl. jours. Mem. Tournament of Roses Com., 1968—; vice chmn. Sister City Com., Pasadena, 1972-84; res. comdr. S. Pasadena Police, 1975-88; pilot-lt. San Bernardino County Sheriff, Rialto, Calif., 1988—. Lt. comdr. USNR, 1950-52. Recipient 50 Yr. award Silver Wings, Cin., 1994. Fellow Am. Acad. Ophthalmology, Current Anthropology; mem. AMA, Calif. Med. Assn., L.A. County Med. Assn., Am. Anthropol. Assn. Office: Pasadena Eye Med Group 595 E Colorado Blvd Pasadena CA 91101

RIFFER, JEFFREY KENT, lawyer, educator; b. Gary, Ind., Sept. 8, 1953; s. Howard and Jeanne (Fischer) R.; m. Catherine Anne Conway, Oct. 22, 1985. BS, Ind. U., 1975, JD, 1978. Bar: Ind. 1978, Calif. 1979, U.S. Ct. Appeals (7th cir.) 1979, U.S. Ct. Appeals (9th cir.) 1981. From assoc. to ptnr. Kadison, Pfaelzer, Woodard, Quinn & Rossi, Los Angeles, 1979-87; ptnr. Jeffer, Mangels, Butler& Marmaro, Los Angeles, 1987—; adj. prof. Pepperdine U., Malibu, Calif., 1981—. Author: Sports and Recreational Injuries, 1985, (jour.) An Overview of Sex Discrimination in Amateur Athletics, 1983. Mem. ABA, Los Angeles County Bar Assn., Order of Coif, Beta Gamma Sigma, Beta Alpha Psi. Republican. Jewish. Office: Jeffer Mangels Butler & Marmaro 10th Flr 2121 Ave of the Stars Los Angeles CA 90067

RIGGS, FRANCIS PORTER, sculptor; b. N.Y.C., May 1, 1922; s. Francis Porter and Margery (Cummings) R.; m. June Rosemary Clarke, Sept. 13, 1945; children: John Prescott, Gillian Anne Brown, Jacqueline June Wahlstrom. Student, Pratt Inst., Bklyn., 1946-48. Indsl. designer Michael Hallward, Boston, 1948-50; sculptor with Alfred Duca, Boston, 1964-66; furniture designer Milo Baughman Design, Wellesley, Mass., 1967-72; instr. Brigham Young U., Provo, Utah, 1969-88; sculptor Ivins, Utah, 1975—. Mem. planning bd. Highland City, Utah, 1985-86. 1st lt. USAF, 1942-45, ETO. Recipient Purchase award Utah Arts Coun., Salt Lake City, 1976, Springville (Utah) Mus., 1989. Home and Studio: 654 Wisteria Way Ivins UT 84738-6316

RIGGS, FRANK, congressman; b. Louisville, Ky., Sept. 5, 1950; m. Cathy Anne Maillard; three children: Ryan, Matthew, Sarah Anne. BA, Golden Gate U. With Veale Investment Properties, until 1987; co-founder (with wife) Duncan Enterprises; mem. 102nd Congress 1st Calif. Dist., 1991-92, mem. 104th Congress, 1995—. With U.S. Army, 1972-75. Republican. Office: US House Reps 114 Cannon House Office Bldg Washington DC 20515-0501*

RIGGS, FRANK LEWIS, foundation executive; b. Indpls., Apr. 1, 1937; s. Frank Lloyd Riggs and Marie Loretta (Shaner) Ellis; m. Gail Evelyn Kershner, July 28, 1960 (div. 1987). BS in Bus. Adminstrn., U. Ariz., 1961, EdD, 1976; MBA, George Washington U., 1964. Mktg. adminstr. TRW Systems, L.A., 1964-67; assn. exec. Electric League Ariz., Phoenix, 1967-68; pub. affairs adminstr. Ariz. Regional Med. program Coll. of Medicine, U. Ariz., Tucson, 1968-73; dir. community affairs Tucson Med. Ctr., 1973-82; dir. pub. rels. Good Samaritan Med. Ctr., Phoenix, 1982-85; pres. The Lew Riggs Co., Phoenix, 1985-88; chief exec. officer Tucson Osteo. Med. Found., Tucson, 1988—; adj. prof. U. Ariz. Coll. Edn., Tucson, 1976-79; cons. to hosps. and physicians in group practice nationally; presenter in field. Editor: Public Relations Handbook, 1982; co-author booklets; contbr. articles to profl. jours. Chmn. pub. rels. Nat. Arthritis Found., Atlanta, 1985-87; participant Ariz. Strategic Planning and Econ. Devel., 1991-92. Lt. col. USAFR, 1987. Recipient Silver Anvil award Pub. Rels. Soc. Am., Golden Mike award Am. Legion Aux., MacEachern citation Acad. Hosp. Pub. Rels., Pres.'s citation Pub. Rels. Soc. Mem. Nat. Assn. Osteo. Founds. (pres. 1991—), Student Osteo. Med. Assn. (found. bd. dirs. 1990—), Acad. Hosp. Pub. Rels. (treas. 1980-81), Rotary. Republican. Methodist. Home: 5050 E South Regency Cir Tucson AZ 85711-3040 Office: Tucson Osteo Med Found 4280 N Campbell Ave Ste 200 Tucson AZ 85718-6585

RIGGS, FRED WARREN, political science educator; b. Kuling, China, July 3, 1917; (parents Am. citizens); s. Charles H. and Grace (Frederick) R.; m. Clara-Louise Mather, June 5, 1943; children: Gwendolyn, Ronald (dec.). Student, U. Nanking, China, 1934-35; BA, U. Ill., 1938; MA, Fletcher Sch. Law and Diplomacy, 1941; PhD, Columbia U., 1948. Lectr. CUNY, 1947-48; rsch. assoc. Fgn. Policy Assn., 1948-51; asst. dir. Pub. Adminstrn. Clearing House, N.Y.C., 1951-55; Arthur F. Bentley prof. govt. Ind. U., 1956-67; dir. Social Sci. Rsch. Inst. U. Hawaii, 1970-73, prof. polit. sci., 1967-87, prof. emeritus, 1987—; vis. asst. prof. Yale U., 1955-56; vis. lectr. Nat. Officials Tng. Inst., Korea, 1956; vis. prof. U. Philippines, 1958-59, MIT, 1965-66, CUNY, 1974-75; vis. scholar Inst. Soc. Studies, The Hague, 1972; sr. specialist East-West Ctr. U. Hawaii, 1962-63. Author: Pressures on Congress: A Study of the Repeal of Chinese Exclusion, 1950, reprinted, 1973, Formosa under Chinese Nationalist Rule, 1952, reprinted, 1972, The Ecology of Public Administration, 1961 (pub. in Portuguese, 1964), Administration in Developing Countries: The Theory of Prismatic Society, 1964 (pub. in Korean, 1966, Portuguese, 1968), Thailand: The Modernization of a Bureaucratic Polity, 1966, Organization Theory and International Development, 1969, Administrative Reform and Political Responsiveness: A Theory of Dynamic Balancing, 1971, Prismatic Society Revisited, 1973 (pub. in Korean, 1987), Applied Prismatics, 1978, (with Daya Krishna) Development Debate, 1987; author: (with others) Contemporary Political Systems: Classifications and Typologies, 1990, Handbook of Comparative and Development Public Administration, 1991, Terminology: Applications in Interdisciplinary Communication, 1993, Parliamentary vs. Presidential Government, 1993, Public Administration in the Global Village, 1994, International Studies Notes, 1994, Comparing Nations: Concepts, Strategies, Substance, 1994, Handbook of Bureaucracy, 1994; co-author, editor: Frontiers of Development Administration, 1971, Tower of Babel: On the Definition and Analysis of Concepts in the Social Sciences, 1975; mem. editorial bd. Pub. Adminstrn. Review, various other jours. Dir. INTERCOCTA project Internat. Social Sci. Coun., 1970-93; chair UNESCO com. INTERCONCEPT project, 1977-79; chair com. conceptual and terminol. analysis Internat. Polit. Sci. Assn., Internat. Sociol. Assn. and Internat. Social Sci. Coun., 1973-79; co-chair N.AM. roundtable on cooperation Social Sci. Info. Mpls., 1979; chair lexicographic terminology com. Dictionary Soc. N.Am., 1983-86. Fellow com. comparative politics Social Sci. Rsch. Inst., 1957-58, Ctr. Advanced Study in Behavioral Scis., 1966-67; honoree Eastern Regional Orgn. Pub. Adminstrn. Conf., 1983; Order of White Elephant conferred King of Thailand, 1986. Mem. COVICO (co-chair csom. on viable constitutionalism), Am. Polit. Sci. Assn., Am. Soc. Pub. Adminstrn. (chair comparative adminstrn. group 1960-71, Dwight Waldo award 1991), Internat. Studies Assn. (chair comparative interdisciplinary studies sect. 1970-74, v.p. 1970-71), Internat. Polit. Sci. Assn., Internat. Sociol. Assn., Assn. Asian Studies (chair com. rsch. materials S.E. Asia 1969-73). Home: 3920 Lurline Dr Honolulu HI 96816-4006 Office: U Hawaii Polit Sci Dept 2424 Maile Way Honolulu HI 96822-2223

RIGGS, HENRY EARLE, college president, engineering management educator; b. Chgo., Feb. 25, 1935; s. Joseph Agnew and Gretchen (Walser) R.; m. Gayle Carson, May 17, 1958; children: Elizabeth, Peter, Catharine. BS, Stanford U., 1957; MBA, Harvard U., 1960. Indsl. economist SRI Internat., Menlo Park, Calif., 1960-63; v.p. Icore Industries, Sunnyvale, Calif., 1963-67, pres., 1967-70; v.p. fin. Measurex Corp., Cupertino, Calif., 1970-74; prof. engring. mgmt. Stanford U., Calif., 1974-88, Ford prof., 1986-88, v.p. for devel., 1983-88; pres. Harvey Mudd Coll., Claremont, Calif., 1988—; bd. dirs. Mutual Funds of Capital Rsch. Group. Author: Accounting: A Survey, 1981, Managing High-Tech Companies, 1983, Financial and Cost Analysis, 1994; contbr. articles to Harvard Bus. Rev. Bd. dirs. Mt. Baldy Coun. Boy Scouts Am., 1993—. Baker scholar Harvard Bus. Sch., Boston, 1959; recipient Gores Teaching award Stanford U., 1980. Mem. Stanford U. Alumni Assn. (bd. dirs. 1990-94, chmn. 1993), Calif. Club, Pauma Valley Club, Sunset Club, Phi Beta Kappa, Tau Beta Pi. Congregationalist. Office: Harvey Mudd Coll Kingston Hall #201 Claremont CA 91711

RIGGS, JACKI PIERACCI, administrator, special education educator; b. San Jose, May 13, 1954; d. Leo A. Pieracci and Laura B. Petersen LaRue; m. Joseph N. Riggs III, Aug. 27, 1978; children: Joseph N. IV, Amanda Marie, Austin Spenser. BS in Child Devel., Brigham Young U., 1981; MA in Spl. Edn., U. N.Mex., 1983, PhD, 1992. Treatment liaison ATASC Project, Albuquerque, 1976-79; dir. alcohol edn. program Juvenile Ct., Albuquerque, 1978-79; tchr. Children's Psychiat. Hosp., Albuquerque, 1985-88; div. dir. Juvenile Facilities, Santa Fe, N.Mex., 1988-89; cabinet sec. N.Mex. Youth Authority, Santa Fe, 1989-90; pvt. practice cons. Albuquerque, 1990—; mem. Gov. Johnson's Transitional Team Children, Youth and Families Dept., 1994. Commr. Youth Authority Commn., Santa Fe, 1988; mem. Gov.'s Substance Abuse Adv. Coun., 1989; mem. Community Corrections Panel, 1988; vol. Bosque Prep. U. N.Mex. fellow, 1986-87, 87-88, 91-92. Mem. NAFE, Coun. for Exceptional Children, Women Execs. in State Govt., Nat. Assn. Juvenile Correctional Adminstrs.

RIGGS, JOHN B., architect; b. Tucson, Ariz., June 26, 1942; s. John Stark and Anna Lee (McAleb) R.; m. Barbara Wynn Bettner, Sept. 1, 1966 (div. Dec. 1976); children—Jeff, Bran; m. Jennifer J. Jewett, June 9, 1979; children—Courtney, Jennifer. B.Arch., U. Ariz., 1966. Registered architect, Ariz., Colo., Utah, Wash., Nev. Draftsman Terry Atkinson, Tucson, 1966-68, CNWC Architects, Tucson, 1968-69; designer Friedman & Jobusch, Tucson, 1969-70; prin., pres. Architecture One, Ltd., Tucson, 1970—; mem. Ariz. State Bd. Tech. Registration, Phoenix, 1980-87, chmn., 1983-84; mem. exam. com. Nat. Council Architectural Registration Bds., 1981-86, asst. coordinator exam. A com., 1984, coordinator, 1985, mem. examination planning com., 1986-87. Bd. dirs., v.p. Ariz. Theatre Co., Tucson, 1980—; adv. com. U. Ariz. Coll. Architecture, 1983—. Recipient numerous awards in field. Mem. AIA (bd. dirs. So. Ariz. chpt. 1976-77), Western Conf. Archtl. Bds. (chmn. 1986-87, bd. dirs., v.p. Ariz. chpt.). Democrat. Methodist. Club: Plaza (bd. govs. 1985—). Office: Architecture One Ltd 6303 E Tanque Verde Rd Ste 200 Tucson AZ 85715-3859

RIGGS, JUNE ROSEMARY, author, interior designer; b. Portishead, Eng., June 28, 1927; came to U.S., 1946; d. Arthur William Edward and Joan Ashworth (Keyte) Clarke; m. Francis Porter Riggs, Sept. 13, 1945; children: John Prescott, Gillian Anne Riggs Brown, Jacqueline June Riggs Wahlstrom. AS, Utah Valley C.C., Provo, Utah, 1974; BS magna cum laude, Brigham Young U., 1976. Interior designer Jordan Marsh, Peabody, Mass., 1964-69; instr. Brigham Young U., Provo, 1970-89. Author: Materials and Components of Interior Arch., 4th edit., 1992. Bd. dirs. S.W. Guild, St. George, Utah, 1992-95. Mem. Am. Soc. Interior Designers (allied), Phi Kappa Phi. Home: 654 Wisteria Way Ivins UT 84738-6316

RIGGS, ROBERT EDWON, law and political science educator; b. Mesa, Ariz, June 24, 1927; s. Lyle Alton and Goldie Esther (Motzkus) R.; m. Hazel Dawn Macdonald, Sept. 1, 1949; children: Robert, Richard, Russel, Rodney, Raymond, Reisa, Preston. BA, U. Ariz., 1952, MA, 1953, LLB, 1963; PhD in Polit. Sci., U. Ill., 1955. Bar: Ariz. 1963. Instr., then asst. prof. polit. sci. Brigham Young U., Provo, Utah, 1955-60, prof. J. Reuben Clark Law Sch., 1975-91, Guy Anderson prof. law, 1991-92; rsch. specialist Bur. Bus. and Pub. Rsch., U. Ariz., 1960-63; assoc. Riggs & Riggs, Tempe, Ariz., 1963-64; mem. faculty U. Minn., 1964-75, prof. polit. sci., 1968-75, dir. Harold Scott Quigley Center Internat. Studies, 1968-70. Author: Politics in the United Nations, 1958, reprinted 1984, The Movement for Administrative Reorganization in Arizona, rev. edit, 1964, (with Jack C. Plano) Forging World Order, 1967, Dictionary of Political Analysis, 1973, 2d edit. (with Jack C. Plano and Helenan S. Robin), 1982, US/UN: Foreign Policy and International Organization, 1971, (with Plano and others) Political Science Dictionary, 1973, (with I. J. Mykletun) Beyond Functionalism: Attitudes toward International Organization in Norway and the U.S, 1979, (with Jack C. Plano) The United Nations, 1988, 2d edit. 1994. Dem. precinct chmn., 1970-72, 76-80, 84-86; mem. Utah Dem. State Ctrl. Com., 1978-82; mayor Golden Valley, Minn., 1972-75; Dem. candidate for U.S. Congress from Minn. 3d dist., 1974; bd. dirs. Minn. UN Assn., 1967-74, Utah Legal Svcs. Corp., 1978-81; chmn. Utah State Adv. Com. to U.S. Commn. on Civil Rights, 1988-92. With AUS, 1945-47. Rotary Found. fellow Oxford (Eng.) U., 1952-53; James W. Garner fellow U. Ill., 1953-55; Rockefeller rsch. fellow Columbia U., 1957-58; NEH rsch. grantee, U. Minn., Brigham Young U. Mem. Phi Beta Kappa, Order of Coif, Phi Kappa Phi, Delta Sigma Rho, Phi Alpha Delta. Mem. Ch. of Jesus Christ of Latter-day Saints (missionary in Eng. 1947-49, in Ariz. 1993-94). Home: 2540 E Camino Mesa AZ 85213-9999

RIGGS, WILLIAM G(ERRY), art gallery director, museum studies educator; b. Frankfurt am Main, Germany, Dec. 12, 1950; (parents Am. citizens); s. William G. and Billie Jean (Johnson) R. BFA in Art, U. Okla., 1979, MLS in Museum Studies, 1987. Preparator U. Okla. Mus. Art, Norman, 1978-79; mgr. collections, preparator Okla. Art Ctr., Oklahoma City, 1979-81, asst. curator, registrar, 1982-84, curator collections, 1985-87; dir. Goddard Ctr. for Performing and Visual Arts, Ardmore, Okla., 1987-90; exhbn. coord. Colorado Springs (Colo.) Art Ctr., 1990, curator fine art, 1991; dir., curator Gallery Contemporary Art, U. Colo., Colorado Springs, 1991—, asst. prof. mus. studies, 1991—; lectr. in field. Author: (essays) Facets of Modern Art from the Oklahoma Art Centr, 1987, (catalog) The Rug Route: From Istanbul to Bokhara, 1990; contbr. articles to profl. publs.; curator Comtemporary Abstraction, 1986, Westheimer Mus. Acquisitions, 1988, Okla. Artists, A Centennial Exhbn., 1990, Art of New West, 1990-91, Colo. Photographers: 10 X 10, 1992, Front Range Revisited, 1992, Tom Wesselmann and Larry Rivers: Graphics and Multiples, 1965-92, also others. Mem. Colorado Springs Arts Commn., 1992—; mem. art and architecture com. USAF Acad., Colorado Springs, 1993—; mem. adv. com. Save Outdoor Sculpture, Colorado Springs Parks and Recreation Dept., 1992-93; mem. art com. Colorado Springs Airport. Mem. Am. Assn. Mus. (surveyor mus. assessment program II 1986-87), Assn. Coll. and Univ. Mus. and Galleries, Colo.-Wyo. Assn. Mus., Nat. Assn. for Mus. Exhbns. (regional rep. 1991-93). Home: 318 Locust Dr Colorado Springs CO 80907-4348 Office: U Colo Gallery Contemporary Art 1420 Austin Bluffs Pky Colorado Springs CO 80918-3733

RIHERD, JOHN ARTHUR, lawyer; b. Belle Plaine, Iowa, Sept. 1, 1946; s. William Arthur and Julia Elizabeth (Swalm) R.; m. Mary Blanche Thielen, July 5, 1969; children: Elizabeth, Teresa. BA, U. Iowa, 1968, JD, 1974; MA, Gonzaga U., 1992. Bar: Wash. 1974, Iowa 1974, U.S. Dist. Ct. (ea. dist.) Wash. 1974, U.S. Ct. Appeals (9th cir.) 1980, U.S. Dist. Ct. (we. dist.) Wash. 1981. Ptnr. Woods & Riherd, Spokane, Wash., 1974-83, Richter-

Wimberley, Spokane, 1983-88, Workland, Witherspoon, Riherd & Brajcich, Spokane, 1988-94; sr. v.p., gen. counsel Med. Svc. Corp. Ea. Wash., 1994—; adj. prof. Whitworth Coll., Spokane, 1988—; bd. dirs. MSC Life Ins. Co. Bd. dirs. Salvation Army, 1976—, Mead Sch. Dist., Spokane, 1986—, pres. 1992-94, Mayor's Leadership Prayer Breakfast, Spokane, 1986-90, Hospice of Spokane, 1984-87, 91—; pres. Spokane County Sch. Dirs. Assn., 1991-92; bd. dirs. MSC Life Ins. Co., 1993—; sr. v.p. Med. Svc. Corp. of Ea. Wash., 1994-95. Mem. ABA, Wash. Bar Assn. (mem. coun. pub. procurement and constrn. law sect. 1986-89, sec.-treas. gen. practice sect. 1989-92), Nat. Health Lawyers Assn., Am. Arbitration Assn. (panel mem. 1988—), North Spokane Exch. Club (pres. 1981), Spokane Country Club. Home: 1309 W Crestwood Ct Spokane WA 99218-2918 Office: Workland Witherspoon Riherd & Brajcich 714 Washington Mut Fin Ctr 601 W Main Ave Spokane WA 99201-0613

RIKELMAN, HERMAN, psychologist; b. N.Y.C., July 25, 1911; s. Max and Jennie (LeShak) R.; m. Augusta Komarow, Oct. 27, 1934; 1 child, Herbert F. BS, Fordham U., 1934; MA, Columbia U., 1936; cert., N.Y. Sch. Social Work, 1940. Lic. clin. psychologist, N.Y. Asst. supr. Jewish Family Svc., N.Y.C., 1938-43; dir. community svcs. Jewish Bd. Guardians, N.Y.C., 1944-55; exec. dir. Karen Horney Clinic, N.Y.C., 1955-64, Family Agent Program, Santa Monica, Calif., 1964-68; hypnotist pvt. practice, Newport Beach, Calif., 1968—, clin. psychologist, 1968—, marriage family therapist, 1968—; Examiner Civil Svc. Commn., N.Y.C., 1955-57, chmn. Community Mental Health Svcs., N.Y.C., 1955-60, mem. Mental Health Com. Govt. Affairs, N.Y.C., 1960-62, Mental Health Workshop Cunard steamship, N.Y.C., Caribbean, 1963. Hon. designee Judea Hall of Fame, 1956. Home: 3010 Park Newport Apt 315 Newport Beach CA 92660-5838

RILES, WILSON CAMANZA, educational consultant; b. Alexandria, La., June 27, 1917; m. Mary Louise Phillips, Nov. 13, 1941; children: Michael, Narvia Riles Bostick, Wilson, Phillip. B.A., No. Ariz. U., 1940; M.A., 1947, LL.D., 1976; LL.D., Pepperdine Coll., 1965, Claremont Grad. Sch., 1972, U. So. Calif., 1975, U. Akron, 1976, Golden Gate U., 1981; L.H.D., St. Mary's Coll., 1971, U. Pacific, 1971, U. Judaism, 1972. Tchr. elem. schs., adminstr. pub. schs. Ariz., 1940-54; exec. sec. Pacific Coast region Fellowship of Reconciliation, Los Angeles, 1954-58; with Calif. Dept. Edn., 1958-83, dep. supt. pub. instrn., 1965-70, supt. pub. instruction, 1971-83; pres. Wilson Riles & Assocs., Inc., 1983—; dir. emeritus Wells Fargo Bank, Wells Fargo Co. Past mem. editorial adv. bd.: Early Years mag. Ex-officio mem. bd. regents U. Calif., 1971-82; ex-officio trustee Calif. State Univs. and Colls., 1971-82; nat. adv. council Nat. Schs. Vol. Program; former mem. council Stanford Research Inst.; former mem. adv. council Stanford U. Sch. Bus.; former mem. adv. bd. Calif. Congress Parents and Tchrs.; former trustee Am. Coll. Testing Program; former mem. Edn. Commn. of States; past 2d v.p. Nat. PTA.; former trustee Found. Teaching Econs.; former mem. Joint Council Econ. Edn.; former mem. Nat. Council for Children and TV. With USAF, 1943-46. Recipient Spingarn medal NAACP, 1973. Mem. Assn. Calif. Sch. Adminstrs., Cleve. Conf., NAACP (Spingarn medal 1973), Nat. Acad. Pub. Adminstrn., Phi Beta Kappa. Office: 400 Capitol Mall Ste 1540 Sacramento CA 95814-4408

RILEY, ANN J., state legislator, technology specialist; b. Memphis, Oct. 27, 1940; m. Ray T. Riley, Apr. 28, 1962. BSBA, U. Albuquerque, 1985; MBA, Webster U., 1988; cert. in pub. policy, Harvard U., 1994. Loan officer Ravenswood Bank, Chgo., 1970-74; mgr. dist. sales Security Lockout, Chgo., 1974-77; owner AR Fasteners, Albuquerque, 1977-82; tech. transfer agt. Sandia Nat. Labs., Albuquerque, 1983—; mem. N.Mex. Senate, Santa Fe, 1993—; resolutions chair energy com. Nat. Order of Women Legil. Nat. Conf. State Legislators. Bd. dirs. All Faiths Receiving Home. Albuquerque, 1989-92, Law Enforcement Acad., Santa Fe, 1991-92; active Leadership Albuquerque, 1991, state federal task force U.S. Office Sci. & Tech., 1995. Pub. Policy Inst. fellow John F. Kennedy Sch. Govt. Harvard U. Democrat. Home: 10201 Karen Ave NE Albuquerque NM 87111-3633

RILEY, ANN L., management professional; b. Mineola, N.Y., July 25, 1950. BA in Ecology, Polit. Sci., Cornell Coll., 1972; M of Landscape Architecture, U. Calif., Berkeley, 1977, PhD in Environ. Planning, 1987. Lobbyist Sierra Club, Washington, 1971; environ. platform researcher, speech writer Senator Dick Clark of Iowa, 1971-72; researcher U.S. Dept. Interior, Washington, 1972; community organizer Hawkeye Area Community Action Program, Cedar Rapids, Iowa, 1972; dir. land use planning program Johnson County Health Dept., Iowa City, 1973-74; contract field worker U.S. Geol. Survey and Wyo. Geol. Survey, 1975; producer environ. projects reports Upper Green River Basin, Wyo., 1975-77; chmn. Nat. Environ. Health Assn. Land Use Com., Calif., 1975-76; developed landscape planning and water conservation program Calif. Dept. Water Resources, Sacramento, 1976-91; program mgr. integrated pest mgmt. program Calif. Dept. Water Resources, 1977-83, staff environ. planner, 1979-82, project mgr. summary report on San Francisco delta, 1983-84, program mgr. statewide stream restoration and flood control program, 1985-88, chief fin. assistance and environ. rev. br., 1988-91; exec. dir. Golden State Wildlife Fedn., Berkeley, 1991-94; exec. dir. S.W. region Coalition to Restore Urban Waters, 1994—; instr. Vista Coll., 1980-81. Founder, leader Orgn. of Women in Landscape, 1976-86; founder Yeast Bay Brewers, 1977-79; founder, mem. steering com. Women's Environ. Network, 1979-85, Coalition to Restore Urban Waters, 1993; founder Urban Creeks Coun., 1982—. Beatrix Farrand Grad. scholar, 1974-75, Nat. Environ. Health Assn. scholar, 1974-75; recipient award for involvement in Wildcat-San Pablo Creek Flood Control Project, 1986, Ann. award East Bay Lesbian/Gay Dem. Club, 1987, Highest Svc. award Urban Creeks Coun., 1989, Honor award Calif. Coun. Landscape Architects, 1989, award fro role in promotion of River Greenways in U.S. from Audubon Soc., 1991; named one of 20 San Francisco Bay Area East Bay Citizens Who Made a Difference by East Bay Express, 1987. Office: Coalition Restoer Urban Wts Ste 107 1250 Addison St Berkeley CA 94702-1706

RILEY, CARROLL LAVERN, anthropology educator; b. Summersville, Mo., Apr. 18, 1923; s. Benjamin F. and Minnie B. (Smith) R.; m. Brent Robinson Locke, Mar. 25, 1948; children: Benjamin Locke, Victoria Smith Evans, Cynthia Winningham. A.B., U. N.Mex., 1948, Ph.D., 1952; M.A., UCLA, 1950. Instr. U. Colo., Boulder, 1953-54; asst. prof. U. N.C., Chapel Hill, 1954-55; asst. prof. So. Ill. U., Carbondale, 1955-60, assoc. prof., 1960-67, prof., 1967-86, Disting. prof., 1986-87, Disting. prof. emeritus, 1987—, chmn. dept., 1979-82, dir. mus., 1972-74; rsch. assoc. lab. anthropology Mus. N.Mex., 1987-90, sr. rsch. assoc., 1990—; rsch. collaborator Smithsonian Instn., 1988—; adj. prof. N.Mex. Highlands U., 1989—. Author: The Origins of Civilization, 1969, The Frontier People, 1982, expanded edit., 1987, Rio del Norte, 1995; editor: Man Across the Sea, 1971, Southwestern Journals of Adolph F. Bandelier, 4 vols., 1966, 70, 75, 84, Across the Chichimec Sea, 1978 and others; contbr. numerous articles to profl. jours. Served in USAAF, 1942-45. Decorated 4 battle stars; grantee Social Sci. Research Council, NIH, Am. Philos. Soc., Am. Council Learned Socs., NEH, others. Home and Office: 1106 6th St Las Vegas NM 87701-4311

RILEY, CHARLES LOGAN (REX RILEY), hospital administrator; b. Toledo, Jan. 20, 1946; s. Charles Allen and Phyllis Mary (Logan) R.; m. Rosemarie Jeanette Webster, Apr. 10, 1971; children: Paul Anthony, Ross Evan. BA, U. Mich., 1968; MHA, U. New South Wales, 1976. Diplomate Am. Coll. Healthcare Execs. Indsl. engr. Internat. Harvester, Melbourne, Victoria, Australia, 1972-74; with Royal Women's Hosp., Melbourne, 1974-79; chief operating officer Preston (Victoria) & Northcote Community Hosp., 1979-84, Valley Children's Hosp., Fresno, Calif., 1989—; chief exec. officer Geelong (Victoria) Hosp., 1984-89; bd. dirs. Hosp. Coun. No. and Cen. Calif., Calif. Hosp. Polit. Action Co.; vice-chmn. Fresno/Madera Hosp. Conf. Mem. Leadership Fresno, 1990-91; mem. exec. com. Combined Health appeal, 1989-90; active Ronald McDonald House, Fresno, 1990-92; vice chair Fresno-Madera Hosp. Conf.; bd. dirs. Hosp. Coun. No. and Ctrl. Calif., Calif. Hosp. PAC. Decorated Navy Commendation medal; scholar Buehler Found., 1964, Health Dept. Victoria, 1973. Fellow Australian Coll. Healthsvc. Execs. (registrar 1983-85, v.p. 1985-87, pres. 1987-88); mem. Am. Coll. Healthcare Execs., Rotary. Home: 2287 W Pinedale Ave Fresno CA 93711-7109 Office: Valley Children's Hosp 3151 N Millbrook Ave Fresno CA 93703-1425

RILEY, DAWN C., educational philosopher, special education educator, researcher; b. Rochester, N.Y., Mar. 18, 1954; d. John Joseph Jr. and June Carol (Cleveland) R. BA in Edn., Polit. Sci., SUNY, 1976; MEd, in Special Edn., summa cum laude, U. Ariz., 1980; PhD, Univ. Calif., Berkeley, 1994. Cert. multiple subject credential (K-Coll.), specialist credential (K-12), Calif., coun. of educators for deaf; elem. permanent credential, N.Y. Elem. sch. tchr., 4th grade Escola Americana do Rio de Janeiro, Brazil, 1975; pvt. practice, comml. artist Rochester, 1972-80; elem. tchr. Rochester City Sch. Dist., 1976-78; rsch. asst., summer vestibule program The Nat. Tech. Inst. for Deaf, 1976-79; tchr. English, 7th-12th grades The Calif. Sch. for Deaf, 1980-94; rsch. asst. to Dr. Richard J. Morris The Univ. Ariz., 1978-80; rsch. asst., Calif. new tchr. support project The Far West Lab. for Ednl. R & D., San Francisco, 1989; chair high sch. English dept. The Calif. Sch. for Deaf, 1990—; coord. & devel. Practical Lang. in Applied Settings Program, 1981-82; chair Computer Curriculum Com., 1982-84, Critical and Creative Thinking Skills Com., 1983-84; coord. Gifted and Talented Program, 1983—. Recipient Kate Navin O'Neill Grad. scholar Univ. of Calif., Berkeley, 1989; University fellow, 1978-80, Evelyn Lois Corey fellow, 1990; Recipient Sustained Superior Accomplishment award Calif. Dept. Edn., 1991. Mem. AAUW, Nat.Coun. Tchrs. of English, Am. Ednl. Rsch. Assn., Am. Assn. Colls. for Tchr. Edn., Philosophy of Edn. Soc., John Dewey Soc., Phi Beta Kappa. Home: 3015 58th Ave Oakland CA 94605-1123 Office: Calif Sch for the Deaf 39350 Gallaudet Dr Fremont CA 94538-2308

RILEY, ERIN LEE, biology educator, forensic scientist; b. Loveland, Colo., June 3, 1963; d. Merlin Blaine Jr. and Lynn Claudette (Hart) R. BS, Colo. State U., 1987; MS, U. Strathclyde, Glasgow, Scotland, 1988. Forensic DNA analysis researcher U.S. Army Criminal Investigation Lab.-Europe, Frankfurt, Fed. Republic of Germany, 1988; instr. biology Merced (Calif.) Coll., 1990; criminalist L.A. Police Dept. Scientific Investigation Div., L.A., 1990—; cons. U.S. Army Criminal Investigation-Europe, Frankfurt, 1988-89; DNA rsch. scientist FBI Acad., Quantico, Va., 1991-92. Fellow Am. Bd. Criminalistics (cert. in criminalistics and molecular biology); mem. AAAS, Am. Acad. Forensic Scis., Forensic Sci. Soc., Internat. Soc. Forensic Scis., Internat. Soc. Haemogenetics, Internat. Assn. Identifications (mem. innovative and gen. techniques com. 1994—), Calif. Assn. Criminalists, So. Calif. DNA Study Group (co-chmn. 1993—), Phi Theta Kappa.

RILEY, HENRY NORTON, computer scientist educator; b. Independence, Mo., Oct. 30, 1932; s. Augustus Mayfield and Elizabeth (Norton) R.; m. Marie Soderstrom, Sept. 7, 1957; children: Michael, Katherine, Elizabeth, Thomas, Patricia. BA in Math., Park Coll., 1954; MS in Computer Sci., Calif. State Polytech. U., 1985; MS in Mgmt. Info. Sys., Claremont Grad. Sch., 1988, PhD in Mgmt. Info. Sys., 1991. Software engr. Burroughs Corp., Chgo., 1957-82; assoc. prof. Calif. State Polytech. U., Pomona, 1981—. Co-author: (with N. Ahituv, A. Neumann) Principles of Information Systems for Management, 4th edit., 1994. Mem. Assn. Computing Machinery. Home: 1237 Oak Mesa Dr La Verne CA 91750-1516 Office: Calif State Polytech U 3801 W Temple Ave Pomona CA 91768-2557

RILEY, JOHN ECKEL, retired academic administrator; b. Haverhill, Mass., Jan. 23, 1909; s. George Duncan and Mary Jane (Oliver) R.; m. Dorcas Mine Tarr, June 1, 1932; children: Jane Noel, Lynn Roberta, Gail Katherine. BA, Ea. Nazarene Coll., 1931, DD, 1950; MA, Boston U., 1931. Ordained Church of the Nazarene, 1933. Pastor Ch. of the Nazarene, Auburn, Maine, 1931-32, Livermore Falls, Maine, 1932-35, New Haven, 1935-38, South Portland, Maine, 1938-42, Toronto, Ont., 1942-44, Nampa, Idaho, 1944-52; faculty N.W. Nazarene Coll., Nampa, 1944-52, pres., 1952-73, pres. emeritus, 1973—; mem. higher commn. N.W. Assn. Secondary and Higher Schs., Seattle, 1954-60; mem. State Commn. on the Arts, Boise, Idaho, 1960-62; edn. cons. Schs. and Colls. of the Dept. World Missions, Kansas City, Mo., 1973-76. Author: The Golden Stairs, 1947, This Holy Estate, 1957, From Sagebrush to Ivy: Story of NNC, 1988, R & R: Recollections and Reflections, 1992; co-author: The Wind Runs Free, 1981. Recipient Disting. Citizen's award Idaho Statesman, Boise. Mem. Nampa (Idaho) Athletic Club, Lions Club, Nampa (Idaho) Indsl. Corp., Nampa C. of C. (life mem.), Nampa Kiwanis Club (hon. mem.). Republican. Home: 207 Mountain View Dr Nampa ID 83686-8867

RILEY, JOHN GRAHAM, economics educator; b. Christchurch, New Zealand, Dec. 8, 1945; came to U.S., 1969; s. Charles Graham and Patricia (White) R.; m. Rita Jane Stulin, July 5, 1971 (div. 1981); m. Beverly Fong Lowe, Oct. 16, 1982; 1 child, Alexandra Lowe Riley. BS, U. Canterbury, Christchurch, 1967, M in Commerce, 1969; PhD, MIT, 1972. Instr. Boston Coll., 1971-72, asst. prof., 1972-73; asst. prof. econs. UCLA, 1973-76, assoc. prof., 1976-80, prof., 1980—, chmn. dept., 1987-90, 92—. Assoc. editor Am. Econs. Rev., 1983-85, co-editor, 1985-87; contbr. numerous articles to profl. jours. Co-chair Ch. and Synagogue Assocs. Inc. Erskine fellow U. Canterbury, 1987; NSF grantee, 1975-89. Fellow Econometrics Soc. Office: UCLA Dept Econs 2263 Bunche Hall Los Angeles CA 90024

RILEY, MARILYN GLEDHILL, communications executive; b. Pitts., Pa., July 17, 1954; d. John Edward and Mary Elizabeth (Ogden) Gledhill; m. John F. Riley Jr. AS with high honors, Community Coll. of Allegheny County, 1981; BS in Bus. Adminstrn. cum laude, Robert Morris Coll., 1985. With MODCOM Assocs., Pitts., 1977-79, asst. account exec., 1979-82, account exec., 1982-84; gen. mgr. MODCOM Advt., Pitts., 1984-90, v.p., gen. mgr., 1989-90; dir. comms. Allegheny County Med. Soc., Pitts., 1990-93; advt. mgr. Intergroup Healthcare Corp., Phoenix, Ariz., 1994; mgr. advt. and media rels. Samaritan Group Inc., Phoenix, 1995—; guest spkr. Pa. State U., Robert Morris Coll., Allegheny C.C., 1987; mem. pub. issues and info. com. adolescent resource network adv. bd. Hosp. Coun. of West Pa., 1990-93; counselor Small Bus. Devel. Ctr., 1995. Mem. editorial bd. Nursing News, 1991; editor: Valley of the Sun Gardener. Communications vol. North Hills Art Festival, McCandless, Pa., 1986-87; judge Jefferson (Pa.) Hosp. Poster Contest, 1987; bd. mgrs. YMCA North Boroughs; reading tutor Greater Pitts. Literacy Coun., 1988-89; bd. dirs. Rachel Carson Homestead Assn. Recipient Communications Mgmt. Honors award Robert Morris Coll. Mem. Bus. and Profl. Advt. Assn. (bd. dirs., v.p. edn.), North Hills C. of C., SMC Pa. Small Bus. Coun., Pitts. Advt. Club, Phoenix Advt. Club, Alpha Tau Sigma. Office: Samaritan Group Inc 3141 N 3rd Ave Phoenix AZ 85013

RILEY, RICHARD LEON, psychiatrist, consultant; b. Omak, Wash., Jan. 31, 1932; s. George Maurer and Lounettie Grace (Chapman) R.; m. Carol Ann Franklin (div. Dec. 1971); children: Kevin, Erin, Brian, Patrick, Michael; m. Renata Karolina Roeber, Dec. 28, 1972; 1 child, Alexandra Elizabeth. Student, El Camino Coll., 1954-56, U. Calif., L.A., 1956-57; BS in Medicine, Duke U., 1960; MD, U. So. Calif., L.A., 1961. Bd. cert. pediatrics; cert. psychiat. examiner, Calif. Pediatric intern L.A. (Calif.) Children's Hosp., 1961-62, pediatric resident, 1962-64, attending physician, 1964-69; pediatric cons. Gen. Hosp., Peace Corp. APIA, Western Samoa, 1969-70; child psychiatry fellowship Pasadena (Calif.) Guidance Clinic, 1971-73, clin. supr., 1973-75; med. dir., acting exec. dir. San Luis Valley Comp. Cmty. Mental Health Ctr., Alamosa, Colo., 1975-77; chief outpatient dept., cons. Humboldt County Dept. Mental Health, 1977-79; pvt. practice psychotherapy and pharmacotherapy, 1979-86; behavioral pediatrician U.S. Army Exceptional Family Member Program, Stuttgart, Germany, 1986-87; chief EFMP U.S. Army Exceptional Family Member Program, Shape, Belgium, 1987-88, evaluator William Beaumont Army Med. Ctr., 1988-91; cons. Indian Health Svc., Portland, 1991—; staff Kaiser-Permanente Med. Group, 1964-69, psychiatrist, supr., 1973-75; asst. clin. prof. pediatrics U. Calif., Irvine, 1967-69; pediatric cons. and lectr. Hope Ship Ceylon, Sri Lanka, 1968; presenter in field. Contbr. articles to profl. jours. With USN, 1950-54. Mem. Am. Psychiat. Assn., Am. Acad. Pediatrics, Am. Acad. Child and Adolescent psychiatry, Wash. State Psychiat. Soc. Home: 7132 W Greenwood Rd Spokane WA 99204-9160 Office: Indian Health Svc PO Box 357 Wellpinit WA 99040-0357

RILEY, STANLEY ROBERT, psychologist; b. Fresno, Calif., Jan. 13, 1928; s. Amos Harvey Riley and Mae Therese (Eickholt) Meek; m. Gloria Joan Riley, June 21, 1953 (dec.); m. Jacquelyn Joy Riley, June 24, 1989; children: Jack David, Michael Patrick, Suzanne Theresa, David Arthur. BA, Fresno (Calif.) State Coll., 1955, MA, 1970; PhD, U. Santa Barbara, 1983. Psychologist Fresno Unified Schs., 1969-89, Jefferson Union H.S., Daly City, Calif., 1989-94, Dept. Edn., State of Hawaii, Maui, Hawaii, 1994—; owner Ed-Psych. Svcs., Fresno, 1975-94. Author: Learning Style Inventory, 1994, Riley Inventory and Basic Learning Skills, 1993, Learning Process Skills, 1988 (diskette) Learning Skills Profile, 1985, (diskettes) Learning Skills Exercises, 1985, Learning Process Skills, 1988, Riley Inventory and Basic Learning Skills, 1993, Learning Style Inventory, 1994, Lose The Brat, Keep The Child, 1995, Behavior Response Activity Test, 1995. Mem. NEA, Calif. Edn. Assn., Am. Psychol. Assn.

RILLERA, MARRI J., publisher, writer; b. Kansas City, Mo., Sept. 15, 1948; d. Frank and Helen (Petrie) Leech; adopted d. Conroy and Helen (Rosenwald) Webster; m. Sandy Baron, 1970 (div. 1974); m. Steve Butch Rillera, June 12, 1976; children: Wendy Morgan, Allison Rillera. BA in Social and Human Ecology, Antioch Coll., Yellow Springs, Ohio, 1976. Founder, pres. Triadoption Libr., Inc., Westminster, Calif., 1978-88; pres. Pure, Inc., Westminster, 1985—. Author: Adoption Search Book: Techniques for Tracing People, 1981, Adoption Encounter: Hurt, Transition, Healing, 1987, Gracini - Twelve Sacred Stones, 1995; author-co-author: Cooperative Adoption, 1985. Dir.-at-large Am. Adoption Congress, Washington, 1982-83; trustee Internat. Soundex Reunion Registry, Carson City, Nev., 1980—; mem. adv. coun., bd. dirs. Concerned United Birth Parents, DesMoines, Iowa, 1983-86. Office: Pure Inc PO Box 638 Westminster CA 92684-0638

RIMA, RICHARD HERBERT, satellite communications engineer; b. Decorah, Iowa, Nov. 21, 1946; s. Earl John Sr. and Marian Lucille (Donald) R.; m. Donna Lee Siska, Aug. 11, 1984. BA in Math. and Econs., Luther Coll., 1969; BS in Elec. Engring., Air Force Inst. Tech., 1974, MS in Elec. Engring., 1974. Commd. 2d lt. USAF, 1969, ret., 1993, advanced through grades to col., 1991; comdr. Detachment 15, 2140th Comm. Group, Levkas, Greece, 1978-79; chief tactical engring. divsn. 2nd Combat Comm. Group, Patrick AFB, Fla., 1979-82; systems integration engr. U.S. Ctrl. Command, MacDill AFB, Fla., 1983-86; comdr. 2134 Comm. Squadron, Sembach Air Base, Germany, 1986-89; chief DSCS Network Mgmt. Divsn. Def. Info. Systems Agy., Arlington, Va., 1989-91; chief C4 Space Systems Divsn. The Joint Staff/J6, Washington, 1991-93, chief CINC Support Divsn., 1993; prin. satellite comm. engr. Femme Comp Inc., Sterling, Va., 1993-94; prin. satellite comm. engr., dep. program mgr. Femme Comp Inc., Colorado Springs, Colo., 1994—. Decorated Def. Superior Svc. medal. Mem. Armed Forces Comm. Electronics Assn., Air Force Assn., The Planetary Soc., Sertoma Club. Republican. Lutheran. Home: 20010 Chisholm Trl Monument CO 80132-8069 Office: Femme Comp Inc 1925 Aerotech Dr Ste 212 Colorado Springs CO 80916-4219

RIMOIN, DAVID LAWRENCE, physician, geneticist; b. Montreal, Que., Can., Nov. 9, 1936; s. Michael and Fay (Lecker) R.; m. Mary Ann Singleton, 1962 (div. 1979); 1 child, Anne; m. Ann Piilani Garber, July 27, 1980; children: Michael, Lauren. BSc, McGill U., Montreal, 1957, MSc, MD, CM, 1961; PhD, Johns Hopkins U., 1967. Asst. prof. medicine, pediatrics Washington U., St. Louis, 1967-70; assoc. prof. medicine, pediatrics UCLA, 1970-73, prof., 1973—, chief med. genetics, Harbor-UCLA Med. Ctr., 1970-86; dir. dept. pediatrics, dir. Med. Genetics and Birth Defects Ctr., 1986—; Steven Spielberg chmn. pediatrics Cedars-Sinai Med. Ctr., L.A., 1989—; chmn. coun. Med. Genetics Orgn., 1993. Co-author: Principles and Practice of Medical Genetics, 1983, 90; contbr. articles to profl. jours., chpts. to books. Recipient Ross Outstanding Young Investigator award Western Soc. Pediatric Research, 1976, E. Mead Johnson award Am. Acad. Pediatrics, 1976. Amllow ACP; mem. Am. Fedn. Clin. Rsch. (sec.-treas. 1972-75), Western Soc. Clin. Rsch. (pres. 1978), Western Soc. Pediatric Residents (pres. 1995), Am. Bd. Med. Genetics (pres. 1979-83), Am. Coll. Med. Genetics (pres. 1991—), Am. Soc. Human Genetics (pres. 1984), Am. Pediatric Soc., Soc. Pediatric Rsch., Am. Soc. Clin. Investigator, Assn. Am. Physicians, Johns Hopkins Soc. Scholars, Inst. Medicine. Office: Cedars-Sinai Med Ctr 8700 Beverly Blvd Los Angeles CA 90048-1804

RIMSZA, SKIP, mayor; b. Chgo.; m. Kim Gill; children: Brian, Jenny. Owner Rimsza Realty; mem. Phoenix City Coun., 1990-94; vice mayor City of Phoenix, 1993, mayor, 1994—; former pres. Bd. Realtors. Mem. several cmty. bds. Office: Office of the Mayor 251 W Washington St Phoenix AZ 85003

RINEHART, CHARLES R., savings and loan association executive; b. San Francisco, Jan. 31, 1947; s. Robert Eugene and Rita Mary Rinehart; married; children: Joseph B., Kimberly D., Michael P., Scott. BS, U. San Francisco, 1968. Exec. v.p. Fireman's Fund Ins. Cos., Novato, Calif., 1969-83; pres., CEO Avco Fin. Services, Irvine, Calif., 1983-89, H.F. Ahmanson & Co., Irwindale, Calif., 1989—; chmn., CEO Home Savs. of Am., Irwindale. Trustee U. San Francisco; mem. adv. com. Drug Use is Life Abuse. Served to 2d lt. U.S. Army, 1968-69. Fellow Casualty Actuarial Soc.; mem. Am. Mgmt. Assn., Am. Acad. Actuaries. Republican. Roman Catholic. Office: Ho Savs Am/H F Ahmanson & Co 4900 Rivergrade Rd Irwindale CA 91706-1404

RINGEL, STEVEN PETER, neurology educator; b. Hamilton, Ohio, Feb. 17, 1943; s. Edward and Hedy (Fried) R.; m. Joan Deutsch, May 29, 1969; children: Andrew, Timothy. MD, U. Mich., 1968. Diplomate Am. Bd. Neurology and Psychiatry. Intern in medicine Rush Presbyn. St. Luke's Hosp., Chgo., 1968-69, resident in neurology, 1969-72; rsch. fellow NIH, NINDS, Bethesda, Md., 1974-76; from asst. to prof. U. Colo., Denver, 1976—; vis. prof. U. Padua, Italy, 1983; dir. Office of Clin. Practice, U. Hosp., Denver, 1994—. Author 4 books; contbr. over 230 articles to profl. jours. Maj. U.S. Army Med. Corps, 1972-74. Robert Wood Johnson Health Policy fellow U.S. Senate, 1991-92; resident scholar Inst. Medicine, 1991-92; recipient Postdoctoral Rsch. fellowship NIH, 1974-76, Rsch. fellowship NATO, 1982-84. Mem. Am. Acad. Neurology (treas. 1989-91, pres.-elect 1995—).

RINGEN, RANDY MARK, editor, writer; b. San Bernardino, Calif., Aug. 3, 1961; s. Randy Ray and Florence (Fitzgerald) R. BA in English, U. Calif., Berkeley, 1983; MA in English, UCLA, 1987. Tchg. asst. UCLA, 1985-86; English instr. Moorpark (Calif.) Coll., 1988, Ventura (Calif.) Coll., 1988-89, Pepperdine U., Malibu, Calif., 1988-89; publs. writer Gen. Dynamics, Rancho Cucamonga, Calif., 1989-91; editor Harvey Mudd Coll. Bull., Claremont, Calif., 1993—. Contbr. Menage: Ventura Coll. Creative Arts Mag., 1984, Blue Moon, 1984, 85, Westwind: UCLA's Jour. of the Arts, 1986, The Best of the Arcade Poetry Project, 1989; performer poetry with music Eastminter Ch., Ventura, Calif., 1987, Arcade Poetry Series, Ventura, 1989-95, Ventura New Music Concert Series, 1993, Carnegie Art Mus., Oxnard, Calif., 1993, Ventura Poetry Festival, 1994. Presbyterian. Home: 6294 Ralston St Ventura CA 93003-6126 Office: Harvey Mudd Coll 301 E 12th St Claremont CA 91711-5901

RINGLER, ROBERT LLOYD, JR., family practice physician, naval officer; b. Raleigh, N.C., Feb. 1, 1957; s. Robert Lloyd and Virginia Marie (Morrow) R.; m. Marie Celeste Crom, Aug. 18, 1979; children: Kimberly Heather, Kristin Nicole, Thomas Robert, Alana Danielle. AB in Chemistry, Duke U., 1978; MD, Uniformed Svcs. U. Health Sci., 1982. Commd. ensign USN, advanced through grades to comdr., 1993; family practice intern Naval Hosp., Charleston, S.C., 1982-83, family practice resident, 1983-85; family practice staff physician, quality assurance physician advisor Naval Hosp., Newport, R.I., 1985-88; asst. dept. head family practice, chair pharmacy and therapeutics com. Naval Hosp., Agana, Guam, 1988-90; family practice teaching staff Naval Hosp., Bremerton, Wash., 1990-93; sr. med. officer USN Support Facility, Diego Garcia, British Indian Ocean Territory, 1993-94; family practice teaching staff Naval Hosp., Bremerton, Wash., 1994—. Lector, lay eucharistic min. Navy Base Chapel, Newport, 1986-88, Agana, 1988-90, Diego Garcia, British Indian Ocean Territory, 1993-94. Mem. AMA, AMSUS, Am. Acad. Family Physicians, Uniformed Svcs. Acad. Family Physicians (bd. dirs. 1990-93, chair membership and svcs. com. 1991-93, 95—), Am. Soc. Colposcopists and Cervical Pathologists. Roman Catholic. Office: Naval Hosp Code 035 Boone Rd Bremerton WA 98312-1898

RINSCH, CHARLES EMIL, insurance company executive; b. Vincennes, Ind., June 28, 1932; s. Emil and Vera Pearl (White) R.; m. Maryann Elizabeth Hitchcock, June 18, 1964; children: Christopher, Daniel, Carl. BS in Stats., Ind. U., 1953; MS in Bus., Butler U., 1959; MBA, Stanford U.,

1960. Budget analyst Chrysler Corp., Indpls., 1955-57; sr. fin. analyst Ford Motor Co., Indpls., 1957-59; budget dir. Nat. Forge Co., Warren, Pa., 1960-61; div. controller and asst. to v.p., fin. Norris Industries, L.A., 1961-65; v.p., treas., sec. Teledyne Inc, L.A., 1965-88; pres., chief exec. officer Argonaut Group Inc., L.A., 1988—. Cubmaster Pack 721, Boy Scouts Am., L.A., 1987-88, treas. 1981-87; mem. dean's adv. coun. Ind. U. Sch. Bus. 1st lt. U.S. Army, 1953-55. Mem. Acad. Alumni Fellows Ind. U. Sch. Bus., L.A. Treas.'s Club. Home: 19849 Greenbriar Dr Tarzana CA 91356-5428 Office: Argonaut Group Inc Ste 1175 1800 Avenue Of The Stars Los Angeles CA 90067-4213

RINSCH, MARYANN ELIZABETH, occupational therapist; b. L.A., Aug. 8, 1939; d. Harry William and Thora Analine (Langlie) Hitchcock; m. Charles Emil Rinsch, June 18, 1964; children: Christopher, Daniel, Carl. BS, U. Minn., 1961. Registered occupational therapist, Calif. Staff occupational therapist Hastings (Minn.) State Hosp., 1961-62, Neuropsychiat. Inst., L.A., 1962-64; staff and sr. occupational therapist Calif. Children's Svcs., L.A., 1964-66, head occupational therapist, 1966-68; researcher A. Jean Ayres, U. So. Calif., L.A., 1968-69; pvt. practice neurodevel. and sensory integraton Tarzana, Calif., 1969-74; pediat. occupational therapist neurodevel. & sensory integration St. Johns Hosp., Santa Monica, Calif., 1991-95; pvt. practice, cons. Santa Monica-Malibu Unified Sch. Dist., 1994—. Mem. alliance bd. Natural History Mus., L.A. County, 1983—; cub scouts den mother Boy Souts Am., Sherman Oaks, Calif., 1986-88, advancement chair Boy Scout Troop 474, 1989-92; mem. vol. League San Fernando Valley, Van Nuys, Calif., 1985-93. Mem. Am. Occupational Therapy Assn., Calif. Occupational Therapy Assn. Home: 19849 Greenbriar Dr Tarzana CA 91356-5428

RIORDAN, GEORGE NICKERSON, investment banker; b. Patchogue, N.Y., May 16, 1933; s. E. Arthur and Constance E. (Whelden) R.; m. Ann Wiggins, Jan. 4, 1958; children—Susan M., Peter G. B.S., Cornell U., 1955; M.B.A., Harvard U., 1960. Vice-pres. Lehman Bros., N.Y.C., 1960-71; mng. dir. Blyth Eastman Paine Webber, Los Angeles and N.Y.C., 1971-81, Prudential-Bache Securities, Los Angeles, 1981-88, Bear Stearns & Co., Inc., L.A., 1988-89, Dean Witter Reynolds Inc., 1989-91; bd. dirs. MacNea Schwnedler Corp., L.A., Pancho's Mexican Buffet, Inc., Ft. Worth, Lewis Galoob Toys, Inc. Served to capt. USAF, 1955-57. Mem. Calif. Club, Quoque Field Club, Athenaeum Club, Valley Hunt Club (Pasadena, Calif.). Office: 3300 Hyland Ave Costa Mesa CA 92626-1503

RIORDAN, JOHN STEPHEN, air force officer; b. Kearny, N.J., July 23, 1965; s. John Joseph and Annie (Minogue) R.; m. Shawn Lynn McGowen, June 8, 1991. BA, Montclair State U., 1987; postgrad., Colo. State U., 1989-91; MBA with honors, Regis U., 1993. Cert. tchr., instr. USAF. Supr. customer svc. BJ's Wholesale Club, East Rutherford, N.J., 1987-88; commd. 2d lt. USAF, 1988, advanced through grades to capt., 1991; combat crew instr. ops. tng. div. 90th Missile Wing, Cheyenne, Wyo., 1988-89, sr. crew instr., 1989-90, missile combat crew comdr. 319th missile squadron, 1990-91, chief programs sect. and quality control sect., 1991-92; instrnl. systems mgr., dir. total quality 90th ops. group 90th Ops. Support Squadron, Cheyenne, Wyo., 1992-94; asst. chief group ops. tng., flight comdr. 2nd space ops squadron 50th Ops. Support Squadron, Faicon AFB, Colo., 1994—; owner, COO Wolf Productivity Mgmt.; assoc. prof. Regis U., Denver, 1994—. Vice chmn. Warren Boosters Assn., Cheyenne, 1992. Mem. ASTD, Am. Soc. Quality Control, Air Force Space Ops. Assn., Air Force Assn., Am. Soc. Tng. and Devel., Toastmasters. Home: 2860 Richmond Dr Colorado Springs CO 80922-1344 Office: 2 SOPS/ DOT Falcon AFB CO 80912

RIORDAN, MICHAEL, author, scientist; b. Springfield, Mass., Dec. 3, 1946; s. Edward John and Evelyn Anna (Hnizdo) R.; m. Linda Michele Goodman, Apr. 10, 1979 (div. Aug. 1988); m. Sandra Lee Foster, Sept. 10, 1988 (div. July 1990). BS in Physics, MIT, 1968, PhD in Physics, 1973. Rsch. assoc. MIT, Cambridge, Mass., 1973-75; editor, publisher Cheshire Books, Inc., Palo Alto, Calif., 1976-85; rsch. scientist U. Rochester, N.Y., 1985-87; sci. info. officer Stanford (Calif.) Linear Accelerator Ctr., 1988-90, asst. to dir., 1992—; asst. to pres. and staff scientist Univs. Rsch. Assn., Inc., Washington, 1990-91; rsch. physicist U. Calif., Santa Cruz, 1995—; treas., dir. Contemporary Physics Edn. Project, Inc., Portola Valley, Calif., 1991-94. Author: The Hunting of the Quark, 1987 (Sci. Writing award Am. Inst. Physics 1988); co-author: The Solar Home Book, 1977, The Shadows of Creation, 1991; editor: The Day After Midnight, 1982. Treas., v.p. Cuesta La Honda (Calif.) Guild, 1986, 87. Mem. Am. Phys. Soc., Nat. Assn. Sci. Writers. Democrat. Home: 4532 Cherryvale Ave Soquel CA 95073-9748 Office: Stanford Linear Accelerator Mail Stop 80 Stanford CA 94309

RIORDAN, RICHARD J., mayor; b. Flushing, N.Y., 1930; m. Eugenia Riordan; 6 children (2 dec.); m. Jill Riordan. Attended, U. Calif., Santa Clara; grad., Princeton U., 1952; JD, U. Mich., 1956. With O'Melveny & Myers, L.A.; owner, operator Original Pantry Cafe; founder Total Pharmaceutical Care, Tetra Tech; mayor L.A., 1993—. Co-founder LEARN, 1991; sponsor Writing to Read computer labs Riordan Found.; active Eastside Boys and Girls Club. Lt. U.S. Army, Korea. Office: Los Angeles City Hall 200 N Spring St Los Angeles CA 90012-4801

RIPARBELLI, CARLO, aerospace engineer; b. Rome, Nov. 15, 1910; came to U.S., 1946, naturalized, 1953; s. Vittorio and Maria (Bernabei) R.; m. Ellen Johnston Dennis, Dec. 20, 1958. DCE, U. Rome, 1933, Dr. Aero Engring., 1934, Libero Docente Costruzioni Aeronautiche, 1940. Research asst. DSSE, Guidonia, Italy, 1937-41; chief designer Aeroplani Caproni, Milan, Italy, 1941-43; research assoc. Princeton (N.J.) U., 1947-48; design specialist Convair, San Diego, 1955-59; design specialist Gen. Atomics div. Gen. Dynamics Corp., San Diego, 1959, mem. research and devel. staff, 1960-65; engring. staff specialist Gen. Dynamics Corp., Pomona, Calif., 1965-72; engring. cons. Aerospace Corp., El Segundo, Calif., 1973-80, Sci. Applications, Inc., La Jolla, Calif., 1973-86; asst. prof. aero. structures U. Rome, 1937-41, Poly. of Milan, 1941-42, asst. prof. Cornell U. Grad. Sch. Aero. Engring., 1949-51; assoc. prof., 1951-55; lectr. U. Calif. San Diego, 1960, 63; cons. Cornell Aero. Lab., Buffalo, 1951, Aeronautica Macchi, Varese, Italy, 1949-55, Bur. Ships, Dept. Navy, 1953-55; participant Allied Govts. Aero. Research and Devel. meeting in Copenhagen, 1958. Contbr. articles to profl. jours.; patentee in field. Served to capt. Italian Air Force, 1936-45, permanent officer, 1938-48. Italo-Am. Com. scholar Princeton U., 1946-47. Fellow AIAA (assoc.); mem. Soc. for Exptl. Stress Analysis, Associazione Italiana di Aeronautica e Astronautica, Inst., Aero Scis. (chmn. com. for sci. meetings San Diego chpt. 1960-61, chmn. programs 1961-62), Sigma Xi. Home and Office: 4429 Arista Dr San Diego CA 92103-1030

RIPINSKY-NAXON, MICHAEL, archaeologist, art historian, ethnologist; b. Kutaisi, USSR, Mar. 23, 1944; s. Pinkus and Maria (Kokielov) R.; m. Agata Dutkiewicz; 1 child, Tariel. AB in Anthropology with honors, U. Calif.-Berkeley, 1966, PhD in Archeology and Art History, 1979. Rsch. asst. Am. Mus. Natural History, N.Y.C., 1964, U. Calif.-Berkeley, 1964-66; mem. faculty dept. anthropology and geography of Near East, Calif. State U.-Hayward, 1966-67; asst. prof. Calif. State U.-Northridge, 1974-75; rschr., assoc. UCLA, 1974-75, sr. rsch. anthropologist Hebrew U., Hadassah Med. Sch., Jerusalem, 1970-71; curator Anthropos Gallery of Ancient Art, Beverly Hills, Calif., 1976-78; chief rsch. scientist Archaeometric Data Labs., Beverly Hills, 1976-78; dir. Ancient Artworld Corp., Beverly Hills, 1979-82; dir. prehistoric studies Mediterranean Rsch. Ctr., Athens, 1989-91; prof., chairperson, Dept. Cultural Studies, Pedagogical U., Kielce, Poland, 1993—; conducted excavations Israel, Egypt, Jordan, Mesopotamia, Mexico, Cen. Am; specialist in the development of early religions and shamanism, phenomenon of origins of domestication and camel ancestry; expert on art works from French Impressionists to ancient Egypt and classical world; research in evolution of consciousness, ethnogenesis and the origins of religion, shamanism and ecstatic states. Author: The Nature of Shamanism, 1993; contbr. articles to sci. and scholarly jours. dir. Cen. Am. Inst. Prehistoric and Traditional Cultures, Belize; chmn. bd. Am. Found. for Cultural Studies. Recipient Cert. of Merit for Sci. Endeavour, Dictionary of Internat. Biography, 1974. Fellow Am. Anthropol. Assn., Royal Asiatic Soc.; mem. Archaeol. Inst. Am. (life), Soc. for Am. Archaeology, Royal Anthropol. Inst., Am. Ethnol. Soc., History of Sci. Soc., Am. Chem. Soc., Assn. for Transpersonal Psychology, Soc. Ethnobiology, Soc. Anthropology of Consciousness, Soc. Archeol. Scis. (life). Office: Ctrl Am Inst, PO Box 59, San Ignacio Cayo Dist, Belize

RIPLEY, EARLE ALLISON, meteorology educator; b. Sydney, N.S., Can., June 29, 1933; s. Edward E. and Hazel M. (Stephens) R.; m. Jean Helen McCrae, May 28, 1966; 1 child, Stephen H. BS, Dalhousie U., Halifax, N.S., Can., 1953; MA, U. Toronto (Can.), 1955. Meteorologist Can. Dept. Transport, Halifax, 1955-60, Nigerian Meteorol. Svc., Lagos, Nigeria, 1960-62; agrometeorologist East African Agr. and Forestry Rsch. Orgn., Nairobi, Kenya, 1962-67; rsch. assoc. U. Sask., Saskatoon, Can., 1968-74; prof. U. Saskatchewan, Saskatoon, Can., 1974—. Author: Environmental Impact of Mining in Canada, 1978. Fellow Royal Meteorol. Soc.; mem. Can. Meteorol. and Oceanographic Soc., Am. Meteorol. Soc. (profl.). Office: U Saskatchewan, Dept Crop Sci & Plant Ecology, Saskatoon, SK Canada S7N 0W0

RIPLEY, ROBERT ELLIOTT, author, psychologist; b. Mpls., Aug. 2, 1930; s. Richard Rolland Elliott and Irma May (Strait) Hanson; m. Lois Johanna Colbiornsen, Oct. 10, 1953 (div. 1968); children: Robert Vincent, Richard Allen, Erika Louise; m. Marie June Schert, Dec. 7, 1968; children: Briana May, Rodrick Elliott. BA, U. Minn., 1957, MA, 1961, PhD, 1967. Cert. psychologist, Minn., S.D., Iowa, Ariz. Stockbroker IDS, Houston, 1958-59; grad. rsch. asst. U. Minn., Mpls., 1959-61, instr., 1965-67; prof. No. State Coll., Aberdeen, S.D., 1961-62, Iowa State U., Ames, 1962-65, Ariz. State U., Tempe, 1967-79; mgmt. trainer, cons. Behavior Tech. Inst., Scottsdale, Ariz., 1979-84; stockbroker, fin. planner Raymond-James, Boca Raton, Fla., 1984-88; freelance author, cons. Carefree, Ariz., 1988—; cons. U.S. Labor Dept., Washington, 1969-72, U.S. Dept. Edn., Washington, 1970-73; sr. mgmt. cons., trainer Motorola, Honeywell, 1974-85. Author: Manage it All! Yourself, Your Company and Others, 1989, Your Child's Age and Stages, 1994, Guiding Your Child to Become an Effective Adult, 1995; contbr. articles to numerous publs.U. Sgt. USAF, 1949-55, Europe. Named Outstanding Man of Phoenix, City of Phoenix, 1973. Mem. ACA (life), Assn. Counselor Educators and Suprs. (life), Iowa Pers. and Guidance Assn. (life), Brit. Literati Club. Republican. Home: PO Box 6105 Carefree AZ 85377-6105

RIPLEY, STUART MCKINNON, real estate consultant; b. St. Louis, July 28, 1930; s. Rob Roy and Nina Pearl (Young) R.; B.A., U. Redlands, 1952; M.B.A., U. Calif., Berkeley, 1959; m. Marilyn Haerr MacDiarmid, Dec. 28, 1964; children—Jill, Bruce, Kent. Vice pres., dir. J.H. Hedrick & Co., Santa Barbara and San Diego, 1958-63; v.p. mktg. Cavanaugh Devel. Co., San Gabriel, Calif., 1963-65; v.p. mktg. dir. Calabasas Park, Bechtel Corp., Calabasas, Calif., 1967-69; v.p. mktg. Avco Community Developers, Inc., La Jolla, Calif., 1969-74; mktg. dir. U.S. Home Corp., Fla. Div., Clearwater, 1974-75; pres., dir. Howard's Camper Country, Inc., National City, Calif., 1975-77; v.p., mktg. dir. Valcas Internat. Corp., San Diego, 1976-77, pres., 1977-79; pres. Stuart M. Ripley, Inc., 1977—, Sunview Realty, Inc., a Watt Industries Co., Santa Monica, Calif., 1979-80; owner Everett Stunz Co., Ltd., La Jolla, 1981—; exec. v.p. Harriman-Ripley Co., Fallbrook, Calif.; avocado/floraculture rancher, subdivider, Fallbrook, 1978—; lectr. UCLA, 1961; pres. Century 21 Coastal, Century 21 Bajamar, Baja California, Mex., 1994—. Served with USN, 1952-55. U. Redlands fellow, 1960—. Mem. Nat. Assn. Homebuilders, Sales and Mktg. Council, Sales and Mktg. Execs., Pi Chi. Republican. Episcopalian. Club: Elks. Home: 13180 Portofino Dr Del Mar CA 92014-3828 Office: 7644 Girard Ave La Jolla CA 92037-4420

RIPPER, RITA JO (JODY RIPPER), strategic planner, researcher; b. Goldfield, Iowa, May 8, 1950; d. Carl Phillip and Lucille Mae (Stewart) Ripper; BA, U. Iowa, 1972; MBA, NYU, 1978. Contracts and fin. staff Control Data Corp., Mpls., 1974-78; regional mgr. Raytheon Corp., Irvine, Calif., 1978-83; v.p. Caljo Corp., Des Moines, Iowa, 1980-84; asst. v.p. Bank of Am., San Francisco, 1984-88; pres. The Northhaven Co., 1988—, The Boardroom Adv. Group, 1990—. Vol. and alt. del. Rep. Party, Edina, Minn., N.Y.C., 1974—; vol. Cancer, Heart, Lung Assns., Edina, N.Y.C., Calif., 1974-78, 84—, Lita, 1986-90. Mem. Amnesty Internat., Internat. Mktg. Assn., World Trade Ctr. Assn., Acctg. Soc. (pres. 1975-76), World Trade Club, Intertel, Mensa, Beta Alpha Psi (chmn. 1977-78), Phi Gamma Nu (v.p. 1971-72) Presbyterian. Clubs: Corinthian Yacht, Mt. Tamalpais Racquet. Home and Office: 501 Oak Lane Dr West Des Moines IA 50265-5146 also: The Northhaven Co PO Box 25145 West Des Moines IA 50265 also: The Boardroom Adv Group 537 Newport Center Dr # 277 Newport Beach CA 92660-6937

RIPPLE, WILLIAM JOHN, forestry researcher, educator; b. Yankton, S.D., Mar. 10, 1952; s. John Franklin and Margaret (Sondergroth) R. BS, S.D. State U., 1974; MS, U. Idaho, 1978; PhD, Oreg. State U., 1984. Geographer S.D. State Planning Bur., Pierre, 1977-81; rsch. assoc. Oreg. State U., Corvallis, 1984-88; asst. prof. Forest Resources Dept. Oreg. State U., Corvallis, 1988-92; assoc. prof. forest resources dept. Oreg. State U., Corvallis, 1992—; dir. Environ. Remote Sensing Applications Lab. Oreg. State U., Corvallis, 1988—; cons. U.S. GAO, Washington, 1989. Editor: GIS for Resource Management, 1987, Fundamentals of GIS, 1989; contbr. articles to profl. jour. Active Corvallis Folklore Soc., treas., 1988-91. Mem. Am. Soc. for Photogrammetry and Remote Sensing (Presdl. Citation for Meritorious Svc. 1987, 88, 90), Columbia River Region (treas. 1987-88, v.p. 1988-89, pres. 1989-90). Home: 1228 NW Dixon St Corvallis OR 97330-4645 Office: Oreg State U Dept Forest Resources Corvallis OR 97331

RIRIE, CRAIG MARTIN, periodontist; b. Lewiston, Utah, Apr. 17, 1943; s. Martin Clarence and VaLera (Dixon) R.; m. Becky Ann Ririe, Sept. 17, 1982; children: Paige, Seth, Theron, Kendall, Nathan, Derek, Brian, Amber, Kristen. AA, San Bernadino Valley Coll., 1966; DDS, Creighton U., 1972; MSD, Loma Linda U., 1978. Staff mem. Flagstaff (Ariz.) Med. Ctr., 1974—; pvt. practice dentistry specializing in periodontics Flagstaff, 1974—; assoc. prof. periodontics No. Ariz. U., Flagstaff, 1979—, chmn. dept. dental hygiene, 1980-81; med. research cons. W.L. Gore, Flagstaff, 1983—. Contbr. articles to profl. jours. V.p. bd. dirs. Grand Canyon coun. Boy Scouts Am., 1991—. Health professions scholarship Creighton U., Omaha, 1969-71; recipient Mosby award Mosby Pub. Co., 1972; research fellowship U. Bergen, Norway, 1978-79. Mem. ADA, Am. Acad. Periodontology (cert.), Western Soc. Periodontology (chmn. com. on research 1982—, bd. dirs. 1983—), No. Ariz. Dental Soc., Am. Acad. Oral Implantologists, Internat. Congress Oral Implantologists, Ariz. Dental Assn., Am. Cancer Soc. (bd. dirs.), Flagstaff C. of C., Rotary. Republican. Mem. LDS Ch. Home: 1320 N Aztec St Flagstaff AZ 86001-3004 Office: 1050 N San Francisco St Flagstaff AZ 86001-3259

RISEBROUGH, DOUG, professional hockey team executive; b. 1954; m. Marilyn Risenbrough; children: Allison, Lindsay. Former player Montreal (Que.) Canadiens, for 8 years; former player Calgary (Alta., Can.) Flames, for 5 years, former asst. coach, 1987-89, asst. gen. mgr., 1989-90, head coach, 1990-92; General Manager Calgary (Alt., Can.) Flames, 1992—. *

RISING, CATHARINE CLARKE, author; b. Berkeley, Calif., Jan. 7, 1929; d. Philip Seymour and Helen Katharine (Davis) Clarke; m. Boardman Rising, Sept. 16, 1950. BS, U. Calif., Berkeley, 1950, PhD, 1987; MA, San Francisco State U., 1979. Cert. cmty. coll. instr., Calif. Author: Darkness at Heart: Fathers and Sons in Conrad, 1990; contbr. articles to profl. jours. Mem. MLA, Joseph Conrad Soc. Am., Phi Beta Kappa.

RISLEY, LARRY L., air transportation executive. CEO, chmn. bd. dirs. Mesa Air Corp. Office: Mesa Airlines 2325 E 30th St Farmington NM 87401-8900*

RISLEY, TODD ROBERT, psychologist, educator; b. Palmer, Alaska, Sept. 8, 1937; s. Robert and Eva Lou (Todd) R.; 1 child, Todd Michael. A.B. with distinction in Psychology, San Diego State Coll., 1960; M.S., U. Wash., 1963, Ph.D., 1966. Asst. prof. psychology Fla. State U., Tallahassee, 1964-65; research assoc. Bur. Child Research, U. Kans., Lawrence, 1965-77, sr. scientist, 1977—, asst. prof. dept. human devel., 1967-69, assoc. prof., 1969-73, prof., 1973-84; prof. psychology U. Alaska, Anchorage, 1982—; pres. Ctr. for Applied Behavior Analysis, 1970-82; dir. Johnny Cake Child Study Ctr., Mansfield, Ark., 1973-74; vis. prof. U. Auckland (N.Z.), 1978; acting dir. Western Carolina Ctr., Morgantown, N.C., 1981; dir. Alaska Div. Mental Health and Devel. Disabilities, 1988-91; cons. in field to numerous orgns. and instns. Co-author: The Infant Center, 1977, Shopping with Children: Advice for Parents, 1978, The Toddler Center, 1979; editor: Jour. Applied Behavior Analysis, 1971-74, Meaningful Differences, 1995; mng. editor: Behavior Therapy, The Behavior Therapist, Behavioral Assessment, 1977-80; mem. editl. bds. of numerous profl. jours.; contbr. revs. and numerous articles. Co-chmn. Fla. task force on use of behavioral procedures in state programs for retarded, 1974—; mem. resident abuse investigating com. div. retardation Fla. Dept. Health and Rehab. Services, 1972—; mem. adv. com. Social Research Inst., U. Utah, 1977—; mem. Alaska Gov.'s Council on Handicapped and Gifted, 1983-88, NIH Mental Retardation Research Com., 1987-88, Alaska Mental Health Bd., 1988. Grantee NIMH, 1971-72, 72-73; research grantee Nat. Ctr. Health Services, 1976-79; grantee Nat. Inst. Edn., 1973, NIH, 1967—. Fellow Am. Psychol. Assn. (coun. of reps. 1982-85, pres. div. 25, 1989); mem. AAAS, Am. Psychol. Soc., Am. Assn. Mental Deficiency, Assn. Advancement of Behavior Therapy (dir. 1975-80, pres. 1976-77, chmn. profl. rev. com. 1977—, series editor Readings in Behavior Therapy 1977—), Soc. Behavioral Medicine, Assn. Behavior Analysis, Sigma Xi. Office: U Alaska-Anchorage Dept Psychology 3211 Providence Dr Anchorage AK 99508-4614

RISLEY-CURTISS, CHRISTINA, social worker, educator; b. Torrington, Conn., Jan. 3, 1948; d. Henry B. and Marjorie Louise (Utz) Risley. BA, U. Conn., 1969; MSSW, U. Tenn., 1980; cert., Cen. Conn. State Coll., 1970; PhD, U. Md. At Balt. Staff devel./tng. cons. Tenn. Dept. Human Svcs., Nashville; social work cons. Cannon Meml. Hosp., Pickens, S.C.; social svc. worker County Dept. Social Svcs., Pickens; social svcs. supr. County Dept. Social Svcs., Laurens, S.C.; dist. dir. social worker Upper Savannah Health Dist. S.C. Dept. Health and Environ. Control, Greenwood; rsch. cons. Westat, Rockville, Md.; asst. rsch. U. Md. at Balt.; instr. U. Md. at Balt. Sch. Social Work; asst. prof. Sch. Social Work Ariz. State U., 1993—; mem. S.C. Gov.'s Juvenile Justice Adv. Coun.; presenter workshops. Contbr. articles to profl. publs. Mem. NASW, Am. Profl. Soc. on the Abuse of Children, Coun. on Social Work Edn.

RISSER, ARTHUR CRANE, JR., zoo administrator; b. Blackwell, Okla., July 8, 1938; s. Arthur Crane and Mary Winn (Stevenson) R.; children: Michelle W., Stephen C., Michael R. BA, Grinnell Coll., Iowa, 1960; MA, U. Ariz., Tucson, 1963; PhD, U. Calif., Davis, 1970. Mus. technician, Smithsonian Instn., Washington, 1963-64; research assoc. Sch. Medicine U. Md., Balt., 1964-65; grad. teaching asst. U. Calif., Davis, 1965-70; asst. prof. biology U. Nev.-Reno, 1970-74; asst. curator birds Zool. Soc. San Diego, 1974-76, curator birds, 1976-81, gen. curator birds, 1981-86; gen. mgr. San Diego Zoo, 1986—; co-chmn. Calif. Condor Working Group on Captive Breeding and Reintroduction, 1983-85; mem. Calif. Condor Recovery Team, 1984-86. Treas., Planned Parenthood, Reno, 1972; bd. dirs. Internat. Found. Conservation Birds, 1979-88, Conservation Rsch. Found. of Papua New Guinea, 1991—. Fellow Am. Assn. Zool. Parks and Aquariums. Office: San Diego Zoo PO Box 551 San Diego CA 92112-0551

RISTINE, JEFFREY ALAN, reporter; b. Ann Arbor, Mich., Apr. 21, 1955; s. Harold G. and Amelia (Schmidt) R. BA, U. Mich., 1977. Reporter The Midland (Mich) Times, 1978-79, Johnstown (Pa.) Tribune-Dem., 1979-80, San Diego Tribune, 1980-92, San Diego Union-Tribune, 1992—. Recipient Appreciation award Am. Planning Assn., San Diego sect., 1988; named Best polit./govt. reporter San Diego Press Club, 1986. Office: San Diego Union-Tribune 350 Camino De La Reina San Diego CA 92108-3003

RISTOW, BRUNNO, plastic surgeon; b. Brusque, Brazil, Oct. 18, 1940; came to U.S., 1967, naturalized, 1981; s. Arno and Ally Odette (von Buettner) R.; student Coll. Sinodal, Brazil, 1956-57, Coll. Julio de Castilhos, Brazil, 1957-58; M.D. magna cum laude, U. Brazil, 1966; m. Urannia Carrasquilla Gutierrez, Nov. 10, 1979; children by previous marriage: Christian Kilian, Trevvor Roland. Intern in surgery Hosp. dos Estrangeiros, Rio de Janeiro, Brazil, 1965, Hospital Estadual Miguel Couto, Brazil, 1965-66, Instituto Aposentadoria Pensão Comerciarios Hosp. for Gen. Surgery, 1966; resident in plastic and reconstructive surgery, Dr. Ivo Pitanguy Hosp. Santa Casa de Misericordia, Rio de Janeiro, 1967; fellow Inst. of Reconstructive Plastic Surgery, N.Y. U. Med. Center, N.Y.C., 1967-68, jr. resident, 1971-72, sr. and chief resident, 1972-73; practice medicine specializing in plastic surgery, Rio de Janeiro, 1967, N.Y.C., 1968-73, San Francisco, 1973—; asst. surgeon N.Y. Hosp., Cornell Med. Center, N.Y.C., 1968-71; clin. instr. surgery N.Y. U. Sch. of Medicine, 1972-73; chmn. plastic and reconstructive surgery div. Presbyn. Hosp., Pacific Med. Center, San Francisco, 1974-92, chmn. emeritus, 1992—. Served with M.C., Brazilian Army Res., 1959-60. Decorated knight Venerable Order of St. Hubertus; Knight Order St. John of Jerusalem; fellow in surgery Cornell Med. Sch., 1968-71; diplomate Am. Bd. Plastic and Reconstructive Surgery. Fellow A.C.S., Internat. Coll. Surgeons; mem. Am. Soc. Aesthetic Plastic Surgery (chmn. edn.), Am. Soc. Plastic and Reconstructive Surgeons, Internat. Soc. Aesthetic Plastic Surgeons, Calif. Soc. Plastic Surgeons, AMA (Physician's Recognition award 1971-83), Calif. Med. Assn., San Francisco Med. Assn. Republican. Mem. Evang. Lutheran Ch. Club: San Francisco Olympic. Contbg. author: Cancer of the Hand, 1975, Current Therapy in Plastic and Reconstructive Surgery, 1988, Male Aesthetic Surgery, 1989, How They Do It: Procedures in Plastic and Reconstructive Surgery, 1990, Middle Crus: The Missing Link in Alar Cartilage Anatomy, 1991, Surgical Technology International, 1992, Aesthetic Plastic Surgery, 1993, Mastery of Surgery: Plastic and Reconstructive Surgery, 1993; Reoperative Aesthetic Plastic Surgery of the Face and Breast, 1994, 95; contbr. articles on plastic surgery to profl. publs. Office: Calif Pacific Med Ctr Pacific Profl Bldg 2100 Webster St Ste 502 San Francisco CA 94115-2381

RITCHIE, ANNE, educational administrator; b. Grants Pass, Oreg., July 1, 1944; d. William Riley Jr. and Allie Brown (Clark) R.; m. Charles James Cooper, Sept. 4, 1968 (div. 1985); children: Holly Anne, Wendy Nicole. BA in Edn. with honors, Calif. State U., Sacramento, 1981. Cert. elem. tchr., Calif. CEO El Rancho Schs., Inc., Carmichael, Calif., 1981—; citizen amb. del. People to People Internat., Russia, Lithuania, Hungary, 1993, China, 1994. Active Sacramento Symphony Assn., Crocker Art Mus.; mem. Rep. Senatorial Inner Circle, Washington, 1995. Mem. AAUW, Nat. Assn. Edn. for Young Children, Profl. Assn. Childhood Educators, Nat. Child Care Assn. Episcopalian.

RITCHIE, CATHERINE D., correctional officer, deputy constable; b. Lynwood, Calif., Aug. 22, 1954; d. Harold Francis and Betty J. (Matlock) R.; m. Walter B. Ritchie Jr., July 21, 1977; children: Jeffrey, Bradley. Bookkeeper, sec. Severy Dental Labs., Orange, Calif., 1972-74, Shell Oil Co., Santa Ana, Calif., 1974-77; owner, ptnr. Vista (Calif.) Chevron Co., 1977-78; sec.-treas. Am. Battery Corp., Escondido, Calif., 1978-85; owner, operator Sophisticated 2ds, Vista, 1983-85, Bridal Elegance, Escondido, 1984-87; sr. correctional officer Humboldt County Sheriff's Dept., Eureka, Calif., 1988—; dep. marshal North Humboldt Jud. Dist., Arcata, Calif., 1991—; sgt. correction divsn. Humboldt County Sheriff's Dept., Arcata, 1991—, jail compliance sgt., 1995—; Co-pub. How to Avoid Auto Repair Rip-offs, 1981. Mem. Nat. Bridal Service (cert., cons.), Nat. Assn. Female Execs., Escondido C. of C., Calif. Farm Bur. Republican.

RITCHIE, C(LAUDE) ALEN, middle school educator, tax preparer; b. Loma Linda, Calif., June 13, 1939; s. Claude Callahan and Alena Lee (Sease) R.; m. Marian Ruth Phillips, Sept. 6, 1960 (div. Sept. 1980); children: Robert Alen, Catherine Elizabeth Ritchie Lynch; m. Jerlynn S. Smith, Feb. 17, 1981 (div. Aug. 20, 1991); m. Carolyn Elliot Hart, June 20, 1992. MusB, U. Redlands, 1961; MA, Calif. State Coll., San Bernardino, 1982. Cert. jr. high tchr., Calif. Tchr. Redlands (Calif.) Unified Sch. Dist., 1961—; choir dir. Presbyn. Ch., Redlands; chair San Gorgonio Svc. Ctr., San Bernardino, 1995—; treas. Citrus Belt Uniserv, Redlands, 1991-93. Treas. Redlands Yucaipa Guidance Clinic, 1971. Recipient Disting. Svc. award Redlands Jaycees, 1972. Mem. NEA (rep. 1988-94), Calif. Tchrs. Assn. (state coun. rep. 1992—), Redlands Tchrs. Assn. (pres. 1990-93), Phi Delta Kappa. Democrat. Presbyterian. Home: 938 Nottingham Dr Redlands CA 92373-6663 Office: Moore Mid Sch 1550 E Highland Ave Redlands CA 92374-5518

RITCHIE, DANIEL LEE, university administrator; b. Springfield, Ill., Sept. 19, 1931; s. Daniel Felix and Jessie Dee (Binney) R. B.A., Harvard U., 1954, M.B.A., 1956. Exec. v.p. MCA, Inc., Los Angeles, 1967-70; pres. Archon Pure Products Co., Los Angeles, 1970-73; exec. v.p. Westinghouse Electric Corp., Pitts., 1975-78; pres. corp. staff and strategic planning Westinghouse Broadcasting Co., 1978-79, pres., chief exec. officer, 1979-81, chmn., chief exec. officer; chmn., chief exec. officer Westinghouse Broadcasting & Cable, Inc., 1981-87; owner Grand River Ranch, Kremmling, Colo., 1977—, Rancho Cielo, Montecito, Calif., 1977—; chancellor U. Denver, 1989—. With U.S. Army, 1956-58. Office: U Denver Office of the Chancellor University Park Denver CO 80208

RITCHIE, DAVID BRIAN, lawyer; b. L.A., Sept. 16, 1958; s. Graham Alastair and Karen Lee (Namson) R.; m. Dana Natalie Israeli, Mar. 14, 1992. BS, Calif. Inst. Tech., 1980; JD, U. So. Calif., 1983. Bar: Calif. 1983, U.S. Patent Office 1984. Atty. Lyon & Lyon, L.A., 1983-93; ptnr. D'Alessandro, Frazzini & Ritchie, L.A., 1993—. Mem. Cal Tech Alumni Assn. (dir. 1991-94). Office: D'Alessandro Frazzini & Ritchie 3521 Yorkshire Rd Ste 1000 Pasadena CA 91107-5432

RITCHIE, ERIC ROBERT DAVID, manufacturing executive; b. Belfast, No. Ireland, Jan. 11, 1942; came to U.S., 1968; BME, Gen. Motors Inst., 1967; MSME, Union Coll., 1972. Registered profl. engr. Iowa, N.Y., Oreg. Process engr. GM of Can. Ltd., 1964-68; mgr. plant engring. GE, Schenectady, N.Y., 1968-73, mgr. internat. facilities, 1973-78; mgr. plant engring. services John Deere Waterloo Works, Waterloo, Iowa, 1978-85; mgr. materials engring. John Deere Component Works, Waterloo, 1985-89; ops. mgr. Garrett Productos Automotrices, Mexicali, Mexico, 1989-90; corp. mfg. engring. mgr. Sulzer Bingham Pumps Inc., Portland, Oreg., 1990-93; corp. materials mgr., 1993—. Active planning and allocation com. Cedar Valley United Way, Waterloo, 1986-89; elder, session leader, State St. Presbyn. Ch., Schenectady, 1972-78, Immanuel Presbyn. Ch., Waterloo, 1979-82, First Presbyn. Ch., Portland, Oreg., 1993—; mem. Mayors Commn. Mcpl. Power, Waterloo, 1987-88. Mem. ASHRAE, Soc. Automotive Engrs., Am. Soc. Metals. Republican. Office: Sulzer Bingham Pumps Inc 2800 NW Front Ave PO Box 10247 Portland OR 97210

RITTER, RUSSELL JOSEPH, mayor, college official; b. Helena, Mont., July 22, 1932; s. Walter A. and SallyC. (Mellen) R.; m. Linaire Wells, Aug. 4, 1956; children—Michael, Leslie, Teresa, Gregory, Daniel. Student Carroll Coll., Helena, 1950-53; A.B. in History, U. Mont.-Missoula, 1957, M.A. in History and Polit. Sci., 1962, postgrad. in History, 1963. Salesman, Capital Ford, 1953-54, 56-57; tchr., coach Billings (Mont.) Central High Sch., 1957-58, Loyola High Sch., Missoula, 1958-62, Flathead High Sch., Kalispell, Mont., 1962-69; dir. devel. and community relations Carroll Coll., Helena, 1969-76, v.p. for coll. relations, 1976-91; dir. Goot Corp.- Rels. Washington Corp., 1991—; commr. City of Helena, 1977-80, mayor pro-tem, 1980, mayor, 1981—; exec. sec.-treas. Carroll Coll. Found., Inc.; owner Danny's Drive In, Kalispell, 1965-69; ptnr. R-B Enterprises, Inc., Kalispell, 1967-71; bd. dirs. Brubaker & Assos., Inc., Kalispell, 1971-74; v.p. Capital Investment, Inc. (KMTX Radio), Helena, 1973-80; pres. Swinging Door Art Gallery, Inc., Helena, 1973—; bd. dirs. Norwest Bank of Helena. Bd. dirs. All Am. Indian Hall of Fame, 1972-78, Jr. Achievement, 1975-79, Mont. Physicians Service, 1984-86, Blue Cross/Blue Shield Mont., 1986—, Mont. C. of C., chmn., Mont. Community Fin. Corp., 1986; bd. govs. Mont. Spl. Olympics, 1984-86; mem. Citizen's Adv. Council, 1975-76; chmn. City-County Bldg., Inc., 1978; mem. Mont. Friendship Force; co-chmn. Mont. CentennialCelebration. Served with USMC, 1953-56. Mem. Helena C. of C. (dir. 1972-75, v.p. 1973, pres. 1974, Ambassador's Club 1976—, chmn. 1978), Mont. Ofcls. Assn., Mont. Ambassadors (Ambassador of Yr. 1986, bd. dirs. 1989, 2d v.p. 1989, pres. 1991). Club: Montana. Lodge: K.C. (4th) degree). Office: PO Box 5476 Helena MT 59604-5476

RITTER, TERRY LEE, electrical engineer, educator; b. St. Paul, Mar. 22, 1952; s. William Henry and Lorraine B. (Jensen) Cole; m. Shamim Siddig, Apr. 21, 1990. BSEE, U. Minn., 1984; MSEE, Stanford U., 1987. Engring. mgr. Intel Inc., Santa Clara, Calif., 1984-88; researcher Apple Computer/Stanford U., Cupertino, Calif., 1988-89; cons., educator various high tech. firms Santa Clara, 1989-90; cons. nCHIP, Fremont, Calif., 1991; researcher Tessera Inc./Sematech, Santa Clara, 1992; cons., v.p. Exec. Financing, Inc.; pres., CEO Exptl. and Applied Scis., 1993-94; v.p. Med-Pro Industries, 1994-95. Co-author: Thin Film MCMs, 1992; contbr. articles to tech. publs. With USN, 1969-77. Mem. IEEE, Internat. Soc. Hybrid Mfrs. Home: 839 Hunter Ln Fremont CA 94539-6265

RITTMANN, PAUL DOUGLAS, health physicist; b. Mpls., Nov. 5, 1949; s. Donald Clarence and Jeanette Alice (Pearce) R.; m. Barbara Ann Behrmann, Oct. 16, 1976; children: Daniel Albert Rittmann, Erika Beth Rittmann. BA in Physics, U. Wis., 1971; MS in Physics, Purdue U., 1973, PhD in Theoretical Physics, 1976. Am. Bd. Health Physics, 1984. Instr. U.S. Naval Nuclear Power Sch., Orlando, Fla., 1976-80; radiological engr. Rockwell Hanford Co., Richland, Wash., 1980-87; prin. engr. Westinghouse Hanford Co., Richland, Wash., 1987—. contbr. articles to profl. jours. Lt. Naval Res. 1976-80. Mem. NRA, Health Physics Soc., IBM and Compatible PC User's Group (Kennewick). Republican. Home: 5001 W Skagit Ave Kennewick WA 99336-1521 Office: Westinghouse Hanford Co PO Box 1970 Richland WA 99352-0539

RITVO, EDWARD ROSS, psychiatrist; b. Boston, June 1, 1930; s. Max Ritvo; m. Riva Golan, Sept. 11, 1989; children: Deborah, Eva, Anne, Matthew, Victoria, Skylre, Max. BA, Harvard U., 1951; MD, Boston U. Sch. Medicine, 1955. Diplomate Am. Bd. Psychiatry and Neurology, Am. Bd. Child Psychiatry. Prof. UCLA Sch. Medicine, 1963—. Author 4 books; contbr. over 150 articles to profl. jours. Capt. U.S. Army, 1959-61. Recipient Blanche F. Ittleson award Am. Psychiat. Assn., 1990. Mem. Nat. Soc. for Autistic Children, Profl. Adv. Bd. (chmn.). Office: UCLA Sch Medicine Dept Psychiatry 760 Westwood Plz Los Angeles CA 90024-8300

RITZ, RICHARD ELLISON, architect, architectural historian, writer; b. Colfax, Wash., Dec. 8, 1919; s. Henry Clay and Katharine Fredericka (Failing) R.; m. Evelyn R. Robinson, Sept. 21, 1940; children: Margaret Karen Ritz Barss, Susan Elizabeth Ritz Williams. Student, Whitman Coll., 1936-37. Registered architect, Oreg. Draftsman, job capt. Pietro Belluschi, Architect, Portland, Oreg., 1946-51; project mgr., chief prodn. Belluschi and Skidmore, Owings & Merrill, Portland, 1951-56; project mgr., then gen. mgr. Skidmore, Owings & Merrill, Portland, 1956-82; pvt. practice architecture Portland, 1982—; founder Greenhills Press, 1991. Author: A History of the Reed College Campus, 1990, An Architect Looks at Downtown Portland, 1991; editor: A Guide to Portland Architecture, 1968; contbr. articles to profl. jours. Bd. dirs. Architecture Found., Portland, 1982-85; mem. Portland Hist. Landmarks Commn., 1987—. Sgt. USAF, 1942-45. Fellow AIA (bd. dirs. Portland chpt. 1975-79, pres. 1978, mem. handbook com. Fin. Mgmt. for Architects 1980); mem. Soc. Archtl. Historians, Oreg. Coun. Architects (del. 1975-79), Portland Art Mus., Oreg. Hist. Soc., Lang Syne Soc., City Club Portland, Univ. Club (Portland), Multnomah Athletic Club. Republican. Presbyterian. Home and Office: 4550 SW Greenhills Way Portland OR 97221-3214

RITZHEIMER, ROBERT ALAN, educational publishing executive; b. Trenton, Ill., Dec. 29, 1931; s. Leslie H. and Hilda M. (Fochtmann) R.; m. Shirley Ann Wharrie, Sept. 11, 1954; children: Kim E. Ritzheimer Chase, Gina C. Ritzheimer Hartle, Scott D., Susan L. Ritzheimer Kelly. BS in Edn., Ill. State Normal U., 1953, MS in Edn., 1960; postgrad., Columbia U., 1955. Cert. tchr., supr., k-12, Ill. Tchr. Bloomington (Ill.) Pub. Schs., 1955-57; prin., elem. and jr. high sch. Wesclin Community Unit #3, New Baden, Ill., 1957-62; ednl. sales rep. Scott Foresman Co., Bradford Woods, Pa., 1962-81; field sales mgr. Scott Foresman Co., Sunnyvale, Calif., 1981-91; mgr. sales support Scott Foresman Co., Sunnyvale, 1992-93; ret., 1993; cons., pub. Calif. State Bd. Edn., Sacramento, 1981-93; guest lectr. Stanford U., Palo Alto, Calif., 1983, Santa Clara (Calif.) U., 1992. Treas. Little League, New Baden, Ill., 1958-62; pres. Ill. Edn. Assn., Kaskaskia Div., E. St. Louis, 1961. With U.S. Army, 1953-55. Mem. ASCD, NEA (life), Calif.Sci. Teachers Assn. Republican. Home: 1566 Deerfield Dr San Jose CA 95129-4707

RIVERS, CHRISTOPHER BEAUMONT, III, newspaper publisher, sales executive; b. San Francisco, Sept. 25, 1964; s. Christopher Beaumont and Elizabeth Jean (Sanderson) R. BA in English, U. Calif., Davis. Intern Ctr. for Investigative Reporting, San Francisco, 1988; news reporter, writer Sonora (Calif.) Union Dem., 1990; editor, pub. Sunset Beacon Newspaper, San Francisco, 1991—; advt. sales mgr. The City Voice Newspaper, 1995—; freelance writer Richmond Rev. Newspaper, San Francisco, 1991-94. Mem. Olympic Club, World Affairs Coun., Media Alliance. Home: 1944 Clement St Apt A San Francisco CA 94121-2217 Office: Sunset Beacon Newspaper 4630 Geary Blvd Ste 200 San Francisco CA 94118-2934

RIVERS, VICTORIA Z., textile design educator, artist; b. Louisville, Sept. 7, 1948; d. Kenneth Clayborn and Ruth Jean (Drillette) Zellich; m. John Gregory Salkin. BFA, Murray State U., 1970, MA in Coll. Teaching, 1974. Prof., grad. adviser in textile arts and costume design U. Calif., Davis, 1980—; mem. crafts adv. panel to Tenn. Arts Commn., 1978-81; vis. artist U. Md. Inst. Sch. Fine Arts, Balt., 1984, U. Colo., Colorado Springs, 1985, Colo. State U., Ft. Collins, 1985, Cranbrook Acad., Bloomfield Hills, Mich., 1986, Old Dominion U., Norfolk, Va., 1988, So. Ill. U., Carbondale, 1989, Concordia U., Montreal, 1989, Akron (Ohio) U., 1990; lectr., presenter and workshop leader numerous colls. and mus. One woman shows include The Am. Embassy, Bern, Switzerland, 1979, Rara Avis Gallery, Sacramento, Calif., 1979, Art Mall Gallery, Mt. Hood Coll., Gresham, Oreg., 1981, Merida Gallery, Louisville, 1980, Art Dept. Gallery, Ctrl. Wash. State U., Ellensburg, 1982, Mus. Neon Art, L.A., 1983, Crocker Art Mus., Tempo Gallery, Sacramento, 1984, Conduit Gallery, Dallas, 1984, 86, Jennifer Pauls Gallery, Sacramento, 1985, 87, 89, Mobilia Gallery, Cambridge, Mass., 1987, Churchill Arts Coun., Fallon, Nev., 1992, Rogue River Gallery, 1993; group shows include Artistic Sass Gallery, Hilton Head Island, S.C., 1978, Huntington (W.Va.) Galleries, 1978, Brooks Meml. Art Gallery, Memphis, 1979, Brunnier Gallery, Ames, Iowa, 1979, 87, Alta Galleries, Sacramento, Calif., 1979, Am. Craft Mus., N.Y.C., 1979, Capricorn Asunder Gallery, San Francisco, 1981, The Louisville Gallery, 1981, Cheney Cowles Mus., Spokane, Wash., 1981, Seipp Gallery, Palo Alto, Calif., 1981, Elaine Potter Gallery, San Francisco, 1983, 86, 88, Gayle Willson Gallery, Southampton, N.Y., 1984, Laguna Beach (Calif.) Art Mus., 1984, Pitts. Ctr. for Arts, 1985, L.A. Mcpl. Art Gallery, 1985, Conduit Gallery, Dallas, 1986, Himovitz/Jensen Gallery, Sancramento, 1987, Mus. Neon Art, L.A., 1988, 91, Mobilia Gallery, Cambridge, 1988, Jennifer Pauls Gallery, 1988, 89, Rockford (Ill.) Art Mus., 1988, Painted Lady Gallery, Sutter Creek, Calif., 1988, 89, Moira-James Gallery, Las Vegas, 1990, Gregory Kondos Art Gallery, Sacramento, 1991, City of Brea (Calif.) Gallery, 1992, Loveland (Colo.) Mus., 1993, Stremmel Gallery, Reno, Nev., 1993, numerous others; contbr. articles to mags., profl. jours. U.S. Govt. fellow, 1972-74, individual artist's fellow Tenn. Arts Commn., 1978-79, visual artist's fellow Nat. Endowment for Arts, 1984-85, Coun. for Internat. Exch. of Scholars, Indo-U.S. Subcommn. on Edn. and Culture Indo-Am. fellow, 1990-91; faculty rsch. grantee U. Calif., 1980—, New Faculty rsch. grantee, 1981-83, Seed grantee, 1992-95. Mem. Surface Design Assn. Office: U Calif Walker Hall Dept Environ Design Davis CA 95616

RIVETT, ROBERT WYMAN, retired pharmaceutical company executive; b. Omaha, Jan. 20, 1921; s. Paul S. and Frances E. (Wyman) R.; m. Myra Jean Bevins, Oct. 18, 1940; children: Suzanne, Teresa, Paul. BS, U. Nebr., 1942, MS, 1943; PhD, U. Wis., 1946. Rsch. microbiologist Abbott Labs., North Chicago, Ill., 1946-48, sect. head antibiotic devel., 1948-57, asst. dir. devel., 1958-59, dir. devel., 1960-64, dir. rsch. adminstrn., 1964-71, dir. corp. quality assurance, 1971-76, dir. quality assurance agr. vet. div., 1976-77; dir. quality assurance Abbott sci. products divsn. Abbott Labs., L.A., 1977-78; v.p. quality assurance Alpha Therapeutic Corp., L.A., 1978-81; cons. chem. and chem. engring. RWR Cons., San Gabriel, Calif., 1982-88. Mem. Waukegan (Ill.) Sch. Bd., 1955-60; former warden Ch. of Our Saviour, San Gabriel. Mem. Am. Chem. Soc., Elk. Republican. Address: 3303 Taos Ct Deming NM 88030-9601

RIZZI, TERESA MARIE, bilingual speech and language pathologist; b. Denver, Aug. 8, 1964; d. Theophilus Marcus and Maudie Marie (Pitts) R. BA in Speech Pathology, U. Denver, 1986, BA in Spanish, 1986; MS in Speech Pathology, Vanderbilt U., 1988. Pediatric speech-lang. pathologist Rose Med. Ctr., Denver, 1988-90; pvt. practice Denver, 1990—; Spanish tchr. Temple Emanual, Denver, 1992-95; owner, operator Niños De Colo., Denver; Spanish tutor and interpreter, Denver, 1988—; bilingual pediatric speech-lang. pathologist The Children's Hosp., Denver, 1994—; presenter in field. G'arin grantee Ctrl. Agy. Jewish Edn., 1993, grantee U. No. Colo. Grad. Sch., 1994. Mem. Am. Speech-Lang.-Hearing Assn. (Continuing Edn. award 1991), Colo. Speech-Lang.-Hearing Assn., Internat. Assn. Orofacial Myology, Phi Sigma Iota. Office: Teresa M Rizzi MS CCC 695 S Colorado Blvd Ste 410 Denver CO 80222-8008

RIZZO, TERRY LEE, physical education educator; b. Chgo., July 2, 1951; s. Albert Ross and Charlene R.; m. Judy L., Jan. 5, 1974; children: Colin Ross, Kyle Ryan. BA with honors, Northeastern Ill. U., 1973; MEd, U. Ariz., 1974; PhD, U. Ill., 1983. Grad. tchg. asst. U. Ariz., Tucson, 1973-74, lectr., 1974-77; phys. edn. tchr. Schubert Elem. Sch., Chgo., 1977-78; rsch. asst. U. Ill., Champaign, 1978-80, lectr., 1980-83, vis. asst. prof., 1983-85; asst. prof. SUNY, Cortland, 1985-88, coord. undergrad. studies, 1987-88; asst. prof. Calif. State U., San Bernardino, 1988-91, assoc. prof., 1991-95, prof., chair dept. of phys. edn., 1995—; part-time phys. edn. tchr. Fenster Coll. Prep. Sch., Tucson, 1974-75; vis. lectr. Northeastern Ill. U., Chgo., 1978; cons. Urbana Pub. Schs., 1982-85, Devel. Svcs. Ctr. Champaign County, Ill., 1982-83, Marriott Motor Hotel, Chgo.; tech. advisor various attys. Contbr. over 20 articles to profl. jours., presenter and reviewer in field; mem . editorial bd. Adapted Phys. Activity Quar., 1993—. Bd. dirs. Easter Seals Soc. Inland Counties, San Bernardino, 1990-93. Mem. AAHPERD (Assn. for Rsch., Adminstrn., Profl. Couns. & Socs.; Nat. Assn. for Sport & Phys. Edn.), Calif. Assn. Post-Secondary Educators of Disabled, Calif. Assn. Health, Phys. Edn., Recreation and Dance, Phi Delta Kappa. Home: 1481 W Cypress Ave Redlands CA 92373-5660 Office: CSU San Bernardino 5500 University Pky San Bernardino CA 92407-2318

RIZZUTO, CARMELA RITA, nursing administrator; b. Waterbury, Conn., Aug. 26, 1942; d. Joseph Anthony and Carmella Rosa R.; m. Thomas Lee Chernesky, Aug. 28, 1982. BS, St. Joseph Coll., 1965; MS, Boston Coll., 1971; EdD, Sch. Edn., UCLA, 1983. RN, Calif. Nursing instr. Samaritan Hosp. Sch. Nursing, Troy, N.Y., 1969; med. nursing coord., clin. specialist Harvard Community Health Plan, Boston, 1971-72; instr. inservice edn. Tufts-New Eng. Med. Ctr., Boston, 1972-73; instr. inservice edn. St. John's Hosp. and Health Ctr., Santa Monica, Calif., 1974-76; asst. clin. prof. Sch. Nursing, UCLA, 1976-79; assoc. dir. nursing edn. St. Francis Hosp. of Santa Barbara, 1981-83; asst. dir. nursing edn. and rsch. Stanford U. Hosp., 1983-90, dir. geriatric patient care grant, 1990-93; rsch. coord. sch. medicine Stanford U., 1994—. Grantee USPHS, NIH, DHHS, USPHS nurse trainee, 1969-71; recipient Chancellor's Patent Fund, UCLA, 1972-73. Contbr. articles to profl. publs. Home: 925 Cascade Dr Sunnyvale CA 94087-4043

ROACH, BEVERLY HYATT, public health clinic manager; b. Provo, Utah, Apr. 27, 1953; d. Edmond Preston and Ora Mae (Sorensen) Hyatt; m. Kenneth David Roach, Dec. 30, 1976; children: David, James, Michelle, Brian. BS in Food Sci. and Nutrition, Brigham Young U., 1975; MS in Pub. Health, U. Utah, 1994. Registered dietitian. Food svc. dir. Canoga Ter. Convalescent Hosp., L.A., 1977-78; cons. nutritionist Am. Nursing Home Mgmt. Co., L.A., 1980-84; clin. dietitian Simi Valley (Calif.) Adventist Hosp., 1985-88, dir. nutrition svcs. dept., 1988-90; nutrition supr. Salt Lake County Health Dept., Salt Lake City, 1990-93, pub. health clinic mgr., 1993—; mem. access to health care com. Salt Lake Cmty. Health Agenda, Salt Lake City, 1993—. Mem. Am. Dietetic Assn., Coun. on Renal Nutrition of So. Calif. (newsletter editor 1986-90, officer 1989), Am. Heart Assn. (nutritional counseling cert. 1989), Utah Pub. Health Assn. (access com. 1992—), Utah Dietetic Assn. Home: 1940 E 5685 S Salt Lake City UT 84121-1343 Office: Salt Lake County Health Dept 3195 S Main St Salt Lake City UT 84115

ROACH, JOHN D. C., manufacturing company executive; b. West Palm Beach, Fla., Dec. 3, 1943; s. Benjamin Browning and Margaret (York) R.; m. Pam Flebbe, Dec. 29, 1967 (div. Aug. 1981); children: Vanessa, Alexandra; m. Elizabeth Louise Phillips, Aug. 28, 1982; children: Bruce Phillips, Bryce Phillips, Brian Phillips. BS in Indsl. Mgmt., MIT, 1965; MBA, Stanford U., 1967. Dir. mgmt. acctg. and info. systems Ventura div. Northrop Corp., Thousand Oaks, Calif., 1967-70; co-founder, mgr. Northrop Venture Capital, Century City, Calif., 1970-71; v.p., dir. Boston Consulting Group, Boston and Menlo Park, Calif., 1971-80; v.p., world-wide strategic mgmt. practice mng. officer Booz, Allen, Hamilton, San Francisco, 1980-82; Houston, 1982-83; vice chmn., mng. dir. Braxton Assocs., Houston, 1983-87; sr. v.p., chief fin. officer Manville Corp., Denver, 1987-88, exec. v.p. ops., 1988-91; pres. Manville Sales Corp., Denver, 1988-90, Manville Mining and Minerals Group, Denver, 1990-91, Celite Corp., Denver, 1990-91; chmn., pres., chief exec. officer Fibreboard Corp., Walnut Creek, Calif., 1991—; bd. dirs. Magma Power Corp. Author: Strategic Management Handbook, 1983; contbr. articles to profl. jours. Bd. dirs. Cystic Fibrosis, Houston, 1986-87, Am. Leukemia Soc., Houston, 1986, Opera Colo., Denver, 1987-91, Bay Area Coun., San Francisco; bd. trustees Alta Bates Med. Ctr.; mem. exec. com. San Francisco Opera Assn. Mem. N.Am. Soc. Strategy Planners, Greater Denver C. of C. (bd. dirs.), Geol. Energy and Minerals Assn. (bd. dirs.), Colo. Forum, Soc. Corp. Planners (charter), Fin. Execs. Inst., Stanford Grad. Sch. Bus. Club, MIT Alumni Club, Met. Racquet Club (Houston), Denver Athletic Club, Cherry Hills Country Club (Englewood, Colo.), Contra Costa Country Club, Claremont Country Club. Home: 125 Guilford Rd Piedmont CA 94611-3804 Office: Fibreboard Corp 2121 N California Blvd Ste 560 Walnut Creek CA 94596-7306

ROACH, MACK, III, radiation oncology educator; b. Palestine, Tex., Sept. 27, 1953; s. Mack Roach, Jr. and Artie Mae (Suber) Bennett; m. Jaclyn C. Imani; 1 child, Imari; m. Deborah A. Roach; 1 child, Sarah. BS in Physics, Morehouse Coll., 1975; MD, Stanford U., 1979. Intern internal medicine Martin Luther King Gen. Hosp., L.A., 1979-80, resident internal medicine, 1980-81; fellow med. oncology U. Calif., San Francisco, 1981-83; chief resident internal medicine Highland Gen. Hosp., Oakland, Calif., 1983-84; resident radiation oncology Stanford (Calif.) U., 1984-87, chief resident radiation oncology, 1987; acting chief radiation oncologist Martinez (Calif.) VA, 1987-88, chief radiation oncologist, 1988-90; asst. prof. radiation oncology U. Calif., San Francisco, 1990-94, assoc. prof. radiation oncology, 1994—; cons. health care related rsch., Lafayette, Calif., 1990; film prodr. Mack Roach III Prodns., Lafayette, 1993—. Recipient Career Devel. award Am. Cancer Soc., 1994—, Healthnet Awareness award U. Calif. San Francisco/Healthnet, 1994. Mem. Am. Soc. Therapeutic Radiation Oncology, Am. Soc. Clin. Oncology, No. Calif. Radiation Oncology Soc., Radiation Therapy Oncology Group. Office: U Calif 505 Parnassus C-75 San Francisco CA 94143-0226

ROARK, DENIS DAREL, college dean; b. Greensboro, N.C., Sept. 10, 1943; s. Russell William Gouge and Edith Marie (Servatius) Roark; m. Glenna Denise Sprakman, Aug. 6, 1973; children: Brian, Staci. BS, Tex. Tech. U., 1966; MS, East Tex. State U., 1969; EdD, U. Ariz., 1985. Libr. Spur (Tex.) Sch. Dist., 1966-67, Dallas (Tex.) Pub. Schs., 1967-68; dir. Learning Resource Ctr. Eastern N.Mex U., Roswell, N.Mex., 1968-85, asst. dean of instrl. support, 1986-88, dean of instrn., 1988—. Contbr. articles to profl. jours. Mem. Assn. for the Study of Higher Edn. (adv. com. N.Mex. commn.), N. Mex. Libr. Assn. (past sec., membership chmn., local arrangements chmn., publs. and mailing chmn., conf. site chmn., treas.), N.Mex. Learning Resource Ctr. Coun., Rotary Internat. Home: 1102 Monterrey Dr Roswell NM 88201-8339 Office: Ea NMex U 58 University Blvd Roswell NM 88201-8435

ROATH, STEPHEN D., pharmaceutical company executive; b. 1941. With Long's Drug Stores Corp., 1964—, exec. v.p. store ops., 1988-91, pres., 1991—. Office: Longs Drug Stores Corp 141 N Civic Dr Walnut Creek CA 94596-3815*

ROBARDS, TIMOTHY ALAN, forester; b. Gary, Ind., July 8, 1963; s. Charles Edwin and Francis Kathleen (Kipling) R.; children: Sarah Robards Sheaks, Corrine Robards Sheaks. BS, Purdue U., 1985; MS, U. Calif., 1988. Researcher U. Calif., Berkeley, 1988-89; programmer/analyst Calif. Dept. Forestry, Sacramento, Calif., 1989-94, forest biometrician, 1994—. Contbr. articles to profl. jours. Mem. Soc. Am. Foresters, Toastmasters Internat. Office: Calif Dept Forestry PO Box 944246 Sacramento CA 94244-2460

ROBB, PEGGY HIGHT, artist, educator; b. Gallup, N.Mex., Sept. 14, 1924; d. John George and Beatrice Allen (Colton) Hight; m. John Donald Robb, Feb. 8, 1946; children: John Donald III, Celeste Robb Nicholson, Ellen Bea, Bradford Hight, George Geoffrey, David MacGregor. BFA, U. N.Mex., 1946, MA, 1960. juror for varied art exhbns., 1987-91; drawing instr. continuing edn. U. N.Mex., 1987—. Works have been exhibited at N.Mex. State Fair, Albuquerque, 1951-90, Jonson Gallery-U. N.Mex., Albuquerque, 1970-81, Guangzhuo (China) Art Inst., 1984, Christians in the Visual Arts, Washington, 1987, Five States Biennial, Los Alamos, N.Mex., 1987, Graham Mus., Wheaton, Ill., 1987-89, Expressions of Faith, Scottsdale, 1988, Civic Ctr. Mus., Phila., 1989, Magnifico Festival Arts, Albuquerque, 1991-93, Peoria (Ill.) Art Guild, 1993, Nat. Christian Fine Arts Exhibit, Farmington, N.Mex., 1994, 95. Mem. Albuquerque United Artists (dir. 1983-84), Fellowship Artists for Cultural Exch., Christians in the Visual Arts, Coll. Fine Arts Alumni (dir. 1989—). Home: 7200 Rio Grande Blvd NW Albuquerque NM 87107-6428

ROBBINS, ANNE FRANCIS See REAGAN, NANCY DAVIS

ROBBINS, CHARLES DUDLEY, III, manufacturing executive; b. Montclair, N.J., Sept. 21, 1943; s. Charles Dudley Robbins Jr. and Elaine (Siebert) Stark; m. Rebecca Lucille Bender; children: Seth A., Evan F., Gwendolyn M., Catherine E., Christopher W. BS in Bus. Adminstrn., U. Phoenix, Irvine, Calif., 1982; MBA, U. Phoenix, Salt Lake City, 1986. Cert. mfg. engr., robotics. Project engr. Mead Paper Corp., Atlanta, 1969-73; engr. McGaw Labs., Glendale, Calif., 1973-75; mgr. tool engring. Weiser Lock Co., South Gate, Calif., 1975-77; chief engr. Bivans Corp., L.A., 1977-79; sr. project engr. Charls Wyle Engring. Corp., Torrance, Calif., 1979-80; automation specialist Mattel Toys Inc., Hawthorne, Calif., 1980-83; dir. automation engring. Deseret Med., Warner Lambert, Sandy, Utah, 1983-88; dir. mfg. Deseret Med., Becton Dickinson, Sandy, 1988-91; dir. Worldwide Mfg., Becton Dickinson Vascular Access, 1991—; chmn. program adv. com. Salt Lake City Cmty. Coll., 1994. Patentee in field. Dist. chmn. Utah Dem. Party, Sandy, 1987-88. Mem. U. Phoenix Alumni Assn., Sandy C. of C. (bd. dirs. 1990-92). Democrat. Episcopalian. Home: 11 S Wolcott St Salt Lake City UT 84102-1815 Office: 9450 State St Sandy UT 84070

ROBBINS, CONRAD W., naval architect; b. N.Y.C., Oct. 11, 1921; s. Girard David and Ethyl Rae (Bergman) R.; m. Danae Gray McCartney, Jan. 8, 1923 (dec. Jan. 1971); children: Lorraine, Linton, Jennifer; m. Melissa Jahn, Apr. 15, 1971 (dec. Mar. 1992). BSE, U. Mich., 1942. Estimator Pacific Electric Co., Seattle, 1946-47; pres. Straus-Duparquet, Lyons-Alpha, Albert Pick, N.Y.C. and Chgo., 1947-67, C.W. Robbins, Inc., Carefree, Ariz., 1967—; cons. in field. Capt. floating drydock USN, 1942-46. Home: 4401 E Mountainview Rd Phoenix AZ 85028 Office: CW Robbins Inc 7500 Stevens Rd Carefree AZ 85377

ROBBINS, JAMES EDWARD, electrical engineer; b. Renovo, Pa., May 11, 1931; s. James Edward and Marguerite Neva (Cleary) R.; m. Elizabeth Anne Caton, 1959 (div. July 1971); children: James, Katherine, Ellen; m. Dorothy Raye Bell, July 23, 1971; stepchildren: Mark, Lori. BEE, Pa. State U., 1958; MS in Math., San Diego State U., 1961. Registered profl. engr., Calif., Ariz. Rsch. engr. Astronautics div. Gen. Dynamics Co., San Diego, 1961-62; mgr. tech. ops. Electronics div. Gen. Dynamics Co., Yuma, Ariz., 1976-82; sr. engr. Kearfott div. Gen. Precision Co., San Marcos, Calif., 1962-65; systems engring. specialist Teledyne Ryan Aerospace Co., San Diego, 1965-76; v.p. Cibola Info. Systems, Yuma, 1982-84; cons. engr. Robbins Engring. Co., Yuma, 1984-85; sr. engring. specialist Gen. Dynamics Svcs. Co., Yuma, Ariz., 1985-90; systems engr. Trimble Navigation, Sunnyvale, Calif., 1990—. Contbr. articles to profl. jours. With USN, 1951-55, Korea. Mem. Inst. Navigation, Nat. Soc. Profl. Engrs., Ariz. Soc. Profl. Engrs. (pres. western div. 1986), Am. Legion, VFW (post comdr. 1963-65), Tau Beta Pi. Home: 704 Le Mans Way Half Moon Bay CA 94019-1437 Office: Trimble Navigation 585 N Mary Ave Sunnyvale CA 94086-2905

ROBBINS, JOHN, foundation executive, writer. Founder EarthSave, Santa Cruz, Calif.; speaker in field for major confs. for Physicians for Social Responsibility, Beyond War, Oxfam, Sierra Club, Humane Soc. U.S., UNICEF, UN Environ. program, also others; guest on Oprah Winfrey, Phil

Donahue, Geraldo Rivera shows. Author: Diet for a New America (Pulitzer Prize nominated), May All Be Fed--Diet for a New World.

ROBBINS, JOHN MICHAEL, JR., mortgage company executive; b. Phoenix, June 16, 1947; s. John Michael and Dorothy Louise (Hollenbeck) R.; m. Laura Hobe, Oct. 5, 1968; children—James S., Deanna M. Student, Phoenix Coll., 1965-66, 70-71. V.p. Colonial Mortgage Co., Phila., 1971-80; regional v.p. Advance Mortgage Co., Southfield, Mich., 1980-82; sr. v.p. Central Fed. Mortgage, San Diego, 1982-83; exec. v.p. Imperial Corp. Am., San Diego, 1983-88; pres., chmn. Am. Residential Mortgage Corp., La Jolla, 1983—; chmn. bd. Am. Mortgage Investment Corp., Fieldstone Co. Zone chmn. Ducks Unltd., San Diego, 1975-78; pres. Encinitas Union Sch. Dist. Ednl. Facilities Corp., 1975-78; bd. dirs. Child Abuse Prevention Found., San Diego YMCA, Polinsky's Children's Ctr., Old Globe Theatre. Mem. Mortgage Bankers Assn. Am. (bd. govs.), San Diego C. of C. (bd. dirs.), Century Club San Diego (bd. dirs. 1992—), Univ. Club San Diego. Republican. Lutheran. Office: Am Residential Mortgage Corp 11119 N Torrey Pines Rd La Jolla CA 92037-1009

ROBBINS, KAREN DIANE, editor; b. Bloomington, Ill., Nov. 25, 1959; d. Harley Edward and Geraldine Elayne (Abell) H; m. Craig Douglas Robbins, May 25, 1992. Cert. Office Adminstrn./Info. Processing, Riverside (Calif.) C.C., 1993, Cert. Graphics Tech., 1993. Temp. Olsten Temp. Svcs., Riverside, 1982-83; inventory auditor RGIS, San Bernardino, Calif., 1984; messenger The Hammond Co., Riverside, 1984-87; data collector grocery stores INFOMAX Retail Auditing Co., Chino, Calif., 1988-90; mktg. auditor RGIS Inventory Specialists, Riverside, Calif., 1988-91. Editor Rat and Mouse Tales, AFRMA Yearbook and Rules and Standards Book. Mem. Am. Fancy Rat and Mouse Assn. (founder). Home: PO Box 2589 Winnetka CA 91396-2589

ROBBINS, NANCY LOUISE See MANN, NANCY LOUISE

ROBBINS, STEPHEN J. M., lawyer; b. Seattle, Apr. 13, 1942; s. Robert Mads and Aneita Elberta (West) R.; m. Nina Winifred Tanner, Aug. 11, 1967; children: Sarah E.T., Alicia S.T. AB, UCLA, 1964; JD, Yale U., 1971. Bar: D.C. 1973, U.S. Dist. Ct. D.C. 1973, U.S. Ct. Appeals (D.C. cir.) 1973, U.S. Ct. Appeals (3d cir.) 1973, U.S. Dist. Ct. (ea. and no. dists.) Calif. 1982, U.S. Dist. Ct. (cen. dist.) Calif. 1983, Supreme Ct. of Republic of Palau, 1994. Pres. U.S. Nat. Student Assn., Washington, 1964-65; assoc. Steptoe & Johnson, Washington, 1972-75; chief counsel spl. inquiry com. on nutrition U.S. Senate, Washington, 1975; v.p., gen. counsel Straight Arrow Pubs., San Francisco, 1975-77; dep. dist. atty. City and County of San Francisco, 1977-78; regional counsel U.S. SBA, San Francisco, 1978-80; spl. counsel Warner-Amex Cable Communications, Sacramento, 1981-82; ptnr. McDonough, Holland and Allen, Sacramento, 1982-84; v.p. Straight Arrow Pubs., N.Y.C., 1984-86; ptnr. Robbins & Livingston, Sacramento, 1986—; gen. legal counsel Govt. of State of Koror, Republic of Palau, Western Caroline Islands, 1994-95. Staff sgt. U.S. Army, 1966-68. Mem. Nat. Inst. Mcpl. Law Officers (assoc.), D.C. Bar, State Bar of Calif., ABA (sect. of urban, state and local govt. law-land use, planning and zoning com., sect. of real property, probate and trust law, sect. natural resources energy, environ. law, forum com. on affordable housing and community devel.), Urban Land Inst. (assoc.), Am. Planning Assn. (planning and law divsn., internat. divsn.), Internat. Urban Devel. Assn., Law Assn. for Asia and the Pacific. Unitarian. Office: Robbins & Livingston 3300 Douglas Blvd Roseville CA 95661-3829

ROBBLEE, RICHARD HOWARD, lawyer; b. Seattle, Apr. 18, 1952; s. John Henry and Florence Lynn (Palmer) R.; m. Nancy Elizabeth Durand, May 15, 1982; children: Elizabeth, Megan. BA magna cum laude, Harvard Coll., 1975; JD cum laude, U. Wash. Law Sch., 1978. Bar: Wash. 1978, U.S. Dist. Ct. (we. dist.) Wash. 1978, U.S. Dist. Ct. (ea. dist.) Wash. 1981, U.S. Ct. Appeals (9th cir.) 1981, U.S. Supreme Ct. 1985. Assoc. Hafer, Cassidy & Price, Seattle, 1978-81; ptnr. Hafer, Price, Rinehart & Schwerin, Seattle, 1982-91, Hafer, Price, Rinehart & Robblee, Seattle, 1992—. Contbr. law rev. comment to profl. jour. Dir. Conway Sch. Dist., Mount Vernon, Wash., 1988—. Named to Order of the Coif, U. Wash., 1978. Mem. Wash. State Bar Assn. Office: Hafer Price Rinehart et al 1100 Olive Way Ste 1600 Seattle WA 98101-1827

ROBECK, CECIL MELVIN, JR., religious studies educator; b. San Jose, Calif., Mar. 16, 1945; s. Cecil Melvin and Berdetta Mae (Manley) R.; m. Patsy Jolene Gibbs, June 14, 1969; children: Jason Lloyd, John Mark, Peter Scott, Nathan Eric. AA, San Jose City Coll., 1967; BS, Bethany Bible Coll., Santa Cruz, Calif., 1970; MDiv, Fuller Theol. Seminary, Pasadena, Calif., 1973, PhD, 1985. Ordained to ministry Assemblies of God, 1973. Instr. religion So. Calif. Coll., Costa Mesa, 1973-74; adminstrv. asst. to dean Fuller Theol. Sem., 1974-77, acting dir. admissions, 1975-77, dir. admissions and records, 1977-79, dir. student svcs., 1979-83, dir. acad. svcs., 1983-85, asst. dean, asst. prof. ch. history, 1985-88, assoc. dean, assoc. prof. ch. history, 1988-92, adj. instr. hist. theology, 1981-85, prof. ch. history ecumenics, 1992—; trustee Bethany Bible Coll., 1985-88, exec. com. 1986-88; exec. com. Internat. Roman Cath. and Pentecostal Dialogue, 1986—, co-chair, 1992—; active Commn. on Faith and Order, Nat. Coun. Chs., 1984—, Sec. Christian World Communions, 1993—; Pentecostal advisor World Coun. Chs., 1989, mem. commn. on faith and order, 1991—; co-chair L.A. Evang. and Roman Cath. Com., 1992—. Author: Prophecy in Carthage, Perpetua, Tertullian and Cyprian, 1992; editor: Charismatic Experiences in History, 1985; contbr. articles to profl. jours. Joseph L. Gerhart scholar, 1969; Assn. Theol. Schs. grantee, 1977. Fellow Wesleyan Holiness Studies Ctr.; mem. Soc. for Pentecostal Studies (1st v.p. 1981-82, pres. 1982-83, editor Pneuma 1984-92), N.Am. Acad. Ecumenists (exec. com. 1989—) N.Am. Patristics Soc. Republican. Home: 1140 N Catalina Ave Pasadena CA 91104-3807 Office: Fuller Theol Sem 135 N Oakland Ave Pasadena CA 91182-0001

ROBECK, MILDRED COEN, early childhood education educator; b. Walum, N.D., July 29, 1915; d. Archie Blane and Mary Henrietta (Hoffman) Coen; m. Martin Julius Robeck, Jr., June 2, 1936; children: Martin Jay Robeck, Donna Jayne Robeck Thompson, Bruce Wayne Robeck. BS, U. Wash., 1950, MEd, 1954, PhD, 1958. Ordnance foreman Sherman Williams, U.S. Navy, Bremerton, Wash., 1942-45; demonstration tchr. Seattle Pub. Schs., 1946-57; reading clinic dir. U. Calif., Santa Barbara, 1957-64; vis. prof. Victoria Coll., B.C., Can., summer 1958, Dalhousie U., Halifax, summer 1964; rsch. cons. State Dept. Edn., Sacramento, Calif., 1964-67; prof., head early childhood edn. U. Oreg., Eugene, Oreg., 1967-86; vis. scholar West Australia Inst. Tech., Perth, 1985; v.p. academic affairs U. Santa Barbara, Calif., 1987-92, exec. faculty, 1992—; trainer evaluator U.S. Office of Edn. Head Start, Follow Thru, 1967-72; cons., evaluator Native Am. Edn. Programs, Sioux, Navajo, 1967-81; cons. on gifted Oreg. Task Force on Talented and Gifted, Salem, 1974-76; evaluator Early Childhood Edn., Bi-Ling. program, Petroleum and Minerology, Dhahran, Saudi Arabia, 1985. Author: Materials KELP: Kgn. Evaluation Learning Pot, 1967, Infants and Children, 1978, Psychology of Reading, 1990; contbr. articles to profl. jours. Evaluation cons. Rosenburg Found. Project, Santa Barbara, 1966-67; faculty advisor Pi Lambda Theta, Eugene, Oreg, 1969-74; guest columnist Oreg. Assn. Gifted and Talented, Salem, Oreg., 1979-81; editorial review bd. ERQ, U.S. Calif., L.A., 1981-91. Recipient Nat. Dairy award 4-H Clubs, Wis., 1934, scholarships NYA and U. Wis., Madison, 1934-35, faculty rsch. grants U. Calif., Santa barbara, 1958-64, NDEA Fellowship Retraining U.S. Office Edn., U. Oreg., 1967-70. Mem. APA, Am. Ednl. Rsch. Assn., Internat. Reading Assn., Phi Beta Kappa, Pi Lambda Theta. Democrat. Home: 95999 Hwy 1015 Yachats OR 97498 Office: U Santa Barbara Executive Faculty Santa Barbara CA 93110

ROBERSON, KELLEY CLEVE, army officer; b. McAlester, Okla., July 11, 1950; s. Cleo Connie and Helen Frances (Sewell) R.; m. Georgia Lee Brown, Jan. 15, 1970; children: Kevin Christopher, Matthew Guy. BBA, Tex. Christian U., 1973; postgrad., U. Md., 1983-88, U. So. Calif., 1991-93. Commd. 2d lt. U.S. Army, 1973, advanced through grades to lt. col., 1992; exec. officer Med. Co., Ft. Carson, Colo., 1974; aviation sect. leader 377th Med. Co., Republic of Korea, 1975-76; ops. officer Aeromed. Evacuation Unit, Ft. Stewart, Ga., 1976-79; exec. officer Aeromed. Evacuation Unit, Grafenwoehr, Germany, 1980-81; comdr. Med. Co. 2nd Armored Div., Garlstedt, Germany, 1981-83; compt. Walter Reed Army Inst. Rsch., Washington, 1983-88; comdr. Aeromed. Evacuation Unit, Hickam AFB, Hawaii, [illegible] chief manpower Tripler Army Med. Ctr., Honolulu, 1990-92; chief resource mgmt., dep. comdr. adminstrn. Letterman U.S. Army Hosp. and Health Clinic, San Francisco, 1992-94; chief resource mgmt. Tripler Army Med. Ctr., Honolulu, 1994—. Pres. Parents Club Damien Meml. High Sch., Honolulu, 1990-91. Mem. ASCD, Am. Soc. Mil. Comptrs., Assn. U.S. Army, Phi Delta Kappa. Methodist. Home: 2417-A Round Top Dr Honolulu HI 96822 Office: Resource Mgmt Divsn Tripler Army Med Ctr Honolulu HI 96859

ROBERTS, ALAN SILVERMAN, orthopedic surgeon; b. N.Y.C., Apr. 20, 1939; s. Joseph William and Fannie (Margolies) S.; BA, Conn. Wesleyan U., 1960; MD, Jefferson Med. Coll., 1966; children: Michael Eric, Daniel Ian. Rotating intern, Lankenau Hosp., Phila., 1966-67; resident orthopaedics Tulane U. Med. Coll., 1967-71; pvt. practice medicine, specializing in orthopedics and hand surgery, Los Angeles, 1971—; mem. clin. faculty UCLA Med. Coll., 1971-76. Served with AUS, 1961. Recipient Riordan Hand fellowship, 1969; Boyes Hand fellowship, 1971. Mem. Riordan Hand Soc., Western Orthopaedic Assn., A.C.S., AMA, Calif., Los Angeles County Med. Assns., Am. Acad. Orthopaedic Surgeons. Republican. Jewish. Contbr. articles to profl. jours.

ROBERTS, ANN BAYARD PRICE, oil painting artist; b. N.Y.C., Aug. 3, 1925; d. John Richard and Edith Adelaide (Quigg) Price; m. John David Roberts, June 24, 1945; 1 child, Susan Jefferson (Mrs. Michael C. O'Brien). Grad., Linden Hall, 1940; degree in advt. design, Pratt Inst., 1943; postgrad., U. So. Calif., 1956, Pasadena City Coll., 1956-91. One-person shows include Gallerie de Ville, Beverly Hills, Calif., Monrovia Libr.; two-person shows include Gallery 8, Pasadena Arts Coun., Pasadena Pub. Libr.; group shows include L.A. County Mus. Art, Pasadena Art Mus., Brand Libr., Glendale, San Bernardino County Mus., Calif. State Fair, Nat. Orange Show-L.A. Art Assn., Gallery de Ville, Beverly Hills, Mishima, Japan, Downey Mus.; represented in permanent collections at Lawry's Foods, Pacific Southwest Portland Cement, T.R.W. Sustaining mem. Assistance League of Pasadena, Calif., 1960—; pres. Rosemary "500", Pasadena, 1992-93; mem. Sycamores Aux., Pasadena. Mem. L.A. Art Assn., Pasadena Soc. Artists (pres. 1989-90), Mus. Sci. and Industry (dir. at large 1994-97), San Marino League (assoc.). Republican. Episcopalian. Home: 2220 Robles Ave San Marino CA 91108-1334

ROBERTS, ANNE CHRISTINE, interventional radiologist, educator; b. Boston, Feb. 20, 1951; d. John D. and Edith Mary (Johnson) R.; m. John Edward Arnold, Feb. 25, 1989. BA, UCLA, 1972, MA, 1973; MD, U. Calif. San Diego, La Jolla, 1982. Diplomate Am. Bd. Radiology, cert. of added qualification interventional radiology, 1994. Clin. fellow radiology Harvard Med. Sch., Boston, 1983-87; asst. prof. radiology U. Calif. San Diego, La Jolla, 1987-93, assoc. prof. radiology, 1993—; chief vascular radiology VA Med. Ctr., La Jolla, 1990-93, acting chief of radiology, 1992-93; chief of radiology Thornton Hosp., U. Calif. San Diego Med. Ctr., La Jolla, 1993. Author: (with others) Current Practice of Interventional Radiology, 1991, Vascular Diseases: Surgical and Interventional Therapy, 1994; contbr. articles to profl. jours. Fellow Am. Heart Assn., Soc. Cardiovascular and Interventional Radiology (sec.-treas., program dir. 1994); mem. Western Angiographic and Interventional Radiology Soc. (sec.-treas. 1994, program dir. 1993), Radiol. Soc. N.Am., Roentgen Ray Soc., Soc. Cardiovascular & Interventional Radiology (program dir. 1994, sec.-treas. 1994-95, chair exec. coun. 1995—). Office: Thornton Hosp/UCSD Med Ctr 9300 Campus Point Dr La Jolla CA 92037

ROBERTS, ARCHIBALD EDWARD, retired army officer, author; b. Cheboygan, Mich., Mar. 21, 1915; s. Archibald Lancaster and Madeline Ruth (Smith) R.; grad. Command and Gen. Staff Coll., 1952; student U.S. Armed Forces Inst., 1953, U. Md., 1958; m. Florence Snure, Sept. 25, 1940 (div. Feb. 1950); children—Michael James, John Douglas; m. 2d, Doris Elfriede White, June 23, 1951; children—Guy Archer, Charles Lancaster, Christopher Corwin. Enlisted U.S. Army, 1939, advanced through grades to lt. col., 1960; served in Far East Command, 1942, 1953-55, ETO, 1943-45, 57-60; tech. info. officer Office Surgeon Gen., Dept. Army, Washington, 1950, Ft. Campbell, Ky., 1952-53, info. officer, Camp Chicamauga, Japan, Ft. Bragg, N.C., Ft. Campbell, Ky., 1953-56, Ft. Campbell, 1956-57, Ft. Benning, Ga., Wurzburg, Germany, 1957-58, spl. projects officer Augsburg, Germany, 1959-60, U.S. Army Info. Office, N.Y.C., 1960-61; writer program precipitating Senate Armed Services Hearings, 1962; ret., 1965; mgr., salesman Nu-Enamel Stores, Ashville, N.C., 1937-38; co-owner, dir. Roberts & Roberts Advt. Agy., Denver, 1946-49; pres. Found. for Edn., Scholarship, Patriotism and Americanism, Inc.; founder, nat. bd. dirs. Com. to Restore Constn., Inc., 1965—. Recipient award of merit Am. Acad. Pub. Affairs, 1967; Good Citizenship medal SAR, 1968; Liberty award Congress of Freedom, 1969; Man of Yr. awards Women for Constl. Govt., 1970, Wis. Legislative and Research Com., 1971; medal of merit Am. Legion, 1972; Speaker of Year award We, The People, 1973; Col. Arch Roberts Week named for him City of Danville, Ill., 1974; recipient Spl. Tribute State of Mich., 1979. Mem. Res. Officers Assn., Airborne Assn., SAR, Sons Am. Colonists. Author: Rakkasan, 1955; Screaming Eagles, 1956; The Marne Division, 1957; Victory Denied, 1966; The Anatomy of a Revolution, 1968; Peace: By the Wonderful People Who Brought You Korea and Viet Nam, 1972; The Republic: Decline and Future Promise, 1975; The Crisis of Federal Regionalism: A Solution, 1976; Emerging Struggle for State Sovereignty, 1979; How to Organize for Survival, 1982; The Most Secret Science, 1984; also numerous pamphlets and articles. Home: 2218 W Prospect PO Box 986 Fort Collins CO 80522-0986

ROBERTS, BARBARA, former governor of Oregon; b. Corvallis, Oreg., Dec. 21, 1936; m. Frank Roberts, 1974; children—Mark, Michael. Mem. Multnomah County Bd. Commrs., Oreg., 1978; mem. Oreg. Ho. of Reps., 1981-85; sec. of state State of Oreg., Salem, 1985-90, gov., 1991-94. Mem. Parkrose Sch. Bd., 1973-83. Fellow Nat. Acad. Pub. Adminstrn. Office: State Capitol Office Of Gov Rm 254 Salem OR 97310

ROBERTS, DARRYL JAY, software engineer; b. Orange, Calif., May 21, 1951; s. Ralph J. and F. Pauline (Little) R.; m. Barbara L. Case, Dec. 14, 1974. BS in Computer Sci., Calif. Polytech. State U., 1974; MSEE, U. Calif., Santa Barbara, 1979. Cert.tchr. C.C., Calif.; microsoft cert. profl. sys. engr., microsoft cert. trainer. Mgr. software engring. Burroughs Corp., Santa Barbara, Calif., 1973-87, Unisys Corp., Camarillo, Calif., 1987-94; cons. Software Engring. Unltd., Ventura, Calif., 1994—. Treas., CFO Ventura Missionary Ch., 1990-93. Recipient Eagle Scout award Boy Scouts Am., 1969, God and Country award, 1968. Mem. IEEE Computer Soc., Assn. Computing Machinery. Republican. Home and Office: PO Box 6476 Ventura CA 93006-6476

ROBERTS, DENNIS WILLIAM, association executive; b. Chgo., Jan. 7, 1943; s. William Owen and Florence Harriet (Denman) R. BA in Journalism, U. N.Mex., 1968; MA in Legal Studies, Antioch U., 1982; MA, St. John's Coll., 1984. Cert. assn. exec. Gen. assignment reporter Albuquerque Pub. Co., 1964, sports writer, 1960-64, advt. and display salesman, 1967-68; dir. info. N.Mex. bldg. br. Asso. Gen. Contractors Am., Albuquerque, 1968-79, asst. exec. dir., 1979-82, dir., 1982—. Active United Way, Albuquerque, 1969-78; chmn. Albuquerque Crime Prevention Council, 1982; bd. dir. ARC (Rio Grande chpt., 1992—). Recipient Pub. Relations Achievement award Assoc. Gen. Contractors Am., 1975, 78. Mem. N.Mex. Pub. Relations Conf. (chmn. 1975, 82-83), Pub. Relations Soc. Am. (accredited, pres. N.Mex. chpt. 1981, chmn. S.W. dist. 1984, chmn. sect. 1988), Am. Soc. Assn. Execs. (cert.), Contrn. Specifications Inst. (Outstanding Industry Mem. 1974, Outstanding Com. Chmn. 1978), Sigma Delta Chi (pres. N.Mex. chpt. 1969). Republican. Lutheran. Clubs: Toastmasters (dist. gov. 1977-78, Disting. Dist. award 1978, Toastmaster of Year 1979-80), Masons, Shriners, Elks. Home: 1709 Hiawatha St NE Albuquerque NM 87112-4519 Office: Assn Gen Contractors 1615 University Blvd NE Albuquerque NM 87102-1717

ROBERTS, DONALD JOHN, economics and business educator, consultant; b. Winnipeg, Man., Can., Feb. 11, 1945; came to U.S., 1967; s. Donald Victor and Margaret Mabel (Riddell) R.; m. Kathleen Eleanor Taylor, Aug. 26, 1967. B.A. (honours), U. Man., 1967; Ph.D., U. Minn., 1972. Instr. dept. managerial econs. and decision scis. J.L. Kellogg Grad. Sch. Mgmt., Northwestern U., Evanston, Ill., 1971-72, asst. prof., 1972-74; assoc. prof. J. L. Kellogg Grad. Sch. Mgmt., Northwestern U., Evanston, Ill., 1974-77; prof. J.L. Kellogg Grad. Sch. Mgmt., Northwestern U., Evanston, Ill., 1977-80, Grad. Sch. Bus., Stanford U., Calif., 1980; Jonathan B. Lovelace prof. grad. sch. bus. Stanford U., 1980—, assoc. dean grad. sch. of bus., 1987-90; dir. exec. program in strategy and orgn., 1992—; prof. dept. econs. Stanford U., 1986—; vis. rsch. faculty U. Catholique de Louvain, Belgium, 1974-75; cons. bus., econs. and antitrust, 1976—; spl. econ. cons. U.S. Dept. Transp., Washington, 1978-79; vis. fellow All Souls Coll., Oxford U., 1995. Assoc. editor: Jour. Econ. Theory, 1977-92, Econometrica, 1985-87, Games and Economics Behavior, 1988—; mem. editorial bd. Am. Econ. Rev., 1991-95, Jour. Econs. and Mgmt. Strategy, 1991—; co-author: Economics, Organization and Management, 1992; contbr. articles to profl. jours. NSF grantee, 1973-93; rsch. fellow Ctr. Ops. Rsch. and Econometrics, Heverlee, Belgium, 1974, fellow Ctr. for Advanced Study in the Behavioral Scis., 1991-92. Fellow Econometric Soc. (mem. coun. 1994—); mem. Am. Econ. Assn., Beta Gamma Sigma. Home: 835 Santa Fe Ave Palo Alto CA 94305-1022 Office: Stanford U Grad Sch Bus Stanford CA 94305

ROBERTS, DWIGHT LOREN, management engineering consultant, novelist; b. San Diego, June 3, 1949; s. James Albert and Cleva Lorraine (Conn) R.; B.A., U. San Diego, 1976, M.A., 1979; m. Phyllis Ann Adair, Mar. 29, 1969; children: Aimee Renee, Michael Loren, Daniel Alexandr. Engring. aide Benton Engring. Inc., San Diego, 1968-73; pres. Robert's Tech. Research Co., also subs. Marine Technique Ltd., San Diego, 1973-76; pres. Research Technique Internat., 1978—; freelance writer, 1979—; owner Agrl. Analysis, 1985-88; constrn. mgr. Homestead Land Devel. Corp., 1988—; sr. engr. cons. Morrison Knudson, 1992—. Served with U.S. Army, 1969-71. Mem. ASTM, AAAS, Nat. Inst. Sci., N.Y. Acad. Scis., Nat. Inst. Cert. in Engring. Techs., Soil and Found. Engr. Assn., Phi Alpha Theta. Baptist. Author: Geological Exploration of Alaska, 1898-1924, Alfred Hulse Brooks, Alaskan Trailblazer, Papaveraceae of the World, Demarchism, Arid Regions Gardening, Visions of Dame Kind: Dreams, Imagination and Reality, Antal's Theory of the Solar System, Science Fair-A Teacher's Manual, Common Ground: Similarities of the World Religions, Black Sheep-Scientific Discoveries From the Fringe, After Manhattan, The Christofilos Effect; contbr. articles to profl. jours. Office: 3111 E Victoria Dr Alpine CA 91901-3679

ROBERTS, ELIZABETH JEAN, environmental studies educator; b. St. Louis, Apr. 29, 1944; d. Gene and Betty J. (Manaska) Deckert; m. John W. Roberts, Aug. 22, 1966 (div. Nov. 1969); 1 child, Kristen M.; m. Elias Velonis Amidon, Apr. 11, 1985. BA, Marquette U., 1966, MA, 1969; EdD, Harvard U., 1982. Coord. White House Conf. on Children & Youth, Washington, 1969-71; dir. children's TV FCC, Washington, 1972-74; pres. Population Edn., Inc., Cambridge, Mass., 1974-80, TV Audience Assessment, Cambridge, 1980-85; prin. Amidon-Roberts Assocs., Boulder, Colo., 1987-94; faculty environ. studies The Naropa Inst., Boulder, 1992—; advisor John D. Rockefeller III, Cambridge, 1974-79; exec. dir. Inst. Deep Ecology, Boulder, 1991-94; writer, tchr., lectr., wilderness guide, Boulder, 1989—; cons. USDA Forest Svc., 1993—; ednl. cons. Environ. Rsch. Lab. U. Ariz., Tucson, 1986-91; advisor Internat. Desert Cities Assn., Phoenix, 1988-90. Editor: Earth Prayers, 1991, Honoring the Earth, 1993. Coord. spiritual retreats for homeless women, Colo., 1992-93; mem. citizens com. UN Conf. on Environment and Devel., 1991; planning advisor UN Confs. on Women, 1975, 80, 85. Recipient design arts award NEA, 1993. Fellow Internat. Execs. Network; mem. Buddhist Peace Fellowship. Democrat. Home: 1314 8th St Boulder CO 80302-5901

ROBERTS, ELIZABETH PORCHER, library director; b. St. Louis, Jan. 17, 1928; d. Francis Davis and Mary (Callaway) Porcher; m. Lorin W. Roberts, June 11, 1949 (div. 1965). AA, William Woods Coll., Fulton, Mo., 1947; BA, U. Mo., 1949; MLS, Emory U., 1956. Reference librarian Emory U. A.W. Calhoun Med. Library, Atlanta, 1954-56; with classified staff sci. library Wash. State U., Pullman, 1957, reference librarian, 1958-62, head serial record sec., 1963-72, acting head sci. library, 1965-66, 69-70, head interlibrary loan, 1970, head sci. library, 1972-76, head Owen Sci. and Engring. Library, 1977—. Contbr. articles to profl. jours. USDA Northwest and Intermountain Regional Document Delivery System grantee, Fred Meyer Chairtable Trust, 1977—. Mem. ALA (sci. tech. sect. com. on comparison of sci. libraries, task for on preconf.), Wash. Library Assn. (com. state interlibrary loan code 1972, com. women's rights 1972), Am. Soc. Engring. Edn. (PNW chmn. engring. sch. libraries div. 1966-68, v.p., program chmn. 1969-70, pres. 1970-71), Am. Soc. Info. Sci. (chmn. mentoring catalyst program 1983-84), Assn. for Faculty Women (chmn. com. on temporary appointments 1984—, faculty status com. 1985—), Assn. Acad. and Rsch. Libraries (sec./treas. 1973, nominating com. 1980), Pacific Northwest Library Assn. Home: 10423 W Ocotillo Dr Sun City AZ 85373-1647 Office: Wash State U Owen Sci and Engring Libr Pullman WA 99164-3200

ROBERTS, FRED LOUIS, technology marketing company executive; b. Sioux City, Iowa, Nov. 4, 1947; s. Fred Louis and Ann (Adamek) R.; m. Patricia A. Miller, Jan. 1982 (div. Jan. 1985). BS, Bradley U., 1971; MBA, St. Mary's Coll., Moraga, Calif., 1991; profl. dir. marketer cert., U. Mo., Kansas City, 1993. V.p. Assn. for Modern Banking, Springfield, Ill., 1977-79; pres. Roberts & Daniels, Washington, 1979-84; ctr. mgr. Compco Computer, San Francisco, 1984-85; corp. account exec. Computer Land Operated Stores, San Francisco, 1985-86; regional account exec. No. Telecom., San Ramon, Calif., 1987-89; v.p. sales and mktg. Diamond Computer Systems, Sunnyvale, Calif., 1989-93; dir. mktg. Chisholm, Campbell, Calif., 1990-93; mng. ptnr. Ams. Tech. Group, Pleasanton, Calif., 1993—. Vice chmn. Peoria County Rep. Ctrl. Com., Peoria, Ill., 1974-76; active Big Bros. and Big Sisters, Springfield, 1978-79. Mem. Pleasanton C. of C., Delta Upsilon (sec. alumni Peoria 1971-80, assoc. editor Quar. 1971). Episcopalian. Home: PO Box 2330 San Ramon CA 94583-7330 Office: Ams Tech Group 5820 Stoneridge Mall Rd Ste 100 Pleasanton CA 94588-3275

ROBERTS, GEORGE CHRISTOPHER, manufacturing executive; b. Ridley Park, Pa., May 27, 1936; s. George H. and Marion C. (Smullen) R.; m. Adriana Toribio, July 19, 1966; children: Tupac A., Capac Y. PhD, Frederico Villareal Nat. U., Lima, Peru, 1989, Inca Garcilosa de la Vega U., Lima, 1992. Sr. engr. ITT, Paramus, N.J., 1960-65; program mgr. Arde Rsch., Mawah, N.J., 1965-67; Space-Life Sci. program mgr., rsch. div. GATX, 1967-69; dir. rsch. and devel. Monogram Industries, L.A., 1969-71; chmn. Inca Mfg. Corp, 1970-72; pres. Inca-One Corp., Hawthorne, Calif., 1972—; pres. Environ. Protection Ctr., Inc., L.A., 1970-76. Bd. dirs., trustee Fairborn Obs.; founder Culver Nat. Bank, 1983; trustee Calif. Mus. Sci. and Industry, 1988-92; trustee Internat. Am. Profl. Photoelectric Photometrists, 1983—, Buckley Sch., 1984-92, Belair Prep Sch., 1992-93; chmn. solar and stellar physics Mt. Wilson Rsch. Corp., 1984-87; bd. dirs. Peruvian Found. 1981, pres. 1986-89, chmn. 1989-91, appt. rep. govt. of Peru in L.A., 1988-91; chmn. Santa Monica Coll. Astronomy Ctr. Found., 1993—; mem. adv. coun. Ctr. Internat. Bus. Edn. & Studies Santa Monica Coll., 1994. Decorated Grade of Amauta Govt. Peru, 1989. Mem. Am. Astron. Soc., Astron. Soc. Pacific. Patentee advanced waste treatment systems, automotive safety systems. Office: 13030 Cerise Ave Hawthorne CA 90250-5523

ROBERTS, GEORGE R., venture capital company executive; married; 3 children. JD, U. Calif., San Francisco. With Bears, Stearns, New York, until 1976; now ptnr. Kohlberg, Kravis, Roberts, San Francisco; dir. Beatrice Co., Chgo., Houdaille Industries Inc., Northbrook, Ill., Malone and Hyde, Memphis, Union Tex. Petroleum Holdings Inc., Houston. Office: Kohlberg Kravis Roberts & Co 2800 Sand Hill Rd Ste 200 Menlo Park CA 94025-7022*

ROBERTS, GERALD JEFFREY, newspaper editor, journalist; b. Cleve., Feb. 1, 1949; s. George and Mary Elizabeth (Andrews) R.; m. Linda J. Kiefer, Aug. 10, 1979; children: Anna, Maggie, Rebecca. AB, Harvard U., 1970. Reporter San Francisco Bay Guardian, 1974-76; writer Calif. Mag., San Francisco, 1976-77; reporter San Francisco Chronicle, 1977-78, capitol corr., 1978-80, asst. city editor, 1981-87, polit. editor, 1987—; polit. commentator Sta. KRON-TV, KQED-TV, San Francisco, 1988—. Recipient Best News Story award, other awards San Francisco Press Club. Mem. Newspaper Guild, Harvard Club San Francisco. Office: San Francisco Chronicle 901 Mission St San Francisco CA 94103-2905

ROBERTS, HOLLY LYNN, artist; b. Boulder, Colo., Dec. 22, 1951; d. Harold Albert Roberts and Emma Jane (Holmes) Evangelos; m. Robert H.

Wilson, Dec. 1, 1989; children: Ramey Wilson, Teal Wilson. Student, Bellas Artes de Mex., San Miguel de Allende, Mex., 1971, U. N.Mex., Quito, Ecuador, 1971-72; BA with spl. distinction, U. N.Mex., 1973; MFA, Ariz. State U., 1981. One woman shows include Roth Art Series, Hobbs, N.Mex., 1980, Harry Wood Gallery, Ariz. State U., Tempe, 1981, Etherton Gallery, Tucson, 1983, 85, 87, Linda Durham Contemporary Art Gallery, Santa Fe, 1986, 87, 89, 91, 95, Jayne H. Baum Gallery, N.Y.C., 1989, 91, Baker Gallery, Kansas City, 1990, Friends of Photography, San Francisco, 1990, Etherton-Stern Gallery, N.Y.C., 1991, 95, Benteler-Morgan Gallery, Houston, 1991, Gallery 210, U. Mo., St. Louis, 1992, Ehlers/Caudill Gallery, Chgo., 1992, 95, Ctr. Photographic Art, Carmel, Calif., 1993, Robert Koch Gallery, San Francisco, 1994, others; group exhbns. include Hunterdon Art Ctr., Clinton, N.J., 1978, U. N.Mex. Art Mus., Albuquerque, 1979, 83, Am. Consulate Gen., Hermosillo, Mex., 1982, Phoenix Art Mus., 1982, 83, 84, Houston Ctr. for Photography, 1983, Robert Freidus Gallery, N.Y.C., 1984, Santa Fe Ctr. for Photography, 1984, John Michael Kohler Arts Ctr., Sheboygan, Wis., 1984, 89, Laurence Miller Gallery, N.Y.C., 1984, Ctr. for Contemporary Arts, Santa Fe, 1985, Mus. Fine Arts, Santa Fe, 1985, 86, 94, Robert Koch Gallery, San Francisco, 1986, Mus. Photographic Art, San Diego, 1987, Mus. Contemporary Photography, Chgo., 1988, Blue Sky Gallery, Portland, Oreg., 1989, Graham Modern, N.Y.C., 1990, Palm Springs (Calif.) Desert Mus., 1990, Pratt-Manhattan Gallery, N.Y.C., 1991, Art Inst. Chgo., 1991. L.A. County Art Mus., 1992, The Light Factory, Charlotte, N.C., 1993; represented in permanent collections Mus. Photographic Art, San Diego, Phoenix Mus. Art, Prudential Ins., Ctr. for Creative Photography, Tuscon, San Francisco Mus. Modern Art, Mus. Fine Arts, Santa Fe, Mus. Fine Arts, Houston, Albuquerque Mus. Art, Monterey (Calif.) Peninsula Mus. Art, Calif. Mus. Photography, Riverside, L.A. Mus. Contemporary Art, Art Inst. Chgo., Green Libr. Stanford U., others. Ferguson grantee Friends of Photography, 1986, grantee Nat. Endowment for Arts, 1986, 88.

ROBERTS, JAMES LEWIS, JR., insurance executive; b. Toledo, Ohio, Nov. 26, 1942; s. James Lewis Sr. and Mary Margaret (Steele) R.; m. Leslie Knutson, Dec. 16, 1967 (div. 1979); children: James III, David Earl. BA, U. Toledo, 1964. CPCU. Spl. agt. Northwestern Mut. Ins. Co., L.A., 1967-68; underwriter Unigard Ins. Group, Huntington Beach, Calif., 1968-70; underwriting mgr. Unigard Ins. Group, Van Nuys, Calif., 1970-72; mktg. mgr. Unigard Ins. Group, Huntington Beach, 1972-75; sales mgr. Am. States Ins. Co., Santa Ana, Calif., 1975-77; ins. agt., v.p. Don Kiger & Assocs., Torrance, Calif., 1977-90; ins. agt., ptnr. Bettis Ins. Svcs., San Pedro, Calif., 1990—. Chpt. pres. Amnesty Internat. USA, Long Beach, Calif., 1985-86, area coord. Los Angeles County, 1992—, case coord. for prisoner of conscience and 1991 Nobelist Aung San Suu Kyi of Myanmar, 1993-95, dist. refugee coord., 1994—; mem. United We Stand America. Lt. USN, 1964-67, Viet Nam. Mem. ACLU, Soc. CPCU, Sigma Phi Epsilon (alumnus). Home: 2215 E 1st St Apt 8 Long Beach CA 90803-2412 Office: Bettis Ins Svcs 1891 N Gaffey St Ste 221 San Pedro CA 90731-1270

ROBERTS, JAMES MCGREGOR, retired professional association executive; b. Moncton, N.B., Can., Nov. 24, 1923; came to U.S., 1949, naturalized, 1956; s. Roland M. and Edith M. (Shields) R.; m. Thelma E. Williams, May 6, 1944; 1 dau., Jana M. B.Commerce, U. Toronto, Ont., Can., 1949. Auditor Citizens Bank, Los Angeles, 1949-54; auditor Acad. Motion Picture Arts and Scis., Hollywood, Calif., 1954—; controller Acad. Motion Picture Arts and Scis., 1956-71, exec. dir., 1971-89, exec. sec. acad. found., 1971-89; exec. cons. Acad. Motion Picture Arts and Scis., Hollywood, Calif., 1989-92; exec. cons., 1990-93, ret., 1994. Served as pilot Royal Can. Air Force, World War II. Home: 4968 Lerkas Way Oceanside CA 92056-7428

ROBERTS, JEAN REED, lawyer; b. Washington, Dec. 19, 1939; d. Paul Allen and Esther (Kishter) Reed; m. Thomas Gene Roberts, Nov. 26, 1958; children: Amy, Rebecca, Nathanial. AB in Journalism, U. N.C., 1966; JD, Ariz. State U., 1973. Bar: Ariz. 1974. Sole practice, Scottsdale, Ariz., 1975—, Jean Reed Roberts, P.C., 1992—; legal dir., advisor to gov. Ariz.-Mex. Commn., 1980-89; judge pro tem Superior Ct., Maricopa County, Ariz., 1979-92; judge pro tem Ariz. Ct. Appeals, 1995—. chmn. Bd. of Adjustment, Town of Paradise Valley, 1984-91; bd. dirs. YWCA, Maricopa County; adv. endowment bd. City of Scottsdale, Ariz., 1994—. Mem. ABA, Charter 100 of Phoenix, Nat. Acad. Elder Law, Scottsdale Bar Assn., Ariz. Bar Assn., Ariz. Women's Town Hall. Democrat. Jewish. Office: 8283 N Hayden Rd Ste 250 Scottsdale AZ 85258-2456

ROBERTS, JERRY, newspaper editor. Polit. editor city desk San Francisco Chronicle, editl. pg. editor, 1995—. Office: San Francisco Chronicle 901 Mission St San Francisco CA 94103-2905

ROBERTS, JERRY KEITH (GERALD KEITH ROBERTS), film critic, author; b. Kittanning, Pa., Oct. 1, 1956; s. Alexander and Ann Louise (Grabowski) R. BA in Journalism, Indiana U. of Pa., 1978. Sports editor Leader-Vindicator, New Bethlehem, Pa., 1978-79, Leader-Times, Kittanning, 1979-80; staff writer Pitts. Post-Gazette, 1980-83; film critic Copley L.A. Newspapers, Torrance, Calif., 1984—. Author: Robert Mitchum: A Bio-Bibliography, 1992, Reading the Rainforest, 1995; co-editor: Movie Talk from the Front Lines, 1994. Recipient honorable mention award Copley Ring of Truth award, 1985, 3d place, 1992. Mem. L.A. Film Critics Assn. (sec. 1989-91, v.p. 1993-95), S.Am. Explorers Club. Office: Copley LA Newspapers 5125 Torrance Blvd Torrance CA 90503-4117

ROBERTS, JOHN ALDEN, lawyer; b. Covina, Calif., Mar. 1, 1955; s. John Howard and Rosemary (Branine) R. BA cum laude, U. La Verne (Calif.), 1977; MFA, Claremont U., 1979; JD, U. La Verne (Calif.), 1986. Bar: Calif. 1986, U.S. Dist. Ct. (so. dist.) Calif. 1986, U.S. Dist. Ct. (cen. dist. Calif. 1987, U.S. Ct. Appeals (9th cir.) 1987. Sole practice Chino, Calif., 1986—. Mem. ABA, San Bernardino County Bar Assn., Am. Art Assn., Delta Theta Phi. Republican. Episcopalian. Home and Office: 15267 Murray Ave Chino Hills CA 91709-2706

ROBERTS, JOHN DERHAM, lawyer; b. Orlando, Fla., Nov. 1, 1942; s. Junius P. and Mary E. (Limerick) R.; m. Malinda K. Swineford, June 11, 1965; 1 child, Kimberlyn Amanda. Cert., Richmond (Va.) Bus. Coll., 1960; BS, Hampden-Sydney (Va.) Coll., 1964; LLB, Washington & Lee U., 1968. Bar: Va. 1968, Fla. 1969, U.S. Supreme Ct. 1969, U.S. Ct. Customs and Patent Appeals 1970, U.S. Tax Ct. 1970, U.S. Ct. Appeals (5th cir.) 1970, U.S. Ct. Appeals (9th cir.) 1974, U.S. Supreme Ct. 1969. Law clk. U.S. Dist. Ct., Jacksonville, Fla., 1968-69; assoc. Phillips, Kendrick, Gearhart & Aylor, Arlington, Va., 1969-70; asst. U.S. Atty. mid. dist. Fla. U.S. Dept. Justice, Jacksonville, 1970-74; asst. U.S. Atty. Dist. of Alaska, Anchorage, 1974-77, U.S. magistrate judge, 1977—. Bd. dirs. Teen Challenge Alaska, Anchorage, 1984-93; chmn. Eagle Scout Rev. Bd., 1993; bd. dirs. Alaska Youth for Christ, 1993—; mem. exec. com. Gov.'s Prayer Breakfast, 1994—. Recipient Citizenship award DAR, Anchorage, 1984, plaque, U.S. Navy, Citizen Day, Adak, Alaska, 1980. Mem. ABA, Nat. Conf. Spl. Ct. Judges (exec. bd. 1985-92), 9th Cir. Conf. Magistrates (exec. bd. 1982-85, chmn. 1984-85), Alaska Bar Assn., Anchorage Bar Assn., Chi Phi, Psi Chi, Phi Alpha Delta. Republican. Office: US Magistrate Judge 222 W 7th Ave #46 Anchorage AK 99513-7504

ROBERTS, JULIA B., banker; b. Great Falls, Mont., May 25, 1953; d. George Clyde and Florence Ethelyn (Snyder) Baldwin; m. William Geoffrey Roberts, Mar. 31, 1973 (div. 1989); children: W. Jay, Zachary W.; m. Bronson B. Smith, Aug. 14, 1992 (div. Dec. 1993). BA cum laude, U. Mont., 1977. Teller Valley Bank Kalispell, Mont., 1977-78, note window supr., 1978-81, money desk mgr., 1981-84, investment officer, 1984-87, investment and security officer, 1987-95. Scorekeeper Pee Wee Baseball, Kalispell, 1989-91; vol. sect. chair United Way Flathead County, Kalispell, 1990-91. Mem. Fin. Women Internat. (v.p. Flathead Valley group 1987-88, pres. 1988-89, state awards and scholarship chmn. 1989-90, group pub. affairs chmn., 1990-91, group pres. 1992-93, state v.p. 1993-94, state pres. 1994-95).

ROBERTS, KENNETH MELVIN, investment advisor; b. Lewiston, Idaho, Aug. 7, 1946; s. Merle Virgil and Ethel Viola (Gooch) R.; m. Sharon Kay Wilson, June 17, 1967; children: Lisa Marie, Michael Lowell. BA in Econs., Whitworth Coll., Spokane, 1968; MBA in Fin., Harvard U., 1971. Security analyst Murphey-Favre, Spokane, 1968-69, security analyst/portfolio mgr., 1971-73; security analyst/stockbroker Foster & Marshall, Spokane, 1973-81; v.p., portfolio mgr. Shearson Asset Mgmt., Spokane, 1981-90; pres., chief investment officer Ken Roberts Adv. Group, Spokane, 1990-94, Ken Roberts Investment Mgmt., 1994—; pres., dir. Ken Roberts Fin. Svcs., 1994——; cons. in investments Whitworth Found., Spokane, 1977—; v.p., dir., Roberts Ranch, Inc., Lewiston, 1974-94; pres., dir. N.W. Asset Mgmt., Spokane, 1991—; bd. dirs. Flow Internat., Kent, Wash., 1991—. Bd. dirs. Whitworth Found., Spokane, 1977-81. Mem. Assn. for Investment Mgmt. and Rsch. Christian.

ROBERTS, LARRY PAUL, broadcasting executive; b. Marengo, Iowa, June 17, 1950; s. Paul V. and Marcheta Jean (Moore) R.; m. Sheryl Irene Delamarter, Aug. 18, 1973; children: Jason, Stacey, Adam. Student, Northwestern U., 1968-69; BS, U. Minn., 1972. Ops. mgr. Sta. WPEO Radio, Peoria, Ill., 1969-70, Sta. WAYL Radio, Mpls., 1970-76; program dir. Sta. KXL and KXL-FM, Portland, Oreg., 1976-82; pres. Sunbrook Broadcasting, Inc. and Sunbrook Communications Corp., licensee of Stas. KDXT and KGRZ, Missoula, Mont., Stas. KQUY, KAAR-FM, KXTL, Butte, Mont., Stas. KBLG, KRKX, KYYA-FM Billings, Mont., 1982—, stas. KAAK, KXGF, Great Falls, Mont., 1982—; licensee Sta. KYSN-FM, East Wenatchee, Wash., Sta. KXAA-FM, Rock Island, Wash. Past pres. bd. dirs. Salvation Army, Pueblo Co.; v.p. United Way, Pueblo; bd. dirs. Rocky Mountain coun. Boy Scouts Am., Wayside Cross Rescue Mission, Pueblo; trustee Western Evang. Sem.; mem. ministerial appointments com., lay minister Columbia River Conf. of Free Meth. Ch. Recipient Outstanding Radio Broadcaster award So. Colo. Press Club, 1986; named Radio Copywriter of Yr., Mont. Broadcasters Assn., 1983, Editorial Writer of Yr., Sigma Delta Chi, 1979, one of Outstanding Young Men in Am., Jaycees, 1980, 85. Mem. Nat. Assn. Broadcasters (bd. dirs.), Lions (past v.p. Portland club 1982), Rotary (v.p. Pueblo club 1982). Republican. Home: 7922 E Woodview Dr Spokane WA 99212-1669 Office: 1212 N Washington St Ste 124 Spokane WA 99201-2401

ROBERTS, LILLIAN, retired principal; b. Albuquerque, Dec. 1, 1927; d. John Wagner and Mattie Rebecca (Beaty) Thomas; m. Vernie Roberts, Aug. 28, 1953 (dec. Sept. 13, 1980); children: Albert, Kenneth, Constance Marie. BA, Calif. State U., Stanislaus, 1964; MA, Fresno (Calif.) Pacific Coll., 1979. Cert. elem. tchr., Calif. Mgr., co-owner Vernie's Barber Shop and Cocktail Lounge, Merced, Calif., 1955-66; tchr. Merced City Sch. Dist., 1962-72, resource tchr., 1972-77, coord. consolidate programs, 1977-92, preschool prin., 1981-92; ret., 1992; pvt. music tchr., Merced, 1960-65; adult edn. tchr. Merced Union High Sch. Dist., 1965-66; chief attendance officer Merced City Sch. Dist., 1981-92, affirmative action officer, title IX officer, 1981-86, mem. blue ribbon boundary task force, 1990-91; adj. instr. Merced Community Coll., 1983-86, seminar leader Early Childhood Devel., 1985, Early Childhood Edn., 1989- 90. Mem. Muir Trail Coun. Girl Scouts U.S.A., 1979-80, 15th Congl. Dist. Constituents Adv. Com., 1987—, Merced Cmty. Concerts, 1972-79; mem. acad. adv. coun. Calif. State U., Stanislaus, 1980; mem. Merced Masterworks Chorale, 1980-85; proctor Merced County Acad. Decathalon; mem. com. Children's Svc. Network Merced County, 1983—, chmn., 1986, also bd. dirs.; exec. dir. Spl. Advs. for Children Merced County, 1992—; bd. dirs. ct. appointed spl. advocates for Abused, Neglected, Abandoned Children (CASA), cons., 1993—. Mem. NEA, Calif. Tchrs. Assn. Merced City Tchrs. Assn., Assn. Calif. Sch. Adminstrn. (charter ret. mems. region IX 1993), Merced Sch. Employees Fed. Credit Union (credit com. 1972-77, bd. dirs 1977-84), Nat. Assn. for the Edn. Young Children, Calif. Assn. for the Edn. Young Children,; Kiwanis Club of Merced. Democrat. Office: Merced City Sch Dist 444 W 23rd St Merced CA 95340-3723 Office: CASA 632 W 13th St Merced CA 95340-5908

ROBERTS, LIONA RUSSELL, JR., electronics engineer, executive; b. Sheffield, Ala., Apr. 9, 1928; s. Liona Russell Sr. and Julia Phillipia (Harrison) R.; m. Norma Jean Walker, Mar. 15, 1952 (div. 1972); children: Laura Lee, Boyd Harrison, John King, Jenna Lynne; m. Carole Jeanne Hedges, 1973. BS in Physics, U. Miss., 1958; MS in Electronics, Navy Postgrad. Sch., Monterey, Calif., 1961; PhD in Mech. Engring., Cath. U. Am., 1977. Cert. amateur radio oper. Commd. ensign USN, 1945, advanced through grades to capt., 1967, ret., 1970; chief scientist Interstate Electronics Corp., Anaheim, Calif., 1970-83; v.p. Enigmatics, Inc., LaHabra, Calif., 1983—. Author: Signal Processing Techniques, 1977; patentee in field, 1987. Mem. IEEE (sr.), Rsch. Soc. Am., Sigma Xi. Home: PO Box 537 New Harmony UT 84757-0537

ROBERTS, MARIE DYER, computer systems specialist; b. Statesboro, Ga., Feb. 19, 1943; d. Byron and Martha (Evans) Dyer; BS, U. Ga., 1966; student Am. U., 1972; cert. systems profl., cert. in data processing; m. Hugh V. Roberts, Jr., Oct. 6, 1973. Mathematician, computer specialist U.S. Naval Oceanographic Office, Washington, 1966-73; systems analyst, programmer Sperry Microwave Electronics, Clearwater, Fla., 1973-75; data processing mgr., asst. bus. mgr. Trenam, Simmons, Kemker et al, Tampa, Fla., 1975-77; mathematician, computer specialist U.S. Army C.E., Savannah, Ga., 1977-81, 83-85, Frankfurt, W. Ger., 1981-83; ops. rsch. analyst U.S. Army Contrn. Rsch. Lab., Champaign, Ill., 1985-87; data base adminstr., computer systems programmer, chief info. integration and implementation div. U.S. Army Corps of Engrs., South Pacific div., San Francisco, 1987-93; computer specialist, IDEF repository coord., Functional Process Improvement Expertise, Defense Info. Systems Agy., Arlington, Va., 1993—. instr. computer scis. City Coll. of Chgo. in Franfurt, 1982-83. Recipient Sustained Superior Performance award Dept. Army, 1983. Mem. Am. Soc. Hist. Preservation, Data Processing Mgmt. Assn., Assn. of Inst. for Cert. Computer Profls., Assn. Women in Computing, Assn. Women in Sci., NAFE, Am. Film Inst., U. Ga. Alumni Assn., Sigma Kappa, Soc. Am. Mil. Engrs. Author: Harris Computer Users Manual, 1983.

ROBERTS, MARY WENDY, state official; b. Champaign, Ill., Dec. 19, 1944; d. Frank and Mary Roberts; m. Richard P. Bullock, Nov. 27, 1976 (div. 1984); 1 child, Alexandra Louise McKay Prentice Bullock. Student Chinese-Japanese Inst., U. Colo., 1964; B.A. in Polit. Sci., U. Oreg., 1965; M.A. in Polit. Sci., U. Wis.-Madison, 1971. Social worker Children's Services Div., Portland, Oreg., 1967-71; counselor Juvenile Ct., Portland, 1971; mem. Oreg. Ho. of Reps., Salem, 1973-75; mem. Oreg. State Senate, Salem, 1975-79; commr. Oreg. Bur. Labor and Industries, Portland, 1979-94; mem. Oreg. adv. com. U.S. Civil Rights Commn.; chmn. Oreg. Apprenticeship and Tng. Council; mem. State Workforce Quality Council; exec. sec. Oreg. Wage and Hour Commn. Oreg. del. democratic Nat. Conv., 1980, 84, co-chmn. Oreg. del., 1984. Mem. Oreg. Women's Polit. Caucus (Mary Riekeway award 1978), Am. Council Young Polit. Leaders, Oreg. Hist. Soc., Portland Art Assn., Nat. Assn. Govt. Labor Ofcls. (nat. bd. dirs.), Women Execs. in State Govt. (founder).

ROBERTS, NORMAN FRANK, English composition and linguistics educator; b. Guilford, Maine, Aug. 18, 1931; s. John Francis and Pearl Estelle (Crozier) R.; m. Shoko Kawasaki, Sept. 18, 1959; children: Norman F. Jr., Kenneth K., Kathryn M. BA, U. Hawaii, 1960, MA, 1963, cert. in linguistics, 1972. Instr. ESL, U. Hawaii, Honolulu, 1962-68; prof. English, linguistics Leeward C.C., Pearl City, Hawaii, 1968-95, prof. emeritus, 1995, chmn. divsn. lang. arts, 1975-81, 92-95; cons. Nat. Coun. Tchrs. English, 1972-94. Author: Model Essay Booklet, 1989; co-author: Community College Library Instruction, 1979; contbr. articles to profl. jours. V.p. Pacific Palisades Community Assn., Pearl City, pres., 1973-74; mem. Aloha coun. Boy Scouts Am., Honolulu, 1972—, dir wood badge course, 1985, chmn. camping promotions, 1989-92. Recipient Dist. award of Merit Boy Scouts Am., 1986. Mem. Hawaii Coun. Tchrs. English (program chmn. 1974), Am. Dialect Soc. (program chmn. Honolulu conf. 1977). Office: Leeward Community Coll Lang Arts Div 96-045 Ala Ike St Pearl City HI 96782-3366

ROBERTS, PAUL DALE, health services administrator; b. Fresno, Calif., Jan. 17, 1955; s. Paul Marceau and Rosemarie Roberts; m. Patricia Mary Mitchell, Mar. 24, 1964; 1 child, Jason Randall Porter. AA, Sacramento City Coll., 1977; diploma in pvt. investigations, Ctrl. Investigation & Security, 1984. Office asst. I Dept. Benefit Payments, Sacramento, Calif., 1976-77; firefighter Calif. Divsn. Forestry, Colfax, 1977; key data operator Dept. Justice, Sacramento, 1977-78; intelligence analyst, spl. forces instr. U.S. Army Mil. Intelligence, Seoul, Korea, 1979-84; law libr. Employment Devel. Dept., Sacramento, 1989-92; office asst. II Dept. Health Svcs., Sacramento, 1992—; disaster courier dept. social svcs. Gov.'s Office of Emergency Svcs., L.A., 1994; chief cert. support Dept. Health Svcs., Sacramento, 1992—. Author: The Cosmic Bleeder, 1991, Madam Zara, Vampiress, 1993, (jour.) Memoirs of Paul Roberts, 1991; prodr.: (book) Villalobos Family, 1993. Sgt. U.S. Army, 1973-76, 79-84. Democrat. Roman Catholic. Home: 60 Parkshore Cir Sacramento CA 95831-3061 Office: Dept Health Svcs Radiologic Health Br 601 N 7th St Sacramento CA 95814-0208

ROBERTS, PETER CHRISTOPHER TUDOR, engineering executive; b. Georgetown, Demerara, Brit. Guiana, Oct. 12, 1945; came to U.S., 1979; s. Albert Edward and Dorothy Jean (Innis) R.; m. Julia Elizabeth Warner, Nov. 10, 1984; children: Kirsta Anne, Serena Amanda, Angelee Julia, Zephanie Elizabeth, Fiona Ann, Emrys Tudor, Peter Christopher Tudor Roberts II. BSc with honors, Southampton (Eng.) U., 1969, PhD in Microelectronics, 1975. Rsch. fellow dept. electronics Southampton U., 1974-77; prof. microcircuit dept. electronics INAOE, Tonantzintla, Mexico, 1977-79; staff scientist Honeywell Systems & Rsch. Ctr., Mpls., 1979-84; dir. advanced tech. Q-Dot Inc. R&D, Colorado Springs, Colo., 1984-86; program mgr. Honeywell Opto-Electronics, Richardson, Tex., 1986; vis. prof. U. N.Mex. CHTM, Albuquerque, 1987; supr. engring. Loral Inc. (formerly Honeywell), Lexington, Mass., 1988-90; mgr. engring. Litton Systems Inc., Tempe, Ariz., 1990—; cons. engr. Q-Dot, Inc. R&D, Colorado Springs, 1982—, pvt. stockholder, 1984—. Author: (with P.C.T. Roberts) Charge-Coupled Devices and Their Applications, 1980; contbr. articles to Boletin del INAGE, IEEE Transactions on Electron Devices, Procs. of the IEE (UK), Procs. of the INTERNEPCON, Internat. Jour. Electronics,IEEE Electron Device Letters, Electronics Letters, Solid State and Electron Devices, IEEE Jour. Solid State Circuits, others. Republican. Home: 1418 N Cliffside Dr Gilbert AZ 85234-2659 Office: Litton Systems 1215 S 52nd St Tempe AZ 85281-6921

ROBERTS, PHILIP JOHN, history educator; b. Lusk, Wyo., July 8, 1948; s. Leslie J. and LaVerne Elizabeth (Johns) R. BA, U. Wyo., 1973, JD, 1977; PhD, U. Wash., 1990. Bar: Wyo. 1977. Editor Lake Powell Chronicle, Page, Ariz., 1972-73; co-founder, co-pub. Medicine Bow (Wyo.) Post, 1977; pvt. practice in law Carbon and Laramie County, Wyo., 1977-84; historian Wyo. State Hist. Dept., Cheyenne, 1979-84; editor Annals of Wyo., Cheyenne, 1980-84, 95—; owner, pub. Capitol Times, Cheyenne, 1982-84, Skyline West Press, Seattle, 1985-90; asst. prof. history U. Wyo., Laramie, 1990—; evaluator Wyo. Coun. for the Humanities, Laramie, 1990—; indexer Osborne McGraw-Hill, Berkeley, 1988—; mem. editl. bd. Annals of Wyo., 1990-95. Author: Wyoming Almanac, 1989 (pub. annually), Buffalo Bones: Stories from Wyoming's Past, 1979, 82, 84, Readings in Wyoming History, 1994; contbr. articles to profl. jours. Mem. Wyo. State Hist. Soc. (life), Wyo. State Bar, Pacific N.W. Historians' Guild, 9th Judicial Cir. Hist. Soc., Western History Assn., Am. Hist. Assn., Orgn. of Am. Historians. Democrat. Office: U Wyo Dept History Laramie WY 82071

ROBERTS, RICHARD HEILBRON, construction company executive; b. Sacramento, Nov. 19, 1925; s. John Montgomery and Mary Lou (Heilbron) R.; m. Jo Anne Sydney Erickson, Feb. 25, 1950; children: Richard, Kurt, Tracy. BSCE, U. Calif., 1949. Registered profl. engr., Calif. Field and resident engr. Calif. Div. Hwys., San Luis Obispo, 1949-51; project and br. mgr. Granite Constrn. Co., Watsonville, Calif., 1951-68, v.p., mgr., 1968-79, pres. engring. constrn. div., 1979-83, exec. v.p., chief operating officer, 1983-89, vice chmn., 1989—, also bd. dirs. Pres. Nellie Thomas Inst. Learning, 1989-90. Served to corp. U.S. Army, 1944-46. Mem. Soc. Am. Mil. Engrs., Beavers (bd. dirs., pres. 1984, Golden Beaver award 1986, Moles Non-mem. award 1988). Republican. Presbyterian. Clubs: Monterey Peninsula Country (Pebble Beach, Calif.); Silverado Country (Napa, Calif.); Pauma Valley (Calif.) Country. Home: 3481 Taylor Rd Carmel CA 93923-8914 Office: Granite Constrn Co PO Box 50085 Watsonville CA 95077-5085

ROBERTS, ROBERT CHADWICK, ecologist, environmental scientist, consultant; b. Yakima, Wash., Jan. 6, 1947. BA in Zoology, Humboldt State Coll., 1969; PhD in Ecology, U. Calif., Davis, 1976. Instr. U. Calif., Davis, 1971-73, 76-77; asst. prof. Western Mich. U., Kalamazoo, 1978-79; ind. cons. Eureka, Calif., 1979-80; instr. Humboldt State U., Arcata, Calif., 1982-83; dir. environ. svcs. Oscar Larson & Assocs., Eureka, 1980—; cons. Nat. Audubon Soc., Sacramento, 1984—, Calif. Native Plant Soc., Sacramento, 1987-89, U.S. Forest Svc., Eureka and Sacramento, 1988—; mem. Outer Continental Shelf Adv. Com., County of Humboldt, 1987-91, Creeks/Wetlands Adv. Com., City of Arcata, 1989-93; chair Calif. steering com. Pacific Coast Venture, N.Am. Waterfowl Plan; expert witness in 6 legal actions, 4 legis. hearings. Contbr. articles to profl. jours., chpts. to books; author, editor numerous tech. reports and environ. documents. Cons. Ballot Proposition 130 Steering Com., Sacramento, 1990. Grantee F.M. Chapman Fund., 1974; sci. trainee NSF, 1970-75. Mem. Ecol. Soc. Am. (cert. sr. ecologist), Soc. Wetland Scientists (cert.), Cooper Ornithol. Soc., Wildlife Soc., Soc. Conservation Biologists, Assn. of State Wetlands Mgrs., Phi Kappa Phi. Office: Oscar Larson & Assocs 317 3rd St Eureka CA 95501-0427

ROBERTS, TIMOTHY WYNELL, journalist; b. French Camp, Calif., Nov. 1, 1957; s. Loron Sr. and Garnola Marie (Wilson) R.; m. Vella Kee Black, July 26, 1986; children: Alaina, Elizabeth, Rachel Marie. BA in Mass Comm., Calif. State U., Hayward, 1979; MS, Northwestern U., 1982. Gen. assignment reporter Hayward Daily Rev., 1979-80; prodr., program coord. Hayward Cable TV 3, 1980-81; TV/radio reporter Medill News Svc., Washington, 1982; gen. assignment reporter, photographer, prodr. KERO TV 23, NBC affiliate, Bakersfield, Calif., 1983; pub. affairs dir. Kaiser Permanente Med. Care Program, Oakland, Calif., 1984-89; cons. pub. rels., video prodr., freelance journalist TWR Enterprises, San Leandro, Calif., 1989—; comm./media specialist Alameda County Social Svcs./Pub. Health Agys., Oakland, Calif., 1993—. Video prodr: Health Care: Antioch Pre-Natal Program, 1989. Mem. adv. bd. Judie Davis African Am. Bone Marrow Donor Recruitment Program, Oakland, Calif., 1993—; treas., past pres., v.p. Hesperian Villas Homeowners Assn., San Leandro, Calif., 1989—. Mem. Soc. Profl. Journalists, Sigma Delta Chi. Home and Office: 24316 Machado Ct Hayward CA 94541

ROBERTS, WESS, author; b. Cedar City, Utah, Oct. 8, 1946; s. Lester Wyatt and Lura Virginia (Russell) R.; m. Cheryl Louise Barron, Mar. 22, 1968; children: Justin, Jaime, Jeremy. BS in Psychology, So. Utah U., 1970; MS in Psychology, Utah State U., 1972, PhD in Psychology, 1974. Project dir. Courseware, Inc., San Diego, 1976-78; project engr., tng. sys. specialist Northrop Svcs., Inc., San Diego, 1978-79; dir. ops. tng. Am. Express, N.Y.C., 1979-81; v.p. human resources Am. Express, Ft. Lauderdale, Fla., 1981-82, Salt Lake City, 1982-85; v.p. human resources devel. Firemans Fund Ins. Cos., Novato, Calif., 1985-91; pvt. practice lectr. Sandy, Utah, 1991—; ad hoc prof. Utah State U., Logan, 1970-73, mem. dean's adv. coun., 1984-85; cons. Utah State U. Devel. Ctr., Logan, 1970-75, INSGROUP, Inc., Huntington Beach, Calif., 1979; mem. evaluation com. Project EVE, Columbus, Ga., 1975; adj. prof. Nova U., Ctr. for the Study of Adminstrn., Ft. Lauderdale, 1981-85; mem. adv. bd. Inst. for Human Resource Mgmt., U. Utah, Salt Lake City, 1983-85; bd. advisors Sch. Profl. Studies, Westminster Coll., Salt Lake City, 1983-85; presenter in field; others. Author: Leadership Secrets of Attila the Hun, 1989, Straight A's Never Made Anybody Rich, 1991, Victory Secrets of Attila the Hun, 1993, Make It So: Leadership Lessons For The Next Generation, 1995; editorial rev. bd.: The Pers. Adminstr., 1982-84; contbr. articles to profl. jours. Trustee The Discovery Ctr., Ft. Lauderdale, 1981-82, The Chord, Inc., Pompano Beach, Fla., 1981-83; mem., loaned exec. Nat. Alliance Bus., Western Region, 1983-85; mem. comm. com. Great Salt Lake United Way, 1984; bd. dirs. Health Plan of the Redwoods, Santa Rosa, Calif., 1987. Maj. U.S. Army, 1973-76. Recipient two Bronze medals Internat. Film and TV Festival of N.Y., 1982, Patriotic Svc. award U.S. Dept. Treasury, Washington, 1984, Silver medal and cert. of merit INTERCOM, Chgo. Internat. Film Festival, 1986, Cert. for Creative Excellence, U.S. Film and Video Festival, 1988, others. Mem. APA, Soc. for Human Resource Mgmt., Am. Ednl. Rsch. Assn.

ROBERTSON, CAREY JANE, musician, educator; b. Culver City, Calif., Apr. 18, 1955; d. Robert Bruce and Marjorie Ellen (Greenleaf) Coker; m. Brian Collins Robertson, June 28, 1975 (div. July 1985); 1 child, Sean Kalen. BMus, Calif. State U., Northridge, 1977; MMus, U. So. Calif., L.A., 1979, PhD of Mus. Arts, 1987. Organist/choir dir. Village Meth. Ch., North

Hollywood, Calif., 1972-75, St. Bede's Episcopal Ch., Mar Vista, Calif., 1975-79; organist interim St. Alban's Episcopal Ch., Westwood, Calif., 1985; organist Covenant Presbyn. Ch., Westchester, Calif., 1985-90; organist/choir dir. St. David's United Ch., West Vancouver, B.C., Can., 1990-91; prin. organist Claremont (Calif.) United Ch. of Christ, 1991—; prof. organ Claremont Grad. Sch., 1991—; concert organist Am. Guild of Organists, throughout U.S. and Can., 1974—; cons. Sch. Theology, U. B.C., 1990. Bd. dirs. Ruth and Clarence Mader Found., Pasadena, Calif., 1993—. Recipient Music Tchrs. Nat. Assn. Wurlitzer Collegiate Artist award, 1980; Irene Robertson scholar, 1977, 78. Mem. Am. Guild Organists (historian, sec. 1985-92, exec. com. 1983-85), Pi Kappa Lambda (Scholastic award 1987). Home: 7514 Pepper St Rancho Cucamonga CA 91730-2125

ROBERTSON, HUGH DUFF, lawyer; b. Grosse Pointe, Mich., Mar. 14, 1957; s. Hugh Robertson and Louise (Grey) Bollinger; m. Lynn Ann Wicker, June 10, 1978. BBA in Fin., U. Wis., Whitewater, 1978; JD, Whittier Coll., 1982. Bar: Calif. 1983, U.S. Tax Ct. 1984. Pres., CEO, A. Morgan Maree Jr. & Assocs., Inc., L.A., 1979—. Mem. ABA (forum com. on entertainment 1982—, forum com. on constrn. industry 1989), State Calif., L.A. County Bar Assn., Beverly Hills Bar Assn., Acad. TV Arts and Scis., Am. Film Inst., Phi ALpha Delta. Republican. Episcopalian. Office: A Morgan Maree Jr & Assocs 4727 Wilshire Blvd Ste 600 Los Angeles CA 90010-3875

ROBERTSON, JACQUELINE LEE, entomologist; b. Petaluma, Calif., July 9, 1947; d. John Lyman and Nina Pauline (Klemenok) Schwartz; m. Joseph Alexander, Sept. 12, 1970 (div. Jan. 1978). BA, U. Calif., Berkeley, 1969, PhD, 1973. Registered profl. entomologist. Research entomologist USDA Forest Service, Berkeley, 1970—. Editor: Jour. Econ. Entomology, 1982—, Can. Entomologist, 1992—; author: Pesticide Bioassays with Arthropods, 1992; contbr. articles to profl. jours.; patentee lab. device, 1982. Mem. Entomol. Soc. Am., Entomol. Soc. Can., AAAS. Democrat. Office: US Forest Svc PSW Sta PO Box 245 Berkeley CA 94701-0245

ROBERTSON, JOSEPH DAVID, lawyer; b. Pitts., Dec. 24, 1944; s. Sinon Joseph and Marie Catherine (Nold) R.; m. Susan Louise Lyon, Apr. 10, 1968; children—Brian, Mark. Student Coll. Steubenville, 1962, U. Md., 1968-69; B.A., Willamette U., 1971, J.D. cum laude, 1974. Bar: Oreg. 1974, U.S. Dist. Ct. Oreg. 1974, U.S. Ct. Appeals (9th cir.) 1976. Shareholder Garrett, Seideman, Hemann, Robertson & De Muniz, P.C., Salem, Oreg., 1974—; mem. Oreg. State Bd. Bar Examiners, Portland, 1983-86; adj. prof. law for trial practice Willamette U. Coll. Law, 1976-78. Contbr. articles to profl. publs. Mem., chmn. Faye Wright local Adv. Com., Salem, 1978-83; mem. Judson local sch. adv. com., Salem, 1984-85; cubmaster Willamette Council Boy Scouts Am., 1979-85, mem. troop com., 1983-85; mem. workers' compensation com. Associated Oreg. Industries, Salem, 1982—; coach Salem Parks & Recreation soccer program, 1979-85; coach Judson Little League, Salem, 1981; mem. disciplinary rev. com. Faye Wright Sch., Salem, 1982. Served with USMC, 1963-67. Recipient Advocacy award Internat. Acad. Trial Lawyers, 1974. Mem. ABA, Workers' Compensation Def. Lawyers Assn., Am. Soc. Law and Medicine, Marion County Bar Assn., Oreg. State Bar Assn. (bd. govs. 1988—; mem. exec. com. litigation sect. 1983-84, bd. govs. 1988—), Oreg. Trial Lawyers Assn. (bd. govs. 1976-78), Oreg. Assn. Def. Counsel. Republican. Club: Salem Tennis and Swim. Office: Garrett Hemann et al Box 749 1011 Commercial St NE Salem OR 97301-1019

ROBERTSON, JOSEPH E., JR., ophthalmologist, educator; b. Jackson County, Ind., July 24, 1952; s. Joseph E. and Virginia Faye (Baxter) R.; m. Margaret Hewitt, Oct. 10, 1976; children: Katherine Faye, Charles Joseph. BS cum laude, Yale U., 1974; MD, Ind. U., 1978. Diplomate Am. Bd. Ophthalmology. Intern Bapt. Med. Ctr., Birmingham, Ala., 1978-79; resident Oreg. Health Sci. U., Portland, 1979-82; pvt. practice Vancouver, Wash., 1982-83; fellow Oreg. Health Sci. U./Devers Hosp./Good Samaritan Hosp., Portland, 1983-84; vitreous surgery fellow Steve Charles, M.D., Memphis, Tenn., 1984-85; asst. prof. Oreg. Health Sci. U., Portland, 1985-92, assoc. prof., 1992—. Contbr. articles to profl. jours., chpts. to books; editor videotapes. Apptd. mem. Oreg. Commn. for the Blind, 1988—; bd. dirs. Oreg. Med. Polit. Action Com., Salem, 1994—. Mem. Am. Acad. Ophthalmology (Oreg. rep. to coun. 1992—, COVE com. 1992—, skills transfer adv. com. 1994—, nat. chair & state coord. Diabetes 2000), Oreg. Acad. Ophthalmology (pres. 1990-91), Oreg. Med. Assn. Democrat. Presbyterian. Office: Casey Eye Inst/OHSU 3375 SW Terwilliger Blvd Portland OR 97201-4146

ROBERTSON, KAREN JEAN, real estate broker, appraiser; b. Boggstown, Ind.; d. James Russell Tillison and Gladys Mae (Lancaster) King; m. Bill Gene Barker, 1961 (dec. 1962); 1 child, Toni Karen Barker; m. Charles Lee Koons, 1971 (dec. 1984); m. William Lenard Robertson, 1991. Real estate cert., Fresno City Coll., 1987; student, U. Calif., Davis, 1986; BA, MBA, Western States U., 1985; grad., Realtors Inst. Calif., 1982. Lic. real estate broker, Calif.; cert. gen. real estate appraiser, Calif.; notary pub., Calif. Telephone operator Ind. Bell Telephone, Indpls., 1954-56; clk., typist Hemphill Noyes & Co., Indpls., 1956-57; tchr. Patricia Stevens Modeling Sch., Indpls., 1957-60; clk., typist RCA, Indpls., 1957-60, City of Fresno, Calif., 1960-61; sr. acctg. clk. Fed. Mktg. Order Grape Crush Adminstrn., Fresno, 1963; clk., typist Calif. Hwy. Patrol, Fresno, 1963-67; radio dispatcher Calif. Dept. Fish and Game, Fresno, 1967-71; real estate agt. various cos., Shaver Lake, Calif., 1974-79; pvt. practice real estate Shaver Lake, 1979—. Mem. Nat. Assn. Realtors, Calif. Assn. Realtors, Fresno Assn. Realtors, Internat. Orgn. Real Estate Appraisers. Democrat. Prebyn. Home: 41617 Tollhouse Rd Shaver Lake CA 93664 Office: PO Box 313 Shaver Lake CA 93664-0313

ROBERTSON, MARIAN ELLA (MARIAN ELLA HALL), small business owner, handwriting analyst; b. Edmonton, Alta., Can., Mar. 3, 1920; d. Orville Arthur and Lucy Hon (Osborn) Hall; m. Howard Chester Robertson, Feb. 7, 1942; children: Elaine, Richard. Student, Willamette U., 1937-39; BS, Western Oreg. State U., 1955. Cert. elem., jr. high. tchr., supt. (life) Oreg.; cert. graphoanalyst. Tchr. pub. schs. Mill City, Albany, Scio and Hillsboro, Oreg., 1940-72; cons. Zaner-Bloser Inc., Columbus, Ohio, 1972-85, assoc. cons., 1985-89; pres. Write-Keys, Scio, 1980-90; owner Lifelines, Jefferson, Oreg., 1991—; tchr. Internat. Graphoanalysis Soc., Chgo., 1979; instr. Linn-Benton Community Coll., 1985-89. Sr. intern 5th Congl. Dist. Oreg., Washington, 1984, mem. sr. adv. coun.; precinct com. mem. Rep. Cen. Com., Linn County, 1986, alt. vice-chair, 1986, parliamentarian, 1988—; candidate Oreg. State Legis., Salem, 1986; del. Northwest Friends Yearly Meeting, Newberg, Oreg., 1990, 91, 92; master gardener vol. Marion County, Oreg. State U. Extension Svc., 1992; floriculture judge Marion County Fair, 1992; master gardener clinic Oreg. State Fair, 1992; clerk Marion Friends Monthly Meeting, 1992-93. Mem. Altrusa Internat. (internat. chmn. 1985-86, chmn. pub. rels. 1989—, corr. sec. 1990-91), Internat. Platform Assn. Republican. Mem. Soc. of Friends. Home: 2757 Pheasant Ave SE Salem OR 97302-3170 Office: Lifelines PO Box 54 Jefferson OR 97352-0054

ROBERTSON, MERLE GREENE, museum administrator; b. Miles City, Mont., Aug. 30, 1919; d. Darrel Irving and Ada Emma (Foote) McCann; m. Wallace McNeill Greene, Dec. 2, 1936 (div. Sept. 1950); children: Barbara Merle Greene Metzler, David Wallace Greene; m. Lawrence William Robertson, Dec. 19, 1966 (dec. May 1981). Student, U. Washington, 1933-35; BA, U. San Francisco, 1952; MFA, U. Guana Guato, Mex., 1963; PhD, Tulane U., 1987. Cert. tchr., Calif. Camp dir. Camp Tapawingo, Sequim, Wash., 1951-53; tchr. San Rafael Mil. Acad., 1952-64; camp dir. Marin County Camp Fire Girls, San Rafael, Calif., 1954-56; expedition dir. Tulane U., New Orleans, 1962—; tchr. Monterey (Calif.) Penninsula Coll., 1974-76, Robert Louis Stevenson Sch., Pebble Beach, Calif., 1967-76; exec. dir. Pre-Columbian Art Rsch. Inst., San Francisco, 1971—; adj. curator H.M. de Young Meml. Art Mus., San Francisco, 1991—, com. mem. pre-Columbian art, 1990—; rsch. assoc. Middle Am. Rsch. Inst./Tulane U., New Orleans, 1976—, U. Calif. Archaeol. Rsch. Facility, Berkeley, 1982—, Calif. Acad. Scis., San Francisco, 1985—; dir. Archaeol. Recording Maya Art in Mex., Gualemala, Belize, Honduras, 1962—. Author: Sculpture of Palenque, 4 vols., 1983-91, Ancient Maya Relief Sculpture, 1967 (Best Design 1967), (CD-ROMS) Merle Greene Robertson's Rubbings of Maya Sculpture; editor: Palenque Round Table, 10 vols., 1973-95; prin. works include over 3000 rubbings of Maya Sculpture. Merle Greene Robertson Sch. named in her honor, Chiapas, Mex., 1981; recipient Order of the Aztec Eagle award Mexican Govt., 1994. Fellow AAAS, The Explorers Club, Soc. for Am. Archaeology; mem. 47th Internat. Cong. Americanists (hon. v.p. 1992), Am. Anthropol. Assn., Assn. de Artistes Mougins. Home: 1100 Sacramento St San Francisco CA 94108-1918 Office: Pre-Columbian Art Rsch Inst 1100 Sacramento St Ste 1004 San Francisco CA 94108-1918

ROBERTSON, SAMUEL HARRY, III, transportation safety research engineer, educator; b. Phoenix, Oct. 2, 1934; s. Samuel Harry and Doris Byrle (Duffield) R.; m. Nancy Jean Bradford, Aug. 20, 1954; children: David Lyle, Pamela Louise. BS, Ariz. State U., 1956; D in Aviation Tech. (hon.), Embry-Riddle Aero. U., 1972. Registered profl. engr. Chief hazards div. Aviation Safety Engring. and Research, Phoenix, 1960-70; pres. Robertson Research Engrs., 1960-70; research prof., dir. Safety Ctr. Coll. Engring. and Applied Scis., Ariz State U., Tempe, 1970-79; pres. Robertson Research Inc., 1970-86, Robertson Aviation Inc., 1977-86, Internat. Ctr. for Safety Edn., 1982-86; pres., chief exec. officer Robertson Research Group, Inc., Tempe, 1986—; airplane design and accident investigator, 1961—; instr. aircrash investigation Internat. Ctr. Safety Edn., 1960—, inst. aerospace safety U. So. Calif., 1962-70, Armed Forces Inst. Pathology, 1970—, Dept. Transp. Safety Inst., 1970-89; pres. Flying R Ranches, 1976—, mem. adv. bd. Rio Salado Bank, Tempe, 1985-94; mem. adv. coun. Ctr. Aerospace Safety Edn., Embry-Riddle Aero. U., Daytona Beach, Fla., 1986—, bd. trustees, 1992—. Contbr. 65 articles to profl. jours. and pubs.; patentee applying plastic to paper, fuel system safety check valves, crash resitant fuel system, safety aircraft seats; holder FAA STC's various fuel systems, fuel system components; designer, developer, mfr. crash resistant fuel systems for airplanes, helicopters, championship racing cars. Served as pilot USAF, 1956-60, Ariz. Army NG 1960-61, 70-74, Ariz. Air NG, 1961-69. Recipient Contbns. Automotive Racing Safety award CNA, 1976, Adm. Luis De Florez Internat. Flying Safety award, 1969, Cert. Commendation Nat. Safety Coun., 1969, Gen. W. Spruance award for safety edn., SAFE Soc., 1982; holder Nat. Speed Record for one class of drag racing car, 1955-62, 5 nat. records for flying model aircraft, 1950-56. Mem. AIAA, Internat. Soc. Air Safety Investigators (Jerome Lederer Aircraft Accident Investigation award, 1981), Aerospace Med. Assn., Exptl. Aircraft Assn., Soc. Automotive Engrs., Am. Helicopter Soc., Nat. Fire Protection Assn., Aircraft Owners and Pilots Assn., U.S. Automobile Club (mem. tech. com.). Office: 1024 E Vista Del Cerro Dr Tempe AZ 85281-5709

ROBESON, DAVID JOHN, patent agent, biotechnology consultant; b. Yorkshire, Eng., Dec. 3, 1948; came to U.S., 1980; s. Sydney Herbert and Doris Barnes (Taylor) R.; m. Maria Theresa Robeson, Dec. 13, 1988. M.I.Biol. in Plant Pathology, The Polytechnic, Wolverhampton, Eng., 1975; PhD, U. Reading, Eng., 1978. Registered patent agt. Rsch. scientist Arco Plant Cell Rsch. Inst., Dublin, Calif., 1983-86; sr. scientist Plant Cell Rsch. Inst., Inc., Dublin, 1987-91; ind. cons./educator biotech. Dublin, 1991—, patent agt., tech. specialist, 1994—. Contbr. articles to profl. jours. Mem. AUTM, Phytochem. Soc. N.Am., Am. Chem. Soc., Assn. Univ. Tech. Mgrs.

ROBINETT, ANN, music educator; b. Soda Springs, Idaho, Aug. 27, 1949; d. Perry and Marcia Elaine (Finlayson) Warner; m. Ronald Roy Robinett, Sept. 12, 1968; children: Jeannine, Randy, Sean. Student, U. Idaho, 1967-68, Idaho State U., 1968. Tchr. music McCammon, Idaho, 1973—. Dir. choir LDS Ch., 1971-92, chmn. music, 1976—, organist, 1989-92; dir. community mus., 1975-86; dir. children's chorus, 1980-86; mem. parent adv. coun. Mt. View Sch. and Lewis and Clark Sch., Pocatello and McCammon, Idaho, 1981-89; bd. mem. Lewis and Clark Sch. PTA, Pocatello and McCammon, 1981-89; pres. Lewis and Clark Sch. PTA, Pocatello, 1984-85; bd. dirs. Pocatello Arts Coun., 1989—. Mem. Idaho Fedn. Music Clubs (pres. 1991-93), Pocatello Music Club (bd. dirs. 1982-92, pres. 1986-89). Republican.

ROBINETT, DEBORA ANN, dietitian; b. Seattle, Jan. 8, 1955; d. Vincent G. and Marie E. Smith; m. Roger Dale Robinett, June 7, 1980 (div. Apr. 1989); children: Rachelle, Dawn, Jason Guy, Jesse Austin; m. William Forrest West IV, May 1, 1993. BS in Nutrition, Oreg. State U., 1977; MA in Orgnl. Sys., Pacific Luth. U., Tacoma, Wash., 1994. Registered dietitian. Dietetic intern Luth. Gen. Hosp., Park Ridge, Ill., 1978; clin. dietitian Virginia Mason Hosp., Seattle, 1978-80, Tacoma Gen. Hosp., 1980-82; owner, dietitian Nutrition Counseling Svc., Tacoma, 1982—; pres., dietitian Health Enhancement Corp., Tacoma, 1990—; dietitian, nutrition cons. Health Comm. Internat., Inc., Gig Harbor, Wash., 1989—. Author: (nutrition workbook) Your Heart Diet Made Simple, 1983; (Body Tailor workbook) Nutrition and Health Workbook, 1990; contbr. articles to newsletters, other publs. Mem. Am. Dietetic Assn., Wash. State Dietetic Assn., So. Puget Sound Dietetic Assn., Nat. Wellness Assn., Am. Heart Assn. (bd. dirs. 1993-95, chair nominating com. 1994), Tacoma Actors Guild (bd. dirs. 1993-95), Rotary (bd. dirs. 1994-96, chair neighborhood harvest com. 1993). Office: Health Enhancement Corp PO Box 99121 Tacoma WA 98499-0121

ROBINETT, RENEÉ MELLO, marketing executive; b. San Jose, Dec. 5, 1964; d. Edward Jesse and Mary Edith (Bledsaw) M. BA in English, San Jose State U., 1987, BS in Politics, 1988. Lic. in real estate, Calif. Swim instr. Decathlon Club, Santa Clara, Calif., 1984-88; with Axlon Toy Co., Sunnyvale, Calif., 1986-87; salesperson Nordstroms, San Jose, 1986-88; exec. mktg. asst. Mass Microsys., Sunnyvale, 1988-89; v.p. mktg./communications UIC Internat. Corp., Santa Clara, 1989-93; mktg. exec. worldwide ops. Photon Dynamics Inc., Milpitas, Calif., 1993—. Newsletter editor Internat. Bus. Assn., Japan, 1990—. Active Republicans Abroad., 1990—; bd. dirs. Santa ClaraUnified Sch. Dist. Edn Found. Mem. NAFE, Fgn. Women Execs. (progs. dir. 1990—). Republican. Roman Catholic. Office: Photon Dynamics Inc 1504 Mccarthy Blvd Milpitas CA 95035-7405

ROBINETT, RUSH DALETH, III, research engineer; b. Albuquerque, July 14, 1960; s. Rush Daleth Jr. and Dorothy (Sohl) R.; m. Laurie Ellen Bowman, Dec. 28, 1993; 1 child Rush Daleth IV. Student, U. Notre Dame, 1978-80; BS magna cum laude, Tex. A&M U., 1982, PhD, 1987; MS, U. Tex., 1984. Teaching asst. U. Notre Dame, South Bend, Ind., 1979-80; rsch. asst. Tex. A&M U., College Station, 1981-82, U. Tex., Austin, 1983-84; rsch. assoc. Ctr. for Strategic Tech., College Station, 1984-87; rsch. engr. Sandia Nat. Lab., Albuquerque, 1988—; student intern NASA Hdqs. Washington, 1981; rsch. engr. Northrop Aircraft Divsn., Hawthorne, Calif., summer, 1983; adj. prof. U. N.Mex., Albuquerque, 1994—; cons. Corning, Elmira, N.Y., 1993—, Albuquerque Pub. Schs. Budget Rev. Bd., 1990; sci. advisor Albuquerque Pub. Schs., 1990-94, sci. instr., summer, 1988-90; presenter, cons. Explora, Albuquerque, 1992. Inventor two-axis hydraulic joint, sway suppressed crane control; contbr. articles to profl. jours. Mentor Valley Acad., Albuquerque, 1989-92. Mem. AIAA (sr., tech. com. 1991-93, student v.p. 1981-82, Best Presentation award 1992), N.Y. Acad. Scis., Am. Helicopter Soc., Phi Kappa Phi, Sigma Gamma Tau. Home: PO Box 1661 Tijeras NM 87059-1661 Office: Sandia Nat Lab MS0310 PO Box 5800 Albuquerque NM 87185

ROBINS, MORRIS JOSEPH, chemistry educator; b. Nephi, Utah, Sept. 28, 1939; s. Waldo George and Mary Erda (Anderson) R.; m. Jerri Johnson, June 11, 1960 (div. July 1972); children: Dayne M., Diane, Douglas W., Debra, Dale C.; m. Jackie Alene Robinson, Aug. 24, 1973; children: Mark K., Janetta A., Tiffany A. BA, U. Utah, 1961; PhD, Ariz. State U., 1965. Cancer rsch. scientist Roswell Park Meml. Inst., Buffalo, 1965-66; rsch. assoc. U. Utah, Salt Lake City, 1966-69; from asst. prof. to prof. chemistry U. Alberta, Edmonton, Can., 1969-86; prof. chemistry Brigham Young U., Provo, Utah, 1987—; vis. prof. medicinal chemistry U. Utah, Salt Lake City, 1981-82; adj. prof. medicine U. Alberta, Edmonton, 1988—; grant evaluation panel Am. Cancer Soc., N.Y.C., 1977-80, Nat. Cancer Inst. Can., Toronto, 1983-86; mem. AIDS & Related Rsch. Study Sect. 4, NIH, Washington, 1995—; cons. in field. Mem. editl. bd. Nucleic Acids Rsch., 1980-83; contbr. articles to profl. jours., chpts. to books; patentee in field. NSF fellow, 1963-64; Rsch. grantee Nat. Cancer Inst. Can., Natural Scis. and Engring. Rsch. Coun. Can., 1969-87, Am. Cancer Soc., NIH, 1987—; named J. Rex Goates prof. Brigham Young U., 1989—. Mem. Am. Assn. for Cancer Rsch., Am. Chem. Soc., Internat. Soc. for Antiviral Rsch. Mem. LDS Ch. Office: Brigham Young Univ Dept Chemistry/Biochemistry Provo UT 84602

ROBINS, ROBERT EDWARD, research scientist; b. Miami, Fla., Aug. 4, 1942; s. Harold Robins and Mildred Arnette Connolly; m. Carol Lynn Belkind Robins, June 12, 1965; 1 child, Joshua Benjamin. BS summa cum laude, Poly. U., Brooklyn, 1964; MS, NYU (Courant Inst.), 1966, U. Wash., 1967-69. Rsch. engr. Boeing Aerospace, Seattle, 1967-68; programmer analyst King County, Seattle, 1970-72; system analyst Puget Sound Govtl. Coun., Seattle, 1972; rsch. scientist Flow Rsch., Inc., Kent, Wash., 1972-80; system analyst Boeing Computer Svcs., Seattle, 1980-81; rsch. scientist Physical Dynamics, Bellevue, Wash., 1981-86, N.W. Rsch. Assocs., Inc., Bellevue, Wash., 1986—. Contbr. articles to profl. jours. Bd. dirs., treas. Seattle Youth Soccer Assn., 1989-93. Grad. fellow NSF, 1964-67. Mem. AIAa, Am. Geophys. Union, Assn. Computing Machinery, Soc. Indsl. and Applied Math. Office: N W Rsch Assocs Inc 300 120th Ave NE Bldg 7 Bellevue WA 98005

ROBINSON, ANNETTMARIE, entrepreneur; b. Fayetteville, Ark., Jan. 31, 1940; d. Christopher Jacy and Lorena (Johnson) Simmons; m. Roy Robinson, June 17, 1966; children: Steven, Sammy, Doug, Pamela, Olen. BA, Edison Tech. U., 1958; BA in Bus., Seattle Community Coll., 1959. Dir. perss. Country Kitchen Restaurants, Inc., Anchorage, 1966-71; investor Anchorage, 1971—; cons. Pioneer Investments, Anchorage, 1983—, M'RAL, Inc. Retail Dry Goods, Anchorage, 1985. Mem. Rep. Presdl. Task Force, Washington, 1984—, Reps. of Alaska, Anchorage, 1987; mem. chmn. round table YMCA, Anchorage, 1986—; active Sta. KWN2, KQLO, Reno, Nev.; active in child abuse issues and prosecution. Named Woman of Yr. Lions, Anchorage, 1989, marksman first class Nat. Rifle Assn., 1953. Mem. NAFE, Spenard Lion's Aux. (past pres.).

ROBINSON, ARNOLD, manufacturing executive; b. N.Y.C., Oct. 27, 1929; s. Louis and Anna (Cohen) R.; m. Gertrude Leah Needleman, Nov. 14, 1954; children: Barry David, Lisa Robinson McConnell, Sanford. BS in Aero. Engring., Poly. Inst. Bklyn., 1951; MS in Aero. Engring., Drexel Inst. Tech., 1955. Registered profl. engr., N.Y., Pa., Fla. Engr. aircraft structures U.S. Naval Aircraft Devel. Ctr., Johnsville, Pa., 1951-54, U.S. Naval Aircraft Factory, Phila., 1954-55; group engr. aircraft structures missiles div. Republic Aviation Corp., Farmingdale, N.Y., 1955-57; asst. chief engr. Omega Aircraft Corp., New Bedford, Mass., 1957-59; v.p., engr., prin. DeVore Aviation Corp. Am., Albuquerque, 1960-91, pres., 1991—. Named Exporter of Yr. NMSBA, 1990; recipient Productivity award N.Mex. Sen. Bingaman, 1989. Mem. AIAA, Am. Helicopter Soc., Internat. Soc. Air Safety Investigators, N.Mex. Entrepreneurs Assn. (treas. 1988-89, pres., 1990—). Office: DeVore Aviation Corp Am 6104B Jefferson St NE Albuquerque NM 87109-3410

ROBINSON, BERNARD LEO, retired lawyer; b. Kalamazoo, Feb. 13, 1924; s. Louis Harvey and Sue Mary (Starr) R.; m. Betsy Nadell, May 30, 1947; children: Robert Bruce, Patricia Anne, Jean Carol. BS, U. Ill., 1947, MS, 1958, postgrad. in structural dynamics, 1959; JD, U. N.Mex., 1973. Rsch. engr. Assn. Am. Railroads, 1947-49; instr. architecture Rensselaer Poly. Inst., 1949-51; commd. 2d lt. Corps Engrs., U.S. Army, 1945, advanced through grades to lt. col., 1965, ret., 1968; engr. Nuclear Def. Rsch. Corp., Albuquerque, 1968-71; admitted to N.Mex. bar, 1973, U.S. Supreme Ct. bar, 1976; practiced in Albuquerque, 1973-85, Silver City, N.Mex., 1985-89, Green Valley, Ariz., 1989-90, Sierra Vista, Ariz., 1990-91; pres. Robinson Fin. Svcs., 1993-94. Dist. commr. Boy Scouts Am., 1960-62. Vice chmn. Rep. Dist. Com., 1968-70. Decorated Air medal, Combat Infantry badge. Mem. ASCE, ABA, Ret. Officers Assn., DAV, Assn. U.S. Army, VFW. Home: 1037 W Eagle Look Ln Tucson AZ 85737-6986

ROBINSON, CALVIN STANFORD, lawyer; b. Kalispell, Mont., Mar. 31, 1920; s. Calvin Alton and Berta Ella (Green) R.; m. Nancy Hanna, Dec. 13, 1945; children: Terrill S., Calvin D., Robert B., Barbara E. B.A., U. Mont., 1944; student U. Wash., U. Calif.; J.D., U. Mich., 1949. Bar: Ill. 1949, Mont. 1949. Assoc. Rooks & Freeman, Chgo., 1949-50; ptnr. Murphy, Robinson, Heckathorn & Phillips and predecessors, Kalispell, Mont., 1950—; dir. Semitool Inc., Kalispell, 1979—, Winter Sports Inc., Whitefish, Mont., 1984—; mem. Mont. Gov.'s Com. Bus. Corp. Laws, Gov's. Revenue Estimating Coun., 1986-88. Mem. Mont. Environ. Quality Council; past vice chmn. Mont. Bd. Housing; past mem. Mont. Bd. Edn., Mont. U. Bd. Regents. Served to lt. USNR, 1942-46. Fellow Am. Coll. Trust and Estate Counsel; mem. ABA, Mont. Bar Assn., N.W. Mont. Bar Assn., Ill. Bar Assn. Mont. State C. of C. (bd. dirs. 1985-93, chmn. 1990-91). Episcopalian. Home: 315 Crestview Rd Kalispell MT 59901-2606 Office: PO Box 759 431 1st Ave NW Kalispell MT 59901-3908

ROBINSON, CHARLES DAVID, financial services executive; b. Warren, Ohio, Sept. 26, 1944; s. Lee Elmo and Dora Mae (Wheeler) R.; m. Sharon Lynn Pemberton, Apr. 8, 1966 (div. July 1979); 1 child, Heather Lynn; m. Sharon Ann Dillon, June 20, 1980. Student, Ventura (Calif.) Jr. Coll., 1962, Harvard U., 1964; BA, Am. U., 1966; MA, Ohio State U., 1979. CFP. Mershon fellow Ohio State U., Columbus, 1966-72; dir. tng. NATPAC-SOUTH Inc., Washington, 1973-74; field underwriter N.Y. Life, Bailey's Cross-Roads, Va., 1974-75; dir. debate W.T. Woodson High Sch., Fairfax, Va., 1975-80; exec. account rep. VALIC, Fairfax, 1980-89, unit mgr., 1981-86; dist. mgr. VALIC, Phoenix, 1990-91, regional mgr., 1991-95; regional v.p. VAMCO, Phoenix, 1991-95; v.p. instl. markets VALIC, Houston, 1995—. Editor, author: (booklet) Mutual Fund Sales Kit, 1992, (brochures) New Mexico Alternative Retirement Plan, 1991, Arizona Optional Retirement Plan, 1991; co-developer: Portfolio Optimizer Asset Allocation Software, 1994. Asst. to chmn. conv. coms. Bush Campaign Republican Nat. Conv., New Orleans, 1988; chmn. Fairfax County Tchrs. for Vivian Watts, Va., 1979. Mem. Inst. Cert. Fin. Planners, Phi Alpha Theta, Alpha Tau Omega. Office: VALIC 2929 Allen Pkwy Houston TX 77019

ROBINSON, CHARLES E., telecommunications industry executive; b. 1933. With Alascom Inc., from 1960, v.p., 1972-76, exec. v.p., 1976-79, pres., from 1979, also bd. dirs.; with Pacific Telecom Inc., Vancouver, Wash., 1982—, formerly pres., chief oper. officer, now pres., chief exec. officer. Office: Pacific Telecom Inc Box 9901 805 Broadway St Vancouver WA 98660-3277

ROBINSON, CHARLES PAUL, nuclear physicist, diplomat, business executive; b. Detroit, Oct. 9, 1941; s. Edward Leonard and Mary Opal (Edmondson) R.; m. Barbara Thomas Woodard; children by previous marriage: Paula S., Colin C. BS in Physics, Christian Bros. U., 1963; PhD in Physics, Fla. State U., 1967. Mem. nuclear test staff Los Alamos (N.Mex.) Nat. Lab., 1967-69, chief test operator, 1969-70, mem. advanced concepts staff, 1971-72, assoc. div. leader, lasers, 1972-76, div. leader, 1976-79, assoc. dir., 1980-85; sr. v.p., bd. dirs. Ebasco Services Inc. subs. Enserch Corp., N.Y.C., 1985-88; ambass. to nuclear testing talks U.S. Dept. State, Geneva, 1988-90; v.p. Sandia Nat. Labs., Albuquerque, 1990-95, pres., lab. dir., 1995—; mem. sci. adv. group Def. Nuclear Agy., Washington, 1981—; mem. nat. security bd. Los Alamos Nat. Lab., 1985—; chmn. Presdl. Tech. Adv. Bd., 1991; mem. U.S. Strategic Command Adv. Bd. Pres. Student Concerts Inc., Los Alamos, 1972-74; instr. U. N.Mex., Los Alamos, 1974-76; exec. bd. Boy Scouts of N.Mex. Mem. AAAS, Am. Phys. Soc., Am. Nuclear Soc., Rotary Internat. Office: Sandia Nat Labs Orgn 4000 PO Box 5800 # 4000 Albuquerque NM 87185

ROBINSON, CHARLES SHERWOOD, consulting geologist; b. East Lansing, Mich., June 23, 1920; s. Charles Summers and Florence (Sherwood) R.; m. Elizabeth Hale, Feb. 10, 1950; children: Virginia C., Charles H., Peter S., Robert S. BS in Chemistry, Mich. Coll. Mines and Tech., 1942; PhD in Geology, U. Colo., 1956. Cert. prof. engr., Colo., Wyo., Mont., Nev., Iowa. Rsch. geologist U.S. Geol. Survey, Denver, 1948-65; pres. Charles S. Robinson & Assocs., Golden, Colo., 1965-80; v.p. Convers Ward Davis Dixion, Golden, 1980-81; gen. mgr. Mineral Systems, Inc., Golden, 1981-90; cons. geol. engr. M.A. Balcar & Assocs., Inc., Denver, 1990-91; gen. mgr. Mineral Systems, Inc., Golden, Colo., 1991—. Author numerous profl. publs.; mem. editorial bd. engring. geology Elsevier Pub., Amsterdam, 1964-94. Dir. Urban Drainage and Flood Control Dist., Denver, 1968-76. Lt. USN, 1942-46. Fellow Geol. Soc. Am.; mem. Soc. for Mining, Metallurgy and Exploration of AIME, Internat. Assn. Engring. Geologists, Soc. Econ. Geologists, Assn. Engring. Geologists. Home: 5265 Mcintyre St Golden CO 80403-1244 Office: Mineral Systems Inc 5265 Mcintyre St Golden CO 80403-1244

ROBINSON, CHARLES WESLEY, energy company executive; b. Long Beach, Calif., Sept. 7, 1919; s. Franklin Willard and Anna Hope (Gould) R.;

m. Tamara Lindovna, Mar. 8, 1957; children: Heather Lynne, Lisa Anne, Wendy Paige. AB cum laude in Econs., U. Calif., Berkeley, 1941; MBA, Stanford U., 1947. Asst. mgr. mfg. Golden State Dairy Products Co., San Francisco, 1947-49; v.p., then pres. Marcona Corp., San Francisco, 1952-74; undersec. of state for econ. affairs Dept. State, Washington, 1974-75, dep. sec. of state, 1976-77; sr. mng. partner Kuhn Loeb & Co., N.Y.C., 1977-78; vice chmn. Blyth Eastman Dillon & Co., N.Y.C., 1978-79; chmn. Energy Transition Corp., Santa Fe and Washington, 1979-82; pres. Robinson & Assocs., Inc., Santa Fe, 1982—; pres. Dyna-Yacht, Inc., Lajolla, Calif., 1982—; bd. dirs. The Allen Group, NIKE, Inc. Patentee slurry transport., Brookings Instn., Washington, 1977—. Served to lt. USN, 1941-46. Recipient Disting. Honor award Dept. State, 1977. Republican. Methodist. Office: Robinson & Assocs Inc PO Box 2224 Santa Fe NM 87504-2224

ROBINSON, DANIELLE E., finance educator; b. Albany, N.Y., Jan. 13, 1942; d. David and Nancy Moore; m. Doug Robinson, Apr. 11, 1970; 1 child, Regina Marie. BBA cum laude, Siena Coll., 1964; MBA, SUNY, Albany, 1966. Asst. prof. econs. Russell Sage Coll., Troy, N.Y., 1966-73, U. Nev., Reno, 1974-83; assoc. prof. econs. UCLA, 1984-90; prof. econs. Portland State U., 1990—, also head econ. dept., 1993—; cons. Werik Ctr., Portland, 1991—. Contbr. articles to profl. jours. Mem. NEA, Calif. Edn. Assn. Democrat. Roman Catholic. Office: The Werik Center 621 SW Alder Ste 700 Portland OR 97205-3622

ROBINSON, DAVID BROOKS, naval officer; b. Alexandria, La., Oct. 26, 1939; s. Donald and Marion (Holloman) R.; m. Gene Kirkpatrick, Aug. 1, 1964; children: Kirk, David. Student, Tex. A&M U., 1958-59; BS, U.S. Naval Acad., 1963; MS in Physics, Naval Postgrad. Sch., Monterey, Calif., 1969. Commd. ensign USN, 1963, advanced through grades to vice admiral, 1993; comdg. officer USS Canon and USS Ready, Guam, 1969-71; adminstrv. aide to Chmn. Joint Chiefs Staff, Washington, 1971-74; comdg. officer USS Luce, Mayport, Fla., 1976-78; surface comdr. assignment officer. and dir. fiscal mgt. and procedural control divsn. Naval Mil. Pers. Cmd., 1979-81; mem. Fgn. Service Inst. Exec. Seminar, Washington, 1982; comdg. officer USS Richmond K. Turner, Charleston, S.C., 1983-84; chief of staff, comdr. Naval Surface Force, Atlantic Fleet, Norfolk, Va., 1984; exec. asst. and sr. aide to vice chief Naval Ops., Washington, 1985, dir. Manpower and Tng. div., 1986, dir. Surface Warfare div., 1987-88; cmdr. cruiser destroyer group 8, 1988-89; vice dir. and subsequently dir. operational plans and interoperability directorate Joint Staff, Washington, 1989-91; dep., chief of staff to comdr. U.S. Pacific Fleet, 1991-93, comdr. naval surface force, 1993—. Decorated Navy Cross, Def. D.S.M., D.S.M., Legion of Merit with 4 gold stars, Bronze Star, Purple Heart. Mem. Optimists (pres. Oakton, Va. 1986-87). Methodist. Office: COMNAVSURFPAC 2421 Vella Lavella Rd San Diego CA 92155-5407

ROBINSON, DAVID E., pharmaceuticals executive; b. 1949. Macquarie U., Sydney, Australia, 1974; BA in Hist. and Polit. Sci., U. New South Wales, Australia, MBA. With Abbott Labs., 1974-84, Adria Labs., Dublin, Ohio, 1984-87; COO Erbamont, Milan, Italy, 1987-89; pvt. practice, cons., 1989-91; pres., CEO Ligand Pharmaceuticals, 1991—. Office: Ligand Pharmaceuticals Inc 9393 Towne Centre Dr San Diego CA 92121-3016*

ROBINSON, DAVID HOWARD, lawyer; b. Hampton, Va., Nov. 24, 1948; s. Bernard Harris and Phyllis (Canter) R.; m. Nina Jane Briscoe, Aug. 20, 1979. B.A., Calif. State U., Northridge, 1970; J.D., Cabrillo Pacific U., 1975. Bar admittee: Calif., 1977, U.S. Dist Ct. (so. dist.) Calif., 1977, U.S. Ct. Claims, 1979, U.S. Supreme Ct., 1980. adminstr. Cabrillo Pacific U. Coll. Law, 1977; assoc. Gerald D. Egan, San Bernardino, Calif., 1977-78, Duke & Gerstel, San Diego, 1978-80, Rand, Day & Ziman, San Diego, 1980-81; sole practice, San Diego, 1981-88; ptnr. Robinson and Rubin, San Diego, 1988—. Mem. San Diego County Bar Assn., San Diego Trial Lawyers Assn.

ROBINSON, DONALD WALLACE, journalist; b. Burns, Oreg., Dec. 30, 1937; s. Wallace Reginald and Esther Berliot (Rognan) R.; m. Deanna Mae Campbell, Mar. 29, 1958; children: Bruce Campbell, Jennifer Jean Robinson Kang. BS in Journalism, U. Oreg., 1959. Reporter Medford (Oreg.) Mail Tribune, summer 1955-58, Leader-Post, Regina, Sask., Can., 1959, La Grande (Oreg.) Observer, 1960, Washington Post, 1966-68; reporter The Register-Guard, Eugene, Oreg., 1960-65, assoc. editor, 1969-77, editorial page editor, 1977—. Recipient Outstanding Reporting of Pub. Affairs award Am. Polit. Sci. Assn.; Congl. fellow Am. Polit. Sci. Assn., 1965-66; Knight fellow Stanford U., 1973-74. Home: 2890 Emerald St Eugene OR 97403-1636 Office: The Register-Guard 975 High St Eugene OR 97401-3204

ROBINSON, FRANK ROBERT, radio station executive; b. Hollywood, Calif., Sept. 17, 1938; s. Frank Robert and Helen Macdonnel (James) R.; m. Ann Katherine Carman, Apr. 24, 1965 (div. 1984); children: Geoffrey Scott, Hilary Ann; m. Dian Winget, July 19, 1991. BS, Westminster Coll., 1967. Gen. mgr. Sta. KLUB and Sta. KISN, Salt Lake City, 1970-85; sta. mgr. KUER, 1986-90; western sales mgr. Custom Bus. Systems, Inc.

ROBINSON, GARY DALE, aerospace company executive; b. Colcord, W.Va., Sept. 9, 1938; s. Samuel Claytor and Madge (Fraley) R. Jr.; m. Lorelei Mary Christl, June 25, 1967; children: John Claytor, Kirk Dean. BA in Latin Am. Econ. History, So. Ill. U., 1964; PhD in Orgn. Behavior, Case Western Res. U., 1977. Program tng. chief The Peace Corps, Washington, 1969-71; cons. self-employed Ohio, 1971-76; health planning advisor USAID, San Salvador, El Salvador, 1976; project dir. Cen. Am. Inst. for Pub. Adminstrn. and Ministry of Health, San Jose, Costa Rica, 1977-78; mgmt. advisor Agy. for Internat. Devel., Santo Domingo, Dominican Republic, 1978-79; indsl. rels. mgr. Boeing Comml. Airplane Co., Everett, Wash., 1979-83; human resource mgr. Boeing Marine Systems, Renton, Wash., 1983-85; indsl. rels. mgr. The Boeing Co., Seattle, 1985-86, internal audit mgr., asst. to v.p. controller, 1986-90, 90—; cons. in field; adj. prof. Cen. Wash. U., Ellensburg, 1984—; mem. adv. bd. Drake, Beam & Moran, Seattle, 1991—; mem. adv. bd. and faculty Sch. of Advanced Studies in Orgnl. Cons., Santiago, chile, 1992—. Contbg. author: International Organizational Behavior, 1986. chmn. Metrocenter YMCA, Seattle, 1990-91; mem. Peace Corps Nat. Adv. Coun., Wash., 1988-89; founding mem. Pacific N.W. Orgn. Devel. Network, Seattle, 1982-86; bd. advisors Nat. Found. for Study Religion & Edn., Greensboro, N.C., 1984-87; mem. edn. com. World Affairs Coun., Seattle, 1987-88; sec., treas. The Edmonds Inst., Lynnwood, Wash., 1989-90; mem. Internat. Rels. Com. Named Paul Harris fellow Rotary Internat., 1989. Mem. The Wash. Ctr. for Mgmt. and Leadership (founder, bd. dirs.), Inst. for Internal Auditors (co-editor Pistas newsletter 1991—), Nat. Orgnl. Devel. Network, Acad. of Mgmt., Earth Svcs. Corps (adv. bd.). Office: The Boeing Co PO Box 3707 M/S 13-20 Seattle WA 98124-2207

ROBINSON, HERBERT HENRY, III, counselor, therapist; b. Leavenworth, Wash., May 31, 1933; s. Herbert Henry II and Alberta (Sperber) R.; m. Georgia Murial Jones, Nov. 24, 1954 (div. 1974); children: Cheri Dean Asbury, David Keith, Peri Elizabeth Layton, Tanda Rene Graff, Gaila Daire. Grad. of Theology, Bapt. Bible Coll., 1959; BA in Philosophy/Greek, Whitworth Coll., 1968; MA in Coll. Teaching, Ea. Wash. U., 1976; postgrad., Gonzaga U., 1980—. Choir dir. Twin City Bapt. Temple, Mishawaka, Ind., 1959-61; min. Inland Empire Bapt. Ch., Spokane, 1961-73; tchr. philosophy Spokane (Wash.) C.C., 1969-72; dir. Alternatives to Violence, Women in Crisis, Fairbanks, Alaska, 1985-87; tchr. pub. rels. U. Alaska, Fairbanks, 1986-87; dir. Alternatives to Violence Men Inc., Juneau, 1988-89; tchr. leadership mgmt. U. Alaska S.E., Juneau, 1988-89; min. Sci. of Mind Ctr., Sandpoint, Idaho, 1989-92; dir., therapist Tapio Counseling Ctr., Spokane, 1991-93; cons. Lilac Blind/Alpha Inc./Marshall Coll., Spokane, 1975-85, Alaska Placer Mining Co., Fairbanks, 1987; tchr. Spokane Falls C.C., Spokane, 1979-85; seminar, presenter Human Resource Devel., Spokane and Seattle, Wash., Pa., 1980; guest trainer United Way/Kellogg Found. Inst. for Volunteerism, Spokane, 1983. First trombone San Diego Marine Band, 1953-56, Spokane Symphony, 1961; bd. dirs. Planned Parenthood, Spokane, 1984, Tanani Learning Ctr., Fairbanks, 1987; mem. consensus bldg. team Sci. of Mind Ctr., Sandpoint, 1989-92. Cpl. USMC, 1953-56. Mem. ACA, Assn. for Humanistic Edn. and Devel., Assn. for Religious Values in Counseling, Internat. Assn. Addictions and Offender Counselors, Internat. Assn. Marriage and Family Counselors, Am. Assn. Profl. Hypnotherapists. Home: 11611 E Maxwell Ave Spokane WA 99206-4867 Office: Tapio Counseling Svcs Yellow Flag Bldg #109 104 S Freya Tapio Ctr Spokane WA 99202

ROBINSON, HERBERT WILLIAM, corporate executive, economist; b. Hull, Yorkshire, Eng., Jan. 2, 1914; came to U.S., 1943, naturalized, 1948; s. Herbert and Mary Elizabeth (Ellis) R.; m. Elsie Caroline Roenfeldt, May 8, 1948; children—Denise Patricia, Keith Brian. BS in Econs. with 1st class hons., U. Coll. Hull (London/ext.), Eng., 1935; PhD, London Sch. Econs., 1937; DPhil, Oxford U., 1939; DSc in Econs. (hon.), U. Hull, 1992. Sr. lectr. math. statistics, econ. theory, trade cycle theory, indsl. orgn. U. Coll., Hull, 1939; asst. to Lord Cherwell, Prime Minister's Pvt. Office, 1939-42; asst. to Lord Layton, Ministry Prodn., 1942-43; Brit. staff mem. Combined Prodn. and Resources Bd., U.S., U.K., Can., 1943-44; dep. dir. statistics, econ. and statistics div. Ministry Agr. and Fisheries, 1945; chief econ. trends VA, 1946; chief operational analysis div. UNRRA Mission to Poland, 1946-47; loan and econs. depts. World Bank, 1947-51; dep. div. dir. Office Program and Requirements, Def. Prodn. Adminstrn., 1951-53; pres. Council Econ. and Industry Research, Inc., Washington, 1954-57; pres. renamed corp. C-E-I-R, Inc., 1958-67, chmn. bd., 1954-67; v.p. Control Data Corp., 1968-70; chmn. Internat. Mgmt. Systems Corp., 1970—. Author: Economics of Building, 1939, Election Issues, 1976, Challenge to Government: Management of a Capitalist Economy, 1991; author articles and reports on econ. subjects. Fellow Royal Statis. Soc. (mem. coun. 1943-44, chartered statistician); mem. Am. Soc. Cybernetics (dir. 1967-75), Am. Econ. Assn., Inst. Mgmt. Scis., Am. Statis. Assn., Royal Econ. Soc., Ops. Rsch. Soc., Econometric Soc., Cosmos Club (Washington), Fountain Hills (Ariz.) Club, Lambda Alpha, Alpha Kappa Psi.

ROBINSON, JOHN THOMAS, arts education administrator, designer; b. Hanford, Calif., Sept. 2, 1944; s. Leroy Lewis and Catherine (Dowd) R. BA, Calif. State U., Fresno, 1965; MFA, Calif. State U., San Francisco, 1972. Art adminstr., educator Palo Alto (Calif.) Unified Sch. Dist., 1965—; visual arts chmn. Calif. State Summer Sch. for the Arts, Sacramento, 1987-95; interior designer Robinson Interiors, San Francisco, 1977-90; part-time art edn. instr. Calif. State U., Hayward, 1971-72; exhbn. designer edn. dept. M. H. DeYoung Mus., San Francisco, 1967-75; tchr. trainer Calif. Arts Project, Sacramento, 1985-88; sch. accreditation team Calif. State Dept. Edn., Sacramento, 1993-94, art cons., 1987; Fulbright Exch. Tchr., England, 1995—. Mem. City of Palo Alto (Calif.) Arts Commn., 1978-79. Fulbright exch. tchr., Eng., 1968-69; RISD summer hon. fellow, 1983; Skidmore Coll. summer fellow, 1987. Mem. Calif. Arts Project, Calif. Art Edn. Assn. (Calif. Secondary Educator of the Yr. award 1992). Home: 709 Shotwell St San Francisco CA 94110-2611 Office: Palo Alto USD 780 Arastradero Rd Palo Alto CA 94306-3827

ROBINSON, LISA HERTZ, public relations consultant; b. Kansas City, Mo., Nov. 13, 1964; d. Frederick Hertz and Judith and Richard Tucker; m. John David Robinson, Nov. 16, 1993. Student, Bowdoin Coll., 1984-85; BA in English Lit. and Composition, Smith Coll., 1987; postgrad., Harvard U. Ext., 1988-90. Asst. dept. devel. and pub. affairs Children's Hosp., Boston, 1987, assoc. level I, 1987-89, assoc. level II, 1989, officer, 1989-90; mgr. pub. rels. Children's Hosp., Denver, 1990; dir. devel. Women's Found. Colo., Denver, 1991-93; pres. Lisa Robinson Cons., Denver, 1994—. Mem. Leadership Denver, 1992-93; founding mem. bd. dirs. Friends of Oneday Found., 1991, chmn. pub. rels., 1991-93; co-chmn. signature event 75th anniversary com. Jr. League Denver, 1992-93, mem. membership mentoring com., 1993-94; pub. rels. liaison Children's Hosp. Gala, 1991, mem. decorations com., 1992, co-chmn. hospitality, 1993. Mem. Nat. Soc. Fund Raising Execs., Pub. Rels. Soc. Am. Jewish. Home: 255 Ash St Denver CO 80220-5620 Office: Rose Found 4567 E 9th Ave Denver CO 80220-3908

ROBINSON, LOUISE EVETTE, marriage family child counselor; b. San Francisco, May 8, 1952; d. Ellis Hart and Doris Sonia (Morris) R.; stepmother Anita Robinson. BA in Psychology, U. Calif., Berkeley, 1973; MA in Psychology, Sonoma State U., 1976. Lic. marriage, family and child counselor. Co-therapist John Champlin M.D., Berkeley, 1976, Jonothon Gross M.D., Napa, Calif., 1976; counselor Buckelew House, Kentfield, Calif., 1975-77, Petaluma (Calif.) Peoples Svcs. Ctr., 1977; intake counselor Youth Advocates C.C. Riders Clinic, Novato, Calif., 1978-80, clin. supr., 1980-82; psychotherapist Robert Cohen M.D., Santa Rosa, Calif., 1984-85; dir., founder Sonoma County Assocs. in Drug Edn., Rohnert Park, Calif., 1982-90; pvt. practice marriage, family and child counseling Kentfield, Rohnert Park and Petaluma, Calif.; speaker Marin Gen. Hosp. Pediatricians, 1981, Chope Hosp. Psychiatry Residents, San Mateo, Calif., 1984; guest speaker Marin County Grand Jury Edn. Com., 1981; instr. Sonoma State U., 1984. Contbr. articles to profl. jours. Mem. Internat. Platform Assn. Democrat. Office: 100 Avram Ave Ste 105 Rohnert Park CA 94928-3100

ROBINSON, MARK LEIGHTON, oil company executive, petroleum geologist, horse farm owner; b. San Bernadino, Calif., Aug. 4, 1927; s. Ernest Guy and Florence Iola (Lemmon) R.; m. Jean Marie Ries, Feb. 8, 1954; children: Francis Willis, Mark Ries, Paul Leighton. AB cum laude in Geology, Princeton U., 1950; postgrad. Stanford U., 1950-51. Geologist Shell Oil Co., Billings, Mont., Rapid City, S.D., Denver, Midland, Tex., 1951-56, dist. geologist, Roswell, N.Mex., 1957-60, div. mgr., Roswell, N.Mex., 1961-63, Jackson, Miss., 1964-65, Bakersfield, Calif., 1967-68, mgr. exploration econs., N.Y.C., 1969; mgmt. advisor BIPM (Royal Dutch Shell Oil Co.), The Hague, The Netherlands, 1966; pres., chmn. bd. dirs. Robinson Resource Devel. Co., Inc., Roswell, 1970—. Campaign chmn. Chaves County Republican Com., Roswell, 1962; mem. alumni schs. com. Princeton U., 1980—. Served with USNR, 1945-46. Mem. Roswell Geol. Soc. (trustee 1972), Am. Assn. Petroleum Geologists, Stanford U. Earth Scientists Assn., Yellowstone Bighorn Research Assn., Am. Horse Shows Assn., SAR, Sigma Xi. Episcopalian. Discovered Lake Como oil field, Miss., 1971, McNeal oil field, Miss., 1973, North Deer Creek Gas Field, Mont., 1983, Bloomfield East Oil Field, Mont., 1986. Home: 1508 Oljato Rd Roswell NM 88201-9300 Office: Robinson Resource Devel Co Inc PO Box 1227 Roswell NM 88202-1227

ROBINSON, PAULETTE JEAN, educational association administrator; b. Duluth, Minn., Dec. 6, 1951; d. James Conrad Lorntson and Donna Lou (Manty) Yang; m. Rodney Joel Baumert, Aug. 14, 1970 (div. Feb. 1990); children: Joel, Kimberly; m. Randall M. Robinson, Aug. 1, 1993. BA in Religious Studies with honors, U. Hawaii Manoa, 1983, MA in Asian Religion, 1985; MNA, U. San Francisco, 1993. Lectr., acad. advisor U. Md. Asian Div., Tokyo, 1986-88; exec. dir. Profl. Engring. Inst., Belmont, Calif., 1989-93; asst. dir. admissions U.S. Internat. U., San Diego, 1994—; lectr. Buddhist Eng. Acad., Tokyo, 1986-87, John Carroll U., 1990; workshop presenter U. Antioch, Santa Barbara, Calif. 1990—; presenter of numerous workshops at ednl. insts. Author: (poetry) Whispers of Asia, 1992. Hospice vol., Manoa, Hawaii, 1983-85. Recipient Teaching Devel. grant U. Hawaii, 1987. Mem. Belmont C. of C. (bd. dirs.), Jewish Community Ctr. Palo Alto, Phi Beta Kappa. Democrat. Jewish. Office: US Internat U 10455 Pomerado Rd San Diego CA 92131-1717

ROBINSON, PETER, paleontology educator, consultant; b. N.Y.C., N.Y., July 19, 1932; s. Edward and Carol Nye (Rhoades) R.; m. Patricia Ellen Fisher, Sept. 11, 1954 (div. Mar. 1980); children: Diane Elizabeth, Nathan; m. Paola D'Amelio Villa, Dec. 8, 1984. BS, Yale U., 1954, MS, 1958, PhD, 1960. Instr. Harpur Coll. SUNY, Binghamton, 1955-57; rsch. assoc. Yale Peabody Mus., New Haven, 1960-61; curator geology U. Colo. Mus., Boulder, 1961—, asst. prof. natural history, 1961-67, assoc. prof., 1967-71, prof., 1971—, dir. mus., 1971-82, prof. geol. sci., 1971—; geologist Colo. Nubian Expdn., Sudan, 1962-66; chief Colo. Paleontol. Expdn., Tunisia, 1967—; mem. geol. adv. group Colo. Bur. Land Mgmt., Denver, 1983—. Mem. AAAS, Soc. Vertebrate Paleontology (pres. 1977-78), Australian Mammal Soc., Soc. Española Paleontologia, Sigma Xi. Democrat. Home: 5110 Williams Fork Trl Apt 204 Boulder CO 80301-3408 Office: Campus Box 315 Mus U Colo Boulder CO 80309

ROBINSON, PHIL ALDEN, director; b. Long Beach, Mar. 1, 1950; s. S. Jesse and Jessie Francis (Roth) Robinson. BA, Union Coll., 1971. Newscaster Stas. WGY/WRGB-TV, Schenectady, 1969-71; freelance filmmaker Los Angeles, 1974—. Screenwriter All of Me, 1984, (with others) Rhinestone, 1984, (TV) 2 episodes Trapper John, M.D., 1981-82; writer, dir. In the Mood, 1987, dir. (TV) 2 episodes George Burns Comedy Week, 1986; screenwriter, dir. Field of Dreams (nomination Writers Guild, Dirs. Guild, Best Picture and Best Screenplay Adaption Acad. award nominations). Served to 1st lt. USAF, 1971-74. Named Screenwriter of Yr. Nat. Assn. Theatre Owners, 1990. Mem. Acad. Motion Picture Arts and Scis., Writers Guild Am. West, Dirs. Guild Am., ASCAP. Office: CAA 9830 Wilshire Bvld Beverly Hills CA 90212

ROBINSON, PHILIP H., lawyer; b. Sandpoint, Idaho, Mar. 17, 1946; s. Daniel W. and Lorna G. (Noah) R.; m. Carol r. Cooper, Dec. 20, 1969; children: Amy E. Robinson Eastlick, Michael W. BS, U. Idaho, 1968, JD, 1970. Bar: Idaho, 1977, U.S. Ct. Mil. Appeals, 1971, U.S. Ct. Appeals (9th cir.) 1991, U.S. Supreme Ct., 1976. Dep. prosecuting atty. Bonner County, Sandpoint, Idaho, 1977-83, prosecuting atty., 1983-93; city atty. City of Sandpoint, 1977—, City of Priest River, Idaho, 1980-93, City of Ponderay, Idaho, 1989—, City of Kootenai, Idaho, 1978-83, 90—; pvt. practice Sandpoint, 1976—; instr. North Idaho Coll., 1978-82, Lewis-Clark Coll., 1980-82; lectr. Nat. Crime Conf., 1988. Founder Bonner County Youth Accountability Bd.; co-chairperson Bonner County Domestic Violence Counsel; mem. Bonner County Child Abuse Protocol Team. Mem. Idaho State Bar Assn., Idaho Prosecuting Attys. Assn. (sec. 1988, treas. 1989, v.p. 1990, pres. 1991), Nat. Assn. of Govt. Attys. in Capital Litigation, Idaho Trial Lawyers Assn. Office: Philip A Robinson 1323 W Michigan St Sandpoint ID 83864-1747

ROBINSON, RICHARD ALLEN, JR., human resources development trainer, consultant; b. Ellensburg, Wash., Aug. 21, 1936; s. Richard Allen and Rosa Adele (Oswald) R.; m. R. Elaine Whitham, Sept. 8, 1956; children: Sharon E. Robinson Losey, Richard Allen, René L. Rivera. BA, U. Wash., 1958; postgrad. U.S. Army Command and Gen. Staff Coll., 1969-70; MA, U. Mo., 1971. Commd. 2d lt. U.S. Army, 1958, advanced through grades to lt. col., 1972, various infantry assignments including command, 1958-72, research and devel. assignments including dep. dir. test of behavioral sci., dep. commandant U.S.A. Organizational Effectiveness, 1975-77, ret., 1979; chief office orgn. and employee devel. Wash. Dept. Social and Health Services, Olympia, 1979—; pvt. practice orgn. and mgmt. devel. cons./trainer, 1979—. Decorated Legion of Merit with oak leaf cluster, Bronze Star. Mem. Am. Soc. Tng. and Devel., Organizational Devel. Network, Mass. Hort. Soc. Contbg. author: Games Trainers Play, vol. II, 1983. Office: DSHS Mail 8425 27th St W Tacoma WA 98466-2722

ROBINSON, RONALD ALAN, oil company executive; b. Louisville, Mar. 23, 1952; s. J. Kenneth and Juanita M. (Crosier) R.; B.S., Ga. Inst. Tech., 1974; M.B.A. with honors, Harvard U., 1978. Staff engr., asst. to exec. v.p. ops. Dual Drilling Co., Wichita Falls, Tex., 1978-80; v.p. Dreco, Inc., Houston, 1980-84, pres., dir. subs. Triflo Industries Internat. Inc.; pres., chief operating officer Ramteck Systems, Inc., 1984-87; chmn. and chief exec. officer Denver Techs. Inc., 1988—. Recipient Optimist Internat. Citizenship award, 1970; Gardiner Symonds fellow, 1977. Mem. Harvard Alumni Assn. Home: 4815 Newstead Pl Colorado Springs CO 80906-5935 Office: Denver Equipment Co 621 S Sierra Madre St Colorado Springs CO 80903-4021

ROBINSON, RONALD HOWARD, aeronautical engineer; b. Boise, Idaho, Oct. 21, 1945; s. Jesse Dwite Robinson and Annie Belle (Baxter) Robinson Bruner; m. Linda Anne Kibble, June 17, 1967; children: James Edward, Kristine Marie. AS, Boise State U., 1966; BSAeroE, U. Wash, 1968; MBA with honors, City U., Seattle, 1980. Registered profl. engr., Wash.; lic. pilot, FAA. Various engring. duties Gen. Electric Corp., Evendale, Ohio, 1969-73; various engring. duties Boeing Co., Seattle, 1966-69, with comml. airplane div., 1973—, aerodynamics tech. engr., 1973-78, flight ops. engr., jet transport ops. cons., 1978-82, spl. projects mgr., 1982-84, tech. requirements mgr., 1984-85, mgr. airline support 7J7 div., 1986-87, mgr. maintenance and reliability advanced programs, 1987-88, mgr. reliability data acquisition and reporting, 1988-89, chief engr. 777 reliability and maintainability, 1990-93, chief engr. 777 test integration, 1993-95, chief engr. 777 test and cert., 1995—. Patentee in field. Mem. No. Assn. Retarded Citizens, Seattle, 1978—, Northwest Gifted Child Assn., 1980, Port of Seattle Joint Com. on Aircraft Overflights, 1983-86; com. mem. Boy Scouts Am., Seattle, 1984-88, chmn. 1988-89. Mem. AIAA (sr.), Aircraft Owners and Pilots Assn., Boeing Mgmt. Assn. Republican. Home: 16813 NE 33d St Bellevue WA 98008 Office: Boeing Comml Aircraft Co MS-02-WC PO Box 3707 Seattle WA 98124-2207

ROBINSON, SAMUEL WILLIS, JR., information sciences specialist; b. Charlotte, N.C., Aug. 6, 1927; s. Samuel Willis and Gladys Pamelia (DeArmon) R.; m. Ramona Del Hatfield, Jan. 27, 1951; children: Sharon, Michael, Susan, Lorraine. BS in Physics, Davidson Coll., 1949; MS in Physics, Clemson U., 1951. Aerospace rsch. scientist Nat. Com. for Aeronautics, Langley AFB, Va., 1951-53; aerospace engr., mgr. Lockheed Ga. Co., Marietta, 1953-70; info. specialist Lockheed Calif. Co., Burbank, 1970-90, computer cost analyst Info. Svcs. div., 1982-90; ret., 1990; regional dir. Simulation Couns., Atlanta, 1960-70; cons. Computer Usage Billing, Burbank, 1987-90. Patentee in field. With USNR, 1945-46. Mem. Phi Beta Kappa, Sigma Pi Sigma. Presbyterian. Home: PO Box 1981 Idyllwild CA 92549-1981

ROBINSON, THEODORE GOULD, golf course architect; b. Long Beach, Calif., May 17, 1923; s. Franklin Willard and Hope (Gould) R.; m. Barbara Henderson, Oct. 28, 1949; children: Theodore G. Jr., Kristine Robinson Monroe, Leigha Robinson Ramsey. BA, U. Calif., Berkeley, 1944; MS, U. So. Calif., 1948. With Gordon Whitnall & Assocs., L.A., 1941-51; prin. Robinson Golf Design, Dana Point, Calif., 1951—. Designer 150 golf courses throughout world. Ensign USN, 1943-46. Recipient awards for best new courses Golf Digest. Mem. Am Soc. Golf Course Architects (pres. 1983). Office: Robinson Golf Designs Inc 33971 Selva Rd Ste 135 Dana Point CA 92629-3788

ROBINSON, THOMAS NATHANIEL, pediatrician, educator, researcher; b. Detroit, May 11, 1960; s. Kenneth J. and Judith R. (Rattner) R. BS in Biol. Scis., Stanford U., 1983, MD with rsch. honors, 1988; MPH in Maternal and Child Health, U. Calif., Berkeley, 1987. Diplomate Nat. Bd. Med. Examiners, Am. Bd. Pediatrics. Intern dept. medicine Children's Hosp. and Harvard Med. Sch., Boston, 1988-89, jr. asst. resident, 1989-90, sr. asst. resident, 1990-91; clin. fellow in pediatric medicine Harvard Med. Sch., Boston, 1988-91; Robert Wood Johnson clin. scholar Sch. Medicine Stanford U., Palo Alto, 1991-93, clin. instr. divsn. gen. pediatrics dept. pediatrics, acting dir. youth studies Ctr. for Rsch. in Disease Prevention Sch. Medicine, 1992-93, acting. asst. prof. divsn. gen. pediatrics dept. pediatrics, co-dir. youth studies Ctr. for Rsch. in Disease Prevention, 1993—; attending physician divsn. gen. pediatrics dept. pediatrics Stanford U. Hosp., Palo Alto, 1992—, Lucile Salter Packard Children's Hosp., Palo Alto, 1992—; clinician scientist Am. Heart Assn., 1993—; presenter in field. Contbr. articles to med. and sci. jours. Alumni Med. scholar Stanford U., 1985; grantee Met. Life Found., 1985-87. Fellow Am. Acad. Pediatrics (sch. health com. No. Calif. dist. 1992—, chair 1993—), Am. Heart Assn. (grantee 1993—, phys. activity subcom. 1993—). Office: Stanford U Sch Med Ctr for Rsch Disease Prevention 1000 Welch Rd Palo Alto CA 94304-1811

ROBISON, BARBARA ANN, retired newspaper editor; b. Portland, Oreg., July 15, 1933; d. Louis Keith and Marjorie (Work) R.; 1 child, Nancy. Student, Coll. Idaho, 1951-54, U. Utah, 1968-70. Reporter Caldwell (Idaho) News Tribune, 1951-54; sports editor LaGrande (Oreg.) Evening-Observer, 1954-55; reporter Idaho Daily Statesman, Boise, 1955-57; asst. women's editor Tacoma (Wash.) News Tribune, 1958-59; lifestyle editor Salt Lake Tribune, 1967-93. Episcopalian. Home: 4210 Caroleen Way Salt Lake City UT 84124-2507

ROBISON, WILLIAM ROBERT, lawyer; b. Memphis, May 5, 1947; s. Andrew Cliffe and Elfrieda (Barnes) R. AB, Boston U., 1970; JD, Northeastern U., 1974. Bar: Mass. 1974, D.C. 1975, U.S. Dist. Ct. Mass. 1975, U.S. Ct. Appeals (1st cir.) 1975, U.S. Dist. Ct. Conn. 1977, U.S. Supreme Ct. 1977, Calif. 1978, U.S. Dist. Ct. (cen. dist.) Calif. 1979, U.S. Ct. Appeals (9th cir.) 1979. Assoc. Meyers, Goldstein, et al, Boston, 1975-76, Cooley, Shrair, et al, Springfield, Mass., 1976-78, Hertzberg, et al, Los Angeles, 1978-79, Marcus & Lewi, Santa Monica, Calif., 1980-81; sole practice Santa Monica, 1981—; lectr. Northeastern U., Boston, 1975-76; judge pro-tem., Mcpl. Ct., Los Angeles, 1984—, Los Angeles Superior Ct., 1987—. Co-author: Commercial Transactions, 1976. Bd. dirs. Boston Legal Asst.

Project, 1972-75, Action for Boston Community Devel., Inc., 1971-75. Mem. ABA, Los Angeles County Bar Assn., Santa Monica Bar Assn. (Cert. of Appreciation 1987). Democrat. Unitarian. Home and Office: 2546 Amherst Ave Los Angeles CA 90064-2712

ROBISON, WILLIAM THOMAS, trade association executive; b. Knoxville, Tenn., Oct. 9, 1924; s. Charles Wilson and Elizabeth Pauline (McGinley) R.; m. Eliza Edwards Lide, Sept. 11, 1948; children: Charlotte Elizabeth, Mary Margaret, Eliza Ann, William Thomas Jr. BS, U. Tenn., 1948; MS, Iowa State Coll., 1949. Asst. extension architect U. Tenn., Knoxville, 1950-51; field rep. Am. Plywood Assn., Atlanta, 1951-63; asst. dir. field services Am. Plywood Assn., Tacoma, 1963-65, dir. field services, 1965-72, v.p. mktg., 1972-81, gen. mgr., 1981-84, pres., 1984—. Served to sgt. USAAF, 1943-46, Natousa. Mem. Am. Soc. Assn. Execs., Alpha Tau Omega. Presbyterian. Club: Firecrest Golf (Tacoma). Office: Am Plywood Assn PO Box 11700 Tacoma WA 98411-0700

ROBLES, ARTURO PERRET, electrical engineer, musician; b. Aguascalientes, Mex., Sept. 18, 1961; came to U.S., 1971; s. Arturo and Maria Fadua Robles; m. Elizabeth Bernadette Perrett, Aug. 20, 1983; 1 child, Esme Simone. BS in Elec. Engring., Calif. State U., Long Beach, 1985. Elec. engr. Caltrans, L.A., 1986-88, Santa Ana, Calif., 1988-91; assoc. transp. elec. engr. Caltrans, Redding, Calif., 1991—; mem. adv. bd. minority engring. program Calif. State U., Fullerton, 1984-85. Course developer, trainer Traffic Safety and Elec. Design. of Signal and Lighting, 1994. Mem. Profl. Engrs. in Calif. Govt., Shasta Blues Soc. Democrat. Roman Catholic. Office: Caltrans Traffic Ops 2247 Court St Redding CA 96001-2529

ROBLES, EMILIO, public relations professional, journalist; b. Madrid, Apr. 21, 1959; came to U.S., 1992; s. Fidel Emilio Robles Ponce and Carmen (Trujillo) R.; m. Wendy Faricy, Jan. 9, 1983; children: Tomas Emilio, Inés May. BA with honours, diploma in edn., U. Wollongong, NSW, Australia, 1982. Journalist The Illawarra Mercury, Wollongong, 1981-87; mgr. corp. affairs Apple Computer Australia, Sydney, 1987-92; sr. pub. rels. mgr. Apple Bus. Sys. div. and personal Apple Computer, Inc., Cupertino, Calif., 1992—. Office: Apple Computer Inc 1 Infinite Loop Cupertino CA 95014-2083

ROBROCK, JAMES LAWRENCE, plastic surgeon; b. Cleve., Aug. 21, 1956; s. Richard Barker and Joan Louise (Peers) R. BA, Kenyon Coll., Gambier, Ohio, 1978; MD, Ohio State U., 1981; cert. in liposuction surgery, Ea. Va. Med. Sch., 1985. Diplomate Am. Bd. Plastic Surgery. Intern in gen. surgery Northwestern U., Chgo., 1981-82, resident in gen. surgery, 1981-84; resident in plastic surgery Rush-Presbyn. St. Luke's Med. Ctr., Chgo., 1984-86; fellow in plastic surgery Maricopa Med. Ctr., Phoenix, 1986-87; pvt. practice Chandler and Phoenix, Ariz., 1987—; instr., attending surgeon Maricopa Med. Ctr., Phoenix, 1988—. Named Humanitarian of Yr., Chgo. Hosp. Coun., 1983, Chandler Vol. of Yr., Am. Cancer Soc., Rotary, Chandler cos., 1990-91, All-Am. in Swimming, NCAA, 1976, 77, 78. Fellow ACS; mem. AMA, Ariz. Soc. Plastic and Reconstructive Surgeons, Ariz. Med. Assn., Am. Soc. Plastic and Reconstructive Surgeons, Maricopa County Med. Soc., Maricopa County Plastic Surgery Soc., Delta Tau Delta. Office: 485 S Dobson Rd Ste 205 Chandler AZ 85224-5604 also: 4950 E Elliot Rd Phoenix AZ 85044-1741

ROCCA, JAMES VICTOR, political science educator; b. Spokane, Wash., Mar. 22, 1930; s. Victer Joseph and Pierina (Balzaretti) R.; m. Hilda Kalchhauser, Jan. 16, 1966. BBA, Gonzaga U., 1952; Absolutorium, U. Vienna, Austria, 1962; Doctorate, U. Vienna, 1964. Claims mgr. Gen. Electric, Oakland, Calif., 1956-58; prof. polit. sci. and polit. econ. N.Mex. Highlands Univ., Las Vegas, N.Mex., 1965—; pres. AAUP, Las Vegas, N.Mex., 1968-70. Author: Imunitaet Von Lokaler Strafgerichtsbarkeit, 1965, Ius Humanitas, 1980; contbr. articles to profl. jours. With U.S. Army, 1952-55. Mem. AAUP (pres. N.Mex. state chpt.), Benevolent Order of Elks.

ROCHA, GUY LOUIS, archivist, historian; b. Long Beach, Calif., Sept. 23, 1951; s. Ernest Louis and Charlotte (Sobus) R. BA in Social Studies and Edn., Syracuse U., 1973; MA in Am. Studies, San Diego State U., 1975; postgrad., U. Nev., 1975—. Cert. archivist Am. Acad. Cert. Archivists. Tchr., Washoe County Sch. Dist., Reno, Nev., 1975-76; history instr. Western Nev. C.C., Carson City, 1976; curator manuscripts Nev. Hist. Soc., Reno, 1976-81, interim asst. dir., 1980, interim dir., 1980-81; state adminstr. archives and records Nev. State Libr. and Archives, Carson City, 1981—; hist. cons. Janus Assocs., Tempe, Ariz., 1980, Rainshadow Assocs., Carson City, 1983—; mem. State Bd. Geographic Names. Co-author The Ignoble Conspiracy: Radicalism on Trial in Nevada, 1986, The Earp's Last Frontier: Wyatt and Virgil Earp in Nevada 1902-1905, 1988; contbr. to book and govt. study; host weekly radio talk show Sta. KPTL, Carson City, 1988—. Ex-officio mem. Nev. Commn. Bicentennial U.S. Constitution, 1986-91. Mem. Washoe Heritage Council, Reno, 1983-85; editorial bd. Nev. Hist. Soc., Reno, 1983—; mem. Washoe County Democratic Central Com., Reno, 1984-87. Mem. Conf. Intermountain Archivists (Council mem 1979-87, v.p. 1984-85, pres. 1985-86), No. Nev. Pub. Adminstrs. Group (pres. 1986-87), S.W. Labor Studies Assn., State Hist. Records Adv. Bd. (dep. coordinator 1984-86, coordinator 1986—), Westerners Internat. Nev. Corral (dep. sheriff 1980-81, sheriff 1984-85, mem. state coordinators steering com. 1985-87, vice chmn. 1986-87), Soc. Am. Archivists, Western History Assn., Nat. Assn. Govt. Archives and Records Adminstrs., Orgn. Am. Historians. Democrat. Home: 1824 Pyrenees St Carson City NV 89703-2331 Office: Nev State Libr & Archives 100 Stewart St Carson City NV 89710

ROCHA, MARILYN EVA, clinical psychologist; b. San Bernardino, Calif., Oct. 23, 1928; d. Howard Ray Gonding and Laura Anne (Johanson) Walker; m. Hilario Ursala Rocha, Mar. 25, 1948 (dec. Feb. 1971); children: Michael, Sherry, Teri, Denise. AA, Solano Jr. Coll., 1970. BA, Sacramento State U., 1973, MA, 1974; PhD, U.S. Internat. U., 1981. Psychologist, Naval Drug Rehab. Ctr., U.S. Navy, San Diego, 1975-85, chief psychologist, 1983-84; staff clin. psychologist Calif. Youth Authority No. Reception Ctr. Clinic, 1985-92, El Paso de Robles Sch., 1992—; dir. Self-Help Agys., San Diego. Author short story. Vol. counselor Hamonium, San Diego, 1976-77; SMRC Planning Group Scripps/Miramar Ranch, 1982-85; leader Vacaville council Cub Scouts Am., Calif., 1957-62, 4-H, also Brownie's. Recipient Outstanding Svc. award CYA, 1993, Woman of the Yr. award CYA, 1995. Mem. APA, PTA (hon., life), Calif. Scholastic Fedn., Am. Assn. Suicidology, Friends of the Libr. (sec.), Bus. and Profl. Women, Kiwanis Internat., Delta Zeta. Democrat. Unitarian. Home: 4625 Ross Dr Paso Robles CA 93446-9379

ROCHA, PEDRO, JR., academic administrator; b. Indé, México, Dec. 25, 1939; came to U.S., 1955; s. Pedro Sr. and Maria (Hernández) R.; m. Maria-Cruz Molina, Dec. 6, 1969; children: Diana-Marie, Delma-Irene, Pedro-Hugo. BA in History, U. Tex., El Paso, 1967, MA in Spanish, 1969; PhD in Edn. Adminstrn., U. Tex., 1981. Cert. secondary tchr., supr., adminstr., supt., Tex. Textbook adminstr. Ysleta Jr. High Sch., El Paso, 1976; secondary tchr. Ysleta Ind. Sch. Dist., El Paso, 1969-77; grad. student asst. U. Tex., El Paso, 1976-77; rsch. assoc. U. Tex., Austin, 1979-80; adminstrv. intern Austin (Tex.) C.C., 1978, substitute assoc. dean, 1981-83; rsch. intern S.W. Ednl. Devel. Lab., Austin, 1980-81; tax examiner div. clk. IRS, Austin, 1982; dir., coord. Cook Community Sch., Austin, 1982-85; from ESL instr. to dir., coord. Brooke Community Sch., Austin, 1985-86; dean Mesabi C.C., Virginia, Minn., 1987-92; v.p. for instrn. Trinidad (Colo.) State Jr. Coll., 1992—; Spanish instr. Vermilion C.C., Ely, Minn., 1990; cons.-evaluator for Commn. on Instns. of Higher Edn. of North Ctrl. Assn. Colls. and Schs.; cons. Raton (N.Mex.) Arts and Humanities Coun., 1993, U. Tex., Austin, 1982-86, Tex. Assn. Chicanos in Higher Edn., Denton, 1982, Mexican Am. Legal Def. & Edn. Fund, San Antonio, 1982, Intercultural Rsch., Inc., El Paso, 1981. Author: Staff Orientation Program: Welcoming the Employee to Our Team. Active mem., bd. dirs. So. Colo. Coal Miners Meml. and Scholarship Fund, 1994-95; pres. Marquette Sch. Bd., Virginia, 1991-92; active San Juan Coun. Cmty. Agencies, Farmington, 1986-87; leader Quarterly Dates Group, Farmington, 1986-87; adv. bd. Austin Cmty. Gardens, 1985-86. With USAF, 1961-65. Richardson fellow U. Tex., 1977-79; nominated and selected for Nat. Cmty. Coll. Hispanic Coun. Leadership Tng. Program for Hispanic C.C. Adminstrs., 1994. Mem. Am. Assn. for Higher Edn., Am. Assn. Cmty./Jr. Coll., Minn. Chief Acad. Adminstrs., Colo. Coun. Acad. deans and Vice Pres., Colo. Ednl. Svcs. Coun., Kiwanis Club (first v.p. Trinidad 1995), Hispanic C. of C. (bd. dirs. Trinidad-Las Animas County Hispanic C. of C., pres. 1995), Kappa Delta Pi, Sigma Delta Pi. Democrat. Roman Catholic. Home: 112 Benedicta Ave Trinidad CO 81082-2002 Office: Trinidad State Jr Coll 600 Prospect St Trinidad CO 81082-2356

ROCHE, CATHERINE MARY, music educator; b. Salt Lake City, Nov. 27, 1922; d. Maurice Augustine and Marie Joanna (Osborne) R. Student, Royal Conservatory Music, Toronto, Can., 1940-43; BA, U. Man., Winnipeg, Can., 1944; B of Sacred Music, Manhattanville Coll., 1965, B of Music Edn., 1967; MA in Edn., U. San Francisco, 1967; postgrad., Ind. U., U. Pacific. Cert. tchr., Que., Ind., Calif.; cert. Kodaly. Tchr. Soc. of Sacred Heart, Montreal, Halifax, Vancouver, and Winnipeg, Can., 1946-68; tchr. music, art Coll. Sophie Barat, Montreal, Que., 1968-70; tchr. music Acad. Sacred Heart, Montreal, Que., 1970-71; tchr. music, art St. Paul's Sch., Montreal, Que., 1971-79; tchr. music Ind. U., Bloomington, 1979-82, Sir Wilfrid Laurier High, Sir William Hingston High, Montreal, 1982-84; pvt. practice Montreal, 1984-89; tchr. music, edn., studio U. Pacific, Stockton, Calif., 1990-95; Kodaly specialist St. George Sch., Stockton, 1991-95; lectr. in field. Recorded Year in Song, 1966; appeared in numerous theatrical prodns. including starring role in (film) Strangers in Good Company, 1988. Organizer, sec. Liturgical Soc., Halifax, Vancouver, 1956-57; organizer edn. projects Filmore Dist., San Francisco, 1966-67; active prison programs Stoney Mountain Prison, Winnipeg, 1967-68. Mem. Am. Assn. Kodaly Educators, Music Educators Nat. Conf., Coll. Music Soc., Internat. Soc. Music Edn., Met. Opera Guild, Pi Kappa Lambda, Phi Delta Kappa. Democrat. Roman Catholic. Home and Studio: CMR Studio 819 Bedford Rd Stockton CA 95204

ROCHE, LISA RILEY, reporter; b. Las Vegas, Nev., Aug. 16, 1958; d. Joseph Thomas and Shirley Arlene (Schulz) Riley; m. Vaughn Stewart Roche, Jan. 1, 1986. BA with honors, U. Nev., 1980. Editor coll. newspaper U. Nev., Las Vegas, 1980-81; newspaper reporter Las Vegas Sun, 1981-84, Las Vegas Rev. Jour., 1984-86, Desert News, Salt Lake City, 1987—. Winner 1st Pl., Nev. State Press Assn., 1984; recipient Spl. merit Desert News, 1989.

ROCHETTE, EDWARD CHARLES, retired association executive; b. Worcester, Mass., Feb. 17, 1927; s. Edward Charles and Lilia (Viau) R.; m. Mary Ann Ruland, July 29, 1978; children by previous marriage—Edward Charles, Paul, Philip. Student, Washington U., St. Louis, Clark U. Exec. editor Krause Publs., Iola, Wis., 1960-66; acting exec. dir. Am. Numismatic Assn., Colorado Springs, Colo., 1967-68, exec. v.p., 1972-87, ret., 1987; editor jour. The Numismatist, Colorado Springs, Colo., 1968-72. Bd. overseers Inst. Philatelic and Numismatic Studies, Adelphi U., Garden City, N.Y., 1979-81; chmn. medals com. Colo. Centennial Bicentennial Commn., 1976; mem. adv. panel Carson City Silver Dollar program Gen. Services Adminstrn., 1979-80; mem. U.S. Assay Commn., 1965. Served with USN, 1944-46. Recipient Gold medal for syndicated column Numismatic Lit. Guild, 1980, 86-88. Mem. Am. Numis. Assn. (life, medal of merit 1972), Am. Soc. Assn. Execs., Colo. Soc. Assn. Execs. (pres. 1988-89). Democrat. Roman Catholic. Lodge: Pikes Peak Kiwanis (pres. 1987-88). Office: Am Numis Assn PO Box 7083 Colorado Springs CO 80933-7083

ROCHWARGER-VERED, MICHELLE, management consultant; b. Buffalo, Mar. 7, 1955; d. Leonard and Arlene Jean Rochwarger. BA, U. Wis., 1977; MBA, U. San Francisco, 1981. Family case worker Salvation Army, Buffalo, 1977; social worker crisis intervention Eric County (N.Y.) Office of Aging, Buffalo, 1977-78; dir. We. Inst. for Tchrs. United Way, Buffalo, 1979; congl. asst. Office Congressman Burton, San Francisco, 1979-80; corp. loan officer Wells Fargo Bank, San Francisco, 1981-83, asst. v.p., tng. mgr., 1983-85; fin. svcs. cons. Omega Performance Corp., San Francisco, 1985-87; pres. Strategic Resources: Cons. Connection, San Francisco, 1987—; cons. Citicorp, San Francisco, 1980-81; mgr. corp. fitness challenge program Wells Fargo Bank, 1983. Bd. dirs. Big Bros./Big Sisters of San Francisco, 1983-85, Florence Crittendon Soc., San Francisco, 1984—, Ct. Apptd. Spl. Advs., San Francisco, 1983-85. Recipient Community Support award United Way, 1984. Mem. NAFE, San Francisco Advtg. Club, Nat. Soc. Performance and Instrn. Democrat. Jewish. Office: Strategic Resources 2040 Polk St Ste 281 San Francisco CA 94109-2520 also: 5319 Univ Dr Ste 403 Irvine CA 92715

ROCK, ARTHUR, venture capitalist; b. Rochester, N.Y., Aug. 19, 1926; s. Hyman A. and Reva (Cohen) R.; m. Toni Rembe, July 19, 1975. BS, Syracuse U., 1948; MBA, Harvard U., 1951. Gen. ptnr. Davis & Rock, San Francisco, 1961-68, Arthur Rock & Assocs., San Francisco, 1969-80; bd. dirs. Argonaut Group, Inc., L.A., Echelon, Palo Alto, Calif., AirTouch Comm., San Francisco; mem. exec. com. Teledyne, Inc., L.A., 1961-94; founder, chmn. exec. com., bd. dirs., past chmn. bd. dirs. Intel Corp., Santa Clara, Calif. Trustee Calif. Inst. Tech.; bd. dirs. San Francisco Opera Assn., 1970-92, San Francisco Mus. Modern Art; mem. vis. com. Harvard U. Bus. Sch., 1982-88. Recipient Medal of Achievement Am. Electronics Assn., 1987, Am. Acad. Achievement, 1989; named to Jr. Achievement Hall of Fame, 1990, Calif. Bus. Hall of Fame, 1990.

ROCK, JAMES MARTIN, economics educator, administrator; b. Plymouth, Wis., Aug. 17, 1935; s. Carroll George and Lillian Augusta (Leverenz) R.; m. Bonnie Kirkland Brown, Aug. 20, 1962; children: Jennifer, Peter, James, Sara. BS in Geography, U. Wis., 1957, MS in Rural Sociology, 1960; PhD in Econs., Northwestern U., 1966. Statistician State of Wis., Madison, 1957-58, U.S. Dept. Agrl., Madison, 1958-60, Purdue U., West Lafayette, Ind., 1960-61; econ. analyst CIA, 1964-66; asst. prof. U. Wis., Oshkosh, 1966-67; prof. U. Utah, Salt Lake City, 1967—, univ. prof., 1990—, dept. chairperson, 1992—; founder Econ. Forum, Salt Lake City, 1969-86; dir. Am. Assn. for Advancement of Core Curriculum, Denver, 1989-94. Author: Wisconsin Aluminum Cookware Industry, 1967, Money, Banking and Macroeconomics, 1977, Keynes's General Theory & My Early Beliefs, 1995; editor, author: Debt and the Twin Deficits Debate, 1991; contbr. articles to profl. jours. Active ACLU, 1968, Juvenile Justice Coun., Salt Lake City, 1983-85; chairperson Sch. Cmty. Coun., Salt Lake City, 1973-75; life mem. PTA, Salt Lake City, 1983—; founder minority scholarship U. Utah, 1986. Recipient Students' Choice award Assoc. Students, U. Utah, 1992, Svc. award Delta Epsilon, U. Wisc., 1957. Mem. Nat. Assn. Colored People (life, treas. 1980, pres. award 1991), Am. Econs. Assn., Alberta Henry Edn. Found. (co-founder, treas. 1967, pres. award 1973), Utah Assn. Acad. Profls. (vice chair 1977), Omicron Delta Epsilon (organizer, advisor 1971, pres. award 1981), Phi Kappa Phi (faculty award 1971). Office: U Utah Dept Economics Salt Lake City UT 84112

ROCKEY, JAY, public relations company executive. Chmn. Rockey Co., Inc., Seattle. Office: Rockey Co Inc 2121 5th Ave Seattle WA 98121-2510

ROCKLIN, EDWARD LAWRENCE, English literature educator, writer; b. N.Y.C., May 27, 1948; s. Ralph Joseph and Helene Clare (Milich) R.; m. M. Kathleen Massey, June 18, 1992. BA magna cum laude, Harvard U., 1970; MA with distinction, Rutgers U., 1974, PhD, 1981. From asst. prof. to assoc. prof. English Clarion U. of Pa., 1981-86; prof. English Calif. State Poly. U., Pomona, 1986—. Contbg. author: A Poet and a Filthy Playmaker, 1988, Teaching the Humanities, 1994; author articles. Mem. adv. bd. Calif. State U. Literacy Project, Pomona, 1993—. ACLS fellow, 1992-93. Mem. MLA, Shakespeare Soc. Am., Marlow Soc. Am., Nat. Coun. Tchrs. English. Office: Calif State Poly U 3801 W Temple Ave Pomona CA 91768-2557

ROCKMAN, ILENE FRANCES, librarian, educator, consultant; b. Yonkers, N.Y., Nov. 9, 1950; d. Leon and Margaret (Klein) R. BA, UCLA, 1972; MS in L.S. U. So. Calif., 1974; MA, Calif. Poly. State U., 1978; PhD, U. Calif., Santa Barbara, 1985. Libr. Wash. State U., Pullman, 1974-75, Calif. Poly. State U., San Luis Obispo, 1975—, assoc. dean, 1994—; adj. prof. Cuesta Coll., San Luis Obispo, 1982-85; abstracter Women Studies Abstracts, Rush, N.Y., 1976-91. Contbr. articles to profl. jours.; editor, Reference Svcs. Rev., 1987—; co-author: BLISS-Basic Library Information Sources and Svcs., 1991. Del. Democratic Nat. Conv., 1984. Recipient scholarship Calif. PTA, L.A., 1973. Mem. ALA, Calif. Libr. Assn. (mem. coun. 1983-86), Assn. Coll. and Rsch. Librs., Am. Ednl. Rsch. Assn., Total Libr. Exchange (pres. 1979-80), Libr. Assocs. Calif. Poly. State U. (exec. sec. 1981-83), Calif. Reading Assn. (exemplary svc. award 1992). Office: Calif Poly State U Libr San Luis Obispo CA 93407

ROCKOFF, S. DAVID, radiologist, physician, educator; b. Utica, N.Y., July 21, 1931; s. Samuel and Sarah (Rattinger) R.; m. Jacqueline Garsh; children—Lisa E., Todd E., Kevin D. A.B., Syracuse U., 1951; M.D., Albany Med. Coll., 1955; M.Sc. in Medicine, U. Pa., 1961. Diplomate: Am. Bd. Radiology. Intern U.S. Naval Hosp., Bethesda, Md., 1955-56; resident and fellow in radiology, USPHS trainee dept. radiology p. of U. Pa., Phila., 1958-61; staff radiologist NIH, Bethesda, Md., 1961-65; asst. prof. radiology Yale U. Sch. Medicine, New Haven, 1965-68; assoc. prof. Yale U. Sch. Medicine, 1968; asst. attending radiologist Yale-New Haven Med. Center, 1965-68; assoc. prof. radiology Washington U. Sch. Medicine, St. Louis, 1968-71; asst. radiologist Barnes and Allied Hosps., St. Louis, 1969-71; cons. radiologist VA Hosp., St. Louis, 1969-71, Homer G. Phillips Hosp., St. Louis, 1968-71; prof. radiology George Washington U. Sch. Medicine, Washington, 1971—; chmn. dept. radiology George Washington U. Sch. Medicine, 1971-77, head pulmonary radiology, 1978—, interim chmn. dept. radiology, 1989-90, prof. emeritus radiology, 1993—; cons. NIH, 1972—; vis. prof. Hadassah U., Beersheba U., Rambam Hosp., Israel, 1977; cons. in radiology VA Hosp., Washington, 1972-77, U.S. Naval Med. Center, Bethesda, 1973-77; mem. diagnostic radiology adv. com. NIH, 1973-76; mem. Cancer Research Manpower Rev. Com., NIH, 1978. Editor-in-chief: Investigative Radiology, 1965-76; editor-in-chief emeritus, 1976—; editor Jour. Thoracic Imaging, 1985; Contbr. numerous articles to med. jours. Served with USN, 1955-58; Served with USPHS, 1961-63. Recipient numerous USPHS grants. Fellow Am. Coll. Radiology (pres.-elect D.C. chpt. 1976), Am. Coll. Chest Physicians; mem. Am. Fedn. Clin. Research, D.C. Med. Soc. (mem. med.-legal com. 1975-78), AMA, Radiol. Soc. N.Am., Assn. Univ. Radiologists, Soc. Thoracic Radiology (pres. 1983-84, exec. dir. 1984-87). Home: PO Box 675650 Rancho Santa Fe CA 92067-5650

ROCKRISE, GEORGE THOMAS, architect; b. N.Y.C., Nov. 25, 1916; s. Thomas S. and Agnes M. (Asbury) R.; m. Margaret Lund Paulson, June 12, 1948 (dec. Aug. 1957); children: Christina, Peter; m. Sally S. Griffin, Dec. 1959 (div.); 1 child, Celia; m. Anneliese Warner, Nov. 27, 1985. B.Arch., Syracuse U., 1938; M.S. in Architecture, Columbia U., 1941. Fellow architecture Columbia U., 1940-41; architect Army and Navy, Panama, 1941-45; designer Edward D. Stone, N.Y.C., 1945-46, UN Hdqrs. Planning Commn., 1946-47; archtl. assoc. Thomas D. Church, San Francisco, 1948-49; pvt. practice architecture San Francisco, 1949-86, Glen Ellen, Calif., 1986-87; chmn. bd. Rockrise, Odermatt, Mountjoy Assocs. (architects and planners); lectr. Sch. Architecture, U. Calif., 1949-53; adviser to faculty com. Sch. Architecture, U. Venezuela, Caracas, 1954; mem. San Francisco Art Commn., 1952-56; cons. architect U.S. Dept. State, Japan, 1957-58, Fed. Republic Germany, Venezuela, Brazil, 1978-80, Bahrain, Brazil, Venezuela, Fed. Republic of Germany, 1981; architect U.S. embassy, Bahrain; vis. lectr. Cornell U., Clemson Coll., 1961, Syracuse U., U. Utah, Stanford U., 1962-65, Nat. U. Mex.; lectr. urban design Spanish Ministry Housing and Devel., Madrid, 1978; mem. San Francisco Planning Commn., 1961-62; adviser to Sec. for design HUD, 1966-67; participant State Dept. AID Urban Seminars Latin Am., 1971; mem. U.S. del. Pan Am. Congress Architects, Caracas, 1980; vis. prof. Universidad Central, Mex., 1985. Mem. pres.'s adv. com. U. Mass., 1971; mem. adv. council San Francisco Planning Urban Renewal Assn.; bd. dirs. Telegraph Hill Dwellers Assn., 1985-86, v.p.; pres. Archtl. Found. No. Calif., 1986; apptd. San Francisco Art Commn., 1986-87. Recipient AIA nat. award for residential work, 1953, 59, prog. architecture award citation, 1956, award of honor and award of merit AIA Homes for Better Living Program, 1956, regional awards for residential architecture AIA, 1957, others; Fulbright fellow in urban design U. Rome, 1978-79. Fellow AIA (pres. No. Calif. chpt. 1961, nat. v.p. from 1969, mem. nat honor awards jury, mem. nat. commn. urban design and planning 1978); mem. Am. Soc. Planning and Housing Ofcls., Am. Inst. Cert. Planners, Am. Soc. Landscape Architects, Nat. Assn. Housing and Redevel. Ofcls., Delta Kappa Epsilon, Tau Sigma Delta, Lambda Alpha. Home: 468 Vallejo St San Francisco CA 94133-4113 Studio: 1280 Hill Rd Glen Ellen CA 95442-9658

ROCKSTROH, DENNIS JOHN, journalist; b. Hermosa Beach, Calif., Feb. 1, 1942; s. Philip Herman and Alicia (Rubio) R.; m. Le Thi Que Huong, May 2, 1970; children: Bryan Benjamin, Paula Kim-Mai. Student, San Luis Rey Coll., 1960-61, El Camino Coll., 1961-62, San Fernando Valley State Coll., 1965-67. Reporter Thousand Oaks (Calif.) News Chronicle, 1966-67; tchr. Girls' High Sch., Qui Nhon, Vietnam, 1967-70; instr. Dalat U./Vietnamese Mil. Acad., 1970-71, Ohlone Coll., Fremont, Calif., 1984—; freelance war corr. Dispatch News Svc., Vietnam, 1967-71; city editor Santa Paula (Calif.) Daily Chronicle, 1972-73, reporter San Jose (Calif.) Mercury News, 1973-90, columnist, 1990—; guest lectr. U. Calif., Berkeley, 1987-91. Vol. Internat. Vol. Svcs., Vietnam, 1967-71; bd. dirs. San Jose unit ARC, 1978, Hope Rehab., San Jose, 1976-77. With U.S. Army, 1962-65, Vietnam. Co-recipient Pulitzer prize for Loma Prieta earthquake coverage, 1989; decorated Army Commendation Medal for Valor, 1965. Mem. Soc. Profl. Journalists, St. Anthony's Sem. Alumni Assn. Roman Catholic. Home: 3573 Tankerland Ct San Jose CA 95121-1244 Office: San Jose Mercury News 39355 California St Ste 305 Fremont CA 94538-1450

ROCKWELL, BURTON LOWE, architect; b. Utica, N.Y., June 3, 1920; s. Burton Lowe and Blanch Louise (Taylor) R.; m. Ruth Aldrich, May 19, 1949; children: Peter Grant, Abbie. BArch, MIT, 1946, MArch, 1947. Registered architect, Calif., N.Y., Vt., Mich., Ind. Project architect John Lyon Reid, Architect, San Francisco, 1947-53; ptnr. John Lyon Reid & Ptnrs., San Francisco, 1953-60, Reid Rockwell Banwell & Tarics, San Francisco, 1960-62, Rockwell & Banwell, San Francisco, 1962-70; pvt. practice Burton Rockwell, FAIA, San Francisco, 1970-88; ptnr. Rockwell, Chatham, Marshall, San Francisco, 1977-88, Rockwell & Rockwell, Architects, San Francisco, 1987—; faculty mem. U. Calif. Berkeley, Coll. Environ. Design, 1962-71; guest prof. MIT, 1969-70; juror Calif. Coalition for Adequate Sch. Housing, Archtl. Competition, 1991; chmn. Calif. Coun. Architects and Engrs., 1965. Architect-designer: Med. Rsch. Facilities, U. Calif., San Francisco, 1968 (AIA honor 1968), ch. sanctuary Lafayette Orinda Presbyn. Ch., 1968 (AIA Bay Area Honor 1974), Ct. House, Govt. Ct., Santa Cruz County, 1967 (Progressive Architecture award); contbr. articles to profl. jours. Bd. dirs. Community Music Ctr., San Francisco, 1972-74, Eastshore Pk. Project, San Francisco, 1975-80, Friends of Recreation and Parks, San Francisco, 1993—; mem. citizens' adv. com. San Francisco Bay Conservation and Devel. Commn., 1966—; mem. archtl. edn. com. Calif. Coun. Higher Edn., Sacramento, 1968-70; mem. bd. examiners Dept. Pub. Works, San Francisco, 1977-78. Served to capt. U.S. Army, 1942-46. Recipient 22 nat. awards for archtl. excellence San Francisco Art Commn., 1953—. Fellow AIA (pres. San Francisco chpt. 1965, bd. dirs., other officers); mem. ASTM, Calif. Coun. Architects (pres. 1968, bd. dirs., other offices 1965—), Constrn. Specification Inst., Am. Soc. Testing and Materials, Internat. Coun. Bldg. Officials. Home: 150 Edgewood Ave San Francisco CA 94117-3713 Office: Rockwell & Rockwell Architects 888 Post St San Francisco CA 94109-6013

ROCKWELL, DON ARTHUR, psychiatrist; b. Wheatland, Wyo., Apr. 24, 1938; s. Orson Arthur and Kathleen Emily (Richards) R.; m. Frances Pepitone-Arreola, Dec. 23, 1965; children: Grant, Chad. BA, Wash. U., 1959; MD, U. Okla., 1963; MA in Sociology, U. Calif., Berkeley, 1967. Diplomate Am. Bd. Psychiatry and Neurology. Intern in surgery San Francisco Gen. Hosp., 1963-64; resident in psychiatry Langley-Porter Neuropsychiatric Inst. U. Calif. Med. Ctr., San Francisco, 1964-67; instr. dept. psychiatry U. Calif. Sch. Medicine, Davis, 1969-70, asst. prof., 1970-74, assoc. prof., 1974-80, acting. assoc., dean curricular affairs, 1979-80, acting assoc. dean student affairs, 1980, assoc. dean student affairs, 1980-82, prof., 1980-84; career tchr. NIMH, 1970-72; assoc. psychiatrist Sacramento Med. Ctr.; med. dir. U. Calif. Med. Ctr., Davis, 1982-84; prof., vice chmn. dept. psychiatry and biobehavioral scis. UCLA, 1984—, dir. univ. Neuropsychiat. Hosp., 1984—, exec. assoc. dir. univ. Neuropsychiat. Inst., 1984—; chief of profl. staff Neuropsychiat. Inst., UCLA, 1984-85; chmn. U. Calif. Hosp. Dirs. Council, 1988-89; cons. Nat. Commn. on Marijuana, Washington, 1971-73. Co-author: Psychiatric Disorders, 1982; contbr. chpts. to books; articles to profl. jours. Bd. dirs. Bereavement Outreach, Sacramento, 1974-84, Suicide Prevention, Yolo County, 1969-84; bd. visitors U. Okla. Sch. Medicine; chmn. hosp. dirs. coun. U. Calif. Hosp.; governing coun. AHA Psychiat. Hosp. Fellow Am. Psychiat. Assn., Am. Coll. Psychiatrists, Am. Coll. Mental Health Adminstrs.; mem. AMA (gov. coun. psych. hosp.), Am. Sociologic Assn., Cen. Calif. Psychiat. Assn. (sec.-pres. 1977-78), U. Okla. Alumni Assn. (trustee 1981-86), Alpha Omega Alpha. Home: 1816 E Las Tunas Rd Santa Barbara CA 93103-1744

ROCKWELL, RICHARD THORNTON, naval engineer; b. Portland, Oreg., Feb. 5, 1946; s. Robert Thornton and Norma Lee (Barron) R.; m. Cheryl Lee Freeman, June 17, 1967; 1 child, Tia Marie. BS Aerospace and Astronautical Engring., U. Wash., 1972; MS in Shipping Mgmt., Ocean Engring., MIT, 1979. Enlisted USN, 1964, commd. ensign, 1972, advanced through grades to comdr., 1986—; type desk officer SRF Subic, Subic Bay, Philippines, 1979-81; LSD-41 project officer Supship Seattle, 1981-85; asst. repair officer Pearl Harbor Navel Shipyard, Hawaii, 1985-87; officer-in-charge Resupship, Pearl Harbor, 1987-89; planning officer Naval Ship Repair Facility, Yokosuka, Japan, 1989-92; mktg. dir. Long Beach (Calif.) Naval Shipyard, 1992-95; retired, 1995; mgr. facilities planning Knott's Berry Farm, Long Beach, 1995—. Mem. Naval Inst., Am. Soc. Naval Engrs. (Brand award 1979), Sigma Xi, Tau Beta Pi.

ROCKWELL, VIRGINIA CONSIDINE, school counselor; b. Fall River, Mass., Dec. 27, 1940; d. John F. and Lucy (Graham) Considine, m. Ralph Edwin Rockwell Jr., Aug. 28, 1965; children: Richard, Katherine. BS in Edn., Bridgewater (Mass.) State U., 1962; MEd, U. Mass., 1965. English tchr. Arcturus Jr. High Sch., Ft. Richardson, Ala., 1962-64; sch. counselor Hopkins Acad., Hadley, Mass., 1964-65; sch. counselor, dept. chair High Point High Sch., Beltsville, Md., 1965-67; employment counselor State of Oreg., Eugene, 1967-69; libr. asst. UCLA, L.A., 1969-70; placement asst. Northwestern U., Evanston, Ill., 1970-71; counselor Swink (Colo.) Sch. Dist., 1982—. Mem. AACD, Am. Sch. Counselor Assn. (recipient Multi Level Sch. Counselor of Yr. Honorable Mention 1991), Colo. Assn. Counseling and Devel., Colo. Sch. Counselor Assn. (recipient Region I Counselor of Yr. Honorable Mention 1986, named Multi Level Sch. Counselor of Yr. 1990), Delta Kappa Gamma. Home: 30 Sierra Dr La Junta CO 81050-3335 Office: Swink Sch 610 Columbia Ave Swink CO 81077-9999

ROCQUE, REBECCA HOMEDEW, mathematics educator; b. Monticello, Utah, July 6, 1954; d. Charles Daniel and Barbara Lucille (Petersen) Homedew; m. Kevin William Rocque, July 22, 1977; children: Heather, Ryan, Brandon, Brent, Dana. BA, Brigham Young U., 1992. Cert. secondary educator, level 4 math and computer sci. endorsement. Substitute tchr. Alpine Sch. Dist., Am. Fork, Utah, 1984-91; pre-sch. tchr. Discovery Days Presch., Lehi, Utah, 1981-91; dir. Sunshine Generation of No. Utah County, Lehi, Utah, 1989-92; tchr. math. Am. Fork (Utah) High Sch., 1991—, Young Mothers' High Sch., Pleasant Grove, Utah, 1991-92; yearbook adviser Am. Fork High Sch., 1992—, swim coach, 1992—, tchr. leader gender equity in edn, 1991—. Girl scout leader Girl Scouts of Am., Lehi, 1986-89; rm. mother PTA, Lehi, 1982-91; soccer coach Lehi Youth Recreation, 1989-90, swim team coach, 1992—; tchr. Community Sch., Lehi, 1983-91. Named one of Outstanding Women of Am., 1991. Mem. NEA, ASCP, Nat. Coun. Tchrs. Math., Am. Assoc. of U., Team Mgmt. Leadership prog., Utah Edn. Assn. Republican. LDS. Home: 755 W 240 S Lehi UT 84043-2516 Office: Am Fork High Sch 510 N 600 E American Fork UT 84003-1914

RODASTA, JOANNE COOK, elementary education educator; b. San Diego, Jan. 11, 1947; d. Roscoe Jepson and Irene Sargent Nielen; m. Philip L. Rodasta, Dec. 27, 1970 (div. July 15, 1982); children: Lisa Novella, Nicolas Christiansen; m. Donald J. Bradford, Feb. 14, 1987. BA, Calif. State U., Long Beach, 1968; MA, U. San Francisco, 1978. Life teaching credential. Elem. educator Buena Park (Calif.) Sch. Dist., 1970—, chair negotiating team, 1982-92; intuitive cons. Spiritsmith, Huntington Beach, Calif., 1988—; nat. trainer critical thinking Project IMPACT, Huntington Beach, Calif., 1985-90; pres. Spiritsmith, Huntington Beach, 1988—. Editor Reflections, 1990-92, Lumaean Letter, 1990—. Pres., founder Havensmith Homes for Neglected Children, Huntington Beach, 1989. Recipient award Calif. Tchr. Assn./NEA, 1985; grantee Bank of Am., 1987. Mem. World Bus. Acad., Triple Nine Soc., Mastergame (bd. dirs. 1990-92), Mensa. Home: 2607 Buckeye St Newport Beach CA 92660-4117

RODDICK, DAVID BRUCE, construction company executive; b. Oakland, Calif., Oct. 31, 1948; s. Bruce Ergo and Hortensia Cabo (Castedo) R.; m. Sharon Ann Belan, May 25, 1975; children: Heather Marie, Christina Dee-Ann. BSCE, U. Calif., Davis, 1971. Engr. Bechtel Corp., San Francisco, 1971-77, contract specialist, 1977-78; subcontract adminstr. Boecon Corp., Richland, Wash., 1978-79; constrn. mgr. BE&C Engrs., Inc., Vancouver, Wash., 1979-81; contracts mgr. Boecon Corp., Tukwila, Wash., 1981-83; sr. constrn. mgr. BE&C Engrs., Inc., Wichita, Kans., 1983-84; v.p. ops. Carl Holvick Co., Sunnyvale, Calif., 1984-88, also sec. bd. dirs.; v.p., gen. mgr. Brookman Co. div. B.T. Mancini Co., Inc., Milpitas, Calif., 1988-92; v.p., sec., CFO B.T. Mancini Co., Inc., 1992—. Mem. devel. com. San Jose (Calif.) Mus. Assn., 1993-95; mem., dir. Constrn. Fin. Mgmt. Assn., 1995—; pres. Reed Sch. PTA, San Jose, 1986-88, San Jose Coun. PTA's, 1988-89; trustee Heart of Valley Bapt. Ch.; bd. dirs. Vinehill Homeowners Assn., 1975-77. Maj. C.E., USAR, 1969—. Decorated Army Achievement medal, 1988, Commendation medal, 1991; recipient Calif. State PTA Hon. Svc. award, 1988. Mem. ASCE, Res. Officers Assn., Am. Arbitration Assn. (mem. panel arbitrators), Engr. Regimental Assn., Calif. Aggie Alumni Assn., Army Engr. Assn., U. Calif.-Davis Century Club, Sigma Nu. Republican. Office: B T Mancini Co Inc 876 S Milpitas Blvd Milpitas CA 95035-6311

RODEFER, JEFFREY ROBERT, lawyer, prosecutor; b. Santa Fe, Mar. 29, 1963; s. Robert Jacob and Joanne D. (Thomas) R. BS, U. Nev., 1985; JD, Willamette U., 1988, cert. dispute resolution, 1988. Bar: Calif. 1990, Nev. 1990, U.S. Dist. Ct. Nev. 1990, U.S. Dist. Ct. (ea. dist.) Calif. 1990, U.S. Ct. Appeals (9th cir.) 1990, Colo. 1991; cert. arbitrator, Nev. Legal intern Willamette U. Legal Aid Clinic, Salem, Oreg., 1987-88; legal rschr. transp. divsn. Nev. Atty. Gen. Office, Carson City, 1989-90, dep. atty. gen. taxation divsn., 1990-93, dep. atty. gen. gaming divsn., 1993—. Author: Nevada Property Tax Manual, 1993; contbr. articles to Nev. Lawyer. Contbg. mem. U. Nev. Coll. Bus. Adminstrn. and Athletic Dept., Reno, 1992, Willamette U. Coll. Law, Ann. Law Fund, Salem, 1992; active Nat. Parks and Recreation Assn., Washington, 1991; mem. First Christian Ch. Mem. Internat. Assn. Gaming Attys., U. Nev. Coll. Bus. Alumni Assn., Am. Inns of Ct. (Bruce R. Thompson chpt.), State Bar Nev. (functional equivalency com. 1994—), Phi Delta Phi. Republican. Office: Nev Atty Gen Office Capitol Complex Carson City NV 89710

RODEFFER, STEPHANIE LYNN HOLSCHLAG, archaeologist, government official; b. Newark, Ohio, Oct. 5, 1947; d. Jerry Bernard and Joan Elizabeth (Dasher) Holschlag; m. Michael Joe Rodeffer, Sept. 11, 1971. BA, U. Ky., 1969; PhD, Wash. State U., 1975. Instr., then asst. prof. anthropology Lander Coll., Greenwood, S.C., 1974-77; archaeologist interagy. archaeol. svcs. Nat. Park Svc./Heritage Conservation and Recreation Svc., Atlanta, 1977-80; archaeologist divsn. cultural programs Heritage Conservation and Recreation Svc./Nat. Park Svc., Albuquerque, 1980-81; archaeologist div. cultural programs Nat. Park Svc., Santa Fe, N.Mex., 1981-82; archaeologist, acting chief preservation planning br. Nat. Park Svc., Phila., 1982-86; chief interagy. archaeol. svcs. br. div. nat. register programs Nat. Park Svc., San Francisco, 1986-90; chief mus. collections repository Western Archaeol. and Conservation Ctr. Nat. Park Svc., Tucson, 1990—. Muster Chmn. Star Ft. Hist. Com., Ninety Six, S.C., 1975. Recipient spl. achievement award Nat. Park Svc., 1980, 82, mgmt. award So. Ariz. Fed. Execs. Assn., 1992; Woodrow Wilson fellow, 1969. Mem. Soc. for Hist. Archeology (membership chmn. 1976-78, sec.-treas. 1978—, Carol Ruppé Disting. Svc. award 1994), Soc. for Am. Archaeology, Soc. Profl. Archaeologists, Phi Beta Kappa. Roman Catholic. Office: Nat Park Svc Western Archaeol-Conservation Ctr 1415 N 6th Ave Tucson AZ 85705-6643

RODGERS, ANTHONY D., hospital administrator. BA, UCLA, 1971, MS in Pub. Health, 1975, postgrad. Rsch. analyst capital projects divsn. L.A. County Dept. Health Svcs., 1973-77; assoc. hosp. adminstr. John Wesley County Hosp., L.A., 1978-79; adminstr. H. Claude Hudson Comprehensive Health Ctr., L.A., 1979-89; chief exec. officer Metro West County Health Ctrs., L.A., 1989; assoc. hosp. adminstr. ops. Olive View Med. Ctr., L.A., 1989-90; chief exec. officer Maricopa Med. Ctr., Phoenix, 1990—; drug testing cons. office commr. Major League Baseball, 1986-87; facility planning cons., Condelli Brown & Assocs., Santa Monica, Calif., 1985-87; program planning con., Omni Corp., Santa Monica, 1980-81; staff planner devel. svc. programs ambulatory care ctrs. Pres. JWCH Inst., Inc., L.A., 1987-89. Mem. Nat. Assn. Pub. Hosps. (exec. bd., fellow), Ariz. Hosp. Assn. (regional coun., bd. dirs. Blue Cross/Blue Shield). Home: 13229 S 48th St Phoenix AZ 85044-5037 Office: Maricopa Med Ctr PO Box 5099 Phoenix AZ 85010-5099

RODGERS, AUDREY PENN, public information officer, public relations consultant; b. Berkeley, Calif., Aug. 8, 1923; d. Lewis August and Edith Harriet (Siler) Penn; m. David Leigh Rodgers, June 13, 1943 (div. Mar. 1982); children: Timothy Leigh, Janice Leigh Rodgers Bracken. AB, U. Calif., Berkeley, 1944. Designer Landscape Design, San Francisco, 1960-70; pres. Campaign Date Svc., Inc., San Francisco, 1970-80; pub. info. dir. East Bay Infiltration Study, Oakland, Calif., 1980-85; pub. info. officer wastewater dept. East Bay Mcpl. Utility Dist., Oakland, 1985—. V.p. devel. Greenbelt Alliance, San Francisco, 1990—; bd. dirs. San Francisco Planning Urban Rsch. Assn., 1970, action chair LWV, San Francisco, 1967. Mem. Pub. Rels. Soc. Am. (chmn. accreditation com. 1984-86, bd. dirs.), Water Polution Control Fedn., Acad. Polit. Sci., Women in Landscape, Calif. Native Plant Soc. (v.p. 1984-85), Sierra Club, Met. Club, Alpha Xi Delta. Democrat. Avocations: swimming, gardening, landscape design, travel, photography. Office: PO Box 24055 Oakland CA 94623-1055

RODGERS, CHRISTINE M., plastic surgeon, educator; b. Phila., Feb. 5, 1951; d. Frank Paul and Irene Ursula (Silwanski) R. BA in Russian, U. Pa., 1973, MD, 1977. Resident in surgery U. Pa./U. Rochester, 1982; resident in plastic surgery Brigham Women's & Children's Hosp., Boston, 1984; asst. prof. plastic surgery N.Y. Med. Coll., Valhalla, 1984-85; chief plastic surgery dept. Lincoln Hosp., Bronx, 1984-86; asst. prof. plastic surgery U. Colo., Denver, 1986—; chief plastic surgery dept. Denver Gen. Hosp., 1986—. Author: Soft Tissue Injuries, 1987. Fellow ACS; mem. Am. Assn. Hand Surgeons, Am. Soc. Maxillofacial Surgeons, Am. Cleft, Palate and Craniofacial Soc., Colo. State Soc. Plastic and Reconstructive Surgery, Am. Soc. Plastic and Reconstructive Surgeons. Home: 455 Eudora St Apt 1101 Denver CO 80220-5126 Office: Rose Med Ctr 4500 E 9th Ave Ste 160 Denver CO 80220-3920

RODGERS, FREDERIC BARKER, judge; b. Albany, N.Y., Sept. 29, 1940; s. Prentice Johnson and Jane (Weed) R.; m. Valerie McNaughton, Oct. 8, 1988; 1 child: Gabriel Moore. AB, Amherst Coll., 1963; JD, Union U., 1966. Bar: N.Y. 1966, U.S. Ct. Mil. Appeals 1968, Colo. 1972, U.S. Supreme Ct. 1974, U.S. Ct. Appeals (10th cir.) 1981. Chief dep. dist. atty., Denver, 1972-73; commr. Denver Juvenile Ct., 1973-79; mem. Mulligan Reeves Teasley & Joyce, P.C., Denver, 1979-80; pres. Frederic B. Rodgers, P.C., Breckenridge, Colo., 1980-89; ptnr. McNaughton & Rodgers, Central City, Colo., 1989-91; county ct. judge County of Gilpin, 1987—; presiding mcpl. judge cities of Breckenridge, Blue River, Black Hawk, Central City, Edgewater, Empire, Idaho Springs and Westminster, Colo., 1978-95; chmn. com. on mcpl. ct. rules of procedure Colo. Supreme Ct., 1984—; mem. gen. faculty Nat. Jud. Coll. U. Nev., Reno, 1990—, elected to faculty coun., 1994—. Author: (with Dilweg, Fretz, Murphy and Wicker) Modern Judicial Ethics, 1992; contbr. articles to profl. jours. Mem. Colo. Commn. on Children, 1982-85, Colo. Youth Devel. Coun., 1989—, Colo. Family Peace Task Force, 1994—. Served with JAGC, U.S. Army, 1967-72; to maj. USAR, 1972-88. Decorated Bronze Star with oak leaf cluster, Air medal. Recipient Outstanding County Judge award Colo. 17th Judicial Dist. Victim Adv. Coalition, 1991; Spl. Community Service award Colo. Am. Legion, 1979. Mem. ABA (jud. adminstrn. div. exec. coun. 1989—, ho. dels. 1993—), Colo. Bar Assn. (bd. govs. 1986-88, 90-92, 93—), Continental Divide Bar Assn., Denver Bar Assn. (bd. trustees 1979-82), First Jud. Dist. Bar Assn., Nat. Conf. Spl. Ct. Judges (chmn. 1989-90), Colo. County Judges Assn. (pres. 1995—), Colo. Mcpl. Judges Assn. (pres. 1986-87), Colo. Trial Judges Coun. (v.p. 1995—), Denver Law Club (pres. 1981-82), Colo. Women's Bar Assn., Am. Judicature Soc., Nat. Coun. Juvenile and Family Ct. Judges, Univ. Club (Denver), Arlberg Club (Winter Park), Marines Meml. Club (San Francisco), Westminster Rotary Club. Episcopalian.

RODGERS, MARILYN CAROL, special education educator; b. Derby, Conn., May 20, 1951; d. Stanley and Mary Irene (Wojiski) Slowik; m. Billy John Rodgers, Oct. 25, 1940; children: David Warner, Merlinna, Jai, Daniel. BA in Psychology, U. Conn., 1973; AMS, Montessori Western Tchr. Prog., Los Alamitos, Calif., 1975. Tchr. Hans Christian Anderson Montessori Sch., Tolland, Conn., 1974-76; breathing therapist Rebirth America, San Francisco, 1977-80; singer Allright Family Band, 1980—; substitute tchr. Hawaii Dept. Edn., Pahoa, 1991—; tutor Hawaii Dept. Edn., Puna, 1992—; underwater birth cons., 1982—; proprietor Opihikao Bed and Breakfast, Hawaii, 1987—; owner Pahoa Swap Shop, 1989-91; lectr. in field. Contbr. articles to profl. jours. Sec. Hawaii Island Theatre, Pahoa. Jehovah's Witness. Home and Office: PO Box 1653 Pahoa HI 96778-1653

RODMAN, ALPINE CLARENCE, arts and crafts company executive; b. Roswell, N.Mex., June 23, 1952; s. Robert Elsworth and Verna Mae (Means) R.; m. Sue Arlene Lawson, Dec. 13, 1970; 1 child, Connie Lynn. Student, Colo. State U., 1970-71, U. No. Colo. Ptnr. Pinel Silver Shop, Loveland, Colo., 1965-68, salesman, 1968-71; real estate salesman Loveland, 1971-73; mgr. Traveling Traders, Phoenix, 1974-75; co-owner Deer Track Traders, Loveland, 1975-85; pres. Deer Track Traders, Ltd., 1985—. Author: The Vanishing Indian: Fact or Fiction?, 1985. Mem. Civil Air Patrol, 1965-72, 87-92, dep. comdr. for cadets, 1988-90; cadet comdr. Ft. Collins, Colo., 1968, 70, Colo. rep. to youth tng. program, 1969, U.S. youth rep. to Japan, 1970. Mem. Bur. Wholesale Sales Reps., Western and English Salesmen's Assn. (bd. dirs. 1990), Internat. Platform Assn., Indian Arts and Crafts Assn. (bd. dirs. 1988-94, exec. com. 1989-92, v.p. 1990, pres. 1991, market chmn. 1992), Crazy Horse Grass Roots Club. Republican. Office: Deer Track Traders Ltd PO Box 448 Loveland CO 80539-0448

RODMAN, SUE ARLENE, wholesale Indian crafts company executive, artist; b. Fort Collins, Colo., Oct. 1, 1951; d. Marvin F. and Barbara I. (Miller) Lawson; m. Alpine C. Rodman, Dec. 13, 1970; 1 child, Connie Lynn. Student Colo. State U., 1970-73. Silversmith Pinel Silver Shop, Loveland, Colo., 1970-71; asst. mgr. Traveling Traders, Phoenix, 1974-75; co-owner, co-mgr. Deer Track Traders, Ltd., Loveland, 1975-85, v.p., 1985—. Author: The Book of Contemporary Indian Arts and Crafts, 1985. Mem. U.S. Senatorial Club, 1982-87, Rep. Presdl. Task Force, 1984-90; mem. Civil Air Patrol, 1969-73, 87-90, pers. officer, 1988—. Mem. Internat. Platform Assn., Indian Arts and Crafts Assn., Native Am. Art Studies Assn., Inc., Western and English Sales Assn., Crazy Horse Grass Roots Club. Mem. Am. Baptist Ch. Avocations: museums, piano, recreation research, fashion design, reading, flying. Office: Deer Track Traders Ltd PO Box 448 Loveland CO 80539-0448

RODNUNSKY, SIDNEY, lawyer, educator, Prince of Kiev, Prince of Trabzon, Prince and Duke of Rodari, Duke of Chernigov, Count of Riga, Count of Saint John of Alexandria; b. Edmonton, Alta., Can., Feb. 3, 1946; s. H. and I. Rodnunsky; m. Teresita Asuncion; children: Naomi, Shawna, Rachel, Tevie, Claire, Donna, Sidney Jr. BEd, U. Alberta, 1966, LLB, 1973; MEd, U. Calgary, 1969, grad. diploma, 1990; BS, U. of State of N.Y., 1988; MBA, Greenwich U., 1990. Served as regional counsel to Her Majesty the Queen in Right of the Dominion of Can.; former gov. Grande Prairie Regional Coll.; now prin. legal counsel Can.; Alta. coord. for gifted children Mensa Can.; past pres. Grande Prairie and Dist. Bar Assn. Author: Breathalyzer Casebook; editor: The Children Speak. Decorated Knight Grand Cross Sovereign and Royal Order of Piast, Knight Grand Cross Order of St. John the Baptist; knight Hospitaller Order St. John of Jerusalem; named to Honorable Order of Ky. Colonels; named adm. State of Tex.; recipient Presidential Legion of Merit. Mem. Law Soc. Alta., Law Soc. Sask., Canadian Bar Assn., Inst. Can. Mgmt. Address: 3 Grandview Garden Ct, 4802-46A Ave, Athabasca, AB Canada T95 IH8

RODOLFF, DALE WARD, sales executive, consultant; b. Casa Grande, Ariz., Aug. 5, 1938; s. Norval Ward and Mary Louise (Grasty) Rodolff; m. Kathleen Pennington, Sept. 3, 1960 (div. July 1983); children: David Ward (dec.), Julia Ann. BS in Mining Engring., U. Ariz.; PMD, U. Cape Town; postgrad., Denver Sem. Registered profl. engr., Republic of South Africa. Supt. smelting and fabricating Inspiration Consol. Copper Co., Claypool, Ariz., 1960-72; smelter and refinery supt. Palabora Mining Co, Phalaborwa, Republic of South Africa, 1972-74; asst. mgr. Empress Nickel Mining Co., Gatooma, Zimbabwe, 1974-77; smelter supt. Magma Copper Co., San Manuel, Ariz., 1977-81; v.p., gen. mgr. Sentinel Mgmt. Corp., Tucson, 1981-82; dir., mgr. metallurgy Outokumpu Engring. Inc., Denver, 1982-86, mgr. N.Am., 1986—, also bd. dirs.; cons., pres. Dale W. Rodolff Cons., 1986—; pres. Bus. Performance Services, Inc., 1986-90,. Contbr. articles to tech. jours.; inventor scrap rod feed system, 1970. Pres. Y Men's Club, Miami, Ariz., 1969. Kennecott scholar U. Ariz., 1959. Mem. AIME (metall. soc., soc. mining engrs., chmn. smelter div. 1970, 71, pyro metall. com. 1973-77). Lodge: Elks. Home: 6527 S Jungfrau Way Evergreen CO 80439-5308 Office: DWRC Corp 6527 S Jungfrau Way Evergreen CO 80439-5308

RODRIGUE, CHRISTINE M(ARY), geography educator, business consultant; b. L.A., Oct. 27, 1952; d. John-Paul and Josephine Genevieve (Gorsky) R. AA in French, German, L.A. Pierce Coll., 1972; BA in Geography summa cum laude, Calif. State U., Northridge, 1973, MA in Geography, 1976; PhD in Geography, Clark U., 1987. Computer analyst Jet Propulsion Labs., Pasadena, Calif., 1977; teaching asst. Clark U., Worcester, Mass., 1976-79, rsch. asst., 1977-78; instr. geography L.A. Pierce Coll., Woodland Hills, Calif., 1981—; cons. Area Location Systems, Northridge, 1984—, tech. writer, 1990—; asst. prof. urban studies and geography Calif. State U., Northridge, 1980-89; asst. prof. geography and planning Calif. State U., Chico, 1989-94, assoc. prof., 1994—; co-dir. Ctr. for Hazards Rsch., 1994—; faculty senator Calif. State U., Chico, 1990-92, grad. geog. adviser, 1992-93; owner Carmel (Calif.) Poster Gallery. Contbr. numerous articles to refereed profl. publs. Recipient Meritorious Performance and Profl. Promise award Calif. State U., 1987, 88, 89, Calif. State U. summer scholar grant, 1990, 92, 94. Mem. AAAS, NOW, Assn. Am. Geographers (chmn. splty. group 1983-84, councillor splty. group 1994—), Capitalism Nature Socialism (mem. editl. bd. 1991—), L.A. Geog. Soc. (v.p. 1987, pres. 1988, editor 1981-84), Union Concerned Scientists, Planetary Soc., Sierra Club, Internat. Arabian Horse Assn., Arabian Horse Registry. Democrat. Office: Calif State U Dept Geography & Planning Chico CA 95929-0425

RODRIGUES, ALFRED BENJAMIN KAMEEIAMOKU, marketing consultant; b. Honolulu, Jan. 23, 1947; s. Alfred Benjamin Kameeiamoku and Ruth Shiegeko (Kameda) R. BA, U. San Francisco, 1969; postgrad. U. Wis., 1977. Pub. info. mgr. Hawaiian Tel.-GTE, Honolulu, 1979-80, pub. affairs program mgr., 1980-84, dir. pub. affairs, 1984-85, dir. mktg. communications, 1986-87, dir. mktg. communications and svcs., 1987-89 sr. v.p., Milici, Valenti and Gabriel Advt., Inc., 1989-91, exec. v.p., 1991-92; pres. Al Rodrigues & Assocs., 1992—. Bd. dirs., pub. rels. chmn. Am. Lung Assn., 1981-88; trustee, v.p. Hawaii Army Mus. Soc., 1982—; bd. dirs. ARC Hawaii, 1983-85; budget com. Aloha United Way. Maj. USAR, 1969-89. Decorated Bronze Star with three oak leaf clusters, Meritorious Svc. medal with oak leaf cluster, Army Commendation medal with 2 oak leaf clusters, Purple Heart with oak leaf cluster, Air medal with oak leaf cluster. Mem. Am. Mktg. Assn. (bd. dirs. Hawaii chpt.), Am. Advt. Fedn., Hawaii Advt. Fedn. (bd. dirs., pres., Advt. Man of Yr., 1989), Pub. Rels. Soc. Am. (pres. Hawaii), Res. Officers Assn., Hawaii C. of C., Rotary. Republican. Roman Catholic.

RODRIGUES, MARK, financial executive, manpower consultant; b. Jhansi, India, Oct. 7, 1948; came to U.S., 1983; s. Basil and Monica (Dasgupta) R.; m. Sandra Williams, Mar. 27, 1976; children: Sarah, Daniel. BTech, Loughborough U., Leicester, Eng., 1970; MBA, Strathclyde U., Glasgow, Scotland, 1971. Cert. Acct., Eng. Fin. analyst Ford Europe, Inc., London, 1971-73; mgmt. cons., London mgr. Mann Judd Mgmt. Cons., 1973-78; pres. Bur. and Industry Svcs. Ltd., London, 1978-81; mng. dir. Indsl. Engring. Svcs., London, 1981-83; v.p. Internat. Staffing Cons., Newport Beach, Calif., 1983-88; pres. Brit. Workforce, Inc., Mission Viejo, Calif., 1988—; pres. Euro Precision Inc., Laguna Hills, Calif., 1992—. Fellow Assn. Cert. Accts.; mem. Royal Oriental Club. Office: Brit Workforce Inc 26002 Marguerite Pky Ste 433 Mission Viejo CA 92692-3262

RODRIGUEZ, DENNIS, electrical engineer; b. Manhattan, N.Y., Oct. 14, 1961; s. Jose and Henrietta (Whitlow) R.; children: Christopher, Rodriguez. BS, NYU, 1987; AS, Cmty. Coll. of Air Force, Maxwell AFB, Ala., 1989. Analytical data specialist Martin Marietta, Waterton Canyon, Colo., 1991-93; asst. to chief engring scis., R & D sect. Mobile Techs. Incorp., Henderson, Nev., 1993—. 1st lt. USAF, 1988-91. Decorated Purple Heart. Democrat.

RODRIGUEZ, LEONARD, foundation administrator; b. Phoenix, Jan. 27, 1944; s. Jesus H. and Manuela (Razo) R.; m. Jo Ann Gama, Jan. 16, 1965 ; 1 child, Lena Teresa. BS in Mktg., Ariz. State U., 1981, MPA, 1995. Cert. tchr., Ariz. Adminstrv. svcs. officer Title XX Adminstrn., Phoenix, 1979-81, Block Grants Adminstrn., Phoenix, 1981-84; property mgmt. mgr. State of Ariz., Phoenix, 1984-86; pres. LTR Mgmt. Svcs., Phoenix, 1986-93; dir. PALS computer literacy program N.W. Resources and Learning Ctr., 1989-91; program cons. City of El Mirage, 1989-91; master tchr. Rio Salado C.C., 1989-91; project dir., exec. dir. Westside Coalition for Substance Abuse Prevention, 1990-91; mem. chpt. svcs. Make-A-Wish Found. of Am., 1993—; adj. clin. instr., faculty assoc. Ariz. State U., 1979-89; cons. Applied Econs. Curriculum, Jr. Achievement of Cen. Ariz., Inc., 1987; nat. tng. cons. Ctr. Substance Abuse Prevention, Housing & Urban Devel., Marco Internat., Washington, 1992—. Chmn. community rels. minority recruitment program Ariz. State U., Tempe, 1985-86; bd. dirs. Concilio Latino de Salud, Inc., pres. 1993-94, vice chmn. Friendly House, Inc., Phoenix, 1982, chmn., 1993, pres., 1987; mem. community problem solving coordinating com. Valley of the Sun United Way, 1988; alliance chmn. Gov.'s Office of Drug Policy, mem. statewide exec. com., 1991; program cons. Cada Uno, Inc., 1990-91; adult literacy coord. Chandler Pub. Libr., 1992-93; tng. cons. Phoenix Fight Back Program, 1992-93; outreach coord. Hemophilia Assn., Ariz., 1992-93. Mem. Ariz. Adminstrs. Assn., Counterparts (founder 1986), Hispanic C. of C., Vesta Club (chmn. scholarship com. 1983), Rotary (pres. 1987-88, voting del. internat. conv. 1987). Home: 6225 N 30th Way Phoenix AZ 85016-2212

RODRIGUEZ, LINDA TAKAHASHI, secondary education educator; b. L.A., June 22, 1941; d. Edward S. and Mary Takahashi; divorced; children: Regina Marie, Marla Sari. AA, Trinidad (Colo.) Jr. Coll., 1961; BA, We. State Coll., Gunnison, Colo., 1963; MA, U. Colo., Denver, 1991. Cert. tchr., adminstr., Colo. Tchr. Stratton (Colo.) Jr./Sr. High Sch., 1964-65, Pikes Peak Elem. Sch., Colorado Springs, 1966-68, Prince Sch., Tucson, 1968-70, Ipava (Ill.) Grade Sch., 1970-72, Macomb (Ill.) Schs., 1972-74, Colchester (Ill.) Jr./Sr. High Schs., 1979-83, Hazel Park (Mich.) Alternative Sch., 1984-85; tchr. 8th grade lang. arts and social studies Denver Pub. Schs., 1986-95, chair lang. dept., 1987-95, tchr. reading resource, 1987-92; creator, dir. Reading Summer Sch., 1987-95; presenter insvcs. Denver Pub. Schs., 1987-94; mentor Alternative Tchr. Cert. Program; mem. bd. dirs. Asian Cultural Ctr. Advisor Asian Edn. Adv. Bd., Denver, 1989-95; bd. dirs. Colo. Youth-at-Risk, Denver, 1992-93. Mem. Landmark Edn. Forum, Highland Park Optimists, Delta Kappa Gamma. Home: 1617 Daphne St Broomfield CO 80020-1155

RODRIGUEZ, MARGARET LOUISE, crisis intervention counselor, community debriefer and trainer; b. San Diego, Aug. 6, 1962; d. John Francis and Justine Margaret (Deggelman) Wurzel; m. Michael Vincent Rodriguez, Sept. 28, 1962. AA in Social Svcs., Pima C.C., Tucson, Ariz., 1992; BA in Psychology, Prescott Coll., Tucson, 1993; MA in Counseling, Chapman U., Tucson, 1994. Lic. domestic violence, critical incident stress debriefing, Ariz. Asst. mgr. TMC Theatres, Tucson, 1978-82; accounts payable clk. P.F. West, Inc., Tucson, 1982-84; dir. accounts payable E.C. Garcia & Co. Inc., Tucson, 1984-87; mediator Our Town Family Ctr., Tucson, 1993—; crisis interventionist Victim Witness, Tucson, 1990—; dir. support program Tucson Fire Dept. F.L.A.M.E.S., Tucson, 1993, 94; trainer crisis intervention Victim Witness, New Zealand, 1994, vol. coord.; debriefer in pub. schs. after fed. bldg. explosion, Oklahoma City, 1995. Mem. ACA, Nat. Orgn. Victim Assistance.

RODRÍGUEZ, PAUL ANTHONY, elementary school educator; b. Pomona, Calif., Sept. 13, 1951; s. Salvador Zuniga and Maria (Fernandez) Rodríguez; m. Doreen Mae Terifaj, Sept. 8, 1989; children: Paul Anthony II, Harmonie Mae, Alexander Faustino. BA, St. Mary's Coll., 1973; BA in Music, History and Lit., Holy Names Coll., 1974; teaching credential, U. La Verne, 1979; MA in Musicology, Calif. State U., Fullerton, 1985. Cert. presch., K-12, adult class, C.C. tchr., Calif. Tchr. Upland (Calif.) Unified Sch. Dist., 1979-85, Chino (Calif.) Unified Sch. Dist., 1985—. Accompanist St. Margaret Mary Cath. Ch., Chino, 1962—, St. Paul the Apostle Cath. Ch., Chino Hills, Calif., 1985—; scout leader, 1988-90. Mem. NEA, Calif.

Assn. for Bilingual Edn. (v.p. 1992—), Calif. Tchrs. Assn., Calif. Music Tcrhs. Assn., Upland Tchrs. Assn., Assoc. Chino Tchrs. Democrat. Roman Catholic. Home: 5031 Independence St Chino CA 91710-1886

RODRIGUEZ, ROMAN, physician, child psychiatrist, educator; b. N.Y.C., Jan. 21, 1951; s. Roman Rodriguez and Margarita (Castillo) Torres. BS in Biology, St. Mary's Coll. of Calif., 1972; MD, U. Calif.-San Francisco, 1976. Diplomate Nat. Bd. Med. Examiners, Am. Bd. Psychiatry and Neurology-Gen. Psychiatry, Am. Bd. Psychiatry and Neurology-Child and Adolescent Psychiatry. Resident in gen. psychiatry Menninger Found., Topeka, 1976-79, fellow in child psychiatry, 1978-80; resident physician Topeka VA Med. Ctr., 1976-79; dir. psychiat. services Youth Ctr. Topeka, 1979-80; assoc. med. dir. Mission/SE Adolescent Day Treatment Ctr., San Francisco, 1980-81; staff psychiatrist, med. advisor Youth Guidance Ctr., San Francisco, 1980-82; clin. dir. Growing Mind Corp., San Rafael, Calif., 1980-85; pvt. practice child psychiatry, San Francisco and San Rafael, Calif., 1980-85; child team leader dept. psychiatry Kaiser Permanente Med. Ctr., South San Francisco, 1985-93, physician well being com., 1990-94, chief dept. psychiatry, 1994—; med. staff Children's Hosp., San Francisco, 1980-85; St. Luke's Hosp., San Francisco, 1981-85; Marin Gen. Hosp., Greenbrae, Calif., 1983-87; asst. clin. prof. U. Calif., San Francisco, 1981—, mem. admissions com. Sch. Medicine, 1980-85; examiner Am. Bd Psychiatry and Neurology, Inc., 1992—. Bd. dirs. Canal Community Alliance, San Rafael, 1985-86, Community Health Ctr. Marin, Fairfax, Calif., 1985-86, Bahia de Rafael Fourplex, San Rafael, 1986, Village in the Park Homeowners Assn., Daly City, 1991-95, trustee Sacred Heart High Sch., 1994—. Mem. Am. Psychiat. Assn., Am. Soc. for Adolescent Psychiatry, Am. Acad. Child and Adolescent Psychiatry, No. Calif. Regional Assn. Child and Adolescent Psychiatry (editor newsletter 1993—), No. Calif. Psychiat. Soc., Calif. Med. Assn., San Mateo County Med. Soc. Republican. Roman Catholic. Home: 116 Cityview Dr Daly City CA 94014-3446 Office: Kaiser Permanente Med Ctr Dept Psychiatry 1200 El Camino Real South San Francisco CA 94080-3208

RODRIQUE, SANDRA GAIL, mental health therapist; b. Tucson, Ariz., Sept. 10, 1966; d. Joseph R. and Ann (Treaddell) R. BA in Applied Psychology, Ea. Wash. U., 1989, BA in Comms., 1989, MS in Counseling Psychology, 1993. Cert. counselor, Wash. Mental health therapist Tillamook (Oreg.) Family Counseling. Mem. ACA, Assn. Specialists in Group Work. Office: Tillamook Family Counseling Ctr 2405 5th St Tillamook OR 97141

ROE, BENSON BERTHEAU, surgeon, educator; b. L.A., July 7, 1918; s. Hall and Helene Louise (Bertheau) R.; m. Jane Faulkner St. John, Jan. 20, 1945; children: David B., Virginia St. John. AB, U. Calif., Berkeley, 1939; MD cum laude, Harvard U., 1943. Diplomate Am. Bd. Surgery, Am. Bd. Thoracic Surgery (dir. 1971-83, chmn. bd. 1981-83, chmn. exam. com. 1978, chmn. long-range planning com. 1980, chmn. program com. 1977). Intern Mass. Gen. Hosp., Boston, 1943-44, resident, 1946-50; nat. rsch. fellow dept. physiology Med. Sch., Harvard U., Boston, Mass., 1947, instr. surgery, 1950; Moseley Traveling fellow Harvard. U. at U. Edinburgh, Scotland, 1951; asst. clin. prof. surgery U. Calif., San Francisco, 1951-58, chief cardiothoracic surgery, 1958-76, prof. surgery, 1966-89, emeritus prof., 1989—; pvt. practice medicine specializing in cardiothoracic surgery San Francisco, 1952-85; cons. thoracic surgery VA Hosp., San Francisco Gen. Hosp., Letterman Army Hosp., St. Lukes Hosp., Blue Shield of Calif., Baxter Labs., Ethicon, Inc.; bd. dirs. Control Laser Corp.; vis. prof. U. Utah, U. Ky., U. Gdansk, Poland, Nat. Heart Hosp., London, U. Ibadan, Nigeria, Sanger Clinic, Charlotte, Rush-Presbyn. Hosp., Chgo., Penrose Hosp., Colorado Springs; bd. dirs. Internat. Bioethics Inst. Mem. editl. bd. Annals of Thoracic Surgery, 1969-82, Pharos; editor 2 med. texts; author 21 textbook chpts.; contbr. 174 articles to profl. jours. Bd. dirs. United Bay Area Crusade, 1958-70, mem. exec. com., 1964-65; bd. dirs. chmn. exec. com. San Francisco chpt. Am. Cancer Soc., 1955-57; bd. dirs. San Francisco Heart Assn., 1964-72, pres., 1964-65, chmn. rsch. com., 1966-71; mem. various coms. Am. Heart Assn., 1967-70; pres. Miranda Lux Found., 1982-94; trustee Avery Fuller Found.; bd. dirs. Internat. Bioethics Inst., Point Reyes Bird Observatory. Served with Med. Svc. Corps, USNR, 1944-46. Fellow Am. Coll. Cardiology, ACS (chmn. adv. coun. thoracic surgery, program chmn. thoracic surgery, cardiovascular com.), Polish Surg. Assn. (hon.); mem. Am. Assn. Thoracic Surgery (chmn. membership com. 1974-75), AMA (residency rev. com. for thoracic surgery), Am. Surg. Assn., Pacific Coast Surg. Assn., Calif. Acad. Medicine (pres. 1974), Calif. Med. Assn., Soc. Univ. Surgeons, Soc. Throacic Surgerons (pres. 1972, chmn. standards and ethics com.), Soc. Vascular Surgery (v.p.). Clubs: Cruising of Am, Pacific Union, St. Francis Yacht, Calif. Tennis. Office: U Calif Div Cardiothoracic Surgery U Calif M593 San Francisco CA 94143-0118

ROE, CHARLES RICHARD, baritone; b. Cleve., May 24, 1940; s. Andrews Rogers and Margaret (Dalton) R.; children by previous marriage—Charles Andrews, Richard Nevins, Robert Arthur; m. Jo Ann Marie Belli, May 21, 1988. B.Mus., Baldwin-Wallace Coll., 1963; M.Mus., U. Ill., 1964. Instr. in music Tex. Tech. U., 1964-68; asst. prof. music Eastern Mich. U., 1968-74; vis. assoc. prof. U. So. Calif., L.A., 1976-77, assoc. prof., 1979-84, prof., 1984-89; prof. U. Ariz., Tucson, 1989—; vis. prof. and artist in residence Western Mich. U., 1978-79; faculty Music Acad. of the West, 1981, 82. Leading singer, N.Y.C. Opera, 1974-81; appeared in leading roles with, Mich. Opera Theater, Sacramento Opera, San Antonio Opera, Ft. Worth Opera, Ky. Opera, Conn. Opera, Utah Opera, Cleve. Opera, Miss. Opera, Lake George Opera, Shreveport Opera, Toledo Opera; appeared with, symphonies: Phila., Cleve., Detroit, Toledo, Wichita, Duluth. Mem. Am. Guild Musical Artists, Actors Equity, Nat. Assn. Tchrs. Singing (S.W. region Singer of Year 1966), AAUP. Office: U Ariz Sch Music Tucson AZ 85721

ROEDER, CHARLES WILLIAM, structural engineering educator; b. Hershey, Pa., Oct. 12, 1942; s. Francis William and Myrtle Marie (Garrison) R.; m. Nancy Lee Newman, June 14, 1969; 1 child, Michael Thomas. BSCE, U. Colo., 1969; MSCE, U. Ill., 1971; PhD, U. Calif., Berkeley, 1977. Mem. gen. constrn. crew Shaffer and Son, Palmyra, Pa., 1960-66; structural engr. J. Ray McDermott, New Orleans, 1971-74; prof. of civil engr. U. Wash., Seattle, 1977—; cons. in field. Editor: Composite and Mixed Construction, 1985; contbr. articles to profl. publs. Chmn. com. Transp. Rsch. Bd., Washington, 1990—. With U.S. Army, 1964-66, Vietnam. Mem. ASCE (chmn. 4 tech. coms., J. James R. Croes medal 1979, Raymond C. Reese Rsch. prize 1984), Am. Welding Soc., Earthquake Engring. Rsch. Inst., Structural Engrs. Assn. Wash., Wilderness Soc., Sierra Club. Home: 5300 NE 67th St Seattle WA 98115-7755 Office: U Wash Box 352700 233 B More Hall FX-10 Seattle WA 98195-2700

ROEHL, JERRALD J(OSEPH), lawyer; b. Austin, Tex., Dec. 6, 1945; s. Joseph E. and Jeanne Foster (Scott) R.; m. Nancy J. Meyers, Jan. 15, 1977; children: Daniel J., Katherine C., J. Ryan, J. Taylor. BA, U. N.Mex., 1968; JD, Washington and Lee U., 1971. Bar: N.Mex. 1972, U.S. Ct. Appeals (10th cir.) 1972, U.S. Supreme Ct. 1977. Practice of Law, Albuquerque, 1972—; pres. Roehl Law Firm P.C. and predecessors, Albuquerque, 1976—; lectr. to profl. groups; real estate developer, Albuquerque. Bd. dirs. Rehab. Ctr. of Albuquerque, 1974-78; mem. assocs. Presbyn. Hosp. Ctr., Albuquerque, 1974-82; incorporator, then treas. exec. com. Ctr. City Coun., 1991—. Recipient award of recognition State Bar N.Mex., 1975, 76, 77. Mem. ABA (award of achievement Young Lawyers div. 1975, council econs. of law practice sect. 1978-80, exec. council Young Lawyers div. 1979-81, fellow div. 1984—, council tort and ins. practice sect. 1981-83), N.Mex. Bar Assn. (pres. young lawyers sect. 1975-76), Albuquerque Bar Assn. (bd. dirs. 1976-79), N.Mex. Def. Lawyers Assn. (pres. 1983-84), Sigma Alpha Epsilon, Sigma Delta Chi, Phi Delta Phi. Roman Catholic. Clubs: Albuquerque Country, Albuquerque Petroleum. Bd. advs. ABA Jour., 1981-83; bd. editors Washington and Lee Law Rev., 1970-71. Home: 4411 Constitution Ave NE Albuquerque NM 87110-5721 Office: Roehl Law Firm PC 300 Central Ave SW Albuquerque NM 87102-3249

ROELKE, ADA (KNOCK-LEVEEN), psychotherapist; b. Cumberland, Md., Aug. 24, 1928; d. George William Knock and Mary Emma (Roelke) Eichelberger; children: Karen Bahnsen, Steven Leveen. BA, Syracuse U., 1950; MSW, San Diego State U., 1967; PhD, Profl. Sch. of Psychol. Studies, 1986. Diplomate Am. Bd. Psychotherapy; bd. cert. social worker; lic. clin. social worker, Calif. Tchr. pub. schs., Syracuse, N.Y., 1960-61; social worker Dept. Pub. Welfare, San Diego, 1964-66; psychiat. social worker State of Calif., Bakersfield, 1967-68; child protection worker Dept. Social Svc., San Diego, 1968-77; pvt. practice psychotherapy La Mesa, Calif., 1969-93; coord., psychotherapist chronic program Grantville Day Treatment Ctr., San Diego, 1977-81; chief social svcs. Edgemoor Geriatric Hosp., Santee, Calif., 1981-88; field supr. Grad. Sch. U. Nev., Reno. Coord. Sr. Help Line Carson City Sr. Ctr. Fellow NASW. Unitarian. Home: 919 Arrowhead Dr Carson City NV 89706-0620

ROEMER, EDWARD PIER, neurologist; b. Milw., Feb. 10, 1908; s. John Henry and Caroline Hamilton (Pier) R.; m. Helen Ann Fraser, Mar. 28, 1935 (dec.); children: Kate Pier, Caroline Pier; m. Marion Clare Zimmer, May 24, 1980. BA, U. Wis., 1930; MD, Cornell U., 1934. Diplomate Am. Bd. Neurology. Intern Yale-New Haven Hosp., 1934-36; resident internal medicine N.Y. Hosp., 1936; resident neurology Bellevue Hosp., N.Y.C., 1936-38; instr. Med. Sch. Yale U., New Haven, 1935-36; asst. prof. neurology Cornell U., N.Y.C., 1936-41; prof. neurology U. Wis., Madison, 1946-64; chief of neurology Huntington Meml. Hosp., Pasadena, Calif., 1964-78; pvt. practice Capistrano Beach, Calif., 1978—; founder, dir. Wis. Neurol. Found., Madison, 1946-64; dir. Wis. Multiple Sclerosis Clinic, Madison, 1946-64; adv. bd. Inst. Antiquities and Christianity, Claremont Grad. Sch., 1970—; dir. found. Univ Good Hope, S.Africa. Contbr. rsch. articles on multiple sclerosis, neuropathies to profl. jours. Lt. col. med. corps U.S. Army, 1941-46, ETO. Fellow ACP, Royal Coll. Medicine, L.S.B. Leakey Found.; mem. Rotary Internat., Annandale Golf Club, El Niguel Country Club, Nu Sigma Nu, Phi Delta Theta. Republican. Home: 35651 Beach Rd Capistrano Beach CA 92624

ROEMER, ELIZABETH, astronomer, educator; b. Oakland, Calif., Sept. 4, 1929; d. Richard Quirin and Elsie (Barlow) R. B.A. with honors (Bertha Dolbeer scholar), U. Calif., Berkeley, 1950, Ph.D. (Lick Obs. fellow), 1955. Tchr. adult class Oakland pub. schs., 1950-52; lab technician U. Calif. at Mt. Hamilton, 1954-55; grad. research astronomer U. Calif. at Berkeley, 1955-56; research asso. Yerkes Obs. U. Chgo., 1956; astronomer U.S. Naval Obs., Flagstaff, Ariz., 1957-66; asso. prof. dept. astronomy, also in lunar and planetary lab. U. Ariz., Tucson, 1966-69; prof. U. Ariz., 1969—; astronomer Steward Obs., 1980—; Chmn. working group on orbits and ephemerides of comets comm. 20 Internat. Astron. Union, 1964-79, 85-88, v.p. comm. 20, 1979-82, pres., 1982-85, v.p. commn. 6, 1973-76, 85-88, pres., 1976-79, 88-91; mem. adv. panels Office Naval Research, Nat. Acad. Scis.-NRC, NASA; researcher and author numerous publs. on astrometry and astrophysics of comets and minor planets including 79 recoveries of returning periodic comets, visual and spectroscopic binary stars, computation of orbits of comets and minor planets. Recipient Dorothea Klumpke Roberts prize U. Calif. at Berkeley, 1950, Mademoiselle Merit award, 1959; asteroid (1657) named Roemera, 1965; Benjamin Apthorp Gould prize Nat. Acad. Scis., 1971; NASA Spl. award, 1986. Fellow AAAS (council 1966-69, 72-73), Royal Astron. Soc. (London); mem. Am. Astron. Soc. (program vis. profs. astronomy 1960-75, council 1967-70, chmn. div. dynamical astronomy 1974), Astron. Soc. Pacific (publs. com. 1962-73, Comet medal com. 1968-74, Donohoe lectr. 1962), Internat. Astron. Union, Am. Geophys. Union, Brit. Astron. Assn., Phi Beta Kappa, Sigma Xi. Office: U Ariz Lunar and Planetary Lab Tucson AZ 85721

ROEMMELE, BRIAN KARL, electronics, publishing, financial and real estate executive; b. Newark, Oct. 4, 1961; s. Bernard Joseph and Paula M. Roemmele. Grad. high sch., Flemington, N.J. Registered profl. engr., N.J. Design engr. BKR Techs., Flemington, N.J., 1980-81; acoustical engr. Open Reel Studios, Flemington, 1980-82; pres. Ariel Corp., Flemington, 1983-84, Ariel Computer Corp., Flemington, 1984-89; pres., chief exec. officer Ariel Fin. Devel. Corp., N.Y.C., 1987-91; pres., CEO Avalon Am. Corp., Temecula, Calif., 1990—; CEO United Credit Card Acceptance Corp., Beverly Hills, 1992—, United ATM Card Acceptance Corp., Beverly Hills, 1992—; pres. MultiPlex Media Corp., Beverly Hills, 1995—; pres., CEO Coupon Book Ltd., 1987-89, Value Hunter Mags., Ltd., AEON Cons. Group, Beverly Hills, Calif.; bd. dirs. Waterman Internat., Whitehouse Station, N.J.; electronic design and software cons., L.A., 1980—. Pub., editor-in-chief: Computer Importer News, 1987—. Organizer Internat. Space Week or Day, 1978-83; lectr. Trenton State Mus., N.J., 1983; chmn. Safe Water Internat., Paris; assoc. dir. World Payment Assn., Geneva. Mem. AAAS, AIAA, ABA, IEEE, Am. Bankers Assn., Bankcard Svcs. Assn., Boston Computer Soc., Ford/Hall Forum, Am. Soc. Notaries, Planetary Soc. Office: Avalon Am Corp PO Box 1615 Temecula CA 92593-1615

ROESCHLAUB, JEAN MARIAN CLINTON, restaurant chain executive; b. Berkeley, Calif.; d. Clifford E. and Nelda M. (Patterson) Clinton; m. David J. Davis III, June 26, 1946 (dec. 1963); children: David J. Davis IV, Diane Davis, Burce Clinton Davis.; m. Ronald Curtis Roeschlaub, Jan. 9, 1965; 1 child, Ronald W. AA, Stephens Coll., 1944. Civilian cons. on loan Q.M. Gen., 1944-45; co-owner, exec. v.p. Clinton's Restaurants, Inc., operators Clinton's Cafeterias, Los Angeles, 1944—. Bd. dirs. Assistance League of So. Calif.; mem. aux. bd. Braille Inst. Am., Los Angeles. Mem. Nat. Restaurant Assn., Calif. State Restaurant Assn., Los Angeles Country Club. Republican. Presbyterian. Home: 222 Monterey Rd Unit 1606 Glendale CA 91206-2071 Office: 515 W 7th St Los Angeles CA 90014-2505

ROESSIG, JOHN ROBERT, financial consultant; b. Omaha, Apr. 14, 1947; s. Allen W. and Frances J. (Evans) R.; m. Barbara L. Schmitz, Aug. 8, 1970; children: Stephanie L., Scott A., Salena M. BS in Pharmacy, Creighton U. Coll. Pharmacy, 1970. CFP. Pharmacist Allen's Self Svc., Grand Island, Nebr., 1970-71; pharmacist U. Nebr. Med. Ctr. Hosp., Omaha, 1971-76, resident in hosp. pharmacy, 1975-76; asst. instr. Coll. Pharmacy U. Nebr., Omaha, 1973-76; pharmacist North Colo. Med. Ctr. Hosp., Greeley, 1976-86; fin. planner Master's Fin. Group, Greeley, 1985—, owner, v.p., 1989—; Facilitator Life Underwrites tng. Coun., Greeley, 1992. Author slide and tape series IV-Admixture technique, 1976. Chmn. Adolescent Health Care Com., Greeley, 1991-92; mem., chmn. nurturing com. Habitat for Humanity, Greeley, 1991—. Mem. Am. Health Ins. Agts. (founder), Greeley Pharmacy Assn. (pres. 1979-80), Kiwanis (sec., bd. dir. Rockies club 1991—, Appreciation award 1991). Republican. Roman Catholic. Office: Master s Fin Group Inc 1521 10th Ave Greeley CO 80631-4725

ROFER, CHERYL KATHRINE, chemist; b. Hackensack, N.J., May 7, 1943; d. Christian and Evelyn Fridericke (Grapatin) R. AB, Ripon Coll., 1963; MS, U. Calif., Berkeley, 1964. Project leader Los Alamos (N.Mex.) Nat. Lab., 1965—. Contbr. articles to profl. jours.; patentee in field. Trustee Ripon Coll., 1992—. Recipient Disting. Alumni citation, Ripon Coll., 1991, Disting. Performance award Los Alamos Nat. Lab., 1990; named to Women of Sci. Hall of Fame, Nat. Atomic Mus. Fellow Am. Inst. Chemists; mem. AAAS, Am. Chem. Soc., N.Y. Acad. Scis., Assn. Women in Sci. Office: Los Alamos Nat Lab PO Box 1663 MS D462 Los Alamos NM 87545

ROGAWAY, BETTY JANE, retired school system administrator, social worker; b. San Francisco, Sept. 8, 1921; d. Irvine and Dorothy (Nathan) Hyman; m. Roderick Matthew Rogaway, Jan. 16, 1945 (dec. Aug. 1964); children: Stephen, Kathryn Rogaway Farrell. BA, U. Calif., Berkeley, 1942; MA, Calif. State U., San Jose, 1968. Lic. social worker, Calif. Social worker Travelers Aid, 1943, ARC, 1943-45, Child Welfare Svcs. Sutter County, Calif., 1945; juvenile welfare officer Palo Alto (Calif.) Police Dept., 1945-49; tchr., cons., coord. Palo Alto Unified Sch. Dist., 1958-82, ret., 1982; cons. HeadStart, San Francisco, 1966, Calif. State Dept. of Edn., Sacramento, 1982. Co-author: Palo Alto: A Centennial History, 1993. Mem. City of Palo Alto Task Force on Child Care, 1973; mem. County Task Force on Reasonable Efforts for Child Abuse Protection, San Jose, 1988-90; mem., pres. Palo Alto Hist. Assn., 1989-92; v.p. Calif. Child Devel. Adminstrs. Assn., Sacramento, 1981-82; pres., mem. Children's Shelter Assn. of Santa Clara County, San Jose, 1983—. Home: 1302 Greenwood Ave Palo Alto CA 94301-3414

ROGERS, BARBARA A., secondary education educator; b. Frackville, Pa., Aug. 25, 1941; d. John R. and Clara M. (Chudzwick) R. BA in Edn., Millersville State Coll., 1963; MA in Chemistry, Bowling Green State U., 1968. Cert. tchr. Scis. tchr. N. Penn High Sch., Lansdale, Pa., 1963-68; sci. tchr. McKinley High Sch., Honolulu, 1968—, chair sci. dept., 1989—; mem. adv. com. Hawaii State Sci. and Engring. Fair, 1983-85, chmn. sci. tour com., 1979-87; coord. Dreyfus Chemistry Workshop, State of Hawaii, 1984-85, ECIA Chpt. 2 Devel. Grant, 1988-89; mem. staff Ann. Student Symposium on Marine Affairs, 1983-90; advanced placement chemistry workshop leader Hawaii Bd. Edn., Col. Bd., 1979, 85; mem. Presdl. Award Selection Com., 1986-90. Mem. Ellison Onizuka Scholarship Com., State of Hawaii, 1986—. Named Sci. Tchr. of Yr., Hawaii Acad. Sci., 1980; recipient NW Regional award High Sch. Chem. Teaching, Am. Chem. Soc., 1987, Presdl. award for Excellence in Sci. and Math. Teaching, Pres. of U.S., 1985, Dedication to Teaching Sci. and Encouragement of Research award Sigma Xi, 1983, Teaching Excellence award Nat. Marine Educators Assn., 1984, 85, 86; grantee NSF, Dreyfus Found. Mem. NEA, Am. Chem. Soc. (sec. Hawaii sect. 1982-84, chair 1984-86, counsilor 1995—, chair HSTA sci. affiliate 1994-95, numerous subcoms., grants, awards), Acad. Alliance in Chemistry (bd. dirs. Hawaii chpt. 1987-89), Nat. Sci. Tchrs. Assn., Hawaii State Tchrs. Assn., Smithsonian, Honolulu Acad. Arts. Democrat. Home: 425 Ena Rd Apt 606C Honolulu HI 96815-1715 Office: McKinley High Sch Sci Dept 1039 S King St Honolulu HI 96814-2113

ROGERS, BRIAN EDWARD, English language educator, stand-up comedian/monologuist; b. Tracy, Calif., June 17, 1964; s. John Patrick and Jo Ellen (Giffen) R.; m. Patricia Phelps Todd, Oct. 5, 1991. BA in English, U. of the Pacific, 1988; MA in English/Creative Writing, San Francisco State U., 1992. Tchr./coord. Kaplan Ednl. Ctr., San Francisco, 1988-91; English instr. City Coll. San Francisco, 1993—, Napa (Calif.) Valley Coll., 1992—; columnist Commuter Times, Corte Madera, CAlif., 1991—; performer over 1200 stand-up comedy performances in U.S., 1988—. Contbr. poetry, essays and non-fictional humor to jours. and popular mags. Del. Calif. Dem. Party, Sacramento, 1992-94; mem. Dem. Ctrl. Com., Marin County, Calif., 1992-94, finance chair, campaign 1992; vol. Bread & Roses, Marin, 1993—. Napa Valley Coll. Title III rsch. grantee, 1994; recipient 1st place Summer Writing Competition, Mill Valley (Calif.) Lit. Rev., 1993. Mem. MLA, Alpha Kappa Lambda. Roman Catholic. Office: Napa Valley Coll 2277 Napa Vallejo Hwy Napa CA 94558-6236

ROGERS, CAMILLE MADELIENE, medical technologist; b. Starbuck, Minn., May 4, 1946; d. Reverend Rue and Margerite (Olsen) Estelina; m. Bernard Rogers, Apr. 6, 1968 (div. Jan. 1977); children: Alan, Drake; life ptnr. Karen Morgan, Jan. 20, 1993. BS in Biology, Calif. Lutheran U., 1968. Med. tech. SMHMC, Santa Monica, Calif., 1972-88; sub. tchr. Eldorado County, Calif., 1988-89; med. tech. Brotman, Culver City, Calif., 1989-90; naturalist Lake Tahoe Basin mgmt. unit USDA Forest Svc., 1988-89; med. tech. U. Calif., San Francisco, 1990—; exec. bd. Iris Ctr. for HIV, San Francisco, 1992-94; steering com. WAVES, Santa Monica, 1989-91. Author: (children's book) Back to the Junkyard, 1964. Mem. Am. Soc. Clin. Pathologists, Bay Area Career Women, Mulberry Union, Connexxus, Hobart Homeowners, Out on the Island Alameda Potluck Soc. Democrat. Office: U Calif 505 Parnassus Ave # 0100 San Francisco CA 94122-2722

ROGERS, DWANE LESLIE, management consultant; b. Maywood, Calif., Oct. 6, 1943; s. Lloyd Donald and Della (McAlister) R.; B.S., Ariz. State U., 1967; M.S., Bucknell U., 1968; m. Doris L. Fantel, Aug. 22, 1970; 1 dau., Valerie Lynn. Successively mktg. research coordinator, customer service analyst, merchandising mgr., product planning mgr., order processing mgr. Samsonite Corp., Denver, 1968-74; dir. adminstrn. WISCO Equipment Co., Inc., Phoenix, 1974-75; dir. discontinued ops. Bowmar Instrument Corp., Phoenix, 1975-77; mgmt. cons., dir. Ariz. ops. Mariscal & Co., Phoenix, 1977-80; mgmt. cons. Ariz. Small Bus. Devel. Center, 1980-81; dir. accounts payable, accounts receivable, crude and finished product acctg. Giant Industries, Phoenix, 1981-92; instr. Maricopa County Community Coll., 1979-83; controller Hawaii Pacific Air, 1993-94; ptnr. Pacific Palms Gift World, 1994—. Mem. Am. Mktg. Assn., Mass Retailing Inst. Republican. Episcopalian. Home: 441 Lewers St Apt 502 Honolulu HI 96815-2449

ROGERS, EARL LESLIE, artist, educator; b. Oakland, Calif., July 8, 1918; s. Robert Ray and Addie Myrtle (Dice) R.; m. Eileen Estelle MacKenzie, Apr. 9, 1945; children: Leslie Eileen, Brian Donald (dec.). Student, L.A. Valley Coll., 1949-52, Northridge State U., 1958-59, UCLA Extension, 1967, Sergei Bongart Sch. Art, 1967-68; AA, Pierce Coll., 1958. Cert. tchr., Calif. Various positions City of L.A., Van Nuys, Calif., 1948-55, Reseda, Calif., 1955-68; pvt. practice Canoga Park, Calif., 1948-68; art tchr. Mariposa (Calif.) County High Sch., 1969-70; art instr. Merced (Calif.) County Coll., 1970—; instr. Earl Rogers Studio Workshop, Mariposa, Calif., 1969—; art dir. Yosemite Nat. Park, Calif., 1973; art instr. Asilomar Conf. Grounds, Pacific Grove, Calif., 1980; juror various art orgns., 1971-95; demonstrator Clovic (Calif.) Art Guild, 1971, 89, Sierra Artists, Mariposa, 1972, 81, 82, 84, 91, Merced Art League, 1976, Yosemite Western Artists, Oakhurst, Calif., 1973, Madera (Calif.) Art Assn., 1978, Chowchilla (Calif.) Art Guild, 1983, 86, 87, 89, 91, Soc. Western Artists, 1981, 89, 93. One-man shows include L.A. City Hall, 1968, Merced Coll., 1969, Mariposa Title Co. Bldg., 1969, Coffee's Gallery, 1970, others; exhibited in group shows include West Valley Artists Assn., 1966-68, L.A. City Hall, 1967, Yosemite Nat. Park, 1973, Soc. Western Artists, 1977-78, Cannon Bldg. Rotunda, Washington, 1982, Mother Lode Gallery, Columbia, Calif., 1977, 78, Arbor Gallery, Merced, 1988, Gold Country Gallery, 1990, 91, Merced Coll., 1969-92, others; represented in permanent collections include John C. Freemont Hosp., Mariposa, Mariposa Family Med. Bldg., Bear Valley (Calif.) Mus., Mariposa County Libr., Mariposa County Arts Coun., Mariposa Mus. and History Ctr. Asst. scout master Boy Scouts of Am., Canoga Park, Calif., 1956-58; art instr. L.A. Recreation Corps, L.A. Parks and Recreation Dept., 1967. Mem. Soc. Western Artists (Neva Rall Meml. award 1978), Mariposa Mus. and Hist. Ctr. (life), Pastel Soc. West Coast. Home and Office: 5323 State Highway 49 N Mariposa CA 95338-9503

ROGERS, GARDNER SPENCER, railroad company executive, retired, consultant; b. Bryn Mawr, Pa., Sept. 16, 1926; s. Gardner Spencer and Frances (Lloyd) R.; m. Margaret Elizabeth Windsor, July 18, 1954; children: Ann Rogers Wilbanks, Barbara Lloyd. Student Episcopal Acad., 1940-44, MIT, 1944-45; BS, U. Colo., 1951. Registered profl. engr., Calif. With Western Pacific R.R. Co., San Francisco, 1947-70, engr. costs, valuation and stats., 1964-69, asst. to gen. mgr. planning and control, 1969, asst. gen. mgr., 1970; gen. mgr. Civil & Mech. Maintenance Pty. Ltd., 1970-77; mgr. Western Australian ops. Fluor Australia Pty. Ltd., 1971-73, gen. mgr. ry. div., 1973-77; gen. mgr. Pilbara Industries, 1971-73; dir. budgets and control Consol. Rail Corp., 1978-79, sr. dir. budgets, planning and control, 1980, dir. corp. planning, 1981-87; cons., 1987—; mem. spl. adv. team R.R. ofcls. to U.S. Govt., 1962; adv. com. on R.R. property ICC, 1966-70. Mng. trustee Daniel B. Gardner Trust, Chgo.; alt. trustee Cathedral Sq. Found., Perth; vestryman Ch. of Eng., 1971-77, mem. synod and provincial synod, 1973-77, mem. diocesan coun., 1974-77, bd. dirs. sch.'s trust, 1975-77; vestryman, chmn. fin. com., sr. warden St. Mary's-by-the-Sea Episc. Ch., Pacific Grove, Calif., 1989-91. Mem. Instn. Engrs. Australia, Am. C. of C. in Australia (bd. dirs., v.p., chmn. Western Australian exec. com. 1976-77), Swanleigh (chmn. exec. com. 1974-77, coun.), Am. Mgmt. Assn., Am. Ry. Engr. Assn. (sec. com. 11 1983-87), Episcopal Diocese of El Camino Real (bd. dirs. 1991-93, lay Eucharistic Min. 1991-94), Diocese of Oreg. (lay Eucharistic Min. 1995—), Ry. and Locomotive Hist. Soc., Soc. of Cin., Mil. Order Loyal Legion (vice comdr.), Colo. Alumni Assn. No. Calif. (pres. 1951-52), Berkeley Tennis Club, Pacific Ry. Club, Commonwealth Club, Australian-Am. Club, Alpha Tau Omega (high coun. 1964-68, 82-90). Republican. Home and Office: 2410 Rogue Valley Manor Dr Medford OR 97504-4512

ROGERS, GARTH WINFIELD, lawyer; b. Fort Collins, Colo., Nov. 4, 1938; s. Harlan Winfield and Helen Marie (Orr) R.; m. Joanne Kathleen Rapp, June 16, 1962; children: Todd Winfield, Christopher Jay, Gregory Lynn, Clay Charles. BS, U. Colo., 1958, LLB, 1962. Bar: Colo. 1962; U.S. Dist. Ct. Colo. 1962. Law clk. to presiding justice U.S. Dist. Ct., Denver, 1962-63; assoc. Allen, Stover & Mitchell, Ft. Collins, 1963-68; ptnr. Allen, Rogers Metcalf & Vahrenwald, Ft. Collins, 1968—. Articles editor Rocky Mountain Law Rev., 1961-62. Bd. advs. Salvation Army, Ft. Collins; past bd. dirs. United Way of Ft. Collins, Trinity Luth. Ch., Ft. Collins, others. Mem. Ft. Collins C. of C. (past bd. dirs.), ABA, Colo. Bar Assn., Larimer County Bar Assn. Office: Allen Rogers Metcalf & Varenwald 125 S Howes St Fort Collins CO 80521-2737

ROGERS, JACK DAVID, plant pathologist, educator; b. Point Pleasant, W.Va., Sept. 3, 1937; s. Jack and Thelma Grace (Coon) R.; m. Belle C. Spencer, June 7, 1958. BS in Biology, Davis and Elkins Coll., 1960; MF, Duke U., 1960; PhD, U. Wis., 1963. From asst. prof. to prof. Wash. State U., Pullman, 1963-72, chmn. dept. plant pathology, 1986—. Contbr. articles to profl. jours. Recipient William H. Weston Teaching Excellence award Mycological Soc. Am., 1992. mem. Mycological Soc. of Am. (pres., 1977-78), Am. Phytopathol. Soc., Botanical Soc. Am., British Mycological Soc.

ROGERS, JANET SUE, nursing administrator; b. Sonora, Calif., Sept. 21, 1951; d. George William Albert and Ona Cleora (Byrum) Creason; m. Jay W. Rogers, July 5, 1969; children: Jason, Jonathan, Jacob. ADN, Sacramento City Coll., 1984. Charge nurse oncology unit Sutter Meml. Hosp., Sacramento, Calif., 1982-86; home care case mgr. Nursing Svcs. Inc., Sacramento, 1986-89; hospice nurse specialist Sutter Hospice, Sacramento, 1989-91; AIDS/Oncology home care specialist Visiting Nurses Assn., Sacramento, 1991-92; dir. nursing svcs. Option Care, Sacramento, 1992—, mem. profl. adv. bd., 1991—, mem. utilization rev. coms., 1986-94; mem. utilization rev. coms. Nursing Svcs. Inc., Sutter Homecare, STAT Nursing, 1986-94; IV therapy cons. Pharmacy Corp. Am. Union City, Calif., 1991-92; designer, instr. Chemo Therapy Cert. Course, 1993; author, spkr. various seminars. Mem. Am. Cancer Soc. (orgnl. advisor 1990-94, breast health facilitator 1991-94, speaker 1991—), Calif. Assn. Home Care, Oncology Nursing Soc. (nat.), Sacramento Assn. Home Care. Office: Option Care 3671 Business Dr Sacramento CA 95820-2165

ROGERS, JEAN CLARK, writer; b. Wendell, Idaho, Oct. 1, 1919; d. John Harvey and Josie Maud (Powers) Clark; m. George William Rogers, Nov. 27, 1942; children: Shelley, Geoffrey, Sidney, Gavin (dec.), Sabrina, Garth. Teaching cert., Albion State Normal Sch., 1939; BA, U. Calif., Berkeley, 1943. Author: (juvenile fiction) Good Bye My Island, 1983, King Island's Christmas, 1985, The Secret Moose, 1985, Dinosaurs are 568, 1988 (Parent's Choice award 1990), Runaway Mittens, 1988, Raymond's Best Summer, 1990. Mem., chmn. Alaska State Pub. Offices Commn., Juneau, 1982-87; mem., v.p. Alaska State Broadcasting Commn., Juneau, 1987-92; hon. lifetime mem. Bartlett Meml. Hosp. Guild, 1994—; mem. Friends of Libr., Juneau Hist. Soc., Friends of Mus., Juneau. Recipient Honored Author Citation, Alaska State Reading Assn., 1982, Golden Apple award for svc. to edn., Delta Kappa Gamma, 1990. Mem. ALA, Alaska State Libr. Assn. (hon. lifetime mem. 1994), Soc. Children's Bookwriters and Illustrators. Home: 1790 Evergreen Ave Juneau AK 99801-1422

ROGERS, KEITH JOHNATHAN, artist; b. Ketchikan, Alaska, Aug. 25, 1940; s. Ralph Dawson and Charlotte Edna (Mercer) R.; m. Nilda Lou Yanke, Oct. 24, 1975 (div. Dec. 1987); children: David Keith, Faline Marie, Nathaniel Aaron. BA, Washington State U., 1976. Represented by Art Concepts Gallery, Tacoma, Wash. One man show East Pike Gallery, Seattle, 1993; exhibited in group shows at Tacoma Mall, Wash. (1st. place, hon. mention), 1968, Carnegie Art Mus., Walla Walla, 1977, Pendleton Art Show (hon. mention) Oreg., 1982, 47th Annual Lake Worth Art League Nat. Art Show, Lake Worth Fla. (1st. place in oils), 1988, Art Concepts Gallery, Tacoma, 1990, Shadowflight Gallery, Seattle, 1991, Annikin Gallery, Friday Harbor, 1994; contbr ink drawings to mags. such as The Artist's and American Artist. Donated paintings to March of Dimes Auction, 1959, others. Puffin Found. grantee, 1991.

ROGERS, MICHAEL ALAN, writer; b. Santa Monica, Calif., Nov. 29, 1950; s. Don Easterday and Mary Othilda (Gilbertson) R.; m. Suzanne Elaine Lavoie, May 21, 1995. BA in Creative Writing, Stanford U., 1972. Assoc. editor Rolling Stone Mag., San Francisco, 1972-76; editor-at-large Outside mag., San Francisco, 1976-78; sr. writer Newsweek mag., San Francisco, 1983—; mng. editor Newsweek Interactive, San Francisco, 1993—; exec. prodr. broadband divsn. The Wash. Post Co., 1995—; vis. lectr. fiction U. Calif., Davis, 1980. Author: Mindfogger, 1973, Biohazard, 1977, Do Not Worry About The Bear, 1979, Silicon Valley, 1982, Forbidden Sequence, 1988; contbr. articles to mags., newspapers. Recipient Disting. Sci. Writing award AAAS, 1976, Best Feature Articles award Computer Press Assn., 1987. Mem. Author Guild, Sierra Club. Office: Wash Post Broadband Divsn 655 Montgomery St Ste 1010 San Francisco CA 94111

ROGERS, MICHELE DENISE, investment consultant; b. Kwang-Ju, South Korea, Aug. 4, 1945; m. Merle Nmi Rogers, Feb. 25, 1970. BA in English, Dankook U., Korea, 1969; BS in Bus. Mgmt., N.H. Coll., 1979. Fin. analyst Raytheon Co., Andover, Mass., 1977-81; fin. cons. Tucker, Anthony, Lawrence, Mass., 1983-88, Sutro, Sacramento, 1988-89; dir., owner Col. Fin. Aid Planners, Woodland, Calif., 1990—; fin. cons. Linsco/Pvt. Ledger, Woodland, Calif., 1990—. Home and Office: 812 Ashley Ave Woodland CA 95695-6809

ROGERS, RICHARD GREGORY, sociology educator; b. Albuquerque, Sept. 14, 1955; s. Calvin B. and Eloise (Wood) R.; m. Cynthia P. Raglin, June 14, 1980; children: Mary, Molly, Stacy. BA, U. N.Mex., 1978; MA, U. Tex., 1982, PhD, 1985. Programmer Cancer Rsch. and Treatment Ctr., Albuquerque, 1979-80; NIH population trainee NIH, Austin, 1981-84; asst. dir. tng. Population Prog., U. Colo., Boulder, 1985—; asst. prof. sociology Population Prog., U. Colo., 1985-92, assoc. prof., 1992—. Contbr. articles to profl. jours.; assoc. editor Jour. Health & Social Behavior, 1989-92. Mem. Am. Pub. Health Assn., Am. Sociol. Assn., Pacific Sociol. Assn., Population Assn. Am., Soc. for Study of Social Biology, So. Demographic Assn. (bd. dirs. 1989-91, v.p. 1991-92), Southwestern Social Sci. Assn., Western Social Sci. Assn. Office: Univ Colo Dept Sociology Campus Box 327 Boulder CO 80309-0327

ROGERS, ROBERT REED, manufacturing company executive; b. Oak Park, Ill., Feb. 22, 1929; s. Glen Charles and Lucile (Reed) R.; m. Barbara June Fain, Feb. 22, 1951 (div.); children: Robin, Janeen, Kevin; m. Celeste Sim, Sept. 29, 1993. BS in Chemistry, Berea Coll., 1951; MBA, Ill. Inst. Tech., 1958, postgrad., 1959-62. Asst. mgr. metallurgy research dept. Armour Research Found., Ill. Inst. Tech., 1955-56, mem. faculty, econs. dept., 1956-62; cons. McKinsey & Co., Inc., 1962-64; mgr. devel. planning, profl. group Litton Industries, Inc., 1964-67; pres. N.Am. subs. Muirhead & Co., Ltd., 1967-68; group v.p. Am. Electric Inc. subs. City Investing Co., 1968-70; pres. Cleartight Corp., 1971-73; pres. Newport Internat. Metals Corp., 1973-76; pres. Kensington Assocs., Inc., Newport Beach, Calif., 1976-83; pres., chmn. bd. Proteus Group, Inc., Newport Beach, 1981-83, pres., chmn. bd. Comparator Systems Corp., Newport Beach, Calif., 1983—. Officer USN, 1951-55. Decorated Knight of Grace Sovereign Order St. John; Machinery and Allied Products Inst. fellow, 1956-62; Berea Coll. grantee, 1947-51. Mem. Navy League, Mensa, Intertel, Ferrari Owners Club, Lido Isle Yacht Club. Republican. Mem. Ch. of Religious Sci. Office: Comparator Systems Corp 4350 Von Karman Ave Ste 180 Newport Beach CA 92660-2041

ROGERS, STUART EAMES, aerospace engineer; b. Seattle, Aug. 27, 1961; s. Kent Raymond and Anne (Streeter) R.; m. Tamara Ann Eastep, May 26, 1984; 1 child, Zachary James. BS in Aerospace Engring., U. Colo., 1983, MS in Aerospace Engring., 1985; PhD, Stanford U., 1989. Rsch. asst. U. Colo., Boulder, 1983-85; rsch. scientist Sterling Fed. Systems, Palo Alto, Calif., 1985-89; aerospace engr. NASA Ames Rsch. Ctr., Moffett Field, Calif., 1989—. Contbr. articles to profl. jours. mem. AIAA (sr.), Tau Beta Pi. Office: NASA Ames Rsch Ctr Mail Stop T27B-1 Moffett Field CA 94035-1000

ROGERS, TED See GRAHAM-ROGERS, CHARLES THEODORE

ROGERS, WILLIAM CORDELL, financial executive; b. Louisville, Apr. 16, 1943; s. Delbert Clifton and Nelle Frances (Grimsley) R.; m. Elaine Elizabeth Nicolay, Apr. 10, 1966; children: William C. II, Erin D., Nicole M., Shannon D. AA, Lincoln Coll., 1969; BS, Ill. State U., 1971; MBA, U. Phoenix, 1993. Exec. Ill. Dept. Revenue, Springfield, 1972-74; fin. dir. Old Heritage Life Ins. Co., Lincoln, Ill., 1974-77; corp. fin. cons. DEN, Inc. CPAs, Tempe, Ariz., 1977-83; v.p., treas. Dahlberg Industries, Scottsdale, Ariz., 1983-91; cons. Act II Printed Cirs. Inc., Tempe, Ariz., 1991-93; cons., Scottsdale, 1977—; instr. econ. Lincoln Coll., 1972-77, real estate taxation, 1978-80. With U.S. Army, 1964-67, Vietnam. Recipient Dow Jones award Dow Jones-Wall St. Jour., 1969. Mem. Nat. Assn. Pub. Accts., Ariz. Soc. Pub. Accts., Rotary (bd. dirs. Scottsdale club 1986—, pres., Paul Harris fellow 1985—). Republican. Home and Office: 8549 E Turney Ave Scottsdale AZ 85251-2831 Office: Internat Profit Assocs Inc 1477 Barclay Blvd Buffalo Grove IL 60089-4537

ROGERS, WILLIAM DARROW, history educator; b. Columbia, Mo., Aug. 1, 1944; s. William Eugene and Aurelia Adreon (Gutman) R.; m. Jean Roberts, Dec. 30, 1978. AB in Govt., Cornell U., 1966; AM in History, U. Mo., 1967, postgrad., 1970-73, 79-85. Tchr. Nova H.S., Redding, Calif., 1967-70; claims rep. U.S. Social Security, San Jose, Calif., 1974-76; self-employed banjo tchr. Palo Alto, Calif., 1976-79; news ops. mgr. KOPN-FM, Columbia, Mo., 1981-83; lectr. U. Mo., Columbia, 1984; reporter Columbia Daily Tribune, 1984-86; tchr. Franklin H.S., Stockton, Calif., 1986—. Mem. Orgn. Am. Historians. Democrat. Office: Franklin H S 300 N Gertrude Ave Stockton CA 95215-4820

ROGGE, RICHARD DANIEL, former government executive, security consultant, investigator; b. N.Y.C., July 5, 1926; s. Daniel Richard and Bertha (Sarner) R.; m. Josephine Mary Kowalewska, June 6, 1948 (dec. June 1995); children: Veronica Leigh Rogge-Erbeznik, Richard Daniel, Christopher Ames, Meredith Ann Rogge-Pierce. BS in Bus. Adminstrn., NYU, 1952. Cert. profl. investigator. Clerical worker FBI, N.Y.C., 1947-52, spl. agt., Phila., 1952-54, Washington, 1954-58, supr., 1958-65, asst. spl. agt. in charge, Richmond, Va., 1965-66, Phila., 1966-67, L.A., 1967-69, inspector, 1969, spl. agt. in charge, Honolulu, 1969-72, Richmond, 1972-74, Buffalo, 1974-77, now security cons., investigator, Calif.; police tng. instr.; writer, lectr. in field. With USMC, 1944-46; PTO. Recipient Order of Arrow award Boy Scouts Am., 1943, Svc. to Law Enforcement awards Va. Assn. Chiefs Police, 1975, N.Y. State Assn. Chiefs Police, 1977, others. Mem. Am. Soc. Indsl. Security, Calif. Assn. Lic. Investigators, Calif. Peace Officers Assn. of Los Angeles County, World Assn. Detectives, Inc., Soc. Former Agts. FBI, Inc., FBI Agents Assn., Am. Legion, K.C., Elks. Republican. Roman Catholic. Home and Office: 32010 Watergate Ct Westlake Village CA 91361-4022

ROGGERO, MIGUEL LEONARDO (MIKE ROGGERO), motion picture company executive, consultant; b. San Diego, May 17, 1962; s. Roland Victor and Dinorah S. (Lopez) R. BS, U. So. Calif., 1984; MBA, U. Pa., 1989. Lic. real estate broker, Calif. Project analyst Stephen J. Cannell Prodns., L.A., 1984-85; sr. analyst Paramount Pictures Corp., L.A., 1985-87; pres., co-founder Prolube, Inc., L.A., 1989—; mgr. fin. Pepsico/Pizza Hut, Inc., 1990-92; dir. bus. devel. Walt Disney Co., 1992—; cons. Oto-Telick Inc., Sherman Oaks, Calif., 1987-88, Mgmt. Info. Network Inc., L.A., 1987-88. Recipient Calif. Masonic Found. scholarship, 1982. Mem. Smithsonian Assocs., U. So. Calif. Alumni Assn., U. So. Calif. Sch. Bus. Alumni Assn., Wharton Club, So. Calif., N.Y. , Sigma Alpha Mu, Beta Gamma Sigma (life mem.). Republican. Home: 1139 Yale St #3 Santa Monica CA 90403

ROGOFF, ARNOLD M., book dealer, publisher, management consultant; b. Oak Park, Ill., Nov. 8, 1930; s. Julius J. and Lucile E. (Wingerhoff) R.; m. Janet E. Percy, July 16, 1968; children: Hilary, Peter. Student, U. Mo., 1948-49, Harvard Coll., 1951; BS, Boston U., 1951. Pres., Opus Prodns., Los Angeles, 1959-61, CGR Labs., Los Angeles, 1961-63; With McGraw-Hill Book Co., N.Y.C., 1963-77, sales mgr. Gregg div., 1974-75, dir. mktg., 1975-77; prin. ptnr. Arnold M. Rogoff & Assocs., Mill Valley, Calif., 1977—; pres. Ethnographic Arts Pubs., Mill Valley, 1978—. Home: 1040 Erica Rd Mill Valley CA 94941-3747 Office: Ethnographic Arts Publs Indsl Ctr Bldg Gate 5 Rd # 108 Sausalito CA 94965-1404

ROGOFF, BARBARA, psychology researcher and educator; b. Brookings, S.D., Jan. 5, 1950; d. William M. and Esther Johanna (Petersen) R.; m. H. Salem Magarian, Oct. 12, 1975; children: Luisa Michelle, Valerie Johanna, David Salem. BA, Pomona Coll., 1971; PhD, Harvard U., 1977. Asst. prof. U. Utah, Salt Lake City, 1977-82, assoc. prof. psychology, 1982-85; prof., 1985-92, coordinator devel. psychology program, 1986-92; prof. U. Calif., Santa Cruz, 1991—. Author: Apprenticeship in Thinking, 1990, Guided Participation in Cultural Activity by Toddlers and Caregivers, 1993; editor: Everyday Cognition, 1984; Children's Learning in the Zone of Proximal Development, 1984, Human Development, 1995—. Recipient Scribner award Am. Ednl. Rsch. Assn., 1993; Kellogg Found. Nat. fellow, 1983-86, Ctr. for Advanced Study in Social and Behavioral Scis./Stanford U. fellow, 1988-89, NSF fellow, 1972-76; NIH grantee, 1983—, Spencer Found. grantee, 1989—, Nat. Inst. Edn. grantee, 1980-82. Fellow Am. Psychol. Assn., Am. Psychol. Soc., Am. Anthrop. Assn.; mem. Soc. for Research in Child Devel. (editor newsletter 1986-91), Soc. for Psychol. Anthropology (sec. 1982-84), Internat. Soc. for Study of Behavioral Devel. Office: U Calif Dept Psychology Social Scis II Santa Cruz CA 95064

ROHDE, JAMES VINCENT, software systems company executive; b. O'Neill, Nebr., Jan. 25, 1939; s. Ambrose Vincent and Loretta Cecilia R.; children: Maria, Sonja, Daniele. BCS, Seattle U., 1962. Chmn. bd. dirs., pres., Applied Telephone Tech., Oakland, 1974; v.p. sales and mktg. Automation Electronics Corp., Oakland, 1975-82; pres., chief exec. officer, chmn. bd. dirs. Am. Telecorp, Inc., 1982—; bd. dirs. Enerlogica, Inc., 1989-91. Chmn. exec. com., chmn. emeritus Pres.'s Coun. Heritage Coll., Toppenish, Wash., 1985—; chmn. No. Calif. chpt. Coun. of Growing Cos., 1990-93; bd. dirs. Ind. Colls. No. Calif., 1991-93. Named Export U.S. Dept. Commerce Exec. Yr. No. Calif., 1993. Mem. Am. Electronics Assn. (bd. dirs. 1992-94, vice chmn. No. Calif. coun. 1992-93, chmn. 1993-94). Republican. Roman Catholic. Office: Am Telecorp Inc 100 Marine Pky Redwood City CA 94065-1031

ROHLA, DRU ALLEN, civic center director; b. York, Nebr., Nov. 23, 1954; s. David Anton and Diane Rohla; m. Pamela Renee, Dec. 28, 1979; children: Ryan David, Kaley Reann. BS, U. Wyo., 1979; MA, U. No. Colo., 1983. Asst. dir. Cheyenne (Wyo.) Civic Ctr., 1985-88, dir., 1988—; bd. dirs. Cheyenne Civic Ctr., 1985—. Pub. rels. dir. City and Mayor of Cheyenne, 1985—. Recipient award Leadership Cheyenne, 1986-87; named one of Outstanding Young Men of Am., 1985, 86, 87, 88, 89. Mem. Cheyenne C. of C. Republican. Methodist. Office: Cheyenne Civic Ctr 2101 Oneil Ave Cheyenne WY 82001-3512

ROHLFING, FREDERICK WILLIAM, lawyer, judge; b. Honolulu, Nov. 2, 1928; s. Romayne Raymond and Kathryn (Coe) R.; m. Joan Halford, July 15, 1952 (div. Sept. 1982); children: Frederick W., Karl A., Brad (dec.); m. Patricia Ann Santos, Aug. 23, 1983. BA, Yale U., 1950; JD, George Washington U., 1955. Bar: Hawaii 1955, Am. Samoa 1978. Assoc. Moore, Torkildson & Rice, Honolulu, 1955-60; ptnr. Rohlfing, Nakamura & Low, Honolulu, 1963-68, Hughes, Steiner & Rohlfing, Honolulu, 1968-71, Rohlfing, Smith & Coates, Honolulu, 1981-84; sole practice Honolulu, 1960-63, 71-81, Maui County, 1988—; dep. corp. counsel County of Maui, Wailuku, Hawaii, 1984-87, corp. counsel, 1987-88; land and legal counsel Maui Open Space Trust, 1992—; prin. Frederick W. Rohlfing III, Honolulu; magistrate judge U.S. Dist. Ct. Hawaii, 1991—. Mem. Hawaii Ho. Reps., 1959-65, 80-84; Hawaii State Senate, 1966-75; U.S. alt. rep. So. Pacific Commn., Noumea, New Caledonia, 1975-77, 1982-84. Capt. USNR, 1951-87. Mem. Hawaii Bar Assn., Fed. Magistrate Judges Assn. Home and Office: RR #1 Box 398 Kekaulike Ave Kula HI 96790

ROHRABACHER, DANA, congressman; b. June 21, 1947; s. Donald and Doris Rohrabacher. Student, L.A. Harbor Coll., 1965-67; BA in History, Long Beach State Coll., 1969; MA in Am. Studies, U. So. Calif., 1976. Reporter City News Svc./Radio West, L.A., 4 yrs.; editorial writer Orange County Register, 1979-80; asst. press. sec. Reagan for Pres. Campaign, 1976, 80; speechwriter, spl. asst. to Pres. Reagan White House, Washington, 1981-88; mem. 101st-103rd Congresses from 45th Calif. dist., 1989-92, 103d Congress from 45th dist. Calif., 1993—; U.S. del. Young Polit. Leaders Conf., USSR; disting. lectr. Internat. Terrorism Conf., Paris, 1985; mem. Internat. Rels. com.; chmn. Sci. subcom. on energy and environ. Recipient Disting. Alumnus award L.A. Harbor Coll., 1987. Office: US House of Reps Rayburn Bldg 2338 Washington DC 20515-0545*

ROHRBACK, MICHAEL DAVID, policy analyst; b. Adrian, Mich., Apr. 30, 1954; s. David Norman and Sara Joyce (Lehman) R.; m. Laura L. Buchan. BA in Econ. with honors, U. Mich., 1980, M of Pub. Policy, 1983, postgrad. Researcher Gt. Lakes Commn., Ann Arbor, Mich., 1982-83; econ. analyst U.S. Dept. State, Washington, 1983; audit mgr. U.S. GAO, Detroit, 1983-89; audit mgr. Far East Office U.S. GAO, Honolulu, 1989-95; sr. evaluator Nat. Security and Internat. Affairs Divsn. U.S. GAO, Washington, 1995—. With USMC, 1972-76. Lutheran. Home: 111 Park Brook Ct Stafford VA 22554 Office: US Gen Acctg Office NS/AD/IA 441 G St NW Washington DC 20548

ROHRBERG, RODERICK GEORGE, welding consultant; b. Minneola, Iowa, Sept. 26, 1925; s. Charles H. and Emma (Minsen) R.; BS in Naval Sci., Marquette U., 1946; BSCE, Iowa State U., 1949; m. Genevieve Mary Sogard, June 19, 1949; children: Karla (Mrs. George H. Witz, Jr.), Roderick K., Cheries (Mrs. Mark Sauer), Timothy, Christopher. Bridge design engr. Alaska Rd. Commn., U.S. Dept. Interior, 1949-51; sr. tech. specialist North Am. Rockwell, rsch., L.A., 1951-69; pres. Creative Pathways, Inc., advanced welding svcs., equipment design and devel., Torrance, Calif., 1969—; pvt. practice, Torrance, Calif., 1972—. Served with USNR, 1944-46. Recipient 1st nat. Airco Welding award, 1966, commendation NASA, 1965, Engring. Profl. Achievement citation Iowa State U., 1973, 3d pl. Von Karman Meml. Grand award, 1974. Registered profl. engr., Calif. Mem. Am. Welding Soc. Lutheran. Patentee in field. Home: 2742 W 234th St Torrance CA 90505-3118 Office: Creative Pathways Inc 3121 Fujita St Torrance CA 90505-4006

ROHRER, GEORGE JOHN, retired lawyer; b. Elmira, N.Y., Oct. 24, 1931; s. George J. and Lois (Hess) R.; m. Martha M. Jacobs, Jan. 6, 1952; children: Jacquelyn M. Berbusse, Michael A., John S. JD with distinction, Pacific Coast U., 1967. Bar: Calif. 1969, U.S. Dist. Ct. (ctrl. dist.) 1969. Incentive dir. Blue Chip Stamp Co., L.A., 1963-69; gen. ptnr. Songer, Leavell Rohrer, Bellflower, Calif., 1969-80; sr. ptnr. Rohrer & Holtz, Anaheim, Calif., 1980-94; ret., 1994; panel atty. Calif. Assn. of Realtors/State, Hotline, Calif. 1977—; Founder/Dir. Midcities Nat. Bank, Bellflower, 1981-90; trustee S.E. area Bar Assn., Norwalk, Calif., 1974-75. Pres. Bellflower Kiwanis Club, 1972-73; dir. Los Cerritos Y.M.C.A., Bellflower, 1977-78; vol. counsel Am. Radio Relay League, 1987-92. Mem. Orange County Bar Assn., Los Angeles County Bar Assn., Orange County Amicus (pro bono), Bellflower C. of C. (pres. 1975-76), Masons, Shriners. Republican.

ROHRER, JANE CAROLYN, gifted education specialist, administrator, consultant; b. Faribault, Minn., July 17, 1940; d. Christian A. and Lydia G. (Hilleboe) R.; children: Paula Eisenrich, Lisa Eisenrich, Peter Eisenrich. BS in English, U. Minn., 1962, MA in English, 1964; MA in Edn., Boise (Idaho) State U., 1976; PhD in Spl. Edn., Gifted, Kent State U., 1992. Cert. tchr. spl. edn./gifted, Ohio, Nev., Idaho. Tchr. English Lompoc (Calif.) High Sch., 1962-63; gifted and talented facilitator Boise Sch. Dist., 1976-84, spl. edn. cons. tchr., 1984-89, spl. edn. adminstrv. intern, 1989-90; faculty Kent (Ohio) State U., 1991-92; dir. Tchr. Edn. Program Sierra Nev. Coll., Incline Village, Nev., 1993—; mem. Nev. Statewide Task Force on Tchr. Edn., English Framework; numerous publs. and conf. presentations. Choir dir., La., Japan, Idaho, Ohio, 1966-70; min. of music Lord of Life Luth.Ch., Chagrin Falls, Ohio, 1990-91. Whittenberger fellow Boise State U., 1975-76. Mem. ASCD, Coun. Exceptional Children (state bd. dirs. 1987-88), Nat. Assn. Gifted Children, S.W. Regional Spl. Edn. Adv. Bd., Idaho Talented and Gifted Assn. (state pres. 1988-89), Mortar Bd., Phi Beta Kappa, Eta Sigma Upsilon, Pi Lambda Theta, Phi Delta Kappa.

ROHRER, REED BEAVER, lawyer; b. Langley AFB, Va., June 15, 1954; s. Richard L. and Elaine (Beaver) R.; m. Penny J. Pylant, June 25, 1977; children: Christopher S., Jennifer R. BBA, U. Hawaii, 1977; JD, Pepperdine U., 1980; LLM in Taxation, U. San Diego, 1981. Bar: Hawaii 1981, U.S. Dist. Ct. Hawaii 1981, U.S. Tax Ct. 1981. Tax specialist Grant Thorton (Alexander Grant), Honolulu, 1981-83; assoc. Oliver, Cuskaden & Lee, Honolulu, 1983-85; corp. counsel Bishop Trust Co. Ltd., Honolulu, 1985-89; v.p., corp. counsel Wall St. Fin. Corp., Irvine, Calif., 1989-92; prin. Law Firm of Reed B. Rohrer, Honolulu, 1992-94; ptnr. Rottenger & Rohrer, Honolulu, 1994—; bd. dirs. Rohrer Investment Corp., Coz U.S.A., Inc., Pacific Mktg. & Investments, Inc.; speaker in field. Author: (with others) Wills and Trusts Formbook, 1987; contbr. articles to profl. jours. Mem. ABA, Hawaii Bar Assn. (chmn. tax sect. 1988, estate and gift tax com.). Republican. Home: 7427 Makaa St Honolulu HI 96825-3125 Office: Rottenger & Rohrer 841 Bishop St Ste 1710 Honolulu HI 96813 also: 733 Bishop St Fl 19 Honolulu HI 96813-4022 also: 2-17-55 Akasaka, Minato-Ku, Tokyo 107, Japan

ROITBLAT, HERBERT LAWRENCE, psychology educator; b. Milw., Apr. 2, 1952; s. Jack and Renee (Siegel) R.; m. Debra Jean Bortel, Aug. 24, 1975; 1 child, Benjamin. BA, Reed Coll., 1974; PhD, U. Calif., 1978. Asst. prof. Columbia U., N.Y.C., 1978-85; prof. U. Hawaii, Honolulu, 1985—. Author: Introduction to Comparative Cognition, 1987; editor: Animal Cognition, 1984, From Animals to Animats 2, 1993, Language and Communication: Comparative Perspectives, 1993; contbr. articles to profl. jours. NSF fellow, 1978. Mem. Am. Psychol. Assn., Internat. Neural Network Soc., Psychonomic Soc. Office: U Hawaii Dept Psychology 2430 Campus Rd Honolulu HI 96822-2216

ROITMAN, JAMES NATHANIEL, chemist; b. Providence, R.I., June 29, 1941; s. Aaron H. and Rose B. R.; m. Esther Thommen, June 8, 1972; 1 child, Thomas B. BA, Brown U., 1963; PhD, UCLA, 1969. Rsch. chemist U.S. Dept. Agr., Albany, Calif., 1969—. Mem. Am. Chem. Soc., Am. Soc. Pharmacognosy. Home: 796 Grizzly Peak Blvd Berkeley CA 94708-1337 Office: USDA WRRC 800 Buchanan St Berkeley CA 94710-1105

ROIZ, MYRIAM, foreign trade marketing executive; b. Managua, Nicaragua, Jan. 21, 1938; came to U.S., 1949; d. Francisco Octavio and Maria Herminia (Briones) R.; m. Nicholas M. Orphanopoulos, Jan. 21, 1957 (div.); children: Jacqueline Doggwiler, Gene E. Orphanopoulos, George A. Orphanopoulos. BA in Interdisciplinary Social Sci. cum laude, San Francisco State U., 1980. Lic. ins. agt. Sales rep. Met. Life Ins. Co., San Francisco, 1977-79; mktg. dir. Europe/Latin Am., Allied Canners & Packers, San Francisco, 1979-83, M-C Internat., San Francisco, 1983-88; v.p. mktg. Atlantic Brokers, Inc., Bayamon, P.R., 1988-92; owner Aquarius Enterprises Internat., San Ramon, Calif., 1992—. Coord. Robert F. Kennedy Presdl. campaign, Millbrae, San Mateo County, local mayoral campaign, Millbrae, 1975; bd. dir., organizer fund-raising campaign for earthquake-devastated Nicaragua; active World Hunger Program Brown U., Children Internat., World Vision, Childhelp USA. Named Outstanding Employee of Yr. Hillsborough City Sch. Dist., 1973; recipient Sales award Met. Life Ins. Co., 1977. Mem. NAFE, World Affairs Coun. Republican. Roman Catholic.

ROJAS, KRISTINE BRIGGS, insurance sales and marketing professional; b. Pocatello, Idaho, July 25, 1947; d. Fergus Jr. and Shirley (Tanner) Briggs; divorced; children: Anthony Ted, Nancy Kristine. Student, Idaho State U., 1965-66. Tech. coord. Farmers Ins. Group, Pocatello, 1971-81; svc. rep. All Seasons Ins. Agy., Ventura, Calif., 1982; sr. comml. underwriting asst. Royal Ins. Co., Ventura, 1982-85; sr. comml. lines underwriter Andreini & Co., Ventura, 1985-88; large comml. account unit coord. Frank B. Hall, Inc., Oxnard, Calif., 1988-93; account exec. Fox Ins. Agy. Inc., Camarillo, Calif., 1993—. Editor (bulletin) News Waves, 1985-87; artist various works specializing in charcoal portraits. Mem. NAFE, Ins. Women Ventura County (treas. 1987-88, v.p. 1988-90, pres. 1990-91, corr. sec. 1991-92, bd. dirs. 1986-87, Woman of Yr. 1989-90), Nat. Assn. Ins.Women. Republican. Baptist. Home: 2197 Brookhill Dr Camarillo CA 93010-2107 Office: Fox Ins Agy Inc 2301 Daily Dr Ste 200 Camarillo CA 93010-6613

ROJHANTALAB, HOSSEIN MOHAMMAD, chemical engineer, researcher; b. Tehran, Iran, Sept. 26, 1944; came to U.S., 1984; s. Mohammad Rojhantalab and Sakineh (Fakhri) Nasser-Ghandi; 1 child, Ayda. MS, Calif. State U., Hayward, 1972; PhD, Oreg. State U., 1976. Asst. prof. Ahwaz (Iran) U., 1976-77, Shiraz (Iran) U., 1977-82; cons., chemist Water-Con Co., Tehran, 1982-84; rsch. assoc. U. Oreg., Eugene, 1985-88; lithography engr. Intel Corp., Hillsboro, Oreg., 1988-91; thin film CVO Tungsten polish engr. Intel Corp., Aloha, Oreg., 1991—; transl. Popular Sci. Pub. Co., Tehran, 1980-83, UNESCO workshop, 1984; editor, CEO, DNA Pub. Co., Tehran, 1982-84; vis. prof. chemistry Ore. State U., 1985. Editor, translator 4 books on genetic code, controlled nuclear fusion to Farsi, 1981-84; contbr. articles to sci. jours. Scholar Calif. State U., 1971-

72; grantee Oreg. State U., 1975-76, CENTO, 1978-79. Mem. Electrochem. Soc. Am. Home: PO Box 6652 Aloha OR 97007-0652

ROKOS, JOHN PAUL, marketing professional; b. L.A., July 21, 1952; s. John C. and Violet Mae R. BS, Wis. U., 1974. Programmer NCR, San Diego, Calif., 1974-76, Ford Motors Co., Mountain View, Calif., 1976-78; mgr. Zentec, Santa Clara, 1978-82, Wyse Tech., San Jose, Calif., 1982—. Mem. Assn. Computing Machinery, IEEE. Office: Wyse Technology San Jose CA 95121

ROLAND, CRAIG WILLIAMSON, architect; b. Lincoln, Nebr., Feb. 20, 1935; s. Harold Eugene and Nell (Williamson) R.; m. Edith Shearman Shaw, July 30, 1960; 1 child, Leah. B.Arch., U. Wash. Pres. Roland/Miller/Assocs., Santa Rosa, Calif., 1966-93; vis. instr. U. Calif.-Berkeley, 1983-84. Mem., chmn. design rev. bd. City of Santa Rosa, 1973-76, mem. planning commn., 1976-78; pres. bd. Sonoma County YMCA, Santa Rosa, 1979—. Served with U.S. Army, 1957-58. Recipient numerous local, state and nat. archtl. design awards. Home: 5441 Buttercup Dr Santa Rosa CA 95404-9628 Office: Craig W Roland Arch 5441 Buttercup Dr Santa Rosa CA 95404-9628

ROLETTA, RICHARD PETER, education administrator; b. L.A., Sept. 19, 1939; s. Pietro Cellini and Rose Mary (Bavero) R.; m. Lucretia Ann Streechon, Apr. 1, 1977. BA in History, U. So. Calif., L.A., 1962; MA in Instructional Media, Calif. State U., Long Beach, 1971. Cert. secondary edn., gen. adminstrn. GATE coord. Dapplegray Intermediate, 1972-82, tchr., 1962-82, asst. prin., 1982-85; asst. prin. Ridgecrest Intermediate, Rancho Palos Verdes, Calif., 1985-87, Rancho Palos Verdes, 1987-91; prin. Dapplegray Intermediate, 1987, Soleado Elem. Sch., Rancho Palos Verdes, 1991—. Dist. membership rep., SASS rep. ACSA; pres. P.V.A.A., 1988-89. Recipient Vol. of Yr. award PTA, 1990, Hon. Svc. award PTA, 1982, Continuing Svc. award PTA, 1990, Golden Apple award PTA, 1982, Calif. pin PTA, 1993, Calif. Silver Bar award 1993.

ROLFES, HERMAN HAROLD, Canadian government official; b. Humboldt, Bask, Sask., Can., July 13, 1936; s. Joseph and Josephine (Heckmann) R.; m. Myrna Josephine Hopfner, Apr. 4, 1961; children: Debora Lynne, Brian Joseph. Student, St. Peter's Coll., Muenster, Sask., Tchrs. Coll. Sask., 1955-56; BA, U. Sask., 1961, BEd, 1965, MEd, 1971. Cert. tchr., Can. Mem. legis. assembly Saskatoon Nutana South, 1971-82, 86—, min. social svcs., 1975-79, min. continuing edn., 1978-79; min. health Sask., 1979-82; now spkr. legis assembly. Saskatoon Nutana South, 1991—. Mem. Sask. Elem. Tchrs. Assn. (past pres.), St. Thomas Moore Alumni Assn., KC. Roman Catholic. Home: 2802 Calder Ave, Saskatoon, SK Canada S7J 1W1 Office: Speaker, Legislative Bldg Rm 129, Regina, SK Canada S4S 0B3

ROLIN, CHRISTOPHER E(RNEST), lawyer; b. Santa Monica, Calif., Feb. 15, 1940; s. Carl A. and Kate (Northcote) R.; m. Debbie Best, April, 1994; children: Whitney, Brett. BA, U. Calif.-Berkeley, 1961; JD, U. So. Calif., 1965. Bar: Calif. 1966. Assoc. Meserve, Mumper & Hughes, L.A., 1966-71, ptnr., 1972; ptnr. Haight, Dickson, Brown & Bonesteel, Santa Monica, Clif., 1977-88; ptnr. Rodi Pollock, L.A., 1990—. Bd. dirs. Legion Lex, 1991—, sec. 1995. Mem. So. Calif. Def. Counsel (bd. dirs. 1981-85), Am. Bd. Trial Advs., L.A. County Bar Assn. (bd. dirs. and vice chmn. law mgmt. sect. 1994, chmn. 1995), Am. Arbitration Assn. (arbitrator 1977—). Republican. Club: Optimists (pres. 1989). Home: 2993 Haddington Dr Los Angeles CA 90064 Office: 801 S Grand Ave Ste 400 Los Angeles CA 90017-4623

ROLL, BARBARA HONEYMAN, anthropologist; b. Portland, Oreg., Apr. 4, 1910; d. Arthur and Carlotta (Parker) Honeyman; m. Scott Alexander Heath, Dec. 23, 1953 (dec. July 1974); m. George Frederick Roll, Mar. 5, 1977. BA, Smith Coll., 1932, LHD (hon.), 1989. Exec. sec. Const. Lab. P&S Med. Ctr., N.Y., 1948-51; rsch. assoc. U. Oreg. Med. Sch., Portland, Oreg., 1951-53; cons. Dr. H. H. Clarke U. Oreg., Eugene, 1957-68; cons. Dr. Margaret Mead AMNH, N.Y., 1966-75; rsch. assoc. U. Pa. Mus., Phila., 1975—; instr. anthropology Community Coll., Monterey, Calif., 1966-74; vis. scholar Inst. Anthropology, Moscow, 1967, 1975. Author: (with J.E.L. Carter) Somatotyping--Development and Applications, 1990, Oral History: Barbara Honeyman Heath Roll: A Woman's Role in Anthropology, 1994; contbr. articles to profl. jours. Fellow AAAS, Am. Assn. Anthropology, NY Acad. Scis.; mem. Coun. Human Biol., Am. Assn. Phys. Anthropology, Inst. Intercultural Studies (sec. 1980-83). Home: 26030 Rotunda Dr Carmel CA 93923-8923

ROLL, JOHN MCCARTHY, lawyer; b. Pitts., Feb. 8, 1947; s. Paul Herbert and Esther Marie (McCarthy) R.; m. Maureen O'Connor, Jan. 24, 1970; children: Robert McCarthy, Patrick Michael, Christopher John. B.A., U. Ariz., 1969, J.D., 1972, LLM U. Va., 1990. Bar: Ariz. 1972, U.S. Dist. Ct. Ariz. 1974, U.S. Ct. Appeals (9th cir.) 1980, U.S. Supreme Ct. 1977. Asst. pros. atty. City of Tucson, 1973; dep. county atty. Pima County (Ariz.), 1973-80; asst. U.S. atty. U.S. Atty.'s Office, Tucson, 1980-87; judge Ariz. Ct. Appeals, 1987-91, U.S. Dist. Ct. Ariz., 1991—; lectr. Nat. Coll. Dist. Attys. U. Houston, 1976-87; mem. criminal justice mental health standards project ABA, 1980-83. Contbr. to Trial Techniques Compendium, 1978, 82, 84, Merit Selection: The Arizona Experience, Arizona State Law Journal, 1991, The Rules Have Changed: Amendments to the Rules of Civil Procedure, Defense Law Journal, 1994. Coach, Frontier Baseball Little League, Tucson, 1979-84; mem. parish coun. Sts. Peter and Paul Roman Catholic Ch., Tucson, 1983-91, chmn., 1986-91; mem. Roman Cath. Diocese of Tucson Sch. Bd., 1986-90. Recipient Disting. Faculty award Nat. Coll. Dist. Attys., U. Houston, 1979, Outstanding Alumnus award U. Ariz. Coll. Law, 1992. Mem. Am. Judicature Soc., Fed. Judges Assn., Pima County Bar Assn. Republican. Lodge: K.C. (adv. coun. 10441). Office: US Dist Ct 55 E Broadway Blvd Tucson AZ 85701-1719

ROLLE, MYRA MOSS (MYRA E. MOSS), philosophy educator, author, translator; b. L.A., Mar. 22, 1937; d. Roscoe and Edith (Wheeler) Moss; m. Andrew Rolle, Nov. 5, 1983. BA, Pomona Coll., 1958; PhD, John Hopkins U., 1965. Asst. prof. U. Santa Clara, Calif., 1970-74; tutor philosophy Claremont (Calif.) McKenna Coll., 1975-82, adj. assoc. prof., 1982-88, adj. prof., 1988-89, prof., 1990—, chairperson, 1993-95, assoc. dir. Gould Ctr. for Humanities, 1992-94. Author: Benedetto Croce Reconsidered, 1987; transl.: Benedetto Croce's Essays on Literature, 1990; contbr. articles, essays, book revs. to profl. jours. and books. Mem. adv. coun. Milton Eisenhower Libr., Johns Hopkins U., 1994—. Mem. Am. Philos. Assn., Am. Soc. for Aesthetics, Am. Soc. for Social Philosophy (bd. dirs. 1983-90, asst. edit. 1988), Am. Soc. for Value Inquiry (assoc. editor jour. 1990—, assoc. editor book series 1990—), Phi Beta Kappa. Office: Claremont McKenna Coll Dept Philosophy Claremont CA 91711

ROLLER, CAROLYN SUE, dietitian; b. Balt., Feb. 19, 1968; d. James Irving and Linda Mildred (Gempp) Crowther; m. Michael David Roller, May 25, 1991; 1 child, Rachel Elizabeth. BS, U. N.Mex., 1990, MS, 1992. Lic. nutritionist, N.Mex.; registered dietitian; cert. aerobics instr. Am. Coun. on Exercise. Weight loss counselor Diet Ctr., Albuquerque, 1989; nutrition asst. St. Joseph's Hosp., Albuquerque, 1990-91; health promotion dietitian FHP Health Care, Albuquerque, 1992-95; spkr. Am. Heart Assn., Albuquerque, 1993-95, program com. mem., 1993—. Mem. Am. Dietetic Assn. (registered dietitian), Albuquerque Dist. Dietetic Assn. Democrat. Presbyterian. Office: FHP Health Care 4300 San Mateo Blvd NE Albuquerque NM 87110-1260

ROLLER, DAVID ISAAC, financial services company executive; b. Bklyn., Jan. 13, 1949; s. Morton and Helen (Deligtiseh) R.; m. Susan Firtle, June 3, 1973; children: Aviva Natanya, Yael Elisheva. BA, L.I. U., 1971; MA, NYU, 1980; PhD, Cleo Soc., Oakland, Mich., 1991; DD, N.W. Ecumenical Inst., Petaluma, Calif., 1992. Ordained rabbi, 1980; cert. religious counselor. Rabbi North Rockland Jewish Cmty. Ctr., Pomona, N.Y., 1980-81; educator, asst. rabbi Old Westbury (N.Y.) Hebrew Congregation, 1982-83; rabbi Beth Emek Congregation, Livermore, Calif., 1983-85; pres., founder Roller Fin. Assocs., Livermore, 1985—; guest rabbi High Holidays, East Bay Chavuarah, Danville, Calif., 1990-93; chaplain Masonic Home for Adults, Union City, Pa., 1992—. Mem. Internat. Assn. Fin. Planners, Am. Coun. Life Underwriters, Am. Assn. Rabbis, East Bay Bd. Rabbis, Masons (chaplain 1985-86), Mensa, Rotary. Republican. Jewish.

ROLLER, SUSAN LORRAYNE, industrial communications specialist, consultant; b. Portsmouth, Va., Sept. 13, 1954; d. Gilbert John Roller and Lois Carolyn (Moore) Logan. BS in Med. Scis., U. Wash., 1976, BA, 1980. Dir. med. programming Omnia Corp., Mpls., 1980-82; program developer Golle & Holmes, Mpls., 1982-83; dir. mktg. Santal Corp., St. Louis, 1983; pres. Fine Line, Ltd., Reno, Nev., 1984—; ind. film prodr., writer. Mem. Reno C. of C., Kappa Kappa Gamma. Republican. Episcopalian.

ROLLINS, ALDEN MILTON, documents librarian; b. Billerica, Mass., July 31, 1946; s. Alden Milton and Agnes Morgan (Simpson) R. BA, Am. U., 1968; MLS, U. R.I., 1973. Documents libr. U. Alaska Libr., Anchorage, 1973—. Author: The Fall of Rome: A Reference Guide, 1983, Rome in the Fourth Century A.D., 1991. With U.S. Army, 1969-71. Mem. ALA, New Eng. Hist. Geneal. Soc., N.H. Hist. Soc., Vt. Hist. Soc. (life), Piscataqua Pioneers (life). Home: 221 E 7th Ave Apt 114 Anchorage AK 99501-3639 Office: U Alaska Libr Govt Documents 3211 Providence Dr Anchorage AK 99508-4614

ROLLINS, JAMES GREGORY, air force officer; b. Vandenberg AFB, Calif., Apr. 6, 1963; s. Clarence Leslie and Mary Ethel (Brooks) R. BS in Bus. Adminstrn., San Jose State U., 1985; MSA in Gen. Adminstrn., Ctrl. Mich. U., 1992; MBA in Aviation Mgmt., Embry-Riddle Aero. U., 1992. Commd. 2d lt. USAF, 1985, advanced through grades to capt., 1989; minuteman intercontinental ballistic missile dep. crew comdr. USAF, Grand Forks AFB, N.D., 1985-86, minuteman intercontinental ballistic missile instr. dep. crew comdr., 1986-87, minuteman intercontinental ballistic missile evaluator dep. crew comdr., 1987-88, strategic air command missile combat competition instr., 1987-88, intercontinental ballistic missile crew comdr., 1988-89, scheduling br. chief ops., 1989-90, order tng. officer emergecy war, 1990-91, intercontinental ballistic missile ops. plans officer, 1991-92; acquisition info. mgr. USAF, L.A. AFB, 1992-93, dep. dir. program control divsn., 1993-94, chief plans and analysis divsn., 1994—. Editor (newsletters) Families First, 1991, Vol. Network, 1990-91. Asst. project officer Project Sandbox fundraiser, 1986; founder Above and Beyond Vol. Tutoring, 1988, cons., 1988—; vol. staff Youth Ctr., Grand Forks AFB, 1988-91, Rebuild L.A. Edn. and Job Tng. Task Force; base project officer Rob's Coats for Kids, 1990, 91; vol. Grand Forks United Way Community Svcs., 1990-91; mem. Nat. Vol. Ctr., 1991—, Minn. Office Vol. Svcs., 1991—, Commdrs. Cmty. Ptnrs. Program, 1994—; project coord. L.A. Works, 1995—; Vol. Habitat for Humanity, 1995—. Decorated Air Force Achievement medal, 1990, Air Force Commendation medal, 1992; named Vol. of Yr., 321st Strategic Missile Wing, 42d Air Divsn., 8th Air Force, Strategic Air Command, 1990; recipient Presdl. award for volunteerism, 1991. Mem. Air Force Assn., Assn. Vol. Adminstrs., Air Force Cadet Officer Mentor Action Program, Performance Mgmt. Assn., Soc. Cost Estimating & Analysis, Tuskegee Airmen, Inc., Assn. of Air Force Missileers, Points of Light Found., Ctr. Corp. Cmty. Rels., Nat. Assn. Ptnrs. in Edn., Torrance C. of C. Home: 4451 Pacific Coast Hwy Apt H-304 Torrance CA 90505-5676 Office: USAF SMC/CW Los Angeles CA 90009

ROLLINS, LANIER, recording company executive; b. New Orleans, Mar. 12, 1937; s. John and Iola Rollins. BA in Music, Chgo. Conservatory Music, 1962; AA in Bus., L.A. Trade Tech. Coll., 1976. Cert. employee plans specialist IRS. Clk., tech. U.S. Postal Svc., Chgo. and L.A., 1959-72; contact rep. Social Security Adminstrn., L.A., 1974-77; employee plans specialist IRS, L.A., 1977-90; pres., prodr. BFN Records, Inc., L.A., 1966-84, Lanier Equity Records, Inc., Atlanta, 1984—; mgmt. analyst VAF Edwards Group, Alta Loma, Calif., 1989—; pub. Ethnicity Connection, Alta Loma, 1989—; Author: The Human Race is a Gang, 1964; pub. (mag.) Ethnicity Connection, 1994. Recipient Music Mony awards ASCAP, N.Y.C., 1976, 81. Mem. Black Entrepreneur Bus. Club (chmn. 1993-94), Rancho Cucamonga (Calif.) C. of C. Home: 10801 Lemon Ave Ste 1321 Alta Loma CA 91737

ROLLINS, LOUIS ARTHUR, editor; b. Cody, Wyo., Sept. 4, 1948; s. George Anthony Rollins and Leslie Vivian (Billings) Lay. BA, Calif. State Coll., 1970. Asst. editor Inst. for Hist. Rev., Torrance, Calif., 1985; editor Loompanics Unltd. (book pub.), Port Townsend, Wash., 1986-94. Author: The Myth of Natural Rights, 1983, Lucifer's Lexicon, 1987. Office: Loompanics Unltd PO Box 1197 Port Townsend WA 98368-0997

ROLLSTIN, GARY RAYMOND, electrical engineer; b. Ephrata, Wash., Jan. 11, 1945; s. Raymond E. and Marie (Danielson) R.; m. Catherine A. Reikofski, June 10, 1971; 1 child, Andrew. BSEE, Colo. State U., 1967, BSBA, 1969. Registered profl. engr., Colo., Ariz., N.Mex. From jr. transmission engr. to substation engr. Tucson Electric Power, Tucson, 1969-74; elec. engr. III City of Grand Island (Nebr.) Utilities, 1974-86; from sr. prodn. engr. to asst. elec. dir. City of Farmington (N.Mex.), 1986—. Judge Dist. Sci. Fair, Farmington, 1990, 91, 92, 93, 94; pres. Lutheran Church ELCA, 1989, 92, 95, v.p. 1988,93. Mem. IEEE. Office: Farmington Elec Utility Sys 101 Browning Pky Farmington NM 87401-7995

ROLSTON, HOLMES, III, theologian, educator, philosopher; b. Staunton, Va., Nov. 19, 1932; s. Holmes and Mary Winifred (Long) R.; m. Jane Irving Wilson, June 1, 1956; children: Shonny Hunter, Giles Campbell. BS, Davidson Coll., 1953; BD, Union Theol. Sem., Richmond, Va., 1956; MA in Philosophy of Sci., U. Pitts., 1968; PhD in Theology, U. Edinburgh, Scotland, 1958. Ordained to ministry Presbyn. Ch. (USA), 1956. Asst. prof. philosophy Colo. State U., Ft. Collins, 1968-71, assoc. prof., 1971-76, prof., 1976—; vis. scholar Ctr. Study of World Religions, Harvard U., 1974-75; lectr. Yale U., Vanderbilt U., others; official observer UNCED, Rio de Janiero, 1992. Author: Religious Inquiry: Participation and Detachment, 1985, Philosophy Gone Wild, 1986, Science and Religion: A Critical Survey, 1987, Environmental Ethics, 1988, Conserving Natural Value, 1994; assoc. editor Environ. Ethics, 1979—; mem. editorial bd. Oxford Series in Environ. Philosophy and Pub. Policy, Zygon: Jour. of Religion and Sci.; contbr. chpts. to books, articles to profl. jours. Recipient Oliver P. Penock Disting. Svc. award Colo. State U., 1983, Coll. Award for Excellence, 1991., Univ. Disting. Prof., 1992; Disting. Russell fellow Grad. Theol. Union, 1991, Disting. Lectr. Chinese Acad. of Social Scis., 1991, Disting. Lectr. Nobel Conf. XXVII. Mem. AAAS, Am. Acad. Religion, Soc. Bibl. Lit. (pres. Rocky Mountain-Gt. Plains region), Am. Philos. Assn., Internat. Soc. for Environ. Ethics (pres. 1989-94), Phi Beta Kappa. Home: 1712 Concord Dr Fort Collins CO 80526-1602 Office: Colo State U Dept Philosophy Fort Collins CO 80523

ROMANOS, NABIL ELIAS, business development manager; b. Roumie, Metn, Lebanon, June 3, 1965; came to U.S., 1982; s. Elias Rachid and Kamale (Salame) R. BA in Econs. and History magna cum laude, Georgetown U., 1986; postgrad., Hautes Etudes Commerciales, France, 1989; MBA, U. Calif., Berkeley, 1989. Rsch. assoc. Am. Fin. Svcs. Assn., Washington, 1986-87; fin. analyst Varian Assocs., Palo Alto, Calif., 1988, sr. fin. analyst, 1989-91; mgr. fin. mkt. analysis Varian Oncology Systems, Palo Alto, 1991-92; mgr. bus. devel. Varian Health Care Systems, Palo Alto, 1992-94, Zug, Switzerland, 1994—. Author: Finance Facts Yearbook, 1987. Vol. tutor for refugees Community Action Coalition, Washington, 1985-86; vol. interpreter emergency room Georgetown U., Washington, 1984-86; internat. vol. Internat. House U. Calif., Berkeley, 1987-89. Scholar Georgetown U., 1985-86, U. Calif., Berkeley, 1987-89. Mem. Phi Alpha Theta. Maronite Catholic. Home: 837 Cowper St Apt F Palo Alto CA 94301-2817

ROMER, ROY R., governor; b. Garden City, Kans., Oct. 31, 1928; s. Irving Rudolph and Margaret Elizabeth (Snyder) R.; m. Beatrice Miller, June 10, 1952; children: Paul, Mark, Mary, Christopher, Timothy, Thomas, Elizabeth. B.S. in Agrl. Econs., Colo. State U., 1950; LL.B., U. Colo., 1952; postgrad., Yale U. Bar: Colo. 1952. Engaged in farming in Colo., 1942-52; ind. practice law Denver, 1955-66; mem. Colo. Ho. of Reps., 1958-62, Colo. Senate, 1962-66; owner, operator Arapahoe Aviation Co., Colo. Flying Acad., Geneva Basin Ski Area; engaged in home site devel.; owner chain farm implement and indsl. equipment stores Colo.; commr. agr. State of Colo., 1975, chief staff, exec. asst. to gov., 1975-77, 83-84, state treas., 1977-86, gov., 1987—; chmn. Gov. Colo. Blue Ribbon Panel, Gov. Colo. Small Bus. Council; mem. agrl. adv. com. Colo. Bd. Agr. Bd. editors Colo. U. Law Rev., 1960-62. Past trustee Iliff Sch. Theology, Denver; mem., past chmn. Nat. Edn. Goals Panel; co-chmn. Nat. Coun. on Standards and Testing. With USAF, 1952-53. Mem. Dem. Gov.'s Assn. (chmn.), Nat. Gov.'s Assn. (former chmn.), Colo. Bar Assn., Order of the Coif. Democrat. Presbyterian. Office: Office of Gov State Capitol Denver CO 80203*

ROMERO, PAUL DAVID, municipal official; b. Cheyenne, Wyo., Sept. 22, 1946; s. Jacob Issau and Mattie Lou (Trammel) R.; m. Joanne Romero, Feb. 1, 1969; children: Jacob, Adam. AA, El Camino Coll., 1968; BS, Calif. State U., Long Beach, 1970, MA, 1975. Instr. Mt. San Jacinto (Calif.) Coll., 1972-79; interpretive specialist Riverside County (Calif.) Parks Dept., 1972-80, dep. dir., 1980-85, dir., 1985—; gen. mgr. Riverside County Regional Park and Open Space Dist., 1990—; cons. Paul Romero & Assocs., Corona, Calif., 1975-79. V.p. program Inland Empire coun. Boy Scouts Am., San Bernadino, Calif., 1990. Named Disting. Alumnus Calif. State U., 1993; recipient Meritorious Svc. award Western Interpreters Assn., 1983, Presdl. Citation Pres.' Commn. on Environ. Quality, 1992. Mem. Nat. Assn. County Park and Recreation Ofcls. (trustee 1991—), Calif. Park and Recreation Soc. (vice chair legis. 1990-92, chair legis. 1992—), County Park and Recreation Dirs. Assn. (pres. 1988-90). Office: County of Riverside Park Divsn 4600 Crestmore Rd Po Box 3507 Riverside CA 92519

ROMERO, PHILIP JOSEPH, economics and policy analyst; b. Abington, Pa., Mar. 22, 1957; s. Joseph John and Mildred Edith (Laundis) R.; m. Lita Grace Flores, Oct. 6, 1984. BA in Econs. and Polit. Sci., Cornell U., 1979; PhD in Policy Analysts, Rand Grad. Sch., 1988. Asst. to mayor Twp. of East Brunswick, N.J., 1977-78; policy analyst Sci. Applications Internat. Corp., Washington, 1980-83; rsch. assoc. RAND Corp., Santa Monica, Calif., 1983-88, assoc. economist, 1988-90; dir. strategic planning United Technologies/Carrier, Hartford, Conn., 1990-91; chief econ. adviser Gov.'s Office, Sacramento, Calif., 1991—, dep. cabinet sec., 1995—; cons. Office of Tech. Assessment, Washington, 1989-90, RAND Corp., Washington, 1990-91, Sec. of Air Forces Sci. Adv. Bd., Washington, 1980-83, Undersec. of Def., Washington, 1985-86; adj. prof. U. So. Calif. and Calif. State U., 1994—; mem. Coun. on Fgn. Rels., 1994—; mem. econ. adv. coun. Calif. Congl. Delegation, 1993—. Co-author: (book) The Deescalation of Nuclear Crises, 1992; contbr. numerous reports and papers to profl. publs. Pres. RAND Grad. Sch. Alumni Assn., Santa Monica, 1989—; founder Adopt-A-School Honors Program, Pacific Palisades, Calif., 1986. Recipient Internat. Affairs fellowship Coun. on Fgn. Rels., N.Y.C., 1989. Mem. The Planning Forum, Am. Econ. Assn., Ops. Rsch. Soc. of Am., Pacific Coun. on Internat. Policy (founding), Acad. Pub. Policy Analysts and Mgmt., Inst. Mgmt. Sci. Home: 1587 Barnett Cir Carmichael CA 95608-5852 Office: Gov's Office State Capitol Sacramento CA 95814

ROMM, JESSICA BETH, management consultant. BA in Social Welfare, U. Calif., Berkeley, 1965; MA, Hunter Coll., 1970; PhD in Pub. Policy and Adminstrn., NYU, 1976. Rsch. asst. Hunter Coll. Urban Rsch. Ctr., N.Y.C., 1968-69; program planning cons. Office Economic Opportunity and Model Cities Program, N.Y.C., 1968-70, 75; project dir. Environ. Resource Assoc., N.Y.C., 1970-72; cons. N.Y. State Office Childrens Svcs./N.Y.C. Family Ct., 1972-74; Fulbright fellow Fulbright Commn., Buenos Aires, 1974-75; asst. dir. edn. fund AFSCME, N.Y.C., 1976-79; mgr. programs C.Am. Planning Assistance, Inc., 1979; market and bus. devel. rep., strategic planning mem. Bechtel Group, Inc., San Francisco, 1980-91; pvt. practice Mill Valley, Calif., 1991—; adj. prof. Golden Gate U. Sch. Pub. Svc. and Internat. Studies, 1991—; cons. UN Devel. Program, Dames & Moore, MacPeople, Bechtel Corp., BPT Properties Foaley Square, Baytrade, Oakland Internat. Trade and Visitor Ctr., San Francisco Redevelopment Agy.; presenter in fields of mktg. biotech., multimedia cos. internat. mkts. Vol. Peace Corps., Santa Cruz, Bolivia, 1965-67. Recipient award of excellence Gov. of Okla., 1987, award of recognition Gov. of Mass., 1987; Fulbright fellow, Buenos Aires, 1974; Internat. Labour Orgn. grantee, 1990. Home and Office: 504 Seaver Dr Mill Valley CA 94941-2249

ROMMEL, YOLANDA ELIZABETH, mental health counselor; b. Lodz, Poland, Jan. 28, 1936; came to U.S., 1960; d. Jan Stanislaw and Helena L. (Paszke) Krysinski; m. Robert Richard Rommel, July 1967 (div. May 1983); children: Peter, Debora Rommel-Woodsome. BA in Comms., Boise State U., 1987; M in Counseling, Idaho State U., 1990. Nat. cert. counselor. Sr. draftsman Reynolds Engring., Mercury, Nev., 1965-69; draftsman various orgns., 1969-82; pvt. practice mental health counseling Ontario, Oreg., 1990—; family therapist Oreg. Human Resources, Ontario, 1990—; counselor Restitution, Treatment, & Tng., Ontario, 1991—. Vol. hospice, Boise, 1976-82, Intermountain Hospice, Pocatello, Idaho, 1989-90. Mem. Nat. Counseling Assn., Orthopsychiatric Assn. Democrat. Home: 1080 SW 5th Ave Ontario OR 97914-3302 Office: Yolanda Rommel Counseling 1001 1st Ave S Payette ID 83661-2808

ROMO, CHERYL ANNETTE, writer, editor; b. Alhambra, Calif., Aug. 21, 1944; d. Howard William and Shirley Marie (Junginger) Barkhurst; m. Rudy George Romo, Feb. 2, 1962 (div. 1969); children: Steven, Sheri, Michael; m. Charles Augustus Roberts, Apr. 25, 1981. B of Pub. Adminstrn., U. San Francisco, 1983. Newspaper reporter, columnist Orange Coast Daily Pilot, Costa Mesa, Calif., 1976-79; news reporter Orange County Register, Santa Ana, Calif., 1979-80; freelance writer Sacramento, 1981-84; editor Sacramento Mag., 1984-86; editor, reporter States News Svc., Washington, 1986-87; editor, dir. publs. Common Cause Mag., Washington, 1987; assoc. editor Pub. Utilities Fortnightly, Alexandria, Va., 1987-89, mng. editor, 1989-90, editor, 1990-92; v.p. Washington Internat. Energy Group, 1992-93; news editor L.A. Daily Jour., 1994—; coord. Taishoff Broadcast Seminar, 1984; mem faculty The Writer's Ctr., Bethesda, Md., 1987-88. Recipient 1st pl. awards for journalism Orange County Press Club, 1978, 79, 80, Calif. State Fair/Sigma Delta Chi, 1983. Mem. Soc. Profl. Journalists (pres. Cen. Calif. chpt. 1984, dep. regional dir. region II 1983-85, v.p. Orange County chpt. 1978-79, 1st pl. award for best editorial Cen. Calif. chpt. 1984). Home: 5215 Sepulveda Blvd Unit 18C Culver City CA 90230-5251 Office: LA Daily Jour 915 E 1st St Los Angeles CA 90012-4050

ROMO, GENE DAVID, municipal official; b. Mora, N.Mex., Jan. 29, 1947; s. Carlos C. and Anna (Nale) R.; m. Frances M. Gutierrez, June 27, 1970; children: Gene Jr., Gabriel, Kathleen. BS in Biology and Health Edn., U. N.Mex., 1970, MS in Health Edn., 1972, PhD in Pub. Health Edn. and Adminstrn., 1987. Exec. dir. Martiurztown Ctr., Albuquerque, 1969-74; health specialist U. N.Mex., Albuquerque, 1974-76, health dir., 1976-78; human services dir. City of Albuquerque, 1978-81, services dept. dir., 1981-84, advisor to chief adminstrv. officer, 1984-85, chief adminstrv. officer, 1985—; adj. prof. U. N.Mex., 1985-86. Author: Herbs of New Mexico, 1984. Bd. dirs. Health and Environment Dept., Santa Fe, 1983-86, United Way Albuquerque. Mem. Internat. City Mgmt. Assn., Am. Soc. for Pub. Adminstrn., Am. Mcpl. Assn., N.Mex. Mcpl. League. Home: 5605 Alta Vista Ct SW Albuquerque NM 87105-3363 Office: City Hall PO Box 1293 Albuquerque NM 87103-1293

RONAGH-LANGROODI, TAHMINEH, dietitian, educator, consultant; b. Langrood, Gilan, Iran, Apr. 9, 1959; came to U.S., 1978; d. Eskandar and Shukufeh (Omidvar) R.-L.; m. David R. Dickens, May 22, 1981; children: Shayda Pauline Dickens, Neemah Alexander Dickens. BA in Chemistry, U. Ky., 1983, MS in Clin. Nutrition, 1985. Registered dietitian; cert. nutrition support dietitian. Instr. U. Nev., Las Vegas, 1985-87; nutrition support dietitian Univ. Med. Ctr. of So. Nev., Las Vegas, 1989—; lectr. parenteral and enteral nutrition, 1989-94, cystic fibrosis and nutrition, 1991, critical care and nutrition, 1990-94. Lectr. I Can Cope Program, Las Vegas, 1989—; instr. Am. Heart Assn., Las Vegas, 1991-92; lectr. Parkinsons Orgn., Las Vegas, 1991-93. Recipient cert. of appreciation Am. Heart Assn., 1989, cert. of achievement Respiratory Conf., 1991, cert. of appreciation Am. Cancer Soc., 1993. Mem. Am. Dietetic Assn., Am. Soc. for Parenteral and Enteral Nutrition, So. Nev. Dietetic Assn. (mem. nominating com. 1991—, chair of lectures 1993-94), Am. Cancer Soc. (chair allied health com. 1992-93). Home: 278 Cordero Dr Henderson NV 89014-5211 Office: Univ Med Ctr of So Nev Nutrition Dept 1800 W Charleston Blvd Las Vegas NV 89102-2329

RONALD, ANN, English literature educator; b. Seattle, Oct. 9, 1939; d. James Quintin and Cleo Elizabeth (Keller) R. BA, Whitman Coll., 1961; MA, U. Colo., 1966; PhD, Northwestern U., 1970. Prof. English lit. U. Nev., Reno, 1970—, acting dean grad. sch., 1988-89, dean Coll. of Arts and

Sci., 1989—. Author: The New West of Edward Abbey, 1982, reprint, 1988, Functions of Setting in the Novel, 1980, Earthtones: A Nevada Album, 1995; editor: Words for the Wild, 1987; mem. editl. bd. Western Am. Lit., 1982—, U. Nev. Press, 1985-94, Studies in Short Fiction, 1988—. Office: U Nev Reno Coll Arts and Scis Reno NV 89557

RONAN, JAMES DOUGLAS, JR., counselor, writer, photographer; b. Oroville, Calif., Oct. 29, 1949; s. James Douglas and Dorothy Ben (Corry) R.; m. Penny Cathyren Wilkerson; m. 2d, Karen Lynn Cook; 1 dau., Terra Rhiannon. A.A., Butte Jr. Coll., 1973; B.A. in Psychology with honors, Sonoma State U., 1976, M.A. in Counseling, 1979. Cert. hypnotherapist. Psychiat. technician Sonoma State Hosp., Eldridge, Calif., 1976-79; counselor Sonoma County Office Edn., 1979; vocat. rehab. counselor VA, San Francisco, 1979-81, coordinator career devel. ctr. VA Regional Office, San Francisco, 1981-83; owner, operator Personal Achievement Career Enrichment Ctr., 1983-86; instr. guidance Santa Rosa Jr. Coll., 1979-85; instr. San Francisco State U. Extension, 1982-83; clin. dir., supr. counseling psychologist Cmty. Counseling Ctr. Dept. Army, Giessen Milcom, West Germany, 1986-89, chief alcohol & drug control program, 1989-90; dir. Quest Vocat. Rehab. Svcs., Eureka, Calif., 1990-92; regional mgr. FAA Aviation Drug Abatement Program, Anchorage, Alaska, 1992—; mem. bd. dirs. European branch Am. Assn. Counseling & Devel., 1989-90. Served to 1st lt. U.S. Army, 1968-71. Decorated Purple Heart, Bronze Star (2) with V device, Combat Infantry badge; recipient Pub. Service award VA Washington, 1983, Spl. Achievement award San Francisco VA, 1982, Dept. Army decoration for Meritious Civilian Svc., 1990; numerous awards for photography. Contbr. articles in field to profl. jours.; contbr. photographs, fiction, poetry, articles pub. various newspapers, mags. Home: PO Box 220230 Anchorage AK 99522-0230

RONCI, CURTIS LEE, marketing professional; b. Dayton, Ohio, Sept. 21, 1955; s. William Lionel and Deyne (Fox) R.; 1 child, Maxwell Lee Ronci. AAS in Comml. Arts, Ferris U., 1975. Freelance graphic artist Curtis Ronci & Assocs., Chgo., 1975-78; account exec. Phase II, Inc., Chgo., 1978-80; ind. talent rep. John Ball & Assocs., Chgo., 1980-83; account exec. Phase II, Inc., Chgo., 1983-90; dir. sales and mktg. Clonetics Corp., San Diego, 1991-94; dir. mktg. comms. Clonetics Corp., 1995; pres., CEO DMD Communications, San Diego, 1995—; academic advisor U. Calif. San Diego International Rels. Pacific Studies, La Jolla, Calif., 1993-94. Mem. AAAS. Office: DMD Communications 6591 Reflection Dr # 207 San Diego CA 92124

RONDEAU, DORIS JEAN, entrepreneur, consultant; b. Winston-Salem, N.C., Nov. 25, 1941; d. John Delbert and Eldora Virginia (Klutz) Robinson; m. Robert Breen Corrente, Sept. 4, 1965 (div. 1970); m. Wilfrid Dolor Rondeau, June 3, 1972. Student Syracuse U., 1959-62, Fullerton Jr. Coll., 1974-75; BA in Philosophy, Calif. State U.-Fullerton, 1976, postgrad., 1976-80. Ordained to ministry The Spirit of Divine Love, 1974. Trust real estate clk. Security First Nat. Bank, Riverside, Calif., 1965-68; entertainer Talent, Inc., Hollywood, Calif., 1969-72; co-founder, dir. Spirit of Divine Love, Huntington Beach, Calif., 1974—; pub., co-founder Passing Through, Inc., Huntington Beach, 1983—; instr. Learning Activity, Anaheim, Calif., 1984—; chmn. bd., prin. D.J. Rondeau, Entrepreneur, Inc., Huntington Beach, 1984—; co-founder, dir. Spiritual Positive Attitude, Inc., Moon In Pisces, Inc., Vibrations By Rondeau, Inc., Divine Consciousness, Expressed, Inc., Huntington Beach, Doris Wilfrid Rondeau, Inc., Huntington Beach, Calif. Author, editor: A Short Introduction To The Spirit of Divine Love, 1984; writer, producer, dir. performer spiritual vignettes for NBS Radio Network, KWVE-FM, 1982-84; author: Spiritual Meditations to Uplift the Soul, 1988. Served with USAF, 1963-65. Recipient Pop Vocalist First Place award USAF Talent Show, 1964, Sigma chpt. Epsilon Delta Chi, 1985, others. Mem. Hamel Bus. Grads., Smithsonian Assocs., Am. Mgmt. Assn., Nat. Assn. Female Execs. Avocations: long-distance running, body fitness, arts and crafts, snorkeling, musical composition.

RONDELL, THOMAS, public relations consultant, marketing communications consultant; b. N.Y.C., Sept. 16, 1933; s. Lester and Florence (Robinson) R.; div.; children: Alexis Sonya, Gabrielle Lee. AB in Sociology, Bard Coll., 1958; postgrad., NYU, 1960. V.p. corp. comm. Citizen Savs. and Loan, San Francisco, 1976-80; pub. rels. cons. Bell Savs., San Mateo, Calif., 1985-88; investor rels. cons. San Francisco Fed. Savs., 1980-88; pub. rels. cons. Cornish and Carey Residential Real Estate, Palo Alto, Calif., 1989—, The Benham Group, Mountain View, Calif., 1992—. V.p., dir. Mental Health Assn. San Francisco, 1982-86, trustee, 1982-86, 94—. With U.S. Army, 1954-56. Mem. Pub. Rels. Soc. Am. (accredited), Nat. Investor Rels. Inst. Home: Condo 21 217 Ada Ave Mountain View CA 94043-4958

RONDORF-KLYM, LOUANN M., clinical investigator, nurse; b. Thief River Falls, Minn., Oct. 27, 1953; d. Eugene LeRoy and Edna Lila (Iverson) Rondorf; m. Michael Allyn Klym, May 16, 1976; children: Trevor William, Matthew Robert. BSN, U. N.D., 1976, MSN, 1990; postgrad., Oreg. Health Scis. U., 1993—. RN, Oreg. Cmty. health nurse Stark County Comty. Health, Dickinson, N.D., 1977-80; DON Dickinson Nursing Ctr., 1980-88; charge nurse St. Luke's Nursing Home, Dickinson, 1988-90; cardiac rehab. nurse St. Joseph's Hosp., Dickinson, 1988-90; DON Oak Villa Care Ctr., Hillsboro, Oreg., 1990-91; clin. investigator Laerdal Mfg. Corp., Tualatin, Oreg., 1991—; mem. ad-hoc com. case-mix sys. N.D. State Human Svcs., 1987-89; mem. ad-hoc com. entry into practice N.D. Assoc. Degree LPN, 1985-86, forum faculty, 1987; team mem. Midwest Alliance in Nursing, 1986; cons. Treasure Valley Living Ctr., Boise, 1989. Author: (video) Med. Center One, 1990; contbr. articles to med. jours. Mem. BLS subcom. Am. Heart Assn., Portland, 1992—, instr. BLS, Calif., N.D. and Oreg., 1976—; vol. Adopt-a-Grandparent King City (Oreg.) Convalescent & Rehab. Ctr., 1992—; mem. govtl. rels. com. N.D. Nurses Assn., Bismarck, 1986-90; vol. Hopkins Elem. Sch., Sherwood, Oreg., 1991—; vol. gardener St. Paul Luth. Ch., Sherwood, 1991—; sec. Badlands Nurses Assn., 1983-85, dir.-at-large, 1985-87, legis. com., 1990, mem. program com., 1990. Mem. ANA (cabinet on edn. N.D. chpt 1987-90), Am. Assn. Med. Instrumentation, Coun. on Cardiopulmonary & Critical Care, Gerontol. Assn. Am. Home: 20730 SW Houston Dr Sherwood OR 97140 Office: Laerdal Mfg Corp 9440 SW Tualatin-Sherwood Tualatin OR 97062

RONEY, JOHN HARVEY, lawyer, consultant; b. L.A., June 12, 1932; s. Harvey and Mildred Puckett (Cargill) R.; m. Joan Ruth Allen, Dec. 27, 1954; children: Pam Peterson, J. Harvey, Karen Louise Hanke, Cynthia Allen Harmon. Student, Pomona Coll., 1950-51; B.A., Occidental Coll., 1954; LL.B., UCLA, 1959. Bar: Calif. 1960, D.C. 1976. Assoc. O'Melveny & Myers, L.A., 1959-67, ptnr., 1967-94, of counsel, 1994—; gen. counsel Pa. Co., 1970-78, Baldwin United Corp., 1983-84; dir. Coldwell Banker & Co., 1969-81, Brentwood Savs. & Loan Assn., 1968-80; spl. advisor to dep. Rehab. of Mut. Benefit Life Ins. Co., 1991-94; cons., advisor to Rehab. of Confederation Life Ins. Co., 1994—; mem. policy adv. bd. Calif. Ins. Commn., 1991-95. Served to 1st lt. USMCR, 1954-56. Mem. ABA, Calif. Bar Assn. (ins. law com. 1991-95, chmn. 1993-94), Los Angeles County Bar Assn., San Francisco Bar Assn., D.C. Bar Assn., N.Y. Coun. Fgn. Rels., L.A. Com. on Fgn. Rels., Conf. Ins. Counsel, Calif. Club, Sky Club (N.Y.). Republican. Home: The Strand Hermosa Beach CA 90254 Office: 400 S Hope St Ste 1600 Los Angeles CA 90071-2899

RONSMAN, WAYNE JOHN, insurance company executive; b. Milw., Jan. 21, 1938; s. Harry Martin and Martha Elizabeth (Popp) R.; m. Joan P. Murphy-Mays, Nov. 30, 1974; children: Allison, Alanna; children by previous marriage: Rosemary, Harry, Martha. Student Marquette U., 1955-58, U. San Francisco, 1960-66. CLU, chartered fin. cons.; cert. fin. planner; registered fin. planner. Acct. Otis McAllister & Co., 1960-62; acct., salesman of data processing Statis. Tabulation Corp., San Francisco, 1962-66; chief acct., gen. mgr. Dillingham Bros. Ltd., Honolulu, 1966-67; ins. salesman Mut. Benefit Life Ins. Co., 1968-91, mgr. Met Life Honolulu, 1991—, gen. agt., Hawaii and Alaska, 1991; v.p. Brenno Assos., Honolulu, 1972-80; prin. Ronsman-Brenno, Anchorage, Alaska, 1980-90; owner Ronsman, Hammond & Assocs., 1991—; bd. dirs. Aloha Nat. Bank, Kihei, Maui, 1989-90; guest lectr. Chaminade U. Law Sch., Honolulu. Mem. Gov's Task Force to Program Correctional Facilities Land, 1970-72; mem. State Bd. Paroles and Pardons, 1972-75; treas. Spl. Edn. Center of Oahu, 1969-78; pres. Ballet Alaska, 1986-87, Maui Ballet Co. Ltd., 1992-93; v.p. devel. Make A Wish Found Hawaii, 1992—. Served with USMCR, 1958-60. Mem. Inst. Mgmt. Acct. (pres. Anchorage chpt. 1989-90), Am. Soc. CLUs, Hawaii Estate Planning Coun. (dir. 1994), Honolulu Assn. Life Underwriters (million dollar round table 1973—), Inst. Mgmt. Accts. (pres. Honolulu 1994-95, 95-96), Hawaii (state editor 1970-71, nat. dir. 1972-73), Kailua (pres. 1968-69) Jaycees, Hawaii C. of C., Nat. Assn. Securities Dealers, Kailua C. of C. (pres. 1977-78). Roman Catholic. Home: Ronsman-Hammond & Assocs 1099 Alaska St Ste # 1500 Honolulu HI 96813 Office: PO Box 336 Honolulu HI 96809-0336

ROODMAN, RICHARD DAVID, hospital administrator; b. St. Louis, Mo., May 13, 1948; s. Milton Harold and Estelle (Pritsker) R.; m. Carol S. Wagner, Aug. 20, 1972; children—Adam, Lindsey, Amanda. B.S. in Fin., U. Mo., 1971, postgrad., 1971—; M.H.A., Wash. U., 1973. Adminstrv. resident Jane Phillips Episcopal Meml. Med. Ctr., Bartlesville, Okla., 1972-73, asst. adminstr., 1974-77, chief exec. officer, 1977-82; chief exec. officer Valley Med. Ctr., Renton, Wash., 1983—. Active various Little Leagues, Bartlesville, 1980-82. Named Boss of Yr. AAUW, Bartlesville, 1980, Emerging Leading in Health Care, Forum Mag., 1985. Mem. Am. Coll. Hosp. Adminstrs. (Outstanding Young Adminstr. of Yr. nominee, Chgo. 1981, 1982), Okla. Hosp. Assn. (various positions), Bartlesville C. of C. (bd. dirs.), Wash. State Hosp. Assn., Seattle Area Hosp. Council (bd. dirs. 1984). Jewish. Lodge: Rotary.

ROOKS, CHARLES S., foundation administrator; b. Whiteville, N.C., June 29, 1937. BA in English, Wake Forest Coll., 1959; Rockefeller Brothers fellow, Harvard U., 1959-60; MA in Polit. Sci., Duke U., 1964, PhD in Polit. Sci., 1968. Rsch. assoc. Voter Edn. Project, Atlanta, 1969-70, dir. tech. assistance programs, 1970-71, dep. dir., 1971-72; exec. dir. Southeastern Coun. of Founds., Atlanta, 1972-78; dir. mem. svcs. Coun. on Founds., Washington, 1979-80, v.p., 1981-82, acting CEO, 1981-82; exec. dir. Meyer Meml. Trust, Portland, Oreg., 1982—; instr. polit. sci. Duke U., Durham, N.C., 1963, 65-67; asst. prof. of govt. Lake Forest Coll., Ill., 1967-69; asst. prof. polit. sci. Clark Coll., Atlanta, 1969-71; bd. dirs. Pacific Northwest Grantmakers Forum; mem. adv. bd. Neighborhood Partnership Fund (Oreg. Cmty. Found.). Contbr. articles to profl. jours. Home: 2706 SW English Ct Portland OR 97201 Office: Meyer Memorial Trust 1515 SW 5th Ave Ste 500 Portland OR 97201-5450*

ROONEY, ALICE GREGOR, art society executive; b. Seattle, July 5, 1926; d. Kaare Arvid and Esther Irene (Neeven) Gregor; m. Robert L. Rooney, Aug. 29, 1953; children: Robin Lee Rooney Cassidy, Scott Corey. BA, U. Wash., 1947. Exec. dir. Allied Arts of Seattle, Seattle, 1960-80; dir. Pilchuch Glass Sch., Seattle, 1980-90; exec. dir. Glass Art Soc., Seattle, 1990—; editor, cons. Nat. Endowment for Arts, Washington, 1977-78, mem. nat. task force on crafts, 1980-81; mem. review panel NEA, Washington, 1984, Seattle Arts Commn., 1989; mem. King County Arts Commn., Seattle, 1982-87, review panel, 1990; mem. task force Coll. of Edn., U. Wash., Seattle, 1978. Recipient Pub. Svc. in Arts award Seattle Arts Commn., 1977, Woman of Achievement award Women in Comm., 1990, Art Svc. award King County Arts Commn., 1991. Mem. Am. Craft Coun. (bd. trustees, chair nominating com. 1991—), Allied Arts Found. (bd. trustees 1980—). Democrat. Office: Glass Art Soc 1305 4th Ave Ste 711 Seattle WA 98101-2401

ROOP, JOSEPH MCLEOD, economist; b. Montgomery, Ala., Sept. 29, 1941; s. Joseph Ezra and Mae Elizabeth (McLeod) R.; B.S., Central Mo. State U., Warrensburg, 1963; Ph.D., Wash. State U., Pullman, 1973; m. Betty Jane Reed, Sept. 4, 1965; 1 dau., Elizabeth Rachael. Economist, Econ. Research Service, U.S. Dept. Agr., Washington, 1975-79; sr. economist Evans Econs., Inc., Washington, 1979-81; staff scientist Battelle Pacific N.W. Labs., Richland, Wash., 1981—; instr. dept. econs. Wash. State U., 1969-71; with Internat. Energy Agy., Paris, 1990-91. Contbr. tech. articles to profl. jours. Served with U.S. Army, 1966-68. Dept. Agr. Coop. State Research Service research grantee, 1971-73. Mem. Am. Econ. Assn., Econometric Soc., Internat. Assn. Energy Economics. Home: 715 S Taft St Kennewick WA 99336-9587 Office: PO Box 999 Richland WA 99352-0999

ROOS, DAVID BERNARD, surgeon; b. Decatur, Ill., Nov. 11, 1928; s. Edmund Carl and Frances (Kuny) R.; m. Edith Julia Edwards, June 10, 1954; children: Steven David, Gary Marshall, Wendy Jeanne, Linda Jennifer, Lisa Alison. AB, Harvard U., 1950; MD, Washinington U., St. Louis, 1954. Diplomate Am. Bd. Surgery. Intern in surgery Cin. Gen. Hosp., 1954-55; fellow in surg. pathology Washington U., St. Louis, 1955; resident in surgery U. Colo. Med. Ctr. and VA Hosp., Denver, 1957-61; pvt. practice Denver, 1962—; instr. in surgery U. Colo. Med. Ctr., Denver, 1960-65, asst. clin. prof. surgery, 1965-75, assoc. clin. prof. surgery, 1975-85, clin. prof. surgery, 1985—. Contbr. chpts. to surg. textbooks, articles to profl. jours. Capt. USAF, 1955-57. Fulbright scholar London, 1959-60. Fellow ACS, Belgian Soc. Surgery (hon.), Soc. Clin. Vascular Surgery (hon.); mem. AMA, Am. Coll. Chest Physicians, Internat. Cardiovascular Surg. Soc., Southwestern Surg. Congress, Soc. for Vascular Surgery, Western Vascular Soc. (founding mem.), Western Surg. Assn. Presbyterian. Office: 1721 E 19th Ave Ste 206 Denver CO 80218-1240

ROOS, GEORGE WILLIAM, physicist; b. Yonkers, N.Y., July 1, 1932; s. George William Jr. and Corinne Elizabeth (Kelly) R.; m. Grace Lennon, Oct. 4, 1958; children: George, John, Edward, Daniel. BS in Physics, Iona Coll., 1953. Physicist Naval Rsch. Lab., Washington, 1953-54; program mgr. electric boat divsn. Gen. Dynamics Co., Groton, Conn., 1957-68, mgr. chg. control, 1968-72, dir. indsl. rels. and mgmt. engring., 1972-77; dir. resource mgmt. Gen. Dynamics Co., Ft. Worth, 1977-79; dir. integrated logistic support Convair divsn. Gen. Dynamics Co., San Diego, 1979-86, v.p. human resources Convair divsn., 1986-92; gen. mgr. Hughes Unmanned Strike Sys., San Diego, 1992-93; chmn. Sandarc, Inc., 1994—. Bd. dirs. ARC, San Diego, 1987-93. Lt. USNR, 1953-57, Korea. Recipient A.A. Loftus award Iona Coll., 1974. Mem. Calif. Mgrs. Assn. (bd. dirs. 1988-93, mem., chmn. exec. com. 1990-92), Corp. Assn. Univ. San Diego (chmn. exec. com. 1995—), U.S. Naval Inst., Navy League, Escondido Country Club. Republican. Roman Catholic. Home: 10726 Vista Valle Dr San Diego CA 92131-1232

ROOS, NESTOR ROBERT, consultant; b. St. Louis, Aug. 19, 1925; s. Maurice and Fannie (Friedman) R.; m. Fay Weil, July 8, 1951; children: Marilyn Roos Hall, Eileen Roos Ruddell, Robert F. BBA, Washington U., St. Louis, 1948; MSBA, Washington U., 1949; D of Bus. Adminstrn., Ind. U., 1959. Instr. bus. La. State U., Baton Rouge, 1949-51; teaching fellow Ind. U., Bloomington, 1951-53; asst. prof. Ga. State U., Atlanta, 1953-55; prof. U. Ariz., Tucson, 1955-86, prof. emeritus, 1986; pres. Risk Mgmt. Pub. Co., Tucson, 1976-90, cons. editor, 1990—; cons., expert witness in field; bd. dirs. Blue Cross-Blue Shield Ariz., sec., 1993-95, vice-chmn., 1995—; mem. Inst. Dirs.' Adv. Com., Phoenix, 1987—, Reverse Mortgage Adv. Com., Tucson, 1988-90. Author: (with others) Multiple Line Insurers, 1970, Governmental Risk Management Manual, 1976, Industrial Accident Prevention, 1980. Bd. dirs. Handmaker Geriatric Ctr., Tucson, 1987-92; pres. Temple Emanu-El, Tucson, 1981-83. With U.S. Army, 1943-45, ETO. Grantee Nat. Inst. Occupational Safety and Health, 1975. Mem. Risk and Ins. Mgmt. Soc., Western Risk and Ins. Assn. (pres. 1972-73), Public Risk and Ins. Mgmt. Assn. (dir. edn. and tng. 1982-89). Democrat. Jewish. Home: 7311 E Camino De Cima Tucson AZ 85715-2212 Office: Risk Mgmt Pub Co 2030 E Broadway Blvd Ste 106 Tucson AZ 85719-5908

ROOT, CHARLES JOSEPH, JR., finance executive, consultant; b. Pierre, S.D., July 26, 1940; s. Charles Joseph and Hazel Ann (Messenger) R.; 1 child from previous marriage, Roseann Marie; m. Sharon Lee, June 24, 1995; stepchildren: Nichole Marie Marcillac, Monique Marie Marcillac. Student, San Francisco Jr. Coll., 1963-65, La Salle Extension U., 1970-71, Coll. of Marin, 1971-72, Am. Coll. Life Underwriters, 1978-82. Registered investment advisor; charter fin. cons.; cert. fin. planner. Estate planner Bankers Life Co., San Francisco, 1966-78; fin. planner Planned Estates Assocs., Corte Madera, Calif., 1978-81; mng. dir. Double Eagle Fin. Corp., Santa Rosa, Calif., 1981—, investment advisor, 1983—; personal bus. mgr., 1987—. V.p. Big Bros. of Am., San Rafael, Calif., 1976-80; treas. com. to elect William Filante, San Rafael, 1978, Cmty. Health Ctrs. of Marin, Fairfax, Calif., 1982-83, Wellspring Found., Philo, Calif., 1981-85; treas., bd. dirs. Ctr. for Attitudinal Healing, Tiburon, Calif., 1989-92; bd. dirs. Pickle Family Circus, San Francisco, 1988, United Way Sonoma Lake, Mendocino Counties, 1993—; bd. dirs. Redwood Empire Estate Planning Coun., Santa Rosa, Calif., 1992—, v.p. programs, 1993, pres. 1995—). Mem. Internat. Assn. Fin. Planners, Coll. Fin. Planning (cert. fin. planner 1988), Registry of fin. Planning, Nat. Assn. Life Underwriters, Marin County Assn. Life Underwriters (v.p. 1971-76, editor newsletter 1976-80), Rotary (Paul Harris Fellow 1980). Republican. Office: Double Eagle Fin Corp 2300 Bethards Dr Ste R PO Box 2790 Santa Rosa CA 95405

ROOT, DORIS SMILEY, portrait artist; b. Ann Arbor, Mich., June 28, 1924; d. George O. and Hazel (Smith) Smiley. Student, Art Inst. of Chgo., 1943-45, N.Y. Sch. Design, 1976-77, Calif. Art Inst., 1984-85. Creative dir. All May Co.'s, L.A., 1962-63; advt. sales pro. dir. Seibu, L.A., 1963-64; v.p. Walgers & Assoc., L.A., 1964-70; owner, designer At The Root of Things, L.A., 1970-73; adv. sales pro. dir. Hs. of Nine, L.A., 1973-74; asst. designer MGM Grand, Reno, Nev., 1974-76; designer, office mgr. Von Hausen Studio, L.A., 1976-82; ABC libr. ABC/Cap Cities, L.A., 1982-89; portrait artist (also known as Dorian), AKA Dorian, art studio, L.A., 1982—. One-man shows include Cookeville, Tenn., 1989, Beverly Hills, Calif., 1991; artist in residence, Cookeville, 1989-90. Republican. Presbyterian.

ROOT, GERALD EDWARD, courts administrator, resource developer; b. Gridley, Calif., May 5, 1948; s. Loris Leo Root and Mary Helen (Wheeler) Murrell; m. Tricia Ann Caywood, Feb. 13, 1981; children: Jason Alexander, Melinda Ann. AA in Bus., Yuba C.C., Marysville, Calif., 1968; BA in Psychology, Calif. State U., Sonoma, 1972; MA in Social Sci., Calif. State U., Chico, 1974; postgrad. in Edn., U. San Francisco, 1991-96. Gen. mgr. Do-It Leisure, Inc., Chico, 1977-80; CETA projects coord. City of Chico, 1980-81; exec. dir. Voluntary Action Ctr., Inc., South Lake Tahoe, Calif., 1981-83; devel. dir. Work Tng. Ctr., Inc., Chico, 1983-92; exec. dir. North Valley Rehab. Found., Chico, 1986-92; resource adminstrn. and devel. Sacramento Superior and Mcpl. Cts., 1992—; project mgr. Juvenile Detention Alternatives Initiative, 1992, Feather River Industries, 1991, Creative Learning Ctr., 1988, Correctional Options-Drug Ct., 1994, Youth & Family Violence Prevention Initiative, 1995, Violence Prevention Resource Ctr., 1995, Delinquency Prevention Initiative, 1995. Bd. dirs. Cmty. Action Agy., Butte County, Calif., 1990, Am. Red Cross, Butte County, 1989; adv. bds. Butte C.C. Dist., 1987-92. With U.S. Army, 1968-70. Mem. Nat. Criminal Justice Assn., Nat. Soc. Fund Raising Execs., Phi Delta Kappa. Office: Sacramento Supr & Mcpl Cts 720 9th St Sacramento CA 95814

ROOT, NILE, photographer, educator; b. Denver, Dec. 11, 1926; s. Victor Nile and Ella May (Holaway) R.; student U. Denver, 1968; MS in Instructional Tech., Rochester Inst. Tech., 1978; m. Abigail Barton Brown, Feb. 5, 1960; 1 child, James Michael. Microphotographer, U.S. Dept. Commerce, Fed. Republic Germany, 1946-48; free-lance photographer, 1949-51; pres. Photography Workshop, Inc., Denver, 1952-60; dir. dept. biophotography and med. illustration Gen. Rose Meml. Hosp., Denver, 1960-70; dir. med. illustration dept. Children's Hosp., Denver, 1970-71; dir. Photography for Sci., Denver, 1971-72; prof. biomed. photog. communications Rochester Inst. Tech. (N.Y.), 1972-86 , chmn. dept., 1974-86, prof. emeritus, 1986—; travel writer, photographer, Japan, China, S.E. Asia, 1986-89; writer, photographer, Tucson, 1989—. dir. HEW project for devel. of field, 1974-77. Served with USN, 1945-46. Recipient numerous awards for sci. photographs; Eisenhart Outstanding Tchr. award Rochester Inst. Tech., 1986; 1st Ann. Faculty fellow Sch. Photog. Arts and Scis., Rochester Inst. Tech., 1979. Fellow Biol. Photog. Assn. (registered, bd. govs. 1977-79, Louis Schmidt award 1986); mem. Ctr. Creative Photography, Friends of Photography, Internat. Mus. Photography. Democrat. Contbr. illustrations to med. textbooks; represented in numerous mus. photog. exhibits. Home and Office: 314 N Banff Ave Tucson AZ 85748-3311

ROOT, ROBERT ALAN, ecologist, project manager; b. Erie, Pa., Mar. 29, 1940; s. Kenneth Melvin and Anne Dorothy (Smith) R.; m. Jill Brainerd, June 25, 1966; children: Michael Shephard, Cynthia Anne. BS, U. Maine, 1963; MS, U. Mont., 1968; PhD, Miami U., Oxford, Ohio, 1971. Rsch. assoc. U. Ill., Urbana, 1971-73; sr. ecologist, project mgr. Dames and Moore, Park Ridge, Ill., 1973-80; project coord. Dames and Moore, Sydney, Australia, 1981-83; lectr. U. Mass., Amherst, 1984; sr. environ. mgr. Battelle Meml. Inst., Columbus, Ohio, 1985-87; dep. program mgr. Battelle Meml. Inst., Springfield, Ill., 1988-92; sr. rsch. scientist Battelle Meml. Inst., Albuquerque, 1993—; adj. asst. prof. botany dept. Ohio State U., Columbus, 1987-92. Co-author: (travel guide) Interstate 90: A Guide to Points You Can See-Without Stopping, 1984. Pres., mem. Dist. 21 Sch. Bd., Wheeling-Buffalo Grove, Ill., 1979-81. Recipient Cert. of Appreciation, U.S. Dept. Energy, 1987. Mem. Ecol. Soc. Am. (sr. ecologist), Nature Conservancy. Office: Battelle Meml Inst 2000 Randolph Rd SE Ste 105 Albuquerque NM 87106-5300

ROOT, WILLIAM DIXON, construction company executive; b. Medford, Oreg., July 27, 1951; s. Earl Merrit and Helen Edith (Dixon) R.; m. Catherine Jeanine Smiraglia, July 10, 1981; children: Stacie Marie, Shawn Dixon. BSBA, U. Nev., Reno, 1978. Contr., sec.-treas. Jensen Elec., Inc., Reno, 1977-82; v.p., sec.-treas. Clark & Sullivan, Inc., Reno, 1982—; v.p., asst. sec. G & S Gen. Inc., Reno, 1986—; v.p., sec., treas. Westech Devel., Reno, 1986—, also bd. dirs.; cons. Micro-Tech., Reno, 1984-93. Mem. Am. Coun. for Constrn. Edn., Assn. Systems Mgrs. Constrn. Fin. Mgrs. Assn. (v.p. 1986-88, pres. 1988-90, chmn., 1990—, nat. bd. dirs., nat. chmn. chpt. formation com., exec. com., vice chmn. conf. planning com., chmn. liaison com. 1995—), Assn. Gen. Contractors, Sierra Nevada IBM Users, Sertoma Club (treas. 1983-88, Centurian award 1986, Tribune award 1989, Disting Svc. award 1989), Rotary (sgt. arms, treas. 1995—), Sierra Challenge Athletics Assn. (pres., past treas). Republican. Home: 2505 Homeland Dr Reno NV 89511-9269 Office: Clark & Sullivan Inc 905 Industrial Way Sparks NV 89431-6009

ROPCHAN, REBECCA G., nursing administrator; b. Decatur, Ill., Apr. 6, 1950; d. Jack R. and Mildred E. (Mecum) Hathaway; m. Jim. R. Ropchan, June 13, 1987. Diploma, St. Lukes Hosp. Sch. Nursing, St. Louis, 1971; BS in Nursing, St. Louis U., 1974, MS in Nursing, 1976. Cardiovascular clin. nurse specialist UCLA Med. Ctr., asst. dir. nursing, assoc. dir. nursing, 1976-91; v.p. City Hope Nat. Med. Ctr., 1991-95; asst. adminstr. ops. Scripps Meml., Encinitas, Calif., 1995—; editorial bd. J.B. Lippencott, Dimesnions in Critical Care Nursing, 1982-89, Aspen Systems, Critical Care Quarterly, 1981—; nat. adv. com. Nursing Profl. Seminar Consultants, Inc., Albuquerque, 1980-88; lectr., cons. in field. Contbr. numerous articles to profl. jours. Recipient Mgmt. & Profl. Staff Incentive award UCLA Med. Ctr., 1989, UCLA Med. Ctr. Spl. Performance award, 1984, Rufus D. Putney Meml. award, 1971, Excellence award Am. Acad. Nurse Practitioners, State of Calif., 1995. Mem. AACN, Am. Orgn. Nurse Execs., Orgn. Nurse Execs. Calif., Oncology Nurse Soc., Am. Acad. Med. Adminstrs., Am. Coll. Oncology Adminstrs., Sigma Theta Tau.

RORABAUGH, WILLIAM JOSEPH, historian; b. Louisville, Dec. 11, 1945; s. Matthew Irvin and Agnes Cecilia (Graf) R. AB in History, Stanford U., 1968; MA in History, U. Calif., Berkeley, 1970, PhD in History, 1976. Asst. prof. history U. Wash., Seattle, 1976-82, assoc. prof., 1982-87, prof., 1987—. Author: The Alcoholic Republic, 1979, The Craft Apprentice, 1986, Berkeley at War: The 1960s, 1989; co-author: America! A Concise History, 1994. NEH fellow, 1981, Nat. Humanities Ctr. fellow, Research Triangle Park, N.C., 1983-84, Sorensen fellow John F. Kennedy Presdl. Libr., Boston, 1992; recipient Book prize Old Sturbridge Village, Sturbridge, Mass., 1987. Mem. Am. Hist. Assn., Orgn. Am. Historians, Soc. for Historians of Early Am. Republic (pres. 1993-94), Alcohol and Temperance History Group. Office: Univ Wash Dept History DP20 Seattle WA 98195

ROSA, EUGENE ANTHONY, sociologist, environmental scientist, educator; b. Canandaigua, N.Y., Sept. 20, 1941; s. Louis Gastaldo and Flora Louise (Brevette) R.; m. Jody Ross, Sept. 7, 1985 (div. 1993). BS, Rochester Inst. Tech., 1967; MA, Syracuse U., 1975, PhD, 1976. Research assoc., instr. Stanford U., 1976-78; from asst. to prof. Wash. State U., Pullman, 1978—; cons. Brookhaven Nat. Lab., Upton, N.Y., 1978—, Nuclear Regulatory Commn., Washington, 1978—; vis. prof. London Sch. Econs., 1988. Editor: Public Reactions to Nuclear Power, 1984, Pub. Reactions to Nuclear Waste, 1993; contbr. articles to profl. jours. Mem. nuclear waste adv. coun. Wash. State, 1987-92. Mem. Am. Sociol. Assn., AAAS, Am. Acad. Polit. and Social Scis., N.Y. Acad. Scis., Internat. Soc. Assn., Soc. for Human

Ecology, Soc. Risk Analysis, Sigma Xi. Home: 1007 NE Alfred Ln Pullman WA 99163-3950 Office: Wash State U Dept Sociology Pullman WA 99164

ROSA, FREDRIC DAVID, residential construction executive; b. Monroe, Wis., Oct. 31, 1946; s. Fredric Carl Rosa and Irene (Sommers) Rosa Figi; m. Melanie A. Downs, May 31, 1986; children: Mark, Katherine. BBA in Mktg., U. Wis., 1968. Dir. mktg. Swiss Colony Stores, Inc., Monroe, 1968-80; pres. Videotape Indsl. Prodns., Inc., Madison, Wis., 1980-82; agt. VR Bus. Brokers, Colorado Springs, Colo., 1982-83; sales rep. NCR Corp., Denver, 1983-85; prin. F. D. Rosa & Assocs., Denver, Aspen and Eagle, Colo., 1985-89; pres. Peak Benefit Cons., Colorado Springs, 1989-95; registered prin. Nexus Fin. Programs, Inc., Colorado Springs, Colo., 1990-92, Nutmeg Securities Ltd., Colorado Springs, 1992-94; sales staff Am. Airlines, Colorado Springs, Colo., 1993-95; cons. Kolb-Lena Cheese Co., Lena, Ill., 1983-85; instr. The Am. Coll., Bryn Mawr, Pa., 1990-91; owner Rosa Constrn., Colorado Springs, 1990-94, Lakewood, Colo., 1995—. Contbr. articles to trade publs. and newspapers. Mem. Am. Soc. CLU and Chartered Fin. Cons., Mensa, Internat. Legion of Intelligence, Delta Sigma Pi (life). Methodist. Home and Office: Rosa Constrn 1270 Cody St Denver CO 80215-4897

ROSALDO, RENATO IGNACIO, JR., cultural anthropology educator; b. Champaign, Ill., Apr. 15, 1941; s. Renato Ignacio and Mary Elizabeth (Potter) R.; m. Michelle Sharon Zimbalist, June 12, 1966 (dec. Oct. 1981); children: Samuel Mario, Manuel Zimbalist; m. Mary Louise Pratt, Nov. 26, 1983; 1 child, Olivia Emilia Rosaldo-Pratt. AB, Harvard U., 1963, PhD, 1971. Asst. prof. cultural anthropology Stanford (Calif.) U., 1970-76, assoc. prof., 1976-85, prof., 1985—, Mellon prof. interdisciplinary studies, 1987-90, dir. Ctr. for Chicano Rsch., 1985-90; chair anthropology, 1994—, Lucie Stern prof. social scis., 1993—. Author: Ilongot Headhunting 1883-1974, 1980, Culture and Truth, 1989. Recipient Harry Benda prize Assn. for Asian Studies, 1983; Guggenheim fellow, 1993. Home: 2520 Cowper St Palo Alto CA 94301-4218 Office: Stanford U Dept Anthropology Stanford CA 94305-2145

ROSALES, SUZANNE MARIE, hospital coordinator; b. Merced, Calif., July 23, 1946; d. Walter Marshall and Ellen Marie (Earl) Potter; children: Anita Carol, Michelle Suzanne. AA, City Coll., San Francisco, 1966. Diplomate Am. Coll. Utilization Review Physicians. Utilization review coord. San Francisco Gen. Hosp., 1967-74; mgr. utilization review/discharge planning UCLA Hosp. and Clinics, 1974-79; nurse III Hawaii State Hosp., Kaneohe, 1979-80; review coord. Pacific Profl. Std. Review Orgn., Honolulu, 1980-81; coord. admission and utilization reviewq The Rehab. Hosp. of the Pacific, Honolulu, 1981-85; coord. Pacific Med. Referral Project, Honolulu, 1985-87; dir. profl. svcs. The Queen's Healthcare Plan, Honolulu, 1987-88; utilization mgmt. coord. Vista Psychiat. Physician Assocs., San Diego, 1989; admission coord. utilization review San Francisco Gen. Hosp., 1989-91, quality improvement coordinator, 1991—; cons. Am. Med. Records Assn. Contbr. articles to profl. jours. Mem. Nat. Assn. Utilization Review Profls. Home: 505 Hanover St Daly City CA 94014-1351 Office: San Francisco Gen Hosp 1001 Potrero Ave San Francisco CA 94110-3518

ROSANDER, ARLYN CUSTER, mathematical statistician, management consultant; b. Mason County, Mich., Oct. 7, 1903; s. John Carl and Nellie May (Palmer) R.; m. Beatrice White, Aug. 26, 1933 (div.); children: Nancy Rosander Peck, Robert Richard Roger (dec.); m. Margaret Ruth Guest, Aug. 15, 1964. BS, U. Mich. 1925; MA, U. Wis., 1928; PhD, U. Chgo., 1933; postgrad. Dept. Agr., 1937-39. Rsch. asst. U. Chgo., 1933-34; rsch. fellow Gen. Edn. Bd. Tech. dir. Am. Youth Commn., Balt. and Washington, 1935-37; chief statistician urban study U.S. Bur. Labor Stats., Washington, 1937-39; sect. and br. chief War Prodn. Bd., Washington, 1940-45; chief statistician IRS, Washington, 1945-61; chief math. and stats. sect. ICC, Washington, 1961-69; cons. Pres.'s Commn. on Fed. Stats., Washington, 1970-71; cons., Loveland, Colo.; lectr. stats. George Washington U., 1946-52. Recipient Civilian War Service award War Prodn. Bd., 1945; Spl. Performance award Dept. Treasury, 1961. Fellow AAAS, Am. Soc. Quality Control (25 yr. honor award 1980, Howard Jones Meml. award 1984, chmn. emeritus svc. industries divsn. 1991, A.C. Rosander award Svc. Industries divsn. 1991); mem. Am. Statis. Assn. Author: Elementary Principles of Statistics, 1951; Statistical Quality Control in Tax Operations, IRS, 1958; Case Studies in Sample Design, 1977; Application of Quality Control to Service Industries, 1985, Washington Story 1985, The Quest for Quality in Services, 1989 (translated into Spanish, 1993, Italian, 1994), Deming's 14 Points Applied to Services, 1991 (translated into Spanish, 1994). Home and Office: 4330 Franklin Ave Loveland CO 80538-1715

ROSE, BARBARA, executive recruiter; b. N.Y.C., Dec. 24, 1932; d. Irving S. and Frieda (Gelband) Feitelson; 1 child, Jason Immanuel. BS, Hunter Coll.; MSW, Columbia U. Pvt. practice psychotherapy N.Y.C., 1958-72, Vt., 1972-79; tech. mgr., supr. and employment cons. various tech. recruitment firms, Calif., 1979-85; founder, exec. recruiter Rose & Assocs., Aptos, Calif., 1985—; exec. recruiter Contingency Search Recruitment, 1985-89; cons. on career transitioning, Aptos, 1990—; leader workshops on stress reduction, goal setting and envisioning for corps.

ROSE, CAROL DENISE, orthopedic unit nurse administrator, educator; b. Las Vegas, Nev., July 31, 1960; d. Howard Elden and Sarah (Haley) Heckethorn; m. Michael Shaun Rose, June 19, 1982; 1 child, Carissa Denise. ADN, U. Nev., Las Vegas, 1981, BSN, 1985. Staff nurse orthopedic unit Univ. Med. Ctr. So. Nev., Las Vegas, 1981-84, acting head nurse, then head nurse orthopedic unit, 1984-88, asst. mgr. orthopedic unit, 1988, orthopedic unit mgr., 1988—; adj. faculty health scis. dept. Clark County C.C., North Las Vegas, Nev.; speaker at profl. confs. Mem. ANA, Nat. Assn. Orthopaedic Nurses (pres. So. Nev. chpt.), Sigma Theta Tau, Phi Kappa Phi. Democrat. Roman Catholic. Office: Univ Med Ctr So Nev 1800 W Charleston Blvd Las Vegas NV 89102-2329

ROSE, CYNTHIA, psychiatrist; b. Boston, Apr. 26, 1936; came to U.S., 1936; d. Irving and Eleanor Lillian (Fox) R.; m. Cameron E. Berry, June 6, 1964 (div. Oct. 1979); children: Scott David,Daniel Irving. AB, Tufts U., 1959; MD, Boston U., 1963. Diplomate Am. Bd. Psychiatry and Neurology. Intern U. Calif. Hosps., San Francisco, 1963-64; resident U. Colo. Health Scis. Ctr., Denver, 1964-67; med. dir. Pikes Peak Mental Health Ctr., Colorado Springs, Colo., 1970-84; psychiat. staff cons. Colo. Coll., Colorado Springs, 1970-77; asst. clin. prof. psychiatry U. Colo. Health Scis. Ctr., Denver, 1975-81, assoc. clin. prof., 1981—; pvt. practice Colorado Springs, 1981—; bd. mem. Psychiatrist's Mut. Ins., Barbados, 1993—. Mem. adv. bd. Head Start, Colorado Springs, 1969-72; mem. Citizens Goals, Colorado Springs, 1978-80. U. Colo. Health Scis. Ctr. child psychiatry fellow, 1967-69. Fellow Am. Psychiat. Assn. (area rep. to assembly 1983-90, exec. com. assembly 1984-90); mem. AMA, Colo. Psychiat. Soc. (sec. 1979-80, pres. 81-82, Spokesperson of Yr. 1991), Colo. Psychiat. Assn., Airplane Owners and Pilots Assn.,Colo. Internat. Women's Forum, Am. Acad. Child and Adolescent Psychiatry, Am. Psychoanalytic Assn. (affiliate). Office: 730 N Cascade Ave Ste 2 Colorado Springs CO 80903-3258

ROSE, DAVID WILLIAM, psychologist, consultant; b. Denver, Oct. 14, 1930; s. Clarence William and Marjorie (Skiff) R.; m. Ruth MacDonald, Dec. 27, 1957 (div. Jan. 1967); children: Scott David, Frederick William, Catharine Jean Hayes; m. Lorretta Espinosa, Oct. 5, 1973; 1 child, Janet Kathleen. BA, U. Colo., 1953; MS, U. Oreg., 1959, PhD, 1964. Lic. clin. psychologist, Colo. Psychologist trainee VA, Roseburg, Oreg., 1958-59, Vancouver, Wash., 1960-61; rsch. asst. U. Oreg., Eugene, 1961-62; clin. trainee USPHS, Eugene, 1962-63; from clin. psychologist to chief psychologist forensic div. Colo. State Hosp., Pueblo, 1963-90; ret., 1990, pvt. practice, , 1990—. Mem. APA, Colo. Psychol. Assn., Rocky Mountain Psychol. Assn., Sr. Counseling Group, Am. Psychology-Law Soc., Am. Soc. Criminology, Am. Correctional Assn. Home: 13 Swift Arrow Ct Pueblo CO 81001-1810 Office: 502 Jackson St Pueblo CO 81004-1834

ROSE, FAYE SCHUMAN, university department director communications; b. Mt. Vernon, Ill.; m. Seymour J. Rose, June 21, 1953 (div. Dec. 1979); children: Lawrence Jay, Susan Alison Rose Verner. BSBA, Washington U., St. Louis, 1952. Pub. affairs asst. San Diego C.C. Dist., 1975-77; pub. affairs writer San Diego State U., 1977-79; dir. comms. San Diego State U. Coll. of Extended Studies, 1979—. Officer LWV. 1965-66; candidate Bd. Edn., San Diego, 1972. Recipient Best Audio/Visual Program award, Internat. Assn. Bus. Comms., 1987. Mem. Pub. Rels. Soc. Am., Pub. Rels. Club San Diego (Best Publicity Program 1989, Best Brochure 1990), San Diego Mus. Art, City Club San Diego, Coun. for Advancement and Support of Edn., San Diego Press Club. Office: San Diego State U 5250 Campanile Dr San Diego CA 92182-1901

ROSE, GREGORY MANCEL, neurobiologist; b. Eugene, Oreg., Feb. 3, 1953; s. Mancel Lee and Ilione (Schenk) R.; m. Kathleen Ann Frye, June 30, 1979; 1 child, Julian Mancel. BS cum laude, U. Calif., Irvine, 1975, PhD, 1980. Research fellow M.P.I. for Psychiatry, Munich, 1976; rsch. assoc. Miescher Labor, M.P.I., Tuebingen, Republic of Germany, 1980-81; regular fellow dept. pharmacology U. Colo. Health Sci. Ctr., Denver, 1981-84, asst. prof., 1984-89, assoc. prof., 1989—; rsch. biologist VA Med. Ctr., Denver, 1981—, co-dir. neurosci. tng. program, 1986-89, assoc. rsch. career scientist, 1989—. Achievements include discovery of importance of stimulus patterning for induction of hippocampal synaptic plasticity. Bd. dirs. Greater Park Hill Community, 1987-90. VA Rsch. Svc. grantee, 1984, 86, 89, 93, NSF grantee, 1988, 90, NIMH grantee, 1989, 94, NIA grantee, 1991. Mem. AAAS, Am. Aging Assn., Soc. Neurosci., Internat. Brain Rsch. Orgn., Soc. Neurosci., N.Y. Acad. Sci. Democrat. Episcopalian. Office: VA Med Ctr Rsch Svc 1055 Clermont St # 151 Denver CO 80220-3808

ROSE, HOWARD D., insurance company executive; b. May 5, 1962. BA in Math., Cornell U., 1984; cert. in systems engring., Electronic Data Systems Corp., 1986. Systems engr. Electronic Data Systems, Dallas, 1985-87; project leader, systems analyst Hughes Aircraft, El Segundo, Calif., 1987-90; I/S project mgr. Farmers Ins. Group, L.A., 1990-94; mgr. SW engring. and system devel. divsn. Prudential Ins., Canoga Park, Calif., 1994—. Author: (with others) Software vol. of Computer Systems Series. Home: 2465 Haring St Apt 5A Brooklyn NY 11235-1810

ROSE, HUGH, management consultant; b. Evanston, Ill., Sept. 10, 1926; s. Howard Gray and Catherine (Wilcox) R.; m. Mary Moore Austin, Oct. 25, 1952; children: Susan, Nancy, Gregory, Matthew, Mary. BS in Physics, U. Mich., 1951, MS in Geophysics, 1952; MBA with highest distinction, Pepperdine U., 1982. Mgr. Caterpillar, Inc., Peoria, Ill., 1952-66; v.p., mktg. mgr. Cummins Engine Co., Columbus, Ind., 1966-69; pres., chief exec. officer Cummins Northeastern, Inc., Boston, 1969-77; pres. Power Systems Assocs., L.A., 1980-83, C.D. High Tech., Inc., Austin, Tex., 1984-87; mgmt. cons. Rose and Assocs., Tucson, 1984, 87—. Contbr. paleontol. articles to various publs. Bd. dirs. Raymond Alf Mus., Claremont, Calif., 1975—, Comstock Found., Tucson, 1988, Environ. Edn. Exch., 1991, Heart Ctr. U. Ariz., Tucson, 1992. With USAAF, WWII. Fellow AAAS; mem. Soc. Vertebrate Paleontology, Beacon Soc. Boston (pres. 1979-80), Algonquin Club Boston (v.p., bd. dirs. 1974-80), Duxbury Yacht Club, Longwood Cricket Club, Delta Mu Delta, Sigma Gamma Epsilon, Beta Beta Beta. Republican. Presbyterian. Office: Rose & Assocs 5320 N Camino Sumo Tucson AZ 85718-5132

ROSE, MASON H., IV, psychoanalyst; b. Charlevoix, Mich., July 4, 1915; s. Mason III and Catharine (DIebel) R.; m. Marlene Alexander, 1990. Student, Philips Exeter, 1932, U. Fla., 1933, Duke U., 1934, U. So. Calif., 1935; B.A., Inst. Religious Sci., 1939; MS, Calif. Inst. Advanced Studies, 1943, PhD, 1946; LL.D. (hon.), Asso. Univs., Hong Kong, 1959. Tennis profl. The Inn, Charlevoix, 1932-35; lectr. Inst. Religious Sci., 1937-43; pvt. practice psychoanalysis Los Angeles, 1941—; exec. dir. Nat. Found. Psychol. Research, 1940-60; psychol. cons. Med. Found. Am., 1948-62; leader Humanist Ch. of Religious Sci., 1957—; v.p., dean undergrad. sch. Calif. Inst. Advanced Study, 1959-65; chancellor Pacific Inst. Advanced Studies, 1965—; pres. Mason Rose & Assocs.; chmn. Gt. Books of Modern World, 1959—; exec dir. Olympic League Am., 1967—; bd. dirs. Ctr. Organic Ecology, 1968—, Everywoman's Village, 1960-70, Disease Prevention and Life Extension Ctr.; cons. World Ecology Corp., 1969—, World Environ. Systems, 1970—. Author: You and Your Personality, 1944, Community Plan for the Returning Serviceman, 1945, Sex Education from Birth to Maturity, 1948, Creative Education, 1953, Humanism as Religion, 1959, The Nutra-Bio-Zyme Soil Management System, 1969, The Nutra-Bio-Zyme Manutrol System, 1970, Bio-N-Gest Sewage Treatment and Water Reclamation System, 1970, Bio-N-Gest Wast Recycling System, 1970, Bio-Dynamics, 1970, The Island Tribe, 1971, New Hopes for the Emotionally Disturbed Child, 1974, 2d edit., 1977, Humanics Health System, 1975, Medical Survey of Nutrition for Pregnancy and Lactation, 1976, How to Provide Optimum Nutrition for You and Your Child, 1978, Suntanning, The World's Most Dangerous Sport, 1979, How to Scare Your Teenager Straight, 1980, Radiant Living, 1986, Multimodal System for the Management of Pain and Stress, 1987, Glasscrete System of Construction, 1987, Macho Manifesto, How to Avoid Rape, 1991, 2nd edit., 1994, Glamorous Hollywood- Fabulous Hollywood, 1994; syndicated newspaper column You and Your Child, 1950-54; TV programs, 1951-52. Mem. AAAS, NAACP, ACLU, Fedn. Am. Scientists, Soc. Social Responsibility in Sci., Aircraft Owners and Pilots Assn., Helms Athletic Found. (life), So. Calif. Olympic Games Com., Philips Exeter Acad. Alumni Assn., PEN, So. Calif. Publicists, Trojan Football Alumni, Athletic Club (L.A.), Press Club (L.A., adv. bd. 1952-75).

ROSE, RAY VINCENT, surgeon; b. St. Paul, May 5, 1921; s. Raymond Charles and Vinnie Kathryn (Falk) R.; m. Elsa Marie Janda, June 25, 1948; children: Steven, Anita, Richard, Laura, Lynnette. BS, U. Minn., 1943, MB, 1946, MD, 1946. Diplomate Am. Bd. Surgery. Intern U. Colo. Med. Ctr., Denver, 1946-47, resident, 1949-51, resident in surgery, 1951-54; pvt. practice Pasco, Wash., 1954—; bd. dirs. Our Lady of Lourdes Hosp., Pasco, 1972-80. Bd. dirs. Wash. divsn. Am. Cancer Soc., Seattle, 1993—, Tri City Cancer Ctr., Wash., 1993—. Capt. USAF, 1947-49. Fellow ACS (past pres. Wash. chpt. 1973-74); mem. Wash. State Med. Assn. (past trustee), AMA, Benton Franklin County Med. Soc. (past pres. 1965). Home: 4508 Riverhaven St Pasco WA 99301-3015 Office: 516 W Margaret St Pasco WA 99301-5273

ROSE, ROBERT E(DGAR), state supreme court justice; b. Orange, N.J., Oct. 7, 1939. B.A., Juniata Coll., Huntingdon, Pa., 1961; LL.B., NYU, 1964. Bar: Nev. 1965. Dist. atty. Washoe County, 1971-75; lt. gov. State of Nev., 1975-79; judge Nev. Dist. Ct., 8th Jud. Dist., Las Vegas, 1986-88; justice Nev. Supreme Ct., Carson City, 1989—, chief justice, 1993-94. Office: Nev Supreme Ct 201 S Carson St Carson City NV 89701

ROSEBERRY, EDWIN SOUTHALL, state agency administrator; b. Roanoke, Va., July 4, 1925; s. Edwin Alexander and Gladys Edmonia (Southall) R.; m. Mary Louise Sprengel, Sept. 2, 1949 (dec. 1978); children: Edwin Jr., David, Kevin; m. Alice Proffit Boger, Dec. 27, 1980; 1 stepdaughter, Elizabeth Leigh Boger. BS in Commerce, U. Va., 1949. Registered sanitarian, Hawaii, Va. Store mgr. Allied Arts, Charlottesville, Va., 1949-51; retail credit sales mgr. B.F. Goodrich Co., Charlottesville, 1951-53; environ. health specialist Dept. of Health, Charlottesville, 1953-84, Dept. of Labor, Honolulu, 1987—; self-employed photographer, Charlottesville, 1949-85, Honolulu, 1985—. Contbr. photographs: The Inward Eye, 1986. Election ofcl. State of Hawaii, Honolulu, 1988—. With USN, 1944-46. Recipient numerous nat. awards Eastman Kodak Co., nat. newspapers, and photography mags., 1951-69. Mem. Am. Indsl. Hygiene Assn., Austrian Hawaiian Club (v.p., bd. dirs. 1985), Antique Auto Assn. (pres. Piedmont region 1964), Hawaii Photo Soc. (v.p. 1989), Elks (tiler and inner guard 1985), Pi Delta Epsilon. Episcopalian. Home: 1101E Kumukumu St Honolulu HI 96825-2602 Office: State of Hawaii DLIR/DOSH 830 Punchbowl St Honolulu HI 96813-5045

ROSEHNAL, MARY ANN, educational administrator; b. Bklyn., July 25, 1943; d. Frank Joseph and Mary Anna (Corso) R.; 1 child, Scott Stoddart. BA in Sociology, San Francisco State U., 1968; M in Sch. Bus. Adminstrn., No. Ariz. U., 1985. Lic. substitute tchr., Ariz.; lic. vocat. nurse, Calif.; cert. sch. bus. mgr., Ariz. Deliquency counselor, Calif., 1969-73; office mgr. Nurses Central Registry, Sun City, Ariz., 1973-75; bus. mgr. Nadaburg sch. dist., Wittmann, Ariz., 1975-78, Morristown (Ariz.) sch. dist., 1978—; served on 1st Assessment Handbook editing task force, Fair Employment Practices Handbook task force, 1979-80; mem. tech. adv. com. Ariz. Dept. Edn., 1993-94; mem. adv. com. Ariz. Auditor Gen. Uniform Sys. Fin. Records; mem. tech. adv. com. Ariz. Dept. Edn. Columnist Wickenburg Sun, 1975—. Clk. Morristown sch. bd., 1974-76; pres. Morristown PTA, 1977-78; sec. Wickenburg area bd., 1979; bd. dirs. Future Frontiers, 1979-81; rep. HUD block grant adv. com., 1979-85; active Wickenburg Friends of Music, 1984—, bd. dirs., 1986—, sec. bd. dirs., 1986-92; sec. Wickenburg Regional Health Care Found., 1989-92, trustee, 1988—. Named to Ariz. Sch. Bd. Assn. Honor Roll, 1976; named Morristown Area Vol. of Yr., 1988. Mem. Assn. Govt. Accts., Ariz. Assn. Sch. Bus. Ofcls. (fin. dir., bd. dirs. 1985-91, v.p. 1991, pres. elect 1992-93, pres. 1993-94, immediate past pres. 1994-95, Gold awards 1986, 87, 88, 90, 91, 92, 93, 94, Silver award 1989), Assn. Sch. Bus. Ofcls. Internat. (mem. pres.'s adv. coun. 1993-94, election com. 1994-95), Morristown Federated Women's Club (edn. chair 1990-94, Wickenburg scenic corridor com. 1990-92), Ariz. Theatre Guild, Wickenberg C. of C. (assoc.). Roman Catholic. Office: PO Box 98 Morristown AZ 85342-0098

ROSELL, SHARON LYNN, physics and chemistry educator, researcher; b. Wichita, Kans., Jan. 6, 1948; d. John E. and Mildred C. (Binder) R. BA, Loretto Heights Coll., 1970; postgrad., Marshall U., 1973; MS in Edn., Ind. U., 1977; MS, U. Wash., 1988. Cert. profl. educator, Wash. Assoc. instr. Ind. U., Bloomington, 1973-74; instr. Pierce Coll. (name formerly Ft. Steilacoom (Wash.) Community Coll.), 1976-79, 82, Olympic Coll., Bremerton, Wash., 1977-78; instr. physics, math. and chemistry Tacoma (Wash.) Community Coll., 1979-89; instr. physics and chemistry Green River Community Coll., Auburn, Wash., 1983-86; researcher Nuclear Physics Lab., U. Wash., Seattle, 1986-88; asst. prof. physics Cen. Wash. U., Ellensburg, 1989—. Lector and dir. Rite of Christian Initiation of Adults, St. Andrew's Ch., Ellensburg, Wash., 1993—, mem. parish coun., 1995—. Mem. Am. Assn. Physics Tchrs. (rep. com. on physics for 2-yr. colls. Wash. chpt. 1986-87, v.p. 1987-88, 94-95, pres. 1988-89, 95-96), Am. Chem. Soc., Math Assn. Am., Internat. Union Pure and Applied Chemistry (allifiate), St. Andrew's Ch. (parish coun.), Ellensburg, Wash., 1995—. Democrat. Roman Catholic. Home: 1100 N B St Apt 2 Ellensburg WA 98926-2570 Office: Cen Wash U Physics Dept Ellensburg WA 98926

ROSELLE, RICHARD DONALDSON, industrial, marine and interior designer; b. Garwood, N.J., Nov. 20, 1916; s. Ernest North and Mary Elizabeth (Donaldson) R.; m. Eunice Calpin, June 28, 1947 (div. Oct. 1981); children: Sheryn, Christina, Gail; m. Judith Marie Bishop, Nov. 13, 1982. Student, St. John's Mil. Acad., 1935, Aurora (Ill.) Coll., 1935-37, Bucknell U., 1937-39. Exec. trainee J.J. Newberry Co., N.Y.C., 1939-41, G. Fox & Co., Hartford, Conn., 1941-42; materials expeditor Pratt & Whitney Aircraft, Hartford, 1942-43; exec. trainee, indsl. engr. TWA Airline, N.Y.C. and Kansas City, 1943-47; with employee rels. staff R.H. Macy, N.Y.C., 1947-49; asst. tng. dir. J.C. Penney Co., N.Y.C., 1949-50; owner Roselle Tile Mfr., Seattle, 1950-56; sr. indsl. designer Walter Dorwin Teague Assocs., Seattle, 1956-63; owner Roselle Design Internat., Inc., Seattle, 1963—; dir. Roselle Design Tours Internat., Seattle, 1967-93; internat. bus. developer via confs., 1993—. Mem. Am. Soc. Interior Design (nat. edn. chair 1972-74), Indsl. Designers Soc. Am. (charter), Internat. Inst. Profl. Designers, Master Resources Coun. Internat. (founder, pres.), Soc. Am. Mil. Engrs., Rotary. Republican. Episcopalian. Office: Roselle Design Internat Camelot Atelier 3854 140th Ave NE Bellevue WA 98005-1451

ROSEME, SHARON DAY, lawyer; b. Sacramento, Aug. 6, 1953; d. George Roseme and Alice Diane Day; m. Daniel George Glenn, June 26, 1982 (div. Nov. 1989); 1 child, Hilary. Student, San Francisco State U., 1971-72; BA, U. Calif., Santa Cruz, 1975; JD, Boalt Hall Sch. of Law, 1978. Jud. staff atty. Calif. State Ct. of Appeal, San Francisco, 1978-80; assoc. Feldman, Waldman & Kline, San Francisco, 1980-82, McDonough, Holland & Allen, Sacramento, 1982—. Contbr. articles to profl. jours. Mem. ABA, State Bar Calif., County Bar Sacramento, County Bar Placer, County Bar San Francisco, Comml. Real Estate Woman Sacramento, Order of Coif. Office: McDonough Holland & Allen 555 Capitol Mall Ste 950 Sacramento CA 95814-4601

ROSEN, ALEXANDER CARL, psychologist, consultant; b. L.A., Feb. 2, 1923; s. Benjamin and Pauline (Katz) R.; m. Florence Friedman, Mar. 18, 1951 (div. Nov. 1973); children: Diane, Judith; m. Susan Margaret Gersbacher, Nov. 4, 1973; 1 child, Rebecca. AA, U. Calif., L.A., 1943; AB, U. Calif., Berkeley, 1946, PhD, 1953. Diplomate clin. psychology Am. Bd. Profl. Psychology; lic. psychologist. Psychologist Contra Costa County, Martinez, Calif., 1953-56; asst. rsch. psychologist Office Naval Rsch. and San Francisco State Coll., 1953-56, UCLA-Neuropsychiat. Inst., L.A., 1956-57; asst. prof. to prof. psychiatry and behavioral sci. UCLA Sch. Medicine, L.A., 1956-89; chief psychology UCLA Neuropsychiatric Inst., L.A., 1958-89; prof. emeritus UCLA Sch. Medicine, L.A., 1989—; pvt. practice psychology cons. L.A., 1973—; instr. San Francisco State Coll., 1955; instr. psychology Calif. Inst. Tech., Pasadena, 1969; staff assoc. Nat. Tng. Lab. Inst. Applied Behavioral Sci., 1962—; cons. tng. U.S. Veteran's Assn., Sepulveda (Calif.) Hosp., 1966—; bd. mem. L.A. Group Psychotherapy Tng. Inst., 1972-75; bd. mem., trustee Calif. Sch. Profl. Psychology, 1974-76, 78; nat. bd., regional bd. Cert. Cons. Internat. Cons. Cons. editor: Jour. Genetic Psychology and Genetic Psychology Monograph, 1984—; contbr. articles to profl. jours. Mem. gov. bd. Hillel Coun., So. Calif.; cons. San Fernando Valley Counseling Ctr., 1991-92, Pacific Ctr. for AIDS, L.A., 1991-94; adv. bd. mem. CSN Valley Youth Orch. Fellow APA, AAAS; mem. Calif. State Psychology Assn. (pres. 1977-78), Western Psychol. Assn. Home: 6247 Sunnyslope Ave Van Nuys CA 91401 :

ROSEN, DAVID ALLEN, manufacturing executive; b. Anchorage, Aug. 4, 1955; s. Harold E. and Marlene (Allen) R.; m. Phyllis A. Romans, Aug. 19, 1980; children: Stephanie, Kevin, Stanford, Alex, Samuel, Kimberly. BS in Bus., Brigham Young U., 1980; MBA, U. Utah, 1990. Coord. Youth Devel. Enterprises, Salt Lake City, 1978-79; instr. Brigham Young U., Provo, 1980; v.p., loan officer Key Bank of Utah, Salt Lake City, 1980-92; dir. of mfg. Larson-Davis Labs., Provo, 1992—; chmn. ATECC adv. com. Mountainland Region Applied Tech. Edn., 1994-95. Mem. fin. com. Greater Salt Lake City Area, YMCA, 1987-91. Mem. Brigham Young Univ. Mgmt. Soc. (Utah County chpt. 1994-95), Kiwanis (pres. 1990-91). Mem. LDS Ch. Home: 124 E 3800 N Provo UT 84604-4510 Office: Larson Davis Labs 1681 W 820 N Provo UT 84601-1341

ROSEN, MANUEL MORRISON, architect, educator; b. Mex., Dec. 2, 1926; came to U.S., 1980; s. Dan Rosen and Rose (Morrison) Konstat; m. Laura Faerman, Dec. 1, 1957; children: Ronald, Karen R. Behar, Dana R. Abed. BArch, Nat. U. Mex., Mexico City, 1953. Owner, pres. Manuel Rosen & Assocs., Mexico City, 1964-80, San Diego, 1985—; dean Sch. Architecture Universidad Iberoamericana; adj. prof. Sch. Environ. Design Calif. Poly. Inst.; pres. Mex. Cultural Inst., San Diego; pres. Technion-Friend, Mexico City, 1960-61, Knoll Furniture, Mexico City, 1960-63, Globus Devel., San Diego, 1987—; cons. Anshen & Allen, San Francisco; advisor New Sch. Architecture, Chula Vista, Calif., 1983; Mexican del. Architecture Congress, Washington; lectr. in field; dean Sch. Architecture U. Iberoamericana Tijuana, B.C.; chair internat. affairs confs., adj. prof. Sch. Architecture Calif. Poly. U., Pomona; prof., chair internat. affairs and lectures New Sch. Architecture, San Diego. Prin. works include Lindavista Area Condominium Bldg., Mexico City, Versalles Condominium Apts., Hillerman Bldg., Mexican Clin. Svcs. Hosp., Benihana's Restaurant, Mexico City, 1971-72, Oaxa (Mex.) Hotel, Hotel Presidente, Acapulco, Mex., Lace Factory, Mexico City, Theatre Ctr., Mexico City, Cultural and Tourist Ctr., Tijuana, Mex., Mus. Fray Anton de Monte Sinos St. Domineo, Dominican Republic, Master Plan Nuevo Vallarta, Mex.; interior designer numerous office bldgs, residences, desgner lamps, rugs, tiles, and other decorative elements; contbr. numerous articles to profl. jours. and newspapers. Bd. dirs. Friends of Tel Aviv Mus., 1982, San Diego Art Ctr., Architecture and Design Group, 1983; bd. govs. YMCA Northwest, La Jolla, Calif., 1983. Recipient numerous archtl. and design awards including 1st award in design for Olympic swimming pool and gymnasium Games of XIX Olympiad, 1968, XX Olympiad, 1972, Ann. prize Mexican Nat. U. Tech. Coun., 1972. Fellow AIA (hon.; chmn. continuing edn. com. 1983, Design award 1988), Mexican Acad. Architecture; mem. Soc. Mexican Architecture, Mexican Soc. Decorators, Mexican Coll. Architects, Nat. Soc. Interior Designers. Home: 7843 E Roseland Dr La Jolla CA 92037-4016 Office: Manuel Rosen 6215 Ferris Sq Ste 140 San Diego CA 92121-3251

ROSEN, MARTIN JACK, lawyer; b. L.A., Sept. 9, 1931; s. Irving and Sylvia (Savad) R.; B.A., UCLA, 1953; J.D., U. Calif.-Berkeley, 1956; m. Joan D. Meyersieck, Oct. 22, 1954; children—Dirk Rosen, Marika. Bar: Calif. 1957. Pvt. practice, Merced, Calif., 1960-62, San Francisco, 1962-82; mem.

Silver, Rosen, Fischer & Stecher, P.C., San Francisco, 1964—. Pres. Trust for Pub. Land, 1979—. Served with USAF, 1958-60. Fellow internat. legal studies U. Calif. Law Sch./Inst. Social Studies, The Hague, 1956-57.

ROSEN, MOISHE, religious organization administrator; b. Kansas City, Mo., Apr. 12, 1932; s. Ben and Rose (Baker) R.; m. Ceil Starr, Aug. 18, 1950; children: Lyn Rosen Bond, Ruth. Diploma, Northeastern Bible Coll., 1957; DD, Western Conservative Bapt. Sem., 1986. Ordained to ministry Bapt. Ch., 1957. Missionary Am. Bd. Missions to the Jews, N.Y.C., 1956; minister in charge Beth Sar Shalom Am. Bd. Missions to the Jews, Los Angeles, 1957-67; dir. recruiting and tng. Am. Bd. Missions to the Jews, N.Y.C., 1967-70; leader Jews for Jesus Movement, San Francisco, 1970-73, exec. dir., 1973—, founder, chmn., 1973—; speaker in field. Author: Saying of Chairman Moishe, 1972, Jews for Jesus, 1974, Share the New Life with a Jew, 1976, Christ in the Passover, 1977, Y'shua, The Jewish Way to Say Jesus, 1982, Overture to Armageddon, 1991, The Universe is Broken: Who on Earth Can Fix It?, 1991, Demystifying Personal Evangelism, 1992. Trustee Western Conservative Bapt. Sem., Portland, Oreg., 1979-85, 86-91, Bibl. Internat. Coun. on Bibl. Inerrancy, Oakland, Calif., 1979-89; bd. dirs. Christian Advs. Serving Evangelism, 1987-91. Office: Jews for Jesus 60 Haight St San Francisco CA 94102-5802

ROSEN, PETER, health facility administrator, emergency physician, educator; b. Bklyn., Aug. 3, 1935; s. Isadore Theodore and Jessie Olga (Solomon) R.; m. Ann Helen Rosen, May 16, 1959; children: Henry, Monte, Curt, Ted. BA, U. Chgo., 1955; MD, Washington U., St. Louis, 1960. Diplomate Am. Bd. Surgery, Nat. Bd. Med. Examiners, Am. Bd. Emergency Medicine; cert. Advanced Cardiac Life Support Instr., Advanced Trauma Life Support Provider. Intern U. Chgo. Hosps. & Clinics, 1960-61; resident Highland County Hosp., Oakland, Calif., 1961-65; assoc. prof. divsn. emergency medicine U. Chgo. Hosps. & Clinics, 1971-73, prof. divsn. emergency medicine, 1973-77; dir. divsn. emergency medicine Denver City Health & Hosps., 1977-86, 87-89; asst. dir. dept. emergency medicine U. Calif., San Diego Med. Ctr., 1989—, dir. edn. dept. emergency medicine, 1989—, dir. emergency medicine residency program, 1991—; attending physician Hot Springs Meml. Hosp., Thermopolis, Wyo., Worland (Wyo.) County Hosp., Basin-Graybull Hosp., Basin, Wyo., 1968-71, U. Chgo. Hosps. & Clinics, 1971-77; dir. emergency medicine residency program, divsn. emergency medicine U. Chgo. Hosps. & Clinics, 1971-77; emergency medicine med. advisor State of Colo., 1977-85; dir. emergency medicine residency program Denver Gen. Hosp., St. Anthony Hosp. Systems, St. Joseph Hosp., 1977-88; clin. prof. divsn. emergency medicine Oreg. Health Scis. U., Portland, 1978-89; prof. sect. emergency medicine, dept. surgery U. Colo. Health Scis. Ctr., 1984-89; dep. mgr. med. affairs Denver Dept. Health & Hosps., 1986-87; med. dir. life flight air med. svc. U. Calif., San Diego Med. Ctr., 1989-91; mem. hosp. staff U. Calif., San Diego Med. Ctr., Tri-City Med. Ctr., Oceanside, Calif., 1989—; base hosp. physician, adj. prof. medicine & surgery U. Calif., San Diego Med. Ctr., 1989—; chair med. ethics com., mem. ethics consult team U. Calif., San Diego Med. Ctr., 1990—, mem. recruitment and admissions com., 1992—; lectr. in field; cons. in field. Author: (with others) Case Reports in Emergency Medicine: 1974-76, 1977, Encyclopedia Brittannica, 1978, 85, Principles and Practice of Emergency Medicine, 1978, 86, Protocols for Prehospital Emergency Care, 1980, 84, Cardiopulmonary Resuscitation, 1982, An Atlas of Emergency Medicine Procedures, 1984, Critical Decisions in Trauma, 1984, Emergency Pediatrics, 1984, 86, 90, Controversies in Trauma Management, 1985, Standardized Nursing Care Plans for Emergency Department, 1986, Emergency Medicine: Concepts and Clinical Practice, 1988, 92, The Clinical Practice of Emergency Medicine, 1991, Essentials of Emergency Medicine, 1991, Current Practice of Emergency Medicine, 1991, Care of the Surgical Patient, 1991, Diagnostic Radiology in Emergency Medicine, 1992, Pediatric Emergency Care Systems: Planning and Management, 1992, The Airway: Emergency Management, 1992; contbg. editor, editor abstracts sect. Jour. Am. Coll. Emergency Physicians, Annals of Emergency Medicine, 1976-83; mem. editorial bd. Topics in Emergency Medicine, 1979-82, ER Reports, 1981-83; consulting editor Emergindex Microindex, 1980—; editor in chief Jour. Emergency Medicine, 1983—; contbr. articles to profl. jours. Capt. USMC, 1965-68, lt. col. Res. inactive. Recipient AMA award, 1970, Am. Hosp. Assn. award, 1973. Fellow Am. Coll. Surgeons, Am. Burn Assn., Am. Coll. Emergency Physicians (chmn. edn. com. 1977-79, bd. dirs. Colo. chpt. 1977-80, pres. Colo. chpt. 1981-82, N.C. chpt. award 1976, Outstanding Contbns. and Leadership in Emergency Medicine award 1977, Silver Tongue Debater award 1980, John. D. Mills Outstanding Contbn. to Emergency Medicine award 1984); mem. Am. Trauma Soc. (founding), Soc. Acad. Emergency Medicine (Leadership award 1990), Alpha Omega Alpha Honor Med. Soc. (grad.), Coun. Emergency Medicine Dirs. Office: U of California-San Diego 200 W Arbor Dr San Diego CA 92103-1911

ROSEN, ROSALIE, association executive; b. Chgo., Mar. 31, 1921; d. Harry and Celia (Minkoff) Singer; m. Joseph Percy Walton, Mar. 12, 1942 (div. 1947); m. Herbert Rosen, June 30, 1949; 1 child, James Robert Rosen. Student, L.A. City Coll., 1941, Santa Monica City Coll. Playground dir. Shenandoah St. Sch., L.A., 1949-56; den mother, advisor Boy Scouts Am., L.A., 1951-56; fundraiser, press and pub. rels. Shenandoah Youth House, L.A., 1951-56; pub. rels. and press chair Calif. Swing Dance, L.A., 1969-73; pub. rels.-press hospitality L.A. Swing Dance Club, 1980-85; pub. rels. and fund raising U.S. Swing Dance Coun., Phoenix, 1987-93, Calif. Swing Dance Hall of Fame, Brea, Calif., 1989—; founder, pres., promoter United Citizens Com. of Am., Inc., L.A., 1972—; mem. adv. bd. Calif. Swing Dance Hall of Fame, 1989—. Mem. PTA (life mem.). Recipient Pride of Nation award L.A. County Bd. Suprs., 1990, Scouter's award, numerous other cmty. svc. awards, Humanitarian award United Citizens Com. of Am., Inc.; named to U.S. Swing Dance Counsel's Nat. Hall of Fame. Mem. L.A. Swing Dance Club (bd. dirs.), U.S. Swing Dance Coun. Jewish.

ROSEN, SANFORD JAY, lawyer; b. N.Y.C., Dec. 19, 1937; s. Alexander Charles and Viola S. (Grad) R.; m. Catherine Picard, June 22, 1958; children: Caren E. Andrews, R. Durelle Schacter, Ian D., Melissa S. AB, Cornell U., 1959; LLB, Yale U., 1962. Bar: Conn. 1962, U.S. Supreme Ct. 1966, D.C. 1973, Calif. 1974. Law clk. to Hon. Simon E. Sobeloff U.S. Ct. Appeals, Balt., 1962-63; prof. sch. law U. Md., Balt., 1963-71; assoc. dir. Coun. on Legal Edn. Opportunity, Atlanta, 1969-70; vis. prof. law U. Tex., Austin, 1970-71; asst. legal dir. ACLU, N.Y.C., 1971-73; legal dir. Mex.-Am. Legal Def. Fund, San Francisco, 1973-75; ptnr. Rosen, Remcho & Henderson, San Francisco, 1976-80, Rosen & Remcho, San Francisco, 1980-82; prin. Law Offices of Sanford Jay Rosen, San Francisco, 1982-86; sr. ptnr. Rosen & Phillips, San Francisco, 1986-89; prin. Rosen & Assocs., San Francisco, 1990; sr. ptnr. Rosen, Bien & Asaro, San Francisco, 1991—; commr. Balt. Community Rels. Commn., 1966-69; mem. com. Patuxent Instn., Balt., 1967-69; ad hoc adminstrv. law judge Calif. Agrl. Labor Rels. Bd., San Francisco, 1975-80; interim monitor U.S. Dist. Ct. (no. dist.) Calif., San Francisco, 1989. Contbr. articles to profl. jours. Mem. Com. on Adminstrn. of Criminal Justice, Balt., 1968; mem. adv. com. HEW, Washington, 1974-75; early neutral evaluator U.S. Dist. Ct. (no. dist.) Calif., San Francisco, 1987—, mediator, 1993—; judge pro tem San Francisco Superior Ct., 1991—; lectr. Balt. State Attys., 1965. Mem. ABA, Assn. Trial Lawyers Am. (chair civil rights sect. 1993-94), D.C. Bar Assn., Calif. Bar Assn., Bar Assn. San Francisco, Calif. Attys. for Criminal Justice. Office: Rosen Bien & Asaro 155 Montgomery St Fl 8 San Francisco CA 94104-4105

ROSEN, SIDNEY MARVIN, lawyer; b. Detroit, June 27, 1939; s. Fred A. and Gertrude (Cole) R.; m. Babette Van Praag, July 3, 1971; children: Jordan, Aviva. BS, U. Ariz., 1961, JD, 1964. Bar: Ariz. 1964, U.S. Dist. Ct. Ariz. 1964, Calif. 1965, U.S. Dist. Ct. (so. dist.) Calif. 1965, U.S. Supreme Ct. 1971. Asst. atty. gen. State of Ariz., Phoenix, 1964-66, spl. asst. atty. gen., 1968-69; assoc. Kirkwood, Kaplan, Russin & Vechi, Bangkok and Saigon, Vietnam, 1967-68; ptnr. Rosen, Ocampo and Fontes, Phoenix, 1970—; co-founder, law instr. Ariz. Bar Rev. Course, 1965-73; prof. internat. law Am. Grad. Sch. of Internat. Mgmt., Phoenix, 1975-76; former gen. counsel Nat. Speakers Assn., 1973-85. Candidate Dem. nomination for atty. gen. State of Ariz., 1974, U.S. Congress, 1976; mem. Ariz.-Mex. Gov.'s Commn., 1974—, counsel commerce and industry sect., 1974—; chmn. campaign Bonds for Israel, Ariz., 1980-85. Baird scholar, University scholar; recipient Speaker Preview Auditions First Pl. award Internat. Platform Assn., 1969-70, Silver Bowl award, 1969-70. Mem. Ariz. Bar Assn. (internat. relations com.), Calif. Bar Assn., Maricopa County Bar Assn., World Assn. Lawyers, Nat. Speakers Assn. (founder, former gen. counsel 1973-85), World Affairs Council, Hospitality Internat. (host), FIABCI (law instr. Internat. Real Estate Fedn. 1985—, gen. counsel Ariz. chpt. 1985—), Ariz. World Trade Assn. (former bd. dirs.), Jaycees (treas. Ariz. chpt. 1969-70, ambassador to Philippine Islands 1969-70), Pan Am. Club of Ariz. (past pres.), Traveler's Century Club, Valley Forward Assn. (bd. dirs.), Phi Alpha Delta (pres. 1963-64). Democrat. Jewish. Lodge: Kiwanis. Home: 2233 N Alvarado Rd Phoenix AZ 85004-1415

ROSENBAUM, JAMES TODD, rheumatologist, educator; b. Portland, Oreg., Sept. 29, 1949; s. Edward E. and David Carol (Naftalin) R.; m. Sandra Jean Lewis, June 27, 1970; children: Lisa Susanne, Jennifer Lewis. AB, Harvard U., 1971; MD, Yale U., 1975. Diplomate Am. Bd. Internal Medicine, Am. Bd. Rheumatology. Intern, resident Stanford (Calif.) Med. Ctr., 1975-78, postdoctoral fellow, 1978-81; from instr. to asst. prof. U. Calif., San Francisco, 1981-83; sr. scientist Kuzell Inst., San Francisco, 1983-85; from asst. prof. to assoc. prof. Oreg. Health Scis. U., Portland, 1985-91, prof., asst. dean rsch., 1991—; bd. dirs. Fund for Arthritis/Infectious Disease Rsch., San Francisco, Oreg. Arthritis Found., Portland, 1986-93, Portland VA Rsch. Found.; mem. spl. rev. panel Nat. Eye Inst., Bethesda, Md., 1992, mem. visual scis. A study sect. Dolly Green scholar Rsch. to Prevent Blindness, N.Y.C., 1986, sr. scholar award, 1994. Mem. Am. Assn. Immunologists, Am. Coll. Rheumatology, Am. Uvetis Soc., Am. Soc. for Clin. Investigation. Home: 5342 SW Hewett Blvd Portland OR 97221-2254 Office: Oregon Health Sci U Casey Eye Inst 3375 SW Terwilliger Blvd Portland OR 97201-4146

ROSENBAUM, LAWRENCE ALAN, evangelist; b. Camp Kilmer, N.J., Jan. 18, 1946; s. Irving and Dorothy Berger Rosenbaum. BA, Yale U., 1967; MA, Brandeis U., 1970. Dir. SOS Ministries, Oakland, Calif., 1980—; adminstrv. dir. Internat. St. and Evangelism Ministries Assn., Oakland, 1985—. Author: You Shall Be My Witnesses, 1986. Office: PO Box 27358 Oakland CA 94602-0358

ROSENBAUM, MICHAEL FRANCIS, securities dealer; b. N.Y.C., Feb. 9, 1959; s. Francis Fels Jr. and Joyce (Keefer) R.; m. Elika Sosnick, Mar. 8, 1986; children: Erin Sosnick, Sarah Greer, Kira Keefer. AB, Princeton U., 1981. Cert. Nat. Assn. Securities Dealers. Product mgr. Sutro & Co., Inc., San Francisco, 1981-84; v.p. sales Pacific Securities, San Francisco, 1984-89; v.p., br. mgr. Rauscher Pierce Resfnes, San Francisco, 1989-92; v.p. sales Smith Mitchell Investment Group, San Francisco, 1992-93; sr. v.p. sales Gruntal & Co., Inc., San Francisco, 1993-94; sr. v.p. taxable fixed income Coast Ptnrs. Securities, San Francisco, 1994—; bd. dirs. S.G. Rosenbaum Found., N.Y.C. Patroller Nat. Ski Patrol, Northstar, Calif., 1988. Democrat. Jewish. Home: PO Box 1104 Ross CA 94957-1104

ROSENBAUM, RICHARD BARRY, neurologist; b. Rochester, Minn., Aug. 17, 1946; s. Edward E. and Davida (Naftalin) R.; m. Lois Peretz Omenn, Apr. 4, 1971; children: Steven, Laura. AB cum laude, Harvard U., 1967, MD cum laude, 1971. Diplomate Am. Bd. Psychiatry and Neurology, Am. Bd. Internal Medicine, Am. Bd. Electrodiagnostic Medicine; lic. MD, Oreg., Calif. Neurologist The Oreg. Clinic, Portland, Oreg., 1977—; clin. prof. neurology Oreg. Health Scis. U., Portland, Oreg., 1992—. Co-author: (book) Carpal Tunnel Syndrome and Other Disorders of the Median Nerve, 1992. With USPHS, 1973-75. Recipient Meritorious Achievement award Oreg. Health Scis. U., 1993. Mem. Am. Acad. Neurology, Am. Assn. Electrodiagnostic Medicine, Alpha Omega Alpha. Office: 5050 NE Hoyt #314 Portland OR 97213

ROSENBERG, ALEX, mathematician, educator; b. Berlin, Germany, Dec. 5, 1926; came to U.S., 1949, naturalized, 1959; s. Theodore and Rela (Banet) R.; m. Beatrice Gershenson, Aug. 24, 1952 (div. Apr. 1985); children: Theodore Joseph, David Michael, Daniel Alex; m. Brunhilde Angun, June 14, 1985. B.A., U. Toronto, 1948, M.A., 1949; Ph.D., U. Chgo., 1951. From instr. to assoc. prof. math. Northwestern U., 1952-61; prof. math. Cornell U., Ithaca, N.Y., 1961-88; chmn. dept. Cornell U., 1966-69; prof., chmn. dept. U. Calif., Santa Barbara, 1986-87, prof., 1986—, prof. emeritus, 1994—; mem. com. undergrad. program math. Math Assn. Am., 1966-76; mem. Inst. Advanced Study, 1955-57; vis. prof. U. Calif., Berkely, 1961, 1979, U. Calif., Los Angeles, 1969-70, 82, U. London, Queen Mary Coll., 1963-64, U. Munich, 1975-76, E.T.H Zurich, 1976, U. Dortmund, 1984-85; trustee Am. Math Soc., 1973-83. Editor: Proc. Am. Math. Soc., 1960-66, Am. Math. Monthly, 1974-77; Contbr. articles to profl. jours. Recipient Humboldt Stiftung Sr. U.S. Scientist award U. Munich, 1975-76, U. Dortmund, 1981. Home: 1225 Plaza Del Monte Santa Barbara CA 93101-4819

ROSENBERG, BARR MARVIN, investment advisor, economist; b. Berkeley, Calif., Nov. 13, 1942; s. Marvin and Dorothy Fraser R.; m. June Diane Weinstock, Sept. 8, 1966. B.A., U. Calif., Berkeley, 1963; M.S. in Econs, London Sch. Econs., 1965; Ph.D., Harvard U., 1968. Asst. prof. Univ. Calif., Berkeley, 1968-74; assoc. prof. Univ. Calif., 1974-77, prof. bus. adminstrn., 1978-83, dir. Berkeley Program in Fin., 1979-81; prin. Barr Rosenberg Assos., Berkeley, Calif., 1975-81; mng. partner Barr Rosenberg Assos., 1981-83, cons., 1983-86; mng. ptnr. Rosenberg Instnl. Equity Mgmt., Orinda, Calif., 1985—. Marshall scholar, U.K., 1963-65. Mem. Am. Econ. Soc., Econometric Soc., Am. Statis. Assn., Am. Fin. Assn., Western Fin. Assn. Office: Rosenberg Instnl Equity Mgmt 4 Orinda Way Bldg E Orinda CA 94563-2515

ROSENBERG, DAN YALE, retired plant pathologist; b. Stockton, Calif., Jan. 8, 1922; s. Meyer and Bertha (Naliboff) R.; AA, Stockton Jr. Coll., 1942; AB, Coll. Pacific, 1949; MS, U. Calif. at Davis, 1952; m. Marilyn Kohn, Dec. 5, 1954; 1 son, Morton Karl. Jr. plant pathologist Calif. Dept. Agr., Riverside, 1952-55, asst. plant pathologist, 1955-59, assoc. plant pathologist, 1959-60, pathologist IV, 1960-63, program supr., 1963-71, chief exclusion and detection, div. plant industry, 1971-76, chief nursery and seed svcs. div. plant industry, 1976-82, spl. asst. div. plant industry, 1982-87; pres. Health, Inc., 1972-73; agrl. cons., 1988—; mem. Citrus Rsch. Adv. com. U. Calif., Riverside, 1992—; mem. Gov.'s Interagy. Task Force on Biotech., 1986—; bd. dirs. Health Inc., Sacramento, 1967, pres., 1971-72, 79-81, 81-83. Served with AUS, 1942-46; ETO. Mem. Am. Phytopath. Soc. (fgn. and regulatory com. 1975—, grape diseases sect. 1977-79, grape pests sect. 1979—), Calif. State Employees Assn. (pres. 1967-69). Contbr. articles to profl. jours. Home and Office: 2328 Swarthmore Dr Sacramento CA 95825-6867

ROSENBERG, DONALD LEE, magazine publisher; b. Atlantic City, N.J., Feb. 22, 1953; s. Sidney J. and Lois Rosenberg; m. Ellen Steiger, Apr. 9, 1979; children: Drew, Evan. BS in Bus. Adminstrn. and Mktg., U. Md., 1976. Gen. mgr. Schwartz Bros., Inc. (SBI Video), Lanham, Md., 1980-86; dir. sales HBO Video, N.Y.C., 1986-87, FOX Home Video, Palatine, Ill., 1987-89; pres. Epic Home Video, L.A., 1989-90, DLR Assocs., Westlake Village, Calif., 1990-91; exec. v.p. Video Software Dealers Assn., Encino, Calif., 1991-94; publ. Video Store Mag., Santa Anna, Calif., 1994—. Office: Video Store Mag 201 Sandpointe Ave Ste 600 Santa Ana CA 92707-8700

ROSENBERG, HOWARD ALAN, manufacturing executive; b. N.Y.C., Nov. 2, 1927; s. Nathan and Anna (Bernstein) R.; m. Carol Hirsch, Feb. 21, 1951; children: Ellen Sue, Robin Jill, Ira Scott. BS, L.I. U., 1949; MA, NYU, 1951. Registered profl. engr. Jr. engr. Wright Aeronaut. Corp., Woodridge, N.J., 1950-52; quality engr. Fairchild Engine Div., Farmingdale, N.Y., 1952-55; quality control mgr. Burndy Corp., Norwalk, Conn., 1955-60; reliability mgr. LFE Corp., Boston, 1960-64; reliability dir. AIL-Cutler Hammer, Comack, N.Y., 1964-69; pres. Western Tech. Assocs., Anaheim, Calif., 1969-80, chief exec. officer, chmn. bd., 1980—; chmn. Printed Cir. Inst. Irvine Valley Coll.; cons. in field; instr. at various colls. Contbr. articles to profl. jours. Chmn. Anti-Defamation League, Santa Ana, Calif., 1984-86, nat. commr.; pres. Orange County Jewish Community Ctr., 1989. 1st lt. infantry USNG, 1949-54. Recipient ADL Civic Commitment award, 1991. Mem. Am. Soc. Quality Control, Calif. Circuits Assn. (bd. dirs. 1970-75), Am. Electroplaters Soc., Am. Legion, Jewish War Vets, Israel Bond Com. (co-chair), Jewish Nat. Fund (com. mem.), B'nai B'rith (mem. youth orgn.). Home: 13592 Carroll Way Tustin CA 92680-1805 Office: Western Tech Assocs 2897 E La Cresta Ave Anaheim CA 92806-1817

ROSENBERG, JANE, author, illustrator; b. N.Y.C., Dec. 7, 1949; d. Abner Emmanuel and Lily (Quittman) R.; m. Robert F. Porter, May 30, 1982; children: Melo Ann Porter, Ava Hermine Porter, Eloise Pearl Porter. BFA, Beaver Coll., 1971; MA in Painting, NYU, 1973. Painter, freelance illustrator N.Y.C., 1974-82; art tchr. Ethical Culture Sch., N.Y.C., 1974-75; art dir. N.Y. News for Kids, N.Y.C., 1979-80; children's book author, illustrator N.Y.C., 1982—. Author, illustrator: Dance Me a Story: Twelve Tales from the Classic Ballets, 1985, Sing Me a Story: The Metropolitan Opera's Book of Opera Stories, 1989, Play Me a Story: A Child's Introduction to Classical Music through Stories and Poems, 1994; one-woman show at Every Picture Tells a Story Gallery, L.A., 1991. Mem. Authors' Guild.

ROSENBERG, JONATHAN BRYAN, software engineer, computer science educator; b. Marysville, Calif., July 30, 1956; s. Irwin K. and Barbara (Fay) R.; m. Carole Ann Hohl, May 30, 1981; children: Brendan, Zachary, Joanna. BA in Math., Kalamazoo Coll., 1978; PhD in Computer Sci., Duke U., 1983. Dir. advanced rsch. and tech. Microelectronics Ctr. of N.C., Research Triangle Park, N.C., 1982-86; rsch. asst. prof. computer sci. dept. Duke U., Durham, N.C., 1986-88; mem. tech. staff MasPar Computer Corp., Santa Clara, Calif., 1988-92; dir. langs. devel. Borland Internat., Scotts Valley, Calif., 1992—. Democrat. Home: 215 Quail Ridge Rd Scotts Valley CA 95066-4822 Office: Borland Internat 100 Borland Way Scotts Valley CA 95066-3248

ROSENBERG, NEIL LLOYD, neurologist; b. Chgo., July 1, 1954; s. Charles B. and Helen (Deitchman) R.; m. Laura J. Watt, Sept. 17, 1977; children: Philip, Rachel. BS in Physiol. Psychology, U. Ill., 1976; MD, Chgo. Med. Sch., 1978. Intern and resident in internal medicine Cook County Hosp., Chgo., 1978-79; resident in neurology Oreg. Health Scis. U., Portland, 1979-82; fellow neuromuscular diseases U. Colo. Sch. Medicine, Denver, 1982-83, asst. prof., 1983-89; neurologist Denver Gen. Hosp., 1983-86; from assoc. investigator to rsch. assoc. VA Med. Ctr., Denver, 1983-89; med. dir. Ctr. for Occupational Neurology & Neurotoxicology Colo. Neurolog. Inst., Englewood, 1989—; med. dir. Neuromuscular Disease Program, 1989—, med. dir. Neuroimmunology Program, 1989—; exec. med. dir. Inst. for Occupational and Environ. Medicine, Englewood, 1989—, Internat. Inst. for Inhalant Abuse, Englewood, 1991—; chmn. rsch. com. Colo. Neruol. Inst., 1990—; vis. prof. Albert Einstein Coll. Medicine, Bronx, N.Y., 1989—; asst. clin. prof. U. Colo. Sch. Med., Denver, 1989—. Author: Frontiers of Neurotoxicology, 1992, Update on Neuroimmunology, 1993, Occupational and Environmental Neurology, 1993; contbr. articles to profl. jours. Recipient Bruno Epstein Intern Achievement award Cook County Hosp., 1979, Rsch. Assoc. award VA, 1986; postdoctoral fellow Muscular Dystrophy Assn., 1982. Mem. AAAS, AMA, Am. Soc. for Neurol. Investigation (pres. 1989-91), Am. Acad. Neurology, Am. Coll. Occupational and Environ. Medicine, Am. Assn. Electrodiagnostic Medicine, N.Y. Acad. Medicine. Office: Colo Neurological Inst 450 W Jefferson Ave Englewood CO 80110-3536

ROSENBERG, RICHARD MORRIS, banker; b. Fall River, Mass., Apr. 21, 1930; s. Charles and Betty (Peck) R.; m. Barbara K. Cohen, Oct. 21, 1956; children: Michael, Peter. B.S., Suffolk U., 1952; M.B.A., Golden Gate Coll., 1962, LL.B., 1966. Publicity asst. Crocker-Anglo Bank, San Francisco, 1959-62; banking services officer Wells Fargo Bank, N.A., San Francisco, 1962-65; asst. v.p. Wells Fargo Bank, N.A., 1965-68, v.p. mktg. dept., 1968, v.p., dir. mktg., 1969, sr. v.p. mktg. and advt. div., 1970-75, exec. v.p., from 1975, vice chmn., 1980-83; vice chmn. Crocker Nat. Corp., 1983-85; pres., chief operating officer Seafirst Corp., 1986-87, also dir.; pres., chief operating officer Seattle First Nat. Bank, 1985-87; vice chmn. bd. BankAm. Corp., San Francisco, 1987-90, chmn., chief exec. officer, 1990—; dir. Airborne Express, Potlatch Corp., Northrop Corp., PacTel; past. chmn. Mastercard Internat. Bd. dirs. Marin Ecumenical Housing Assn.; trustee Calif. Inst. Tech., U. So. Calif. Jewish. Office: BankAm Corp Dept 3001 PO Box 37000 San Francisco CA 94137-0002

ROSENBERG, SHAWN WILLIAM, political psychologist, educator; b. Winnipeg, Manitoba, Canada, Mar. 25, 1951; s. Harry and Florence (Loffman) R.; children: Angele, Phillip. BA, Yale U., 1972; postgrad., Harvard U., 1975-76; MLitt, Oxford U., 1982. Lectr. Yale U., New Haven, Conn., 1979-81; prof., dir. polit. psychology program U. Calif., Irvine, 1988—. Author: Political Reasoning and Cognition, 1987, Reason, Ideology and Politics, 1988; editl bd. Western Polit. Quarterly, Polit. Psychology, Jour. Polit. Ideologies; contbr. articles to profl. jours. Fellow Canada Coun., 1972-76; recipient Outstanding Book award Nat. Assn. Univ. and Coll. Librs., 1989. Mem. Am. Polit. Sci. Assn. (sect. chair 1993), Internat. Soc. Polit. Psychology (governing coun. 1990-92, Outstanding Early Achievement award), Soc. for Rsch. on Child Development. Office: U Calif Sch Social Scis Irvine CA 92717

ROSENBERG, SYDNEY J., security company executive; b. San Francisco, Sept. 3, 1914; s. Morris and Gussie (Kaufman) R.; m. Joyce Wexler, Nov. 15, 1939 (div. Mar. 1968); children: Brad, Jill Rosenberg Hughes, Todd; m. 2d Jaclyn Barde, Mar. 22, 1968; stepchildren: Gregg Cobarr, Glenn Cobarr. B.A., Stanford U., 1936; M.B.A., Harvard U., 1938. Pres., chief exec. officer Am. Bldg. Maintenance Industries, Los Angeles, from 1938; now chmn. bd. Am. Bldg. Maintenance Industries, San Francisco; chmn. ABM Security Svcs.; bd. dirs. Craig Corp., AMPCO Parking Svcs., AMTECH Elevator Svcs., AMTECH Lighting Svcs., Comm. Air. Mech. Svcs., Easterday Supply Co., Rose Pest Control Co.; pres. OPTIC Fund. Bd. govs. Performing Arts Council; bd. govs. Los Angeles Music Ctr.; trustee Jewish Big Bros.; mem. dirs. council Children's Orthopaedic Hosp. Mem. Chief Execs. Orgn., Urban Land Inst., World Bus. Council. Republican. Jewish. Clubs: Hillcrest (Los Angeles); Big Canyon (Newport, Calif.). Office: American Building 50 Fremont St San Francisco CA 94105-2230

ROSENBERGER, PATRICIA HIRT, psychology educator, researcher; b. Grosse Pointe, Mich., Feb. 12, 1955; d. Rudolph Alvin and Evelyn Ruth (Mutersbaugh) Hirt; m. Dale Brian Rosenberger, Aug. 20, 1977; children: Greta Hirt, Lise Karin. BA, U. Mich., 1977; MA, U. Ill., 1984, PhD, 1987. Lic. psychologist. Rsch. assoc. Yale U., New Haven, Conn., 1978-79; rsch. asst. dept. psychology U. Ill., Urbana, 1980-84, teaching asst. dept. psychology, 1984-85; intern psychology dept. psychiatry Ohio State U., Columbus, 1985-86, lectr. dept. psychology, 1986-91, asst. prof., cons. dept. psychiatry, 1987-89, rsch. psychologist dept. psychiatry, 1989-93; psychologist Rehab Ctr., Columbus, 1990-91; asst. prof. psychology dept. Colo. State U., 1993-95. Contbr. articles to profl. jours. Bd. mem. Downtown Playsch., Columbus, 1985-90. Regent scholar U. Mich., 1973, James B. Angell scholar, 1975; dissertation rsch. grantee U. Ill., 1984, AIDS grantee Ohio State U., 1989-94. Mem. APA, Nat. Register Health Providers Psychol., Colo. Psychol. Assn., Mortar Board, Phi Kappa Phi. Office: Colo State Univ 3400 16th St Bldg 5 Ste YY Greeley CO 80631

ROSENBLATT, ALLAN D., psychiatrist; b. St. Louis, June 18, 1926. PhB and BS in Physiology, U. Chgo., 1945, MD, MS in Neurophysiology, 1948. Diplomate Am. Bd. Psychiatry and Neurology in Psychiatry. Intern L.A. (Calif.) County Gen. Hosp., 1948-49; resident in psychiatry Bellevue Hosp., 1949-50; USPH fellow, resident in psychiatry N.Y. State Psychiat. Inst., 1950-51; psychoanalytic tng. Columbia U. Psychoanalytic Ctr., 1950-53; clin. asst. Child Guidance Clinic Mt. Sinai Hosp., N.Y.C., 1951-52; adj. psychiatrist Child Guidance Clinic Hosp. for Joint Disease, N.Y.C., 1952-53; pvt. practice N.Y.C., 1951-53, San Diego, 1955—; pres. San Diego Soc. Psychiatry and Neurology, 1956-59, San Diego Assn. Psychiatry and Psychology, 1958-60, San Diego Psychoanalytic Found., 1966-71; chmn. governing coun. San Diego Acad. Behavioral Scis., 1960-63; chmn. bd. dirs. San Diego Psychoanalytic Inst., 1980-83, dir. and chmn. edn. com., 1977-80, 83-86, tng. and supervising analyst, sr. instr.; clin. prof. psychiatry U. Calif., Sch. Medicine, San Diego; cons. in field. Editor: Am. Psychoanalytic Assn. Newsletter, 1982-84; consulting editor Psychoanalytic Inquiry; contbr. articles to profl. jours. Lt. USNR, 1951-53. Fellow Am. Psychiat. Assn. (life, cons. quality assurance com.), Am. Coll. Psychoanalysts; mem. Am. Psychoanalytic Assn. (life, fellow bd. profl. standards 1974-80, 83-86, exec. councilor 1980-83, 91—, exec. councilor-at-large 1987-91, mem. task force on certification 1991-92, chair com. on appts., chair external credentialing com., co-chair com. on socs.), San Diego Psychoanalytic Soc., San Diego Psychiat. Soc., San Diego County Med. Soc. Home: 1689 Los Altos Rd San Diego CA 92109-1357 Office: 3252 Holiday Ct Ste 205 La Jolla CA 92037-1808

ROSENBLATT, GERD MATTHEW, chemist; b. Leipzig, Germany, July 6, 1933; came to U.S., 1935, naturalized, 1940; s. Edgar Fritz and Herta (Fisher) R.; m. Nancy Ann Kaltreider, June 29, 1957 (dec. Jan. 1982); children: Rachel, Paul; m. Susan Frances Barnett, Nov. 23, 1990. BA, Swarthmore Coll., 1955; PhD, Princeton U., 1960; Doctorate in Physics (hon.), Vrije Universiteit Brussel, 1989. Chemist Lawrence Radiation Lab., Univ. Calif., 1960-63, cons., guest scientist, 1968-84; from asst. to assoc. prof. chemistry Pa. State U., University Park, 1963-70, prof., 1970-81; assoc. div. leader Los Alamos (N.Mex.) Nat. Lab., 1981-82, chemistry div. leader, 1982-85; dep. dir. Lawrence Berkeley (Calif.) Lab., 1985-89, sr. chemist, 1985—; lectr. U. Calif., Berkeley, 1962-63; vis. prof. Vrije U. Brussels, 1973; vis. fellow Southampton U., 1980, King's Coll., Cambridge, 1980; adj. prof. chemistry U. N.Mex., 1981-85; cons. Aerospace Corp., 1979-85, Solar Energy Rsch. Inst., 1980-81, Xerox Corp., 1977-78, Hooker Chem. Co., 1976-78, Los Alamos Nat. Lab., 1978, mem. external adv. com. Ctr. for Materials Sci., 1985-93; mem. rev. com. chemistry divsn., 1985; mem. rev. com. for chem. engring. divsn. Arbonne Univ. Assn., 1974-80, chmn., 177-78; mem. rev. com. for chem. sci. Lawrence Berkeley Lab., 1984; chmn. rev. com. for chem. and material sci. Lawrence Livermore Nat. Lab., 1984-91; mem. bd. advs. Combustion Rsch. Facility, Sandia Nat. Lab., 1985-89; mem. bd. advs. R&D divsn. Lockheed Missiles & Space Co., 1985-87; chmn. chemistry III panel Internat. Sci. Found., 1994; mem. U.S. Nat. Com., Com. on Date for Sci. and Tech., 1986-92, Internat. Union of Pure and Applied Chemistry, 1986-92; mem. basic scis. lab. program panel energy, 1985-89; sec. IUPAC Commn. on High Temperature and Solid State Chemistry, 1992—. Editor: (jour.) Progress in Solid State Chemistry, 1977—; mem. editorial bd. High Temperature Sci., 1979—; contbr. articles to profl. jours. Du Pont grad. fellow, Princeton U., 1957-58; fellow Solvay Inst., 1973, U.K. Rsch. Coun., 1980. Fellow AAAS; mem. Am. Chem. Soc., Am. Phys. Soc., Electrochem. Soc., Nat. Rsch. Coun. (chmn. high temperature sci. and tech. com. 1977-79, 84-85, panel on exploration of materials sci. and tech. for nat. welfare 1986-88, sci. and tech. info. bd. 1990-91, chmn. numerical data adv. bd. 1986-90, solid state scis. com. 1988-91, chmn. western regional materials sci. and engring. meeting 1990, panel on long-term retention of selected sci. and tech. records of fed. govt. 1993). Home: 1177 Miller Ave Berkeley CA 94708-1754 Office: Lawrence Berkeley Lab U Calif Berkeley CA 94720-0001

ROSENBLATT, PAUL GERHARDT, federal judge. AB, U. Ariz., 1958, JD, 1963. Asst. atty. gen. State of Ariz., 1963-66; adminstrv. asst. to U.S. Rep., 1967-72; sole practice, Prescott, 1971-73; judge Yavapai County Superior Ct., Prescott, 1973-84; judge, U.S. Dist. Ct. Ariz., Phoenix, 1984—. Office: US Dist Ct US Courthouse & Fed Bldg 230 N 1st Ave Ste 7012 Phoenix AZ 85025-0007

ROSENBLUM, CARLA NADINE, travel agent, retirement community executive; b. Seattle, Apr. 25, 1937; d. Carl August and Nadine Chaffa (Schwartz) Mahne; m. A. Leon Rosenblum, Feb. 28, 1965; 1 child, Sara Lynnette. BS, Mills Coll., Oakland, Calif., 1959. Buyer, stationery City of Paris Dept. Store, San Francisco, 1959-63, Diamond's Dept. Store, Phoenix, 1963-65; corp. buyer Arkwright Corp., L.A., 1965-66; mgr. various travel agys. San Jose, Calif., 1977-84; supr. Incentive Journeys, San Jose, Calif., 1984-86, Internat. Passages, Santa Clara, Calif., 1986—; ptnr. Willow Glen Villa, San Jose; with Marisan Travel, Santa Clara, 1989-92; coord. vacation svcs. Wagons-Lits Traves, U.S.A., 1992-94, Carlson Wagonlit Travel, 1994—. Mem. San Jose Pacific Area Travel Assn., Travelarians San Jose, Assn. Retail Travel Agts. Democrat. Jewish. Home: 15999 Bohlman Rd Saratoga CA 95070-6340 Office: Willow Glen Villa 15999 Bohlman Rd Saratoga CA 95070-6340

ROSENBLUM, RICHARD MARK, utility executive; b. N.Y.C., Apr. 28, 1950; s. Victor Sigmund and Julia (Kessler) R.; m. Michele E. Cartier, Aug. 30, 1979; children: Gialisa, Jeremy Scott. BS, MS, Rensselaer Poly. Inst., 1973. Registered profl. engr., Calif. Startup engr. Combustion Engring. Inc., Windsor, Conn., 1973-76; engr. So. Calif. Edison Co., Rosemead, 1976-82, project mgr. San Onofre Nuclear Generating Sta., 1982-83, tech. mgr., 1983-84, nuclear safety mgr., 1984-86, mgr. quality assurance, 1986-89, mgr. nuclear regulatory affairs, 1989-93, v.p. Engring. and Tech. Svcs., 1993—. N.Y. State Regents scholar, 1968-73. Office: 2244 Walnut Grove Ave Rosemead CA 91770-3714

ROSENBLUTH, MURRAY JOSEPH, chemical engineer; b. Phila., June 6, 1931; s. Louis and Fannie S. (Pinkowitz) R.; m. Adele E. Goldman, June 28, 1953; children: Harry J., Ellen P., Joshua H. BSChemE, Drexel U., 1953, MSChemE, 1959. Registered profl. engr., Calif., Pa., Ohio, Tex., Fla. Tech. engr. to sect. head Procter and Gamble Co., 1960-79, sect. head, 1979-81, engring. compt. dept. spl. assignment, 1981-82, process tech. sect. head, 1982-85, project mgmt. sect. head, 1985-87, project mgr., 1987-90; sr. tech. project engr., project mgr. IPC Sys. Engring., Inc., Oxnard, Calif., 1990 . Dir. Cancer Share, Cin., 1989; ctrl. com. Dem. Party, Cin., 1970. 1st lt. U.S. Army, 1953-55. Jewish. Home: 2591 Northstar Cv Port Hueneme CA 93041-1568 Office: IPC Sys Engring Inc 1901 Solar Dr Ste 265 Oxnard CA 93030-2643

ROSENFELD, RON GERSHON, pediatrics educator; b. N.Y.C., June 22, 1946; s. Stanley I. and Deborah (Levin) R.; m. Valerie Rae Spitz, June 16, 1968; children: Amy, Jeffrey. BA, Columbia U., 1968; MD, Stanford U., 1973. Intern Stanford (Calif.) U. Med. Ctr., 1973-74, resident in pediatrics, 1974-75, chief resident pediatrics, 1975-76; pvt. practice Santa Barbara, Calif., 1976-77; postdoctoral fellow Stanford U. Sch. Medicine, 1977-80, from asst. to assoc. prof. pediatrics, 1980-89, prof. pediatrics, 1989-93; chmn., prof. pediatrics Oreg. Health Scis. U., 1993—; physician-in-chief Doernbecher Children's Hosp., 1993—; cons. Genentech Inc., South San Francisco, 1980—, Kabi Pharmacia, Inc., Stockholm, 1990—, Novo Nordisk, Inc., Copenhagen, 1991—, Diagnostic Systems Labs., Webster, Tex., 1991—, Serono, Norwell, Mass., 1992—. Editor: Growth Abnormalities, 1985, Turner Syndrome, 1987, Turner Syndrome: Growth, 1990, Growth Regulation; editorial bd.: Jour. Clin. Endocrinology and Metabolism, Growth Factors, Clin. Pediatric Endocrinology, Growth and Growth Factors, Growth Regulation. Recipient Ross Rsch. award Ross Laboratories, 1985. Mem. Endocrine Soc., Soc. for Pediat. Rsch., Lawson Wilkins Pediat. Endocrine Soc. (pres.-elect 1996—), European Soc. for Pediat. Endocrinology, Diabetes Soc. Office: Oreg Health Scis Univ Dept Pediatrics 3181 SW Sam Jackson Park Rd Portland OR 97201-3011

ROSENFELD, SANDRA KAYE, elementary school educator; b. Portland, Oreg., Aug. 6, 1953; d. Howard Wayne and Ruth Eileen (Russell) Darling; m. Stephen Barry Rosenfeld, June 25, 1983; 1 child, Austin Harrison. BS in Edn., Portland State U., 1975, MS in Edn., 1983. Ticket agt. Meml. Coliseum, Portland, 1971-93, Civic Stadium, Portland, 1975—; early childhood educator Portland Pub. Schs., 1975—; mem. parent involvement com., sabbatical leave com., dislocated workers com., Portland Pub. Sch. System, 1992—; mem. consortium Concordia Coll., 1992—. Dir. youth and edn. Congregation Neveh Shalom, 1987-94. Mem. NEA, Oregon Edn. Assn. (mem. jud. panel), Portland Assn. Tchrs. (mem. contract maintenance com., sec. exec. bd., co-chair Impact II, mem. instrnl. profl. devel. com., head bldg. rep., chair site coun.), Theatrical Employees Union Local B-20 (bus. agt., past pres.), Women's League for Conservative Judaism (regional chmn., past pres.), Coalition of Alternatives in Jewish Edn, Hadassah. Home: 6837 SW 11th Dr Portland OR 97219-2149 Office: James John Sch 7439 N Charleston Ave Portland OR 97203-3706

ROSENFIELD, JAMES STEVEN, real estate developer; b. L.A., June 22, 1962; s. Robert Allan and Elyse Harriet (Bernstein) R. BA in Polit. Sci., U. Calif., Berkeley, 1984. Polit. cons. Senator John Tunney, L.A., 1985—; assoc. Cloverleaf Group, Inc., L.A., 1985-87; pres. J.S. Rosenfield & Co., L.A., 1987—; ptnr. John V. Tunney & Assocs., L.A., 1991—; developer Sears Roebuck & Co. stores, Fresno and Modesto, Calif. Coro Found. fellow, 1985. Mem. Internat. Coun. Shopping Ctrs., Univ. Art Mus. at Berkeley. Democrat. Jewish.

ROSENKILDE, CARL EDWARD, physicist; b. Yakima, Wash., Mar. 16, 1937; s. Elmer Edward and Doris Edith (Fitzgerald) R.; m. Bernadine Doris Blumenstine, June 22, 1963 (div. Apr. 1991); children: Karen Louise, Paul Eric; m. Wendy Maureen Ellison, May 24, 1992. BS in Physics, Wash. State Coll., 1959; MS in Physics, U. Chgo., 1960, PhD in Physics, 1966. Postdoctoral fellow Argonne (Ill.) Nat. Lab., 1966-68; asst. prof. math. NYU, 1968-70; asst. prof. physics Kans. State U., Manhattan, 1970-76, assoc. prof., 1976-79; physicist Lawrence Livermore (Calif.) Nat. Lab., 1979-93, lab. assoc., 1994-95, cons., 1974-79; chief scientist C.R. Sci., 1993—. Contbr. articles on physics to profl. jours. Woodrow Wilson fellow, 1959, 60. Mem. Am. Phys. Soc., Am. Astron. Soc., Soc. for Indsl. and Applied Math., Am. Geophys. Union, Acoustical Soc. Am., Math. Assn. Am., Phi Beta Kappa, Phi Kappa Phi, Phi Eta Sigma, Sigma Xi. Republican. Presbyterian. Club: Tubists Universal Brotherhood Assn. (TUBA). Current Work: Nonlinear wave propagation in complex media. Subspecialties: Theoretical physics; Fluid dynamics.

ROSENKRANTZ, LINDA, writer; b. N.Y.C., May 26, 1934; d. Samuel H. and Frances (Sillman) R.; m. Christopher Finch, Feb. 2, 1973; 1 child, Chloe. BA, U. Mich., 1955. Founding editor Auction Mag., N.Y.C., 1967-72; columnist Copley News Svc., San Diego, 1986--. Author: Talk, 1968; co-author: Gone Hollywood, 1979, SoHo, 1981, Beyond Jennifer and Jason, 1988, Beyond Charles and Diana, 1992, Beyond Shannon and Sean, 1992, Beyond Sarah and Sam, 1992, The Last Word on First Names, 1995.

ROSENSTEIN, ALLEN BERTRAM, electrical engineering educator; b. Balt., Aug. 25, 1920; s. Morton and Mary (Epstein) R.; m. Betty Lebell; children: Jerry Tyler, Lisa Nan, Adam Mark. B.S. with high distinction, U. Ariz., 1940; M.S., UCLA, 1950, Ph.D., 1958. Elec. engr. Consol. Vultee Aircraft, San Diego, 1940-41; sr. elec. engr. Lockheed Aircraft Corp., Burbank, Calif., 1941-42; chief plant engr. Utility Fan Corp., Los Angeles, 1942-44; prof. engring. UCLA, 1946—; founder, chmn. bd. Inet, Inc., 1947-53, cons. engr., 1954—; founder, chmn. bd. dirs. Pioneer Magnetics, Inc., Pioneer Research Inc., Anadex Instruments Inc.; dir. Internat. Transformer Co., Inc., Fgn. Resource Services; cons. ednl. planning UNESCO, Venezuela, 1974-76. Author: (with others) Engineering Communications, 1965, A Study of a Profession and Professional Education, 1968; contbr. articles to profl. jours.; patentee in field. Bd. dirs. Vista Hill Psychiat. Found. Served with USNR, 1944-46. Fellow IEEE (com. on competitiveness); mem. AAAS, NSPE (coun. on competitiveness), Am. Soc. Engring. Edn., N.Y. Acad. Scis., Am. Electronics Assn. (competitiveness steering com.), Sigma Xi, Phi Kappa Phi, Delta Phi Sigma, Tau Beta Pi. Home: 314 S Rockingham Ave Los Angeles CA 90049-3638

ROSENSTEIN, LEONARD, real estate company executive; b. Phila., Aug. 4, 1922; s. Benjamin and Esther (Zibulski) R.; m. Eleanor M. Peterson, Mar. 11, 1960; children: Elissa L., Risa B., Tedd B. BS in Pharmacy, Temple U., 1943; BS in Pharmacy (hon.), New Orleans. Lic. pharmacist, Pa., N.J. Pres. Lincoln Pharmacy, Atlantic City, N.J., 1947-69, Mercy Ambulance, Las Vegas, Nev., 1971-73, Nev. Devel. and Realty Co., Las Vegas, 1973—, am. Mgmt. Co., Las Vegas, 1973—; chmn. Players Express Travel, Las Vegas, 1990—. Editor: Temple University Apothecary, 1943. Chmn. Downtown Improvement Authority, Atlantic City, N.J., 1982-84; pres. N.J. Pharm. Assn., 1960; chmn., pres. Nat. Assn. Retail Druggists, Washington, 1969; commr. So. Nev. Regional Housing Bd., Las Vegas, 1993-94.; mem. Beth Sholem Congregation, 1971—. Cpl. U.S. Army, 1943-46, ETO. Recipient award Am. Legion, 1940, E.R. Squibb, 1960, Bowl of Hygea, A.H. Robbins, 1965; named Ky. Col., 1965—. Mem. Greater Las Vegas Realtor Assn., Inst. Real Estate Mgmt., Jewish War Vets, Am. Legion, Elks, Alpha Zeta Omega. Home: 909 Cashman Dr Las Vegas NV 89107-4429 Office: Nev Devel & Realty Co 2980 Meade Ave Las Vegas NV 89102

ROSENSTEIN, ROBERT BRYCE, lawyer, financial advisor; b. Santa Monica, Calif., Feb. 26, 1954; s. Franklin Lee and Queen Esther (Shall) R.; m. Resa Shanee Brookler, Nov. 30, 1980; children: Shaun Franklin, Jessica Laney, Madeline Frances. BA, Calif. State U., Northridge, 1976; JD, Southwestern U., 1979. Bar: Calif. 1979, U.S. Dist. Ct. (cen. and no. dists.) Calif. 1980, U.S. Tax Ct. 1981; registered environ. assessor. Service rep. Social Security Adminstrn., Los Angeles, 1974-77; tax cons. Am. Tax Assocs., Los Angeles, 1970-78, ptnr., 1978; prin., pres. Robert B. Rosenstein, PC, Los Angeles, 1979-84; ptnr. Rosenstein and Werlin, Los Angeles, 1984-87; pres. Robert Bryce Rosenstein Ltd., Temelula, 1987—; chief fin. officer BSE Mgmt. Inc., Los Angeles, 1987-90, corp. counsel, 1987-92, sr. v.p. corp. devel., acquisitions, 1990-92; corp. counsel, 1995—; bd. dirs. BSE Mgmt. Inc, Sirius Computer Corp., Spartan Computer, Unicomp, Inc., Diagnostic Engring. Inc.; pres. Will Find Inc., 1986-87. Recipient Am. Jurisprudence award Bancroft Whitney; Order of Cheviler. Mem. ABA (taxation and environ. coms., vice chmn. gen. bus. sect.), Assn. Trial Lawyers Am., L.A. Bar Assn. Democrat. Jewish. Lodges: Masons, Ionic, Composite. Office: 27450 Ynez Ste 222 Temecula CA 92591

ROSENTHAL, ALAN JAY, psychiatry educator; b. Detroit, Sept. 4, 1938; married; 3 children. AB magna cum laude, Wayne State U., 1960; MD, U. Mich., 1963. Diplomate Am. Bd. Psychiatry and Neurology in Psychiatry, Am. Bd. Child Psychiatry. Intern Kaiser Found. Hosp., San Francisco, 1963-64; resident in psychiatry U. Mich. Med. Ctr., Ann Arbor, 1964-65; resident in child psychiatry Stanford (Calif.) U. Med. Ctr., 1967-68, instr., chief resident in child psychiatry, 1968-69, asst. prof. dept. psychiatry, 1969-75, dir. child psychiatry, 1970-73, dir. child psychiatry resident tng. program, 1970-75, clin. assoc. prof. dept. psychiatry, 1975-88, clin. prof. dept. psychiatry, 1988—; dir. Children's Health Coun. Mid-Peninsula, Palo Alto, Calif., 1973—; bd. dirs. Children's Health Coun., Palo Alto Adolescent Svcs. Corp.; cons. in field; presenter, lectr. in field. Mem. AMA, Am. Psychiat. Assn., Am. Acad. Child Psychiatry, Assn. Mid-Peninsula (bd. dirs. family svc.), Victor Vaughn Soc., Delta Sigma Rho, Phi Beta Kappa. Home: 75 Old Spanish Trl Portola Valley CA 94028

ROSENTHAL, DONNA, broadcast producer; b. El Paso, Tex., Jan. 6, 1950; d. Morris and Elinor (Greene) R.; m. Joe Lurie, 1986. BA, U. Calif., Berkeley, 1969; MSc, London Sch. Econs., 1977. Lectr. Sophia U., Tokyo, 1970-71; prodr. Israel TV, Jerusalem, 1972-74, Veronica TV, The Netherlands, 1979-85, Sta. KRON-TV, San Francisco, 1986; journalist The Atlantic, Newsweek, The L.A. Times, The Washington Post, The Boston Globe, 1986—; reporter The New York Daily News, 1986. Author: (screenplay) Snakehead, 1995. Mem. NATAS, Soc. Profl. Journalists.

ROSENTHAL, EMILY SARAH, television producer; b. N.Y.C., Sept. 19, 1967; d. Robert Kenneth and Esther Lowell (Zamore) R. BA in Econs. and Cmty. Health cum laude, Tufts U., 1989; postgrad., Am. Grad. Sch. Internat. Mgmt., 1994—. Edtl. asst. The Internat. Economy, Washington, 1989-90; corp. comms. asst. Smick Medley Internat., Washington, 1990; White House producer, assignment editor NHK-Japan Broadcasting, Washington, 1990-91; producer Conus Comms., Washington, 1991; producer, sta. rels. liaison Potomac TV/Comms., Inc., Washington, 1991; ops. mgr. Pyramid Video, Washington, 1991-94. Mem. Nat. Press Club. Jewish.

ROSENTHAL, JACK, broadcasting executive; b. Chgo., Aug. 7, 1930; s. Samuel J. and Celia (Weinberg) R.; m. Elaine Lois Brill, May 2, 1954; children: Michael Bruce, Robert Joseph, Richard Scott. BA in History, U. Wyo., 1952, LLD (hon.), 1993. Sec., treas. Buffalo Theatre Corp., 1952-57, No. Wyo. Broadcasting Corp., 1957-64; v.p., gen. mgr. Sta. KTWO Radio and TV, Casper, Wyo., 1964-69; exec. v.p. Harriscope Broadcasting Corp., 1969-77; pres. broadcast div. Harriscope Broadcasting Corp., Los Angeles, 1977-87; pres. Wyo. Radio Network, 1987—, Clear Channel Radio, Inc., 1988—; chmn. Wyo. industry adv. com. FCC; dir. Wyo. Nat. Bank, Affiliated Bank Corp. of Wyo.; dir. TV Info. Office, 1984; designer U.S. Postage stamps 15 cent Buffalo Bill Cody, 1988, 25 cent Wyo. Centennial Commemorative, 1990, 29 cent Oreg. Trail Commemorative, 1993; mem. ct. of honor World Stamp Expo '89, World Columbian Expo 1992, ct. of honor, Granada, Spain, 1992. Producer (TV film) Conrad Schwiering-Mountain Painter (Western Heritage award 1974). Mem. Wyo. Travel Commn., 1969-71, Wyo. Land and Water Commn., 1965-66, Yellowstone Nat. Park Centennial Commn., 1972, Wyo. Coun. Arts, 1969, City of Casper Art Fund, 1979-80; bd. dirs. Milward Simpson Endowment, U. Wyo. Found., 1970—; adv. Nat. Park Svc. Dept. Interior, 1974-76; mem. jud. planning com. Wyo. Supreme Ct., 1976-77; mem. citizens stamp adv. com. U.S. Postal Svc., 1985-89, chmn. 1990-92; trustee The Philatelic Found.; advisor, Nat. Postal Mus. Smithsonian Inst., 1993—. Served to 1st lt. U.S. Army, 1952-54, Korea. Recipient Alfred I. DuPont Found. award broadcast journalism, 1965, U.S. Conf. Mayors award for outstanding community service, 1966, Disting. Alumnus award U. Wyo., 1982, Commendation Casper C. of C., 1984, Disting. Alumnus award Coll. Arts and Scis., U. Wyo., 1991, chmn. football centennial, 1993; named hon. mem. Shoshoni and Arapahoe Indian Tribes, 1965. Mem. Nat. Assn. Broadcasters (nat. chmn. TV and radio polit. action com. 1977-79, Grover C. Cobb meml. award 1983), Wyo. Assn. Broadcasters (pres. 1963), Fedn. Rocky Mountain States Ednl. TV Com. Office: 150 Nichols Ave Casper WY 82601-1816

ROSENTHAL, JOHN DAVID, dentist; b. Portland, Oreg., Feb. 26, 1950; s. Lawrence A. and H. Bertha (Klein) R.; m. Barbara J. Loomis, Apr. 1, 1977; children: Kristin, Benjamin. BS, U. Oreg., 1973; DMD, U. Oreg. Health Sci. U., 1976. Dentist Rosenthal & Rosenthal, DMD, Portland, 1976-79; pvt. practice Portland, 1979—. Dental chmn. United Way of Oreg., Portland, 1985; mem. membership com. Temple Beth Israel, Portland, 1984-87; mem. adv. com. Robison Retirement Home, Portland, 1986—. Fellow Am. Coll. Dentists, Acad. Gen. Dentistry, Acad. Dentistry Internat.; mem. Oreg. Soc. Dentistry for Children, Western Soc. Periodontology, Multnomah Dental Soc. (bd. dirs. 1979-81, pres. 1986), Oreg. Dental Assn. (membership chmn. 1984-88, chmn. mem. svcs. coun. 1988-91, Svc. award 1991), Oreg. Acad. Gen. Dentistry (bd. dirs. 1986-90, sec.-treas. 1990-91, pres. 1991-92), Oreg. Health Sci. U. Sch. Dentistry Alumni Assn. (bd. dirs. 1987-90), Theta Chi. Home: 6565 SW 88th Pl Portland OR 97223-7273

ROSENTHAL, PAUL, physical therapist; b. Bklyn., Jan. 7, 1952; s. Irving and Mary M. (Benjamin) R.; m. April Marie Cosloy, July 20, 1985; children: Alec, Chloe. BA in Physiology, San Francisco State U., 1974; BS in Phys. Therapy, U. Calif., San Francisco, 1977. Lic. in phys. therapy, Oreg., Calif. Staff phys. therapist Seton Med. Ctr., Daly City, Calif., 1977-80, West Bay Home Health, Daly City, 1980-83; chief phys. therapist St. Catherine Hosp. on HMB, Moss Beach, Calif., 1983-85; phys. therapist Valley Phys. Therapy, Pittsburg, Calif., 1985-87; owner, chief phys. therapist Coastal Phys. Therapy, Brookings, Oreg., 1987—; owner Fifth St. Health and Fitness, Brookings, 1993—; ptnr. The Heritage Group, Brookings, 1989—. Mem. 17C Sch. Budget Com., Brookings, 1990—. Mem. Am. Phys. Therapy Assn., Oreg. Phys. Therapy Assn., Oreg. Phys. Therapists in Ind. Practice, Am. Coll. Sports Medicine. Office: Coastal Phys Therapy 580 5th St Ste 600 Brookings OR 97415-9702

ROSENTHAL, PHILIP, gastroenterologist; b. Bayshore, N.Y., Oct. 18, 1949; m. Sherrin Jean Packer; children: Seth, Aaron. BS, SUNY, Albany, 1971; MD, SUNY, Bklyn., 1975. Asst. prof. pediatrics Coll. of Physicians and Surgeons Columbia U., N.Y.C., 1981-83; asst. prof. pediatrics U. So. Calif., L.A., 1983-89, tenured assoc. prof. pediatrics, 1989; dir. pediatrics and nutrition, med. dir. pediatric liver transplant program Cedars-Sinai Med. Ctr., L.A., 1989—; assoc. prof. UCLA, 1989-95; prof. pediat. and surg. U. Calif. San Francisco Med. Ctr., 1995—; asst. attending physician Presbyn. Hosp./Vanderbilt Clinic, N.Y.C., 1981-83, Babies Hosp./Columbia U., 1981-83, Children's Hosp. of L.A., 1983-89; with Vanderbilt Clinic/Columbia U., 1981-83; attending physician Harlem Hosp. and Med. Ctr., N.Y.C., 1981-83, L.A. County/U. So. Calif. Med. Ctr., 1988-89. Vol. City of L.A. Marathon, 1989-90; v.p. Westside Jewish Community Ctr., L.A., 1989-92, bd. dirs. program com., 1987, Children's Liver Found., 1986; mem adv. bd. Jewish Activities Mus., 1990—. Nat. Inst. Arthritis grantee, 1978-81, Children's Hosp. of L.A. grantee, 1984-86, 86-87, Abbott Labs. grantee, 1984-85, Children's Liver Found. grantee, 1985-86. Mem. Am. Acad. Pediatrics, N.Am. Soc. Pediatric Gastroenterology and Nutrition. Office: U Calif San Francisco Med Ctr MU4 East 500 Parnassus Ave San Francisco CA 94143-0136

ROSENTHAL, RICHARD JAY, real estate consultant, mediator, educator; b. N.Y.C., Mar. 10, 1940; s. David and Laura Rosenthal. BBA, Hofstra U., 1961; postgrad., U. So. Calif., 1966, NYU, 1978, U. Pa., 1976. Lic. real estate broker, Calif. Pres., designated broker MDR Investment Co., L.A.; broker owner R.J. Rosenthal & Assocs., Realtors, L.A., 1975; CEO The Rosenthal Co., Real Estate Cons., L.A., 1975; mng. ptnr. The Rosenthal Group Real Estate Consultants, Mediators and Educators, L.A., 1990—; vis. lectr. State of Calif. Pers. Devel. Ctr.; guest lectr. Sch. Law, Whittier Coll.; master instr. Calif. Assn. Realtors; adj. prof. real estate Sch. Bus. Adminstrn., Calif. State U., Sacramento; chmn. exec. bd. Real Estate and Land Use Inst., Calif. State U.; cert. instr. for continuing edn. State of Calif. State of Hawaii; mediator L.A. Superior Ct. Panel, La. Supreme Ct. Panel, Calif. Assn. Realtors Panel; speaker in field. Contbr. articles to profl. jours. Commr. County of L.A., 1984—, chmn. commn. on local govt. svcs., 1992—; mediator L.A. Superior Ct. Panel, La. Supreme Ct. Panel, Calif. Assn. Realtors Panel. Recipient spl. honor and highest commendation, Calif. State Assembly, 1979, 86, commendation for Outstanding Leadership and Svc. to the People of Calif. and the Real Estate Industry, Senate Rules Com., 1986, Outstanding Svc. to the Community and Real Estate Industry, Bd. of Suprs., 1979, Outstanding Leadership and Svc. to Community and Field of Real Estate, 1985, Dedicated Svc. to County of Los Angeles, 1987, Mayor's Cert. of Appreciation, 1986, and others. Mem. ABA, Am. Soc. Real Estate Counselors, Nat. Assn. Realtors (bd. dirs. 1984—, regional vice pres. Calif., Hawaii and Guam 1991), Nat. Coun. Exchangors, Nat. Inst. for Dispute Resolution, Realtors Nat. Mktg. Inst., Calif. Real Estate Educators Assn., Calif. Assn. Realtors (bd. dirs. 1978—, pres. 1986), So. Calif. Mediation Assn., No. Calif. Mediation Assn., Los Angeles County Bar Assn., L.A. Bd. Realtors, Palm Desert-Rancho Mirage Bd. Realtors, Palm Springs Bd. Realtors, Beverly Hills Bd. Realtors, Los Angeles County Trial Lawyers Assn. (assoc.), Soc. Profls. in Dispute Resolution, Real Estate Educators Assn., Lambda Alpha Internat., Soc. Profls. in Dispuite Resolution, Nat. Inst. for Dispute Resolution, Southern Calif. Mediation Assn., No. Calif. Mediation Assn. and others. Office: The Rosenthal Group Real Estate Cons PO Box 837 Venice CA 90294-0837

ROSENTHAL, SETH A., radiologist, oncologist; b. Bucks County, Pa., July 9, 1961; s. Isadore and Corinne Rosenthal; children: Ruth, Eli. BA in Chemistry and History, Wesleyan U., Middletown, Conn., 1982; MD, Yale U., 1987. Diplomate Nat. Bd. Med. Examiners, Am. Bd. Radiology. Medicinal chemist Merck Sharp & Dohme, West Point, Pa., 1982-83; intern Yale New Haven (Conn.) Hosp., 1987-88; resident in radiation oncology U. Pa., Phila., 1988-90, chief resident in radiation oncology, 1990-91; asst. prof. in residence in radiation oncology U. Calif. San Francisco, 1991-93; asst. clin. prof. surgery U. Calif. Davis, Sacramento, 1993—; asst. clin. prof. radiation oncology U. Calif., San Francisco, 1993—; attending physician Radiation Oncology Ctrs., Sacramento, 1993—. Recipient Young Oncologist award Am. Radium Soc., 1982. Mem. Phi Beta Kappa. Office: Sutter Radiation Oncology Ctr 5271 "F" St Sacramento CA 95819

ROSENTHAL, SOL, lawyer; b. Balt., Oct. 17, 1934; s. Louis and Hattie (Getz) R.; m. Diane Myra Sackler, June 11, 1961; children: Karen Abby, Pamela Margaret, Robert Joel. AB, Princeton U., 1956; JD, Harvard U., 1959. Bar: Md. 1959, Calif. 1961. Law clk. to chief judge U.S. Ct. Appeals, 4th cir., Balt., 1959-60; assoc. Kaplan, Livingston, Goodwin, Berkowitz & Selvin, Beverly Hills, Calif., 1960-66, ptnr., 1966-74; ptnr. Buchalter, Nemer, Fields & Younger, L.A., 1974—; bd. dirs. Playboy Enterprises, Inc., Chgo.; arbitrator Dirs. Guild Am., L.A., 1976—, Writers Guild Am., L.A., 1976—, Am. Film Mktg. Assn., 1989—; negotiator Writers Guild-Assn. Talent Agts., L.A., 1978—. Founder Camp Ronald McDonald for Good Times, L.A., 1985; charter founder Mus. Contemporary Art, L.A., 1988. Mem. ABA, Calif. Bar Assn., L.A. County Bar Assn. (trustee 1981-82), L.A. Copyright Soc. (pres. 1973-74), Acad. TV Arts and Scis. (bd. govs. 1990-92), Beverly Hills Bar Assn. (pres. 1982-83), Phi Beta Kappa. Office: Buchalter Nemer et al Ste 2400 1801 Century Park E Los Angeles CA 90067-2326

ROSENWASSER, RENA SUE, poet; b. N.Y.C., Jan. 19, 1950; d. Emanuel and Florence (Compaine) R. BA, Sarah Lawrence Coll., 1971; MA, Mills Coll., 1979. Founding mem. Kelsey St. Press, Berkeley, Calif., 1974-84, dir., 1984—. Author: Isle, 1993 (Pen West nomination), Unplace Place, 1994, Simulacra, 1986; editor: Under Flag, 1991 (Multi-cultural Pubs. award). Democrat. Office: Kelsey St Press 2718 9th St Berkeley CA 94710-2606

ROSENZWEIG, CAROL BARBARA, writer, art publisher; b. N.Y.C.; d. Sidney and Sadie (Greenberg) Kupersmith; m. Saul Louis Rosenzweig, Feb. 11, 1961; children: Davy, Laurance. BA, Pa. State U., 1951. Acct. exec., v.p. Pub. Relations Research Inc., Pitts., 1951-60; freelance writer St. Louis, Los Angeles, Palm Springs, Calif., 1961-80; pres. Rosebranch, Inc., Los Angeles, 1980-86, Artist Editions Ltd., Beverly Hills, Calif., 1985—; v.p. R.Z. Group, Inc., Los Angeles, 1986—. Author: (TV shows) House Husband, 1983, 21 Days of America, 1985 (Heritage award), Women of the World, 1987. Chmn. emeritus Young Talent award com. Los Angeles County Mus. Art, 1985—; pres. Carol and Saul Rosenzweig Family Found., Los Angeles, 1987. Mem. Women in Film, Royal TV Soc., Modern and Contemp. Art Council (bd. dirs. 1976-85). Jewish. Club: Mountaingate (Los Angeles). Office: RZ Group Inc 1081 Westwood Blvd Los Angeles CA 90024-2911

ROSENZWEIG, MARK RICHARD, psychology educator; b. Rochester, N.Y., Sept. 12, 1922; s. Jacob and Pearl (Grossman) R.; m. Janine S.A. Chappat, Aug. 1, 1947; children: Anne Janine, Suzanne Jacqueline, Philip Mark. B.A., U. Rochester, 1943, M.A., 1944; Ph.D., Harvard U., 1949; hon. doctorate, U. René Descartes, Sorbonne, 1980. Postdoctoral research fellow Harvard U., 1949-51; asst. prof. U. Calif., Berkeley, 1951-56; assoc. prof. U. Calif., 1956-60, prof. psychology, 1960-91, assoc. research prof., 1958-59, research prof., 1965-66, prof. emeritus, 1991—; vis. prof. biology Sorbonne, Paris, 1973-74; mem. exec. com. Internat. Union Psychol. Sci., 1972—, v.p., 1980-84, pres., 1988-92, past pres. 1992-96; mem. U.S. Nat. Com. for Internat. Union Psychol. Sci., NRC Nat. Acad. Sci., 1984—, chmn., 1984-88. Author: Biologie de la Mémoire, 1976, (with A.L. Leiman) Physiological Psychology, 1982, 2d edit., 1989, (with M.J. Renner) Enriched and Impoverished Environments: Effects on Brain and Behavior, 1987, (with D. Sinha) La Recherche en Psychologie Scientifique, 1988; editor: (with P. Mussen) Psychology: An Introduction, 1973, 2d edit., 1977, (with E.L. Bennett) Neural Mechanisms of Learning and Memory, 1976, International Psychological Science: Progress, Problems, and Prospects, 1992; co-editor: (with L. Porter) Ann. Rev. of Psychology, 1968-94; contbr. articles to profl. jours. Served with USN, 1944-46. Recipient Disting. Alumnus award U. Rochester; Fulbright research fellow; faculty research fellow Social Sci. Research Council, 1960-61; research grantee NSF, USPHS, Easter Seal Found., Nat. Inst. Drug Abuse. Fellow AAAS, APA (Disting. Sci. Contbn. award 1982), Am. Psychol. Soc.; mem. NAS, NAACP (life), Am. Physiol. Soc., Am. Psychol. Soc., Internat. Brain Rsch. Orgn., Soc. Exptl. Psychologists, Soc. for Neurosci., Société Française de Psychologie, Sierra Club (life), Common Cause, Fulbright Assn. (life), Phi Beta Kappa, Sigma Xi. Office: U Calif Dept Psychology 3210 Tolman Hall Berkeley CA 94720-1650

ROSETT, ANN DOYLE, librarian; b. Valdosta, Ga., Jan. 9, 1955; d. David Spencer Doyle and Lois Annette Gray; m. Robert Allen Richardson, Aug. 1, 1976 (div. June 1981); children: Caitlin Ann, Brendan Wesley; m. John David Rosett, Aug. 6, 1983. Student, Kenyon Coll., 1972-75, U. Dayton, 1974, U. Ala., Birmingham, 1978; BA, Shepherd Coll., 1982; MLS, U. Wash., 1988. Cert. profl. libr., Wash. College libr. Northwest Coll., Kirkland, Wash., 1988—. Mem. ALA, Assn. Christian Librs. (dir.-at-large 1992-93), Assn. Coll. and Rsch. Librs., Am. Theol. Lib. Assn., N.W. Assn. Christian Librs. (treas. 1989-91, pres. 1991-93). Democrat. Office: NW Coll DV Hurst Libr PO Box 579 5520 108th Ave NE Kirkland WA 98033-7523

ROSETT, ARTHUR IRWIN, lawyer, educator; b. N.Y.C., July 5, 1934; s. Milton B. and Bertha (Werner) R.; m. Rhonda K. Lawrence; children: David Benjamin, Martha Jean, Daniel Joseph. A.B., Columbia U., 1955, LL.B., 1959. Bar: Calif. 1968, N.Y. State 1960, U.S. Supreme Ct. 1963. Law clk. U.S. Supreme Ct., 1959-60; asst. U.S. atty. So. Dist. N.Y., 1960-63; practice law N.Y.C., 1963-65; assoc. dir. Pres.'s Commn. on Law Enforcement and Adminstrn. Justice, 1965-67; acting prof. law UCLA, 1967-70, prof., 1970—. Author: Contract Law and Its Application, 1971, 5th revised edit., 1994, (with D. Cressey) Justice by Consent, 1976, (with E. Dorff) A Living Tree, 1987. Served with USN, 1956-58. Mem. Am. Law Inst. Home: 641 S Saltair Ave Los Angeles CA 90049-4134 Office: UCLA Law Sch 405 Hilgard Ave Los Angeles CA 90024-1301

ROSHONG, DEE ANN DANIELS, dean, educator; b. Kansas City, Mo., Nov. 22, 1936; d. Vernon Edmund and Doradell (Kellogg) Daniels; m. Richard Lee Roshong, Aug. 27, 1960 (div.). BMusEd., U. Kans., 1958; MA in Counseling and Guidance, Stanford U., 1960; postgrad. Fresno State U., U. Calif.; EdD, U. San Francisco, 1980. Counselor, psychometrist Fresno City Coll., 1961-65; counselor, instr. psychology Chabot Coll., Hayward, Calif., 1965-75; coord. counseling services Chabot Coll., Valley Campus, Livermore, Calif., 1975-81, asst. dir. student pers. svcs., 1981-89, Las Positas Coll., Livermore, Calif., 1989-91, assoc. dean student svcs., 1991-94, dean student svcs., 1994—; writer, coord. I, A Woman Symposium, 1974, Feeling Free to Be You and Me Symposium, 1975, All for the Family Symposium, 1976, I Celebrate Myself Symposium, 1977, Person to Person in Love and Work Symposium, 1978; The Healthy Person in Body, Mind and Spirit Symposium, 1979, Feelin' Good Symposium, 1980, Change Symposium, 1981, Sources of Strength Symposium, 1982, Love and Friendship Symposium, 1983, Self Esteem Symposium, 1984, Trust Symposium, 1985, Prime Time: Making the Most of This Time in Your Life Symposium, 1986, Symposium on Healing, 1987, How to Live in the World and Still Be Happy Symposium, 1988, Student Success is a Team Effort, Sound Mind, Sound Body Symposium, 1989, Creating Life's Best Symposium, 1990, Choices Symposium, 1991, Minding the Body, Mending the Mind Symposium, 1992, Healing through Love and Laughter Symposium, 1993, Healing Ourselves Changing the World Symposium, 1994, Finding Your Path Symposium, 1995; mem. cast TV prodns. Eve and Co., Best of Our Times, Cowboy; chmn. Calif. C.C. Chancellor's Task Force on Counseling, Statewide Regional Counseling Facilitators, 1993-95, Statewide Conf. on Emotionally Disturbed Students in Calif. C.C.s, 1982—, Conf. on the Under Represented Student in California C.C.s, 1986, Conf. on High Risk Students, 1989. Mem. Assn. Humanistic Psychologists, Western Psychol. Assn., Nat. Assn. Women Deans and Counselors, Assn. for Counseling and Devel., Calif. Assn. Community Colls. (chmn. commn. on student services 1979-84), Calif. Community Colls. Counselors Assn. (Svc. award 1986, 87, award for Outstanding and Disting. Service, 1986, 87, Spl. Svc. award for outstanding svc Calif. advocated for re-entry edn., 1991), Alpha Phi. Author: Counseling Needs of Community Coll. Students, 1980. Home: 1856 Harvest Rd Pleasanton CA 94566-5456 Office: 3033 Collier Canyon Rd Livermore CA 94550-9797

ROSICH, RAYNER KARL, physicist; b. Joliet, Ill., Aug. 28, 1940; s. Joseph F. and Gretchen (Cox) R.; BS in Physics cum laude with honors, U. Mich., 1962, MS in Physics, 1963; PhD, U. Colo., 1977; MBA, U. Denver, 1982; m. Judy Louise Jackson, Aug. 20, 1966; children: Heidi Ann, Kimberly Ann, Dawn Ann. Teaching fellow and rsch. asst. U. Mich., Ann Arbor, 1962-67; staff, Argonne (Ill.) Nat. Lab. Applied Math. Div., summers 1961-63; physicist, project leader Inst. for Telecommunication Sci., U.S. Dept. Commerce, Boulder, Colo., 1967-80; sr. scientist and program mgr. Electro Magnetic Applications, Inc., Denver, 1980-82; applications mgr. Energy Systems Tech., Inc., Denver, 1982-83, mgr. R&D, 1983; prin. scientist, program mgr. Contel Info. Systems, Inc., Denver, 1983-84, dir. tech. audits, 1985, dir. basic and applied R&D, 1986; lab. scientist for systems engring. lab. Hughes Aircraft Co., Denver, 1986, lab. scientist for data systems lab, 1986-90, lab. scientist for systems lab., 1990-92; prin. engr., Advanced System Techs., Inc., Denver, 1992-95; project mgr. Evolving Systems, Inc., 1995—. instr. math. Arapahoe Cmty. Coll., 1987—. Vol. judo instr., county recreation dist., 1976-77. Recipient Spl. Achievement award U.S. Dept. Commerce, 1974, Outstanding Performance award, 1978, Sustained Superior Performance award, 1979; Libbey-Owens-Ford Glass Co./U. Mich. Phoenix Meml. fellow, 1964-66; NSF Summer fellow, 1965. Mem. Am. Phys. Soc., AAAS, IEEE, Assn. Computing Machinery, Applied Computational Electromagnetics Soc., Soc. Computer Stimulation, Sigma Xi, Phi Kappa Phi. Home: 7932 W Nichols Ave Littleton CO 80123-5558 Office: Evolving Systems Inc 8000 E Maplewood Ave Englewood CO 80111

ROSIER, DAVID LEWIS, investment banker; b. Sioux City, Iowa, Mar. 22, 1937; s. Orel Lewis and Jewell May (Palmer) R.; m. Jackie Dodd, July 1965 (div. 1973); 1 child, Michele, m. Carol Mary Byre, Nov. 25, 1982. BSBA, U. Denver, 1960. V.p., mgr. mktg. Hertz Internat., Ltd., N.Y., 1970-71; regional v.p. Amtrak, N.Y., 1971-73; mng. ptnr. Rosier & Assocs., Ltd., San Diego, 1969—; sr. v.p. for strategic mktg. Am. Prins. Holdings, Inc., San Diego, 1979-84; v.p., registered prin. Am. Diversified Equity Corp., Costa Mesa, Calif., 1984-85; pres. Glen Eagle, Inc., 1986-87; sr. v.p. Western Region Cozad Investment Svcs. Inc., San Diego, 1987-88; dir. corp. fin. Brookstreet Securities Corp., Irvine, Calif., 1993—. Appeared as speaker on nat. TV and at various industry conferences. Bd. dirs. Nautical Heritage Soc. (Hamburg award 1988). Mem. Oceanside Rotary (Paul Harris fellow, benefactor), Kona Kai Internat. Yacht Club (commodore 1987), Internat. Order of the Blue Gavel (founder and past chmn. bd. trustees Humanities Found.), Big Band Jazz Hall of Fame Found. (founder, treas., dir.).

ROSIN, MORRIS, real estate, land development company executive; b. San Antonio, Feb. 21, 1924; s. Berco and Leia (Dupchansky) R.; student Tex. A&M U., 1942, St. Mary's U., 1941, 45-47; m. Ethel Rosenberg; children—Susan, Charles, Lindsay. Sec.-treas. Bimbi Mfg. Co., 1949-67; pres. Bimbi Shoe Co. div. Athlone Industries, San Antonio, 1970-72; v.p. Athlone Industries, Parsippany, N.J., 1967-72; pres. Ardo Pro, San Antonio, 1966-74, Yoakum Bend Corp., San Antonio, 1968—, Broadway Devel. Corp., 1984-90; sec.-treas. R & R Corp., San Antonio, 1970-72. Served with USAAF, 1942-45. Clubs: Masons (32 deg.), Shriners. Home: 7477 Avenida De Palais Carlsbad CA 92009-6909

ROSKY, BURTON SEYMOUR, lawyer; b. Chgo., May 28, 1927; s. David T. and Mary W. (Zelkin) R.; m. Leatrice J. Darrow, June 16, 1951; children: David Scott, Bruce Alan. Student, Ill. Inst. Tech., 1944-45; BS, UCLA, 1948; JD, Loyola U., L.A., 1953. Bar: Calif. 1954, U.S. Supreme Ct 1964, U.S. Tax Ct 1964; C.P.A., Calif. Auditor City of L.A., 1948- 51; with Beidner, Temkin & Ziskin (C.P.A.s), L.A., 1951-52; supervising auditor Army Audit Agy., 1952-53; practiced law L.A., Beverly Hills, 1954—; ptnr. Duskin & Rosky, 1972-82; s Rosky, Landau & Fox, 1982-93; ptnr. Rosky, Landau, Stahl & Sheehy, Beverly Hills, 1993-94; lectr. on tax and bus. problems; judge pro tem Beverly Hills Mcpl. Ct., L.A. Superior Ct.; mem. L.A. Mayor's Community Adv. Council. Contbr. profl. publs. Charter supporting mem. Los Angeles County Mus. Arts; contbg. mem. Assocs. of Smithsonian Instn.; charter mem. Air and Space Mus; mem. Am. Mus. Natural History, L.A. Zoo; supporting mem. L.A. Mus. Natural History; mem. exec. bd. So. Calif. coun. Nat. Fedn. Temple Brotherhoods, mem. nat. exec. bd. With USNR, 1945-46. Walter Henry Cook fellow Loyola Law Sch. Fellow Jewish Chautauqua Soc. (life mem.); mem. Am. Arbitration Assn. (nat. panel arbitrators), Am. Assn. Attys.-CPAs (charter mem. pres. 1968), Calif. Assn. Attys.-CPAs (charter mem., pres. 1963), Calif. Soc. CPAs, Calif., Beverly Hills, Century City, Los Angeles County bar assns., Am. Judicature Soc., Chancellors Assocs. UCLA, Tau Delta Phi, Phi Alpha Delta.; mem. B'nai B'rith. Jewish (mem. exec. bd., pres. temple, pres. brotherhood). Club: Mason. Office: Rosky Landau & Fox 8383 Wilshire Blvd Beverly Hills CA 90211

ROSNER, ROBERT ALLAN, advocate; b. Lincoln Park, N.J., Nov. 2, 1956; s. Henry and Katherine (Kravitt) R.; m. Robin Simons, May 20, 1989. BS, U. Puget Sound, 1980; MBA, U. Wash., 1992. Restaurant mgr. Eatery, Phila., 1976-78; pub. rels. mgr. Big Brothers/Sisters, Tacoma, Wash., 1979; pub. affairs dir. Sta. KNBQ, Tacoma, 1980; exec. dir. Safety Assistance from the Elderly, Seattle, 1981-82, Smoking Policy Inst., Seattle, 1982-93; dep. campaign chair United Way of King County, 1993-94; COO The Sci. Club, 1995; bd. dirs., chmn. bd. Giraffe Project, Langley, Wash., 1989, Coming of Age in Am., Seattle, 1989; adj. prof. Heritage Inst./Antioch, Seattle, 1988, Seattle Pacific U. Grad. Sch. Bus., 1993; radio program host KOMO radio. Author: U.S. Environmental Protection, 1990, Guide to Workplace Smoking Policies, 1990; contbr. articles to profl. jours. Bd. dirs. Salvation Army, Seattle, 1992. Recipient Gen. News Reporting award, Soc. Profl. Journalists, 1980, Emerald award Internat. TV and Video Assn., Seattle, 1986, Surgeon Gen.'s medallion, 1988. Mem. Seattle Downtown Rotary. Office: 9187 Mandus Olson NE Bainbridge Island WA 98110

ROSS, ALEXANDER DUNCAN, art librarian; b. N.Y.C., Aug. 3, 1941; s. Donald Duncan and Anita (Petersen) R.; m. Susan Dixon Getman, July 29, 1967 (div. 1977); m. Eleanore Saunders Stewart, June 22, 1985. B.A., Columbia U., 1966, M.S., 1968, M.A., 1971. Asst. art librarian Columbia U., N.Y.C., 1968-71; assoc. librarian Cleve. Mus. Art, 1971-75; head art librarian Stanford U., Calif., 1975—. Contbr. articles to profl. jours. Mem. Art Libraries Soc. N. Am. Home: 4175 Wilkie Way Palo Alto CA 94306-4159 Office: Stanford U Art & Arch Libr 102 Cummings Art Bldg Stanford CA 94305

ROSS, ALVIN, manufacturing executive; b. Minot, N.D., Apr. 4, 1922; s. Samuel and Goldie (Perlin) R.; m. Barbie Wechsler, Apr. 14, 1946; children: Talby W., Gelb, Elyse M. Piper, Mark W. Ross. BA, U. Wash., 1946, Master degree, 1958. Sales mgr. midwest H.D. Lee Co., Mission, Kans., 1963-72; v.p. Wrangler Boys div. Midwest Blue Bell Corp. (Wrangler Co.), Greensboro, N.C., 1972-85; pres. Opportunity Mktg., City of Industry, Calif., 1990—; pres. Opportunity Mktg. Co. consulting Apparel Industry, Palm Desert, Calif., 1991; v.p. mktg. Jaime L'amour Sportswear divsn. Summit Ridge Corp., 1994—. Office: Opportunity Mktg Co 11110 NE 41st Dr # 44 Kirkland WA 98033-7729

ROSS, CHARLES ALEXANDER, geologist; b. Champaign, Ill., Apr. 16, 1933; s. Herbert Holdsworth and Jean (Alexander) R.; m. June Rosa Pitt Phillips, June 27, 1959. BA, U. Colo., 1954; MS, Yale U., 1958, PhD, 1959. Rsch. assoc. Peabody Mus., Yale U., New Haven, 1959-60; asst., assoc. geologist Ill. State Geol. Survey, Urbana, 1960-64; asst., assoc., full prof. dept. geology Western Wash. U., Bellingham, 1964-82, chair dept. geology, 1977-82; sr. staff geologist Gulf Oil Co., Tech. Exploration Ctr., Houston, 1982-83, dir., mgr., 1983-85; biostratigrapher Chevron USA, Houston, 1985-92, GeoBioStrat, Bellingham, Wash., 1992—; rsch. assoc. dept. geology Western Wash. U., 1992—; sec., treas. Soc. Econ. Paleontologists and Mineralogists, Tulsa, 1982-84; pres. Cushman Found. for Foraminiferal Rsch., 1983-84, 90-91. Author, co-author and editor of 8 books; contbr. over 175 articles to profl. jours. 1st lt. U.S. Army, 1954-56. Recipient Best Paper award 1967 Jour. Palontology, 1968. Fellow Geol. Soc. Am., Cushman Found. for Foraminiferal Rsch.; mem. AAAS, Am. Assn. Petroleum Geologists, Soc. Sedimentary Geology (hon. mem., hon. mem. Permian Basin Sect.). Office: GeoBioStrat 600 Highland Dr Bellingham WA 98225-6410

ROSS, DAVID EDWARD, software engineer; b. L.A., Aug. 5, 1941; s. Sydney Harold and Lillian (Weiss) R.; m. Evelyn Rita Rappaport, Oct. 25, 1964; children: Allen Michel, Heather Michelle. BA in Math., UCLA, 1964, cert. in numerical analysis, 1965. Computer programmer UCLA, 1962-66, Computer Applications, Inc., L.A., 1966-69; software engr. Unisys Corp., Santa Monica, Camarillo, Calif., 1969-93; computer software engr. Sci. Applicatoins Internat. Corp., Camarillo, 1993—. Reviewer Computing Revs., 1981—. Mem. Mcpl. Adv. Coun., Oak Park, Calif., 1974-81; mem. sch. bd. Oak Park Unified Sch. Dist., 1981-89; mem. Parks and Recreation Planning Com., Oak Park, 1978-79, 85-86, 90-92, 94—; trustee, pres. Cmty. Found. Oak Park, 1980—. Mem. Assn. Computing Machinery. Jewish. Office: Sci Applications Internat 5151 Camino Ruiz Camarillo CA 93012-8601

ROSS, DEBORAH LYNN (DEBBIE ROSS), reporter, photographer; b. Pitts., Mar. 29, 1961; d. David William and Joan Muriel (Reinhardt) R. BS in Journalism, Ball State U., 1984. Reporter, photographer High Country Ind. Press, Belgrade, Mont., 1986-87, Dillon (Mont.) Tribune-Examiner, 1987—. Recipient first prizes for best sports photo and best editorial page Mont. Newspaper Assn., 1987, third place award Nat. Newspaper Assn., 1988. Mem. Nat. Press Photographer's Assn. (best photo 1983, 1984), Mont. Press Assn. Democrat. Presbyterian. Office: Dillon Tribune-Examiner Dillon MT 59725

ROSS, DOUGLAS ARTHUR, electrical engineering educator, consultant; b. Seattle, May 6, 1942; s. Don Ray and Sylvia (Forey) R.; m. Nicholl Louise Dorsey Ross; children: Donald Raymond, Margaret Louise, Sarah Elizabeth. BSEE, Seattle U., 1965; MSEE, 1966; PhD, U. Washington, 1969. Teaching asst. Seattle U., 1965-66; teaching asst. U. Washington, 1966-67, rsch. asst., 1967-69; lectr. Elec. Engring. Queen Mary Coll. U. London, 1969-82; assoc. prof. Elec. Engring. U. Colo., Denver, 1982-85, assoc. chmn. Computer Sci., 1989-90, assoc. prof. Elec. Engring., 1985—; numerous presentations in field. Author: (with others) Sound Reception in Fish, 1976, Optoelectronic Devices and optical Imaging Techniques, 1979, Geometric Theory of Diffraction, 1981, Light Scattering in Biological Materials, 1981, Analysis of Organic and Biological Surfaces, 1984, Optical Particle Sizing, 1988; contbr. articles to profl. jours.; patentee in field. Mem. IEEE, Pi Mu Epsilon, Tau Beta Pi, Sigma Xi. Home: 121 W 8th St Leadville CO 80461-3527 Office: Univ Colorado at Denver 1200 Larimer St Denver CO 80204-5300

ROSS, FRANCES MARGARET, medical technologist, artist; b. Brockport, N.Y., Nov. 20, 1950; d. Benjamin Berlin and Marjorie Lou (Wilder) R. BA in Bacteriology, U. Calif., L.A., 1976. Cert. med. technologist. Med. technologist Oreg. Med. Labs, Eugene, 1978—. Artist numerous watercolor paintings, 1991—; exhbns. include 152nd Ann. Exhibit and travelling exhbn. Am. Watercolor Soc., 1994, Watercolor West Ann. Exhbn., 1994-95. Recipient Grumbacher Bronze medal N.W. Watercolor Soc., 1992, Award of Excellence, Sacramento Fine Arts Ctr. Nat. Open Exhibit, 1991, People's Choice award Beaverton Arts Commn., 1991, Best in Show and Judge's Choice award Lane County Fair, 1990, 92. Mem. Watercolor Soc. Oreg. (Bronze Merit award 1992, Silver Merit award 1993, Gold Merit award 1994), Eugene Concert Choir (graphic artist, Spl. Recognition award 1991, 92). Home: 170 E 33rd Ave Eugene OR 97405-3821

ROSS, GERALDINE YVONNE, biologist, educator; b. Avonmore, Pa., Nov. 18, 1934; d. Peter Louis and Marian Faye (Prusack) DeGrazia; m. Peter Anthony Ross, June 21, 1958; children: Eric Peter, Christopher Allan, Bryan Mitchell. BA, Seton Hill Coll., 1956; MS, Northwestern U., 1957; postgrad., U. Wis., 1957-60, U. Wash., 1974-77. Teaching asst. Northwestern U., Evanston, Ill., 1956-57; rsch. fellow U. Wis., Madison, 1957-60; instr. Bellevue (Wash.) C.C., 1968-89; prof. Highline C.C., Des Moines, Wash., 1980—; sec. faculty senate Highland C.C., Des Moines, Wash., 1990-94; co-organizer critical thinking workshops; textbook reviewer. Author: Study Guide to Accompany Microbiology by Cano and Colome, 1985; coauthor: Instructor's Resource Manual for Starr and Taggart's Biology, 1989, 92, 95, Instructor's Resource Manual for Starr's Biology, 1991, 94; contbr. revs to profl. jours. Active Directions for the '70's Bellevue Sch. Dist., 1969, sci. adv. com., 1970-73. Recipient Excellence in Teaching award Nat. Instn. for Staff and Orgnl. Devel., 1992, Sullivan Class prize Seton Hill Coll., 1954, 56, Disting. Teaching award Phi Theta Kappa, 1990. Mem. Human Anatomy and Physiology Soc., N.W. Biology Instrs. Orgn., Puget Sound Microbiologists, N.Am. Biology Tchrs. Assn., Sigma Xi, Alpha Lambda Delta, Kappa Gamma Pi. Office: Highline CC PO Box 98000 Des Moines WA 98198-9800

ROSS, GLYNN, opera administrator; b. Omaha, Dec. 15, 1914; s. Herman and Ida (Carlson) R.; m. Angelamaria Solimene, Nov. 15, 1946; children: Stephanie, Claudia, Melanie, Anthony. Student, Leland Powers Sch. Theater, Boston, 1937-39. founder O.P.E.R.A. Am.; bd. dirs. Nat. Opera Inst., Soc. for Germanic Music Culture; founder, dir. Pacific N.W. Festival, 1975—. Opera stage dir., U.S., Can., 1939-63, debut, San Francisco Opera, 1948, gen. dir., founder Seattle Opera Assn., Inc., 1963-83; dir. Ariz. Opera, 1983—; founder Pacific N.W. Ballet. Served to 1st lt. AUS, 1942-47. Office: Ariz Opera Assn 3501 N Mountain Ave Tucson AZ 85719-1925

ROSS, HUGH COURTNEY, electrical engineer; b. Dec. 31, 1923; s. Clare W. and Jeanne F. Ross; m. Sarah A. Gordon (dec.); m. Patricia A. Malloy; children: John C., James G., Robert W. Student, Calif. Inst. Tech., 1942, San Jose State U., 1946-47; BSEE, Stanford U., 1950, postgrad., 1954. Registered profl. elec. engr., Calif. Instr. San Benito (Calif.) High Sch. and Jr. Coll., 1950-51; chief engr. vacuum power switches Jennings Radio Mfg. Corp., San Jose, Calif., 1951-62; chief engr. ITT Jennings, San Jose, Calif., 1962-64; pres. Ross Engring. Corp., Campbell, Calif., 1964—. Contbr. articles to tech. jours.; patentee in field. Fellow IEEE (life) (chmn. Santa Clara Valley subsect. 1960-61); mem. Am. Vacuum Soc., Am. Soc. Metals. Office: 540 Westchester Dr Campbell CA 95008-5012

ROSS, HUGH NORMAN, astronomer; b. Westmount, Can., July 24, 1945; came to U.S., 1973; s. James Stewart Alexander and Dorothy Isabel (Murray) R.; m. Kathleen Ann Drake, July 30, 1977; children: Joel Stephen, David Michael. BS in Physics, U. B.C., Vancouver, Can., 1967; MS in Astronomy, U. Toronto, Ont., Can., 1968, PhD in Astronomy, 1973. Rsch. fellow in radio astronomy Calif. Inst. Tech., Pasadena, 1973-78; min. evangelism Sierra Madre (Calif.) Congl. Ch., 1975-86, min. apologetics, 1986—; pres. Reasons To Believe, Pasadena, Calif., 1986—. Author: The Fingerprint of God, 1989, 2d edit., 1991, The Creator and the Cosmos, 1993, 2d edit., 1995, Creation and Time, 1994; also articles, videos, audiotapes and tape albums. Grantee Murdock Charitable Trust, 1990. Mem. Christian Edn. Assn., Am. Sci. Affiliation (cons. commn. for integrity in sci. edn. 1986—). Office: Reasons To Believe PO Box 5978 Pasadena CA 91117-0978

ROSS, JAMES CARL, aerospace engineer; b. Santa Monica, Calif., July 27, 1955. BSME, UCLA, 1973; MEngring., Calif. Poly. State U., 1980; PhD in Aerospace Engring., Iowa State U., 1987. Aerospace engr. in basic fluid mechanics group NASA Ames Rsch. Ctr., Moffett Field, Calif., 1980-82, 84-89, leader low-speed aerodynamics group, 1989—; grad. asst. Iowa State U., 1982-83; aerodynamics cons. America 3, Boston, 1990-91; bd. dirs. Pacific Inverter, Spring Valley, Calif., 1988—; presenter in field. Contbr. articles to profl. publs.; patentee in field. Mem. AIAA, Soc. Automotive Engrs. Office: NASA Ames Rsch Ctr MS 247-2 Moffett Field CA 94035

ROSS, JANET, retired English language educator; b. Duluth, Minn., Apr. 19, 1914; d. Guy Whittier Chadbourn and Helen (Mason) Ross. Student, Carleton Coll., 1931-32; BA, U. Minn., 1935, MA, 1940; PhD, U. Iowa, 1960. Asst. prof. English Fla. State U., Tallahassee, 1949-52, Macalester Coll., St. Paul, 1957-60; instr. English U. Iowa, Iowa City, 1952-54, 55-57, U. B.C. (Can.), Vancouver, 1960-62; prof. English, coord. MA teaching English as fgn. lang. Ball State U., Muncie, Ind., 1961-80; prof. emeritus Ball State U., Muncie, 1980—; vis. prof. U. Colo., Boulder, summers 1956-58, 60, 71-72, 83-85, Pontificia U. Rio Grande do Sul, Porto Alegre, Brazil, 1973; guest lectr. Montgomery (Md.) Community Coll., 1977, U. Saga (Japan), 1980, U. Panama, Panama City, 1981. Co-author: Language and Life in the U.S.A., 1961, 4th edit., 1982, To Write English, 1965, 3rd edit., 1984; author: Understanding English, 1982. Fulbright fellow, Netherlands, 1954-55; Danforth Found. grantee U. Mich., 1964; Nat. Assn. Fgn. Student Affairs travel study grantee Yale U., 1962, travel grantee, France, 1966. Mem. Tchrs. English to Speakers Other Langs. (regional sec. 1976-80), Colo. Authors League (sec. 1987—). Home: 500 Mohawk Dr Apt 606 Boulder CO 80303-3757

ROSS, JOHN, physical chemist, educator; b. Vienna, Austria, Oct. 2, 1926; came to U.S., 1940; s. Mark and Anna (Krecmar) R.; m. Virginia Franklin (div.); children: Elizabeth A., Robert K.; m. Eva Madarasz. BS, Queens Coll., 1948; PhD, MIT, 1951; D (hon.), Weizmann Inst. Sci., Rehovot, Israel, 1984, Queens Coll., SUNY, 1987, U. Bordeaux, France, 1987. Prof. chemistry Brown U., Providence, 1953-66; prof. chemistry MIT, Cambridge, 1966-80, chmn. dept., 1966-71; chmn. faculty of Inst. MIT, 1975-77; prof. Stanford (Calif.) U., 1980—, chmn. dept., 1983-89; cons. to industries, 1979—; mem. bd. govs. Weizmann Inst., 1971—. Author: Physical Chemistry, 1980; editor Molecular Beams, 1966; contbr. articles to profl. jours. 2nd lt. U.S. Army, 1944-46. Recipient medal Coll. de France, Paris. Fellow AAAS, Am. Phys. Soc.; mem. NAS, Am. Acad. Arts and Scis., Am. Chem. Soc. (Irving Langmuir Chem. Physics prize 1992). Home: 738 Mayfield Ave Palo Alto CA 94305-1044 Office: Stanford U Dept Chemistry Stanford CA 94305-5080

ROSS, JOHN J., petroleum products company executive. BA, U. Okla, 1951; LLB, U. Denver, 1958. Bar: Colo. 1958. Gen. tax counsel Chevron Corp., San Francisco. Office: Chevron Corp 555 Market St San Francisco CA 94105-2801

ROSS, JONATHAN, film writer, producer, director; b. N.Y.C., July 17, 1961; s. Peter and Carol Angela (Barnes) R. BA, Columbia U., 1983. Investment banker Paine Webber Inc., N.Y.C., 1983-86; creative exec. 20th Century Fox Film Corp., L.A., 1986-87; pres. JR Prodns., L.A., 1987—. Prodr.: (short film) ...And Then I Woke Up, 1994, (play) Unbeatable Harold, 1991, Terry Neal's Future, 1988; prodr. TV commls., 1987—. Coord. Achilles Track Club for People with Disabilities, So. Calif., 1988—; advisor Crippled Children's Soc., L.A., 1992. 1994 L.A. Marathon honoree, KCOP-TV. Mem. Krav Maga Assn.

ROSS, JUNE ROSA PITT, biologist; b. Taree, May 2, 1931; came to U.S., 1957; d. Bernard and Adeline Phillips; m. Charles Alexander, June 27, 1959. BS with honors, U. Sydney, New S. Wales, Australia, 1953, PhD, 1959, DSc, 1974. Research assoc. Yale U., New Haven, 1959-60, U. Ill.,

Urbana, 1960-65; research assoc. Western Wash. U., Bellingham, 1965-67, assoc. prof., 1967-70, prof. biology, 1970—, chair dept. biology, 1989-90; pres. Western Wash. U. Faculty Senate, Bellingham, 1984-85; conf. host Internat. Bryozoology Assn., 1986. Author: (with others) A Textbook of Entomology, 1982, Geology of Coal, 1984; editor (assoc.) Palaios, 1985-89; contbr. articles to profl. jours. Grantee NSF; recipient Western Wash. U. Outstanding Educator award, 1973, Western Wash. U. Research award, 1986. Mem. Australian Marine Scis. Assn., The Paleontol. Soc. (councillor 1984-86, treas. 1987-93), U.K. Marine Biol. Assn. (life), Microscopy Soc. of Am., Internat. Bryozoology Assn. (pres. 1992-95). Office: Western Wash U Dept Biology Bellingham WA 98255-9060

ROSS, KATHLEEN ANNE, college president; b. Palo Alto, Calif., July 1, 1941; d. William Andrew and Mary Alberta (Wilburn) R. BA, Ft. Wright Coll., 1964; MA, Georgetown U., 1971; PhD, Claremont Grad. Sch., 1979; LLD (hon.) Alverno Coll. Milw., 1990, Dartmouth Coll., 1991, Seattle U., 1992; LHD (hon.) Whitworth Coll., 1992, LLD (hon.) Pomona Coll., 1993. Cert. tchr., Wash. Secondary tchr. Holy Names Acad., Spokane, Wash., 1964-70; dir. rsch. and planning Province Holy Names, Wash. State, 1972-73; v.p. acads. Ft. Wright Coll., Spokane, 1973-81; rsch. asst. to dean Claremont Grad. Sch., Calif., 1977-78; assoc. faculty mem. Harvard U., Cambridge, Mass., 1981; pres. Heritage Coll., Toppenish, Wash., 1981—; cons. Wash. State Holy Names Schs., 1971-73; coll. accrediting assn. evaluator N.W. Assn. Schs. and Colls., Seattle, 1975—; dir. Holy Names Coll., Oakland, Calif., 1979—; cons. Yakima Indian Nation, Toppenish, 1975—; speaker, cons. in field. Author: (with others) Multicultural Pre-School Curriculum, 1977, A Crucial Agenda: Improving Minority Student Success, 1989; Cultural Factors in Success of American Indian Students in Higher Education, 1978. Chmn. Internat. 5-Yr. Convocation of Sisters of Holy Names, Montreal, Que., Can., 1981; TV Talk show host Spokane Council of Chs., 1974-76. Recipient E.K. and Lillian F. Bishop Founds. Youth Leader of Yr. award, 1986, Disting. Citizenship Alumna award Claremont Grad. Sch., 1986, Golden Aztez award Washington Human Devel., 1989, Harold W. McGraw Edn. prize, 1989, John Carroll award Georgetown U., 1991, Holy Names medal Ft. Wright Coll., 1981, Pres. medal Eastern Washington U., 1994; named Yakima Herald Rep. Person of Yr. 1987, First Annual Leadership award Region VIII Coun. Advancement and Support Edn., 1993; Wash. State Medal of Merit, 1995; numerous grants for projects in multicultural higher edn., 1974—. Mem. Nat. Assn. Ind. Colls. and Univs., Am. Assn. Higher Edn., Soc. Intercultural Edn., Tng. and Research, Sisters of Holy Names of Jesus and Mary. Roman Catholic. Office: Heritage Coll Office of Pres 3240 Fort Rd Toppenish WA 98948-9562

ROSS, KERRY LYNN, secondary education educator; b. Augsburg, Germany, Mar. 25, 1960; came to U.S., 1960; d. James Kyle and Janet (Bean) Parker; m. Brent Derek Ross, Dec. 31, 1981; children: Parker Andrew, Garett Corbin. BFA, Ea. N.Mex. U., 1981, U. Tex., 1984; postgrad., Ea. N.Mex. U., 1987-89. Cert. tchr., Tex., N.Mex., Colo. Tchr. theatre Midland (Tex.) Freshman H.S., 1982-86; theatre dir. Clovis (N.Mex.) H.S., 1986-90; theatre tchr., yearbook advisor Eaglecrest H.S., Aurora, Colo., 1990—; cons. Clovis High Sch. Student Assistance Team, 1987-90, chairperson Clovis Schs. Curriculum Guide, 1987-90; mem. EHS assessment team; co-chair Cherry Creek Schs. Fine Arts Curriculum review com., 1992—; mem. Eaglecrest High Sch. Needs Assesment Com., 1992—, Proficiency Com., 1993—. Vol. Am. Cancer Soc., Midland, 1984, Clovis, 1988; block chairperson March of Dimes, Midland, 1983; bd. dirs. Ctrl. Christian U., Clovis, 1988-90; jr. ch. coord. S.E. Christian Ch., Englewood, Colo., 1992-94. Mem. NEA, ASCD, Internat. Platform Assn., Alliance for Colo. Theatre (treas. 1994—), Ednl. Theatre Assn., Colo. Edn. Assn. Republican. Home: 6312 S Emporia Cir Englewood CO 80111-5528

ROSS, LANSON CLIFFORD, JR., religion educator, pastor, author; b. Killdeer, N.D., June 23, 1936; s. Lanson Charles and Mabel (Smith) R.; children: David F., Lanson III. BA in Biblical Studies, Seattle Pacific U., 1960; M. Sacred Theology, Internat. Coll., 1984; D of Ministries, 1986. Pres. PAC RIM Coll; founder Planned Living Seminars; pastor Quilcene Bible Ch.; pres. Pacific Rim Grad. Sch. Theology. Club: Seattle Yacht. Author: Total Life Prosperity, 1983; Give Your Children a Target, 1985, Take Charge of Your Life, 1986, The Bubble Burst, 1987; producer 5 vol. video seminar A Planned Life Style, 1986, and film A Time to Grow (J.C. Mc Pheeters award 1988). Office: PO Box 546 Quilcene WA 98376-0546

ROSS, LEABELLE I. (MRS. CHARLES R. ROSS), retired psychiatrist; b. Lorain, Ohio, Feb. 11, 1905; d. Charles E. and Harriet (Dobbie) Isaac; AB, Western Res. U., 1927, MD, 1930; m. Charles R. Ross, Sept. 23, 1941; children: Charles R., John Edwin. Surg. intern Lakeside Hosp., Cleve., 1931-32; resident obstetrics and gynecology Iowa State U. Hosp., 1932-33; resident obstetrics and surgery N.Y. Infirmary, N.Y.C., 1933-34; pvt. practice, Cleve., 1935-40; staff physician Cleve. State Hosp., 1938-42; dir. student health Bowling Green (Ohio) State U., 1942-45; psychiatrist Bur. Juvenile Rsch., Columbus, Ohio, 1946-47; psychiat. cons., 1948-51; psychiatrist Mental Hygiene Clinic, Columbus VA, 1951-55; dir. med. svcs. Juvenile Diagnostic Ctr., 1955-59, acting supt., 1958, 61-62, dir. psychiat. svcs., 1959-62, clin. dir., 1962-70. Mem. Am. Psychiat. Assn., Ohio Psychiat. Assn., Am. Group Psychotherapy Assn., Tri-State Group Psychotherapy Soc., Neuropsychiat. Assn. Ctrl. Ohio, Assn. Physicians Div. Mental Hygiene and Correction (pres. 1963-64), Alpha Sigma Rho, Nu Sigma Phi. Club: Soroptimist. Home: 1085 Tasman Dr #200 Sunnyvale CA 94089

ROSS, MARIE HEISE, retired librarian; b. N.Y.C., June 19, 1930; d. Henry Albert and Sophie Elizabeth (Stoever) Heise; m. Leon T. Stark, Aug. 9, 1952 (div. 1977); children: Antony A. Stark, Kathy T. Stark, Leslie Stark Wolff; m. David H. Ross, May 2, 1982; 1 stepchild, Randolph E. BA, CUNY, 1952, MLS, 1969. Cert. libr., N.Y. Sr. libr. Queens Borough Pub. Libr., Jamaica, N.Y., 1969-82, 83-85; libr., indexer H.W. Wilson Co., Bronx, N.Y., 1986-92, ret., 1992. Home: 14304 Stalgren Ct NE Albuquerque NM 87123-2209

ROSS, MARY BETH, academic administrator; b. Bklyn., July 8, 1942; d. Norman and Eleanor (Desmond) R.; m. Richard Patrick Roth, Aug. 22, 1964 (div. Feb. 1981); children: Geoffrey Davitt, Melissa Desmond. AB in English, Le Moyne Coll., 1964; MA in English, Syracuse U., 1969, PhD in English, 1973; postgrad., U. Coll. London, 1985-86. Cert. secondary English tchr., N.Y.; dual citizen Republic of Ireland, 1989. Asst. prof. English SUNY Upper-Div. Coll., Utica, 1973-75; founder, dir. The Women's Writers' Ctr., Cazenovia, N.Y., 1975-79; speech writer Office of the Mayor, Syracuse, N.Y., 1986-93; sr. program officer The Nat. Faculty, Seattle, Wash., 1993—; adj. faculty Syracuse U., 1979-85, Syracuse U. Coll. Law, 1979-85, Le Moyne Coll., Syracuse, 1979-85. Author: The Maid of Chepstow: A Fable, 1992; guest editor-in-chief Mademoiselle Mag., 1964. Mem. Women's Dem. Club, Syracuse, 1986-93; surrogate speaker coord. Dem. Presdl. Campaign, Ctrl. N.Y., 1988. Recipient Unsung Heroine Spl. award of honor NOW, 1992. Mem. MLA. Democrat. Roman Catholic.

ROSS, MOLLY OWINGS, gold and silversmith, jewelry designer, small business owner; b. Ft. Worth, Feb. 5, 1954; d. James Robertson and Lucy (Owings) R. BFA, Colo. State U., 1976; postgrad., U. Denver, 1978-79. Graphic designer Amber Sky Illustrators and Sta. KCNC TV-Channel 4, Denver, 1977-79; art dir. Mercy Med. Ctr., Denver, 1979-83, Molly Ross Design, Denver, 1983-84; co-owner Deltex Royalty Co., Inc., Colorado Springs, Colo., 1981—, LMA Royalties, Ltd., Colorado Springs, 1993—; art dir., account mgr. Schwing/Walsh Advt., Mktg. and Pub. Rels., Denver, 1984-87, prodn. mgr., 1987-88; jewelry designer Molly O. Ross, Gold and Silversmith, Denver, 1988—. Pres. Four Mile Hist. Park Vol. Bd., Denver 1985-87; bd. dirs. Four Mile Hist. Park Assn., 1985-86, Hist. Denver, Inc., 1986-87, Denver Emergency Housing Coalition, 1989-90; coun. mem. feminization of poverty critical needs area coun. Jr. League Denver, 1989-90, chmn. children in crisis/edn. critical needs area, 1990-91, project devel., 1991-92, co-chmn. Done in a Day Cmty. Project 75th Anniversary Celebration, 1991-93, mem. bd. dirs., 1993-94, v.p. cmty. projects, 1993-94; co-chmn. Project IMPACT, 1994-95; exec. v.p. external affairs Jr. League of Denver, 1995—; mem. bd. dirs. Denver Area Prep., 1994—. Named Vol. of Month (March), Jr. League Denver, 1990, Vol. of Yr., Four Mile Hist. Pk., 1988; recipient Gold Peak Mktg. award-team design Am. Mktg. Assn., 1986, Silver Peak Mktg. award-team design Am. Mktg. Assn., 1986, Gold Pick award-art dir. Pub. Rels. Soc. Am., 1980-81. Mem. Natural Resources Def. Coun., Physicians for Social Responsibility, Am. Farmland Trust, Nat. Trust for Hist. Preservation, Sierra Club, Environ. Def. Fund.

ROSS, RENAE LYNN, marketing professional; b. Conneaut, Ohio, June 5, 1962; d. Richard Edward and Patricia Ann (Sanford) R. BS, Ohio State U., 1985; postgrad., U. So. Calif., 1994—. Programmer E I du Pont de NeMours, Circleville, Ohio, 1984-85, IBM Corp., Lexington, Ky., 1985-86; software engr. Rolm Corp., Santa Clara, Calif., 1986-87; software team leader IBM Corp., Boca Raton, Fla., 1987-88; product planner IBM Corp., Boca Raton, 1988-89; mktg. rep. IBM Corp., L.A., 1989-93; sr. sales rep. Worldtalk, Corp., Los Gatos, Calif., 1993-94; vendor rels. mgr. 4th Dimension Software, Irvine, Calif., 1994-95; cons. Mission Viejo, Calif., 1995—. Mem. Profl. Assn. Diving Instrs. (master scuba diver trainer), Nat. Ski Patrol (Alpine patrol), Mensa. Office: Ste 160 27758 Santa Margarita Pky Mission Viejo CA 92691

ROSS, ROBERT JOSEPH, head professional football coach; b. Richmond, Va., Dec. 23, 1936; s. Leonard Aloysius and Martha Isabelle (MMiller) R.; m. Alice Louise Bucker, June 13, 1959; children: Chris, Mary Catherine, Teresa, Kevin, Robbie. BA, Va. Mil. Inst., 1959. Tchr., head football coach Benedictine High Sch., Richmond, 1959-60; tchr., coach Colonial Heights (Va.) High Sch., 1962-65; asst. football coach Va. Mil. Inst., Lexington, 1965-67, Coll. William and Mary, Williamsburg, Va., 1967-71, Rice U., Houston, 1971-72, U. Md., College Park, 1972-73; head football coach The Citadel, Charleston, S.C., 1973-77; head coach U. Md., College Park, 1982-87; head football coach Ga. Inst. Tech., Atlanta, 1987-91; asst. coach Kansas City (Mo.) Chiefs, 1978-82; head coach San Diego Chargers, 1992—. 1st lt. U.S. Army, 1960-62. Named Coach of Yr., Washington Touchdown Club, 1982, Kodak Coach of Yr., 1990, Bobby Dodd Coach of Yr., 1990, Bear Bryant Coach of Yr., 1990, Scripps-Howard Coach of Yr., 1990, Nat. Coach of Yr., CBS Sports, 1990, Coach of Yr., Walter Camp Football Found., 1990, NFL Coach of Yr. UPI, 1992, Pro Football Weekly, 1992, Pro Football Writers' Assn., 1992, Football News, 1992, Football Digest, 1992, Maxwell Football Club, 1992, AFC Coach of Yr. Kansas City 101 Banquet. Mem. Am. Football Coaches Assn., Coll. Football Assn. (coaching com. 1988-92). Roman Catholic. *

ROSS, ROBERT KING, retired educator; b. Manti, Utah, Jan. 27, 1927; s. Clarence King Ross and Annamae Plant Nielson; m. Patsy Ruth Tattu, Dec. 25, 1947 (dec. 1988); children: Scott, Barbara, Richard, Michael. BA in Secondary Edn., Ea. Wash. Coll. Edn., 1951. Cert. master tchr., Wash. Tchr. Reardon (Wash.) High Sch., 1951-52; microphotography specialist U.S. Atomic Energy Commn., Richland, Wash., 1952-54; mgr. St. Paul br. Dakota Microfilm Svc., 1954-61; system specialist 3M Co., Seattle, 1961-64; prin., tchr. U.S. Bur. Indian Affairs, Shungnak, Alaska, 1964-68; tchr. Port Angeles (Wash.) Sch. Dist., 1968-89, ret., 1989; mem. Wash. State Newspaper in Edn. Com., Tacoma, 1970-92; instr. record ann. tchrs. seminars. Contbr. articles to profl. jours. With USMC, 1945-47. Recipient Cert. of Appreciation Seattle P.I. Newspaper, 1980. Fellow Elks; mem. DAV, VFW. Home: 324 E 11th St Port Angeles WA 98362-7932

ROSS, ROGER, publishing executive; b. Jan. 6, 1929; s. George and Sophia (Peck) R.; m. Lila Levy, Dec. 18, 1953; 1 child, Anthony. Student, Carnegie Mellon U., 1948; BS, Columbia U., 1950, MIA, 1952. Comptr. Coun. on Fgn. Rels., N.Y.C., 1952-58; dir. LTB Printing & Pub., Rio de Janeiro, 1958-65; dir., cons. Graphic Controls Corp., Buffalo, Brazil, 1965-77; pres., chief exec. officer Editora Tradicao/Opera Mundi, Rio de Janiero, 1965-77; chief exec. officer, mng. dir. Morrison & Gibb, Edinburgh, Scotland, 1977-81; dep. chmn., chief oper. officer British Printing Copr., Eng., Italy, Spain, Portugal, 1981-82; cons. Longman Pub. Group, Eng., Scotland, 1982; exec. v.p., chief oper. officer The Book Press, Brattleboro, Vt., 1983-84; pres. Roger Ross Assocs., Scottsdale, Ariz., 1984—; exec. dir. Ctr. de Biblioteca-Franklin Book Programs, Rio de Janeiro, 1964-65; rep. of Brazil Nobel Prize ceremonies, Stockholm, 1974; lectr. in field. Editor in chief Jour. Internat. Affairs; contbr. articles to profl. jours. Vice chmn. joint meeting Essex and Union City, Elizabeth, N.J., 1987-91; village pres. City of South Orange, 1987-91. Mem. Coun. Fgn. Rels., Soc. Graphical and Allied Trades (hon.). Home and Office: 8519 E San Daniel Dr Scottsdale AZ 85258-2583

ROSS, ROGER SCOTT, lawyer; b. Columbus, Ohio, Oct. 25, 1946; s. Donald William and Iris Louise (Smith) R.; m. Lynn Louise Patton, July 29, 1967; 1 child, Anastacia Lynn. Student, Ohio State U., 1964-66; BS in Laws, Western State U., Fullerton, Calif., 1983; JD, Western State U., 1985. Bar: Calif. 1985, U.S. Dist. Ct. (cen. dist.) Calif. 1985. Office mgr. Dial Fin. Co., Buena Park, Calif., 1970-78; asst. br. mgr., loan officer Calif. 1st Bank, Rolling Hills Estates, 1978-79; asst. v.p., loan officer Lloyds Bank, Monterey Park, Calif., 1979-85; pvt. practice law Tustin, Calif., 1985-86; ptnr. Anderson & Ross, El Toro, Calif., 1986-87; pvt. practice Orange, Calif., 1987-90, Bellflower, Calif., 1990-94, Anaheim, Calif., 1994—; atty., coach Constnl. Rights Found. of Orange County, 1987—. Mem. ABA, Calif. Bar Assn., L.A. County Bar Assn., Assn. Trial Lawyers Am., Orange County Trial Lawyers Assn., Nat. Forensic Club, Rotary. Republican. Office: 401 N Brookhurst Ste 100 Anaheim CA 92801

ROSS, SANDRA K., critical care nurse; b. Ellensburg, Wash., Mar. 18, 1951; d. Charles Vernon and Thalia Kathleen (Collias) La Due; m. Leon T. Ross, Nov. 21, 1982; 1 child, Traci Kathleen. ADN, San Joaquin Delta Coll., Stockton, Calif., 1985; BS, Wash. State U., Pullman, 1973. Cert. critical care nurse. Sr. staff nurse San Joaquin Gen. Hosp., Stockton; staff nurse St. Joseph's Med. Ctr., Stockton; staff nurse ICU St. Dominic's Hosp., Manteca, Calif. With U.S. Army, 1974-76. Mem. AACN, Alpha Xi Delta, River City Quilters Guild. Home: 4867 Bridgewater Cir Stockton CA 95219-2014

ROSS, STAN, accounting firm executive; b. 1939. With Kenneth Leventhal & Co., L.A., 1964—, now mng. ptnr. Office: Kenneth Leventhal & Co 2049 Century Park E Los Angeles CA 90067-3101

ROSS, STEVEN CHARLES, business administration educator, consultant; b. Salem, Oreg., Jan. 14, 1947; s. Charles Reed and Edythe Marie (Calvin) R.; m. Meredith Lynn Buholts, June 15, 1969; children: Kelly Lynn, Shannon Marie. BS, Oreg. State U., 1969; MS, U. Utah, 1976, PhD, 1980. Cons. IRS Tng. Staff, Ogden, Utah, 1977-80; asst. prof. Marquette U., Milw., 1980-88; assoc. prof. Mont. State U., Bozeman, 1988-89, Western Washington U., Bellingham, 1989—; govt. and industry cons.; cons. editor microcomputing series West Pub. Co. Author 30 books and several articles in computer systems field. Mem. adv. com. Milwaukee County Mgmt., 1981-85, Port of Bellingham, 1990—. Capt. U.S. Army, 1969-75. Recipient rsch. fellowship, U. Utah, 1977-79, Marquette U., 1981-84. Mem. Acad. Mgmt., Decision Scis. Inst., Inst. Mgmt. Scis., Assn. for Computing Machinery, Assn. Computer Educators, Bellingham Yacht Club (trustee 1992-93, sec. 1993-94, rear cmdr. 1994-95). Office: Coll Bus and Econs Western Wash U Bellingham WA 98225

ROSS, SUEELLEN, artist; b. Oakland, Calif., July 12, 1941; d. Eugene Paul Burton and Edith Ellen (Metcalf) Burille; m. Paul Louis Ross, Oct. 20, 1976 (div. 1989); m. Richard A. Lyon, Nov. 7, 1993. BA in Speech Arts, U. Calif., Berkeley, 1969, postgrad., 1978-79. Educator various jr. and sr. high schs. Calif., N.Y. and P.R., Calif., 1966-71; publicist and publicity dir. N.Y.C., Seattle, 1971-80; artist, 1980—; judge painting and drawing Anacortes Art Fair, Wash., 1989, Edmonds Art Fair, 1994; judge painting, drawing and sculpture Pacific Rim Wildlife Art Show, 1987-89, 91-94. Exhibited works in numerous shows including Leigh Yawkey Woodson Art Mus., Wausau, Wis., 1987, 89, 91, 92, 93, 94, 95, Nat. Park Found., Jackson Hole, Wyo., 1991, 92, N.W. Watercolor Soc. Ann. Show, Kirkland, Wash., 1991, 92, 94, Howard/Manville Gallery, Kirkland, 1993, 94, 95, others; works represented in numerous pub. collections including Leigh Yawkey Woodson Art Mus., Mpls. Savs. and Loan, Safeco Ins. Co., Seattle, SeaFirst Bank, Seattle, Shell Oil Co., Houston, Signature. Mem. N.W. Watercolor Soc. Home and Office: 1909 SW Myrtle St Seattle WA 98106-1646

ROSS, TERENCE WILLIAM, architect; b. Saginaw, Mich., Sept. 27, 1935; s. Oran Lewis and Drucilla (Chadman) R.; BArch, U. Mich., 1958; m. Patricia Ann Marshall, Sept. 27, 1974; children by previous marriage: Deborah, David. Designer, Roger W. Peters Constrn. Co., Fond du Lac, Wis., 1958-62; draftsman Kenneth Clark, Arch., Santa Fe, N.Mex., 1962-63, Holien & Buckley, Archs., Santa Fe, 1963-64; office mgr. Philippe Register, Architect, Santa Fe, 1964-68; prin. Register, Ross, & Brunet architects, engrs., Santa Fe, 1968-71, Luna-Ross & Assoc., 1971-77; staff CNWC Archs., Tucson, to 1981, ADP Architects, 1981-89; sr. architect U. Calif., 1989—. Vice chmn. N.Mex. R.R. Authority, 1969-74, sec., 1970-72. Bd. dirs. Colo., N.Mex. Soc. Preservation of Narrow Gauge, El Dorado Western Narrow Gauge Railway Found. Recipient award for hist. preservation N.Mex. Arts Commn., 1971, award for outstanding svcs. to cmty. Santa Fe Press Club, 1972; named col. aide-de-camp State of N.Mex., 1968, hon. mem. staff atty. gen. Mem. AIA (chpt. pres. 1970, dir.), Constrn. Specifications Inst., N.Mex. Soc. Architects (dir. 1972), Ariz. Soc. Archs., N.Mex. R.R. Authorities (chmn. joint exec. com. 1970-74), Sacramento Valley Garden Ry. Soc. (pres. 1993, dir. 1994), San Gabriel Hist. Soc. (hon.), Alpha Rho Chi, Sashay Rounders Sq. Dance Club (pres. 1974), Diamond Squares Sq. Dance Club, Railroad Club (pres. N.Mex. 1969, 70, dir.). Author: Track of the Cats. Home and Office: 2813 57th St Sacramento CA 95817-2403

ROSS, WAYNE ANTHONY, lawyer; b. Milw., Feb. 25, 1943; s. Ray E. and Lillian (Steiner) R.; m. Barbara L. Ross, June 22, 1968; children: Gregory, Brian, Timothy, Amy. BA, Marquette U., 1965, JD, 1968. Bar: Wis. 1968, Alaska 1969. Asst. atty. gen. State Alaska, 1968-69; trustee, standing master Superior Ct. Alaska, 1969-73; assoc. Edward J. Reasor & Assocs., Anchorage, 1973-77; prin. Wayne Anthony Ross & Assocs., 1977-83; ptnr. Ross, Gingras & Frenz, Anchorage and Cordova, Alaska, 1983-84, Ross & Gingras, Anchorage and Cordova, 1985; pres. Ross and Miner, P.C., Anchorage, 1986-93; pres. Ross and Miner P.C., Anchorage, 1993—; COL, I.G. Alaska State Def. Force; pres. Tyone Mountain Syndicate, Inc. Alaska Rep. Nat. Committeeman. Mem. NRA (bd. dirs. 1980-92, 94—, benefactor), Alaska Bar Assn. (Stanley award), Anchorage Bar Assn., Alaska Gun Collectors Assn. (pres. emeritus), Ohio Gun Collectors Assn. (hon. life), Smith and Wesson Collectors Assn., 49th Territorial Guard Regiment (pres.), Alaska Territorial Cavalry (sec.), State Guard Assn., Military Vehicle Preservation Assn. (v.p.), Alaska Peace Officers Assn. Roman Catholic. Home: PO Box 101522 Anchorage AK 99510-1522 Office: Ross & Miner 327 E Fireweed Ln Ste 201 Anchorage AK 99503-2110

ROSSBACH, CAROLETTA, art consultant; b. Fremont, Mich., Jan. 9, 1942; d. Robert Henry and Mary Viola (Ball) Curley; m. Sept. 17, 1966 (div. Jan. 1991). BA in Music, UCLA, 1964; MA in Music, Calif. State U., Northridge, 1979. Cert. tchr., Calif. Admin. asst. Musician's Union, L.A., 1964-66; tchr. St. Joseph's Elem. Sch., Carpinteria, Calif., 1968; music tchr. La Colina Jr. High Sch., Santa Barbara, Calif., 1968-78, San Marcos H. S., Santa Barbara, Calif., 1980; owner, developer Delphine Art Gallery, Santa Barbara, Calif., 1979-92; art cons. Letty Rossbach Fine Art, Santa Barbara, Calif., 1992—; pres. women's bd. Santa Barbara (Calif.) Mus. Art, 1993-94, mem. collector's coun., 1994—; v.p. women's bd. Mus. Acad. of West, Santa Barbara, Calif., 1986-87, bd. trustees Santa Barbara Chamber Orch., 1992-94. Mem. Soroptimist Internat.

ROSSER, JAMES MILTON, university president; b. East St. Louis, Ill., Apr. 16, 1939; s. William M. and Mary E. (Bass) R.; 1 child, Terence. B.A., So. Ill. U., 1962, M.A., 1963, Ph.D., 1969. Diagnostic bacteriologist Holden Hosp., Carbondale, Ill., 1961-63; research bacteriologist Eli Lilly & Co., Indpls., 1963-66; coordinator Black Am. studies, instr. health edn. So. Ill. U., Carbondale, 1968-69; asst. prof. Black Am. studies dir. So. Ill. U., 1969-70, asst. to chancellor, 1970; asso. vice chancellor for acad. affairs U. Kans., Lawrence, 1970-74; assoc. prof. edn., pharmacology and toxicology U. Kans., 1971-74; vice chancellor dept. higher edn. State of N.J., Trenton, 1974-79; acting chancellor State of N.J., 1977; pres., prof. health care mgmt. Calif. State U., Los Angeles, 1979—; mem. tech. resource panel Ctr. for Research and Devel. in Higher Edn., U. Calif., Berkeley, 1974-76; mem. health maintenance orgn. com. Health Planning Coun., State of N.J., 1975-79; mem. standing com. on research and devel. bd. trustees Ednl. Testing Service, 1976-77; mem. steering com. and task force on retention of minorities in engring. Assembly of Engring. NRC, 1975-78; mem. Bd. Med. Examiners, State of N.J., 1978-79; vis. faculty mem. Inst. Mgmt. of Lifelong Edn., Grad. Sch. Edn., Harvard U., 1979; mem. Calif. State U. Trustees Spl. Long Range Fin. Planning Com., 1982-87; mem. Am. Coun. on Edn., 1979—, AFL/CIO Labor Higher Edn. Coun., 1983—, Nat. Commn. Higher Edn. Issues, 1981-82; mem. The Calif. Achievement Coun., 1983-89, strategic adv. counc. Coll. and Univs. Systems Exchange, 1988-91; bd. dirs. Am. Humanities Coun., So. Calif. Am. Humanics, Inc. Coun., Sanwa Bank Calif., 1993—, Edison, Fedco, Inc. Author: An Analysis of Health Care Delivery, 1977. Mem. exec. bd., chmn. varisty scouting program L.A. area coun. Boy Scouts Am., 1980—; bd. dirs. Hispanic Urban Ctr., L.A., 1979—, L.A. Urban League, 1982—, Cmty. TV of So. Calif., Sta. KCET, 1980-89, United Way, L.A., 1980-91, Orthopaedic Hosp., 1983-86; mem. Citizen's Adv. Coun. Congl. Caucus Sci. and Tech., 1983—; bd. dirs. L.A. Philharm. Assn., 1986—; mem. performing arts coun./edn. coun. Music Ctr., 1984—; mem. minority bus. task force Pacific Bell, 1985-86; mem. bd. govs. Nat. ARC, 1986-91, Mayor's Blue Ribbon Task Force on Drugs, City of L.A., 1988; Nat. Adv. Coun. on Aging, 1989-93; bd. dirs. Nat. Health Found., 1990—, Calif. C. of C., 1993—; bd. trustees Woodrow Wilson Nat. Fellowship Found., 1993—. NSF fellow, 1961; NDEA fellow, 1967-68; recipient award of recognition in Edn. Involvement for Young Achievers, 1981, Pioneer of Black Hist. Achievement award Brotherhood Crusade, 1981, Alumni Achievement award So. Ill. U., 1982, Friend of Youth award Am. Humanics, Inc., 1985, Leadership award Dept. Higher Edn. Ednl. Equal Opportunity Fund Program, 1989, Medal of Excellence Gold State Minority Found., 1990, Take Charge of Learning Success award Inst. for Redesign of Learning. Mem. Calif. C. of C. (bd. dirs. 1993—), Alhambra C. of C. (bd. dirs. 1979—), Los Angeles C. of C. (bd. dirs. 1985-90), Am. Assn. State Colls. and Univs., Kappa Delta Pi, Phi Kappa Phi. Roman Catholic. Office: Calif State Univ Office of the Pres 5151 State University Dr Los Angeles CA 90032-8500*

ROSSI, AMADEO JOSEPH, chemist; b. Seattle, Sept. 23, 1954; s. Amadeo Joseph and Maria Asilia (Chinella) R.; m. Frances Marie Stotts, Sept. 19, 1981; children: Anthony Joseph, Matthew Christopher, Brian Michael. BS in Wood and Fiber Sci., U. Wash., 1979, MS in wood chemistry, 1987. Research aide U. Wash., Seattle, 1978-79; environ. engr. Georgia-Pacific Corp., Eugene, Oreg., 1980; engr., dir. hazardous waste remediation projects Foster Wheeler Environ. Corp., Seattle, 1981—. Contbr. articles to profl. jours. Mem. Am. Chem. Soc., Air Pollution Control Assn., Forest Products Rsch. Soc., Xi Sigma Pi, Sigma Xi. Office: EBASCO Svcs Inc 10900 NE 8th St Bellevue WA 98004-4405

ROSSI, GUY ANTHONY, publishing executive; b. Binghamton, N.Y., Aug. 12, 1952; s. Anthony J. and Mary L. (Cannavino) R. Assoc. Liberal Arts, Broome Community Coll., 1973; BA, N.Mex. State U., 1977. Chief exec. officer, owner Inter Gen. Pub., Mesilla, N.Mex., 1977—; pub. Mesilla Valley Courier, 1977-81; graphic artist Las Cruces (N.Mex.) Sun News, 1981-85; profl. stamp dealer Rossi's Cinderellas, Mesilla, 1985—; art dir. Hynes Advt., Las Cruces, 1986-89; graphic artist, printing and duplicating N.Mex. State U., Las Cruces, 1977; graphic artist Larry Edwards Advt., Las Cruces, 1991-92; art dir. Las Cruces Sun News, 1992—; print media cons. N.Mex. Farm and Ranch Mag., Las Cruces, 1980-89. Pub., editor historic map: The Mesilla Map, 1977-81; artist commemorative envelopes and U.S. Postal Svc. postmarks, 1977—. Fellow Am. Philatelic Soc., Am. Revenue Assn., Am. Topical Assn., Cinderella Stamp Club of Eng., N.Mex. Philatelic Assn.; mem. Mesilla Valley Stamp Club (charter mem., pres., bd. dirs., 1990-91, graphic and print media cons., 1977—). Democrat. Office: Rossi's Cinderellas Inter Gen Pub PO Box 367 Mesilla NM 88046-0367

ROSSI, MARIO ALEXANDER, architect; b. Chgo., Apr. 9, 1931; s. Gastone J. and Irma (Giorgi) R.; m. Jo Ann Therese Kneip, Apr. 12, 1958; children: John Vincent, Lyn Ann, Paul Alexander, Mara Ann. BArch, Ill. Inst. Tech., 1955. Architect Omnimetrics, L.A., 1967-78; pvt. practice Seal Beach, Calif., 1975—. Prin. works include fin. models for Calif. Fed. Bank, L.A., First Nat. City Bank, N.Y.C., Glendale (Calif.) Fed. Bank, Wailea, Alexander and Baldwin, Hawaii. Lt. (j.g.) USN, 1955-58. Home and Office: 1721 Catalina Ave Seal Beach CA 90740-5710

ROSSIN, HERBERT YALE, television broadcaster; b. Phila., May 15, 1936; s. Jack Rossin and Edna Wolinsky; m. Meryl Ann Barsky, Nov. 15,

1965; children: Abby Rae, Shane J.P. Degree, Journalism Price Sch., Phila., 1957; student, Temple U., 1958. Gen. mgr. KIKU TV/13, Honolulu, 1968-70; br. mgr. Columbia Pictures, Las Vegas, 1970-74; ptnr. Internat. TV Concepts, Las Vegas, 1974-78; sta. mgr. KUAM AM/FM/TV, Agana, Guam, 1978-80; v.p. Tag Mktg. and Advt., Cherry Hill, N.J., 1981-83; gen. mgr. WLXI-TV/61, Greensboro, N.C., 1983-85; v.p., gen. mgr. WHLL-TV/27, Boston, 1986-87; v.p. Home Shopping Network, L.A., 1987-88; owner A.S.A.P. Multi-Corp., Las Vegas, 1988—; broadcast cons. Fashion Channel-Video Mall, L.A., 1987-88; scriptwriter Four Star Pictures, L.A., 1988-89; network cons. Las Vegas TV Network, 1992; pres. Video Music TV Stas. Am., 1984-88, named Broadcaster of Yr., 1985. Producer motion picture Miss Conduct, 1957; creator TV shows New Millionaires, Wireless Wonder; editor Israel Mag., 1960. Producer telethon Heart Fund Am., Las Vegas, 1972. With U.S. Air N.G., 1954-58. Recipient Edn. award Albert Einstein Hebrew Acad., 1974, People Law Sch. award Nev. Trial Lawyers, 1992 Citizenship award Govt. of Guam, 1979, others. Mem. Nat. Assn. TV Program Execs. Home and Office: ASAP Multi Corp 7704 Musical Ln Las Vegas NV 89128-4082

ROSSMANN, ANTONIO, lawyer, educator; b. San Francisco, Apr. 25, 1941; s. Herbert Edward and Yolanda (Sonsini) R.; m. Kathryn A. Burns, Oct. 6, 1991. Grad. Harvard U., 1963; JD, 1971. Bar: Calif. 1972, D.C. 1979, U.S. Supreme Ct. 1979, N.Y. 1980. Law clk., Calif. Supreme Ct., 1971-72; assoc. Tuttle & Taylor, Los Angeles, 1972-75; pub. advisor Calif. Energy Commn., 1975-76; sole practice, San Francisco, 1976-82, 85—; exec. dir. Nat. Center for Preservation Law, 1979-80; mem. McCutchen, Doyle, Brown & Enersen, San Francisco, 1982-85; adj. prof. law Hastings Coll. Law, 1981-84; vis. prof. UCLA Sch. Law, 1985-88; adj. prof. Stanford Law Sch., 1989-90, U. Calif. Sch. Law, 1991—. Bd. dirs. Planning and Conservation League, 1984—, Calif. Water Protection Council, 1982-83, San Francisco Marathon, 1982-90; pres. Western State Endurance Run, 1986—; pres., bd. dirs. Toward Utility Rate Normalization, 1976-79. Served to lt. comdr. USN, 1963-68. Fulbright lectr., U. Tokyo, 1987-88. Mem. Calif. State Bar (chmn. com. on environment 1978-82), Assn. Bar City of N.Y., U.S. Rowing Assn., U.S. Soccer Fed. (state referee), L.A. Athletic Club, Harvard Club (San Francisco, N.Y.C.). Contbr. articles to legal jours.; editor Harvard U. Law Rev., 1969-71. Office: 380 Hayes St San Francisco CA 94102-4421

ROSSO, LOUIS T., scientific instrument manufacturing company executive; b. San Francisco, 1933; married. A.B., San Francisco State Coll., 1955; M.B.A., U. Santa Clara, 1967. Product specialist Spinco div. Beckman Instruments, Fullerton, Calif., 1959-63, mktg. mgr., 1963-69, mgr. Spinco div., 1969-70, mgr. clin. instruments div., 1970-74, corp. v.p., mgr. analytical instruments group, 1974-80, corp. sr. v.p., 1980-83, pres., 1983—, now also chmn., chief exec. officer; also bd. dirs. Beckman Instruments, Inc.; v.p. SmithKline Beckman Corp., Phila. Office: Beckman Instruments Inc 2500 N Harbor Blvd Fullerton CA 92635-2607*

ROSTAD, KENNETH LEIF, provincial government official; b. Yorkton, Sask., Can., Sept. 7, 1941; s. Leif and Mary Katherine (McLennan) R.; m. Shirley Gail Tien, May 19, 1979; children: Kyle, Kelsy, Karsten. B Commerce, U. Saskatoon, Sask., 1967, LLB, 1979. With Royal Bank Can., 1959-60, Shell Can. Ltd., 1967-69, Sears Can. Inc., 1969-76; ptnr. Gaede Fielding Rostad & Syed, Camrose, Alta., Can., 1979-86; solicitor gen. Govt. Alta., Edmonton, 1986-88, min. responsible for housing, 1987-89, min. responsible for native affairs, 1987-91, atty. gen., 1988-92, apptd. min. justice and atty. gen., 1993-94; min. responsible for govt. reorganization secretariat Govt. Alta., 1993—; apptd. min. fed. and intergovernmental affairs Govt. Alta., Edmonton, 1994—. Alderman City of Camrose, 1985-86; mem. legis. assembly Province Alta., 1986—. Mem. Law Soc. Alta. (hon. bencher), Can. Bar Assn., Lions Internat. (pres.). Progressive Conservative. Lutheran. Office: Min Fed & Intergovernmental, Legislature Bldg Rm 404, Edmonton, AB Canada T5K 2B6

ROSTEN, DAVID BRUCE, international investment advisor; b. Long Branch, N.J., July 28, 1953; s. Philip Rosten and Leila June Freeman; m. Kristin Brigetta West, Jan. 10, 1993. BA, U. Calif., Irvine, 1982; student, U. Copenhagen; JD, Oxford (Eng.) U., 1984; JD in Internat. Law and Politics, U. San Diego, 1984. Dir. Wilshire Savs. and Loan, L.A., 1986-88; owner Rosten Realty, Newport Beach, Calif., 1986-93; owner, pres. Rosten Capital, Newport Beach, 1994—. Office: Rosten Capital 1009 W Balboa Blvd Newport Beach CA 92661-1003

ROSTOKER, MICHAEL DAVID, micro-electronics company executive, lawyer; b. Quincy, Mass., Mar. 15, 1958; s. David and E. Louise (Berleue) R. Student, Carnegie-Mellon U., 1976-78; BS in Indsl. Engring., U. Pitts., 1980; JD, Franklin Pierce Law Ctr., 1984; PhD in Indsl. Engring., City U., L.A., 1992. Bar: U.S. Patent and Trademark Office 1983, N.H. 1984, U.S. Dist. Ct. N.H. 1984, Mass. 1985, Pa. 1985, U.S. Dist. Ct. D.C. 1985, U.S. Ct. Appeals (D.C. cir.) 1985. Lectr. in computer sci. Point Park Coll., Pitts., 1979-80; sys. analyst GE, Fitchburg, Mass., 1980-81; patent atty. Rines and Rines, Boston and Concord, N.H., 1983-85; patent counsel Schlumberger Well Svcs., Houston, 1985-87; sr. counsel intellectual property Intel Corp., Santa Clara, Calif., 1987-88; v.p. strategic alliances LSI Logic Corp., Milpitas, Calif., 1988—; cons. in field, Concord, 1981-85; mem. faculty computer sci. and math. Franklin Pierce Coll., Rindge, N.H., 1981-85; mem. adj. faculty law Franklin Pierce Law Ctr., 1983-85; edtl. bd. Software Protection Reporter, 1984-94; lectr. seminars in field. Author: Computer Jurisprudence: Legal Responses to the Information Revolution, 1985, Technology Management: Licensing and Protection for Computers in the World Market, 1993; contbr. articles to profl. jours.; patentee in field. Mem. ABA (patents, sci. and tech., litigation sects.), Am. Trial Lawyers Assn., Am. Intellectual Property Assn. Republican. Jewish. Home: 108 McPherson Ct Boulder Creek CA 95006-9203 Office: LSI Logic Corp 1525 Mccarthy Blvd Milpitas CA 95035-7424

ROSTVOLD, GERHARD NORMAN, economist, consultant; b. Nashwauk, Minn., Oct. 15, 1919; s. Arndt and Olive Mathilda (Ness) R.; m. Virginia Fay Faubion, Feb. 3, 1945; children—Roger Mark, Laura Ann, Christine Marie, Ellen Alicia. A.B. in Econs.-Accountancy with great distinction, Stanford, 1948, M.A. in Econs, 1949, Ph.D. in Econs, 1955. Instr. Stanford U., 1949-51; prof. econs. and acctg. Pomona Coll., Claremont, Calif., 1952-66; cons. Urbanomics Rsch. Assoc., Laguna Hills, Calif., 1966—; adj. prof. econs. Pepperdine U.; econ. newscaster Sta. KHJ-TV, L.A., 1978-82; econ. cons. to govt., industry; trustee Mortgage & Realty Trust. Author: The Southern California Metropolis—1980, 1960, Financing California Government, 1967, The Economics of Energy, 1975, Economics and the Environment, 1975, The Economics of the Public Utility Enterprise, 1976, Understanding How the Economic System Works, 1976, Teacher's Instructional Program for Understanding How the Economic System Works, 1976, Charting Your Path to Economic and Financial Survival in the 1980's, 1979, How to Stretch your Dollars to Cope with the Inflation of the 1980's, 1981; co-author: California Local Finance, 1960, Garcia-Rostvold Work Experience Education Series, 1974, (with Thomas J. Dudley) Congressional report, New Perspectives on Grazing Fees and Public Land Management in the 1990s, 1992; social sci. editor: Stone/Leswing Social Sci. Series; editor: Rostvold Econ. Outlook and Personal Money Mgmt. Newsletter; contbr. articles to profl jours. Chmn. nat. adv. bd. Coun. Pub. Lands; mem. Calif. advisory bd., mem. Calif. Coun. Econ. Edn. Served with USAAF, 1942-45. NSF fellow Stanford U., 1965-66; recipient Wig Disting. Professorship award Pomona Coll., 1962; Conservation award Dept. Interior, 1975. Mem. Am. Econ. Assn., Western Econ. Assn. (pres. 1966-67), Nat. Tax Assn. (pres.), Lambda Alpha. Home: 4 Montpellier Laguna Niguel CA 92677-5432 Office: Urbanomics Rsch 23276 S Pointe Dr Laguna Hills CA 92653-1432

ROSVALL, GENE HOWARD, elementary education educator; b. Salt Lake City, Nov. 16, 1941; s. Oran Howard and Cecile (Humphreys) R.; m. Faye Elton, Nov. 20, 1964 (dec. Aug. 1969); children: Robert, Todd; m. Patricia Harvey, Apr. 3, 1970; 1 child, Jennifer. BS, U. Utah, 1977, MEd, 1979. Cert. tchr. elem. edn. K-8, Utah. Elem. tchr. Granite Sch. Dist., Salt Lake City, 1977-95. Author: A Walk In Their Shoes, 1993, (short story) The Crystal Palace, 1993. City coun. mem. Murray (Utah) City Govt., 1984-89; coun. chairperson Murray City Coun., 1986; v.p. Murray Redevelopment Agy., 1987; candidate Utah State Legislature, 1988. Recipient Resolution of Appreciation, Murray City Govt., 1987. Mem. NEA (nat. rep. assembly), Granite Edn. Assn. (rep. 1985-88, exec. bd. mem. 1988-95), League of Cities and Towns, People to People Internat. Student Ambassador Program (teacher-leader 1990-95). LDS. *Died March 22, 1995.*

ROSVALL, PATRICIA LYNN, biology educator; b. Salt Lake City, Feb. 20, 1944; d. William Mack and La Veta (Mangum) Harvey; m. Gene Howard Rosvall, Apr. 3, 1970; children: Robert, Todd, Jennifer. ADN, Weber State Coll., 1983; BS, Westminster Coll., 1986. RN, Utah; cert. biology educator, Utah. Flight attendant United Airlines, San Francisco, 1965-70; biology tchr. Granite Sch. Dist., West Valley City, Utah, 1987—. Implemented new sci. course for school dist., 1994-95. Docent Hogle Zoo, Salt Lake City, 1981-83; state conv. rep. Rep. Party, Salt Lake City, 1988, county conv. rep., 1988; rep. Utah Edn. Assn. House of Dels., 1988-93; com. mem. Ptnrs. in Edn., 1990-91; mem. Centennial Sch. Com., West Valley, 1993-94. Mem. Granite Edn. Assn. (rep. 1988-93), People to People Internat. Student Ambassador Program. LDS. Office: John F Kennedy Jr High Sch 4495 South 4800 West West Valley City UT 84120

ROSZTOCZY, FERENC ERNO, business executive; b. Szeged, Hungary, Aug. 16, 1932; came to U.S., 1957, naturalized, 1962; s. Ferenc Lipot and Edith Jolan (Kunzl) R.; m. Diane Elder, Dec. 21, 1963; children: Thomas Ferenc, Robert Anthony, Stephanie Elder, Edward Joseph. MS, U. Szeged, 1955; PhD, U. Calif., Berkeley, 1961. Phys. chemist Stanford Research Inst., Menlo Park, Calif., 1961-64; mem. tech. staff Bell Labs., Murray Hill, N.J., 1964-68; mgr. semicondr. materials Bell & Howell, Pasadena, Calif., 1968-69; mgr. semicondr. crystal growth and device engring. Varian Assos., Palo Alto, Calif., 1969-75; dir. Ariz. Machinery Co., Avondale, 1974—, pres., 1975—, chmn. bd., 1976—; pres. Stotz Farms, Inc., 1979—; dir. Ariz. Indsl. Machinery Co., 1975-91; cons. Siltec Corp., Menlo Park, Calif., 1971-72; mem. agribusiness adv. bd. 1st Interstate Bank Ariz., 1995—. Bd. trustees Agua Fria High Sch., 1981-89, pres. 1986-87. Mem. United Dairymen Ariz. (dir. 1985—). Roman Catholic. Club: Wigwam Country. Contbr. articles to profl. jours. Patentee in field. Home: 1010 E Acacia Cir Litchfield Park AZ 85340-4529 Office: Ariz Machinery Co 11111 W McDowell Rd Avondale AZ 85323

ROTENBERG, SUSAN, association administrator; b. Seattle, May 25, 1943; d. Samuel and Jean (Pass) R.; children: Brandon Landworth, Ryan Landworth. BA in English, U. Wash.; BS in Psychology, Western Wash. U.; M in Psychology, Antioch U. Cmty. corrections officer King County (Wash.) Dept. Corrections; correctional mental therapist Spl. Offender Ctr., Monrow, Wash.; cmty. corrections psychiat. social worker Wash. Corrections Ctr., Shelton; exec. dir., founder Nat. Coalition for Mentally Ill in Criminal Justice System; coord. panel subcom. on human resources U.S. Ho. Reps.; prin. coord. breakfast and briefing U.S. Congress, Washington, 1991, 93, 94, State Policy Design Acad., 1993, others; presenter, speaker in field; tech. asst. to teams from Govs.' offices, Nat. Inst. Corrections, 1992, Substance Abuse and Mental Svc. Adminstrn., Ctr. for Mental Health Svcs. Author forwards for 3 books in field; contbr. articles to profl. jours.; producer tng. videos Bridging the Gap, Mental Illness in Prisons; writer legislation in field State of Wash., 1992. Bd. dirs. King County Mental Health Bd.; mem. corrections mental health adv. com. Dept. Corrections/U. Wash., 1993; adv. bd. dept. cmty. psychiatry U. Wash.; mem. ad hoc work group Nat. Alliance for Mentally Ill Forensic Network Exec. Com.; past bd. dirs. Cmty. Action for Mentally Ill Offender, Wash. Recipient cert. for Contbn. in Outstanding Svc. Gov. Booth Gardner, Wash., 1989, Disting. Svc. award Nat. Assn. Counties, 1990. Office: NCMI 2470 Westlake Ave N Ste 101 Seattle WA 98109-2282

ROTH, FREDERIC HULL, JR., secondary education educator; b. Cleve., July 27, 1941; s. Frederic Hull and Emmy Alice (Braun) R.; m. Kathleen Marie Keady, Nov. 15, 1962; children: Frederic Hull III, Kimberley Adrienne, Lara Hilary. BA, Yale U., 1963; MA, Columbia U., 1967; PhD, U. Va., 1973. English instr. Robert Louis Stevenson Sch., Pebble Beach, Calif., 1963-65, chmn. dept. English, 1991—; English instr. Landon Sch., Bethesda, Md., 1966-68; coord. pres.'s youth opportunity program Walter Reed Army Med. Ctr., Washington, summer 1968; asst. prof. English Hamilton Coll., Clinton, N.Y., 1971-77; chmn. dept. English Cranbrook Kingswood Sch., Bloomfield Hills, Mich., 1977-91; chmn., co-founder, bd. dirs. Clinton (N.Y.) ABC Program, 1974-76. Keynote lectr. Cranbrook Elderhostel, Bloomfield Hills, Mich., summers 1980-90; bd. dirs. Detroit Film Soc., 1986-91. Travel/rsch. grantee NEH, 1974. Mem. MLA, SAR, Nat. Coun. Tchrs. of English, World Affairs Coun., Founders & Patriots, Union Club Cleve., Detroit Econ. Club. Episcopalian. Home: 135 Littlefield Rd Monterey CA 93940-4917 Office: Robert Louis Stevenson Sch PO Box 657 Pebble Beach CA 93953

ROTH, JOHN KING, philosopher, educator; b. Grand Haven, Mich., Sept. 3, 1940; s. Josiah V. and Doris Irene (King) R.; m. Evelyn Lillian Austin, June 25, 1964; children: Andrew Lee, Sarah Austin. BA, Pomona Coll., 1962; student, Yale U. Div. Sch., 1962-63; MA, Yale U., 1965, PhD, 1966; LHD, Ind. U., 1990. Asst. prof. philosophy Claremont McKenna Coll., Calif., 1966-71, assoc. prof., 1971-76, Russell K. Pitzer prof. philosophy, 1976—; vis. prof. philosophy Franklin Coll., Lugano, Switzerland, 1973; Fulbright lectr. Am. studies U. Innsbruck, Austria, 1973-74; vis. prof. philosophy Doshisha U., Kyoto, Japan, 1981-82; vis. prof. Holocaust studies U. Haifa, Israel, 1982; Fulbright lectr. in Am. studies Royal Norwegian Ministry of Edn., Oslo, Norway, 1995—. Author: Freedom and the Moral Life, 1969, Problems of the Philosophy of Religion, 1971, American Dreams, 1976, A Consuming Fire, 1979, (with Richard L. Rubenstein) Approaches to Auschwitz, 1987, (with Frederick Sontag) The American Religious Experience, 1972, (with Frederick Sontag) The Questions of Philosophy, 1988, (with Robert H. Fossum) The American Dream, 1981, (with Fossum) American Ground, 1988, (with Rubenstein) The Politics of Latin American Liberation Theology, 1988, (with Michael Berenbaum) Holocaust: Religious and Philosophical Implications, 1989, Ethics, 1991, (with Carol Rittner) Memory Offended, 1991, (with Creighton Peden) Rights, Justice, and Community, 1992, (with Carol Rittner) Different Voices, 1993, American Diversity, American Identity, 1995. Spl. advisor U.S. Holocaust Meml. Coun., Washington, 1980-85, mem., 1995—. Danforth grad. fellow, 1962-66; Graves fellow, 1970-71; NEH fellow, 1976-77; Faculty Pairing grantee Japan-U.S. Friendship Commn., 1981-83; named U.S. Prof. of Yr. Coun. Advancement and Support of Edn. and Carnegie Found. Advancement of Tchg., 1988. Mem Am. Philos. Assn., Am. Acad. Religion, Am. Studies Assn., Calif. Coun. for Humanities, Phi Beta Kappa. Presbyterian. Home: 1648 N Kenyon Pl Claremont CA 91711-2905 Office: Claremont McKenna Coll 850 Columbia Ave Claremont CA 91711-3901

ROTH, MICHAEL JAMES, magazine publisher; b. Burbank, Calif., Feb. 24, 1952; s. Murray M. and Frances (Ackerman) R. BS, Calif. State U., Northridge, 1978; MBA, Calif. State U., San Francisco, 1983. Regional mgr. Cass Advt., San Francisco, 1979-82, Media Networks, Inc., San Francisco, 1982-83; pub. Golden State Mag., San Francisco, 1983-89; assoc. pub. Aloha Mag., Honolulu, 1990-92; pres. Roth Comms., Honolulu, 1992—; founder Wailea (Hawaii) Mag., 1991-94, Golden State Mag., 1984—. Pub.: (vis. guide) Discover the Californias, 1988 (Belding award 1988); mktg. dir.: (vis. guides) Islands of Aloha, 1992 (Pele award 1992), Golf Hawaii, The Complete Guide, 1994 (Pele award 1994); project mgr. (vis. guide) Wailea Mag., 1993 (Belding award 1993). Haul-out mgr. Waikiki Yacht Club, Honolulu, 1992-94; skipper Trans Pacific Yacht Race, San Francisco-Honolulu, 1990; mem. U.S. Sailing race com., 1993-94; commr. of Yachting Aloha State Games, 1994. 1st place trimmer, St. Francis Yacht Club Big Boat Series, 1990. Mem. St. Francis Yacht Club, Waikiki Yacht Club. Home: 1717 Mott Smith Dr Apt 1608 Honolulu HI 96822-2825

ROTH, ROBERT CHARLES, lawyer; b. Racine, Wis., Feb. 6, 1945; s. Robert Charles and Lucille (Holy) R.; m. Karen Trombley, May 18, 1974; children: David, Michael. BBA, St. Nobert Coll., 1967; JD, Marquette U., 1970; postgrad. course in law, George Washington U., 1972. Bar: Wis. 1970, U.S. Dist. Ct. (ea. dist.) Wis. 1970, U.S. CT. Mil. Appeals 1970, U.S. Army Ct. Mil Rev. 1971, Colo. 1974, U.S. Dist. Ct. Colo. 1974, U.S. Ct. Appeals (10th cir.) 1974, U.S. Ct. Appeals (5th cir.) 1979, U.S. Ct. Claims 1980. Atty. Shaw & Coghill, Denver, 1974-76; ptnr. Shaw, Spangler & Roth, Denver, 1976—; bd. dirs. Love Oil Co., Denver; pub. arbitrator Nat. Assn. Securities Dealers. Served as capt. U.S. Army, 1970-74. Mem. ATLA, ABA, Colo. Bar Assn., Denver Bar Assn., Wis. Bar Assn., Fed. Bar Assn., Colo. Trial Lawyers Assn., Greenwood Athletic Club.

ROTH, SANFORD HAROLD, rheumatologist, health care administrator, educator; b. Akron, Ohio, June 12, 1934; s. Charles and Rose Marie (Zelman) R.; m. Marcia Ann, June 9, 1957; children: Shana Beth, Sari Luanne. B.Sc., Ohio State U., 1955, M.D., 1959. Intern Mt. Carmel, Columbus, Ohio, 1959-60; fellow Mayo Grad. Sch. Medicine, 1962-65; pvt. practice medicine specializing in rheumatology Phoenix, 1965—; med. dir. Arthritis Ctr., Ltd., Phoenix, 1983—; dir. Arthritis Program Healthwest Regional Medical Ctr., Phoenix, 1987-89; med. dir. Arthritis/Orthopedic Ctr. for Excellence Humana Hosp., Phoenix, 1989—; dir. arthritis rehab. program St. Luke's Hosp., Phoenix, 1978-87; med. research dir. Harrington Arthritis Research Ctr., Phoenix, 1984-88; prof., dir. aging and arthritis program Coll. Grad. Program, Ariz. State U., Tempe, 1984—; dir. medicine Ariz. Insts., Phoenix, 1985—; past state chmn. Gov.'s Conf. on Arthritis in Ariz., 1967; cons., rep. arthritis adv. com. FDA, 1982—, chmn. anti-rheumatic new drug guidelines, 1984—; cons. Ciba-Geigy, 1983—, Upjohn, 1985-87, Pennwalt, 1985-88, Arthritis Found. Clinics, 3M-Riker Labs, Inc., 1981-89, VA, 1970-87, FTC, 1980—, Boots Pharm. Co., 1980-87, Greenwich Pharm., 1986-87, Hoffman-LaRoche, 1986—, FDA Office Compliance, 1987—, G.D. Searle, 1987—; prin. investigator Coop. Systematic Studies of Rheumatic Diseases; vis. scholar in rheumatology Beijing Med. Coll., People's Republic China, 1982; proctor, vis. scholar program U.S.-China Edn. Inst., 1982—; med. research dir., exec. bd., trustee Harrington Arthritis Research Ctr., 1983-88; co-chair PANLAR Collaborative Clin. Epidemiol. Group, 1989—; mem. com. on revision U.S. Pharmacopeial Conv., 1990—; mem. antirheumatic drug task force WHO-Internat. League Against Rheumatism, 1991—. Author: New Directions in Arthritis Therapy, 1980; Handbook of Drug Therapy in Rheumatoloy, 1985; med. contbg. editor RISS, Hosp. Physician, 1960-68, Current Prescribing, 1976-80; hon. internat. cons. editor Drugs, 1977—; editor in chief Arthron, 1982-85; editor, contbg. author: Rheumatic Therapeutics, 1985; med. cons. editor Update: Rheumatism, 1985, AMA Drug Evaluations, 6th edit., 1986, 7th edit., 1990; mem. editorial bd. VA Practitioner, 1985—, Comprehensive Therapy, 1987; mem. internat. editorial bd. Jour. Drug Devel., 1988—, Practical Gastroenterology, 1989—; contbr. numerous articles to profl. jours., chpts. to books. Fellow Am. Coll. Rheumatology (founding, liaison com. to regional med. program 1974-76, co-dir. med. info. system ARAMIS, computer com., chmn. antiinflammatory drug study club 1974—, com. on clubs and councils 1977-80, western regional co-chmn. 1977—, therapeutic and drug com. 1979—, glossary com. 1981-83, ad hoc com. on future meeting sites 1983); mem. AMA, ACP (regional program com., ann. Philip S. Hench lectureship chmn. 1978-79), Arthritis Found. (dir. central Ariz. chpt. 1982-83, past chmn. med. and sci. com. 1967-72), Lupus Found. Am. (bd. 1981—), Internat. Soc. Rheumatic Therapy (sec.-gen. 1990—, bd. dirs. 1987—, pres. 1992—), Maricopa County Med. Soc. (rehab. com.), Am. Soc. Clin. Rheumatology (past pres. exec. council), Am. Coll. Clin. Pharmacology, Soc. Internal Medicine, Mayo Clinic Alumni Assn., Mayo Clinic Fellows Assn. (sec. 1964-65), Argentine Rheumatology Soc. (hon.), Mayo Clinic Fellows Rheumatology Soc. (pres. 1964-65), Mayo Clinic Film Soc. (bd. dirs. 1964-65), Pan Am. League Against Rheumatism (chmn. clin. trials com. 1987—). Office: Arthritis Ctr Ltd 3330 N 2nd St Ste 601 Phoenix AZ 85012-2371

ROTH, STEVEN D., mental health counselor; b. Sandusky, Ohio, Feb. 10, 1952; s. Charles A. and Betty J. Roth; m. Gerilyn F. Sekela, Oct. 25, 1975; 1 child, Linsday M. BA, Bowling Green State U., 1974, MA, 1979. Case mgr. Erie County Welfare Dept., Sandusky, Ohio, 1974-78; job placement/procurement specialist Double S Industries, Sandusky, 1978-80; coord. resident svcs., staff devel. Luther Home of Mercy, Williston, Ohio, 1980-86; coord. psychosocial devel. Ruth Ide Mental Health Ctr., Toledo, Ohio, 1986-89; dir. program evaluation Wood County Mental Health Bd., Bowling Green, Ohio, 1989-90; behavior mgmt. specialist Wood County Bd. of Mental Retardation, Bowling Green, 1991-92; instr. U. Toledo, 1992; quality assurance mgr. Charter Hosp., Toledo, 1992; coord., therapist No. Wyo. Mental Health Ctr., Sheridan, Wyo., 1992—; statis. cons. St. Vincent's Hosp., Toledo, 1984; instr. psychology Sheridan Coll., 1993—. Mem. APA (student affiliate), ACA, Am. Mental Health Counselors Assn., Nat. Coun. Self-Esteem, Elks. Episcopal. Home: 81 Davis Tee Sheridan WY 82801-6024 Office: Supported Independence Project 101 W Brundage St Sheridan WY 82801-4217

ROTHBARD, MURRAY NEWTON, economics educator; b. N.Y.C., Mar. 2, 1926; s. David and Ray (Babushkin) R.; m. Jo Ann Beatrice Schumacher, Jan. 16, 1953. AB, Columbia U., 1945, MA in Econs., 1946, PhD in Econs., 1956. Instr. econs. Baruch Coll., N.Y.C., 1948-49; sr. analyst William Volker Fund, Burlingame, Calif., 1956-62; assoc. prof. econs. Polytech Inst., Bklyn., 1966-70; prof. Polytech U., Bklyn., 1970-86; S.J. Hall Disting. prof. econs. U. Nev., Las Vegas, 1986—; v.p. acad. affairs L.V. Mises Inst. Auburn (Ala.) U., 1982—; bd. dirs. Ctr. Libertarian Studies, Burlingame; v.p. John Randolph Club, Burlingame, 1990—. Author: Man, Economy and State, 1962, America's Great Depression, 1963, For A New Liberty, 1973, Conceived in Liberty, 1979, Ethics of Liberty, 1981; editor Rev. Austrian Econs., 1986—, Jour. Libertarian Studies, 1976—. Found. Fgn. Affairs grantee, Chgo., 1962-66. Mem. History of Econs. Assn., Soc. Historians Am. Republic (rep. 1987—). Republican. Office: U Nev Las Vegas Dept Econs 4505 S Maryland Pky Las Vegas NV 89154-9900

ROTHBLATT, DONALD NOAH, urban and regional planner, educator; b. N.Y.C., Apr. 28, 1935; s. Harry and Sophie (Chernofsky) R.; m. Ann S. Vogel, June 16, 1957; children: Joel Michael, Steven Saul. BCE, CUNY, 1957; MS in Urban Planning, Columbia U., 1963; Diploma in Comprehensive Planning, Inst. Social Studies, The Hague, 1964; PhD in City and Regional Planning, Harvard U., 1969. Registered profl. engr. N.Y. Planner N.Y.C. Planning Commn., 1960-62, N.Y. Housing and Redevel. Bd., 1963-66; research fellow Ctr. for Environ. Design Studies, Harvard U., Cambridge, Mass., 1965-71; teaching fellow, instr., then asst. prof. city and regional planning Harvard U., 1967-71; prof. urban and regional planning, chmn. dept. San Jose State U., Calif., 1971—; Lady Davis vis. prof. urban and regional planning Hebrew U., Jerusalem and Tel Aviv U., 1978; vis. scholar Indian Inst. Architects, 1979, vis. scholar, rsch. assoc. Inst. Govtl. Studies, U. Calif., Berkeley, 1980—; cons. to pvt. industry and govt. agys. Author: Human Needs and Public Housing, 1964, Thailand's Northeast, 1967, Regional Planning: The Appalachian Experience, 1971, Allocation of Resources for Regional Planning, 1972, The Suburban Environment and Women, 1979, Regional-Local Development Policy Making, 1981, Planning the Metropolis: The Multiple Advocacy Approach, 1982, Comparative Suburban Data, 1983, Suburbia: An International Assessment, 1986, Metropolitan Dispute Resolution in Silicon Valley, 1989, Good Practices for the Congestion Management Program, 1994; editor: National policy for Urban and Regional Development, 1974, Regional Advocacy Planning: Expanding Air Transport Facilities for the San Jose Metropolitan Area, 1975, Metropolitan-wide Advocacy Planning; Dispersion of Low and Moderate Cost Housing in the San Jose Metropolitan Area, 1976, Multiple Advocacy Planning: Public Surface Transportation in the San Jose Metropolitan Area, 1977, A Multiple Advocacy Approach to Regional Planning: Open Space and Recreational Facilities for the San Jose Metropolitan Area, 1979, Regional Transpotation Planning for the San Jose Metropolitan Area, 1981, Planning for Open Space and Recreational Facilities in the San Jose Metropolitan Area, 1982, Regional Economic Development Planning for the San Jose Metropolitan Area, 1984, Planning for Surface Transportation in the San Jose Metropolitan Area, 1986, Expansion of Air Transportation Facilities in the San Jose Metropolitan Area, 1987, Provision of Economic Development in the San Jose Met. Area, 1988, Metropolitan Governance: American/Canadian Intergovernmental Perspectives, 1993; contbr. numerous articles to profl. jours.; dir.: Pub. TV series Sta. KTEH, 1976. Served to 1st lt. U.S. Army Corps of Engrs., 1957-59. Rsch. fellow John F. Kennedy Sch. Govt. Harvard U., 1967-69; William F. Milton rsch. fellow, 1970-71; faculty rsch. grantee, NSF, 1972-82, Calif. State U., 1977-88; grantee Nat. Inst. Dispute Resolution, 1987-88, Can. Studies Enrichment Program, 1989-90, Can. Studies Rsch. Program, 1992-93, Univ. Rsch. and Tng. Program grantee Calif. Dept. Transp., 1993-95; recipient Innovative Teaching award Calif. State U. and Coll., 1975-79; co-recipient Best of West award Western Ednl. Soc. for Tele-communication, 1976; recipient award Internat. Festival of Films on Architecture and Planning, 1983, Meritorious Performance award San Jose State U., 1986, 88, 90. Mem. Assn. Collegiate Schs. of Planning (pres. 1975-76), Am. Inst. Cert. Planners, Am. Planning Assn., Planners for Equal Opportunity, Internat. Fedn. Housing and Planning, AAUP, Calif. Edn. Com. on Architecture and Landscape, Architecture and Urban and

Regional Planning (chmn. 1973-75). Office: Urban and Regional Planning Dept San Jose State U San Jose CA 95192

ROTHENBERG, HARVEY DAVID, educational administrator; b. Fort Madison, Iowa, May 31, 1937; s. Max and Cecelia Rothenberg; A.A., Wentworth Mil. Acad., 1957; B.B.A., State U. Iowa, 1960; M.A., U. No. Colo., 1961; postgrad. Harris Tchrs. Coll., 1962-63, St. Louis U., 1962-63; Ph.D., Colo. State U., 1972; m. Audrey Darlynne Roseman, July 5, 1964; children—David Michael, Mark Daniel. Distributive edn. tchr. Roosevelt High Sch., St. Louis, 1961-63, Proviso West High Sch., Hillside, Ill., 1963-64, Longmont (Colo.) Sr. High Sch., 1964-69, 70-71; supr. research and spl. programs St. Vrain Valley Sch. Dist., Longmont, Colo., 1971-72; chmn. bus. div. Arapahoe Community Coll., Littleton, Colo., 1972-75; dir. vocat., career and adult edn. Arapahoe County Sch. Dist. 6, Littleton, 1975—; instr. Met. State Coll., Denver, part-time, 1975—, Arapahoe Community Coll., Littleton, 1975—, Regis Coll., 1979—; vis. prof. U. Ala., Tuscaloosa, summer 1972; dir. Chatfield Bank, Littleton, 1974-83, Yaak River Mines Ltd., Amusement Personified Inc.; pres. Kuytia Inc., Littleton, 1975—; co-owner Albuquerque Lasers, profl. volleyball team. Mem. City of Longmont Long-Range Planning Commn., 1971-72, pres. Homeowners Bd., 1978-80. Recipient Outstanding Young Educator award St. Vrain Valley Sch. Dist., 1967, Outstanding Vocational Educator, Colo. 1992, We. Region U.S., 1993. Mem. Am., Colo. (mem. exec. com. 1966-68, treas. 1972-73) vocat. assns., Littleton C. of C., Colo. Assn. Vocat. Adminstrs, Colo. Educators For and About Bus., Delta Sigma Pi, Delta Pi Epsilon, Nat. Assn. Local Sch. Adminstrs., Colo. Council Local Sch. Adminstrs. Clubs: Elks, Masons, Shriners. Home: 7461 S Sheridan Ct Littleton CO 80123-7084 Office: Arapahoe County Sch Dist 6 5776 S Crocker St Littleton CO 80120-2012

ROTHENBERG, MARCY MIROFF, public relations consultant; b. Hollywood, Calif., Dec. 23, 1950; d. Victor and Eugenie Alice (Wankel) Miroff; m. Peter Jay Rothenberg, June 22; 1 child, Valerie Jill. AB, UCLA, 1973; MA, U. So. Calif., 1977. Publicity coord. Ruben for Assembly Com., Van Nuys, Calif., 1971-72; staff writer dept. pub. rels. Prudential Ins. Co. Am., L.A., 1973-74; pub. rels. cons. to econ. devel. program Mayor's Office, City of L.A., 1974-75; staff writer dept. pub. affairs ARCO, L.A., 1975-78; comm. rep. divsn. pub. affairs So. Calif. Gas Co., L.A., 1978-79; dir. bus. devel. Meserve, Mumper & Hughes, L.A., 1979-80; account supr. Hill and Knowlton, Inc., L.A., 1980-82; asst. prof. Sch. Journalism U. So. Calif., L.A., 1986-89; owner Rothenberg Comm., Porter Ranch, Calif., 1982—. Author: (study guides) Something Ventured, 1991, The Sales Connection, 1992. Pub. rels. cons. PRIDE (Porter Ranch is Developed Enough!), 1989-91; mem. shared decision making coun. Castlebay Lane Elem. Sch., Porter Ranch, 1990-92, Frost Mid. Sch., Granada Hills, Calif., 1992-94. Recipient Bronze Quill award of Merit (2nd pl.), L.A. chpt. Internat. Assn. Bus. Communicators, Bronze Quill award of Excellence (1st pl.), 1985, ACE award of Excellence, 1989, 1st pl. award of Excellence, Med. Mktg. Assn., 1985, 86. Mem. Pub. Rels. Soc. Am. (accredited, bd. dirs. L.A. chpt. 1989, mem. nat. profl. devel. com. 1978-79, mem. nat. social responsibility com. 1980-81), Publicity Club L.A., UCLA Alumni Assn., U. So. Calif. Journalism Alumni Assn., Phi Beta Kappa. Democrat. Jewish. Office: Rothenberg Comm 19041 Braemore Rd Porter Ranch CA 91326-1202

ROTHERHAM, LARRY CHARLES, insurance executive; b. Council Bluffs, Iowa, Oct. 22, 1940; s. Charles Sylvester and Edna Mary (Sylvanus) R.; m. Florene F. Black, May 29, 1965; children: Christopher Charles, Phillip Larry, Kathleen Florene. Student, Creighton U., 1959-61; BSBA, U. Nebr., 1965; postgrad., Am. Coll., Bryn Mawr, Pa., 1985, 87. CPCU, CLU, ARM. Claims rep. and underwriter Safeco Ins. Co., Albuquerque, New Mex., 1965-69; br. mgr. Ohio Casualty Group, Albuquerque, 1969—; assoc. in risk mgmt. Ins. Inst. Am., 1976—. Mem. PTA Collet Park Elem. Sch., Albuquerque, 1963-82, Freedom H.S., Albuquerque, 1982-86; bd. chmn. N.M. Property Ins. Program. Mem. New Mex. Soc. Chartered Property & Casualty Underwriters (charter mem., pres. 1975-77), New Mex. Soc. Chartered Life Underwriters, New Mex. Ins. Assn. Democrat. Roman Catholic. Home: 2112 Gretta St NE Albuquerque NM 87112-3238 Office: Ohio Casualty Group 10400 Academy Rd NE Ste 200 Albuquerque NM 87111-1229

ROTHHAMMER, CRAIG ROBERT, social worker, consultant; b. San Francisco, May 17, 1954; s. Robert Charles and Gloria Lee (Molloy) R.; m. Dawn Alicia Alvarez, 1988. BA, U. Calif., Santa Barbara, 1976; MSW, San Diego State U., 1979. Lic. clin. social worker, Calif. Social work asst. Mercy Hosp., San Diego, 1977; psychiat. social worker Lanterman State Hosp., Pomona, Calif., 1979-83, Sonoma State Hosp., Eldridge, Calif., 1983-84; children's social worker County Adoption Service, San Bernardino, Calif., 1984-86; psychiatric social worker Patton State Hosp., 1987-88; psychiat. soc. worker II Crisis Outpatient Services Riverside (Calif.) County Mental Health, 1988-90; mental health svcs. supr. Interagy. Svcs. for Families, Riverside County Mental Health, 1990—; expert examiner Behavioral Sci. Examiners, Calif.; pvt. practice (part time) social work Redlands, Calif., 1986-89; field instr. MSW program Calif. State U., San Bernardino, 1989—, marriage, family & child counselor program Loma Linda (Calif.) U., 1993. Vol. Social Advs. for Youth, Santa Barbara, Calif., 1974-76, Am. Diabetes Assn., San Diego, 1978-79, San Diego Assn. For Retarded, 1978-80; liason Adoptive Family Assn., San Bernardino, 1986. Mem. NASW, Acad. Cert. Social Workers (diplomate in clin. social work). Democrat. Office: Interagy Svcs for Families 9890 County Farm Rd Ste 1 Riverside CA 92503-3518

ROTHLISBERG, ALLEN PETER, librarian, educator, deacon; b. Jamaica, N.Y., Nov. 15, 1941; s. Allen Greenway and Agnes Clare (Donohoe) R.; m. Linda Lee Lillie, Oct. 17, 1964; children: Bethanie Lynn, Craig Allen. AB, San Diego State U., 1963; MLS, Our Lady of the Lake U., 1970. Cert. tchr., Ariz.; ordained deacon Episcopal Ch., 1989. Libr. dir. Prescott (Ariz.) Pub. Libr., 1963-75; dir. learning resources, head libr. Northland Pioneer Coll., Holbrook, Ariz., 1975-92; libr. dir. Chino Valley (Ariz.) Pub. Libr., 1992—; libr. media instr. Northland Pioneer Coll., Holbrook, Ariz., 1978—. Author: Dance to the Music of Time: Second Movement, 1972; contbr. articles to profl. pubs. Recreation dir. Town of Chino Valley, 1993—, pub. access TV dir., 1993—; Episcopal deacon St. George's Ch., Holbrook, 1989-92, St. Luke's, Prescott, 1992—. Recipient Libr. of Yr. Ariz. State Libr. Assn., 1966. Mem. Elks, Masons. Democrat. Episcopalian. Office: Chino Valley Pub Libr PO Box 1188 Chino Valley AZ 86323-1188

ROTHMAN, FRANK, lawyer, motion picture company executive; b. Los Angeles, Dec. 24, 1926; s. Leon and Rose (Gendel) R.; m. Mariana Richardson, Aug. 7, 1985; children: Steven, Robin, Susan. B.A., U. So. Calif., 1949, LL.B., 1951. Bar: Calif. 1952, D.C., U.S. Dist. Ct. (cen. dist.) Calif. 1951. Dep. city atty. City of Los Angeles, 1951-55; mem. law firm Wyman, Bautzer, Rothman, Kuchel & Silbert, Los Angeles, 1956-82; chmn. bd., chief exec. officer MGM-UA Entertainment Co., Culver City, Calif., 1982-86; ptnr. Skadden Arps Slate, L.A., 1986—. Bd. editors U. So. Calif. Law Rev., 1948. Served with USAAF, 1945-46. Fellow Am. Coll. Trial Lawyers; mem. L.A. Bar Assn., Calif. Bar Assn., Univ. Club. Democrat. Home: 10555 Rocca Pl Los Angeles CA 90077-2904 Office: Skadden Arps Slate 300 S Grand Ave Bldg 3400 Los Angeles CA 90071-3144

ROTHMAN, JUDITH ELLEN, associate dean; b. Bklyn., Sept. 12, 1946; d. Benjamin and Shirley (Finkelstein) Siegel; m. Elliott charles Rothman, Jan. 1, 1983; children by previous marriage: Reed Adam Slatas, Kimberly Joy Slatas. BS in Acctg., Fairleigh Dickinson U., 1976, postgrad., 1976-77; postgrad., UCLA, 1986-87. Acct. Interpace Corp., Parsippany, N.J., 1976-77; mgr. fin. planning Blue Cross So. Calif., Woodland Hills, 1977-82; asst. dir. fin. Cedars-Sinai Med. Ctr., L.A., 1982-87; assoc. dean fin. and bus. affairs, Sch. Medicine UCLA, Westwood, 1987-94; sr. assoc. dean fin. and adminstrn. Sch. Medicine UCLA, L.A., 1994—. Mem. Calif. Abortion Rights Action League, Friends of Calif. Spl. Olympics. Mem. NAFE, Assn. Am. Med. Colls. (region sec. 1992, region pres. 1993), Med. Group Mgmt. Assn., UCLA Anderson Mgmt. Alumni Assn. Office: UCLA Sch Medicine 12-138CHS 10833 Le Conte Ave Los Angeles CA 90024

ROTHMAN, JULIUS LAWRENCE, retired English language educator; b. N.Y.C., Sept. 22, 1920; s. Samuel and Bessie (Kantor) R.; m. Stella Lambert, June 23, 1948. BSS, CCNY, 1941; MA, Columbia U., 1947, PhD, 1954. Lectr. Hunter Coll., N.Y.C., 1947-50, Rutgers U., New Brunswick, N.J., 1950-53; tech. writer Olympic Radio & TV, L.I. City, N.Y., 1951-61; prof. English Nassau Community Coll., Garden City, N.Y., 1962-86, prof. emeritus, 1986—; broadcaster, talk show host weekly program Sta. WHPC, 1974-82; deputy dir. gen. Internat. Biographical Ctr., Cambridge, England, 1992—. Editor, contbg. author The Cabellian, 1968-72; contbr. sects. to books on folklore and legend; contbr. articles to profl. jours. Mem. Nat. Com. to Preserve Social Security and Medicare, Arthritis Found.; mem. adv. bd. 9th Senatorial Dist. N.Y., 1984-88; seat sponsor Ariz. State U. Sundome Performing Arts Assn. Named Internat. Man of Year 1991-92, Internat. Biographical Ctr., Cambridge. Mem. Cabell Soc. (founder 1967, exec. v.p. 1968-72), Ret. Pub. Employees Assn., Nat. Wildlife Fedn., Nat. Ret. Tchrs. Assn., Columbia U. Alumni Assn. Methodist.

ROTHMAN, PAUL ALAN, publisher; b. Bklyn., June 26, 1940; s. Fred B. and Dorothy (Regosin) R.; m. Mary Ann Dalson, July 28, 1966 (div. 1992); children: Deborah, Diana. BA, Swarthmore Coll., 1962; JD, U. Mich., 1965; LLM in Taxation, NYU, 1967. Bar: N.Y. 1965. Assoc. Dewey, Ballentine, Busby, Palmer & Wood, N.Y.C., 1965-67; v.p. Fred B. Rothman & Co., Littleton, Colo., 1967-85, pres., 1985—; chmn. bd. Colo. Plasticard, Littleton, 1983-95. Editor Mich. Law Rev., 1963-65. Home: 25437 Stanley Park Rd Evergreen CO 80439-5512 Office: Fred B Rothman & Co 10368 W Centennial Rd Littleton CO 80127-4205

ROTHMAN, STEVEN ISAIAH, oil explorationist, consultant; b. Greenwich, Conn., Dec. 23, 1947; s. Sidney and Florence Ann (Russakoff) R.; m. Barbara Jane Grower, June 29, 1969. BSEE in Computer Sci., Rensselaer Polytech. U., 1969; MSEM in Ops. Rsch., Northeastern U., 1972. Mem. tech. staff. Lincoln Labs. The MITRE Corp., Bedford, Mass., 1969-72; mem. tech. staff. NASA The MITRE Corp., Houston, 1972-74; mem. tech. staff. NORAD The MITRE Corp., Colorado Springs, 1974-75; mem. tech. staff. Energy Rsch. Devel. Adminstn. The MITRE Corp., Washington, 1975-76; v.p. Kilovolt Corp., Hackensack, N.J., 1976-79; owner Copper Creek Systems, Glenwood, N.Mex., 1979—; chmn. bd. Bravo Resources, Glenwood, 1982—; vice chmn. Zavanna L.L.C., Denver, 1994—; cons. Innuit Indians, Goose Bay, Labrador Canada, 1990-91. Author in field. Chmn. Sonic Booms Citizens Com., Glenwood, 1979—; tech. adv. Western N.Mex. U. Math. Dept., Silver City, N.Mex., 1980-81; part owner Catron County Courier, Reserve, N.Mex., 1987-90. Recipient Plaque of Appreciation award Catron County Govt., Reserve, 1985. Mem. N.Mex. Ornithol. Soc., Nature Conservancy, Amnesty Internat., Childreach. Jewish. Office: Bravo Resources Inc 1000 Catwalk Rd Glenwood NM 88039

ROTHSCHILD, HELENE, marriage/family therapist and author; b. Bklyn., Oct. 11, 1940. BS in Health Edn., Bklyn. Coll., 1962, MS in Health Edn., 1965; MA in Marriage/Family/Child Counseling, U. Santa Clara, Calif., 1980. Lic. marriage, family and child counselor; lic. tchr., Calif., N.Y. Founder, dir. Inst. for Creative Therapy, Sedona, Ariz., 1982-86, dir. tng., 1982—; pvt. practice marriage, family therapy, Sedona, 1980—; health edn. tchr. Lafayette High Sch., Bklyn., 1961-65, 73-76; part-time health edn. tchr. in pvt. elem. schs., Bklyn., 1966-73. Host TV show Creative Therapy with Helene Rothschild, radio show Hello Helene, KEST, San Francisco; author 10 tapes, 2 books, 5 booklets, 10 posters, 5 cards, 48 articles; lectr. in field; facilitator hundreds of seminars and workshops; appeared numerous times on TV, radio; addressed numerous mags., newspapers, convs., corps. Author: Free to Fly-Dare to be a Success; prodr. tapes: Free to Fly-Dare to be a Success, Dare to be Thin, I Deserve It All, Successful Parenting, Fantastic Relationships, Dare to be Prosperous; contbr. articles to profl. jours. Home and Office: PO Box 10419 Sedona AZ 86339-8419

ROTHSTEIN, BARBARA JACOBS, federal judge; b. Bklyn., Feb. 3, 1939; d. Solomon and Pauline Jacobs; m. Ted L. Rothstein, Dec. 28, 1968; 1 child, Daniel. B.A., Cornell U., 1960; LL.B., Harvard U., 1966. Bar: Mass. 1966, Wash. 1969, U.S. Ct. Appeals (9th cir.) 1977, U.S. Dist. Ct. (we. dist.) Wash. 1971, U.S. Supreme Ct. 1975. Pvt. practice law Boston, 1966-68; asst. atty. gen. State of Wash., 1968-77; judge Superior Ct., Seattle, 1977-80; judge Fed. Dist. Ct. Western Wash., Seattle, 1980—, chief judge, 1987-94; faculty Law Sch. U. Wash., 1975-77, Hastings Inst. Trial Advocacy, 1977, N.W. Inst. Trial Advocacy, 1979—; mem. state-fed. com. U.S. Jud. Conf., chair subcom. on health reform. Recipient Matrix Table Women of Yr. award Women in Communication, Judge of the Yr. award Fed. Bar Assn., 1989; King County Wash. Women Lawyers Vanguard Honor, 1995. Mem. ABA (jud. sect.), Am. Judicature Soc., Nat. Assn. Women Judges, Fellows of the Am. Bar, Wash. State Bar Assn., U.S. Jud. Conf. (state-fed. com., health reform subcom.), Phi Beta Kappa, Phi Kappa Phi. Office: US Dist Ct 705 US Courthouse 1010 5th Ave Seattle WA 98104-1130

ROTKIN, MICHAEL ERIC, community studies educator, city official; b. N.Y.C., Sept. 17, 1945; s. Irving Jacob and Esther (Repps) R.; m. Karen Frost Rian, June 15, 1968 (div. Aug. 1983); m. Madelyn Suzanne McCaul, Sept. 17, 1989. BA summa cum laude, Cornell U., 1969; PhD in History of Consciousness, U. Calif., Santa Cruz, 1992. Vol. VISTA, Fla., 1965-66; teaching asst. U. Calif., Santa Cruz, 1969-73, lectr. community studies 1973—, dir. field studies, 1977—; mem. Santa Cruz City Council, 1979-88, 92—, mayor, 1981-82, 85-86. Co-author: Revolutionary Theory, 1983. Editor Socialist Rev., 1970-79. Contbr. numerous articles to mags. and newspapers. Mem. nat. com. New Am. Movement, Chgo., 1978-79; bd. dirs. Met. Transit Dist., Santa Cruz, 1979-88, 92—, chmn. bd., 1983, 88; chief negotiator UC-AFT, 1989—; bd. dir. Food and Nutrition, Inc., 1988-92, Santa Cruz Community Credit Union, 1988-92; chair Santa Cruz Action Network, 1988-92. Woodrow Wilson fellow, 1969. Democrat. Jewish. Office: U Calif Community Studies Dept Santa Cruz CA 95064

ROTMAN, MORRIS BERNARD, public relations consultant; b. Chgo., June 6, 1918; s. Louis and Etta (Harris) R.; m. Sylvia Sugar, Mar. 1, 1944; children: Betty Ruth, Jesse, Richard. Student, Wright Jr. Coll., 1936-37, Northwestern U., 1937-39. Editor Times Neighborhood publs., Chgo., 1938-40; asst. editor City News Bur., 1940-42; mng. editor Scott Field Broadcaster, USAAF, 1942-43; publicity dir. Community and War Fund of Met. Chgo., 1943-45; v.p. William R. Harshe Assocs., 1945-49, pres., 1949-66; chmn. bd., chief exec. officer (name changed to Harshe-Rotman & Druck, Inc.), 1966-81; pres. Ruder Finn & Rotman, Inc. (merger of Harshe-Rotman & Druck and Ruder & Finn), 1982, ret.; founder Morris B. Rotman & Assocs., Chgo., 1989—; adj. prof. Coll. of Desert, Palm Desert, Calif. Chmn. solicitations pub. rels. div. Community Fund Chgo., 1948-49, spl. events chmn., 1953; chmn. communications div. Jewish Fedn. Chgo., 1965, Combined Jewish Appeal,1 966; life dir. Rehab. Inst. Chgo.; U.S. dir. The Shakespeare Globe Centre (N.Am.) Inc.; trustee Roosevelt U. (emeritus). Recipient Prime Minister Israel medal, 1969. Mem. Pub. Rels. Soc. Am. (past dir.), Chgo. Presidents' Orgn. (pres. 1970-71), Acad. Motion Picture Arts and Scis. (assoc.), Chief Execs. Orgn., Chgo. Press Vets. Assn., Mid-Am. Club, Standard Club, Publicity Club, Bryn Mawr Country Club, Tamarisk Country Club (Palm Springs), Headline Club, Desert Rats (Palm Springs; chair), Sigma Delta Chi. Home (winter): 3 Columbia Dr Rancho Mirage CA 92270-3149

ROTTER, JEROME ISRAEL, medical geneticist; b. L.A., Feb. 24, 1949; s. Leonard L. and Jeanette (Kronenfeld) R.; m. Deborah Tofield, July 14, 1970; children: Jonathan Moshe, Amy Esther, Samuel Alexander. BS, UCLA, 1969, MD, 1973. Intern Harbor-UCLA Med. Ctr., Torrance, Calif., 1973-74; fellow in med. genetics Harbor-UCLA Med. Ctr., Torrance, 1975-78, asst. research pediatrician, 1978-79, faculty div. med. genetics, 1978-86; resident in medicine Wadsworth VA Hosp., Los Angeles, 1974-75; asst. prof. medicine and pediatrics Sch. Medicine UCLA, 1979-83, assoc. prof. Sch. Medicine, 1983-87, prof. Sch. Medicine, 1987—; dir. divsn. med. genetics and co. dir. med. genetics birth defect ctr. Cedars-Sinai Med. Ctr., 1986—; key investigator Ctr. for Ulcer Rsch. and Edn., L.A., 1980-89; dir. genetic epidemiology core Ctr. for Study of Inflammatory Bowel Disease, Torrance, 1985-91; assoc. dir. Cedars-Sinai Inflammatory Bowel Disease Ctr., L.A., 1992—; dir. Stuart Found. CSMC Common Disease Risk Assessment Ctr., 1986—; dir. genetic epidemiology core project molecular biology of arteriosclerosis UCLA, 1987—. Mem. bd. govs. Cedars-Sinai, chair med. genetics, 1990—. Recipient Regents scholarship UCLA, 1966-73; recipient Richard Weitzman award Harbor-UCLA, 1983, Ross award Western Soc. for Pediatric Rsch., 1985. Mem. Am. Heart Assn., Am. Soc. Human Genetics, Am. Gastroent. Assn., Am. Diabetes Assn., Soc. for Pediatric Research, Western Soc. for Clin. Investigation (mem. council 1985-88), Am. Fedn. for Clin. Rsch., Western Assn. Physicians, Am. Soc. for Clin. Investigation. Jewish. Office: Cedars-Sinai Med Ctr Div Med Genetics 8700 Beverly Blvd Los Angeles CA 90048-1804

ROTTER, PAUL TALBOTT, retired insurance executive; b. Parsons, Kans., Feb. 21, 1918; s. J. and LaNora (Talbott) R.; m. Virginia Sutherlin Barksdale, July 17, 1943; children—Carolyn Sutherlin, Diane Talbott. B.S. summa cum laude, Harvard U., 1937. Asst. mathematician Prudential Ins. Co. of Am., Newark, 1938-46; with Mut. Benefit Life Ins. Co., Newark, 1946—; successively asst. mathematician, asso. mathematician, mathematician Mut. Benefit Life Ins. Co., 1946-59, v.p., 1959-69, exec. v.p., 1969-80, ret., 1980. Mem. Madison Bd. Edn., 1958-64, pres., 1959-64; Trustee, mem. budget com. United Campaign of Madison, 1951-55; mem. bd., chmn. advancement com. Robert Treat council Boy Scouts Am., 1959-64. Fellow Soc. Actuaries (bd. govs. 1965-68, gen. chmn. edn. and exam. com. 1963-66, chmn. adv. com. edn. and exam. 1969-72); mem. Brit. Inst. Actuaries (asso.), Am. Acad. Actuaries (v.p. 1968-70, bd. dirs., chmn. edn. and exam. com. 1965-66, chmn. rev. and evaluation com. 1968-74), Asso. Harvard Alumni (regional dir. 1965-69), Actuaries Club N.Y. (pres. 1967-68), Harvard Alumni Assn. (v.p. 1964-66),Am. Lawn Bowls Assn. (pres. SW div.), Phi Beta Kappa Assos., Phi Beta Kappa. Clubs: Harvard N.J. (pres. 1956-57); Harvard (N.Y.C.); Morris County Golf (Convent, N.J.); Joslyn-Lake Hodges Lawn Bowling (pres. 1989-90). Home: 18278 Canfield Pl San Diego CA 92128-1002

ROTTSCHAEFER, WILLIAM ANDREW, philosophy educator; b. Tulsa, June 20, 1933; s. Dirk and Clara (Linsmeyer) R.; m. Marie Therese Schickel. BA, St. Louis U., 1956, MA, 1957, Licentiate in Sacred Theol., 1966; MS, U. Ill., 1969; PhD, Boston U., 1973. Asst. prof. philosophy SUNY, Oswego, 1972-73, Plattsburgh, 1973-75; asst. prof. philosophy Lewis & Clark Coll., Portland, Oreg., 1975-79, assoc. prof. philosophy, 1979-85, prof. philosophy, 1985—. Contbr. articles and revs. to profl. jours.; referee for several scholarly periodicals. Mem. Philosophy of Sci. Assn., Am. Philos. Assn., Inst. for Religion in an Age of Sci., Ctr. for Theology and the Natural Scis. (assoc.), Am. Acad. Religion. Office: Lewis and Clark Coll 0615 SW Palatine Hill Rd Portland OR 97219-7879

ROTZ, MARTA LYNNE, small business owner; b. Portland, Oreg., Mar. 12, 1947; d. Eugene Paul and Louise Elizabeth (Cutter) Hiney; m. Dennis Lee Parr, Aug. 2, 1966 (div.); children: Martin Lee, Darlene Leslie; m. Kerry Val Rotz, Feb. 2, 1980. Grad. high sch., Milwaukie, Oreg. Purchasing agt., ctrl. receiving coord. Bend (Oreg.) Meml. Clinic, 1982-93; proprietor Rotz's Maintenance Svc., Bend, 1982—; cons. Parr Excellence Creative Car Audio, Bend, 1992—. Democrat. Roman Catholic. Office: Rotzs Maintenance Svc PO Box 6933 Bend OR 97708-6933

ROUBAL, WILLIAM THEODORE, biophysicist, educator; b. Eugene, Oreg., Dec. 20, 1930; s. Frank J. and Irene I. (Ellenberger) R.; m. Carol Jean, Sept. 6, 1953; children: Diane Jeanette Roubal Daniel, Linda Ann Roubal Myrick, Sandra Mae Roubal, Cathy Roubal Hoover. BS, Oreg. State U., 1954, MS, 1959; PhD, U. Calif.-Davis, 1965. Chemist dept. entomology Oreg. State U., Corvallis, 1958-60; rsch. chemist Pioneer Rsch. Lab., Dept. Interior, Seattle, 1960-70; rsch. scientist Dept. Commerce, Seattle, 1970-75; sr. scientist NOAA, NMFS, Seattle, 1976—; biophysicist Environ. Conservation div. Nat. Marine Fisheries Svc., Seattle, 1968-75; assoc. prof. Sch. Fisheries, U. Wash., Seattle, 1976—; ednl. specialist Seattle Central Community Coll., 1974-85; instr., lectr. in field. Head usher Haller Lake United Methodist Ch., Seattle, 1974-89; workshop dir. Seattle YMCA Summer Family Camp, Seabeck, Wash., 1979—. Served as 1st lt. U.S. Army, 1954-56. Recipient award Seattle Central Community Coll., 1980. Mem. Am. Chem. Soc., Am. Oil Chemists' Soc. (A.E. MacGee award 1964), Am. Sci. Glassblowers Soc. (abstracts chmn. 1964-65). Home: 17840 Wayne Ave N Seattle WA 98133-5142 Office: NOAA NMFS EC Div 2725 Montlake Blvd E Seattle WA 98112-2013

ROULEAU, MARK LOUIS, financial executive; b. Washington, Nov. 13, 1956; s. David William and Florence Louise (Walters) R.; m. Lisa Wyckoff, Jan. 10, 1995. BS in Bus. Mgmt., Cornell U., 1978; MBA, Calif. State U., Long Beach, 1984; JD, Loyola U., L.A., 1990. Staff acct. Blue Cross/Blue Shield, Chgo., 1978-79, Informatics, Inc., L.A., 1979-81; controller/treas. Specialty Restaurants Corp., Long Beach, Calif., 1981-85; dir. fin. Davidson & Assocs., Inc., Torrance, Calif., 1985-89; v.p., CFO, gen. counsel Assoc. Hosts, Inc., Tarzana, Calif., 1989-92, pres., CEO, 1993—. Mem. State Bar Calif. Office: Associated Hosts Inc 18801 Ventura Blvd # 200 Tarzana CA 91356-3343

ROUNDS, DONALD MICHAEL, public relations executive; b. Centralia, Ill., May 9, 1941; s. Donald Merritt and Alice Josephine (Soulsby) R.; m. Alma Genevieve Beyer, Dec. 13, 1975. BS in History, Polit. Sci., Colo. State U., 1963. Police reporter, night city editor The Rocky Mountain News, Denver, 1960-70; mgr. Don M. Rounds Co., Denver, 1970-75; sr. editor Western Oil Reporter, Denver, 1975-80; energy writer The Rocky Mountain News, Denver, 1980-87; sr. media rels. advisor Cyprus Minerals Co., Englewood, Colo., 1987-92, media and community rels. mgr., 1992-93; media and community rels. mgr. Cyprus Amax Minerals Co., Englewood, 1994-95, dir. coms., 1995—; adv. bd Colo. State Minerals, Energy, and Geology (appointed by gov.), 1992—. Contbr. articles to mags. and newspapers. Sec. covenant com. Ken Caryl Ranch Master Assn., Littleton, Colo., 1980-84. Recipient 1st place spl. news series AP, 1987, 1st place news sweepstakes, 1987, Margolin award U. Denver Coll. Bus., 1986, Betty McWhorter Commendation of Honor Desk & Derrick Club of Denver, 1987, Journalism award Rocky Mountain Assn. Geologists, 1985, Citizen Svc. award Denver Police Dept., 1969, Pub. Svc. award Englewood Police Dept., 1967. Mem. Nat. Mining Assn. (pub. rels. com.), Soc. Profl. Journalists, Sigma Delta Chi, Denver Press Club (bd. dirs. 1987). Republican. Methodist. Home: 8220 S San Juan Range Rd Littleton CO 80127-4011 Office: Cyprus Amax Minerals Co 9100 E Mineral Cir Englewood CO 80112-3401

ROUNDS, LINNEA PAULA, library administrator; b. Gary, Ind., Feb. 12, 1944; d. Paul and S. Dolly (Fudaley) Korpita; m. Keith Rounds, Aug. 17, 1968; children: Daniel K., Paula L. B.A. in Journalism, Marquette U., 1965. Pub. relations asst. Wis. Heart Assn., Milw., 1963-66; pub. info. asst. Wyo. Hwy. Dept., Cheyenne, 1966-68; writer, operator AP, Cheyenne, 1969; account exec. Media, Inc., Cheyenne, 1969-71; communications specialist Sch. Dist. 1, Cheyenne, 1971-73; free-lance writer, 1973-77; pub. programs, publs. and mktg. mgr. Wyo. State Library, Cheyenne, 1977—. Editor Outrider, 1977—. Den leader Longs Peak council Cub Scouts, Boy Scouts Am., 1980, 81, pack liaison, 1982-83; bd. dirs. United Way of Laramie County, Cheyenne, 1981-84. Recipient Best of Show award ALA, 1985. Mem. Nat. Fedn. Press Women (sec. 1989-91, 3d v.p. 1991-93, 2nd v.p. 1993—, Comm. Contest award 1974, 85, 86, 87), Wyo. Press Women (pres. 1983-85, writing contest awards 1970-95, Communicator of Achievement 1989, Woman of Achievement 1990 Wyo. Commn. Women), Wyo. Library Assn., LWV, Wyo. Info. Officers Coop. (chmn., co-founder 1980-83). Democrat. Roman Catholic. Clubs: Zonta (Cheyenne) (bd. dirs., rec. sec. 1975-76, chmn. scholarship com. 1985, pres. 1988-89, area dir. dist. 12 1988-90, Zontian of Yr. 1991); Madame Curie Circle, Polish Nat Alliance. Home: 7413 Willshire Blvd Cheyenne WY 82009-2090 Office: Wyo State Library 2301 Capitol Ave Cheyenne WY 82002-0009

ROUSSEAU, DAVID, agricultural products executive; b. 1961. Ptnr. Rousseau Farming Co. I, Litchfield Park, Ariz., 1979—; with Rousseau Farming Co., 1979—. Office: Rousseau Farming Co II 2315 S 105th Ave Tolleson AZ 85353-9217*

ROUSSEAU, WILL, agricultural products executive; b. 1958. Ptnr. Rousseau Farming Co. I, Litchfield Park, Ariz., 1979—; with Rousseau Farming Co., 1979—. Office: Rousseau Farming Co II 2315 S 105th Ave Tolleson AZ 85353-9217*

ROUTSON, CLELL DENNIS, manufacturing company executive; b. Elkhart, Ind., Oct. 8, 1946; s. Clell Dean and Olene Maize (Replogle) R.; m. Paula Leone McLallin, Sept. 2, 1967 (div. June 1988); children: Clell Dustin, Courtney Trevor; m. Suazann Kay Brown, 1995. BSBA, Ball State U., Muncie, Ind., 1971. With Proctor & Gamble, Cin., 1971-74; nat. sales mgr. Palmer Instruments, Inc., Cin., 1974-76; with Nordson Corp., Amherst,

Ohio, 1976-81, MCC Powers, Cleve., Chgo., Singapore, 1981-86; sales mgr., v.p., pres. Burgess, Inc., Freeport, Ill., 1986-89; mgr. mktg. and sales, v.p. sales and mktg. Kloppenberg & Co., Englewood, Colo., 1990-92; v.p. ops., gen. mgr. T.E.I. Engineered Products, Englewood, 1992—; mng. dir. Resource Dynamics, Singapore, Chgo., 1985-86; bd. dirs. T.E.I. Engring Products, Englewood. Contbr. articles to profl. jours. Mem. Metropolitan Club (Denver). Republican. Methodist. Office: TEI Engineered Products Inc 6920 S Jordan Rd Englewood CO 80112-4248

ROUX, ANN TAYLOR, gifted/talented education educator; b. Seattle, Nov. 4, 1946; d. Woodrow L. and Marguerite (Myers) Taylor; m. Leo Roux, June 26, 1994; children; Mark, Madeleine. BA in History, U. Wash., 1970; MA in Gifted/Talented Edn., U. Denver, 1992. Tchr. Los Altos (Calif.) Sch. Dist., 1970-73, Jefferson County Sch. Dist., Golden, Colo., 1974, 85—. Pres. Children's Hosp. Aux., Denver, 1977—; bd. dirs. Evergreen (Colo.) Chamber Orch., 1989-93. Mem. LWV (pres. 1975-85), Jr. League Denver. Democrat.

ROUZBAHANI, LOTFOLLAH, cytogeneticist; b. Tehran, Iran, June 20, 1949; came to U.S., 1985; s. Hossein Rouzbahani and Mahjabin Faryadras; m. Mansooreh Shadkamian, Sept. 21, 1975; children: Ashkan, Faraz. DVM, Tehran U., 1979, PhD in Cytology, 1981; postgrad., Pasteur Inst., Lyon, France, 1979, Razi Inst., Tehran, 1982, The Genetics Inst., 1992. Lab. dir. Terhan Cytogenetics Ctr., 1979-85, Biogene, Riverside, Calif., 1991-92; dir. cytogenetics lab. Iranian Ministry Pub. Health, Tehran, 1980-85; tchr. Paramed. Inst. Tehran, 1980-85, Shafa, Farah Nursing Colls., Tehran, 1980-85; asst. prof. Iranian Med. Assn. Ctr., Tehran, 1982-85, Terhan U. Med. Sch., 1982-85; cytogeneticist Genetics Inst., Pasadena, Calif., 1986—; genetics cons. several hosps., Tehran, 1982-85; lab. dir. Genetics Clinic of Dr. Farhud, Tehran, 1982-85; chmn. Sci., Tech. Med, Aids of Tehran, 1983-85; cytogeneticist Genetic Ctr., Orange, Calif., 1988-90, Loma Linda (Calif.) U., 1989-92. Author: Human Genetic Counseling, 1981 (award 1984, 88), Hereditary, Environment and Child Health, 1985 (awards 1988, 91), Genetics and Woman Disease, 1986 (award 1990), Techniques of the Chromosome Laboratory, 1990; contbr. over 50 articles to profl. jours. Sec. Persian Cultural and Social Soc., 1988-91; bd. dirs. Zarathushtrian Assembly, Anaheim, Calif., 1986—, Nat. Iranian Resistance Movement, Claremont, Calif., 1985—; mem. Sci. Teaching Bd. of Inst. of Mothers and Newborns, 1979-85. Named to Honor Bd., Sci. Mag. of Iran, 1983. Mem. So. Calif. Profl. Group, Am. Soc. Human Genetics, Assn. Cytogenetic Technologists, Med. Lab. Workers Soc., Internat. Sterility Soc., Ancient Iran Cultural Soc. Home: 443 Lewis Ct Claremont CA 91711-5132 Office: Alfigen/The Genetics Inst 111 W Del Mar Blvd Pasadena CA 91105

ROVEN, ALFRED NATHAN, surgeon; b. Czechoslovakia, Apr. 6, 1947; came to the U.S., 1949.; BA in Psychology, Calif. State U., Northridge, 1969; MD, U. So. Calif., 1977. Diplomate Am. Bd. Plastic and Reconstructive Surgery, Am. Bd. Otolaryngology. Resident in otolaryngology U. So. Calif., 1977-82; past clin. chief plastic surgery Cedars Sinai Med. Ctr., L.A.; resident in plastic and reconstructive surgery U. N.C., 1982-84; clin. chief burns Cedars Sinai Med. Ctr., L.A.; clin. chief hands Cedars Sinai Med. Ctr.; qualified med. examiner State of Calif. Contbr. articles to profl. jours. Physician L.A. Free Clinic, 1995—. Mem. Am. Registry of Arbitrators, Am. Soc. Head and Neck Surgery, L.A. County Med. Assn. (com. environ. health), Calif. Med. Assn., Am. Pain Soc., Am. Burn Assn., Am. Soc. Plastic and Reconstructive Surgeons, Internat. Confedn. Plastic Surgery, Fed. Issues Emergency Task Force, Nathan A. Womack Surg. Soc. Office: 444 S San Vicente Blvd # 600 Los Angeles CA 90048-4171

ROVIRA, LUIS DARIO, state supreme court justice; b. San Juan, P.R., Sept. 8, 1923; s. Peter S. and Mae (Morris) R.; m. Lois Ann Thau, June 25, 1966; children—Douglas, Merilyn. B.A., U. Colo., 1948, LL.B., 1950. Bar: Colo. 1950. Now chief justice Colo. Supreme Ct., Denver.; mem. Pres.'s Com. on Mental Retardation, 1970-71; chmn. State Health Facilities Council, 1967-76. Bd. dirs YMCA, 1969-78, Children's Hosp.; trustee Temple Buell Found. With AUS, 1943-46. Mem. ABA, Colo. Bar Assn., Denver Bar Assn. (pres. 1970-71), Colo. Assn. Retarded Children (pres. 1968-70), Alpha Tau Omega, Phi Alpha Delta. Clubs: Athletic (Denver), Country (Denver). Home: 4810 E 6th Ave Denver CO 80220-5137

ROWAN, RONALD THOMAS, lawyer; b. Bozeman, Mont., Nov. 6, 1941; s. Lawrence Eugene and Florence M.; m. Katherine Terrell Sponenberg, Sept. 4, 1964; children: Heather, Nicholaus, Matthew. BA, Wichita U., 1964; JD, U. Denver, 1969. Bar: Colo. 1969, U.S. Dist. Ct. Colo. 1969. Asst. city atty. City of Colorado Springs, Colo., 1969-71; asst. dist. atty. 4th Jud. Dist., Colorado Springs, 1971-79; gen. counsel U.S. Olympic Com., Colorado Springs, 1979—, dir. legal affairs, 1986—. Chmn. CSC, Colorado Springs, 1975—; chmn. Criminal Justice Adv. Bd., 1983—; chmn. El Paso Criminal Justice Adv. Com.; bd. dirs. Crimestoppers, 1982-87, past pres. 1985-87, Internat. Anti-counterfeiting Coalition; chmn. Community Corrections Bd., 1981, 86, 87. Mem. ABA, Colo. Bar Assn., El Paso County Trial Lawyers (pres. 1972), El Paso County Bar Assn., U. Denver Law Alumni (chmn.), Colo. Trial Lawyers Assn., Pikes Peak or Bust Rodeo Assn. (Ramrod 1989). Republican. Roman Catholic. Home: 2915 Nevermind Ln Colorado Springs CO 80917-3544 Office: US Olympic Com One Olympic Plz Colorado Springs CO 80909

ROWE, CARL OSBORN, municipal offical; b. Colorado Springs, Colo., Feb. 3, 1944; s. Prentiss Eldon and Jo Ann (Osborn) R.; m. Dale Robin Oren, Apr. 12, 1984; 1 child, Stefanie Osborn. BA in Govt. cum laude, George Mason U., 1972; M Urban Affairs, Va. Poly. Inst. and State U., 1976. Cert. pub. housing mgr. Spl. clk. FBI, Washington, 1968-71; mgmt. analyst ICC, Washington, 1972-75; dir. policy and mgmt. U.S. Bur. Reclamation, Washington, 1975-82; exec. dir. City of Las Vegas Housing Authority, 1990-94; pres. Rowe Bus. Consulting, Las Vegas, Nev., 1982-90, 94—; exec. dir. So. Nev. Housing Corp., 1994-95; assoc. Success Strategies, Las Vegas, 1995; bd. dirs. Flowtronics, Inc., Phoenix, Sportstech, Inc., Scottsdale, Ariz., MSP Sys., Inc., Scottsdale. Columnist Las Vegas Bus. Press, 1989-90, 94—. Exec. dir. So. Nev. Housing Corp., So. Nev. Reinvestment and Affordable Housing Com.; founding bd. dirs., CEO Family Cabinet of So. Nev., Affordable Housing Inst. So. Nev.; bd. dirs. Opportunity Village, LLV Alumni Found.; active So. Nev. Homeless Coalition; mem. exec. bd. Pacific S.W. Regional Conf., Oasis So. Nev. Cmty. Svc. Guild, Las Vegas Cmty. Empowerment Commn. Decorated USAF Commendation medal; named one of Top 50 over 50 in Las Vegas, Prime Mag. Mem. Am. Soc. Pub. Adminstrn. (mem. governing coun.), Nat. Assn. Housing and Redevel. Ofcls. (mem. exec. bd.), Pub. Housing Authorities Dirs. Assn. (mem. exec. bd.), No. Calif./Nev. Exec. Dirs. Assn. (mem. exec. bd.), Leadership Las Vegas, Las Vegas C. of C., LLV Alumni Found. (pres.), Phi Theta Kappa. Office: Success Strategies 4820 Alpine Pl Ste B102 Las Vegas NV 89107

ROWE, DAVID ALAN, magazine publisher; b. La Jolla, Calif., Feb. 8, 1956; s. Harold Derwood and Carmen Alida (Chenier) R.; m. Danette Leslee Nordick, July 31, 1982; 1 child, Evan Christopher. BA, U. Calif. San Diego, La Jolla, 1979. Dir. pub. rels. Cath. Cmty. Svc., San Diego, 1979-80; editor Hare Publs. Inc., Carlsbad, Calif., 1980-82; pub., editor-in-chief Harcourt Brace Jovanovich, Inc., Irvine, Calif., 1982-87; pub., pres. Video Software Mag./VSP Publs., Inc., L.A., 1987-91; pub., exec. v.p. Oreg. Bus. Mag./ Mediamerica, Inc., Portland, 1991—; mktg. rsch. cons. Mem. mktg. com. United Way, Portland, 1992-94; dir. Associated Oreg. Industries, Salem, 1992-93; chmn. Oreg. Enterprise Forum, Portland, 1994; dir. Portland C. of C., 1994. Recipient Maggie award for best entertainment publ., L.A., 1990, 91, 92; named Media Adv. of Yr., U.S. Small Bus. Adminstrn., Oreg., 1993, Pacific N.W. region, 1993, Maggie award for Best Managerial and Profl. Pub., 1995. Mem. Am. Bus. Press, Western Publs. Assn., Portland Met. C. of C. (dir. 1994—). Roman Catholic. Office: Oreg Bus Mag 610 Broadway Ste 200 Portland OR 97205

ROWE, DEE, vintner. Acct. Touche Ross and Co., 1960-72; officer Belcor, Inc., 1972-80; contr. Consol Industries, Inc., Clovis, Calif., 1980—. Office: Consol Industries Inc 2148 E Copper Ave Clovis CA 93611-9128*

ROWE, MARJORIE DOUGLAS, retired social services administrator; b. Bklyn., July 29, 1912; d. Herbert Lynn and Mary Manson (Hall) Douglas; m. Richard Daniel Rowe, July 29, 1937; 1 child, Richard Douglas. AB cum laude, Whitman Coll., 1933; MS in Social Adminstrn., Case Western Res. U., 1936. Caseworker Children's Svcs., Cleve., 1933-36, supr., 1937-39; dir. Adoption Svc. Bur., Cleve., 1940-41; social work supr., psychiat. social work cons. Ea. State Hosp., Medical Lake, Wash., 1962-67; dir. social svcs. Interlake Sch.for Developmentally Disabled, Medical Lake, 1967-74, supt., 1975-82. Pres. chpt. R.P.E.O., Spokane, Wash., 1949, Spokane Alumnae chpt. Delta Delta Delta, 1955-57; chpt. mem. ARC, Orofino, Idaho, 1941-45, Orofino chpt. chmn., 1945-46; sec. Idaho state chpt. AAUW, 1945-46. Mem. Am. Assn. for Mental Deficiency (region I chmn. 1976-77, social work chmn. 1971-73), NASW (gold card mem.), P.E.O. (pres. Spokane Reciprocity 1950), Acad. Cert. Social Workers, Spokane Women of Rotary (pres. 1960-61), Phi Beta Kappa, Delta Sigma Rho, Mortar Bd. Episcopalian. Home: 946 E Thurston Ave Spokane WA 99203-2948

ROWE, MARY SUE, accounting executive; b. Melrose, Kans., Aug. 31, 1940; d. Gene and Carmen (Glidewell) Woffard; m. Edward Rowe, Nov. 27, 1985; children from previous marriage: Denise, Dynell, Dalene, Denette. Student, MTI Bus. Coll., 1968, Calif. State U., Fullerton, 1969, Broome (N.Y.) Community Coll., 1974-76; cert. Sch. Bus. Mgmt., Calif. State U., San Bernardino, 1986. Variou bookkeeping and secretarial, 1968-76; asst. mgr., acct. RM Dean Contracting, Chenango Forks, N.Y., 1976-80; acctg. asst. Hemet (Calif.) Unified Sch. Dist., 1981-86; dir. acctg. Desert Sands Unified Sch. Dist., Indio, Calif., 1986-91; bus. svcs. cons. ednl. div. Vicenti, Lloyd & Stutzman, CPA, La Verne, Calif., 1991—. Bd. dirs. Family Svcs. Assn., Hemet, 1982-83, PTA Officer, 1993-95. Mem. NAFE, Calif. Assn. Bus. Ofcls. (acctg. com., R*D com., vice chmn. 1988-90, chmn. 1990-91, state acctg. adv. com. 1990-92), Riverside Assn. Chief Accts. (co-chmn. 1986-88), Coalition for Adequate Sch. Housing. Republican. Home: 2668 Grand Teton Ave Hemet CA 92544-3200 Office: Vicenti Lloyd & Stutzman 2100A Foothill Blvd La Verne CA 91750-2947

ROWE, RANDY ROLAND, nonprofit organization executive, consultant; b. Redmond, Oreg., Aug. 23, 1955; s. Melvin Charles and Myrna Louise (Carlson) R.; m. Dana Fawn Nimmons, Apr. 26, 1980; children: Jered Randall, Jeremy James. BA, Northwest Coll., 1979; MA, U. No. Colo., 1982; PhD, Internat. Sem., 1992. Ordained to ministry Assemblies of God, 1982. Asst. farm mgr. Carlson Farms, Boardman, Oreg., 1974-75; farm prodn. mgr. Rowe Farms, Mesa, Wash., 1975-79; dir. Teen Challenge of the Rocky Mountains, Denver, 1979-84; adminstr. Teen Challenge of the Rocky Mountains, Sundance, Wyo., 1984-91; exec. dir. Teen Challenge of Wyo., Inc., Sundance, Wyo., 1991—; charter bd. mem. Life Challenge, Inc., Ramona, Calif., 1988-92; treas. Happy Trails Unltd., Inc., Cripple Creek, Colo., 1991-94; tng. com. mem. Teen Challenge Nat., Inc., Springfield, Mo., 1994. Author: The Nature of Life-Controlling Sin Among Christians, 1992. Elected officer Vista West Improvement and Svcs. Dist., Crook County, Wyo., 1984-94. Recipient Most Ednl. Presentations award Crook County Family Violence, Sundance, 1986. Mem. ACA (profl. mem.), Am. Assn. Christian Counselors (charter mem.), Christian Mgmt. Assn. (regional dir. 1990-94), Assn. Christian Schs. Internat., Kiwanis Internat. Office: Teen Challenge of Wyo Inc 303 Vista West Rd PO Box 1160 Sundance WY 82729

ROWE, RUSSELL MARC, executive staff member; b. Syosset, N.Y., Jan. 30, 1967; s. Harold C. and Evelyne M. (Valerie) R. BA in Political Science, U. Nev., 1990. Legis. asst. Congressman James H. Bilbray, Washington, D.C., 1991-93; legis. rep. Mirage Resorts, Inc., Las Vegas, 1993; exec. asst. Congressman James H. Bilbray, Las Vegas, 1994; mem. bd. dirs. UNLV Alumni Assn., 1994—. Mem. Sigma Chi Fraternity Alumni Assn. (mem. exec. bd. 1993, Grand Consul citation 1994). Roman Catholic.

ROWE, SANDRA MIMS, newspaper editor; b. Charlotte, N.C., May 26, 1948; d. David Lathan and Shirley (Stovall) Mims; m. Gerard Paul Rowe, June 5, 1971; children—Mims Elizabeth, Sarah Stovall. BA, East Carolina U., Greenville, N.C., 1970; postgrad., Harvard U., 1991. Reporter to asst. mng. editor The Ledger-Star, Norfolk, Va., 1971-80, mng. editor, 1980-82; mng. editor The Virginian-Pilot and The Ledger Star, Norfolk, Va., 1982-84, exec. editor, 1984-86, v.p., exec. editor, 1986-93; editor The Oregonian, Portland, 1993, 1994—; mem. nominating jury for Pulitzer Prize in Journalism, 1986, 87, mem. Pulitzer Prize Bd., 1994—. Bd. visitors James Madison U., Harrisonburg, Va., 1991—. Named Woman of Yr. Outstanding Profl. Women of Hampton Rds., 1987. Mem. Am. Soc. Newspaper Editors (bd. dirs. 1992—, sec. 1995), Va. Press Assn. (bd. dirs. 1985-93). Episcopalian. Office: The Oregonian 1320 SW Broadway Portland OR 97201-3469

ROWE, VIKKI DENAE, mental health therapist; b. Lynwood, Calif., Mar. 19, 1960; d. Edward James and Karen Gayle (McElhinney) Woodworth; m. Brian Edward House, June 11, 1977 (div. Jan. 1982); 1 child, Jason Edward House; m. Jerry Arthur Rowe, Apr. 9, 1983. BA, Eastern Wash. U., Cheney, 1990, MS in Counseling Psychology, 1992. Cert. counselor. Counseling intern Crisis Residential Ctr., Spokane, 1991-92; therapist Excelsior Youth Ctr., Spokane, 1992-94; counselor Asbell Profl. Group, Spokane, 1994—; mem. Nat. Bd. for the Certification of Counselors, 1992—. Mem. ACA, Action Women's Exch., Psi Chi (treas. 1989-90), Am. Mental Health Counselors Assn. Office: Asbell Profl Group 140 S Arthur St Ste 690 Spokane WA 99202-2220

ROWEN, HARVEY ALLEN, investment company executive; b. Chgo., Sept. 21, 1943. BS in Acctg., UCLA, 1964; JD, U. Calif., Berkeley, 1967; MBA in Mktg. & Fin., NYU, 1981. Bar: Calif., D.C., N.Y. Pvt. practice Beverly Hills, Calif., 1967-68; counsel Securities & Exch. Commn., Washington, 1968-71, Com. Energy & Commerce, U.S. Congress, Washington, 1971-75; sr. cons. SRI Internat. (formerly Stanford Rsch. Inst.), Palo Alto, 1975-77; asst. to pres. Merrill Lynch, Pierce, Fenner & Smith, Inc., N.Y.C., 1977-80, v.p. corp. planning, 1980-81; v.p. corp. planning Merrill Lynch & Co., Inc., N.Y.C., 1981-83, v.p. banking devel., banking divsn., 1983-84; exec. v.p. Merrill Lynch Bank & Trust Co., N.Y.C., 1984-85, pres., 1985-88; chmn. trust com. Merrill Lynch Trust Co., N.Y.C., 1987-90; prin. Harvey Rowen & Assocs., Newport Beach, Calif., 1990-91; pres., CEO The Charles Schwab Trust Co., S.F., 1992—; sr. v.p. Schwab Instl. Svcs. to Corps. Charles Schwab & Co., Inc., 1992—; mem. dean's adv. bd. Haas Sch. Bus., U. Calif., Berkeley; lectr. in field. Author: The Securities Acts Amendments of 1975, 1975, The Securities Acts Amendments of 1975: A Legislative History, 1976, The Emerging Financial Services Industry, 1983; author: (with others) The Deregulation of the Banking and Securities Industries 305, 1979; mem. editorial adv. bd. Banking Expansion Reporter. Mem. ABA (bus. sect., banking com., fed. regulation securities com., chmn. product and svc. devels. subcom. of com. devels. in investment svcs. 1985-87), Am. Bankers Assn., Calif. Bankers Assn., Calif. Bar Assn. Office: The Charles Schwab Trust Co 1 Montgomery St Fl 7 San Francisco CA 94104-5522

ROWEN, MARSHALL, radiologist; b. Chgo.; s. Harry and Dorothy (Kasnow) R.; m. Helen Lee Friedman, Apr. 5, 1952; children: Eric, Scott, Mark. AB in Chemistry with highest honors, U. Ill., Urbana, 1951; MD with honors, U. Ill., Chgo., 1954, MS in Internal Medicine, 1954. Diplomate Am. Bd. Radiology. Intern Long Beach (Calif.) VA Hosp., 1955; resident in radiology Los Angeles VA Hosp., 1955-58; practice medicine specializing in radiology Orange, Calif., 1960—; chmn. bd. dirs. Moran, Rowen and Dorsey, Inc., Radiologists, 1969—; asst. radiologist L.A. Children's Hosp., 1958; assoc. radiologist Valley Presbyn. Hosp., Van Nuys, Calif., 1960; dir. dept. radiology St. Joseph Hosp., Orange, 1961—, v.p. staff, 1972; dir. dept. radiology Children's Hosp. Orange County, 1964—, chief staff, 1977-78, v.p., 1978-83; asst. clin. prof. radiology U. Calif., Irvine, 1967-70, assoc. clin. prof., 1979-72, clin. prof. radiology and pediatrics, 1976-95, pres. clin faculty assn., 1980-81, v.p., trustee Children's Hosp. Orange County, 1990-91, 1992-95; trustee Choc. Padrinos; sec. Choco Health Svcs., 1987-89, v.p., 1990-93, trustee, 1995—; trustee Found. Med. Care Orange County, 1972-76, Calif. Commn. Adminstrn. Svcs. Hosp., 1975-79, Profl. Practice Systems, 1990-92, Med. Specialty Mgrs., 1990-95, St. Joseph Med. Corp., 1993-95; v.p. Found Med. Care Children's Hosp., 1988-89; v.p., bd. dirs. St. Joseph Med. Corp. IPA; bd. dirs Orange Coast Managed Care Svcs., 1995, Paragon Med. Imaging, 1993-95, Calif. Med. Imaging, 1994-95. Mem. editorial bd. Western Jour. Medicine; contbr. articles to med. jours. Founder Orange County Performing Arts Ctr., mem. Laguna Art Mus., Laguna Festival of Arts, Opera Pacific, S. Coast Reportory, Am. Ballet Theater, World Affairs Council. Served to capt. M.C., U.S. Army, 1958-60. Recipient Rea sr. med. prize U. Ill, 1953; William Cook scholar U. Ill., 1951. Fellow Am. Coll. Radiology; mem. AMA, Am. Heart Assn., Soc. Nuclear Medicine (trustee 1961-62), Orange County Radiol. Soc. (pres. 1968-69), Calif. Radiol. Soc. (pres. 1978-79), Radiol. Soc. So. Calif. (pres. 1976), Pacific Coast Pediatric Radiologists Assn. (pres. 1971), Soc. Pediatric Radiology, Calif. Med. Assn. (chmn. sect. on radiology 1978-79), Orange County Med. Assn. (chmn. UCI liason com. 1976-78), Cardioradiology Soc. So. Calif., Radiol. Soc. N.Am., Am. Roentgen Ray Soc., Am. Coll. Physician Execs., Soc. Chmn. Radiologists Children Hosp., Rams Booster Club, Center Club, Sequoia Athletic Club, Phi Beta Kappa, Phi Eta Sigma, Omega Beta Phi, Alpha Omega Alpha. Office: 1201 W La Veta Ave Orange CA 92668-4213

ROWLAND, FRANK SHERWOOD, chemistry educator; b. Delaware, Ohio, June 28, 1927; m. Joan Lundberg, 1952; children: Ingrid Drake, Jeffrey Sherwood. AB, Ohio Wesleyan U., 1948; MS, U. Chgo., 1951, PhD, 1952, DSc (hon.), 1989; DSc (hon.), Duke U., 1989, Whittier Coll., 1989, Princeton U., 1990, Haverford Coll., 1992; LLD (hon.), Ohio Wesleyan U., 1989, Simon Fraser U., 1991. Instr. chemistry Princeton (N.J.) U., 1952-56; asst. prof. chemistry U. Kans., 1956-58, assoc. prof. chemistry, 1958-63, prof. chemistry, 1963-64; prof. chemistry U. Calif., Irvine, 1964—, dept. chmn., 1964-70, Aldrich prof. chemistry, 1985-89, Bren prof. chemistry, 1989-94, Bren rsch. prof., 1994—; Humboldt sr. scientist, Fed. Republic of Germany, 1981; chmn. Dahlem (Fed. Republic of Germany) Conf. on Changing Atmosphere, 1987; vis. scientist Japan Soc. for Promotion Sci., 1980; co-dir. western region Nat. Inst. Global Environ. Changes, 1989-93; del. Internat. Coun. Sci. Unions, 1993—; fgn. sec. NAS, 1994—; lectr., cons. in field. Contbr. numerous articles to profl. jours. Mem. ozone commn. Internat. Assn. Meteorology and Atmospheric Physics, 1980-88, mem. commn. on atmospheric chemistry and global pollution, 1979-91; mem. acid rain peer rev. panel U.S. Office of Sci. and Tech., Exec. Office of White House, 1982-84; mem. vis. com. Max Planck Insts., Heidelberg and Mainz, Fed. Republic Germany, 1982—; ozone trends panel mem. NASA, 1986-88; chmn. Gordon Conf. Environ. Scis.-Air, 1987; mem. Calif. Coun. Sci. Tech., 1989—, Exec. Com. Tyler Prize, 1992—. Recipient numerous awards including John Wiley Jones award Rochester Inst. of Tech., 1975, Disting. Faculty Rsch. award U. Calif., Irvine, 1976, Profl. Achievement award U. Chgo., 1977, Billard award N.Y. Acad. Sci., 1977, Tyler World Prize in Environment Achievement, 1983, Global 500 Roll of Honor for Environ. Achievement UN Environment Program, 1988, Dana award for Pioneering Achievements in Health, 1987, Silver medal Royal Inst. Chemistry, U.K., 1989, Wadsworth award N.Y. State Dept. Health, 1989, medal U. Calif., Irvine, 1989, Japan prize in Environ. Sci., 1989, Dickson prize Carnegie-Mellon U., 1991; Guggenheim fellow, 1962, 74, Albert Einstein prize of World Cultural Coun., 1994. Fellow AAAS (pres. elect 1991, pres. 1992, chmn. bd. dirs. 1993), Am. Phys. Soc. (Leo Szilard award for Physics in Pub. Interest 1979), Am. Geophys. Union (Roger Revelle medal 1994); mem. NAS (bd. environ. studies and toxicology 1986-91, com. on atmospheric chemistry 1987-89, com. atmospheric scis., solar-terrestial com. 1979-83, co-DATA com. 1977-82, sci. com. on problems environment 1986-89, Infinite Voyage film com. 1988-92, Robertson Meml. lectr. 1993, chmn. com. on internat. orgns. and programs 1993—, chmn. officer internat. affairs 1994—), Am. Acad. Arts and Scis., Am. Chem. Soc. (chmn. divsn. nuclear sci. and tech. 1973-74, chmn. divsn. phys. chemistry 1974-75, Tolman medal 1976, Zimmermann award 1980, E.F. Smith lectureship 1980, Environ. Sci. and Tech. award 1983, Esselen award 1987, Peter Debye Phys. Chem. award 1993), German Am. Acad. Coun., Am. Philos. Soc. Home: 4807 Dorchester Rd Corona Del Mar CA 92625-2718 Office: U Calif Irvine Dept of Chemistry 571 PS1 Irvine CA 92717

ROWLAND, RUTH GAILEY, hospital official; b. Salt Lake City, Dec. 7, 1922; d. Frederick George and Lucy Jane (Hill) N.; m. Joseph David Gailey, Apr. 9, 1942 (dec. July 1984); children: Sherylynne Harris-Roth, Joseph David Jr., Robert Nelson; m. Joseph Brigham Rowland, Oct. 14, 1986. Student, Felt-Tarrant Community Coll., Salt Lake City, 1941-42, U. Utah. Dir. vol. svcs., pub. rels. dir. Lakeview Hosp., Bountiful, Utah, 1961-92. Mem. com. Women's State Legis. Coun., Salt Lake City, 1970-92; mem. legis. com. Utah Comprehensive Planning Agy., Salt Lake City; mem. Farmington (Utah) Bd. Health, 1979-85; mem. Davis County Adv. Bd. Volunteerism; mem. social svcs. com. LDS Ch. Recipient Total Citizen award Utah C. of C., 1992. Mem. Assn. Dirs. Vol. Svcs. of Am. Hosp. Assn., Utah Assn. Vol. Auxs. (pres.), Utah Dirs. Vol. Svcs. (pres.), Salt Lake Dental Aux. (pres.), Bountiful C. of C. (bd. dirs. 1975-80), Sorompimists. Republican. Home: 871 S 750 E Bountiful UT 84010-3824 Office: Lakeview Hosp 630 E Med Dr Bountiful UT 84010

ROWLAND, SUSAN BLAKE, English language educator; b. Balt., Feb. 9, 1946; d. Walter True and Susan Elizabeth (Stoll) B.; m. Bertram I. Rowland, Nov. 30, 1974; stepchildren: Shawn, Celia, Kevin. BA, Western Coll., Oxford, Ohio, 1968; postgrad., Columbia U., 1968; MA, San Francisco State U., 1976. Instr. Am. Lang. Inst., San Francisco, 1975-76; tchr. Burlingame (Calif.) Adult Sch., 1976-77; sr. lectr. ESL Coll. of Notre Dame, Belmont, Calif., 1977—; substitute tchr. San Mateo (Calif.) Adult Sch., 1977—. Co-author: Academic Reading and Study Skills for International Students, 1985. Mem. Tchrs. English to Speakers Other Langs., Calif. Assn. Tchrs. English to Speakers Other Langs. Home: 1420 Southdown Rd Hillsborough CA 94010-7252 Office: Coll of Notre Dame 1500 Ralston Ave Belmont CA 94002-1908

ROWLEY, WILLIAM ROBERT, surgeon; b. Omaha, June 7, 1943; s. Robert Kuhlmeyer and Dorothy Eleanor (Larson) R.; m. Eileen Ruth Murray, Aug. 11, 1968; children: Bill II, Jeff, Jill. BA in Psychology, U. Minn., 1966, MD, 1970. Diplomate Am. Bd. Surgery. Commd. lt. USN, 1972, advanced through grades to rear admiral, 1994; intern U. Calif., San Diego, 1970-71, gen. surgery resident, 1971-72; gen. surgery resident Naval Regional Med. Ctr., Phila., 1973-76; peripheral vascular surgery fellow Naval Regional Med. Ctr., San Diego, 1977-78; staff surgeon Naval Regional Med. Ctr., Phila., 1977; staff vascular surgeon Naval Regional Med. Ctr., San Diego, 1978-85, chmn. dept. surgery, 1985-88, dir. surg. svcs., 1987-88; asst. chief of staff for plans and ops. Naval Med. Command S.W. Region, San Diego, 1988-89; dep. comdr. Nat. Naval Med. Ctr., Bethesda, Md., 1989-91; comdg. officer Naval Hospital, Camp Pendleton, Calif., 1991-93; dep. asst. chief for health care ops. Navy Bur. of Medicine and Surgery, Washington, 1993-94, asst. chief for plans, analysis and evaluation, 1994-95; cmdr. Naval Med. Ctr., Portsmouth, Va., 1995—; program dir. vascular surgery fellowship Naval Hosp., San Diego, 1980-85, gen. surgery residency, 1985-89; assoc. prof. surgery Uniformed Svcs. U. for Health Scis., Bethesda, 1985—. Fellow ACS; mem. AMA, Am. Coll. Physician Execs., Internat. Soc. Cardiovascular Surgery.

ROY, ASIM, business educator; b. Calcutta, India, May 5, 1948; came to U.S., 1975; s. Samarendra Nath and Chhaya (Mukherjee) R.; m. Suchandra Mukherjee, Feb. 10, 1974; 1 child, Sion Roy. B.E., Calcutta U., 1971; M.S. (scholar), Case Western Res. U., 1977; Ph.D., U. Tex., 1979. Foreman, Guest, Keen, Williams, Calcutta, 1972-74; mgr. optimization group Execucom Systems Corp., Austin, 1980-82; asst. prof. U. Nebr., Omaha, 1983, Ariz. State U., Tempe, 1983-89, assoc. prof., 1989—; vis. prof. Stanford (Calif.) U., 1991; cons. Mid-Am. Steel Corp., 1976-77, Fabri-Centre, Inc., Cleve., 1976; pres., chief exec. officer Decision Support Software, Inc. Author software: IFPS/Optimum and Maxima. Contbr. articles to profl. jours. Calcutta U. Merit scholar, 1967; U. Tex. rsch. scholar, 1978-80; grantee NSF. Mem. Inst. Mgmt. Sci. (program chmn. 1990), Ops. Rsch. Soc. Am. (gen. chmn. 1993), Internat. Neural Network Soc. Hindu. Home: 5771 W Gail Dr Chandler AZ 85226-1232 Office: Ariz State U Sch of Business Tempe AZ 85287

ROY, CATHERINE ELIZABETH, physical therapist; b. Tucson, Jan. 16, 1948; d. Francis Albert and Dorothy Orme (Thomas) R.; m. Richard M. Johnson, Aug. 31, 1968 (div. 1978); children: Kimberly Anne, Troy Michael. BA in Social Sci. magna cum laude, San Diego State U., 1980; MS in Phys. Therapy, U. So. Calif., 1984. Staff therapist Sharp Meml. Hosp., San Diego, 1984-89, chairperson patient and family edn. com., 1986-87, chairperson sex edn. and counselling com., 1987-89, chairperson adv. bd. for phys. therapy, asst. for edn. program, 1987-89; mgr. rehab. phys. therapy San Diego Rehab. Inst., Alvarado Hosp., 1989-91; dir. therapeutic svcs. VA Med. Ctr., San Diego, 1991—; lectr. patient edn., family edn., peer edn.; mem. curriculum rev. com. U. So. Calif. Phys. Therapy Dept., 1982; bd. dirs. Ctr. for Edn. in Health; writer, reviewer licensure examination items for phys. therapy Profl. Examination Services.. Tennis coach at clinics Rancho Penasquitos Swim and Tennis Club, San Diego, 1980-81; active Polit. Activities Network, 1985; counselor EEO, 1992-95. Mem. Am. Phys. Therapy Assn. (rsch. presenter nat. conf. 1985, del. nat. conf. 1986-94, rep. state conf. 1987-89, 92-94, Mary McMillan student award 1984, mem. exec. bd. San Diego dist. 1985-88, 92-94), AAUW, NAFE, Am. Congress Rehab. Medicine, Phi Beta Kappa, Phi Kappa Phi, Chi Omega. Home: 5067 Park West Ave San Diego CA 92117-1048 Office: San Diego VA Med Ctr Spinal Cord Injury Svc 3350 La Jolla Village Dr San Diego CA 92161-0002

ROY, RAYMOND, bishop; b. Man., Can., May 3, 1919; s. Charles-Borromé e and Zephirina (Milette) R. B.A. in Philosophy and Theology, U. Man., 1942; student, Philos. Sem., Montreal, 1942-43, Major Sem., Montreal, 1943-46, Major Sem. St. Boniface, 1946-47. Ordained priest Roman Catholic Ch. 1947. Asst. pastor, then pastor chs. in Man., 1947-50, 53-66; chaplain St. Boniface (Man.) Hosp., 1950-53; superior Minor Sem., St. Boniface, 1966-69; pastor Cathedral Parish, St. Boniface, 1969-72; ordained bishop, 1972; bishop of St. Paul, Alta., Can., 1972—. Club: K.C. Address: 4410 51st Ave Box 339, Saint Paul, AB Canada T0A 3A0*

ROY, RAYMOND ALBERT, JR., pharmacist; b. Matewan, W.Va., Mar. 3, 1954; s. Raymond Albert and Mary (Howerton) R. B.S. in Pharmacy, W.Va. U., 1977. Registered pharmacist, Va., W.Va., N.C., S.C., Nev. Pharmacist Strosnider Drug Co., Williamson, W.Va., 1977-78; pharmacy mgr. Rite Aid Pharmacy, Morgantown, W.Va., 1978-80; pharmacist in charge, pharmacy mgr. K Mart Pharmacy, Lynchburg, Va., 1980-88, Las Vegas, 1988—; elder care and child care pharmacist Park-Davis Pharms., Morris Plains, N.J., 1985—. Recipient Pharmacy Edn. Program award Burroughs Wellcome Co., 1982. Mem. Am. Pharm. Assn., Nev. Pharmacist Assn. Roman Catholic. Home: 2713 Saint Clair Dr Las Vegas NV 89128-7296 Office: K Mart Pharmacy 3680 3760 E Sunset Rd Las Vegas NV 89120-3233

ROY, WILLIAM GLENN, sociology educator; b. Rochester, N.Y., Mar. 22, 1946; s. James Rider and Nona Alice (Monks) R.; m. Alice Madeleine Royer, Apr. 3, 1976; children: Margaret Alice, Joseph Edward. BA, Emory U., 1968; PhD, U. Mich., 1977. Prof. UCLA, 1976—. Woodrow Wilson fellow, 1968; rsch. grantee NSF, 1987. Mem. Phi Beta Kappa. Office: UCLA Dept Sociology Los Angeles CA 90024

ROYBAL-ALLARD, LUCILLE, congresswoman; b. Boyle Heights, Calif., June 12, 1941; d. Edward Roybal; m. Edward T. Allard; 4 children. BA, Calif. State U., L.A. Former mem. Calif. State Assembly; mem. 103rd Congress from 33rd Calif. dist., 1993—; mem. Banking and Fin. Svcs., Budget Com. Office: Ho of Reps 324 Cannon Washington DC 20515*

ROY-BYRNE, PETER PAUL, psychiatrist, educator; b. N.Y.C., May 1, 1951; s. Gerard Joseph and Viola (Lo Prest) Byrne; m. Janice Maria Roy, May 5, 1978; children: Jordan, Reed. BA in Psychology, Vassar Coll., 1974; MD, Tufts U., 1978. Diplomate Am. Bd. Psychiatry and Neurology. Resident in psychiatry UCLA Neuropsychiat. Inst., L.A., 1979-82; fellow in biologic psychiatry NIMH, Bethesda, Md., 1982-85, spl. asst. to dir., 1985-86; assoc. prof. psychiatry U. Wash. Med. Sch., Seattle, 1986-90, prof. psychiatry, 1992—, vice-chmn. dept. psychiatry, 1992—; chief of psychiatry Harborview Med. Ctr., Seattle, 1992—; mem. subcoms. on panic and generalized anxiety Diagnostic and Statistical Manual, 4th edit., 1989-93; tech. advisor clin. practice guidelines on panic/anxiety Assn. for Health Care Policy and Rsch. Editor: Anxiety: New Findings for the Clinician, 1988, Benzodiezepines in Clinical Practice: Risks and Benefits, 1991; contbr. numerou sci. articles to profl. jours.; jour. referee 13 sci. jours., 1986—; mem. editl. bd. Video Jour. of Psychiatry, 1993—. Rsch. grantee (3) NIMH, 1987-93. Mem. Am. Psychiat. Assn., Soc. for Biologic Psychiatry, Am. Coll. Neuropsychophemenology. Roman Catholic. Office: Harborview Med Ctr 325 9th Ave Seattle WA 98104-2420

ROYCE, EDWARD R. (ED ROYCE), congressman; b. Los Angeles, Oct. 12, 1951; m. Marie Porter. BA, Calif. State U., Fullerton. Tax mgr. Southwestern Portland Cement Co.; mem. Calif. Senate, 1983-93, 103rd Congress from 39th dist. Calif., 1993—; vice chmn. Public Employment and Retirement Com.; mem. Bus. and Profs. com., Indsl. Rels. com.; legis. author, campaign co-chmn. Proposition 15 Crime Victims/Speedy Trial Initiative; author nation's 1st felony stalking law, bill creating Foster Family Home Ins. Fund, legis. creating foster parent recruitment and tng. program; mem. Banking and Fin. Svcs. Com., Internat. Rels. Com. Named Legis. of Yr. Orange County Rep. Com., 1986, Child Adv. of Yr. Calif. Assn. Svc. for Children, 1987. Mem. Anaheim C. of C. Republican. Office: US Ho of Reps 1113 Longworth Ho Office Bldg Washington DC 20515-0539*

ROYER, THEODORE HENRY, real estate sales, property management; b. Norwood, Colo., May 30, 1936; s. Dwight J. and Sarah Jane (Garner) R.; m. Mary Rene Hull, May 30, 1954; children: Eric, David, Bruce, Curtis. MA in Bus. and Acctg., Western State Coll., 1975. Mem. San Miguel County Rep. Party (chmn. 1982-84, treas. 1984—). Mormon. Served with U.S. Army, 1955-57. Home: 1425 Harris Ln 102 # 3 Blanding UT 84511

ROYER, VICTOR HENRY, marketing consultant, author; b. Prague, Czech Republic, June 6, 1955; s. Georgina Sidonia Lukas Royer. BA in Philosophy, U. Melbourne, Australia, 1978; MA in Philosophy, U. Wollongong, Australia, 1982. Advt. asst. Melbourne, Australia, 1972-73; sales exec., 1974; writer/prodr./personality ABC Radio, 1975-76; writer/prodr./presenter radio show, 1978; advt. cons., writer/designer Fairfax Press, Australia, 1981-83, Olympic Games fgn. corres., 1984; staff writer Sta. KCOP-13 TV, L.A., 1984; art dir. L.A. Songwriters Showcase, 1984; mgr. creative svcs., writer promotional material Beverly Hills, Calif., 1985-86; prodn. coord. and buyer Ridesharing Orgn., L.A., 1986-89; pres., ptnr. Premier Gaming, Las Vegas, Nev., 1994—; pres. MRM Entertainment, Inc., Hollywood, Calif., 1989-90; creative and mktg. cons. Weddle/Caldwell Advt. Agy., Las Vegas, Nev., 1990; comml. mktg. cons. and writer/prodr./dir. TV commls., comml. video, Las Vegas, 19990—; gaming corr., nat. gaming mags., 1985—; gaming cons. and spkr., Las Vegas, 1993—; judge prime time Emmy awards Acad. TV Arts and Scis., Hollywood, 1987-94. Author: Play Smart and Win, 1994; contbr. numerous articles to profl. jours. Home: 257 El Camino Verde Henderson NV 89014 Office: MRM Entertainment Inc 9016 Wilshire Blvd Ste 146 Beverly Hills CA 90211-1891

ROYLANCE, LYNN MICHELLE, electrical engineer; b. San Francisco, Nov. 27, 1951; d. Jack Clifton and Alice Helen (Gordh) R.; m. Julian Payne Freret Jr., June 21, 1979; children: Morgan Elizabeth Freret, Taylor Susanne Freret. BSEE, BS in Physics, MIT, 1972; MSEE, Stanford U., 1973, PhD in Elec. Engring., 1978. Instr. Stanford U., Stanford, Calif., 1974; mem. tech. staff Hewlett-Packard Labs., Palo Alto, Calif., 1977-81; project mgr. Hewlett-Packard Labs., Calif., 1981-87, project mgr. Cir. Tech. Group R & D, 1987-89; sect. mgr. Cir. Tech. Group R & D, 1989—; Mem. program com. Internat. Symposium on Very Large Scale Integration Tech., 1982-85. Contbr. articles to profl. jours. NSF fellow, 1972-75. Mem. IEEE, Am. Mgmt. Assn., Phi Beta Kappa, Sigma Xi, Tau Beta Pi (program com., No. Calif. Electronic Material Symposium 1981, chmn. 1983-84, treas. No. Calif. section 1985-87). Home: 1160 Laureles Dr Los Altos CA 94022-1012 Office: Hewlett-Packard 5301 Stevens Creek Blvd Santa Clara CA 95051-7201

RUBALD, TERRY ELLEN, state official; b. Riverton, Wyo., Nov. 12, 1953; d. Dale Brice Trubey and Elizabeth Frances (Sheldon) Knapp; m. Timothy Mark Rubald, July 1, 1978; 1 child, Lawrence Sheldon. BSBA with honor, U. Wyo., 1976. Cert. permanent property tax appraiser, Wyo. Adminstr. lease records Am. Nuclear Corp., Casper, Wyo., 1977-79; land agt. Gulf Mineral Resources, Denver, 1979-80; owner, operator Mateo Village, Sundance, Wyo., 1980-89; county assessor Crook County, Sundance, 1987-91; mem. Wyo. Bd. Equalization, Cheyenne, 1991—, chmn., 1995—. Past pres. Crook County Rep. Women; current 1st v.p. Laramie County Rep. Women; chmn. Crook County Rep. Ctrl. Com.; bd. dirs., treas., past pres. Devils Tower Tourism Assn.; treas. troop 116 Boy Scouts Am., Cheyenne, 1994-95; pub. rels. com. Cheyenne Frontier Days, 1994-95. Recipient Honor Book for excellence in field mgmt. bus. adminstrn. dept. U. Wyo.; scholar Wyo. H.H., Bugas law scholar. Mem. Internat. Assn. Assessing Officers, Wyo. County Assessors Assn. (pres.), U. Wyo. Alumnae Assn. (bd. dirs. 1985-89). Methodist. Office: Wyo Bd Equalization PO Box 448 122 W 25th St Cheyenne WY 82001-3096

RUBAYI, SALAH, surgeon, educator; b. Baghdad, Iraq, Oct. 1, 1942; came to U.S., 1981; s. Abdulla Mossa Rubayi and Fatma (Ibriham) Al-Jarah; m. Cecile-Rose, June 23, 1985. MD, U. Baghdad, Iraq, 1966; LRCP and LRCS, Royal Coll. Surgeons and Physicians, Scotland, 1974. Lic. physician and surgeon, Calif. Surgeon burn and reconstructive surgery Birmingham Accident Hosp., Eng., 1978-81; fellow burn unit Los Angeles County/U. So. Calif. Med. Ctr., 1981-82; fellow plastic surgery Rancho Los Amigos Med. Ctr., Downey, Calif., 1982-85, mem. attending staff in plastic and reconstructive surgery, chief pressure ulcer mgmt. service, 1985—; chmn. Laser Safety Com. Rancho Los Amigos Med. Ctr., 1985—; asst. prof. surgery U. So. Calif. Contbr. articles to profl. jours. Fellow ACS, Internat. Coll. Surgeons, Am. Soc. Laser Medicine and Surgery; mem. Internat. Soc. Burn Injury, Am. Burn Assn., Internat. Soc. Paraplegia. Office: Rancho Los Amigos Med Ctr HB121 7601 Imperial Hwy # Hb121 Downey CA 90242-3456

RUBENSTEIN, LEONARD SAMUEL, communications executive, ceramist, painter, sculptor, photographer; b. Rochester, N.Y., Sept. 22, 1918; s. Jacob S. and Zelda H. (Gordon) R.; widowed May 28, 1983; children—Carolinda, Eric, Harley. B.F.A. cum laude, Alfred U., 1939; student Western Reserve, 1938; postgrad. U. Rochester, 1940-41. Creative dir. Henry Hempstead Advt. Agy., Chgo., 1949-55; v.p., exec. art dir. Clinton E. Frank Advt. Agy., Chgo., 1955-63; v.p., nat. creative dir. Foster & Kleiser div. Metromedia, Inc., Los Angeles, 1967-73, v.p. corp. creative cons., Metromedia, Inc., Los Angeles, 1973-88; guest lectr. U. Chgo.; instr. Columbia Coll., Chgo.; past. pres. Art Dirs. Club Chgo. (spl. citation); instr. Fashion Inst., Los Angeles; lectr. in field. Mem. Soc. Typog. Arts (past dir.), Am. Ceramic Soc. (design chpt.), Am. Craft Coun., Inst. Outdoor Advt. (past plans bd.), Los Angeles County Mus. Art, Mus. Contemporary Art of L.A. (charter), Palos Verdes (Calif.) Art Ctr., Phi Epsilon Pi. Lodge: B'nai B'rith. Author: (with Charles Hardison) Outdoor Advertising; contbr. articles in field to profl. publs. One-man show: Calif. Mus. Sci. and Industry, 1970; two-person exhibition of porcelains, Palos Verdes Art Ctr., 1987; numerous juried nat. and regional group shows; creator concept for Smithsonian exhibition Images of China: East and West, 1982; writer-producer (ednl. video) Paul Soldner, Thoughts on Creativity, 1989, (video documentary) High-Tech/Low-Tech: The Science and Art of Ceramics, 1994; porcelains in permanent collections of 3 mus., 1992. Home and Office: 30616 Ganado Dr Palos Verdes Peninsula CA 90275-6223

RUBENSTEIN, MARTIN DONALD, hematologist; b. L.A., Aug. 16, 1950; s. Solomon I. and Sylvia (Fein) R.; m. Peggy Jane Bosset, Oct. 7, 1979; children: Aaron Michael, Nathan Edward. BS with distinction, Stanford U., 1972, MD, 1976. Diplomate Am. Bd. Internal Medicine, Am. Bd. Hematology. Intern, resident Stanford (Calif.) U. Hosp., 1976-79, fellow in hematology, 1979-81; pvt. practice hematology & oncology Southbay Oncology-Hematology Ptnrs., Campbell, Calif., 1981—; pres. med. staff O'Connor Hosp., San Jose, Calif., 1993-94, med. dir. Cancer Care Ctr., 1991—; chmn. med. adv. com. No. Calif. region ARC, San Jose, 1990—; clin. assoc. prof. medicine Stanford U. Sch. Medicine. Fellow ACP; mem. Am. Soc. Hematology, Calif. Med. Assn., Santa Clara County Med. Soc. Office: 50 E Hamilton Ave Ste 200 Campbell CA 95008-0251

RUBENSTEIN, MICHAEL ALAN, architect; b. St. Louis, July 18, 1944; s. Melvin Paul and Miriam (Schwartz) R. BArch, Wash. U., 1966, MArch, 1968. Registered architect, Calif. Designer Skidmore, Owings, Merrill, N.Y.C., 1967-68, Helmuth, Obata, Kassabaum, St. Louis, 1968-69, Peckham/Guyton Assocs., St. Louis, 1969-70, B.A. Berkus, L.A., 1970-71, Gruen Assocs., L.A., 1971-72; design cons. Gruen Assocs., N.Y.C., 1971, Studio Works, N.Y.C., 1972; design cons., mem. staff Experiments in Art and Tech., L.A., 1972-73; pvt. practice architecture Healdsburg, 1975-86; ptnr. Anderson & Rubenstein, Santa Rosa, 1986-87; prin. Rubenstein Architects, AIA, Santa Rosa, 1987—. Exhibited Eugenia Butler Gallery, Los Angeles, 1970, Calif. 101, Monterey Design Conf., 1980, Cultural Arts Council Sonoma County, 1986. Mem. Design Rev. Com., Healdsburg, Calif., 1978-80, chmn. 1980-83; mem. Steering Com., Healdsburg, 1981-83; coordinator Regional Urban Design Assistance Team, Healdsburg, 1982; chmn. Cultural Resource Survey Rev. Com., Healdsburg, 1982-83. Recipient Gold Nugget award Pacific Coast Builders Conf., 1989, Western Red Cedar Lumber Assn. Merit award, Quivira Vineyards Winery, 1990. Mem. AIA (bd. dirs. Redwood Empire chpt., v.p., pres. elect Redwood Empire chpt. 1986, pres. 1987, past pres., bd. dirs. 1988, Honor award 1984, Design awards, Plaza St. Cafe Merit award 1984, 86), Metal Constrn. Assn. (Honor award 1988), Quivira Winery.

RUBENSTEIN, STEVEN PAUL, newspaper columnist; b. L.A., Oct. 31, 1951; s. Victor Gerald and Florence (Fox) R.; m. Caroline Moira Grannan, Jan. 1, 1989; children: William Laurence, Anna Katherine. BA, U. Calif., Berkeley, 1977. Reporter L.A. Herald Examiner, 1974-76; reporter San Francisco Chronicle, 1976-81, columnist, 1981—. Office: San Francisco Chronicle 901 Mission St San Francisco CA 94103-2905

RUBIN, CHARLES ALEXIS, writer; b. L.A., Dec. 4, 1953; s. Herbert Bernard and Jacqueline (Bashor) R.; m. Doris Sara Villalobos, July, 23, 1978; 1 child, Daniel Charles. BA in English magna cum laude, San Francisco State U., 1978, MA in English, 1980. Communications supr. Am. Protective Services, Oakland, Calif., 1982-83; assoc. editor Personal Computing mag., San Jose, 1983-84; free-lance writer Oakland, 1984—; sr. assoc. Waterside Assocs., Fremont, Calif., 1986-87; editorial cons. Televisual Market Strategies, Saratoga, 1985-86. Author: The Endless Apple, 1984, Thinking Small: The Buyer's Guide to Portable Computers, 1984, Appleworks: Boosting Your Business with Integrated Software, 1985, Command Performance: Appleworks, 1986, Microsoft Works, 1986, Macintosh Hard Disk Management, 1988, Running Microsoft Works, 1990, The Macintosh Bible (What Do I Do Now?), 1990, The Macintosh Bible Guide to System 7, 1991, The Macintosh Bible Guide to File Maker Pro, 1991, The Macintosh Bible Guide to Clarisworks, 1993, The Little Book of Computer Wisdom, 1994, Guerrilla Marketing Online, 1995. Democrat. Jewish. Home: 125 San Patricio Dr Sedona AZ 86336-4701

RUBIN, JONATHAN, government relations consultant; b. Topeka, Kans., Feb. 19, 1949; s. Sidney and Claire (Bodian) R.; m. Diane Kefauver, Dec. 27, 1981; children: Benjamin Estes, David Bodian. BA, Syracuse U., 1971. Mem. nat. field staff McGovern for Pres., 1972; pvt. cons. Calif., 1972-76; field staff dir. Carter for Pres., Calif., 1976, 80; polit. dir. Calif. Dem. Party, 1978-81; pres. Rubin/Kefauver Assocs., San Francisco, 1981-87; chief of staff State Senator Quentin Kopp, Sacramento, 1988-91; ptnr. Bay Rels., San Francisco, 1991—; bd. dirs. CalTrain/Joint Powers Bd., 1992—, commr. Met. Transp. Commn., 1995—. Creator, commentator TV for San Francisco Giants It Came From Left Field mag. show, 1988, 89; film and theater reviewer San Francisco Bus. Times, 1977-78. Bd. dirs. Bread and Roses, Mill Valley, Calif., 1989-93. Mem. Masons (3 deg.).

RUBIN, KENNETH HOWARD, geochemistry educator, artist; b. Sherman Oaks, Calif., July 11, 1962; s. Sheldon and Ann Rene (Lustgarten) R. BA in Chemistry, U. Calif., San Diego, 1984, MS in Oceanography, 1985, PhD in Earth Sci., 1991. Rsch. asst. Scripps Inst. Oceanography U. Calif.-San Diego, La Jolla, 1984-91, postdoctoral rschr. Scripps Inst. Oceanography, 1991-92; asst. rschr. Sch. Ocean and Earth Sci. and Tech. U. Hawaii, Honolulu, 1992-94, asst. prof. Sch. Ocean and Earth Sci. and Tech., 1994—; vis. scientist Lawrence Livermore (Calif.) Nat. Lab., 1988-90; rschr. Hawaii Ctr. for Volcanology, Honolulu, 1992—; mem. NSF-RIDGE program, 1991—. Two person show Mandeville Gallery, U. Calif., San Diego, 1984, group show, 1984. Mem. numerous environ. orgns., 1984—. Rsch. grantee NSF, 1993, 94, State of Hawaii, 1993, 94. mem. Am. Geophys. Union, Geol. Soc. Am., Am. Chem. Soc. Office: U Hawaii Sch Ocean/Earth Sci/Tech 2525 Correa Rd Honolulu HI 96822-2219

RUBIN, LAWRENCE IRA, podiatrist; b. Buffalo, Dec. 19, 1945; s. Harold Philip and Rose (Kaiser) R.; m. Janis Bernstein, Sept. 12, 1970 (div. Apr. 1986); children: Alison Meredith, Stacy Heather; m. Linda Sleeth, Apr. 30, 1989. Student, Am. U., 1963-65; D of Podiatric Medicine, N.Y. Coll. of Podiatric Medicine, 1969. Diplomate Am. Bd. Podiatric Surgery. Resident in podiatry Kensington Hosp., Phila., 1970; pvt. practice medicine specializing in podiatry Clarence, N.Y., 1970-76; chief podiatric surgery and medicine Meml. Hosp. of Gardena, Calif., 1977-88; cons. South Bay Free Clinic, Gardena, 1979—. Bd. trustee Calif. Coll. Podiatric Medicine. Fellow Am. Coll. Foot Surgeons, Am. Coll. Podiatric Med. Rev.; mem. Calif. Podiatric Med. Assn. (peer rev. com., chmn. patient and ins. rels. com. 1993-94), L.A. County Podiatric Med. Soc. (pres. 1983-84, parliamentarian 1985-95, mem. at large 1995—, chmn. seminar com. 1980-82, 87-90, Pres.'s award 1984), Am. Acad. Podiatric Sports Medicine (assoc.), Masons (master mason 1974—). Democrat. Jewish. Office: Gardena Podiatrist's Group 1141 W Redondo Beach Blvd Gardena CA 90247-3586

RUBIN, LILLIAN BRESLOW, sociologist; b. Phila., Jan. 13, 1924; d. Sol and Rae (Vinin) Breslow; m. Seymour Katz, Mar. 6, 1943 (div. Oct. 1961); m. Henry M. Rubin, Mar. 4, 1962; 1 child, Marci R. BA, U. Calif., Berkeley, 1967, MA, 1968, PhD, 1971; LHD, SUNY, Albany, 1992. Rsch. sociologist Inst. for Study of Social Change U. Calif., Berkeley, 1971—; alumni prof. interpretive sociology Queens Coll., CUNY, 1988-94. Author: (book) Worlds of Pain, 1976, Intimate Strangers, 1983, Just Friends, 1985, Families on the Fault Line, 1994. Recipient Woodrow Wilson Honorable Mention, 1968. Mem. Am. Sociol. Assn., Calif. Assn. Family Therapists, Nat. Coun. on Family Rels., Am. Orthopsychiat. Assn., Phi Beta Kappa. Democrat. Jewish. Office: U Calif Inst for Study of Social Change 2420 Bowditch Berkeley CA 94720

RUBIN, SANDRA MENDELSOHN, artist; b. Santa Monica, Calif., Nov. 7, 1947; d. Murry and Freda (Atliss) Mendelsohn; m. Stephen Edward Rubin, Aug. 6, 1966. BA, UCLA, 1976, MFA, 1979. Instr. Art Ctr. Coll. Design, Pasadena, Calif., 1980, UCLA, 1981. One-woman exhbns. include L.A. County Mus. Art, 1985, Fischer Fine Arts, London, 1985, Claude Bernard Gallery, N.Y.C., 1987, L.A. Louver Gallery, L.A., 1992; group exhbns. include L.A. County Mus. Artm 1977, 82, 83, L.A. Mcpl. Art Gallery, 1977, 83, 93, L.A. Contemporary Exhbns., 1978, L.A. Inst. Contemporary Arts, 1978, Newport Harbor Art Mus., Newport Beach, Calif., 1981, Odyssia Gallery, N.Y.C., 1981, Nagoya (Japan) City Mus., 1982, Long Beach (Calif.) Mus. Art, 1982, Brooke Alexander Gallery, N.Y.C., 1982, Laguna Beach (Calif.) Mus. Art, 1982, Jan Baum Gallery, L.A., 1984, San Francisco Mus. Art, 1986, Claude Bernard Gallery, 1986, Struve Gallery, Chgo., 1987, Boise (Idaho) Mus., 1988, Judy Youen's Gallery, London, 1988, Tatistscheff Gallery, Inc., Santa Monica, Calif., 1989, Tortue Gallery, Santa Monica, 1990, Contemporary Arts Forum, Santa Barbara, Calif., 1990, San Diego Mus. Art, 1991, Fresno (Calif.) Met. Mus., 1992, Jack Rutberg Fine Arts, L.A., 1993. Recipient Young Talent Purchase award L.A. County Mus. Art, 1980; Artist's Fellowship grant NEA, 1981, 91.

RUBIN, SHELDON, aerospace engineer; b. Chgo., July 19, 1932; s. George and Elsie (Braid) R.; m. Ann Renee Lustgarten, July 3, 1955; children—Geoffrey, Kenneth, Beth. B.S., Calif. Inst. Tech., 1953, M.S., 1954, Ph.D., 1956. Registered profl. engr., Calif. Research engr. Lockheed Aircraft, Burbank, Calif., 1956-58; sect. head Hughes Aircraft, Culver City, Calif., 1958-62; disting. engr. The Aerospace Corp., El Segundo, Calif., 1962—; cons. in field; former vis. prof. UCLA. Contbr. articles to profl. jours.; patentee in field. Recipient Trustees Disting. Achievement award, Aerospace Corp., 1981, Outstanding Accomplishment award, 1979, 86; Shuttle Flight Cert., NASA, 1981. Fellow AIAA (assoc.), Soc. Automotive Engrs. (com. chmn.). Jewish.

RUBIO, IVAN PATRICIO, engineering executive; b. San Felipe, Chile, Apr. 9, 1948; came to U.S., 1977; s. Jilberto Hector Rubio and Emilia Abarca; m. Yolanda Ines Leiva, Oct. 6, 1976; children: Patricia Pineda, Cynthia Rubio. BBA, U. Chile, 1971. Inspection supr. Consolidated Casting Corp., Dallas, 1978-80, quality control mgr., 1980-83; quality control mgr. Unicast, Manchester, N.H., 1983-84, Precision Castparts Corp., Portland, Oreg., 1984-89; project engring. mgr. Precision Cast Parts Corp., Portland, Oreg., 1989-91, process support engring. mgr., 1991-93, engring. program mgr., 1993—; pres. Andes Internat., Inc., Portland, 1992—. Office: Precision Castparts Corp 4600 SE Harney Dr Portland OR 97206-0825

RUBLE, ANN, minister; b. Seattle, Oct. 26, 1953; d. Monte Rahe and Stella (Terefinko) R.; m. Francis Michael Trotter, Aug. 29, 1984. Cert. sec., Met. Bus. Coll., Seattle, 1972. Ordained to ministry Ch. of Scientology, 1980. Minister Ch. of Scientology, Seattle, 1980—, dir. pub. affairs, 1983; pres. Ch. of Scientology of Wash. State, Seattle, 1984-88, dir., 1989—. Bur. chief Jour. Freedom News, 1984-88. Mem. Citizen's Commn. Human Rights, Seattle, 1984—, Com. on Religious Liberties, Seattle, 1985—; bd. dirs. Denny Regrade Crime Prevention Coun., 1994—. Office: Ch Scientology Washington State 2226 3rd Ave Seattle WA 98121-2019

RUBY, CHARLES LEROY, law educator, lawyer, civic leader; b. Carthage, Ind., Dec. 28, 1900; s. Edgar Valentine and Mary Emma (Butler) R.; certificate Ball State U., 1921-22; AB, Cen. Normal Coll., 1924, LLB, 1926, BS, 1931, BPE, 1932; MA, Stanford, 1929; JD, Pacific Coll. of Law, 1931; PhD, Olympic U., 1933; m. Rachael Elizabeth Martindale, Aug. 30, 1925; children: Phyllis Arline (Mrs. Norman Braskat), Charles L., Martin Dale. Prin., Pine Village (Ind.) High Sch., 1923-25; Glenwood (Ind.) Pub. Schs., 1925-26; tchr. El Centro (Calif.) Pub. Sch., 1926-27, Fresno Cen. (Calif.) Union High Sch., 1927-29; prof. law Fullerton Coll., 1929-66; prof. edn. Armstrong Coll., summer 1935, Cen. Normal Coll., summers 1929-33; admitted to Ind. bar, 1926, U.S. Supreme Ct. bar, 1970; pres. Ret. Service Vol. Program, North Orange County, Calif., 1973-76, 83-84; dir. North Orange County Vol. Bur., Fullerton Sr. Citizens Task Force. Life trustee, co-founder Continuing Learning Experiences program Calif. State U., Fullerton, hon. chmn. fund com. Gerontology Bldg; founder, dir. Fullerton Pub. Forum, 1929-39; founder Elks Nat. Found.; co-founder, benefactor Gerontology Ctr. Calif. State U., Fullerton; pres. Fullerton Rotary, 1939-40, hon. mem., 1983—; mem. U.S. Assay Commn., 1968—; mem. Orange County Dem. Cen. Com., 1962-78; bd. dirs. Fullerton Sr. Multi-purpose Ctr., 1981—; bd. dirs. Orange County Sr. Citizens Adv. Council; mem. pres.'s com. Calif. State U., Fullerton. Recipient Medal of Merit, Am. Numis. Assn., 1954, Spl. Commendation Calif. State Assembly, 1966, 88, Calif. State Senate, 1978, 86, Commendation Ind. Sec. of State, 1984, Commendation Bd. Suprs. Orange County, 1985, Commendation Fullerton City Council, 1986, 88, Commendation Orange County Bd. Supervisors, 1986, Commendation Calif. State Senate, 1986, Commendation Exec. Com. Pres. Calif. State U., Fullerton, 1986, Commendation Calif. gov., 1988; Charles L. and Rachael E. Ruby Gerontology Ctr. named in his and late wife's honor, Calif. State U., Fullerton. Fellow Ind. Bar Found.; mem. Pres. Assocs. Calif. State U. Fullerton, Fullerton Coll. Assocs. (named Spl. Retiree of Yr. 1986, Commendation 1986), Calif. (life, pres. So. sect. 1962-63, treas. 1964-65, pres. 1960-61, dir. 1956-65), pres. Fullerton Secondary Tchrs. Assn., Orange County Tchrs. Assn. (pres. 1953-55), Fullerton Coll. (pres. 1958-60) Tchrs. Assn., NEA (life), Ind. Bar Assn., Stanford U. Law Soc., Calif. State Council Edn., Am. Numismatic Assn. (gov. 1951-53, life adv. bd.), Ind. Bar Assn. (hon. life, Golden Career award 1983), Calif. Bus. Educators Assn. (hon. life), Calif. Assn. Univ. Profs., Pacific S.W. Bus. Law Assn. (pres. 1969-70, life), Numismatic Assn. So. Calif. (life, pres. 1961), Calif. Numis. Assn., Indpls. Coin Club (hon. life), Los Angeles Coin Club (hon. life), U.S. Supreme Ct. Hist. Soc., Calif. Town Hall, North Orange County Mus. Assn. (life, benefactor dir.), Stanford U. Alumni Assn. (life), Old Timers Assay Commn. (life), Fullerton Archeology (hon. life, benefactor dir.). Methodist. Clubs: Elks, Fullerton Coll. Vets. (hon. life). Contbr. articles in field to profl. jours. Home: 308 N Marwood Ave Fullerton CA 92632-1139

RUBY, LAWRENCE, nuclear science educator, engineer; b. Detroit, July 25, 1925; s. Irving Morris and Rose Ruby ; m. Judith Ruby, Apr. 8, 1951; children: Jill, Peter, Frederick. AB in Physics, UCLA, 1945, MA in Physics, 1947, PhD in Physics, 1951. Registered profl. engr., Calif. Physicist Lawrence Berkeley (Calif.) Lab., 1950-87; lectr. in nuclear engring. U. Calif., Berkeley, 1959-61, assoc. prof. nuclear engring., 1961-66, prof. nuclear engring., 1966-87; prof. nuclear sci. Reed Coll., Portland, 1987-91; adj. prof. applied physics & elec. engring. Oreg. Grad. Inst. Sci. & Tech., Portland, 1991—; cons. Lawrence Livermore (Calif.) Nat. Lab., 1955-87. Mem. Am. Phys. Soc., Am. Assn. Physics Tchrs., Am. Nuclear Soc., Sigma Xi. Home: 663 Carrera Ln Lake Oswego OR 97034-1674 Office: Oreg Grad Inst Sci and Tech PO Box 91000 20000 NW Walker Rd Portland OR 97291-1000

RUCH, CHARLES P., university official; b. Longbranch, N.J., Mar. 25, 1938; s. Claud C. and Marcella (Pierce) R.; m. Sally Joan Brandenburg, June 18, 1960; children: Cheryl, Charles, Christopher, Cathleen. BA, Coll. of Wooster, 1959; MA, Northwestern U., 1960, PhD, 1966. Counselor, tchr.

Evanston (Ill.) Twp. High Sch., 1960-66; asst. prof. U. Pitts., 1966-70, assoc. prof., dept. chmn., 1970-74; assoc. dean sch. edn. Va. Commonwealth U., Richmond, 1974-76, dean sch. edn., 1976-85, interim provost, v.p., 1985-86, provost, v.p., 1986-93; pres. Boise (Idaho) State U., 1993—; cons. various univs., govtl. agys., ednl. founds. Author or co-author over 50 articles, revs., tech. reports. Mem. Am. Psychol. Assn., Am. Ednl. Research Assn., Phi Delta Kappa. Office: Boise State U 1910 University Dr Boise ID 83725-0001

RUCH, WAYNE EUGENE, microlithography engineer; b. Sewickly, Pa., Nov. 24, 1946; s. Eugene Herbert and Marian Adelle (Moreth) R. BS in Chemistry, Carnegie Mellon U., Pitts., 1968; MS in Chemistry, U. Fla., 1975. Sr. engr. Harris Corp., Palm Bay, Fla., 1975-80, lead engr., 1980-85, staff engr., 1985-91; microlithography inspection staff engr., cons. KLA Instruments, San Jose, Calif., 1991-93, sr. applications devel. engr., 1993—; adj. prof. chemistry Fla. Inst. Tech., Melbourne, Fla., 1979-85. Contbr. articles to profl. jours. With U.S. Army, 1969-71. Decorated Bronze Star with oak leaf cluster. Mem. N.Y. Acad. Scis., Am. Chem. Soc. Home: 15100 Fern Ave Boulder Creek CA 95006-9776

RUCINSKI, ROBERT D., environmental company executive; b. Wisconsin Rapids, Wis., Apr. 22, 1943; s. Donald C. and Bertha M. (Krueger) R.; married; children: Christopher, Vicki. BS, U. Wis., Stevens Point, 1972; MPA, Brigham Young U., 1978. Cert. profl. contract mgr. Procurement intern U.S. Army Aviation Systems, St. Louis, 1972-73; supr. contracts U.S. Army Tooele (Utah) Army Depot, 1973-78; contract mgr. U.S. Corps of Engrs., Winchester, Va., 1978-79; mgr. acquisitions U.S. Dept. Energy, Laramie (Wyo.) Energy Tech. Ctr., 1979-83; v.p. U. Wyo. Rsch. Corp., Western Rsch. Inst., Laramie, 1983-88; pres., chmn. Resource Tech. Corp., Laramie, 1988—; mem. supervisory com. Univ. Wyo. Credit Union, Laramie, 1987—; mem. Am. Chem. Soc. adv. com. for Environ. Buyers Guide. Mem. com. State Rep. Party, Laramie, 1990. With USN, 1964-68. Mem. VFW (life), Am. Legion, DAV (life), Nat. Ski Patrol (dir. 1983-84), Elks. Roman Catholic. Home: 1814 Arnold St Laramie WY 82070-8130 Office: R T Corp PO Box 1346 Laramie WY 82070-1346

RUCKER, THOMAS DOUGLAS, purchasing executive; b. Ottumwa, Iowa, Aug. 30, 1926; s. Everett Henry and Harriett Mary (Evans) R.; A.B., Loyola U., 1951; postgrad. St. Patrick's Coll., 1950-52; m. Rita Mary Rommelfanger, Apr. 18, 1953; children—David, Theresa, Martin, Paul. Asst. purchasing agt. Radio TV Supply, Los Angeles, 1952-53; buyer Consol. Western Steel div. U.S. Steel, Commerce, Calif., 1953-64, S.W. Welding & Mfg. Co., Alhambra, Calif., 1964-70; dir. purchasing Southwestern Engring., Commerce, Calif., 1970-87, ret. Served with USAAF, 1945-46. Home: 650 Tamarack Ave Apt 2611 Brea CA 92621-3240 Office: Southwestern Engring 5701 S Eastern Ave Ste 300 Los Angeles CA 90040-2934

RUDAT, DAVID L., fire chief; b. Oceanside, Calif., Apr. 13, 1952; m. Carol Ann Senator, July 21, 1973; children: Stephanie, Catherine, Brandon. BS in Bus. Adminstrn., Calif. State U., Long Beach, 1977; MPA, U. So. Calif., 1995. Firefighter City of Orange Fire Dept., Calif., 1972—, paramedic, 1973-84, fire engr., 1982-83, capt., 1983-90, battalion chief, 1990-92, asst. chief, 1992-94, chief, 1994-95. Chmn. svc. team Boy Scouts Am., Orange County, 1992-95; mem. cmty. support team Orange YMCA, 1991-95. Recipient Firefighter Adminstrv. Excellence award Orange Rotary, 1986. Mem. Calif. Fire Chiefs Assn. (legis. chair 1994-95), Orange County Fire Chiefs Assn. Office: Orange Fire Dept PO Box 449 Orange CA 92666-0449 Office: Fire Dept 176 S Grand Orange CA 92666

RUDD, GERALD RAY, retail food and drug company executive; b. Kinsley, Kans., Oct. 6, 1929; s. Linford L. and Bertha Viola (Workman) R.; m. Nicole Cardoso-Ayres, Oct. 4, 1930; children: Christian, Derek. BA, George Washington U., 1958; grad. Program for Mgmt. Devel., Harvard U., 1968. Mgmt. intern AEC, Washington, 1958-59; labor relations mgr. Albertsons, Inc., Boise, Idaho, 1959-62, dir. indsl. relations, 1962-70, v.p. personnel and indsl. relations, 1970-74, sr. v.p. human resources, 1974—. Served to lt. USN, 1951-55. Mem. Am. Soc. Personnel Adminstrn. (Profl. of Yr. awards Boise chpt. 1984, nat. soc. 1986). Republican. Mormon. Club: Hillcrest Country (Boise). Home: 1101 S Owyhee St Boise ID 83705-2208 Office: Albertson's Inc 250 E Parkcenter Blvd Boise ID 83706-3940

RUDDELL, ALYSA ANN, clinical psychologist; b. Ellensburg, Wash., Nov. 11, 1949; d. Clyde Ruddell and Helen May (Ponath) Bostrom; m. Abdelmajid Azzedine, Sept. 15, 1989; children: Mostefa Azzedine. BA, Western Wash. U., 1972; MA, U.S. Internat. U., 1982, PhD, 1986. Counselor Salvation Army, Door of Hope, San Diego, 1982-84; psychology intern Cuyamaca Outpatient Clinic, San Diego, 1984, Southwood Adolescent Psychiat., San Diego, 1985; counselor Community Rsch. Found., San Diego, 1984-87; sexual assault counselor Women's Resource Ctr., San Luis Rey, Calif., 1986-87; mental health specialist Evergreen Counseling Ctr., Aberdeen, Wash., 1987-88; clin. psychologist Ruddell & Assocs., Aberdeen, 1988—, Federal Way, Wash., 1988—; clin. cons. health dept. St. Joseph Hosp. Aberdeen, 1987-90; clin. supr. Cath. Community Svcs., Tacoma, Wash., 1992-94; expert witness Tech. Adv. Svc. for Attys., 1988—; guest radio talk shows, 1987-94. Dir. Camps Farthest Out, Wash., 1990; pres. of bd. Grays Harbor Rape Crisis, Aberdeen, 1987-90. Named for Spl. Contbns., Bellingham (Wash.) C. of C., 1979, for Outstanding Svc., YWCA, Bellingham, 1974. Mem. APA, Am. Bd. Forensic Examiners, Wash. State Psychol. Assn., Internat. Soc. for the Study of Dissociation, Child Abuse Prevention Resources. Home: 6222 25th St NE Tacoma WA 98422-3306 Office: Ruddell & Assocs 402 S 333rd St Federal Way WA 98003-6309

RUDER, MELVIN HARVEY, retired newspaper editor; b. Manning, N.D., Jan. 19, 1915; s. Moris M. and Rebecca (Friedman) R.; m. Ruth Bergan, Feb. 10, 1950; 1 dau., Patricia E. Morton. B.A., U. N.D., 1937, M.A., 1941; grad. student, Northwestern U., 1940. Asst. prof. journalism U. N.D., 1940; indsl. relations specialist Westinghouse Electric Co., Sharon, Pa., 1940-41; pub. relations with Am. Machine & Foundry Co., N.Y.C., 1946; founder, editor Hungry Horse News, Columbia Falls, Mont., 1946-78; editor emeritus Hungry Horse News, 1978—. Chmn. adv. coun. Flathead Nat. Forest, Dist. 6 Sch. Bd., 1967-70. Served to lt. (s.g.) USNR, 1942-45. Recipient Pulitzer prize for gen. local reporting, 1965. Mem. Mont. Press Assn. (pres. 1957), Flathead Associated C. of C. (pres. 1971), Glacier Natural History Assn. (pres. 1983). Home: Buffalo Hill Terr 40 Claremont Kalispell MT 59901

RUDIN, ANNE NOTO, former mayor, nurse; b. Passaic, N.J., Jan. 27, 1924; m. Edward Rudin, June 6, 1948; 4 children. BS in Edn., Temple U., 1945, RN, 1946; MPA, U. So. Calif., 1983; LLD (hon.), Golden Gate U., 1990. RN, Calif. Mem. faculty Temple U. Sch. Nursing, Phila., 1946-48; mem. nursing faculty Mt. Zion Hosp., San Francisco, 1948-49; mem. Sacramento City Council, 1971-83; mayor City of Sacramento, 1983-92. Pres. LWV, Riverside, 1957, Sacramento, 1961, Calif. Elected Women's Assn., 1973—; mem. Calif. bd. dirs. Common Cause; bd. trustees Golden Gate U.; adv. bd. U. So. Calif., Army Depot Reuse Commn.; bd. dirs. Sacramento Theatre Co., Sacramento Symphony. Recipient Women in Govt. award U.S. Jaycee Women, 1984, Woman of Distinction award Sacramento Area Soroptimist Clubs, 1985, Civic Contbn. award LWV Sacramento, 1989, Woman of Courage award Sacramento History Ctr., 1989, Peacemaker of Yr. award Sacramento Mediation Ctr., 1992, Regional Pride award Sacramento Mag., 1993, Humanitarian award Japanese Am. Citizen's League, 1993, Outstanding Pub. Svc. award Am. Soc. Pub. Adminstrn., 1994; named Girl Scouts Am. Role model, 1989. Mem. Japan Soc. No. Calif.

RUDIN, NORAH, forensic DNA consultant, science writer; b. N.Y.C., Nov. 10, 1957; d. Benjamin and Jenny (Sadovsky) R. BA, Pomona Coll., 1979; PhD, Brandeis U., 1987. Postdoctoral fellow Lawrence Berkeley Lab., Berkeley, Calif., 1987-90; cons. Calif. Dept. Justice DNA Lab., Berkeley, 1990-93; freelance sci. writer and forensic DNA cons. Richmond, Calif., 1994—; commentator, DNA expert TV and radio. Co-author: DNA Demystified, 1994; contbr. articles to profl. jours.; reviewer Jour. Forensic Scis. Goldwyn fellow, 1981-85; NIH grantee, 1983-85. Mem. AFTRA. Home and Office: 452 Key Blvd Richmond CA 94805-2428

RUDINSKY, NORMA LEIGH, English language educator, translator; b. Cedar City, Utah, Oct. 23, 1928; d. Wilford Webster and Anna Mae (Langford) Leigh; m. Julius A. Rudinsky, June 12, 1954 (dec. 1980); children: Helen Ann, Alexander John, Stephen Anthony, Paul Joseph, Michael Francis, Mary Louise. AB in English, Stanford (Calif.) U., 1950, AM in English, 1953; certs. in Slovak lang., Comenius U., Bratislava, Slovakia, 1981, 82, 84, 90. Sr. instr. English Oreg. State U., Corvallis, 1966—; lectr. in field. Author: Incipient Feminists, 1991; translator: Seven Slovak Stories by Martin Kukucin, 1980, That Alluring Land: Slovak Stories By Timrava, 1992 (Heldt Prize for Transl. 1993). Internat. Rsch. & Exch. Bd. fellow, 1982, 84, 86-87, Humanities Ctr. fellow, 1988. Mem. Am. Assn. Advancement Slavic Studies, Czechoslovak History Conf., Slovak Studies Assn. (v.p. 1984-86), Slovak Inst. Roman Catholic. Office: Oreg State U Dept Of English Corvallis OR 97331

RUDISILL, RICHARD, museum curator, educator; b. Butte, Mont., Jan. 17, 1932; s. Darl Cole and Margaret (White) R. A.A., Sierra Coll., 1950; B.A. in English, Sacramento State Coll., 1952, M.A. in English, 1957; Ph.D. in Am. Studies, U. Minn., 1967. Instr., Am. studies and English U. Minn., Mpls., 1959-67, research grantee grad. sch., 1964-65; prof. art U. N.Mex., Albuquerque, 1968-71, adj. prof. art and art history, 1987—; research assoc., vis. specialist photog. history Mus. N.Mex., Santa Fe, 1971-73; curator photog. history Mus. N.Mex., 1974—; prof. photog. studies Art Inst. Chgo., 1973-74. Author: Mirror Image: The Influence of the Daguerreotype on American Society, 1971, Photographers of the New Mexico Territory 1854-1912, 1973, Directories of Photographers: An Annotated World Bibliography, 1991; contbr. articles on photog. history to The World Book Ency. and profl. jours. Served with AUS, 1953-55. Recipient McKnight Humanities award Am. History, 1967; Nat. Endowment Arts vis. specialist grantee, 1972-73. Democrat. Lutheran. Address: Mus of NMex Photo Archives PO Box 2087 Santa Fe NM 87504-2087

RUDISIN, GERARD JOHN, marketing executive; b. Pitts., Nov. 8, 1953; s. John and Marion (Donnelly) R.; m. Valerie L. Shalin, Aug. 10, 1980 (div. Jan. 1986); m. Andrea M. Fabrega, Dec. 26, 1987. BS, MIT, 1975; MS, UCLA, 1980. Sr. software architect Western Digital, Pitts., 1981-83; engring. mgr. Tartan Labs., Pitts., 1983-86; v.p. mktg. Alsys, Inc., Boston, 1986-91, Rational Software Corp., Santa Clara, Calif., 1991—. Mem. Assn. for Computing Machinery, Sigma Xi. Office: Rational Software Corp 2800 San Tomas Expy Santa Clara CA 95051-0951

RUDOLPH, RONALD ALVIN, human resources executive; b. Berwyn, Ill., May 12, 1949; s. Alvin J. and Gloria S. (Nicoletti) R. BA, U. Calif., Santa Cruz, 1971. Sr. cons. De Anza Assocs., San Jose, Calif., 1971-73; pers. adminstr. McDonnell Douglas Corp., Cupertino, Calif., 1974-75; employment rep. Fairchild Semiconductor, Mountain View, Calif., 1973-74, 75; compensation analyst Sperry Univac, Santa Clara, Calif., 1975-78; mgr. exempt compensation div. Intel Corp., Santa Clara, 1978-79, compensation mgr., 1979-82; dir. corp. compensation Intel Corp., 1982-85; v.p. human resources UNISYS Corp., San Jose, 1985-91, ASK Group Inc., Mountain View, Calif., 1991—; cons. Rudolph Assocs., Cupertino, 1982—; bd. dirs. Dynamic Temp. Svcs., Sunnyvale, Calif. Mem. Spl. Com. for Parolee Employment, Sacramento, 1973-75; bd. dirs. Jr. Achievement, San Jose, 1987-88. Mem. Am. Soc. Pers. Adminstrs., Am. Compensation Assn., No. Calif. Human Resources Coun. Office: ASK Computer Systems Inc PO Box 58013 2880 Scott Blvd Santa Clara CA 95050-2554

RUDOLPH, ROSS, surgeon, researcher, educator; b. Reading, Pa., Nov. 25, 1940; m. Nancy Taylor; children: Daniel, Rebecca, David, Susan. BA in Philosophy, Yale U., 1962; MD, Columbia U., 1966. Cert. Am. Bd. Plastic Surgery, Am. Bd. Surgery, Nat. Bd. Med. Examiners. Intern Hosp. of the U. of Pa., Phila., 1966-67; resident plastic and gen. surgery U. Hosp. of Cleve. and Case Western Res. U., 1969-74; asst. prof. plastic surgery Med. Coll. Wis., Milw., 1974-75; asst. prof. plastic surgery in residence U. Calif., San Diego, 1975-79, assoc. prof. plastic surgery in residence, 1979-80, assoc. adj. prof. plastic surgery, 1980-84, assoc. clin. prof. plastic surgery, 1984—; chief divsn. plastic surgery VA Hosp., San Diego, 1975-80; operating rm. com., pharmacy com. VA Hosp., La Jolla, 1976-79, tissue com., 1978-80; electives com., com. on edn. policy U. Calif. San Diego Sch. Medicine, 1976-79; cons. plastic surgery San Diego (Calif.) Zoo, 1977-79; med. risk mgmt. com. Univ. Hosp., 1977-79; rehab. com. Sharp Meml. Hosp., 1983-84; edn. com. Childrens Hosp., 1985-88; vis. prof. com. Plastic Surgery Ednl. Found., 1987-88; operating rm. com. Green Hosp. Scripps Clinic, 1987; reviewer various jours.; others. Contbr. articles to profl. jours. Chmn. health and scis. com. Torrey Pines dist. Boy Scouts Am., 1977-79; trustee San Diego (Calif.) Opera, 1990-92. With USPHS, 1967-69. Grantee Adria Labs., 1975—, Ednl. Found. Am. Soc. Plastic and Reconstructive Surgeons, 1975-76, 84-85, 90, VA, 1976-78, 77-80, 81-83, McGhan Corp., 1977—, Dow-Corning Corp., 1977-79, NIH, 1978-80, Orthopedic Rsch. and Edn. Found., 1981-82, M. Larry Lawrence Found., 1990. Fellow ACS; mem. AAAS, Am. Assn. Plastic Surgeons (local arrangements com. 1984-85, audit com. 1986-87, program com. 1987-88, 90-91, 93-94, program chmn. 1994—), Am. Cleft Palate Assn. (time and place com. 1978-79), Am. Soc. for Aesthetic Plastic Surgery (sci. rsch. com. 1989—, vice chmn. silicone implant rsch. com. 1992, candidate group, symposium com. 1992), Am. Soc. Plastic and Reconstructive Surgeons (program com. 1979-80), Calif. Soc. Plastic Surgeons (mem. com. 1980-82, 89-90), Plastic Surgery Rsch. Coun., San Diego Plastic Surgery Assn., Soc. Univ. Surgeons, Wis. Soc. Plastic Surgeons, Phi Gamma Delta, Phi Beta Kappa, Alpha Omega Alpha, others. Office: Scripps Clinic & Rsch Found 10666 N Torrey Pines Rd La Jolla CA 92037-1027

RUDOLPH, THOMAS KEITH, aerospace engineer; b. Jamestown, N.D., Oct. 4, 1961; s. Arthur John and Melinda Magdelina (Nehlich) R. BS in Aerospace Engring., Iowa State U., 1983. Registered profl. engr., Wash. Engr. Boeing Mil. Airplanes, Seattle, 1984-88, sr. engr., 1988-90; sr. engr. Boeing Comml. Airplanes, Seattle, 1990-91, specialist engr., 1991-94; specialist engr. Boeing Mil. Airplanes, Seattle, 1994—; chmn. weight improvement program Boeing B-2 Program, Seattle, 1986-88. Mem. AIAA (sr.), Soc. Allied Weight Engrs. (sr., chmn. activities com. 1985-86, treas. 1986-87, facilities chmn. internat. conf. 1987, v.p. 1987-88, pres. 1991-92), Iowa State U. Alumni Assn. (life), Marston Club (life). Republican. Methodist. Office: Boeing Mil Airplanes M/S 4E-48 PO Box 3707 Seattle WA 98124

RUDOLPH, WALTER PAUL, engineering research company executive; b. Binghamton, N.Y., Aug. 17, 1937; s. Walter Paul and Frieda Lena (Hennemann) R.; m. Leila Ortencia Romero, Dec. 18, 1960; children: Jonathan, Jana, Catherine. BEE, Rensselaer Poly. Inst., 1959; MSBA, San Diego State U., 1964. Elec. engr. Gen. Dynamics/Astronautics, San Diego, 1959-62; ops. research analyst Navy Electronics Lab., San Diego, 1962-64; mem. profl. staff Gen. Electric Tempo, Honolulu, 1964-70, Ctr. for Naval Analysis, Arlington, Va., 1970-77; pres. La Jolla (Calif.) Research Corp., 1977—. Served to Capt. USNR, 1959-92. Republican. Presbyterian. Home: 1559 El Paso Real La Jolla CA 92037-6303 Office: La Jolla Rsch Corp PO Box 1207 La Jolla CA 92038-1207

RUEBE, BAMBI LYNN, interior, environmental designer; b. Huntington Park, Calif., Nov. 13, 1957; d. Leonard John Ruebe and Vaudis Marie Powell. BS, UCLA, 1988. Millwright asst. Kaiser Steel Corp., Fontana, Calif., 1976-79; electrician Fleetwood Enterprises, Riverside, Calif., 1977; fashion model internat., 1977-85; free-lance draftsman, 1982-83; project coord. Philip J. Sicola Inc., Culver City, Calif., 1982-83; prin. designer Ruebe Inclusive Design, Highland, Calif., 1983-89, Ventura, Calif., 1990—; cons. mfg. design Burlington Homes New Eng. Inc., Oxford, Maine, 1987-90, DeRose Industries, Chambersburg, Pa., 1984, Skyline Corp., Redlands, Calif., 1982-84; cons. lighting Lightways Corp., L.A., 1984-87; mem. design rev. bd. San Bernardino (Calif.) Downtown Main St. Redevel. Com., 1987-89. Motion picture project designer, lighting design for the movie Deceptions, 1990. Mem. World Affairs Coun., Inland So. Calif., 1986—; mem. Citizens adv. com. Highland Calif. Gen. Plan, 1988-90; co-chmn. civil rights com. AFL-CIO, Fontana, 1978-79. Recipient Cert. Merit Scholastic Art award Scholastic Mags. Inc., Southeastern Calif., 1974, Dirs. Incentive award for Archtl. Design City of Ventura, Calif., 1990. Mem. Nat. Trust for Hist. Preservation. Democrat. Office: Ruebe Inclusive Design 50 N Oak St Ventura CA 93001-2631

RUETER, TOM WILLIAM, water transportation executive; b. Renton, Wash., July 15, 1955; s. William and Mary Elizabeth (Eccles) R.; m. Toshiko Takamitsu, Oct. 23, 1983; children: Lea Sarah, Mari Kristen. Translator, tour guide Am. and Pacific Tours, Inc., Anchorage, 1974-76, ops. mgr., 1976-87; translator, ops. mgr. Alaska Gen. Trade, Inc., Anchorage, 1977-87; steamship agy. ops. profl. North Star Terminal and Stevedore Co., Anchorage, 1987-88, v.p. agy., 1988—. Mem. Propeler Club of Am. Office: North Star Terminal and Stevedore Co 790 Ocean Dock Rd Anchorage AK 99501-1164

RUGE, NEIL MARSHALL, retired law educator; b. Washington, Dec. 28, 1913; s. Oscar Gustave and Ruth (Jones) R.; m. Madeleine Filhol, Jan. 1942 (dec. May 1944); m. Helga Maria Kley, July 23, 1949; children: Carl, Madeleine. Student, Calif. Inst. Tech., 1931-33; A.B., Stanford U., 1935; J.D., U. Calif. at Berkeley, 1938; postgrad., Harvard U. Grad. Sch. Bus. Adminstrn., 1946-47. Bar: Calif. 1938, U.S. Supreme Ct. 1962. Practiced law in Tulare, Calif., until 1941; joined U.S. fgn. service, 1947; assigned to Palermo, Italy, 1947-49, Casablanca, 1950-55, London, 1956, Cardiff, 1956-58; security and personnel officer State Dept., 1958-62; dep. prin. officer Munich, 1962-68; 1st sec. Am. embassy Guatemala, 1968-69; prof. law Calif. State U., Chico, 1969-80. Contbr. articles to profl. jours. Served to maj. AUS, 1941-46; colonel res. Mem. Sierra Club, Phi Beta Kappa. Home: 936 Bryant Ave Chico CA 95926-2818

RUGENSTEIN, ROBERT WAYNE, clothing designer; b. Indpls., Dec. 4, 1921; s. August Carl and Dorothy Jane (Wuellner) R.; m. Ida May Vazzano; children: Mark, Dominick, Warren, Connie, Kathryn. Lineman Alaska Hwy. telephone line Miller Constrn. Co., 1942-43; designer Ft. Wayne (Ind.) Tailors Co., 1946-63, Craddock Uniform Co., Kansas City, Mo., 1963-67, Hayes Garment Co., Nashville, 1967-69, Fechheimer Co., Cin., 1969-70, Campus Sweater and Sportswear, Paramus, N.Y., 1970-78; v.p. prodn., design Cherokee Apparel Corp., Venice, Calif., 1978-82; internat. clothing cons. Rugida Apparel Svc., Orovilla, Calif., 1982—. Patentee adjustable die cutter, solar energy home, solar energy builders; author: Revelation House, 1992. With U.S. Army, 1943-46, India. Recipient award Nat. Inventor's Soc., 1962, David Rockefeller Spirit of Svc. award Internat. Exec. Svc. Corp., 1992. Mem. Internat. Exec. Svc. Corp. (vol. exec.), Vols. in Tech. Assistance' Mensa, Shriners. Republican. Home and Office: 3229 Rugida Rd Oroville CA 95965-9762

RUGG, DAVID LEWIS, software engineer; b. Roseburg, Oreg., Jan. 16, 1936; s. Thomas Arthur and Dorothy Margaret (Lewis) R.; m. Fran Talmage, Sept. 8, 1958; children: Molly Ann Rugg Cooley, Kenneth Robert Rugg, Daniel Eugene Rugg. Student, U. Redlands, 1955-58, San Diego State Coll., 1958-60; BA, Chapman Coll., 1976; postgrad., Chico State Coll., 1979-86. Tech. writer Ryan Aero, San Diego, 1960-61, Comarco, Ridgecrest, Calif., 1961-74; tech. writer Naval Weapons Ctr. (USN), China Lake, Calif., 1974-77, configuration mgmt. specialist, 1977-80, product assurance engr., 1980-81, head software engring. br., 1981-90, software quality assurance specialist, 1990-92; head A6-E Naval Air Weapons Ctr. Weapons Divsn. (formerly NWC), China Lake, 1992-94, internal cons., 1994—. Contbr. articles to profl. jours. With USAF, 1960. Mem. IEEE, Assn. of Computing Machinery. Home: 9500 Zelzah Ave # 168 Northridge CA 91325-2001 Office: NAWCWPNS Code CO28 1 Admin Cir Bldg 117 China Lake CA 93555

RUGGERI, ZAVERIO MARCELLO, medical researcher; b. Bergamo, Italy, Jan. 7, 1945; came to U.S., 1978; s. Giovanni and Anna (Dolci) R.; m. Rosamaria Carrara, June 12, 1971. MD magna cum laude, U. Milan, 1970; degree in Clin. and Exptl. Hematology magna cum laude, U. Pavia, Italy, 1973, degree in Internal Medicine magna cum laude, 1981. Asst. clin. prof. hematology U. Milan, 1972-80; assoc. dir. hemophilia ctr. Policlinico Hosp., Milan, 1980-82; vis. investigator Scripps Clinic and Research Found., La Jolla, Calif., 1978-82, asst. mem., 1982-89; assoc. mem. Scripps Clinic and Rsch. Found., La Jolla, Calif., 1989-93; mem. Scripps Rsch. Inst., 1993—; dir. Roon Ctr. for Arteriosclerosis and Thrombosis, 1989—; head div. Exptl. Thrombosis and Hemostasis, 1989—; vis. investigator St. Thomas/St. Bartholomews Hosps., London, 1974-76. Editor: Clinics in Haematology, 1985; mem. editorial bds. Blood, 1988-92, Peptide Research, 1988—, Haematologica, 1990—, Jour. Biological Chemistry, 1993—; contbr. articles to profl. jours., chpts. to books. Research scholar Italian Ministry of Edn., 1970, Italian Hemophilia Found., 1970-72. Mem. AAAS, Assn. Am. Physicians, Italian Hemophilia Found., Am. Soc. Clin. Investigation, Italian Soc. Thrombosis and Hemostasis, Internat. Soc. Thrombosis and Hemostasis, Am. Heart Assn. (council on thrombosis), World Fedn. Hemophilia, Am. Fedn. Clin. Research, N.Y. Acad. Scis., Am. Soc. Hematology. Office: Scripps Rsch Inst 10666 N Torrey Pines Rd La Jolla CA 92037-1027

RUGGILL, SOLOMON P., psychologist; b. N.Y.C., Sept. 29, 1906; s. Abraham and Sarah (Silverberg) R.; m. Sophie Stock, June 8, 1938; children: Robert Zachary, Peter Alan. BS, CCNY, 1927; MA in Edn., Columbia U., 1930, PhD in Psychology, 1934. Lic. psychologist, N.Y. Tchr. elem. and jr. high sch. Bd. of Edn. of N.Y.C., 1929-59, psychologist, Bur. of Child Guidance, 1959-62; psychologist Baro Civic Ctr. Clinic, Bklyn., 1961-62; assoc. prof. L.I. U., Bklyn., 1962-69, prof., 1969-79, prof. emeritus, 1979—, acting chmn. dept. guidance and counseling, 1972-73; dir. Flatback Progressive Sch., Bklyn., 1943-45, Camp Kinderwelt, Fraternal Order Farband, N.Y.C., 1959-60; lectr. in gerontology to various orgns., Tucson, 1980—, Keeping Mentally Alert classes Sr. Day Ctrs., 1985—. Pres. Chancy Meml. Found., N.Y.C., 1961-63; mem. adv. council Pima Council on Aging, Tucson, 1987—. Mem. N.Y. Acad. Pub. Edn., N.Y. State Guidance Assn., Jewish Tchrs. Assn. (life). Jewish. Home: 425 W Paseo Redondo Apt 7E Tucson AZ 85701-8262

RUHL, ROGER DONALD, JR., minister; b. Pasadena, Calif., Dec. 1, 1957; s. Roger Donald Ruhl and Sandra Colleen (French) Hills; m. Kerri Lee Handy, Feb. 25, 1978; children: Traci, Stephanie, Melissa. Degree, So. Calif. Sch. Evangelism, 1980. Min. Ch. of Christ, Long Beach, Calif., 1980-83, Klamath Falls, Oreg., 1983—. Editor: Balance of Truth and Freedom, 1987; author, editor The Bible Meditator mag., 1990—; contbr. articles to religious publs. Republican. Home: 201 Jefferson St Klamath Falls OR 97601-3147 Office: Ch of Christ 2521 Nile St Klamath Falls OR 97603-6913

RUHLMAN, TERRELL LOUIS, business executive; b. Warren, Pa., Nov. 13, 1926; s. Ross L. and Gertrude R.; m. Phyllis E., Jan. 15, 1951; children—Robyn Ruhlman Dempsey, Randall L., Heather Ruhlman Martin, Mark A. BS, Pa. State U., 1949; JD, George Washington U., 1954; postgrad., Duquesne U. Grad. Bus. Sch., 1966-68. Bar: D.C. bar. Patent counsel Joy Mfg. Co., Pitts., 1954-59; gen. counsel Joy Mfg. Co., 1959-62, asst. to pres., 1962-69; v.p. oilfield ops. Joy Mfg. Co., Houston, 1969-73; gen. mgr. Reed Tool Co., Houston, 1973-74; pres., chief operating officer Reed Tool Co., 1974-76, dir., 1975-76; v.p., dir. Baker Internat. Corp., 1975-76, pres. mining group, 1976; pres., chief exec. officer, dir. Ansul Co., Marinette, Wis., 1976-80; pres. Wormald Americas, Inc., Scottsdale, Ariz., 1980-88; chmn., chief exec. officer Cade Industries, Inc., Scottsdale, 1988—, also bd. dirs.; bd. dirs. Environ. Engring. Concepts Inc. With USAF. Served with USAF. Home: 9710 E La Posada Cir Scottsdale AZ 85255-3716 Office: # 114 8711 E Pinnacle Peak Rd # 114 Scottsdale AZ 85255-3555

RUIZ, ANTHONY, organizational development consultant, educator; b. L.A., Apr. 15, 1943; s. Gustavo and Rafaela (Loya) R.; m. Irene Pardo, June 1, 1968; 1 child, Michael Anthony. BSBA, Calif. State U., L.A., 1970; MPA, U. So. Calif., L.A., 1976; EdD, Seattle U., 1990. Asst. exec. dir. Eastland Cmty. Youth Ctrs., L.A., 1967-70; asst. dir. Epic program Calif. State U., L.A., 1970-72, dir. Epic program, 1972-75; dir. manpower programs Maravilla Found., L.A., 1975-77; asst. dir. continuing edn. Western Washington U., Bellingham, Wash., 1977-81; exec. asst. to pres. South Seattle C.C., 1981-84, assoc. dean instrn., 1984-92; asst. to vice chancellor Seattle C.Cs., 1992-94; pres., CEO Ruiz & Assocs., Bellevue, Wash., 1994—; mem. occupl. edn. adv. com. Seattle Pub. Schs., 1984-90; mem. adv. bd. King 5 TV, Seattle, 1990—. Bd. dirs. Sc. Ctr. West Seattle, 1983-87, Ch. Coun. Greater Seattle, 1986-91, Consejo Mental Health Ctr., 1986-90, Seattle Sister City Program, 1988—, Vols. of Am., Seattle, 1990—, United Way King County, Seattle, 1994—, also chair project lead, 1988-93; mem. adv. bd. Seattle Housing Authority, 1988-92. Mem. Kiwanis Club (bd. dirs. West Seattle 1981-92, bd. dirs. Stadium Way 1993—). Democrat. Roman Catholic. Home: 13604 SE 54th Pl Bellevue WA 98006-4218

RUIZ, LUIS RAFAEL, investment and financial planning consultant; b. Mayaguez, P.R., Jan. 18, 1946; s. Louis Rafael and Aida Luz (Reteguis) R.; m. P. Eneida Sanchez, Aug. 26, 1967; children: Kristina M., Michael L. AA, Bronx C.C., 1976; BA, CCNY, 1978; postgrad, U. Phoenix, Brea, Calif., 1982-84. Registered prin. NASD; registered investment advisor SEC. Supr. Thomson McKinnon, N.Y.C., 1968-69, Reynolds and Co., N.Y.C., 1969-70; mgr./supr. Weiss Voison, N.Y.C., 1970-72; mgr. W.E. Hutton, N.Y.C., 1972-74; investment cons. in pvt. practice Orange, Calif., 1969—; ops. mgr., v.p. Paine Webber, N.Y.C., 1974-84; ops. mgr., v.p., asst, mgr. Shearson Lehman, Beverly Hills, Calif., 1984-86; compliance officer, v.p. Assoc. Securities Co., L.A., 1987—; dir., v.p. Assoc. Securities Corp. of Nev., Reno, 1992—; registered investment advisor Assoc. Planners, L.A., 1987—; arbitrator, panelist NASD, PSE, NYSE, NFA, Washington, 1987—, notary pub., Calif. Troop leader Boy Scouts Am., Orange, 1987-92; bd. dirs., coach Little League, Orange, 1985-92; fin. planner, counsel La Purisima Ch. and Sch., Orange, 1985-92, St. Jeanne's Sch., Tustin, Calif., 1983-87. Sgt. USAF, 1964-68. Democrat. Roman Catholic. Home: 7412 E White Oak Rdg Orange CA 92669-4519 Office: Assoc Securities Corp 5933 W Century Blvd Fl 9 Los Angeles CA 90045-5471

RULE, DANIEL RHODES, opera company executive; b. L.A., Aug. 25, 1940; s. Rhodes Elmore and Maud Justice (Edwards) R. BA, Occidental Coll., 1962. Asst. music adminstr. N.Y.C. Opera, 1965-70, assoc. mng. dir., 1970-79, mng. dir., 1980-83; gen. mgr. Central City Opera, Denver, 1984—; cons. Ohio State Arts Coun., Columbus, 1984, 86. Bd. dirs. Colo. Children's Chorale, Denver, Colo. Lawyers for Arts. Ford Found. fellow, N.Y., 1966-68. Mem. Am. Guild Mus. Artists (employer chmn. pension and health fund), Denver Athletic Club. Republican. Mem. Christian Ch. (Disciples of Christ). Office: Central City Opera House Assn 621 17th St Ste 1601 Denver CO 80293-1601

RULEY, STANLEY EUGENE, cost analyst; b. Akron, Ohio, Jan. 24, 1934; s. Royal Lovell and Opal Lenora (McDougall) R.; m. Annie Adam Patterson, Dec. 15, 1962; children: Cheryl Ann, Janice Lynn. Student, Kent State U., 1951-53; BSBA, Ohio State U., 1955. Registered profl. engr., Calif. Indsl. engr. Gaffers & Satler Inc., Hawthorne, Calif., 1961-62; mfg. engr. data systems div. Litton Industries Inc., Van Nuys, Calif., 1962-65; contract price analyst Naval Plant Rep. Office Lockheed, Burbank, Calif., 1966-72; contract negotiator Naval Regional Procurement, Long Beach, Calif., 1972-75; cost/price analyst Def. Contract Adminstrn. Services, Van Nuys, 1975-82; chief of contract pricing, dir. contracting Air Force Flight Test Ctr., Edwards AFB, Calif., 1982-89; cons. engr., Northridge, Calif., 1971—. Served as sgt. U.S. Army, 1956-59. Recipient Sustained Superior Performance award Air Force Flight Test Ctr., 1984, Excellent Performance award Air Force Flight Test Ctr., 1982-83, Outstanding Performance award NAVPRO Lockheed, 1970. Mem. Am. Inst. Indsl. Engrs., IBM Computer User Group (Madison, Wis., Conn., San Fernando Valley), Air Force Assn. (life), Nat. Contract Mgmt. Assn. Republican. Presbyterian. Clubs: Lockheed Employee Recreation (treas. Gem and Mineral 1976, pres. 1976), Camper (Burbank) (pres. 1974). Lodge: Masons (past master, 1992). Home: 18751 Vintage St Northridge CA 91324-1529 Office: Indsl Engring Svcs 18751 Vintage St Northridge CA 91324-1529

RULIFSON, JOHNS FREDERICK, computer company executive, computer scientist; b. Bellefontaine, Ohio, Aug. 20, 1941; s. Erwin Charles and Virginia Helen (Johns) R.; m. Janet Irving, June 8, 1963; children: Eric Johns, Ingrid Catharine. BS in Math., U. Wash., 1966; PhD in Computer Sci., Stanford U., 1973. Mathematician SRI, Internat., Menlo Park, Calif., 1966-73; scientist Xerox Rsch., Palo Alto, Calif., 1973-80; mgr. ROLM, Santa Clara, Calif., 1980-85; scientist Syntelligence, Sunnyvale, Calif., 1985-87; exec. Sun Microsystems, Mountain View, Calif., 1987—. Fellow Assn. for Computing Machinery (System Software award 1990); mem. IEEE. Home: 3785 El Centro Ave Palo Alto CA 94306-2642 Office: Sun Microsystems 2550 Garcia Ave Mountain View CA 94043-1109

RULLKOETTER, JILL E., museum education administrator; b. St. Louis, Oct. 2, 1953; d. Robert Carl Rullkoetter and Evelyn K. (Herrman) Stacy; m. William L. Hurley, Jr., Sept. 1, 1985; 1 child, Nicholas Rullkoetter Hurley. BA in Art History, U. Mo., 1976; MA, U. Wash., 1984. Rsch. asst. Mus. Art & Archaeology U. Mo., Columbia, 1975-76; curatorial asst. Henry Art Gallery U. Wash., Seattle, 1978-79, teaching asst. dept. art history, 1979-80; coord. edn. program Seattle Art Mus., 1982-85, head edn., 1986—; staff liason architect selection com. Seattle Mus. Art; speaker and panelist in field. Author (guide booklet) Treasures from the National Museum of American Art. A Family Guide, 1986 Trustee Seattle Archtl. Found., 1990-92. Mem. Am. Assn. Mus. (chmn. edn. com. western region 1985-87, bd. dirs. 1994—), Wash. Mus. Assn., Western Mus. Assn. (bd. dirs., sec. 1988-92, 2d v.p. 1992-94, pres. 1994—), N.W. Inst. Architecture and Urban Studies in Italy (bd. dirs. 1981-91, 2d v.p. 1987-88). Office: Seattle Art Mus PO Box 22000 Seattle WA 98122-9700

RUMACK, CAROL MASTERS, radiologist; b. Washington, June 10, 1943; m. Barry H. Rumack, June 20, 1964; children: Rebecca, Marc. BS, U. Chgo., 1965; BS, MD, U. Wis., 1969. Diplomate Am. Bd. Diagnostic Radiology. Intern U. Md., 1969-70; resident in radiology U. Colo., Denver, 1971-74; mem. staff St. Anthony Hosp., 1975-76, Denver Gen. Hosp., 1976-80, U. Colo. Health Scis. Ctr., Denver, 1980—; chief diagnostic radiology Sch. Medicine U. Colo., Denver, 1987—, instr. radiology, 1976-78, asst. prof. radiology, pediatrics, 1978-81, assoc prof. radiology, pediatrics, 1987—; dir. pediatric radiology Sch. Med. U. Colo., Denver, 1987—. Mem. editorial bd. Pediatric Radiology, Diagnostic Radiology; contbr. articles to profl. jours. Fellow Am. Coll. Radiology, 1984, Am. Inst. Ultrasound Med. 1986; recipient research award U. Colo. Health Scis. Ctr. Dept. Radiology, 1984. Mem. Am. Assn. Women Radiologists (pres. 1981-82), Am. Coll. Radiology (com. pub. info. 1984—, various others coms.), Am. Inst. Ultrasound Med. (bd. govs. 1984—, mem. various coms.), Am. Med. Women's Assn. (regional gov. of reg. XI, 1984-85), Am. Roentgen Ray Soc., Assn. U. Radiologists, Colo. Radiological Soc.(radiation protection com. 1976—, various other coms.), Midwestern Pediatric Radiologist Assn., Radiological Soc. N.Am., Rocky Mt. Radiological Assn., Soc. Pediatric Radiology (sec.), Soc. Radiologists Ultrasound, Am. Acad. Pediatrics (nomination com. sect. radiology, 1981-85). Office: U Colo Health Scis Ctr 4200 E 9th Ave # 030A Denver CO 80220-3706

RUMBAUGH, CHARLES EARL, lawyer, corporate executive; b. San Bernardino, Calif., Mar. 11, 1943; s. Max Elden and Gertrude Maude (Gulker) R.; m. Christina Carol Pinder, Mar. 2, 1968; children: Eckwood, Cynthia, Aaron, Heather. BS, UCLA, 1966; JD, Calif. Western Sch. Law, 1971; cert. in Advanced Mgmt., U. So. Calif., 1993. Bar: Calif. 1972, U.S. Dist. Ct. (cen. dist.) Calif. 1972, U.S. Ct. Appeals (9th cir.) 1972. Engr. Westinghouse Electric Corp., Balt., 1966-68; legal counsel Calif. Dept. of Corps., L.A., 1971-77; legal counsel Hughes Aircraft Co., L.A., 1977-84, asst. to corp. dir. contracts, 1984-89, asst. to corp. v.p. contracts, 1989-95; corp. dir. contracts/pricing Lear Astronautics Corp., 1995—; arbitrator comml., franchise, real estate and constrn. panels Am. Arbitration Assn., L.A., 1989—; mem. arbitration and mediation panels Franchise Arbitration and Mediation, Inc., 1994—, Arbitration and Mediation Internat., 1994—, Ctr. for conflict Resolution, L.A., 1990—, Los Angeles County Superior Ct., 1993; speaker to profl. and trade assns.; adj. prof. West Coast U. Contbr. articles to profl. jours. Counselor Boy Scouts Am., L.A., 1976—; mem. City of Palos Verdes Estates (Calif.) Stables Planning Com., 1986-90; judge pro tem Los Angeles County Superior Ct., L.A., 1991—. Fellow Nat. Contract Mgmt. Assn. (cert. profl. contracts mgr., nat. bd. advisors, nat. v.p. southwestern region 1993-95, nat. dir. 1992-93, pres. L.A./South Bay chpt. 1991-92, Outstanding Fellows award 1994); mem. ABA (forum on franchising, forum on constrn. industry), Nat. Security Indsl. Assn. (vice chmn. west coast legal subcom. 1994—), Fed. Bar Assn. (pres. chpt. 1992-93), State Bar Calif. (franchise law com. 1992-95, Wiley W. Manual award 1992), Los Angeles County Bar Assn., South Bay Bar Assn., Soc. Profls. in Dispute Resolution, Aerospace Industries Assn. (chmn. procurement techniques com. 19987-88, 93-94), Christian Legal Soc. Office: PO Box 2636 Rolling Hills CA 90274

RUMMERFIELD, PHILIP SHERIDAN, medical physicist; b. Raton, N. Mex., Feb. 27, 1922; s. Lawrence Lewis and Helen Antoinette (Roper) R.; m. Mary Evelyn Kubick, Dec. 29, 1979; children: Casey Regan, Dana Jay. BSME, Healds Coll., 1954; MSc, U. Cin., 1964, DSc, 1965. Registered profl. engr., safety, nuclear, Calif. Piping engr. Morrison Knudsen Co., Surabaja, E. Java, 1956-57; civil engr. State of Calif., San Francisco, 1957-59, constn. and radiation engr., 1959-63; hosp. physicist and radiation safety officer U. Calif., San Diego, 1966-73; prin. Applied Radiation Protection Svc., Encinitas, Calif., 1973—. Contbr. articles to Science, Bull. Atomic Scientists, Occupational Health Nursing, Health Physics Jour., Internat. Jour. Applied Radiation & Isotopes. Candidate for City Coun., Carlsbad, Calif., 1984. Grantee Teaching grant NSF, 1969-71. Mem. Am. Nuclear Soc., Calif. Soc. Profl. Engrs., Am. Indsl. Hygiene Assn., Am. Assn. Physicists in Medicine (pres. So. Calif. chpt. 1971-72), Calif. Soc. Profl. Engrs., Health Physics Soc. (pres. So. Calif. chpt. 1973-74). Democrat. Home: 3303 Dorado Pl Carlsbad CA 92009-7706 Office: Applied Radiation Protection Svcs 700 2nd St Ste C Encinitas CA 92024-4459

RUNICE, ROBERT E., retired corporate executive; b. Fargo, N.D., Aug. 20, 1929; s. E.M. and Ruth (Soule) R.; m. Geraldine Kharas, June 26, 1954; children: Michael, Christopher, Paul, Karen. B.S., N.D. State U., 1951. Sr. v.p. Northwestern Bell Tel. Co., Omaha, Nebr., 1945-81; v.p. Am. Tel. & Tel. Co.-Info. Systems, Morristown, N.J., 1981-83; v.p., pres. comml. devel. div. US West, Inc., Englewood, Colo., 1983-91; bd. dirs. Bombay Co., Ft. Worth, Tandy Brands Accessories, Arlington, Tex., Utilx Corp., Kent, Wash. Trustee Colo. Symphony Assn. Republican. Episcopalian. Home: Box 503 10940 S Parker Rd Parker CO 80134-7440 Office: 9785 S Maroon Cir Ste 332 Englewood CO 80112-5918

RUNKLE, ETHEL MONA, artist; b. Davenport, Iowa, Dec. 4, 1921; d. Louis and Agnes (Jungjohann) Behrens; m. Karl Ehresman Runkle, Jan. 25, 1947; children: Carol Ann, Richard Louis. Grad., Shimer Coll., Mt. Carroll, Ill., 1942; student, St. Ambrose Coll., Davenport, Iowa, 1943, Chgo. Art Inst., 1945, N.Y. Sch. Interior Design, 1955. Cert. Nat. Watercolor Soc. Illustrator Rock Island (Ill.) Arsenal, 1942-44; stewardess United Air Lines, Chgo., 1944-46; craft dir. Westbury (N.Y.) Country Club, 1967; owner, operator Polynesian Fashions, Huntington, N.Y., 1967-71, The Woodshed, Escondido, Calif., 1975-77; art dir. Holland-Am. Lines, Seattle, 1986-87; artist San Diego, 1983—; operator Hawaii Condo Rentals, San Diego, 1964—; art demonstrator San Marcos Art Assn., Calif., 1987, Escondido Art Assn., Calif., 1987, La Jolla Art Assn., La Jolla, Calif., 1986. illustration San Diego, 1987; executed mural, 1987; represented in pvt. collections; exhibited in group show of Nat. Watercolor Soc., L.A., 1987. Historian Clipped Wings, San Diego, 1985-86, Lloyd Harbor Hist. Assn., N.Y., 1966-71, Huntington Hist. Soc., N.Y., 1963-71, Soc. Preservation L.I. Antiquities, N.Y., 1967-70. Recipient Pres.'s Citation of Merit, Nat. Soc. Paint Casein & Acrylic, N.Y., 1988, second place award Escondido Art Assn., 1987. Mem. Am. Soc. Marine Artists, Internat. Soc. Women Marine Artists, Nat. Watercolor Soc. (rep. Alaska and Hawaii 1987-88), USCG Art Program, Clairmont Art Guild, San Diego Watercolor Soc. (pres. 1987-88, 3rd pl. award 1988), La Jolla Art Assn., Nat. Soc. of Painters in Casein and Acrylic. Republican. Lutheran. Summer home: 13604 Valle de Lobo Way Poway CA 92064 Winter home: 22612 N Via De La Caballa Sun City West AZ 85375

RUNNELLS, DONALD DEMAR, geochemist, consultant; b. Eureka, Utah, Dec. 30, 1936; s. Raymond DeMar and Cleo Cecil (Beckstead) R.; m. Erika Anna Bahe, Sept. 3, 1958; children: Timothy, Suzanne. BS with high honors, U. Utah, 1958; MA, Harvard U., 1960, PhD, 1963. Rsch. geochemist Shell Devel. Co., Houston and Miami, 1963-67; asst. prof. U. Calif.-Santa Barbara, 1967-69; assoc. prof. geochemistry U. Colo., Boulder, 1969-75, prof., 1975-92, chair dept. geol. sci., 1990-92; pres. Shepherd Miller, Inc., Ft. Collins, Colo., 1993—. cons. geochemistry to cos., and govt. agys. Mem. water sci. and tech. bd. NRC/NAS, 1989-92. Contbr. articles to profl. publs. NSF fellow, 1958-62. Fellow Geol. Soc. Am.; mem. Am. Chem. Soc., Assn. Exploration Geologists (pres. 1990-91), Geochemical Soc., Assn. Ground-water Scientists and Engrs. Home: 8032 Allott Ave Fort Collins CO 80525-4269 Office: Shepherd Miller Inc 1600 Specht Point Rd Ste F Fort Collins CO 80525-4311

RUNNICLES, DONALD, conductor; b. Edinburgh, Scotland, Nov. 16, 1954. Student, Edinburgh U., Cambridge U., London Opera Ctr. Repetiteur Mannheim, Germany, Nat. theater, from 1980, Kapellmeister, from 1984; prin. condr. Hanover, from 1987; numerous appearances with Hamburg Staatsoper; former gen. music dir. Stadtische Buhnen, Freiburg/Breisgau; mus. dir. San Francisco Opera, 1992—; appearances with Met. Opera include Lulu, 1988, The Flying Dutchman, 1990, The Magic Flute; condr. Vienna Staatsoper, 1990-91; debut at Glyndebourne with Don Giovanni, 1991, condr. London Symphony Orch., Orch. de Paris, Israel Philharm., Rotterdam Philharm., Seattle Symphony, Pitts. Symphony, Chgo. Symphony; rec. Hansel und Gretel (Humperdinck); also numerous symphonic engagements. Office: San Francisco Opera War Meml Opera House San Francisco CA 94102 also: Stadtische Buhnen, Bertoldstr 46, W-7800 Freiburg/Breisgau Germany

RUNYON, STEVEN CROWELL, university administrator, communications educator; b. San Rafael, Calif., June 20, 1946; s. Charles A. and Katherine C. (Pease) R.; m. Lynna Lim, Mar. 9, 1974; 1 child, Wendy Victoria. BA in Econs., U. San Francisco, 1971, postgrad., 1978—; MA in Radio and TV, San Francisco State U., 1976. Radio producer Sta. KGO, San Francisco, 1965-68; engr., announcer Stas. KSFR, KSAN, San Francisco, 1966-68; publicist Kolmar Assocs./Chuck Barris Prodns., San Francisco, 1970; instructional media technician U. San Francisco, 1968-72; technician, archivist, mgr. Wurster, Bernardi & Emmons, San Francisco, 1972-73; projectionist So. Pacific R.R., San Francisco, 1974; broadcast ops. engr. Stas. KPEN, KIOI, KIQI, San Francisco, 1968-74, public and community affairs program producer, 1971-74, AM transmitter engr., 1974; lectr. communication arts, U. San Francisco, 1974—, gen. mgr. Sta. KUSF-FM, 1974—, dir. mass media studies program, 1975—, acting chmn. communication arts dept., 1976; TV historian; producer, engr., cons. radio and TV programs; communications and audiovisual cons. Author: A Study of the Don Lee Broadcasting Systems' Television Activities, 1930-41, 1976, Educational Broadcast Management Bibliography, 1974; contbr. articles to profl. jours. Grantee Calif. Coun. Humanities in Public Policy, Rockefeller Found., Father Spieler Meml. Trust, NSF; recipient cert. of merit for documentary radio series Peninsula Press Club, 1979, Diploma of Honor, Internat. Robert Stolz Soc., 1981, Fr. Dunne award U. San Francisco, 1986, Coll. Svc. award Coll. Arts and Scis. U. San Francisco, 1988; lic. gen. class radiotelephone operator FCC. Mem. Soc. Broadcast Engrs., Broadcast Edn. Assn., Assn. Communication Adminstrs., Assn. for Edn. in Journalism and Mass Communication, Assn. Recorded Sound Collections, Pres.'s Ambassadors of U. San Francisco, Internat. Communication Assn., Com. Ethics in Pub. Affairs Broadcasting. Office: U San Francisco 2130 Fulton St San Francisco CA 94117-1080

RUOTOLO, LUCIO PETER, English language educator; b. N.Y.C., Mar. 14, 1927; s. Onorio and Lucia (Sperling) R.; m. Marcia Mauney, June 11, 1960; children: Cristina, Vanessa, Peter. BA, Colgate U., 1951; MA, Columbia U., 1954, PhD, 1960. Part-time lectr. Hofstra Coll., Hempstead, N.Y., 1956-57; lectr. New Sch. for Social Rsch., N.Y.C., 1957; acting instr., prof. English Stanford (Calif.) U., 1957—; cons. panelist NEH, Washington, 1974-75; reader Nat. Humanities Ctr., N.C., 1986; film editor Christianity and Crisis, N.Y.C., 1965-66. Author: Six Existential Heroes, 1973 (Wilson prize 1972), The Interrupted Moment: A View of Virginia Woolf's Novels, 1986; editor: Virginia Woolf's Freshwater, 1976; founding editor Virginia Woolf Miscellany, 1973—. Co-chmn. Stanford/Palo Alto (Calif.) Dem. Club, 1968; co-pres. bd. Palo Alto Chamber Orch., 1980; bd. dirs. Peninsula Drama Guild, Palo Alto, 1964-67. Rsch. grantee NEH, 1973. Mem. MLA, Virginia Woolf Soc. (founding, pres. 1983-87). Presbyterian. Office: Stanford U Dept English Stanford CA 94305

RUOTSALA, JAMES ALFRED, historian, writer; b. Juneau, Alaska, Feb. 17, 1934; s. Bert Alfred and Eva (Karppi) E.; m. Janet Ann Whelan, July 31, 1987; stepchildren: Theresa Cowden, Douglas Whelan, Peggy MacInnis, Michael Whelan, Bruce Whelan. Student, U. Md., 1960-61, Basic Officers Sch., Maxwell AFB, 1964, Air U., Maxwell AFB, 1985; AA, U. Alaska, Kenai, 1990. Asst. div. mgr. Macmillan Pub. Co., 1964-80; mgr. Denny's Restaurants, 1980-82; dir. mktg. and sales Air Alaska, 1982-89; state security supr., lt. Knightwatch Security, Juneau, Alaska, 1990—; archival dir. Alaska Aviation Heritage Mus., 1987-90. Author: Lockheed Vegas in Southeast Alaska, 1980, We Stand Ready, 1986, Eielson, Father of Alaskan Aviation, 1986; Alaska's Aviation Heritage Air Alaska newspaper; contbr. articles to profl. jours. Journalist 1st cl. USN, 1951-56; sgt. U.S. Army, 1958-64; 1st sgt. USAR, 1983-94; ret. USAR, 1994; lt. col. ASDF, 1985—. Decorated Korean Svc. medal with 2 combat stars, Korean Presdl. unit citation, UN Svc. medal, Nat. Def. Svc. medal, Vietnam Svc. medal, Meritorious Svc. medal with 2 oak clusters, Army Commendation medal with 4 oak lead clusters; recipient USAF Brewer Aerospace award, Grover Leoning award, Paul E. Garber award, 1984-85, State of Alaska Gov.'s Cert. Appreciation, 1983, Mayor's Pub. Svc. award, Anchorage, 1985, Commendation from Gov. of Alaska, 1993, 94, 18th Session Alaska Legis. Cert. Recognition, 1993, 94. Mem. VFW (sr. vice comdr. 1995), Res. Officers Assn. (pub. affairs officer 1985—), U.S. Naval Inst., Aviation and Space Writers Assn., Am. Aviation Hist. Soc., Am. Legion (historian), Pioneers of Alaska (sec. 1988, v.p. 1989, pres. 1990, Igloo 33, treas. 1994-95, Igloo 6, Cert. Appreciation 1988), Rotary. Methodist. Home: 2723 John St Juneau AK 99801-2020 Office: Knightwatch Security PO Box 33251 Juneau AK 99803-3251

RUPE, DALLAS GORDON, III, real estate property manager, securities arbitrator; b. Dallas, Dec. 10, 1934; s. Dallas Gordon and Ruby Lee (Landers) R.; m. Ann Walker Caldwell, Mar. 12, 1983; children: Robin, Sean, Amy, Dallas IV. BA, So. Meth. U., 1957; student, Northwestern U., 1959. V.p., dir. Rupe Investment Corp., Dallas, 1955—; v.p. Quinn & Co., Inc., Albuquerque, 1981-86, Underwood Neuhause, Inc., Houston, 1986-87; pres. The Market, Inc., Taos, N.Mex., 1987-89, The Rupe Cos., Inc., Ontario, Oreg., 1989—; bd. dirs. Big D. Prodns., Inc., Dallas, Rupe Capital Corp., Dallas, Moore Investment Co., Dallas, Moore Royalty Co., Dallas. Bd. dirs. Ontario Devel. Corp.; trustee Rupe Found., Dallas, 1955—. Mem. Ontario C. of C. (bd. dirs.), Treasure Valley Rental Assn., Kappa Sigma. Office: The Rupe Cos Inc 93 SW 4th Ave Ontario OR 97914

RUPP, JEAN LOUISE, communications executive, author; b. Portland, Oreg., Aug. 29, 1943; d. Edward Howard and Dorothy Eugenia (Ross) Brown; m. Herbert Gustav Rupp, July 4, 1987. BA in English, Portland State U., 1965. Cert. tchr., Oreg. Tchr., dept. head Beaverton (Oreg.) Sch. Dist., 1967-88; pres., founder Write Communications, Portland, 1988—; adj. faculty Portland C.C., Concordia U., Portland State U.; nat. trainer, cons.State of Oreg., City of Portland, Nike, Inc., Oreg. Health Scis. U., Oreg. Mil. Acad., Oreg. Fin. Instns. Assn., Freightliner, Automated Data Processing, others, 1988—; spkr. Tektronix, Fred Meyer, Pacific Power, Am. Inst. of Banking, Utah Power, Pacific Telecom, Inc., other; writing dir. U.S. Army C.E., USDA Forest Svcs., PacifiCare, others, 1989-90. Author: Grammar Gremlin: An Instant Guide to Perfect Grammar for Everybody in Business, 1994; TV appearances include Stas. KATU-TV and KGW-TV. Vol. Dove Lewis Emergency Vet. Clinic, Portland, 1989—, Doerbecher Children's Hosp., Oreg. Humane Soc. Mem. ASTD, Oreg. Speakers Assn. (sec., bd. dirs. 1991—), Nat. Speakers Assn., Ctr. for Marine Conservation. Republican. Office: Write Comm 8885 SW Canyon Rd Ste 201 Portland OR 97225-3455

RUPP, SIGRID LORENZEN, architect; b. Bremerhaven, Germany, Germany, Jan. 3, 1943; came to U.S., 1953; d. Harry Wilhelm and Mary Sophie (Gernert) Lorenzen; m. Steven Rupp, June 8, 1963 (div. 1976). BArch, U. Calif., Berkeley, 1966. Registered architect, Calif., Mont., Mass., Colo., Wash., Utah, Ariz., Idaho. Assoc. Spencer Assocs., Palo Alto, Calif., 1971-76; pres. SLR Architects, Palo Alto, 1976—; mem. Arch. Rev. Bd., Palo Alto, 1971-77, chmn., 1975-77. Trustee Theatre Artaud, 1988—; bd. dirs. Diablo Ballet, 1995. Mem. AIA, Constrn. Specification Inst., Calif. Women in Environ. Design (pres. 1992-94), Orgn. Women Architects. Democrat.

RUPP, VIRGIL WILLIAM, journalist, editor; b. Marshall, Minn., Aug. 26, 1929; s. Iliff William and Alice (McLain) R.; m. Rosemary Ann Bracken, Apr. 26, 1929; children: Linda Ann, Eric William. Student, U. Minn., 1947-78, 53-54. Reporter, columnist The Bull., Bend, Oreg., 1955-59; copyeditor, columnist Duluth (Minn.) Herald & News-Tribune, 1959-63; reporter, photographer East Oregonian, Pendleton, Oreg., 1963-83; editor Agri-Times N.W., Pendleton, 1983—. Author: Let'er Buck, 1985, PGG--A History of a Co-op, 1982; contbr. short story to Reader's Digest. Bd. dirs. Am. Heart Assn., Pendleton, 1991-92, Pendleton Friends of Libr., 1992—, Round-Up Hall of Fame, Pendleton, 1992—; mem. N.E. Nev. Hist. Soc., Umatilla County Hist. Soc. Staff sgt. U.S. Army MC, 1951-52, Korea. Home: 514 NW Furnish Ave Pendleton OR 97801-1344 Office: J/A Pub 206 SE Court Ave Pendleton OR 97801-2349

RUPPERT, JOHN LAWRENCE, lawyer; b. Chgo., Oct. 7, 1953; s. Merle Arvin and Loretta Marie (Ford) R.; m. Katharine Marie Tarbox, June 5, 1976. BA, Northwestern U., 1975; JD, U. Denver, 1978; LLM in Taxation, NYU, 1979. Bar: Colo. 1978, U.S. Dist. Ct. Colo. 1978, Ill. 1979, U.S. Tax Ct. 1981. Assoc. Kirkland & Ellis, Denver, 1979-84, ptnr., 1984-88; ptnr. Ballard, Spahr, Andrews & Ingersoll, Denver, 1988—; lectr. U. Denver Coll. Law, fall, 1984-92, adj. prof. law grad. tax program, 1993—. Contbr. articles to profl. jours. Mem. ABA, Colo. Bar Assn. (exec. coun. tax sect. 1985-89), Denver Bar Assn., Equipment Leasing Assn. Am. Office: Ballard Spahr Andrews & Ingersoll 1225 17th St Ste 2300 Denver CO 80202-5523

RUPPERT, SIEGFRIED, scientist; b. Langenschwarz, Germany, Oct. 2, 1958; came to U.S., 1991; s. Roland and Lina (Krug) R. Diploma degree in Biology, U. Heidelberg, Germany, 1984, PhD, 1989. Postdoctoral fellow U. Heidelberg, 1989-91, U. Calif., Berkeley, 1991-94; scientist Genentech, Inc., South San Francisco, Calif., 1994—; cons. Biopharm, GmbH, Heidelberg, Germany, 1988-91. Contbr. articles to profl. jours. Rsch. fellow German Cancer Rsch. Ctr., 1988, 90; hon. fellow Boehringer Ingelheim, 1991-93; long-term fellow EMBO, 1991-93; fellow Howard Hughes Med. Inst., 1993-94. Home: 4150 17th St # 7 San Francisco CA 94114 Office: Genentech Inc 460 Point San Bruno Blvd South San Francisco CA 94080

RUSCH, PATRICIA HULL, dietitian; b. Long Beach, Calif., Oct. 27, 1946; d. Donald Benjamin and Jeanne Marie (Cullin) Hull; m. Dale Allen Williamson, July 21, 1969 (div. Mar. 1983); children: Cary Lynn, Sandra Lee; m. Robin Alan Rusch, June 27, 1987. BS in Dietetics, Calif. State U., L.A., 1969; MPH Nutrition, U. Calif., L.A., 1970. Registered dietitian. Metabolic dietitian City of Hope Med. Ctr., Duarte, Calif., 1971-73; clin. dietitian St. Agnes Med. Ctr., Fresno, Calif., 1974; food svc. dir. Bel Haven Conv. Hosp., Fresno, 1974-76; pvt. practice cons. dietitian Fresno, 1976-79; pres., bd. dirs. Dietary Directions, Inc., Fresno, 1979—; keynote spkr. Spring Meeting Calif. Dietetic Assn., L.A., 1973. Author: Diet Manual for Long-term, 1980, 85, 90. Recipient Kitchen Layout and Design award So. Calif. Gas Co., L.A., 1970. Mem. Am. Dietetic Assn., Cons. Dietitians of Calif. (chmn., editor 1986—), Ctrl. Valley Dietetic Assn. (sec., chmn. various coms. 1973—), Dietitians in Psychology/Diabilities), Sea Knights Dive Club (pres. editor 1986—). Republican. Office: Dietary Directions Inc 2350 N Chestnut Ave # 111 Fresno CA 93703-2807

RUSCONI, LOUIS JOSEPH, marine engineer; b. San Diego, Calif., Oct. 10, 1926; s. Louis Edward and Laura Ethelyn (Salazar) R.; m. Virginia Caroline Bruce, Jan. 1, 1972. BA in Engring. Tech., Pacific Western U., 1981, MA in Marine Engring. Tech., 1982; PhD in Marine Engring. Mgmt., Clayton U., 1986. Cert. nuclear ship propulsion plant operator, surface and submarine. Enlisted USN, 1944, electrician's mate chief, 1944-65, retired, 1965; marine electrician planner U.S. Naval Shipyard, Vallejo, Calif., 1965-72; marine elec. technician Imperial Iranian Navy, Bandar Abbas, Iran, 1974-79; marine shipyard planner Royal Saudi Navy, Al-Jubail, Saudi Arabia, 1980-86; cons. in marine engring., 1986—. Author: Shipyards Operations manual, 1980, poetry (Golden Poet award 1989, Silver Poet award 1990). Mem. Rep. Presdl. Task Force, Washington, 1989-90, trustee, 1991. Mem. IEEE, U.S. Naval Inst., Soc. of Naval Architects and Marine Engrs. (assoc. mem.), Fleet Res., Nat. Geographic Soc. Home: 949 Myra Ave Chula Vista CA 91911-2315

RUSH, ANDREW WILSON, artist; b. Detroit, Sept. 24, 1931; s. Harvey Ditman and Mary Louise (Stalker) R.; m. Jean Cochran, Apr., 1957; children: Benjamin, Samuel, Joseph, Margaret; m. Ann Woodin, Oct., 1978. B.F.A. with honors, U. Ill., 1953; M.F.A., U. Iowa, 1958. Asso. prof. art U. Ariz., 1959-69; co-dir. Rockefeller Found. Indian Arts Project, 1960-

64; vis. artist, artist-in-residence Ohio State U., 1970, U. Ark., 1972, Colo. Coll., 1973-74; resident mem. Rancho Linda Vista, Community of the Arts, Oracle, Ariz., 1969—. One-man shows include Carlin Galleries, Ft. Worth, 1973, Graphics Gallery, Tucson, 1972, 75, Tucson Art Inst., 1984; exhibited in group shows at World's Fair, N.Y.C., 1964, USIS exhbns., Europe, Latin Am., 1960-65; represented in permanent collections Libr. of Congress, Uffizzi Mus., Dallas Mus., Ft. Worth Mus., Seattle Mus., Free Libr., Phila.; illustrator: Andrew Rush on Oliver Wendell Holmes, 1973, Rule of Two (Ann Woodin), 1984, Voice Crying in the Wilderness (Edward Abbey), 1990, Ask Marilyn, 1992. Served with USMC, 1953-55. Fulbright grantee, 1958-59. Address: Rancho Linda Vista O M Star Rte 2360 Oracle AZ 85623

RUSH, DOMENICA MARIE, health facilities administrator; b. Gallup, N.Mex., Apr. 10, 1937; d. Bernardo G. and Guadalupe (Milan) Iorio; m. W. E. Rush, Jan. 5, 1967. Diploma, Regina Sch. Nursing, Albuquerque, 1958. RN N.Mex.; lic. nursing home adminstr. Charge nurse, house supr. St. Joseph Hosp., Albuquerque, 1958-63; dir. nursing Cibola Hosp., Grants, 1960-64; supr. operating room, dir. med. seminars Carrie Tingley Crippled Children's Hosp., Truth or Consequences, N.Mex., 1964-73; adminstr. Sierra Vista Hosp., Truth or Consequences, 1974-88, pres., 1980-89; clin. nursing mgr. U. N.Mex. Hosp., 1989-90; adminstr. Nor-Lea Hosp., Lovington, N.Mex., 1990-94; with regional ops. divsn. Presbyn. Healthcare Svcs., Albuquerque, 1994—, regional ops., 1994—; bd. dirs. N.Mex. Blue Cross/Blue Shield, 1977-88, chmn. hosp. relations com., 1983-85, exec. com. 1983—; bd. dirs. Region II Emergency Med. Svcs. Originating bd. SW Mental Health Ctr., Sierra County, N.Mex., 1975; chmn. Sierra County Personnel Bd., 1983—. Named Lea County Outstanding Woman, N.Mex. Commn. on Status of Women; Woman of Yr. for Lea County, N.Mex., 1993. Mem. Am. Coll. Health Care Adminstrs., Sierra County C. of C. (bd. dirs. 1972, 75-76, svc. award 1973, Businesswoman of the Yr. 1973-74), N.Mex. Hosp. Assn. (bd. dirs., sec.-treas., pres.-elect, com. chmn., 1977-88, pres. 1980-81, exec. com., 1980-83, 84-85, recipient meritorius svc. award 1988), N.Mex. So. Hosp. Coun. (sec. 1980-81, pres. 1981-82), Am. Hosp. Assn. (N.Mex. del. 1984-88, regional adv. bd. 1984-88). Republican. Roman Catholic. Home: 1100 N Riverside Truth Or Consequences NM 87901

RUSHER, WILLIAM ALLEN, writer, commentator; b. Chgo., July 19, 1923; s. Evan Singleton and Verna (Self) R. AB, Princeton, 1943; JD, Harvard, 1948; DLit (hon.), Nathaniel Hawthorne Coll., 1973. Bar: N.Y. bar 1949. Assoc. Shearman & Sterling & Wright, N.Y.C., 1948-56; spl. counsel fin. com. N.Y. Senate, 1955; assoc. counsel internal security subcom. U.S. Senate, 1956-57; pub., v.p. Nat. Review mag., N.Y.C., 1957-88, also bd. dirs.; Disting. fellow The Claremont Inst, 1989—; mem. Adv. Task Force on Civil Disorders, 1972. Author: Special Counsel, 1968 (with Mark Hatfield and Arlie Schardt) Amnesty?, 1973, The Making of the New Majority Party, 1975, How to Win Arguments, 1981, The Rise of the Right, 1984, The Coming Battle for the Media, 1988; editor: The Ambiguous Legacy of the Enlightenment, 1995; columnist Universal Press Syndicate, 1973-82, Newspaper Enterprise Assn., 1982—; played role of Advocate in TV program The Advocates, 1970-73. Bd. dirs. Media Rsch. Ctr., Washington; chmn. bd. advisors Ashbrook Ctr., Ashland, Ohio; past vice chmn. Am. Conservative Union; past trustee Pacific Legal Found., Sacramento; trustee, treas. Wilbur Found., Santa Barbara. Recipient Disting. Citizen award NYU Sch. Law, 1973. Mem. ABA, U. Club (N.Y.C. and San Francisco), Met. Club (Washington). Anglican. Home and Office: 850 Powell St San Francisco CA 94108-2051

RUSHING, DON G., lawyer; b. Terrell, Tex., June 2, 1948. BS, U.S. Air Force Acad., 1970; MBA, U. So. Calif., 1973; JD, UCLA, 1978. Bar: Colo. 1978, Calif. 1979. Co-chair, CEO Gray, Care, Ware & Friedenrich, San Diego. Assoc. editor UCLA Law Review, 1976-78; contbr. articles to law reviews. Mem. ABA, Colo. Bar Assn., San Diego County Bar Assn., Phi Kappa Phi, Beta Gamma Sigma. Office: Gray Care Ware & Freidenrich 401 B St Ste 1700 San Diego CA 92101-4240

RUSK, LAUREN, editor; b. Boston, Oct. 22, 1948; d. Henry G. and Olga (Wester) Russell. BA, Reed Coll., 1980; PhD, Stanford U., 1995. English instr. Stanford (Calif.) U., 1981-82, 84-85, writing cons. Engring. Sch., 1985—, instr. western culture, 1987-88, editor geophysics dept., 1990—; devel. editor Addison-Wesley Pub. Co., Reading, Mass., 1993—; contract editor Ctr. for the Future of Children, Packard Found., Palo Alto, Calif., 1994—. Contbr. articles, poems to profl. publs., chpts. to books. Stanford fellow, 1980-84. Mem. MLA, Soc. for Study of Multi-Ethnic Lits. of U.S. Democrat. $D. Home and Office: 2256 Bowdoin St Palo Alto CA 94306-1214

RUSSELL, BILL, former professional basketball team executive, former professional basketball player; b. Monroe, La., Feb. 12, 1934. Grad., San Francisco State Coll., 1956. Player, NBA Boston Celtics Profl. Basketball Club, 1956-69, coach, 1966-69; sportscaster ABC-TV, 1969-80, CBS-TV, 1980-83; coach NBA Seattle Supersonics, 1973-77; coach NBA Sacramento Kings, 1987-88, v.p. basketball ops., then exec. v.p., 1988-89; mem. U.S. Olympic Basketball Team (Gold medal), 1956. Appeared in: TV series Cowboy in Africa; also commls.; co-host: The Superstars, ABC-TV, 1978-79; Author: Second Wind: Memoirs of an Opinionated Man, 1979. Inducted into Basketball Hall of Fame, 1974; mem. 11 NBA championship teams. Office: Sacramento Kings 1 Sports Pky Sacramento CA 95834-2300*

RUSSELL, CARINA BOEHM, interior designer; b. Livingston, Mont., Dec. 21, 1954; d. Edward and Pia Maria (Fondelli) Boehm; m. John N. Russell, Dec. 14, 1978; children: Cara, Evan. BS, Mont. State U., 1977. Pvt. practice Rocky Mountain Design-Interiors, Livingston, 1978—. Active com. Livingston Comprehensive Plan, 1993-94; v.p. Livingston Youth Soccer League, 1993—. Mem. Am. Soc. Interior Designers (profl.), Soroptimists (pres. 1992—), Livingston C. of C. (bd. dirs. 1993—). Episcopalian. Office: Rocky Mountain Design 601 W Park St Livingston MT 59047-2531

RUSSELL, CARL LLOYD, computer systems analyst; b. Hayward, Calif., Oct. 12, 1950; s. Carl John Russell and Janet Modenia (Schaeffer) Martin; children: Kristina Yvonne, Kathleen Marie. BA, Northwest Nazarene Coll., Nampa, Idaho, 1976. Computer operator Meredian Wood Products, Nampa, 1978-80; computer programmer Latah, Inc., Boise, Idaho, 1980-82; computer programmer Cougar Mountain Software, Boise, 1982-86, mgr. of rsch. and devel., 1986—. Author computer software, 1978. With USN, 1968-69. Republican. Nazarene. Home: 1304 Eldoran Nampa ID 83651 Office: Cougar Mountain Software 9180 Potomac Dr Boise ID 83704

RUSSELL, CAROL ANN, personnel service company executive; b. Detroit, Dec. 14, 1943; d. Billy an dIris Koud; m. Victor Rojas (div.). BA in English, Hunter Coll., 1993. Registered employment cons. Various positions in temp. help cos. N.Y.C., 1964-74; v.p. Wollborg-Michelson, San Francisco, 1974-82; co-owner, pres. Russell Staffing Resources, Inc., San Francisco and Sonoma, 1983—; media guest, spkr., workshop and seminar leader in field; host/cmty. prodr. Job Net program for Viacom Cable T.V.; pres. bd. Russell Ctr. for Career Skills. Pub. Checkpoint Newsletter; contbr. articles to profl. publs. Named to the Inc. 500, 1989, 90. Mem. Soc. to Preserve and Encourage Radio Drama Variety and Comedy, Internat. Platform Assn., No. Calif. Human Resources Coun., Soc. Human Resource Mgmt., Calif. Assn. Pers. Cons. (pres. Golden State chpt. 1984-85), Calif. Assn. Temp. Svcs., Bay Area Pers. Assn. (pres. 1983-84), Pers. Assn. Sonoma County. Office: Russell Pers Svcs Inc 120 Montgomery St San Francisco CA 94104-4303

RUSSELL, DANA, small business operator; b. Tuba City, Ariz., Aug. 2, 1949; s. Rudolph and Peggy (Sangster) R.; m. Caroline Ann Harrison; children: Grey Noel, Brian Haley-Allen, Grant David, Stephen Bradley. BBA, Cen. State U., 1972. Adminstr. community edn. Navajo Nation, Window Rock, Ariz., 1973-78; adminstr. higher edn. Navajo Community Coll., Tsaile, Ariz., 1978-90; pres., operator West Canyon Boiler, Inc., Flagstaff, Ariz., 1990-93; pres., owner Canyon Tng. and Sales, Flagstaff, 1993—; coun. mem. Navajo Nation - Pvt. Industry Coun., Window Rock, 1986-90. Office: Canyon Tng & Sales 2710 N Fremont Blvd Flagstaff AZ 86001-0708

RUSSELL, DAVID E., federal judge; b. Chicago Heights, Ill., Mar. 19, 1935; s. Robert W. and Nellie (Petkus) R.; m. Denise A. Hurst, Apr. 1, 1968 (div. 1978); children: Dirk, Kent, Laura, Rachel; m. Sandra M. Niemeyer, Oct. 31, 1982; children: Jeff Ahrens, Penny, Stacy. BS in Acctg., U. Calif., Berkeley, 1957, LLB, 1960. Bar: Calif. 1961, U.S. Dist. Ct. (no. dist.) Calif. 1961, U.S. Tax Ct. 1967; CPA, Calif. Staff acct. Lybrand, Ross Bros. & Montgomery, San Francisco, 1960-64; assoc. Robert C. Burnstein, Esquire, Oakland, Calif., 1964-65; ptnr. Russell & Humphreys, Sacramento, 1965; ptnr. Russell, Humphreys & Estabrook, Sacramento, 1966-70, prin., 1971-73; shareholder Russell, Jarvis, Estabrook & Dashiell, Sacramento, 1974-86; bankruptcy judge U.S. Dist. Ct. for Ea. Dist. Calif., Sacramento, 1986—. Office: US Bankruptcy Ct 650 Capitol Mall Rm 8038 Sacramento CA 95814-4706

RUSSELL, FINDLAY EWING, physician; b. San Francisco, Sept. 1, 1919; s. William and Mary Jane (Findlay) R.; m. Marilyn Ruth Jenkins, Apr. 12, 1975; children—Christa Ann, Sharon Jane, Robin Emily, Constance Susan, Mark Findlay. BA, Walla Walla (Wash.) Coll., 1941; MD, Loma Linda (Calif.) U., 1950; postgrad. (fellow), Calif. Inst. Tech., 1951-53; PhD, U. Santa Barbara, Calif., 1974, LLD (hon.), 1989. Intern White Meml. Hosp., Los Angeles, 1950-51; practice medicine specializing in toxinology and toxicology Los Angeles, 1953—; mem. staff Los Angeles County-U. So. Calif. Med. Center, Loma Linda U. Med. Center, U. Ariz. Med. Ctr.; physiologist Huntington Inst. Med. Research, 1953-55; dir. lab. neurol. research Los Angeles County-U. So. Calif. Med. Center, 1955-80; mem. faculty Loma Linda U. Med. Sch., 1955—; prof. neurology, physiology and biology U. So. Calif. Med. Sch., 1966-81; prof. pharmacology and toxicology U. Ariz., 1981—; cons. USPHS, NSF, Office Naval Rsch., WHO, U.S. Army, Walter Reed, USAF, Brooks AFB. Author: Marine Toxins and Venomous and Poisonous Marine Animals, 1965, Poisonous Marine Animals, 1971, Snake Venom Poisoning, 1980; co-author: Bibliography of Snake Venoms and Venomous Snakes, 1964, Animal Toxins, 1967, Poisonous Snakes of The World, 1968, Snake Venom Poisoning, 1983, Bibliography of Venomous and Poisonous Marine Animals and Their Toxins, 1984; editor: Toxicon, 1962-70. Served with AUS, 1942-46. Decorated Purple Heart, Bronze Star; recipient award Los Angeles County Bd. Suprs., 1960; award Acad. Medicine Buenos Aires, 1966; Skylab Achievement award, 1974; Jozef Stefan medal Yugoslavia, 1978. Fellow A.C.P., Am. Coll. Cardiology, Royal Soc. Tropical Medicine, N.Y. Acad. Scis.; mem. Internat. Soc. Toxinology (pres. 1962-66, Francisco Redi medal 1967), Royal Soc. Medicine, Am. Soc. Physiology, Western Soc. Pharmacology (pres. 1973). Office: U Ariz Coll Pharmacy Tucson AZ 85721

RUSSELL, FRANCIA, ballet director, educator; b. Los Angeles, Jan. 10, 1938; d. W. Frank and Marion (Whitney) R.; m. Kent Stowell, Nov. 19, 1965; children: Christopher, Darren, Ethan. Studies with, George Balanchine, Vera Volkova, Felia Doubrouska, Antonina Tumkovsky, Benjamin Harkarvy; student, NYU, Columbia U. Dancer, soloist N.Y.C. Ballet, 1956-62, ballet mistress, 1965-70; dancer Ballets USA/Jerome Robbins, N.Y.C., 1962; tchr. ballet Sch. Am. Ballet, N.Y.C., 1963-64; co-dir. Frankfurt (Fed. Republic Germany) Opera Ballet, 1976-77; dir., co-artistic dir. Pacific N.W. Ballet, Seattle, 1977—; affiliate prof. of dance U. Wash. Dir. staging over 100 George Balanchine ballet prodns. throughout world, including the Soviet Union and People's Republic of China, 1964—. Named Woman of Achievement, Matrix Table, Women in Communications, Seattle, 1987, Gov.'s Arts award, 1989. Mem. Internat. Women's Forum. Home: 2833 Broadway E Seattle WA 98102-3935 Office: Pacific NW Ballet 301 Mercer St Seattle WA 98109-4600

RUSSELL, GARY, broadcast executive; b. Winnepeg, Man., Can., Dec. 17, 1948; s. Raymond Anthony Wakefield and Florence Margret (Willson) Vidler; m. Deborah Kim Finnson, Oct. 10, 1984; children: Amanda, Charles. Grad., Kelvin High Sch., Winnepeg, 1967. Radio announcer Sta. CHLO, St. Thomas, Ont., 1967, Sta. CKOM, Saskatoon, Sask., 1968-69, Sta. CJME, Regina, Sask., 1969, Sta. CKLW, Windsor, Ont., 1970; radio announcer Sta. CKLG, Vancouver, B.C., 1970-73, program dir., 1975-85; program dir. Sta. CKY, Winnepeg, 1975-86; nat. program dir. Moffat Comm., Winnepeg, 1986-89; v.p., gen. mgr. 54 Rock, Ottawa, 1990-92, Sta. CJAY, Calgary, Alta., 1992—. Office: Standard Radio Inc, Box 2750 Station M, Calgary, AB Canada T2P 4P8

RUSSELL, JAMES SARGENT, retired naval officer; b. Tacoma, Mar. 22, 1903; s. Ambrose J. and Loella Janet (Sargent) R.; m. Dorothy Irene Johnson, Apr. 13, 1929 (dec. Apr. 1965); children: Donald Johnson, Kenneth McDonald (dec. 1993); m. 2d, Geraldine Haus Rahn, July 12, 1966. BS, U.S. Naval Acad., 1926; MS, Calif. Inst. Tech., 1935. Served with U.S. Mcht. Marine, 1918-22; commd. ensign U.S. Navy, 1926, advanced through grades to adm., 1958; naval aviator, 1929-65; comdg. officer aircraft sqdn. VP 42, Aleutians and Alaska, 1941-42; chief of staff to comdr. Carrier Div. Two, Pacific campaigns of Palau, P.I., Iwo Jima, Okinawa, 1944-45; bombing survey, Japan, 1945; comdg. officer U.S.S., Bairoko, 1946-47, U.S.S. Coral Sea, 1951-52; with aircraft carrier desk Bur. Aero., 1939-41, dir. mil. requirements, 1943-44; dept. dir. mil. application AEC, 1947-51; dir. air warfare div. Office Chief Naval Ops., 1952-54; comdr. carrier div. 17 & 5, Pacific Fleet, 1954-55, chief Bur. of Aero., 1955-57; dep. comdr. Atlantic Fleet, 1957-58, vice chief Naval Ops., 1958-61; comdr. NATO forces in So. Europe, 1962-65, ret., 1965; recalled to active duty, 1967, 68, Vietnam; mem. various Navy adv. bds.; cons. Boeing Co., 1965-79. Decorated D.S.M. with oak leaf cluster, Legion of Merit with two oak leaf clusters, D.F.C., Air medal (U.S.); grand cross Royal Order King George I (Greece); Grand Ofcl. Order Republic of Italy; comdr. Legion of Honor (France); Gt. Cross Peruvian Cross of Naval Merit; Grand Officer Order of Naval Merit (Brazil); recipient Collier-Trophy, 1956, Russell Trophy Order of Daedalians; named to Nat. Mus. of Naval Aviation Hall of Honor, 1990. Fellow AIAA. Home: 7734 Walnut Ave SW Tacoma WA 98498-5223

RUSSELL, JAMES T., physicist and inventor; b. Bremerton, Wash., Feb. 23, 1931; m. Barbara Ann Giblett, Sept. 12, 1953; children: Janet, James C., Kristen. BA, Reed Coll., Portland, Oreg., 1953. Physicist GE Co., Richland, Wash., 1953-65; sr. scientist Battelle Meml. Inst./Pacific N.W. Labs., Richland, 1965-80; v.p. Digital Recording Corp., Salt Lake City, 1981-85; pres. Russell Assocs., Inc., Bellevue, Wash., 1985—; v.p. Info. Optics Corp., Issaquah, Wash., 1989—. Patentee (40) in field. Recipient IR-100 award Internat. Rsch. Mag., 1974. Mem. IEEE, Am. Phys. Soc., Optical Soc. Am., Soc. Photographic and Instrumentation Engrs. Home: 14589 SE 51st St Bellevue WA 98006-3509

RUSSELL, JAY D., marketing executive; b. Milw., Dec. 20, 1950; s. John Frank and Veronica Cecilia (Jones) R.; m. Carol Jean Croft, Feb. 14, 1976 (div. 1980); 1 stepchild, Kirsten Jean. BS, Ariz. State U., 1984, MBA, 1987. Prin. Southwest Casting Corp., Albuquerque, 1973-77; exec. v.p. Creative Constrn. Inc., Albuquerque, 1977-78; ops. supt. Demas Constrn. Inc., Alameda, N.M., 1978-81; adminstrv. mgr. Investment and Retirement Systems Inc., Phoenix, 1984-85; research asst. dept. communications Ariz. State U., Tempe, Ariz., 1985-86; grad. asst. Ariz. State U., 1986-87; project coordinator CHR Interiors, Scottsdale, Ariz., 1987-88; assoc. CHR Equipment and Space Planning, Scottsdale, 1988-89; prin. AJR Equipment Co., Scottsdale, 1985-90; pres., CEO AJR Equipment Co., Inc., Scottsdale, 1991—; research intern Gov's Office State of Ariz., Phoenix, 1986; mktg. intern Chase Bank Ariz., cons. 1988—, Fin. Ctr., Scottsdale, 1987; grad. liaison Econ. Club of Phoenix, Tempe, 1986-87. Named Outstanding Grad. Student Fin., Wall St. Jour., 1987; Exxon Edni. Found. scholar, 1986. Mem. Ariz. State U. Alumni Assn., Sigma Iota Epsilon, Phi Kappa Phi, Beta Gamma Sigma. Roman Catholic. Club: Econ. (Phoenix). Office: AJR Equipment Co Inc 8010 E Mcdowell Rd Ste 114 Scottsdale AZ 85257-3868

RUSSELL, JOHN DRINKER, legal educator and administrator, consultant; b. Portland, Oreg., Sept. 19, 1911; s. Charles Bert and Alice Eleanor (Drinker) R.; m. Lucille Erica Umbreit, July 11, 1953. B.A., Stanford U., 1931, M.A., 1941; LL.B., Northwestern Sch. Law, Lewis and Clark Coll., 1935. Bar: Oreg. 1935, U.S. Dist. Ct. Oreg. 1936. Ptnr. Berg, Jones & Russell, Portland, 1935-38; counselor, instr. Menlo Coll., Menlo Park, Calif., 1938-42, dir. admissions, registrar, 1946-55, prof. domestic and internat. comml. law, 1946-77, dir. top acad. adminstr., 1955-77, part time prof. law and internat. bus., 1977-81, prof. emeritus, 1981—. Active Menlo Park Master Plan Com., 1955-56. Served to comdr. USNR, 1942-63. Mem. ABA, Inter-Am. Bar Assn., Internat. Bar Assn., Oreg. State Bar, Am. Legion, Am. Assn. Ret. Persons, Res. Officers Assn., Ret. Officers Assn., Delta Sigma Pi, Delta Theta Phi, Phi Delta Kappa. Republican. Presbyterian. Club: Rotary (pres. Menlo Park 1952-53, chmn. Rotary Found. scholarships com. Dist. 513 1981-89). Home: 850 Webster St Apt 714 Palo Alto CA 94301-2838 Office: Menlo Coll Menlo Park CA 94025

RUSSELL, MARJORIE ROSE, manufacturing company executive; b. Welcome, Minn., Sept. 3, 1925; d. Emil Frederick and Ella Magdalene (Sothman) Wohlenhaus; m. Kenneth Kollmann Russell, Sept. 15, 1947 (div. May 1973); children: Jennie Rose, Richard Lowell, Laura Eloise, James Wesley. Student, Northwestern Sch., Mpls., 1944-45, St. Paul Bible Inst., 1946-47. Cook U. Minn., Mpls., 1943-45; maintenance person U. Farm Campus/N.W. Schs., St. Paul, 1945-46; clk. Kresge Corp., Mpls., 1945; cook, waitress, mgr. Union City Mission Bible Camp, Mpls., 1944-47; caterer for v.p. Gt. No. R.R., St. Paul, 1947; custodian Old Soldiers Home, St. Paul, 1946; nurse Sister Elizabeth Kenney Polio Hosp., St. Paul, 1946; seamstress Hirsch, Weis, White Stag, Pendleton, Mayfair, Portland, Oreg., 1960-72; owner, operator, contract mgr., creative designer The Brass Needle, Portland, 1972—; contractor Forrester's Sanderson Safety, Scotsco, Nero & Assocs., Gara Gear, Portland, 1972—, Columbia Sportswear; tchr. Indo Chinese Cultural Ctr., Portland, 1982; mfr. of protective chaps and vests for the Pacific Northwest hogging industry. Designer, producer Kisn Bridal Fair, 1969; composer: He Liveth in Me, 1968; prodr. Safety Chaps for Loggers. Sec. Model Cities Com., Portland, 1969; com. mem. Neighborhood Black Christmas Parade, Portland, 1970; custume designer Local Miss Jr. Black Beauty Contest, Portland, 1973; nominating com. Nat. Contract Mgmt. Assn., Portland, 1978; mem. nominating com. Multi-Cultural Sr. Adv. Com., 1988-91. Mem. NAFE, Urban League, Urban League Guild (historian 1991-92), Am. Assn. Ret. Persons, Nat. Contract Mgmt. Assn. Democrat. Mem. United Ch. of Christ. Home and Office: The Brass Needle 2809 NE 12th Ave Portland OR 97212-3219

RUSSELL, MARLOU, psychologist; b. Tucson, June 2, 1956; d. William Herman and Carole Eleanor (Musgrove) McBratney; m. Jan Christopher Russell, Sept. 9, 1989. BA U. Ariz., 1981; MA Calif. Grad. Inst., 1983, PhD, 1987. Lic. psychologist, marriage, family and child counselor. Asst. to pres. Western Psychol. Svcs., L.A., 1978-81; crisis counselor Cedars-Sinai Med. Ctr., L.A., 1980-84; counselor South Bay Therapeutic Clinic, Hawthorne, Calif., 1982-84; psychotherapist PMC Treatment Systems, L.A., 1984-85, Beverly Hills Counseling Ctr., 1984-85, Comprehensive Care Corp., L.A., 1985-86; pvt. practice, L.A., 1986—; counselor Brotman Med. Ctr., L.A., 1982-83, Julia Ann Singer Ctr., L.A., 1984; bd. dirs. Los Angeles Commn. Assaults Against Women, 1987-89. Mem. Internat. Assn. Eating Disorders Profls, Women in Health, Women's Referral Svc., Calif. State Psychol. Assn., Calif. Assn. Marriage & Family Therapists (bd. dirs. 1993-94), Am. Adoption Congress, Westside Bus. Womens Assn. (bd. dirs. 1993-94). Democrat. Office: 1452 26th St Ste 103 Santa Monica CA 90404-3042

RUSSELL, NEWTON REQUA, state senator; b. L.A., June 25, 1927; s. John Henry and Amy (Requa) R.; m. Diane Henderson, Feb. 12, 1953; children: Stephen, Sharon, Julia. BS, U. So. Calif., 1951; postgrad. UCLA, Georgetown U. Spl. agt. Northwestern Mut. Life Ins. Co., Calif., 1954-64; mem. Calif. State Assembly, 1964-74, Calif. Senate, 1974—; vice-chmn. com. on energy, utilities and comm., mem. com. on local govt., vice chmn. com. on fin. and investment, internat. trade, mem. com. on transp., com. ins., joint com. on rules, com. on Pub. Employment and Retirement, select com. on Calif.'s wine industry, mem. Com. on Legis. Ethics, Joint Oversight Com. on Lowering the Cost of Electric Svcs, senate select com. mediation. Mem. Rep. State Central Com. Served with USN, 1945-46. Recipient Outstanding Legislator award Calif. Rep. Assembly, 1968, 76, 81, Mayor's commendation City of Burbank, 1978, Disting. Service award County Suprs. Assn. Calif., 1980, Nat. Rep. Legislator of Yr., 1981, Legislator of Yr. award Los Angeles County Fedn. Rep. Women, 1982, Legislator of Yr. award Calif. Credit Union League, 1983, Paul Harris Fellow award Rotary Found. Rotary Internat., numerous honors from cmty. orgns. and instns. Mem. Rotary Internat., Am. Legion, Delta Tau Delta, Alpha Kappa Phi. Mem. Church on the Way. Office: Office of State Senate 401 N Brand Blvd Ste 424 Glendale CA 91203-2307

RUSSELL, PATRICK JAMES, priest; b. Boise, Idaho, May 10, 1959; s. Glenn Edward and Doralea (Trumble) R. BA, Boise U., 1982; MDiv, St. Patrick's Sem., 1986. Ordained priest Roman Catholic Ch., 1986. Assoc. pastor St. Marks Cath. Ch., Boise, 1986-91; chaplain Chateau de Boise, 1991—, Bishop Kelly H.S., 1993—. Active Nat. Cath. Office for Persons With Disabilities, 1991—, Idaho Vocations Bd., 1992—; founder, dir. Father Russell Charity Golf Scramble for Persons with Chronic Illnesses, 1986—. Named Idaho Handicapped Student of Yr., 1974, Best Actor, Boise Little Theatre, 1979-80, Outstanding Young Man of Am., 1983, 84, 86, 87, Outstanding Youth in Achievement, Cambridge, U.K., Internat. Man of Yr., Cambridge, 1995. Mem. Am. Film Inst., Amnesty Internat., Nat. Theatre Comm. Group (charter), Internat. Soc. Poets (life, award), Internat. Biog. Ctr., Right to Life/Spl. Olympics, Sigma Phi Epsilon. Democrat.

RUSSELL, PAUL EDGAR, electrical engineering educator; b. Roswell, N.Mex., Oct. 10, 1924; s. Rueben Matthias and Mary (Parsons) R.; m. Lorna Margaret Clayshulte, Aug. 29, 1943; children: Carol Potter, Janice Russell Cook, Gregory. BSEE, N.Mex. State U., 1946, BSME, 1947; MSEE, U. Wis., 1950, PhDEE, 1951. Registered elec. engr., Ariz., Minn., S.C. From instr. to asst. prof. elec. engring. U. Wis., Madison, 1947-52; sr. engr., design specialist Gen. Dynamics Corp., San Diego, 1952-54; from prof. to chmn. elec. engring. dept. U. Ariz., Tucson, 1954-63; dean engring. Kans. State U., Manhattan, 1963-67; prof. Ariz. State U., Tempe, 1967-90; dir. engring. Ariz. State U. West, Phoenix, 1985-88; dir. Sch. Constrn. and Tech. Ariz. State U., Tempe, 1988-90; cons. in field, 1954—; programs evaluator, mem. engring. commn. Accreditation Bd. for Engring. and Tech., N.Y.C., 1968-81. Contbr. articles to jours. and chpts. to books. Served as sgt. U.S. Army, 1944-46. Recipient Disting. Service award N.Mex. State U., 1965. Fellow IEEE (life, chmn. Ariz. sect. 1960), Accreditation Bd. Engring. and Tech.; mem. Am. Soc. Engring. Educators. Home: 5902 E Caballo Ln Paradise Valley AZ 85253

RUSSELL, PHILIP COURTNEY, computer consultant; b. Monroe, Maine, Aug. 7, 1925; s. Emmet and Amy Melvina (Dyer) R.; m. Bolette Grant, Sept. 11, 1947; 1 child, Jane Ann. Student, Wheaton (Ill.) Coll., 1942-43. Commd. USN, 1942-62, advanced through grades to sr. chief journalist, ret., 1962; pub. affairs officer USN Civil Svc., various locations, 1962-80; pub. rels. cons. Camarillo, Calif., 1980-83; computer cons. Waldport, Oreg., 1984—. Author: Job Interviewing for Women, 1978, Can You Start Monday, 1980, Mouse Droppings Book of Macintosh Hints, vols. I and II, 1986-88; author booklet: Women and Federal Jobs, 1977; contbr. articles to profl. jours. Recipient Outstanding Svc. awards, USN, 1969-80, Freedom Found. award, 1963-70; named Journalist of the Yr. Dept. of Navy, 1965. Mem. corvallis Macintosh Users Group (editor, 1984-92, bd. dirs. 1992—). Democrat. Home: 1420 SW Crest Cir Waldport OR 97394-9726

RUSSELL, THOMAS ARTHUR, lawyer; b. Corona, Calif., Aug. 2, 1953; s. Larry Arthur Russell and Patricia Helena (Collins) Heath; m. Mary Ellen Leach, June 20, 1992; 1 child, Trevor James Russell. BS, U. Calif., Berkeley, 1976; JD, U. So. Calif., 1982. Bar: Calif. 1983, U.S. Dist. Ct. (cen. dist.) Calif. 1983, U.S. Ct. Appeals (9th cir.) 1986, U.S. Supreme Ct. 1988. Law clk. Calif. Ct. Appeal, L.A., 1981; assoc. Graham & James, Long Beach, Calif., 1982-88; ptnr. Williams Woolley Cogswell Nakazawa & Russell, Long Beach, 1988—; speaker, panelist Nat. Marine Bankers Assn., Chgo. 1987—; bd. dirs., Ctr. Internat. Comml. Arbitration, 1991—, Internat. Bus. Assn. So. Calif., 1989—, pres. 1994—; lectr. Pacific Admiralty Seminar, 1992. Author: (with others) Benedict on Admiralty, 1995, Recreational Boating Law, 1992. Mem. ABA (Bronze Key award 1982, maritime fin. subcom., chmn. 1994—), Maritime Law Assn. U.S. (proctor, fin. and recreational boating coms., chmn. subcom. on recreational boating edn. 1991—), Calif. Bar Assn., L.A. County Bar Assn., Long Beach Bar Assn., Legion of Lex. Am. Inn of Ct. (barrister). Republican. Roman Catholic. Home: 7 Mustang Rd Rancho Palos Verdes CA 90275-5250

RUSSI, JOHN JOSEPH, priest, educational administrator; b. San Francisco, Oct. 27, 1939; s. Frank John and Catherine Mary (Carroll) R. BA, Chaminade U., 1962; STL, U. Fribourg, Switzerland, 1967; MA, U. San Francisco, 1978; PhD, Kennedy We. U., 1993. Cert. secondary tchr., jr.

coll. tchr., marriage, family, child counselor, Calif. Tchr. St. Louis Sch., Honolulu, 1961-62, pres., 1988—; tchr. Riordan High Sch., San Francisco, 1962-63; tchr., counselor, prin., pres. Archbishop Mitty High Sch., San Jose, Calif., 1967-88; regent Archbishop Mitty High Sch., 1990—, Chaminade U., Honolulu, 1988—; bd. dirs. St. Anthony Sch., Wailuku, Hawaii, 1989—. Bd. dirs. Kukui Gardens, Honolulu, 1988. Mem. Waialae Country Club. Democrat. Roman Catholic. Home: 3140 Waialae Ave Honolulu HI 96816-1510 Office: St Louis Sch 3142 Waialae Ave Honolulu HI 96816-1510

RUSSIN, ROBERT ISAIAH, sculptor, educator; b. N.Y.C., Aug. 26, 1914; s. Uriel and Olga (Winnett) R.; m. Adele Mutchnick, May 21, 1937; children: Joseph Mark, Lincoln David, Uriel Robin. BA, CCNY, 1933, MS, 1935; postgrad. (Inst. fellow), Beaux Arts Inst. Design, 1935-36. Tchr. sculpture Copper Union Art Inst., N.Y.C., 1944-47; prof. art U. Wyo., Laramie, 1947-86; prof., artist-in-residence U. Wyo., 1976-85, Disting. prof. emeritus, 1985—. One-man shows Tucson Fine Arts Ctr., 1966, Colorado Springs (Colo.) Fine Arts Ctr., 1967, Palm Springs (Calif.) Desert Mus., Chas. G. Bowers Meml. Mus., Judah L. Magnes Meml. Mus., Berkeley, Calif.; retrospective one-man exhbn. Nat. Gallery Modern Art, Santo Domingo, Dominican Republic, 1976, Tubac Ctr. of the Arts, Ariz., 1987, Riggins Gallery, Scottsdale, Ariz., 1989, Fine Arts Mus., U. Wyo., 1991; sculpture commns. include 2 8-foot metal figures, Evanston (Ill.) Post Office, 1939, three life-size carved figures, Conshohocken (Pa.) Post Office, 1940, Benjamin Franklin Monument, U. Wyo., 1957, Bust of Lincoln, Lincoln Mus., Washington, (now in Gettysburg Mus.), 1959, Lincoln Monument atop summit Lincoln Hwy., (now U.S. Interstate 80), Wyo, 1959, monumental bas-relief bronze Cheyenne (Wyo.) Fed. Bldg, 1966, two carved wood walls, Denver Fed. Bldg., 1966, monumental fountain, City of Hope Med. Ctr., Los Angeles, 1966-67, statue, Brookhaven (N.Y.) Nat. Lab., 1968, life-size bronze sculpture fountain, Pomona Coll., 1969, monumental bronze sculpture Prometheus Natrona County (Wyo.) Pub. Library, 1974, Man and Energy, Casper (Wyo.) C. of C., 1974, 12-foot marble carving Menorah Med. Ctr., Kansas City, Mo., 1975, Einstein and Gershwin medals Magnes Meml. Mus, Berkeley, Nat. Mus. Art, Santo Domingo, Dominican Republic, 1975, monumental fountain, Galleria d'Arte Moderna, Santo Domingo, 1977, Duarte Monument, Santo Domingo, 1977, 30 foot steel and water fountain monument City Hall, Casper, 1980, marble and bronze monument, Lincoln Centre, Dallas, 1982, acrylic steel and bronze monument, Herschler State Office Bldg., Cheyenne, 1984, marble monument, U. Wyo., Laramie, 1985, portrait head Charles Bluhdorn, chmn. Gulf & Western, 1975, portrait bust Pres. J. Balaguer of Dominican Republic, 1975, portrait head G. Wilson Knight, Shakespearean actor and scholar, 1975, 2 12-foot bronze figures The Greeting and the Gift for Bicentennial Commn., Cheyenne, 1976, monumental marble head of Juan Pablo Duarte liberator Dominican Republic, Santo Domingo, 1976, marble sculpture Trio, U. Wyo., 1985, Isaac B. Singer medal for Magnes Mus., 1983, monumental Holocaust Figure Tucson Jewish Community Ctr., 1989, granite monument Chthonodynamis, Dept. Energy Bldg., Washington, 1992, bust Hon. Milward Simpson, 1993, bust James Forest U. Wyo., 1993, bronze statue Univ. Med. Ctr., Tuscon, 1995; contbr. articles to profl. jours. Recipient awards sec. fine arts U.S. Treasury, 1939, 40, Lincoln medal U.S. Congress, 1959, Alfred G.B. Steel award Pa. Acad. Fine Arts, 1961, medal of Order of Duarte Sanchez y Mella, Dominican Republic, 1977; Ford Found. fellow, 1953. Mem. Nat. Sculpture Conf. (exec. bd.), Sculptors Guild, Nat. Sculpture Soc., AIA, AAUP, Coll. Art Internat. Inst. Arts and Letters, Phi Beta Kappa (hon.). Home: 61 N Frk Rd Centennial WY 82055 also: 1160 Placita Salubre Green Valley AZ 85614

RUSSO, ALVIN LEON, obstetrician/gynecologist; b. Buffalo, Dec. 2, 1924; s. Anthony Joseph and Sarah (Leone) R.; m. Mary Rose Hehir, Sept. 19, 1953; children: Mary B., Sally A. Silvestri, Daniel J., Jeanne Wotherspoon, Margaret Battaile, Terri A., Anthony A. Student, Baylor U., Waco, Tex., 1943-44, U. Iowa, 1944; MD, U. Kans., Kansas City, 1949. Diplomate Am. Bd. Obstetrics and Gynecology. Intern, then resident E. J. Meyer Meml. Hosp., Buffalo, 1949-55; Fellow in gynocological oncology Roswell Park Meml. Inst., Buffalo, 1955; pvt. practice ob/gyn. San Bernardino, Calif., 1955-89; med. dir. San Bernardino Community Hosp., 1989-92; ret., 1992; bd. dirs. San Bernardino Community Hosp., 1982-89, chmn. bd., 1982-85. Pres. San Bernardino unit Am. Cancer Soc., 1961-62; bd. dirs. More Attractive Community Found. Capt. USAF, 1951-53. Knight, St. John of Jerusalem, 1986--; recipient Distinguished Member award Boy Scouts Am., 1987. Fellow Am. Coll. Ob-Gyns.; mem. AMA, Calif. Med. Assn., N.Y. Acad. Scis., S.W. Ob-Gyn. Soc. (coun. mem. 1989—, v.p. 1992), San Bernardino-Riverside Ob-Gyn. Soc. (pres. 1966), Lions Internat. (dep. dist. gov. 1962-63), Serra Club (pres. San Bernardino chpt.), Arrowhead Country Club (bd. dirs., pres.). Republican. Roman Catholic. Home: 3070 Pepper Tree Ln San Bernardino CA 92404-2313

RUSSO, LAURA, gallery director; b. Waterbury, Conn., Mar. 7, 1943; d. Lawrence and Lillian A. (Russo) Kaplan; m. John I. Lawrence, May 6, 1962 (div. 1974); children: Maia Giosi, Dylan Russo. Cert., Pacific N.W. Coll. Art, 1975. Art instr. Tucker Maxon Oral Sch., Portland, Oreg., 1970-74, Pacific N.W. Coll. of Art, Portland, 1977-78; assoc. dir. Fountain Fine Arts, Seattle, 1981-82; asst. dir. The Fountain Gallery of Art, Portland, 1975-86; owner, dir. The Laura Russo Gallery, Portland, 1986—; lectr. Seattle Art Mus., 1987, Portland State Coll., 1992; juror Oreg. Sch. Design, Portland, 1988, Western Oreg. State Coll. 1992, Beaverton Arts Commn., 1992; com. mem. Oreg. Com. for Nat. Mus. Women in Arts, 1988; lectr. Oregon Hist. Soc., 1990. Mem. com. award and grants Met. Arts Commn., Portland, 1988, 89; mem. P.N.C.A.; juror Art in Pub. Schs. Program, 1990. Mem. Alumni Friends, Contemporary Arts Coun. (program chmn., v.p. 1989-91), Portland Art Mus. (search com. 1993-94), Oreg. Art Inst., Friends Print Soc., Oreg. Art Inst., L.A. Mus. Contemporary Art, Seattle Art Mus. Democrat. Office: Laura Russo Gallery 805 NW 21st Ave Portland OR 97209-1408

RUST, JOHN LAURENCE, manufacturing company executive; b. Normal, Ill., June 23, 1925; married. Student, Ill. Wesleyan U., 1943; BA, U.S. Mil. Acad., West Point, N.Y., 1949. Enlisted U.S. Army, 1943; resigned from active duty Ill. Army N.G., 1954; owner, mgr. Chevrolet dealership, Bloomington, Ill., 1954-60; pres. Rust Tractor Co., Albuquerque, 1960—; chmn. Rust Equipment Co., Albuquerque, 1967—; bd. dirs. Sunwest Bank Albuquerque, Mountain States Mut. Casualty Co., Fed. Home Loan Bank Dallas. Campaign chmn. United Community Fund, Albuquerque, 1965, pres., 1967-68; bd. regents N.Mex. Mil. Inst., Roswell, 1962-74; vice chmn. Presbyn. Healthcare Services, Albuquerque, 1968-82, chmn., trustee, 1982-83; pres. U. N.Mex. Found., Inc., 1980-84, bd. dirs. 1980—; vice chmn. Southwest Community Health Services, Albuquerque, 1981-83, chmn., 1983—. Served to col. USAR, ret. Home: 3550 Tucson Ct NW Albuquerque NM 87120-1124 Office: Rust Tractor Co 4000 Osuna Rd NE Albuquerque NM 87109-4423

RUSTAD, BILLIE JO, check recovery business owner; b. Anaconda, Mont., Jan. 30, 1971; d. Philip Roy and Betty Lou (Wolfe) Schaff; m. Lenny Rustad, May 15, 1993; children: Cody Allen, Bryson Alexander. Grad., high sch., 1989. Sec. McKeon Law Firm, Anaconda, Mont., 1989-91; legal sec. Haxby & Somers, Butte, Mont., 1991-93; owner, operator Check Patrol, Anaconda, 1993—; owner/operator B & L Collections, Anaconda, 1993—. Home: 820 Birch St Anaconda MT 59711-2444 Office: Check Patrol 307 E Park St Rm 310A Anaconda MT 59711-2300

RUSTAGI, JAGDISH SHARAN, statistics educator; b. Sikri, India, Aug. 13, 1923; came to U.S., 1961; s. Chhotey Lal and Mora Devi (Rustagi); m. Kamla Rastogi, June 12, 1949; children: Pradip, Pramod, Madhu. B.S., Delhi U., 1944, M.S., 1946; Ph.D., Stanford U., 1956. Lectr. Hindu Coll., Delhi U., 1946-52; research asst. Stanford U., 1952-55; asst. prof. Carnegie Inst. Tech., 1955-57, Mich. State U., 1957-58; reader Aligarh U., 1958-60; asst. dir. biometrics U. Cin., 1960-63; assoc. prof. Ohio State U., 1963-65, prof. math., 1965-70, prof. statistics, 1970-88, chmn. dept. stats., 1979-83, 84-88, chmn., prof. emeritus, 1988—; vis. prof. U. Philippines, 1988-89; vis. scientist Advanced Mfg. Process Control, IBM, 1990-92. Stanford U. fellow, 1952-53. Fellow Am. Statis. Assn., Inst. Math. Statistics, Indian Soc. Med. Statistics; mem. Internat. Statistics Inst., Sigma Xi. Home: 18531 Oak Dr Monte Sereno CA 95030-3125

RUSTAM, MARDI AHMED, film and television producer, publisher; b. Kirkuk, Iraq, Nov. 25, 1932; came to U.S., 1954; s. Ahmed Baker and Fatima (Behram) R.; m. Sarah Alice Shoup, Apr. 15, 1960; children: Sandra Nesreen, Karima Marguerite. BFA, Art Inst. Chgo., 1960; MFA, U. So. Calif., 1973. Free-lance film editor L.A., 1962-69, free-lance motion picture technician, 1962-72; film producer Mars Prodns. Corp., L.A., 1972—; pub. The Tolucan, Toluca Lake, Calif., 1984—. Cons. Nat. Assn. Arab Ams., Washington, 1980—, Am. Arab Anti-Discrimination Com., Washington, 1984—. Recipient Best Horror Film award, 1977, Outstanding Film of Yr. award London Film Festival, 1977, Golden Scroll Merit award Acad. Sci. Fiction, Fantasy and Horror, 1984, Svc. award, 1993, Saturn award Acad. Sci. Fiction, Fantasy and Horror, 1995. Mem. L.A. Press Club, Calif. Newspaper Pubs. Assn., Toluca Lake C. of C. (bd. dirs., Bus. of Yr. award Tolucan Newspaper 1994), Lions, Elks. Office: Mars Prodns Corp 10215 Riverside Dr Toluca Lake CA 91602-2501

RUSZKIEWICZ, CAROLYN MAE, newspaper editor; b. Tucson, Nov. 10, 1946; d. Robert Frank and Charlotte Ruth (Hadley) Knapton; m. Joseph Charles Ruszkiewicz, July 11, 1969. BA, Calif. State U., Long Beach, 1971, MA, 1973. Reporter Long Beach (Calif.) Press-Telegram, 1968-85, consumer editor, 1985-86, lifestyle editor, 1986-89, regional news editor, 1989-91, city editor, 1991-95, asst. mng. editor, 1995—. Office: Long Beach Press-Telegram 604 Pine Ave Long Beach CA 90844-0003

RUTES, WALTER ALAN, architect; b. N.Y.C., Sept. 21, 1928; s. Jack and Sarah (Ogur) R.; m. Helene Darville, Apr. 2, 1952; children: Daniel J., Linda Lee. B.Arch. (Sands Meml. medal 1950), Cornell U., 1950; fellow city planning, MIT, 1951; postgrad., Harvard U. Grad. Sch. Design, 1978. Cert. Nat. Council Archtl. Registration Bds. Assoc. ptnr. Skidmore, Owings & Merrill, N.Y.C., 1951-72; v.p. John Carl Warnecke & Assocs., N.Y.C., 1972-74; staff v.p. Intercontinental Hotels Corp., N.Y.C., 1974-80; dir. architecture Holiday Inns, Inc., Memphis, 1980-83; dir. design The Sheraton Corp., Boston, 1983-85; chmn 9 Tek Ltd. Hotel Cons., 1985—; chmn. adv. bd. Hult Fellowships for Constrn. Industry, 1968-75, Architects and Engrs. Com. New Bldg. Code, 1968; mem. zoning adv. com. N.Y.C. Planning Commn., 1970; lectr. in field, 1968—; mem. steering com. UNESCO Council Tall Bldgs. and Urban Habitat, 1980—; vis. prof. Cornell-Essec Grad. Program; vis. prof. Nova U. Author: Hotel Planning and Design, New Trends in Resort Design and Development; (software system) SHAPE, Megatrends and Marketecture; contbr. articles to profl. jours.; prin. works include Lincoln Center Library for Performing Arts, N.Y.C., 1967, Am. Republic Ins. Co. Nat. Hdqrs., Des Moines, 1967, HUD Apts., Jersey City, 1972, Merrill Lynch Bldg., N.Y.C., 1973, Tour Fiat, Paris, 1974, Aid Assn. for Luths. Nat. Hdqrs., Appleton, Wis., 1976, Semiramis Intercontinental Hotel, Cairo, 1985, Intercontinental, Jeddah, 1983, Embassy Suites Internat., 1985, Universal City Hotel Complex, L.A., 1986, TechWorld Conv. Hotel, Washington, 1986, Sheraton Fairplex Conv. Ctr., L.A., 1992, Orlando Conv. Ctr. Hotel, 1993, Winter Olympiad Media Complex, Norway, 1993, Ephesus Resort Complex, Turkey, 1986, Royal Christiania Hotel, Oslo, Norway, 1991, EuroFrance Leisure Park Complex, Cannes, 1993, Kuna Hills Multi Resort, Guam, 1994. Recipient Platinum Circle award Hotel Design Industry, 1988. Fellow AIA; mem. Ethical Culture Soc. Office: 8501 N 84th Pl Scottsdale AZ 85258-2419 also: 25 Richbell Rd White Plains NY 10605-4110

RUTH, CRAIG, business executive; b. July 18, 1930; s. Clarence Miller and Kathryn Dorothy (Buch) R.; m. Marion Nelson, Apr. 19, 1958; children: Robert Nelson, Lee Kathryn, William Walter, Ann Alva. BA, Muskingum Coll., 1952; postgrad., Northwestern U., 1956. Tchr., coach N.Y.C. and Chgo., 1955-66; dir. mktg. Great Lakes Carbon Co., Los Angeles, 1966-68; exec. v.p. Ketchum, Peck & Tooley, Los Angeles, 1968-75; pres. Tooley & Co., Los Angeles, 1975—; mgr. Two Rodeo Dr., Beverly Hills; bd. dirs. Los Angeles Internat. Bus. Ctr.; council mem. Urban Land Inst., 1982—. Bd. dirs. Bldg. Owner & Mgrs. Assn.; chmn. Elgin Baylor & Jerry West Nights Los Angeles Lakers, Ed Sherman Night, Muskingum Coll., Los Angeles, Muskingum Coll. Reunion Com.; vice chmn. USMC Scholarship Ball. Capt. USMC, 1953-55. Named one of Outstanding Men of Am. C. of C., 1965; recipient Humanitarian award Nat. Conf. Christians and Jews, 1988. Mem. Internat. Assn. Corp. Real Estate Execs., Spinal Cord Soc., 3rd Marine Divsn. (life), Japan Am. Cultural Coun., Beverly Hills Econ. Devel. Coun., Bus. Devel. Coun. (beverly Hills chpt.), Big Ten Club. Republican. Presbyterian. Home: 4045 Miraleste Dr Rancho Palos CA 90275-6574 Office: Tooley & Co 11150 Santa Monica Blvd Ste 20 Los Angeles CA 90025-3386

RUTHER, CHRISTINE L., biomedical engineer; b. Dayton, Ohio, May 17, 1963; d. Frank J. and Nancy L. (Patten) R.; m. Gregory R. Adams, Sept. 1992. BS in Physics, Xavier U., Cin., 1985; MS in Biomed. Engring., Ohio State U., 1990. Physics and math tchr. Chaminade-Julienne High Sch., Dayton, 1985-86, chmn. dept. sci., 1986-87; teaching assoc. Ohio State U., Columbus, 1987-90; rsch. asst. Bionetics for NASA, Kennedy Space Ctr., Fla., 1991; clin. engr. William Beaumont Hosp., Royal Oak, Mich., 1991-92, Biomed. Cons. Svcs., Irvine, Calif., 1993-95; dir. product devel. and regulatory affairs AirBed Corp., Anaheim, Calif., 1995—. Mem. IEEE, Assn. for Women in Sci.

RUTHERFORD, GEORGE WILLIAMS, III, preventive physician; b. San Diego, Apr. 6, 1952; s. G. Williams and Anna Gwyn (Dearing) R.; m. Lisa Anderson, Aug. 24, 1974 (div. 1984); children: Alicia Gwyn, George Williams IV; m. Mary Workman, Feb. 23, 1985; children: Alexandra Catherine, Anne Elizabeth Martha, Hugh Thomas Gwyn. AB in Classics, Stanford U., 1975, BS in Chemistry, 1975, AM in History, 1975; MD, Duke U., 1978. Diplomate Am. Bd. Pediatrics, Nat. Bd. Med. Examiners; cert. physician, surgeon, Calif., lic. physician, surgeon, N.Y. Intern U. Calif. Med. Ctr., San Diego, 1978-79; resident U. Calif. Med. Ctr., Hosp. for Children, San Diego, 1979-80, Hosp. for Sick Children, Toronto, 1980-81; chief resident Children's Hosp. and Health Ctr., San Diego, 1981-82; EIS officer divsn. viral diseases, divsn. field svcs Epidemology Office Ctrs. for Disease Control, Atlanta, 1982-84; dir. divsn. immunization, acting dir. divsn. tropical disease N.Y.C. Dept. Health, 1983-85; med. epidemologist AIDS program Ctrs. for Disease Control, San Francisco Dept. Pub. Health, 1985-87; from med. dir. to dir. AIDS office San Francisco Dept. Pub. Health, 1986-90; chief, infectious disease br. and state epidemologist Calif. Dept Health, Berkeley, 1990-92, dep. dir. prevention svcs. and state epidemologist, 1992—, state health office, 1993-95; assoc. dean adminstrn., prof. epidemiology/health adminstrn. Sch. Pub. Health, U. Calif., Berkeley, 1995—; transport physician Children's Hosp. and Health Ctr., San Diego, 1981; clin. asst. prof. pediatrics Emory U., Atlanta, 1982-83, Cornell U., N.Y.C., 1984-85, U. Calif., San Francisco, 1986-92, asst. clin. prof. epidemology and biostats., 1987-92, family and cmty. medicine, 1988-90; assoc. adj. prof. epidemology, biotstats. and pediatrics, 1992—; assoc. clin. prof. cmty. health U. Calif., Davis, 1981—; cons. Pan-Am. Health Orgn., S.Am., 1986-89, Ctrs. Disease Control, Atlanta, 1987—, WHO, 1988-90. Contbr. numerous articles to profl. jours., chpts. to books; co-translator cardiology teaching manual, other Spanish med. articles; editor in chief Calif. Morbidity, 1990-92; mem. editl. bd. Calif. AIDS Update, 1988—, Current Issues in Pub. Health, 1993—; referee: AIDS, 1988—, Am. Jour. Pub. Health, 1989—, Brit. Med. Jour., 1994—, Internat. Jour. Epidemology, 19916, Jour. Acquired Immune Deficiency Syndrome, 1989—, New Eng. Jour. Medicine, 1989—, Western Jour. Medicine, 1989—. Mem. numerous profl. adv. coms., task forces, etc. which aid govt. and charitable orgns. in work against infectious disease, especially AIDS. Commdr. USPHS, 1982—. Fellow Am. Acad. Pediatrics; mem. APHA, Am. Assn. for History of Medicine, Am. Soc. Tropical Medicine and Hygiene, Bay Area Communicable Disease Exch., Calif. Med. Assn., Infectious Diseases Soc. Am., No. Calif. Pub. Health Assn., Internat. AIDS Soc., Soc. for Epidemiol. Rsch., Soc. for Pediatric Epidemiol. Rsch., Calif./Baja Calif. Binat. Health Coun., Conf. of State and Territorial Epidemiologists, Assn. State and Territorial Health Ofcls., U.S.-Mex. Border Health Assn., others. Republican. Episcopalian. Office: U Calif Berkeley Sch Pub Health 140 Warren Hall Berkeley CA 94720

RUTHERFORD, REID, finance company executive; b. Morristown, N.J., Dec. 30, 1952; s. Clinton Homer and Bonnie Beth (Bergner) R.; m. Beth Ann Husak, Apr. 3, 1977; children: Ian Michael, Laurel Bryce, Corinne Leigh, Alyse Allyne. BA, Pepperdine U., 1975; MBA, Stanford U., 1981. Exec. v.p. Analytics, Inc., N.Y.C., 1976-79; pres. Softlink Corp., Santa Clara, Calif., 1981-83, Research Applications for Mgmt., Menlo Park, Calif., 1984-85, Concord Growth Corp., Palo Alto, Calif., 1985—; with EXXE Data Corp., Palo Alto, 1993—. Contbr. articles to profl. jours. Office: EXXE Data Corp 1170 E Meadow Dr Palo Alto CA 94303-4234

RUTHERFORD, THOMAS TRUXTUN, II, state senator, lawyer; b. Columbus, Ohio, Mar. 3, 1947; s. James William and Elizabeth Whiting (Colby) R.; m. Linda Sue Rogers, Aug. 28, 1965 (div.); 1 child, Jeremy Todd. BBA, U. N.Mex., 1970, JD, 1982. Page, reading clk. N.Mex. State Legislature, 1960-65; mem. N.Mex. Atty. Gen. Environ. Adv. Commn., 1972; radio broadcaster Sta. KOB Radio and TV, 1963-72; mem. N.Mex. Senate, Albuquerque, 1972—, majority whip, 1978-88, chmn. rules com., 1988—, chmn. econ. devel. and new tech. interim com., mem. sci. and new tech. oversight com.; pres. Rutherford & Assocs., Albuquerque, 1978-83; pvt. practice, Albuquerque, 1983—; former bd. dirs. Union Savs. Bank, Albuquerque; past chmn. Albuquerque Cable TV adv. bd.; mem. Southwest Regional Energy Council, N.Mex. Gov.'s Commn. on Public Broadcasting; bd. dirs., v.p. Rocky Mountain Corp. for Pub. Broadcasting; mem. Am. Council Young Polit. Leaders, del. mission to Hungary, Austria, Greece, 1983; mem. Fgn. Trade Adv. Com. Bd. Econ. Devel. and Tourism; trade del. to People's Republic of China, 1985. N.Mex. Broadcasting Assn. scholar, 1970. Home: 4719 Marquette Ave NE Albuquerque NM 87108-1267 also: PO Box 1610 Albuquerque NM 87103-1610

RUTHERFORD, WILLIAM DRAKE, investment executive, lawyer; b. Marshalltown, Iowa, Jan. 14, 1939; s. William Donald and Lois Esther (Drake) R.; m. Janice W. Rutherford, Feb. 4, 1965 (div. Mar. 1982); children: Wayne Donald, Melissa Drake; m. Karen Anderegg, Jan. 2, 1994. B.S., U. Oreg., 1961; LL.B., Harvard U., 1964. Bar: Oreg. 1964, U.S. Dist. Ct. Oreg. 1966. Assoc. Maguire, Kester & Cosgrave, Portland, Oreg., 1966-69; house counsel May & Co., Portland, 1969-70, pvt. practice, 1970-71; pvt. practice McMinnville, Oreg., 1971-84; mem. Oreg. Ho. of Reps., Salem, 1977-84; state treas. State of Oreg., Salem, 1984-87; chmn. Oreg. Investment Coun., Salem, 1986-87; exec. v.p., dir. U.S. and Australia ops. ABD Internat. Mgmt. Corp., N.Y.C., 1987-88, pres., chief exec. officer, bd. dirs., 1988-89; pres., bd. dirs. Societé Gen. Touche Remnant, 1990-93; dir. spl. projects Metallgesellschaft Corp., N.Y.C., 1994—. 1st lt. U.S. Army, 1964-66. Recipient Contbn. to Individual Freedom award ACLU, 1981. Mem. Nat. Assn. State Treas. (exec. v.p. 1985, 86, pres. western region 1985, 86), Nat. Assn. State Auditors, Comptr. and Treas. (exec. com. 1987). Republican. Home: 6978 SW Foxfield Ct Portland OR 97225-6054

RUTLAND, HENRY LEE, educational administrator, consultant; b. San Mateo, Calif., Mar. 5, 1947; s. Samuel Peter and Inez (Thomas) R.; children: Erik, Adam. BA in Am. History, U. Calif., Berkeley, 1969, postgrad., 1970-74. Student affairs officer, dir. ednl. opportunity program Calif. State U., Chico, 1975-78; dir. spl. svcs. U. Calif., Berkeley, 1978-81; coord. devel. Phoenix Recycling Svc., Newark, Calif., 1981-83; exec. dir. Willie Mays "Say Hey" Found., Inc., Redwood City, Calif., 1982-83; tech. recruiter Seigal and Bishop, Inc., San Francisco, 1983-85, Tech Search, San Francisco, 1985-86; dir. employment and tng. svcs. San Diego Urban League, 1986-87; fundraiser La Mesa, Calif., 1987-88; dir. grad. student affirmative action, asst. to grad. dean U. Calif., San Diego, 1988-92; exec. dir. Young Black Scholars Program 100 Black Men of L.A., Inc., 1992-93; cons. Peterson's Guides Inc., 1993, U. Calif. San Francisco, 1993, U. Medicine and Dentistry N.J., Newark, 1991. Bd. dirs. Paradise Valley Hosp. Found., San Diego, 1986, Outward Bound San Diego, 1988-89.

RUTLEDGE, ALBERT HENRY, architectural engineer, architect; b. Nashville, June 11, 1928; s. Albert Henry and Emma Jame (Hughes) R.; m. Naomi L. Jenkins, May 9, 1954 (div. July 1965); children: Albert Henry III, Darryl Walker; m. Iva D. Goodwin, Nov. 10, 1965. Student, Cleve. Engring. Inst., 1950-52, John Carrol U., 1954-57; BS in Engring. and Mgmt., Calif. U., Long Beach, 1972. Cert. plant engr. Am. Inst. Plant Engrs.; registered profl. engr., Calif. Piping designer, engr. Fluor Corp., Irvine, Calif., 1966-70; engr. City of Compton, Calif., 1971-73, R.M. Parsons Co., Pasadena, Calif., 1973-76; facilities engr. GE, Mojave, Calif., 1979-87; arch., engr. A.H. Rutledge & Assocs., California City, Calif., 1987—. Mem., deacon First Missionary Bapt. Ch., Ridgecrest, Calif., 1993; mem., usher First Bapt. Ch., Calif., 1994; active Concern Citizens, California City, 1994. Mem. Free and Accepted Masons (worshipful master). Home: 7742 Dogbane Ave California City CA 93505-1818

RUTLEDGE, JOE, pathologist, scientist; b. Lewisburg, Tenn., Aug. 18, 1950; s. Edward and Geraldine (Cathey) R.; m. Ellen Armistead, May 15, 1976; children: Jack, Rosemary. BS, Rhodes Coll., 1972; MD, Vanderbilt U., 1976. Diplomate Am. Bd. Pediatric Pathology, Am. Bd. Anatomic and Clin. Pathology. Asst. prof. pathology Univ. Tex. Southwestern Medical Sch., Dallas, 1980-88; assoc. prof. lab. medicine U. Washington, Seattle, 1988—; mem. adv. bd. Human Developmental Anatomy Ctr., Washington, 1992—; collaborative rschr. Oak Ridge (Tenn.) Nat. Lab., 1982—. Contbr. chpts. to books; contbr. articles to profl. jours. Adv. bd. Healthcare Profl. West Washington, Seattle, 1992—, March of Dimes. Fellow Coll. Am. Pathology (practice com. 1980-95); mem. Soc. for Pediatric Pathology (coun. 1988-94), Am. Assn. Clin. Chemistry (pediatric com. 1980-94), Am. Soc. Clin. Pathology, Am. Soc. Human Genetics. Office: Childrens Hosp & Med Ctr Lab Ch 37 4800 Sand Point Way NE Seattle WA 98105-3901

RUTLEDGE, WILLIAM P., manufacturing company executive; b. 1942. BS, Lafayette Coll., 1963; MS, George Washington U., 1967. With Bethlehem Steel Corp., 1963-68, foreman; with Stamco Sales Co., 1968-71, sales engr.; successively bus. planner, works mgr., dir. planning, div. mgr. FMC Corp., 1971-86; with Teledyne Inc., 1986—, group exec., v.p., 1987-88, sr. v.p., 1988-90, pres., 1990-91, pres., CEO, 1991—, now also chmn., bd. dirs. Office: Teledyne Inc 1901 Avenue Of The Stars Los Angeles CA 90067-6001*

RUTTENCUTTER, BRIAN BOYLE, holding company/manufacturing company executive; b. Long Beach, Calif., June 15, 1953; s. Wayne Andrew and Florence Mae (Heckman) F.; m. Marilyn Ruth Grubb, Sept. 9, 1978; children: Christi Anne (dec.), Melissa Lyn. BS in Bus. Adminstrn. and Acctg., Biola U., 1976; MBA, Calif. State U., Long Beach, 1983. Cert. mgmt. acct. Controller Fuller Theol. Sem., Pasadena, Calif., 1976-80; dir. gen. acctg. Air Calif., Newport Beach, 1980-84; corp. controller PBS Bldg. Systems, Inc., Anaheim, Calif., 1984-88, v.p. fin. and adminstrn., 1988-93; CFO, v.p. fin. For Better Living, Inc., and The Quikset Orgn., Auburn and Irvine, Calif., 1993—; chmn., vice chmn., fin. commn. City Irvine, Calif., 1990-94. Mem. Drivers for Hwy. Safety, Irvine, Calif., 1986; bd. dirs. Grace Brethren Ch., Long Beach, 1978-80; bd. dirs. Woodbridge Cmty. Ch., Irvine, 1986-88, 91-92, vice chmn., 1991, chmn., 1992; v.p. Greater Irvine Rep. Assembly, 1990—, treas., 1991. Mem. Inst. Cert. Mgmt. Accts., Inst. Mgmt. Accts., Fin. Execs. Inst. (dir. Orange County chpt.). Republican. Baptist. Home: 14262 Wyeth Ave Irvine CA 92714-1838 Office: 17791 Fitch Ave Irvine CA 92714

RUTTER, DEBORAH FRANCES, orchestra administrator; b. Pottstown, Pa., Sept. 30, 1956; d. Marshall Anthony and Winifred (Hitz) R. BA, Stanford U., 1978; MBA, U. So. Calif., 1985. Orch. mgr. L.A. Philharm., 1978-86; exec. dir. L.A. Chamber Orch., 1986-92, Seattle Symphony, 1992—. Bd. dirs. AIDS project L.A., 1985-92; active Jr. League L.A., 1982-92. Mem. Am. Symphony Orch. League, Assn. Calif. Symphony Orchs. (pres. 1988-91), Assn. N.W. Symphony Orchs. (bd. dirs. 1993—), Chamber Music Soc. L.A. (bd. dirs. 1987-92), Ojai Festival (pres.'s coun.). Democrat. Episcopalian. Office: Seattle Symphony Ctr House 305 Harrison St Fl 4 Seattle WA 98109-4623*

RUTTER, MARSHALL ANTHONY, lawyer; b. Pottstown, Pa., Oct. 18, 1931; s. Carroll Lennox and Dorothy (Tagert) R.; m. Winifred Hitz, June 6, 1953 (div. 1970); m. Virginia Ann Hardy, Jan. 30, 1971 (div. 1992); children: Deborah Frances, Gregory Russell, Theodore Thomas; m. Terry Susan Knowles, Dec. 19, 1992. BA, Amherst (Mass.) Coll., 1954; JD, U. Pa., 1959. Bar: Calif 1960. Assoc. O'Melveny & Myers, Los Angeles, 1959-65; assoc. Flint & MacKay, Los Angeles, 1965-67, ptnr., 1967-72; ptnr. Rutter, O'Sullivan, Greene & Hobbs, Los Angeles, 1973—. Gov. The Music Ctr. of L.A. County, 1978-86, 89-92; bd. dirs. Chorus Am., Phila., 1987—, pres., 1993-95; bd. dirs., pres. L.A. Master Chorale Assn., 1963-92, chmn., 1992—; vestryman All Saints Ch., Beverly Hills, Calif., 1983-86, 88-90. Mem. ABA, Assn. Bus. Trial Lawyers (bd. dirs. 1980-82), L.A. County Bar Assn.,

Beverly Hills Bar Assn., Century City Bar Assn., English-Speaking Union (various offices L.A. chpt. 1963-91), L.A. Jaycees (bd. dirs. 1964-67). Democrat. Episcopalian. Home: 460 S Oakland Ave Apt 112 Pasadena CA 91101-4003 Office: Rutter O'Sullivan Greene & Hobbs Ste 2700 1900 Avenue Of The Stars Los Angeles CA 90067-4508

RUYBALID, LOUIS ARTHUR, social worker, community development consultant; b. Allison, Colo., Apr. 6, 1925; s. Mike Joseph and Helen Mary (Rodriguez) R.; m. Seraphima Alexander, June 12, 1949; children: Mariana, John. BA, U. Denver, 1946-49, MSW, 1951; PhD, U. Calif., Berkeley, 1970; Professor Ad-Honorem (hon.), Nat. U., Caracas, Venezuela, 1964. Social worker Ariz., Calif., Colo., 1951-62; advisor community devel. Unitarian Service Com., Caracas, 1962-64, U.S. Agy. for Internat. Devel., Rio de Janeiro, Brazil, 1964-66; area coordinator U.S. Office Econ. Opportunity, San Francisco, 1966-68; prof., dept. head U. So. Colo., Pueblo, 1974-80; licensing analyst State of Calif., Campbell, 1984—; prof. sch. of social work Highlands U., Las Vegas, N.Mex., 1988-89; cons. UN, Caracas, 1978, Brazilian Govt., Brazilia, 1964-66, Venezuelan Govt., Caracas, 1962-64. Author: (books) Favela, 1970, Glossary for Hominology, 1978, (research instrument) The Conglomerate Hom., 1976. Mem. exec. com. Pueblo (Colo.) Regional Planning Com., 1974-79, Nat. Advisory com. The Program Agy. United Presbyn. Ch., 1978-79. Served with USN, 1944-46. Recipient Pro Mundo Beneficio medal Brazilian Acad. Human Sci., Sao Paulo, 1976; United Def. Fund fellow U. Calif., Berkeley, 1961-62, Cert. World Leadership Internat. Leaders of Achievement, 1988-89. Mem. NASW (cert.), Ethnic Minority Commn., IMAGE (nat. edn. chair), Am. Hominol. Assn. (nat. pres. 1975-79), U. Calif. Alumni Assn., AARP (minority spokesperson), Phi Beta Kappa, Phi Sigma Iota. Democrat. Home and Office: Ruybalid Assoc Inc 129 Calle Don Jose Santa Fe NM 87501-2364

RUYTER, NANCY LEE CHALFA, dance educator; b. Phila., May 23, 1933; d. Andrew Benedict Chalfa and Lois Elizabeth (Strode) McClary; m. Ralph Markson (div.); m. Hans C. Ruyter, Dec. 7, 1968. BA in History, U. Calif., Riverside, 1964; PhD in History, Claremont Grad. Sch., 1970. Tchr. theater dept. Pomona Coll., 1965-72; instr. dance program U. Calif., Riverside, 1972-76, acting chair dance program, 1974-75; instr. dance dept. UCLA, 1976; instr. phys. edn. dept. Orange Coast Coll., 1976-77; asst. prof. dept. phys. edn. and dance Tufts U., 1977-78; asst. prof. phys. edn. dept. Calif. State U., Northridge, 1978-82; asst. prof., then assoc. prof. dance dept. U. Calif., Irvine, 1982—, assoc. dean Sch. Fine Arts, 1984-88, chair dept. dance, 1989-91; presenter in field. Appeared with Jasna Planina Folk Ensemble, 1972-77, 78-79, Di Falco and Co., 1955-57; choreographer, dir. numerous coll. dance prodns.; contbr. articles, revs. to profl. publs.; author: Reformers and Visionaries: The Americanization of the Art of Dance, 1979. Mem. Am. Soc. Theatre Rsch., Bulgarian Studies Assn., Congress on Rsch. in Dance (bd. dirs. 1977-80, pres. 1981-85), Folk Dance Fedn., Internat. Fedn. Theatre Rsch., Soc. Dance Rsch., Soc. Ethnomusicology, Soc. Dance History Scholars (steering com. 1980-81), Spanish Dance Soc., Theatre Libr. Assn. Office: U Calif-Irvine Dept Dance Irvine CA 92717

RYALS, CONNIE, state government department administrator; b. Nampa, Idaho, June 6, 1952; d. Samuel Wesley and Elaine Louise (Pace) Beeson; m. Steven Elden Ryals, April 20, 1969. Audit clerk Albertson's Inc., Boise, Idaho, 1970-73, adminstrv. sec., 1973-75, staff acct., 1975, coord. accts. payable, 1975-78, acctg. supr. pvt. label, 1978-82, mgr. sales audit dept., 1982-87; adminstr. internal ops. Idaho Dept. Adminstrn., Boise, Idaho, 1987-91; dir. Idaho Dept. of Employment, Boise, Idaho, 1991—; mem. bd. dirs. Idaho Total Quality Inst., 1991—, Interstate Conf. of Employment Security Adminstrs., Washington, 1993—; mem. strategic planning com. Boise State U., 1993; mem. steering com. State Employee Compensation Com., Boise, 1993—. Chmn. Govt. Andrus/Robert Redford Fund Raiser, Boise, 1989. Mem. Idaho Total Quality Inst. (dir. 1991—). Office: Employment Dept 317 Main St Boise ID 83735-0001

RYAN, BUDDY (JAMES RYAN), professional football coach; b. Frederick, Okla., Feb. 17, 1931; m. Doris Ward, children: Jim, Rex, Rob, (div. 1966); m. Joanie Clark. Ed., Okla. State U. Football coach, athletic dir. Gainesville, H.S., Gainesville, Okla., 1959-60; defensive coordinator U. Buffalo, 1961-65, Vanderbilt U., Nashville, 1965-66, U. of Pacific, Stockton, Calif., 1966-67; mem. defensive staff N.Y. Jets, 1968-75; defensive line coach Minn. Vikings, 1976-77; defensive coordinator Chgo. Bears, 1978-86; head coach Phila. Eagles, 1986-91; defensive coordinator Houston Oilers, 1993-94; head coach, gen. manager Arizona Cardinals, 1994—; horse breeder Lawrenceburg, Ky., 1977—. Master Sergeant, US Army, Korean War. former Baptist, now Roman Catholic. Office: Arizona Cardinals PO Box 888 Phoenix AZ 85001-0888*

RYAN, CATHRINE SMITH, publisher; b. Calif.; d. Owen W. and Margarette D. Griffin; A.A., Bellevue Jr. Coll., Denver, 1948; grad. Barnes Sch. Commerce, Denver, 1950; student N.Y. Ballet Acad., 1954. Dir. Ballet Workshop, Enumclaw, Wash., 1958-64; dir. confs. and seminars San Francisco Theol. Sem., 1977-80; pres., dir. Cathi, Ltd., pub. and cons. office orgn. and mgmt., San Francisco, 1980—; freelance travel photographer, 1968-80; guest instr. in field; guest lectr. on German rsch. Recipient various certs. of recognition. Republican. Mormon. Author: Face Lifting Exercises, 1980, Sullivan's Chain, 1986; contbr. articles to procedure and policy manuals, geneal. rsch., family histories; translator old German script. Avocation: scuba diving.

RYAN, CLARENCE AUGUSTINE, JR., biochemistry educator; b. Butte, Mont., Sept. 29, 1931; s. Clarence A. Sr. and Agnes L. (Duckham) R.; m. Patricia Louise Meunier, Feb. 8, 1936; children: Jamie Arlette, Steven Michael (dec.), Janice Marie, Joseph Patrick (dec.). BA in Chemistry, Carroll Coll., 1953; MS in Chemistry, Mont. State U., 1956, PhD in Chemistry, 1959. Postdoctoral fellow in biochemistry Oreg. State U., Corvallis, 1959-61, U.S. Western Regional Lab., Albany, Calif., 1961-63; chemist U.S. Western Regional Lab., Berkeley, Calif., 1963-64; asst. prof. biochemistry Wash. State U., Pullman, 1964-68, assoc. prof., 1968-72, prof., 1972—, Charlotte Y. Martin disting. prof., 1991—, chmn. dept. agrl. chemistry, 1977-80, fellow Inst. Biol. Chemistry, 1980—; faculty athletics rep. to PAC-10 & NCAA Wash. State U., 1991-94; vis. scientist dept. biochemistry U. Wash., 1981, Harvard U. Med. Sch., 1982; cons. Kemin Industries, Des Moines, 1981—, Plant Genetics, Davis, Calif., 1987-89; research adv. bd. Frito-Lay, Inc., Dallas, 1982, Plant Genetic Engring. Lab., N.M. State U., Las Cruces, 1986-89; mem. NRC rev. bd. Plant Gene Exptl. Ctr., Albany, Calif., 1990-93; mgr. biol. stress program USDA Competitve Grants Program, Washington, 1983-84; former mem. adv. panels for H. McKnight Found., Internat. Potato Ctr., Lima, Peru, Internat. Ctr. Genetic Engring. and Biotech., New Delhi, Internat. Ctr. Tropical Agr., Cali, Columbia, Internat. Tropical Agr., Ibandan, Africa; mem. grant rev. panels NSF, USDA, DOE, NIH; co-organizer Internat. Telecommunications Symposium on Plant Biotech. Mem. edit. bd. several biochem. and plant physiology jours.; contbr. articles to profl. publs., chpts. to books; co-editor 2 books. Grantee USDA, NSF, NIH, Rockefeller Found., McKnight Found.; recipient Merck award for grad. rsch. Mont. State U., 1959, career devel. awards NIH, 1964-74, Alumni Achievement award Carroll Coll., 1986, Pres.'s Faculty Excellence award in rsch. Wash. State U., 1986; named to Carroll Coll. Alumni Hall of Fame, 1981, Carroll Coll. Basketball Hall of Fame, 1982. Mem. AAAS, Nat. Acad. Scis. (elected 1986), Am. Chem. Soc. (Kenneth A. Spencer award 1992), Am. Soc. Plant Physiologists (Steven Hales Prize 1992), Am. Soc. Exptl.Biology, Biochem. Soc., Internat. Soc. Chem. Ecology, Internat. Soc. Plant Molecular Biology (bd. dirs.), Phytochem. Soc. N.Am., Nat. U. Continuing Assn. (Creative Programming award 1991), Phi Kappa Phi (Recognition award 1976, selected 1 of 100 centennial disting. alumni Mont. State U. 1993). Democrat. Office: Wash State Univ Inst Biol Chemistry Pullman WA 99164

RYAN, EVONNE IANACONE, financial planner; b. Buffalo, Aug. 30, 1949; d. Raphael and Mary (Silvaroli) Ianacone; m. Thomas William Ryan, July 11, 1981; children: Christine Irving, Thomas William IV. Student, U. Buffalo, 1970-72; BS in Edn., So. Ill. U., 1974, postgrad., 1975-78; postgrad., U. Mo., 1989-91, Coll. Fin. Planning, 1993—. Registered securities prin. Spl edn. tchr. Belleville (Ill.) Pub. Sch., 1974-78; research dir. Mo. Pub. Interest Research Group, St. Louis, 1978-79, exec. co-dir., 1979-83; corp. trainer, producer, dir. cmty. access coordination Storer Cable Communications, Florissant, Mo., 1983-85; prodn. mgr. Storer Cable Communications, Florissant, 1985-86; employee devel. and cmty. rels. dir. Cencom Cable TV, St. Louis, 1987-88; stockbroker Edward D. Jones & Co., Littleton, Colo., 1989-93, SunAmerica Securities, Littleton, 1993-94; co-founder Fin. & Tax Strategies, Inc., Littleton, 1994—. Contbr. articles to profl. publs. Recipient award for cable excellence Nat. Acad. Cable Programming, 1988, Emmy award, 1988. Mem. Women in Cable (v.p. St. Louis chpt. 1988-89), Rotary (Littleton). Home: 144 Willowleaf Dr Littleton CO 80127-3572 Office: 5944 S Kipling Ste 206 Littleton CO 80127

RYAN, FREDERICK JOSEPH, JR., lawyer, public official; b. Tampa, Fla., Apr. 12, 1955; s. Frederick Joseph and Cordelia Beth (Hartman) R.; m. Genevieve Ann McSweeney, Dec. 28, 1985; children: Genevieve Madeline, Madeline Elizabeth. BA, U. So. Calif., 1977, JD, 1980. Bar: Calif. 1980, D.C. 1986. Assoc. Hill, Farrer and Burrill, Los Angeles, 1980-82; dep. dir. then dir. presdl. appointments and scheduling The White House, Washington, 1982-87, dir. pvt. sector initiatives, 1985-87, asst. to the Pres., 1987-89; chief of staff Office of Ronald Reagan, L.A., 1989-95; vice chmn. Allbritton Comm. Co., Washington, 1995—; mem. staff Reagan-Bush Campaign, Los Angeles, 1980; dir. Internat. Conf. on Pvt. Sector Initiatives, Paris, 1986, Italian-Am. Conf. on Pvt. Sector Initiatives, 1987, Brit.-Am. Conf. on Pvt. Sector Initiatives, 1988. Author (column) Legal Briefs, 1980-82. Chmn. Monterey Park (Calif.) Community Rels. Commn., 1977-78; bd. dirs. Fordi Theater, Washington, Town Hall of Calif., L.A., Nancy Reagan Found.; trustee Ronald reagan Presdl. Found. Recipient Presdl. Commendation for pvt. sector initiatives Pres. Ronald Reagan, 1986, Medal of Arts and Letters, Govt. of France, 1986, Golden Ambrosiana medal of Milan, Italy, 1987, The Lion of Venice medal, Italy, 1987, Comdr. of the Order of Merit of Republic of Italy, 1992. Mem. ABA, Jonathan Club (L.A.). Presbyterian. Office: Allbritton Comm Co 800 17th St NW Washington DC 20006-3903

RYAN, GEORGE WESLEY, III, aerospace engineer; b. Kansas City, Mo., Feb. 19, 1966; s. George Wesley Jr. and Gloria Sue (Roach) R.; m. Carol Elaine Willey, Apr. 25, 1992. BS in Aerospace Engring., U. Kans., 1989, MS in Aerospace Engring., 1992. Flight test engr. Kohlman Sys. Rsch., Lawrence, Kans., 1988-91; dynamics and controls engr. PRC Inc., Edwards AFB, Calif., 1992—. Contbr. articles to profl. jours. Mem. AIAA (programs officer 1993-94, chmn. local sect. 1995-96, 2d Pl. Design Competition 1989), Soc. Flight Test Engrs., Am. Sailing Assn., Sigma Alpha Epsilon. Republican. Office: PRC Inc PO Box 273 Edwards CA 93523-0273

RYAN, JAMES See RYAN, BUDDY

RYAN, JOAN, sportswriter; b. Sept. 20, 1959; m. Barry Tompkins; 1 child. BS in Journalism with honors, U. Fla., 1981. Copy editor Orlando (Fla.) Sentinel, 1981-82, copy editor sports, 1982-83, sports writer, 1983-85; sports columnist San Francisco Examiner, 1985—. Recipient Fla. Sports Columnist of Yr. award, 1984, numerous AP Sports Editors awards, AP 1st place enterprise reporting award, 1993, Nat. Headliner award sports writing, 1990, Women's Sports Found. Journalism award, 1992. Office: San Francisco Examiner PO Box 7260 110 5th Ave San Francisco CA 94120

RYAN, JODELL, fine artist; b. Fresno, Calif., Oct. 13, 1932. Student with various artists. Exhibited Fresno Art Mus., Hall of Flowers, San Francisco, Don Price Gallery, Commonwealth Club, San Francisco, Fresno Art Ctr., Fresno Dist. Fair Fine Art Show, others. Recipient Best of Show award S.W.A. Spring Show, Best of Show award Clovis Old West Show, 1st Pl. award 53rd Ann. Statewide Exhbn., Santa Cruz, Judges Choice award 24th Ann. Open Representational Art Show, 1995, more than 50 other awards. Mem. Soc. Western Artists, Pastel Soc. of West Coast, Pastel Soc. of Am., Knickerbocker Artists.

RYAN, JOHN EDWARD, federal judge; b. Boston, Jan. 22, 1941; s. Howard Frederick and Mary (Burke) R.; m. Terri Reynolds; children: Valerie, Jennifer, Keely. BSEE, U.S. Naval Acad., 1963; LLB, Georgetown U., 1972; MS, Pacific Christian U., 1979. Assoc. Hale and Dorr, Boston, 1972-76, C.F. Braun, Alhambra, Calif., 1976-77; gen. counsel Altec Corp., Anaheim, Calif., 1977-79; v.p., sr. atty. Oak Industries, San Diego, 1979-82; sr. v.p. Oak Media, San Diego, 1982-84; ptnr. Dale and Lloyd, La Jolla, Calif., 1984-85, Jennings, Engstrand and Henrikson, San Diego, 1985-86; bankruptcy judge U.S. Bankruptcy Ct., Santa Ana, Calif., 1986—; ex officio dir. Orange County Bankruptcy Forum; exec. com. 9th Cir. conf. With USN, 1963-69. Mem. Mass. Bar Assn., Calif. Bar Assn., Orange County Bar Assn., Bankruptcy Judges Assn. Republican. Roman Catholic. Home: 3155 Summit Dr Escondido CA 92025-7529 Office: US Bankruptcy Ct PO Box 12600 Santa Ana CA 92712-2600*

RYAN, KEVIN DURWOOD, retail executive; b. Syracuse, N.Y., Jan. 9, 1961; s. William Durwood and Sally Ann (Foelker) R. AA in Bus., Allen Hancock Coll., 1983, AS in Mgmt., 1986, AS in Acctg., 1986. Recreation supr. Santa Maria (Calif.) Recreation Dept., 1975-81; sales mgr. Bulders Emporium, Santa Maria, 1979-84; mgr. Los Padres Theatres, Inc., Santa Maria, Calif., 1980-90; gen. mgr. Grossmans Inc., Novato, Calif., 1987-92; mgr. Mrs. Fields Co., San Ramon, Calif., 1992; gen. mgr. Hollywood Entertainment Corp., Pleasant Hill, Calif., 1993-95; pres. Ryan Enterprises, Pleasant Hill, 1993—. Recipient award Dept. Social Svcs. for Handicapped, Archdiocese L.A., 1978, Home Improvement Specialist award Wickes Corp., 1980, 82, 84. Mem. KTEH Founders Soc., Vallejo Police and Fireman Benefit Assn., Diablo Valley AIDS Soc., Solano County AIDS Task Force, K.C. Republican. Roman Catholic. Home: PO Box 23561 Pleasant Hill CA 94523-0561

RYAN, MARY GENE, military officer, occupational health nurse; b. Corona, Calif., Sept. 11, 1953; d. Robert James and Genevieve Louise (Kubilis) Guzinski; m. Robert Eldon Ryan III, June 9, 1979; children: Michael Warren, Jessica Gene, Matthew James. BSN, So. Conn. State Coll., 1975; MPH, U. Tex., 1980. Commd. 2d lt. USAF, 1976, advanced through grades to lt. col., 1995; staff nurse obstetrics U. Conn. Med. Ctr., Farmington, 1975-76; med.-surgical staff nurse Williams AFB (Ariz.) Hosp., 1976-77; flight nurse instr. 2d Aeromed. Evacuation Squadron, Rhein Main, Fed. Republic of Germany, 1977-79; officer in charge environ. health Wilford Hall Med. Ctr., Lackland AFB, Tex., 1980-84; chief environ. health AFSC Hosp., Edwards AFB, Calif., 1984-88; dir. occupational health Peterson Med. Clinic, Oxnard, Calif., 1988-89; mgr. health and safety County of Ventura (Calif.)/Gen. Svcs. Agy., 1989—; cons. environ. health L.A. AFB, 1984-88; chief nurse Calif. Air Nat. Guard 146 Med. Sqd., 1992—. Contbr. articles to profl. jours. Mem. choir, soloist, lay eucharistic min. Edwards AFB Cath. Chapel, 1984-88, mem. religious edn. com., 1984-85, lectr., commentator, 1986-87, marriage encounter counselor, 1991—; team mom for various sports, 1989—; AIDS educator, Edwards AFB, 1986-88. Recipient Meritorious Svc. medals USAF, Clin. award Am. Assn. Occupational Health Nurses, 1991. Mem. APHA (occupational health sect.), Am. Assn. Occupational Health Nurses, Calif. Assn. Occupational Health Nurses, Calif. Ctrl. Coast Occupational Health Nurses Assn. (pres. 1993—), Ventura County Med. Aux. Office: County Ventura/Gen Svcs Agy Risk Mgmt/HSLP 800 S Victoria Ave CA #1070 Ventura CA 93009-0001

RYAN, MICHAEL LOUIS, controller; b. Corning, Iowa, Feb. 22, 1945; s. Leo Vincent and Elda May (Lawrence) R. AAS in Constrn. Tech., Iowa State U., 1965; BS in Acctg., Drake U., 1972. CPA, Iowa, Wyo. Acct. Ernst & Ernst, Des Moines, 1972-75, Becker, Herrick & Co., Pueblo, Colo., 1975-78; pvt. practice acctg. Gillette, Wyo., 1978-81; acct. Karen M. Moody, CPAs, Sheridan, Wyo., 1981-85; contr. T-C Investments, Inc., Sheridan, 1985—; ptnr. WHG Partnership, Sheridan, 1991—; v.p. Bosley-Ryan Constrn., Inc., Sheridan, 1993—. With spl. forces U.S. Army, 1966-68, Vietnam. Mem. AICPA (tax div.), Wyo. Soc. CPAs, Am. Legion (fin. officer 1977-81), Lodge (sec. Sheridan club 1982-90, pres. 1989), Phi Kappa Phi, Beta Alpha Psi, Beta Gamma Sigma. Democrat. Roman Catholic. Home: 735 Canby St Sheridan WY 82801-4907 Office: T-C Investments Inc 856 Coffeen Ave Sheridan WY 82801-5318

RYAN, RANDEL EDWARD, JR., airline pilot; b. N.Y.C., Jan. 11, 1940; s. Randel Edward and Ann Augusta (Horwath) R.; m. Pamela Michael Wiley, May 12, 1962; children: Katherine, Gregory. BS in Sci., Trinity Coll., 1961. Quality control supr. Ideal Toy Corp., Jamaica, N.Y., 1961-62; airline pilot United Airlines, San Francisco, 1967—. Editor: The Lowdown, 1980-83. Pres., Highlands Community Assn., San Mateo, Calif., 1975; chmn. Com. to Re-elect County Supr., San Mateo, 1976; mediator San Mateo County, 1986—; arbitrator Better Bus. Bureau, 1988—; rep. Highlands Community Assn., San Mateo, 1970-86; coach Little League and Babe Ruth Baseball, San Mateo, 1979-83. Served to capt. USAF, 1962-68. Recipient Vandor award San Mateo PTA, 1976, awards of merit United Airlines, San Francisco, 1975, 79. Mem. Air Line Pilots Assn. (chmn. speakers panel 1983-86, community rels com. 1983-86, bd. dirs. 1986-89, 91-93, chmn. coun. 34 1991-93, vice-chmn. 1986-89, editor newspaper The Bayliner 1984-86, mem. contract study com. 1984-86, vice-chmn. MEC grievance com. 1989-91, chmn. MEC grievance rev. 1993—, mem. nat. hearing bd. 1994—).Democrat. Club: Highland Tennis (San Mateo). Home: 1768 Lexington Ave San Mateo CA 94402-4025 Office: United Airlines San Francisco Internat Airport San Francisco CA 94128

RYAN, READE HAINES, JR., lawyer; b. Plainfield, N.J., Jan. 4, 1937; s. Reade Haines and Anne Mary (Moment) R.; m. Joan Louise Larson, June 16, 1966; children: Reade Haines III, Rebecca Marie. AB, Princeton U., 1959; LLB, Harvard U., 1965. Bar: N.Y. 1966, Calif. 1985. Assoc. Shearman & Sterling, N.Y.C., 1965-73; ptnr. Shearman & Sterling, 1973—; lectr. Practicing Law Inst., 1977-88, Am. Law Inst.-ABA, 1979-94, Calif. Continuing Edn. of the Bar, 1995. Lt. USN, 1959-62. Mem. ABA, Internat. Bar Assn., Calif. State Bar Assn. (fin. instns. com.), N.Y. State Bar Assn., Assn. of Bar of City of N.Y., L.A. County Bar Assn., The Calif. Club. Republican. Office: 599 Lexington Ave New York NY 10022-6030

RYAN, ROBERT W., retired air force officer, aeronautical engineer; b. Nov. 15, 1952. BS, USAF Acad., 1975; grad., USAF Test Pilot Sch., 1979, USAF Squadron Officer Sch., 1983; student, USAF Air Command and Staff Coll., 1986; MS in Aero. Engring., Air Force Inst. Tech., 1987. Commd. 2d lt. USAF, 1975, advanced through grades to lt. col.; flight test engr. Air Force Flight Test Ctr., Edwards AFB, Calif., 1975-79, project flight test engr., 1979-83; chief flight test engr. Ogden ALC, Hill AFB, Utah, 1983-86; sect. leader aero. engring. Air Force Inst. Tech., Wright-Patterson AFB, Ohio, 1986-87; chief engr. officer Hdqs. AFSC, Andrews AFB, Md., 1988-89, aircraft/armament test program and policy mgr., 1989-91; chief engring. divsn. 412 Test Wing, Edwards AFB, 1991-94; chief investments reliance planning AFFTC SFTC Office, Edwards AFB, 1994-95; group engr. Raythcon Aircraft Corp., Witchita, Kans., 1995—. Office: USAF 195 E Popson Edwards CA 93524-6801

RYAN, STEPHEN JOSEPH, JR., ophthalmology educator, university dean; b. Honolulu, Mar. 20, 1940; s. S.J. and Mildred Elizabeth (Farrer) F.; m. Anne Christine Mullady, Sept. 25, 1965; 1 dau., Patricia Anne. A.B., Providence Coll., 1961; M.D., Johns Hopkins U., 1965. Intern Bellevue Hosp., N.Y.C., 1965-66; resident Wilmer Inst. Ophthalmology, Johns Hopkins Hosp., Balt., 1966-69, chief resident, 1969-70; fellow Armed Force Inst. Pathology, Washington, 1970-71; instr. ophthalmology Johns Hopkins U., Balt., 1970-71, asst. prof., 1971-72, assoc. prof., 1972-74; prof., chmn. dept. ophthalmology Los Angeles County-U. So. Calif. Med. Ctr., L.A., 1974-95; prof. dept. ophthalmology L.A. and U. So. Calif. Med. Ctr., L.A., 1974—; acting head ophthalmology div., dept. surgery Children's Hosp., L.A., 1975-77; med. dir. Doheny Eye Inst. (formerly Estelle Doheny Eye Found.), L.A., 1977-86; chief of staff Doheny Eye Hosp., L.A., 1985-88; dean U. So. Calif. Sch. Medicine, L.A., 1991—; mem. advisory panel Calif. Med. Assn., 1975—. Editor: (with M.D. Andrews) A Survey of Ophthalmology--Manual for Medical Students, 1970, (with R.E. Smith) Selected Topics on the Eye in Systemic Disease, 1974, (with Dawson and Little) Retinal Diseases, 1985, (with others) Retina, 1989; assoc. editor: Ophthalmol. Surgery, 1974-85; mem. editorial bd. Am. Jour. Ophthalmology, 1981—, Internat. Ophthalmology, 1982—, Retina, 1983—, Graefes Archives, 1984—; contbr. articles to med. jours. Recipient cert. of merit AMA, 1971; Louis B. Mayer Scholar award Research to Prevent Blindness, 1973; Rear Adm. William Campbell Chambliss USN award, 1982. Mem. Wilmer Ophthal. Inst. Residents Assn., Am. Acad. Ophthalmology and Otolaryngology (award of Merit 1975), Am. Ophthal. Soc., Pan-Am. Assn. Ophthalmology, Assn. Univ. Profs. of Ophthalmology, L.A. Soc. Ophthalmology, AMA, Calif. Med. Assn., Los Angeles County Med. Assn., Pacific Coast Oto-Ophthal. Soc., L.A. Acad. Medicine, Pan Am. Assn. Microsurgery, Macula Soc, Retina Soc., Nat. Eye Care Project, Rsch. Study Club, Jules Gonin Club, Soc. Scholars of Johns Hopkins U. (life). Office: U So Calif Sch of Medicine Doheny Eye Inst 1450 San Pablo St Los Angeles CA 90033

RYAN, SYLVESTER D., bishop; b. Catalina Island, Calif., Sept. 3, 1930. Grad., St. John's Sem., Camarillo, Calif. Ordained priest Roman Cath. Ch., 1957, titular bishop of Remesiana. Aux. bishop L.A., 1990-92; bishop Monterey, Calif., 1992—. Office: Chancery Office PO Box 2048 580 Fremont St Monterey CA 93940-3216*

RYBARSKI, MICHAEL ANTON, publishing company executive; b. Chgo., Apr. 4, 1949; s. Walter Frank and Dorothy Grace (Zak) R.; m. Jan Marie Plummer, Jan. 19, 1991. A.B., Providence Coll., 1971; M.A., U. Chgo., 1972, M.B.A., 1981. Asst. editor Scott, Foresman & Co., Glenview, Ill., 1972-74; assoc. editor Open Court Pub. Co., LaSalle, Ill., 1974-75, dir. planning and ops., 1975-77, asst. gen. mgr., 1977-81; v.p., dir. Houghton Mifflin Co., Boston, 1981-85; chmn. VideoTours, Inc., Simsbury, Conn., 1985-89; sr. v.p. pub. Age Ware, Inc., Emeryville, Calif., 1989—. Mem. exec. bd. Big Bros., 1969-71; v.p. Providence Film Soc., 1970-71. Mem. Assn. Am. Pubs. (fin. com.). Episcopalian. Home: 790 Crossbrook Dr Moraga CA 94556-1239 Office: Age Wave Inc 1900 Powell St Emeryville CA 94608-1811

RYDELL, AMNELL ROY, artist, landscape architect; b. Mpls., Sept. 17, 1915; s. John S. and Josephine Henrietta (King) R.; m. Frances Cooksey, Jan. 24, 1942. BFA, U. So. Calif., 1937; postgrad., Atelier 17, Paris, 1938, U. Calif., Berkeley, 1939-40, U. Calif., Santa Cruz, 1988. Instr. engring. Douglas Aircraft, El Segundo, Calif., 1940-46; ind. artist, designer San Francisco, 1946-48; ind. artist, designer Santa Cruz, 1948—, ind. landscape architect, 1958-91. Author, cons.: Low Maintenance Gardening, 1974. Pres. Santa Cruz Hist. Soc., 1978-79, Rural Bonny Doon Assn., 1955-56, Santa Cruz Orgn. for Progress and Euthenics, 1977-78; mem. vision bd. City of Santa Cruz, 1991-92; mem. task force Ctr. for Art and History, 1986-94; bd. dirs. Santa Cruz Hist. Trust, 1978-94, Art Mus. Santa Cruz County, 1982-94; donor advisor Roy and Frances Rydell Visual Arts Fund, Greater Santa Cruz County Cmty. Found.; archivist pers. hist. archives, spl. collections Libr. U. Calif., Santa Cruz. Mem. Am. Soc. Landscape Architects (emeritus), William James Assn. (vice chair bd. 1979—), Art Forum (chair 1983-90), Art League. Home: 201 Pine Flat Rd Santa Cruz CA 95060-9708

RYDER, HAL, theatre educator, director; b. Evanston, Ill., Aug. 21, 1950; s. Lee Sigmund and Katherine (Philipsborn) Rosenblatt; m. Caroline Margaret Ogden, Nov. 17, 1976 (div. 1991). Student, U. Ariz., 1968-72, U. Miami, summer 1971; cert. in drama, Drama Studio London, 1973; BA in Drama, U. Wash., 1987. Drama specialist Rough Rock (Ariz.) Demonstration Sch., 1971-72; artistic dir. Mercury Theatre, London, 1973-75, Fringe Theatre, Orlando, Fla., 1976-79; dir. Drama Studio London, 1980-82, interim adminstrv. dir., 1985; artistic dir. Alaska Arts Fine Arts Camp, Sitka, 1987, Shakespeare Plus, Seattle, 1983-92; instr. Cornish Coll. Arts, Seattle, 1982—, producer theatre, 1987—, acting-chmn. theatre dept., 1990; artistic dir. Open Door Theatre, 1992—, Snoqualmie Falls Forest Theatre, 1992-94; creative cons. Sea World Fla., Orlando, 1979; lit. mgr. Pioneer Square Theatre, Seattle, 1983; space mgr. Seattle Mime Theatre, 1986-87. Author: Carmilla, 1976, (with others) Marvelous Christmas Mystery, 1978; editor: Will Noble BLood Die, 1987, The New Emperor's Premier, 1990; dir. over 125 stage plays; appeared in over 40 prodns. Recipient Faculty Excellence award Seafirst Bank, Seattle, 1988. Mem. SAG, AFTRA, Am. Fedn. Tchrs. (Cornish chpt.). Democrat. Jewish. Home: 1012 NE 62nd St Seattle WA 98115-6604 Office: Cornish Coll Arts 710 E Roy St Seattle WA 98102-4604

RYDER, VIRGINIA PINKUS, retired school system administrator; b. L.A., Sept. 22, 1922; d. Frederick Ball and Dorothy (Cloud) Pinkus; m. William V. Ryder Jr., June 10, 1943 (div. 1948). BA, San Francisco State Coll., 1953, MA, 1969. Cert. elem. tchr., high sch. tchr., jr. coll. tchr., Calif. Tchr., adminstr. San Francisco Unified Schs., 1953-77. Author: Ethnic Cooking, Easy Meals, Comorants Landing, Travels of an Olive Eater, 3

Monkey Saves the Day. Mem. Internat. Palm Soc., Internat. Waterlily Soc. Home: 620 Lombardy Ln Laguna Beach CA 92651-2911

RYDOLPH, SIMMIE TOMMY, middle school educator; b. Refugio, Tex., Oct. 25, 1939; s. Simmie T. and Agnes G. Polk. BA, U. Calif., Berkeley, 1969, SUNY, Albany, 1988; MA in Liberal Studies, Wesleyan U., 1988. Cert. tchr., Alaska. Tchr. English Kumasi (Ghana) Secondary Tech. Sch., 1971-73; group counselor Contra Costa County Juvenile Facility, Martinez, Calif., 1970, 73-79; social studies tchr. Gruening Mid. Sch., Eagle River, Alaska, 1983—; mem. Social Studies Textbook Com., Anchorage, 1992—. Pianist 1st Bapt. Ch., Lualualei, Hawaii, 1963-65; pianist, organist, vocalist 1st Meth. Ch., Wasilla, Alasks, 1985-92; tutor Anchorage Literacy Project, Anchorage, 1990, Concerned Advocates R Everywhere, Anchorage, 1990-93; workshop presenter Anchorage Sch. Dist., Rotary, Ch. Jesus Christ Latter Day Sts., Wasilla. With USN, 1963-65, res. Fulbright-Hayes fellow, 1991; NEH scholar, 1990, 92, 94, Wesleyan U. scholar, 1971-73. Mem. Nat. Coun. Social Studies (mem. acad. freedom, ethics and equity com. 1994-95), Rotary (music dir. 1984—). Home: 3965 Grey Wolf Cir Wasilla AK 99654-1848

RYE, DAVID BLAKE, television news anchor; b. Norfolk, Va., Oct. 4, 1943; s. C. Glenn and Shirley Jean (Frye) R.; m. Gay Ann Darkenwald, Apr. 17, 1971; 1 child, Ian Glenn. BA in English, U. Mont., 1970. On-air personality Sta. KLTZ, Glasgow, Mont., 1969, Sta. KYLT, Missoula, Mont., 1970-71, Sta. KKGF, Great Falls, Mont., 1971-72, Sta. KGRC-FM, Hannibal, Mo., 1972, Sta. KUDI, Great Falls, 1972-74, Sta. KEIN, Great Falls, 1974; news dir. Sta. KFBB-TV, Great Falls, 1974-78; spl. asst. U.S. Hou. Rep. Ron Marlenee, Washington, 1978-80; news anchor Sta. KULR-TV, Billings, Mont., 1980-90, 93—; elected to Mont. State Senate, 1990. Pres. City of Billings Animal Control Bd., 1987; bd. dirs. Horizon Home for the Sexually Abused, Billings, 1987; Mont. State senator, 1991-95. Served as sgt. U.S. Army, 1967-69, Vietnam. Named Newsperson of Yr. Billings Jaycees, 1985. Mem. Mont. Assn. Press Broadcasters (pres. 1985-87, Radio Programmer of Yr. 1972, TV Broadcaster of Yr. 1984, 86), Radio and TV News Dirs. Assn., Hilands Golf Club (Billings), Order of DeMolay, Kiwanis (pres. Billings chpt. 1988-89). Republican. Lutheran. Home: 2016 Rehberg Ln Billings MT 59102-6542 Office: Sta KULR-TV 2045 Overland Ave Billings MT 59102-6454

RYGIEWICZ, PAUL THADDEUS, plant ecologist; b. Chgo., Feb. 19, 1952; s. Sigismund Thaddeus and Regina (Korpalski) R. BS in Forestry, U. Ill., 1974; MS in Wood Sci., U. Calif., Berkeley, 1976; PhD in Forest Resources, U. Wash., 1983. Research wood technologist ITT Rayonier, Inc., Shelton, Wash., 1977; research assoc. Centre National de Recherches Forestières, Nancy, France, 1983-84; research soil microbiologist U. Calif., Berkeley, 1984-85; rsch. ecologist, global climate change project leader EPA, Corvallis, Oreg., 1985—; asst. prof. dept. forest sci. Oreg. State U., 1987—. Contbr. articles to profl. jours.; rsch. on reforestation of tropical forests in Brazil, global climate changes on forests. Vol. Big Bros. of Am., Urbana, Ill., 1972-74. Fellow Regents U. Calif., Berkeley, 1973-74, Weyerhaeuser U. Calif., Berkeley, 1978-79, Inst. Nat. de la Recherche Agronomique, France, 1983-84, French Ministry of Fgn. Affairs, 1983-84. Mem. Ecol. Soc. Am., Am. Soc. Plant Physiologists, Soil Ecology Soc., Forestry Club (Urbana and Berkeley), Portland Wheelmen Touring Club, Sigma Xi, Gamma Sigma Delta, Xi Sigma Pi (officer 1973-74). Office: EPA 200 SW 35th St Corvallis OR 97333-4902

RYLANDER, ROBERT ALLAN, financial service executive; b. Bremerton, Wash., Apr. 8, 1947; s. Richard Algot and Marian Ethelyn (Peterson) R.; m. Donna Jean Marks, June 28, 1984; children: Kate, Josh, Erik, Meagan. BA in Fin., U. Wash., 1969; postgrad., U. Alaska, 1972-74. Controller Alaska USA Fed. Credit Union, Anchorage, 1974-77, mgr. ops., 1977-80, asst. gen. mgr., 1980-83, exec. v.p., chief operating officer, 1983—; chmn. Alaska Home Mortgage, Inc., Anchorage, 1992—, Alaska Option Svcs. Corp., Anchorage, 1983—; bd. dirs. Alaska USA Ins., Inc., Anchorage. Served to capt. USAF, 1969-74. Mem. Credit Union Execs. Soc. Home: PO Box 220587 Anchorage AK 99522 Office: Alaska USA Fed Credit Union PO Box 196613 Anchorage AK 99519-6613

RYLES, GERALD FAY, private investor, business executive; b. Walla Walla, Wash., Apr. 3, 1936; s. L. F. and Janie Geraldine (Bassett) R.; m. Ann Jane Birkenmeyer, June 12, 1959; children—Grant, Mark, Kelly. B.A., U. Wash., 1958; M.B.A., Harvard U., 1962. With Gen. Foods Corp., White Plains, N.Y., 1962-65, Purex Corp., Ltd., Lakewood, Calif., 1966-68; cons. McKinsey & Co., Inc., Los Angeles, 1968-71; with Fibreboard Corp., San Francisco, 1971-79, v.p., 1973-75, group v.p., 1975-79; with Consol. Fibres, Inc., San Francisco, 1979-88, exec. v.p., 1979-81, pres., dir., 1981-86, chief exec. officer, 1986-88; cons. Orinda, Calif., 1988-90; with Interchecks Inc., 1990-92, pres., CEO, 1990-92; bus. exec., pvt. investor, 1992-94; chmn. bd., CEO Microserv, Inc., Kirkland, Wash., 1994—; bd. dirs. Morning Sun, Inc., Tacoma, Wash. Mem. adv. com. entrepreneur and innovation program U. Wash. Bus. Sch. Served to capt. U.S. Army, 1958-66. Mem. Harvard Bus. Sch. Assn., Univ. Wash. Alumni Assn., World Trade Club (San Francisco), Orinda Country Club, Wash. Athletic Club. Republican. Episcopalian. Home: 2625 90th Ave NE Bellevue WA 98004-1601

RYMAR, JULIAN W., manufacturing company executive; b. Grand Rapids, Mich., June 29, 1919; student Grand Rapids Jr. Coll., 1937-39, U. Mich., 1939-41, Am. Sch. Dramatic Arts, 1946-47, Wayne U., 1948-52, Rockhurst Coll., 1952-53; Naval War Coll., 1954-58; m. Margaret Macon Van Brunt, Dec. 11, 1954; children: Margaret Gibson, Gracen Macon, Ann Mackall. Entered USN as aviation cadet, 1942, advanced through grades to capt., 1964; chmn. bd., chief exec. officer, dir. Grace Co., Belton, Mo., 1955—; chmn. bd. dirs. Shock & Vibration Research, Inc., 1956-66; chmn. bd., CEO Bedtime Story Fashions; bd. dirs. Am. Bank & Trust; comdg. officer Naval Air Res. Squadron, 1957-60, staff air bn. comdr., 1960-64. Mem. Kansas City Hist. Soc.; bd. dirs. Bros. of Mercy, St. Lukes Hosp.; adv. bd. dirs. St. Joseph Hosp.; trustee Missouri Valley Coll., 1969-74; pres. Rymar Found. Active Sch. Am. Rsch., Inst. Am. Arts, Mus. N.Mex. Found., Spanish Colonial Art Soc. Mem. Mil. Order World Wars, Navy League U.S. (pres. 1959-60, dir. 1960-70), Rockhill Homes Assn. (v.p.) Friends of Art (pres., chmn. bd. govs. 1969-70, exec. bd. 1971-74), Soc. of Fellows of Nelson Gallery Found. (exec. bd. 1972-77), Soc. Profl. Journalists, Press Club, Univ. of Mich. Club, Arts Club of Washington, Sch. of Am. Rsch., Santa Fe Symphony, Inst. Am. Indian Art, Mus. NMex. Found., Mus. Indian Arts & Culture, Mus. Internat. Folk Art, Mus. Fine Arts, Spanish Colonial Arts Soc., Quiet Birdman Club, Sigma Delta Chi. Episcopalian (dir., lay reader, lay chalice, vestryman, sr. warden, diocesan fin. bd., parish investment bd.).

RYMER, PAMELA ANN, federal judge; b. Knoxville, Tenn., Jan. 6, 1941. AB, Vassar Coll., 1961; LLB, Stanford U., 1964; LLD (hon.), Pepperdine U., 1988. Bar: Calif. 1966, U.S. Ct. Appeals (9th cir.) 1966, U.S. Ct. Appeals (10th cir.), U.S. Supreme Ct. V.p. Rus Walton & Assoc., Los Altos, Calif., 1965-66; Assoc. Lillick McHose & Charles, L.A., 1966-72, ptnr., 1973-75; ptnr. Toy and Rymer, L.A., 1975-83; judge U.S. Dist. Ct. (cen. dist.) Calif., L.A., 1983-89, U.S. Ct. Appeals (9th cir.), L.A., 1989—; faculty The Nat. Jud. Coll., 1986-88; mem. com. summer ednl. programs Fed. Jud. Ctr., 1987-88; chair exec. com. 9th Cir. Jud. Conf., 1990; mem. com. criminal law Jud. Conf. U.S., 1988-93, Ad Hoc com. gender-based violence, 1991-94, fed.-state jurisdiction com., 1993—. Mem. editorial bd. The Judges' jour., 1989-91; contbr. articles to profl. jours. and newsletters. Mem. Calif. Postsecondary Edn. Commn., 1974-84, chmn., 1980-84; mem. L.A. Olympic Citizens Adv. Commn.; bd. visitors Stanford U. Law Sch., 1986—, chair, 1993—, exec. com.; bd. visitors Pepperdine U. Law Sch., 1987—; mem. Edn. Commn. of States Task Force on State Policy and Ind. Higher Edn., 1987-89; bd. dirs. Constnl. Rights Found., 1985; Jud. Conf. U.S. Com. Fed.-Sttae Jurisdiction, 1993, Com. Criminal Law, 1988-93, ad hoc com. gender based violence, 1991-94; chair exec. com. 9th cir. jud. conf., 1990-94. Recipient Outstanding Trial Jurist award L.A. County Bar Assn., 1988. Mem. ABA (task force on civil justice reform 1991—), State Bar Calif. (antitrust and trade regulation sect., exec. com. 1990-92), L.A. County Bar Assn. (chmn. antitrust sect. 1981-82), Assn. of Bus. Trial Lawyers (bd. govs. 1990-92), Stanford Alumni Assn., Stanford Law Soc. Soc. Calif., Vassar Club So. Calif. (past pres.). Office: US Ct Appeals 9th Cir 125 S Grand Ave Ste 600 Pasadena CA 91105-1652

RYMER, THÉRÈSE ELIZABETH, family practice nurse practitioner; b. New London, Conn., Dec. 5, 1947; d. Kenneth Frank and Ursula Kathleen (O'Reilly) Gmeiner; m. Timothy Charles Rymer, Dec. 29, 1973; children: Gerard, Andrew, Deirdre. Diploma, St. Joseph's Coll. Nursing, 1969; cert. nurse practitioner, U. Calif., San Diego, 1976, cert. occupational health nurse, 1990. RN, Calif.; cert. Am. Bd. Occupational Health Nurses. Staff nurse ICU Marin Gen. Hosp., San Rafael, Calif., 1969-70, Pacific Med. Ctr., San Francisco, 1970-71; staff nurse, charge nurse Mercy Hosp., San Diego, 1972-75; family practice nurse practitioner U. Calif. San Diego Med. Ctr., 1976-83, employee health nurse, coord., then dir. employee health, 1983-91; dir. clin. svc. U. Calif. San Diego Ctr. Occupational and Environ. Medicine, 1991—; Exec. steering com., mem. med. planning bd. St. Vincent de Paul/Joan Kroc Med. Clinic, San Diego. Mem. editorial bd. Jour. Hosp. Occupational Health, 1993—; contbr. articles to profl. jours. Mem. disaster med. assistance team Nat. Disaster Med. System. Mem. Calif. State Assn. Occupational Health Nurses (bd. dirs. 1992-94, membership chair San Diego chpt. 1991-92), Assn. Hosp. Employee Health Profls. (pres. San Diego chpt. 1988-89). Roman Catholic. Office: U Calif Ctr Occupational & Environ Med 3500 5th Ave Ste 102 San Diego CA 92103-5020

RYMER DAVIS, CAROL ANN, radiologist; b. Denver, Nov. 28, 1944; d. Charles Albert and Marion (Reinhart) Rymer; m. John Charles Davis IV, May 10, 1969; children: Heather Mead, Marne Anne. BS, Colo. Coll., 1965; MD, U. Colo., 1969. Bd. cert. radiology and nuclear medicine. Intern U. N.Mex., Albuquerque, 1969-70, resident radiology, 1971-74, fellow nuclear medicine, 1974; resident gen. surgery Lovelace Med. Ctr., Albuquerque, 1970-71, staff physician, chief nuclear medicine, 1974-91; staff physician Fitzsimmons Med. Ctr., Denver, 1991; staff physician, chief nuclear medicine St. Joseph Hosp., Denver, 1991—, chief breast imaging, 1992—. Safety officer, chief safety officer Albuquerque Internat. Balloon Fiesta, Albuquerque, 1990-91. Col. U.S. Army. Recipient Pres. Recognition award Greater Albuquerque Med. Assn., 1988; named Woman of Yr. Zonta Club Albuquerque, 1989; set 14 world records in hot air ballooning. Mem. Internat. Women's Forum (Woman That Makes a Difference 1991). Episcopalian. Home: 1158 S Vine St Denver CO 80210-1831

RYNIKER, BRUCE WALTER DURLAND, industrial designer, manufacturing executive; b. Billings, Mont., Mar. 23, 1940; s. Walter Henry and Alice Margaret (Durland) R.; B. Profl. Arts in Transp. Design (Ford scholar), Art Ctr. Coll. Design, Los Angeles, 1963; grad. specialized tech. engring. program Gen. Motors Inst., 1964; m. Marilee Ann Vincent, July 8, 1961; children: Kevin Walter, Steven Durland. Automotive designer Gen. Motors Corp., Warren, Mich., 1963-66; mgmt. staff automotive designer Chrysler Corp., Highland Park, Mich., 1966-72; pres., dir. design Transform Corp., Birmingham, Mich., 1969-72; indsl. designer, art dir. James R. Powers and Assocs., Los Angeles, 1972-75; sr. design products mgr. Mattel Inc., El Segundo, Calif., 1975—; dir. design and devel. Microword Industries, Inc., Los Angeles, 1977-80, also dir.; exec. mem. Modern Plastics Adv. Council, 1976-80; elegance judge LeCercle Concours D'Elegance, 1976-77; mem. nat. adv. bd. Am. Security Council, 1980; cons. automotive design, 1972—. Served with USMC, 1957-60. Mem. Soc. Art Ctr. Alumni (life), Mattel Mgmt. Assn., Second Amendment Found., Am. Def. Preparedness Assn., Nat. Rifle Assn. Designer numerous exptl. automobiles, electric powered vehicles, sports and racing cars, also med. equipment, electronic teaching machines, ride-on toys. Home: 21329 Marjorie Ave Torrance CA 90503-5443

RYPKA, EUGENE WESTON, microbiologist; b. Owatonna, Minn., May 6, 1925; s. Charles Frederick and Ethel Marie (Ellerman) R.; m. Rosemary Speeker, June 1, 1967. Student, Carleton Coll., 1946-47; BA, Stanford U., 1950, PhD, 1958. Prof. microbiology, systems, cybernetics U. N.Mex., Albuquerque, 1957-62; bacteriologist Leonard Wood Meml. Lab. Johns Hopkins U., Balt., 1962-63; sr. scientist Lovelace Med. Ctr., Albuquerque, 1963-71, chief microbiologist, 1971-93; adj. prof. U. N.Mex., 1973—; cons. Hoffmann-LaRoche Inc., 1974—, Airline Pilots Assn., Washington, 1976, Pasco Lab., Denver, 1983—; advisor Nat. Com. Clinic Lab. Standards, Pa., 1980-84. Contbr. articles to profl. jours. and chpts. in books. Served with USNR, USMC 1943-46. Fellow AAAS; mem. IEEE, Internat. Soc. Systems Sci. Republican. Presbyterian. Home: 8345 Highland Sta Albuquerque NM 87198

SA, JULIE, mayor, restaurant chain owner; b. Korea, Dec. 15, 1950; came to US, 1970;; married;. Degree in Polit. Sci., Dong-A U., Korea. Owner restaurant chain; councilwoman City of Fullerton, Calif., 1992-94, mayor, 1994—; rep. bd. Orange County Sanitation Dists. Mem. Fullerton C. of C., Orange County Korean C. of C., Orange County Chinese C. of C. Office: Office of the Mayor 303 W Commonwealth Ave Fullerton CA 92632

SA, LUIZ AUGUSTO DISCHER, physicist; b. Lages, Brazil, Sept. 28, 1944; came to U.S., 1983; s. Catulo J.C. and Maria (Discher) S. MSc in Physics, Carnegie Mellon U., 1969; PhD in Elec. Engring., Stanford U., 1989. Asst. prof. Cath. U. of Rio, Rio de Janeiro, 1969-72, Fed. U. of Rio, Rio de Janeiro, 1973-83; post-doctoral scholar Stanford (Calif.) U., 1990-91, rsch. scientist, 1991—; rsch. scientist SOI/MDI project Themdi instrument will be flown in SOHO spacecraft NASA, 1992—. Contbr. articles to Jour. of Applied Physics, Jour. Geophys. Rsch., Proc. of 4th SOHO Workshop on Helioseismology, ESA, 1995. Recipient of Recognition award NASA, 1994. Mem. Am. Astronomical Soc., Am. Geophysical Union, Sigma Xi. Roman Catholic. Office: CSSA HEPL Annex-A Stanford CA 94305

SAAD, MOHAMMED FATHY, medical educator; b. Kom Hamada, Behaira, Egypt, Jan. 23, 1952; came to the U.S., 1981; s. Hassaneen Hilmy and Faiza S. (Younis) S. MBBCh with honors, U. Alexandria, Egypt, 1975, M of Medicine, 1979, MD, 1986; MS in Biomedical Scis., U. Tex., Houston, 1984. Intern Alexandria U. Hosp., 1976-77, resident dept. medicine, 1977-80; asst. lectr. Alexandria U., 1980-81, instr., 1984-86, asst. prof. medicine and endocrinology, 1986-87; fellow sect. endocrinology, dept. medicine U. Tex., Anderson Hosp. and Tumor Inst., Houston, 1981-84; staff physician Sacaton (Ariz.) Indian Hosp., 1987-91, Phoenix Indian Med. Ctr., 1988-91; attending physician dept. medicine Rancho Los Amigos Med. Ctr., L.A., 1991—; attending physician dept. medicine U. So. Calif.-Los Angeles County Med. Ctr., L.A., 1991—, assoc. prof. medicine, 1991—; vis. assoc. Phoenix epidemiology and clin. rsch. br. Nat. Inst. Diabetes and Digestive and Kidney Diseases, NIH, 1987-91; vis. endocrinologist Maricopa Med. Ctr., Phoenix, 1988-91. Author: (with others) Fundamentals of Surgical Oncology, 1986; subeditor sect. endocrine tumors Year Book Cancer, 1985-88; reviewer Am. Jour. Physiology, Diabetes, Diabetes Care, European Jour. Clin. Investigations, Jour. Lipid Rsch., Obesity Rsch., Ethnicity & Disease; contbr. articles to profl. jours. Recipient Egyptian State prize and medal of honor Nat. Acad. Sci., 1985; grantee Ariz. Kidney Found., 1989-90, Nat. Heart, Lung and Blood Inst., 1991—, Genentech, Inc., 1992-93, 94—. Mem. Am. Diabetes Assn. (grantee 1989-90, 93—), Am. Fedn. Clin. Rsch., Royal Coll. Physicians U.K., Am. Heart Assn. (mem. high blood pressure coun.), Egyptian Med. Assn., European Assn. Study Diabetes, Endocrine Soc. Office: U So Calif Med Sch Divsn Endocrinology 1200 N State St Rm 8250 Los Angeles CA 90033-4525

SAAR, FREDERICK ARTHUR, data processing executive; b. Scranton, Pa., Aug. 30, 1946; s. Frederick Arthur and Mary (Gray) S.; m. Mary-Em C. Suitor. Sr. programmer Fed. Reserve Bank, Charlotte, 1967-74; EDP auditor First Commerce Corp., New Orleans, 1974-76; audit dir. First Interstate Bancorp, Phoenix, 1976-84; mgr. info. resource mgmt. First Interstate Bank, Phoenix, 1984-90, cons. sys. devel. divsn., 1990—; computer mgmt. 1st Interstate Bank divsn. 1st Interstate Bancorp, 1991—; pres. Hogan Users Group, Dallas, 1983-84. Served with U.S. Army, 1964-67, Vietnam. Named Auditor of Yr. Inst. Internal Auditors, Phoenix chpt., 1981-82. Mem. EDP Auditors Assn. (cert. info. systems auditor, pres. Phoenix chpt. 1985), Inst. Cert. Computer Profls. (cert. systems profl.). Republican. Episcopalian. Office: First Interstate Bank 734 W Alameda Ste 101 Tempe AZ 85282

SAARI, ALBIN TOIVO, electronics engineer; b. Rochester, Wash., Mar. 16, 1930; s. Toivo Nickoli and Gertrude Johanna (Hill) S.; m. Patricia Ramona Rudig, Feb. 1, 1958; children: Kenneth, Katherine, Steven, Marlene, Bruce. Student, Centralia Community Coll., Wash., 1950-51; AS in Electronic Tech., Wash. Tech. Inst., Seattle, 1958; BA in Communications, Evergreen State Coll., Olympia, Wash., 1977. Electronic technician Boeing Co., Seattle, 1956-59; field engr. RCA, Van Nuys, Calif., 1959-61; tv engr. Gen. Dynamics, San Diego, 1961-65, Boeing Co., Seattle, 1965-70; mgr. electronic maintenance and engring. Evergreen State Coll., Olympia, Wash., 1970—; mem. adv. bd. KAOS-FM Radio, Olympia, 1979-82, New Market Vocat. Skills Ctr., Tumwater, Wash., 1985—, South Puget Sound Cmty. Coll., Olympia. Soccer coach King County Boys Club, Federal Way, Wash., 1968-70, Thurston County Youth Soccer, Olympia, 1973-78. With USAF, 1951-55. Recipient Merit award for electronic systems design Evergreen State Coll., 1978. Mem. Soc. Broadcast Engrs. (chmn. 1975-77), Soc. of Motion Picture and TV Engrs., IEEE, Audio Engring. Soc., Tele-Communications Assn., Assoc. Pub. Safety Communications Officers. Lutheran. Home: 6617 Husky Way SE Olympia WA 98503-1433 Office: Evergreen State Coll Media Engring # L1309 Olympia WA 98505

SAAVEDRA, CHARLES JAMES, banker; b. Denver, Nov. 2, 1941; s. Charles James and Evangeline Cecilia (Aragon) S.; m. Ann Helen Taylor, 1967; children: Michael, Kevin, Sarah. BSBA, Regis U., Denver, 1963; postgrad. U. Calif., San Francisco, 1964-66. Vice-pres., Western States Bankcard Assn., San Francisco, 1969-77; dir. info. systems World Airways, Inc., Oakland, Calif., 1977-79; v.p. computer services First Nationwide Bank, San Francisco, 1979-83; sr. v.p. Wells Fargo Bank, San Francisco, 1983-92; sr. v.p. Union Bank, San Francisco, 1992—; instr. Programming & Systems Inst., San Francisco, 1968-69; lectr. Am. Mgmt. Assn., 1984—; pres. Right Direction Project of Contra Costa County; bd. dirs. No. Calif. Family Ctr. With USNR, 1963-64. Mem. Data Processing Mgrs. Assn. (bd. dirs., chmn. program com. 1981), Am. Nat. Standards Inst., Am. Bankers Assn., San Francisco Jaycees, Alpha Delta Gamma. Clubs: Commonwealth of Calif.; Lake Lakewood Assn. Home: 210 Lakewood Rd Walnut Creek CA 94598-4826 Office: Union Bank 350 California St San Francisco CA 94104-1402

SABALIUS, ROMEY, foreign language and literature educator; b. Lubeck, Germany, Mar. 9, 1963; came to U.S., 1984; m. Atscaux Kagami. BA, U. Mainz, Germany, 1984; MA, U. So. Calif., L.A., 1986, PhD, 1992; Magister, U. Munich, Germany, 1989. Vis. prof. Vassar Coll., Poughkeepsie, N.Y., 1992; asst. prof. German lit. Utah State U., Logan, 1992-95; asst. prof., German coord. San Jose (Calif.) State U., 1995—. Author: The Dream Never Becomes Reality, 1994, Die Romane Hugo Loetschers, 1995; contbr. articles to profl. jours. Utah State U. grantee, 1993-95; Quadrille Ball Found. scholar, 1986-87, Friedrich-Ebert Found. scholar, 1983-89. Mem. MLA, Am. Assn. Tchrs. German, German Studies Assn., Philol. Assn. Pacific Coast, Rocky Mountain MLA, Internat. Vereinigung der Germanisten. Office: San Jose State U Dept Fgn Langs 1 Washington Sq San Jose CA 95192-0091

SABANAS-WELLS, ALVINA OLGA, orthopedic surgeon; b. Riga, Latvia, Lithuania, July 30, 1914; d. Adomas and Olga (Dagilyte) Pipyne; m. Juozas Sabanas, Aug. 20, 1939 (dec. Mar. 1968); 1 child, Algis (dec.); m. Alfonse F. Wells, Dec. 31, 1977 (dec. 1990). MD, U. Vytautas The Great, Kaunas, Lithuania, 1939; MS in Orthopaedic Surgery, U. Minn., 1955. Diplomate Am. Bd. Orthopaedic Surgery. Intern Univ. Clinics, Kaunas, 1939-40; resident orthopaedic surgery and trauma Red Cross Trauma Hosp., Kaunas, 1940-44; orthopaedic and trauma fellow Unfall Krankenhous, Vienna, Austria, 1943-44; intern Jackson Park Hosp., Chgo., 1947-48; fellow in orthopaedic surgery Mayo Clinic, Rochester, Minn., 1952-55; assoc. orthopaedic surgery Northwestern U., 1956-72; asst. prof. orthopaedic surgery Rush Med. Sch., 1973-76; pvt. practice orthopaedic surgery Sun City, Ariz., 1976-89; pres. cattle ranch corp. Contbr. articles to profl. jours. Fellow ACS; mem. Am. Acad. Orthopaedic Surgery, Physicians Club Sun City, Mayo Alumni Assn. Mem. U. Minn. Alumni Assn., Ruth Jackson Orthopedic Soc. Republican. Mem. Evang. Reformed Ch. Home: 3101 Skipworth Dr Las Vegas NV 89107-3241

SABATELLA, ELIZABETH MARIA, clinical therapist, educator, mental health facility administrator; b. Mineola, N.Y., Nov. 9, 1940; d. D. F. and Blanche M. (Schmetzle) S; 1 child, Kevin Woog. BS, SUNY, Brockport, 1961; MA, SUNY, Stony Brook, 1971, MSW, 1983. Lic. social worker, N.Y., N.Mex.; cert. tchr., N.Y., N.Mex.; registered clin. social worker, Calif. Tchr. physical edn. Comseqogue Sch. Dist., Port Jefferson, N.Y., 1968-73, 84-87, 88-91; clin. therapist Cibola Counseling Svcs., Grants, N.Mex., 1991-95, regional dir., 1993-95; clin. therapist Family Growth Counseling Ctr., Encinitos, Calif., 1995—; therapist for adolescents, 1973-84; therapist for abused children Farmingville Mental Health Clinic; therapist for alcoholics Lighthouse Ctr.; mem. Family Systems Network for Continuing Edn., Calif., Colo., 1978-80; mem. biofeedback and mediation com. McLean Hosp., Boston, 1978; mem. therapeutic touch team East and West Ctr., N.Y.C., 1980-84, sexual abuse treatment coord., 1992-95. Art and photographs exhibited at group show N.Mex. Art League, 1991; contbr. poetry and children's story to various publs. Recipient Editor's Choice award and Best New Poet award Nat. Libr. Poetry, 1988, Merit award and Place Winner for Poetry, Iliad Press, 1993. Mem. NASW, Writers Assn., Sierra Club. Home: 3852 Jewell St Apt 208 San Diego CA 92109

SABATINI, JOSEPH DAVID, librarian; b. Bronx, N.Y., Oct. 25, 1942; s. Amadeo Sabatini and Victoria (Azriel) Curry; m. Mary Helena Budinger, Nov. 11, 1972; 1 child, Robert Amadeo. BA, UCLA, 1964, MLS, 1965. Vol. Vol. in Svc. to Am., various locations, 1965-67; asst. libr. Sch. Law Libr., U. N.Mex., Albuquerque, 1968-72; head info. svcs. Albuquerque Pub. Libr., 1973-76, cmty. resources specialist, 1977-80, head main libr., 1980—. Mem. N.Mex. Libr. Assn. (chair various coms., chair legis. com., pres. 1980-81). Home: 3514 6th St NW Albuquerque NM 87107-2419 Office: Albuquerque Pub Libr 501 Copper Ave NW Albuquerque NM 87102-3129

SABATINI, LAWRENCE, bishop; b. Chgo., May 15, 1930; s. Dominic and Ada (Piloi) S. Ph.L., Gregorian U., Rome, 1953, S.T.L., 1957, J.C.D., 1960; M.S. in Edn., Iona Coll., 1968. Ordained priest, Roman Catholic Ch., 1957, bishop, 1978. Prof. canon law St. Charles Sem., S.I., N.Y., 1960-71; pastor St. Stephen's Parish, North Vancouver, B.C., Canada, 1970-78; provincial superior Missionaries of St. Charles, Oak Park, Ill., 1978; aux. bishop Archdiocese Vancouver, B.C., Can., 1978-82; bishop Diocese Kamloops, B.C., Can., 1982—; procurator, adviser Matrimonial Tribunal, N.Y.C., 1964-71; founder, dir. RAP Youth Counseling Service, S.I., N.Y., 1969-71; vice ofcl. Regional Matrimonial tribunal of Diocese Kamloops, 1978-82; chmn. Kamloops Cath. Pub. Schs., 1982—. Named Man of Yr. Confratellanza Italo-Canadese, 1979. Mem. Can. Canon Law Soc., Canon Law Soc. Am., Can. Conf. Cath. Bishops. Office: Diocese of Kamloops, 635A Tranquille Rd, Kamloops, BC Canada V2B 3H5*

SABATINI, WILLIAM QUINN, architect; b. Pitts.; s. William L. and Lydia M. (Contento) S.; m. Carol Anne Christoffel, Feb. 26, 1972; children: Quinn, Jay, Jillian. BA, Franklin & Marshall Coll., 1971; MArch, U. N.Mex., 1978. Registered arch., N.Mex., Nev.; cert. Nat. Coun. Archtl. Registration Bds. Intern Jess Holmes, Arch., Albuquerque, 1974-78; project mgr. Jack Miller & Assocs., Las Vegas, 1978-81; sr. design arch. HNTB, Kansas City, Mo., 1981-84; prin. Holmes Sabatini Assocs. Arch., Albuquerque, 1984—. Prin. works include Ctrl. Campus Bookstore U. N.Mex. (Merit award N.Mex. Soc. Archs. 1977), Luna County Courthouse, Deming, N.Mex. (Honor award N.Mex. Hist. Preservation Soc. 1978), James R. Dickinson Libr. U. Nev., Las Vegas (Merit award AIA 1981, Honor award Nev. Soc. Arch. 1981), Reno Conv. Ctr. (Merit award Nev. Soc. Archs. 1983), Corp. Hdqs. Nev. Power Co., Las Vegas (Honor award Nev. Soc. Archs. 1983), YMCA, Las Vegas (Honor award Nev. Soc. Archs. 1983), Sanctuary Remodel St. Johns United Meth. Ch., Albuquerque (Best Interiors award N.Mex. Bus. Jour. 1986), The Presidio Office Bldg., Albuquerque (Best Bldgs. award and Best Interiors award N.Mex. Bus. Jour. 1987, Project of Yr. award Assoc. Gen. Contractors N.Mex. 1987), Suarez Residence, Albuquerque (Merit award N.Mex. Soc. Am. 1988), Fire Sta. Number 13 and Fire Marshall's Office, Albuquerque (Merit award Albuquerque Conservation Soc. 1987, Best Bldgs. award N.Mex. Bus. Jour. 1988), Santa Fe Imaging Ctr. (Citation of Excellence, Modern Health Care Mag., AIA com. on healthcare 1989, Best Bldgs. award N.Mex. Bus. Jour. 1989), Health Scis. Bldg. U. N.Mex. (Best Bldgs. award N.Mex. Bus. Jour. 1989), U.S. Port of Entry, Columbus, N.Mex. (Best Bldgs. award N.Mex. Bus. Jour. 1989, Honor award N.Mex. Soc. Archs. 1990, GSA Design award U.S. Gen. Svcs. Adminstrn. 1990), Student Svcs. Bldg., Albuquerque TVI (Best Bldgs. award N.Mex. Bus. Jour. 1989, Merit award Albuquerque Conservation Soc. 1990), Expansion and Renovation Albuquerque Conv. Ctr. (Best Bldgs. award N.Mex. Bus. Jour. 1990), Lovelace Multi-Specialty Clinic Facility, Albuquerque (Merit award N.Mex. Soc. Archs. 1991), Pete's Playground U. N.Mex. Hosp. (Honor award N.Mex. Soc. Archs. 1992, Best Bldgs. Spl. award N.Mex. Bus. Jour. 1993), Nursing Unit Remodel U. N.Mex. Hosp. (Excellence award Am. Soc. Interior Designers 1992), 3.5 Meter Telescope Kirtland AFB, N.Mex. (Honor award AIA 1993). Bd. dirs. Albuquerque Chamber Orch., 1988, Hospice Rio Grande, 1992—; mem. adv. bd. Balloon Mus., 1989—; v.p., mem. adv. bd. St. Pius High Sch., 1993—. With USAR, 1971-78. Mem. AIA (bd. dirs. Albuquerque chpt. 1986-87). Roman Catholic. Office: Holmes Sabatini Assocs Archs West Courtyard 202 Central Ave SE Albuquerque NM 87102-3428

SABEY, J(OHN) WAYNE, academic administrator, consultant; b. Murray, Utah, Dec. 10, 1939; s. Alfred John and Bertha (Lind) S.; m. Marie Bringhurst, Sept. 10, 1964; children: Clark Wayne, Colleen, Carolyn, Natasha Lynne. BA in Asian Studies, Brigham Young U., 1964, MA in Asian History, 1965; PhD in East Asian History, U. Mich., 1972. Teaching asst. Brigham Young U., Provo, 1964-65, rsch. asst., 1965, adj. prof. history, 1988-89; rsch. asst. U. Mich., Ann Arbor, 1966; from instr. to asst. prof. history U. Utah, Salt Lake City, 1970-80; v.p. Western Am. Lang. Inst., Salt Lake City, 1980-84, dir., 1984-86, pres., 1986—; exec. v.p. Pacific Rim Bus. Coords., Salt Lake City, 1993—, also bd. dirs., 1993—; assoc. dir. exch. program between U. Utah and Nagoya Broadcasting Network of Japan, 1973-79; lectr. in field, Superior award in extemporaneous speaking, 1956. Author essay, contbr. articles to ency. Chmn. bd. trustees Western Am. Lang. Inst., 1986—, sec. to bd. trustees, 1980-86; chmn. bd. trustees Found. for Internat. Understanding, 1982—; mem. internat. adv. coun. Salt Lake C.C., 1988-94; mem. bd. advisors Consortium for Internat. Edn., 1972-77. Horace H. Rackham Sch. grad. studies fellow, 1969-70, Fulbright-Hays rsch. fellow (Japan), 1968-69, U.S. Nat. Def. fgn. lang. fellow, 1965-68. Mem. Assn. for Asian Studies (gen. chairperson, chairperson local arrangements western conf. 1970-72), Phi Kappa Phi. Home: 8710 Oakwood Park Cir Sandy UT 84094

SABHARWAL, RANJIT SINGH, mathematician; b. Dhudial, India, Dec. 11, 1925; came to U.S., 1958, naturalized, 1981; s. Krishan Ch and Devti (An) S.; m. Pritam Kaur Chadha, Mar. 5, 1948; children—Rajinderpal, Amarjit, Jasbir. B.A. with honors, Punjab U., 1944, M.A., 1948; M.A. U. Calif, Berkeley, 1962; Ph.D., Wash. State U., 1966. Lectr. math. Khalsa Coll., Bombay, India, 1951-58; teaching asst. U. Calif., Berkeley, 1958-62; instr. math. Portland (Oreg.) State U., 1962-62, Wash. State U., 1963-66; asst. prof. Kans. State U., 1966-68; mem. faculty Calif. State Hayward, 1968—, prof. math., 1974—. Author papers on non-Desarguesian planes. Mem. Am. Math. Soc., Math. Assn. Am., Sigma Xi. Address: 27892 Adobe Ct Hayward CA 94542-2102

SABIN, JACK CHARLES, engineering and construction firm executive; b. Phoenix, June 29, 1921; s. Jack Byron and Rena (Lewis) S.; B.S., U. Ariz., 1943; B in Chem. Engring., U. Minn., 1947; m. Frances Jane McIntyre, Mar. 27, 1950; children—Karen Lee, Robert William, Dorothy Ann, Tracy Ellen. With Standard Oil Co. of Calif., 1947-66, sr. engr., 1966—; pres., dir. Indsl. Control & Engring., Inc., Redondo Beach, Calif., 1966—; owner/mgr. Jack C. Sabin, Engr.-Contractor, Redondo Beach, 1968—; staff engr. Pacific Molasses Co., San Francisco, 1975-77; project mgr. E & L Assocs., Long Beach, Calif., 1977-79; dir. Alaska Pacific Petroleum, Inc., 1968—, Marlex Petroleum, Inc., 1970, 71—, Served with U.S. Army, 1942-46; capt. Chem. Corps, Res., 1949-56. Registered profl. engr., Calif., Alaska; lic. gen. engring. contractor, Ariz., Calif. Mem. Nat. Soc. Profl. Engrs., Ind. Liquid Terminals Assn., Conservative Caucus, Calif. Tax Reduction Com., Tau Beta Pi, Phi Lambda Upsilon, Phi Sigma Kappa. Republican. Clubs: Elks; Town Hall of Calif. Address: 151 Camino De Las Colinas Redondo Beach CA 90277-5828 also: 4421 NE Wistaria Dr Portland OR 97213

SABSAY, DAVID, library consultant; b. Waltham, Mass., Sept. 12, 1931; s. Wiegard Isaac and Ruth (Weinstein) S.; m. Helen Glenna Tolliver, Sept. 24,1 966. AB, Harvard U., 1953; BLS, U. Calif., Berkeley, 1955. Circulation dept. supr. Richmond (Calif.) Pub. Library, 1955-56; city libr. Santa Rosa (Calif.) Pub. Library, 1956-65; dir. Sonoma County Library, Santa Rosa, 1965-92; libr. cons., 1992—; coordinator North Bay Coop. Library System, Santa Rosa, 1960-64; cons. in field, Sebastopol, Calif., 1968—. Contbr. articles to profl. jours. Commendation, Calif. Assn. Library Trustees and Commrs., 1984. Mem. Calif. Library Assn. (pres. 1971, cert. appreciation 1971, 80), ALA. Club: Harvard (San Francisco). Home and Office: 667 Montgomery Rd Sebastopol CA 95472-3020

SACHS, LOREN ALLEN, magnetic resonance imaging technology specialist; b. Tacoma, Wash., Nov. 24, 1962; s. Neil Russell and Annette Marie (Harvey) S.; m. Denise Yurie Nakamura, Apr. 11, 1992; 1 child, Alyssa. AA, L.A. Harbor Cmty Coll., Wilmington, Calif., 1990; BA, Calif. State U., 1994. Cert. Radiologic Tech., Am. Registry of Radiologic Tech. Radiologic tech. Harbor-UCLA Medical Ctr., Torrance, Calif., 1983-85; MR tech., CT tech. Harbor-UCLA Diagnostic Imaging Ctr., Torrance, Calif., 1985-91; MR tech. mktg. rep. MRI Cen. Glendale, Calif., 1991—. Author: Illustrated Guide to MRI Positioning, 1992; contbr. articles to profl. jours. Recipient Young Am. award Calif. News Youth Found., 1976. Mem. Am. Soc. Radiologic Technologists, Calif. Soc. Radiologic Technologists (sec. 1989-90, v.p. 1990-91). Home: 21111 Dolores St # 50 Carson CA 90745-1323 Office: MRI Healthcare Ctr of Glendale 1109 S Central Ave Glendale CA 91204-2212

SACKETT, TIMOTHY DAVID, information systems specialist; b. Portland, OR, Sept. 1, 1955; s. Stanley McKennon and Lurah Louise (Slocum) S.; m. Leslie Elizabeth Porterfield, July 21, 1979; children: Stewart McKennon, Andrey Elizabeth. Student, Portland State U., 1973-76, Linfield Coll., 1993—. Mgmt. trainee U.S. Bank Oreg., 1973-77, br. officer ops./loans, 1977-80, liaison analyst info. processing divsn., 1980-83, info. resource mgmt. specialist III, 1983-84; sr. software specialist Info. Ctr. Nike, Inc., 1984-85, office systems adminstr., 1986-87; sr. info. ctr. analyst Info. Ctr. Fred Meyer, Inc., Portland, Oreg., 1987-89, decision support supr., 1989, project coord., 1989-91, project mgr. tech. svcs., 1991-94; network mgr. Columbia Mgmt. Co., Portland, 1994—; instr. Portland C.C., 1989-91; mem. adv. bd. continuing edn. program Linfield Coll., Portland, 1990; ind. bus. cons., 1991—. Mem. vestry St. Michael & All Angels Ch., Portland, 1991-94. Mem. Data Processing Mgmt. Assn. (pres. Portland chpt. 1989-90), Portland Personal Computer Club. Democrat. Episcopalian. Office: Columbia Mgmt Co 1301 SW 5th Ave Portland OR 97201-5601

SACKHEIM, ROBERT LEWIS, aerospace engineer, educator; b. N.Y.C., N.Y., May 16, 1937; s. A. Frederick and Lillian L. (Emmer) S.; m. Babette Freund, Jan. 12, 1964; children: Karen Holly, Andrew Frederick. BSChemE, U. Va., 1959; MSChemE, Columbia U., 1961; postgrad., UCLA, 1966-72. Project engr. Comsat Corp., El Segundo, Calif., 1969-72; project mgr. TRW, Redondo Beach, Calif., 1964-69, sect. head, 1972-76, dept. mgr., 1976-81, mgr. new bus., 1981-86, lab. mgr., 1986-90, dep. ctr. dir., 1990-93, ctr. dir., 1993—; instr. UCLA engring. ext., 1986; mem. adv. bds. NASA, Washington, 1989—; mem. peer rev. bd. various univs. and govtl. agys., 1990—; mem. Nat. Rsch. Coun./Aeronautics and Space Engring. Bd., 1994—; guest lectr. various univs. and AIAA short courses. Author: Space Mission Analysis and Design, 1991, Space Propulsion Analysis and Design, 1995; contbr. over 70 papers to profl. jours., confs. Mem. adv. bd. L.A. Bd. Edn., 1990-92; fund raiser March of Dimes, L.A., 1970-90, YMCA, San Pedro, Calif., 1974-86. Capt. USAF, 1960-63. Recipient Group Achievement award NASA, 1970, 78, 86. Fellow AIAA (chmn. com. 1980-83, J.H. Wyld Propulsion award 1992, Shuttle Flag award 1984). Office: TRW Space & Elects Group Bldg 01/RM 2010 1 Space Park Blvd Rm 2010 Redondo Beach CA 90278-1001

SACKS, ARTHUR BRUCE, environmental and liberal arts educator; b. N.Y.C., Apr. 21, 1946; s. Fred and Lillian Pearl (Levy) S.; m. Normandy Roden, May 17, 1987; children: Rachel, Erica. BA, Bklyn. Coll., 1967; MA, U. Wis., 1968, PhD, 1975. Teaching asst. dept. English, U. Wis., Madison, 1968-72, asst. to assoc. dean for student acad. affairs, 1972-76, lectr. dept. English, 1975, sr. lectr. Inst. for Environ. Studies, 1976-90, coord. acad. programs, 1976-78, asst. to dir., asst. dir., then assoc. dir., 1983-85, acting dir., then dir., 1985-90, assoc. mem. dept. urban and regional planning, 1985-93, adminstr. acad. programs, 1978-85; sr. spl. asst. to dean grad. sch. U. Wis., 1990-93; assoc. mem. Russian and East European studies U. Wis., Madison, 1992-93, acting dir. internat. faculty and staff svcs., 1993; dir., prof. internat. studies Colo. Sch. Mines, Golden, 1993—; mem. adj. faculty Ohio State U., Columbus, 1992-94; prof. environ. sci. Internat. U., Moscow, 1992—. Bd. dirs. Friends of Waisman Ctr. on Mental Retardation and Human Devel., 1991-93; mem. Emergency Med. Svcs. Commn., 1992-93. Recipient blue ribbon for poetry Am. Assn. Interpretive Naturalists, 1983. Mem. AAAS, Am. Assn. Higher Edn., N.Am. Assn. Environ. Edn. (adv. group internat. rels. com. 1991-94, rep. to jour. 1988—, nominating com. 1989-90, pres. 1984-85, pres.-elect 1983-84, sec. 1982-83, exec. com. 1982-86, chmn. devel. com. 1986-94, liaison to Friends of the UN Environ. Programme, chmn. participation World Decade of the Environ., 1982-92, bd. dirs. 1980-84, chmn. environ. studies sect. 1980-82, program com. confs., publs. com. 1978-83, chmn. 1981-83, polit. strategies com. 1982-83, sec.-treas. environ. studies sect. 1978-80, chmn. con. on establishing jour. environ. studies 1978, mem. spl. task force on mission, membership and orgnl. structure 1977-78, mem. planning group nat. comm. environ. edn. rsch. 1979-80), Internat. Soc. Environ. Edn., World Conservation Union. Office: Colo Sch Mines 301 Stratton Hall Golden CO 80401

SACKS, ROBERT NEIL, lawyer; b. Oberlin, Ohio, Oct. 29, 1960; s. Norman and Miriam Sacks; m. Gabrielle Gopin, July 18, 1992. BA, U. Wis., 1981; JD, UCLA, 1986. Bar: Calif. 1986. Assoc. Morrison & Foerster, L.A., 1986-91; ptnr. Ross, Sacks & Glazier, L.A., 1991—; arbitrator L.A. Superior Ct., 1993—; judge pro tem L.A. Mcpl. Ct., 1993—; speaker on estate and trust litigation topics, L.A., 1994. Mem. ABA, L.A. County Bar Assn., Beverly Hills Bar Assn. Office: Ross Sacks & Glazier 300 S Grand Ave Ste 3900 Los Angeles CA 90071-3149

SACKTON, FRANK JOSEPH, university official, lecturer, retired army officer; b. Chgo., Aug. 11, 1912; m. June Dorothy Raymond, Sept. 21, 1940. Student, Northwestern U., 1936, Yale, 1946, U. Md., 1951-52; B.S., U. Md., 1970; grad., Army Inf. Sch., 1941, Command and Gen. Staff Coll., 1942, Armed Forces Staff Coll., 1949, Nat. War Coll., 1954; M.Pub. Adminstrn., Ariz. State U., 1976. Mem. 131st Inf. Regt., Ill. N.G., 1929-40; commd. 2d lt. U.S. Army, 1934, advanced through grades to lt. gen., 1967; brigade plans and ops. officer (33d Inf. Div.), 1941, PTO, 1943-45; div. signal officer, 1942-43, div. intelligence officer, 1944, div. plans and ops. officer, 1945; sec. to gen. staff for Gen. MacArthur Tokyo, 1947-48; bn. comdr. 30th Inf. Regt., 1949-50; mem. spl. staff Dept. Army, 1951; plans and ops. officer Joint Task Force 132, PTO, 1952; comdr. Joint Task Force 7, Marshall Islands, 1953; mem. gen. staff Dept. Army, 1954-55; with Office Sec. Def., 1956; comdr. 18th Inf. Regt., 1957-58; chief staff 1st Inf. Div., 1959; chief army Mil. Mission to Turkey, 1960-62; comdr. XIV Army Corps, 1963; dep. dir. plans Joint Chiefs Staff, 1964-66; army general staff mil. ops., 1966-67, comptroller of the army, 1967-70, ret., 1970; spl. asst. for fed./state relations Gov. Ariz., 1971-75; chmn. Ariz. Programming and Coordinating Com. for Fed. Programs, 1971-75; lectr. Am. Grad. Sch. Internat. Mgmt., 1973-77; vis. asst. prof., lectr. public affairs Ariz. State U., Tempe, 1976-78; founding dean Ariz. State U. Coll. Public Programs, 1979-80; prof. public affairs Ariz. State U., 1980—, finance educator, v.p. bus. affairs, 1981-83, dep. dir. intercollegiate athletics, 1984-85, dir. strategic planning, 1987-88. Contbr. articles to public affairs and mil. jours. Mem. Ariz. Steering Com. for Restoration of the State Capitol, 1974-75, Ariz. State Personnel Bd., 1978-83, Ariz. Regulatory Coun., 1981-93. Decorated D.S.M., Silver Star, also Legion of Merit with 4 oak leaf clusters, Bronze Star with 2 oak leaf clusters, Air medal, Army Commendation medal with 1 oak leaf cluster, Combat Inf. badge. Mem. Ariz. Acad. Public Adminstrn., Pi Alpha Alpha (pres. chpt. 1976-82). Clubs: Army-Navy (Washington); Arizona (Phoenix). Home: 12000 N 90th St Apt 2071 Scottsdale AZ 85260-8600 Office: Ariz State U Sch Pub Affairs Tempe AZ 85287

SADAVA, DAVID ERIC, biology educator; b. Ottawa, Ont., Can., Mar. 14, 1946; came to U.S., 1967; s. Samuel and Ruth (Bloom) S.; m. Angeline Douvas, June 15, 1972; 1 child, Dana Louise. BS, Carleton U., Ottawa, 1967; PhD, U. Calif. San Diego, La Jolla, 1971. Prof. biology Scripps Coll., Claremont, Calif., 1972—, chmn. Joint Sci. Program, 1980—; vis. prof. dept. pediatrics U. Colo., Denver, 1979—, dept. molecular biology, 1981—. Author: Cell Biology: Organelle Structure and Function, 1993; co-author: Plants, Food, People, 1977, Plants, Genes and Agriculture, 1994; contbr. articles to profl. jours. Woodrow Wilson Found. fellow, 1968. Office: Claremont McKenna Coll Joint Sci Dept Claremont CA 91711

SADILEK, VLADIMIR, architect; b. Czechoslovakia, June 27, 1933; came to U.S., 1967, naturalized, 1973; s. Oldrich and Antoine (Zlamal) S.; Ph.D. summa cum laude in City Planning and Architecture, Tech. U. Prague, 1957; m. Jana Kadlec, Mar. 25, 1960; 1 son, Vladimir, Jr. Chief architect State Office for City Planning, Prague, 1958-67; architect, designer Bank Bldg. Corp., St. Louis, 1967-70, assoc. architect, San Francisco, 1970-74; owner, chief exec. officer Bank Design Cons., San Mateo, Calif., 1974-81, West Coast Development Co., San Mateo, 1975—; pres., chief exec. officer Orbis Devel. Corp., San Mateo, 1981—. Served with Inf. of Czechoslovakia, 1958. Recipient awards of excellence from Bank Building Corp. and AIA for planning and design of fin. instns. in Hawaii, Calif. (1971), Ariz., N.Mex., Tex. (1972), Colo., Wyo. (1973), Idaho, Oreg., Washington (1974); lic. architect, 28 states. Republican. Roman Catholic. Home: 80 Orange Ct Burlingame CA 94010-6516 Office: 1777 Borel Pl San Mateo CA 94402-3509

SADLER, GRAHAM HYDRICK, library administrator; b. Sikeston, Mo., Aug. 17, 1931; s. Philip Landis and Montie Pearl (Hydrick) S.; m. Betty A. Grugett, Nov. 22, 1950; children—Graham Hydrick, Lee, Susan, Harrison. B.S., S.E. Mo. State Coll., 1952; M.L.S., Emory U., 1957. Asst. libr. S.E. Mo. State Coll., Cape Girardeau, 1954-61; adminstrv. libr. Kinderhook Regional Libr., Lebanon, Mo., 1961-66; dir. Fort Lewis Coll. Libr., Durango, Colo., 1966-67; assoc. prof. librarianship Kans. State Tchrs. Coll., Emporia, 1967-69; asst. libr., dir. community svc. Denver Pub. Libr., 1970-77; dir. County of Henrico Pub. Libr., Richmond, Va., 1978-94, ret., 1994; mem. adv. com. Office of Library Service to Disadvantaged, 1978-91. Mem. ALA (membership com. 1989-92), Southeastern Libr. Assn., Va. Libr. Assn.

SADOW, TIM N., distribution center executive; b. Phila., Dec. 28, 1957; s. Jay Walter and Edith (Sipser) S.; m. Joyce Lynn Munroe; children: Kelly, Shawn, Nathan. BA in Advt. and Pub. Rels., Temple U., 1979. Ops. mgr. WTC Air Frt., Phoenix, 1981-82; gen. mgr. Hi Tech Distbn., Tempe, Ariz., 1982—. Violinist, Met. Pops Orch., Phoenix, 1993-94. Recipient Recognition award Motorola, Inc., Mesa, Ariz., 1984, Performance award, 1990, TCS award, 1992, Safety awards State Comp. Fund, Phoenix, 1989, 90.

SADRI, FEREYDOON, medical company executive; b. Kermanshah, Iran, July 28, 1950; came to U.S., 1977; s. Ahmad and Kohar (Rahmani) S.; m. Mariam Joy Hemmons, June 9, 1994. BS, Razi U., Kermanshah, 1976; MS, U. Akron, 1980; PhD, Kent State U., 1984. Postdoctoral fellow biomed. engring. U. Akron, Ohio, 1984-85; dir. cardiovascular lab. Gulf South Rsch. Ins., New Orleans, 1986-87; dir. R&D T.O.P.S. Med. Corp., Bellevue, Wash., 1987-92, Bio-Rsch. Lab., Redmond, Wash., 1992-94; v.p., sci. dir. Bio-Preserve Med., Redmond, 1994—. Patentee organ preservation and treatment device. Grantee Am. Heart Assn., 1985, Eagl Club, 1985. Home: 1641 233rd Pl NE Redmond WA 98053-4451

SADRUDDIN, MOE, oil company executive, consultant; b. Hyderabad, India, Mar. 3, 1943; came to U.S., 1964; m. Azmath Oureshi, 1964; 3 children. BSME, Osmania U., Hyderabad, 1964; MS in Indsl. Engring., NYU, 1966; MBA, Columbia U., 1970. Cons. project engr. Ford, Bacon & Davis, N.Y.C., 1966; staff indsl. engr. J.C. Penney, N.Y.C., 1966-68; sr. cons. Drake, Sheahan, Stewart & Dougall, N.Y.C., 1968-70, Beech-Nut Inc. subs. Squibb Corp., N.Y.C., 1970-72; founder, pres. Azmath Constrn. Co., Englewood, N.J., 1972-77; crude oil cons., fgn. govt. rep., 1977—; pres. A-One Petroleum Co., Fullerton, Calif., 1985—; govt. advisor Puerto Rico, 1980-82, Dominica, 1983-84, St. Vincent, 1981-82, Kenya, 1983-84, Belize 1984-85, Costa Rica 1983-86, Paraguay 1984-87. Mem. Los Angeles World Affairs Council. Mem. Internat. Platform Assn. Address: A-One Petroleum Co 2656 N Camino Del Sol Fullerton CA 92633-4806

SADUN, ALFREDO ARRIGO, neuro-ophthalmologist educator; b. New Orleans, Oct. 23, 1950; s. Elvio H. and Lina (Ottoleghi) S.; m. Debra Leigh Rice, Mar. 18, 1978; children: Rebecca Eli, Elvio Aaron, Benjamin Maxwell. BS, MIT, 1972; PhD, Albert Einstein Med. Sch., Bronx, N.Y., 1976, MD, 1978. Intern Huntington Meml. Hosp. U. So. Calif., Pasadena, 1978-79; resident Harvard U. Med. Sch., Boston, 1979-82, HEED Found. fellow in neuro-ophthalmology Mass. Eye and Ear Inst., 1982-83, instr. ophthalmology, 1983, asst. prof. ophthalmology, 1984; dir. residential tng. U. So. Calif. Dept. Ophthalmology, L.A., 1984-85, 90—; asst. prof. ophthalmology and neurosurgery U. So. Calif., L.A., 1984-87, assoc. prof., 1987-90; full prof. U. So. Calif., 1990—; prin. investigator Howe Lab. Harvard U., Boston, 1981-84, E. Doheny Eye Inst., L.A., 1984—; examiner Am. Bd. Ophthalmology; mem. internal rev. bd. U. So. Calif. Author: Optics for Opthalmologists, 1988, New Methods of Sensory Visual Testing, 1989; contbr. articles to profl. jours. and chpts. to books. James Adams scholar, 1990-91; recipient Pecan D. award, 1988-92. Fellow Am. Acad. Ophthalmology, Neuro-Ophthalmologists; mem. NIH (Med. Scientist Tng. award 1972-78), Am. Assn. Anatomists, Assn. Univ. Prof. Ophthalmology (assoc.), Soc. to Prevent Blindness, Nat. Eye Inst. (New Investigator Rsch. award 1983-86, ROI awards 1988-91, 1993—), Soc. Neuroscis., Assn. Rsch. in Vision and Ophthalmology, N.Am. Neuro-Ophthal. Soc. (chmn. membership com. 1990—, v.p. 1994—). Home: 2478 Adair St San Marino CA 91108-2610 Office: U So Calif E Doheny Eye Inst 1450 San Pablo St Los Angeles CA 90033-4615

SAEGER, DANIEL PAUL, insurance company sales executive; b. Ada, Okla., Jan. 28, 1956; s. Harold Paul and Patricia Louise (Behrens) S.; m. Renée M. Mullin, June 21, 1980; children: Stephen Louis, Michael Joseph. BS in Mgmt., U. No. Colo., Greeley, 1978; MBA, U. Phoenix, Denver, 1992. Asst. v.p. Capitol Life, Denver, 1980-84; account mgr. Alexander & Alexander, Denver, 1984-86; account exec. CIGNA, Denver, 1987-91; group mgr. N.Y. Life Ins. Co., Denver, 1991—. Mem. Colo. Group Ins. Assn. (bd. dirs. 1987, 88, 94, coord. ins. reform legislation 1994), Greenwood Athletic Club. Republican. Home: 6220 S Krameria St Englewood CO 80111-4243 Office: NY Life Ins 2260 S Xanadu Way Ste 290 Aurora CO 80014-1373

SAFDAR, SYED MOHAMMED, quality assurance engineer; b. Karachi, Sind, Pakistan, Apr. 4, 1956; s. Ahsan Mohammed and Raisa Begum Syed; m. Naureen Hasan Beg, Apr. 20, 1985; children: Sana S., Fahd S. BEEE, NED U. Engring. and Tech., Pakistan, 1979; MSEE, Miss. State U., 1982. Quality engring. supr. Advanced Micro Devices, Inc., Sunnyvale, Calif., 1982-87; reliability and quality assurance mgr. Fairchild Semiconductor, Milpitas, Calif., 1987; quality engring. mgr. Integrated Device Tech., Inc., Salinas, Calif., 1988—. Contbr. articles to profl. jours. Recipient First prize Univ. Sci. Exhbn., 1978, Tough Minded Bus. award Southwestern Co., 1980. Mem. Soc. Electronic Engr. (publs. editor). Office: Integrated Device Tech Inc 1566 Moffett St Salinas CA 93905-3342

SAFERITE, LINDA LEE, library director; b. Santa Barbara, Calif., Mar. 25, 1947; d. Elwyn C. and Polly (Frazer) S.; m. Andre Doyon, July 16, 1985. BA, Calif. State U., Chico, 1969; MS in Library Sci., U. So. Calif., 1970; cert. in Indsl. Relations, UCLA, 1976; MBA, Pepperdine U., 1979. Librarian-in-charge, reference librarian Los Angeles County Pub. Libr. System, 1970-73, regional reference librarian, 1973-75, sr. librarian-in-charge, 1975-78, regional adminstr., 1978-80; libr. dir. Scottsdale (Ariz.) Pub. Libr. System, 1980-93, Fort Collins (Colo.) Pub. Libr., 1993—; task force del. White House Conf. on Libr. and Info. Svcs., 1992—, rep. Region V, 1982-94. Bd. dirs. Scottsdale-Paradise Valley YMCA, 1981-86, Ariz. Libr. Friends, 1990-92; bd. dirs. AMIGOS, 1990, chmn., 1992-93; mem. Class 5, Scottsdale Leavership, 1991. Recipient Cert. Recognition for efforts in civil rights Ariz. Atty. Gen.'s Office, 1985, Libr. award Ariz. Libr. Friends, 1988, Women of Distinction award for Edn., 1989; named State Libr. of Yr., 1990. Mem. ALA, Ariz. State Libr. Assn. (pres. 1987-88), Ariz. Women's Town Hall AlumniAssn., Met. Bus. and Profl. Women (Scottsdale, pres. 1986-87), Soroptimist (pres. 1981-83). Republican. Office: Fort Collins Pub Libr 201 Peterson St Fort Collins CO 80524-2919

SAGE, RODERICK DUNCAN, dermatologist, educator; b. Iowa City, Iowa, Feb. 13, 1926; s. Erwin Carlton and Katherine (Miles) S.; m. Jacquelin Irene Price, June 14, 1952; children: Jonathan S., Jefferson D., Rowan F., Andrew E. BA, U. Iowa, 1949; MD, Stanford U., 1954. Diplomate Am. Bd. Dermatology. Intern Med. Coll. Va., Richmond, 1953-54; med. resident Dartmouth Coll., Hanover, N.H., 1954-55; resident in dermatology Stanford Hosp., San Francisco, 1955-58; pvt. practice Reno, Nev., 1958—; prof. U. Nev. Med. Sch., Reno, 1971—; lectr. Stanford (Calif.) Med. Sch., 1966—; lectr., cons. in field. Contbr. articles to profl. publs. With USN, 1943-46. Office: 975 Ryland St Reno NV 89502-1667

SAGER, DONALD ALLEN, insurance company executive; b. Cleve., Sept. 13, 1930; s. Albert Allen and Dolores Vera (Stone) S.; m. Shirley T. Sager, Dec. 23, 1951; children: Donald A. II, David Allen. BA, U. Md., 1958; postgrad., U. Md. Law Sch., 1958-60. Sr. underwriter Monumental Life Ins. Co., Balt., 1958-64; v.p. Am. Health & Life Ins. Co., Balt., 1964-77; asst. v.p. Univ. Life Ins. Co., Indpls., 1977-81; v.p. Vulcan Life Ins. Co., Birmingham, Ala., 1981-84, Modern Pioneers' Life Ins. Co., Phoenix, 1984-87, Old Reliance Ins. Co., Phoenix, 1987—. Dir. Hearing and Speech Agy., Balt., 1974-77; treas. Essex Recreational Coun., Balt., 1966-73; bd. dirs. Arthritis Found., Phoenix, 1988-91; precinct capt. Rep. Party, Phoenix, 1990—; dir. City of Phoenix Pacific Rim adv. coun., mem. Abraham Lincoln Soc.; bd. dirs. Ariz. Dept. Ins. Small Group Reinsurance Bd., mem. examination com. Ariz. Dept. Ins. License. With U.S. Army, 1951-53, Korea. Decorated Bronze Star. Mem. Assn. Health Underwriters (legis. com. 1992—), Masons, Shriners, Moose, Elks, Order of De Molay (cert., N.D. gov. 1988-90). Lutheran. Home: 5429 E Charter Oak Rd Scottsdale AZ 85254-4217 Office: Old Reliance Ins Co 1433 N 3rd Ave Phoenix AZ 85003-1201

SAGER, NANCY WYNNE, special education consultant; b. Chgo., Apr. 21, 1948; d. Bertram William and Natalie Inez (Hill) S.; m. Donald Harry Ruggles Jr., Oct. 7, 1990; stepchildren: Chloe, Derek. BA in Elem. Edn. and Sociology, Monmouth Coll., 1970; MA in Spl. Edn., U. No. Colo., 1976; student, U. Houston, 1978; cert. in spl. edn. adminstrn., U. No. Colo., 1985. Tchr. Greeley (Colo.) Pub. Schs., 1972-73, St. Vrain Valley (Colo.) Schs., 1973-74, Brighton (Colo.) Pub. Schs., 1974-75, Denver Pub. Schs., 1975-76; referral coord. Houston Ind. Schs., 1976-80; tchr. Aurora (Colo.) Pub. Schs., 1980-81; edn./behavior cons. Cherry Creek (Colo.) Schs., 1981—; cons. and speaker in field. Author: (with others) Bully-Proofing Your School, 1994; contbr. articles to profl. jorus. Participant defining significant identifiable emotional behavioral disorders Colo. Dept. Edn., 1982-83; pres. Colo. Fedn. Coun. Exceptional Children, 1986-87. Verne F. Shelley scholar, 1991. Home: 1802 S Uinta Way Denver CO 80231-2914

SAGMEISTER, EDWARD FRANK, business owner, hospitality industry executive, civic official, retired fund raiser consultant, career officer; b. N.Y.C., Dec. 10, 1939; s. Frank and Anna (Unger) S.; m. Anne Marie Ducker, Aug. 18, 1962; children: Cynthia Anne, Laura Marie, Cheryl Suzanne, Eric Edward. BS, U. San Francisco, 1962; MBA, Syracuse U., 1968; postgrad., Air Command and Staff Coll., 1977, Air War Coll., 1981. Commd. 2d lt. USAF, 1963, advanced through grades to lt. col., pers. officer, 1963, aide-de-camp, 1965; dir. pers. sys. Alaskan Air Command, 1968; sys. design program analysis officer HQ USAF, The Pentagon, 1971; spl. asst. sec. Air Force Pers. Coun., USAF, 1975; dir. pers. programs and assignments HQUSAF Europe, 1979; Air Force dep. asst. inspector gen., 1982; ret. USAF, 1984; dir. devel. Am. Cancer Soc., Riverside, Calif., 1984-87; cons. Redlands, Calif., 1987-92; chmn. of bd., pres., CEO Hospitality Pub and Grub, Inc., San Bernardino, Calif., 1992—; instr. Am. Internat. U., L.A., 1987; program dir. Am. Radio Network, L.A., 1987; ptnr., owner Midway Med. Ctr., San Bernardino, 1990-91. Foreman pro tem San Bernardino County Grand Jury, 1990-91; mem. Redlands 2000 Com., 1988; campaign cabinet mem. Arrowhead United Way, San Bernardino, 1986-87, loaned exec., 1985; exec. dir. Crafton Hills Coll. Found., Yucaipa, Calif., 1988; vol. San Bernardino County Dept. Probation, 1985-88; mem. Redlands Cmty. Chorus, 1988-90; vice-chmn., charter mem. Redlands Human Rels. Commn., 1994—; mem. Redlands Youth Accountability Bd., San Bernardino County, 1994—. Mem. San Bernardino C. of C., Redlands C. of C., Ret. Officers Assn., Nat. Soc. Fundraising Execs., (dir., charter mem. Inland Empire chpt. 1987-88), Empire Singers (v.p. 1987). Republican. Roman Catholic. Home: 503 Sunnyside Ave Redlands CA 92373-5629 Office: Hospitality Pub and Grub Inc 1987 Diners Ct San Bernardino CA 92408-3330

SAGRAVES, MICHELLE KAYE, nursing administrator; b. Moses Lake, Wash., July 21, 1958; d. Robert K. and Patricia (Church) Rugg; m. Scott Gary Sagraves, June 9, 1990; children: Tayler, Kimberly, Nicholas, Jordann. ADN, N.Mex. State U., Carlsbad, 1987. Cert. CEN, ACLS instr. Staff nurse Guadalupe Med. Ctr., Carlsbad, 1987-89; staff nurse emergency dept. New Britain (Conn.) Gen. Hosp., 1989-90; charge nurse emergency dept. Edgewater Med. Ctr., Chgo., 1990-91, nurse mgr., 1991-93; staff RN Maricopa Med. Ctr., Phoenix, 1993—. Mem. Emergency Nurses Assn. Home: 15435 S 45th St Phoenix AZ 85044-4932 Office: Maricopa Med Ctr 2601 E Roosevelt St Phoenix AZ 85008-4973

SAHATJIAN, MANIK, nurse, psychologist; b. Tabris, Iran, July 24, 1921; came to U.S., 1951; d. Dicran and Shushanig (Der-Galustian) Mnatzaganian; m. George Sahatjian, Jan. 21, 1954; children: Robert, Edwin. Nursing Cert., Am. Mission Hosps.-Boston U., 1954; BA in Psychology, San Jose State U., 1974, MA in Psychology, 1979. RN, Calif., Mass. Head nurse Am. Mission Hosp., Tabris, 1945-46; charge nurse Banke-Melli Hosp., Tehran, 1946-51; vis. nurse Vis. Nurse Assn., Oakland, Calif., 1956-57; research asst. Stanford U., 1979-81, Palo Alto (Calif.) Med. Research Found., 1981-84; documentation supr. Bethesda Convalescent Ctr., Los Gatos, Calif., 1985-86; sr. outreach worker City of Fremont (Calif.) Human Svcs., 1987-90, case mgr., 1990—; guest rsch. asst. NASA Ames Lab., Mountain View, Calif., summers 1978, 79. Author (with others) psychol. research reports. Fulbright scholar, 1951; Iran Found. scholar, 1953. Mem. AAUW, Western Psychol. Assn. Democrat. Mem. St. Andrew Armenian Church. Home: 339 Starlite Way Fremont CA 94539-7642

SAHS, MAJORIE JANE, art educator; b. Altadena, Calif., Aug. 27, 1926; d. Grayson Michael and Janie Belle (Aaron) McCarty; m. Eugene Otto Sahs, July 21, 1949; children: Victoria, Stephen, Jeffry. Student, Emerson Coll., Boston, 1945; BA, Sacramento State U., 1970; MA in Art Edn., Calif. State U., Sacramento, 1972, postgrad., 1973-79. Cert. secondary tchr., Calif. Tchr. art Sacramento County Schs., 1971-80; cons. Whole Brain Learning Modes, Sacramento, 1980-84; tng. specialist Art Media, Sacramento, Calif., 1983—; instr. Found. for Continuing Med. Edn., Calif., 1985; presenter Nat. Art Edn. Conf., Chgo., 1992, 93, Asian Pacific Conf. on Arts Edn., Franklin, Australia, Internat. Conf., Montreal, Can., 1993; cons. and lectr. in field; judge U.S. Treas., 1994, 95, Dept. of Calif. Student Art. Prodr., writer guide and video Gesture Painting Through T'ai Chi, 1992; editor, pub. Calif.'s state newspaper for art edn., 1987-90; editor: Crocker Museum Docent Guide, 1990; mem. editl. bd. Jour. for Nat. Art Edn. Assn., 1990—; editor (newsletter) U.S. Soc. for Edn. Through Art, 1994; designer of ltd. edits. scarves and cards for Nat. Breast Cancer Rsch. Fund, Exploration Inspiration '95. Del. Calif. Arts Leadership Symposium for Arts Edn., 1979, Legis. Coalition Through The Arts, Calif., 1989, 95; judge Calif. State Fair Art Show, 1989, Fed. Treasury Poster Contest, 1994, 95; organizer and host art show and fundraiser for women candidates, 1992. Recipient State award of Merit. Mem. Internat. Assn. Edn. through Art, U.S. Soc. Edn. through Art (editor newsletter 1994-96), Nat. Art Edn. Assn. (mem. editl. bd. jour. 1990—, Nat. Outstanding Newspaper Editor award 1988, 89), Calif. Art Edn. Assn. (mem. state coun., mem. area coun., editor state paper, State Award of Merit), Calif. Children's Homes Soc. (pres. Camellia chpt. 1990-91), Asian Pacific Arts Educators Assn., Art Ctr. L.A. Alumni. Home and Office: 1836 Walnut Ave Carmichael CA 95608-5417

SAILOR, J. DOUGLAS, engineering consultant; b. Elkhart, Ind., Nov. 14, 1927; s. Clifford Earl and Mildred Marie (Scholl) S.; m. Florence Margaret Magee, Aug. 30, 1960; children: Brian Scott, Craig Randall. BSEE, Purdue U., 1950, MSEE, 1951. Project engr. Wright Air Devel. Ctr., Dayton, Ohio, 1951-55, U.S. Army White Sands (N.Mex.) Signal Corp., 1955-56; mgr. systems engring. Lockheed Missiles & Space Co., Sunnyvale, Calif., 1957-92; pvt. cons. Morgan Hill, Calif., 1993—. Author: Space System Engineering, 1962, System Engineering Management Guide, 1983, System Engineering Manual, 1985. Pfc. U.S. Army, 1955-56. Fellow AIAA (assoc., chmn. San Francisco Bay area, Engr. of Yr. award 1986), Am. Astro. Soc. (chmn. San Francisco Bay area 1964), Nat. Coun. System Engrs. Home: 14125 Sycamore Dr Morgan Hill CA 95037-9405

SAINI, SUBHASH, computer scientist; b. New Delhi, Oct. 13, 1948. PhD, U. So. Calif., 1986. Asst. prof. physics Rajdhani Coll., New Delhi, 1972-75, chmn. dept. physics, 1975-81; teaching/rsch. asst. U. So. Calif., L.A., 1981-85, lectr., 1985; rsch. assoc. UCLA, 1986-87; rsch. staff mem. Lawrence Livermore (Calif.) Nat. Lab., 1987-89; sr. computer scientist for numerical aerodynamic simulation NASA, Moffett Field, Calif., 1989—; supercomputing cons. U. So. Calif., 1987-89; vis. prof. physics U. Delhi, 1976-77. Contbr. over 50 articles to profl. jours. Mem. IEEE, Soc. for Indsl. and Applied Math., Assn. Computing Machinery. Office: NASA Ames Rsch Ctr Mail Stop T27A-1 Moffett Field CA 94035

ST. AMAND, PIERRE, geophysicist; b. Tacoma, Wash., Feb. 4, 1920; s. Cyrias Z. and Mable (Berg) St. A.; m. Marie Pöss, Dec. 5, 1945; children: Gene, Barbara, Denali, David. BS in Physics, U. Alaska, 1948; MS in Geophysics, Calif. Inst. Tech., 1951, PhD in Geophysics and Geology, 1953; Dr. honoris causa, U. De Los Altos, Tepatitlan, Mex., 1992. Asst. dir. Geophys. Lab., U. Alaska, also head ionospheric and seismologic investigations, 1946-49; physicist U.S. Naval Ordnance Test Sta., China Lake, Calif., 1950-54; head optics br. U.S. Naval Ordnance Test Sta., 1955-58; head earth and planetary sci. div. U.S. Ordnance Test Sta., 1961-78, now cons. to tech. dir., head spl. projects office, 1978-88; fgn. service with ICA as prof. geol. and geophys. Sch. Earth Scis., U. Chile, 1958-60; originator theory rotational displacement Pacific Ocean Basin; pres. Saint-Amand Sci. Services; adj. prof. McKay Sch. Mines, U. Nev., U. N.D.; v.p., dir. Covillea Corp.; v.p., dir. tech. Muetal Corp.; cons. World Bank, Calif. Div. Water Resources, Am. Potash & Chem. Co., OAS; mem. U.S. Army airways communications system, Alaska and Can., 1942-46; cons. Mexican, Chilean, Argentine, Philipines, Can. govts.; mem. Calif. Gov.'s Com. Geol. Hazards; mem. com. magnetic instruments Internat. Union Geodesy and Geophys., 1954-59, Disaster Preparation Commn. for Los Angeles; charter mem. Sr. Exec. Service. Adv. bd. GeoScience News; contbr. 100 articles to scientific jours. Chmn. bd. dirs. Ridgecrest Community Hosp.; chmn. bd. dirs. Indian Wells Valley Airport Dist.; v.p. bd. dirs. Kern County Acad. Decathlon. Decorated knight Mark Twain, Mark Twain Jour.; recipient cert. of merit OSRD, 1945, cert. of merit USAAF, 1946, letter of commendation USAAF, 1948, Spl. award Philippine Air Force, 1969, Diploma de Honor Sociedad Geologica de Chile, Disting. Civilian Svc. medal USN, 1968, L.T.E. Thompson medal, 1973, Thunderbird award Weather Modification Assn., 1974, Disting. Pub. Svc. award Fed. Exec. Inst., 1976, Meritorious Svc. medal USN, 1988, Disting. Alumnus award U. Alaska, 1990; Fulbright rsch. fellow France, 1954-55. Fellow AAAS, Geol. Soc. Am., Earthquake Engr. Rsch. Inst.; mem. Am. Geophys. Union, Weather Modification Assn., Am. Seismol. Soc., Sister Cities (Ridgecrest-Tepatitlan) Assn. (pres.), Rotary (past pres., Paul Harris fellow), Footprinters Internat. (mem. grand bd., pres.), Sigma Xi. Home: 1748 W Las Flores Ave Ridgecrest CA 93555-8635

SAINT-AUBIN, ARTHUR FLANNIGAN, French language educator, writer; b. Eutaw, Ala., Aug. 14, 1953; s. James Flannigan and Annabelle Saint-Aubin. BA, Swarthmore, 1973; MA, Johns Hopkins, 1976, PhD, 1979; student, L.A. Psychoanalytic Inst., 1988-92. Instr. Loyola Coll., Balt., 1976-78; asst. prof. Hampton U., Va., 1978-79; asst. prof. Occidental Coll., L.A., 1979-85, assoc. prof., 1985-94, prof., 1994—; maître asst. Université de Rennes, France, 1984-86; dir. Oxy-in-France, 1983-88; editl. adv. Jour. of Hist. of Sexualite, Chgo., 1992—. Author: The Disorders of Love, 1982, History & Literature, 1983; translator Mme de Villedieu. Mem. Nat. Orgn. of Men Against Sexism, 1989—. Recipient Ford Fdn. award, 1978, Lilly Fdn. award, 1979. Mem. Assn. French Tchrs., Coll. Lang. Assn., Mens' Studies Assn., Am. Mens' Studies (treas. 1993—). Office: Occidental Coll 1600 Campus Rd Los Angeles CA 90041

ST. CLAIR, SHANE SCOTT, communications and international health specialist; b. Salem, Oreg., Feb. 27, 1965; s. Leo Christian and Cecelia Loraine (Hall) St. C.; m. Carol Lynn Stewart, Apr. 4, 1993. Student, La Sierra U., 1983, Crafton Hills Coll., 1987-89, Sierra Coll., 1990. Dir. Sale Away, Grand Terrace, Calif., 1986-90; capt. Canvasback Mission Inc., Benicia, Calif., 1991-94, devel. dir., 1993-94; exec. dir. Search for One, Inc., 1994—. Contbr. articles to profl. jours. Charter pres. Jr. C. of C., Benicia, 1993-94. Capt. U.S. Merchant Marine. Mem. Toastmasters Internat. (1st pl. Internat. Speech award 1994). Office: PO Box 833 Angwin CA 94508

ST. JEAN, GARRY, professional basketball coach; m. Mary Jane St. Jean; children: Emily, Gregory. B in Phys. Edn., Springfield (Mass.) Coll., 1973, M in Phys. Edn., postgrad. cert. Head coach Chicopee (Mass.) High Sch., 1973-80; coll. scout, asst. bench coach, asst. dir. player pers. Milw. Bucks, 1980-86; asst. coach, asst. player pers. dir. N.J. Nets, 1986-88; asst. coach Golden State Warriors, 1988-92; head coach Sacramento Kings, 1992—. Office: Sacramento Kings One Sports Pkwy Sacramento CA 95834*

ST. JOHN, EUGENE LOGAN, labor union director; b. Everett, Wash., Dec. 2, 1947; s. Huston Hopkins and Rena (Guillette) St. John; m. Carolyn Sue Crabb, July 15, 1978; children: Jeannine, Jordan, Michael, Matthew. BA, Western Wash. U., 1970; postgrad., U. Wash., 1978. VISTA vol. U.S. Govt. OEO, Ft. Lauderdale, Fla., 1970-71; organizer Internat. Fedn. Profl. and Tech. Engrs. Local 17 AFL-CIO, Seattle, 1972-74, bus. rep., 1974-80, program dir., 1980-82; exec. dir. Wash. Pub. Employees Assn., Olympia, 1982—. Bd. dirs. Evergreen State Coll. Labor Ctr., Olympia, 1988-90; mem. Pub. Employees Retirement Sys. Adv. Com., Olympia, 1984-85; bd. dirs. Wash. Citizen Action, Seattle, 1990-94, People for Fair Taxes, Olympia, 1986-90, Thurston County Child Care Action Coun., Olympia, 1988-90. Mem. Wash. Soc. Assn. Execs., Indsl. Rels. Rsch. Assn., Wash. State Grange, Third House Lobbyist Orgn. Democrat. Office: Wash Pub Employees Assn 124 10th Ave SW Olympia WA 98501-1203

ST. LOUIS, NENA, artist, performance artist; b. St. Louis, Sept. 17, 1951; d. Hughes Hannibal and Lela Nuna (Knox) Shanks; m. Michael Barton Lewis, July 30, 1987. Student, Macalester Coll., 1972-73; BA, U. Nebr., 1974; postgrad., U. Calif., Berkeley, 1988-90, Lorraine Hansberry Theatre, San Francisco, 1991-93. Playwright Lorraine Hansberry Theatre, San Francisco, 1991-93; s. One woman plays include Mace Space for Art, San Francisco, 1991-93, Morphos Gallery, San Francisco, 1992, Solo Mio, San Francisco, 1993, Sole Search, San Francisco, 1993, Lorraine Hansberry Theatre, San Francisco, 1994, Taking Shape, San Francisco, 1994, African-Am. Performance Art Festival, 1994; exhibited in groups shows at Images, A Gallery, San Francisco, 1988-89, Mace Space for Art, 1991-92, Bomani Gallery, San Francisco, 1992—, Jewish Mus. San Francisco, 1993, 94, Laney Coll., 1995; playwright: Indigo Lady, 1993, Essays on Anger and Custard Pie, 1994. Bd. dirs. 11th St. Gallery, Lincoln, Nebr., 1985; arts-in-sch. rev. panelist Nebr. Arts Coun., 1987-88. Recipient Best Sculpture award Emerald City Art Competition, 1985. Mem. Theatre Bay Area, Artists Equity (bd. dirs. No. Calif.). Democrat. Office: 547 Hayes St # 1 San Francisco CA 94102-4234

ST. PE, GERALD J., manufacturing company executive. Student, Loyola U. With Litton Industries Inc., Beverly Hills, Calif., 1961—, various mgmt. positions, 1961-85; pres. Ingalls Shipbldg. Div., Pascogoula, Miss., 1985—, sr. v.p. parent co., 1985—. Office: Ingalls Shipbuilding PO Box 149 Pascagoula MS 39568-0149 also: Litton Industries 360 N Crescent Dr Beverly Hills CA 90210-4802

SAITO, FRANK KIYOJI, import-export firm executive; b. Tokyo, Feb. 28, 1945; s. Kaoru and Chiyoko S.; LL.B., Kokugakuin U., 1967; m. Elaine Tamami Karasawa, Feb. 22, 1975; children—Roderic Kouki, Lorine Erika. With import dept. Trois Co. Ltd., Tokyo, Japan, 1967-68; founder import/export dept. Three Bond Co., Ltd., Tokyo, 1968-71; sales mgr. Kobe Mercantile, Inc., San Diego, 1971-76; pres. K & S Internat. Corp., San Diego, 1976—. Office: K & S Internat Corp K & S Bldg 8015 Silverton Ave San Diego CA 92126-6383

SAITO, PAUL MAKOTO, landscape architect; b. Los Angeles, Oct. 2, 1936; s. William Taketora and Mabel Hiro (Ono) S.; m. Gloria Katsuko Takehashi, June 1, 1963; 1 child, Naomi Kikuko. A.A., Pierce Coll.; B.S., Calif. Poly. Inst. Landscape architect asst. Recreation and Parks Dept., Los Angeles, 1959-64; landscape architect Anaheim Recreation and Parks Dept., Calif., 1964-72; pres. Recreation Land Planners Inc., Placentia, Calif., 1972-76, Saito-Sullivan Assocs., Brea, Calif., 1976-80, Saito Assocs., Fresno, Calif., 1980—. Served with Air N.G., 1968-74. Recipient Daisy award Calif. Landscape Contractors Assn., 1975; Cert. Recognition, Calif. Poly. Alumni Assn., 1981; award of Merit, Calif. Garden Club, 1985. Fellow Am. Soc. Landscape Architects, Am. Inst. Landscape Architects (internat. pres. 1971-73), Council Landscape Architects (pres. 1985), State Bd. Landscape Architects (pres. 1984—). Democrat. Baptist. Office: Saito Assocs 2904 N Blackstone Ave Ste C Fresno CA 93703-1014

SAITO, WILLIAM HIROYUKI, software company executive; b. L.A., Mar. 23, 1971; s. Toshiyuki and Yoko S. BS in Biochemistry, BA in Polit. Sci., U. Calif., Riverside, 1992. Cert. EMT. Programmer Merrill Lynch, Burbank, Calif., 1985-86; instr. Calif. Poly. U., Pomona, 1985-87; staff cons. computer sci. dept. U. Calif., Rancho Cucamonga, Tokyo, 1988-92; ptnr. I/O Software, Walnut, Calif., 1987-90; pres. I/O Software, Riverside, Calif., 1990-91; pres., CEO, I/O Software, Inc., Cucamonga, Calif., 1991—; CEO, Japan I/O Software, K.K., Tokyo, 1991—, chmn. bd., 1992—; cons. IBM, Riverside, 1986-87, Japan IBM, Tokyo, 1988-90, Japan NEC, Tokyo, 1987-89, ASCII, Tokyo, 1988-90. Mem. IEEE, AMA, AAAS, Mensa. Republican. Roman Catholic. Office: I/O Software Inc 10970 Arrow Route Rancho Cucamonga CA 91730-4838 also: Japan I/O Software KK Matex, 1-9-10 Matsugaya 9th Fl Bldg 2, Taito-ku Tokyo 111, Japan

SAKAMOTO, KATSUYUKI, college chancellor, psychology educator; b. L.A., Oct. 24, 1938; m. Edna Christine Sakamoto; children: David Katsu, Bryce Yoshio. BA in Psychology, Calif. State U., Fresno, 1961, MA in Psychology, 1968; PhD in Exptl. Social Psychology, So. Ill. U., Carbondale, 1971; postgrad., Carnegie Mellon U., 1984. Acting dir. Army Edn. Ctr., Munich, 1962-63; dir. social svcs. Salvation Army, Fresno, Calif., 1964-66; assoc. prof. psychology Keuka Coll., Keyka Park, N.Y., 1971-78; prof. social psychology Ea. Oreg. State Coll., La Grande, 1978-85, assoc. dean, then acting dean, 1980-82, 84, assoc. dean acad. affairs, 1982-85; prof. psychology Ind. U. East, Richmond, 1985-91, vice chancellor for acad. affairs, 1985-90, spl. asst. to chancellor, 1990-91; prof., chancellor Calif. Sch. Profl. Psychology, Alameda, 1991—; lectr. So. Ill. U., 1970-71; vis. prof. SUNY, Binghamton, 1973; adj. prof. Alfred (N.Y.) U., 1972-76, Nazareth Coll. Rochester, N.Y., 1975-78, Eisenhower Coll., Seneca Falls, N.Y., 1975-77; evaluator Western Assn. Schs. and Colls., 1991—; commr.-at-large North Ctrl. Assn. Colls. and Schs., 1989-91, educator, cons., 1986-91; mem. exec. bd. for study ctrs. in Japan, China and Korea, campus dir. Oreg. Sys. Higher Edn., 1980-85; bd. visitors Newark (N.Y.) Devel. Ctr., 1975-77; presenter in field. Contbr. articles to profl. jours. Bd. dirs. troop 119 Boy Scouts Am., Richmond, 1986-91, Project 100001, Townsend Cmty. Ctr., Richmond, 1987-89, Alameda Girls Club, Inc., 1992—, Asian Cmty. Mental Health Svcs., 1991—, Found. for Ednl. Excellence, Alameda, 1993—; pres., bd. dirs. Whitewater Opera Co., Richmond, 1987-91, Leadership Wayne County, Richmond, 1988-91; cons. teaching mini-grant program Richmond Cmty. Schs., 1988-91; mem. citizens adv. bd. Wayne County Sheriff's Dept., 1989-91. Mem. APA, Am. Assn. for Higher Edn., Am. Assn. State Colls. and Univs., Am. Assn. Univ. Adminstrs. (nat. v.p. 1990-92, bd. dirs. Found. 1991—), Am. Assn. for Higher Edn. (founding mem. Asian Am. caucus), Asian Am. Psychol. Assn. (treas., membership officer 1983-91, pres. 1988-91), Calif. Psychol. Assn., Nat. Assn. Acad. Affairs Adminstrs., Nat. Coun. Schs. Profl. Psychology, Rotary (bd. dirs. Alameda 1993—). Home: 2837 Brown St Alameda CA 94502-7949 Office: Calif Sch Profl Psychology 1005 Atlantic Ave Alameda CA 94501-1148

SAKAMOTO, NORMAN LLOYD, civil engineer; b. Honolulu, May 22, 1947; s. Shuichi and Fusa (Hayashi) S.; m. Penelope A. Hayasaka, July 12, 1970; children: David H., Gregory F., Katherine E. BSCE, U. Hawaii, 1969; MSCE, U. Ill., 1970. Registered profl. engr., Calif., Hawaii; lic. spl. inspector, Hawaii; lic. contractor, Hawaii. Engr. storm drain City of L.A., 1970-71, engr. streets and frwys., 1972-73; engr. hydrology C.E., 1971-72; v.p. S & M Sakamoto, Inc., Honolulu, 1973-85; pres. SC Pacific Corp., Ewa Beach, Hawaii, 1985—; bd. dirs. Bldg. Industry Assn., Honolulu, spl. appointee, 1991-92, pres.-elect, 1993, pres., 1994; bd. dirs. City Contractors Assn., Honolulu; trustee Home Builders Inst., 1993—. Scoutmaster Honolulu area Boy Scouts Am., 1989-92. Named Remodeler of Month Bldg. Industry Assn., 1990, 91, Remodeler of Yr., 1991. Mem. ASCE, Nat. Assn. Home Builders (dir. 1992—), Internat. Fellowship Christian Businessmen, Constrn. Industry Legis. Assn., C. of C. Evangelical. Office: SC Pacific Corp 91-178 Kalaeloa Blvd Kapolei HI 96707-1819

SAKIN, LARRY ALBERT, shop owner; b. Tucson, Feb. 24, 1960; s. Larry and Doris W. (Glenn) S. AA, Pima C.C., 1984; BS in Bus. Adminstrn., Kennedy We. U., Thousand Oaks, Calif., 1995. Owner Awareness Music Prodn., Tucson, 1979-82; sales rep. Alphagraphics Inc., Tucson, 1984-85; owner Kept in the Dark Records, Tucson, 1986—; ptnr. PDQ Records and Tapes, Tucson, 1988—; co-chairperson Simon Peter Inc., Tucson, 1979; co-founder, dir. Retail Employers Against Censorship, Tucson, 1991-94. Author: "Networks"; A Resource Manual for Viral Illness Patients, 1994. Mem. urgent action network Amnesty Internat., Tucson, 1993—; co-founder, chair United Fedn. Viral Illness Orgns., 1989-93; mem. Citizens Transp. Adv. Coun., 1994. Recipient Roger Baldwin Medal of Liberty nominee ACLU, 1992. Democrat. Office: Kept in the Dark Records 7151 E Speedway Ste 105 Tucson AZ 85710

SAKKAL, MAMOUN, architect, interior designer; b. Damascus, Syria, Dec. 31, 1950; came to U.S., 1978; s. Lutfi Sakkal and Dourieh Khatib; m. Seta K. Sakkal, Mar. 13, 1980; children: Aida, Kindah. BArch with honors, U. Aleppo, Syria, 1974; MArch, U. Wash., 1982, cert. urban design, 1982. Registered architect, Wash., Syria; lic. interior designer, U.S. Archtl. designer MCE, Damascus, 1974-75; dir. design MCE, Aleppo, 1975-76; prin. Sakkal & Assocs., Aleppo, 1976-78; archtl. designer Arch. Assocs., Seattle, 1978-82; sr. designer RD&S, Bellevue, Wash., 1982-84; prin. Restaurant/Hotel Design, Seattle, 1984—, Sakkal Design, Bothell, 1991—; lectr. U. Aleppo, 1974-75, Applied Arts Inst., 1977-78, affiliate instr. U. Wash., 1990—. Author: Geometry of Muquarnas in Islamic Architecture, 1981; designer Oct. Mus., Damascus, Syria, 1977 (1st prize Syrian Ministry Dev.); one man shows include Nat. Mus. Aleppo, Syria, 1969, U. Aleppo, 1984, U. Wash., 1979, 80, 90, 91, U. Cambridge, Eng., 1990, Islamic Soc. N.Am. Conv., Chgo., 1994; contbr. articles to profl. jours. Recipient Best Logo Design award Arab Union Sports, 1976, Best Project Design award Aleppo Ministry of Culture, 1975, Best Modernization Project award Holiday Inns System, 1986, Best Lounge Renovation award Bowlers Jour. Ann. Design Contest, 1987, 1st award in Kufi style 3d Internat. Calligraphy Competition, Rsch. Ctr. for Islamic History, Art and Culture, Istanbul, Turkey, 1993. Office: Sakkal Design 1523 175th Pl SE Bothell WA 98012-6460

SAKURAI, JENNIFER M., editor, writer; b. Seattle, Nov. 21, 1965; d. Fred Yutaka and Toshiko (Shindo) s. Student, Smith Coll., 1983-84; BA, Pepperdine U., 1987; postgrad. studies in journalism Japanese, U. Calif., L.A., 1990—. Editor Parker Publs., Commerce, Calif., 1989; asst. prodn. editor Price, Stern, Sloan, L.A.; from assoc. editor to mng. editor Bobit Publishing, Redondo Beach, Calif., 1990—; prin. R.J. Mgmt. Counsulting, Santa Monica, Calif., 1993—. Author: Outrageous Activity Crosswords, 1989, Rules of the Game (4 vols.), 1990. Mem. concert com. Harbor Found. for the Retarded, Harbor City, Calif., 1994—; mem. Chadwick Sch. Alumni Coun., 1993—. Mem. Smith Coll. Club (applicant interviewer L.A. 1993—). Office: Bobit Publishing 2512 Artesia Blvd Redondo Beach CA 90278

SALAITA, GEORGE NICOLA, physicist; b. Madaba, Jordan, Apr. 22, 1931; came to U.S., 1954; s. Nicola J. and Azizeh (Shamas) S.; m. Linda Masou, July 30, 1959; children: Nicholas, John, Nadya. BS in Physics, Millikin U., 1957; MS in Physics, Tex. A&M, 1959; PhD, Va. Polytech. Inst. & State U., 1966. Rsch. tech. Mobil Rsch., Dallas, 1959-62; asst. prof., assoc. prof., prof. So. Meth. U., Dallas, 1966-81; sr. rsch. scientist Chevron Petroleum Tech. Co., LaHabra, Calif., 1981—; cons. Gearhart Inc., Ft. Worth, 1970-80; chmn. numerous IEEE, Soc. Petroleum Engrs. and Soc. Profl. Well Log Analysts symposia. Editor: The Log Analyst, 1988-89; contbr. tech. articles to profl. jours. Mem. Soc. Petroleum Engrs., Soc. Profl. Well Log Analysts, Am. Nuclear Soc., Sigma Xi. Office: Chevron Pet Tech Co 1300 S Beach Blvd La Habra CA 90631-6374

SALAMAN, MAUREEN KENNEDY, nutritionist; b. Glendale, Calif., Apr. 4, 1936; d. Ted and Elena (Peters) Kennedy; 1 child, Sean. West Coast Report, Sta. WMCA-AM, N.Y.C., 1980—; hostess Maureen Salaman's Accent on Health Sta. KFCB, Concord, Calif.; pres. Nat. Health Fedn., Monrovia, Calif., 1982—; cons., lectr., rschr. on cancer rsch. and metabolic medicine, nutrition; freedom of choice lobbyist. Author: Foods That Heal, Nutrition: The Cancer Answer, 1983, The Diet Bible, The Light at the End of the Refrigerator, Health Freedom News, 1982-85. Contbr. articles to profl. jours.; hostess TV show Maureen Salaman's Maximize Your Life. Developer nutrition programs for radio and TV. Office: Nat Health Fedn PO Box 688 Monrovia CA 91017-0688 also: Maureen Kennedy Salaman Inc 1259 El Camino Real Ste 1500 Menlo Park CA 94025-4227

SALAMON, MIKLOS DEZSO GYORGY, mining educator; b. Balkany, Hungary, May 20, 1933; came to U.S., 1986; s. Miklos and Sarolta (Obetko) S.; m. Agota Maria Meszaros, July 11, 1953; children: Miklos, Gabor. Diploma in Engring., Polytech U., Sopron, Hungary, 1956; PhD, U. Durham, Newcastle, England, 1962; doctorem honoris causa, U. Miskolc, Hungary, 1990. Research asst. dept. mining engring. U. Durham, 1959-63; dir. research Coal Mining Research Controlling Council, Johannesburg, South Africa, 1963-66; dir. collieries research lab Chamber of Mines of South Africa, Johannesburg, 1966-74, dir. gen. research org., 1974-86; disting. prof., dir. Ctr. for Advanced Mining Sys. Colo. Sch. Mines, Golden, 1986-94, head dept. mining engring., 1986-90, dir. Colo. Mining and Mineral Resources Rsch. Inst., 1990-94; 22d Sir Julius Wernher Meml. lectr., 1988; hon. prof. U. Witwatersrand, Johannesburg, 1979-86; vis. prof. U. Minn., Mpls., 1981, U. Tex., Austin, 1982, U. NSW, Sydney, Australia, 1990, 91—; mem. Presdl. Commn. of Inquiry into Safety and Health in South African Mining Industry, 1994-95. Co-author: Rock Mechanics Applied to the Study of Rockbursts, 1966, Rock Mechanics in Coal Mining, 1976; contbr. articles to profl. jours. Mem. Pres.'s Sci. Adv. Council, Cape Town, South Africa, 1984-86, Nat. Sci. Priorities Com., Pretoria, South Africa, 1984-86. Recipient Nat. award Assn. Scis. and Tech. Socs., South Africa, 1971. Fellow South African Inst. Mining and Metallurgy (hon. life, v.p. 1974-76, pres. 1976-77, gold medal 1964, 85, Stokes award 1986, silver medal 1991), Inst. Mining and Metallurgy (London); mem. AIME, Internat. Soc. Rock Mechanics. Roman Catholic. Office: Colo Sch of Mines Dept Of Mining Engring Golden CO 80401

SALAMONE, GARY P. (PIKE SALAMONE), newspaper editor-in-chief, cartoonist; b. Rochester, N.Y., Aug. 26, 1950. BA, St. John Fisher Coll., 1972; MA, San Diego State U., 1979. Editor, pub. Inkslinger's Review, San Diego, 1981—; founder, news dir. Continental News Svc., San Diego, 1985—; pub., columnist Continental Newstime, San Diego, 1987—; founder, editor-in-chief Continental Features/Continental News Svc., San Diego and Washington, 1988—; pub., cartoonist Kids' Newstime, San Diego, 1992—. Author: An Examination of Alexander Hamilton's Views on Civil Liberty, 1979. Vol. radio announcer, reader Nat. Pub. Radio Affiliate Sta. KPBS, San Diego, 1976-81; founder Fisher Recycling, Rochester, N.Y., 1971; pres. Young People's Conservation Com., Webster-Penfield, N.Y., 1971; high sch. coord. Ecology Centre, San Diego, 1976; vol. pub. info. asst. Cleve. Nat. Forest, San Diego. Mem. Phi Alpha Theta, Pi Sigma Alpha. Democrat. Office: Continental Features Continental News Svc 341 W Broadway Ste 265 San Diego CA 92101-3802

SALAND, LINDA CAROL, anatomy educator, researcher; b. N.Y.C., Oct. 24, 1942; d. Charles and Esther (Weingarten) Gewirtz; m. Joel S. Saland, Aug. 16, 1964; children—Kenneth, Jeffrey. B.S., CCNY, 1963, Ph.D. in Biology, 1968; M.A. in Zoology, Columbia U., 1965. Research assoc. dept. anatomy Columbia U. Coll. Physicians and Surgeons, N.Y.C., 1968-69; sr. research assoc. dept. anatomy Sch. Medicine, U. N.Mex., Albuquerque, 1971-78, asst. prof., 1978-83, assoc. prof., 1983-89, prof., 1989—. Mem. editorial bd. Anat. Record, 1980—; contbr. articles to profl. jours. Predoctoral fellow NDEA, 1966-68; research grantee Nat. Inst. on Drug Abuse, 1979-83, NIH Minority Biomed. Research Support Program, 1980—; NIH research grantee, 1986—. Mem. AAAS, Am. Assn. Anatomists, Soc. for Neurosci., Women in Neuroscience (chair steering comm. 1991-93), Am. Soc. Cell Biology, Sigma Xi. Office: U NMex Sch Medicine Dept Anatomy Basic Med Sci Bldg Albuquerque NM 87131

SALAPATA, GEORGIA (GINA), archaeologist; b. Argos, Greece, Mar. 3, 1960; came to U.S., 1983; d. Ioannis and Sophia (Kyriakidou) S.; m. Reza M. Ghezelbash, Dec. 8, 1990; 1 child, Philip Salapata Ghezelbash. BA, U. Athens, Greece, 1982; MA, U. Pa., 1986, PhD, 1992. Lectr. univ. mus. edn. dept. U. Pa., Phila., 1988-90; instr. modern Greek Lingual Inst., Phila., 1990; grad. intern dept. antiquities J. Paul Getty Mus., Malibu, Calif., 1992-93; lectr. in classical studies Massey U., Palmerston North, New Zealand, 1995—; trench supr., excavator various sites in Greece, 1981-93 (summers). Contbr. articles to profl. jours. Mem. Am. Inst. Archaeology. Office: Massey U, English Dept, Palmerston North New Zealand

SALAZAR, LUIS ADOLFO, architect; b. New Orleans, Sept. 17, 1944; s. Gustavo Adolfo and Luz Maria (Florez) S.; m. Sandra Kay Bucklew, May 30, 1969 (div. Jan. 1984); 1 child, Staci Dahnal. AA, Harbor Coll., 1966; BArch, Ariz. State U., 1971. Registered architect, Ariz., Calif., N.Mex. Area architect Peace Corps, Sierra Leone, 1971-73; project architect Van Sittert Assocs., Phoenix, 1973-77; pres., owner Salazar Assoc. Architects, Ltd., Phoenix, Inc., Inc., 1977—; Prin. works include bldg. design Kenema Cathedral, Kenema, Sierra Leone, West Africa, 1980, U.S. West Foothills Switching Ctr., Phoenix, Celebration Luth. Ch., Phoenix. Bd. dirs. Community Behavioral Services, Phoenix, 1983-85; Phoenix Meml. Hosp., 1984-94, Terraco Properties. mem. Subcom. on Bond Election, Phoenix, 1984; mem. Visual Improvement Awards Com., City of Phoenix, 1985-88. Mem. AIA (chmn. program com., honor award Ariz. chpt. 1984, visual improvement awards coms. 1985, 86), Inst. Architects. Roman Catholic. Office: Salazar Assocs Architects Ltd 313 E Thomas Rd Ste 208 Phoenix AZ 85012-3238

SALAZAR, OLGA, brewery official; b. Las Vegas, Nev., May 10, 1957; d. Joel and Mary Chillson Salazar. BA, U. Colo., 1979; Masters, Denver U., 1994. Import negotiator United Bank Denver, 1979-80; sales mgr. Sta. KBNO Latino Broadcasting Corp., Denver, 1980-83; account exec. Group One Broadcasting, Denver, 1983-84; regional advt. supr. McDonald's Corp., Houston, 1984-86; advt. mgr. Coors Brewing Co., Golden, Colo., 1986-90, asst. nat. program mgr., 1990-93, nat. program mgr., 1993—. Office: Coors Brewing Co 311 10th St Golden CO 80401-5811

SALAZAR, WAYNE HARDY, arts and social services administrator; b. N.Y.C., May 17, 1960; s. Oscar René and Barbara Sloan (Hardy) S. Student, Cornell U., 1978-80; BFA, Sch. Visual Arts, N.Y.C., 1984. Prodn. designer Mirror on the Moon Prodns., N.Y.C., 1983; non-theatrical sales mgr. First Run Features, N.Y.C., 1983-85; graphic designer Forty Acres and a Mule Filmworks, Bklyn., 1984-87; mgr. spl. projects Cinecom Entertainment Group, N.Y.C., 1985-90; producer, dir. Wayne Salazar Video, Bklyn., 1987-91; dir. Latino Collaborative, Bklyn., 1988-91; film coord. Hawaii Internat. Film Festival, Honolulu, 1990-92; exec. dir. Visual Aid, San Francisco, 1992—; panelist N.Y. State Coun. on Arts, N.Y.C., 1990-91; prodn. asst. Character Generators Video, N.Y.C., 1986-90; lectr. U. Hawaii/Manoa, Honolulu, 1990; festival programmer Adam Baran Honolulu Gay and Lesbian Film Festival, 1991-93, cons., 1994—; cons. EBS Prodns., San Francisco, 1992—. Contbr. film revs., essays to profl. publs. Recipient Bd. Dirs. award Cable Car Awards, 1993. Mem. Artist's Equity. Home: 787A Castro St San Francisco CA 94114-2849

SALDAÑA, JOHNNY, theatre educator, researcher; b. Austin, Tex., Aug. 20, 1954; s. Isabel Martinez and Dominga (Olivo) S. BFA, U. Tex., 1976, MFA, 1979. Cert. K-12 theatre tchr., Ariz. Asst. prof. Wash. State U., Pullman, 1979-81; prof. theatre Ariz. State U., Tempe, 1981—; cons. New Orleans Pub. Schs., 1989, 91; instr. Northwestern U., Evanston, Ill., 1990, Ariz. Artist-Tchr. Inst., Phoenix, 1993-95. Author: Drama of Color; co-author: (plays) I Didn't Know That!, 1978, Flashback!, 1979; contbr. articles to profl. jours. Recipient Burlington Resources Found. Faculty Achievement award Ariz. State U., 1991, Coll. of FIne Arts Disting. Faculty award, 1995. Mem. Am. Alliance for Theatre and Edn. (conf. chmn. 1993-94, creative drama award 1989), Ednl. Theatre Assn., Ariz. Theatre Educators Assn. Democrat. Office: Ariz State U Dept Theatre PO Box 872002 Tempe AZ 85287-2002

SALDICH, ANNE RAWLEY, counseling psychologist; b. Orange, N.J., Nov. 20, 1933; d. William and Mary (Burke) Rawley; divorced; 1 child, Alan George. BA in English Lit., U. Detroit, 1956; postgrad., U. Calif., Berkeley, 1961-62; MA in Polit. Sci., Wayne State U., 1962; PhD in Sociology, U. Paris, Sorbonne, 1971; MA in Counseling Psychology, U. Calif., San Francisco, 1990. Lectr. San Jose (Calif.) State U., 1972, U. Santa Clara, Calif., 1973; freelance writer, 1971-84; lectr. U. Calif., Berkeley, 1972-77; instr. govt. French Press Inst., Paris, 1984; asst. editor Stanford U. Jour. Econ. Lit., 1980-85; intern in counseling Miramonte Mental Health Ctr., Palo Alto, 1988-89, New Day Residential Treatment Ctr., East Palo Alto, 1989, Family Svc. Agy., Burlingame, Calif., 1989-90, Growth and Leadership Ctr., Mountainview, 1991-92, Palo Alto Psychol. Svcs., Palo Alto, 1992. Author: Electronic Democracy: Television's Impact on The American Political Process, 1979; contbr. articles to profl. jours. Chmn., mediator Palo Alto Rental Housing Mediation Task Force, 1978-79; co-chmn. com. on environ., Palo Alto Futurecast Com. for the Yr. 2001, 1986; mem. publicity and fundraising com. Career Action Ctr., 1987-88; founder, mgr. internat. visitors com. Hospitality Ctr., 1988-89, co-founder mentoring program for girls St. Elizabeth Seton Sch., Palo Alto; bd. dirs. Neighbors Abroad, 1994. Woodrow Wilson fellow, 1962. Mem. AAUW (chmn. bus. and profls. group), Internat. Inst. Comm., Calif. Assn. Marriage and Family Therapists, Experience Corps, Chi Sigma Iota. Home and Office: 2585 Park Blvd Z-100 Palo Alto CA 94306

SALDICH, ROBERT JOSEPH, electronics company executive; b. N.Y.C., June 7, 1933; s. Alexander and Bertha (Kasakove) S.; m. Anne Rawley, July 21, 1963 (div. Nov. 1979); 1 child, Alan; m. Virginia Vaughan, Sept. 4, 1983; stepchildren: Tad Thomas, Stan Thomas, Melinda Thomas, Margaret Thomas. BSChemE, Rice U., 1956; MBA, Harvard U., 1961. Mfg. mgr. Procter & Gamble Mfg. Co., Dallas, Kansas City, Kans., 1956-59; rsch. asst. Harvard Bus. Sch., Boston, 1961-62; asst. to pres. Kaiser Aluminum & Chem. Corp., Oakland, Calif., 1962-64; mgr. fin. and pers., then gen. mgr. various divs. Raychem Corp., Menlo Park, Calif., 1964-83, with office of pres., 1983-87, sr. v.p. telecommunications and tech., 1988-90, pres., CEO, 1990—; pres. Raynet Corp. subs. Raychem Corp., 1987-88. Chair mfg. com. adv. bd. Leavy Sch. Bus. and Adminstrn., Santa Clara U. Mem. Calif. Roundtable (dir. Bay Area Coun.), San Francisco Com. on Fgn. Rels. Jewish. Office: Raychem Corp Mailstop 120/7815 300 Constitution Dr Menlo Park CA 94025-1140*

SALDIN, THOMAS R., consumer products company executive, corporate lawyer; b. 1946. BA, Carleton Coll., 1968; JD, Cin. Coll. Law, 1974. Law clk. to presiding justice U.S. Dist. Ct. (so. dist.) Ohio, 1974-76; assoc. Benjamin, Faulkner & Tepe & Sach, Cin., 1976-78; asst. gen. counsel Albertson's Inc., Boise, Idaho, 1978-81, v.p., gen. counsel, 1981-83, sr. v.p. gen. counsel, 1983—. Office: Albertson's Inc 250 E Parkcenter Blvd Boise ID 83706-3940

SALDIVAR, JOSÉ DAVID, humanities educator; b. Brownsville, Tex., July 12, 1955; s. Ramón and Maria Alicia (Treviño) S.; m. Laura Escoto, Mar. 28, 1981; 1 child, David Xavier. BA in Comparative Lit., Yale U., 1977; PhD in English, Stanford U., 1983. Asst. prof. English Ariz. State U., Tempe, 1981-83, U. Houston, 1983-85; asst. prof. lit. U. Calif., Santa Cruz, 1986-94; prof. ethnic studies U. Calif., Berkeley, 1994—. Editor: The Rolando Hinojosa Reader, 1985, Criticism in the Borderlands, 1991; author: The Dialectics of Our America, 1991; editl. bd. The Americas Rev., 1993—, Am. Lit. History, 1993—. Recipient Stanford Humanities William Rice Kimball award, 1985-86; U. Calif. Pres.'s Humanities grantee, 1990-91. Mem. Am. Studies Assn. (program com.). Office: Univ of calif Dept Ethnic Studies 508 Barrows Hall Berkeley CA 94720

SALE, GEORGE EDGAR, physician; b. Missoula, Mont., Apr. 18, 1941; s. George Goble and Ruth Edna (Polleys) S.; m. Joan M. Sutliff, 1989; children: George Gregory Colby, Teo Marie Jonsson. AB, Harvard U., 1963; MD, Stanford U., 1968. Intern U. Oreg., Portland, 1968-69; sr. asst. surgeon USPHS, Albuquerque, 1969-71; resident in pathology U. Wash., Seattle, 1971-75, instr. pathology, 1975-78, asst. prof., 1978-81, assoc. prof., 1981-88, prof., 1988—; asst. mem. faculty, dept. oncology Hutchinson Cancer Ctr., Seattle, 1975-88, assoc. mem., 1988-91, mem., 1991—. Author, editor: Pathology of Bone Marrow Transplantation, 1984, Pathology of Transplantation, 1990. Mem. AASS, Internat. Acad. Pathology, Coll. Am. Pathologists, Am. Assn. Investigative Pathologists, Physicians for Social Responsibility. Home: 12146 Sunrise Dr NE Bainbridge Island WA 98110-4304 Office: Fred Hutchinson Cancer Rsh Ctr 1124 Columbia Seattle WA 98104

SALERNO, JOSEPH MICHAEL, air cargo company executive; b. Port Washington, N.Y., Jan. 12, 1917; s. Angelo and Anna Marie (Fasano) S.; m. Edith Evangeline Fields, Apr. 2, 1949; children: Linda Marie, Bruce Charles, Paul Michael, David Brian. BS, Tri-State Coll., 1943. Flight engr. Pan Am. World Airways, Inc., San Francisco, 1943-77; owner, pres. Salair, Inc., Seattle, 1980—, also bd. dirs. Pres. Horizon View Community, Bellevue, Wash., 1958-63; mem. Bellevue Citizens Sch. Adv. Coun., 1964; pres. Eastgate Elem. Sch. PTA, Bellevue, 1963. Republican. Roman Catholic. Home: 14560 SE 51st St Bellevue WA 98006-3510 Office: Salair Inc Spokane Internat Airport Salair Inc Hngr 745 Spokane WA 99204

SALESKY, WILLIAM JEFFREY, manufacturing company executive; b. Boston, June 12, 1957; s. Harry Michael Salesky and Eleanor Faith (Stutman) Spater; m. Cherri Lynne DeGreek, Nov. 27, 1982; 1 child, Joshua Steven. BS, U. Calif., Davis, 1978; MS, U. Calif., Berkeley, 1980, PhD, 1982. Co-op engr. Bechtel Corp. Inc., San Francisco, 1977-78; engr. U. Calif., Davis, 1978-79; rsch. assoc. Lawrence Berkeley Lab., 1979-82; project mgr. Smith Internat., Irvine, Calif., 1982-89; dir. engring. & quality assurance Mark Controls, Long Beach, Calif., 1989-94; v.p. engring. Stamet Inc., Gardena, Calif., 1994—; cons. Printnonix Corp., Irvine, Calif., 1988, Metal Alloys Inc., Irvine, 1986-88, Ceracon Inc., Irvine, 1984-86; chmn. L.A. Conf. on Fugitive Emissions from Valves, 1993. Patentee in field. Mgr. Irvine Baseball Assn., 1990; grad. asssembly rep. U. Calif., Berkeley, 1980-81; mem. race com. Internat. Am.'s Cup Class World Championship; mem. San Diego Crew Classic Race Com., 1992-95; mem. Am.'s Cup Race Com., 1992, 95. Recipient Meritorious award Petroleum Engr. mag., 1988, award for outstanding contbns. Valve Mfrs. Assn. Am., 1993. Mem. ASTM, Am. Soc. Metals Internat. (bd. dirs. 1988-90, Earl Parker fellow 1981), Soc. Petroleum Engrs., Am. Petroleum Inst., South Shore Yacht Club (CFO 1989-91, bd. dirs. 1991-93). Office: Stamet Inc 17244 S Main St Gardena CA 90248-3101

SALETTA, CHARLES ANTHONY, JR., architect. BS, USAF Acad., 1965; MArch, Harvard U., 1976; MBA, Vanderbilt U., 1980. Registered arch., Ariz. Commd. 2d lt. USAF, 1965, advanced through grades to lt. col., ret., 1993; pres. Charles A. Saletta Jr., A.I.A., Arch., Phoenix. Mem. AIA (emeritus), Soc. Am. Mil. Engrs., Res. Officers Assn., Ret. Officers Assn., Harvard Club Am., Air Force Acad. Assn. Grads., Air Force Assn., Am. Legion. Office: Charles A Saletta Jr AIA 334 W Granada Rd Phoenix AZ 85003-1153

SALINGER, JOAN ADAH, computer graphics, photography and art educator; b. Detroit, 1951. Student, U. Wis., 1969-71; BFA in Art magna cum laude, U. Mich., 1973; MFA in Photography, Cranbrook Acad. Art, 1976. Calif. cmty. coll. instr. credential. Resident artist Artist in Schs., Flint, Mich., 1976-77; assoc. prof. computer graphics, photography, art Orange Coast Coll., Costa Mesa, Calif., 1980—; part time instr. Cerritos Coll., Art Inst. So. Calif., Santa Ana Coll., Saddleback Coll., Chapman Coll., East L.A. Coll., Otis Art Inst. Parsons Sch. Design, L.A. Valley Coll., Pasadena City Coll., C.S. Mott Coll., Andover H.S. Works exhibited at Joslyn Ctr. of the Arts, Torrance, Calif., Moreau Gallery-St. Mary's Coll., Notre Dame, Ind., Orange Coast Coll., Costa Mesa, Otis Art Inst. Parsons Sch. Design, L.A., Laguna Beach (Calif.) Sch. Art, Cerritos Coll., Norwalk, Calif., GMB Gallery, Birmingham, Mich., B.C. Space Gallery, Laguna Beach, Assn. Internat. Photo Art Dealers Exposition, N.Y.C., Ikono Photo Gallery, Venice, Italy, others; represented in numerous pub. collections. Grantee Nat. Endowment for the Arts, Mich. Coun. of the Arts, C.S. Mott Found. Mem. Assn. Computing Machinery, SIGGRAPH Interest Group Graphics (nat. and L.A. chpt.), NCGA, L.A. Ctr. for Photographic Studies, Phi Delta Kappa, Sigma Epsilon Sigma. Office: Orange Coast Coll 2701 Fairview Rd Costa Mesa CA 92626-5563

SALISBURY, DAVID FRANCIS, newspaper, television science writer; b. Seattle, Feb. 24, 1947; s. Vernon H. and Lurabelle (Kline) S. BS, U. Wash., 1969. Sci. editor Christian Sci. Monitor, Boston, 1972-76; correspondent Christian Sci. Monitor, Los Angeles, Boulder (Colo.) and San Francisco, 1976-85; sci. and tech. writer U. Calif., Santa Barbara, 1985-93, Stanford (Calif.) U., 1993—; mem. research adv. com. Pub. Service Electric and Gas Co., Newark, N.J., 1979-83. Author: Money Matters, 1982. contbr. many articles to popular mags. and tech. jours. Recipient sci. writing awards, NSPE, 1978, Aviation Space Writers Assn., 1981, Grand Gold medal and Bronze medal Coun. for Advancement and Support of Edn., 1988. Mem. AAAS (sci. writing award 1976), Nat. Assn. Sci. Writers (Sci-in-Soc. award 1974). Christian Scientist. Office: Stanford U News Svc Press Courtyard Santa Teresa St Stanford CA 94305

SALLEE, WESLEY W(ILLIAM), nuclear chemist; b. Perry, Okla., June 5, 1951; s. Jimmie Richard and Nadine A. (Barnes) S.; m. Exine Mamie Clark, Mar. 21, 1979; children: Rachel Nadine, Daniel Mason. BS in Chemistry, Okla. State U., 1974; PhD in Chemistry, U. Ark., 1983. Commd. 1st lt. USAF, 1976, advanced through grades to capt., 1978, resigned, 1979; nuclear physicist U.S. Army White Sands Missile Range, 1983—. Author technical reports and symposium papers; contbr. articles to profl. jours. Mem. ASTM. Republican. Home: 1515 Dorothy Cir Las Cruces NM 88001-1625 Office: Nuclear Effects Lab PO Box 333 White Sands Missile Range NM 88002

SALLMAN, JEANNE LARRAINE, volunteer, administrator; b. Indianola, Iowa, May 14, 1941; d. George E. and Minnie Olean (Rhoades) Freeborn; m. Richard A. Sallman, May 24, 1958 (div. Mar. 1983); children: Ronald Richard, Steven Gene. Grad. with nursing degree, Des Moines Area Community Coll. Publicity chmn., den mother, rm. mother Boy Scouts Am., Indianola; publicity chmn. Grow & Glow Garden Club, Indianola; pres. PTA, Indianola, 1975; mem. Nat. Odd Shoe Exchange, 1953—, also dir.; organizer nat. handicap agy. for foot-handicapped people in Taipei, Taiwan. Office: 7102 N 35th Ave Ste 2 Phoenix AZ 85051-8312

SALLOUM, GLENN RICHARD, film company assistant; b. Hameranck, Mich., Jan. 1, 1965; s. Richard Joseph and Maria Luisa (Marchesi) S. BS, Mich. State U., 1987; postgrad., Columbia Coll., 1990. Film experience includes, Drop Zone, 1992-93, Speed, 1993-94, Godzilla, 1994—, Twister, 1995. Office: Graces Prodns PO Box 4016 Los Angeles CA 90078-4016

SALMON, MATT, congressman; b. Salt Lake City, Jan. 21, 1958; s. Robert James and Gloria (Aagard) S.; m. Nancy Huish, June, 1979; children: Lara, Jacob, Katie, Matthew. BA in English Lit., Ariz. State U., 1981; MA in Pub. Adminstrn., Brigham Young U., 1986. Mgr. pub. affairs U.S. West, Phoenix, 1988—; mem. Ariz. Senate, Mesa, 1990-94, 104th Congress, Washington, 1995—; congressman, Ariz. U.S. House of Reps., Washington, D.C., 1995—. Bd. dirs. Mesa United Way, 1990—, Ariz. Sci. Mus., 1992—. Recipient Outstanding Svc. award Ariz. Citizens with Disabilities, 1991, Excellence in Govt. award Tempe Ctr. for Handicapped, 1992; named Outstanding Young Phoenician, Phelps Dodge/Phoenix Jaycees, 1990, Outstanding Legislator, Mesa United Way, 1991. Republican. Mormon. Office: 104th Congress Cannon 115 House Office Bldg Washington DC 20515

SALMON, MERLYN LEIGH, laboratory executive; b. Macksville, Kans., June 24, 1924; s. Kenneth Elbert and Inez Melba (Prose) S.; student U. Kans., 1943-44; BS, U. Denver, 1951, MS, 1952; m. Flora Charlotte Sievers, Mar. 20, 1948; children: Charla Lee, Merlyn Leigh. Rsch. engr. Denver Rsch. Inst., U. Denver, 1951-56; owner-operator Fluo-X-Spec Lab., Denver, 1956-92; ret. 1992; cons. in field. With AUS, 1943-45, 45-47. Mem. Am. Chem. Soc., Soc. for Applied Spectroscopy (Outstanding Svc. award 1970), Am. Soc. Metals, Sigma Xi, Tau Beta Pi, Phi Lambda Upsilon. Omicron Delta Kappa. Democrat. Contbr. articles to profl. jours. Address: 718 Sherman St Denver CO 80203

SALMON, SYDNEY ELIAS, medical educator, director; b. S.I., N.Y., May 8, 1936; m. Joan; children: Howard, Julia, Laura, Stewart, Russell. BA cum laude, U. Ariz., 1958; MD, Washington U., St. Louis, 1962. Intern, then resident in medicine Strong Meml. Hosp., Rochester, N.Y., 1962-64; rsch. fellow in immunology dept. pediats. Harvard U. Med. Sch., Boston, 1965-66; rsch. fellow dept. medicine Medicine and Cancer Rsch. Inst. U. Calif., San Francisco, 1966-68, asst. prof. medicine dept. medicine, 1968-72; assoc. prof. medicine U. Ariz., Tucson, 1972-74, head sect. hematology and oncology, 1972-81, prof. medicine, 1974-89, founding dir. Ariz. Cancer Ctr., 1976—, regents prof. medicine, 1989—; NIH spl. fellow Cancer Rsch. Inst., U. Calif., San Francisco, 1966-68, rsch. assoc., 1968-72; mem. nat. cancer adv. bd. Nat. Cancer Inst., 1990—; founding sci. Selectide Corp., 1990; mem. sci. adv. bds. Amplimed Corp., SUGEN Corp.; bd. dirs. Synergen Devel. Corp., Repligen Devel. Corp. Editor: Cloning of Human Tumor Cells, Human Tumor Cloning, Adjuvant Therapies of Cancer, 1982, Clinics of Haematology, 1982; mem. adv. bd. Cancer Treatment Reports, 1979-82; mem. editl. bd. Stell Cells, Jour. Clin. Oncology; patentee in field; contbr. articles to profl. jours. Surgeon USPHS, 1964-66. Recipient Lectureship award Gold Headed Cane Soc., 1979, Alumni Achievement award U. Ariz., 1986. Mem. AAAS, Am. Soc. Hematology, Am. Soc. Clin. Investigation, Am. Soc. Clin. Oncology (pres. 1984-85), Am. Cancer Soc. (bd. dirs. Ariz. divsn.), Leukemia Soc. Am., Am. Assn. Cancer Rsch., Assn. Am. Cancer Insts. (pres. 1988-89). Office: U Ariz Cancer Ctr 1515 N Campbell Ave Tucson AZ 85724-0001*

SALMON, WILLIAM IRWIN, writer; b. Washington, Jan. 20, 1942; s. Harry Irwin and Corinne (Wall) S.; m. Lydia Susan Smith, Aug. 25, 1962; 1 child, Edward Lee. BS in Chemistry, Coll. of William and Mary, 1963; PhD in Phys. Chemistry, Iowa State U., 1971. Owner The Photographic Lab., Salt Lake City, 1974-81; sec.-treas. Light Source, Inc., Salt Lake City, 1980-83; instr. computer sci. dept. U. Utah, Salt Lake City, 1981-85, adj. asst. prof. computer sci. dept., 1985-91; pres. Interactive Ednl. Systems, Salt Lake City, 1990—; adj. assoc. prof. computer sci. dept. U. Utah, Salt Lake City, 1991—; cons. on computing various sch. dists. in Utah, Salt Lake City, Park City, 1986—. Co-author: Computing for Engineers and Scientists with FORTRAN 77, 1988, A Second Course in Computer Science with Modula-2, 1987; author: Structures and Abstractions, 1991, The Structures and Abstractions Labs, 1992. Mem. IEEE, Assn. for Computing Machinery, Sigma Xi, Phi Beta Kappa, Phi Kappa Phi. Home and Office: Interactive Ednl Systems 2135 Wellington St Salt Lake City UT 84106-4116

SALONEN, ESA-PEKKA, conductor; b. Helsinki, Finland, June 30, 1958. Student, Sibelius Acad., Helsinki; studies with, Rautavaara and Panula. Condr. Finnish Radio Symphony, 1979; guest condr. orchs., London, Berlin, Paris, L.A., Phila., Minn.; prin. condr. Swedish Radio Symphony Orch., 1985—; prin guest condr. Philharmonia Orch., London, 1985-94, Oslo Philharm. Orch., 1985-90; artistic advisor Stockholm Chamber Orch., 1986—; music dir. L.A. Philharm. Orch., 1992—. Office: VanWalsum Mgmt, 26 Wadham Rd, London SW15 2LR, England also: Los Angeles Philharm Orch 135 N Grand Ave Los Angeles CA 90012-3013 also: Swedish Radio Symphony, Sveriges Radio, S-105 10 Stockholm Sweden*

SALSIG, DOYEN, photographer, photography studio owner; b. San Diego, Jan. 17, 1923; d. Felix and Fay (Doyen) Johnson; m. Budd Salsig, June 11, 1943; children: Winter, Kristin, Fay, Ben. AA, San Diego City Coll., 1965; BA in Biology, U. Calif., San Diego, 1970. Owner West Wind Studio, Flagstaff, Ariz., 1972—; photo workshop leader Mus. of No. Ariz., Flagstaff, 1978-93. Author: Parole: Quebec; Counter-sign: Ticonderoga, 1980 (grand prize Coconino County Women of the Arts 1985); contbr., photos and photographic essays to profl. jours. Bd. dirs., v.p. Grand Canyon (Ariz.) Natural History Assn., 1988—; vice chmn. Coconino County Rep. Com., Flagstaff, 1990—; pres. Rep. Women's Club, Flagstaff, 1989-91; docent Mus. No. Ariz., Flagstaff, 1975-82; mem. Ariz. Humanities Coun., 1991-94; del. Rep. Nat. Conv., 1992. Home and Office: 428 E Birch Ave Flagstaff AZ 86001-5226

SALSKI, ANDRZEJ M., journalist, editor; b. Warsaw, Poland, Jan. 16, 1948; came to U.S., 1987; s. Zbigniew and Kazimiera (Muszynski) S.; m. Elzbieta Piwdwarczyk, Sept. 23, 1975 (div. Jan. 1990); children: Alicja, Andrzej J.; m. Izabella Staroscinska, June 29, 1991. BA, U. Warsaw, 1977, MA in Journalism, 1982. Adminstrv. asst. PAX, pub. house, Warsaw, 1965-71, Polish Press Agy., Warsaw, 1971-74; asst. mgr. R & D Inst., Warsaw, 1974-76; journalist Polish Press Agy. (PAP), Warsaw, 1976-82; editor-in-chief Cen. Union of Coops. of Folk Art and Fine Arts, Warsaw, 1982-85; dir. pub. rels. Dem. Party, Warsaw, 1985-88; asst. editor Monitor, Silicon Valley Polish Am. Assn., San Jose, Calif., 1990-92; editor-in-chief Nasze Wiadomosci, Polish Am. Congress, San Francisco, 1992-93; editor-in-chief The Summit Times, Calif., 1993—. Contbr. numerous articles to various publs. Dir. pub. rels. Polish Am. Congress No. Calif., San Francisco, 1992—. Recipient Golden Siren, Coun. of Warsaw, 1987, Silver Cross of Merit, State Coun. of Poland, Warsaw, 1987. Mem. Polish Inst. Arts and Scis. Am., Am. Coun. for Polish Culture, Polish Am. Hist. Assn., Inst. of J. Pilsudski. Home: 1116 The Alameda Berkeley CA 94707

SALTARELLI, THOMAS RICHARD, lawyer; b. Beaver, Pa., Apr. 22, 1947; s. Dominic J. and Lena M. (Setting) S.; m. Donna Perry, Oct. 20, 1979; children: Grant, Anna. BS, Pa. State U., 1969; MBA, U. So. Calif., 1975; JD, Western State U. Coll., 1978. Bar: Calif. 1981, D.C. 1992, U.S. Dist. Ct., U.S. Mil. Ct. Appeals, U.S. Supreme Ct. With Am. Hosp. Supply Corp., Irvine, Calif., 1972-76; sales rep. Cenco Med., L.A., 1976-78; pres. Dacion Corp., Irvine, 1978-81; pvt. practice lawyer Newport Beach, Calif., 1981-85; ptnr. Wildish, Boehmer & Saltarelli, Orange, Calif., 1985-87, King & Saltarelli, Irvine, 1987-89, Saltarelli & Steponovich,, Irvine, 1989-94, Saltarelli Law Corp., Newport Beach, 1994—; dir. AEI Corp., Irvine, 1989—. Mayor, city coun. City of Tustin, Calif., 1992—. Lt. USN, 1969-72, Vietnam. Republican. Roman Catholic. Home: 2212 Palermo Tustin CA 92680-8707 Office: Saltarelli Law Corp 4350 Von Karman Ave Ste 450 Newport Beach CA 92660

SALTER, JAMES, writer; b. Passaic, N.J., June 10, 1925; m. Ann Altemus, June 6, 1951 (div. 1976); children: Allan Conard, Nina Tobe, Claude Cray, James Owen; m. Kay Eldredge; 1 child, Theo Shaw. BS, USMA, 1945; M in Internat. Affairs, Georgetown U., 1950. Author: The Hunters, 1957, The Arm of Flesh, 1961, A Sport and a Pastime, 1967, Light Years, 1976, Solo Faces, 1981, Dusk and Other Stories, 1989 (Pen, Faulkner prize 1989). Lt. Col. USAF, 1960. Home: 500 N St Aspen CO 81611-1253 Office: Farrar Straus & Giraux Inc 19 Union Sq W New York NY 10003-3307

SALTER, ROBERT BRYAN, wildlife biologist; b. Bradenton, Fla., Aug. 21, 1952; s. Robert Bryan and Ruby Marie (Sikes) S.; children: Joshua, Zachary, Moriah. BS, Tenn. Technol. U., 1978. Field rsch. asst. Tenn. Technol. U., Cookeville, 1975-78; park naturalist Tenn. State Parks, Jamestown, 1978; reclamation specialist Tenn. Dept. of Conservation, Monteagle, 1978-83; reclamation specialist N.Mex. Energy & Minerals Dept., Santa Fe, 1983-90, bur. chief, 1984-90; wildlife biologist U.S. Forest Svc., Pecos, N.Mex., 1990-91; mining specialist Mineral Policy Ctr., Bozeman, Mont., 1991-92; water resource specialist N.Mex. Environment Dept., Santa Fe, 1992—. Author: Chamisa Dreams, 1994. Adv. bd. mem. Amigos Bravos, Taos, N.Mex., 1993-94; organizer, adv. N.Mex. Mining Coalition, Santa Fe, 1992-93, Mont. Hard Rock Working Group, Bozeman, 1991. With U.S. Army, 1970-72.

SALTMAN, PAUL DAVID, educational administrator, biologist; b. Los Angeles, Apr. 11, 1928; s. David J. and Sadie (Solotoy) S.; m. Barbara June Golden, July 3, 1949; children—David Percy, Joshua Fred. B.S., Calif. Inst. Tech., 1949, Ph.D., 1953; grad. research, Coll. de France, Paris, 1949-50. From instr. to prof. biology U. So. Calif., 1953-67; vis. prof. U. Copenhagen, 1960-61; provost Revelle Coll., U. Calif., San Diego, 1967-72; vice chancellor acad. affairs Revelle Coll., U. Calif., 1972-80, prof. biology, 1967—. Named Alumnus of Year Calif. Inst. Tech., 1973; sr. Fulbright fellow Australia, 1981; recipient Intra Sci. Research award, 1980. Mem. AAAS, AAUP, Am. Chem. Soc., Am. Soc. Biol. Chemists, Am. Soc. Plant Physiology, Fedn. Am. Scientists, Pacific Slope Biochem. Soc., Am. Inst. Nutrition, Am. Coll. Nutrition, Sigma Xi. Home: 9704 Blackgold Rd La Jolla CA 92037-1113 Office: U Calif Dept Biology La Jolla CA 92093-0322

for Disease Control, Atlanta, 1986-87; cons. Emergency Med. Svcs. Bureau, Helena, 1977, Devel. Disabilities Tng. Inst., Helena, 1977-78; mem. injury prevention profls. New Eng. Network to Prevent Childhood Injuries, Newton, Mass., 1988—; mem. core faculty devel. trauma sys. tng. program U.S. Dept. Transp., Washington, 1989—, tech. assistance team mem. EMS, 1991-93; EMS instr. and program coord. Great Falls Vocat. Tng. Ctr., 1991-93; rsch. asst. inst. for cmty. studies U. Mo., Kansas City, 1983—; pres. elect interim exec. com. Intermountain Regional EMS Children Coord. Coun., Salt Lake City, 1994—. Editor and tech. cons.: Workbook for Prehospital Care and Crisis Interventions, 4th edit., 1992, 5th edit., 1993, Instructor Resource Manual for Prehospital Care and Crisis Intervention, 4th edit., 1992, Workbook for First Responder, 1990; contbg. editor Jour. of Prehospital Care, 1984-85, The EMT Jour., 1980-81; editl. cons. Am. Acad. Orthopaedic Surgeons, 1980-81; contbr. numerous articles to profl. jours.; video prodr. and presenter in field. Mem. Park County DUI Task Force, Livingson, 1993—; inaugural coord. Mont. Safe Kids Coalition, Big Timber, 1988-90; adv. com. Nat. Significance Project for Respite Care, 1977-78; mem. basic life support com. of Mont., Mont. Heart Assn., 1977-82. Recipient Golden award for humanity ARC, 1976, 500 Hour award, 1976, Outstanding Svc. award Nat. Coun. State EMS Tng. Coords., 1979, Leadership award, 1981, Charter Membership award, 1984, J.D. Farrington award for excellence Nat. Assn. Emergency Med. Technicians, 1981, Jeffrey S. Harris award, 1985, Outstanding Svc. award Am. Heart Assn., 1982, Appreciation cert. for paramedic emergency care U.S. Dept. Transp., 1984. Mem. Nat. Registry EMTs, Mont. Bd. Med. Examiners. Democrat. Home: 317 N 2nd St Livingston MT 59047-1901 Office: Critical Illness Trauma P O Box 1249 301 W 1st Ave Big Timber MT 59011

SANDE, BARBARA, interior decorating consultant; b. Twin Falls, Idaho, May 5, 1939; d. Einar and Pearl M. (Olson) Sande; m. Ernest Reinhardt Hohener, Sept. 3, 1961 (div. Sept. 1971); children: Heidi Catherine, Eric Christian; m. Peter H. Forsham, Apr. 1990. BA, U. Idaho, 1961. Lic. designer, Calif. Asst. mgr., buyer Home Yardage Inc., Oakland, Calif., 1972-76; cons. in antiques and antique valuation, Lafayette, Calif., 1977-78; interior designer Neighborhood Antiques and Interiors, Oakland, Calif., 1978-86; owner, Claremont Antiques and Interiors, Lafayette, Calif., 1987-94; assoc. Neiman-Marcus, San Francisco, 1994—; cons. Benefit Boutique Inc., Lafayette; cons., participant antique and art fair exhibits, Orinda and Piedmont, Calif., 1977—. Decorator Piedmont Christmas House Tour, 1983, 88, 89, Oakland Mus. Table Setting, 1984, 85, 86, Piedmont Showcase Family Room, 1986, Piedmont Showcase Music Room, 1986, Piedmont Kitchen House Tour, 1985, Santa Rosa Symphony Holiday Walk Benefit, 1986, Piedmont Benefit Guild Showcase Young Persons Room, 1987, Piedmont Showcase Library, 1988, Peidmont Showcase Solarium, 1989, Jr. League Table Setting, Oakland-East Bay, 1989, 90. Bd. dirs. San Leandro Coop. Nursery Sch., 1967; health coord. parent-faculty bd., Miramonte High Sch., Orinda, 1978, Acalanes Sch. Dist., Lafayette, Calif., 1978; bd. dirs. Orinda Community Ctr. Vols., 1979; originator Concerts in the Park, Orinda, 1979; cons. not-for-profit Benefit Boutigue, Inc., Lafayette, Calif, 1991. Mem. Am. Soc. Interior Design (assoc.), Am. Soc. Appraisers (assoc.), Am. Decorative Arts Forum, De Young Mus., Nat. Trust Historic Preservation, San Francisco Opera Guild, San Francisco Symphony Guild. Democrat. Avocations: travel, hiking.

SANDER, SUSAN BERRY, environmental planning engineering corporation executive; b. Walla Walla, Wash., Aug. 26, 1953; d. Alan Robert and Elizabeth Ann (Davenport) Berry; m. Dean Edward Sander, June 3, 1978. BS in Biology with honors, Western Wash. U., 1975; MBA with honors, U. Puget Sound, 1984. Biologist, graphic artist Shapiro & Assocs., Inc., Seattle, 1975-77, office mgr., 1977-79, v.p., 1979-84, pres., owner 1984—, also bd. dirs. Merit scholar Overlake Service League, Bellevue, Wash., 1971, Western Wash. U. scholar, Bellingham, 1974-75, U. Puget Sound scholar, 1984; named Employer of Yr. Soc. Mktg. Profl. Svcs. 1988, Small Bus. of Yr. City of Seattle, Environ. Cons. of Yr., King County, Entrepreneur of Yr., Inc. Mag. Mem. UN U.S.A. Mem. Seattle C. of C., Soroptimist Internat. (bd. dirs.), Exec. Officers Club. Avocations: swimming, hiking, traveling, painting. Office: Shapiro & Assocs Inc 1201 3rd Ave Ste 1700 Seattle WA 98101-3000

SANDERLIN, TERRY KEITH, counselor; b. Ashland, Oreg., Aug. 5, 1950; s. Calvin Carney and Myrtle Estell (Cope) S.; m. Theresa Emma Garcia, Jan. 19, 1969 (div. Feb. 1976); 1 child, Sean Eric; m. Margaret Lillian Lutz, Dec. 26, 1987. B in Bus., U. N.Mex., 1982, M in Counseling, 1983, EdD, 1993. Lic. clin. mental health, N.Mex.; cert. hypnotherapist Internat. Assn. Counselors and Therapists. Unit supr. Bernalillo County Juvenile Detention Ctr., Albuquerque, 1978-80; counselor Independence Halfway House, Albuquerque, 1980-81; mental health worker Bernalillo County Mental Health Ctr., Albuquerque, 1981-82; probation parole officer N.Mex. Probation/Parole, Albuquerque, 1982-87; dist. supr. N.Mex. Probation/Parole, Gallup, 1987-88; vocat. counselor Internat. Rehab. Assn., Albuquerque, 1989-91; counseling psychologist VA, Albuquerque, 1991—; owner, dir. Counseling and Tng. Specialist, Albuquerque, 1988—; counselor Albuquerque (N.Mex.) Counseling Specialist, 1983-86; guest lectr. sociology dept. U. N.Mex., Albuquerque, 1992; presenter 5th Annual S.W. Substance Abuse Conf., Albuquerque, 1992; presenter N.Mex. Corrections Dept., Santa Fe, 1993. Author: (video tapes) Breathing Free & Good, 1991, Understanding Adolescent Satanism, 1991, (manual) Social Skills and Anger Management, 1993. Vol. counselor Adult Misdemeanor Probation, Albuquerque, 1974-76; panel mem. Cmty. Corrections Selection Panel, Albuquerque, 1987-90. With U.S. Army, 1969-72, Vietnam. Recipient Outstanding Citizenship, Albuquerque (N.Mex.) Police Dept., 1974. Mem. ACA, Am. Corrections Assn., Am. Legion. Democrat. Office: Counseling & Tng Specialist 5215 Grand Albuquerque NM 87108

SANDERS, ADRIAN LIONEL, education consultant; b. Paragould, Ark., Aug. 3, 1938; s. Herbert Charles and Florence Theresa (Becherer) S.; m. Molly Jean Zecher, Dec. 20, 1961. AA, Bakersfield Coll., 1959; BA, San Francisco State U., 1961; MA, San Jose State U., 1967. 7th grade tchr. Sharp Park Sch., Pacifica, Calif., 1961-62; 5th grade tchr. Mowry Sch., Fremont, Calif., 1962-64; sci. tchr. Blacow Sch., Fremont, Calif., 1964-76; 5th grade tchr. Warm Springs Sch., Fremont, 1977-87, 5th grade gifted and talented edn. tchr., 1987-94; edn. cons., 1994—. Mem. San Jose Hist. Mus. Assn., 1980—, Nat. Geog. Soc., Washington, 1976—, Alzheimer's Family Relief Program, Rockville, Md., 1986; vol. 7 km. Race for Alzheimer's Disease Willow Glen Founders Day, San Jose, 1988-92. Named Outstanding Young Educator, Jr. C. of C., Fremont, Calif., 1965. Mem. Smithsonian Assocs., U.S. Golf Assn. Home and Office: 15791 Rica Vista Way San Jose CA 95127-2735

SANDERS, AUGUSTA SWANN, retired nurse; b. Alexandria, La., July 22, 1932; d. James and Elizabeth (Thompson) Swann; m. James Robert Sanders, Jan. 12, 1962 (div. 1969). Student, Morgan State U., 1956. Pub. health nurse USPHS, Washington, 1963 64; mental health counselor Los Angeles County Sheriff's Dept., 1972-79; program coordinator Los Angeles County Dept. Mental Health, 1979-88; program dir. L.A. County Dept. Health Svcs., 1989-92; ret., 1992; appointee by Calif. Gov. Jerry Brown to 11th Dist. Bd. Med. Quality Assurance, 1979-85; health cons., legal, 1994—. Mem. Assemblyman Mike Roo's Commn. on Women's Issues, 1981—, Senator Diane Watson's Commn. on Health Issues, 1979—; chmn. Commn. Sex. Equity Los Angeles Unified Sch. Dist., 1984-90. Mem. NAFE, L.A. County Employees Assn. (v.p. 1971-72), So. Calif. Black Nurses Assn. (founding mem.), Internat. Fedn. Bus. and Profl. Women (pres. L.A. Sunset dist. 1988-89, dist. officer 1982-89), Internat. Assn. Chemical Dependency Nurses (treas. 1990-92), Chi Eta Phi. Democrat. Methodist.

SANDERS, CHARMAINE YEVETTE, pharmacist; b. Greenville, Miss., Dec. 7, 1966; d. Booker Taliferro and Georgia Louise (Settle) Anderson; m. Sherard Dale Sanders, Aug. 11, 1990. BS in Pharmacy, U. Miss., 1990. Registered pharmacist, Miss. Staff pharmacist Tripler Army Med. Ctr., Tripler AMC, Hawaii, 1993—; supr. outpatient pharmacy svcs., Ft. Stewart, Ga., 1992; supr. TAMC Pharmacy, Ft. Stewart, 1994. Mem. Officer's Wives Club, Ft. Stewart, 1990—. Mem. Am. Pharmacists Assn., Miss. Pharmacists Assn.

SANDERS, DAVID BRUCE, physics and astronomy educator; b. Washington, May 1, 1947; s. George Washington and Marie Elizabeth (Temple) S.; m. Maria Dulce Dulalia Justiniani, Sept. 12, 1974; 1 child, David Michael. BS in Physics with distinction, U. Va., 1970; MS in Physics, Cornell U., 1972; PhD in Astrophysics, SUNY, Stony Brook, 1981. NSF Presdl. fellow Ctr. for Naval Analyses, Arlington, Va., 1972-76; rsch. asst. SUNY, Stony Brook, 1976-81; rsch. assoc. Five Coll. Radio Astronomy Obs., U. Mass., Amherst, 1982-83; rsch. fellow, sr. rsch. fellow Calif. Inst. Tech., 1984-86, 87-88; asst. prof. Inst. for Astronomy, U. Hawaii, Honolulu, 1989-91; assoc. prof. U. Hawaii, Honolulu, 1991-94, prof., 1995—; assoc. dir. for rsch. support Inst. for Astronomy, U. Hawaii, Honolulu, 1993—; prof. U. Hawaii, Honolulu, 1995—. Author book chpts, sci. articles, rev. articles and popular articles. Recipient acad. fellowships Dept. Def., 1968-69, U. Va., 1966-67, NSF, 1972-74; grantee NASA, 1989-94, NSF, 1990-93. Mem. AAAS, Internat. Astron. Union (commns. 28 and 40), Am. Astron. Soc., Sigma Xi, Sigma Pi Sigma (v.p. U. Va. chpt. 1968-69). Office: Inst for Astronomy 2680 Woodlawn Dr Honolulu HI 96822-1839

SANDERS, DAVID CLYDE, management and marketing consultant; b. Lubbock, Tex., Oct. 8, 1946; s. Jasper Clyde and Mary Jo (Baber) S.; m. Barbara Ann Huck 1976 (div. July 1983); m. Marcia Lynn Fik, Nov. 20, 1983; children: Ashton Harrison, Geoffrey Davidson. Student, U. Tex., 1964; BA, Tex. Tech. U., 1969; postgrad., So. Meth. U., 1969-70, U. Tex., 1970-71. Exec., auditor Ch. Scientology Tex., Austin, 1971-75; exec., cons. Expansion Consultants, L.A., 1975-77; cons. pub. relations Exec. Mgmt. Specialists, L.A., 1977-80; exec. dir. Inst. for Fin. Independence, Glendale, Calif., 1980-83; mktg. dir. Michael Baybak & Co., Beverly Hills, Calif., 1983-85; sr. cons., ptnr. Mgmt. Tech. Consultants, L.A., 1985-86; sr. cons. Sterling Mgmt. Systems, Glendale, 1986-93, sr. v.p., 1988-89, exec. coun. mem., exec. establishment officer, 1988-89, advanced cons., 1989-93; spkr., ptnr. JPR & Assocs., L.A., 1985-88; pres. Prosperity Assocs., 1990—; direct distbr. Ruby Direct Distbn. Amway Corp., 1991-93; sr. cons. Mgmt. Success, 1993—. Author, Sanders Newsletter, 1983-88. Co-founder, pres. Bus. Adv. Bur. So. Calif., Huntington Beach, 1977-79; founder, exec. dir. Bus. Adv. Bur. Internat., 1995; mem., contbr. Citizen's Commn. on Human Rights, L.A., 1976—; co-founder Vol. Ministers L.A., 1977-78. Mem. World Inst. Scientology Enterprises (chartered), Itnernat. Hubbard Ecclesiastical League of Pastors, Citizens for Alternative Tax System (sustaining), Friends of Narconon Chilocco New Life Ctr., Alpha Phi Omega (sec. Tex. Tech. U. chpt. 1965-69), Internat. Assn. Scientologists (founder). Republican. Home: 4648 Lasheart Dr La Canada CA 91011-2125 Office: Ste 100 200 N Maryland Ave Glendale CA 91206-4262

SANDERS, JAMES JOSEPH, architect; b. Clearwater, Kans., 1936. BS in Architecture, U. Wash., 1963; MS in Architecture, Columbia U., 1964. Registered arch., Wash., 1968, Mont., 1993; cert. Nat. Coun. Archtl. Registration Bd. Designer Jerome Menell/Charles Eames, N.Y.C., 1963-64; designer/draftsman Foote Okerlund and Zieger, Seattle, 1964-65; assoc., designer, project arch. Naramore Bain Brady and Johanson, Seattle, 1965-68; asst. prof., lectr. dept. architecture U. Wash., Seattle, 1968-76; prin. James J. Sanders Arch. and Urban Designer, Seattle, 1968-76; project dir., designer TRA Architecture Engring. Planning Interiors Ltd., Seattle, 1977—; prin. TRA Architecture Engring. Planning Interiors Ltd., 1991—. Prin. works include Farm Products Rsch. Lab. at U. Wash., Bellevue (Wash.) C.C., Pike St. Hill Climb, Seattle, UNICO, Seattle, Doha (Qatar) Internat. Airport, McCarran Internat. Airport, Las Vegas, Dulles Internat. Airport, Washington, Wash. State Conv. and Trade Ctr., Seattle, Providence Conv. Ctr., New Denver Internat. Airport Concourses, Wash. State Patrol Hdqrs. Bldg., others. Chmn. Pike Pl. Market Hist. Commn., 1981; past bd. dirs. Allied Arts of Seattle; active Leschi Improvement Coun., Seattle, Madrona Cmty. Coun., Seattle; profl. soccer referee WSSA, 1974-85. Grad. scholar Columbia U. Fellow AIA (past chmn. Honor awrds com., pre. Seattle chpt. 1993-94, recipient Student Gold medal, Scholar for Design, Home awards); mem. Seattle Architecture Found. (bd. dirs.). Office: TRA Seattle 215 Columbia St Seattle WA 98104-1551

SANDERS, JERRY, protective services official; b. San Pedro, Calif., July 14, 1950; m. Rana Sampson; children: Jamie, Lisa. AA, Long Beach City Coll., 1970; BA in Pub. Adminstrn., Nat. U., 1988; postgrad., San Diego State U. Cert. P.O.S.T mgmt. Police officer San Diego Police Dept., 1973-93, chief of police, 1993—. Bd. dirs. Second Chance, NCCJ, San Diego State U. Cmty. Adv. Bd., Children's Initiative, Youth Econ. Enterprise Zones; mem. cmty. leaders adv. bd. ElderHelp of San Diego. Recipient Headliner of Yr. award San Diego Press Club, 1984, 93, Exceptional Performance citation for SWAT leadership, 1986. Office: San Diego Police Dept 1401 Broadway San Diego CA 92101-5729*

SANDERS, ROBERTA MAE, secondary educator; b. Albuquerque, Dec. 30, 1954; d. Joseph Najeeb and Cecilia Mae (Reid) Rockos; m. George Wayne Sanders. BS in Vocat. Home Econs., Edn., U. N.Mex., 1977, cert. in health edn., 1987. Cert. home econs. tchr., N.Mex. Instr., demonstrator Amana Corp., Albuquerque, 1976-77; tchr. home econs. Moriarty (N.Mex.) Mcpl. Schs., 1977-79, Harrison Mid. Sch., 1979-92, West Mesa High Sch., 1992—; mem. prin. selection com. Albuquerque Pub. Schs., 1992, mem. textbook evaluation com., 1989-90; com. mem. N.Mex. Mid. Sch. Curriculum Guide for Home Econs. Edn., 1987-88. Recipient Focus on Excellence award Albuquerque ASCD, 1990, tchr. enrichment awards N.Mex. Dept. Edn., 1988-90. Mem. NEA, Am. Vocat. Assn., Am. Home Econs. Assn., N.Mex. Home Econs. Assn. (planning com., exhibit chmn. ann. meeting 1979-81), N.Mex. Vocat. Assn., N.Mex. Vocat. Home Econs. Tchrs. Assn. (conf. exhibit com. 1987-92), Home Econs. Edn. Assn. Roman Catholic. Office: West Mesa High Sch 6701 Fortuna Rd NW Albuquerque NM 87121-1306

SANDERS, WALTER JEREMIAH, III, electronics company executive; b. Chgo., Sept. 12, 1936. BEE, U. Ill., 1958. Design engr. Douglas Aircraft Co., Santa Monica, Calif., 1958-59; applications engr. Motorola, Inc., Phoenix, 1959-60; sales engr. Motorola, Inc., 1960-61; with Fairchild Camera & Instrument Co., 1961-69; dir. mktg. Fairchild Camera & Instrument Co., Mountain View, Calif., 1961-68, group dir. mktg. worldwide, 1968-69; pres. Advanced Micro Devices Inc., Sunnyvale, Calif., until 1987, chmn. bd., chief exec. officer, 1969—; dir. Donaldson, Lufkin & Jenrette. Mem. Semicondr. Industry Assn. (co-founder, dir.), Santa Clara County Mfg. Group (co-founder, dir.). Office: Advanced Micro Devices Inc PO Box 3453 One AMD Pl Sunnyvale CA 94086-3453*

SANDERS, WILLIAM JOHN, research scientist; b. Detroit, July 10, 1940; s. John William and Charlotte Barbara (Linsday) Steele; m. Gary Roberts, Sept. 12, 1961; children: Scott David, Susan Deborah. BS, U. Mich., 1962; MSEE, U. Calif., Berkeley, 1964. Sr. rsch. scientist Stanford (Calif.) U., 1967—; Pres. Computers in Cardiology, 1990-93, bd. dirs., 1978—. Inventor cardiac probe; contbr. articles to profl. jours. Mem. IEEE Computer Soc., Assn. Computing Machinery. Home: 3980 Bibbits Dr Palo Alto CA 94303-4531 Office: Stanford U Med Ctr Cardiovasc Medicine Stanford CA 94305

SANDERS, WYMAN, psychiatrist, pediatrician, educator; b. Boston, Oct. 4, 1931; s. Russell and Sabra (Hood) S.; m. Cathrine Sammon, Nov. 28, 1965 (div. Feb., 1975); children: James, Robert. BA, Williams Coll., 1957; MD, U. Rochester, N.Y., 1958; pediatric residency, Harvard U., 1961; psychiatric residency, UCLA, 1971. Diplomate Nat. Bd. Med. Examiners, Am. Bd. Psychiatry and Neurology; cert. sex counselor Am. Assn. Sex. Edn., Counseling and Therapy. Instr. dept. psychiatry, dept. pediatrics UCLA, 1970-72, asst. prof., 1972-75; asst. clin. prof. dept. psychiatry UCLA, 1976-78, assoc. clin. prof., 1978—; assoc. clin. prof. dept. psychiatry Univ. So. Calif., L.A., 1980-82; med. dir. The Bresler Ctr. Med. Group, Inc., L.A., 1981-87; assoc. mem. UCLA Jonsson Comprehensive Cancer Ctr., L.A., 1983—; pres., founder Optimal Health Mgmt., Inc., L.A., 1987—; resident in pediatrics Mass. Gen. Hosp., Boston, 1959-60; pediatric fellow dept.psychiatry Children's Hosp. Med. Ctr., Boston, 1964-65; adj. pediatrician Well Baby Clinics, Cambridge, Mass., 1965-66, residency gen. psychiatry Harbor Gen. Hosp., Torrance, Calif., 1967-68, chief clin. svcs., 1975-76; dir. child psychiatry-pediatrics liason svc. UCLA Sch. Medicine, 1970-72, jr. attending psychiatrist UCLA Ctr. Health Scis., 1970-75; sr. staff psychiatrist Kennedy Child Study Ctr. Santa Monica, 1981. Contbr. articles to profl. jours. Examiner on Qualifications Panel for Pub. Health Nurse positions, 1971—; v.p. Sch. bd. St. Matthews, L.A., 1972-75; psst mem. external assessment team State of Calif. Commn. for Teacher preparation and licensing; dir. h.s. protestant chapel program Augsburg, Gemany, 1962-64. Capt. U.S. Army, 1961-64. Recipient Physicians Recognition award Am. Med. Soc., 1969. Fellww Am. Orthopsychiatric Assn.; mem. Am. Psychiatric Assn., Mass. Med. Soc., Nat. Wellness Soc., Soc. for Pub. Health Edn., So. Calif. Psychiatric Soc. (past mem. com. on child and adolescent psychiatry, past mem. of desgregation subcom., preventive psychiatry com.), So. Calif. Soc. for Child Psychiatry. Home and Office: Optimal Health Mgmt Inc 3326 SE 7th Ave Portland OR 97202-2702

SANDERSON, DAVID R., physician; b. South Bend, Ind., Dec. 26, 1933; s. Robert Burns and Alpha (Rodenberger) S.; divorced, 1978; children: David, Kathryn, Robert, Lisa; m. Evelyn Louise Klunder, Sept. 20, 1980. BA, Northwestern U., 1955, MD, 1958. Cons. in medicine Mayo Clinic, Rochester, Minn., 1965-87, chmn. dept. Thoracic Disease, 1977-87; cons. in medicine Mayo Clinic Scottsdale, Ariz., 1987—, chmn. dept. internal medicine, 1988—, vice chmn. bd. govs., 1987-94; assoc. dir. Mayo Lung Project, Nat. Cancer Inst., Rochester. Contbr. articles to profl. jours. Recipient Noble award, Mayo Found., Rochester, "Significant Sig" award, Sigma Chi Fraternity, Ill., 1989, Chevalier Jackson award, Am. Bronchoesophagologic Assn., Fla., 1990. Fellow ACP, Am. Coll. Chest Physicians (gov. for Minn. 1981-87); mem. Am. Bronchoesophagologic Assn., World Assn. for Bronchology, Internat. Bronchoesophagologic Assn., Internat. Assn. Study of Lung Cancer, AMA. Presbyterian. Home: 10676 E Bella Vista Dr Scottsdale AZ 85258-6086 Office: Mayo Clinic Scottsdale 13400 E Shea Blvd Scottsdale AZ 85259-5404

SANDERSON, RICHARD ALEXANDER, health facility administrator; b. L.A., Sept. 30, 1943; s. Bruce Andrew MD and Dorothy Marie (McIntyre) Sanderson; m. Hilary Joy Walton, Aug. 26, 1968. BA, Loma Linda U., 1967, MPH, 1974. Adminstr. trainee Calif. Dept. of Mental Health, Sacramento, 1969-70; community health planner Community Health Plan Assn., San Diego, 1970-71; exec. dir. San Diego Biomedical Research Inst., 1971-73; caridac monitor tech. Loma Linda U. Med. Ctr., 1973-74; admin. residency Riverside Gen. Hosp., Riverside, Calif., 1974-75; adminstr. and chief exec. officer Burbank Community Hosp., Burbank, Calif., 1975-83, W. Covina Hosp., W. Covina, Calif., 1983-86, Woodland Park Hosp., Portland, Oreg., 1987-88; pres. Hil-Rich Inc., Clackamas, Oreg., 1988-93; trustee Bruce and Dorothy Sanderson Family Trust, Bonita, Calif., 1992—; dir. Hosp. Council of S. Calif., Los Angeles, 1981-83; pres. Verdago Hills VNA, Glendale, Calif., 1982-84; treas. at Home Health Services, La Canada, Calif., 1985-87; v.p. Consortium Hosps. Orgn. in Cooperative Efforts, Burbank, 1982-83. Bd. dirs. Alliance for Habitat Conservation, San Diego, 1994—. Mem. Am. Coll. Healthcare Adminstrs. Office: PO Box 1166 Bonita CA 91908-1166

SANDFORD, PAUL ALLAN, biomedical laboratory director, biochemist; b. Milford, Mich., Nov. 24, 1939; s. Federick Tom and Alice Ruth (Howland) S.; m. Caryl Ann Needham, Aug. 26, 1961; children: Thad Arthur, Amy Kathleen Sandford-Alcorn. AB in Chemistry and Math., Albion Coll., 1962; PhD in Biochemistry, U. Ill., 1967. Sr. rsch. scientist Ag. Rsch. Svc. NRRC, Peoria, 1967-77; rsch. fellow, mgr. new ventures Kelco (divsn. of Merck & Co.), San Diego, 1977-86; dir. bioapplications Protan, Inc., Woodinville, Wash., 1986-90; v.p., tech. devel. Vivo Rx, Inc., Santa Monica, 1990—; pres. P. A. Sandford & Affiliates, Del Mar, Calif., 1985—; chmn. Gordon Rsch. Conf. Chemistry Carbohydrates, 1979-81. Editor: Exocellular Microbial Polysaccharides, 1978, Fungal Polysaccharides, 1980, Chitin and Chitosan, 1989, Advances in Chitin and Chitosan, 1992, Internat. Jour. Carbohydrate Polymers, 1982—; contbr. numerous articles to sci. jours.; copatentee in field. NIH fellow, 1962-67. Mem. Am. Chem. Soc. (chmn. Peoria sect. 1977-78, chmn. carbohydrate divsn. 1978-79, chmn. San Diego sect. 1981-82), Am. Chitosci. Soc. (co-founder). Home: 2822 Overland Ave Los Angeles CA 90064-4218 Office: Vivo Rx Inc 3212 Nebraska Ave Santa Monica CA 90404-4214

SANDHU, FATEJEET SINGH, radiologist, educator; b. Jullunder, Punjab, India, Dec. 19, 1961; came to the U.S., 1966; s. Shingara Singh and Jatinder Kaur (Jallienwalla) S.; m. Maury Ellen Schear, May 23, 1992. BA in Chemistry magna cum laude, Duke U., 1982; MD cum laude, Emory U., 1986. Bd. cert. radiology. Intern internal medicine Yale U. Sch. Medicine, New Haven, 1986-87; resident radiology U. Calif., San Francisco, 1987-91; fellowship U. Calif., San Francisco (Calif.) Gen. Hosp., 1991-92, Emory U. Sch. Medicine, Emory Hosp., Grady Hosp., Atlanta, 1992-93; clin. instr. dept. radiology U. Calif., San Francisco, 1991-92, asst. prof. radiology in residence dept. radiology, 1993—; chief interventional radiology dept. radiology San Francisco (Calif.) Gen. Hosp., dir. imaging fellowship dept. radiology, asst. dir. Vascular Access Clinic; med. staff San Francisco (Calif.) Gen. Hosp., VA Med. Ctr., San Francisco; mem. various coms. U. Calif., San Francisco; presenter and lectr. in field. Contbr. articles to profl. jours. Mem. Soc. Cardiovascular and Interventional Radiology (ednl. materials com. 1992—), Phi Eta Sigma, Phi Beta Kappa, Alpha Omega Alpha. Office: San Francisco Gen Hosp 1001 Potrero Ave San Francisco CA 94110-3518

SANDHU, GURTEJ SINGH, engineer, reseacher; b. London, Eng., Oct. 24, 1960; came to U.S., 1985; s. Sarjit S. and Gurmit K. (Minhas) S.; m. Sukesh Guleria, June 21, 1987; children: Gureet, Suntej. MS, Indian Inst. Tech., Delhi, 1985; PhD, U. N.C., Chapel Hill, 1989. Process devel. engr. Micron Semiconductor Inc., Boise, Idaho, 1989-91, sr. engr., 1991-93, sect. head, 1993—. Contbr. more than 40 articles to profl. jours.; patentee in field. Mem. IEEE, Electrochem. Soc., Am. Phys. Soc., Materials Rsch. Soc. Office: Micron Semiconductor Inc 2805 E Columbia Rd Boise ID 83706-9624

SANDIFER, SANDRA ANN, moving image educator; b. Ringgold, La., Mar. 31, 1957; d. Glynn Lawrence and Annie Mae (Caskey) S.; m. Kendall Richard Griggs, Feb. 5, 1983 (div. Dec. 1989). BA in English, La. State U., 1989; BA in Film, Coll. Santa Fe, 1993. Mgr. Rockower Bros., Shreveport, La., 1975-81; dental asst. Paul Wood DDS, Shreveport, La., 1981-88, Erick Carlgren DDS, Santa Fe, N.Mex., 1990-92, Kerry Tramontanas DDS, Santa Fe, N.Mex., 1992-94; instr. Coll. Santa Fe, 1994—. Author: (screenplay) Star Light, Star Bright, 1993. Coll. Santa Fe Moving Image Dept. scholar, 1991; recipient Sony Corp. award, 1991. Mem. Omicron Delta Kappa, Phi Kappa Phi. Office: Coll Santa Fe Moving Image Dept St Michaels Dr Santa Fe NM 87505

SANDIFUR, CANTWELL PAUL, SR., mortgage company executive; b. Decatur, Ill., Jan. 15, 1903; s. Frank Noah and Claira Louise (Iles) S.; m. Jenny Evelyn Duling, Dec. 4, 1940; children: C. Paul Jr., Mary Louise, William F., Ann Elizabeth. LLB, Lewis and Clark Coll., 1930. Ins. agt. Prudential Life Ins., Newark, 1925-27, West Coast Life Ins. Co., Seattle, Spokane, Wash., 1929-38; owner various businesses, Spokane, 1938-54; chm. bd. Met. Mortgage and Securities Co. Inc., Spokane, 1954—; bd. dirs. subs. Met. Mortgage & Securities Co. Inc. Chair established in his name Ea. Wash. U. Coll. Bus. Aminstrn., 1991. Mem. Manito Lions Club, Spokane Club. Republican. Methodist. Office: Met Mortgage & Securities W 929th Sprague Ave Spokane WA 99204

SANDLER, HERBERT M., savings and loan association executive; b. N.Y.C., Nov. 16, 1931; s. William B and Hilda (Schattan) S.; m. Marion Osher, Mar. 26, 1961. BSS, CCNY, 1951; JD, Columbia U., 1954. Bar: N.Y. 1956. Asst. counsel Waterfront Commn. N.Y. Harbor, 1956-59; partner firm Sandler & Sandler, N.Y.C., 1960-62; pres., dir., mem. exec. com. Golden West Savs. & Loan Assn. and Golden West Fin. Corp., Oakland, Calif., 1963-75; chmn. bd., co-chief exec. officer, dir., mem. exec. com. World Savs. & Loan Assn. and Golden West Fin. Corp., Oakland, 1975—; charter mem. thrift instns. adv. coun. to Fed. Res. Bd., 1980-81; former chmn. legis. and regulation com. Calif. Savs. and Loan League. Pres., trustee Calif. Neighborhood Services Found.; chmn. Urban Housing Inst.; mem. policy adv. bd. Ctr. for Real Estate and Urban Econs. U. Calif., Berkeley. With U.S. Army, 1954-56. Office: Golden W Fin Corp 1901 Harrison St Oakland CA 94612-3574

SANDLER, MARION OSHER, savings and loan association executive; b. Biddeford, Maine, Oct. 17, 1930; d. Samuel and Leah (Lowe) Osher; m. Herbert M. Sandler, Mar. 26, 1961. BA, Wellesley Coll., 1952; postgrad., Harvard U.-Radcliffe Coll., 1953; MBA, NYU, 1958; LLD (hon.), Golden Gate U., 1987. Asst. buyer Bloomingdale's (dept. store), N.Y.C., 1953-55; security analyst Dominick & Dominick, N.Y.C., 1955-61; sr. fin. analyst Oppenheimer & Co., N.Y.C., 1961-63; sr. v.p., dir. Golden West Fin. Corp.

and World Savs. & Loan Assn., Oakland, Calif., 1963-75, vice chmn. bd. dirs., CEO, mem. exec. com., dir., 1975-80, pres., co- chief exec. officer, dir., mem. exec. com., 1980-93, chmn. bd. dirs., CEO, mem. exec. com., 1993—; pres., chmn. bd. dirs., CEO Atlas Assets, Inc., Oakland, 1987—, Atlas Advisers, Inc., Oakland, 1987—, Atlas Securities, Inc., Oakland, 1987—; mem. adv. com. Fed. Nat. Mortgage Assn., 1983-84. Mem. Pres.'s Mgmt. Improvement Coun., 1980, Thrift Insts. Adv. Coun. to Fed. Res. Bd., 1989-91, v.p., 1990, pres., 1991; mem. policy adv. bd. Ctr. for Real Estate and Urban Econs. U. Calif., Berkeley, 1981—, mem. exec. com. policy adv. bd., 1985—; mem. ad hoc com. to rev. Schs. Bus. Adminstrn. U. Calif., 1984-85; vice chmn. industry adv. com. Fed. Savs. and Loan Ins. Corp., 1987-88, Ins. Corp., 1987-88; bd. overseers NYU Schs. Bus., 1987-89; mem. Glass Ceiling Commn., 1992-93. Mem. Phi Beta Kappa, Beta Gamma Sigma. Office: Golden W Fin Corp 1901 Harrison St Oakland CA 94612-3574

SANDLER, MAURICE, urologist; b. N.Y.C., Dec. 13, 1937; married; 3 children. BA, NYU, 1957; PhD, Emory U., 1961, MD, 1964. Diplomate Am. Bd. Urology. Intern in surgery Bronx Mcpl. Hosp. Ctr., Albert Einstein Coll. Medicine, 1964-65; jr. asst. resident in surgery Upstate Med. Ctr., Syracuse, N.Y., 1965-66, fr. asst. resident in urology, 1966-67, asst. resident in urology, 1967-68, chief resident in urology, 1968-69; assoc. attending physician Upstate Med. Ctr., Syracuse, 1969-72, Crouse-Irving Meml. Hosp., Syracuse, 1972; attending physician Brookside Hosp., San Pablo, Calif., 1972—, Dr.'s Hosp., Pinole, Calif., 1972, Richmond (Calif.) Hosp., 1972, Herrick Hosp., Berkeley, Calif., 1972; staff physician VA Hosp., Syracuse, 1972; chief of staff Dr.'s Hosp., chief surgery; chief surgery Brookside Hosp.; med. dir. West Contra Corto Urological Surg. Med. Group Inc.; adj. assoc. prof. dept. zoology Syracuse U., 1966; assoc. prof. dept. urology Upstate Med. Ctr., 1969-72; rsch. assoc. dept. anatomy Emory U., 1960-64; cons. in field. Fellow ACS, Internat. Coll. Angiology; mem. Soc. Univ. Urologists, Am. Urol. Assn., Am. Nephrology Soc., Internat. Soc. Nephrology, So. Anatomical Soc., Am. Anatomical Soc., Histochem. Soc., Sigma Xi. Office: 2089 Vale Rd Ste 25 San Pablo CA 94806-3849

SANDLIN, MARLON JOE, planned giving director, financial planner; b. Berkeley, Calif., Jan. 14, 1953; s. Ernest L. and Eunice (Knouf) S.; m. Sheryll L. Ballard, July 14, 1979; children: Chelsea, Kelly. AA, Diablo Valley Coll., Pleasant Hill, Calif., 1973; BA, U. Calif., Berkeley, 1975; MDiv, Fuller Theol. Sem., 1979. Cert. fin. planner. Assoc. dir. ch. rels. Fuller Theol. Sem., Pasadena, 1979-81; dir. ch. rels. Fuller Theol. Sem., 1981-84; assoc. dir. resource devel. Compassion Internat., Colorado Springs, Colo., 1984-95; v.p. Mission Aviation Fellowship Found., Redlands, Calif., 1995—. Bd. dirs. San Gorgonio Girl Scout Coun. Mem. Christian Estate Planners of Calif., Planned Giving Roundtable of So. Calif., Inst. CFPs. Republican. Presbyterian. Home: 9363 Shamouti Dr Riverside CA 92508-6463 Office: Mission Aviation Fellowship Found PO Box 3202 Redlands CA 92373

SANDLIN, STEVEN MONROE, power company contracts executive; b. Lebanon, Ind., May 9, 1935; s. Alva Rogers and Bertha Marie (Spiedel) S.; m. Joann Dana Borke, Aug. 9, 1957; children: Suzann, Sharyln, Syndi, Steven. BS in Aero Engring., Purdue U., 1957; MA in Edn., Roosevelt U., 1961; AA in Bus., De Anza Coll., 1977. Registered Profl. engr., Wash. Commd. ensign USN, 1957; naval constructor USN Civil Engr. Corps, 1957-67; contracts mgr. A.G. Schoonmaker Co., Sausalito, Calif., 1967-70; contracts and program mgr. Hewlett-Packard Co., Cupertino, Calif., 1970-78; bus. mgr. Wash. Pub. Power Supply System, Richland, 1978-94, U.S. Dept. of Energy, Richland, Wash., 1994—; v.p. Reno Holiday Club, Cupertino, 1975-78; mktg. mgr. Pennywhistle Prodns., Richland, 1980-85. Author (pamphlet) U.S. Naval Institute Proceedings, 1965, U.S. Civil Engineer, 1960. Mem. Richland Planning Devel. Commn., 1986; chmn. Richland Libr. Bd., 1985. Fellow Nat. Mgmt. Assn. (v.p. 1984, pres. 1992); mem. Nat. Contract Mgmt. Assn. (chmn. 1990), Wash. Army N.G., Am. Mil. Insignia Collectors Club, Co. Mil. Historians, Am. Polar Soc. Republican. Home: 2250 Davison Ave Richland WA 99352-1919 Office: US Dept of Energy 3050A George Washington Way Richland WA 99352-1617

SANDO, EPHRIAM, English language educator; b. Chgo., Mar. 1, 1934; s. Samuel Saul and Frieda Gardenia (Kolinsky) S. BA with highest honors, UCLA, 1956, MA, 1958, PhD, 1962. Asst. in English UCLA, 1958-62; asst. prof. U. Iowa, Iowa City, 1962-67; asst. prof. Calif. State U.-Dominguez Hills, Carson, 1967-68, assoc. prof., 1968-73, prof. English, 1973—; acting chair English Calif. State U., Dominguez Hills, Carson, 1971-72; dir. Susan E. Barrett Poetry award, Carson. Co-translator: The Alhambra, 1968, High Wedlock Then Be Honoured, 1970; contbr. criticism and poetry to profl. jours. Recipient Found. Rsch. award Found. Com., Carson, 1987, Meritorious Performance awards Awards Com., Carson, 1987-88. Democrat. Jewish. Home: 704 E Elsmere Dr Carson CA 90746-2317 Office: Calif State U 1000 E Victoria St Carson CA 90747-0001

SANDOR, JOHN ABRAHAM, state agency administrator; b. Buckley, Wash.; m. Lenore Barbat, 1956; children: Mary, Janet. BA in Forestry, Wash. State U., 1950; MPA, Harvard U., 1959. Dep. regional forester U.S. Forest Svc., Milw., 1972-76; regional forester U.S. Forest Svc., Juneau, Alaska, 1976-84; cons. Alaska-Pacific Rim Enterprises, Juneau, 1984-88; exec. dir. Alliance Juneau's Future, Inc., 1988-90; commr. Alaska Dept. Environ. Conservation, Juneau, 1990-94; ret., 1995. 2d lt. M.C., U.S. Army, 1945-46. Paul Harris fellow Rotary; named Conservationist of Yr., Alaska Wildlife Conservation and Sportsmen Coun., 1979; recipient Superior Svc. award U.S. Dept. Agriculture, 1983. Fellow Soc. Am. Foresters (coun. 1985-86). Methodist.

SANDRICH, JAY H., television director; b. L.A., Feb. 24, 1932; s. Mark R. and Freda (Wirtschafter) S.; m. Nina Kramer, Feb. 11, 1952 (div.); children: Eric, Tony, Wendy; m. Linda Green Silverstein, Oct. 4, 1984. BA, UCLA, 1953. Producer (TV show) Get Smart, 1965; dir. (TV shows) He and She, 1967, Mary Tyler Moore Show, 1970-88, Soap, 1977-79, Cosby Show, 1984-92; dir. (films) Seems Like Old Times, 1980, For Richer, For Poorer (HBO), 1992. Served to 1st lt. Signal Corps U.S. Army, 1952-55. Mem. Dirs. Guild Am. (award 1975, 85, 86), TV Acad. Arts and Scis. (Emmy award 1971, 73, 85, 86).

SANDRIN, COLLEEN LOUISE, healthcare philanthropist; b. Litchfield, Ill., Oct. 28, 1953; d. Elmer Sandrin and Bernadine Mary (Kline) Buffington. Student, U. Colo., 1971-74; BA, U. No. Colo., 1977. Staff asst. judiciary Sen. Floyd K. Haskell, Washington, 1974-75; title IX coord. U. No. Colo., Greeley, 1976; pub. rels. dir. Pikes Peak United Way, Colorado Springs, Colo., 1978-79, assoc. campaign dir., 1979-81; dir. resource and fund devel. Sacramento Area United Way, 1981-83; exec. dir. Am. Cancer Soc., Sacramento, 1983-87; exec. v.p. Woodland (Calif.) Meml. Health Found., 1987—. Bd. dirs. Woodland C. of C., v.p. for econ. devel., exec. com. mem. Named Big Sister of Month, Big Bros./Big Sisters Program, 1985; recipient Innovative Program of Yr. award Calif. Assn. Pub. Hosps., 1989; 1st place award (grantsmanship category) Assn. Healthcare Philanthropy Showcase, 1990; The Healthcare Forum outreach and edn. grantee, 1991. Mem. Assn. Healthcare Philanthropy, Nat. Com. Planned Giving, Planned Giving Roundtable, Woodland Rotary Club. Democrat. Episcopalian. Office: Woodland Meml Health Found 1325 Cottonwood St Woodland CA 95695-5131

SANDS, SHARON LOUISE, graphic design executive, art publisher, artist; b. Jacksonville, Fla., July 4, 1944; d. Clifford Harding Sands and Ruby May (Ray) MacDonald; m. Jonathan Michael Langford, Feb. 14, 1988. BFA, Cen. Washington U., 1968; postgrad, UCLA, 1968. Art dir. East West Network, Inc., L.A., 1973-78, Daisy Pub., L.A., 1978; prodn. dir. L.A. mag., 1979-80; owner, creative dir. Carmel Graphic Design, Carmel Valley, Calif., 1981-85; creative dir., v.p. The Video Sch. House, Monterey, Calif., 1985-88; graphic designer ConAgra, ConAgra, Nebr., 1988; owner, creative dir. Esprit de Fleurs, Ltd., Carmel, Calif., 1988—; lectr. Pub. Expo, L.A., 1979, panelist Women in Mgmt., L.A., 1979; redesign of local newspaper, Carmel, Calif., 1982. Contbr. articles to profl. mags. Designer corp. ID for Carmel Valley C. of C., 1981, 90, redesign local newspaper, Carmel, Calif., 1982. Recipient 7 design awards Soc. Pub. Designers, 1977, 78, Maggie award, L.A., 1977, 5 design awards The Ad Club of Monterey Peninsula, 1983, 85, 87, Design awards Print Mag. N.Y., 1986, Desi awards, N.Y., 1986, 88. Mem. NAFE, Soc. for Prevention of Cruelty to Animals, Greenpeace. Democrat. Home and Office: 15489 Via La Gitana Carmel Valley CA 93924-9669

SANDSTEDT, LYNN ALFRED, foreign language and humanities educator; b. Snyder, Colo., Oct. 19, 1932; s. Reuben Alfred and Enda (Bartram) S.; m. Phyllis M. Troudt, June 24, 1961; children: Todd E., Scott D. BA in Spanish Edn., U. No. Colo., 1954; MA in Spanish Lang. and Lit., U. Colo., 1964, PhD in Spanish Lang. and Lit., 1973. Life tchg. cert., Colo. Tchr. Brighton (Colo.) H.S., 1956-57; H.S. tchr., supr. fgn. langs. Dist. 6, Greeley, Colo., 1957-72; prof. Spanish lang. and lit., chair dept. Hispanic studies U. No. Colo., Greeley, 1972—. With U.S. Army, 1954-56. Recipient NDEA award U. Ariz., Guadalajara, Mexico, 1964, Anthony Papalia award, 1994, Founders award Cen. State Conf., 1995; Fulbright Study grantee U. Valladolid, Burgos, Spain, 1962; named Outstanding Educator, State Dept. Edn., Colo., 1987, Outstanding Coll. Tchr., S.W. Conf. on the Tchg. Fgn. Langs., N.Mex., 1989. Mem. MLA, Am. Assn. Tchrs. Spanish and Portuguese (pres. 1984-86, exec. dir. 1993—, Disting. Svc. award), Am. Coun. on the Teaching of Fgn. Lang. (pres. 1990-92, Florence Stiener award, Anthony Papalia award), Colo. Congress Fgn. Lang. Tchrs. (pres. 1964-66, Svc. award, Scholarship award, Genevieve Overman award). Office: U No Colo Dept Hispanic Studies Greeley CO 80639

SANDSTROM, ALICE WILHELMINA, accountant; b. Seattle, Jan. 6, 1914; d. Andrew William and Agatha Mathilda (Sundius) S. BA, U. Wash., 1934. CPA, Wash. Mgr. office Star Machinery Co., Seattle, 1935-43, Howe & Co., Seattle, 1943-46; pvt. practice acctg., Seattle, 1945-85; controller Children's Orthopedic Hosp. and Med. Ctr., Seattle, 1948-75, assoc. adminstr. fin., 1975-81; lectr. U. Wash., Seattle, 1957-72. Mem. Wash. State Title XIX Adv. Com., 1975-82, Wash. State Vendors Rate Adv. Com., 1980-87, Mayor's Task Force for Small Bus., 1981-83; bd. dirs. Seattle YWCA, 1981—, pres., 1986-88; bd. dirs. Sr. Svcs. Seattle King Co., 1989-95, bd. dirs. Sr. Services Seattle/King County, 1985, treas., 1986, pres. 1988-90; bd. dirs. Children's Orthopedic Hosp. Found., 1982-90. Fellow Hosp. Fin. Mgmt. Assn. (charter, state pres. 1956-57, nat. treas. 1963-65, Robert H. Reeves Merit award 1970, Frederick T. Muncie award 1985), Wash. State Hosp. Assn. (treas. 1956-70), Am. Soc. Women Accts. (pres. Seattle chpt. 1946-48), Am. Soc. Women CPAs, Wash. Soc. CPAs, Women's Univ. Club (Seattle), City Club (Seattle, charter mem.). Home and Office: 5725 NE 77th St Seattle WA 98115-6345

SANDSTROM, ROBERT EDWARD, physician, pathologist; b. Hull, Yorkshire, Eng., Apr. 4, 1946; came to U.S., 1946; s. Edward Joseph and Ena Joyce (Rilatt) S.; m. Regina Lois Charlebois (dec. May 1987); children: Karin, Ingrid, Erica. BSc, McGill U., Montreal, 1968; MD, U. Wash., 1971. Diplomate Am. Bd. Pathology, Am. Bd. Dermatopathology. Internship Toronto (Can.) Gen. Hosp., 1971-72; resident pathologist Mass. Gen. Hosp., Boston, 1974-78; clin. fellow Harvard U. Med. Sch., Boston, 1976-78; cons. King Faisel Hosp., Riyadh, Saudi Arabia, 1978; pathologist, dir. labs. St. John's Med. Ctr., Longview, Wash., 1978—; v.p. Intersect Systems Inc., Longview, Wash., 1990—; chmn. bd. Cowlitz Med. Svc., Longview, 1988; participant congl. sponsored seminar on AIDS, Wash., 1987. Script writer movie Blood Donation in Saudi Arabia, 1978; contbr. articles to profl. jours. Surgeon USPHS, 1972-74. Fellow Coll. Am. Pathologists, Royal Coll. Physicians; mem. Cowlitz-Wahkiakum County Med. Soc. (past pres.). Roman Catholic. Home: 49 View Ridge Ln Longview WA 98632-5556 Office: Lower Columbia Pathologists 1606 E Kessler Blvd Ste 100 Longview WA 98632-1841

SANDVIG, KIPP RAY, physical education educator; b. Wausau, Wis., Apr. 26, 1956; s. Melvin Carl and Betty Lou (Hoeft) S.; m. Sandra Marie Gerner, Dec. 22, 1978; children: Katherine Rebecca, Megan Elizabeth. BS in Phys. Edn., Carthage Coll., 1978. Cert. tchr., Wis. Tchr. Herzl Sch., L.A., 1978-82, Our Lady of Grace Sch., Encino, Calif., 1982-83, Newbridge Sch., L.A., 1983-90, St. Michael and All Angels Sch., Studio City, Calif., 1990—; coach Defiance (Ohio) Blue Dolphins, 1975-79, Burbank (Calif.) YMCA, 1980-81, Beverly Hills (Calif.) YMCA, 1981-82, Crescenta-Canada YMCA, La Canada, Calif., 1986-89, Palisades-Malibu YMCA, Pacific Palisades, Calif., 1989-90, Culver-Palms YMCA, Culver City, Calif., 1992-93, Glendale (Calif.) YMCA, 1993-94, Arcadia (Calif.) Swim Club, 1994—; cons. Merrill Pub., Columbus, Ohio, 1989-90. Fellow GTE 1986. Mem. NSTA, Nat. Coun. Tchrs. Math., Am. Swim Coaches Assn., So. Calif. Swimming Assn. (all-star coach 1989-94). Home: 400 E Live Oak St Apt 30 San Gabriel CA 91776-1525

SANELLO, FRANK ANTHONY, journalist, columnist; b. Joliet, Ill., May 17, 1952; s. Frank Anthony and Evelyn Justine (Stiglic) S. BA with honors, U. Chgo., 1974; MA, UCLA, 1976. Mng. editor Eastside Sun, L.A., 1977; tech. writer Litton Data Systems, Van Nuys, Calif., 1977-79; columnist Cashbox mag., Hollywood, Calif., 1979, United Features Syndicate, L.A., 1986—; film crtic Daily News, Van Nuys, 1982-84; reporter UPI, L.A., 1984, People mag., L.A., 1984—. Mng. editor Real Estate Illustrated, Van Nuys, 1980. Democrat. Home: 1127 N Genesee Ave # 1 Los Angeles CA 90046-6210

SANFORD, ALLAN ROBERT, research seismologist, educator; b. Pasadena, Calif., Apr. 25, 1927; s. Roscoe Frank and Mabel Aline (Dyer) S.; m. Alice Elaine Carlson, Aug. 31, 1956; children: Robert Allan, Colleen Ann. BA, Pomona, 1949; MS, Caltech, 1954, PhD, 1958. Asst. prof. New Mex. Tech., Socorro, N.M., 1957-64; assoc. prof. New Mex. Tech., Socorro, 1964-68, coord. Geophysics program, 1978—, prof., 1968—. Contbr. articles to profl. jours. With USN, 1945-46. Recipient Disting. Rsch. award New Mex. Tech., 1985. Mem. Am. Geophysical Union, Am. Assn. Advancement Sci. (fellow 1964), Soc. Exploration Geophysicists, Seismological Soc. Am., Sigma Xi. Home: 1302 North Dr Socorro NM 87801-4442 Office: New Mex Tech Geoscience Dept Socorro NM 87801

SANFORD, KATHLEEN DIANE, nursing administrator; b. San Diego, Oct. 4, 1952; d. Donald Brown and JoAlice (Robertson) Smith; m. William Mack Sanford, May 11, 1974; children: Jonathan Mack, Michael Andrew, Stephanie Alyse. BSN, U. Md., 1974; MA, Pepperdine U., 1977; MBA, Pacific Lutheran U., Tacoma, Wash., 1983; D in Bus. Adminstrn., Nova U., Ft. Lauderdale, Fla., 1993. Officer U.S. Army Nurse Corps, Ft. Belvoir, Va., 1974-78; supr. Eden Hosp., Castro Valley, Calif., 1978-80; clin. coord. St. Joseph Hosp., Tacoma, 1980-83; v.p. nursing Harrison Meml. Hosp., Bremerton, Wash., 1983—; tchr. Pacific Luth. U., 1994—. Contbr. articles to profl. jours; columnist Community Style Newspaper. Mem. nursing adv. bd. Olympic Coll., Bremerton, 1988; bd. dirs. Kitsap County United Way; chairperson South Kitsap Cub Scouts, Olalla, Wash., 1988; active Am. Heart Assn., bd. dirs., 1988. Capt. U.S. Army, 1974-78; lt. comdr. Wash. Army N.G. Walter Reed Army Inst. Nursing scholarship U.S. Army, 1970; named Am.'s New Traditional Homemaker Frozen Food Industry, N.Y.C., 1986. Mem. Am. Bus. Women's Assn. (Woman of Yr. award 1988, 93, The Am. Bus. Woman of Yr. award 1994), Nat. League for Nursing, Am. Orgn. Nurse Execs., Wash. Orgn. Nurse Execs. (pres. 1993). Republican. Methodist. Office: Harrison Meml Hosp 2520 Cherry Ave Bremerton WA 98310-4229

SANFORD, LEROY LEONARD, rancher; b. Sanford Ranch, Wyo., June 24, 1934; s. Claude Leonard and Herminnie May (Brockmeyer) S.; m. Barbara Jo Shackleford, June 15, 1965 (dec. Oct. 1965); stepchildren: Christina Pedley, Marlena McCollum, Diana Sumners; 1 foster child, Catherine Frost. Cert. satellite geodecy, Johns Hopkins U., 1971; cert. astron. geodecy, U.S. Geol. Survey-Branch R & D, 1971. Cert. Geodesic Surveyor. Rancher Sanford Ranch, Douglas, Wyo., 1952-57; topographer, photogrametrist U.S. Geol. Survey-Topog. Divsn.-Hdqs., Denver, 1957-81; rancher Sanford Ranch, Douglas, 1981—; speaker various schs. and community orgns. Congl. Svc. medal U.S. Congress, 1972. Mem. NRA (endowment), Am. Solar Energy Soc., Antarctican Soc., Wyo. Farm Bur. Republican. Home: 400 Windy Ridge Rd Douglas WY 82633-0145

SANG, FUH-CHING, computer science educator; b. Taiwan, July 27, 1961; m. Shih-An Chu, Dec. 17, 1993. BS, Tunghai U., Taiwan, 1983; MA, U. Tex., Dallas, 1986, PhD, 1990. Programmer Honeywell Info. Sys., Taiwan, 1983-84; computer lab. cons. U. Tex., Dallas, 1985-86, rsch. asst., tchg. asst., 1986-90; asst. prof. Calif. State Poly. U., Pomona, 1990—. Office: Calif State Poly U 3801 W Temple Ave Pomona CA 91768-2557

SANKAR, SUBRAMANIAN VAIDYA, aerospace engineer; b. New Delhi, India, June 22, 1959; came to U.S. 1982; s. V.S.S. and Bala (Sankar) Narayanan; m. Asha Govindarajan, July 31, 1988; 1 child, Sitara Sankar. B.Tech., Indian Inst. Tech., Madras, 1982; MSAE, Ga. Inst. Tech., Atlanta, 1983; PhD, Ga. Inst. Tech., 1987. R & D dir. Aerometrics, Inc., Sunnyvale, Calif., 1987—. Contbr. articles to profl. jours. J.N. Tata scholar, India. Mem. AIAA, Nat. Geog. Soc., AAAS. Home: 34211 Petard Ter Fremont CA 94555-2611 Office: Aerometrics Inc 550 Del Rey Ave Unit A Sunnyvale CA 94086

SANKOVICH, JOSEPH BERNARD, cemetery management consultant; b. Johnstown, Pa., Feb. 6, 1944; s. Joseph George and Helen Mary (Kasprzyk) S. Student, St. Francis Sem., 1964-68; BA, St. Francis Coll., 1966; postgrad., St. John Provincial Sem., 1968-69; MA, U. Detroit, 1973. Cert. cemetery exec., cath. cemetery exec., profl. cons. Assoc. pastor St. Mary's Ch., Nanty Glo, Pa., 1970-71, Sacred Heart Ch., Dearborn, Mich., 1971-74; dir. Mt. Kelly Cemetery, Dearborn, 1972-84; admissions counselor U. Detroit, 1974-81; dir. religious edn. St. James Ch., Ferndale, Mich., 1981-84; exec. Diocesan Cemetery Cons., Wyoming, Pa., 1984-86; dir. cemeteries Archdiocese of Seattle, 1986-91; mgmt. cons., owner Joseph B. Sankovich & Assocs., Edmonds, Wash., 1991—; cons. Archdiocese St. Paul and Mpls., 1990—, Diocese San Diego, 1991—, Archdiocese Santa Fe, 1991—, Diocese Tucson, 1991—, Diocese Toledo, 1992—, Diocese Saginaw, 1992—, Archdiocese Edmonton, Alta., Can., 1993—, Diocese Monterrey, 1993—, Diocese Fresno, 1994—; mem. Task Force on Cremation of Bishops Com. on Liturgy Nat. Conf. Cath. Bishops, 1990-92; instr. Am. Cemetery Assn. Univ. Ops./Maintenance, 1994. Author, editor: Directory of Western Catholic Cemeteries, 1992, 94; author mgmt. assessments, sales programs, market analyses, 1986—; contbr. articles to profl. jours. Mem. Am. Cemetery Assn., Nat. Cath. Cemetery Conf., Wash. Interment Assn. (bd. dirs. 1990-91), Cath. Cemeteries of the West (founder 1987, governancy com. 1987-90). Address: Joseph B Sankovich & Assocs 24006 92d Ave W Edmonds WA 98020

SANNA, LUCY JEAN, writer; b. Menomonie, Wis., Apr. 20, 1948; d. Charles Albert and Margaret Sheila (McGee) S.; m. Peter Lawrence Frisch, Jan. 2, 1971, 1 child, Katherine Sanna. BA., St. Norbert Coll., 1969; postgrad. U. Wis., Madison, 1970-74. Asst. editor Scott Foresman & Co., Glenview, Ill., 1970-73; freelance editor, Palo Alto, Calif., 1973-75; editor FMC Corp., San Jose, Calif., 1975-78; supr. corp. advt. Memorex Corp., Santa Clara, Calif., 1978-79, exec. presentations adminstr., 1979; mgr. communications svc. Electric Power Rsch. Inst., Palo Alto, 1980-87, exec. speech writer, 1988-89; mgr. exec. communications, 1989—. Author: How to Romance the Woman You Love, 1995. Office: Electric Power Rsch Inst PO Box 10412 Palo Alto CA 94303-0813

SANNER, MONTY RAY, nonprofit organization administrator; b. Riverside, Calif., Oct. 11, 1953; s. Russell Ray and Rose-Marie (Took) S.; m. Jackie Ora Damon, Sept. 11, 1976; children: Kristen, Adam, Kaci. BA in Sociology, Ea. Ky. U., 1976; MA in Communications, Regent U., 1989. With customer svc. United Airlines, Chgo., 1978-80; account exec. Evergreen Internat. Airlines, Chgo., 1980-81, Coca Cola, Lenexa, Kans., 1981-82; asst. dir. advt. Thomas Nelson Pubs., Nashville, 1984-85; dir fundraising Logoi Ministries, Miami, Fla., 1985-86; account exec. South Cen. Bell, Nashville, 1986-87; dir. customer svc. Compassion Internat., Colorado Springs, Colo., 1987—. Contbr. articles to profl. jours. Mem. Internat. Customer Svc. Assn., Am. Soc. Travel Agts., Internat. Platform Assn., Phi Kappa Alpha. Republican. Episcopalian. Home: 12235 Lazy H Way Colorado Springs CO 80908-4111 Office: Compassion Internat 3955 Cragwood Dr Colorado Springs CO 80918-7859

SANNWALD, WILLIAM WALTER, librarian; b. Chgo., Sept. 12, 1940; s. William Frederick and Irene Virginia (Stanish) S.; children: Sara Ann, William Howard. B.A., Beloit Coll., 1963; M.A.L.S., Rosary Coll., River Forest, Ill., 1966; M.B.A., Loyola U., Chgo., 1974. Mktg. mgr. Xerox Univ. Microfilms, 1972-75; assoc. dir. Detroit Public Library, 1975-77; dir. Ventura (Calif.) County Library, 1977-79; city libr. San Diego Public Libr., 1979—; vis. instr. mktg. San Diego State U. Author: Checklist of Library Building Design Considerations, 2d edit., 1992; chairperson editorial adv. bd. Pub. Librs. Pres. Met. Libraries Sect., 1989. Recipient Outstanding Prof. award and Outstanding Mktg. Prof. award, 1985; Award of Merit AIA San Diego chpt., 1988. Mem. ALA, Calif. Library Authority for Systems and Services (pres. congress of mems. 1980), Calif. Library Assn. Roman Catholic. Home: 1201990 Calle De Medio El Cajon CA 92019-4905 Office: San Diego Pub Libr 820 E St San Diego CA 92101-6416*

SANO, ROY I., bishop. Ordained to ministry United Meth. Ch., later consecrated bishop; appointed Bishop Rocky Mountain Conf., United Meth. Ch., Denver. Office: PO Box 6006 Pasadena CA 91102-6006*

SANQUIST, NANCY JOHNSON, international facility management professional; b. Muncie, Ind., Aug. 31, 1947; d. Charles Elof and Pauline Lydia (Murphy) S.; m. James M. Johnson, Dec. 1988. BA, UCLA, 1970; MA, Bryn Mawr Coll., 1973; MS, Columbia U., 1978. Instr. Lafayette Coll., Easton, Pa., 1973-74, Muhlenberg Coll., Bethlehem, Pa., 1974-75, Northampton Area Community Coll., Bethlehem, 1974-75; dir. Preservation Office City of Easton, 1977-78; cons. El Pueblo de Los Angeles State Historic Park, 1978-79; dir. restoration Bixby Ranch Co., Long Beach, Calif., 1979-82; mgr. computer applications Cannel-Heumann & Assoc., Los Angeles, 1982-84; dir. Computer-Aided Design Group, Marina del Rey, Calif., 1984-93, Strategic Asset Mgmt. PAE Inc., L.A., 1993—; adj. instr. UCLA, 1979-86, Grad Sch. Calif. State U., Dominguez Hills, 1981. Author numerous tech. articles and manuals. Bd. dirs. Historic Easton, Inc., 1977-78, Simon Rodia's Towers in Watts, Los Angeles, 1979-81, Los Angeles Conservancy, 1982-86, Friends of Schindler House, West Hollywood, Calif., 1978—, pres., 1982-85. Recipient Outstanding Contbn. award Nat. Computer Graphics Assn., 1987. Mem. Internat. Facility Mgmt. Assn. (seminar leader, lectr. N.Am., Asia, Australia, Europe and Mid. East 1987—).

SANSWEET, STEPHEN JAY, journalist, author; b. Phila., June 14, 1945; s. Jack Morris and Fannie (Axelrod) S. BS, Temple U., 1966. Reporter Phila. Inquirer, 1966-69; reporter Wall Street Jour., Phila., 1969-71, Montreal, Que, Can., 1971-73; reporter Wall Street Jour., L.A., 1973-84, dep. bur. chief, 1984-87, bur. chief, 1987—; lectr. bus. journalism U. So. Calif., L.A., 1984-87. Author: The Punishment Cure, 1976, Science Fiction Toys and Models, 1981, Star Wars: From Concept to Screen to Collectible, 1992, Tomart's Guide to Worldwide Star Wars Collectibels, 1994; consulting editor: Star Wars Galaxy, 1993, 2d series, 1994, 3d series, 1995. Recipient award for best fire story Phila. Fire Dept., 1968, Pub. Svc.-Team Mem. award Sigma Delta Chi, 1977; finalist Loeb award, 1990. Mem. Soc. Profl. Journalists. Office: Wall Street Jour 6500 Wilshire Blvd Ste 1500 Los Angeles CA 90048-4935 also: The Wall Street Journal 200 Liberty St New York NY 10281-1003

SANTEE, DALE WILLIAM, lawyer, air force officer; b. Washington, Pa., Mar. 28, 1953; s. Robert Erwin and Elsbeth Emma (Bantleon) S.; divorced; 1 child, Enri De'Von; m. Junko Mori, June 2, 1992. BA, Washington & Jefferson Coll., 1975; MA, U. No. Ariz., 1982; JD, U. Pitts., 1978. Bar: Pa. 1978, U.C. Ct. Mil. Appeals 1979, Calif. 1989. Floor mgr., commn. salesman J.C. Penney Co., Washington, Pa., 1971-76; asst. mgr. Rach Enterprises, Charleroi, Pa., 1977-78; legal intern Washington County Pub. Defender; commd. 2d lt. USAF, 1979, advanced through grades to major, 1989; from asst. staff judge advocate to area def. counsel Luke Air Force Base, Ariz., 1979-81; claims officer 343 Combat Support Group/Judge Advocate, Eielson AFB, Alaska, 1981-83; sr. staff legal adviser Dept. Vet. Affairs, Washington, 1983-89; asst. staff judge advocate Mil. Justice div. Air Force Judge Advocate Gen.'s Office, Washington, 1986-89, 63CSG/Judge Advocate, Norton Air Force Base, Calif., 1989-91; dep. pub. defender Juvenile div. San Diego County, 1990-93, dep. alt. pub. defender, 1993—; staff judge advocate 452 AMW/Judge Advocate, March AFB, Calif., 1991—; v.p. Neuer Enterprises, Nanjemoy, Md., 1983-89; participant Mgmt. Devel. Seminar, 1988. Mem. San Diego County Rep. Party; pres., co-chmn. legis. com. PTA Zamorano Elem. Sch., San Diego, chmn. SITE com.; mem. San Diego County Child Abuse Coord. Coun., San Diego County Commn. on Children and Youth, San Diego County Juvenile Ct. Mental Health Task Force, San Diego County Unified Sch. Dist. Parent Adv. Coun., San Diego County Youth Ct. Com. Decorated Air Force Commendation medal, 1981, 89, Air Force Meritorious Svc. medal, 1991; named Outstanding Young Man of Am., U.S. Jaycees, Montgomery, Ala., 1981; acad. scholar Washington &

Jefferson Coll., 1971-75, Beta scholar Washington & Jefferson Coll., 1974, Pa. Senatorial scholar Pa. Senate, 1975, 76, 77, 78. Mem. Pa. Bar Assn., Calif. Bar Assn., San Diego County Bar Assn., San Diego County Psych-Law Soc. Home: 1156 Corrales Ln Chula Vista CA 91910-7956

SANTILLAN, ANTONIO, financial company executive; b. Buenos Aires, May 8, 1936; naturalized, 1966; s. Guillermo Spika and Raphaella C. (Abaladejo) S.; children: Andrea, Miguel, Marcos. Grad., Morgan Park Mil. Acad., Chgo., 1954; BS in Psychology, Coll. of William and Mary, 1958. Cert. real estate broker. Asst. in charge of prodn. Wilding Studios, Chgo., 1964; pres. Adams Fin. Services, Los Angeles, 1965—. Writer, producer, dir. (motion pictures) The Glass Cage, co-writer Dirty Mary/Crazy Harry, Viva Knievel; contbg. writer Once Upon a Time in America; TV panelist Window on Wall Street; contbr. articles to profl. fin. and real estate jours. Served with USNR, 1959. Recipient Am. Rep. award San Francisco Film Festival, Cork Ireland Film Fest, 1961. Mem. Writer's Guild Am., L.A. Bd. Realtors, Beverly Hills Bd. Realtors (income/investment divsn. steering com.), Westside Realty Bd. (bd. dirs.), L.A. Ventures Assn. (bd. dirs.), Jonathan Club (L.A.), Rotary, Roundtable, Toastmasters Internat., Wilshire Country Club. Office: Adams Fin Svcs Inc 425 N Alfred St West Hollywood CA 90048-2504

SANTOR, KEN, state treasurer. Real estate developer, gen. contractor, treas. state of Nev., 1987—. Served with USMC, Korea. Office: Office of State Treas Capitol Bldg Carson City NV 89710

SANTRY, BARBARA LEA, venture capitalist; b. Key West, Fla., Jan. 20, 1948; d. Jere Joseph and Frances Victoria (Appel) S. BS in Nursing, Georgetown U., 1969; MBA, Stanford U., 1978. Program analyst, br. chief U.S. Dept. HEW, Washington, 1973-76; mgr. cons. div. Arthur Andersen and Co., San Francisco, 1978-80; asst. v.p. Am. Med. Internat., Washington, 1980-83; v.p. Alex Brown and Sons, Inc., Balt., 1983-86; ptnr. Wessels, Arnold and Henderson, Mpls., 1986-88; v.p. Dain Bosworth Inc., Mpls., 1988-90, sr. v.p., 1990-91; ptnr. Pathfinder Venture Capital Funds, Menlo Park, Calif., 1991—. Served to lt. USNR, 1967-72. Office: 3000 Sand Hill Rd Ste 255 Menlo Park CA 94025-7116

SANTUCCI, SELENE MARIE, artist, educator; b. Seattle, 1950. BA with distinction, Wash. State U., 1972, MS, 1975, MFA, 1983; BFA with distinction, Mass. Coll. Art, 1981. Exhbns. include River Run Gallery, Ketchum, Idaho, 1995, Mia Gallery, Seattle, 1995, Pacific Arts Ctr., Seattle, 1994, Gango Gallery, Portland, Oreg., 1994, Holter Art Mus., Helena, Mont., 1994, Prichard Gallery, Moscow, Idaho, 1994, Tacoma (Wash.) Art Mus., 1993, Boise State U. Gallery of Art, Idaho, 1993, Bellevue (Wash.) Art Mus., 1993, numerous others; work collected at Continental Mortgage Bank, Seattle, Wash. State Arts Commn./Wash. State U., Vancouver, Creston (Wash.) Sch., others; articles. Office: Mia Gallery 512 1st Ave South Carnation WA 98014

SANWICK, JAMES ARTHUR, mining executive; b. Balt., Feb. 15, 1951; s. Alfred George and Catherine Anne (von Sas) S.; m. Brenda Julia Tietz, Sept. 20, 1980; children: Luke Graham, Sierra Catherine. AS, Catonsville (Md.) Community Coll., 1975; BS, U. No. Colo., 1976; M in Pub. Administn., U. Alaska S.E., 1985. Recreation therapist Md. Sch. for the Blind, Balt., 1974; dir. camp New Horizon United Cerebral Palsy Md., Balt., 1975; sub-dist. mgr. Nat. Park Svc., various, 1976-82; freelance mgmt. cons. Juneau, Alaska, 1982-84; regional mgr. div. labor standards Alaska Dept. Labor, Juneau, 1983-88; adj. faculty sch. bus. and pub. administrn. U. Alaska S.E., Juneau, 1985-93; mgr. Alaska Productivity Improvement Ctr., Juneau, 1989-93; mgr. human resources and pub. affairs Greens Creek Mining Co., Juneau, 1989-93; mgr. human resources Rawhide Mining Co., Fallon, Nev., 1993—; bd. dirs. Gov.'s Com. on Employment Disabled Persons, Alaska Acad. Decathalon Inc.; chmn. Job Svc. Employer Com., Alaska, 1989-93; bd. advisors Inst. Mine Tng. U. Alaska S.E., 1989-93. Co-author: (info. phamphlet) Blue Water Paddling in Alaska, 1980; editor: (film) Green's Creek Project, 1990; photographic editor: Inside Passage Mag., 1982, 83; photographer: (book) Death Valley, 1977. Patrolman Nat. Ski Patrol System, Juneau, 1978-83; instr., trainer ARC, Alaska, Utah, Ariz., 1979-82; v.p. bd. dirs. Alaska Acad. Decathlon. Sgt. USMC, 1970-73. Recipient Nat. New Svc. award United Cerebral Palsey, 1975; named Candidate of Yr. Nat. Ski Patrol System, 1979. Mem. Nev. Mining Assn. (human resources com. 1993—), Soc. Human Resources Mgmt., Juneau Ski Club. Office: Rawhide Mining Co PO Box 2070 Fallon NV 89407-2070

SAPOCH, JOHN CRIM, JR., management consultant; b. Allentown, Pa., Feb. 1, 1937; s. John Crim and Dorothy Salome (Rems) S.; m. Betty Katherine Wingert, Aug. 9, 1958 (div.); children: John Crim III, William Martin; m. Ava Helena Anttila, Jan. 9, 1991. AB, Princeton U., 1958; MBA, U. Pa., 1964. Tchr., coach, dean students Kent (Conn.) Sch., 1958-61; asst. to dean admissions U. Pa., Phila., 1961-62; sec. for alumni assns. Princeton (N.J.) U., 1962-65, dir. Princeton U. Conf., 1965-66; adminstrv. dir., treas., gen. mgr., exec. v.p. J.P. Cleaver Co., Inc., Princeton, 1966-78; also pres. subs., bd. dirs. J.P. Cleaver Co. Inc., Princeton, 1966-78; chmn., pres., treas., bd. dirs. SINC, Princeton, 1978—, Princeton Pacific Inc., Manhattan Beach, Calif., 1980—. Author tng. manuals. Vice pres., pres. class of 1958, Princeton U., 1958-68; bd. dirs., treas. Princeton Youth Ctr., 1966-70; founder, trustee Princeton Youth Fund, 1967-68; founder, bd. dirs. Princeton Midget Football League, 1968-73; chmn. Friends Princeton U. Football, 1974-78; founder, chmn. Friends Princeton High Sch. Athletics, 1978-80. Named hon. mem. Princeton High Sch. Class of 1980. Mem. Princeton U. Alumni Assn., Wharton Grad. Sch. Alumni Assn., Wharton Club of So. Calif., Princeton Alumni Club (founder, treas. 1965), U. Pa. Alumni Assn. So. Calif., Princeton Area Alumni Assn., Princeton Club (N.Y.C., So. Calif.), Ivy Club (Princeton), 200 Club (Trenton, N.J.), Torrequebrada County Club, L.A. Athletic Club, Finnish Am. C. of C. Home: 4003 The Strand Manhattan Beach CA 90266-3184 Office: Princeton Pacific Inc PO Box 279 Manhattan Beach CA 90267-0279

SAPONTZIS, STEVE F., philosophy educator, writer; b. N.Y.C., Feb. 9, 1945; s. Zissis Peter and Lea Marie (Vial) S.; m. Jeanne Marie Gocker, Dec. 25, 1992. BA, Rice U., 1967; postgrad., U. Paris, 1967-68; MPhil, Yale U., 1970, PhD, 1971. From asst. to full prof. philosophy Calif. State U., Hayward, 1971—; lectr. Stanford U., Palo Alto, Calif., 1986. Author: Morals Reason and Animals, 1987; co-editor: Between the Species Jour., 1984—; mem. bd. editl. advisors Am. Philos. Quar., 1991-94. Mem. animal welfare rsch. com. Lawrence Berkeley (Calif.) Lab., 1986-90; pres. Hayward Friends of Animals Humane Soc., 1985—; bd. dirs. Paw Pac Animal Welfare, Sacramento, 1984—. Fulbright fellow U.S. Govt., 1967-68, Woodrow Wilson Found. fellow Yale U., 1968-69; NEH grantee, 1976, Am. Coun. Learned Socs. grantee, 1988. Mem. Am. Philos. Assn., Internat. Soc. for Environ. Ethics, Soc. for Study Ethics and Animals (bd. dirs. 1984—). Democrat. Office: Calif State U Dept Philosophy Hayward CA 94542

SAPP, DONALD GENE, minister; b. Phoenix, Feb. 27, 1927; s. Guerry Byron and Lydia Elmeda (Snyder) S.; m. Anna Maydean Nevitt, July 10, 1952 (dec.); m. Joann Herrin Mountz, May 1, 1976; children: Gregory, Paula, Jeffrey, Mark, Melody, Cristine. AB in Edn., Ariz. State U., 1949; MDiv, Boston U., 1952, STM, 1960; D Ministry, Calif. Grad. Sch. Theology, 1975. Ordained to ministry Meth. Ch., 1950. Dir. youth activities Hyde Park (Mass.) Meth. Ch., 1950-52; minister 1st Meth. Ch., Peabody, Mass., 1952-54, Balboa Island (Calif.) Community Meth. Ch., 1954-57, Ch. of the Foothills Meth., Duarte, Calif., 1957-63; sr. minister Aldersgate United Meth. Ch., Tustin, Calif., 1963-70, Paradise Valley (Ariz.) United Meth. Ch., 1970-83; dist. supt. Cen. West Dist. of Desert S.W. Conf. United Meth. Ctr., Phoenix, 1983-89. Editor Wide Horizons, 1983-89; contbr. articles to profl. jours. Chaplain City of Hope Med. Ctr., Duarte, 1957-63; trustee Plaza Community Ctr., L.A., 1967-70; corp. mem. Sch. Theology at Claremont, Calif., 1972-80; pres. Met. Phoenix Commn., 1983-85; del. Western Jurisdictional Conf. United Meth. Ch., 1984, 88; bd. dirs. Coun. Chs., L.A., 1963-67, Orange County (Calif.) Human Rels. Coun., 1967-70, Interfaith Counseling Svc. Found., 1982-89, Wesley Community Ctr., Phoenix, 1983-89; mem. gen. conf. United Meth. Ch., 1988. With USN, 1945-46. Mem. Ariz. Ecumenical Coun., Bishops and Exec. Roundtable, Rotary (pres.), Kappa Delta Pi, Tau Kappa Epsilon. Democrat. Home: 5225 E Road Runner Rd Paradise Valley AZ 85253

SAPSOWITZ, SIDNEY H., entertainment and media company executive; b. N.Y.C., June 29, 1936; s. Max and Annette (Rothstein) Sapsowitz; m. Phyllis Skopp, Nov. 27, 1957; children: Donna Dawn Chazen, Gloria Lynn Aaron, Marsha Helene Gleit. BBA summa cum laude, Paterson (N.J.) State Coll., 1980. Various fin. and oper. systems positions Metro Goldwyn Mayer, Inc., N.Y.C., 1957-68; exec. v.p. Penta Computer Assoc. Inc., N.Y.C., 1968-70, Cons. Actuaries Inc., Clifton, N.J., 1970-73; CFO Am. Film. Theatre, N.Y.C., 1973-76; exec. v.p., CFO Cinema Shares Internat Dristb. Corp., N.Y.C., 1976-79; sr. cons. Solomon, Finger & Newman, N.Y.C., 1979-80; exec. v.p., chief fin. officer Metro Goldwyn Mayer, Inc., L.A., 1980-85; various positions leading to exec. v.p. fin. and adminstrn., CFO MGM/UA Entertainment Co., Culver City, Calif., 1985-86; also bd. dirs. MGM/UA Entertainment Co., L.A.; fin. v.p.; chief bus. and ops. officer, Office of Pres., dir. United Artists Corp., Beverly Hills, Calif., 1986-87; chmn. bd., CEO MGA/UA Telecommunications Corp., Beverly Hills, 1986-89; sr. exec. v.p., dir., mem. exec. com. MGA/UA Communications Co., 1986-89; chmn., CEO Sid Sapsowitz & Assocs., Inc., 1989—. Pres., Wayne Conservative Congregation, N.J., 1970-77. Mem. Am. Mgmt. Assn., Am. Film Inst., Acad. Motion Picture Arts and Scis., Fin. Exec. Inst., TV Acad. Arts and Scis., KP (chancellor comdr.).

SARAFIAN, ARPI, English language educator; b. Beirut, Sept. 10, 1943; came to U.S., 1976; d. Hagop and Ouriz (Yeretz) Kouyoumjian; m. Vartan Sarafian; children: Sevag, Hourig. PhD, U. So. Calif., L.A., 1991. Cert. tchr., Calif. Lectr. Calif. State U., L.A., 1978—, Loyola Marymount U., L.A., 1991—. Contbr. essays and revs. to Armenian Observer, 1977—; assoc. editor Virginia Woolf Studies Ann. Office: Calif State U Dept English 5151 State University Dr Los Angeles CA 90032

SARAVO, ANNE COBBLE, clinical psychologist, mental health administrator; b. Atlanta, Feb. 23, 1938; d. William Edwin and Iris Benny (Norman) Cobble; m. James Vincent Saravo, June 13, 1958; children: Stacy Anne, Lisa Ames Furmanek. BA, Tex. Tech. U., 1959; MS, U. Mass., 1964, PhD, 1965; postgrad., Regional Health Authority, London, 1978-79, U. So. Calif., 1980-81. Lic. psychologist, Calif. Assoc. prof. psychology Antioch Coll., Yellow Springs, Ohio, 1966-69; cons. Winchester (Eng.) Day Treatment Nursery Sch., 1971-73; sch. psychologist Muroc Unified Sch. Dist., Edwards AFB, Calif., 1974-75; clinical psychologist Antelope Valley Hosp., Lancaster, Calif., 1975-76, Farnborough Hosp., Kent, Eng., 1978-80, Orange County (Calif.) Mental Health Svc., 1981-84; pvt. practice clin. psychology Seal Beach, Calif., 1981—; chief adult out-patient svc. Orange County (Calif.) Mental Health Svc., 1984-87, chief adult inpatient svcs., 1987—; bd. dirs. High Hopes Neurol. Recover Group, Costa Mesa, Calif., chair profl. adv. bd., 1988—; oral examination commr. Calif. Bd. Psychology, 1989—; geriatric coord. Orange County Mental Health Svcs., 1985-87; profl. adv. bd. Orange County Caregiver Resource Ctr., 1989—; mem. Alzheimers Disease rev. panel Calif. Dept. Mental Health, 1990—. Contbr. articles to profl. jours. Chairperson Conf. Geriatric Mental Health, Asilomar, Calif., 1986, So. Calif. Geriatric Mental Health Coordinators, 1985-87. U.S. Pub. Health fellow Fels Research Inst., 1966-67. Mem. APA, Calif. Psychol. Assn. (chair medicare/pub. sector subcom. 1990—), Nat. Acad. Neuropsychology (grad.), Brit. Psychol. Soc. Office: Orange County Mental Health Svc 515 N Sycamore St Santa Ana CA 92701-4637 also: 550 Pacific Coast Hwy # 203 Seal Beach CA 90740

SARCHET, FRED CHARLES, peace and environmental activist; b. Milnerton, Alta., Can., Dec. 23, 1903; came to U.S., 1917; s. Thomas Ulysses and Minnie (Newton) S.; m. Agnes Margaret Johnson, Jan. 1, 1932; children: Jeremy, Helen Ann, Fred L. BS in Elec. Engring. cum laude, Wash. State Coll., Pullman, 1925. From student engr. to quality control engr. Gen. Electric Corp., Schenectady, 1925-50; project engr. Eastern Engring. Co., New Haven, 1951-54; prin. sales engr. Balteau Electric Corp., Stamford, Conn., 1954-63, western div. sales mgr., 1962-63; sales engr. La Mar Industries, Long Beach, Calif., 1963-64, Indsl. Filtration Co., San Pedro, Calif., 1964; zone mgr. Investors Diversified Svcs., Inc., 1964; stock and bond trader Dempsey-Tegeler & Co., Inc., 1964-67; rep. J. Henry Helser & Co., Investment Mgrs., L.A., 1967-68; a prin. founder, treas. Whittier Area Peace Coalition, 1979—; activist for peace and a sustainable environment, chmn. The Whittier (Calif.) Environ. Coun., 1990—; coord. Gt. Decisions Discussion Program in Whittier, 1975—; mem., coord. Whittier chpt. Gray Panthers, 1978-84. del. Internat. Population and Devel. Conf., Cairo, 1994; presenter RSVP Meals-on-Wheels, 1971; active Whittier Sr. Mixed Chorus. Recipient Cert. of Commendation as Dem. of Yr., Los Angeles County Dem. Party, 1993, others. Mem. UN Assn. (bd. dirs. Whittier chpt. 1972—, treas. 1972-78, environ. liaison 1989—, Peace medal 1980). Democrat. Unitarian. Home: 13250 Philadelphia St Apt 412 Whittier CA 90601-4317

SARFEH, JAMES IRAJ, surgery educator; b. Tehran, Iran, Nov. 2, 1940; s. Rostam K. and Valentina Sarfeh; m. Sharon Lynnette Haney, Apr. 23, 1983; children: Jennifer Alexandra, Jilian Valerie, Colin Rustam. BA, NYU, 1964; MD, Albany Med. Coll., 1968. Intern Albany Med. Ctr., 1968-69, resident, 1969-71, 72-73, chief resident, 1973-74, instr. surgery, 1973-74, asst. prof., 1974-77, assoc. prof., 1977-80; asst. prof. surgery U. Calif., Irvine, 1980-83, assoc. prof., 1983-89, prof., 1989—; attending surgeon Albany Med. Ctr., 1974-80, U. Calif., Irvine, 1981—; staff surgeon Long Beach (Calif.) VA Med. Ctr., 1981—; cons. Albany Va Med. Ctr., 1974-80; cons. surgeon St. Joseph Hosp., Orange, Calif., 1983—; vis. prof. Gloucester Royal Infirmary, England, 1984, U. N.Mex., 1985, U. Iowa, 1986, U. Ariz., 1987, U. Mich., 1988, Borwn U., R.I. Hosp. Program, 1990, Med. Coll. Ohio, 1991, U. Ill., Chgo., 1993, others; speaker, presenter and researcher in field. Author: Gastrointestinal Bleeding: Diagnosis and Management, 1977; contbr. chpts. to books and 87 articles to profl. jours. Fellow Am. Coll. Surgeons; mem. Am. Assn. Study Liver Disease, Am. Gastroenterological Assn., Am. Surgery Liver Group, Am. Surg. Assn., Assn. Acad. Surgery, Ctrl. Surg. Assn., Collegium Internat. Chirurgiae Dogestive, Internat. Soc. Surgery, L.A. Surg. Soc., Pacific Coast Surg. Assn., Soc. Surgery Alimentary Tract, Soc. Univ. Surgeons, Western Surg. Assn., So. Calif. Chpt. Am. Coll. Surgeons.

SARGENT, DIANA RHEA, corporate executive; b. Cheyenne, Wyo., Feb. 20, 1939; d. Clarence and Edith (de Castro) Hayes; grad. high sch.; m. Charles Sargent, Apr. 17, 1975 (div. 1991); children: Rene A. Coburn, Rochelle A. Rollins, Clayton R. Weldy, Christopher J. IBM proof operator Bank Am., Stockton, Calif., 1956-58, gen. ledger bookkeeper, Modesto, Calif., 1963-66; office mgr., head bookkeeper Cen. Drug Store, Modesto, 1966-76; pres. Sargent & Coburn, Inc., Modesto, 1976—; ptnr. R.C.D. Farms (almond ranch). Mem. Stanislaus Women's Ctr., NOW, San Francisco Mus. Soc., Modesto Women's Network, Yerba Buena Art Ctr. Office: 915 14th St Modesto CA 95354-1010

SARGENT, HARRY TOMPKINS, professional golfer; b. San Diego, Mar. 30, 1947; s. Marston Cleves and Grace Charlotte (Tompkins) S.; m. Debra Kay Sponnoble, Sept. 19, 1981; children: Lucas Jon, Samantha Ann. BA in French and History, San Diego State U., 1970. Asst. golf prof. Carlton Oaks Country Club, Santee, Calif., 1973-76; mini-tour player various golf tours, 1974-76; head golf profl. Yorba Linda (Calif.) Country Club, 1978—. Mem. PGA (v.p. 1991, v.p. So. Calif. sect. 1988-90, pres. 1993-94, jr. golf leader award 1983, 84, leader award 1989, 91, tchr. of yr. award So. Calif. sect. 1986, 93, nat. jr. golf leader award 1989, Horton Smith award 1990, Golf Profl. of Yr. 1991), PGA Jr. Golf Assn. (pres. 1991, 92, 93, 94, Bill Bryant award 1985). Home: 3805 Singingwood Dr Yorba Linda CA 92686-6909 Office: 19400 Mountain View Ave Yorba Linda CA 92686-5530

SARGENT, MURRAY, III, physicist, educator, software engineer; b. N.Y.C., Aug. 18, 1941; s. Murray Jr. and Lucy (Garfield) S.; m. Helga Reineke, May 21, 1967; children: Nicole, Christine. BS in Physics, Yale U., 1963, MS, 1964, PhD, 1967. Postdoctoral researcher Yale U., New Haven, Conn., 1967; mem. tech. staff Bell Telephone Labs., Holmdel, N.J., 1967-69; prof. optical sci. U. Ariz., Tucson, 1969—; sr. software design engr. Microsoft, Redmond, Wash., 1992—; vis. prof. U. Stuttgart, 1975-76, Max Planck für Festkorperforschung, 1975-76, Max Planck für QuantenOptik, 1982-92, U. Toronto, 1991; pres. Scroll Systems, Inc., Tucson, 1981—. Author: Laser Physics, 1977, Interfacing Microcomputers, 1981, IBM PC from Inside Out, 1984, Elements of Quantum Optics, 1991, Semiconductor Laser Physics, 1993, The PC from the Inside Out, 1994. Recipient U.S. Sr. Scientist award Humboldt Stiftung, 1975. Fellow Optical Soc. Am.; mem. Am. Phys. Soc., Sigma Xi. Republican. Office: Microsoft One Microsoft Way Redmond WA 98052

SARGENT, WALLACE LESLIE WILLIAM, astronomer, educator; b. Elsham, Eng., Feb. 15, 1935; s. Leslie William and Eleanor (Dennis) S.; m. Anneila Isabel Cassells, Aug. 5, 1964; children: Lindsay Eleanor, Alison Clare. B.Sc., Manchester U., 1956, M.Sc., 1957, Ph.D., 1959. Research fellow Calif. Inst. Tech., 1959-62; sr. research fellow Royal Greenwich Obs., 1962-64; asst. prof. physics U. Calif., San Diego, 1964-66; mem. faculty dept. astronomy Calif. Inst. Tech., Pasadena, 1966—; prof. Calif. Inst. Tech., 1971-81, Ira S. Bowen prof. astronomy, 1981—; Thomas Gold lectr. Cornell U., 1994-95. Contbr. articles to profl. jours. Alfred P. Sloan fellow, 1968-70. Fellow Am. Acad. Arts and Scis., Royal Soc. (London); mem Am. Astron. Soc. (Helen B. Warner prize 1969, Dannie Heineman prize 1991), Royal Astron. Soc. (George Darwin lectr. 1987), Astron. Soc. Pacific (Bruce Gold medal 1994), Internat. Astron. Union. Club: Athenaeum (Pasadena). Home: 400 S Berkeley Ave Pasadena CA 91107-5062 Office: Calif Inst Tech Astronomy Dept 105-24 Pasadena CA 91125

SARICH, VINCENT M., anthropologist, educator; b. Chicago, Ill., Dec. 13, 1934; s. Matt and Manda Saric; m. Jorjan Snyder; children: Kevin, Tamsin. BS, Ill. Inst. Tech., 1955; PhD, U. Calif., Berkeley, 1967. Instr. anthropology Stanford U., Berkeley, Calif., 1965; asst. prof. anthropology U. Calif. Berkeley, Berkeley, Calif., 1967-80; assoc. prof. U. Calif. Berkeley, 1970-81; prof., 1981—. Office: U Calif Dept of Anthropology 232 Kroebel Hall Berkeley CA 94720

SARICIFTCI, NIYAZI SERDAR, physicist; b. Konya, Turkey, Mar. 19, 1961; came to U.S., 1992; s. Ibrahim and Sükran (Cetintürk) S. MS, U. Vienna, 1986, PhD, 1989. Rsch. scientist U. Vienna, 1985-89, U. Stuttgart, Germany, 1989-92, U. Calif., Santa Barbara, 1992—. Mem. Am. Phys. Soc., German Phys. Soc., Austrian Phys. Soc.

SARKAR, DIPAK KUMAR, physiologist, educator; b. Calcutta, India, Aug. 25, 1950; came to U.S., 1980; s. Joydeb Chandra and Aruna (Mondal) S.; m. Shirley Ann Sanderson, May 4, 1984; children: Abby Joya, Sophie Dipti. BSc, Calcutta U., 1970, MSc, 1973, PhD, 1975; DPhil, Oxford (Eng.) U., 1979. Vis. postdoctoral assoc. Sch. of Medicine Yale U., New Haven, 1979; rsch. assoc. Mich. State U., East Lansing, 1980-83; asst. prof. U. Calif., San Diego, 1983-88; assoc. prof. Wash. State U., Pullman, 1988—, adj. assoc. prof. pharmacology and toxicology, 1989—, adj. assoc. prof. genetics and cell biology, 1989—; ad hoc grant reviewer NSF, Washington, 1987, 91; mem. rsch. rev. com. NIAAA/Pub. Health Svcs., Bethesda, Md., 1991—; invited speaker at nat. and internat. confs., various insts. Editor: Reproductive Neuroendocrinology of Aging and Drug Abuse; mem. editl. bd. Endocrinology, 1989—, Neuroendocrinology, 1987-90; contbr. chpt. to Neuroendocrinology of Aging, 1983; contbr. articles, abstracts to profl. publs. Grantee Andrew Mellon Found., 1983-86, San Diego Reproductive Medicine Rsch. and Edn. Found., 1985-87, March of Dimes, 1985-87, NIH/NIA, 1985-89, NIH/NICHD, 1986-89, Wash. State U., 1988-91, NIH/NIAAA, 1991—. Mem. AAAS, N.Y. Acad. Scis., Soc. for Neurosci., Internat. Soc. Neuroendocrinology, Internat. Brain Rsch. Orgn., Soc. Endocrinology (U.K.), Endocrine Soc. Office: Wash State Univ 215 Wegner Pullman WA 99164

SARKISIAN, PAMELA OUTLAW, artist; b. Spokane, Sept. 26, 1941; d. Willard Clinton and Frances (Montieth) Outlaw; m. Ronald Edward Sarkisian, Nov. 11, 1960; children: Ronald Abraham, Michelle Suzanne. Grad. high sch., Stockton, Calif. Art student Oceanside, Calif., 1972-80; founder Palette 'N Easel Studio, Oceanside, Calif., 1980—, operator, mgr., 1980-85; art tchr. in residence Palette 'N Easel Studio, Oceanside, 1985-95. Designer floral collector plate series Danbury Mint/MBI, Inc.; creator greeting card images; represented in Laura Larkin Gallery, Del Mar, Calif., 1993-94, Charles Hecht Galleries, Tarzana and Palm Desert, Calif., 1993-94, 95, Lou Martin Gallery, Laguna Beach, Calif., 1994, Charles Hecht Gallery, La Jolla, Calif., 1995. Pres. Zonta Internat., Oceanside, 1980-81; mem. Emblem Club #177, Oceanside, 1971-91; princess Daughters of the Nile, San Diego, 1974; bd. dirs. Oceanside Girls Club, 1980. Recipient 1st Pl. award San Dieguito Art Guild, 1978, 85, 2nd Pl. award, 1983, 89, 3rd Pl. award, 1983, 1990. Mem. North County Art Assn. (founder), Carlsbad Oceanside Art League, 1978, San Dieguito Art Guild, Fallbrook Art Assn., San Diego Art Inst., Assn. pour Promotion Artiste Français, ARTISPHERE. Office: Palette 'N Easel Studio 1021 S Coast Hwy Oceanside CA 92054-5004

SARLAT, GLADYS, public relations consultant; b. Elizabeth, N.J., July 22, 1923; d. Max and Dora (Levin) S. BS, U. Wash., 1946. Asst., Kay Sullivan Assocs. N.Y.C., 1949-50; fashion dir. Warsaw & Co., N.Y.C., 1950-54; asst. fashion coordinator Emporium Dept. Store, San Francisco, 1955-56; asst. prodn. mgr. Cunningham & Walsh Advt., San Francisco, 1958-59; v.p., pub. rels. dir. Harwood Advt. Inc., Tucson and Phoenix, 1959-68; v.p., dir. Waller & Sarlat Advt. Inc., Tucson, 1968-69; pres. Godwin & Sarlat Pub. Rels., Inc., Tucson, 1970-87; counsel, Godwin Sarlat Pub. Rels., 1987-88, cons., 1988—; of counsel Liess Peck & Godwin, Tuscon, 1993—; cons. in field. Mem. adv. com. Downtown Devel. Corp., 1979-85, Festival in the Sun; bd. dirs. Tuscon Conv. and Visitors Bur., 1993—. Named Woman of Yr. for Bus., Ariz. Daily Star, 1963; recipient Lulu award L.A. Woman in Advt., 1962. Mem. Pub. Rels. Soc. Am. (past bd. mem., counselors acad.), Fashion Group, Tucson Met. C. of C. (v.p., dir. 1976-85, chmn bd. 1986-87), Tucson Trade Bur. (dir. 1977-80). Republican. Jewish. Home: 5530 N Camino Arenosa Tucson AZ 85718-5417 Office: 177 N Church Ave Ste 608 Tucson AZ 85701-1118

SARLEY, JOHN G., broadcast executive, writer; b. Cleve., Mar. 1, 1954; s. Edward James and Ann Sarley. BA, Cleve. State U., 1977. Writer, producer Marschalk Co. Advt., Cleve., 1977-80, DOCSI Corp., Hollywood, Calif., 1980—; pres. Sarley, Bigg & Bedder Inc., Hollywood, 1981—. Recipient multiple Clio awards. Mem. Broadcast Promotion and Mktg. Execs., Hollywood C. of C. Office: Sarley Bigg & Bedder Inc 1644 N Stanley Ave Hollywood CA 90046-2713

SARNAT, HARVEY BARRY, pediatric neurology educator; b. Chgo., Dec. 19, 1941; s. Bernard David and Sylvia Joan (Dietsch) S.; m. Margaret Ione Strom, Dec. 27, 1967; children: Naomi Beth Sarnat, Daryl Jacob Sarnat. BS, U. Ill., 1962; MS, U. Ill., Chgo., 1965, MD, 1966. Intern, resident in pediatrics U. Ill. Hosp., Chgo., 1966-68; resident in neurology, fellow in neuropathology U. Va., Charlottesville, 1970-73; Asst. prof. St. Louis U., 1973-76; cons. U. Western Australia, Perth, 1976-77; assoc. prof. St. Louis U., 1977-78, U. Ark., Little Rock, 1978-81; assoc. prof. U. Calgary (Can.), 1981-86, prof., 1986-92; prof., head divsn. pediatric neurology U. Washington, Seattle, 1992—. Author: 3 med. textbooks; editor: 3 med. textbooks; contbr. 150 rsch. articles to various med. jours. Mem. WHO com. for revision of internat. classification of diseases UN, 1989-92. Capt. M.C., USAF, 1968-70. Recipient Carrell-Krusen award for neuromuscular rsch. U. Tex. S.W., 1994; Sarkowsky prof. of child neurology (endowed chair) U. Washington, 1993—. Mem. Child Neurology Soc., Am. Assn. Neuropathologists, Am. Neurol. Assn., Internat. Child Neurol. Assn. (exec. com. 1976—), Canadian Assn. Pediatric Neurology. Office: Children's Hosp CH-49 4800 Sand Point Way NE Seattle WA 98105-3901

SARSAM, MUMTAZ BASHIR, bridge engineer; b. Mosul, Iraq, Jan. 18, 1933; came to the U.S., 1956; s. Bashir H. and Naima A. (Hafez) S.; m. Vivian Miller, July 29, 1961; children: Mark C., Samir M. BSc in Civil Engring., S.D. State U., 1960, MSc in Civil & Structural Engring., 1972. Registered profl. engr., Ariz. Bridge design squad leader S.D. Dept. Transp., Pierre, 1960-68; asst. instr. civil engring. S.D. State U., Brookings, 1968-72; bridge maintenance engr. S.D. Dept. Transp., Pierre, 1972-83; transp. rsch. engr. Ariz. Transp. Rsch. Ctr., Tempe, Ariz., 1984-85; transp. maintenance engr. Ariz. Dept. Transp., Phoenix, 1986, transp. bridge maintenance engr., 1986-93, bridge design leader, 1994-95; bridge maintenance engr., 1995—. Mem. ASCE. Republican. Mem. Orthodox Ch. Office: Ariz Dept Transp 635 E 205 S 17th Ave Phoenix AZ 85007-3212

SARSON, JOHN CHRISTOPHER, television producer, director, writer; b. London, Jan. 19, 1935; s. Arnold Wilfred and Annie Elizabeth (Wright) S.; m. Evelyn Patricia Kaye, Mar. 25, 1963; children: Katrina May, David

Arnold. BA with honors, Trinity Coll., Cambridge, Eng., 1960, MA, 1963. Dir. Granada TV, Manchester, Eng., 1960-63; producer, dir. Sta. WGBH-TV, Boston, 1963-73; pres. Blue Penguin, Inc., Boulder, Colo., 1974—; v.p. TV programming Sta. WYNC-TV, N.Y.C., 1989-90; dir. Pub. Broadcasting Assocs., Newton, Mass.; cons. to numerous pub. TV stations. Creator, producer MAsterpiece Theatre, PBS, 1970-73, Zoom, PBS, 1971-73; producer Live From the Met, PBS, 1977-79, Kid's Writes, Nickelodeon, 1982-83, American Treasure, a Smithsonian Journey, 1986, Spotlight Colorado, 1991, PArenting Works, 1993, Club 303, 1994. Served with Royal Navy, 1956-57. Recipient Emmy award, 1973, 74, Peabody award Ohio State U., 1978, Internat. Emmy award, 1983, Nat. Acad. TV Arts and Scis. Gov.'s award, 1991. Mem. Dirs. Guild Am., Nat. acad. TV Arts and Scis. (gov. Heartland chpt.). Home and Office: 3031 5th St Boulder CO 80304-2501

SARTINI, RICHARD LEE, retired internist; b. Meriden, Conn., June 23, 1946; s. Silvio Joseph and Lena Josephine Sartini. AB in French, Coll. Holy Cross, 1968; MD, Tufts U., 1972. Intern and resident Cin. Gen. Hosp., 1972-75; intern Alexian Bros. Hosp., San Jose, Calif., 1976-78; pulmonary fellow U. Calif., Irvine, 1978-80; staff physician, chief respiratory medicine San Clemente (Calif.) Hosp., 1980-88; staff physician Mission Community Hosp., Mission Viejo, Calif., 1980-88, Saddleback Hosp., Laguna Hills, Calif., 1980-88, South Coast Hosp., Laguna Beach, Calif., 1980-88. Fellow Am. Coll. Chest Physicians; mem. ACP, Orange County Med. Assn., AMA, Calif. Med. Assn., Nat. Assn. Med. Dirs. Respiratory Care. Roman Catholic. Home and Office: 169 High Dr Laguna Beach CA 92651-1833

SARTOR, LUIGI, chemical engineering researcher, consultant; b. Pordenone, Italy, Jan. 16, 1962; came to U.S., 1979; BA in Chem. Engring., Manhattan Coll., 1984; PhD in Chem. Engring., U. Minn., 1990. Rsch. asst. U. Minn., Mpls., 1984-90; rsch. engr. Avery Dennison, Pasadena, Calif., 1990-91, sr. rsch. engr., 1991-93, rsch. assoc., 1993—. Sec. Tau Beta Pi N.Y.C., 1983-84; sec., v.p. Calif. Rose Ct. Assn., Pasadena, 1993-94. Named Dean's list Manhattan Coll., N.Y.C., 1980, 81, 83, 84; recipient 1993 Honorary award Avery Dennison Tech. Dirs., Concord, Ohio, 1993. Office: Avery Dennison Avery Rsch Ctr 2900 Bradley St Pasadena CA 91107-1560

SARTORIS, DAVID JOHN, radiologist; b. Chgo., Nov. 25, 1955; s. Cornelius Ugo and Helen Louise (Lesjak); m. Cyd Clariza Grepo. BS, Stanford U., 1976, MD, 1980. Diplomate Am. Bd. Radiology. Intern, diagnostic radiology Stanford (Calif.) Univ. Med. Ctr., 1980-81; resident, diagnostic radiology Stanford U. and Affil. Hosps., 1981-84; fellow, musculoskeletal radiology U. Calif. and Affil. Hosps., San Diego, 1984-85; asst. prof. radiology U. Calif., San Diego, 1985-87, assoc. prof. radiology, 1987-94, prof. radiology, 1994—; chief, musculoskeletal IMG U. Calif. San Diego Med. Ctr., 1985-91, chief, quantitative bone densitometry, 1985—; lectr. in field; cons. Rsch. and Edn. Fund/Radiol. Soc. North Am.; vis. prof. numerous univs. including Creighton U. Med. Ctr., Omaha, 1993, U. Pitts., 1990, VA Med. Ctr., Long Beach, Calif., 1990, U. Ottawa/Ottawa Gen. Hosp., Ont., Can., 1987, others; served on numerous coms. in field. Contbr. over 400 articles to profl. jours., numerous chpts. to books in field; editorial adv. bd. Chem. Rubber Co. Pres., Inc., Boca Raton, Fla., Diagnostic Imaging mag., 1987, Thieme Med. Pubs., Inc., N.Y.C., Year Book Med. Pubs., Chgo., Applied Radiology Jour.; asst. editor: AJR/musculoskeletal sect., 1987-88; reviewer jours. Rsch. grantee The Arthritis Soc., Toronto, Ont.; recipient Silver Spoon awards from residents at U. Calif., San Diego, 1986, 93, 94, others. Mem. Am. Coll. Radiology, Am. Roentgen Ray Soc., Assn. U. Radiologists, Radiol. Soc. N. Am., Calif. Radiol. Soc., Physicians for Social Responsibility, Internat. Skeletal Soc. (Youngest-Ever New Mem. award 1987, Pres.'s medal 1989), So. Calif. Bone and Mineral Club, New Bone Densitometry Soc., Bone Dysplasia Soc., Phi Beta Kappa. Office: UCSD Med Ctr Dept Radiology 350 Dickinson St San Diego CA 92103-1913

SARWAR, BARBARA DUCE, school system administrator; b. Mpls., Aug. 9, 1938; d. Harold Taylor and Barbara (Thayer) Duce; m. Mohammad Sarwar, Dec. 28, 1972; children: Barbara, Sarah, Franklin. BS, U. Colo., 1972; M Spl. Edn., Ea. N.Mex. U., 1975, Edn. Specialist, 1979. Cert. tchr., adminstr., N.Mex. Tchr. 2d grade, English as 2d lang. Lake Arthur (N.Mex.) Mcpl. Schs., 1972-74; tchr. spl. edn. Artesia (N.Mex.) Pub. Schs., 1974-79, ednl. diagnostician, 1979-88, dir. spl. edn., 1988—. Contbr. to profl. publs. Pres. Altrusa Club Artesia, 1981-82, 86-87, The Arc of Artesia, 1990-92. Named Employee of Yr. Arc of N.Mex., 1994. Mem. NEA, Artesia Edn. Assn. (pres. 1978-79), Internat. Reading Assn. (pres. Pecos Valley chpt. 1975-76, sec. N.Mex. unit 1977-78), Nat. Assn. Sch. Psychologists, N.Mex. Sch. Adminstrs. Assn., Phi Kappa Phi, Phi Delta Kappa. Home: PO Box 1493 Artesia NM 88211-1493 Office: Artesia Pub Schs 1106 W Quay Ave Artesia NM 88210-1857

SASAKI, DARRYL YOSHIO, research chemist; b. Honolulu, July 9, 1962; s. Charles Daigaku and Grace Hisako (Fujinaka) S.; m. Yukiko Takada, Mar. 22, 1991; 1 child, Dayne. BS, UH Manoa, 1984; MS in Organic Chemistry, U. Calif., Irvine, 1986, PhD in Organic Chemistry, 1989. Sr. mem. tech. staff Sandia Nat. Labs Org. 1811, Albuquerque, 1994—. Contbr. articles to profl. jours.; patentee in field. Mem. AAAS, Am. Chem. Soc., Soc. of Polymer Sci. Office: Sandia Nat Labs MS 1407 Albuquerque NM 87185

SASAKI, Y. TITO, business services company executive; b. Tokyo, Feb. 6, 1938; came to U.S., 1967, naturalized, 1983; s. Yoshinaga and Chiyoko (Imada) S.; m. Janet Louise Cline, June 27, 1963; 1 child, Heather N. BS, Chiba U., 1959; postgrad. Royal Coll. Art, London, 1961, U. Oslo, 1962; MS, Athens Tech. Inst., Greece, 1964; postgrad. U. Calif., Berkeley, 1969. Chief designer Aires Camera Industries Co., Tokyo, 1958-59; tech. officer London County Council, 1961-62; researcher Athens Ctr. Ekistics, 1964-66; sr. researcher Battelle Inst., Geneva, 1966-68; project engr. Marin County Transit Dist., San Rafael, Calif., 1968-69; chief planning, research Golden Gate Bridge Dist., San Francisco, 1969-74; pres. Visio Internat. Inc., Somona, Calif., 1973—; chmn. steering com. Kawada Industries Inc., Tokyo, 1974-82; chief exec. officer Quantum Mechanics Corp., Somona, 1981—; bd. dirs., v.p. Sonoma Skypark, Inc., 1986-89. Mem. ASME, AIAA, Am. Soc. Testing and Materials, Am. Welding Soc., Am. Inst. Cert. Planners, World Soc. Ekistics, Am. Vacuum Soc., Aircraft Owners and Pilots Assn. Roman Catholic. Office: Visio Internat Inc PO Box 1888 Sonoma CA 95476-1888

SASENICK, JOSEPH ANTHONY, health care company executive; b. Chgo., May 18, 1940; s. Anthony E. and Caroline E. (Smicklas) S.; m. Barbara Ellen Barr, Aug. 18, 1962; children: Richard Allen, Susan Marie, Michael Joseph. BA, DePaul U., 1962; MA, U. Okla., 1966. With Miles Labs., Inc., Elkhart, Ind., 1963-70; product mgr. Alka-Seltzer, 1966-68, dir. mktg. grocery products div., 1968-70; with Gillette Corp., Boston, 1970-79; dir. new products/new ventures, personal care div. Gillette Corp., 1977; v.p. diversified cos. and pres. Jafra Cosmetics Worldwide, 1977-79; mktg. dir. Braun AG, Kronberg, W. Ger., 1970-73; chmn. mng. dir. Braun U.K. Ltd., 1973-77; with Abbott Labs., North Chicago, 1979-84; corp. v.p., pres. consumer products div. Abbott Labs., 1979-84; pres., chief exec. officer Moxie Industries, 1984-87, Personal Monitoring Technologies, Rochester, N.Y., 1987; pres. Bioline Labs., Ft. Lauderdale, Fla., 1988; mng. dir., ptnr. Vista Resource Group, Newport Beach, Calif., 1988-90; pres., CEO, Alcide Corp., Redmond, Wash., 1991-92, CEO, 1992—. Mem. Knollwood Club, El Niguel Club, Landmark Club, Wash. Athletic Club. Home: 1301 Spring St Seattle WA 98104-1354 Office: Alcide Corp 8561 154th Ave NE Redmond WA 98052-3557

SASMOR, JAMES CECIL, publisher representative, educator; b. N.Y.C., July 29, 1920; s. Louis and Cecilia (Mockler) S.; 1 child from previous marriage: Elizabeth Lynn; m. Jeannette L. Fuchs, May 30, 1965. BS, Columbia U., 1942; MBA, Calif. Western U., 1977, PhD, 1979. Cert. Am. Bd. Med. Psychotherapists, sex educator Am. Assn. Sex Educators, Counselors and Therapists, Healthcare Risk Mgr. Am. Inst. Med. Law, diplomate Am. Bd. Sexology. Advt. sales exec. 1946-59; registered rep. Nat. Assn. Security Dealers, 1956-57; founder, owner J.C. Sasmor Assocs. Publishers' Reps., N.Y.C., 1959-89; co-founder, pres., dir. adminstrn. Continuing Edn. Cons., Inc., 1976—; pub. cons., 1959—; clin assoc., U. So. Fla. Coll. of Medicine, 1987-89; adj. faculty Coll. Nursing, 1980-89, dir. Ednl. Counseling Comprehensive Breast Cancer Ctr., U. So. Fla. Med. Ctr., 1984-89, client librn. mental health inst., 1979-89. Team tchr. childbirth edn. Am. Soc. Childbirth Educators; bd. dirs. Tampa chpt. ARC; bd. dirs. Ariz. divsn. Am. Cancer Soc., pub. edn. com., co-chmn. adult edn. com. Sedona (Ariz.) unit; county nursing ednl. cons. ARC. With USN, 1942-58, PTO; lt. USNR ret. Recipient cert. appreciation ARC, 1979, Dept. Health and Rehab. Svcs. award for Fla. Mental Health Inst. Svc., 1980, Cert. of Appreciation Am. Fgn. Svc. Assn., 1988. Internat. Coun. of Sex Edn. and Parenthood Am. U. fellow, 1981—. Mem. NAACOG (bd. dirs. Tampa chpt.), Nat. Assn. Pubs. Reps. (pres. 1965-66), Am. Soc. Psychoprophylaxis in Obstetrics (dir. 1970-71), Am. Soc. Childbirth Educators (co-founder, dir. 1972—), Internat. Coun. Women's Health Issues (chmn. resources com.), Health Edn. Media Assn., Nursing Educators Assn. Tampa, Lions (bd. dirs. Found. Ariz., pres. Sedona club). Author: Economics of Structured Continuing Education in Selected Professional Journals'; contbr. chpts. to Childbirth Education: A Nursing Perspective; contbr. articles to profl. jours. Home: 235 Arrowhead Dr Sedona AZ 86351-8900 Office: PO Box 2282 Sedona AZ 86339-2282

SASMOR, JEANNETTE LOUISE, educational consulting company executive; b. N.Y.C., May 17, 1943; d. Sol and Willmyra J. (Reilly) Fuchs; m. James C. Sasmor, May 30, 1965. BS, Columbia U., 1966, MEd, 1968, EdD, 1974; adult primary care nurse practitioner, U. Md., Balt., 1982; MBA, U. South Fla., 1990. Cert. adult primary care nurse practitioner; cert. women's health nurse practitioner; cert. risk mgr. Coord. ANA Div. Maternal Child Health, N.Y.C., 1972-73; maternal child health cons. test constrn. div. Nat. League for Nursing, N.Y.C., 1973; prof., dir. continuing nursing edn. U. South Fla., Tampa, 1973-89; v.p. and dir. edn. Continuing Edn. Cons. Inc., Tampa, Fla., 1976-89, Sedona, Ariz., 1989—; maternal child health coord. 2nd yr. nursing curriculum in maternal child health Yavapai Coll., Prescott, Ariz., 1994—; dir. internat. study tours USSR, 1986, New Zealand/Australia, 1990, Scandinavia, 1992; mem. scope practice com. Ariz. Bd. Nursing, 1994—. Author: What Every Husband Should Know About Having a Baby, 1972, Father's Labor Coaching Log and Review Book, 1972, 82, Childbirth Education: A Nursing Perspective, 1979. Del. White House Conf. on Children and Youth, 1970, White House Conf. on Families, 1980; bd. dirs. Ariz. divsn. Am. Cancer Soc., 1992—;. Am. Acad. Nursing fellow, 1977, Robert Wood Johnson Nurse faculty fellow in Primary Care, 1981-82; recipient NEAA Nursing Practice award Tchr.'s Coll. Columbia U., 1992, Vol. of Yr. award Sedona-Oak Creek unit. Am. Cancer Soc., 1992, Outstanding Cmty Leader award Lambda Omicron chpt. Sigma Theta Tau, 1994. Mem. Internat. Coun. on Women's Health Issues (pres. 1986-90), Am. Soc. Childbirth Educators (pres. 1972-78), Fla. Nurses Assn. (pres. dist. 4 1976-77), Ariz. Nurses Assn. (continuing edn. review com. 1990—), Ariz. Bd. Nursing (scope of practice com. 1994—), Lions (treas. Sedona-Oak Creek Canyon club 1990—), One Good Turn Inc. (pres. 1992-95), Phi Theta Kappa, Pi Lambda Theta, Sigma Theta Tau (chpt. treas. 1992—, newsletter editor 1991-94), Kappa Delta Pi. Office: Yavapai Coll 1100 E Sheldon St Prescott AZ 86301-3220

SASSO, GIUSEPPE, systems analyst; b. Capri, Italy, July 6, 1952; came to U.S., 1982; s. Paolo and Flora Scotto (Di Santolo) Sasso; m. Eliane Siqueira, June 6, 1976; 1 child, Chiara Francesca Perin Di Santolo. Student, Caracciolo Inst., Napoli, Italy, 1972, Salerno (Italy) U., 1973-75, Catholic Pontiff U., Rio de Janeiro, 1977; BS in Maths., St. Ursula U., Rio de Janeiro, 1981. Systems analyst UN, Rio de Janeiro, 1977-79, Getulio Vargas Found., Rio de Janeiro, 1978-82, Union Carbide, Rio de Janeiro, 1982, Software System Installations, L.A., 1984-85; sr. staff cons. Mmgt. Info. Sys. Internat., L.A., 1985-90; system analyst Farmers Ins. Group, L.A., 1990-91; sr. program analyst L.A. County, L.A., 1991—. Home: 102 Via Sevilla Redondo Beach CA 90277-6749 Office: Los Angeles County 9150 Imperial Hwy Downey CA 90242-2835

SASSOON, VIDAL, hair stylist; b. London, Jan. 17, 1928; s. Nathan and Betty (Bellin) S.; divorced 1980; children—Catya, Elan, Eden, David. Student, NYU. Founder, former chmn. bd. Vidal Sassoon, Inc. (beauty treatment products, appliances), Europe and Am.; pres. Vidal Sassoon Found.; lectr. in field. Author: autobiography A Year of Beauty and Health, 1976. Served with Palmach Israeli Army. Recipient award French Ministry of Culture, award for services rendered Harvard Bus. Sch.; Intercoiffure award Cartier, London, 1978; Hair Artists Internat. fellow. Clubs: Anabelle (London, Eng.), Ambassadeurs (London, Eng.), Claremont (London, Eng.); Le Club (N.Y.C.). Office: Vidal Sassoon Inc 505 S Beverly Dr #1077 Beverly Hills CA 90212

SATALOFF, RONALD ARTHUR, small business owner; b. Phila., Dec. 22, 1951; s. Joseph and Sylvia (Brown) S. BA in Sociology, Rutgers U., 1974; postgrad., U. Mass., 1974-75. Adminstrv. asst. Phila. 76ers, 1973-74; dir. group sales Md. Arrows, Landover, 1975-76; asst. ticket mgr. Phila. Phillies, 1976-77; regional mgr. Amfax Comms., S. Weymouth, Mass., 1977-80; sales mgr. Graphic Products Corp., West Hartford, Conn., 1980-81; pres. World Features Syndicate, Inc., La Jolla, Calif., 1981—.

SATER, WILLIAM FREDERICK, history educator, writer; b. N.Y.C., Nov. 17, 1937. AB in History, Stanford U., 1959; MA, UCLA, 1964, PhD, 1968. Prof. history Calif. State U., Long Beach, 1967—; cons. Rand Corp., Calif., 1977-90, Mellon Fellowship Found., 1982-88, NEH, 1983, ABC Cilo, 1985—, Libr. Congress, 1988—; book rev. editor The New World, 1984-90; guest lectr. Peace Corps, L.A., 1967, U. Chile, Santiago, 1968, UCLA, 1972, U. Concepcion, Chile, 1975, Cath. U., Santiago, 1980, U. Calgary, 1983, 87, Western Can. Mil. Soc., 1983; papers presented at Am. Hist. Assn., 1972, 76, Pacific Coast Conf. L.Am. History, 1972, Nat. Assn. Pvt. Schs., 1983, Conf. on Independence of Mex., U. Calif., Irvine, 1987, Can. Hist. Assn., 1990, 94, Rocky Mountain Conf. L.Am. History, Soc. for Mil. History, Ont., 1993. Editor, assoc. editor, book rev. editor The History Tchr., 1972-85; mng. editor TVI Report, 1984—; author: The Revolutionary Left and Terrorist Violence in Chile, 1986, Puerto Rican Terrorists: A Possible Threat to U.S. Energy Installations?, 1981, The Heroic Image in Chile, 1973, The History Teacher, 1981, The Research Guide to Andean History, 1981, The Southern Cone Nations, 1984, Chile and the War of the Pacific, 1986, Chile and the United States, 1990; contbr. articles to profl. jours. 1st lt. U.S. Army, 1959-60. Fellow U. Calif.-U. Chile, 1965-66, Orgn. Am. States, 1974-75; recipient Barros Arana Internat. Contest on Chilean History, Chilean Hist. Assn., 1984. Mem. Chilean Acad. History (corr.), Pacific Coast of L.Am. Studies (bd. govs., Hubert Herring award), Conf. on L.Am. History (chmn. com. teaching and teaching materials, chmn. andean studies com.), Am. Hist. Assn. Office: Calif State U Dept History Long Beach CA 90840

SATEREN, TERRY, theater technical production; b. Madison, Wis., Dec. 5, 1943; s. Leland Bernhard and Eldora (Johnson) S. BA, Augsburg Coll., 1968. Tech. prodn. dir. Guthrie Theatre, Mpls., 1974-78, dir. prodn., 1985-87; dir. exhibits Sci. Mus. Minn., St. Paul, 1978-85; tech. prodn. dir. Seattle Repertory Theatre, 1987—; cons. acad. and community theaters and museums, 1974—, U. Minn., 1992; Master class lectr. U. Wash., Seattle, 1989-91; adj. prof. U. Wash., 1991-92. Designer: (operas) Three Penny Opera, 1972, Newest Opera in the World, 1972, Don Giovanni, 1973; commd. sculptor numerous inds., chs. and acad. instns., 1966—. Pres.'s scholar Valparaiso (Ind.) U., 1967. Mem. U.S. Inst. Theatre Tech. Home: 7341 23rd Ave NW Seattle WA 98117-5661 Office: Seattle Repertory Theatre 155 Mercer St Seattle WA 98109-4639

SATHER, GLEN CAMERON, professional hockey team executive, coach; b. High River, Alta., Canada, Sept. 2, 1943. Former professional hockey player; pres., gen. mgr. Edmonton Oilers, Nat. Hockey League, Alta., Can., coach, 1977-89, now alt. gov.; coach winning team in Stanley Cup competition, 1987. Recipient Jack Adams Award for NHL Coach of the Yr., 1986. Office: care Edmonton Oilers, Northlands Coliseum, Edmonton, AB Canada T5B 4M9*

SATO, IRVING SHIGEO, education consultant; b. Honolulu, Sept. 4, 1933; s. Jusaku and Matsuyo (Uchida) S.; m. Helen Hatsuko, Aug. 18, 1956. B.Ed. with honors, U. Hawaii, 1955; M.S., U. So. Calif., 1962. Tchr. high sch., Honolulu, 1957-58; tchr., chmn. English and history Pasadena High Sch., Calif., 1958-66; cons. gifted and creative student programs Colo. Dept. Edn., Denver, 1966-68; cons. edn. mentally gifted Calif. Dept. Edn., Los Angeles, 1968-72; dir. Nat. State Leadership Tng. Inst. on Gifted and Talented, Los Angeles, 1972-93; instr. U. Denver, 1966-67, U. Colo., 1967-68, U. So. Calif., 1970-75, Widener U., Pa., 1981-91; cons. on gifted programs to numerous sch. dists., states, fgn. countries, 1966—; conf. speaker. Editor: (with James A. Gallagher and Sandra N. Kaplan) Promoting the Education of the Gifted/Talented: Strategies for Advocacy, 1983; co-editor (newsletter) The Gifted Pupil, 1968-72. Contbr. articles to profl. jours. Served to 1st lt. U.S. Army, 1955-57. Recipient cert. of recognition Office Gifted and Talented, U.S. Office Edn., 1974. Mem. Coun. State Dirs. Programs for Gifted (pres. 1969-71), Assn. for Gifted (exec. bd. 1972-79, pres. 1977-78), Nat. Assn. for Gifted Children (bd. govs. 1977-88, cert. of merit 1973, disting service award 1982), Calif. Assn. Gifted (Educator of Yr. award 1976), Assn. Supervision and Curriculum Devel., Phi Delta Kappa, Phi Kappa Phi. Home: 1744 Via Del Rey St South Pasadena CA 91030-4128

SATO, MILES MASAKAZE, computer programmer, systems analyst; b. Honolulu, May 14, 1950; s. Seigi and Michie Sato; m. Miriam H. Nitta, Aug. 12, 1978; children: Matthew, Michael. AB in Exptl. Psychology, Grinnell Coll., 1972; MSPH in Biostats., U. Hawaii, 1976, MPH in Health Svcs. Adminstrn., 1978. Rsch. assoc. Pacific Biomed. Rsch. Ctr., Honolulu, 1973-75; sr. data reduction analyst U.S. Army Strategic Def. Command (tech. support contractors), Kwajalein Missile Range, Honolulu, 1978-92; programmer/analyst, LAN adminstr. Hawaii Employers Coun., Honolulu, 1992—. Contbr. articles to profl. jours. Mem. IEEE, APHA, Am. Statis. Assn., Assn. for Computing Machinery, Nat. Systems Programmers Assn. Lutheran. Office: Hawaii Employers Coun 2682 Waiwai Loop Honolulu HI 96819-1938

SATO, TADASHI, artist; b. Maui, Hawaii, Feb. 6, 1923. Student, Honolulu Sch. Art, Bklyn. Mus. Art Sch., New Sch. Soc. Rsch. Exhbns. include Guggenheim Mus., N.Y.C., 1954, Honolulu Acad. Arts, 1957, Pacific Heritage Exhibit, L.A., 1963, McRoberts and Tunnard Ltd., London, 1964, White House Festival Arts, Washington, 1965, Berlin Art Festival, 1967, Japanese C. of C., Honolulu, 1993-94, Maui Cmty. and Cultural Assn., 1994; represented in permanent collections Albright-Knox Art Gallery, Buffalo, Guggenheim Mus., Whitney Mus. Am. Art, N.Y.C., Honolulu Acad. Arts, U. Art Gallery, Tucson, (mosaic) Hawaii State Capitol Bldg., State Libr. Aina Haina, Oahu, State Hosp., Kea-lakekua, Hawaii, Wailulu War Meml. Gymnasium, Maui, Krannert Art Mus., Ill., U. Nebr.; executed murals Halekulani Hotel, Honolulu, (mosaic) West Maui Recreation Ctr., (oil) Bay Club, Kapalua, Maui; retrospective Hui No Eau, Makawao, Maui, 1992. Office: PO Box 476 Lahaina HI 96767-0476

SATRE, RODRICK IVERSON, environmental consultant, business developer; b. Geneseo, N.Y., July 14, 1951; s. Roy Ingvold Jr. and Patricia Ruth (Holder) S.; m. Bonita Daley, Sept. 30, 1978. BS in Chem. Engring., Clarkson U., 1973; MBA in Internat. Bus., John F. Kennedy U., 1989. Plant engr., then operating asst. Chevron Chem. Co., Richmond, Calif., 1974-78, area supr., 1978-80; sr. analyst Chevron Chem. Co., San Francisco, 1980-85; group leader, then sr. rsch. engr. Chevron Chem. Co., Richmond, 1985-89; mgr. Internat. Tech. Corp., Martinez, Calif., 1990—; prin. SSD Consulting, Point Richmond, Calif., 1990-92; gen. mgr. Internat. Tech. Corp., Houston, 1992-93; mng. prin. engr. Harding Lawson Assocs., Novato, Calif., 1993—; prin. assoc. Kertesz Internat., Inc., San Francisco, 1990—. Patentee in field. Sci. judge Richmond Unified Sch. Dist., 1985—. Mem. Cons. Engrs. and Land Surveyors of Calif., Hazardous Waste Assn. Calif., Berkeley Ski Club (v.p. 1978-79, pres. 1981-82). Republican.

SATTER, RAYMOND NATHAN, judge; b. Denver, Oct. 19, 1948; s. Charles Herbert and Muriel Vera (Tuller); m. Suzanne Elizabeth Ehlers, May 28, 1977. BA, U. Denver, 1970; JD, Cath. U., 1973. Bar: Colo. 1973, U.S. Dist. Ct. Colo. 1973, U.S. Ct. Appeals (10th cir.) 1973, U.S. Supreme Ct. 1976, U.S. Tax Ct. 1981. Assoc. Wallace, Armatas & Hahn, Denver, 1973-75; ptnr. Tallmadge, Wallace & Hahn, Denver, 1975-77; pvt. practice Denver, 1978-87; Denver County judge, 1987—; gen. counsel Satter Dist., Denver, 1977-78; assoc. mcpl. judge City of Englewood, Colo., 1985-86; mem. Colo. Supreme Ct. Com. on Civil Rules. Pres. Young Artists Orch. Denver, 1985-87; sec. Denver Symphony Assn., 1985-86. Mem. Colo. Bar Assn. (ethics com.), Denver Bar Assn. (Jud. Excellence award 1992, 95). Office: Denver County Ct 108 City & County Bldg 1437 Bannock St Denver CO 80202-5308

SATTER, SUSAN EDEL, medical consultant; b. Mason City, Iowa, Mar. 4, 1949; d. Elmer William and Madonna Josephine (Feeney) Edel; 1 child, Chelsea Lauren. B in Gen. Studies, U. Iowa, 1981, BA in Edn., 1983; MBA, U. Phoenix, 1992. Rsch. asst. Coll. Medicine U. Iowa, Iowa City, 1970-73, rsch. asst. Coll. of Botany, 1973-75, rsch. scientist Coll. of Dentistry, 1975-78; pvt. cons. in electron microscopy, 1979-83; lab. mgr. Valleylab Pfizer, Inc., Boulder, Colo., 1984-94. Mem. steering com. for nat. conf. Exploring div. Boy Scouts Am., Boulder, 1990. Mem. AAAS, Am. Assn. Med. Instrumentation (mem. nat. standard working group 1991), N.Y. Acad. Scis. Office: Satter & Assocs 4143 Sunrise Ct Boulder CO 80304-0958

SATTIN, ALBERT, psychiatry and neuropharmacology educator; b. Cleve., Oct. 5, 1931; s. Sam and Edith (Stolarsky) S.; m. Renee Schnider, Dec. 16, 1962; children—Rebecca Lee, Michael M. B.S., Western Reserve U., 1953, M.D., 1957. Diplomate Am. Bd. Psychiatry and Neurology. Intern Washington U., St. Louis, 1957-58; resident in psychiatry Case-Western Reserve U., Cleve., 1958-62; fellow Dept. Biochemistry, U. London, 1965-66; instr., sr. instr. Case-Western Res. U. Sch. Medicine, 1965-1970, asst. prof. psychiatry and pharmacology, 1970-77; assoc. prof. psychiatry Ind. U. Sch. Medicine, Indpls., 1977-84, assoc. prof. psychiatry and neurobiology, Ind. U. Grad. Sch., 1984-91; assoc. prof. psychiatry and biobehavioral scis. UCLA, 1991—; chief Antidepressant Neuropharmacology Lab, West L.A. and Sepulved VA Med. Ctrs., 1991—; psychiat. cons. Olive View L.A. County Med. Ctr., 1991—. Contbr. articles to profl. jours. Grantee NIMH, NSF, VA; Am. Psychiat. Assn. fellow, 1969. Mem. Am. Psychiat. Assn., Soc. for Neurosci. Soc. Biol. Psychiatry, Internat. Soc. Neurochemistry. Office: 116 A/11 DVA Sepulveda Med Ctr 16111 Plummer St Sepulveda CA 91343-2036

SATUREN, BEN B., oceanic wildlife artist; b. Somerset, Pa., Dec. 10, 1948; s. I. M. and B. R. Saturen; m. Colleen A. Francis, Dec. 28, 1967. BS in Landscape Architecture, Iowa State U., 1970; postgrad., Calif. Coll. of Arts & Crafts, 1985-86. Exhibited in group shows at The Oakland (Calif.) Mus., 1987, San Bernardino County Mus., Redlands, Calif., 1987, Leigh Yawkey Woodson Art Mus., Wausau, Wis., 1989, Boston Mus. of Sci., 1989-90, Art League of Daytona Beach, Fla., 1990, Open Studios of San Francisco, 1990, Snake Lake Nature Ctr., Tacoma, 1990, Vt. Inst. of Natural Sci., Woodstock, Vt., 1990, Transco Energy Co. & Rice Media Ctr., Houston, 1990-93, World Wildlife Fund Stamp & Cachet Collection, 1991, Can. Mus. Nature, Ottawa, Ont., 1991, Commonwealth of Va. Mus. Natural History, 1991, Roger Tory Peterson Inst., Jamestown, N.Y., 1992-93, Bell Mus. Natural History, Mpls., 1993, Houston Mus. Natural Sci, 1993, 95, Oshkkosh Pub. Mus., Wis., 1993, Ctrl. Pk. Wildlife Conservation Ctr., N.Y.C., 1993-94, Petaluma Wildlife and Natural Sci. Mus. (outdoor mural), Calif., 1994 (selected project Reefkeeper's Artist of the Yr., 1994); pub. Nature Discovery Press. Named Project Reefkeeper's Artist-of-the-Year, 1994. Mem. Soc. of Animal Artists, Artists Guild of San Francisco.

SAUER, DAVID ANDREW, writer, computer consultant; b. Urbana, Ill., Feb. 25, 1948; s. Elmer Louis and Frances (Hill) S. BA, Northwestern U., 1970; MS, Simmons Coll., 1975. Reference libr. Boston U., 1976-78, bibliographer, 1978-84, sci. bibliographer, 1984-88, head Stone Sci. Libr., 1988-94. Co-author: Internet for Windows, 1994, WinComm Pro: The Visual Learning Guide, 1995, ProComm Plus V2 for Windows: The Visual Learning Guide, 1995. Mem. S.W. Corridor Project, Boston, 1977-87, Forest Hills Neighborhood Improvement Assn., Boston, 1977-90, Forest Hills/Woodbourne Neighborhood Group, 1991-94. Mem. ALA, Spl. Librs. Assn., Assn. Coll. and Rsch. Librs., Geoscience Info. Soc., N.E. Map Orgn., San Diego Computer Soc. Democrat. Home and Office: 1034 La Tierra Dr San Marcos CA 92069-4617

SAUER, HENRY JACK, elementary school educator, small business owner; b. Portland, Oreg., Oct. 23, 1946; s. Henry Jack and Pauline Catherine (Rahn) S.; B.A., Wash. State U., 1970, M.Ed., 1981; m. Nancy Lee Lauber, July 25, 1970. Tchr., coach schs. in Wash., 1970—; learning mgr. experienced based career edn. Kennewick Sch. Dist., 1979-80, project mgr. CETA employer-edn. demonstration project, 1980-81, project dir. CETA employer-edn. project, 1981-82; asst. prin. Desert Hills Middle Sch., 1982-90; ednl. cons., instr. grade 4 Sunset View Elem. Sch., 1990—; pres. Fine Wine Line, Inc., 1993—; cons. social studies. Patentee apparatus for carrying or storing bottles. Active local United Way, Boy Scouts Am. Mem. Wash. Assn. Sch. Adminstrs., Assn. Supervision and Curriculum Devel., Phi Delta Kappa. Lutheran. Club: Kiwanis. Home and Office: 2306 S Anderson Pl Kennewick WA 99337-2918

SAUER, JAMES EDWARD, JR., hospital administrator; b. Sanborn, N.D., Feb. 14, 1934; s. James Edward and Rose Marie (Grafton) S.; m. Sharon Ann Groom, Aug. 18, 1962; children—Scott Michael, Jeffrey William, Steven Douglas. B.S. in Bus. Adminstrn., U. N.D., 1956; M.H.A., U. Minn., 1964. Administrv. asst. Meth. Hosp., Madison, Wis., 1961-62; adminstrv. resident San Jose Hosp. and Health Ctr., Calif., 1963-64; asst. adminstr. Providence Hosp., Portland, Oreg., 1967-69, assoc. adminstr., 1969-73; pres., exec. dir. Calif. Hosp. Med. Ctr., Los Angeles, 1973-79; adminstr. St. Joseph Med. Ctr., Burbank, Calif., 1979—; mem. hosp. adv. com. Blue Cross So. Calif., 1976-79. Trustee, Sisters of Providence in Calif., 1979—; mem. exec. com. retirement bd. Sisters of Providence, 1983—. Contbr. articles to profl. jours. Served to capt. USAF, 1956-62. Fellow Am. Coll. Hosp. Adminstrs.; mem. Am. Hosp. Assn. (chmn. 1982-84), Oreg. Conf. Cath. Hosps. Assn. (pres. 1973-74), Hosp. Council So. Calif. (bd. dirs. 1975-81, exec. com. 1977-81, chmn. 1979-80), Calif. Hosp. Assn. (trustee 1979-84, chmn. 1983, Walker Fellow 1983), Calif. Assn. Cath. Hosps. (trustee 1981-82), Am. Arbitration Assn. (Los Angeles adv. council), Hollywood Acad. Medicine, Central Area Teaching Hosps. (bd. dirs. 1976-79). Lodge: Rotary. Office: Alexander & Alexander 55 S Lake Ave Ste 500 Pasadena CA 91101-2626

SAULNESS, FIONA, real estate executive; b. Manchester, Eng., Jan. 15, 1956; came to U.S., 1956; d. Douglas Munro Masters and Joan Elina (Gerrard) Hall; m. Robert Paul Saulness, July 11, 1981. Grad. high sch., Seattle. Legal sec. Foster, Pepper and Riviera, Seattle, 1974-78; salesperson, mgr. West Coast Homes Real Estate Co., Seattle, 1978-84; salesperson, trainer Home Realty, Inc., Seattle, 1984-88; sales assoc. Windermere Real Estate, Seattle, 1988—. Episcopalian. Office: Windermere Real Estate 10004 Aurora Ave N Ste 10 Seattle WA 98133-9349

SAULPAUGH, CHRISTOPHER FRANCIS, publishing executive; b. West Point, N.Y., Apr. 1, 1962; s. Richard R. and Susan T. (Tadahira) S. BS in Bus. Adminstrn., Calif. State U., San Bernardino, 1992. Sys. engr. Computer Connection, Victorville, Calif., 1990-93; tech. svcs. mgr. Roger Wagner Pub., El Cajon, Calif., 1993—; owner Future Tech. Sys., Apple Valley, Calif., 1992-94. Cons.: (book) Hyperstudio in an Hour, 1993; software developer. Vol. Calif. Dept. Forestry, San Bernardino, 1988-93; mortar platoon sect. leader Calif. Nat Guard, San Bernardino, 1986-93. Sgt. U.S. Army, 1982-86. Mem. IEEE, NRA (life), Am. Legion, Apple Valley Gun Club (v.p. 1986—). Office: Roger Wagner Pub Inc 1050 Pioneer Way Ste P El Cajon CA 92020-1943

SAULT, NICOLE LANDRY, anthropologist and educator; b. St. Paul, 1952; m. Peter C. Reynolds. BA in Anthropology and English, U. Calif., Santa Barbara, 1970; MA in Anthropology, UCLA, 1975, PhD in Anthropology, 1985. Vis. asst. prof. anthropology Santa Clara (Calif.) U., 1977—. Author and editor: Many Mirrors: Body Image and Social Relations, 1994; contbr. articles to profl. jours. Recipient Sisterhood is Powerful award Santa Clara U., 1994; Irvine Found. grantee, 1992; Fulbright-Hays scholar, 1989. Mem. Am. Anthropol. Assn., Amnesty Internat., Greenpeace, Phi Beta Kappa. Roman Catholic. Office: Santa Clara Univ Dept Anthropology Santa Clara CA 95053

SAUNDERS, BRIAN KEITH, consulting company executive; b. Columbus, Ohio, June 4, 1961. BSEE, Purdue U., 1983; MBA, Dartmouth U., 1988. Asst. mgr. engring. New Eng. Telephone, Boston, 1983-85, asst. product mgr., 1985-86; assoc. Booz Allen & Hamilton, N.Y.C., 1987-90; dir. strategy and planning Pacific Bell, San Ramon, Calif., 1991-92; gen. mgr. Compus Svcs. Corp., Pleasanton, Calif., 1993-94; prin. cons., designer BKS Design, San Ramon, Calif., 1994—; prin. Regis McKenna Inc., Palo Alto, Calif., 1995—; bd. dirs. Children's Media Lab., Berkeley, Calif., 1993—, Family Stress Ctr., Concord, Calif., 1995—; mem. industry coun. Mt. Diablo Coll., Pleasant Hill, Calif., 1993—; mem. exec. coun. Tuck MBEP Alumni Assn. Dartmouth Coll., Hanover, N.H., 1994—. Mem. IEEE, Assn. for Computing Machinery, Joint Ctr. for Polit. and Econ. Studies (assoc.), World Affairs Coun., Armed Forces Comms. and Electronics Assn. Office: BKS Design 152 Victory Circle San Ramon CA 94583

SAUNDERS, DEBRA J., columnist; b. Newton, Mass., Dec. 8, 1954. BA in Latin and Greek, U. Mass., Boston, 1980. Asst. dir. Arnold Zenher Assocs., 1982-83; writer/rschr., account exec. Todd Domke Assocs., Sacramento, 1983-84, Russo Watts & Rollins, Sacramento, 1985-86; asst. to Rep. Leader Calif. Legislature, Sacramento, 1987-88; columnist, editl. writer L.A. Daily News, 1988-92; columnist San Francisco Chronicle, 1992—; leader study group on polit. speechmaking Harvard U., Cambridge, Mass., 1984; tchr. editl. and column writing UCLA Ext., 1992. Office: San Francisco Chronicle 901 Mission St San Francisco CA 94103-2905

SAUNDERS, JAMES, management and training consultant; b. Chgo., Sept. 22, 1924; s. James Windam and Carrie Evelyn (Cox) S.; m. Gwendolyn Haithcox, Oct. 21, 1945 (dec. May 1971); children: Patricia Ann, Kathryn Lynn; m. Anita Joanne Laster, Sept. 16, 1972 (div. Oct. 1977); m. Bettye Jean Ricks, Apr. 18, 1981. BS in Math., Roosevelt U., 1953. Quality assurance rep. Dept. Army and Signal Corps., Chgo., 1945-63; dep. dir. quality assurance U.S. Naval Ordnance Plant, Forest Park, Ill., 1963-70; quality systems mgr. Gen. Foods Corp., Chgo., 1970-82; pres. Saunders and Assocs., Peoria, Ariz., 1982-91; councilman, vice mayor City of Peoria, 1985-91; examiner Ariz. Govs. Alliance for Quality, 1995. Bd. dirs., sec. Ariz. Retirement Ctrs., Peoria, 1984-85; chmn., bd. dirs., founder Peoria Econ. Devel. Group, 1987-91, dir. emeritus, 1991—; mem. Peoria Personnel Bd., 1984-85, Maricopa County Pvt. Industry Coun., 1984-89, chmn., 1988-89, exec. com. Westside Transp. Coalition, Peoria, 1988-89. Recipient Black Achiever of Industry award Chgo. YMCA, 1977, Image Govt. award NAACP, 1989, also various other awards. Mem. Peoria C. of C. (v.p., bd. dirs. 1985), Westside Coalition Chambers Commerce, Lions (sec., v.p. Peoria chpt. 1983-86), Kiwanis, Masons, Alpha Phi Alpha. Home: 18847 N 88th Dr Peoria AZ 85382-8528

SAUNDERS, JAMES HARWOOD, accountant; b. Carlsbad, N.Mex., Apr. 2, 1948; s. Eugene C. and Ruth (Powelson)S.; m. Kathleen Sue Matson, Jan. 26, 1974 (div. Apr. 1982); m. Bette Kim McCutcheon, Sept. 4, 1982; children: James C., Carl J., William K. AA in Adminstrn. Justice, Glendale Coll., Glendale, Ariz., 1975; BSBA, Ariz. State U., 1978. CPA, N.M., Ariz., Colo., Nev., Utah; lic. funeral dir. and embalmer; cert. fraud examiner. Embalmer Denton Funeral Home, Carlsbad, 1964-69; clk., trainee Sears & Roebuck Co., Dallas and Albuquerque, 1969-71, Phoenix, 1971-73; police sgt. spl. ops. Phoenix Police Dept., 1973-80; staff acct. various CPA firms, Carlsbad, 1980-83; owner James H. Saunders Acctg., Carlsbad, 1983-86; pvt. practice acctg. Eagar, Ariz., 1987—; auditor, mgmt. advisor to several Ariz. municipalities, 1987—; bd. dirs. Ariz. Lion Eye Bank. Vol. fireman Carlsbad Fire Dept., 1965-68; reserve dep. Bermallio County Sheriff Dept., Albuquerque, 1969-70. Mem. AICPA, Ariz. Soc. CPAs, N.Mex. Soc. CPAs, N.Mex. Assn. Funeral Dirs., Lions (sec. Carlsbad chpt. 1985-87, pres. Springerville, Ariz. chpt. 1987-91). Office: PO Box 1270 74 N Main Eagar AZ 85925

SAUNDERS, KAREN ESTELLE, secondary education educator; b. San Carlos, Ariz., June 13, 1941; d. Walter Carl and Irma Marie (Gallmeyer) Sorgatz; m. John Richard Saunders, Dec. 27, 1962 (div. Nov. 1981). BA, Ariz. State U., 1964, MA, 1968, postgrad., 1982—. Tchr., chair fine arts dept. McClintock High Sch., Tempe, Ariz., 1964-77; tchr., chair art dept. Corona del Sol High Sch., Tempe, 1977—, chair fine arts dept., 1987—; tchr., chair art dept. McClintock High Sch., Tempe, 1964-77; coord. artists-in-schs. program Tempe Union H.S., 1975-80, program adminstr. travel/study program, 1976-78, 80, Corona del Sol H.S., 1994-95; program chair Four Corners Art Educators Conf., Scottsdale, Ariz., 1982; co-chair S.W. Indian Art Collectibles Exhbn., Carefree, Ariz., 1982, also editor, designer catalogue; adv. editorial bd. Sch. Arts Mag., 1989—; artist-in-schs. coord. Corona del Sol High Sch., 1994-95. Editorial bd. Jour. Art Edn., 1982-85. Mem. State Art Guide Com., Tempe, 1975-77; mem. planning com. Sheldon Lab. Systems Facilities, 1980-83; chmn. Tempe Sculpture Competition, Fine Arts Ctr., 1983; mem. Ariz. Scholastic Art Adv. Bd., Phoenix, 1983-87; judge Mill Ave. Arts Festival, Tempe, 1989, 1991-94. Recipient Vincent Van Gogh award Colo. Alliance for Arts Edn., 1978, Ariz. Art Educator of Yr. award Ariz. Art Edn. Assn., 1979, Leadership award Four Corners Art Educators Conf., 1982, Lehrer Mel. award Ariz. State U. Sch. Art, 1986, Tempe Diablos Ednl. Excellence awards, 1991; Ariz. State U. fellow, 1967-68. Mem. NEA, Nat. Art Edn. Assn. (v.p., bd. dirs. 1980-82, chmn. leadership workshop 1979, Pacific Secondary Art Educator of Yr. award 1985, co-chair Pres.' Day 1992-95 Conv.), Assn. Secondary Curriculum Devel., Ariz. Alliance for Arts Edn. (bd. dirs. 1976-81, co-chmn. western regional conf. 1978), Tempe Secondary Edn. Assn., Ariz. Art Edn. Assn. (pres. 1976-78), Tempe Sister Cities Orgn. (exch. tchr. Regensburg, Germany 1992), Women's Image Now Club, Mortar Bd., Phi Delta Kappa, Alpha Phi. Home: 930 S Dobson Rd Unit 22 Mesa AZ 85202-2912 Office: Corona del Sol High Sch 1001 E Knox Rd Tempe AZ 85284-3204

SAUNDERS, RAYMOND JENNINGS, artist, educator; b. Pitts., Oct. 28, 1934. Student (Nat. Scholastic scholar), Pa. Acad. Fine Arts, U. Pa., Barnes Found.; B.F.A., Carnegie Inst. Tech., 1960; M.F.A., Calif. Coll. Arts and Crafts. Teaching asst. Calif. Coll. Arts and Crafts, 1960-61; resident Am. Acad. in Rome, 1964-66; art and urban affairs cons. N.Y.C. Bd. Edn. and Human Resources Adminstrn., 1967; mem. faculty Calif. Coll. Arts and Crafts, Oakland, 1988—. Vis. artist, R.I. Sch. Design, 1968, artist-in-residence, vis. artist and critic at various art schs., univs., 1968—; subject of profl. articles.; show Stephen Wirtz Gallery, 1989; one-man shows include San Francisco Mus. Modern Art, 1971, Seattle Art Mus., 1981, Pa. Acad. Fine Arts, 1990, Tampa Mus. Art, 1992, Stephen Wirtz Gallery, San Francisco, 1993, Galerie Resche, Paris, 1993, Oakland Mus., 1994, M.H. de Young Meml. Mus., San Francisco, 1995; represented in permanent collections, Mus. Modern Art, N.Y.C., Whitney Mus. Am. Art, N.Y.C., Phila. Mus. Art, Chrysler Mus., Va.; author: Black is a Color, 1968. Served with U.S. Army, 1957-59. Recipient Thomas Eakins prize, Schwabacher-Frey award San Francisco Mus. Art Ann., 1961, award Nat. Inst. Arts and Letters, 1963, Prix de Rome Am. Acad. in Rome, award City of Phila., Atwater Kent award Soc. Four Arts, 1970, Granger Meml. award Pa. Acad. Fine Arts, 1972, Art award KQED, 1975, Guggenheim award, 1976, Nat. Endowment for Arts award, 1977, 84; Cresson European traveling scholar. Address: 49 Geary St Fl 3 San Francisco CA 94108-5729

SAUNDERS, SHARON, media director; b. Provo, Utah, Apr. 17, 1946; d. Lynn Furlong and Beulah (Hatch) Olsen; m. Kevin Forrest Saunders, Aug. 9, 1986; 1 child, Kelsey. AA, BYU, 1966. Media buyer, planner Tracy-Locke, Denver, 1977-80; sr. media buyer The Gap, San Francisco, 1983; media dir. Dakis Concern, Orinda, Calif., 1985-86; pres., owner Media Mentor, San Francisco, 1984—. Sponsor advt. team softball league, 1993—. Office: Media Mentor 642 Chenery St San Francisco CA 94131

SAUSE, HELEN, redevelopment executive; b. Reedsport, Oreg., June 13, 1934; d. Howard Forrest and Blanche Irene (Cope) Perkins; m. Samuel Hunter Sause, Feb. 29, 1964; children: David, Paula, Carole. BA, U. Calif., Hayward, 1976. Loan officer, office mgr. Scott Built Homes, Eugene, Oreg., 1957-60; dep. dir. Eugene (Oreg.) Urban Renewal, 1960-62, Seaside (Calif.) Urban Renewal, 1962-64; assoc. Whisler/Patri Assoc., Planning and Archtl. Firm, San Francisco, 1964-68; asst. to dir., corp. sec. San Francisco (Calif.) Redevel. Agy., 1968-80, project dir. for Yerba Buena Ctr., 1980—. Chair econ. devel. commn. City of Alameda, Calif., 1990—; active Devel. Fund, 1990—; vestry mem., stewardship chair Christ Ch. Episcopal, 1992—; treas. Citizens Housing Corp., 1993—. Recipient award Mayors Fiscal Adv. Com., San Francisco, 1993, 94. Mem. Nat. Assn. Housing and Redevel. Ofcls. (pres. 1987-89, chair internat. com. 1989—, Lange award 1994), Lambda Alpha (exec. com. 1992). Democrat. Office: San Francisco Redevel Agy 770 Golden Gate Ave San Francisco CA 94102-3120

SAUSMAN, KAREN, zoological park administrator; b. Chgo., Nov. 26, 1945; d. William and Annabell (Lofaso) S. BS, Loyola U., 1966; student, Redlands U., 1968. Keeper Lincoln Park Zoo, Chgo., 1964-66; tchr. Palm Springs (Calif.) Unified Sch., 1968-70; ranger Nat. Park Svc., Joshua Tree, Calif., 1968-70; zoo dir. The Living Desert, Palm Desert, Calif., 1970—; natural history study tour leader internat., 1974—; part-time instr. Coll. Desert Natural History Calif. Desert, 1975-78; field reviewer conservation grants Inst. Mus. Svcs., 1987—, MAP cons., 1987—, panelist, 1992—; internat. studbook keeper for Sand Cats, 1988—, for Cuvier's Gazelle, Mhorr Gazelle, 1990—; co-chair Arabian Oryx species survival plan propogation group, 1986—; spkr. in field. Author Survival Captive Bighorn Sheep, 1982, Small Facilities- Opportunities and Obligations, 1983; wildlife illustrator books, mags, 1970—; editor Fox Paws newsletter Living Desert, 1970—, ann. reports, 1976—; natural sci. editor Desert Mag., 1979-82; compiler Conservation and Management Plan for Antelope, 1992; contbr. articles to profl. jours. Past bd. dirs., sec. Desert Protective Coun.; adv. coun. Desert Bighorn Rsch. Inst., 1981-85; bd. dirs. Palm Springs Desert Resorts Convention and Visitors Bur., 1988-94; bd. dirs., treas. Coachella Valley Mountain Trust, 1989-92. Named Woman Making a Difference Soroptomist Internat., 1989, 93. Fellow Am. Assn. Zool. Parks and Aquariums (bd. dirs., accredation field reviewer, desert antelope taxon adv. group, caprid taxon adv. group, felid taxon adv. group, small population mgmt. adv. group, wildlife conservation and mgmt. com., chmn. ethics com. 1987, mem. com., internat. rels. com., ethics task force, pres'. award 1972-77, outstanding svc. award 1983, 88, editor newsletter, Zool. Parks and Aquarium Fundamentals 1982); mem. Internat. Species Inventory System (mgmt. com., policy adv. group 1980-88), Calif. Assn. Mus., Calif. Assn. Zoos and Aquariums, Internat. Union Dirs. Zool. Gardens, Western Interpretive Assn. (so. Calif. chpt.), Am. Assn. Mus., Arboreta and Botanical Gardens So. Calif. (coun. dirs.), Soc. Conservation Biology, Nat. Audubon. Soc., Jersey Wildlife Preservation Trust Internat., Nature Conservancy, East African Wildlife Soc., African Wildlife Found., Kennel Club Palm Springs (past bd. dirs., treas. 1978-80), Scottish Deerhound Club Am. (editor SCottish Deerhounds in N.A., 1983, life mem. U.K. chpt.). Office: The Living Desert 47 900 Portola Ave Palm Desert CA 92260

SAUSSER, ROBERT GARY, retired army officer; b. St. Benedict, Pa., Apr. 6, 1941; s. Robert Jacob and Maxine Larue (Earley) S.; married Nov. 2, 1963; 1 child, Geoffrey Robert. BS, U.S. Mil. Acad., West Point, N.Y., 1963; MS, Ind. U., 1971. Commd. 2d lt. U.S. Army, 1963, advanced through grades to brig. gen., 1989; ops. officer 25th Div. Arty., Schofield Barracks, Hawaii, 1977-78; comdr. 1st Bn., 8th F.A., Schofield Barracks, 1978-80; pers. officer 7th Inf. Div., Ft. Ord, Calif., 1980-83; student U.S. Army War Coll., Carlisle Barracks, Pa., 1983-84; comdr. 25th Div. Arty., Schofield Barracks, 1984-86; exec. asst. to Comdr. in Chief, Combined Forces Command, Seoul, Republic of Korea, 1986-88; chief of staff U.S. Army I Corps, Ft. Lewis, Wash., 1988-89; chief U.S. Mil. Assistance Group, Manila, 1989-92; dep. comdr. U.S. Army Pacific, Ft. Shafter, Hawaii, 1992; asst. divsn. comdr. 6th Inf. Divsn. U.S. Army Pacific, Ft. Richardson, Alaska, 1992-93; ret., 1993; bd. dirs. Army, Air Force Exch. Svc., Dallas, 1992-93. Decorated Bronze Star, Legion of Merit, D.S.M., Def. Superior Svc. medal. Mem. Assn. U.S. Army, U.S. Army F.A. Assn., West Point Alumni Assn. Republican.

SAUTE, ROBERT EMILE, drug and cosmetic consultant; b. West Warwick, R.I., Aug. 18, 1929; s. Camille T. and Lea E. (Goffinet) S.; m. Arda T. Darnell, May 18, 1957; children: Richard R., Steven N., Allen K. BS, R.I. Coll. Pharmacy, 1950; MS, Purdue U., 1952, PhD, 1953. Registered pharmacist. Tech. asst. to pres. Lafayette (Ind.) Pharmacal, 1955-56; sr. rsch. and devel. chemist H.K. Wampole Denver Chem. Co., Phila., 1956-57; supt. Murray Hill (N.J.) plant Strong Cobb Arner Inc., 1957-60; adminstrv. dir. rsch. and devel. Avon Products Inc., Suffern, N.Y., 1960-68; dir. rsch. and devel. toiletries div. Gillette Co., Boston, 1968-71; group v.p. Dart Industries, L.A., 1972-75; pres. Saute Cons., Inc., L.A., 1975—; bd. dirs. Joico Labs., Inc., Cosmetics Enterprises, Ltd. Contbr. to books; patentee in field. With U.S. Army, 1953-55. Fellow Soc. Cosmetic Chemists (bd. dirs. 1987-89, chmn. Calif. chpt. 1986); mem. AAAS, N.Y. Acad. Scis., Soc. Investigative Dermatology, Am. Assn. Pharm. Scientists, Sigma Xi, Rho Chi.

SAUVAGE, LESTER ROSAIRE, health facility administrator, cardiovascular surgeon; b. Wapato, Wash., Nov. 15, 1926; s. Lester Richard Sauvage and Laura Marie Brouillard; m. Mary Ann Marti, June 9, 1956; children: Lester Jr., John, Paul, Helen, Joe, Laura, William, Mary Ann. Student, Gonzaga U., 1942-43, DSc (hon.), 1982; MD, St. Louis U., 1948; Honoris Causa (hon.), Seattle U., 1976. Diplomate Nat. Bd. Med. Examiners, Am. Bd. Surgery, Am. Bd. Thoracic Surgery. Intern King County Hosp., Seattle, 1948-49, surg. resident, 1949-50, sr. resident, 1955-56; sr. resident Children's Med. Ctr., Boston, 1956-58; rsch. assoc. dept. surgery U. Wash., Seattle, 1950-52; sr. resident in thoracic surgery Boston City Hosp., 1958; pvt. practice Pediatric and Cardiovascular Surgeons, Inc., Seattle, 1959-91; founder, med. dir. Hope Heart Inst. (formerly Reconstructive Cardiovascular Rsch. Ctr.), Seattle, 1959—; clin. prof. surgery sch. medicine U. Wash.; chmn. dept. surgery, dir. surg. edn. Providence Med. Ctr., Seattle; dir. cardiac surgery Children's Orthopedic Hosp. and Med. Ctr.; presenter in field, 1974—. Author: Prosthetic Replacement of the Aortic Valve, 1972; mem. editorial bd. Annals Vascular Surgery; contbr. over 200 rsch. papers to profl. jours. Capt. M.C., U.S. Army, 1952-54. Recipient Vocat. Svc. award Seattle Rotary Club, 1977, Humanitarian award Human Life Found., 1977, Brotherhood award Nat. Conf. Christians and Jews, 1979, Clemson award Soc. Biomaterials, 1982, Jefferson award Am. Inst. Pub. Svc., Seattle Post-Intelligencer, 1983, Gov.'s Disting. Vol. award, 1983, Spotlight award Am. Soc. Women Accts., 1985, Wash. State Medal of Merit, 1987, Seattle 1st Citizen award, 1992. Mem. AMA, Am. Acad. Pediatrics (surg. sect.), Am. Assn. Thoracic Surgery, Am. Coll. Cardiology, Am. Coll. Chest Physicians, Am. Coll. Surgeons, Am. Heart Assn., Am. Pediatric Surg. Assn., Neurovascular Soc. N.Am. (founding mem.), Wash. State Heart Assn., Wash. State Med. Assn., North Pacific Pediatric Soc., North Pacific Surg. Soc., N.W. Soc. Clin. Rsch., Pacific Assn. Pediatric Surgeons, Pacific Coast Surg. Assn., New Eng. Soc. Vascular Surgery (hon.), Seattle Surg. Soc., King County Med. Soc., Internat. Cardiovascular Soc., Soc. Artificial Internal Organs, Soc. Clin. Vascular Surgery (hon.), Soc. Vascular Surgery, Acad. Surg. Rsch., Alpha Omega Alpha, Alpha Sigma Nu. Roman Catholic.

SAVAGE, JAMES CRAMPTON, geophysicist; b. Dallas, Sept. 18, 1926; s. John Francis and Georgia (Williford) S.; m. Jane Farish, Dec. 28, 1992. BS, U. Ariz., 1950; PhD, Calif. Inst. Tech., 1957. Asst. prof. U. B.C., Vancouver, Can., 1958-64; assoc. prof. U. Minn., Mpls., 1964-65, U. Toronto, Ont., Can., 1965-69; geophysicist U.S. Geol. Survey, Menlo Park, Calif., 1969—. With U.S. Army, 1944-46. Fellow Am. Geophys. Union (Whitten medal 1989, pres. tectonophysics sect. 1980-82); mem. AAAS, Seismology Soc. Am. (pres. 1978-79). Democrat. Home: 451 Menlo Oaks Dr Menlo Park CA 94025-2345 Office: US Geol Survey 345 Middlefield Rd Menlo Park CA 94025-3561

SAVAGE, KARLEEN SUE, small business owner; b. San Diego, Oct. 16, 1963; d. Joseph Conrad Olayan and Terri Eileen Anderson; m. Donald Edward Savage, Nov. 11, 1988; children: Shendileen, Loraleen, Donald Jr., Anderson, Shaileen, Morgan. Cert. legal sec., Cascade Bus. Coll., 1985. Loan svc. rep. Mellon Fin., Bellingham, Wash., 1985-86; office mgr. to Dr. Austin McGreal D.D.S. Upland, Calif., 1987-88; mgr. Expectation Party Sales, Riverside, Calif., 1991-92; owner Prime Affaire, Riverside, 1992—; lectr. in field. tchr. relief soc. Latter Day Saints, Bloomington, Calif., 1991, primary counselor, 1993, nursery leader, Riverside, 1994; pres., v.p., mem. PTA, Bloomington. Pres.'s award PTA, Bloomington, 1989, 90. Republican. Office: Prime Affaire 231 E Alessandro Blvd # A-338 Riverside CA 92508-6039

SAVAGE, SANDRA HOPE SKEEN, mathematics educator, curriculum writer; b. Charleston, W.Va., Apr. 4, 1938; d. Raymond and Freda (Burgess) Skeen; m. Steven William Savage, Aug. 17, 1963; 1 child, Samantha. BS in Secondary Edn. Math and English, Bob Jones U., 1960; MS in Math., Ill. Inst. Tech., 1966; EdD in Math. Edn., Columbia U., 1976. Cert. tchr., Calif., N.Y., Ill., Fla., W.Va., Minn. Math. tchr. S. Charleston Jr. High Sch., 1960-61, Citrus Grove Jr. High Sch., Miami, Fla., 1961-62, Skiles Jr. High Sch., Evanston, Ill., 1962-65, Evanston Twp. High Sch., 1965-67, White Plains (N.Y.) High Sch., 1967-68; chmn. math. dept. The Scarborough Sch., Scarborough-on-Hudson, N.Y., 1968-71; math. tchr. Alexander Ramsey High Sch., Roseville, Minn., 1971-72, Minnehaha Acad., Mpls., 1971-72; lectr. math. Pace U., Westchester County, N.Y., 1972-73; team leader, math. tchr. Fox Lane Mid. Sch., Bedford, N.Y., 1973-74; prof. math. Orange Coast Coll., Costa Mesa, Calif., 1977—; lectr. math. edn. North Park Coll., Chgo., 1965; judge Odyssey of the Mind Competition, 1995; math. media cons. Annenberg Found., Washington, 1991; cons Business Link, Costa Mesa, 1990—. Speaker Expanding Your Horizons Women's Conf., Irvine, Calif., 1984-87; guild mem. Orange County Performing Arts Ctr., Costa Mesa, 1985-87; asst. troop leader Girl Scouts Am., Laguna Niguel, Calif., 1985-87; active Geneva Presbyn. Ch., Laguna Hills, Calif., 1983—. Recipient Cert. Merit, Nat. Merit Scholarship Corp., 1956, Tchr. of Yr. award Orange County Tchrs., 1994, Nat. Inst. for Staff and Orgn. Devel. awrd U. Tex., 1993, U.S.A. Today Teaching Excellence award, 1993; Dept. Edn. Nat. Workplace Literacy Program grantee, 1995. Fellow NSF (grantee 1983); mem. AAUW, Am. Math. Assn. Two Yr. Colls., Math. Assn. Am., Assn. for Women in Sci., Calif. Math. Coun., Orange County Math. Assn. (sec. 1982-83), Phi Delta Kappa (pres. Trabuco chpt. 1986-87, 95—). Democrat. Home: 12 Novilla Laguna Beach CA 92677-8915 Office: Orange Coast Coll PO Box 5005 2701 Fairview Rd Costa Mesa CA 92626-5561

SAVAGE, TERRY RICHARD, information systems executive; b. St. Louis, Oct. 21, 1930; s. Terry Barco and Ada Vanetta (Cochran) S.; m. Gretchen Susan Wood, Sept. 26, 1964; children: Terry Curtis, Christopher William, Richard Theodore. AB, Washington U., St. Louis, 1951, MA, 1952; PhD, U. Pa., 1954. Mgr. system software IBM Rsch., Yorktown Heights, N.Y., 1956-63; dir. data processing Documentation Inc., Bethesda, Md., 1963-64; mgr. info. systems Control Data Corp., Rockville, Md., 1964-67; dir. rsch. Share Rsch. Corp., Santa Barbara, Calif., 1967-68; computer-aided acquisition and logistic support program mgr. TRW, Redondo Beach, Calif., 1968-92; ret., ind. cons. pvt. practice, 1992—; expert witness U.S. Congress, 1981, 84, 88, 89. Contbr. articles to profl. jours. Bd. dirs. ABC-Clio Press, Santa Barbara, 1970-75, Help the Homeless Help Themselves, Rancho Palos Verdes, Calif., 1988—, ChorusLiners, Rancho Palos Verdes, 1983—. Mem. Cosmos Club. Home and Office: 30000 Cachan Pl Palos Verdes Peninsula CA 90275-5412

SAVAGE, THOMAS WARREN, engineering manager; b. Morgantown, W.Va., Feb. 6, 1959; s. Thomas Louis Savage and Sandra Mabel (Ferguson) Crawford; m. Cydney Ellen Fry, May 8, 1981; children: Jessica Louise, Kristin Anne, Thomas Dylan. BS in Computer Engring., Santa Clara U., 1993. Electronic technician ITT North, Galion, Ohio, 1977-79; electronic test engr. Fairchild Test Systems, San Jose, Calif., 1979-82; design engr. Tandem Computers, Cupertino, Calif., 1982-94; engring. mgr. Tandem Computers, Cupertino, 1994—. Patentee in field. Home: 4998 Harwood Rd San Jose CA 95124-5208 Office: Tandem Computers 10555 Ridgeview Ct Cupertino CA 95014-0710

SAVARA, ARUN MADAN, engineering executive, management educator; b. Bombay, India, Dec. 4, 1947; s. Madan and Sheela S.; m. Mira Savara, May 3, 1976; children: Siddarth, Aditya, Varun. B in Techol., Indian Inst. Tech., Bombay, India, 1971; MS, Cornell U., 1973; PhD, Purdue U., 1989. Exec. Tata Engring., India, 1976-82; CEO Tata Engring. Svcs., Singapore, 1982-85; teaching asst. Purdue U., W. Lafayette, Ind., 1985-88; dir. devel. Verifone, Miliani, Hawaii, 1989-91, MIS dir., 1991-93, dir. ops. audit, 1993—. Co-editor: International Strategic Management, 1989. Office: Verifone 100 Kahelu Ave Mililani HI 96789-3914

SAVEN, ALAN, oncologist, hematologist; b. Oct. 1, 1958; married; 2 children. MD, U. Cape Town (South Africa), 1977-82. Diplomate in internal medicine, med. oncology and hematology Am. Bd. Internal Medicine; lic. physician, Calif., Pa., Gt. Britain. Rotating intern U. Cape Town, 1983; resident Albert Einstein Med. Ctr., Phila., 1984-87; fellow in hematology and oncology Scripps Clinic and Rsch. Found., La Jolla, Calif., 1990-94; staff physician, chief neurol. oncology svc. Scripps Clinic and Rsch. Found., La Jolla, 1990—, chief clin. drug devel. program, 1992—, assoc. dir. clin. rsch. Ida M. & Cecil H. Green Cancer Ctr., 1993—; chief leukemia and lymphoma svc. Scripps Clinic and Rsch. Found., 1992—; adj. asst. mem. Scripps Rsch. Inst., 1992—; lectr. in field. Contbr. numerous chpts. to books, articles to profl. jours. Guy Elliot rsch. fellow U. Cape Town, 1984. Fellow ACP; mem. Am. Soc. Clin. Oncology, Am. Soc. Hematology, Cancer and Leukemia Group B. Office: Scripps Clin and Rsch Found Div Hematology and Oncology 10666 N Torrey Pines Rd La Jolla CA 92037-1027

SAVITRIPRIYA, SWAMI, religious leader, author; b. Apr. 1, 1930; divorced; three children. Ordained Hindu nun, Holy Order of Sannyas, 1975. Psychotherapist, 1970-75; founder, spiritual dir. Shiva-Shakti Kashmir Shaivite Hindu Ch., Ashram, Marin County, Calif., 1975-77, Shiva-Shakti Ashram, Oakland, Calif., 1978, Convent of the Divine Mother, Kona, Hawaii, 1979-80, Holy Mountain Monastery and Retreat Ctr., Groveland, Calif., 1984-92, Holy Mountain U., Groveland, Calif., 1985-92; founder, spiritual dir. Inst. for New Life, Groveland, Calif., 1990-92, Santa Cruz, Calif., 1992-95; founder, spiritual dir. Shiva-Shakti Ashram, Lake Chapala, Jalisco, Mex., 1995—. Author (books) Kundalini-Shakti: From Awakening to Enlightenment, 1980, The Psychology of Mystical Awakening: The Yoga Sutras, 1991, The Cloud of the Universe, 1986, The Worlds of the Chakras, 1987, Arising Woman, 1988, Arising Man, 1988, Tantras of Personal and Spiritual Unfoldment, 1989, New World Hinduism, 1990, others; translator: Bhagavad Gita, 1974, Narada Bhakti Sutras, 1976, Upanishads, 1981, Shiva Sutras, 1984, Pratyabhijnahridayam, 1987, Vijnana Bhairava, 1989, others. Home and Office: Shiva-Shakti Ashram 9297 Siempre Viva Rd Ste 71-270 San Diego CA 92173

SAVONA, MICHAEL RICHARD, physician; b. N.Y.C., Oct. 21, 1947; s. Salvatore Joseph and Diana Grace (Menditto) S.; m. Dorothy O'Neill, Oct. 18, 1975. BS summa cum laude, Siena Coll., 1969; MD, SUNY, Buffalo, 1973. Diplomate Am. Bd. Internal Medicine. Intern in internal medicine Presbyn. Hosp. Columbia U., N.Y.C., 1973-74, resident in internal medicine, 1974-76; vis. fellow internal medicine Delafield Hosp./Columbia U. Coll. Physicians and Surgeons, N.Y.C., 1974-76; practice medicine specializing in internal medicine Maui Med. Group, Wailuku, Hawaii, 1976-87, gen. practice medicine, 1987—; dir. ICU, Maui Meml. Hosp., also dir. respiratory therapy, CCU., chmn. dept. medicine, 1980—; clin. faculty John A. Burns Sch. Medicine, U. Hawaii, asst. prof. medicine, 1985—, asst. rsch. prof., 1989—. Bd. dirs. Maui Heart Assn.; dir. profl. edn. Maui chpt. Am. Cancer Soc.; mem. Maui County Hosp. Adv. Commn.; mem. coun. Community Cancer Program of Hawaii. Recipient James A. Gibson Wayne J. Atwell award, 1970, physiology award, 1970, Ernest Whitebsky award, 1971, Roche Lab. award, 1972, Pfiser Lab. award, 1973, Phillip Sang award, 1973, Hans Lowenstein M.D. Meml. award, 1973. Mem. AMA, Am. Thoracic Soc., Hawaii Thoracic Soc., Maui County Med. Assn. (past pres.), Hawaii Med. Assn., Hawaii Oncology Group, ACP, SW Oncology Coop. Group, Alpha Omega Alpha, Delta Epsilon Sigma. Office: 1830 Wells St Wailuku HI 96793-2365

SAVRUN, ENDER, engineering executive, researcher, engineer; b. Adana, Turkey, July 29, 1953; came to U.S., 1978; s. Yusuf and Nemide Savrun; m. Canan Erdamar, Oct. 23, 1979; 1 child, Altay. BS, Istanbul (Turkey) Tech. U., 1976, MS, 1978; PhD, U. Wash., 1986. Rsch. engr. Charlton Industries, Redmond, Wash., 1984-85; rsch. scientist Flow Industries, Kent, Wash., 1985-87, Photon Scis., Bothell, Wash., 1987-88; mgr. rsch. Keramont Rsch. Corp., Tucson, 1988-89; v.p. R & D Keramont Corp., Tucson, 1989-92; founder, pres. Sienna Rsch., Inc., Tucson, 1992—. Contbr. articles to profl. jours.; patentee in field. Turkish Govt. scholar, 1979. Mem. ASME, Am. Soc. for Metals, Am. Ceramic Soc. Office: Sienna Rsch Inc 9004 Inverness Dr NE Seattle WA 98115-3980

SAWYER, GERALD, interior designer; b. L.A., Nov. 7, 1938; s. W. L. and Hazel Elizabeth (Duncan) S.; m. Mary L. Long, Feb. 18, 1966. BA, Northeastern State Coll., 1960; MA, Calif. State U., Fullerton, 1972. Tchr. Tulsa (Okla.) Unified Sch. Dist., 1960-64, Garden Grove (Calif.) Unified Sch. Dist., 1964-81; freelance artist Sunriver, Oreg., 1981-84; designer Village Interiors, Sunriver, 1985-87; designer, ptnr. Sawyer & Sawyer Interior Design, Sunriver, 1987—. Bd. dirs. Sunriver (Oreg.) Music Festival, 1983-87, Sunriver (Oreg.) Art Assn., 1984-85, Ctrl. Oreg. Arts Assn., Bend, Oreg., 1985-86, Regional Arts Coun. Ctrl. Oreg., 1987-88. Named Most Outstanding Speech Tchr., State of Okla., 1961. Mem. Am. Soc. Interior Designers (allied mem.). Office: Sawyer & Sawyer Interior Design PO Box 3282 15 Camas Ln Sunriver OR 97707

SAWYER, GRANT, lawyer; b. Twin Falls, Idaho, Dec. 14, 1918; s. Harry William and Bula Bell (Cameron) S.; m. Bette Norene Hoge, Aug. 1, 1946; 1 child, Gail. BA, Linfield Coll., 1939; student, U.Nev., Reno, 1940-44; JD, Georgetown U., 1948. Bar: Nev. 1948, D.C. 1948, U.S. Dist. Ct. Nev. 1967, U.S. Ct. Appeals (9th cir.) 1974, U.S. Supreme Ct. 1959. Pvt. practice Elko, Nev., 1948-50; dist. atty. Elko County, Nev., 1950-58; gov. State of Nev., 1959-67; sr. ptnr. Lionel Sawyer & Collins, Las Vegas, 1967—. Author books and articles on gaming. Mem. bd. regents U. Nev., 1957-58; Dem. nat. committeeman for Nev., 1968-88; chmn. Nev. Commn. on Nuclear Projects, 1985-95; mem. adv. bd. Aid for Aids of Nev., 1987—; trustee Bluecoats, Inc., 1987—; mem. exec. com. U. Nev. Las Vegas Found., 1988—; mem. nat. adv. coun. ACLU, 1988—; bd. dirs. Nat. Jud. Coll., 1991-94. Pvt. to 1st lt. U.S. Army, 1942-46, PTO. Mem. ABA, Nev. Bar Assn., D.C. Bar Assn., Am. Judicature Soc., Phi Delta Phi. Office: Lionel Sawyer & Collins 300 S 4th St Stop 1700 Las Vegas NV 89101-6014

SAWYER, THOMAS EDGAR, management consultant; b. Homer, La., July 7, 1932; s. Sidney Edgar and Ruth (Bickham) S.; BS, UCLA, 1959; MA, Occidental Coll., 1969; PhD, Walden U., 1990; m. Joyce Mezzanatto, Aug. 22, 1954; children—Jeffrey T., Scott A., Robert J., Julie Anne. Project engr. Garrett Corp., L.A., 1954-60; mgr. devel. ops. TRW Systems, Redondo Beach, Calif., 1960-66; spl. asst. to gov. State of Calif., Sacramento, 1967-69; prin., gen. mgr. Planning Rsch. Corp., McLean, Va., 1969-72; dep. dir. OEO, Washington, 1972-74; assoc. prof. bus. mgmt. Brigham Young U., 1974-78; pres. Mesa Corp., Provo, 1978-82, chmn. bd., 1978-82; pres. and dir. Sage Inst. Internat., Inc., Provo, Utah, 1982-88; chmn. bd., CEO Pvt. Telecom Networks, Inc. (name changed to Nat. Applied Computer Techs., Inc.), Orem, Utah, 1988—; chief tech. officer GST Telecommunications (formerly Greenstar Telecomm., Inc.), San Francisco, 1993—; also bd. dirs., Vancouver, Wash., 1995—; dir. Intechna Corp., HighTech Corp., Indian Affiliates, Inc., Greenstar USA, Inc., San Francisco, 1994—. Chmn. Nat. Adv. Council Indian Affairs; chmn. Utah State Bd. Indian Affairs; mem. Utah Dist. Export Coun.; mem. Utah dist. SBA Council; chmn. So. Paiute Restoration Com.; mem. adv. coun. Nat. Bus. Assn.; mem. Utah Job Tng. Coordinating Coun. Served with USMC, 1950-53. Mem. Am. Mgmt. Assn., Am. Soc. Public Adminstrn., Utah Coun. Small Bus. (dir.), Utah State Hist. Soc. (bd. dirs. 1993—). Republican. Mormon. Club: Masons. Author: Assimilation Versus Self-Indentity: A Modern Native American Perspective, 1976, Computer Assisted Instruction: An Inevitable Breakthrough, Current Challenges of Welfare: A Review of Public Assistance As Distributive Justice, 1989, Impact of Failure By Senior Executives to Receive Accurate Critical Feedback on Pervasive Change, 1990, The Promise of Funding a New Educational Initiative Using the Micrcomputer, 1988, New Software Models for training and Education delivery, 1989, New Organizations: How They Deviate from Classical Models, 1989, Increasing Productivity in Organizations: The Paradox, 1989, An Introduction and Assessment of Strategic Decision Making Paradigms in Complex Organizations, 1989, The Influence of Critical Feedback and Organizational Climate on Managerial Decision Making, 1990, Future of Technology in Education, 1989. Home: 548 W 630 S Orem UT 84058-6154 Office: Nat Applied Computer Techs Inc 744 S 400 E Orem UT 84058-6322

SAWYER, THOMAS WILLIAM, air force officer; b. Turlock, Calif., Nov. 19, 1933; s. Everett Edward and Marie Georgine (Gunderson) S.; m. Faith Barry Martin, Feb. 16, 1957; children: William Everet, John Martin, Susan Quincy. BS in Mil. Sci., U. Nebr., 1965; MS in Internat. Rels., George Washington U., 1974. Enlisted U.S. Air Force, 1952, commd. and advanced through grades to maj. gen., 1983; comdr. 57th Fighter Squadron, Keflavik, Iceland, 1971-73; chief internat. relations div. Hdqrs. U.S. Air Force, Washington, 1974-77; vice comdr. 20th Air Div., Fort Lee, Va., 1977-78; mil. asst. to Sec. Air Force, 1978-80; comdr. 26th Air Div., Luke AFB, Ariz., 1980-82; dep. ops. NORAD and Space Command, Colorado Springs, Colo., 1982-86; retired USAF, 1986; founder, pres. Aerospace Network Inc., 1986. Bd. dirs. Pikes Peak chpt. ARC, Colo./Wyo. chpt. Am. Def. Preparedness Assn. Decorated Disting. Service medal, Def. Disting. Service medal, Legion of Merit with 2 oak leaf clusters, Silver Star (2). Mem. Phoenix C. of C. (bd. dirs. 1980-82), Colorado Springs C. of C. Home: 10 W Cheyenne Mountain Blvd Colorado Springs CO 80906-4335 Office: Aerospace Network Inc 10 W Cheyenne Mountain Blvd Colorado Springs CO 80906-4335

SAX, HERBERT, financial planner; b. N.Y.C., Nov. 5, 1929; s. Murray and Rose (Rifkin) S.; m. Carolyn Tambor, Jan. 20, 1952; children: Jeffrey F., Edward J. BA in Psychology, Bklyn. Coll., 1950; postgrad., Bernard Baruch Sch. Bus. Adminstrn., 1953-59, Coll. for Fin. Planning, 1986-88. CPA; cert. fin. planner; registered investment adviser. Asst. office mgr. Arrow Metal Products, N.Y., 1953-54; acct. Samuel Arlow & Co., N.Y., 1954-56, Morris R. Feinsod & Co., N.Y., 1956-60; contr., treas., v.p. fin. Ehrenreich Photo-Optical Industries and Nikon Inc., Garden City, N.Y., 1960-73, pres., chief exec. officer, 1973-84; exec. dir. Coalition to Preserve Integrity Am. Trademarks, Washington, 1984-85; pres. Herbert Sax & Assocs., Woodland Hills, Calif., 1986—; bd. dir. Internat. Photographic Coun., N.Y. Cpl. U.S. Army, 1951-53. Mem. AICPA, N.Y. State Soc. CPAs, Internat. Bd. Standards and Practices for Cert. Fin. Planners.

SAXENA, AMOL, podiatrist, consultant; b. Palo Alto, Calif., June 5, 1962; s. Arjun Nath and Veera Saxena; m. Karen Ann Palermo, Aug. 11, 1985; children: Vijay, Tara Ann. Student, U. Calif., Davis, 1980-82; BA, Washington U., St. Louis, 1984; D in Podiatric Medicine, William Scholl Coll. Podiatric Medicine, 1988. Diplomate Am. Bd. Podiatric Surgery; lic. podiatrist, Calif., Ill. Resident in podiatric surgery VA Westside Br., Chgo., 1988-89; cons. Puma U.S.A., Inc., Framingham, Mass., 1986—; pvt. practice Mountain View, Calif., 1989-93; with dept. sports medicine Palo Alto Med. Found., 1993—; dir. Puma Sports Medicine, Framingham; mem. podiatry team St. Frances/Gunn Los Altos (Calif.) High Sch., Palo Alto, 1989—, Stanford (Calif.) U., 1989—; mem. med. staff El Camino Hosp., 1989—, team podiatrist Stanford U., 1989—. Guest editor The Lower Extremity; contbr. articles to profl. jours. Vol. coach Gunn High Sch. Track and Cross County, Palo Alto, 1989—; podiatrist U.S. Olympic Track and Field Trials, New Orleans, 1992, 1993. Fellow Am. Acad. Podiatric Sports Medicine, Am. Coll. Foot and Ankle Surgeons; mem. Am. Podiatric Med. Assn., Calif. Podiatric Med. Assn., Am. Med. Soccer Assn., Aggie Running Club. Republican. Office: 1197 E Arques Ave Sunnyvale CA 94086-3904 also: 913 Emerson St Palo Alto CA 94301-2415

SAXENA, NARENDRA K., marine research educator; b. Agra, India, Oct. 15, 1936; came to U.S., 1969; s. Brijbasi Lal and Sarbati Saxena; m. Cecilia H. Hsi, Mar. 21, 1970; Sarah Vasanti, Lorelle Sarita. Diploma Geodetic Engring., Tech. U., Hanover, Fed. Republic Germany, 1966; D in Tech Scis., Tech. U., Graz, Austria, 1972. Research assoc. geodetic sci. Ohio State U., Columbus, 1969-74; asst. prof. U. Ill., Urbana, 1974-78; asst. prof. U. Hawaii, Honolulu, 1978-81, assoc. prof., 1981-86, prof., 1986—, dept. chmn., 1994—; adj. research prof. Naval Postgrad. Sch., Monterey, Calif., 1984—; co-chmn. Pacific Congresses on Marine Tech., Honolulu, 1984, 86, 88; pres. Pacon Internat. Inc., 1987—. Editor Jour. Marine Geodesy, 1976—. Mem. Neighborhood Bd., Honolulu, 1984. Fellow Marine Tech. Soc. (various offices 1974—); mem. ASCE, Am. Geophys. Union, The Tsunami Soc. (sec. 1985—). Office: U Hawaii Dept Civil Engring Honolulu HI 96822

SAXON, ROBERTA P., chemical physicist; b. Chgo., July 19, 1946; s. Alfred and Blanche (Fine) Pollack. BA, Cornell U., 1967; PhD, U. Chgo., 1971. Research assoc. Argonne (Ill.) Nat. Lab., 1972-73, U. Wash., Seattle, 1973-74; chem. physicist SRI Internat., Menlo Park, Calif., 1974-79, sr. chem. physicist, 1979-91, dep. dir. phys. sci. divsn., 1991—. Editor: Electronic and atomic Physics, 1986; contbr. articles to profl. jours. Collaborative Research grantee NATO, 1984. Fellow Am. Phys. Soc.; mem. Am. Chem. Soc. Office: SRI Internat 333 Ravenswood Ave Menlo Park CA 94025-3453

SAXTON, LLOYD, psychologist and author; b. Loveland, Colo., Sept. 28, 1929; s. Oliver George and Alice Augusta (Andersen) S.; m. Nancy Alison Roberts, Dec. 17, 1955; children: Perry Brent, Jay Ronald, Barbara Jean. AB in English, U. Calif., Berkeley, 1950, BS in Psychology, 1954; MS in Psychology, San Francisco State U., 1955; PhD in Psychology, U. of the Pacific, Stockton, Calif., 1957. Lic. psychologist, Calif., 1958. Intern in clin. psychology Chilldren's Hosp., San Francisco, 1955-56; teaching fellow U. Pacific, San Francisco, 1955-57, instr. psychology, 1957-58, asst. prof. psychology, 1958-60; assoc. prof. psychology Am. Acad. of Asian Studies, San Francisco, 1960-62, prof. psychology, 1962-65; chmn. dept. psychology Coll. of San Mateo, Calif., 1965-75, prof. psychology, 1975-92; pvt. practice San Francisco/Larkspur, 1958—. Author: Individual, Marriage and the Family, 1968, Individual, 9th edit., 1995; author/editor: A Marriage Reader, 1970, The American Scene, 1970. Mem. APA, AAAS, AAUP, Am. Assn. Marriage and Family Therapists, Western Psychol. Assn., Am. Mensa. Democrat. Home and Office: 57 Hatzic Ct Larkspur CA 94939-1971

SAXTON, MARY JANE, management educator; b. Syracuse, N.Y., Mar. 3, 1953; d. John Cook and Florence (Cooper) S.; m. Paul Hood. BA, SUNY, Cortland, 1975; MBA, U. Pitts., 1979, PhD, 1987. Counselor Methadone Mgmt. Svcs., Inc., N.Y.C., 1975-76; resident mgr. Crossroads Svcs., Inc., Jackson, Miss., 1976; outreach worker Jackson Mental Health Ctr., 1977-78; cons. Organizational Design Cons., Inc., Pitts., 1982-83, mktg. dir., 1984-86; asst. prof. mgmt. U. Houston, 1988-93; lectr. mgmt. U. Colo., Denver, 1994—, U. Denver, 1994—; part-time lectr. Sch. Indsl. Adminstrn., Carnegie Mellon U., Pitts., 1986, U. Pitts., 1983-87; cons. Wessex, Ctr. for Creative Comm., Children's Hosp., Pullman Swindell, Westinghouse Elec. Corp. Co-editor: Gaining Control of the Corporate Culture, 1985; co-author: The Kilmann-Saxton Culture-Gap Survery, 1983; contbr. articles to profl. jours. Mem. Greater Houston Women's Found., 1991-93. U.S.-Soviet Joint Ventures grantee U. Houston, 1990. Mem. Acad. of Mgmt., Am. Soc. Tng. and Devel., Colo.-Wyo. Assn. Psychologists, Inst. Ops. Rsch. and Mgmt. Svcs.

SAYANO, REIZO RAY, electrochemical engineer; b. Los Angeles, Dec. 15, 1937; s. George Keiichiro and Miyo (Nakao) S.; m. Tamiko Shintani, May 28, 1967; children—Kiyomi Coleen, Naomi Jennifer. A.A., Los Angeles Community Coll., 1958; B.S., UCLA, 1960, M.S., 1962, Ph.D., 1967. Research asst. electrochem. and shock tube research dept. engring. UCLA, 1961-66; mem. staff TRW Systems, corrosion and advanced battery research and devel. Redondo Beach, Calif., 1966-78; dir. engring. Intermedics Intraocular Inc., Pasadena, Calif., 1978-80, dir. research and devel., 1980-82, v.p. engring. devel. and research, 1982-84; v.p. research and devel. Interpore Internat. Inc., 1984-85; dir. research and devel., product process devel. IOLAB Corp. subs. Johnson & Johnson Co., Claremont, Calif., 1985-87, dir. new tech., research and devel., 1987-88; v.p., gen. mgr. Nidek Techs., Inc., Pasadena, Calif., 1988—. NASA predoctoral trainee, 1964-65. Mem. Electrochem. Soc., Nat. Assn. Corrosion Engrs., AAAS, Am. Mgmt. Assn., Sigma Xi. Office: 675 S Arroyo Pky Ste 330 Pasadena CA 91105-3264

SAYKALLY, RICHARD JAMES, chemistry educator; b. Rhinelander, Wis., Sept. 10, 1947; s. Edwin L. and Helen M. S. BS, U. Wis., Eau Claire, 1970; PhD, U. Wis., Madison, 1977. Postdoctoral Nat. Bur. Standards, Boulder, Colo., 1977-79; asst. prof. U. Calif., Berkeley, 1979-83, assoc. prof., 1983-86, prof., 1986—, vice chmn. dept. chemistry, 1988-91; Bergman Lectureship Yale U., 1987; Merck-Frost lectr. U. B.C., 1988; Bourke Lectureship Royal Soc. Chemistry, 1992, L.J. Bircher Lectureship, Vanderbilt U., 1993; prin. investigator Lawrence Berkeley Lab., 1983-91; prin. investigator Lawrence Berkeley Lab., 1983-91; prin. investigator program Sci. for Sci. NSF; mem. Laser Sci. Topical Group Fellowship Com., 1993—; mem. internat. steering com. 12th Internat. Conf. on Laser Spectroscopy, 1995; lectr. U. Alta. (Can.), 1995. Contbr. over 160 articles to profl. jours.; editl. rev. bd. Jour. Chem. Physics, 1993-95, Molecular Physics, 1983—, Chem. Physics Letters, 1987—, Spectroscopy Mag., 1986—, Rev. of Sci. Instruments, 1987-90. Dreyfuss Found. fellow, 1979; Churchill fellow Cambridge U., 1995; presdl. investigator NSF, 1984-88; recipient Bomem Michelson prize for spectroscopy, 1989, E.K. Plyler prize for molecular spectroscopy, 1989, Disting. Alumnus award U. Wis., Eau Claire, 1987, E.R. Lippincott medal OSA, SAS, 1992, Disting. Tchg. award U. Calif., Berkeley, 1992, Humboldt Sr. Scientist award, 1995; Harry Emmett Gunning lectureship U. Alberta, 1995. Fellow Am. Phys. Soc., Royal Soc. Chem., Am. Acad. Arts and Scis.; mem. AAAS, AAUP, Optical Soc. Am., Am. Chem. Soc. (Harrison Howe award 1992). Office: University of California Dept of Chemistry 419 Latimer Hall #1460 Berkeley CA 94720-1460

SAYRE, EDWARD CHARLES, librarian; b. Longview, Wash., Aug. 15, 1923; s. Kenneth C. Sayre and Clare (Davis) Clingan; m. Virginia A. Hoy, June 9, 1951; children: Steven Anthony, Sabrina Karen. BA, Coll. of Gt. Falls, 1955; MA, U. Idaho, 1961; MLS, U. Md., 1968. Coordinator library services Thomas Nelson Community Coll., Hampton, Va., 1968-69; dir. Roswell Pub. Library, N.Mex., 1969-70; cons. N.Mex. State Library, Santa Fe, 1970-72; dir. Central Colo. Library System, Denver, 1972-78, Serra Coop. Library System, San Diego, 1978-79, Los Alamos County (N.Mex.) Library System, 1979-88; county adminstr. Los Alamos County, 1988-89; cons., 1976—, ret., 1989. Contbr. articles to profl. jours. Served to maj. USAF, 1951-67. HEA Title II fellow, 1968. Mem. ALA, N.Mex. Library Assn. (pres.-elect 1972), Beta Phi Mu (dir. 1973-74). Democrat. Unitarian. Home: 3 Timber Ridge Rd Los Alamos NM 87544-2317

SAYRE, JOHN MARSHALL, lawyer, former government official; b. Boulder, Colo., Nov. 9, 1921; s. Henry Marshall and Lulu M. (Cooper) S.; m. Jean Miller, Aug. 22, 1943; children: Henry M., Charles Franklin, John Marshall Jr., Ann Elizabeth Sayre Taggart (dec.). BA, U. Colo., 1943, JD, 1948. Bar: Colo. 1948, U.S. Dist. Ct. Colo. 1952, U.S. Ct. Appeals (10th cir.) 1964. Law clk. trust dept. Denver Nat. Bank, 1948-49; asst. cashier, trust officer Nat. State Bank of Boulder, 1949-50; ptnr. Ryan, Sayre, Martin, Brotzman, Boulder, 1950-66, Davis, Graham & Stubbs, Denver, 1966-89, of counsel, 1993—; asst. sec. of the Interior for Water and Sci., 1989-93. Bd. dirs. Boulder Sch. Dist. 3, 1951-57; city atty. City of Boulder, 1952-55; gen. counsel Colo. Mcpl. League, 1956-63; prin. counsel No. Colo. Water Conservancy Dist. and mcpl. subdist., 1964-87, spl. counsel, 1987, bd. dirs. dist., 1960-64; former legal counsel Colo. Assn. Commerce and Industry. Lt. (j.g.) USNR, 1943-46. Decorated Purple Heart. Fellow Am. Bar. Found. (life), Colo. Bar Found; mem. ABA, Colo. Bar Assn., Boulder County Bar Assn. (pres. 1959), Denver Bar Assn., Nat. Water Resources Assn. (Colo. dir. 1980-89, 93—, pres. 1984-86), Denver Country Club, Denver Club, Mile High Club, Phi Gamma Delta, Phi Beta Kappa. Republican. Episcopalian. Office: Davis Graham & Stubbs PO Box 185 Denver CO 80201-0185 Home: 355 Ivanhoe St Denver CO 80220-5841

SAYWARD, JENNY, cultural organization executive; b. Kennewick, Wash., Sept. 5, 1952; d. Russell Elwood and Elizabeth (Wilson) Nelson. BA in History, Conn. Coll., 1974; AA in Interpreting for the Deaf, Seattle Ctrl. C.C., 1988; cert. elem. teaching, Antioch U., 1991. Cert. elem. tchr. Family planning educator Family Planning of N.H., Dover, 1975-77; owner Open Arms Child Care, Seattle, 1981-87; interpreter Riverview Sch. Dist., Carnation, Wash., 1988-90; support group facilitator Lesbian Resource Ctr., Seattle, 1989-90; exec. dir. Lesbian Mothers Nat. Def. Fund, Seattle, 1991—. Author: (pamphlet series) Information for Lesbian Families, 1994; editor: (newsletter) Mom's Apple Pie, 1991—. Mem. NOW, Mensa. Office: Lesbian Mothers Nat Def Fnd PO Box 21567 Seattle WA 98111-3567

SAYWELL, WILLIAM GEORGE GABRIEL, foundation administrator; b. Regina, Sask., Can., Dec. 1, 1936; s. John Ferdinand Tupper and Vera Marguerite S.; m. Helen Jane Larmer; children: Shelley Jayne, William James Tupper, Patricia Lynn. BA, U. Toronto, 1960, MA, 1961, PhD, 1968; LLD, U. B.C., 1994. Asst. prof. dept. East Asian studies U. Toronto, Ont., Ont., Can., 1963-69; asst. prof. U. Toronto, Ont., Can., 1969-71, assoc. prof., 1971-82, prof., 1982-83, chmn. dept., 1971-76; prof. dept. history, pres. Simon Fraser U., Burnaby, B.C., Can., 1983-93; pres., chief exec. officer Asia Pacific Found. of Can., Vancouver, B.C., 1993—; sinologist and 1st sec. Can. Embassy, Peking, 1972-73; dir. U. Toronto-York U. Ctr. Modern East Asia, 1974-75; prin. Innis Coll., 1976-79; vice provost U. Toronto, 1979-83; dir. Westcoast Energy, Spar Aerospace. Author articles and revs. on Chinese affairs to profl. jours. Decorated Order B.C. Office: Asia Pacific Found Can, 666-999 Canada Pl, Vancouver, BC Canada V6C 3E1

SCAFE, LINCOLN ROBERT, JR., sales executive; b. Cleve., July 28, 1922; s. Lincoln Robert and Charlotte (Hawkins) S.; student Cornell U., 1940-41; m. Mary Anne Wilkinson, Nov. 14, 1945; children—Amanda Katharine, Lincoln Robert III. Service mgr. Avery Engring. Co., Cleve., 1946-51; nat. service mgr. Trane Co., LaCrosse, Wis., 1951-57; service and installation mgr. Mech. Equipment Supply Co., Honolulu, 1957-58; chief engr. Sam P. Wallace of Pacific, Honolulu, 1958-62; pres. Air Conditioning Service Co., Inc., Honolulu, 1962-84; sales engr. G.J. Campbell & Assocs., Seattle, 1984-89. Served with USNR, 1942-45; PTO. Mem. ASHRAE, Alpha Delta Phi. Clubs: Cornell Hawaii (past pres.); Outrigger Canoe. Republican. Author tech. service lit. and parts manuals; contbr. articles to trade publs. Home: 10721 SW 112th St Vashon WA 98070-3044 Office: GJ Campbell and Associates 11613 Rainier Ave S Seattle WA 98178-3945

SCAGLIONE, CECIL FRANK, marketing executive, publisher; b. North Bay, Ont., Can., Dec. 2, 1934; came to U.S., 1967, naturalized, 1982; s. Frank and Rose (Aubin) S.; m. Mary Margaret Stewart, Nov. 11, 1954 (div. 1982); children: Cris Ann, Michael Andrew, Patrick Andrew; m. Beverly Louise Rahn, Mar. 25, 1983; student North Bay Coll., 1947-52, Ryerson Tech. Inst., Toronto, Ont., 1955-56, San Diego State U. Inst. World Affairs, 1979. Fin. writer Toronto Telegram, 1955; reporter Sarnia (Ont.) Observer, 1956-57; reporter, editor Kitchener-Waterloo (Ont.) Record, 1957-61; reporter, editor, analyst Windsor (Ont.) Star, 1961-67; writer, editor, photo editor Detroit News, 1967-71; reporter, assoc. bus. editor San Diego Union, 1971-80; mgr. corp. communications Pacific Southwest Airlines, San Diego, 1981-83; sr. v.p. media rels. Berkman & Daniels, Inc., San Diego, 1984-87, prin. Scaglione Mktg. Comm., 1987—; pres., CEO Mature Life Features, 1990—. Mem. adv. coun. SBA, Accredited Pub. Rels. Soc. Am. Recipient award B.F. Goodrich Can., Ltd., 1962, 66, Spl. Achievement award Nat. Assn. Recycling Industries, 1978, award SBA, 1980; Herbert J. Davenport fellow, 1977 U. Mo.; Can. Centennial grantee, 1966. Mem. San Diego Press Club (hon. life, past pres.) awards 1978, 80, 84, Airline Editors Forum awards 1982, 83, Soc. Profl. Journalists, Internat. Food, Wine & Travel Writers Assn. Roman Catholic. Founding editor-in-chief Aeromexico mag., 1973; contbr. articles, columns and photographs to various publs.

SCALA, JAMES, health care industry consultant, author; b. Ramsey, N.J., Sept. 16, 1934; s. Luigi and Lorene (Hendrickson) S.; m. Nancy Peters, June 15, 1957; children: James, Gregory, Nancy, Kimberly. B.A., Columbia U., 1960; Ph.D., Cornell U., 1964; postgrad., Harvard U., 1968. Staff scientist Miami Valley Labs., Procter and Gamble Co., 1964-66; head life scis., dir. fundamental research Owens Ill. Corp., 1966-71; dir. nutrition T.J. Lipton Inc., 1971-75; dir. health scis. Gen. Foods Corp., 1975-78; v.p. sci. and tech. Shaklee Corp., San Francisco, 1978-85, sr. v.p. sci. affairs, 1986-87; lectr. Georgetown U. Med. Sch., U. Calif.-Berkeley extension. Author: Making the Vitamin Connection, 1985, The Arthritis Relief Diet, 1987, 89, Eating Right for a Bad Gut, 1990, 92, The High Blood Pressure Relief Diet, 1988, 90, Look 10 Years Younger, Feel 10 Years Better, 1991, 93, Prescription for Longevity, 1992, 94, If You Can't/Won't Stop Smoking, 1993; editor: Nutritional Determinants in Athletic Performance, 1981, New Protective Roles for Selected Nutrients, 1989; columnist Dance mag.; contbr. articles on nutrition and health scis. to profl. publs. With USAF, 1953-56. Disting. scholar U. Miami, Fla., 1977, Fla. Atlantic U., 1977. Mem. AAAS, Am. Inst. Nutrition, Am. Coll. Nutrition, Brit. Nutrition Soc., Sports Medicine Coun., Am. Soc. Cell Biology, Inst. Food Technologists, Astron. Soc. Pacific (bd. dirs., chmn. devel. coun.), Am. Dietetic Assn., Olympic Club (San Francisco), Oakland Yacht Club, Sigma Xi. Republican.

SCALISE, GEORGE MARTIN, electronics company executive; b. Warren, Pa., May 1, 1934; m. Dorothea K. McDonald, Apr. 28, 1962; children: Kathleen Marie, George Edward, Craig Thomas. B.S.M.E., Purdue U., 1956. Engr. CBS Electronics, Lowell, Mass., 1958-61; asst. gen. mgr. Motorola, Phoenix, 1961-67; gen. mgr. Motorola, Geneva, 1968; group dir., adminstrn. Fairchild, Mountain View, Calif., 1968-70, v.p., gen. mgr., 1970-74; v.p. adminstrn. and internat. ops. Advanced Micro Devices, Sunnyvale, Calif., 1974-81, sr. v.p., 1981-87; pres., chief exec. officer Maxtor Corp., San Jose, Calif., 1987—; dir. Microelectronics & Computer Tech. Corp.; chmn. bd. Semicondr. Research Corp., Research Triangle Park, N.C.; adviser U.S.-Japan Work Group on High Tech. Industries, 1983, U.S.-Japan Common Market Businessmen Adv. Group; adv. panel Tech. and Am. Econ. Transition, Office of Tech. Assessment. Mem. adv. council Engring. Found., U. Tex.-Austin Served with U.S. Army, 1956-58. Mem. Semicondr. Industry Assn. (chmn. pub. policy com. 1982—). Roman Catholic. Office: Maxtor Corp 211 River Oaks Pky San Jose CA 95134-1913

SCANLAN, JOHN JOSEPH, retired bishop; b. Ihiscarra, County Cork, Ireland, May 24, 1906; came to U.S., 1930; s. Peter Scanlan and Katherine Coleman. Student, Hallows Coll., Dublin, Ireland, 1923-30; LLD (hon.), Portland U., 1966; LHD (hon.), U. Hawaii, 1980. Ordained priest Roman Cath. Ch., 1930. Asst. pastor Archiodese of San Francisco, 1930-50, pastor, 1950-54; aux. bishop Diocese of Honolulu, 1954-67, ordinary bishop, 1968-81, adminstr., 1981-82, ret., 1982; dir. archdiocesan coun. cath. men Archdiocese of San Francisco, 1952-54; mem. Cath. Philosophic Assn., San Francisco, 1940-50. Mem. Nat. Coun. Cath. Bishops. Home: Nazareth House 245 Nova Albion Way San Rafael CA 94903

SCANLON, DERALEE ROSE, registered dietitian, educator, author; b. Santa Monica, Calif., Aug. 16, 1950; d. Stanley Ralph and Demba (Runkle) S.; m. Alex Spataru, July 20, 1970 (div. 1974). AA, Santa Monica Coll., 1968; accred. med. record tech., East L.A. Coll., 1980; BS, U. Calif., L.A., 1984. Registered Dietitian. V.p. corp. sales, nutrition dir. LIfeTrends Corp., Carlsbad, Calif., 1984-86; dir. media, nutrition Irvine Ranch Farmers Markets, L.A., 1987-88; spokesperson for media Calif. Milk Adv. Bd., San. Diego, 1986; nutrition reporter Med-NIWS, L.A., 1990-91; dietitian Sta. ABC-TV The Home Show, L.A., 1991-92, Sta. NBC-TV David Horowitz Fight Back, L.A., 1991-92; dietitian, nutrition reporter Sta. KTTV-TV Good Day L.A., 1994—; co-host talk radio show Light and Lively, KABC, 1994—; media spokesperson Lifetime Food Co., Seaside, Calif., 1992—, Interior Design Nutritionals, Provo, Utah, 1993—, Weight Watchers, 1993; contbr. writer L.A. Parent Mag., Burbank, Calif., 1991—; syndicated nutrition reporter Live N'Well TV Series, Utah, 1992—; nutrition educator Emeritus Coll. Sr. Health, Santa Monica, 1990-92; nutrition lectr. Princess Cruises, L.A., 1987; nutrition video host AMA Campaign Against Cholesterol, 1989; lectr. on nutrition and health to various orgns., 1993—; leader seminar series on I.B.S. UCLA Med. Ctr., 1994—. Author: The Wellness Book of IBS, 1989, Diets That Work, 1991, revised edit., 1992, 93; newspaper columnist: Ask The Dietitian, 1990—; columnist Natural Way Mag; contbr. articles to profl. jours. Mem. AFTRA, Dietitians in Bus./Comms. (regional rep. 1990-92, So. Calif. chairperson 1991-92, editor nat. newsletter 1994—), Am. Dietetic Assn. (pub. rels. chair 1985-87), Calif. Dietetic Assn. (Dietitian of Yr. in Pvt. Practice, Bus. and Comm. 1993), Soc. for Nutrition Edn., Nat. Speakers Assn. Home and Office: 10613 Eastborne Ave Los Angeles CA 90024-5920

SCANLON, MICHAEL PATRICK, medical legal researcher; b. Santa Monica, Calif., Feb. 22, 1946; s. Michael Patrick Scanlon and Rose Ann (Lance) Marchu; m. Terumi Okuma, Mar. 3, 1968; children: Sean, Justine, Ty. Student, Loyola U., Westchester, Calif., 1964-66; AA, Pierce Coll., 1975; BA, Calif. State U., Northridge, 1980. Dental lab. technician Santa Maria, Calif., 1961-62, Dr. Petrasick DDS, Seattle, Wash., 1962-63, Dr. Ludwig DDS, Encino, Calif., 1963-65; op. room technician Encino Hosp., 1969-72, cardiac catherization technician, 1972-73; neurosurg. asst. Kenneth J. Richland Neurosurgeon, Encino, 1973-86, Joel Singer MD Neurosurgeon, West Hills, Calif., 1980-86; orthopedic asst. San Fernando Valley Orthopedic Group, Northridge, Calif., 1986-89; owner, med. legal researcher Scanlon Med. Specialties, Moorpark, Calif., 1979-94; head soccer coach Moorpark (Calif.) High Sch., 1984-94. Bd. dirs. Moorpark Athletic Cmty. Complex, 1992-94; head coach Moorpark Express Soccer Club, 1994; asst. scoutmster Troop 156 Boy Scouts Am., Van Nuys, Calif., 1963-66; asst. men's soccer coach Moorpark Coll., 1994—. With U.S. Army, 1966-69, Vietnam, Japan. Coach Boys Soccer Champions, Calif. Interscholastic Fedn., Cerritos, 1994; High Sch. Coach of the Yr., Frontier League, Ventura, Calif., 1993, 94; Moorpark Coach of Yr., Moorpark High Sch. Boosters, 1993, 94. Democrat.

SCANNELL, FAYE NAOMI, art educator; b. Halifax, Pa., May 6, 1947; d. Paul Frederick and Emma Ellen (Lebo) Snyder; m. John Robert Scannell, July 11, 1969; children: Michelle Deborah, Amanda Jeanne, Rebecca Susan, Benjamin David. BS in Art Edn., Kutztown U. Pa., 1969; postgrad., various colls. in Pa. and Wash., 1970-93; MEd in Integrated Arts, Lesley Coll., 1995. Cert. tchr. K-12, Pa., Wash. Art tchr. Nazareth (Pa.) Schs., 1969-70, Upper Dauphin Schs., Elizabethville, Pa., 1970-71, Halifax (Pa.) Area Schs., 1971-72; supr.- book restoration U. Wash. Rare Collections, Seattle, 1972-77; art specialist Bellevue (Wash.) Schs., 1977—; adj. prof. Seattle Pacific U., 1980-83; mem. adv. bd., program designer, instr. Bellevue Art Mus., 1985—; lead art tech. tchr. eastern dist. State of Wash., 1990—; cons. Microsoft Home Products, Redmond, Wash., 1992—; writer Glencoe/Macmillan/McGraw-Hill, Columbus, Ohio, 1993—; presenter integrated curriculum & tech. at local, state and regional convs. Contbg. writer Classroom Creativity Cards, 1994, Digital Chisel/Multimedia Tool Kit, 1994-95. Leader Girl Scouts Am., Bothell, Wash., 1988—, del. Contemporary Issues Conv., Seattle, 1994. Computer Aided Art Instrn. grantee Washington State, 1990. Mem. Nat. Art Edn. Assn., Wash. Art Edn. Assn. (Wash. Art Educator of Yr. 1993), Wash. Art Alliance, Northwest Coun. Computer Edn., Bellevue Art Mus., Seattle Art Mus. Home: 22627 7th Dr SE Bothell WA 98021

SCANNELL, WILLIAM EDWARD, aerospace company executive, consultant, psychologist; b. Muscatine, Iowa, Nov. 11, 1934; s. Mark Edward and Catharine Pearson (Fowler) S.; m. Barbara Ann Hoemann, Nov. 23, 1957; children: Cynthia Kay, Mark Edward, David Jerome, Terri Lynn, Stephen Patrick. BA in Gen. Edn., U. Nebr., 1961; BS in Engring., Ariz. State U., 1966; MS in Systems Engring., So. Meth. U., 1969; PhD, U.S. Internat. U., 1991. Commd. 2d lt. USAF, 1956, advanced through grades to lt. col., 1972; B-47 navigator-bombardier 98th Bomb Wing, Lincoln Air Force Base, Nebr., 1956-63; with Air Force Inst. of Tech., 1963-65, 68-69; chief mgmt. engring. team RAF Bentwaters, England, 1965-68; forward air contr. 20th Tactical Air Support Squadron USAF, Danang, Vietnam, 1970-71; program mgr. Hdqrs. USAF, Washington, 1971-74, staff asst. Office of Sec. Def., 1974-75, ret., 1975; account exec. Merrill Lynch, San Diego, 1975-77; program engring. chief Gen. Dynamics, San Diego, 1977-79, engring. chief, 1979-80, program mgr., 1980-83; mgr. integrated logistics support Northrop Corp., Hawthorne, Calif., 1984-88; mgr. B-2 program planning and scheduling Northrop Corp., Pico Rivera, Calif., 1988-91; pres. Scannell and Assocs., Borrego Springs, Calif., 1991—; mem. adj. faculty U.S. Internat. U., San Diego. Decorated DFC with three oak leaf clusters, Air medal with 11 oak leaf clusters. Mem. APA, Calif. Psychol. Assn., Soc. Indsl. and Orgnl. Psychology, Inst. Indsl. Engrs., Coronado Cays Yacht Club, Psi Chi. Republican. Roman Catholic. Home: 717 Anza Park Trail Borrego Springs CA 92004 Office: Scannell and Assocs PO Box 2392 Borrego Springs CA 92004-2392

SCARBROUGH, ERNEST EARL, stockbroker, financial planner; b. Memphis, Jan. 7, 1947; s. Earl Carson and Mary Lillian (Keileber) S.; m. Cindy Cowley, Sept. 22, 1973; children: Michael E., William E. AA, Phoenix Coll., 1974; BA, Ottawa U., 1993; MBA, U. Phoenix, 1995. Cert. fin. planner. Profl. pilot, airline transport rating, flight instr. various gen. aviation cos., Memphis and Phoenix, 1968-72; transp. analyst leasing and sales Rollins Leasing Co., Phoenix, 1971-73; cost analyst Ariz. Pub. Service Co., Phoenix, 1973-75; air traffic contr. FAA, Ariz. and Calif., 1975-81; account exec. E.F. Hutton & Co., Phoenix, 1982-83, asst. v.p., 1984-86, v.p., 1987; v.p., portfolio mgr. Prudential-Bache Securities, Inc., Phoenix, 1988-90; v.p. Esplanade Office Dean Witter Reynolds, Phoenix, 1990-95; mng. dir. investments, asst. br. mgr. Piper Jaffray, Phoenix, 1995—. Corp. chmn. Phoenix chpt. climb-the-mountain campaign Am. Cancer Soc., 1986; chmn. stewardship, vice-chmn. fin. Cross in Desert United Meth. Ch., Phoenix, 1987-88; bd. dirs. Sojourner Ctr., 1988—, pres. bd., 1989-91, chmn. adv. bd., 1991-94; jr. achievement tchr. cons., 1992—. With USAF, 1966-70. Mem. Internat. Assn. for Fin. Planning, Internat. Assn. CFPs, Profl. Air Traffic Contrs. Orgn. (local pres. 1975-81), Ctrl. Ariz. Estate Planning Coun., Rotary (v.p. Phoenix chpt. 1987, pres.-elect 1988). Republican. Home: 2419 E Sunnyside Dr Phoenix AZ 85028-1103 Office: Piper Jaffray 2525 E Camelback Rd Ste 900 Phoenix AZ 85016

SCATENA, LORRAINE BORBA, rancher, women's rights advocate; b. San Rafael, Calif., Feb. 18, 1924; d. Joseph and Eugenia (Simas) de Borba; m. Louis G. Scatena, Feb. 14, 1960; children: Louis Vincent, Eugenia Gayle. BA, Dominican Coll., San Rafael, 1945; postgrad., Calif. Sch. Fine Arts, 1948, U. Calif., Berkeley, 1956-57. Cert. elem. tchr., Calif. Tchr. Dominican Coll., 1946; tchr. of mentally handicapped San Anselmo (Calif.) Sch. Dist., 1946; tchr. Fairfax (Calif.) Pub. Elem. Sch., 1946-53; asst. to mayor Fairfax City Recreation, 1948-53; tchr., libr. U.S. Dependent Schs., Mainz am Rhine, Fed. Republic Germany, 1953-56; translator Portugal Travel Tours, Lisbon, 1954; bonding sec. Am. Fore Ins. Group, San Francisco, 1958-60; rancher, farmer Yerington, Nev., 1960—; hostess com. Caldecott and Newbury Authors' Awards, San Francisco, 1959; mem. Nev. State Legis. Commn., 1975; coord. Nevadans for Equal Rights Amendment, 1975-78, rural areas rep., 1976-78; testifier Nev. State Senate and Assembly, 1975, 77; mem. adv. com. Fleischmann Coll. Agr. U. Nev., 1977-80, 81-84; speaker Grants and Rsch. Projects, Bishop, Calif., 1977, Choices for Tomorrow's Women, Fallon, Nev., 1989. Trustee Wassuk Coll., Hawthorne, Nev., 1984-87; mem. Lyon County Friends of Libr., Yerington, 1971—, Lyon County Mus. Soc., 1978; sec., pub. info. chmn. Lyon County Rep. Women, 1968-73, v.p. programs, 1973-75; mem. Lyon County Rep. Cen. Com., 1973-74; mem. Marin County Soc. Artists, San Anselmo, Calif., 1948-53; charter mem. Eleanor Roosevelt Fund Women and Girls, 1990, sustaining mem., 1991—; Nev. rep. 1st White House Conf. Rural Am. Women, Washington, 1980; participant internat. reception, Washington, 1980; mem. pub. panel individual presentation Shakespeare's Treatment of Women Characters, Nev. Theatre for the Arts, Ashland, Oreg. Shakespearean Actors local performance, 1977. Recipient Outstanding Conservation Farmer award Mason Valley Conservation Dist., 1992, Soroptimist Internat. Women Helping women award 1983, invitation to first all-women delegation to U.S.A. from People's Republic china, U.S. House Reps., 1979; Public Forum Travel grantee Edn. Title IX, Oakland, Calif., 1977; fellow World Lit. Acad., 1993. Mem. Lyon County Ret. Tchrs. Assn. (unit pres. 1979-80, 84-86, v.p. 1986-88, Nev. div. Outstanding Svc. award 1981, state conv. gen. chmn. 1985), Rural Am. Women Inc., AAUW (br. pres. 1972-74, 74-76, chair edn. found. programs, 1983—, state convention gen. chmn. 1976, 87, state div. sec. 1970-72, state div. legis. program chmn. 1976-77, state div. chmn. internat. rels. 1979-81, state div. pres. 1981-83, br. travelship, discovering women in U.S. history Radcliffe Coll. Div. Humanities award 1975, Future Fund Nat. award 1983), Mason Valley Country Club, Italian Cath. Fedn. Club (pres. 1986-88), Uniao Portuguesa Estado da Calif. Roman Catholic. Home: PO Box 247 Yerington NV 89447-0247

SCATES, STEVEN MICHAEL, hematologist, oncologist; b. Ceres, Calif., Feb. 27, 1955; s. Michael Floyd S. and Teresa (Baraggio) Welsh; m. Karen Dianne, Sept. 29, 1990. AA in Biology, Modesto Jr. Coll., 1975; BS in Bacteriology, U. Calif., Davis, 1978; MD, Washington U. St. Louis, 1985. Cert. Am. Bd. Internal Medicine; cert. hematology, med. oncology. Intern UCLA Med. Ctr., 1986-88, asst. prof. divsn. hematology-oncology, 1991-92; hematologist, oncologist pvt. practice, Morgan Hill, Calif., 1992—; chmn. dept. medicine St. Louise Hosp., 1994, chmn. bioethics com., 1994, dir. cardiopulmanary svcs., 1995—, chmn. critical care, 1995—, sec. treas. med. staff, 1995—; researcher in field. Contbr. chpts. to books and articles to profl. jours. Hematology-Oncology fellow UCLA Med. Ctr., 1988-91, McDonnell Rsch. fellow, Washington U., St. Louis, 1982, Am. Cancer Soc. Clin. Oncology fellow, 1989, Revlon Rsch. fellow, 1990; recipient Am. Cancer Soc. Career Devel. award, 1992. Mem. AAAS, Am. Coll. Physicians, Am. Soc. Clin. Oncology, Am. Soc. Hematology, Assn. No. Calif. Oncologists, Calif. Med. Assn., Santa Clara Med. Assn., Mensa. Home: PO Box 635 Morgan Hill CA 95038-0635 Office: 18511 Mission View Dr Morgan Hill CA 95037-2902

SCAVEN, GREGORY JOSEPH, chemical engineer; b. Phila., Apr. 9, 1963; s. Joseph Charles and Josephine Marie (Rocco) S.; m. Lorraine Robbins Gilmore, Sept. 29, 1990; 1 child, Victoria Leigh Scaven. BS in Engring., Lehigh U., 1985; MS in Engring., U. Pa., 1987. Project engr. Talley Def. Systems, Mesa, Ariz., 1991—. Contbr. articles to profl. jours. Capt. U.S. Army, 1985-91. Mem. AICE, Am. Chem. Soc., Am. Def. Preparedness Assn., Internat. Pyrotechnics Soc. Home: 2037 E Hermosa Vista Dr Mesa AZ 85213-2211 Office: Talley Def Systems 3500 N Greenfield Rd Mesa AZ 85215-9117

SCEPANSKI, JORDAN MICHAEL, librarian, administrator; b. Yonkers, N.Y., Nov. 21, 1942; s. Michael James and Margaret (Witko) S.; m. H. Lea Wells, Apr. 18, 1981; children—Kathryn Mary, Jordan Wells, Jennifer Elizabeth. BS, Manhattan Coll., 1964; MLn, Emory U., 1967; postgrad., U. N.C., Charlotte, 1976-77; M.B.A., U. Tenn., Nashville, 1982. Vol. Peace Corps, Turkey, 1964-66; adult services librarian Uniondale Pub. Library, N.Y., 1967-68; various profl. staff positions ALA, Chgo., 1970-73; asst. dir. library, asst. prof. U. N.C., Charlotte, 1974-78; dir. central library Vanderbilt U., Nashville, 1978-84; dir. univ. library and learning resources Calif. State U., Long Beach, 1984—; mgmt. intern Joint Univ. Librs., Nashville, 1977-78; cons./trainer Assn. Rsch. Librs., 1979-80; Fulbright lectr. Hacettepe U., Ankara, Turkey, 1981-82; cons. Coll. Charleston, S.C., No. Ky. U., Highlands Heights, Elon Coll., N.C.; facilitator, trainer U. Notre Dame, South Bend, Ind., U. Nebr., Lincoln, U. Wyo.; founding mem. IBM Informa; bd. dirs. VTLS Inc. Contbr. articles to profl. jours. cons. Calif. State U., L.A. Served with U.S. Army, 1968-70. Recipient K.G. Saur award Coll. and Research Libraries publ., 1988; sr. fellow UCLA, 1983; faculty/librarian coop. research grantee Council on Library Resources, 1983. Mem. ALA (chair internat. rels. round table 1990-91), Western Assn. Schs. and Colls. (accreditation vis. team), Freedom to Read Found., Fulbright Alumni Assn., Jane Austen Soc. N.Am., Jane Austen Soc., S.W. Am.-Turkish Assn. So. Calif., Beta Phi Mu, Phi Beta Delta. Democrat. Roman Catholic. Home: 6714 E Los Arcos St Long Beach CA 90815-2409 Office: Calif State U-Long Beach U Libr Long Beach CA 90840

SCEPER, DUANE HAROLD, lawyer; b. Norfolk, Va., Nov. 16, 1946; s. Robert George and Marion Eudora (Hynes) S.; m. Sharon Diane Cramer, July 4, 1981; stepchildren: Karin Stevenson, Diane Stevenson. BS in Law, Western State U., 1979, JD, 1980. Bar: Calif. 1982, U.S. Dist. Ct. (so. dist.) Calif. 1982. Field engr. Memorex/Tex. Instruments, San Diego, 1968-70; computer programmer San Diego, 1970-81; atty. Allied Ins. Group, San Diego, 1981-85; sole practice San Diego, 1985-87; ptnr. Zybelman, Paluso, Alter, Graham and Sceper, San Diego, 1987—; cons. computers 1980—; lectr. estate planning various orgns. Patentee in field. Active Com. to Elect King Golden to Congress, San Diego, 1978. Served with USAF, 1965-68. Recipient Am. Jurisprudence award, 1979. Mem. ABA, San Diego County Bar Assn., Assn. Trial Lawyers of Am., Calif. Trial Lawyers Assn., San Diego Trial Lawyers Assn., Am. Subrogation Attys. Assn. of Ins. Def. Counsel, So. Calif. Defense Counsel, Delta Theta Phi. Democrat. Home: 2641 Massachusetts Ave Lemon Grove CA 91945-3149 Office: Zybelman Paluso Alter Graham & Sceper 707 Broadway Ste 1100 San Diego CA 92101-5300

SCHAAF, MIV, writer, graphic designer, composer; b. Oct. 3, 1920; m. Alfred Musso, 1959; 1 chld, Gia Musso. BA, Mich. State U., 1943; postgrad., Humboldt State U., 1988—. Owner Miv Schaaf Assocs., 1954—; seminar tchr. UCLA, U. Calif. Irvine, Scripps Coll., 1977—; del. White House Conf. Librs., 1979; judge Robert B. Campbell book collection UCLA, 1980; speaker in field. Author: Who Can Not Read About Crocodiles, 1988; columnist L.A. Times, 1972-87; writer North Coast Jour., 1993—; writer 156 poems; composer some 160 songs, including Songs of Age and Songs of Rage. Pres. Archtl. Panel, L.A., 1951-69; founder Pasadena Cultural Heritage Commn., 1973. Recipient Premier award Pasadena Heritage, 1977, Met. Coop. Libr. System and Calif. Libr. Assn. award, 1982, Gold Crown award Pasadena Arts Coun., 1983. Home: 83 Wilson Ln Fieldbrook CA 95519

SCHAAFSMA, CURTIS FORREST, archaeologist; b. Vallejo, Calif., Jan. 22, 1938; s. Harold Fye Schaafsma and Gertrude Alpha (Iverson) Offutt; m. Polly Avis Dix, Sept. 28, 1958; children: Hoski, Pieter. BA, U. Colo., 1962; MA, U. N.Mex., 1971. Archaeologist Ft. Burgwin Rsch. Ctr., Taos, N.Mex., 1964-65; park ranger U.S. Nat. Park Svc., Kayenta, Ariz., 1966; archaeologist U. Utah, Salt Lake City, 1970, State Planning Office, Santa Fe, 1971, MAPCO, Inc., Tulsa, 1972-73; survey archaeologist Colo. State Archaeologist, Boulder, 1974, U. N.Mex., Albuquerque, 1972; rsch. archaeologist Sch. Am. Rsch., Santa Fe, 1974-79; state archaeologist Mus. N.Mex., Santa Fe, 1979-92, curator anthropology, 1992—. With USN, 1956-58. Mem. Am. Soc. Conservation Archaeology (pres. 1984-88), Soc. Am. Archaeology, Nat. Assn. State Archaeologists (sec., treas. 1979-81), Archaeol. Soc. N.Mex. (bd. dirs. 1979—), N.Mex. Archaeol. Coun., N.Mex. Assn. Mus. Office: Mus NMex PO Box 2087 Santa Fe NM 87504-2087

SCHABER, GORDON DUANE, law educator, former judge; b. Ashley, N.D., Nov. 22, 1927; s. Ronald and Esther (Schatz) S. A.B. with distinction, Sacramento State Coll., 1949; J.D. with honors, U. Calif. at San Francisco, 1952; LL.D., McGeorge Sch. Law, 1961, John Marshall Law Sch., 1983, Widener U., Del. Law Sch., 1984; LLD, Southwestern U., 1994. Bar: Calif. 1953. Pvt. practice Sacramento, 1953-65; ptnr. firm Schaber & Cecchettini, Sacramento, 1953-65; prof., asst. dean McGeorge Coll. of Law (now McGeorge Sch. Law of U. Pacific), Sacramento, 1953-56, asst. dean, 1956, acting dean, dean, prof. law, 1957-91, univ. counsellor, disting. prof. law, 1991—; presiding judge Superior Ct. Sacramento County, 1965-70; dir. Air Calif., 1974-81, Westgate Corp., 1979-82, Sacramento Cablevision, 1980-82, Capitol Bank of Commerce, vice chmn., 1987-90; chmn. bd. dirs. River City Cablevision Inc.; mem. Calif. Bd. Control, 1962-64; chmn. Greater Sacramento Plan Com., 1970; cons. on establishment Sch. Law at U. Puget Sound, 1970-71; cons. study on jud. workload Jud. Council Calif., 1971-72; mem. Adv. Com. to Chief Justice Calif. on Superior Ct. Mgmt., 1971; cons. vehicle theft study Calif. Hwy. Patrol, 1972; panelist Sacramento Bee Secret Witness Program, 1971-90; mem. adv. com. to Calif. Office Econ. Opportunity, Calif. Legal Services Expt., 1972; vice chmn. Calif. Ednl. Facilities Authority, 1978—; bd. dirs. Nat. Center Adminstrv. Justice, 1978; mem. President's Adminstrn. Justice Task Force, 1980; mem. Joint Task Force on Student Fin. Aid Com. and Govt. Rels., 1988-90, Com. to Study the Law Sch. Process, 1989-90, Ind. Law Sch. Com., 1989-90. Author: Contracts in a Nutshell, 1975, 3d rev. edit., 1990, Procedural Guide for the Evaluation and Accreditation of Court Facilities, 1977, (with others) The Twentieth Century and the Courthouse, 1977; contbr. articles to profl. jours., book reviewer. Mem. Sacramento-San Joaguin chpt. Muscular Dystrophy Assn. Telethon Gift com. 1980, Sierra Found. for Health (One Hundred Million Dollar Health Trust), 1987—, adv. bd. Performing Arts Fund, Sacramento Bee, 1987—, exec. com. Sacramento Area Commn. on Mather Conversion, 1989-90, law sch. admission coun., Fin. Aid Svcs. Com., 1989-90; past mem., bd. advisors Mental Health Soc. Sacramento, Better Bus. Bur., League of Women Votors; trustee Stanford Homes Found., 1980-87; bd. dirs. Sacramento Regional Foundation, 1982-87, Sutter Hosps. of Sacramento, 1978; mem. bd. advisors Coll. Public Interest Law, Pacific Legal Found., 1974—; vice chmn. Calif. Edn. Facilities Authority, 1978; chmn. Sacramento County Democratic Central Com., 1960-64; mem. Dem. State Central Com., 1960-64, 74-82; trustee Sierra Found. for Health, 1987—, Hon. Lorenzo Patino Scholarship trust, 1984; active numerous other civic coms. Named Sacramento County Young Man of Yr., 1962, Trial Judge of Yr. Calif. Trial Lawyers Assn., 1969, Humanitarian of Yr. Sacramento County Bar Assn., 1990, Sacramentan of Yr. Sacramento C. of C., 1994, Outstanding Alumnus Hastings Coll., 1994; recipient Legal Edn. and Jud. award Am. Trial Lawyers Assn., 1965, Order of Hornet Calif. State U., Sacramento, 1972, award Citizenship and Law Related Edn. Ctr., 1994, Silver Hope award Multiple Sclerosis Soc., 1994. Fellow Am. Bar Found.; mem. ABA (council sect. legal edn. and admissions to bar 1975, chmn. 1981, sec. 1982-92, adv. com. pres.-elect on competence of lawyers continuing edn. 1978, numerous other coms., Robert J. Kutak award 1991), Sacramento Bar Assn. (v.p. 1970), State Bar Calif. (mem. com. legislation 1969-89, spl. com. appellate cts. 1970-72, long range adv. planning com. 1972-89, vice chmn. com. law sch. edn. 1973, chmn. 1974, mem. commn. to study bar examination processes 1976-80, Merit Selection Com., others), Am. Judicature Soc., Order of Coif, Phi Delta Phi. Clubs: Commonwealth, Comstock, Sutter, Sacramento/Capitol, many others. Home: 937 Piedmont Dr Sacramento CA 95822-1701 Office: U Pacific McGeorge Sch Law 3200 5th Avecramento CA 95817-2705

SCHABOW, JOHN WILLIAM, accountant; b. Chgo., Mar. 30, 1937; s. William John and Mary V. (Brink) S.; m. Gail P. Ekren, Oct. 17, 1959; children: Robin, John R. Student, Davis Elkins Coll., 1955-58, Ariz. State U., 1972-74. Accredited tax advisor Accreditation Coun. for Accountancy & Taxation. Cost clk. G.D. Searle, Skokie, Ill., 1958-60; acct. Sugarcreek Foods, Chgo., 1960-63, Arlington Park Rack Track, Chgo., 1963-65, G. Heiss & Assocs., Chgo., 1965-69, Murray & Murray CPA's, Phoenix, 1969-70, Wm. R. Schulz & Assocs., Phoenix, 1970-73; pres., owner John W. Schabow, Ltd., Phoenix, 1973—; registered rep. H.D. Vest Investment Securities, Inc., Phoenix, 1985—, adv. bd. dirs. Mem. editorial adv. bd. Accounting Today, 1993—. Bd. dirs. Inst. for Partially Sighted, Phoenix, 1986-87. Served with U.S. Army, 1961-62. Mem. Ariz. Soc. Practicing Accts. (pres. 1987-88, co-founder), Nat. Soc. Pub. Accts. (state dir. 1983-87, bd. govs. 1988-92, chmn. nat. affairs com. 1995—). Republican. Lutheran. Home: 4440 W Bluefield Ave Glendale AZ 85308-1613 Office: 11725 N 19th Ave Phoenix AZ 85029-3500

SCHACHT, LINDA JOAN, broadcast journalist; b. Berkeley, Calif., Sept. 11, 1944; d. Henry Mevis and Mary (Turnbull) S.; m. John Burdette Gage, May 1, 1976; children: Peter Turnbull, Katharine Burdette. BA, U. Calif., Berkeley, 1966, MJ, 1978. Reporter Sta. KQED-TV, San Francisco, 1974-76, Sta. KPIX-TV, San Francisco, 1976—; vis. faculty Grad. Sch. Journalism U. Calif., Berkeley, 1990—. Reporter Dem. conv., 1980 (Emmy award 1981), investigative article on second mortgage brokers, 1977 (Emmy award), on children as witnesses, 1984 (Calif. State Bar award 1985, ABA award 1986). Mem. Nat. Acad. TV Arts and Scis.

SCHADE, CHARLENE JOANNE, adult and early childhood education educator; b. San Bernardino, Calif., June 26, 1935; d. Clarence George Linde and Helen Anita (Sunny) Hardesty; m. William Joseph Jr., Apr. 12, 1958 (div., 1978); children: Sabrina, Eric, Camela, Cynthia; m. Thomas Byron Killens, Sept. 25, 1983. BS, UCLA, 1959. Tchr. dance & pe L.A. Unified Secondary Schs., Calif., 1959-63; dir., instr. (Kindergym) La Jolla YMCA, Calif., 1972-76; instr. older adult San Diego Community Colls., 1977—; artist in residence Wolf Trap/Headstart, 1984-85; workshop leader S.W. Dance, Movement and Acro-Sports Workshop, prime-time adult activities coord., 1988—, Am. Heart Assn., Arthritis Found., Am. Lung Assn., AAHPERD (S.W. dist.), Calif. Assn. Health, Phys. Edn., Recreation and Dance, Head Start, San Diego Assn. Young Children, Calif. Assn. Edn. Young Child, Calif. Kindergarten Assn., Assn. Childhood Edn. Internat., IDEA Internat. Assn. Fitness Profls., San Diego C.C., Am. Soc. on Aging, 1977—; cons. to Calif. Gov.'s Coun. on Phys. Fitness, 1993; feature guest Sta. KFMB and KPBS TV shows, San Diego, 1980-88. Author: Move With Me From A to Z, 1982, Move With Me, One, Two, Three, 1988; co-author: Prime Time Aerobics, 1982, Muevete Conmigo, uno, dos, tres, 1990; co-writer: Guide for Physical Fitness Instructors of Older Adults, Grant Project, 1990, The Empowering Teacher, 1990, Handbook for Instructors of Older Adults, 1994. Dir. We Care Found., San Diego, 1977-79, Meet the Author programs San Diego County Schs., 1988—; founder SOLO, San Diego, 1981-83; adminstr., v.p. ODEM chpt. Toastmasters, San Diego, 1982; chmn. People with Arthritis Can Exercise com. San Diego chpt. Arthritis Found., 1994-95; trainer PACE instrs. Nat. Arthritis Found., 1995—. Grantee Video Showcase of Exercises for Older Adults, 1992-93. Mem. AAPHERD (workshop leader), Calif. Assn. Health, Phys. Edn., Recreation and Dance (workshop leader). Office: Exer Fun/Prime Time Aerobic 3089C Clairemont Dr Ste 130 San Diego CA 92117-6802

SCHAEFER, DAN L., congressman; b. Gutenberg, Iowa, Jan. 25, 1936; s. Alvin L. and Evelyn (Everson) S.; m. Mary Margaret Lenney, 1959; children: Danny, Darren, Joel, Jennifer. B.A., Niagara U., 1961, LLD (hon.), 1986; postgrad., Potsdam State U., 1961-64. Pub. relations cons., 1967-83; mem. Colo. Gen. Assembly, 1977-78; mem. Colo. Senate, 1979-83, pres. pro tem, 1981-82, majority whip, 1983; mem. 98th-103rd Congresses from 6th dist. Colo., Washington, 1983—; mem. house small bus. com., 1983, govt. ops. com., 1983, energy and commerce com., 1984-86 (subcom. on fossil and synthetic fuels; commerce, transp. and tourism; oversight/investigations), environ. and energy study com., 1987— (subcoms. on Transp. and Hazardous materials, Telecom. and Fin.), Energy and Commerce ranking Rep Oversight and Investigations, 1993—, Rep. study com.; mem. house sci. and high tech. task force, mil. reforms caucus, congl. grace caucus; mem. adv. com., com. of concern for Soviet Jewry; mem. exec. bd. Environ. and Energy Study Conf., 1995; chmn. Subcom. on Energy and Power House Commerce Com.; mem. Subcom. on Telecom. in Fin., House Vet. Affairs Com., Subcom. on Edn., Training, Employment and Housing. Pres. Foothills Recreation Bd., 1973-76; sec. Jefferson County Republican Party, Colo., 1975-76. Served with USMCR, 1955-57. Recipient Colo. Park and Recreation citation, 1976; named Elected Ofcl. of Yr., Lakewood/South Jeffco C. of C., 1986, 88, 90, Leadership award U.S. Congl. Adv. Bd., Am. Security Coun. Found.; Taxpayers Friend award Nat. Taxpayer's Union,

1985-86, 88, 90, 91, 92, Golden Bulldog award Watchdog of Treasury, 1985-86, 86-87, 87-88, 88-89, 89-90, 91-92. Mem. C. of C., Beta Theta Pi. Roman Catholic. Lodge: Rotary. Office: House of Representatives 2353 Rayburn House Office B Washington DC 20515*

SCHAEFER, GEORGE LOUIS, theatrical producer and director, educator; b. Wallingford, Conn., Dec. 16, 1920; s. Louis and Elsie (Otterbein) S.; m. Mildred Trares, Feb. 5, 1954. BA magna cum laude, Lafayette Coll., 1941, LittD, 1963; postgrad., Yale Drama Sch., 1942; LHD, Coker Coll., 1973. Producer, dir. TV series Hallmark Hall of Fame, 1955-68; freelance producer, dir., 1945—; assoc. dean sch. theater, film and TV UCLA, 1986-91; artistic dir. N.Y.C. Ctr. Theatre Co., 1949-52; dir. Dallas State Fair Musicals, 1952-58; pres. Compass Prodns., Inc., 1959-86. Dir. Broadway prodns. G.I. Hamlet, 1945, Man and Superman, 1947, The Linden Tree, 1948, The Heiress (revival), 1949, Idiot's Delight (revival), 1950, Southwest Corner, 1955, The Apple Cart, 1956, The Body Beautiful, 1958, Write Me a Murder, 1961, The Great Indoors, 1966, The Last of Mrs. Lincoln, 1972, Mixed Couples, 1980; co-producer Broadway and London prodns. The Teahouse of the August Moon, 1953; dir., co-producer Zenda for Los Angeles Civic Light Opera Co., 1963; producer To Broadway with Love for N.Y. World's Fair, 1964; producer, dir. TV spls. Do Not Go Gentle into That Good Night, 1967, A War of Children, Sandburg's Lincoln, 1974-76, In This House of Brede, 1975, Truman at Potsdam, Amelia Earhart, 1976, Our Town, 1977, First You Cry, Orchard Children, 1978, Blind Ambition, Mayflower, 1979, The Bunker, 1981, Jean Harris Trial, 1982, A Piano for Mrs. Cimino, 1982, Deadly Game, 1983, Answers, 1983, Right of Way, 1983, Children in the Crossfire, 1984, Stone Pillow, 1985, Mrs. Delafield Wants to Marry , 1986, Laura Lansing Slept Here, 1988, Let Me Hear You Whisper, 1990, The Man Upstairs, 1992; dir. films An Enemy of the People, Generation, Doctor's Wives, Pendulum, Macbeth; dir. Los Angeles prodn. Leave It To Jane, 1987. Mem. Nat. Council on the Arts, 1983-88. Recipient Emmy awards, 1959, 60, 61, 68, 73, Dirs. Guild Am. TV awards, 1961, 64, 67, 68, Dinneen award Nat. Cath. Theatre Conf., 1964; named Dir. of Yr., Radio-TV Daily, 1957, 60, 63, 65; Am. Theatre fellow, 1995. Mem. Dirs. Guild Am. (v.p. 1961-79, pres. 1979-81), Phi Beta Kappa.

SCHAEFER, HARRY GEORGE, utilities company executive; b. Calgary, Alta., Can., Oct. 18, 1936. B.S. in Commerce, U. Alta., Can., 1957. Chartered accountant Can., 1959. Sr. auditor Riddell Stead Graham & Hutchison, Montreal, Que., Can., 1957-61; lectr. acctg. Sir George Williams U., Can., 1961-63; asst. controller TransAlta Utilities Corp. (formerly Calgary Power Ltd.), Alta., Can., 1963-70, dir. fin., 1970-73, treas., dir. fin., 1973-75, v.p. fin., chief fin. officer, 1975-80, sr. v.p. fin., 1980-81; sr. v.p. fin. and corp. planning TransAlta Utilities Corp. (formerly Calgary Power Ltd.), Calgary, Alta., Can., 1981; pres., dir. TransAlta Resources Corp., Calgary, Alta., Can., 1981—, vice chmn. bd., chief fin. officer, dir., 1985-89, chmn., chief fin. officer, 1989, 1990—; v.p. fin., dir. AEC Power Ltd.; bd. dirs. Can. N.W. Energy Ltd., Keyword Office Tech. Ltd., TransCan. Pipelines Ltd., Sun Life Trust, Telus Corp., Microelectronics Centre. Mem. bus. adv. council U. Alta.; bd. dirs. Can. Energy Rsch. Inst.; past. bd. dirs. Alta. Children's Prov. Gen. Hosp. Mem. Can. Inst. Chartered Accountants, Can. Elec. Assn. (acctg. and fin. sect.), Fin. Execs. Inst. (past pres. Calgary chpt., past chmn. Can.), Northwest Electric Light and Power Assn., Alberta Inst. Chartered Accts. Clubs: Ranchmen's, Winter (Calgary). Avocations: badminton; squash; tennis. Office: TransAlta Utilities Corp, 110-12th Ave SW Box 1900, Calgary, AB Canada T2P 2M1

SCHAEFER, JAMES BRUCE, insurance company executive; b. Chgo., Jan. 19, 1954; s. Edward N. and Kathleen A. (Dahlin) S.; m. Laurie A. Biggins; children: James Bruce II, Nicholas Edward. AA, Rio Hondo Coll., 1980; BA, Calif. State U., 1982; MBA, Pepperdine U., 1993. Acct. exec. John Hancock Mutual Ins., L.A., 1982-86; cons. Fred S. James, Irvine, Calif., 1986-88; asst. v.p. Johnson & Higgins, Costa Mesa, Calif., 1988-91; regional mgr. Mutual of Omaha, Orange, Calif., 1991—. Bd. dirs. Christian Children's Fund, 1991—. Mem. Nat. Skeet Shooting Assn., Indsl. League Orange County, Orange County Benefits Coun., San Diego Benefits Coun. Republican. Roman Catholic. Home: 4741 Elder Ave Seal Beach CA 90740-3002

SCHAEFER, (ALBERT) RUSSELL, physicist; b. Oklahoma City, Oct. 13, 1944; s. Albert R. and Marcella (Russell) S.; m. Judith Ann Bracewell, Jan. 19, 1968; children: Amy M., Brandon M. BS in Physics, U. Okla., 1966, PhD in Atomic and Molecular Physics, 1970. Physicist Nat. Bur. Standards, Washington, 1970-86; chief scientist Western Rsch. Corp., San Diego, 1986-87; sr. scientist Sci. Applications Internat. Corp., San Diego, 1987—; adj. prof. physics Montgomery Coll., Rockville, Md., 1974-86; presenter in field. Contbr. articles to profl. jours. Co-founder, bd. dirs. Greater Laytonville (Md.) Civic Assn., 1975. Recipient Bronze medal U.S. Dept. Commerce, 1981; NSF fellow, 1966-70. Mem. Soc. Photo-Optical Instrumentation Engrs., Optical Soc. Am. (teller com. 1976), Phi Beta Kappa, Sigma Xi. Methodist. Office: Sci Application Internat 4161 Campus Point Ct San Diego CA 92121-1513

SCHAEFER, SAUL, cardiologist; b. Tel Aviv, Israel, Dec. 6, 1947; came to U.S., 1952; s. Rudi and Gertrude S.; m. Sylvia Lopez, July 14, 1985; children: Jonathan, Adam. B of Engring., The Cooper Union, 1968; postgrad., U. So. Calif., 1968-69, UCLA, 1970-76; MD, U. Calif., Davis, 1981. Diplomate Am. Bd. Internal Medicine, Am. Bd. Internal Medicine (Cardiovascular Disease), Nat. Bd. Med. Examiners; lic. MD, Calif.; profl. cert. in bioengring.; Calif. State teaching credential. Tchr. secondary level L.A. Unified Sch. Dist., 1970-76; residency internal medicine U. Calif., San Francisco, 1981-84; fellow cardiology U. Tex. Southwestern Med. Ctr., Dallas, 1984-87; asst. dir. echocardiography VA Med. Ctr., San Francisco, 1987-90; asst. prof. medicine and radiology in residence U. Calif., San Francisco, 1987-91; dir. interventional cardiology VA Med. Ctr., San Francisco, 1990-91; dir. interventional cardiology U. Calif., Davis, 1991-94, assoc. prof. medicine, 1991—. Contbr. numerous articles to profl. jours. and chpts. to books. Recipient N.Y. State Regents scholarship, 1964, Mosby Scholarship award, 1981, Award for Excellence in Diagnostic Radiology, 1981, NIH Clin. Investigator award, 1987, Am. Heart Assn., Calif. Affiliate, Grant-in-Aid, 1988, 90, 93, Hibbard E. Williams Rsch. award, 1992, Deans grant U. Calif. Davis, 1993, Best Doctors in Am. award, 1994. Fellow Am. Coll. Cardiology; mem. Am. Coll. Cardiology, Am. Fedn. Clin. Rsch., Soc. Magnetic Resonance in Medicine, Am. Soc. Echocardiography, Am. Hearts Assn. Office: U Calif Cardiovascular Medicine TB 172 Bioletti Way Davis CA 95616

SCHAEFER, WILLIAM DAVID, English language educator; b. Dighton, Mass., May 11, 1928; s. Louis and Elsie K. (Otterbein) S.; m. Josephine R. Lamprecht, Aug. 8, 1958; 1 dau., Kimberly. B.A., NYU, 1957; M.S., U. Wis., 1958, Ph.D., 1962. Mem. faculty UCLA, 1962-90, prof. English, 1970-90, chmn. dept., 1969-71, exec. vice chancellor, 1978-87. Author: James (BV) Thomson: Beyond the City, 1965, Speedy Extinction of Evil and Misery, 1967, Education Without Compromise: From Chaos to Coherence in Higher Education, 1990; contbr. articles to profl. jours., short stories to literary mags. Served with AUS, 1954-56. Fulbright fellow Eng., 1961-62. Mem. MLA (exec. dir. 1971-78). Home: 164 Stagecoach Rd Bell Canyon CA 91307-1044 Office: UCLA 405 Hilgard Ave Los Angeles CA 90024-1301

SCHAEFFER, COLLEEN DIANE, English language educator; b. Culver City, Calif., Apr. 29, 1956; d. James William and Pamela Lorraine (Lacey) Johnson; m. Douglas Arthur Schaeffer, Aug. 27, 1977. BA in English summa cum laude, Calif. State U., Northridge, 1990, MA in English with distinction, 1993. Acting br. mgr. U.S. Life Savs. and Loan, San Fernando, Calif., 1980-81; tech. writer Great Western Bank, Northridge, 1990; tchg. assoc. Calif. State U., Northridge, 1991-93, English instr., 1993-94; English instr. Antelope Valley Coll., Lancaster, Calif., 1993—; tutor, cons., Panorama City, Calif., 1991—; copy editor, Panorama City, 1991—; guest lectr. composition com. Calif. State U., Northridge, 1992, 93; guest speaker, organizer grad. studies Calif. State U./Sigma Tau Delta, 1991, 92, 93. Author: Pragmatic Sequencing: A Case Study, 1993; editor, author Verbatim newsletter, 1991-92; assoc. editor periodical New Voices, 1994—; speaker, presenter in field. Mem. Greenpeace, 1984—. Recipient Cert. of Merit, Sigma Tau Delta, 1993. Mem. MLA, Nat. Coun. Tchrs. and Educators, Conf. of Composition and Comm. Democrat. Office: Calif State Univ 18111 Nordhoff St Northridge CA 91330-0001

SCHAEFFER, REINER HORST, air force officer, retired librarian, foreign language professional; b. Berlin, Lichterfelde, Fed. Republic Germany, Jan. 13, 1938; came to U.S., 1958; s. Immanuel Emil and Wilhelmine (Fahrni) Frei-S.; m. Cathy Anne Cormack, Apr. 6, 1966; 1 child, Brian Reiner. Nat. Cert., Bus. Sch., Thun, Switzerland, 1957; B.G.S. in Bus., U. Nebr., 1970; M.P.A. in Orgnl. Behavior, U. Mo., 1972; Ph.D. in Fgn. Lang. Edn., Ohio State U., 1979. Commd. officer USAF, 1958, advanced through grades to lt. col.; instr. German, French USAF Acad., Colorado Springs, Colo., 1975-77, assoc. prof., 1979-81, chmn. German, 1981, dir. librs., 1982-86, prof., 1986-92, dir. Acad. Librs., 1986—. Mem. People to People, Colorado Springs; bd. dirs. Friends of AF Acad. Librs. Named Disting. Grad. Air Force Inst. Tech, Wright-Patterson AFB, Ohio, 1979; recipient 5 Meritorious Service medals, 5 Air Force Commendation medals. Mem. Am. Assn. Tchrs. of German, Swiss Club (pres. Colorado Springs chpt. 1990—, chmn. Lewis Palmer High Sch. accountability com.), Pi Alpha Alpha, Alpha Sigma Alpha. Republican. Home: 515 Celtic Ct Colorado Springs CO 80921-1807 Office: Fgn Lang Ctr LLC 315 E Willamette Ave Colorado Springs CO 80903-1115

SCHAFER, GERALD LEWIS, librarian; b. El Paso, Tex., Apr. 20, 1949; s. Norman Oscar and Clarice S. BA, U. Tex., El Paso, 1971; MLS, U. Denver, 1973. Info. specialist Denver Rsch. Inst., 1973-75; area mgr. Denver Pub. Libr., 1975-80; dir. profl. communications Skidmore, Owings & Merrill, Denver, 1981-84; coord. collection devel. svcs. Auraria Libr., Denver, 1984—. Editor: Master Plan-U.S. Air Force Academy, 1984. Chair collections task force Colo. State Libr., Denver, 1993-94. Mem. ALA, Colo. Libr. Assn. Home: 2054 Clarkson St Denver CO 80205-5117 Office: Auraria Libr Lawrence At 11th St Denver CO 80204

SCHAFFER, JEFFREY LEE, nonprofit organization executive; b. L.A., Oct. 28, 1958; s. Mervin Bernard and Zena Harriet (Lindsay) S.; m. Reina Maria Alonso, Sept. 9, 1989, children: Philip Santos, Jacob José. BA, U. Calif., Berkeley, 1980; MPA, U. So. Calif., 1987. Field rep. Office Congressman A.C. Beilenson, Washington, L.A., 1980-82; mcpl. devel. advisor Peace Corps, Kosrae, Ea. Caroline Islands, 1982-84; staff asst. CARE, Washington, 1985; rsch. asst. Office Treasurer, State of Calif., Sacramento, 1986; account exec. Braun & Co., L.A., 1986-89; assoc. dir. Shelter Partnership, L.A., 1989—. Editor Homeless Reporter newsletter, 1989-90; exec. prodr. video Neighbors in Need, 1990. Group leader Operation Crossroads Africa, Kithumula Kenya, 1986; bd. dirs. Friends of Coro, L.A., 1990-91, Los Angeles Countywide Coalition for Homeless, L.A., 1991-93; pres., bd. dirs. Peace Corps Svc. Coun., L.A., 1990-91; mem. met. bd. Jewish Fedn. Coun., L.A., 1990-92; active New Leaders Project, L.A., 1992; chmn. Ams. with Disabilities Act com. L.A. Emergency Food and Shelter Local Bd., 1992—; sec. Asian Pacific Islander Planning Coun., San Fernando Valley; trainer Kellogg Tng. Ctr., 1994—. Mem. U. Calif. Alumni Assn., UCLA Internship Assn., Friends of Micronesia, Sigma Delta Pi (life). Democrat. Office: Shelter Partnership 523 W 6th St Ste 616 Los Angeles CA 90014

SCHAFFER, JOEL LANCE, dentist; b. Bklyn., Oct. 18, 1945; s. Martin Alter and Irene Natalie (Shore) S.; m. Susan Anne Swearingen, Feb. 14, 1980 (div.); 1 child, Jericho Katherine. BS, L.I. U., 1967; DDS, Howard U., 1971. Dental intern Eastman Dental Ctr., Rochester, N.Y., 1971-72; gen. practice dentistry, Boulder, Colo., 1973—; evaluator Clin. Rsch. Assocs.; lectr. in field, 1972—. Contbr. articles to dental jours; patentee in field. Advisor Boulder Meals on Wheels; mem. Boulder County Com. for Persons with Disabilities. Named outstanding clinician Boulder County Dental Forum, 1979. Mem. ADA, Am. Acad. Oral Implantology, Boulder County Dental Soc., Am. Soc. Dental Aesthetics, Tau Epsilon Phi, Alpha Omega. Jewish. Home: 4171 S Hampton Cir Boulder CO 80301-1793 Office: 2880 Folsom St Boulder CO 80304-3739

SCHAFFER, ROBERT WARREN, state senator; b. Cin., July 24, 1962; s. Robert James and Florence Ann (Bednar) S.; m. Maureen Elizabeth Menke, Feb. 8, 1986; children: Jennifer, Emily, Justin. BA in Polit. Sci., U. Dayton, 1984. Legis. asst. State of Ohio, Columbus, 1985; majority adminstrv. asst. Colo. Senate, Denver, 1985-87; Colo. senator representing Dist. 14 Ft. Collins, 1987—; chmn. state affairs com., 1995—; commr. Colo. Advanced Tech. Inst., 1988—; proprietor No. Front Range Mktg. and Distbn., Inc. Mem. Mental Health Bd. Larimer County, 1986-87, Bus. Affairs, Edn., Nat. Conf. State Legislatures Com. on Econ Devel. Commerce; campaign co-chair Arnold for Lt. Gov., Larimer and Weld Counties, 1986; head coach Ft. Collins Youth Baseball, 1986—; chmn. Senate Fin. Com.; Republican candidate for lt. gov., 1994. Mem. Colo. Press Assn., Colo. Press Club, Jaycees (Mover and Shaker award, 1989), KC. Republican. Roman Catholic. Home: 3284 Silverthorne Dr Fort Collins CO 80526-2766 Office: The State Senate State Capitol Denver CO 80203

SCHAFFER, THOMAS RAY, waste management executive; b. Inglewood, Calif., Apr. 7, 1955; s. Charles T. and Marilyn L. (Yost) S.; m. Lynitta M. Gerbert, Oct. 12, 1982; 1 child, Christopher. BS, UCLA, 1977; MS, Loyola Marymount, 1980. Registered profl. civil engineer, Calif., Ariz. Water resource control engineer Calif. Regional Water Quality Control, L.A., 1977-80; sr. environ. engr. Jacobs Engring., Pasadena, Calif., 1980-84, Lee and Ro Consulting Engrs., Pasadena, 1984; sr. civil engr. County Sanitation Dists. L.A. County, Whittier, Calif., 1984-90; wastewater mgr. City of Sedona, Ariz., 1990-94; constrn. mgr., engr. Town of Silverthorne, Colo., 1995—. Fellow U.S. Govt., 1978. Mem. LWV, Water Environ. Fedn., Ariz. Water Pollution Control Assn. Home: 226 Sunlight Dr Dillon CO 80435 Office: Town of Silverthorne PO Box 1309 Silverthorne CO 80498

SCHAFFNER, IRVING, physician, researcher; b. Chgo., Sept. 10, 1930; s. Samuel and Mary (Kanter) S.; m. Charlotte Elaine Schaffner, June 24, 1951; children: Daniel, Rivka, John. BS in Biochem., Roosevelt U., 1951; MD, The Chgo. Med. Sch., 1956; D of Oriental Medicine (hon.), Union U., 1985. Pres. Thousand Oaks (Calif.) Med. Group, 1958—; founder, Conejo Valley Community Hosp., Thousand Oaks, 1964; pres. Interfaith Crusade for World Health Found., Thousand Oaks, 1991—; assoc. prof. Drew Postgrad. Med. Sch., L.A., 1982-92; clin. asst. ptof. family medicine Coll. Osteopathic Medicine of the Pacific, Pomona, Calif., 1992—; pres. Angola-Am. Found., Thousand Oak, 1990—, bd. dirs.; med. dir. Grumman Aerospace West, Pt. Aueneme, Calif., 1977-92; dir. Med. Bd. Calif. Physicians Assts., 1980-92; med. cons. Semtech Corp., North American Rockwell, Burroughs Corp., So. Calif. Gas, So. Calif. Edison; med. rschr. Phillips Pharm.; bd. dirs. Hollywood Film Sch., Westlake Village, Calif.; med. editor Thousand Oaks Broadcasting Co., former owner 1965-70; owner semi-pro football club; advisor Kisekka Found. Hosp., Uganda; v.p. Alpha Pharmaceuticals; med. advisor, bd. dirs. Uganda Missions. Inventor ozone device for med. sterilization. Bd. dirs. Hemophilia Found. So. Calif., 1951-83, Conejo Valley Art Mus., Thousand Oaks, 1988—. Hon. rsch. fellow, Chgo. Med. Sch. 1952-56; recipient Outstanding Citizens award City of Thousand Oaks, 1991, Man of Action award Conejo Valley Times Newspaper, Achievement award Am. Cancer Soc., Laymans award Kiwanis, Thousand Oaks. Mem. FAA (sr. examiner), Calif. Med. Assn., Ventura County Med. Soc., Conejo Valley C. of C. (bd. dirs. 1980), Phi Beta Kappa. Republican. Home: 705 Warrendale Simi Valley CA 93065 Office: Thousand Oaks Med Group 246 Lombard St Thousand Oaks CA 91360-5806

SCHALLER, JOANNE FRANCES, nursing consultant; b. Columbus, Ga., July 15, 1943; d. John Frank and Ethel Beatrice (Spring) Lanzendorfer; m. Robert Thomas Schaller, Jan. 22, 1977; 1 child, Amy. BS, Pacific Luth. U., 1969; M in Nursing, U. Wash., 1971. House supr. UCLA Hosp., 1971-72; outpatient supr. Harborview Hosp., Seattle, 1973-75; outpatient clinic and emergency room supr. U. Wash. Hosp., Seattle, 1975-77; co-author, researcher with Robert Schaller MD Seattle, 1977-87; prin. Nursing Expert-Standards of Care, Seattle, 1987—; cons. Wash. State Trial Lawyers, Wash. Assn. Criminal Def. Lawyers, 1989—; founder, CEO Present Perfect, Seattle, 1991—. Contbr., editor articles to profl. jours. Bd. dirs. Pacific Arts Ctr., 1992—; vol. guardian ad litem King County Juvenile Ct., 1978—; vol. Make a Wish Found. U.S. Bank, 1984—, Multiple Sclerosis Assn., 1986—, Am. Heart Assn., 1986—, Internat. Children's Festival, 1987—, Seattle Children's Festival, 1987—, Seattle Dept. Parks and Recreation Open Space Com., 1990—, Pacific N.W. Athletic Congress, 1991—, Wash. Fed. Garden Clubs Jr. Advisor, 1992—, Fred Hutchison Cancer Rsch. Ctr., 1993—; mem. parent coun. Seattle Country Day Sch., 1986—; mem. Photo Coun. Seattle Art Mus., 1986—, Native Am. Coun., 1989—; mem. N.W. coun. Seattle Mus., 1992—, mem. NAOO Coun., 1989—, Plestcheeff Inst. Decorative Arts, 1992—; mem. fundraiser Children's Hosp. Med. Ctr., 1977—, Breast Cancer Fund, 1994—, Susan G. Komen Breast Cancer Found., 1994—. Named 1st Migrant Health Care Nurse, State of Wash., 1969, 1st Am. nurse visiting China, 1974. Mem. AAUW, ANA, Wash. State Nurses Assn., U. Wash. Alumni Assn. Home and Office: 914 Randolph Ave Seattle WA 98122-5267

SCHANDER, MARY LEA, police official; b. Bakersfield, Calif., June 11, 1947; d. Gerald John Lea and Marian Lea Coffman; B.A. (Augustana fellow) Calif. Luth. Coll., 1969; M.A., U. Calif., Los Angeles, 1970; m. Edwin Schander, July 3, 1971. Staff aide City of Anaheim (Calif.) Police Dept., 1970-72, staff asst., 1972-78, sr. staff asst., 1978-80; with Resource Mgmt. Dept., City of Anaheim, 1980-82; asst. to dir. Pub. Safety Agy., City of Pasadena Police Dept., 1982-85, spl. asst. to police chief, 1985-88, adminstrv. comdr., 1988-92, police comdr., 1992—; freelance musician; publisher Australian Traditional Songs, 1985, Songs in the Air of Early California, 1994; lectr. Calif. Luth. Coll.; cons. City of Lodz, Poland, Internat. Assn. Chiefs of Police; assessor Nat. Commn. on Accreditation for Law Enforcement Agencies; speaker, panelist League of Calif. Cities, Pasadena Commn. on Status of Women; mcpl. mgmt. asst. CLEARS. Producer (cable TV program) Traditional Music Showcase. Contbr. articles in field to profl. jours. Bd. dirs. Women At Work, Pasadena Pops Orch. Recipient Women at Work Medal of Excellence, 1988. Mem. Nat. Womens Political Caucus, Nat. Ctr. for Women in Policing, Pasadena Arts Coun., L.A. County Peace Officers, Internat. Assn. Chiefs of Police. Home: PO Box 50151 Pasadena CA 91115-0151 Office: Pasadena Police Dept 207 N Garfield Ave Pasadena CA 91101-1748

SCHAPIRA, MOREY RAEL, electronics sales executive; b. Chgo., Jan. 4, 1949; s. Julius and Rose (Schwartz) S; m. Barbara Stein, May 29, 1977; children: Rachel, Deborah, Michael. BS in Physics cum laude, Case Western Res. U., 1970; MBA, Harvard U., 1977. Rsch. scientist rsch. div. Raytheon Co., Waltham, Mass., 1970-75; cons. scientist Lincoln Labs., MIT, Lexington, 1976; product mktg. engr. microwave semicondr. div. Hewlett Packard Co., San Jose, Calif., 1977-80; domestic sales mgr. optoelectronics div. Hewlett Packard Co., Palo Alto, Calif., 1980-81, distbr. mktg. mgr. optoelectronics div., 1981-83; corp. distbn. mgr. Hewlett Packard Components, San Jose, Calif., 1983-85; nat. distbr., sales mgr. Micro Power Systems, Santa Clara, Calif., 1985-87; nat. sales mgr. Network Gen. Corp., Menlo Park, Calif., 1987-89, v.p. worldwide sales, 1989-90, gen. mgr. Asia/Ams. sales, 1991-93; v.p. mktg. Digital Link Corp., Sunnyvale, Calif., 1993—. Editor-in-chief, then pub. A Guide to Jewish Boston, 1974-77; pub., editor-in-chief HarBus News, 1976-77. gen. mgr. network gen. Asia, Ams. Div. chmn. United Way Campaign., 1978; nat. v.p. Union of Councils for Soviet Jews, 1979-84, nat. pres., 1984-86; pres. Bay Area Council on Soviet Jewry, San Francisco, 1980-84. Mem. Am. Mgmt. Assn., No. Calif. Venture Capital Assn., Harvard Bus. Sch. Assn. No. Calif., Am. Phys. Soc., Churchill Club. Home: 1154 Crespi Dr Sunnyvale CA 94086-7039 Office: Digital Link Corp 217 Humboldt Ct Sunnyvale CA 94089-1300

SCHAPP, REBECCA MARIA, museum director; b. Stuttgart, Fed. Republic Germany, Dec. 12, 1956; came to U.S., 1957; d. Randall Todd and Elfriede Carolina (Scheppan) Spradlin; m. Thomas James Schapp, May 29, 1979. AA, DeAnza Coll., 1977; BA in Art, San Jose State U., 1979, MA in Art Adminstrn., 1985. Adminstrv. dir. Union Gallery, San Jose, Calif., 1979-82; mus. coordinator de Saisset Mus. Santa Clara (Calif.) U., 1982-86, asst. dir., 1984, acting dir., 1986-87, asst. dir., 1987-89, dep. dir., 1989-92, dir., 1993—. Mem. San Francisco Mus. Modern Art; bd. dirs. Works of San Jose, v.p. 1983-85. Mem. Non-Profit Gallery Assn. (bd. dirs.). Democrat. Office: De Saisset Museum Santa Clara Univ 500 El Camino Real Santa Clara CA 95050-4345

SCHARF, BARRY W., artist. BFA, East Carolina U., 1973; MFA, Otis Art Inst., L.A., 1975; postgrad., Advt. Ctr. Painter, sculptor, represented by Nikai Gallery, B.C., Can., Waterworks, Friday Harbor, Wash., Ron Segal Gallery, Seattle; creative dir. Water Forest Design, Inc., Redmond, Wash., 1995—; art instr. Citurs Coll., Azusa, Calif., 1978, Studio 2034, 1984-93; founding dir. L.A. Contemporary Exhbns., 1977; evaluator King County Arts Commn, Wash., 1995. Solo shows include Ivey Gallery, L.A., Linda's on Melrose Ave., L.A., Baker Gallery, Mission Viejo, Calif., The Greenpeace Gallery, L.A., Ron Segal Gallery, Seattle, 1994; exhibited in group shows Mus. Sci. and Industry, L.A., The Experience Ctr. Gallery, Costa Mesa, Calif., DOR Gallery, Venice, Calif., L.A. Mcpl. Art Gallery, Ojai (Calif.) Arts Ctr.; represented in collections at East Carolina U., Robert Fox Enterprises, Netherlands Bank of Calif., others; subject of articles. Mem. Coll. Art Assn., Internat. Sculpture Ctr., Soc. Illustrators, Graphic Artists Guild, North Western Sculptors Assn. Address: 2810 233d Pl NE Redmond WA 98053

SCHARF, ROBERT LEE, lawyer; b. Chgo., May 13, 1920; s. Charles A. and Ethel Virginia (McNabb) S.; m. Jacqueline B. Scharf, Nov. 2, 1940; children: Bonnie Scharf Heald, Mary Ellen Pinero, Robert L. Jr. JD, Loyola U., 1948. Bar: Ill. 1949, Calif. 1972; lifetime teaching credential Calif. Community Colls. With FBI, 1940-73; dep. city atty. City of L.A., 1973-84; atty. Mitsui Mfrs. Bank, L.A., 1984-85; 2d lt. U.S. Army, 1944-46. Mem. L.A. County Bar Assn., San Fernando Valley Bar Assn., Soc. Former FBI Agts. Office: PO Box 260123 Encino CA 91426-0123

SCHATT, PAUL, newspaper editor; b. N.Y.C., Aug. 31, 1945; divorced; children: Suzannah, Andrew. BA with distinction Polit. Sci., English, Ariz. State U., 1967. Editor Ariz. Republic, 1964-66, reporter, 1965-74, urban affairs editor, 1974-75, asst. city editor, 1975-79, chief asst. city editor, 1979-82, asst. met. editor, 1985-86, met. editor, 1986-88, editor edit. pages, 1993—; asst. editor Ariz. Mag., 1981-82, editor, 1982-85; editor edit. pages Phoenix Gazette, 1988-93, The Ariz. Republic, 1993—; vis. lectr. Pub. Affairs Journalism, Ariz. State U., 1976—, instr. Mass. Comm. Dept., 1974-76; dir. Eugene C. Pulliam Fellowship. Phoenix program, 1990—; writing coach, 1989; del. Pre White House Conf. Librs., 1991. v.p. Crisis Nursery, 1984-87, bd. dirs. 1980-87; exec. bd. Hospice of the Valley, 1980-87; pres. Friends of Phoenix Pub. Libr., 1985-86, bd. dirs. 1986—; bd. trustees 1st Amendment Congress, 1989—; bd. dirs. Camelback Hosps. 1982-89, chmn. bd. dirs. 1986-87, Cactus Pine Coun. Girl Scouts Am., 1988-89, Sun Sounds Inc., 1982-89, Valley Leadership Inc., 1991—, alum. assn., 1985-89, Ariz. Zool. Soc., 1991—, Barrow Neurol. Found., 1991—, Kids Voting, 1991-93, Barry Goldwater Inst., 1991-93, Ariz. Club, 1991—. With Ariz. Nat. Guard, 1966-79. Recipient Montgomery award Outstanding Svc. to Community Friends of Phoenix Pub. Libr., 1989; profl. Journalism fellow Stanford U., 1970-71. Mem. Am. Soc. Newspaper Editors, Soc. Profl. Journalists (pres. Valley of Sun chpt. 1974-75, 83-84, exec. bd. 1988-92), Sigma Delta Chi (co-chair nat. convention 1974). Office: The Ariz Republic Editorial Dept 120 E Van Buren St Phoenix AZ 85004-2227

SCHATZ, HOWARD, ophthalmologist; b. Chgo.; s. Lawrence and Beatrice Schatz; m. Beverly Ornstein; children: Jacqueline, Jessica. MD, U. Ill., Chgo. Diplomate Am. Bd. Ophthalmology, Nat. Bd. Med. Examiners. Intern Cook County Hosp., Chgo.; resident ophthalmology Ill. Eye and Ear Infirmary, U. Ill., Chgo.; fellowship med. retina Wilmer Eye Inst., Johns Hopkins U. Sch. Medicine, Balt., fellowship surg. retina; dir., staff mem. Retina Rsch. Fund, St. Mary's Hosp. and Med. Ctr., San Francisco; clin. prof. ophthalmology U. Calif., San Francisco; presenter and lectr. in field. Editor: Retina-Am. Jour. Retinal and Vitreal Diseases, (with others) Laser Photocoagulation of Retinal Disease, 1988; author: Fundus Fluorescein Angiography: A Composite Slide Collection, 1975, 2d edit., 1976, (with T.C. Burton, L.A. Yannuzzi, M.F. Rabb) Intrepretation of Fundus Fluorescein Angiography, 1978, (with L.A. Yannuzzi, K.A. Gitter) The Macula, 1979, Laser Treatment of Fundus Disease: A Comprehensive Text and Composite Slide Collection, 1980, Essential Fluorescein Angiography: A Compendium of 100 Classic Cases, 1983, California Resource Directory for the Blind and Visually Impaired, 1991; contbr. articles to jours. With USAF, 1969-71. Recipient Honor award Am. Acad. Ophthalmology and Otolaryngology, 1977, Arlo A. Morrison Lectr. award Calif. Assn. Ophthalmology, 1988, Second Annual Vallotton Lectr. award Med. U. S.C., Charleston, 1990, Paul Chandler Professorship Lectr. award Harvard Med. Sch., Boston, 1991; USPHS grantee Nat. Inst. Neurol. Diseases and Blindness, 1968, 69. Mem. AMA (Physicians Recognition awards 1974, 81, 84, 88, Dr. William

Beaumont award 1981), Calif. Med. Assn., San Francisco Med. Soc., Retina Soc., Am. Macula Soc. (Paul Henkind Lectr. award 1994), Am. Fluorescein Angiography Club, Western Retina Study Club. Home: PO Box 640345 San Francisco CA 94164 Office: One Daniel Burnham Ct # 210C San Francisco CA 94109

SCHATZ, MONA CLAIRE STRUHSAKER, social worker, educator; b. Phila., Jan. 4, 1950; d. Milton and Josephine (Kivo) S.; m. James Fredrick Struhsaker, Dec. 31, 1979; 1 child, Thain Mackenzie. BA, Metro State Coll., 1976; postgrad., U. Minn., 1976; MSW, U. Denver, 1979; D in Social Work/Social Welfare, U. Pa., 1986. Teaching fellow U. Pa., Phila., 1981-82; asst. prof. S.W. Mo. State U., Springfield, 1982-85; rschr. Colo. State U., Ft. Collins, 1979—, assoc. prof., 1985—, dir. non-profit agy. adminstrn. program, field coord., 1986-88, project dir. Fostering Families and the Colo. Human Svcs. Tng. and Rsch. Inst. and Consortium, 1987—, dir. youth agy. adminstrn. program Am. Humanics, 1988-90; cons. Mgmt. and Behavioral Sci. Ctr., The Wharton Sch. U. Pa., 1981-82; resource specialist So. N.J. Health Systems Agy., 1982; adj. faculty mem. U. Mo., Springfield, 1984; med. social worker Rehab. and Vis. Nurse Assn., 1985-90; mem. Colo. Child Welfare Adv. Com., Family Preservation Initiative. Contbr. articles to profl. jours. Cons., field rep. Big Bros./Big Sisters of Am., Phila., 1979-83; acting dir., asst. dir. Big Sisters of Colo., 1971-78; owner Polit. Cons. in Colo., Denver, 1978-79; active Food Co-op, Ft. Collins, Foster Parent, Denver, Capital Hill United Neighbors, Adams County (Denver) Social Planning Coun., Co., Colo. Justice Coun., Denver, Regional Girls Shelter, Springfield; bd. dirs. Crisis Helpline and Info. Svc. Scholar Lilly Endowment, Inc., 1976, Piton Found., 1978; recipient Spl. Recognition award Big Bros./Big Sisters of Am., 1983, Recognition award Am. Humanics Mgmt. Inst., 1990. Mem. Inst. Internat. Connections (bd. dirs.), Coun. Social Work Edn., Group for Study of Generalist Social Work, Social Welfare History Group, Nat. Assn. Social Workers (nominating com. Springfield chpt., state bd. dirs., No. Colo. rep.), Student Social Work Assn. Colo. State U. (adv. 1986-89), Permanency Planning Coun. for Children and Youth, NOW (treas. Springfield chpt. 1984-85), Student Nuclear Awareness Group (advisor), Student Social Work Assn. (advisor), Har Shalom, Alpha Delta Mu. Democrat. Jewish. Office: Colo State U Social Work Dept Fort Collins CO 80523

SCHATZ, WAYNE ARDALE, middle school educator; b. Cody, Wyo., July 27, 1947; s. Albert R. and Leona Mildred (Johnston) S.; m. Roanne Longwith, Dec. 16, 1966; children: Heidi Edith, Robert, Leon, Dale, Anne. BS, Ea. Mont. Coll., 1969; MEd, Lesley Coll., 1987. Cert. Elem. tchr., Wyo. Tchr. Coffeen Elem. Sch., Sheridan, Wyo., 1969-78, Woodland Park Elem., Sheridan, 1978-87; computer tchr. Cen. Mid. Sch., Sheridan, 1987-94; in-svc. instr. Sch. Dist. #2, Sheridan, 1987—, sch. dist. #2 tech. coord., 1994—; extension instr. U. Wyo., Laramie, 1989—. Bd. dirs. Bighorn Audobon Soc., Sheridan, 1966-77, pres., 1977-80; active Sheridan County Red Cross, Sheridan. Mem. Sheridan Cen. Edn. Assn. (pres. 1979-80, Tchr. of the Month 1988, 92, Tchr. of Yr. 1992), Wyo. Edn. Assn. (bd. dirs. 1980-82, treas. 1982-84), Wyo. Ednl. Computing Coun. (pres. 1989-92). Republican. Mem. LDS Ch. Home: 955 Lewis St Sheridan WY 82801-3423 Office: 620 Adair Ave Fl 3 Sheridan WY 82801-3507

SCHAU, HARVEY CHARLES, physicist; b. Kalamazoo, Dec. 19, 1949; s. Harvey Charles and Evelyn Opal (Wheeler) S.; m. Sharron Rhonda Solomon Goldstein, Aug. 23, 1973 (div. Sept. 1984); 1 child, Jennifer Blake. BS, Fla. Atlantic U., 1972, MS, 1973; PhD, U. Fla., 1975. Physicist Gen. Dynamics Corp., Pomona, Calif., 1976-78; engr. Martin Marietta Corp., Orlando, Fla., 1978-80; physicist Exxon Corp., Orlando, 1980-82, Naval Rsch. Lab., Orlando, 1983-89, Hughes Missile Sys. Co., Tucson, 1990—; pres. Schau Assocs., Tucson, 1980—. Contbr. articles to profl. jours. Mem. IEEE, Internat. Soc. Optical Engrs. Home: 160 N Pantano Rd Apt 2098 Tucson AZ 85710-2389 Office: Hughes Missile Sys Co PO Box 11337 Tucson AZ 85734-1337

SCHAUER, TONE TERJESEN, lawyer; b. Arendal, Norway, Jan. 1, 1941; came to U.S., 1958; d. Haakon and Signe (Andersen) Terjesen; children from previous marriage: Randi Vargas, Shawn Wilson, Kristina Schauer; m. John Richilano; 1 child, Jamie. BA, Colo. State U., 1969, M in French Lit., 1971; JD, U. Colo., 1977. Bar: Colo. 1977, U.S. Ct. Appeals (10th cir.) 1977. Dep. pub. defender State of Colo., Denver, 1977-83; pvt. practice Boulder, Colo., 1983-90, Denver, 1990—. Mem. ABA, Colo. Bar Assn., Denver Bar Assn. Democrat. Home: 356 Marion St Denver CO 80218-3928 Office: 150 E 10th Ave Denver CO 80203-2740

SCHAUFELE, ROGER DONALD, aircraft company executive; b. Mar. 30, 1928; s. Franklin A. and Josephine (Schmidt) S.; m. Barbara Powell Harkness, Oct. 8, 1949; children—Margaret Jo, Roger Donald Jr. B.S. in Aeros., Rensselaer Poly. Inst., 1949; M.S. in Aeros., Calif. Inst. Tech., 1952. With Douglas Aircraft Co., Santa Monica, Calif., 1949-51; with Douglas Aircraft Co., Long Beach, Calif., 1955—, asst. chief aerodynamics, comml. programs, DC-10 dep. dir. aerodynamics, 1967-71, dir. tech., 1971-76, dir. advanced engring, 1976-79, dir. aircraft design, 1979-81, v.p. engring., 1981-87; v.p., gen. mgr. comml. advanced products Douglas Aircraft, Long Beach, Calif., 1987-89, cons., 1989—; mem. aero. adv. com. NASA, Washington, 1981-87; mem. aero. and space engring. bd. NRC, Washington, 1982-85; mem. U. engring. adv. and devel. council Calif. State U.-Long Beach, 1983—; mem. aero. engring. tech. indsl. adv. bd. Ariz. State U., Tempe, 1983-86; mem. com. on sci. and tech. U.S. Ho. Reps., Congl. Adv. Com. on Aeronautics, Washington, 1984-87;. Patentee in field. Fellow AIAA, Inst. for Advancement of Engring.; mem. ASME, Soc. Automotive Engrs. (tech. bd. 1983-85, bd. dirs. 1990—), Aero. Club of So. Calif., Tau Beta Pi, Gamma Alpha Rho. Home: 13112 Wheeler Pl Santa Ana CA 92705-1826 Office: Douglas Aircraft Co 3855 Lakewood Blvd M/C 18A-61 Long Beach CA 90846

SCHAWLOW, ARTHUR LEONARD, physicist, educator; b. Mt. Vernon, N.Y., May 5, 1921; s. Arthur and Helen (Mason) S.; m. Aurelia Keith Townes, May 19, 1951; children: Arthur Keith, Helen Aurelia, Edith Ellen. BA, U. Toronto, Ont., Can., 1941, MA, 1942, PhD, 1949, LLD (hon.), 1970; DSc (hon.), U. Ghent, Belgium, 1968, U. Bradford, Eng., 1970, U. Ala., 1984, Trinity Coll., Dublin, Ireland, 1986; DTech (hon.), U. Lund, Sweden, 1987; DSL (hon.), Victoria U., Toronto, 1993. Postdoctoral fellow, research asso. Columbia, 1949-51; vis. assoc. prof. Columbia U., 1960; research physicist Bell Telephone Labs., 1951-61, cons., 1961-62; prof. physics Stanford U., 1961-91, also J.G. Jackson-C.J. Wood prof. physics, 1978, prof. emeritus, 1991—, exec. head dept. physics, 1966-70, acting chmn. dept., 1973-74. Author: (with C.H. Townes) Microwave Spectroscopy, 1955; Co-inventor (with C.H. Townes), optical maser or laser, 1958. Recipient Ballantine medal Franklin Inst., 1962, Thomas Young medal and prize Inst. Physics and Phys. Soc., London, 1963, Schawlow medal Laser Inst. Am., 1982, Nobel prize in physics, 1981, Nat. Medal of Sci., NSF, 1991, Arata award High Temperature Soc. Japan, 1994; named Calif. Scientist of Yr., 1973, Marconi Internat. fellow, 1977. Fellow Am. Acad. Arts and Scis., Am. Phys. Soc. (coun. 1966-70, chmn. div. electron and atomic physics 1974, pres. 1981), Optical Soc. Am. (hon. mem. 1983, dir.-at-large 1966-68, pres. 1975, Frederick Ives medal 1976); mem. NAS, IEEE (Liebmann prize 1964), AAAS (chmn. physics sect. 1979), Am. Philos. Soc., Royal Irish Acad. (hon.). Office: Stanford U Dept Physics Stanford CA 94305

SCHECHTER, CLIFFORD, financial executive, lawyer; b. N.Y.C., Feb. 14, 1958; s. Howard and Diana D. (Eiss) S.; m. Niely Okonsky, June 17, 1979; children: Dana Ann, Adam Hillel, Talia Beth. BS summa cum laude, U. R.I., 1979; JD, Fordham U. Sch. Law, 1982; MBA, L.I. U., 1988. Bar: N.Y. 1983, U.S. Tax Ct. 1983, U.S. Supreme Ct. 1986, D.C. 1990, U.S. Dist. Ct. (so. and ea. dists.) N.Y. 1983; lic. gen. securities prin., fin. and ops. prin. Nat. Assn. Securities Dealers; CFP; registered investment advisor. Tax supr. Touche Ross & Co., Jericho, N.Y., 1982-86; sr. v.p., dir. taxes L.F. Rothschild & Co. Inc., N.Y.C., 1986-91, chief fin. officer, dir. adminstrn. and taxes, 1991-93; pres. Royal Fin. Svcs. Inc., San Diego, 1993—; adj. prof. Adelphi U., Garden City, N.Y., 1983-91, Pace U., N.Y.C., 1991-93. Bd. dirs. P.A.D. Pub. Svc. Ctr., Washington, 1986—, Congregation Chabad of Rancho Bernardo and Poway. Recipient Uniroyal Found. Fellowship award, 1978, Am. Jurisprudence award Scholastic Excellence in Estate Planning, 1982. Mem. ABA, N.Y. State Bar Assn., D.C. Bar Assn., Bar Assn. Nassau County, Internat. Assn. Fin. Planning, Fin. Mgmt. Assn., Securities Industry Assn., Wall St. Tax Assn., Profl. Fraternity Assn. (bd. dirs. 1994—), Phi Alpha Delta (internat. proctor 1986-88, marshal 1988-90, historian 1990-92, treas. 1992-94, internat. vice justice 1994—, dist. XV justice 1984-86, Outstanding Active mem. award 1982, Stan P. Jones Meml. award 1985, Outstanding Alumnus mem. Wormser chpt. 1982-85), Beta Gamma Sigma, Phi Kappa Phi. Republican. Jewish. Home: 14376 Twisted Branch Rd Poway CA 92064-1461 Office: Royal Fin Svcs Inc 2111 Palomar Airport Rd Ste 330 Carlsbad CA 92009-1418

SCHECHTER, ROBERT JAY, ophthalmic surgeon; b. Bklyn., Dec. 20, 1949; s. Abraham and Vivian (Pall) S. BS, Yale U., 1970, MD, 1974. Diplomate Nat. Bd. Med. Examiners; bd. cert. Am. Bd. Ophthalmology. From clin. instr. to clin. asst. prof. ophthalmology Jules Stein Eye Inst. of UCLA Sch. Medicine, 1978-88, clin. assoc. prof. ophthalmology, 1988—; clin. attending physician Long Beach VA Hosp., 1979-88; clin. asst. prof. ophthalmology U. Calif.-Irvine Sch. Medicine, 1983-92; cons. Long Beach VA Hosp., 1988—; mem. L.A. Kaiser-Permanente Med. Care Evaluation Com., 1983-87; sec. med. staff L.A. Kaiser-Permanente Hosp., 1984, v.p. med. staff, 1985, pres. med. staff, 1986, chmn. exec. com., 1986, quality assurance coord. for ophthalmology, 1987—, med. computing com., 1987—, adminstrv. coun., 1987—; lectr. and presenter in field. Contbr. articles to profl. jours. Fellow ACS (chmn. ophthalmology sect. regional meeting 1988, co-chmn. ophthalmology sect. regional meeting 1989, 90, 91, 92, program dir. ophthalmology sci. session 1988, assoc. program dir. ophthalmology sci. session 1989, 90, 91, 92), Am. Acad. Ophthalmology (basic and clin. sci. course com. sect. III-optics, refraction and contact lenses 1991-92).

SCHECHTMAN, VICKI LYNN, neurophysiologist; b. Willimantic, Conn., July 27, 1955; d. George Bernard and Marilyn (Baum) S.; m. Bruce Bon; 1 child, Michael. BA in Psychology, Ariz. State U., 1978; MA in Psychology, Calif. State U., 1982; PhD in Neurosci., UCLA, 1987. Teaching asst. dept. psychology Calif. State U., Long Beach, 1980-82; lab. asst. dept. anatomy Sch. Medicine UCLA, 1983-85, EEG technologist Sleep Disorders Lab. Neuropsychiatric Inst., 1986-87, rsch. asst. dept. anatomy Sch. Medicine, 1985-87, postdoctoral rschr. Brain Rsch. Inst. Sch. Medicine, 1987-90, asst. rsch. physiologist Brain Rsch. Inst. Sch. Medicine, 1990—; invited lectr. Assn. Profl. Sleep Socs., Mpls., 1990, Toronto, 1991, Children's Hosp., L.A., 1991; cons. BRSG, 1990-91; co-investigator NICHD, 1989—; co-prin. investigator March of Dimes, 1991-93. Consulting reviewer Sleep, Pediatric Rsch.; contbr. articles to med. jours. Recipient Scholl award Nat. Sudden Infant Death Syndrome Found., 1986; felow mental health tng. program NIMH, 1985-87. Mem. Am. Physiol. Soc., Internat. Brain Rsch. Orgn., Sleep Rsch. Soc., Assn. Women in Sci., Soc. Psychophysiol. Rsch., Fedn. Behavioral, Psychol. and Cognitive Scis., Soc. Neurosci. Home: 8550 Noble Ave North Hills CA 91343-6009 Office: UCLA Sch Medicine Brain Rsch Inst Los Angeles CA 90024-1761

SCHEER, JANET KATHY, mathematics educator; b. Bklyn., Apr. 22, 1947; d. Seymour and Hilda (Shoer) S. BA, Bklyn. Coll., 1968; MS, Syracuse (N.Y.) U., 1969; PhD, Ariz. State U., 1977. Cert. tchr., N.Y., Ariz.; cert. prin., Ariz. Math. tchr. Jamesville (N.Y.) DeWitt Middle Sch., 1969-72; math. tchr., middle sch. coordinator Am. Internat. Sch., Kfar Shmaryahu, Israel, 1972-74; from asst. prof. to assoc. prof. So. Ill. U., Carbondale, 1977-88; nat. product devel. specialist Scott, Foresman and Co., Glenview, Ill., 1989-90; dir. field svcs. for math. Scott, Foresman and Co., 1991; exec. dir. Create A Vision, Mountain View, Calif., 1992—; cons. in field, 1977—; sr. nat. math. cons. Holt, Rinehart & Winston, N.Y.C., 1986-89, Harcourt Brace-Jovanovich/Holt, 1989. Editor Ill. Math. Tchr. jour., 1980-83; author: Manipulatives in Mathematics Unlimited, 1987; contbr. to textbooks and profl. jours. Named one of Outstanding Young Women Am., 1978, 81-85, Outstanding Tchr. Yr. So. Ill. U., 1978-79; recipient numerous grants. Mem. Nat. Council Tchrs. Math., Research Council for Diagnostic and Prescriptive Math. (charter mem., v.p. 1984-86), Ill. Council Tchrs. Math. (various offices), Phi Delta Kappa, Kappa Delta Pi. Office: Create A Vision 1300 Villa St Mountain View CA 94041-1197

SCHEFCIK, JERRY ALLEN, art gallery administrator, university official; b. Alliance, Nebr., Sept. 15, 1952; s. Robert and Verna Mae (Woodworth) S.; m. Tamara Dawn Forsyth, Apr. 24, 1979; children: Annie, David, Catherine. BA in Art and Design, Brigham Young U., 1979; MA in Art History, U. Denver, 1982. Instr. Spanish, Brigham Young U., Provo, Utah, 1979-80; mus. asst. Springville (Utah) Mus. Art, 1979-80; asst. curator Sch. Art Slide Libr., then grad. tchg. asst. U. Denver, 1981-82; curator Francis King Collection Western Art, Sangre de Cristo Arts and Conf. Ctr., Pueblo, Colo., 1982, curator visual arts, 1982-84; curator art Amarillo (Tex.) Art Ctr., 1984-89; curator Donna Beam Fine Art Gallery, U. Nev., Las Vegas, 1989-90, dir., 1991—, curator Metcalf Gallery, Tam Alumni Ctr., 1989—; curator Nev. Inst. for Contemporary Art, 1991—, interim dir., 1990-91; lectr. in field, 1983; cons. S.E. Colo. Arts Coun., Lamar, 1984, Marsh Media, Inc., Amarillo, 1986-87; book reviewer Harcourt Brace Jovanovich, Inc., San Diego, 1989; grant evaluator Nev. Coun. on Arts, 1989-90; mem. adv. panel Las Vegas Neon Mus., 1993; mem. arts adv. subcom. for Nev. artists for McCarran Art Gallery, McCarran Internat. Airport, 1990-94. Curator over 150 exhbns., including Julian Onderdonk: A Texas Tradition traveling exhbn., 1984, Georgia O'Keefe and Her Contemporaries, 1985, Divine Images and Magic Carpets: The Asian Art Collection of Dr. and Mrs. William T. Price, 1987, John Marin Watercolors, 1988, Figuratively Speaking: Art of the Human Form, 1991, ZOOID, 1993, Art—In, On and Out of the Bag, 1993, From New York: Recent Thinking in Comtemporary Photography, 1993; editor exhbn. catalogues and brochures. Bd. dirs. Area Arts Found., Amarillo, 1988-89; mem. adv. panel visual arts curriculum Las Vegas Acad., 1993. Mem. Am. Assn. Mus., Western Mus. Conf. (ann. meeting local arrangements com. 1991). Democrat. Mem. LDS Ch. Office: U Nev Las Vegas Donna Beam Fine Art Gallery 4505 S Maryland Pky Las Vegas NV 89154

SCHEID-RAYMOND, LINDA ANNE, property management professional; b. Rochester, N.Y., Aug. 13, 1953; d. Arthur F. and Anna M. Scheid; m. Dan Raymond, June 27, 1987. BFA, U. Colo., 1975. Leasing agt. Richard E. Rudolph, Boulder, Colo., 1975-77; adminstrv. asst., co-mgr. Harsh Investment Corp., Denver, 1977-83; property mgr. A.G. Spanos Mgmt., Colorado Springs, Colo., 1984-85, Carmel Devel. and Mgmt., Denver, 1985-88, Property Asset Mgmt., Denver, 1989—. Contbr. photographs to profl. mags.

SCHEIMER, JANICE SCHAEFER, financial consultant, planner; b. Alva, Okla., Sept. 21, 1948; d. Andrew August and Ruth Ida (Boyce) Schaefer; m. Gary Lee Scheimer, Aug. 10, 1968; children: Scott Allen, Eric Lee. BS, Ariz. State U., 1971, MBA, 1972. Cert. fin. planner. Rate analyst Northwest Pipeline, Salt Lake City, 1976-78; mktg. mgr. Western Fed. Savs., Colorado Springs, 1979-82; fin. cons. Shearson, Lehamn, Hutton/Am. Express, Gimsbach, Fed. Republic Germany, 1982-83, Colorado Springs, Fed. Republic Germany, 1982-83, 1985—; fin. cons. Integrated Resources, Gimsbach, Fed. Republic Germany, 1983-85; v.p., treas. Golden Horizons, Inc., Cheyenne Wells, Colo., Fed. Republic Germany, 1979—; sec., treas. Schaefer Farms, Inc., Cheyenne Wells, Colo., Fed. Republic Germany, 1985—; v.p. to pres. S.S. & N., Inc., Cheyenne Wells, Colo., Fed. Republic Germany, 1985—; pres. Schaeffer Farms Inc., 1985-92; mgr. Linsco Pvt. Ledger, Colorado Springs, Colo., 1991; instr. U. Md., Fed. Republic Germany, 1984-85; lectr. Meml. Hosp. Women's Ctr.; cons. Pro-Trac, 1984; mem. internat. affairs com. Bus. and Profl. Women, Colorado Springs. Soccer team mother Am. Youth Assn., Ramstein, Fed. Republic Germany, 1982-85; mem. Homebuilders Assn., Colorado Springs, 1985—; mem. econ. devel. com. City of Colorado Springs. Mem. NAFE, Inst. Cert. Fin. Planners, Speakers' Bur. Networking Assn., Christian Bus. Women., Profl. Bus. Women (Colo. Springs world affairs com.), Officers Wives Club (Ramstein) (treas. 1984-85). Republican. Home: 2340 Oak Hills Dr Colorado Springs CO 80919-3473 Office: Linsco/Pvt Ledger 630 Southpointe Ct Ste 101 Colorado Springs CO 80906-3800

SCHEINBAUM, DAVID, photography educator; b. Bklyn., Apr. 14, 1951; s. Louis and Rhoda (Feerman) S.; m. Vicki Golden, May 30, 1973 (div. 1975); m. Janet Ann Goldberg-Russek, Mar. 21, 1982; stepchildren: Jonathan Russek, Andra Russek; 1 child, Zachary. BA, CUNY, 1973. Instr. photography Pace U., N.Y.C., 1974-75, LaGuardia (N.Y.) Community Coll., 1975-78; assoc. prof. art Coll. Santa Fe, 1979-81, 82—, assoc. prof. of art photography, 1981—; printer, asst. to Beaumont Newhall, Santa Fe, 1980-93; printer to Eliot Porter, Santa Fe, 1980-90; co-dir. Scheinbaum & Russek, Ltd., Santa Fe, 1979—. Author: (photographs) Bisti, 1987, Miami Beach: Photographs of an American Dream, 1990; photography exhbns. include Pace U., 1974, Midtown Y Gallery, N.Y., 1977, Santa Fe Gallery for Photography, 1979, 81, The Armory for the Arts, Santa Fe, 1980, 1981, Sea Breeze Gallery, Block Island, R.I., 1982, Highlands U., Las Vegas, N.Mex., 1982, Gov's. Gallery, Santa Fe, 1982, Santa Fe Festival for the Arts, 1982, Coll. Santa Fe, 1983, Dem. Conv., San Francisco, 1984, Mus. Natural History, Albuquerque, Bisti/Miami Beach Photogroup Coral Gables, Fla., 1990, Ctr. Met. Studies U. Mo., St. Louis, 1988, Earthscope Expo '90 Photo Mus., Osaka, Japan, 1990, Jamestown C.C., N.Y., 1990, Neikrug Photo Gallery Internat., Tokyo, 1987; in permanent collections Norton Gallery Mus., West Palm Beach, Fla, Amon Carter Mus., Ft. Worth, N.Mex. State U., Las Cruces, Ctr. Creative Photography, Tucson, Ariz., Mus. Fine Arts, Santa Fe, Bklyn. Mus., U. Okla., Norman, Bibliothèque Nationale France, Paris, Gernsheim Collection. U. Tex., Austin, Albuquerque Mus., Rockwell Mus., Corning, N.Y., Chase Manhattan Bank, N.Y. Pub. Libr., Fogg Art Mus., Harvard U., Met. Mus. Art, N.Y.C., Frito-Lay Collection, Kans. City, Expo 90 Photo Mus., Osaka, Coll. Art Gallery, SUNY, New Paltz, N.Y., Univ. Art Mus., U. N.Mex. Inducted Wall of Fame Kingsborough C.C., N.Y., 1994. Mem. N.Mex. Coun. on Photography (founder, v.p., bd. dirs.), Santa Fe Ctr. Photography (bd. dirs. 1978-85). Jewish. Home: 369 Montezuma Ave # 345 Santa Fe NM 87501-2626 Office: Coll Santa Fe Saint Michaels Dr Santa Fe NM 87501

SCHELAR, VIRGINIA MAE, chemistry educator, consultant; b. Kenosha, Wis., Nov. 26, 1924; d. William and Blanche M. (Williams) S. BS, U. Wis., 1947, MS, 1953; MEd, Harvard U., 1962; PhD, U. Wis., 1969. Instr. U. Wis., Milw., 1947-51; info. specialist Abbott Labs., North Chgo., Ill., 1953-56; instr. Wright Jr. Coll., Chgo., 1957-58; asst. prof. No. Ill. U., DeKalb, 1958-63; prof. St. Petersburg (Fla.) Jr. Coll., 1965-67; asst. prof. Chgo. State Coll., 1967-68; prof. Grossmont Coll., El Cajon, Calif., 1968-80; cons. Calif., 1981—. Author: Kekule Centennial, 1965; contbr. articles to profl. jours. Active citizens adv. coun. DeKalb Consol. Sch. Bd.; voters svc. chair League Women Voters, del. to state and nat. convs., judicial chair, election laws chair. Standard Oil fellow, NSF grantee; recipient Lewis prize U. Wis. Fellow Am. Inst. Chemists; mem. Am. Chem. Soc. (membership affairs com., chmn. western councilor's caucus, exec. com., councilor, legis. counselor, chmn. edn. com., editor state and local bulletins).

SCHELL, FARREL LOY, transportation engineer; b. Amarillo, Tex., Dec. 14, 1931; s. Thomas Phillip and Lillian Agnes (McKee) S.; m. Shirley Anne Samuelson, Feb. 6, 1955; children: James Christopher, Maria Leslyn Schell Peter. BS, U. Kans., 1954; postgrad., Carnegie-Mellon U., 1974. Registered profl. engr., Calif., Colo. Resident engr. Sverdrup & Parcel, Denver, 1957-61; project engr. Bechtel Corp., San Francisco, 1961-62, Parsons, Brinckerhoff-Tudor-Bechtel, San Francisco, 1962-67; mgr. urban transp. dept. Kaiser Engrs., Oakland, Calif., 1967-78; program dir. San Francisco Mcpl. Rwy I.C., 1978-80; project mgr. Houston Transit Cons., 1980-83, Kaiser Transit Group, Miami, 1983-85; mgr. program devel. Kaiser Engrs., Oakland, 1985-87; project mgr. O'Brien-Kreitzberg & Assocs., San Francisco, 1987-89; sr. project mgr. Bay Area Rapid Transit Dist., Oakland, Calif., 1989—; dir. Schelter Devel. Corp., Piedmont, Calif., 1982—. Contbr. articles to profl. jours. Lt. (j.g.) USN, 1954-57, PTO. Mem. ASCE, ASME, Nat. Soc. Profl. Engrs., Nat. Coun. Engring. Examiners, Am. Planners Assn., Am. Pub. Transit Assn., Lakeview Club, Scarab Club, Pachacamac Club, Sigma Tau, Tau Beta Pi. Home: 24 York Dr Piedmont CA 94611-4123 Office: Bay Area Rapid Transit Dist 800 Madison St Oakland CA 94607-4730

SCHELLER, ERIN LINN, publishing company executive; b. Port Arthur, Tex., Dec. 25, 1942; d. Truman Edward Jr. and Margaret Jane (Imhoff) Linn; m. Herman Scheller, Oct. 19, 1983; 1 child, Christopher Wayne Levy. Student, Barat Coll., 1960-61; BS, U. Tex., 1964. Tchr. Cath. Sch. Dist., Houston, 1965-67; owner, pres. The Pub.'s Mark, Incline Village, Nev., 1982—; pres., chmn. bd. EduVision Inc., computer software co., Incline Village, 1994—; guest lectr. death edn. related orgns., U.S., 1982—. Author: Children Are Not Paper Dolls, 1982, I Know Just How You Feel, 1986, Dear Teacher, 1988, 150 Facts About Grieving Children, 1990, Premonitions, Visitations and Dreams, 1991. Advisor Mo. Bapt. Children's Group, St. Louis, 1980-81; chpt. leader The Compassionate Friends, Denver, 1980-81, Greeley, Colo., 1981-83; 2nd v.p. Republican Women's Club, Incline Village, 1987-90; mem. AAUW, Incline Village, 1987-89; pres. Teester's Ladies Golf Assn., Incline Village, 1987-90; mem. Assn. for Death. Edn. and Counseling, 1985—, Grief Edn. Inst., 1981—, The Compassionate Friends, 1980—. Named Honored Author, Ill. Libr. Exposition, 1985. Republican. Lutheran. Home and Office: The Publishers Mark PO Box 6300 Incline Village NV 89450-6300

SCHELLER, JAMES CHARLES, patent lawyer; b. Balt., Oct. 8, 1956; s. James Charles and Mary Dora (Naglieri) S.; m. Myung-Hee Lee, Sept. 8, 1984. BA in Biophysics, Johns Hopkins U., 1978; MBA, Carnegie-Mellon U., 1980; JD, U. Calif., Los Angeles, 1983. Patent atty. Blakely, Sokoloff, Taylor and Zafman, Sunnyvale, Calif., 1982—. Editor UCLA jour. of Environ. Law and Policy, 1981-83. Mem. ABA, AAAS. Office: Blakely Sokoloff Taylor & Zafman 1279 Oakmead Pky Sunnyvale CA 94086-4040

SCHELLINGER, JAMES RAYMOND, advertising sales executive; b. Casper, Wyo., Apr. 18, 1963; s. William Joseph and Trina Louise (Cundall) S.; m. Cheryl Lynne Wentz, June 27, 1987; 1 child, Cody Lee. AAS, N.W. C.C., Powell, Wyo., 1984; BS, Black Hills State Coll., Spearfish, S.D., 1986. Operator, roustabout Valentine Constrn., Inc., Glenrock, Wyo., 1980-86; resident asst. N.W. C.C., 1982-84, Black Hills State Coll., 1984-86; sales mgr. Sta. KWIV and KATH, Douglas, Wyo., 1987-89; account exec. Sta. KROE, Sheridan, Wyo., 1989—. Bd. dirs. Am. Heart Assn., Douglas, 1987-89, Hugh O'Brian Youth Found.; info. coord. Am. Cancer Soc., Douglas, 1988-89; mem. Sheridan Youth Steering Com., 1990-91; city councilman City of Sheridan, 1995—. Mem. U.S. Jr. C. of C. (bd. dirs. 1991-92, Hamilton award 1991, Frost award 1992), Wyo. Jaycees (regional bd. dirs. 1989-90, v.p. 1990-91, pres. 1991-92, Officer of Yr. award 1990, 91), Sheridan Area C. of C. (chmn. retail com. 1989-92), Phi Beta Lambda (state pres. 1985-86). Republican. Roman Catholic. Home: 735 Clarendon Ave Sheridan WY 82801-3517 Office: Sta KROE 1716 Kroe Ln Sheridan WY 82801-9681

SCHELLMAN, JOHN A., chemistry educator; b. Phila., Oct. 24, 1924; s. John and Mary (Mason) S.; m. Charlotte Green, Feb. 10, 1954; children: Heidi M., Lise C. AB, Temple U., 1948; MS, Princeton U., 1949, PhD, 1951; PhD (hon.), Chalmers U., Sweden, 1983, U. Padua, Italy, 1990. USPHS postdoctoral fellow U. Utah, 1951-52, Carlsberg Lab., Copenhagen, 1953-55; DuPont fellow U. Minn., Mpls., 1955-56; asst. prof. chemistry U. Minn., 1956-58; assoc. prof. chemistry Inst. Molecular Biology, U. Oreg., Eugene, 1958-63; prof. chemistry, rsch. assoc. Inst. Molecular Biology, U. Oreg., 1963—; vis. Lab. Chem. Physics, Nat. Inst. Arthritis and Metabolic Diseases, NIH, Bethesda, Md., 1980; vis. prof. Chalmers U., Sweden, 1986, U. Padua, Italy, 1987. Contbr. articles to profl. jours. Served with U.S. Army, 1943-46. Fellow Rask-Oersted Found., 1954, Sloan Found., 1959-63, Guggenheim Found., 1969-70. Fellow Am. Phys. Soc.; mem. NAS, Am. Chem. Soc., Am. Soc. Biochemistry and Molecular Biology, Am. Acad. Arts and Scis., Biophys. Soc., Phi Beta Kappa, Sigma Xi. Democrat. Home: 780 Lorane Hwy Eugene OR 97405-2340 Office: Univ Oreg Inst Molecular Biology Eugene OR 97403

SCHENDEL, WINFRIED GEORGE, insurance company executive; b. Harpstedt, Germany, June 19, 1931; s. Willi Rudolf Max and Anna Margarete (Sassen) S.; came to U.S., 1952, naturalized, 1956; B.S. in Elect. and Indsl. Engring., Hannover-Stadthagen U., Hannover, W. Germany, 1952; m. Joanne Wiiest, Aug. 24, 1953; children—Victor Winfried, Bruce Lawrence, Rachelle Laureen. Elec. draftsman Houston Lighting & Power Co., 1954-57; elec. draftsman, corrosion technician Transcontinental Gas Pipeline Co., Houston, 1957-59; elec. engr. Ken R. White Cons. Engrs., Denver, 1959-61; sales engr. Weco div. Food Machinery & Chem. Corp., various locations, 1961-64; ins. field underwriter N.Y. Life Ins. Co., Denver, 1964-66, asst. mgr., 1966-70, mgmt. asst., 1970-71, gen. mgr., 1971-77, mgr., 1979-85, field underwriter, 1985—; ind. gen. agt., Denver, 1978-79. Instl. rep., advancement chmn. Denver Area council Boy Scouts Am., Lakewood, Colo., 1968-72; precinct chmn. Republican Party, Jefferson County, Colo., 1976, 78; founder, mem. (life) Sister City Program, Lakewood, Colo.; chmn. adv. bd.

ARC, Jefferson County, Colo., 1986-88. Recipient Centurion award, 1966; Northwestern Region Leader Manpower Devel. award N.Y. Life Ins. Co., 1968, Salesman of Yr. award Jefferson County Salesman with a Purpose Club, 1983, Top awards ARC, 1988-89. Mem. Nat. Assn. Life Underwriters, Gen. Agents and Mgrs. Assn. (recipient Conf. Nat. Mgmt. award, 1975), Colo. Life Underwriters Assn. (reg. v.p. Denver Metro area 1989-90), Mile High Assn. Life Underwriters (pres. 1986-87, nat. com. 1988, 91), Lakewood C. of C. (pres. people-to-people, Trailblazer of Yr. award 1982, 83, Trail Boss of Yr. 1983). Presbyterian (elder). Clubs: Lions, Edelweiss, Internat. Order Rocky Mountain Goats, N.Y. Life Star (leading asst. mgr. Continental region 1980), Masons, Rotary (Paul Harris award, 1995, Golden Rotary), Shriners. Home: 13802 W 20th Pl Golden CO 80401-2104 Office: NY Life Ins Co 13802 W 20th Pl Golden CO 80401-2104

SCHENK, DALE BERNARD, neuroscientist; m. Maria Torres, Sept. 9, 1978; children: Anais, Sara. BA cum laude, U. Calif., San Diego, 1979, PhD, 1984. Scientsit Scios/Nova, Mountain View, Calif., 1984-87; sr. scientist and project leader Athena Neurosci., South San Francisco, 1987-90, sr. scientist, dir. immunochemsitry, 1990-93, project leader, mgr., 1993-94, dir. neurobiology, 1994—; presenter in field. Ad Hoc reviewer jours.; contbr. numerous articles to profl. jours.; patentee in field. Grantee Am. Liver Found., 1983, NIH, 1986, 89, 90. Mem. AAAS, Am. Soc. Hypertension (fouder), U.S. Chess Fedn. Home: 605 Sharp Park Rd Pacifica CA 94044-2459 Office: Athena Neuroscis Inc 800 Gateway Blvd South San Francisco CA 94080-7021

SCHENK, RAY M(ERLIN), electronics company executive; b. Logan, Utah, Dec. 18, 1946; s. Merlin F. and Thelma E. (Birch) S. BS in Acctg. magna cum laude, Utah State U., 1969. CPA, Utah. Staff acct. Haskins and Sells, Phoenix, 1969, Salt Lake City, 1969-71; controller Kimball Electronics, Salt Lake City, 1971—. Recipient Scholastic Achievement cert. Phi Kappa Phi, 1967, 68; 1st Security Found. scholar, 1968; Alpha Kappa Psi scholarship award, 1969; CPA medallion, 1970. Mem. AICPAs, Inst. Mgmt. Accts., Am. Acctg. Assn., Utah Assn. CPAs. Home: 5044 Boabab Dr Salt Lake City UT 84117-6807 Office: Kimball Electronics 350 Pierpont Ave Salt Lake City UT 84101-1711

SCHENK, SUSAN KIRKPATRICK, geriatric psychiatry nurse; b. New Richmond, Ind., Nov. 29, 1938; d. William Marcius and Frances (Kirkpatrick) Gaither; m. Richard Dee Brown, Aug. 13, 1960 (div. Feb. 1972); children: Christopher, David, Lisa; m. John Francis Schenk, July 24, 1975 (widowed Apr. 1995). BSN, Ind. U., 1962; postgrad., U. Del., 1973-75. RN, PHN, BCLS; cert. community coll. tchr., Calif. Staff nurse, then asst. dir. nursing Bloomington (Ind.) Hosp., 1962-66; change nurse Newark (Del.) Manor, 1967-69; charge nurse GU Union Hosp., Terre Haute, Ind., 1971-72; clin. instr. nursing Ind. State U., Terre Haute, 1972-73; clin. instr. psychiatric nursing U. Del., Newark, 1974-75; psychiatric nursing care coord. VA Med. Ctr., Perry Point, Md., 1975-78; nurse educator Grossmont Hosp., La Mesa, Calif., 1978-90, community rels. coord., 1990-91; dir. sr. behavioral health svcs. Scripps Hosp. East County, El Cajon, Calif., 1991—; tech. advisor San Diego County Bd. Supervisors, 1987; tech. cons. Remedy Home and Health Care, San Diego, 1988; expert panelist Srs. Speak Out, KPBS-TV, San Diego, 1988; guest lectr. San Diego State U., 1987. Editor: Teaching Basic Caregiver Skills, 1988; author, performer tng. videotape Basic Caregiver Skills, 1988. Mem. patient svcs. com. Nat. Multiple Sclerosis Soc., San Diego, 1986-89; bd. dirs. Assn. for Quality and Participation, 1989. Adminstrn. on Aging/DHHS grantee, 1988. Mem. Am. Psychiat. Nurses Assn., Ind. U. Alumni Assn. (life), Mensa, Sigma Theta Tau. Home: 9435 Carlton Oaks Dr # D Santee CA 92071-2588 Office: Scripps Hosp East County 1688 E Main St El Cajon CA 92021-5204

SCHENK, WILLIAM HENRY, mechanical engineer; b. Arlington Heights, Ill., Apr. 19, 1961; s. Richard Roy and Elizabeth June (Autem) S.; m. Karen Lee Prunier, Apr. 29, 1989; children: Elizabeth Hannah, Laura Kathryn. BSME, U. Ill., 1983. Assoc. mech. engr. Shugart Corp., Sunnyvale, Calif., 1983-85; mech. engr. Priam Corp., San Jose, Calif., 1985-87, Plus Devel., San Jose, 1987-89; sr. mech. engr. Grid Systems Corp., Fremont, Calif., 1989-93, Cisco Systems Corp., San Jose, Calif., 1993—. Mem. ASME. Republican. Roman Catholic. Home: 36853 Capistrano Dr Fremont CA 94536-6421 Office: Cisco Systems Corp 170 W Tasman Dr San Jose CA 95134

SCHENKKAN, ROBERT FREDERIC, writer, actor; b. Chapel Hill, N.C., Mar. 19, 1953; s. Robert Frederic Sr. and Jean (McKenzie) S.; m. Mary Anne Dorward, Dec. 1, 1984; children: Sarah Victoria, Joshua McHenry. BA in Theatre Arts, U. Tex., 1975; MFA in Acting, Cornell U., 1977. Author: (plays) Final Passages, 1981, Derelict, 1982, Intermission, 1982, Lunchbreak, 1982, The Survivalist, 1982 (Best of the Fringe award Edinburgh Festival 1984), Tachinoki, 1987, Tall Tales, 1988 (Playwrights Forum award 1988, Best One Act Plays 1993), Heaven on Earth, 1989 (Julie Harris Playwright award Beverly Hills Theatre Guild 1989), The Kentucky Cycle, 1991 (Pulitzer Prize for drama 1992, L.A. Drama Critics Circle Best Play award 1992, Penn Ctr. West award 1993, Best Play Tony award nominee 1993, Best Play Drama Desk award nominee 1993), Conversations with the Spanish Lady and Other One Act Plays, 1993; actor (TV) Father Brown Detective, 1979, Murder in Cowetta County, 1980, George Washington, 1983, Kane and Abel, 1984, Nutcraker, 1987, (films) Act of Vengeance, 1974, Sweet Liberty, 1986, The Manhattan Project, 1986, Bedroom Window, 1987. Grantee Vogelstein Found., 1982, Arthur Found., 1988, Fund for New Am. Plays grantee 1990, Calif. Arts Coun. grantee, 1991. Mem. SAG, Writers Guild, Dramatists Guild, Actors Equity, Ensemble Studio Theatre.

SCHEPP, GEORGE PHILLIP, JR., research consultant; b. L.A., Apr. 14, 1955; s. George Phillip and Mary Opal (Andrews) S. BSBA, El Camino Coll., Torrance, Calif., 1976. Mktg. cons. Rockwell Internat., L.A., 1977-79; with promotional sales and rsch. dept. N.W. Surplus, Inc., Seattle, 1979-81; v.p. incentive premium and promotions Bear Images Internat., Inglewood, Calif., 1981-91; sales promotions rsch. cons. Gifthouse Internat., Cypress, Calif., 1989—; spl. advisor internat. sales, mktg. promotional rsch. divsn. Wade Ceramics Ltd., Stohe-on-Trent, U.K., 1990—; advisor mail order mktg. div. new product devel., promotion Collectors Corner, Arvada, Colo., 1991-94; prodn. cons. spl. video mktg. prodn. Crystal Blue Videos div. L.C.P. Prodns., Ltd., 1992. Republican. Methodist. Office: British Internat Import Ltd PO Box 1578 Inglewood CA 90308-1578

SCHERER, PHIL, airport terminal executive; b. 1941. Dir. acctg. and adminstrn. All Trans Express, San Francisco, 1965-73; dir. acctg. Pacific Intermountain Express Co., Walnut Creek, Calif., 1973-82; CFO, COO Three Way Corp., Sunnyvale, Calif., 1982-90; with MCN Enterprises Inc., 1990—. Office: M C N Enterprises Inc 270 Lawrence Ave South San Francisco CA 94080-6817*

SCHERICH, ERWIN THOMAS, civil engineer, consultant; b. Inland, Nebr., Dec. 6, 1918; s. Harry Erwin and Ella (Peterson) S.; student Hastings Coll., 1937-39, N.C. State Coll., 1943-44; B.S., U. Nebr., 1946-48; M.S., U. Colo., 1948-51; m. Jessie Mae Funk, Jan. 1, 1947; children—Janna Rae Scherich Thornton, Jerilyn Mae Scherich Dobson, Mark Thomas. Civil and design engr. U.S. Bur. Reclamation, Denver, 1948-84, chief spillways and outlets sect., 1974-75, chief dams br., div. design, 1975-78, chief tech. rev. staff, 1978-79, chief div. tech. rev. Office of Asst. Commr. Engring. and Rsch. Ctr., 1980-84; cons. civil engr., 1984—. Mem. U.S. Com. Internat. Commn. on Large Dams. Served with AUS, 1941-45. Registered profl. engr., Colo. Fellow ASCE; mem. NSPE (nat. dir. 1981-87, v.p. southwestern region 1991-93), Profl. Engrs. Colo. (pres. 1977-78), Jefferson County West C. of C. Republican. Methodist. Home and Office: 3915 Balsam St Wheat Ridge CO 80033-4449

SCHERTZ, MORRIS, library director; b. N.Y.C., May 3, 1929; s. Jacob Schertz and Frieda (Kerschner) S.; m. Marcia Ruth Lang, Aug. 4, 1959; children—Hannah, Owen, Bonnie, Jessica, Peter. B.A., NYU, 1952; M.L.S., Pratt Inst., 1956. Librarian Bklyn. Pub. Library, Bklyn., 1956-58; curator Colby Coll., Waterville, Maine, 1958-62; dir. library SUNY-Buffalo, 1962-64; assoc. dir. library U. Mass., Amherst, 1964-69; dir. library U. Denver, 1969—. Contbr. articles to profl. jours. Mem. ALA, Colo. Library Assn., Colo. Alliance of Research Libraries (bd. dirs., treas., Denver, 1973—). Office: U Denver University Blvd Denver CO 80208-0001

SCHEUER, PAUL JOSEF, chemistry educator; b. Heilbronn, Germany, May 25, 1915; came to U.S., 1938; s. Albert and Emma (Neu) S.; m. Alice Elizabeth Dash, Sept. 5, 1950; children: Elizabeth E., Deborah A., David A., Jonathan L.L. BS with high honors, Northeastern U., Boston, 1943; MA, Harvard U., 1947, PhD, 1950. Asst. prof. chemistry U. Hawaii, Honolulu, 1950-55, assoc. prof. chemistry, 1956-61, prof. chemistry, 1961-85, prof. chemistry emeritus, 1985—; vis. prof. Orsted Inst., U. Copenhagen, 1977, 89; Toyo Suisan vis. prof. U. Tokyo, 1992. Author: Chemistry of Marine Natural Products, 1973; editor: (12 series) Marine Natural Products, 1978-93; contbr. 250 articles to profl. jours. Spl. agt. U.S. Army, 1944-46, ETO. Recipient Rsch. Achievement award Am. Soc. Pharmacognosy, 1994; named P.J. Scheuer award Marine Chemists, 1992; NATO fellow, 1975. Fellow AAAS, Royal Soc. Chemistry; mem. Am. Chem. Soc. (sect. chair 1956, 87, Guenther award 1994), Northeastern U. Alumni Assn. (Disting. Alumni award 1984). Office: U Hawaii Chemistry Dept 2545 The Mall Honolulu HI 96822-2233

SCHEUNEMAN, DANA LYNN, school counselor; b. Denver, Nov. 20, 1964; d. Eleanor Louise (Linn) S.; m. Stephen Blane Durrance, Dec. 18, 1993. BA in Psyche Communication, U. Colo., 1988, MA in Psychology, 1993. Rsch. asst. U. Colo. Health Scis. Ctr., Denver, 1988-91; counselor Rape Assistance and Awareness Program, Denver, 1990-93; instr. U. Colo., Denver, 1991-93; therapist Human Svcs. Inc. Counseling Svcs., Denver, 1992-93; sch. counselor Florence Crittenton Sch., Denver, 1993—; contract therapist Carolyn Bushong Psychotherapy Assocs., Denver, 1994—; mem. Denver Partnership for Adolescent Concerns and Successes, 1993—. Contbr. articles to profl. jours. Recipient Excellence in Rsch. award Psi Chi Nat. Honor Soc. in Psychology, 1987; named Outstanding Young Woman of Am., Outstanding Am. Program, 1988. Mem. Am. Counseling Assn., Internat. Order of Ea. Star. Office: Florence Crittenton Sch 2880 W Holden Pl Denver CO 80204-3353

SCHICK, JANELLE KEYSAR, interior designer; b. Camden, Ark., Mar. 19, 1946; d. Wayne Clyde Keysar and Mary Frances (Stansel) Ernst; m. Richard Henry Schick, July 24, 1976; children: Sheri L., Zachary R. AA in Interior Design, Scottsdale (Ariz.) C.C., 1980. Asst. designer Don Beams & Assocs., Phoenix, 1980-81; interior designer Peter Lendrum & Assocs., Phoenix, 1981-82, Tulliani Interiors, Scottsdale, 1982-83; assoc. Design Concepts, Scottsdale, 1983-86, Lara & Rowlands, Scottsdale, 1986-90, Pat Bacon & Assocs., Scottsdale, 1990-91; dir. mktg. and residential design Hart Interiors, Tempe, Ariz., 1991; jr. ptnr. Inter Plan Design Group, Scottsdale, 1991—; vis. faculty Scottsdale C.C., 1985-86. Dir. Scottsdale chpt. Am. Field Svc. Internat., 1980-87, host parent students from Belgium, 1984-85, students from New Zealand, 1994. Mem. Am. Soc. Interior Designers (profl., chmn. mktg. com. Ariz. chpt. 1992-95, allied mem. rep. bd. dirs. Ariz. North chpt. 1992-94, Presdl. citation 1989, 93, 94), Homebuilders Assn. Ctrl. Ariz. (assoc., mem. allied com. 1993-95). Office: Inter Plan Design Group 7373 N Scottsdale Rd Ste A17B Scottsdale AZ 85253

SCHIELE, PAUL ELLSWORTH, JR., educational business owner, writer; b. Phila., Nov. 20, 1924; s. Paul Ellsworth Sr. and Maud (Barclay) S.; m. Sarah Irene Knauss, Aug. 20, 1946; children: Patricia Schiele Tiemann, Sandra Schiele Kicklighter, Deborah Schiele Hartigan. AT, Temple U., 1949; BA, LaVerne U., 1955; MA, Claremont Associated Colls., 1961; PhD, U.S. Internat. U., San Diego, 1970. Cert. sec. tchr., Calif. 1961. Tchr. sci. and math. Lincoln High Sch., Phila., 1956-57, Ontario (Calif.) Sch. Dist., 1957-65; math. and sci. cons. Hacienda La Puente U. Sch. Dist., Calif., 1965-75; asst. prof. Calif. State U., Fullerton, 1975-83; pres., owner Creative Learning Environments and Resources, Glendora, Calif., 1983—, cons. sci. curriculum, 1985—; dir. title III project ESEA, 1974-75, cons. for project, 1975-77; cons. in field. Author: Primary Science, 1972, 2d edit., 1976; editor: A Living World, 1974, 2d edit., 1986; writer 9 sound filmstrips, model units for sci. and math. activity books, 10 sci. activities for L.A. Outdoor Edn. Program, 1980; editor 21 sci. and math. activity books; writer, co-dir. (TV) Marine Biology Series, 1970-71; contbr. numerous articles to profl. magazines, 1960-85; writer and designer of 2 sci. ednl. games; designer in field. Apptd. adv. com. Sci. and Humanities Symposium Calif. Mus. Sci. and Industry, 1974; mem. State Sci. Permit Com., Tide Pools of Calif. Coast, 1974-75; active Playhouse 90, Pasadena (Calif.) Playhouse; mem. Friends of Libr., Friends Libr. Found. Mem. Internat. Platform Assn., ABI Rsch. Assn. (bd. govs.), Calif. Elem. Edn. Assn. (hon.), Nat. PTA (hon.), Calif. Inter-Sci. Coun. (pres., chmn. 1971, 72), Elem Sch. Scis. Assn. (past pres., bd. dirs.), Phi Delta Kappa (chartered). Republican. Lutheran. Home: 231 Catherine Park Dr Glendora CA 91741-3018

SCHIELL, CHARLES RANDALL, leasing company executive; b. Aurora, Colo., Nov. 15, 1952; s. Charles and Audrey Mary (Parsons) S.; m. Janelle Marie Norris, Dec. 28, 1974; children: Charles Christopher, Angela Janelle. BA, U. Colo., 1975; MBA, Colo. State U., 1985. Br. mgr. Gen. Fin. Corp., Ft. Collins, Colo., 1977-78; collection mgr. 1st Nat. Bank, Ft. Collins, 1978-79; mgr. ops. Tri Continental Leasing Corp., Englewood, Colo., 1979-82; credit mgr. Colo. Nat. Leasing Corp., Golden, 1982-83, v.p. credit and ops., 1983-84; v.p. ops, treas. 1st Centennial Leasing Corp., Denver, 1984-89; v.p. ops., treas. 1st Concord Acceptance Corp., 1990-92, sr. v.p. ops., 1992—. Precinct committeeman Denver County Dem. Com., 1976, 77, Jefferson County Dem. Com., 1990—; precinct committeeman Arapahoe County Dem. Com., 1984-86, dist. capt., 1986-88; bd. dirs., treas. Lake Crest Met. Dist., 1990—; bd. dirs. Standley Lake Homeowners Assn., 1991—. Mem. Equipment Leasing Assn., Western Assn. Equipment Lessors. Presbyterian. Home: 12172 W 84th Pl Arvada CO 80005-5167 Office: 1st Concord Acceptance Corp 1515 Arapahoe St Ste 1095 Denver CO 80202-2117

SCHIFF, GUNTHER HANS, lawyer; b. Cologne, Germany, Aug. 19, 1927; came to U.S., 1936; s. Hans and Alice (Goldstein) S.; m. Katharine MacMillan, Jan. 27, 1950 (div. 1957); children: Eric Alan, Mary Alice; m. JoAnn R. Schiff; children: Jage, Hans Judson. B.S.F.S., Georgetown U., 1949, J.D., 1952. Bar: D.C. 1952, Calif. 1953. Assoc., ptnr. various firms, Beverly Hills, Calif., 1954—; sec. Los Angeles Copyright Soc., Beverly Hills, 1975-76. Contbr. articles to profl. jours. Pres. Beverly Hills Civil Svc. Commn., 1984-85, 88-89; pres. Free Arts for Abused Children, 1993-94, dir.; chmn. Rent Control Rev. Bd., Beverly Hills, 1980-84; trustee Young Musicians Found. With USNR, 1945-46. Mem. Beverly Hills Bar Assn. (chmn. Resolutions Com. 1977-78), Los Angeles County Bar Assn., ABA, U.S. Copyright Soc., Los Angeles Copyright Soc. Clubs: Lake Arrowhead Country, Calif. Yacht. Home: 612 N Foothill Rd Beverly Hills CA 90210-3404 Office: Law Office Gunther H Schiff 9430 W Olympic Blvd Beverly Hills CA 90212-4552*

SCHIFF, LAURIE, lawyer; b. Newark, Apr. 24, 1960; d. Norman Nathan and Claire Jane (Schott) S.; m. Ralph Conrad Shelton II, 1992. BS in Law, We. State U., Fullerton, Calif., 1987, JD, 1988. Bar: Calif. 1989. Ptnr. Schiff Mgmt., Newport Beach, Calif., 1983-89; pvt. practice Schiff & Assocs., Irvine, Calif., 1989-91; ptnr. Schiff & Shelton, 1991—; probation monitor State Bar Ct. Calif., 1991—. Producer: (record album) Boys Just Want to Have Sex, 1984. Bd. dirs. Jewish Family Svcs. of Orange County, 1994—. Mem. ABA, Orange County Bar Assn., Am. Mensa, Am. Polocrosse Assn., Saddlebrook Polocrosse (treas. 1991), Am. Quarterhorse Assn., Internat. Cat Assn., Tonks West (v.p. 1994—). Democrat. Jewish. Office: Schiff & Shelton 3 Hutton Centre Dr Ste 400 Santa Ana CA 92707-5736

SCHIFF, LEONARD NORMAN, electrical engineer; b. N.Y.C., Dec. 7, 1938; s. Milton and Elsie (Sternberg) S.; m. Marilyn Claire Leiner, July 14, 1962; children: Michael, Laura. BEE, CCNY, 1960; MSEE, N.Y.U., 1962; PhD in Elec. Engring., Bklyn. Polytechnic Inst., 1968. Mem. tech. staff Bell Labs., Holmdel, N.J., 1960-67, RCA Labs., Princeton, N.J., 1967-78; group head RCA Labs., Princeton, 1978-83, lab. dir., 1983-87; lab. dir. David Sarnoff Rsch. Ctr., Princeton, 1987-93; v.p. tech. Qualcomm, San Diego, 1993—. Patentee in field. Mem. IEEE (sr.), Eta Kappa Nu, Tau Beta Pi, Sigma Xi. Home: 13689 Winstanley Way San Diego CA 92130-1412 Office: Qualcomm 6455 Lusk Blvd San Diego CA 92121-2779

SCHIFF, STEVEN HARVEY, congressman, lawyer; b. Chicago, Ill., Mar. 18, 1947; s. Alan Jerome and Helen M. (Ripper) S.; m. Marcia Lewis, Nov. 8, 1968; children: Jaimi, Daniel. BA, U. Ill., Chgo., 1968; JD, U. N.Mex., 1972. Bar: N.Mex. 1972, U.S. Dist. Ct. N.Mex. 1972, U.S. Ct. Appeals (10th cir.) 1980. Asst. dist. atty. Dist. Atty.'s Office, Albuquerque, 1972-77, sole practice, 1977-79; asst. city atty. City of Albuquerque, 1979-81; dist. atty. State of N.Mex., Albuquerque, 1981-89; mem. 101st-104th Congresses from 1st N.Mex. dist., Washington, D.C., 1989—; mem. govt. reform & oversight com. U.S. House of Reps., mem. judiciary com. and standards of ofcl. conduct com., chmn. sci. subcom. on basic rsch.; lectr. U. N.Mex., Albuquerque, 1981—. Chmn. Bernalillo County Rep. Party Conv., Albuquerque, 1984, 87, staff judge adv. N.Mex. Air N.G. Col. JAGC, USAFR. Recipient Law Enforcement Commendation medal SR, 1984. Mem. ABA, Albuquerque Bar Assn., N.Mex. Bar Assn. Republican. Jewish. Club: Civitan. Lodge: B'nai Brith (pres. 1976-78). Home: 804 Summit Ave NE Albuquerque NM 87106-2045 Office: House of Reps 2404 Rayburn Washington DC 20515-3101 also: 625 Silver Ave SW Ste 140 Albuquerque NM 87102

SCHIFF BERNARD, ELLIE, political and nonprofit fundraiser; b. Saginaw, Mich.; d. William Clifford and Margaret (Adolfino) Bragg; children: David S., Andrew L.; m. George W. Bernard, Aug. 24, 1986. BA, Calif. State U. Exec. dir. Jimmy Stewart Marathon St. John's Hosp., Santa Monica, Calif., 1985-86; fundraiser Barbara Boxer (candidate U.S. Senate), L.A., 1991-92; west coast coord. The Woman's Legal Defense Fund, Washington, 1992-93; fin. dir. so. Calif. Delaine Eastin Com., L.A., 1994; assoc. dir. Women Vote Project, L.A., 1994; dir. Major Gifts, City of Hope, La., 1994—. Mem. Nat. Soc. Fund Raising Execs. Democrat.

SCHIFFNER, CHARLES ROBERT, architect; b. Reno, Sept. 2, 1948; s. Robert Charles and Evelyn (Keck) S.; m. Iovanna Lloyd Wright, Nov. 1971 (div. Sept. 1981); m. Adrienne Anita McAndrews, Jan. 20, 1983. Student, Sacramento Jr. Coll., 1967-68, Frank Lloyd Wright Sch. Architecture, 1968-77. Registered architect, Ariz., Nev., Wis. Architect Taliesin Associated Architects, Scottsdale, Ariz., 1977-83; pvt. practice architecture Phoenix, 1983—; adj. prof. The Frank Lloyd Wright Sch. of Architecture, 1994, 95. Named one of 25 Most Promising Young Americans Under 35, U.S. mag., 1979; recipient AIA Honor award Western Mountain Region, 1993, Western Home awards Sunset Mag., 1989, 91, AIA Ariz. Merit award, 1993 and numerous others. Home: 5202 E Osborn Rd Phoenix AZ 85018-6137 Office: Camelhead Office Ctr 2600 N 44th St # 208 Phoenix AZ 85008-1521

SCHIFFNER, JOAN LESSING, consultant; b. Hollywood, Calif., Nov. 26, 1944; d. Lessing Robert and Ruth Isabel (Chamberlain) Sattler; children: Robert Garrett, Gregory Garrett, Laura Garrett. BA, San Jose State U., 1970, postgrad.; postgrad., U. Calif. Cert. in non-profit orgn.mgmt. Cons. to health and human svc. govtl. and non-profit orgns. Civilian Pers. Office, Fort Ord, Calif., 1993—; ptnr. Millson, Schiffner and Assocs.; bd. dirs. Growth and Opportunity, Inc, Am. Red Cross, 1990—; cons. Saving Our Libr.'s Excellence Com. 1992-93. Pub. info. officer San Benito County (Calif.) United Way, bd. dirs., 1988-90; founding mem. San Benito County Vol. Ctr. Task Force, San Benito County Cable Access Commn., 1987-90; co-founder San Benito County Action Team; vice chair San Benito County Voluntary Orgns. Active in Disasters, 1990-91; appointed to cen. com. ARC No. Calif. Earthquake Relief and Preparedness Project, 1991; pres. Network of San Benito, 1988-90; mem. San Benito County Econ. Group, Mex. Am. Com. on Edn., 1970—, Hollister Sister Cities Assn., 1989—; sec. bd. dirs. Econ. Devel. Corp.; exec. dir. San Benito County Interfaith, 1990-91; mem. adv. bd. San Benito Health Found., 1991—; pub. rels. chair San Benito County AIDS Project, 1992-94; active numerous non-profit and civic orgns.; bd. dirs ARC. Mem. AAUW, San Benito County C. of C., Phi Alpha Theta, Psi Chi, Alpha Kappa Delta. Democrat. Roman Catholic. Home: 845 Helen Dr Hollister CA 95023-6613

SCHILBRACK, KAREN GAIL, system analyst; b. Tomahawk, Wis., Sept. 28; d. Edward Richard and Irene Angeline (Ligman) S. Student U. Calif.-Santa Barbara, 1967-69; BA in Anthropology, U. Calif.-Davis, 1971; postgrad. in Edn. and Archeology, Calif. State Poly. U., San Luis Obispo, 1971-72. Cert. tchr., computer specialist, data processing; lic. cosmetologist. Computer specialist Facilities Systems Office, Port Hueneme, Calif., 1975-78, sr. computer specialist, 1978-80, project mgr. U.S. Naval Constrn. Bn. Ctr., 1980-89, imaging systems computer specialist Comptr. Office, 1989-92; fiscal quality specialist Dept. Def. Finance and Acctg. Svc., DAO, Port Hueneme, 1992—; tng. cons. FACSO, 1981, 82; curriculum cons. Ventura Community Coll., Calif., 1981-89; instr. U.S. Navy, Port Hueneme, 1983, 91, Civil Service Commn., Port Hueneme, 1978-80. Author: AMALGAMAN Run Procedures, 1976; Cobol Programming Efficiencies, 1978, Imaging System UserManual, 1991; co-author, editor: Training Manual for Direct Data Entry System, 1983. Mem. Vols. for Camarillo State Hosp., Camarillo, 1978-88, coord. Ventura County, 1981; chmn. scholarship fund drive Ventura, Santa Barbara, Los Angeles, Counties, 1980. Named Young Career Woman of Yr., Calif. Bus. and Profl. Women, 1979. Mem. Young Ladies Inst. (pres. Santa Paula, dist. dep. Ventura/Santa Barbara Counties), Am. Biog. Inst. Research Assn. (lifetime dep. gov.). Lodge: Toastmistress. Home: 6993 Wheeler Canyon Rd Santa Paula CA 93060-9759 Office: Compt Office Code 24-A USNCBC Port Hueneme CA 93042

SCHILLER, HERBERT IRVING, social scientist, author; b. N.Y.C., Nov. 5, 1919; s. Benjamin Franklin and Gertrude (Perner) S.; m. Anita Rosenbaum, Nov. 5, 1946; children: Daniel T., P. Zachary. B in Social Sci., CCNY, 1940; MA, Columbia U., 1941; PhD, NYU, 1960. Teaching fellow CCNY, 1940-41, lectr. econs., 1949-59; economist U.S. Govt., 1941-42, 46-48; mem. faculty Pratt Inst., Bklyn., 1950-63; prof. econs., chmn. dept. social studies Pratt Inst., 1962-63; research asso. prof. Bur. Econ. and Bus. Research, U. Ill. at Urbana, 1963-65, research prof., 1965-70; prof. communication U. Calif., San Diego, 1970-90, prof. emeritus, 1990—; lectr. Bklyn. Acad. Music, 1961-66; vis. fellow Inst. Policy Studies, Wash., 1968; vis. prof. U. Amsterdam, The Netherlands, 1973-74; Thord-Gray vis. lectr. U. Stockholm, 1978; vis. prof. comms. Hunter Coll., CUNY, 1978-79, Am. U., 1991-93, NYU, 1993-95. Author: Mass Communications and American Empire, 1969, rev. edit., 1992, Superstate: Readings in the Military-Industrial Complex, 1970, The Mind Managers, 1973, Communication and Cultural Domination, 1976, Who Knows: Information in the Age of the Fortune 500, 1981, Information and the Crisis Economy, 1984, Culture Inc.: The Corporate Takeover of Public Expression, 1989, (with others) Hope and Folly: The U.S. and UNESCO, 1945-85, 1989; editor Quar. Rev. Econs. and Bus., 1963-70; co-editor: Triumph of the Image: The Media's War in the Persian Gulf, 1992, Beyond National Sovereignty: International Communication in the 1990s, 1993. Served with AUS, 1942-45, MTO. Mem. AAAS, Internat. Assn. Mass Communication Research (v.p.), Internat. Inst. Communications (trustee 1978-84), AAUP (sec. Ill. U.), Phi Beta Kappa. Home: 7109 Monte Vista Ave La Jolla CA 92037-5326 Office: U Calif San Diego La Jolla CA 92093

SCHILLER, JOHANNES AUGUST, clergyman, educator; b. Gaylord, Kans., June 17, 1923; s. Johann Carl and Adele Dorothea (Kirchoff) S.; m. Aleen B. Linhardt, Aug. 26, 1946; children: Paul Omar, Samuel Robert. BA, Capital U., 1945; cand. theology, Evangel. Luth. Theol. Sem., 1947; MA, U. Mo., 1959; PhD in Sociology, U. Wash., 1967. Ordained to ministry Am. Luth. Ch., 1947. Pastor Peace Luth. Ch., Sterling, Colo., 1947-49, Trinity-St. Paul Parish, Malcolm, Iowa, 1949-51, Immanuel Luth. Ch., Beatrice, Nebr., 1951-56, Salem Luth. Ch., Lenexa, Kans., 1956-58; asst. prof., assoc. prof., now prof. sociology Pacific Luth. U., Tacoma, Wash., 1958-91; prof. emeritus Pacific Luth. U., Tacoma, 1991—; regency prof. Pacific Luth. U., Tacoma, Wash., 1976—, chair dept. sociology, 1956-71, 86-88, dean div. social scis., 1969-76, 88-91, dir. grad. programs div. social scis., 1977-82, dir. Ctr. Social Rsch. and Pub. Policy, 1987-90; chaplain Beatrice State Home, 1953-56; adj. prof. San Francisco Theol. Sem., San Anselmo, Calif., 1978-89. Editor: The American Poor, 1982; contbr. articles to profl. publs. Mem. Am. Sociology Assn., Pacific Sociology Assn., Nat. Coun. Family Rels., Wash. State Sociol. Assn. Home: 1217 Wheeler St S Tacoma WA 98444-3843

SCHILLER, NELSON BENJAMIN, physician, cardiologist; b. Buffalo, Apr. 20, 1940; s. Arthur and Belle (Shroder) S.; m. Ellen Jane Wile, Aug. 29, 1964; children: Laura, Emily. BS, Union Coll., Schenectady, N.Y., 1962;

MD, SUNY, Buffalo, 1966. Diplomate Am. Bd. Internal Medicine, sub-bd. Cardiology. Intern Ochsner Med. Found., 1966-67; resident in internal medicine U. Calif., San Diego, 1969-71; USPHS fellow in cardiology U. Calif., San Francisco, 1971-73, prof. medicine and radiology, 1988-92, prof. medicine, radiology and anesthesiology, 1992—, dir. echocardiography lab., 1973—. Assoc. editor Jour. Am. Coll. Cardiology, 1992—; author more than 200 sci. papers and book chpts. Lt. comdr. USPHS, 1967-69. NIH grantee. Fellow Am. Coll. Cardiology. Office: U Calif Med Ctr Box 0214 San Francisco CA 94143-0214

SCHILLING, DEAN WILLIAM, manufacturing executive; b. Waverly, Iowa, Apr. 25, 1944; s. Alvin Louis and Etta Christine (Poppe) S.; m. Betty Ann (Homeister), Aug. 5, 1962; children: Angela Marie, Christine Ann. AS, Iowa State U., 1964, BS, 1969. Engr. Systems Genetics, Clarksville, Iowa, 1970-81; sr. tech. support Hewlett Packard, Sunnyvale, Calif., 1983-85; pres. Cryo Genetic Technology, Soquel, Calif., 1985—. Inventor biol. devices and methods to remedy human infertility; holder 3 patents. Mem. Am. Fertility Soc., Soc. Cryobiology, Iowa State Alumni. Lutheran. Lodge: Order of Knoll (founders club 1988).

SCHILLING, EDWIN CARLYLE, III, lawyer; b. Baton Rouge, Apr. 5, 1943; s. Edwin Carlyle and Ann (LeTarde) S.; m. Lanell Holder, Dec. 18, 1964; children: Joel, Daniel. BA in Physics/Math., Baylor U., 1966; JD, La. State U., 1969. Bar: La. 1969, Colo. 1989, Alaska 1990, U.S. Supreme Ct. 1982, U.S. Ct. Mil. Appeals 1981, U.S. Tax Ct. 1982, U.S. Ct. Appeals (Fed. cir.) 1982. Commd. USAF, 1969-89, advanced through grades to lt. col.; assoc. prof. law USAF Acad., Colo., 1972-76; staff judge advocate Kunsan AB, Korea, 1976-77, Myrtle Beach (S.C.) AFB, 1977-80; dir. USAF Legal Assistance Program, Washington, 1980-83; with Air War Coll., 1983-84; staff judge advocate Elemdorf AFB, Alaska, 1984-87; asst. staff judge advocate Air Force Acctg. and Fin. Ctr., Lowry AFB, Colo., 1987-89; pvt. practice law Aurora, Colo., 1989—. Co-author book: Survival Manual for Women in Divorce, 1990, Survival Manual for Men in Divorce; co-author video tape/manual: How to Successfully Manage Military Divorce, 1990. Sec. Eastridge Civic Assn., Aurora, 1988—; bd. dirs. Consumer Credit Counseling Svc., Anchorage, 1985-87, Myrtle Beach Fed. Credit Union, 1978-81. Mem. ABA (exec. mem. fed. procedures and legislation com.), La. Bar Assn., Colo. Bar Assn., Alaska Bar Assn. Republican. Presbyterian. Office: 2767 S Parker Rd Ste 230 Aurora CO 80014-2701

SCHILLING, FREDERICK AUGUSTUS, JR., geologist, consultant; b. Phila., Apr. 12, 1931; s. Frederick Augustus and Emma Hope (Christoffer) S.; m. Ardis Ione Dovre, June 12, 1957 (div. 1987); children: Frederick Christopher, Jennifer Dovre. BS in Geology, Wash. State U., 1953; PhD in Geology, Stanford U., 1962. Computer geophysicist United Geophys. Corp., Pasadena, Calif., 1955-56; geologist various orgns., 1956-61, U.S. Geol. Survey, 1961-64; underground engr. Climax (Colo.) Molybdenum Co., 1966-68; geologist Keradamex Inc., Anaconda Co., M.P. Grace, Ranchers Exploration & Devel. Corp., Albuquerque and Grants, N.Mex., 1968-84, Hecla Mining Co., Coeur d'Alene, Idaho, 1984-86, various engring. and environ. firms, Calif., 1986-91; prin. F. Schilling Cons., Canyon Lake, Calif., 1991—. Author: Bibliography of Uranium, 1976. Del. citizen amb. program People to People Internat., USSR, 1990-91. With U.S. Army, 1953-55. Fellow Explorers Club; mem. Geol. Soc. Am., Am. Assn. Petroleum Geologists, Soc. Mining Engrs., Internat. Platform Assn., Adventurers' Club Inc. L.A., Masons, Kiwanis, Sigma Xi, Sigma Gamma Epsilon. Republican. Presbyterian. Office: F Schilling Cons 30037 Steel Head Dr Canyon Lake CA 92587-7460

SCHILLING, JANET NAOMI, nutritionist, consultant; b. North Platte, Neb., Mar. 1, 1939; d. Jens Harold and Naomi Frances (Meyer) Hansen; children: Allan Edward III, Karl Jens. BS, U. Neb., 1961; MS, Ohio State U., 1965; MPH, U. Calif., Berkeley, 1991. Registered dietitian. Tchr. home econs. Peace Corps., Dimbokro, Ivory Coast, 1962-64; cons. nutrition Wis. Divsn. Health, La Crosse, 1966-67, 69; dietary cons. Cozad (Neb.) Community Hosp., 1968; instr. Viterbo Coll., La Crosse, 1974-81; lectr. U. Wis., La Crosse, 1982-84; teaching asst. ESL Sch. Dist. La Crosse, 1984-87; nutrition educator Women, Infant, and Children Program, 1988-89; nutrition cons. Vis. Nurses, LaCrosse, 1987-89; dietitian Merrithew Meml. Hosp., Martinez, Calif., 1992; pub. health nutrition cons. Women Infant & Childrens Program Policy and Compliance Unit, Sacramento, 1995; nutrition cons. Wis. Winnebago Nation, 1991; pediatric dietitian in Romanian Orphanges thru World Vision, 1993; nutritionist Contra Costa Head Start & Child Devel., 1994. Author: Life in the Nutrition Community, 1980, Life in the Nutrition Cycle II, 1980; co-author: Nutrition Activities, 1984, Recipe Book of Nutritious Snacks, 1985. Mem. LaCrosse Sch. Dist. Nutrition Task Force, 1976-88, Sunday sch. tchr., supr. Our Savior's Luth. Ch., 1975-86, chmn., Mobile Meals, 1982-86; v.p. membership booster club Ctrl. High Sch. LaCrosse, 1985-87, pres., 12987-88; bd. dirs. YMCA, LaCrosse, 1982-88; mem. No. Calif. Returned Peace Corps Vols., 1990—. Mem. AAUW (pres. 1978-80, Named Grant scholar 1981), APHA, LaCrosse Area Dietetic Assn. (1st pres. 1968-69, Outstanding Dietitian Yr. 1985), Wis. Dietetic Assn. (chmn. educators 1983-85), No. Wis. Dietetic Assn. (pres. 1982), Am. Dietetic Assn. (educators practice group 1978-90), LaCrosse Jaycees (Carol award 1973), Calif. Dietetic Assn. Democrat. Home: 1604 Roger Ct El Cerrito CA 94530-2028

SCHILLING, JOLYON DAVID, vascular and general surgeon; b. Oklahoma City, Oct. 10, 1958; s. John Albert and Lucille Olive (West) S.; m. Diane Helina Schilling, Apr. 2, 1994. BS, U. Wash., 1981, MD, 1986. Resident gen. surgery U. Tex. S.W. Med. Sch., Dallas, 1986-91; fellow vascular surgery U. Ariz. Sch. Medicine, Tucson, 1991-93; pvt. practice Southwestern Surgery Assocs., Tucson, 1993—; clin. asst. prof. dept. surgery U. Ariz., Tucson, 1994—; flight surgeon 162d F.G. Ariz. Air Nat. Guard, Tucson, 1993—. Fellow Am. Coll. Angiology, S.W. Surg. Assn.; mem. ACS (assoc.). Office: Southwestern Surg Assocs 5300 E Erickson Dr Ste 108 Tucson AZ 85712-2809

SCHILLING, VIVIAN, novelist, screenwriter and actress; b. Wichita, Kans.; d. Donald A. and Lou (Nichols) Schilling; m. Eric Parkinson. Student in theatre arts, Wichita State U., 1982. Actress with leading roles in Soultaker, The Legend of Wolf Mountain, In A Moment of Passion, Future Shock, Savage Land, others. Screenwriter, co-prodr. films: Terror-Eyes, 1990, Soultaker, 1991, Future Shock, 1993; author: Sacred Prey, 1994 (Golden Scroll award for outstanding achievement in lit. 1994). Recipient Saturn award Acad. Sci. Fiction, 1992. Mem. Women in Film (hon.), Screen Actors Guild, Authors Guild. Office: Truman Press Inc 15445 Ventura Blvd Ste 905 Sherman Oaks CA 91403-3005

SCHIMMEL, WALTER P., aerospace engineer, educator; b. Chgo.; s. Walter P. Sr. and Ruth Ann-Margaret (Herzan) S.; m. Jacqueline Pica, Dec. 29, 1962; children: Lisa N., Stephen P., Nadja A. BSME, Purdue U., 1965; MSME, U. Notre Dame, 1966, PhD, 1969. Mem. profl. staff Sandia Nat. Labs., Albuquerque, 1969-82; chief of svc. Hydro-Que. Rsch. Inst., Montreal, 1982-85; dept. chmn., prof. aerospace engring. Embry-Riddle U., Daytona Beach, Fla., 1985-93; tech. transfer mgr. Sandia Nat. Labs., Albuquerque, 1993—; pres. Performances Assocs., 1970—. Contbr. articles to profl. jours. Served with U.S. Army, 1954-62. Fellow ASME; mem. AIAA, Am. Bd. Engring./Tech. Accreditation, Sigma Xi, Tau Beta Pi, Pi Tau Sigma.

SCHINDLER, KEITH WILLIAM, software engineer; b. Selma, Calif., May 27, 1959; s. George Junior and Doris Angelynn (Young) S. BSEE in Computer Sci. with honors, U. Calif., Berkeley, 1982. Programmer Summit Group, Berkeley, 1979-81; jr. programmer Control Data, Inc., Sunnyvale, Calif., 1983; assoc. mem. tech. staff Symbolics, Inc., Chatsworth, Calif., 1987-88; sr. mem. tech. support Graphics div. Symbolics, L.A., 1988-90; software engr. Sidley, Wright & Assoc., Hollywood, Calif., 1990-92; cons. Out-Takes, Inc., L.A., 1992—; ptnr. Schindler Imaging, West Hollywood, Calif., 1992—; tech. dir. Sidley-Wright & Assoc., Hollywood, 1990-92, Movie Time Cable Channel, Hollywood, 1990, Video Image, Marina Del Rey, Calif., 1990; cert. developer Apple Computer, Inc., 1991—, Truevision, Inc., 1990—; developer software Out-Takes' Digital Photography System; creator The Matte Machine. Patentee in field. Mem. IEEE Computer Soc., Assn. for Computing Machinery (spl. interest group graphics), Soc. Motion Picture and TV Engrs., Tau Beta Pi. Democrat. Office: Schindler Imaging 28276 Rey De Copas Ln Malibu CA 90265-4461

SCHINE, WENDY WACHTELL, foundation administrator; b. White Plains, N.Y., May 5, 1961; d. Thomas and Esther Carole (Pickard) Wachtell; m. Jonathan Mark Schine, Sept. 2, 1990; children: Jameson Myer, Bradley Thomas. BA, Wellesley Coll., 1983; MA in Journalism, U. So. Calif., L.A., 1987. Legis. asst. U.S. House Reps., Washington, 1983-85; varied positions KCBS-TV, L.A., 1986-88; v.p. Joseph Drown Found., L.A., 1988—; bd. dirs. Arts, Inc., L.A., L.A. Urban Funders, L.A. Cities in Schs.; advisor Psychol. Trauma Ctr., L.A., 1988—, Ctr. for Talented Youth, Glendale, Calif., 1989—. Mem. oversight com. Pathways Project, Big Sisters, L.A. Office: Joseph Drown Found Ste 1930 1999 Avenue Of The Stars Los Angeles CA 90067-6051

SCHIPPER, MERLE, art historian and critic, exhibition curator; b. Toronto, Ont., Can.; came to U.S., 1943; d. Leon J. and Libby (Genesove) Solway; m. Bernard Schipper, May 22, 1943 (div. Jan. 1980); children: Lee, Amy Schipper Howe. BA, U. Toronto, 1943; MA, UCLA, 1970, PhD, 1974. Instr. extension UCLA, 1974-78, 83-84, lectr. summer session, 1977-79, 84; vis. artist grad. sch. Claremont (Calif.) U., 1979; lectr. U. So. Calif., L.A., 1985; corr. L.A. ARTNews, N.Y.C., 1985-87; columnist ARTScene, L.A., 1987—; project dir. Santa Monica (Calif.) Arts Found., 1987-89; art book reviewer L.A. Daily News, 1990-91; organizer Congress Internat. Assn. Art Critics, 1991; mem. pub. art panel Santa Monica Arts Commn., 1993—; mem. artist selection panel Met. Transp. Assn., Chinatown Sta., 1993. Panelist, mem. grants com. Art Orgn. Dept. Cultural Affairs, L.A., 1984-85; mem. selection com. of sculpture installation Calif. Med. Ctr., L.A., 1986; mem. Rev. Com. Hist. Resources Survey Project, L.A., 1978-85, So. Calif. Com. for Contemporary Art Documentation, L.A., 1985-89. Rsch. fellow Indo-U.S. Subcommn., 1988; travel grantee Ptnrs. of Ams., 1989. Mem. Coll. Art Assn., Internat. Assn. Art Critics. Home and Office: 835 Grant St Apt 3 Santa Monica CA 90405-1328

SCHIRMER, HENRY WILLIAM, architect; b. St. Joseph, Mo., Dec. 8, 1922; s. Henry William and Asta (Hansen) S.; m. Jane Irene Krueger; children: Andrew Lewis, Monica Sue, Daniel F. Carr. AS, St. Joseph Jr. Coll., 1942; BArch Design, U. Mich., 1949. Staff architect Eugene Meier, Architect, St. Joseph, 1939, Neville, Sharp & Simon, Kansas City, Mo., 1946, 49, Ramey & Himes, Wichita, Kans., 1950-57; ptnr. Schaefer & Schirmer, Wichita, 1957-60, Schaefer, Schirmer & Eflin, Wichita, 1960-72, Schaefer, Schirmer & Assocs. P.A., Wichita, 1972-76; prin. Henry W. Schirmer, Topeka, 1976-92, Green Valley, 1993—. Editor: Profile Ofcl. Directory of AIA, 1978, 80, 83, 85, 87, 89-90, 91-92, pub., 1985-92; contbr. AIA Handbook; works include Burn Ctr. U. Kans. Med. Ctr., Allen County Community Jr. Coll., Iola, Kans., Rainbow Mental Health Ctr., Kansas City, Kans., Capitol Area Plaza Project, Topeka. Pres. East Br. YMCA, 1954—; bd. dirs. Wichita YMCA, 1956-73; bd. dirs. San Ignacio Heights H.O.A., 1995—. With C.E. U.S. Army, ETO. Decorated Purple Heart. Fellow AIA (past pres. Kans. chpt., seminar leader, chmn. nat. com. office mgmt.1976, nat. bd. dirs. 1979-81, treas. 1982-86, fin. com. 1988, nat. documents com. 1978, chmn. nat. com. on project mgmt. 1977, Edward C. Kemper medal 1990); mem. Kans. Bd. Tech. Professions (chmn. bd. 1985, 87), Nat. Coun. Archtl. Registration Bds. (profl. conduct com. 1986-89, procedures and documents com. 1990), Tau Sigma Delta. Lutheran. Home: 4191 S Emelita Dr Green Valley AZ 85614-5614

SCHIRRA, WALTER MARTY, JR., business consultant, former astronaut; b. Hackensack, N.J., Mar. 12, 1923; s. Walter Marty and Florence (Leach) S.; m. Josephine Cook Fraser, Feb. 23, 1946; children: Walter Marty III, Suzanne Karen. Student, Newark Coll. Engring., 1940-42; B.S., U.S. Naval Acad., 1945; D. Astronautics (hon.), Lafayette Coll., U. So. Calif., N.J. Inst. Tech. Commd. ensign U.S. Navy, 1945, advanced through grades to capt., 1965; designated naval aviator, 1948; service aboard battle cruiser Alaska, 1945-46; service with 7th Fleet, 1946; assigned Fighter Squadron 71, 1948-51; exchange pilot 154th USAF Fighter Bomber Squadron, 1951; engaged in devel. Sidewinder missile China Lake, Calif., 1952-54; project pilot F7U-3 Cutlass; also instr. pilot F7U-3 Cutlass and FJ3 Fury, 1954-56; ops. officer Fighter Squadron 124, U.S.S. Lexington, 1956-57; assigned Naval Air Safety Officer Sch., 1957, Naval Air Test Ctr., 1958-59; engaged in suitability devel. work F4H, 1958-59; joined Project Mercury, man-in-space, NASA, 1959; pilot spacecraft Sigma 7 in 6 orbital flights, Oct. 1962; in charge operations and tng. Astronaut Office, 1964-69; command pilot Gemini 6 which made rendezvous with target, Gemini 7, Dec. 1965; comdr. 11 day flight Apollo 7, 1968; ret., 1969; pres. Regency Investors, Inc., Denver, 1969-70; chmn., chief exec. officer ECCO Corp., Englewood, Colo., 1970-73; chmn. Sernco, Inc., 1973-74; with Johns-Manville Corp., Denver, 1974-77; v.p. devel. Goodwin Cos., Inc., Littleton, Colo., 1978-79; ind. cons., 1979-80; dir. Kimberly Clark, 1983-91. Decorated D.F.C.(3), Air medal (2), Navy D.S.M.; recipient Distinguished Service medal (2), also; Exceptional Service medal NASA. Fellow Am. Astronautical Soc., Soc. Exptl. Test Pilots. Home and Office: PO Box 73 Rancho Santa Fe CA 92067-0073

SCHLADOR, PAUL RAYMOND, JR., insurance agent; b. Riverside, Calif., Oct. 16, 1934; s. Paul Raymond Sr. Schlador and Lois Geraldine (Burrus) Kaeding; m. Evangeline Kathern, Aug. 19, 1955; children: Debora Lynn TeSam, Cheryl Jean Bastian, Bonnie Kay Tucker. Student, San Diego City Jr. Coll., 1954-55, Ins. Industry, San Diego, 1960-62, Am. Coll., San Diego, 1970-74. CLU. Agt. Bankers Life of Nebr., San Diego, 1959-63; agt./ mgr. Southwestern Life Ins. Co., San Diego, 1959—; ind. agt. State Farm Ins. Co., San Diego, 1978—. With USNG, 1952-60. Mem. San Diego Assn. Life Underwriters (pres. 1989-90, legis. v.p. 1988), Kiwanis Club El Cajon Valley. Republican. Methodist. Home: 1267 Oakdale Ave # C El Cajon CA 92021-6454 Office: State Farm Ins 7800 University Ave # 1A La Mesa CA 91941-4928 also: BPOE Lodge # 1812 El Cajon CA 92021

SCHLAX, SHARON LYNN NEWELL, physical education educator; b. Oxnard, Calif., Feb. 14, 1950; d. Ruth Nana (Pool) Horton; 1 child, Amber Lynn Gould. BA, Calif. Bapt. Coll., Riverside, 1971; MS, Azusa Pacific U., 1985. Cert. tchr., Calif. Tchr. phys. edn. Mission Mid. Sch., Riverside, 1971—, dept. head, 1987—; tchr. spl. edn. Summer Sch., Riverside County Schs., 1989—; tchr. Teens Learn Choices Mission Mid. Sch., 1986—; tennis coach; softball, track and intramural sports coach. Democrat. Home: 21409 Webster Ave Perris CA 92570 Office: Mira Loma Mid Sch 5051 Steve St Riverside CA 92509

SCHLEGEL, JOHN PETER, university president; b. Dubuque, Iowa, July 31, 1943; s. Aaron Joseph and Irma Joan (Hingtgen) S. BA, St. Louis U., 1969, MA, 1970; BDiv, U. London, 1973; DPhil, Oxford U., 1977. Joined Soc. of Jesus, 1963, ordained priest Roman Cath. Ch., 1973. From asst. prof. to assoc. prof. Creighton U., Omaha, 1976-79, asst. acad. v.p., 1978-82; dean Coll. Arts and Scis. Rockhurst Coll., Kansas City, Mo., 1982-84, Marquette U., Milw., 1984-88; exec. and acad. v.p. John Carroll U., Cleve., 1988-91; pres. U. San Francisco, 1991—; cons. Orgn. for Econ. Devel. and Cooperation, Paris, 1975-76. Author: Bilingualism and Canadian Policy in Africa, 1979; editor: Towards a Redefinition of Development, 1976; contbr. articles to profl. jours. Mem. Milwaukee County Arts Coun., 1986-88, Mo. Coun. on Humanities, Kansas City, 1984; trustee St. Louis U., 1985-91, Loyola U. Chgo., 1988-95, Loyola U. New Orleans, 1995—, St. Ignatius H.S., Cleve., 1990-91, Loyola Coll. in Md., 1992—; bd. dirs. San Francisco ARC, 1991-94, Coro Found., Commonwealth Club Calif. Oxford U. grantee, 1974-76; Govt. of Can. grantee, 1977-78. Mem. Am. Coun. on Edn., Can. Studies in U.S., Olympic Club, Univ. Club, Bohemian Club. Office: U San Francisco Office of Pres 2130 Fulton St San Francisco CA 94117-1080

SCHLEH, EDWARD CARL, business analyst; b. St. Paul, Nov. 2, 1915; s. Edward G. and Augusta (Seltz) S.; m. Myra Adelle Oberschulte, June 7, 1941; children: Jeanne, John, Richard, Elizabeth, Robert. BBA, U. Minn., 1937. Placement officer U. Minn. Employment Office, Mpls., 1937-39, Ells Employment Svc., Mpls., 1939-40; mgr. personnel rsch. 3-M Co., St. Paul, 1940-48; pres. Schleh Assocs., Inc., Mpls. and Palo Alto, Calif., 1948-95; U.S. del. to internat. mgmt. confs. in Chile, France, Germany, Australia, Japan; bd. Exec. Svc. Corps., San Francisco; adv. bd. Santa Clara U. Bus. Sch.; bd. dirs. Coun. Internat. Progress in Mgmt.; presenter seminars, speeches for profit orgns. U.S. and abroad. Author: Successful Executive Action, Management by Results, Effective Management of Personnel, The Management Tactician, How to Boost Your Return on Management; contbr. articles to profl. publs. Mem. Soc. Advancement of Mgmt. (Frederick Taylor Key award), Am. Mgmt. Assn. (wall of fame). Home: 368 Selby Ln Menlo Park CA 94027-3933

SCHLEICHER, ROBERT EARL, economist; b. Livington, Mont., Dec. 16, 1960. BS in Bus., Mont. State U., 1984, MPA, 1986. Grad. teaching asst. Mont. State U., Bozeman, 1985-86; aide, adminstrv. asst. Gov.'s Office, Helena, Mont., 1987-89; rsch. specialist Mont. Dept. Labor and Industry, Helena, Mont., 1989—. Budget chair, treas. Helena Citizens' Coun., Helena, 1993, chair, 1994. Mem. Am. Soc. Pub. Adminstrn., Internt. Assn. Pers. Employment Svcs. Home: 1823 E Broadway St Helena MT 59601-4711 Office: Mont Dept Labor & Industry 1301 Lockey Helena MT 59624

SCHLENKER, EDGAR ALBERT, business director, educator, entrepreneur; b. Sacramento, June 4, 1961; s. Albert and Irmgard (Hess) S.; m. Adele Margaret Gibbons, Jan. 8, 1983 (div.); 1 child, Margaret Adele. BS in econ./fin., Calif. State U., Sacramento, 1986; MBA, U. Calif., Berkeley, 1988. Founder Precious Gifts Ltd., Sacramento, 1983-86; prin. RSA Cons., Berkeley, 1986-88; assoc. Dowdell Investment Banking, San Rafael, Calif., 1988-89; dir. mktg. and sales Info Store, Inc., San Francisco, 1988-90; dir. Solano County Small Bus. Devel. Ctr., Suisun, Calif., 1990—; chmn. Internat. Reprint Corp., Berkeley, 1988—; pres. IRC Med. Pub., Benicia, Calif. chmn. Internat. Reprint Corp., Berkeley, 1988—; pres. IRC Med. Pub., Benicia, Calif. Elected to Solano County Bd. Suprs., 2d Dist., 1992. Fellow Inst. Dirs.; mem. U. Calif.-Berkeley Alumni Assn. Republican. Home: PO Box 1576 Benicia CA 94510 Office: Solano County Small Bus Devel Ctr 320 Campus Ln Suisun City CA 94585-1400

SCHLESINGER, ROBERT JACKSON, business administration educator; b. N.Y., Dec. 5, 1927; s. Robert B. and Corrine Marie (Jackson) S.; m. Sylvia Barbara Tiersten, Dec. 24, 1980; children: Lisa Roberta, Karen Ann. BSEE, U. Conn., 1953; MS in Ops. Rsch., West Coast U., 1972; PhD, Brunel U., Eng., 1984. Registered profl. engr., Calif. Design engr. GE Co., Syracuse, N.Y., 1953-55; mem. tech. staff Ramo-Wooldridge, L.A., 1955-58; mem. corp. staff Gen. Dynamics Corp., San Diego, 1958-61; v.p. mktg. and systems ITT, Calif. and N.J., 1961-65; dir. R&D Packard Bell divsn. Teledyne, Newbury Park, Calif., 1965-68; mem. tech. staff Cal-Tech.'s JPL, Pasadena, Calif., 1968-70; pres., CEO Rho Sigma Inc., L.A., 1970-80; prof. info. and decision systems dept. San Diego State U., 1984—; lectr. in field. Author: Principles of Electronic Warfare, 1961; contbr. articles to profl. publs., chpts. to books. Mem. IEEE, Sigma Xi. Home: PO Box 3457 La Mesa CA 91944-3457 Office: San Diego State U College Ave San Diego CA 92182-0127

SCHLESINGER, RUDOLF BERTHOLD, lawyer, educator; b. Munich, Germany, Oct. 11, 1909; s. Morris and Emma (Aufhauser) S.; m. Ruth Hirschland, Sept. 4, 1942; children: Steven, June, Fay. Dr. Jur., U. Munich, 1933; LLB, Columbia U., 1942; Dr. Jur. (hon.), U. Trento, 1994. Bar: N.Y. 1942, U.S. Supreme Ct. 1946. Law sec. to Chief Judge Irving Lehman, N.Y. Ct. Appeals, 1942-43; confidential law sec. Judges N.Y. Ct. Appeals, 1943-44; asso. Milbank, Tweed, Hope & Hadley, N.Y.C., 1944-48; asso. prof. Cornell U., 1948-51, prof., 1951-75, William N. Cromwell prof. internat. and comparative law, 1956-75; prof. Hastings Coll. Law, U. Calif., 1975—, vis. prof., 1974; Cons. N.Y. State Law Rev. Commn., 1949—; mem. adv. com. internat. rules of jud. procedure, 1959-66; vis. prof. Columbia, 1952, Salzburg Seminar, 1964; Charles Inglis Thomson disting. vis. prof. U. Colo., summer 1976. Author: Cases, Text and Materials on Comparative Law, 4th edit., 1980, (with Baade, Damaska and Herzog) 5th edit., 1988, (with Baade, Herzog and Wise) Supplement to 5th edit., 1994; Formation of Contracts: A Study of the Common Core of Legal Systems, 2 vols., 1968, others; editor-in-chief Columbia Law Rev., 1941-42; bd. editors Am. Jour. Comparative Law; author articles on legal topics. Trustee Cornell U., 1961-66. Carnegie Corp. Reflective year fellowship, 1962-63. Mem. Am. Law Inst. (life), Am. Bar Assn., Internat. Acad. Comparative Law, Phi Beta Kappa, Order of Coif. Home: 1333 Jones St San Francisco CA 94109-4179 Office: U Calif Hastings Coll of Law 200 Mcallister St San Francisco CA 94102-4707

SCHLESINGER, RUTH HIRSCHLAND, art curator, consultant; b. Essen, Germany, Mar. 11, 1920; came to U.S., 1936; d. Kurt M. and Henriette (Simons) Hirschland; m. Rudolf B. Schlesinger, Sept. 4, 1942; children: Steven, June, Fay. BA cum laude, Wheaton Coll., Norton, Mass., 1942; intern, Met. Mus. of Art, N.Y.C., 1941. Dir. Upstairs Gallery, Ithaca, N.Y., 1960-67; curatorial asst. Andrew D. White Mus. Cornell U., Ithaca, N.Y., 1967-70; curator of prints Herbert F. Johnson Mus. Cornell U., 1970-75; art curator Hastings Coll. of the Law U. Calif., San Francisco, 1978—. Author: (mus. catalog) 15th and 16th Century Prints of No. Europe from the Nat. Gallery of Art-Rosenwald Collection, 1973, other catalogs. Mem. UN World Centre founding com., 1979-84; mem. art adv. com. N.Y. State Fair, Syracuse, 1973; cons. Gallery Assn., State of N.Y., 1972-74. Recipient History of Art prizes Wheaton Coll., 1941, 42. Home: 1333 Jones St Apt 810 San Francisco CA 94109-4112 Office: U Calif Hastings Coll of Law 200 McAllister San Francisco CA 94102

SCHLOSE, WILLIAM TIMOTHY, health care executive; b. West Lafayette, Ind., May 16, 1948; s. William Fredrick and Dora Irene (Chitwood) S.; m. Linda Lee Fletcher, June 29, 1968 (div. 1978); children: Vanessa Janine Schlose Hubert, Stephanie Lynn; m. Kelly Marie Martin, June 6, 1987; 1 child, Taylor Jean Martin-Schlose. Student, Bowling Green State U., 1966-68, Long Beach City Coll., 1972-75; teaching credential, UCLA, 1975. Staff respiratory therapist St. Vincent's Med. Ctr., L.A., 1972-75; cardio-pulmonary chief Temple Community Hosp., L.A., 1975-76; adminstrv. dir. spl. svcs. Santa Fe Meml. Hosp., L.A., 1976-79; mem. mktg. and pub. rels. staff Nat. Med. Homecare Corp., Orange, Calif., 1979-81, Medtech of Calif., Inc., Burbank, Calif., 1981-84; regional mgr. Mediq Health Care Group Svcs., Inc., Chatsworth, Calif., 1984-88; pres. Baby Watch Homecare, Whittier, Calif., 1988-90, Tim Schlose and Assocs., Orange, Calif., 1990—; staff instr., Montebello (Calif.) Adult Schs. Author: Fundamental Respiratory Therapy Equipment, 1977. With USN, 1968-72. Mem. Am. Assn. Respiratory Care, Calif. Soc. Respiratory Care (past officer), Nat. Bd. Respiratory Care, Nat. Assn. Apnea Profls., Am. Assn. Physicians Assts., L.A. Pediatric Soc., Calif. Perinatal Assn., Porsche Owners Club L.A., Porsche Club Am. Republican. Methodist. Office: Tim Schlose and Assocs 910 E Chapman Ave Orange CA 92666

SCHLOTTER, WALLY, chamber of commerce executive, television director; b. San Diego. AA in Bus., Grossmont Jr. Coll., 1972; BS in Telecommunications and Film, San Diego State U., 1975; student, Nat. Acad. TV Arts and Scis., 1974. With KPBS-TV, San Diego, 1973-75; asst. to exec. producer Police Story NBC Columbia Pictures TV, San Diego, 1975-76; production coord. nat. TV commls. San Diego, writer, production assistant, production coord., location scout, location mgr., assoc. producer/dir.; assoc. dir., dir. Motion Picture and TV Bur., San Diego; v.p. Greater San Diego C. of C. Creator, producer many fundraisers including San Diego EMMY Awards broadcast to benefit Nat. Acad. TV Arts and Scis. scholarship fund, 1978, 79, Kids Day at the Movies for orphaned children, Oscar Nite Variety Club fundraiser for children. Bd. govs. Muscular Dystrophy Assn.; trustee San Diego Festival of Arts; bd. dirs. Young Friends of the Symphony; active Multiple Sclerosis Soc., Socail Advocates for Youth, others. Recipient Nat. Best of West Producer award, 1975, San Diego Emmy citation for assoc. dir., 1976, Green Derby award Simon and Simon campaign, 1982, Appreciation award SAG, 1985, Headliner of Yr. award, 1986, Outstanding Young Alumnus award, 1986, Outstanding Young Citizen award, 1988, numerous others. Mem. Nat. Acad. TV Arts and Scis. (bd. govs., past v.p., co-founder/chmn. scholarship fund), Am. Film Inst., Variety Club (bd. govs., past chmn. spl. events, past. v.p.), Ad Club. Home: 5551 Candlelight Dr La Jolla CA 92037-7713 Office: 402 W Broadway Ste 1000 San Diego CA 92101-8507

SCHLOTTMAN, JAMES L., not-for-profit organization executive, consultant; b. Hayward, Calif., Dec. 20, 1943; s. Victor Louis and Marcella Ruth Schlottman; m. Barbara Lee Houtsma, Dec. 23, 1966; children: Tadd Cornell, Tara Brooke. BA, Sioux Falls Coll., 1966. Art instr. Rapid City (S.D.) Pub. Sch. System, 1966-70; dir. alumni affairs Sioux Falls (S.D.) Coll., 1970-76; planning and devel. coord. University Hills Christian Living Ctr., Denver, 1976-78; dir. resource devel. Swedish Med. Ctr. Found., Englewood,

Colo., 1978-79; dir. maj. gifts and alumni rels., dir. ann. funds U. Colo. Health Scis. Ctr., Denver, 1980-84; v.p., campus dir. devel. U. Colo. Found., Denver, 1984-87; v.p. instl. advancement and comms. Colo. Christian U., Lakewood, 1987-89; cons. Schlottman and Assocs., Aurora, Colo., 1987—; exec. dir. Bethesda Found., Denver, 1990—. Bd. dirs. Netherlands Am. Soc. of the Rockies, Denver, 1994. Fellow Assn. for Healthcare Philanthropy (regional officer, mem. nat. conf. com.),; mem. Nat. Soc. Fund Raising Execs. (dir. Colo. chpt. 1980—, pres. 1987), Colo. Planned Giving Roundtable, Kiwanis South Denver. Office: Bethesda Found 4400 E Iliff Ave Denver CO 80222

SCHLUETER, JEFFREY J., marketing executive; b. Wichita, Kans., Apr. 7, 1964; s. John J. and K. Melissa (Harrell) S.; m. Paula Michele Benoit, Mar. 5, 1994. BA with distinction, U. Colo., 1986; M of Internat. Mgmt. with distinction, Am. Grad. Sch. Internat. Mgmt., 1990. Gen. mgr. Alpine Camera, Inc., Breckenridge, Colo., 1988-90; market rsch. mgr. US WEST Strategic Mktg., Englewood, Colo., 1991-93; mgr. market intelligence US WEST Enhanced Svcs., Denver, 1993-94, market mgr., 1994—. Recipient Worldwide scholarship Am. Grad. Sch., 1990. Mem. Phi Beta Kappa. Home: 1699 S Trenton St Apt 59 Denver CO 80231-5602

SCHMALENBERGER, JERRY LEW, pastor, seminary administrator; b. Greenville, Ohio, Jan. 23, 1934; s. Harry Henry and Lima Marie (Hormel) S.; m. Carol Ann Walthall, June 8, 1956; children: Stephen, Bethany Allison, Sarah Layton. BA, Wittenberg U., 1956, DDiv (hon.), 1984; MDiv, Hamma Sch. Theology, Springfield, Ohio, 1959, D of Ministry, 1976. Ordained to ministry Luth. Ch., 1959. Dir. Camp Mowana, Mansfield, Ohio, 1958-59; pastor 3d Luth. Ch., Springfield, 1959-61, 1st Luth. Ch., Bellefontaine, Ohio, 1961-66; sr. pastor 1st Luth. Ch., Tiffin, Ohio, 1966-70, Mansfield, 1970-79; sr. pastor St. John's Luth. Ch., Des Moines, 1979-88; pres., prof. parish ministry Pacific Luth. Theol. Sem., Berkeley, Calif., 1988—; co-dir. Iowa Luth. Hosp. Min. of Health Program, Des Moines, 1986-88; Roland Payne lectr. Gbarnga (Liberia) Sch. Theology, 1987; lectr. Luth. Theol. Sem., Hong Kong, 1994, The United Theol. Coll., Kingston, Jamaica, 1994. Author: Lutheran Christians' Beliefs Book One, 1984, Book Two, 1987, Iowa Parables and Iowa Psalms, 1984, Saints Who Shaped the Church, 1986, Stewards of Creation, 1987, Nights Worth Remembering, 1989, The Vine and the Branches, 1992, Call to Witness, 1993, Plane Thoughts on Parish Ministry, 1994, Invitation to Discipleship, 1995; columnist Rite Ideas, 1987-88. Bd. dirs. Grand View Coll., Des Moines, 1980-88, Wittenberg U., Springfield, Ohio, 1974-87, Luth. Social Services of Iowa, 1980-87, chmn. pre fund drive, 1988; bd. dirs. Planned Parenthood of Mid-Iowa, Des Moines, 1987-88; dir. Evang. Outreach/Luth. Ch. Am., 1983-85; mem. Iowa Luth. Hosp. Charitable Trust, 1986-88; chair Com. for Homeless Fund, Des Moines, 1986. Named Outstanding Alumni Wittenberg U., 1965, Young Man of Yr. Tiffin Jaycees, 1965, Man of Yr. Bellefontaine Jaycees, Disting. Alumni award Trinty Sem., Columbus, 1989. Mem. NAACP, Acad. Preachers, Acad. Evangelists (organizer 1986—), Kiwanis, Rotary. Home & Office: 2770 Marin Ave Berkeley CA 94708-1530

SCHMALTZ, ROY EDGAR, JR., artist, art educator; b. Belfield, N.D., Feb. 23, 1937; s. Roy and Mercedes (Martin) S.; m. Julia Mabel Swan, Feb. 1, 1958; children: Liese Marlene, Jennifer Lynn, Gregory Jason. Student Otis Art Inst., Los Angeles, 1959-60, U. Wash., 1960-61, Akademie der Bildenden Kunste, Munich, W. Ger., 1965-66; B.F.A., San Francisco Art Inst., 1963, M.F.A., 1965. Lectr. art Coll. of Notre Dame, Belmont, Calif., 1968-70, M. H. De Young Meml. Art Mus., San Francisco, 1968-70; prof. art St. Mary's Coll. of Calif., Moraga, 1969—, chmn. dept. art; mem. artists' bd. San Francisco Art Inst., 1989-92; exhbns. include: Seattle Art Mus., 1959, M. H. De Young Meml. Art Mus., 1969, Frye Art Mus., Seattle, 1957, San Francisco Mus. Modern Art, 1971, U. Calif.-Santa Cruz, 1977, Fine Arts Mus. of San Francisco, 1978, Oakland Art Mus., 1979, Rutgers U., Camden, N.J., 1979, Springfield (Mo.) Art Mus., 1980, Butler Inst. Am. Art, Youngstown, Ohio, 1981, Huntsville (Ala.) Mus. Art, 1982, Haggin Mus., Stockton, Calif., 1982, U. Hawaii-Hilo, 1983, Alaska State Mus., Juneau, 1981, Tex. State U., San Marcos, 1980, Crocker Art Mus., Sacramento, 1982, Hearst Art Gallery, 1986; group exhbns. include San Francisco Internat. Airport Gallery, 1987, Solano Coll., Fairfield, Calif., 1988, U. Del., Newark, 1988, San Francisco Art Inst., 1989, Natsoulas Gallery, Davis, Calif., 1989, Bedford Regional Ctr. Arts, Walnut Creek, Calif., 1989, Contemporary Realist Gallery, San Francisco, 1994, Hearst Art Gallery, Moraba, Calif., 1995; represented in permanent collections: Richmond Art Ctr. (Calif.), U. Hawaii-Hilo, Las Vegas Art Mus. (Nev.), Hoyt Mus. and Inst. Fine Arts, New Castle, Pa., Frye Art Mus., San Francisco Art Inst., M. H. De Young Meml. Art Mus., Mills Coll., Oakland, Amerika-Haus, Munich, Contra Costa County Art Collection, Walnut Creek, Calif., Western Wash. U., Bellingham, Clemson U., S.C.; dir. Hearst Art Gallery, St. Mary's Coll.; vis. artist lectr. Academie Art Coll., San Francisco, 1971, grad. program Lone Mountain Coll., San Francisco, 1973-74. Coach Little League Baseball Team, Concord, Calif., 1982; mem. artist's bd. San Francisco Art Inst., 1989-93. Fulbright fellow, 1965-66; Frye Art Mus. traveling fellow, 1957; recipient Painting award All Calif. Ann., 1965; Nat. Watercolor award Chautauqua Inst., 1980; Seattle Art Assn. Painting award, 1957; San Francisco Art Inst. award, 1961; Otis Art Inst. award, 1959; Walnut Creek Civic Art Ctr. award, 1982, San Francisco Art Commn. award, 1985, Calif. State Fair Art award, 1985, Sears award for excellence in leadership, 1989-90. Mem. Coll. Art Assn., Fine Arts Mus. of San Francisco, AAUP, San Francisco Art Inst. Alumni Assn. Home: 1020 Whistler Dr Suisun City CA 94585-2929 Office: Saint Marys Coll Dept Art Moraga CA 94575

SCHMALZ, CHARLES JOSEPH, artist, photographer, creative consultant; b. Indpls., Nov. 3, 1947; s. Charles Joseph and Mary Ann (Eberle) S. BFA in Visual Comm., Advt. Design, Pratt Inst., Bklyn., 1971. Tchr. Sacred Heart Elem. Sch., Indpls., 1964-65; spl. projects art dir. Random House, Knopf, Inc., N.Y.C., 1970-73; art dir. Klemtner Advt., N.Y.C., 1973-76; v.p. group art dir. Medigraphics, Wm. D. McAdams, N.Y.C., 1976-79; exec. art dir. Vicom Assocs., San Francisco, 1980-81; creative dir. Rainoldi, Kerzner & Radcliffe, San Francisco, 1981-87; author, tchr. basic layout Acad. of Art Coll., San Francisco, 1989-90; prin. Charles Schmalz Creative Svcs., San Francisco, 1990—. Photographer: solo exhibitions include Galleria U. Calif. Extension, San Francisco, 1992, Davis Art Ctr. The Hallway Gallery Davis, Calif., 1993, LCR Gallery, Weed, Calif., 1994, Palos Verdes Art Ctr., Ranchos Palos Verdes, Calif., 1995, Merced (Calif.) Coll. Art Gallery, 1995; group exhibitions include Lilian Paley Ctr. for Visual Arts, Oakland, 1992, Orange County Ctr. for Contemporary Art, Santa Ana, Calif., 1993, Paris Gibson Sq. Mus. of Art, Gt. Falls, Mont., 1993, Hoyt Nat. Art Show, 1993, Univ. of Toledo Ctr. for the Visual Arts, Nat. Juried Exhibit, 1993, Alexandria (La.) Mus. of Art, 1994, Dadian Gallery, The Ctr. for Arts and Religion, Washington, 1995. Exec. dir., founder Fresh Start reintegration process for the homeless, 1989-90. Recipient Merit award 15th Ann. N.D. Nat. Juried Exhibition U. N.D., 1992, 1st Pl. award 89th Open Juried Exhibit, Long Beach Arts, Calif., 1993, People's Choice award, 9th Ann. Photo Show, Mus. Anthropology Calif. State U., Chico, 1993, Gallery Choice award, Gallery 57, Fullerton, Calif., 1993, Purchase award S.W. Tex. State U., San Marcos, 1994, Univ. Gallery, U. Del., 1994; also numerous awards for work in advertising and design., 1969—. Mem. ACLU, Amnesty Internat., Greenpeace, Artists Equity, Am. Inst. Graphic Arts. Home and Studio: 271 Santa Rosa Ave San Francisco CA 94112-1906

SCHMALZ, ROCHELLE PERRINE, library director; b. Syracuse, N.Y., Jan. 12, 1944; d. Roy Seal Henderson and Ramona Magdalena (Leitner) Perrine; m. Warner Henry Schmalz, June 22, 1962; children: Gregory, Kirsten Leitner. BA in History, U. Calif., Berkeley, 1974, MLS, 1975. Health ctr. libr. Kaiser-Permanente Med. Ctr., Oakland, Calif., 1976-81; dir. Resource Ctr. Planetree, San Francisco, 1981-86; dir. libr. and AV svcs. St. Mary's Med. Ctr., San Francisco, 1987—; cons. primary prevention program, Geneva, 1987, various hosps. and health resource ctrs. First author classification scheme Planetree Classification Scheme for Consumer Health, 1988. Mem. Med. Libr. Assn., No. Calif./Nev. Med. Libr. Group (pres. 1995—). Democrat. Presbyterian. Office: St Marys Med Ctr 450 Stanyan St San Francisco CA 94117-1079

SCHMAUSS, STEPHEN ANTHONY, retired computer programmer; b. L.A., June 1, 1940; s. Kenneth and Doris (Armstrong) S. Student, UCLA, 1975, Mt. San Antonio Coll., 1989. Programmer Centaur Computer Sys., Glendale, Calif., 1970-75, Kaynar Industries, Fullerton, Calif., 1975-82; sr. systems programmer Shiley Inc., Irvine, Calif., 1982-94; ret., 1994; cons. J.P.L., Pasadena, Calif., 1975, FiServ, Spokane, Wash., 1994. With USN, 1958-63. Democrat.

SCHMEIR, FRED TITUS, social worker; b. Durango, Colo., May 27, 1947; s. Henry Edward and Lois Louise (Titus) S.; m. Bobbe Jo Dougherty, Oct. 23, 1969 (div. May 1987); children: Rory, Shelly, Kiley. BA, Ft. Lewes Coll., Durango, 1969; MA, U. No. Colo., Greeley, 1980. Social worker Dept. Human Svcs., Pagosa Springs, Colo., 1971-74, Durango, 1974-76; dir. Dept. Human Svcs., Pagosa Springs, 1976-80; dir. human svcs. Dept. Human Svcs., Monte Vista, Colo., 1980-86; cons. Dept. Human Svcs., Monte Vista, 1986-87; adminstr. Dept. Human Svcs., Ft. Morgan, Colo., 1987-89; dir. human svcs. Dept. Human Svcs., Lamar, Colo., 1989—; bd. dirs. S.E. Colo. region Family Guidance and Mental Health, 1989—; mem. state policy adv. bd. Dept. Social Svcs., Denver, 1980, 82, 84, mem. placement alternative bd., Lamar, 1989—; pres. Child Protection Team, Monte Vista, 1980-86. Author: (poetry) Passings, 1970, (short story) Red Light/Green Light, 1994, (tng. manual) Orientation to Human Services, 1990. Recipient grants Colo. State Dept. social Studies, 1990-94. Mem. Nat. Assn. Counties, Exec. Dirs. Com., Am. Pub. Welfare Assn., Elks. Republican. Methodist. Home: 806 Yucca Dr Apt 2 Lamar CO 81052-4064 Office: Dept Human Resources 1001 S Main St Lamar CO 81052-3813

SCHMID, INGRID, medical researcher; b. Treibach, Austria, Oct. 24, 1952; came to U.S., 1982, permanent resident, 1982; d. Ernst and Anny (Navratil) Dobrovolny; m. Peter Schmid, Dec. 23, 1981; 1 child, Ernst Walter. M in Pharmacy, U. Vienna, Austria, 1976. Lic. pharmacist, Austria. Intern pharmacist Pub. Pharmacy, Vienna, 1977-79; quality control mgr., head drug registration dept. Co. Substantia (Parke Davis Austria), Vienna, 1979-81; vol. lab. of Dr. George Fareed UCLA Molecular Biology Inst., 1982; staff rsch. assoc. lab. of Dr. John Fahey UCLA Dept. Microbiology and Immunology, 1983-87; staff rsch. assoc. lab. of Dr. Janis Giorgi UCLA Sch. Medicine, 1987-93, supr. flow cytometry core facility Jonsson Cancer Ctr., 1989—, acad. staff rsch. specialist, 1993—, flow cytometry instr., 1991—; nat. tech. cons. for flow cytometry on the Multictr. AIDS Cohort Study, 1989-90; presenter UCLA, 1988, 7th Ann. Clin. Applications of Cytometry meeting, Charleston, S.C., 1992. Author: (with others) Vaccines, 1990; contbr. articles to profl. jours. Mem. Internat. Soc. for Analytical Cytology, UCLA Adminstrs. and Suprs. Assn. Office: UCLA Sch Medicine Dept Medicine/CIA/CIC 12-236 Factor Bldg Los Angeles CA 90024-1745

SCHMID, RUDI (RUDOLF SCHMID), internist, educator, university official; b. Switzerland, May 2, 1922; came to U.S., 1948, naturalized, 1954; s. Rudolf and Bertha (Schiesser) S.; m. Sonja D. Wild, Sept. 17, 1949; children: Isabelle S., Peter R. B.S., Gymnasium Zurich, 1941; M.D., U. Zurich, 1947; Ph.D., U. Minn., 1954. Intern U. Calif. Med. Center, San Francisco, 1948-49; resident medicine U. Minn., 1949-52, instr., 1952-54; research fellow biochemistry Columbia U., 1954-55; investigator NIH, Bethesda, Md., 1955-57; assoc. medicine Harvard U., 1957-59, asst. prof., 1959-62; prof. medicine U. Chgo., 1962-66; prof. medicine U. Calif., San Francisco, 1966-91, prof. emeritus, 1991—, dean Sch. Medicine, 1983-89, assoc. dean internat. rels., 1989-95; Cons. U.S. Army Surgeon Gen., USPHS, VA. Mem. editorial bd. Jour. Clin. Investigation, 1965-70, Blood, 1962-75, Gastroenterology, 1965-70, Jour. Investigative Dermatology, 1968-72, Annals Internal Medicine, 1975-79, Proceedings Soc. Exptl. Biology and Medicine, 1974-84, Chinese Jour. Clin. Scis., Jour. Lab. Clin. Medicine, 1991—, Hepatology Comm. Internat. (Japan), 1993—; cons. editor Gastroenterology, 1981-86. Served with Swiss Army, 1943-48. Master ACP; fellow AAAS, N.Y. Acad. Scis., Royal Coll. Physicians; mem. NAS, Am. Acad. Arts and Scis., Assn. Am. Physicians (pres. 1986), Am. Soc. Clin. Investigation, Am. Soc. Biol. Chemists, Am. Soc. Hematology, Am. Gastroenterol. Assn., Am. Assn. Study Liver Disease (pres. 1965), Internat. Assn. Study Liver (pres. 1980), Swiss Acad. Med. Scis. (mem. senate), Leopoldina, German-Am. Acad. Coun. Home: 211 Woodland Rd Kentfield CA 94904-2631 Office: U Calif Med Sch Office of Dean PO Box 0410 San Francisco CA 94143-0410

SCHMID-SCHOENBEIN, GEERT WILFRIED, biomedical engineer, educator; b. Albstadt, Baden-Wurttemberg, Germany, Jan. 1, 1948; came to U.S., 1971; s. Ernst and Ursula Schmid; m. Renate Schmid-Schoenbein, July 3, 1976; children: Philip, Mark, Peter. Vordiplom, Liebig U., Giessen, Germany, 1971; PhD in Bioengrng., U. Calif., San Diego, 1976. Staff assoc. dept. physiology Columbia U., N.Y.C., 1976-77, sr. assoc., 1977-79; asst. prof. dept. applied mechs. & engrng. scis. U. Calif., San Diego, 1979-84, assoc. prof., 1984-89, prof., 1989—. Editor: Frontiers in Biomechanics, 1986, Physiology and Pathophysiology of Leukocyte Adhesion, 1994. Recipient Melville medal ASME, 1990. Fellow Am. Inst. for Med. & Biol. Engrng., Am. Heart Assn.; mem. Biomed. Engrng. Soc. (pres. 1991-92), Am. Microcirculatory Soc., European Microciculatory Soc., Am. Physiol. Soc. Office: U Calif San Diego Dept Bioengineering La Jolla CA 92093-0412

SCHMIDT, ALAN FREDERICK, consulting cryogenic engineer; b. Chgo., Mar. 21, 1925; s. Ethan Warner and Lucille (Bouilly) S.; m. Jane Theresa Baker, Mar. 17, 1951; children: Rae Lynn, Liane. BSME, Ill. Inst. Tech., 1951; MSME, U. Colo., 1953. Project engr. Nat. Bur. Standards, Boulder, Colo., 1952-63, cons., 1963-76; prin. Alan F. Schmidt, cons., cryogenics engrng., Boulder, 1976—. Co-author: Liquid Cryogens: Liquefaction, Storage and Handling, 1982; contbr. articles on cryogenic engrng., chpt. to book. Staff sgt. inf. AUS, 1943-46, ETO. Fellow Tex. Co., 1951-52. Mem. ASME, Sci. Rsch. Soc. Am., Sigma Xi. Home and Office: 133 Elk Rd Lyons CO 80540-8149

SCHMIDT, CAROL SUZANNE, hospital administrator; b. River Rouge, Mich., Aug. 8, 1936; d. J. T. Grant Vaden and Virginia Jean (Senker) Vaden Webster; m. Ronald Lee Schmidt, Aug. 18, 1957; children: Karen Suzanne Corsilius, Linda Martin, Ronald Lee. RN diploma Hinsdale Hosp. Sch. Nursing, Ill., 1958; BS in Nursing cum laude, Met. State Coll., Denver, 1981; M.A. cum laude, Webster U.-Denver, 1984. RN, Colo. Operating room nurse Porter Meml. Hosp., Denver, 1961-69, charge relief nurse, 1975-76, adminstrv. supr., 1976-77, head nurse ortho/neuro unit, 1977-82; disease control nurse Vis. Nurse Assn., Denver, 1961-63; nurse Denver Gen. Hosp., 1966-67; office mgr., bookkeeper Timber Ridge Constrn., Evergreen, Colo., 1967-79; asst. dir. nursing Boulder Meml. Hosp., Colo., 1982-83, dir. nursing, 1984-89; v.p., chief clin. officer Avista Hosp., 1989—. Tchr. Seventh Day Adventist Ch., Boulder and Denver, 1958-85; vol. Colo. Health Fair, Denver, 1979, 80; tchr. basic life support Am. Heart Assn., Denver, 1980-82; mem. Colo. Women's Forum Health Adminstrn., 1990—. Recipient Dist. Nurse of Yr. award Colo. Nurse Assn., 1975. Mem. Am. Coll. Hosp. Execs. of Am. Hosp. Assn., Am. Orgn. Nurse Execs., Assn. Seventh Day Adventist Nurses (bd. dirs. 1984-86), Colo. Soc. Nurse Execs. (active image of nursing 1985), Bus. and Profl. Women (legis. com. 1985), Colo. Fedn. Nursing Orgns. Avocations: needlework; travel. Office: Avista Hosp 100 Health Park Dr Louisville CO 80027-9583

SCHMIDT, CHRISTOPHER VAN ALST, systems programmer; b. Burlingame, Calif., Apr. 18, 1960; s. Werner F. and Mary Jane (Lodge) S.; m. Margret Buckley, Dec. 28, 1990. BS in Computer Sci., Yale U., 1982. Sys. programmer SUMEX Computer Project, 1982-90; developer Petaluma, Calif., 1991-93; editor San Mateo Libertarian, 1993—. Mem. Nat. Space Soc., Nat. Wildlife Fedn., Nat. Taxpayers Union, Nature Conservancy, Greenpeace, Space Studies Inst., ACLU Peninsula Humane Soc., Internat. Fund for Family Planning, Natural Resources Def. Coun., Computer Profls. for Social Responsibility, Assn. for Computing Machinery, Drug Policy Found., Zero Population Growth, Assn. for Vol. Surg. Contraception. Libertarian.

SCHMIDT, CYRIL JAMES, librarian; b. Flint, Mich., June 27, 1939; s. Cyril August and Elizabeth Josephine S.; m. Martha Joe Meadows, May 22, 1965; children: Susan, Emily. BA, Cath. U. Am., 1962; MSLS, Columbia U., 1963; Ph.D., Fla. State U., 1974. Asst. bus. and industry dept. Flint Pub. Library, 1963-65; reference librarian Gen. Motors Inst., Flint, 1965; asso. librarian S.W. Tex. State U., San Marcos, 1965-67; head undergrad. libraries, asst. prof. Ohio State U., 1967-70; dir. libraries SUNY, Albany, 1972-79; also mem. faculty SUNY (Sch. Library and Info. Sci.); univ. librarian Brown U., Providence, 1979-81; exec. v.p. Rsch. Libraries Group, Stanford, Calif., 1981-89; prin. cons. Schmidt & Assocs., Palo Alto, Calif., 1989—; univ. prof., libr. San Jose (Calif.) State U., 1992—. Author papers in field. Libr. Svcs. Act fellow, 1962-63, Higher Edn. Act fellow, 1970-72. Mem. ALA, ACLU, Pi Sigma Alpha, Beta Phi Mu. Home: 244 Forest Ave Palo Alto CA 94301-2510 Office: San Jose State U 1 Washington Sq San Jose CA 95112-3613

SCHMIDT, DIANA GAIL, paralegal; b. Olney, Tex., Dec. 5, 1946; d. Ernest B. and Helen N. (Wright) Perkins; m. Lail William Schmidt, Jr., Aug. 14, 1974 (div. 1986); 1 child, Andrea. Student, U. Okla., 1965-67; mktg. cert., U. Phoenix, 1992, BA in Mgmt., 1993. Real estate lic., Colo. Owner DG Ventures, Lakewood, Colo., 1984-85; realtor Century 21 Profls., Lakewood, 1987-89; paralegal Attys. Svc. Ctr., Denver, 1987-92; paralegal specialist Resolution Trust Corp., Denver, 1992—. Dir. 6th Ave. Townhome Assn., Golden, Colo., 1993—; pres. Union Sq. Community Assn., Lakewood, 1988; chair mentor program Toastmasters Internat., Lakewood, 1990; speaker MADD, Denver, 1990, The Jungle Lady, Denver, 1994. Recipient Take Pride in Am. award U.S. Dept. of Interior, Washington, 1989, Community award City Coun., Lakewood, 1989. Republican. Home: 444 Gladiola St Golden CO 80401-5250 Office: Resolution Trust Corp 707 17th St Ste 3800 Denver CO 80202-3438

SCHMIDT, EDWIN STEVEN, nursing educator; b. Cin., June 25, 1953; s. Edwin John and Rose Ann (Manzi) S. ADN, Long Beach City Coll., Calif., 1986; BSN, U. Phoenix, 1993. Cert. pub. health nurse, 1993. Grad. nurse technician VA Med. Ctr., Long Beach, Calif., 1986, staff nurse, 1987-88; intensive care nurse Kaweah Delta Dist. Hosp., Visalia, Calif., 1988-89; RN team leader FHP Long Beach, 1989, home health nurse, 1990-91; hospice nurse FHP Hawaiian Gardens, Calif., 1991, GI nurse, 1991-92; clin. coord. FHP Long Beach, Calif., 1992-93; hospice nurse Meml. Med. Ctr., Long Beach, Calif., 1993; utilization mgmt. nurse SCAN Health Plan, Long Beach, Calif., 1993; pain control cons. pvt. practice, Long Beach, Calif., 1991—. With USN, 1972-81, Vietnam. Recipient Long Beach City Coll. Viking award, 1986. Mem. Nat. League for Nursing, Assn. for Advancement of Nursing, Sci. and Rsch. Home: 1110 Ohio Ave Long Beach CA 90804-3601

SCHMIDT, FRANK BROAKER, executive recruiter; b. Shamokin, Pa., Aug. 8, 1939; s. Frank Wilhelm and Doris (Maurer) S.; children by previous marrage: Susan E., Tracie A.; m. Elizabeth Mallen, Mar. 18, 1989; children: Alexandra M., Frank W.M. BS, U. Pa., 1962; MBA, Case Western Res. U., 1969; cert. brewmaster, Siebel Inst. Brewing Tech., Chgo., 1964. With Carling Brewing Co., Cleve., 1964-69, mgr. sales and advt. div., brand mgr., 1969-70; advt. and merchandising mgr. The Pepsi-Cola Co., Purchase, N.Y., 1970-71, dir. mktg. programs, then dir. mgmt. devel., 1971-74; mgr. sales and mktg. The Olga Co., Van Nuys, Calif., 1974-75; pres. F.B. Schmidt, Internat., L.A., 1975—; chmn. Mediterranean Properties, 1994—. Author: Draft Beer Manual, 1967, Assn. Nat. Advertisers Computerized Media System, 1970. Pres. Morrison Ranch Estates Homeowners Assn., 1993-94, chmn., 1995—. Mem. Calif. Exec. Recruiters Assn., Wharton Alumni Assn., Personnel Cons. Am. (region chmn. 1981-83, chmn. 92-95), Am. Mktg. Assn. Republican. Office: 30423 Canwood St Ste 239 Agoura Hills CA 91301-4318

SCHMIDT, JOHN WESLEY, advanced engineer, environmental scientist; b. Pendleton, Oreg., Aug. 26, 1954; s. Earl B. and Mary C. (Eaton) S.; m. Julia Anne Hampton, Nov. 23, 1988. AA, Columbia Basin Coll., 1985, AAS in Nuclear Technology, 1985; BSME, Wash. State U., 1991. Health physics technician Rockwell Hanford Co., Richland, Wash., 1985-87; health physics technician Westinghouse Hanford Co., Richland, Wash., 1987-90, advanced engr., 1990—. Mem. Assn. N.W. Environ. Profls., Health Physics Soc., Tri Cities Enological Soc., Columbia Basin Health Physics Soc., Richland Rod and Gun Club. Office: Westinghouse Hanford Co PO Box 1970 H6-30 Richland WA 99352

SCHMIDT, JOSEPH DAVID, urologist; b. Chgo., July 29, 1937; s. Louis and Marian (Fleigel) S.; m. Andrea Maxine Herman, Oct. 28, 1962. BS in Medicine, U. Ill., 1959, MD, 1961. Diplomate Am. Bd. Urology. Rotating intern Presbyn. St. Luke's Hosp., Chgo., 1961-62, resident in surgery, 1962-63; resident in urology The Johns Hopkins Hosp., Balt., 1963-67; faculty U. Iowa Coll. Medicine, Iowa City, 1969-76; faculty U. Calif., San Diego, 1976—, prof., head div. urology, 1976—; cons. U.S. Dept. Navy, San Diego, 1976—; attending urologist Vets. Affairs Dept., San Diego, 1976—. Author, editor: Gynecological and Obstetric Urology, 1978, 82, 93. Capt. USAF, 1967-69. Recipient Francis Senear award. U. Ill., 1961. Fellow Am. Coll. of Surgeons; mem. AMA, Am. Urol. Assn. Inc., Alpha Omega Alpha. Office: U Calif Med Ctr Divsn Urology 200 W Arbor Dr San Diego CA 92103-8897

SCHMIDT, L(AIL) WILLIAM, JR., lawyer; b. Thomas, Okla., Nov. 22, 1936; s. Lail William and Violet Kathleen (Kuper) S.; m. Diana Gail (div. May 1986); children: Kimberly Ann, Andrea Michelle; m. Marilyn Sue, Aug. 11, 1990. BA in Psychology, U. Colo., 1959; JD, U. Mich., 1962. Bar: Colo. 1962, U.S. Dist. Ct. Colo. 1964, U.S. Tax Ct. 1971, U.S. Ct. Appeals (10th cir.) 1964. Ptnr. Holland & Hart, Denver, 1962-77, Schmidt, Elrod & Wills, Denver, 1977-85, Moye, Giles, O'Keefe, Vermeire & Gorrell, Denver, 1985-90; of counsel Mankoff, Hill, Held & Goldburg, Dallas, 1989—; pvt. practice law Denver, 1990—; lectr. profl. orgns. Author: How To Live--and Die--with Colorado Probate, 1985, A Practical Guide to the Revocable Living Trust, 1990; contbr. articles to legal jours. Pres. Luth. Med. Ctr. Found., Wheat Ridge, Colo., 1985-89; pres. Rocky Mountain Prison and Drug Found., Denver, 1986—; bd. dirs. Luth. Hosp., Wheat Ridge, 1988-92; bd. dirs. Denver Planned Giving Roundtable, Bonfils Blood Ctr. Found. Fellow Am. Coll. Trust and Estate Counsel (Colo. chmn. 1981-86); mem. ABA, Am. Judicature Soc., Rocky Mtn. Estate Planning Coun. (founder, pres. 1970-71), Greater Denver Tax Counsel Assn., Am. Soc. Magicians, Denver Athletic Club, Phi Delta Phi. Republican. Baptist. Office: 1050 17th St Ste 1700 Denver CO 80265 also: Law Offices of Gregory J Morris 300 S 4th St Las Vegas NV 89101-6014

SCHMIDT, PATRICIA FAIN, nurse educator; b. Chgo., June 17, 1941; d. Lawrence D. and Catherine B. (Schira) Fain; m. Donald W. Schmidt, July 16, 1966; children: Kathryn, Kristine, Michael. BSN, Coll. of St. Teresa, 1963; MSN, Marquette U., 1965; EdD, U.S. Internat. U., 1981. Instr. Coll. of St. Teresa, Winona, Minn.; asst. prof. San Diego State U.; interim dean for mathematics and natural and health scis. Palomar Coll., San Marcos, Calif. Mem. Sigma Theta Tau. Home: 12573 Utopia Way San Diego CA 92128-2229

SCHMIDT, RUTH A(NNA) M(ARIE), geologist; b. Bklyn., Apr. 22, 1916; d. Edward and Anna M. (Range) S. AB, NYU, 1936; MA, Columbia U., 1939, PhD, 1948. Cert. profl. geologist. Geologist U.S. Geol. Survey, Washington, 1943-56; dist. geologist U.S. Geol. Survey, Anchorage, 1956-63; prof., chmn. geology dept. U. Alaska, Anchorage, 1959-84; cons. geologist Anchorage, 1964—; lectr. Elder Hostels, Alaska Pacific U., Anchorage, 1988-89, U. Alaska, Anchorage, 1994; coord. Engrng. Geol. Evaluating Group, Alaskan 1964 Earthquake, Anchorage, 1964; environ. cons. Trans Alaska Pipeline, Office of Gov., Anchorage, 1975-76. Editor: Alaska geology field trip guide books, 1984, 89; contbr. articles to profl. jours. Trustee, pres. Brooks Range Libr., Anchorage, 1979-91; bd. dirs., com. chmn. Anchorage Audubon Soc., 1989—; mem. exec. bd., chmn. various coms. Alaska Cen. Environment, Anchorage. Fellow AAAS, Arctic Inst. N.Am. (bd. govs. 1983-94), Geol. Soc. Am.; mem. Am. Inst. Profl. Geologists (charter), Am. Assn. Petroleum Geologists, Internat. Geol. Congress (del.), Alaska Geol. Soc. (hon. life mem., bd. dirs. 1993-95), Sigma Xi.

SCHMIDT, STANLEY EUGENE, retired speech educator; b. Harrington, Wash., Dec. 14, 1927; s. Otto Jacob and Ella Genevieve (Wilson) S.; m. Randall Lee, Stephen Douglas. BS in Edn., U. Idaho, 1956; MEd in Adminstrn., U. Oreg., 1958; MA in Speech, Wash. State U., 1975. Supt., tchr., coach Rose Lake (Idaho) Sch. Dist. # 35, 1949-55; forensics coach, speech tchr. Jefferson H.S., Portland, Oreg., 1955-65; dir. forensics Portland C.C., 1965-93, lead speech instr., 1979-82, subject area chmn., 1986-90; adj. prof. speech U. Portland, 1987-93; ret., 1993; subject-area chmn., 1986-90, parliamentarian faculty senate, 1975-80. Co-author anthology: The Literature of the Oral Tradition, 1963. Chmn., precinct committeeman Rep. Party, Kootenai County, Idaho, 1951-53; mem. Easter Seal Soc., Portland, 1980—; pres. Kootenai County Tchrs. Assn., 1953-54, North Idaho Edn. Assn., 1954-55, Oreg. Speech Assn., 1960-61, Oreg. C.C. Speech Assn., 1971-72. Recipient Excellence award U.S. Bank, Portland, 1993, Merit award N.W.

Forensic Assn., 1992. Mem. Portland Rose Soc., Royal Rosarian, Masons (jr. grand deacon 1990-91, jr. grand steward 1991-92, grand orator 1992-93, 94—, dist. dep. 1986-90, 32d deg. Scottish Rite, comdr. 1989-90), Cryptic Masons of Oreg. (grand orator 1994-95), Tualitin Valley Shrine Club (dir. of the work 1989-95), Shriners (pres. 1991, bd. dirs. 1989—), Red Cross of Constantine (St. Laurence conclave). Baptist. Home: 5460 SW Palatine St Portland OR 97219-7259 Office: Portland CC Speech Dept PO Box 19000 Portland OR 97219

SCHMIDT, TERRY LANE, health care executive; b. Chgo., Nov. 28, 1943; s. LeRoy C. and Eunic P. S.; children: Christie Anne, Terry Lane II. B.S., Bowling Green State U., 1965; M.B.A. in Health Care Adminstrn, George Washington U., 1971. Resident in hosp. adminstrn. U. Pitts. Med. Center, VA Hosp., Pitts., 1968-69; adminstrv. asst. Mt. Sinai Med. Center, N.Y.C., 1969-70; asst. dir. Health Facilities Planning Council of Met. Washington, 1970-71; asst. dir. dept. govtl. relations A.M.A., Washington, 1971-74; pres. Terry L. Schmidt Inc. Physician Svcs. Group, San Diego, 1974—; exec. dir., chief operating officer Emergency Health Assocs. P.C., Phoenix, 1989-91, Charleston Emergency Physicians, S.C., 1990-95, Joplin Emergency Physican Assocs., 1991-92, Big Valley Med. Group, 1991-92, Blue Ridge Emergency Physicians, P.C., 1992-93, Berkeley Emergency Physicians, P.C., 1992-93; pres. Med. Cons. Inc., 1983-84; v.p. Crisis Communications Corp. Ltd., 1982-90; pres. Washington Actions on Health, 1975-78; partner Washington counsel Medicine and Health, 1979-81; pres. Ambulance Corp. Am., La Jolla, Calif., 1984-87; chmn., pres. Univ. Inst., 1992—; lectr., part-time faculty dept. health care adminstrn. George Washington U., 1969-84, preceptor, 1971-84; adj. prof. grad. sch. Pub. Health San Diego State U., 1989—, preceptor, 1989—, clin. prof., 1995—; asst. prof. Nat. Naval Sch. Health Care Adminstrn., 1971-73; faculty CSC Legis. Insts., 1972-76, Am. Assn. State Colls. and U. Health Tng. Insts.; mem. adv. com. ambulatory care standards Joint Commn. Accreditation of Hosps., 1971-72; guest lectr. health care adminstrn. Nat. U., San Diego, 1992—; adj. prof. Bus. Adminstrn. U.S. Internat. U., San Diego, 1994-95. Author: Congress and Health: An Introduction to the Legislative Process and the Key Participants, 1975, A Directory of Federal Health Resources and Services for the Disadvantaged, 1976, Health Care Reimbursement: A Glossary, 1983; mem. editl adv. bd.: Nation's Health, 1971-73; contbr. articles to profl. jours. Bd. dirs. Nat. Eye Found., 1976-78. Mem. Am. Hosp. Assn., Med. Group Mgmt. Assn., Hosp. Fin. Mgmt. Assn., Med. Group Mgrs., Assn. Venture Capital Groups (bd. dirs. 1984-89), Med. Adminstrs. of Calif., San Diego Venture Group (chair 1984-87), U. Calif. San Diego Venture Group (chair 1984-87), U. Calif. San Diego Faculty Club, University Club (life), Nat. Dem. Club (life), Nat. Rep. Club (life), Capitol Hill Club (life), Alpha Phi Omega (pres. Bowling Green alumni chpt. 1967-70, sec.-treas. alumni assn. 1968-71). Office: 9191 Towne Center Dr Ste 360 San Diego CA 92122

SCHMIDT, WALDEMAR ADRIAN, pathologist, educator; b. L.A., Aug. 22, 1941; s. Waldemar Adrian and Mary Charlotte (Parker) S.; m. Karmen LaVer Bingham, Feb. 1, 1963; children: Rebecca, Sarah, Waldemar, Diedrich. BS, Oreg. State U., 1965; PhD, U. Oreg., 1969, MD, 1969. Intern U. Oreg. Hosps. and Clinics, Portland, 1969-70, resident, 1970-73; pathologist LDS Hosp., Salt Lake City, 1973-77; prof. pathology U. Tex. Med. Sch., Houston, 1977-91, Oreg. Health Sci. U. and VA Med. Ctr., Portland, 1991—. Author: Principles and Techniques of Surgical Pathology, 1982; editor Cytopathology Annual, 1991—. Asst. scoutmaster Boy Scouts Am., Houston, 1982-91. Maj. U.S. Army, 1970-76. Mem. Coll. Am. Pathologists (program com.), Sigma Xi, Alpha Omega Alpha. Office: VA Med Ctr 3710 SW US Veterans Hosp Rd Portland OR 97207

SCHMIDT-DOWLER, VALERIE WOOD, retired mental health nurse; b. Chgo., July 12, 1915; d. Walter Arthur and Ebba Amanda (Stubbs) Wood; m. Frederick Schmidt, June 15, 1940 (dec. Apr. 1978); children: Frederick W. Schmidt, Carol Lorenzen, Dianne Wiest; m. G.L. Dowler, Feb. 14, 1982. Diploma, Evanston (Ill.) Sch. Nursing, 1938. RN, Calif. Nurse on surg. ward, also mental health clinic Queens Hosp., Honolulu, 1938-41; office nurse Escondido, Calif., 1960-85. Mem. Order Eastern Star (past matron), White Shrine of Jerusalem (worthy high priestess), Daus. of the Nile, Felicita Ct. Order of the Aramanth. Republican. Methodist. Home: 1540 Birch Ave Escondido CA 92027-4602

SCHMIEDER, CARL, jeweler; b. Phoenix, Apr. 27, 1938; s. Otto and Ruby Mable (Harkey) S.; m. Carole Ann Roberts, June 13, 1959; children: Gail, Susan, Nancy, Amy. Student Bradley Horological Sch., Peoria, Ill., 1959-61; BA, Pomona Coll., 1961; Owner timepiece repair svc., Peoria, 1959-61; clock repairman Otto Schmieder & Son, Phoenix, 1961-65, v.p., 1965-70, pres., 1970—, chief exec. officer, 1970—. Mem. subcom. Leap Commn., 1966; area rep. Pomona Coll., 1972-76. Cert. jeweler; cert. gemologist, gemologist appraiser; recipient Design award Diamonds Internat., 1965, Cultured Pearl Design award, 1967, 68, Diamonds for Christmas award, 1970; winner Am. Diamond Jewelry Competition, 1973; bd. dirs. Lincoln Hosp., 1983—, Ariz. Mus., 1984-88; delegate White House Conf. on Small Bus., 1986, 95; chmn. Gov.'s Conf. on Small Bus., 1988-91; col. Confederate Air Force. Mem. Am. Gem. Soc. (dir. 1973-86, nat. chmn. nomenclature com. 1975-77, chmn. membership com. 1977-81, officer 1981-86), Ariz. Jewelers Assn. (Man of Yr. 1974), Jewelers Security Alliance (dir. 1974-78), Jewelers Vigilance Com. (dir. 1981-87), Jewelry Industry Council (dir. 1982-88), 24 Karat Club So. Calif., Exptl. Aircraft Assn., Warbirds of Am. (dir. 1990—), Deer Valley (Ariz.) Airport Tenants Assn. (dir. 1980-90, pres. 1983-90), Ariz. C. of C. (bd. dirs. 1985-89), Small Bus. Council (bd. dirs. 1985-89, chmn. 1988, del. to White House Conf., 1986, 95, chmn. Govs. Conf. on small bus. 1988-89), Nat. Small Bus. United (bd. dirs. 1990-94), Kiwanis (pres. Valley of Sun chpt. 1975-76), Friends of Iberia, Rotary. Republican. Methodist. Home: 537 W Kaler Dr Phoenix AZ 85021-7244 Office: Park Ctrl Phoenix AZ 85013

SCHMITT, CATHERINE LAURA, academic career counselor; b. Santa Barbara, Calif., May 5, 1967; d. David R. and Harriet L. (Holland) S. Student, Santa Barbara C.C., 1987; BA in Social Ecology, U. Calif., Irvine, 1990; MS in Counseling, Calif. State U., Fullerton, 1993. Team facilitator knowledge and social responsibilty program U. Calif., Irvine, summer 1989, assoc. students commr., career paraprofl. counselor, 1989-90; peer counselor Ednl. Opportunity Program Irvine Valley C.C., 1991, specialist aide Cmty. Outreach, 1991-92, counseling intern Disabled Students Program and Svcs., 1991-93; career and workability program coord. Career Ctr. Calif. State Polytechnic U., Pomona, 1993—, mem. univ. diversity com., 1994—. Pres. Nat. Alliance for Blind Students, Washington, 1991-93; mem. bd. publs., membership com. Claif. Coun. of the Blind, Burbank, 1992—; treas., bd. dirs. Nat. Issues Forum of Orange County, 1992-93; mem. adv. bd. spl. needs in transit com. Orange County Transp. Authority, Garden Grove, Calif., 1992-93; conf. program selection com. AHEAD, 1994—. Recipient Vol.-in-People (VIP) award Vol. Ctr. of Greater Orange County, 1993. Mem. NAFE, Am. Counseling Assn., Toastmasters Internat. Office: Calif Polytechnic U Career Ctr Bldg 97 3801 W Temple Ave Pomona CA 91768-2557

SCHMITT, GEORGE HERBERT, hospital executive; b. Dallas, Dec. 16, 1939; s. Herbert S. and Regina T. (King) S.; m. Sue Ann Klein, Jan. 29, 1966; children: George Michael, Kristin Sue (dec.), Joseph Christopher, Susanne Nicole, Elizabeth Theresa. AB, Cardinal Glennon Coll., St. Louis, 1961; postgrad., Kenrick Sem., St. Louis, 1961-63; MHA, U. Minn., 1967; ScD, Maryville Coll., 1978. Gen. acct. Ameron Corp., St. Louis, 1965-66; asst. dir. Stanford Med. Ctr., Palo Alto, Calif., 1966-68; assoc. adminstr., dir. planning and devel. St. Joseph Infirmary, Louisville, 1968-70, exec. dir., 1970-74; pres., chief exec. officer Forbes Health System, Pitts., 1974-88, Main Line Health, Inc., Radnor, Pa., 1988-91, George H. Schmitt & Assocs., Health Sector Advisors, Villanova, Pa., 1991-92, F-O-R-T-U-N-E Cons. of Allegheny, Pitts., Pitts., 1992-93; sr. v.p. Calif. Healthcare System, Inc., San Francisco, 1993—. Bd. dirs. BeneSys, Inc.; past vice-chmn. Joint Commn. on Accreditation of Healthcare Orgns.; founding bd. dirs. Am. Healthcare Systems, Holy Cross Health Systems; past chmn. bd. dirs. Meritcare Inc. Mem. Am. Hosp. Assn. (past bd. mem.). Home: 683 Ironbark Cir Orinda CA 94563-2410 Office: Calif Healthcare System Inc 1 California St Fl 15 San Francisco CA 94111-5401

SCHMITT, NANCY CAIN, public and corporate relations executive, writer; b. Fayetteville, N.C., June 12, 1942; d. Carlton White and Cleo Margaret (Parnell) Cain; m. Louis Dennis Schmitt, July 13, 1974 (div.). BA, Wake Forest U., 1960-64. Reporter Gastonia (N.C.) Gazette, 1964-66; copy editor, reporter Twin City Sentinel, Winston-Salem, N.C., 1966-67; entertainment editor Fayetteville (N.C.) Observer, 1967-78; lifestyle editor Anchorage (Alaska) Times, 1978-83; pub. rels. specialist Multivisions Cable TV Co., Anchorage, 1983-84; editor Alaska Jour. of Commerce, Anchorage, 1984-85; sr. comms. specialist U.S. Postal Svc., 1985—. Author: How to Care for Your Car: A Women's Guide to Car Care in Alaska, 1978 (award 1979); mem. editorial bd. Episc. Diocean of Alaska, Fairbanks, 1983-86; contbr. articles to profl. jours. and nat. publs. Recipient Asst. Postmaster Gen.'s award for excellence. Mem. Nat. Fedn. Press Women (bd. mem. 1990-91), Pub. Rels. Soc. Am., Alaska Press Women (pres. treas., sec., communicator of achievement, recipient numerous awards), Alaska Press Club (recipient 3 awards), Rotary Internat. (bd. dirs. 1991-92). Home: 6716 E 16th Ave Apt A Anchorage AK 99504-2513 Office: U S Postal Svc Corp Rels 3720 Barrow St Anchorage AK 99599-0041

SCHMITT, PAUL JOHN, history educator; b. Pitts., Jan. 25, 1951; s. Phillip John and Adeline Marie (Barnhart) S.; m. Ruth Margaret Glass, June 20, 1987. BS, Ariz. State U., 1976, BA in Edn., 1978; MA, U. Nev., Las Vegas, 1994. Registration clk. Hermosa Inn Resort, Scottsdale, Ariz., 1978-79, asst. mgr., 1979-82; convention svc. mgr. Carefree (Ariz.) Inn Resort, 1982-84; tchr. Tonopah (Nev.) High Sch., 1984-85; reservation clk. Desert Inn Country Club and Spa, Las Vegas, Nev., 1985-92; prof. history C.C. of So. Nev., Las Vegas, 1992—. Mem. Assn. Am. Geographers, Am. Western History Assn., Orgn. Am. Historians, Phi Alpha Theta, Gamma Theta Upsilon. Office: CC So Nev Cheyenne Campus Dept Regional Studies 3200 E Cheyenne Ave S2C North Las Vegas NV 89030

SCHMITT, RICHARD GEORGE, industrial engineer; b. St. Cloud, Minn., June 18, 1948; s. George William and Viola Theresa (Mechenich) S.; m. Ligia Marie Pereira, Aug. 29, 1970; children: Christopher Michael, Scott Andrew. B in Indsl. Engring. with honors, Gen. Motors Inst., 1971. Indsl. engr. Gen. Motors, Fremont, Calif., 1966-78; sr. indsl. engr. Gen. Motors, Oklahoma City, 1978-80; indsl. engring. mgr. Shugart Assocs., Sunnyvale, Calif., 1980-81; mfg. tech. mgr. Magnex Corp., San Jose, Calif., 1981-82, prodn. mgr., 1982-83; facilities mgr. Apple Computer, Fremont, 1983, indsl. engring. mgr., 1984-85, robotics mgr., 1985-86, new product ops. mgr., 1987, Pacific logistics ops. mgr., 1988-93; Pacific phys. logistics mgr. Apple Computer, Cupertino, Calif., 1987—, pacific ops. dir., 1993, Pacific supply chair design mgr., 1994-95. Transp. chmn. Mt. Hamilton dist. Boy Scouts Am., 1984, asst. scoutmaster, 1986-92; chief YMCA Indian Guides, San Jose, 1977-83. Mem. Am. Assn. Indsl. Engrs. (sr.), Soc. Mfg. Engrs. (sr.), Coun. Logistics Mgmt., Am. Prodn. Inventory Control Soc., Lions (scholar 1966). Democrat. Roman Catholic. Home: 1963 Wave Pl San Jose CA 95133-1127 Office: Apple Computer 20330 Stevens Creek Blvd Cupertino CA 95014-2239

SCHMITT, ROMAN AUGUSTINE, educator, researcher; b. Johnsburg, Ill., Nov. 13, 1925; s. Joseph Stephen and Mary B. (Freund) S.; m. Jean. M. Vertovec, Dec. 28, 1954; children: Joseph, Mary, Peter, Katherine. MS, U. Chgo., 1950, PhD, 1953. Postdoctoral fellow U. Ill., Champaign, 1953-56; scientist Gen. Atomic Inc., San Diego, 1956-66; prof. chemistry, oceanography, & geology Oreg. State U., Corvallis, 1966-93, prof. emeritus, 1993—. Assoc. editor Geochimica et Cosmochimica Acta, 1974—; contbr. numerous articles to profl. jours. With U.S. Army, 1944-46, ETO. Recipient George Merrill award NAS, 1972. Roman Catholic. Home: 1830 NW Hawthorn Pl Corvallis OR 97330-1835 Office: Oreg State U Radiation Ctr Corvallis OR 97331-5901

SCHMITZ, CHARLES EDISON, evangelist; b. Mendota, Ill., July 18, 1919; s. Charles Francis Schmitz and Lucetta Margaret (Foulk) Schmitz Kaufmann; m. Eunice Magdalene Ewy, June 1, 1942; children: Charles Elwood, Jon Lee. Student, Wheaton Coll., 1936-37, 38, 39; BA, Wartburg Coll., Waverly, Iowa, 1940; BD, Wartburg Theol. Sem., Dubuque, Iowa, 1942, MDiv, 1977. Ordained to ministry Luth. Ch., 1942. Founding pastor Ascension Luth. Ch., L.A., 1942-48, Am. Evang. Luth. Ch., Phoenix, 1948-65; dir. intermountain missions, founding pastor 14 Evang. Luth. Parishes, Calif., Ariz., N.Mex., Fla., 1948-65; evangelist Am. Luth. Ch., Mpls., 1965-73; sr. pastor Peace Luth. Ch., Palm Bay, Fla., 1973-89; pastor-at-large Am. Evang. Luth. Ch., Phoenix, 1989—; charter mem. Navajo Luth. Mission, Rock Point, Ariz., 1960—; pastoral advisor Ariz. Luth. Outdoor Ministry Assn., Prescott, 1958-65, 89—; Kogudus Internat. Retreat master and chaplain, Fla., Berlin and Marbach, Germany, 1990; mem. transition team Fla. Synod Evang. Luth. Ch. Am., 1985-89. Author: Evangelism for the Seventies, 1970; co-author: ABC's of Life, 1968; assoc. editor Good News mag., 1965-71. Founder, chmn. Ariz. Ch. Conf. on Adult and Youth Problems, 1956-65; vice chmn. synod worship & ch. music com. Am. Luth. Ch., Mpls., 1960-66; chmn. Space Coast Luth. Retirement Ctr., Palm Bay, Fla., 1985-89; chaplain Ariz. chpt. Luth. Brotherhood, 1991—. Named Citizen of Yr., Palm Bay C. of C., 1979. Mem. Nat. Assn. Evangelicals, German Am. Nat. Congress (nat. chaplain), Lions (officer Phoenix and Palm Bay clubs 1952—, Ariz. Dist. 21A chaplain 1994—), Kiwanis (bd. dirs. L.A. chpt. 1942-48). Republican. Home: 12444 W Toreador Dr Sun City West AZ 85375-1926

SCHMITZ, DENNIS MATHEW, English language educator; b. Dubuque, Iowa, Aug. 11, 1937; s. Anthony Peter and Roselyn S.; m. Loretta D'Agostino, Aug. 20, 1960; children—Anne, Sara, Martha, Paul, Matthew. B.A., Loras Coll., 1959; M.A., U. Chgo., 1961. Instr. English Ill. Inst. Tech., Chgo., 1961-62, U. Wis., Milw., 1962-66; asst. prof. Calif. State U., Sacramento, 1966-69, assoc. prof., 1969-74, prof., 1974—; poet-in-residence, 1966—. Author: We Weep for Our Strangeness, 1969, Double Exposures, 1971, Goodwill, Inc., 1976, String, 1980, Singing, 1985, Eden, 1989, About Night: Selected and New Poems, 1993. Recipient Discovery award Poetry Center, N.Y.C., 1968; winner First Book Competition Follett Pub. Co., 1969; di Castagnola award Poetry Soc. Am., 1986; Shelley Meml. award Poetry Soc. Am., 1987; NEA fellow, 1976-77, 85-86, 92-93, Guggenheim fellow, 1978-79. Mem. PEN, Assoc. Writing Programs. Roman Catholic. Office: Calif State U Dept English 6000 J St Sacramento CA 95819-2605

SCHMITZ, VINCENT HERMAN, healthcare facility executive, finance executive; b. Bakersfield, Calif., Aug. 12, 1946; s. Walfred Nicholas and Mildred Telitha (Sparks) S.; m. Frances Conrad, Mar. 21, 1970 (div. Jan. 1980); children: Phoenix, Ingrid; m. Sondra Lynn Brown, Oct. 14, 1983; 1 child, Michael John. BA, U. Calif., Santa Barbara, 1968; MBA, Calif. State U., Sacramento, 1971. Acct. Tenneco, Bakersfield, 1971, Kern Union High Sch. Dist., Bakersfield, 1972; chief acct. Mercy Hosp., Bakersfield, 1972-73, chief fin. officer, 1973-87; exec. v.p., chief fin. officer Mercy Healthcare Sacramento, 1987—. Mem. Rotary Internat., Bakersfield, 1978-87, Paul Harris fellow, 1984. Mem. Am. Coll. Healthcare Execs., Health Care Fin. Mgmt. Assn. (pres. No. Calif. chpt. 1986), Rotary (Sacramento chpt.). Home: 3 Still Shore Ct Sacramento CA 95831-5567 Office: Mercy Health Care 10540 White Rock Rd Rancho Cordova CA 95670-7984

SCHMUDE, JUDY GAIL, health care administrator; b. Kenosha, Wis., Mar. 2, 1939; d. Howard D. and Joycelyn V. (Correll) Ohlgart; divorced; children: Frederick E., Randall H. BS, U. Wis., Whitewater, 1962, MS, 1971; MT, Kenosha Mem. Hosp., 1971; PhD, Marquette U., 1983. Cert. tchr. Tchr. gen. sch. Kenosha Unified Schs., 1962-67; instr. sci. Gateway Tech. Inst., Kenosha, 1967-75; edn. coordinator Kenosha Mem. Hosp., 1975-80, dir., 1980-86; v.p. women's care St. Joseph's Hosp. and Med. Ctr., Phoenix, 1986—, v.p. maternal and child health, 1989-90, v.p. ambulatory svcs., 1990—, v.p. patient svcs., 1994—; adj. faculty U. Phoenix, 1986—; faculty Cardinal Stritch Coll., Milw., 1985-86; cons. Kenosha Mem. Hosp., 1983-86. Author: Quality Assurance Nursing Schools, 1985, Politics in Health Care Administration, 1988; contbr. articles to profl. jours. Pres. Wish. Health Edn., 1986, Am. Cancer Soc., Kenosha, 1985; elected mem. Ariz. Women's Town Hall, 1987, 88, 89, panel chair, 1989, 91, 92; state chair Airz. Prenatal Care Coaliition, 1988-89, 93, 94. Mem. Am. Coll. Hosp. Execs., Ariz. Hosp. Assn., Squaw Peak Hiking Club, Phi Delta Kappa. Democrat. Lutheran. Office: St Josephs Hosp Med Ctr 350 W Thomas Rd Phoenix AZ 85013-4409

SCHNACK, GAYLE HEMINGWAY JEPSON (MRS. HAROLD CLIFFORD SCHNACK), corporate executive; b. Mpls., Aug. 14, 1926; d. Jasper Jay and Ursula (Hemingway) Jepson; student U. Hawaii, 1946; m. Harold Clifford Schnack, Mar. 22, 1947; children: Jerrald Jay, Georgina, Roberta, Michael Clifford. Skater, Shipstad & Johnson Ice Follies, 1944-46; v.p. Harcliff Corp., Honolulu, 1964—, Schnack Indsl. Corp., Honolulu, 1969—, Nutmeg Corp., Cedar Corp.; ltd. ptnr. Koa Corp. Mem. Internat. Platform Assn., Beta Sigma Phi (chpt. pres. 1955-56, pres. city council 1956-57). Established Ursula Hemingway Jepson art award, Carlton Coll., Ernest Hemingway creative writing award, U. Hawaii. Office: PO Box 3077 Honolulu HI 96802-3077 also: 1200 Riverside Dr Reno NV 89503

SCHNAPP, ROGER HERBERT, lawyer; b. N.Y.C., Mar. 17, 1946; s. Michael Jay and Beatrice Joan (Becker) S.; m. Candice Jacqueline Larson, Sept. 15, 1979; 1 child, Monica Alexis. BS, Cornell U., 1966; JD, Harvard U., 1969; postgrad. Pub. Utility Mgmt. Program, U. Mich., 1978. Bar: N.Y. 1970,, U.S. Ct. Appeals (2d cir.) 1970, U.S. Supreme, 1974, U.S. Dist. Ct. (so. dist.) N.Y. 1975, U.S. Ct. Appeals (4th and 6th cirs.) 1976, U.S. Ct. Appeals (7th cir.) 1977, U.S. Dist. Ct. (so. dist.) N.Y. 1975, U.S. Dist. Ct. (no. dist.) Calif. 1980, U.S. Ct. Appeals (8th cir.) 1980, Calif., 1982, U.S. Dist. Ct. (cen. dist.) Calif. 1982, U.S. Ct. Dist. (ea. dist.) Calif., 1984. Atty. CAB, Washington, 1969-70; labor atty. Western Electric Co., N.Y.C., 1970-71; mgr. employee rels. Am. Airlines, N.Y.C., 1971-74; labor counsel Am. Electric Power Svc. Corp., N.Y.C., 1974-78, sr. labor counsel, 1978-80; indsl. rels. counsel Trans World Airlines, N.Y.C., 1980-81; sr. assoc. Parker, Milliken, Clark & O'Hara, L.A., 1981-82; ptnr. Rutan & Tucker, Costa Mesa, Calif., 1983-84, Memel, Jacobs, Pierno, Gersh & Ellsworth, Newport Beach, Calif., 1985-86, Memel, Jacobs & Ellsworth, Newport Beach, 1986-87; pvt. practice, Newport Beach, 1987—; bd. dirs. Dynamic Constrn., Inc., Laguna Hills, Calif., 1986—; commentator labor rels. Fin. News Network; commentator Sta. KOCN Radio, 1990-91; lectr. Calif. Western Law Sch., Calif. State U.-Fullerton, Calif. State Conf. Small Bus.; lectr. collective bargaining Pace U., N.Y.C.; lectr. on labor law Coun. on Edn. in Mgmt.; N.E. regional coord. Pressler for Pres., 1979-80. Mem. bus. rsch. adv. coun. U.S. Dept. Labor; trustee Chapman U., 1991—. Mem. Calif. Bar Assn., Am. Arbitration Assn. (adv. com. Orange County area, cons. collective bargaining com.), Conf. R.R. and Airline Labor Lawyers, Balboa Bay Club, The Ctr. Club. Republican. Jewish. Author: Arbitration Issues for the 1980s, 1981, A Look at Three Companies, 1982; editor-in-chief Indsl. and Labor Rels. Forum, 1964-66; columnist Orange County Bus. Jour., 1989-91; contbr. articles to profl. publs. Office: PO Box 9049 Newport Beach CA 92658-1049

SCHNEBLY, F(RANCIS) DAVID, aerospace and electronics company executive; b. San Francisco, May 1, 1926; s. Frederick Dorsey and Mary Florence (Blake) S.; m. Miriam Louise Ford, Aug. 27, 1949; children: Mary Diane, Linda Marie, Anne Louise, David Albert, Kathleen Marie. BE in Areo. Engring., U. So. Calif., 1950; cert. advanced mgmt., Harvard U., 1970. Project engr. Hiller Aircraft Corp., Palo Alto, Calif., 1950-55, mgr. ops. rsch., 1955-58; mgr. ops. analysis Lockheed Missiles & Space Co., Sunnyvale, Calif., 1958-63, mgr. mil. programs, 1963-65, asst. dir. advanced programs, 1965-67, project mgr. advanced aircraft, 1967-70, dir. airborne systems, 1970-76, dir. remotely piloted vehicles, 1976-83; pres. F. David Assocs., Inc., Santa Rosa, Calif., 1983—; v.p. devel., bd. dirs. Command Systems Group, Inc., Torrance, Calif.; mem. panel U.S. Army Sci. Adv. Bd., Washington, 1965-66; presenter seminars in field. Author: Helicopter Performance Analysis Method, 1955. Pres. Hiller Mgmt. Club, Palo Alto, 1957; capt. Mounted Patrol San Mateo County, Woodside, Calif., 1976. Recipient award U.S. Army Aviation Rsch. and Tech. Labs. Mem. Am. Unmanned Systems Orgn., Am. Assn. Profl. Mgrs., Shack Riders (bd. dirs. 1983-87), Alpha Eta Rho (pres. Iota chpt. 1949). Republican. Home and Office: 1160 Pine St # B Menlo Park CA 94025-3407

SCHNECK, STUART AUSTIN, neurologist, educator; b. N.Y.C., Apr. 1, 1929; s. Maurice and Sara Ruth (Knapp) S.; m. Ida I. Nakashima, Mar. 2, 1956; children—Lisa, Christopher. B.S. magna cum laude, Franklin and Marshall Coll., 1949; M.D., U. Pa., 1953. Diplomate Am. Bd. Psychiatry and Neurology (bd. dirs., sec. 1990-91, v.p. 1991-92, pres. 1992-93). Intern Hosp. U. Pa., Phila., 1953-54; resident in medicine U. Colo. Med. Center, Denver, 1954-55, 57-58, resident in neurology, 1958-61; instr. neurology U. Colo. Sch. Medicine, 1959-61; instr. neuropathology Columbia U., N.Y.C., 1961-63; vis. fellow in neurology Vanderbilt Clinic, Columbia-Presbyn. Med. Center, N.Y.C., 1961-63; asst. prof. neurology and pathology U. Colo., 1963-67, assoc. prof., 1967-70, prof., 1970—, assoc. dean clin. affairs Sch. Medicine, 1984-89; cons. Fitzsimons Army Hosp., VA, Nat. Jewish Hosp.; pres. med. bd. Univ. Hosp., Denver, 1983-89, bd. dirs., 1989-90. Contbr. articles to profl. jours. Served with USAF, 1955-57. USPHS fellow, 1961-63. Mem. AAAS, Denver Med. Soc., Am. Acad. Neurology, Am. Assn. Neuropathologists, Am. Neurol. Assn., Colo. Assn. Clin. Neurologists, Alpha Omega Alpha (bd. dirs. 1979-89, treas., pres. 1990-93). Office: 4200 E 9th Ave Denver CO 80220-3706

SCHNEEWEIS, HAROLD NATHAN, security specialist; b. N.Y.C., May 23, 1938; s. Theodore and Rae (Knopf) S.; m. Diane Lenore Ackerman, June 26, 1960; children: Scott Bryan, David Michael, Richard Alan, Beth Lynn. BA, NYU, 1959; postgrad., Brooklyn Law Sch., 1959-61; MA, Sam Houston State U., 1972; student, FBI Acad., 1974; Mgmt. degree, Nat. War Coll., 1980. Commd. U.S. Army, 1959, advanced through grades to col., 1980; commdg. officer U.S. Army Correctional Facility, Ft. Hood, Tex., 1972-73; staff officer hdqs. Dept. of Army, Washington, 1974-75; commdg. officer 519th Military Police Battalion, Washington, 1975-77; staff officer Joint Chiefs of Staff, Washington, 1977-79; dir. ops. hdqs. U.S. Army Criminal Investigation Com., Washington, 1980-82; commdg. officer 6th region U.S. Army Criminal Investigation Com., San Francisco, 1982-85; ret. U.S. Army, 1985; chief MILSTAR security Lockheed Space & Missle Co., Sunnydale, Calif., 1985-86; supervising security rep. Pacific Gas & Electric Co., San Francisco, 1986—; ind. security cons., San Francisco, 1985—. Decorated Air medal, Bronze Star, Legion of Merit. Mem. Am. Soc. Indsl. Security, FBI Nat. Acad. Assocs., U.S. Army CID Agents Assn., Calif. Peace Officers Assn. Republican. Jewish. Home: 2528 Laguna Vista Dr Novato CA 94945-1526 Office: Pacific Gas & Electric Co 123 Mission St San Francisco CA 94105-1551

SCHNEIBEL, VICKI DARLENE, human resources administrator; b. Astoria, Oreg., Mar. 11, 1946; d. Howard Stanley and Sally (Thompson) Brandt; m. Lawrence Walter Schneibel, Mar. 18, 1967. AAS, Anchorage Community Coll., 1986; BA, Alaska Pacific U., 1991, MAT, 1994. Cert. profl. sec. Clk. typist The Oregonian, Portland, Oreg., 1964-67; statis. typist Rader Pneumatics, Inc., Portland, Oreg., 1967-71; sec., bookkeeper Larry's Custom Remodeling, Portland, Oreg., 1971-73; bookkeeper Tualatin Hills Pk. & Recreation Dist., Portland, Oreg., 1973-74; pvt. sec. Aloha (Oreg.) Community Bapt. Ch., 1974-79; exec. sec. Hyster Sales Co., Tigard, Oreg., 1979-83, 1st Nat. Bank of Anchorage, 1983-84; office mgr. Control Data Alaska, Anchorage, 1984-86; human resource adminstr. Westmark Hotels, Inc., Anchorage, 1986—. Author: Let Sleeping Moose Lie, Good Dog!, 1994. Active Anchorage Women's Commn., 1995—, Alaska Worksite Wellness Alliance. Mem. ASTD, Am. Mgmt. Assn., Soc. For Human Resource Mgmt. Lutheran. Home: 6646 Cimarron Cir Anchorage AK 99504-3945 Office: Westmark Hotels Inc 880 H St Ste 101 Anchorage AK 99501-3450

SCHNEIDER, CALVIN, physician; b. N.Y.C., Oct. 23, 1924; s. Harry and Bertha (Green) S.; A.B., U. So. Calif., 1951, M.D., 1955; J.D., LaVerne (Calif.) Coll., 1973; m. Elizabeth Gayle Thomas, Dec. 27, 1967. Intern Los Angeles County Gen. Hosp., 1955-56, staff physician, 1956-57; practice medicine West Covina, Calif., 1957—; staff Inter-Community Med. Ctr., Covina, Calif. Cons. physician Charter Oak Hosp., Covina, 1960—. With USNR, 1943-47. Mem. AMA, Calif., L.A. County med. assns. Republican. Lutheran. Office: 224 W College St Covina CA 91723-1902

SCHNEIDER, EDWARD LEE, botanic garden administrator; b. Portland, Oreg., Sept. 14, 1947; s. Edward John and Elizabeth (Mathews) S.; m. Sandra Lee Alfarone, Aug. 2, 1968; children: Kenneth L., Cassandra L. BA, Cen. Wash. U., 1969, MS, 1971; PhD, U. Calif., Santa Barbara, 1974. From asst. to assoc. prof. botany S.W. Tex. State U., San Marcos, 1974-84, prof., 1984-94, chmn. biology dept., 1984-89, dean sci., 1989-92; dir. Santa Barbara (Calif.) Botanic Garden, 1992—. Co-author: The Botanical World; contbr. articles to profl. jours. NSF grantee, 1980, 90; recipient Presdl. Rsch. award S.W. Tex. State U., 1985. Fellow Tex. Acad. Sci. (pres. 1992-93); mem. Internat. Water Lily Soc. (bd. dirs., sec. 1989—), Internat. Pollination Congress, Nat. Coun. Deans, Tex. Assn.Deans. Home: 1140 Tunnel Rd Santa Barbara CA 93105-2134 Office: Santa Barbara Botanic Garden 1212 Mission Canyon Rd Santa Barbara CA 93105-2126

SCHNEIDER, EDWARD LEWIS, medicine educator, research administrator; b. N.Y.C., June 22, 1940; s. Samuel and Ann (Soskin) S. BS, Rensselaer Poly. Inst., 1961; MD, Boston U., 1966. Intern and resident N.Y. Hosp.-Cornell U., N.Y.C., 1966-68; staff fellow Nat. Inst. Allergy and Infectious Diseases, Bethesda, Md., 1968-70; research fellow U. Calif., San Francisco, 1970-73; chief, sect. on cell aging Nat. Inst. Aging, Balt., 1973-79, assoc. dir., 1980-84, dep. dir., 1984-87; prof. medicine, dir. Davis Inst. on Aging U. Colo., Denver, 1979-80; dean Leonard Davis Sch. Gerontology U. So. Calif., L.A., 1986—, exec. dir. Ethel Percy Andrus Gerontology Ctr., 1986—, prof. medicine, 1987—, William and Sylvia Kugel prof. gerontology, 1989—; sci. dir. Buck Ctr. for Rsch. in Aging, 1989—; cons. MacArthur Found., Chgo., 1985-93, R.W. Johnson Found., Princeton, N.J., 1982-87, Brookdale Found., N.Y.C., 1985-89. Editor: The Genetics of Aging, 1978, The Aging Reproductive System, 1978, Biological Markers of Aging, 1982, Handbook of the Biology of Aging, 1985, 95, Interrelationship Among Aging Cancer and Differentiation, 1985, Teaching Nursing Home, 1985, Modern Biological Theories of Aging, 1987, The Black American Elderly, 1988, Elder Care and the Work Force, 1990. Med. dir. USPHS, 1968—. Recipient Roche award, 1964. Fellow Gerontology Soc., Am. Soc. Clin. Investigation; mem. Am. Assn. Retired Persons, U.S. Naval Acad. Sailing Squadron (coach 1980-86). Office: U So Calif Andrus Gerontology Ctr Los Angeles CA 90089-0191

SCHNEIDER, GARY PAUL, accountant educator; b. Cin., July 16, 1952; s. Anthony J. and Elaine M. (Silbernagel) S. BA, U. Cin., 1973; postgrad., U. Cin, 1979-83; MBA, Xavier U., Cin., 1975; PhD, U. Tenn., 1993. CPA, Ohio. Trust officer Provident Bank, Cin., 1975-76; pvt. practice acctg. Cin., 1976-89; adj. asst. prof. Xavier U., 1985-89; asst. prof. U. San Diego, 1992—; bd. dirs. Morrison Greenhouses, Inc., Loveland, Ohio, 1983-86. Author: Building Accounting Systems: A Transaction Cycle Approach, 1995, Fundamentals of Estate Planning, 1980; contbg. editor: (book series) Solutions to the Uniform CPA Examination, 1979, 80, 81, 82. Sch. bd. mem. Univ. San Diego H.S., 1993-95. Mem. Am. Acctg. Assn. (doctoral consortium fellow 1991), Am. Inst. CPA's, Mensa, Beta Gamma Sigam, Beta Alpha Psi. Home: 904 Glen Arbor Dr Encinitas CA 92024-1955 Office: U San Diego 5998 Alcala Park San Diego CA 92110-2429

SCHNEIDER, GERALD L., plastic surgeon; b. Mechanicsburg, Pa., Oct. 25, 1945; s. Gordon Henry and Pauline Emma (Rife) S.; m. Patricia Davis, July 15, 1978; 1 child, Ross Roberts. BS, No. Ariz. U., 1968; MD, U. Ariz., 1973. Intern Naval Regional Med. Ctr., San Diego, 1973-74; resident in gen. surgery U.S. Naval Hosp., San Diego, 1974-78; resident in plastic surgery U.S. Naval Hosp., Portsmouth, Va., 1978-80; staff surgeon divsn. plastic surgery U.S. Naval Hosp., San Diego, 1981-83, chief divsn. plastic surgery, 1983-84; pvt. practice Flagstaff, Ariz., 1984-90; staff surgeon La Jolla (Calif.) Cosmetic Surgery Ctr., 1990-91; surgeon Scripps Clinic & Rsch. Found., La Jolla, 1991—. Capt. USNR. Fellow ACS; mem. Am. Soc. Plastic and Reconstructive Surgeons, Lipoplasty Soc. North Am. Avocation: golf. Office: Scripps Clinic & Rsch Found 10666 N Torrey Pines Rd La Jolla CA 92037

SCHNEIDER, JERRY ALLAN, pediatrics educator; b. Detroit, Nov. 14, 1937; s. Benjamin and Sarah (Dorfman) S.; m. Elaine Barbara Bergner, Dec. 8, 1963; children: Danielle, Jane. Student, U. Mich., 1955-58; BS, Northwestern U., 1959, MD, 1962. Intern, resident Johns Hopkins Hosp., Balt., 1962-65; postdoctoral fellow NIH, Bethesda, Md., 1965-69, CNRS, Gif-sur-Yvette, France, 1969-70; from asst. prof. to assoc. prof. Pediatrics U. Calif., San Diego, 1970-77, prof. Pediatrics, 1977—. Guggenheim fellow Imperial Cancer Rsch. Found., London, 1977-78, Fogarty Internat. fellow, 1983-84. Office: U Calif San Diego Pediatrics 0609-F La Jolla CA 92093-0609

SCHNEIDER, JOSEPH FRANCIS, journalism educator, editor; b. Louisville, Aug. 26, 1932; s. John M. and Sarah A. (Weatherly) S.; m. Lenore T. Sharpley, Nov. 14, 1953; children: Stephen, Thomas. BA, U. Louisville, 1955; MA, Sophia U., Tokyo, 1972. Sports editor Va.-Tennessean, Bristol, Va., 1955-56; law enforcement reporter Evansville (Ind.) Courier, 1956-57, Fla. Times-Union, Jacksonville, 1957-58; asst. state editor Greensboro (N.C.) Daily News, 1958-62; S.E. Asia/Vietnam bur. chief Pacific Stars & Stripes, Tokyo, 1962-66, asst. editorial/feature editor, 1968-73; asst. mil. editor Stars & Stripes, Darmstadt, Fed. Republic Germany, 1966-68; asst. metro editor San Diego Union-Tribune, 1973—; instr. investigative reporting San Diego State U., 1975—; instr. journalism U. San Diego, 1992—. Mem. Soc. Profl. Journalists, Asian Am. Journalists Assn., San Diego Hist. Soc., Investigative Reporters and Editors, Kappa Tau Alpha, Pi Kappa Phi. Democrat. Roman Catholic. Office: San Diego Union-Tribune 350 Camino De La Reina San Diego CA 92108-3003

SCHNEIDER, TAMMI JOY, archaeology educator; b. Detroit, Dec. 28, 1962; d. Edward Schnedier and Ruth Helene (Litwak) Aaron. BA, U. Minn., 1984; PhD in Ancient History, U. Pa., 1991. Coord. Middle East Ctr. U. Pa., Phila., 1991-93; asst. prof. The Claremont (Calif.) Grad. Sch., 1993—; asst. field dir. The Miqne/Ekron Archaeol. Execs., Jeruselem, 1986-94, dir. Tel Safi Excavation, 1994; project dir. Instity for Antiquity Christianity, Calremont, Calif., 19936; rsch. asst. Sumerian Dictionary Project, Phila., 1989-91; co-curator Temple Mus. Keneseth Israel, Elkins Park, Pa., 1990. Contbr. articles to profl. jours. Ancient History fellowship U. Pa., 1988-91, grantee, 1989-90; Dorot Travel grantee Dorot Found., 1986; Fletcher Jones Grant, 1995. Mem. Israel Exploration Soc., Am. Oriental Soc., Corp. of Am. Schs. of Oriental Rsch. (sec. 1994—), Ancient Biblical Manuscript Ctr. (adv. bd.), Assn. of Ancient Historians. Office: The Claremont Grad Sch Harper Hall Rm 22 Claremont CA 91711

SCHNEIDER, WOLF, magazine editor, writer; b. N.Y.C., Mar. 5, 1953; d. Mortimer Stanley and Helene Carol (Werner) S. BA, CCNY, 1975; MA, U. So. Calif., 1976. Disc jockey Sta. KNCN-FM, Corpus Christi, Tex., 1977-78; producer Sta. KMET-FM, L.A., 1980-85; editor Videopreview mag., L.A., 1986; film reporter The Hollywood Reporter, L.A., 1987-88; dir. pub. rels. Showtime Networks, L.A., 1989-90; editor Am. Film Mag., L.A., 1990-92; film columnist L.A. Weekly, 1995—; panel moderator NCTA Conv., 1985, panel moderator Billboard Am. Film Inst. Video Conf., L.A., 1987; guest lectr. Assn. of Film Commrs. Cineposium, L.A.1988; awards judge Nat. Cable Forum Ace awards, L.A., 1986, 88; course instr. Am. Film Inst., L.A., 1991, 92. Contbr. articles to profl. jours., popular mags. Mem. publicity com. IFP West, L.A., 1989-90. Mem. PEN/West, 1990—, AFI, 1989—. Office: LA Weekly 6715 W Sunset Blvd Los Angeles CA 90028-7107

SCHNEITER, GEORGE MALAN, golfer, development company executive; b. Ogden, Utah, Aug. 12, 1931; s. George Henery and Bernice Slade (Malan) S.; B. Banking and Fin., U. Utah, 1955; m. JoAnn Deakin, Jan. 19, 1954; children: George, Gary, Dan, Steve, Elizabeth Ann, Michael. With 5th Army Championship Golf Team U.S. Army, 1955-56; assoc. golf pro Hidden Valley Golf Club, Salt Lake City, 1957; golf pro Lake Hills Golf Club, Billings, Mont., 1957-61, sec., 1957-61, pres., 1964—; pres. Schneiter Enterprises, Sandy, Utah, 1974—; developer Schneiter's golf course, 1973—, and subdiv., 1961—; player PGA tour 1958-78; sr. player PGA tour, 1981—. With U.S. Army, 1955-56. Winner Utah sect. Sr. Championship, Wyo. Open Super Sr. Championship, Salt Lake City Parks Tournament, Vernal Brigham Payson Open, Yuma Open, Ariz.; named U.S. Army Ft. Carson Post Golf Champ, 5th Army Championship Golf Team, 1955-56. Mem. PGA, Am. Mormon, Salt Lake City C. of C., Internat. Golf Course Supertaints Assn. Office: 8969 S 1300 E Sandy UT 84094

SCHNELL, ROGER THOMAS, retired military officer, state official; b. Wabasha, Minn., Dec. 11, 1936; s. Donald William and Eva Louise (Barton) S.; m. Barbara Ann McDonald, Dec. 18, 1959 (div. Mar. 1968); children: Thomas Allen, Scott Douglas; m. Young H. Kim, Sept. 25, 1987 (div. Nov. 1993); children: Eunice, Candice. A in Mil. Sci., Command and Gen. Staff Coll., 1975; A in Bus. Administn., Wayland Bapt. U., 1987. Commd. 2d lt. Alaska N.G., 1959, advanced through grades to col., 1975; shop supt. Alaska N.G., Anchorage, 1965-71, personnel mgr., 1972-74, chief of staff, 1974-87, dir. logistics, 1987; electrician Alaska R.R., Anchorage, 1955-61, elec. foreman, 1962-64; dir. support personnel mgmt. Joint Staff Alaska N.G., 1988-92, ret.; personnel mgr. State of Alaska, 1992; asst. commr. dept. mil. and vets. affairs State of Alaska, Ft. Richardson, 1992-95, dep. commr. dept. mil. and vets. affairs, 1995—. Bd. dirs. Meth. Trust Fund. Mem. Fed. Profl. Labor Relations Execs. (sec. 1974-75), Alaska N.G. Officers Assn. (pres. 1976-78, bd. dirs. 1988—), Am. Legion, Amvets. Republican. Methodist. Lodge: Elks. Home: 6911 Hunt Ave Anchorage AK 99504-1891 Office: Dept Mil and Vets Affairs State of Alaska PO Box 5800 Camp Denali Bldg #4900 Fort Richardson AK 99505-0800

SCHNELL, RUSSELL CLIFFORD, atmospheric scientist, researcher; b. Castor, Alta., Can., Dec. 12, 1944; s. Henry Emmanuel and Anna (Traudt) S.; m. Suan Neo Tan, May 25, 1974; children: Alicia, Ryan. BSc with distinction, U. Alta. (Can.), Edmonton, 1967; BSc, Meml. U., St. John's, Nfld., Can., 1968; MSc, U. Wyo., 1971, PhD, 1974. Research scientist U. Wyo., Laramie, 1971-74, Nat. Ctr. Atmospheric Research and NOAA, Boulder, Colo., 1974-76; dir. Mt. Kenya study World Meteorol. Orgn. div. UN, Nairobi, Kenya, 1976-78; research scientist U. Colo., Boulder, 1979-82, dir. Arctic Gas and Aerosol Sampling Program, 1982-92, fellow Coop. Inst. Research in Environ. Scis., 1985-92; dir. Mauna Loa Observatory, Hilo, Hawaii, 1992—; mem. aerobiology com. Nat. Acad. Sci., 1976-79; cons. UN, Geneva, 1977-80, Shell Devel., Modesto, Calif., 1978-79, Holme, Roberts & Owen, 1990-92; mem. adv. bd. Frost Tech., Norwalk, Conn., 1983-85; bd. dirs. TRI-S Inc., Louisville, Colo., Magee Sci.,. Editor Geophys. Research Letters, Arctic Haze Edit., 1983-84; discovered bacteria ice nuclei, 1969; patentee in field; contbr. articles to profl. jours. Bd. dirs. Boulder Valley Christian Ch., 1978-91; chmn. Boulder Council Internat. Visitors, 1983-85. Rotary Internat. fellow, 1968-69. Mem. Am. Geophys. Union, AAAS, Am. Meteorol. Soc. (cert. cons. meteorologist), Internat. Assn. Aerobiology, Soc. Cryobiology, Sigma Xi, Sigma Tau. Home: 1 Kahoa Rd Hilo HI 96720-2205 Office: Mauna Loa Observatory PO Box 275 Hilo HI 96721-0275

SCHNELLER, EUGENE S., sociology educator; b. Cornwall, N.Y., Apr. 9, 1943; s. Michael Nicholas and Anne Ruth (Gruner) S.; m. Ellen Stauber, Mar. 24, 1968; children: Andrew Jon, Lee Stauber. BA, L.I. U., 1967; AA, SUNY, Buffalo, 1965; PhD, NYU, 1973. Rsch. asst. dept. sociology NYU, N.Y.C., 1968-70; project dir. Montefiore Hosp. and Med. Ctr., Bronx, N.Y., 1970-72; asst. prof. Med. Ctr. and sociology Duke U., Durham, N.C., 1973-75; assoc. prof., chmn. dept. Union Coll., Schenectady, 1975-79, assoc. prof., dir. Health Studies Ctr., 1979-85; prof., dir. Sch. Health Adminstrn. and Policy, Ariz. State U., Tempe, 1985-91, assoc. dean rsch. and adminstrn. Coll. Bus., 1992-94; dir. L. William Seidman Rsch. Ctr., Tempe, 1992-94, counselor to pres. for health profl. edn., 1994—; vis. rsch. scholar Columbia U., N.Y.C., 1983-84; chmn. Western Network for Edn. in Health Adminstrn., Berkeley, Calif., 1987-92; mem. Ariz. Medicaid Adv. Bd., 1990-92, Ariz. Data Adv. Bd., 1989-91, Ariz. Health Care Group Adv. Bd., 1989; mem. health rsch. coun. N.Y. State Dept. Health, 1977-85; fellow Accrediting Commn. on Edn. for Health Svcs. Adminstrn., 1983-84. Author: The Physician's Assistant, 1980; mem. editorial bd. Work and Occupations, 1975-93, Hosps. and Health Svcs. Adminstrn., 1989-92, Health Adminstrn. Press, 1991—; contbr. articles to profl. jours., chpt. to book. Trustee Barrow Neurol. Inst., Phoenix, 1989—. Mem. APHA, Am. Sociol. Assn., Assn. Univ. Health Programs Health Adminstrn. (bd. dirs. 1990—, chmn. bd. dirs. 1994-95). Home: 9600 N 96th St Apt 282 Scottsdale AZ 85258-5165 Office: Ariz State U Office of Provost Adminstrn Bldg Tempe AZ 85287

SCHNITZER, ARLENE DIRECTOR, art dealer; b. Salem, Oreg., Jan. 10, 1929; d. Simon M. and Helen (Holtzman) Director; m. Harold J. Schnitzer, Sept. 11, 1949; 1 child, Jordan. Student, U. Wash., 1947-48; BFA (hon.) Pacific NW Coll. Art., 1988. Founder, pres. Fountain Gallery of Art, Portland, Oreg., 1951-86; exec. v.p. Harsch Investment Corp., 1951—. Apptd. to Oreg. State Bd. Higher Edn., 1987-88; former bd. dirs. Oreg. Symphony Assn., v.p. Oreg. Symphony; former bd. dirs. U.S. Dist. Ct. Hist. Soc.; former bd. dirs. Boys and Girls Club, 1988—; mem. Gov.'s Expo '86 Commn., Oreg.; mem. exec. com., former bd. dirs. Artquake; former mem. adv. bd. Our New Beginnings; past bd. dirs. Artists Initiative for a Contemporary Art Collection; former trustee Reed Coll., 1982-88; mem. exec. com. bd. dirs. N.W. Bus. Com. for Arts.; trustee, mem. exec. com. Oreg. Health Scis. Univ. Found.; mem. arts acquisition and collections com. Portland Art Mus.; mem. Nat. Com. for the Performing Arts, Kennedy Ctr., 1995—. Recipient Aubrey Watzek award Lewis and Clark Coll., 1981, Pioneer award U. Oreg., 1985, Met. Arts Commn. award, 1985, White Rose award March of Dimes, 1987, Disting. Svc. award Western Oreg. State Coll. 1988, Oreg. Urban League Equal Opportunity award 1988, Gov's. award for Arts, 1987, Woman of Achievement award YWCA, 1987, Disting. Svc. award U. Oreg., 1991, SAFECO Art Leadership award ArtFair/Seattle, 1994; honored by Portland Art Assn., 1979. Mem. Univ. Club, Multnomah Athletic Club, Portland Golf Club. Office: Harsch Investment Corp 1121 SW Salmon St Portland OR 97205-2000

SCHNITZLER, BEVERLY JEANNE, designer, art educator, writer; b. Berkeley, Calif.; children: Erich Gregory. BS, Ariz. State U., 1954; MA, Calif. State U., L.A., 1959; postgrad., Claremont Grad. Sch., 1956-59, Chouinard Art Inst., L.A., 1960-63. Spl. art tchr. and cons. Alhambra (Calif.) City Sch. Dist., 1958-60; prof. art Calif. State U., L.A., 1960—; cons. in art and creative fabric art Calif. State U., L.A., 1960—; lectr. in field; Calif. State U. del. for internat. acad. exch. guidelines to Yunnan Art Inst., Kunming, China, 1993. Author: New Dimensions in Needlework, 1978; project dir. and head designer heraldic banners Calif. State U., L.A., 1986-87; exhibiting artist in fiber art. Participant student/prof. exch. program Kunming, 1993. Calif. State U. L.A. instl. grantee, 1978, 79; AAUW Found. grantee, 1988; recipient Award for Outstanding Artistic Merit, Calif. State U. L.A. Assoc. Students, 1987; scholar conf. Spain and Portugal of the Navagators: The Age of Discovery to the Enlightenment, Georgetown U., 1990, scholar conf. participant Portugal and Spain of the Navigators: The Age of Exploration, George Washington U., 1992; recipient Emily Gates Nat. Alumna Achievement award Sigma Sigma Sigma, 1995. Mem. Nat. Surface Design Assn., Costume and Textile Coun. of L.A. County Mus., Internat. Designers Assn., Internat. World Conf. of Educators, AAUW, Am. Craftsman's Coun., Fine Art Club of Pasadena. Office: Calif State U Art Dept 5151 State University Dr Los Angeles CA 90032

SCHOBER, ROBERT CHARLES, electrical engineer; b. Phila., Sept. 20, 1940; s. Rudolph Ernst and Kathryn Elizabeth (Ehrisman) S.; m. Mary Eve Kanuika, Jan. 14, 1961; children: Robert Charles, Stephen Scott, Susan Marya. BS in Engring. (Scott Award scholar), Widner U., 1965; postgrad., Bklyn. Poly. Extension at Gen. Electric Co., Valley Forge, Pa., 1965-67, U. Colo., 1968-69, Calif. State U.-Long Beach, 1969-75, U. So. Calif., 1983-84. Engr. Gen. Electric Co., Valley Forge, 1965-68, Martin Marietta Corp., Denver, 1968-69; sr. engr. Jet Propulsion Lab., Pasadena, Calif., 1969-73, sr. staff, 1986—; mem. tech. staff Hughes Semiconductor Co., Newport Beach, Calif., 1973-75; prin. engr. Am. Hosp. Supply Corp., Irvine, Calif., 1975-83; sr. staff engr. TRW Systems, Redondo Beach, Calif., 1983-84; cons. Biomed. LSI, Huntington Beach, Calif. Mem. IEEE (student br. pres. 1963-65), Soc. for Indsl. and Applied Math., Assn. for computing Machinery, Tau Bea Pi. Republican. Patentee cardiac pacemakers. Current Work: Develop large scale integrated circuits for computer, spacecraft, and military, as well as commercial applications; design high speed signal processing integrated circuits; instrumental in starting the quest for low power integrated circuits; actively persuing the advancment of ultra low power technology; provides dissemination through public domain distribution of a low power MOSIS cell library, workshops and publications. Subspecialties: application specific microprocessor architecture design; ultra low power analog and digital systems and integrated circuits; integrated circuit design; focal plane electronic signal processing arrays, neural networks; synchro converter electronics; sigma-delta analog to digital converters and signal processing electronics; implantable medical devices including cardiac pacemakers, defibulators and hearing aids. Office: Jet Propulsion Lab 4800 Oak Grove Dr Pasadena CA 91109-8001

SCHOCH, DAVID HENRY, real estate executive; b. N.Y.C., May 21, 1947; s. Theodore W. and Carol (Malmquist) S. AB, Syracuse U., 1968; MBA, UCLA, 1971. Cost analyst So. Pacific, San Francisco, 1971-72; acct. Peat Marwick Mitchell & Co., San Francisco, 1972-76; fin. analyst Rocor Internat., Palo Alto, Calif., 1976-77; v.p. property sales McNeil Corp., San Mateo, Calif., 1977-84; v.p. real estate fin. Metric Realty, Foster City, Calif., 1984—. Mem. Am. Fin. Assn., Nat. Assn. Bus. Economists, Bay Area Mortgage Assn. Republican. Lutheran. Office: Metric Realty 1 California St San Francisco CA 94111

SCHOEN, EDGAR JACOB, pediatrician, pediatric endocrinologist; b. Bklyn., Aug. 10, 1925; s. Irving I. and Mathilda (Jacobs) S.; m. Fritzi M. Puehringer, May 15, 1960; children: Melissa, Eric. BS, U. Ill., 1946; MD, NYU, 1948. Intern Lincoln Hosp., N.Y.C., 1948-49; pediatric resident Mass. Gen. Hosp., Boston, 1949-50, 52-54, endocrinology fellow, 1944-50; pediatric and endocrine staff Kaiser Permanente, Oakland, Calif., 1954—; clin. prof. pediatrics U. Calif. Med. Ctr., San Francisco, 1960—; chief pediatrics Kaiser Permanente, Oakland, Calif., 1966-90. Contbr. over 90 articles to profl. jours. Lt. USN, 1952-54. Home: 2309 Bywood Dr Oakland CA 94602-2012 Office: Kaiser Permanente Med Ctr 280 W Macarthur Blvd Oakland CA 94611-5642

SCHOEN, STEVAN JAY, lawyer; b. N.Y.C., May 19, 1944; s. Al and Ann (Spevack) S.; m. Cynthia Lukens; children: Andrew Adams, Anna Kim. BS, U. Pa., 1966; JD, Cornell U., 1969; MPhil in Internat. Law, Cambridge U. (Eng.), 1979. Bar: N.Mex. 1970, N.Y. 1970, U.S. Dist. Ct. N.Mex. 1973, U.S. Supreme Ct. 1976, U.S. Tax Ct. 1973, U.S. Ct. Internat. Trade 1982. Nat. dir. Vista law recruitment U.S. OEO, Washington, 1970-71; atty. Legal Aid Soc. of Albuquerque, 1971-73; chief atty. N.Mex. Dept. Health and Social Svcs., Albuquerque, 1973-77; atty. Brennan, Schoen & Eisenstadt, 1979-88, Messersmith, McNeill & Schoen, 1989—; probate judge, Sandoval County, 1990—; arbitrator, NYSE. mem. N.Mex. Supreme Ct. Appellate Rules Com., 1982-92; chmn. rules com. Com. on Fgn. Legal Cons., 1993, Jud. Edn. Planning Com.; mem. Children's Code Rules Com., 1976-78. Bd. dirs., officer, Placitas Vol Fire Brigade, 1973-86; mem. Albequerque Adv. Com. on Fgn. Trade Zone. Recipient Cert. for Outstanding Svc. to Judiciary N.Mex. Supreme Ct., 1982, cert. of Appreciation, N.Mex. Supreme Ct., 1992, Cert. of Appreciation, N.Mex. Sec. of State, 1980, Cert. of Appreciation, U.S. OEO, 1971, Pro Bono Pub. Svc. award 1989, cert. Recognition Legal Aid, 1994. Mem. Am. Judges Assn., Nat. Coll. Probate Judges, State Bar N.Mex. (past chmn. real property, probate and trust sect. 1989, Outstanding Contbn. award 1989, task force on regulation of advt. 1990-91, past chmn. appellate practice sect. 1991, past chmn. internat. law sect. 1991-92, commn. on professionalism 1992—, organizing com. U.S.-Mex. law inst. 1992), N.Mex. Probate Judges Assn. (chmn. 1993-95), Oxford-Cambridge Soc. N.Mex. (sec.), N.Mex. Assn. Counties (adv. bd.). Home: 14 Rainbow Valley Rd Placitas NM 87043-8801 Office: 5700 Harper Dr NE Ste 430 Albuquerque NM 87109-3573

SCHOENDORF, JUDSON RAYMOND, allergist; b. New Orleans, Jan. 13, 1942; s. John Adam and Thelma Elizabeth (Verges) S. BA, Tulane U., 1962; MD, La. State U., 1966; MBA, Pepperdine U., 1992. Lic. physician, La., Calif.; cert. Am. Bd. Med. Mgmt. Intern Charity Hosp. of La., New Orleans, 1966-67; resident in pediatrics L.A. County/U. So. Calif. Med. Ctr., 1969-70; fellow UCLA/Harbor Gen. Hosp., 1970-72; allergist Russell T. Spears, M.D., Long Beach, 1972-76, The Harriman Jones Med. Group, Long Beach, 1976—; chief exec. officer The Harriman Jones Med. Group, 1989-91; pres., chief exec. officer The Harriman Jones Med. Found., 1992—; staff Kaiser Hosp, Bellflower, 1970-72, Children's Hosp., Long Beach, 1972—, Bauer/St. Mary's Hosp., Long Beach, 1972—, UCLA Hosp., 1972—, Community Hosp., Long Beach, 1977—; faculty UCLA, 1972—, Harbor Gen. Hosp., 1972—, others. Contbr. articles to profl. jours. Bd. dirs. Long Beach Children's Clinic, 1976-81, pres., 1978-81; bd. dirs. Long Beach Symphony Orch., 1985-89; bd. dirs. Am. Lung Assn. Calif., 1985—, exec. com., 1988—; adv. coun. phys. edn. dept. Calif. State U., Long Beach, 1985—; mem. Civil Svc. Commn., City of Long Beach, 1981-89, pres., 1982-83, 85-86; bd. dirs. Long Beach Civic Light Opera, 1986-88; mem. Redevel. Agy., City of Long Beach, 1989—; chair, RDA, 1993—; mem. cultural steering com. Pub. Corp. Arts, Long Beach; bd dirs. Adv. Com. Pub. Art, 1992—; mem. Mayor's Econ. Coun., 1994—, Joint Powers Authority Spring St. Corridor-Long Beach/Singal Hill, 1994—. Lt. USN, 1967-69, capt. USNR, 1985—. Decorated Navy Achievement Medal, Republic of Viet Nam Campaign Medal, Vietnamese Cross of Gallantry, others; recipient Katherine White Humanitarian award Long Beach Kiwanis, 1995. Mem. Calif. Med. Assn., L.A. County Med. Assn., Long Beach Med. Assn., Acad. Allergy, L.A. Soc. Allergy and Immunology, Am. Acad. Physician Execs. Office: Harriman Jones Med Group 2600 Redondo Ave Long Beach CA 90806-2325

SCHOENFELD, LAWRENCE JON, jewelry manufacturing company executive, travel industry consultant; b. Los Angeles, Nov. 30, 1945; s. Donald and Trudy (Libizer) S.; Carol Sue Gard, Aug. 24, 1969. AA, Los Angeles Valley Coll., Van Nuys, Calif., 1963; BBA, Wichita State U., 1969, MSBA, 1970; grad., US Army Command/Gen Staff Sch., Ft. Leavenworth, Kans., 1988. Cert. tchr., Calif.; lic. real estate broker, Calif. Asst. treas. Advance Mortgage, Los Angeles, 1970-72; v.p. ops. Unigem Internat., Los Angeles, 1972—; pres. L. & C. Schoenfeld Corp.; bd. dirs. The Schoenfeld Constrn. Co., Telecom Group, Uniorr Corp., Execucentre-West, Schoenfeld & Co., Customer Ground Handling Svc. Corp.; co-developer Bay-Osos Mini Storage Co., San Luis Obispo, Calif., El Mercadero World Trade Show, Guatemala, 1986, Santiago, 1987, Bahai, 1988, Paraguay, 1989, El Mercado, Costa Rica, 1990, Los Osos Mini Storage Co., Quito, 1991, Santa Cruz, 1993; pres. Accents on Beverly Hills, Accents at the Biltmore, Santa Barbara, 1995. Mem. Improvement Commn., Hermosa Beach., Calif. 1976-78. Served to maj. US Army Med. Service Corps, 1970-72, lt. col. with res. 1972—. Mem. South Am. Travel Assn., World Trade Assn. (assoc.), Town Hall, Wichita State U. Alumni Assn. (nat. dist. rep.), Res. Officers Assn., Brit. Am. C. of C. Jewish. Office: Unigem Internat 350 S Beverly Dr Ste 350 Beverly Hills CA 90212-4817

SCHOENGARTH, R(OBERT) SCOTT, life insurance company executive; b. L.A., June 27, 1949; s. Bruce William and Barbara Agnes (Wiggins) S.; m. Margaret Kathleen Maguire, Nov. 29, 1986; children: Tobey, Mandy. Student, Glendale (Calif.) Coll., 1970; BA in Journalism, Calif. State U., Northridge, 1973. News and sports writer Sta. KFWB, Hollywood, Calif., 1971-72; sports writer Sta. KMPC, L.A., 1973-74; sr. writer, rsch. analyst, asst. dir. sales promotion Transam./Occidental Life Ins. Co., L.A., 1974-79; dir. mktg. svcs. Gt. Am. Life Ins. Co., Beverly Hills, Calif., 1979-81; asst. v.p., dir. mktg. communications Sunset Life Ins. Co., Olympia, Wash., 1981—; workshop host, meeting planner Olympia Visitors and Conv. Bur., 1989, lst v.p., 1988. Pres. parish coun. Sacred Heart Ch., Lacey, Wash., 1980-85; chmn. credit com. Essell Credit Union, Olympia, 1987-95; lector, eucharistic min., choir leader St. Michael's Ch., Olympia, 1990—; chmn. Sunset Life's United Way Campaign; bd. dirs. United Way Thurston County. Recipient Advt. Excellence award Nat. Underwriter Mag., 1992. Mem. Life Communicators Assn. (exec. com. 1989-90, chmn. ann. meeting 1989, media chmn. 1990-91, award of excellence 1986, 90, 94, Best of Show award 1988, Morgan Crockford award 1989, Spl. Recognition award 1992, ann. meeting arrangements chmn. 1992), Ins. Conf. Planners Assn. Republican. Office: Sunset Life Ins Co 3200 Capitol Blvd S Olympia WA 98501-3304

SCHOENI, DOUGLAS EUGENE, wholesale distribution executive; b. Mt. Holly, N.J., Aug. 18, 1957; s. Donald Dean and Donna Eugene (Summers) S. Student, U. Kans., 1976-78. Asst. mgr. Rusty's IGA, Lawrence, Kans., 1978-82; dept. mgr. Willards IGA, Osawatomie, Kans., 1982-83; store mgr. Bonner Springs (Kans.) IGA, 1983-87; sales rep. Tombstone Pizza Corp., Medford, Wis., 1988-89; br. mgr. Saxton Inc., Denver, 1990—. Mem. Optimist, Bonner Springs, 1987; vol. United Way Big Brothers Program. Office: Saxton Inc 3950 Nome St Unit H Denver CO 80239-3362

SCHOENSTEIN, JOSEPH ROY, accountant; b. Jamaica, N.Y., Nov. 30, 1957; s. Leroy Joseph and Carolyn Nelda (Richrod) S.; m. Sherry Ann McMullen, Sept. 1, 1979. BSBA, Ohio State U., 1979; MBA, U. Dayton, 1991. Staff acct., SCOA Industries, Inc., Columbus, Ohio, 1979-81, sr. acct., 1984-86; supr. acctg. SCA Internat., Inc., Columbus, Ohio, 1981-84; supr. gen. acctg. Warner Cable Communications, Dublin, Ohio, 1986-88, mgr. gen. acctg., 1988-92; v.p., fin. and contr. Bakersfield (Calif.) div. Time Warner Cable, 1992—; bd. dirs., treas. Kern County Econ. Opportunity Corp., 1993. Home: 2428 Moffitt Way Bakersfield CA 93309-4391

SCHOESLER, MARK GERALD, state legislator, farmer; b. Ritzville, Wash., Feb. 16, 1957; s. Gerald E. and Dorothy (Heinemann) S.; m. Ginger J. Van Aelst, Apr. 8, 1978; children: Veronica, Cody. AA, Spokane (Wash.) C.C., 1977. Mem. Wash. Ho. of Reps., Olympia, 1992—; asst. majority floor leader, mem. rules, agr. and ecology, fin., and corrections coms. Pres. Wash. Friends Farms and Forests, 1991-92; mem. Cmty. Econ. Revitalization Bd. Mem. Wash. Assn. Wheat Growers (dir. 1990-92). Republican. Mem. United. Ch. Christ. Home: Rte 1 Box 151 Ritzville WA 99169

SCHOETTGER, THEODORE LEO, city official; b. Burton, Nebr., Sept. 2, 1920; s. Frederick and Louise Cecelia (Gierau) S.; m. Kathlyn Marguerite Hughey, June 3, 1943; children—Gregory Paul, Julie Anne. B.S. in Bus. Adminstrn. with Distinction, U. Nebr., 1948. C.P.A., Calif. Sr. acct. Haskins & Sells, Los Angeles, 1948-55; controller Beckman Instruments, Inc., Fullerton, Calif., 1955-58; corp. chief acct. Beckman Instruments, Inc., 1958-60; treas. Docummun Inc., Los Angeles, 1960-77; fin. dir. City of Orange, Calif., 1977-93. Mem. fin. com., treas., bd. dirs. Childrens Hosp. Served to lt. USNR, 1942-45. Mem. Calif. Soc. CPA's (nat. dir., v.p., past pres. Los Angeles chpt.), Fin. Execs. Inst., Mcpl. Fin. Officers Assn., Beta Gamma Sigma, Alpha Kappa Psi. Methodist. Clubs: Jonathan, Town Hall. Home: 9626 Shellyfield Rd Downey CA 90240-3418

SCHOFIELD, JAMES ROY, computer programmer; b. Reedsburg, Wis., Aug. 16, 1953; s. G. C. Schofield and Margaret (Collies) Tverberg. BA, Carleton Coll., 1976. Programmer Brandon Applied Systems, San Francisco, 1977-78, Rand Info. Systems, San Francisco, 1979-83; systems programmer IBM, San Jose, Calif., 1983-91; programmer Office of Instnl. Rsch./U. Calif., Berkeley, 1991-94, Datis Corp., San Mateo, Calif., 1994—. Mem. Assn. for Computing Machinery, Assn. for Computing Machinery Spl. Interest Group in Computers and Soc., Phi Beta Kappa. Home: PO Box 25143 San Mateo CA 94402-5143 Office: Datis Corp 1875 S Grant St San Mateo CA 94402-2669

SCHOFIELD, KEITH, research chemist; b. Derby, England, July 27, 1938; came to U.S., 1963; s. Kenneth Schofield and Peggy (Hewitt) Furniss; divorced; children: Jeremy N., Clare, Susan A. BA, Cambridge U., 1960, MA and PhD, 1964. Rsch. scientist Nat. Ctr. Atmospheric Rsch., Boulder, Colo., 1965-67; rsch. physicist Cornell Aeronautical Rsch. Lab., Buffalo, 1967-68; sr. staff scientist GM Rsch. Lab., Santa Barbara, Calif., 1968-74; rsch. assoc. Quantum Inst. U. Calif., Santa Barbara, 1974-90; rsch. dir. Chemdata Rsch., Santa Barbara, 1974—; rsch. assoc. chemistry dept. U. Calif., Santa Barbara, 1991—; cons. GM Corp., Santa Barbara, 1975-88, Arnold Engring. Devel. Ctr., Arnold AFB, Tenn, 1988-92. Contbr. articles to profl. jours. Chmn. conservation Los Padres Chpt. Sierra Club, Santa Barbara, 1990-92; bd. dirs. Las Positas Friendship Park, Santa Barbara, 1993—. Postdoctoral Rsch. fellow U. Calif., 1964-65; U.K. State and Major scholar, Cambridge, 1957-60. Mem. Am. Chem. Soc., Am. Physical Soc., Combustion Inst. Home: PO Box 40481 Santa Barbara CA 93140-0481

SCHOLL, ALLAN HENRY, retired school system administrator, education consultant; b. Bklyn., May 6, 1935; s. Joseph Arnold and Edith (Epstein) S.; m. Marina Alexandra Mihailovich, July 3, 1960. BA, UCLA, 1957; MA, U. So. Calif., 1959, PhD in History, 1973. Lic. gen. secondary tchr. (life), administrv. svcs. (life), jr. coll. tchr. (life) Calif. Tchr. social studies L.A. Unified Sch. Dist., 1960-82, adviser social studies sr. high schs. div., 1982-84, dir. secondary social studies Office Instrn., 1984-91; instr. history L.A. City Coll., 1966-69, U. So. Calif., L.A., 1968-69, Community Coll., Rio Hondo, Calif., 1972-74, Cerritos (Calif.) Coll., 1973-74; dir. Almar Ednl. Cons., Pasadena, Calif., 1991—; curriculum writer interactive TV and history teaching and resource guides; cons. Pasadena Unified Sch. Dist., 1987-88, Coll. Bd., 1980-88; edn. cons. Am. Odyssey, 1991; cons. h.s. govt. and U.S. history textbooks, 1987. Author: United States History and Art, 1992; co-author: History of the World, 1990, History of the World: The Modern Era, 1991, 20th Century World History: The Modern Era, 1993, People of African Descent in Nazi Occupied Europe, 1995, Timeline of the Holocaust: A Teaching Guide for Secondary Scools, Rescuers and Rescued: A Holocaust Teaching Guide; Cont. Anne Frank in Historical Perspective; contbr. articles to profl. jours. Bd. dirs. Pasadena Chamber Orch., 1977-78, Pasadena Symphony Orch., 1984-85, Pasadena Centennial Com., 1985; mem. exec. bd., chmn. edn. com. Martyrs Meml. and Mus. of Holocaust of L.A., 1992—; mem. ednl. adv. bd. Gene Autry Western Heritage Mus., 1992—. With U.S. Army, 1958-59. NDEA fellow Russian lang. studies, 1962; Chouinard Art Inst. scholar, 1952. Mem. Am. Hist. Assn., Nat. Coun. Social Studies, Calif. Coun. Social Studies, So. Calif. Social Studies Assn. (bd. dirs. 1982-84), Assoc. Adminstrs. L.A. (legis. coun. 1984-86), Nat. History Hon. Soc., Crohn's and Colitis Found. Am., Phi Alpha Theta.

SCHOLNICK, JOSEPH B., public relations executive, journalist; b. Bklyn, Dec. 28, 1921; s. Philip and Esther (Kemper) S.; m. Lynne Okon, Aug. 22, 1948; children—Tina M., Eric Nils, Nadia Franzeska. AB, U. Miami, 1950; MS, Northwestern U., 1951; postgrad. in gen. mgmt. Am. Mgmt. Assn., 1958-59. Mem. staff Buffalo Evening News, 1951-56; dir. pub. relations Brown-Forman Distillers Corp., Louisville, 1956-62; contbg. editor Argosy Mag., 1962-65; v.p. pub. relations and communications Calif. World's Fair, Long Beach, 1963-65; gen. mgr. internat. expositions div. Am. Express Co., N.Y.C., 1965-69; pres. Communications Workshop, Long Beach, Internat. Group, Long Beach, 1969—, Creative Travel Svcs. Corp., Long Beach, 1973-89; mng. dir. admissions mktg. Pacific 21 Council, Century City, Los Angeles, 1974-75; dir. advance admissions mktg. Expo 74, Spokane, Wash., 1973-74; dir. mktg. Lion Country Safari, Inc., 1975-77; exec. v.p., chief exec. officer LA 200 Corp., 1977-82; pub. relations liaison U.S. and Can., Mex. Nat. Tourist Council, 1978-84; columnist, travel editor Capitol News Service of Sacramento, 1983—. Served with USAAF, 1942-45. Mem. Internat. Pub. Relations Assn., Pub. Relations Soc. Am., Sigma Delta Chi. Clubs: Nat. Press, Overseas Press, Greater Los Angeles Press. Home: 412 N Bellflower Blvd Unit 121 Long Beach CA 90814-2002

SCHOLTEN, PAUL, obstetrician/gynecologist, educator; b. San Francisco, Oct. 14, 1921; s. Henry Francis and Gladys (Lamborn) S.; m. Marion Lucy O'Neil, Feb. 7, 1948; children: Catherine Mary (dec.), Anne Marie, Pauline Marie, Joseph, Stephen, John. AB, San Francisco State U., 1943; postgrad., Stanford U., 1946-47; MD, U. Calif., San Francisco, 1951. Diplomate Am. Bd. Ob-Gyn. Intern San Francisco Gen. Hosp., 1951-52; resident in ob-gyn U. Calif., San Francisco, 1952-55; pvt. practice specializing in ob-gyn San Francisco, 1955-80; coll. physician Student Health Svc. San Francisco State U., 1956-80, dir. women's svcs. Student Health Svc., 1980-91; pvt. practice San Francisco, 1991—; part-time ship's surgeon Delta Lines, 1980-84; assoc. clin. prof. Med. Sch., U. Calif., San Francisco, 1955—, assoc. clin. prof. Nursing Sch., 1987—; preceptor Med. Sch., Stanford U., 1989-91; lectr. on health and wine at numerous univs., profl. groups. Contbr. articles to profl. publs., chpts. to books. Cons. U.S. Wine Inst.; sci. advisor Calif. State Adv. Bd. on Alcohol-Related Problems, 1980-86; bd. dirs. A.W.A.R.E., Century Coun. Sgt. U.S. Army, 1944-46. Mem. AMA, Calif. Med. Assn., Pan Am. Med. Assn., San Francisco Med. Soc. (editor 1971—, historian), San Francisco Gynecol. Soc., Am. Coll. Ob-Gyn., Soc. Med. Friends of Wine (bd. dis. 1955—, past pres.), San Francisco Wine and Food Soc. (bd. dirs. 1960—, past pres.), Internat. Wine and Food Soc. (gov. 1989—, Bronze medal 1989), San Francisco State U. Alumni Assn. (bd. dirs. 1962—), German Wine Soc., Sierra Club. Republican. Roman Catholic. Home and Office: 121 Granville Way San Francisco CA 94127-1133

SCHOLZ, GARRET ARTHUR, financial executive; b. Bridgeport, Conn., Sept. 22, 1939; s. Edward G. and Ann E. (Dineson) S.; m. Jeanne L. LaBorde; children: Michael, Stephen, Christopher. B.B.A., U. Oreg., 1961, M.B.A., 1965. Security analyst Equitable Life Assurance, N.Y.C., 1966-68; fin. mgr. Olin Corp., New Haven, 1968-73; asst. treas. McKesson Corp., San Francisco, 1973-81, treas., 1982-90, v.p. fin., 1990—; bd. dirs. Golden State Ins. Co., Hamilton, Bermuda; v.p., treas., ArmorAll Products, Inc., P.C.S., Inc.; bd. dirs. Sunbelt Beverage Corp., Medis Health and Pharm. Svcs. Corp. Trustee McKesson Found., San Francisco; bd. dirs. San Francisco Met. YMCA; bd. dirs. Edgewood Children's Ctr.; mem. adv. com. San Francisco Found. 1st lt. U.S. Army, 1961-64. Mem. Fin. Execs. Inst., Fin. Officers of No. Calif., Bankers Club, Olympic Club , Commonwealth Club. Office: McKesson Corp 1 Post St San Francisco CA 94104-5203

SCHOMER, HOWARD, retired clergyman, educator, social policy consultant; b. Chgo., June 9, 1915; s. Frank Michael and Daisy (Aline) S.; m. Elsie Pauline Swenson, Mar. 23, 1942; children: Karine, Mark, Paul, Ellen. B.S. summa cum laude, Harvard U., 1937, postgrad., 1939-40; student, Chgo. Theol. Sem., 1938-39, 40-41, D.D., 1954; LL.D., Olivet Coll., 1966. Ordained to ministry Congl. Ch., 1941. Student pastor Fitzwilliam, N.H., Oak Park, Ill.; asst. dean U. Chgo. Chapel., 1940-41; counsellor Am. history Harvard U., 1939-40; civilian pub. service Am. Friends Service Com., 1941-45; Am. Bd. Mission fellow to chs. of Europe Chambon-sur-Lignon, France, 1946-55; history tchr., work camp dir. Coll. Cevenol; founder internat. conf. center Accueil Fraternel, Permanent Conf. Protestant Chs. in Latin Countries of Europe; asst. to rapporteur UN Commn. on Human Rights, UN Econ. and Social Council, 1947-48; inter-church aid sec. for Europe World Council Chs., Geneva, 1955-58; pres., prof. ch. history Chgo. Theol. Sem., 1959-66; exec. dir. dept. specialized ministries Div. Overseas Ministries, Nat. Council Chs., N.Y.C., 1967-70; participant integration demonstrations in Ala., Ga., Washington, Chgo., SCLC, 1960-66; world issues sec. United Ch. Bd. World Ministries, 1971-80; Indochina liaison officer World Council of Chs., 1970-71; United Ch. of Christ officer for social responsibility in investments, 1972-81; founder, dir. Corp. Adv. Services, 1980-90; founder, mem. United Ch. Christ Working Group with United Ch. in German Democratic Rep. and Fed. Rep. of Germany, 1977-86; vis. prof. religion and society Andover Newton Theol. Sch., 1981; vis. lectr. Manchester Coll., St. John's U.; Woodrow Wilson vis. fellow Drew U., 1981; pres. Internat. Fellowship of Reconciliation, 1959-63, v.p., 1963-65; participant 1st-3d assemblies World Council Chs., Amsterdam, 1948, Evanston, 1954, New Delhi, 1961; rep. UN non-govt. orgn. UNIAPAC, 1979-85; pastoral assoc. First Congl. Ch. (United Ch. Christ), Montclair, N.J., 1983-89; delegated observer Vatican Council II, 1963; v.p. Am. Friends Coll. Cevenol., 1981-89; bd. dirs. Interfaith Center for Corp. Responsibility, 1973-81; chmn. exec. com. Freedom of Faith - A Christian Com. for Religious Rights, 1978-81; mem. nat. adv. bd. N.Y. State Martin Luther King Jr. Inst. for Nonviolence, 1989-92. Translator: The Prayer of the Church Universal (Marc Boegner), 1954; editor: The Oppression of Protestants in Spain, 1955, the Role of Transnational Business in Mass Economic Development, 1975; editor-at-large Christian Century, 1959-70; contbr.; Business, Religion and Ethics-Inquiry and Encounter, 1982, Aspects of Hope, 1993; articles to religious and interdisciplinary publs.; corr. in U.S. for Évangile et Liberté, 1988—. Past co-chmn. Chgo. Com. for Sane Nuclear Policy; bd. dirs. World Conf. on Religion and Peace, 1974-84, sec. for Kampuchea issues, 1979-81; former trustee Am. Waldensian Aid Soc.; mem. internat. council Internat. Ctr. Integrative Studies, 1984-91, bd. dirs., 1987-91; trustee Internat. Inst. for Effective Communication, 1987-93; bd. dirs. Alternative Lifelong Learning, 1992—, Cambodian Found. for Justice, Peace and Devel., 1993—. Mem. ACLU, Wider Quaker Fellowship, Fellowship Reconciliation, Ctr. for Theology and the Natural Scis., Outlook Club (Berkeley), Harvard Club San Francisco, Phi Beta Kappa. Home: 1012 Contra Costa Dr El Cerrito CA 94530-2710

SCHONBERGER, HOWARD, news reporter; b. Pottawattamie County, Iowa, Mar. 9, 1921; s. Edward Hermann and Anna (Hazel) S.; m. Virginia Harcum, June 10, 1945 (div. Jan. 1962); 1 child, Howard; m. Ottley Briggs Smith, Jan. 30, 1967; children: Kathy Smith, Mark Smith, Gary Smith. BS in Journalism, Northwestern U., 1948, MS in Journalism, 1949. Intern AP Bur., Chgo., 1940-41; editor, columnist Gorrell Publs. Vets. Report, Washington, 1946-47; advt. dir. Palo Alto (Calif.) Times, 1949-79; mktg. dir., columnist Jour. of San Juan Islands, Friday Harbor, Wash., 1985—; instr. graphic arts Medill Sch., Northwestern U., Evanston, 1946. Columnist Ferry Home Companion, 1988—; artist; editor and pub. for Newspaper Promotion Assn., Chgo., 1974. Vice-pres. Palo Alto C. of C., 1965-68; trustee Palo Art Club, 1965-79; fireman Sunset Point Fire Sta., San Juan Island, Wash., 1979-89. 1st lt. infantry, U.S. Army, 1942-46, 50-52, PTO and Korea. Recipient Advt. Wank award Advt. Club, San Francisco Bay, 1960. Mem. Arts and Crafts Guild (bd. dirs. 1982—), Lions (bd. dirs., v.p. 1953—), San Juan Golf and Country Club, San Juan Island Yacht Club, Calif. Newspaper Advt. Assn. (pres., bd. dirs. 1962-67, Advt. Excellence awards 1960-79), Sigma Delta Chi. Home: 1585 Wilks Way Friday Harbor WA 98250-9544 Office: Journal San Juan Islands Box 519 Friday Harbor WA 98250

SCHONBRUN, RENA, librarian; b. Jamaica, N.Y., Nov. 3, 1940; d. Henry and Madeline (Kapelsohn) S. BS in Chemistry, CUNY, 1962; MLS, Case Western Reserve U., 1963. Lit. chemist Libr., Lederle Lab, Pearl River, N.Y., 1963-67, info. chemist, 1967-68; librarian-systems devel. Nat. Agrl. Libr., Beltsville, Md., 1968-70, systems analyst, 1970-71; libr. Western Regional Rsch. Ctr., U.S. Dept. Agr., Albany, Calif., 1971—. Bd. dirs. SPV Homeowners' Assn., San Pablo, Calif., 1983—. Mem. Am. Chem. Soc., Spl. Librs. Assn. (various local and div. offices), N.Am. Series Interest Group, Beta Phi Mu. Office: Libr Western Regional Rsch Ctr US Dept Agr 800 Buchanan St Albany CA 94710

SCHONEBAUM, ALFRED, food company executive; b. Dortmund-Horde, Westfalen, Germany, Nov. 27, 1914; came to U.S., 1947; s. Emil and Bertha (Muller) S.; m. Margaret Karliner, July 13, 1939; 1 child, Reuben-Max. Abitur, Real Gymnasium, Dortmund-Horde, 1930. Dept. mgr. Wollwaren House Saxonia, Dresden, Germany, 1934-35, buyer, 1936-38; sales rep. Import Firm, Soerabaia, Java, 1938-40; exec. Import Firm, Semarang, Java, 1940-47; dept. mgr. textile firm N.Y.C., 1948-52; exec. Specialty Food Co., N.Y.C., 1952-80; cons. in field. Pres. condo bd., Jackson Heights, N.Y., 1986-93; vol. Light House, Rego Park, N.Y., 1980-94. Recipient Mgmt. Achievement award N.Y. Habitat, 1988. Mem. Coun. N.Y. Coops. Democrat. Jewish. Home: 18755 W Bernardo Dr #1347 San Diego CA 92127

SCHONER, STEVEN RONALD, park ranger; b. L.A., Jan. 28, 1951; s. Eugene Harry and Nancy Ann (Truscello) S.; m. Diane Herman, July 30, 1978; 1 child, Anna Rachel. BS in Philosophy, No. Ariz. U., 1975. Lectr., tour guide Lowell Obs., Flagstaff, Ariz., 1971-74; machinist Mack Corp., Flagstaff, 1978-82, W. L. Gore and Assocs., Flagstaff, 1982-86; park svc. ranger Nat. Park Svc., Flagstaff, 1988—; dir., founder Am. Meteorite Survey, Flagstaff, 1978—. Dir. Right to Vote Com., Flagstaff, 1981-84. Mem. Gold Prospectors Assn. Am. Republican. Home: 3 N Bonito St Flagstaff AZ 86001-5333 Office: Nat Park Svc 2717 N Steves Blvd # 3 Flagstaff AZ 86004-3959

SCHOOLEY, ROBERT T., educator; b. Denver, Nov. 10, 1949; s. Robert Enoch and Lelia Francis (Barnhill) S.; m. Pamela Owen Cook, Mar. 29, 1972; children: Kimberly Dana, Elizabeth Kendall. BS, Washington & Lee U., 1970; MD, Johns Hopkins U., 1974. Diplomate Am. Bd. Internal Medicine. Instrn Johns Hopkins Hosp., Balt., 1974-75, resident, 1975-76; clin. assoc. lab. clin. investigation Nat. Inst. Allergy & Infectious Deisease, NIH, Bethesda, Md., 1976-77; chief clin. assoc. lab. clin. investigation Nat. Inst. Allergy & Infectious Disease, NIH, Bethesda, Md., 1977-78; men. officer lab. clin. investigation Nat. Inst. Allergy & Infectious Deisease, NIH, Bethesda, Md., 1978-79; from instr. to assoc. prof. medicine Harvard Med. Sch., Boston, 1979-90; prof. medicine U. Colo., Denver, 1990—; cons. internal medicine Mass. Eye and Ear Infirmary, Boston, 1980-85, cons. infectious diseases Harvard U. Health Svcs., Cambridge, Mass., 1982-90. mem. editorial bd. Anrimicrobial Agts. and Chemotherapy, 1987—, Biotherapy, 1987—, Jour. Acquired Immune Deficiency Syndromes, 1988—, Clin. and Diagnostic Lab. Immunology, 1992; contbr. articles to profl. jours. Clin. and rsch. fellow Infectious Disease Unit, Mass. Gen. Hosp., Boston, 1979-81; rsch. fellow Medicine Harvard Med. Sch., 1979-81. Fellow Infectious Disease Soc. Am.; mem. AAAS, Am. Assn. Immunologists, Am. Soc. Clin. Investigation, Am. Assn. Physicians, Omicron Delta Kappa. Office: U Colo Health Sci Ctr 4200 E 9th Ave B-168 Denver CO 80262

SCHOONMAKER, ROBERT CADBURY, management consultant; b. Northampton, Mass., June 26, 1944; s. John Warder and Ann Pitkin (Palmer) S.; m. Kama Sue Conger, Jan. 22, 1968; children: Rachael, Melanie, Trista, Tara, Tania, Robert J., Trent, Benjamin, Joshua, Nicole, Jeremy. BS in History, Brigham Young U., 1968, M. Accountancy, 1973. Cert. in mgmt. acctg. Dir. regulatory affairs Gen. Telephone Co. of Ill., Bloomington, Ill., 1979-81; acctg. dir. Gen. Telephone Co. of Mich., Muskegon, 1981; contr. Gen. Telephone Co. of Ind., Ft. Wayne, 1981-82; v.p. revenue requirements Gen. Telephone Co. of the Midwest, Grinnell, Iowa, 1982-84; v.p. GVNW Inc./Mgmt., Colorado Springs, Colo., 1984-90; v.p. fin. Fidelity Comms., Sullivan, Mo., 1990-91; v.p. GVNW Inc./Mgmt., Colorado Springs, 1991—. With U.S. Army, 1969-72. Mem. LDS Church. Home: 5317 Miranda Rd Colorado Springs CO 80918-2319 Office: GVNW Inc/ Mgmt 2270 La Montana Way Colorado Springs CO 80918-6900

SCHOPPA, ELROY, accountant, financial planner; b. Vernon, Tex., Aug. 25, 1922; s. Eddie A. and Ida (Foerster) S.; m. Juanita C. Young, Aug. 11, 1956 (div.); children: Karen Marie, Vickie Sue; m. Gail O. Evans, May 12, 1984; stepchildren: Veronica, Vanessa. BBA, Tex. Tech U., 1943; postgrad. Law Sch., U. Tex., 1946-47; MA, Mich. State U., 1950. CPA, Tex., Calif.; cert. real estate broker; cert. ins. agt. Mem. faculty Tex. Tech U., Lubbock, 1943, U. Tex., Austin, 1946-47, Mich. State U., East Lansing, 1947-50; auditor Gen. Motors Corp., 1950-56; dir. systems and procedures Fansteel Metall. Corp., 1956-59; gen. auditor Consol. Electro Dynamics Corp., 1959-60; auditor, sr. tax acct. Beckman Inst. Inc., Fullerton, Calif., 1960-70; pres. Elroy Schoppa Acctg. Corp., La Habra, Calif., 1960—; fin. planner Nat. Assn. Stock Dealers; cons. to bus. Treas. La Habra Devel. Corp.; organizer, pres. 4-H Club, Vernon; adviser Jr. Achievement, Waukegan, Ill.; bd. dirs. Klein Ctr. for Prevention of Domestic Violence; asst. football and basketball coach, Manzanola, Colo.; coach Am. Girls Sport Assn., La Habra. Served with USN, 1942-46; USNR, 1946-62. Mem. Calif. Soc. CPA's, Alpha Phi Omega, Theta Xi. Republican. Lutheran. Club: Phoenix (Anaheim, Calif.). Avocations: hunting, fishing, camping, traveling. Office: 801 E La Habra Blvd La Habra CA 90631-5531

SCHOPPE, JAMES HENRY, printing company executive; b. Des Moines, Feb. 27, 1936; s. John Everett Sr. and Mary Lucile (Heizer) S. Grad. high sch., Gresham, Oreg. Founder, proprietor Schoppe Printing Co., Portland, Oreg., 1960—; pub. Schoppe Bookcrafters, Portland, 1992—. Editor: Hope Chimes, 1951-67; author: The Supreme Peacemakers, 1991; news writer The Vanguard (USAF Air Base newspaper), 1957; news editor: The Vanguard (Portland State U.), 1959. Precinct committeeman Rep. party, 1960-69. Presbyterian. Office: Schoppe Printing Co 6509 N Interstate Ave Portland OR 97217-4835

SCHORB, JODI RENE, market researcher; b. Buffalo, Apr. 22, 1966; d. Brian Lee and Judith (Christopher) S. BA in English Lit., Northwestern U., 1988; MA in English Lit., San Francisco State U., 1994; postgrad., U. Calif., Davis, 1994—. Asst. canvass dir. Pub. Interest Rsch. Group, Boston, 1988-89; exec. asst. Evans Rsch. Assocs., San Francisco, 1989—. Mem. MLA, Philol. Assn. Pacific Coast (conf. speaker 1994). Mem. Green Party. Office: Evans Rsch Assocs 120 Howard St Ste 660 San Francisco CA 94105-1620

SCHORR, ALAN EDWARD, librarian, publisher; b. N.Y.C., Jan. 7, 1945; s. Herbert and Regina (Fingerman) S.; m. Debra Genner, June 11, 1967; 1 son, Zebediah. BA, CUNY, 1966; MA, Syracuse U., 1967; postgrad., U. Iowa, 1967-71; MLS, U. Tex., 1973. Tchr., rsch. asst. dept. history U. Iowa, 1967-70; govt. publs. and map libr., asst. prof. Elmer E. Rasmuson Libr., U. Alaska, 1973-78; assoc. prof., dir. libr. U. Alaska, Juneau, 1978-84; prof., dean univ. libr. Calif. State U., Fullerton, 1984-86; pres. The Denali Press, Juneau, 1986—; freelance indexer and bibliographer; vis. lectr. Birmingham (Eng.) Poly., 1981; mem. Alaska Ednl. Del. to China, 1975. Author: Alaska Place Names, 1974, 4th edit., 1991, Directory of Special Libraries in Alaska, 1975, Government Reference Books, 1974-75, 1976, 1976-77, 1978, Government Documents in the Library Literature 1909-1974, 1976, ALA RSBRC Manual, 1979, Federal Documents Librarianship 1879-1987, 1988, Hispanic Resource Directory, 1988, 3d edit., 1995, Refugee and Immigrant Resource Directory, 1990, 92, 94; editor: The Sourdough, 1974-75, Directory of Services for Refugees and Immigrants, 1987, 3d edit., 1993, Guide to Smithsonian serial publs., 1987 ; book reviewer, columnist: S.E. Alaska Empire, 1979—, L.A. Times; contbr. articles to profl. jours. Mem. Auke Bay (Alaska) Vol. Fire Dept.; mem. Juneau Borough Cemetery Adv. Com., 1980-81, Juneau Borough Libr. Adv. Com., 1981-82, Am. Book Awards Com., 1980; mem. strategic com. Juneau Sch. Bd., Juneau Bd. Edn., 1991—, chmn. facilities com., 1994—. Mem. ALA (reference and subscription books rev. com. 1975-86, reference and adult services div. publs. com. 1975-77, Nat. Assn. Hispanic Publications, Mudge citation commn. 1977-79, 84-86, Dartmouth Coll. Medal Commn., Governing Council 1977-84, Dewey medal com. 1984-85, Denali Press award), Alaska Library Assn. (exec. bd. 1974-75, nominating com. 1977-79), Pacific N.W. Library Assn. (rep. publs. com. 1973-75), Assn. Coll. and Research Libraries (publ. com. 1976-80), Spl. Libraries Assn. (assoc. editor geography and map div. bull. 1975-76), Soc. for Scholarly Pub., Internat. Assn. Ind. Pubs (bd. dirs. 1990—), Pub. Mktg. Assn., PEN Ctr. USA West, Amnesty Internat., Explorers Club N.Y., No. Pub. Consortium (regional rep. 1993—). Office: PO Box 1535 Juneau AK 99802

SCHORR, MARTIN MARK, forensic psychologist, educator, writer; b. Sept. 16, 1923; m. Dolores Gene Tyson, June 14, 1952; 1 child, Jeanne Ann. Student Balliol Coll., Oxford (Eng.) U., 1945-46; AB cum laude, Adelphi U., 1949; postgrad., U. Tex., 1949-50; MS, Purdue U., 1953; PhD, U. Denver, 1960; postgrad., U. Tex. Diplomate in psychology, Diplomate Am. Bd. Profl. Disability Cons., Diplomate Am. Bd. Forensic Examiners; lic. clin. psychologist. Chief clin. psychol. svcs. San Diego County Mental Hosp., 1963-67; clin. dir. human services San Diego County, 1963-76; pvt. practice, forensic specialist San Diego, 1962—; forensic examiner superior, fed. and mil. cts., San Diego, 1962—; prof. abnormal psychology San Diego State U., 1965-68; chief dept. psychology Center City (Calif.) Hosp., 1976-79; cons. Dept. Corrections State of Calif., Minnewawa, 1970-73, Disability Evaluation Dept. Health, 1972-75, Calif. State Indsl. Accident Commn., 1972-78, Calif. Criminal Justice Adminstrn., 1975-77, Vista Hill Found., Mercy Hosp. Mental Health, Foodmaker Corp., Convent Sacred Heart, El Cajon, FAA Examiner. Author: Death by Prescription, 1988; dir.: Alpha Centauri Prodns. Recipient award for aid in developing Whistle Blower Law Calif. Assembly, 1986. Fellow Internat. Assn. Soc. Psychiatry, Am. Bd. Forensic Examiners, Am. Coll. Forensic Examiners (life); mem. AAAS, PEN, APA, Am. Acad. Forensic Scis., Qualified Med. Evaluator, Internat. Platform Assn., World Mental Health Assn., Mystery Writers Am., Nat. Writers' Club, Mensa. Home: University City 2970 Arnoldson Ave San Diego CA 92122-2114 Office: 275 F St Chula Vista CA 91910-2820

SCHOTT, DAVID PRESTON, lawyer; b. York, Pa., Apr. 27, 1949; s. Clarence Lenwood and Beverly Elizabeth (Runkle) S. BA, San Jose State U., 1975; JD, Santa Clara (Calif.) U., 1983. Program dir. Cmty. Living Experiences, San Jose, 1975-78; legal asst. SCCBA Pub. Interest Law Found., San Jose, 1978-80; exec. dir. Housing for Ind. People, San Jose, 1980-85; pvt. practice law San Jose, 1986-88; dep. dist. atty. Monterey County Dist. Atty.'s Office, Salinas, Calif., 1988-92; dist. counsel Monterey Bay Unified Air Pollution Control Dist., Monterey, Calif., 1992—. Pres. Cmty. Devel. Assn. San Jose, 1982-84; bd. dirs. Mental Health Assn., Santa Clara, Calif., 1980-84; mem. Commn. on Developmental Disabilities, San Jose, 1983-87, Moss Landing (Calif.) Harbor Dist., 1990-91, Monterey County Transp. Commn., 1991-92; grad. Leadership Monterey Peninsula, 1991-92. Recipient Outstanding Svc. Commendation, Human Rels. Commn., Santa Clara County, 1984, Creative Housing award No. Calif. Assn. for Non-Profit Housing, San Francisco, 1983; Berkeley Law Found. fellow, 1985. Office: Monterey Bay Unified Air Pollution Control Dist 24580 Silver Cloud Ct Monterey CA 93940-6536

SCHOTTERS, BERNARD WILLIAM, communications company executive; b. Indpls., Nov. 25, 1944; s. Bernard William and Virginia (Hubbard) S.; m. Nancy Fraze, Nov. 13, 1953; children: Payson T., Ian McKiney. BSBA, Washington U., 1967; MBA, Northwestern U., 1968. With Am. Nat. Bank and Trust Co. Chgo., 1972-74; v.p. Wells Fargo Bank, Los Angeles, 1974-83; dir. fin. Tele-Communications, Inc., Denver, 1983-85, v.p. fin., 1985—, dir. subs.; pres. ARP Cable (formerly Group W Cable), N.Y.C., 1987. Served to lt. USN, 1968-72. Club: Denver Cable. Office: Tele-Communications Inc 4643 S Ulster St Denver CO 80237

SCHOW, DUANE (JACK) RIVERS, manufacturing company executive; b. Lovell, Wyo., Aug. 7, 1936; s. Eugene Butler Schow and Irene Grace (Rivers) Mills; m. Liv Johansen, Aug. 30, 1960; children: Jan Erik, Einar, Lyle, Mark, David, Lynnette, Geir, Derek. Cert. of Completion, Weber Coll., 1956; BS in Mfg. Engring., Utah State U., 1963; postgrad., Santa Clara (Calif.) U., 1964-65; MS in Indsl. Edn., Brigham Young U., 1970. Tech. staff mem. Sandia Corp., Livermore, Calif., 1963-64; mfg. engr. Hewlett-

Packard Corp., Palo Alto, Calif., 1964-65; spl. instr. Brigham Young U., Provo, Utah, 1965-70; mfg. engring. mgr. Tandbergs Radiofabrik A/S, Oslo, Norway, 1970-77; project mgr. A/S Elektrisk Bur., Billingstad, Norway, 1977-78; assoc. prof. Brigham Young U., Provo, 1978-81; cons. Schow Engring. & Machine Co., Sandy, Utah, 1981-89; rsch. engr. Hercules Composite STructures, Magna, Utah, 1989-92; owner, cons. Schow Devel. Co., Sandy, Utah, 1992—. Patentee adjustable stroke eccentric. Industry adv. bd. mem. Tinius Olsen Skole, Kongsburg, Norway, 1971-78. Named Outstanding Sr. engr. Utah State U., 1963. LDS.

SCHOW, TERRY D., state official; b. Ogden, Utah, Dec. 14, 1948; s. Hugh Stuart Sloan and Minnie Aurelia (Ellis) Mohler; m. June Hansen, Feb. 14, 1973; children: Amy, Jason. AD, Honolulu C.C., 1975; BA, Chaminade U., 1975. Cert. in mgmt., Utah. Spl. and criminal investigator State of Utah, Ogden, 1976-83, lead investigator, 1984-92; investigator Fed. Govt., Salt Lake City, Denver, 1983-84; mgr. State of Utah, Ogden, 1992—. Mem. Gov.'s Coun. on Vets. Issues, 1989—, chmn., 1990—; mem. State of Utah Privatization Policy Bd., 1989-92; chmn. 1st Congressional Dist. Utah Rep. Party, 1982-83, mem. state exec. com., 1982-83; chmn. legis. dist Weber County Rep. Party, Ogden, 1987-91, 93—; trustee Utah's Vietnam Meml., Salt Lake City, 1988—; leader Boy Scouts Am., Ogden, 1985—. Sgt. U.S. Army, 1967-70, 72-76; Vietnam. Decorated Bronze Star, 1970, Combat Inf. Badge, 1970; recipient Championship Team Trophy Pistol U.S. Army, 1975. Mem. DAV (life Weber chpt. 4, comdr. 1993—, state 3d jr. vice comdr. 1992, state 2d jr. vice comdr. 1993—, state sr. vice comdr. 1994, state comdr. 1995—), NRA (life), VFW, AL, Utah Peace Officers Assn., Utah Pub. Employees Assn. (bd. dirs. 1988-89, v.p. 1989-92, pres. 1992-93, chmn. Ogden Valley dist.), Kiwanis (Ogden chpt. pres. 1992-93, pres. Layton chpt. 1985-86, named Kiwanian of Yr. 1982-83, lt. gov. divsn. 3 ut/ld dist. Kiwanis internat. bd. dirs., 1995—, homeless vets. fellow Ogden 1992—, Weber County vets. meml. com. 1994—). Republican. Mormon. Home: 4045 Bona Villa Dr Ogden UT 84403-3203 Office: State of Utah Office Recoveries 2540 Washington Blvd Fl 4 Ogden UT 84401-3112

SCHRADER, HARRY CHRISTIAN, JR., retired naval officer; b. Sheboygan, Wis., Aug. 4, 1932; s. Harry Christian and Edna Flora (Stubbe) S.; m. Carol Joan Gossman, June 23, 1956; 1 child, Mary Clare. BS, U.S. Naval Acad., 1955; MS, U.S. Naval Postgrad. Sch., 1963. Commd. ensign USN, 1955, advanced through grades to vice adm., 1982; comdr. U.S.S. Tawasa, 1963-64, U.S.S. A. Hamilton, 1970-72, U.S.S. Jackson, 1972-73, U.S.S. Gilmore, 1973-75, U.S.S. Long Beach, 1975-78; dir. MLSF Amphibious, Mine Warfare and Advanced Vehicles div. Office Naval Ops., Washington, 1978-80; comdr. Cruiser Destroyer Group One, San Diego, 1980-82, Naval Surface Forces, U.S. Pacific Fleet, San Diego, 1982-85; ret. USN, 1985; mgr. Middle East/NATO programs, autonetics div. Rockwell Internat., Anaheim, Calif., 1985-87; pres. Coronado (Calif.) Tech. Internat., 1987. Mem. Am. Def. Preparedness Assn., San Diego Oceans Found. (mem. adv. bd.), Sigma Xi.

SCHRADER, LAWRENCE EDWIN, plant physiologist, educator; b. Atchison, Kans., Oct. 22, 1941; s. Edwin Carl and Jenna Kathryn (Tobiason) S.; m. Elfriede J. Massier, Mar. 14, 1981. BS, Kans. State U., 1963; PhD, U. Ill., 1967; grad., Inst. Ednl. Mgmt., Harvard U., 1991. Asst. prof. dept. agronomy U. Wis., Madison, 1969-72; assoc. prof. U. Wis., 1972-76, prof., 1976-84; prof., head dept. agronomy U. Ill., Urbana, 1985-89; dean Coll. Agr. and Home Econs. Wash. State U., Pullman, 1989-94, prof. dept. horticulture, 1994—; chief competitive rsch. grants office Dept. Agr., Washington, 1980-81; trustee, treas. Agrl. Satellite Corp., 1991-94. Contbr. chpts. to books, articles to profl. jours. Active Consortium for Internat. Devel., 1989-94, chair fin. com., vice chair exec. com., 1990-92, trustee 1989-94; mem. exec. com. Coun. Agrl. Heads of Agr., 1992-94. Capt. U.S. Army, 1967-69. Recipient Soybean Researchers Recognition award 1983, Disting. Service award in Agriculture Kansas State U., 1987; Romnes Faculty fellow U. Wis., 1979. Fellow AAAS (mem. steering group, sect. agr. 1991-95, chair-elect sect. on agriculture, food and renewable resources 1995—), Am. Soc. Agronomy, Crop Sci. Soc. Am.; mem. Am. Soc. Plant Physiologists (sec. 1983-85, pres. elect 1986, pres. 1987), Am. Chem. Soc., Sigma Xi, Gamma Sigma Delta, Phi Kappa Phi, Phi Eta Sigma, Blue Key, Alpha Zeta. Methodist. Home: 3504 Crestview Rd Wenatchee WA 98801-9668 Office: Wash State U Tree Fruit Rsch & Extension Ctr 1100 N Western Ave Wenatchee WA 98801-1230

SCHRADER, WILLIAM P., organization executive, farmer; b. Phoenix; m. Bondena; children: Alissa Schrader Urshel, William P. Jr., Larry, Travis. Student, Ariz. State U. Bd. dirs. Salt River Project, Phoenix, 1964-90, v.p. bd., 1990-94, pres., 1994—; pres. Schrader Farms, Inc. Bd. dirs. Greater Phoenix Econ. Coun., Groundwater Users Adv. Coun.; mem. Maricopa C.C.'s Found., East Valley Partnership, Scottsdale (Ariz.) Mcpl. Corp.; former mayor and mem. city coun. City of Scottsdale; 1st chmn. Parada del Sol, Scottsdale Rodeo. Named to Scottsdale Hall of Fame; named Citizen of Yr., City of Scottsdale. Mem. Am. Pub. Power Assn., Am. Mgmt. Assn., Nat. Water Resources Assn., Colorado River Water Users Assn., Scottsdale C. of C., Scottsdale Jr. C. of C. (life, Disting. Svc. award), Scottsdale Charros (life), White Mountain Country Club, Ariz. Club, Mesa Country Club (Ariz.). Methodist. Home: 5611 Calle Camelia Phoenix AZ 85018-4617 Office: Salt River Project PO Box 52025 Phoenix AZ 85072-2025

SCHRAG, PETER, editor, writer; b. Karlsruhe, Germany, July 24, 1931; came to U.S., 1941, naturalized, 1953; s. Otto and Judith (Haas) S.; m. Melissa Jane Mowrer, June 9, 1953 (div. 1969); children: Mitzi, Erin Andrew; m. Diane Divoky, May 24, 1969 (div. 1981); children: David Divoky, Benaiah Divoky; m. Patricia Ternahan, Jan. 1, 1988. A.B. cum laude, Amherst Coll., 1953. Reporter El Paso (Tex.) Herald Post, 1953-55; asst. sec., asst. dir. publs. Amherst Coll., 1955-66, instr. Am. Studies, 1960-64; asso. edn. editor Sat. Rev., 1966-68, exec. editor, 1968-69; editor Change mag., 1969-70; editor at large Saturday Rev., 1969-72; contbg. editor Saturday Review/Education, 1972-73; editorial adv. bd. The Columbia Forum, 1972-75; editorial bd. Social Policy, 1971—; contbg. editor More, 1974-78, Inquiry, 1977-80; editorial page editor Sacramento Bee and McClatchy Newspapers, 1978—; vis. lectr. U. Mass. Sch. Edn., 1970-72; fellow in profl. journalism Stanford U., Palo Alto, Calif., 1973-74; lectr. U. Calif. at Berkeley, 1974-78, 90—; Pulitzer Prize juror, 1988-89. Author: Voices in the Classroom, 1965, Village School Downtown, 1967, Out of Place in America, 1971, The Decline of the Wasp, 1972, The End of the American Future, 1973, Test of Loyalty, 1974, (with Diane Divoky) The Myth of the Hyperactive Child, 1975, Mind Control, 1978; contbr. articles. Mem. adv. com. Student Rights Project, N.Y. Civil Liberties Union, 1970-72; mem. Com. Study History, 1958-72; trustee Emma Willard Sch., 1967-69; bd. dirs. Park Sch., Oakland, Calif., 1976-77, Ctr. for Investigative Reporting, 1979-81; bd. visitors Claremont Grad. Sch. Guggenheim fellow, 1971-72; Nat. Endowment for Arts fellow, 1976-77. Office: Sacramento Bee 21st And Q St Sacramento CA 95852

SCHRAMM, WILLFRIED, biochemist; b. Koenigsberg, Germany, Jan. 22, 1944; came to U.S., 1979; s. Gerhard and Elsa (Gasenzer) S.; m. Gudrun Huebener, Sept. 21, 1968; children: Frauke, Antje. MS, U. Rostock (Germany), 1970; PhD, U. Hamburg (Germany), 1977. Rsch. assoc. U. Rostock, 1970-76; sr. rsch. assoc. Med. Sch., Luebeck, Germany, 1977-79, Worcester Found. Exptl. Biology, Shrewsbury, Mass., 1979-82; rsch. scientist U. Mich., Ann Arbor, 1982—; v.p. rsch. and devel. BioQuant, Inc., Ann Arbor, 1985-93, Saliva Diagnostic Systems, Vancouver, Wash., 1993—; cons. for numerous biotechnology cos., 1984-86; mem. adv. bd. Inst. Biochemistry and Biotech., Oakland (Mich.) U., 1989-91; mem. faculty U. Mich., 1982-93. Contbr. articles to profl. jours. Recipient Career Devel. award Deutsche Forschungsgemeinschaft, Germany, 1979; rsch. grantee NIH, 1985-93, NIDA, 1989-93, pvt. founds., U.S. Army, 1982-90. Mem. AAAS, Am. Chem. Soc., Am. Assn. Clin. Chemists, N.Y. Acad. Scis., Soc. for Study of Reprodn. Office: Saliva Diagnostic Systems 11719 NE 95th St Vancouver WA 98682-2444

SCHREIBER, ANDREW, psychotherapist; b. Budapest, Hungary, Aug. 1, 1918; s. Alexander and Bella (Gruen) S.; m. Mona Schreiber, Aug. 6, 1950; children: Julie, Brad, Robin. BA, CCNY, 1941, MEd, 1943; MSW, Columbia U., 1949; PhD, Heed U., 1972. Diplomate Am. Bd. Sexology; lic. psychotherapist, Calif. Pvt. practice Belmont, Calif., 1970—; sales mgr. vibro ceramics dir. Gulton Industries, Metuchen, N.J., 1949-57; mktg. mgr. Weldotron Corp., Newark, 1957-63; head dept. spl. edn. San Mateo (Calif.) High Sch. Dist., 1964-70; mem. faculty Heed U., 1970-71, advisor to doctoral candidates on West Coast, 1971; lectr. spl. edn. U. Calif.-Berkeley, 1973; cons. on hypnotherapy Psoriasis Rsch. Inst., Palo Alto, Calif., 1993—. Art Students League of N.Y. scholar, 1933-35, San Francisco State U. grantee. Fellow Am. Acad. Clin. Sexology; mem. NEA, AACD, Learning Disabilities Assn., Am. Assn. Sex Educators, Counselors and Therapists, Calif. Assn. Marriage and Family Therapists, Calif. Tchrs. Assn. Home: 2817 San Ardo Way Belmont CA 94002-1341

SCHREIBER, DARREN MATTHEW, law clerk; b. Victorville, Calif., Sept. 13, 1970; s. Joseph Conrad and Diane Carol (Zabel) S. BA in Politics, Philosophy/Govt., Claremont McKenna Coll., 1992; postgrad., U. Calif., Davis. Polit. cons. Jerry Bakke for Congress, San Pedro, Calif., 1990; cons. Inst. for Social Justice, San Bernardino, Calif., 1989-92; sr. rsch. asst. Rose Inst. of State and Local Govt., Claremont, Calif., 1989-92; law clk. King Hall Civil Rights Clinic, Davis, 1994—. Publ. asst. Atlas of South Cen. Los Angeles/Demographic Change in the San Gabriel Valley, 1992. Pub. interest grantee King Hall Legal Found., 1994; fellow George H. Moyr Found., 1992, J. Cleveland McKenna Found., 1992; mem. Trial Practic Hons. Bd., King Hall, 1994. Republican. Presbyterian. Home: 2950 Portage Bay West # 220A Davis CA 95616

SCHREIBER, EDWARD, computer scientist; b. Zagreb, Croatia, Mar. 17, 1943; came to U.S., 1956, naturalized, 1960; s. Hinko and Helen (Iskra) S.; m. Barbara Nelson, 1967 (div. 1969); m. Lea Lusia Hausler, Nov. 7, 1983. BSEE, U. Colo., Denver, 1970. Registered profl. engr. Colo.; cert. data processor. Sr. software scientist Autotrol, Denver, 1972-78; software engr. Sigma Design, Englewood, Colo, 1979-82; founder, v.p. Graphics, Info., Denver, 1982-86; chmn. Schreiber Instruments, 1987—; instr. computer sci. U. Colo., Denver, 1971-72, Colo. Women's Coll., Denver, 1972-73, U. Denver, 1983. Contbr. articles on computer graphics to profl. jours. Trustee 1st Universalist Ch., Denver, 1972-78; Dem. candidate for U.S. Ho. of Reps., 1980. Served with U.S. Army, 1960-66. Mem. IEEE, Assn. for Computing Machinery, Nat. Computer Graphics Assn., Mensa. Office: Schreiber Instruments Inc 4800 Happy Canyon Rd Ste 250 Denver CO 80237-1074

SCHREIBER, EVERETT CHARLES, JR., chemist, educator; b. Amityville, N.Y., Nov. 13, 1953; s. Everett Charles Sr. and Mary Elizabeth (Johnston) S.; m. Jane Karen Sklenar, July 19, 1980. BS, Pace U., 1975; PhD, U. Nebr., 1980. Rsch. assoc. SUNY, Stony Brook, 1980-82; asst. dir. rsch. Muscular Dystrophy Assn., N.Y.C., 1983-84; rsch. assoc. SUNY, 1984-86; spectroscopist G.E. NMR Instruments, Fremont, Calif., 1986-87; quality assurance engr. Varian NMR Instruments, Palo Alto, Calif., 1987-89, tech. tng. specialist, 1989-95, sr. tech. support chemist, 1995—. Author of tng. texts in engring. and computers; editor Megabytes. V.p. Old Bailey Pl. Home Owners Assn., Fremont, 1989, pres., 1990-93, bd. mem., 1994—; treas. Young Life, Mission Valley, Fremont, 1993-95. Mem. Am. Chem. Soc., Biophys. Soc., N.Y. Acad. Sci., Soc. Magnetic Resonance in Medicine. Republican. Roman Catholic. Office: Varian NMR Instruments 3120 Hansen Way Palo Alto CA 94304-1030

SCHREIBER, OTTO WILLIAM, retired manufacturing company executive; b. Greenwood, Wis., July 4, 1922; s. Otto Waldemar and Meta Wilhelmina (Suemnicht) S. BSEE, U. Wis., Madison, 1944. Electroacoustic scientist Navy Electronics Lab., San Diego, 1946-56; electronics engr. then mgr. electronic engring. dept., ordnance div. Libascope, Sunnyvale, Calif., 1956-65; chief engr. Teledyne Indsl. Electronics Co., San Jose, Calif., 1965-68; exec. v.p. Marcom Corp., San Francisco, 1969; test mgr. MB Assocs., San Ramon, Calif., 1970-71; ops. mgr. Am. Svc. Products, Inc., Newhall, Calif., 1972-75; mfg. mgr. UTI, Inc., Sunnyvale, Calif., 1975-80; dir. mfg. Hi-Shear Ordnance/Electronics, Torrance, Calif., 1980-82; tech. writing supr. Westinghouse Marine divsn., Sunnyvale, 1980-92; ret., 1992. Lt. comdr. USNR, 1944-59. Mem. IEEE (life), Soc. Tech. Communication, Eta Kappa Nu, Kappa Eta Kappa. Republican. Lutheran. Home: 2180 Akard Ave Redding CA 96001-2704

SCHREIMAN, HOWARD LESLIE, special education educator; b. L.A., Oct. 11, 1954; s. R. Robert Schreiman and Janet Ellen (Noble) Mondry. AA, L.A. City Coll., 1974; BA, UCLA, 1977, MEd, 1984; resource specialist cert., U. Calif., Riverside, 1990. Learning handicapped and severely handicapped credential, secondary social studies credential. Pres., CEO Mar-Tel Industries Inc., L.A., 1984-86; spl. day class instr. Palm Springs (Calif.) H.S., 1986-89, resource specialist, 1989—, dept. chair spl. edn., 1994—; pres. faculty senate Palm Springs H.S., 1990-91; mem. Comm. Task Force, Palm Springs, 1988-89; mentor tchr. Palm Springs Unified Sch. Dist., 1989-90, workability job coach developer, 1989-93. Mem. UCLA Alumni Scholarship Com., Coachella Valley, 1992—, dist. chair, 1989-91; mem. steering com. Young Leadership of the Desert, Jewish Fedn., Palm Springs, 1994—. Mem. Palm Springs Tchrs. Assn. (mem. budget com. 1993—, mem. by-laws com. 1994, bldg. rep. 1988-90, 92—, parliamentarian 1993—), UCLA Club of the Desert, Phi Delta Kappa, Alpha Kappa Delta, Pi Gamma Mu. Democrat. Jewish. Office: Palm Springs HS 2248 E Ramon Rd Palm Springs CA 92264-7917

SCHREINER, GEORGE FREDERIC, pharmaceutical executive, medical researcher; b. N.Y.C., May 9, 1949; s. George Elmer and Joanne (Baker) S.; m. Kathryn Kerry McDade, Jan. 1, 1988; children: George Alexander, Jocelyn Overton, Colin Fields. AB, Harvard U., 1971, MD, 1977, PhD, 1977. Diplomate Am. Bd. Internal Medicine with subspecialty in nephrology. Asst. prof. medicine Harvard Med. Sch., Boston, 1983-85; asst. prof. medicine and pathology Washington U., St. Louis, 1985-89, assoc. prof. medicine, 1989-93; cons. prof. medicine Stanford U., Palo Alto, Calif., 1993—; v.p. med. sci. CV Therapeutics, Palo Alto, 1993—; established investigator Am. Heart Assn., 1989—. Asst. editor Am. Jour. Kidney Disease, 1992—. Mem. Am. Assn. Immunologists, Am. Soc. Nephrology, Am. Assn. Pathologists, Internat. Soc. Nephrology, Am. Fedn. Clin. Rsch. (chmn. pub. policy com. 1991-92, chmn. Midwest sect. 1989-90), Am. Clin. and Climatol. Assn. Office: CV Therapeutics 3172 Porter Dr Palo Alto CA 94304-1212

SCHREMPF, DETLEF, professional basketball player; b. Leverkusen, Germany, Jan. 21, 1963. Student, U. Washington. Forward Dallas Mavericks, 1985-89, Indiana Pacers, 1989-93, Seattle Supersonics, 1993—; player West German Olympic Team, 1984, 92. Recipient Sixth Man award NBA, 1991, 92; mem. NBA All-Star team, 1993.

SCHROEDEL, JEAN REITH, political science educator; b. Seattle, July 25, 1951; d. Robert Harry and Genevieve Dale Schroedel; m. Frederick Elwood Saling, Aug. 24, 1972 (div. June 1980); m. Paul Peretz, June 22, 1984; 1 child, John Alexander. BA in Polit. Sci., U. Wash., 1981; PhD in Polit. Sci., MIT, 1990. Bus., govt., and soc. program lectr. U. Wash., Seattle, 1986-88; asst. prof. polit. sci. Yale U., New Haven, 1989-91; asst. prof. Ctr. for Politics and Econs. Claremont (Calif.) Grad. Sch., 1991-94, assoc. prof., 1995—; book reviewer Jour. Health Politics, 1985, Polit. Sci. Quar., 1991, Women and Politics, 1993, Policy Rsch. Quar., 1994, Am. Polit. Sci. Rev., 1995; papers presented at Am. Polit. Sci. Assn., 1984, 91, 92, 93, Women in Trades Conf., Seattle, 1986, APA, 1989, Western Polit. Sci. Assn., 1990, 91, 93, 3d Women's Policy Rsch. Conf., 1992, Symposium on Clinton's First 100 Days, Calif. State U., 1993; jour. and grant reviewer for Legis. Studies Quar., Women and Politics, Policy Rsch. Quar., Am. Polit. Sci. Rev., State and Local govt. Rev., Bunting Inst. Author: Alone in a Crowd: Women in the Trades Tell Their Stories, 1985, Congress, the President and Policymaking: A Historical Analysis, 1994; contbr. articles to profl. jours. and mags. Assoc. Murray Rsch. Ctr., Radcliff Coll. Recipient Internat. Assn. of Machinists and Aerospace Workers Nat. scholarship, 1980-81; grantee Ctr. for Investigative Journalism Rsch., 1984; rsch. grantee Social Svc. Faculty, 1990-91, Fletcher Jones Found., 1992-93, 93-94. Mem. Am. Polit. Sci. Assn. (best dissertation on women and politics com. 1993-94), Women's Caucus for Polit. Sci., Western Polit. Sci. Assn. (program com. 1991-92, Betty A. Nesvold prize com. 1993-94, Pi Sigma Alpha Best Paper award 1992), Nat. Women's Studies Assn. Democrat. Office: Claremont Grad Sch Ctr for Politics and Econs 170 E 10th St Claremont CA 91711-5909

SCHROEDER, ARNOLD LEON, mathematics educator; b. Honolulu, May 27, 1935; s. Arnold Leon and Wynelle (Russell) S.; BS in Math., Oreg. State U., 1960, MS in Stats., 1962; NSF Insts. at UCLA, 1964, U. So. Calif., 1965; m. Maybelle Ruth Walker, Nov. 9, 1956; children: Steven, Michael, Wendy. Assoc. prof. math. Long Beach (Calif.) C.C., 1962—; computer cons. McDonnell-Douglas Corp., 1966-74, statis. researcher in med. and social sci., 1976-80; cons. statis. software including SPSS, BMDP, and Fortran, 1980—; dir. Schroeder's Statis. Svcs. Author: Statistics/Math Note's for Colleges, 1986—. Chmn. bd. elders Grace Bible Ch., South Gate, Calif., 1985-92. Served with USAF, 1953-57. Mem. Faculty Assn. Calif. C.C., C.C. Assn., Am. Bowlers Tour (life). Home: 5481 E Hill St Long Beach CA 90815-1923 Office: 4901 E Carson St Long Beach CA 90808-1706

SCHROEDER, CHERYL ANN, health and educational consultant; b. Cheyenne, Wyo., June 3, 1955; d. Milan Berry and Mary Clare (Gleason) Finley; m. David Paul Schroeder, July 14, 1979; children: Stacy Ann, Stephanie Ann. BA, U. Wyo., 1977, MEd, 1982, EdD, 1986. Cert. tchr., ednl. adminstr., Wyo., Nebr. Tchr. Lincoln (Nebr.) Pub. Schs., 1977-81; rsch. asst. U. Wyo., Laramie, 1982-83, 85, instr. reading and math. Lab. Sch., 1983-84, dir. Early Childhood Spl. Edn. Projects, 1986-87, project coord. Sch. Nursing, 1988-90, prin. investigator, chmn. Wyo. Task Force Infant Mortality, 1990-92, instr., 1990-92, dir. Wyo. Perinatal Substance Abuse Prevention Program, 1990-93, faculty Sch. Phys. and Health Edn., 1993; pres. Creative Cons., Inc., Laramie, 1993—; owner The Learning Ctr., Laramie; instr. Laramie County C.C., 1984, 85, 86; dir. The A.D.A.M. Project, Laramie, 1986-88, co-facilitator parent group, 1988; presenter numerous workshops, seminars for univs., pub. schs., confs. and civic assns.; expert witness Wyo. Protection and Advocacy, Cheyenne, 1993; evaluator Intensive Family Preservation Svcs. Pilot Program, 1994—, Healthy Infants-Capable Adolescents Program, Cheyenne, 1991-93. Author: Modern Concepts in Fetal Alcohol Syndrome and Fetal Alcohol Effects, 1994; contbr. numerous articles to profl. jours. Mem. Albany County Sch. Bd., Laramie, 1993—; vice-chmn. Well Aware, 1992—, chmn. Women's Health Month, 1993, 94; edn. com. Coun. Regional Networks for Genetic Svcs., 1993—; exec. com. Wyo. chpt., March of Dimes, 1989-91, mem. health profls. adv. com., 1987-93, chmn., 1989-91; exec. com. Medicine Bow chpt. March of Dimes, 1984-87; co-chmn. perinatal conf. March of Dimes, 1985, planning com. mem., 1987, chmn. Mothers March, 1984-86; bd. dirs. The Open Sch., Laramie, mem., 1984-88, sec., 1985-86, pres., 1986-87; vol. Lincoln (Nebr.) Planned Parenthood, 1977-80. Grantee Office Rural Health, Licensed Beverage Info. Coun., 1992, Office Substance Abuse Prevention, 1990, Union Pacific Railroad Found., 1986-87, 87-88, 89-90, Criminal Justice, 1987-88, Cmty. Svcs., 1986, 88, City of Laramie, 1988, Mountain States Regional Genetic Svcs. Network, 1987-88, March of Dimes, 1986; recipient Outstanding Prevention Demonstration Program award Ctr. Substance Abuse Prevention, 1993. Mem. Nat. Sch. Bd. Assn., Wyo. Sch. Bd. Assn., Nat. Assn. Perinatal Addiction Rsch. and Edn., Mountain States Regional Genetic Svcs. Network (chmn. edn. com. 1993—, chmn. confs. and spl. projects grants 1989—, mem. steering and planning com. 1993—, mem. edn. com. 1987—), Nat. Perinatal Assn. (edn. com. 1992—), Zontas Internat. (exec. bd. 1992-94), Kappa Delta Pi, Phi Delta Kappa, Alpha Epsilon Delta. Roman Catholic. Home: 1154 Frontera Dr Laramie WY 82070-5024 Office: Creative Consultants Inc PO Box 6023 Laramie WY 82070-9003

SCHROEDER, GLENN CARL, lawyer, educator; b. Ann Arbor, Mich., Mar. 21, 1953; s. Glenn A. Schroeder and Monnie C. (Hamling) Phillips; m. Janet S. Wong, Jan. 1, 1990. BA, U. Calif., L.A., 1975; MA, U. Ill., 1976; JD, Yale U., 1979. Bar: Calif. 1979. Assoc. Loeb and Loeb, L.A., 1979-86, ptnr., 1987; gen. counsel, sr. v.p. Sta. KCET Community TV of So. Calif., L.A., 1987—; adj. prof. Loyola U. Law Sch., L.A., 1982, Whittier Coll. Sch. of Law, L.A., 1988—. Bd. dirs. Asian Rehab. Svcs., L.A., 1989-90. Mem. L.A. County Bar Assn. (exec. com. of intellectual property sect. 1988-92), L.A. Copyright Soc. Office: Community TV of So Calif Sta KCET 4401 W Sunset Blvd Los Angeles CA 90027-6017

SCHROEDER, MARY MURPHY, federal judge; b. Boulder, Colo., Dec. 4, 1940; d. Richard and Theresa (Kahn) Murphy; m. Milton R. Schroeder, Oct. 15, 1965; children: Caroline Theresa, Katherine Emily. B.A., Swarthmore Coll., 1962; J.D., U. Chgo., 1965. Bar: Ill. 1966, D.C. 1966, Ariz. 1970. Trial atty. Dept. Justice, Washington, 1965-69; law clk. Hon. Jesse Udall, Ariz. Supreme Ct., 1970; mem. firm Lewis and Roca, Phoenix, 1971-75; judge Ariz. Ct. Appeals, Phoenix, 1975-79, U.S. Ct. Appeals (9th cir.), Phoenix, 1979—; vis. instr. Ariz. State U. Coll. Law, 1976, 77, 78. Contbr. articles to profl. jours. Mem. Am. Bar Assn., Ariz. Bar Assn., Fed. Bar Assn., Am. Law Inst., Am. Judicature Soc. Democrat. Club: Soroptimists. Office: US Ct Appeals 9th Cir 6421 Courthouse & Fed Bldg 230 N 1st Ave Phoenix AZ 85025-0230*

SCHROEDER, PATRICIA SCOTT (MRS. JAMES WHITE SCHROEDER), congresswoman; b. Portland, Oreg., July 30, 1940; d. Lee Combs and Bernice (Lemoin) Scott; m. James White Schroeder, Aug. 18, 1962; children: Scott William, Jamie Christine. B.A. magna cum laude, U. Minn., 1961; J.D., Harvard U., 1964. Bar: Colo. 1964. Field atty. NLRB, Denver, 1964-66; practiced in Denver, 1966-72; hearing officer Colo. Dept. Personnel, 1971-72; mem. faculty U. Colo., 1969-72, Community Coll., Denver, 1969-70, Regis Coll., Denver, 1970-72; mem. 93d-104th Congresses from 1st Colo. dist., 1973—; co-chmn. Congl. Caucus for Women's Issues, 1976—; mem. Ho. of Reps., ranking minority mem. judiciary subcom. on the Constitution, mem. Nat. Security Com. Congregationalist. Office: US Ho of Reps 2307 Rayburn House Office Washington DC 20515

SCHROEDER, RITA MOLTHEN, retired chiropractor; b. Savanna, Ill., Oct. 25, 1922; d. Frank J. and Ruth J. (McKenzie) Molthen; m. Richard H. Schroeder, Apr. 23, 1948 (div.); children—Richard, Andrew, Barbara, Thomas, Paul, Madeline. Student, Chem. Engring., Immaculate Heart Coll., 1940-41, UCLA, 1941, Palmer Sch. of Chiropractic, 1947-49; D. Chiropractic, Cleve. Coll. of Chiropractic, 1961. Engring.-tooling design data coordinator Douglas Aircraft Co., El Segundo, Santa Monica and Long Beach, Calif., 1941-47; pres. Schroeder Chiropractic, Inc., 1982-93; dir. Pacific States Chiropractic Coll., 1978-80, pres. 1980-81. Recipient Palmer Coll. Ambassador award, 1973. Parker Chiropractic Research Found. Ambassador award, 1976, Coll. Ambassador award Life West Chiropractic Coll. Mem. Internat. Chiropractic Assn., Calif. Chiropractic Assn., Internat. Chiropractic Assn. Calif., Assn. Am. Chiropractic Coll. Presidents, Council Chiropractic Edn. (Pacific State Coll. rep.), Am. Pub. Health Assn., Royal Chiropractic Knights of the Round Table. Home: 8701 N State Highway 41 Spc 18 Fresno CA 93720-1010 Office: Schroeder Chiropractic Inc 2535 N Fresno St Fresno CA 93703-1831

SCHROEDER, WILLIAM JOHN, electronics executive; b. Havre de Grace, Md., June 9, 1944; s. William Martin and Dorothy Jeanne (McLaughlin) S.; m. Marilee Jane Alne, May 28, 1966; children: Kristen, Kari Britt, Kimberley. BSEE, Marquette U., 1966, MSEE, 1968; MBA, Harvard U., 1972. Devel. engr. Honeywell Inc., Mpls., 1968-70; mgmt. cons. McKinsey & Co., Los Angeles, 1972-76; mgr. product planning Memorex Corp., Santa Clara, Calif., 1976-78; pres. Priam Corp., San Jose, Calif., 1978-85, chmn., 1985-86; pres. Conner Peripherals, Inc., San Jose, 1986-89, vice chmn., 1989-94; CEO Arcada Software Inc., a Conner Co., 1993-94; pres., CEO Diamond Multimedia Systems, Inc., San Jose, Calif., 1994—; bd. dirs. Xircom Corp., Thousand Oaks, Calif. Office: Diamond Multimedia Systems Inc 2880 Junction Ave San Jose CA 95134-1922

SCHROEDER, WILLIAM ROBERT, actor, graphic designer, linguist; b. L.A., July 9, 1941; s. Robert Manville and Miriam Ruth (Sloop) S.; m. Marie Paule Fautrel, Sept. 7, 1963. BA, UCLA, 1964; BFA, Art Ctr. Coll. Design, Pasadena, Calif., 1971. Mailman U.S. Post Office, Santa Monica, Calif., 1967-71; art dir., producer N.W. Ayer/West, Los Angeles, 1971-75; pres., gen. mgr. Advt. Ctr., Los Angeles, 1976-77, Alouette Internat., Santa Monica, Calif., 1972—; free-lance woodcarver, Santa Monica, 1981—; free-lance actor, Hollywood, Calif., 1983—; appeared in feature films King of the Streets, 1983, The Forbidden Tome, 1984, The End of Innocence, 1985, Poltergeist II, 1986. Producer TV commercials, 1972-75; author, creator computerized lang. courses Mattel Intellivision, 1980-82; real estate developer, 1989—. Publicity mgr. Concerned Homeowners of Santa Monica, 1981-82. Recipient 1st Pl. award Belding award for Excellence in Advt., Los Angeles, 1974; Cert. of Merit, Art Dirs. Club Los Angeles, 1972. Mem. Am. Fedn. Radio and TV Artists, Santa Monica C. of C., Mensa (Los Angeles), Combat Pilots Assn., Orange County Squadron, Internat. Plastic Modelers

Soc., The Found. Brain Rsch., Astronomical Soc. Pacific, Internat. Soc. Philosophical Inquiry, Internat. Legion of Intelligence, Santa Monica Theatre Guild, The Air Mus. Libertarian. Office: Alouette Internat 1626 Montana Ave Santa Monica CA 90403-1808

SCHROETER, VERNON WALTER, chiropractor; b. New London, Conn., July 16, 1956; s. Walter George Jr. and Marilyn Helen (Beatrice) S. AA, Moheagan C.C., 1979; D of Chiropractic, Plamer Coll. Chiropractic, 1984. Chiropractor All Chiropractic Care, Mesa, Ariz., 1983—. Author: From Conception to Birth and Beyond, 1994, Textbook of Self Defense Using Human Biomechanics, 1993; producer (videotape) Dr. Schroeter's Ultimate Self-Defense, 1990. Office: All Chiropractic Care 54 S Sirrine Mesa AZ 85210-1431

SCHROFF, WILLIAM K., real estate professional, business consultant; b. N.Y.C., Mar. 1, 1947; s. William L. and Kathleen (McDonnell) S.; m. Karen M. Zeanah, June 1968 (div. 1977); children: Zachary, William. BBA, Stetson U., 1968, MBA, 1969. V.p. N. Donald & Co., Denver, 1981-82; pres., dir. Westfin Corp., Denver, 1982-83; chmn., exec. v.p., dir. Vantage Securities, Emglewood, Colo., 1983-85; pres., dir. Dunhill Investments Ltd., Englewood, 1985-88; assoc. Prudential Hampton Realtors, Palm Springs, Calif., 1989-90; prin., v.p. Empowerment Housing, Denver, 1992-93; prin. Electra Holdings, Denver, 1991-93; mng. dir. West World Properties, Palm Springs, 1990-92; v.p. Nat. Relocation Corp., Denver, 1993-94; pres., bd. dirs. Realty Resources, Inc., Denver, 1994—; dir. Computer Periph. Prods, Denver, 1985—; cons. Electra 2000, Denver, 1991-92; com. chmn. Palm Springs Bd. Realtors (prin. Nat. Relocation Corp. 1993—, v.p., dir. Realtor to Realtor Svcs., Inc. 1994—, top com. award 1992). Dir. GLAD, Cathedral City, Calif., 1991-92, pres. Log Cabin Fedn., Riverside County, 1991-92; del. LIFE Lobby Sacramento, 1992; mem. com. Colo. Coalition for Homeless. Mem. Nat. Assn. Realtors, Calif. Assn. Realtors, Colo. Assn. Realtors, Denver Profl. Men's Club (mem. exec. com., chmn. membership com.), Log Cabin Club Colo. (founder, pres.), Equality PAC (treas.). Office: Nat Relocation Corp 910 15th St Ste 1066 Denver CO 80202

SCHRYVER, BRUCE JOHN, safety engineer; b. Newark, Aug. 14, 1944; s. Francis Henry and Ann Laura (Hart) S.; m. Lorraine Patricia Simodis, Oct. 8, 1966; children: Holly Lynn, Wendy Marie. BA in Occupational Safety and Health, Western States U., 1984, MS in Safety Mgmt., 1989, PhD in Safety Mgmt., 1989. Cert. safety profl.; cert. products safety mgr.; cert. hazard control mgr.; cert. hazardous materials mgr.; cert. healthcare safety profl. Inspector Lansing B. Warner Inc., Chgo., 1968-69; engring. rep. Glens Falls Ins. Co., Newark, 1969; safety dir. Hillside Metal Products, Newark, 1969-70; loss prevention specialist Warner Ins. Group, Chgo., 1970-79, regional loss control mgr., 1979-82, nat. loss control coordinator, 1982-85; mgr., asst. v.p. loss control svcs. Ins. Co. of the West, San Diego, 1985-90; v.p. loss control svcs. Ins. Co. of the West, 1990—; v.p. mcpl. law enforcement svcs. Ins. Co. of the West, San Diego, 1992—. Inventor Emergency Light Mount, 1971. Mem. Town of Clay (N.Y.) Pub. Safety Com., 1976-78, Beacon Woods East Homeowners Assn., Hudson, Fla., 1979-85, Meadowridge Homeowners Assn., La Costa, Calif., 1986—; cons. Town of Clay Police Dept., 1975-78. With USCG, 1964-68. Recipient lettter of appreciation Town of Clay, 1977, cert. of appreciation DAV, 1968, Golden State award, 1990. Mem. Am. Soc. Safety Engrs., Soc. Fire Protection Engrs., Nat. Safety Mgmt. Soc., Vets. Safety, Nat. Fire Protection Assn., San Diego Safety Coun., Calif. Conf. Arson Investigators. Republican. Roman Catholic. Home: 3047 Camino Limero Carlsbad CA 92009-4525 Office: Ins Co of the West 10140 Campus Point Dr San Diego CA 92121-1520

SCHUBERT, ANNE MAUREEN, industrial waste administrator; b. Martinez, Calif., Oct. 19, 1954; d. James Benjamin and Mariel Ann (Phillips) Schubert; div.; children: Amara Victoria, Joseph Benjamin, Odinn Glenn, Aaron Dean. AS in Life Sci., Allan Hancock Coll., 1982, AA in Liberal Arts, 1982. Registered environ. assessor, Calif.; cert. indsl. waste insp. grade IV, collection systems maintenance grade II, lab. analysis grade I. Indsl. waste insp. City of Santa Maria (Calif.), 1984-86; mgr. indsl. pretreatment program, collection systems Simi Valley (Calif.) County Sanitation Dist., 1986-91, state pub. edn. com., indsl. hazardous waste com., 1986-91, source control mgr., divsn. head pretreatment, storm water mgmt., hazardous materials mgmt. program, 1991—. Chair City Simi Valley Hazardous Materials Mgmt. Task Force, 1989-90; sec., chmn. Tri Counties Voluntary Cert. Com., State Voluntary Cert. Com., Tri Counties Pub. Edn.; indsl./hazardous waste com., pub. edn. com. Calif. Water Pollution Control Assn., 1986-91, Water Pollution Control Fedn., bd. dirs. Tri Counties chpt., 1991-92; mem. Ventura County Hazardous Waste Mgmt., supr. adv. com.; mem. Hazardous Waste Assn. Calif., Hazardous Materials Control Rsch. Inst., Ventura County storm water task force, 1991—, quality mgmt. com., 1993; chair Bus. Outreach Illicit Discharge Control subcom., 1992—. Recipient Merit award Indsl. Waste Insp. Tech., 1986, Disting. Leadership award, 1987. Mem. Keepers of the Flame fraternity. Republican. Roman Catholic. Office: Simi Valley County Sanitation Dist 500 W Los Angeles Ave Simi Valley CA 93065-1644

SCHUBERT, GERALD, planetary and geophysics educator; b. N.Y.C., Mar. 2, 1939; s. Morris and Helen (Nelson) S.; m. Joyce Elaine Slotnick, Jan. 16, 1960; children: Todd, Michael, Tamara. BS in Engring. Physics, MS in Aero. Engring., Cornell U., 1961; PhD in Aero. Sci. Engring., U. Calif., Berkeley, 1964. Head heat transfer dept. U.S. Naval Nuclear Power Sch., Mare Island, Calif., 1961-65; mem. tech. staff Bell Telephone Research Labs., Whippany, N.J., 1965; asst. prof. planetary and geophysics UCLA, 1966-70, assoc. prof., 1970-74, prof., 1974—. Co-author: Geodynamics, 1982; contbr. articles to profl. jours. Served to lt. USN, 1961-65. Alexander von Humboldt fellow, 1969, Guggenheim fellow, 1972, Berman fellow Hebrew U. Jerusalem, 1982-83, Nat. Acad. Scis. Nat. Research Council fellow, Cambridge, Eng., 1965-66. Fellow Am. Geophys. Union (James B. Macelwane fellow 1975); mem. AAAS, Div. Planetary Sci. Am. Astron. Assn. Office: UCLA Dept Earth and Space Sci Los Angeles CA 90024

SCHUBERT, RONALD HAYWARD, retired aerospace engineer; b. Bklyn., Aug. 25, 1932; s. John and Joan Sarah (Hayward) S.; m. Dorothy May Smith, Mar. 5, 1953 (div. 1961); children: Marcus H., Malcolm F., Ronald J. (dec.), Ann E.; m. Linda Jane van der Ploeg, Mar. 6, 1961 (div. 1988). BA cum laude, Ohio State U., 1956. Assoc. engr. Hughes Aircraft Co., Fullerton, Calif., 1957-61; physicist Nat. Cash Register Co., Dayton, Ohio, 1962-63; sr. research engr. Lockheed Missiles and Space Co., Sunnyvale, Calif., 1963-90. Served as staff sgt. USMC, 1951-54. Recipient Hon. mention Woodrow Wilson Fellowship Com. Mem. Phi Beta Kappa. Democrat. Roman Catholic. Home: 201 W California Ave Apt 1023 Sunnyvale CA 94086-5035

SCHUBERT, RUTH CAROL HICKOK, artist, educator; b. Janesville, Wis., Dec. 24, 1927; d. Fay Andrew and Mildred Wilamette (Street) Hickok; m. Robert Francis Schubert, Oct. 20, 1946; children: Stephen Robert, Michelle Carol. Student DeAnza Coll., 1972-73; AA, Monterey Peninsula Coll., 1974; BA with honors, Calif. State U.-San Jose, 1979. Owner, mgr. Casa De Artes Gallery, Monterey, Calif., 1977-86; dir. Monterey Peninsula Mus. Art Council, 1975-76; leader painting workshops, demonstrator, lectr. and judge in U.S., Can. and New Zealand. One woman shows include Aarhof Gallery, Aarau, Switzerland, 1977, Degli Agostiniani Recolletti, Rome, 1977, Wells Fargo Bank, Monterey, 1975, 78, 79, Seaside (Calif.) City Hall Gallery, 1979, 89, Village Gallery, Lahaina, Hawaii, 1983, 86, 89, 93, Portola Valley Gallery, 1984, 85, Rose Rock Gallery, Carmel, 1984-86, Taupo (N.Z.) Arts Soc., 1988, Geyserland Art Mus., Rotorua, N.Z., 1988, Wanganui (N.Z.) Art Soc., 1988, Rogue Gallery, Medford, Oreg., 1989, 94, Hallie Brown Ford Gallery, Roseburg, Oreg., 1991, 95, Collection of Ann Cunningham, Carmel, Calif., 1993-95; catalog nat. group juried shows include Sierra Nev. Mus. Art, Reno, 1980, Bard Hall Gallery, San Diego, 1980, San Diego Nat. Watercolor Show, Mid-West Nat. Watercolor Show, Rahr-West Mus, Manitowoc, Wis., 1980, Rosicrucian Mus., San Jose, 1981, 84, Calif. State Agri-Images, Sacramento, 1984; XVII Watercolor West, Brea Civic Cultural Ctr., 1985, Watercolor West XXIII Brand Art Galleries, Glendale, Calif., 1991, Watercolor West XXV Riverside (Calif.) Art Mus., 1993, Nat. Pen Women at Marjorie Evans Gallery, Carmel, Calif., 1986, Monterey County Juried Expo, Monterey Peninsula Mus. Art, Monterey, Calif., 1986, 87, Am. Artists Group Exhbn., 1993, 94, 95, Gallery Hirose, Tsukuba, Ibaragi, Japan; Internat. Art Show for End of World Hunger, Ashland, Oreg., 1990, biann. art exhbn. Sumner Mus., Washington, 1992, State of the Art, New Eng. Fine Arts, Boston, 1993, N.W. Wildlife, Nightingale Gallery, Ea. Oreg. Coll., La Grande, 1993, N.W. Visual Arts Ctr. 19th Ann., Panama City, Fla., 1993, NWWS Waterworks N.W. Julie Tolles Gallery, Mercer Island, Wash., 1994; represented in permanent collections: Monterey Calif. Peninsula Mus. Art, Nat. Biscuit Co. subs. RJR Nabisco, San Jose, Waikato Mus. Art, Hamilton, N.Z., Muscular Dystrophy Assn., San Francisco, Nanoose Bay, Old Sch. House Mus., Qualicum Bay, Vancouver Island Brit. Columbia, USS George Washington, Pres. Bill Clinton, Barbara Bush, also numerous pvt. collections. Recipient 1st prize Monterey County Fair, 1979, Jade Fon Watercolor award Hall of Flowers, San Francisco, 1980, 1st Nat. Art Show N.Y. Am. Artist mag., 1980 Nat. Art Appreciation, 1984, Norcal State Art Fair, 1985, Watercolor award 25 Ann. Aqueous Media Show, Salem, Oreg., 1990, Watercolor transparent award Oreg. State U., 1991; numerous other awards for watercolor paintings. Mem. Artists Equity Assn., Am. Watercolor Soc. (assoc.), Nat. Watercolor Soc. (assoc.), Watercolor Soc. Oreg., LaHaina Arts Soc., Rogue Valley Art Gallery, Monterey Peninsula Watercolor Soc., N.W. Watercolor Soc. (signature), Watercolor West (signature), Arts coun. So. Oreg., Mid-West Watercolor Soc., Cen. Coast Art Assn. (pres. 1977-78), Nat. League Am. Penwomen (pres. 1983-84, 86-87), Art Alumni San Jose State U., Nat. Mus. Women in Arts, Women Artists Registry N.Am. Contbr. to profl. publs. Home: 2462 Senate Way Medford OR 97504-8538

SCHUCHAT, SAMUEL PRICE, professional society administrator; b. Washington, Feb. 19, 1960; s. Theodor and Bertha (Moscou) S.; m. Ilana DeBare; 1 child, Rebecca. BA, Williams Coll., Williamstown, Mass., 1983; MPA, San Francisco State U., 1989. Promotion dir. The Data Ctr., Oakland, Calif., 1987-88; dep. dir. Sacramento ATDS Found., 1989-90; devel. dir. Children Now, Oakland, 1992; exec. dir. Calif. League Conservation Voters, San Francisco, 1992—; cons. in field. Office: Calif League Conservation Voters 965 Mission St # 625 San Francisco CA 94013

SCHUCKIT, MARC ALAN, psychiatry educator, researcher; b. Milw., Mar. 5, 1944; s. Samuel Bernard and Lillian (Ginsberg) S.; m. Judith Schrinsky, July 2, 1967; children: Dena Leigh, Jordan Daniel. BS, U. Wis., 1965; MD, Wash. U., 1968. Diplomate Am. Bd. Psychiatry, Am. Bd. Neurology. Intern Cedars-Sinai Hosp., L.A., 1968-69; chief resident in psychiatry U. Calif., San Diego, 1971-72, asst. prof. psychiatry, 1974-75, prof., 1978—; spl. asst. alcohol studies USN Naval Health Research Ctr., San Diego, 1972-74; dir. alcohol and drug abuse inst. U. Wash., Seattle, 1975-78; dir. alcoholism research ctr. VA Hosp., San Diego, 1978—. Author: Drug and Alcohol Abuse, 4th edit., 1995, Educating Yourself about Alcohol and Drugs: A People's Primer, 1995; contbr. 350 articles to psychiat. jours. Author: Drug and Elcohol Abuse, 4th edit., 1995, Educating Yourself about Alcohol and Drugs: A People's Primer, 1995; editor Jour. of Studies in Alcohol, 1994—; contbr. 350 articles to psychiat. jours. Recipient Diego's Young Man of Yr. award Friendly Sons of St. Patrick, 1982, Disting. Rschr. award Rsch. Soc. Alcoholism, 1993, Isaacson award Internat. Soc., 1994. Fellow Am. Psychiat. Assn. (Hofheimer award 1972), Am. Coll. Neuropsychopharmacology; mem. Research Soc. Alcoholism, Internat. Soc. Biomed. Research in Alcoholism, Am. Med. Soc. on Alcoholism. Office: VA Med Ctr 3350 La Jolla Village Dr # 116A San Diego CA 92161

SCHUELE, DONNA CLARE, lawyer, educator; b. June 26, 1957; d. Donald Edward and Clare Ann (Kirchner) S.; m. Charles L. Valdez. BA, Case Western Res. U., 1979; JD, U. Calif., Berkeley, 1985; postgrad., U. Calif., 1985—. Bar: Calif. 1985, U.S. Dist. Ct. (no. dist.) Calif. 1985. Tchr. math. Beachwood (Ohio) High Sch., 1979, De La Salle High Sch., Concord, Calif., 1981-85; systems engr. IBM Corp., San Francisco, 1979-81; atty. Bowles & Verna, Walnut Creek, Calif., 1986-87; prof. law Whittier Coll., L.A., 1988-90; mem. Calif. State Bar Com. on History of Law in Calif., 1990-91; lectr. history polit. sci. law & soc. U. Calif., Santa Barbara, Calif., 1993—. Democrat. Roman Catholic.

SCHUETT, STACEY LYNN, writer, illustrator; b. Elmhurst, Ill., Oct. 9, 1960; d. Marvin Donald Schuett and Rita Cecile (Hassenhauer) Kimball. AA, Sierra Coll., 1981; BA, U. Calif., Davis, 1983. Illustrator: Lights Around the Palm, 1987, The Moon Comes Home, 1989, Watch Me, 1990, Is It Dark? Is It Light?, 1991, I'll See You in My Dreams, 1993, If You Want to Find Golden, 1993, When Spring Comes, 1993, Beginnings, 1994, Outside the Window, 1994, The Feather-Bed Journey, 1995; author, illustrator: Somewhere in the World, Right Now, 1995. Mem. Graphic Artists Guild, Soc. Children's Writers and Illustrators. Home and Office: PO Box 15 Duncans Mills CA 95430-0015

SCHUETZ, JOHN MICHAEL, sales executive; b. Chgo., Apr. 16, 1947; s. Henry Albert and Ann Delores (Kunst) S.; m. Jacqueline Claire Furneaux, Apr. 22, 1972; children: Michael Richard, Sean David. BS in Advt., Marquette U., Milw., 1969. Gen. field mgr. Ford Motor Co., San Jose, 1972-85; v.p. we. region IVECO Trucks of N.Am., Huntington Beach, Calif., 1985-91; nat. dealer mgr. Wynnoil Co., 1992-94; v.p., CEO Ben's Oil, Inc., Toro, Calif., 1994—; bd. dirs. Forsyte Research Group, Santa Rosa, Calif., 1988—. Leader Boy Scouts Am., El Toro, Calif., 1988—; coach Am. Youth Soccer Orgn., Saddleback Valley. Lt. USN, 1969-72. Mem. Sun and Sail Club, Phi Theta Psi. Republican. Roman Catholic. Home: 21821 Ticonderoga Ln El Toro CA 92630-2313

SCHUH, MARY LOUISE, geologist; b. Valders, Wis., June 25, 1956; d. Norbert Edward and Janet Marie (Wagner) S. BS, U. Wis., Oshkosh, 1978; MS, No. Ill. U., 1981. Staff geologist White Pine (Mich.) Copper Co., 1979-80; petroleum geologist Gulf Oil Corp., various, 1981-85; staff geologist Chevron, USA, various, 1985—. Bd. dirs. West Washington Pk. Neighborhood, Denver, 1988-92. Recipient Bd. Regents fellowship No. Ill. U., 1980. Mem. Am. Assn. Petroleum Geologists, Soc. Sedimentary Geology. Home: 701 Lake St Rangely CO 81648-3113 Office: Chevron 100 Chevron Rd Rangely CO 81648-9746

SCHULDT, EVERETT ARTHUR, engineer, consultant; b. Newark, Oct. 29, 1938; s. Arthur John and Ruby Ellen (Warner) S.; m. Georgiana Louise Benson, Sept. 24, 1960; children: David Arthur, Carl Everett. BSME, Rensselaer Poly. Inst., 1960. Lic. profl. engr., Ohio, Calif., Fla., Washington. Mfg. mgr. Procter & Gamble Co., N.Y.C., 1960-70; engr. Procter & Gamble Co., Cin., 1970-72, group leader, 1972-76, sr. engr., 1976-85, tech. section head, 1985-93; ret., 1993. Mem. Am. Soc. of Mech. Engrs., Am. Inst. of Chemical Engrs., Natl. Soc. of Profl. Engrs., Am. Welding Soc., Soc. of Naval Architects & Marine Engrs., Am. Boat & Yacht Coun., Nat. Marine Mfrs. Assn. Republican. Presbyterian. Home and Office: 8037 Brooklyn Ave NE Seattle WA 98115-4311

SCHULER, ALISON KAY, lawyer; b. West Point, N.Y., Oct. 1, 1948; d. Richard Hamilton and Irma (Sanken) S.; m. Lyman Gage Sandy, Mar. 30, 1974; 1 child, Theodore. AB cum laude, Radcliffe Coll., 1969; JD Harvard U., 1972. Bar: Va. 1973, D.C. 1974, N.Mex. 1975. Assoc. Hunton & Williams, Richmond, Va., 1972-75; asst. U.S. atty. U.S. Atty's. Office, Albuquerque, 1975-78; adj. prof. law U. N.Mex., 1983-85, 90; ptnr. Sutin, Thayer & Browne, Albuquerque, 1978-85, Montgomery & Andrews, P.A., Albuquerque, 1985-88; sole practice, Albuquerque, 1988—. Bd. dirs. Am. Diabetes Assn., Albuquerque, 1980-85, chmn. bd. dirs., 1984-85; bd. dirs. June Music Festival, 1980—, pres., 1983-85, 93-94; bd. dirs. Albuquerque Conservation Trust, 1986-90, N.Mex. Osteo. Found., 1993—; chairperson Albuquerque Com. Fgn. Rels., 1984-85; mem. N.Mex. Internat. Trade and Investment Coun., Inc., 1986—; mem. coun. and v.p. St. Lukes Luth. Ch., 1992, pres. 1993—. Mem. Fed. Bar Assn. (coord.), ABA, Va. Bar Assn., N.Mex. State Bar Assn. (chmn. corp., banking and bus. law 1982-83, bd. dirs. internat. and immigration law sect. 1987—, chmn. 1993-94), Harvard U. Alumni Assn. (mem. fund campaign, regional dir. 1984-86, v.p. 1986-89, chmn. clubs com. 1985-88, chmn. communications com. 1988-91), Radcliffe Coll. Alumnae Assn. Bd. Mgmt. (regional dir. 1984-87, chmn. communications com. 1988-91, Harvard-Radcliffe Club (pres. 1980-84). Home: 632 Cougar Loop NE Albuquerque NM 87122-1808 Office: 5700 Harper Dr NE Ste 430 Albuquerque NM 87109-3573

SCHULLERY, PAUL DAVID, editor, writer, consultant; b. Middletown, Pa., July 4, 1948; s. Stephen Emil and Judith Catherine (Murphy) S.; m. Dianne Patricia Russell, June 11, 1983 (div. Dec. 1988). BA in Am. History, Wittenberg U., 1970; MA in Am. History, Ohio U., 1977. Ranger, naturalist Nat. Park Service, Yellowstone Park, Wyo., 1972-77 (summers); historian, archivist Nat. Park Service, Yellowstone Park, 1974-77 (winters); exec. dir. Am. Mus. Fly Fishing, Manchester, Vt., 1977-82; freelance writer Livingston, Mont., 1982-86; assoc. editor Country Jour., Harrisburg, Pa., 1986—; v.p. comm. Fedn. Fly Fishers, West Yellowstone, Mont., 1983-84, sr. advisor, 1982-85; mem. coun. advisors Nat. Parks and Conservation Assn., Washington, 1987—; environ. protection specialist rsch. divsn. Yellowstone Nat. Park, 1988-90, resource naturalist, 1990-92, acting chief cultural resources, 1992-94; adj. prof. Am. Studies U. Wyo., 1991—; affiliate prof. History Mont. State U., 1991—. Author: The Bears of Yellowstone, 1980, 3d edit., 1992 (named one of Best Books of 1986 Mont. mag.), Mountain Time, 1984, American Fly Fishing: A History, 1987 (named one of Best Books of Last 30 Yrs. Trout mag.), The Bear Hunter's Century, 1988, Pregnant Bears and Crawdad Eyes, 1991, Yellowstone's Ski Pioneers, 1995; co-author: (with Austin Hogan) The Orvis Story, 1981, (with John D. Varley) Freshwater Wilderness: Yellowstone Fishes and Their World, 1983 (1st pl. award Competition of Conf. Nat. Park Coop. Assns. 1984, Overall Award for Excellence in Interpretive Pubs. Nat. Park Svc. 1984), (with Conger Beasley Jr., C.W. Buchholtz and Stephen Trimble) The Sierra Club Guides to the National Parks of the Rocky Mountains and the Great Plains, 1984, (with Don Despain, Douglas Houston and Mary Meagher) Wildlife in Transition: Man and Nature on Yellowstone's Northern Range, 1986, (with Bud Lilly) Bud Lilly's Guide to Western Fly Fishing, 1987, A Trout's Best Friend, 1988, (with William Sontag and Linda Griffin) The National Parks: A Seventy-Fifty Anniversary Album, 1991; editor: Old Yellowstone Days, 1979, The Grand Canyon: Early Impressions, 1981, American Bears: Selections from the Writings of Theodore Roosevelt, 1983, The National Parks, 1986, Theodore Roosevelt: Wilderness Writings, 1986, Island in the Sky: Pioneering Accounts of Mt. Rainier, 1986, Yellowstone Bear Tales, 1991; contbr. articles to profl. jours. and mag. Trustee Am. Mus. Fly Fishing,. 1982-91, emeritus, 1991—. Recipient Design Excellence awards Printing Industries Am. Assn., 1981, 83, Award of Recognition Consol. Papers Inc., 1981. Mem. AAAS, Am. Inst. Biol. Scis., Theodore Roosevelt Assn. Greater Yellowstone Coalition, Trout Unltd., Yellowstone Grizzly Found., Internat. Assn. for Bear Rsch. and Mgmt., Gt. Bear Found., Phi Alpha Theta. Lutheran. Office: PO Box 168 Yellowstone National Park WY 82190-0168

SCHULMAN, ELIZABETH WEINER, financial consultant; b. Tucson, Nov. 17, 1950; d. Leonard and Doris (Goldman) Weiner; m. Steven Andrew Schulman, Aug. 15, 1981. BA, Brandeis U., 1972; postgrad., U. Ariz., 1976-78. Office mgr. Assocs. in Periodontics and Endodontics, Tucson, 1973-78; campaign cons. various polit. campaigns Tucson, 1978-79; asst. v.p. Merrill Lynch Pvt. Client Group, Tucson, 1979—. Bd. dirs. Catalina coun. Boy Scouts of Am., Tucson, 1987-90, adv. coun., 1990-92; bd. dirs. Jewish Community Found., Tucson, 1989-91; mem. alumni admissions coun. Brandeis U., 1990—. Mem. Investment Mgmt. Cons. Assn. (bd. dirs. 1991—, chmn. cert. com. 1989—, treas. 1993-94, v.p. 1994), Jr. League of Tucson (coun. sec. 1989-90), Hadassah (spl. gifts. chmn. 1989-91). Office: Merrill Lynch 5460 E Broadway Blvd Ste 350 Tucson AZ 85711-3728

SCHULTE, HENRY GUSTAVE, college administrator; b. Seattle, Oct. 14, 1920; s. John Henry and Alma (Winter) S.; m. Joan Noel Burton, Aug. 20, 1949; children—Steven Craig, Scott John, Jane Martha. B.A. in Econs. and Bus., U. Wash., 1948. With D.K. MacDonald & Co., Seattle, 1952-67, asst. treas., 1957-60, treas., 1960-67; bus. mgr. legal firm Bogle, Gates, Dobrin, Wakefield & Long, Seattle, 1967; adminstr. Child Devel. and Mental Retardation Ctr. U. Wash., Seattle, 1968-86; mem. steering com. mental retardation research ctrs. group Nat. Inst. Child Health and Human Devel., 1971-85. Mem. exec. bd., treas. Assn. Univ. Affiliated Facilities, 1974-77. Served with AUS, 1940-45. Mem. Soc. Research Adminstrs. (mem. exec. com. 1971-72), Am. Assn. Mental Deficiency. Office: U Wash WJ-10 Seattle WA 98195

SCHULTZ, JAMES MICHAEL, nonprofit marketing administrator; b. Mt. Pleasant, Mich., Dec. 9, 1953; s. James Henery and Lorraine Helen (Conklin) S.; m. Shirley Jean Loesch, Nov. 25, 1988; 1 child, Luke Rumnan. AA, Grand Rapids Jr. Coll., 1977; BS in Sociology, Grand Valley State Colls., 1977; MS in Urban Policy Analysis, So. Ill. State U., 1982; profl. devel. cert., Portland State U., 1991. Edn. coord. Utah Navajo Devel. Coun., Blanding, 1979-81; dir. of ops. Careco, Inc., Ft. Myers, Fla., 1983-85; exec. dir. S.E. Asian Refugee Ctr., Vancouver, Wash., 1986; sr. assoc. United Way Columbia-Willamette, Portland, Oreg., 1987-91, dir. mktg., 1991—. Coauthor: Portland Community Profile Report, 1989. Mem. Multnomah County Citizen Involvement Com., Portland, 1989-93, chmn., 1991-93; mem. Multnomah County Cen. Citizen Budget Adv. Com., Portland, 1991; VISTA vol. Dept. Action, Ute Indian Reservation, 1978-79; mem. Willamette Valley Devel. Officers, Portland, 1991—. Mem. Am. Mktg. Assn. (bd. dirs. Oregn. chpt. 1992—, sec. Oreg. chpt. 1992—, pres. 1995—, R. G. Ru Lund award Oreg. chtp. 1993), Oreg. Peace Inst. (bd. dirs., chair resource devel. com. 1994—), Nat. Soc. Fundraising Execs. (Oregon chpt. 1994—). Democrat. Roman Catholic. Home: 2714 NE Bryce St Portland OR 97212-1638 Office: United Way Columbia-Willame 619 SW 11th Ave Portland OR 97205-2646

SCHULTZ, KAREN LEE, fire and water restoration company executive; b. Hempstead, N.Y., June 24, 1953; d. Odd Andre and Irene Mae (Cortez) Solbakken; 1 child, Miakoda Li. Sr. recreation therapist Posada del Sol, Tucson, 1977-81; pres., owner Intimate Luxury, Tucson, 1981-85; gen. mgr. Global Restoration, Tucson, 1985-86; pres., owner A&D Restoration, Tucson, 1986—; owner, sec., treas. Ariz. Quality Refinishing, Inc., 1988-89; owner, qualifying party A&D Carpet and Floorcovering, 1989—, A&D/Karoco Svcs., 1990—; owner Ednl. Resources Assocs., 1991—. Pres. Activities Dirs. Assn. Tucson, 1979-80; mem. candidate evaluation com. C. of C., Tucson, 1984-86; asst. leader Girl Scouts U.S.A., 1984-85. Mem. NAFE, Tucson Bus. and Profl. Women, (pres., chmn. Trade Fair 1985-86), Tucson Women's Symposium, So. Ariz. Claims Adjusters. Democrat. Office: A&D Restoration Inc 1665 E 18th St Ste 108 Tucson AZ 85719-6808

SCHULTZ, KENNETH W., engineering executive. B in Aeronautics, N.Y.U., 1950; MBA, George Washington U., 1960. Exec. v.p. Xonics Inc., Van Nuys, Calif., 1975-80; with Xantech, Inc., 1980—, now pres. Office: Xontech Inc 6862 Hayvenhurst Ave Van Nuys CA 91406-4717*

SCHULTZ, RICHARD ALLEN, geological engineering educator; b. Glen Ridge, N.J., July 23, 1957; s. Arthur Franklin and Viola Grace (Stover) S.; m. Rosemary Legner Schultz, Oct. 16, 1988. BS, Rutgers U., 1979; MS, Ariz. State U., 1982; PhD, Purdue U., 1987. Instr. Purdue U., West Lafayette, Ind., 1987; postdoctoral rsch. fellow Goddard Space Flight Ctr., Greenbelt, Md., 1988-90; asst. prof. geol. engring. U. Nev., Reno, 1990-95, assoc. prof., 1995—; pres. Orion Geomechanics, Reno, 1991—; co-chair 35th U.S. Symposium on Rock Mechanics, Lake Tahoe, Calif., 1994-95. Assoc. editor Jour. Geophys. Rsch., 1993—; contbr. articles to profl. jours. Bd. dirs. Old Washoe Estates Homeowners Assn., Carson City, Nev., 1994. Grantee NASA, NSF, Dept. Energy. Mem. Am. Geophys. Union, Geol. Soc. Am., Assn. Engring. Geologists. Office: U Nev Mackay Sch Mines/172 Reno NV 89557-0138

SCHULTZ, THOMAS ROBERT, hydrogeologist; b. Van Wert, Ohio, July 2, 1946; s. Robert Roland and Mary Avanell (Davies) S.; m. Sandra Lee Pound, Aug. 29, 1968; children: Lindsay D., Zachary T. BS in Geology, Ohio State U., 1969, MS in Geology, 1972; Phd in Hydrology, U. Ariz., 1979. Cert. profl. hydrogeologist Am. Inst. Hydrology. Hydrologist Ariz. State Land Dept., Phoenix, 1977-79, U.S. Office Surface Mining, Denver, 1979-80; sr. hydrogeologist Wahler Assocs., Denver, 1980-82, Kaman Scis. Tempo, Denver, 1983-84; sr. project hydrogeologist Woodward Clyde Cons., Denver, 1984-87; sr. assoc. hydrogeologist Harding Lawson Assocs., Denver, 1987-92, Haley & Aldrich, 1992—; advisor Environ. Tech. Program, Colo. Mountain Coll., Leadville, 1985—, chmn. adv. bd., 1992-93. Contbr. articles to profl. jours. 2d lt. Ohio Nat. Guard, 1969-75. Mem. Nat. Water Well Assn., Colo. Ground Water Assn., Colo. Hazardous Waste Mgmt. Soc. Office: Haley & Aldrich 1600 Broadway Ste 1125 Denver CO 80202-4911

SCHULTZE, ERNST EUGENE, marketing communications executive; b. Columbia, Mo., Jan. 20, 1944; s. Andrew Byron and Jeanne V. (Homsley) S.; m. Marlene Diane Finke, June 7, 1964 (div. 1981); 1 child, Nicole Johanna

Dove. BA, Nebr. Wesleyan U., 1968; MBA, San Diego State U., 1975; lifetime teaching credential, Calif. Community Colls. Mktg. coord. Ektelon Corp., San Diego, 1976-79, ops. project mgr., 1979-80; exec. v.p. Mktg. Group, San Diego, 1980-83; v.p. Jack Lewis Agy., San Diego, 1983-84; mktg. strategist Gable Agy., San Diego, 1984-85; pres. Schultze & Wilson, San Diego, 1985—; pres. Nat. Mgmt. Assn., 1979; mktg. com. Gaslamp Quarter Coun., San Diego, 1988-98; bd. dirs. MedEquip Ams., Inc. Contbr. articles to profl. jours. Counsel Schulze City Coun. campaign, San Diego, 1975, Killea City Coun. campagin, San Diego, 1981. Recipient Golden State award, 1989; named Big Hitter in Bus. City San Diego. Mem. Am. Mktg. Assn., Phi Kappa Tau. Republican.

SCHULTZE, WILLIAM ANDREW, political science educator; b. Washington, Mo., Feb. 13, 1937; s. Andrew Byron and Jeanne Via (Homsley) S.; m. Sharon Petersen, Apr. 10, 1960 (div. Sept. 1983); children: Blair, David, Carol; m. Desiree Ann Scott. BA, Nebr. Wesleyan U., 1959; MA, Rutgers U., 1964, PhD, 1967. Ins. inspector Retail Credit Co., Lincoln, Nebr., 1959-60; govtl. researcher New Brunswick (N.J.)-Raritan Valley C. of C., 1962-63; instr. Rutgers U., New Brunswick, 1963-64, Valparaiso (Ind.) U., 1964-66; asst. prof. Kans. State U., Manhattan, 1966-68; asst. prof., assoc. prof., prof. polit. sci. San Diego State U., 1968—. Author: Urban Politics: A Political Economy Approach, 1985, State and Local Politics, 1988, others. Campaign treas. Bob Filner for Sch. Bd., San Diego, 1978; advisor Yes on Prop. "C", 1980. Fulbright fellow, France, 1976-77; Prof. Associe Sorbonne-U. de Nice, French Ministry Higher Edn., 1980-81. Mem. Am. Polit. Sci. Assn., Western Polit. Sci. Assn. (editorial bd. Western Polit. Quar. 1978-79). Home: 4543 E Talmadge Dr San Diego CA 92116-4828 Office: San Diego State U Dept Polit Sci San Diego CA 92182

SCHULZ, RAYMOND ALEXANDER, medical marketing professional, consultant; b. Paris, June 2, 1946; s. Helmut W. and Colette (Prieur) S.; m. Dixie Lee Suzanne Specht, Apr. 9, 1977 (div. Dec. 1990); children: Christopher, William. BA in Physics, W.Va. U., 1970; MS in Computer Sci., Columbia U., N.Y.C., 1975. Sr. programmer Meml. Sloan Kettering Cancer Ctr., N.Y.C., 1972-74; program coord. Neurol. Inst. Columbia Presbyn. Hosp., N.Y.C., 1974-76; engring. mgr. EMI Med. Systems, Northbrook, Ill., 1976-78; product mgr. Johnson & Johnson (Technicare), Solon, Ohio, 1978-80; group product mgr. Siemens Corp., Iselin, N.J., 1980-82; mktg. mgr. Toshiba Am. Med. Systems (formerly Diasonics MRI), South San Francisco, 1983-92; dir. mktg. Voxel, Laguna Hills, Calif., 1992—. Contbr. over 30 papers on the application of holography to a variety of med. specialties to profl. publs. Recipient First prize Roeutgen Centenary Congress, 1995. Mem. Am. Assn. Physicists in Medicine, N.Y. Acad. Scis., Soc. for Magnetic Resonance, Larchmont Yacht Club, Commonwealth Club of Calif., Eta Kappa Nu. Office: Voxel 26081 Merit Circle Ste 117 Laguna Hills CA 92653

SCHULZ, RENATE ADELE, German studies and second language acquisition educator; b. Lohr am Main, Germany, Feb. 24, 1940; came to U.S., 1958; 1 child, Sigrid Diane. BS, Mankato State Coll., 1962; MA, U. Colo., 1967; PhD, Ohio State U., 1974. Edn. officer U.S. Peace Corps, Ife Ezinihitte, Nigeria, 1963-65; asst. prof. Otterbein Coll., Westerville, Ohio, 1974-76, State U. Coll. N.Y., Buffalo, 1976-77; from asst. to assoc. prof. U. Ark., Fayetteville, 1977-81; from assoc. to prof. U. Ariz., Tucson, 1981—, chair PhD program in second lang. acquisition and teaching, 1994—; disting. vis. prof. USAF Acad., Colorado Springs, Colo., 1990-91. Author: Options for Undergraduate Foreign Language Programs, 1979, Lesen, Lachen, Lernen, 1983, Aktuelle Themen, 1987, Im Kontext: Lesebuch zur Landeskunde, 1990; mem. editorial bd. Modern Lang. Jour., 1985—. Recipient Creative Tchg. award U. Ariz. Found., Tucson, 1984, Stephen A. Freeman award N.W. Conf. Tchg. Fgn. Langs., 1984, Bundesverdienstkreuz, Fed. Govt. Germany, 1990. Mem. Am. Coun. Tchg. Fgn. Langs. (exec. coun. 1979-81, Florence Steiner award 1993), Am. Assn. Tchrs. German (v.p. 1988-90, pres. 1990-91, editor Die Unterrichtspraxis 1980-85), MLA (del. 1989-91), Tchrs. of ESL, Am. Assn. Applied Linguistics, Am. Assn. Tchrs. French. Office: Univ of Ariz Dept German Studies Tucson AZ 85721

SCHULZ, ROBERT ADOLPH, management educator, management consultant; b. Long Branch, N.J., Aug. 20, 1943; s. Robert Adolph and Anna Elizabeth (Fuga) S. BA in Math., St. Vincent Coll., Latrobe, Pa., 1965; BS in Mech. Engring., U. Notre Dame, 1966; MBA, U. Pitts., 1967; PhD in Bus. Adminstrn., Ohio State U., 1971. Rsch. asst. Tech. and Bus. Svcs., Ohio State U., Columbus, 1967-68; teaching asst. dept. mktg. Ohio State U., 1968-70; sr. assoc. Mgmt. Horizons, Inc., Columbus, 1970-71; dir. tech. edn. Mgmt. Horizons Data Systems, Columbus, 1971-72, dir. edn., 1972-73; assoc. prof., Faculty of Mgmt. U. Calgary, Alta., Can., 1973-88, acad. dir. petroleum land mgmt., 1983—, prof. mgmt., 1988—, univ. coord. teaching devel. office, 1991—; pres. Myosymmetries Internat. Inc., 1994—; pres. Scenario Mgmt. Cons. Ltd., Calgary, 1987—; pres. Myosymmetries Internat. Inc., 1994—. Chmn. Align to 21st Century Task Force, Calgary Econ. Devel. Authority, 1989-92, bd. govs., 1994—; chmn. coordinating com. Calgary Cath. Diocese Synod, 1990-94, co-chmn. implementation com., 1994—; bd. dirs. Calgary Sponsor and Refugee Soc., 1981-83. Recipient awards for teaching and coaching acad. teams, Hon. Life Mem. award U. Calgary Students' Union, 1991, Order of U. Calgary, 1994, City of Calgary award for edn., 1995. Mem. Soc. for Teaching and Learning in Higher Edn., Can. Assn. Petroleum Landmen (hon.). Home: 24-1815 Varsity Estates Dr NW, Calgary, AB Canada T3B 3Y7 Office: U Calgary, Faculty of Mgmt, Calgary, AB Canada T2N 1N4

SCHULZKE, MARGOT SEYMOUR, artist, educator; b. San Francisco; d. Charles R. and Helen (Spande) Seymour; m. Ernest F. Schulzke, 1959; children: Kurt, Kristen, Eric, Kari, Stuart. BA in Art, Brigham Young U., 1959; studied with, Albert Handell and others. Tchr. art and English Washington Sch., Chicago Heights, Ill., 1960-62; instr. Maude I. Kerns Art Ctr., Eugene, Oreg., 1963-64; lectr. Brigham Young U. Edn. Weeks., Provo, Utah, 1966-68; instr. Roseville (Calif.) Art Ctr., 1985—; instr. painting workshops. Exhibited in shows at Nat. Art Club, N.Y.C., New Orleans, San Francisco, Colo., Oreg., Nev., Calif., others; at Mus. Ill., N.J., Utah (numerous awards); contbr. articles to profl. jours. Bd. dirs. Friends of Moldova Relief, Sacramento, 1992-93. Mem. Pastel Soc. Am., Pastel Soc. West Coast (bd. dirs. 1985—, adv. bd. 1988—, founding pres. 1985-88, ways and means chmn. 1985-94), Degas Pastel Soc. New Orleans, Knickerbocker Artists of Am., Degas Pastel Soc. Mem. LDS Ch. Studio: PO Box 3322 Auburn CA 95604-3322

SCHUMACHER, BARBARA FINTON, apparel executive; b. Little Rock, Feb. 5, 1951; d. Malcolm Wilson and Wilma (Terry) Finton; m. Paul Sommer, Apr. 19, 1980 (div. Dec. 1985); m. Scott Alan Schumacher, Aug. 31, 1991; 1 child, Katherine Meihui. BS in Psychology, U. Ark., 1973. Sales svc. mgr. Levi Strauss & Co., Little Rock, 1974-76; spls. mgr. Levi Strauss & Co., San Francisco, 1976-79, sundries mgr., 1979-82, inventory & prodn. planning mgr., 1982-89; asst. gen. mgr. distbn. Levi Strauss & Co., Florence, Ky., 1989-91; gen. mgr. distbn. Levi Strauss & Co., Fife, Wash., 1991-94; transition mgr. Levi Strauss & Co., San Francisco, 1994—, v.p. customer fulfillment ea. region, 1995—. Bd. dirs. Big Bros./Big Sisters, Cin., 1990-91. Mem. AAUW, Warehouse Edn. & Rsch. Coun.

SCHUMACHER, FREDERICK RICHMOND, lawyer; b. N.Y.C., Sept. 4, 1930; s. Frederick William and Anna De Rose Elizabeth (Richmond) S.; AB, Princeton U., 1952; JD, Cornell U., 1957; postgrad. in law, cert. in taxation, U. So. Calif., 1959-61; m. Birte Vestel, Dec. 1, 1973; children: Anna Lisa, Ian, Eric. Admitted to N.Y. bar, 1957, Calif. bar, 1960; assoc. firm Clark, Carr & Ellis, N.Y.C., 1957-59, firm Thelen, Marrin, Johnson & Bridges, Los Angeles, 1960-62; individual practice law, 1963—, pres. Frederick R. Schumacher, Ltd., Newport Beach, Calif., 1982, Colorado Springs, Colo., 1992—; of counsel Lewis, D'Amato Brisbois & Bisgaard, 1991-92; cons. fed. and internat. taxes. Active Republican Nat. Com., 1981—. Served with USMC, 1952-54. Mem. Calif. Bar Assn., Hunting Hall of Fame Found. (charter mem.), 1st Marine Divsn. Assn. (life). Author: International Letters of Credit, 1960. Office: 630 Southpointe Ct Ste 100 Colorado Springs CO 80906

SCHUMACHER, HENRY JEROLD, former career officer, business executive; b. Torrance, Calif., June 17, 1934; s. Henry John and Rene (Wilcox) S.; m. Barbara Howell, Aug. 24, 1958; children: Sheri Lynn, Henry Jerold II. Student, Stanford U., 1953; B.S., U.S. Mil. Acad., 1957; M.S., Northeastern U., Boston, 1965; M.B.A., Auburn U., 1977. Commd. lt. U.S. Army, 1958, advanced through grades to maj. gen., 1982; army attaché Moscow, 1969-71; chief communications ops. Vietnam, 1971-72; exec. officer Office Chief of Staff, 1972-75; comdr. U.S. Army Communications Command, Panama, 1977-79; dir. network integration, Office Asst. Chief of Staff Automation and Communications, Dept. Army, 1979-81; comdr. The White House Communications Agy., Washington, 1981-82; chief U.S. Army Signal Corps, 1981-83; ret., 1983; sr. v.p. Visa Internat., 1983-86; chief oper. officer Fuel Tech., Inc., Stamford, Conn., 1986-87; pres. IMM Systems, Phila., 1987-89; exec. v.p. Cylink Corp., Sunnyvale, Calif., 1990-95; exec. dir. Hiller Mus., 1995—. Decorated Def. D.S.M., D.S.M., Legion of Merit. Home: 156 Normandy Ct San Carlos CA 94070-1519 Office: Hiller Mus 1300 Hancock St Redwood City CA 94063

SCHURMANN, GERARD, composer, conductor; b. Kertosono, Dutch East Indies, The Netherlands, Jan. 19, 1924; came to U.S., 1981; s. Johan Gerard and Elvire Stephanie Adeline (Dom) S.; m. Vivien Hind, Sept. 1948 (div. 1972); 1 child, Karen; m. Carolyn Mary Nott, May 26, 1973. Studied composition with Alan Rawsthorne (in Eng.), piano with Kathleen Long (in Eng.), and conducting with Franco Ferrara (in Italy). Cultural attaché Embassy of The Netherlands, London, 1945-48; resident conductor Dutch Radio, Hilversum, Holland, 1948-50; composer, conductor various orgns., London, 1950-81, L.A., 1981—. Music compositions include: (orchestral) Six Studies of Francis Bacon, 1968, Variants, 1970, Attack and Celebration, 1971, Piano Concerto, 1972-73, Violin Concerto, 1975-78, The Gardens of Exile, 1989-90, Concerto for Orch., 1991-95; (chamber and instrumental) Bagatelles-for piano, 1945, Fantasia-for cello and piano, 1967, Sonatina-for flute and piano, 1968, Serenade-for violin solo, 1969, Contrasts-for piano, 1973, Leotaurus-for piano, 1975, Two Ballades-for piano, 1981-83, Duo-for violin and piano, 1983-84, Quartet for Piano and Strings, 1986, Ariel-oboe solo, 1987; (vocal and choral) Chuench'i-for high voice and piano, 1966, Chuench'i-for high voice and orchestra, 1967, Summer is Coming, 1970, The Double Heart, 1976, Opera-Cantata Piers Plowman, 1979-80, Slovak Folk Songs-for high voice and piano, 1987, Slovak Folk Songs-for soprano, tenor and orchestra, 1988; composer of over 40 feature films which include: Not in Vain, The Third Key, The Long Arm, Man in the Sky, Lease of Life, Camp on Blood Island, The Two-Headed Spy, The Ruthless One, Horrors of the Black Musuem, Konga, The Headless Ghost, Cone of Silence, The Living Earth, Dr Syn, The Ceremony, The Bedford Incident, Attack on the Iron Coast, The Lost Continent, Claretta; orchestrator of films including: Lawrence of Arabia (Winner Academy Award), Exodus (Winner Academy Award), The Vikings, Cross of Iron; composed music for theatre including: The Old Vic Theatre, London (Shakespeare), La Comedie Francaise, Paris (Racine, Moliere), TNP, Paris (Shakespeare), Commedia Dell'arte, Rome (Pirandello, Shakespeare). Lt. Royal Air Force, Eng., 1941-45. NEA grantee, 1984, Bursary award British Arts Coun., 1973, Internat. Music awardBritish Coun., 1980, Vis. Fellowship award U.S. State Dept., 1980, National Endowment for the Arts grant, 1985-86. Mem. ASCAP, Acad. Motion Pictures, Arts and Scis., Brit. Acad. Film and TV Arts, Assn. Profl. Composers, Composers Guild of Great Britain, Performing Right Soc., Assn. Composers and Pub., Phyllis Court Club. Home: 3700 Multiview Dr Los Angeles CA 90068-1226

SCHURTER, BETTE JO, realtor; b. Salem, Oreg., July 7, 1932; d. Walter Robert and Dixie Wayne (Gayman) Haverson; m. John J. Schurter, Oct. 2, 1954; children: John Thomas, Steven Robert, Brian Douglas. BS, Portland State U., 1980. Mgr. Ball, Ball & Brosamer, Danville, Calif., 1982-87; realtor Stan Wiley, Inc. Realtors, Wilsonville, Oreg., 1988—. Mem. Draft Bd., Aurora, Oreg., 1980—. Mem. AAUW, Clackamas County Bd. Realtors, Clackamas County Million Dollar Club, Wilsonville C. of C., Aurora Colony Hist. Soc. Home: 24979 NE Pr Dr Aurora OR 97002 Office: Stan Wiley Inc 8750 SW Citizens Dr Wilsonville OR 97070-6404

SCHUSSEL, ALAN LEWIS, rehabilitation counselor; b. Bklyn., Oct. 27, 1963; s. Erwin Marvin and Suellen (Kleppel) S.; m. Clarice Ann West, June 9, 1991; children: Zachary Terence, Marni Amber. BA, Gallaudet U., 1989; MA, U. Ariz., 1994. Cert. rehab. counselor. Resident advisor Rochester (N.Y.) Inst. Tech., 1983-87; resident advisor Gallaudet U., Washington, 1987-89, tutor, 1987-92; residential counselor Family Svcs. Found., Landover, Md., 1989; case mgr. People Encouraging People, Balt., 1990-92; rehab. counselor dept. econ. security State of Ariz., Tucson, 1993—; bd. dirs. Cmty. Outreach Program for Deaf, Rehab. Counselor Dir. Search, Ariz. Coun. for Hearing Impaired, 1994—; mem. preconf. com. Am. Deafness and Rehab. Assn., San Francisco, 1992-93; mem. Statewide Interpreter Planning Com., Phoenix, 1993—, chair subcom. interpreter preparation planning, 1994—; mem. Com. on Real Time Captioning Project, 1995—; dir. New Agy. Planning Project, 1995—; rep. to bd. Ariz. Assn. of the Deaf; panelist on deaf culture, 1992—. Active Silent Protest, U. Ariz., 1993, Deaf Pres. Now, Gallaudet U., Washington, 1988, Empowerment for the Deaf, Phoenix, 1994, Project Pride Cmty. Outreach, Tucson, 1992-93; com. mem. Christopher City Elections, Tucson, 1992. Mem. ACA, Nat. Rehab. Assn., Ariz. Rehab. Assn., Am. Sign Lang. Club (treas. 1992-93), Kappa Sigma. Democrat. Jewish. Home: 16960 W Falcon Ln Marana AZ 85653-9199 Office: State of Ariz Vocat Rehab 899 N Wilmot Ste D-3 Tucson AZ 85711

SCHUSTER, PHILIP FREDERICK, II, lawyer; b. Denver, Aug. 26, 1945; s. Philip Frederick and Ruth Elizabeth (Robar) S.; m. Barbara Lynn Nordquist, June 7, 1975; children: Philip Christian, Matthew Dale. BA, U. Wash., 1967; JD, Willamette U., 1972. Bar: Oreg. 1972, U.S. Dist. Ct. Oreg. 1974, U.S. Ct. Appeals (9th cir.) 1986, U.S. Supreme Ct. 1986. Dep. dist. atty. Multnomah County, Portland, Oreg., 1972; title examiner Pioneer Nat. Title Co., Portland, 1973-74; assoc. Buss, Leichner et al, Portland, 1975-76; from assoc. to ptnr. Kitson & Bond, Portland, 1976-77; pvt. practice Portland, 1977—; arbitrator Multnomah County Arbitration Program, 1985—. Contbr. articles to profl. jours. Organizer Legal Aid Svcs. for Community Clinics, Salem, Oreg. and Seattle, 1969-73; Dem. committeeman, Seattle, 1965-70. Mem. ABA, Multnomah Bar Assn. (Vol. Lawyers Project), NAACP (exec. bd. Portland,Oreg. chpt. 1979—), ACLU, Internat. Platform Assn., Alpha Phi Alpha. Office: 1500 NE Irving St Ste 540 Portland OR 97232-4209

SCHUSTER, ROBERT PARKS, lawyer; b. St. Louis, Oct. 25, 1945; s. William Thomas Schuster and Carolyn Cornforth (Daugherty) Hathaway; 1 child, Susan Michele. AB, Yale U., 1967; JD with honors, U. of Wyo., 1970; LLM, Harvard U., 1971. Bar: Wyo. 1971, U.S. Ct. Appeals (10th cir.) 1979, U.S. Supreme Ct. 1984, Utah 1990. Dep. county atty. County of Natrona, Casper, Wyo., 1971-73; pvt. practice law, Casper, 1973-76; assoc. Spence & Moriarity, Casper, 1976-78; ptnr. Spence, Moriarity & Schuster, Jackson, Wyo., 1978—. Trustee U. Wyo., 1985-89; Wyo. Dem. nominee for U.S. House of Reps., 1994; polit. columnist Casper Star Tribune, 1987-94. Ford Found. Urban Law fellow, 1970-71; pres. United Way of Natrona County, 1974; bd. dirs. Dancers Workshop, 1981-83; chair Wyo. selection com. Rhodes Scholarship, 1989—; mem. bd. visitors Coll. Arts and Scis., U. Wyo., 1991—; mem. planning com. Wyo. Dem. Party; mem. platform com. Dem. Nat. Conv. 1992—; mem. Dem. Nat. Com., 1992—; mem. Wyo. Public Policy Forum, 1992—; bd. dirs. Community Visual Art Assn.; nom. U.S. House of Reps., 1994. Mem. ABA, Assn. Trial Lawyers Am., Wyo. Trial Lawyers Assn. Home: PO Box 548 Jackson WY 83001-0548 Office: Spence Moriarity & Schuster 15 S Jackson St Jackson WY 83001

SCHUSTER-ARTIS, NANCY MARIE, medical/surgical nurse; b. Tuscola, Ill., May 14, 1961; d. Robert George and Elizabeth (Birkner) Schuster; m. David Michael Artis, Aug. 8, 1987. AA, Springfield (Ill.) Coll., 1982; diploma in nursing, St. John's Sch. Nursing, Springfield, 1982; BSN, Sangamon State U., 1984. RN, Calif., Ill. Med.-surg. staff nurse, relief charge nurse St. John's Hosp., Springfield, 1982-88; med.-surg. staff nurse, relief charge nurse Covenant Med. Ctr., Urbana, Ill., 1988-91, unit quality assurance rep., 1989-91, quality assurance dept. co-chair, 1990-91, mem. nursing coun., 1990; infection control liaison, med.-surg. nurse Sierra Hosp., Fresno, Calif., 1991-94, mem. nurse practice coun., diabetic educator, 1991—, mem. totaly quality mgmt. teams, 1993—, svc. coord. med.-surg., 1995—; nutritional counselor Nutri/System, Champaign, Ill., 1988-89; lab. instr. Parkland Coll., Champaign, 1990. Nurse ARC, Ill., 1982—; advisor Springfield Area Nursing Explorer Post 727, 1985-88; mem. State Nurses Active in Politics in Ill., Springfield, 1982-87. Mem. Nat. League for Nursing (advocacy com. 1991—), Ill. Nursing Assn. (corr. sec. 9th dist. 1982-87), Profl. Nurse Forum. Home: 28700 Long Hollow Ct S Coarsegold CA 93614-9629 Office: Sierra Community Hosp 2025 E Oakota Ave Fresno CA 93726

SCHÜTRUMPF, ECKART ERNST, classical languages and philosophy educator; b. Marburg, Hesse, Germany, Feb. 3, 1939; came to U.S., 1987; s. Hans Justus and Margarethe (Wetz) S.; m. MaryAnne Leaver, Dec. 21, 1971; children: Fleming, Caroline, Helene, Justin. PhD, Philipps U., Marburg, 1966, Habilitation, 1976. Lectr. Philipps U., Marburg, 1966-81; pvt. docent Philips U., Marburg, 1979-83; sr. lectr. U. Cape Town, 1983-85, prof., 1985-87; prof. classics U. Colo., Boulder, 1987-93. Author: Die Bedeutung des Wortes ethos in der Poetik des Aristoteles, 1970, Die Analyse der polis durch Aristoteles, 1980, Xenophon Poroi, Vorschläge zur Beschaffung von Geldmitteln, 1982, Aristoteles Politik Buch I-III (2 vols.), 1991, (with H.J. Gehfke) vol.3, 1995; contbr. 40 articles to profl. publs. Rsch. scholar Deutsche Forschungsgemeinschaft, 1973-75, Exch. scholar British Coun., 1979, Rsch. scholar Volkswagenwerk Found., 1981-83. Mem. APA, Classical Assn. Mid West and South, Mommsen Gesellschaft. Office: U Colo Classics Dept Campus Box 248 Boulder CO 80309

SCHUTZ, JOHN ADOLPH, historian, educator, former university dean; b. L.A., Apr. 10, 1919; s. Adolph J. and Augusta K. (Gluecker) S. AA, Bakersfield Coll., 1940; BA, UCLA, 1942, MA, 1943, PhD, 1945. Asst. prof. history Calif. Inst. Tech., Pasadena, 1945-53; assoc. prof. history Whittier (Calif.) Coll., 1953-56, prof., 1956-65; prof. Am. history U. So. Calif., L.A., 1965-91; chmn. dept. history U. So. Calif., 1974-76, dean social scis. and communication, 1976-82. Author: William Shirley: King's Governor of Massachusetts, 1961, Peter Oliver's Origin and Progress of the American Rebellion, 1967, The Promise of America, 1970, The American Republic, 1978, Dawning of America, 1981, Spur of Fame: Dialogues of John Adams and Benjamin Rush, 1980, A Noble Pursuit: A Sesquicentennial History of the New England Historic Genealogical Society, 1995; joint editor: Golden State Series; contbg. author: Spain's Colonial Outpost, 1985, Generations and Change: Genealogical Perspectives in Social History, 1986, Making of America: Society and Culture of the United States, 1990, rev. edit., 1992. Trustee Citizens Rsch. Found., 1985—. NEH grantee, 1971; Sr. Faculty grantee, 1971-74. Mem. Am. Hist. Assn. (pres. Pacific Coast br. 1972-73), Am. Studies Assn. (pres. 1974-75), Mass. Hist. Soc. (corr.), New Eng. Hist. Geneal. Soc. (trustee 1988—, editor, author intro. book Boston Merchant Census of 1789, 1989, recording sec. 1995—), Colonial Soc. Mass. (corr.). Home and Office: 1100 White Knoll Dr Los Angeles CA 90012-1353

SCHUTZKY, MARILYN HORSLEY, artist; b. Soda Springs, Idaho, July 13, 1936; d. Earl James and Alta (Bollwinkel) Horsley; m. Victor Sergay Schutzky, Oct. 11, 1957; children: Allen Victor, Sandra Kristin. Student, U. Calif., Berkeley, 1954-55, U. Utah, 1955-57. Free-lance artist, 1957—. One-woman shows include Design Concepts, Alamo, Calif., 1991, Harbor Studio Gallery, Gig Harbor, 1991, Back Bay Gardens Gallery, Corte Madera, Calif., 1988, St. Paul Towers, Oakland, Calif., 1988, Marin Arts Guild, Larkspur, Calif., 1986, Two Birds, Forest Knolls, Calif., 1983, Avoir Gallery, Kirkland, Wash., 1993, 94; exhibited in groups shows at Waterworks '92, Seattle Conv. Ctr., Grand Exhbn. '92, Akron (Ohio) Soc. of Artists, Howard Mandeville Gallery, Kirkland, 1992, The Nut Tree, 1991, Kaiser Gallery, 1991, Ariz. Aqueous, Tubac, 1993, 95, Suncities Mus., Phoenix, Ariz., 1994, Western Fedn. Watercolor Socs., Phoenix, 1994, and others. Recipient 1st award Frye Art Mus., 1990, James Copley Purchase award San Diego Watercolor Soc., 1988, 2d Pl. award The Artist's Mag., 1993, Excellence award Western Fedn. Watercolor Socs., 1993. Mem. N.W. Watercolor Soc. (Past Pres.'s award 1992, Signature award 1992, Merit award 1993), Marin Soc. Artists, Ariz. Watercolor Assn. (awarded Coatimundi Soc. membership), Eastbay Watercolor Soc. (Signature award 1989), Fedn. Can. Artists, Marin County Watercolor Soc., Watercolor West. Home and Studio: 8915 N Harborview Dr # 103 Gig Harbor WA 98332-2179 also: Marilyn Schutzky Studio 7340 E Turquoise Ave Scottsdale AZ 85258-1220

SCHWAB, CHARLES R., brokerage house executive; b. Sacramento, 1937; m. Helen O'Neill; 5 children. Stanford U., 1959, Postgrad., 1961. Formerly mut. fund mgr. Marin County, Calif.; founder brokerage San Francisco, 1971; now chmn., CEO Charles Schwab & Co., Inc. Author: How to be Your Own Stockbroker, 1984. Republican. Office: Charles Schwab & Co Inc 101 Montgomery St San Francisco CA 94104-4122*

SCHWAB, HOWARD JOEL, judge; b. Charleston, W.Va., Feb. 13, 1943; s. Joseph Simon and Gertrude (Hadas) S.; m. Michelle Roberts, July 4, 1970; children: Joshua Raphael, Bethany Alexis. BA in History with honors, UCLA, 1964, JD, 1967. Bar: Calif. 1968, U.S. Dist. Ct. (cen. dist.) Calif. 1968, U.S. Ct. Appeals (9th cir.) 1970, U.S. Supreme Ct. 1972. Clk. legal adminstrn. Litton Industries, L.A., 1967-68; dep. city atty. L.A., 1968-69; dep. atty. gen. State of Calif., L.A., 1969-84; judge Mcpl. Ct. L.A. Jud. Dist., 1984-85; judge Superior Ct. Superior Ct. L.A. County, L.A., 1985—; mem. faculty Berkeley (Calif.) Judicial Coll., 1987—. Contbr. articles to profl. jours. Recipient CDAA William E. James award Calif. Dist. Atty.'s Assn., 1981. Mem. San Fernando Valley Bar Assn., Inn. of Ct., Phi Alpha Delta. Democrat. Jewish. Office: LA Superior Ct 6230 Sylmar Ave Van Nuys CA 91401-2712

SCHWABE, MARCUS CHRISTOPHER, college administrator; b. Winnipeg, Man., Can., Dec. 20, 1960; s. Lothar and Hanna (Ludwinski) S.; m. Lorie Ann Bustard, Aug. 16, 1986; children: Adam, Noah, Kayleigh. BS, U. Alta., 1982, BEd, 1984. High sch. tchr. Strathcona County, Sherwood Park, Alta., Can., 1985-87; real estate sales Re/Max Real Estate, Edmonton, Alta., Can., 1987-88; dir. alumni and ch. rels. Augusta Univ. Coll. (formerly Camrose Luth. U. Coll.), Camrose, Alta., 1988-92, dir. alumni, 1992—; owner Lifecare, 1985—; cons., presenter Lifecare, 1985—. Editor Kaluko mag., 1988-90, 94—. Mem. coms. Evang. Luth. Ch. Can., chairperson synod youth com., 1992-88, mem. Alta. and the Ters. synod stewardship com., chairperson Office for Resource Devel., mgr. convs., coach slow pitch baseball team. Mem. Assn. Univs. and Colls. Can., Assn. Can. Alumni Adminstrn., Can. Coun. for Advancement of Edn., Coun. for Advancement and Support of Edn., Assn. Alta. Fund-Raising Execs. (program chair), Augustana Univ. Coll. Alumni Assn. (exec. dir., bd. dirs.). Home: 4504 13th Ave, Edmonton, AB Canada T6L 4A3 Office: Augustana Univ Coll, 4901 46th Ave, Camrose, AB Canada T4V 2R3

SCHWABE, PETER ALEXANDER, JR., judge; b. Portland, Oreg., July 23, 1935; s. Peter Alexander and Evelyn (Zingleman) S.; A.B., Stanford, 1958; J.D., Willamette U., 1960; m. Bonnie Jean LeBaron, June 21, 1958; children: Mark, Karen, Diane, Patricia, Kurt. Admitted to Oreg. bar, 1960; pvt. practice, Portland, 1960-76; fed. adminstrv. law judge, 1976—. Mem. ABA, Oreg. State Bar Assn., Beta Theta Pi, Phi Delta Phi. Home: 4366 Dorking Ct Sacramento CA 95864-6150 Office: 2031 Howe Ave Sacramento CA 95825-0176

SCHWANBECK, VICTOR RAYMOND, lawyer, civilian military employee; b. Roswell, N.Mex., Jan. 23, 1944; s. Raymond Victor and Melouise (Johnson) S.; m. Betty Gale Wilcox, Sept. 14, 1979; children: Tracy, Kimberly. BA, Ariz. State U., 1966; JD, U. Ariz., 1969. Bar: Ariz. 1969, U.S. Ct. Appeals (fed. cir.) 1984, U.S. Ct. Mil. Appeals 1971, U.S. Supreme Ct. 1974. Commd. 2d lt. USAF, 1966, advanced through grades to brigadier gen., 1993; lawyer Pima County Pub. Def., Tucson, 1972; assoc. Miller Pitt & Feldman, Tucson, 1972-74; ptnr. Cannon & Schwanbeck, Tucson, 1974-78, Schwanbeck & Present, Tucson, 1978—. Asst. adjutant gen. Ariz. Nat. Guard. Decorated Meritorious Svc. medal, Air Force Commendation medal with 1 oak leaf cluster, Air Force Achievement medal. Mem. Ariz. Bar Assn., Ariz. Trial Lawyers, Pima County Bar Assn., Rotary, Elks, Sertoma (pres. 1976O-77). Office: Schwanbeck & Present 627 N Swan Rd Tucson AZ 85711-2101

SCHWANTES, CARLOS ARNALDO, history educator, consultant; b. Wilmington, N.C., Mar. 7, 1945; s. Arnaldo and Frances (Casteen) S.; m. Mary Alice Dassenko, Sept. 4, 1966; children: Benjamin, Matthew. BA, Andrews U., 1967; MA, U. Mich., 1968, PhD, 1976. From instr. to prof. Walla Walla Coll., College Place, Wash., 1969-85; prof. history U. Idaho, Moscow, 1984—; cons. TV History of Idaho, 1988. Author: Coxey's Army: An American Odyssey, 1985, The Pacific Northwest: An Interpretive History, 1989, In Mountain Shadows: A History of Idaho, 1991, Railroad Signatures Across the Pacific Northwest, 1993; also author or editor 7 other books; mem. editl. bd. Pacific N.W. Quar., 1982—, Idaho Yesterdays, 1987—, Forest and Conservation History, 1988—, Pacific Hist. Rev., 1991—; contbr. articles to profl. jours. NEH fellow, 1982-83, rsch. fellow Idaho Humanities Coun., 1989-90; Idaho State Bd. Edn. rsch. grantee, 1990-91. Mem. Orgn. Am. Historians, Western History Assn., Mining History Assn. (coun. 1990—), Lexington Soc., Idaho State Hist. Soc. Republican. Seventh-day Adventist. Office: U Idaho Dept History Moscow ID 83843

SCHWANZ, JUDITH ANN, seminary educator; b. Cleve., Apr. 19, 1955; d. Roger Alan and Jane Marie (Forsberg) Munson; m. Keith Duane Schwanz, June 28, 1975; children: Karla Kimberlee, Jason Andrew. MA in Counseling, Western Evang. Sem., 1987; MS in Psychology, Portland State U., 1994. Lic. profl. counselor, Oreg.; ordained minister Ch. of the Nazarene, 1989. In-patient staff counselor Christian Therapy Program, Portland, Oreg., 1987-89; counselor Christian Counseling Inst., Portland, 1987-90; adj. faculty mem. Western Evang. Sem., Portland, 1987-89, prof., 1989—. Dir. women's ministry Ch. of the Nazarene, 1979-88, 92—. Mem. APA, ACA. Home: 7700 SE Strawberry Ln Portland OR 97267-5469

SCHWARTZ, ARTHUR SOLOMON, research psychologist; b. N.Y.C., June 12, 1924; s. Aaron and Elsie (Silverstein) S.; m. Eileen Hannigan, June 2, 1951; children—Amy, Andrew, Jainah, Beth, Nancy. B.A., NYU, 1950; Ph.D., U. Buffalo, 1957, postdoctoral fellow, UCLA, 1956-58. Research psychologist NIH, Washington, 1958-62, Barrow Neurol. Inst., Phoenix, 1962—; adj. assoc. prof. Ariz. State U., Tempe, 1962—; cons. in field. Contbr. articles to profl. jours. Served with U.S. Army, 1943-46. Grantee NIH, NSF. Mem. Soc. Neorosci., Internat. Neuropsychology Soc., Democrat. Jewish. Office: Barrow Neurol Inst 350 W Thomas Rd Phoenix AZ 85013-4409

SCHWARTZ, BETTY BARSHA, secondary education educator, writer, artist; b. Bklyn., Dec. 3, 1932; d. John Barsha and Daisy (Lack) Ferrari; m. Arthur Nathaniel Schwartz, Jan. 13, 1968 (div. Feb. 1980); 1 child, Jonathan Matthew. BA, Syracuse U., 1954; MPA, Calif. State U., Northridge, 1994. Ind. researcher, writer L.A., 1980-85; acct. exec. AT&T, L.A., 1985-92; policy analyst L.A. County Met. Transp. Authority, L.A., 1993; spl. events coord. Taiwan program Ctr. for Internat. Tng. and Devel., USC Sch. Pub. Adminstrn., 1994; mem. tchg. staff William S. Hart H.S., Santa Clarita, Calif., 1994—; project cons., guest lectr. Pasadena City Coll.; mem. scholar and adv. com. MTA Red Line Project, Ea. ext., 1994. Author: Tracking Transit Art, 1994, Art on Track, 1994; one-woman shows include Paideia Gallery, L.A., 1964, 1966, Orange County Art Assn., Fullerton, Calif., 1964; exhibited in group shows at Paideia Gallery, L.A., 1963, 64, 65, L.A. Art Assn., 1964, 65, Calif. State Coll., Long Beach, 1965, Bakersfield (Calif.) Coll., 1966, Long Beach Mus. Art, 1967, Fine Arts Fedn., Burbank, Calif., 1982, Orange County Art Assn., Brea, Calif., 1983, 86, Riverside (Calif.) Art Mus., 1987; represented in pvt. collections. Media relations vol. Stevenson Ranch (Calif.) Town Coun., 1992; campaign vol. Clinton campaign, Santa Clarita Valley Dem. Club, 1992, Senator Roberti's No on Recall, N. Hollywood, 1994. Recipient Second award modern oil All Calif. Art Exhibit, Riverside, 1966, Honorable Mention award Joslyn Ctr. of Arts, Torrance, Calif., 1984. Mem. Am. Soc. Pub. Adminstrn. Home: 25124 Steinbeck Ave Apt G Santa Clarita CA 91381-1213

SCHWARTZ, CHERIE ANNE KARO, storyteller; b. Miami, Fla., Feb. 24, 1951; d. William Howard and Dorothy (Olesh) Karo; m. Lawrence Schwartz, Aug. 12, 1979. BA in Lit., The Colo. Coll., 1973; MA in Devel. Theater, U. Colo., 1977. Tchr. English, drame, mime, creative writing, speech coach South High Sch., Pueblo, Colo., 1973-76; tchr. drama St. Mary's Acad., Denver, 1979-81; tchr. English and drama Rocky Mountain Hebrew Acad., Denver, 1981-83; full-time profl. storyteller throughout N.Am., 1982—; storyteller, docent, tchr. tng., mus. outreach Denver Mus. Natural History, 1982—; trainer, cons., performer, lectr, keynote speaker various orgns., synagogues, instns., agys., confs. throughout the country, 1982—; co-founder, chairperson Omanim b'Yachad: Artists Together, Nat. Conf. Celebrating Storytelling, Drama, Music and Dance in Jewish Edn., Denver, 1993. Storyteller: (audio casette tapes) Cherie Karo Schwartz Tells Stories of Hanukkah from Kar-Ben Books, 1986, Cherie Karo Schwartz Tells Stories of Passover From Kar-Ben Books, 1986, Miriam's Trambourine, 1988, Worldwide Jewish Stories of Wishes and Wisdom, 1988; storyteller, actor: (video tape) The Wonderful World of Recycle, 1989; author: (book) My Lucky Dreidel: Hanukkah Stories, Songs, Crafts, Recipes and Fun for Kids, 1994; author numerous stories in anthologies of Jewish literature. Title III grantee State of Colo. Edn., Pueblo, 1975-76. Mem. Coalition for Advancement of Jewish Edn. (coord. Jewish Storytelling Conf. 1989—, coord. Nat. Jewish Storytelling Network), Nat. Assn. for Preservation and Perpetuation of Storytelling, Nat. Storytelling Assn. (Colo. state rep. and liaison), Rocky Mountain Storytelling Guild. Democrat. Jewish. Home: 996 S Florence St Denver CO 80231-1952

SCHWARTZ, DAVID MARCUS, magazine editor-in-chief; b. Fort Wayne, Ind., Sept. 27, 1949; s. Isaac Ralph and Eleanor (Cohen) S. BS in Indsl. Engring., Purdue U., 1971; MBA, Ind. U., 1972. Assoc. pub. Musician's Industry Mag., Berkeley, Calif., 1979-81, Electronic Musician Mag., Berkeley, 1985-88; exec. pub. HyperMedia Mag., Berkeley, 1987-88; editor-in-chief Mix Mag., Emeryville, Calif., 1977—; exec. editor Fox Mag., 1993—; dir. devel. Act III Publishing, 1992—; exec. producer San Francisco Music Fair, 1985-90, Music and Multimedia Festival, 1994; exec. producer 1993 Tech. Excellence and Creativity Awards. Editor: Studio Life, 1982, Hal Blaine and the Wrecking Crew, 1990. Mem. Audio Engring. Soc., NARAS (v.p. 1990). Office: Mix Mag 6400 Hollis St Ste 12 Emeryville CA 94608-1052

SCHWARTZ, ERIC ROBERT, aerospace engineer; b. Phila., July 17, 1959; s. Donald Jay Schwartz and Arlene Judith (Kline) Zieve; m. Patricia Ann Tate. BS in Aerospace Engring., Pa. State U., 1981; MS in Aerospace Engring., Calif. State U., Long Beach, 1988. Sr. engr. McDonnell Douglas, Long Beach, 1981-87, mgr. advanced engring., 1987-92, program mgr. advanced engring., 1992—; tech. advisor NATO, Brussels, 1994—; tech. advisor safety com. FAA, Washington, 1993—. Author: Aircraft Characteristics Prediction Methods, 1988. Pilot Am. Med. Support Flight Team, Santa Monica, Calif., 1991—. FAA rsch. grantee, 1993. Mem. AIAA (co-chmn. survivability tech. com. 1994—), Aircraft Owners and Pilots Assn., Tau Beta Pi. Home: 514 Oceanhill Dr Huntington Beach CA 92648-3748 Office: McDonnell Douglas 3855 N Lakewood Blvd Long Beach CA 90846-0003

SCHWARTZ, JANICE BLUMENTHAL, cardiologist; b. N.Y.C., Apr. 27, 1949; d. Martin Blumenthal and Frances (Multach) Cove; m. Jerry C. Griffin, Apr. 25, 1981. Grad., Newcomb Coll., 1970; MD, Tulane U. Sch. Medicine, 1974. Diplomate Am. Bd. Internal Medicine. Intern in medicine U. So. Calif., L.A., 1974-75; resident in medicine Cedar-Sinai Med. Ctr., L.A., 1975-77; clin. fellow cardiology Cedar-Sinai Med. Ctr., 1977-78; fellow in cardiology Stanford (Calif.) U., 1978-81; instr. medicine Baylor Coll. Medicine, Houston, 1981-82; asst. prof. medicine Baylor Coll. Medicine, 1982-84; asst. prof. medicine U. Calif., San Francisco, 1984-90, assoc. prof. medicine, 1990—; fellow in geriatrics U. Calif., L.A., 1990; assoc. staff cardiovascular rsch. inst. U. Calif., San Francisco, 1986—, affiliated faculty inst. for health and aging, 1989—; mem. study sect. biol. and clin. aging rev. com. Nat. Inst. Aging, 1990-94; chair ad hoc site visit review com. tchg. nursing home project Albert Einstein Coll. Medicine, 1992; adv. panel on geriatrics USP Pharm. Conv., 1990—; lectr. univs., colls., assns. Fellow Am. Coll. Cardiology (ednl. programs com. 1994—), Coun. Geriatric Cardiology (bd. dirs. 1991—, publs. com.); mem. AAAS, Am. Heart Assn. (fellow coun. clin. cardiology), Am. Fedn. Clin. Rsch., Am. Soc. Clin. Pharmacology & Therapeutics (co-chmn. sec. geriatric clin. pharmacology 1988-90, chmn. 1991-94, nominating com. 1990—, coordinating com. 1988—, bd. dirs. 1993—), Am. Geriatric Soc., Am. Soc. Pharmacology & Exptl. Therapeutics (exec. com. 1991—), Western Soc. Clin. Investigation. Office: U Calif M 1186 San Francisco CA 94143-0124

SCHWARTZ, JEFFREY ALAN, fundraising executive; b. L.A., Jan. 29, 1966; s. Robert Harris and Sandra Joan (Leanse) S.; m. Sizanne Leslie Davis, Feb. 14, 1993. BA, U. Southern Calif., 1988; MA, Univ. Reading, 1989, U. Southern Calif., 1991; D in philosophy, U. Southern Calif., 1993. Analyst Santa Monica Mountains Conservancy, Malibu, Calif., 1990; teaching asst. U. Southern Calif., L.A., 1991; rsch. analyst Citizens' Rsch. Found., L.A., 1992; devel. dir. Alliance for Children's Rights, L.A., 1993—. Author: Public Funding of State Elections, 1992; contbr. articles to profl. jours. Dir. Venice Family Clinic, 1994; vol. Jewish Cmty. Ctrs. Assn., 1994; dir. Jewish Fedn. Coun. of Greater L.A., 1994. Mem. Nat. Soc. Fundraising Execs., Am. Pol. Sci. Assn., L.A. Jr. C. of C. Home: 4050 Ellenita Ave Los Angeles CA 91356 Office: Alliance for Childrens Rights 3600 Wilshire Blvd Ste 1904 Los Angeles CA 90010

SCHWARTZ, JOHN ANDREW, surgeon; b. Lorain, Ohio, June 19, 1952; s. William Marvin and Joan Marie (Nellis) S.; 1 child, Lauren Caroline. BS, Xavier U., 1974; MD, U. Cin., 1978. Diplomate Am. Bd. Surgery. Internship gen. surgery U. Ill., 1978-79, residency in gen. surgery, 1979-84; fellowship vascular surgery N.C. Meml. Hosp., 1984-86; asst. prof. U. South Fla., Tampa, 1986-89; surgeon Medford (Oreg.) Clinic, 1989—; instr. surgery U. Ill., Chgo., 1980-84; clin. instr. surgery U. N.C., Chapel Hill, 1984-86; attending surgeon Ashland Community Hosp., Providence Hosp., Rogue Valley Med. Ctr., 1990; co-dir. vascular lab. U. South Fla. Med. Clinic, 1986-89; chmn. Surg. ICU Com., James A. Haley VA Hosp., 1986-89. Contbr. numerous articles to profl. jours. Recipient The Peter B. Samuels Essay award, 1986. Fellow ACS; mem. Internat. Soc. for Cardiovasc. Surgery, Western Vascular Soc., Nathan A. Womack Surg. Soc., Southeastern Surg. Congress, The Warren H. Cole Soc., So. Assn. for Vascular Surgery, Oreg. Med. Assn., Jackson County Med. Soc. Office: Medford Clinic 555 Black Oak Dr Medford OR 97504-8311

SCHWARTZ, JOHN BENJAMIN, telecommunications and real estate executive; b. N.Y.C., July 19, 1950; s. Jerome Stephen and Anne (Simmons) S.; m. Diane Roberta Markrow, Jan. 12, 1985; children: Brendan, Jonathan. Student, Stanford U., 1969-70. Co-founder, gen. mgr. WYEP-FM, Pitts., 1972-75; founder, pres. KBDI-TV, Broomfield, Colo., 1976-80; telecom. cons. Boulder, Colo., 1980—; pres. Instrnl. Telecom. Found., Boulder, 1983—; gen. ptnr. J-K Realty Ptnrs., Boulder, 1983—; pres. The 90's Channel, Boulder, 1989—; chief bureaucrat The 90's, Chgo., 1989-92; bd. dirs. Inst. for Alternative Journalism, Sta. WYBE-TV, Phila.; pres., dir. Sta. KRZA-FM, Alamosa, Colo., 1982-84, hon. dir., 1984—. Contbr. articles to profl. jours. Mem. adv. bd. Ctr. for Media Edn., Washington, 1993—. English Spkg. Union scholar, 1969. Democrat. Office: Instrnl Telecom Found PO Box 6060 Boulder CO 80306-6060

SCHWARTZ, JOHN CHARLES, chemical engineer; b. Seattle, Apr. 30, 1939; s. Charles and Elizabeth Mercy (Dougherty) S.; m. Sandra Helene Waroff, Aug. 20, 1960 (div. Sept. 1982); children: Barry, Allan, Craig. BS in Chemistry, U. Okla., 1960; MS in Chemistry, Rutgers U., 1968. Research chemist FMC Corp., Carteret and Princeton, N.J., 1962-74; sr. process engr. FMC Corp., Green River, Wyo., 1974-94; ret., 1994; technologist phosphorous chem. divsn. FMC Corp., Green River, Wyo., 1989-94; lab. stockroom operator U. Okla., Norman, 1956-60. Contbr. articles to prof. jours.; patentee in field. Co-founder Cong. Beth Israel of Sweetwater County, Wyo., Wyo. chpt. Nat. Alliance for Mentally Ill, pres. Sweetwater County, Wyo. chpt. Capt. Chem. Corps, U.S. Army, 1960-66. Mem. VFW, AIChe, Am. Legion, Am. Chen. Soc. (pres. U. Okla. chpt. 1957), Nat. Mental Health Consumer's Assn., Alpha Epsilon Pi, Alpha Chi Sigma, Phi Lambda Upsilon, Phi Eta Sigma. Democrat. Jewish. Lodge: Eagles. Home: PO Box 648 Green River WY 82935-0648 Office: FMC Wyo Corp PO Box 872 Green River WY 82935-0872

SCHWARTZ, JOHN THEODORE, orthopedic surgeon; b. Rochester, Minn., Oct. 13, 1957; s. John Theodore Sr. and Dolores (Pencavage) S. BS, U. Md., 1980, MD, 1984. Diplomate Nat. Bd. Med. Examiners, Am. Bd. Orthopedic Surgery. Intern in gen. surgery U. Md. Hosp., Balt., 1984-85; resident in orthopedic surgery U. Md. Hosp., 1985-89; fellow Brigham & Women's Hosp./Children's Hosp. Med. Ctr., Boston, 1989-90; orthopedic surgeon Webster Orthopedic Med. Group, San Ramon, Calif., 1990—. Mem. AMA, AAAS, Am. Acad. Orthopedic Surgery, So. Med. Assn., Mass. Med. Soc., Mass Med. Benevolent Soc., Med. Alumni Assn. U. Md., Anderson Orthopedic Rsch. Inst., U. Md. Surgical Soc. Office: Webster Orthopedic Med Group Ste 140 5201 Norris Canyon Rd San Ramon CA 94583

SCHWARTZ, LAWRENCE JAY, ophthalmologist; b. Bklyn., May 24, 1943; s. Nathan and Rita Joan (Smolensky) S.; m. Sandra Berlin, Dec. 21, 1969; children: Andria, Richard, Marla. BA, Cornell U., 1964; MD, SUNY, Buffalo, 1968. Diplomate Am. Bd. Ophthalmology. Intern L.A. County-U. So. Calif. Med. Ctr., L.A., 1968-69, resident in internal medicine, 1969; resident in ophthalmology Pacific Med. Ctr., San Francisco, 1970-72; ophthalmologist in pvt. practice, L.A., 1974—; ophthalmology cons. L.A. Olympics, 1984; assoc. dir. Ellis Eye Ctr., L.A., 1983—; mem. med. exec. com. Cedars-Sinai Med. Ctr., L.A., 1990-93. Co-author textbook chpt. Bd. dirs. Crittenton Ctr., L.A., 1984-88. Served to maj. U.S. Army, 1973-74. Fellow Am. Acad. Ophthalmology, Phi Delta Epsilon (pres. 1986-87). Republican. Jewish. Office: 8635 W 3d St Ste 390W Los Angeles CA 90048

SCHWARTZ, LOUIS, radiologist; b. N.Y.C., Sept. 19, 1940; s. Abraham and Paula (Hojmon) S.; m. Marilyn Carole Altman, Aug. 28, 1965; children: Debra, Steven, Susan. BS magna cum laude, Adelphi Coll., 1961; MD, Albert Einstein Coll. Medicine, 1965. Radiologist Riverside (Calif.) Gen. Hosp., 1971—; radiologist Parkview Community Hosp., Riverside, 1972—, chief radiology, 1979—; pres. Arlington Radiol. Med. Group Inc., Riverside, 1982—; chief of staff Parkview Community Hosp., Riverside, 1990-91. Mem. AMA, Am. Coll. Radiology, Calif. Radiol. Soc., Inland Radiol. Soc. (pres. 1979), Riverside County Med. Assn. Office: Arlington Radiol Med Group Inc 3900 Sherman Dr Riverside CA 92503-4005

SCHWARTZ, MARTIN LERNER, physician; b. Newport News, Va., 1945. PhD in Biochemistry, Duke U., 1972, MD, 1973. Resident Bess Kaiser Hosp., Portland, Oreg., 1973-77, mem. staff, 1977—. Home: 3325 N Interstate Ave Portland OR 97227-1020 also: 4347 SW Donner Way Portland OR 97201-1598

SCHWARTZ, MICHAEL WARREN, physician investigator; b. Durham, N.C., Oct. 3, 1954; s. Theodore B. and Mrs. Schwartz; m. Patricia Shannon, June 30, 1984; children: Jay Wesley, Anne Shannon. BA in Biology, U. Colo., 1978; MD, Rush Med. Coll., 1983. Intern U. Wash. Sch. Medicine, Seattle, 1983-84, resident, 1984-86; acting instr. divsn. metabolism, endocrinology & nutrition U. Wash. Dept. Medicine & VA Med. Ctr., Seattle, 1990-92, acting ass.t prof., 1992-93, asst. prof., 1993—. Contbr. articles to profl. jours. Sr. Rsch. fellow in endocrinology and nutrition U. Wash. Sch. Medicine and VA Med. Ctr., 1987-89; recipient Nathan M. Freer award, 1983, NIH Rsch. Svc. award, 1987-90, Dept. Vets. Affairs Assoc. Investigator award, 1989, Pilot and Feasibility award, U. Wash., 1991, NIH Physician Scientist award, 1992, others. Mem. AMA, Am. Coll. Physicians, Am. Diabetes Assn., Am. Fedn. Clin. Rsch., N.Am. Assn. Study Obesity, Endocrine Soc., Alpha Omega Alpha, Sigma Xi. Office: VA Med Ctr Dept Medicine 1660 S Columbian Way Seattle WA 98108-1532

SCHWARTZ, MILTON LEWIS, federal judge; b. Oakland, Calif., Jan. 20, 1920; s. Colman and Selma (Lavenson) S.; m. Barbara Ann Moore, May 15, 1942; children: Dirk L., Tracy Ann, Damon M., Brooke. A.B., U. Calif. at Berkeley, 1941, J.D., 1948. Bar: Calif. bar 1949. Research asst. 3d Dist. Ct. Appeal, Sacramento, 1948; dep. dist. atty., 1949-51; practice in Sacramento, 1951-79; partner McDonough, Holland, Schwartz & Allen, 1953-79; U.S. dist. judge Eastern Dist. Calif., U.S. Dist. Ct., Calif., 1979—; prof. law McGeorge Coll. Law, Sacramento, 1952-55; mem. Com. Bar Examiners Calif., 1971-75. Pres. Bd. Edn. Sacramento City Sch. Dist., 1961; v.p. Calif. Bd. Edn., 1967-68; trustee Sutterville Heights Sch. Dist. Served to maj. 40th Inf. Divsn. AUS, 1942-46, PTO. Named Sacramento County Judge of Yr., 1990; Milton L. Schwartz Am. Inn of Court named in his honor, Davis, Calif. Fellow Am. Coll. Trial Lawyers; mem. State Bar Calif., Am. Bar Assn., Am. Bd. Trial Advocates, Anthony M. Kennedy Am. Inn of Ct. (pres. 1988-90, pres. emeritus 1990—). Office: US Dist Ct 1060 US Courthouse 650 Capitol Mall Sacramento CA 95814-4708

SCHWARTZ, MODEST EUPHEMIA, real estate company executive; b. Chgo., Dec. 14, 1915; d. Giles E. and Evelyn (Tomczak) Ratkowski; m. Edward Joseph Schwartz, Feb. 9, 1946 (dec. July 1979); children: Kathryn Ann, Edward Thomas. BA, UCLA, 1936, MA, 1938; libr. credential, Immaculate Heart Coll., L.A., 1958. Cert. tchr., libr., Calif. Tchr. Alhambra (Calif.) City Schs., 1938-58, libr., 1958-72; v.p. Fremont Svc., Alhambra, 1959-83, pres., 1983-86; v.p. Moulding Supply Co., Alhambra, 1967-83, pres., 1983-85; v.p., bd. dirs. Sequoia Mgmt. Co., Alhambra, 1969-86; mng. ptnr. SRSH Realty Ptnrs., Alhambra, 1986-89. Bd. dirs. Found. for Cardiovasc. Rsch., Pasadena, Calif., 1973-85, Progressive Savs., Alhambra, 1979-85; mem. Ret. Sr. Vol. Program, Alhambra, 1979—; mem. Alhambra Cmty. Hosps. Aux., 1987—, med. libr., 1990—; mem. Friends of Alhambra Pub. Libr., 1981—, treas., 1993—; pres. bd. trustees Alhambra Pub. Libr., 1981-83, 89-91, mem., 1976-83, 85-93; pres. Alhambra Pub. Libr. Found., 1990—; mem. Los Angeles County Art Mus., Met. Mus., N.Y.C. Mem. ALA, NEA, AAUW (life, Edn. Found. grant in her name 1988, br. treas. 1986-88, 89-91, corr. and rec. sec. 1992-93, co-chair ways-and means com. 1993—, auditor 1995—), Calif. Ret. Tchrs. Assn. (co-chair hospitality 1991—, membership chmn., 2d v.p. membership Pasadena-Foothill divsn. 1993-95, chmn. neighborhood group Pasadena-Foothill divsn. 1995—), UCLA Alumni Assn., Women's City Club. Home: 1117 N Stoneman Apt K Alhambra CA 91801

SCHWARTZ, ROBERT JOHN, landscape contractor, landscape designer; b. Elkhorn, Wis., June 14, 1954; s. Robert Knilans and Mary Cosella (Fleming) S. 2 BS degrees cum laude, U. Wis., Stevens Point, 1976; AA in Landscape Design ad hoc, U. Minn., 1985; AA, Calif. Poly. Inst., Pomona. Lic. landscape contractor, Calif. Real estate broker, salesman McKy-Ellis Realtors Madison Wis., Janesville, Wis., 1979-80; sole proprietor Teutonic Landscapes Co., Milw., 1982-85, Rialto, Calif., 1985—. Supporter St. Joseph's Indian Sch., Chamberlain, S.D., 1986—, Mercy Home for Boys and Girls, Chgo., 1986—, Asian Relief, Inc., Riverdale, Md., 1986—, So. Poverty Law Ctr., Montgomery, Ala., 1991-93; active The Heritage Found., Washington, 1992—, The Wall of Liberty Nat. Found., Washington, 1993—, Am. Conservative Union, Washington, 1993—. Recipient City Hall Coun. citations City of Claremont, Calif., 1986-87, City of Upland, Calif., 1989. Republican. Home and Office: 1018 N Ash Ave Rialto CA 92376-4578

SCHWARTZ, STEVEN MICHAEL, cardiothoracic surgeon; b. L.A., Oct. 14, 1955; s. Gary Howard and Ethel (Feiler) S.; m. Debra Charlen Durbin, Feb. 20, 1983; children: Rachel, Elise, Amanda. BS, U. Calif., Irvine, 1977, MD, 1981. Diplomate Am. Bd. Surgery, Am. Bd. Thoracic Surgery. Intern U. Calif. Med. Ctr., Irvine, 1981-82; resident surgery U. Hawaii, Honolulu, 1983-87, chief resident surgery, 1986-87, asst. prof. surgery, 1987-89; chief resident cardiac surgery U. Calif. San Diego Med. Ctr., 1989-91; pvt. practice San Jose (Calif.) Cardiac Surgery Group, 1991—. Contbr. articles to profl. jours. Grantee NSF, Irvine, 1975; Hawaii Heart Assn. fellow, Honolulu, 1987-89. Fellow ACS (assoc.), Am. Coll. Cardiology, Am. Coll. Chest Physicians, Soc. Thoracic Surgeons; mem. Calif. Med. Assn. Office: San Jose Cardiac Surgery Group 3803 S Bascom Ave #100 Campbell CA 95008

SCHWARTZMAN, ARNOLD MARTIN, film director, graphic designer; b. London, England, Jan. 6, 1936; came to U.S., 1978; s. David and Rose S.; m. Isolde, Oct. 17, 1980; 1 child, Hannah. Student, Canterbury Coll. Art, 1953, Nat. Diploma in Design, 1955. Sr. designer Associated Rediffusion TV, London, England, 1959-65; concept planning exec. Erwin-Wasey Advt., London, England, 1965-68; dir. Conran Design Group, London, England, 1968-69; prin. Designers Film Unit, London, England, 1969-78; film dir. The Directors Studio, London, England, 1969-78; design dir. Saul Bass and Assoc. Inc., L.A., 1978-79; pres. Arnold Schwartzman Prod., L.A., 1979—; dir. design Olympic Games, L.A., 1982-83. Author, photographer: Graven Images, 1993; author: Phono-Graphics, 1993; co-author: Airshipwreck, 1978, Code Name: The Long Sobbing, 1994, Anglafile: The Best of British in Los Angeles, 1994. Recipient Oscar Acad. award, Acad. Motion Picture Arts and Scis., 1982, Silver award, Designers and Art Dirs. Assn. London, 1969, 71, 75. Mem. Acad. Motion Picture Arts and Scis. (documentary exec. com.), Alliance Graphique Internationale, Brit. Acad. Film and TV Arts (bd. dirs.), Am. Inst. Graphic Arts (mem. adv. bd.). Home: 317 1/2 N Sycamore Ave Los Angeles CA 90036-2689

SCHWARY, RICHARD JOSEPH, investment company executive; b. L.A., Dec. 7, 1944; s. Joseph Louis and Mary (Koury) S.; m. Rose Ann Martin, June 10, 1978; children: Kristen Rose, Brandon Richard. BS, Calif. State U., Long Beach, 1973. With. Hughes Aircraft, El Segundo, Calif., 1973-76; v.p. JCI Inc., Ingelwood, Calif., 1976-80; pres. Calif. Numis. Investments, Inc., Redondo Beach, Calif., 1980—; chmn. bd. Am. Numis. Exch., Newport Beach, Calif., 1988-92; expert witness FTC, FBI, L.A., 1988—. Contbr. author United States Pattern: Experimental and Trial Pieces, 7th edit., 1982, A Guide Book of United States Coins, 44th edit. With USAF, 1965-69. Mem. Profl. Numismatists Guild. Republican. Roman Catholic. Office: Calif Numis Investments Inc 525 W Manchester Blvd Inglewood CA 90301

SCHWARZ, GERARD, conductor, musician; b. Weehawken, N.J., Aug. 19, 1947; s. John and Gerta (Weiss) S.; m. Jody Greitzer, June 23, 1984; children: Alysandra, Daniel, Gabriella, Julian. BS, Juilliard Sch., 1972, MA, 1972; DFA (hon.), Fairleigh Dickinson U., Seattle U.; DMus (hon.), U. Puget Sound. Trumpet player Am. Symphony Orch., 1965-72, Am. Brass Quintet, 1965-73, N.Y. Philharm., 1973-77; trumpet player, guest condr. Aspen Music Festival, 1969-75, bd. dirs., 1973-75; music dir. Erick Hawkins Dance Co., 1967-72, SoHo Ensemble, 1969-75, Eliot Feld Ballet Co., N.Y.C., 1972-78; prin. condr. Waterloo Festival, 1975-93, Music Sch. Princeton (N.J.) U.; music dir. N.Y. Chamber Symphony, 1977—, L.A. Chamber Orch., 1978-86, White Mountains (N.H.) Music Festival, 1978-80, Music Today at Merkin Concert Hall, N.Y.C., 1988-89; music advisor Mostly Mozart Festival, Lincoln Ctr., N.Y.C., 1982-84, music dir., 1984—; music advisor Seattle Symphony, 1983-84, prin. condr., 1984-85, music dir., 1985—; artistic advisor Tokyu Bunkamura's Orchard Hall, Japan, 1994—; mem. faculty Juilliard Sch., N.Y.C., 1975-83, Mannes Coll. Music, 1973-79, Montclair (N.J.) State Coll., 1975-80; guest condr. various orchs. including Phila. Orch., L.A. Philharmonic, St. Louis, Buffalo, Detroit, San Francisco, Atlanta, Houston, Pitts., Minn., Jerusalem Symphony, Israel Chamber Orch., Moscow Philharmonic, Moscow Radio Orch., Orch. Nat. de France, Paris, London Symphony Orch., Frankfurt Radio, Stockholm Radio, Helsinki Philharm., Ensemble InterContemporain, Monte Carlo Philharm., Nat. Orch. Spain, English Chamber Orch., London Symphony, Scottish Chamber Orch., City of Birmingham (Eng.) Symphony, Nouvel Orchestre Philharmonique, Sydney (Australia) Symphony, Melbourne (Australia) Symphony, Orchestre National de Lyon, France, Orchestre Philharm. de Montpellier, France, Washington Opera, Da Capo Chamber Players, 20th Century Chamber Orch., Chamber Music Soc. Lincoln Ctr., San Francisco Opera, Seattle Opera, Tokyu Bunkamura, Japan, Residentie Orch. of The Hague, The Netherlands, St. Louis Symphony, London Mozart Players, Kirov Orch., St. Petersburg, Russia, Tokyo Philharm., Royal Liverpool (Eng.) Philharm., Vancouver (Can.) Symphony Orch., City of London Symphonia, Evian Festival in France, 1994; also numerous appearances on TV; rec. artist Columbia, Nonesuch, Vox, MMO, Desto, Angel, Delos records; record: Seattle Symphony 1994-95 Season, 1995. Bd. dirs. Naumburg Found., 1975—. Recipient award for concert artists Ford Found., 1973, Grammy award nominee, Mumms Ovation award, Record of Yr. awards, Ditson Condrs. award Columbia U., 1989; named Condr. of Yr., Musical Am. Internat. Directory of Performing Arts, 1994. Office: NY Chamber Symphony 1395 Lexington Ave New York NY 10128-1647

SCHWARZ, GLENN VERNON, editor; b. Chgo., Nov. 24, 1947; s. Vernon Edward and LaVerne Louise (Schuster) S.; m. Cynthia Frances Meisenhoelder, June 17, 1984; 1 child, Chloe. BA, San Francisco State U., 1970. Sports writer San Francisco Examiner, 1970-87, sports editor, 1988—. Fundraiser San Francisco Zoological Soc., 1987—. Mem. AP Sports Editors, Baseball Writers Assn. Am. (bd. dirs. 1986-87). Office: San Francisco Examiner 110 5th St San Francisco CA 94103-2918

SCHWARZ, I. GENE, psychiatry educator; b. N.Y.C., Nov. 20, 1930; married; 3 children. BS, Wagner Coll., 1951, MA, 1953; MD, Med. Coll. Ga., 1960. Diplomate Am. Bd. Pschiatry and Neurology; cert. psychoanalyst. Instr. psychiatry U. Cin. Coll. Medicine, 1964-68; pvt. practice psychiatry, 1964—, pvt. practice psychoanalysis, 1965—; asst. prof. psychiatry U. Cin.

Coll. Medicine, 1968-70; asst. dir. psychiatry Cin. Gen. Hosp., 1968-70; instr. Denver Inst. Psychoanalysis U. Colo. Sch. Medicine, 1970-71, asst. clin. prof. dept. psychiatry, 1970-84, assoc. clin. prof., 1984-92, clin. prof., 1992—; psychology specialist U.S. Army, 1953-55; sch. psychologist Richmond County Bd. Edn., Augusta, Ga., 1955-56; staff mem. Colo. Gen. Hosp., U. Colo. Health Scis. Ctr., Denver, 1970—; inst. assoc. Denver Inst. Psychoanalysis, U. Colo. Sch. Medicine, 1971-73, faculty mem., 1973—, assoc. tng. and supervising analyst, 1974-76, tng. analyst, 1976—, supervising analyst, 1979—; treas., 1983-86, assoc. dir., 1986-89, dir., 1989-92; cons. in field. Contbr. articles to profl. jours. Recipient Commendation, Chief Justice Pringle, Supreme Ct. of State of Colo., 1978, Svc. award Supreme Ct. Grievance Com. of State of Colo., 1978. Fellow Am. Psychiat. Assn., Colo. Psychiat. Assn.; mem. Internat. Psychoanalytic Assn., Am. Psychoanalytic Assn. (membership com. 1983-86, fellow to bd. of profl. standards 1984-92, com. for non-med. clin. tng. 1988), Denver Psychoanalytic Soc. (sec. 1973-75, chmn. membership com. 1982-85, v.p. 1985-87). Office: 4900 Cherry Creek South Dr Denver CO 80222-2283

SCHWARZ, JOSEPH RICHARD, engineering manager; b. Pomona, Calif., Dec. 7, 1954; s. Robert Joseph and Edith M. (Varian) S.; m. Pamela Anne Galligan, Apr. 8, 1978 (div. June 1983). BSEE magna cum laude, Calif. State Polytech. U., Pomona, 1977. Digital systems engr. Metron Corp., Upland, Calif., 1977-78; installation mgr. Hughes Aircraft, Denmark, Hawaii and Fed. Republic Germany, 1978-88; co-owner Penrose Gallery, Big Bear Lake, Calif., 1988-90; system engr. Gen. Dynamics, Pomona, Calif., 1989-91; ops. mgr. Amacron/Cycad Corp., Rancho Cucamonga, Calif., 1991-94; sr. system engr. Sysecca Inc., Marina del Rey, Calif., 1995—. Telephone counselor Garden Grove (Calif.) Community Ch., 1984-90. Mem. ACLU, L.A. Music Ctr., Sierra Club, Toastmasters, Eta Kappa Nu, Tau Beta Pi. Republican. Home: 611 Opal Ct Upland CA 91786-6525

SCHWARZ, MICHAEL, lawyer; b. Brookline, Mass., Oct. 19, 1952; s. Jules Lewis and Estelle (Kosberg) S. BA magna cum laude, U. No. Colo., 1975; postgrad. U. N.Mex., 1977, JD, 1980; Rsch. reader in Negligence Law, Oxford U., 1978; diploma in Legal Studies, Cambridge U., 1981. Bar: N.Mex. 1980, U.S. Dist. Ct. N.Mex. 1980, U.S. Ct. Appeals (10th, D.C., and Fed. cirs.) 1982, U.S. Ct. Internat. Trade, 1982, U.S. Tax Ct. 1982, U.S. Supreme Ct. 1983, N.Y. 1987. VISTA vol., Albuquerque, 1975-77; rsch. fellow N.Mex. Legal Support Project, Albuquerque, 1978-79; supr. law Cambridge (Eng.) U., 1980-81; law clk. to chief justice Supreme Ct. N.Mex., Santa Fe, 1981-82; pvt. practice law, Santa Fe, 1982—; spl. prosecutor City of Santa Fe, 1985; spl. asst. atty. gen., 1986-88; mem. editorial adv. com. Social Security Reporting Svc., 1983-95. Author: New Mexico Appellate Manual, 1990, 2nd. edit., 1994; contbr. articles to profl. jours. Vice dir. Colo. Pub. Interest Rsch. Group, 1974; scoutmaster Great S.W. Area coun. Boy Scouts Am., 1977-79; mem. N.Mex. Acupuncture Licensing Bd., 1983. Recipient Cert. of Appreciation Cambridge U., 1981, Nathan Burkan Meml. award, 1980, N.Mex. Supreme Ct. Cert. Recognition, 1992, 93. Mem. ABA (litigation com. on profl. responsibility, litigation com. on pretrial practice and discovery), Assn. Trial Lawyers Am., Am. Arbit. Assn., State Bar N.Y., N.Mex. State Bar (bd. dirs. employment law sect. 1990—, chair employment law sect. 1991-92), N.Y. Bar Assn., First Jud. Dist. Bar Assn. (treas. 1987-88, sec. 1988-89, v.p. 1989-1990, pres. 1990-91, local rules com. mem. 1989-92), N.Mex. Supreme Ct. (standing com. on profl. conduct 1990—, hearing officer, reviewing officer disciplinary com. 1993—), Am. Inns. of Ct. N.Mex. (barrister), Nat. Employment Lawyers Assn. (Nat. chpt., N.Mex. chpt.), Sierra Club, Amnesty Internat., Nat. Audubon Soc. Home and Office: PO Box 1656 Santa Fe NM 87504-1656

SCHWEBACH, MARTHA KEENE, nurse practitioner; b. Pratt, Kans., Feb. 3, 1939; d. Samuel Sidney and Alice Katherine (Sanko) Keene; m. Donald E. Schwebach, Sept. 3, 1960; children: Douglas, Cynthia, Daryl, Dean. Dominican Sch. of Nursing, 1960, U. N.Mex., 1968; Fellow, U. N.Mex., 1968-69. Cert. family nurse practitioner, 1977. Lectr., co-author, fellow dept. epidemiology, cmty. medicine U. N.Mex. Sch. of Medicine, Albuquerque, 1968-72; pilot project U. N.Mex., 1969-72; adminstr. Hope Med. Ctr., Inc., Estancia, N.Mex., 1970-77, Moriarty (N.Mex.) Med. Clinic, 1977-82, Ctrl. N.Mex. Med. Ctr., Inc., Moriarty, 1982-91; family nurse practitioner Family Health Clinic, Moriarty, 1992—; established not-for-profit med. organ. with later expansion to urgent care ctr.; cons. for establishment of rural clinics; grant writer in field. Contbr. numerous publs. to profl. jours. Guest lectr. for AMA, Am. Hosp. Assn., Josiah Macy Jr. Found., Dept. Health, Edn. and Welfare. Recipient formal recognition for nurses where practice reflects high profl. stds.; honored by Pres. Gerald R. Ford at Oval Office of White House, 1974; named N.Mex. Outstanding Young Woman of Yr., 1974, 90, one of Outstanding Young Women of Am., 1974; first family nurse practitioner in U.S. Mem. ANA, Am. Nurses Credentialing Ctr., ANA Coun. on Advanced Practice, N. Mex. Nurses Assn., N. Mex. Nurse Practitioner Council. Home: PO Box 327 901 Martinez Rd Moriarty NM 87035 Office: Family Health Clinic 1108 Rt 66 SW Moriarty NM 87035

SCHWEHR, ROBERT FREDERICK, software/hardware development professional; b. Menomonie, Wis., May 24, 1946; s. Frederick E. and Barbara J. (Wagner) S.; m. Linda Ellen Berigan, June 8, 1968; children: Kurt, Kiley. BSEE, U. Wis., 1969; MSEE, Stanford (Calif.) U., 1973. Design engr. Hewlett Packard, Palo Alto, Calif., 1969-73; project mgr. Hewlett Packard, Cupertino, Calif., 1973-87, sect. mgr., 1987—. Sgt. U.S. Army Nat. Guard, 1970-76. Mem. IEEE Computer Soc. Home: 414 Distel Dr Los Altos CA 94022-1715 Office: Hewlett Packard 47LA 19410 Pruneridge Ave # 47la Cupertino CA 95014-0610

SCHWEIGERT, LYNETTE AILEEN, interior designer, consultant; b. Sacramento, July 6, 1949; d. Marvin Gerhardt and Aileen Helen (Velcoff) S.; m. Alan H. Randolph, May 1, 1976; 1 child, Tyler Mason Randolph. BS in Design, U. Calif., Davis, 1971. Display designer Weinstock's, Sacramento, 1971-72, Roos-Atkins, Sacramento, 1972-73; prin., project designer Randolph-Schweigert & Co., Reno, 1975-93; owner, project designer Hospitality Design Group, Reno, 1985—; prin. Design Ctr. Cons., Reno, 1982-86; cons. interior design Dan Carne AIA, Reno, 1980—, Paul Huss AIA, Reno, 1985-89, U.S. West Investments, Reno, 1984-89; cons. space planning Family Cousneling Svc. of No. Nev., Reno, 1986-91; instr. interior deisgn U. Nev., Reno, 1994—. Named one of Top 60 Restaurant Designers, Contract Mag., 1985; recipient Finalist prize Sierra Arts Found., Reno, 1980, Cert. Recognition for Participation in Preprofessional Internship Program U. Nev., 1987. Mem. Inst. Bus. Designers (affiliate). Office: Hospitality Design Group 2346 Palmer Ct Reno NV 89502-9746

SCHWEIKER, MAXINE AYNES, magagine editor; b. Des Moines, Nov. 7, 1915; d. Charles William and Bertha Abigail (Davidson) Aynes; m. J. Herman Schweiker, Oct. 7, 1938 (dec. Oct. 1989); children: James, Thomas, Daniel, Susan Schweiker Stavros. Student, Drake U., 1934-37. Supr. secs. Iowa Ho. of Reps., Des Moines, 1960-70; contbg. editor Home Mags., 1980-85; regional editor Better Homes & Gardens, also others Meredith Publs., Des Moines, 1975-94; bd. dirs. China Mist, Scottsdale, Ariz., Thornwood Products, Scottsdale; former field editor S.W. Sampler, Spirit of the West. Contbr. articles to Phoenix Home & Garden. Bd. dirs. Parents Anonymous, Des Moines, 1980-85, Convalescent Home for Children, Des Moines, 1983-87, World Affairs Coun., Scottsdale, 1992-93. Mem. Am. Soc. Interior Designers (press affiliate), Nat. League Am. Pen Women (sec.), PEO (past pres., sec.), Phoenix Writers Club (pres. 1992-94). Home: 7710 E Thornwood Dr Scottsdale AZ 85251-1639

SCHWEITZER, RAYMOND D., city manager, author; b. Dodge City, Kans., Jan. 16, 1936; s. Howard R. and Mary Mildred (Montgomery) S.; m. Jean Barker, May 30, 1966. AA, Dodge City Jr. Coll., 1961; AB in Polit. Sci., Ft. Hays (Kans.) State U., 1963; postgrad., Kans. U., 1964-66. Asst. city mgr. City of Oak Ridge, Tenn., 1965-68; city mgr. City of Alcoa, Tenn., 1968-71, City of Prescott, Ariz., 1971-72; adminstr. City of Morristown, Tenn., 1972-76; city mgr. City of North Las Vegas, Nev., 1976-82; dep./city adminstr. City of San Bernardino, Calif., 1982-88; freelance author, 1988-89; city mgr. City of Banning, Calif., 1989—. Author: (novel) The Elder's Avenger, 1989, Tattletale Heart, 1990, The Elder's Avenger Part II, 1991. Mem. Internat. City Mgrs. Assn., Banning C. of C. (bd. dirs. 1989-92), Kiwanis. Home: 1319 Fairway Oaks Ave Banning CA 92220-6417

SCHWERIN, KARL HENRY, anthropology educator, researcher; b. Bertha, Minn., Feb. 21, 1936; s. Henry William and Audrey Merle (Jahn) S.; m. Judith Drewanne Altermatt, Sept. 1, 1958 (div. May 1975); children: Karl Frederic, Marguerite DelValle; m. Partha Louise Hake Buell, Jan. 25, 1979; stepchildren: Tamara, Brent, Taryn. BA, U. Calif., Berkeley, 1958; PhD, UCLA, 1965. Instr. Los Angeles State Coll., 1963; asst. prof. anthropology U. N.Mex., Albuquerque, 1963-68, assoc. prof., 1968-72, prof., 1972—, asst. chmn. dept. anthropology, 1983-85, chmn. dept. anthropology, 1987-93; prof. invitado Inst. Venezolano de Investigaciones Cientificas, Caracas, 1979. Author: Oil and Steel Processes of Karinya Culture Change, 1966, Antropologia Social, 1969, Winds Across the Atlantic, 1970; editor: Food Energy in Tropical Ecosystems, 1985; contbr. articles to profl. jours. V.p. Parents without Ptnr., Albuquerque, 1976-77. Grantee Cordell Hull Found., Venezuela, 1961-62, N.Y. Zool. Soc., Honduras, 1981; Fulbright scholar Cañar, Ecuador, 1969-70, Paris, 1986. Fellow Am. Anthrop. Assn.; mem. Am. Ethnol. Soc., Am. Soc. Ethnohistory (pres. 1975), Southwestern Anthropol. Assn. (co-editor Southwestern Jour. Anthropology 1972-75), N.Mex. Cactus and Succulent Soc. (v.p. 1970-71), Maxwell Mus. Assn. (bd. dirs. 1984-85), Internat. Congress of Americanists (35th-40th, 43d, 46th, 48th), Sigma Xi (chpt. pres. 1980-81). Office: U NMex Dept Anthropology Albuquerque NM 87131

SCHWICHTENBERG, DARYL ROBERT, drilling engineer; b. nr. Tulare, S.D., Nov. 8, 1929; s. Robert Carl and Lillian Rose (Hardie) S.; m. Helen M. Spencer, 1955 (div. Jan. 1971); children: Helayne, Randall, Hyalyn, Halcyon, Rustan; m. Helen Elizabeth Doehring, Nov. 11, 1971 (div. May 1982); 1 child, Suzanne. Student, U. Wyo., 1954-55; BSME, S.D. Sch. Mines and Tech., 1957; postgrad., Alexander Hamilton Inst., N.Y.C., 1962-63. Lic. pilot, rated AMEL. Office engr. Ingersoll-Rand Co., Mpls., 1957-58; sub br. mgr. Ingersoll-Rand Co., Duluth, Minn., 1959-60; product engr. Ingersoll-Rand Co., N.Y.C., 1960-63, devel. engr., 1964; sales mgr. Ingersoll-Rand Co., Phillipsburg, N.J., 1965; pres., founder Daryl Drilling Co., Inc., Flagstaff, Ariz., 1965-82; pres. Silent Rose Mining Co., Fallon, Nev., 1982-85; sr. design engr. Nev. Test Site Fenix & Scisson, 1985-90; prin. project engr. Raytheon Svcs. Nev., 1990-95; project mgr. Raytheon Svcs. Nev., Nev. Test Site, 1995—; co-owner, mgr. Dead Shot Ranch, Bondurant, Wyo., 1977-82. Inventor electronic subtitling for opera patrons. 1st lt. U.S. Army, 1950-54, Korea. Decorated Bronze Star. Mem. ASME, NRA, VFW, Inst. Shaft Drilling Tech. (speaker, instr. 1986—), Am. Legion, Mensa. Republican. Office: Raytheon Svcs Nev PO Box 328 Mercury NV 89023-0328

SCHWIER, EDWARD GEORGE, naval officer; b. Cin., Oct. 3, 1947; s. George Walter and Alma Catherine (Lubbe) S.; m. Donna Marie Hesselbrook, June 7, 1969 (div.); children: Michael Edward, Andrew George, Melissa Marie; m. Lois Jean Faulkner, Dec. 24, 1994; stepchildren: Lisa Marie Arnold, Tricia Diane Arnold. BS in Aeronautical Engring., Naval Academy, 1969; MS in Weapons Systems Tech., Naval Postgrad. Sch., 1980. Commd. ensign USN, 1969, advanced through grades to capt., 1989; main propulsion asst. USS Eugene A. Greene, 1970-72; engr. officer USS Reasoner, 1973-75; staff commdr. Destroyer Squadron 15 USN, Yokosuka, Japan, 1975-78; exec. officer USS Estocin, 1980-82; flag sec. and aide Commander Naval Surface Force Atlantic Fleet, 1982-84; dir. ops. staff of Commander Joint Task Force Middle East, 1989-90; from comptroller to comptroller, bus. officer Naval Shipyard, Norfolk & Charleston, 1990-93; commanding officer Naval Welfare Assessment Divsn., Corona, Calif., 1993—. Mem. KC, Am. Soc. Military Comptrollers (pres. 1992-93. Comptroller of Yr. 1993), Am. Soc. Naval Engrs., Toastmasters, Mensa. Roman Catholic. Home: 2115 Highpointe Dr Apt 212 Corona CA 91719-5961 Office: Naval Warfare Assessment Divsn PO Box 5000 Corona CA 91718-5000

SCHWINDEN, TED, former governor of Montana; b. Wolf Point, Mont., Aug. 31, 1925; s. Michael James and Mary (Preble) S.; m. B. Jean Christianson, Dec. 21, 1946; children: Mike, Chrys, Dore. Student, Mont. Sch. Mines, 1946-47; B.A., U. Mont., 1949, M.A., 1950; postgrad., U. Minn., 1950-54. Owner grain farm Roosevelt County, Mont., 1954—; land commr. State of Mont., 1969-76, lt. gov., 1977-80, gov., 1981-89; disting. prof. pub. affairs, 1989—; mem. U.S. Wheat Trade Mission to Asia, 1968; dir. Stillwater Mining Co. Chmn. Mont. Bicentennial Adv. Council, 1973-76; mem. Mont. Ho. of Reps., 1959, 61, Legis. Council, 1959-61, Wolf Point Sch. Bd., 1966-69, Pub. Employees Retirement System Bd., 1969-74. Served with inf. AUS, 1943-46. Decorated Combat Inf. badge. Mem. Mont. Grain Growers (pres. 1965-67), Western Wheat Assos. (dir.). Democrat. Lutheran. Clubs: Masons, Elks. Home: 1335 Highland St Helena MT 59601-5242

SCHWINKENDORF, KEVIN NEIL, nuclear engineer; b. Newberg, Oreg., Mar. 11, 1959; s. Waldemar Adolf and Hattie Bertha (Baumgarten) S. BS, Oreg. State U., 1981, MS, 1983; postgrad., U. Wash. Reg. profl. engr., Wash. Advanced engr. UNC Nuclear Industries, Richland, Wash., 1983-84, engr., 1986-87; sr. engr. Westinghouse Hanford Co., Richland, 1987—; v.p. numerical methods, Analyst Devel. Corp., Scappoose, Oreg., 1990—. Designer: (ballistics software) PC-Bullet-ADCs, 1990 (Best Paper award 1992); author tech. publ. in field. Participant March of Dimes Walk-a-Thon, Richland, 1989, 90. Mem. Am. Nuclear Soc., NSPE, NRA, Soc. Computer Simulation, Safari Club Internat., Tau Beta Pi. Republican. Home: 1121 Pine St Richland WA 99352-2135 Office: Nuc Analysis and Characterization Devel Dept WHC PO Box 1970 MSIN HO-38 Richland WA 99352

SCHWORTZ, BARRIE MARSHALL, video/film producer; b. Pitts., Sept. 12, 1946; s. Nathan Schwortz and FLorence T. (Rosenfeld) Black; m. Erin J. Gallant, Sept. 11, 1971 (div.); 1 child, David Henry. BA, Brooks Inst., Santa Barbara, 1971. Owner Barrie Schwortz Studios, Santa Barbara, 1971-85; pres., founder Ednl. Video, Inc., Santa Barbara, 1978-88; owner Barrie Schwortz Prodns., L.A., 1985—; imaging cons. Cedars-Sinai Med. Ctr., L.A., 1990—; documenting photographer Shroud of Turin Rsch. Project, 1978-88; faculty mem. Brooks Inst. Photography, Santa Barbara, 1975-85. Producer: (videotape program) Shroud of Turin Symposium, 1984; writer, producer: (videotape program) The Complete Birth, 1985, New Tools for an Ageold Task, 1989; dir.: Money, History in Your Hands, 1995. With USN, 1965-69. Recipient Merit awards Art Direction Mag., 1979, 81, 84, San Francisco Art Dirs., 1984, 87, N.Y. Art Dirs. Club, 1982, 87, 88. Mem. Santa Barbara Video Assn. (pres., founder 1984). Jewish. Home and Office: Barrie Schwortz Prodns 3003 Glendale Blvd Los Angeles CA 90039-1803

SCHWYN, CHARLES EDWARD, accountant; b. Muncie, Ind., Oct. 12, 1932; s. John and Lela Mae (Oliver) S.; m. Mary Helen Nickey, May 25, 1952 (dec.); children: Douglas, Craig, Beth; m. Madelyn Steinmetz. BS, Ball State U., 1957. CPA, Calif., D.C. With Haskins, Sells & Orlando, Chgo., Orlando, Fla., 1958-67; mgr. Deloitte, Haskins & Sells, Milan, Italy, 1967-70, San Francisco, 1970-80; with Deloitte, Haskins & Sells (now Deloitte & Touche), Oakland, Calif., ptnr. in charge, 1980-92, ret., 1992. Bd. dirs. Jr. Ctr. Art and Sci., 1982-89, pres., 1987-88; bd. dirs., trustee Oakland Symphony, 1982-86, 89-91; bd. dirs. Oakland Met. YMCA, 1984-89, Oakland Police Activities League, 1981-91, Joe Morgan Youth Found., 1982-91, Summit Med. Ctr., 1989-94; bd. dirs. Marcus A. Foster Ednl. Inst., 1986-95, pres., 1991-93; mem. adv. bd. Festival of Lake, 1984-89, U. Oakland Met. Forum, 1992—; co-chmn. Commn. for Positive Change in Oakland Pub. Schs.; mem. campaign cabinet United Way Bay Area, 1989; bd. regents Samuel Merritt Coll., 1994—. With USN, 1952-56. Recipient Cert. Recognition Calif. Legis. Assembly, 1988, Ctr. for Ind. Living award, Oakland Bus. Arts award for outstanding bus. leader Oakland C. of C., 1992; date of job retirement honored in his name by Oakland mayor. Mem. AICPA (coun. 1987-90), Oakland C. of C. (chmn. bd. dirs. 1987-88, exec. com. 1982-89), Calif. Soc. CPAs (bd. dirs. 1979-81, 83-84, 85-87, pres. San Francisco chpt. 1983-84), Nat. Assn. Accts. (pres. Fla. chpt. 1967), Claremont Country Club (treas., bd. dirs. 1989—), Lakeview Club (bd. govs. 1987-92), Oakland 100 Club (pres. 1994), Rotary (bd. dirs. Oakland club 1986-88, 91-92, treas. 1984-86, pres. 1991-92). Office: Deloitte & Touche 2101 Webster St Fl 20 Oakland CA 94612-3027

SCIAME, DONALD RICHARD, computer systems analyst, dentist, magician, locksmith; b. Bklyn., Sept. 10, 1945; s. Mario and Ruth Marie (Kozell) S.; m. Kathy Ann Thamann, Mar. 17, 1987. AB, Rutgers U., 1967; DMD, N.J. Coll. Medicine & Dentistry, 1971; MAPA, U. N.Mex., 1984; cert. locksmith, electronic security, NRI Schs., 1988. Dep. chief svc. unit dental program USPHS Indian Hosp., Whiteriver, Ariz., 1971-73; chief svc. unit dental program USPHS Indian Hosp., Sacaton, Ariz., 1973-76, Santa Fe, 1976-88; systems analyst USPHS Area Office, Albuquerque, 1988-90; dir. div. info. mgmt. svcs. USPHS-IHS Area Office, Albuquerque, 1990—. Contbr. articles to profl. jours. Mem. IHS Dental Profl. Specialty Group, IHS Dental Computer Users Group, ADA, Internat. Coll. Dentists, Psi Omega Dental Fraternity, N.J. Dental Sch. Alumni Assn., USPHS Commn. Officers Assn., Albuquerque Area Dental Soc. Indian Health Svcs., Mumps User's Group, Soc. Am. Magicians. Home: 1914 Conejo Dr Santa Fe NM 87505-6108 Office: IHS Area Office 505 Marquette Ave NW Ste 1506 Albuquerque NM 87102-2163

SCIARONI, LINDA GILLINGHAM, middle school educator; b. Torrance, Calif., Feb. 15, 1962; d. Robert Edward and Dorathea Ellenor (Dixon) Gillingham; m. Daniel Martin Sciaroni, Feb. 14, 1987. BA, Whitworth Coll., Spokane, Wash., 1983; MA in Spl. Edn.: Gifted, Calif. State U., L.A., 1995. Tchr. Belvedere Jr. High Sch. L.A. Unified Sch. Dist., 1984—, chair dept. sci., 1992—, gifted coord., 1986—, Title IX coord., 1993—. Sci-Mat fellow Coun. Basic Edn., 1993, Eleanor Roosevelt fellow AAUW, 1990, May V. Seagoe scholar Calif. Assn. for Gifted, 1993. Mem. AAUW, AAAS, Nat. Sci. Tchr. Assn., Calif. Sci. Tchr. Assn., Greater L.A. Sci. Tchrs. Assn., Calif. Assn. for the Gifted, Phi Delta Kappa.

SCIOTTO, COSIMO GINO, pathologist, hematopathologist; b. Veszprem, Hungary, Aug. 2, 1945; came to U.S., 1956; s. Vincent and Camilla (Udvary) S.; m. Susan E. Skinner, July 20, 1968; children: Carina Marie Sciotto-Kelly, Elisabeth Ann. BS, Case Inst. Tech., Cleve., 1968; MS, Cleve. State U., 1969; PhD, Case Western Res. U., 1976, MD, 1976. Dir. hematology Denver VA Hosp., 1979-81; staff pathologist Penrose Hosp., Colorado Springs, Colo., 1981—, dir. pathology, 1993—. Trustee Colo. Assn. for Continuing Med. Lab. Edn., Denver, 1981-92. Fellow Coll. Am. Pathologists, Hematopathology Soc., Am. Assn. Clin. Chemists; mem. Colo. Soc. Clin. Pathologists (pres. 1986), El Paso Med. Soc., Colo. Med. Soc. Office: Penrose Hosp Dept Pathology 2215 N Cascade Ave Colorado Springs CO 80907-6799

SCLAR, DAVID ALEXANDER, medical policy educator; b. Columbus, Ohio, Dec. 31, 1954. B Pharmacy cum laude, Wash. State U., 1985; PhD in Pharmacy and Bus. Adminstrn., U. S.C., 1988. Assoc. prof. health policy and adminstrn./Ingelheim Scholar Wash. State U. Coll. Pharmacy; advisor U.K. Dept. Health and Social Svcs., China Bur. of Drugs and Biologicals, U.S. Senate Select Com. on Aging; mem. FDA Rev. Com. on pharm. mktg. practice. Contbr. articles to profl. jours.; editoriabl bd.: Hospital Formulary. Grantee in field. Mem. Am. Assn. Pharm. Scientists, Am. Pharm. Assn., Am. Soc. Hosp. Pharmacists, Am. Pub. Health Assn., Am. Assn. Colls. of Pharmacy, Assn. Health Svcs. Rsch. Home: SE 1005 Spring St Pullman WA 99163 Office: Coll of Pharmacy Wash State Univ Pullman WA 99164

SCOFIELD, LARRY ALLAN, civil engineer; b. Niskyuna, N.Y., Mar. 23, 1952; s. Jack Dewayne and Edythe Mae (Van Wie) S. BSE, Ariz. State U., 1975, MSE, 1981. Registered profl. engr., Ariz. Engr.-in-tng. Ariz. Dept. of Transp., Phoenix, 1976-78, constrn. project engr., 1978-80, pavement design engr., 1980-81, resident engr., 1981-82, geologic and found. invest. engr., 1982-84, transp. engr. supr., 1984-94, mgr. transp. rsch., 1994—; mem. panel Nat. Coop. Hwy. Rsch. Program, Washington, 1986—; mem. Transp. Rsch. Bd. Com., Washington, 1990—; mem. expert task group Strategic Hwy. Rsch. Program, Washington, 1989—; mem. adv. panel Fed. Hwy. Adminstrn., Washington, 1986—. Contbr. articles to profl. jours. Mem. ASCE, ASTM, Asphalt Paving Technologists. Republican. Baptist. Home: 807 W Keating Ave Mesa AZ 85210-7611

SCOLES, EUGENE FRANCIS, legal educator, lawyer; b. Shelby, Iowa, June 12, 1921; s. Sam and Nola E. (Leslie) S.; m. R. Helen Glawson, Sept. 6, 1942; children—Kathleen Elizabeth, Janene Helen. A.B., U. Iowa, 1943, J.D., 1945; LL.M., Harvard U., 1949; J.S.D., Columbia U., 1955. Bar: Iowa 1945, Ill. 1946. Assoc. Seyfarth-Shaw & Fairweather, Chgo., 1945-46; asst. prof. law Northeastern U., 1946-48, assoc. prof., 1948-49; assoc. prof. U. Fla., 1949-51, prof., 1951-56; prof. U. Ill., Champaign, 1958-68; Max Rowe prof. law U. Ill., 1982-89, prof. emeritus, 1989—; vis. prof. McGeorge Law Sch. U. Pacific, Sacramento, 1989-92; prof. U. Oreg., 1968-82, dean Sch. Law, 1968-74, disting. prof. emeritus, 1982—; vis. prof. Khartoum U., Sudan, 1964-65. Author: (with H.F. Goodrich) Conflict of Laws, 4th edit., 1964, (with R.J. Weintraub) Cases and Materials on Conflict of Laws, 2d edit., 1972, (with E.C. Halbach, Jr.) Problems and Materials on Decedents' Estates and Trusts, 5th edit., 1993, Problems and Materials on Future Interests, 1977, (with P. Hay) Conflict of Laws, 2d edit., 1992; contbr. articles to profl. jours.; notes and legislation editor Iowa Law Rev., 1945; reporter Uniform Probate Code Project, 1966-70; mem. joint editorial bd. Uniform Probate Code, 1972—. Mem. ABA, Soc. Pub. Tchrs. Law, Am. Law Inst., Ill. Bar Assn., Assn. Am. Law Schs. (pres. 1978), Order of Coif. Home: 1931 Kimberly Dr Eugene OR 97405-5849 Office: U Oreg Sch of Law 11th And Kincaid Eugene OR 97403

SCORA, RAINER WALTER, botanist; b. Mokre, Silesia, Poland, Dec. 5, 1928; came to U.S., 1951; s. Paul Wendelin and Helene (Nester) S.; m. Christa Maria Fiala, June 24, 1971; children: George Alexander, Katharina Monarda, Peter Evan. BS, DePaul U., 1955; MS, U. Mich., 1958, PhD, 1964. From asst. prof. to prof. botany U. Calif., Riverside, 1964—. Author over 100 sci. publs. With U.S. Army, 2d Div., Signal Corps, 1955-57. Alfred P. Sloan fellow, 1959; recipient Cooley award Am. Inst. Biological Scis., 1968. Mem. Am. Inst. Biol. Scis., Botanical Soc. Am., Phytochem. Soc. N.Am., Internat. Assn. Plant Taxonomists, Internat. Orgn. Plant Biosystematists, Gamma Sigma Delta, Sigma Xi. Republican. Roman Catholic. Office: Univ Calif Dept Botany Plant Scis Riverside CA 92521

SCORSINE, JOHN MAGNUS, lawyer; b. Rochester, N.Y., Dec. 3, 1957; s. Frank and Karin (Frennby) S.; m. Susan Nauss, May 31, 1980 (div.); m. Theresa A. Burke, Dec. 17, 1988; 1 child, Jennifer E. BS, Rochester Inst. Tech., 1980; JD, U. Wyo., 1984. Bar: Wyo. 1984, U.S. Dist. Ct. Wyo. 1984, U.S. Ct. Appeals (10th cir.) 1989, U.S. Army Ct. Criminal Appeals 1995. Part-time deputy sheriff Monroe County (N.Y.), 1978-80; police officer Casper (Wyo.) Police Dept., 1980-81; intern U.S. Atty. Office, Cheyenne, Wyo., 1983-84; sole practice Rock Springs, Wyo., 1984-85; ptnr. Scorsine and Flynn, Rock Springs, 1986; prin. Scorsine Law Office, Rock Springs, 1986—; commr. Dist. and County Court, 1986—; ptnr. Sunset Advt., 1987-89; chmn. bd. dirs. Youth Home Inc., Rock Springs, 1987-88; treas. Sweetwater County Community Corrections Bd., 1990—; mem. Nat. Ski Patrol, 1976—. Leader Medicine Bow Ski Patrol, Laramie, Wyo., 1983; legal advisor Rocky Mountain div. Nat. Ski Patrol, 1984; asst. patrol leader White Pine Ski Area, Pinedale, Wyo., 1986; avalanche advisor Jackson Hole Snow King Ski Patrol, 1987—, avalanche instr. 1993—; sect. chief Teton sect. Nat. Ski Patrol, 1991-94; mem. Sweetwater County Search and Rescue, 1989—, tng. officer, 1993—; mem. Sweetwater County Emergency Dive Team, 1990—, mem. Sweetwater County Fire Dept., 1992-94, Reliance Vol. Fire Dept., 1994—; mem. Am. N. Peary Land Expdn., 1989; scoutmaster Boy Scouts Am., 1987-93; pres. Sweetwater County Vol. Fire Assn., 1993-94. Capt. JAG, USAR, 1991—. Recipient Yellow Merit star Nat. Ski Patrol, 1993, Fritch Volunteerism award, 1993. Mem. ABA, Wyo. State Bar, Wyo. Trial Lawyers Assn., Assn. Am. Trial Lawyers, Rock Springs C. of C., Res. Officers Assn. (nat. councilman 1993—, state pres. 1994). Democrat. Lutheran. Lodge: Rotary. Home: 519 Wasatch Cir Rock Springs WY 82901-4586 Office: Scorsine Law Office 2706 Ankeny Way Rock Springs WY 82901-5649

SCOTT, CHARLES KENNARD, state senator, cattle rancher; b. Oreg., Aug. 19, 1945; s. Oliver Kennard and Deborah Ann (Hubbard) S.; m. Elaine Fenton, Dec. 20, 1975; children—Daniel, Abigail. A.B., Harvard Coll., 1967; M.B.A., Harvard U., 1969. Analyst, HEW and EPA, 1969-74; v.p., mgr. Bates Creek Cattle Co., Casper, Wyo., 1974—; mem. Wyo. Ho. of Reps., 1979-82; mem. Wyo. Senate, 1982—; chmn. Labor, Health and Social Svc. Com.

SCOTT, DAVID IRVIN, minister; b. Yakima, Wash., Dec. 5, 1947; s. Jack Phillip and Betty Lucille (Paronto) S.; m. Jill Louise Baker, June 23, 1982 (div. May 1991). AA, Monterey Peninsula Coll., Calif., 1975. Accredited resident mgr., Inst. Real Estate Mgmt., 1987. Courier Gallery Hawaii, Inc., Honolulu, 1981; acting resident mgr. Fairway Gardens, Honolulu, 1981;

resident mgr. Waimalu Park, Honolulu, 1981-83, Waikiki Skyliner, Honolulu, 1983-84, Bishop Gardens, Honolulu, 1985-86, Plaza Landmark, Honolulu, 1986-88, Westlake Apts., Honolulu, 1988, Fairway Gardens, Honolulu, 1988—; condo mgmt. cons.; pres. Inner Man Ministries. Mem. Honolulu Bd. Realtors, Inst. Real Estate Mgmt., Alpha Gamma Sigma. Office: Inner Man Ministries 1290D Maunakea St # 201 Honolulu HI 96817-4119

SCOTT, DONALD MICHAEL, educational association administrator, educator; b. Los Angeles, Sept. 26, 1943; s. Bernard Hendry and Barbara (Lannin) S.; m. Patricia Ilene Pancoast, Oct. 24, 1964 (div. June 1971); children: William Bernard, Kenneth George. BA, San Francisco State U., 1965, MA, 1986. Cert. tchr. Calif. Tchr. Mercy High Sch., San Francisco, 1968-71; park ranger Calif. State Park System, Half Moon Bay, 1968-77; tchr. adult div. Jefferson Union High Sch. Dist., Daly City, Calif., 1973-87; dir. NASA-NPS Project Wider Focus, Daly City, 1983-90; dir. Geo.S. Spl. Projects Wider Focus, San Francisco, 1990—; also bd. dirs. Wider Focus, Daly City; nat. park ranger/naturalist Grant-Kohrs Ranch Nat. Hist. Site, Deer Lodge, Mont., 1987-88; nat. park ranger pub. affairs fire team Yellowstone Nat. Park, 1988; nat. park ranger Golden Gate Recreation Area, 1988-92; rsch. subject NASA, Mountain View, Calif., 1986-90; guest artist Yosemite (Calif.) Nat. Park, 1986; nat. park ranger Golden Gate Nat. Recreation Area, Nat. Park Svc., San Francisco, 1986, nat. park svc. history cons. to Bay Dist., 1988-94; adj. asst. prof. Skyline Coll., 1989-94, Coll. San Mateo, 1992-94; aerospace edn. specialist NASA/OSU/AESP, 1994—. Contbr. articles, photographs to profl. jours., mags. Pres. Youth for Kennedy, Lafayette, calif., 1960; panelist Community Bds. of San Francisco, 1978-87; city chair Yes on A com., So. San Francisco, San Mateo County, Calif., 1986; active CONTACT Orgn., 1991—, bd. dirs. 1995—. Mem. Yosemite Assn. (life), Wider Focus, Friends of George R. Stewart, Nat. Sci. Tchrs. Assn., Nat. Coun. of Tchrs. of Math., Internat. Tech. Edn. Assn., Smithsonian Air and Space Planetary Soc. (charter mem.). Democrat. Home and Office: MST12A NASA Ames Rsch Ctr Moffett Field CA 94035-1000

SCOTT, G. JUDSON, JR., lawyer; b. Phila., Nov. 16, 1945; s. Gerald Judson and Jean Louise (Evans) S.; m. Ildiko Kalman, Mar. 21, 1971; children: Nathan Emory, Lauren Jean. AA, Foothill Jr. Coll., Los Altos, Calif., 1965; BA, U. Calif.-Santa Barbara, 1968; JD cum laude, U. Santa Clara, 1975. Bar: Calif. 1975, U.S. Dist. Ct. (no. dist.) Calif. 1975, U.S. Ct. Appeals (9th cir.) 1975, U.S. Supreme Ct. 1981. Assoc. Feldman, Waldman & Kline, San Francisco, 1975-76, Law Offices John Wynne Herron, San Francisco, 1976-80; of counsel firm Haines & Walker, Livermore, Calif., 1980; ptnr. Haines Walker & Scott, Livermore, 1980-84; officer, dir., shareholder firm Smith, Etnire, Polson and Scott, Pleasanton, Calif., 1984-88; pvt. practice, 1988—; judge pro tem Livermore-Pleasanton Mcpl. Ct., 1981—; lectr. Calif. Continuing Edn. of Bar. Contbg. author: Attorneys' Guide to Restitution, 1976; editor: The Bottom Line, 1989-91. Pres. Walnut Creek Open Space Found., Calif., 1981-83. Capt. USNR, 1968—. Mem. Assn. Trial Lawyers Am. (sustaining), Consumer Attys. Calif., Ea. Alameda County Bar Assn. (v.p. 1981-82), Calif. State Bar (standing com. on lawyer referral svcs. 1985-88, exec. com. law practice mgmt. sect. 1988-93, chair-elect 1991-92, chair 1992-93), Alameda County Bar Assn. (chmn. law office econs. com. 1986-87), Alameda-Contra Costa County Trial Lawyers Assn., Livermore C. of C. (past chmn. growth study 1983), Pleasanton C. of C. Republican. Episcopalian. Office: Ste 125 6140 Stoneridge Mall Rd Pleasanton CA 94588-3232

SCOTT, GEORGE LARKHAM, IV, architect; b. Bloomington, Ill., Aug. 11, 1947; s. George Larkham III and Marilyn Louise (Bouseman) S.; m. Patricia Jean Gregurich, Aug. 1, 1969; 1 child, Matthew Larkham. B in Archtl. Studies, Wash. State U., 1973, BArch, 1974. Dir. facilities planning County of Spokane, Wash., 1978-79; project architect Skidmore, Owings & Merrill, Portland, Oreg., 1981-82; owner George L. Scott, Architect and Planner, Portland, Oreg., 1982—. Prin. works include masterplan Rancho Seco Nuclear Power Sta., Sacramento, Calif., masterplan Boeing Comml. Airplane Co., Portland, high tech. clean room facilities for nat. and internat. clients, helistop atop 42 story U.S. Bancorp Tower, U.S. Bancorp Office Bldg., Portland, Oreg., on-base family housing complex Trident Submarine Base, Bangor, Wash., interior archtl. design and space plan of Bonneville Power Adminstrn. 550,000 S.F. hdqrs. bldg., Portland; designer 2 130 foot ocean going motor yachts; lectr., contbr. articles on clean room tech. to profl. jours. Chmn. Task Force on Community Devel., Spokane, 1977; active Committee to Elect Gov. Ray, Wash., 1977-78, City of Spokane Planning Commn., 1977-78. Home and Office: 11445 SW Lanewood St Portland OR 97225-5301

SCOTT, GLORIA, publishing marketing consultant; b. N.Y.C., May 22, 1927; d. Matthew and Ethel Lindenberg; m. Sidney Steinberg, Mar. 2, 1947 (dec. 1969); children: Marcy Lea Chessler, Cindy Ann Sachs; m. John Lenard Scott, Dec. 1, 1974 (div. May 1991). BBA, CCNY, 1947; MEd, Temple U., 1963. Adminstr. Rahmani Trading Corp., N.Y.C., 1947-50; acct. Pola Stout Corp., Phila., 1950-54; adminstr. Bristol Twp. Police Dept., Pa., 1954-58; acct. Odora Corp., N.Y.C., 1958-59, Middletown Twp., Neshaminy, Pa., 1959-60; tchr., chmn. social studies dept. Pennsbury Schs., Falls Twp., Pa., 1960-70; mktg. dir., dir. profit ctr. Bantam Books, N.Y.C., 1970-77; exec. officer Infocom Broadcast Svc., Hawley, Pa., 1977-89; ind. mktg. cons. Bantam, Doubleday, Dell Publishing Group, Random House, Assn. Am. Pubs., World Book Inc., N.Y.C., 1989—; ptnr. Scott/Satz Group, Walnut Creek, Calif., 1991—, LetterLink, Walnut Creek, Calif., 1992—; mem. negotiating team Pa. Tchrs. Assn., 1963-67. Contbr. articles to profl. jours. Active Pa. Bd. Edn. Mem. AAUW, LWV, Nat. Women's Polit. Caucus, Great Books Club (sec. 1986—), Walnut Creek C. of C., Rotary Internat. Avocations: running, aerobics, reading. Home and Office: 539 Monarch Ridge Dr Walnut Creek CA 94596-2955

SCOTT, GREGORY KELLAM, state supreme court justice; b. San Francisco, July 30, 1943; s. Robert and Althea Delores Scott; m. Carolyn Weatherly, Apr. 10, 1971; children: Joshua Weatherly, Elijah Kellam. BS in Environ. Sci., Rutgers U., 1970, EdM in Urban Studies, 1971; JD cum laude, Ind. U., Indpls., 1977. Asst. dean resident instrn. Cook Coll. Rutgers U., 1972-75; trial atty. U.S. SEC, Denver, 1977-79; gen. counsel Blinder, Robinson & Co., Inc., Denver, 1979-80; asst. prof. coll. law U. Denver, 1980-85, assoc. prof., 1985-93, assoc. prof. emeritus, 1993—, chair bus. planning program, 1986-89, 92-93; justice Colo. Supreme Ct., Denver, 1993—; of counsel Smith & Radford, Indpls., 1987-92; v.p., gen. counsel Comml. Energies, Inc., 1990-91; presenter in field. Author: (with others) Structuring Mergers and Acquisitions in Colorado, 1985, Airport Law and Regulation, 1991, Racism and Underclass in America, 1991; contbr. articles to profl. jours. Mem. ABA, Nat. Bar Assn., Nat. Assn. Securities Dealers, Inc., Nat. Arbitration Panel (arbitrator), Colo. Bar Found., Sam Cary Bar Assn., Am. Inn Ct. (founding mem. Judge Alfred A. Arraj inn).

SCOTT, GWENDOLYN HARRISON, educator, consultant; b. Sheridan, Wyo., Mar. 11, 1927; d. Leonard Elliott and Danora (Smith) Harrison; m. Harold R. Scott Sr., Jan. 22, 1951 (div. Apr. 15, 1978); children: Victoria Vitatoe, Claudia Hinds, Harold Roy Jr. BFA, U. Denver, 1948, MA, 1968. Cert. secondary tchr., Colo. Elem. tchr. Kansas City Pub. Schs., Kans., 1948-50; art tchr. Children's Mus., Denver, 1953-58; elem. tchr. Denver Pub. Schs., 1964-69; social sci. instr. Loretto Heights Coll., 1969-70; high sch. social sci. tchr. Denver Pub. Schs., 1970-86; free-lance lectr. Blacks in the west, 1986—; cons., facilitator Anti-Defamation League, Denver, 1989—; adj. instr. C.C. of Aurora (Colo.), 1990—. Author: (curriculum) Comparative Study of Am. and Kenyan Women, 1985; co-author: A World of Difference Colorado Guide, 1989, Teaching the Film Schindler's List, 1994. Coun. bd. mem. Colo. Com. for Women's History, 1993—; bd. dirs. Denver Sister Cities Interant., 1992—; congl. dist. rep. Colo. Coun. for Libr. Devel., Colo. State Libr. Dept., 1990—, exec. bd. mem., 1992—. Fulbright scholar Washington, 1980, India, 1980, Kenya, 1985; women's studies grantee Southwest Inst. for Women's Rsch., Ariz. U., 1983-84; NEH grantee Kansas State U., 1977; recipient Altera M. Bryant award Women United the World, Denver, 1992. Mem. Nat. League Am. Pen Women (treas. Denver br. 1989—, svc. award 1994), Colo. Coun. for Social Studies (urban reg. dir. 1982-84, svc. award 1984), Black Educator United (outstanding sec. tchr. award 1977), Delta Kappa Gamma (v.p. 1988-92, rose award 1994). Democrat. Home: 6632 E Asbury Ave Denver CO 80224-2314

SCOTT, HOWARD WINFIELD, JR., temporary help services company executive; b. Greenwich, Conn., Feb. 24, 1935; s. Howard Winfield and Janet (Lewis) S.; B.S., Northwestern U., 1957; m. Joan Ann MacDonald, Aug. 12, 1961; children: Howard Winfield III, Thomas MacDonald, Ann Elizabeth. With R.H. Donnelly Corp., Chgo., 1958-59; sales rep. Masonite Corp., Chgo. also Madison, Wis., 1959-61; sales rep. Manpower Inc., Chgo., 1961-63, br. mgr., Kansas City, Mo., 1963-65, area mgr., Mo. and Kans., 1964-65, regional mgr. Salespower div., Phila., 1965-66; asst. advt. mgr. soups Campbell Soup Co., Camden, N.J., 1966-68; pres. PARTIME, Inc., Paoli, Pa., 1968-74; dir. marketing Kelly Services Inc., Southfield, Mich., 1974-78; pres. CDI Temporary Services, Inc., 1978-91; pres. Dunhill Pers. System, Inc., Woodbury, N.Y., 1991-94; v.p. S.O.S. Temporary Svcs., Salt Lake City, 1994; pres. S.O.S. Staffing Svcs., Salt Lake City, 1995—. Trustee Internat. House Phila, 1995—. Served with AUS, 1957-58. Mem. Nat. Assn. Temporary Services (sec. 1970-71, pres. 1971-73, bd. dirs. 1982-91), Kappa Sigma. Republican. Home: 4030 Saddleback Rd Park City UT 84060-4809 also: 1204 Annapolis Sea Colony E Bethany Beach DE 19930 Office: SOS Staffing Svcs 1415 S Main Salt Lake City UT 84115

SCOTT, J. BRIAN, sales executive; b. Chgo., Dec. 12, 1963; s. Joe and Marilyn (Fant) S.; m. Sandra L. McGinnis, Sept. 5, 1987. BS in Engring., U. Ill., 1985; MBA, City U., Bellevue, Wash., 1993. Applications engr. Grasso, Inc., Evansville, Ind., 1985; sales rep. Grasso, Inc., Grand Rapids, Mich., 1985; applications engr. FMC Corp., Hoopeston, Ill., 1987-89; dist. sales mgr. FMC Corp., Columbus, Wis., 1989-90; area sales mgr. FMC Corp., Vancouver, Wash., 1990-93. Mem. Midwest Food Processors, Assn. Allied Industries (exec. treas. 1990), N.W. Food Processors Assn.

SCOTT, JACQUELINE DELMAR PARKER, educational association administrator, business administrator, consultant, fundraiser; b. L.A., May 18, 1947; d. Thomas Aubrey and Daisy Beatrice (Singleton) Parker (div.); children: Tres Mali, Olympia Ranee, Stephen Thomas. AA in Theatre Arts, L.A. City Coll., 1970; BA in Econs., Calif. State U., Dominquez Hills, Carson, 1973; MBA, Golden Gate U., 1979. Cert. parenting instr. Sales clk. Newberry's Dept. Store, L.A., 1963-65; long distance operator Pacific Telephone Co., L.A., 1965-66; PBX operator Sears, Roebuck & Co., L.A., 1966-68; retail clk. Otey's Grocery Store, Nashville, 1968-69; collector N.Am. Credit, L.A., 1970-71; office mgr. Dr. S. Edward Tucker, L.A., 1972-74; staff coord. sch. edn. dept. Calif. State U., 1973-74; bank auditor Security Pacific Bank, L.A., 1974-76, corp. loan asst., 1976-77; dist. credit analyst Crocker Nat. Bank, L.A., 1977-78, asst. v.p., 1978-80; capital planning adminstr. TRW, Inc., Redondo Beach, Calif., 1980-82, ops. bus. adminstr., 1982-84, lab. sr. bus. adminstr., 1984-86, project bus. mgr., 1986-87, div. sr. bus. adminstr., 1987-92; ptnr., co-author, co-facilitator, cons. Diversified Event Planners, Inc., L.A., 1990-93; asst. area devel. dir. United Negro Coll. Fund, L.A., 1993—. Co-founder career growth awareness com. TRW Employees Bootstrap, Redondo Beach, Calif., 1980, pres., 1983-84; role model Inglewood High Sch., TRW Youth Motivation Task Force, Redondo Beach, 1981-83, Crozier Jr. High Sch., 1981-83, Monroe Jr. High Sch., Redondo Beach, 1981-83, Frank D. Parent Career Day, TRW Affirmative Action Com., Redondo Beach, 1987, St. Bernard's Career Day, 1991; chairperson community involvement com., 1981, chairperson disaster com., 1989-90; chairperson gen. and local welfare com. TRW Employees Charitable Orgn., 1989-90, disaster com. chair, 1988-89, bd. dirs. 1987-89; pres. Mgmt. Effectiveness Program Alumnae, L.A., 1982-83, TRW Employees Bootstrap Program Alumnae, 1983-84; group leader Jack & Jill of Am., Inc., South L.A., 1980-81, parliamentarian, 1986-87, v.p., 1981-82, chpt. pres., 1984-86, regional dir., 1987-89, nat. program dir., 1992—, liaison to Young Black Scholars Program, 1986—; bd. dirs. Adolescent Pregnancy Child Watch, 1993—, Jack & Jill Am. Found., 1992—; L.A. mem. Nat. Black Child Devel. Inst., 1994—; vol. ARC, 1994—; parenting instr. Am. Red Cross, 1994—. Recipient commendation NAACP, 1985, United Negro Coll. Fund, 1986, United Way, 1988, Austistic Children's Telephon, 1980, Inglewood Sch. Dist., 1981, Pres. award Harbor Area Chpt. Links, Inc., 1985, Women of Achievement award City of L.A., Black Pers. Assn., 1994. Mem. Black Women's Forum (sponsor), Delta Sigma Theta.

SCOTT, JAMES MICHAEL, artist, filmmaker; b. Wells, England, July 9, 1941; came to U.S., 1989; s. William George and Hilda Mary Scott; m. Anna Katherine Partridge, Feb. 19, 1966 (div. 1976); children: Paloma, Alexander, Rosie; m. Yolanda Orozco, 1995. Art scholar, Bryanston Sch., Sorbonne, Paris, 1959; student painting and theatre design, Slade Sch. Fine Art, London, 1960-61, Slade Sch. Fine Art, Berlin, 1964. Ind. filmmaker Maya Film Prodns., London, 1964-70; film prodr. and dir. Flamingo Pictures, London, 1980-88; artist Santa Monica, 1989—; tchr., lectr. cinema Bath Acad. Art, U.K., Maidstone Coll. Art, U.K., Royal Coll. Art, London, Nat. Film Sch., U.K., U. So. Calif. Writer, dir.: (feature films) The Sea, 1962, Adult Fun, 1972, Coilin and Platonida, 1976, Loser Takes All, 1989, (films about artists) Love's Presentation, 1966, R.B. Kitaj, 1967, Richard Hamilton, 1969, The Great Ice Cream Robbery, 1970, Antoni Tapies, 1974, Chance, History, Art..., 1979; dir.: (TV films) Every Picture Tells a Story, 1984, Getting Even, 1985, Inspector Morse - The Last Enemy, 1988, (documentaries) Night Cleaners, 1974, Hajj 75, 1975, '36 to '77, 1978, (shorts) The Rocking Horse, 1962, In Separation, 1965, A Shocking Accident (Acad. award best short film 1983, Brit. Acad. award nominee best live action short film 1983), People Are the Same the Universe Over, 1987, Crime in the City, 1987, (info. films and commls.) Ejectoret, Stamp Exhibition - Olympia, Patrick McGrath; writer: (screenplays) Circle of Fear, Darkroom Window, Dibs, Someone, Somewhere. Recipient Silver Boomerang award Melbourne, Australia, 1979. Mem. Am. Acad. Motion Picture Arts, Dirs. Guild Am., Dirs. Guild Great Britain, Brit. Acad. Film and TV Arts, Assn. Cinematograph and Allied Techs. Home and Office: PO Box 10003 Santa Monica CA 90410-1003

SCOTT, JOHN CARLYLE, gynecologist, oncologist; b. Mpls., Sept. 24, 1933; s. Horace Golden and Grace (Melges) S.; m. Beth Krause, 1958 (div. 1977); m. Paola Maria Martini, Feb. 8, 1986; children: Jeff, David, Suzanne, Danielle. AB, Princeton U., 1956; BS, MD, U. Minn., 1961. Diplomate Am. Coll. Ob-gyn., Pan Am. Ob-gyn. Soc. Intern Sch. Medicine Marquette U., Milw., 1961-62, resident Sch. Medicine, 1962-66; resident Harvard Med. Sch., Boston, 1965; Am. Cancer fellow Marquette Med. Sch., Milw., 1966-67, instr. ob-gyn., 1966-67; clin. instr. ob-gyn. U. Wash. Med. Sch., Seattle, 1968-75, clin. asst. prof., 1975-85, clin. assoc. prof., 1985—; mem. faculty adv. com. dept. ob-gyn. U. Wash., Seattle, 1973—. Author: First Aid for N.W. Boaters, 1977; author Am. Jour. Ob-Gyn., 1970, 75, 77. Bd. dirs. Renton (Wash.) Handicapped Ctr., 1968-70, March of Dimes, 1974-79; bd. dirs. enabling sys. U. Hawaii, Honolulu, 1977-80. Capt. U.S. Army, 1950-52, Korea. Decorated U.S. senate Medal of Freedom, Bronze and Silver Stars. Fellow Royal Soc. Medicine (gynecology and oncology sects.), Am. Coll. Obb-Gyns, Internat. Coll. Surgeons (sec. U.S. sect. 1994, v.p. worldwide); mem. Pan Am. Ob-gyn. Soc., S.W. Oncology Group, N.W. Oncology Group, Puget Sound Oncology Group, Seattle Gynecol. Soc. (pres. 1978), Baker Channing Soc., Sigma Xi. Home: 726 16th Ave E Seattle WA 98112 Office: 9730 4th Ave NE Ste 202 Seattle WA 98115

SCOTT, JUDITH MYERS, elementary education educator; b. Loredo, Mo., Dec. 29, 1940; d. Wilbur Charles and Dora Emma (Frazier) Myers; m. David Ronald Scott, Dec. 18, 1965; children: Russell Myers, Geoffrey Douglas. BA in Edn., Ariz. State U., 1962, MA in edn., 1970. Cert. tchr., Ariz. Tchr. 2d grade Scottsdale (Ariz.) Elem. Dist., 1962-64; tchr. 1st grade Cahuilla Sch., Palm Springs, Calif., 1965, Palm Crest Sch., La Canada, Calif., 1968-69; tchr. Ak Chin Community Sch., Maricopa, Ariz., 1969-70; grad. asst. Ariz. State U., Tempe, 1970-71; pvt. tutor Tempe, 1970-77; tchr. Dayspring Presch., Tempe, 1978-83; tchr. 3d grade Waggoner Elem. Sch., Kyrene, Ariz., 1984-86; reading specialist Tempe Elem. Sch. Dist., 1986-90, tchr., trainer collaborative literacy intervention program, 1990—; exec. dir. Beauty for All Seasons, Tempe, 1982-86; presenter in field. Coord. New Zealand Tchr. Exch., Tempe Sister Cities, 1992—. Mem. NEA, ASCD, IRA, ARA, Ariz. Sch. Adminstrs., Ariz. Edn. Assn. Methodist. Home: 1940 E Calle De Caballos Tempe AZ 85284-2507 Office: Tempe Elem Sch Dist 3205 S Rural Rd Tempe AZ 85282-3853

SCOTT, JUDY HASLEE, computer systems analyst; b. Denver, May 7, 1949; d. Leland Howard and June Marie (Selman) Haslee; m. Randon B. Tompkins, June 14, 1969 (div. Aug. 1972); 1 child, Adrian Scott; m. John H.S. Scott; 1 child, Jillene Linay. Student, Graceland Coll., 1967-69; BS magna cum laude, Met. State Coll., 1983. Various positions Denver Pub. Schs., 1972-81, programmer/analyst, 1984-90, sr. analyst, 1991—; programmer EMI, Littleton, Colo., 1983-84; state technology plan com. Colo. Dept. Edn., Denver, 1993-94. Adv. bd. data processing Emily Griffith Opportunity Sch., Denver, 1991. Mem. Assn. for Info. Mgmt. in Edn. (bd. dirs. 1993-94, pres. 1994—), Colo. Ednl. Tech. Coun. (pres. bd. dirs. 1994—). Mem. Ch. RLDS. Office: Denver Pub Schs Dept Technology Svcs 780 Grant St Denver CO 80203-3509

SCOTT, KELLY, newspaper editor. Mng. editor sunday calendar The L.A. Times. Office: LA Times Times Mirror Sq Los Angeles CA 90012-3816

SCOTT, KENNETH CRAIG, artist; b. L.A., Mar. 19, 1955; s. Carl E. and Lois C. Scott. instr. stained glass U. Hawaii, Honolulu, 1985-90. One-man shows include The Croisanterie, Honolulu, 1987, Live Art Gallery, San Francisco, 1992, Caffe Valentino, Waikiki, Honolulu, 1993-94; group exhbns. include The Stained Glass Assn. Hawaii, Honolulu, 1985, 86, 87, Honolulu Acad. Arts, 1990, Live Art Gallery, San Francisco, 1992, 93, Ala Moana Ctr. Exhibit Hall, Honolulu, 1993, Linekona Ctr., Acad. Arts, Honolulu, 1993, Waikiki Gallery, Honolulu, 1994. Mem. Hawaiian Craftsmen Assn. (adminstrv. v.p. 1993-94). Home: PO Box 235024 Honolulu HI 96823

SCOTT, KENNETH EUGENE, lawyer, educator; b. Western Springs, Ill., Nov. 21, 1928; s. Kenneth L. and Bernice (Albright) S.; m. Viviane H. May, Sept. 22, 1956 (dec. Feb. 1982); children: Clifton, Jeffrey, Linda; m. Priscilla Gay, July 30, 1989. BA in Econs., Coll. William and Mary, 1949; MA in Polit. Sci., Princeton U., 1953; LLB, Stanford U., 1956. Bar: N.Y. 1957, Calif. 1957, D.C. 1967. Assoc. Sullivan & Cromwell, N.Y.C., 1956-59, Musick, Peeler & Garrett, L.A., 1959-61; chief dep. savs. and loan commr. State of Calif., L.A., 1961-63; gen. counsel Fed. Home Loan Bank Bd., Washington, 1963-67; Parsons prof. law and bus. Stanford (Calif.) Law Sch., 1968—; mem. Shadow Fin. Regulatory Com., 1986—; bd. dirs. Benham Capital Mgmt. Mut. Fund, Mountain View, Calif., RCM Capital Funds, San Francisco. Author: (with others) Retail Banking in the Electronic Age, 1977; co-editor: The Economics of Corporation Law and Securities Regulation, 1980. Mem. ABA, Calif. Bar Assn., Phi Beta Kappa, Order of Coif, Pi Kappa Alpha, Omicron Delta Kappa. Home: 610 Gerona Rd Stanford CA 94305-8453 Office: Crown Quadrangle Stanford Law Sch Stanford CA 94305-8610

SCOTT, LATAYNE COLVETT, writer; b. Santa Fe, Mar. 11, 1952; d. Bennie Leo Colvett and Rose Anne (Cates) Hensley; m. Daniel G. Scott, Dec. 27, 1973; children: Ryan Virgil, Celeste Anne. BS, U. N.Mex., 1980; MSL, Trinity Theol. Sem., 1994, postgrad. Author: The Mormon Mirage, 1979, 88, Open Up Your Life: A Woman's Workshop on Hospitality, 1984, To Love Each Other: A Woman's Workshop on 1 Corinthians 13, 1985, 92, Time Talents Things: A Woman's on Christian Stewardship, 1987, Crisis: Crucible of Praise, 1989, 92, Why We Left Mormonism: Eight People Tell Their Stories, 1990, Why We Left A Cult: Six People Tell Their Stories, 1993, After Mormonism: What? Reclaiming the Ex-Mormon's World View for Christ, 1994; author (with Glen Greenwood) A Marriage Made in Heaven, 1990; contbg. editor, book reviewer Release Ink; editor The Voice; scrip writer videos The Acappella Co.; author radio play The Hummingbird Feeder, 1994, Letters to God, 1994; contbd. articles to numerous mags. Recipient Disting. Christian Svc. award Pepperdine U., 1990. Mem. PEN, U.S. Gospel Music Assn., S.W. Writers Workshop.

SCOTT, LORETTA BERNADETTE, newspaper editor; b. Bklyn., Apr. 2, 1945; d. Cornelius George and Marcella Helen (Riley) Greaney; m. Robert B. Scott, Sept. 21, 1969 (div. 1975); m. C. Kenneth Miller, Jr., Mar. 17, 1983. BA, St. John's U., Queens, N.Y., 1968. Cert. secondary English tchr. Editorial asst. Crawdaddy Mag., N.Y.C., 1969; pers. asst. Amerace-Esna Corp., N.Y.C., 1969-70; tchr. English Wallkill (N.Y.) High Sch., 1970-71, Ellenville (N.Y.) High Sch., 1971-72; editor New Times, Ithaca, N.Y., 1972-75; editor, reporter New Times, Syracuse, N.Y., 1975-77; freelance writer Miami, Fla., 1978; reporter Hollywood (Fla.) Sun-Tattler, 1978-79, asst. city editor, 1979-80; Gannett Found. grad. fellow U. Hawaii, Honolulu, 1980-81; reporter Press-Enterprise, Riverside, Calif., 1981-82, copy editor, 1982-83, food editor, 1983—. Editor: Foodspell, 1990. Mem. Am. Inst. Wine and Food, Assn. Food Journalists (regional co-dir. 1988-90). Office: Press-Enterprise 3512 14th St Riverside CA 92501-3814

SCOTT, MARK RICHARD, information services executive; b. Milw., June 28, 1955; s. Richard Edward and Suzanne A. (Rohling) S.; m. Jacqueline Kay Kalisiak, Sept. 26, 1986; children: Katie and Kelly (twins.). BSBA, Drake U., 1977. Sales exec. Xerox Corp., Des Moines, 1977-82; sales mgr. Xerox Corp., Denver, 1982-86; br. mgr. Wang Labs., Denver, 1986-89, Mead Data Ctrl., Denver, 1989—; speaker in field. Mem. benefactors com. Colo. Bar Assn. Barrister Ball, Denver, 1989—, Maricopa County Barrister Ball, Phoenix, 1992—. Mem. Sigma Alpha Epsilon. Republican. Home: 3980 Nassau Cir W Cherry Hl Vlg CO 80110-5125 Office: Mead Data Ctrl 1801 California St Ste 4310 Denver CO 80202-2643

SCOTT, MARY LOUISE, educator, writer; b. Ft. Worth, Tex., Oct. 15, 1932; d. Edward Hughes and Gertrude Elizabeth (Wiltshire) S. AB, U. San Diego, 1955; MA, San Diego State U., 1961; JD, U. San Diego, 1970. Bar: Calif. Tchr. San Diego Unified Sch. Dist., 1955-89; rsch. assoc. San Diego Aerospace Mus., 1989-94, edn. specialist, 1994—; curriculum writer San Diego City Schs., 1972, 73, 80-89. Author: San Diego: Air Capital of the West, 1991; co-author: Young Adults in the Marketplace (2 vols.), 1979; contbr. articles to profl. jours. Recipient Citation of Honor Diocese of San Diego, 1955, cert. of appreciation San Diego State U., 1985, recognition Calif. State Assembly, 1991; ednl. mentor Old Globe Theatre, San Diego, 1987, 88, 89. Mem. Am. Aviation Hist. Soc., U.S. Naval Inst., Navy League U.S., Zool. Soc. San Diego, San Diego Natural History Soc. Democrat. Roman Catholic. Home: 4702 Norma Dr San Diego CA 92115-3136 Office: San Diego Aerospace Mus Balboa Park 2001 Pan American Plz San Diego CA 92101

SCOTT, MORRIS DOUGLAS, ecologist; b. Mason City, Iowa, Sept. 8, 1945; s. Morris William and Maxine Imogene (Eppard) S.; m. Suvi Annikki Lehtinen, Aug. 12, 1983. BS, Iowa State U., 1967; PhD, Auburn U., 1971. Instr. zoology Auburn U., Ala., 1971-72; asst. prof. So. Ill. U., Carbondale, 1972-74; sr. ecologist Amax Coal Co., Indpls., 1974-75, environ. mgr., Billings, Mont., 1975-77; rsch. assoc. Mont. State U., Bozeman, 1977-80, dir. Inst. Natural Resources, 1980-86; biologist, rsch. div. Yellowstone Nat. Park, Wyo., 1986—; cons. mining industry. Author: Heritage from the Wild, Familiar Land and Sea Mammals of the Northwest. Editor Conf. Proceedings Plains Aquatic Research, 1983. Contbr. articles to profl. jours. Bd. dirs. Bridger Canyon Property Owners Assn., Bozeman, 1984—. Auburn U. fellow, 1970. Mem. Ecol. Soc. Am., Wildlife Soc., Animal Behavior Soc., Gamma Sigma Delta. Current work: Land use planning systems for microcomputers; wildlife mgmt. on reclaimed surface mines; behavioral ecology of feral dogs; ecology of waterfowl and grouse; biology of pronghorn antelope. Home: 16257 Bridger Canyon Rd Bozeman MT 59715-8286

SCOTT, NORMAN JACKSON, JR., biologist, zoologist, educator, researcher; b. L.A., Sept. 30, 1934; s. Norman Jackson and Marion Lucille (Riley) S.; m. Joan Barbara Mattson, Sept. 1, 1956; children: Brian Edward, Elena Maria. BS, Humboldt State U., 1956, MS, 1962; PhD, U. So. Calif., 1969. Course coord. Orgn. for Tropical Studies, Costa Rica, 1968-70; asst. prof. U. Conn., Storrs, 1968-74; zoologist U.S. Fish and Wildlife Svc., Albuquerque, 1974-92, San Simeon, Calif., 1992-93; zoologist Nat. Biol. Svc., San Simeon, Calif., 1993—; adj. prof. U. N.Mex., Albuquerque, 1974—, U. Calif., Santa Barbara, 1993—. Editor: Herpetological Communities, 1983; contbr. articles to profl. jours. With USAFR, 1957-63. Named Disting. Alumnus Humboldt State U., 1988. Mem. AAAS, Am. Soc. Ichthylogists and Herpetologists, Am. Soc. Zoologists, Am. Inst. Biol. Sci., Soc. Study Amphibians and Reptiles (dir. 1982-84, pres. 1987), Soc. Systematic Biologists, Soc. for Study Evolution, Ecol. Soc. Am., Soc. Conservation Biology, Assn. Tropical Biology, Sigma Xi. Home: 3655 Lindquist Ln Creston CA 93432

SCOTT, OTTO, writer; b. N.Y.C., May 26, 1918; s. Otto Felix and Katherine (McGivney) S.; m. Rose Massing (div. 1952); 1 child, Katherine;

m. Nellie Mouradian (div. 1963); children: Mary, Philipa; m. Anna Barney Scott, Apr. 29, 1963; 1 child, Ann Elizabeth. MA in Polit. Sci., Valley Christian U., Fresno, Calif., 1985. Mem. staff United Features Syndicate, N.Y.C., 1939-40; v.p. Globaltronix de Venezuela, Caracas, 1954-56, Mohr Assocs., N.Y.C., 1957-59, Becker, Scott & Assocs., N.Y.C., 1960-63; editor Bill Bros., N.Y.C., 1964-67; asst. to chmn. Ashland (Ky.) Oil, Inc., 1968, 69; edn. writer, reviewer San Diego Union Tribune, 1970; sr. writer Chalcedon Found., Vallecito, Calif., 1982-94; cons. Ashland Oil, Inc., 1972—; editor, pub. Otto Scott's Compass, Seattle, 1990—. Author: History Ashland Oil (The Exception) 1968, Robespierre: Voice of Virtue (History French Revolution), 1974, The Professional: Biography of J.B. Saunders, 1976, The Creative Ordeal: History of Raytheon Corporation, 1976, James I: The Fool as King, 1976, 86, Other End of the Lifeboat (History of South Africa), 1985, Buried Treasure: The Story of Arch Mineral, 1987, The Secret Six: The Fool as Martyr, 1987, The Great Christian Revolution, 1991. With U.S. Merchant Marine, 1941-47. Mem. Author's Guild, Overseas Press Club, Com. for Nat. Policy, Com. for Monetary Rsch. and Edn., The Southern League. Presbyterian. Office: Otto Scotts Compass Uncommon Books 828 S 299th Pl Federal Way WA 98003-3749

SCOTT, PATRICIA JEAN, educational telecommunications administrator; b. Tacoma, Wash., Oct. 30, 1946; d. Donald Matthew and Gladys Myrtle (Olson) Gregurich; m. George Larkham Scott IV, Aug. 1, 1969; 1 child, Matthew Larkham. BA, Wash. State U., 1968; MA in Instrl. TV, Gonzaga U., 1975; PhD in Ednl. Policy and Mgmt., U. Oreg., 1994. Cert. secondary tchr., Wash. Tchr. secondary Moses Lake (Wash.) Schs., 1968-70; project dir. Wash. Commn. for Humanities, Spokane, 1975-77; adminstrv. asst. for telecourses Spokane Falls Community Coll., 1977; adminstrv. asst. Oreg. Community Coll. Telecommunications Consortium, Portland, 1983-89; intern to dir. of edn. policy and planning, govs. office State Oreg.; intern to commr. for community colls. State Dept. of Edn., Salem, 1988; grant writer Riggs Inst., Beaverton, Oreg., 1986-88; tchr. adult literacy, Portland, 1986—. Fundraiser St. Mary of the Valley Cath. Sch., Beaverton, 1982-83; precinct com. person Spokane County, 1976-80; mem. Catlin Gabel Sch. Auction com., Portland, 1983-86. Mem. Women in Communications Internat., Nat. Assn. Female Execs. Home: 11445 SW Lanewood St Portland OR 97225-5301

SCOTT, PETER, JR., vintner; b. 1953. Grad., U. Calif., Berkeley, 1976. With Touche Ross, San Francisco, 1976-84, Edgar Dunn & Conover, San Francisco, 1984-91, Kendall Jackson Winery, 1991—. Office: Kendall-Jackson Winery LTD 421 Aviation Blvd Santa Rosa CA 95403-1069*

SCOTT, PETER BRYAN, lawyer; b. St. Louis, Nov. 11, 1947; s. Gilbert Franklin and Besse Jean (Fudge) S.; m. Suzanne Rosalee Wallace, Oct. 19, 1974; children: Lindsay W., Sarah W., Peter B. Jr. A.B., Drury Coll., 1969; J.D., Washington U., St. Louis, 1972, LL.M., 1980. Bar: Mo. 1972, Colo. 1980; diplomate Ct. Practice Inst. Sole practice, St. Louis, 1972-80; assoc. firm McKie and Assocs., Denver, 1980-81; ptnr. firm Scott and Chesteen, P.C., Denver, 1981-84, Veto & Scott, Denver, 1984-92; pvt. practice atty., Denver, 1992—; tchr. Denver Paralegal Inst., Red Rocks Community Coll. Mem. Evergreen Christian Ch., Disciples of Christ. Capt. USAR, 1971-79. Mem. ABA, Mo. Bar Assn., Colo. Bar Assn., Denver Bar Assn. Republican. Home: 26262 Wolverine Trl Evergreen CO 80439-6203 Office: Peter B Scott PC 6595 W 14th Ave Denver CO 80214-1998

SCOTT, PETER DALE, writer, retired English language educator; b. Montreal, Quebec, Can., Jan. 11, 1929; s. Francis Reginald and Marian Mildred (Dale) S.; m. Mary Elizabeth Marshall, June 16, 1956; children: Catherine Dale, Thomas, John Daniel; m. Ronna Kabatznick, July 14, 1993. BA, McGill U., Montreal, Que., Can., 1949, PhD, 1955; postgrad, Inst. d'Etudes Politiques, Paris, 1950, Univ. Coll., Oxford, Eng., 1950-52. Fgn. service officer Canadian Dept. External Affairs, Ottawa, Ont., 1957-61; asst. prof. speech U. Calif., Berkeley, 1961-66, from asst. prof. to assoc. prof. English, 1966-80, prof., 1980-94; ret., 1994. Author: The War Conspiracy, 1972, Crime and Cover-Up, 1977, Coming to Jakarta, 1988, Listening to the Candle, 1992, Deep Politics and the Death of JFK, 1993, Crossing Borders, 1994; co-author: The Assassinations, 1976, The Iran-Contra Connection, 1987, Cocaine Politics, 1991. Fellow Internat. Ctr. Devel. Policy (Freedom award 1987). Mem. Assn. for Responsible Dissent (bd. dirs. 1988). Office: U Calif Dept English Berkeley CA 94720

SCOTT, ROBERT KEITH, economic development executive; b. Tegucigalpa, Honduras, Nov. 1, 1947; came to U.S., 1956; s. Virgil Everett and Olive (Halldorson) S.; m. Nancy Jean Moore Scott, July 4, 1970; children: Tracy, Leslie, Ann. BS in Electrical Engring., Colo. State U., 1969. cert. Econ. Developer Am. Econ. Devel. Coun. Engring. project mgr. U.S. Army, Ft. Meade, Md., 1970-74, Nat. Security Agency, Ft. Meade, Md., 1975-79; real estate sales, mgmt. various, 1980-88; CEO Colo. Springs (Colo.) Econ. Devel., 1989—; dir. Colo. Springs C. of C., Colo. Econ. Devel. Coun. Former mem. adv. bds. Colo. Commn. on Higher Edn., U. Colo. Coll. of Engring., U. Colo. Coll. of Bus.; dir. Japan Am. Soc. of Colo., Colo. Inst. of Tech. Transfer, Colo. Springs Sports Corp., Pub. Edn. Coalition, Tradition of Excellence Fdn., Fdn. for Colo. Springs Future. Capt. U.S. Army, 1970-74. Mem. Country Club of Colo., Broadmoor Golf Club. Office: Colorado Springs Econ Devel Corp 90 S Cascade Ave Ste 1050 Colorado Springs CO 80903

SCOTT, SANDRA LYNN (SANDY SCOTT), artist, sculptor, printmaker; b. Dubuque, Iowa, July 24, 1943; d. Jim and Dolly (Dillon) S. Student, Kansas City (Kans.) Art Inst., 1962-63. Animation background artist Calvin Motion Pictures, 1963-65; freelance portrait artist, illustrator Kona Coast, Hawaii, 1969, San Francisco, 1969; instr. Scottsdale Artists Sch., Ariz., 1987, Loveland Acad. Fine Art, 1992, The Fechin Inst., Taos, N.Mex., 1995. One woman shows include: Nat. Cowboy Hall Fame, 1978, Pen & Brush, N.Y., 1988; group shows include: Cheyenne Frontier Days Governor's Invitational Western Art Show, 1992, 93, 94, 95, Loveland Rotary's Colo. Invitational Art Show, 1992, 93, 94, 95, Nat. Wildlife Mus. Art Show, 1992, 93, 94, 95, Nat. Acad. Western Art, 1993, 94, Am. Women Artist Art Show, 1993, The West Show Tucson Mus. Art, 1993, Artist of Am. Denver Rotary Show, 1993, 94, 95, Nat. Cowboy Hall Fame, 1995, Western Art Exhibit, China; private collections include: Nat. Cowboy Hall Fame, Trammell Crow Corp., Mus. Arts and Crafts, Opryland Hotel, Miramichi Salmon Mus., Sebastiani Vineyards Collection, El Pasco Zoo, Vickers Oil Corp., Mustang Oil Corp., Ritz Carlton Hotel, Hillsdale Coll., Nat. Wildlife Mus., City Fort Collins, Brookgreen Gardens. Recipient Ann Huntington Sculpture award Catherine Lorillard Wolfe Art Club, 1982, Merit Sculpture award Northwest Rendezvous Group, 1987, 88, Hubbard Art Excellence award, 1991, Sculpture award Am. Profl. Artists League, 1991; recipient Sculpture prize Allied Artists, 1983, Catherine Lorillard Wolfe Art Club, 1983, Salmagundi Club, 1983, Am. Artists Profl. League, 1982, 83, Pen and Brush, 1984, Knickerbocker Artists, 1984, Ellen P. Speyer prize Nat. Acad. Design, 1988; recipient Gold medal for Sculpture Nat. Acad. Western Art, 1992.. Mem. Soc. Animal Artists, Am. Artist Profl. League, Pen & Brush, Northwest Rendezvous Group, Catherine Lorillard Wolfe Art Club. Home: 200 Gregory Rd Fort Collins CO 80524

SCOTT, WILLIAM ARTHUR, III, treasurer, swami; b. L.A., Apr. 10, 1949; s. William Arthur Jr. and Mary Lyndal (Dutton) S. BA, Occidental Coll., 1971; MA, Stanford (Calif.) U., 1972; postgrad., UCLA, 1973-76. Cert. tchr., Calif. Tchr. Quartz Hill (Calif.) High Sch., 1972-78; treas. Vedanta Soc. of So. Calif., Hollywood, 1984—; swami Ramakrishna Order of India, Belur, Calcutta, 1990—; treas. Sidewalk Astronomers. Composer operatta Claudia & Alexander, Vivekananda Oratorio. Nat. Merit scholar, 1967. Mem. Calif. Rare Fruit Growers, So. Calif. Iris Soc., Am. Iris Soc., Aril Soc. Internat. (pres. 1979-89), Phi Beta Kappa, Phi Mu Alpha Sinfonia (pres. Eta Kappa chpt. 1969-71). Republican. Home: 1946 Vedanta Pl Los Angeles CA 90068-3920

SCOTT, WILLIAM CORYELL, medical executive; b. Sterling, Colo., Nov. 22, 1920; s. James Franklin and Edna Ann (Schillig) S.; m. Jean Marie English, Dec. 23, 1944 (div. 1975); children: Kathryn, James, Margaret; m. Carolyn Florence Hill, June 21, 1975; children: Scott, Amy Jo, Robert. AB, Dartmouth Coll., 1942; MD, U. Colo., 1944, MS in OB/GYN, 1951. Cert. Am. Bd. Ob-Gyn., 1956, 79, Am. Bd. Med. Mgmt., 1991. Intern USN Hosp., Great Lakes, Ill., 1945-46, Denver Gen. Hosp., 1946-47; resident Ob-Gyn St. Joseph's Hosp., Colo. Gen. Hosp., Denver, 1946-51; practice medicine specializing in Ob-Gyn Tucson, 1951-71; assoc. prof. emeritus U. Ariz. Med. Sch., Tucson, 1971-94, 1994; v.p. med. affairs U. Med. Ctr., Tucson, 1984-94. Contbr. articles to med. jours. and chpt. to book. Pres. United Way, Tucson, 1979-80, HSA of Southeastern Ariz., Tucson, 1985-87; chmn. Ariz. Health Facilities Authority, Phoenix, 1974-83. Served to capt. USNR, 1956-58. Recipient Man of Yr. award, Tucson, 1975. Fellow ACS, Am. Coll. Ob-Gyn, Pacific Coast Ob-Gyn Soc., Ctrl. Assn. of Ob-Gyn; mem. AMA (coun. on sci. affairs 1984-93, chmn. 1989-91), Am. Coll. Physician Execs., Am. Coll. Health Care Execs., Ariz. Med. Assn., La Paloma Country Club. Republican. Episcopalian. Home: PO Box 805 Sonoita AZ 85637-0805

SCOTT, WILLIAM HERBERT, state agency administrator; b. Estancia, N.Mex., Mar. 19, 1925; s. Chester Ray and Elizabeth Bryan (McNama) S.; m. Maryann Mavis Munro, Dec. 26, 1952 (div. 1980); children: Jean Ann, Megan Lynne; m. Dorothy Caroline Caster, Apr. 16, 1980. BS in Civil Engring., U. N.Mex., 1949, BBA in Acctg., 1949. CPA, Alaska. Field engr., office mgr. Kincaid & King Constrn., Anchorage, 1949-50; office mgr. M-B Contracting Co., Inc., Anchorage, 1951-52; staff acct. R.L. Rettig, CPA, Anchorage, 1952-54; ptnr. Rettig, Scott & Co., CPAs, Anchorage, 1955-60; mng. ptnr. Scott, McMahon & Co., CPAs, Anchorage, 1960-61, Peat, Marwick Mitchell & Co., Anchorage, 1961-83; cons., 1983-91; exec. dir. Alaska Indsl. Devel., Anchorage, 1991-92, Alaska Permanent Fund Corp., Juneau, 1992-94; sec. Alaska Bd. Pub. Accountancy, 1963-65. Mem. Com. on Operation U.S. Senate, Washington, 1976; honorary consul Denmark, Anchorage, 1963-88. Lt. j.g. USNR, 1942-46, PTO. Named Knight of Dannebrog Queen of Denmark, 1973, 83. Mem. Am. Arbitration Assn. (panel 1984—), Alaska Soc. CPAs (pres., founder 1961-62), AICPA (coun. 1961-62), Anchorage C. of C. (pres. 1966), Alaska State C. of C. (pres. 1968), Alaskan Air Command Civilian Affairs, Sigma Chi.

SCOTT, W(ILLIAM) RICHARD, sociology educator; b. Parsons, Kan., Dec. 18, 1932; s. Charles Hogue and Hildegarde (Hewit) S.; m. Joy Lee Whitney, Aug. 14, 1955; children: Jennifer Ann, Elliot Whitney, Sydney Brooke. AA, Parsons Jr. Coll., 1952; AB, U. Kans., 1954, MA, 1955; PhD, U. Chgo., 1961. Asst. prof. to assoc. prof. sociology Stanford (Calif.) U., 1960-69, prof., 1969—, chair dept. sociology, 1972-75; courtesy prof. Sch. Medicine, Stanford U., 1972—, Sch. Edn., Grad. Sch. Bus., 1977—; fellow Ctr. for Advanced Study in Behavioral Scis., 1989-90; dir. Orgns. Rsch. Tng. Program, Stanford U., 1972-89, Ctr. for Orgns. Rsch., 1988—; mem. adv. panel Sociology Program NSF, Washington, 1982-84; mem. epidemiol. and svc. rsch. rev. panel NIMH, Washington, 1984-88; mem. Commn. on Behavioral and Social Scis. and Edn., NAS, 1990—. Author: (with O.D. Duncan et al) Metropolis and Region, 1960, (with P.M. Blau) Formal Organizations, 1962, Social Processes and Social Structures, 1970, (with S.M. Dornbusch) Evaluation and the Exercise of Authority, 1975, Organizations: Rational, Natural and Open Systems, 1981, rev. edit., 1992, (with J.W. Meyer) Organizational Environments: Ritual and Rationality, 1983, edit., 1992, (with A.B. Flood) Hospital Structure and Performance, 1987, (with J.W. Meyer), Institutional Environments and Organizations: Structural Complexity and Individualism, 1994, Institutions and Organizations: Theory and Research, 1995; editor Ann. Rev. of Sociology, 1986-91. Fellow Woodrow Wilson, 1954-55; mem. Nat. Commn. Nursing, 1980-83; chair Consortium Orgns. Rsch. Ctrs., 1989-91; elder First Presby. Ch., Palo Alto, Calif., 1977-80, 83-86. Social Sci. Research Council fellow, U. Chgo., 1959; named Edmund P. Learned Disting. Prof., Sch. Bus. Adminstrn., U. Kans, 1970-71; recipient Cardinal Citation for Disting. Service, Labette Community Coll, Parsons, 1981, Disting. Scholar award Mgmt. and Orgn. Theory div. Acad. Mgmt., 1988. Mem. Inst. Medicine, Am. Sociol. Assn. (chmn. sect. on orgns. 1970-71, mem. coun. 1989-92), Acad. Mgmt., Sociol. Rsch. Assn., Macro-Organizational Behavior Soc., Phi Beta Kappa. Democrat. Presbyterian. Home: 940 Lathrop Pl Stanford CA 94305-1060 Office: Stanford U Dept Sociology Bldg 120 Stanford CA 94305

SCOTTON, BRUCE WARREN, psychiatrist, educator; b. Champaign, Ill., Nov. 7, 1947; s. Donald W. and Beverly J. (Warren) S.; m. June Yokell, July 19, 1981; children: David, Lauren. BS in Zoology magna cum laude, U. Ill., 1964-68; MD, Columbia U., 1972; analytic tng., C.G. Jung Inst., 1978-87. lic. DEA; lic. surgeon and physician, Calif.; cert. Jungian analyst, forensic examiner Nat. Bd. Forensic Examiners, 1994. Internal medicine intern Kaiser Found. Hosp., San Francisco, 1972-73; psychiatric resident U. Calif., San Francisco, 1973-75, 76-77; emergency room physician and surgeon Calif. Emergency Physicians, Oakland, 1974-78; interdisciplinary team leader inpatient treatment and rsch. Langley Porter Psychiatric Inst., U. Calif., San Francisco; pvt. practice San Francisco, 1977—; researcher in field, Liberia, India, Nepal, Zurich, and others, 1972—;. Editorial bd. mem. Transpersonal Review, 1993—; contbr. articles to profl. jours. Bd. govs. C.G. Jung Inst. San Francisco, 1980-81. Office: 322 Clement St San Francisco CA 94118-2316

SCRIBNER, DOROTHY NESBITT, community relations executive, consultant; b. San Francisco, June 21, 1938; d. John and Freda (Keller) Nesbitt; children: Diana Lynne Vaughn, Karen Elizabeth Weber, Matthew Joseph Duffy. Exec. sec. East Bay Zool. Soc., Oakland, Calif., 1968-73; field coord. San Francisco Bay Girl Scout Coun., San Leandro, Calif., 1975-77; owner, operator Specialty Svcs., Pleasanton, Calif., 1972-85, Design Works Ltd., Pleasanton, 1980-82, Star Coffee Svc., Pleasanton, 1985-86; exec. dir. Danville (Calif.) Area C. of C., 1985-86; mgr. downtown project Town of Danville, 1986-89; event coord. Valley Vol. Ctr., Pleasanton, 1990; investor, bus. owner Pleasanton, 1990-93. Contbg. editor (newsletters) Zoo's News, 1969-73, Progress, 1985-86. Chmn. Evergreen br. Childrens Hosp., 1979-80, treas., 1991, bd. dirs., treas, Oakland, 1982-85; chmn. Downtown Assn. Heritage Days Celebration, Pleasanton, 1990-91; active Alameda County Libr. Commn., Oakland, 1991; vice-mayor City of Pleasanton, 1992—, city coun. mem. 1990-94, chair downtown task force, 1991-93; chair League Calif. Cities Econ. Devel. Tools Sub-com., 1994. Mem. Stockwatchers Club, Nat. Trust Hist. Preservation.

SCRIMSHAW, GEORGE CURRIE, retired plastic surgeon; b. Canajoharie, N.Y., Nov. 10, 1925; s. George and Margaret Eleanor (Salkeld) S.; m. Erna Christine Adam, Sept. 20, 1957 (div. 1982); m. Helen Irene Mott, Dec. 4, 1982; children: Katherine, Kristen, Kirby, Tracy. BA, Harvard U., 1948; MD cum laude, Tufts U., 1952. Diplomate Am. Bd. Plastic Surgery. Intern N.Y. Hosp./Cornell Med. Ctr., N.Y.C., 1952-53, resident in surgery, 1953-54; resident in surgery New England Med. Ctr., Boston, 1954-55; resident in plastic surgery Franklin Hosp./U. Calif., San Francisco, 1955-57; pvt. practice Fresno, Calif., 1957-58, Quincy, Mass., 1958-62; chief dept. plastic surgery Permanente Med. Group, Oakland, Calif., 1962-88, ret., 1988; cons., attending plastic surgeon Faulkner Hosp., Southshore Hosp., Quincy Hosp., 1959-62. Contbr. articles to profl. jours. With U.S. Army, 1944-46. Mem. ACS (life), Am. Cleft Palate Assn. (life), Am. Soc. of Plastics and Reconstructive Surgery (life), Calif. Soc. of Plastic Surgeons (life), Am. Soc. of Aesthetic Surgery (life), Alpha Omega Alpha (life).

SCRITSMIER, JEROME LORENZO, light fixture manufacturing company executive; b. Eau Claire, Wis., July 1, 1925; s. Fredrick Lorenzo and Alvera Mary (Schwab) S.; B.S., Northwestern U., 1950; m. Mildred Joan Lloyd, June 27, 1947; children—Dawn, Lloyd, Janet. Salesman, Sylvania Elec. Products, Los Angeles, 1951-69; chmn. Cameron Properties Inc.; chief fin. officer Environ. Lighting for Architecture Co., Los Angeles, 1973—. Served with USAAF, 1943-46. Mem. Apt. Assn. (pres., dir. Los Angeles County). Republican. Club: Jonathan (Los Angeles). Home: 2454 Cameron Ave Covina CA 91724-3921 Office: 17891 Arenth St La Puente CA 91748

SCRIVEN, MICHAEL, philosopher, evaluator; b. Beaulieu, United Kingdom, Mar. 28, 1928. BA in Math. with honors, U. Melbourne, Australia, 1948; MA in Math. and Philosophy, U. Melbourne, 1950; DPhil, Oxford (Eng.) U., 1956. Teaching asst. math. dept. U. Melbourne, 1949; instr. philosophy dept. U. Minn., 1952-56, rsch. assoc. Minn. Ctr. for Philosophy of Sci., 1953-56; asst. prof. philosophy Swarthmore Coll., 1956-60; prof. history and philosophy of sci. Ind. U., 1960-66; prof. philosophy U. Calif., Berkeley, 1966-78, spl. asst. to vice-chancellor, 1975-77, prof. edn., 1975-78; fellow Inst. Higher Studies, Santa Barbara, 1976-90; univ. prof., dir. Evaluation Inst. U. San Francisco, 1978-82; prof. dept. edn. U. Western Australia, 1982-90, dir. Ctr. Tertiary Edn. Studies, 1983-90; prof., dir. Evaluation Inst. Pacific Grad. Sch. Psychology, Palo Alto, Calif., 1989-92; fellow Ctr. Advanced Study in Behavioral Scis., Stanford, Calif., 1963; Alfred North Whitehead fellow for advanced study in edn. Harvard U., 1970-71; sr. nat. lectr. in evaluation Nova U., Ft. Lauderdale, Fla., 1973-90; disting. vis. scholar Ctr. for Advanced Study in Theoretical Psychology, U. Alta., Edmonton, Can., 1965, 80, Ednl. Testing Svc., Princeton, N.J., 1970; dir. model tng. program for evaluators Nat. Inst. Edn., 1972-73; cons. prof. Grad. Sch. Edn., Stanford U., 1990-92; adj. prof. philosophy Western Mich. U., 1990-94; sr. fellow in evaluation NSF, 1992-93. Co-author: The Gas Turbine in Automobile Design, 1956, Psychology, 1960, How to Buy a Word Processor: Electronic Typewriters, Personal Computer Systems and Dedicated Systems, 1982, Word Magic: Evaluating and Selecting Word Processing, 1983, Russian edit., 1987; author: Applied Logic: An Introduction to Scientific Method, 1965, Primary Philosophy, 1966, Philosophy of Science, 1970, Evaluation: A Study Guide for Educational Administrators, 1974, Reasoning, 1976, Evaluation Thesaurus, 1977, 4th edit., 1991, The Logic of Evaluation, 1981; editor: (with H. Feigl) The Foundations of Science and the Concepts of Psychology and Psychoanalysis, vol. 1, 1956, (with H. Feigl and G. Maxwell) Concepts, Theories and the Mind-Body Problem, vol. 2, 1958, Collected Papers of Eugene R. Wigner, 1966, Statistics as a Spectator Sport by R. Jaeger, 1982, (with George Madaus and Daniel Stufflebean) Evaluation Models, 1983; mem. editl. bd., editl. rev. panels and editorships to numerous jours. and mags. Grantee Nuffield Found., 1951-52, Carnegie Corp., 1960-61, NSF, 1965, 1966-71, 74-75, 80, 92-93, U.S. Office Edn., 1971-72; recipient Pres.'s Prize Competition, Evaluation Network, 1980, Lazarsfeld prize Am. Evaluation Soc., 1986; hon. fellow Nat. Acad. Social Scis. Home: 415 Drakes View Dr Inverness CA 94937-9708

SCRIVER, ROBERT MACFIE, sculptor; b. Browning, Mont., Aug. 15, 1914; s. Thaddeus Emery and Ellison Scriver; m. Mary Helen Strachan, Nov. 27, 1966 (div. Nov. 1970); m. Lorraine, Aug. 15, 1972. Student, Dickinson State Tchr's Coll., N.D., 2 years; Bachelor's degree, Vandercook Sch. Music, Chgo., 1935, Master's degree, 1941; postgrad., Northwestern Univ., summer 1937, U. Wash., summer 1938; D.Arts hon., Carroll Coll. mem. C.M. Russell Adv. Bd., Great Falls, Mont., 1983—. Group of works includes No More Buffalo, 1983 (gold medals 1983), An Honest Try (gold medals), Bob Scriver Hall of Bronze Mus. Mont. Wildlife, 1989; author: No More Buffalo, 1983 (pub. awards 1983), An Honest Try (pub. awards), The Blackfeet, Artists of the Northern Plains, 1990 (pub. awards). Justice of the peace Glacer County, Mont.; city magistrate City of Browning. Served to sgt. USAAF, 1940. Recipient Gold and Silver medals Cowboy Artists Am., Phoenix, Gold and Silver medals Nat. Acad. Western Arts, Oklahoma City, Mont. State Gov.'s award, 1990; honoree Bob Scriver Day State Mont., Helena. Mem. Nat. Sculpture Soc., Nat. Acad. Western Art, Soc. Animal Artists, Browning C. of C. (pres.); mem. emeritus Cowboy Artists Am. Republican. Native American. Lodge: Masons. Office: Museum Mont Wildlife Junction Hwys 2 & 89 Browning MT 59417

SCRONCE, RONALD GUY, academic counselor; b. Wilmington, N.C., Jan. 1, 1943; s. Warren Clampitt and Virginia Grace (Wilkinson) S.; 1 child, Ami Caroline. BABA, Catawba Coll., Salisbury, N.C., 1965; MA in Edn., East Carolina U., 1973. Nat. cert. counselor. Program officer East-West Ctr., Honolulu, 1979-82; edn. counselor, specialist Dept of U.S. Army Continuing Edn. System, Schofield Barracks, Hawaii, 1982-87, 91—; edn. counselor USAF Edn. Svc., Yokota Air Base, Japan, 1987-88; edn. svcs. oficer USN Edn.Support System, Yokosuka Naval Base, Japan, 1988-90. Mem. ACA (del. to conv. 1971), Hawaii Counseling Assn. (pres. 1985-86), Hawaii Assn. for Counselors and Educators in Govt. (charter, pres. 1993-94), Phi Delta Kappa (sec. 1971). Home: 716A Olokele Ave Apt D Honolulu HI 96816-1019

SCRUGGS, H. E., JR., political science educator; b. Columbus, Ga., June 5, 1957; s. Herbert Eugene and Mary Ellen (Wilkie) S.; m. Shirley Johnson, Dec. 15, 1978; children: Angela, David, Elliot, Camilla, Lydia, Dallin. BA in Polit. Sci., Brigham Young U., 1982, JD, 1984. Counsel U.S. Senate Judiciary Com., Sub-com. on Constitution, Washington, 1984-85; CEO Pub. Affairs Adv. Group, Salt Lake City, 1985-88; chief of staff Gov. of Utah, Salt Lake City, 1988-91; asst. prof. polit. sci. Brigham Young U., Provo, Utah, 1991—. Republican. Mem. Ch. LDS. Office: Brigham Young Univ 745 Swkt Provo UT 84602-1130

SCUDDER, DAVID BENJAMIN, economist, foundation administrator; b. Evanston, Ill., July 30, 1923; s. Guy and Ruth Marilla (Benjamin) S.; m. Marjorie Adell Buckland, Dec. 27, 1946; children: David Foster, Rexford Guy. BS, Bowling Green State U., 1948; AM, U. Chgo., 1950, postgrad., 1950-51. Economist CIA, Washington, 1951-81, econ. cons., 1981-84; editor, co-pub. World Amateur Dancer, McLean, Va., 1982-84; treas. The Scudder Assn., Inc., Arlington, Va., 1990-92, Boise, Idaho, 1992—. Editor quarterly newsletter The Scudder Assn. Inc, 1989—; contbr. articles and reports to jours. Active Springfield Civic Assn., Fairfax County, Va., 1956-61. With USAF, 1943-45, ETO. Home: 1031 Strawberry Ln Boise ID 83712-7726

SCUDDER, HENRY JOHNSTON, aerospace scientist; b. Bklyn., Sept. 26, 1935; s. Henry Johnston and Margaret (Hail) S.; m. Constance Theodora Falconer, Jan. 10, 1985; children: Rebecca Sue, Michael Johnston, Melissa Lynn, Matthew Peter, Althea Gengenbach. B Engring. Physics, Cornell U., 1958, MSEE, 1960; PhDEE, U. Calif., Berkeley, 1964. Registered profl. engineer, N.Y. Info. scientist GE R & D Ctr., Schenectady, 1964-84; assoc. prof. mfg. engring. Boston U., 1985-90; rocket scientist Rocketdyne, Canoga Park, Calif., 1991—; pres. Stochastic Enterprises, Canoga Park, 1973—. Author: Introduction to Computerized Tomography, 1978. Hon. bishop Soc. for Creative Anachronisms, Rensselaer, N.Y., 1981. Mem. Am. Soc. Non-Destructive Testing (Most Significant Devel. of Yr. award 1983). Office: Rocketdyne 6633 Canoga Ave Canoga Park CA 91303-2703

SCUDDER, THAYER, anthropologist, educator; b. New Haven, Aug. 4, 1930; s. Townsend III and Virginia (Boody) S.; m. Mary Eliza Drinker, Aug. 26, 1950; children: Mary Eliza, Alice Thayer. Grad., Phillips Exeter Acad., 1948; A.B., Harvard U., 1952, Ph.D., 1960; postgrad., Yale U., 1953-54, London Sch. Econs., 1960-61. Research officer Rhodes-Livingstone Inst., No. Rhodesia, 1956-57; sr. research officer Rhodes-Livingstone Inst., 1962-63; asst. prof. Am. U., Cairo, 1961-62; research fellow Center Middle East Studies, Harvard U., 1963-64; asst. prof. Calif. Inst. Tech., Pasadena, 1964-66; assoc. prof. Calif. Inst. Tech., 1966-69, prof. anthropology, 1969—; dir. Inst. for Devel. Anthropology, Binghamton, N.Y., 1976—; cons. UN Devel. Program, FAO, IBRD, WHO, Ford Found., Navajo Tribal Coun., AID, World Conservation Union, Lesotho Highlands Devel. Authority, South China Electric Power Joint Venture Corp. Author: The Ecology of the Gwembe Tonga, 1962; co-author: Long-Term Field Research in Social Anthropology, 1979, Secondary Education and the Formation of an Elite: The Impact of Education on Gwembe District, Zambia, 1980, No Place to Go: The Impacts of Forced Relocation on Navajos, 1982, For Prayer and Profit: The Ritual, Economic and Social Importance of Beer in Gwembe District, Zambia, 1950-1982, 1988, The IUCN Review of the So. Okavango Integrated Water Development Project, 1993. John Simon Guggenheim Meml. fellow, 1975. Mem. Am. Anthrop. Assn. (1st recipient Solon T. Kimball award for pub. and applied anthropology 1984, Edward J. Lehman award 1991), Soc. Applied Anthropology, Am. Alpine Club. Office: Calif Inst Tech # 228-77 Pasadena CA 91125

SCULLY, JOHN KENNETH, engineering executive, consultant; b. N.Y.C., Nov. 19, 1935; s. Francis Joseph and Dorothy Bonita (Cadley) S.; m. Roxanne Allison Glaser, Feb. 12, 1966; children: Roxanne Allison, Rebecca Suzanne. BS in Physics, Hofstra U., 1959; MS in Engring., UCLA, 1962; postgrad., Poly. Grad. Ctr., Farmingdale, N.Y., 1962-64. Engr. Sperry Corp., Great Neck, N.Y., 1956-60; sr. engr. Northrop Corp., Anaheim, Calif., 1960-62; dept. mgr. Harris Corp., Syosset, N.Y., 1962-72; sr. mem. tech. staff Litton Industries, Woodland Hills, Calif., 1972-80; pres. JKS Systems Ltd., Westlake Village, Calif., 1980—; spl. asst. to pres. GTT Industries, Inc., Westlake Village, 1991—; mng. dir. Adam-Tech. Group, Geneva, 1991—; chmn. R&D subtask Industry/Joint Svcs., 1979. Contbr. over 30 tech. papers to prof. jours. Mem. IEEE. Office: GIT Industries Inc 5655 Lindero Canyon Rd Ste 421 Westlake Village CA 91362

SCULLY, VINCENT EDWARD, sports broadcaster; b. Bronx, N.Y., Nov. 29, 1927; s. Vincent Aloysius and Bridget (Freehill) S.; m. Sandra Hunt,

Nov. 11, 1973; children: Michael, Kevin, Todd, Erin, Kelly, Catherine Anne. B.A., Fordham U., 1949. Sports announcer Bklyn. Dodgers Profl. Baseball Team, 1950-57, L.A. Dodgers Profl. Baseball Team, 1957—, CBS-TV, 1975-82, NBC-TV, 1982-89. Served with USNR, 1944-45. Recipient TV award Look mag., 1959; named Sportscaster of Year in Calif., 1959, 60, 63, 69, 71, 73-75; Nat. Sportscaster of Year, 1966, 78, 82; named to Fordham U. Hall of Fame, 1976. Mem. AFTRA, Screen Actors Guild, Catholic Actors, TV Acad. Arts and Scis. Roman Catholic. Clubs: Lambs (N.Y.C.); Bel Air Country, Beach. Office: LA Dodgers 1000 Elysian Park Ave Los Angeles CA 90012-1112

SEABERG, ERIC DAYLE, audio engineer; b. San Diego, Oct. 20, 1953; s. William Eric and Marilyn Carolyn (Oberg) S.; m. Nancy Ellen Amerian-Omachi, Feb. 24, 1973 (div. 1984); children: Robin Eric, Sean Arthur; m. Deborah Ellen Harris, June 1, 1992. Grad., Fresno (Calif.) High Sch., 1971. Chief audio engr. Kenjo Audio, Inc., Fresno, 1971-79; chief engr., ptnr. Triad Recorders, Fresno, 1979-83, chief engr., 1983-85; chief engr. Maximus Recording, Fresno, 1985-88; owner, operator Seaberg Audio Svcs., Fresno, 1988—. Mem. Audio Engring. Soc., Soc. Motion Picture and TV Engrs., NARAS. Home: 705 E Spruce Fresno CA 93720 Office: 1809 N Helm Ave Ste 1 Fresno CA 93727-1629

SEABORG, GLENN THEODORE, chemistry educator; b. Ishpeming, Mich., Apr. 19, 1912; s. H. Theodore and Selma (Erickson) S.; m. Helen Griggs, June 6, 1942; children: Peter, Lynne Seaborg Cobb, David, Stephen, John Eric, Dianne. AB, UCLA, 1934; PhD, U. Calif.-Berkeley, 1937; numerous hon. degrees; LLD, U. Mich., 1958, Rutgers U., 1970; DSc, Northwestern U., 1954, U. Notre Dame, 1961, John Carroll U., Duquesne U., 1968, Ind. State U., 1969, U. Utah, 1970, Rockford Coll., 1975, Kent State U., 1975; LHD, No. Mich. Coll., 1962; DPS, George Washington U., 1962; DPA, U. Puget Sound, 1963; LittD, Lafayette Coll., 1966; DEng, Mich. Technol. U., 1970; ScD, U. Bucharest, 1971, Manhattan Coll., 1976, U. Pa., 1983. Rsch. chemist U. Calif., Berkeley, 1937-39, instr. dept. chemistry, 1939-41, asst. prof., 1941-45, prof., 1945-71, univ. prof., 1971—, leave of absence, 1942-46, 61-71, dir. nuclear chem. research, 1946-58, 72-75, asso. dir. Lawrence Berkeley Lab., 1954-61, 71—; chancellor Univ. (U. Calif.-Berkeley), 1958-61; dir. Lawrence Hall of Sci. U. Calif., Berkeley, 1982-84, chmn. Lawrence Hall of Sci., 1984—; sect. chief metall. lab. U. Chgo., 1942-46; chmn. AEC, 1961-71, gen. adv. com., 1946-50; research nuclear chemistry and physics, transuranium elements.; chmn. bd. Kevex Corp., Burlingame, Calif., 1972-87, Advanced Physics Corp., Irvine, Calif., 1988—; mem. Pres.'s Sci. Adv. Com., 1959-61; mem. nat. sci. bd. NSF, 1960-61; mem. Pres.'s Com. on Equal Employment Opportunity, 1961-65, Fed. Radiation Council, 1961-69, Nat. Aeros. and Space Council, 1961-71, Fed. Council Sci. and Tech., 1961-71, Nat. Com. Am.'s Goals and Resources, 1962-64, Pres.'s Com. Manpower, 1964-69, Nat. Council Marine Resources and Engring. Devel., 1966-71; chmn. Chem. Edn. Material Study, 1959-74, Nat. Programming Council for Pub. TV, 1970-72; dir. Ednl. TV and Radio Center, Ann Arbor, Mich., 1958-64, 67-70; pres. 4th UN Internat. Conf. Peaceful Uses Atomic Energy, Geneva, 1971, also chmn. U.S. del., 1964, 71; U.S. rep. 5th-15th gen. confs. IAEA, chmn., 1961-71; chmn. U.S. del. to USSR for signing Memorandum Cooperation Field Utilization Atomic Energy Peaceful Purposes, 1963; mem. U.S. del. for signing Limited Test Ban Treaty, 1963; mem. commn. on humanities Am. Council Learned Socs., 1962-65; mem. sci. adv. bd. Robert A. Welch Found., 1957—; mem. Internat. Orgn. for Chem. Scis. in Devel., UNESCO, 1981-92, pres., 1981-92, pres. emeritus, 1992—; mem. Nat. Commn. on Excellence in Edn., Dept. Edn., 1981-83; co-discoverer elements 94-102 and 106: plutonium, 1940, americium, 1944-45, curium, 1944, berkelium, 1949, californium, 1950, einsteinium, 1952, fermium, 1953, mendelevium, 1955, nobelium, 1958, seaborgium, 1974; co-discoverer nuclear energy isotopes Pu-239, U-233, Np-237, other isotopes including I-131, Fe-59, Te-99m, Co-60; originator actinide concept for placing heaviest elements in periodic system. Author: (with Joseph J. Katz) The Actinide Elements, 1954, The Chemistry of the Actinide Elements, 1957, (with Joseph J. Katz and Lester R. Morse) 2d ed. Vols. I & II, 1986, The Transuranium Elements, 1958, (with E.G. Valens) Elements of the Universe, 1958 (winner Thomas Alva Edison Found. award), Man-Made Transuranium Elements, 1963, (with D.M. Wilkes) Education and the Atom, 1964, (with E.K. Hyde, I. Perlman) Nuclear Properties of the Heavy Elements, 1964, (with others) Oppenheimer, 1969, (with Ben Loeb) Stemming the Tide, 1987, (with W.R. Corliss) Man and Atom, 1971, Nuclear Milestones, 1972, (with Ben Loeb) Kennedy, Khruschev and the Test Ban, 1981, (with Walt Loveland) Elements beyond Uranium, 1990, (with Ben Loeb) The Atomic Energy Commission Under Nixon, 1992, (with Ray C. Colvig) Chancellor at Berkeley, 1994, (with Ronald L. Kathren, Jerry B. Gough, Gary T. Benefiel) The Plutonium Story: The Journals of Professor Glenn T. Seaborg 1939-1946, 1994; editor: Transuranium Elements: Products of Modern Alchemy, 1978, (with W. Loveland) Nuclear Chemistry, 1982, Modern Alchemy: The Seleced Papers of Glenn T. Seaborg, 1994; assoc. editor Jour. Chem. Physics, 1948-50; mem. editorial adv. bd. Jour. Inorganic and Nuclear Chemistry, 1954-82, Indsl. Rsch., Inc, 1967-75; mem. adv. bd. Chem. and Engring. News, 1957-59; mem. editorial bd. Jour. Am. Chem. Soc, 1950-59, Ency. Chem. Tech., 1975—, Revs. in Inorganic Chemistry, 1977—; mem. hon. editorial adv. bd. Internat. Ency. Phys. Chemistry and Chem. Physics, 1957—, Nuclear Sci. and Techniques, Chinese Nuclear Soc., 1989—; mem. panel Golden Picture Ency. for Children, 1957-61; mem. cons. and adv. bd. Funk and Wagnalls Universal Standard Ency, 1957-61; mem. Am. Heritage Dictionary Panel Usage Cons., 1964-80; contbr. articles to profl. jours. Trustee Pacific Sci. Ctr. Found., 1962-77, Sci. Svc., 1965, pres., 1966-68, chmn., 1988—; trustee Am.-Scandinavian Found., 1968—, Ednl. Broadcasting Corp., 1970-72; bd. dirs. Swedish Coun. Am., 1976—, chmn. bd. dirs., 1978-82; bd. dirs. World Future Soc., 1969—, Calif. Coun. for Environ. and Econ. Balance, 1974-83; bd. govs. Am. Swedish Hist. Found., 1972—; hon. chair spl. panel Protection and Mgmt. Plutonium, 1994—. Decorated officer Legion of Honor (France); recipient John Ericsson Gold medal Am. Soc. Swedish Engrs., 1948; Nobel prize for Chemistry (with E.M. McMillan), 1951, John Scott award and medal City of Phila., 1953, Perkin medal Am. sect. Soc. Chem. Industry, 1957, U.S. AEC Enrico Fermi award, 1959, Joseph Priestley Meml. award Dickinson Coll., 1960, Sci. and Engring. award Fedn. Engring. Socs., Drexel Inst. Tech., Phila., 1962; named Swedish Am. of Year, Vasa Order of Am., 1962; Franklin medal Franklin Inst., 1963; 1st Spirit of St. Louis award, 1964; Leif Erikson Found. award, 1964; Washington award Western Soc. Engrs., 1965; Arches of Sci. award Pacific Sci. Center, 1968; Internat. Platform Assn. award, 1969; Prometheus award Nat. Elec. Mfrs. Assn., 1969; Nuclear Pioneer award Soc. Nuclear Medicine, 1971; Oliver Townsend award Atomic Indsl. Forum, 1971; Disting. Honor award U.S. Dept. State, 1971; Golden Plate award Am. Acad. Achievement, 1972, Daniel Webster medal, 1976, John R. Kuebler award Alpha Chi Sigma, 1978; Founders medal Hebrew U. Jerusalem, 1981; Great Swedish Heritage award, 1984, Ellis Island Medal of Honor, 1986, Seaborg medal UCLA, 1987, Vannevar Bush award NSF, 1988, Nat. Medal of Sci. NSF, 1991, Royal Order of the Polar Star Sweden, 1992, Profl. Fraternity Assn. Career Achievement award, 1993; Minor Planet 4856-Asteroid Seaborg named in his honor, 1995. Fellow Am. Phys. Soc., Am. Inst. Chemists (Pioneer award 1968, Gold medal award 1973), Chem. Soc. London (hon.), Royal Soc. Edinburgh (hon.), Am. Nuclear Soc. (hon. chair Spl. Panel on Protection and Mgmt. of Plutonium 1994—, Henry DeWolf-Smyth award 1982, Seaborg award 1984, hon. chair Spl. Panel on Protection and Mgmt. of Plutonium 1994—), Calif. Acad. Scis., N.Y. Acad. Scis., Washington Acad. Scis., AAAS (pres. 1972, chmn. bd. 1973), Royal Soc. Arts (Eng.); mem. Am. Chem. Soc. (award in pure chemistry 1947, William H. Nichols medal N.Y. sect. 1948, Charles L. Parsons award 1964, Gibbs medal Chgo. sect. 1966, Madison Marshall award No. Ala. sect. 1972, Priestley medal 1979, pres. 1976, George C. Pimentel award in chem. edn., 1994), Am. Philos. Soc., Royal Swedish Acad. Engring. Scis. (adv. council 1980), Am. Nat., Argentine Nat., Bavarian, Polish, Royal Swedish, USSR acads. scis., Royal Acad. Exact, Phys. and Natural Scis. Spain (acad. fgn. corr.), Soc. Nuclear Medicine (hon.), World Assn. World Federalists (v.p. 1980), Fedn. Am. Scis. (bd. sponsors 1980—), Deutsche Akademie der Naturforscher Leopoldina (East Germany), Nat. Acad. Pub. Adminstrn., Internat. Platform Assn. (pres. 1981-86), Am. Hiking Soc. (bd. dirs. 1979-84, v.p. 1980, adv. com. 1984—), Phi Beta Kappa, Sigma Xi, Pi Mu Epsilon, Alpha Chi Sigma (John R. Kuebler award 1978), Phi Lambda Upsilon (hon.); fgn. mem. Royal Soc. London, Chem. Soc. Japan, Serbian Acad. Sci. and Arhemian (San Francisco); Chemists (N.Y.C.); Cosmos (Washington), University (Washington); Faculty (Berkeley). Office: U Calif Lawrence Berkeley Lab 1 Cyclotron Rd Berkeley CA 94720

SEAGER, FLOYD WILLIAMS, medical educator; b. Ogden, Utah, July 1, 1921; s. Roy Alfred and Florence (Williams) S.; m. Beth Anne Seager, Feb. 6, 1943 (div. June 1965); m. Dauna Gayle Olsen, July 7, 1973; children: Stephen, Nancy, Candice, Pamela, Kevin, Karen. AS, Weber State U., 1941; BS in Chemistry, U. Utah, 1943; MD, Hahnemann U., 1947. Diplomate Nat. Bd. Med. Examiners. Pvt. practice Ogden, 1949-51; founder Ogden Clinic, 1951; chief of staff McKay Hosp., Ogden, 1979-81, trustee, 1989—; clin. prof. medicine U. Utah Med. Sch., Salt Lake City, 1990—. Editor: (med. jours.) Sub Q, 1980—, Ad Libitum, 1989. Capt. USMC, 1951-53, Korea. Dr. Seager Day named in his honor Mayor of Ogden, 1991; named Dr. of Yr., Utah State Med. Soc., 1993, Quiet Pioneer, Gov. Utah, 1991; recipient Point of Light award Pres. Bush, 1992. Mem. Am. Legion, Rotary Club Ogden, Elks. Republican. Mormon. Home and Office: 4046 S 895 E Ogden UT 84403-2416

SEALE, JAMES RICHARD, structural engineer; b. Rock Springs, Wyo., Dec. 28, 1953; s. James and Florence (Zamboni) S. BSCE, U. Wyo., 1976, MSCE, 1978. Registered profl. engr., Utah, Wyo., Calif., Conn., Md., N.J., Fla. Engr. I Eimco Processing Equipment Co., Salt Lake City, 1978-82, engr. II, 1982-86, engr. III, 1986-93, sr. engr. III, engring. tech. and standard divsn., 1993—. Sr. advisor Jr. Achievement, 1982-83. Mem. NSPE, ASCE, Utah Soc. Profl. Engrs., Am. Inst. Steel Constrn., Am. Concrete Inst., Elks. Democrat. Roman Catholic. Home: 5614 Laurelwood Dr Salt Lake City UT 84121-1217 Office: Eimco Processing Equipment 616 2nd Ave Salt Lake City UT 84103-3405

SEALE, ROBERT L., state treasurer; b. Inglewood, Calif., Oct. 4, 1941; m. Judy Seale (dec.). BSA, Calif. Poly. U. Former contr. and sr. fin. officer Rockwell Internat.; sr. accountant Ernst & Ernst, L.A.; mng. ptnr. Pangborn & Co., Ltd. CPA's, 1985-88; now state treas. State of Nev.; bd. dirs. Pub. Radio, Las Vegas, Pub. TV, Reno. Former treas. Nev. Rep. Party. Office: Office of State Treas Capital Complex Carson City NV 89710

SEALE, ROBERT MCMILLAN, office services company executive; b. Birmingham, Ala., Feb. 1, 1938; s. Robert McMillan and Margaret Sutherland (Miller) S.; B.A., Emory U., 1959. With N.Y. Life Ins. Co., San Francisco, 1960-67; with Dictaphone Office Services div. Dictaphone Corp., San Francisco, 1967-69; pres. Am. Profl. Service, Inc., Dictation West, Miss Jones' Word Processing, San Francisco, Pleasant Hill, South San Francisco, Calif., Los Angeles, Beverly Hills, Riverside, Portland, Phoenix, Las Vegas, Orange County, Calif. and Denver, 1969-93, Environments West, 1980-86, Los Arcos Properties, 1980—; founder Seale Orgn., 1993; bd. dirs. The Rose Resnic Ctr. for Blind and Handicapped, Computer Based Patient Record Inst.; med. word processing cons. to hosps., health care insts., office equipment mfrs.; lectr. in field. Contbr. articles in field to profl. jours. Chmn. San Francisco Mayor's Com. for Employment of Handicapped, 1971-73; mem. Calif. Gov.'s Planning and Adv. Com. for Vocat. Rehab. Planning, 1968-69; pres. Calif. League for Handicapped, 1968-70, bd. dirs., 1966-73, 84-89, adv. council, 1973-77; v.p. Stebbins Found., 1980—89; pres Stebbins Housing Corp., 1980-89; assoc. St. Francis Hosp. Found., 1990—. Recipient Spoke and Spark award U.S. Jr. C. of C., 1967; KABL Outstanding Citizen's award, 1965, 71. Mem. Am. Health Info. Mgmt. Assn., Adminstrv. Mgmt. Soc., Sales and Mktg. Execs. Assn., Am. Assn. Med. Transcription (Disting. Service award 1985), Med. Transcription Industry Alliance, Emory U. Alumni Assn., Emory Lamplighters Soc., U.S. C. of C., Delta Tau Delta. Republican. Office: 280 W Camino Sur Palm Springs CA 92262-4303

SEAMAN, ARLENE ANNA, musician, educator; b. Pontiac, Mich., Jan. 21, 1918; d. Roy Russell and Mabel Louise (Heffron) S. BS, life cert., Ea. Mich. U., 1939; MMus, Wayne State U., 1951; postgrad., Colo. Coll., 1951-52, Acad. Music, Zermatt Switzerland, 1954, 58, U. Mich. guest conductor Shepherds and Angels, Symphonie Concertante, 1951; asst. conductor Detroit Women's Symphony, 1960-68; adjudicator Mich. State Band and Orch. Festivals, Solo and Ensemble Festivals, 1950-70, Detroit Fiddler's Band Auditions, 1948-52, Mich. Fedn. Music Clubs, 1948-55; tchr. Ea. Mich. U., 1939-42, Hartland Sch. Music, 1939-42, Pontiac (Mich.) Pub. Schs., 1942-45, Detroit Pub. Schs., 1945-73, pvt. studio, 1973-90. Performer cello South Oakland Symphony, 1958-65, Detroit Women's Symphony, 1951-68, Riviera Theatre Orch., 1959, 60, Masonic Auditorium Opera, Ballet Seasons, 1959-65, Toledo Ohio Symphony, 1963-70, others; performer trumpet Detroit Brass Quartet, 1974-78; piano accompanist various auditions, recitals, solo and ensemble festivals; composer: Let There Be Music, 1949, Fantasy for French Horn and Symphonic Band, 1951. Mem. Quota Internat., Delta Omicron. Home: 14650 N Alamo Canyon Dr Tucson AZ 85737-8812

SEARBY, DANIEL MACLEOD, venture capitalist; b. Milw., June 24, 1934; s. Edmund Wilson and Muriel Marjorie (MacLeod) S.; m. Joan Innes Hinsch, June 16, 1960 (div. 1974); children: Daniel MacLeod, David Porter, Bruce Hamilton; m. Catharine Ann Rollins, Jan. 31, 1976; 1 child, Katharine MacLeod. AB, Dartmouth Coll., 1957; MS, Columbia U., 1958. Group product mgr. Procter & Gamble Co., Cin., 1958-69; fin. dir. OPIC, Washington, 1970-72; dep. asst. sec. Dept. State, Washington, 1973-74; sr. v.p. Triad, Los Altos, Calif., 1974-76; pres. Kearns Internat., San Francisco, 1976-83, MacLeod Investments, Palo Alto, Calif., 1984—; bd. dirs. Internat. Diplomacy Coun. Contbr. articles to profl. jours. Cpl. USMC, 1959-64. Republican. Episcopalian. Home: 459 Walsh Rd Atherton CA 94027-6438 Office: MacLeod Investments 2471 E Bayshore Rd # 525 Palo Alto CA 94303-3206

SEARIGHT, MARY DELL (MRS. PAUL JAMES SEARIGHT), nursing educator; b. Cordell, Okla., Jan. 4, 1918; d. John Quitman and Grace Jewel (Giles) Williams; diploma St. Francis Hosp. Sch. Nursing, 1940; B.S. with honors, U. Calif. at Berkeley, 1960; M.S., U. Calif. at San Francisco, 1961; Ed.D., U. San Francisco, 1980; m. Paul James Searight, June 12, 1953; children—Gregory Newton, Sara Ann. Clin. nursing in various hosps., clinics, industries, drs. offices, 1940-59; instr. nursing Merritt Coll., Oakland, Calif., 1961-66; lectr. U. Calif. at San Francisco Sch. Nursing, 1966-68; nursing cons. regional med. programs, lectr. U. Minn., Mpls., 1968-71; chmn. dept. Sonoma State U., 1971-77, prof. nursing, 1971-87, prof. emeritus, 1987—; mem. acad. senate, 1972-75, cons. nursing edn., 1972-77; project dir. Nat. 2d Step Project, 1978-81; cons. Bur. Health Resources Devel., San Francisco, 1973-75; mem. chancellor's liaison com. nursing edn. Calif. State U. and Colls. Office of Chancellor, Los Angeles, 1973-76; chmn. Sonoma County Health Facilities Planning Com., Santa Rosa, Calif., 1970-72; mem. planning com. Sonoma Health Services/Edn. Activities, Santa Rosa, 1972; mem. exec. com., bd. dirs. Sonoma County Comprehensive Health Planning Com., 1970-72. Mem. Nat. League Nursing, Am. Assn. Colls. Nursing, Am., Calif. (Lulu Hassenplug award 1975) Nurses Assns., Santa Rosa Symphony League, Sigma Theta Tau. Author: Your Career in Nursing, 1970, 2d edit., 1977; editor, contbg. author: The Second Step, Baccalaureate Education for Registered Nurses (Book of Year, Am. Jour. Nursing), 1976; contbr. articles to profl. jours. Address: 5555 Montgomery Dr Apt C-1 Santa Rosa CA 95409

SEARIGHT, PATRICIA ADELAIDE, retired radio and television executive; b. Rochester, N.Y.; d. William Hammond and Irma (Winters) S. BA, Ohio State U. Program dir. Radio Sta. WTOP, Washington, 1952-63, gen. mgr. info., 1964; radio and TV cons., 1964-84; ret., 1984; producer, dir. many radio and TV programs; spl. fgn. news corr. French Govt., 1956; v.p. Micro Beads, Inc., 1955-59; sec., dir. Dennis-Inches, Corp., 1955-59; exec. dir. Am. Women in Radio and TV, 1969-74; fgn. service officer U.S. Dept. State, ret., AEC, ret. Mem. pres.'s coun. Toledo Mus. Art. Recipient Kappa Kappa Gamma Alumna achievement award. Mem. Am. Women in Radio and TV (program chmn.; corrs. sec.; dir. Washington chpt.; pres. 1958-60, nat. membership chmn. 1962-63, nat. chmn. Industry Info. Digest 1963-64, Mid-Eastern v.p. 1964-66), Soc. Am. Travel Writers (treas. 1957-58, v.p. 1958-59), Nat. Acad. TV Arts and Scis., Women's Advt. Club (Washington, pres. 1959-60), Nat. Press Club, Soroptimist, Kappa Kappa Gamma. Episcopalian. Home: 9498 E Via Montoya Scottsdale AZ 85255-5074

SEARS, ALAN EDWARD, lawyer; b. Chattanooga, Oct. 31, 1951; s. Edward Lee and Anna Marie (Shepperd) S.; m. Paula Scott Lebeau, Nov. 11, 1988; children: Kelley, Shelby, Anna Marie, Rebecca. BA, U. Ky., 1974; JD, U. Louisville, 1977. Bar: Ky. 1977, U.S. Supreme Ct. 1980, Ariz. 1987, D.C. 1989, Calif. 1990, U.S. Dist. Ct. (we. and ea. dists.) Ky., U.S. Dist. Ct. Ariz., U.S. Dist. Ct. D.C., U.S. Ct. Appeals (D.C., 4th, 5th, 6th, 7th, 9th, 11th and D.C. cirs.), U.S. Tax Ct., U.S. Dist. Ct. (ctrl. & so. dists.) Calif. Asst. corp. counsel City of Ashland, Ky., 1977-78; assoc. Johnson, Dunnagan & Martin, Ashland, 1977-79, Amshoff & Amshoff, Louisville, 1979-81; chief criminal div., asst. U.S. atty. U.S. Dept. Justice, Louisville, 1981-85; exec. dir. atty. gens. commn. on pornography U.S. Dept. Justice, Washington, 1985-86; assoc. solicitor U.S. Dept. Interior, Washington, 1986-87; exec. dir. Children's Legal Found., Phoenix, 1987-90; assoc. Snell & Wilmer, Phoenix, 1990; exec. dir., gen. counsel Nat. Family Legal Found., Phoenix, 1990-91; asst. U.S. atty. U.S. Dept. Justice, 1991-93; pres., gen. counsel Alliance Def. Fund, 1993—; cons. and pub. speaker to numerous organizations. Co-author: Time, Place & Manner Regulation, 1989, Prosecution & Trial of Obscenity Case, 1988; contbr. chpts. to books. Dir. Ariz. Family Rsch. Inst., Phoenix, 1988—, Lincoln Caucas Ednl. Corp., Phoenix, 1990—. Mem. ABA, Ariz. Lawyers Div. Federalist Soc. (dir. 1988—), Calif. Bar Assn., Ariz. Bar Assn., Ky. Bar Assn., D.C. Bar Assn. Office: Alliance Def Fund 11811 N Tatum Blvd P184 Phoenix AZ 85028

SEARS, STEVEN LEE, screenwriter, consultant; b. Ft. Gordon, Ga., Dec. 23, 1957; s. Richard Bruce Sr. and Marian (Dean) S. AA, U. Fla., 1976; BA in Theater cum laude, Fla. State U., 1980. Writer Stephen J. Cannell Prodns., Hollywood, Calif., 1984-88, story editor, 1987-88; story editor VIACOM/Hargrove/Silverman Prodns., 1988; writer A. Shane Prodns., Superboy Prodns., 1989; exec. story cons. Highwayman Glen Larson/New West Prodns., Universal City, Calif., 1988; writer TV pilots Columbia Pictures Television, 1990. Writer (TV shows) Riptide, 1984-86, Hadcastle & McCormick, 1985, The A-Team, 1986-87, Stingray, 1987, Jesse Hawkes, 1989, Superboy, 1989, Grand Slam, 1989, Hardball, 1989, Who Gets Harry?, 1989, Robin's Hoods, 1994, Walker, Texas Ranger, 1994, (TV pilots) Harry O'Fell-Detective from Hell, 1990, The Inquisitor, 1990, (screenplay) Endangered Species, (interactive movie) Dreadnought, 1995, (TV show) Itsy Bitsy Spider, 1995; story editor TV shows J.J. Starbuck, 1987-88, The Father Dowling Mysteries, 1988; co-producer (TV show) Swamp Thing, 1991; producer (TV show) Raven, 1992-93; supervising prodr. (TV show) Xena Warrior Princess, 1995; exec. prodr. (feature) The Last Perfect Wave, 1995. Mem. AFTRA, SAG, Writers Guild Am. Democrat.

SEASTONE, BRIAN ARTHUR, protective services official, consultant; b. Boulder, Colo., May 27, 1957; s. Walter Gene and Elizabeth Joyce (Cronland) S. BA, U. Phoenix, 1987; MEd, No. Ariz. U., 1994. Dep. sheriff, evidence technician Boulder (Colo.) County Sheriff's Dept., 1974-80; officer U. Ariz. Police Dept., Tucson, 1980-84, pub. info. officer, cpl., 1984-87, sgt., 1987-89, adminstrv. sgt., 1989—; faculty senator U. Ariz., 1990-92, 94-95. Tech. advisor (video) Date Rape What Could Happen?, 1988 (Cert. of merit 1989). Recipient Outstanding Citizen award Boulder C. of C., 1973, Greek Achievement award Western Regional Greek Conf., 1992, Presdl. Cert. of Merit, 1993; named Ariz. Crime Prevention Officer of Yr., Ariz. Crime Prevention Assn., 1987, 88. Mem. Internat. Assn. Campus Law Enforcement Adminstrs. (assoc.), Ariz. Accreditation PAC, So. Ariz. Alumni Assn. (v.p. 1989-90, pres. 1990-93), Kappa Alpha (advisor). Democrat. Roman Catholic. Office: U Ariz Police Dept 1200 E Lowell Tucson AZ 85721

SEAU, JUNIOR (TIANA SEAU, JR.), professional football player; b. Samoa, Jan. 19, 1969. Student, U. So. Calif. Linebacker San Diego Chargers, 1990—; player Super Bowl XXVIV, 1994. Named to Sporting News Coll. All-Am. Team, 1989, to Pro Bowl Team, 1991, 92, 93,to Sporting News NFL All Pro Team, 1992, 93. Office: San Diego Chargers PO Box 609609 San Diego CA 92160-9609*

SEAWELL, DONALD RAY, lawyer, publisher, arts center executive, producer; b. Jonesboro, N.C., Aug. 1, 1912; s. A.A.F. and Bertha (Smith) S.; m. Eugenia Rawls, Apr. 5, 1941; children: Brook Ashley, Donald Brockman. A.B., U. N.C., 1933, J.D., 1936, D.Litt., 1980; L.H.D., U. No. Colo., 1978. Bar: N.C. 1936, N.Y. 1947. With SEC, 1939-41, 45-47, Dept. Justice, 1942-43; chmn. bd., dir., pub., pres. Denver Post, 1966-81; chmn. bd., dir. Gravure West, L.A., 1966-81; dir. Swan Prodns., London; of counsel firm Bernstein, Seawell, Kove & Maltin, N.Y.C., 1979—; chmn. bd., chief exec. officer Denver Ctr. for Performing Arts, 1972—; ptnr. Bonfils-Seawell Enterprises, N.Y.C.; bd. vis. U. N.C. Chmn. bd. ANTA, 1965—; mem. theatre panel Nat. Coun. Arts, 1970-74; bd. govs. Royal Shakespeare Theatre, Eng.; trustee Am. Acad. Dramatic Arts, 1967—, Hofstra U., 1968-69, Cen. City Opera Assn., Denver Symphony; bd. dirs., chmn. exec. com. Air Force Acad. Found., Nat. Inst. Outdoor Drama, Walter Hampden Meml. Library, Hammond Mus.; pres. Helen G. Bonfils Found., Denver Opera Found.; dir. Found. for Denver Ctr. for Performing Arts Complex, Population Crisis Com.; bd. dirs. Family Health Internat., Found. for Internat. Family Health; bd. visitors N.C. Sch. Arts, 1992—. With U.S. Army, WW II. Recipient Am. Acad. Achievement award, 1980, Tony award for producing On Your Toes, 1983, Voice Research and Awareness award Voice Found., 1983. Mem. Bucks Club (London), Dutch Treat Club (N.Y.C.), Denver Country Club, Denver Club, Cherry Hills Country Club, Mile High Club (Denver), Garden of Gods Club (Colorado Springs, Colo.). Office: Denver Ctr for Performing Arts 1050 13th St Denver CO 80204-2157

SECKINGER, GERALD EDWIN, investor; b. Manchester, Mich., May 28, 1925; s. Joseph Edward and Myrta Mae (Weber) S.; widowed; children: Marianne Leitereg, Mark Bernard, Margo Lynn Guzman, Martin Neil, Martha Jean Toffol, Michael John, Matthew Joseph. BA, Mich. State U., 1950. Gen. mgr. Del Mar Hotel, Sault Ste. Marie, Mich., 1950-52; food svc. dir. Montgomery Ward & Co., Chgo., 1952-82; food svc. cons., pres. Seckinger Assocs., Glenview, Ill., 1982-87; pvt. investor Gerald Seckinger, Scottsdale, Ariz., 1987—. Civil def. officer U.S. Govt., Glenview, Ill., 1962-64. 1st lt. U.S. Army Air Corps, 1943-46. Mem. McCormick Ranch POA, Am. Legion, Foodsvcs. Cons. Soc. Internat., KC. Republican. Roman Catholic. Home: 7806 E Via De La Entrada Scottsdale AZ 85258-4119

SECONDO, MITCHELL R., food products executive; b. 1941. With Bud Antle, Inc., 1962—. Office: Bud Antle Inc 639 Sanborn Pl Salinas CA 93901-4517*

SEDLANDER, JOHN WINGATE, controller; b. Detroit, July 26, 1946; s. E.J. and Mary Elizabeth (Wingate) S.; m. Jean Marie Whiteside, Aug. 17, 1968 (div. 1979); 1 child, Nathan John; m. Ellen Flanagan, Nov. 17, 1979; children: Mark, Erica. BA, U. Mich., 1968, MBA, 1970. Compensation analyst Jos. Schlitz Brewing Co., Milw., 1970-72, fin. analyst, 1972-73; mgr. purchasing and distbn. Geyser Peak Winery, Geyserville, Calif., 1973-78; dir. fin. planning CBS Specialty Stores, Emeryville, Calif., 1978-80; mgr. fin. planning Harris Corp., San Carlos, Calif., 1980-86, mgr. gen. acctg., 1986-87, credit mgr., 1987-88; mgr. fin. planning Sola Optical, Petaluma, Calif., 1988-92, contr., 1992—. Bd. dirs. The Endowment Bd., Oakland, Calif., 1980-93, Com. on the Shelterless, Petaluma, 1992—. Democrat. Lutheran. Home: 1629 Cerro Sonoma Cir Petaluma CA 94954-5768 Office: Sola Optical 1500 Cader Ln Petaluma CA 94954-5665

SEDLOCK, JOY, psychiatric social worker; b. Memphis, Jan. 23, 1958; d. George Rudolph Sedlock and Mary Robson; m. Thomas Robert Jones, Aug. 8, 1983. AA, Ventura (Calif.) Jr. Coll., 1978; BS in Psychology, Calif. Luth. U., 1980; MS in Counseling and Psychology, U. LaVerne, 1983; MSW, Calif. State U., Sacramento, 1986. Research asst. Camarillo (Calif.) State Hosp., 1981, tchr.'s aide, 1982; sub. tchr. asst. Vertura County Sch. Dist., 1981; teaching asst. Ventura Jr. Coll., 1980-82, tchr. adult edn., 1980-84; psychiatric social worker Yolo County Day Treatment Ctr., Broderick, Calif., 1986, Napa (Calif.) State Hosp., 1986—. Bd. dirs. Napa County Humane Soc. Mem. NOW. Home: PO Box 1095 Yountville CA 94599-1095 Office: Napa State Hosp Napa/Vallejo Hgwy Napa CA 49558

SEEBA, HINRICH CLAASSEN, foreign language educator; b. Hannover, Germany, Feb. 5, 1940; came to U.S., 1967; s. Hinrich and Irmgard (Witte) S. Student, Göttingen, Zürich, Tübingen univs., 1960-67; staatsexamen, U. Tübingen, Fed. Republic of Germany, 1966, PhD, 1967. Asst. prof. German U. Calif., Berkeley, 1968-72, assoc. prof., 1972-76, prof., 1976—, chmn. dept. German, 1977-81, 89-91; vis. prof. Free U. Berlin, 1992, Stanford (Calif.) U., 1994. Author: Kritik des ästhetischen Menschen, 1970, Die Liebe zur Sache, 1973; author, editor: Kleist: Dramen I, 1987, II, 1991; co-editor Politzefs, 1975, Brinkmanns, 1981; contbr. scholarly papers on German lit. to jours.; editorial bd. Lessing Yearbook, 1979—, Eighteenth Century Studies, 1982-85, The German Quar., 1988-92, 94—, South Cen. Rev., 1988—; adv. bd.

German Studies Rev., 1990—, Zeitschrift für Germanistik, 1991—, U. Calif. Press Modern Philology Series, 1992—. Studienstiftung fellow, 1963-68, Guggenheim Found. fellow, 1970-71. Mem. MLA, Am. Assn. Tchrs. German, German Studies Assn., Philol. Assn. of Pacific, Lessing Soc. (pres. 1985-87), Heine Soc., Grillparzer Gesellschaft, Herder Gesellschaft. Lutheran. Office: U Calif Dept German Berkeley CA 94720

SEEBACH, LYDIA MARIE, physician; b. Red Wing, Minn., Nov. 9, 1920; d. John Henry and Marie (Gleusen) S.; m. Keith Edward Wentz, Oct. 16, 1959; children: Brooke Marie, Scott. BS, U. Minn., 1942, MB, 1943, MD, 1944, MS in Medicine, 1951. Diplomate Am. Bd. Internal Medicine. Intern Kings County Hosp., Bklyn., 1944; fellow Mayo Found., Rochester, Minn., 1945-51; pvt. practice Oakland, Calif., 1952-60, San Francisco, 1961—; asst. clin. prof. U. Calif., San Francisco, 1981—; mem., vice chmn. Arthritis Clinic, Presbyn. Hosp., San Francisco, 1961-88, pharmacy com., 1963-78; chief St. Mary's Hosp. Arthritis Clinic, San Francisco, 1968-72; exec. bd. Pacific Med. Ctr., San Francisco, 1974-76. Contbr. articles to med. jours. Fellow ACP; mem. AMA, Am. Med. Womens Assn. (pres. Calif. chpt. 1968-70), Am. Rheumatism Assn., Am. Soc. Internal Medicine, Pan Am. Med. Womens Assn. (treas.), Calif. Acad. Medicine, Calif. Soc. Internal Medicine, Calif. Med. Assn., San Francisco Med. Soc., San Francisco Med. Assn., San Francisco Soc. Internal Medicine, No. Calif. Rheumatism Assn., Internat. Med. Women's Assn., Mayo Alumni (bd. dirs. 1983-89), Iota Sigma Pi. Republican. Lutheran. Office: 490 Post St Ste 939 San Francisco CA 94102-1410

SEEGALL, MANFRED ISMAR LUDWIG, retired physicist, educator, real estate executive; b. Berlin, Germany, Dec. 23, 1929; s. Leonhard and Vera Antonie (Vodackova) S.; came to U.S., 1952, naturalized, 1957; m. Alma R. Sterner Clarke; 2 stepchildren: James, Mark. BS magna cum laude, Loyola Coll., 1957; MS, Brown U., 1960; PhD, Stuttgart (Germany) Tech. U., 1965. Research engr. Autonetics Corp. div. N.Am. Aviation, Downey, Calif., 1959-61; physicist Astronautics div. Gen. Dynamics, Inc., San Diego, 1961-62; research scientist Max Planck Inst., Stuttgart, 1962-65; instr. stats. and algebra San Diego City Coll., 1966; sr. research engr. Solar div. Internat. Harvester Co., San Diego, 1967-73; research cons. in energy and pollution, San Diego, 1974-83; part-time evening instr. Mesa Coll., San Diego, 1980-81; instr. Grossmont Coll., El Cajon, Calif., 1981; sr. scientist Evaluation Research Corp., San Diego, 1981-82, RCS analyst Teledyne Micronetics, San Diego, 1983-84, sr. design specialist Alcoa Defense Systems, San Diego, 1984-87, cons. phys scis., 1987-89; ind. contractor in tech. writing, engring. rsch. and real estate, 1990-92, freelance writer, 1993—. Mem. IEEE (sr.), Internat. Platform Assn., Calif. Parapsychology Found. (pres. 1994—), Cottage of Czechoslovakia of House of Pacific Rels., Rosicrucian Order, Loyola Coll., Brown U. alumni assns. Republican. Club: San Diego Lodge AMORC. Contbr. articles on acoustics, pollution and temp. measurement methods to tech. jours.; patentee in field. Address: 8735 Blue Lake Dr San Diego CA 92119-3512

SEEGER, SONDRA JOAN, artist; b. L.A., May 27, 1942; d. Reinhold Josheph and Bertha Catherine (Monese) S.; m. Richard John Pahl, Aug. 18, 1961 (div. 1974); children: Catherine Marie, Douglas Richard, Angela Gay, Susan Joan; m. David Ernest Matteson, Apr. 25, 1990. Student, Marylhurst Coll., 1960. Pvt. practice musician various locations, 1973-81; security guard MGM Hotel, Las Vegas, 1981-82; real estate salesperson Century 21, Kent, Wash., 1983-85; mgr. Viera Land & Cattle, Inc., La Grande, Oreg., 1984-92; freelance artist, Casper, Wyo., 1991—; ptnr. Old West Saddle Shop, Casper, 1989-93, Casper, Wyo., 1993—; com. mem. Oreg. State Forest Practices Com., N.E. Region, 1990-91. Named Union Co. Tree Farmer of Yr., Am. Tree Farm System, 1987. Mem. NRA, Allied Artists, Cider Painters of Am., Australian Soc. of Miniature Art, Small Woodlands Assn., Knickerbocker Artists (assoc.), United Pastelists of Am., The Art League of Alexandria, Va., Miniature Art Soc. Fla., Oil Painters Am., Wyo. Artists Assn., Cody Country Art Guild, Am. Soc. Classical Realism, Gen. Artist Mem., Internat. Platform Assn., Oreg. Forest Resources Inst., Am. Artists' Profl. League. Republican. Home and Office: Old West Saddle Shop PO Box 4300 Casper WY 82604-0300

SEEKINS, ANNA MARIE, manufacturing executive; b. Lexington, Nebr., Oct. 22, 1948; d. Frederick Reo and Doris Louise (Hollibaugh) Green; m. James Lee Seekins, Jan. 3, 1969; children: Heidi Anne, Amy Marie. Grad. Westminster High Sch., Colo., 1966. With Forsythe & Dowis Carnival, 1950-64, Green's Amusements, 1964-68; collator, Jeppesen Time-Mirror, Denver, 1967-73; typesetter AAA Marking, Colorado Springs, Colo., 1975-78; seamstress Camp 7, Longmont, Colo., 1978-80; co-owner Westco Rep, Inc., Longmont, 1980—; order clk. Staydynamics, Longmont, 1982-84. Vol., Army Community Svc. Ctr., Colorado Springs. Republican. Baptist. Home: 305 Stinson Ave Cheyenne WY 82007-1110 Office: Westco Rep Inc 305 Stinson Ave Cheyenne WY 82007-1110

SEELENFREUND, ALAN, distribution company executive; b. N.Y.C., Oct. 22, 1936; s. Max and Gertrude (Roth) S.; m. Ellyn Bolt; 1 child, Eric. BME, Cornell U., 1959, M. in Indsl. Engring., 1960; PhD in Mgmt. Sci., Stanford U., 1967. Asst. prof. bus. adminstrn. Grad. Sch. Bus. Stanford U., Palo Alto, Calif., 1966-71; mgmt. cons. Strong, Wishart and Assocs., San Francisco, 1971-75; various mgmt. positions McKesson Corp., San Francisco, 1975-84, v.p., chief fin. officer, 1984-86, exec. v.p., chief fin. officer, 1986-89, chmn., chief exec. officer, 1989—, also bd. dirs.; bd. dirs. Armor All Products Corp., Pacific Gas and Electric Co. Bd. dir. Golden Gate Nat. Park Assn. Mem. World Affairs Coun. No. Calif., Bus. Roundtable, Bay Area Coun., Calif. Bus. Roundtable, Bankers Club, St. Francis Yacht Club, Villa Taverna Club, Pacific Union Club. Office: McKesson Corp 1 Post St San Francisco CA 94104-5203*

SEETHALER, WILLIAM CHARLES, international business executive, consultant; b. N.Y.C., Dec. 4, 1937; s. William Charles and Catherine Frances (Flaherty) S. Student, Quinnipiac Coll., Conn., 1955-56, Ohio State U., 1956-58; BSBA, U. San Francisco, 1977; MBA, Pepperdine U., 1982. Asst. to v.p. sales T. Sendzimir, Inc., Waterbury, Conn. and Paris, 1960-66; mgr. internat. ops. Dempsey Indsl. Furnace Co., East Longmeadow, Mass., 1966-67; mgr. internat. sales Yoder Co., Cleve., 1967-74; mng. dir., owner Seethaler & Assocs., Palo Alto, Calif.; owner, chief exec. officer Seethaler Internat. Ltd., Palo Alto, Calif., 1974—; ptnr. DFS Computer Assocs., San Jose, Calif., 1976-87. Bd. dirs. Palo Alto Fund, 1979-93, chmn., 1986-88; comty. rels. advisor Stanford U., 1986—. Mem. Inst. Indsl. Engrs. (sr., v.p. profl. rels. Peninsula chpt. 1988-90, del. to Silicon Valley Engring. Coun. 1991—, bd. dirs.), Joint Venture: Silicon Valley (bd. dirs. 1992—), Assn. Iron and Steel Engrs., Assn. MBA Execs., Palo Alto C. of C. (v.p. orgn. affairs 1976-77, pres. 1977-78, bd. dirs. 1975-79), U. San Francisco Alumni Assn., Stanford U. Alumni Assn., Pepperdine U. Alumni Assn., Stanford Diamond Club. Office: 701 Welch Rd Bldg 323 Palo Alto CA 94304-1709

SEFF, KARL, chemistry educator; b. Chgo., Jan. 23, 1938; s. Joseph and Rose (Hauser) S. BS, U. Calif., Berkeley, 1959; PhD, MIT, 1964. Rsch. assoc. UCLA, 1965-67; asst. prof. chemistry U. Hawaii, Honolulu, 1968-73, assoc. prof. chemistry, 1973-75, prof. chemistry, 1975—; cons. Filtrol Corp., L.A., 1966-73, Mitsubishi Heavy Industry, Nagasaki, Japan, 1992-94; vis. scholar Princeton (N.J.) U., 1974-75, Oxford (Eng.) U., 1988, 89; assoc. rschr. U. Mex, 1981-82; vis. prof. Dartmouth U., 1989; lectr. Tokyo Inst. Tech., 1980, 91, U. Salford, Eng., 1983, U. N.Mex., 1985, U. P.R., 1985, U. Bristol, 1988, ETH, Zurich, Switzerland, 1988, Goethe U., Frankfort, Germany, 1988, Imperial Coll., London, 1989, Cambridge U., 1989, Kyungpook Nat. U., Korea, 1990, Acad. Sci. Leningrad, 1990, Pusan Nat. U., Korea, 1990, Northwestern U., 1994, others. Contbr. more than 160 articles to profl. jours. NATO sr. fellow, NSF, 1975, Rsch. Travel award, 1988-90; grantee Army Rsch. Office, 1969-72, NIH, 1972-75, 75-78, NSF, 1973-76, 75, 77, 78-81, Petroleum Rsch. Fund, 1974-76, 95—, Gordon Conf., 1976, U.S.-Korea Coop. Rsch., NSF, 1982, 84-86, Mitsubishi Industries, 1992-93. Mem. Am. Chem. Soc. (local sect. chair, award 1983, councilor 1992-94), Am. Crystallographic Assn., Vegetarian Soc. Honolulu (exec. com. 1993—), Sigma Xi. Democrat. Office: U Hawaii Dept Chemistry 2545 The Mall Honolulu HI 96822-2233

SEGAL, CARL MICHAEL, electronics company executive; b. N.Y.C., Feb. 6, 1930; s. Michael Carl and Frances (Brandon) S.; m. Shirley Theresa Benz Nipotti, Jan. 10, 1953 (div. July 1981); children: Michael Carl, Paul Anthony, Carol Ann; m. Arona Helene Weiner, May 12, 1991. Student, El Camino Coll., 1947-48; grad., DeVry Tech. Inst. Mktg. rep. Source 2, Santa Clara, Calif., 1981-84; gen. sales mgr. Integrated Electronics, San Jose, Calif., 1984-85; dist. sales mgr. Raytheon Co., Mountain View, Calif., 1985-87; area sales mgr. Wellex Corp., Fremont, Calif., 1987-88; sales mgr. Sonictron, San Jose, 1988-89; dist. sales mgr. Assembly Shop Inc., San Diego, 1989-90; sales mgr. IPAC Mfg., Carlsbad, Calif., 1990-91; mfr.'s rep. Profl. Sales Co., San Diego, 1991-94; dir. sales/mktg. Western Radio Electronics, San Diego, 1994—. Chmn. Adat Ami Synagogue, 1990—, usher chmn., 1992. Sgt. U.S. Army, 1948-52, Korea. Mem. Ranch Breakfast Club. Republican. Jewish. Home: 6955 Caminito Curva San Diego CA 92119-2421 Office: Western Radio Electronics 5555 Kearny Villa Rd San Diego CA 92123-1107

SEGAL, D. ROBERT, publishing and broadcast company executive; b. Oshkosh, Wis., Oct. 30, 1920; s. Morris Henry and Ida (Belond) S.; m. Kathryn McKenzie; children: Jonathan McKenzie, Janet Elizabeth Crane. Currently pres., chief exec. officer, dir. Freedom Newspapers, Inc., Irvine, Calif.; pres. Freedom Communications, Inc., Orange County Cable News, Kinston (N.C.) Free-Press, New Bern (N.C.) Sun Jour., Burlington (N.C.) Times-News, Jacksonville (N.C.) Daily News, WLNE-TV, New Bedford, Mass. and Providence, KFDM-TV, Beaumont, Tex., WTVC-TV, Chattanooga, WRGB-TV, Schenectady, Freedom Newspapers of Fla., Inc., Crawfordsville Jour.-Rev. (Ind.), Greenville (Miss.) Delta Dem. Pub. Co., Dothan (Ala.) Progress.; mng. ptnr. Clovis News-Jour. (N.Mex.), Rio Grande Valley Newspaper Group (Tex.), Gastonia Gazette (N.C.), Lima News (Ohio), Odessa Am. (Tex.), Pampa Daily News (Tex.), Orange County Cablenews Network. Trustee Children's Hosp of Orange County, Calif., Boy Scout Council of Orange County. Served with USAAF, 1942-45. Office: Freedom Newspapers Inc 17666 Fitch Irvine CA 92714-6022*

SEGAL, MORTON, public relations executive; b. N.Y.C., Mar. 3, 1931. BA, Kenyon Coll., England, 1953; MFA in Dramatic Lit., Columbia U., 1956. Mgr. publicity Paramount Pictures, 1961-63; dir. worldwide publicity and pub. rels. 20th Century Fox, 1963-65; v.p. advt. and publicity MGM, 1965-72; with Allen, Ingersoll, Segal and Henry, 1973-75; prin. ICPR, 1975-79, pres., 1978-85; vice chmn., prin. Dennis Davidson Assocs., 1986—; with L.A. Internat. Film Exposition, 1982-84. Mem. Acad. Motion Picture Arts and Scis. Office: Dennis Davidson Assocs Inc 5670 Wilshire Blvd Ste 700 Los Angeles CA 90036-5607

SEGAL, STEVEN PAUL, social work educator; b. Bklyn., Jan. 13, 1943; married, 2 children. BA, Hunter Coll., Bronx, 1965; MSW, U. Mich., 1967; PhD, U. Wis., 1972. Caseworker N.Y. Bur. Child Welfare, N.Y.C., 1965; social group worker Windsor Group Therapy Project, Ont., 1965-66; unit supr. Fresh Air Soc., Detroit, 1966; caseworkr Lansing (Mich.) Cons. Ctr., 1966-67, Jewish Family & Children's Svcs., Detroit, 1967; asst. to assoc. prof. and rsch. social worker U. Calif., Berkeley, 1972-88; prin. investigator Inst. Sci. Analysis, Berkeley, 1982-94; assoc. dir. Ctr. for Rsch. on Orgn. and Financing, Western Consortium, Berkeley, 1988-92; dir. Mental Health and Social Welfare Rsch. Group U. Calif., Berkeley, 1973—; prof. sch. social welfare and pub. health U. Calif., 1988—; dir. Ctr. Self Help Rsch., 1990—; lectr. in field; conductor workshops in field. Contbr. numerous articles to profl. jours. Recipient Medal of Brescia, Italy, 1987, Western European Regional Rsch. Fulbright award, 1986-87; NIMH traineeships, 1965, 66, 67, 68, 69, 70-72; N.Y. State Rsch. fellow in psychiat. epidemiology, 1969-71, others. Mem. NASW, APHA, Am. Sociol. Assn., Am. Psychol. Assn. Home: 733 Santa Barbara Rd Berkeley CA 94707-2045 Office: Sch Social Welfare 120 Haviland Hall U of Calif Berkeley CA 94720

SEGALL, MARK M., physician, colon and rectal surgeon; b. Far Rockaway, N.Y., Jan. 20, 1948; s. Solomon Kief and Sylvia Tina (Stangel) S.; m. Nikki Forbes, Feb. 18, 1978; children: Jeremy, Eli, Leah, Noah. Student, Wayne State U., 1965-66, U. Mich., 1966-68; MD, U. Mich., 1972. Diplomate Am. Bd. Surgery, Am. Bd. Colon and Rectal Surgery. Intern in surgery UCLA, 1972-73; physician Kaiser, W. L.A., 1973-75; resident in surgery William Beaumont Hosp., Royal Oak, Mich., 1975-79; colon and rectal surgery fellow U. Minn., Mpls., 1979-80; pvt. practice surgeon Southfield, Mich., 1980-83, Los Gatos, Calif., 1983—; clin. instr. Wayne State U. Sch. Medicine, Detroit, 1980-84, Stanford U. Sch. Medicine, Palo Alto, Calif., 1984—; clin. asst. prof. Dept. Surgery Stanford U. Sch. Medicine, 1990—. Contbr. articles to profl. jours. Active Little Learners, 1986—. Recipient Profl. Vol. of Yr. award Am. Cancer Soc., 1988. Fellow Southwestern Surg. Cong., Am. Coll. Surgeons, Am. Soc. Colon and Rectal Surgeons (Ohio Valley Proctologic Soc. award); mem. Soc. Am. Gastrointestinal Endoscopic Surgeons, San Jose Surg. Soc., Santa Clara Surg. Soc., N.W. Soc. Colon and Rectal Surgeons, No. Calif. Soc. Colon and Rectal Surgeons, Santa Clara County Med. Soc., Calif. Med. Assn., Am. Med. Assn. Democrat. Jewish. Office: 15195 National Ave # 202 Los Gatos CA 95032-2631

SEGALMAN, RALPH, sociology educator; b. N.Y.C., July 15, 1916; s. Samuel and Celia S.; m. Anita Cohen, Aug. 25, 1940; children: Robert, Ruth, Daniel. AB in Zoology, Sociology, U. Mich., 1937, MSW, 1944; PhD in Social Psychology, NYU, 1966. Lic. clin. social worker, Calif.; lic. marriage, family, child counselor, Calif. Social worker, exec. dir. various Jewish fedns., community couns., social svc. programs, Sioux City, Iowa, Waterbury, Conn., El Paso, Tex., 1940-65; from asst. to assoc. prof. Grad. Sch. Social Work U. Tex., El Paso, 1965-69, assoc. prof., asst. dean Grad. Sch. Social Work, 1967-69; vis. prof. social work U. Wis., Madison, 1969-70; prof. sociology Calif. State U., Northridge, 1970-86, emeritus prof. sociology, 1986—; cons. on social policy, family, public welfare and other issues; keynote spkr. with Alfred Himelson at sessions on the future of the family, Profs. World Peace Acad., Seoul, Korea, 1994. Author: Dynamics of Social Behavior and Development, 1978, The Swiss Way of Welfare, Lessons for the Western World, 1986, (with Asoke Basu) Poverty in America: The Welfare Dilemma, 1981 (Scholarly Work award Calif. State U. 1982), (with David Marsland) Cradle to Grave: Comparative Perspectives on the State of Welfare, 1989; founding consulting editor Jour. of Sociology and Social Welfare; affiliated assoc. editor Jour. Am. Behavioral Sci. Recipient State Israel award, 1963. Fellow AAAS, Found. Jewish Culture, Council Jewish Fedns. and Welfare Funds; mem. Am. Sociol. Assn. Home and Office: 18723 Sunburst St Northridge CA 91324-3828

SEGEL, KAREN LYNN JOSEPH, tax professional, lawyer; b. Youngstown, Ohio, Jan. 15, 1947; d. Samuel Dennis and Helen Anita Joseph; m. Alvin Gerald Segel, June 9, 1968 (div. Sept. 1976); 1 child, Adam James. BA in Soviet and East European Studies, Boston U., 1968; JD, Southwestern U., 1975. Cert. tax profl. Adminstrv. asst. Olds Brunel & Co., N.Y.C., 1968-69, U.S. Banknote Corp., N.Y.C., 1969-70; tax acct. S.N. Chilkov & Co. CPA's, Beverly Hills, Calif., 1971-74; intern Calif. Corps. Commr., 1975; tax. sr. Oppenheim Appel & Dixon CPA's, L.A., 1978, Fox, Westheimer & Co. CPA's, L.A., 1978, Zebrak, Levine & Mepos CPA's, L.A., 1979; ind. cons. acctg., taxation specialist Beverly Hills, 1980—; bd. dirs. World Wide Motion Pictures Corp., L.A. Editorial adv. bd. Am. Biog. Inst. High sch. amb. to Europe People-to-People Orgn., 1963. Named 1991, 93 Woman of Yr., Am. Biog. Inst. Mem. Nat. Soc. Tax Profls., Nat. Trust for Hist. Preservation, Am. Mus. Natural History, Winterthur Guild, Women's Inner Circle of Achievement.

SEGGER, MARTIN JOSEPH, museum director, art history educator; b. Felixtowe, Eng., Nov. 22, 1946; s. Gerald Joseph and Lillian Joan (Barker-Emery) S.; m. Angele Cordonier, Oct. 4, 1968; children: Cara Michelle, Marie-Claire, Margaret Ellen. B.A., U. Victoria, 1969, Diploma in Edn., 1970; M. in Philosophy, U. London, 1973. Prof. art history U. Victoria, B.C., 1970-74; museologist Royal B.C. Mus., Victoria, 1974-77; dir. Maltwood Art Mus., prof. art history U. Victoria, B.C., 1977—; cons. Nat. Mus. Corp., Ottawa, 1977, UNESCO, O.E.A., Cairo, 1983. Author: exhbn. catalogue House Beautiful, 1975, Arts of the Forgotten Pioneers, 1971, Victoria: An Architectural History, 1979, (commendation Am. Assn. State and Local History 1980), This Old House, 1975, This Old Town, 1979, British Columbia Parliament Buildings, 1979, The Heritage of Canada, 1981, Samuel Maclure: In Search of Appropriate Form, 1986 (Hallmark award 1987), (a guide) St. Andrew's Cathedral, 1990, The Development of Gordon Head Campus, 1988, An Introduction to Museum Studies, 1989, An Introduction to Heritage Conservation, 1990, Botswana Live, 1994; editl. bd. mem. Managing Leisure: an International Journal, U.K., 1994—. Bd. govs. Heritage Can. Found., 1979-83; chmn. City of Victoria Heritage Adv. Com., 1975-79; bd. dirs. Heritage Trust, 1977-86, B.C. Touring Coun., Sta. CFUV Radio, B.C. Govt. House Found., 1987-93; mem. B.C. Heritage Adv. Bd., 1973-83; councillor City of Victoria, 1987-93; vice-chair Provincial Capital Commn., 1991—; pres. Assn. Vancouver Island Municipalities, 1993-94. Decorated knight Equestrian Order of Holy Sepulchre of Jerusalem; recipient award Heritage Can. Communications, 1976, Heritage Conservation award Lt. Gov. B.C., 1989, Harley J. McKee award Assn. Preservation Technology, 1994. Fellow Royal Soc. Arts; mem. Can. Mus. Assn. (counsellor 1975-77), Internat. Coun. Mus. (exec.), Internat. Coun. Monuments and Sites (bd. dirs. 1980-92), Soc. Study Architecture Can. (bd. dirs. 1979-81), Authors Club (London), Can. Mus. Dirs. Orgn., Canarvon Club. Roman Catholic. Home: 1035 Sutlej St, Victoria, BC Canada V8V 3P2 Office: U Victoria, PO Box 3025, Victoria, BC Canada V8W 2P2

SEGRE, EUGENE JOSEPH, drug development consultant, physician; b. Torino, Italy, Sept. 12, 1932; came to U.S., 1940; s. Ernesto and Anna (Jona) S.; m. Zina Cecilia Camarda, June 8, 1956; children: David, Paul, Lisa. BA, Cornell U., 1953, MD, 1956. Diplomate Am. Bd. Internal Medicine, Nat. Bd. Med. Examiners. Staff scientist Worcester Found., Shrewsbury, Mass., 1962-64; assoc. med. dir. Syntex Corp., Palo Alto, Calif., 1964-66; dir. clin. pharmacology Syntex Corp., Palo Alto, 1966-67; assoc. dir. Inst. of Medicine Syntex Corp., Palo Alto, 5, 1967-77, v.p., dir. Inst. of Medicine, 1977-80, sr. v.p. devel. rsch., 1980-90; cons. Palo Alto, 1990—; mem., chair sci. adv. bds. Hana Biologics, Berkeley, Calif., 1990-92, Pharmagenesis, 1991—, Acea Pharms., 1991—, Calydon, 1991—; asst. clin. prof. Stanford U. Med. Sch., Palo Alto, 1965-84, emeritus, 1993—. Author: Androgens, Virilization and the Hirsute Female, 1967; contbr. chpts. to books, more than 50 articles to profl. jours.; patentee in field. Capt. USAF, 1957-59, 61-62. Fellow ACP; mem. Am. Soc. for Clin. Pharmacology and Therapeutics, Phi Beta Kappa, Alpha Omega Alpha. Home and Office: 470 Santa Rita Ave Palo Alto CA 94301-3943

SEHEULT, MALCOLM MCDONALD RICHARDSON, solicitor; b. Port of Spain, Trinidad, July 18, 1949; s. Errol Andre and Laura (Laltoo) S.; m. Robin Lynn Montanye; children: Kristie, Julie, Laura, Aimée. BA in Sociology magna cum laude, U. Toronto, 1971, BEd, 1972, MA, 1973; LLB, U. Toronto, Ottawa, 1976; DJuris, Kensington U., 1988. Bar: Ontario, Can. 1978, N.Y. 1987; cert. tchr., Toronto, Can. Pvt. practice Toronto, 1978-85; assoc. Outerbridge, Barristers & Solicitors, Mississauga, Ont., Can., 1985-86, Don Brown, Mississauga, 1986—; lectr. numerous profl. and community groups and orgns. Producer, editor Where Is Tomorrow?, 1969; editor Ottawa Law Rev.; also articles. Mem. Justice for Children, Vanier Inst. of Family, Ont. Sch. Tchrs. Fedn.; bd. dirs. North York Branson Hosp. Mem. ABA, N.Y. State Bar Assn., Can. Bar Assn., Assn. Trial Lawyers Am., Law Soc. Upper Can., Medico-Legal Soc., Lawyers Club, Can. Civil Liberties Union, Royal Soc. Arts (fellow 1979), Mensa Internat., Can. Sociology and Anthropology Assn., Nat. Directory Sociology of Edn. and Ednl. Sociology, Am. Philatelic Soc., Phi Kappa Phi. Home: 25623 State St Loma Linda CA 92354-2443 Address: 2638 Victoria Park Ave, Willowdale, ON Canada M2J 4A6

SEIBEL, ERWIN, oceanographer, educator; b. Schwientochlowitz, Germany, Apr. 29, 1942; came to U.S., 1952. BS, CCNY, 1965; MS, U. Mich., 1966, PhD, 1972. Asst. research oceanographer U. Mich., Ann Arbor, 1972-75, assoc. research oceanographer, 1975-78, asst. dir. sea grant, 1975-78; environ. lab dir. San Francisco State U., 1978-81, chmn. dept. geoscis., 1981-88, dean undergraduate studies, 1988—. commr. Calif. Commn. on Tchr. Credentialing; sr. scientist cruises U. Mich., 1971-78; mem. sea grant site rev. teams Nat. Sea Grant Program, Washington, 1978—; bd. govs. Moss Landing Marine Labs., Calif., 1981—; mem. adv. com. Ctr. Advancement Mercantile Spacefaring; coord. Biology Forum Calif. Acad. Scis., 1988-89; exec. sec. Oceans 83 Marine Tech. Soc., IEEE, San Francisco, 1982-83; coord. Symposium for Pacific AAAS El Nino Effect, 1983-84; dir. environ. monitoring nuclear power plant, 1972-78; mem. sci. adv. panel Calif. Commn. Tchr. Credentialing, 1988-93; mem. steering com. Pacific Basin Studies Ctr., 1990-93; commr. Calif. Commn. on Teaching Credentialing, 1993—. Contbr. articles to profl. jours.; developer photogrammetric technique for continuous shoreline monitoring. Advisor MESA program for Minority Students, San Francisco area, 1981-88; vol. San Francisco Bay Area council Girl Scouts U.S., 1982-86. Served to capt. U.S. Army, 1967-71, Vietnam. Grantee Am. Electric Power Co., 1972-78, Gt. Lakes Basin Commn., 1975-76, Calif. Div. Mines and Geology, 1986-88, Am. Coun. Edn. and Ford Found., 1990-94. Recipient Exceptional Merit Service award San Francisco State U., 1984. Fellow AAAS, Calif. Acad. Scis., Geol. Soc. Am.; mem. N.Y. Acad. Scis., Am. Geophys. Union, Marine Tech. Soc. (pres. San Francisco Bay chpt. 1982-83), Western Assn. Schs. and Colls. (mem. student learning and teaching effectiveness task force 1994-95), U. Mich. Alumni Assn., Gold Key (hon.), Sigma XI (pres. San Francisco State U. chpt. 1982-84, 90-92, Chautauqua coord. 1989—, faculty athletic rep. NCAA, NCAC, 1991-93). Office: San Francisco State U Dean of Undergrad Studies 1600 Holloway Ave San Francisco CA 94132-1722

SEIDE, MARILYN BERNSTEIN, mental health administrator; b. Bklyn., Dec. 25, 1930; d. Louis and Hannah Rose (Bistrong) Bernstein; m. Ray Seide, Nov. 20, 1960; children: Jared David, Liam Evan. BA, Bennington Coll., 1952; MA, New Sch. Social Rsch., 1973; PhD, Union Inst., 1981. Mental health specialist, rsch. assoc. Juvenile Justice Inst., N.Y.C., 1973-79; supr. compliance monitoring Div. Criminal Justice Svcs., N.Y.C., 1979-80; assoc. dir. North Cen. Bronx (N.Y.) Hosp., 1980-87; program dir. Psychiatric Pavillion Bergen Pines City Hosp., Paramus, N.J., 1988-91; mgr. adult svcs. Riverside (Calif.) County Dept. Mental Health, 1991—; mem. adv. bd. Patton State Hosp., 1993—. Contbr. articles to profl. jours. Pres. bd. vis. Manhattan Children's Psychiat. Ctr., 1977-91; adv. bd. Commn. on Quality Care, 1977-90; mem. Mental Health Advocacy Group for Children and Youth, 1984-91; pres. bd. trustees Walden Sch., 1988-90. Fellow Am. Orthopsychiatric Assn.; mem. APHA, Am. Coll. Healthcare Execs., Assn. Mental Health Adminstrs. Office: Riverside County Dept Mental Health PO Box 7549 Riverside CA 92503

SEIDEL, GEORGE ELIAS, JR., animal scientist, educator; b. Reading, Pa., July 13, 1943; s. George E. Sr. and Grace Esther (Heinly) S.; m. Sarah Beth Moore, May 28, 1970; 1 child, Andrew. BS, Pa. State U., 1965; MS, Cornell U., 1968, PhD, 1970; postgrad., Harvard U. Med. Sch., Boston, 1970-71. Asst. prof. physiology Colo. State U., Ft. Collins, 1971-75, assoc. prof., 1975-83, prof., 1983—; vis. scientist Yale U., 1978-79, MIT, 1986-87; mem. bd. on agr. NRC. Co-editor: New Technologies in Animal Breeding, 1981; contbr. articles to profl. jours. Recipient Alexander Von Humboldt award, N.Y.C., 1983, Animal Breeding Research award Nat. Assn. Animal Breeders, Columbia, Mo., 1983, Clark award Colo. State U., 1982, Upjohn Physiology award, 1986; Gov's. award for Sci. and Tech., Colo., 1986. Mem. AAAS, NAS, Am. Dairy Sci. Assn., Am. Soc. Animal Sci. (Young Animal Scientist award 1983), Soc. for Study of Reprodn., Internat. Embryo Transfer Soc. (pres. 1979). Home: 3101 Arrowhead Rd Laporte CO 80535-9374 Office: Animal Reprodn Lab Colo State U Fort Collins CO 80523

SEIDEL, JOAN BROUDE, stockbroker, investment advisor; b. Chgo., Aug. 16, 1933; d. Ned and Betty (Treiger) Broude; m. Arnold Seidel, Aug. 18, 1957; children: David, Craig. BA, UCLA, 1954; postgrad., N.Y. Inst. Fin. Registered prin., investment advisor Morton Seidel & Co. Inc., L.A., 1970-74, v.p., 1974-93; pres., 1993—; also bd. dirs. Morton Seidel & Co. Inc., L.A.; instr. UCLA Extension, 1979-84. Treas. City of Beverly Hills, Calif., 1990—, chmn. rent adjustment bd., 1989-90, mem., 1983-89; mem. investment com. YWCA, L.A., 1987—, chmn. bd. dirs., 1989—, treas. Greater L.A., 1992—; bd. dirs. Discovery Fund for Eye Rsch., L.A., 1987—. Named Citizen of Yr. Beverly Hills C. of C., 1993. Fellow Assn. for Investment Mgmt. and Rsch.; mem. Nat. Assn. Security Dealers (dist. bus. conduct com. 25 1993—), L.A. Soc. Fin. Analysts, Orgn. Women Execs., Women in Bus., City Club, Bond Club, Phi Sigma Alpha. Home: 809 N Bedford Dr Beverly Hills CA 90210-3023 Office: Morton Seidel & Co Inc 350 S Figueroa St Bldg 499 Los Angeles CA 90071-1203

SEIDENSTICKER, EDWARD GEORGE, Japanese language and literature educator; b. Castle Rock, Colo., Feb. 11, 1921; s. Edward George and Mary Elizabeth (Dillon) S. B.A., U. Colo., 1942; M.A., Columbia U., 1947; postgrad., Harvard U., 1947-48; LittD (hon.), U. Md., 1991. With U.S. Fgn.

Service, Dept. State, Japan, 1947-50; mem. faculty Stanford U., 1962-66, prof., 1964-66; prof. dept. Far Eastern langs. and lit. U. Mich., Ann Arbor, 1966-77; prof. Japanese Columbia U., 1977-85, prof. emeritus, 1986—. Author: Kafu the Scribbler, 1965, Japan, 1961, Low City, High City, 1983, Tokyo Rising, 1990, Very Few People Come This Way, 1994; transl.: (by Murasaki Shikibu) The Tale of Genji, 1976. Served with USMCR, 1942-46. Decorated Order of Rising Sun Japan; recipient Nat. Book award, 1970; citation Japanese Ministry Edn., 1971; Kikuchi Kan prize, 1977; Goto Miyoko prize, 1982; Japan Found. prize, 1984; Tokyo Cultural award, 1985; Yamagata Banto prize, 1992.

SEIERSTAD, ALBERTA JUNE, chemist; b. Cumberland, Wis., June 21, 1949; d. Albert Martin and Violette Anna (Peterson) S. BS in Chemistry and Math., U. Wis., River Falls, 1971; postgrad., Iowa State U., 1971-72, U. Nebr., 1972-74. Lab. asst. U. Wis., River Falls, 1969-71; teaching asst. Iowa State U., Ames, 1971-72, U. Nebr., Lincoln, 1972-74; rsch. asst. Utah Water Rsch. Lab., Logan, 1977-79, rsch. chemist, 1980-84, lab. supr., 1984-86; lab. mgr. Portland (Oreg.) Water Bur., 1987—; quality assurance lab. cons. Ecosystems Rsch. Inst., Logan, 1982. Co-author/editor lab. procedures manual: Analytical Procedures for Selected Water Quality Parameters, 1981. Mem. APHA, Am. Water Wks. Assn. (standard methods com. 1980—), Am. Chem. Soc. Home: 39920 Hall Ct Sandy OR 97055-9387 Office: Portland Water Bur 2010 N Interstate Ave Portland OR 97227-1756

SEIFEL, ELIZABETH MARGARET, business owner; b. Boston, Apr. 23, 1956; d. Norman and Mary Elizabeth (Gill) S.; m. Steve Melnikoff (div. Dec. 1990.). BS in Urban Studies, Mass. Inst. Tech., 1978, M in City Planning, 1979. Exec. dir. Tent City Corp., Boston, 1979-81; planner, economist Blayney-Dyett, San Francisco, 1981-82; assoc.-in-charge Williams-Kuebelbeck, Belmont, Calif., 1982-89; prin. Seifel Assocs., San Francisco, 1990—; mem. Contra Costa County Home Tech. Adv. Commn., 1994—. Dir. Women's Philharmonic, San Francisco, 1990-94; mem. Leadership Calif., 1994—. Mem. Am. Inst. Cert. Planners, Calif. Redevel. Assn., Urban Land Inst., Non-Profit Housing Assn., MIT Alumni Assn. No. Calif. (officer 1982-94, dir. 1993-94, nat. selection com. 1994—, pres. 1995—). Office: Seifel Assocs 100 Bush St Ste 400 San Francisco CA 94104

SEIFERT, GEORGE, professional football coach; b. San Francisco, Jan. 22, 1940; m. Linda Seifert; children: Eve, Jason. Grad., U. Utah, 1963. Asst. football coach U. Utah, 1964; head coach Westminster Coll., 1965; asst. coach U. Iowa, 1966, U. Oreg., 1966-71; secondary coach Stanford U., 1972-74; head coach Cornell U., 1975-76; from secondary coach to defensive coord. San Francisco 49ers, 1980-89, head coach, 1989—. With AUS, 1963. Office: San Francisco 49ers 4949 Centennial Blvd Santa Clara CA 95054-1229*

SEIFERT, MIKI, scriptwriter, producer; b. Bethlehem, Pa., Mar. 20, 1958; d. Conrad Harry and Jeanette Elmira (Funk) S.; m. William Franco, Dec. 28, 1986. BA in French and in Political Sci., Moravian Coll., 1981. Writer, producer Speckled Gekko Prodns., San Diego, 1987—; prodn. technician KNSD TV, San Diego, 1988-90. Producer Summerdance, 1988, Impressions of the Border, 1990, The Foundling (Southwestern Regional Emmy), 1991, Odi's Story, 1991, Ramona Birth of a Mis-ce-ge-Nation, 1991, To My Sister's Husband (CINE Eagle award, Cert. Merit, Southwestern Regional Emmy, Gold Seal, Duisberger Medaille), 1992, Public Works, 1992. Mem. Film & Video Artists Assn. San Diego (co-founder, dir., sec. 1992-94). Home: 3853 1st Ave San Diego CA 92103-3013 Office: Speckled Gekko Prodns 3852 1st Ave San Diego CA 92103

SEIFERT, STEPHEN WAYNE, lawyer; b. Washington, May 25, 1957; s. Arthur John and Frances E. (Smith) S. BA summa cum laude, Yale U., 1979; JD, Stanford U., 1982. Bar: Colo. 1982, U.S. Dist. Ct. Colo. 1982, U.S. Ct. Appeals (10th cir.) 1982, U.S. Ct. Appeals (5th cir.) 1987, U.S. Supreme Ct. 1988. Ptnr.. Fairfield and Woods P.C., Denver, 1982—; mng. dir. Fairfield & Woods P.C., Denver, 1990-92, 95—. Author: Colorado Creditors' Remedies--Debtors' Relief, 1990; contbg. author: Colorado Methods of Practice; contbr. articles to profl. jours. Chmn. bd. Opera Colo., 1989-92; bd. trustees Denver Pub. Libr. Friends Found. Mem. ABA, Am. Bankruptcy Inst., Colo. Bar Assn., Denver Bar Assn. Law Club Denver (v.p. 1992-93, pres. 1993-94), Yale-Harvard Regatta Com. (bd. dirs.), Allied Arts Inc. (program chmn. Denver World Affairs coun.), Phi Beta Kappa, Univ. Club. Episcopalian. Office: Fairfield & Woods PC 1700 Lincoln St Ste 2400 Denver CO 80203-4524

SEIFFERT, GERALD NORMAN, sales executive; b. St. Paul, Feb. 11, 1939; s. Marvin Frank and Lorraine Ellen (Miller) S.; m. Pamela Morris. Grad. bus. adminstrn., Macalester Coll., 1962. Comml. credit analyst First Nat. Bank, St. Paul, 1963-66; loan supr., asst. cashier, br. mgr. internat. divsn. Bank of Am. Nat. Trust & Savs. Assn., San Francisco, 1966-71; mgr. internat. br. Anquilla (West Indies) br. Bank of Am. NT & SA, San Francisco, 1968-70; owner, operator J. Norman Gallery, Ketchum, Idaho, 1971-88; sales agt. Caldwell Banker, Sun Valley, Idaho, 1989—; pres., exec. com. Idaho Mountain Express, 1989—; adj. faculty mem., instr. cmty. fire protection and master planning Nat. Fire Acad., Emmitsburg, Md., 1991—. Mayor, City of Ketchum, Idaho, 1975-88; mem. Gov.'s Blue Ribbon Local Govt. Task Force, 1977-78; third v.p. Assn. Idaho Cities, 1977-80; chmn. bd. Ketchum (Idaho) Area Rapid Transit Bus Sys., 1979-88; bd. mem. Blaine County Airport Commn., 1980-88; candidate U.S. Congress, Idaho, 1991-92. With USAR, 1962-68. Recipient Peace and Friendship medal U.S. State Dept. Home: PO Box 759 Ketchum ID 83340-0759

SEIGEL, DANIEL A., retail executive. With Thrifty Corp., pres., COO, 1990, pres., CEO, also bd. dirs.; also exec. v.p. Pacific Enterprises. Office: Thrifty Corp 3424 Wilshire Blvd Los Angeles CA 90010-2241*

SEILER, STEVEN LAWRENCE, health facility administrator; b. Chgo., Dec. 30, 1941; married. B. U. Ariz., 1963; M, U. Iowa, 1965. Adminstrv. resident Rush-Presbyn.-St. Luke's Med. Ctr., Chgo., 1965, adminstrv. asst., 1965-68; asst. adminstr. Lake Forest (Ill.) Hosp., 1968-71, adminstr., 1971-73, pres., 1973-86; exec. v.p Voluntary Hosps. Am., Park Ridge, Ill., 1987-89, sr. v.p., 1986-92; CEO Good Samaritan Regional Med. Ctr., Phoenix, 1992—; adj. prof. Contbr. articles to profl. jours. Mem. AHA (svc. com.), Ill. Hosp. Assn. (chair 1980-81). Home: 3930 E Rancho Dr Paradise Vly AZ 85253-5025 Office: Good Samaritan Regional Med Ctr 1111 E Mcdowell Rd Phoenix AZ 85006-2612

SEITZ, WALTER STANLEY, cardiovascular research consultant; b. L.A., May 10, 1937; s. Walter and Frances Janette (Schleef) S. BS in Physics and Math., U. Calif., Berkeley, 1959; PhD in Biophysics, U. Vienna, 1981, MD, 1982. Health physicist U. Calif. Radiation Lab., 1959-61; rsch. assoc. NIH at Pacific Union Coll., 1961-63; physicist Lockheed Rsch. Labs., Palo Alto, Calif., 1961-63; staff scientist Xerox Corp., Pasadena, Calif., 1963-66; sr. scientist Applied Physics Cons., Palo Alto, 1966-75; instr. clin. sci. U. Ill Coll. Medicine, Urbana, 1983-84; cons. cardiology Cardiovascular Rsch. Inst. U. Calif. Sch. Medicine, San Francisco, 1987—; sr. scientist Inst. Med. Analysis and Rsch., Berkeley, 1987—. Contbr. articles to profl. jours. Postdoctoral Rsch. fellow, U. Calif. San Francisco, 1984. Fellow Am. Coll. Angiography; mem. AAAS, Royal Soc. Medicine London, N.Y. Acad. Scis., Physicians for Social Responsibility. Office: IMAR Cons Inc 38 Panoramic Way Berkeley CA 94704-1828

SEKAYUMPTEWA, LOREN, social worker; b. Winslow, Ariz., Mar. 23, 1950; s. Dayton Aquilla and Myra (Nez) S.; m. Mary A. Billiman (dec.); children: Lorie L., Carrie L., Christina L., Tracey M., Shaandiin C.; m. Marilyn J. Gishie; 1 child, Andrea L. AA, Brigham Young U., 1971, BS, 1973; MSW, U. Utah, 1981-83, postgrad. Cert. social worker, Utah. Social svc. rep. Bur. Indian Affairs, Keams Canyon, Ariz., 1973-74; dir. social svcs. Hopi Ctr. for Human Devel., Second Mesa, Ariz., 1975-76, human svcs. cons., 1974-75; counselor Navajo Community Coll., Tsaile, Ariz., 1975-76, dir. counseling, 1975-76, dean of students, 1977-81; chief adminstr. Hotevilla (Ariz.)-Bacavi Community Sch., 1983-84; exec. dir. Dine Ctr. for Human Svcs., Tsaile, 1984-87; clin. dir. Toyei Industries, Inc., Ganado, Ariz., 1987-91; exec. dir. Navajo Nation Pub. Sch. Bd. Assn., Window Rock, Ariz., 1991—; cons. linguistics anthropology dept. U. Utah, Salt Lake City, 1973-74; cons. edn. Toyei Industries, Inc., Ganado, Ariz., 1985-87, Utah Navajo Devel. Corp., Blanding, 1985-87; mem. bd. rev. Western Region Indian Alcoholism Ctr., Salt Lake City, 1974-75. Chairperson Gov.'s Coun. on Devel. Disabilities, State of Ariz., Phoenix; pres. No. Ariz. Health Edn. Ctr., Flagstaff, 1985-90; vice chmn. Ariz. Mental Health Planning Coun., Phoenix, 1986-90; pres. Native Am. Rsch. and Tng. Ctr., U. Ariz., Tucson, 1984-90. NIMH scholar, 1973-75. Navajo. Office: Navajo Nation Pub Sch Bds Assn PO Box 1909 Saint Michaels AZ 86511

SEKINE, DEBORAH KEIKO, systems analyst, programmer; b. Honolulu, Dec. 1, 1952; d. Yoshiteru and Yaeko (Matsuda) Isa; m. Andrew K. Sekine, May 8, 1993. BA in Math. with distinction, U. Hawaii, 1974, BEd with distinction, 1974, MS in Computer Sci., 1976, MBA, 1987. Data analyst, engr. in-charge Kentron, Honolulu, 1977-81; sys. analyst Am. Savs., Honolulu, 1981-82; analyst, programmer City and County of Honolulu, 1982—; cons. Am. Savs., Honolulu, 1982. Contbr. articles to profl. jours. Vol. Hawaii Dem. Conv., Honolulu, 1984, Mayoral campaign, 1988, 92; com. co-chair Hui Makaala, Honolulu, 1989—; caregiver Makiki Christian Ch., Honolulu, 1991—. Mem. IEEE, Assn. for Computing Machinery, Am. Fedn. State County Mcpl. Employees, U. Hawaii MBA Alumni Assn., Phi Kappa Phi. Mem. United Ch. of Christ. Home: 3322 George St Honolulu HI 96815-4319

SELBY, JEROME M., mayor; b. Wheatland, Wyo., Sept. 4, 1948; s. John Franklin and Claudia Meredith (Hudson) S.; m. Gloria Jean Nelson, June 14, 1969; children: Tyan, Cameronn, Kalen. BS in Math., Coll. Idaho, 1969, MA in Ednl. Adminstrn., 1974; MPA, Boise State U., 1978. Assoc. engr. Boeing Co., Seattle, 1969-71; dir. evaluation WICHE Mountain States Regional Med. Program, Boise, 1971-74; dir. rsch., evaluation Mountain States Health Corp., Boise, 1974-76, with health policy analysis and accountability, 1976-78; dir. health Kodiak (Alaska) Area Native Assn., 1978-83; mgr. Kodiak Island Borough, 1984-85, mayor, 1985—; proprietor Kodiak Tax Svc., 1978—, Registered Guide, Kodiak, 1987—; cons. Nat. Cancer Inst., Washington, 1973-78, others. Contbr. articles to profl. jours. Treas. ARC, Kodiak, 1978-93, bd. dirs., 1978-95, chmn., 1989-90, mem. western ops. hdqrs. adv. bd., 1986-92, mem. group IV and V nat. adv. com., 1986-89, nat. bd. govs., 1989-95, chmn. chpt. rels. com., 1994-95; pres. S.W. Alaska Mcpl. Conf., Anchorage, 1988-89, v.p., 1986-87, bd. dirs., 1986—; pres. Alaska Mcpl. League Investment Pool, Inc., 1992—; v.p. Alaska Mcpl. League, 1988-90, pres., 1990-91, bd. dirs., 1988—; mem. Alaska Resource Devel. Coun., 1987—, exec. com., 1989—; mem. policy com. of outer continental shelf adv. bd. U.S. Dept. Interior, 1990—; co-chair Alaska Task Force, 1995; mem. com. on Oil Pollution Act, 1995; mem. Nat. Assn. Counties, Cmty. and Econ. Devel. Steering Com., 1990—, Alaska govtl. roles task force, 1991-92; chmn. Kodiak Island Exxon Valdez Restoration Com., 1991—; dir. Kodiak Health Care Found., 1992—; co-chmn. Arctic Power, 1993—; mem. bd. dirs. Western Interstate Region Nat. Assn. of Counties, 1993—. Paul Harris fellow, 1987, 88, 91, 92; recipient Outstanding Contbn. award Alaska Mcpl. League, 1994. Mem. Alaska Conf. Mayors, Nat. Soc. Tax Profls., Acad. Polit. Sci., Alaska Mcpl. Mgrs. Assn., Kodiak C. of C. (dir. 1983—), Rotary (bd. dirs. 1989—, treas. 1989-93, v.p. 1993-94, pres. 1995-96, pres. 1995—). Office: Kodiak Island Borough 710 Mill Bay Rd Kodiak AK 99615-6340

SELBY, NAOMI ARDEAN, women's health nurse, medical/surgical nurse; b. Duncan, Okla., Jan. 17, 1946; d. Orbie J.N. Sr. and Dorothy Naomi (Foster) S. BSN, Tex. Woman's U., 1969. Staff nurse, head nurse labor and delivery Meth. Med. Ctr., Dallas; cons., staff nurse ob-gyn. Southeastern Meth. Hosp., Dallas, staff nurse, operating room; head nurse ob-gyn. Yukon Delta Regional Hosp./USPHS/Indian Health Svc., Bethel, Alaska; nurse mgr. cen. supply rm./oper. rm. Yukon Kuskokwim Delta Regional Hosp./USPHS Indian Health Svc. Mem. NAACOG, Assn. Operating Room Nurses. Home: PO Box 287 Unit 3114 Bethel AK 99559-0287

SELDNER, BETTY JANE, environmental engineer, consultant, aerospace company executive; b. Balt., Dec. 11, 1923; d. David D. and Miriam M. (Mendes) Miller; m. Warren E. Gray, June 20, 1945 (div. 1965); children: Patricia, Deborah; m. Alvin Seldner, Nov. 15, 1965; children: Jack, Barbara. BA in Journalism, Calif. State U., Northridge, 1975, MA in Communications, 1977. Dir. pub. info. United Way, Van Nuys, Calif., 1958-63; dir. edn. United Way, Los Angeles, 1963-68; dir. pub. relations, fin. San Fernando Valley Girl Scout Council, Reseda, Calif., 1968-73; asst. dir. pub. info. Calif. State U., Northridge, 1973-75; dir. environ. mgmt. HR Textron Corp., Valencia, Calif., 1975-87; environ. engr. Northrop Aircraft, Hawthorne, Calif., 1987-92, EMCON Assocs., Burbank, Calif., 1992-93, Atkins Environ., 1992-93, Seldner Environ., Valencia, Calif., 1993—. Author non-fiction. Mem. Santa Clarita Valley Environ. Mgrs. Soc. (chmn. bd. dirs. 1984), San Fernando Valley Round Table (pres. 1971-72), Hazardous Materials Mgrs.' Assn., Zonta Internat. Republican. Jewish.

SELF, SUSAN CAROLYN, technical writer; b. Oakland, Calif., May 11, 1949; d. Charles William and Caroline Lillian (Omo) S. BA in English, Am. Lit., U. Calif., San Diego, 1972, PhD in Comparative Lit., 1982. Tech. editor Indsl. Software Components, San Diego, 1983-86, TechFoss, San Diego, 1986-94; TeleSoft Tele Soft, San Diego, 1984-93; tech. writer Alsys, San Diego, 1993-94, Thomson Software Products, San Diego, 1995—. Author and editor: (anthology) Creative VOM, 1994. Vol. writer, editor, proofreader San Diego Earth Times, 1991-95; editor Zero Population Growth San Diego Newsletter, 1992-95, Save Our Forests and Ranchlands, San Diego, 1992; vol. Peter Navarro Campaign, San Diego, 1992, 93. Mem. IEEE (assoc.). Soc. for Tech. Comm. (sr.). Democrat. Office: Thomson Software Products 10251 Vista Sorrento Pky San Diego CA 92121-2700

SELF, VICKI JOYE, advertising executive; b. Ft. Worth, Apr. 8, 1969; d. Jack Henry and Debbie (Maddox) S. BS in Mktg. and Advt., Ind. U., 1991. Banking svcs. counselor Lincoln Nat. Bank, Ft. Wayne, Ind., 1991-93; mktg. coord. Patterson Riegel Assocs., Ft. Wayne, 1993; client svcs. mgr. Omoto Advt., Denver, 1993-94; account exec. Deutsch, Shea & Evans/TMP, Denver, 1994—. Mem. com., pub. rels. advisor Denver Art Mus., 1994; com. chair pub. affairs ARCC, Ft. Wayne, 1993; mem. pub. rels. com. Allen County Collaborative for Edn., Ft. Wayne, 1993. Home: 508 S Corona St Denver CO 80209-4404

SELIGMAN, THOMAS KNOWLES, museum administrator; b. Santa Barbara, Calif., Jan. 1, 1944; s. Joseph L. and Peggy (Van Horne) S.; children: Christopher, Timothy, Dylan. BA, Stanford U., 1965; BFA with honors, San Francisco Acad. Art, 1967; MFA, Sch. Visual Art, N.Y.C., 1968. Tchr., mus. dir. Peace Corps, Liberia, 1968-70; curator dept. Africa, Oceania and Ams. Fine Arts Museums, San Francisco, 1971-88; dep. dir. edn. and exhbns. Fine Arts Museums, 1972-88, dep. dir. ops. and planning, 1988-91; dir. Stanford (Calif.) U. Mus. Art, 1991—; mem. cultural property adv. com. USIA, 1988-92, Nat. Endowment for Art Indemnity Panel, 1992-95. Author mus. catalogues, articles in field. Trustee Internat. Coun. Mus./Am. Assn. Mus., 1990-94, Am. Fedn. Arts; mem. adv. coun. Acad. Art Coll. Grad. Program. Fellow Nat. Endowment Arts, 1974-75, 87. Mem. Assn. Art Mus. Dirs., Am. Assn. Mus., Leaky Found. Address: Stanford U Mus Art Stanford CA 94305-5060

SELIGSON, MARCIA SUE, journalist; b. N.Y.C., Apr. 27, 1937; d. Philip Crystal and Pauline (Henoch) S.; m. Thomas Martin Drucker, Feb. 28, 1982. Student, Columbia U., 1959. Publicity dir. Dell Pub., N.Y.C., 1966-67, New Am. Libr., 1967-68; contbg. editor New Times Mag., N.Y.C., 1973-75, New West Mag., L.A., 1977-79, Lears Mag., N.Y.C., 1991-94; v.p. Ctr. for Corp. Innovation, Marina Del, Calif., 1990—; cons. Allstate, Hewlett Packard, Playboy, 1987-93. Author: Eternal Bliss Machine, 1973, Options, 1978; contbr. articles to various mags. Founder, exec. dir. End Hunger Network, 1979-81; mem. steering com. Women Against Gun Violence, L.A., 1993—, Hollywood Women's Polit. Com., L.A., 1989-90; mem. adv. bd. Americans for Peace Now, 1994—. Office: Ctr For Corp Innovation 520 Washington Blvd # 430 Marina Del Rey CA 90292

SELL, JOHN VICTOR, computer architect; b. Seattle, Aug. 19, 1950; s. John A. and Solvieg P. (Fiske) S. BS in Engring., Harvey Mudd Coll., 1972; MS in Elec. Engring. and Computer Sci., U. Calif., Berkeley, 1973. Project mgr. Hewlett-Packard Co., Palo Alto, Calif., 1973-80; founder, v.p. Ridge Computers, Inc., Santa Clara, Calif., 1980-88; design engr. Apple Computer, Inc., Cupertino, Calif., 1988-92; v.p., fellow The 3DO Co., Redwood City, Calif., 1992—. Office: The 3DO Co 600 Galveston Dr Redwood City CA 94063-4721

SELL, ROBERT EMERSON, electrical engineer; b. Freeport, Ill., Apr. 23, 1929; s. Cecil Leroy and Ona Arletta (Stevens) S.; m. Ora Lucile Colton, Nov. 7, 1970. B.S., U. Nebr., 1962. Registered profl. engr., Nebr., Mo., Ill., Ind., Ohio, W.Va., Ky., Ark., Tex., Oreg., Wash., Calif. Chief draftsman Dempster Mill Mfg. Co., Beatrice, Nebr., 1949-53; designer-engr. U. Neb., Lincoln, 1955-65; elec. design engr. Kirkham, Michael & Assos., Omaha, 1965-67; elec. design engr. Leo A. Daly Co., Omaha, St. Louis, 1967-69; mech. design engr. Hellmuth, Obata, Kassabaum, St. Louis, 1969-70; chief elec. engr. Biagi-Hannan & Assos., Inc., Evansville, Ind., 1971-74; elec. project engr. H.L. Yoh Co., under contract to Monsanto Co., Creve Coeur, Mo., 1974-77; elec. project engr. Dhillon Engrs., Inc., Portland, Oreg., 1978-85; project coordinator Brown-Zammit-Enyeart Engring., Inc., San Diego, 1985-88; elec. engr. Morgen Design, Inc., San Diego, 1988; lead elec. engr. Popov Engrs., Inc., San Diego, 1988-89; mech. and elect. specialist Am. Engring. Labs., Inc. div. Prof. Svc. Industries, Inc., San Diego, 1990—; instr. Basic Inst. Tech., St. Louis, 1971. Mem. ASHRAE, IEEE. Home: PO Box 261578 San Diego CA 92196-1578 Office: AEL/PSI 7940 Arjons Dr Ste A San Diego CA 92126-6303

SELLARS, PETER, theater director; b. Sept. 27, 1957. B.A. magna cum laude, Harvard U., 1980. Dir. Boston Shakespeare Co., 1983-84; dir., chief operating officer Am. Nat. Theater at J.F. Kennedy Ctr., Washington, 1984—. Theater and opera dir.: The Death of Klinghoffer, Nixon in China, Mozart/Da Ponte Trilogy (Don Giovanni, Le nozze di Figaro, Cosi fan tutte), Magic Flute, Ajax, Zangezi. MacArthur Found. fellow, 1983; recipient Emmy Award Outstanding Classical Program in the Performing Arts (Nixon in China), 1988. Office: Boston Opera 300 Massachusetts Ave Boston MA 02115-4544 also: CAA 9830 Wilshire Blvd Beverly Hills CA 90212-1804

SELLER, GREGORY EROL, marketing executive, writer; b. Denver, Oct. 4, 1953; s. Otto Gustave and Dolores Louise (Crawford) S. BBA, U. Colo., 1975. Account exec. Gt.-West Life, L.A., 1975-79; asst. v.p. group devel. Gt.-West Life, Denver, 1980-84; v.p. sales and nat. accts. Great-West Life, L.A., 1988—; pres., chief exec. officer Benefits Communication Corp., Denver, 1985-87; bd. dirs. Benefits Communication Co. Editor newsletter Focus on 457, 1988—; mem. editorial bd., 457 Ind. Info. Svcs., 1990—. Mem. vestry, treas. St. Thomas Episc. Ch., Hollywood, Calif., 1989-93. Mem. Delta Upsilon. Democrat. Home: 37 New York Ct Monarch Beach CA 92629-4524 Office: Great-West Life 18101 Von Karman Ave Ste 1460 Irvine CA 92715-1010

SELLERY, J'NAN MORSE, English and American literature educator; b. Oakland, Calif., Jan. 3, 1928; d. Raymond Stephen and Minna Esther (Bourus) Morse; m. Austin R. Sellery, Aug. 30, 1947; children: Stephen Brooke, Edward Austin, Margaret Joan, John Merritt. BA, U. Calif., Riverside, 1965; MA, U. Calif., 1967, PhD, 1970. Asst. prof. Harvey Mudd Coll., Claremont, Calif., 1970-74, assoc. prof. Claremont grad. sch., 1974-80, prof. English Claremont grad. sch., 1980—, Louisa & Robert Miller chair prof. humanities, 1989—; coord. women's studies Claremont Coll., 1988-91; cons. UMI Press, 1989, Conn. Rev., 1988. Books co-editor: Faust Part I, 1969, The Scapegoat, 1972, Bibliography of Elizabeth Bowen, 1981; editor (jours.) Women's Voices, 1986, Gender, 1990; sr. editor Psychol. Perspectives, 1969—; contbr. articles and poetry to mags. and profl. jours. NDEA fellow U. Calif., 1967-70; rsch. grantee Harvey Mudd Coll., 1971-90, NEH summer grantee Yale U., 1979, Mellon grantee in curriculum Claremont Colls., 1989; vis. humanities scholar U. Calgary, Can., 1992. Mem. AAUW (nat. bd. mem. 1982-83, mem. fellowship panel 1989-93), MLA, Nat. Women's Studies Assn. (coord. coun. 1989-92, cons. jour. and book awards 1991—). Office: Harvey Mudd Coll Kingston Hall Claremont CA 91711

SELVIN, PETER SAM, lawyer; b. L.A., Dec. 1, 1953. BA with highest honors, U. Calif., San Diego, 1975; MA, U. Chgo., 1976; JD, UCLA, 1980. Bar: Calif. 1980, U.S. Dist. Ct. (cen. dist.) Calif. 1981, U.S. Dist. Ct. (no. dist.) Calif. 1990, U.S. Ct. Appeals (9th cir.) 1987. Clk. to presiding justice Calif. Ct. Appeals (2d Appellate Dist., Divsn. 5), 1979; assoc. Loeb and Loeb, L.A., 1980-87, ptnr., 1987—, chair litigation dept., 1994—. Contbr. articles to profl. jours. Mem. Calif. State Bar Assn. (com. on adminstrn. justice 1992-93, co-chair tech. subcom. state bar litigation sect. 1992-93), L.A. County Bar Assn. (litigation sect.), Fin. Lawyers Conf., Fed. Bar Assn., Assn. Bus. Trial Lawyers. Office: Loeb and Loeb 1000 Wilshire Blvd Ste 1800 Los Angeles CA 90017-2475

SELZER, KENNETH A., neurologist, editor; b. N.Y.C., Mar. 2, 1954; s. Milton C. and Sylvia (Bennett) S.; m. Lynn Dunbar, Mar. 2, 1955; 1 child, Jenna Nicole. BA in Chemistry, SUNY, 1976; MD, UCLA, 1982; postgrad., Harvard Bus. Sch., 1987-90. Diplomate Am. Bd. UR/QA Physicians. Internship St. Mary's Hosp., Long Beach, Calif., 1982-83; med. dir. Mercy Carepoint Family Med. Group, San Diego, 1983-88; pres., CEO Integrated Healthcare Svcs., Inc., San Diego, 1983-88; gen. ptnr. La Jolla Cons. Group, San Diego, 1989-90; resident in neurology Vanderbilt U., Nashville, 1991-93; pub. Neuropractice, San Diego, 1993—; bd. dirs. Healthwatch, Inc., Denver, Biomed. Rsch. Inst., San Diego; prin. investigator TPA trial for acute treatment Ischemic Strokes Vanderbilt U., 1992; biomed. rsch. asst. SUNY, Binghamton, 1974-76. N.Y. State Regents scholar, 1972-76; Study Rsch. grantee San Diego Biomed. Rsch. Soc., 1980-82; Rsch. fellow Scripps Clinic and Rsch. Found., 1978. Mem. AMA, ACP (assoc.), Am. Coll. Emergency Physicians, Am. Acad. Neurology, Am. Acad. Med. Dirs., Am. Coll. Sports Medicine, Calif. Med. Assn., Undersea Med. Soc., San Diego Assn. for Corp. Growth. Home: 4062 Moratalla Ter San Diego CA 92130-2282 Office: Neuropractice 3525 Del Mar Heights Rd Ste 196 San Diego CA 92130-2123

SELZER, STEPHEN RASHAW, healthcare administrator; b. Alvin, Tex., Feb. 7, 1952; s. Ardine and Kathryn Eileen (Rashaw) S.; m. Robbynn Ellen Krenz, Aug. 10, 1974; children: Daniel Rashaw, Lucy Maegan, Margaret Lee. BS in Sociology and Biology, Stephen F. Austin State U., Nacogdoches, Tex., 1974; MS in Healthcare Adminstrn., U. Houston at Clear Lake City, 1977. Lic. nursing home adminstr., Colo. Asst. adminstr. Sharpstown Gen. Hosp., Houston, 1977, Shoal Creek Hosp., Austin, Tex., 1979-80; adminstr. Lockhart (Tex.) Hosp., 1977-79, Grant Buie Hosp., Hillsboro, Tex., 1981-84, HCA Cross Timbers Cmty. Hosp., Ft. Worth, 1984-85; assoc. adminstr. Eastwood Hosp., El Paso, Tex., 1980-81; v.p. Wesley regional network HCA Wesley Med. Ctr., Wichita, Kans., 1985-89; adminstr. Montezuma County Hosp. Dist., Cortez, Colo., 1989—; mem. regional adv. coun. Colo. Found. for Med. Care, Denver, 1992—. Mem. adv. bd. S.W. Campus, Pueblo (Colo.) C.C., 1992—; bd. dirs. Hospice of Montezuma County; chmn. fin. com. 1st United Meth. Ch., Cortez, 1993—, mem. adminstrv. bd. Staff sgt. USAFR, 1971-77. Named Outstanding Fund Raiser, Kiwanis, Hillsboro, Tex., Outstanding Employer of Yr. Colo. group Am. Legion, 1993. Mem. Colo. Hosp. Assn. (bd. dirs. 1993—), Am. Coll. Healthcare Execs. (assoc.), Cortez Area C. of C. (bd. dirs., co-pres. 1994). Office: Montezuma County Hosp Dist 1311 N Mildred Rd Cortez CO 81321-2231

SEMEL, GEORGE HERBERT, plastic surgeon; b. N.Y.C., Apr. 20, 1938; s. Louis Bennett and Sara Sonja (Eutis) S. AB, Columbia U., 1959; MD, Boston U., 1963. Diplomate Am. Bd. Plastic Surgery. Intern L.A. County Gen. Hosp., 1963-64; resident gen. surgery Long Beach (Calif.) VA Hosp., 1964-67; residency in plastic surgery Mayo Clinic, Rochester, Minn., 1967-69; chief resident plastic surgery Med. U. S.C., Charleston, 1969-70; pvt. practice L.A., 1970—. Founder L.A. Music Ctr., 1978, Mus. Contemporary Art, 1980. With Calif. NG, 1964-69, USNG, 1969-73. Mem. AMA, Am. Soc. Plastic Surgery, Am. Lipoplasty Soc., L.A. Soc. Plastic Surgeons, L.A. County Med. Soc., Phi Gamma Delta. Office: 450 S Beverly Dr Beverly Hills CA 90212-4415

SENDRA-ANAGNOST, TERESA AMOR, nurse practitioner, writer; b. Mt. Pleasant, N.Y., Nov. 20, 1935; d. Fernando Miralles Sendra and Hazel Ellene (Rice) Estruch; div. Oct. 1985; children: James Christopher, Karen Ellen, Andrew John. AA cum laude, Los Angeles Valley Coll., 1971; BS, Calif. State U., Northridge, 1979. Registered nurse practitioner, Calif. Staff nurse So. Calif. Permanente Med. Group, Panorama City, 1971-75, 1975-88, nurse practitioner, 1988—. Active Am. Cancer Soc. Project Outreach, L.A.,

1986-87. Mem. United Nurses Assn. Calif., ANA (nat. cert.), Calif. Coalition of Nurse Practitioners, Am. Acad. Nurse Practitioners (cert.). Home: 5630 Ranchito Ave Van Nuys CA 91401-4710 Office: So Calif Permanente Med Group 13652 Cantara St Panorama City CA 91402-5423

SENDZIKAS, ALDONA MARIJA, museum curator; b. Toronto, Ont., Can., Dec. 23, 1963. BA, U. Toronto, 1986, MA, 1990; cert. mus. studies, Humber Coll.; doct. student, U. Hawaii. Mil. interpreter Hist. Fort York, Toronto, 1986-87, curatorial asst., 1988-89, asst. curator, 1989-91; exhibit specialist USS Bowfin Submarine Mus. and Park, Honolulu, 1991-92, mus. curator, 1992—; organizing com. mem. War Along the Niagara Symposium, Buffalo, N.Y., St. Catharines, Ont., 1988, Western Mus. Assn. annual conf., 1994; lectr. in field. Contbr. articles to profl. jours. Judge state and local competitions Hawaii History Day, 1993, 94, 95. Mem. Hawaii Mus. Assn., Ontario Mus. Assn., Coun. on Am.'s Mil. Past. Office: USS Bowfin Sub Mus & Park 11 Arizona Memorial Rd Honolulu HI 96818-3145

SENEVIRATNE, SONAL JERARD, systems analyst. BS in Biol. Scis., U. So. Calif., 1986; MS in Sys. Mgmt., 1989. Teaching asst. Programming and Data Processing U. So. Calif., 1984-86, info. mgr., 1986-88; cons. Citadel Rsch. Group, L.A., 1987-90; programmer, systems analyst U. So. Calif., 1988—. Mem. ASPA, Inst. Mgmt. Sci., Ops. Rsch. Soc. Am., Acad. Mgmt. Office: U So Calif 3550 Trousdale Pkwy Los Angeles CA 90089

SENGUPTA, MRITUNJOY, mining engineer, educator; b. Cuttack, Orissa, India, Oct. 24, 1941; came to U.S., 1968; s. Chandi P. and Bani S.; m. Nupur Bagchi, Jan. 15, 1981; children: Shyam S. ME, Columbia U., 1971, MS, 1972; PhD, Colo. Sch. of Mines, 1983. Mining engr. Continental Oil Co., Denver, 1977-78, United Nuclear Corp., Albuquerque, 1978-80, Morrison-Knudson Co., Boise, Idaho, 1975-77, 80-82; assoc. prof. U. Alaska, Fairbanks, 1983-88, prof., 1989—; cons. UN Devel. Program, 1987. Author: Mine Environmental Engineering, vols. I and II, 1989, Environmental Impacts of Mining, 1992; contbr. articles to profl. publs. Recipient Gold medal Mining Metall. Inst. of India, 1976, Nat. Merit scholarship Govt. of India, 1959-63. Mem. NSPE, So. Mining Engrs. Home: 421 Cindy Dr Fairbanks AK 99701-3220 Office: U Alaska Fairbanks AK 99775

SENGUPTA, SAILES KUMAR, engineering researcher, statistical consultant; b. Bankura, India, Jan. 1, 1935; came to U.S., 1963; s. Bhabani Charan and Pratima Gupta Sen; m. Sumedha Chouhury Sengupta, Aug. 8, 1969; children Dyuti, Chaitee. BSc, Calcutta U., India, 1953, MSc, 1956; PhD, U. Calif., 1969. Asst. prof. math. U. Mo., Kansas City, 1969-76; assoc. prof. math. S.D. Sch. of Mines, Rapid City, 1976-81, prof. math. and computer sci., 1981-90; sr. fellow Naval Rsch. Lab., Monterey, Calif., 1990-91; electronics engr. Lawrence Livermore Lab., Livermore, Calif., 1991—; consulting statistician Inst. Atmospheric Rsch., S.D. Sch. of Mines, Rapid City, 1985-91, Lawrence Livermore Nat. Lab., 1992—; cloud field classifier Naval Oceanographic Atmospheric Rsch. Lab., Monterey, 1990-91; sr. vis. fellow Univ. Corp. Atmospheric Rsch. Lab., Boulder, Colo., 1990. Co-editor: Automated Pattern Analysis in Petroleum Exploration, 1992; contbr. numerous articles to profl. jours. Recipient Univ. Gold medal, Calcutta U., 1956. Mem. IEEE Sig. Processing Soc., Am. Stats. Assn., Sigma Xi. Hindu. Office: Lawrence Livermore Nat Lab Engring Rsch Divsn EE Dept L 156 Livermore CA 94550

SENSABAUGH, GEORGE FRANK, JR., forensic sciences educator; b. Palo Alto, Calif., June 8, 1941; s. George Frank and Elizabeth Katherine (Ake) S.; m. Linda Sallander, Aug. 30, 1963; children: Jeffrey, Laura. BA, Princeton U., 1963; D of Criminology, U. Calif., Berkeley, 1969. Researcher U. Calif., San Diego, 1969-71, Nat. Inst. Med. Rsch., London, 1971-72; from. asst. prof. to prof. U. Calif., Berkeley, 1972—. Contbr. articles to profl. jours. Fulbright scholar, 1993. Fellow Am. Acad. Forensic Scis. (Paul L. Kirk award 1987); mem. Am. Chem. Soc., Am. Soc. Human Genetics, Calif. Assn. Criminalists, N.Y. Acad. Scis. Office: U Calif Sch Pub Health Berkeley CA 94720

SENUNGETUK, VIVIAN RUTH, lawyer; b. Syracuse, N.Y., Sept. 27, 1948; d. George Albert and Ethel Margaret (Hearl) Bender; children: Adam George Moore, William Guugzhuk Senungetuk. BA, SUNY, Binghamton, 1968; MAT, U. Alaska, 1972; JD, Boston U., 1984. Bar: Alaska 1985, Mass. 1985, U.S. Dist. Ct. Alaska 1985, N.Y. 1995. Adminstr. Indian Edn., Sitka, Alaska, 1974-76, Cook Inlet Native Assn., Anchorage, 1977-80; assoc. Erwin, Smith & Garnett, Anchorage, 1984-86; sole practice Anchorage, 1986-94; adj. prof. constitutional law U. Alaska, Anchorage, 1986-88. Author: A Place for Winter, 1987. Mem. Assn. Trial Lawyers Am., Alaska Acad. Trial Lawyers. Democrat. Pentecostal. Home: 803 Oakwood St Fayetteville NY 13066

SEOANE, MARTA HEBE, demographer, social scientist; b. Canelones, Uruguay, May 11, 1943; came to U.S., 1964; d. Joaquin Raul and Felipa Josefa (Scaglione) S.; m. Kingsley Davis, Nov. 5, 1985; 1 child, Austin Alexander Seoane Davis. BA in Sociology, Calif. State U., Northridge, 1976; MA in Sociology, U. So. Calif., 1983, PhD in Sociology, 1988. Pres., cons. Demographic Rsch., Stanford, Calif., 1989—; sr. demographer Hispanic Market Connections, Inc., Los Altos, Calif., 1992-94; ctr. assoc. Internat. Population Ctr., U. Calif., San Diego, 1991—; adj. prof. San Diego State U., 1992—. Author: Hispanic Market Handbook, 1995. Recipient Hubert B. Herring Meml. award for best dissertation Pacific Coast Coun. on Latin Am. Studies, 1989. Mem. Am. Sociol. Assn., Latin Am. Assn., Population Assn. Am., Calif. Sociol. Assn., Pacific Coast Coun. on Latin Am. Studies. Home: 975 Wing Pl Stanford CA 94305-1028 Office: 975 Wing Pl Palo Alto CA 94305

SEPPI, EDWARD JOSEPH, physicist; b. Price, Utah, Dec. 16, 1930; s. Joseph and Fortunata S.; m. Betty Stowell, Aug. 25, 1953; children: Duane Joseph, Kevin Darrell, Cynthia Rae. BS, Brigham Young U., 1952; MS, U. Idaho, 1956; PhD, Calif. Inst. Tech., 1962. Staff physicist Gen. Electric Co., Richland, Wash., 1952-58; rsch. fellow Calif. Inst. Tech., Pasadena, 1962; staff physicist Inst. for Def. Analysis, Washington, 1962-64; rsch. area dept. head SLAC, Stanford, Calif., 1966-68, head exptl. facility dept., 1968-74; mgr. med. diagnosis Varian Assocs., Palo Alto, Calif., 1974-76, sr. scientist, 1980-90; sr. scientist Superconducting Super Collider, Dallas, 1990-91; with Varian Assocs., Palo Alto, Calif., 1991-93; prin. scientist Ginston Rsch. Ctr. Varian, Palo Alto, 1993—. Author: (with others) The Stanford Two-Mile Accelerator, 1968; contbr. articles to more than 82 sci. publs.; holder more than 20 patents, including med. instrumentation. Asst. scoutmaster Boy Scouts Am., Menlo Park, Calif., 1969-75; bd. dirs. Ladera Community Assn., 1988-90. Mem. Am. Phys. Soc. Home: 320 Dedalera Dr Portola Valley CA 94028

SEQUIN, CARLO H., computer science educator; b. Winterthur, Switzerland, Oct. 30, 1941; came to U.S., 1970; s. Carl R. and Margarit (Schaeppi) S.; m. Margareta Frey, Oct. 5, 1968; children: Eveline, Andre. B.S., U. Basel, Switzerland, 1965, Ph.D., 1969. Mem. tech. staff Bell Labs., Murray Hill, N.J., 1970-76; vis. Mackay lectr. U. Calif.-Berkeley, 1976-77, prof. elec. engring. computer scis., 1977—, assoc. chmn. computer sci., 1980-83. Contbr. 150 articles to profl. jours.; author first book on charge-coupled devices; patentee integrated circuits. Fellow IEEE; mem. Assn. Computing Machinery, Swiss Acad. Engring. Scis. Office: U Calif Dept EECS Computer Scis Divsn Berkeley CA 94720-1776

SERAFINE, MARY LOUISE, psychologist, educator, lawyer; b. Rochester, N.Y., July 2, 1948. B.A. with honors in music, Rutgers U., 1970; Ph.D., U. Fla., 1975; JD, Yale U., 1991. Bar: Calif., D.C.; U.S. Tax Ct. Teaching and research fellow U. Fla., Gainesville, 1970-76; vis. asst. prof. U. Tex.-San Antonio, 1976-77; asst. prof. U. Tex.-Austin, 1977-79; postdoctoral fellow dept psychology Yale U., New Haven, 1979-83, lectr., 1981-83; asst. prof. dept. psychology Vassar Coll. Poughkeepsie, N.Y., 1983-88; with O'Melveny & Myers, L.A., 1988—. Author: Music as Cognition: The Development of Thought in Sound, 1988. Contbr. articles to profl. jours. Editorial reviewer Child Devel., Devel. Psychology, Am. Scientist, Jour. Experimental Child Psychology, Jour. Applied Developmental Psychology, Yale Law Jour. Grantee State of Fla., 1974-75, U. Tex.-Austin, 1977, Spencer Found., 1979-85. Office: O'Melveny & Myers 1999 Avenue Of The Stars Los Angeles CA 90067-6022

SERAFINI, VICTOR RENATO, aerospace engineer; b. Chgo., June 9, 1934; s. Renato Victor and Stella (Koch) S.; m. Donetta Werre. BS in Aero. Engring., U. Ill., 1957, postgrad., 1957-65; postgrad., UCLA, 1957-65. Rsch. and project engr. Rocketdyne Div. N.Am. Aviation, Canoga Park, Calif., 1957-67; program/project mgr. TRW Inc., Redondo Beach, Calif., 1967-78; dir. spacecraft engring. Comms. Satellite Corp. (now Comsat Corp.), El Segundo, Calif., 1978-94; aerospace cons., pres. S.T.D. Assocs., El Segundo, Calif., 1995—; bd. dirs., cont. Autobahn West, Westlake Village, Calif.; mgmt. cons. Westoaks Realty, Weatlake Village, 1975—; pres. STD Assocs., Rancho Palos Verdes, Calif., 1965—. Recipient award of recognition TRW Inc., 1965, Recognition of Outstanding Effort award NASA and TRW, 1963-64, Outstanding Contbn. award to recovery stranded Intelsat VI 603 satellite Intelsat Orgn., 1992. Mem. AIAA (liquid rocket tech. com. 1985-86). Mem. Christian Ch. Home: PO Box 2665 Palos Verdes Peninsula CA 90274-8665

SERBEIN, OSCAR NICHOLAS, business educator, consultant; b. Collins, Iowa, Mar. 31, 1919; s. Oscar Nicholas and Clara Matilda (Shearer) S.; m. Alice Marie Bigger, Sept. 16, 1952; children: Mary Llewellyn Serbein Parker, John Gregory. BA with highest distinction, U. Iowa, 1940, MS, 1941; PhD, Columbia U., 1951. Grad. asst. math. U. Iowa, Iowa City, 1940-41; clk. Met. Life Ins. Co., N.Y.C., 1941-42; lectr. U. Calif., Berkeley, summer 1948, 50; lectr., asst. prof., assoc. prof. Columbia U., N.Y.C., 1947-59; prof. ins. Stanford (Calif.) U., 1959-89, dir. doctoral program Grad. Sch. Bus., 1960-64, prof. emeritus ins., 1989—; cons. Ins. Info. Inst., N.Y.C., 1971-78, N.Am. Re-Assurance Life Service Co., Palo Alto, 1973, SRI Internat., Menlo Park, Calif., 1980-81, other bus.; cons., expert witness various law firms. Author: Paying for Medical Care in the U.S., 1953, Educational Activities of Business, 1961; co-author: Property and Liability Insurance, 4 ed., 1967, Risk Management: Text and Cases, 2 ed., 1983; also articles. Bd. dirs. Sr. Citizens Coord. Coun., Palo Alto, 1986-89, dir. emeritus, 1990—. Maj. USAF, WWII. Decorated Bronze Star, 1944. Mem. Am. Risk and Ins. Assn., Western Risk and Ins. Assn., Phi Beta Kappa, Sigma Xi, Beta Gamma Sigma. Democrat. Methodist. Club: Stanford Faculty. Home: 731 San Rafael Ct Stanford CA 94305-1007 Office: Stanford U Grad Sch Business Stanford CA 94305

SERES, JOEL LEONARD, neurosurgeon; b. Bronx, N.Y., Mar. 10, 1933; s. Joseph Charles and Gussie (Brodat) S.; m. Sandra Lamer, Sept. 18, 1988; children: David Stuart, Barbara Ellen Harrington, Steven Paul, Andrew Carl. BS in Chemistry, U. Del., 1954; MD, Jefferson Med. Coll., 1958. Diplomate Am. Bd. Neurological Surgery; lic. physician Alaska, Del., Oregon. Intern Del. Hosp., Wilmington, 1958-59; resident Del. Med. Ctr., Wilmington, U. Oreg. Med. Sch., Portland; gen. surgery physician Del. Hosp., Wilmington, 1961-63; pvt. practice Newark, 1959-61; neurosurgeon U. Oreg. Med. Sch., 1963-67; pvt. practice Portland, Oreg., 1967—; founder, dir. N.W. Occupational Medicine Ctr., Portland, Oreg., 1972—; clin. prof. neurosurgery U. Oreg. Health Scis. Ctr., Portland, 1990—; bd. dirs. Commn. on Accreditation Rehab. Facilities, Tucson; govs. psychosurgery bd. State of Oreg., 1973-82; subcom. on acupuncture Oreg. State Bd. Med. Examiners 1973—, chmn. 1979—; staff Good Samaritan Hosp. & Med. Ctr., Portland, Emanuel Hosp., Portland, Woodland Park Hosp., Portland., St. Vincent Hosp. & Med. Ctr., Portland, Providence Med. Ctr., Portland, Holladay Park Hosp., Portland, Oreg. Health Scis. U., Portland. Contbr. articles to profl. jours. Dir. Congregation Beth Israel, Portland, 1989—. Recipient Oliver J. Nesbit award for outstanding vol. faculty Oreg. Health Scis. U., 1971-75. Fellow ACS, Am. Coll. Pain Medicine; mem. AMA, Am. Pain Soc. (founding mem.), Am. Acad. Pain Medicine (founding mem., pres. 1985-86), Am. Assn. Neurolog. Surgeons (vice-chmn. sect. on pain 1988-89, chmn., 1990-91), Internat. Assn. for the Study of Pain (founding mem.), Western USA Pain Soc. (founding mem., pres. 1982-83), Oreg. Neurosurg. Soc. (v.p. 1975-76), Oreg. Med. Assn., Multnomah County Med. Soc., Congress Neurolog. Surgeons. Office: NW Occupl Med Ctr 15862 SW 72nd Ave Portland OR 97224-7974

SERFAS, RICHARD THOMAS, architecture educator, urban planner, county official; b. Reading, Pa., Nov. 24, 1952; s. Clifford Donald and Helen Catherine (McGovern) S. Student, Jacksonville U., 1970-72; BA, Colo. State U., 1974; MPA, Pa. State U., 1977; MS in Real Estate Devel., Columbia U., 1995. Project coord. ACTION Peace Corps, VISTA, Gary, Ind., 1974-75; city adminstr. City of Beverly Hills, Mo., 1975; grad. rsch. asst. dept. pub. adminstrn. Pa. State U., Middletown, 1976-77; community planner St. Louis County Dept. Planning, 1977-78; mgmt. analyst Clark County Sanitation Dist., Las Vegas, Nev., 1978-79; environ. planner Clark County Dept. Comprehensive Planning, Las Vegas, 1979-80, prin. planner, 1980-84, asst. coord. planning, 1984-85, coord. advance planning, 1985-89, asst. dir., 1989-94; instr. U. Nev. Sch. Architecture, Las Vegas, 1989—; student advisor Las Vegas chpt. AIA, 1989—. Staff advisor Clark County Comprehensive Plan Steering Com., 1980—, Environ. Task Force, Las Vegas, 1984—, Archtl. Design Task Force, Las Vegas, 1984—, Devel. Sector Task Force, Las Vegas, 1984—; mem. Transit Tech. Com., Las Vegas, 1989—. Recipient achievement award Nat. Assn. Counties, 1983-90. Mem. Am. Inst. Cert. Planners, Urban Land Inst., Nat. Assn. Corp. Real Estate Execs., Nat. Coun. for Urban Econ. Devel., Am. Planning Assn. (treas. Nev. chpt. 1979-91, pres. 1992—, Appreciation award 1981, 83, 85, 87, 89, 91, Outstanding Pub. Sector Planning Accomplishment award 1987, 88, 90, 91), Cmty. Assns. Inst. So. Nev. (bd. dirs. 1990-92, sec. 1993—). Democrat. Roman Catholic. Home: 2713 Brookstone Ct Las Vegas NV 89117-2442

SERNA, JOE, JR., mayor; b. Stockton, Calif.; m. Isabel Serna; children: Phillip, Lisa. BA in Social Sci., Govt., Sacramento State Coll., 1966; postgrad., U. Calif., Davis. Vol. Peace Corps., Guatemala, 1966; edn. advisor Lt.-Gov. Mervyn Dymally, 1975-77; prof. govt. Calif. State U., Sacramento, 1969—; mayor City of Sacramento, 1992—. Mem. Sacramento City Coun. 5th Dist., 1981-92, law and legis. com., 1989-92, Housing & Devel. Commn., Sacramento, chmn. budget and fin. com., 1981-89, transp. and cmty. devel. com., 1989-92; dir. United Farmworkers Am.'s Support Com. in Sacramento County, 1970-75; co-trustee Crocker Art Mus. Assn.; founder Thursday Night Market, Mayor's Summer Reading Camp; mem. Sacramento Housing & Devel. Commn.; bd. dirs. Regional Transit. Office: Office of the Mayor 915 I St Sacramento CA 95814-2608

SERNAQUE, JOSE DAVID, cardiothoracic and vascular surgeon; b. Chiclayo, Peru, Sept. 10, 1944; came to U.S., 1973; s. David and Juana Maria (Tesen) S.; m. Clara Isabel Alcantara; children: David Antonio, Jose Manuel. MD, U. San Marcos, Lima, Peru, 1991. Lic. physician, Md., Ill., Calif. Intern U. San Marcos Affiliated Hosps., 1969-70, resident in cardiology, 1970-72; resident in gen. surgery Luth. Hosp. Md., Balt., 1973-77; resident in cardiovascular and thoracic surgery U. Ill. Med. Ctr., Chgo., 1977-79; pvt. practice cardiovascular and thoracic surbery, 1981—; mem. staff L.A. Cmty. Hosp., East L.A. Drs. Hosp., Santa Martha Hosp., Charter Suburban Hosp., Beverly Hosp, Montebello. Contbr. articles to med. jours. Fellow Am. Coll. Angiology, Internat. Coll. Surgeons; mem. Am. Heart Assn. (sci. coun. in cardiovascular surgery), Los Angeles County Med. Assn., InterAm. Coll. Physicians and Surgeons, Peruvian Am. Med. Soc. Office: 16660 Paramount Blvd Ste 203 Paramount CA 90723-5458

SEROT, DAVID ELLIOT, economist, consultant; b. Fresno, Calif., Nov. 24, 1944; s. Nathan and Queenie Rosalie (Feldman) S. BA, UCLA, 1966; MA, 1968; PhD, U. Calif., 1976. Economist U.S. Dept. Energy, Washington, 1976-86; rsch. economist Pacific Northwest Labs., Richland, Wash., 1986-90; prin. DES Research, Richland, Wash., 1990—. Contbr. articles to profl. jours. Mem. Tri-City Indsl. Devel. Coun., Kennewick, Wash., 1993—. With U.S. Army, 1968-70, Vietnam. Mem. Am. Economic Assn., Nat. Assn. Bus. Economists. Jewish. Home: 616 Fuller St Richland WA 99352-1819 Office: DES Research 2000 Logston Blvd Richland WA 99352-5309

SERTNER, ROBERT MARK, producer; b. Phila., Oct. 7, 1955; s. Morton I. Sertner and Laurie (Hymes) Blicker. BBA, U. Tex., 1977. Ptnr. von Zerneck/Sertner Films, Los Angeles, 1985—. Producer over 50 TV movies including Hostage Flight, Too Young To Die? (INH Best Movie award), The Courtmartial of Jackie Robinson, Combat High, To Heal A Nation, 1987 (Best Picture Internat. TV Movie awards), Trouble in the City of Angels, Celebration Family, Proud Men, Gore Vidal's Billy the Kid (winner Houston Film Festival), Man Against the Mob, Maybe Baby, Robin Cook's Mortal Fear, Take Me Home Again, Outbreak, (mini series) The Big One: The Great Los Angeles Earthquake, Queenie, Jackie Collins' Lady Boss, TNT's Native American Miniseries, incl. Geronimo, 1993, The Broken Chain, 1993, Lakota Woman, 1994, (theater) Living in Oblivion (nominated best picture Sundance Film Festival), 1994, God's Lonely Man, 1994. Mem. Acad. TV Arts and Scis., Hollywood Radio and TV Soc., Nat. Acad. Cable Programming, Mus. of Broadcasting Creative Coun., Caucus for Producers, Writers and Dirs. Office: von Zerneck/Sertner Films 12001 Ventura Pl Ste 400 Studio City CA 91604-2629

SERVOSS, MARCUS EDWARD, public relations executive; b. Council Bluffs, Iowa, Feb. 21, 1940; s. Clair E. and Catherine (Nason) S.; m. Deborah Radman, June 30, 1984; children: Robert, Tracy. BA, U. S. D., 1965; MA, American U., 1967. Press aide Congressman John Hansen, Washington, 1965-66, U.S. Dept. HUD, Washington, 1967-73; pres. Darcy Comms., Denver, 1973-81; pres., CEO Servoss Pub. Rels., Denver, 1981—; pres. Pinnacle Worldwide, Mpls., 1993, chmn., 1994. Mem. Colo. Bus. Com. for the Arts, 1991—, chmn., 1991-92; mem. adv. bd. Keep Denver Beautiful. Mem. Pub. Rels. Soc. Am. (counselors acad. credentials chmn. 1992-93), Denver C. of C. (comms. coun. 1991-94). Office: Servoss Pub Rels 455 Sherman St Denver CO 80203-4400

SERWINT, NANCY JEAN, classical archaeologist, educator; b. Chgo., May 7, 1951; d. Stanley Anthony and Gertrude Rose (Radkiewicz) S. BA in Classics, U. Ill., 1973; MA in Art History, U. Chgo., 1977; MA in Classical Archaeology, Princeton U., 1982, PhD in Classical Archaeology, 1987. Asst. prof. art Ariz. State U., Tempe, 1988-92; assoc. prof. art Ariz. State U., 1993—; trustee Cyprus Am. Archaeological Rsch. Inst., Nicosia, 1993—; alumni coun. Am. Sch. Classical Studies at Athens, Greece, 1991-94; asst. dir. Princeton-Cyprus Archaeological Expedition, Marion, 1983—. NEH fellow, 1992-93, Am. Sch. Classical Studies at Athens fellow, 1983-84, 85-86, Samuel Kress Found. fellow, 1984-85. Mem. Am. Schs. Oriental Rsch., Archaeological Inst. Am., Egypt Exploration Soc., N.Am. Soc. Sports Historians, Women's Classical Caucus. Office: Ariz State U Sch Art Tempe AZ 85287-1505

SESTINI, VIRGIL ANDREW, biology educator; b. Las Vegas, Nov. 24, 1936; s. Santi and Merceda Francesca (Borla) S. BS in Edn., U. Nev., 1959; postgrad., Oreg. State U., 1963-64; MNS, U. Idaho, 1965; postgrad., Ariz. State U., 1967, No. Ariz. U., 1969; cert. tchr., Nev. Tchr. biology Rancho High Sch., 1960-76; sci. chmn., tchr. biology Bonanza High Sch., Las Vegas, 1976-90; ret., 1990; co-founder, curator exhibits Meadows Mus. Nat. History, 1993-94; part-time tchr. Meadows Sch., 1987-94; ret., 1994; edn. specialist, cell biologist SAGE Rsch., Las Vegas, 1993. Served with USAR, 1959-65. Recipient Rotary Internat. Honor Tchr. award, 1965, Region VIII Outstanding Biology Tchr. award, 1970, Nev. Outstanding Biology Tchr. award Nat. Assn. Biology Tchrs., 1970, Nat. Assn. Sci. Tchrs., Am. Gas Assn. Sci. Teaching Achievement Recognition award, 1976, 1980, Gustov Ohaus award, 1980, Presdl. Honor Sci. Tchr. award, 1983; Excellence in Edn. award Nev. Dept. Edn., 1983; Presdl. award excellence in math. and sci. teaching, 1984, Celebration of Excellence award Nev. Com. on Excellence in Edn., 1986, Hall of Fame award Clark County Sch. Dist., 1988, Excellence in Edn. award, Clark County Sch. Dist., 1987, 88, Spl. Edn. award Clark County Sch. Dist., 1988, NSEA Mini-grants, 1988, 89, 92, World Decoration of Excellence medallion World Inst. Achievement, 1989, Cert. Spl. Congl. Recognition, 1989, Senatorial Recognition , 1989, mini-grant Jr. League Las Vegas., 1989, Excellence in Edn. award, Clark County Sch. Dist., 1989; named Nev. Educator of Yr., Milken Family Found./Nev. State Dept. Edn., 1989; grantee Nev. State Bd. Edn., 1988, 89, Nev. State Edn. Assn., 1988-89. Author: Lab Investigations For High School Honors Biology, 1989, Microbiology: A Manual for High School Biology, 1992, Laboratory Investigations in Microbiology, 1992; co-author: A Biology Lab Manual For Cooperative Learning, 1989, Metrics and Science Methods: A Manual of Lab Experiments for Home Schoolers, 1990, Experimental Designs in Biology I: Botany and Zoology, 1993, Designs in Biology: A Lab Manual, 1993, Integrated Science Lab Manual, 1994; contbr. articles to profl. jours. Mem. AAAS, NEA, Nat. Assn. Taxidermists, Nat. Sci. Tchrs. Assn. (life, Nev. State chpt. 1968-70), Nat. Assn. Biology Tchrs. (life, OBTA dir. Nev. State 1991—), Am. Soc. Microbiology, Coun. for Exceptional Children, Am. Biographic Inst. (rsch. bd. advisors 1988), Nat. Audubon Assn., Nat. Sci. Suprs. Assn., Am. Inst. Biol. Scis., So. Nev. Scale Modelers (region VIII coord. Modeloberfest, 1995). Avocations: scale models, military figures, scale model circus, photography, chess. Office: Sage Rsch 2250 E Tropicana Ave Ste 19 452 Las Vegas NV 89119

SETCHKO, EDWARD STEPHEN, minister, theology educator; b. Yonkers, N.Y., Apr. 27, 1926; s. Stephen John and Mary Elizabeth (Dulak) S.; m. Penelope Sayre, Nov. 18, 1950; children—Marc Edward, Kip Sherman, Robin Elizabeth, Jan Sayre, Dirk Stephen. B.S., Union Coll., 1948; M.Div. cum laude, Andover Newton Theol. Sch., 1953, S.T.M., 1954; Th.D., Pacific Sch. Religion, 1962. Ordained to ministry United Ch. of Christ, 1954; cert. profl. hosp. chaplain. Psychometrician, Union Coll. Character Research Project, Schenectady, N.Y., 1947-50; asst. pastor Eliot Ch., Newton, Mass., 1950-54; clin. tng. supr. Boston City Hosp., 1951-54; intern, chaplain Boston State Mental Hosp., 1953-54; univ. campus minister U. Wash., Seattle, 1954-58; Danforth grantee, 1958-59; grad. fellow in psychotherapy Pacific Sch. Religion, Berkeley, Calif., 1959-60, instr. dept. pastoral psychology, 1960-61, grad. fellow, lectr. theology and psychology, 1961-62, asst. prof. psychology and counseling, 1962-63, dir. continuing theol. edn., 1962-63; clin. psychologist Calif. Correctional Facility, Vacaville, Calif., 1961-62; field research sec. laity div. United Ch. Christ, Berkeley, Calif. and N.Y.C., 1963-68; vis. prof. psychology and sociology Starr King Ctr. for Religious Leadership, Berkeley, 1967-69; assoc. prof. religion and soc. Starr King Ctr., Grad. Theol. Union, Berkeley, Calif., 1969-71, prof., 1971-83; career counselor The Ctr. for Ministry, Oakland, Calif., 1986-89; mem. faculty, chmn. curriculum and faculty com. Layman's Sch. Religion, Berkeley, 1960-67; cons. and lectr. in field. Del. voter registration delegation, Miss., 1965; mem. peace del., Mid-East, 1983; lectr. Internat. Conf. on the Holocaust and Genocide, Tel Aviv, 1982, Nuclear Disarmament Conf., W.Ger., 1980, 81, 82, Internat. Ctr. for Peace in the Middle East, Resource Ctr. for Non-Violence, Clergy & Laity Concerned, Ecumenical Peace Inst., Internat. Peace Acad.; World Policy Inst., Inst. Peace and World Order, Am. Friends Service Com. (bd. dirs.), Berkeley Ctr. for Human Interaction, Ristad Found., Am. Friends Golan Heights, Pacific Inst. of Criminal Justice; dir. The Project for Peace and Reconciliation in the Middle East (non-profit Calif. Found. 1983-89); vol. South Berkeley Cmty. Ch. hunger project Alta Bates Hospice. Lt. (j.g.) USNR, 1944-46, WW II. Mem. Am. Psychol. Assn. (cert.), Calif. State Psychol. Assn., Assn. Clin. Pastoral Edn., World Future Soc., Soc. Sci. Study of Religion, Inst. Noetic Scis., Com. for Protection Human Subjects (U. Calif.-Berkeley). Democrat. Contbr. articles to profl. jours.; condr. seminars: Futurology; Intricacies of Being Human, Images of Women and Men; Changing Values in Roles Between the Sexes in a Technological Society, Cybernetics and Humanization of Man; developer curriculum: Peace and Conflict Studies (U. Calif., Berkeley).

SETENCICH, ELI JOHN, columnist; b. Sacramento, Apr. 10, 1924; s. Joko Ilija and Jovanka (Ljescovic) S.; m. Elizabeth Jackson (div.); m. Yvonne Dillon, Sept. 4, 1965; children: Stephen, Amy Lynn. BA in Journalism, U. Calif., Berkeley, 1952. Reporter Walnut Creek (Calif.) Sun, 1952-54, KFRE radio-TV, Fresno, Calif., 1954-61; polit. writer Fresno Bee, 1961-80, columnist, 1980—. Author: Fresno, California's Heartland, 1993. Capt. USAF, 1942-45, ETO. Office: The Fresno Bee 1626 E St Fresno CA 93706-2006

SETEROFF, SVIATOSLAV STEVE, management and logistics information systems consultant; b. Shanghai, People's Republic of China, Oct. 6, 1937; came to U.S., 1949; s. Leo G. and Olga D. (Pankova) S.; m. Deanna Catherine Rogers (div. 1964); children: Steven James, Richard Aubrey; m. Joyce Eileen Schieldge, Feb. 22, 1965; children: Barbara Lynn Seteroff Anderson, Leanne Marie Seteroff DeBroeck. AA, Chapman Coll., 1974, BA cum laude, 1975; MBA, U. Puget Sound, 1983. Enlisted USN, 1955-75, commd. warrant officer, 1976-85; sr. analyst McDonnell Douglas Astronautics Co., Rockville, Md., 1985-87; program mgr. Anadac, Inc., Arlington, Va., 1987; v.p. Systems Mgmt. Am. Corp., San Diego, 1987-89; project mgr. info. systems, logistics, sr. ops. analyst MERIT Systems, Inc., Bremerton, Wash., 1989-91; founder, owner Mgmt. and Logistics Assocs., 1990—; instr. Residence Edn. Ctr., Chapman U., Bangor, Wash., 1985—.

Developer Scrivener Masonic Lodge Mgmt. Program, 1992. Mem. Am. Soc. Naval Engrs. (nat. chmn. logistics symposium 1991-93, Pres. award 1993), Am. Soc. Logistics Engrs. (symposium presenter, chmn. advanced tech. steering group 1994—), Ret. Officers Assn., Masons. Office: 12890 Old Military Rd NE Poulsbo WA 98370-7972

SETLIN, ALAN JOHN, entrepreneur; b. N.Y.C., Oct. 27, 1933; s. Samuel and Alyce (Inginito) S.; children: Susan Marie, Peggy Ann, Gina Marie, Alycia Ruth, Alana Jean; m. Deborah Ann Kozlowski, Oct. 14, 1986. Student, U. Miami. CLU. V.p. Figurette, Ltd., Miami, Fla., 1956-60; ptnr. Robins & Clarke, N.Y.C., 1960-63; leading agt. Equitable Life Ins. Co., N.Y.C., 1963; gen. agt. Madison Life Ins. Co., N.Y.C., 1963-66, Beneficial Nat. Life Ins. Co., N.Y.C., 1967-72; pres., chief exec. officer Alliance Assoc., Inc., Beverly Hills, Calif., 1972—; ptnr. McMutry & Bell, Inc., Beverly Hills, 1982—; chief exec. officer Emergency Help, Inc., Beverly Hills, 1989—; COO, dir. Clinica Medica Familiar, L.A.; bd. dirs. Six Million Dollar Forum, 1979-80. Mem. Rep. Senatorial Inner Circle, 1988-90. Sgt. AUS, 1952-54. Mem. Nat. Assn. Life Underwriters (fed. legis. chmn. Western States div. 1980-81, pres. L.A. chpt. 1979-80), CLU Assn. (pres. county chpt. 1979-80), Million Dollar Round Table (life), Golden Key (nat. com.). Roman Catholic. Office: Clinica Medica Familiar 600 Wilshire Blvd Ste 700 Los Angeles CA 90017-3219

SETO, JOSEPH TOBEY, virologist, educator; b. Tacoma, Aug. 3, 1924; s. Toraichi and Kiyo Morita Seto; m. Grace K. Nakano, Aug. 9, 1959; children: Susan L., Steven F. BS, U. Minn., 1949; MS, U. Wis., 1955, PhD, 1957. Postdoctoral fellow UCLA, 1958-59; asst. prof. San Francisco State U., 1959-60; prof. microbiology Calif. State U., L.A., 1960-88, prof. emeritus, 1988; cons. U.S. Naval Biology Lab., Oakland, Calif., 1959-61; vis. prof. Inst. Virology, Giessen, Fed. Republic Germany, 1965-66, 72-73, 79-80, 86-87, NATO sr. scientist, 1972, WHO Exchange Worker, 1972. Sgt. U.S. Army, 1945-46. United Health Found. fellow, 1965; recipient Humboldt Found. award 1972, 86, Humboldt Found. medal 1991. Fellow Am. Soc. Microbiology; mem. AAAS, Microscopy Soc. Am., Sigma Xi. Office: Calif State U-Los Angeles Dept Microbiology Los Angeles CA 90032-8201

SETZEKORN, WILLIAM DAVID, architect, consultant; b. Mt. Vernon, Ill., Mar. 12, 1935; s. Merrett Everet and Audrey (Ferguson) S.; m. Georgia Sue Brown, Feb. 4, 1958 (div. 1968); children: Jeffrey Merle, Timothy Michael. BArch, Kans. State U., 1957; cert. in computer graphics, Harvard U., 1968; BA with MA equivalency in Humanities, Western Ill. U., 1982. Registered arch., Calif. Coord. design and constrn. Cal-Expo, Sacramento, 1968; pvt. practice Los Altos and Seattle, Calif., 1968-85; cons. Contra Costa County, Martinez, Calif., 1985-89, El Dorado County, Placerville, Calif., 1985-89, Somerset, Calif., 1989—; cons. Fed. Emergency Mgmt. Agy., The Presidio, San Francisco, 1989—. Author: Formerly British Honduras: A Profile of the New Nation of Belize, 1975, 4 other titles; contbr. articles to mags. Dir. alumni affairs Pi Kappa Alpha Alumni chpts., Manhattan, Kans. and Davis, Calif., 1957—. Recipient Ofcl. Commendation, State of Calif., 1968, U.S. Presdl. Medal of Merit, Ronald Reagan, 1988. Fellow Augustan Soc. (bd. dirs. 1994); mem. Noble Co. of the Rose (knight 1979), numerous other internat. orders of chivalry. Republican. Home: PO Box 706 Somerset CA 95684-0706

SEVER, LOWELL ENYEART, epidemiologist; b. Yakima, Wash., Sept. 22, 1939; s. Ralph Wesley and Virginia Love (Enyeart) S.; m. Susan Curry Carter, Dec. 18, 1965; children: Jeremy Carter, Alison Mary. AA, Wenatchee Valley Coll., 1959; BA, U. Wash., 1966; MA, U. Wis., Milw., 1968; PhD, U. Wash., 1973. Rsch. assoc. U. Wash., Seattle, 1972-74; asst. prof. U. Calif., L.A., 1974-79; sr. rsch. scientist Battelle Pacific Northwest Labs., Richland, Wash., 1979-84; asst. dir. for sci. div. of birth defects Ctrs. for Disease Control, Atlanta, 1984-89; staff scientist Battelle Pacific Northwest Labs., Richland, 1989-95; program mgr. Battelle Ctrs. for Pub. Health Rsch. and Evaluation, Seattle, 1995—; summer faculty New England Epidemiology Inst., Medford, Mass., 1985—; affiliate prof. U. Wash. Sch. of Pub. Health, Seattle, 1990—. Contbr. articles to profl. jours. Exec. com. March of Dimes Birth Defects Found., Richland, 1980-84, Atlanta, 1985-89, Seattle, 1990—. Recipient Spl. Recognition award USPHS, 1988. Fellow Am. Coll. Epidemiology; mem. Soc. for Pediatric Epidemiologic Rsch. (pres. 1989-90), Am. Epidemiol. Soc., Soc. for Epidemiologic Rsch., Am. Pub. Health Assn., Teratology Soc. Office: Battelle Seattle Rsch Ctr 4000 NE 41st St Seattle WA 98105-5428

SEVERINSEN, DOC (CARL H. SEVERINSEN), conductor, musician; b. Arlington, Oreg., July 7, 1927; m. Emily Marshall, 1980; children—Nancy, Judy, Cindy, Robin, Allen. Ptnr. Severinsen-Akwright Co.; pops condr. The Phoenix (Ariz.) Symphony Orchestra. Mem., Ted Fio Rito Band, 1945, Charlie Barnet Band, 1947-49, then with, Tommy Dorsey, Benny Goodman, Norro Morales, Vaughn Monroe; soloist network band: Steven Allen Show, NBC-TV, 1954-55; mem., NBC Orch. Tonight Show, 1962-67 , music dir., 1967-92 ; past host of: NBC-TV show The Midnight Special; recs., RCA Records, including; albums: Brass Roots, 1971, Facets, 1988, The Tonight Show Band, Night Journey. Address: care Thomas Cassidy Inc 366 Horseshoe Dr Basalt CO 81621-9104 also: c/o William Morris Agency 151 S El Camino Dr Beverly Hills CA 90212-2704 also: The Phoenix Symphony Orch Symphony Hall 2498 3707 N 7th St Phoenix AZ 85014-5059*

SEVETSON, DONALD JAMES, minister, church administrator; b. Oak Park, Ill., Oct. 4, 1933; s. Earl Winfred and Lillian Ione (Anderson) S.; m. Mary Louise Frank, Nov. 30, 1957; children: Philip Curtis, Andrea Lyle, Erika Linnea. BA, Macalester Coll., 1954; BDiv, Chgo. Theol. Sem. and U. Chgo., 1957. Ordained to ministry Congl. Ch., 1958. Minister Raymond Congl. Ch., Franksville, Wis., 1959-62; assoc. minister 1st Congl. Ch., Mpls., 1957-59, Dekalb, Ill., 1962-65, Appleton, Wis., 1965-69; minister Parkview United Ch. of Christ, White Bear Lake, Minn., 1969-73; assoc. conf. minister Minn. Conf. United Ch. of Christ, Mpls., 1973-80; conf. minister Ctrl. Pacific Conf. United Ch. of Christ, Portland, Oreg., 1980—; chairperson coun. conf. ministers United Ch. of Christ, Cleve., 1994—, chairperson, bd. dirs. office of comm., 1989-93. Author: The First Century, 1994. Chair Oreg. Holocaust Resource Ctr., Portland, 1989-91, bd. dirs., 1984-91, 94—; trustee Pacific U., Forest Grove, Oreg., 1989—. Mem. NAACP, Urban League, Chgo. Theol. Sem. Alumni Assn. (pres. 1962-64). Democrat. Office: United Ch of Christ Ctrl Pacific Conf 0245 SW Bancroft St Ste E Portland OR 97201

SEVEY, ROBERT WARREN, retired broadcasting executive, journalist; b. Mpls., Dec. 6, 1927; s. Benjamin Warren and Helen Margaret (Benham) S.; m. Rosalie Fergueson Thomas, Jan. 28, 1950; children: Michael Warren, David Ellis. BA, U. Calif., Santa Barbara, 1951. Announcer, newscaster WOI and KASI, Ames, Iowa, 1947-49; sports dir. KIST, Santa Barbara, 1949-51; prodn. asst. CBS-TV, Hollywood, Calif., 1951-52; producer, announcer KPHO-TV, Phoenix, 1952-54; prodn. mgr. KULA-TV, Honolulu, 1954-57; prodn. mgr. radio-TV Holst & Male Inc., Honolulu, 1957-59; sta. mgr. KGMB-TV, Honolulu, 1959-61; news dir. Sta. KHVH-TV, Honolulu, 1961-65, Sta. KGMB-TV, Honolulu, 1966-86; v.p. news/corporate affairs Heftel Broadcasting Co., Honolulu, 1987-90; with Heftel Broadcasting Co., L.A., 1990-91; ret., 1991. S/sgt. U.S. Army, 1945-47. Mem. Radio-TV News Dirs. Assn., Honolulu Press Club (pres. 1969-70, mem. Hall of Fame 1987—).

SEVILLA, CARLOS A., bishop; b. San Francisco, Aug. 9, 1935. Ed., Gonzaga U., Santa Clara U., Jesuiten Kolleg, Innsbruck, Austria, Cath. Inst. Paris. Ordained priest Roman Cath. Ch., 1966, bishop, 1989. Titular bishop Mina, 1989—; aux. bishop San Francisco, 1989—. Office: Archdiocese San Francisco 445 Church St San Francisco CA 94114-1720*

SEWELL, CHARLES ROBERTSON, geologist, exploration company executive, investor; b. Malvern, Ark., Feb. 7, 1927; s. Charles Louis and Elizabeth (Robertson) S.; m. Margaret Helen Wilson, Dec. 26, 1953 (dec. July 1985); children: Michael Stuart, Charles Wilson, Marion Elizabeth; m. Louise T. Worthington, Nov. 29, 1985; 1 child, Ginger B. BS, U. Ark.-Fayetteville, 1950; MA, U. Tex.-Austin, 1955, postgrad., 1961-64. Registered geologist, Calif., Ariz. Well logging engr. Baroid, Houston, 1950; asst. metallurgist Magcobar, Malvern, Ark., 1951; geologist Socony-Mobil Petroleum Co., Roswell, N.Mex., 1955; sr. geologist Dow Chem. Co., Freeport, Tex., 1956-61; spl. instr. U. Tex., Austin, 1962-65; pvt. practice cons. geologist, Austin, 1962-65; dist. geologist, mgr. Callahan Mining Corp., Tucson, 1965-68; owner, cons. geologist Sewell Mineral Exploration, worldwide, 1968—, extensive work USSR-CIS, 1988—. Contbr. articles to profl. jours. Elder, Presbyn. Ch., Tucson, 1973—. With USN, 1944-46, 51-53. NSF grantee, 1962-64, 63. Mem. AIME, Ariz. Geol. Soc., Mining Found. Southwest (bd. govs. 1982-86, 90—, pres. 1984). Republican. Lodge: Masons. Discoverer/co-discoverer numerous metallic and non-metallic ore deposits. Home and Office: 260 S Sewell Pl Tucson AZ 85748-6700

SEYBERT, JANET ROSE, lawyer, military officer; b. Cin., Feb. 7, 1944; d. Peter Robert and Helen Rose (Young) S. BA in Classics, BS in Edn., U. Cin., 1966; MA in Classics, U. Iowa, 1968; JD, Chase Coll. Law, 1975; ML, Army JAG Sch., 1984. Bar: Ohio 1975, U.S. Ct. Mil. Appeals 1975, Colo. 1981, U.S. Ct. Claims 1985; cert. mortgage investor; cert. profl. clown. Instr. Latin, ancient history Salem Coll., Winston-Salem, N.C., 1968-70; instr. N.C. Gov.'s Sch., Winston-Salem, N.C., 1969; instr. phys. edn., Latin Kemper Hall, Kenosha, Wis., 1970-71; instr. in Latin Carthage Coll., Kenosha, Wis., 1970-71; commd. 2d lt. USMC, 1972; completed interservice transfer to USAF, 1978, advanced through grades to maj., 1982; lawyer USAF Acad. USAF, Colorado Springs, Colo., 1978-81; chief civil law Sheppard AFB, Tex., 1981-84; dep. staff judge adv., chief mil. justice Homestead AFB, Fla., 1984-88; chief civil law Lowry AFB, Colo., 1988-91; ret., 1991—, pvt. practice environ. law, 1991—; owner, pres. The Seybert Funding Cos., 1991—; atty., notary The Seybert Funding Cos., S & K Ent., 1994—; legal advisor Armed Forces Disciplinary Control Bd., Child and Family Advocacy Coun. USAF, Homestead AFB, 1984-88. Vol. Muscular Dystrophy Assn., Colorado Springs, 1978-81; contbr. Ellis Island Resoration Program, Homestead AFB, 1985-88; active Nat. Mus. Women in Arts, Nat. Air and Space Mus.; officer in charge Lowry Silver and Blue Choir; charter mem. Women in Military Svc. to Am. Meml. Mem. ABA, Judge Adv. Assn., Edn. Profl. Assn., Ohio Bar Assn., Fed. Bar Assn., Colo. Bar Assn., Colo. Women's Bar Assn., Am. Bus. Women's Assn. (chmn. audit com. Homestead charter chpt., hist. com. 1987, pres. Visions charter chpt. 1990-91, 91-92, Top 10 Bus. Women 1987, Woman of Yr. 1987), Phi Beta Kappa, Kappa Delta Pi. Home: 378 Florence St Aurora CO 80010-4223

SEYBOLD, STEVEN JON, entomologist; b. Madison, Wis., Oct. 14, 1959; s. Robert Russel and Patricia Jane (Sovinec) S. BS in Forestry, U. Wis., 1983; PhD in Entomology, U. Calif., Berkeley, 1992. Nat. resources asst. Forest Pest Mgmt. Unit Wis. Dept. Natural Resources, Madison, 1982; forest practitioner Swedish Forest Svc., Hedemora, Sweden, 1983; grad. rsch. asst. Dept. Entomol. Scis., U. Calif., Berkeley, 1984-92; postdoctoral rsch. entomologist Forest Svc., USDA, Albany, Calif., 1992-93; entomologist dept. biochemistry U. Nev., Reno, 1993—. Literacy tutor Marin County Literacy Project, 1986-87; van pool coord. Larkspur Vanpool, Marin County, 1989-93; mem. Dept. Entomol. Scis. Grad. Adv. Com., Berkeley, 1987, Bioscis. Libr. Adv. Com., U. Calif., Berkeley, 1988-92. NSF fellow, 1985-88, rsch. grantee, 1990; USDA postdoctoral rsch. grantee/postdoctoral fellow in biochemistry U. Nev., 1993-95. Mem. Entomol. Soc. Am., Internat. Soc. Chem. Ecology, Am. Chem. Soc., Sigma Xi, Phi Beta Kappa (merit scholar 1989), Gamma Sigma Delta, Xi Sigma Pi, Phi Kappa Phi. Office: U Nev Dept Biochemistry MS 330 Reno NV 89557-0014

SEYFER, ALAN ERIC, surgeon; b. Ft. Smith, Ark., Aug. 15, 1945; s. Robert Paranteau and Maria Teresa (Ortiz) S.; m. Glenna Lee Stuart, Oct. 26, 1968; children: Tara Lee, Jessie Lynn. BS in Engring., U.S. Mil. Acad., 1967; MD, La. State U., 1973. Diplomate Am. Bd Surgery, Am. Bd. Plastic Surgery, Am. Bd. Hand Surgery and Plastic Surgery. U.S. army officer Artillery/Missiles, U.S.A., Asia, 1967-69; surg. internship Fitzsimons Army Med. Ctr., Denver, 1973-74, gen. surg. residency, 1974-78; plastic surg. residency Walter Reed Army Med. Ctr., Washington, 1978-81, hand microsurg. fellowship, 1979-80; hand microsurg. fellowship Duke U., Durham, N.C., 1979-80; chief plastic surgery svc. and dir. residency Walter Reed Army Med. Ctr., Washington, 1983-89, chief orthpaedic hand surgery, 1985-89; prof. surgery, head divsn. plastic surgery Oreg. Health Scis. U., Portland, 1989—; dir. plastic surgery tng. Oreg. Health Scis. U., Portland, 1989—; cons. NIH, Bethesda, Md., 1988—. Author: Atlas of Chest Wall Construction, 1986; editor: Chest Wall Reconstruction, 1989, Depuytren's Contracture, 1991, Bone Repair and Regeneration, 1994; assoc. editor Annals of Plastic Surgery, 1993—; contbr. articles to profl. jours. and chpts. to books. Recipient Rsch. grants, Vis. professorships, Arthur Garnes lectureship Columbia U., 1991, Best Tchr. award Oreg. Health Scis. U., 1993. Fellow Am. Coll. Surgeons; mem. Soc. Univ. Surgeons, Am. Assn. Plastic Surgeons. Office: Oreg Health Scis U L352A Divsn Plastic Surgery 3181 SW Sam Jackson Park Rd Portland OR 97201-3011

SEYFERT, HOWARD BENTLEY, JR., podiatrist; b. Clifton Heights, Pa., July 10, 1918; s. Howard Bentley and Mabel (Ashenbach) S.; m. Anna Mary van Roden, June 26, 1942; 1 child, Joanna Mary Irwin. D of Podiatric Medicine, Temple U., 1940. Cert. Nat. Bd. Podiatry Examiners (past pres.), Ariz. State Bd. Podiatry Examiners (past pres.). Pvt. practice podiatry Phoenix, 1950-82, Sedona, Ariz., 1982—; mem. med. staff Marcus J. Lawrence Meml. Hosp., Cottonwood, Ariz. Served to capt. USAAF, 1942-46, ETO, lt. col. Res. ret. Decorated Bronze Star. Fellow Acad. Ambulatory Foot Surgery, Am. Coll. Foot Surgeons; mem. Ariz. Podiatric Med. Assn. (past pres.), Am. Podiatric Med. Assn. Republican. Presbyterian. Clubs: OakCreek Country (Sedona); Fairfield Flagstaff Country (Flagstaff, Ariz.). Home: Air Force Village W 21364 Westover Circle Riverside CA 92518

SEYL, EDITH J., occupational therapist; b. Lancaster, Pa., Feb. 27, 1950; d. Frank Lydston Seyl and Jean Morton (Sanders) Seyl Dorsey; m. Fred William Cook, Aug. 26, 1972 (div. May 1977). Activities dir. Franklin Care nursing home, Gladstone, Oreg., 1977-80; pvt. practice nursing homes and pvt. practice, Vancouver, Wash., 1980—; massage therapist Home Health, Portland, Oreg., 1987-88, Home Health-Willamette Falls, Oregon City, Oreg., 1992—; dir. occupational therapy Eastmoreland Hosp., Portland, Oreg., 1988-92; occupational therapist Willamette Falls Home Health, 1992—; dir. Weaver's Tale Retreat Ctr., Portland, 1992—. Mem. Am. Occupational Therapy Assn., Occupational Therapy Assn. Oreg. Office: Weaver's Tale Retreat Ctr 4112 SE Pine St Portland OR 97214-2037

SEYLE, ROBERT HARLEY, artist, educator; b. National City, Calif., Oct. 9, 1937; s. Robert Van and Kristine (Aam) S.; children: Preston Van Seyle, Bryn Leigh Seyle. Student, Loma Linda U., 1956-58, 59-60; BFA, Otis Art Inst., L.A., 1961, MFA, 1966; postgrad., Clairmont (Calif.) Coll., 1978. Tchr. painting and sculpture Camarillo (Calif.) Cmty. Ctr., 1970, Shasta Coll. Ext. Program, Hynpalm, Calif., 1974; faculty painting, design, sculpture, drawing Loma Linda U., Riverside, Calif., 1976-79; tchr. drawing and painting West Union (W.Va.) Cmty. Ctr., 1982; faculty ceramics, sculpture, drawing, design/composition Pacific Union Coll., Angwin, Calif., 1991—; one-man shows include Ankrum Gallery, L.A., 1968, Palm Springs Desert (Calif.) Mus., 1974; works in permanent collections at Palm Springs Desert Mus., MGM Studios, Hollywood, Calif., Otis Art Inst., Beneficial Ins. Group, Storm King Art Mus., N.Y., La Jolla Art Mus., San Pedro and Peninsula YMCA, Calif. and many pvt. collections. Exhibited in group shows at Calif. Mus. Sci. and Industry, 1966, Otis Art Inst., 1966, Krannert Mus., U. Ill., 1967, Calif. Design X, 1968, Calif. Expo, Sacramento, 1968, Newport Harbor Mus., Calif., 1969, La Jolla (Calif.) Art Mus., 1969, Sacramento Capitol Bldg., 1974, San Bernardino County Mus., Calif., 1978, 79, Riverside (Calif.) Art Ctr., 1978, Ankrum Gallery, 1978, I. Wolk Gallery, St. Helena, Calif., 1992, Luther Burbank Ctr. for Arts, 1993, The Artful Eye, Calistoga, Calif., 1994. With U.S. Army, 1961-63. Home and Office: 545 Howell Mountain Rd Angwin CA 94508-9757

SEYMOUR, JEFFREY ALAN, governmental relations consultant; b. L.A., Aug. 31, 1950; s. Daniel and Evelyn (Schwartz) S.; m. Valerie Joan Parker, Dec. 2, 1973; 1 child, Jessica Lynne. AA in Social Sci., Santa Monica Coll., 1971; BA in Polit. Sci., UCLA, 1973, MPA, , 1977. Councilmanic aide L.A. City Coun., 1972-74; county supr.'s sr. dep. L.A. Bd. Suprs., 1974-82; v.p. Bank of L.A., 1982-83; prin. Jeffrey Seymour & Assocs., L.A., 1983-84; ptnr. Morey/Seymour & Assocs., 1984—; mem. comml. panel Am. Arbitration Assn., 1984—. Chmn. West Hollywood Parking Adv. Com., L.A., 1983-84; chmn. social action com. Temple Emanuel of Beverly Hills, 1986-89, bd. dirs. 1988-93, v.p., 1990-93; v.p. Congregation N'vay Shalom, 1994-95; mem. Pan Pacific Park Citizens Adv. Com., L.A., 1982-85; bd. dirs. William O'Douglas Outdoor Classroom, L.A., 1981-88; exec. sec. Calif. Fedn. Young Dems., 1971; mem. Calif. Dem. Cen. Com., 1979-82; pres. Beverlywood-Cheviot Hills Dem. Club, L.A., 1978-81; co-chmn. Westside Chancellor's Assocs. UCLA, 1986-88; mem. L.A. Olympic Citizens Adv. Com.; mem. liaison adv. commn. with city and county govt. for 1984 Olympics, 1984; v.p. cmty. rels. metro region, Jewish Fedn. Coun. of L.A., 1985-87, co-chmn. urban affairs commn., 1987-89, vice chmn., 1989-90, subcom. chmn. local govt. law and legislation commn., 1990—, chmn. campus outreach task force, 1994—; mem. adv. bd. Nat. Jewish Ctr. for Immunology & Respiratory Medicine, 1991—; bd. dirs. Hillel Coun. of L.A., 1991—; mem. platform on world peace and internat. rels. Calif. Dems., 1983; pres. 43d Assembly Dist. Dem. Coun., 1975-79; arbitrator BBB, 1984—; trustee UCLA Found., 1989—; pres. UCLA Jewish Alumni, 1992-95; mem. Santa Monica Mountains Com., 1995—; mem. cabinet Jewish Cmty. Rels. Com. Greater L.A., 1994—, chair campus outreach task force, 1994—; mem. adv. bd. L.A. Peace Now. Recipient Plaques for services rendered Beverlywood Cheviot Hills Dem. Club, L.A., 1981, Jewish Fedn. Coun. Greater L.A., 1983; Certs. of Appreciation, L.A. Olympic Organizing Com., 1984, County of L.A., 1984, City of L.A., 1987; commendatory resolutions, rules com. Calif. State Senate, 1987, Calif. State Assembly, 1987, County of L.A., 1987, City of L.A., 1987. Mem. Am. Soc. Pub. Adminstrn., Am. Acad. Polit. and Social Scis., Town Hall of Calif., So. Calif. Planning Congress, Urban Land Inst., UCLA Alumni Assn. (mem. govtl. steering com. 1983—, chair, 1995—, bd. dirs. 1995—). Office: Morey/Seymour and Assocs 233 Wilshire Blvd Ste 290 Santa Monica CA 90401-1206

SFERRAZZA, PETER JOSEPH, mayor, lawyer; b. N.Y.C., Apr. 30, 1945; s. Peter Joseph and Jane S. (Terry) S.; m. Vivian Ann Canty, 1968 (div.); children—Jessica, Joey. BA, Mich. State U., 1967; JD, U. Wis., 1972. Bar: Wis. 1972, Nev. 1977. Legal intern Wis. Judicare, Madison, 1971-72; staff atty. Wis. Judicare, Wausau, 1972-75, Dane County Legal Services, Wausau, 1972; sole practice Wausau, 1975-76; dir. Nev. Indian Legal Service, Carson City, 1976-79; ptnr. Howard, Cavallera & Sferrazza, Reno, 1979-81; sole practice Reno, 1981—; mayor City of Reno, 1983—; tribal judge Washoe Tribe, Carson City, 1979-80. Alderman city of Wausau, 1976; councilman City of Reno, 1981-83; del. Nat. Democratic conv., 1984; chmn. Nev. Dem. Conv., 1984. Roman Catholic. Office: City of Reno Office of Mayor 490 S Center St Reno NV 89501-2105*

SHACKELFORD, GORDON LEE, JR., physics educator; b. South Bend, Ind., Apr. 7, 1948; s. Gordon Lee and Leatha Mae (Andrews) S.; m. Janis Elizabeth Mead, Apr. 6, 1974. BS in Physics, San Diego State U., 1970, MS in Radiol. Physics, 1974. Electronic designer for physics dept. San Diego State U., 1969-70; electronic engr. Naval Electronics Lab., Point Loma, Calif., 1970; electronic engr. product design Info. Machine Corps., Santee, Calif., 1970-71; lectr. physics San Diego State U., 1971—, asst. dir. alumni and devel. Coll. of Scis., 1980-81, assoc. dean scis., external rels., 1981—, project mgr. Biomass Power Plant, 1984-87, 89—; project mgr. SDSU 100 Telescope, 1989—, Tijuana River Tidal Wetlands Restoration Project, chmn. faculty senate athletic sub-com.. Mem. quality life bd. City of San Diego, 1989-90; vice-chmn. Lakeside Community Planning Group. Home: 9716 Red Pony Ln El Cajon CA 92021-2343 Office: San Diego State U Physics Dept San Diego CA 92182

SHACKLEY, DOUGLAS JOHN, fire alarm company executive; b. Oakland, Calif., Sept. 21, 1938; s. Floyd H. and Margaret I. Shackley; student San Jose State U., 1957, Chabot Coll., 1962-63; diploma in bus. mgmt. LaSalle Extension U., 1972; m. Chloe Jeanne Olson, Sept. 11, 1965; children—Derek Todd, Darren James, Daniel John, Christina Louise. Office mgr. service dept. Am. Dist. Telegraph Co., Oakland, 1961-67; office mgr. Pacific Aux. Fire Alarm Co., San Francisco, 1967-69, mgr., 1969-73, pres., gen. mgr., 1973—, also dir.; contbg. mem. Alarm Industry Telecommunications Com. Pres., Chabot Sch. Dad's Club, 1969-70, Chabot Sch. Parent's Club, 1971-72; moderator Eden United Ch. of Christ, 1980-81, vice moderator 1987-88; mem. Eden Area YMCA, San Francisco YMCA, Boy Scouts Am.; sustaining mem. Calif. Republican Com.; mem. Rep. Presdl. Task Force; San Francisco Fire Dept. 3rd Party Cert. Task Force, 1994-95. Served with USMC, 1957-61. Mem. Nat. Fire Prevention Assn., Calif. Automatic Fire Alarm Assn. (bd. dirs. 1986-87, 94, 95, pres. 1988-89, v.p. for No. Calif. 1987-88), Lake Mont Pine Home Owner Assn. (bd. dirs. 1988-89), San Francisco C. of C. (code com.), Rotary. Home: 1380 Carlton Pl Livermore CA 94550-6400 Office: Pacific Aux Fire Alarm Co 95 Boutwell St San Francisco CA 94124-1903

SHACTER, DAVID MERVYN, lawyer; b. Toronto, Ont., Can., Jan. 17, 1941; s. Nathan and Tillie Anne (Schwartz) S. BA, U. Toronto, 1963; JD, Southwestern U., 1967. Bar: Calif. 1968, U.S. Ct. Appeals (9th cir.) 1969, U.S. Supreme Ct. 1982. Law clk., staff atty. Legal Aid Found., Long Beach, Calif., 1967-70; asst. city atty. City of Beverly Hills, Calif., 1970; ptnr. Shacter & Berg, Beverly Hills, 1971-83, Selwyn, Capalbo, Lowenthal & Shacter Profl. Law Corp., 1984—; del. State Bar Conf. Dels., 1976—; lectr. Calif. Continuing Edn. of Bar, 1977, 82, 83, 86; judge pro tem L.A. and Beverly Hills mcpl. cts.; arbitrator L.A. Superior Ct., 1983—, also judge pro tem; disciplinary examiner Calif. State Bar, 1986. Bd. dirs. and pres. Los Angeles Soc. Prevention Cruelty to Animals, 1979-89. Mem. Beverly Hills Bar Assn. (bd. govs. 1985—, editor-in-chief jour., sec. 1987-88, treas. 1988-89, v.p. 1989-90, pres.-elect 1990-91, pres. 1991-92), Los Angeles County Bar Assn., Am. Arbitration Assn. (nat. panel arbitrators), City of Hope Med. Ctr. Aux., Wilshire C. of C. (bd. dirs., gen. counsel 1985-87). Office: Selwyn Capalbo Lowenthal & Shacter Profl Law Corp 8383 Wilshire Blvd Ste 510 Beverly Hills CA 90211

SHADDOCK, PAUL FRANKLIN, SR., human resources director; b. Buffalo, Apr. 7, 1950; s. William Edmund and Rhea (Riester) S.; m. Linda Jeannine Bauer, July 19, 1980; children: Paul Jr., Jessica. BS, State U. Coll. N.Y., Buffalo, 1973; MBA, SUNY, Binghamton, 1975. Warehouse mgr. Ralston Purina Co., Denver, 1976-77; prodn. supr. Samsonite Corp., Denver, 1978-79, labor rels. rep., 1979-83; dir. human resources NBI, Inc., Denver, 1984-89, United Techs. Corp., Colorado Springs, Colo., 1990—. Mem. Colo. Alliance of Bus., Denver, 1983-85, 90—, exec. com. U. Colo., Colorado Springs, 1990—. Mem. Assn. of Quality Participation, Am. Personnel Assn., Colo. Human Resource Assn., Human Resource Electroncis Group, Mountain States Employers Coun., Rocky Mountain Human Resources Group, Colorado Springs C. of C. Republican. Roman Catholic. Home: 2360 Shiprock Way Colorado Springs CO 80919-3859

SHADE, LINDA BUNNELL, academic administrator; m. William Shade. BA in English and Comm., Baylor U., 1964; MA in English Lang. and Lit., U. Colo., 1967; PhD in English Lit., Colo. U., 1970. Asst. prof. English, acting assoc. dean Coll. Humanities U. Calif., Riverside, 1970-77; dean acad. affairs for acad. programs and policy studies Calif. State U., 1977-87, asst. dean acad. program improvement, 1977-87; vice chancellor for acad. programs U. Colo., Colorado Springs, 1987-93, chancellor, 1993 ; chair Chief Acad. Officers of Sys. of Higher Edn.; active Minn. Women's Econ. Round Table, 1989. Bd. dirs. St. Paul chpt. ARC; active St. Paul Chamber Orch. Task Force, Baylor U. Coun. Sesquicentennial Coun. of 150, 1990, Grace Episcopal Ch., Colorado Springs. Woodrow Wilson Dissertation fellow Colo. U.; recipient Baylor U. Men and Women of Merit award Omicron Delta Kappa, 1992. Office: U Colo 1420 Austin Bluffs Pkwy Colorado Springs CO 80933*

SHADEGG, JOHN B., congressman; b. Phoenix, Oct. 22, 1950; s. Stephen and Eugenia Shadegg; m. Shirley Shadegg; children: Courtney, Stephen. BA, U. Ariz., 1972, JD, 1975. Advisor U.S. Sentencing Commn.; spl. asst. atty. gen. State of Ariz., 1983-90; spl. counsel Ariz. Ho. Rep. Caucus, 1991-92; pvt. practice; mem. 104th Congress from 4th Ariz. dist., 1995—, mem. various coms., asst. whip; mem. Victims Bill of Rights Task Force, 1989-90; mem. Fiscal Accountability and Reform Efforts Com., 1991-92; counsel Arizonian's for Wildlife Conservation, 1992; chmn. Proposition 108-Two-Thirds Tax Limitation Initiative, 1992. Rep. Party Ballot Security chmn., 1982; active Corbin for Atty. Gen., 1982-86; Rep. Precinct committeeman; chmn. Ariz. Rep. Caucus, 1985-87; chmn. Ariz. Lawyers for Bush-Quayle, 1988; mem. steering com., surrogate spkr. Jon Kyl for Congress, 1988-92; former pres. Crime Victim Found.; founding dir. Goldwater Inst. Pub. Policy; chmn. Ariz. Juvenile Justice Adv. Coun.; mem. adv. bd. Salvation Army; mem. vestry Christ Ch. of Ascension, 1989-91; mem. class II Valley

Leadership; bd. dirs. Ariz. State U. Law Soc. Office: US House Reps 503 Cannon House Office Bldg Washington DC 20515-0304*

SHADRACH, (MARTHA) JEAN HAWKINS, artist; b. La Junta, Colo., Nov. 7, 1926; d. Lloyd Marion Hawkins and Martha May (Hawkins) Sudan; widowed, 1987; children: John M., Karolyn Sue Shadrach Green. BA, U. Colo., 1948. Owner Artique, Ltd. Gallery, Anchorage, Alaska, 1971-87; instr. Foothills Art Ctr., Golden, 1988-89, Prince William Sound C.C., Homer, Alaska, 1993, Kachemak Bay C.C., Homer, 1994; facilitator mktg. art seminars; guest lectr. Cunard Cruise Lines, 1988-90, 95. Bd. dirs. Bird Treatment and Learning Ctr., Anchorage, 1994, Anchorage Art Selection Com., 1984. Recipient gov.'s award for excellence in art, Anchorage, 1970, drawing award All Alaska Juried Show, 1970, 1st prize Fairbanks Watercolor Soc., 1987, Paul Schwartz Meml. award Sumi-e Soc. Am., 1993. Mem. Alaska Watercolor Soc. (v.p. 1994—, award 1988). Home and Studio: 3530 Fordham Dr Anchorage AK 99508-4558

SHAEFFER, CLAIRE BRIGHTWELL, writer, educator; b. Weston, Ga., Dec. 2, 1939; d. Louie and Juanita (Sumner) Brightwell; m. Charlie W. Shaeffer, Jr., Feb. 24, 1959; children: Charlie W. III, James Robert. AA with honors, Laney Coll., 1968; BA summa cum laude, Old Dominion U., 1974. Floor supt. Famous Barr, St. Louis, 1960-64; tchr. Montgomery County (Md.) Adult Edn., 1969-70; cons. Portsmouth (Va.) City Schs., 1972-74; tchr. Coll. of the Desert, Palm Desert, Calif., 1975—; lectr. various cities in U.S. and Europe various cities in U.S. and London, 1984—. Author: 101 Sewing Shortcuts, 1978, The Complete Book of Sewing Short Cuts, 1981, Sew Successful, 1984, Sew A Beautiful Gift, 1986, Price It Right: An Alterations Pricing Guide, 1986, Claire Shaeffer's Sewing S.O.S., 1989, Claire Shaeffer's Fabric Sewing Guide, 1989, Sew Any Patch Pocket, 1992, Sew Any Set-in Pocket, 1994, Couture Sewing Techniques, 1993 (with others) Great Sewn Clothes, 1991, Jackets, Coats, and Suits, 1992, Distinctive Details, Beyond the Pattern, 1995; contbr. articles to profl. jours. Pres. Navy Officer's Wives, Portsmouth Naval Hosp., 1971-72; v.p. Assistance League Palm Springs Desert Area, 1976-77, pres., 1977-78; bd. dirs. Riverside County (Calif.) Heart Assn., 1978-82, sec., 1979-81; chmn. ann. mtg. Calif. Heart Assn., Burlingame, 1982. Recipient Second Place award Nat. Fedn. Press Women, 1989, Third Place award, 1993, First Place award 1994; First Place award Calif. Press Women, 1989, 93, 94, Third Place award, 1993, Second Place award, 1995. Mem. Fashion Group Internat. (sec. 1992-94), Profl. Assn. Custom Clothiers, Calif. Press Women. Office: PO Box 157 Palm Springs CA 92263-0157

SHAEFFER, THELMA JEAN, primary school educator; b. Ft. Collins, Colo., Feb. 1, 1949; d. Harold H. and Gladys June (Ruff) Pfeif; m. Charles F. Shaeffer, June 12, 1971; 1 child, Shannon Emily. BA, U. No. Colo., 1970, MA, 1972. Cert. profl. tchr., type B, Colo. Primary tchr. Adams County Dist #12 Five Star Schs., Northglenn, Colo., 1970-84; chpt. I (lang. arts) tchr. Adams County Dist #12 Five Star Schs., Northglenn, 1984-92, chpt. I, read succed tchr., 1992—; mem. policy coun. Adams County Dist. # 12 Five Star Schs., Northglenn, 1975-79, dist. sch. improvement team, 1987-89; presenter Nat. Coun. Tchrs. of English, 1990. Vol. 1992 election, Denver, alumni advisor for Career Connections U. No. Colo., 1993—. Mem. Colo. Tchrs. Assn. (del. 1992), Dist. Tchrs. Edn. Assn. (exec. bd. mem. 1991-93), Internat. Reading Assn. (pres. Colo. coun. 1988), Internat. Order of Job's Daughters (coun. mem.), Order of Eastern Star, Delta Omicron. Episcopalian. Home: 6502 Perry St Arvada CO 80003-6400 Office: Hulstrom Elem Sch 10604 Grant Dr Northglenn CO 80233-4117

SHAEUMIN, MINAYA, customer service representative; b. San Francisco, July 11, 1928; d. John Jesse and Helen Elizabeth (Forsyth) McNeil; m. Maurice Loren Turner, July 28, 1949 (div. Nov. 1955); 1 child, Colleen Ann; m. Rayee Shaeumin, Feb. 13, 1973. Student, Santa Rosa (Calif.) Jr. Coll., 1958-60; AA, Tanana Valley C.C., Fairbanks, Ark., 1987; BS in Anthropology, Oreg. State U., 1992. Lic. life ins. agt., health and accident agt. Intern tchr. 2d grade Primrose Elem. Sch., Santa Rosa, 1961-62; floor clk. surg. wing Santa Rosa Meml. Hosp., 1962; lab. technician Optical Coating Labs., Santa Rosa, 1962-63; live-in practical nurse, housekeeper, sch. tchr. Healsburg, Calif., 1963-65; saleslady, mgr. cosmetic dept. Empire Drug Store, Santa Rosa, 1965-67; cmty. ctr. aide, coord. Cmty. Ctr., Ukiah, Calif., 1968-69; picture framer New Horizons Art Gallery, Fairbanks, Alaska, 1985; seed analyst Oreg. State U. Seed Lab., Corvallis, 1988; owner, operator Best Publs., 1991-92; customer svc. rep. Prequest Co., 1993—; agt., rep. Bus. Network Comms. Inventor matchbook holder-dispensor; inventor-designer free standing mag. rack; writer songs. Active mem. Pro-Choice Orgn., 1991—; mem. The Planetary Soc., 1989-91, Nat. Space Soc., 1990-91; mem. gold club North Shore Animal League, N.Y., 1985—. Recipient Benefactor award North Shore Animal League, 1991, Cert. of Appreciation, Nat. Cm. to Preserve Social Security and Medicare, 1991. Mem. Amnesty Internat. USA, Ams. to Limit Congl. Terms, Am. Policy Inst. "We the People", LWV, Srs. Coalition, So. Poverty law Ctr., Nat. Com. to Preserve Social Security and Medicare. Home: 205 NW 11th St Apt 2 Corvallis OR 97330-6048

SHAFER, DALLAS EUGENE, psychology gerontology educator, minister; b. Holyoke, Colo., Jan. 26, 1936; s. Howard C. and Mary M. (Legg) S.; m. Opal Iline Bruner, Aug. 22, 1954; children: Kim, Jana, Amy. BA, Nebr. Christian, 1958; postgrad., U. Colo., Colorado Springs, 1968-72, U. So. Calif., L.A., 1973; PhD, Walden U., 1978. Cert. clin. pastoral counseling; ordained to ministry Christian Ch., 1958. Minister Christian Ch., Colorado Springs, 1960-62, Julesburg, Colo., 1962-67; instr. of honors program U. Colo., Colorado Springs, 1974, 75; instr. psychology-gerontology Coll. of St. Francis, Colorado Springs, 1982, 84, 93; adj. grad. prof. U. Colo., Colorado Springs, 1992—; sr. minister counseling Christian Ch., Security, Colo., 1967-93; prof. psychology/gerontology Pikes Peak C.C., Colorado Springs, 1969—, dept. chair psychology/gerontology, 1969-92, pres. faculty assn., 1992-94, 95—; vice chair devel. team Westley White Rehab. Ctr., Julesburg, 1966-67; trainer-cons. Pikes Peak Hospice, Colorado Springs, 1980-81; cons. St. Thomas Moore Hospice, Canon City, Colo., 1982, Sante Christo Hospice, Pueblo, Colo., 1983-84; trainer for grief teams in U.S. mil. pers., Hawaii, Japan, 1994. Author: Approaches to Palliative Care, 1978, 92, Delphi-80-Study of Ministry, 1981; contbr. articles to Christian Standard. Sr. min. counseling Christian Ch. Security, 1967-93; bd. dirs. Colo. State Bd. Examiner for Nursing Home, Denver, 1977-83, chmn., 1981-83; moderator Conf. on Prevention of Violence-Sch. Dist. #3, Security, 1992. Mem. Colo. Edn. Assn. (mem. higher edn. com. 1992-94). Office: Pikes Peak CC 5675 S Academy Blvd Colorado Springs CO 80906-5422

SHAFER, JAMES ALBERT, health care administrator; b. Chgo., Aug. 26, 1924; s. James Earl and Kathleen (Sutterland) S.; m. Irene Jeanne Yurcega, June 20, 1948; children: Kathleen Mary, Patricia Ann. Technician Zenith Radio Corp., Chgo., 1946-47; owner, operator Eastgate Electronics, Chgo., 1947-61; applications engr. Perfection Mica Co., Bensenville, Ill., 1961-71; pres. Electronics Unltd., Northbrook, Ill., 1972-73, Ariz. Geriatric Enterprises Inc., Safford, 1974-86; sec.-treas. Saguaro Care Inc., 1988—; bd. dirs. Mt. Graham Community Hosp., Safford. Republican. Roman Catholic. Home: Skyline Ranch 10729 W Cottonwood Rd Pima AZ 85543-0630 Office: Saguaro Care Inc PO Drawer H Pima AZ 85543

SHAFER, SUSAN WRIGHT, elementary education educator; b. Ft. Wayne, Dec. 6, 1941; d. George Wesley and Bernece (Spray) Wright; 1 child, Michael R. BS, St. Francis Coll., Ft. Wayne, 1967, MS in Edn., 1969. Tchr. Ft. Wayne Community Schs., 1967-69, Amphitheatre Pub. Schs., Tucson, 1970—; odyssey of the mind coord. Prince Elem. Sch., Tucson, 1989-91, future problem solving, 1991-94. Tchr. Green Valley (Ariz.) Cmty. Ch., Vacation Bible Sch., 1987-89, dir. vacation bible sch., 1989-93. Mem. AAUW, NEA (life), Delta Kappa Gamma (pres. Alpha Rho chpt.), Alpha Delta Kappa (historian Epsilon chpt. 1990—), Phi Delta Kappa (life, Tucson chpt.). Republican. Methodist. Home: 603 W Placita Nueva Green Valley AZ 85614-2827 Office: Prince Elem Sch 125 E Prince Rd Tucson AZ 85705-3635

SHAFF, BEVERLY GERARD, educational administrator; b. Oak Park, Ill., Aug. 16, 1925; d. Carl Tanner and Mary Frances (Gerard) Wilson; m. Maurice A. Shaff, Jr., Dec. 20, 1951 (dec. June 1967); children: Carol Maureen, David Gerrard, Mark Albert. MA, U. Ill., 1951; postgrad., Colo. Coll., 1966, 73, Lewis and Clark Coll., 1982, Portland State U., 1975-82. Tchr. Haley Sch., Berwyn, Ill., 1948-51; assoc. prof. English, Huntingdon Coll., Montgomery, Ala., 1961-62; tchr. English, William Palmer High Sch., Colorado Springs, Colo., 1964-67, 72-76, dir., 1967-72; tchr. English, Burns (Oreg.) High Sch., 1976-78; tchr. English as 2d lang. Multnomah County Ednl. Svc. Dist., Portland, Oreg., 1979-85; coord. gen. studies Portland Jewish Acad., 1984-90; with Indian Edn. Prog./Student Tng. Edn. Prog. (STEP) Portland Pub. Schs., 1990-92; tchr. St. Thomas More Sch., Portland, 1992—. Del. Colorado Springs Dem. Com., 1968, 72; active Rainbow Coalition, Portland. Mem. Nat. Assn. Admnstrs., Nat. Assn. Schs. and Colls., Nat. Coun. Tchrs. Math., Nat. Coun. Tchrs. English. Home: 1 Jefferson Pky Apt 125 Lake Oswego OR 97035-8810

SHAFFER, AUDREY JEANNE, medical records administrator, educator; b. Hutchinson, Minn., Nov. 24, 1929; d. Floyd R. and Edna C. (Seppman) Kleiman; m. Frank L. Shaffer, July 15, 1948; 1 child, Cynthia Louise Shaffer Wilkinson. BS, Loma Linda U., 1973; MA, Central Mich. U., 1982. Registered records adminstr. Med. records clk. San Bernardino County Hosp., Calif., 1948-50; radiology receptionist White Meml. Med. Ctr., Los Angeles, 1950-52; med. records clk. Portland Adventist Hosp., Oreg., 1952-53; med. record mgr. Tempe Community Hosp., Ariz., 1953-54; faculty Loma Linda U., Calif., 1975—; dir. med. info. services Corona Community Hosp., Calif., 1973-89 ; med. records cons. Calif., Utah, Fla. and Philippines, 1981-92, China, 1993—, pilot and med. asst. Liga Internat., Mex., 1964-68; chmn. Corona Blood Bank, 1957-68; chmn. vols. Corona Community Hosp. Aux., 1965-68; archaeology supr. Caesarea Expdn., Am. Schs. Oriental Research, Israel, summers 1974—. Recipient Vol. Service award Corona Community Hosp., 1968, Congeniality award Caesarea Archeol. Expdn., 1975, Alumna of Yr. award Sch. Allied Health Professions Loma Linda U. Mem. Loma Linda U. Med. Record Alumni (pres. 1979-81), Am. Health Info. Mgmt. Assn., Calif. Health Info. Assn. (mem. quality assurance com. 1980-81, pub. rels. com. 1988-91), Inland Area Health Info. Assn. (pres. elect 1991, pres. 1992-93), Nat. Assn. Healthcare Quality, Archeol. Inst. Am., Inland Quality Assurance Network (pres. 1988). Clubs: Women's Improvement (program chmn. 1960-61), Corona Flying (sec. 1960-68) (Corona). Home: 6473 Valley Dr Riverside CA 92505-2068

SHAFFER, DALLAS YOUNG, library administrator; b. Spokane, June 18, 1940; s. George Wendell and Phyllis Louella (Jansen) Y.; children: Erika, Ursula. BA in History, Stanford U., 1962; MLA, U. Wash., Seattle, 1965. Children's libr. King County Libr., Seattle, 1965-66; freelance researcher, indexer Washington, 1966-70; libr. Nebr. Libr. Commn., Lincoln, 1970-73; acquisitions editor Congl. Info. Svc., Bethesda, Md., 1973-74; exec. asst. Prince George's County Libr., Hyattsville, Md., 1974-78, info. svcs. officer, 1978-81, area mgr., 1981-87; dir. Monterey County Free Librs., Salinas, Calif., 1987—. Contbr. articles to profl. publs. Pres. Md. Libr. Assn., Balt., 1980-81; mem. Monterey County Affirmative Action Adv. Commn., 1987-93. Melcher scholar, 1964. Mem. ACLU, Libr. Adminstrn. and Mgmt. Assn. (pres. 1989-90), Calif. County Librs. Assn. (pres. 1993—). Office: Monterey County Free Librs 26 Central Ave Salinas CA 93901-2628

SHAFFER, WAYNE ALAN, lawyer; b. Reno, Oct. 15, 1954; s. William V. and Shirley Joy (Perry) S.; m. Robin E. Sprung, Jan. 7, 1978. BA, U. Nev., 1977; JD magna cum laude, Calif. Western Sch. Law, 1981. Bar: Nev. 1981, U.S. Dist. Ct. Nev. 1981, Calif. 1982. Dep. dist. atty. Washoe County, Reno, 1981-82; assoc. Lionel, Sawyer & Collins, Reno, 1982-84, Law Office Eugene J. Wait Jr., Reno, 1985-89; ptnr. Wait & Shaffer, Reno, 1989—; instr. Old Coll. Sch. Law, Reno, 1982. Mem. ABA, Nev. Bar Assn., Calif. Bar Assn., Assn. Def. Counsel No. Nev., Assn. Def. Counsel No. Calif. Republican. Office: Wait & Shaffer 305 W Moana Ln Ste D Reno NV 89509-4905

SHAGAM, MARVIN HÜCKEL-BERRI, private school educator; b. Monongalia, W.Va.; s. Lewis and Clara (Shagam) S. AB magna cum laude, Washington and Jefferson Coll., 1947; postgrad., Harvard Law Sch., 1947-48, Oxford (Eng.) U., 1948-51. Tchr. Mount House Sch., Tavistock, Eng., 1951-53, Williston Jr. Sch., Easthampton, Mass., 1953-55, Westtown (Pa.) Sch., 1955-58, The Thacher Sch., Ojai, Calif., 1958—; dept. head Kurasimi Internat. Edn. Centre, Dar-es-Salaam, Tanzania, 1966-67, Nkumbi Internat. Coll., Kabwe, Zambia, 1967-68; vol. visitor Prisons in Calif., 1980—, Calif. Youth Authority, 1983—; sr. youth crisis counsellor InterFace, 1984—. 1st lt. M.I. res. U.S. Army, 1943-56. Danforth Found. fellow, 1942; Coun. for the Humanities fellow, Tufts U., 1983. Mem. Western Assn. Schs. and Colls. (accreditation com.), Great Teaching (Cooke chair 1977—), Phi Beta Kappa, Delta Sigma Rho, Cum Laude Soc. Republican.

SHAH, ABHAY, business educator, marketing consultant; b. Almora, India, June 5, 1956; came to the U.S., 1982; s. Jagdish and Madhuri Shah. BA in Econs. with honors, Calcutta U., 1979; MBA, U. Evansville, 1983; PhD in Mktg., Okla. State U., 1991. Sales rep. Richardson Vicks India, Calcutta, 1980; property cons. A.K. Property Cons., Calcutta, 1980-82; tchg. assoc. Okla. State U., Stillwater, 1985-88; MBA dir., assoc. prof. U. So. Colo., Pueblo, 1988—; mktg. cons. So. Colo. Mktg. Rsch., Pueblo, 1990—. Mem. Am. Mktg. Assn., World Wildlife Fund. Home: 247 Bonnymede Rd Pueblo CO 81001-1333 Office: Univ So Colo 2200 Bonforte Blvd Pueblo CO 81001-4901

SHAH, BHAILAL MORARJI, pharmacist; b. Koday-Kutch, Gujarat, India, Jan. 18, 1945; came to U.S., 1969; s. Morarji T. and Laxmiben M. (Lalan) S.; m. Neela B. Gala, Dec. 21, 1975; children: Monali, Jatin. Diploma in Pharmacy, Bombay (India) Coll. Pharmacy, 1966; B. in Pharmacy, U. Shivaji, Karad, India, 1969; BS in Pharmacy, U. Kans., 1971. Registered pharmacist Ariz., Kans., Calif. Staff pharmacist St. Joseph Hosp., Kansas City, Mo., 1971-73, Rsch. Med. Ctr., Kansas City, 1974-75; in-charge of out patient clinic pharmacy Good Samaritan Regional Med. Ctr., Phoenix, 1976—. Mem. India Assn., Phoenix, 1981—. Mem. Ariz. Pharmacy Assn., Am. Hosp. Pharmacy Soc. Home: 8734 E San Esteban Dr Scottsdale AZ 85258-2603 Office: Good Samaritan Reg Med Ctr 1111 E Mcdowell Rd Phoenix AZ 85006-2612

SHAH, DEVANG KUNDANLAL, software engineer; b. Mombasa, Kenya, Oct. 2, 1963; s. Kundan B. and Saryu K. (Mehta) S. BTech Electronics Engrng. with honors, Inst. Tech. Banaras Hindu U., Varanasi, India, 1985; MA in Computer Sci., U. Tex., 1989. Software engr. Tata Consultancy Svcs., Bombay, India, 1985-86; mem. tech. staff SunSoft, Inc. subs. Sun Microsystems, Inc., Mountain View, Calif., 1990—; Sun Microsystems rep. to Unix Internat. multiprocessor working group, Parsippany, N.J., 1990. Author tech. papers in field. Mem. IEEE (tech. com. on oper. systems & stds. 1990-91, stds. com. on threads ext. for portable oper. systems), Assn. for Computing Machinery. Home: 1031 Foster City Blvd Apt B Foster City CA 94404-2328 Office: SunSoft Inc 2550 Garcia Ave # 5 40 Mountain View CA 94043-1109

SHAH, GIRISH POPATLAL, data processing services company executive; b. Junagadh, India, Apr. 11, 1942; came to U.S., 1963; s. Popatlal Gulabchand and Lalitaben Popatlas (Kamdar) S.; m. Devmani Manilal Jhaveri, June 18, 1968; children: Nivisha, Munjal, Bhavin. B in Tech., Indian Inst. Tech., Bombay, 1963; MS, U. Calif., Berkeley, 1965. Project analyst IBM Corp., Palo Alto, Calif., 1965-67; v.p. Optimun Systems, Inc., Palo Alto, 1967-72; pres. Banking Systems Internat. Corp., Jakarta, Indonesia and Campbell, Calif., 1972-76; dir. software services Tymshare Transactions Services, San Francisco, 1980-83; sr. scientist McDonnell Douglas Corp., Fremont, Calif., 1984-86; dir. corp. devel. Sysorex Internat., Inc., Cupertino, Calif., 1986-87; v.p. Sysorex Internat., Inc., Mountain View, Calif., 1987—; sr. v.p. Sysorex Info. Systems Inc., Mountain View, 1987-91. Mem. adv. bd. Goodwill Industries, San Francisco; bd. dirs. Gujarate Cultural Assn., 1982; chmn. temple bd. Jain Ctr., 1990-94; co-chmn. Jaina Conv., 1991-94; city gov. Fedn. Indo-Am. Assns., Fremont, Calif., 1991—; pres.'s coun. Fedn. Jain Assoc. N.Am., 1995—; mem. Jaina charitable trust, 1995—. J.N. Tata Trust nat. scholar, 1963. Mem. Ops. Research Soc. Am., Assn. Indians in Am. (v.p. 1980). Democrat. Home: 4048 Twyla Ln Campbell CA 95008-3721 Office: Sysorex Info Systems Inc 335 E Middlefield Rd Mountain View CA 94043-4003

SHAH, SURESH CHANDRA, anesthesiologist; b. India, June 1, 1951; m. Vishaka Shah; children: Shalini, Amy, Neal. MD, U. Gujarat, Ahmedabad, India, 1973. Diplomate Am. Bd. Anesthesiology, Am. Bd. Pain Medicine; bd. cert. pain mgmt. Am. Bd. Anesthesiology. Intern V.S. Gen. Hosp., Ahmedabad, India, 1973-74; resident dept. surgery St. Catherine's Hosp., Tralee, Ireland, 1974-75; jr. resident dept. anesthesiology West-Wales (Eng.) Gen. Hosp., Carmathen, 1976-77; sr. resident dept. anesthesiology North Middlesex Hosp., London, 1976-77; resident in anesthesiology and pain mgmt. Temple U. Hosp., Phila., 1977-79; assoc. anesthesiologist Mercy Hosp., Wilkes-Barre, Pa., 1979-83; attending anesthesiologist Hollywood Presbyn. Hosp., L.A., 1983—, John F. Kennedy Meml. Hosp., Indio, Calif., 1984—; med. dir. S.W. Pain Control and Sports Therapy Ctr., Palm Desert, Calif., 1986—. Mem. Am. Congress Rehab. Medicine, Am. Assn. for Study of Headaches, Calif. Med. Assn., Riverside County Med. Soc., Am. Acad. Pain Medicine, Internat. Assn. for Study of Pain, Am. Pain Soc., Calif. Soc. Anesthesiologists, Am. Heart Assn. (bd. dirs. 1980—), Am. Soc. Regional Anesthesia, Am. Soc. Anesthesiologists, Internat. Anesthesia Rsch. Soc. Home: 40-530 Morningstar Rd Rancho Mirage CA 92270-4044 Office: SW Pain Control 73-345 Us Highway 111 Palm Desert CA 92260-3924

SHAHIN, THOMAS JOHN, dry cleaning wholesale supply company executive; b. Buffalo, July 30, 1943; s. Thomas Mark and Marie (Colletto) S.; m. Laraine Edna Clements, Feb. 25, 1967; 1 child, Lori Lynn. BSBA, Calif. State U., L.A., 1966. Asst. v.p. stock brokerage div. United Calif. Bank, L.A., 1969-76; v.p., gen. mgr., treas. Newhouse Splty. Co. Inc., Santa Ana, Calif., 1976—, also bd. dirs. Patentee belt buckle. Officer USN, 1966-69, Vietnam. Mem. Textile Care Allied Trade Assn., Laundry and Drycleaners Suppliers, Internat. Fabricare Inst., Internat. Drycleaners Congress, Calif. Fabricare Inst., Beta Gamma Sigma. Republican. Roman Catholic. Office: Newhouse Splty Co Inc 2619 Oak St Santa Ana CA 92707-3720

SHAKMAN, ROBERT ALLAN, public health physician. BA in History with honors, U. Pa., 1965; MD, Northwestern U., 1969; MPH, U. Calif., Berkeley, 1972. Diplomate Am. Bd. Preventive Medicine, Nat. Bd. Med. Examiners; lic. physician, surgeon Calif., Oreg. Intern Evanston Hosp., Northwestern U. Med. Ctr., Evanston, 1969-70; pub. health physician Alameda (Calif.) and Contra Costa County Health Depts., 1972, Ventura County, 1970-72, 76-77; physician Permanente Med. Group, Walnut Creek, Lancaster, Calif., 1972-75; pvt. practice Ojai, Calif., 1973; environ. health cons. Ojai, Ventura, Calif., 1973-77; dir. occupational and environ. health program Navy Missile Test Ctr. and Air Base, Point Mugu, Calif., 1977-80; med. affairs dir. Vetco Offshore, Inc., Ventura, Calif., 1980-85; med. cons. Calif. Dept. Health Svcs., L.A., 1985-86; med. dir. so. region Calif. Med. Rev., Inc., Bakersfield, 1986-87; asst. med. dir. Blue Cross of Calif., L.A., 1987-90, med. dir., 1990-93; v.p., med. dir. Blue Cross of Calif., 1993—; bd. dirs. Am. Lung Assn., Ventura County, Calif., 1981-88, pres. 1986-87; clin. assoc. prof. preventive medicine U. So. Calif., L.A.,. Author: Poison Proof Your Body: Food, Pollution and Your Health, 1980; Where You Live May Be Hazardous to Your Health: A Health Index to American Communities, 1979.; contbr. articles and abstracts to profl. jours. Med. mem. Ventura County Air Pollution Hearing Bd., (past vice chmn., chmn.). Fellow Am. Coll. Preventive Medicine; mem. AMA, Ventura County Med. Assn., Calif. Med. Assn., Western Occupational Med. Assn., Am. Pub. Health Assn. Office: Blue Cross of Calif 21555 Oxnard St Woodland Hills CA 91367-4943

SHALACK, JOAN HELEN, psychiatrist; b. Jersery City, Mar. 6, 1932; d. Edward William and Adele Helen (Karski) S.; m. Jerome Abraham Sheill. Student, Farleigh Dickinson U., 1950-51; BA cum laude, NYU, 1954; MD, Women's Med. Coll. Pa., 1958. Intern Akron (Ohio) Gen. Hosp., 1958-59; resident in psychiatry Camarillo (Calif.) State Hosp., 1959-62; resident in physchiatry UCLA Neuropsychiat. Inst., 1962, U. So. Calif., L.A., 1963; pvt. practice Beverly Hills, Calif., 1963-83, Century City L.A., Calif., 1983-86, Pasadena, Calif., 1986—; pres., chair bd. dirs. Totizo Inc., Beverly Hills, 1969-71; mem. staff Westwood Hosp., 1970-75. Mem. AMA, Calif. Med. Assn., L.A. County Med. Assn., Physicians for Social Responsibility, Union of Concerned Scientists, Phi Beta Kappa, Mu Chi Sigma. Home and Office: 1405 Afton St Pasadena CA 91103-2702

SHALINSKY, DAVID RAY, pharmacologist; b. Glendale, Calif., June 21, 1958; s. Theodore S. and Louise Kathleen (Wolfson) Shalin; m. Janet Louise Milligan, Aug. 16, 1980; children: Emily Louise, Claire Morgan. BA in Social Welfare, Calif. State U., Chico, 1980, BA in Psychology, 1980; PhD in Pharmacology, Tulane U., 1988. Lab., pharmacology supr. U. Calif., San Diego, 1988-92. Mem. Ch. Coun. Coll. Luth. Ch., San Diego, 1990-92; co-founder Bridges for Peace, New Orleans, 1983. Recipient Nat. Rsch. Svc. award NIH, 1991. Mem. Am. Assn. Cancer Rsch., Sci. Democrat. Home: 12888 Meadowdale Ln San Diego CA 92131-2297 Office: Ligand Pharms Inc 11149 N Torrey Pines Rd La Jolla CA 92037-1031

SHAM, LU JEU, physics educator; b. Hong Kong, Apr. 28, 1938; s. T.S. and Cecilia Maria (Siu) Shen; m. Georgina Bien, Apr. 25, 1965; children: Kevin Shen, Alisa Shen. GCE, Portsmouth Coll., Eng., 1957; BS, Imperial Coll., London U., Eng., 1960; PhD in Physics, Cambridge U., Eng., 1963. Asst. rsch. physicist U. Calif. at San Diego, La Jolla, 1963-66, assoc. prof., 1968-76, prof., 1975—, dean div. natural scis., 1985-89; asst. prof. physics U. Calif. at Irvine, 1966-67; rsch. physicist IBM Corp., Yorktown Heights, N.Y., 1974-75; reader Queen Mary Coll., U. London, 1967-68. Assoc. editor Physics Letters A., 1992—; contbr. sci. papers to profl. jours. Recipient Churchill Coll. studentship, Eng., 1960-63, Sr. U.S. Scientist award Humboldt Found., Stuttgart, Germany, 1978; fellow Guggenheim Found., 1984. Fellow Am. Phys. Soc.; mem. AAAS. Democrat. Office: U Calif San Diego Dept Physics 0319 La Jolla CA 92093-0319

SHAMBAUGH, STEPHEN WARD, lawyer; b. South Bend, Ind., Aug. 4, 1920; s. Marion Clyde and Anna Violet (Stephens) S.; m. Marilyn Louise Pyle; children: Susan Wynne Shambaugh Hinkle, Kathleen Louise Shambaugh Thompson. Student San Jose State Tchrs. Coll., 1938-40, U. Ark., 1951; LLB, U. Tulsa, 1954. Bar: Okla. 1954, Colo. 1964. Mem. staff Reading & Bates, Inc., Tulsa, 1951-54; v.p., gen. mgr., legal counsel Reading & Bates Drilling Co. Ltd., Calgary, Alta., Can., 1954-61; sr. ptnr. Bowman, Shambaugh, Geissinger & Wright, Denver, 1964-81; sole practice, Denver, 1981—; dir., fin. counsel various corps. Col. USAF ret. Mem. ABA, Fed. Bar Assn., Colo. Bar Assn., Okla. Bar Assn., Denver Bar Assn., P-51 Mustang Pilots Assn., Masons, Shriners, Elks, Spokane Club, Petroleum Club of Bakersfield, Phi Alpha Delta.

SHAMGOCHIAN, THERON, food products executive; b. 1947. BSBA, Stanislaus State Coll., 1970. Prin. Monte Cristo Packing Co., Livingston, Calif., 1970-88; pres. Shamgochian Theron Inc., Livingston, 1973—. Office: Shamgochian Theron Inc 11173 Mercedes Ave Livingston CA 95334-9707*

SHANAHAN, MICHAEL GEORGE, police officer; b. Seattle, Oct. 14, 1940; s. Raymond Roderick and Carletta (Anderson) S.; m. Jo-Anne Genevieve David, Sept. 16, 1961; children: Patrick, Matthew, Raymond. BA in Psychology, Stanford U., 1962. Asst. police chief U. Wash., Seattle, 1970-71, police chief, 1971—; mem. law enforcement task force interim mcpl. com. Wash. State Legis., 1970-71, campus law enforcement task force-higher edn. com., 1970-71; co-chmn. Wash. Law Enforcement Standards Task Force; founding chmn. Washington Law Enforcement Exec. Forum, 1981, Operation Bootstrap, 1985, others. Author: Private Enterprise and the Public Police: The Professionalizing Effects of a New Partnership, 1985; contbr. articles to profl. jours. Mem. nat. exploring com. Boy Scouts Am., 1977, exec. bd., chief Seattle council, 1984-88; mem. Blanchet High Sch. Bd., Seattle, 1978-79, Gov.'s Coun. on Criminal Justice, 1980-81, Gov.'s Coun. Food Assistance, 1983-86. Major U.S. Army, 1963-70, Vietnam. Decorated Bronze Star; recipient award for pub. svc. U.S. Dept. Transp., 1984, Humanitarian award Seattle chpt. NCCJ, 1985, Silver Beaver award Boy Scouts Am., 1986, St. Matthew award Northwest Harvest, 1987, Paul J. Breslin award Internat. Security Mgrs. Assn., 1990, Criminal Justice award of excellence Wash. State U., 1989. Mem. FBI Nat. Acad. Assocs., Nat. Inst. Justice (peer rev. program), Internat. Assn. Chiefs of Police (bd. officers 1983-84, gen. chmn. divsn. state assns. 1983-84, co-chmn. pvt. sector liaison com.), Police Exec. Rsch. Forum, Wash. Assn. Sheriffs and Police Chiefs, Rotary Internat. (pres. Univ. Rotary Club Seattle 1985-86, founding chmn. Rotary Op. First Harvest, Svc. Above Self award 1988). Roman Catholic. Lodge: Rotary (pres. Univ. club. Seattle 1985-86). Office: U Wash Police Dept 1117 NE Boat St Seattle WA 98105-6709

SHANAHAN, R. MICHAEL, securities dealer; b. 1939. Stanford U., 1960. With Capital Rsch. & Mgmt. Co., Inc., L.A., 1964—; with AMCAP Fund,

Inc., 1970—, now pres. Office: AMCAP Fund Inc 333 S Hope St Los Angeles CA 90071-1406*

SHANE, WILLIAM WHITNEY, astronomer; b. Berkeley, Calif., June 3, 1928; s. Charles Donald and Mary Lea (Heger) S.; B.A., U. Calif., Berkeley, 1951, postgrad., 1953-58; Sc.D., Leiden U. (Netherlands), 1971; m. Clasina van der Molen, Apr. 22, 1964; children—Johan Jacob, Charles Donald. Research asso. Leiden (Netherlands) U., 1961-71, sr. scientist, 1971-79; prof. astronomy, dir. Astron. Inst., Cath. U. Nijmegen, Netherlands, 1979-88; guest prof. astronomy Leiden U., The Netherlands, 1988-93; C.H. Adams fellow Monterey (Calif.) Inst. Rsch. Astronomy, 1994—. Served with USN, 1951-53. Mem. Internat. Astron. Union (commns. 33, 34), Am. Astron. Soc., Astron. Soc. Netherlands, Astron. Soc. of the Pacific, AAAS, Phi Beta Kappa. Research on structure and dynamics of galaxies, radio astronomy. Home: 9095 Coker Rd Prunedale CA 93907-1401 Office: Monterey Inst Rsch Astronomy 900 Major Sherman Ln Monterey CA 93940-4633

SHANGRAW, CLARENCE FRANK, museum official; b. Burlington, Vt., Aug. 9, 1935; s. Eugene and Hazel Bernice (Fuller) S.; m. Sylvia Chen, Dec. 23, 1961 (dec.); children—Lea Lihsia, Lin Ethan. Grad., Yale U. Inst. Far Eastern Langs., 1955; A.B. with high honors, U. Calif.-, Berkeley, 1963, M.A., 1965. Tchr. U. Calif.-, Berkeley, 1964-65; art research asst. M.H. de Young Mus., 1965; asst. curator Avery Brundage Collection, 1966-68; sr. curator Asian art Asian Art Mus. San Francisco, 1968-85, acting dir., chief curator, 1985, chief curator, 1986-89, dep. dir., chief curator, 1989-92, chief curator emeritus, 1992; dir. Tsui Mus. Art, Hong Kong, 1992-93; Asian art cons., 1993—; adj. prof. Sch. Mus. Studies John F. Kennedy U., 1980—. Author: Origins of Chinese Ceramics, 1978, Masterworks of Ming: 15th Century Chinese Blue and White Porcelains, 1985, Marvels of Medieval China: Those Lustrous Song and Yuan Lacquers, 1986; co-author: Chinese Blue and White Porcelains from the Voyages of Drake and Cermeno Found at Drakes Bay, California, 1982; editor: Legacy of Chenghua, Hong Kong, 1993; contbr. sect.: Chinese, Japanese and Korean Sculptures in the Avery Brundage Collection, 1974, 5,000 Years of Korean Art, 1979, The Art of Japan: Masterworks in the Asian Art Mus. of San Francisco, 1991, Vol. I, Tsui Museum of Art: Early Chinese Ceramics, Reflections on Early Chinese Ceramics, 1992; contbr.: catalog Treasures from the Shanghai Museum: 6, 000 Years of Chinese Art, 1983, Looking at Asian Art Patronage, 1989, Beauty, Wealth, and Power: Jewels and Ornaments of Asia, 1992, Some Reflections on the Beginnings of China's Ceramic Traditions, 1993; contbr. numerous articles to profl. jours. Served with USAF, 1954-58. Mem. Am. Assn. Mus., Internat. Council Mus., Oriental Ceramics Soc. London, Am. Inst. Archaeology, Assn. Asian Studies. Republican. Conglist. Home: 5517 Diamond Heights Blvd San Francisco CA 94131-2642 Office: Asian Art Mus Golden Gate Park San Francisco CA 94118

SHANHOUSE, BILL, sculptor, educator; b. Rockford, Ill., July 10, 1926; s. Louis Jacob and Lois Francis (Miller) S.; m. Linda Joyce Fillingham; children: Susan, Laurie, Robin, Barbara, Nancy, Jennifer. Grad., U.S. Naval Acad., 1949; BSEE, Northwestern U.; postgrad., Hofstra U., Corcoran Sch. of Art, Washington. Chief engr. S.S. Hunter; pres. Internat. Sys. Rsch. Corp.; v.p. ops. Renwell Industries; v.p. corp. devel. P&F Industries; v.p. student affairs Hofstra U.; v.p. adminstrv. svcs. U. Iowa; GS-12 engring. supr. Office Naval Rsch.; dir. employment programs City of N.Y.; cons. Dept. State, Nat. Bur. Stds., Nat. Endowment of the Arts, Md. State Legis., Tex. Commn. on the Arts; lectr. U. Iowa, George Washington U., Hofstra U., Am. Mgmt. Assn., Am. Assn. Indsl. Mgmt.; writer Washington Post, King Features Syndicate, Jossey-Bass. Inventor metering and measuring equipment, navigational instrumentation, and relative motion devices; sculpture installations Mitchell Mus., Lowe Mus., U. Tex., Fordham U., Morehead State U., Phila. Internat. Gardens; one-man shows include Arts Coun., Grapeville, Tex., Dallas Design Ctr., Carroll Sch., Southlake, Tex., U. Tex., Dallas, Dallas Symphony Showhouse, Paige Gallery, Dallas, Md. Coll. Art, Silver Spring, Bloomingdale's, McLean, Va., Lakeforest, Gaithersburg, Md., Montgomery County Delegation, Annapolis, Md., Slavin Gallery, Washington, Montgomery Mall, Bethesda, Md., Community Fed. Assn., Washington, Fordham U., N.Y.C., Lincoln Ctr., N.Y.C., Diane Brown Gallery, Washington; exhibited in group shows at Hofstra Mus., Hempstead, N.Y., Wright Gallery, Dallas, Dimensions, Lenexa, Kans., Edith Baker Gallery, Dallas, Dallas Mus. Art, Britt-Neman, Stenhamra, Sweden, Republic Pl., Austin, Tex., D'Art, Dallas, Kelton Mathis, Arlington, Tex., LTV Ctr., Dallas, Frito-Lay, Plano, Tex., Montage, Dallas, Mitchell Mus., Mt. Vernon, Ill., Tex. Sculpture Assn., Dallas, Signature Pl., Dallas, Sculpture Resources Inc., Dallas, Samuell Grand Park, Dallas, Athena Gallery, N.Y.C., Dallas Design Ctr., Paige Gallery, Dallas, Morehead State U., Ky., Carrier Found., Belle Mead, N.J., Swimmer Gallery, Mt. Kisco, N.Y., numerous others. Bd. dirs. U. Iowa Mus. Art, Columbia Visual Arts Coll., Sculpture Resources, Inc., Tex. Sculpture Assn., Tex. Arts Alliance, Studio Theatre. With USN, 1943-52. Home and Office: PO Box 578 Angel Fire NM 87710

SHANK, BRYAN LEIGH, marketing executive; b. St. Louis, July 13, 1954. B Journalism, U. Mo., 1976; MS in Advt., Northwestern U., 1984. Various advt. and pub. positions, 1976-83; from asst. account exec. to sr. account exec., mktg. exec. Ross Roy, Inc., Detroit, 1984-88; account supr. Hyundai Dealer Advt. Assns. Hyundai Dealer Advt. Assns. Backer Spielvogel Bates, Irvine, Calif., 1988-90; sr. account dir. Pacific Region Mazda Dealer Assn. Foote, Cone & Belding, Santa Ana, Calif., 1990-91; mgr. market planning luxury automobile divsn. launch Amati divsn. Mazda Motor of Am., Irvine, 1991-92; dir. mktg. Orange County Register, Santa Ana, 1993—.

SHANK, MAURICE EDWIN, aerospace engineering executive, consultant; b. N.Y.C., Apr. 22, 1921; s. Edwin A. and Viola (Lewis) S.; m. Virginia Lee King, Sept. 25, 1948; children: Christopher K., Hilary L. Shank-Kuhl, Diana L. Boehm. B.S. in Mech. Engring., Carnegie-Mellon U., 1942; D.Sc., MIT, 1949. Registered profl. engr., Mass. Assoc. prof. mech. engring. MIT, Cambridge, 1949-60; with Pratt & Whitney, East Hartford, Conn., 1960-87, dir. engine design and structures engring., 1980-81, dir. engring. tech., 1981-85, dir. engring. tech. assessment, 1985-86; v.p. Pratt Whitney of China, Inc., East Hartford, 1986-87; pvt. exec. cons. to industry and govt., 1987—; cons. editor McGraw-Hill Book Co., N.Y.C., 1960-80; adv. com. to mechanics div. Nat. Bur. Standards, Washington, 1964-69; vis. com. dept. mech. engring. Carnegie-Mellon U., Pitts., 1968-78; corp. vis. coms. depts. materials sci. and engring., dept. aeros. and astronautics MIT, 1968-74, 79-92; mem. rsch. and tech. adv. coun. com. on aero. propulsion NASA, Washington, 1973-77, mem. aero. adv. com., 1978-86; mem. aero. and space engring. bd. NRC, 1989-92; lectr. in field. Contbr. articles to profl. jours. Served to maj. U.S. Army, 1942-46. Fellow AIAA, ASME, AIME, Am. Soc. Metals; mem. Nat. Acad. Engring., Conn. Acad. Sci. and Engring. Episcopalian. Club: Cosmos.

SHANK, THOM LEWIS, real estate executive, entertainment consultant; b. Butler, Pa., Apr. 23, 1953; s. Berdyne Delmont and Florence Elizabeth (Glasser) S. BA in Sociology, U. Pa., 1974; MBA, Pepperdine U., 1981. Negotiator Worldmark Travel, N.Y.C. and Phila., 1971-76; retail ops. mgr. Just Plants, Inc., Roxborough, Pa., 1973-79; founder, mgr. The Best-direct mail sales, Edgemoor, Del., 1974-79; property mgr. Moss and Co., Westwood, Calif., 1977-82; talent mgr. Thom Shank Assocs., Brentwood, Calif., 1979-84; pres., founder The Great Am. Amusement Co., Palm Desert, Calif., 1979-84; sales exec. Fred Sands Realtors, Brentwood, 1981-85; sales and mktg. dir. Coldwell Banker, Newport Beach, Calif., 1985-86, Great Western Ranches, Burbank, Calif., 1988—; dist. and regional mgr. E.R.A. Real Estate, Pasadena, Calif., 1986; owner Century 21 Realtors, Tarzana, Calif., 1987-89. Lutheran. Office: 4910 Birch St Newport Beach CA 92660

SHANKLAND, SCOTT EDWIN, mortgage company executive; b. Portland, Oreg., Jan. 25, 1949; s. Glenn A. and Elizabeth M. (Abolin) S.; m. Gloria A. Goetz, July 5, 1973; children: Stephanie, Leslie. BS in Indsl. Engring., Oreg. State U., 1971. Lic. gen. mortgage broker, real estate broker. Sales assoc. Stan Wiley, Inc. Realtors, Portland, Oreg., 1972-75; with Cason-West Constrn. Co., Portland, 1975-76; assoc. broker, sales assoc., br. mgr. Shelter Properties Corp., Lake Oswego, Oreg., 1976-80; sole propr. IGR Mortgage Co., Lake Oswego, 1982-83; pres. IGR Mortgage Co., Portland, 1992—; v.p., gen. mgr. Mainlander Svcs. Corp (divsn. IGR Mortgage Co.), Portland, 1984-92. Office: IGR Mortgage Co 4700 SW Macadam Ave Ste 300 PO Box 69126 Portland OR 97201

SHANNAHAN, WILLIAM PAUL, lawyer; b. Detroit, Mich., Nov. 21, 1934; s. William and Jean (Boyle) S.; m. Saracia L. Price, Sept. 24, 1983; children: MeglynAnne, Michael-Padraic. AB, U. Detroit, 1956; JD, Georgetown U., 1958. Bar: D.C. 1958, Mich. 1958, Calif. 1962. Ptnr. Higgs, Fletcher & Mack, La Jolla, Calif., 1967-81, Aylward, Kintz, et al.2, La Jolla, Calif., 1981-87, pvt. practice, La Jolla, Calif., 1987—. with U.S. Army, 1959-60. Democrat. Roman Catholic. Office: 1200 Prospect St Ste 425 La Jolla CA 92037-3608

SHANNON, BERNARD JOSEPH, optometrist, vision care company executive; b. Mpls., Aug. 15, 1930; s. Bernard Joseph and Theresa E. (Murphy) S.; m. Edith Joanne Davis, Sept. 4, 1964; children: Sean, Maurya, Erin. BS, Ill. Coll., Chgo., 1954; OD, Ill. Coll. Optometry, Chgo., 1956; cert., Wharton Grad. Sch., Phila., 1976, U. Mo., 1991. Pvt. practice in clin. optometry Mauston, Wis., 1956-76; dir. profl. svcs. Bausch & Lomb, Inc., Rochester, N.Y., 1976-79, dir. internat. distbn., 1979-82; exec. dir. Ciba Vision Corp., Atlanta, 1983-92; v.p. PBH, Phoenix, 1992—; pres. North Cen. States Coun., Mpls., 1967-68; cons. U.S. Army Surgeon Gen., Washington, 1973-76. Co-author: (manpower study) Optometric Man Power, 1974; The Leader and, 1975; contbr. articles to profl. jours. Chmn. City Planning Commn., Wis., 1967, City Housing Authority, Wis., 1969; pres. Kiwanis Club, Wis., 1960; bd. dirs. State of Wis.-Regional Mgr., 1974. With USN, 1952-54. Mem. Am. Optometric Found. (past bd. dirs.), Am. Acad. Optometry, Am. Optometric Assn. (pres. 1974-75, Disting. mem.), Wis. Optometric Assn. (pres. 1966-67, Disting. mem., OD of Yr.), Tomb and Key, Beta Sigma Kappa. Roman Catholic. Home: 30068 N 77th Pl Scottsdale AZ 85262-2143

SHANNON, BRIAN LEE, artist, education educator; b. Detroit, Feb. 24, 1962; s. David Lee and Wanda Sue (Ross) S. BFA magna cum laude, U. Mich., 1984; MFA, Cranbrook Acad. of Art, Bloomfield Hills, Mich., 1987. Asst. prof. Pacific Northwest Coll. of Art, Portland, Oreg., 1991—; adjunct asst. prof. Portland State U., Oreg., 1993; asst. prof. Oreg. Sch. of Arts and Crafts, Portland, Oreg., 1994—; printmaking cons. Nike, Inc., Beaverton, Oreg., 1994. Recipient Commissioned Patron Print, Portland Art Mus., 1993-94; named Artist-In-Residence Oreg. Sch. Arts and Crafts, Portland, 1987-88. Mem. Coll. Art Assn. Home: 2135 SE Ankeny St Portland OR 97214-1623 Office: Off-Ramp Studios 237 NW 14th Ave Portland OR 97209-2602

SHANNON, EDFRED L., JR., gas and oil drilling company executive; b. 1926; (married). B.S., U. Calif., Berkeley, 1951. Petroleum engr. Union Oil Co. of Calif., 1951-53; with Santa Fe Internat. Corp., Alhambra, 1953—, v.p., 1960-63, chmn., from 1963, chief exec. officer, from 1963, pres., from 1986, also dir. Office: Santa Fe Internat Corp Box 4000 1000 S Fremont Ave Alhambra CA 91802

SHANNON, PATRICK KAVANAUGH, finance manager; b. Aurora, Colo., Dec. 22, 1955; s. Lawrence Kavanaugh and Dorothy Berneice (Holtry) S. BSBA cum laude, U. Colo., 1978; MBA, U. Denver, 1990. Assoc. analyst estimating Lockheed/Martin Marietta Corp., Denver, 1978-79; fin. specialist estimating Martin Marietta Corp., Denver, 1979-81, sr. fin. specialist estimating, 1981-83, fin. adminstr. estimating, 1983-86, chief maj. proposals, 1986-88, mgr. maj. proposals, 1988-89, mgr. overhead control, 1989-92, mgr. fin. planning and analysis, 1992-94; mgr. ind. estimating ATLAS Fin. Analysis, 1994—; treas., bd. dirs. Red Rocks Fed. Credit Union, Littleton, Colo., 1993, vice-chmn. bd. dirs., 1994—. Treas. bd. dirs. Rue Royale Homeowners Assn., Denver, 1982-91; del. Colo. State Conf. Dem. Party, Denver, 1984; del. Denver County Assembly, 1984, 90, precinct committeeman, 1984-90. Mem. Beta Gamma Sigma. Presbyterian. Home: 809 Fillmore St Denver CO 80206-3849 Office: Martin Marietta Astronautics MS DC 2811 PO Box 179 Denver CO 80201

SHANNON, RICHARD STOLL, III, financial executive; b. N.Y.C., Mar. 22, 1943; s. Richard Stoll Jr. and Margaret (Cather) S.; m. Ann Wright Schmidt, June 14, 1965; children: Clea Cather, Kathryne Baltzelle, Arianna Wright. BA, Stanford U., 1966, MA, 1969; PhD, Harvard U., 1973. Asst. prof. U. Mich., Ann Arbor, 1973-78; mgr., trustee, gen. ptnr. various family trusts, partnerships and corps. Englewood, Colo., 1978-84; pres. Shannon Mgmt. Corp., Englewood, 1985—; bd. dirs. Escalante Internat. Corp., Denver. Author: The Arms of Achilles, 1975; editor (with others) Oral Literature and The Formula, 1976. Bd. dirs. Cherryvale Sanitation Dist., Englewood, 1984—, pres., 1986-93; regional chmn. Stanford Ann. Fund/Keystone Project, 1985—; mem. Rackham Advancement Coun., U. Mich., 1992—. Teaching fellow Harvard U., 1970-73. Mem. Am. Philol. Assn., Denver C. of C., Cherry Creek Commerce Assn., Cherry Hills Country Club, Denver Petroleum Club, Phi Beta Kappa. Office: Shannon Mgmt Corp 3098 S Pennsylvania St Englewood CO 80110-1649

SHANNON, ROBERT RENNIE, optical sciences center administrator, educator; b. Mt. Vernon, N.Y., Oct. 3, 1932; s. Howard A. and Harriebell (Rennie) S.; m. Helen Lang, Feb. 13, 1954; children: Elizabeth, Barbara, Jennifer, Amy, John, Robert. B.S., U. Rochester, 1954, M.A., 1957. Dir. Optics Lab., ITEK Corp., Lexington, Mass., 1959-69; prof. Optical Scis. Ctr., U. Ariz., 1969—, dir., 1983-92, prof. emeritus, 1992—; cons. Lawrence Livermore Lab., 1980-90; trustee Aerospace Corp., 1985-94; mem. Air Force Sci. Adv. Bd., 1986-90; mem. NRC Commn. on Next Generation Currency, 1992-94; mem. com. on def. space tech. Air Force Studies Bd., 1989-93, Hubble Telescope recovery panel, 1990; bd. dirs. Precision Optics Corp., Schott Glass Techs. Editor: Applied Optics and Optical Engineering, Vol. 7, 1980, Vol. 8, 1981, Vol. 9, 1983, Vol. 10, 1987, Vol. 11, 1992. Fellow Optical Soc. Am. (pres. 1985, mem. engring. coun. 1989-91), Soc. Photo-Optical Instrumentation Engrs. (pres. 1979-80, recipient Goddard award 1982); mem. NAE, Tucson Soaring Club (past pres.), Sigma Xi. Home: 7040 E Taos Pl Tucson AZ 85715-3344 Office: U Ariz Optical Scis Ctr Tucson AZ 85721

SHANNON, THOMAS FREDERIC, German language educator; b. Cambridge, Mass., Mar. 16, 1948; m. Christine D. Höner. BA in German summa cum laude, Boston Coll., 1969; MA in German Lit., SUNY, Albany, 1973; MA in Theoretical Linguistics, Ind. U., 1975, PhD in Germanic Linguistics, 1982. Instr. in German Boston Coll., 1969-70; teaching fellow in German SUNY, Albany, 1971-73; univ. fellow Ind. U., Bloomington, 1973-74, assoc. instr., 1974-76, 1979-80; acting asst. prof. in Germanic linguistics U. Calif., Berkeley, 1980-82, asst. prof., 1982-87, assoc. prof., 1987-94, prof., 1994—, dir. lang. lab., 1989-92, assoc. dir. Berkeley Lang. Ctr., 1994-95; co-organizer Berkeley Confs. on Dutch Lang. & Lit., 1987, 89, 91, 93, 95; econs., presenter, speaker in field. Contbr. articles to profl. jours. With USAR, 1970-76. Grantee U. Calif.-Berkeley, 1983-84, 94-95, Am. Coun. Learned Socs., 1987, Internat. Assn. Netherlandic Studies, 1988, 91, 94, Fulbright Found., 1979; NDEA fellow, 1969; Fulbright rsch./lectr. grantee Rijksuniversiteit Groningen, Netherlands, 1992-93. Mem. MLA (exec. com. discussion group in Germanic philology 1989-94, discussion group for Netherlandic Studies 1995—, divsn. on lang. change 1995), Am. Assn. Netherlandic Studies (exec. com. 1988—, editor newsletter 1989—, series editor publs. 1994—), Am. Assn. Tchrs. German, Assn. Computers and Humanities, Internat. Assn. Netherlandic Studies, Internat. Assn. Germanstik, Internat. Soc. Hist. Linguistics, Linguistic Soc. Am., Netherlands Am. U. League, Philol. Assn. Pacific Coast, European Linguistic Soc., Soc. Germanic Philology (v.p. 1991-92, 95—), Alpha Sigma Nu. Home: 770 Rose Dr Benicia CA 94510-3709 Office: U Calif Dept German 5317 Dwinelle Hall Berkeley CA 94720-3243

SHANOR, CLARENCE RICHARD, clergyman; b. Butler, Pa., Dec. 26, 1924; s. Paul L. and Marion (McCandless) S.; B.A., Allegheny Coll., 1948; S.T.B., Boston U., 1951, Ph.D., 1958; m. Anna Lou Watts, June 23, 1948; 1 son, Richard Watts. Ordained to ministry Methodist Ch., 1950; pastor Meth. Ch., South Hamilton, Mass., 1951-54; research asso. Union Coll., Schenectady, 1954-55; prof. Christian edn. Nat. Coll., Kansas City, Mo., 1956-58; asso. minister First United Meth. Ch., St. Petersburg, Fla., 1958-61, First United Meth. Ch., Fullerton, Calif., 1961-66; coord. Metro dept. San Diego dist. United Meth. Union, San Diego, 1966-87, ret., 1987; pres. Human Svcs. Corp., 1972-77. Treas. San Diego County Ecumenical Conf., 1970-71, pres., 1975-77; chmn. Coalition Urban Ministries, 1970-71, Cultural and Religious Task Force Rancho San Diego, 1970-74; chmn. western jurisdiction Urban Network United Meth. Ch., 1978. Chmn. San Diego Citizens Com. Against Hunger, 1969-72; bd. dirs. Interfaith Housing Found., chmn., 1979, pres. 1988—; v.p. North County Interfaith Coun., 1987—; mem. Gaslamp Quarter Project Area Com., San Diego, 1978, mem. coun., 1980-84; chmn. bd. Horton House Corp., 1978; mem. Mayor's Task Force on the Homeless, 1983-84; chmn. Downtown Coordinating Coun., 1983-84; mem. regional Task Force on Homeless, 1986-87; vice-chmn. Community Congress, 1987, ret., 1987; bd. dirs. North County Interfaith Coun., 1987-92, Redwood Ter. Town Ct., 1995—; pres., bd. dirs. North County Housing Found., 1987—. Chmn. Calif. State Commn. for Rev. of Master Plan Higher Edn.; Recipient San Diego Inst. for Creativity award, 1969, Boss of Yr. award Am. Bus. Women's Assn., 1972, Christian Unity award Diocesan Ecumenical Commn., 1984, Congl. Disting. Svc. award, 1984, Helen Beardsley Human Rights award, 1986, Mayor O'Connor's Seahorse award 1989, Ecumenical Conf. award San Diego County, 1991, Vol. Extraordinaire award No. County Interfaith Coun., 1993. Author: (with Anna Lou Shanor) Kindergartner Meet Your World, 1966. Home: 1636 Desert Gln Escondido CA 92026-1849

SHANSBY, JOHN GARY, investment banker; b. Seattle, Aug. 25, 1937; s. John Jay and Jule E. (Boyer) S.; m. Joyce Ann Dunsmore, June 21, 1959 (div.); children: Sheri Lee, Kimberly Ann, Jay Thomas; m. Barbara Anderson De Meo, Jan. 1, 1983 (div.); m. Jane Robinson Dettner, May 1, 1990. B.A., U. Wash., 1959. Sales exec. Colgate-Palmolive Co., N.Y.C., 1959-67; subs. pres. Am. Home Products Corp., N.Y.C., 1968-71; v.p. Clorox Co., Oakland, Calif., 1972-73; ptnr. Booz, Allen & Hamilton, San Francisco, 1974-75; chmn. bd., chief exec. officer, dir. Shaklee Corp., San Francisco, 1975-86; mng. gen. ptnr. The Shansby Group, San Francisco, 1986—. Chmn. Calif. State Commn. for Rev. of Master Plan Higher Edn.; founder J. Gary Shansby chair mktg. strtegy U. Calif., Berkeley; trustee Calif. State U. Mem. San Francisco C. of C. (past pres.), Villa Traverna Club, Silverado Country Club, Lincoln Club of No. Calif., Pennask Lake Fishing Club (B.C.), St. Francis Yacht Club, Sky Club of N.Y.C., Sigma Nu. Republican. Office: The Shansby Group 250 Montgomery St San Francisco CA 94104-3401

SHANSTROM, JACK D., federal judge; b. Hewitt, Minn., Nov. 30, 1932; s. Harold A. and Willian (Wendorf) S.; m. June 22, 1957; children: Scott S., Susan K. BA in Law, U. Mont., 1956, BS in Bus., 1957, LLB, 1957. Atty. Park County, Livingston, Mont., 1960-65; judge 6th Jud. Dist. Livingston, 1965-82; U.S. magistrate Billings, Mont., 1983-90, U.S. Dist. judge, 1990—. Capt. USAF, 1957-60. Office: US Dist Ct PO Box 985 Billings MT 59103-0985

SHAPERO, HARRIS JOEL, pediatrician; b. Winona, Minn., Nov. 22, 1930; s. Charles and Minnie Sara (Ehrlichman) S.; m. Byong Soon Yu, Nov. 6, 1983; children by previous marriage: Laura, Bradley, James, Charles. AA, UCLA, 1953; BS, Northwestern U., 1954, MD, 1957. Diplomate and cert. specialist occupational medicine Am. Bd. Preventive Medicine; cert. aviation medicine FAA. Intern, L.A. County Harbor Gen. Hosp., 1957-58, resident in pediatrics, 1958-60, staff physician, 1960-64; attending physician Perceptually Handicapped Children's Clinic, 1960-63; disease control officer for tuberculosis, L.A. County Health Dept., 1962-64; pvt. practice medicine specializing in pediatrics and occupational medicine, Cypress, Calif., 1965-85; pediatric cons. L.A. Health Dept., 1963-85, disease control officer sexually transmitted diseases, 1984-85; emergency room dir. AMI, Anaheim, Calif., 1968-78; mem. med. staff Anaheim Gen. Hosp., Beach Cmty. Hosp., Norwalk Cmty. Hosp.; courtesy staff Palm Harbor Gen. Hosp., Bellflower City Hosp.; pediatric staff Hosp. de General, Ensenada, Mex., 1978—; primary care clinician Sacramento County Health, 1987-88; pvt. practice medico-legal evaluation, 1986-92; founder Calif. Legal Evaluation Med. Group; apptd. med. examiner in preventive and occupational medicine State of Calif. Dept. of Indsl. Rels., 1989; health care provider, advisor City of Anaheim, City of Buena Park, City of Cypress, City of Garden Grove, Cypress Sch. Dist., Magnolia Sch. Dist., Savanna Sch. Dist., Anaheim Unified Sch. Dist., Orange County Dept. Edn.; pediatric and tuberculosis cons. numerous other orgns.; FAA med. examiner, founder Pan Am. Childrens Mission. Author: The Silent Epidemic, 1979. Named Headliner in Medicine Orange County Press Club, 1978. Fellow Am. Coll. Preventive Medicine; mem. L.A. County Med. Assn., L.A. County Indsl. Med. Assn., Am. Pub. Health Assn., Mex.-Am. Border Health Assn. Republican. Jewish. Avocations: antique books and manuscripts, photography, graphics, beekeeper. Home: PO Box 228 Wilton CA 95693-0228

SHAPIRO, ALICE KUBERNICK, dietitian, consultant; b. Chgo., Apr. 26, 1946; d. Sidney Kubernick and Ethel Ruth (Hyman) Shonman; m. Roy David Goldman, Nov. 22, 1967 (dec. May 1976); 1 child, Samuel A. Kubernick; m. Howard Harvey Shapiro. Life teaching credential, Calif. State U., Hayward, 1968; BA in History, U. Calif., Berkeley, 1967; BA in Biology, U. Calif., Riverside, 1972; MS in Biol. Sci., U. Calif., Irvine, 1974. Registered dietitian. Prof. biology Cypress (Calif.) C.C., 1973-92; coord. teen program Siuslaw Pub. Libr., Florence, Oreg., 1992-93; dietitian Peace Harbor Hosp., Florence, 1993—; biology tchr. Siuslaw H.S., Florence, 1995—; cons. Long Beach (Calif.) Pub. Health, 1985-86; lectr. Inst. for Natural Resources, Berkeley, 1990-92. Co-author: (tng. manual) VIM Program, 1986. Bd. dirs. Oreg. Fedn. Dem. Women. Mem. Oreg. Diabetes Educators.

SHAPIRO, ALISON ESTHER, software engineer; b. Newton, Mass., Dec. 6, 1963; d. Murray L. and Dorothy E. (Nebergall) S. BS in Math., U. Chgo., 1984, MS in Computer Sci., 1985; postgrad., U. Denver, 1994. Engr. Carnegie Group, Inc., Pitts., 1985-89, sr. engr., 1989-92; sr. engr. Carnegie Group, Inc., Denver, 1992-94, prin. knowledge engr., 1994—; presenter 4th Re-engring. Forum, 1994. Patentee in field. Bd. dirs Tues. Night Folk Dancers, Pitts., 1991-92. Mem. IEEE Computer Soc., Assn. for Computing Machinery (treas. Pitts. chpt. 1991-92), Am. Assn. Artificial Intelligence, Sierra Club (outing leader 1991-92). Office: Carnegie Group Inc 707 17th St Ste 2100 Denver CO 80202-3404

SHAPIRO, LARRY JAY, pediatrician, scientist, educator; b. Chgo., July 6, 1946; s. Philip and Phyllis (Krause) S.; m. Carol-Ann Uetake; children: Jennifer, Jessica, Brian. A.B., Washington U., St. Louis, 1968, M.D., 1971. Diplomate Am. Bd. Pediatrics, Am. Bd. Med. Examiners, Am. Bd. Med. Genetics. Intern St. Louis Children's Hosp., 1971-72, resident, 1971-73; research assoc. NIH, Bethesda, Md., 1973-75; asst. prof. Sch. Medicine, UCLA, 1975-79, assoc. prof., 1979-83, prof. pediatrics and biol. chemistry, 1983-91; investigator Howard Hughes Med. Inst., 1987-91; prof., chmn. dept. pediat. U. Calif.-San Francisco Sch. Medicine, 1991—, chief pediat. svcs. U. Calif. San Francisco Med. Ctr., 1991—. Contbr. numerous articles to profl. publs. Served to lt. comdr. USPHS, 1973-75. Fellow AAAS, Am. Acad. Pediatrics (E. Mead Johnson award in research 1982); mem. Nat. Acad. of Arts & Scis., Soc. Pediatric Research (council 1984-87, pres. 1991-92), Western Soc. for Pediatric Research (council 1983-87, Ross award in research 1981, pres. 1989-90), Soc. for Inherited Metabolic Disease (council 1983-88, pres. 1986-87), Assn. Am. Physicians, Inst. Medicine, Nat. Acad. Scis., Am. Soc. Human Genetics (council 1985-88), Am. Soc. Clin. Investigation, Am. Pediatric Soc., Am. Acad. Arts & Scis. Office: U Calif Third Ave & Parnassus San Francisco CA 94143

SHAPIRO, MATTHEW SCOTT, orthopaedic surgery educator, athletic team physician; b. Bklyn., Nov. 6, 1958; s. Alvin and Helen Francis (Rosenberg) S.; m. Alison Joan Erde, Dec. 6, 1992. BA in Biochemistry, Cornell U., 1979; MD, Columbia U., 1983. Diplomate Nat. Bd. Med. Examiners. Resident in gen. surgery Maine Med. Ctr., Portland, 1983-85; resident and Annie C. Kane fellow in orthopaedic surgery N.Y. Orthopaedic Hosp., Columbia-Presbyn. Med. Ctr., N.Y.C., 1985-88; rsch. and clin. fellow in sports medicine, asst. clin. prof. orthopaedic surgery UCLA Med. Ctr., 1988-90; asst. team physician UCLA Athletic Dept., 1988—; asst. prof. orthopaedic surgery UCLA Med. Ctr., 1988—; mem. med. bd. Musculoskeletal Transplant Found., Holmdel, N.J., 1993—; cons. physician Wadsworth VA Med. Ctr., L.A., 1989—; vis. prof. Al Falah Mil. Hosp., Abu Dhabi, United Arab Emirates, 1993; presenter in field. Author: (chpt.) Sports Induced Inflammation, 1990, Diagnostic Imaging of the Shoulder, 1990, Biomechanics of Diarthrodial Joints, 1990; contbr. articles to profl. jours. Recipient Harrison L. McLaughlin award for excellence in orthopaedic surgery, 1988, Orthopedic Rsch. and Edn. Fund grant, NIH grant, 1994. Fellow Am. Acad. Orthopedic Surgeons. Home: 816 Hanley

Ave Los Angeles CA 90049 Office: UCLA Med Ctr Orthopedic Surgery CHS 76-119 10833 Le Conte Ave Los Angeles CA 90024

SHAPIRO, PHILIP, psychiatrist, consultant; b. Chgo., July 14, 1943; s. Edward and Dorothy (Spector) S.; m. Sharon Whitney, Mar. 21, 1974; children: Jon, David. BS, U. Mich., 1965; MD, U. Ill., 1969; M in pub. health, Columbia U., 1982. Diplomate Am. Bd. Psychiatry and Neurology. Intern Jewish Hosp. St. Louis, 1969-70; lt. commander and gen. medical officer U.S. Pub. Health Svc. Outpatient Clinic, Portland, Oreg., 1970-72; physician trainee Shri Hans Humanitarian Svcs., N.Y.C., 1972-73; chief clinician Methadone Maintenance treatment program St. Mary's Hosp., Bedford, Stuyvesant, N.Y., 1973-74; psychiatric resident Albert Einstein Coll. Medicine, N.Y.C., 1974-75, Kings County Hosp., N.Y., 1975-77; staff psychiatrist South Beach Psychiat. Ctr., Ft. Hamilton, N.Y., 1977-78; dir. div. mental health and development disabilties State of Alaska, 1983-84; chief medical officer Oregon State Hosp., 1984-91; clin. dir. legal offender unit Western State Hosp., Steilacoom, Wash., 1991-92; staff psychiatrist Family Counseling Ctr., St. Helen's, Oreg., 1992—; assoc. attending psychiatrist Harlem Hosp. Ctr., 1978-82, asst. clinical prof. psychiatry Columbia Univ., 1978-82; attending psychiatrist Alaska Psychiatric Inst., 1982-83; cons. Joint Commn. Accredition of Health Orgns., 1990—; cons. in the field, 1992—. Contbr. articles to profl. jours. Mem. Am. Psychiatric Assn., Oregon Psychiatric Assn., Acad. Occupational and Organization Psychiatry. Home and Office: 2712 SW Patton Rd Portland OR 97201-1651

SHAPIRO, RICHARD STANLEY, physician; b. Moline, Ill., June 11, 1925; s. Herbert and Esther Dian (Grant) S.; BS, St. Ambrose Coll., 1947; BS in Pharmacy, U. Iowa, 1951, MS in Preventive Medicine and Environ. Health, 1951, M.D., 1957; m. Arlene Blum, June 12, 1949; children: Michele Pamela, Bruce Grant, Gary Lawrence; m. Merry Lou Cook, Oct. 11, 1971. Pharmacist, Rock Island, Ill., 1951-53; research asst. U. Iowa Coll. Medicine, Iowa City, 1950-51, 53-57; practice medicine specializing in allergy, Beverly Hills, Calif., 1958-62, Lynwood, Calif., 1962—; attending physician Good Hope Found. Allergy Clinic, Los Angeles, 1958-62, Cedars of Lebanon Hosp., Hollywood, Calif., 1959-68, U. So. Calif.-Los Angeles County Med. Center, 1962—; physician St. Francis Hosp., Lynwood, 1962—; assoc. clin. prof. medicine U. So. Calif., 1978-84, emeritus, 1984—. Bd. dirs. Westside Jewish Community Center, 1961-65, Camp JCA, 1964-65. Served with USNR, 1943-45; PTO. Diplomate Am. Bd. Allergy and Immunology. Fellow Am. Geriatric Soc., Am. Coll. Allergy, Am. Assn. Clin. Immunology and Allergy; mem. Am. Soc. Tropical Medicine and Hygiene, Am. Acad. Allergy, Los Angeles Allergy Soc., AMA, Calif., Los Angeles County med. assns., West Coast Allergy Soc., AAAS, Am., Calif. socs. internal medicine, Calif. Soc. Allergy, Am. Heart Assn., Sierra Club, Sigma Xi. Jewish. Mason; mem. B'nai B'rith. Contbr. articles to profl. jours. Office: 8301 Florence Ave Ste 104 Downey CA 90240-3946

SHAPIRO, SUMNER LEROY, psychoanalyst; b. Boston, May 15, 1926; s. Harry Alexander and Eva (Goldberg) S.; m. widowered; children: Paul Steven, Carolyne Amy, Leslie Susan. AB, Harvard U., 1946, MA, 1947; MD, Boston U., 1953. Intern New Eng. Ctr. Hosp., 1955-56; resident Worcester State Hosp., 1958-60; with L.A. Psychoanalytic Inst., 1960—; psychoanalyst pvt. practice, L.A., 1967—; various teaching positions, UCLA. Author: Moment of Insight, 1969, Beyond Insight, 1973, Beyond Case Histories, 1984, Well-Kept Secrets, 1993. Home and office: 16780 Oak View Dr Encino CA 91436-3238

SHAPIRO, YANINA, psychology educator; b. Moscow, Russia, Aug. 2, 1948; came to the U.S., 1975; p. Boris Yakoulevich and Irina Dmitrievna (Churikova) S. BS, Moscow Bauman U., MS in Mech. Engring.; EdM in Human Devel., Harvard U., 1986, EdD in Human Devel. and Psychology, 1991; BA in English, Coll. Fgn. Langs., Moscow; Cert. of German Studies, Vienna U., postgrad., 1981-82. Editor Inst. Info., Moscow, 1975, Gulf Pub. Co., Houston, 1975-76; engr. Ford Motor Co., Dearborn, Mich., 1976-79, Dowland Bach Co., Anchorage, Alaska, 1979; tech. cons. Exxon Rsch. and Engring., N.Y.C., 1980-81; engring. instr. dept. engring. Tufts U., Mass., 1982-83; engr. Dept. Transp., Cambridge, Mass., 1983-87; asst. prof. psychology St. Francis Coll., Loretto, Pa., 1992-93, Ea. Oreg. State Coll., La Grande, 1993-94. Contbr. articles to profl. jours. Mem. AAAS, APA, Am. Psychol. Soc., Soc. for Neurosci. Democrat.

SHARIAT, HORMOZ, pastor; b. Teheran, Iran, Sept. 9, 1955; came to U.S., 1979; s. Javad and Shamsi (Rastegar) S.; m. Donnell Jean Roper, Oct. 23, 1977; children: Hanniel Mina, Jonathan Navid, Michelle Mojdeh. BSEE, Arya Mehr U., Tehran, Iran, 1978; MSEE, U. So. Calif., 1981, PhD, 1986; BS, San Jose Christian Coll., 1993. Ordained minister Iranian Christian Ch., 1991. Mem. technical staff Rockwell Internat., Seal Beach, Calif., 1981-87; rsch. scientist Lockheed Artificial Intelligence Ctr., Menlo Park, Calif., 1987-91; pastor Iranian Christian Ch., San Jose, Calif., 1991—; founding pastor Iranian Christian Ch., Walnut Creek, Calif., 1992—; adj. prof. San Jose Christian Coll., 1993—. Author: (with others) Motion Understanding: Robot and Human Vision 1988; contbr. articles profl. jours. Sec. to bd. dirs. Radio Voice of Christ, Portland, Oreg., 1983-88; lectr. Fellowship of Iranian Christians, L.A., 1983-87; mem. exec. bd. The Worldwide Alliance of Iranian Christian Orgns., Chs. and Groups, 1988—, pres., 1991—. Home: 1026 Whitebick Dr San Jose CA 95129-3049 Office: Iranian Christian Ch 4265 Kirk Rd San Jose CA 95124-4816

SHARIFF, ASGHAR J., geologist; b. Haft Kel, Iran, July 28, 1941; came to U.S., 1964, naturalized, 1978; s. Abdulwahab and Sakineh (Kamiab) S.; m. Kay L. Schoenwald, Aug. 9, 1969; 1 child, Shaun. B.Sc., Calif. State U., Northridge, 1971, M.Sc., 1983. Cert. profl. geologist, Va., Wyo. Petroleum geologist Iranian Oil Exploration and Producing Co., Ahwaz, 1971-74; geol. cons. D.R.L., Inc., Bakersfield, Calif., 1974-76, Strata-log, Inc., 1976-79, Energy Log, Inc., Sacramento, 1979-80; geologist U.S. Dept. Energy, Washington, 1980-81, Bur. Land Mgmt. Dept. Interior, Washington, 1981-89, asst. dist. mgr., Rawlins, Wyo., 1989-93, chief reservoir mgmt. team, Casper, Wyo., 1993—. Contbr. articles to profl. jours. Mem. Am. Assn. Petroleum Geologists, Soc. Profl. Well Log Analysts, Soc. Petroleum Engrs.

SHARKEY, RICHARD DAVID, product designer, architect, musician; b. Columbus, Ohio, May 8, 1957; s. John David and Beatrice Diane (Ziesler) S.; m. Melissa Duke Smith, Dec. 21, 1980 (div. 1995); children: Flax Allistair Linden, Ambrosia Rose Ashley. Student, U. No. Colo., 1975-77, Emporia State U., 1977-78, U. Denver, 1978-81. Music tchr., pvt. studio, piano, cello, composition theory Evergreen, Colo., 1978-82; pvt. bus., period residential restoration Sharkey and Assocs., Evergreen and Denver, 1978-86; stair apprentice Denver Stair Co., 1985-86; stair master Heidelberg Stair Co., Evergreen, 1986; pvt. bus., designer period staircases, millwork O'Searcaigh, Ltd., Evergreen and Denver, 1986-90; with Archtl. Artworks, Englewood, Colo., 1993—; cons. stair and millwork design, Heidelberg Stair, Evergreen, Frank's Woodworking, Lyons, Colo., Pierce Segerberg & Spaeh Architects, Vail, Colo., Charles Cunnifree & Assoc., Aspen, Colo., numerous manufacturers, contractors, architecture, design firms, 1987—; cons. archtl. design period features. Composer/music: numerous piano compositions, 1972—; designer: numerous architecture, millwork and interior designs; inventor: woodworking tools and accessories, and building products, 1986—; works featured in numerous mags. Recipient scholarship Outward Bound Colo., Optimist Club of Evergreen, 1973, music grant, U. No. Colo., Greeley, 1975-76, Emporia (Kans.) U., 1977; scholar U. No. Colo., 1976. Mem. Internat. Soc. Archtl. Artisans (pres., founder 1988—), Denver Cherry Creek Club (charter mem.), Rotary. Mem. Christian Science Ch. Home: 3313 S Santa Fe Dr Ste G Englewood CO 80110-2150 Office: Archtl Artworks PO Box 1241 Englewood CO 80150-1241

SHARMA, ARJUN DUTTA, cardiologist; b. Bombay, June 2, 1953; came to U.S., 1981; s. Hari D. and Gudrun (Axelsson) S.; m. Carolyn D. Burleigh, May 9, 1981; children: Allira, Eric, Harison. BSc, U. Waterloo, Ont., Can., 1972; MD, U. Toronto, Ont., 1976. Intern Toronto Gen. Hosp., 1976-77, resident in medicine, 1978-80; resident in medicine St. Michael's Hosp., Toronto, 1980-81; residency medicine Toronto Gen. Hosp., 1977-78; Rsch. assoc. Washington U., St. Louis, 1981-83; asst. prof. pharmacy and toxicology U. Western Ont., London, 1985-89, asst. prof. medicine, 1983-89, assoc. prof. medicine, 1989-90; dir. interventional electrophysiology Sutter Meml. Hosp., Sacramento, 1990-95; abstract reviewer, faculty of ann. sci. sessions N.Am. Soc. for Pacing and Electrophysiology, 1993; assoc. clin. prof. U. Calif., Davis, 1988-95; cons. Medtronic Inc., Mpls., 1985—, Telectronics Pacing Sys., Inc., 1990-94; mem. rsch. com. Sutter Inst. Med. Rsch.; mem. exec. com. Sutter Heart Inst., 1992. Reviewer profl. jours., including Circulation, Am. Jour. Cardiology; contbr. articles to profl. publs. Mem. coun. for basic sci. Am. Heart Assn., chmn. ann. sci. session, 1989; active Crocker Art Mus. Recipient John Melady award, 1972, Dr. C.S. Wainwright award, 1973-75, Rsch. prize Toronto Gen. Hosp., 1979, 80, Ont. Career Scientist award Ont. Ministry of Health, 1983-89; Med. Rsch. Coun. Can. fellow, 1981-83. Mem. Am. Fedn. Clin. Rsch., Sacramento Med. Soc., Eldorado Med. Soc. Office: 3941 J St Ste 260 Sacramento CA 95819-3633

SHARMA, BRAHAMA DATTA, chemistry educator; b. Sampla, Punjab, India, June 5, 1931; naturalized Am. citizen; s. Des Raj and Kesara Devi (Pathak) S.; m. Millicent M. Hewitt, Dec. 22, 1956; children: Nalanda V. Sharma Bowman, Renuka D. BS with honors, U. Delhi, India, 1949, MS, 1951; PhD, U. So. Calif., 1961. Chemist Govt. Opium Factory, Ghazipur, India, 1951-52; lab. assoc., sci. asst. Nat. Chem. Lab., Poona, India, 1952-55; lab. assoc. U. So. Calif., L.A., 1955-61; research fellow Calif. Inst. Tech., Pasadena, 1961-65; asst. prof. chemistry U. Nev., Reno, 1963-64, Oreg. State U., Corvallis, 1965-70; asst. prof. chemistry Calif. State U., Northridge, 1973-75, assoc. prof., 1975-76; prof. L.A. Pierce Coll., Woodland Hills, Calif., 1976—; part-time assoc. prof. chemistry Calif. State U., L.A., 1973-85, prof., 1985—; vis. assoc. Calif. Inst. Tech., 1979, 82; pres. L.A. Pierce Coll. Senate, 1981-82, chmn. profl. and acad. stds., 1989-92. Contbr. articles to profl. jours. Grantee E.I. duPont de Nemours, L.A., 1961, Am. Chem. Soc. Petroleum Rsch. Fund, Washington, 1965-69, NSF, Washington, 1967-69. Mem. AAAS (chmn. on edn. com. So. Calif. chpt. 1981-82), ACS, Royal Soc. Chemistry (chartered chemist), Am. Crystallography Assn., Am. Inst. Parliamentarians (sec., adminstr., lt. gov. region VII), Nat. Assn. Parliamentarians, Calif. State Assn. Parliamentarians (pub. rels. chmn., statewide edn. chmn. So. area, pres. Calif. Sigma unit), Sigma Xi. Office: LA Pierce Coll Woodland Hills CA 91371

SHARMAN, WILLIAM, professional basketball team executive; b. Abilene, Tex., May 25, 1926; m. Joyce Sharman; children by previous marriage: Jerry, Nancy, Janice, Tom. Student, U. So. Calif. Basketball player Washington Capitols, 1950-51, Boston Celtics, 1951-61; coach Los Angeles/Utah Stars, 1968-71; coach Los Angeles Lakers, 1971-76, gen. mgr., 1976-82, pres., 1982-88, spl. cons., 1991—. Author: Sharman on Basketball Shooting, 1965. Named to Nat. Basketball Assn. All Star First Team, 1956-59, 2d Team, 1953, 55, 60, All League Team, 7 times; named Coach of Year Nat. Basketball Assn., 1972, Naismith Basketball Hall of Fame, 1976. Home: 4511 Roma Ct Marina Dl Rey CA 90292-7704 Office: LA Lakers PO Box 10 3900 W Manchester Blvd Inglewood CA 90306

SHARON, TIMOTHY MICHAEL, physicist; b. Portsmouth, Va., Aug. 21, 1948; s. Lester Clark and Ruth May (Banister) S.; student Santa Ana Coll., 1966-68; B.A., U. Calif.-Irvine 1970, M.A., 1972, Ph.D., 1976; m. Carla Deon Colley, Dec. 17, 1977. Jr. specialist solid state theory U. Calif.-Irvine, 1976, research asst. radiation physics Med. Center and Sch. Medicine, 1976-77, cons. to attending staff Research and Edn. Found., 1976-77; mktg. physicist Varian Assos., Irvine, 1977-78; prin. engr., program mgr. Spectra Research Systems, Newport Beach, Calif., 1977-82; v.p. Brewer-Sharon Corp., Newport Beach, 1981-86, Micor Instruments, Inc., Irvine, Calif., 1983-86; pres., chief exec. officer Medelec Instruments Co., Inc., Newport Beach, 1986-88; pres. Pacific Crest Enterprises, El Toro, Calif., 1988-91; pres., chief exec. officer Novus Group NA, Irvine, Calif., 1991—; adj. faculty physics and engring. Columbia Pacific U., San Rafael, Calif., 1981-87; dean Sch. Engring., Newport U., Newport Beach, Calif., 1983-87; mem. adv. panel on pub. Am. Inst. Physics, 1974-75. Brython P. Davis univ. fellow, 1973-74. Mem. AAAS, Am. Phys. Soc., Brit. Interplanetary Soc. (asso. fellow), Am. Assn. Physicists in Medicine, IEEE, Assn. Advancement Med. Instrumentation, Smithsonian Instn., Am. Film Inst., Nat. Hist. Soc., Nat. Geog. Soc., Festival of Arts Laguna Beach, Mensa, Intertel, Sigma Pi Sigma, Phi Theta Kappa, Alpha Gamma Sigma. Clubs: Acad. Magical Arts, Club 33. Contbr. articles to profl. jours.

SHARP, LAURENCE NEWTON, diagnostic company executive; b. Providence, Dec. 4, 1932; s. Henry Freeman and Harriet Beth (Smira) S.; m. Nancy Ann Adle Sharp, June 8, 1963; 1 child, Theodore Douglas Sharp. BA, Boston U., 1954; MA, U. Kans., 1956. Salesman VW&R, Braun Div., Phoenix, 1956-59; regional mgr. VW&R, Braun Div., Tucson, 1959-63; clin. sales mgr. VW&R, Braun Div., L.A., 1963-66; mktg. mgr. B-D Labs., Cockeysville, Md., 1966-69; v.p. sales and mktg. Internat. Equipment Co., Needham Heights, Mass., 1969-70; gen. sales mgr. Micromedic Sys., Phila., 1970-74; gen. mgr. Micromedic Sys., Toronto, Can., 1974-84; dir. internat. sales ICN Biomedics, Costa Mesa, Calif., 1985-89, v.p. sales Asia/Pacific, 1989—; pres. Novercal Consulting, Toronto, Can., 1981-83. Mem. Young Reps., Phoenix, 1956-59. Mem. Am. Air Mail Soc. Republican. Methodist. Office: ICN Biomedicals 3300 Hyland Ave Costa Mesa CA 92626-1503

SHARP, PAMELA ANN, quality assurance engineer; b. Pullman, Wash., Dec. 20, 1950; d. Robert Melvin and Vivian Lois (Steele) Olson; m. David William Sharp, June 16, 1973; children: Jaime David, Erik Scott. Student, Big Bend C.C., Moses Lake, Wash., 1969-70; BS in Zoology, Wash. State U., 1973; postgrad., Portland State U., 1976. Lab. technician The Carter Mining Co., Gillette, Wyo., 1977-79, lab. supr., 1979-80, quality control supr., 1980-81, engring. analyst, 1982-88; engr. quality control The Carter Mining Co., Gillette, 1988-89; owner Sharp Consulting, Gillette, 1989—, Landscape Design, 1993—; leader auditor tng. ISO 9000; obedience dog tng. instr., 1990—. Supt. Campbell County Fair, Gillette, 1985-87. Mem. AIME, ASTM (proximate analysis chmn. 1985—, chmn. on-line analysis com.), Am. Water Ski Assn. (regular judge 1974-91, eastern regional water ski trick record 1975, 3d nat. trick title 1962, state champion in tricks Wash., Idaho, Mont. 1961-73, 2d 1987 Western region women's III tricks). Republican. Presbyterian. Office: Sharp Consulting 2406 Hillcrest Dr Gillette WY 82718-5641

SHARP, ROBERT LEE, aerospace engineering consultant, test pilot; b. Indpls., Ind., Jan. 18, 1925; s. Floyd Neal and Nancy L. (Collett) S.; m. Margaret Maxine Deputy, June 28, 1947; children: Richard, Roger, William. BS in Aeronautics Engring., Purdue U., 1950, student, 1950. Fighter pilot USAF & Ind. ANG., 1944-63; test pilot McDonnell Aircraft Corp., St. Louis, 1956-62; chief spacecraft engr. pilot McDonnell Douglas Corp., St. Louis, 1962-74; sr. group engr. BDM Corp., Albuquerque, 1975-81; cons. Albuquerque, 1981-84; aerospace systems mgr. Gen. Dynamics Corp., San Diego, 1984-87; pres. Sharp Aerospace Assocs., Albuquerque, 1987—. Designer Gemini & Skylab Spacecraft Crew Stations, 1962-74. Maj. USAF & ANG. Recipient various awards NASA, 1965-74. Mem. AIAA. Home and Office: Sharp Aerospace Assocs 12324 Eastridge Dr NE Albuquerque NM 87112-4605

SHARP, ROBERT PHILLIP, geology educator, researcher; b. Oxnard, Calif., June 24, 1911; s. Julian Hebner Sharp and Alice Sharp Darling; m. Jean Prescott Todd, Sept. 7, 1938; adopted children—Kristin Todd, Bruce Todd. B.S., Calif. Inst. Tech., Pasadena, 1934, M.S., 1935; M.A., Harvard U., Cambridge, Mass., 1936, Ph.D., 1938. Asst. prof. U. Ill., Urbana, 1938-43; prof. U. Minn., Mpls., 1946-47; prof. Calif. Inst. Tech., Pasadena, 1947-79, chmn., 1952-67, prof. emeritus, 1979—. Author: Glaciers, 1960, Field Guide-Southern California, 1972, Field Guide-Coastal Southern California, 1978, Living Ice-Understanding Glaciers and Glaciation, 1988, (with A.F. Glazner) Geology Under Foot in Southern California, 1993. Served to capt. USAF, 1943-46. Recipient Exceptional Sci. Achievement medal NASA, 1971, Nat. Medal Sci., 1989, Charles P. Daly medal Am. Geog. Soc., 1991; Robert P. Sharp professorship Calif. Inst. Tech., 1978. Fellow Geol. Soc. Am. (councillor, Kirk Bryan award 1964, Penrose medal 1977), Am. Geophys. Union; hon. fellow Internat. Glaciological Soc.; mem. NAS. Republican. Home: 1901 Gibraltar Rd Santa Barbara CA 93105-2326 Office: Calif Inst Tech 1200 E California Blvd Pasadena CA 91106

SHARPE, ROLAND LEONARD, retired engineering company executive, earthquake and structural engineering consultant; b. Shakopee, Minn., Dec. 18, 1923; s. Alfred Leonard and Ruth Helen (Carter) S.; m. Jane Esther Steele, Dec. 28, 1946; children: Douglas Rolfe, Deborah Lynn, Sheryl Anne. BS in Civil Engring., U. Mich., 1947, MSE, 1949. Registered civil engr. and structural engr., Calif. Designer, Cummins & Barnard, Inc., Ann Arbor, Mich., 1947-48; instr. engring. U. Mich., 1948-50; exec. v.p. John A. Blume & Assocs., engrs., San Francisco, 1950-73; chmn., founder Engring. Decision Analysis Co., Inc., Cupertino, 1974-87; cons. earthquake engr., 1987—; mng. dir. EDAC, GmBH, Frankfurt, Germany, 1974-82; dir. EDAC; pres. Calif. Devel. & Engring. Co., Inc., Las Vegas, Nev., 1973-81; mem. nat. earthquake hazard reduction program adv. com. overviewing Fed. Emergency Mgmt. Agy., U.S. Geol. Survey, NSF and Nat. Inst. Stds. and Tech., 1990-93. Author: (with J. Blume, E.G. Kost) Earthquake Engineering for Nuclear Facilities, 1971. Mem. Planning Commn., Palo Alto, 1955-60; mng. dir. Applied Tech. Coun., Palo Alto, 1973-83; dir. Earthquake Engring. Rsch. Inst., 1972-75, now mem.; project dir., editor Tentative Provisions for Devel. of Seismic Regulations for Buildings, 1978; tech. mgr., contbr., editor Data Processing Facilities: Guidelines for Earthquake Hazard Mitigation, 1987. Served with USMC, 1942-46. Author, co-author over 200 engring. papers and reports; author of chpts.: (with others) Seismic Safety Guide, 1995; contbr. chpts. book. Fellow ASCE (hon. mem., chmn. dynamic effects com., 1978-80, exec. com. structural div. 1980-84, 89-93, chmn. 1983, mgmt. group B 1989-93, Earnest O. Howard award 1994); mem. Japan Structural Cons. Assn. (hon. mem. 1992), Structural Engrs. Assn. Calif. (dir. 1971-73, chmn. seismology com. 1972-74), Structural Engrs. No. Calif. (dir. 1969-71, life mem.), Am. Concrete Inst. (life). Recipient citation for contbn. to constrn. industry Engring. News Record, 1978-79, 86-87; chmn. U.S. Joint Com. on Earthquake Engring., 1982-88. Home: 10320 Rolly Rd Los Altos CA 94024-6520

SHARPE, SHANNON, professional football player; b. Chgo., June 26, 1968. Student, Savannah State U. Tight end Denver Broncos, 1990—; player AFC Championship Game, 1991. Named to Pro Bowl Team, 1992, 93, Sporting News NFL All-Pro Team, 1993. Office: Denver Broncos 13655 E Broncos Pkwy Englewood CO 80112

SHARPE, WENONAH FINCH, writer, educator, editor; b. Penicton, B.C., Can., July 22, 1926; d. Sidney Gordon and Mabel Marguerite (Callaghan) Finch; m. Grant William Sharpe, Apr. 3, 1948; children: Christopher, Kathryn, Charles, Loretta, Paul, Patrick, Fred, Rosemary, Lena. BA, U. Wash., 1982. Corr. studies instr. U. Wash., Seattle, 1978-93. Co-author: (with others) Introduction to Park Management, 1983, Introduction to Advanced Park Management, 1994, Introduction to Advanced Forestry, 5th edit., 1986, Introduction to Forest and Renewable Resources, 6th edit., 1995. Mem. Wash. Women in Timber, Phi Beta Kappa.

SHARPE, WILLIAM FORSYTH, economics educator; b. Cambridge, Mass., June 16, 1934; s. Russell Thornley Sharpe and Evelyn Forsyth (Jillson) Maloy; m. Roberta Ruth Branton, July 2, 1954 (div. Feb. 1986); children: Deborah Ann, Jonathan Forsyth; m. Kathryn Dorothy Peck, Apr. 5, 1986. AB, UCLA, 1955, MA, 1956, PhD, 1961. Economist Rand Corp., 1957-61; asst. prof. econs. U. Wash., 1961-63, assoc. prof., 1963-67, prof., 1967-68; prof. U. Calif., Irvine, 1968-70; Timken prof. fin. Stanford U., 1970-89, Timken prof. emeritus, 1989-92; prin. William F. Sharpe Assocs., 1986-92; prof.fin. Stanford U., 1993-95, STANCO 25 prof. of fin., 1995—. Author: The Economics of Computers, 1969, Portfolio Theory and Capital Markets, 1970; co-author: Fundamentals of Investments, 1989, 2d edit., 1993, Investments, 5th edit., 1995. With U.S. Army, 1956-57. Recipient Graham and Dodd award Fin Analysts' Fedn., 1972, '73, '86-88. Nicholas Molodovsky award, 1989. Nobel prize in econ. scis., 1990. Mem. Am. Fin. Assn. (v.p. 1979, pres. 1980), Western Fin. Assn. (Enduring Contbn. award 1989), Ea. Fin. Assn. (Disting. Scholar award 1991), Am. Econ. Assn., Phi Beta Kappa.

SHARPSTONE, LEWIS EDWARD, accountant; b. London, Oct. 14, 1960; came to U.S., 1986; s. Stanley and Angela (Lawrence) S.; children: Jaimie Tessa, Samuel David. BSc in Computer Sci. and Math., U. Manchester, Eng., 1982. Chartered acct., U.K.; CPA, Calif. Sr. acct. Price Waterhouse, London, 1982-86; mgr. Price Waterhouse, L.A., 1986-89; mgr. Singer Lewak Greenbaum & Goldstein, L.A., 1989-93, ptnr., 1993—; mem. faculty Ctr. for Non-Profit Mgmt., L.A., 1991—; chmn. Corp. Coun., L.A., 1993-94; speaker, presenter seminars in field. Contbr. articles to profl. publs. Mem. AICPA, Calif. Soc. CPAs, Assn. Chartered Accts. in Eng. and Wales. Jewish. Office: Singer Lewak Greenbaum & Goldstein 10960 Wilshire Blvd # 1100 Los Angeles CA 90024

SHARPTON, THOMAS, physician; b. Augusta, Ga., July 15, 1949; s. Thomas and Elizabeth (Dozier) S. BA, Northwestern U., 1971; MS, Stanford U., 1973, MD, 1977. Intern Martinez (Calif.) VAMC, 1977-78, resident, 1978-80; mem. staff Kaiser Permanente Med. Group, Oakland, Calif., 1980—; asst. clin. prof. medicine U. Calif., San Francisco, 1994—; cons. Berkeley (Calif.) Free Clinic, 1977—; chmn. peer review Kaiser Permanente Med. Group, Oakland, 1985-86; clin. mem. faculty U. Calif., San Francisco, 1992, asst. clin. prof., 1994. Mem. Alameda County Profl. Adv. Com., Oakland, 1984-88, Alameda County AIDS Task Force, Oakland, 1985-88. Fellow ACP; mem. Calif. Med. Assn., Alameda-Contra Costa Med. Assn., Mensa, Sigma Pi Sigma, Phi Beta Kappa. Democrat. Club: Phi Beta Kappa of No. Calif. Office: Kaiser PMG 280 W Macarthur Blvd Piedmont CA 94611-5642

SHARROW, MARILYN JANE, library administrator; bd. Oakland, Calif.; d. Charles L. and H. Evelyn S.; m. Lawrence J. Davis. BS in Design, U. Mich., 1967, MALS, 1969. Librarian Detroit Pub. Libr., 1968-70; head fine arts dept. Syracuse (N.Y.) U. Librs., 1970-73; dir. libr. Roseville (Mich.) Pub. Libr., 1973-75; asst. dir. librs. U. Wash., 1975-77, assoc. dir. librs., 1978-79; dir. libraries U. Man., Winnipeg, Can., 1979-82; chief libr. U. Toronto, Can., 1982-85; univ. libr. U. Calif., Davis, 1985—. Recipient Woman of Yr. in Mgmt. award Winnipeg YWCA, 1982; named Woman of Distinction, U. Calif. Faculty Women's Rsch. Group, 1985. Mem. ALA, Assn. Rsch. Librs. (bd. dirs., v.p., pres-elect 1989-90, pres. 1990-91, chair sci. tech. work group 1994—, rsch. collections com. 1993—), Online Computer Libr. Ctr.-Rsch. Librs. Adv. Com. (vice chmn. 1992-93, chair 1993-94). Office: U Calif Shields Lib Davis CA 95616

SHATNEY, CLAYTON HENRY, surgeon; b. Bangor, Maine, Nov. 4, 1943; s. Clayton Lewis and Regina (Cossette) S.; m. Deborah Gaye Hansen, Apr. 5, 1977; children: Tony, Andy. BA, Bowdoin Coll., 1965; MD, Tufts U., 1969. Asst. prof. surgery U. Md. Hosp., Balt., 1979-82; assoc. prof. U. Fla. Sch. Medicine, 1982-87; clin. assoc. prof. Stanford (Calif.) U. Sch. Medicine, 1987—; dir. traumatology Md. Inst. Emergency Med. Svcs., Balt., 1979-82; dir. trauma U. Hosp., Jacksonville, 1982-85; assoc. dir. trauma Santa Clara Valley Med. Ctr., 1992—; cons. VA Coop. Studies Program, Washington, 1980—. Editl. bd. Circulatory Shock, 1989—; writer, actor med. movie. Maj. U.S. Army, 1977-79. State of Maine scholar Bowdoin Coll., 1961-65. Fellow ACS, Southeastern Surg. Congress, Southwestern Surg. Congress, Soc. Surg. Alimentary Tract, Am. Assn. Surg. Trauma, Soc. Critical Care Medicine, Soc. Internat. de Chirurgie, Western Surg. Assn., Pacific Coast Surg. Assn., Phi Kappa Phi. Home: 900 Larsen Rd Aptos CA 95003-2640 Office: Valley Med Ctr Dept Surgery 751 S Bascom Ave San Jose CA 95128-2604

SHAU, HUNGYI, immunologist; b. Chanhua, Taiwan, Sept. 25, 1952; came to U.S., 1977; s. Ming-Je and Ton-Kuei (Lin) S.; m. Ching-Ching Lin, Sept. 13, 1956; children: Carol, Calvin. BS, Nat. Taiwan U., 1975; PhD, Duke U., 1982. Postdoctoral fellow Duke U., Durham, N.C., 1982-83, UCLA, 1983-85; rsch. asst. prof. U. So. Calif., L.A., 1985-86; asst. rsch. oncologist UCLA, 1986-88, adj. asst. prof., 1988-91, asst. prof., 1991-94; assoc. prof., 1994—. Contbr. articles to profl. jours., chpts. to books. Mem. Am. Assn. Immunologists, Am. Assn. Cancer Rsch. Office: Div Surg Oncology UCLA Sch Medicine 54-140 CHS Los Angeles CA 90095-1782

SHAVER, CARL HUTCHENS, retail company executive; b. Richland, Oreg., June 10, 1913; s. Charles Jacob and Minne (Mary) S.; m. Georgia Bruce, Oct. 17, 1934 (dec. Apr. 1980); children—Carl B., Dennis G.; m. Laura Frazier, Aug. 12, 1983. Student N.W. Nazarene Coll., Nampa, Idaho, 1931-32. Clk., Stockwells, Nampa, 1935-36, mgr., Donnelly, Idaho, 1936-41; mgr. Shavers, Donnelly and New Meadows, Idaho, 1941-53; pres. Shaver's Inc., Boise, Idaho, 1953-80, chmn. bd., 1980—; pres. Boise Wholesale Drygoods Co., Inc., 1953-77; chmn. bd. Citizens Nat. Bank, Boise, 1981—; vice-chmn. Associated Food Stores, also bd. dirs.; bd. dirs., v.p. Shore Club

Lodge Inc., McCall, Idaho. Bd. dirs. United First Meth. Ch., Boise, 1968-74. Named Small Businessman of Yr., State of Idaho, 1973; recipient Disting. Citizen award Idaho Daily Statesman, 1984. Mem. Nat. Assn. Textile and Apparel Wholesalers (bd. dirs. 1962-74, pres. 1974-76), Idaho Retailers (pres. 1951), Greater Boise C. of C. (bd. dirs. 1965-71). Republican. Clubs: Hillcrest Country, Arld (bd. dirs.) (Boise). Lodges: Masons, Shriners. Home: 3100 Crescent Rim Dr Apt 401 Boise ID 83706-2868 Office: Shavers Inc 705 S 8th PO Box 7278 Boise ID 83707-1278 other: Associated Food Stores Inc 3100 Crescent Rim Dr Boise ID 83706-2873

SHAVER, PHILLIP ROBERT, psychologist, educator; b. Iowa City, Iowa, Sept. 7, 1944; s. Robert Richard and Frances Magdalene (Quinn) S. BA in Psychology, Wesleyan U., Middletown, Conn., 1966; PhD in Social Psychology, U. Mich., 1971. Asst. prof. psychology Columbia U., N.Y.C., 1971-75; assoc. prof. NYU, 1975-80; assoc. prof. U. Denver, 1980-84, prof. psychology, 1984-87; prof. psychology SUNY, Buffalo, 1988-92; prof. psychology, dept. chair U. Calif., Davis, 1992—; coord. doctoral program in personality and social psychology NYU, 1978-80; pres. Societal Data Corp., N.Y.C., 1977-82; head experimental and social areas dept. psychology U. Denver, 1981-84, 87—; vis. prof. U. Hawaii, Manoa, 1986; mem. grad. fellowship evaluation panel NSF, 1990—; cons. to numerous orgns. Editorial bd.: Jour. Social and Personal Relationships, 1988—, Personality and Social Psychology Bull., 1985—, Rev. Personality and Social Psychology, 1979-82, 86—, Jour. Personality and Social Psychology, 1978-80, 85—, Behavioral Sci., 1972-80, Jour. Experimental Social Psychology, 1972-75; contbr. reviews and articles to profl. jours. Fundraiser Arthritis Found., Buffalo, 1991. Grantee NIMH, Russell Sage Found., Spencer Found., NSF, Nat. Inst. Alcoholism, Nat. Ctr. for Child Abuse and Neglect; Woodrow Wilson fellow, NSF fellow. Fellow Am. Psychol. Assn., Am. Psychol. Soc.; mem. Eastern Psychol. Assn., Soc. for Exptl. Social Psychology, Soc. for Psychol. Study Social Issues, Internat. Soc. for Rsch. on Emotion, Internat. Soc. for Study Personal Relationships, Internat. Network Personal Relationships, Phi Beta Kappa, Phi Kappa Phi, Sigma Xi. Democrat. Home: 2409 Merlot Dr Napa CA 94558-2599 Office: U Calif Dept Psychology Park Hall Davis CA 95616-8686

SHAW, A. PARK, III, commercial real estate broker; b. Hartford, Conn., May 1, 1947; m. Cassandra Claire Hudson, May 1, 1982. BA in Geol. Scis., Amherst Coll., 1974. Field/exploration geologist Union Carbide Corp., 1974-76; project geologist Chapman Wood & Griswold, Albuquerque, 1976-80; owner, mgr. Element of Time, Albuquerque, 1980-84; broker assoc. The Vaughan Co., Albuquerque, 1986-88; v.p. Hooten/Stahl Comml. Investment, Inc., Albuquerque, 1988—. Judge N.Mex. Sci. and Engring. Fair, 1975—, mem. bd. advisors, 1992; master gardener N.Mex. dept. Agr., 1984, 85; bd. dirs. Albuquerque Boys Club, 1979-84; pres. Albuquerque Jaycees, 1981; J.C.I. senator # 34705, pres. senate N.Mex. Jr. Chamber Internat., 1983, nat. v.p., 1985; dir. mktg. Albuquerque/S.W. Airlines Air Show, 1991; grad. Leadership Albuquerque, 1992, bd. dirs., 1993—; chmn. N.Mex. Bus. Assistance Coun., 1992-95. With U.S. Army, 1967-70. Named Outstanding Vol. of N.Mex., Gov. of N.Mex., 1982, Mover and Shaker N.Mex. Bus. Jour., 1990, 93. Mem. Nat. Assn. Realtors (cert. comml. investment mem.), Nat. Eagle Scout Assn. (life), N.Mex. Assn. Commerce and Industry (bd. dirs. 1992-94), South Valley C. of C. (founder, pres. 1988-91), N.Mex. Vine and Wine Soc. (pres. Mid Rio Grande chpt. 1989), Nat. Assn. Watch and Clock Collectors (founding, pres. 1985), Albuquerque Geol. Soc. (pres. 1980), Albuquerque C. of C. (amb. 1987—), SAR, DAV (life), Nat. Rifle Assn. (life), Children Am. Revolution (sr. pres. N.Mex. Soc. 1977), Masons. Home: 2809 Chanate Ave SW Albuquerque NM 87105-6827

SHAW, CAROLE, editor, publisher; b. Bklyn., Jan. 22, 1936; d. Sam and Betty (Neckin) Bergenthal; m. Ray Shaw, Dec. 27, 1957; children: Lori Eve Cohen, Victoria Shaw Locknar. BA, Hunter Coll., 1962. Singer Capitol Records, Hilton Records, Rama Records, Verve Records, 1952-65; TV appearances Ed Sullivan, Steve Allen, Jack Paar, George Gobel Show, 1957; owner The People's Choice, L.A., 1975-79; founder, editor-in-chief Big Beautiful Woman mag., Beverly Hills, Calif., 1979—; creator Carole Shaw and BBW label clothing line for large-size women. Author: Come Out, Come Out Wherever You Are, 1982. Office: BBW Mag PO Box K-298 Tarzana CA 91356

SHAW, CHARLES ALDEN, engineering executive; b. Detroit, June 8, 1925; s. Fred Alden and Amy (Ellis) S.; m. Barbara Loveland, Mar. 9, 1963 (div. 1979); children: Amy Elizabeth, Polly Nicole; m. Jeanne Steves Partridge, Apr. 22, 1989. BS, Harvard U., 1945; MSEE, Syracuse U., 1958. Test and design engr. G.E., Syracuse-Schenectady, N.Y., 1947-51; chief engr. Onondaga Pottery Co., Syracuse, 1951-60; mgr. semiconductor div. G.E., Syracuse-Schenectady, 1960-66; cons. to gen. dir. Bull-G.E., Paris, 1966-69; mgr. CAD sect. integrated cir. product dept. G.E., Syracuse, 1969-71, mgr. CAD ctr. solid state applied ops., 1971-78, mgr. computer support solid state applied ops., 1978-81; dir. CAD G.E. Intersil, Cupertino, Calif., 1981-88; cons. in field Cupertino, 1988-89; mgr. tech. program Cadence Design Systems, Santa Clara, Calif., 1989—. Trustee Hidden Villa, Los Altos Hills, Calif., 1986-92; vol. tech. KTEH Channel 54 pub. TV, 1984—. With USN, 1942-45, PTO. Mem. IEEE, Assn. Computing Machinery (chmn. spl. interest group SIGDA 1986-91), Design Automation Conf. (exec. bd. 1985—), Harvard Club of Peninsula. Democrat. Unitarian. Home: 4925 Monaco Dr Pleasanton CA 94566-7671 Office: 555 River Oaks Pky San Jose CA 95134-1917

SHAW, CHRISTOPHER WILLIAM, geologist; b. Bozeman, Mont., Jan. 3, 1961; s. Carlton William and Sarah Jane (Johnson) S. BS in Geology, Mont. State U., 1984; MS, U. Idaho, 1988. Kayak guide Alaska Mountain Treks, Moose Pass, 1983; drivers helper North of 60 Trucking, Whitehorse, Alaska, 1983; geologist Geomax, Bozeman, 1984; forestry aide U.S. Forest Svc., Wise River, Mont., 1985; forestry tech. minerals U.S. Forest Svc., Sheridan, Mont., 1988; geologist Idaho Geol. Survey, Moscow, 1987-88, John Childs Cons. Geologist, Bozeman, 1988, Noranda Exploration Inc., Denver, 1988; exploration geologist Pegasus Gold Corp., Butte, Mont., 1989—. Mem. leadership team 4-H, Bozeman, 1978-79. Mem. Geol. Soc. Am., Am. Assn. Petroleum Geologists, Mont. Mining Assn., Tobacco Root Geol. Soc. Home: 9660 Fish Hatchery Rd Bozeman MT 59715-9350 Office: Pegasus Gold Corp PO Box 330 Imlay NV 89418

SHAW, DAVID LYLE, journalist, author; b. Dayton, Ohio, Jan. 4, 1943; s. Harry and Lillian (Walton) S.; m. Alice Louise Eck, Apr. 11, 1965 (div. Sept. 1974); m. Ellen Torgerson, July 17, 1979 (dec.); stepchildren: Christopher, Jordan; m. Lucy Stille, Apr. 14, 1988; 1 child, Lucas. BA in English, UCLA, 1965. Reporter Huntington Park Signal (Calif.), 1963-66, Long Beach Independent (Calif.), 1966-68; reporter L.A. Times, 1968-74, media critic, 1974—. Author: WILT: Just Like Any Other 7-Foot, Black Millionaire Who Lives Next Door, 1973, The Levy Caper, 1974, Journalism Today, 1977, Press Watch, 1984; contbr. numerous articles to mags. including Gentlemen's Quar., Esquire, TV Guide, New York. Recipient Mellet Fund Nat. award, 1983, PEN West award, 1990, Calif. Bar Assn. Gold Medallion, 1990, Pulitzer Prize for disting. criticism, 1991. Office: LA Times Times Mirror Sq Los Angeles CA 90012

SHAW, ELEANOR JANE, newspaper editor; b. Columbus, Ohio, Mar. 23, 1949; d. Joseph Cannon and Wanda Jane (Campbell) S. BA, U. Del., 1971. With News-Jour. newspapers, Wilmington, Del., 1970-82, editor HEW desk, asst. met. editor, 1977-80, bus. editor, 1980-82; topics editor USA Today, 1982-83; asst. city editor The Miami Herald, 1983-85; projects editor The Sacramento Bee, 1985-87, news editor, 1987-91, exec. bus. editor, 1991-93, editor capitol bureau news, 1993—. Bd. dirs. Del. 4-H Found., 1978-83. Mem. Calif. Soc. Newspaper Editors (bd. dirs. 1990—), No. Calif. Wine Soc. (v.p. 1987-93, pres. 1993—). Office: The Sacramento Bee PO Box 15779 Sacramento CA 95852-0779

SHAW, HENRY FRANCIS, geochemist; b. Boston, June 5, 1955; s. Henry Francis Jr. and Elizabeth (Cavaliere) S. BA in Geology, Amherst Coll., 1977; MS in Geology, Calif. Inst. Tech., 1978, PhD in Geology/Chemistry, 1984. Vis. assoc. Calif. Inst. Tech., Pasadena, 1983-84; postdoctoral fellow Lawrence Livermore (Calif.) Nat. Lab., 1983-85, geochemist, task leader, 1985-87, tech. area leader, 1987-90, assoc. head earth scis. dept., 1990—. Contbr. articles to profl. jours. Fellow Anthony Inst., Calif. Inst. Tech., 1977. Mem. Am. Mineral Soc., Am. Geophys. Union, Am. Geochem. Soc., Sigma Xi. Office: Lawrence Livermore Nat Lab # L201 Livermore CA 94550

SHAW, LILLIE MARIE KING, vocalist; b. Indpls., Nov. 27, 1915; d. Earl William and Bertha Louise (Groth) King; m. Philip Harlow Shaw, June 26, 1940. Student, Jordan Conservatory Music, Indpls., 1940-43; BA, Ariz. State U., 1959; MA, Denver U., 1962; pvt. vocal study, 1944-70. Educator, libr. Glendale (Ariz.) Schs., 1959-67; lectr. libr. sci. Ariz. State U., Tempe, 1962-68. Concertizing, oratorio, symphonic soloist, light opera, 1965-82; soloist First Ch. of Christ Scientist, Sun City West, Ariz., 1980—. Monthly lectr. Christian Women's Fellowship, Phoenix, 1989—; World Conf. del. Soc. of Friends, 1967. Mem. Nat. Soc. Arts and Letters (sec. 1990-94, nat. del. 1992), Am. Philatelic Assn. (life), Am. Topical Assn., Phoenix Philatelic Soc., Auditions Guild Ariz. (sec. 1989-92), Phoenix Opera League, Phoenix Symphony Guild (bd. mem. youth activities 1986—), Sigma Alpha Iota Alumnae (Phoenix chpt., life, treas. 1988-94, Sword of Honor 1972, Rose of Honor 1982, Rose of Dedication 1995). Republican. Home: 6802 N 37th Ave Phoenix AZ 85019-1103

SHAW, MARK HOWARD, lawyer, business owner, entrepreneur; b. Albuquerque, Aug. 26, 1944; s. Brad Oliver and Barbara Rae (Mencke) S.; m. Ann Marie Brookreson, June 29, 1968 (div. 1976); adopted children: Daniel Paul, Kathleen Ann, Brian Andrew; m. Roslyn Jane Ashton, Oct. 9, 1976; children: Rebecca Rae, Amanda Leith. BA, U. N.Mex., 1967, JD, 1969. Bar, N.Mex. 1969. Law clk. to presiding justice N.Mex. Supreme Ct., Santa Fe, 1969-70; ptnr. Gallagher & Ruud, Albuquerque, 1970-74, Schmidt & Shaw, Albuquerque, 1974-75; sr. mem. Shaw, Thompson & Sullivan P.A., Albuquerque, 1975-82; chief exec. officer United Ch. Religious Sci. and Sci. Mind Publs., L.A., 1982-91; atty., bus. owner, entrepreneur Santa Fe, N.Mex., 1991—. Trustee 1st Ch. Religious Sci., Albuquerque, 1974-77, pres. 1977; trustee Sandia Ch. Religious Sci., Albuquerque, 1980-82, pres. 1981-82; trustee United Ch. Religious Sci., Los Angeles, 1981-82, chmn. 1982; trustee Long Beach (Calif.) Ch. Religious Sci., 1983-86, chmn. 1983-86; chmn. Bernalillo County Bd. Ethics, Albuquerque, 1979-82. Served as sgt. USMCR, 1961-69. Mem. N.Mex. Bar Assn., Pres.'s Assn., Am. Mgmt. Assn. Home and Office: 2724 Puerto Bonito Santa Fe NM 87505-6534

SHAW, MORGAN ALBERT, architect, consultant; b. Ogden, Utah, Dec. 3, 1916; s. William Henry and Elizabeth (Johns) S.; m. Ramona Story, Sept. 28, 1940 (dec. Apr. 1990). Student, Corcoran Art Sch., Washington, 1937-39; cert., Art Students' League, N.Y.C., 1939-41; BArchwith honors, U. Calif., Berkeley, 1949. Lic. architect. Designer, draftsman Walter Wagner, Architect and Engr., Fresno, Calif., 1949-50, Skidmore, Owings & Merrill, San Francisco, 1950-51; job capt. Falk & Booth, San Francisco, 1951-52; owner, prin. Morgan Shaw, Architect, Berkeley, 1953—; instr. U. Calif., San Francisco, 1966-67. Contbr. articles to profl. jours. 1st lt. USAF, 1942-45, ETO. Mem. Phi Beta Kappa. Home: 2500 Hillegass Ave Apt 15 Berkeley CA 94704-2936

SHAW, RICHARD EUGENE, cardiovascular researcher; b. Springfield, Ohio, Jan. 20, 1950; s. Eugene Russell and Marjorie Catherine (Lewe) S.; m. Christine Elizabeth Costa, Nov. 26, 1976; children: Matthew, Brian. BA, Duquesne U., 1972; MA, U.S. Internat. U., San Diego, 1977; PhD, U. Calif., San Francisco, 1984. Cert. nuclear med. technologist. Staff nuclear med. technician Scripps Meml. Hosp., La Jolla, Calif., 1975-79; rsch. asst. U. Calif. San Francisco Sch. Medicine, 1980-85; mgr. rsch. programs San Francisco Heart Inst., Daly City, Calif., 1985-87, dir. rsch., 1988-90, dir. rsch. and ops., 1991—; sr. advisor steering com. for databases Daus. of Charity Nat. Health Systems, St. Louis, 1993—; cons. for data elements Calif. Heart Network, San Diego, 1991—. Editor-in-chief Jour. Invasive Cardiology, King of Prussia, Pa., 1989—; contbr. more than 200 articles and book chpts. to med. lit. Coach Am. Youth Soccer Orgn., Burlingame, Calif., 1990—. Fellow Am. Coll. Cardiology; mem. Am. Heart Assn., Soc. for Clin. Trials, N.Y. Acad. Scis., Am. Statis. Assn., Soc. Behavioral Medicine. Office: San Francisco Heart Inst at Seton Med Ctr 1900 Sullivan Ave Daly City CA 94015-2200

SHAW, RICHARD MELVIN, gemologist, gold company executive; b. Los Angeles, Jan. 14, 1947; s. Melvin and Harriet Louise (Hammond) S.; m. Deanna Lee Revel, Mar. 9, 1968 (div. 1973); 1 child, Katharine Lillian; m. Janet Lynne Gribble, Dec. 31, 1981; 1 child, Jacquelyn Louise. Student L.A. Valley Coll.-Van Nuys, 1965-67; grad. Gemological Inst. Am., 1976. Design coordinator Foxy Jon's Smokehouse Cabins, Inc., L.A., 1968-71; Pantera specialist, used car mgr. Bricker Lincoln-Mercury, L.A., 1971-74; designer Melvin Shaw & Assos., Santa Monica, Calif., 1974-76; instr. Gemological Inst. Am., Santa Monica, 1976-79, dir. rsch. and devel., 1979-82; ptnr., dir. sales and mktg. N.W. Gold Mktg., Woodland Hills, Calif., 1982-83; exec. v.p. Nat. Gold Distbr., Ltd., Canoga Park, Calif., 1983-86; pres., CEO Campbell Shaw, Inc., Woodland Hills, 1986—; founder, ptnr. Rick Shaw & Co., 1982—. Developer, designer Diamond Pen instrument; gemelogical cons., 1988; developer of standardized microscope grading method. Mem. L.A. County Mus. Alliance, Mineral. Soc. So. Calif., Nat. Assn. Underwater Instrs., Instrument Soc. Am.

SHAW, STANFORD J., history educator; b. St. Paul, May 5, 1930; s. Albert G. Shaw and Belle (Paymar) Jaffey; m. Ezel Kural, June 15, 1938; 1 child, Wendy Miriam Kural. BA, MA, Stanford U., 1952; MA, PhD, Princeton U., 1958; MA (hon.), Harvard U., 1966; PhD (hon.), Bosporus U., Istanbul, Turkey, 1986. Asst. prof. Turkish history Harvard U., Cambridge, Mass., 1960-65, assoc. prof. Turkish history, 1965-68; prof. Turkish and Judeo-Turkish history UCLA, 1968—; vis. prof. U. Bosporus, 1990-91. Author: Between Old and New, 1971, History of the Ottoman Empire and Modern Turkey, 2 vols., 1976-77, Turkey and The Holocaust, 1992, The Jews of the Ottoman Empire and the Turkish Republic, 1992; editor-in-chief Jour. Mid. East Studies, 1967-80; contbr. articles to profl. jours. Recipient Medal of Honor, Am. Friends of Turkey, 1992, Medal of Honor, Rsch. Ctr. on Islamic History, Art and Culture, Istanbul, 1990, Guggenheim fellowship, 1966-67, NEH fellow, 1972-73, 78-80. Fellow Inst. Turkish Studies (sr.); mem. AAUP, Am. Hist. Soc., Turkish Hist. Soc. Jewish. Office: UCLA Dept History 405 Hilgard Ave Los Angeles CA 90024-1301

SHAW, WILLIAM VAUGHAN, architect; b. Los Angeles, Apr. 12, 1924; s. Norman Tooker and Elizabeth Allison (Kennedy) S.; m. Mary Morse, Sept. 14, 1967; stepchildren: Susan Osborne, Charles D. Osborne, Polly Osborne, Ellen Osborne. BA in Architecture, U. Calif. at Berkeley, 1950. Practice architecture Carmel, Calif., 1951-55; partner Walter Burde, Burde Shaw & Assos., Carmel, 1955-69; founder, prin. Will Shaw & Assos., Monterey, Calif., 1969—; trustee Monterey Bay Aquarium. (Recipient Calif. Gov.'s award in environmental design for Shell Ser. Sta., Carmel 1964, Urban Renewal Design Award Progressive Architecture mag. 1973). Pres. Calif. 7th Agr. Dist., 1964-65; founder, pres. Monterey County Citizens Planning Assn., 1960-65; chmn. design adv. com. Monterey County, 1960-65; exec. dir. Found. Environmental Design, 1963-69; chmn. exec. com. Monterey Found., 1965-67, pres., 1972-73; bd. dirs. Pebble Beach Corp., 1976—; pres., founding mem. Big Sur Found., 1977—. Served to lt. USNR, 1944-47, PTO. Fellow Am. Acad. in Rome, 1968. Fellow AIA (pres. Monterey chpt. 1964, AIA Honor award for Merchant Built houses 1968). Clubs: Old Capital (Monterey), Pacific Biol. Lab. (Monterey). Office: 225A Cannery Row Monterey CA 93940-1436

SHAW-COHEN, LORI EVE, magazine editor; b. Manhattan, N.Y., Apr. 22, 1959; d. Ray and Carole (Bergenthal) Shaw; m. Robert Mark Cohen, Sept. 20, 1981; children: Joshua Samuel, Drew Taylor, Logan Shaw. BA in Journalism, U. So. Calif., 1981. Editorial asst., writer BBW: Big Beautiful Woman Mag., Los Angeles, 1979-80; editorial asst., writer Intro Mag., Los Angeles, 1980-81; mng. editor 'Teen Mag., Los Angeles, 1981-86; writer, interviewer Stan Rosenfeld & Assocs. Pub. Relations, Los Angeles, 1980-81; cons. BBW: Big Beautiful Woman Mag., Los Angeles, 1981—, Media Research Group, Los Angeles, 1984; condr. seminars Women in Communication, Los Angeles, 1983, Pacific N.W. Writers Conf., Seattle, 1984. Patentee children's toy, 1971; lyricist for songs, 1977—; contbr. articles and poems to profl. jours. and mags. Office: BBW: Big Beautiful Woman Mag 19528 Ventura Blvd # 298 Tarzana CA 91356-2917

SHAY, ROSHANI CARI, political science educator; b. Milw., Oct. 5, 1942; d. Walter John and Dorothee May (Dahnke) O'Donnell; 1 child, Mark Sather. Student, Willamette U., 1960-63; BA, U. Oreg., 1968, MA, 1971, PhD, 1974. Adminstrv. asst. Dept. of Youth Svcs., Lubbock, Tex., 1963; teaching asst., instr. U. Oreg., Eugene, 1969-72; vis. asst. prof. Oreg. State U., Corvallis, 1973-74, Willamette U., Salem, Oreg., 1973-79, Lewis and Clark Coll., Portland, Oreg., 1976, 78; from asst. prof. to prof. Western Oreg. State Coll., Monmouth, 1979—, chair history, polit. sci., pub. adminstrn. dept., 1991-94; chair social sci. divsn., 1994—. Author: (with others) The People of Rajneeshpuram, 1990, Annual Yearbook on the Sociology of Religion, 1995, (simulation) European Unity Project, 1982. Cofounder, v.p., sec.-treas. Ind. Opportunities Unltd., Salem, 1986—; cofounder, sec. Inst. for Justice and Human Rights, San Francisco, 1988-94; bd. dirs. Oreg. UN Assn., Portland, 1982—, Salem UN Assn., 1982-91; v.p., pres., bd. dirs. Garten Found. for Disabled, Salem, 1989—; pres. Assn. Oreg. Faculties, 1989-91; mem. adv. bd. Connections Program for Disabled Deaf, Salem, 1989—; pres., bd. dirs. Model UN of the Far West, San Diego, 1981-84, 86-88, 95-96; mem. Oreg. Women's Polit. Caucus. Danforth Found. fellow, 1968-74; named Woman of Achievement YWCA Tribute, Salem, 1990. Mem. Am. Fedn. Tchrs. (v.p., legis. oficer local 2278 1982-88), Western Polit. Sci. Assn., Communal Studies Assn., Mental Health Assn. Oreg., Oreg. Acad. Sci., Oreg. Internat. Coun., Phi Kappa Phi (hon.), Oreg. Rehab. Assn. (Bd. Mem. of Yr. 1995). Democrat. Home: 348 S Main St Falls City OR 97344-9763 Office: Western Oreg State Coll 345 Monmouth Ave N Monmouth OR 97361-1314

SHCOLNIK, ROBERT MILTON, insurance company executive; b. South Bend, Ind., Aug. 21, 1938; s. Harry and Esther (Baim) S.; m. Linda K. Egleberry, Aug. 10, 1972; children: Scott, Keith, Carin. BS in Bus., Ariz. State U., 1960; student, Am. Savings & Loan Inst., 1961; diploma in ins., Hartford Ins. Group Ins. Group, 1965. Loan officer, branch mgr., asst. to the pres. Home Savings & Loan Assn., 1959-61; pres. Harris/Shcolnik & Assocs., Inc., Phoenix, 1961—; ptnr. Harris/Shcolnik Properties; v.p., bd. dirs. My Florist, Inc., 1970—; guest lectr. in ins. Phoenix Coll.; speaker Ind. Ins. Agts. Am. Contbr. articles to profl. jours.; designer interface minicomputer concept. Mem. nat. presidents circle Ctrl. Mutual Ins. Co., intercircle, 1975, 76, 94, Ariz. Jonathan Trumbull Coun., Hartford Ins., 1979-80, Nat. Product Devel. Com. Hartford Inst., 1993-94, Nat. Great Am. Ins. Agts. Adv. Coun., 1979-81, chmn., 1979, Pacer (agts. coun., chmn. regional comml. lines, nat. coun. lines com. 1990-93), CNA group, agts. coun. Cigna Inst.; mem. Key Club, Continetnatl Assurance Co., 1970-75; past pres. Am. Savs. and Loan Inst., Ariz.; bd. dirs. Jewish Cmty. Ctr., 1980-86, v.p., exec. com., 1983-85; mem. combined ops. coun. Jewish Ctrs. Greater Phoenix, 1987-88; mem. Mayro's Task Force on Graffiti, 1993-95. Named Outstanding Agt. of Yr. Maricopa County Assn. Independent Ins. Agts., 1973, 76-78; recipient Jewish Community Ctr. Disting. Svc. award, 1981, 83, 85. Mem. Ind. Ins. Agts. Ariz. (pres. 1985), Phoenix Cmty. Alliance (bd. dirs., exec. com. 1992-95). Republican. Jewish. Office: Harris Shcolnik & Assocs 4808 N Central Ave Phoenix AZ 85012-1714

SHEA, B(ARBARA) CHRISTINE, communications educator, consultant; b. Washington, Nov. 28, 1961; d. Edward Vincent and Micheline Marie (Simplicio) S. BA summa cum laude, Towson State U., 1983; MA, Ohio U., 1985; PhD, U. Calif., Santa Barbara, 1995. Teaching assoc. Ohio U., Athens, 1983-84; instr. Clarion U. Pa., 1985; lectr. Calif. Poly. State U., San Luis Obispo, 1985—; cons. for corp. non-profit and ednl. orgns., 1984—, presenter in field. Assoc. editor Cross-Exam. Debate Yearbook, 1986-92; contbr. articles to scholarly jours., chpts. to books and procs. Regents fellow U. Calif., 1994-95. Mem. AAUP, Internat. Comm. Assn., Internat. Soc. for Study Argumentation, Orgn. for Study Comm., Lang. and Gender, Speech Comm. Assn., Western States Comm. Assn., Acad. Mgmt., Nat. Coun. for Rsch. on Women, Phi Kappa Phi. Office: Calif Poly Speech Comm Dept San Luis Obispo CA 93407

SHEAFFER, RICHARD ALLEN, electrical engineer; b. Bronxville, N.Y., May 30, 1950; s. Harold Aumond and Carol Lois (Henry) Sweet; children: Alan Michael Sheaffer, Russell Logan Sheaffer, Neil Andrew Sheaffer. BSEE, Pa. State U., 1972; MSEE, U. So. Calif., 1975. Registered profl. engr., Calif., Fla. Elec. engr. So. Calif. Edison Co., Rosemead, 1973-79, 80-90, Harris Controls div., Melbourne, Fla., 1979-80; cons. to elec. utility industry, 1990-91; sr. engr. San Diego Gas & Electric, 1991—; project leader nomogram study for Pacific and S.W. transfer subcom. Western Systems Coordinating Coun., 1988, 91. Author: 1984 West-of-the-River Operating Study, 1985, December 22, 1982 Disturbance Study, 1983. Mem. IEEE (Power Engring. Soc., Engring. Mgmt. Soc.), Phi Eta Sigma. Episcopalian.

SHEARER, CAROLYN JUANITA, secondary education educator; b. Heber Springs, Ark., May 20, 1944; d. James A. and Juanita Ruth (Wallace) S. BS, U. Colo., Boulder, 1966, MA, 1972. Cert. tchr., Colo. Tchr. Aurora (Colo.) Pub. Schs., reading resource tchr.; presenter writing process workshops. Author curriculum materials. Mem. PTA. Mem. NEA, ASCD, Colo. Edn. Assn., Aurora Edn. Assn. (bd. dirs., bargaining support team), Internat. Reading Assn., Colo. Reading Assn., Aurora Reading Assn. Pi Lambda Theta (v.p. Denver Metro chpt.). Democrat. Methodist. Office: West Mid Sch 10100 E 13th Ave Aurora CO 80010-3302

SHEARING, MIRIAM, justice; b. Waverly, N.Y., Feb. 24, 1935. BA, Cornell U., 1956; JD, Boston Coll., 1964. Bar: Calif. 1965, Nev. 1969. Justice of peace Las Vegas Justice Ct., 1977-81; judge Nev. Dist. Ct., 1983-92, chief judge, 1986; justice Nevada Supreme Ct., Carson City, 1993—. Mem. ABA, Am. Judicature Soc., Nev. Judges Assn. (sec. 1978), Nev. Dist. Ct. Judges Assn. (sec. 1984-85, pres. 1986-87), State Bar Nev., State Bar Calif., Clark County Bar Assn. Democrat.

SHEARING, STEVEN PAUL, ophthalmic surgeon; b. N.Y.C., Aug. 12, 1934; m. Miriam E. Shearing; children: Robert, Laura, Leslie. BA, Cornell U., 1956; MD, Boston U., 1964. Diplomate Am. Bd. Ophthalmology. Intern Long Beach Meml. Hosp., 1965; resident in ophthalmology U. Calif., San Francisco, 1965-68; med. dir. Shearing Eye Inst., Las Vegas, Nev., 1968—; Fulbright scholar Free U., Berlin, 1956-57; lectr. Am. Soc. Cataract and Refractive Surgery conv., Boston, 1994; lectr. and participant in confs. and demonstrated numerous surgeries worldwide. Past mem. editl. bd. Jour. Am. Soc. of Cataract Refractive Surgery, Internat. Jour. Cataract Surgery; mem. editl. bd. Ocular Surgery News; contbr. articles to profl. jours. Recipient Disting. House Staff Alumnus award Long Beach Meml. Hosp. Med. Ctr., 1970-80, Disting. Alumnus award Boston U. Sch. Medicine, 1987; named Phako Pioneer, Ho. of Reps., Congress, 1987; inducted into Nev. Inventors Hall of Fame, 1989; Steven P. Shearing chair of ophthalmology established U. Calif., San Francisco, 1993. Mem. Las Vegas Ophthalmol. Soc. (past pres.), Am. Soc. Cataract Refractive Surgery (Innovator's award 1986). Office: Shearing Eye Inst and Surgery Ctr 2575 Lindell Rd Las Vegas NV 89102

SHECHTER, ISHAIAHU, biochemistry researcher, educator; b. Tel Aviv, July 29, 1940; came to U.S., 1964; s. Israel and Judith (Levine) S.; m. Bracha Freiman; children: Toby-Yael, Donna-Ruth, Jonathan-Roy. BS in Biochemistry, Hebrew U., Jerusalem, 1964; PhD in Biochemistry, UCLA, 1969; postgrad., Harvard U., 1969-72. Postdoctoral fellow Harvard U., Cambridge, Mass., 1969-72; from lectr. to prof. Tel Aviv U., 1972-91; VIP scientist UCLA Sch. Medicine, L.A., 1979-80; vis. scientist Dupont Rsch. Inst., Wilmington, Del., 1985-86; vis. prof. Sandoz Rsch. Inst., East Hanover, N.J., 1988-89; sr. vis. scientist Gladston Inst.-U. Calif., San Francisco, 1989-90; sr. fellow Eleanor Roosevelt Inst., Denver, 1991—; adj. prof. biochemistry U. Colo., Denver, 1992—; cons. Sandoz Pharms., East Hanover, 1989-92. Postdoctoral fellow NIH, 1969-72; rsch. grantee NIH, 1972-93. Office: Eleanor Roosevelt Inst 1899 Gaylord St Denver CO 80206-1210

SHEDENHELM, WILLIAM REX CHARLES, writer; b. L.A., Mar. 18, 1924; s. Charles Walter and Jeanne DeEarl (Williamson) S.; m. Geri Fleming, 1959 (div. 1960); m. Shirley Joan Sayers, July 30, 1965; 1 child, Richard Scott. AA, L.A. City Coll., 1948; BS, Columbia U., 1952; MA, Calif. State U., Dominquez Hills, 1985. Seismic chief computor Western Geophys. Co., 1954-55; petroleum geologist Tex. Petroleum, Venezuela, 1956-58; mng. editor Trailer Life Mag., L.A., 1959, MotoRacing, L.A., 1959-61, Sports Car Graphic Mag., L.A., 1961-68; sr. editor Rock & Gem Mag., Ventura, Calif., 1970-93; geology tchr. Elderhostel, Ventura, Calif., 1990-93. Author ten books on auto repair, backpacking, rockhounding, stained glass work, travel. With U.S. Army, 1943-46, ETO, S.W. PTO. Mem. NRA, E Clampus Vitus. Office: 5260 Elmhurst St Ventura CA 93003-3938

SHEEHAN, LAWRENCE JAMES, lawyer; b. San Francisco, July 23, 1932. AB, Stanford U., 1957, LLB, 1959. Bar: Calif. 1960. Law clk. to chief judge U.S. Ct. Appeals 2d Cir., N.Y.C., 1959-60; assoc. O'Melveny & Myers, L.A., 1960-68, ptnr., 1969-94, of counsel, 1995—; bd. dirs. Van Kamper, Am. Capital Mut. Funds, FPA Mut. Funds, TCW Convertible Securities Fund Inc., Source Capital, Inc. Mem. ABA, Los Angeles County Bar Assn., Calif. Bar Assn., Order of Coif. Office: O'Melveny & Myers 1999 Avenue Of The Stars Los Angeles CA 90067-6022 also: O'Melveny & Myers 400 S Hope St Los Angeles CA 90071-2801

SHEEHAN, MICHAEL JARBOE, archbishop; b. Wichita, Kans., July 9, 1939; s. John Edward and Mildred (Jarboe) S. MST, Gregorian U., Rome, 1965; D of Canon Law, Lateran U., Rome, 1971. Ordained priest Roman Cath. Ch., 1964. Asst. gen. sec. Nat. Coun. Cath. Bishops, Washington, 1971-76; rector Holy Trinity Sem., Dallas, 1976-82; pastor Immaculate Conception Ch., Grand Prairie, Tex., 1982-83; bishop Diocese of Lubbock, Tex., 1983-93; archbishop Archdiocese of Santa Fe, Albuquerqe, N.Mex., 1993—; past chmn. Am. Bd. Cath. Missions, 1989-91; trustee Cath. Relief Svcs., 1992—. Contbr. articles to New Cath. Ency. Trustee St. Mary Hosp., Lubbock, 1983-89; bd. dirs. Tex. Conf. of Chs. Mem. Serra Club (chaplain 1983-93). Office: Archdiocese of Santa Fe 4000 Saint Josephs Pl NW Albuquerque NM 87120-1714*

SHEEM, SANG KEUN, fiber optics engineering professional; b. Seoul, Korea, Mar. 20, 1944; s. Eung-Taek and Ki-Jik (Oh) S.; m. Susan Kim, Mar. 22, 1970; children: Edward J., Shana J. MS in Engring., U. Calif., 1973, PhD in Engring., 1975. Rsch. physicist U.S. Naval Rsch. Lab., Washington, 1976-81; mgr. Rockwell Internat., Dallas, 1981-86; mgr. sensor program Lawrence Livermore (Calif.) Nat. Lab., 1986—; mem. corp. optical panel Rockwell Internat., Dallas, 1982-86; cons. Kaptron Fiber Optic Co., Palo Alto, Calif., 1987-88, Amaco Rsch. Ctr., Naperville, Ill., 1986-87; pres. Berkeley Optics Co., Livermore, 1994—. Contbr. articles, referee to profl. jours. Mem. IEEE, Optical Soc. Am., Korean Scientist and Engr. Assn. (pres. No. Calif. chpt. 1990-91), Internat. Platform Assn. Office: Lawrence Livermore Nat Lab 7000 East Ave L-407 Livermore CA 94550

SHEEN, PORTIA YUNN-LING, retired physician; b. Republic of China, Jan. 13, 1919; came to U.S., 1988; d. Y. C. and A. Y. (Chow) Sheen; m. Kuo, 1944 (dec. 1970); children: William, Ida, Alexander, David, Mimi. MD, Nat. Med. Coll. Shanghai, 1943. Intern, then resident Cen. Hosp., Chungking, Szechuan, China, 1943; with Hong Kong Govt. Med. and Health Dept., 1948-76; med. supt. Kowloon (Hong Kong) Hosp., 1948-63, Queen Elizabeth Hosp., Kowloon, 1963-73, Med. and Health Hdqrs. and Health Ctr., Kowloon, 1973-76, Yan Chai Hosp., New Territories, Hong Kong, 1976-87. Fellow Hong Kong Coll. Gen. Practitioners; mem. AAAS, British Med. Assn., Hong Kong Med. Assn., Hong Kong Pediatric Soc., N.Y. Acad. Sci. Methodist. Home: 1315 Walnut St Berkeley CA 94709-1408

SHEERAN, ANGELA MAUREEN, information specialist; b. Laredo, Tex., Apr. 3, 1961; d. Patrick Ritter and Elizabeth (Hornburg) S. BJ, U. Tex., 1983. Reporter, assignments editor The Daily Tex. U. Tex., Austin, 1983; reporter El Campo (Tex.) Leader-News, 1984, The South Jetty Newspaper, Port Aransas, Tex., 1984-85; adminstrv. asst. to city mgr. City of Port Aransas, 1985-86; devel. dir., dep. dir. Com. to Aid Abused Women, Sparks, Nev., 1988-94; information specialist Nat. Coun. Juvenile and Family Ct. Judges, Reno, 1994—; vol. grant writer Nev. AIDS Found. Recipient 1st place award Gulf Coast Press Assn., 1984, 3d place award, 1984; recipient scholarship Leadership Reno, Class of 1992. Mem. Nat. Soc. Fund Raising Execs. (chair Philanthropy Day 1993, v.p. Sierra chpt. 1994), Nev. Network Against Domestic Violence. Home: 632 Marsh Ave Reno NV 89509-1419 Office: Nat Coun Juvenile and Family Ct Judges Reno NV 89509

SHEERAN, MICHAEL JOHN LEO, priest, college administrator; b. N.Y.C., Jan. 24, 1940; s. Leo John and Glenna Marie (Wright) S. AB, St. Louis U., 1963, PhL, 1964, AM in Polit. Sci., 1967, AM in Theology, 1971, STL, 1971; PhD, Princeton U., 1977. Joined Soc. Jesus, 1957; ordained priest Roman Catholic Ch., 1970. Exec. editor Catholic Mind, N.Y.C., 1971-72; assoc. editor Am. mag., N.Y.C., 1971-72; assoc. chaplain Aquinas Inst., Princeton, N.J., 1972-75; asst. dean Regis Coll., Denver, 1975-77, dean of Coll., 1977-82, v.p. acad. affairs, 1982-92, acting pres., 1987-88, pres., 1993—; retreat dir., cons. on governance for religious communities, 1970—. Author: Beyond Majority Rule, 1984. Contbr. articles and editorials to publs. Trustee Rockhurst Coll., Kansas City, Mo., 1982-91, Creighton U., Omaha, 1985-95, U. San Francisco, 1985-94, Loyola U., New Orleans, 1994—, Rocky Mountain Coll. of Art and Design, 1994—; active Mile High United Way, 1995—. Ford Found. scholar, 1963. Democrat. Home: 3333 Regis Blvd Denver CO 80221-1099 Office: Regis U 3333 Regis Blvd Denver CO 80221-1099

SHEFI, ELLEN LESLIE, acupuncturist, nutritionist; b. Lorain, Ohio, Mar. 9, 1954; d. Albert Freedman and Sally Ann Bernes; divorced; 1 child, Liora. BS in Human Nutrition, U. Mich., 1976; postgrad., Nat. Coll. Naturopathic Med., 1985-88, East-West Coll. Massage, 1987; MA in Oriental Medicine, Oreg. Coll. Oriental Medicine, 1989. Registered dietitian, Israel; cert. iridology, Calif., cert. advanced iridology and clin. nutrition, Calif.; lic. massage technician, Oreg., 1987, lic. acupuncturist, Oreg., 1989; diplomate in acupuncture Nat. Commn. Certification of Acupuncturists. Dietetic intern Tel HaShomer Med. Ctr., Tel Aviv, 1976-77; head dietitian Afula HaEmek Hosp., Afula, Israel, 1978-79; pub. lectr. on nutrition Israel, 1978-85; instr. dietetics and nutrition Ohel Sara C.C., Israel, 1981-82, Sherman Nursing Sch., Afula HaEmek Hosp., Israel, 1981-82; apprentice in naturopathic medicine Dr. Zeev Pechtholt, Tel Aviv, 1982-83; herbalist for natural herbal tincture bus. Eclectic Inst., Portland, Oreg., 1986-87; massage therapist Family Natural Health Ctr., Portland, 1987-89; pvt. practice specializing in acupuncture Multnomah Acupuncture Clinic, Portland, 1989-90; acupuncturist Hooper Detoxification Ctr., Portland, 1989-90; acupuncturist and pvt. practice Portland Addictions Acupuncture Ctr., 1990-92; owner pvt. acupuncture Sylvan Acupuncture Ctr., Portland, 1991—; nutrition contbr. Interactive Body/Mind Info. Sys. computer program, 1992; cons. nutritionist Moshav Moledet, Kibbutz Merhavia, Kibbutz Ein Harod Ihud and Me'Uhad, others, Israel, 1981-85; planner nutrition program for pre-sch. and elem. edn. Ministry of Health, Dept. Health Edn., Jerusalem, 1984; cons. nutritionist Parent Child Svcs., HeadStart Program, Portland, 1987-93; guest lectr. Oreg. Coll. Oriental Medicine, Portland, 1989-93; acupuncture dir. court ordered diversion program for alcohol and drug treatment InAct, 1992-94; guest speaker acupuncture and AIDS Nat. Acupuncture Detoxification Assn. Nat. Conf., 1992, acupuncture for drug addiction treatment in Multnomah County prison and jail Alcohol and Drug Problems Assn. 5th Nat. Conf. on Women's Issues, 1991. Mem. Am. Assn. Acupuncture and Oriental Medicine, Nat. Acupuncture Detoxification Assn., Oreg. Acupuncture Assn. Office: Sylvan Acupuncture Ctr # 207 2041 SW 58th Ave Ste 207 Portland OR 97221-1333

SHEH, ROBERT BARDHYL, environmental management company executive; b. N.Y.C., July 29, 1939; s. Talat and Nedime (Karali) S.; m. Mary Cheney Fleming, Dec. 29, 1961; children—Andrea K., Jonathan C., Robert R., Elisabeth F., Theresa N. BS in Civil Engring, Rennselaer Poly. Inst., 1960; grad. program for Mgmt. Devel., Harvard U., 1974. With The Ralph M. Parsons Co., 1971—; sr. v.p., mgr. petroleum, chem., mining and metall. div. The Ralph M. Parsons Co., Pasadena, Calif., 1981-88, pres., 1989-92, also bd. dirs.; pres., CEO Internat. Tech. Corp., Torrance, Calif., 1992—; mem. adv. bd. Sch. Chem. Engr. U. Calif., Berkeley, 1986—; bd. dirs. Davidson Assocs. Bd. regents Marymount Internat. Sch., London, 1979; bd. trustees Harvey Mudd Coll., 1992—. With USNR, 1960-64. Mem. Calif. Club (L.A.), Annandale Golf Club (Pasadena), L.A. Country Club. Office: Internat Tech Corp 23456 Hawthorne Blvd Torrance CA 90505-4716

SHEIDLEY, WILLIAM EDWARDS, English language educator; b. Kansas City, Mo., May 29, 1940; s. Hubert O. and Betsey Josephine (Edwards) S.; m. Harlow W. Sheidley, June 19, 1962; children: Jennifer L., Nathaniel J. AB, Stanford U., 1962, AM, 1966, PhD, 1968. Asst. prof. English U. Conn., Storrs, 1966-72, assoc. prof. English, 1972-81, prof. English, 1981-93; asst. prof. English U.S. Air Force Acad., Colo., 1993-94; assoc. prof. and chair English and fgn. langs. U. So. Colo., Pueblo, 1994-95; prof., chair English and fgn. langs. U. So. Colo., Pueblo, 1995—; dir. Conn. Writing Project, Storrs, 1982-87; cons. Bedford Books, Boston, 1982—, Prentice-Hall, Englewood Cliffs, 1983—, St. Martin's Press, N.Y., 1985—; vis. lectr. English U. So. Colo., Pueblo, 1992-93. Author: Barnabe Googe, 1981; co-editor: Children's Literature jour., 1974-77; contbr. articles to profl. jours. Mem. MLA, Nat. Coun. Tchrs. English, Marlowe Soc. Am., Spenser Soc. Democrat. Home: 4307 Meadowview Ct Colorado Springs CO 80918-4313 Office: Univ So Colo English and Fgn Langs 2200 Bonforte Blvd Pueblo CO 81001-4901

SHEKHAR, STEPHEN S., obstetrician, gynecologist; b. New Delhi, India, Jan. 13, 1944; s. S.P. Jain and Shakuntala Mithal; m. Claudette Dorita, Jan. 6, 1978; children—Sasha, Stephen. M.B., B.S., Govt. Med. Coll., Punjabi U., Patiala, 1966. Came to U.S., 1972. Intern, Columbia U. Coll. Phys. and Surgeons-Roosevelt Hosp. N.Y.C., 1972-73; surgeon, Nat. Health Service U.K., 1966-72; resident in ob-gyn St. Clare's Hosp.-Margaret Hauge Maternity Hosp., N.Y.C. and N.J., 1973-76, Columbia U., Harlem Hosp., N.Y.C., 1976-77; practice medicine specializing in ob-gyn, North Hollywood, Calif., 1977—; mem. staff Los Angeles County-U. So. Calif. Med. Sch.; assoc. prof. clin. Ob-Gyn L.A. county U. So. Calif. Sch. Medicine. Fellow Am. Coll. Ob-Gyn, ACS, Los Angeles Soc. Ob-Gyn; mem. Calif. Med. Assn., Los Angeles County Med. Assn., AMA. Jain. Office: 1510 San Pablo St # 104 Los Angeles CA 90033

SHELDON, LARRY F., physician assistant; b. Kalispell, Mont.; s. Lester Francis Sheldon and Florence Bell (Holbert) Hermanson. Degree in allied health, Everett C.C., 1982; bd. cert. primary care and surgery, U. Wash., 1992. Physician asst. cardiothoracic surgery U. Wash., Seattle, 1991—, mem. faculty dept. surgery, 1991—; teaching assoc. Medex N.W., U. Wash., Seattle, 1991—. With USN/USNR, 1973-82. Fellow Am. Acad. Physician Assts. in Cardiovascular Surgery, Am. Acad. Physician Assts.

SHELDON, MARK SCOTT, research engineer; b. Orange, Calif., May 19, 1959; s. Howard Lezurn and Vida Louise (Winegar) S.; m. Marti Reisman, Aug. 8, 1986. BS in Engring. and Applied Sci., Calif. Inst. Tech., 1981; MSME, Cornell U., 1985. Rsch. engr. Energy and Environ. Rsch. Corp., Irvine, Calif., 1985-91, sr. rsch. engr., 1991—. Mem. ASME (assoc.). Mem. Reorganized LDS Ch. Office: Energy and Environ Rsch Corp 18 Mason Irvine CA 92718-2706

SHELDON, MARTI REISMAN, software engineer; b. Miami, Fla., Sept. 28, 1961; d. Murray and Eleanor (Orton) Reisman; m. Mark Scott Sheldon, Aug. 8, 1986. BS in Computer Sci., Cornell U., 1983; MS in Computer Sci., UCLA, 1989. Sr. project engr. Hughes Aircraft Co., L.A., 1981—. Mem. IEEE, Assn. Computer Machinery, Tau Beta Pi, Alpha Phi Omega. Democrat. Jewish. Office: Hughes Aircraft Co PO Box 902 El Segundo CA 90245-0902

SHELDON, SUSAN FRANCES, data administration manager; b. Portland, Oreg., Dec. 3, 1948; d. Arthur John and Mary Frances (Blake) Tonsing; 1 child, Stephanie Koren. BS in Edn. with honors, U. Oreg., 1970; postgrad., Portland Community Coll., 1973-75, 74-76. Bus. analyst Fred Meyer Inc., Portland, 1970-76; supr. payroll services Am. Data Services, Portland, 1976-77; systems analyst Meier & Frank subs. May Co., Portland, 1977-79; systems analyst Nike Inc., Beaverton, Oreg., 1979-83, data adminstr., 1983-88; data administration manager SAIF Corp., Salem, Oreg., 1988-90, project mgr., 1991—. Group leader, sponsor Beaverton Alcoholics Anonymous programs, 1985-87; mem. Info. Tech. Commn., City of Salem, 1989-90. Mem. Data Adminstrn. Mgmt. Assn. (founder, sec. Portland chpt. 1984-86), Nat. Assn. Female Execs. Republican. Episcopalian. Home: 1846 Kamela Dr S Salem OR 97306-2244 Office: SAIF Corp 400 High St SE Salem OR 97312-0700

SHELLEDY, JAMES EDWIN, III, editor; b. Spencer, Iowa, Nov. 11, 1942; s. James E. Jr. and Patricia L. (Cornwall) S.; m. Susan Emily Thomas, Mar. 7, 1986; 1 child, Ian Whittaker. BA, Gonzaga U., 1966. Reporter Spkesman-Rev., Spokane, Wash., 1963-66; tchr., coach Kootenai High Sch., Harrison, Idaho, 1967-71; reporter AP, Boise, Idaho, 1971-72; reporter, editor Lewiston (Idaho) Morning Tribune, 1973-80; editor, pub. Idahonian, Moscow, Idaho, 1981-91, Daily News, Pullman, Wash., 1981-91; editor The Salt Lake Tribune, Salt Lake City, 1991—; juror Pulitzer Prize Com., Columbia U., 1987-88; dir. Investigative Reporters and Editors, 1978-82; bd. dirs. New Directions for News, 1989—, Newspaper Agy. Corp., 1994—; mem. AP audit com., N.Y.C., 1982-91. Dir. Idaho Parks Found., Boise, 1976-78, Idaho-Washington Symphony, Pullman, Wash., 1986-89; commr. Idaho Lottery Commn., Boise, 1990-91; adv. bd. Utah YWCA, 1992—. Roman Catholic. Office: The Salt Lake Tribune 143 S Main St Salt Lake City UT 84111-1917

SHELLHORN, RUTH PATRICIA, landscape architect; b. L.A., Sept. 21, 1909; d. Arthur Lemon and Lodema (Gould) S.; m. Harry Alexander Kueser, Nov. 21, 1940. Student dept. landscape architecture, Oreg. State Coll., 1927-30; grad. landscape architecture program, Cornell U. Coll. Architecture, 1933. Pvt. practice landscape architecture, various cities Calif., 1933—; exec. cons. landscape architect Bullocks Stores, Calif., 1945-78, Fashion Sqs. Shopping Ctrs., Calif., 1958-78, Marlborough Sch., L.A., 1968—, El Camino Coll., Torrance, Calif., 1970-78, Harvard Sch., North Hollywood, Calif., 1974-90; cons. landscape architect, site planner Disneyland, Anaheim, Calif., 1955, U. Calif., Riverside Campus, 1956-64, numerous others, also numerous gardens and estates; landscape architect Torrance (Calif.) City Goals Com., 1969-70; cons. landscape architect City of Rolling Hills (Calif.) Community Assn., 1973-93. Contbr. articles to garden and profl. publs.; subject of Oct. 1967 issue Landscape Design & Constrn. mag. Named Woman of Year, Los Angeles Times, 1955, Woman of Year, South Pasadena-San Marino (Calif.) Bus. Profl. Women, 1955; recipient Charles Goodwin Sands medal, 1930-33, Landscape Architecture award of merit Calif. State Garden Clubs, 1984, 86, Horticulturist of the Yr. award So. Calif. Hort. Inst., numerous nat., state, local awards for excellence. Fellow Am. Soc. Landscape Architects (past pres. So. Calif. chpt.), Phi Kappa Phi, Kappa Kappa Gamma (Alumni Achievement award 1960). Home and Office: 362 Camino De Las Colinas Redondo Beach CA 90277-6435

SHELTON, JOEL EDWARD, clinical psychologist; b. Havre, Mont., Feb. 7, 1928; s. John Granvil and Roselma Fahy (Ervin) S.; m. Maybelle Platzek, Dec. 17, 1949; 1 child, Sophia. AB, Chico (Calif.) State Coll., 1951; MA, Ohio State U., 1958, PhD, 1960. Psychologist Sutter County Schs., Yuba City, Calif., 1952-53; tchr., vice prin. Lassen View Sch., Los Molinos, Calif., 1953-55; tchr. S.W. Licking Schs., Pataskala, Ohio, 1955-56; child psychologist Franklin Village, Grove City, Ohio, 1957; clin. psychologist Marion (Ohio) Health Clinic, 1958; intern Children's Mental Health Ctr., Columbus, Ohio, 1958-59; acting chief research psychologist Children's Psychiat. Hosp., Columbus, 1959-60; cons. to supt. schs. Sacramento County, Calif., 1960-63; mem. faculty Sacramento State Coll., 1961-69; clin. psychologist DeWitt State Hosp., Auburn, Calif., 1965; exec. dir. Children's Ctr. Sacramento, Citrus Heights, Calif., 1963-64, Gold Bar Ranch, Garden Valley, Calif., 1964-72; clin. psychologist El Dorado County Mental Health Ctr., Placerville, Calif., 1968-70, Butte County Mental Health Dept., Oroville, Calif., 1970-94; dir. dept. consultation, edn. and community services Butte County Mental Health Ctr., Chico, 1974-85, outpatient supr., 1986-94; mgmt. cons., 1972-94; advisor to pres. Protaca Industries, Chico, 1974-80; exec. sec. Protaca Agrl. Rsch., 1974-80; small bus. cons., 1983—; cons. on coll. scholarships and funding, 1991-92, computer cons., 1994—. Mem. APA, Western Psychol. Assn. Home: 1845 Veatch St Oroville CA 95965-4787

SHELTON, PHILIP ANDERSON, criminal investigator, writer; b. Coeur d'Alene, Idaho, July 3, 1938; s. Philip Anderson and Mildred Evelyn (Wendt) S.; m. Sharon Lee Hopkins, Feb. 15, 1973 (div. Sept. 1985); 1 child, Thane Kevit. Student, Chico (Calif.) State Coll., 1957, U. Calif., Davis, 1960-62, Sacramento State U., 1973-75. Cert. criminal investigator, Calif.; lic. pvt. investigator, Calif. Fraud investigator U.S. Fidelity & Guarantee Co., Sacramento, 1960-64; owner, operator Philip A. Shalton Profl. Investigations, Sacramento, 1964-77; chief investigator Yolo County Conflict Def., Woodland, Calif., 1966-69; investigator Fed. Pub. Defender, Sacramento, 1975; chief investigator Fed. Pub. Defender, Fresno, 1977-78, Santa Barbara (Calif.) County Pub. Defender, 1978—. Author short stories and novella. Bd. dirs. Santa Barbara Mus. of Art, 1980-84; founding mem. G.A.T.E. Sch. Program, Santa Barbara, 1980-85; mem., group leader City/County Disaster Svcs., Santa Barbara, 1980-89. Recipient Honor for Bravery World Secret Svc. Orgn., 1960; grantee Calif. Cattlemen's Assn., 1956, Fed. Defender Program, Washington, 1978. Mem. World Assn. Detectives, Assn. Brit. Detectives, Coun. Internat. Investigators, Calif. Assn. Lic. Investigators (cofounder 1966, Svc. award 1969), Inst. Personal Injury Investigators (dir., cofounder 1966—), Def. Investigators Assn. Office: Santa Barbara County Pub Defender 1100 Anacapa 3d Fl Santa Barbara CA 93101

SHELTON, ROBERT CHARLES, electronics engineer; b. L.A., July 31, 1934; s. Weir Mitchell and Martalena (Scavarda); BSEE, Calif. State Poly. U., 1961; divorced; 1 son, Kevin Lyle. Ops. mgr. Halcyon, Palo Alto, Calif., 1971-74; mfg. mgr. Programmed Power, Menlo Park, Calif., 1974-78; pres. Shelton Electronics, Menlo Park, 1976—. Bd. dirs. Herbert Hoover Boys Club, Menlo Park; vol. Peninsula Meml. Blood Bank, St. Anthony Padua Dining Rm. Served with USN, 1952-56. Mem. IEEE, Profl. and Tech. Cons. Assn. Clubs: Elks (chmn. Palo Alto public relations); Rotary (bd. dirs., pres. 1981-82) (Menlo Park). Roman Catholic. Rsch. and publs. in telecommunication microwave and high energy physics, small computer systems and data communications; patentee various cryogenic and computer devices. Address: PO Box 2573 Menlo Park CA 94026-2573 Office: 1259-351 El Camino Real Menlo Park CA 94025-4227

SHELTON, ROBERT NEAL, physics educator, researcher; b. Phoenix, Oct. 5, 1948; s. Clark B. and Grace M. (McLaughlin) S.; m. Adrian Ann Millar, Aug. 30, 1969; children: Christian, Cameron, Stephanie. BS, Stanford U., 1970; MS, U. Calif., San Diego, 1973, PhD, 1975. Postdoctoral researcher U. Calif.-San Diego, La Jolla, 1975-76, asst. rsch. physicist, 1976-78; asst. prof. Iowa State U., Ames, 1978-81, assoc. prof., 1981-84, prof. physics, 1984-87; prof. physics, chmn. dept. U. Calif.-Davis, 1987-90, vice chancellor for rsch., 1990—. Contbr. over 200 articles to profl. jours. Mem. Am. Phys. Soc., Sigma Xi. Office: U Calif Dept Physics Davis CA 95616

SHELWOOD, HOWARD RAYMON, military officer; b. Bay Springs, Miss., Oct. 30, 1956; s. Howard Malaci Shelwood and Gettie Mae Moffett; m. Debra Ann Wicker, June 12, 1982. BS, Tenn. State U., 1980; MA, Webster U., 1988, Naval War Coll., 1993. Commd. 2d lt. USAF, 1980, advanced through grades to maj., 1992; officer-in-charge propulsion br. Field Maintenance Squadron, Norton AFB, Calif., 1982-83; officer-in-charg flight line br. Orgn. Maintenance Squadron, Norton AFB, Calif., 1982-84; officer-in-charge Field Maintenance Squadron, McChord AFB, Wash., 1984-85, asst. maintenance supr., 1985, maintenance supr., 1985-86; chief C-17 system maintenance sect. HQ Mil. Airlift Command, Scott AFB, Ill., 1986-89, chief C-17 logistics sect., 1989-91; dep. comdr. maintenance Air Rescue Squadron, Osan AB, South Korea, 1991-92; comdr. 602d Aircraft Generation Squadron, Travis AFB, Calif., 1994—. Mem. Air Force Assn., Airlift/Tanker Assn., Maintenance Officer Assn., Tudkegee Airmen Inc., Presidio Yacht Club. Home: 862 Christine Dr Vacaville CA 95687-4642 Office: 602d Aircraft Generation Sq 180 Goodall St Travis AFB CA 94535-2901

SHEMER, MARTHA EVVARD, investment company executive; b. Ames, Iowa, Apr. 19, 1919; d. John Marcus and Martha (Cooper) Evvard; m. Jack Corvin Shemer, June 24, 1937 (dec. 1967); children: Jack Evvard, William Barry Pioneer of properties, Phoenix, Scottsdale, Ariz., LaJolla, Calif. and Del Mar, Calif., 1941-75; pres. Shemer Enterprises, Phoenix, 1975-83, Shemer Investment Co., Phoenix, 1975—. History columnist Paradise Valley Ind. newspaper, 1987. Benefactor Shemer Art Ctr. and Mus. to City of Phoenix, 1984. Martha Evvard Shemer Day proclaimed by City of Phoenix, 1994; recipient Quill and Scroll nat. contest award, 1936. Republican. Avocations: helping humanity, writing, travel, inventing, needlepoint.

SHEN, GENE GIIN-YUAN, organic chemist; b. Taipei, Taiwan, Apr. 12, 1957; came to U.S., 1981; s. Chi and Su-Chin Shen; m. Grace Hsiao-Fen Shen, July 31, 1982; 1 child, Jennifer Iting. BS in Chemistry, Nat. Taiwan U., 1979; PhD in Organic Chemistry, U. Calif., Riverside, 1986. Postdoctoral fellow U. Calif., Riverside, 1986-87; rsch. chemist Nucleic Acid Rsch. Inst. ICN, Costa Mesa, Calif., 1987-88; prin. investigator Pharm-Eco Labs., Inc., Simi Valley, Calif., 1988-91; prin. scientist Beckman Instruments, Inc., Brea, Calif., 1991—. Contbr. articles to Jour. Am. Chem. Soc., Jour. Steroid Biochemistry and Molecular Biology, Tetrahetron Letters, Nucleosides and Nucleotides, others. Mem. Am. Chem. Soc., Phi Beta Kappa. Office: Beckman Instruments Inc 200 S Kraemer Blvd Brea CA 92621-6208

SHEN, HSIEH WEN, civil engineer, consultant, educator; b. Peking, China, July 13, 1931; s. Tsung Lien and Bick Men (Jeme) S.; m. Clare Tseng, Oct. 20, 1956; children: Eveline, Anthony. BS, U. Mich., 1953, MS, 1954; PhD, U. Calif.-Berkeley, 1961. Hydraulic engr. Harza Engring. Co., Chgo., 1961-63; mem. faculty Colo. State U., Ft. Collins, 1964-86; prof. civil engring. U. Calif., Berkeley, 1986—; cons. World Bank, UN, Harza, Stone & Webster, U.S. Army C.E. Author, editor: River Mechanics 1971; Sedimentation, 1973; Modeling of Rivers, 1979. Recipient Horton award Am. Geophys. Union, 1976, Joan Hodges Queneau award Am. Assn. Engring. Socs. and Nat. Audubon Soc., 1992; Guggenheim Found. fellow, 1974. Mem. U.S. Nat. Acad. Engring., Internat. Assn. Hydraulic Research (pres. fluvial hydraulics 1984-86), ASCE (Freeman scholar 1966, chmn. probability approach 1983-84, Einstein award 1990). Office: U Calif 412 Obrien Hall Berkeley CA 94720-1703

SHEN, JIANPING, acoustical engineer; b. Huzhou, Zhejiang, China, Feb. 25, 1945; came to U.S., 1980; s. Shaotian and Sujin (Chen) S.; m. Yiyun Zheng, Feb. 1, 1976; children: Feimo, Yijing. BS, Nanjing U., China, 1968; MS, UCLA, 1982, PhD, 1990. Machinist/technician Hongsheng Equip. Factory, Ji-an, China, 1968-73, translator, 1974-76; instr. Huzhou Sr. H.S., 1976-80; teaching assoc. UCLA, 1981-85, postgrad. rschr., 1986-90, postdoctoral fellow, 1991—; mech. design cons. A.J. Rassey Engring., L.A., 1992; tech. equip. analyst PMS Sys. Corp., Santa Monica, Calif., 1993-95; engring. cons. Hersh Acoustical Engring., Westlake Village, Calif., 1994-95. Translator (book): Electroacoustics, 1975. Vice pres. Chinese Students and Scholars Assn., L.A., 1990-91. Mem. Am. Phys. Soc., Acoustical Soc. Am. Home: 2027 Beloit Ave Los Angeles CA 90025-6217

SHEN, MASON MING-SUN, medical center administrator; b. Shanghai, Jiang Su, China, Mar. 30, 1945; came to U.S., 1969; s. John Kaung-Hao and Mai-Chu (Sun) S.; m. Nancy Hsia-Hsian Shieh, Aug. 7, 1976; children: Teresa Tao-Yee, Darren Tao-Ru. BS in Chemistry, Taiwan Normal U., 1963-67; MS in Chemistry, S.D. State U., 1971; PhD in Biochemistry, Cornell U., 1977; MS in Chinese Medicine, China Acad., Taipei, Taiwan, 1982; OMD, San Francisco Coll Acupuncture, 1984; AMD (hon.), Asian Am. Acupuncture Coll., San Diego, Calif., 1985; MD (Medicina Alternativa), Internat. U., Colombo, Sri Lanka, 1988, MD, 1988. Diplomate Nat. Commn. for Cert. of Accupuncturists; lic. acupuncturist. Rsch. assoc. Lawrence Livermore (Calif.) Lab., 1979-80; assoc. prof. Nat. Def. Med. Coll., Taipei, 1980-82; prof. Inst. of Chinese Medicine China Acad., Taipei, 1981-82, San Francisco Coll. Acupuncture, 1983-85; chief acupuncturist Acupuncture Ctr. of Livermore, Calif., 1982-93; prof. Acad. Chinese Culture & Health Scis., Oakland, Calif., 1985-86; chief acupuncturist Acupuncture Ctr. of Danville, Calif., 1985-89; dir. Pain & Stress Mgmt. Ctr., Danville, Calif., 1989-90; adminstr. Ea. Med. Ctr., Pleasanton, Calif.; chmn. adminstrn. subcom., 1991-92, acupuncture com. State of Calif., 1988-92. Contbr. articles to profl. jours. Rep. Rep. Party, Danville, 1988-93; bd. dirs. Asian Rep. Assembly, 1989—. 2d lt. Rep. of China Army, 1966-69. Recipient Nat. Rsch. Svc. award NIH, 1977. Mem. AAAOM, N.Y. Acad. Sci., Calif. Cert. Acupuncturists Assn. (bd. dirs. 1984-88, pres. 1984-85), Acupuncture Assn. Am. (bd. dirs. 1986-90, v.p. 1987-89), Am. Assn. Acupuncture and Oriental Medicine (bd. dirs. 1987-92, pres. 1989-90), Nat. Acupuncture Detoxification Assn. (cons. 1987—), Presdl. Round Table (presdl. adv. com.), Hong Kong and Kowloon Chinese Med. Assn. (hon. life pres. 1985). Republican. Home: 3240 Touriga Dr Pleasanton CA 94566-6966 Office: Eastern Med Ctr 3510 Old Santa Rita Rd Ste D Pleasanton CA 94588-3466

SHEN, NELSON MU-CHING, fiber optics communications scientist; b. Taiwan, Sept. 2, 1946; came to U.S., 1971; s. Mao-Chang and Ching (Chang)

S.; m. Jane Chu; children: Helen Diana, Basil Francis. BS in Physics, Chung Yuan Christian U., Taiwan, 1969; MS in Physics, North Western State U., La., 1972; PhD in Physics, U. Tex., Dallas, 1977. Rsch. assoc. U. So. Calif., L.A., 1977-79; chief scientist, dir. techs. Kaptron corp., Palo Alto, Calif., 1979-81; sr. engr. GTE Corp., Mountain View, Calif., 1981-82; sr. scientist Raychem Corp., Menlo Park, Calif., 1982—. Patentee in fiber optics; contbr. papers to profl. publs. Chmn. bd. trustee, Canaan Ch., Mountain View, 1986—. Mem. Optical Soc. Am., Internat. Soc. for Optical Engring. Home: 4131 Old Trace Rd Palo Alto CA 94306-3728 Office: Raychem Corp 300 Constitution Dr Menlo Park CA 94025-1140

SHEN, YUEN-RON, physics educator; b. Shanghai, China, Mar. 25, 1935; came to U.S., 1956; BS, Nat. Taiwan U., 1956; MS, Stanford U., 1959; PhD, Harvard U., 1963. Rsch. asst. Hewlett-Packard Co., Palo Alto, Calif., 1959; rsch. fellow Harvard U., Cambridge, Mass., 1963-64; asst. prof. U. Calif., Berkeley, 1964-67, assoc. prof., 1967-70, full prof., 1970—; prin. investigator Lawrence Berkeley Lab., 1964—. Author: The Principles of Nonlinear Optics, 1984. Sloan fellow, 1966-68; recipient Guggenheim Found. fellowship, 1972-73, Charles Hard Townes award, 1986, Arthur L. Schawlow prize Am. Phys. Soc., 1992, Alexander von Humboldt award, 1984, Outstanding Rsch. award DOE-MRS Rsch., 1983, Sustained Outstanding Rsch. award, 1987. Fellow Am. Phys. Soc. (disting. traveling lectr. Laser Sci. Topical Group 1994—), Optical Soc. Am., Photonics Soc. Chinese-Ams.; mem. AAAS, NAS, Academia Sinica. Office: U Calif Berkeley Dept Physics Berkeley CA 94720

SHENG, TSE CHENG (TED C. SHENG), natural resources educator; b. Chia-Hsing, China, Oct. 16, 1924; came to U.S. 1984; s. Tsu Ming and Chen Hwa (Sze) S.; m. Chuan Shen, June 1, 1947; children: Tom Sze-Tsan, Richard Van. BSc, Nat. Chekiang U., 1947; MSc, Colo. State U., 1966. Soil conservation specialist Chinese-Am. Joint Commn. on Rural Reconstruction, Taipei, Republic of China, 1953-68; expert advisor Food and Agrl. Orgn. of UN, Rome, 1968-84; prof. watershed mgmt. Colo. State U., Ft. Collins, 1985—; internat. cons. UN Devel. Programme, N.Y.C., 1987—; cons. Computer Assisted Devel. Inc., Ft. Collins, 1988—. Author: Watershed Conservation I & II, 1986-90, Soil Conservation for Small Farmers in the Humid Tropics, 1989, Watershed Survey and Planning, 1990; editor: Conservation Policies for Sustainable Hillslope Farming, 1992. Recipient award Crown Zellerbach Found., 1965, Hugh Hammond Bennett award, 1991. Mem. Soil and Water Conservation Soc. (life, vice chair internat. affairs com. 1994-95), World Assn. Soil and Water Conservation, Chinese Soil and Water Conservation Soc. (bd. dirs. 1966-68). Home: 636 S Shields St Fort Collins CO 80521 Office: Dept of Earth Resources Colo State Univ Fort Collins CO 80523

SHENG, Y. SHERRY, zoological park administrator; b. Taipei, Taiwan, Nov. 14, 1950; came to U.S., 1973; BS in Zoology, Nat. Taiwan U., 1973; MS in Fisheries Biology, U. Wash., 1977. Fisheries biologist Alaska Dept. Fish and Game, Juneau, 1976-77; tour guide Seattle Aquarium, 1977, aquarium naturalist, 1977-80, acting curator of programs, 1980-81, curator of programs, 1981-85, dir., 1985-88; dir. Met. Wash. Park Zoo, Portland, Oreg., 1988—; adj. prof. Seattle Pacific U., 1978-81. Bd. dirs. Portland Vis. Assn., 1990—, Oreg. State Bd. Forestry, 1990—. Nat. Forest Found., 1992—, mem. exec. com., 1992—; mem. adminstrv. rev. com. Oreg. State Bd. Higher Edn., 1992-93; mem. Gov.-Elect Transit Team, 1994-95. Recipient Women of Achievement award Oreg. Commn. for Women, 1990, Excellence in Mgmt. award Seattle Mgmt. Assn., 1987; Wilbert McLeod Chapman scholar U. Wash., 1976. Fellow Am. Leadership Forum (sr.); mem. Am. Zoo and Aquarium Assn. (profl.), Internat. Union Dirs. Zool. Gardens, Rotary Club Portland (bd. dirs.). Office: Metro Wash Park Zoo 4001 SW Canyon Rd Portland OR 97221-2705

SHENK, HOWARD FRED, association executive; b. Greenville, S.C., Feb. 14, 1939; s. Donald Hugh and Ruth Aletha (Swartz) S. BSBA, U. Ala., 1961. Gen. mgr. H & R Block Co., Honolulu, 1967-71; v.p. ops. E. K. Fernandez Shows, Honolulu, 1971-75; pres. Micrographics Ltd., Honolulu, 1975-78; pres. Colo. Indsl. Communications, Denver, 1978-83; exec. dir. Arabian Horse Owners Found., 1983—; dir. So. Ariz. Internat. Livestock Assn., The World Crabbet Trust; devel. and spl. events cons. Nat. Western Stock Show and Rodeo, So. Ariz. Internat. Livestock Assn., 1984—; dir. Fred Graham Communications Ltd., Frank C. Howard Holdings Ltd., Micrographics Ltd. Chmn. Hawaii State Fair, 1970; chmn. Equine Studies Adv. Com. Pima C.C. Pres. Tucson Children's Mus., 1995. Served with USAF, 1962-67. Mem. Kings Alley Mchts. Assn. (pres. 1976-78), SAR, Internat. Assn. Amusement Parks and Attractions, Outdoor Amusement Bus. Assn., Internat. Arabian Horse Assn., Therapeutic Riding Tucson (pres.), Tucson Childrens Mus. (dir.), Am. Horse Shows Assn., Royal Hawaiian Showmen. Republican. Presbyterian. Office: 4101 N Bear Canyon Rd Tucson AZ 85749

SHENKAR, ODED, human resources management educator; b. Jerusalem, Israel, Dec. 16, 1951; came to the U.S., 1977; s. Joshua and Bluma (Karklinsky) S.; m. Miriam Stessel, July 23, 1980; children: Keshet S. Shenkar, Joshua Shenkar. BA, Hebrew U., Jerusalem, 1976, MS in Sociology, 1978; M.Phil., Columbia U., 1979, PhD, 1981. Prof. Tel-Aviv U., Israel, 1982—; prof. U. Hawaii, Honolulu, 1988—; mem. adv. bd. China Rev. Internat., Honolulu, editl. bd. Organization Studies, Cambridge, U.K., Mgmt. Internat. Rev., Hohenheim, Germany, Jour. Internat. Bus. Studies, London, Ont., Can. Editor: Global Perspectives on Human Resources, 1994, Management in China 1979-90, 1991; co-editor: International Business in China, 1993. Lt. Israel Def. Forces, 1970-72. Arthur Andersen fellow Judge Inst. of Mgmt. U. Cambridge, Eng., 1995; vis. examiner Chinese U. of Hong Kong, 1994. Office: U Hawaii at Manoa CBA 2404 Maile Way Honolulu HI 96822-2223

SHEP, ROBERT LEE, editor, publisher, textile book researcher; b. Los Angeles, Feb. 27, 1933; s. Milton and Ruth (Miller) Polen S. B.A., U. Calif.-Berkeley, 1955; student Royal Acad. Dramatic Art, London, 1956; B.Fgn. Trade, Am. Inst. Fgn. Trade, 1960. Asst. area mgr. fgn. dept. Max Factor, Hollywood, Calif., 1960-65; editor, pub. The Textile Booklist, Lopez Island, Wash., 1980-84; free-lance writer, book reviewer, library appraiser, book repairer. Author: Cleaning and Repairing Books, 1980, Cleaning and Care for Books, 1983, Bhutan - Fibre Forum, 1984, Civil War Gentleman, 1994; co-author: (annotated edit.) The Costume or Annals of Fashion, 1986, Dress and Cloak Cutter: Womens Costume 1877-1882, 1987; editor: The Handbook of Practical Cutting, 2d rev. edit., 1986; pub. Ladies' Guide to Needle Work, 1986, Edwardian Ladies' Tailoring, 1990. Art of Cutting and History of English Costume, 1987; editor, pub. Tailoring of the Belle Epoque, 1991, Late Georgian Costume, 1991, Civil War Cooking, 1992, Art in Dress, 1993, Minister's Complete Guide to Practical Cutting, 1993, Freaks of Fashion, 1993; pub. Civil War Era Etiquette, 1988, Ladies Self Instr., 1988; mem. editorial rev. bd. The Cutter's Rsch. Jour. Bd. dirs AIDS Care and Edn. Svcs., Pacific Textiles. Mem. Costume Soc. (London), Costume Soc. Am. (bd. dirs. 1985-87), Costume Soc. Ont., Mendocino County HIV Consortium (mem. steering com.), Australian Costume and Textile Soc., U.S. Inst. Theatre Tech. Home: PO Box 668 Mendocino CA 95460-0668

SHEPARD, EARL ALDEN, retired government official; b. Aurora, Ill., Sept. 30, 1932; s. Ralph George and Marcia Louise (Phelps) S.; m. Carolyn Mae Borman, Sept. 1, 1959; 1 son, Ralph Lyle. AS in Bus. Adminstrn. magna cum laude, Southea. U., 1967, BSBA magna cum laude, 1969; MBA, U. Chgo., 1974. Chief program budget divsn. U.S. Army Munitions Command., Joliet, Ill., 1971-73; comptr., dir. adminstrn. U.S. Navy Pub. Works Ctr., Gt. Lakes, Ill., 1973-77; dep. comptr. U.S. Army Electronics Command/U.S. Army Communications Electronics Materiel Readiness Command, Ft. Monmouth, N.J., 1977-79; dir. resource mgmt., comptr., dir. programs U.S. Army, White Sands Missile Range, N.Mex., 1979-92; bd. dirs. 1st Nat. Bank of Dona Ana County, 1987—; mem. adv. com. Rio Grande Bancshares/First Nat. Bank of Dona Ana County, 1983-84; founding mem. White Sands Missile Range Hist. Found., 1992—. Mem. bd. govs. Southea. U. Ednl. Found., 1969-71; founding mem. White Sands Millile Range Hist. Found., 1992—; chmn. fin. com. No. Va. Assn. for Children with Learning Disabilities, 1966-67, treas., 1968-70; pres. West Long Branch (N.J.) Sports Assn., 1979. Fed. and local govt. employee scholar, 1967, Ammunition Procurement Supply Agy. fellow, 1974. Republican. Home: 2712 Topley Ave Las Cruces NM 88005-1334

SHEPARD, KENNETH SIHLER, physician, surgeon; b. Des Moines, Iowa, Oct. 21, 1922; s. Kenneth Eglin and Dorothy Marie (Sihler) S.; m. Helen Reis (dec. Oct. 1982); children: Ann, Helen, Kenneth, Mary, David; m. Colleen Gay Braker, Dec. 24, 1982; children: Christopher, Kevin. AB, BS, Duke U., 1943, MD, 1947. Diplomate Am. Bd. Pediatrics; ordained to ministry Episcopal Ch. as deacon, 1982. Intern St. Francis Hosp., Evanston, Ill.; resident in contagious disease Willard Parket Hosp., N.Y.C.; resident in pediatrics Duke U. Sch. Medicine, Durham, N.C.; resident in pathology Boston Children's Hosp.; fellow in psychosomatic pediatrics Duke U. Sch. Medicine, Durham; fellow in perinatology U. Vt., Burlington; commd. 2d lt. U.S. Army Air Corps, 1943, advanced through grades to col., 1950; flight surgeon, cons. in pediat. to USAF surgeon gen., 1965-77; chief dep. warden Calif. Med. Facility, Vacaville, Calif., 1987-92, med. dir. Calif. Med. Ctr., 1987-92; clin. dir. Calif. Youth Authority, 1993—; deacon Epiphany Episcopal Ch., Vacaville, Calif., 1982—. Contbr. numerous articles to profl. jours.; presenter in field. Fellow Royal Acad. Health, Royal Acad. Pediatrics; mem. AMA, Assn. Am. Med. Authors, World Congress Pediatrics, Internat. Pediatric Soc., Aerospace Med. Soc., Am. Acad. Pediatrics, Soc. Air Force Physicians, Soc. Air Force Physicians, Aerospace Med. Assn., Soc. for Adolescent Medicine, Ill. Med. Soc., Chgo. Med. Soc., Cook County Med. Soc., Howland Pediatric Soc., Chgo. Pediatric Soc., Colston Soc. Med. Rsch. (Eng.), Univ. Club Evanston, Tex. Pediatric Soc., Lions, numerous others. Home: 124 Viewmont Ln Vacaville CA 95688 Office: CSP Sacramento PO Box 29 Represa CA 95671-7129

SHEPARD, ROBERT CARLTON, English language educator; b. Akron, Ohio, Dec. 20, 1933; s. Robert and Mildred Lucille (Stewart) S.; m. Marjorie Alma Mackey, June 9, 1956; children: Robert Lincoln, Donald Ward. BA, U. Oreg., 1970, MA, 1971; postgrad., England, 1979, 1991. Prof. English Southwestern Oreg. C.C., Coos Bay, 1971-94, chair divsn. English, 1976-78, prof. emeritus, 1994—; liaison Oreg. Com. for Humanities, 1985-86; judge statewide writing contests Nat. Coun. Tchrs. English, Urbana, Ill., 1987-88; founder Willamette Valley Vineyards, Turner, Oreg., 1991; co-founder Willamette Valley Brewing Co., Portland, 1993, Breweries Across Am., Portland, 1994. Author, photographer, producer: (multi-image show) Christmas Fiestas of Oaxaca (Mexico), 1985; developer ednl. software, 1993—. With USMCR, 1954-58. Grad. Teaching fellow U. Oreg., 1970-71. Democrat. Home: 3280 Sheridan Ave North Bend OR 97459-3043

SHEPARD, WILLIAM WAYNE, editor; b. Danville, Ill., Oct. 7, 1926; s. Carl Wayne and Mildred Leota (Ellingwood) S.; m. H. Joanne North, Nov. 1946; children: Gregory W., Mark W., Sue K. Portugal, Melinda A. Waltermire. BS, U. Ill., 1950. Advt. staff The Coloradoan, Fort Collins, 1950-52; co-pub. Espanola (N.Mex.) Valley News, 1952-53; advt. staff Sacramento Union, 1953-54; advt. staff, reporter Daily Dem., Woodland, Calif., 1954-63; info. specialist U. Calif., Davis, 1963-69; editor Rajo Publs., Mill Valley, Calif., 1969-80; editor Calif. Horse Rev. Paint Horse Jour., Sacramento and Ft. Worth, 1980-91; exec. dir., newsletter editor Livestock Publs. Coun., Eureka, Calif., 1991—. Author: (booklet) Root and Crown Diseases of Deciduous Fruit and Nut Trees, 1968; co-author: (booklet) News Photography for Extension Workers, 1966. Cpl. U.S. Army, 1945-46, PTO. Mem. Outdoor Writers Assn. Am., Outdoor Writers Assn. Calif. Democrat. Home and Office: 2631 Garland St Eureka CA 95501-3574

SHEPERSKY, MIMI, probate examiner; b. Portland, Oreg., Oct. 12, 1964; d. Sigman Roe and June Kim; m. Douglas M. Shepersky; children: Matthew Aaron, Katherine Ann, Grace Lee. Grad. high sch., Rancho Palos Verdes, Calif.; cert. legal asst. with honors, U. San Diego, 1989. Paralegal, office mgr. Law Offices Thomas Kagy, L.A., 1983, Law Office Tong S. Suhr, L.A., 1983-84; head litigation sect., paralegal def. litigation Wells Fargo Bank, N.A., L.A., 1984-85; paralegal bankruptcy and fed. litigation Pachulski, Stang & Ziehl, P.C., L.A., 1985-88; paralegal, office mgr. Law Offices Donald H. Glaser, San Diego, 1989—; paralegal probate, computer cons. Village Law Ctr., San Marcos, 1990-91; paralegal, probate, trust adminstrn. Law Offices Arthur S. Brown, Carlsbad, Calif., 1992-93, Higgs, Fletcher & Mack, San Diego, 1993-94. Editor newsletter Noteworthy, 1984-85. Sec.-elect Korean Am. Coalition, L.A., 1983-84; counselor Korean Am. Youth Found., 1974-82. Mem. San Diego Assn. Legal Assts., Nat. Notary Assn. (founding co-chair North County com.). Republican. Presbyterian. Home: 1503 Sundale Rd El Cajon CA 92019 Office: Superior Ct County San Diego 201 W Broadway San Diego CA 92101

SHEPHERD, KAREN, former congresswoman, legislative staff member; b. Silver City, N.Mex., July 5, 1940; m. Vincent P. Shepherd. BA, U. Utah, 1962, MA, Brigham Young U., 1963. Former instr. Brigham Young U., Am. U., Cairo; former pres. Webster Pub. Co.; former adminstr. David Eccles Sch. Bus., U. Utah; former dir. Salt Lake County Social Svcs., Utah; former dir. continuing edn. Westminster Coll.; former mem. Utah Senate; mem. 103d Congress from 2d Utah dist., Washington, 1993-95, Nat. Common Cause Governing Bd., Washington, 1995—; founding mem. Utah Women's Polit. Caucus, Project 2000. Former mem. Untied Way, Pvt. Industry Coun.; former mem. adv. bd. U.S. West Sch. Social Work; trustee Westminster Coll., co-chair. Recipient Women in Bus. award U.S. Small Bus. Assn., Woman of Achievement award, Pathfinder award, 1st place award Nat. Assn. Journalists. Fellow Inst. Politics Kennedy Sch Govt.; Salt Lake Area C. of C. (pub. rels. com.). Home: 1261 2nd Ave Salt Lake City UT 84103-4342 Office: US Ho Reps 414 Cannon Bldg Washington DC 20515-0003

SHEPHERD, THOMAS IRVIN, mining specialist, electrical engineer; b. Riverton, Wyo., Feb. 11, 1953; s. Marion Thomas and Berethe Patricia (Bergstrom) S.; m. Carol Ann Fuoss, Aug. 12, 1978; children: Sara Elaine, Andrew Thomas. BSEE, U. Wyo., 1976. With elec. maintenance dept. AMAX Coal Co./Belle Ayr Mine, Gillette, Wyo., 1976-79, AMAX Coal Co./Eagle Butte Mine, Gillette, 1979-80; elec. engr. scales dept. We. div. AMAX Coal Co., Gillette, 1980-89, dryer supr., 1989-93, supr. engring. syss., 1993-94, maintenance supr., 1994—. Co-inventor electronic coupled-in-motion railroad track scale. Sponsor Luth. Youth Fellowship, Gillette, 1977; den leader Boy Scouts Am., Gillette, 1990-92, asst. scout master, 1992—; coach Little League Baseball, Gillette, 1990-92. Mem. IEEE, Indsl. Computing Soc., Luth. Layman's League, Instrument Soc. Am. Republican. Home: 1217 Shipwheel Ln Gillette WY 82716-4828 Office: AMAX Coal Co Belle Ayr Mine PO Box 3005 Gillette WY 82717-3005

SHEPHERD, WILLIAM C., pharmaceutical company executive; b. 1939. With Allergan Inc., Irvine, Calif., 1964—, pres., chief oper. officer, 1984—, pres., CEO, 1992—, bd. dirs. Office: Allergan Inc PO Box 19534 2525 Dupont Dr Irvine CA 92715-1531*

SHEPP, ALAN, artist, educator; b. Cleve., 1935. BA, Bowling Green State U., 1957; BFA, Cleve. Inst. Art, 1958; MFA, U. Wash., 1963. Instr. U. London Goldsmiths Coll., 1964-66, Mpls. Coll. Art, 1966-70, U. Victoria, B.C., Can., 1970, Calif. State U., Hayward, 1971—. One-man shows include Mpls. Inst. Art, 1967, 70, Neill Gallery, N.Y.C., 1978, 79, Stephen Wirtz Gallery, San Francisco, 1982, 85, 90, 92, Monterey (Calif.) Peninsula Mus. Art, 1991; group shows include Mpls. Inst. Art, 1967, Contemporary Mus. Art, Chgo., 1970, Mus. Modern Art, Tel Aviv, 1971, San Francisco Mus. Modern Art, 1978, Palm Springs Desert Mus., 1986, Richmond (Calif.) Art Ctr., 1990; represented in permanent collections Seattle Art Mus., Cleve. Mus. Art, Walker Art Ctr., Mpls., others. Address: 49 Geary St San Francisco CA 94108-5705

SHEPPARD, JACK W., retired air force officer; b. Parkersburg, W.Va., Aug. 8, 1931; s. James Lee and Audrey Irene (Heiney) S.; m. Norma Ann Stutler, Sept. 4, 1953; children—Bradley, Gregory. B.A.C., U. Akron, Ohio, 1955; M.A. in Pub. Adminstrn., George Washington U., 1965. Commd. lt. U.S. Air Force, 1955, advanced through grades to maj. gen.; vice comdr. 60 Mil. Airlift Wing, USAF, Travis AFB, Calif., 1977-79; comdr. 1606 Air Base Wing, USAF, Kirtland AFB, N.Mex., 1979-81; dir. internat. staff Inter Am. Def. Bd., USAF, Washington, 1981-82; dep. chief staff for personnel USAF Mil. Airlift Command, Scott AFB, Ill., 1982-83, chief of staff, 1983-85; comdr. Twenty First Air Force, McGuire AFB, N.J., 1985-87; asst. dep. chief staff programs and resources Hdqrs. USAF, Washington, 1987-88, ret., 1988. Mem. Order of Daedalians, Air Force Assn., Airlift Assn., Theta Chi. Presbyterian. Home: PO Box 908 21 Beaver Ln Cedar Crest NM 87008-9433

SHERBURN, EARL FRANKLIN, community arts director, tour consultant; b. Van Wert, Ohio, May 28, 1943; s. Carl Edwin and Esther Edith (Rager) S. MusB, U. Mich., 1965, MusM, 1970; D in Mus. Arts, U. So. Calif., 1984. Pvt. instr. music Van Wert City Schs., summers 1962-64; dir. music Virginia City (Mont.) Players, summer 1965, Burroughs High Sch., Ridgecrest, Calif., 1965-69; dir. vocal music Bakersfield Jr. Coll., Ridgecrest, 1967-69; teaching asst. U. Mich., Ann Arbor, 1969-70; dir. instrumental music Palmdale (Calif.) High Sch., 1970-86; teaching asst. U. So. Calif., L.A., 1977-78; dir. art ctr. Dept. Cultural Affairs, L.A., 1986-90; dir. community arts, 1990—; cons. Tours of L.A. Area, Glendale, Calif., 1986—; v.p. Glendale Regional Arts Coun., 1990-92. Arranger various jazz ensemble compositions. Prin. percussionist Antelope Valley Symphony Orch., Lancaster, Calif., 1970-86; city councilman City of Palmdale, 1978-86; mem. arts com. Calif. Contract Cities Assn., El Monte, 1978-86; founding chair Antelope Valley Found., Palmdale, 1984-86; asst. dir. Founders Cathedral Choir, L.A., 1986-90; mem. L.A. County Mus. Art, Mus. Contemporary Art, Natural History Mus. Mem. U. So. Calif. Alumni Assn., U. Mich. Alumni Club (L.A. chpt.), Phi Delta Kappa, Pi Kappa Lambda, Kappa Kappa Psi. Democrat. Mem. Ch. Religious Sci. Office: Dept Cultural Affairs 433 S Spring St Fl 10 Los Angeles CA 90013-2048

SHERIDAN, GEORGE EDWARD, manufacturing company executive; b. Emporia, Kans., July 4, 1915; s. George and Josephine Frances (Benson) S.; m. Edith Joye Card, July 4, 1940; 1 dau., Phyllis Lynne. Liberal arts student Coll. of Emporia, 1934-36; engring. student Nat. Schs., 1936-37, Los Angeles City Jr. Coll., 1937-38. Cert. mfg. engr.; registered profl. engr., Calif. With Douglas Aircraft, Santa Monica, Calif., 1939-40, Northrop Aircraft, Hawthorn, Calif., 1940-45; pres. Sheridan Products, Inc., Inglewood, Calif., 1940-87; ret., 1987. Active, YMCA, Inglewood, 1960—. Mem. Soc. Mfg. Engrs. (life, award 1979-80, Industrialist of Yr. 1982 past chmn.), U.S. Power Squadron, Am. Ordnance Def. Preparedness Assn., Nat. Rifle Assn., Smithsonian Assos., Cutting Tool Mfg. Assn., Nat. Fedn. Ind. Bus., Mech. Bank Collectors Am., Antique Toy Collectors Am. Republican. Quaker. Patentee double edge scraper. Home: 27692 Via Rodrigo Mission Viejo CA 92692-2019

SHERIDAN, JOHN BRIAN, librarian; b. N.Y.C., Aug. 20, 1947; s. John Bernard and Margaret Ann (Hefferon) S.; m. Dindy Reich, Aug. 20, 1972; children: Molly, Jonah, Liz Mary. BA in Classics, CCNY, 1970; AM in Classical Studies, Ind. U., 1972; MLS, U. Wis., Milw., 1973. Cataloguer, acquisitions librarian Kearney (Nebr.) State Coll., 1973-75; head tech. services Knox Coll., Galesburg, Ill., 1975-77; head librarian Transylvania U., Lexington, Ky., 1977-84, The Colo. Coll., Colorado Springs, 1984—; chmn. Colo. Council of Acad. Librarians, 1987-88. Contbr. articles to profl. jours. Commr. Environ. Improvement Commn., Lexington, 1978-81; coach Colorado Springs Youth Soccer and Basketball Assn., 1984-92; bd. dirs. North End Homeowners Assn., Colorado Springs, 1985-90, pres., 1988-90; adv. com. Lulac Nat. Ednl. Svcs. Ctr., 1991—; mem. Balbas Bandeleros Riding Club. Fellow U. Wis., Milw., 1972; recipient Ward medal in Latin, CCNY, 1970; Regents scholar, CCNY, 1965-69. Mem. ALA (councilor 1987-91, sec. social responsibilities roundtable 1984-85, chmn. 1985-86), Colo. Libr. Assn. (pres. Coll. and Univ. divsn. 1992-94), Rothman Rooters Club. Democrat. Home: 1731 N Nevada Ave Colorado Springs CO 80907-7456 Office: Colo Coll Charles Leaming Tutt Libr 1021 N Cascade Ave Colorado Springs CO 80903-3252

SHERMAN, ALAN ROBERT, psychologist, educator; b. N.Y.C., Nov. 18, 1942; s. David R. and Goldie (Wax) S.; m. Llana Helene Tobias, Aug. 14, 1966 (div. 1989); children: Jonathan Colbert, Relissa Anne. BA, Columbia U., 1964; MS, Yale U., 1966, PhD, 1969. Lic. psychologist, Calif. Faculty psychology U. Calif., Santa Barbara, 1969—; clin. psychologist in pvt. practice Santa Barbara, 1981—; cons. in field. Author: Behavior Modification, 1973; contbr. articles to profl. jours. and chpts. in books. Pres. Santa Barbara Mental Health Assn., 1978, 84-85, 91, Mountain View Sch. Site Coun., Santa Barbara, 1978-84. NIMH predoctoral rsch. fellow, 1964-69; recipient vol. of yr. award Santa Barbara Mental Health Assn., 1979, tchg. excellence awards Delta Delta Delta, Alpha Chi Omega, Gamma Phi Beta, Santa Barbara; grantee in field. Fellow Behavior Therapy and Rsch. Soc.; mem. APA, AAUP (chpt. pres. 1978-79), Calif. Psychol. Assn., Assn. for Advancement of Behavior Therapy, Santa Barbara County Psychol. Assn. (pres. 1985), Phi Beta Kappa (chpt. pres. 1977-78), Sigma Xi, Psi Chi (chpt. faculty advisor, 1979—). Office: Univ of Calif Dept Psychology Santa Barbara CA 93106-9660

SHERMAN, DONALD H., civil engineer; b. Jackson, Wyo., May 14, 1932; s. Howard M. and Dorothy (Turner) S.; children: D. John, Cynthia Lynn Pierceall, Richard L., Sheila L. Bufmack; m. Patricia A. Hoffman, June 26, 1993. AA in Engring., Fullerton Jr. Coll., 1953; diploma in surveying and mapping, I.C.S., 1955; BS in Geology, U. Wyo., 1960, BS in Civil Engring., 1968. Registered profl. engr., Wyo., Colo. Geophysicist Texaco Geophysical, Casper, Wyo. and Billings, Mont., 1960-63; surveyor Wyo. Hwy. Dept., Jackson, 1963-64; engring. geologist Wyo. Hwy. Dept., Cheyenne, 1964-66, hydraulics engr., 1968-72; civil engr., rotation trainee U.S. Bur. Reclamation, Denver, 1972-73; civil engr. D.M.J.M.-Phillips-Reister-Haley, Denver, 1973-79, Stearns Roger, Inc., Glendale, Colo., 1980-82, Centennial Engring., Arvada, Colo., 1983-85; civil engr. land devel. York Assocs., Denver, 1986-87; civil engr. City of Colo. Springs, 1987—; owner Valley View Trailer Park, Jackson, 1965-95; advisor to U.S. Sen. Clifford Hansen on Black 14 incident, 1969. Recipient Presdl. Legion of Merit Rep. Nat. Com., 1992-95, Presdl. Commn., Rep. Nat. Com., 1992-95, Cert. of Award Presdl. Adv. Commn., 1991-92, 94. Mem. Citizens Against Govt. Waste (charter), Concerned Women of Am., Nat. Right to Life, Nat. Republican Congressional Com., Nat.Republican Senatorial Com. Republican. Home: 131 N Roosevelt St Colorado Springs CO 80909-6547 Office: City Engring 30 S Nevada Ave Rm 403 Cab Colorado Springs CO 80903-1825

SHERMAN, ERIC, director, writer, educator; b. Santa Monica, Calif., June 29, 1947; s. Vincent and Hedda (Comorau) S.; m. Eugenia Blackiston Dillard, Apr. 1, 1978; children: Cosimo, Rocky. BA cum laude, Yale U., 1968. Film producer, dir., writer, photographer and editor; films include: Charles Lloyd-Journey Within, 1968; Paul Weiss-a Philosopher in Process, 1972; Waltz, 1980; Inside Out, 1982; Measure of America, 1983; Michael Reagan's Assault on Great Lakes, 1983, Futures, 1990 (Peabody Broadcast award 1990); represented in film festivals N.Y.C. Cine Golden Eagle, Melbourne, Australia, Bilbao, Spain, others; books include: (with others) The Director's Event, 1970; Directing the Film, 1976; Frame by Frame, 1987, Selling Your Film, 1990; pres. Film Transform; film tchr. Art Ctr. Coll. Design, Pepperdine U., UCLA; guest lectr. Yale, Calif. Inst. Tech., U. So. Calif.; Andrew Mellon lectr. on arts Calif. Inst. Tech., 1977; chief cons. (motion picture industry) Gallup Orgn.; contbr. numerous articles to film publs. and distbn. catalogues, book dedication; works include three oral histories for Am. Film Inst. under Louis B. Mayer Found. grant. Trustee Am. Cinematheque; bd. dir. Film Forum. Mem. Soc. Motion Picture and TV Engrs. (asso.), Assn. Ind. Video and Filmmakers, Univ. Film Assn., Assn. Visual Communicators, Nat. Alliance Media Arts Ctrs. Home and Office: 2427 Park Oak Dr Los Angeles CA 90068-2539

SHERMAN, FREDERICK HOOD, lawyer; b. Deming, N.Mex., Aug. 9, 1947; s. Benjamin and Helen (Hood) S.; m. Janie Carol Jontz, Oct. 23, 1973; children: Jerah Elizabeth, Frederick Jakub. BBA, Southern Meth. U., 1970, JD, 1972. Bar: Tex. 1972, N.Mex. 1973, U.S. Dist. Ct. N.Mex. 1973, U.S. Dist. Ct. (we. dist.) Tex. 1974, U.S. Supreme Ct. 1979; cert. mediator; bd. cert. civil trial advocate Nat. Bd. Trial Advocacy. Assoc. Sherman & Sherman, Deming, 1973-74, ptnr., 1974-78; prin. Sherman & Sherman P.C., Deming, 1978—; assoc. prof. Western N.Mex. U., Silver City, 1975-77; mem. specialization com. N.Mex. Supreme Ct., 1986—; mem. jud. selection com. State Bar N.Mex., 1985-88, legal retreat com. 1986-88, co-chair, 1986-87, alternative dispute resolution com., 1980-91; owner Rio Mimbres Wine. Contbr. articles to profl. jours. Chmn. Luna County Planning Commn., Deming, 1976-78; apptd. visitor to U. N.Mex. Law Sch., 1983—; treas. Luna County Econ. Devel. PSS, 1987-88, also bd. dirs.; mem. bd. visitors U. N.Mex. Law Sch., 1983—; bd. dirs. Luna County Hosp., 1991-94; bd. mem. Deming Pub. Sch., 1991—, pres., 1991—; liaison Workers Compensation Bd. Supreme Ct., 1991-93; chmn. bd. dirs. Luna County Charitable Found., 1991—; hon. dir. Deming Art Coun. Named cert. civil trial advocate Nat. Bd. Trial Advocacy. Mem. N.Mex. Bar Assn., State Bar N.Mex. (coomr.

1978-86, com. on alt. dispute resolutions practice 1980-90, jud. selection com. 1985, com. for legal retreat 1989-89), Tex. Bar Assn., 6th Jud. Bar Assn., Assn. Trial Lawyers Am. (notably large award 1983, 84, 85), N.Mex. Trial Lawyers Assn. (bd. dirs. 1986—, sec. 1989), Am. Inns of Ct. (master atty. 1995). Democrat. Roman Catholic. Office: Sherman & Sherman PC PO Box 850 Deming NM 88031-0850

SHERMAN, KATHLEEN A., public relations executive; b. LeMars, Iowa, July 19, 1947; d. James Herbert and Virginia Lister (Irwin) S. Student, Loyola Marymount U., Calif. State U., Northridge, UCLA. Head pub. rels. William O'Neil & Co., L.A., 1970-84, also bd. dirs.; head of pub. rels./ promotions Investor's Bus. Daily Show, L.A., 1984—; owner The Gift Boutique, Marina Del Rey, Calif.; bd. dirs. Data Analysis, Marina Del Rey. Assoc. prodr.: (TV show) Investor's Business Daily Show, 1984-88, (video) Investor's Business Daily Story; editor, contbr.: How to Make Money in Stocks, 1984. Vol. Save a Heart Fedn., L.A., 1990; fundraiser Steve Saltzman Campaign, Santa Monica, Calif., 1988. Republican. Methodist. Office: Investor's Bus Daily 12655 Beatrice St Los Angeles CA 90066-7300

SHERMAN, LETITIA REID, dietitian; b. L.A., Aug. 23, 1938; d. Jack Tawney and Letitia (Lytle) Reid; m. George C. Sherman, Aug. 2, 1974 (div. Aug. 1992); children: Jane P., Frank W., Letitia Kelly Hill, Robert Emmett Kelly. BS, U. Calif., Davis, 1960; MEd, Phillip U., 1970. Registered dietitian Am. Dietetics Assn.; cert. culinary educator Am. Culinary Fedn. Tchr. Albuquerque Tech. Vocat. Inst.; dietitian lobbyist N.Mex. Dietetics Assn.; edn. cons. Zanios Foods, Albuquerque; dietitian cons. Montabello, Albuquerque, El Centro Villa, Albuquerque, Manorcare, Albuquerque; educator Albuquerque Cultural Arts Ctr.; educator Santa Fe (N.Mex.) Chefs Assn., Taos (N.Mex.) Chefs Assn., Las Cruces (N.Mex.) Chefs Assn. Am. Culinary Fedn. scholar, 1989, Sch. Am. Chefs scholar, 1989. Mem. Albuquerque C. of C. Home and Office: 9317 Guadalupe Trl NW Alameda NM 87114-1719

SHERMAN, LINDA ARLENE, immunologist; b. N.Y.C., Feb. 27, 1950; d. Theodore and Helen (Tannenbaum) S.; m. Norman R. Klinman, June 18, 1978; children: Theodore, Matthew. BA, Barnard Coll., 1971; PhD, MIT, 1976. Postdoctoral fellow Albert Einstein Coll. Medicine, Bronx, 1976-77, Harvard Med. Sch., Boston, 1977-78; asst. mem. Scripps Clinic and Rsch. Found., La Jolla, Calif., 1978-85, assoc. mem., 1985—; adv. rev. panel NSF, Washington, 1985-89, Am. Cancer Soc., 1991-92; sci. adv. bd. Synbiotics, San Diego, 1988-90; mem. immunobiology study sect. NIH, 1992—. Section editor Jour. of Immunology, Bethesda, Md., 1990-94; contbr. articles to profl. jours. Rsch. grantee, Nat. Inst. on Aging, 1990—, NCI, 1989—, 1990—. Mem. Am. Assn. Immunologists. Home: 7766 Hillside Dr La Jolla CA 92037-3944 Office: Scripps Rsch Inst 10666 N Torrey Pines Rd La Jolla CA 92037-1027

SHERMAN, RANDOLPH, plastic and reconstructive surgeon, educator; b. St. Louis, May 27, 1951; s. Leon and Pearl (Lichtenfeld) S.; m. Sandra Lee Wackerman, May 3, 1992; 1 child, Max Lassen. BA, U. Rochester, 1973; MD, U. Mo., 1977. Intern in gen. medicine U. Wis., Madison, 1978; intern in surgery U. Calif., San Francisco, 1978-79, resident in surgery, 1979-81; resident in surgery SUNY, Syracuse, 1981-83; fellow in plastic and reconstructive surgery UCLA, 1983-85; asst. prof. plastic and orthopedic surgery U. So. Calif. Sch. Medicine, L.A., 1985-90, assoc. prof. plastic, orthopedic and neurol. surgery, 1990-95, chmn. divsn. plastic and reconstructive surgery, 1994—. Editor: Orthopedic Clinics, 1993; contbr. articles to profl. jours. Founder L.A. chpt. Operation Smile Internat., 1993—; med. dir. Op. Second Chance, L.A., 1994-95. Recipient L.A. Humanitarian award Calif. Hosp., 1994. Fellow ACS, Am. Assn. Plastic Surgeons, Am. Assn. Hand Surgeons (bd. dirs. 1991-95), Am. Soc. Hand Surgery, Am. Soc. Reconstructive Microsurgery, Calif. Soc. Plastic Surgery. Office: U So Calif Divsn Plastic Surgery 1450 San Pablo St Los Angeles CA 90033-4680

SHERMAN, ROBERT B(ERNARD), composer, lyricist, screenwriter; b. N.Y.C., Dec. 19, 1925; s. Al and Rosa (Dancis) S.; student UCLA, 1943; BA, Bard Coll., 1949; MusD (hon.) Lincoln U., 1990; m. Joyce Ruth Sasner, Sept. 27, 1953; children: Laurie Shane, Jeffrey Craig, Andrea Tracy, Robert Jason. Popular songwriter, 1950-60, including Tall Paul, Pineapple Princess, You're Sixteen (Gold Record); songwriter Walt Disney Prodns., Beverly Hills, Calif., 1960-68, for 29 films including The Parent Trap, 1961, Summer Magic, 1963, Mary Poppins, 1964, That Darn Cat, 1965, Winnie The Pooh, 1965, Jungle Book, 1967, Bedknobs and Broomsticks, 1971; co-composer song It's A Small World, theme of Disneyland and Walt Disney World, Fla.; composer, lyricist United Artists, Beverly Hills, 1969—, songs for film Chitty, Chitty, Bang, Bang, 1969, Snoopy, Come Home!, 1972; song score Charlotte's Web, 1972; composer for Walt Disney's Wonderful World of Color, TV, 1961—; co-producer NBC-TV spl. Goldilocks, 1970; v.p. Musi-Classics, Inc.; co-producer, composer, lyricist stage musical Victory Canteen, 1971; composer-lyricist Broadway show Over Here, 1975, Busker Alley, 1995; screenplay and song score Tom Sawyer, United Artists, 1972, Huckleberry Finn, 1974, The Slipper and the Rose, 1977, The Magic of Lassie, 1978. Served with inf. AUS, 1943-45; ETO. Decorated Purple Heart; recipient 2 Acad. awards best score for Mary Poppins, 1964, best song for Chim Chim Cheree, 1964; Grammy award, 1965; Christopher medal, 1965, 74; nine Acad. award nominations; Acad. award nomination for song score Bedknobs and Broomsticks, 1971, for best song The Age Of Not Believing, 1971, others; 16 golden, 4 platinum and one diamond record album, 1965-83; first prize best composer song score Tom Sawyer, Moscow Film Festival, 1973, B.M.I. Pioneer award, 1977; Golden Cassette awards for Mary Poppins, Jungle Book, Bed Knobs and Broomsticks, 1983, Mouscar award Disney Studios, Disney Legend award, 1990, BMI Richard Kirk Achievment award, 1991. Mem. Acad. Motion Picture Arts and Scis. (exec. bd. music br. 12 yrs.), AFTRA, Nat. Acad. Rec. Arts and Scis., Composers and Lyricists Guild (exec. bd.), Dramatists Guild, Authors League. Office: 9030 Harratt St West Hollywood CA 90069-3858

SHERMAN, ROBERT DEWAYNE, radiologic technologist, entrepreneur; b. Concord, Calif., May 31, 1949; s. Chester Josiah and Bette Louise (Elrod) S.; m. Cora Sue Donahue, June 15, 1968 (div. 1973); 1 child, Eric James; m. Virginia Marie Mayer, July 27, 1975 (div. 1988); 1 child, Jana Marie. AA, Foothill Coll., Los Altos, Calif., 1970. Cert. radiol. technologist, Calif. Staff technologist Palo Alto (Calif.) Med. Found., 1971-74, CT technologist, 1974-76, CT supr., 1976—, angiography team, 1982—, MRI staff, 1989-93; pvt. business exec. Newark, Calif., 1994—. Office: 37037 Magnolia St Apt 124 Newark CA 94560-3662

SHERMAN, SIGNE LIDFELDT, securities analyst, former research chemist; b. Rochester, N.Y., Nov. 11, 1913; d. Carl Leonard Broström and Herta Elvira Maria (Thern) Lidfeldt; m. Joseph V. Sherman, Nov. 18, 1944 (dec. Oct. 1984). BA, U. Rochester, 1935, MS, 1937. Chief chemist Lab. Indsl. Medicine and Toxicology Eastman Kodak Co., Rochester, 1937-43; chief rsch. chemist Chesebrough-Pond's Inc., Clinton, Conn., 1943-44; ptnr. Joseph V. Sherman Cons., N.Y.C., 1944-84; investment strategist Signe L. Sherman Holdings, Troy, Mont., 1984—. Author: The New Fibers, 1946. Fellow Am. Inst. Chemists; mem. AAAS, AAUW (life), Am. Chem. Soc., Am. Econ. Assn., Am. Assn. Ind. Investors (life), Fedn. Am. Scientists (life), Union Concerned Scientists (life), Western Econ. Assn. Internat., Earthquake Engrng. Rsch. Inst., Nat. Ctr. for Earthquake Engrng. Rsch., N.Y. Acad. Scis. (life), Internat. Platform Assn., Cabinet View Country Club. Office: Signe L Sherman Holdings Angel Island 648 Halo Dr Troy MT 59935-9415

SHERMAN, ZELDA CHARLOTTE, artist; b. L.A., June 18, 1924; d. Jacob and Celia (Knopow) Pynoos; m. Lawrence James Sherman, Dec. 17, 1943; children—Susan Meyers, Daniel Michael. Student UCLA, 1945-47, Otis Art Inst., Los Angeles, 1947-50, Kann Art Inst., Los Angeles, 1950-52. Exhibited in group shows at Sao Paulo Biennial, Brazil, 1961, Heritage Gallery, Los Angeles, 1963-94, D'Allesio Gallery, N.Y.C., 1965-66, Grand Prix Internat. de Deauville, Paris, 1972, Priz de Rome, Palais des Beaux Artes, Rome, 1973, Heritage Gallery, Los Angeles, 1962-95; represented in permanent collections Mcpl. Art Gallery, Los Angeles, Palm Springs Mus., Winthrop Rockefeller Found., Laguna Mus. Art, Calif., Container Corp., Vincent Price Gallery, L.A. Am. Recipient award Phelan Found., 1961, Pasadena Mus., 1961, All City Exhbn. award Barnsdale, 1963, 65. Mem. Nat. Watercolor Soc. Home: 1300 Chautauqua Blvd Pacific Palisades CA 90272-2606 Office: Heritage Gallery 708 N La Cienega Blvd Pacific Palisades CA 90272

SHERR, MORRIS MAX, lawyer; b. Marysville, Calif., Oct. 3, 1930; s. Alfred and Alice Carrie (Peters) S.; m. Bobbie Gray, June 27, 1954; children—David, Rodney. B.A., Calif. State U., 1952; J.D., U. Calif.-San Francisco, 1956. Bar: Calif. 1956. Prin. elem. sch., Stanislaus County, Calif., 1952-54; instr. Golden Gate Coll., 1954-55; instr. Calif. State U.-San Francisco, 1955-56; asst. prof. Calif. State U.-Fresno, 1956-59; assoc. Thompson & Rose, C.P.A.s, Fresno, Calif., 1959-61; ptnr. Blumberg, Sherr & Kerkorian, Fresno, Calif., 1961-84, Morris M. Sherr & Assocs., Fresno, 1984—. Mem. adv. council St. Agnes Hosp. Found., 1978-83. Mem. Am. Inst. C.P.A.s, Fresno Estate Planning Council (dir. 1977-79), Fresno County Bar, Christian Legal Soc., Calif. State Bar (cert. tax specialist). Baptist (chmn. trustees 1967-69, deacon 1969-73). Mem. Am. Baptist Chs. of West (moderator). Clubs: Fresno Kiwanis, Elks, Masons, Shriners. Office: 6051 N Fresno St Ste 200 Fresno CA 93710-5280

SHERRARD, RAYMOND HENRY, retired government official; b. Chgo., Mar. 8, 1944; s. Henry Loren and Minnie Valeria (Elrod) S.; m. Marsha L. McDermid, 1967 (div. 1971). AA, Long Beach City Coll., 1965; BA, Calif. State U., 1967; grad., Treasury Dept. Law Enforcement, Washington, 1970. Spl. dep. U.S. Marshal, L.A., 1970; pres. RHS Enterprises, Cypress, Calif., 1981-95; criminal investigator criminal investigation div. IRS, Santa Ana, Calif., 1969-94; story cons. Charles Fries Prodns., Hollywood, Calif., 1976—; instr. Fed. Law Enforcement Tng. Ctr., Glynco, Ga., 1977—; screenwriter Orion TV, Century City, Calif., 1984—; tech. advisor Paramount Pictures, Hollywood, 1987—; dir. speaker panel IRS, Laguna Niguel, Calif., 1984-92. Author: Federal Law Enforcement Patches, 1983, vol. 2, 1987, About Badges, 1987, Badges of the United Marshals, 1990; columnist Police Collector News; contbr. articles to profl. jours. Recipient Presidential Commendation, Pres. U.S.A., Washington, 1980, Spl. Act award U.S. Treasury Dept., L.A., 1978, 87. Mem. Nat. Assn. Treasury Agts. (v.p. 1995), Fed. Criminal Investigators Assn. (life, regional v.p. 1978-80), Assn. Fed. Investigators, Fed. Law Enforcement Officers Assn., Calif. Narcotic Officers Assn. (life, sec. 1974). Republican. Home: PO Box 5779 Garden Grove CA 92645-0779

SHERRATT, GERALD ROBERT, college president; b. Los Angeles, Nov. 6, 1931; s. Lowell Heyborne and Elva Genevieve (Lamb) S. B.S. in Edn., Utah State U., 1953, M.S. in Edn. Adminstrn., 1954; Ph.D. in Adminstrn. Higher Edn., Mich. State U., 1975. Staff assoc. U. Utah, Salt Lake City, 1961-62; dir. high sch. relations Utah State U., Logan, 1962-64, asst. to pres., 1964-77, v.p. for univ. relations, 1977-81; pres. So. Utah U., Cedar City, 1982—; dir. Honeyville Grain Inc., Utah; mem. council pres. Utah System Higher Edn., 1982—; chmn. bd. Utah Summer Games, Cedar City, 1984—; chmn. pres.'s council Rocky Mountain Athletic Conf., Denver, 1984-85. Author hist. pageant: The West: America's Odyssey, 1973 (George Washington Honor medal 1973). Chmn. Festival of Am. West, Logan, Utah, 1972-91; chmn. bd. Utah Shakespearean Festival, Cedar City, 1982-86; chmn. bd. dirs. Salt Lake City Branch of the Federal Reserve Bank of San Francisco. Served to 1st lt. USAF, 1954-57. Recipient Editing award Indsl. Editors Assn., 1962, Robins award Utah State U., 1967, Disting. Alumnus award Utah State U., 1974, So. Utah U., 1991, Total Citizen award Cedar City C. of C., 1993; named to Utah Tourism Hall of Fame, 1989. Mem. Am. Assn. State Colls. and Univs., Cache C. of C. (bd. dirs. 1980-82), Phi Kappa Phi, Phi Delta Kappa, Sigma Nu (regent 1976-78). Mem. LDS Ch. Lodge: Rotary. Home: 331 W 200 S Cedar City UT 84720-3101 Office: So Utah U 351 W Center St Cedar City UT 84720-2470

SHERRIFFS, RONALD EVERETT, communications and film educator; b. Salem, Oreg., Apr. 10, 1934; s. Robert William and Margaret Kathleen (Tutt) S.; m. Mary Lona West, July 9, 1960; children: Ellen, Matthew. BA, San Jose State U., 1955, MA, 1957; PhD, U. So. Calif., 1964. Instr. theater Mich. State U., East Lansing, 1960-61; asst. prof. broadcasting Tex. Tech U., Lubbock, 1964-65; asst. prof. speech U. Oreg., Eugene, 1965-70, assoc. prof., 1970-79, prof. telecommunications and film, 1979-92, chmn. dept. speech, 1978-84, 88-90, prof. journalism and comm., 1993—. Author: (with others) Speech Communication via Radio and TV, 1971, TV Lighting Handbook, 1977, Small Format TV Production., 1985, 3d edit., Video Field Production and Editing, 1994; producer, dir. TV programs, 1965—. Mem. Oreg. Pub. Broadcasting Policy Adv. Bd., 1980-88. Served to lt. comdr. USNR, 1957-68, PTO. Faculty enrichment program grantee Can., 1984, 91. Mem. Speech Communication Assn. Am., AAUP, Western States Communication Assn. Clubs: Oreg. Track; McKenzie Flyfishers (Eugene). Office: U Oreg Eugene OR 97403

SHERSHER, ZINOVY ISRAIL, artist; b. Birobidjan, USSR, Apr. 12, 1947; came to U.S., 1980; s. Israil and Adel (Schkliar) S.; m. Irina Levinson, Feb. 5, 1977; children: Roman, Lawrence. Student, Sch. of Fine Arts and Design, Kursk, Russia, 1962-65; MA, U. Fine/Applied Arts, Kursk, Russia, 1970; MusB, Mus. Coll., Kursk, Russia, 1975; student, Sch. of Visual Arts, N.Y.C., 1981-82. Fine artist various art galleries, 1980-91, Inspiration Art Studio, Hollywood, Calif., 1991—. One-man shows include Am.-Israeli Friendship Club, Bklyn., 1980, Metropol, Bklyn., 1985, Sherberg Gallery, L.A., 1989-90, Art Expo Calif. '90, L.A., 1990, Window Gallery, Beverly Hills, Calif., 1992, Security Pacific Bank, North Hollywood, Calif., 1992, Birch Gallery, L.A., 1993, pvt. show, Santa Barbara, Calif., 1993; exhibited in group shows All City Art Show, Oreol, USSR, 1973, Young Artist Group Show, Moscow, 1978, Regal Art Gallery, Bklyn., 1982-85, Installation One Gallery, Encino, Calif., 1989, Finegood Gallery, West Hills, Calif., 1989, Sherberg Gallery, L.A., 1989-90, Mussavi Gallery, South Hampton, N.Y., 1990, George Mayers Gallery, L.A., 1991, Ulf Breed Gallery, Munich, 1992, Barakat Gallery, Beverly Hills, Calif., 1992, Salmagundi Club, N.Y.C., 1992, others; represented in pvt. and pub. collections. Contbr. art Assn. for Breast Cancer Studies, Woodland Hills, Calif., 1994, Big Sisters Guild, L.A., 1994. Recipient Award of Appreciation, City of L.A., 1992, Internat. Inst. award, 1992. Mem. Oil Pastel Assn. Home: 6260 Morse Ave North Hollywood CA 91606-2920 Office: Inspiration Art Studio 1666 N Mccadden Pl Hollywood CA 90028-6110

SHERWIN, GARY CRAIG, media relations director, convention executive; b. Glendale, Calif., Feb. 28, 1961; s. Gerald Neil and Constance Marie (Santry) S.; m. Elizabeth Teri, Feb. 21, 1987; 1 child, Lauren Michele. BA in Comms., Calif. State U., Fullerton, 1983. Reporter Daily News Tribune, Fullerton, Calif., 1981-82; intern reporter L.A. Times, 1982-83; news bureau mgr. Palm Springs (Calif.) Conv. and Visitors Bur., 1984-86; dir. mktg. comms. Fort Worth (Tex.) Conv. and Visitors Bur., 1986-90; dir. media rels. L.A. Convention and Visitors Bureau, 1990—; dir. comms. com. Hollywood Entertainment Mus., 1992—. Mem. L.A. Cen. City Assn., 1991—; grad. mem. Leadership Fort Worth, 1988. Named Outstanding Journalism Student, Calif. Newspaper Pubs. Assn., 1981, Outstanding Grad., Soc. Profl. Journalists, 1983. Mem. PRSA (accredited, charter mem. Fort Worth chpt.), Soc. Am. Travel Writers (assoc., chmn. pub. rels. com.). Office: LA Convention & Vis Bureau 633 W 5th St Ste 6000 Los Angeles CA 90071-2088

SHERWOOD, ALLEN JOSEPH, lawyer; b. Salt Lake City, Sept. 26, 1909; s. Charles Samuel and Sarah (Abramson) Shapiro; m. Edith Ziff, Jan. 19, 1941; children—Mary (Mrs. John Marshall), Arthur Lawrence. Student, UCLA, 1927-30; AB, U. So. Calif., 1933, LLB, 1933. Bar: Calif. 1933, U.S. Supreme Ct. 1944. Pvt. practice law L.A., 1933-54, Beverly Hills, 1954—; legal counsel Internat. Family Planning Rsch. Assn., Inc., 1970-76; bd. dirs. Family Planning Ctrs. Greater L.A., Inc., 1968-84, pres., 1973-76. Mem. editorial bd. So. Calif. Law Rev., 1932-33. Contbr. articles to profl. jours. Mem. Calif. Atty. Gen.'s Vol. Adv. Coun. and its legis. subcom., 1972-78. Mem. Med.-Legal Soc. So. Calif. (bd. dirs. 1966-74), ABA, L.A. County Bar Assn., Beverly Hills Bar Assn., State Bar of Calif., Am. Arbitration Assn. (nat. panel arbitrators 1965—), Order of Coif, Tau Delta Phi, Brentwood Country Club (L.A.), Masons. Home: 575 Moreno Ave Los Angeles CA 90049-4840 Office: 12424 Wilshire Blvd Bldg 900 Los Angeles CA 90025-1043

SHERWOOD, ANNE LESLEY, molecular biologist; b. Chgo., May 10, 1954; d. William Milton and Maryon Renee (Bilodeau) Zilbersher; m. Yoshihide Sakuragi, July 25, 1981 (div. June 1989). BA, Kenyon Coll., 1976; MS, U. Ark., 1978; PhD, Purdue U., 1987. Rsch. microbiologist Cities Svc. Oil Co., Tulsa, Okla., 1976-77; rsch. asst. in immunology U. Ark., Fayetteville, 1979-81; postdoct. sr. fellow Dept. Biochemistry, U. Wash., Seattle, 1987-89; rsch. assoc. Dept. Biochem. Oncology, Pacific N.W. Rsch. Found., Seattle, 1989—. Contbr. articles to profl. jours. Del. Wash. Dem. Party, Seattle, 1992; musician Seattle Philharm. Orch., 1987—; mem. St. Thomas Singers. Mem. AAAS, Assn. Women in Sci., Washington Yacht Club. Episcopalian. Home: 5304 228th St SW Mountlake Terrace WA 98043-3933 Office: Pacific NW Rsch Found 720 Broadway Seattle WA 98122-4327

SHI, WENYUAN, microbiologist; b. Hangzhou, Zhejiang, China, June 26, 1962; came to U.S., 1985; s. Zhuxian Shi; m. Hanjing Yang, Sept. 3, 1987; 1 child, Jamie Young. BS in Genetics, Fudan U., Shanghai, China, 1984; PhD in Genetics, U. Wis., 1992. Rsch. asst. U. Wis., Madison, 1985-92; rsch. scientist U. Calif., Berkeley, 1992-95; prof. UCLA, 1995—. Author: Methods in Molecular Microbiology, 1994; contbr. articles to profl. jours. Pres. SOS China Edn. Fund, Calif., 1992-93, gen. sec., 1994; pres. Smargen Hitechland, Calif., 1994—. Mem. Am. Soc. Microbiology. Home: 7011 Kentwood Ave Los Angeles CA 90045 Office: Sch Medicine and Dentistry Ctr for Health Scis 10833 Le Conte Ave Los Angeles CA 90024-1668

SHIBLEY, GAIL ROSE, state legislator; b. North Bend, Oreg., Apr. 7, 1958; d. Lyle Donald and Rosemarie Elizabeth (Duban) S.; life ptnr. Kelly Sue Rogers. BA, U. Oreg., 1980. Congrl. aide U.S. rep. Jim Weaver U.S. Ho. Reps., Washington and Eugene, Wash., 1980-86; acct. exec. Ryan, Hutchins, Southwick, Portland, 1987-90; program mgr. City of Portland, Oreg., 1990—; mem. Oreg. Ho. Reps., Portland, 1991—; mem. Multi County Community Action Com., Portland, 1992—, Gov.'s Coun. DUII, Portland, 1992—, Breast and Cervical Cancer Coalition, Portland, 1992—. Dem. precinct leader, Multnomah County, Oreg., 1991—; fundraiser, mem. Right ot Privacy, Oreg., 1985—; mem. Gay and Lesbian Victory Fund, 1992—; trustee No On 13 Com., Oreg., 1994—; bd. dirs. Neighborhood Partnership Fund, Portland, 1994. Recipient Legis. Excellence award Multnomah County Community Action Agy., 1991, Nan Wood Honeyman award Oreg. Women's Polit. Caucus, 1991, Torch award Human Rights Campaign Fund, 1992; named to Legis. Honor Roll Oreg. Environ. Coun., 1991. Fellow Am. Leadership Forum, 1994-95, Oreg. Women's Polit. Caucus, Oreg. Hist. Soc., City Club Portland. Democrat. Home: PO Box 6805 Portland OR 97228-6805 Office: Oreg Ho of Reps H-395 State Capitol Salem OR 97310

SHIDELER, ROSS PATRICK, foreign language and comparative literature educator, author, translator, poet; b. Denver, Apr. 12, 1936. B.A., San Francisco State U., 1958; M.A., U. Stockholm, 1963; Ph.D., U. Calif., Berkeley, 1968. Instr. in comparative lit. U. Calif., Berkeley, 1967-68; asst. prof. English Hunter Coll., N.Y.C., 1968-69; asst. prof. Scandinavian lang. and comparative lit. UCLA, 1969-73, assoc. prof., 1973-79, prof., 1979—; chmn. program in comparative lit., 1979-86, 92—. Author: (monograph) Voices Under The Ground: Themes and Images in the Poetry of Gunnar Ekelof, 1973, Per Olov Enquist-A Critical Study, 1984; translator: (play) The Night of the Tribades (Per Olov Enquist), 1977, The Hour of the Lynx, 1990 (Per Olov Enquist), 1990; U.S. assoc. editor Swedish Book Rev., 1984—. Fellow NDFL, 1964; fellow NDEA, 1965; Fulbright-Hays fellow, 1966-67. Mem. MLA (exec. com. divsn. Scandinavian Langs. and Lits. 1993—), Soc. for Advancement Scandinavian Studies (exec. coun. 1985-89), Am. Comparative Lit. Assn., Assn. Depts. and Programs Comparative Lit. (exec. com. 1993-94, 94—). Office: UCLA Dept Comparative Lit Los Angeles CA 90024

SHIEH, JAE-HUNG, research scientist; b. Taipei, Taiwan, May 6, 1955; came to U.S., 1982; m. Hsiao-Liang Pai; 2 children. BS, Nat. Tsing Hua U., 1979; MS, Nat. Taiwan U., 1977; PhD, U. North Tex., 1987. Rsch. fellow Meml. Sloan-Kettering Cancer Ctr., N.Y.C., 1987-92; rsch. scientist Amgen Inc., Thousand Oaks, Calif., 1993—. Mem. Am. Soc. Hematology, Internat. Soc. Exptl. Hematology. Office: Amgen Inc 1860 De Havilland Dr Thousand Oaks CA 91320-1701

SHIELDS, MARLENE SUE, elementary school educator; b. Denver, Apr. 7, 1939; d. Morris and Rose (Sniderman) Goldberg; m. Charles H. Cohen, Dec. 22, 1957 (dec.); children: Lee, Richard, Monica; m. Harlan Shields. BA magna cum laude, Met. State Coll., 1980; MA, U. No. Colo., 1986. Preschool tchr. Temple Emanuel, Denver, 1970-75; tchr. Kindergarten Temple Sinai, Denver, 1975-80; tchr. pre-Kindergarten St. Mary's Acad., Englewood, Colo., 1980-83; tchr. Beach Court Elem., Denver, 1983-86, Valverde Sch., Denver, 1984-85; tchr. third grade Brown Elem., Denver, 1985-86; tchr. learning disabilities Cowell Elem. Sch., Denver, 1986-87, Sabin Elem. Sch., Denver, 1987-88; tchr. second grade Sabin Elem., Denver, 1988—; mem. curriculum com. Denver Pub. Sch., 1989—, pers. subcom., 1991—; citizen amb. Spain joint tchr. conf. Mem. Colo. Copun. Internat. Reading Assn., Nat. Assn. for Young Children, Nat. Tchrs. Colo. Math., Internat. Reading Assn., Carousel of Intervention, Delta Kappa Gamma (sec.), PRIDE (lang. curriculum com., math. curriculum com., impact com., CDM rep. 1994-95). Home: 5800 Big Canon Dr Englewood CO 80111-3516

SHIELDS, WILLIAM DONALD, neurologist, educator; b. Salt Lake City, Oct. 29, 1941; s. F. Alburn and Ruth (Clawson) S.; m. Virginia Mary Howell, May 19, 1970; children: Stephen Christopher, Justin Michael, Christine Rebecca. B.A., U. Utah, 1967, MD, 1971. Diplomate Am. Bd. Pediatrics, Am. Bd. Psychiatry and Neurology. Resident in pediatrics Los Angeles County-U. So. Calif. Med. Ctr., L.A., 1971-73; fellow in neurology U. Utah, Salt Lake City, 1973-76; asst. prof. UCLA Sch. Medicine, 1976-83, chief pediatric neurology, 1980—, assoc. prof., chief, 1983-90, prof., 1990—. dir. pediatric epilepsy program UCLA, 1994—. Contbr. med. articles to profl. publs. Mem. profl. adv. bd. Epilepsy Found. Am., 1983—. Recipient Teaching award UCLA Dept. Pediatrics, 1977, 79, Teaching award UCLA Dept. Neurology, 1994; USPHS Nat. Inst. Child Health grantee, 1980-83, Calif. Inst. Cancer Rsch. grantee, 1982, NINDS program project grantee, 1992—. Fellow Am. Acad. Pediatrics; mem. Profs. of Child Neurology, Am. Acad. Neurology, Am. Epilepsy Soc., Los Angeles County Epilepsy Soc. (chmn. profl. adv. bd. 1981-86, pres. 1986—), Nat. Inst. Neurologic Disease and Stroke. Mormon. Office: UCLA Sch Medicine 10833 Le Conte Ave Los Angeles CA 90024

SHIERS, FRANK ABRAM, lawyer; b. Marlboro, Mass., Oct. 23, 1920; s. Frank and Sarah (Chalk) S.; m. Sylvia A. Broz, Mar. 27, 1954; children: Frank A., Jane Marie Shiers Bryce. BA, Western Wash. U., 1942; JD, U. Wash., 1949. Bar: Wash. 1949, U.S. Dist. Ct. (we. dist.) Wash. 1950, U.S. Supreme Ct. 1969. Pvt. practice law Port Orchard, Wash., since 1949; ptnr. Greenwood & Shiers, Port Orchard, since 1950; now sr. ptnr. Shiers, Chrey, Cox & Caulkins, Port Orchard. Mem. Kitsap County Estate Planning Coun. Mem. Wash. State Bar Assn. (com. on profl. legal svcs. to armed forces and fee arbitration bd.), Kitsap County Bar Assn., VFWW, Am. Legion, Kitsap County-Wash. State Trial Lawyers Assn., Navy League (past pres. Bremerton coun.), Young Men's Bus. Club (past pres. Wash. chpt.), Elks (by-laws chmn. Wash. chpt.). Office: Shiers Chrey Cox & Caulkin 600 Kitsap St Ste 202 Port Orchard WA 98366-5394

SHIFFER, JAMES DAVID, utility executive; b. San Diego, Mar. 24, 1938; s. Kenneth Frederick and Thelma Lucille (Good) S.; m. Margaret Edith Rightmyer, Sept. 5, 1959 (div. July 1986); children: James II, Elizabeth Gonzales, Russell; m. Esther Zamora, Sept. 13, 1986; stepchildren: Bryan Boots, Jeremy Hellier, Marisol Boots. BS ChemE, Stanford U., 1960, MS ChemE, 1961. Registered profl. engr., Calif. Nuclear engr. Pacific Gas & Electric Co., Humboldt Bay Power Plant, Eureka, Calif., 1961-71; tech. mgr. Pacific Gas & Electric. Co., Diablo Canyon Power Plant, Avila Beach, Calif., 1971-80; mgr. nuclear ops. Pacific Gas & Electric Co., San Francisco, 1980-84, v.p. nuclear power generation, 1984-90, sr. v.p., gen. mgr. nuclear power generation bus. unit, 1990-91, exec. v.p. elec. supply, nuclear power generation bus. units, 1991—, also bd. dirs; exec. v.p. Pacific Gas & Electric, San Francisco, 1994—; pres., CEO PG&E Enterprises, San Francisco, 1994—, also bd. dirs.; bd. dirs. Nuclear Energy Inst.; bd. control U.S. Generating Co., U.S. Oper. Svcs. Co. Mem. AIChE, Commonwealth Club of Calif. (bd. govs.). Republican. Episcopalian. Home: 2550 Royal Oaks Dr Alamo CA 94507-2227 Office: Pacific Gas & Electric Co PO Box 770000 77 Beale St B32 San Francisco CA 94177

SHIFFMAN, LESLIE BROWN, management executive; b. Fresno, Calif., Dec. 9, 1936; d. Albert Brown and Marion Jean (Riese) Brown-Propp; married, Jan. 20, 1957 (div. 1972); m. Sydney Shiffman, July 4, 1993; children: Susan, Steven, David, Thomas. BS, U. So. Calif., 1958. Office mgr.

pvt. practice physician, Long Beach, Calif., 1971-73; cost acct. Panavision, Inc., Tarzana, Calif., 1974-76; exec. sec. Hartman Galleries, Beverly Hills, Calif., 1976-78; adminstrv. asst. Galanos Originals, L.A., 1978—. Named L.A. Alumnae Panhellenic Assn. Women of Yr., 1977. Mem. Alpha Epsilon Phi (nat. pres. 1985-89, trustee, sec. found. 1990-91, pres. found. 1991-95, Woman of Distinction award 1993). Republican. Jewish. Home: 1745 S Bentley Ave # 1 Los Angeles CA 90025-4323 Office: Galanos Originals 2254 S Sepulveda Blvd Los Angeles CA 90064-1812

SHIH, MARIE, metaphysical healer; b. Florence, Ariz., Jan. 24, 1959; d. John Cecil and Josephine Marie (Carter) Lewis; m. Ravi Sundervardan Candadai, Aug. 13, 1982 (div. Aug. 1984); m. Tony Hu-Tung Shih, July 11, 1987 (div. Sept. 1991); m. Jack Hunter Caldwell, Jan. 2, 1995; 1 child, John Lewis Caldwell; step-children: Trevor Hunter, Levi Robert. BA, U. Ariz., 1982, postgrad., 1982-84. Musician, writer, illustrator, Tucson and Seattle, 1978—; front desk clk. Ghost Ranch Lodge, Tucson, 1982-83; adminstrv. sec. Starnet Corp., Seattle, 1985-86; vol. U.S. Peace Corps, Mbalmayo, Cameroun, Africa, 1986; practitioner Christian Science Ch., 1994—; ind. team mgr. Noevir Natural Herbal Cosmetics, Seattle, 1987-92, author, editor mo. newsletter, 1989-92, attended nat. convs., 1989-92; lectr. So. Seattle Cmty. Coll., 1990-92. Author press releases, bus. forms local orgns., Tucson, Seattle, 1978-93; editor letters, speeches local orgns., Seattle; author, editor, designer mo. newsletter Fairmount News and Views, 1993-94; contbr. articles to jours. Bd. dirs., com. chmn. S.W. Seattle Liberacy Coalition, 1989-90; active ArtsWest, United Way, West Seattle Totem Theatre, 1990-94; bus. sponsor West Seattle Hi-Yu, 1991; active 6th Ch. of Christ, Scientist, Seatle, 1987—, 1st reader, 1991-94; active 1st Ch. of Christ, Scientist, Boston, 1990—; mem. steering com. Constellation Park and Marine Res. at Ritchey Viewpoint, 1993-94; founding mem. Fairmount Ravine Preservation Group, 1993-94. Mem. NAFE, West Seattle C. of C. (area dir. 1990-91, com. mem. 1990-93, com. chair 1992-93), Neighborhood Promotion Com. Republican. Address: 582 Winston Creek Rd # C Mossyrock WA 98564-9635

SHILL, VICTOR LAMAR, architect; b. Phoenix, July 6, 1933; s. Victor David and Olive (Nielsen) S.; m. Patsy Ann Nelson, Nov. 7, 1952; children: Michael, Wayne, Mark, Curt, Tracy. BArch, Ariz. State U., 1955. Registered architect, Ariz. Architect Kistner, Wright & Wright, Los Angeles, 1955-56, Horlbeck, Hickman & Assocs., Mesa, Ariz., 1956-63; pres. Shill, Judd, Richards & Johnson Architects, Inc., Mesa, 1963—. Prin. works include Mesa Police Bldg., Mesa Cts. Bldg., Dobson Jr. High Sch., Mesa (Lighting award 1981), Rhoder Jr. High Sch., Mesa (AIA award 1978), Ariz. State U. Student Health Bldg., Tempe, Ea. Ariz. Coll. Fine Arts Ctr., Thatcher, Shepherd Jr. High Sch., Brimhall Jr. High Sch., Dobson High Sch., Mohave High Sch., River Valley High Sch., over 100 ch. projects throughout Ariz. Mem. AIA. Republican. Mormon. Home: 2550 N Gilbert Rd Mesa AZ 85203-1304 Office: Shill Judd Richards & Johnson 1045 E Mckellips Rd Mesa AZ 85203-3001

SHILLINGTON, KEITH ALLAN, software engineer; b. Palo Alto, Calif., Apr. 13, 1955; s. Dennis Frederick and Mary S. BA in Computer Sci., U. Calif., San Diego, 1978. Mgr. software distbn. U. Calif.-San Diego Inst. Info. Systems, 1977-78; operational and orgnl. designer, customer cons. SofTech Microsystems, San Diego, 1979-80; instr. Ada courses, designer software tools, mgr. validation testing & mktg. data TeleSoft, San Diego, 1980-90; instr. Ada courses, contractor Fastrak Tng. Inc., San Diego, 1992—; cons. Sci. Applied Internat. Corp. Editor: UCSD Pascal Users Manual, 1978-80; author Ada Compiler Validation Capability tests. Ind. contractor, Ada instr. and system troubleshooter, office mgr. San Diego Earth Day, 1990-91, bd. dirs., 1993—. Mem. IEEE, Assn. for Computing Machinery.

SHIMABUKURO, ELTON ICHIO, sales professional; b. Hilo, Hawaii, Oct. 26, 1950; s. Hideo and Chieko (Hanashiro) S.; m. Lily Yuriko Fujimoto, May 3, 1980; 1 child, Kelli. BEd, U. Hawaii, Honolulu, 1974. CLU; chartered fin. cons. Sales rep. Sun Fin. Group, Honolulu, 1974-79, sales mgr., 1979—. Pres. Greenview Condominium Assn. of Apt. Owners, Honolulu, 1980-82; bd. dirs. Honolulu Japanese Jr. C. of C., 1983-84, Hawaii Lupus Found., Inc., 1990. With USAR, 1968-77. Mem. Am. Soc. CLUs and ChFCs, Internat. Assn. Fin. Planners, Gen. Agts. and Mgrs. Conf., West Honolulu Assn. Life Underwriters (bd. dirs. Honolulu chpt. 1984-86, treas. 1986-88, Life Ins. Profl. of Yr. 1989), Hawaii State Assn. Life Underwriters (chair membershp com. Honolulu chpt. 1979-80, chmn. pub. rels. com. 1981-82), Kiwanis, Rotary of Alamoana. Office: Sun Fin Group 711 Kapiolani Blvd Ste 1100 Honolulu HI 96813-5249

SHIMODA, JERRY YASUTAKA, national historic park administrator; b. Haleiwa, Hawaii, Mar. 21, 1930; s. Tamotsu and Sasai Shimoda; m. Clara H. Segawa, Aug. 7, 1954; children: Karen Marie K., Randall T., Shaun T., Teri Ellen H., Jacqueline Y., David Y. BA in Govt., U. Hawaii, 1952, MA in Far Ea. Area Studies, 1957; postgrad., St. Louis U., 1957-59. Historian Jefferson Nat. Expansion Meml. Nat. Hist. Site, St. Louis, 1957-60; chief historian, in charge hist. rsch. and visitor svcs. Saratoga Nat. Hist. Park, Stillwater, N.Y., 1960-66; chief historian Home of Franklin D. Roosevelt Nat. Hist. Site and, Frederick Vanderbilt Nat. Hist. Site, Hyde Park, N.Y., 1966-69; instr. Nat. Park Svc. Stephen T. Mather Tng. Ctr., Harpers Ferry, W.Va., 1969-72; supt. Pu'uhonua o Honaunau (Hawaii) Nat. Hist. Park, 1972—, Puukohola Heiau Nat. Hist. Site, Honaunau, 1972—; lectr. environ. edn. Pa. State U., U. W.Va., Shepherd Coll., 1969-72; acting supr. Kaloko-Honokohau Nat. Hist. Park, 1988-90; instr. environ. edn., interpretive and basic instructing techniques U. Hawaii, Hilo, Kapiolani C.C.; U.S. del. U.S.-Japan Panel on Nat. Parks and Equivalent Res., 1968—, World Conf. on Marine Parks, Tokyo, 1975; Japanese translator U.S. Nat. Park Svc.; mem. internat. bd. dirs. Heritage Interpretation Internat.; numerous presentations at confs. and tng. courses. Author booklets on nat. parks, mgmt. and history; contbr. numerous articles to profl. publs., mags. and newspapers. Bd. dirs. Volcano Art Ctr.; mem. adv. com. Wailoa State Ctr.; mem. Hawaii Gov.'s Task Force on Ocean and Recreation; chmn. restoration com. St. Benedict's Ch., Honounau, 1982-95. Recipient spl. achievement award Nat. Park Svc., 1964, 68, 70, resolution W.Va. Senate, 1971, Hawaii Ho. of Reps., 1982, sec.'s cert. Dept. Interior, 1971, Exec. of Yr. award West Hawaii chpt. Profl. Secs. Internat., 1981, cert. Govt. of Japan, 1981, staff plaque Pu'uhonua o Honaunau Nat. Hist. Park, Puukohola Heiau Nat. Hist. Site and Kaloko-Honokohau Nat. Hist. Park, 1988, cert. Japan Nat. Parks Assn., 1989, cert. of appreciation South Kona Aloha Lions Club, 1990, also others. Mem. Hawaii Mus. Assn. (bd. dirs. 1988-92), Kona Hist. Soc. (bd. dirs. 1988-92), Big Island Ocean Recreation and Tourism Assn. (exec. com.), Kona Judo Club (pres. 1977—), Rotary (pres. Kona Nauka 1978-79, Paul Harris fellow 1991, Disting. Svc. award 1992). Office: Pu'uhonua o Honaunau Nat Hist Pk PO Box 129 Honaunau HI 96726-0129

SHIMOGORI, KOTARO, designing company executive; b. Tokyo, Jan. 6, 1960; s. Mamoru and Tomoko (Otaki) S.; m. Mary Jeanne Thompson, June 22, 1994. BA, Calif. Inst. Arts, Valencia, 1982. Graphic designer Collagrpahics, L.A., 1978-88; dir. internat. affairs musee Internationale, L.A., 1989-90; dir. design Yamada Lighting Co., L.A., 1989-91; pres. Kotaro Shimoqori, Inc., L.A., 1990—; pres. indsl. design Isosceles, Inc., L.A., 1983-85, Platypus, Inc., L.A., 1985-88; pres. Indsl. Design and Tech., L.A., 1993—; creative dir. Clegg Industries, Inc., L.A., 1993—, Personalized Graphics Inc., L.A., 1994—; lectr. Calif. Inst. Arts, Valencia, 1985-89, Otis Parsons, L.A., 1986-89, UCLA, 1990. Author, designer furniture; producer architectural LA Style, 1992; patentee in field. Recipient Good Design award Japanese Govt., 1990, Roscoe award Interior Design Mag., 1993. Office: Kotaro Shimogori Inc 600 Flower Ave Venice CA 90291-2725

SHIMONKEVITZ, RICHARD PHILLIP, immunologist; b. Bellevue, Nebr., Dec. 4, 1954; s. William Francis and Adeline Helene (Demboski) S.; m. Christa Helen Rheindt, Dec. 19, 1981; children: Lisa Helen, Christian William. BS in Biology, Utah State U., 1977; MS in Immunology, Colo. State U., 1981; PhD in Immunology, U. Colo., 1984. Postdoctoral scientist Ludwig Inst. for Cancer Rsch., Epalinges, Switzerland, 1984-86, Rsch. Inst. of Scripps Clinic, LaJolla, Calif., 1986-88; rsch. scientist Cytel Corp., LaJolla, 1988-89, Rocky Mountain Multiple Sclerosis Ctr., Englewood, Colo., 1989-93, 95—, Supragen Inc., Lakewood, Colo., 1993-95. Reviewer Jour. of Immunology, 1988—; contbr. articles to profl. jours. Rsch. grant Nat. Multiple Sclerosis Soc., 1989, Colo. Neurol. Soc., 1989, NIH, 1993. Mem. Am. Assn. of Imunologists. Office: Rocky Mountain Multiple Sclerosis Ctr 501 E Hampden Ave Englewood CO 80110

SHIMPFKY, RICHARD LESTER, bishop; b. Albuquerque, Oct. 18, 1940; m. Jamel Shimpfky, 1966; children: Trevor, Allison, Joshua. Grad., U. Colo., 1963, Va. Theol. Seminary, 1970. Ordained to diaconate Episc. Ch., 1970. With William L. Philips Found., Richmond, Va., 1963-67; curate St. Peter's Ch., Arlington, 1970-72; vicar All Saints' Sharon Chapel, Alexandria, Va., 1972-73, rector, 1973-77; rector Christ Ch., Ridgewood, N.J., 1977-90; bishop Diocese El Camino Real, Monterey, Calif., 1990—. *

SHIN, EDWARD SUNG-SHIK, bilingual education educator; b. Seoul, Aug. 26, 1960; Came to U.S., 1977; s. Hyun-Woo and Sai-Shin (Jahng) S.; m. Rachel Youn-Kyung, Apr. 11, 1992; children: Calvin Joon Ho, Sarah Yerin. BA, UCLA, L.A., 1986; MEd, Harvard U., 1990. Cert. tchr., adminstrv. svcs., bilingual instr., Calif. Site/program dir. YMCA, L.A., 1984-86; bilingual tchr. L.A. Unified Sch. Dist., 1986—; chair faculty Overland Ave. Sch., L.A., 1991-92; tchr. Korean lang. L.A. Christian Reformed Ch., 1987-90. Singer Olympic Honor Choir, L.A., 1984; group leader, counselor UCLA, 1985; vol. Neuropsychiatric Inst. UCLA, 1986. Chancellor's scholar UCLA, 1980; grantee Harvard Grad. Sch. Edn., 1989-90. Mem. ASCD, Assn. Calif. Sch. Adminstrs., United Teachers of L.A. Korean Presbyterian.

SHIN, JAI MOO, biochemistry researcher; b. Seoul, Republic of Korea, July 15, 1958; came to U.S., 1990; s. Deok D. and Yeon S. (Hwang) S.; m. Bo Mee Chang, Feb. 1, 1986; 1 child, Jung Hyun. BSc, Seoul Nat. U., 1981; MS, Korea Adv. Inst. Sci. & Tech., Seoul, 1983, PhD, 1986. Tchg. asst., rsch. asst. Korea Advanced Inst. Sci. and Tech., 1981-86; sr. rschr. Hamil Pharm. Co., Seoul, 1986-91; rschr. Sch. Medicine UCLA, 1990—. Author: Annals of the New York Academy of Science, 1992; contbr. articles to profl. jours. including Jour. Biol. Chem.; patentee in field. Mem. Am. Chem. Soc., N.Y. Acad. Sci. Home: 3700 S Sepulveda Blvd Apt 135 Los Angeles CA 90034-6842 Office: VA Med Ctr Membrane Biology Bldg 113 Rm 324 11301 Wilshire Blvd Los Angeles CA 90073

SHIN, SUK-HAN, geography educator, director Korean-American affairs; b. Seoul, Korea, Aug. 28, 1930; came to U.S., 1964; s. Kee Duk and Jung Sook (Shin) S.; m. Myung Jah Kim, Dec. 30, 1958; children: Yong Wook, Soo Hyun. BA, Seoul Nat. U., 1954; MA, Clark U., 1967; PhD, U. Pitts., 1975. Tchr. Jin Myung Girls Sr. High Sch., Seoul, 1954-61; urban planner Chonghab Architect Rsch. Ctr., Seoul, 1961-62; asst. planner S.W. Pa. Regional Planning Commn., Pitts., 1968; rsch. fellow Korea Rsch. Inst. of Human Settlements, Seoul, 1980; environ. cons. Engring.-Sci., Inc., Pasadena, Calif., 1982; prof. geography Ea. Wash. U., Cheney, 1969-92, prof. emeritus, 1992—; dir. Inst. Korean-Am. Affairs, Ea. Wash. U., Spokane, Wash. Author: Journal of Environmental Conservation, 1977, Impact of Industrial Development, 1980, Environment: Conservation Management and B/C, 1983; (chpt. in book) Themes and Research Methods, 1983. Mem. Adv. Coun. on Peaceful Unification of Republic of Korea, Seoul, 1982-87, 91-93, Spokane Internat. Coordinating Coun., Spokane, 1986-88; pres. Spokane Korean Assn., 1978-84, Spokane Korean-Am. Citizens Assn., 1989-92; chmn. Seoul Olympic Supporting Com. of Spokane, 1986-88. Donnelly fellow Clark U., 1965-66; grantee Korea Rsch. Found.; recipient City Medal of Seoul, 1980, Disting. Korean Scientist Abroad, Min. Sci. and Tech., ROK, 1980, Cert. of Appreciation Korea Rsch. Inst. Human Settlements, 1981, Minister of Environ., Republic of Korea, 1983, Cert. of Achievement, Korean Consul Gen., 1986. Mem. Assn. Am. Geographers (session chmn., 1983, '84, '91), Assn. Pacific Coast Geographers (session chmn. 1984), N.W. Sci. Assn. (chmn. soc. sci. 1975-76), Western Regional Sci. Assn. (session chmn. 1983, '84), Korean Geog. Soc., Korean Sci. and Engring. Assn., Am. Regional Sci. Assn. Mailing: 15134 Matisse Cir La Mirada CA 90638-4738

SHIN, SUNG SIK, pathologist, educator, researcher; b. Pusan, Korea, Jan. 29, 1956; came to U.S., 1984; MD, Seoul Nat. U., 1980. Diplomate in anat. and clin. pathology and hematology Am. Bd. Pathology. Resident in pathology Rush Med. Ctr., Chgo., 1984-88; fellow in hematopathology City of Hope Med. Ctr., Duarte, Calif., 1988-90, staff pathologist, 1990-91; staff pathologist Kaiser Found. Hosp., Fontana, Calif., 1991-92, U. Calif. San Diego Med. Ctr., 1992—; assoc. prof. pathology U. Calif. San Diego Sch. Medicine, 1992—. Contbr. articles to med. jours. Am. Cancer Soc. clin. oncology fellow, 1990. Mem. U.S. and Can. Acad. Pathology, Calif. Med. Assn., San Diego County Med. Soc. Office: U Calif San Diego Med Ctr 200 W Arbor Dr San Diego CA 92103-1911

SHINBO, ROBERT, landscape architect; b. Seattle, June 20, 1948; s. Hachiro and May (Asai) S.; m. Sharron Chin, Feb. 25, 1968; 1 child, Roberta. B Landscape Architecture, U. Wash., 1971; M, Harvard U., 1973. Registered landscape architect Calif., Wash. Designer Sakuma James Peterson, Seattle, 1970-71; research asst. Harvard U., Cambridge, Mass., 1972-73; designer Sasaki Assocs., Watertown, Mass., 1973-76, SWA Group, Irvine, Calif., 1976-77; sr. assoc. Edaw Co., Newport Beach, Calif., 1977-78; prin. Robert Shinbo Assocs., Seattle, 1978—. Commr. Pike Place Market Hist. Commn., Seattle, 1988—; mem. King County Affordable Housing Task Force, 1986; fund-raiser U. Wash. Coll. Architecture and Urban Planning. Recipient Nat. award Program for Energy Innovation of Wash. State Energy Office, 1986. Mem. Am. Soc. Landscape Architects (pres. Wash. chpt. 1985, Merit award 1986), Urban Land Inst., Am. Planning Assn., Lambda Alpha. Office: Robrt Shinbo Assocs 89 Virginia St Seattle WA 98101-1012

SHINK, SHARI FRANCINE, lawyer, legal administrator; b. Greensburg, Pa., Dec. 3, 1948; d. John Anton and Frances Marie (Ursic) S. BS in Psychology, U. Pitts., 1970; JD, Rutgers U., 1975. Bar: Pa., U.S. Dist. Ct. Colo., U.S. Dist. Ct. (we. dist.) Pa., U.S. Supreme Ct. Neighborhood legal svcs. atty. Child Advocacy Legal Aid, Pitts., 1975-77, staff atty., 1977-79, mng. atty., 1979-81; exec. dir. Colo. Guardian Ad Litem Project, Denver, 1981-84; founder, exec. dir. Children's Legal Clinic, Denver; mem. Gov.'s Commn. to Study Children's Code, Denver, 1983-84; mem. Task Force to Recodify Children's Code, 1994; field instr. U. Denver Coll. Law and Sch. Social Work, 1982—; instr. legal rights of children Met. State Coll., Denver; coord. Colo. Supreme Ct. Task Force on Permanent Families for Children, 1986-89; chair subcom. on child custody Colo. Legis. Task Force on Children's Issues, 1991-92; mem. steering com. Nat. Com. for Rights of the Child/Legal Action Project Adv. Bd., Colo. Coalition for Protection of Children Policy Com., Denver Children's Network, Child Abuse Coalition of Weld County, Ctr. for People of Capital Hill, Denver; cons. Inst. for Child Abuse and Neglect U. No. Colo., Greeley; presenter, spkr. in field. Bd. dirs. Met. Child Protection Coun., 1982-84, Chrysalis Teen Group Home, 1982-83; appointed to Jack Hogan Charitable Found. Task Force, 1987. Scholar-in-residence C. Henry Kempe Nat. Ctr. for Prevention and Treatment of Child Abuse and Neglect, 1978; recipient Internat. Legis. Svc. award Parents Without Ptnrs., 1993; named One of Best of New Generation Who Are Changing America, Esquire Mag., 1984. Mem. ABA (mem. task force on children), NAFE, Nat. Assn. Counsel for Children (v.p., dir. 1979-81), Nat. Assn. Ct. Appointed Spl. Child Advocates, Pa. Bar Assn., Colo. Bar Assn. (mem. steering com. juvenile law forum). Democrat. Roman Catholic. Club: Colo. Mountain. Lodge: Nat. Slovene Benefit Soc.

SHINN, CRAIG WAGNER, public administration educator, consultant; b. Reedley, Calif., Sept. 9, 1951; s. Ridgway F. and Clarice (Wagner) S.; m. Kathleen Anne Cox, Sept. 30, 1978; children: Karrie Lark Pelling, Erin Jakob Ridgway, Caitlin Anne. BS in Forestry, U. Maine, 1974; MPA, Lewis & Clark U., 1984; PhD in Forest Mgmt., U. Wash., 1993. Hist. agriculturist Old Sturbridge (Mass.) Village, 1973-74; hist. agrl. researcher Colonial Pa. Plantation, Edgemont, 1974-75; grower Breezeland Orchards, Warren, Mass., 1975-77; researcher Crown Zellerbach Corp., Wilsonville, Oreg., 1977-85; prin. N.W. Resources, Canby, Oreg., 1985—; rsch. asst. Ctr. for Nat. Forest Products U. Wash., Seattle, 1988-90; asst. prof. pub. adminstrn. Portland (Oreg.) State U., 1991-92; asst. prof. pub. adminstrn. Lewis & Clark Coll., Portland, 1992—; adj. prof. pub. adminstrn. Seattle U., 1990-91. Author: British Columbia Log Expert Policy, 1993; co-author: Rural Resource Management, 1994. Mem. planning commn. City of Canby, Oreg., 1981-85; spokesperson South Canby Neighborhood Assn., 1980-83; bd. dirs., founder Portland County Dance Cmty., 1978-84. Mem. ASPA (pres. Portland chpt. 1993—), Soc. Am. Foresters, Am. Sociol. Assn., Acad. Polit. Sci. Democrat. Unitarian. Office: NW Resource 645 NE 22nd Ave Canby OR 97013-2002

SHINN, DUANE K., music publisher; b. Auburn, Calif., Nov. 13, 1938; s. Archie W. and Iola E. (Eisley) S.; m. Beverly J. Luman; children: Kurt, Kendra, Garin, Garth. BS, So. Oreg. State Coll., 1970, MS, 1977. Prin. Keyboard Workshop/Duane Shinn Pubs., Medford, Oreg., 1965—. Author, pub. instructional audio and video cassettes on piano playing, including: Piano Improvising, 1985, How to Dress Up Naked Music, 1988, Keyboard by Chords, 1982, Piano Tricks: author: Will Herk Go to Hell for Biting the Avon Lady, 1980. Office: Duane Shinn Publs PO Box 700 Medford OR 97501-0047

SHIOTA, TAKAO, telecommunication research company executive; b. Tokyo, Feb. 16, 1950; s. Takeo and Masako (Matsusita) S.; m. Keiko Anna Akagi, March 15, 1981; children: Kentaro, Shinjiro, Sachiko. BS, Chiba U., Japan, 1972. Engr. Japan Distillation Industry, Inc., Chiba, 1972-73; engr. R & D Fujikura Ltd., Tokyo, 1973-83; mgr. R & D Fujikura Ltd., Chiba, 1983-91; group leader Optical Tech. Rsch. Corp. Noll Rsch. Group, Tsukuba, Japan, 1987-91; pres. Fujikura Tech. Am. Corp., Sunnyvale, Calif., 1991—. Author: Fundamentals and Application of MicroOptics, 1987, Handbook of Advanced Electronics Material, 1990; editor: Japan Jour. of Applied Physics, 1988-91. Mem. Optical Soc. of Am., Internat. Soc. for Optical Engring., Soc. Cable TV En grs. Office: Fujikura Tech Am Corp 3001 Oakmead Village Dr Santa Clara CA 95051-0811

SHIPLEY, VETA FERN WILSON, personnel recruiting company executive; b. Manchester, Okla., Sept. 29, 1921; d. Charles C. and Oma (Ready) Wilson; m. David M. Shipley, Jan. 21, 1943 (div. Nov. 1968); children—Davon David Shipley, Sondra Fern Busch. Student U. Colo., 1961-62. Cons., Cartwright Employment Agy., Boulder, 1969-71, head cons., 1973-77; mgr. Western Permanent Services, Boulder, 1972; owner, mgr. Shipley Personnel Recruiting, Boulder, 1978-85. Currently doing exec. recruiting book research. Fund raiser Mountain View Methodist Ch., 1960; tchr. Sunday Sch., Meth. Ch., 1954-56, chmn. Bible Sch., 1954; leader, Colo. Muscular Dystrophy Research Fund Drive, 1955; mgr. telethon drive, Boulder, 1955. Republican. Avocations: Travel; sewing; oil painting; interior design; swimming. Died June 20, 1995. Home: 7205 Ballygar Way Elk Grove CA 95758-4476

SHIPMAN, KEITH BRYAN, sportscaster; b. Puyallup, Wash., Apr. 26, 1961; s. Richard James and Carol Esther (Christianson) S.; m. Julie Anne Poppe, June 30, 1984; children, Alicia Bryanne, Gregory Dane. BA in Comms., Wash. State U., 1983. Sportscaster/producer KOMO Radio/TV, Seattle, 1983-85; sports/pub. affairs dir. KCPQ TV, Tacoma-Seattle, 1986—; AM drive sports host KJR Radio, Seattle, 1991-93; play by play announcer RayCom Sports, Charlotte, N.C., 1992—; disc jockey KPUG AM/KNWR FM Radio, Bellingham, Wash., 1978-81; play-by-play announcer Tri-Cities Triplets Baseball, KAFR-FM Radio, Richland, Wash., 1985; baseball guide track announcer Turner Broadcasting System, Atlanta, 1990; host/producer "The Chuck Knox Show", Anderson/Baer Prodns., Bainbridge Island, Wash., 1987-88; host "The Chuck Knox Show", Andersen Ent., Bellevue, Wash., 1985-88, various other free-lance work. Pres. bd. dirs. Plaza Hall, Tacoma, Wash., 1989-94; exec. com. Muscular Dystrophy Assn., Seattle, 1989-91; vol. Boys and Girls Club of King County, Seattle and Whatcom County, Bellingham, 1988—, Children's Hosp., Seattle, 1992—. Named Sportscaster of the Yr. for Wash., Nat. Sportscasters and Sportswriters Assn., 1986, 87, 88; recipient Emmy award NATAS, 1990, 92, 94. Mem. Nat. Sportscasters and Sportswriters Assn. (bd. dirs. 1989—), NATAS, Radio TV News Dirs. Assn. Office: KCPQ TV 4400 Steilacoom Blvd SW Tacoma WA 98499-4002

SHIPP, DAN SHACKELFORD, lawyer; b. Yazoo City, Miss., Jan. 6, 1946; s. Dan Hugh and Anora Nona (Shackelford) A.; m. Carolyn Julie Perry, Nov. 30, 1974; children: Perry Lee, Clay Alexander. AA, Holmes Jr. Coll., 1966; BA, Miss. State U., 1968; JD, U. Miss., 1971. Bar: Miss. 1971, U.S. Dist. Ct. (no. dist.) Miss. 1971, U.S. Dist. Ct. (so. dist.) Miss. 1976, Colo. 1986, U.S. Ct. Appeals (5th cir.) 1982, U.S. Ct. Appeals (10th cir.) 1986, U.S. Dist. Ct. Colo. 1986. Pvt. practice Yazoo City, Miss., 1974-83, Aspen, 1986—; speaker in field. Recipient Master Advocate Cert. award Nat. Inst. for Trial Advocacy, 1993. Mem. ABA, Colo. Trial Lawyers Assn. (bd. dirs. 1986-88), Assn. Trial Lawyers Am., Colo. Bar Assn., Toastmasters Internat. Grand Champions Club. Office: 407 J AABC PO Box 8629 Aspen CO 81612-8629

SHIPP, JAMES P., systems engineer. BS in Info. Mgmt., Brigham Young U., 1989. Intern Brigham Young U. Network, 1989; systems engr. WordPerfect Corp., Orem, Utah, 1990-93, network systems engr., 1994—; network intern Brigham Young U., 1989; tech. editor Drake Tng. and Technologies, 1993. Mem. Assn. Computing Machinery, IEEE, CNEPA. Home: 1856 Heather Dr Orem UT 84057-2260

SHIPP, JOSEPH CALVIN, physician, educator; b. Northport, Ala., Feb. 10, 1927; s. Ezra Jonah and Nora (Earnest) S.; m. Marjorie Madeline Morris, Nov. 25, 1961; children: Joseph Calvin, Sherise, Dana, Michele. BS, U. Ala., 1948; MD, Columbia U., 1952. Diplomate Am. Bd. Internal Medicine. Asst. prof. medicine Harvard Med. Sch., Boston, 1958-60; rsch. scientist Oxford U., Eng., 1958-59; assoc. prof. medicine U. Fla., Gainesville, 1960-65; prof. medicine U. Fla., 1965-70; prof. and chmn. dept. medicine U. Nebr., Omaha, 1970-80; regent's disting. prof. medicine U. Nebr., 1980-86; prof. medicine U. Calif. San Francisco, Fresno, 1986—; cons. NIH, 1965-85, Fulbright-Hayes Internat. Medicine, 1976—. Contbr. over 250 articles to profl. jours. in field of diabetes and medicine. Pres. U. Calif. Found., San Francisco-Fresno, 1994—; bd. trustees, mem. Sansum Med. Rsch. Found. Fulbright-Hayes awardee, 1977. Fellow ACP; mem. Am. Diabetes Assn., Endocrine Soc., Am. Soc. Clin. Investigation, Assn. Am. Physicians, Rotary (chmn. internat. activities com. 1988-89), Alpha Omega Alpha, Phi Beta Kappa, Masons, Elks. Republican. Roman Catholic. Home: 7463 N Laguna Vista Ave Fresno CA 93711-0231 Office: U Calif San Francisco 445 S Cedar Ave Fresno CA 93702-2907

SHIPPER, TODD JEFFREY, communications executive; b. Detroit, Nov. 18, 1946; s. Norman N. Shipper and Evaline (Spring) Krasner; m. Sherry E. Brown, May 30, 1968 (div. 1969). AA, L.A. Valley Coll., 1970; student, Calif. State U., Northridge, 1970-72. Announcer various radio stas., 1967-73; salesman, mgr. Standard Shoes, Encino, Calif., 1973-76; asst. mgr. K-Mart, Westminster, Calif., 1976-77; salesman Contractors Lic. Sch., Van Nuys, Calif., 1977-80; dir. mktg. Columbia Sch. Broadcasting, Hollywood, Calif., 1980-84; owner, operator Nat. Broadcasting Sch., Sacramento, Portland, Seattle, 1984-92, Las Vegas, 1984-94; owner, operator NBS Travel Tng. Sch., 1989-92, Nat. Career Tng. Ctr., Las Vegas, 1992-94; prin. Sound Ideas, Inc., Las Vegas, 1994—; prin. Nat. Advt. Agy., Las Vegas, 1986—, Nat. Ednl. Cons., Las Vegas, 1986—. With USAF, 1965-67. Mem. Nat. Assn. Trade and Tech. Schs., Assn. Broadcasters. Democrat. Jewish. Office: Sound Ideas Inc 3678 Nicole St Las Vegas NV 89120-2225

SHIPPEY, LYN, reading center director; b. Childress, Tex., Mar. 6, 1927; d. Robert Coke and Alta (Timmons) Elliott; m. James George Shippey, Mar. 29, 1947; children: James Robert, Deborah Shippey Meyer, Marilyn Shippey Buron. BS, U. Corpus Christi, 1963; MA in Edn., San Diego State U., 1977; EdD, U. San Diego, 1993. Cert. tchr., reading specialist, tchr. of learning handicapped, Calif. Substitute tchr. Dept. Edn., Guam, 1958-61; tchr. counselor Robstown Ind. Sch. Dist., Tex., 1964-65; elem. tchr. Cupertino Union Sch. Dist., Calif., 1965-68, tchr., secondary, 1968-71; dir. PIRK Reading Center, Poway, Calif., 1973—; cons., workshop presenter PIRK Reading Programs, Calif., Tex., 1974—. Author: Perceptual Integration Reading Kits, 1971, PIRK Reading Program, 1977, rev. 1987. Mem. Coun. for Exceptional Children, Alcala Soc. U. San Diego (scholar), Orton Dyslexia Soc., Learning Disabilities Assn., Coun. for Learning Disabilities. Office: PIRK Reading Center 16957 Cloudcroft Dr Poway CA 92064-1306

SHIPPEY, SANDRA LEE, lawyer; b. Casper, Wyo., June 24, 1957; d. Virgil Carr and Doris Louise (Conklin) McC.; m. Ojars Herberts Ozols, Sept. 2, 1978 (div.); children: Michael Ojars, Sara Ann, Brian Christopher; m. James Robert Shippey, Jan. 13, 1991. BA with distinction, U. Colo., 1978; JD magna cum laude, Boston U., 1982. Bar: Colo. 1982, U.S. Dist. Ct. Colo. 1985. Assoc. Cohen, Brame & Smith, Denver, 1983-84, Parcel, Meyer, Schwartz, Ruttum & Mauro, Denver, 1984-85, Mayer, Brown & Platt, Denver, 1985-87; counsel western ops. GE Capital Corp., San Diego,

1987-94; assoc. Page, Polin, Busch & Boatwright, San Diego, 1994—. Active Pop Warner football and cheerleading. Mem. Phi Beta Kappa, Phi Delta Phi. Republican. Mem. Ch. of Christ. Home: 11878 Glenhope Rd San Diego CA 92128-5002 Office: Page Polin Busch & Boatwright 350 W Ash St Ste 900 San Diego CA 92101-3440

SHIRAI, SCOTT, communications executive; b. Honolulu, June 5, 1942; s. George Yoshio and Thelma Takeko (Tominaga) M.; children: Todd, Kimberly, Lance, Lyle. MusB, U. Hawaii, 1983; exec. dir. news, reporter Sta. KHON-TV, Honolulu, 1974-81; asst. gen. mgr. Vanguard Investments, Berkeley, Calif., 1976-79; newscaster Sta. KPOI, Honolulu, 1979-80; news dir. Sta. KGU, Honolulu, 1981-82; owner Visual Perspectives, 1981—; dir. pub. rels. Hawaiian Electric Co., Honolulu, 1982-90; dir. community rels., Hawaiian Electric Industries, 1990—; instr. U. Hawaii, 1984—; dir. BBB of Hawaii. Bd. dirs., sec. Hawaii Com. For Freedom of Press, 1982—; bd. dirs. Mental Health Assn. in Hawaii, 1981—, Moanalua Gardens Found., 1981-84, Health and Community Services Council, 1982-86, Friends of Father Damien, 1986; v.p. Mele Nani Singers, 1986—; mem. Mayors Adv. Com. on Mcpl. TV, 1987, Office of Hawaiian Affairs Pub. Rels. Adv. Com., 1987, (all Honolulu); sec., dir. Pro Geothermal Alliaance, 1990-91. Recipient Jefferson award Honolulu Advertiser, 1985, Gold award Audio-Visual Producers Assn. Am., 1985, Audio-Visual Dept. of Yr. award Videography mag., 1986, Award of Excellence Nat. Hospice Orgn., 1987, Intre award Inst. Teleradial Atica Puerto Rico, Inc., 1988. Mem. ASTD, Internat. TV Assn. (pres. 1983—), Am. Film Inst., AFTRA (bd. dirs. 1980-83), Pub. Rels. Soc. Am. (immediate past pres. and del. 1995—), Hawaii Speakers Assn., Hawaii Film Bd., Honolulu Cmty. Media Council, Hawaii Cmty. TV Assn. (pres. 1990—). Clubs: Honolulu Press (bd. dirs. 1984—), Hui Luna (bd. dirs. 1986-90) (Honolulu). Avocations: martial arts, singing. Office: Hawaiian Electric Industries PO Box 730 1001 Bishop St Ste 811 Honolulu HI 96813

SHIRASAWA, RICHARD MASAO, systems analyst and coordinator; b. Cleve., Jan. 18, 1948. BS, Mich. State U., 1970; MPA, U. So. Calif., 1992. Lab. technician Litton Bionetics, Bethesda, Md., 1971-73; biologist NIH, Washington, 1973-79; mgmt. intern Dept. HHS, Washington, 1979-81; systems coord. Health Care Financing Adminstrn., San Francisco, 1981—. Mem. Toastmasters Internat. (named Competent Toastmaster 1988). Office: Health Care Fin Adminstrn 75 Hawthorne St San Francisco CA 94105-3919

SHIRE, HAROLD RAYMOND, law educator, author, social scientist; b. Denver, Nov. 23, 1910; s. Samuel Newport and Rose Betty (Herman) S.; m. Cecilia Goldhaar, May 9, 1973; children: David, Darcy, Esti. MBA, Pepperdine U., 1972; LLD (hon.), 1975; JD, Southwestern U., L.A., 1974; M in Liberal Arts, U. So. Calif., 1977; PhD in Human Behavior, U.S. Internat. U., San Diego, 1980. Bar: Calif. 1937, U.S. Dist. Ct. (so. dist.) Calif. 1939, U.S. Supreme Ct. 1978. Dep. dist. atty. L.A. County, Calif., 1937-38; asst. U.S. atty. So. Dist. Calif., L.A. and San Diego, 1939-42; pvt. practice, L.A., 1946-56; pres., chmn. bd. Gen. Connectors Corp., U.S. and Eng., 1956-73; prof. mgmt. and law Pepperdine U., Malibu, Calif., 1974-75, U.S. Internat. U., San Diego, 1980-83; dir. Bestobell Aviation, Eng., 1970-74. Advisor U. S.C. Gerentology, Andrus Ctr., pre-retirement tng., 1976-80; bd. dirs. Pepperdine U., 1974-80; nat. bd. govs. Union Orthodox Jewish Congregations Am., 1973—. With U.S. Army, 1942-46. Author: Cha No Yu and Symbolic Interactionism: Method of Predicting Japanese Behavior, 1980; The Tea Ceremony, 1984. Patentee aerospace pneumatics; invented flexible connectors. Pres. Jewish Nat. Fund Legion of Honor, 1991—; mem. Presdl. Roundtable, Washington, 1989-93. Decorated chevalier du vieux moulin (France); companion Royal Aero. Soc. (U.K.); recipient Tea Name Grand Master Soshitsu Sen XV Urasenke Sch., Kyoto, Japan, 1976, Medal of Honor Jewish Nat. Fund, 1991, Legion of Honor, 1991. Mem. Am. Legion (svc. officer China #1), Masons (32 degree, Hiram award 1994), Royal Arch, Shrine. Republican. Achievements include designing and mfg. fluidic sys. flexible integrity for Saturn IV and welding in Apollo XI Landing on moon, 1969. Office: PO Box 1352 Beverly Hills CA 90213-1352

SHIREMAN, JOAN FOSTER, social work educator; b. Cleve., Oct. 28, 1933; d. Louis Omar and Genevieve (Duguid) Foster; m. Charles Howard Shireman, Mar. 18, 1967; 1 child, David Louis. BA, Radcliffe Coll., 1956; MA, U. Chgo., 1959, PhD, 1968. Caseworker N.H. Children's Aid Soc., Manchester, 1959-61; dir. research Chgo. Child Care Soc., 1968-72; assoc. prof. U. Ill., Chgo., 1972-85; prof. Portland (Oreg.) State U., 1985—, dir. PhD program, 1992—; interim exec. dir. Partnership for Rsch., Tng. and Grad. Edn. in Child Welfare, 1994; research cons. child welfare orgns., Ill., 1968-85, Oreg. 1985—; lectr. U. Chgo., 1968-72. Co-author: Care and Commitment: Foster Parent Adoption Decisions, 1985; mem. editorial bd. Jour. Sch. Social Work, 1978-81, Social Work Rsch. and Abstracts, 1990-93, Children and Youth Svcs. Rev., Jour. of Social Work Edn., 1990—; contbr. chpts. to books and articles to profl. jours. Bd. dirs. Oreg. chpt. Nat. Assn. for Prevention of Child Abuse, 1985-87, Friendly House, Portland, 1992—; mem. adv. com. Children's Svcs. div. State of Oreg., 1985—. Grantee HEW, 1980-82, Chgo. Community Trust, 1982-86, Oreg. Children's Trust Fund, 1991—. Mem. Nat. Assn. Social Workers, AAUP, Citizens for Children, Acad. Cert. Social Workers, Council on Social Work Edn., Phi Beta Kappa. Home: 2535 SW Sherwood Dr Portland OR 97201-1679 Office: Portland State U Grad Sch Social Work PO Box 751 Portland OR 97207-0751

SHIRILAU, MARK STEVEN, utilities executive; b. Long Beach, Calif., Dec. 13, 1955; s. Kenneth Eugene and Marjorie Irene (Thorvick) Shirey; m. Jeffery Michael Lau, Nov. 25, 1984 (dec. Aug. 1993). BSEE, U. Calif., Irvine, 1977, MS Bus. Adminstrn., 1980; M in Engring., Calif. Poly. State U., 1978; Diploma in Theology, Episc. Theol. Sch., Claremont, Calif., 1984; MA in Religion, Sch. Theology at Claremont, 1985; PhD, U. Calif., Irvine, 1988. Ordained priest Ecumenical Cath. Ch., 1987; consecrated bishop, 1991. Grad. asst. Electric Power Inst., 1977-78; pres., chief exec. officer M.S.E., Santa Ana, Calif., 1977-87; adminstrv. mgr. EECO Inc., Santa Ana, Calif., 1979-83; fin. engr. So. Calif. Edison Co., Rosemead, 1983-84, conservation engr., 1984-85, conservation supr., 1985-89; exec. v.p. Aloha Systems, Inc., 1989-93, pres., 1993—, bd. dirs.; bd. dirs. Ewing Consolidated Corp., Outrider Trucking, Inc.; part-time instr. Santa Ana Coll., 1982-84; lectr. engring. West Coast U., Orange, Calif., 1984-91; bd. dirs. Am. Electronics Assn. Credit Union. Sweetwater Springs Water Dist., Heat Pump Coun. So. Calif., AIDS Interfaith Network Sonoma County. Archbishop, primate Ecumenical Cath. Ch. Mem. IEEE (sr. mem.), Assn. Energy Engrs. (sr. mem.), Assn. Demand-Side Mgmt. Profls. (bd. dirs., charter mem., exec. v.p.), Pacific Bears Club (v.p.), Dignity Integrity (life mem.), Eta Kappa Nu. Democrat. Author: Triune Love: An Insight into God, Creation, and Humanity, 1983, Salvation, Scripture and Sexuality, 1992, History of the Ecumenical Church, 1993. Home: 20200 River Blvd Monte Rio CA 95462-9709 Office: PO Box 32 Villa Grande CA 95486-0032

SHIRLEY, COURTNEY DYMALLY, nurse; b. Trinidad, July 17, 1937; came to U.S., 1960; d. Andrew Hamid Dymally; m. Adolph Shirley, Apr. 8, 1960; children: Ingrid, Robyne, Andrea, Kirk, Sandra. Cert. mgmt./adminstrn. health facilities, UCLA, 1978; BBA, Calif. Coast U., 1980, MBA, 1983. Cert. critical care nurse, advanced critical care nurse, nursing home adminstr. Head nurse med. unit Prince of Wales Gen. Hosp., London, 1959-60; asst. head nurse, CCU staff nurse Cedars-Sinai Hosp., L.A., 1962-73; asst. dir. nursing, dir. in-svc. edn., staff nurse Beverly Glen Hosp., 1973-75; supr. ICU/CCU/house Imperial Hosp., 1975-76; house supr. Med. Ctr. of North Hollywood, 1976-77; dir. nursing Crenshaw Ctr. Hosp., 1977-78, Mid-Wilshire Convalescent, 1978-79; supr. ICU/CCU, coord. utilization rev. Temple U., 1979-80; house supr. East L.A. Doctors' Hosp., 1980-81; pvt. nurse various hosps. and homes, 1981-86; utilization rev. coord. Managed Care Resources, L.A., 1986-88; profl. rev. systems utilization rev. coord. Nat. Med. Enterprises, Santa Monica, Calif., 1988—, cert. case mgr., 1993—. Mem. AACN, Internat. Case Mgmt. Assn., Sci. of Mind, Toastmasters (sgt. at arms 1990). Office: Nat Med Enterprises 2700 Colorado Ave Santa Monica CA 90404-3521

SHIRLEY, JOHN JEFFERY, manufacturing executive; b. Dallas, Jan. 28, 1955; s. John Albert Jr. and Margaret Louise (Webb) S.; m. Kathe Wright Hildreth, Sept. 20, 1978. BS in Computer Sci., Nat. U., 1987, MS in Software Engring., 1989. Engr. 3M Co., San Diego, 1973-82; sr. engr. Grumman Aerospace, Virginia Beach, Va., 1982-85; computer specialist Grumman Aerospace, San Diego, 1985-89, dir. computer ops. Western area, 1989—; owner Digital Concepts, San Diego, 1978—; instr. P.D. Pruden Votech, Chesapeake, Va., 1982-83; assoc. prof. Nat. U., San Diego, 1989—; instr. U. Calif., San Diego, 1989—. Republican. Office: Grumman Aircraft Svcs PO Box 366 San Diego CA 92112-0366

SHIRLEY, MICHAEL JAMES, ski area executive; b. Flagstaff, Ariz., Oct. 25, 1941; s. James Watson and Lorraine Elizabeth (Thomson) S.; m. Gloria Marie Bruni, Aug. 20, 1966; children: Brian Michael, Cynthia Marie. BS, No. Ariz. U., Flagstaff, 1969; MBA, U. Ariz., 1970. Sr. acct. Morrison-Knudsen Co., Inc., Boise, Idaho, 1970-72; asst. treas. Morrison-Knudsen Co., Inc., 1972-74, corp. treas., 1974-75, v.p. adminstrn., 1975-85; v.p. adminstrn. Morrison Knudsen Corp., 1985-89, v.p. fin., treas., 1989-91; gen. mgr. Bogus Basin Ski Area, Idaho, 1991—. Bd. dirs. United Way Ada County, 1975-81; bd. dirs. Jr. Achievement of S.W. Idaho, 1978-86, pres., 1983-86; mem. Idaho Coun. Econ. Edn., 1978—; bd. dirs. Boise Philharm. Assn., 1982-85, Bogus Basin Recreation Assn., 1984—. Staff sgt. USAF, 1963-67. Recipient Wall St. Jour. award No. Ariz. U., 1969, Alumni Achievement award, 1978. Mem. Boise Area C. of C. (bd. dirs. 1985-89). Republican.

SHIRLEY, ROBERT CLARK, university president, strategic planning consultant, educator; b. Jacksonville, Tex., July 1, 1943; s. James Cullen and Mary Jim (Clark) S.; m. Terrie Thomas, June 17, 1967; children: Robin, Deron. B.B.A., U. Houston, 1965, M.B.A., 1967; Ph.D., Northwestern U., 1972. Asst. dean faculties U. Houston, 1974-76; asst. to pres. SUNY-Albany, 1976-77, assoc. v.p. acad. affairs, 1977-79; assoc. prof. Central U. Iowa, Pella, 1979-81; prof. Trinity U., San Antonio, 1981-84; pres. U. So. Colo., Pueblo, 1984—; cons. on strategic planning and mgmt. to numerous colls. and univs. Author: Strategy and Policy Formation, 1981; contbr. articles to profl. publs. Mem. Pueblo Econ. Devel. Bd. Bill Laufman Meml. scholar U. Houston, 1965-66; Northwestern U. fellow, 1969-71; HEW research asst. grantee, 1971, 72; La. State U. Found. grantee, 1972, 73. Mem. Acad. Mgmt., Soc. Coll. and Univ. Planning, Pueblo C. of C. Presbyterian. Lodge: Rotary. Office: U So Colo 2200 Bonforte Blvd Pueblo CO 81001-4901*

SHIRTCLIFF, JOHN DELZELL, business owner, oil jobber; b. Roseburg, Oreg., Mar. 2, 1948; s. Henry Marion and Sheila Nell (Delzell) S.; m. Connie Lee Cantrell, June 13, 1975; children: Darcie, Danielle, Andrew. BS, Oregon State U., 1970. Pres. Shirtcliff Oil Co., Myrtle Creek, Oreg., 1971—. Engr. Myrtle Creek (Oreg.) Vol. Fire Dept., 1971—, emergency technician, 1981—; mem. Rep. Cen. Com., Roseburg, Oreg., 1982-88; chmn. Umpqua Community Coll. Budget Com., Roseburg, 1983—; bd. dirs. Mercy Hospice, Roseburg, 1988—. 2nd lt. U.S. Army, 1970-71. Named Citizen of Year, Myrtle Creek City, 1986, Vol. of Year, Douglas County C. of C., 1987. Mem. Petroleum Marketers Assn. Am. (dir. Oreg. 1988), Oreg. Petroleum Marketers Assn. (v.p. legis. chmn. 1986, pres. 1987, PMAA dir. 1988), Pacific Oil Conf. (bd. dirs., v.p. 1995), Lions, Elks, Masons, Shriners. Republican. Office: Shirtcliff Oil Co 283 SW Western Ave PO Box 6003 Myrtle Creek OR 97457-0051

SHISHIDO, CALVIN M., special services administrator; b. Honolulu, Aug. 24, 1933; s. Isamu and Kane (Seto) S.; children: Dale, Neala. BS, Florence State, 1961. Spl. agt. IRS, Pitts., 1962-65, FBI, Washington, 1965-84; pvt. investigator Honolulu, 1987-88; spl. asst. to deputy dir. Harbors Div Dept. of Transp., Hawaii, 1988-90; sheriff State of Hawaii, 1990-91, spl. projects mgr. dept. pub. safety, 1991—. Sgt. USAF, 1952-57. Mem. Soc. Former Spl. Agts. of FBI (chpt. chmn. Honolulu 1987-88), Lions (program chmn. San Francisco 1970-71), Jr. C. of C.

SHISHIDO, FUMITAKE, transportation company executive; b. Tokyo, Mar. 3, 1960; came to U.S., 1985; s. Osamu and Miyoko (Sugiue) S.; m. Kayoko Matsubara, June 21, 1986. BA, Waseda U., Tokyo, 1982; MBA, Columbia U., N.Y.C., 1987. Line mgr. Nippon Yusen Kaisha, Tokyo, 1982-84, investment analyst, 1984-85, project team mem., 1987-88; dir. fin. and asst. sec. Crystal Cruises, Inc., L.A., 1988-92, v.p., treas., 1993—; asst. mgr. NYK Line Europe Divsn. Tokyo, 1993—. Mem. Columbia Bus. Sch. Club Japan, Beta Gamma Sigma (N.Y.). Office: NYK Line, 2-3-2 Marunouchi, Chiyodabu, Tokyo 100, Japan

SHIVELY, JUDITH CAROLYN (JUDY SHIVELY), office assistant, contract administrator; b. Wilkinsburg, Pa., Jan. 30, 1962; d. John Allen and Edith (Crowell) S. BA in English, U. Nev., Las Vegas, 1984. Circulation aide Charleston Heights Libr., Las Vegas, 1979-86; asst. food editor Las Vegas Sun Newspaper, 1985-88, asst. horse racing editor, 1985-90, features writer, page editor, 1988-89, editor youth activities sect., 1989-90; racebook ticket writer, cashier Palace Sta. Hotel Racebook, Las Vegas, 1989-92; contract adminstr., gen. office asst. Loomis Armored, Inc., Las Vegas, 1992—; horse racing historian, researcher, Las Vegas, 1985—; vol. rsch. asst. Dictionary of Gambling and Gaming, 1982-84; part-time clk. Hometown News, Las Vegas, 1994—. Staff writer horse race handicaps, columns, articles, feature stories Las Vegas Sun Newspaper, 1985-90; freelance writer for monthly horse racing publ. Inside Track, 1992-94. Mem. Phi Beta Kappa. Republican. Home: PO Box 26426 Las Vegas NV 89126-0426

SHKURKIN, EKATERINA VLADIMIROVNA (KATIA SHKURKIN), social worker; b. Berkeley, Calif., Nov. 20, 1955; d. Vladimir Vladimirovich and Olga Ivanovna (Lisenko) S. Student, U. San Francisco, 1972-73; BA, U. Calif., Berkeley, 1974-77; MSW, Columbia U., 1977-79; postgrad., Union Grad. Sch., 1986. Cert. police instr. domestic violence, Alaska. Social worker Tolstoy Found., N.Y.C., 1978-79, adminstr., 1979-80; program supr. Rehab. Mental Health Ctr., San Jose, Calif., 1980-81; dir. svc. counselor Kodiak (Alaska) Crisis Ctr., 1981-82; domestic violence counselor Abused Women's Aid in Crisis, Anchorage, 1982-85; pvt. practice social work specializing in feminist therapy Susitna Therapy Ctr., Anchorage, 1985—; pvt. practice, 1985-89; field instr. Abused Women's Aid in Crisis, Anchorage, 1983-88, Divsn. Family and Youth Svcs., State of Alaska, 1989-91, South Cen. Found.-Dena A. Coy Prematernal Alcohol Treatment Ctr., 1991-92; expert witness Anchorage Mcpl. Cts., 1982—; interim faculty mem. U. Alaska, Anchorage, summer 1985, fall 1988—, LaVerne U., Anchorage, 1986—; family therapist Anchorage Ctr. for Families, 1994—. Coordinator Orthodox Christian Fellowship, San Francisco, 1972-76; pub. speaker Abused Women's Aid in Crisis, Anchorage, 1982—; active nat. and local election campaigns, 1968—. Mem. NASW (cert.). Democrat. Russian Orthodox. Home and Office: 3605 Arctic Blvd # 768 Anchorage AK 99503-5789

SHLIMAK, YAN, office assistant, home healthcare provider; b. Moscow, Apr. 16, 1971; came to U.S., 1989; s. Vladimir and Tanya (Rozenbaum) S. Spl. diploma, Med. Vocal. Sch., Moscow, 1989; student, Santa Monica Coll., 1989-92, UCLA, 1992—. Trans. aid person Moscow Med. Hosp. #4, 1986-87; lab. technician Epidemiology Sta., Moscow, 1987-88; office asst. Cardiology Ctr., L.A., 1992-94, area dental office, L.A., 1990—; home care provider In-Home Supportive Svcs., Bur. Spl. Ops., L.A., 1990—; ind. rschr. targeted controlled drug delivery sys., L.A., 1991—. Contbr. articles to profl. publs. Vol. area podiatric office, L.A., 1991-92, UCLA Med. Ctr., summer 1993, Acculturation and Social Adaptation Program for Fgn. Sr. Citizens, L.A., 1992-94. Citizen's Scholarship Found. Am. scholar, 1994. Mem. AAAS, N.Y. Acad. Sci., Golden Key. Jewish. Home: # 202 1351 N Crescent Heights Los Angeles CA 90046

SHMAVONIAN, GERALD S., association executive; b. L.A., June 26, 1945; s. Sarkis Neshan and Berje-Lucia (der Hareutunyan) S. Student, U. Calif., Berkeley, 1964-70. Leader archaeol. excavation team Guatemala, Turkey, 1970-75; pub. City Mags., 1975-80; special advisor Bicentennial Commission, Washington, D.C., 1987; chmn. Am. Nationalities Coun., Stanford U., 1983—. Mem. Calif. Scholarship Fedn. (life, pres. 1963), Nat. Forensic League (pres. 1963, degree of honor), Statesmen's Club. Home: 6219 N Prospect Ave Fresno CA 93711-1658 Office: 10940 Wilshire Blvd Fl 15 Los Angeles CA 90024-3915

SHNEIDER, JEFFREY A., architect; b. Lincoln, Nebr., Apr. 29, 1948; s. Sam and Rose (Block) S.; m. Anne Louise Shockley, Feb. 21, 1971; children: Sarah, Max. BS, U. Wis., 1971; MArch, U. Nebr., 1974. Pres. CSHQA Archs./Planners, Boise, Idaho, 1974-94. Active Leadership Boise, 1980-81; dir., exec. com. Boise Area Econ. Devel. Coun.; past. pres. Boise Art Mus. Recipient outstanding young man award, 1981, Mgmt. Magic for Design Profls. Profl. Svcs. Mgmt. Jour. Seminar, 1987. Mem. Am. Inst. Archs. (pres. 1977—), Ada Planning Assn. Office: CSHQA Archs/Planners Ctrl Sta 200 N 6th Boise ID 83702

SHNEIDMAN, EDWIN S., psychologist, educator, thanatologist, suicidologist; b. York, Pa., May 13, 1918; s. Louis and Manya (Zukin) S.; m. Jeanne E. Keplinger, Oct. 1, 1944; children: David William, Jonathan Aaron, Paul Samuel, Robert James. A.B., UCLA, 1938, M.A., 1940; M.S., U. So. Calif., 1947, Ph.D., 1948. Diplomate: Am. Bd. Examiners Profl. Psychology (past v.p.). Clin. psychologist VA Center, Los Angeles, 1947-50; chief research VA Center, 1950-53; co-dir. Central Research Unit for Study Unpredicted Deaths, 1953-58; co.-dir. Suicide Prevention Center, Los Angeles, 1958-66; chief Center Studies Suicide Prevention NIMH, Bethesda, Md., 1966-69; vis. prof. Harvard U., 1969; fellow Ctr. Advanced Study in Behavioral Scis., 1969-70; clin. assoc. Mass. Gen. Hosp., 1969, Karolinska Hosp., Stockholm, 1978; prof. med. psychology UCLA, 1970-75, prof. thanatology, 1975-88, emeritus, 1988—; vis. prof. Ben Gurion U. of Negev, Beersheva, 1983. Author: Deaths of Man, 1973, Voices of Death, 1980; Definition of Suicide, 1985, Suicide as Psychache, 1993; editor: Thematic Test Analysis, 1951; editor: (with N.L. Farberow) Clues to Suicide, 1957, The Cry for Help, 1961, Essays in Self-Destruction, 1967, (with M. Ortega) Aspects of Depression, 1969, On the Nature of Suicide, 1969, (with N.L. Farberow, L.E. Litman) Psychology of Suicide, 1970, Death and the College Student, 1972, Death: Current Perspectives, 1976, 80, 84, Suicidology: Contemporary Developments, 1976, Endeavors in Psychology: Selections From The Personology of Henry A. Murray, 1981, Suicide Thoughts and Reflections, 1981. Served to capt. USAAF, 1942-45. Recipient Harold M. Hildreth award Psychologists in Pub. Service, 1966; Louis I. Dublin award Am. Assn. Suicidology, 1969; Disting. Profl. Contbn. to Pub. Service award Am. Psychol. Assn., 1987. Mem. Am. Assn. Suicidology (founder, past pres.), Am. Psychol. Assn. (past div. pres.), Soc. Projective Techniques (past pres.), Melville Soc. Office: UCLA Neuropsychiat Inst 760 Westwood Plz Los Angeles CA 90024-8300

SHNEOUR, ELIE ALEXIS, biochemist; b. Neuilly-sur-Seine, France, Dec. 11, 1925; came to U.S., 1941, naturalized, 1944; s. Zalman and Salomea (Landau) S.; m. Polly M. Henderson, 7 Sept. 1990; children from previous marriage: Mark Zalman, Alan Brewster. B.A., Columbia U., 1947; DSc (hon.), Bard Coll., 1969; M.A., U. Calif., Berkeley, 1955; Ph.D., UCLA, 1958. Teaching., research fellowship U. Calif., Berkeley, 1953-55, Am. Heart Assn. research fellow, 1958-62; teaching., research fellowship U. Calif., L.A., 1958; research fellow Nat. Cancer Inst., 1956-57; Am. Heart Assn. research fellow N.Y.U., 1958-59; research assoc. genetics Stanford U., 1962-65; assoc. prof. biology and neurosciences U. Utah, 1965-69; research neurochemist City of Hope Nat. Med. Ctr., Duarte, Calif., 1969-71; dir. rsch. Calbiochem., 1971-75; pres. Biosystems Insts., Inc., 1975—; dir. Biosystems Rsch. Inst., 1979—; mem. exec. com. Nat. Acad. Sci. Study Group on Biology and the Exploration of Mars, 1964; chmn. Western Regional coun. Rsch. in Basic Bioscis. for Manned Orbiting Missions, Am. Inst. Biol. Scis., NASA, 1966-69. Author: Extraterrestrial Life, 1965, (with Eric A. Ottesen) National Academy of Sciences, National Rsch. Coun., 1966, (with S. Moffat) Life Beyond the Earth, 1966, The Malnourished Mind, 1974; contbr. numerous articles to sci. and lay jours. Chmn. citizens adv. coun. San Diego Pub. Schs., 1971-72; mem. adv. coun. Cousteau Soc., 1977—; bd. dirs. Am.-Ukraine Trade Coun., 1991—, Lunar Power System Coalition, 1993—, Transinnova S.A. France, 1990—; chmn. sci. adv. bd. County of San Diego, 1995—. With U.S. Army, 1944-45. Recipient William Lockwood prize, 1947. Mem. IEEE, AAAS (chmn. So. Calif. Skeptics soc. Pacific divsn. 1988-90), Am. Chem. Soc., N.Y. Acad. Scis., Am. Inst. Biol. Scis., Am. Soc. for Biochemistry and Molecular Biology (chmn. sci. advisors program 1973-75, mem. com. on pub. policy 1974-76, congl. liaison 1992—), Am. Soc. Neurochemistry (mem. coun. 1971-73), Soc. Neurosci., Internat. Soc. Neurochemistry, U.S. C. of C. (bd. dirs. 1993—), La Jolla Chamber Music Soc. (bd. dirs. 1994—), Sigma Xi, Phi Sigma. Office: Biosystems Insts Inc 700 Front St San Diego CA 92101-6000

SHOCTOR, JOSEPH HARVEY, barrister, producer, civic worker; b. Edmonton, Alta., Can., Aug. 18, 1922. BA, LLB, U. Alta., 1946, LLD (hon.), 1981; diploma in theatre adminstrn. (hon.), Grant McEwan Coll., 1986. Named to Queens Counsel, 1960. Barrister, solicitor, sr. counsel Duncan & Craig, Edmonton, 1993—; bd. dirs. Saxony Investments, Inc., Desa Stores Ltd.; pres., exec. officer Harvey Holdings Ltd. Prodr. Broadway plays including Peter Pan, 1965, Henry, Sweet Henry, 1967, Billy, 1969, Hamlet, 1969; founder, pres., exec. producer, bldg. chmn., campaign chmn. Citadel Theater; producer Circle 8 Theatre, Civic Opera, Red Cross Entertainment; panelist pub. affairs talk show and sports forum. Active United Cmty. Fund, 1968—; chmn. Downtown Devel. Corp., Edmonton, 1986; mem. Edmonton Jewish Welfare Bd.; past pres. Edmonton Jewish Cmty. Coun.; past nat. sec. Federated Zionist Orgn.; past nat. v.p. United Israel Appeal, Inc.; past bd. dirs. Can. Coun. Jewish Welfare Funds; chmn. divsn. Brit. Commonwealth Games Found., 1978; bd. govs. Nat. Theatre Sch. of Can., officer Order of Can., 1986. Inducted into Cultural Hall of Fame, 1987; named Man of Hr., Sta. CFRN-TV, 1966, Citizen of Yr., B'nai B'rith, 1966, one of Twelve Top Albertans of the 70's, The Alberta Report, U. Alberta Alumni Wall of Recognition, 1995, Disting. Citizen Grant MacEwan C.C., 1995; recipient Performing Arts award City of Edmonton, 1972, Theatre Arts Achievement award Province of Alta., 1975, Prime Minister's medal State of Israel, 1978, Builder of Cmty. award City of Edmonton, 1979, Queen's Silver Jubilee medal, 1977, City of Edmonton Silver Ribbon award, 1985, Great Canadian award, 1992, Commemorative medal for 125th Anniversary Canadian Confederation, 1992; The Shoctor Theatre named in his honor, 1976; Alta. Order of Excellence. Mem. Edmonton C. of C. Clubs: The Edmonton, The Centre, Eskimo Football (founder, past sec.-mgr.). Office: Duncan & Craig, 10060 Jasper Ave 2800, Edmonton, AB Canada T5J 3V9

SHOE, STEPHEN CHARLES, marketing professional; b. Kansas City, Mo., Oct. 12, 1935; s. Charles Arthur and Mary Margaret (Skaggs) S.; m. Patricia Carmen Williams, Mar. 9, 1958; children: David Mark, Peggy Jo, Rebecca Lynn. BA, U. North Colo., 1958, MA, 1961. Tchr. art & advt. Borah (Idaho) High Sch., 1960-66; account exec. KEST Radio, Boise, Idaho, 1966-68, KBIO & KGDN Radio, Seattle, 1968-70; dir. sch. svcs. Nat. Assn. Christian Sch., Wheaton, Ill., 1970-73, dir., 1973-74; pub. rels. dir. Wheaton (Ill.) Christian High Sch., 1974-75; pub. relations dir. Rockmont Coll. (now Colo. Christian U.), Lakewood, 1975-78; cons. Lakewood, 1978—; pres. Railroad Promotions, 1990—; with pub. rels. dept. Georgetown Loop Railroad, 1984-94. Contbr. articles to profl. jours. Named Model Railroad Industry Person of Yr., 1993. Mem. Model R.R. Industry Assn. (exec. dir. 1987—), South Lakewood Optimist Club (past pres.), Seattle Optimist Club (past pres.). Republican. Home: 12235 W Texas Dr Lakewood CO 80228-3619

SHOEMAKER, BILL (WILLIAM LEE SHOEMAKER), retired jockey, horse trainer; b. Fabens, Tex., Aug. 19, 1931; s. B. B. and Ruby (Call) S.; m. Cynthia Barnes, Mar. 7, 1978; 1 dau., Amanda Elisabeth. Jockey, 1949-90, ret., 1990, trainer, 1990—. Author: Stalking Horse, 1994. Office: Care Vincent Andrews Mgmt 315 S Beverly Dr Ste 216 Beverly Hills CA 90212-4310*

SHOEMAKER, CAMERON DAVID JAMES, dean, educator; b. Honolulu, Dec. 15, 1940; s. John James and Belle Bird (Kellogg) S.; m. Catherine LaMoyne Prevost, May 23, 1966 (div. 1969); 1 child, David James; m. Leona Martha Wohlwend, May 18, 1972; 1 child, Jennifer Lee. BA in Polit. Sci., The Citadel, 1963; MA in History, San Jose State U., 1973; EdD, U. San Francisco, 1990. Commd. 2d lt. U.S. Army, 1963, advanced through grades to maj., 1971; fgn. area officer U.S. Army, U.S., Korea, Germany and Vietnam, 1972-84; ret. U.S. Army, 1984; mgmt. analyst Def. Lang. Inst., Monterey, Calif., 1985; ednl. tech. project mgr. Def. Lang. Inst., Monterey, 1985-86, dir. info. resources mgmt., 1986-90; evening coll. adminstr., instnl. researcher Monterey Peninsula Coll., 1990-92; dean of bus. Sacramento (Calif.) City Coll., 1992—; instr., Chapman Coll., Monterey, 1982-84, Monterey Inst., 1987; chmn. Asian Employment Program Com., Monterey, 1983-84; guest lectr., Naval Postgrad. Sch., Monterey, 1986-87; mem. Handicapped Individual Program Com., Monterey, 1986-90, treas., 1989-90. Contbr. articles to various publs. Pres., Creekside Community Assn.,

Salinas, Calif., 1985-86; mem. County Svc. Area Adv. Bd., Salinas, 1985-87, Flood Control Dist. Planning Com., Salinas, 1986-87; active Leadership Monterey Peninsula, grad., 1992. Decorated Silver Star medal; recipient Comdrs. award for Civilian Svc. Dept. of Army, 1990; Carl D. Perkins fellow, 1993. Mem. Royal Asiatic Soc., Monterey Peninsula Scottish Soc. (treas. 1986-92), Caledonian Club of Sacramento (treas. 1994—), Los Ricos Mgmt. Assn. (pres. 1995-96), Phi Delta Kappa. Republican. Roman Catholic. Home: 22315 Capote Dr 11577 Melones Cir Gold River CA 95670-7738 Office: Sacramento City Coll 3835 Freeport Blvd Sacramento CA 95822-1318

SHOEMAKER, CLARA BRINK, retired chemistry educator; b. Rolde, Drenthe, The Netherlands, June 20, 1921; came to U.S., 1953; d. Hendrik Gerard and Hendrikje (Smilde) Brink; m. David Powell Shoemaker, Aug. 5. 1955; 1 child, Robert Brink. PhD, Leiden U., The Netherlands, 1950. Instr. in inorganic chemistry Leiden U., 1946-50, 51-53; postdoctoral fellow Oxford (Eng.) U., 1950-51; rsch. assoc. dept. chemistry MIT, Cambridge, 1953-55, 58-70; rsch. assoc. biochemistry Harvard Med. Sch., Boston, 1955-56; project supr. Boston U., 1963-64; rsch. assoc. dept. chemistry Oreg. State U, Corvallis, 1970-75, rsch. assoc. prof. dept. chemistry, 1975-82, sr. rsch. prof. dept. chemistry, 1982-84, prof. emerita, 1984—. Sect. editor: Structure Reports of International Union of Crystallography, 1967, 68, 69; co-author chpts. in books; author numerous sci. papers. Bd. dirs. LWV, Corvallis, 1980-82, bd. dirs., sec., Oreg., 1985-87. Fellow Internat. Fedn. Univ. Women, Oxford U., 1950-51. Mem. Metall. Soc. (com. on alloy phases 1969-79), Internat. Union of Crystallography (commn. on structure reports 1970-90), Am. Crystallographic Assn. (crystallographic data com. 1975-78, Fankuchen award com. 1976), Sigma Xi, Iota Sigma Pi (faculty adv. Oreg. State U. chpt. 1975-84), Phi Lambda Upsilon. Office: Oreg State U Dept Chemistry Corvallis OR 97331

SHOEMAKER, EUGENE MERLE, geologist; b. L.A., Apr. 28, 1928; s. George Estel and Muriel May (Scott) S.; m. Carolyn Jean Spellmann, Aug. 18, 1951; children: Christine Carol, Patrick Gene, Linda Susan. B.S., Calif. Inst. Tech., 1947, M.S., 1948; M.A., Princeton U., 1954, Ph.D., 1960; Sc.D., Ariz. State Coll., 1965, Temple U., 1967, U. Ariz., 1984. Geologist U.S. Geol. Survey, 1948-93, scientist emeritus, 1993—, exploration uranium deposits and investigation salt structures Colo. and Utah, 1948-50, regional investigations geochemistry, volcanology and structure Colorado Plateau, 1951-56, research on structure and mechanics of meteorite impact and nuclear explosion craters, 1957-60, with E.C.T. Chao, discovered coesite, Meteor Crater, Ariz., 1960, investigation structure and history of moon, 1960-73, established lunar geol. time scale, methods of geol. mapping of moon, 1960, application TV systems to investigation extraterrestrial geology, 1961—, geology and paleomagnetism, Colo. Plateau, 1969—, systematic search for planet-crossing asteroids and comets, 1973-94; with C.S. Shoemaker and D.H. Levy discovered Periodic Comet Shoemaker-Levy 9, 1993; Trojan asteroids U.S. Geol. Survey, 1985-94, geology of satellites of Jupiter, Saturn, Uranus and Neptune, 1978—, investigating role of large body impacts in evolution of life, 1981—; impact craters of Australia, 1983—; organized br. of astrogeology U.S. Geol. Survey, 1961; co-investigator TV expt. Project Ranger, 1961-65; chief scientist, center of astrogeology U.S. Geol. Survey, 1966-68; prin. investigator geol. field investigations in Apollo lunar landing, 1965-70, also television expt. Project Surveyor, 1963-68; prof. geology Calif. Inst. Tech., 1969-85, chmn. div. geol. and planetary scis., 1969-72; sci. team leader Clementine Mission to the Moon, 1993-94; staff mem. Lowell Observatory, Flagstaff, Ariz., 1993—. Recipient (with E.C.T. Chao) Wetherill medal Franklin Inst., 1965; Arthur S. Flemming award, 1966; NASA medal for exceptional sci. achievement, 1967; honor award for meritorious service U.S. Dept. Interior, 1973; Disting. Service award, 1980; Disting. Alumni award Calif. Inst. Tech., 1986, co-recipient Rittenhouse medal, 1988, Nat. Medal of Sci. President Bush, 1992. Mem. NAS, Internat. Astron. Union, Am. Acad. Arts and Scis., Geol. Soc. Am. (Day medal 1982, Gilbert award 1983), Mineral Soc. Am., Soc. Econ. Geologists, Geochem. Soc., Am. Assn. Petroleum Geologists, Am. Geophys. Union (Whipple award 1993), Am. Astron. Soc. (Kuiper prize 1984), Meteoritical Soc. (Barringer award 1984, Leonard medal 1985). Home: RR 4 Box 998 Flagstaff AZ 86001-8346 Office: US Geol Survey 2255 N Gemini Dr Flagstaff AZ 86001-1637

SHOEMAKER, HAROLD LLOYD, infosystem specialist; b. Danville, Ky., Jan. 3, 1923; s. Eugene Clay and Amy (Wilson) S.; A.B., Berea Coll., 1944; postgrad. State U. Ia., 1943-44, George Washington U., 1949-50, N.Y. U., 1950-52; m. Dorothy M. Maddox, May 11, 1947 (dec. Feb. 1991). Research physicist State U. Ia., 1944-45, Frankford Arsenal, Pa., 1945-47; research engr. N.Am. Aviation, Los Angeles, 1947-49, Jacobs Instrument Co., Bethesda, 1949-50; asso. head systems devel. group The Teleregister Corp., N.Y.C., 1950-53; mgr. electronic equipment devel. sect., head planning for indsl. systems div. Hughes Aircraft Co., Los Angeles, 1953-58; dir. command and control systems lab. Bunker-Ramo Corp., Los Angeles, 1958-68, v.p. Data Systems, 1968-69, corp. dir. data processing, 1969-75; tech. staff R & D Assocs., Marina Del Rey, Calif., 1975-85; info. systems cons., 1985—. Served with AUS, 1945-46. Mem. IEEE. Patentee elec. digital computer. Home: PO Box 3385 Granada Hills CA 91394-0385

SHOEMAKER, JOAN, mayor; b. Hartford, Conn., Feb. 20, 1935; d. Jean George and Olive Irene (Clifford) Hauet; m. Warner D. Dalton, Nov. 8, 1956 (div. Apr. 1960); children: Lori, Robert; m. Steven R. Shoemaker, Dec. 18, 1965; children: Mike, Marsi, Jennifer, Douglas. Mayor City of El Cajon, Calif., 1990—. Planning commr. City of El Cajon, 1979-83, councilwoman, 1983-90. Republican. LDS. Office: City of El Cajon 200 E Main St El Cajon CA 92020-3912

SHOEN, EDWARD JOSEPH, transportation and insurance companies executive; s. Leonard and Anna (Carty) S. MBA, Harvard U. Pres., chmn. Amerco Nev. Corp., Phoenix; pres. U-Haul Internat., Inc., Phoenix. Office: Amerco Nev Corp PO Box 21502 Phoenix AZ 85036-1502 also: Amerco 1325 Airmotive Way Reno NV 89502-3201

SHOJI, JUNE MIDORI, import and export trading executive; b. Long Beach, Calif., June 21, 1957; d. Sam Masatsugu and Tomiyo (Kinoshita) S. BA in Psychology and Econs., UCLA, 1975-79; cert. Japanese, Waseda U., Tokyo, 1980-82; Grad. Gemologist, Gemol. Inst., Santa Monica, Calif., 1984. Mktg. rep. IBM Corp., L.A., 1982-84, Xerox Corp., El Monte, Calif., 1984-86; adminstrv. drilling analyst Arco Internat. Oil & Gas, L.A., 1986-89; buyer OEM components & machinery Honda Trading Am., Torrance, Calif., 1989-94, asst. mgr. OEM components machinery and non-ferrous metals, 1994—. Home: 1865 W 166th St Gardena CA 90247-4664

SHOKEIR, MOHAMED HASSAN KAMEL, medical geneticist, educator; b. Mansoura, Egypt, July 2, 1938; emigrated to Can., 1969, naturalized, 1974; s. Hassan Sayed and Lolia Nora (Kira) S.; m. Donna Jean Nugent, Feb. 27, 1968; children: Marc Omar, Vanessa May. MB, BCh in Medicine and Surgery, Cairo U., 1960, ChD, 1963, ChD in Orthopedics, 1964; MS, U. Mich., 1965, PhD, 1969. Intern Cairo U. Hosps., 1960-61, resident, 1961-64; Fulbright rsch. scholar dept. human genetics U. Mich., 1964-69; asst. prof. pediatrics U. Sask., Saskatoon, 1969-71, assoc. prof., 1971-73, prof., 1977—, dir. div. med. genetics, 1975—, head dept. pediatrics, 1979—; head dept. pediatrics Saskatoon Dist. Health Bd., 1993—; head sect. clin. genetics U. Man., Winnipeg, 1973-75; mem. staffs Univ. Hosp., Saskatoon City Hosp., St. Paul's Hosp.; cons. Winnipeg Health Scis. Centre, Regina Gen. Hosp. Contbr. articles to profl publs. Mem. Acad. Freedom and Tenure Com., Ottawa, Ont., Can., 1980-90, Queen Elizabeth II scientist, 1969-75. Med. Rsch. Coun. grantee, 1970-79; Canadian Coll. Med. Geneticists Found. fellow, 1975—. Fellow Can. Coll. Med. Geneticists, Can. Soc. Clin. Investigation (councillor 1974-76), Can. Med. Assn. (chmn., mem. adv. com. 1987—); mem. Assn. Med. Sch. Pediatric Dept. Chairmen, Assn. Canadian Univ. Dept. Chairmen, Am. Pediatric Soc., Soc. Pediatric Research, N.Y. Acad. Scis., Am. Geriatrics Soc., Am. Fedn. Clin. Research, Mid-Western Soc. Pediatric Research, Western Pediatric Soc., Am. Soc. Human Genetics, Genetics Soc. Am., Genetics Soc. Can., Am. Genetic Assn., Am. Pub. Health Assn. Home: 108 Riel Crescent, Saskatoon, SK Canada S7J 2W6 Office: U Sask, Dept Pediatrics, Saskatoon, SK Canada S7N 0X0

SHOLTIS, JOSEPH ARNOLD, JR., corporation executive, nuclear aerospace engineer, consultant; b. Monongahela, Pa., Nov. 28, 1948; s. Joseph and Gladys (Frye) S.; m. Cheryl Anita Senchur, Dec. 19, 1970; children: Christian Joseph, Carole Lynne. BS in Nuc. Engring. (Disting. Mil. Grad.), Pa. State U., 1970; diplomas Air Univ., 1975, 78; MS in Nuclear Engring., U. N.Mex., 1977, postgrad., 1978-80. Lic. sr. reactor operator NRC, 1980-84. Mathematician, statistician, mine safety analyst U.S. Bur. Mines, Pitts., 1968-70; commd. 2d lt. USAF, 1970, advanced through grades to lt. col. 1988, ret., 1993; nuclear rsch. officer Fgn. Tech. Div., USAF, Wright-Patterson AFB, Ohio, 1971-74; chief space nucl. sys. safety sect. Air Force Weapons Lab., Kirtland AFB, N.Mex., 1974-78; mil. mem. tech. staff, project officer Sandia Nat. Labs., Albuquerque, 1978-80; chief radiation sources div., reactor facility dir. Armed Forces Radiobiology Rsch. Inst., Bethesda, Md., 1980-84; program mgr. SP-100 space reactor power sys. tech. devel. program Air Force Element U.S. Dept. Energy, Germantown, Md., 1984-87; chief analysis and evaluation br. Air Force Safety Agy., Kirtland AFB, N.Mex., 1988-91, chief nuc. power and sources div., 1991-92, chief nuc. energy systems, 1992-93; dir. rsch. and engring., gen. mgr. N.Mex. ops. Oakton Internat. Corp., Va., 1993—; cons. Internat. Corp., 1993—, in field; space shuttle nuclear payload safety assessment officer Air Force Weapons Lab., Kirtland AFB, 1976-78; instr. med. effects nuc. weapons Armed Forces Radiobiology Rsch. Inst., Bethesda, 1980-85, mem. reactor and radiation facility safety com., 1980-85; faculty, lectr. Uniformed Svcs. Univ. Health Scis., Bethesda, 1982-87; chmn. Power System Subpanel Interagency Nuclear Safety Rev. Panel risk assessments of Galileo, Ulysses and Cassini nuclear-powered space missions, 1987-92; Dept. of Def. chmn. Interagency Nuclear Safety Rev. Panel evaluation of Ulysses, Cassini nuclear-powered space missions for the office of the pres., 1989-93; mem. power system subpanel Interagency Nuc. Safety Rev. Panel for evaluation of Cassini, Mars Pathfinder, Mars Survey, and Pluto Express nuc.-powered space missions, 1993—; instr. Inst. for Space Nuc. Power Studies U. N.Mex., 1987-91; U.S. del., tech. advisor UN Sci. and Tech. Subcom. and Legal Subcom. Working Group on Nuclear Power Sources in Outer Space, 1984-88; mem. U.S. contingent U.S. and U.S.S.R. discussions on nuclear space power system safety, 1989-90; mem. adv. com., tech. program com. Symposia on Space Nuclear Power and Propulsion, U. N.Mex., 1989—; mem. Multimegawatt Space Reactor Power Project safety working group, 1988-91; mem. SP-100 Space Reactor Project safety adv. com., 1990-93; mem. space exploration initiative Nuclear Safety Policy Working Group, 1990-91; mem. Air Force Thermionic Space Power Program Safety com., 1990-93; mem. Strategic Def. Initiative Orgn. Ind. Evaluation Group, 1991-93; mem., ind. advisor U.S. Dept. Energy Ind. Safety Assessment of TOPAZ-II space reactor power system, 1993; mem. Ind. Rev. Team recert. evaluation Cassini space mission, 1994; mem. program com. Reactor Safety Divsn. Am. Nuclear Soc., 1992-94; lectr. N.Mex. Acad. of Sci. Vis. Scientist Program, 1991—. Author: (with others) LMFBR Accident Delineation, 1980, Military Radiobiology, 1987, Power System Subpanel Report for Galileo Space Mission, 1989, Power System Subpanel Report for Ulysses Space Mission, 1990, Safety Evaluation Report for Ulysses Space Mission, 1990, A Critical Review of Space Nuclear Power and Propulsion 1984-1993, 1994; contbr. articles, chpts. in books. Charter mem. N.Mex. Edn. OutreachCom., 1989—; USGA rules official Sun Country Amateur Golf Assn., N.Mex., 1993—. Decorated Def. Meritorious Svc. medal (2), Air Force Meritorious Svc. medal (2) Air Force Commendation medal (3), Nat. Def. Svc. medal (2), U.S. Army Reactor Comdr. Badge, U.S. Air Force Missileman Badge, Air Force Master Space Systems Badge, Nat. Aeronautics and Space Administration ment awards (3); recipient White House citation. Mem. Am. Nuclear Soc. (Best Paper 1977), ASME, AIAA, AAAS, N.Mex. Acad. Scis., Sigma Xi. Republican. Avocations: hunting, fishing, camping, golfing, motorcycle touring. Office: PO Box 910 Tijeras NM 87059-0910

SHONK, ALBERT DAVENPORT, JR., advertising executive; b. L.A., May 23, 1932; s. Albert Davenport and Jean Spence (Stannard) S.; BS in Bus. Adminstrn., U. So. Calif., 1954. Field rep. mktg. div. Los Angeles Examiner, 1954-55, asst. mgr. mktg. and field supr. mktg. div. 1955-56, mgr. mktg. div., 1956-57; account exec. Hearst Advt. Svc., Los Angeles, 1957-59; account exec., mgr. Keith H. Evans & Assos., San Francisco, 1959-65; owner, pres. Albert D. Shonk Co., L.A., 1965—; gen. ptnr. Shonk Land Co. LTD, Charleston, W.Va., 1989—; pres. Signet Circle Corp., Inc., 1977-81, dir., 1962-81, hon. life dir., 1981—, treas., 1989—. Bd. dirs. Crittenton Ctr. for Young Women and Infants, sec., 1978, 1st v.p., 1978-79, exec. v.p., 1979-81, pres., 1981-83, chmn. bd., 1983-85, hon. life dir., 1986—; co-chair centennial com., founding chmn. Crittenton Assocs. Recipient Medallion of Merit Phi Sigma Kappa, 1976, Founders award, 1961,NIC Interfraternal award, 1989 . Mem. Advt. Club Los Angeles, Bus. and Profl. Advt. Assn., Pubs. Rep. Assn. of So. Calif., Nat. Assn. Pubs. Reps. (past v.p. West Coast 1981-83), Jr. Advt. Club L.A. (hon. life, dir., treas., 1st v.p.), Trojan Club, Skull and Dagger, U. So. Calif., U. S.C. Commerce Assocs. (nat. bd. 1991-, treas. 1995—), U. S.C. Assocs., Inter-Greek Soc. (co-founder, hon. life mem. and dir., v.p. 1976-79, pres. 1984-86), Phi Sigma Kappa (dir. grand council 1962-70, 77-79, grand pres. 1979-83, chancellor 1983-87, 90-91, v.p. meml. found. 1979-84, pres. 1984, trustee pres. Phi Sigma Kappa found. 1984-94), Alpha Kappa Psi, Town Hall. Home: 3460 W 7th St Apt 806 Los Angeles CA 90005-2312 Office: Albert Shonk Co 3156 Wilshire Blvd Ste 7 Los Angeles CA 90010-1209

SHOOK, DALE ALFORD, JR., minister; b. Wichita Falls, Tex., May 19, 1945; s. Dale Alford and Betty (Rushing) S.; m. Jane Bradley, July 17, 1970; children: Joy, Brad. BA in Religious Edn., Hardin-Simmons U., 1967; MDiv, Southwestern Bapt. Sem., Ft. Worth, 1970. Ordained to ministry So. Bapt. Conv., 1970. Youth min. 1st Bapt. Ch., Merkel, Tex., 1965-68, Mineral Wells, Tex., 1968-71; assoc. pastor 1st Bapt. Ch., Albuquerque, 1971-80; assoc. pastor, adminstr. Taylor Meml. Bapt. Ch., Hobbs, N.Mex., 1980—; vice chmn. exec. bd..Mex. Bapt. State Conv., 1983-85, chmn., 1986. Contbr. articles to profl. jours. Bd. dirs. Young Assocs. Hardin-Simmons U., 1970-80, pres. alumni, 1985; mem. Coun. on Aging, Hobbs, 1988-90. Fellow Nat. Assn. Bus. Adminstrn., So. Bapt. Bus. Adminstrn., So. Bapt. Religious Edn. Assn. (vice chmn. 1988, v.p. 1987-88, bd. dirs. 1990—), So. Bapt. Assn. (moderator 1988). Office: Taylor Meml Bapt Ch 1700 E Yeso Dr Hobbs NM 88240-4217

SHORE, DIANA KAY, nutritionist; b. Parkersburg, W.Va., May 28, 1949; d. James Dana and Viola Mary (Bowen) McClanahan; m. Philip Shore, 1982; children: Adam, Allison. BGS, Ohio U., 1971, BS in Edn., 1972, PhD, 1989; MS, Murray State U., 1979. Registered dietitian, Ohio, Calif.; cert. elem., secondary, vocat. tchr. Grad. asst. Murray (Ky.) State U., 1978-80, Ohio State U., Columbus, 1980-81, 82-83; instr. Morehead (Ky.) State U., 1987-88; dietitian Women, Infants and children, Huntington, W.Va., 1985-87; dietitian wellness Carmel Hosp., Columbus, 1990-94; dietitian Shore Med. Ctr., Chatsworth, Calif., 1991-94; instr. L.A. Valley Coll., 1994—. Mem. nominating com. L.A. Med. Aux., 1994—; steering com. Granada Hills (Calif.) Hosp. Found., 1993—; art docent Parent Faculty Assn. Round Meadow Sch., 1992—. Mem. Am. Dietetic Assn., L.A. Dietetic Assn. (chair pub. rels. 1993-94, Com. Chair of Yr. 1994), Toastmasters (CTM award). Office: Shore Med Ctr 10324 Mason Ave Chatsworth CA 91311-3305

SHORE, JOHN JAMES, III, materials and environmental engineering consultant; b. Rivesville, W.Va., July 27, 1930; s. John James II and Mary Elisbeth (Radcliffe) S.; m. Verne Jean Ashcraft, July 2, 1955 (div. 1978); children: Kimberlee, Leslie, Holly, John IV; m. Melba Odesa Beall, July 21, 1979. BSChemE, W.Va. U., 1955; student in engring. and mgmt. sch., U. Calif., L.A., 1989. Cert. hazardous materials responder, Calif; cert. in hazardous waste mgmt. U.S. EPA. Rural carrier U.S. Postal Dept., Rivesville, 1951-53; quality control engr. E.I. DuPont de Nemours, Parkersburg, W.Va., 1955-57; materials engr. Aerojet Gen., Sacramento, Calif., 1957-79; materials engr. Gen. Dynamics, Pomona, Calif., 1979-85, sect. head materials tech., 1985-92; sr. environ. engring. specialist Hughes Missile Systems, Pomona, Calif., 1992-94, ret., 1994; pvt. cons. Claremont, Calif., 1994—. Contbr. articles to profl. jours. and reports; co-patentee in field. Trailblazer, chief YMCA Indian Guides, Orangevale, Calif., 1971-74; adult leader YMCA Grey Y, Orangevale, 1974-76. With U.S. Army, 1950-51. Mem. Aerospace Industries Assn. (materials and structures com.), Soc. of Automotive Engring. (polymers, composites and elastomers coms. 1985—), Elks, Sigma Phi Omega, Phi Lambda Upsilon. Republican. Home and Office: 641 Rockford Dr Claremont CA 91711-2909

SHORS, SUSAN DEBRA, lawyer; b. Detroit, Nov. 23, 1954; d. Clayton Marion and Arlene Lois (Towle) S.; m. Brian F. Connors; 1 child, Ian Shors Connors. BA, Pitzer Coll., 1976; JD, Golden Gate U., 1984. Bar: Calif. Extern, Calif. Supreme Ct., San Francisco, 1983; rsch. atty. Calif. Ct. Appeals, San Francisco, 1984-85; appellate atty., San Francisco, 1985—; staff atty. 6th dist. Appellate Program, 1988-89. Sr. editor Golden Gate Law Rev. Notes and Comments, 1985; mem. editorial bd. Barrister's Club Mag., 1986-89. Atty. Lawyers Com. for Urban Affairs/Asylum Project, San Francisco, 1986. Mem. ACLU, Calif. Bar Assn., Bar Assn. San Francisco (mem. appellate com. 1986—), Calif. Attys. for Criminal Justice. Democrat. Office: Law Offices 1795 Union St San Francisco CA 94123-4427

SHORT, JAMES FRANKLIN, JR., sociology educator, researcher; b. Sangamon County, Ill., June 22, 1924; s. James Franklin and Ruth L. (Walbaum) S.; m. Kelma E. Hegberg, Dec. 27, 1947; children: Susan Elizabeth, James Michael. Student, Shurtleff Coll., Alton, Ill., 1942-43; B.A., Denison U., 1947, hon. degree, 1975; M.A., U. Chgo., 1949, Ph.D., 1951. Instr. Ill. Inst. Tech., 1950, Ind. U., South Bend extension, 1950-51; mem. faculty Wash. State U., Pullman, 1951—; prof. sociology Wash. State U., 1963-94, prof. emeritus, 1994—; dir. Sociol. Research Lab., 1962-65; dean Grad. Sch., 1964-68; dir. Social Research Center, 1970-85; vis. assoc. rsch. prof. U. Chgo., 1959-62; vis. prof. law and sociology Stanford, 1975; vis. scholar Inst. of Criminology, Cambridge U., 1976; disting. vis. prof. U. Colo., summer 1986; disting. vis. prof. (Hooker prof.) McMaster U., fall 1987, Beto chair prof. Criminal Justice Ctr. Sam Houston State U., spring, 1990; co.-dir. rsch. Nat. Commn. on Causes and Prevention of Violence, 1968-69; fellow Ctr. for Advanced Study in the Behavioral Scis., Stanford, 1969-70; cons. NIMH, 1961-76, mem. behavioral scis. fellowship rev. panel, 1963-66, mem. behavior sci. review panel, tng. grant br., 1967-71, chmn., 1970-71; mem. assembly behavioral and social scis. NRC, 1973-75, mem. com. on rsch. on law enforcement and adminstrn. of justice Commn. on Behavioral Scis. and Edn., 1984-89, mem. panel on understanding violence, 1989-92; Am. Sociol. Assn. rep. to NAS, 1970-72; cons. NSF, 1970—, mem. social adv. com., 1971-72, rsch. adv. com., 1973; cons. Ford Found., 1962-64. Author: (with A.F. Henry) Suicide and Homicide, 1954, (with F.L. Strodtbeck) Group Process and Gang Delinquency, 1965, 2d edit., 1974; Delinquency and Society, 1990; also articles chpts. in books; editor: Gang Delinquency and Delinquent Subcultures, 1968, Modern Criminals, 1970, 2d edit., 1973, The Social Fabric of Metropolis, 1971, (with Marvin Wolfgang) Collective Violence, 1972; editor, contbr. Delinquency, Crime and Society, 1976, The State of Sociology, 1981, The Social Fabric, 1986, (with Lee Clarke) Organizations, Uncertainties, and Risk, 1992; asso. editor Am. Sociol. Rev, 1960-63, 70-71; editor, 1972-74; asso. editor Social Problems, 1958-61, 67-69, Am. Jour. Sociology, 1964-72; adv. editor Jour. Life Threatening Behavior, 1971-75; mem. adv. bd. Jour. Rsch. in Crime and Delinquency, 1980—, Am. Sociologist, 1967-68, Jour. Criminal Law and Criminology, 1976—; assoc. editor Ann. Rev. Sociology, 1980-87; adv. editor Deviant Behavior, Sociol. Inquiry, contbr. to encys., yearbooks. Chmn. nat. peer rev. com. Clark County (Nev.) Nuclear Waste Divsn., 1991-95. 2d lt. USMCR, 1943-46, PTO. Faculty Rsch. fellow Social Sci. Rsch. Coun., 1953-56; Guggenheim fellow, 1976, fellow Inst. Criminology and Kings Coll., Cambridge U., 1976, Centre for Socio-Legal Studies and Wolfson Coll., Oxford, 1986; NIMH, NSF grantee; recipient Regents Faculty Excellence award for rsch. Wash. State U., 1987, Outstanding Faculty Achievement award Coll. Sci. and Art, 1988; Bruce Smith award Acad. Criminal Justice Scis., 1987. Fellow Japan Soc. for Promotion Sci., Am. Soc. Criminology (Edwin Sutherland award 1979), AAAS; mem. Western Soc. Criminology (Paul Tappan award 1977), mem. Am. Sociol. Assn. (chmn. research com. 1963, mem. council 1967-70, 76-80, com. on exec. office and budget 1971, 76-80, chmn. 1977-80, mem. publs. com. 1972-74, 76-80, sec. 1977-80, pres.-elect 1982-83, pres. 1983-84, Found. bd. trustees 1985-89, pres. 1989, chair adv. com. 1990—, sect. on environ. and tech. Outstanding Achievement award 1990), Pacific Sociol. Assn. (pres. 1966-67), Soc. Study Problems (exec. com. 1965-66), Western Assn. Grad. Schools (exec. com. 1965-67), Sociologists for Women in Soc., Law and Soc. Assn. (trustee 1978-80), Sociol. Research Assn. (sec.-treas. 1982, pres. 1983), Phi Beta Kappa (hon.), Phi Kappa Phi (hon.). Home: 425 SE Dexter St Pullman WA 99163-2312

SHORT, JAY MILTON, biotechnology company executive; b. Lebanon, Ind., Mar. 5, 1958; s. Roy Milton and Patricia Ann (Brewer) S.; m. Heidi Patrice Messinger, July 26, 1980; children: Ryan Milton, Cole Evan. BA in Chemistry with honors, Taylor U., Upland, Ind., 1080; PhD in Biochemistry, Case Western Res. U., 1985. Tchg. asst. Taylor U., 1978-80, Kent (Ohio) State U., 1981, Case Western Res. U., Cleve., 1981-85; staff scientist R & D, Stratagene Cloning Systems, La Jolla, Calif., 1985-88, sr. staff scientist, 1988-89, v.p. long term rsch. and biol. ops., 1989-92, v.p. long term rsch. and ops., 1992-94; pres. Stratcyte, Inc., La Jolla, 1992-94; chief tech. officer Recombinant Brocatalysis, Inc., La Jolla, Calif., 1994—; also bd. dirs. Recombinant Brocatalysis, Inc., La Jolla; bd. dirs. Stressgen, Inc., Invitrogen, Indsl. Biocatalysis, Inc.; reviewer human genome project and patenting DNA sequences U.S. Congl. Office Tech. Assessment; chmn., ofcl. Instnl. Animal Care and Use Com.; mem. peer rev. com. Nat. Inst. Environ. Health Scis.; ewciwque Peoxa, NAS, Genetic Analysis Techniques, Analytical Biochemistry, Nucleic Acids Rsch.; cons. on transgenic toxicology testing EEC, 1991-94; lectr. in field; mem. adj. faculty U. Calif., San Diego, 1991; lectr. Ctr. for Drug Evaluation and Rsch., FDA, 1992, others. Editor Mutation Rsch.; contbr. numerous articles and abstracts to sci. jours.; numerous patents in field, including sys. for regulation of eukaryotic genes, methods for phenotype creation from multiple gene populations, transgenic non-human animals carrying test DNA sequences, mutagenesis testing using transgenic non-human animals carrying test DNA sequences, polycos mutagenesis sys., use of trans-acting proteins for devel. in situ expression screening system. Recipient 1st place award for innovation and entrepreneurship in biotech. U. Calif., 1990, 91; numerous grants including Nat. Inst. Environ. Health Scis., 1989-94, NIH, 1990-94, Nat. Cancer Inst., 1992-95. Mem. AAAS, Am. Soc. Biochemistry and Molecular Biology, Am. Soc. Microbiology, Environ. Mutagenesis Soc., Soc. Toxicology (chmn. conf. discussion group 1993), Japanese Environ. Mutagen Soc., N.Y. Acad. Scis. Office: Recombinant Biocatalysis Inc 505 S Coast Blvd 4th fl La Jolla CA 92037

SHORT, RAY EVERETT, minister, sociology educator emeritus, author, lecturer; b. Coffeyville, Kans., Jan. 5, 1919; s. Franklin Marion and Jennie (Messersmith) S.; m. Jeannette Louise Stephens, June 12, 1954; children: Glenn Alan, Linda Louise, Kenneth Ray, Timothy Wesley, Karen Amy; 1 stepdau., Mary Jennings. AB, Willamette U., 1944; postgrad., U. Chgo., 1946; BD, Duke, 1948, PhD, 1961; postgrad., U. Idaho, 1950-51. Ordained to ministry Meth. Ch., 1946. Dir. Westminster Found., Duke, 1944-46; co-pastor Interracial Meth. Ch., Durham, N.C., 1947; asst. prof. religion, dir. chapel programs Fla. So. Coll., Lakeland, 1947-48; exec. dir. Fla. br. United World Federalists, 1948-51; dir. Intermountain Region, 1953-54, Wesley Found., U. Idaho, 1950-51; exec. dir. Student YMCA-YWCA, U. Denver, 1951-53; pastor Fairmont Meth. Ch., Lockport, Ill., 1954-56; grad. asst. sociology Duke, 1956-57; assoc. prof. religion, head divsn. religion and philosophy, chaplain Tenn. Wesleyan Coll., 1957-60; assoc. prof. sociology and religion, head dept. sociology U. Dubuque, Iowa, 1960-65, acting chmn. div. social sci., 1962-65; assoc. prof. sociology, head dept. sociology and anthropology U. Wis., Platteville, 1965-70, prof. sociology, 1966-87, prof. emeritus, 1987—; prof. sociology and anthropology Copenhagen Study Ctr. U. Wis., spring 1974, nat. lectr., 1975—; chmn. Peace and World Order divsn. North Iowa Meth. Conf., 1963-69; rep. U.S. Jr. C. of C. in testimony before U.S. Senate Com. on Fgn. Rels., 1950; Midwest region rep. Nat. Coun. World Federalist Assn., 1964-73, pres. Midwest region, 1967-69, chmn. nat. coun., 1971-72, nat. v.p., 1991—; mem. spl. Wis. Conf. called with Pres's Commn. for Observance of 25th Anniversary of UN, 1970-87; mem. Wis. U. Meth. Bd. on Ch. and Soc., 1973-80, chmn. World Peace divsn., mem. exec. com., 1975-80. Author: Sex, Love or Infatuation: How Can I Really Know?, 1978, on videocassette, 1987, 2nd edit., 1990, Sex, Dating and Love: Questions Most Often Asked, 1984, 2nd edit., 1994; contbr. articles to profl. jours. Dem. candidate for Wis. 3rd Dist. Congl. Seat, 1970, 72; del. Dist. and State Convs., 1969-87, mem. state platform com., 1975-87; bd. dirs. Dubuque Salvation Army, 1961-65; mem. nat. bd. Am. Freedom Assn.; nat. v.p. Campaign for UN Reform, 1983-87, 1st v.p., 1989—; dir., founder Wis. Ann. High Sch. World Peace Study Program, 1975-87. Recipient NSF grant Anthropology Inst., Fairmont State Coll., W.Va., 1962. Fellow Am. Sociol. Assn.; mem. AAUP, Nat. Coun. on Family Rels., Fedn. Am. Scientists, Nat. United Meth. Men (mem. peace adv. task force 1990—). Home: 505 S Miller Ave Lafayette CO 80026-1545

SHORTLIFFE, EDWARD HANCE, internist, medical information science educator; b. Edmonton, Alta., Can., Aug. 28, 1947; s. Ernest Carl and Elizabeth Joan (Rankin) S.; m. Linda Marie Dairiki, June 21, 1970; children: Lindsay Ann, Lauren Leigh. AB, Harvard U., 1970; PhD, Stanford U., 1975, MD, 1976. Diplomate Am. Bd. Internal Medicine. Trainee NIH, 1971-76; intern Mass. Gen. Hosp., Boston, 1976-77; resident Stanford Hosp., Palo Alto, Calif., 1977-79; asst. prof. medicine Stanford U. Sch. Medicine, Palo Alto, 1979-85, assoc. prof., 1985-90, prof., 1990—, chief div. gen. internal medicine, 1988—; pres. SCAMC, Inc. (Symposium on Computer Applications in Med. Care), Washington, 1988-89; assoc. chair medicine Primary Care, 1993—; bd. dirs. Smart Valley, Inc.; advisor Nat. Bd. Med. Examiners, Phila., 1987-93; mem. Nat. Fed. Networking Adv. Coun., NSF, 1991-93; mem. computer sci. and telecomm. bd. NRC, 1991—. Editor: Rule-Based Expert Systems, 1984, Readings in Medical Artificial Intelligence, 1984, Medical Informatics: Computer Applications in Health Care, 1990; developer several medical computer programs including MYCIN, 1976 (Grace M. Hopper award Assn. Computing Machinery). Recipient Young Investigator award Western Soc. Clin. Investigation, 1987, rsch. career award Nat. Libr. of Medicine, 1979-84; scholar Kaiser Family Found., 1983-88. Fellow Am. Assn. Artificial Intelligence, Am. Coll. Med. Informatics (pres. 1992-94); mem. Soc. for Med. Decisionmaking (pres. 1989-90), Inst. Medicine, Am. Soc. for Clin. Investigation, Am. Med. Informatics Assn., Assn. Am. Physicians, Am. Clin. and Climatol. Assn. Office: Stanford U Sch Medicine Sect on Med Informatics 300 Pasteur Dr Palo Alto CA 94304-2203

SHOSTAK, G. SETH, astronomer; b. Norfolk, Va., July 20, 1943; s. Arnold Aaron and Bertha (Gortenburg) S.; m. Karen Ann Claffey, Apr. 28, 1984. BA in Physics, Princeton U., 1965; PhD in Astronomy, Calif. Inst. Tech., 1972. Research assoc. Nat. Radio Astronomy Obs., Charlottesville, Va., 1972-74; sr. systems analyst Penn Cent. R.R., Phila., 1974-75; research assoc. State U., Groningen, Netherlands, 1975-85; dir. DIGIMA Computer Animation, Groningen, Netherlands, 1985—; bd. dirs. Found. Computer Animation, Groningen, 1987-88; pub. programs scientist Search for Extraterrestrial Intelligence Inst., Mountain View, Calif., 1989—. Contbr. articles to profl. jours. Recipient Cindy award, 1975. Mem. Netherlands Assn. Sci. Film and TV (J.S. Niewenhuis 1984, Wubbo Ockels prize 1988), Soc. Motion Picture and TV Engrs. Jewish. Home: 1372 Cuernavaca Circle Mountain View CA 94040 Office: SETI Inst 2035 Landings Dr Mountain View CA 94043-0818

SHOTTS, WAYNE J., nuclear scientist, federal agency administrator; b. Des Plaines, Ill., Mar. 20, 1945; s. Norman Russell Shotts and Winnifred Mae (Averill) Shotts Goeppinger; m. Melinda Maureen Antilla, June 24, 1967 (dec. Feb. 1975); children: Kenneth Wayne Shotts, Jeffrey Alan Shotts; m. Jacquelyn Francyle Willis, Aug. 11, 1979. BA in Physics, U. Calif., Santa Barbara, 1967; PhD, Cornell U., 1973. Rsch. physicist E.I. duPont deNemours & Co., Wilmington, Del., 1973-74; physicist U. Calif., Livermore, Calif., 1974—; physicist Lawrence Livermore Nat. Lab., Livermore, Calif., 1974-79, group leader, thermonuclear design divsn., 1979-85, divsn leader, nuclear chemistry, 1985-86, divsn. leader, prompt diagnostics, 1986-88, prin. dep. assoc. dir., military applications, 1988-92, prin. dep. assoc. dir. def. and nuclear techs., 1992—. Recipient Ernest Orlando Lawrence Meml. award U.S. Dept. Energy, Washington, 1990. Mem. Am. Phys. Soc., Am. Assn. Advancement Sci. Office: Lawrence Livermore Nat Lab PO Box 808 Livermore CA 94551-0808

SHOUP, TERRY EMERSON, university dean, engineering educator; b. Troy, Ohio, July 20, 1944; s. Dale Emerson and Betty Jean (Spoon) S.; m. Betsy Dinsomore, Dec. 18, 1966; children: Jennifer Jean, Matthew David. BME, Ohio State U., 1966, MS, 1967, PhD, 1969. Asst. prof. to assoc. prof. Rutgers U., New Brunswick, N.J., 1969-75; assoc. prof. to prof. U. Houston, 1975-80; asst. dean, prof. Tex. A&M U., College Sta., 1980-83; dean, prof. Fla. Atlantic U., Boca Raton, 1983-89; dean, Sobrato prof. Santa Clara (Calif.) U., 1989—; cons., software specialist Numerical Methods in Engring. Author: (books) A Practical Guide to Computer Methods for Engineers, 1979, Resheniye Ingenyernikh Zadach NA EVM Prakticheskoye rukovodstvo, 1982, Narichnik Po Izchislitelni Methodi Za Ingeneri, 1983, Numerical Methods for the Personal Computer, 1983, Applied Numerical Methods for the Microcomputer, 1984, (with L.S. Fletcher) Introduction to Engineering with FORTRAN Programming, 1978, Solutions Manual for Introduction to Engineering Including FORTRAN Programming, 1978, Introduccion a la ingenieria Incluyendo programacion FORTRAN, 1980, (with L.S. Fletcher and E.V. Mochel) Introduction to Design with Graphics and Design Projects, 1981, (with S.P. Goldstein and J. Waddell) Information Sources, 1984, (with Carl Hanser Verlag) Numerische Verfahren fur Arbeitsplatzrechner, 1985, (with F. Mistree) Optimization Methods with Applications for Personal Computers, 1987; (software) Numerical Methods for the Personal Computer-Software User's Guide, Version 2, 1983, Optimization Software for the Personal Computer, 1986; editor in chief Mechanism and Machine Theory, 1977—; contbr. more than 100 articles to profl. jours. Fellow ASME (chmn. Design Engring. div. 1987-88, Mech. Engring. div. 1980-81, Centennial medal 1980, Gustus Larson award 1981); mem. Am. Soc. for Engring. Edn. (Dow Outstanding Faculty award 1974, Western Electric award 1984), Fla. Engring. Soc. Home: 1310 Quail Creek Cir San Jose CA 95120-4162 Office: Santa Clara U Coll Engring Office Of The Dean Santa Clara CA 95053

SHOVALD, ARLENE ELIZABETH, newspaper reporter; b. Stambaugh, Mich., Apr. 14, 1940; d. William Lawrence and Dorothy Mary (Scott) Mellstrom; m. Robert Paul Shovald, June 20, 1959; children: Robert, Terri, Richard, Anne. AA, Colo. Mountain Coll., 1992. Freelance writer, 1959—; editor The Reporter, Iron River, Mich., 1974-79; nurse aide and sec. to nursing svcs., 1979-81; reporter, photographer The Mountain Mail, Salida, 1981-87; reporter The Mountain Mail, Salida, Colo., 1989—; corr. The Pueblo (Colo.) Chieftain, 1987-89; creative writing tchr. Colo. Mountain Coll., Salida, 1992, West Iron County Community Schs., Iron River, 1970s. Author: (book) Kill the Competition, 1987; author numerous newspaper and mag. articles (award: Colo. Domestic Violence Coalition Commendation for Outstanding Work on Behalf of Victims of Domestic Violence). Mem. Chaffee County Emergency, Med. Svcs. Coun., Salida, 1990-93; mem., publicist Salida Steam Plant Com., 1991-94. Mem. Colo. Author's League, Colo. Press Assn. Home: 1124 D St Salida CO 81201-2739 Office: The Mountain Mail 125 Second St Salida CO 81201

SHRAIRMAN, RUTH, computer scientist, company executive; b. St. Petersburg, Russia, Mar. 29, 1947; came to the U.S., 1986; d. Miron and Riva (Belotserkovskaya) S.; m. Leonid Glotstein (div. Mar. 1966); m. Alexander Livshitz Landau, June 5, 1971; children: Igor, Daniel. MSc summa cum laude in Control and Optimization, Inst. Chem. Machine Engring., Moscow, 1964; diploma in Numerical Methods and Computer Programming, Inst. Advanced Tng. of Rschrs. and Mgrs., Moscow, 1973; MSc in Computer Sci., U. Colo., 1990, postgrad., 1990—. Sr. rsch. engr. All-Union Sci. Rsch. Vitamin Inst., Moscow, 1965-77; sr. scientist Ministry of Comm., Telecom. Rsch. Ctr., Israel, 1978-86; rsch. assoc. Coll. Bus. and Adminstrn. U. Colo., Boulder, 1986-87, tchg. asst. dept. computer sci., 1987-89; sys. analyst AMICS Enterprises, Inc., 1989-90; chmn., founder VeriFax Corp., 1990—; tchg. asst. Tel-Aviv U., Sch. Math., 1984-85; lectr. and presenter in field. Contbr. articles to profl. jours.; patentee in field. Recipient NSF award, 1993. Mem. Assn. for Computing Machinery. Office: Univ Colo Computer Sci Dept PO Box 430 Boulder CO 80309-0430

SHREEVE, JEAN'NE MARIE, chemist, educator; b. Deer Lodge, Mont., July 2, 1933; d. Charles William and Maryfrances (Briggeman) S. BA, U. Mont., 1953, DSc (hon.), 1982; MS, U. Minn., 1956; PhD, U. Wash., 1961; NSF postdoctoral fellow, U. Cambridge, Eng., 1967-68. Asst. prof. chemistry U. Idaho, Moscow, 1961-65; assoc. prof. U. Idaho, 1965-67, prof., 1967-73, acting chmn. dept. chemistry, 1969-70, 1973, head dept., and prof., 1973-87, vice provost rsch. and grad. studies, prof. chemistry, 1987—; Lucy W. Pickett lectr. Mt. Holyoke Coll., 1976, George H. Cady lectr. U. Wash., 1993; mem. Nat. Com. Standards in Higher Edn., 1965-67, 69-73. Mem. editl. bd. Jour. Fluorine Chemistry, 1970—, Jour. Heteroatom Chemistry, 1988—, Accounts Chem. Rsch., 1973-75, Inorganic Synthesis, 1976—; contbr. articles to sci. jours. Mem. bd. govs. Argonne (Ill.) Nat. Lab., 1992—. Recipient Disting. Alumni award U. Mont., 1970; named Hon. Alumnus, U. Idaho, 1972; recipient Outstanding Achievement award U. Minn., 1975, Sr. U.S. Scientist award Alexander Von Humboldt Found., 1978, Excellence in Teaching award Chem. Mfrs. Assn., 1980; U.S. hon. Ramsay fellow, 1967-68, Alfred P. Sloan fellow, 1970-72. Mem. AAAS (bd. dirs. 1991-95), AAUW (officer Moscow chpt. 1962-69), Am. Chem. Soc. (bd. dirs. 1985-93, chmn. fluorine divsn. 1979-81, Petroleum Rsch. Fund adv. bd. 1975-77, women chemists com. 1972-77, Fluorine award 1978, Garvan medal 1972, Harry and Carol Mosher award Santa Clara Valley sect. 1992), Phi Beta Kappa. Office: U Idaho Rsch Office 111 Morrill Hall Moscow ID 83843

SHRESTHA, PRANAYA, electrical engineer, consultant; b. Kathmandu, Nepal, July 19, 1966; came to the U.S., 1976; s. Bishnu Bahadur and Sabita S.; m. Megha. BSEE, U. Colo., 1989. Mgr. Neighborhood Grocery, Denver, 1987-90; project engr. Colo. Springs Utilities, Colo. Springs, 1991; elec. engr. Elcon Assocs., Inc., Portland, 1991—. Mem. IEEE. Home: 17039 Wellington Dr Parker CO 80134

SHREVE, PEG, state legislator, retired elementary educator; b. Spencer, Va., July 23, 1927; d. Hubert Smith and Pearl (Looney) Adams; m. Don Franklin Shreve, June 17, 1950 (dec. Sept. 1970); children: Donna, Jennifer, John, Don. BA, Glenville State U., 1948. Cert. elem. tchr., Va., Wyo. Reading tchr. Wood County Bd., Parkersburg, W.Va., 1948-50; elem. tchr. Mt. Solon, Va., 1950-52, Bridgewater, Va., 1952-53, Cody, Wyo., 1970-86; mem. Wyo. Ho. of Reps., 1983—, chmn.. com. travel, recreation and wildlife, 1983-91, majority whip, 1992-94, speaker pro tem, 1995—. Mem. coun. Girl Scouts U.S.A., White Sulpher Springs, W.Va., 1962-65; co-chmn. Legis. Exec. Conf., Wyo., 1987; mem. Nat. Com. State Legislatures, 1982—. Named Legislator of Yr., Wyo. Outfitters Assn., 1989, Ofcl. of Yr., Wyo. Wildlife Assn., 1990, Alumna of Yr., Glenville State Coll., 1994. Mem. AAUW (exec. bd.), Nat. Women Legislators, Soroptimists (Women Helping Women award 1985), Beta Sigma Phi (Lady of Yr. award 1986). Republican. Presbyterian. Home: PO Box 2257 Cody WY 82414-2257

SHREVE, THEODORE NORRIS, construction company executive; b. St. Louis, Feb. 14, 1919; s. Truxtun Benbridge and Beulah (Dyer) S.; m. Caroline Prouty, Jan. 7, 1943; children: Sara Ann Caile, Suzanne Foster Shreve, Theo Carol. BS, U. Colo., 1942. Sec., treas. Trautman & Shreve, Inc., Denver, 1946-68, pres., 1965-86, chmn. bd., 1984—; pres. 4030 Corp., 1984—. Mem. Colo. U. Found. Bd., 1988—; Rep. County Assembly, 1962. Served with USNR, 1942-45. Registered profl. engr., Colo. Mem. Mech. Contractors Assn., Colo. Soc. Profl. Engrs., Rotary, Gyro Club, Denver Country Club, Sigma Phi Epsilon. Republican. Episcopalian. Home: 1510 E 10th Ave Apt 13W Denver CO 80218-3101 Office: Trautman & Shreve 4406 Race St Denver CO 80216-3818

SHRONTZ, FRANK ANDERSON, airplane manufacturing executive; b. Boise, Idaho, Dec. 14, 1931; s. Thurlyn Howard and Florence Elizabeth (Anderson) S.; m. Harriet Ann Houghton, June 12, 1954; children: Craig Howard, Richard Whitaker, David Anderson. Student, George Washington U., 1953; LLB, U. Idaho, 1954; MBA, Harvard U., 1958; postgrad., Stanford U., 1969-70. Asst. contracts coordinator Boeing Co., Seattle, 1958-65, asst. dir. contract adminstrn., 1965-67, asst. to v.p. comml. airplane group, 1967-69, asst. dir. new airplane program, 1969-70, dir. comml. sales operations, 1970-73, v.p. planning and contracts, 1977-78; asst. sec. Dept. Air Force, Washington, 1973-76, Dept. Def., Washington, 1976-77; v.p., gen. mgr. 707/727/737 div. Boeing Comml. Airplane Co., Seattle, 1978-82, v.p. sales and mktg., 1982-84; pres. Comml. Airplane Co. Boeing Div., Seattle, 1986—; pres., chief exec. officer The Boeing Co., Seattle, 1986—, chmn., chief exec. officer, 1988—; bd. dirs. Citicorp, Boise Cascade Corp., 3M Co.; mem. The Bus. Coun., 1987; vice chmn. New Am. Schs. Devel. Corp. Mem., bus. policy com. Bus. Roundtable; trustee Smithsonian Instn. 1st lt. AUS, 1954-56. Mem. Phi Alpha Delta, Beta Theta Pi. Clubs: Overlake Golf and Country, Columbia Tower. Office: Boeing Co PO Box 3707 Mail Stop 10-21 Seattle WA 98108-2207*

SHROPSHIRE, DONALD GRAY, hospital executive; b. Winston-Salem, N.C., Aug. 6, 1927; s. John Lee and Bess L. (Shouse) S.; m. Mary Ruth Bodenheimer, Aug. 19, 1950; children: Melanie Shropshire David, John Devin. B.S., U. N.C., 1950; Erickson fellow hosp. adminstrn., U. Chgo., 1958-59; LLD (hon.), U. Ariz., 1992; EdD (hon.), Tucson U., 1994. Personnel asst. Nat. Biscuit Co., Atlanta, 1950-52; asst. personnel mgr. Nat. Biscuit Co., Chgo., 1952-54; adminstr. Eastern State Hosp., Lexington, Ky., 1954-62; assoc. dir. U. Md. Hosp., Balt., 1962-67; adminstr. Tucson Med. Ctr., 1967-82, pres., 1982-92, pres. emeritus, 1992—; pres. Tucson Hosps. Med. Edn. Program, 1970-71, sec., 1971-86; pres. So. Ariz. Hosp. Council, 1968-69; bd. dirs. Ariz. Blue Cross, 1967-76, chmn. provider standards com., 1972-76; chmn. Healthways Inc., 1985-92; bd. dirs. 1st Interstate Bank Ariz., Tucson, Tucson Med. Found. Bd. dirs. Health Planning Coun. Tucson, 1992, mem. exec. com., 1969-74; chmn. profl. divsn. United Way, Tucson, 1969-70, vice chmn. campaign, 1988, Ariz. Health Facilities Authority, 1992—, bd. dirs., 1992—; chmn. dietary svcs. com., vice chmn., 1988 Md. Hosp. Coun., 1966-67; bd. dirs. Ky. Hosp. Assn., 1961-62, chmn. coun. profl. proactice, 1960-61; past pres. Blue Grass Hosp. Coun.; trustee Assn. Western Hosps., 1974-81, pres., 1979-80; mem. accreditation Coun. for Continuing Med. Edn., 1982-87, chair, 1986; bd. govs. Pima C.C., 1970-76, sec., 1973-74, chmn., 1975-76, bd. dirs. Found., 1978-82, Ariz. Bd. Regents, 1982-90, sec., 1983-86, pres., 1987-88; mem. Tucson Airport Authority, 1987—, bd. dirs., 1990—, pres., 1995; v.p. Tucson Econ. Devel. Corp., 1977-82; bd. dirs. Vol. Hosps. Am., 1977-88, treas., 1979-82; mem. Ariz. Adv. Health Coun. Dirs., 1976-78; bd. dirs. Tucson Tomorrow, 1983-87, Tucson Downtown Devel. Corp., 1988-95, Rincon Inst., 1992—, Sonoran Inst., 1992—; dir. Mus. No. Ariz., 1988—; nat. bd. advisors Coll. Bus. U. Ariz., 1992—, chmn. Dean's Bd. Fine Arts, 1992—; pres. Ariz. Coun. Econ. Edn., 1993—; vis. panel Sch. Health Adminstrn. & Policy Ariz. State U., 1990—. Named to Hon. Order Ky. Cols.; named Tucson Man of Yr. 1987; recipient Disting. Svc. award Anti-Defamation League B'nai B'rith, 1989. Mem. Am. Hosp. Assn. (nominating com. 1983-86, trustee 1975-78, ho. dels. 1972-78, chmn. coun. profl. svc. 1973-74, regional adv. bd. 1969-78, chmn. joint com. with NASW 1963-64, Disting. Svc. award 1989), Ariz. Hosp. Assn. (Salisbury award 1982, bd. dirs. 1967-72, pres. 1970-71), Ariz. C. of C. (bd. dirs. 1988-93), Assn. Am. Med. Colls. (mem. assembly 1974-77), Tucson C. of C. (bd. dirs. 1968-69), United Comml. Travelers, NLN, Ariz. Town Hall (bd. dirs. 1982-93, chmn. 1990-92, treas. 1985), Pima County Acad. Decathlon Assn. (dir. 1983-85), Tucson Community Coun., Rotary Club (pres. 1993-94), Nat. Assn. Schs. and Pub. Affairs, Pi Alpha Alpha. Baptist (ch. moderator, chmn. finance com., deacon, ch. sch. supt., trustee, bd. dirs. ch. found.). Home: 6734 N Chapultepec Circle Tucson AZ 85750 Office: Tucson Med Ctr 2195 E River Rd Ste 202 Tucson AZ 85718-6586

SHROPSHIRE, HELEN MAE, historian; b. Prosser, Nebr., May 7, 1909; d. William Pearl and Dicy Belle (Myer) Stafford. Grad., Rogers Bus. Coll., Everett, Wash., 1928. Co-owner Camera Exchange, Pacific Grove, Calif., 1947-62; co-owner, photographer, writer Shropshire Film Prodns., Pacific Grove, 1950-76; pilot, co-owner Monarch Aviation, Monterey, Calif., 1962-63; co-founder, mgr. Calif. Heritage Guides, Monterey, Calif., 1971—. Mem. Ninety Nines Inc. (life). Republican. Home: 1623 Josselyn Canyon Rd Monterey CA 93940-5273 Office: Calif Heritage Guides 10 Custom House Plz Monterey CA 93940-2430

SHUBART, DOROTHY LOUISE TEPFER, artist, educator; b. Ft. Collins, Colo., Mar. 1, 1923; d. Adam Christian and Rose Virginia (Ayers) Tepfer; m. Robert Franz Shubart, Apr. 22, 1950; children: Richard, Lorenne. Grad., Cleve. Inst. Art, 1944-46; AA, Colo. Women's Coll., 1944; grad., Cleve. Inst. Art, 1946; student, Western Res. U., 1947-48; BA, St. Thomas Aquinas Coll., 1974; MA, Coll. New Rochelle, 1978. Art tchr. Denver Mus., 1942-44, Cleve. Recreation Dept., 1944-50; ind. artist, portrait painter Colo., Cleve., N.Y., and N.Mex., 1944—; adult edn. art tchr. Nanuet (N.Y.) Pub. Schs., 1950-65, Pearl River (N.Y.) Adult Edn., 1950-51; rec. sec. Van Houten Fields Assn., West Nyack, N.Y., 1969-74. Exhbns. include Hopper House, Rockland Ctr. for Arts, CWC, Cleve. Inst. Art, Coll. New Rochelle, Rockland County Ann. Art Fair, 1970-89. Leader f-H Club, Nanuet, 1960-80, Girl Scouts, Nanuet, 1961-68; mem. scholarship and gen. com. PTA, Nanuet, 1964-68; mem. arterial rd. planning com. Eldorado (Santa Fe) Cmty. Improvement Assn., 1992-94; capt. Neighborhood Watch, local organizer El Dorado chpt.; worked for Jim Baca Gov.'s campaign, 1994. Gund scholar Cleve. Inst. Art, 1946. Mem. AAUW, NOW, Wilderness Club, El Dorado Arterial Road Planning Com., Delta Tau Kappa, Phi Delta Kappa. Democrat. Home: 8 Hidalgo Ct Santa Fe NM 87505-8898

SHUBB, WILLIAM BARNET, lawyer; b. Oakland, Calif., May 28, 1938; s. Ben and Nellie Bernice (Fruechtenicht) S.; m. Sandra Ann Talarico, July 29, 1962; children: Alisa Marie, Carissa Ann, Victoria Ann. AB, U. Calif., Berkeley, 1960, JD, 1963. Bar: Calif., 1964, U.S. Ct. Internat. Trade 1981, U.S. Customs Ct. 1980, U.S. Ct. Appeals (9th cir.) 1964, U.S. Supreme Ct. 1972. Law clk. U.S. Dist. Ct., Sacramento, 1963-65; asst. U.S. atty., Sacramento, 1965-71; chief asst. U.S. atty. (ea. dist.) Calif., 1971-74; assoc. Diepenbrock, Wulff, Plant & Hannegan, Sacramento, 1974-77, ptnr., 1977-80, 81-90; U.S. atty. Eastern Dist. Calif., 1980-81; judge U.S. Dist. Ct. (ea. dist.) Calif., 1990—; chmn. com. drafting of local criminal rules U.S. Dist. Ct. (ea. dist.) Calif., 1974, mem. speedy trial planning com., 1974-80; lawyer rep. 9th Cir. U.S. Jud. Conf., 1975-78; mem. faculty Fed. Practice Inst., 1978-80; instr. McGeorge Sch. Law, U. Pacific, 1964-66. Mem. ABA, Fed. Bar Assn. (pres. Sacramento chpt. 1977), Calif. Bar Assn., Assn. Def. Counsel, Am. Bd. Trial Advs., Sacramento County Bar Council. Office: US Courthouse 650 Capitol Mall Sacramento CA 95814-4708*

SHUGART, ALAN F., electronic computing equipment company executive; b. L.A., Sept. 27, 1930. BS in Engring. and Physics, U. Redlands, 1951. Dir. engring. IBM, San Jose, Calif., 1952-69; v.p. Memorex Corp., Sunnyvale, Calif., 1969-73; pres. Shugart Assocs., 1973-78; chmn., chief exec. officer Seagate Tech., Scotts Valley, Calif., 1978—, also bd. dirs., also pres., COO. Office: Seagate Tech 920 Disc Dr Scotts Valley CA 95066-4544*

SHUKLA, PRADIP KANTILAL, academic administrator, educator, consultant; b. Ahmedabad, Gujarat, India, Sept. 7, 1956; came to U.S., 1961; s. Kantilal T. and Manju K. (Vyas) S.; m. Yatri P. Thaker, Jan. 6, 1983; children: Monica, Amy. BSc in Bus. Adminstrn., Calif. State U., Long Beach, 1978, BA in Econs., 1978, MBA, 1979; MSc in Bus. Adminstrn., U. So. Calif., 1983; MEd, UCLA, 1983, PhD in Ednl. Adminstrn., 1990. Cert. prodn. and inventory mgr. Coord. tutoring ctr. Compton (Calif.) Coll., 1976, instr. bus. and law, 1980-86, adminstrv. analyst, 1982-83, dir. instnl. rsch., 1986-88, asst. to pres., 1990—; night libr. Lynwood (Calif.) Adult Sch., 1974-78; lectr. in mgmt. Calif. State U., Long Beach, L.A., Northridge, 1978-91; mgmt. cons. P.K. Shukla & Assocs., Orange, Calif., 1979—; assoc. prof. mktg. and mgmt. Chapman U., Orange, 1985—; cons. various corps. and colls., Calif., 1979—; internat. cons. and speaker import/export ventures. Adv. bd. St. Francis Med. Ctr., Lynwood, Calif., 1979-81, Santa Ana (Calif) Zoo, 1988—; community breakfast chairperson City Lynwood, 1980; polit. cons. various candidates local and statewide, Calif., 1979—. Scholar Bank of Am., Soc. Calif. Edison Co., UCLA Grad. Sch. Mgmt.; grantee U.S. Dept. Edn., Compton Coll., Chapman U. Mem. Internat. Acad. Mgmt. Mktg., Internat. Acad. Bus. & Soc. (charter), Computer Using Instrs., Western Acad. Mgmt. (program reviewer, arrangements com., program com.), Western Mktg. Educators Assn. (program reviewer, session chmn.), Am. Mktg. Assn., Acad. Mgmt. (program reviewer). Republican. Home: 10492 Park Villa Cir Villa Park CA 92667-5318 Office: Chapman U 333 N Glassell St Orange CA 92666-1011

SHULER, SALLY ANN SMITH, telecommunications, computer services and software company executive; b. Mt. Olive, N.C., June 11, 1934; d. Leon Joseph and Ludia Irene (Montague) Simmons; m. Henry Ralph Smith Jr., Mar. 1, 1957 (div. Jan. 1976); children: Molly Montague, Barbara Ellen, Sara Ann, Mary Kathryn; m. Harold Robert Shuler, Aug. 2, 1987. BA in Math., Duke U., 1956; spl. studies, U. Liège, Belgium, 1956-57; postgrad. in bus. econs., Claremont Grad Sch., 1970-72. Mgr. fed. systems GE Info. Svcs. Co., Washington, 1976-78; mgr. mktg. support GE Info. Svcs. Co., Rockville, Md., 1978-81; dir. bus. devel. info. tech. group Electronic Data Systems, Bethesda, Md., 1981-82; v.p. mktg. optimum systems div. Electronic Data Systems, Rockville, 1982-83; v.p. planning and communications Electronic Data Systems, Dallas, 1983-84; exec. dir. comml. devel. U.S. West Inc., Englewood, Colo., 1984-90; v.p. mktg. devel. Cin. Bell Info. Systems Inc., 1990-92; mgmt. cons. in mergers and acquisitions Denver, 1992-93; v.p. major accounts U.S. Computer Svcs., Denver, 1993—. Recipient GE Centennial award, Rockville, 1978. Mem. Women in Telecommunications, Rotary (fellow Internat. Found.), Phi Beta Kappa, Tau Psi Omega, Pi Mu Epsilon. Democrat. Presbyterian. Office: US Computer Svcs 1626 S Syracuse St Denver CO 80231-2691

SHULMAN, MICHAEL GEOFFREY, pharmaceutical researcher; b. Paterson, N.J., May 8, 1940; s. Raymond C. and Clara C. (Schneider) S.; m. Peggy M. Alterman, Dec. 27, 1961 (div. Oct. 1991); children: Lori B., Shelly C. Grad. Pre-Med., U. N.C., 1961; MD, Columbia U., 1965. Diplomate Am. Bd. Internal Medicine. Assoc. dir. Babington Regl. Kidney Ctr., Berkeley, Calif., 1972-73; med. co-dir. Northside Dialysis Ctr., Atlanta, 1974-91; med. dir. Regl. Dialysis of Anniston, Ala., 1986-90; assoc. dir. immunohematology Sandoz Pharm. Corp., East Hanover, N.J., 1991-92, assoc. dir. cardiovascular, 1992-94; assoc. dir. Mycophenolate Mofetil clin. transplant program Syntex Rsch., Palo Alto, Calif., 1994—; chmn. med. adv. com. Greater Atlanta Lupus Found., Atlanta, 1988-90; med. dir. nutritional support team, St. Joseph's Hosp., Atlanta, 1986-88. Author book chpt. Systemic Lupus, 1985. Maj. U.S. Army, 1969-72, Germany. Recipient Disting. Svc. award Greater Atlanta Chpt., Lupus Found., 1990. Mem. Am. Soc. Transplant Physicians, Am. Soc. Nephrology, Am. Soc. Internal Medicine, Am. Heart Assn. (Coun. on the Kidney), Am. Soc. Hypertension. Jewish. Office: Syntex Rsch A4IID 3401 Hillview Ave PO Box 10850 Palo Alto CA 94303

SHULTZ, FRED TOWNSEND, geneticist, biologist; b. Grinnell, Iowa, Mar. 3, 1923; s. J. Gordon and Katharine Lucia (Townsend) S.; m. Carolyn Covell June 24, 1961; children: Trina, Rebecca, Daniel, Brian. AB in Biol. Sci., Stanford U., 1947; PhD in Genetics, U. Calif.-Berkeley, 1952. Geneticist, biologist Animal Breeding Cons., Sonoma, Calif., 1952—; pres. Avian Allure; chmn. bd. dirs. Biol. Frontiers Inst. Inventor new life forms and prodn. systems. Served to 2nd lt. USAF, 1942-45. Recipient Poultry Sci. Research award Poultry Sci. Assn., 1954. Mem. Genetic Soc. Am., Am. Genetics Assn., Genetic Soc. Can., Poultry Sci. Assn., World Poultry Sci., World Aquaculture Soc., Am. Fisheries Soc., Nat. Shellfisheries Assn., Calif. Acad. Sci., Am. Soc. Agrl. Cons. Republican. Home: 19443 Marna Ln Sonoma CA 95476-6309 Office: Animal Breeding Cons PO Box 313 Sonoma CA 95476

SHULTZ, GEORGE PRATT, former secretary of state, economics educator; b. N.Y.C., Dec. 13, 1920; s. Birl E. and Margaret Lennox (Pratt) S.; m. Helena M. O'Brien, Feb. 16, 1946; children: Margaret Ann Shultz Tilsworth, Kathleen Pratt Shultz Jorgensen, Peter Milton, Barbara Lennox Shultz White, Alexander George. BA in Econs., Princeton U., 1942; PhD in Indsl. Econs., MIT, 1949; hon. degrees, U. Notre Dame, Loyola U., U. Pa., U. Rochester, Princeton U., Carnegie-Mellon U., Baruch Coll., N.Y.C., Northwestern U., Yeshiva U., U. Tel Aviv, Technion-Israel Inst. Tech. Mem. faculty M.I.T., 1949-57; assoc. prof. indsl. relations MIT, 1955-57; prof. indsl. relations Grad. Sch. Bus., U. Chgo., 1957-68, dean sch., 1962-68; fellow Ctr. for Advanced Study in Behavioral Scis., 1968-69; U.S. sec. labor, 1969-70; dir. Office Mgmt. and Budget, 1970-72; U.S. sec. treasury, also asst. to Pres., 1972-74; chmn. Council on Econ. Policy, East-West Trade Policy com.; exec. v.p. Bechtel Corp., San Francisco, 1974-75, pres., 1975-77; vice chmn. Bechtel Corp., 1977-81; also dir.; pres. Bechtel Group, Inc., 1981-82; prof. mgmt. and pub. policy Stanford U., 1974-82, prof. internat. econs., 1989-91, prof. emeritus, 1991—; chmn. Pres. Reagan's Econ. Policy Adv. Bd., 1981-82; U.S. sec. of state, 1982-89; disting. fellow Hoover Instn., Stanford, 1989—; bd. dirs. Bechtel Group, Inc., Ziff-Davis Pub. Co., GM, Gulfstream Aerospace Corp., AirTouch Comms.; chmn. J.P. Morgan Internat. Coun.; chmn. adv. coun. Inst. Internat. Studies, Gov.'s Econ. Policy Adv. Bd. State of Calif. Author: Pressures on Wage Decisions, 1951, (with Charles A. Myers) The Dynamics of a Labor Market, 1951, (with John R. Coleman) Labor Problems: Cases and Readings, 1953, (with T.L. Whisler) Management Organization and the Computer, 1960, (with Arnold R. Weber) Strategies for the Displaced Worker, 1966, (with Robert Z. Aliber) Guidelines, Informal Controls and the Market Place, 1966, (with Albert Rees) Workers and Wages in the Urban Labor Market, 1970, Leaders and Followers in an Age of Ambiguity, 1975, (with Kenneth W. Dam) Economic Policy Beyond the Headlines, 1977, Turmoil and Triumph: My Years as Secretary of State, 1993; also articles, chpts. in books, reports, and essays.

Served to capt. USMCR, 1942-45. Mem. Am. Econ. Assn., Indsl. Relations Research Assn. (pres. 1968), Nat. Acad. Arbitrators. Office: Stanford U Hoover Instn Stanford CA 94305

SHULTZ, JOHN DAVID, lawyer; b. L.A., Oct. 9, 1939; s. Edward Patterson and Jane Elizabeth (Taylor) S.; m. Joanne Person, June 22, 1968; children: David Taylor, Steven Matthew. Student, Harvard Coll., 1960-61; BA, U. Ariz., 1964; JD, Boalt Hall, U. Calif., Berkeley, 1967. Bar: N.Y. 1968, Calif. 1978. Assoc. Cadwalader, Wickersham & Taft, N.Y.C., 1968-77; ptnr. Lawler, Felix & Hall, L.A., 1977-83, mem. exec. com., chmn. planning com., co-chmn. recruiting and hiring com.; ptnr. Morgan, Lewis & Bockius, L.A., 1983—, chmn. mgmt. com., mem. lateral entry com.; chmn. profl. evaluation com., chmn. bus. plan com., chmn. practice devel. com., chmn. recruiting com. Trustee St. Thomas Ch., N.Y.C., 1969-72, Shore Acres Point Corp., Mamaroneck, N.Y., 1975-77; mem. adv. bd. Internat. and Comparative Law Center, Southwestern Legal Found., 1981—; active Practicing Law Inst. Adv. Bd., Corp. and Securities Law, 1992—. Mem. ABA, Assn. Bar City N.Y., State Bar Calif., N.Y. State Bar Assn., Jonathan Club (L.A.), Phi Delta Phi, Sigma Chi. Episcopalian. Office: Morgan Lewis & Bockius 801 S Grand Ave Los Angeles CA 90017-4613

SHULTZ, KIM TODD, municipal official; b. Honolulu, Feb. 3, 1952; s. Harold Creed and Susan Louise (Privara) S.; m. Patrizia Materassi, May 16, 1985; children: Pierre Luigi, GianCarlo Materassi. BA in Sociology and Polit. Sci., U. Hawaii, 1977; MA in Urban Planning, UCLA, 1984. Chief rschr., adminstrv. aide to vice chair gen. plan com. State of Hawaii Ho. of Reps., 1979-81; with environ. svcs. dept. City of West Covina, Calif., 1981-82; with rent control adminstrn. dept. City of Santa Monica, Calif., 1982-83; cons. various orgns., 1983-84; with pub. works agy. City of Santa Ana, Calif., 1985-89; with Bechtel Corp., Riverside, Calif., 1989-91, City of Ontario, Calif., 1991—. V.p. ops. Leadership Connection, Upland, Ontario, Calif., 1993-95; bd. dirs. Planning Network, 1982-84, Life of the Land, Honolulu, 1978-80, Urban Innovations Group, L.A., 1981-83. Mem. Am. Planning Assn., Am. Assn. Profl. Adminstrs., Hydrogen Soc., Union Concerned Scientists, Intelligent Transp. Sys.-Am. Home: 5125 Camino Real Riverside CA 92509-5407

SHUMAKER, JEANETTE ROBERTS, English language educator; b. Salinas, Calif., Dec. 24, 1958; d. Claude Herschel III and Dorothea Eileen (Hayes) Roberts; m. Andrew David Shumaker, July 26, 1985; 1 child, Nicholas. BA, U. Redlands, 1981; higher diploma, Trinity Coll., Dublin, Ireland, 1983; M English, Claremont Grad. Sch., 1985, PhD in English, 1990. Lectr. in writing programs UCLA, 1989-90; asst. prof. English Elizabethtown (Pa.) Coll., 1990-91, U. Tex.-Permian Basin, Odessa, 1991-92; asst. prof. English San Diego State U.-Imperial Valley, Calexico, Calif., 1992—, dir. activity 1 title III, 1993—, faculty chair, 1994—. Contbr. articles to profl. jours. Recipient Outstanding Faculty Contbn. award San Diego State U. Alumni Assn., 1994; Rotary Internat. fellow, 1982-83, George Eliot fellow. Mem. MLA, Soc. for Study of Narrative Lit., Am. Coun. Irish Studies, Interdisciplinary 19C Studies Assn., Philol. Assn. of Pacific Coast. Democrat. Office: San Diego State U Imperial Valley 720 Heber Ave Calexico CA 92231

SHUMAN, JAMES BURROW, writer, consultant; b. N.Y.C., Sept. 8, 1932; s. Ik and Elizabeth Frances (Davies) S.; m. Victoria Grove, Oct. 4, 1958 (div. 1976); children: James Burrow Jr., Robert Grove. BA, Wesleyan U., 1954. Reporter The Sharon (Pa.) Herald, 1956-60, UPI, Washington, 1960-61; assoc. editor The Reader's Digest, Washington and Pleasantville, N.Y., 1961-71; cons. to John D. Rockefeller 3d, N.Y.C., 1971-73; pvt. practice writer, cons. Lahaska, Pa., 1973-75; asst. press sec. The White House, Washington, 1975-77; cons. Gerald R. Ford, Palm Springs, Calif. and Washington, 1977-80; pres. Allegheny Found., Pitts., 1980-81; chmn. James B. Shuman and Assocs., Lahaska, N.Y.C., Washington, L.A., 1981—. Author: (with others) The Kondratieff Wave, 1972, In Constant Fear, 1974; contbr. numerous articles to mags. Lt. (j.g.) USN, 1954-56. Recipient Best Spot News Story award Pa. Newspaper Pubs. Assn., 1959. Mem. Phillips Mill Assn., Lav Club Paris, Gilgit Polo Club (Pakistan). Republican. Mem. Soc. of Friends. Home and Office: 914 Westwood Blvd # 517 Los Angeles CA 90024-2905

SHUMAN, THOMAS ALAN, correctional operations executive, consultant; b. Fairmont, W.Va., Dec. 31, 1946. BA, N.Mex. State U., 1969, 73; postgrad., U. N.Mex., 1988. Mgr. Drum Appliance, Inc., Las Cruces, N.Mex., 1971-75; classification supr. N.Mex. Corrections Dept., Santa Fe, 1976-80, mgmt. analyst supr., 1981-83, dir. classification, 1983-84, dep. sec., 1984-87; pres. Correctional Data Systems, Santa Fe, 1987—; owner Desktop Publ. Co., Santa Fe, 1988—; dir. N.Mex. Corrections Tng. Acad., 1991-95, probation, parole dir., 1995—; pres. Silicon Wizard Corp., 1989—; cons. Nat. Inst. Corrections, Washington, 1988, Am. Correctional Assn., Md., 1987—. Mem. Smithsonian Inst., U.S. Naval Inst. Served to lt. U.S. Army, 1969-71, Vietnam. Decorated Bronze Star, Presdl. Commendation. Mem. NRA, N.Mex. State U. Alumni Assn. Republican. Presbyterian.

SHUMATE, CHARLES ALBERT, retired dermatologist; b. San Francisco, Aug. 11, 1904; s. Thomas E. and Freda (Ortmann) S.; B.S., U. San Francisco, 1927, H.H.D., 1976; M.D., Creighton U., 1931. Pvt. practice dermatology, San Francisco, 1933-73, ret., 1973; asst. clin. prof. dermatology Stanford U., 1956-62; pres. E Clampus Vitus, Inc., 1963-64; hon. mem. staff St. Mary's Hosp. Mem. San Francisco Art Commn., 1964-67, Calif. Heritage Preservation Commn., 1963-67; regent Notre Dame Coll. at Belmont, 1965-78, trustee, 1977-93; pres. Conf. Calif. Hist. Socs., 1967; mem. San Francisco Landmarks Preservation Bd., 1967-78, pres., 1967-69; trustee St. Patrick's Coll. and Sem., 1970-86; dir. U.S. Catholic Hist. Soc., 1988—. Served as maj. USPHS, 1942-46. Decorated knight comdr. Order of Isabella (Spain); knight Order of the Holy Sepulchre, knight of St. Gregory, knight of Malta. Fellow Am. Acad. Dermatology; mem. U. San Francisco Alumni Assn. (pres. 1955), Calif. Book Club (pres. 1969-71), Calif. Hist. Soc. (trustee 1958-67, 68-78, pres. 1962-64), Soc. Calif. Pioneers (dir. 1979—), Drum Found. (v.p. 1986—). Clubs: Bohemian, Olympic, Roxburghe (pres. 1958-59) (San Francisco); Zamorano (Los Angeles). Author: Life of George Henry Goddard; The California of George Gordon, 1976, Jas. F. Curtis, Vigilante, 1988, Francisco Pacheco of Pacheco Pass, 1977; Life of Mariano Malarin, 1980; Boyhood Days: Y. Villegas Reminiscences of California 1850s, 1983, The Notorious I.C. Woods of the Adams Express, 1986, Rincon Hill and South Park, 1988, Captain A.A. Ritchie, Pioneer, 1991, Stormy Life of Major William Gouverneur Morris, 1993. Mem. St. Andrew Soc. (hon. mem.). Home: 1901 Scott St San Francisco CA 94115-2613 Office: 490 Post St San Francisco CA 94102-1401

SHURTLEFF, AKIKO AOYAGI, artist, consultant; b. Tokyo, Jan. 24, 1950; d. Kinjiro and Fumiyo (Sugata) Aoyagi; m. William Roy Shurtleff, Mar. 10, 1977 (div. 1995); 1 child, Joseph Aoyagi. Grad., Women's Coll. Art, Tokyo, 1971; student, Acad. Art, San Francisco, 1991-92. Fashion designer, illustrator Marimura Co. and Hayakawa Shoji, Inc., Tokyo, 1970-72; co-founder, art dir. Soyfoods Ctr. consulting svcs., Lafayette, Calif., 1976-94; freelance illustrator, graphic designer; lectr. U.S. Internat. Christian U., Tokyo, 1977, Japanese Tofu Mfrs. Conv., Osaka, 1978; presenter cooking demonstrations, tchr. cooking classes. Co-author, illustrator: The Book of Tofu, 1975, The Book of Miso, 1975, The Book of Kudzu, 1977, Tofu and Soymilk Production, 1979, The Book of Tempeh, 1979, Miso Production, 1979, Tempeh Production, 1980; illustrator: Spirulina (by L. Switzer), 1982, The Book of Shiatsu-The Healing Art of Finger Pressure (by S. Goodman), 1990, Staying Healthy with Nutrition (by E. Haas), 1992, Culinary Treasures of Japan (by John and Jan Belleme), 1992, Yookoso, An Invitation to Contemporary Japanese, Vols. 1 & 2 (by Hasu-Hiko Tohsaku), 1994-95, Blue Collar & Beyond (by Yana Parker), 1995, Damn Good Ready to Go Resumes, 1995, Homework (by Peter Jeswald), 1995. Office: Akiko Aoyagi Shurtleff PO Box 443 Lafayette CA 94549-0443

SHURTLEFF, WILLIAM ROY, food products executive; b. Oakland, Calif., Apr. 28, 1941; s. Lawton Lothrop and Barbara Anne (Reinhardt) S.; m. Akiko Aoyagi, Mar. 10, 1977; 1 child: Joseph Aoyagi. BS in Indsl. Engring. and Physics, Stanford U., 1962, MEd, 1966. Indsl. engr. U.S. Steel Corp., Pittsburg, Calif., 1963; with Peace Corps, Nigeria, 1964-66; founder, dir. Esalen program in human awareness Stanford (Calif.) U., 1967-68; founder, dir. Soyfoods Ctr., Lafayette, Calif., 1976—; speaker in field. Author: The Book of Tofu, 1983, The Book of Miso, 1983, Miso Production, 1981, The Book of Tempeh, 1985, Tofu and Soymilk Production, 1984, Tempeh Production, 1986, Soyfoods Industry and Market: Directory and Databook, 1984, Soymilk Industry and Market: Worldwide and Country-by-Country Analysis, 1984, History of Tempeh, 1985, Tofutti and Other Soy Ice Creams: Non-dairy Frozen Dessert Industry and Market, 1985, Thesaurus for SoyaScan, 1986, and others; compiler over 45 bibliographies on soybeans and soyfoods; prodr. computerized bibliographic database SoyaScan. Mem. Soyfoods Assn. Am. (bd. dirs.), Tofu Standards Com. (co-chair 1984-86), Earthsave Found. (bd. dirs.), Tau Beta Pi. Home and Office: 1021 Dolores Dr Lafayette CA 94549-2907 also: PO Box 234 Lafayette CA 94549-0234

SHUSTER, ALVIN, journalist, newspaper editor; b. Washington, Jan. 25, 1930; s. Fred and Dora (Levy) S.; m. Miriam Schwartz, June 22, 1952; children: Fred, Jessica, Beth. AB, George Washington U., 1951. Reporter Washington Bur. N.Y. Times, 1952-61, asst. news editor, 1961-66, reporter London Bur., 1967-70; bur. chief Saigon, Vietnam, 1970-71, London, 1971-75, Rome, 1975-77; dep. editor editorial pages L.A. Times, 1977-83, fgn. editor, 1983—; pres. Fgn. Corrs. Assn., London, 1973-74; trustee Monterey (Calif.) Inst. Internat. Studies, 1983—. Editor: The Witnesses, 1964, Washington: The New York Times Guide to the Nations' Capital, 1967. Nieman fellow Harvard U., 1966-67. Mem. Reform Club (London). Office: Los Angeles Times Times Mirror Sq Los Angeles CA 90012

SHWAYDER, ELIZABETH YANISH, sculptor; b. St. Louis; d. Sam and Fannie May (Weil) Yaffe; m. Nathan Yanish, July 5, 1944 (dec.); children: Ronald, Marilyn Ginsburg, Mindy; m. M.C. Shawayder, 1988. Student, Washington U., 1941, Denver U., 1960; pvt. studies. One-woman shows include Woodstock Gallery, London, 1973, Internat. House, Denver, 1963, Colo. Women's Coll., Denver, 1975, Contemporaries Gallery, Santa Fe, 1963, So. Colo. State Coll. Pueblo, 1967, others; exhibited in group shows: Salt Lake City Mus., 1964, 71, Denver Art Mus., 1961-75, Oklahoma City Mus., 1969, Joslyn Mus., Omaha, 1964-68, Lucca (Italy) Invitational, 1971, others; represented in permanent collections include Colo. State Bank, Bmh Synagogue, Denver, Colo. Women's Coll., Har Ha Shem Congregation, Boulder, Colo., Faith Bible Chapel, Denver, others. Chmn. visual arts Colo. Centennial-Bicentennial, 1974-75; pres. Denver Council Arts and Humanities, 1973-75; mem. Mayor's Com. on Child Abuse, 1974-75; co-chmn. visual arts spree Denver Pub. Schs., 1975; trustee Denver Center for the Performing Arts, 1973-75; chmn. Concerned Citizens for Arts, 1976; pres. Beth Israel Hosp. Aux., 1985-87; organizer Coat Drive for the Needy, Denver and N.Y.C., 1982-87, Common Cents penny dirve for homeless, 1991-93; bd. dirs. Mizel Mus., Srs., Inc.; active Mayor's Com. on Cultural Affairs, Nat. Mus., Women in the Arts Mus., Freedom Found. at Valley Force, Hospice of Metro Denver. Humanities scholar Auraria Librs.-U. Colo.; recipient McCormick award Ball State U., Muncie, Ind., 1964, Purchase award Color Women's Coll., Denver, 1963, Tyler (Tex.) Mus., 1963, 1st prize in sculpture 1st Nat. Space Art Show, 1971, Humanitarian award Milehi Denver Sertoma, 1994, The Gleitsman Found., 1994, Svc. to Mankind awards Freedom Found. at Valley Forge, Mile Hi Sertoma Club, Minoruyasui Found., Gleitsman Found. Mem. Artists Equity Assn., Rocky Mountain Liturgical Arts, Allied Sculptors Colo., Allied Arts Inc. Hist. Denver, Symphony Guild, Parks People, Beth Israel Aux. Home: 131 Fairfax St Denver CO 80220-6331

SIART, WILLIAM ERIC BAXTER, banker; b. Los Angeles, Dec. 25, 1946; s. William Ernest and Barbara Vesta (McPherson) Baxter; m. Noelle Ellen Reid, Sept. 17, 1966; children—Shayne Allison, Tiffany Ann. B.A. in Econs., U. Santa Clara, 1968; M.B.A., U. Calif., Berkeley, 1969. With Bank of Am., 1969-78; v.p. corp. banking Bank of Am., Brussels, 1977-78; sr. v.p. charge mktg. Western Bancorp, Los Angeles, 1978-81; pres., chief operating officer First Interstate Bank of Nev. N.A., Reno, 1981-82; pres., chief exec. officer First Interstate Bank of Nev. N.A., 1982-84, chmn. bd., pres., chief exec. officer, 1984; formerly chmn., pres., chief exec. officer First Interstate Bank Calif., L.A., also bd. dirs.; pres. First Interstate Bancorp, L.A., 1990—, CEO, 1994—. Trustee U. Nev.-Reno Found.; bd. dirs. Sierra Arts Found. Mem. Am. Bankers Assn. (mem. govt. relations council), Reno-Sparks C. of C. (dir.). Republican. Roman Catholic. Office: First Interstate Bancorp 633 W 5th St Los Angeles CA 90071-2005*

SIBITZ, MICHAEL WILLIAM, school superintendent; b. San Francisco, July 22, 1937; s. Michael Jacob and Erna Anna Elsa (Altendorf) S.; m. Marilyn Joyce Pricco, Nov. 19, 1966; children: Elizabeth, Ryan. BA, San Francisco State U., 1959, MA, 1964, EdD, U. San Francisco, 1980; postgrad. Notre Dame U. of Calif., Stanford U. Tchr., Pacifica, Calif., 1959-64, Dept. Def., 1964-65; tchr. Belmont, Calif., 1965-70, specialist, 1970-71, adminstr., 1971-80; supr. instruction, prin., Los Altos, Calif., 1980-84; asst. supt. Sylvan Union Sch. Dist., Modesto, Calif., 1984—, supt., pres.; bd. dirs. Modesto Symphony, 1993. Mem. Stanislaus Arts Commn.; past pres. United Way Stanislaus County, Stanislaus Country Industry Edn. Council. Served with U.S. Army, 1960-66. Mem. Assn. Calif. Sch. Adminstrs. (charter), NEA (life), Assn. Supervision and Curriculum Devel., Kiwanis, Phi Delta Kappa. Roman Catholic. Contbr. articles to profl. jours. Home: 2019 Woodhaven Cir Riverbank CA 95367-2106 Office: Sylvan Union Sch Dist 605 Sylvan Ave Modesto CA 95350-1517

SICILIAN, JAMES MICHAEL, research engineer; b. Bronx, N.Y., May 25, 1947; s. Leonard James and Veronica Patricia (Reinwald) S. BS, MIT, 1969; MS, Stanford U., 1970, PhD, 1973. Tech. editor C.S. Draper Lab., Cambridge, Mass., 1968-69; research analyst Savannah River Lab., Aiken, S.C., 1973-76; staff Los Alamos (N.Mex) Scientific Lab, 1976-79, asst. group leader, 1979-80; sr. scientist Flow Science, Inc., Los Alamos, 1980—, sec. of corp., 1980—, v.p., 1990—. Mem. Cultural Ctr. adv. com., Los Alamos, 1987-89; vice chmn. Park and Recreation Bd., Los Alamos, 1989-90; treas. N.Mex. Theater Assn., 1983-85; pres. Los Alamos Little Theater, 1978-79; sec. Los Alamos Light Opera, 1990-91. Recipient AEC spl. fellowship, U.S. AEC, 1969-72. Mem. AAAS, ASME, Sigma Xi. Office: Flow Science Inc 1325 Trinity Dr Los Alamos NM 87544-3217

SICILIANO, ROCCO CARMINE, institute executive; b. Salt Lake City, Mar. 4, 1922; s. Joseph Vincent and Mary (Arnone) S.; m. Marion Stiebel, Nov. 8, 1947; children: Loretta, A. Vincent, Fred R., John, Maria. B.A. with honors, U. Utah, 1944; LL.B., Georgetown U., 1948; LHD, Hebrew Union Coll. Bar: D.C. bar 1949. Legal asst. to bd. mem. NLRB, Washington, 1948-50; asst. sec.-treas. Procon Inc., Des Plaines, Ill., 1950-53; asst. sec. labor charge employment and manpower Dept. Labor, Washington, 1953-57; spl. asst. to Eisenhower for personnel mgmt., 1957-59; ptnr. Wilkinson, Cragun & Barker, 1959-69; pres. Pacific Maritime Assn., San Francisco, 1965-69; undersec. of commerce Washington, 1969-71; pres., chmn. bd., chief exec. officer Ticor, Los Angeles, 1971-84; chmn., exec. com. Ticor, 1984-85; of counsel Jones, Day, Reavis & Pogue, 1984-87; chmn. bd., chief exec. officer Am. Health Properties, Inc., 1987-88; chmn. Dwight D. Eisenhower World Affairs Inst., Washington, 1991—; chmn. Ctr. for Govtl. Studies, 1992—; commr. Calif. Citizens Budget Commn., 1993-; bd. dirs. United TV, Inc.; mem. Fed. Pay Bd., 1971-73; trustee J. Paul Getty Trust. Bd. dirs. Eisenhower Inst., L.A. Philharm. Assn.; past chmn. Calif. Bus. Roundtable; trustee Com. for Econ. Devel.; co-chmn. Calif. Commn. on Campaign Financing; bd. govs. Cedars-Sinai Med. Ctr. 1st lt. AUS, 1943-46, MTO, ETO. Decorated Bronze Star; Order of Merit (Italy). Mem. Nat. Acad. Pub. Adminstrn., Met. Club (Washington), Calif. Club (L.A.). Home: 612 N Rodeo Dr Beverly Hills CA 90210-3208 Office: 918 16th St NW Ste 501 Washington DC 20006-2902 also: PO Box 2249 Beverly Hills CA 90213-2249

SICKEL, JOAN SOTTILARE, foundation administrator; b. Jersey City, Dec. 29, 1941; d. Peter S. and Rose M. (Maresca) Sottilare; m. Walter F. Sickel Jr., Jan. 4, 1964 (div. July 1979); children: Walter F. III (dec.), Linda Hilaire. AB, Georgian Ct. Coll., 1963. Dir. ann. giving Tucson Med. Ctr. Found., 1980-87; dir. devel. and pub. rels. Ariz. Children's Home, Tucson, 1987-93; exec. dir. Ariz. Children's Home Found., Tucson, 1993-94; curator edn. program devel. Ariz. Aerospace Found., Tucson, 1995—. Mem. women's studies adv. coun. U. Ariz. Mem. Nat. Soc. Fund Raising Execs., Nat. Assn. for Hosp. Devel., Pub. Rels. Soc. Am., Planned Giving Round Table of So. Ariz., AAUW, Ariz. Assn. for Hosp. Devel. (treas. 1986-88), U. Ariz. Presidents Club, U. Ariz. Wildcat Club, Soroptimists Internat. (chair fin. com. 1985). Home: 4151 N Camino Ferreo Tucson AZ 85715-6358 Office: 6000 E Valencia Tucson AZ 85706

SICULAR, GEORGE MYER, civil engineer, educator, consultant; b. N.Y.C., Aug. 15, 1921; s. Theodore and Sophie (Reisner) S.; m. Alice Greene, July 20, 1948; children: Terry, Lawrence. BCE, Cooper Union, 1949; MSCE, Columbia U., 1953; Engrs. degree, Stanford U., 1971. Jr. tool designer Mergen Thaler Linotype Co., N.Y.C., 1941, 42; structural designer Kennedy-VanSaun Engrs., N.Y.C., 1948; asst. prof. CCNY, N.Y.C., 1949-54; part-time cons. engr. Structures and Hydraulics, N.Y., N.J., 1949-54; from asst. prof. to prof. civil engring. San Jose (Calif.) State U., 1954-94, prof. emeritus, 1994—; cons. civil engr. San Francisco Bay area, 1954—; resident engr. Reconstruction of Grafenwöhr Mil. Base, Bavaria, 1946; civil engring. advisor Project India, U. Roorkee, USAID, 1963-64, Project Singapore, U. Singapore, Ford Found., 1967-69; chmn. mission and goals com. San Jose State U., 1971-72; acad. senator Calif. State U. Sys., 1975-85; conductor feasibility studies, Gilroy, Calif. Reservoir, Upper Llagas Reservoir, Calif., flood studies on various streams, design of energy dissipators, restoration of streams; expert witness in many cases resulting from floods. Contbr. articles to profl. jours. Bd. dirs. Jewish Fedn. San Jose, 1973-77; mem. pub. affairs com. Santa Clara County Med. Assn., 1978; mem. Jewish Pub. Affairs Calif., treas. 1983-84; comdr. post 52 Palo Alto Am. Legion, 1988-89; chmn. adult edn. com. Temple Bethel, Aptos, Calif., 1993-94; mem. tech. adv. com. Pajaro Valley Water Mgmt. Agy., Watsonville, Calif., 1993-94; chair tech. adv. com. Groundwater Guardian Com., Pajaro Valley, Watsonville, Calif., 1994. 2nd Lt. C.E., U.S. Army, 1942-46. Grad. fellow NSF, 1961, 62. Fellow ASCE; mem. United Profs. of Calif. (pres. San Jose State U. chpt. 1973-76, no. v.p. 1980-82). Democrat. Jewish. Home and Office: 387 California St Watsonville CA 95076-3916

SIDELLS, ARTHUR F., architect; b. Warren, Ohio, July 4, 1907; s. Byron T. and Mabel Ellen (Luce) S.; m. June Marie Isaly, Nov. 5, 1932; children: Stephen A., Stuart F. BArch, Carnegie Inst. Tech, 1931. Registered architect, Ohio, Pa., Fla., Calif. Pvt. practice Menlo Park, Calif.; vis. lectr. Kent State U.; alumni counselor Carnegie-Mellon U.; mem. Ohio State Bd. Examiners of Architects, 1961-72, pres., 1965, 66, 71; mem. Nat. Coun. Archtl. Registration Bds., 1964-68, chmn. pub. rels. com., chmn. nominating com, exam. com.; mem. Nat. Architect Accrediting Bd., 1967-74, pres., 1972-73, past pres., 1973-74. Prin. works include W.D. Packard Music Hall, Trumbull Regional Campus, Kent State U., Warren Western Reserve High Sch., Riverview Housing for Elderly, St. Joseph Hosp., Second Nat. Bank and Office Tower, Union Savings & Trust Eastwood Br.; contbr. articles to profl. jours. Charter pres. Warren Jaycees, 1933, 1st v.p. Ohio Jaycees, 1937; pres. Warren Rotary Club, 1950, Warren Community Chest, 1950-52. Recipient Sch. Exhibit awards AASA Convs., 1956-61, Spl. citation Pub. Edn., Geneva, Award of Merit Ohio Prestressed Concrete Assn., 1970, Thomas Jefferson medal Nat. Architect Accrediting Bd., 1985; established (with Stephen A. Sidells and Stuart F. Sidells) Carnegie Tradition Scholarship, Carnegie-Mellon U., 1986; Arthur F. Sidells Collection accepted into architecture archives, Carnegie-Mellon U., 1987. Fellow AIA (Ea. Ohio chpt. Gold medal award 1983); mem. SAR, The Buckeye Club (life, pres. 1958). Office: Arthur F Sidells Architect 1330 University Dr Apt 64 Menlo Park CA 94025-4242

SIDHU, GURMEL SINGH, geneticist, researcher; b. Jullundur, Punjab, India, May 23, 1944; came to U.S., 1980; s. Naranjan Singh and Kartar Kaur (Hoti) S.; m. Baljit Aulakh, Mar.21, 1979; children: Vikramjit, Rupinderpal. BS, Punjab U., 1960, MS, 1966; PhD, U. B.C., Vancouver, Can., 1974. Postdoctoral fellow Simon Fraser U., Burnaby, B.C., 1973-75, rsch. scientist, 1975-80; asst. prof. genetics U. Nebr., Lincoln, 1980-86; rsch. scientist Calif. State U., Fresno, 1987-89, prof. plant pathology, 1989—; rsch. dir. Germain's Inc., Fresno, 1992—. Editor: Genetics of Pathogenic Fungi, 1989; assoc. editor: (jours.) Phytopathology, 1980-86, Crop Improvement Sci., 1980—. Pres. Punjab Literacy Assn. Calif., 1994. Rsch. fellow U. Wis., 1986-87. Mem. AAAS, Phytopathology Soc. Am., Genetics and Cytology Soc. Can. Home: 1637 Gettysburg Ave Clovis CA 93611-4509 Office: Calif State U Shaw and Cedar Fresno CA 93740

SIDHU, MOHAN, anesthesiologist; b. India, June 15, 1950; came to U.S., 1975; s. Gurdial and Bachan S.; m. Gurpreet Brar, 1979; children: Simren, Jasmin, Sonya. MBBS, Christian Med. Sch., Ludhiana, India, 1973. Diplomate Am. Bd. Anesthesiology. Dir. outpatient anesthesia U. Calif. Irvine Med. Ctr., Orange, Calif., 1982-84; chief anesthesia Women's Hosp., Long Beach, Calif., 1987—; assoc. clin. prof. U. Calif. Irvine. Fellow Am. College Anesthesiologists. Office: Women's Hosp 2801 Atlantic Ave Long Beach CA 90806-1737

SIDHU, VICTOR S., investment executive; b. Pitts., Nov. 23, 1938; s. S. S. and Mary Elizabeth (Homoney) S.; m. Nancy Dayton; 1 child, Mary Sidhu Pittman. Student, Princeton U., 1956-59; BA, U. Chgo., 1961; MA, U. Ill., 1967. Chartered fin. analyst. Asst. to chmn. of dept. U. Ill., Champaign, 1963-65; account exec. Dean Witter Co., Chgo., 1967-70; pres., founder RMI Corp., Winnetka, Ill., 1970-72; investment mgr. Lincoln Nat. Investment Advisors, Chgo., 1972-73; lectr. Northeastern Ill. U., Chgo., 1971-73; v.p., div. mgr. Harris Bank, Chgo., 1973-87; v.p., chief investment officer First Interstate Bank of Calif., L.A., 1987-90; sr. v.p. Capital Rsch. and Mgmt. Co., L.A., 1990—. Bd. advisors Salvation Army, Santa Monica, Calif., 1988—; bd. dirs. U. Chgo. Alumni Assn., L.A., 1989-90. Fellow Fin. Analysts Fedn.; mem. L.A. Soc. Fin. Analysts (pres. 1992-93, gov. 1989—), Am. Fin. Assn. (life), Am. Mgmt. Assn., Inst. Chartered Fin. Analysts, Jonathan Club. Republican. Congregationalist. Home: 39 Sea Colony Dr Santa Monica CA 90405-5322 Office: Capital Rsch & Mgmt Co 333 S Hope St Los Angeles CA 90071-1406

SIDMAN, SALLY, emergency physician; b. Flora, Ill., Mar. 21, 1960; d. Cecil Dale Brown and Marjoria Alice (Dyer) Carnahan; m. Daniel J. Favello; children: Melinda Jean Sidman, Daniel Ray Sidman. BSN, St. Louis U., 1982; MD, Loma Linda U., 1991. RN Clay County Hosp., Flora, Ill., 1982-84, St. Francis Hosp., Miami, 1984-89; RN Loma Linda (Calif.) U., 1989-91, physician emergency medicine, 1991—; physician emergency medicine Kaiser Fontana (Calif.) Med. Ctr., 1992-94; owner, mgr. Dream Seekers Publ., Inc., Newburgh, Ind., 1994—; instr. Am. Heart Assn., Loma Linda, 1991—, Am. Coll. of Emergency Physicians, Calif. chpt., 1992—; songwriter Broadcast Music Inc., Nashville, 1994. Contbg. author: Medicine Made Easy, 1992. Community assistance organizer Bayshore Luth. Ch., Miami, 1984-89; sponsor Children Internat., Kansas City, Mo., 1992—; contbr. Emergency Medicine Found., Dallas, 1993—, City of Hope, L.A., 1993—. Mem. AMA, Am. Coll. of Emergency Physicians, Calif. Med. Assn., Fla. Med. Assn., Am. Heart Assn. (sec. Clay County chpt., 1983-84), Sigma Theta Tau. Lutheran. Office: 3700 Washington Ave Evansville IN 47750

SIEBERT, DIANE DOLORES, author, poet; b. Chgo., Mar. 18, 1948; m. Robert William Siebert, Sept. 21, 1969. RN. Author: Truck Song, 1984 (Notable Children's Book award ALA, 1984, Sch. Libr. Jour. one of Best Books 1984, Outstanding Children's Book award N.Y. Times Book Rev. 1984, Reading Rainbow Selection book 1991), Mojave, 1988 (Children's Editor's Choice 1988, Internat. Reading Assn. Tchrs.' Choice award 1989, others), Heartland, 1989 (award Nat. Coun. for Social Studies/Children's Book Coun. 1989, on John Burroughs List Nature Book for Young Readers 1989, award Ohio Farm Bur. Women 1991), Train Song, 1990 (Notable Children's Book award ALA, 1990, Redbook Mag. one of Top Ten Picture Books 1990, one of Best Books award Sch. Libr. Jour. 1990, others), Sierra, 1991 (Outstanding Sci. Trade Book for Children award Nat. Sci. Tchrs.' Assn. 1991, Notable Children's Trade Book in Field Social Studies award Nat. Coun. Social Studies 1991, Beatty award Calif. Libr. Assn. 1992), Plane Song, 1993 (Outstanding Sci. Trade Book for Children 1994, Tchrs.' Choice award Internat. Reading Assn. 1994, Platinum award Oppenheim Toy Portfolio). Home: PO Box 758 Terrebonne OR 97760-0758

SIEBERTS, JAN KRISTIAN, bank executive; b. Portland, Oreg., Aug. 26, 1942; s. Ned Alworth and Solveig (Storkersen) S.; m. Gail Ann Smith, Dec. 28, 1971; children: Solveig Kara, Soren K. BS, U. Oreg., 1967. Mgr. Master-Charge 1st Nat. Bank, Anchorage, 1968-75; sr. v.p. Nat. Bank of Alaska, Anchorage, 1975—. Bd. dirs. Anchorage Neighborhood Housing Svcs. Served with U.S. Army, 1962-64; Korea. Mem. Mortgage Bankers Assn.

Office: Nat Bank of Alaska 301 W Northern Lights Blvd Anchorage AK 99503-2603

SIECK, GREG R., advertising executive; b. L.A., June 12, 1956; s. David Wieboldt and Ruth Helen (Rodgers) S.; m. Barbara Marcellyn Flanders, Oct. 29, 1989. BA, U. So. Calif., 1978. Sr. v.p. J. Walter Thompson, N.Y.C., 1982-89; v.p. J. Walter Thompson, San Francisco, 1989-91, Foote, Cone & Belding Advt., L.A., 1991—. Office: Foote Cone & Belding Advt PO Box 2505 Santa Ana CA 92707-0505

SIEFER, STUART B., architect; b. Detroit, Nov. 28, 1942; s. Louis and Esther (Ressler) S.; m. Nancy Ann Feldman, Apr. 23, 1967; children: Eric S., Jeremy M., Ted B. BA, Wayne State U., 1965; postgrad., U. Detroit, 1965-68; BArch, Ariz. State U., 1971. Registered architect, Ariz. Designer, draftsman various firms, Detroit, 1966-68; rschr. Detroit Bd. Edn., 1967; archtl. designer Peace Corps, Tegucigalpa, Honduras, 1968-70; designer, job capt. various firms, Phoenix, 1970-73; prin. Siefer Assocs., Tempe, Ariz., 1973—. Bd. dirs. Downtown Tempe Community, Inc., 1993—; vol. bd. mem. Tempe Ctr. for Habilitation, 1993—; mem. Ariz. Town Hall, Phoenix, 1993—. Recipient 11 design awards Tempe Beautification Com., 1975—, merit & Crescordia award Valley Forward Assn. AIA Ariz., 1988, 93, Beautification award City of Mesa, Ariz. Mem. AIA (pres. Rio Salado chpt.), Rio Salado Architecture Found. (exec. mem.), Tempe C. of C. (pres. 1992-93) Found. (founding bd. mem. 1995).

SIEGEL, BROCK MARTIN, chemist; b. Binghamton, N.Y., Aug. 25, 1947; s. Samuel Joseph and Clara Louise (Davenport) S.; m. Catherine Sandra Bloomfield, Dec. 19, 1978; children: Justin, Aaron, Rachael. BS, Syracuse U., 1969; PhD, U. Ill., 1974. Postdoctoral assoc. Columbia U., N.Y.C., 1974-76; asst. prof. U. Minn., Mpls., 1976-79; tech. dir. Henkel Corp., Mpls., 1979-86, Henkel Rsch. Corp., Santa Rosa, Calif., 1986-90; mgr. MilliGen/Biosearch, Novato, Calif., 1990-91; dir. Applied Biosys. divsn. Perkin Elmer, Foster City, Calif., 1991—. Author: Nucleic Acids, 1975; contbr. articles to profl. jours.; patentee vitamin E chemistry. Bd. dirs. Camp Chai, Santa Rosa, 1987-91. NIH fellow, 1972-74, NIH fellow, 1975, DuPont Found. fellow U. Minn., 1978. Mem. Am. Chem. Soc., N.Y. Acad. Sci. Office: Applied Biosystems Inc 850 Lincoln Centre Dr Foster City CA 94404-1128

SIEGEL, CHARLOTTE DOUGLAS, marketing research professional; b. Winfield, Kans., July 8, 1951; d. Charles Henry and Betty Lee (Darnell) Douglas; m. Terry Siegel, Apr. 13, 1980; 1 child, Shannon. Student, Wichita State U., 1972-74; Assoc. Bus., Mesa C.C., 1988; BS in Bus. Adminstrn., U. Phoenix, 1994. Franchising asst. Times Mirror Cable TV, Phoenix, 1980-82; pres., cons. CDS Cons., Inc., Phoenix, 1982-90; mgr. market rsch. Cox Comms., Phoenix, 1990—. Designer, implementer market rsch. project Strategy Planning Through Analysis of Geocoded System Activity, 1993; author market segmentation case study Saving Advt. Dollars, 1994, pay-per-view case study Phoenix Suns PPV Tracking Case Study, 1994. Mem. Cable TV Adminstrn. and Mktg. Soc. (awards 1993, 94), Valley of the SunCable Club (treas. 1983-85), Women in Cable (membership chair 1982-83). Republican. Jewish. Office: Cox Comms 17602 N Black Canyon Hwy Phoenix AZ 85023-1936

SIEGEL, MO J., beverage company executive; b. Salida, Colo., Nov. 21, 1949; s. Joe E. and Betty Siegel; children—Gabriel, Sarah, Megan, Kate, Luke. Founder Celestial Seasonings Herb Tea Co., Boulder, Colo.; pres., chief exec. officer Celestial Seasonings Herb Tea Co., until 1984, Celestial Seasonings div. Dart and Kraft, 1984-86; founder, pres. Earthwise Corp., 1990; pvt. investor, lectr., TV talk show guest; CEO Celestial Seasonings Herb Tea Co., 1991—, chmn. bd.; bd. dirs. numerous orgns. Author numerous articles. Founder, pres. Inst. Advancement Internat. Fedn. Democracies, Jesusonian Non Profit Found.; founder Coors Classic Bicycle Race (formerly Red Zinger Bicycle Classic). named One of Best of New Generation, Esquire Mag.; Celestial Seasonings named One of 100 Best Cos. to Work For. Mem. Young Pres.' Orgn. *

SIEGEL, RICHARD LEWIS, political science educator; b. N.Y.C., Oct. 21, 1940; s. Samuel and Clara Siegel; children: Naomi Siegel Morse, Daniel, Jordan. BA, Brandeis U., 1961; PHD, Columbia U., 1967. From instr. to prof. U. Nev., Reno, 1965—, chairperson dept. polit. sci., 1988-92. Author: Employment and Human Rights, 1994, Evaluating the Results of Foreign Policy, 1969, (with others) Comparing Public Policies, 1977; contbr. articles to profl. jours. Nat. bd. dirs. ACLU, 1975-88. Recipient Hazel Erskine Lifetime Achievement award ACLU, 1989. Mem. Internat. Studies Assn., Am. Polit. Sci. Assn., Policy Studies Orgn. Democrat. Jewish. Office: Dept Polit Sci U Nev Reno NV 89557

SIEGEL, SHELDON C., physician; b. Mpls., Jan. 30, 1922; s. Carl S.; m. Priscilla Rikess, Mar. 3, 1946; children—Linda, Nancy. A.A., Va. Jr. Coll., 1940; B.A., B.S., U. Minn., 1942, M.D., 1945. Intern U. Minn. Hosp., 1946, resident in pediatrics, 1947-48; fellow in pediatric allergy Rochester, N.Y., 1949-50; practice medicine specializing in pediatric allergy and pediatrics St. Paul, 1950-52, San Antonio, 1952-54, Los Angeles, 1954—; clin. instr. pediatrics U. Rochester, 1949-50, U. Minn., 1950-51; asst. prof. pediatrics U. Tex., 1952-54; asst. clin. prof. U. Calif. at Los Angeles Med. Sch., 1955, clin. asso. prof., 1957-62, clin. prof., 1963—, co-chief pediatric allergy clinic, 1957—; mem. staff Harbor Gen. Hosp., Torrance, Calif., Daniel Freeman Hosp., Inglewood, Calif., Centinela Valley Community Hosp., Inglewood, Hawthorne (Calif.) Community Hosp. Editorial bd.: Jour. Allergy, 1973-75; contbr. articles to med. jours. Fellow Am. Acad. Allergy (pres. 1974), Am. Coll. Allergists, Am. Acad. Pediatrics; mem. AMA, Allergy Found. Am. (pres. 1976), Calif., Los Angeles County med. assns., Los Angeles Pediatric Soc., Calif., Los Angeles socs. allergy, Western Pediatric Research Soc., Am. Bd. Med. Specialists, Sigma Xi. Office: 11620 Wilshire Blvd Los Angeles CA 90025-1706

SIEGEL, STUART ELLIOTT, physician, pediatrics educator, cancer researcher; b. Plainfield, N.J., July 16, 1943; s. Hyman and Charlotte Pearl (Freinberg) S.; m. Linda Wertkin, Jan. 20, 1968; 1 child, Joshua. BA, MD, Boston U., 1967. Diplomate Am. Bd. Pediatrics, Am. Bd. Pediatric Oncology. Intern U. Minn. Hosp., Mpls., 1967-68, resident, 1968-69; clin. assoc. NIH, Bethesda, Md., 1969-72; asst. prof. pediatrics U. So. Calif. Sch. Medicine, Los Angeles, 1972-76, assoc. prof., 1976-81, prof., 1981—; head div. hematology-oncology Children's Hosp. of Los Angeles, 1976—, dep. physician-in-chief, 1987-90, assoc. chair dept. pediatrics, 1994—; mem. clin. cancer program project com. NIH, Nat. Cancer Inst., HEW, Bethesda, Md., 1978-82; pres. So. Calif. Children's Cancer Services, Los Angeles, 1977—. Bd. dirs. Nat. Leukemia Broadcast Coun., 1987—, Ronald McDonald Children's Charities, 1988—, Make-A-Wish Found., 1987—, Children's Hosp. L.A. Found., 1994—. Surgeon USPHS, 1969-72. Fellow Am. Acad. Pediatrics. Office: Childrens Hosp Los Angeles Div Hematology Oncology PO Box 54700 Los Angeles CA 90054-0700

SIEGFRIED, WILLIAM, chemist; b. Phila., July 4, 1925; s. Howard and Sadie L. (Wolverton) S.; m. Brenda M. Bowen, Jan. 2, 1948 (div. Jan. 1964); children: Patricia, Michael; m. Katherine Ann Delia, Feb. 29, 1964. BS in Chemistry, Bucknell U., 1950. Chemist Ohio Apex div. F.M.C. Corp, Nitro, W.Va., 1950-52; chief chemist Kindt-Collins Co., Cleve., 1952-58, 60-64; dir. rsch. Munray Product div. Fanner, Cleve., 1958-60, Victrylit Candle Co., Oshkosh, Wis., 1964-68; chief chemist Freeman Mfg. Co., Cleve., 1968-79; mng. dir. R&D Blended Waxes, Inc., Oshkosh, 1979-85; chief chemist J.F. McCaughin Co., Rosemead, Calif., 1985—. Patentee in field. With USN, 1943-46, PTO. Home: 1409 N Tamar Dr La Puente CA 91746-1123 Office: J F McCaughin 2628 River Ave Rosemead CA 91770-3302

SIEGLER, RICHARD LOUIS, pediatric nephrologist, educator; b. Vallejo, Calif., May 5, 1939; s. Alfred Charles and Loyola Ann (Wolf) S.; m. Karen Koenig, June 25, 1963; children: Mark, Matthew, Amy. BA in Life Sci., Calif. State U., Sacramento, 1961; MD, Creighton U., 1965. Diplomate Am. Bd. Pediats., Am. Bd. Pediat. Nephrology. Intern in mixed medicine-pediatrics Creighton Meml. - St. Joseph's Hosp., Omaha, Nebr., 1965-66, resident in pediatrics, 1966-67; resident in pediatrics U. Utah Med. Ctr., 1969-71; fellowship in nephrology Dept. Medicine, U. Utah Med. Ctr., 1971-72; chief pediat. nephrology dept. pediats. Sch. Medicine, U. Utah, Salt Lake City, 1972—, acting chmn. dept. pediats., 1982-83, vice chair clin. affairs, 1983-87; mem. exec. com. Primary Children's Med. Ctr., Salt Lake City, 1982-83; dir. pediat. renal disease program U. Utah Health Scis. Ctr., Salt Lake City, 1982—. Contbr. articles to profl. jours., book chpts. Bd. trustees Utah Children, Salt Lake City, 1989-90. Capt. U.S. Army, 1967-68, Viet Nam. Decorated Bronze Star; recipient Rsch. awards So. Ariz. Found., 1990-91; Thrasher Rsch. Fund grantee, 1978-79, 82-85. Fellow Am. Acad. Pediats. (mem. exec. com. Utah chpt. 1986-90, pres. Utah chpt. 1988-90, chair legis. com. 1990-92); mem. Am. Soc. Nephrology, Am. Soc. Pediat. Nephrology, Internat. Soc. Nephrology, Internat. Soc. Pediat. Nephrology, Soc. Pediat. Rsch. Office: Divsn Nephrology Dept Pediats U Utah Health Scis Ctr 50 N Medical Dr Salt Lake City UT 84132-0001

SIEKMAN, GRACE ANNE, nursing administrator; b. Nebr., Aug. 1, 1952; d. Frank E. and Lucille C. (Wegehoeft) Cherry; m. Dana M. Siekman, Jan. 7, 1972; children: Meredith, Michelle, Marlayna. LPN, S.E. Community Coll., 1974; ADN, SUNY, 1986; BSN, U. Phoenix, 1994. RN, Colo.; cert. ACLS instr., BLS instr., EMT instr.; cert. neonatal resuscitation instr., ABLS trauma care nurse, EMT-intermediate. Staff nurse Teamsters Hosp., Anchorage, 1975-77, Westside Manor, Lexington, Nebr., 1978-80; neonatal nurse Good Samaritan Hosp., Kearney, Nebr., 1980-81; staff nurse, Lamaze instr. Jennie Melham Meml. Med. Ctr., Broken Bow, Nebr., 1981-85, Med. Ctr., Holyoke, Colo., 1985-87; charge nurse, Lamaze instr. Chase County Hosp., Imperial, Nebr., 1987-88; charge nurse med./surg. Kit Carson County Hosp., Burlington, Colo., 1988-93, home health coord., 1993, obstetrics supr., 1993—; paraprofl. Stratton Schs., 1989-92; EMT instr. Morgan Community Coll., Ft. Morgan, 1989—. Vol. EMT-I Stratton Ambulance Svc., 1988—; pianist, organist Stratton Meth. Ch., 1988—. Named Outstanding Nurse of Yr., Kit Carson County, 1991, 92; recipient Northeastern Plains Nurse award, 1993. Mem. Assn. Women's Health, Obstetrics and Neonatal Nurses, Emergency Med. Assn. Colo. (EMT Intermediate of Yr. 1991), Order Eastern Star.

SIEMIONOW, MARIA, hand surgeon, microsurgeon; b. Poznan, Poland, May 3, 1950; came to U.S., 1989; d. Bronislaw and Zofia (Jackowska) Kusza; m. Wlodzimierz Siemionow, Apr. 26, 1975; 1 child, Krzysztof. MD, Med. Acad., Poznan, 1974, degree in Orthopedics, 1981, PhD in Microsurgery, 1985, DSc in Microcirculation, 1992. Asst. clin. instr. Inst. Orthopedics/Rehab. Medicine, Poznan, 1978-81, sr. asst. lectr., 1982-86, adj. orthopedics, hand and microsurgery, 1987-90; rsch. assoc. prof., rsch. dir. U. Utah, Salt Lake City, 1990—; vis. prof. U. Guadalajara, Mex., 1986, U. Monastir, Tenesia, 1989, Mount Vernon Hosp., London, 1992, Chang Gung Meml. Hosp, Taipei, Taiwan, 1994. Editl. bd. Jour. Investigative Surgery, 1991-93; contbr. articles to sci. jours. Christine Kleinert Hand Surgery fellow, 1985. Mem. Am. Soc. Reconstructive Microsurgery (pres. 1992), Internat. Soc. Reconstructive Microsurgery (pres. 1993), Plastic Surgery Rsch. Coun., Physicians for Peace (pres. 1993), Interplast-Turkey (pres. 1993). Office: U Utah 50 N Med Dr 3C127 Salt Lake City UT 84132

SIEMON-BURGESON, MARILYN M., education administrator; b. Whittier, Calif., Nov. 15, 1934; d. John Roscoe and Louise Christina (Secoy) Mason; m. Carl J. Siemon, Aug. 18, 1956 (div. Oct. 1984); children: Timothy G., Melanie A. Siemon Imes; Troy M.; m. James K. Burgeson, Jan. 24, 1987. BA, U. Redlands, 1956; MA, Pacific Oaks Coll., 1975; postgrad., Point Loma Coll., 1979-80. Cert. elem. and early childhood tchr. Tchr., administr. Sierra Madre (Calif.) Community Nursery Sch., 1970-77; tchr. parent edn. and music Pasadena (Calif.) Unified Schs., 1977-79, project coordinator, 1980-82, tchr. curriculum resource dept., 1982-83, head tchr., Washington Children's Ctr., 1983—; endorsed trainer High Scope Found. Register, 1990—; trainer Program for Infant/Toddler Caregivers. Active Arcadia (Calif.) Bicentennial Commn., 1974-76; mem. policy coun. for cmty. housing svcs. Pasadena Head Start, 1992—; life mem. Sierra Madre Sch. PTA; mem. Child Care Coalition, Pasadena. Ednl. Professions Devel. fellow Pacific Oaks Coll., Pasadena, 1969. Mem. Nat. Assn. Edn. Young Children (grantee 1970), Child Care Info. Svc. (bd. dirs., chmn. parent edn. and family affairs 1986—), Women Ednl. Leadership (asst. program v.p.), AAUW (past pres., co-chmn. Math.-Sci. Conf. 1983, chair Coll./Univ. Rels. 1988—, grantee 1982, 83), Pasadena Coun. Women's Clubs (pres. 1995—), Delta Kappa Gamma (pres. 1986-88, 92-94). Republican. Episcopalian. Home: 2266 Kinclair Dr Pasadena CA 91107-1022 Office: Washington Children's Ctr 130 E Penn St Pasadena CA 91103-1828

SIERRA, RUBEN ANGEL GARCIA, professional baseball player; b. Rio Piedras, P.R., Oct. 6, 1965. Grad. high sch., Rio Piedras, P.R. Baseball player Tex. Rangers, 1982-92, Oakland Athletics, 1992—. Named Am. League Player of Yr., Sporting News, 1989, recipient Silver Slugger award, 1989; named to All-Star team, 1989, 91-92, 94; Am. League RBI Leader, 1989. Office: Oakland-Alameda County Coliseum 7000 Coliseum Way Oakland CA 94621-1945*

SIEWERT, SAM BURK, aerospace engineer; b. Berkeley, Calif., Apr. 14, 1967; s. Howard Richard and Virginia Lee (Burk) S.; m. Michelle Lisa Shugert, Dec. 30, 1989; 1 child, David Maxwell. Student, U. Calif., Berkeley, 1984-85; BS in Aerospace Engring., U. Notre Dame, 1989; postgrad., U. Houston, 1989—; MS in Computer Sci., U. Colo., Boulder, 1993; postgrad., U. Colo., 1994—. Engr. specialist guidance, navigation and control div. McDonnell Douglas Space Systems Co., Houston, 1989—; mem. Aeroassist Flight Experiment Mission Ops. Panel, Houston, 1991; mem. tech. point of contact models assessment team Johnson Space Ctr., Houston, 1990-91; mem. Space Shuttle Mission Control Ctr. Guidance and Procedures Officer Software Devel. Team, Houston, 1991-92; mem. Pluto Express Mission Ops. Design Team, Boulder, 1993—. Tutor Vols. in Pub. Schs., Houston, 1989-91, Literacy Advance, Houston, 1990. Mem. AIAA, ACM. Office: U Colo Space Grant Coll Engring Ctr ME-014 Boulder CO 80309

SIFFERMAN, THOMAS RAYMOND, speciality chemical researcher; b. Chgo., July 28, 1941; s. Joseph A. and Mary B. S.; m. Rose Mary Murphy, June 8, 1968; children: Nancy A., Joseph J., Laura M. BME, Marquette U., 1964; MSME, Purdue U., 1966, PhD, 1970. Registered profl. engr., Okla. Teaching/rsch. asst. Purdue U., W. Lafayette, Ind., 1968-70; rsch., sr. rsch. scientist Conoco, Ponca City, Okla., 1970-81; vis. assoc. prof. U. Tulsa, 1981-82; rsch. assoc. Mobil Rsch. - DRL, Dallas, 1982-87; activity leader Mobil Rsch.-CRL, Princeton, N.J., 1987-88; rsch. assoc. Mobil Rsch.-DRL, Dallas, 1988-91; planning assoc. Mobil Rsch. - DRL, Dallas, 1991-92; rsch. assoc. Mobil Rsch.-DRL, Dallas, 1992; rsch. fellow Kelco Rsch., San Diego, 1992—; cons. in field. Contbr. articles to profl. jours.; patentee in field. Mem. ASME, Soc. Petroleum Engrs. (sect. chmn. 1974), Soc. Rheology, Sigma Xi, Tau Beta Pi, Pi Mu Epsilon, Pi Tau Sigma. Roman Catholic. Office: Kelco 8225 Aero Dr San Diego CA 92123-1716

SIFFORD, BENTON ALEXANDER, III, energy consultant; b. Evanston, Ill., Sept. 20, 1955; s. Benton Alexander Jr. and Gail Byrd (Sollender) S.; m. Saralynn Baker, Nov. 6, 1982. BA in Geography, U. Calif., Santa Barbara, 1978; MS in Geography, U. Idaho, 1984. Mgr. Oak Tree Antiques, London, 1978-80; geothermal specialist Idaho Office Energy, Boise, 1980; sr. assoc. Eliot Allen & Assocs., Salem, Oreg., 1981-84; program mgr. Oreg. Dept. Energy, Salem, 1984-95; pvt. practice Sifford Energy Svcs., Neskowin, Oreg., 1995—; pres. Wood Energy Coordination Group, Portland, 1988—. Author: Geothermal Resources Council Transactions, Vol. 7, 1984, Vol. 14, 1990, Bioenergy Conversion Opportunities, 1988; also articles. Pres. Neskowin (Oreg.) Cmty. Assn., 1989-94; commr. Neskowin Regional Water Dist., 1993—. Recipient cert. of appreciation USDA Forest Svc., 1988, 89, Lions Internat., Salem, 1990. Mem. Geothermal Resources Coun. (pres. Pacific N.W. sect. 1985-88, bd. dirs. 1988-90), Assn. Pacific Coast Geographers, Internat. Dist. Heating Assn. Home: PO Box 870 Neskowin OR 97149-0870 Office: Sifford Energy Svcs Box 900 Neskowin OR 97149-0900

SIGAL, SANFORD DAVID, real estate developer; b. L.A., Jan. 28, 1964; s. Martin Irving and Gloria (Blatter) S.; m. Cindy Sisino, Mar. 12, 1988; children: Hayden Joshua, Thea Samantha. BS, UCLA, 1987. Pres., CEO West Venture Cos., Burbank, Calif., 1984—; developer Firestone Shopping Ctr., Norwalk, Calif., 1990, Norwalk Sq. Shopping Ctr., 1989, Azusa (Calif.) Promenade, 1989, La Mirada (Calif.) Ctr., 1988, Bonnie Brae Retail Shopping Ctr., L.A., 1987; residential home builder, L.A., San Bernardino, Riverside and Ventura Counties. Mem. Econ. Devel. Commn., Alusa. Mem. Internat. Coun. Shopping Ctrs., Pres'. Club. Republican. Jewish. Office: West Venture Cos 300 E Magnolia Blvd Ste 400 Burbank CA 91502-1154

SIGHOLTZ, SARA O'MEARA, nonprofit organization executive; b. Knoxville, Tenn.; m. Robert Sigholtz; children: John; stepchildren: Taryn, Whitney. Attended, Briarcliff Jr. Coll.; BA, The Sorbonne, Paris. Co-founder, chmn. bd., CEO CHILDHELP USA/Internat. (formerly Children's Village USA), Woodland Hills, Calif., 1974—. Bd. dirs. Internat. Soc. Prevention Child Abuse and Neglect, Children to Children, Inc.; hon. com. mem. Learning Disabilities Found., Inc.; mem. Mayor's adv. bd., Defense for Children Internat., Nat. Soc. Prevention Cruelty to Children, World Affairs Coun.; adv. bd. mem. Ednl. Film Co.; bd. dirs. Internat. Alliance on Child Abuse and Neglect; sustaining mem. Spastic Children's League, past pres.; mem., past recording sec. Assistance League So. Calif. Recipient Cross of Merit, Knightly Order of St. Brigitte, 1967, Victor M. Carter Diamond award Japan-Am. Soc., 1970, Dame Cross of Merit of Order of St. John of Denmark, 1980, Official Seal of 34th Gov. Calif., 1981, Woman of Achievement award Career Guild, 1982, Women Making History award Nat. Fedn. Bus. Profl. Women's Clubs, 1983, Disting. Am. award for svc., 1984, Humanitarian award Nat. Frat. Eagles, 1984, Nat. Recognition award outstanding leadership Am. Heritage Found., 1986, Notable Am. award svc. to Calif., 1986, Dove of Peace award Pacific Southwest and Ctrl. Pacific Regions B'nai B'rith, 1987, Paul Harris fellow award Rotary Found., 1989, Love and Help the Children award, 1990, Presdl. award, 1990, Hubert Humphrey award Touchdown Club Washington, 1994, numerous others. Mem. SAG, AFTRA, Victory Awards (exec. com.), Am. Biographical Inst. (nat. bd. advisors), Alpha Delta Kappa (hon.). Office: Childhelp USA 6463 Independence Ave Woodland Hills CA 91370

SIGLER, MARJORIE DIANE, computer programming executive, analyst; b. Fullerton, Calif., Sept. 19, 1943; d. Earl Lawrence Whipple and Ruth Juanita (Long) Purcell; children: Stephen, Deborah; m. William A. Sigler, June 19, 1995; Grad computer programming LaSalle U., Chgo., 1973; BSBA U. Phoenix, 1994. Computer programmer Los Alamos (N.Mex.) Nat. Lab., 1972-81, cons. control data, 1984-89, sr. analyst, programmer, 1989—; contract programmer Computer Assistance, Inc., Tulsa, 1981-82; profl. svcs. analyst Control Data Corp., Denver, 1982-84, Los Alamos, 1984-89. Mem. Order Eastern Star (past matron), Toastmasters Internat. Home: 950 Santa Clara Pl Los Alamos NM 87544-3209

SIGMAN, MELVIN MONROE, psychiatrist; b. N.Y.C., Dec. 15, 1935; s. Irving and Lillian (Pearlman) S. BA, Columbia U., 1956; MD, SUNY, N.Y.C., 1960; postgrad., William Alanson White Analytic Inst., N.Y.C., 1969. Staff psychiatrist Hawthorne (N.Y.) Cedar Knolls Sch., 1966-68; pvt. practice psychiatry N.Y.C., 1966-72, Fresno, Calif., 1974-87; staff psychiatrist Fresno County Dept. of Health, 1974-87, Psychol. Svcs. for Adults, L.A., 1987-93; psychiatrist pvt. practice, L.A., 1993—; attending staff psychiatry Bellevue Hosp., N.Y.C., 1966-68; cons. N.Y. Foundling Hosp., N.Y.C., 1966-72; assoc. attending staff Roosevelt Hosp., N.Y.C., 1967-72; asst. clin. prof U. Calif. San Francisco, Fresno, 1977; chmn. cen. Calif. com. Columbia Coll. Nat. Alumni Secondary Schs. Served to capt. USAF, 1961-63. Fellow Royal Soc. Health, Am. Orthopsychiat. Assn.; mem. Holiday Spa Clif., Fresno Racquet Club. Fresno Racquet. Office: 10780 Santa Monica Blvd Ste 250 Los Angeles CA 90025-4749

SIGNOROVITCH, DENNIS JAMES, communications executive; b. Norristown, Pa., July 23, 1945; s. James and Regina S.; m. Susan E. McLaughlin, 1968; children: James Edward, Sarah Elizabeth. BS in Fgn. Svc., Georgetown U., 1967; MA, Old Dominion U., 1972; postgrad., U. Toledo., 1972. Instr. U. Toledo, 1972-77; writer/editor Doehler Jarvis div. NL Industries, Toledo, 1977-78; mgr. pub. rels. Eltra Corp., N.Y.C., 1979, mgr. planning, 1980; spl. assignment staff Allied Corp., Morristown, N.J., 1981; dir. pub. affairs Eltra Corp., Morristown, 1981-82; dir. pub. affairs Allied Info. Systems, Trumbull, Conn., 1982-83, dir. pub. affairs indsl. and tech. sector, 1983-86, dir. corp. communications, 1986-90, staff v.p. communications, 1990-92; v.p. pub. affairs AlliedSignal Aerospace, Torrance, Calif., 1992—. With U.S. Army, 1967-70. Decorated Bronze Star with oak leaf cluster. Mem. Torrance C. of C. (bd. dirs. 1993), The Conf. Bd. (corp. comm. coun. 1991), Vol. Ctr. of South Bay (bd. dirs. 1994), L.A. Music Ctr. Unified Fund (aerospace com. mem. 1992, 93). Office: Allied Signal Aerospace 2525 W 190th St Torrance CA 90504-6061

SIGOLOFF, SANFORD CHARLES, retail executive; b. St. Louis, Sept. 8, 1930; s. Emmanuel and Gertrude (Breliant) S.; m. Betty Ellen Greene, Sept. 14, 1952; children: Stephen, John David, Laurie. B.A., UCLA, 1950. Cons. AEC, 1950-54, 57-58; gen. mgr. Edgerton, Germeshausen & Grier, Santa Barbara, Calif., 1958-63; v.p. Xerox Corp., 1963-69; pres. CSI Corp., Los Angeles, 1969-70; sr. v.p. Republic Corp., Los Angeles, 1970-71; chief exec. officer Kaufman & Broad, Inc., Los Angeles, 1979-82; chmn., pres., chief exec. officer Wickes Cos. Inc., Santa Monica, 1982—. Contbr. articles on radiation dosimetry to profl. jours. Bd. govs. Cedars-Sinai Hosp. Served in USAF, 1954-57. Recipient Tom May award Nat. Jewish Hosp. and Research Ctr., 1972. Mem. AAAS, Am. Chem. Soc., AIAA, Am. Nuclear Soc., IEEE, Radiation Research Soc. Office: Wickes Cos Inc 3340 Ocean Park Blvd Santa Monica CA 90405-3204

SIGURDSON, EDWIN D., small business owner; b. Port Townsend, Wash., May 3, 1942; s. Clarence E. and Beverly Mabel S. BA in Bus. Adminstrn., Oreg. State U., 1970. CPA, Oreg. Regional controller Arcata Communications Co., Portland, Oreg., 1971-73; acct. Ed Luoma CPA, Astoria, Oreg., 1973-75; sr. utility auditor Oreg. Pub. Utility Commn., Salem, Oreg., 1975-84; owner Formula 1 Computers, Salem, 1981—, Willamette Systems Integration, Inc., Salem, 1991-93; cons. Oreg. Computer Resource, Inc., Salem, 1985—; instr. Chemeketa C.C., 1986—. Served with U.S. Army, 1964-66. Mem. Oreg. Soc. CPAs, PHi Theta Kappa, Beta Alpha Psi. Office: Oreg Computer Resource Inc 3074 Lancaster Dr NE # 265 Salem OR 97305-1396

SIKAND, GEETA, dietitian; b. Udaipur, Rajasthan, India, Sept. 2, 1951; came to U.S., 1971; d. Anand Prakash and Shanti Devi Ahluwalia; m. Sharanpal Singh Sikand, June 6, 1971; children: Vikram, Kabir, Sunjeev. BS in Dietetics, Calif. State U., Long Beach, 1975, MS in Nutrition, 1976. Registered dietitian, Calif. Teaching dietitian St. Mary Med. Ctr., Long Beach, 1976-79; cons. dietitian Orange County Weight REduction Group, Anaheim, Calif., 1981, Los Alamitos (Calif.) Med. Ctr., 1981; teaching dietitian Baylor Coll. Medicine, Houston, 1981-86; clin. instr. medicine U. Calif., Irvine, 1989—; lipid rsch. dietitian U. Calif.-Irvine/VA Med. Ctr., Long Beach, 1989—; cons. dietitian San Clemente (Calif.) Hosp., 1986-93, Mission Viejo, Calif., 1989—. Chair Heart Fest com. Am. Heart Assn., Irvine, 1992-94; sec. United India Assn., Orange, Calif., 1991-92, v.p., 1992-94. Mem. Am. Dietetic Assn., Calif. Dietetic Assn. (treas. 1993—, chair fundraising com. 1992-93). Hindu. Home: 25201 Exmoor Mission Viejo CA 92692-2890

SIKES, CYNTHIA LEE, actress, singer; b. Coffeyville, Kans., Jan. 2, 1954; d. Neil and Pat (Scott) S.; m. Alan Bud Yorkin, June 24, 1989. Student, Am. Conservatory Theater, San Francisco, 1977-79. Appeared in TV series St. Elsewhere, 1981-83, L.A. Law, 1989; TV movies include His Mistress, s1990; films include Man Who Loved Women, That's Life, Arthur On The Rocks, Love Hurts, 1988; also Broadway show Into The Woods, 1988-89. Active Hollywood Women's Polit. Com. Recipient Gov.'s Medal of Merit, Kans., 1986. Mem. Environ. Media Assn. (bd. dirs.). Democrat.

SIKORA, JAMES ROBERT, educational business administrator; b. Sacramento, July 8, 1945; s. George Robert and Marian Frances (Fears) S.; m. Marie Lynore Nyarady, June 22, 1968. BEE, U. Santa Clara, 1967; postgrad., U. Calif.-Santa Cruz, 1979—. Electronic engr. GTE-Sylvania, Santa Cruz, 1967-69; systems analyst GTE-Sylvania, 1969-71; sr. support analyst GTE-Sylvania, Mt. View, Calif., 1971-73; bus. systems coordinator Santa Clara County Office Edn., San Jose, Calif., 1973-76; dir. dist. payroll, personnel svcs. Santa Clara County Office Edn., 1976-85, dir. dist. bus. svcs., 1985-95; self-employed sch. bus. cons. Omniserve, 1995—; cons. records mgmt. County of Santa Clara, San Jose, 1982; vice chair exec. bd. Edn. Mandated Cost Network, 1991-95; mem. Sch. Fin. Svcs. Subcom., 1987-94. Author, co-editor Howdy Rowdy Memorial, 1979. Sponsor San Jose/Cleveland Ballet, Santa Cruz County Symphony, Dixieland Monterey, Monterey

Bay Aquarium Patrons Cir., Long Marine Lab., San Jose Repertory Theater, Ctr. Photog. Arts, Napa Valley Wine Libr., Silver Chancellor's Cir., U. Calif. Santa Cruz; mem. Team Shakespeare, Shakespeare Santa Cruz, Omni Found. Mem. Pub. Agy. Risk Mgmt. Assn., Am. Diabetes Assn., Calif. Assn. Sch. Bus. Ofcls. (subsect. pres. 1984-85, sect. bd. dirs. 1987-93, sect. pres. 1991-92, state bd. dirs. 1991-92, state legis. com. 1989—, state strategic planning com. 1994), Norwegian Elkhound Assn. (pres. 1977-79), Wine Investigation for Novices and Oenephiles, Amnesty Internat., Calif. Trout, Calif. State Parks Found., Am. Dog Owners Assn., Sierra Club (life). Libertarian. Roman Catholic. Home and Office: 400 Coon Heights Rd Ben Lomond CA 95005-9711

SILBERGELD, ARTHUR F., lawyer; b. St. Louis, June 1, 1942; s. David and Sabina (Silbergeld) S.; m. Carol Ann Schwartz, May 1, 1970; children: Diana Lauren, Julia Kay. BA, U. Mich., 1968; M City Planning, U. Pa., 1971; JD, Temple U., 1975. Bar: N.Y. 1976, Calif. 1978, D.C. 1983, U.S. Ct. Appeals (2d, 9th and D.C. cirs.). Assoc. Vladeck, Elias, Vladeck & Lewis, N.Y.C., 1975-77; field atty. NLRB, Los Angeles, 1977-78; ptnr., head employment law practice group McKenna, Conner & Cuneo, L.A., 1978-89; ptnr., head labor and employment law practice group Graham & James, L.A., 1990—; instr. extension divsn. UCLA, 1981-89. Author: Doing Business in California: An Employment Law Handbook, 1989, Advising California Employers, 1990, 91, 93 supplements; contbr. articles to profl. jours. Founding mem. L.A. Mus. Contemporary Art; mem. Mus. Modern Art, N.Y., Art Inst. Chgo.; bd. dirs. Bay Cities unit Am. Cancer Soc., Calif., 1981-85, Jewish Family Svc. L.A., 1981-85, So. Calif. Employment Round Table, 1990—. Mem. ABA (com. on devel. law under NLRA 1975—), L.A. County Bar Assn. (exec. bd. labor law sect. 1984—). Office: Graham & James 801 S Figueroa St Fl 14 Los Angeles CA 90017-2573

SILBERMAN, IRWIN ALAN, public health physician; b. Newport News, Va., Sept. 1, 1932; s. Henry and Toby (Weiss) S.; m. Mitsue Fukuyama, May 7, 1964 (div. July 1984); children: Denise, Donn, Daniel, Dean, Dana; m. Andrea George, 1983. BA, U. Calif., Berkeley, 1953; MD, U. Calif., San Francisco, 1956; MS, U. No. Colo., 1980. Intern L.A. County Harbor Gen. Hosp., Torrance, Calif., 1956-57; resident ob-gyn. Harbor/UCLA Med. Ctr., Torrance, 1957-61; commd. USAF, 1961, advanced through grades to col., 1971; staff obstetrician-gynecologist Tachikawa (Japan) Air Base, 1963-65; chief ob-gyn. Mather Air Force Base, Sacramento, 1965-66; chief aeromed. services Yokota Air Base, Tokyo, 1966-68; dir. base med. services Itazuke Air Base, Fukuoka, Japan, 1968-70, Kirkland Air Force Base, Albuquerque, 1970-72; chief hosp. services USAF Hosp. Davis-Monthan, Tucson, 1972-81; ret. USAF, 1981; med. dir. CIGNA Healthplan of Fla., Tampa, 1981-83; chief women's clinic H.C. Hudson Comprehensive Health Ctr., L.A., 1983-85; dir. maternal health and family planning programs Los Angeles County Dept. Health Svcs., L.A., 1985-91, dir. family health programs, maternat and child health, 1991—; mil. cons. to surgeon-gen. USAF, 1980-81; bd. dirs. L.A. Regional Family Planning Coun.; pres. Perinatal Adv. Coun. of L.A. Comtys., 1993-94. Chmn. health profls. adv. com. March of Dimes, Los Angeles, 1988; camp physician Boy Scouts Nat. Jamboree, Fort Hill, Va., 1985. Recipient Meritorious Service medal, USAF, 1972, 81, Air Force Commendation medal, 1980, Air medal, 1969. Fellow Am. Coll. Obstetricians and Gynecologists, Am. Coll. Physician Execs., Am. Coll. Preventive Medicine; mem. APHA, Am. Acad. Med. Dirs., So. Calif. Pub. Health Assn. (governing coun. 1988—). Home: 3716 Beverly Ridge Dr Sherman Oaks CA 91423-4509 Office: LA County Dept Health Svcs 241 N Figueroa St Los Angeles CA 90012-2693

SILBERMAN, MILES LOUIS, research and exploration geologist; b. N.Y.C., Sept. 25, 1940; s. David and Ida Clair (Raffloer) S.; m. Karen Wenrich, June 25, 1983; children: Daryl, Kevin. BS, Queens Coll., 1963; MS, U. Rochester (N.Y.), 1967, PhD, 1971. Registered geologist, Calif. Rsch. geologist U. S. Geol. Survery, Menlo Park, Calif., 1967-82; sr. exploration geologist Anaconda Minerals, Reno, Nev., 1982-83; rsch. geologist U.S. Geol. Survey, Denver, 1983-95; cons. econ. geologist Golden, 1995—; vis. prof. U. Nev., Reno, 1977; tech. adv. U.S. Geol. Survey, Israel, China, Mex., 1975, 77-88. Adv. editor Isochran West, Socorro, N.Mex., 1971-90; contbr. numerous articles to profl. jours. Fellow Soc. Econ. Geologists; mem. Assn. Exploratin Geochemistry, Geol. Soc. Nev., Sigma Xi. Home: 63 S Devinney St Golden CO 80401-5314

SILBERT, AMY FOXMAN, clinical art therapist; b. Augusta, Ga., July 11, 1953; d. Elliott and Anita Foxman; m. Philip Silbert, Sept. 6, 1987; children: Sean Kenneth, Karen Debra, Samantha Danielle. BA in Design, UCLA, 1976; MA, Loyola Marymount U., 1990. Art dir., advt. mgr. Unico Am. Corp., L.A., 1976-78; freelance graphic artist, art specialist, tchr., 1979-82; vol. coord., tchr. Craft and Folk Art Mus., L.A., 1983-86; art specialist Art Reach, UCLA Calif. Arts Coun., 1983-84; editor in chief Grad. Achievement Preparation Svc., Santa Monica, Calif., 1985-87; tchr. coordinator art exhibit Hebrew Union Coll., Los Angeles, 1984; guest children's TV programs, 1970-84. Gov. intern U.S. Congress, Washington, 1973. Recipient 1st Place award traffic light design City Monterrey, Calif., 1973. Democrat. Jewish. Home: 760 Briercliff Ln Lake Oswego OR 97034

SILER, PATRICK WALTER, drawing and ceramics educator; b. Spokane, Wash., 1939. BA, Wash. State U., 1961; MA in Painting, U. Calif., Berkeley, 1963. Teaching asst. U. Calif., Berkeley, 1967-71; artist-in-residence, instr. U. S.D., Vermillion, 1968; guest lectr. Coll. San Mateo, Calif., 1969; instr. ceramics U. Calif., Berkeley, 1971; prof. Wash. State U., Pullman, 1973—; Lectr. various workshops, colls. and orgns. One-man shows include S.W. Craft Ctr., San Antonio, 1990, Spokane (Wash.) Falls C.C., 1990, Whatcom Mus., Bellingham, Wash., 1991, U. Puget Sound, Tacoma, Wash., 1991, Bemis Found. Alternative Worksite, Omaha, 1992; exhibited in group shows at Wash. State U. Mus. Art, 1991, Sybaris Gallery, Royal Oak, Mich., 1991, Moira-James Gallery, Las Vegas, Nev., 1992, Jennifer Pauls Gallery, 1992; also pvt. collections; contbr. articles and artwork to profl. jours.; featured in numerousarticles. Recipient metal of excellence Internat.Ceramic Exposition, Calgary, Alta., Can., 1972, award of residence Alternative Workspace, Bemis Project/Artist Colony, Omaha, 1986-87; Wash. State Arts Commn. fellow, 1986, NEA fellow in ceramic sculpture, 1990. Home: NW 325th Dillon Pullman WA 99163

SILFLOW, RONALD MARK, animal scientist, microbiologist; b. Kendrick, Idaho, May 25, 1956; s. Emil F. and Doris M. (Hereth) S.; m. Laura Ann Stillman, June 14, 1980; children: Jennifer Lynn, Caleb John, Zachary James. BS in Animal Sci., U. Idaho, 1979; MS in Vet. Sci., Wash. State U., 1989, PhD in Animal Sci., 1992; BA in Biblical Studies, Living Faith Fellowship, Ministry Tng. Ctr., Pullman, Wash., 1989. Rsch. technician Wash. State U., Pullman, 1983-91, rsch. assoc., 1991-94, instr., 1994—; prin. investigator BioTracking, Moscow, Idaho, 1994. Contbr. articles to profl. jours. Student rsch. awardee Wildlife Disease Assn., 1988, Terry Amundson award, 1991, rsch. award Foun. for North Am. Wild Sheep, 1994. Mem. Am. Assn. Animal Scientists, Soc. for Leukocyte Biology. Republican. Home: SW210 Kimball Pullman WA 99163 Office: Dept Animal Science Wash State Univ Pullman WA 99164

SILLIMAN, KATHRYN, nutrition educator; b. L.A., July 30, 1960; d. Edmund Neal and Beverly Jean (Martin) S.; m. Stephen Farrar Riley, Sept. 1, 1990; 1 child, Audrey Hypatia Silliman. BS in Nutrition and Food Sci., Simmons Coll., Boston, 1984; MS in Nutrition, U. Calif. Berkeley, 1986, PhD in Nutrition, 1990. Registered dietician. Teaching asst. U. Calif. Berkeley, 1985-90; asst. prof. Calif. State U., Chico, 1990—. Author: Nutrition and Fitness, 1993; author: (book chpt.) Sugars and Sweeteners, 1991; contbr. articles to profl. jours. Recipient Ellsworth C. Dougherty prize U. Calif. Berkeley, 1990. Mem. Am. Dietetic Assn. (New Researchers award 1992), Calif. Dietetic Assn. (Zellmer Scholarship award 1994, leg. liaison 1993—), North Valley Dietetic Assn. (cmty. nutrition officer 1991-92, pres. 1992-93, legis. liaison 1993—), Calif. Nutrition Coun. Democrat. Office: Dept Biol Scis Calif State U Chico Chico CA 95929-0515

SILVA, ED, food products executive; b. 1943. Prin. Dairy Bus., Gonzalis, Calif., 1964-75; pres. Silva Harvesting, Inc., Gonzalis, Calif., 1975—. Office: Silva Harvesting Inc River Rd Gonzales CA 93926*

SILVA, ERNEST R., visual arts educator, artist. BFA, U. R.I., 1971; MFA, Tyler Sch. Art, 1974. Instr. U. R.I., Kingston, 1977-79; lectr. dept. visual arts U. Calif. San Diego, La Jolla, 1979-87, prof. dept. visual arts, 1987—; represented by Jan Baum Gallery, L.A., Lenore Gray Gallery, Providence, R.I., Porter Randall Gallery, La Jolla; bd. dirs. Installation Gallery, San Diego, mem. arts adv. bd., 1992—, exec. com., 1993—; lectr. Phila. Coll. Art, 1973, U. R.I., 1974, 84, 91, RISD, 1977, Tyler Sch. Art, Elkins Park, Pa., 1979, U. Calif. Irvine, 1981, Southwestern Coll., Chula Vista, 1982, San Diego State U., 1985, Nat. Soc. Arts and Letters, Washington, 1986, Friends of Jung, San Diego, 1991. One-person exhbns. include Inst. Contemporary Art, Boston, 1972, Artists Space, N.Y.C., 1975, Anyart Contemporary Art Ctr., Providence, R.I., 1976, Lenore Gray Gallery, Providence, 1978, 79, 92, Roy Boyd Gallery, L.A., 1982, 84, 87, Quint Gallery, San Diego, 1982, 83, 86, Jan Baum Gallery, L.A., 1989, 91, Tuttle Gallery, McDonogh, Md., 1990, Porter Randall Gallery, La Jolla, 1994, many others; group exhbns. include Mus. Phila. Civic Ctr., 1973, Cheltenham (Pa.) Art Ctr., 1973, Pratt Graphic Ctr., N.Y.C., 1975, Corcoran Art Gallery, Washington, 1975, Ft. Worth Art Mus., 1976, Baker Gallery, La Jolla, 1980, Ind. Contemporary Exhbns., L.A., 1982, Navy Pier, Chgo., 1983, 84, 85, Roy Boyd Gallery, Chgo., 1983, 85, 86, Heckscher Mus. Art, Huntington, N.Y., 1984, Indpls. Mus. Art, 1984, Forum Internat. Kunstmesse, Zurich, Switzerland, 1984, Nat. History Mus., San Diego, 1985, Visual Arts Ctr. Alaska, Anchorage, 1985, San Francisco Airport Mus., 1985, Sonrisa Gallery, L.A., 1985, Alaska State Mus., Juneau, 1986, Foire Internat. De L'Art Contemporain, Nice, France, 1986, Lyceum Theatre, San Diego, 1987, Installation Gallery, San Diego, 1986, 87, 88, Chgo. Internat. Art Exposition, 1987,L.A. Convention Ctr., 1987, Cmty. Arts, San Francisco, 1989, 90, Annex Gallery, La Jolla, 1990, Bill Bace Gallery, N.Y.C., 1991, David Lewinson Gallery, Del Mar, Calif., 1991, Southwestern Coll. Art, Chula Vista, Calif., 1992, Boehm Gallery Palomar Coll, San Marcos, Calif., 1993, Porter Randall Gallery, La Jolla, 1992, numerous others; represented in permanent collections Fogg Art Mus. Harvard U., Cambridge, Mass., Grand Rapids (Mich.) Art Mus., La Jolla Mus. Contemporary Art, Laguna Mus. Art, De Saisset Mus. U. Santa Clara, Newport Harbor Art Mus., Newport Beach, Calif., Mus. Contemporary Art, San Diego, La Jolla, San Jose Mus. Art, San Diego Mus. Art; subject reviews, articles, 1974—. Office: U Calif San Diego Visual Arts 0327 La Jolla CA 92093

SILVA, EVELYN, food products executive; b. 1947. V.p. Silva Harvesting Inc., Gonzales, Calif., 1975—. Office: Silva Harvesting Inc River Rd Gonzales CA 93926*

SILVA, JOANNA KONTAXIS, dietitian; b. Psari Trifilias, Greece, Nov. 19, 1940; came to U.S., 1967; d. George Demetrios and Sophia George (Naisopoulos) Kontaxis; m. Michael Andrew Silva, Oct. 4, 1969; children: Mark Alexander, Paul Richard. BA, Harokopios Coll., Kalithea, Athens, Greece; BS, U. Calif., Berkeley. Chief clin. dietitian A.H.E.P.A. Hosp., Salonika, Greece, 1961-67; clin. dietitian Providence Hosp., Oakland, Calif., 1967-92; renal dietitian B.M.A. Berkeley Dialysis Unit, 1990—; cons. dietitain Calif. Hosp., Oakland, 1976-81, C.D.C. Dialysis Unit, Vallejo, Claif., 1993—, C.A.P.D. Dietitien for Total Renal Care, Walnut Creek, Calif., 1992—. Mem. Am. Dietetic Assn. (registered), Bay Area Dietetic Assn. (hospitality chmn. 1979-87), Calif. Dietetic Assn., Daus. of Penelope (pres. 1990-92). Greek Orthodox. Home: 4 Rita Way Orinda CA 94563-4132 Office: BMA Dialysis 3017 Telegraph Ave Berkeley CA 94705-2013

SILVA, JOHN PHILIP COSTA, newspaper editor; b. Providence, Jan. 19, 1951; s. Silvano Costa and Florence Josephine (Russo) S.; m. Deborah Helen Radovsky, May 8, 1977; children: Daniel David, Matthew Philip. BA in Journalism, U. R.I., 1973. Staff writer Providence Jour.-Bull., 1973-79; staff writer Miami (Fla.) News, 1979-81, asst. city editor, 1981-82; spl. corr. The Wall St. Jour., Miami, 1980-81; city editor Lexington (Ky.) Herald-Leader, 1982-84; night city editor L.A. Herald Examiner, 1984-85, assignment editor, 1985-87; asst. mng. editor Ariz. Daily Star, Tucson, 1987—. Recipient 1st place for spot news UPI Newspapers New Eng., 1977. Mem. Nat. Assn. Hispanic Journalists, Investigative Reporters and Editors Assn. Home: 9433 N Albatross Dr Tucson AZ 85741-5126 Office: Ariz Daily Star 4850 S Park Ave Tucson AZ 85714-1637

SILVA, LADON GAY, dietitian; b. Ft. Campbell, Ky., Oct. 22, 1954; d. Smiles Manning and Martha Jane (Porter) S.; m. Richard Peter Saval, Feb. 14, 1991. BS, Calif. Poly. State U., 1977; MBA, U. Redlands, 1994. Dir. food services Cottonwood (Calif.) Union Sch. Dist., 1977-78; dietetic intern U. Calif. Hosps. and Clinics, San Francisco, 1978-79; clin. dietician Bakersfield (Calif.) Meml. Hosp., 1979-89; pediat. territory specialist Wyeth-Ayers Labs., Buena Park, Calif., 1989—; cons. Centre for Neuroskills, Bakersfield, 1980-85, Dr. Shivinder Deol, Bakersfield, 1985-86, Bakersfield Cmty. Hosp., 1984-86, Kern Valley Hosp., Colonial Hosp., Hilltop Convalescent Hosp., 1985-86, Charter Hosp., Bakersfield, 1988-94. Mem. Bakersfield Rep. Assembly, 1987—. Mem. Am. Dietetic Assn., Calif. Sch. Food Service Assn. (v.p. Shasta Cascade chpt. 1978), Calif. Dietetic Assn. (rep. legisl. info and pub. policy com. 1986-87), Diabetic Educators Assn., Cons. Nutritionists Assn., Kern County Nutrition Council. Methodist. Home: 4213 Homer Ln Bakersfield CA 93311-1220 Office: Wyeth-Ayerst Labs 6530 Altura Blvd Buena Park CA 90620-1040

SILVA, ROBERT OWEN, retired protective service official; b. La Junta, Colo., Sept. 5, 1935; s. Owen Delbert and Gertrude H. (Kerr) S.; m. Meredith Ann Ginn, Dec. 18, 1953; children—Edward, Andrew, Colleen. Student Pueblo Jr. Coll., 1953, FBI Nat. Acad., 1975, Police Found. Exec. Program, 1979-80. Cert. peace officer, Colo. Police officer Pueblo Police Dept., Colo., 1958-66, sgt., 1966-72, capt., 1972-77, chief of police, 1977-92, ret. dir. Colo. Police Officers Standards and Tng. Bd. dirs. Salvation Army, Pueblo, Easter Seals Soc., Pueblo, Community Corrections Bd., Pueblo, Served with U.S. Army, 1955-57; apptd. by gov. Colo. Crim. Justice Comsn., 1990. Mem. Pueblo Community Coll. Criminal Justice Adv. Bd., Leadership Pueblo Steering Com., Pikes Peak Community Coll. Criminal Justice Program (chmn. adv. bd. 1981), Organized Crime Strike Force (bd. dirs. 1977-84, chmn. 1982, 83, 84); Colo. Assn. Chiefs of Police (pres. 1984-85), Rocky Mountain Info. Network (chmn. bd. dirs. 1986—), Presbyterian (elder). Lodges: Kiwanis (bd. dirs. 1982-84), Elks.

SILVA, YVONNE JOAN, writer; b. Bloomfield, Nebr.; d. Leslie and Rosamond (Stephens) Downie; m. Robert Silva, Mar. 28, 1950 (div. Aug. 1973); children: Diane, Robert, Gregory; m. Ralph M. Kniseley, Oct. 16, 1973. Student, U. Oreg., 1949-50, U. Tenn., 1963-66. Freelance writer Oak Ridge, Tenn., 1958-73, Vienna, Austria, 1973-75, Emmett, Idaho, 1975—; organizer Thursday Writers Group, Vienna, 1973-75. Author: Attila, 1976; editor, pub. (literary mag.) The Signal, 1987-92; contbr. articles, essays and poetry to profl. publs. Active Cmty. Rels. Coun., Oakridge; facilitator Mothers United Sexual Abuse Program, Boise; organizer, facilitator Women's Conciousness Raising Group, Boise and Emmett, 1990-94. Named Poet of the Yr., Idaho Writer's League, 1989. Mem. NOW, Nat. Writers Union, Nat. Writers Assn., Poets and Writers Inc. Democrat. Home: PO Box 67 Emmett ID 83617-0067

SILVAS-OTTUMWA, SALLY, publishing executive; b. San Juan, P.R., May 1, 1950; d. Hector Juan and Eulencia Regina (Mariposa) S.; m. William Ottumwa, May 1, 1975 (div. 1989). BA, Vassar Coll., 1973; MA, Columbia U., 1978, MLS, 1985. Pub. asst. Random House, N.Y.C., 1973-76; editorial asst./assoc. Princeton U. Press, Princeton, N.J., 1978-82; asst. editorial dir. Addison-Wesley Publs., Reading, Mass., 1985-87; assoc. editorial dir. The Denali Press, Juneau, Alaska, 1988—. Mem. Reading (Mass.) Human Rights Commn., 1987. Recipient Fleckman award, Columbia U., N.Y.C., 1978. Mem. Assn. Am. Publishers, Latinos in Publishing, Hispanic Women in the Media (sec. 1985-87, exec. bd. 1990-92). Office: The Denali Press PO Box 021535 Juneau AK 99802-1535

SILVEIRA, RONALD LOUIS, video company executive; b. San Diego, Sept. 29, 1948; s. Oliver L. and Leoma E. (Singmaster) S.; m. Annaliz Durham, Nov. 17, 1984. BA in Biol. Scis., U. Calif., Berkeley, 1971; M of Mgmt., Willamette U., 1977. Adminstrv. mgr. Video Prodn. Services Inc., Berkeley, 1977-80; gen. mgr. Astin Zappia Post-Prodn., Los Angeles, 1980-84; sales mgr. Compact Video Services, Inc., Burbank, Calif., 1984-86; v.p. sales and mktg. Compact Video Services, Burbank, 1986-88; pres. Compact Video Svcs. & Image Transform, 1988-90, Unitel Video, L.A., 1990—; chmn. Hollywood Radio and TV Soc., Internat. Broadcast Awards com., 1985, 86. Adminstrv. asst. to rep. Jay Haskell, Harrisburg, Pa., 1974. Mem. Internat. Teleprodn. Soc. (pres. So. Calif. chpt. 1991-93), Acad. TV Arts and Scis.

SILVER, BARNARD JOSEPH STEWART, mechanical engineer, consultant; b. Salt Lake City, Mar. 9, 1933; s. Harold Farnes and Madelyn Cannon (Stewart) S.; m. Cherry Bushman, Aug. 12, 1963; children: Madelyn Stewart Palmer, Cannon Farnes, Brenda Picketts Call. BS in Mech. Engring., MIT, 1957; MS in Engring. Mechanics, Stanford U., 1958; grad. Advanced Mgmt. Program, Harvard U., 1977. Registered profl. engr., Colo. Engr. aircraft nuclear propulsion div. Gen. Electric Co., Evandale, Ohio, 1957; engr. Silver Engring. Works, Denver, 1959-66, mgr. sales and tech. svcs., 1966-71; chief engr. Union Sugar div. Consol. Foods Co., Santa Maria, Calif., 1971-74; directeur du complexe SODESUCRE, Abidjan, Côte d'Ivoire, 1974-76; supt. engring. and maintenance U and I, Inc., Moses Lake, Wash., 1976-79; pres. Silver Enterprises, Moses Lake, 1971-88, Silver Energy Systems Corp., Moses Lake, 1980—, Salt Lake, 1990— ; pres., gen. mgr. Silver Chief Corp., 1983—; pres. Silver Corp., 1984-86, 93—; chmn. bd. Silver Pubs., Inc., 1986-87, 89—; chmn. bd. Agronomics Internat., McLean, Va., 1994—; v.p. Barnard J. Stewart Cousins Land Co., 1987-88, 92—; dir. Isle Piquant Sugar Found., 1993-94; mem. steering com. World Botanical Inst., 1993—; instr. engring. Big Bend C.C., 1980-81. Explorer adviser Boy Scouts Am., 1965-66, 89-90, chmn. cub pack com., 1968-74, 94—, chmn. scout troop com., 1968-74, vice chmn. Columbia Basin Dist., 1986-87; pres. Silver Found., 1971-84, v.p., 1984—; ednl. counselor MIT, 1971-89; pres. Chief Moses Jr. H.S. Parent Tchr. Student Assn., 1978-79; missionary Ch. of Jesus Christ of Latter-day Saints, Can., 1953-55, West Africa, 1988, Côte d'Ivoire, 1988-89, Zaire, 1989, Holladay North Stake, 1991, dist. pres. No. B.C., No. Alberta, Yukon and N.W. Ters., 1955; stake high counselor, Santa Maria, Calif., 1971-72, Moses Lake, Wash., 1977-79; presiding elder Côte d'Ivoire, 1974-76, 88; 2d counselor Moses Lake Stake Presidency, 1980-88; bd. dirs. Columbia Basin Allied Arts, 1986-88; mem. Health Sci. Coun. U. Utah, 1991—; mem. Sunday sch. gen. bd. Ch. of Jesus Christ of Latter-Day Saints, 1991-93, com. for mems. with disabilities, 1992-93, choice adv. bd., 1993—; emergency preparedness dir. Holladay North Stake, 1993—. Served with Ordnance Corps, U.S. Army, 1958-59. Decorated chevalier Ordre National (Republic of Côte d'Ivoire). Mem. ASME, Assn. Energy Engrs., AAAS, Am. Soc. Sugar Beet Technologists, Internat. Soc. Sugar Cane Technologists, Am. Soc. Sugar Cane Technologists, Environ. Engrs. & Mgrs. Inst., Sugar Industry Technicians, Nat. Fedn. Ind. Bus.; Utah State Hist. Soc. (life), Mormon Hist. Assn., G.P. Chowder and Marching Soc., Western Hist. Assn., Sons of Utah Pioneers, Univ. Archeol. Soc. (life), Kiwanis, Cannon-Hinckley Study Group, Sigma Xi (life, sec., treas. Utah chpt. 1994—), Pi Tau Sigma, Sigma Chi, Alpha Phi Omega. Republican. Mormon. Home: 4391 Carol Jane Dr Salt Lake City UT 84124-3601 Office: Silver Energy Systems Corp 13184 Rd 3 NE Bldg 1 Ste B Moses Lake WA 98837 also: Silver Enterprises 4391 South 2275 E Carol Jane Dr Salt Lake City UT 84124-3601 also: Silver Publishers Inc PO Box 17755 Salt Lake City UT 84117-0755 also: Silver Chief Corp 1433 S Skyline Dr Moses Lake WA 98837-2417 also: Agronomics Internat 6928 Butternut Ct Mc Lean VA 22101-1506 also: Silver Pubs Inc 2275 E Carol Jane Dr Salt Lake City UT 84124-3601

SILVER, JAMES ALLEN, former military physician; b. Tracy, Minn., Apr. 7, 1933; s. Bernard J. and Nora J. (Bustad) S.; m. Regina Alohanohea Lover, June 15, 1964; children: Maile, Moana, Gregory, Telu, James K. BA, St. John's U., 1955; BS, MD, U. Minn., 1958; MPH, U. Mich., 1973. Diplomate Am. Bd. Occupational Medicine. Asst. med. dir. Marathon Oil Co., Findlay, Ohio, 1973-74; commd. USAF, 1974, advanced through grades to col., 1976; chief preventive medicine HQPACAF, Hickam AFB, Hawaii, 1974-78; comdr. USAF Hosp., Kirtland AFB, N.Mex., 1978-83; dir. med. inspection div. HQAFISC, Norton AFB, Calif., 1983-85; dir. environ. health ops. HQAFLC, Wright-Patterson AFB, Ohio, 1985-88; with 15 Med GP/SG, Hickam AFB, Hawaii, 1988-93; ret., 1993. Fellow Am. Coll. Preventive Medicine; mem. Am. Acad. Occupational Medicine, Aerospace Med. Assn., Soc. Air Force Flight Surgeons. Republican. Roman Catholic. Lodge: ELks. Home: 2840 Cooper Creek Dr Henderson NV 89014-6911

SILVER, MONTE S., elementary education educator, consultant; b. N.Y.C., Sept. 5, 1949; s. Hy Joseph and Norma Rose (Leventhal) S.; m. Mindy Sue Ring, Apr. 17, 1977 (div. 1980); m. Barbara Carol Nield, Apr. 18, 1984; children: Tony Charles Printy, Jason Sebastian Printy. BA in Polit. Sci., SUNY, Binghamton, 1970; MA in Elem. Edn., Hunter Coll., 1971. Tchr. grades 4-6 Oakland (Calif.) Unified Sch. Dist., 1977—; ind. resource specialist, 1988; Foss sci. cons. Ency. Britannica, Calif., 1993—. Home: 5010 Flicker Way Garden Valley CA 95633-9206

SILVERBERG, LEWIS HENRY, management consultant; b. L.A., Nov. 1, 1934; s. Milton Henry and Marjorie Vella (Coates) S.; m. Amelia Francis Backstrom, June, 9, 1959 (div. 1979); children: Stephen, Richard, Donna; m. Alice Ellen Deakins, Mar. 9, 1979. BA, Pomona Coll., 1955; JD, UCLA, 1958. Bar: Calif. 1959, U.S. Supreme Ct. 1966. Pvt. practice San Diego, 1959-89; exec. v.p., dir. Liquor Barn, Inc., San Diego, 1989-93; bus. cons. San Diego, 1993—; referee Calif. inheritance tax and probate, 1972-88. Trustee San Diego Zool. Soc.; active various pub., charitable and ednl. orgns. Republican. Office: PO Box 90947 San Diego CA 92169-2947

SILVERBERG, STUART OWEN, obstetrician, gynecologist; b. Denver, Oct. 14, 1931; s. Edward M. and Sara (Morris) S.; BA, U. Colo., 1952, MD, 1955; m. Joan E. Snyderman, June 19, 1954 (div. Apr. 1970); children: Debra Sue Owen, Eric Owen, Alan Kent; m. 2d, Kay Ellen Conklin, Oct. 18, 1970 (div. Apr. 1982); 1 son, Cris S.; m. 3d, Sandra Kay Miller, Jan., 1983. Intern Women's Hosp. Phila., 1955-56; resident Kings County Hosp., Bklyn., 1958-62; practice medicine specializing in obstetrics and gynecology, Denver, 1962—; mem. staff Rose Med. Ctr., N. Suburban Med. Ctr., U. Hosp., St. Anthony Hosp.; med. exec. bd., chmn. dept. obstetrics and gynecology, 1976-77, 86-87, dir. Laser Ctr., 1994-95; clin. instr. U. Colo. Sch. Medicine, Denver, 1962-72, asst. clin. prof., 1972-88, assoc. clin. prof., 1989—, dir. gynecol. endoscopy and laser surgery, 1988-90; v.p. Productos Alimenticos, La Ponderosa, S.A.; dir., chmn. bd. Wicker Works Video Prodns., Inc., 1983-91; cons. Ft. Logan Mental Health Ctr., Denver, 1964-70; mem. Gov.'s Panel Mental Retardation, 1966; med. adv. bd. Colo. Planned Parenthood, 1966-68, Am. Med. Ctr., Spivak, Colo., 1967-70. Mem. Colo. Emergency Resources Bd., Denver, 1965—. Served to maj. AUS, 1956-58; Germany. Diplomate Am. Bd. Obstetrics and Gynecology, Am. Bd. Laser Surgery. Fellow Am. Coll. Obstetrics and Gynecologists, Am. Soc. Laser Medicine and Surgery, ACS; mem. Am. Internat. fertility socs., Colo. Gynecologists and Obstetricians Soc., Hellman Obstet. and Gynecol. Soc., Colo. Med. Soc. (bd. dirs. 1987-95, speaker of the house 1989—), Clear Creek Valley Med. Soc. (trustee 1978, 80, 87, 93—, pres. 1995), Phi Sigma Delta, AMA, Flying Physicians Assn., Aircraft Owners and Pilots Assn., Nu Sigma Nu, Alpha Epsilon Delta. Jewish. Mem. editorial rev. bd. Colo. Women's Mag.; editor in chief First Image, Physicians Video Jour., 1984-86. Office: 8300 N Alcott St Ste 301 Westminster CO 80031

SILVERMAN, ALAN H., lawyer; b. N.Y.C., Feb. 18, 1954; s. Melvin H. and Florence (Green) S.; m. Gretchen E. Freeman, May 25, 1986; children: Willa C.F., Gordon H.F. BA summa cum laude, Hamilton Coll., 1976; MBA, U. Pa., 1980, JD, 1980. Bar: N.Y. 1981, U.S. Dist. Ct. (so. and ea. dist.) N.Y. 1981, U.S. Ct. Internat. Trade 1981, D.C. 1986, U.S. Supreme Ct. 1990. Assoc. Hughes, Hubbard & Reed, N.Y.C., 1980-84; asst. counsel Newsweek, Inc., N.Y.C., 1984-86; v.p., gen. counsel, sec., dir. adminstrn. Post-Newsweek Cable, Phoenix, 1986—. Contbr. articles to profl. jours. Mem. prevention adv. com. Gov. Pa. Justice Commn., 1975-79; bd. dirs. Lawyers' Alliance for N.Y., 1982-85, N.Y. Lawyers Pub. Interest, 1983-85, Nat. Assn. JD-MBA Profls., 1983-85, Bus. Vols. for Arts, Inc., Phoenix, 1989-93, Ariz. Vol. Lawyers for the Arts, Inc., 1994—; mem. Maricopa County Citizens Jud. Adv. Coun., 1990-93. Mem. ABA, Assn. of Bar of City of N.Y., D.C. Bar Assn., Phi Beta Kappa. Home: 5222 N 34th Pl Phoenix AZ 85018-1521 Office: Post-Newsweek Cable 4742 N 24th St Ste 270 Phoenix AZ 85016-4860

SILVERMAN, ANTHONY, securities trader, dealer; b. 1943. Stock broker Minn. Stock Brokers, Mpls., 1966-77; pres. Anthony Investment Co., 1977-87, Paradise Valley Securities, Inc., Phoenix, 1987—. Office: Paradise Valley Securities Inc 11811 N Tatum Blvd Phoenix AZ 85028-1614*

SILVERMAN, FREDRICK LEE, mathematics educator; b. Hot Springs, Ark., Mar. 3, 1946; s. Bernard Max and Olivia (Levinger) S.; m. Barbara Zarin Silverman, Jan. 2, 1977; 1 child, Adam Neil. BA, So. Meth. U., Dallas, 1968; MA in Teaching Math., U. Chgo., 1970; EdD, U. Houston, 1978. Cert. tchr. Secondary math. tchr. L.G. Pinkston High Sch., Dallas, 1973-74; asst., assoc. prof. La. State U., Shreveport, 1978-84; prof. U. No. Colo., Greeley, 1984—, faculty senate chmn., 1990-91; coord. elem. edn., 1992-93, co-dir. elem. math./sci. project, 1993—; faculty trustee U. No. Colo., Greeley, 1991-92; mem. nat. bd. advisor MATHTEQ-Lawrence Hall Sci., Berkeley, Calif., 1987-90; cons. math. edn. Fayetteville (N.C.) State U., 1988, N.C. Dept. Pub. Instrn., Raleigh, 1989, East Carolina U., 1990. Bd. mem. Greeley Chamber Orch., 1985—. 1st lt. USAF, 1970-72. Mem. Nat. Coun. Tchrs. Math., Internat. Reading Assn., Am. Ednl. Rsch. Assn., Colo. Coun. Tchrs. Math., Internat. Study Group on Ethnomathematics. Democrat. Jewish. Home: 2010 46th Ave Apt F-2 Greeley CO 80634-3255 Office: U No Colo Mckee Hall Greeley CO 80639

SILVERMAN, GREGG JOSHUA, physician, scientist; b. Perth Amboy, N.J., Nov. 21, 1955; s. Melvin and Irma Lee (Horowitz) S.; m. Eileen Sabena Gallagher, May 16, 1991; 1 child, Perry Elan. BA in Biochemistry cum laude, Brandeis U., 1977; MD, Rutgers Med. Sch., 1981. Diplomate Am. Bd. Internal Medicine. Intern and resident in medicine Uni. Hosp., San Diego, 1981-84; clin. fellow div. rheumatology Scripps Clinic and Rsch. Found., La Jolla, Calif., 1985-87, rsch. fellow div. clin. immunology, dept. basic clin. rsch., 1985-87, sr. rsch. assoc. div. clin. immunology, 1988-90; asst. prof. dept. medicine U. Calif. San Diego, La Jolla, 1990—; adj. asst. memd. dept. molecular and esptl. medicine Scripps Clinic and Rsch. Found., La Jolla., 1990—. Contbr. numerous articles to profl. jours., chapters to books. NIH Clin. Ctr. fellow, Bethesda, Md., 1978, 79, ARA Western Regional Outstanding Rsch. fellow, 1985, Arthritis Foundation Postdoct. fellow 1987-88, Lupus Found. of Am. Inc. fellow 1992; recipient ARA Sr. Rheumatology Scholar award, 1987, Biomed. Rsch. award Arthritis Found., 1993-96. Fellow Am. Coll. Rheumatology; mem. Am. Assn. Immunologists, Alpha Omega Alpha. Office: U Calif 9500 Gilman Dr La Jolla CA 92093-5003

SILVERMAN, NORMAN HENRY, cardiologist, educator; b. Johannesburg, South Africa, Sept. 29, 1942; came to U.S., 1972; s. Simon Cecil and Jean (Krawitz) S.; m. Heather Silverman. DSc in Med., U. Witwatersrand, Johannesburg, 1985; postgrad., U. Witwatersrand. Diplomate Am. Bd. Pediatrics. Asst. prof. pediatrics Stanford U., Palo Alto, Calif., 1974-75; asst. prof. pediatrics U. Calif., San Francisco, 1975, assoc. prof. radiology, 1979, prof., 1985—. Co-author: Two Dimensional Echocardiography, 1982, Congenital Heart Disease, 1990; author: Pediatric Echocardiography, 1993. Lt. South African Def. Force, 1968-69. Grantee March of Dimes, 1977-79, Am. Heart Assn., 1978-80, 90-92. Fellow Am. Coll. Cardiology, Am. Acad. Pediatrics, Coll. of Physicians of South Africa, Soc. of Pediatric Rsch., Am. Pediatric Soc.; mem. Univ. Club (Palo Alto). Office: U Calif San Francisco CA 94143-0214

SILVERMAN, STEVEN LEE, aerospace engineer; b. Boston, Dec. 23, 1953; s. Benjamin K. and Beverly (Miller) S. BS, U. Va., 1977, MS, 1981. Cert. netware adminstr. Project scientist Princeton U., 1972-77; aerospace engr. Naval Surface Weapons Ctr., Dahlgren, Va., 1979-80; project engr. Rockwell Internat. Corp., Downey, Calif., 1981-85; rschr. Rockwell Internat. Corp., Seal Beach, Calif., 1985-87; project engr. Rockwell Internat. Corp., Downey, Calif., 1987—; pres. Capricorn Computing, Downey, 1981-84; CEO Sports Line Sys., Seal Beach, 1983-90. Mem. AIAA (2nd prize regional meeting 1977, 1st prize regional meeting 1981).

SILVERN, LEONARD CHARLES, retired engineering executive; b. N.Y.C., May 20, 1919; s. Ralph and Augusta (Thaler) S.; m. Gloria Marantz, June 1948 (div. Jan. 1968); 1 child, Ronald; m. Elisabeth Beeny, Aug. 1969 (div. Oct. 1972); m. Gwen Taylor, Nov. 1985. BS in Physics, L.I. U., 1946; MA, Columbia U., 1948, EdD, 1952. Registered profl. consulting engr., Calif. Tng. supr. U.S. Dept. Navy, N.Y.C., 1939-49; tng. dir. exec. dept. N.Y. Div. Safety, Albany, 1949-55; resident engring. psychologist Lincoln Lab. MIT for Rand Corp., Lexington, 1955-56; engr., dir. edn., tng., rsch. labs. Hughes Aircraft Co., Culver City, Calif., 1956-62; dir. human performance engring. lab., cons. engring. psychologist to v.p. tech. Northrop Norair, Hawthorne, Calif., 1962-64; cons. engr., 1969-95; prin. sci., v.p., pres. Edn. and Tng. Cons. Co., L.A., 1964-95, Sedona, Ariz., 1980, pres. Systems Engring. Labs. div., 1980-95; ret., 1995; cons. hdqrs. Air Tng. Command USAF, Randolph AFB, Tex., 1964-68, Electronic Industries Assn., Washington, 1963-69, Edn. R and D Ctr., U. Hawaii, 1970-74, Ctr. Vocat. and Tech. Edn., Ohio State U., 1972-73, Coun. for Exceptional Children, 1973-74, Canadore Coll. Applied Arts and Tech., Ont., Can., 1974-76, Centro Nacional de Productividad, Mexico City, 1973-75, N.S. Dept. Edn., Halifax, 1975-79, Aeronutronic Ford-Ford Motor Co., 1975-76, Nat. Tng. Systems Inc., 1976-81, Nfld. Pub. Svc. Commn., 1978, Legis. Affairs Office USDA, 1980, Rocky Point Techs., 1986; adj. prof. edn., pub. adminstrn. U. So. Calif. Grad. Sch., 1957-65; vis. prof. computer scis. U. Calif. Extension Div., L.A., 1963-72. Dist. ops. officer, disaster communications svc. L.A. County Sheriff's Dept., 1973-75, dist. communications officer, 1975-76; bd. dirs. SEARCH, 1976—; mem. adv. com. West Sedona Community Plan of Yavapai County, 1986-88; councilman City of Sedona, 1988-92; rep. COCOPAI, 1988-89; vol. earth team Soil Conservation Svc., U.S. Dept Agr., 1989-92; Verde Resource Assn., 1988-90, Group on Water Logistics, 1989-90; chair publs. com. Ariz. Rural Recycling Conf., 1990. With USN, 1944-46. Mem. IEEE (sr.), APA, Am. Radio Relay League (life), Nat. Solid Waste Mgmt. Symposium (chmn. publs. com. 1988-89), Ariz. Rural Recycling Conf. (chair publs. com. 1990), Friendship Vets. Fire Engine Co. (hon.), Soc. Wireless Pioneers (life), Quarter Century Wireless Assn. (life), Sierra Club (treas. Sedona-Verde Valley Group 1991-93), Assn. Bldg. Coms., Vox Pop (chmn. bd. dirs. Sedona, 1983-93, dir. 1993-95), Nat. Parks and Conservation Assn., Wilderness Soc., Ariz. Ctr. Law in Pub. Interest. Contbg. editor Ednl. Tech., 1968-73, 81-85; reviewer Computing Revs., 1962-92. Contbr. numerous articles to profl. jours. Office: PO Box 2085 Sedona AZ 86339-2085

SILVERS, ABRAHAM, biostatistician, researcher; b. N.Y.C., Apr. 28, 1934; s. Jack and Shirley (Glassman) S.; m. Joan Martha Siegel, Dec. 15, 1963; children: Miriam Golden, Martha Rome, Jonathan. BS, UCLA, 1956, PhD, 1964. Assoc. prof. math. Calif. State U., L.A., 1964-68; sr. scientist Stanford (Calif.) U., 1966-74; rsch. assoc., metrician U. Calif., San Francisco, 1974-76; dir. cancer stats. rsch. Mayo Clinic, Rochester, Minn., 1976-78; assoc. prof. exptl. sci. Baylor Coll. Medicine, Houston, 1978-82; sr. project mgr. Electric Power Rsch. Insts., Palo Alto, Calif., 1982—; adj. prof. biostatistics U. Calif., San Francisco, 1986-88; dir. biostatistical core cancer ctr.; pres. BioTech Rsch. Assoc., Inc., Palo Alto, 1993—; dir. stats. Stanford Heart Disease Prevention Program, 1970-74; dir. stats. rsch. and demonstration Nat. Ctr. Heart Disease, Houston, 1978-82; pres. BioTech Rsch. Assocs., Inc. Contbr. articles to peer-reviewed jours. Fellow Am. Statis. Assn. (pres. San Francisco Bay chpt. 1988-89, disting. medal in environ. statistics 1993). Office: BioTech Rsch Assocs Inc Ste 283 3790 El Camino Real Palo Alto CA 94306

SILVERS, E. RANDALL, computer system manager; b. Somerville, N.J., July 8, 1951; s. William Joseph Silvers Sr. and Edna Rebecca (Pysher) Silvers-Brennan; m. Cynthia Lee Mulch, Aug. 6, 1974; children: Benjamin Judah, Deborah Lynn. AA summa cum laude, Palomar Coll., 1979; ASBA, Thomas Nelson Coll., 1984, AAS in Data Processing, 1984; postgrad., Christopher Newport, Newport News, Va., 1984-85. Cert. nat. registry EMT. Maintenance chief Escondido (Calif.) Convalescent Ctr., 1977-79; registrar, instr. Profl. Med. Inst., Hampton, Va., 1980-81; corps asst. Salvation Army, Logansport, Ind., 1985-88; computer system mgr. info. liason Salvation Army Harbor Light, L.A., 1988—; rep. divisional computer bd. (MIS) Salvation Army So. Calif., L.A., 1991—. Arranger orchestration for cantata; composer march; author poem. Scoutmaster Boy Scouts Am., San Diego, 1972-75, Camp Pendleton, Calif., 1975-76, Hampton, Va., 1980-84, Huntington Park, Calif., 1990-92, Whittier, Calif, 1992-94; commr., San Diego County, Calif., 1976-79; bandmaster Salvation Army, San Diego, 1970-71, 72-73, Escondido, 1974-77, Hampton, 1979-85, Logansport, 1985-88, Huntington Park, Calif., 1988-92, Long Beach Temple, 1994—; asst. dir., prin. euphonium Peninsula Community Band, Newport News, 1980-85; instr./trainer ARC, Langley AFB, Va., 1979-85, 1st aid/CPR chmn., 1981-84. Sgt. USMC, 1969-77, Vietnam. Named Vol. of Month and Yr., ARC, 1980; decorated Air Force Achievement medal. Mem. Students Vets. Assn. (pres. 1982-84), Am. Legion (sgt. at arms 1974, 2d vice comdr. 1972—), VFW, Alpha Micro Users Soc., Phi Beta Lambda (parliamentarian 1983-84). Republican. Office: Salvation Army Harbor Light 809 E 5th St Los Angeles CA 90013-2112

SILVERSTEIN, RICHARD MARK, fundraiser; b. N.Y.C., Oct. 1, 1952; s. Jule and Gloria (Shapiro) S. B in Hebrew Lit., Jewish Theol. Sem., 1975; BA, Columbia U., 1975; MA, U. Calif., L.A., 1979; PhD, U. Calif., Berkeley, 1983. Exec. dir. Leo Baeck Temple, L.A., 1986-87, City of Hope Nat. Med. Ctr., L.A., 1988-90; dir. devel. Western region Brandeis U., L.A., 1990-92; campaign dir. Jewish Fedn. Orange County, Tustin, Calif., 1993—. Contbr. articles to profl. jours. Recipient N.Y. State Regents scholarship, 1970-75, Sir Simon Marks fellowship, 1979-80, Nat. Found. for Jewish Culture Doctoral fellowship, 1979-80. Mem. Nat. Soc. Fund Raising Execs., Columbia U. Alumni Assn., UCLA Alumni Assn. Democrat. Office: Jewish Fedn Orange County 1385 Warner Ave Ste A Tustin CA 92680-6442

SILVERSTEIN, ROBERT LOUIS, aerospace executive; b. Balt., June 22, 1944; s. Solis Maurice and Bessie (Brager) S.; m. Ellen Charlotte Cohen, Feb. 27, 1965; children: Seth Michael, Rachel Joy, Alison Beth. BS in Aero. and Astron. Engring., MIT, 1965; MS in Aero. and Astron. Engring., NYU, 1966. Mem. program mgmt. and tech. staff TRW Sys. Group, McLean, Va., 1966-73; dep. dir. Intelligence Cmty. Staff, Washington, 1973-76; v.p., dir. analysis ctr. Northrop Corp., Arlington, Va., 1976-84; v.p. bus. devel. and adminstrn. B-2 divns. Northrop Corp., Pico Rivera, Calif., 1984-90, Northrop Grumman Corp., Hawthorn, Calif., 1990—; v.p., gen. mgr. electronics sys. divsn. Hawthorne Site; cons. Undersec. Policy OSD, 1977-85, USN, 1981—, Dep. Dir. CIA, Washington, 1981-85, Office Mgmt. & Budget, Washington, 1981-83, Pres. Sci. Advisor, Washington, 1981-88, Naval Rsch. Adv. Coun., Washington, 1982-91; bd. dirs., cons. Naval Studies Bd. NAS, Washington, 1991—. Active Reagon Transition Team, Washington, 1981. Office: Northrop Grummon Corp 2301 W 120th St Hawthorne CA 90250

SILVERSTEIN, STEVEN B., oil company executive; b. Cleve., Sept. 21, 1951; s. Fred R. and Norma (Gillett) S.; m. Mary C. Straley, Aug. 6, 1988; children: Zachariah, Alisha. Student, Syracuse U., 1969-70, U. Rochester, 1972-73. Purchasing and warehouse mgr. Arctic Catering, Anchorage, 1979-80, field supr., 1980-82; freight auditor, then dir. in-bound logistics JB Gottstein Co., Anchorage, 1982-86; sr. logistics specialist, sr. supply mgmt. specialist ARCO Alaska, Inc., Anchorage, 1986—; speaker Atlanta Internat. Intermodal Expo, 1989, 91. Bd. dirs. Anchorage Ctr. for Performing Arts, 1993—. Mem. Am. Soc. Transp. and Logistics (cert., pres. 1982-88, Best Small Chpt. award 1986), Anchorage Concert Assn. (v.p., treas., bd. dirs. 1980—, now pres.), Coun. Logistics Mgmt. Jewish. Home: 1210 N St Anchorage AK 99501-4272

SILVERTHORN, LEE JAMES, clinical psychology; b. Atlanta, Nov. 27, 1929; m. Alma Inez, Aug. 28, 1971; children: Lee J. III, Judith A. BA, U. Mich., 1950; MA, U. Kans., 1953, PhD, 1957. Instr. U. Kans. Extension divsn., Leavenworth City and Fed. Prison, 1957-60; asst. chief psychology svc. VA Med. Ctr., Leavenworth, 1957-66; asst. prof. U. Kans., 1963-66; chief psychology svc. VA Med. Ctr., Memphis, 1967-75; Fulbright prof. U. Chiengmia, Thailand, 1966-67; ass. to assoc. prof. divsn. psychology Dept. Psychiatry, U. Tenn. Ctr. for Health Scis., Memphis, 1968-75; staff psychologist VA Med. Ctr., Palo Alto, Calif., 1975-85, cons., 1985—; forensic examiner Superior Ct. of Santa Clara county, San Mateo County, 1982—; pvt. practice, 1961—; cons. psychologist N.E. Kans. Guidance Ctr., Atchison, Kans., 1957-64; chief psychology svc. VA Hosp., Jefferson Barracks, St. Louis, 1966; adj. prof. dept. of psychology Memphis State U., 1967-75; mem. vice-chmn. Tenn. Bd. of Exminers in Psychology, 1972-75; presenter in field. Fellow AAS, Am. Psychol. Soc.; mem. Calif. State Psychol. Assn., Sigma Xi. Home and Office: 3339 Kenneth Dr Palo Alto CA 94303-4216

SILVESTRI, PHILIP SALVATORE, lawyer; b. San Francisco, Nov. 10, 1944; s. Philip and Olga (Difilipo) S.; m. Dianne Loveland, June 22, 1968; children: Lauren, Steven, Karin. BA, U. San Francisco, 1966, JD, 1969. Bar: Calif. 1969; cert. family law specialist State Bar Calif. Assoc. Goth, Dennis & Aaron, Redwood City, Calif., 1969-84; ptnr. Goth, Aaron & Silvestri, Redwood City, 1984-87, Goth & Silvestri, A.P.C., Redwood City, 1987—. With N.G., 1969-75. Republican. Office: Goth & Silvestri APC 1000 Marshall St Ste B Redwood City CA 94063-2027

SILVIA, RAYMOND ALAN, librarian; b. Gustine, Calif., Apr. 10, 1950; s. Antonio and Mary (Viveiros) S.; m. Doris Elizabeth Newcomb, Jan. 9, 1972; children: Mary, Paul, Hilary, Dominic, Elizabeth. AA in English, Modesto (Calif.) Jr. Coll., 1970; BA in English summa cum laude, Calif. State U., Fresno, 1972, MA in English with distinction, 1982; MLS, San Jose State U., 1985. Cert. cmty. coll. tchr., Calif. Lectr. Calif. State U., Fresno, 1980-82; investor Clovis, Calif., 1982—; ref. libr./supr. King's County Libr., Hanford, Calif., 1986-90; libr./sr. libr. Calif. State Dept. Corrections, Sacramento, 1990-94, supervising libr., 1994—, spkr./trainer, mem. statewide correcitonal law libr. task, 1994; spkr./panel mem. Calif. Libr. Assn. 96th Ann. Conf., Anaheim, 1994. Contbr. articles to profl. jours. Chmn. ref. com. San Joaquin Valley Libr. Sys., Fresno, 1989-90; mem. Secular Franciscan Order, Fresno, 1975—, novice master, 1984. Mem. MLA, Spl. Librs. Assn., Calif. State U. Fresno Alumni Assn., Phi Kappa Phi. Republican. Roman Catholic.

SILVIUS, DONALD JOE, educational consultant; b. Kingman, Kans., July 30, 1932; s. Henry Edgar and Gladys Mae (Beaty) S.; m. Jean Anne Able, Aug. 30, 1951; children: Laurie Dawn Silvius Gustin, Steven Craig, Jonathan Mark, Brian James. Student So. Calif. Coll., 1949-52; AA, Bakersfield Coll., 1962; BA, Fresno State Coll., 1963, MA, 1968. Radio/TV announcer, musician, music arranger and copyist, life ins. underwriter, other positions, 1953-62; jr. high sch. English tchr., elem. and jr. high counselor, child welfare, attendance and guidance supr., supr. pupil personnel svcs. Standard Sch. Dist., Oildale, Calif., 1963-92; ret. 1992; edn., guidance and computer cons., 1992—; tchr. counseling/guidance and spl. edn. various colls. Recipient Standard PTA-Hon. Service award, Bakersfield "Up With People" Appreciation award, Golden Apple Service award Standard Sch. Dist. Tchrs. Assn., Innovations award Calif. Tchrs. Assn., Hon. Service award Kern chpt. Calif. Assn. Sch. Psychologists, Outstanding Ednl. Leader award West Kern chpt. Assn. Calif. Sch. Adminstrs., 1977-78, 7th Dist. PTA-Silver Service award, Continuing Service award Highland-Wingland PTA, Outstanding Community Service for Developmentally Disabled award. Mem. NEA, Calif. Tchrs. Assn., North of the River C. of C., Calif. Assn. Supervision of Child Welfare and Attendance, Assn. Calif. Sch. Adminstrs., Am. Assn. Curriculum Devel., Am. Assn. Counseling and Devel., ACES, ASCD, AMECD, ARVIC, Mental Health Assn. (Calif. exec. bd.), Assn. Kern County, Mensa, PTA, Calif. Assn. Counseling and Devel., CACES, CACAE, CAMECD, CARVIC, Oildale Lions Club, Phi Delta Kappa

SIM, JANET MAO, dietitian, food management and dietetics educator; b. Shanghai, Nov. 25, 1940; came to U.S., 1959; d. Feng Siang and Wei Fong (Wong) Mao; m. James See-Yuen Sim, June 5, 1965; children: Judith K.L., Andrea K.C. BS in Dietetics, U. Colo., 1969; MS in Foods and Nutrition, Iowa State U., 1966; EdD in Curriculum and Instrn., U. San Francisco, 1989; postgrad., U. Toronto, Can., 1979-80. Asst. dir. Dairy Coun., Buffalo, 1967-68; dir. dietary dept. Somers (N.Y.) Manor, 1969-72; adj. prof. Rochester (N.Y.) Inst. Tech., 1972-74, asst. prof., 1974-78, assoc. prof., 1978; instr. U. Ill., Chgo., 1982-84; lectr. San Francisco State U., 1986-87, asst. prof., 1987-90, assoc. prof., 1990-93, prof., 1994—; dietitian Grasslands Hosp., Valhalla, N.Y., 1968; cons. foodservice mgmt., 1984-86; dir. dietary svcs. St. Francis Convalescent Hosp., Daly City, Calif., 1986; dietetics program coord. Rochester Inst. Tech., 1974-78; dietetics program dir. San Francisco State U., 1992—, curriculum writer new undergrad. program, 1990; panelist, presenter various profl. assn. confs. Co-author: Handbook of Food Preparation, 9th edit., 1993, Case Studies in Foodservice Management Services, 1993; mem. editorial rev. bd. Hospitality and Tourism Educator, 1988-91; contbr. articles to profl. jours. Heinz grad. degree fellow, 1988-89; HEW grantee, 1975. Mem. Am. Dietetic Assn. (mem. editorial rev. bd. 1989-90, 93—), Coun. Hotel, Restaurant and Instnl. Edn. (mem. editorial rev. bd. 1988-91), Am. Home Econ. Assn. (foods and nutrition coun. 1992-93). Office: San Francisco State Univ 1600 Holloway Ave San Francisco CA 94132-1722

SIMARD, MARIE FRANÇOISE, endocrinologist; b. Montreal, Que., Can., Dec. 16, 1955; came to U.S., 1991; d. Jean-Yvon and Fleurette Lucie (Charbonneau) S.; m. William Tupper Couldwell, Sept. 15, 1987; children: Mitchell, Sandrine, Geneviève. BS, Coll. Sainte-Foy, Quebec, Can., 1975; MD, Laval U., Quebec, Can., 1980. Diplomate Am. Bd. Internal Medicine, Am. Bd. Endocrinology, Diabetes and Metabolism. Intern Royal Victoria Hosp., McGill U., Montreal, 1980-81, resident in internal medicine, 1981-84, rsch. fellow in reproductive endocrinology, 1984-85; clin./rsch. fellow in endocrinology Wadsworth VA Med. Ctr., UCLA, 1985-87; clin. pediatric endocrinology fellow Saint-Justine Pediatric Hosp., U. Montreal, 1989-90; endocrinology rsch. fellow divsn. endocrinology Montreal Children's Hosp., McGill U., 1990-91; clin. asst. prof. medicine dept. internal medicine U. So. Calif., 1991—; vis. asst. prof. endocrinology dept. internal medicine U. So. Calif., 1991-92; endocrinology cons. dept. internal medicine Kern Med. Ctr., Calif., 1993-94. Contbr. articles to profl. jours. Recipient Rsch. award Que. Health Rsch. Funding Assn., 1984, Rsch. award Med. Rsch. Coun. Can., 1990-92; Profl. Staff Assn. Rsch. grantee U. So. Calif., 1991; Endocrinology/Molecular Biology Rsch. fellow U. So. Calif., 1991-92. Mem. Profl. Physician's Corp. Que., Endocrine Soc. Home: 3860 Valley Lights Dr Pasadena CA 91107-1344

SIMARD, RODNEY, literature and communications educator, media consultant; b. Ft. Smith, Ark., June 18, 1952; s. Houston H. and Dorothy (Turner) S. BA, U. Memphis, 1974; MA, Miss. State U., 1976; PhD, U. Ala., 1982. Instr. lit. Birmingham-So. Coll., 1981-82; instr. lit. and communications Calif. State U., Bakersfield, 1982-86; asst. prof. lit. Calif. State U., San Bernardino, 1986-92, assoc. prof., coord. Am. Studies program, 1992—. Author: Postmodern Drama, 1984, The Whole Writer's Catalog: An Introduction to Advanced Composition, 1992; gen. editor series American Indian Studies, 1989-93, Studies in American Indian Literatures, 1993; assoc. editor Furniture Methods and Materials, 1973-74; editor Black Warrior Review, 1979-80, Showtime, 1983-84, Tribal Discourse: Proceedings of the Symposium on the Status of American Indians in the CSU; cons. editor Elan, 1988-89; faculty editor Pacific Review, 1988-89; contbg. editor The Variorum Edition of the Poetry of John Donne, 1982-88; contbr. articles to profl. jours., anthologies, other publs. Tribal mem. Cherokee Nation of Okla.; bd. dirs., v.p., mem. profl. adv. coun. Riverside (Calif.) and San Bernardino County Am. Indian Ctr. Mem. MLA, Inland Area Native Am. Assn. (adv. coun., cons. editor assn. newsletter), NAACP, ACLU, Gay Am. Indians, Sigma Tau Delta, Phi Gamma Delta. Office: Calif State U Dept English San Bernardino CA 92407

SIMBURG, EARL JOSEPH, psychiatrist, psychoanalyst; b. Vonda, Sask., Can., Mar. 21, 1915; came to U.S., 1941; s. Joseph E. and Liza (Yurovsky) S.; m. Virginia Ronan, Feb. 10, 1958; children by previous marriage: Arthur, Melvyn, Sharon. Cert. medicine, U. Sask., Saskatoon, 1935; MDCM, McGill U., Montreal, Que., Can., 1938; grad., San Francisco Psychoanal. Inst., 1959. Diplomate Am. Bd. Psychiatry and Neurology. Intern Royal Victoria Hosp., Montreal, 1938-39; sr. physician Brandon (Can.) Hosp. Mental Diseases, 1939-41; resident Grace New Haven Hosp., 1941-43; pvt. practice psychiatry and psychoanalysis Berkeley, Calif., 1947—; mem. faculty San Francisco Psychoanalytic Inst.; instr. psychiatry Yale U., New Haven, 1941-43, U. Calif., San Francisco, 1949-59; cons. Calif. Dept. Health, Berkeley, 1975-76; pres. med. staff Herrick Hosp. and Health Ctr., 1985; active med. staff Alta-Bates Med. Ctr., Earl J. Simburg lectr. Contbr. articles to the Jour. of the Am. Psychoanalytic Assn. Served to major M.C. USAF, 1943-47. Earl J. Simburg Lecture given annually in his honor Alta Batesa Med. Ctr. Fellow Am. Psychiat. Assn. (life), AAAS; mem. AMA, Am. Psychoanalytic Assn. (life, cert.), Calif. Med. Assn., Alameda Contra Costa County Med. Assn., Am. Geriatrics Soc., Am. Assn. for Geriatric Psychiatry. Home: 86 Tamalpais Rd Berkeley CA 94708-1949 Office: 2006 Dwight Way Berkeley CA 94704-2633

SIMEROTH, DEAN CONRAD, chemical engineer; b. Marysville, Calif., Mar. 21, 1946; s. Raphael Conrad and Mary Beatrice (Watson) S.; m. Phyllis Deborah Minakowski, Feb. 7, 1971 (div. Nov. 1994); 1 child, Brian Conrad. BS in Chem. Engring., U. Calif., Davis, 1968. From air pollution specialist to chief engr. evaluation br. Calif. Air Resources Bd., Sacramento, 1969-87; chief criteria pollutant br. Calif. Air Resources Bd., 1987—. Served in U.S. Army, 1969-71, Korea. Mem. AIChE, Air Waste Mgmt. Assn., Kiwanis (treas. Woodland, Calif. chpt. 1988—). Democrat. Roman Catholic. Office: Calif Air Resources Bd PO Box 2815 2020 L St Sacramento CA 95812

SIMINI, JOSEPH PETER, accountant, financial consultant, author, former educator; b. Buffalo, Feb. 15, 1921; s. Paul and Ida (Moro) S.; BS, St. Bonaventure U., 1940, BBA, 1949; MBA, U. Calif.-Berkeley, 1957; DBA, Western Colo. U., 1981; m. Marcelline McDermott, Oct. 4, 1968. Insp. naval material Bur. Ordnance, Buffalo and Rochester, N.Y., 1941-44; mgr. Paul Simini Bakery, Buffalo, 1946-48; internal auditor DiGiorgio (Fruit) Corp., San Francisco, 1950-51; tax accountant Price Waterhouse & Co., San Francisco, 1953; sr. accountant Richard L. Hanlin, C.P.A., San Francisco, 1953-54; prof. accounting U. San Francisco, 1954-79, emeritus prof., 1983—; mem. rev. bd. Calif. Bd. Accountancy, 1964-68. Mem. council com. Boy Scouts Am., Buffalo, San Francisco, 1942-65, Scouters Key, San Francisco council; bd. dirs. Nat. Italian Am. Found., Washington, 1979-85. Served to ensign USNR, 1944-46. Recipient Bacon-McLaughlin medal St. Bonaventure U., 1940, Laurel Key, 1940; Outstanding Tchr. award Coll. Bus. Adminstrn., U. San Francisco, 1973; Disting. Tchr. award U. San Francisco, 1975, Joseph Peter Simini award, 1977. Crown Zellerbach Found. fellow, 1968-69; Gold Medal Associazione Piemontese nel Mondo, Turin, Italy, 1984; decorated Knight Order of Merit, Republic of Italy, 1982. CPA, Calif. Mem. Am. Inst. C.P.A.s, Calif. Soc. C.P.A.s (past chmn. ednl. standards, student relations com. San Francisco chpt.), Inst. of Mgmt. Accts. (past pres. San Francisco chpt.), Am. Acctg. Assn., Am. Mgmt. Assn. (lectr. 1968-78), Am. Arbitration Assn. (comml. arbitrator), Delta Sigma Pi (past pres. San Francisco alumni club), Beta Gamma Sigma. Roman Catholic. Clubs: Serra (past pres. Golden Gate chpt.), Il Cenacolo (past pres.), Toastmasters (past pres. Magic Word). Lodges: K.C., Rotary (past pres. Daly City). Author: Accounting Made Simple, 1967, 2d rev. edit., 1987, Cost Accounting Concepts for Nonfinancial Executives, 1976, Become Wealthy! Using Tax Savings and Real Estate Investments, 1982, Balance Sheet Basics for the Nonfinancial Managers, 1989, Petals of the Rose, 1990, Wealth-Building Basics Letter, 1990. Tech. editor, Accounting Essentials, 1972. Patentee Dial-A-Trig and Verbum Est card game. Home: 977 Duncan St San Francisco CA 94131-1800 Office: PO Box 31420 San Francisco CA 94131-0420

SIMKHOVICH, BORIS ZALMAN, biochemist, researcher; b. Riga, Latvia, July 26, 1947; came to U.S., 1989; s. Zalman Israel and Sofia (Lipkina) S.; m. Mara Adamsky, May 30, 1991; 1 stepchild, Larry Adamsky. MD, Riga Med. Inst., 1971, PhD, 1974; DMS, Inst. for Gen. Pathology, Moscow, 1988. Rsch. assoc. Inst. of Organic Synthesis, Riga, 1975-85, head rsch. lab., 1985-89; rsch. assoc. U. So. Calif., L.A., 1989-90; dir. biochemistry Heart Inst. Good Samaritan Hosp., L.A., 1990—. Contbr. scientific papers to profl. jours.; reviewer for rsch. jours. in the field of cardiology. Recipient 1st prize Annual Scientific award Latvian Acad. of Scis., 1985. Mem. Internat. Soc. for Heart Rsch. (Am. sect.), Am. Heart Assn. Office: Good Samaritan Hosp 1225 Wilshire Blvd Los Angeles CA 90017

SIMMEL, EDWARD CLEMENS, psychology educator, consultant; b. Berlin, Jan. 30, 1932; s. Ernst and Herta Helen (Brüügemann) S.; m. Marilyn Simmel (div. July 1980), children: Gregg, Cassandra, Kristina; m. Wendy Taylor, Jan. 4, 1983. BA, U. Calif., Berkeley, 1955; PhD, Wash. State U., 1960. Asst. prof. Western Wash. U., Bellingham, 1960-62, Calif. State U., L.A., 1962-65; asst. prof. Miami U., Oxford, Ohio, 1965-67, assoc. prof., 1967-71, prof., 1971-90, prof. emeritus, 1990—; cons. Human Factors in Aviation Safety, Borrego Springs, Calif., 1990—; vis. investigator Jackson Lab., Bar Harbor, Maine, 1970, 73, 75, 81. Editor: Perspectives in Behavior Genetics, 1986; mem. editorial bd. Behavior Genetics Jour., 1980-90; contbr. numerous articles to profl. jours. With USAF, 1951-52. NSF grantee, 1972-73. Fellow Am. Psychol. Soc.; mem. Assn. Aviation Psychologists, Western Psychol. Assn., Aircraft Owners and Pilots Assn., Aerospace Med. Assn.,

Sigma Xi (pres. Miami U. chpt. 1971-72, Outstanding Rsch. award 1976). Home: PO Box 759 Borrego Springs CA 92004-0759

SIMMONS, BRADLEY WILLIAMS, pharmaceutical company executive; b. Paterson, N.J., Apr. 16, 1941; s. John Williams and Grace Law (Van Hassel) S.; m. Diane Louise Simmons, June 6, 1964 (div. May 1986); children: Susan, Elizabeth, Jonathan. AB, Columbia U., 1963, BSChemE, 1964; MBA, NYU, 1974. Chem. engr. Pfizer, Inc., N.Y.C., 1969-73, analyst, 1973-76, dir. planning, 1976-79; dir., bus. analysis Bristol-Myers, N.Y.C., 1979-82, v.p., 1982-85; pres. Oncogen subs. Bristol-Myers, Seattle, 1985-87, sr. v.p. adminstrn., 1987—; adj. prof. Farleigh Dickinson U., Teaneck, N.J., 1974-84; v.p. Empty Space Theatre, Seattle, 1991—, also bd. dirs.. Coun. mem. Borough of Allendale, N.J., 1977-82; mem. Bergen County (N.J.) Com., 1974-82; bd. dirs. Washington Exhibition Sci. and Tech., 1989—; v.p., bd. dirs. Empty Space Theatre, 1991—. Mem. Wash. State Biotech. Assn. (chmn. external rels. com. 1989-90, vice-chmn., bd. dirs. 1990-91), Wash. Exhbn. Sci. and Tech. (bd. dirs.). Republican. Mem. Unity Ch.

SIMMONS, CHRISTOPHER LAIRD, graphic designer, art director; b. Iowa City, Iowa, Jan. 12, 1962; s. Jerry Laird and Nola Ann (Cox) S.; m. Paula Joan Polchert, July 25, 1992; 1 child, Abby Marie. Owner, graphic designer S.U. Graphics, Redondo Beach, Calif., 1978-82; prodn. mgr., art dir. Photoventures Graphics, Long Beach, Calif., 1982-87; owner, creative dir. Mindset Graphics, Manhattan Beach, Calif., 1987-92; advt. and mktg. mgr. Creative Computers, Torrance, Calif., 1992-94; dir. mktg. comms. NovaQuest Infosystems/DirectWare, Torrance, Calif., 1995—. Editor: Galaxy Class, 1987-93; composer (theme music TV programs) Viewpoints on Video, 1988, KidVid Co., 1989, colorist: (comic book) Triad Universe, 1994; art dir. Computer Player Mag., 1994-95. Recipient Apple Computers Inc. ARPL Design/1st pl. award 1994, 2 Harvey Rsch. Orgn. Communications awards, 1994. Mem. Art Dirs. Club L.A., L.A. Macintosh User Group, Direct Mktg. Assn. Independent.

SIMMONS, CLEDA MARIE, artist; b. Douglas, Wyo., June 24, 1927; d. Neil and Hulda Louise (Anderson) Diehl; m. Alfred Allen Simmons, May 9, 1951 (dec. Dec. 1987); children: Alfred Allen Jr., Barry Neal, Nina Marie. Student, Casper (Wyo.) Jr. Coll., 1946-47, U. N.Mex., Albuquerque, 1947-51. Painter, illustrator, graphic artist Vista, Calif., 1978—; graphic artist Epsilon Sigma Alpha Women Internat., Ft. Collins, Colo., 1969-70; art editor ESA Women Int., Ft. Collins, Colo., 1970-73, art dir., 1973-77; artistic dir. Vista Iniatitive for Visual Arts, 1990-94, bd. dirs.; artistic dir. Murals of Vista, 1994-95. Illustrator Our Government, 1969, Beneath the Peaks, 1973; co-author: Art of Editorship, 1972; author: Design and Your World, 1995; one-woman shows include Ateneo de Belles Artes, Madrid, 1955-90 (Purchase award 1955), Art Ways-Design Ctr., San Diego, 1991, Creative Art Ctr., Burbank, Calif., 1986, Mark Reuben Gallery, San Francisco, 1985, Gallery of World Art, Newton Upper Falls, Mass., 1982, Ahmed's Gallery Lounge, Cambridge, Mass., 1981, The Catseye, Wellesley, Mass., 1979, Loveland (Colo.) Mus., 1978, and numerous others 1954—. Exhbn. dir. Women's Caucus for the Arts, L.A., 1985, Women Exhbns. in Boston, 1980-83. Home and Office: 724 Osborne St Vista CA 92084-1804

SIMMONS, CLYDE, professional football player; b. Lanes, S.C., Aug. 4, 1964. Student, Western Carolina. Former defensive end Phila. Eagles, 1986-94; with Ariz. Cardinals, 1994—. Named NFL All-Pro team defensive end, The Sporting News, 1991. Office: Ariz Cardinals PO Box 888 Phoenix AZ 85001-0888

SIMMONS, DONNA MARIE, neuroscientist, neurobiology researcher, histotechnologist; b. Hartford, Conn., Oct. 13, 1943; d. John Henry and Ellen Louise (Meehl) Strayer; m. Corvin Gale Simmons, Sept. 17, 1964. Student, U. Wash., Western Wash. State U.; postgrad. U. Southern Calif., 1994—. Histologic technician, instr. Tacoma Gen. Hosp. Sch. Med. Tech., Tacoma, Wash., 1963; lab. technician Med. Sch. U. Wash., 1964; histologic technician Northgate Med. Lab., Seattle, 1964-67; rsch. technologist in neuroanatomy Regional Primate Rsch. Ctr., U. Wash., 1967-82; rsch. asst. Devel. Neurobiology Lab. Salk Inst., La Jolla, Calif., 1982-85; sr. technician, lab. mgr. Neural Systems Lab. Howard Hughes Med. Inst. at Salk Inst., 1985-90; rsch. assoc. dept. of biol. scis.-neurobiology, U. So. Calif., L.A., 1990—; cons., lectr. in field.; judge Greater San Diego Sci. and Engring. Fair, 1987-89, Calif. Sci. Fair, 1992, 95; leader sci. del. to People's Rep. of China, 1986; chair China Scientist Exchange Fund, 1986-87; mem. Swiss Histology Meeting Exch., 1990. Author tech. articles, revs. in field; mem. editorial bd. Jour. histotech. Recipient Diamond Cover award Jour. of Histotech., 1990; various svc. awards; best non-clin. pub. in field, 1985. Mem. AAAS, Am. Soc. Clin. Pathologists (affiliate), Wash. State Histology Soc. (past pres., histology liaison Am. Soc. Med. Tech.), Nat. Soc. Histotech. (charter mem., regional dir. 1980-82, jud. chair 1983-86), Calif. Soc. Histotech. (San Diego dir. protem 1985-86), Assn. Women in Sci. (San Diego charter mem., bd. dir. 1985-90), Soc. for Neurosci., Swiss Soc. for Histotech., Women in Neurosci., N.Y. Acad. Sci., NOW, Am. Alpine Club, J.B. Johnston Club. Office: U So Calif Hedco Neurosci Bldg MC 2520 Los Angeles CA 90089

SIMMONS, DWAYNE DEANGELO, biology educator; b. Toledo, Oct. 31, 1959; s. Johnnie Clarance Simmons and Carleen Reid; m. D'Nisa Dell Hoover. BS, Pepperdine U., 1980; PhD, Harvard U., 1986. Harvard teaching fellow Harvard U., Cambridge, Mass., 1982-85; Harvard resident tutor Harvard U., Cambridge, 1983-85; asst. prof. biology Pepperdine U., Malibu, Calif., 1985-90, UCLA, 1990—; physiol. scis. prof., 1994—; guest lectr. L.A. Elem. Schs., 1986; trustee Mission Jour.; participant seminars Harvard U., Mich. State U., Swarthmore Coll., Calif. Inst. Tech., Duke U. Med. Sch., Montpellier Cedex, France; mem. review com. NOH, 1993—, NSF, 1995; mem. postgrad. com. Ford Found., 1995—. Contbr. articles to profl. jours. Sci. Team Leader Lynwood Unified Sch. Dist., 1991—, part-time min. Recipient minority rsch. initiation award NSF, 1987, NSF grant awards, 1988, 91; Soc. Neurosci. travel fellow, 1987; Alfred P. Sloan rsch. fellow, 1990; recipient NIH 1st award, 1992, Christian svc. award Pepperdine U. Alumni, 1993. Mem. Pepperdine U. Alumni Bd. (assoc., sec. 1986), Assn. Research in Otolaryngology, Scientific Research Soc., Soc. for Neurosci., N.Y. Acad. of Sci., Sigma Chi, Alpha Chi. Mem. Ch. of Christ. Office: UCLA Dept Biology Dept Physiol Sci Los Angeles CA 90095

SIMMONS, GLORI LOUISE, nonprofit development officer; b. Pomona, Calif., Dec. 18, 1966; d. John Louis and Kathy Louise (Thompson) S. BA in English Lit., U. Wash., 1989. English tchr. Geos Lang. Sys., Tokyo, 1989-91; devel. asst. Seattle Repertory Theatre, 1991—; devel. coord. Wash. Alliance Concerned with Sch. Age Parents, Seattle, 1993—. Bd. dirs. Cmty. Progress Alliance, Seattle, 1993—; mem. Wash. Alliance Concerned with Sch. Age Parents, Seattle, 1993—; vol., facilitator El Centro de la Raza, Seattle, 1994—. Mem. N.W. Devel. Officers Assn.

SIMMONS, LYNDA MERRILL MILLS, educational administrator; b. Salt Lake City, Aug. 31, 1940; d. Alanson Soper and Madeline Helene (Merrill) Mills; m. Mark Carl Simmons, Nov. 17, 1962; children: Lisa Lynn Simmons Morley, William Mark, Jennifer Louise, Robert Thomas. BS, U. Utah, 1961, MS, 1983. Cert. sch. adminstr., Utah. Tchr. Wasatch Jr. H.S./ Granite Dist., Salt Lake City, 1961-64, Altamont (Utah) H.S./Duchesne Dist., 1964-66; tchr. spl. edn. Park City (Utah) H.S., 1971-73; resource tchr. Eisenhower Jr. H.S., Salt Lake City, 1979-88; tchr. specialist Granite Sch. Dist., Salt Lake City, 1985-90; asst. prin. Bennion Jr. H.S., Salt Lake City, 1990-93; prin. Hartvigsen Sch., Salt Lake City, 1993—; adj. prof. spl. edn. U. Utah, Salt Lake City, 1987—, Utah Prin. Acad., 1994-95, co-chair Utah Spl. Educators for Computer Tech., Salt Lake City, 1988-90; mem. adv. com. on handicapped Utah State Office Edn., 1990-93; presenter at confs. Author: Setting Up Effective Secondary Resource Program, 1985; contbr. articles to profl. publs. Dist. chmn. Heart Fund, Cancer Dr., Summit Park, Utah, 1970-82; cub pack leader Park City area Boy Scouts Am., 1976-80; bd. dirs. Jr. League Salt Lake City, 1977-80; cookie chmn. Park City area Girl Scouts U.S., 1981; dist. chmn. March of Dimes, 1982—. Recipient Amb. award Salt Lake Conv. and Vis. Bur., 1993. Mem. Nat. Assn. Secondary Sch. Prins., Park City Young Women's Mut. (pres. 1989-93, family history cons. 1993—), Women's Athanaeum (v.p. 1990-93, pres. 1994—), Coun. for Exceptional Children (pres. Salt Lake chpt. 1989-90, pres. Utah Fedn. 1991-93, Spl. Educator of Yr.), Granite Assn. Sch. Adminstrs. (sec.-treas. 1992-94). Mem. LDS Ch. Office: Hartrigsen Sch 350 E 3605 S Salt Lake City UT 84115

SIMMONS, NED LEE, landscape artist, art dealer, consultant; b. Carmel, Calif., Mar. 15, 1939; s. Ned Lee, Sr. and Grace Lucille (Sinclair) S.; m. Barbara June Yocom Simmons, Dec. 31, 1968 (div. June 1989); children: Valerie, Gaylene. BS in Forest Mgmt., Humboldt State U., Arcata, Calif., 1964; MS in Forest Mgmt., 1973. Cert. profl. forester, Calif. Cons. forester Western Timber Svcs., Inc., Arcata, Calif., 1965-89; pvt. practice Trinidad (Calif.) Art, 1989—. Editor: the Volunteer Trinidadian, 1988; author: A Trinidad Story, 1989, 93, Rainbow Ridge, 1991. Fireman Trnindad (Calif.) Vol. Fire Dept., 1989—. Mem. Trinidad Mus. Soc., Humboldt North Coast Landtrust, Redwood Art Assn., Trinidad C. of C. Home and Office: Trinidad Art PO Box 1233 Trinidad CA 95570-1233

SIMMONS, NOEL ALEXANDER, human resources executive, consultant; b. San Francisco, Dec. 28, 1947; s. Clifford Edgar and Mildred (Malchow) S.; m. Elaine Diane Meyer, July 27, 1974; children: Carly Michelle, Rebecca Marie. BA, U. Calif., Berkeley, 1971; MBA, San Francisco State U., 1973. Regional acctg. mgr. ITT Continental Bakery, San Francisco, 1973-75; regional personnel mgr. VWR Sci. Corp., San Francisco, 1976-79; indsl. rels. mgr. Signetics Corp., Sunnyvale, Calif., 1979-81; human resources dir. Eaton Corp., Sunnyvale, 1981-89; human resources cons. The Simmons Group, Belmont, Calif., 1989—. Mem. No. Calif. Football Officials Assn., Calif., 1971-75; advisor Jr. Achievement, San Mateo County, Calif., 1976-79; sec. Redwood City (Calif.) Shores Homeowners Assn., 1983. Capt. USAF, 1973-79. Mem. Labor Adjustment Bd., Am. Soc. Personnel Adminstrs., No. Calif. Human Resources Coun., Calif. Unemployment Ins. Coun., Santa Clara (Calif.) Valley Personnel Assn., Peninsula Employee Rels. Coun. Home: 645 Spar Dr Redwood City CA 94065-1151 Office: Simmons Group 951-2 County Rd Ste 136 Belmont CA 94002

SIMMONS, RANDALL CRAIG, librarian, bookseller; b. Canyonville, Oreg., June 8, 1951; s. Ray and Vera Lorraine (Moore) S.; m. Leola Joy Bailey, June 14, 1973 (div. Apr. 1992); children: Jeffrey, Mason. AB in Pre-Sem. Studies, N.W. Nazarene Coll., 1973; MLS, U. Oreg., 1975; postgrad., Olivet Nazarene Coll., 1978-79; PhD in Libr. and Info. Sci., U. Ill., 1986. Clk. typist Caldwell (Idaho) Pub. Libr., 1973-74; libr. asst. N.W. Christian Coll., 1975-76; asst. prof., asst. libr. Olivet Nazarene Coll., 1976-80; grad. asst. U. Ill., Champaign, 1984-85; prof. N.W. Nazarene Coll., 1982-93; reference libr. N.W. Nazarene Coll., 1982-86, dir., 1987-93, dir. archives, 1992-93; propr. Roads Less Traveled Enterprises, Boise, Idaho, 1994—; libr. cons. Idaho State Libr., 1995—, mem. statewide strategy focus groups; presenter in field. Contbr. articles, revs. to profl. publs. N.W. Nazarene Coll. Alumni-Faculty grantee, 1984; Josie B. Houchens fellow, 1985, Elizab Luehm Latzer fellow, 1986. Mem. ALA, Assn. Coll. and Rsch. Librs., Idaho Libr. Assn. (chair acad. and spl. librs. divsn. 1988-90, 2nd v.p. 1991-92, ann. conf. chair 1992-93, 1st v.p., pres. elect 1992-93, pres. 1993-94, past pres. 1994-95), Beta Phi Mu, Phi Delta Lambda. Democrat. Methodist. Office: Roads Less Traveled 3017 W State St Boise ID 83703

SIMMONS, RICHARD BRYAN, finance executive; b. Oklahoma City, Aug. 17, 1947; s. Richard H. and Bonnie L. (Bryan) S.; m. Pamela Bond, Dec. 31, 1972 (div. Sept. 1992); children: Chris, Tally. MBA, U. Kans., 1972, 0BS, 1970. Sr. fin. analyst Frito Lay Corp., Dallas, 1972-76; asst. treas., contr. Gen. Recreation, Inc., Boulder, Colo., 1976-79; v.p. fin. Sentinel Pub. Co., Denver, 1979-86, Lehman Comm Corp., Longmont, Colo., 1986—; newsprint chmn. Colo. Press Assn., Denver, 1992, 93. Author, editor: (textbook) Principles of Marketing, 1972. Pres. Rotary, Broomfield, Colo., 1987. Capt. U.S. Army, 1972. Mem. Beta Sigma Phi. Home: 1621 Belero St Broomfield CO 80020-3522 Office: Lehman Comm Corp 350 Terry St Longmont CO 80501-5440

SIMMONS, ROBERT MICHAEL, lawyer; b. Milw., Jan. 27, 1948; s. Keith Rexford and June Antoinette (Schimmels) S.; m. Judy Ann Whelan, July 6, 1978; children: Paul Michael, Michael David. BA in Econs., U. Wis., 1970, JD, 1973; ML, George Washington U., 1979. Bar: D.C. 1973, U.S. Supreme Ct. 1976, U.S. Claims Ct. 1978. Atty. advisor USDA, Washington, 1973-78; atty. advisor USDA, Portland, Oreg., 1978-85, asst. regional atty., 1985-87; regional atty. USDA, San Francisco, 1987—; mem. Sr. Exec. Svc., 1989—. Recipient Superior Service award USDA, 1985. Mem. ABA (forest resources subcom, vice chmn. 1986), Fed. Bar Assn. (v.p. 1986-87), Fed. Legal Coun. (v.p. 1988, pres. 1989). Office: USDA Office of Gen Counsel 211 Main St Rm 1060 San Francisco CA 94105-1924

SIMMONS, ROBERT WAYNE, synthetics and coating manufacturing company executive; b. Sayre, Okla., July 1, 1946; s. Ova Wayne Simmons and Verna L. Simmons-Harris; m. Mari Melissa Reeves, Aug. 2, 1974; children—Tia Michelle, Ashley Megan. A.A., Bacone Jr. Coll., Muskogee, Okla., 1967; B.S. in Zoology, Northeastern Okla. State U., 1970. Drilling fluid engr. Baroid Engring. Co., Houston, 1970-71; sales rep. GAF Corp., Cape Girardeau, Mo., 1971-79, product engr., N.Y.C., 1979-80, assoc. prodn. mgr., 1980, mktg. mgr., 1980-81; midwest regional sales mgr. Gen. Tire & Rubber Co., Toledo, 1981-81, nat. sales mgr., bldg. products group mgr., 1983-85, dir. mktg. coated fabric group, 1985, 86; nat. mktg. mgr., gen. mgr. Pleko Products Corp., 1986-88; pres. chief exec. officer RW Simmons & Assocs., Inc. Served with USMC, 1968-69. Recipient Pres. Club award GAF Corp., 1976; named hon. capt. Girardeau Navy, 1979. Mem. Constrn. Specification Inst., Roofing Industry Ednl. Instn., Am. Mgmt. Assn., Phi Sigma Epsilon. Democrat. Lutheran. Lodges: Rotary (sec./treas. Cape Girardeau club 1978), Masons, Shriners, Elks. Author: Super System, Maintenance & Repair, Roofing Manual, 1981. Patentee roofing system application. Office: RW Simmons & Assocs Inc 31849 Pacific Hwy S Ste 159 Federal Way WA 98003-5400

SIMMONS, RONNY MICHAEL, dentist; b. New Orleans, Sept. 1, 1951; s. Warren and Rebecca (Aboutboul) S.; m. Nancy Dru Bryant, Nov. 29, 1986. BS, La. State U., 1974, DMD, 1978. Diplomate Fed. Svcs. Bd. Dentistry. Commd. capt. USAF, 1978, advanced through grades to lt. col., 1990; dentist USAF, Cannon AFB, N.Mex., Okinawa, Japan, 1978-80, Tyndall AFB, Fla., 1980-81, Mountain Home AFB, Idaho, 1982-84, Upper Heyford, England, 1984-86, England AFB, L.A., 1986-89, Keesler AFB, Miss., 1989-91, Fairchild AFB, Wash., 1991-94, Cannon AFB, N. Mex., 1994—. Mem. ABA, Acad. Gen. Dentistry, Phi Kappa Phi, Omicron Kappa Upsilon. Jewish.

SIMMONS, TED CONRAD, writer; b. Seattle, Sept. 1, 1916; s. Conrad and Clara Evelyn (Beaudry) S.; m. Dorothy Pauline Maltese, June 1, 1942; children: lynn, Juliet. Student U. Wash., 1938-41, UCLA and Los Angeles State U., 1952-54, Oxford (Eng.) U., 1980. Drama critic Seattle Daily Times, 1942; indsl. writer, reporter-editor L.A. Daily News, 1948-51; contbr. Steel, Western Metals, Western Industry, 1951—; past poetry dir. Watts Writers Workshop; instr. Westside Poetry Center; asst. dir. Pacific Coast Writers Conf., Calif. State Coll. Los Angeles. Served with USAAF, 1942-46. Author: (poetry) Deadended, 1966; (novel) Middlearth, 1975; (drama) Greenhouse, 1977, Durable Chaucer, 1978, Rabelais and other plays, 1980, Dickeybird, 1981 (nominated TCG Plays-in-Progress award 1985), Alice and Eve, 1983, Deja Vu, Deja Vu, 1986, The Box, 1987, Ingrid Superstar, 1988, Three Quarks for Mr. Marks, 1989, Ingrid: Skier on the Slopes of Stromboli, 1990, A Midsummer's Hamlet, 1991, Hamlet Nintendo, After Hours, Dueling Banjoes, Viva el Presidente, Climate of the Sun, 1992, Nude Descending Jacob's Ladder, 1993, Almost an Opera, 1994, Landscape with Inverted Tree and Fred Astaire Dancing, 1995, O.J. Othello, Fast Track; writer short story, radio verse; book reviewer Los Angeles Times; contbr. poetry to The Am. Poet, Prairie Wings, Antioch Rev., Year Two Anthology; editor: Venice Poetry Company Presents, 1972. Grantee Art Commn. King County, 1993.

SIMMONS, VICTOR J., real estate and insurance broker; b. Vallejo, Calif., June 17, 1945; s. Victor J. Simmons; children: Miriam Victoria, Jonathan Victor. BA, U. Nev., 1968. Bid coord. Dietary Products div. Am. Hosp. Supply Corp., Irvine, Calif., 1972-73; loan officer, appraiser Brentwood Savs., L.A., 1973-77; loan cons. Union Fed. Savs., L.A., 1978-79; real estate broker Far West Mortgage, L.A., 1980-81; ins. agt. Met. Life Ins., L.A., 1981-84; real estate broker Far West Mortgage, L.A., 1984-85; loan cons. Coast Savs., Beverly Hills, Calif., 1985-90; dist. agt., rep. Prudential Life Ins. Co., El Segundo, Calif., 1990-92; mortgage loan cons. Great Western Bank, Torrance, Calif., 1992-94; loan cons. Western Fin. Savings Bank, Beverly Hills, Calif., 1994-95; assessment appeals hearing officer L.A. County, L.A., 1995—. Contbr. articles to profl. jours., 1967-71. 1st lt. USMCR, 1968-71. Democrat. Baptist. Home: 3503 W 85th St Inglewood CA 90305-1616 Office: PO Box 78281 Los Angeles CA 90016

SIMMS, JULIA ANN, public relations executive; b. Coronado, Calif., Nov. 2, 1960; d. James C. Frampton and Julia A. (Brandley) Gale; m. Michael T. Simms, apr. 2, 1988; children: Ann Elizabeth, Mary Frances. Attended, Pitzer Coll., San Diego State U. Pub. rels. account exec. Frampton & Assocs., San Diego, 1983-88; pub. rels. dir. Larsen & Assoc., San Diego, 1988-90; asst. v.p. pub. rels. McMillin Cos., National City, Calif., 1990—. Pub. rels. com. Make A Wish Found., San Diego, 1993-94. Recipient Best Pub. Rels. Campaign award Bldg. Industry Assn., San Diego, 1987, 90, 91, 92, 94. Mem. Pub. Rels. Soc. Am. (accredited), Press Club of San Diego, Sales and Mktg. Coun. (pres. 1994, bd. dirs. 1988-95). Office: McMillin Cos 2727 Hoover Ave National City CA 91950-6625

SIMMS, MARIA ESTER, health services administrator; b. Bahia Blanca, Argentina; came to U.S., 1963; d. Jose and Esther (Guays) Barberio Esandi; m. Michael Simms, July 15, 1973 (Aug. 1993); children: Michelle Bonnie Lee Carla, Michael London Valentine, Matthew Brandon. Degree medicine, Facultad del Centenario, Rosario, Argentina, 1962; Physician Asst. Cert. (hon.), U. So. Calif., 1977. Medical diplomate. Pres. Midtown Svcs. Inc., L.A., 1973—. Chmn. bd. dirs. Am.'s Film Inst., Washington; chmn. bd. trustees World Film Inst. Fellow Am. Acad. Physicians' Assts.; mem. Bus. for Law Enforcement (northeast divsn.), Physicians for Social Responsibility, Mercy Crusade Inc., Internat. Found. for Survival Rsch., Noetic Scis. Soc., Inst. Noetic Scis., So. Calif. Alliance for Survival, Supreme Emblem Club of U.S., Order Eastern Star, Flying Samaritans, Shriners.

SIMMS, MARIA KAY, publishing and computer services executive; b. Princeton, Ill., Nov. 18, 1940; d. Frank B. and Anna (Haurberg) S.; m. Neil F. Michelsen, Oct. 2, 1987 (dec. 1990); children: Shannon Sullivan Stillings, Molly A. Sullivan, Elizabeth Maria Jossick. BFA, Ill. Wesleyan U., 1962. Cert. cons. profl. astrologer; ordained min. L.A. Cmty. Ch. of Religious Sci. Art tchr. elem. and jr. high pub. schs., Dundee, Northbrook, Ill., 1962-65; high sch. art tchr. Danbury, Conn., 1975-76; self employed gallery painter various cities, 1962-77, free-lance comml. illustrator, 1972-74, 86-87; shop, gallery, café owner Conn., 1976-79; art dir. ACS Pubs., Inc., San Diego, Calif., 1987-90; pres. Astro Comm. Svcs., Inc. (formerly ACS Pubs.), San Diego, 1990—; conf. lectr. United Astrology Congress, Washington, 1992, Am. Fedn. Astrologers Internat. Conv., Chgo., 1992. Author: Twelve Wings of the Eagle, 1988, Dial Detective, 1989; co-author: Search for the Christmas Star, 1989, Circle of the Cosmic Muse, 1994, Your Magical Child, 1994; contbr. numerous articles to mags. High priestess Cir. of the Cosmic Muse; chairperson pub. outreach focus group Wiccan Ind. Network. Recipient numerous art awards. Mem. Nat. Assn. Women Bus. Owners, Nat. Coun. Geocosmic Rsch. Inc. (dir., pubs. dir. 1981-92, editor jour. 1984-92), Am. Fedn. Astrologers, Internat. Soc. Astrol. Rsch., New Age Pubs. Assn. Office: Astro Comm Svcs Inc 5521 Ruffin Rd San Diego CA 92123-1314

SIMMS, STEVEN RODNEY, anthropology educator; b. Tujunga, Calif., Dec. 12, 1951; s. Rodney Melvin and Isabel Marie (Eastlack) S.; m. Marina Lorraine Hall, Dec. 6, 1989. BA, U. Utah, 1973, PhD, 1984; MA, U. Nev., 1976; postgrad., U. Pitts., 1978. Assoc. instr. U. Utah, Salt Lake City, 1981-84; asst. prof., dir. archaeol. technician program Weber State Coll., Ogden, Utah, 1985-87; asst. prof. Utah State U., Logan, 1988-90, assoc. prof., 1991—; dir. archaeol. field schs. Weber State Coll., Utah State U., 1985-92; co-investigator Petra (Jordan) Ethnoarchaeol. Project, 1986-90. Author: Behavioral Ecology and Hunter-Gatherer Foraging, 1987; contbr. chpts. to books and articles to profl. jours. Mem. Antiquities Task Force, Salt Lake City, 1992, Utah Govs. Adv. Com. on Native Am. Burials, Salt Lake City, 1990-91, Utah Govs. Com. on Historic Preservation, Salt Lake City, 1984-85. Recipient numerous grants NSF, LS.B. Leakey Found., Am. Ctr. for Oriental Rsch. and others, 1981—. Mem. Utah Profl. Archaeol. Coun. (pres. 1992-94, v.p. 1989-91), Soc. for Am. Archaeology, Utah Statewide Archaeol. Soc. (Archaeology Preservation award 1988, Landscape Preservation award Cache Valley Hist. Soc. 1994), Sigma Xi. Office: Dept Sociology Social Work & Anthropology Utah State U Logan UT 84322-0730

SIMMS, THOMAS HASKELL, chief of police; b. Yuma, Ariz., Sept. 3, 1945; s. Jessie Lee and Mary Elizabeth (Servos) S.; m. Oct. 12, 1966 (div. July 1981); m. Virginia Lee David, Mar. 26, 1988; children: Thomas Haskell Jr., Julie Marie. BA, St. Mary's Coll., Moraga, Calif., 1981; MA, Calif. Poly., Pomona, 1991. Officer Mountain View (Calif.) Police Dept., 1972-76; police sgt. East Bay Parks, Oakland, Calif., 1976-79; police lt. Town of Moraga, Calif., 1979-84, chief police, 1984-87; chief police City of Piedmont, Calif., 1987-91; chief of police City of Roseville, Calif., 1991—. Bd. dirs. Piedmont coun. Boy Scouts Am., 1988-89. Maj. U.S. Army, 1967-71, Vietnam. Mem. Calif. Chiefs Police Assn., Calif. Peace Officers Assn., Rotary, Kiwanis (pres. Moraga 1982-83, Kiwanian of Yr. award 1983). Presbyterian. Office: Roseville Police Dept 311 Vernon St Roseville CA 95678-2634

SIMON, CATHY JENSEN, architect; b. Los Angeles, Sept. 30, 1943; d. Bernard Everett and Bitten Hanne (Smith) S.; m. Michael Palmer, Nov. 23, 1972; 1 child, Sarah Marina. B.A. Wellesley Coll., 1965; M. Arch., Harvard U., 1969. Registered architect, Calif. 1974, N.Y. 1988, Mass. 1988. Architect Cambridge 7 Assocs., Mass., 1968-69, Building Systems Devel., San Francisco, 1970-72, Mackinlay Winnacker McNeil, Oakland, Calif., 1973-74; prin. Marquis Assocs., San Francisco, 1974-85; prin. Simon Martin-Vegue Winkelstein Moris, 1985—; sr. lectr. architecture U. Calif., Berkeley, 1982-85, vis. lectr., 1973-82; teaching coordinator Women's Sch. Planning and Arch., Santa Cruz, Calif., 1976; speaker ALA Nat. Conv., 1992, Les Grandes Bibliotheques de L'Avenin, Paris, 1991. Prin. works include Yerba Buena Gardens Retail and Entertainment Complex, San Francisco, Mus. N.Mex. Master Plan, Santa Fe, San Francisco Ballet Pavilion, Lick Wilmerding High Sch. Master Plan, San Francisco, Bothell Br. Campus, Bothell, Wash., San Francisco New Main Libr., Oceanside Water Pollution Control Project, San Francisco, Newport Beach (Calif.) Ctrl. Libr., Coll. 8 U. Calif., Santa Cruz, Olin Humanities Bldg. Bard Coll., N.Y., San Francisco Day Sch., Fremont (Calif.) Main Libr., Peter J. Shields Libr. U. Calif., Davis, Elena Baskin Visual Art Studios U. Calif., Santa Cruz, Primate Discovery Ctr., San Francisco Zoo, Braun Music Ctr., Stanford U. The Premier, La Jolla Colony, La Jolla, Calif. Mem. exec. com. San Francisco Mus. Modern Art; active Leadership Commn. Design Industry; mem. tech. assistance com., San Francisco Redevel. Agy., San Francisco, 1982—; mem. adv. panel Calif. Bd. Archtl. Examiners; bd. dirs. Golden Gate Nat. Park Assn. Recipient Calif. Preservation award Chambord Apartments, 1984, Adaptive Re-use award Engr. Offices, Am. Soc. Interior Designer, 1982, Commodore Sloat Sch. Honor award Nat. Sch. Bds. Assocs., 1980, Marcus Foster Mid. Sch. Honor award East Bay AIA, 1980; NEA grantee 1983. Mem. Orgn. Women Architects (founding 1972), San Francisco chpt. AIA, AIA (jury mem. nat. honor awards 1980, Los Angeles chpt. awards jury 1984). Home: 265 Jersey St San Francisco CA 94114-3822 Office: Simon Martin-Vegue Winkelstein Moris 501 2nd St # 701 San Francisco CA 94107-1431

SIMON, KAREN JORDAN, retail executive; b. Bridgeport, Conn., Feb. 11, 1953; d. John Francis and Mary (Kirlik) J.; m. James Lawrence Simon, Aug. 12, 1977. BA, So. Conn. U., 1974. Asst. buyer Gimbels Dept. Store, Bridgeport, Conn., 1970-77; buyer Foremost Div./McKesson June Foods Co., Secaucus, N.J., 1977-79; gen. mgr. Charrette Corp., Woburn, Mass., 1979-80; dir. purchasing Cumberland Farms Inc., Canton, Mass., 1980-88; corp. v.p. Dairy Mart Inc., Enfield, Conn., 1988-90; sr. v.p. Circle K Corp., Phoenix, 1990-92; pres. FISCO Farm and Home Stores, Stockton, Calif., 1993—. Mem. Nat. Assn. Convenience Stores (exec. coun. 1990-92), Ariz. Retailers Assn. (bd. dirs. 1991-92). Office: FISCO 4554 Qantas Ln Ste 1 Stockton CA 95206-4919

SIMON, MATTHEW JAMES, dean, educator, educational facilities planner; b. Indpls., Mar. 9, 1948; s. Max and Janet (Frisch) S.; m. Sharon Mae Kowaloff, Nov. 28, 1973; children: Katherine Dana, Reid Scott. AB, Ind. U., 1970, MLS, 1973, MA, 1975. Libr. Ind. U., Bloomington, 1971-73; govt. documents libr. Kean Coll. N.J., Union, 1973-74; instr. Hunter Coll. CUNY, 1974-75, prof., chief libr. Queens Coll., 1980-93; chemistry libr. Columbia U.,

N.Y.C., 1975-77, Herbert Lehman libr., 1977-80; dean univ. librs. U. Nev., Las Vegas, 1993—; planner, archtl. cons. 24 librs. and univ. and sch. bldgs., 1982-94; pres. Matthew Simon Planning, Las Vegas, 1986—, Simon Archtl. Svcs. Contbr. articles to profl. jours. Recipient Albert S. Bard award City Club N.Y., 1988. Mem. ALA, AIA. Jewish. Office: Matthew Simon Planning PO Box 70746 Las Vegas NV 89170-0746

SIMON, MAURYA, poet, educator; b. N.Y.C., Dec. 7, 1950; d. Robert Leopold Simon and Baila Goldenthal; m. Robert Edward Falk; children: Naomi Falk, Leah Falk. BA with honors, Pitzer Coll., 1980; MFA in English, U. Calif., Irvine, 1984. Lectr. in Creative Writing U. Calif., Riverside, 1984-90, asst. prof. in Creative Writing, 1991-94, assoc. prof. in Creative Writing, 1995—; vis. poet Calif. Inst. Tech., Pasadena, 1991-94. Author: The Enchanted Room, 1986, Days of Awe, 1989, Speaking in Tongues, 1990, The Golden Labyrinth, 1995; contbr. poetry to various periodicals including The Georgia Review, Poetry, TriQuarterly, The Southern Review, Ironwood, Grand Street, The Kenyon Review, Salmagundi, The Hudson Review, The Missouri Review, Verse, The Gettysburg Review. Councilwoman San Antonio Canyon Town Hall, Mt. Baldy, Calif., 1988-92, mayor-moderator, 1992-93. Indo-Am. fellow Fulbright Found., Bangalore, India, 1990-91; recipient Gibbs Smith Poetry award Gibbs Smith Books, 1990. Mem. Poetry Soc. Am., Acad. Am. Poets, Poets & Writers. Home: PO Box 203 Mount Baldy CA 91759-0203 Office: Creative Writing dept Calif 2116 Watkins Hal # U Riverside CA 92521

SIMON, NANCY RUTH, lawyer; b. Gary, Ind., Apr. 25, 1960; d. Norbert Fred and Elizabeth Anna (Laird) S. BSEE, Iowa State U., 1985; MBA, U. Dallas, 1988; JD, So. Meth. U., 1991. Bar: Tex., 1991, Calif., 1994. Elec. engr. Tex. Instruments, Dallas, 1986-88; law clk. to pvt. law firms Dallas, 1989-91; law clk. U.S. Attys. Office, 1991; assoc. Felsman, Bradley, Gunter & Dillon, LLP, Ft. Worth, 1991-93; patent counsel Apple Computer, Inc., Cupertino, Calif., 1993—. Co-author: Attorneys' Fees in IPL Cases; mem. So. Meth. U. Law Rev. Jour. of Air Law and Commerce, 1990-91. Mem. ABA, State Bar Tex., State Bar Calif., Mensa Iowa State U. Student Alumni Assn. (mem. career awareness com. 1984-85), Sigma Iota Epsilon, Zeta Tau Alpha (social chmn. 1982-83, house mgr. 1983-84, chmn. jud. bd. 1984-85), Phi Delta Phi. Office: Apple Computer Inc 1 Infinite Loop Cupertino CA 95014-2083

SIMON, RENEE BLATT, communications executive; b. N.Y.C., Mar. 25, 1928; d. Irving and Fanny (Miller) Blatt; m. Harry J. Simon, Mar. 22, 1949 (dec. Oct. 1977); children: Joel, Amy Simon Weiner, Matthew. BA, Adelphi U., 1947; MS, Stanford U., 1949; MLS, UCLA, 1966. Cert. tchr. jr. coll. Dir. med. libr. Comty. Hosp., Long Beach, Calif., 1966-72; elected mem. City Coun., Long Beach, 1972-78; prof. pub. adminstrn. Calif. State U., Long Beach, 1978-80; dep. dir. transp. So. Calif. Assn. Govts., L.A., 1980-87; pres. Inst. Mgmt. Comms., Long Beach, 1987—; bd. dirs. FHP Found., Long Beach, CRI Found. Articles editor: (jour.) Western Govtl. Researcher, 1988-92; contbr. feature columns to various bus. jours. and newspapers, articles to mags. Mem., past vice-chair Redevel. Agy., Long Beach, 1988—; bd. dirs. Housing Devel. Corp., Long Beach, 1991—, Internat. City Theater, Long Beach, 1992—, Long Beach Symphony Guild, 1994-95, fin. sec.; bd. dirs. Long Beach Heritage Coalition, 1989-90, pres. Recipient Ann. Susan B. Anthony award NOW, 1975, Disting. Achievement award Pi Alpha Alpha, 1981, Humanitarian award NCCJ, 1989. Mem. Am. Soc. Pub. Adminstrn. (bd. dirs., sec. 1991-92), Calif. Elected Women's Assn. for Edn. and Rsch. (founding mem.), Soroptimist Internat. (dir. comty. svc. 1993). Office: Inst Mgmt Comms # 242 6475 E Pacific Coast Hwy # 242 Long Beach CA 90803

SIMON, RONALD I., financial consultant; b. Cairo, Nov. 4, 1938; came to U.S., 1942; s. David and Helene (Zilkha) S.; m. Anne Faith Hartman, June 19, 1960; children: Cheryl, Eric, Daniel. BA, Harvard U., 1960; MA, Columbia U., 1962, PhD, 1968. V.p. Harpers Internat., N.Y.C., 1959-62; fin. analyst Amerace Corp., N.Y.C., 1965-66; v.p. Am. Foresight Inc., Phila., 1966-67; asst. to pres. Avco Corp., Greenwich, Conn., 1967-70; exec. v.p. Avco Community Developers Inc., La Jolla, Calif., 1970-73; pres. Ronald I. Simon Inc., La Jolla, 1973—, Delta Data Systems Corp., Phila., 1980-81; exec. v.p. Towner Petroleum Corp., Houston, 1983-85; mng. dir., chief fin. officer The Henley Group Inc., La Jolla, 1986-90; pvt. practice fin. cons. La Jolla, 1990—; chmn. Sonant Corp., San Diego; bd. dirs. Craig Corp., L.A., Reading Co., Phila. Bd. dirs. San Diego Opera Co., 1988-90; bd. dirs. Mandeville Art Gallery U. Calif., San Diego. Ford Found. fellow, 1963-65; recipient Ann. award Nat. Comml. Fin. Conf., 1963. Mem. University Club (N.Y.C.). Office: 1020 Prospect St Ste 410C La Jolla CA 92037-4148

SIMON, SHELDON WEISS, political science educator; b. St. Paul, Jan. 31, 1937; s. Blair S. and Jennie M. (Dim) S.; m. Charlann Lilwin Scheid, Apr. 27, 1962; 1 child, Alex Russell. BA summa cum laude, U. Minn., 1958, PhD, 1964; MPA, Princeton U., 1960; postgrad., U. Geneva, 1962-63. Asst. prof., then prof. U. Ky., 1966-75; prof. polit. sci. Ariz. State U., 1975—, chmn. dept., 1975-79, dir. Ctr. Asian Studies, 1980-88; vis. prof. George Washington U., 1965, U. B.C. Can., 1972-73, 79-80, Carleton U., 1976, Monterey Inst. Internat. Studies, 1991, Am. Grad. Sch. Internat. Mgmt., 1991-92; cons. USIA Rsch. Analysis Corp., Am. Enterprise Inst. Pub. Policy Rsch., Hoover Instn., Orkand Corp., Nat. Bur. Asian Rsch. Author: Asian Neutralism and U.S. Policy, 1975, The ASEAN States and Regional Security, 1982, The Future of Asian-Pacific Security Collaboration, 1988; editor: The Military and Security in the Third World, 1978, East Asian Security in the Post-Cold War Era, 1993; also others; contbr. articles to profl. jours., chpts. to books. Mem. Com. Fgn. Relations, Phoenix, 1976—; bd. dirs. Phoenix Little Theater, 1976-79. Grantee Am. Enterprise Inst., 1974, Earhart Found., 1979, 81, 82, 84, 88, U.S. Inst. Peace, 1994—; Hoover Instn. fellow, 1980, 85. Mem. Am. Polit. Sci. Assn., Assn. Asian Studies, Internat. Studies Assn. (profl. ethics com. 1987-91, v.p. 1991-93), Asia Soc. (contemporary affairs com. 1987—), U.S. Coun. for Asia-Pacific Security, Phi Beta Kappa. Democrat. Jewish. Home: 5630 S Rocky Point Rd Tempe AZ 85283-2134 Office: Ariz State U Polit Sci Dept Tempe AZ 85287

SIMON, STEVEN ADAM, sculptor, educator; b. Encino, Calif., Apr. 16, 1959; s. Alvin Leonard and Simone Arlene (Hyman) S. BA in Polit. Sci., Calif. State U., Northridge, 1981, BA in 3-D Art, 1983. Pres. Monkey Man Press Pub. Co., L.A., 1980—; mem. staff tch. sculpture lab. UCLA, 1985—. One man show at Alexander Gallery, Studio City, Calif., 1987; exhibited in group shows at Orlando Gallery, Sherman Oaks, Calif., 1985, Karl Bornstein Gallery, Santa Monica, Calif., 1987, Found. for Art Resources, L.A., 1993, Venice, Calif., 1994; prin. works at Villa Buenaventura Sculpture Garden, San Juan Cosala, Mex., David Bermant Collection, Santa Ynez, Calif., Moorpark (Calif.) Coll., Cermak Plaza, Berwyn, Ill., Fitzgerald's Park, Cork, Ireland; author: (poems) I'm Not Sure What You're Saying, But I Can Relate, 1980, Brace For The Impact, 1986. Recipient Ann. Conv. award Am. Lung Assn., 1986. Studio: 17945 Topham St Encino CA 91316-7125 Office: UCLA Dept Art 405 Hilgard Ave Los Angeles CA 90095

SIMON, WILLIAM LEONARD, film and television writer and producer, author; b. Washington, Dec. 3, 1930; s. Isaac B. and Marjorie (Felsteiner) S.; m. Arynne Lucy Abeles, Sept. 18, 1966; 1 child, Victoria Marie; 1 stepson, Sheldon M. Bermont. BEE, Cornell U., 1954; MA in Ednl. Psychology, Golden State U., 1982, PhD in Communications, 1983. Writer features and TV movies, documentary and indsl. films, TV programs, 1958—; lectr. George Washington U., Washington, 1968-70; juror Coun. on Nontheatrical Events Film Festival, 1975-90, Cindy Festival Blue Ribbon Panel, 1985—; jury, chmn., bd. dirs. CINE film festival, 1990—. Writer over 600 produced works for motion pictures and TV, including (screenplays) Fair Woman Without Discretion, Majorca, Swindle, A Touch of Love, (teleplays and documentaries) From Information to Wisdom, Flight of Freedom II, Missing You, (home video) Star of India at Sea, Combat Vietnam series; writer, producer The Star of India: Setting Sail; author: Profit from Experience-The Story of Transformation Management, 1995. Pres. Foggy Bottom Citizens Assn., 1963-65, mem. exec. bd., 1965-69; v.p. Shakespeare Summer Festival, 1966-67, trustee, 1965-70; mem. interview com. Cornell U., 1987-88. Lt. USN, 1954-58. Recipient 10 Golden Eagle awards Cine Film Festival, gold medal N.Y. Internat. Festival, gold medal Freedoms Found., IFPA Gold Cindy; awards Berlin, Belgrade and Venice film Festivals, numerous others. Mem. Nat. Acad. TV Arts and Scis. (gov. D.C. chpt. 1970-73), Writers Guild Am., Am. Film Inst., Internat. Documentary Assn., Rotary (bd. dirs., program chmn.), Eta Kappa Nu (chpt. pres. 1953-54), Tau Beta Pi. Republican. Home: 6151 Paseo Delicias PO Box 2048 Rancho Santa Fe CA 92067-2048

SIMONDS, JOHN EDWARD, newspaper editor; b. Boston, July 4, 1935; s. Alvin E. and Ruth Angeline (Rankin) S.; m. Rose B. Muller, Nov. 16, 1968; children—Maximillian P., Malia G.; children by previous marriage—Rachel F., John B. B.A., Bowdoin Coll., 1957. Reporter Daily Tribune, Seymour, Ind., 1957-58, UPI, Columbus, Ohio, 1958-60; reporter, asst. city editor Providence Jour. Bull., 1960-65, Washington Evening Star, 1965-66; corr. Gannett News Svc., Washington, 1966-75; mng. editor Honolulu Star Bull., 1975-80, exec. editor, 1980-87, sr. editor, editorial page editor, 1987-93; exec. Hawaii Newspaper Agy., Honolulu, 1993—. Served with U.S. Army, 1958. Mem. Am. Soc. Newspaper Editors, AP Mng. Editors, Soc. Profl. Journalists, Nat. Conf. Editorial Writers. Home: 5316 Nehu Pl Honolulu HI 96821-1941 Office: Hawaii Newspaper Agy 605 Kapiolani Blvd Honolulu HI 96813-5129

SIMONE, VERA SUZANNE, political science educator; b. Breslau, Germany, Dec. 19, 1937; came to U.S., 1939; d. Hans and Elizabeth (Redner) S.; m. Ismith Khan (div.); 1 child, Jameen Khan. BA, Queens Coll., 1958; MA, PhD, U. Mich., 1971. Lectr. Queens Coll., N.Y.C., 1964-70; prof. polit. sci. Calif. State U., Fullerton, 1972—. Author: China in Revolution, 1968, The Asian Pacific: Political and Economic Development in a Global Context, 1995. Mem. Internat. Studies Assn., Am. Sociol. Assn., Assn. for Asian Studies, Phi Beta Kappa. Jewish. Office: Calif State U 800 N State College Blvd Fullerton CA 92631-3547

SIMONEIT, BERND ROLF TATSUO, geochemistry educator; b. Heilbronn, Republic of Germany, Sept. 7, 1937; came to U.S., 1952; s. Kurt Erich and Anna (Dietrich) S.; m. Lynda J. Wells, June 17, 1961 (div. Mar. 1966); m. Doreen Joy Gee, Sept. 7, 1968; 1 adopted child, Amanda Jane Houlding. BS, U. R.I., 1960; postgrad., MIT, 1961, 64; PhD, U. Bristol, Eng., 1975. Chemist A.C. Lawrence Leather Co., Peabody, Mass., 1962-63; spectroscopist space sci. lab. U. Calif., Berkeley, 1965-70, assoc. specialist space sci. lab., 1970-72, specialist space sci. lab., 1972-73; assoc. rsch. geochemist UCLA, 1976-81; assoc. prof. sch. oceanography Oreg. State U., Corvallis, 1981-83, prof. coll. oceanography, 1983—; cons. EG&G Idaho, Inc., Idaho Falls, 1983-92, Refineria de Petroleo, SA, Concon, Chile, 1990—, Chevron Petroleum Tech. Co., La Habra, 1992—; mem. NASA Exobiology Adv. Panel, Washington, 1980-85; mem., chmn. deep sea drilling project Joint Oceanographic Instns. for Deep Earth Sampling Orgn. Geochemistry Adv. Panel, Washington, 1978-83. Editor: Organic Geochemistry, 1982-87, 90—, Applied Geochemistry, 1992—; co-editor: Gulf and Peninsular Province of the Californias, 1990; contbr. articles to profl. jours. Recipient Best Paper of Yr. award Geochemical Soc., 1977, 81. Mem. AAAS, Internat. Assn. Geochemistry and Cosmochemistry, Am. Assn. for Aerosol Rsch., Internat. Soc. for the Study of the Orgin of Life, Am. Assn. Petroleum Geologists, Am. Chem. Soc., Am. Geophys. Union, Am. Soc. for Mass Spectrometry, European Assn. for Geochemistry. Office: Oreg State Univ Coll Oceanic and Atmospheric Scis Oceanography Adminstrn Bldg 104 Corvallis OR 97331-5501

SIMONIAN, DEBRA LYN, dietitian, educator; b. Fresno, Calif., Sept. 27, 1951; d. Johnny Oscar and Louise Peggy (Nahabedian) S. BA in Home Econs., Calif. State U., Fresno, 1975, MBA, 1987. Registered dietitian. Staff dietitian, dietetic/nutrition svcs. Valley Children's Hosp., Fresno, 1978-80, asst. dir. dietetic/nutrition svcs., 1980-83, dir. dietetic/nutrition svcs., 1983—; lectr. Calif. State U., Fresno, 1988-93; instr. Kings River C.C., Reedley, Calif., 1992-93; self-employed lectr. and cons., Fresno, 1987—; sec.-treas. Calif. Dietetic Assn. Found., Playa del Rey, 1994—. Author: Hunger in Fresno County, 1986, How to Start a Business in Fresno County, 1987; editor: Dietitian's Pediatric Handbook, 1990. Mem. Fresno Women's Network, 1987, Jr. League of Fresno, 1989. Mem. Calif. Dietetic Assn. (sec.-treas. 1994—, awards com. 1993-94), Calif. Dietetic Assn./Ctrl. Valley Dist. (pres. 1989-91). Democrat. Office: Valley Children's Hosp 3151 N Millbrook Ave Fresno CA 93703

SIMONS, ANNETTE, performing company executive; b. N.Y.C., June 7, 1953; d. Eloy and Mary (Quiñones) S. BA, Loyola-Marymount U., 1975; MFA, Bklyn. Coll., CUNY, 1990. Legal specialist Pettit & Martin, L.A., 1977-88; devel. adminstr. N.Y.C. Ballet, 1988-90; dir. grant writing The Music Ctr., L.A., 1990-93; mng. dir. L.A. Baroque Orch., Santa Monica, 1993—; permissions specialist Calliope Media, Santa Monica, 1995—. Commr. Santa Monica Arts Commn., 1992—. Office: LA Baroque Orch 1223 Wilshire Blvd # 686 Santa Monica CA 90403-5400

SIMONS, LYNN OSBORN, state education official; b. Havre, Mont., June 1, 1934; d. Robert Blair and Dorothy (Briggs) Osborn; BA, U. Colo., 1956; postgrad. U. Wyo., 1958-60; m. John Powell Simons, Jan. 19, 1957; children: Clayton Osborn, William Blair. Tchr., Midvale (Utah) Jr. High Sch., 1956-57, Sweetwater County Sch. Dist. 1, Rock Springs, Wyo., 1957-58, U. Wyo., Laramie, 1959-61, Natrona County Sch. Dist. 1, Casper, Wyo., 1963-64; credit mgr. Gallery 323, Casper, 1972-77; Wyo. state supt. public instrn., Cheyenne, 1979-91; sec.'s regional rep. region VIII U.S. Dept. Edn., Denver, 1993—; mem. State Bds. Charities and Reform, Land Commrs., Farm Loan, 1979-91; mem. State Commns. Capitol Bldg., Liquor, 1979-91; Ex-officio mem. bd. trustees U. Wyo., 1979-91; ex-officio mem. Wyo. Community Coll. Commn., 1979-91; mem. steering com. Edn. Commn. of the States, 1988-90; mem. State Bd. Edn., 1971-77, chmn., 1976-77; advisor Nat. Trust for Hist. Preservation, 1980-86. Mem. LWV (pres. 1970-71). Democrat. Episcopalian. Office: US Dept Edn 1244 Speer Blvd Ste 310 Denver CO 80204-3582

SIMONS, MARLENE J., state legislator, rancher; b. Deadwood, S.D., July 1, 1935; d. Royal B. Mills and Elsie M. Snook; m. Frank Simons, Sept. 24, 1951; children: Greg, Linda, Sully. Grad. high sch., Sundance, Wyo. Pres. Outdoors Unltd., Kaysville, Utah; mem. Wyo. Ho. of Reps., 1979-94, appropriation com., 1994—; mem. rules com., chmn. agrl. com., mem. appropriations com., mem. western legis. state conf. com., mem. water policy com.; vice chmn. Pub. Lands Adv. Coun., 1986—; stockgrower Farm Bur., Wyo., 1969—; rancher, outfitter. Pres. Wyo. Multiple Use Coalition, Ranch A Restoration Found.; sec. Black Hills Multi-Use Coalition; mem. Madison water steering com. Black Hills Hydrology Study; leader 4-H. Republican. Home: Windy Acres Ranch 5480 Hwy 14 Beulah WY 82712 Office: Outdoors Unltd PO Box 373 Kaysville UT 84037-0373

SIMONS, STEPHEN, mathematics educator, researcher; b. London, Aug. 11, 1938; came to U.S., 1965; s. Jack Isidore Simons and Ethel Esther (Littman) Harris; m. Jacqueline Mania Berchadsky, Aug. 13, 1963; 1 son, Mark. BA, Cambridge U., Eng., 1959, PhD, 1962. Instr. U. B.C., Vancouver, Can., 1962-63; asst. prof. U. BC, Vancouver, Can., 1964-65; asst. prof. U. Calif., Santa Barbara, 1965-67, assoc. prof., 1967-73, prof., 1973—, chmn. dept., 1975-77, 88-89; trustee Math. Scis. Rsch. Inst., Berkeley, Calif., 1988-94. Peterhouse rsch. fellow, Cambridge U., 1963-64. Mem. Am. Math. Soc., The Inst. Mgmt. Scis. Office: Univ Calif Dept Math Santa Barbara CA 93106

SIMONSON, SUSAN KAY, hospital administrator; b. La Porte, Ind., Dec. 5, 1946; d. George Randolph and Myrtle Lucille (Opfel) Menkes; m. Richard Bruce Simonson, Aug. 25, 1973. BA with honors, Ind. U., 1969; MA, Washington U., St. Louis, 1972. Perinatal social worker Yakima Valley Meml. Hosp., Yakima, Wash., 1979-81, dir. patient support and hospice program, 1981—, dir. social svc., 1982—; instr. Spanish, ethnic studies, sociology Yakima Valley Coll., Yakima, Wash., 1981—; pres. Yakima Child Abuse Council, 1983-85; developer nat. patient support program, 1981. Contbr. articles to profl. jours. Mem. Jr. League, Yakima; mem. adv. council Robert Wood Johnson Found. Rural Infant Health Care Project, Yakima, 1980, Pregnancy Loss and Compassionate Friends Support Groups, Yakima, 1982—, Teen Outreach Program, Yakima, 1984—. Recipient NSF award, 1967, discharge planning program of yr. regional award Nat. Glasrock Home Health Care Discharge Planning Program, 1987; research grantee Ind. U., 1968, Fulbright grantee U.S. Dept. State, 1969-70; Nat. Def. Edn. Act fellowship, 1970-73. Mem. AAUW, Soc. Med. Anthropology, Soc. Hosp. Social Work Dirs. of Am. Hosp. Assn. (regional award 1989), Nat. Assn. Social Workers, Phi Beta Kappa. Office: Yakima Valley Meml Hosp 2811 Tieton Dr Yakima WA 98902-3761

SIMPSON, ALAN KOOI, senator; b. Cody, Wyo., Sept. 2, 1931; s. Milward Lee and Lorna (Kooi) S.; m. Ann Schroll, June 21, 1954; children—William Lloyd, Colin Mackenzie, Susan Lorna. BS, U. Wyo., 1954, JD, 1958; LLD (hon.), Calif. Western Sch. of Law, 1983, Colo. Coll., 1986, Notre Dame U., 1987; JD (hon.), Am. U., 1989. Bar: Wyo. 1958, U.S. Supreme Ct. 1964. Asst. atty. gen. State of Wyo., 1959; city atty. City of Cody, 1959-69; partner firm Simpson, Kepler, and Simpson, Cody, Wyo., 1959-78; mem. Wyo. Ho. of Reps., 1964-77, majority whip, 1973-75, majority floor leader, 1975-77, speaker pro tem, 1977; legis. participant Eagleton Inst. Politics, Rutgers U., 1971; mem. U.S. Senate from Wyo., 1978—, asst. majority leader, 1985-87, asst. minority leader, 1987-95, chmn. vets. affairs com., chmn. fin. subcom. on Social Security and Family Policy, chmn. subcom. on immigration and refugee policy; mem. Sen. Rep. Policy Com. Spec. Com. on Aging; guest lectr. London exchange program Regent's Coll., London, 1987. Formerly v.p., trustee N.W. C.C., Powell, Wyo., 1968-76; trustee Buffalo Bill Hist. Ctr., Cody, Grand Teton Music Festival; del. Nat. Triennial Episcopal Ch. Conv., 1973, 76. With U.S. Army, 1954-56. Recipient Nat. Assn. Land Grant Colls. Centennial Alum award U. Wyo., 1987, Lifetime Svc. award Vietnam Vets. Am., 1993. Mem. Wyo. Bar Assn., Park County Bar Assn., Fifth Jud. Dist. Bar Assn., Am. Bar Assn., Assn. Trial Lawyers Am., U. Wyo. Alumni Assn. (pres. 1962, 63, Disting. Alumnus award 1985), VFW (life), Am. Legion, Amvets. (Silver Helmet award). Lodges: Eagles, Elks, Masons (33 deg.), Shriners, Rotary (pres. local club 1972-73). Office: US Senate 105 Dirksen Senate Bldg Washington DC 20510-5002

SIMPSON, ANDREA LYNN, energy communications executive; b. Altadena, Calif., Feb. 10, 1948; d. Kenneth James and Barbara Faries Simpson; m. John R. Myrdal, Dec. 13, 1986; 1 child, Christopher Ryan Myrdal. BA, U. So. Calif., 1969, MS, 1983; postgrad. U. Colo., Boulder Sch. Bank Mktg., 1977. Asst. cashier United Calif. Bank, L.A., 1969-73; asst. v.p. mktg. 1st Hawaiian Bank, Honolulu, 1973-78; v.p. corp. comm. BHP Hawaii, Inc. (formerly Pacific Resources, Inc.), Honolulu, 1978—. Bd. dirs. Arts Coun. Hawaii, 1977-81, Hawaii Heart Assn., 1978-83, Coun. Pacific Girl Scouts U.S., 1982-85, Child and Family Svcs., 1984-86, Honolulu Symphony Soc., 1985-91, Sta. KHPR Hawaii Pub. Radio, 1988-92, Kapiolani Found., 1990-95, Hanahauoli Sch., 1991—; bd. dirs., 2nd. v.p. Girl Scout Coun. Hawaii, 1994—; trustee Hawaii Loa Coll., 1984-86, Kapiolani Women's and Children's Hosp., 1988—, Hawaii Sch. For Girls at LaPietra, 1989-91, Kapiolani Med. Ctr. at Pali Momi, 1994—; commr. Hawaii State Commn. on Status of Women, 1985-87, State Sesquecentennial of Pub. Schs. Commn., 1990-91; bd. dirs. Hawaii Strategic Devel. Corp., 1991—, Hawaii Children's Mus., 1994—, Pacific Asian Affairs Coun., 1994—, Girl Scout Coun. Hawaii, 1994—; adv. dir. Hawaii Kids at Work, 1991—, Hawaii Mothers Against Drunk Driving, 1992—. Named Panhellenic Woman of Yr. Hawaii, 1979, Outstanding Woman in Bus. Hawaii YWCA, 1980, Outstanding Young Woman of Hawaii Girl Scouts Coun. of the Pacific, 1985, 86, Hawaii Legis., 1980. Mem. Am. Mktg. Assn., Pub. Rels. Soc. Am. (bd. dirs. Honolulu chpt. 1984-86, Silver Anvil award 1984, Pub. Rels. Profl. Yr. 1991), Pub. Utilities Communicators Assn. (Communicator of Yr. 1984), Honolulu Advt. Fedn. (Advt. Woman of Yr. 1984), U. So. Calif. Alumni Assn. (bd. dirs. Hawaii 1981-83), Outrigger Canoe Club, Pacific Club, Kaneohe Yacht Club, Rotary (pub. rels. chmn. 1988—, Honolulu chpt.), Alpha Phi (past pres., dir. Hawaii), Hawaii Jaycees (Outstanding Young Person of Hawaii 1978). Office: BHP Hawaii Inc 733 Bishop St Ste 2700 Honolulu HI 96813-4022

SIMPSON, ANN MARCOUX, sports marketing executive; b. Jackson, Mich., Oct. 12, 1954; d. William Joseph and Kae Marie Marcoux; m. David Ritchie Simpson, Jan. 4, 1975. BA, U. Mich., 1976. Dept. mgr. Jacobsons, Ann Arbor, Mich., 1976-78; mktg. Braniff, Dallas, 1978-79; customer rels. Dillards, Dallas, 1979-80; mktg. cons. Imagery, Seattle, 1980-85; pub. rels. Sundance Cruiseline, Seattle, 1985-86; account exec. Sammers & Conner, Seattle, 1986-88; dir. Airborne Express, Seattle, 1988-94; sport mktg. exec. Puget Sound Golf Club, Seattle, 1994—; pres. mktg. com. exec. internat., 1992-93; speaker in field. Contbr. articles to profl. jours. Campaign chair Rep. House, Mich., 1972-78; com. chair Poncho, Washington, 1980-90. Mem. Internat. Assn. Bus. Commn. (pres. 1986-87, 6th dist. dir. 1986-89), Internat. Com. Am. Electronics Assn. Office: Puget Sound Golf Club PO Box 19212 Seattle WA 98109-1212

SIMPSON, BARCLAY, manufacturing company executive; b. Oakland, Calif., May 25, 1921; s. Walter Chapin and Jessie B. (Smith) S.; m. Joan Devine Simpson, Oct. 10, 1945 (div. 1971); children: John, Anne, Jean; m. Sharon Elizabeth Hanley, June 8, 1984; children: Jeffrey, Julie, Amy, Elizabeth. BSBA, U. Calif., Berkeley, 1966. Chmn. Simpson Mfg. Co. Inc., Pleasanton, Calif., 1980—; owner, dir. Barclay Simpson Fine Arts Gallery, Lafayette, Calif., 1981—; bd. dirs. Civic Bank of Commerce, Oakland, Calif., McFarland Energy Corp., Santa Fe Springs, Calif., Calender-Robinson Ins., San Francisco. Author: (exhbn. catalogue) Rembrandt, 1989. Bd. dirs. Bay Area Rapid Transit, Oakland, 1977-88, pres., 1977; trustee John Muir Hosp., Walnut Creek, 1967-75, Univ. Art Mus., Berkeley, Calif., 1988—, Calif. Coll. Arts & Crafts, Oakland, 1987—. Sr. lt. USN, 1942-46, PTO.

SIMPSON, BOB GENE, quality assurance professional; b. DeWitt, Ark., Feb. 20, 1932; s. Fearmon Lambert Simpson and Myrtle Elsie (Lowrance) Simpson Palmer. BS in Physics., U. Ctrl. Ark., 1962. Quality/reliabilty engr. Motorola Inc., Phoenix, 1963-70; reliability engr. Motorola Inc., Mesa, Ariz., 1973-74; component engr. Control Data Corp., Tucson, 1971-73; mgr. quality assurance Engineered Sys. Inc., Tempe, 1976-90, supr. of quality assurance, 1991—. With USN, 1951-55; with AEC Contractor, 1957-59. Mem. Ch. of God Internat. Home: 1457 W University Dr Mesa AZ 85201-5426

SIMPSON, C. DENE, clinical neuropsychologist, psychophysiologist; b. Ashland, Ky., Sept. 16, 1936; s. Curtis Zotto and Clarice Lorrine Simpson; m. Margaret Louise Cline, Aug. 17, 1956; children: René, Michelle, Yvonne. BA, Bethany Nazarene Coll., 1958; MA, U. Kans., 1962; PhD, U. Okla., Oklahoma City, 1974. Lic. psychologist, Idaho, Okla. Statis. analyst Ford Motor Co., Claycomo, Mo., 1959-63; prof. N.W. Nazarene Coll., Nampa, Idaho, 1963-66, head Dept. of Psychology, 1970-88; prof. Bethany (Okla.) Nazarene Coll., 1966-67; rsch. psychologist Okla. Med. Rsch. Found., Oklahoma City, 1967-68, Okla. Ctr. for Alcohol Related Studies, Oklahoma City, 1968-70; clin. neuropsychologist Boise, Idaho, 1976—; pres. Human Tech., Inc., Boise, 1985—; cons. VA Med. Ctr., Boise; vis. prof. U. St. Andrews, Scotland, 1988; cons. neuropsychologist Intermountain Hosp. of Boise, 1983—. Contbr. sci. articles to profl. jours. Mem. The Nature Conservancy, 1988—, The Perringrine Fund, Boise, 1988—, World Ctr. for Birds of Prey. Fellow NSF-U. Mo., 1967, Nat. Def. Edn. Act-U. Okla., 1968-70; equipment grantee Nat. Sci. Found.-N.W. Nazarene Coll., 1978-79. Fellow Idaho Psychol. Assn. (pres. 1974-77, exec. bd. 1988); mem. Am. Psychol. Assn., Western Psychol. Assn., Internat. Neuropsychology Soc., N.Y. Acad. Scis., Internat. Assn. for the Study of Traumatic Brain Injury, Assn. for Applied Psychophysiology and Biofeedback. Republican. Mem. Ch. of the Nazarene. Home: 979 Strawberry Ln Boise ID 83712-7724 Office: 317 Allumbaugh St Boise ID 83704-9208

SIMPSON, CHARLES ROBERT, marketing professional. BS in Bus. Adminstrn., U. Tenn., 1971; MBA in Mktg., Bloomfield Coll., 1973. Gen. ptnr. Simpson Constrn. and Restoration, Paterson, N.J., 1972-79; v.p. sales and mktg. The Jim Walter Corp., Tampa, Fla., 1979-83; v.p. franchise mktg. Comml. Credit/Control Data, Mpls., 1983-84; v.p. acquisitions Equity Program Investment Corp., Falls Church, Va., 1984-85; pres., gen. mgr. Simpson Mktg. Group, Chandler, Ariz., 1985-87; v.p. mktg. and sales Hooker U.S.A., L.J. Hooker Homes, L.J. Hooker Internat., Phoenix, Atlanta, Dallas, 1987-91; cons. Resolution Trust Corp.-Oversight Bd., Phoenix, Denver, 1991—; lectr. Ariz. State U., Tempe, Harvard U. Grad. Sch. Bus. Contbg. editor of rsch. recommendations in weekly publs. Mem. Habitat for Humanities; adv. bd. Resolution Trust Corp.; mem. Greenspeace; past mem. bd. dirs. Verde Valley Sch., Sedona, Ariz. Recipient Pacesetter award Nat. Assn. Homebuilders, 1989, MIRM designation, 1988, MAME award in a career total of 21 categories, 1987-90, Nat. MIRM award, 1988. Mem. Nat. Trust for Hist. Preservation, Nat. Park and Wildlife Fedn., Benevolent Protective Order of Elks, Univ. Club, Essex County Hist. Soc. (past pres.). Office: PO Box 31203 Phoenix AZ 85046-1203

SIMPSON, DAVE, radio producer; b. Rantoul, Ill., Oct. 5, 1960; s. Ronald James and Janet Kay (Smith) S.; m. Karen Wilson, Nov. 3, 1984; children: Katherine, Allison. BS in Quantitative Psychology, UCLA, 1984. Program dir. Sierra Ski and Pack Club, L.A., 1983-88; co-dir. KVMR Broadcast Tng. Course, Nevada City, Calif., 1992—; ind. producer Nat. Pub. Radio Pub. Radio Satellite, Washington, 1993—. Producer, host The Morning Show, Mediawatch, Required Reading, Late Night Eclectica KVMR-FM, Nevada City, 1988—; author: KVMR Broadcaster Handbook, 1993, KVMR Standard Operating Manual, 1993, The Art and Technique of Radio Broadcasting, 1993; contbr. articles to KVMR Program Guide, 1991—. Mem. Media Alliance, Western Pub. Radio, Assn. Ind. Producers. Office: KVMR-FM PO Box 1327 Nevada City CA 95959-1327

SIMPSON, GARY LAVERN, public health medical director; b. St. Louis, Jan. 3, 1947; m. Sandra Cheryl Lapham; children: Cassandra Alyn, Courtney Meredith. BS, U. Ill., 1969, MS, 1970, PhD, 1973; MD, Rush Med. Coll., Chgo., 1974; MSc in Clin. Medicine, U. Oxford, Eng., 1977; MPH in Tropical Pub. Health, Harvard U., 1978. Diplomate Mass. Bd. Med. Examiners, Am. Bd. Internal Medicine, Calif. Bd. Med. Examiners, N.Mex. Bd. Med. Examiners. Intern Peter Bent Brigham Hosp., Boston, 1974-75, resident, 1975-76; sr. registrar in internal medicine/infectious diseases U. Oxford, Clin. Med. Sch., Radcliffe Infirmary, Eng., 1976-77; fellow infectious diseases divsn. infectious diseases Stanford (Calif.) U., 1978-79; asst. prof. medicine divsn. infectious diseases U. N.Mex., Albuquerque, 1979-83, clin. assoc. prof. medicine, 1983-88; attending physician Presbyn. Healthcare Svcs., Albuquerque, 1987-89; med. dir. infectious diseases Pub. Health divsn. Dept. Health, State of N.Mex., Santa Fe, 1992—; teaching asst. U. Ill., Champaign-Urbana, 1969-70, rsch. assoc., 1970-72; rsch. cons. U. N.Mex., Albuquerque, 1973-74, adj. assoc. prof. dept. biology, 1986-87; rsch. scientist Rush Med. Sch., 1973-74; clin. fellow Harvard Med. Sch., Boston, 1974-76; dir., chief medicine Raymond Hosp., Wrentham, Mass., 1976; staff physician Children's Hosp. Med. Ctr., Boston, 1976; vis. prof. Instituto Nacional de Salud, Bogota, Colombia, 1979-80; attending physician U. N.Mex. Hosp., 1979-87, VA Med. Ctr., Albuquerque, 1980-87; assoc. scientist Lovelace Med. Found., Albuquerque, 1983-86; med. dir. Cottonwood de Albuquerque, Residential Treatment Ctr., Los Lunas, N.Mex., 1983-84, Jim Kelly Counseling Assocs., Albuquerque, 1984-86, Presbyn. Alcohol and Drug Treatment Ctr., Northside Presbyn. Hosp., Albuquerque, 1987-89; sr. cons. bur. communicable diseases AID, Dept. State, Washington, 1984—; cons. Am. Inst. Biol. Scis., Washington, 1984—; Eagleson lectr. Am. Biol. Safety Assn. 36th Annual Conf., Albuquerque, lectr. in field; vis. prof. dept. med. microbiology and sec. of infectious diseases Faculty of Medicine U. Manitoba, Winnipeg, Can. Contbr. articles to profl. jours. Recipient Cert. award U.S. Indian Health Svc., 1995; Robert Wood Johnson fellow, 1977, Agy. for Internat. Devel. Edn. fellow, 1978, Palo Alto Med. Rsch. Found. fellow, 1979; hon. I award U. Ill. Fellow ACP; mem. AAAS, Oxford Med. Soc., Royal Soc. Tropical Medicine and Hygiene, Am. Soc. Microbiology, Am. Soc. Tropical Medicine and Hygiene, Am. Fedn. Clin. Rsch., Infectious Diseases Soc. Am., Am. Soc. Addiction Medicine (cert.). Home: 18 Senda Aliento Placitas NM 87043

SIMPSON, JOCELYN YVETTE, pediatric medical/surgical and hematology/oncology nurse; b. L.A., Oct. 29, 1966; d. James Earl and Elena Jane (Rowland) S. BA in Biol. Scis., U. Calif., Santa Barbara, 1988; ADN, Santa Barbara City Coll., 1991; BS in Health Care Mgmt., U. La Verne, 1995. RN, Calif.; cert. PALS. Lab. asst. U. Calif. Santa Barbara Student Health Svcs., 1985, asst. Eye Clinic, 1987-88; med. asst. Santa Barbara Med. Found. Clinic, 1988-89, Children's Med. Clinic Santa Barbara, 1989-91; staff nurse Children's Hosp. L.A., 1991—. Scholar Ventura County Black Nurses Assn. Mem. NAFE, Nat. Coun. Negro Women Inc., U. Calif.-Santa Barbara Alumni Assn., U. Calif.-Santa Barbara Black Alumni Club.

SIMPSON, PATRICK J., lawyer; b. Glendale, Calif., Sept. 26, 1944. AB, U. Calif, Berkeley, 1967, JD, 1971. Bar: Oreg. 1971. Mem. Perkins Coie, Portland, Oreg. Address: Perkins Cole 1211 SW 5th Ave Ste 1500 Portland OR 97204-3715

SIMPSON, PATRICK KENNETH, research and development engineer, engineering company executive; b. Cordova, Alaska, Jan. 13, 1964; s. Kenneth Miles Joseph and Verna Ann (Franklin) S.; m. Christalyn Marie Beane, June 14, 1986; children: Zachary Patrick, James Patrick. BA in Computer Sci., U. Calif., San Diego, 1986. Engr. UNISYS, San Diego, 1986-87; sr. engr. Ball Systems Engrng. div., San Diego, 1987-88; engrng. specialist Electronics div. Gen. Dynamics, San Diego, 1988-91; prin. engr. ORINCON, 1994; pres. Sci. Fishery Sys., Inc., San Diego, 1994—; instr. U. Calif., San Diego Extension, 1988-89, UCLA Extension, 1990, Applied Tech. Inst., San Diego, 1990—; lectr. NATO, Europe and U.S., 1991. Author: Artificial Neural Systems, 1990, (with others) Certification in Knowledge Engineering Manual, 1989, Handbook of Neural Network Applications, 1990, Neural Networks, 1991; editor: Neural Networks: Technology and Applications, 2 vols., 1995; editor, book revs. Jour. Neural Network Computing, 1989-91; editor IEEE Transactions on Neural Networks, 1991-94, Australian Jour. Intelligent Information Processing Systems, 1994—; contbr. articles to profl. jours. Vol. Cystic Fibrosis Found., San Diego, 1988—. Mem. IEEE (chmn. San Diego chpt. 1988, treas. neural networks coun. 1990-91, chmn. program and steering com. 1990—, v.p. 1992-93, pres. 1994), Soc. Photo Optical and Instrumentation Engrs. (session chmn. 1990-94), Internat. Assn. of Knowledge Engrs. (session chmn. 1989), Internat. Neural Network Soc. Home: 17436 Ashburton Rd San Diego CA 92128-3939 Office: Sci Fishery Systems Inc 5011 Kearny Villa Rd 17436 Ashburton Rd San Diego CA 92128

SIMPSON, PETER KOOI, university official; b. Sheridan, Wyo., July 31, 1930; s. Milward Lee and Lorna Helen (Kooi) S.; m. Lynne Alice Livingston, June 18, 1960; children: Milward Allen, Margaret Ann, Peter Kooi Jr. BA, U. Wyo., 1953, MA, 1962; PhD, U. Oreg., 1973. Pres. Western Hills, Inc., Billings, Cody, Wyo., 1959-61; asst. prof. history Ea. Oreg. Coll., La Grande, Oreg., 1962-65, Lane Community Coll., Eugene, Oreg., 1968-69, 70-72; instr. U. Oreg., Eugene, 1969-70; asst. to pres. Casper (Wyo.) Coll., 1974-77, coord. U.Wyo.-Casper Coll. upper div., 1976-77; dean instrn. Sheridan Coll., 1977-83, asst. to pres. for devel., dean instrn., 1983-84; v.p. for devel., alumni and univ. rels., exec. dir. Found., U. Wyo., Laramie, 1984-89; v.p. for institutional advancement, 1989—. Author: The Community of Cattlemen, 1987; also articles. Mem. Wyo. Ho. of Reps., 1980-84; rep. candidate for Gov. of Wyo., 1986; bd. dirs. Wyo. Vol. Assistance Corp., Laramie, 1985-89, Casper Troopers, 1988—. Lt. USNR, 1954-60. Recipient award for signal contbn. to hist. preservation Wyo. Conservation Com., 1989; grantee Oreg. Edn. Coordinating Coun., 1971; named outstanding educator Am. Fuller and Dees, 1975, exemplary alumni U. Wyo. Coll. Arts & Scis., 1993. Mem. SAG, Wyo. Hist. Soc., Cowboy Joe Club (exec. com. 1984—), Rotary (chmn. Found. 1990-92), Masons (32 degree, K.C.C.H.), Shriners, Jesters. Episcopalian. Home: 812 Grand Ave Laramie WY 82070-3942 Office: U Wyo Found PO Box 3963 Laramie WY 82071-3963

SIMPSON, RICHARD JOHN, police detective, municipal official; b. Greensburg, Pa., Oct. 23, 1953; s. Henry Theodore and Marceline (Krempasky) S.; m. Gail Montgomery, Jan. 10, 1977 (div. May 1981); m. Jeri Anne Sheely, July 10, 1981; children: Jessica Ann, Alexander Richard, Allison Dawn. BA, Calif. U. Pa., 1976, 78; cert., Pa. Police Acad., 1978. Asst. security supt. Rouse Svc. Co., Greensburg, 1971-77; asst. police chief Ellsworth (Pa.) Borough Police Dept., 1977-78; police officer Fallowfield Twp. Police Dept., Charleroi, Pa., 1978-80; police detective, trainer, instr., coord. field tng., supr. sex crimes unit Rock Springs (Wyo.) Police Dept., 1980—; rsch. asst. centennial com. Rock Springs Police Dept.; police instr. State of Wyo, 1982—; actor, cons. tng. films series theater dept. Western Wyo. Coll., Rock Springs, 1987-88. Editor quar. newsletter Blue Knights News Wyo., 1986-92. Asst. basketball coach Spl. Olympics, Rock Springs, 1987. Recipient numerous commedations Rock Springs Police Dept., 1980—, Outstanding Law Enforcement Officer award, 1985, Disting. Svc. medal, 1987, Svc. medal 1988. Mem. Nat. Assn. Field Tng. Officers, Police Protective Assn. (v.p. 1984-85, treas. 1990-94), Western Alliance Police Officers (v.p. 1985-87), Calif. U. Pa. Alumni Assn., Intermountain World War II Reenactment Assn., Shooting Stars Motorcycle Club (pres. 1980-84), Blue Knights Internat. Law Enforcement Motorcycle Club (pres. Wyo. chpts. 1985-92, bd. dirs. Wyo. chpt. 1 1992—), High Desert Riders, Motorcycle Club (legis. officer 1991-94). Home: 103 Agate St Rock Springs WY 82901-6601 Office: Rock Springs Police 221 C St Rock Springs WY 82901-6220

SIMPSON, ROBERT HOUSER, orthodontist; b. Pratt, Kans., Aug. 14, 1938; s. George and Ruby Ethel (Houser) S.; m. Sally Marie Carney, Aug. 13, 1960; children: Erin Lynne, Jennifer Ashling. BA in Psychology, U. Kans., 1960; DDS, U. Mo., Kansas City, 1965, MS, 1968. Pvt. practice, orthodontist Englewood, Colo., 1968—. Past. trustee U. Mo. at Kansas City Sch. Dentistry. Mem. Am. Assn. Orthodontists, Pierre Fauchard Acad., Am. Dental Assn., Met. Denver Dental Soc. (past bd. dirs.), Arapahoe County Dental Soc. (past pres.), Rocky Mountain Dental Study Club (past pres.), Colo. Orthodontic Assn. (past pres.), U. Mo. at Kansas City Dental Sch. Alumni Assn. (past pres. Colo. chpt.), Phi Gamma Delta, Omicron Delta Kappa, Omicron Kappa Upsilon, Psi Omega Dental. Office: 7200 E Dry Creek Rd Ste A105 Englewood CO 80112-2556

SIMPSON, ROD REX, city planner; b. Ft. Knox, Ky., Jan. 14, 1962; s. Kenny Rex and Phyllis Ann (Kirk) S.; m. Janice Segars, May 19, 1990. BA in Sociology, Calif. State U.-Stanislaus, Turlock, 1985. Social worker Hemodialysis Inc., Glendale/Pasadena, Calif., 1986-88; program mgr. San Joaquin Valley Health Devel. Coun., Modesto, Calif., 1988-89; planning technician City of Patterson, Calif., 1989-90, city planner, 1990-92, planning dir., 1992—; mem., vice chair Downtown Task Force, Turlock, 1992-93; mem. consol. planning com. Stanislaus Area Assn. Govts., 1991—, mem. expressway project com., 1994—. Mem. Am. Planning Assn., Stanislaus Planning Dirs. Assn., Kiwanis Club of Patterson. Home: 882 Whispering Pines Dr Turlock CA 95382-0458 Office: City of Patterson 33 S Del Puerto Ave Patterson CA 95363-2517

SIMPSON, STEVEN QUINTON, physician, researcher; b. Miami, Okla., Aug. 17, 1957; s. Dallas James and Carolyn Sue (Moberly) S.; m. Pamela Janette Nicklaus, May 20, 1989; children: Nathan Edward, Andrew Dallas. BS, Baker U., 1979; MD, U. Kans., 1983. Diplomate Am. Bd. Internal Medicine, Am. Bd. Pulmonary Disease, Am. Bd. Critical Care Medicine; cert. Nat. Inst. Occupational Safety and Health. Intern in internal medicine Kans. U. Med. Ctr., Kansas City, 1983-84, resident in internal medicine, 1984-86; fellow in pulmonary and critical care medicine Rush-Presbyn. St. Luke's Med. Ctr., Chgo., 1986-89, instr. medicine Divsn. Pulmonary and Critical Care Medicine, 1986-89, asst. prof. Divsn. Pulmonary and Critical Care Medicine, 1989-90; asst. prof. Divsn. Pulmonary and Critical Care Medicine U. N.Mex., 1990—; attending physician Rush-Presbyn. St. Luke's Med. Ctr., Chgo., 1989-90, U. N.Mex. Hosp., Albuquerque, 1990—; adj. scientist Inhalation Toxicology Rsch. Inst., Lovelace Biomed. and Environ. Rsch. Inst., Albuquerque, 1991—; consulting physician Miner's Colfax Med. Ctr., Raton, N.Mex., 1990—, dir. Cardiopulmonary Outreach Program and Black Lung Clinic, 1992—; attending physician Albuquerque VA Med. Ctr., 1992—, dir. med. ICU, 1993—; presenter 19th Ann. Am. Thoracic Soc. Lung Disease Symposium, N.Mex., 1991, 94, U. N.Mex., 1993, Soc. of Critical Care Medicine, 1994. Author: (with others) The Physiologic and Pathologic Effects of Cytokines, 1990; contbr. articles to profl. jours. Grantee Chgo. Lung Assn., 1989-91, Am. Lung Assn., 1991-93, Miner's Colfax Med. Ctr., 1992—, N.Mex. Dept. Health, 1993-94. Mem. AAAS, ACP (Cecile Lehman Mayer Rsch. award finalist 1988, 92, Alfred Soffer Rsch. award 1992, DuPont Young Investigator award 1993), Am. Coll. Chest Physicians, Am. Thoracic Soc. (sec.-treas. N.Mex. chpt. 1994-95, pres. 1995—), Am. Fedn. for Clin. Rsch., N.Y. Acad. Scis., Soc. Critical Care Medicine, Blue Key Nat. Honor Soc., Alpha Delta Sigma. Office: U N Mex Dept Med Pulmonary Divsn 2211 Lomas Blvd NE # 5-acc Albuquerque NM 87106-2745

SIMPSON, VELMA SOUTHALL, insurance agent; b. Denver, Jan. 29, 1948; d. Herbert Eugene and Gladys Jane (Pasquale) Southall; m. Stephen Wayne Simpson, Aug. 24, 1968; children: Sarah, Anna, Benjamin. BA, Colo. State U., 1971; postgrad., U. Denver, 1975-76. Agt. Allstate Ins. Co., Longmont, Colo., 1983—. Active St. Vrain Hist. Soc., Longmont, Theatre Co., 1st Congl. Ch.; bd. dirs. Mountain Prairie Girl Scouts U.S.A. Democrat. Home: 13966 N 75th St Longmont CO 80503-9219 Office: Allstate Ins Co 1600 Hover Rd C-1 Longmont CO 80501-2440

SIMPSON, WILLIAM ARTHUR, insurance company executive; b. Oakland, Calif., Feb. 2, 1939; s. Arthur Earl and Pauline (Mikalasic) S.; m. Nancy Ellen Simpson, Mar. 31, 1962; children—Sharon Elizabeth, Shelley Pauline. B.S., U. Calif.-Berkeley, 1961; postgrad. Exec. Mgmt. Program, Columbia U. C.L.U. V.p. mktg. Countrywide Life, L.A., 1973-76; v.p. agy. Occidental Life of Calif., L.A., 1976-79; pres., CEO Vol. State Life, Chattanooga, 1979-83; exec. v.p. Transam. Occidental Life Ins. Co., L.A., 1983-86, pres., 1986-88, pres., CEO, 1988-90, also bd. dirs.; dir. USLIFE Corp., N.Y.C., 1990—; pres., CEO All Am. Life Ins. Co., Pasadena, Calif., 1990-94, USLIFE Life Ins. div. USLIFE Corp., 1994, pres., CEO USLIFE Corp., 1995—, mem. Office of Chmn., 1995—. Pres. Chattanooga coun. Boy Scouts Am., 1982, bd. dirs., L.A., 1983, v.p., 1983-85, vice-chmn L.A. area, 1989, chmn., 1989; pres. bd. councillors L.A. County Am. Cancer Soc.; trustee Verdugo Hills Hosp. Found. 1st lt. U.S. Army, 1961-64. Mem. Am. Soc. CLUs, Life Ins. Mktg. and Rsch. Assn. (bd. dirs. 1986-89). Republican. Presbyterian. Lodge: Rotary. Office: USLIFE Corp 125 Maiden Ln New York NY 10038

SIMPSON, WILLIAM BRAND, economist, educator; b. Portland, Oreg., Nov. 30, 1919; s. John Alexander and Janet Christie (Brand) S.; m. Ruth Laura Decker, June 12, 1957. B.A. in Math., Reed Coll., 1942; M.A. in Stats., Columbia U., 1943; Ph.D. in Econs., Claremont Grad. Sch., 1971. Cons. Nat. Def. Mediation Bd., 1941-42, U.S. Dept. Interior, 1942, U.S. War Dept., Tokyo, 1947; head econ. sect. Counter-Intelligence Office, Manila, 1945; spl. rep. Supreme Commander Allied Powers, Japan, 1945-46; exec. dir. Cowles Commn. Research Econs., U. Chgo., 1948-53; co-founder, bd. dirs. Inst. Social and Personal Rels., Oakland, Calif., 1955-61; prof. econs. Calif. State U., L.A., 1958—; econs. cons. higher edn.; cons. Am. Acad. Asian Studies Grad. Sch., San Francisco, 1956, Japanese Assn. for Rsch. on Forcibly Brought Chinese, 1991—, Japan Pub. TV, 1993; mentor Reed Coll., 1991—, mem. nat. adv. coun., 1994—. Author: Cost Containment for Higher Education, 1991, Special Agent in the Pacific, WWII, 1995, Philosophy of a Concerned Academic, 1995; mng. editor, co-editor Econometrica, 1948-53; editor Managing With Scarce Resources, 1993; contbr. articles to profl. jours. Mem. Philippine arts coun. Pacific-Asia Mus., also mem. Japanese arts coun. Fellow Nat. Social Sci. Rsch. Coun. Mem. ACLU, Econometric Soc. (internat. sec. 1948-52), AAUP (state pres. 1975-76, mem. com. econ. status acad. profession 1976-79, nat. council 1978-81, com. govt. rels. 1982-88, state chmn. com. issues and policy 1981—), Am. Econs. Assn. (chmn. panel polit. discrimination 1978-80), Am. Assn. Higher Edn., Congress Faculty Assns., Soc. Coll. and U. Planning, United Scottish Socs. So. Calif., Sierra Club (L.A. chpt.), Claremont Grad. Sch. Alumni (coun. 1993—), Phi Beta Kappa. Democrat. Home: PO Box 41526 Los Angeles CA 90041-0526 Office: Calif State U Los Angeles CA 90032

SIMS, BERNARD, food products executive; b. 1949. Grad., Gonzage U., 1971. With Virgil Hastings CPA, Moses Lake, Wash., 1971-72, Seattle First Nat. Bank, Seattle, Wash., 1972-73; v.p.-fin., adminstrn. Snokist Growers, Yakima, Wash., 1973—. Office: Snokist Growers 18 W Mead Ave Yakima WA 98902-6026*

SIMS, DARCIE DITTBERNER, grief management specialist, psychotherapist, clinical hypnotherapist; b. Milw., May 20, 1947; d. Van F. and Alicia (Haake) Dittberner; m. Robert A. Sims, Aug. 19, 1970; children: Alicia, Austin (dec.). BA in Journalism, U. N.Mex., 1969, MEd, 1971; MA in Mental Health Counseling, St. Mary's U., San Antonio, 1980; PhD, LaSalle U., 1991. Cert. counselor, N.Mex., Mich., Kans., Mo., La.; nationally cert. grief counselor, clin. hypnotherapist. Adj. prof. death and dying No. Mich. U., Marquette, 1978-79; cons. crisis mgmt. Northside Ind. Sch. Dist., San Antonio, 1981-82; adj. prof. sociology McMurry Coll., Abilene, Tex., 1983; psychotherapist Pastoral Care & Counseling Ctr., Abilene, 1983-84; dir. social svc. Hospice Abilene, 1983-84; counselor, therapist Albuquerque Pub. Sch. System, 1984-85, mental health specialist, 1985-88; dir. prevention program Crittenton Children's Psychotherapy Ctr., Kansas City, Mo., 1988-89; pvt. practice Slidell, La., 1989-91; pvt. practice, trainer N.D., 1991-92; pvt. practice, psychotherapist Albuquerque, 1992-94; hypnotherapist, psychotherapist Wenatchee, Wash., 1994—; v.p. nat. bd. dirs. Compassionate Friends, Inc., Chgo.; dir. Big A and Co. Cons., Albuquerque; bd. v.p. Widowed Person's Svc. D. Dirs., Kansas City; co-chmn., keynote speaker World Gathering on Bereavement, Seattle, 1991; nat. trustee Nat. Cath. Ministries to the Bereaved, 1992—; v.p. EduVisions, Inc.; cons. in field. Author: Why Are the Casseroles Always Tuna?, 1990, Footsteps Through the Valley, 1993, Touchstones, 1993, The Other Side of Grief, 1993, Finding Your Way Through Grief, 1993, If I Could Just See Hope, 1994; author: (with others) Dear Parents; We Need Not Walk Alone, 1990, Young People and Death, 1991; author monthly column Bereavement Mag.: Grief and Humor Dept., 1987—. Troop cons. Girl Scouts Am.; state sec. Associated Care Children's Health, Albuquerque, 1985-87. Named Vol. of Yr. USAF Family Svcs., 1975. Mem. AACD, Am. Mental Health Counselor Assn., Assn. for Death Edn. and Counseling (cert. grief counselor 1983—, bd. dirs. neonatal 1995—), Make Today Count Inc. (cons. 1975—, Nat. Appreciation award 1988). Office: Big A & Company PO Box 4181 Wenatchee WA 98807-4181

SIMS, JACK, marketing professional; b. 1943. Officer, dir. David baker Assoc., London, 1969-76; officer Sims, Freeman, O'Brien Elmsford, Elmsford, N.Y., 1976-92, chmn. bd., 1991—. Office: Alcone Sims O'Brien 15 Whatney Irvine CA 92718-2808*

SIMS, JOHN CARY, law educator; b. Cleve., Feb. 21, 1949; s. Cary William and Mary Jane (Corcoran) S.; m. Nancy Suzanne Drabble, June 12, 1982. AB, Georgetown U., 1971; JD, Harvard U., 1974. Bar: Mass. 1974, D.C. 1975, Calif. 1986. Law clk. to chief judge U.S. Ct. Appeals (1st cir.), Portland, Maine, 1974-75; atty. Pub. Citizen Litigation Group, Washington, 1975-86; assoc. prof. McGeorge Sch. Law U. of Pacific, Sacramento, 1986-89, prof., 1989—. Home: 2716 11th Ave Sacramento CA 95818-4421 Office: U of Pacific McGeorge Law Sch 3200 5th Ave Sacramento CA 95817-2705

SIMS, LINDA GERALDINE, therapist, educator; b. L.A., Dec. 22, 1946; d. Douglas A. and Geraldine E. (Rainwater) Westmoreland; m. David A. Myers, July 30, 1966 (div. Jan. 1973); 1 child, Kenneth David; m. LeBron Sims, Sept. 4, 1976; 1 child, Jennifer Louise. BA in Psychology, San Diego State U., 1977; MEd in Pastoral Counseling, U. Puget Sound, 1987. Clin. intern Christian Counseling Svc., Tacoma, Wash., 1985-87, resident, 1987-88; clin. staff counselor N.W. Pastoral Counseling (formerly Christian Counseling Svc.), Tacoma, Wash., 1988—, dir. adminstrn., 1990—; workshop presenter N.W. Pastoral Counseling, Tacoma, Wash., 1988—; workshop presenter Assoc. Ministries, Tacoma, 1989-94. Mem. Am. Counseling Assn., Internat. Assn. Marriage and Family Counselors, Assn. for Spiritual, Ethical and Religious Values in Counseling, Wash. Counseling Assn., Wash. Mental Health Counselors Assn. Democrat. Presbyterian. Office: NW Pastoral Counseling 3549 Bridgeport Way W Tacoma WA 98466-4429

SIMS, PAUL KIBLER, geologist; b. Newton, Ill., Sept. 8, 1918; s. Dorris Lee and Vere (Kibler) S.; m. Dolores Carsell Thomas, Sept. 15, 1940; children: Thomas Courtney, Charlotte Ann. AB, U. Ill., 1940, MS, 1942; PhD, Princeton, 1950. Spl. asst. geologist Ill. Geol. Survey, 1942-43; geologist U.S. Geol. Survey, 1943-61; prof. geology, dir. Minn. Geol. survey U. Minn., 1961-73; research geologist U.S. Geol. Survey, 1973—; pres. Econ. Geology Pub. Co., 1979—; Bd. dirs. North Star Research and Devel. Inst., Mpls., 1966-73. Co-editor: Geology of Minnesota, 1972, 75th anniversary vo.. Economic Geology, 1981. Adviser Minn. Outdoor Recreation Resources Commn., 1963-67. Served with USNR, 1943-46. Recipient Meritorious Service award U.S. Dept. Interior, 1984; Goldich medal Inst. on Lake Superior Geology, 1985, Disting. Svc. award U.S. Dept. Interior, 1991. Fellow Geol. Soc. Am., Soc. Econ. Geologists (councilor 1965-68, pres. 1975, Ralph W. Marsden award medal 1989); mem. Internat. Assn. on Genesis of Ore Deposits, Internat. Union Geol. Sci. (subcom. Precambrian stratigraphy, sec. 1976-84), Assn. Am. State Geologists (hon.), Colo. Sci. Soc. (hon.). Home: 1315 Overhill Rd Golden CO 80401-4238

SIMS, ROBERT REYNOLD, civil engineer; b. Milw., Aug. 22, 1939; s. Robert Forest and Ada (Pankow) S.; m. Nevette Mary Seaman, June 3, 1967. BSCE, U. Wis., 1963. Registered profl. engr., Calif., Nev., Ariz., Hawaii, Guam. Civil engr. assoc. County of L.A. Pub. Works, 1963-68; project mgr. VTN, Van Nuys, Calif., 1968-72; gen. mgr., exec. v.p. ESCO Internat., Guam, 1973-76; exec. v.p. Engrng. Svc. Corp., Culver City, Calif., 1976-92; pres. Robert R. Sims P.E., Inc., Rolling Hills Estates, Calif., 1991—, Land Design Cons., Inc., Pasadena, Calif., 1992—. Councilman L.A. Citizens Planning Coun., 1985—. Recipient Merit award San Fernando Valley Bay Coun., 1980. Fellow Inst. for Advancement of Engrng.; mem. NSPE, ASCE, Am. Cons. Engrs. Coun., Nat. Acad. Forensic Engrs., Calif. Soc. Profl. Engrs. (chpt. pres., state dir., state treas., Pres.'s award 1991, Outstanding Svc. award 1992), Calif. Soc. Profl. Engrs. Edn. Found. (founding bd. dirs. 1986-92, Outstanding Contbn. to Engrng. in Sci. Cmty. award 1989). Republican. Home: 127 Cottonwood Cir Rolling Hills CA 90274-3430 Office: Land Design Cons Inc Ste 500 201 S Lake Ave Pasadena CA 91101

SIMUNICH, MARY ELIZABETH HEDRICK (MRS. WILLIAM A. SIMUNICH), public relations executive; b. Chgo.; d. Tubman Keene and Mary (McCamish) Hedrick; m. William A. Simunich, Dec. 6, 1941. Student Phoenix Coll., 1967-69, Met. Bus. Coll., 1938-40. Exec. sec. sales mgr. Sta. KPHO radio, 1950-53; exec. sec. mgr. Sta. KPHO-TV, 1953-54; account exec. Tom Rippey & Assos., 1955-56; pub. rels. dir. Phoenix Symphony, 1956-62; co-founder, v.p. Paul J. Hughes Pub. Rels., Inc., 1960-65; owner Mary Simunich Pub. Rels., Phoenix, 1966-77; pub. rels. dir. Walter O. Boswell Meml. Hosp., Sun City, Ariz., 1969-85; pub. rels. cons., 1985—; pres. Darci PR, Phoenix, 1994—, Cityscape, Inc. (formerly Citynet, Inc.), 1994—; instr. pub. rels. Phoenix Coll. Evening Sch., 1973-78. Bd. dirs. Anytown, Ariz., 1969-72; founder, sec. Friends Am. Geriatrics, 1977-86. Named Phoenix Advt. Woman of Year, Phoenix Jr. Advt. Club, 1962; recipient award Blue Cross, 1963; 1st Pl. award Ariz. Press Women, 1966. Mem. NAFE, Women in Comm., Internat. Assn. Bus. Communicators (pres. Ariz. chpt. 1970-71, dir.), Pub. Rels. Soc. Am. (sec., dir. 1976-78), Am. Soc. Hosp. Pub. Rels. (dir. Ariz. chpt. 1976-78), Nat., Ariz. Press Women. Home: 4133 N 34th Pl Phoenix AZ 85018-4771 Office: Darci Group 2425 E Camelback Ste 450 Phoenix AZ 85016-4236

SINCLAIR, SARA VORIS, health facility administrator, nurse; b. Kansas City, Mo., Apr. 13, 1942; d. Franklin Defenbaugh and Inez Estelle (Figenbaum) Voris; m. James W. Sinclair, June 13, 1964; children: Thomas James, Elizabeth Kathleen, Joan Sara. BSN, UCLA, 1965. RN, Utah; lic. health care facility adminstr.; cert. health care adminstr. Staff nurse UCLA Med. Ctr. Hosp., 1964-65; charge nurse Boulder (Colo.) Meml. Hosp., 1966, Boulder (Colo.) Manor Nursing Home, 1974-75, Four Seasons Nursing Home, Joliet, Ill., 1975-76; dir. nursing Home Health Agy of Olympia Fields, Joliet, Ill., 1977-79; dir. nursing Sunshine Terr. Found., Inc., Logan, Utah, 1980, asst. adminstr., 1980-81, adminstr., 1981-93; dir. divsn. health systems improvement Utah Dept. Health, Salt Lake City, 1993—; mem. long term care profl. and tech. adv. com. Joint Commn. on Accreditation Healthcare Orgns., Chgo., 1987-91, chmn., 1990-91; mem. adj. clin. faculty Weber State U., Ogden, Utah; moderator radio program Healthwise, Sta. KUSU-RM, 1985-93; spkr. Nat. Coun. Aging, 1993, Alzheimer's Disease Assn. Ann. Conf., 1993; chmn. dept. Health Ethics Instnl. Rev. Bd., 1995—; rep. Congressman James V. Hansen White House Conf. on Aging, 1995; presenter in field. Contbg. author: Associate Degree Nursing and The Nursing Home, 1988. Mem. dean's adv. coun. Coll. Bus. Utah State U., Logan, 1989-91, mem. presdl. search com., 1991-92; chmn., co-founder Cache Cmty. Health Coun., Logan, 1985; chmn. bd. Hospice of Cache Valley, Logan, 1986; mem. Utah State Adv. Coun. on Aging, 1986—; apptd. chmn. Utah Health Facilities Com., 1989—; mem. Utah Adv. Coun. on Aging, 1987—; chmn. Bear River Dist. Adv. Coun. on Aging, 1989-91; chmn. health and human svcs. subcom. Cache 2010, 1992-93; chair ethics com. Utah Dept. Health, 1995—; rep. White House Conf. on Aging, 1995. Recipient Disting. Svc. award Utah State U., 1989. Fellow Am. Coll. Health Care Adminstrs. (presenter 1992-93, 95, v.p. Utah chpt. 1992-94, convocation and edn. coms. 1992-94, region IX vice gov. 1994—); mem. Am. Healthcare Assn. (non-proprietary v.p. 1986-87, region v.p. 1987-89, presenter workshop conv. 1990-93, presenter ann. convocation 1995, exec. com. 1993—), Am. Coll. Health Care Adminstrs. (vice gov. region 9 1994—), Utah Health Care Assn. (pres. 1983-85, treas. 1991-93, Disting. Svc. award 1991), Utah Gerontol. Soc. (bd. dirs. 1992-93, 95—, chmn. nominating com.

1993-94), Cache C. of C. (pres. 1991), Logal Bus. and Profl. Women's Club (pres. 1989, Woman of Achieve,ent award 1982, Woman of Yr. 1982), Rotary (Logan chpt., chair cmty. svc. com. 1989-90). Office: Utah Dept Health Divsn Health Systems Improvement 288 N 1460 W Salt Lake City UT 84116-3100

SINCLAIR, WILLIAM DONALD, church official, fundraising consultant, political activist; b. L.A., Dec. 27, 1924; s. Arthur Livingston and Lillian May (Holt) S.; m. Barbara Jean Hughes, Aug. 9, 1952; children: Paul Scott, Victoria Sharon. BA cum laude, St. Martin's Coll., Olympia, Wash., 1975; postgrad. Emory U., 1978-79. Commd. 2d lt. USAAF, 1944, advanced through grades to col., USAF, 1970; served as pilot and navigator in Italy, Korea, Vietnam and Japan; ret., 1975; bus. adminstr. First United Methodist Ch., Colorado Springs, Colo., 1976-85; bus. adminstr. Village Seven Presbyn. Ch., 1985-87; bus. adminstr. Sunrise United Meth. Ch., 1987-89; vice-chmn. council fin. and adminstrn. Rocky Mountain conf. United Meth. Ch., U.S.A., 1979-83. Bd. dirs. Chins-Up Colorado Springs, 1983—; chmn. bd. dirs. Pikes Peak Performing Arts Ctr., 1985-92; pres. Pioneers Mus. Found., 1985—; Rep. candidate for Colo. State Chmn., 1992-93. Decorated Legion of Merit with oak leaf cluster, D.F.C., Air medal with 6 oak leaf cluster, Dept. Def. Meritorious Service medal, Vietnam Cross of Gallantry with Palms. Fellow Nat. Assn. Ch. Bus. Adminstrs. (nat. dir., regional v.p., v.p. 1983-85, pres. 1985-87; Ch. Bus. Adminstr. of Yr. award 1983, inducted hall of fame 1995), Colo. Assn. Ch. Bus. Adminstrs. (past pres.), United Meth., Assn. Ch. Bus. Admins. Adminstrs. (nat. sec. 1978-81), Christian Ministries Mgmt. Assn. (dir. 1983-85), USAF Acad. Athletic Assn. Clubs: Colorado Springs Country, Garden of the Gods, Met. (Denver), Winter Night Club. Lodge: Rotary (pres. Downtown Colorado Springs club 1985-86), Order of Daedalians. Home: 3007 Chelton Dr Colorado Springs CO 80909-1008

SINCOFF, STEVEN LAWRENCE, science administrator, scientist; b. N.Y.C., Apr. 17, 1948; s. Murray B. and Lillian (Goldberg) S.; m. Marcella Seay, June 12, 1993; children by previous marriage: Kristina Lynne, Carolyn Suzanne. BSChemE, N.J. Inst. Tech., 1969, MSChemE, 1972; PhD in Analytical Chemistry, Ohio State U., 1980. Commd. 2d lt. USAF, 1969, advanced through grades to lt. col., 1987, retired, 1991; fuels mgmt. officer USAF, Albuquerque and Galena, Alaska, 1970-74; chem. engr. Aero. Systems Div., Wright-Patterson AFB, Ohio, 1974-77; assoc. prof. chemistry USAF Acad., Colorado Springs, Colo., 1980-84, dir. continuing edn. dept. chemistry, 1982-84; chief gas analysis lab. McClellan (AFB) Cen. Lab., Calif., 1984-88; exec. officer to comdr. Tech. Ops. Div. McClellan AFB, Calif., 1988-89, chief info. officer, 1989-91; gen. mgr. ChemWest Analytical Lab., Sacramento, 1991-92; dir. ops. Barringer Labs., Inc., Golden, Colo., 1992-94; instr. chemistry C.C. Aurora, Colo., 1995—; reviewer chemistry textbooks Saunders Pub., Phila., 1983-84. Mem. Am. Chem. Soc., Air Force Assn. Jewish. Home and Office: 9757 W Nova Ave Littleton CO 80127-3932

SINES, RANDY DWAIN, business executive; b. Spokane, Jan. 16, 1948; s. Myron Jones and Paula Inez (Walls) S.; student Wash. State U., 1966-67, U. Wash., 1968-69; m. Irene Cheng, Mar. 18, 1981. With Boeing Co., 1967; with Winchell's Donut House, Inc., Seattle, 1968-71; owner, mgr. bakeries, Wash. and Mont., 1972-78; owner, mgr. Sonsine Inc., Great Falls, Mont., 1976-79; pres. Gardian Port Corp., Oxnard, Calif., 1980-82; pres., chmn. SNS Motor Imports, Inc., Oxnard, 1982-86; chmn. Karakal Corp. of Ams., Ventura, Calif., 1986-89; chief exec. officer, chmn. Steel Stix, U.S.A., 1990—; chmn. Mitt USA Corp., 1991—; mng. ptnr. Sharps Internat., 1993—. Recipient alumni grant Wash. State U., 1967; lic. water well contractor, Wash., Mont. Patentee sports apparatus, over 20 patents worldwide. Home and Office: 4056 S Madelia St Spokane WA 99203-4227

SINGER, ELYSE JOY, physician; b. N.Y.C., June 26, 1952; d. Herman and Charlotte (Grossman) S.; m. Bradley A. Manning, Sept. 17, 1989. BA, SUNY, Buffalo, 1973; MD, U. South Ala., 1978. Diplomate Am. Bd. Psychiatry and Neurology. Intern in internal medicine West LA VA Med. Ctr., 1979, resident in adult neurology, 1979-82; fellow UCLA Pain Mgmt. Ctr., 1982-84; med. staff fellow NIH, Bethesda, Md., 1984-86; rsch. physician West L.A. VA Med. Ctr., 1987—; asst. prof. UCLA Sch. Med., 1987—; assoc. prof. Sch. Medicine, UCLA, 1994; neurology co-investigator L.A. Men Study, 1991—; neurologist UCLA AIDS Clin. Trials Group, 1987—. Mem. Internat. Assn. for the Study Pain, Am. Pain Soc., Am. Acad. Neurology. Office: West LA VA Medical Ctr Dept Neurology W127 Wilshire & Sawtelle Blvds Los Angeles CA 90073

SINGER, FRANK J., insurance company executive, lawyer; b. N.Y.C., Mar. 12, 1944; s. Frank James and Margaretta (Barnes) S.; m. Christine Heins, Feb. 14, 1987; children: Frank, Blake, Cole, Deborah, Victoria. BS, Calif. Western U., 1983, MBA, 1987; JD, La Salle U., 1994. Cert. ins. counselor. Sales mgr. Liberty Mut. Ins. Co., Boston, 1963-74; v.p. Sentry Ins., Stevens Point, Wis., 1974-87; pres., CFO Comml. Acceptance Ins. Co., Sacramento, 1987—; chmn., CFO, Artisan Contractors Assn. Am., Sacramento, 1989—. With U.S. Army, 1962-65. Mem. Mensa. Republican. Office: Comml Acceptance Ins Co 2150 Professional Dr Ste 170 Roseville CA 95661-3732

SINGER, JANICE GAIL, psychotherapist, consultant; b. Chgo., Aug. 14, 1947; d. Harold and Dorothy (Kagen) S.; 1 child, Rachael Jacqueline. BA, U. Toledo, 1969; MSW, U. Wis., Milw., 1977; postgrad., Gestalt Inst., Cleve., 1982, Dreikers Relationship Ctr., Boulder, Colo., 1985; Reiki II, Nancy Retzlaff R.M., Milw., 1986. Program evaluator, project cons. Mental health Planning Council of Milw., 1976-78; counselor abortion WomanCare-West, Milw., 1978; treatment foster care worker Children's Service Soc. of Wis., Milw., 1978-81; mental health coordinator, primary psychotherapist Bread and Roses Women's Health Ctr., Inc., Milw., 1981-84; originator Friends' Psychotherapy Collective, Milw., 1984—; Santa Barbara Counseling Ctr., Calif., 1992-93, Family Therapy Inst., Santa Barbara, 1992—; radio talk show host Santa Barbara, 1994—; group facilitator for vols. Santa Barbara AIDS/CAP Retreat, 1991—; trainer Family Harmony Inst., Ojai, Calif., 1991; workshop presenter U. Calif. Santa Barbara Women's Ctr. Women's Spirituality Seminars, 1992; facilitator People to People, Waukesha, Wis., 1976-80; mem. coalition sexual misconduct by psychotherapists, Wis., 1984-86, 88-91; cons. Women to Women, Inc., Milw., 1981-92. Author: Women's Spirituality: Goddess & Native American Rituals & Traditions, 1992, Victim to Victim: Women Recovering from Childhood Sexual Abuse, 1992; co-author: (consumer guide) Making Therapy Work for You, 1986, revised, 1991; creator therapy mode Action Oriented Therapy, 1983; co-creator: (workshops) Living Your Goodness Enhancing Self-Esteem Thru Action, 1988, Living in Balance-Integrating Male & Female Energy, 1987, Grieving: The Benefits of Being a Cry Bavy, 1988, Seeking the Spirit-A Shamanic Tradition, 1989, Working With Abusive, Noncompliant, Obnoxious Patients, What Your Body's Saying Whether Your Lips are Moving or Not, 1989, Co-dependency: When Your Drug of Choice is Anyone But You, 1989, Discovering Your E/Sensual Body-Being Sensual is Essential to Life, 1989, Celebration in Living!, 1984, Living Beyond AIDS, 1987, Transforming Body Image, 1987, Finding Peace in Your Body, others. Co-creator, co-facilitator Santa Barbara Hearts, Hands, and Voices Metaphysical Healing Group for HIV Affected Persons, 1991-92; bd. dirs. Santa Barbara Rape Crisis Ctr., 1991—; chair health com. Santa Barbara Women's Polit. Com., 1991—; workshop leader Milw. AIDS Project, 1987; co-creator workshops Celebration in Living, 1984, Living Beyond AIDS, 1987, Transforming Body Image, 1987; active Maple Dale Sch. Human Sexuality, Milw., 1983-86; curriculum com. Nicolet High Sch. Human Sexuality, 1987. Mem. Feminist Therapy Network (pres. 1984-87), Nat. Assn. Social Workers, Assn. for Human Animal Bonding, Wis. Assn. Outpatient Mental Health Facilities (mem. ethics com. 1981-86). Democrat. Home and Office: 638 Calle De Los Amigos Santa Barbara CA 93105-4455

SINGER, JEFFREY ALAN, surgeon; b. Bklyn., Feb. 2, 1952; s. Harold and Hilda (Ginsburg) S.; m. Margaret Sue Gordon, May 23, 1976; children: Deborah Suzanne, Pamela Michelle. BA cum laude, Bklyn. Coll., 1973; MD, N.Y. Med. Coll., 1976. Diplomate Am. Bd. Surgery. Intern Maricopa County Gen. Hosp., Phoenix, 1976-77, resident, 1977-81, mem. teaching faculty, 1981—; trauma cons. John C. Lincoln Hosp., Phoenix, 1981-83; pvt. practice Phoenix, 1981-87; group pvt. practice Valley Surg. Clinics, Ltd., Phoenix, 1987—; sec.-treas med. staff Humana Desert Valley Hosp., Phoenix, 1987-89, chief surgery, 1985-87, 91-93, exec. com., 1993—. Assoc. editor Ariz. Medicine. Rep. precinct committeeman, Phoenix, 1986—. Fellow ACS, Internat. Coll. Surgeons, Southwestern Surg. Congress, Am. Soc. Abdominal Surgeons; mem. AMA, Ariz. Med. Assn. (bd. dirs. polit. com. 1985, chmn. bd. dirs. polit. com. 1991-93, legis. com. 1986—), Alpha Omega Alpha. Office: Valley Surg Clinics Ltd 16601 N 40th St Ste 105 Phoenix AZ 85032-3353

SINGER, KURT DEUTSCH, news commentator, author, publisher; b. Vienna, Austria, Aug. 10, 1911; came to U.S., 1940, naturalized, 1951; s. Ignaz Deutsch and Irene (Singer) S.; m. Hilda Tradelius, Dec. 23, 1932 (div. 1954); children: Marian Alice Birgit, Kenneth Walt; m. Jane Sherrod, Apr. 9, 1955 (dec. Jan. 1985); m. Katherine Han, Apr. 8, 1989. Student, U. Zürich, Switzerland, 1930, Labor Coll., Stockholm, Sweden, 1936; Ph.D., Div. Coll. Metaphysics, Indpls., 1951. Escaped to Sweden, 1934; founder Ossietzky Com. (successful in release Ossietzky from concentration camp); corr. Swedish mag. Folket i Bild, 1935-40; founder Niemöller Com.; pub. biography Göring in Eng. (confiscated in Sweden), 1940; co-founder pro-Allied newspaper Trots Allt, 1939; corr. Swedish newspapers in, U.S., 1940; editor News Background, 1942; lectr. U. Minn., U. Kans., U. Wis., 1945-49; radio commentator WKAT, 1950; corr. N.Am. Newspaper Alliance, N.Y.C., 1953—; pres. Singer Media Corp., 1987—; dir. Oceanic Press Service, San Clemente, Calif. Author, editor: underground weekly Mitteilungsblätter, Berlin, Germany, 1933; author: The Coming War, 1934, (biog.) Carl von Ossietzky, 1936 (Nobel Peace prize), Germany's Secret Service in Central America, 1943, Spies and Saboteurs in Argentina, 1943, Duel for the Northland, 1943, White Book of the Church of Norway, 1944, Spies and Traitors of World War II, 1945, Who are the Communists in America, 1948, 3000 Years of Espionage, 1951, World's Greatest Women Spies, 1952, Kippie the Cow; juvenile, 1952, Gentlemen Spies, 1953, The Man in the Trojan Horse, 1954, World's Best Spy Stories, 1954, Charles Laughton Story; adapted TV, motion pictures, 1954, Spy Stories and Asia, 1955, More Spy Stories, 1955, My Greatest Crime Story, 1956, My Most Famous Case, 1957, The Danny Kaye Saga; My Strangest Case, 1958, Spy Omnibus, 1959, Spies for Democracy, 1960, Crime Omnibus Spies Who Changed History, 1961, Hemmingway-Life and Death of a Giant, 1961, True Adventures in Crime, Dr. Albert Schweitzer, Medical Missionary, 1962, Lyndon Baines Johnson-Man of Reason, 1964, Ho-i-man; juveniles, 1965; Kurt Singer's Ghost Omnibus, 1965; juvenile Kurt Singer's Horror Omnibus; The World's Greatest Stories of the Occult, The Unearthly, 1965, Mata Hari-Goddess of Sin, 1965, Lyndon Johnson-From Kennedy to Vietnam, 1966, Weird Tales Anthology, 1966, I Can't Sleep at Night, 1966, Weird Tales of Supernatural, 1967, Tales of Terror, 1967, Famous Short Stories, 1967, Folktales of the South Pacific, 1967, Tales of The Uncanny, 1968, Gothic Reader, 1968, Bloch and Bradbury, 1969, Folktales of Mexico, 1969, Tales of the Unknown, 1970, The House in the Valley, 1970, Hablan Los Artistas, 1970, Tales of the Macabre, 1971, Three Thousand Years of Espionage, 1971, El Mundo de Hoy, 1971, Cuentos Fantasticos del Mas, 1971, Aldous Huxley, El Camino al Infierno, 1971, Ghouls and Ghosts, 1972, The Unearthly, 1972, The Gothic Reader, 1972, Satanic Omnibus, 1973, The Plague of the Living Dead, 1973, Gothic Horror Omnibus, 1974, Dictionary of Household Hints and Help, 1974, Supernatural, 1974, They are Possessed, 1976, True Adventures into the Unknown, 1980, I Spied-And Survived, 1980, Great Adventures in Crime, 1982, The Oblong Box, 1982, Shriek, 1984, First Target Book of Horror, 1984, 2d, 1984, 3d, 1985, 4th, 1985, Solve A Crime, 1994, The Ultimate Quiz Book, 1994, The Complete Guide to Career Advancement, 1994, The Sex Quiz Book, 1994, The Marriage Quiz Book, The Psychology Quiz Book, The Teenage Quiz Book, Success Secrets, 1995; editor: UN Calendar, 1959-58; contbr. articles to newspapers, popular mags., U.S., fgn. countries, all his books and papers in Boston U. Library-Spl. Collections. Mem. UN Speakers Research Com., UN Children's Emergency Fund, Menninger Found. Mem. Nat. Geog. Soc., Smithsonian Assos., Internat. Platform Assn. (v.p.), United Sch. Assemblies (pres.). Address: Singer Media Corp Seaview Business Pk 1030 Calle Cordillera # 106 San Clemente CA 92673-6234

SINGER, MICHAEL HOWARD, lawyer; b. N.Y.C., Nov. 22, 1941; s. Jack and Etta (Appelbaum) S.; m. Saundra Jean Kupperman, June 1, 1962; children: Allison Jill, Pamela Faith. BS in Econs., U. Pa., 1962; JD, NYU, 1965, LLM in Taxation, 1968. Bar: N.Y. 1965, U.S. Ct. Claims 1968, U.S. Supreme Ct. 1969, U.S. Ct. Appeals (6th cir.) 1970, D.C. 1972, U.S. Tax Ct. 1972, Nev. 1973, U.S. Ct. Appeals (9th cir.) 1973. Law asst. Appellate Term Supreme Ct., N.Y.C., 1965-68; trial lawyer Ct. Claims Tax Div., Washington, 1968-72; tax lawyer Beckley, DeLanoy & Jemison, Las Vegas, 1972-74; ptnr. Oshins, Singer, Segal & Morris, Las Vegas, 1974-87; pvt. practice law Las Vegas, 1987; ptnr. Michael H. Singer Ltd., Las Vegas, 1987—. Pres. Las Vegas chpt. NCCJ, 1980-82. Mem. ABA, ABI, Nev. Bar Assn., Las Vegas Country Club. Democrat. Jewish. Home: 4458 Los Reyes Ct Las Vegas NV 89121-5341 Office: Michael H Singer Ltd 520 S 4th St Fl 2 Las Vegas NV 89101-6524

SINGER, RICHARD LOUIS, chamber of commerce executive; b. Chgo., Feb. 21, 1943; s. Bernard Edward and Lillian (Glassner) S.; m. Sandra Lee Skaug, Dec. 8, 1963 (div. Apr. 1981); children: Cathy Jo, David Jeremy; m. Janet Susan Pack, Aug. 19, 1982. AA, L.A. City Coll., 1963; BA, Stanford U., 1965; MA, Harvard U., 1967. Mng. editor The Daily News, Whittier, Calif., 1969-80; divsn. editor Highlander Publs., Walnut, Calif., 1980-82; editor, assoc. publ. Star News, Pasadena, Calif., 1982-87; editor, publ. This Week, Whittier, Calif., 1988-90; exec. v.p. Monrovia (Calif.) C. of C., 1990—. Author: Americans by Destiny, 1974, City Lites, 1980 (Pulitzer prize 1981), Biography of John Kruissink, 1987 (Peabody award 1987).

SINGER, ROBERT, plastic surgeon; b. Buffalo, Oct. 22, 1942; s. Murray and Fay Singer; m. Judith Harris. Student, SUNY, Buffalo, 1960-63; MD, SUNY, 1967. Lic. physician, Calif.; diplomate Am. Bd. Plastic and Reconstructive Surgery. Resident in gen. surgery Stanford Med. Ctr., Palo Alto, Calif., 1967-69, Santa Barbara Cottage and Gen. Hosp., 1972-74; resident in plastic surgery Vanderbilt U., 1974-76; pvt. practice specializing in emergency and trauma San Diego, 1971-72; pvt. practice plastic, reconstructive and aesthetic surgery La Jolla, Calif., 1976—; prior asst. clin. prof. plastic surgery U. Calif., San Diego; sr. staff, chief plastic surgery Scripps Meml. Hosp., La Jolla, 1980-86, vice chmn. dept. surgery, 1989-91. Contbr. articles to profl. jours. Active San Diego Opera, San Diego Mus. of Man, La Jolla Playhouse, Voices for Children, San Diego Zoo, Mus. Photog. Arts, KPBS, others; mem. exec. com. Anti-Defamation League. Fellow ACS; mem. AMA, Calif. Med. Assn., San Diego County Med. Soc., San Diego Internat. Soc. Plastic Surgeons (pres. 1988-89), Calif. Soc. Plastic Surgeons (pres. 1995), Am. Soc. Aesthetic Plastic Surgeons (pres. 1994-95), Internat. Soc. Clin. Plastic Surgeons, Am. Soc. Plastic and Reconstructive Surgeons, J.B. Lynch Soc., Royal Soc. Medicine, Am. Assn. for Accreditation of Ambulatory Surgery Facilities (v.p. 1994), San Diego Plastic Surgery Soc. (pres. 1989-90). Jewish. Office: 9834 Genesee Ave Ste 100 La Jolla CA 92037-1214

SINGH, ANITA, statistician; b. Delhi, India, Apr. 28, 1952; came to U.S., 1973; d. Mohan Lal and Magan Devi Jain; m. Ashok Kumar Singh, Mar. 30, 1978; children: Aditi, Arjun. MS in Math. Stats., Delhi U., 1973; MS in Stats., Purdue U., 1976, PhD in Stats., 1978. Statistician Wyman Gordon Co., Worcester, Mass., 1978-80; from asst. to assoc. prof. N.Mex. Inst. Mining and Tech., Socorro, 1980-85; staff statistician Lockheed, Las Vegas, Nev., 1990—. Contbr. articles to profl. jours. Mem. Am. Statis. Assn., Indian Statis. Assn., Internat. Environmetrics Soc., Internat. Chemometrics Soc. (N.Am. chpt.), Caucus for Women in Statistics. Hindu. Home: 413 Pyramid St Henderson NV 89014-4020 Office: Lockheed 980 Kelly Johnson Dr Las Vegas NV 89119-3716

SINGH, MAHENDRA PRATAP, manufacturing executive; b. Allahabad, India, Aug. 23, 1950; came to U.S. 1971; s. Rajendra Prasad and Shanti Singh; m. Usha Rani Singh, July 16, 1977; children: Niharika, Namita, Deepti. BS, Indian Inst. Tech., Kanpur, 1971; MS, Case Western Res. U., 1974; MBA, U. Ill., 1976. Registered profl. engr., Wis. Research asst. Case Western Res. U., Cleve., 1971-73; rsch. asst. dept. econs., survey rsch. lab. U. Ill.-Champaign, 1974-75; mgr. application engring. AFL Industries, West Chicago, Ill., 1976-79; product mgr. Dana Corp., Elgin, Ill., 1979-80; product mgr. Reliance Electric Co., Greenville, S.C., 1980-88, gen. mgr., Seattle, 1988—. Tech. reviewer Am. Soc. Heating, Refrigerating and Air-Conditioning Engrs. Jour.; contbr. numerous articles to profl. lit.; patentee control for variable speed drives. NASA rsch. grantee, 1972-73; EPA rsch. grantee, 1974. Mem. ASHRAE, Am. Mktg. Assn., Toastmasters (past pres.). Home: 7809 SE 75th Pl Mercer Island WA 98040-5501 Office: Reliance Electric Co PO Box 81085 Seattle WA 98108-1085

SINGH, RAJESH KUMAR, psychiatrist; b. 1948. MD, U. Santo Tomas, Manila, The Philippines. Diplomate Am. Bd. Psychiatry. Now with Las Encinas Hosp., Pasadena, Calif. Mem. APA, Soc. Calif. Psychiat. Assn. Office: 977 Holly Vista Dr Pasadena CA 91105-1221

SINGH, RAKESH, computer engineer. B in Tech. in Elec. Engring., Inst. Tech., India, 1988; MS in Computer Engring., U. Calif., Santa Barbara, 1990; postgrad., U. Calif., Berkeley, 1993—. Software cons. Citicorp Overseas Software Ltd., Bombay, India, 1988; software devel. engr. Sunsoft, Mountain View, Calif., 1990-91; database performance engr. Sun Microsystems Comp. Corp., Mountain View, Calif., 1991—; cons. engr. Migration Software Systems, Ltd., San Jose, Calif. Chancellors fellow U. Calif., Irvine. Mem. Assn. for Computing Machinery.

SINGH, TARA, research chemist; b. Kotdata, Punjab, India, June 11, 1921; came to U.S., 1966; naturalized, 1972; s. Nand and Isar (Kaur) Singh; m. Rani Surinder, Dec. 29, 1954; children: Nina, Roopinder, Sylvia, Sonya. BS with honors, Punjab U., 1944, MS with 1st class honors, 1946; AM, Harvard U., 1949, PhD, 1950. Post doctorate fellow with Prof. R.B. Woodward Harvard U., 1950-51; Post doctorate fellow NRC, Can., 1953-54; prof. chemistry govt. colls., Punjab, India, 1954-58; prin. govt. colls., India, 1958-64; rsch. and devel. chemist PEBOC Ltd., Northolt, Eng., 1964-65, Unilever Rsch. Lab., Isleworth, Eng., 1965-66, Aldrich Chem.Co., Milw., 1966-76, Polyscis., Inc., Warrington, Pa., 1976-88, Calbiochem, La Jolla, Calif., 1989—. Author many books; contbr. numerous articles to profl. jours. Mem. Am. Chem. Soc. Home: 4202 Appleton St San Diego CA 92117-1901

SINGLETON, ALBERT OLIN, III, physician; b. Galesburg, Ill., Feb. 16, 1946; s. Albert Olin Jr. and Eliz Joan (Anderson) S.; m. Ann Terrell, Mar. 30, 1975; children: Terrell Albert Olin IV, Caroline, Sidney Elizabeth. BA in English, U. Tex., 1969; MD, U. Tex., Galveston, 1973. bd. cert. Gen. Psychiatry, 1981, Geriatric Psychiatry, 1994. Gen. psychiatry intern, resident U. Tex. Med. Branch, 1973-76, child and adolescent psychiatry fellow, 1976-78; instr. U. Tex. Med. Br., Galveston, 1978—, Colo. Health Sci. Ctr., Denver, 1993—; pres. Titus Harris Clinic, Galveston, 1982-93; asst. chief psychiatry, asst. chief med. staff Colo. Mental Health Inst., Pueblo, 1994-95, chief med. staff, chief psychiatry, 1995—; bd. dirs. Gulf Health Network, Galveston, 1991-93. Chmn. bd. Ctr. for Transp. and Commerce, Galveston, 1990-92; S.W. region dir. AAPRCO, Washington, 1992—. Mem. Galveston County Med. Soc. (pres. 1993). Episcopalian. Office: 2989 Broadmoor Valley Rd Colorado Springs CO 80906-4467

SINGLETON, FRANCIS SETH, dean; b. Phila., July 13, 1940; s. William Francis and Anna A. (Setian) S.; m. Margaret Neff, June 14, 1962 (div. 1983); children: William, Andrew; m. Charlotte T. Kennedy, Jan. 16, 1988. AB, Harvard U., 1962; MA, Yale U., 1963, PhD, 1968. Budget examiner Bur. of Budget, Washington, 1964-65; dean Pearson Coll. Yale U., New Haven, 1966-69; lectr. U. Dares Salaam, Tanzania, 1969-70; asst. prof. U. Alta., Edmonton, Can., 1970-71; from assoc. prof. to prof., chair politics and govt. Ripon (Wis.) Coll., 1972-83; rsch. assoc. Russian Ctr., Harvard U., Cambridge, Mass., 1983-84; dean arts and scis. Pacific U., Forest Grove, Oreg., 1984-91, prof. govt., 1991—; academic dean Espiritu Santo U., Guayaquil, Ecuador, 1994—; ampart lectr. U.S.I.A., Africa, 1983, 90; bd. dirs. Oreg. Internat. Coun., Salem, 1986—; lectr. Ural U., Russia, 1991; cons. Russia Fedn. Govt., 1992. Author: Africa in Perspective, 1968; contbr. articles to profl. publs., chpts. to books. Bd. dirs. Com. Fgn. Rels., Portland, 1989—; mem. adv. com. Light Rail Tri-Met, Portland, Oreg., 1989—. Grantee Rockefeller Found., 1969-70, Nat. Coun. Soviet and E. Europe Rsch., 1983-84. Home: 2580 SW 3rd St # A Corvallis OR 97333-1636 Office: Pacific U 2043 College Way Forest Grove OR 97116-1756

SINGLETON, HAROLD CRAIG, music educator; b. Decatur, Ala., Sept. 5, 1950; s. Harold Millard and Evelyn Marion (Lumpkin) S.; m. Margaret Elizabeth Stephenson, Feb. 22, 1974; children: Stephen Mark, William Craig. BA, Samford U., 1973; M in Ch. Music, So. Bapt. Sem., Louisville, 1976, D in Musical Arts, 1980; M in Music Edn., Holy Names Coll., 1990. Prof. ch. music Golden Gate Bapt. Sem., Mill Valley, Calif., 1980—; min. music Tiburon Bapt. Ch., Calif., 1985—; condr. Golden Gate Choral Soc., Mill Valley, 1987—. Mem. Nat. Assn. Tchrs. Singing, Hymn Soc. Am., Am. Choral Dirs. Assn., Orgn. Am. Kodály Educators, So. Bapt. Ch. Music Conf. (v.p. 1984—). Democrat. Office: Golden Gate Sem 201 Seminary Dr Mill Valley CA 94941-3197

SINGLETON, HENRY EARL, industrialist; b. Haslet, Tex., Nov. 27, 1916; s. John Bartholomew and Victoria (Flores) S.; m. Caroline A. Wood, Nov. 30, 1942; children: Christina, John, William, James, Diana. S.B., S.M., Mass. Inst. Tech., 1940, Sc.D., 1950. V.p. Litton Industries, Inc., Beverly Hills, Calif., 1954-60; CEO Teledyne Inc., Los Angeles, 1960-86; chmn. Teledyne Inc., 1960-91, Singleton Group, Beverly Hills, Calif., 1988—; chmn. exec. com. Teledyne, Inc., L.A., 1991—. Home: RR 3 Box 32 Santa Fe NM 87505-9802 Office: 335 N Maple Dr Ste 177 Beverly Hills CA 90210-3858*

SINGLETON, JAMES KEITH, federal judge; b. Oakland, Calif., Jan. 27, 1939; s. James K. and Irene Elisabeth (Lilly) S.; m. Sandra Claire Hoskins, Oct. 15, 1966; children: Matthew David, Michael Keith. Student, U. Santa Clara, 1957-58; AB in Polit. Sci., U. Calif., Berkeley, 1961, LLB, 1964. Bar: Calif. 1965, Alaska, 1965. Assoc. Delaney Wiles Moore and Hayes, Anchorage, 1963, 65-68, Law Offices Roger Cremo, Anchorage, 1968-70; judge Alaska Superior Ct., Anchorage, 1970-80, Alaska Ct. Appeals, Anchorage, 1980-90, U.S. Dist. Ct. for Alaska, Anchorage, 1990—; chmn. Alaska Local Boundary Commn., Anchorage, 1966-69. Chmn. 3d Dist. Rep. Com., Anchorage, 1969-70. Mem. ABA, Alaska Bar Assn., Phi Delta Phi, Tau Kappa Epsilon. Office: US Dist Ct 222 W 7th Ave Unit 41 Anchorage AK 99513-7504*

SINHA, ALOK KUMAR, software design engineer; b. Hazaribagh, Bihar, India, Apr. 7, 1963; came to U.S., 1985; s. Ajit Kumar and Chinmoyee (Ghosh) S. B in Tech., Banaras Hindu U., 1984; MS in Mining Engring., U. Alaska, 1987, MS in Computer Sci., 1989. Systems engr. Computer Maintenance Corp., Calcutta, India, 1984-85; VAX systems adminstr. U. Alaska, Fairbanks, 1988-89; product support engr. Microsoft Corp., Redmond, Wash., 1989-90; software design engr. Microsoft Corp., Redmond, 1990—; X.500/Distributed File sys. test team lead Microsfot, Redmond, 1990—; sys. engr. Directory Svc. in Windows NT, 1993-94; engr. interactive TV software. Contbr. articles to profl. jours. Vol. Wash. Spl. Summer Olympics for Disabled Athletes, Wash., 1990—. Mem. Assn. for Computing Machinery (spl. invest group on computer comm.), Phi Kappa Phi. Office: Microsoft One Microsoft Pl Redmond WA 98053

SINISHTA, GJON, pastoral associate; b. Podgorica, Montenegro, Apr. 8, 1930; came to U.S., 1965; s. Prenk and Viktoria (Gjokaj) S.; m. Maria Theresa Amaya, Jan. 3, 1968; 1 child, Michael John. Degree in radio broadcasting-journalism, Journalist Broadcasting Sch., Belgrade, Yugoslavia, 1947; student, Colombiere Coll., Clarkston, Mich., 1966-67, John Carroll U., 1967-68, U. Santa Clara, 1973-74. Broadcaster, translator, writer Yugoslav Broadcasting Inst., Belgrade, 1947-56; imprisoned for anti-communist propaganda, 1956-61; acct. Zagreb (Croatia) Textile Co., 1961-63; escaped from Yugoslavia, in refugee camps in Italy, 1963-64; assembler Ford Motor Co., Wixom, Mich., 1965-66; pressman GM, Cleve., 1967-68; asst. food mgr. U. Santa Clara, Calif., 1968-71, dir. Mission Ch., 1971-77; pastoral assoc. St. Ignatius Ch., U. San Francisco, 1977-95; exec. sec. Albanian Cath. Inst. Univ. San Francisco, 1970-93; editor Albanian Cath. Bull., San Francisco, 1980-95. Author: The Fulfilled Promise: A Documentary Account on Religious Persecution in Albania, 1976; co-author: (booklet) Sacrifice for Albania, 1966, Mediterranean Europe Phrasebook, 1992; tranlator: Banishing God in Albania, 1988. Lt. Yugoslav Army, 1951-52. Recipient Naim Frasheri medal Pres. Sali Berisha of Albania, 1994. Mem. Amnesty Internat. Democrat. Roman Catholic. *Died May 8, 1995.*

SINNETTE, JOHN TOWNSEND, JR., research scientist, consultant; b. Rome, Ga., Nov. 4, 1909; s. John T. Sinnette and Katherine Alice Lyon. BS, Calif. Inst. Tech., 1931, MS, 1933. Chemist Met. Water Dist., Banning, Calif., 1937-39, Boulder City, Nev., 1939-40; physicist U.S. Bur. Reclamation, Boulder City, 1940-41; rsch. scientist Nat. Adv. Com. for Aeronautics, Langley Field, Va., 1941-43, Cleve., 1943-51; cons. physicist U.S. Naval Ordnance Test Sta., Pasadena, Calif., 1951-58, Cleve. Pneumatic Industries, El Segundo, Calif., 1958-60; tech. dir. Hydrosystems Co., El Segundo, 1960-62; physicist Thrust Systems Corp., Costa Mesa, Calif., 1963-64; lectr. compressor design Case Inst. Tech., 1946-48; cons. many firms in aeronautical and related industries, 1950-79. Contbr. papers to sci. meetings and confs. Vol. Am. Cancer Soc., Costa Mesa, Calif., 1976-80, Cancer Control Soc., 1979-82; contbr. Action on Smoking and Health, Washington, 1985-95. Mem. AAAS, Am. Statistical Assn., Am. Math Soc., Nat. Health Fed. Democrat. Home: 135 N B St Tustin CA 92680-3110

SINNEX, CEIL, nonprofit foundation founder, newsletter publisher; b. Washington, Dec. 31, 1944; d. John Robertson and Mary Elizabeth (Titsworth) Deatherage; m. W. John McCormick, Feb. 16, 1985. BA, U. Tenn., 1966. Reporter local weekly papers, Washington, 1967, Houston Post, 1968-70; Washington correspondent small news burs., Washington, 1970-75; staff writer AP, Honolulu, 1975-76; pub. info. specialist East-West Ctr., Honolulu, 1978-82; prin. Ceil Sinnex Comm., Paauilo, Hawaii, 1983—; founder, exec. dir. Ovarian Cancer Prevention and Early Detection Found., Paauilo, Hawaii, 1991; speaker to various orgns. on ovarian cancer, 1991—. Editor: (newsletter) Ovarian Plus, 1995—; commr. (TV pub. svc. announcement) Silent Killer, 1992 (Telly award 1993); contbr. articles to publs. Bd. dirs. Friends of the Waikiki Aquarium, Honolulu, 1980-90, Honolulu unit, Am. Cancer Soc., 1984-89. Recipient Outstanding Svc. cert. Montgomery County (Md.) Commn. on Status of Women, 1975, Jonquils award for efforts in the Fight Against Cancer, Duke U. Comprehensive Cancer Ctr., Durham, N.C., 1994.

SINOTO, YOSIHIKO H., archaeologist, educator; b. Tokyo, Sept. 3, 1924; came to U.S., 1954; s. Yosito and Yosie (Yanagimoto) S.; m. Kazuko Sato, Apr. 24, 1949; 1 child, Akihiko. BA in Anthropology, U. Hawaii, 1958; DSc, U. Hokkaido, Sapporo, Japan, 1962. Archaeologist Archaeol. Inst. Japan, Chiba Prefecture, 1949-54; fellow in anthropology Bishop Mus., Honolulu, 1958-61, anthropologist, 1962-89, chmn. dept. anthropology, 1970-89, sr. anthropologist, Kenneth Pike Emory disting. chair, 1990—; affiliate faculty Grad. Sch. U. Hawaii, Honolulu, 1962—; cons. Marshall Islands Historic Places Rev. Bd., 1986-94; mem. Hawaii Historic Places Rev. Bd., 1986—; assoc. Micronesia Area Rsch. Ctr., U. Guam, 1988—. Grantee Nat. Geographic Soc., 1973, 74, 79, Ter. Govt. French Polynesia, 1982, 84, 86, numerous others; recipient Imperial award of Japan Order of the Rising Sun, Gold and Silver Rays, 1995. Mem. Japanese Archaeol. Assn., Polynesian Soc., Soc. Am. Archaeology, Indo-Pacific Prehistory Assn., Soc. Oceanists. Office: Dept Anthropology Bishop Mus PO Box 19000A Honolulu HI 96817-0916

SINTON, PETER, newspaper editor, journalist. Bus./fin. editor The San Francisco Chronicle, sr. bus. writer, 1995—. Office: Chronicle Pub Co 901 Mission St San Francisco CA 94103-2905

SINTON, WILLIAM MERZ, astronomer, educator; b. Balt., Apr. 11, 1925; s. Robert Nelson and Alma Merz (Summers) S.; m. Marjorie Anne Korner, June 4, 1960; children: Robert William, David Theodore, Alan Nelson. AB, Johns Hopkins U., 1949, PhD, 1953. Rsch. assoc. Johns Hopkins U., Balt., 1953-54; rsch. assoc., lectr. Harvard U., Cambridge, Mass., 1954-57; astronomer Lowell Obs., Flagstaff, Ariz., 1957-66; prof. physics and astronomy U. Hawaii, Honolulu, 1966-90; ret., 1990; adj. astronomer Lowell Obs., Flagstaff, Ariz., 1989—. Co-author: Tools of the Astronomer, 1961; contbr. articles to sci. jours. Sgt. U.S. Army, 1943-46, ETO. Fellow Optical Soc. Am. (Adolph Lomb medal 1954); mem. Am. Astron. Soc. (committeeman div. planetary sci. 1971-73), Am. Geophys. Union. Home: 850 E David Dr Flagstaff AZ 86001-4731

SIRI, JEAN BRANDENBURG, citizen advocate; b. Lakota, N.D., Mar. 11, 1920; d. Tunis Orville and Edith Marion (Molloy) Brandenburg; m. William E. Siri, Dec. 3, 1947; children—Lynn, Ann. B.S., Jamestown Coll., 1942; postgrad., U. Calif.-Berkeley, 1945-46, U. Calif., San Francisco, 1944. Biologist, Donner Lab., U. Calif., Berkeley, 1945-52. mem. State Solid Waste & Resource Recovery Adv. Coun., Sacramento, 1973-75; dir., chmn. Stege Sanitary Dist., El Cerrito, Calif., 1975-79; elected bd. dirs. ward 1 East Bay Regional Park, 1993—; coun. mem. El Cerrito City Coun., 1980-85, 87-91, mayor, 1982-83, 88-89. Mem. Save San Francisco Bay Assocs., Contra Costa Hazardous Waste Task Force, 1985-86, County Environ. Health Coordinating Council, 1985-88, County Hazardous Materials Commn., 1986-92, County Pub. and Environ. Health Adv. Bd., 1987—; founder, chmn. West County Toxics Coalition, 1986—; alternate solid waste West Contra Costa Joint Powers Authority, 1988-89. Served to lt. USNR, 1942-44. Recipient Sol Feinstone Environ. award U. Syracuse, 1977, Clean Air award Lung Assn. Santa Clara, 1976, Get Tough on Toxics Environ. award, 1986, Spl. award Homeless and Hungry Volunteers of Am., 1987. Mem. LWV, NAACP, Gray Panthers, Native Plant Soc., Sierra Club (city rep. to county homeless adv. com. 1988-93, Scope Environ. award 1986), Calif. State Local Emergency Planning Com. (rep. 1990-92), Audubon Soc., West Contra Costa Conservation League (pres.), League of Conservation Voters (dir 1978-79), West Contra Costa Transp. Joint Powers Authority. Democrat.

SIRI, KASEMSAN, power electronics researcher; b. Suphanburi, Thailand, Jan. 31, 1959; came to the U.S., 1981; s. Chamrus and Sudsanguan Siri; m. Ketnapa Sema-Ngern, Dec. 13, 1989; children: Natsha, Thirapit, Thiratham. BEE, Chulalongkorn U., 1981; MEE, U. Ill., Chgo., 1985, PhD, 1991. Rsch. asst. Power Electronics Rsch. Lab. U. Ill., Chgo., 1985-87, 88-91; R&D engr. Cyberpak Co., Burr Ridge, Ill., 1987-88; assoc. dir. Ill. Power Applications Ctr. I. Ill., Chgo., 1991-92; power electronics rschr. Rockwell Internat. Corp., Canoga Park; sr. rsch. and devel. engr. Hughes Power Products, El Segundo, Calif., 1992—; cons. engr. Qualitek Co., Addison, Ill., 1991-92. Contbr. articles to profl. jours. Mem. IEEE, Thai Engring. Assn. Ill., Assn. Thai Profls. in Am. and Can. Home: 16523 Purche Ave Torrance CA 90504-1837 Office: Hughes Power Products RC Bldg R50 M/S J512 6775 S Centinela Ave Culver City CA 90230-6303

SIRIGNANO, WILLIAM ALFONSO, aerospace and mechanical engineer, educator; b. Bronx, N.Y., Apr. 14, 1938; s. Anthony P. and Lucy (Caruso) S.; m. Lynn Haisfield, Nov. 26, 1977; children: Monica Ann, Jacqueline Hope, Justin Anthony. B.Aero.Engring., Rensselaer Poly. Inst., 1959; Ph.D., Princeton U., 1964. Mem. research staff Guggenheim Labs., aerospace, mech. scis. dept. Princeton U., 1964-67, asst. prof. aerospace and mech. scis., 1967-69, assoc. prof., 1969-73, prof., 1973-79, dept. dir. grad. studies, 1974-78; George Tallman Ladd prof., head dept. mech. engring. Carnegie-Mellon U., 1979-85; dean Sch. Engring., U. Calif.-Irvine, 1985-94; cons. industry and govt., 1966—; lectr. and cons. NATO adv. group on aero. research and devel., 1967, 75, 80; chmn. nat. and internat. tech. confs.; chmn. acad. adv. council Indsl. Research Inst., 1985-88; mem. space sci. applications adv. com. NASA, 1985-90, chmn. combustion sci. microgravity disciplinary working group, 1987-90; chmn. com. on microgravity rsch. space studies bd. NRC. Assoc. editor: Combustion Sci. and Tech, 1969-70; assoc. tech. editor Jour. Heat Transfer, 1985-92; contbr. articles to nat. and internat. profl. jours., also research monographs. United Aircraft research fellow, 1973-74; Disting. Alumni Rsch. award U. Calif. Irvine, 1992. Fellow AIAA (Pendray Aerospace Lit. award 1991, Propellants and Combustion award 1992), ASME (Freeman Scholar award 1992), IDERS (Oppenheim award 1993), AAAS; mem. Combustion Inst. (treas. internat. orgn., chmn. ea. sect.), Soc. Indsl. and Applied Math., Orange County Engring. Coun. (Excellence award 1994), Am. Electronics Assn. (recognition 1994). Office: U Calif Sch Engring S 3202 Engring Gateway Irvine CA 92717

SISCO, DENNIS G., marketing professional. BA in Econs., We. Md. Coll., 1946. Syss. programmer IBM Corp., 1968; syss. analyst, programmer Am. Can Co., 1970-71; dir. corp. devel. Nat. CSS, Inc., 1971-79; v.p. Turnkey Syss., Inc., 1971-79; v.p. ops., CFO Data Switch Corp., 1981-83; gen. ptnr. Oak Investment Pntrs., 1983-86; pres. The Stepstone Corp., 1986-88; with Dun & Bradstreet Corp., 1988—; also pres. D & B Enterprises, 1993—. Lt. U.S. Army, 1968-70. Office: Dataquest Incorporated 1290 Ridder Park Dr San Jose CA 95131-2304*

SISEMORE, CLAUDIA, educational films and videos producer, director; b. Salt Lake City, Sept. 16, 1937; d. Darrell Daniel and Alice Larril (Barton) S. BS in English, Brigham Young U., 1959; MFA in Filmmaking, U. Utah, 1976. Cert. secondary tchr., Utah. Tchr. English, drama and writing Salt Lake Sch. Dist., Salt Lake City, 1959-66; tchr. English Davis Sch. Dist., Bountiful, Utah, 1966-68; ind. filmmaker Salt Lake City, 1972—; filmmaker-in-residence Wyo. Coun. for Arts and Nat. Endowment for Arts, Dubois, Wyo., 1977-78; prodr., dir. ednl. films Utah Office Edn., Salt Lake City, 1979-93, Canyon Video, 1993—. Prodr., dir. Beginning of Winning, 1984 (film festival award 1984), Dancing through the Magic Eye, 1986, Se Hable Espanol, 1986-87; writer, dir., editor (film) Building on a Legacy, 1988, (videos) Energy Conservation, 1990, Alternative Energy Sources, 1990, Restructuring Learning, 1991, Kidsercise, 1991, Traditional Energy Sources, 1992, A State Government Team, 1992, Problem Solving Using Math Manipulatives, 1993, Canyon Video, 1993—; videos Western Mountains and Basins, 1994, Bikes, Boards and Blades, 1994; exhibited (abstract paintings) in group show Phillips Gallery; represented in numerous pvt. and pub. collections. Juror Park City (Utah) Arts Festival, 1982, Utah Arts Festival, Salt Lake City, 1982, Am. Film Festival, 1985-86, Best of West Film Festival, 1985-86; bd. dirs. Utah Media Ctr., Salt Lake City, 1981-87; mem. multi-disciplinary program Utah Arts Coun., Salt Lake City, 1983-87. Recipient award Utah Media Ctr., 1984, 85; Nat. Endowment for Arts grantee, 1978, Utah Arts Coun. grantee, 1980. Mormon.

SISSON, CAROLE MCDONALD, interior designer; b. Compton, Calif., Oct. 29, 1945; d. Charles B. and A. Jean (West) McDonald; m. Gary Allen Sisson, Oct. 30, 1965; children: Todd Allen, Tanya Danielle. BA in English Edn., S.D. State U., 1967. Designer Furniture World, Rapid City, S.D., 1976-78, Vaughan's, Bozeman, Mont., 1978-80; owner, designer Carriage Shoppe Ltd., Rapid City, 1973-76, Kent Interiors Ltd., Bozeman, 1980-85, Carol Sisson Designs, Bozeman, 1985—. Ball chmn. Mus. of Rockies; bd. dirs. Bozeman Symphony; chmn. Cmty. Corrections Bd. Mem. ASID (treas. intermountain chpt. 1993-95). Republican. Presbyterian. Office: 117 E Main St Bozeman MT 59715-4761

SIT, CHUNG SHEUNG, quality engineer; b. Hong Kong, Mar. 5, 1957; came to the U.S., 1976; s. Shung Sip and Nui-Ching (Chan) S. BS in Indsl. Engring., U. Wis., Milw., 1980, MS, 1982. Quality assurance engr. I Vendo Co., Fresno, Calif., 1983-84, mfg. engr. II, 1984-87; project engr. Blue Diamond Growers, Sacramento, Calif., 1987-90; sr. indsl. engr. FMC Corp., Madera, Calif., 1990-92; indsl. engr. Paramount Farms, Bakersfield, Calif., 1992-93; sr. quality engr. Grundfos Pumps Corp., Clovis, Calif., 1993—. Mem. Am. Soc. Quality Control. Republican. Home: 1585 E Omaha Ave Fresno CA 93720-2305

SITILIDES, JOHN, government relations executive; b. Jersey City, Feb. 8, 1962; s. Louis and Frances (Sagiroglou) S. B, Queens Coll., N.Y.C., 1983; M Internat. and Pub. Affairs, Columbia U., 1986. Dep. press sec. D'Amato for Senate, N.Y.C., 1986; exec. dir. Maltese for State Senate, Middle Village, N.Y., 1988; comm. mgr. D'Amato for Senate, N.Y.C., 1992; exec. asst. comm. Sen Alfonse D'Amato, N.Y.C., 1986-93; founder The Sitilides Group, Sacramento, Calif., 1993—; chmn. The Western Policy Ctr., Sacramento, 1994—. V.p. devel. World Affairs Coun., Sacramento, 1994; mem. Nat. Rep. Com., Washington, 1984. Mem. Nat. Wilderness Inst., Young Execs. Am., U.S. C. of C. Republican. Greek Orthodox. Office: The Sitilides Group 7700 College Town Dr Ste 101 Sacramento CA 95826-2303

SIUZDAK, GARY EDWARD, chemist, consultant; b. Pawtucket, R.I., Dec. 29, 1961; s. Edward Stanley and Doris Gertrude (Corbett) S.; m. Milena Pamela Frieden, Apr. 8, 1989. BA in Applied Math., R.I. Coll., 1985, BS in Chemistry, 1985; PhD in Phys. Chemistry, Dartmouth Coll., 1990. Dir. Mass Spectrometry Lab. The Scripps Rsch. Inst., La Jolla, Calif., 1990—. Author: Mass Spectrometry in Biotechnology, 1995. Alexander von Humboldt postdoctoral fellow, 1990, Deutscher Akademischer Austausch Dienst, 1990; recipient Phys. Scis., Ronald J. Boruch award, 1985, Chemistry Achievement award CRC Press, 1982. Mem. Am. Soc. for Mass Spectrometry. Office: The Scripps Rsch Inst MB 10-A 10666 N Torrey Pines Rd La Jolla CA 92037-1027

SIVADAS, IRAJA (WILLIAM SHEPARD WATKINS), mathematics educator; b. Palo Alto, Calif., Aug. 6, 1950; s. Charles Edward and Wilma Barbara (Comstock) Watkins; m. Ophelia Nuñez, June 9, 1979. AS in Math., Cabrillo Community Coll., 1975; BA in Math., U. Calif., Santa Cruz, 1978, MA in Math., 1987; postgrad., San Jose State U., 1981-83. Prodn. head backward wave oscillator Watkins-Johnson, Scotts Valley, Calif., 1978-80; supr. final quality assurance Intel, Santa Cruz, Calif., 1980-81; instr. math. Cabrillo Community Coll., Aptos, Calif., 1983-87, Kauai Community Coll., Lihue, Hawaii, 1987—. Co-author: Hawaiian Profiles in Non-Violence, Kauai County Energy Self-Sufficiency Report. U.S. del. Finastras Peace Conf., San Salvador, El Salvador, 1985; mem. energy adv. bd. Kauai County, 1989—; mem. Spark Matsunaga Inst. Peace, 1988—, exec. com., 1989—; 28th Dist. Dem. sec., Calif., 1986-88; participant Vets. Fast for Life (fasted 23 days on water), 1986. With USN, 1969-72, Vietnam. Mem. Am. Math. Soc., Math. Assn. Am., Hawaiian Acad. Scis., U. Hawaii Profl. Assembly, Naval Order, VFW (post 5888, liaison Nicaraguan Govt. 1984-86, Santa Cruz chmn. 1984-87, commdr. 1987, awards 1986, 87). Hindu. Home: PO Box 607 Hanapepe HI 96716-0607 Office: Kauai Community Coll 3-1901 Kaumualii Hwy Lihue HI 96766-9500

SIYAN, KARANJIT SAINT GERMAIN SINGH, software engineer; b. Mauranipur, India, Oct. 16, 1954; came to U.S., 1978; s. Ahal Singh and Tejinder Kaur (Virdi) S.; m. Dei Gayle Cooper, Apr. 8, 1987. B in Tech. Electronics, Indian Inst. Tech., 1976, M in Tech. Computer Sci., 1978; MS in Engring., U. Calif., Berkeley, 1980; PhD of Computer Sci., Kennedy-Western U., Berkeley, 1994. Cert. enterprise netware engr.; cert. microsoft profl. Sr. mem. tech. staff Rolm Corp., San Jose, Calif., 1980-84; cons. Siyan Cons. Svcs., L.A., 1985-86, Emigrant, Mont., 1987—. Author, sr. instr.: Learning Tree Internat., 1985—; author: Internat Firewalls and Network Security, Netware-The Professional Reference, Windows NT-The Professional Reference, Migrating to Netware 4, Netware Training Guide-Network 4 Update, Netware 4 Training Guide-Netware 4 Administration, CNE Training Guide-TCP/IP and NFS; co-author: Implementing Internet Security, Downsizing Netware, LAN Connectivity, Netware 4 for Professionals, Banyan Vines-The Professional Reference; author seminars on Novell Networking, TCP/IP Networks, Windows NT, Solaris-PC Network Integration. Mem. IEEE, ACM, Enterprise, Network Profl. Assn., Kappa Omicron Phi.

SIZEMORE, KENNETH LEE, county official; b. Salt Lake City, June 22, 1954; s. Allen DeVar and Myrna Lee (Syme) S.; m. Barbara Lynn Zolman, Dec. 18, 1975; children: Audrey, Jacob, Sarah, Kaye, Lance, Richard, Lee. BA, Utah State U., 1977, postgrad., 1979-83. Cert. econ. devel. fin. profl. Nat. Devel. Coun. Asst. county planner Cache County, Logan, Utah, 1977-80, county planner, 1980-86; dep. dir. Five County Assn. Govts., St. George, Utah, 1986—; Utah state rep. The Western Planner, Casper, Wyo., 1977-87, mem. editorial bd., 1994—. Co-author: Levels of Analysis in River Basin Planning, 1979, Integrating Water Resources and Land Use Planning, 1979. Voting dist. chmn. Rep. Com., Logan, Utah, 1975-77; chmn. Providence Utah Bd. Adjustment, 1985-86. Staff sgt. Utah Army N.G., 1984-93, with USAR, 1993—. Named Outstanding Young Men of Am., U.S. Jaycees, 1980; recipient Allen Stokes Conservation award Bridgerland Audubon Soc., 1986. Mem. Am. Planning Assn. (chpt. sec. 1984-86), Nat. Assn. County Planning Dirs. (Utah state rep. 1983-85). Republican. Mormon. Home: 2500 Arch Cir Santa Clara UT 84765-5538 Office: Five County Assn Govts 906 N 1400 W Saint George UT 84770-4989

SIZEMORE, NICKY LEE, computer scientist; b. N.Y.C., Feb. 13, 1946; d. Ralph Lee and Edith Ann (Wangler) S.; m. Frauke Julika Hoffmann, Oct. 31, 1974; 1 child, Jennifer Lee Sizemore; 1 stepchild, Mark Anthony Miracle. BS in Computer Sci., SUNY, 1989. Sgt. first class U.S. Army, 1964-68, 70-86; computer operator UNIVAC, Washington, 1968-69, programmer, 1969-70; programmer/analyst Ultra Systems, Inc., Sierra Vista, Ariz., 1986-87; computer scientist Comarco, Inc., Sierra Vista, 1987-92, ARC, Profl. Svcs. Group, Sierra Vista, 1992-93, Computer Scis. Corp., Ft. Huachuca, Ariz., 1994; sr. cons. Inference Corp., 1995—; speaker numerous confs., seminars, symposia. Mem. AIAA (mem. artificial intelligence standard com.), Computer Soc. IEEE, Am. Assn. for Artificial Intelligence (co-dir. workshop on verification, validation, and test of knowledge-based sys. 1988), Assn. for Computing Machinery, Armed Forces Comms.-Electronics Assn., Am. Def. Preparedness Assn. Home: 880 E Charles Dr Sierra Vista AZ 85635-1611 Office: Inference Corp 550 N Continenta Blvd Ste 300 El Segundo CA 90245

SJOLANDER, GARY WALFRED, physicist; b. Bagley, Minn., Dec. 5, 1942; s. Tage Walfred and Evelyn Mildred (Kaehn) S.; m. Joann Lorraine Tressler, June 18, 1966; 1 child, Toby Ryan. BS in Physics, U. Minn., 1970, MS in Physics, 1974, PhD in Physics, 1975. Rsch. assoc. U. Minn., Mpls., 1975-76; rsch. scientist Johns Hopkins U., Balt., 1977-78, sr. physicist, 1978-82; sr. engr. Westinghouse Electric Corp., Annapolis, Md., 1982-85; sr. staff engr. Lockheed Martin Astronautics, Denver, 1985—; pres. Cypress Improvement Assn., Inc., Severna Park, Md., 1984-85; advisor Inroads/Denver, Inc., 1986-88. Author numerous articles in field. With USAF, 1960-64. Mem. Am. Phys. Soc., Am. Geophys. Union, AIAA, The Planetary Soc. Lutheran. Home: 811 W Kettle Ave Littleton CO 80120-4443 Office: Lockheed Martin Astronautic PO Box 179 Denver CO 80201-0179

SJOSTROM, JOAN SEVIER, travel consultant; b. Denver, Nov. 10, 1931; d. George Field and Martha Watson (Turnbull) Sevier; m. Rex William Sjostrom, Mar. 16, 1952; children: Sandra, Anne, John, Sharon. Student, Colo. State U., 1949-51. Bookkeeper U.S. Nat. Bank, Denver, 1951-52, First Nat. Bank, Ft. Collins, Colo., 1952, Larimer County Credit Assn., Ft. Collins, 1953-55, Fox Drug, Castle Rock, Colo., 1974-86; owner, mgr. Travel Haus Inc., Castle Rock, 1984—. Vol. Swedish Emergency Ctr., 1976-82, Douglas County Schs. Spl. Edn. Program, 1980-84; mem. Interfaith Task Force Bd., 1987-88; mem. Douglas County Bd. Edn., 1978-88; mem. Douglas County Placement Alternative Commn., Castle Rock., 1984—; mem. D.C. Schs. Sr. Program, Castle Rock, 1992—. Mem. Castle Rock Rotary (v.p. 1992—, pres. 1993-94, dist. scholarship 1991, 92, 93). Republican. Lutheran. Home: 2072 W Wolfensberger Rd Castle Rock CO 80104-9635 Office: Travel Haus Inc 741 Wilcox St Castle Rock CO 80104-1740

SKAAR, SARAH HENSON, editor; b. Bryan, Tex., June 19, 1958; d. James Bond Henson and Evie Leone (Callihan) Miller; m. Kent Skaar, Apr. 7, 1990. BS, Wash. State U., 1983, M in Adult and Continuing Edn., 1986. Asst. prof. U. Idaho Coop. Extension System, 1984-91; editor Intermountain Horse and Rider, Idaho Falls, 1994—. Author: Risk Management: Strategies for Managing Volunteer Programs, 1988. Recipient Pub. Info. award Nat. Assn. County Agrl. Agts., 1989.

SKAGGS, DAVID E., congressman; b. Cin., Feb. 22, 1943; s. Charles and Juanita Skaggs; m. Laura Locher, Jan. 3, 1987; 1 child, Matthew; stepchildren: Clare, Will. BA in Philosophy, Wesleyan U., 1964; student law, U. Va., 1964-65; LLB, Yale U., 1967. Bar: N.Y. 1968, Colo. 1971. Assoc. Newcomer & Douglass, Boulder, Colo., 1971-74, 77-78; chief of staff Congressman Tim Wirth, Washington, 1975-77; ptnr. Skaggs, Stone & Sheehy, Boulder, 1978-86; mem. 100th-104th Congresses from 2d Colo. dist., Washington, 1987—; mem. Appropriations com., subcoms. Commerce and Justice, Interior; mem. Colo. Ho. of Reps., Denver, 1980-86, minority leader 1982-85. Former bd. dirs. Rocky Mountain Planned Parenthood, Mental Health Assn. Colo., Boulder County United Way, Boulder Civic Opera. Served to capt. USMC, 1968-71, Vietnam; maj. USMCR, 1971-77. Mem. Colo. Bar Assn., Boulder County Bar Assn., Boulder C. of C. Democrat. Congregationalist. Office: US House of Reps 1124 Longworth Bldg Washington DC 20515-0602 also: 9101 Harlan St Unit 130 Westminster CO 80030-2925

SKAGGS, L. SAM, retail company executive; b. 1922; married. With Am. Stores Co., Salt Lake City, 1945—, chmn. bd., chief exec. officer, 1962-89, chmn., 1989—, also bd. dirs.; chmn. Sav-On Drugs, Anaheim, Calif., bd. dirs. Served with USAAF, 1942-45. Office: Am Stores Co 709 E South Temple Salt Lake City UT 84102-1205*

SKALAGARD, HANS MARTIN, artist; b. Skuo, Faroe Islands, Feb. 7, 1924; s. Ole Johannes and Hanna Elisa (Fredriksen) S.; came to U.S., 1942, naturalized, 1955. Pupil Anton Otto Fisher, 1947; m. Mignon Diana Haack Haegland, Mar. 31, 1955; 1 child, Karen Solveig Sikes. Joined U.S. Mcht. Marine, 1942, advanced through grades to chief mate, 1945, ret., 1965; owner, operator Skalagard Sq., Rigger Art Gallery, Carmel, 1966—; libr. Mayo Hays O'Donnel Libr., Monterey, Calif., 1971-73; painter U.S. Naval Heritage series, 1973—; exhibited in numerous one-man shows including Palace Legion of Honor, San Francisco, 1960, J.F. Howland, 1963-65, Fairmont Hotel, San Francisco, 1963, Galerie de Tours, 1969, 72-73, Pebble Beach Gallery, 1968, Laguna Beach (Calif.) Gallery, 1969, Arden Gallery, Atlanta, 1970, Gilbert Gallery, San Francisco, Maritime Mus. of Monterey, Calif., 1993, Rigger Art Gallery, Carmel, Calif., Stanton Ctr., Monterey, 1993, St. Francis Yacht Club, San Francisco, 1995; group shows: Am. Artists, Eugene, Oreg., Robert Louis Stevenson Exhibit, Carmel Valley Gallery, Biarritz and Paris, France, David Findley Galleries, N.Y.C. and Faroe Island, Europe, Martime Mus., Calif, 1993, 94, 95, Pacific Coast Lumber Schooners, 1994, numerous others; represented in permanent collections; Naval Post Grad. Sch. and Libr., Allen Knight Maritime Mus., Salvation Army Bldg., Monterey, Calif., Robert Louis Stevenson Sch., Pebble Beach, Anenberg Art Galleries, Chestlibrook Ltd., Skalagard Art Gallery, Carmel, 1984; work represented in numerous boosk including Modern Masters of Marine Art, 1993; profiled in profl. jours.; lectr. Bd. dirs. Allen Knight Maritime Mus., 1973—, mem. adv. and acquisition coms., 1973-77; founder Skalagard Square Rigger Gallery; chairperson Mayor's Choice Exhibit Carmel, Calif., 1995; co founder Carmel Gallery Alliance. Recipient Silver medal Tommaso Campanella Internat. Acad. Arts, Letters and Scis., Rome, 1970, Gold medal, 1972, Gold medal and hon. life membership Academia Italia del Arti e del Honoro, 1980, Gold medal for artistic merit Academia d'Italia. Mem. Navy League (bd. dir. Monterey), Internat. Platform Assn., Sons of Norway (cultural dir. 1974-75, 76-77). Subject of cover and article Palette Talk, 1980, Compass mag., 1980. Home: 25197 Canyon Dr Carmel CA 93923-8329 Office: PO Box 6611 Carmel CA 93921-6611 also: Dolores At 5th St Carmel CA 93921

SKALAK, RICHARD, engineering mechanics educator, researcher; b. N.Y.C., Feb. 5, 1923; s. Rudolph and Anna (Tuma) S.; m. Anna Lesta Allison, Jan. 24, 1953; children: Steven Leslie, Thomas Cooper, Martha Jean, Barbara Anne. BS, Columbia U., 1943, CE, 1946, PhD, 1954; MD (hon.), Gothenburg U., Sweden, 1990. Instr. civil engring. Columbia U., N.Y.C., 1948-54, asst. prof., 1954-60, assoc. prof., 1960-64, prof., 1964-77, James Kip Finch prof. engring. mechanics, 1977-88, emeritus, 1988—, dir. Bioengring. Inst., 1978-88; prof. bioengring. U. Calif., San Diego, 1988—, dir. Inst. for Mechs. and Materials, 1992—; Hunter lectr. Clemson U., 1994; mem. panel Gov.'s Conf. on Sci. and Engring., R&D, 1989-90. Contbr. articles to sci. jours. Bd. dirs. Biotech. Inst., Gothenburg, Sweden, 1978—; mem. adv. bd. Ctr. for Biomed. Engring., N.Y.C., 1994—. Recipient Great Tchr. award Columbia Coll. Soc. of Older Grads., 1972, Merit medal Czechoslovakian Acad. Scis., 1990. Fellow AAAS, ASME (Centennial medal 1980, Melville medal 1990, editor jour. 1984), Am. Acad. Mechanics, Soc. Engring. Sci., Am. Inst. Med. and Biol. Engring. (founding); mem. NAE, Soc. Rheology, Am. Heart Assn., Microcirculatory Soc., Internat. Soc. Biorheology (Poiseuille medal 1989), Biomed. Engring. Soc. (Alza medal 1983), Cardiovascular System Dynamics Soc., Am. Soc. for Engring. Edn., Tau Beta Pi, Sigma Xi. Democrat. Presbyterian. Office: U Calif San Diego Ames Dept Bioengring La Jolla CA 92093-0412

SKARDA, RICHARD JOSEPH, clinical social worker; b. Santa Monica, Calif., Jan. 2, 1952; s. Robert Ralph and Cathryn Marie (Tourek) S. AA, Los Angeles Valley Coll., Van Nuys, Calif., 1976; BA, U. Calif., Berkeley, 1978; MSW, UCLA, 1980. Lic. clin. social worker, Calif.; Diplomate Am. Bd. Clin. Social Workers. Children's services worker Los Angeles County Dept. Children's Services, Panorama City, Calif., 1980-82; police service rep. Los Angeles Police Dept., 1982; psychiatric social worker Penny Lane, Sepulveda, Calif., 1983; children's services worker Ventura (Calif.) County Pub. Social Services Agy., 1983-85; head social work dept. Naval Med. Clinic, Port Hueneme, Calif., 1985-94. Mem. dean's coun. UCLA Sch. Social Welfare. With USN, 1970-74. Fellow Calif. Soc. Clin. Social Work; mem. Nat. Assn. Social Workers (diplomate), Acad. Cert. Social Workers.

SKARIAH, MATTHEW, religious organization administrator; b. Punnackad, Kerala, India, Feb. 21, 1945; arrive in Canada; s. Mathai Skariah and Aleyamma (Chacko) Mathai; m. Susamma Mathew, Oct. 18, 1976; 1 child, Annie Susan. LLB, Blackstone Sch. Law, 1970, JD, 1972; DD, Am. Sch. of Bible, 1971. Ordained. Founder, dir. Outreach for Youth Internat., Inc., Tulsa, 1973-78; founder, dir. World Prayer Band, Tulsa, 1978-89, Roswell, N.Mex., 1978—. Author: Crispy Christians, 1984, Free But Not Cheap, 1985, Talk Less and Pray More, 1988, Inspirational Nuggets, 1994. Ordained minister Bapt. Ch., 1971. Republican. Baptist. Office: World Prayer Band 200 W 1st St Ste 531 Roswell NM 88201-4676

SKEEN, JOSEPH RICHARD, congressman; b. Roswell, N.Mex., June 30, 1927; s. Thomas Dudley and Ilah (Adamson) S.; m. Mary Helen Jones, Nov. 17, 1945; children: Mary Elisa, Mikell Lee. B.S., Tex. A&M U., 1950. Soil and water engr. Ramah Navajo and Zuni Indians, 1951; rancher Lincoln County, N.Mex., 1952—; mem. N.Mex. Senate, 1960-70, 97th-103rd Congresses from 2nd N.Mex. dist., Washington, D.C., 1981—; mem. appropriations com., subcom. agr., chmn. appropriations com., subcom. def. Chmn. N.Mex. Republican Party, 1963-66. Served with USN, 1945-46; Served with USAFR, 1949-52. Mem. Nat. Woolgrowers Assn., Nat. Cattle Growers Assn., N.Mex. Woolgrowers Assn., N.Mex. Cattle Growers Assn., N.Mex. Farm and Livestock Bur. Republican. Club: Elks. Office: House of Representatives Washington DC 20515

SKEFF, KELLEY MICHAEL, health facility administrator; b. Center, Colo., 1944. MD, U. Chgo., 1970. Diplomate Am. Bd. Internal Medicine. Intern Harbor Gen. Hosp., Torrance, Calif., 1970-71; resident in internal medicine U. Colo. Med. Ctr., Denver, 1974-75; resident in internal medicine Stanford (Calif.) U. Hosps., 1975-76, fellow in internal medicine, 1976; program dir. Stanford U. Recipient Alpha Omega Alpha award Assocs. Am. Med. Coll., 1994. Office: Stanford U Dept Med 300 Pasteur Dr Palo Alto CA 94304-2203

SKELTON, DAVID LEE, lawyer; b. Windom, Minn., Apr. 9, 1947; s. Donald P. and Lois L. (Olson) S. BA, U. Minn., 1969; JD, U. San Diego, 1980, LLM in Taxation, 1986. Bar: Calif. 1980. Instrnl. designer tng. courses Northrop Worldwide Aircraft Svcs., 1977-78; tng. analyst computer-assisted instrn. Control Data Corp., 1979-80; pvt. law practice, 1981; ptnr. Ashfield & Skelton, 1981-82; chpt. 13 trustee So. Dist. Calif., San Diego, 1982—. Lt. USN, 1969-76. Mem. Nat. Assn. Chpt. 13 Trustees, San Diego County Bar Assn. Office: Chpt 13 Trustee 620 C St Ste 413 San Diego CA 92101-5312

SKELTON, DOUGLAS H., architect; b. Cottage Grove, Oreg., Apr. 17, 1939; s. Harry Edward and Mary Jane (Caldwell) S.; m. Bonita L. Baker, June 17, 1961; children: Paul D., Cynthia J., Justin D. Student, Oreg. State U., 1957-59; degree in architecture, U. Oreg., 1963. Registered architect, Oreg. Draftsman Payne & Struble Architecture, Medford, Oreg., 1965-66; intern architect Wayne Struble Architect, Medford, Oreg., 1966-70, assoc., 1973-78; project architect William Seibert Architect, Medford, Oreg., 1970-73; ptnr. Struble & Skelton Architects, Medford, Oreg., 1978-83; owner Douglas Skelton Architect, Medford, Oreg., 1983-89; ptnr. Skelton, Straus & Seibert Architects, Medford, Oreg., 1989—; mem. law rev. com. State Bd. Architects, Oreg., 1991. Design bldg. renovation (911 Mag. award 1991). Chmn. Hist. and Archtl. Rev. Commn., City of Jacksonville, 1992—; bd. dirs. Rogue Valley Christian Ch., 1994. Recipient Outstanding Sch. Bldg. award Am. Sch. and Univ. mag., 1987. Mem. AIA (v.p. So. Oreg. chpt. 1972, pres. 1973), Architects Coun. Oreg. (del., treas. 1989), Medford/Jackson C. of C. (devel. com. 1992—), Rotary (bd. dirs. Jacksonville/Applegate chpt. 1994). Office: Skelton Straus & Seibert 26 Hawthorne St Medford OR 97504-7114

SKELTON, ELIZABETH ANNE, foreign language educator; b. Youngstown, Ohio, Aug. 19, 1966; d. Ritchie Blaine and Marianne (Leifheit) S.; m. M. Peter McCarville, May 17, 1991. BA in German, Colo. Coll., 1989; MA in secondary edn./TESOL, U. N.Mex., 1994. Cert. tchr., Colo., N.Mex. Tchr. German/speech Liberty H.S., Colorado Springs, Colo., 1989-92; tchr. ESL/German Highland H.S., Albuquerque, 1992-95; tchr., program coord. ESL Olathe Middle & H.S., Moorhead, Minn., 1995—. Editor: Concordia Language Villages, 1992. Boettcher scholarship Boettcher Found., 1984. Mem. Tchrs. of ESL, ASCD, Am. Assn. for Tchrs. of German. Office: Montrose County Sch Dist RE-IJ University Blvd Albuquerque NM 87108

SKELTON, JOHN EDWARD, computer technology consultant; b. Amarillo, Tex., May 10, 1934; s. Floyd Wayne and Lucille Annabelle (Padduck) S.; m. Katherine Dow, Mar. 22, 1959; children: Laura Ann, Jeanette Kay, Jeffrey Edward. BA, U. Denver, 1956, MA, 1962, PhD, 1971. Mathematician U.S. Naval Ordnance Lab., Corona, Calif., 1956-59; various sales support and mktg. positions Burroughs Corp., Denver, Detroit, Pasadena, Calif., 1959-67; asst. prof. U. Denver, 1967-74; dir. Computer Ctr., U. Minn., Duluth, 1974-85; prof., dir. computing svcs. Oreg. State U., Corvallis, 1985-94; cons. World Bank, China, 1988, Educom Cons. Group, 1985. Author: Introduction to the Basic Language, 1971; co-auhtor: Who Runs the Computer, 1975; also articles. Mem. Assn. for Computing Machinery (pres. Rocky Mountain chpt. 1971, faculty advisor U. Minn. 1980-82, peer rev. team 3 regions 1981-90), Assn. for Spl. Interest Group on Univ. Computing (bd. dirs. 1987-91), Rotary (dist. youth exch. com. 1991—), Sigma Xi (chpt. pres. 1983-84), Phi Kappa Phi (chpt. pres. 1989-90). Episcopalian.

SKEWES-COX, BENNET, accountant, educator; b. Valparaiso, Chile, Dec. 12, 1918; came to U.S., 1919, naturalized, 1943; s. Vernon and Edith Page (Smith) S-C.; B.A., U. Calif., Berkeley, 1940; M.A., Georgetown U., 1947; B.B.A., Golden Gate Coll., 1953; m. Mary Osborne Craig, Aug. 31, 1946; children: Anita Page McCann, Pamela Skewes-Cox Anderson, Amy Osborne Skewes-Cox (Mrs. Robert Twiss). Asst. to press officer Am. Embassy, Santiago, Chile, 1941-43; state exec. dir. United World Federalists of Calif., 1948-50; pvt. practice acctg., San Francisco, 1953—; asst. prof. internat. relations San Francisco State U., 1960-62; grad. researcher Stanford (Calif.) U., 1962-63, Georgetown U., Washington, 1963-65; pres. Acad. World Studies, San Francisco, 1969—; sec. Alpha Delta Phi Bldg. Co., San Francisco, 1957—; lectr. in field. Mem. Democratic state central com. Calif., 1958-60, fgn. policy chmn. Calif. Dem. Council, 1959-61, treas. Marin County Dem. Central Com., 1956-62; founder, 1st. chmn. Calif. Council for UN Univ., 1976—; compiler World Knowledge Bank; bd. dirs. Research on Abolition of War; treas. Marin Citizens for Energy Planning. Served as lt. (j.g.), USNR, 1943-46. Mem. Assn. for World Edn. (internat. council 1975—), Am. Soc. Internat. Law, Am. Polit. Sci. Assn., San Francisco Com. Fgn. Relations, Am. Acctg. Assn., Calif. State Univ. Profs., AAUP, Nat. Soc. Public Accts., Fedn. Am. Scientists, UN Assn., Internat. Polit. Sci. Assn. World Federalists Assn., World Govt. Orgns. Coalition (treas.). Clubs: University, Commonwealth of Calif., Lagunitas Country. Author: The Manifold Meanings of Peace, 1964; The United Nations from League to Government, 1965; Peace, Truce or War, 1967. Home: Monte Alegre PO Box 1145 Ross CA 94957-1145 Office: Acad World Studies 2806 Van Ness Ave San Francisco CA 94109-1426

SKHISOV, EDUARD, office project assistant; b. Odessa, Ukraine, Aug. 29, 1971; came to the U.S., 1992; s. Yakov and Yevgeniya (Katsel) S. Student, Odessa Poly. U., 1988-91, Santa Monica Coll., 1992-93; BS in Computer Sci., Calif. State U., L.A., 1994. Software engr. Odessa (Ukraine) Inst. Power Engring. and Design, 1990-91; office project asst. Calif. State U., L.A., 1993—. Mem. Assn. for Computing Machinery, Golden Key Honor Soc., Phi Kappa Phi. Jewish. Home: 1019 N Hayworth Ave Apt 5 Los Angeles CA 90046-6139

SKIDMORE, DAVID THEODORE, service executive; b. Williamson, W.Va., July 31, 1952; s. Theodore Roosevelt and Frances Margaret (Shamblin) S.; m. Donna Joy Burgess, Feb. 6, 1970; children: Suzette Lynn, Christopher David. Lineman C & P Telephone Co., Huntington, W.Va., 1970-71, splicer, 1971-76, engr., 1976-78; engr. Tesinc, Columbia, S.C., 1978-79, area mgr., 1979-80; engr. Volt Info. Scis., N.Y.C., 1981-82, regional mgr., 1982-88, div. mgr., 1988-92; exec. v.p. The Maxima Corp., Lanham, Md., 1991-93; corp. v.p., bd. dirs., officer corp., 1992-93; COO Maxima Network Svcs., Inc., Rancho Cucamonga, Calif., 1993—. Recipient Glass Fiber Splicer award Anaconda Corp., 1984. Mem. Am. Mgmt. Assn., Assn. Field Svc. Mgrs. Home: 20 Canyon Island Dr Newport Beach CA 92660

SKIDMORE, DONALD EARL, JR., government official; b. Tacoma, Apr. 27, 1944; s. Donald E. and Ingeborg (Johnsrud) S.; BSc, Evangel Coll., 1968. With Dept. Social and Health Svcs., State of Wash., Yakima, 1967-74; quality rev. specialist Social Security Adminstrn., Seattle, 1974-76, program analyst, Balt., 1976-79, Seattle, 1979-81, quality assurance officer, mgr. Satellite office, Spokane, Wash., 1981-84, program analyst, Seattle, 1984-90, mgmt. analyst, 1990—. Pres., bd. dirs. Compton Court Condo Assn., 1980-81; v.p., trustee Norwood Village, 1987-90; vice chair ops. subcom., mem. citizen's adv. com. METRO, 1987-89; mem. citizen's adv. com. land use planning, Bellevue, Wash., 1988-90. Grad. Bellevue Police Citizen's Acad., 1992. Office: 2201 6th Ave Ste 400 Seattle WA 98121-1834

SKIDMORE, ERIC DORR, information systems manager; b. Sangley Point Naval Base, Philippines, May 28, 1960; parents Am. citizens; s. Ellis Dee and Elaine Nadine (Hoffman) S.; married; two children. Student, Oreg. State U., 1978-80; BS in Bus. and Econs., Eastern Oreg. State Coll., LaGrande, 1983. Programmer JAHL Data Systems, Klamath Falls, Oreg., 1980-83, v.p. customer support, 1983-85; programming/support supr. Kennewick (Wash.) Indsl., 1985-86, data div. mgr., 1986-89; info. systems mgr. Bright Wood Corp., Madras, Oreg., 1989—; bd. dirs. Jefferson County Devel. Corp., Madras, 1992—; mem. bus. adv. coun., bus. dept. Madras Sr. High Sch., 1991—. Bd. dirs. Jefferson County chpt. ARC, 1994—. Mem. Portland Area Novell Users Group, Future Bus. Leaders Am./Phi Beta Lambda. Republican.

SKIDMORE, REX AUSTIN, social work educator; b. Salt Lake City, Dec. 31, 1914; s. Charles H. and Louise (Wangsgaard) S.; m. Knell Spencer, Aug. 31, 1939; children: Lee Spencer, Larry Rex. BA, U. Utah, 1938, MA, 1939; PhD, U. Pa., 1941. Instr. sociology U. Pa., 1940-41, Utah State Agrl. Coll., Logan, 1941-42; spl. agt. FBI, Miami, Fla., San Francisco, San Antonio, 1943-45; dir. bur. student counsel U. Utah, 1947-57, asso. prof., 1947-50, prof., 1950-85, dean Grad. Sch. Social Work, 1956-75. Author: Mormon Recreation: Theory and Practice, 1941, Building Your Marriage, 1951, 3d edit., 1964, Marriage Consulting, 1956, Introduction to Social Work, 1964, 6th edit., 1994, Introduction to Mental Health, 1979, Social Work Administration, 1983, 3d edit., 1995; contbr. articles to sociol. jours. Chmn. Western Mental Health Council, Western Interstate Commn. Higher Edn., 1964-65; mem. Nat. Adv. Council Nat. Manpower and Tng. Recipient distinguished service awards Community Service Council, Nat. Assn. Social Work, 1975, distinguished service awards Utah Conf. on Human Services, 1976. Mem. Coun. on Social Work Edn., Phi Kappa Phi, Pi Kappa Alpha, Pi Gamma Mu. Mem. Ch. of Jesus Christ Latter-Day Saints. Home: 1444 S 20th E Salt Lake City UT 84108

SKIDMORE, THOMAS ERNEST, automotive and communications company executive; b. Vancouver, B.C., Can., Oct. 20, 1949; s. Arthur and Frances Elsie (McLellan) S.; m. Lorraine Goodman; 2 children. Various positions TCG Internat., Inc., Burnaby, B.C., 1967—, vice chmn. fin. and investments, CEO comm. group; vice chmn., pres., CEO Glentel, Inc., Burnaby, 1990—; bd. dirs. TCG Internat. Inc., Glenayre Techs., Inc., N.Y.C., Glentel Inc., Franann Holdings Ltd., Burnaby, Autostock Inc., Montreal, PQ, Speedy Auto Glass, Inc., Seattle, Trans Am. Glass, Inc. Office: TCG Internat Inc, 4710 Kingsway 28th Fl, Burnaby, BC Canada V5H 4M2

SKIELLER, CHRISTIAN, manufacturing executive; b. Copenhagen, Mar. 23, 1948; came to U.S., 1979; s. Erik C. and Vibeke (Tvilstegaard) S.; m. Kathleen E. Christman, Jan. 11, 1986; children: Claudia Christman, Christina Christman. MSc, Tech. U. Denmark, Copenhagen, 1971; MBA, Stanford U., Calif., 1981. Mgr. mfg. ops. Schou Mfg., Copenhagen, 1972-76; systems engr. IBM, Copenhagen, 1976-79; partner, gen. mgr. CSMC, Menlo Park, Calif., 1982-84; mfg. mgr. Oximetrix/Abbott Labs., Mountain View, Calif., 1984-87; prin. cons. Christian Skieller Cons., Menlo Park, 1987-90; v.p. ops. ABAXIS, Mountain View, 1990-91; v.p. mfg. Medtronic Cardio-Rhythm, San Jose, Calif., 1992—. Mem. Am. Prodn. and Inventory Control Soc. Home: 55 Black Fox Way Woodside CA 94062-4103

SKILES, VIOLET DENICE, artist; b. Toppenish, Wash., Apr. 24, 1954; d. Clarence Herman and Hazel Emma (Middleton) Johnson; m. Randall Kent Skiles, Oct. 2, 1976; children: Brandon, Megan. Grad., Grandview H.S., Wash., 1972; studied with Judi Betts, Frank Webb, Barbara Nechls and Al Brouillette. Exhbns. include solo show: Edmonds (Wash.) Art Festival Mus., 1992, two-person show: Tolles Gallery, Mercer Island, Wash., 1995, group shows: Allied Artists of Am. 73d Internat. Show, N.Y.C., 1986, Am. Watercolor Soc. 120th Internat. Show, N.Y.C., Women Painters of Wash., Kobe, Japan, 1987, Tokyo, 1987, Rhine, Germany, 1989, San Diego (Calif.) Watercolor Soc. Internat. Soc. Shows, 1989, 90, N.W. Watercolor Soc. Show, Kirkland, Wash., 1991, 93. Recipient Purchase award Seattle (Wash.) Telco Fed. Credit Union Competition, 1987, Pacific N.W. Arts and Crafts Fair award, Bellevue (Wash.) Art Mus., 1988, Watercolor West award San Diego Watercolor Soc. Internat. Exhbn., 1989, Painting Competition finalist Artist Mag., 1992. Mem. N.W. Watercolor Soc. (signature), Women Painters Wash. (Elizabeth Everett Memnl. award 1988), Christians in the Visual Arts. Home: 3206 174th Ave NE Redmond WA 98052-5733

SKILLIN, THERESE JENO, elementary school educator; b. San Jose, Calif., Feb. 16, 1956; d. Joseph John and Eloise Martha (Holden) Jeno; m. Robert Hance Skillin, Sept. 28, 1985;; children: Paul Holden, Julia Rose, Anna Katherine. BA, San Francisco State U., 1978, MA, 1983. Cert. Calif. multiple subject life tchr. Tchr. Lost Hills (Calif.) Union Sch., 1979-81, Panama Unified Sch. Dist., Bakersfield, Calif., 1981-85, Santa Paula (Calif.) Sch. Dist., 1985-90; adult literacy tutor Family Literacy Aid to Reading Program, Bakersfield, 1986, 87; cons. Ventura (Calif.) County Farm Bus., 1987-88, Ventura County Supt. County Schs.; sci. specialist, chair Ventura County Environ. and Energy Edn. Coun., 1990; originator, presenter Farm Day, Kern and Ventura Counties; presenter Ventura County Creative Arts Seminar, 1990, Calif. Kindergarten Conf., San Francisco, 1995; tchr. agrl. seminar, Ker County, 1992-94. Author children's books. Mem. AAUW (mem. Camarillo Creative Arts Workshop 1988), Ventura County Reading Assn., Northern Calif. Kindergarten Assn., So. Calif. Assn. Sci. Specialists, Wasco Jr. Woman's Club (sec. 1982-83, v.p. 1983-84, dir. Annual Fun Run, named Woman of Yr. 1982), Santa Barbara Cactus and Succulent Soc. (cons.), Petroleum Wives Assn. (com. chairperson 1993-94). Democrat. Roman Catholic. Home and Office: 2901 22nd St Bakersfield CA 93301-3237

SKILLING, DAVID VAN DIEST, manufacturing executive; b. St. Louis, Sept. 16, 1933; s. David Miller Jr. and Eloise Margaret (van Diest) S.; m. Barbara Jo Chaney, Aug. 4, 1956; children: Kimberly Alice, Mark Chaney. BS, Colo. Coll., 1955; MBA, Pepperdine U., 1977. With TRW, Inc., Los Angeles, 1970-83, Cleve., 1983-93, Orange, Calif., 1993—; dir. mktg. energy group TRW, Inc., Los Angeles, 1978-83, v.p. planning and devel., indsl. and energy sector, 1983-86, v.p. corp. planning and devel., 1987-89, exec. v.p., gen. mgr. infosystems and svcs., 1989—; bd. dirs. Lamson & Sessions, Cleve. Bd. dirs. ISI, 1995—; bd. trustees The Colo. Coll., 1994—, Nat. Commn. on Children. Mem. Nat. Assn. Mfrs. (bd. dirs. 1988-93), Assn. for Corp. Growth, Calif. Bus. Roundtable (exec. com. 1994—). Republican. Office: TRW Inc 505 City Pkwy W Orange CA 92608

SKINNER, DAVID COOPER, school administrator, educator; b. Jersey City, Nov. 4, 1947; s. Samuel James and Elaine (Cooper) S.; 1 child, Ethan. AB, Grinnell Coll., 1969; MA, Northeastern U., 1973. Owner, operator Rebecca's Oven restaurant, North Bennington, Vt., 1971-72, Movie Madness Cinema Bookstore, Cambridge, Mass., 1977-79, David Skinner Baseball Cards, various locations, 1980-87; lab. mgr. L.C. Optical Svc., Cambridge, 1973-77; asst. mgr. Ctrl. Sq. Cinemas, Cambridge, 1979, Brattle Theatre, Cambridge, 1979-80, Harvard Sq. Theater, Cambridge, 1980; instr. Cochise Coll., Sierra Vista, Ariz., 1987-92; dir., tchr. Wood Canyon Sch., Bisbee, Ariz., 1992—. Contbr. articles to profl. publs.; assoc. prodr., scriptwriter, on-air personality The Club, WGBH-TV, Boston, 1979. Bd. dirs. Bisbee Food Coop., 1987-89. Mem. Soc. for Am. Baseball Rsch., Negro Leagues Baseball Mus., Native Seeds/Search, Seed Savers Exch., Ayurvedic Inst. Home: PO Box 777 Bisbee AZ 85603-0777 Office: Wood Canyon Sch PO Box 781 Bisbee AZ 85603

SKINNER, E. MORGAN, JR., broadcast executive; b. Logan, Utah, Apr. 28, 1940; s. Earnest M. and Mabel Clarinda (Peterson) S.; m. Darlene Anice Coppinger, Aug. 31, 1986; children: Brad, Randy, Matthew, Suzanne, Earnest, Elizabeth, Jenifer, Ryan, Aaron. BA in Journalism, Ariz. State U., 1964; postgrad., U. Utah, 1964-67; JD, LaSalle U., 1970. Prodn. sales rep. Sta. KBRV Radio, Soda Springs, Idaho, 1956-58; program dir. Sta. KMOR Radio, Salt Lake City, 1964-65; news/agriculture divsn. Sta. KSL Radio-TV, Salt Lake City, 1965-66; news, pub. affairs rep. Sta. WNYW-WRFM, N.Y.C., 1966-69, Sta. KBIG AM/FM, L.A., 1969-72; sales mgr., sta. mgr. Sta. KOOL Radio-TV, Phoenix, 1972-79; pres. Sta. ABM Internat., Phoenix, 1979-81; v.p., gen. mgr. Sta. KORK AM/FM, Las Vegas, 1981-83; pres., gen. mgr. Frontier Media, Las Vegas, 1983-86; v.p. ops. Am. Mus. Hist. Documents, Las Vegas, 1986-89; pres., CEO Beehive Broadcasting Corp., St. George, Utah, 1989—. Named Outstanding News Dir. AP, 1990-92, Best News and Sports Utah Broadcasters, 1992-93; recipient Disting. Svc. award Utah Sch. Bd. Assn., 1994. Mem. Rotary Internat., Boy Scouts Am., Utah Broadcasters Assn., Nat. Assn. Broadcasters. Mem. Ch. LDS. Office: Beehvie Broadcasting Corp PO Box 1450 Saint George UT 84771-1450

SKINNER, KNUTE RUMSEY, poet, English educator; b. St. Louis, Apr. 25, 1929; s. George Rumsey and Lidi (Skjoldvig) S.; m. Jeanne Pratt; 1953; divorced 1954; 1 child, Frank; m. Linda Kuhn, Mar. 30, 1961 (div. Sept. 1977); children: Dunstan, Morgan; m. Edna Kiel, Mar. 25, 1978. Student, Culver-Stockton Coll., 1947-49; B.A., U. No. Colo., 1951; M.A., Middlebury Coll., 1954; Ph.D., U. Iowa, 1958. Instr. English U. Iowa, Iowa City, 1955-56, 57-58, 60-61; asst. prof. English Okla. Coll. for Women, 1961-62; lectr. creative writing Western Wash. U., Bellingham, 1962-71; asso. prof. English Western Wash. U., 1971-73, prof. English, 1973—; pres. Signpost Press Inc., nonprofit corp., 1983-95. Author: Stranger with a Watch, 1965, A Close Sky Over Killaspuglonane, 1968, 75, In Dinosaur Country, 1969, The Sorcerers: A Laotian Tale, 1972, Hearing of the Hard Times, 1981, The Flame Room, 1983, Selected Poems, 1985, Learning to Spell "Zucchini," 1988, The Bears and Other Poems, 1991, What Trudy Knows and Other Poems, 1994; editor: Bellingham Rev., 1977-83, 93-95; contbr. poetry, short stories to anthologies, textbooks, periodicals. Nat. Endowment for the Arts fellow, 1975. Mem. Am. Conf. Irish Studies, Wash. Poets Assn. Office: Western Washington U HU 323 Bellingham WA 98225-9055

SKINNER, NANCY JO, municipal recreation executive; b. Ogallala, Nebr., Nov. 5, 1956; d. Dale Warren Skinner and Beverly Jane (Fister) Berry. AA, Platte Community Coll., 1977; BS, U. Ariz., 1981; MBA, U. Phoenix, 1990; diploma, Nat. Exec. Devel. Sch., 1992. Cert. leisure profl. Sports specialist YWCA, Tucson, 1981, asst. dir. summer day camp, 1981, dir. health, phys. edn. and recreation, 1981-82; sr. recreation specialist Pima County Parks and Recreation Dept., Tucson, 1983, recreation program coord., 1983-90; recreation coord. III Phoenix Parks, Recreation and Libr. Dept., 1990-94, recreation supr., 1994—; labor mgmt. quality of work life rep. Pima County Govt., 1987; dist. coord. Atlantic Richfield Co. Jesse Owens Games, Tucson, 1986-89; adv. Pima County Health Dept. Better Health Through Self Awareness, 1982-83. Dir. tournament Sportsman Fund-Send a Kid to Camp, Tucson, 1984, 85, 86; mem. labor mgmt. quality of working life com. Pima County Govt., 1987; dist. coord. Nat. Health Screening Coun., Tucson, 1982-85; event coord. Tucson Women's Commn. Saguaro Classic, 1984; com. mem. United Way, Tucson, 1982-83; panelist Quality Conf. City of Phoenix, 1992. Musco/APRf Grad. scholar; recipient City of Phoenix Excellence award, 1994. Mem. Nat. Recreation and Parks Assn., Ariz. Parks and Recreation Assn. (cert., treas. dist. IV 1987, pres. 1988, 89, state treas. 1990, pub. rels. chair 1993, Tenderfoot award 1984, co-chair state conf. ednl. program com. 1995), Delta Psi Kappa. Democrat. Methodist. Office: Phoenix Pks Recreation & Libr Dept 3901 W Glendale Ave Phoenix AZ 85051-8132

SKINNER, NATHAN LESTON, development chemist; b. Longview, Wash., Jan. 11, 1937; s. Nathan Leston and Lena (Gideon) S.; m. Sandra Celestine Hubka, July 1, 1959 (div. Jan. 1976); 1 child, Shannon Elizabeth; m. Susan Kay Brunkhorst, May 23, 1981; children: Niles Bentley, Kelci Nicole. Student, Lower Columbia Coll., 1955-56, Santiago Coll., 1956-57, Orange Coast Coll., 1957-64. Lab. technician Narmco, Costa Mesa, Calif., 1956-59, Crys-Tech., Santa Ana, Calif., 1960-61; engr. Western Semicondr., Santa Ana, 1962-66, Semco, Westminster, Calif., 1965-67; sr. rsch. asst. Hughes Rsch. Lab., Malibu, Calif., 1967-70; engr. Santa Barbara Rsch. Ctr., Goleta, Calif., 1970-76; rsch. dir., co-owner Sexwax, Inc., Carpinteria, Calif., 1970—; scientist III EG&G/EM, SBO, Goleta, 1976-91; tech. dir. Xsirius, Inc., Santa Barbara, Calif., 1991—; co-owner, rsch. dir. Sumus Co., Santa Barbara, 1990—, Microchem. Co., Carpinteria, 1991—; VCG sci. lead S.L.3 NASA, Marshall, Ala., 1978-85; invited speaker Nat. Tng. Inst. Pilot Program on Sci. and Tech., Albuquerque, 1991. Inventor surfboard wax, 1970, process for removing impurities from zone refined materials, 1975, direct vapor/solid synthesis of mercuric iodide using compounds of mercury and iodine, 1990; contbr. tech. papers to profl. jours. including Jour. Crystal Growth, 1988, Nuclear Instruments and Methods in Physics Rsch., 1989, NASA Conf. Publ., Jour. Spacecraft and Rockets 16, 1979. Founder REACTS (Rediscovery Educational Activities Create Tomorrow's Scientists)Goleta, 1990, exec. dir., 1990-93, resource leader; vol. sci. educator, demonstrator Santa Barbara County Schs., 1971—. Recipient Letter of Commendation, NASA, 1985; Spl. Recognition award Adopt-a-Sch. com. Santa Barbara Industry Edn. Coun., 1990. Mem. Am. Chem. Soc., Mensa. Office: Xsirius Inc 815-A E Mason St Santa Barbara CA 93103

SKINNER, STANLEY THAYER, utility company executive, lawyer; b. Fort Smith, Ark., Aug. 18, 1937; s. John Willard and Irma Lee (Peters) S.; m. Margaret Olsen, Aug. 16, 1957; children—Steven Kent, Ronald Kevin. B.A. with honors, San Diego State U., 1960, M.A., U. Calif., Berkeley, 1961, J.D., 1964. Bar: Supreme Ct. Calif. bar 1965, U.S. Circuit Ct. Appeals for 9th Circuit bar 1965, 10th Circuit bar 1966. Atty. Pacific Gas and Electric Co., San Francisco, 1964-73; sr. counsel Pacific Gas and Electric Co., 1973, treas., 1974-76, v.p. fin., 1976, sr. v.p., 1977, exec. v.p., 1978-86, exec. v.p., chief fin. officer, 1982-85, vice chmn. bd., 1986-91, pres., chief oper. officer, 1991-94; pres., CEO Pacific Gas and Electric Co., San Francisco, 1994—, also chmn. bd. dirs.; chmn. bd. dirs., CEO Pacific Gas and Electric Co., 1995—; bd. dirs. Pacific Gas Transmission Co., Elec. Power Rsch. Inst. Bd. dirs. United Way of Bay Area, campaign chmn., 1992; trustee, former chmn. bd. dirs. Golden Gate U.; bd. dirs. Bay Area chpt. ARC. Mem. Calif. State Bar Assn., Pacific Coast Elec. Assn. (bd. dirs.), Pacific Coast Gas Assn., Calif. State C. of C. (bd. dirs.), San Francisco C. of C. (bd. dirs.), Bankers Club San Francisco, Moraga Country Club. Republican. Presbyterian. Office: Pacific Gas & Electric Co 77 Beale St San Francisco CA 94105-1814

SKIPP, TRACY JOHN, legal support service company owner; b. Bourne, Mass., Feb. 10, 1966; s. Herbert Bucklin and Nanette Marie (Fisher) S.; m. Karyn Shayann Brennan, Nov. 24, 1986; children: Tracy John Jr., Brennan Ross Anthony, Megan Shaylynn. Paralegal grad., Albuquerque Career Inst., 1989; B. Univ. Studies, U. N.Mex., 1995. Med. asst. pvt. psychiat. practice, Albuquerque, 1987-89; owner Skipp's Legal Support Resources, Albuquerque, 1990-95. Co-author, illustrator: The Gift of the Apple, The Birth of a Star. Sustaining mem. Rep. Nat. Com., Washington, 1988—; rep. gen. honors coun., internat. affairs coun. Associated Stuents U. N.Mex., co-chmn. U. N.Mex. Vol. Svc. Coalition; med. missionary to Mex. St. Mark's United Meth. Ch. of El Paso; participant in 1996 Rolex Awards for Enterprise. Named Man of the Yr., Am. Biog. Inst., 1995; L.B. Reeder scholar, Dudley Wynn Honors Ctr. scholar, 1992—. Fellow Internat. Order of Merit, Am. Bio. Inst.; mem. Internat. Platform Assn., Am. Freedom Coalition, Nat. Notary Assn., Legal Assts. N.Mex., Nat. Fedn. Paralegal Assn., Arnold Air Soc., N.Mex. Acad. Sci., Blue Key, Phi Beta Delta, Epsilon Sigma Alpha, Phi Delta Kappa. Republican. Methodist. Office: Skipp's Legal Support Resources 604 Dorado Pl SE Albuquerque NM 87123-3827

SKIRVIN, WILLIAM DAVID, artist, art director; b. Barstow, Calif., Mar. 8, 1952; s. Orval and Sylvia (Reynolds) S.; div.; children: Donovan Steven, Sarah Michelle, Dylan Thomas. Grad. high sch., Barstow. Tech. illustrator McDonnell Douglas Corp., Lemoore, Calif., 1973-80; freelance artist San Francisco, Calif., 1980—; fine artist, 1992—; art dir. Virgin Interactive Entertainment, Irvine, Calif., 1992—; art dir. Sierra On-Line, Inc., Oakhurst, Calif., 1987-91. Pvt. collections include USN, Hewlett Packard, Apple Computers, and others. Republican.

SKLADAL, ELIZABETH LEE, elementary school educator; b. N.Y.C., May 23, 1937; d. Angier Joseph and Julia May (Roberts) Gallo; m. George Wayne Skladal, Dec. 26, 1956; children: George Wayne Jr., Joseph Lee. BA, Sweet Briar Coll., 1958; EdM, U. Alaska, 1976. Choir dir. Main Chapel, Camp Zama, Japan, 1958-59, Ft. Lee, Va., 1963-65; choir dir. Main Chapel and Snowhawk, Ft. Richardson, Alaska, 1968-70; tchr. Anchorage (Alaska) Sch. Dist., 1970—. Active Citizens' Adv. Com. for Gifted and Talented, Anchorage, 1981-83, music com. Anchorage Sch. Dist., 1983-86; soloist Anchorage Opera Chorus, 1969—, Community Chorus, Anchorage, 1986-80; mem. choir First Presbyn. Ch., Anchorage, 1971—, deacon, 1988—; participant 1st cultural exch. from Anchorage to Magadan, Russia with Alaska Chamber Singers, 1992. Named Am. Coll. Theater Festival winner Amoco Oil Co., 1974; recipient Cmty. Svc. award Anchorage U. Alaska Alumni Assn., 1994-95. Mem. AAUW, Anchorage Concert Assn. Patron Soc. (assocs. coun. of dirs.), Alaska Chamber Singers, Am. Guild Organists (former dean, former treas.). Republican. Presbyterian. Home: 1841 S Salem Dr Anchorage AK 99508-5156

SKLANSKY, JACK, electrical and computer engineering educator, researcher; b. N.Y.C., Nov. 15, 1928; s. Abraham and Clara S.; m. Gloria Joy Weiss, Dec. 24, 1957; children: David Alan, Mark Steven, Jeffrey Paul. BEE, CCNY, 1950; MSEE, Purdue U., 1952; D in Engring. Sci., Columbia U., 1955. Research engr. RCA Labs., Princeton, N.J., 1955-65; mgr. Nat. Cash Register Co., Dayton, Ohio, 1965-66; prof. elec. and computer engring. U. Calif., Irvine, 1966—; pres. Scanicon Corp., Irvine, 1980-89. Author: (with others) Pattern Classifiers and Trainable Machines, 1981; editor: Pattern Recognition, 1973, (with others) Biomedical Images and Computers, 1982; editor-in-chief: Machine Vision and Applications, 1987. Recipient best paper award Jour. Pattern Recognition, 1977; rsch. grantee NIH, 1971-84, Army Rsch. Office, 1984-91, NSF, 1992—. Fellow IEEE, Internat. Assn. for Pattern Recognition; mem. ACM. Office: U Calif Dept Elec & Computer Engring Irvine CA 92717

SKLAR, LOUISE MARGARET, service executive; b. L.A., Aug. 12, 1934; d. Samuel Baldwin Smith and Judith LeRoy (Boughton) Nelson; m. Edwynn Edgar Schroeder, Mar. 20, 1955 (div. July 1975); children: Neil Nelson, Leslie Louise Schroeder Grandclaudon, Samuel George; m. Martin Sklar, Oct. 17, 1983. Student, U. So. Calif., 1952-54, UCLA, 1977-79. Acct. Valentine Assocs., Northridge, Calif., 1976-78, programmer, 1978-79; contr. Western Monetary, Encino, Calif., 1979-81; pres. Automated Computer Composition, Chatsworth, Calif., 1984—. Mem. Assn. L.A. County Bridge Units (bd. dirs. 1990—, sec. 1984-86), Am. Contract Bridge League (bd. govs. 1993—, mem. nat. charity com. 1982), Conn. Soc. Generalogists, Ky. Hist. Soc., So. Calif. Assistance League, Heart of Am. Geneal. Soc., Chatsworth C. of C., Greater L.A. Zoo Assn., Zeta Tau Alpha. Republican. Office: Automated Computer Composition Inc 21356 Nordhoff St Chatsworth CA 91311-5818

SKLAR, RICHARD LAWRENCE, political science educator; b. N.Y.C., Mar. 22, 1930; s. Kalman and Sophie (Laub) S.; m. Eva Molineux, July 14, 1962; children: Judith Anne, Katherine Elizabeth. A.B., U. Utah, 1952; M.A., Princeton U., 1957, Ph.D., 1961. Mem. faculty Brandeis U., U. Ibadan, Nigeria, U. Zambia; mem. faculty SUNY-Stony Brook; now prof. emeritus polit. sci. UCLA; mem. fgn. area fellowship program Africa Nat. Com., 1970-73; Simon vis. prof. U. Manchester, Eng., 1975, Fulbright vis. prof. U. Zimbabwe, 1984; Lester Martin fellow Harry S. Truman Rsch. Inst., Hebrew U. Jerusalem, 1979; fellow Africa Inst. of South Africa, 1994—. Author: Nigerian Political Parties: Power in an Emergent African Nation, 1963, Corporate Power in an African State, 1975; co-author: Postimperialism: International Capitalism and Development, 1987, African Politics and Problems in Development, 1991; contbr. articles to profl. jours. Served with U.S. Army, 1952-54. Rockefeller Found. grantee, 1967. Mem. Am. Polit. Sci. Assn., African Studies Assn. (dir. 1976-78, 80-83, v.p. 1980-81, pres. 1981-82), AAUP (pres. Calif. Conf. 1980-81). Home: 1951 Holmby Ave Los Angeles CA 90025-5905

SKLOVSKY, ROBERT JOEL, pharmacology educator; b. Bronx, N.Y., Nov. 19, 1952; s. Nathan and Esther (Steinberg) S. BS, Bklyn. Coll., 1975; MA in Sci. Edn., Columbia U., 1976; PharmD, U. of Pacific, 1977; D in Naturopathic Medicine, Nat. Coll. Naturopathic Medicine, 1983. Intern Tripler Army Med. Ctr., Honolulu, 1977; prof. pharmacology Nat. Coll. Naturopathic Medicine, Portland, Oreg., 1982-85; pvt. practice specializing in naturopathic medicine Milwaukie, Oreg., 1983—; cons. State Bd. Naturopathic Examiners, Oreg., Hawaii, Clackamas County Sherriff's Dept.; cons. Internat. Drug Info. Ctr., N.Y.C., 1983—; cons. Albert Roy Davis Scientific Research Lab, Orange Park, Fla. 1986. Recipient Bristol Labs. award, 1983. Fellow Am. Coll. Apothecaries; mem. Am. Assn. Naturopathic Physicians, Oreg. Assn. Naturopathic Physicians, N.Y. Acad. Sci. Office: 6910 SE Lake Rd Portland OR 97267-2196

SKOGEN, HAVEN SHERMAN, investment company executive; b. Rochester, Minn., May 8, 1927; s. Joseph Harold and Elpha (Hemphill) S.; m. Beverly R. Baker, Feb. 19, 1949; 1 child, Scott H. BS, Iowa State U., 1950; MS, Rutgers U., 1954, PhD, 1955; MBA, U. Chgo., 1970. Registered profl. engr., Wis. Devel. engr. E.I. duPont, Wilmington, Del., 1955-57; prof. Elmhurst (Ill.) Coll., 1957-58; chief engr. Stackpole, St. Marys, Pa., 1958-62; plant mgr. Magnatronics, Elizabethtown, Ky., 1962-65; mgr. Allen-Bradley, Milw., 1965-70; v.p. Dill-Clithrow, Chgo., 1970-74; oil co. exec. Occidental Oil Co., Grand Junction, Colo., 1974-92; ptnr. H&B Investment CO., 1992—. Author: Synthetic Fuel Combustion, 1984; inventor radioactive retort doping, locus retorting zone. Naval Rsch. fellow, 1951-55. Fellow Am. Inst. Chemists; mem. Internat. Platform Assn., Masons, Elks, Sigma Xi, Phi Beta Kappa, Phi Lambda Upsilon. Republican. Home: 3152 Primrose Ct Grand Junction CO 81506-4147 Office: PO Box 2399 Grand Junction CO 81502-2399

SKOGLUND, ELIZABETH RUTH, marriage, child and family counselor; b. Chgo., June 17, 1937; d. Ragnar Emmanuel and Elizabeth Alvera (Benson) S. BA, UCLA, 1959; MA, Pasadena Coll., 1969. Cert. tchr., Calif.; cert. marriage, family and child counselor, Calif. Tchr. Marlborough Sch., Los Angeles, 1959-61; tchr., counselor Glendale (Calif.) High Sch., 1961-72; pvt. practice family counseling Burbank, Calif., 1972—. Author: over 20 books including It's OK to Be a Woman Again, 1988, Making Bad Times Good, 1991, Safety Zones, 1991, Harold's Dog Horace is Scared of the Dark, 1992, The Welcoming Hearth, 1993, Amma: The Life and Words of Amy Carmichael, 1994. Mem. Calif. Assn. Marriage and Family Therapists, Simon Wiesenthal Ctr. Republican.

SKOK, PAUL JOSEPH, lawyer; b. Tarrytown, N.Y., Nov. 3, 1947; s. Paul Joseph Skok and Anna S. (Ruscigno) Barlow. BS, Purdue U., 1970; MA, Ball State U., 1974; JD, U. Denver, 1984. Bar: Colo. 1985, U.S. Dist. Ct. Colo. 1985. Assoc. Skaalerud and Price, Denver, 1985-86, Law Office Paul Joseph Skok, Denver, 1986—; lectr. in law U. Denver, 1990. Author: Trial Attorney's Guide to Insurance Coverage and Bad Faith, 1994, supplement edit., 1994. Corp. counsel Have a Heart, Denver, 1987. Mem. ABA, Colo. Bar Assn., Denver Bar Assn., Assn. Trial Lawyers Am., Colo. Trial Lawyers Assn., Delta Tau Delta (chpt. advisor, alumni supr. U. Colo. 1977-83, 88). Roman Catholic. Home: 7660 Knox Ct Westminster CO 80030-4540 Office: 303 E 17th Ave Ste 700 Denver CO 80203-1260

SKOLNIKOFF, ALAN ZACHARY, psychiatrist; b. N.Y.C., Aug. 25, 1932. MD, SUNY, 1959. Intern Madigan Gen. Hosp., Tacoma, Wash., 1959-60; resident Langley Porter, San Francisco, 1963-66; candidate San Francisco Psychoanalyst Inst., 1965-73; fellow Community Psychiat. Tng. Ctr., Berkeley, Calif., 1966-68; pvt. practice San Francisco; assoc. clin. prof. U. Calif.; tng. supr. analyst San Francisco Psychoanalytic Inst. Contbr. articles to profl. jours. Fellow Am. Psychiatric Assn.

SKOOG, WILLIAM ARTHUR, former oncologist; b. Culver City, Calif., Apr. 10, 1925; s. John Lundeen and Allis Rose (Gatz) S.; m. Ann Douglas, Sept. 17, 1949; children: Karen, William Arthur, James Douglas, Allison. AA, UCLA, 1944; BA with gt. distinction, Stanford U., 1946, MD, 1949. Intern medicine Stanford Hosp., San Francisco, 1948-49, asst. resident medicine, 1949-50; asst. resident medicine N.Y. Hosp., N.Y.C., 1950-51; sr. resident medicine Wadsworth VA Hosp., Los Angeles, 1951, attending specialist internal medicine, 1962-68; practice medicine specializing in internal medicine, Los Altos, Calif., 1959-61; pvt. practice hematology and oncology Calif. Oncologic and Surg. Med. Group, Inc., Santa Monica, Calif., 1971-72; pvt. practice med. oncology, San Bernardino, Calif., 1972-94; assoc. staff Palo Alto-Stanford (Calif.) Hosp. Center, 1959-61, U. Calif. Med. Center, San Francisco, 1959-61; asso. attending physician U. Calif. at Los Angeles Hosp. and Clinics, 1961-78; vis. physician internal medicine Harbor Gen. Hosp., Torrance, Calif., 1962-65, attending physician, 1965-71; cons. chemistry Clin. Lab., UCLA Hosp., 1963-68; affiliate cons. staff St. John's Hosp., Santa Monica, Calif., 1967-71, courtesy staff, 1971-72; courtesy attending med. staff Santa Monica Hosp., 1967-72; staff physician St. Bernardine (Calif.) Hosp., 1972-94, hon. staff, 1994—; staff physician San Bernardino Community Hosp., 1972-90, courtesy staff, 1990-94; chief sect. oncology San Bernardino County Hosp., 1972-76; cons. staff Redlands (Calif.) Community Hosp., 1972-83, courtesy staff, 1983-94, hon. staff, 1994; asst. in medicine Cornell Med. Coll., N.Y.C., 1950-51; jr. research physician UCLA Atomic Energy Project, 1954-55; instr. medicine, asst. research physician dept. medicine UCLA Med. Center, 1955-56, asst. prof. medicine, asst. research physician, 1956-59; clin. asso. hematology VA Center, Los Angeles, 1956-59; co-dir. metabolic research unit UCLA Center for Health Scis., 1955-59, 61-65; co-dir. Health Scis. Clin. Research Center, 1965-68, dir., 1968-72; clin. instr. medicine Stanford, 1959-61; asst. clin. prof. medicine, assoc. research physician U. Calif. Med. Center, San Francisco, 1959-61; lectr. medicine UCLA Sch. Medicine, 1961-62, assoc. prof. medicine, 1962-73, assoc. clin. prof. medicine, 1973—. Served with USNR, 1943-46, lt. M.C., 1951-53. Fellow ACP; mem. Am., Calif. med. assns., So. Calif. Acad. Clin. Oncology, Western Soc. Clin. Research, Am. Fedn. Clin. Research, Los Angeles Acad. Medicine, San Bernardino County Med. Soc., Am. Soc. Clin. Oncology, Am. Soc. Internal Medicine, Calif. Soc. Internal Medicine, Inland Soc. Internal Medicine, Phi Beta Kappa, Alpha Omega Alpha, Sigma Xi, Alpha Kappa Kappa. Episcopalian (vestryman 1965-70). Club: Redlands Country. Contbr. articles to profl. jours. Home: 1119 Kimberly Pl Redlands CA 92373-6786

SKOOR, JOHN BRIAN, art educator, art consultant; b. Mount Vernon, Wash., Dec. 14, 1939; s. George Nephi and Marie Elizabeth (Collins) S.; m. Susan Diane Waugh, June 17, 1972; children: Marie Elizabeth, Christine Elaine. AA in Edn., Graceland Coll., Lamoni, 1960; BA in Art, Cen. Wash. U., 1962, BA in Edn., 1965, MA in Art, 1969. Art instr. Delta (Mich.) Coll., Saginaw, 1977-79; instr. Renton (Wash.) Vocat. Tech. Inst., 1981-83; art instr. Green River (Wash.) Community Coll., Auburn, 1988—; cons. staff and development instr. various Seattle sch. dists., 1988—; art instr. Higline Community Coll., Seattle, 1990—; adj. faculty Cen. Wash. U., 1984—, Seattle Pacific U., 1986—; dir. sr. programs Highline C.C., 1992—; guest speaker Wash. Art Educators Assn. Conv., 1990. Illustrator of religious curriculum texts, 1978-80; exhibited acrylic theol. paintings show, Independence, Mo., 1980. Guest speaker Alma (Mich.) Art Dept., 1977, Nat. Camping Assn., Detroit, 1979, Wash. Art Tchrs. Assn., 1990; coord. sr. programs Highline C. of C., 1992—; elder Reorganized Ch. of Jesus Christ of Latter Day Saints, Seattle, 1966—, pastor, 1987—, bd. dirs. creative arts festival, Mich., 1977. Mem. Wash. Alliance for Arts Edn. (commn. chmn. 1987—), Richland Art Tchrs. Assn. (pres. 1965-66), Tri-City Art Tchrs. Assn. (pres. 1966-67), Nat. Art Educators Assn. Home and Studio: 4830 S Morgan St Seattle WA 98118

SKOPIL, OTTO RICHARD, JR., federal judge; b. Portland, Oreg., June 3, 1919; s. Otto Richard and Freda Martha (Boetticher) S.; m. Janet Rae Lundy, July 27, 1956; children: Otto Richard III, Casey Robert, Shannon Ida, Molly Jo. BA in Econs., Willamette U., 1941, LLB, 1946, LLD (hon.), 1983. Bar: Oreg. 1946, IRS, U.S. Treasury Dept., U.S. Dist. Ct. Oreg., U.S. Ct. Appeals (9th cir.), U.S. Supreme Ct. 1946. Assoc. Skopil & Skopil, 1946-51; ptnr. Williams, Skopil, Miller & Beck (and predecessors), Salem, Oreg., 1951-72; judge U.S. Dist. Ct., Portland, 1972-79; chief judge U.S. Dist. Ct., 1976-79; judge U.S. Ct. Appeals (9th cir.), Portland, 1979—; chmn. com. adminstrn. of fed. magistrate sys. U.S. Jud. Conf., 1980-86; co-founder Oreg. chpt. Am. Leadership Forum; chmn. 9th cir. Jud. Coun. Magistrates Adv. Com., 1988-91; chmn. U.S. Jud. Conf. Long Range Planning Com., 1990-95. Hi-Y adviser Salem YMCA, 1951-52; appeal agt. SSS, Marion County (Oreg.) Draft Bd., 1953-66; master of ceremonies 1st Gov.'s Prayer Breakfast for State Oreg., 1959; mem. citizens adv. com., City of Salem, 1970-71; chmn. Gov.'s Com. on Staffing Mental Instns., 1969-70; pres., bd. dirs. Marion County Tb and Health Assn., 1958-61; bd. dirs. Willamette Valley Camp Fire Girls, 1946-56, Internat. Christian Leadership, 1959, Fed. Jud. Ctr., 1979; trustee Willamette U., 1969-71; elder Mt. Park Ch., 1979-81. Served to lt. USNR, 1942-46. Recipient Oreg. Legal Citizen of Yr. award, 1986, Disting. Alumni award Willamette U. Sch. Law, 1988. Mem. ABA, Oreg. Bar Assn. (bd. govs.), Marion County Bar Assn., Am. Judicature Soc., Oreg. Assn. Def. Counsel (dir.), Def. Research Inst., Assn. Ins. Attys. U.S. and Can. (Oreg. rep. 1970), Internat. Soc. Barristers, Prayer Breakfast Movement (fellowship council). Clubs: Salem, Exchange (pres. 1947), Illahe Hills Country (pres., dir. 1964-67). Office: US Ct Appeals 232 Pioneer Courthouse 555 SW Yamhill St Portland OR 97204-1336

SKORA, WAYNE PHILIP, retired air force officer; b. Chgo., Jan. 16, 1944; s. Felix Anthony Skora and Lillie (Goshko) St. Thomas; m. Dorothy Mae Barrett, June 13, 1966; children: Tanya Christine, Christopher Michael. BS in Engring. Sci., USAF Acad., 1966; MS in Human Resource Mgmt., U. Utah, 1976. Commd. 2d lt. USAF, 1966, advanced through grades to col., 1988; F-4 pilot USAF, various locations, 1967-69, 71-79; flight safety officer Hdqrs. Tactical Air Command, Langley AFB, Va., 1979-82; chief safety, A-10 pilot 23d Tactical Fighter Wing, England AFB, La., 1982-84; chief Office Mil. Cooperation, Am. Embassy, Manama, Bahrain, 1984-87; asst. chief logistics 507th Tactical Air Control Wing, Shaw AFB, S.C., 1987-88; dep. comdr. for ops. So. Air Div., Howard AFB, Panama, 1988-90; dep. for safety Air Force Devel. Test Ctr., Eglin AFB, Fla., 1990-92. Decorated Legion of Merit, DFC with oak leaf cluster, Air medal with 21 oak leaf clusters, Def. Meritorious Svc. medal, AF Meritorious Svc. medal with oak leaf cluster, AF Commendation medal with oak leaf cluster. Mem. Order of Daedalians (sec. 1988-90). Roman Catholic. Home: 24 Luxury Ln Colorado Springs CO 80921-3300

SKORUPSKI, DIANE CHRISTINE, school library media specialist; b. Southbridge, Mass., Mar. 24, 1948; d. Axel Hector and Naomia Maxine (Willis) Johnson; m. Alfred Robert Skorupski, Oct. 9, 1971; children: Kurt (dec.), Gregory R., Kayle J. BS in Edn., North Adams State Coll., 1970; MLS, U. Ariz., 1988. Tchr., Libr., Ariz. Tchr. Town of Dudley, Mass., 1970-71, Sowest Supervisory Sch. Union, Bennington, Vt., 1971-73; sch. libr. media specialist Sunnyside Sch. Dist. # 12, Tucson, 1987—; bd. mem. Sch. Libr. Media Divsn., 1988-91, pres.-elect, 1992-93, pres. 1993-94. Contbr.: Information Literacy: Educating Children for the 21st Century, 1994. Brownie/Jr. Scout Leader Sahuaro Girl Scout Coun., Tucson, 1985-92. Grantee Tech. for Tchg. US West, Am. Assn. Sch. Adminstrs., Autodesk, AT&T, 1991-93. Mem. ALA, NEA, Am. Assn. Sch. Librs., Ariz. Libr. Assn., Ariz. Reading Assn., Tucson Area Reading Coun. (v.p. elect 1995—). Home: 7810 N Rasmussen Ave Tucson AZ 85741-1448 Office: Liberty Elem School 5495 S Liberty Ave Tucson AZ 85706

SKOTHEIM, ROBERT ALLEN, museum administrator; b. Seattle, Jan. 31, 1933; s. Sivert O. and Marjorie F. (Allen) S.; m. Nadine Vail, June 14, 1953; children—Marjorie, Kris, Julia. BA, U. Wash., 1955, MA, 1958, PhD, 1962; LLD (hon.), Hobart and William Smith Colls., Geneva, N.Y., 1975; LittD (hon.), Whitman Coll., 1988; LHD (hon.), Coll. Idaho, 1988, Occidental Coll., 1989, Ill. Wesleyan U., 1990; DFA (hon.), Willamette U., 1989. Prof. history U. Wash., 1962-63; prof. history Wayne State U., Detroit, 1963-66; prof. UCLA, 1966-67, U. Colo., Boulder, 1967-72; provost, dean faculty Hobart and William Smith Colls., 1972-75; pres. Whitman Coll., Walla Walla, Wash., 1975-88, Huntington Libr., Art Collections & Bot. Gardens, San Marino, Calif., 1988—. Author: American Intellectual Histories and Historians, 1966, Totalitarianism and American Social Thought, 1971; Editor: The Historian and the Climate of Opinion, 1969; co-editor: American Social Thought: Sources and Interpretations, 2 vols, 1972. Guggenheim fellow, 1967-68. Mem. Phi Beta Kappa (hon.). Office: Huntington Library Art Collections & Bot Gardens 1151 Oxford Rd San Marino CA 91108-1299

SKOUSEN, ROYAL JON, linguist; b. Cleve., Aug. 5, 1945; s. Leroy Bentley and Helen Louise (McCarty) S.; m. Sirkku Unelma Härkönen, June 24, 1968; children: Mikko, Lawrence, Angela, Christina, Nathaniel, Benjamin, Stephen. BA in English, Brigham Young U., 1969; MA in Linguistics, U. Ill., 1971, PhD in Linguistics, 1972. Instr. in linguistics U. Ill., Urbana, 1970-72; asst. prof. linguistics U. Tex., Austin, 1972-79; asst. prof. English Brigham Young U., Provo, Utah, 1979-81, assoc. prof. English, 1981-86, prof. English, 1986—; vis. prof. linguistics U. Calif., San Diego, 1981; Fulbright lectr. in linguistics U. Tampere, Finland, 1982; cons. Houghton Mifflin Pubs., Boston, 1978-82, WordPerfect Corp., Orem, Utah, 1984. author: Substantive Evidence in Phonology, 1975, Analogical Modeling of Language, 1989, Analogy and Structure, 1992; editl. bd. Computers and the Humanities, 1987—, Jour. of Quantitative Linguistics, 1993—. Spencer Found. rsch. grantee, 1974; James L. Barker lectr. Brigham Young U., 1985-86. Mem. Internat. Soc. Quantitative Linguistics (founding mem.), Found. for Ancient Rsch. and Mormon Studies (editor), Deseret Lang. and Linguistics Soc. (editor, pres. 1980-82). Mem. LDS Ch. Office: Brigham Young U Dept English Provo UT 84602

SKRATEK, SYLVIA PAULETTE, mediator, arbitrator, dispute systems designer; b. Detroit, Dec. 23, 1950; d. William Joseph and Helen (Meskauskas) S.; m. John Wayne Gullion, Dec. 21,1984. BS, Wayne State U., 1971; MLS, Western Mich. U., 1976; PhD, U. Mich., 1985. Media specialist Jackson (Mich.) Pub. Schs., 1971-79; contract specialist Jackson County Edn. Assn., 1976-79; field rep. Mich. Edn. Assn., E.Lansing, 1979-81; contract adminstr. Wash. Edn. Assn., Federal Way, 1981-85, regional coord., 1985-88, program adminstr., from 1988; dir. mediation svcs. Conflict Mgmt. Inst., Lake Oswego, Ore., 1986-87; exec. dir. N.W. Ctr. for Conciliation, 1987-88; served in Wash. State Senate, 1990-94; tng. cons. City of Seattle 1986—; trustee Group Health Coop. of Puget Sound, Wash., 1984-87; sole proprietor Skratek & Assocs., 1980—; pres. Resolutions Intenat., 1990—. Contbr. articles to legal jours. Mem. Soc. for Profls. in Dispute Resolution, Indsl. Rels. Rsch. Assn.

SKROCKI, EDMUND STANLEY, II, health fair promoter, executive; b. Schenectady, N.Y., Sept. 6, 1953; s. Edmund Stanley I and Lorraine (Nocian) S.; m. Diane Carolyn Sittig, Sept. 6, 1976 (div. 1992); children: Carolyn, Michelle, Edmund III; life ptnr. Leslee Erickson; 1 child, Johnathon Edmund. AA, LaValley Coll., 1981; BA, Sonoma State U., 1982, MA, 1987; postgrad., Am. Inst. Hypnotherapy. Pres. Skrocki's Philos. Svc., Lakeview Terrace, Calif., 1971-81; pres., CEO Skrocki's Superior Svc., Lakeview Terrace, 1971-76; pres., chief exec. officer Skrocki's Superior Svc., Redding, Calif., 1976—; pres., CEO, promoter Redding (Calif.) Health Faire, 1991—. Bd. govs., deancon Ch. of Universal Knowledge, 1991—. Named one of Outstanding Young Men Am., 1980. Mem. Shasta Submarine Soc. (pres. 1984—). Home and Office: 755 Quartz Hill Rd Redding CA 96003-2118

SKROMEDA, STEVE, investment company executive; b. 1957. BS, Calif. State U., 1982. CFO Kennedy Cabot & Co., Beverly Hills, Calif., 1983—. Office: Kennedy Cabot & Co Inc 9470 Wilshire Blvd Beverly Hills CA 90212-2707*

SKUD, BERNARD EINAR, marine biologist; b. Ironwood, Mich., Jan. 31, 1927; s. Ferdinand and Elma (Hendrickson) S.; m. Patricia Ruth Duffin, Aug. 20, 1950; children: Timothy, Ferd, Eric. BS, U. Mich., 1949, MS, 1950; postgrad., U. Wash., 1951-53; Fellow of Pub. & Internat. Affairs, Princeton U., 1968. Grad. asst. U. Mich., Ann Arbor, 1949-50; rsch. biologist U.S. Fish and Wildlife Svc., Seattle, 1950-56; supervisory fishery biologist U.S. Bur. Comml. Fisheries, Boothbay Harbor, Maine, 1956-58; asst. dir. U.S. Bur. Comml. Fisheries, Galveston, Tex., 1958-61; dir. U.S. Bur. Comml. Fisheries, Boothbay Harbor, 1961-70; dir. investigations Internat. Pacific Halibut Commn., Seattle, 1970-78; divsn. chief U.S. Nat. Marine Fisheries Svc., Washington, 1978-79; sr. scientist U.S. Nat. Marine Fisheries Svc., Narragansett, R.I., 1980-85; dir. Internat. North Pacific Fisheries Commn., Vancouver, B.C., Can., 1986-91; CEO Sisu Consulting, Oak Harbor, Wash., 1991—; affiliate prof. U. Wash., Seattle, 1971-78, U. R.I., Kingston, 1980-86. Editor (bull.) Internat. Pacific Halibut Commn. Scientific Reports, 1970-78, Jour. N.W. Atlantic Fishery Science, 1985-86. Bd. dirs. St. Andrews Hosp., Boothbay Harbor, 1965-70. With USN, 1945-46. Fellow Am. Inst. Fishery Rsch. Biologists (pres. 1981-83); mem. Am. Fisheries Soc. (book rev. editor 1965-70). Home: 11435 115th St NW Oak Harbor WA 98277 Office: Sisu Consulting 11435 115th St NW Oak Harbor WA 98277-2201

SKYLSTAD, WILLIAM S., bishop; b. Omak, Wash., Mar. 2, 1934; s. Stephen Martin and Reneldes Elizzbeth (Danzl) S. Student, Pontifical Coll., Josephinum, Worthington, Ohio; M.Ed., Gonzaga U. Ordained priest Roman Catholic Ch., 1960; asst. pastor Pullman, Wash., 1960-62; tchr. Mater Cleri Sem., 1961-68, rector, 1968-74; pastor Assumption Parish, Spokane, 1974-76; chancellor Diocese of Spokane, 1976-77; ordained bishop, 1977; bishop of Yakima, Wash., 1977-90, Spokane, Wash., 1990—. Office: Diocese of Spokane PO Box 1453 1023 W Riverside Ave Spokane WA 99201-1103 Home: 1025 W Cleveland Ave Spokane WA 99205-3320*

SLABACH, STEPHEN HALL, lawyer; b. Oklahoma City, Nov. 15, 1934; s. Carl Edward and Alvine A. (Woellner) S.; m. Elizabeth Havard Cartwright, Feb. 15, 1958; children: Elizabeth Slabach Schmit, Stephen Edward, William Cartwright. BSME, Northwestern U., 1957; postgrad. George Washington U. Sch. Law, 1957-59; LLB, Stanford U., 1961. Bar: Calif. 1962, U.S. Dist. Ct. (no. dist.) Calif. 1962, U.S. Ct. Appeals (9th cir.) 1973, U.S. Supreme Ct. 1976. Law clk. to judge Calif. First Dist. Ct. Appeal, San Francisco, 1961-62; assoc. Cooley, Crowley, Gather, Godward, Castro & Huddleson, San Francisco, 1962-65; assoc. Cushing, Cullinan, Hancock & Rothert, San Francisco, 1965-73, ptnr., 1973-75; sole practice, Burlingame, Calif., 1975-88, San Mateo, 1975—; Legal aid vol. San Mateo County; trustee San Mateo County Law Libr. Com., 1993—; pres. Pacific Locomotive Assn., 1988-90, gen. counsel, 1980—; bd. dirs. Notre Dame H.S., Belmont, Calif., 1976-84, pres., bd., 1981-82. Mem. State Bar Calif., ABA, Am. Judicature Soc., Kiwanis (Burlingame). Republican. Episcopalian. Office: 520 S El Camino Real Ste 700 San Mateo CA 94402-1720

SLACK, DONALD CARL, agricultural engineer, educator; b. Cody, Wyo., June 25, 1942; s. Clarence Ralbon and Clara May (Beightol) S.; m. Marion Arline Kimball, Dec. 19, 1964; children: Jonel Marie, Jennifer Michelle. BS in Agrl. Engring., U. Wyo., 1965; MS in Agrl. Engring., U. Ky., 1968, PhD in Agrl. Engring., 1975. Registered profl. engr., Ky., Ariz. Asst. civil engr. City of Los Angeles, 1965; research specialist U. Ky., Lexington, 1966-70; agrl. engring. advisor U. Ky., Tha Phra, Thailand, 1970-73; research asst. U. Ky., Lexington, 1973-75; from asst. prof. to assoc. prof. agrl. engring. U. Minn., St. Paul, 1975-84; prof. U. Ariz., Tucson, 1984—, head dept. agrl. and biosystems engring., 1991—; tech. advisor Ariz. Dept. Water Resources, Phoenix, 1985—; cons. Winrock Internat., Morrilton, Ark., 1984, Water Mgmt. Synthesis II, Logan, Utah, 1985, Desert Agrl. Tech. Systems, Tucson, 1985—, Portek Hermosillo, Mex., 1989—, World Bank, Washington, 1992—; dep. program support mgr. Rsch. Irrigation Support Project for Asia and the Near East, Arlington, Va., 1987-94. Contbr. articles to profl. jours. Fellow ASCE (Outstanding Jour. Paper award 1988); mem. Am. Soc. Agrl. Engrs. (Ariz. sect. Engr. of Yr. 1993), Am. Geophys. Union, Am. Soc. Agronomy, Soil Sci. Soc. Am., Am. Soc. Engring. Edn., SAR, Brotherhood of Knights of the Vine (master knight), Sigma Xi, Tau Beta Pi, Alpha Epsilon, Gamma Sigma Delta. Democrat. Lutheran. Home: 9230 E Visco Pl Tucson AZ 85710-3167 Office: U Ariz Agrl Biosystems Engrin Tucson AZ 85721

SLADICH, HARRY HAMILL, university administrator; b. Anaconda, Mont., Jan. 9, 1938; s. Joseph Francis and Caroline (Hamill) S.; m. Marguerite Dill, June 18, 1960; children: Harry G., Jennifer M., Suzanne. BBA, Gonzaga U., 1959, MBA, 1967. Asst. prof. Gonzaga U., Spokane, Wash., 1963—, dir. adminstrv. services, 1962-71, asst. to pres., 1972-83, v.p. adminstrn. and planning, 1983—. Bd. dirs. ARC, Spokane, 1978—, chmn., 1981-83, adv. council western ops., Burlingame, Calif., 1983-86; mem. com. on nominations ARC, Washington, 1991-92; mem. exec. com. adv. bd. Wash. State Higher Edn. Bd., 1986-87; bd. dirs. Wash. State Catholic Conf., Seattle, 1980-84, Mus. Native Am. Culture, Spokane, 1989-92; chmn. edn. div. United Way, Spokane, 1983, bd. dirs. 1991—, v.p. adminstrn., 1995—. Roman Catholic. Home: 1103 W 17th Ave Spokane WA 99203-1108 Office: Gonzaga U 502 E Boone Ave Spokane WA 99258-1774

SLATER, DON AUSTIN, shipyard executive, consultant; b. Bay City, Mich., May 27, 1938; s. William Stuart and Inez Fern (Hagen) S.; m. Sara Belva Sanford, Feb. 3, 1962; children: Shandra Sanford, Nathan Dorman. BS in Naval Architecture and Marine Engring., U. Mich. Naval architect Western Boat Bldg. Corp., Tacoma, 1964; exec. v.p. and gen. mgr. Star Marine Industries, Tacoma; gen. mgr. Shipyard div. Marine Iron Works, Tacoma; pres., CEO Marine Industry N.W., Inc., Tacoma, 1976—; cons. to various law firms, Wash. and N.J., 1975—; arbitrator Am. Arbitration Assn., 1985—. 1st v.p. Va. V Found., Settlem 1986; bd. dirs. Puget Sound Marine Hist. Soc., 1978-80. Home: 30720 43rd Ave SW Federal Way WA 98023-2164 Office: Marine Industries NW Inc 313 E F St # 1275 Tacoma WA 98421-1821

SLATER, JAMES MUNRO, radiation oncologist; b. Salt Lake City, Jan. 7, 1929; s. Donald Munro and Leone Forestine (Fehr) S.; m. JoAnn Strout, Dec. 28, 1948; children: James, Julie, Jan, Jerry, Jon. B.S. in Physics, U. Utah, Utah State U., 1954; M.D., Loma Linda U., 1963. Diplomate: Am. Bd. Radiology. Intern Latter Day Saints Hosp., Salt Lake City, 1963-64; resident in radiology Latter Day Saints Hosp., 1964-65; resident in radiotherapy Loma Linda U. Med. Ctr., White Meml. Med. Center, Los Angeles; fellow in radiotherapy Loma Linda U. Med. Ctr., White Meml. Med. Center, 1967-68, U. Tex.-M.D. Anderson Hosp. and Tumor Inst., Houston, 1968-69; mem. faculty Loma Linda (Calif.) U., 1975—, prof. radiology, 1979—, chmn. radiation scis. dept., 1979-89, dir. nuclear medicine, 1970—, dir. radiation oncology, 1975-79, chmn. dept. radiation oncology, 1990—, dir. Cancer Inst., 1993—, exec. v.p. Med. Ctr., 1994—; treas. med. ctr., 1995—; treas. Med. Ctr., 1995—; co-dir. cmty. radiology oncology program L.A. Country-U. So. Calif. Comprehensive Cancer Ctr., 1978-83; mem. cancer adv. coun. State of Calif., 1980-85; clin. prof. U. So. Calif., 1982—; founding mem. Proton Therapy Coop. Group, 1985—, chmn. 1987-91; cons. charged particle therapy program Lawrence Berkeley Lab., 1986—; cons. R&D monoclonal antibodies Hybritech Inc., 1985-94, bd. dirs., 1985-94; mem. panel cons. Internat. Atomic Energy Agy. UNA, 1994—; cons. Sci. Applications Internat. Corp., 1979—. Bd. dirs. Am. Cancer Soc., San Bernardino/Riverside, 1976—, exec. com., 1976—; pres. Inland Empire chpt., 1981-83. NIH fellow, 1968-69; recipient exhbn. awards Radiol. Soc. N.Am., 1973, echbn. awards European Assn. Radiology, 1975, exhbn. awards Am. Soc. Therapeutic Radiologists, 1978, Alumnus of Yr. award, 1993, 94. Fellow Am. Coll. Radiology; mem. AMA, ACS (liaison mem. to commn. on cancer 1976-84), Am. Radium Soc., Am. Soc. Clin. Oncology, Am. Soc. Therapeutics Radiologists, Assn. Univ. Radiologists, Calif. Med. Assn., Calif. Radiol. Soc., Gilbert H. Fletcher Soc. (pres. 1981-82), Loma Linda U. Med. Sch. Alumni Assn., Radiol. Soc. N.Am., San Bernardino County Med. Soc., Bernardino County Med Soc., Soc. Chairmen Of Acad. Radiation Oncology Programs, Alpha Omega Alpha. Home: 1210 W Highland Ave Redlands CA 92373-6659 Office: Loma Linda U Radiation Medicine Loma Linda CA 92350

SLATER, LEONARD, writer, editor; b. N.Y.C., July 15, 1920; s. Max and Jean (Lenobel) S.; m. Betty Moorsteen, 1946; children: Amy, Lucy. BA in Polit. Sci., U. Mich., 1941. Reporter, writer, White House and Pentagon NBC News, Washington, 1941-44; corr. Washington bur., White House and Pentagon Time mag., 1945-47; assoc. editor Newsweek mag., N.Y.C., 1947-60, corr. Eastern Europe and Middle East; bur. chief Newsweek mag., Los Angeles; sr. editor, columnist McCalls' mag., N.Y. and Europe, 1961-64; free-lance writer, editor, 1964—. Author: Aly, 1965, The Pledge, 1970, Ella & Her Teenage Cats, 1993; contbr. articles to mags. Mem. Authors League of Am. Home: 4370 Arista Dr San Diego CA 92103-1029 also: Binicalaf Minorca, Balearic Islands Spain

SLATER, MANNING, broadcasting consultant; b. Springfield, Mass., Aug. 29, 1917; s. Ely and Sarah Deenah (Hurwitz) Slotnick; m. Anita Norman, July 1, 1977; children—Gary Edward, Richard Stuart. B.A., Am. Internat. Coll., 1939. Pres. Community Markets, Springfield, Mass., 1939-46; v.p., treas. Bridgeport Broadcasting Co., Conn., 1947-58; pres., chmn. bd. Hercules Broadcasting Co., Sacramento and Seattle, 1959—; also Slater Broadcasting Co.; pres. Slater Investment Co. Bd. govs. Mercy Hosp., Sacramento. Named Man of Yr. State of Israel Bonds, 1989. Mem. Nat. Assn. Broadcasters, Radio Advt. Bur., Sacramento C. of C., B'nai B'rith. Democrat. Jewish. Clubs: University, Comstock Club Sacramento. Home: 48635 Sundrop Ct Palm Desert CA 92260-6646 also: 48 635 Sundrop Ct Palm Desert CA 92260 Office: 1337 Howe Ave Ste 110 Sacramento CA 95825-3361

SLATER, SHELLEY, document and training manager; b. Ogden, Utah, June 26, 1959; d. Lynn Russell and Darlene (Allen) Slater; m. Dale Thomas Hansen, Jan. 26, 1977 (div. Feb. 1979); 1 child, Thomas Arthur; m. Eugene Allan DuVall, Mar. 8, 1981 (div. Dec. 1985); 1 child, Gregory Allan; m. Steven Blake Allender, June 9, 1990 (div. May 1993). BBA cum laude, Regis U., 1992, postgrad., 1992—. Installation, repair technician MT Bell, Clearfield, Utah, 1977-81; ctrl. office technician MT Bell, Salt Lake City, 1981-83, engring. specialist, 1983-86; engring. specialist U.S. West Comm., Englewood, Colo., 1986-93; network analyst, documentation and tng. mgr. Time Warner Comm., Englewood, Colo., 1993—; documentation and tng. mgr., 1995—; bus. cons. Jr. Achievement, Denver, 1988-89. Day capt. AZTEC Denver Mus. of Natural History, 1992; loaned exec. Mile High United Way, 1993. Democrat. Home: 9618 S Cordova Dr Hghlnds Ranch CO 80126-3788 Office: Time Warner Comm 160 Inverness Dr W Englewood CO 80112-5001

SLATES, ROGER DUANE, II, lawyer, sole practitioner; b. Garden Grove, Calif., Nov. 13, 1964; s. Roger D. Sr. and Marlette Marie (Parsch) S.; m. Lisa Marie Whiteman, Jan. 25, 1993. BS in Fin. Mgmt., Calif. State U., Long Beach, 1987, BS in Investments, 1987, BS in Real Estate, 1987; JD, U. Calif., Berkeley, 1990. Bar: Calif., 1990. Real estate salesperson R.D. Slates & Assocs., Huntington Beach, Calif., 1983-87; city atty. internship City Atty.'s Office, Huntington Beach, Calif., 1988; atty. Miller, Starr & Regalia, Oakland, Calif., 1989-92, sole practitioner, Oakland, Calif., 1992—. Youth del. Rep. Nat. Conv., Dallas, 1984; vol. Radio Amateur Civil Emergency Svcs., 1990—; comm. vol. ARC; former res. dep. Contra Costa Sheriffs Dept., Martinez, Calif., 1991-93. Recipient Am. Jurisprudence award Boalt Hall Law Sch., 1987, Cert. of Merit, Orange County Bd. Suprs., 1990. Mem. Orange County Bar Assn., Orange County Barristers Assn., Am. Radio Relay League. Republican. Home: 822 13th St Huntington Beach CA 92648-3435 Office: R D Slates II PO Box 244 Huntington Beach CA 92648-0244

SLATTERY, CHARLES WILBUR, biochemistry educator; b. La Junta, Colo., Nov. 18, 1937; s. Robert Ernest Slattery and Virgie Belle (Chamberlain) Tobin; m. Arline Sylvia Reile, June 15, 1958; children: Scott Charles, Coleen Kay. BA, Union Coll., 1959; MS, U. Nebr., 1961, PhD, 1965. Instr. chemistry Union Coll., Lincoln, Nebr., 1961-63; asst. prof., assoc. prof. chemistry Atlantic Union Coll., South Lancaster, Mass., 1963-68; rsch. assoc. biophysics MIT, Cambridge, 1967-70; asst. prof., then prof. biochemistry Loma Linda U., Calif., 1970-80, prof. biochemistry-pediatrics, 1980—, chmn. dept., 1983—; vis. prof. U. So. Calif., L.A., 1978-79. Contbr. articles to profl. jours. NIH grantee, 1979-82, 86-89, Am. Heart Assn. (Calif.), 1981-83, 83-84. Mem. AAAS, Am. Chem. Soc. (biochemistry div.), Am. Dairy Sci. Assn., Am. Heart Assn. Thrombosis Coun., N.Y. Acad. Scis., The Protein Soc., Am. Soc. Biochemistry and Molecular Biology. Internat. Soc. for Rsch. on Human Milk and Lactation, Sigma Xi. Office: Loma Linda U Sch of Medicine Dept of Biochemistry Loma Linda CA 92350

SLAUGHTER, ANNE MARIE, biologist; b. Vallejo, Calif., Mar. 15, 1969; d. Dennis Robert and Penny Mary (Graf) S. BS in Zoology, BS in Marine Biology, Humboldt State U., 1992. Lab technician dept. oceanography U. Hawaii, Oahu, 1992-93; teaching assoc. Humboldt State U., Arcata, Calif., 1993—. Vol. judge sci. fair Eureka (Calif.) Bd. Edn., 1994. Mem. AAAS. Office: Humboldt State U Dept Biology Arcata CA 95521

SLAUGHTER, JOHN BROOKS, university president; b. Topeka, Mar. 16, 1934; s. Reuben Brooks and Dora (Reeves) S.; m. Ida Bernice Johnson, Aug. 31, 1956; children: John Brooks, Jacqueline Michelle. Student, Washburn U., 1951-53; BSEE, Kans. State U., 1956, DSc (hon.), 1988; MS in Engring., UCLA, 1961; PhD in Engring. Scis, U. Calif., San Diego, 1971; D Engring. (hon.), Rensselaer Poly. Inst., 1981; DSc (hon.), U. So. Calif., 1981, Tuskegee Inst., 1981, U. Md., 1982, U. Notre Dame, 1982, U. Miami, 1983, U. Mass., 1983, Tex. So. U., 1984, U. Toledo, 1985, U. Ill., 1986, SUNY, 1986; LHD (hon.), Bowie State Coll., 1987; DSc (hon.), Morehouse Coll., 1988, Kans. State U., 1988; LLD (hon.), U. Pacific, 1989; DSc (hon.), Pomona Coll., 1989; LHD (hon.), Alfred U., 1991, Calif. Luth. U., 1991, Washburn U., 1992. Registered profl. engr., Wash. Electronics engr. Gen. Dynamics Convair, San Diego, 1956-60; with Naval Electronics Lab. Center, San Diego, 1960-75, div. head, 1965-71, dept. head, 1971-75; dir. applied physics lab. U. Wash., 1975-77; asst. dir. NSF, Washington, 1977-79; dir. NSF, 1980-82; acad. v.p., provost Wash. State U., 1979-80; chancellor U. Md., College Park, 1982-88; pres. Occidental Coll., Los Angeles, 1988—; bd. dirs., vice chmn. San Diego Transit Corp., 1968-75; mem. com. on minorities in engring. Nat. Rsch. Coun., 1976-79; mem. Commn. on Pre-Coll. Edn. in Math., Sci. and Tech. Nat. Sci. Bd., 1982-83; bd. dirs. Monsanto Co., ARCO, Avery Dennison Corp., IBM, Northrop Grumman Corp.; chmn. advancement com. Music Ctr. of L.A. County, 1989-93. Editor: Jour. Computers and Elec. Engring, 1972—. Bd. dirs. San Diego Urban League, 1962-66, pres., 1964-66; mem. Pres.'s Com. on Nat. Medal Sci., 1979-80; trustee Rensselaer Poly. Inst., 1982; chmn. Pres.'s Com. Nat. Collegiate Athletic Assn., 1986-88; bd. govs. Town Hall of Calif., 1990; bd. dirs. L.A. World Affairs Coun., 1990. Recipient Engring. Disting. Alumnus of Yr. award UCLA, 1978, UCLA medal, 1989, Roger Revelle award U. Calif.-San Diego, 1991, Disting. Svc. award NSF, 1979, Svc. in Engring. award Kans. State U., 1981, Disting. Alumnus of Yr. award U. Calif.-San Diego, 1982; Naval Electronics Lab. Ctr. fellow, 1969-70; elected to Topeka High Sch. Hall of Fame, 1983, Hall of Fame of Am. Soc. Engring. Edn., 1993; named Kansan of Yr. by Kans. Native Sons and Daus., 1994. Fellow IEEE (chmn. com. on minority affairs 1976-80), Am. Acad. Arts and Scis.; mem. NAE, Nat. Collegiate Athletic Assn. (chmn. pres. commn.), Am. Soc. for Engring. Edn. (inducted into Hall of Fame 1993), Phi Beta Kappa (hon.), Tau Beta Phi, Eta Kappa Nu. Office: Occidental Coll 1600 Campus Rd Los Angeles CA 90041-3384

SLAUGHTER, PAUL DAMIEN, photojournalist; b. Louisville, Nov. 8, 1938; s. Thomas Booker and Lucretia (Katra) S.; m. Inee Yang, Jan. 8, 1984; 1 child, Alexander Sasha Yang. Chief photographer L.A. Olympic Organizing Com., 1984; official production photographer L.A. Internat. Theater Festival, 1987; freelance photographer, 1970—. Exhibited in shows at World Trade Ctr. Club Hong Kong, Image Bank; represented in premanent collections of Occidental Petroleum, Prudential Ins., L.A. Pub. Library, Community Redevel. Agy. L.A., Am. Soc. Mag. Photographers Archive at George Eastman House; contbr. editor Photographic Mag. Recipient Steuben Glass award, Eastman Kodak, Gold award, Art Directors Club. Mem. Am. Soc. Mag. Photographers. Office: Paul Slaughter Photography 1300 Calle Giraso Santa Fe NM 87501-8906

SLEDGE, REGINALD LEON, industry and compliance analyst; b. Balt., July 8, 1954; s. Herbert Clifton and Juanita (Brantley) S. Grad., Lawrence Acad., 1972; student, Dartmouth Coll., 1968; BS, Boston U., 1976; MBA, Columbia U., 1984, student, 1988; postgrad. Fin. analyst West Point-Pepperell, Inc., N.Y.C., 1976-77; fin. futures trader European Am. Bank, N.Y.C., 1978-82; portfolio mgr. Fuji Bank, N.Y.C., 1984-85; fin. cons. Control Assocs., N.Y.C., 1986-87; acct., fin. analyst Spicer & Oppenheim, N.Y.C., 1987-88; compliance analyst BankAm. Bus. Credit Inc., San Diego, 1988—; mem. Columbia Bus. Sch. Alumni Counseling Bd. Mem. Rep. Nat. Com., 1986—. Mem. Assn. for Investment Mgmt. and Rsch., Fin. Analysts Fedn., Columbia Bus. Sch. Club N.Y. (past v.p.). Republican. Roman Catholic. Home: 5225 Fiore Ter Apt D117 San Diego CA 92122-5647 Office: BankAm Bus Credit Inc 10124 Old Grove Rd San Diego CA 92131-1649

SLEEPER, ANDREW DUKE, electrical engineer, statistician; b. Oklahoma City, Okla., Mar. 21, 1959; s. Harold G. and Ann Sleeper; m. Julie Nguyen Phuoc Xuan Phuong, Nov. 2, 1981; children: Kim, Minh, Pascal. BSEE summa cum laude, Rice U., 1981; MS in Statistics, Colo. State U., 1994. Registered profl. engr., Colo. Engr. Hewlett-Packard Co., Corvallis, Oreg., 1981-87, Woodward Gov. Co., Loveland, Colo., 1987—; consulting statistician, 1991—; presenter Euro-EM '94, 1994. Contbr. articles to profl. jours. Precinct committeeman Rep. Orgn., Ft. Collins, Colo., 1988—. Mem. IEEE, Am. Soc. for Quality Control (cert. quality engr., cert. reliability engr.; trainer in statistics and quality engring. 1987—). Home: 1502 Mathews Fort Collins CO 80524 Office: Woodward Gov Co 3800 N Wilson Ave Loveland CO 80538

SLETTEN, JOHN ROBERT, construction company executive; b. Gt. Falls, Mont., Sept. 19, 1932; s. John and Hedvig Marie (Finstad) S.; m. Patricia Gail Thomas, Dec. 16, 1962; children: Leighanne, Kristen Gail, Erik John. BS in Archtl. Engring., Mont. State U., 1956. Estimator Sletten Constrn. Co., Gt. Falls, 1956-63; v.p., area mgr. Sletten Constrn. Co., Las Vegas, Nev., 1963-65; pres., chief exec. officer Sletten Constrn. Co., Gt. Falls, 1969—; bd. dirs. 1st Banks, Gt. Falls, Blue Cross-Blue Shield, Helena, Mont. Chmn. Gt. Falls Mil. Affairs Com., 1985; pres. President's Cir., Mont. State U., Bozeman, 1986; trustee Mont. Hist. Soc., Helena, 1987. with USMC, 1950-52. Mem. Mont. Contractors Assn. (bd. dirs. 1969-75, pres. 1974), Mont. C. of C. (chmn. 1984), Pachyderm Club, Rotary (bd. dirs. Gt. Falls), Elks. Republican. Lutheran. Office: Sletten Inc 1000 25th St N PO Box 2467 Great Falls MT 59403-2467

SLETTEN, KENNETH G., construction executive; b. 1929. BS in Engring., U. Colo.; MBA, Stanford U. Pres. Rudolph & Sletter, Inc., Foster City, Calif., 1961—. Office: Rudolph & Sletten Inc PO Box 4637 989 E Hillside Blvd Foster City CA 94404*

SLIDER, MARGARET ELIZABETH, elementary education educator; b. Spanish Fork, Utah, Nov. 27, 1945; d. Ira Elmo and Aurelia May (Peterson) Johnson; m. Richard Keith Slider, Oct. 25, 1968; children: Thomas Richard, Christopher Alan. AA, Chaffey Coll., 1966; BA, Calif. State U., San Bernardino, 1968, MEd in English as Second Lang., 1993. Cert. elem. tchr., Calif. Tchr. Colton (Calif.) Unified Sch. Dist., 1968—; lead sci. tchr. McKinley Sch., 1994—; mem. kindergarten assessment com. Colton Joint Unified Sch. Dist., Colton, 1988-90, dist. math. curriculum com., 1992-94; trainer Calif. State Dept. Edn. Early Intervention for Sch. Success, 1993—, demonstrator on-site classroom, 1994. Treas. McKinley Sch. PTA, Colton, 1989-91. Mem. NEA, ASCD, AAUW, Calif. Tchrs. Assn., Calif. Elem. Edn. Assn., Calif. Assn. of Tchrs. of English to Students of Other Langs., Calif. Mathematics Coun., Assn. Colton Educators, Pi Lambda Theta. Home: 1628 Waterford Ave Redlands CA 92374-3967 Office: Colton Unified Sch Dist 1212 Valencia Dr Colton CA 92324-1731

SLIKER, TODD RICHARD, accountant, lawyer; b. Rochester, N.Y., Feb. 9, 1936; s. Harold Garland and Marion Ethel (Caps) S.; BS with honors (Ford Found. scholar), U. Wis., 1955; PhD, Cornell U., 1962; MBA, Harvard, 1970; JD, U. Denver, 1982; m. Gretchen Paula Zeiter, Dec. 27, 1963; children: Cynthia Garland, Kathryn Clifton. Bar: Colo. 1983. With Clevite Corp., Cleve., 1962-68, head applied physics sect., 1965-68; asst. to pres. Granville-Phillips Co., Boulder, Colo., 1970; v.p., gen. mgr. McDowell Electronics, Inc., Metuchen, N.J., 1970-71; pres. C.A. Compton, Inc., mfrs. audio-visual equipment, Boulder, 1971-77; chief acct. C&S Inc., Englewood, Colo., 1977-80, v.p., 1980-82; sole practice law, Boulder, 1983-88; mgmt. real estate, 1972—. Del., Colo. Rep. Assembly, 1974, 76; Rep. dist. fin. coordinator, 1974-75; precinct committeeman, 1974-86, 92-94; chmn. Boulder County Rep. 1200 Club, 1975-79; mem. Colo. Rep. State Cen. Com., 1977-81, asst. treas., 1979-87; sect. corr. Harvard U., 1981—. Served to 1st lt. USAF, 1955-57. Recipient paper award vehicular communication group IEEE, 1966. Lic. real estate salesman, securities salesman; CPA, Colo. Mem. Colo. Soc. CPAs (govt. relations task force 1983-86), Colo. Bar Assn. (publs. com. 1982-84), Am. Phys. Soc., Optical Soc. Am. (referee Jour.), Colo. Harvard Bus. Sch. Club, Hist. Boulder Club, Rotary, Sigma Xi, Phi Kappa Phi, Theta Chi, Beta Alpha Psi. Contbr. articles to profl. jours. Patentee in field. Home: 12500 Oxford Rd Longmont CO 80501-8436

SLINKER, JOHN MICHAEL, academic director; b. Lafayette, Ind., Jan. 8, 1952; s. William Guy Mahan and Betty Lucille (Utterback) and Richard Earl Slinker; m. Pamela Jo Pickering, Mar. 15, 1975. BS, Ea. N.Mex. U., 1974, MA, 1979; EdD, No. Ariz. U., 1988. Asst. sports infor. dir., news writer Ea. N.Mex. U., Portales, 1970-74, news svcs. dir., sports info. dir., 1974-82; dir. univ. news and publs. No. Ariz. U., Flagstaff, 1982-86; dir. pub. affairs Humboldt State U., Arcata, Calif., 1988-92, dir. univ. rels., 1992—; cons. Calif. Dept. Parks and Recreation, Sacramento, 1989-90. Vol. Boy Scouts Am., Eureka, Calif., 1991-93, dist. commr., 1991-92. Mem. Coun. for Advancement and Support of Edn. (Bronze medal), Sigma Nu (div. comdr. 1976-81, chpt. advisor, Outstanding Alumnus 1976, 79, 81, 82). Republican. Methodist. Home: 1221 West Ave # A Eureka CA 95501-1234 Office: Humboldt State U Office Univ Rels Arcata CA 95521

SLOAN, EARLE DENDY, JR., chemical engineering educator; b. Seneca, S.C., Apr. 23, 1944; s. Earle Dendy and Sarah (Bellotte) S.; m. Marjorie Nilson, Sept. 7, 1968; children: Earle Dendy III, John Mark. BSChemE, Clemson U., 1965, MSChemE, 1972, PhD in Chem. Engring., 1974. Engr. Du Pont, Chattanooga, 1965-66, Seaford, Del., 1966-67; cons. Du Pont, Parkersburg, W.Va., 1967-68; sr. engr. Du Pont, Camden, S.C., 1968-70; postdoctoral fellow Rice U., 1975; prof. chem. engring. Colo. Sch. Mines, Golden, 1976—, Gaylord and Phyllis Weaver dist. prof. chem. engring., 1992—; pres. faculty senate, Colo. Sch. Mines, 1989-90. Author: Clathrate Hydrates of Natural Gases, 1990; chmn. pub. bd. Chem. Engring. Edn., 1990—. Scoutmaster local Cub Scouts, 1978-81; elder Presbyn. Ch., Golden, Colo., 1977-79, 92-94. Fellow AIChE (chmn. area Ia thermodynamics and transport 1990-93), mem. Am. Soc. for Engring. Edn. (chmn. ednl. rsch. methods divsn. 1983-85), Am. Chem. Soc. Home: 2121 Washington Ave Golden CO 80401-2374

SLOAN, F(RANK) BLAINE, lawyer, educator; b. Geneva, Nebr., Jan. 3, 1920; s. Charles Porter and Lillian Josephine (Stiefer) S.; m. Patricia Sand, Sept. 2, 1944; children—DeAnne Sloan Riddle, Michael Blaine, Charles Porter. AB with high distinction, U. Nebr., 1942, LLB cum laude, 1946; LLM in Internat. Law, Columbia U., 1947. Bar: Nebr. 1946, N.Y. 1947. Asst. to spl. counsel Intergovtl. Com. for Refugees, 1947; mem. Office Legal Affairs UN Secretariat, N.Y.C., 1948-78, gen. counsel Relief and Works Agy. Palestine Refugees, Beirut, 1958-60, dir. gen. legal div., 1966-78, rep. of Sec. Gen. to Commn. Internat. Trade Law, 1969-78, rep. to Legal Sub-com. on Outer Space, 1966-78; rep. UN Del. Vietnam Conf., Paris, 1973; rep UN Conf. on Carriage of Goods by Sea, Hamburg, 1978; prof. internat. law orgn. and water law Pace U., 1978-87, prof. emeritus, 1987—. law lectr. Blaine Sloan Internat., 1988—. Author: United Nations General Assembly Resolutions in Our Changing World, 1991; contbr. articles to legal jours. Cons. UN Office of Legal Affairs, 1983-84, UN Water Resources Br., 1983; supervisory com., Pace Peace Ctr. Navigator AC, U.S. Army, 1943-46. Recipient Outstanding Prof. award Pace Law Sch., 1987. Decorated Air medal. Mem. Am. Soc. Internat. Law, Am. Acad. Polit. and Social Sci., Am. Arbitration Assn. (panel of arbitrators), Order of Coif, Phi Beta Kappa, Phi Alpha Delta (hon.). Republican. Roman Catholic. Home: HCR-68 Box 72 Foxwind-Forbes Park Fort Garland CO 81133 Office: 78 N Broadway White Plains NY 10603-3710

SLOAN, JERRY (GERALD EUGENE SLOAN), professional basketball coach; b. Mar. 28, 1942; m. Bobbye; 3 children: Kathy, Brian, Holly. Student, Evansville Coll., Evansville, Ind. Professional basketball player, Baltimore, 1965-66, Chicago Bulls, NBA, 1966-76; head coach Chicago Bulls, 1979-82; scout Utah Jazz, NBA, Salt Lake City, 1983-84, asst. coach, 1984-88, head coach, 1988—; player 2 NBA All-Star games; named to NBA All-Defensive First Team, 1969, 72, 74, 75. Office: care Utah Jazz Delta Ctr 301 West South Temple Salt Lake City UT 84101-1105*

SLOAN, LANNY GENE, municipal official; b. Denver, Aug. 30, 1945; s. Vincent Eugene and Leta Valma (Atwood) S.; m. Janet Cellen, July 5, 1968 (div. 1973); m. Patti Stucker, 1990. Student, U. Utah, 1963-68; BA in Bus. Mgmt., Lewis-Clark State Coll., 1990. Registered land surveyor, Idaho. Engr.'s technician Idaho Dept. Transp., Jerome, 1970-77; land surveyor Edwards-Howard-Martens, Engrs., Twin Falls, Idaho, 1977-80; project supt. J. Holley Constrn., Wells, Nev., 1981—; dir. pub. works City of Jerome, 1982-90, City of Coos Bay (Oreg.), 1990-93; city adminstr. City of Salmon, Idaho, 1993—; mem. adv. bd. N.W. Tech. Transfer Ctr., Olympia, Wash. Chmn. bd. dirs. Jerome City Libr., 1986-90; bd. trustees Coos Bay Libr., 1991—; bd. dirs. Jerome City Airport, 1986-90, Bay Area Rehab., 1990—. Mem. Am. Pub. Works Assn., Am. Water Works Assn. (trustee intermountain sect. 1987—), Pacific N.W. Pollution Control Assn., Green Drake Soc. Office: City of Salmon 200 Main St Salmon ID 83467-4111

SLOAN, MICHAEL DANA, information systems specialist; b. Santa Monica, Calif., Sept. 30, 1960; s. Avery and Beverly Rae (Krantz) S.; m. Barbara Rogers; 1 child, Ashley Harrison. BS in Bus. Adminstrn., Calif. State U., Northridge, 1983; MBA, Pepperdine U., 1987. Programmer/ analyst TICOR, Inc., L.A., 1979-80; data processing analyst Deluxe Check Printers, Inc., Chatsworth, Calif., 1980-83; fin. systems analyst Wismer & Assocs., Inc., Canoga Park, Calif., 1983-84; sr. systems analyst Coast Savs. & Loan, Granada Hills, Calif., 1984-86; microcomputer systems specialist Litton Industries, Woodland Hills, Calif., 1986-87; systems mgr., info. resources mgr. TRW, Inc.- Space and Def., Redondo Beach, Calif., 1987-93; project mgr. Health Net, Woodland Hills, 1993-95; mgr. fin. systems Merisel Ams. Inc., El Segundo, Calif., 1995—; cons. Data Most, Inc., Chatsworth, 1982-83, Home Savs. & Loan, North Hollywood, Calif., 1987, Micro Tech., L.A., 1987, TRW, Inc.-Space and Def., Redondo Beach, Calif., 1993—. Mem. IEEE Computer Soc., Salle Gascon Fencing Club, U.S. Fencing Assn., Delta Sigma Pi. Republican. Office: TRW Space and Defense One 1 Space Park Blvd # 2828 Redondo Beach CA 90278-1001

SLOAN, ROSALIND, nurse, military officer; b. New Haven, Apr. 22, 1953; d. Paul and Blanche (Kopp) S. BSN, U. Conn., 1976; M of Ednl. Adminstrn., San Diego State U., 1993. Staff nurse Peter Bent Brigham Hosp., Boston, 1976-79; commd. officer USN, 1979, advanced through grades to comdr., 1988; staff nurse Portsmouth (Va.) Naval Hosp., 1979-83, Charleston (S.C.) Naval Hosp., 1983-85; charge nurse labor and delivery U.S. Naval Hosp., Subic Bay, Philippines, 1985-88; instr. Basic Hosp. Corps Sch.-Naval Sch. Health Scis., San Diego, 1988-90, asst. dir., 1990-91; asst. officer-in-charge, acad. officer Naval Sch. Dental Assisting and Tech., San Diego, 1991-92; dept. head command edn. and tng. Naval Med. Ctr., Oakland, Calif., 1993—. Recipient Naval Commendation medal USN, Subic Day, 1988, Naval Commendation medal Naval Sch. Health Scis., San Diego, 1991. Mem. Nat. Nursing Staff Devel. Orgn., Nat. Holistic Nursing Assn., Bay Area Soc. Health Edn. and Tng. (treas.), Coun. Coll. and Mil. Educators, Phi Kappa Phi.

SLOANE, BEVERLY LEBOV, writer, consultant; b. N.Y.C., May 26, 1936; d. Benjamin S. and Anne (Weinberg) LeBov; m. Robert Malcolm Sloane, Sept. 27, 1959; 1 child, Alison Lori Sloane Gaylin. AB, Vassar Coll., 1958; MA, Claremont Grad. Sch., 1975, doctoral study, 1975-76; cert. in exec. mgmt., UCLA Grad. Sch. Mgmt., 1982, grad. exec. mgmt. program., UCLA 1982; grad. intensive bioethics course Kennedy Inst. Ethics, Georgetown U., 1987, advanced bioethics course, 1988; grad. sem. in Health Care Ethics, U. Wash. Sch. Medicine, Seattle, summer 1988-90, 94; grad. Summer Bioethics Inst. Loyola Marymount U., summer, 1990; grad. Annual Summer Inst. on Teaching or Writing, Columbia Tchrs. Coll., summer 1990; grad. Annual Summer Inst. on Advanced Teaching of Writing , summer, 1993, Annual Inst. Pub. Health and Human Rights, Harvard U. Sch. Pub. Health, 1994, grad. exec. refresher course profl. pub. Stanford U., 1994; cert. Exec. Mgmt. Inst. in Health Care, U. So. Calif., 1995, cert. advanced exec. program Grad. Sch. Mgmt. UCLA, 1995; cert. in ethics corps tng. program, Josephson Inst. of Ethics, 1991, cert. ; ethics fellow Loma Linda U. Med. Ctr., 1989; cert. clin. intensive biomedical ethics, Loma Linda U. Med. Ctr., 1989. Circulation libr. Harvard Med. Libr., Boston, 1958-59; social worker Conn. State Welfare, New Haven, 1960-61; tchr. English, Hebrew Day Sch., New Haven, 1961-64; instr. creative writing and English lit. Monmouth Coll., West Long Branch, N.J., 1967-69; freelance writer, Arcadia, Calif., 1970—; v.p. council grad. students, Claremont Grad. sch., 1971-72, adj. dir. Writing Ctr. Speaker Series Claremont Grad. Sch., 1993—; mem. adv. coun. tech. and profl. writing Dept. English, Calif. State U., Long Beach, 1980-82; mem. adv. bd. Calif. Health Rev., 1982-83; mem. Foothill Health Dist. Adv. Coun. L.A. County Dept. Health Svcs., 1987-93, pres., 1989-91, immediate past pres., 1991-92. Ann. Key Mem. award, 1990. Author: From Vassar to Kitchen, 1967, A Guide to Health Facilities: Personnel and Management, 1971, 2nd edit. 1977, 3d edit., 1992. Mem. pub. relations bd. Monmouth

County Mental Health Assn., 1968-69; chmn. creative writing group Calif. Inst. Tech. Woman's Club, 1975-79; mem. ethics com., human subjects protection com. Jewish Home for the Aging, Reseda, Calif., 1994—, Santa Teresita Hosp., 1994—; mem. task force edn. and cultural activities, City of Duarte, 1987-88; mem. strategic planning task force com., campaign com. for pre-eminence Claremont Grad. Sch., 1986-87, mem. alumni coun., 1993—, bd. dirs., governing bd.. alumni assn., 1993—, mem. alumni coun., mem. steering com. annual alumni day 1994—, mem. alumni awards com., 1994—, mem. alumni events com., 1994—, mem. vol. devel. com., 1994—; Vassar Coll. Class rep. to Alumnae Assn. Fall Coun. Meeting, 1989,, class corr. Vassar Coll. Quarterly Alumnae Mag., 1993—; co-chmn. Vassar Christmas Showcase New Haven Vassar Club, 1965-66, rep. to Vassar Coll. Alumnae Assn. Fall Coun. Meeting, 1965-66; co-chmn. Vassar Club So. Calif. Annual Book Fair, 1970-71; chmn. creative writing group Yale U. Newcomers, 1965-66, dir. creative writing group Yale U. Women's Orgn., 1966-67; grad. AMA Ann. Health Reporting Conf., 1992, 93; mem. exec. program network UCLA Grad. Sch. Mgmt., 1987—; trustee Ctr. for Improvement of Child Caring, 1981-83; mem. League Crippled Children, 1982—, bd. dirs., 1988-91, treas. for gen. meetings, 1990-91, chair hostesses com., 1988-89, pub. rels. com., 1990-91; bd. dirs. L.A. Commn. on Assaults Against Women, 1983-84; v.p. Temple Beth David, 1983-86; mem. cmty. rels. com. Jewish Fedn. Council Greater L.A., 1985-87; del. Task Force on Minorities in Newspaper Bus., 1987-89; cmty. rep. County Health Ctrs. Network Tobacco Control Program, 1991. Recipient cert. of appreciation City of Duarte, 1988, County of L.A., 1988; Coro Found. fellow, 1979; named Calif. Communicator of Achievement, Woman of Yr. Calif. Press Women, 1992. Fellow Am. Med. Writers Assn. (pres. Pacific So 1987-89, dir. 1980-93, Pacific S.W. del. to nat. bd. 1980-87, 89-91, chmn. various conv. coms., chmn. nat. book awards trade category 1982-83, chmn. Nat. Conv. Networking Luncheon 1983, 84, chmn. freelance and pub. relations coms. Nat. Midyr. Conf. 1983-84, workshop leader ann. conf. 1984-87, 90-92, nat. chmn. freelance sect. 1984-85, gen. chmn. 1985, Asilomar Western Regional Conf., gen. chmn. 1985, workshop leader 1985, program co-chmn. 1987, speaker 1985, 88-89, program co-chmn. 1989, nat. exec. bd. dirs. 1985-86, nat. adminstr. sects. 1985-86, pres.-elect Pacific S.W. chpt. 1985-87, pres. 1987-89, immediate past pres. 1989-91, bd. dirs., 1991-93, moderator gen. session nat. conf. 1987, chair gen. session nat. conf., 1986-87, chair Walter C. Alvarez Meml. Found. award 1986-87, Appreciation award for outstanding leadership 1989, named to Workshop Leaders Honor Roll 1991); mem. Women in Comm. (dir. 1980-82, 89-90, v.p. cmty. affairs 1981-82, N.E. area rep. 1980-81, chmn. awards banquet 1982, sem. leader, speaker ann. nat. profl. conf., 1985, program adv. com. L.A. chpt. 1987, v.p. activities 1989-90, chmn. L.A. chpt. 1st ann. Agnes Underwood Freedom of Info. Awards Banquet 1982, recognition award 1983, nominating com. 1982, 83, com. Women of the Press Awards luncheon 1988, Women in Comm. awards luncheon 1988), Am. Assn. for Higher Edn., AAUW (legis. chmn. Arcadia br. 1976-77, books and plays chmn. Arcadia br. 1973-74, creative writing chmn. 1969-70, 1st v.p. program dir. 1975-76, networking chmn. 1981-82, chmn. task force promoting individual liberties 1987-88, named Woman of Yr., Woman of Achievement award 1986, cert. of appreciation 1987), Coll. English Assn., APHA, Am. Soc. Law, Medicine and Ethics, Calif. Press Women (v.p. programs L.A. chpt. 1982-85, pres. 1985-87, state pres. 1987-89, past immediate past state pres. 1989-91, chmn. state speakers bur. 1989—, del nat. bd. 1989—, moderator ann. spring conv., 1990, 92, chmn. nominating com. 1990-91, Calif. lit. dir. 1990-92, dir. state lit. com. 1990-92, dir. family literacy day Calif., 1990, Cert. of Appreciation, 1991, named Calif. Communicator of Achievement 1992), AAUP, Internat. Comm. Assn., N.Y. Acad. Scis., Ind. Writers So. Calif. (bd. dirs. 1989-90, dir. Specialized Groups 1989-90, dir. at large 1989-90, bd. dirs. corp. 1988-89, dir. Speech Writing Group, 1991-92), Hastings Ctr., AAAS, Nat. Fedn. Press Women, (bd. dirs. 1987-93, nat. co-chmn. task force recruitment of minorities 1987-89, del. 1987-89, nat. dir. of speakers bur. 1989-93, editor of speakers bur. directory 1991, cert. of appreciation, 1991, 93, Plenary of Past Pres. state 1989—, workshop leader-speaker ann. nat. conf. 1990, chair state women of achievement com. 1986-87, editor Speakers Bur. Addendum Directory, 1992, editor Speakers Bur. Directory 1991, 92, named 1st runner up Nat. Communicator of Achievement 1992), AAUW (chpt. Woman of Achievement award 1986, chmn. task force promoting individual liberties 1987-88, speaker 1987, Cert. of Appreciation 1987, Woman of Achievement-Woman of Yr. 1986), Internat. Assn. Bus. Communicators, Soc. for Tech. Comm. (workshop leader, 1985, 86), Kennedy Inst. Ethics, Soc. Health and Human Values, Assoc. Writing Programs, Authors Guild. Clubs: Women's City (Pasadena), Claremont Colls. Faculty House, Pasadena Athletic, Town Hall of Calif. (vice chair cmty. affairs sect. 1982-87, speaker 1986, faculty-instr. Exec. Breakfast Inst. 1985-86, mem. study sect. coun. 1986-88), Authors Guild. Lodge: Rotary (chair Duarte Rotary mag. 1988-89, mem. dist. friendship exch. com. 1988-89, mem. internat. svc. com. 1989-90, info. svc. com. 1989-90) Home and Office: 1301 N Santa Anita Ave Arcadia CA 91006-2419

SLOANE, ROBERT MALCOLM, hospital administrator; b. Boston, Feb. 11, 1933; s. Alvin and Florence (Goldberg) S.; m. Beverly LeBov, Sept. 27, 1959; 1 dau., Alison. A.B., Brown U., 1954; M.S., Columbia U., 1958. Adminstrv. resident Mt. Auburn Hosp., Cambridge, Mass., 1957-58; med. adminstr. AT&T, N.Y.C., 1959-60; asst. dir. Yale New Haven Hosp., 1961-67; assoc. adminstr. Monmouth Med. Center, Long Branch, N.J., 1967-69; adminstr. City of Hope Nat. Med. Center, Duarte, Calif., 1969-80; pres. Los Angeles Orthopedic Hosp., Los Angeles Orthopedic Found., 1980-86; pres., CEO Anaheim (Calif.) Meml. Hosp., 1986-94; pres. Vol. Hosp. Am. West, Inc., Anaheim, 1995—; mem. faculty Columbia U. Sch. Medicine, 1958-59, Yale U. Sch. Medicine, 1963-67, Quinnipiac Coll., 1963-67, Pasadena City Coll., 1972-73, Calif. Inst. Tech., 1973-85, U. So. Calif., 1976-79, clin. prof., 1987—, UCLA, 1985-87; chmn. bd. Health Data Net, 1971-73; bd. dirs. Intervalley Health Plan; pres. Anaheim (Calif.) Meml. Hosp., 1986-94, Anaheim Meml. Devel. Found., 1986-94. Author: (with B. L. Sloane) A Guide to Health Facilities: Personnel and Management, 1971, 3d edit., 1992; mem. editorial and adv. bd. Health Devices, 1972-90; contbr. articles to hosp. jours. Bd. dirs. Health Systems Agy. Los Angeles County, 1977-78; bd. dirs. Calif. Hosp. Polit. Action Com., 1979-87, vice chmn., 1980-83, chmn., 1983-85. Served to lt. (j.g.) USNR, 1954-56. Fellow Am. Coll. Hosp. Adminstrs. (regent 1989-93, nominations com., 1994—); mem. Am. Hosp. Assn., Hosp. Council So. Calif. (bd. dirs., sec. 1982, treas. 1983, chmn. elect 1984, chmn. 1985, past chmn. 1986, 89), Calif. Hosp. Assn. (bd. dirs., exec. com. 1984-86, 89), Vol. Hosps. Am. (bd. dirs. west region 1986—, vice-chmn. 1990-93, chmn 1993-94, pres. 1995—), Anaheim C. of C. (bd. dirs. 1994). Home: 1301 N Santa Anita Ave Arcadia CA 91006-2419 Office: 12555 W Jefferson Blvd Ste 325 Los Angeles CA 90066-7000

SLOCUM, MICHAEL SCOTT, satellite systems design engineer; b. Anderson, Ind., Jan. 13, 1969; s. Michael Faye Sipes and Donna Lou (McCord) Slocum; m. Leora Colleen Harris, Feb. 8, 1990; children: Micaiah Christopher, Hosannah Michal. BSEE with honors, U. Md., Munich, Germany, 1991; MSEE, MIT, 1992; PhD in Elec. Engring. with honors, U.S. Army Intelligence Coll., Ft. Devens, Mass., 1994. Design engr. MEC, Costa Mesa, Calif., 1992-93, sr. design engr., 1993—; ptnr. Engring. Scis., Chino Hills, Calif., 1993—; adv. bd. IEW, Darmstadt, Fed. Republic Germany, 1990-92; mem. Engring. Coun., Darmstadt, 1991-92. Author: IEW Electro-Mechanical System Utilization, 1990, Special Purpose Counter-Measures Set AN/MLQ-34, 1991, Mean Time Between Failures, 1992, Oxidation and Migration of Copper on Special Geometries, 1994. Jr. high tchr. Calvary Chapel Chino Hills, 1992—. With U.S. Army, 1987-92. IEW rsch. grantee, Frankfurt, Fed. Republic Germany, 1990. Mem. AIAA, IEEE, Soc. Mfg. Engrs., Inst. Indsl. Engring., Am. Soc. Quality Control, Planetary Soc., Space Soc., Sigma Xi. Republican. Office: MEC 3160 Pullman St Costa Mesa CA 92626-3315

SLOMANSON, WILLIAM REED, law educator, legal writer; b. Johnstown, Pa., May 1, 1945; s. Aaron Jacob and Mary Jane (Reed) S.; m. Anna Maria Valladolid, June 24, 1972; children: Lorena, Michael, Paul, Christina. BA, U. Pitts., 1967; JD, Calif. Western U., 1974; LLM, Columbia U., N.Y.C., 1975. Bar: Calif. 1975. Assoc. Booth, Mitchel, Strange & Smith, L.A., 1975-77; prof. law Western State U., San Diego and Fullerton, Calif., 1977—; judge Provisional Dist. World Ct., L.A., 1990—; mem. bd. advisors San Diego Community Coll. Dist., 1989—. Author: (reference book) International Business Bibliography, 1989, (textbooks) Fundamental Perspectives on International Law, 1990, 2d edit., 1995, California Civil Procedure, 1991, California Civil Procedure in a Nutshell, 1992, (practitioner's treatise) The Choice Between State and Federal Courts in California, 1994. Lt. USN, 1967-71, Vietnam. Mem. Am. Soc. Internat. Law (chair, editor newsletter on UN decade of internat. law), San Diego County Bar Assn. (co-chair internat. law sect. 1988-92). Office: Western State U 2121 San Diego Ave San Diego CA 92110-2905

SLONE, RONALD RICH, academic consultant; b. Cin., July 1, 1943; s. Roy E. and Myrtle I. (Stephens) S.; m. Marilyn Norma Hornemann, Mar. 14, 1982. BSBA, Miami (Ohio) U., 1965; MBA, U. Cin., 1966. Isntr. bus. Ind. State U., Terre Haute, 1966-69; asst., assoc. dir. accreditation Am. Assembly Collegiate Schs. Bus., St. Louis, 1969-73, dir. accreditation, 1976-83; cons. Fla. Bd. Regents, Tallahassee, 1983-84; dir. rsch. and planning Coll. Bus. Coll. Bus. Boise (Idaho) State U., 1984-92; pres. Strategic Directions, Boise, 1993—. Mem. Beta Gamma Sigma (mng. dir. 1973-78). Presbyterian. Home and Office: 330 Fall Dr Boise ID 83706-4820

SLONIMSKY, NICOLAS, conductor, composer; b. St. Petersburg, USSR, Apr. 27, 1894; came to U.S., 1923, naturalized, 1931; s. Leonid and Faina (Vengerova) S.; m. Dorothy Adlow, July 30, 1931; 1 dau., Electra. Ed., Conservatory of Music, St. Petersburg; D.F.A. (hon.), Northwestern U., 1980. Condr. Pierian Sodality, Harvard, 1928-30; instr. Eastman Sch. Music, Rochester, N.Y., 1923-25, Boston Conservatory Music, 1925-45; instr. Slavic langs. and lits. Harvard U., 1946-47; vis. prof. Colo. Coll., summer 1940, 47-49; lectr. music Simmons Coll., 1947-49, Peabody Conservatory, 1956-57, U. Calif. at Los Angeles, 1964-67; guest condr., Paris, Berlin, Budapest, Havana, San Francisco, Los Angeles, Hollywood, 1931-33, S.A., 1941-42. Concert tours as pianist, Europe, 1921-22, U.S., 1923—, S.Am., 1941-42; wrote for ballet, orch., piano, voice.; author: Music since 1900, 5th edit., 1994, Music of Latin America, 4th edit., 1972, Lexicon of Musical Invective, 1953, Perfect Pitch: A Life Story, 1988, Lectionary of Music, 1989; editor: Internat. Cyclo. of Music and Musicians, 4th-8th edits., 1946-58, Baker's Biog. Dictionary of Musicians, 5th edit., 1958, 6th edit., 1978, 7th edit., 1984, 8th edit., 1991, Concise Baker's Biographical Dictionary of Musicians, 1988, 93; mem. Am. music editorial bd.: Ency. Brit., 1958—; contbr.: ann. music surveys to Ency. Brit. Year Books, 1950-68. Mem. (hon.) Am. Acad. Inst. Arts and Letters. Home: 2630 Midvale Ave Los Angeles CA 90064-4214

SLOSKY, LEONARD C., environmental consultant; b. Colo. Springs, Colo., Sept. 18, 1952; s. Harry and Shirley Mae (Hoffman) S. BA, U. Colo., 1975. Registered environ. assessor, Calif. Staff asst. Colo. Gov's. Office, Denver, 1975-77; staff dir. Intergovtl. Sci., Engring. & Tech. Adv. Panel Natural Resources Task Force Exec. Office of the Pres., Washington, 1978-81; asst. to the Gov. Colo. Gov.'s Office, Denver, 1981-85; pres. Slosky & Co., Inc., Denver, 1985—; exec. dir. Rocky Mountain Low-Level Radioactive Waste Bd., Denver, 1983—; mem. Waste Isolation Pilot Plant blue ribbon com., Washington, 1989-91. Mem. Greater Denver C. of C. (co-chairperson, mem. environ. com. 1992). Office: Slosky & Co Inc 1675 Broadway Ste 1400 Denver CO 80202-4614

SLOUBER, JAMES KIRK, accountant; b. Chgo., Feb. 12, 1952; s. Robert James and Doris Marie (Olson) S.; m. Kerry Perry, Oct. 24, 1981; children: Erika, Kirsten, Bradon. BA in Acctg., Econs., and Bus., Augustana Coll., Rock Island, Ill., 1974; MS in Taxation, DePaul U., 1978. CPA, Calif., Ill. Acct. Procon, Inc., Des Plaines, Ill., 1974-75; tax supervising sr. Peat, Marwick, Mitchell & Co., Chgo., Newport Beach, Calif., 1977-80; tax mgr. Price Waterhouse, West Los Angeles, Calif., 1980-83; sr. tax mgr. Price Waterhouse, Washington, 1983-84; sr. mgr. in charge tax dept. Price Waterhouse, Riverside, Calif., 1984-89; tax ptnr. in charge Pannell Kerr Forster, L.A., 1989-91, Goldfarb, Whitman & Cohen, L.A., 1991-94; ptnr. Parks Palmer Turner & Yemenidjian, L.A., 1994—; mem. citizens univ. com. U. Calif., Riverside, 1985-89. Author: (booklet) Interest Expense Rules After Tax Reform, 1989; contbr. 7 articles to profl. jours. Bd. dirs. United Way Inland Valleys, Riverside, 1986-90, Luth. Sch. Foothills, 1993—. Mem. AICPA (tax divsn., treas. tax exempt orgns. com.), Calif. Soc. CPAs, Ill. Soc. CPAs, L.A. City Hdqrs. Assn., Kiwanis, Canyon Crest Country Club. Republican. Lutheran. Home: 9426 Carlynn Pl Tujunga CA 91042-3319 Office: Parks Palmer Turner & Yemenidjian 1990 S Bundy Dr 6th Fl Los Angeles CA 90025-5291

SLOVER, ARCHY F., chemist; b. Oshkosh, Wis., July 8, 1920; s. Archie F. and Josephine Petronella (Zindler); BA, UCLA, 1947; m. Mary Beatrice Corkill, May 25, 1946 (dec. June 17, 1987); 1 child, Mary Kay Slover Eckhardt. Devel. chemist Kelite Products Co., L.A., 1946-49; v.p., gen. mgr. Delco Chems. Inc., L.A., 1949-57; mgr. indsl. spltys. Pennwalt Corp., L.A., 1957-74; chemist Custom Chem. Formulators Inc., Cudahy, Calif., 1974—, mgr. Cherokee Chem. Co., Inc., Compton, Calif., 1976-89; cons. in field. Capt. U.S. Army, 1942-46. Fellow AAAS, Am. Inst. Chemists; mem. Nat. Assn. Corrosion Engrs., Am. Chem. Soc., Am. Electroplaters Soc., USAF Assn., Soc. Advancement Material Process Engrs., Res. Officers Assn., Sigma Alpha Epsilon, Ky. Cols. Patentee in field. Address: 21 Hacienda Dr Arcadia CA 91006-2347

SLOVIC, STEWART PAUL, psychologist; b. Chgo., Jan. 26, 1938; s. Jacob S. and Blanche (Cohen) S.; m. Roslyn Judith Resnick, Aug. 30, 1959; children: Scott, Steven, Lauren, Daniel. BA, Stanford U., 1959; MA, U. Mich., 1962, PhD, 1964. Rsch. assoc. Oreg. Rsch. Inst., Eugene, 1964-76; rsch. assoc. Decision Rsch., Eugene, 1976-86, pres., 1986—; prof. dept. psychology U. Oreg., Eugene, 1986—; bd. sci. dirs. Risk Sci. Inst., Washington, 1987-91; cons. EPA, Washington, 1987-90; adviser WHO, Geneva, 1991; bd. dirs. Nat. Coun. Radiation Protection and Measurement. Author: Acceptable Risk, 1981; editor: Judgment Under Uncertainty, 1982; contbr. articles to profl. publs. J.S. Guggenheim fellow, 1986-87; recipient Oreg. Acad. of Sci. Outstanding Contbn. to Sci. award, 1995. Fellow AAAS, APA (Disting. Sci. Contbn. award 1993), Am. Psychol. Soc. (charter), Soc. Risk Analysis (pres. 1983-84, Disting. Contbn. award 1991). Office: Decision Rsch 1201 Oak St Eugene OR 97401-3519

SLUSSER, ROBERT WYMAN, aerospace company executive; b. Mineola, N.Y., May 10, 1938; s. John Leonard and Margaret McKenzie (Wyman) S.; BS, MIT, 1960; MBA, Wharton, 1962; ERC, Ft. Belvior Def. Systems Mgmt. Sch., 1977; AMP, Claremont, 1982; m. Linda Killeas, Aug. 3, 1968; children: Jonathan, Adam, Robert, Mariah. Assoc. adminstr.'s staff NASA Hdqrs., Washington, 1962-65; with Northrop Corp., Hawthorne, Calif., 1965—, adminstr. Space Labs., 1965-68, mgr. bus. and fin. Warnecke Electron Tubes Co. div., Chgo., 1968-71, mgr. bus. adminstrn. YF-17 Program Aircraft Div., 1971-75, mgr. adminstrn. F-18/Cobra programs, also mgr. F-18 design to cost program, 1975-79, mgr. engring. adminstrn., 1980-82, acting v.p. engring., 1982, v.p. info. resources, 1983-91, mgr. long range planning, 1991-93; program mgr.-bus. F/A-18E/F program, 1994—. CFO, bd. dirs. So. Calif. Hist. Aviation Found., 1987-90, chmn. of bd., pres., 1990—; bd. dirs., contracting officer, PDES, 1988-91; mem. dirs. adv. bd. S.C. Rsch. Authority, 1991-95. Grumman Aircraft Engring. scholar, 1956-60. Fellow AIAA (assoc.); mem. So. Calif. Soc. Info. Mgnt., (mem. exec. com. 1987-91), Northrop Mgmt. Club (bd. dirs. 1992-93, Man of Yr. 1991-92). Home: 7270 Berry Hill Dr Palos Verdes Peninsula CA 90275-4402 Office: Northrop Aircraft Div 1 Northrop Ave Hawthorne CA 90250-3236

SLUTZ, DONALD RAY, computer scientist; b. Oak Park, Ill., Sept. 25, 1942; s. Donald Pierce and Edith Lillian (Bergstrom) S.; m. Jonine Carmelle Gotelli, Dec. 30, 1981; children: Regina, Cynthia, David. BSEE, U. Wis., 1964; SMEE, MIT, 1965, PhD in Elec. Engring., 1968. Mem. rsch. staff IBM Rsch., San Jose, Calif., 1968-81; sr. designer Esvel, Campbell, Calif., 1981-84; software designer Tandem Computers, Cupertino, Calif., 1984—. Contbr. articles to profl. jours. Pres., bd. dirs. Aromas (Calif.) Water Dist., 1977-79. Fellow Assn. for Computing Machinery; mem. IEEE. Office: Tandem Computers LOC 251-05 10100 Tantau Ave Cupertino CA 95014-3542

SMALL, JONATHAN ANDREW, lawyer; b. Balt., June 30, 1959; s. Marvin Myron and Suzanne (Bierstock) S. AA, Foothill Jr. Coll., 1980; BS in Math. with honors, Calif. Poly. State U., 1983; JD, U. Santa Clara, 1986. Bar: Calif. 1987, U.S. Dist. Ct. (no. and so. dists.) Calif. 1987, U.S. Patent Office 1987, U.S. Ct. Appeals (fed. cir.) 1987. Patent atty. Townsend & Townsend, San Francisco, 1986-89, Xerox Corp., Palo Alto, Calif., 1989-92; assoc. Weil, Gotshal & Manges, Menlo Park, Calif., 1992-93; chief patent counsel, asst. corp. sec. Komag Inc., Milpitas, Calif., 1993-94; also gen counsel Komag Inc., Milpitas, 1994—. Editor-in-chief Santa Clara Computer and High-Tech. Law Jour., 1985-86; contbr. articles to legal jours. Mem. ABA, Am. Intellectual Proerty Law Assn. Office: Komag Inc 275 S Hillview Dr Milpitas CA 95035-5417

SMALL, KENNETH ALAN, economics educator; b. Sodus, N.Y., Feb. 9, 1945; s. Cyril Galloway and Gertrude Estelle (Andrews) S.; m. Adair Bowman, June 8, 1968; 1 child, Gretchen Lenore. BA, BS, U. Rochester, 1968; MA, U. Calif., Berkeley, 1972, PhD, 1976. Asst. prof. Princeton (N.J.) U., 1976-83; rsch. assoc. Brookings Inst., Washington, 1978-79; assoc. prof. U. Calif., Irvine, 1983-86, prof. econs., 1986—, assoc. dean social sci., 1986-92, chmn. econs., 1992-95; vis. prof. Harvard U., Cambridge, Mass., 1991-92; cons. N.Y. State Legislature, Albany, 1982-83, Rand Corp., Santa Monica, Calif., 1985-86, ECO N.W., Eugene, Oreg., 1987—, World Bank, Washington, 1990—, Port Authority of N.Y. and N.J., 1994; mem. adv. coun. South Coast Air Quality Mgmt. Dist., El Monte, Calif., 1989-92; mem. study com. on urban transp. congestion pricing NRC, 1992-94. Co-author: Futures for a Declining City, 1981, Urban Decline, 1982, Road Work, 1989; Author: Urban Transportation Economics, 1992; co-editor: Urban Studies Glasgow, Scotland, 1992—, Kluwer Acad. Publs. book series, Dordrecht, The Netherlands, 1993—; assoc. editor Regional Sci. and Urban Econs., Amsterdam, The Netherlands, 1987—; editorial bd. Jour. Urban Econs., San Diego, 1989—, Transportation, Dordrecht, 1993—; contbr. articles, book revs. to profl. jours. Grantee NSF, 1977-87, Inst. Transp. Studies U. Calif., 1984-89, Haynes Found., L.A., 1987-88, U.S. and Calif. Depts. Transp., 1988—. Mem. Am. Econ. Assn., Econometric Soc., Transp. Rsch. Bd., Royal Econ. Soc., Regional Sci. Assn., Am. Real Estate and Urban Econs. Assn. Office: Univ Calif Dept Econs Irvine CA 92717

SMALL, ROBERT E., architect, architecture educator; b. N.Y.C., Mar. 10, 1927; s. James J. and Elsie K. (Kohrs) S.; m. Charity V. Williams, Aug. 21, 1955; children—Thomas, Catherine, John. B.S. in Archtl. Engring., Kans. State U., 1952; M.Arch., U. Oreg., 1955. Registered architect, Wash., Kans. Prin. Robert E. Small and Assocs., Architects, Seattle, 1968—; chmn. dept. architecture U. Wash., Seattle, 1982—; Cons. to various agencies on design for elderly and disabled including U.S. Nat. Bur. Standards, Wash. State, Alaska State, Seattle Housing Authority, 1974—. Author: Site Planning for Housing, 1976; Designing Accessable Environments, 1976. Served with USN, 1944-46, PTO. Recipient numerous research grants HUD, Nat. Bur. Standards, others. Mem. AIA, Assoc. Coll. schs. of Architects. Home: 13110 70th Ln NE Kirkland WA 98034-1603 Office: U Wash Coll Architecture and Urban Planning Dept Architecture Seattle WA 98105

SMALLEY, TOPSY NEHER, librarian; b. Boston, Dec. 5, 1943; d. H. Victor and Sara Elizabeth (Yoder) Neher; 1 child, Brian. BA, Pomona Coll., 1966; MLS, UCLA, 1967; MA in Liberal Studies, SUNY, Plattsburgh, 1982. Head libr. Greenville (Pa.) Pub. Libr., 1967-70; asst. libr. Feinberg Libr. SUNY, 1970-76, assoc. libr., 1980-84; asst. dir. Clinton C.C. Libr., Plattsburgh, 1978-79; head pub. svcs. Monterey (Calif.) Peninsula Coll. Libr., 1984-88, Cabrillo Coll. Libr., Aptos, Calif., 1988—. Contbg. author: Theories of Bibliographic Education, 1982; also articles. Mem. ALA. Democrat. Home: 4810 Porter Gulch Rd Aptos CA 95003-2728 Office: Cabrillo Coll Libr 6500 Soquel Dr Aptos CA 95003-3119

SMALLMAN, GAIL ELIZABETH, entrepreneur; b. Buffalo, N.Y., Mar. 24, 1953; d. Lemuel James and Beverly Ann (Waldron) S.; m. Ronald Hugh Strasser, 1974 (div. 1975). Student, Oreg. State U., 1971-72, Portland State, 1972-74, City U., Seattle, 1979. Word processor Atty. Gen.'s Consumer Protection, Portland, Oreg., 1974-75, Lane Powell Moss & Miller, Seattle, 1978-79; sec. Carney, Probst & Levak, Portland, 1975-76, Jones, Lang, Klein, et al., Portland, 1978; office mgr. Corl & Willis, Corvallis, Oreg., 1976-77; adminstrv. asst. Reed McClure Moceri et al., Seattle, 1978-80; systems mgr. Lane Powell Spears et al., Seattle, 1980-94; owner Sunrise Place Bed & Breakfast, Bainbridge Island, Wash., 1994—; v.p. Wang/Informatics special interest group VS Legal Users' Group, Sacramento, 1990-91. Active Residents Opposed to Aircraft ReRouting, 1991. Scholar Oregon State U., 1971. Mem. Am. Mgmt. Assn., LawNet Inc. (v.p., bd. dirs. 1991-93), Bainbridge Island C. of C., Bainbridge Island Bed & Breakfast Assn., Bremerton/Kitsap County Visitors & Conv. Bur. Democrat. Episcopalian. Home and Office: 10245 NE Sunrise Pl Bainbridge Island WA 98110

SMALLWOOD, BETTY, lawyer; b. Eagle Pass, Tex., Nov. 27, 1946; d. Charles Augustus and Helen Elizabeth (Stanford) S. BA, U. Tex., 1968, BS, 1970; grad., Med. Tech. Sch., 1970; JD, U. San Diego, 1986. Bar: Tex. 1992, Nev. 1987; lic. real estate agt. Nev.; cert. med. technologist. Med. technologist VA Med Ctr., Denver and Houston, 1977-83; atty. Clark & Sacco, Las Vegas, Nev., 1987-88, Jeffrey Burr & Assocs., Las Vegas, 1988-91; pvt. practice Henderson, Nev., 1991—; instr., coord. U. Nev. Las Vegas Ctr. for Internat. Bus., 1992. Exec. editor U. San Diego Law Rev., 1985-86. Campaign worker Nev. U.S. Senator, 1988, Clark County Attys. for Nev. Atty. Gen., Las Vegas, 1990; girls day vol. Las Vegas Boys and Girls' Club, 1991; bd. dirs. United Cerebral Palsey of South Nev., 1992-93. Named Disting. Women So. Nev. Careline Inc., 1990, 91. Mem. ABA, So. Nev. Internat. Bus. Coun. (bd. dirs. 1994), Am. Bus. Women's Assn., So. Nev. Assn. of Women Attys. (sec. 1989-90), State Bar Nev., State Bar Tex., Henderson C. of C. (amb. corps 1992-93). Office: 153 W Lake Mead Dr Ste 104 Henderson NV 89015-7044

SMARANDACHE, FLORENTIN, mathematics researcher, writer; b. Balcesti-Vilcea, Romania, Dec. 10, 1954; came to U.S., 1990; s. Gheorghe and Maria (Mitroiescu) S.; m. Eleonora Niculescu; children: Mihai-Liviu, Silviu-Gabriel. MS, U. Craiova, 1979; postgrad., Ariz. State U., 1991. Mathematician I.U.G., Craiova, Romania, 1979-81; math. prof. Romanian Coll., 1981-82, 1984-86, 1988; math. tchr. Coop. Ministry, Morocco, 1982-84; French tutor pvt. practice, Turkey, 1988-90; software engr. Honeywell, Phoenix, 1990-95. Author: Nonpoems, 1990, Only Problems, Not Solutions, 1991, numerous other books; contbr. articles to profl. jours. Mem. U.S. Math. Assn., Romania Math. Assn., Zentralblatt fur Math. (reviewer). Home: 2456 S Rose Peak Dr Tucson AZ 85710-9999

SMATHERS, JAMES BURTON, medical physicist, educator; b. Prairie du Chien, Wis., Aug. 26, 1935; s. James Levi and Irma Marie (Stindt) S.; m. Sylvia Lee Rath, Apr. 20, 1957; children—Kristine Kay, Kathryn Ann, James Scott, Ernest Kent. B.Nuclear Enging., N.C. State Coll., 1957, M.S., 1959; Ph.D., U. Md., 1967. Diplomate Am. Bd. Radiology, Am. Bd. Med. Physics, Am. Bd. Medical Physics; cert. in radiation oncology physics; registered profl. engr., D.C., Tex., Calif. Research engr. Atomics Internat., Canoga Park, Calif., 1959, Walter Reed Army Inst. Research, Washington, 1961-67; prof. nuclear engring. Tex. A. and M. U., College Station, 1967-80; prof., head bioengring. Tex. A. and M. U., 1976-80; prof., head med. physics, dept. radiation oncology UCLA, 1980—; cons. U.S. Army, Dept. Energy, also pvt.; industry. Served with U.S. Army, 1959-61. Recipient Excellence in Teaching award Gen. Dynamics, 1971; Excellence in Research award Tex. A. and M. U. Former Students Assn., 1976. Mem. Am. Nuclear Soc., Health Physics Soc., Am. Assn. Physcists in Medicine, Am. Soc. Engring. Edn. (Outstanding Tchr. award in nuclear engring. div. 1972), Radiation Research Soc., Nat. Soc. Profl. Engrs., Calif. Soc. Profl. Engrs., Sigma Xi, Sigma Pi Sigma, Phi Kappa Phi. Home: 18229 Minnehaha St Northridge CA 91326-3427 Office: UCLA Dept Radiation Oncology B265 200 UCLA Med Plz Los Angeles CA 90095

SMEAD, BURTON ARMSTRONG, JR., lawyer; b. Denver, July 29, 1913; s. Burton Armstrong and Lola (Lewis) S.; m. Josephine McKittrick, Mar. 27, 1943; children: Amanda Armstrong, Sydney Hall. BA, U. Denver, 1934, J.D., 1950; grad. Pacific Sch. Banking Trust Sch., 1955. Bar: Colo., 1950. With Norwest Bank Denver (formerly Denver Nat. Bank), 1934-78, trust officer, 1955-70, v.p. and trust officer, 1970-78, sec. bd. dirs.,; pvt. practice law, Englewood, Colo., 1978—; of counsel Buchanan & Thomas, Lakewood, Colo., 1985—; bd. dirs., trust counsel, Resources Trust Co., Englewood, Colo. Author: History of the Twelfth Field Artillery Battalion in the European Theater of Operations, 1944-45, Captain Smead's Letters to Home, 1944-45; editor: Colorado Wills and Estates, 1965. Pres., trustee Stebbins Orphans Home Assn. Chmn. bd. dirs. Am. Cancer oc., N.Y.C., Colo. div., 1961-68. Maj. U.S. Army, 1941-45; ETO. Decorated Bronze Star, Croix de Guerre (France). Mem. ABA, Arapahoe Bar Assn., Colo. Bar Assn. (treas. 1970-88, chmn. probate and trust law sect. 1967-68, exec. coun., bd. govs.

1970-88, coun. bd. gov. 1970-88, hon. 1989—, award of merit 1979), Denver Estate Planning Coun. (co-founder, pres. 1971-72), Univ. Club (Denver). Republican. Episcopalian. Home and Office: 3130 Cherryridge Rd Englewood CO 80110-6057

SMELICK, ROBERT MALCOLM, investment bank executive; b. Phoenix, Mar. 27, 1942; s. Valentine and Mary Helen (McDonald) S.; m. Gail Paine Sterling, Dec. 10, 1979; children: Christopher Paine, Alexandra McBryde, Gillian Sterling. BA, Stanford U., 1964; MBA, Harvard U., 1968; postgrad. U. Melbourne (Australia), 1965-66. v.p. Kidder Peabody & Co., Inc., N.Y.C. and San Francisco, 1968-79; mng. dir. First Boston Corp., San Francisco, 1979-89; mng. prin., founder Sterling Payot Company, San Francisco, 1989—; bd. dirs. Willamette Industries, Portland, Oreg., AdExpress Co., San Francisco, Metricom, Inc., Los Gatos, Calif.; chmn. bd. trustees Town Sch. for Boys, chair, San Francisco. Republican. Episcopalian. Office: 222 Sutter St Fl 8 San Francisco CA 94108-4445

SMELSER, NEIL JOSEPH, sociologist; b. Kahoka, Mo., July 22, 1930; s. Joseph Nelson and Susie Marie (Hess) S.; m. Helen Thelma Margolis, June 10, 1954 (div. 1965); children: Eric Jonathan, Tina Rachel; m. Sharin Fateley, Dec. 20, 1967; children: Joseph Neil, Sarah Joanne. B.A., Harvard U., 1952, Ph.D., 1958; B.A., Magdalen Coll., Oxford U., Eng., 1954; M.A., Magdalen Coll., Oxford U., 1959; grad., San Francisco Psychoanalytic Inst., 1971. Mem. faculty U. Calif., Berkeley, 1958-94, prof. sociology, 1962—, asst. chancellor ednl. devel., 1966-68; assoc. dir. Inst. of Internat. Studies, Berkeley, 1969-73, 80-89; Univ. prof. sociology U. Calif., Berkeley, 1972-94; prof. emeritus, 1994—; dir. edn. abroad program for U. Calif., Berkeley, 1977-79, spl. advisor Office of Pres., 1993-94, dir. Ctr. for Advanced Study in Behavioral Scis., 1994—; bd. dirs. Found. Fund for Rsch. in Psychiatry, 1967-70, Social Sci. Rsch. Coun., 1968-71, chmn., 1971-73; trustee Ctr. for Advanced Study in Behavioral Scis., 1980-86, 87-93, chmn., 1984-86, Russell Sage Found., 1990—; mem. subcom. humanism Am. Bd. Internal Medicine, 1981-85, 89-90; mem. com. econ. growth Social Sci. Rsch. Coun., 1961-65; chmn. sociology panel Behavioral and Social Scis. survey NAS and Social Sci. Rsch. Coun., 1967-69; mem. com. on basic rsch. in behavioral and social scis. NRC, 1980-89, chmn., 1984-86, co-chmn., 1986-89. Author: (with T. Parsons) Economy and Society, 1956, Social Change in the Industrial Revolution, 1959, Theory of Collective Behavior, 1962, The Sociology of Economic Life, 1963, 2d edit., 1975, Essays in Sociological Explanation, 1968, Sociological Theory: A Contemporary View, 1971, Comparative Methods in the Social Sciences, 1976, (with Robin Content) The Changing Academic Market, 1980, Sociology, 1981, 2d edit., 1984, 3d edit. 1987, 4th edit. 1991, 5th edit., 1995, Social Paralysis and Social Change, 1991, Effective Committee Service, 1993, Sociology, 1994; editor: (with W.T. Smelser) Personality and Social Systems, 1963, 2d edit., 1971, (with S.M. Lipset) Social Structure and Mobility in Economic Development, 1966, Sociology, 1967, 2d edit., 1973, (with James Davis) Sociology: A Survey Report, 1969, Karl Marx on Society and Social Change, 1973, (with Gabriel Almond) Public Higher Education in California, 1974, (with Erik Erikson) Themes of Work and Love in Adulthood, 1980, (with Jeffrey Alexander et al) The Micro-Macro Link, 1987, Handbook of Sociology, 1988, (with Hans Haferkamp) Social Change and Modernity, 1992, (with Richard Munch) Theory of Culture, 1992, (with Richard Swedberg) The Handbook of Economic Sociology, 1994; editor Am. Sociol. Rev., 1962-65, 89-90; adv. editor Am. Jour. Sociology, 1960-62. Rhodes scholar, 1952-54; jr. fellow Soc. Fellows, Harvard U., 1955-58; fellow Russell Sage Found., 1989-90. Mem. Am. Sociol. Assn. (coun. 1962-65, 67-70, exec. com. 1963-65, v.p. 1973-74), Pacific Sociol. Assn., Internat. Sociol. Assn. (exec. com. 1986-94, v.p. 1990-94), Am. Acad. Arts and Scis. (hon.), Am. Phils. Soc. (hon.), Nat. Acad. of Scis. (hon.). Home: 890 Robb Rd Palo Alto CA 94306-3729

SMETS, TOBIAS CHARLES, elementary education educator; b. Flagstaff, Ariz., Aug. 8, 1964; s. Russell James Smets; m. Michele Suzanne Blum, Feb. 10, 1989; 1 child, Alexander. BS in Criminology, No. Ariz. U., 1986; MEd, Ariz. State U., 1991. Cert. tchr. K-8. Recreation coord. Gilbert (Ariz.) Parks and Recreation, 1984—; tech. writer, corp. sec. Engring. and Surveying of Ariz., Inc., Mesa, 1986-91; tchr. Tempe (Ariz.) Elem. Sch. Dist., 1991—; aquatic safety instr. ARC, Phoenix, 1982—. Author: An Old Cherished Photograph, 1992, Timothy Tycoon, 1993. Mem. Nat. Horological Soc., Phi Theta Kappa, Phi Kappa Phi, Phi Alpha Delta (treas. 1985-86). Christian. Home: 727 W 2nd Pl Mesa AZ 85201-6414

SMILEY, ROBERT WILLIAM, industrial engineer; b. Phila., Oct. 18, 1919; s. Albert James and Laura Emma (Hoiler) S.; children from previous marriage: Robert, James, Lauralee, Mary; m. Gloria Morais, Jun. 30, 1990; stepchildren: Deborah, Sheila, Vicki, James, Sonja, Michelle. Certificate in Indsl. Engring, Gen. Motors Inst., 1942; student, U. Rochester, 1948; student mgmt. program for execs., U. Pitts. Grad. Sch. Bus., 1968; student, San Jose State Coll., 1969; BSBA, Coll. Notre Dame, Belmont, Calif., 1972, MBA, 1974. Registered profl. engr., Calif. With A.S. Hamilton (cons. engrs.), Rochester, N.Y., 1946-48; commd. lt. comdr. USN, 1952, advanced through grades to comdr., 1960; engaged in tech. contract mgmt. (Poseidon/Polaris and Terrier Missile Programs), 1952-64; officer in charge (Polaris Missile Facility Pacific), Bremerton, Wash., 1964-66; resigned, 1966; mgr. product assurance Missile Systems div. Lockheed Missiles and Space Co., Sunnyvale, Calif., 1966-72; mgr. materiel Missile Systems div. Lockheed Missiles and Space Co., 1972-77; mgr. product assurance McDonnell Douglas Astronautics, 1977-78; dir. product assurance Aerojet Tactical Systems, Sacramento, 1978-83; dir. quality assurance Aerojet Solid Propulsion Co., Sacramento, 1984-92, Tahoe Surg. Instruments, Inc., 1992—; frequent guest lectr. at colls. on quality control and reliability; chmn. Polaris/Minuteman/Pershing Missile Nondestruct Test Com., 1958-64; quality control cons. Dragon Missile Program, U.S. Army, 1971. Contbr. articles to sci. jours., chpt. to Reliability Handbook, 1966, Reliability Engineering and Management, 1988. Served with USNR, 1942-46, 51-52; now capt. ret. Recipient letters of Commendation for work on Polaris/Poseidon Sec. of Navy, 1960, certificate of Honor Soc. for Nondestructive Testing, 1966. Fellow Am. Soc. Quality Control (chmn. San Francisco sect. 1969-70, exec. bd. 1966—, chmn. reliability divsn. 1971, 81, nat. v.p. 1984-85; mem. SCORE (chmn. Sacramento chpt. 1993—), Aircraft Industries Assn. (chmn. quality assurance com.), Navy League, AAAS, Am. Mgmt. Assn. Home and Office: 9144 Green Ravine Ln Fair Oaks CA 95628-4110

SMISSON, DAVID CLAYTON, physician; b. Ft. Valley, Ga., Oct. 23, 1933; s. Hugh Franklin Sr. and Emily Carolyn (Wright) S.; m. Joan Patricia Fox, Sept. 24, 1960; children: David Clayton Jr., Richard Michael, Anne Marie, Sharon Lynn, Angela Jane, Victoria Leah. BS in Pre-Medicine, The Citadel, 1954; MD, Johns Hopkins U., 1958. Intern Med. Ctr. U. Colo., Denver, 1958-59; resident in surgery Med. Ctr. U. Kans., Kansas City, 1959-61; resident in internal medicine Med. Coll. Ga., Augusta, 1963-65, fellow in cardiology, 1965-66; pvt. practice St. Joseph's Hosp., Minot, N.D., 1966-90; chief med. svc. VA Med. Ctr., Miles City, Mont., 1990—. Author: (monograph) Transvenous Pacemaker Implantation Techniques: Recommendations Based on 20 Years of Experience, 1989. Capt. U.S. Army, 1961-63. Fellow ACP, Am. Coll. Cardiology; mem. N.Am. Soc. Pacing and Electrophysiology. Episcopalian. Home: 105 Lynam Dr Miles City MT 59301-4748 Office: VA Med Ctr 210 S Winchester Ave Miles City MT 59301-4742

SMITH, ALBERT CROMWELL, JR., investments consultant; b. Norfolk, Va., Dec. 6, 1925; s. Albert Cromwell and Georgie (Foreman) S.; m. Laura Thaxton, Oct. 25, 1952; children: Albert, Elizabeth, Laura. BS in Civil Engring., Va. Mil. Inst., 1949; MS in Govtl. Adminstrn., George Washington U., 1965; MBA, Pepperdine U., 1975; PhD in Bus. Adminstrn. LaSalle U., 1994. Enlisted USMC, 1944, commd. 2d lt., 1949, advanced through grades to col., 1970; comdr. inf. platoons, companies, landing force; variously assigned staffs U.K. Joint Forces, U.S. Sec. Navy, Brit. Staff Coll., Marine Staff Coll., U.K. Staff Coll., U.K. Latimer Staff Coll.; adviser, analyst amphibious systems; ret., 1974; pres. A. Cromwell-Smith, Ltd., Charlottesville, Va., 1973, head broker, cons. A. Cromwell Smith, Investments, La Jolla and Coronado, Calif., 1975—. Bd. dirs. Reps. La Jolla, 1975-76; vestryman St. Martin's Episcopal Ch., 1971-73. Decorated Legion of Merit with oak leaf cluster with V device, Bronze Star with V device with oak leaf cluster, Air medal with 2 oak leaf clusters, Purple Heart, Vietnamese Galantry cross with gold star. Mem. ASCE, SAR, Nat. Assn. Realtors, Calif. Assn. Realtors, San Diego Bd. Realtors, Coronado Bd. Realtors, Stockbrokers Soc., So. Calif. Options Soc., Mil. Order Purple Heart. Club: Kona Kai. Author: The Individual Investor in Tomorrow's Stock Market, 1977, The Little Guy's Stock Market Survival Guide, 1979, Wake Up Detroit! The EVs Are Coming, 1982, The Little Guy's Tax Survival Guide, 1984, The Little Guy's Sailboat Success Guide, 1986, The Little Guy's Business Success Guide, 1988, Little Guy's Real Estate Success Guide, 1990, Little Guy's Stock Market Success Guide, 1992, Little Guy's Stock Market Future Effectiveness, 1994, Semper Fidelis in Peace and War, 1995; contbr. articles to civilian and mil. publs. Office: PO Box 180192 1001 B Ave Ste 319/320 Coronado CA 92178

SMITH, ALEXIS, artist; b. L.A., Aug. 24, 1949; d. Dayrel Driver and Lucille Lloyd (Doak) S.; married, June 11, 1990. BA, U. Calif, Irvine, 1970. Represented by Margo Leavin Gallery, L.A.; tchr. Calif. Inst. Arts, Valencia, 1975; tchr. U. Calif., Irving, 1976, San Diego, 1977-78; tchr. UCLA, 1979-82, 85-88, Skowhegan (Maine) Sch. Painting and Sculpture, 1990; selection panelist Conceptual Art, NEA Fellowship Awards, 1980; trustee L.A. Contemporary Exhbns., 1985-86; jurist fellowship awards Chgo. Art Inst., 1986; lectr. and vis. artist numerous colls. and galleries including Western Ill. State U., Macomb, 1976, Coll. Art Assn. Conf., L.A., 1977, U. Calif., Santa Barbara, Coll. Creative Studies, 1978, San Francisco Art Inst., 1979, Cuesta Coll., San Luis Obispo, Calif., 1980, Women's Caucus for Art, 1982, U. Hawaii at Manoa, Honolulu, 1983, Art Ctr. Coll. of Design, Pasadena, 1986, Los Angeles County Mus. Art, UCLA Wight Gallery, L.A., 1989, Mus. Contemporary Art, L.A., 1990. Co-author: (with Amy Gerstler) Past Lives, 1989; one woman shows include Whitney Mus. Am. Art, N.Y.C., 1975, 91, Mandeville Art Gallery, San Diego, 1976, Holly Solomon Gallery, N.Y.C, 1977, 78, 79, 81, Rosamund Felsen Gallery, L.A., 1978, 80, 82, L.A. County Mus. Art, 1981, Margo Leavin Gallery, L.A., 1982, 85, 88, 90, 93, 94, Walker Art Ctr., Mpls., 1986, Aspen (Colo.) Art Ctr., 1987, Bklyn. Mus., 1987-88, Santa Monica Mus. Art, 1989; exhibited in group shows at Whitney Mus. Am. Art, N.Y., 1975, 79, 81, 83, 89-90, 92, Mus. Modern Art, N.Y.C., 1976, 80, 84, L.A. County Mus. Art, 1976, 81, 83, 87, Musee d'art Modern, Paris, 1977, Hirshhorn Mus. and Sculpture Garden, Washington, 1983, Mus. Contemporary Art, L.A., 1986-88, Triton Mus. Art, Santa Clara, Calif., 1988, Fresno (Calif.) ARt Mus., 1988, Margo Leavin Gallery, 1991, Centro Cultural Art Contemporaneo, Mexico City, Musee d'Art Moderne et d'Art Contemporain, Nice, France, 1991, numerous others; commd. works include The Grand, Grand Centerm Grand Rapids, Mich., 1983, Snake Path, Stuart Collection, U. Calif. San Diego, La Jolla, 1992, terrazzo floor designs L.A. Convention Ctr. Expansion Project, 1993; subject of articles in Artforum, 1976, 79, 85, 87, 90, The Village Voice, 1982, N.Y. Times, 1983, 91, L.A. Times, 1991, Jour. Art, 1991, Jour. Contemporary Art, 1991, House and Garden, 1991, Portfolio Magazine, 1980, others. Mem. artist adv. coun. Mus. of Contemporary Art, L.A. 1979—; mem. arts pub. policy project NEA, 1987; gov. Skowhegan Sch., 1990-93. Recipient New Talent award L.A. County Mus. Art, 1974, 4th Councilman Dist. Svc. award L.A. City Count., 1986, Key to City, City of Grand Rapids, Mich., 1983; NEA fellow, 1976, 87. Address: Margo Leavin Gallery 812 N Robertson Blvd Los Angeles CA 90069

SMITH, ALICE MURRAY, civic worker, mathematician; b. Buffalo, Apr. 23, 1930; d. Robert Leslie and Alice Emma (Bennett) Murray; m. Robert Crellin Smith, Feb. 21, 1953 (dy. 1988); children: William Stewart, Peter Crellin, Edward Bennett. AB, Smith Coll., 1951. Mathematician U.S. Govt., Las Cruces, N.Mex., 1951-52. Contbr. articles to profl. jours. Pres. Phoenix Rep. Women, 1967, Arizonans for Nat. Security, Phoenix, 1983-87, 89-91, Ariz. Coordinating Coun. Rep. Women, 1991-93; mem. Ariz. Rep. Com., 1992—; mem. curriculum com. All Saints Day Sch., Phoenix, 1968-71. Republican.

SMITH, ARTHUR KITTREDGE, JR., university official, political science educator; b. Derry, N.H., Aug. 15, 1937; s. Arthur Kittredge and Rena Belle (Roberts) S.; m. June Mary Dahar, Nov. 28, 1959; children: Arthur, Valerie, Meredith. B.S., U.S. Naval Acad., 1959; M.A., U. N.H., 1966; Ph.D., Cornell U., 1970. Vis. prof. El Colegio de Mexico, Mexico City, 1968-69; asst. prof. polit. sci. SUNY-Binghamton, 1970-74, assoc. prof., 1974-84, prof., 1984-88, provost for grad. studies and research, 1976-83, v.p. for adminstrn., 1982-88; prof. govt. and internat. studies U. S.C., Columbia, 1988-91, exec. v.p. for acad. affairs, provost, 1988-90, 91, interim pres., 1990-91; pres., prof. polit. sci. U. Utah, Salt Lake City, 1991—. Author: (with Claude E. Welch, Jr.) Military Role and Rule: Perspectives on Civil-Military Relations, 1975; contbr. articles to profl. jours. Active Am. Stores Co., First Security Corp. Served with USN, 1959-65. Lehman fellow, 1966-69, NDEA fellow, 1969-70. Mem. Am. Polit. Sci. Assn., L.Am. Studies Assn., Inter-Univ. Sem. on Armed Forces and Soc., Am. Coun. on Edn., World Affairs Coun. (pres. Binghamton chpt. 1976-76), Phi Beta Kappa, Pi Sigma Alpha, Omicron Delta Kappa, Phi Delta Kappa, Beta Gamma Sigma, Phi Kappa Phi. Home: 1480 Military Way Salt Lake City UT 84103-4455 Office: U Utah Office of the Pres 203 Park Building Bldg Salt Lake City UT 84112-1201

SMITH, BARBARA BARNARD, music educator; b. Ventura, Calif., June 10, 1920; d. Fred W. and Grace (Hobson) S. B.A., Pomona Coll., 1942; Mus.M., U. Rochester, 1943, performer's cert., 1944. Mem. faculty piano and theory Eastman Sch. Music, U. Rochester, 1943-49; mem. faculty U. Hawaii, Honolulu, 1949—; assoc. prof. music U. Hawaii, 1953-62, prof., 1962-82, prof. emeritus, 1982—; sr. fellow East-West Center, 1973; lectr.-recitals in Hawaiian and Asian music, U.S., Europe and Asia, 1956—; field researcher Asia, 1956, 60, 66, 71, 80, Micronesia, 1963, 70, 87, 88, 90, 91, Solomon Islands, 1976. Author publs. on ethnomusicology. Mem. Internat. Soc. Music Edn., Internat. Musicol. Soc., Am. Musicol. Soc., Soc. Ethnomusicology, Internat. Coun. for Traditional Music, Asia Soc., Am. Mus. Instrument Soc., Coll. Music Soc., Soc. for Asian Music, Music Educators Nat. Conf., Pacific Sci. Assn., Assn. for Chinese Music Rsch., Phi Beta Kappa, Mu Phi Epsilon. Home: 581 Kamoku St Apt 2004 Honolulu HI 96826-5210

SMITH, BENJAMIN ERIC, venture capitalist, executive; b. L.A., Mar. 22, 1915; s. Jesse Oliver and Clara Louise (Ferris) S.; m. Donelle Ray, Jan. 6, 1956 (div. 1971); children: Lee Fleming, Deidre Ray Folsom. BA, U. Redlands, 1937; postgrad., Yale U., 1938-39; MA, U. So. Calif., 1940. Mgr. Birch-Smith Storage Co., L.A., 1940-42; div. mgr. Bekins Van & Storage Co., L.A., 1946-50; nat. sales mgr. Meletron Corp., L.A., 1952-56; v.p. Leo G. MacLaughlin Co., Pasadena, Calif., 1956-57; sr. cons. Barry & Co., L.A., 1957-65; pres. Benjamin E. Smith & Assoc., L.A., 1965—, Lancer Pacific Inc., Carlsbad, Calif., 1973-79, Aries Group, San Diego, 1979—; mem., dir. Corp. Fin. Coun., San Diego, 1976—; faculty mem. Southwestern U., L.A., 1941-42, U. So. Calif., 1959-60; mem. San Diego in the Global Economy Com., San Diego, 1990-91. Author: Love, War, and Laughter, 1995, Two Paths, 1995; columnist West Coast Cmty. Newspapers, 1985-92; contbr. articles to profl. jours. Chmn. 57th Assembly Dist. Rep. Cen. Com., Hollywood, 1958-62; exec. dir. L.A. County Cen. Com., 1957. Lt. col. U.S. Army, 1942-46, 50-52. Republican. Episcopalian. Home: 3017 Azahar Ct Carlsbad CA 92009-8301 Office: Aries Group 5841 Mission Gorge Rd Ste B San Diego CA 92120-4015

SMITH, BERNALD STEPHEN, retired airline pilot, aviation consultant; b. Long Beach, Calif., Dec. 24, 1926; s. Donald Albert and Bernice Merrill (Stephens) S.; m. Marilyn Mae Spence, July 22, 1949; children: Lorraine Ann Smith Foute, Evelyn Donice Smith DeRoos, Mark Stephen, Diane April (dec.). Student, U. Calif., Berkeley, 1944-45, 50-51. Cert. airline transport pilot, flight engr., FAA. Capt. Transocean Air Lines, Oakland (Calif.) and Tokyo, 1951-53, Hartford, Conn., 1954-55; 1st officer United Air Lines, Seattle, 1955, San Francisco, 1956-68; tng. capt. United Air Lines, Denver and San Francisco, 1961-68; capt. United Air Lines, San Francisco, 1968-86, 2d officer, 1986-93, ret., 1993; founder, v.p. AviaAm., Palo Alto, Calif., 1970-72, AviaInternat., Palo Alto, 1972-74; cons. Caproni Vizzola, Milan, 1972-84; prin., cons. Internat. Aviation Cons. and Investments, Fremont, Calif., 1985—; instr. aviation Ohlone Coll., Fremont, 1976; founder Pacific Soaring Coun.; founder, trustee AirSailing, Inc., 1970—, Soaring Safety Found., 1985—. Author/editor: American Soaring Handbook, 1975, 80; contbr. articles to profl. jours. Trustee Nat. Soaring Mus., 1975—, pres. 1975-78; mem. RTCA, SSA del., 1992—. Comdr. USNR, 1944-75. Mem. AIAA (pub. bd. 1977-94), Soaring Soc. Am. (pres. 1969-70, chmn. pub. bd. 1971-84, chmn. ins. com. 1975-93, bd. dirs. 1963—, Warren Eaton Meml. Trophy 1977, Exceptional Svc. award 1970, 75, 82, 88, 91, named to Hall of Fame 1984), Soc. Automotive Engring., Nat. Aero. Assn., Exptl. Aircraft Assn., Aircraft Owners and Pilots Assn., Airline Pilots Assn., Seaplane Pilots Assn., Orgn. Scientifique et Technique Internat. du Vol a Voile (bd. dirs., U.S. del. 1981—), Fedn. Aeronatique Internat. (Paul Tissandier Diplome 1992, Lilienthal medal 1993, Highest Soaring award, U.S. del. 1991—), Commn. de Vol A Voile (U.S. del. 1970-71, 78, 85—, v.p. 1988—), U. Calif. Alumni Assn. (life). Democrat. Methodist. Office: Internat Aviation Cons Investments PO Box 3075 Fremont CA 94539-0307

SMITH, BERNARD JOSEPH CONNOLLY, civil engineer; b. Elizabeth, N.J., Mar. 11, 1930; s. Bernard Joseph and Julia Susan (Connolly) S.; B.S., U. Notre Dame, 1951; B.S. in Civil Engring., Tex. A&M U., 1957; M.B.A. in Fin., U. Calif.-Berkeley, 1976; m. Josephine Kerley, Dec. 20, 1971; children—Julia Susan Alice, Teresa Mary Josephine, Anne Marie Kathleen. Asst. Bernard J. Smith, cons. engr. office, Dallas, 1947-57; hydraulic engr. C.E., U.S. Army, San Francisco, 1957-59, St. Paul dist., 1959-60, Kansas City (Mo.) dist., 1960-63, Sacramento dist., 1963-65; engr. Fed. Energy Regulatory Commn., San Francisco Regional Office, 1965—. Served with U.S. Army, 1952-54. Registered profl. engr., Calif., Mo.; lic. real estate broker, Calif. Mem. ASCE (sec. power div. San Francisco sect. 1969), Soc. Am. Mil. Engrs. (treas. Kansas City post 1962), Res. Officers Assn. (chpt. pres. 1973). Club: Commonwealth of Calif. Home: 247 28th Ave San Francisco CA 94121-1001 Office: Fed Energy Regulatory Commn 901 Market St San Francisco CA 94103-1729

SMITH, BETTY DENNY, county official, administrator, fashion executive; b. Centralia, Ill., Nov. 12, 1932; d. Otto and Ferne Elizabeth (Beier) Hasenfuss; m. Peter S. Smith, Dec. 5, 1964; children: Carla Kip, Bruce Kimball. Student, U. Ill., 1950-52; student, L.A. City Coll., 1953-57, UCLA, 1965, U. San Francisco, 1982-84. Freelance fashion coordinator L.A., N.Y.C., 1953-58; tchr. fashion Rita LeRoy Internat. Studios, 1959-60; mgr. Mo Nadler Fashion, L.A., 1961-64; showroom dir. Jean of Calif. Fashions, L.A., 1965—; freelance polit. book reviewer for community newspapers, 1961-62; staff writer Valley Citizen News, 1963. Bd. dirs. Pet Assistance Found., 1969-76; founder, pres., dir. Vol. Services to Animals L.A., 1972-76; mem. County Com. To Discuss Animals in Research, 1973-74; mem. blue ribbon com. on animal control L.A. County, 1973-74; dir. L.A. County Animal Care and Control, 1976-82; mem. Calif. Animal Health Technician Exam. Com., 1975-82, chmn., 1979; bd. dirs. L.A. Soc. for Prevention Cruelty to Animals, 1984-94, Calif. Coun. Companions Animal Advocates, 1993; dir. West Coast Regional Office, Am. Humane Assn., 1988—; CFO Coalition for Pet Population Control, 1987-92; mem. Calif. Rep. Cen. Com., 1964-72, mem. exec. com., 1971-73; mem. L.A. County Rep. Cen. Com., 1964-70, mem. exec. com., 1966-70; chmn. 29th Congl. Cen. Com., 1969-70; sec. 28th Senatorial Cen. Com., 1967-68, 45th Assembly Dist. Cen. Com., 1965-68; mem. speakers bur. George Murphy for U.S. Senate, 1970; campaign mgr. Los Angeles County for Spencer Williams for Atty. Gen., 1966; mem. adv. com. Moorpark Coll., 1988—; mem. adv. bd. Wishbone Prodn., 1995—. Mem. Internat. Platform Assn., Mannequins Assn. (bd. dirs. 1967-68), Motion Picture and TV Industry Assn. (govt. rels. and pub. affairs com. 1992—), Lawyers' Wives San Gabriel Valley (bd. dirs. 1971-74, pres. 1972-73), L.A. Athletic Club, Town Hall, Delta Gamma, Pi Phi Theta. Home: 1766 Bluffhill Dr Monterey Park CA 91754-4533

SMITH, CARIN A., veterinarian, writer; b. Moses Lake, Wash., Sept. 3, 1958; d. William and Katherine Smith; m. Jay Bender, May 19, 1990. BS in Microbiology, Oreg. State U., 1980; DVM, Oreg. State U., Wash. State U., 1984. Pres. Smith Vet. Svcs., Albuquerque, 1986-90, Leavenworth, Wash., 1990—; co-founder Childless by Choice, Leavenworth, 1992—. Author: Easy Health Care for Your Horse, 1990, Relief Veterinarian's Manual, 1990, Employer's Guide to Hiring, 1992, Get Rid of Fleas and Ticks, 1993, rev. edit., 1995, 101 Training Tips for Your Cat, 1994; editor: (newsletter) Childless by Choice, 1992—. Pres. bd. dirs. Leavenworth Libr., 1994-95. Recipient 1st Place nonfiction book award Southwest Writers Workshop, 1989. Mem. Am. Vet. Med. Assn., Women Vets. Assn., Am. Endurance Ride Conf. Office: Childless by Choice PO Box 695 Leavenworth WA 98826-0695 Also: SmithVet Svcs PO Box 254 Leavenworth WA 98826-0254

SMITH, CARTER BLAKEMORE, broadcaster; b. San Francisco, Jan. 1, 1937; s. Donald V. and Charlotte M. (Nichols) S.; children: Carter Blakemore, Clayton M. AA, City Coll. San Francisco, 1958; BA, San Francisco State U., 1960; postgrad. N.Y. Inst. Finance, 1969-70; Assoc. in Fin. PLanning, Coll. for Fin. Planning, 1984. Announcer, Sta. KBLF, Red Bluff, Calif., 1954-56; personality Sta. KRE-KRE FM, Berkeley, Calif., 1958-63, Sta. KSFO, San Francisco, 1963-72, Sta. KNBR, San Francisco, 1972-83, Sta. KSFO, San Francisco, 1983-86, Sta. KFRC, San Francisco, 1986-91, 93-94; mem. faculty radio-TV dept. San Francisco State U., 1960-61. Mem. adv. bd. Little Jim Club Children's Hosp., 1968-71; bd. dirs. Marin County Humane Soc., 1968-73, San Francisco Zool. Soc., 1980-90; trustee Family Svc. Agy. Marin, 1976-85; mem. alumni bd. Lowell High Sch. Recipient award San Francisco Press Club, 1965; named one of Outstanding Young Men in Am. U.S. Jaycees, 1972. Mem. Amateur Radio Relay League (life), Quarter Century Wireless Assn., Alpha Epsilon Rho.

SMITH, CATHLEEN LYNNE, psychology educator; b. Salt Lake City, Mar. 17, 1947; d. Dasil Clawson and Melba (Fairbourn) S. BA with honors, U. Utah, 1968, MA, 1972, PhD, 1976. Asst. prof. of psychology Portland (Oreg.) State U., 1975-79, assoc. prof. psychology, 1979-83, prof. psychology, 1983—. Contbr. articles to profl. jours. Chair Portland Foster Grandparent Program Adv. Coun., 1983-86. Mem. APA, Western Psychol. Assn., Gerontol. Soc. Am., Soc. for Rsch. in Child Devel., Oreg. Ethics Commons (bd. dirs.), Phi Beta Kappa, Phi Kappa Phi, Sigma Xi (Portland State U. chpt. pres. 1992-93). Democrat. Home: 2518 SW Vista Ave Portland OR 97201-1775 Office: Dept Psychol Portland State U PO Box 751 Portland OR 97207

SMITH, CHARLES ANTHONY, businessman; b. Santa Fe, Sept. 16, 1939; s. Frances (Mier) Vigil; student various adminstrv. and law courses; m. Paula Ann Thomas, June 26, 1965; 1 dau., Charlene Danielle. Circulation mgr. Daily Alaska Empire, 1960-63; agt. Mut. of N.Y. Life Ins. Co., Juneau, Alaska, 1964-65; mng. partner Future Investors in Alaska and Cinema Alaska, Juneau, 1961-62; SE Alaska rep. K & L Distbrs., 1966-68; mgr. Alaska Airlines Newspapers, SE Alaska, 1969; dep. Alaska Retirement System, Juneau, 1970-71; apptd. dir. hwy. safety, gov.'s hwy. safety rep., Juneau, 1971-83; pres. Valley Service Ctr., Inc., 1984—. Alaska pres. Muscular Dystrophy Assn. Am.; pres. SE Alaska Emergency Med. Services Council, 1965-72. Served to major Army N.G., 1964-88. Named Alaska Safety Man of Yr., 1977. Mem. Am. Assn. Motor Vehicle Adminstrs., Alaska Peace Officers Assn., Nat. Assn. Gov.s' Hwy. Safety Reps., N.G. Assn., Internat. Platform Assn. Roman Catholic. Club: Elks (Juneau). Author various hwy. safety manuals and plans, 1971—. Home: PO Box 32856 Juneau AK 99803-2856 Office: Pouch N Juneau AK 99811

SMITH, CHARLES CONARD, refractory company executive; b. Mexico, Mo., Feb. 10, 1936; s. Charles Adelbert and Waldine (Barnes) S.; m. Constance Nagel, Oct. 6, 1962; children: Stewart Ashley, Graham Prior. BS in Ceramic Engring., Iowa State U., 1958; MBA, Stanford U., 1962. Process engr. Kaiser Refractory divsn. Kaiser Aluminum, Moss Landing, Calif., 1962-65; materials mgr. Kaiser Refractory divsn. Kaiser Aluminum, Mexico, Mo., 1965-67; divsn. planning Kaiser Refractory divsn. Kaiser Aluminum, Oakland, Calif., 1967-69; v.p., gen. mgr. Kaiser Refractories Argentina, Buenos Aires, 1969-74; with divsn. planning Kaiser Refractories divsn. Kaiser Aluminum, Oakland, 1974-77, mktg. mgr., 1977-80, gen. mgr. mfg., 1980-82, v.p., gen. mgr. refractories divsn., 1982-85; chmn., pres., CEO Nat. Refractories and Mineral Corp., Livermore, Calif., 1985—. Patentee in refractory field. Lt. USNR, 1958-60. Mem. Refractories Inst. (past chmn., exec. com.). Republican. Home: 63 Lincoln Ave Piedmont CA 94611-3830

SMITH, CHARLES LEWIS, retired naval officer and association executive; b. Clarkston, Ga., Oct. 27, 1920; s. Robert Clyde and Emelyn (Bloodworth) S.; m. Mildred Lee Stilley, Sept. 5, 1947; children: Jan, Robert Eugene. Student, Ga. Sch. Tech., 1938-39. Enlisted USN, 1937, advanced through grades to comdr., 1968; various assignments including comdg. officer USS Chickasaw (ATF 83), 1962-64; leadership devel. officer Amphibious Force U.S. Pacific Fleet, 1964-66; comdg. officer USS Tioga County (LST 1158), 1966-68; dept. head Amphibious Sch. U.S. Naval

Amhibious Base, Coronado, Calif., 1968-70, ret., 1970; dir. pub. rels. and fin. San Diego County coun. Boy Scouts Am., 1971-80, dir. pub. rels., 1980-82, dir. planned giving, 1982-85, ret., 1985; mem. nat. adv. bd. Am. Security Coun., 1994—. Trustee God Bless Am. Week, Inc., 1972-80, pres., 1977-78, co-chmn. San Diego Bicentennial Pageant, 1976; mem. adv. bd. Commd. Officers Mess (Open) U.S. Naval Sta., 1973-89; bd. dirs. Boys Club Chula Vista, Calif., 1985-87; devel. com. Alvarado Health Found., Alvarado Hosp. Med. Ctr., 1986-87; charter rev. com. City of Chula Vista, 1986-88; mem. accolades com. City of San Diego, 1988-90; rsch. bd. advisors Am. Biog. Inst., 1988—; vol. Boy Scouts Am. 1935-71, 85—; scout commr. San Diego County coun. 1969-71, mem. internat. rels. com. 1985-92, bd. dirs., 1995—, scoutmaster 7th Nat. Jamboree, Farragut State park, Idaho, 1969, 13th World Jamboree, Japan, 1971, mem. nat. staff Nat. Jamboree, Ft. A.P. Hill, Va., 1986. Recipient svc. award Civitan Internat., 1968, Community Svc. resolution Calif. Senate, 1970, Southwestern Coll., 1973, Silver Beaver award Boy Scouts Am., 1965, Svc. to Youth resolution Calif. Senate, 1985, award Armed Forces YMCA Century Club, 1988, Appreciation award United Way San Diego, 1974-82, citation for heroism Sheriff of San Diego, 1991, Recognition award San Diego Rotary Club, 1991, citation for svc. City of San Diego Accolades Com. 1992; Scouter Chuck Smith Day proclaimed by City of San Diego, 1985; flagpole dedicated to Scouter Chuck Smith San Diego County Coun. BSA, 1992; named to Honorable Order Ky. Cols., 1985. Mem. VFW (mem. nat. adv. bd. 1990—, Cert. of Appreciation 1995), Nat. Soc. Fund Raising Execs. (bd. dirs. San Diego chpt., 1975-80, 84-85, hosp. com. 1984-85), UN Assns. (bd. dirs. San Diego chpt. 1972-85), Ret. Officers Assn. (life, bd. dirs. Sweetwater chpt. 1972-92, pres. 1975, 81), Navy League U.S. (bd. dirs. 1984—, greeters 1983—, Appreciation award 1985, Cert. of Merit 1991), Mil. Order World Wars (comdr. 1989-90, nat. citations 1987, 91, 92, Outstanding Chpt. Comdr. award Dept. So. Calif. 1990), Am. Legion, Crazy Horse Meml. Found., Clarkston Civitan Club (founding bd. dirs.), Eagle Scout Alumni Assn. (founder 1973, bd. dirs. 1986-88, life mem. 1985—), Hammer Club San Diego, Kiwanis (bd. dirs. 1984-88, chmn. fellowship com. 1983-84, boys and girls com. 1984-85, planned giving com. 1988-89), Order of the Arrow (vigil, Cross Feathers award 1968), Masons, Shriners, Order of Ea. Star (life). Methodist.

SMITH, CHARLES RICHARD, marketing executive; b. Covington, Ohio, Nov. 5, 1932; s. Richard Weller and Harriet Rosalind (Minton) S.; m. Margaret Jean Porter, Aug. 7, 1954; children: David Paul, Kevin Richard, Jennifer Perlee, Melinda Jean. BA, Ohio Wesleyan U., Delaware, 1954; B Chem. Engring., Ohio State U., 1960. Product engr. Dow Corning Corp., Midland, Mich., 1960-63; tech. pub. rels. mgr. Clyde Williams & Co., Columbus, Ohio, 1963-66; dir. pub. rels. Chem. Abstracts Svc., Columbus, 1966-68; v.p. sales/mktg. Ventron Corp., materials div., Bradford, Pa., 1968-73; v.p. sales/svc. Applied Materials, Inc., Santa Clara, Calif., 1973-77; gen. mgr. Gyrex Corp., Santa Barbara, Calif., 1977-81; pres., CEO Auto/Recognition Systems, Santa Barbara, 1982-84; v.p. mktg./sales Tylan Corp., Torrance, Calif., 1984-85, Benzing Tech., Santa Clara, Calif., 1985-88; v.p. sales High Yield Tech., Sunnyvale, Calif., 1988-91; cons. Internat. Remote Imaging Systems, Chatsworth, Calif., 1981-82, Hakuto Co. Ltd., Tokyo, 1989—; dir. Micropulse Systems, Santa Barbara, Benzing Tech., Santa Clara; founder Action Pro Tem internat. bus. cons. co. Author: Plasma Jet Technology, 1962; contbr. articles to profl. jours. Mem. U.S. English, Washington, Citizens Against Waste, Washington. With USAF, 1955-57. Mem. Semiconductor Equipment and Materials Internat. (chmn. stds. group 1970-71, chmn. sales exec. coun. 1988-90, W.C. Benzing award 1990), Marines' Meml. Assn., Soc. Photo Optical Instrumentation Engrs., Churchill Club. Republican. Home: 7933 Caledonia Dr San Jose CA 95135-2112 Office: Action Pro Tem 3315 San Felipe Rd # 7 San Jose CA 95135-2000

SMITH, CHARLES VINTON, mayor, retired electrical engineer; b. Frankfort, Ohio, July 21, 1932; s. Vinton Jay and Bernice Louetta (Blue) S.; m. Nancy Carol Johnson, Apr. 9, 1960; children: Robin, Jeffrey, Stacy, Scott. BEE, Ohio State U., 1959. Mem. tech. staff Hughes Aircraft, Culver City, Calif., 1959-61; rsch. engr. N.Am. Aviation, Anaheim, Calif., 1961-63, sr. rsch. engr., 1963-65; engring. supr. N.Am.-Rockwell, Anaheim, Calif., 1965-76; project engr. Rockwell Internat., Anaheim, 1976-90, ret., 1990; mayor City of Westminster, Calif., 1988—; v.p., treas. Merit Micro Software Corp., Oklahoma City, 1983-87; v.p. SDS Land Corp., Chillicothe, Ohio, 1976-70; gen. ptnr. Caloh, a ltd. partnership, Westminister, Calif., 1969—; pres., broker S & A Realty and Investment, Garden Grove, Calif., 1978—. Planning commr. Westminster Planning Commn., Westminster, 1978-84; city councilman Westminster City Coun., 1984-88; life mem. Westminster Community Theater, 1979. Sgt. USMC, 1950-54. Mem. IEEE, Westminister Lions Club (pres. 1982-83), Masons (master mason 1960-90, Ohio chpt.), West Orange County Bd. of Realtors. Republican. Home: 8761 Tamarisk Cir Westminster CA 92683-6840 Office: City of Westminster 8200 Westminster Blvd Westminster CA 92683-3366

SMITH, CHARLES Z., state supreme court justice; b. Lakeland, Fla., Feb. 23, 1927; s. John R. and Eva (Love) S.; m. Eleanor Jane Martinez, Aug. 20, 1955; children: Carlos M., Michael O., Stephen P., Felica L. BS, Temple U., 1952; JD, U. Wash., 1955. Bar: Wash. 1955. Law clk. Wash. Supreme Ct., Olympia, 1955-56; dep. pros. atty., asst. chief criminal div. King County, Seattle, 1956-60; ptnr. Bianchi, Smith & Tobin, Seattle, 1960-61; spl. asst. to atty. gen. criminal div. U.S. Dept. Justice, Washington, 1961-64; judge criminal dept. Seattle Mcpl. Ct., 1965-66; judge Superior Ct. King County, 1966-73; former assoc. dean, prof. law U. Wash., 1973; now justice Wash. Supreme Ct., Olympia. Mem. adv. bd. NAACP, Seattle Urban League, Wash. State Literacy Coun., Boys Club, Wash. Citizens for Migrant Affairs, Medina Children's Svc., Children's Home Soc. Wash., Seattle Better Bus. Bur., Seattle Foundation, Seattle Symphony Orch., Seattle Opera Assn., Community Svc. Ctr. for Deaf and Hard of Hearing, Seattle U., Seattle Sexual Assault Ctr., Seattle Psychoanalytic Inst., The Little Sch., Linfield Coll., Japanese Am. Citizens League, Kawabe Meml. Hous, Puget Counseling Ctr, Am. Cancer Soc., Hutchinson Cancer Rsch. Ctr., Robert Chinn Found.; pres. Am. Bapt. Chs. U.S.A., 1976-77, lt. col. ret. USMCR. Mem. ABA, Am. Judicature Soc., Washington Bar Assn., Seattle-King County Bar Assn., Order of Coif., Phi Alpha Delta, Alpha Phi Alpha. Office: Wash Supreme Ct Temple of Justice (AV-11) PO Box 40929 Olympia WA 98504*

SMITH, CHESTER, broadcasting executive; b. Wade, Okla., Mar. 29, 1930; s. Louis L. and Effie (Brown) S.; m. Naomi L. Crenshaw, July 19, 1959; children: Lauri, Lorna, Roxanne. Country western performer on Capitol records, TV and radio, 1947-61; owner, mgr. Sta. KLOC, Ceres-Modesto, Calif., 1963-81, Sta. KCBA-TV, Salinas-Monterey, Calif., 1981-86; owner, gen. ptnr. Sta. KCSO-TV, Modesto-Stockton-Sacramento, Sta. KCVU-TV, Paradise-Chico-Redding, Calif., Sta. KTA-TV, Santa Maria, Calif., Sta. KO9UF-TV, Morro Bay, Calif., 1986—; co-owner Sta. KBVU-TV, Eureka, Calif., 1990—; owner Sta. KNSO-TV, Merced-Fresno, KDS TV, Chico, Calif. Mem. Calif. Broadcasters Assn. Republican. Mem. Christian Ch. original rec. Wait A Little Longer Please Jesus; inducted Country Music Hall of Fame, Nashville, 1955, inductee Western Swing Hall of Fame, Sacramento, 1988.

SMITH, CHRISTOPHER ALLEN, technology company executive, marketing professional; b. Rockford, Ill., Nov. 16, 1961; s. Robert Lee and Martha Ann (Moody) S.; m. Mary G. Meany, Apr. 13, 1991. BA, Ind. U., 1983, postgrad., 1983; postgrad., Golden Gate U., 1986-87. Rates analyst North American Van Lines, Ft. Wayne, Ind., 1984-85; mgr., investor rels. BRAE Corp., San Francisco, 1985-87; fin. analyst CIS Corp., San Francisco, 1987-89; dir., corp. devel. Affiliated Computer Systems, Inc., San Francisco, 1989—. Contbr. articles to profl. jours. Vol. Rep. Party, Foster City, Calif., 1988; apptd. dir. Pvt. Industry Coun. Contra Costa County. With USMCR, 1982-83. Mem. Equipment Leasing Assn. Am. (Jour. award 1991), Ind. U. Alumni Assn. Republican. Roman Catholic. Office: Affiliated Computer Systems 525 Market St San Francisco CA 94105-2708

SMITH, CHRISTOPHER CASE, newspaper editor; b. Honolulu, July 22, 1934; s. Dudley Wall and Elizabeth McLean (Case) S.; m. Marjorie Anne Nurse, June 21, 1959; children: Suzanne Elizabeth, Patricia Louise (dec.), Sandra Kathleen. AB, Princeton U., 1956; MA, Stanford U., 1959. Adminstrv. asst. Calif. Assn. Ins. Agts., Berkeley, 1960-62; fin. writer The San Diego Union, 1962-68; asst. editor Bus. Week, Los Angeles, 1968-71; fin. writer The Honolulu Advertiser, 1971—. Bd. dirs. Friends of the Cancer Rsch. Ctr. Hawaii, 1984—. Served to lt. j.g., USNR, 1956-58. Recipient first prize media awards for econ. understanding Dartmouth Amos Tuck Sch., 1978. Mem. Am. Soc. Profl. Journalists. Office: The Honolulu Advertiser 605 Kapiolani Blvd Honolulu HI 96813-5129

SMITH, CINDY JEAN, secondary education educator, coordinator; b. Los Alamos, N.Mex., Oct. 11, 1959; d. Robert Earl and Joyce Helen (Pamplin) S. BS, ENMU, 1982; MA, U. N.Mex., 1986. Cert. tchr., N.Mex. Tchr. 7-8 Conn. Jr./Sr. H.S., Crownpoint, N.Mex., 1982-87; tchr. 6th grade Bernallio (N.Mex.) Med. Sch., 1987-88; tchr. 1st-5th grade Chruch Rock N.Mex. Sch., 1988-91; tchr. sci. 8th grade Zuni (N.Mex.) Middle Sch., 1991—; northern regional coord. N.Mex. Math., Engring. Sci. Achievement; advisor, design com. N.Mex. Mesa Inc., U. N.Mex., 1990—; tchr. mem. Tchr. Opportunities to Promote Sci./Los Alamos Nat. Labs., 1993—; earth shuttle educator N.Mex. State Dept. of Edn., Santa Fe, 1994—. Author: From A Lifetime of Octobess, 1990. Mem. N.Mex. Dem. Party, 1979—. Math./Sci. grantee SIMSE/DOE, 1994. Mem. Planetary Soc., Zuni United Sch. Employees (v.p. 1993—), Ednl. Field Studies (trip coord. 1993—), Order of the Ea. Star. Episcopalian. Office: Zuni Middle Sch PO Box 447 Zuni NM 87327-0447

SMITH, CLAY TAYLOR, geology educator; b. Omaha, June 30, 1917; s. Dean Taylor and Gertrude Maude (Taylor) S.; m. Sarah Gwendolyn Austin, May 19, 1940; children: Dean Austin, Stanley Dickinson. B.S. in Sci., Calif. Inst. Tech., 1938, M.S., 1940, Ph.D., 1943. Jr. geologist U.S. Geol. Survey, Washington, 1940-42; exploration geologist Con. Mining and Smelting, Trail, B.C., 1943; party chief Union Mines Devel. Corp., Grand Junction, Colo., 1943-46; field geologist U.S. Vanadium Corp., Winnemucca, Nev., 1946-47; prof., dean admissions N.Mex. Inst. Mining and Tech., Socorro, 1947-82, dir. alumni rels., 1983-86, prof. emeritus, 1986—; cons. geologist, 1947—. Contbr. articles to profl. jours. Named Outstanding Tchr. N.M., N.M. Acad. Sci., 1972; Golden Deeds award Exchange Club, 1983; Appreciation award N.Mex. Sci. Tchrs. Assn., 1972. Fellow AAAS, Geol. Soc. Am., Soc. Econ. Geologists; mem. N.Mex. Geol. Soc. (hon. mem., pres. 1956-57), Am. Inst. Profl. Geologists, Nat. Assn. Geology Tchrs., Lions Club (pres. 1956, 94-95). Republican. Presbyterian. Home: 1205 Vista Dr Socorro NM 87801-4445 Office: Geoscience Dept N Mex Inst Mining and Tech Socorro NM 87801

SMITH, CLIFFORD NEAL, business educator, writer; b. Wakita, Okla., May 30, 1923; s. Jesse Newton and Inez Lane (Jones) S.; m. Anna Piszczan-Czaja, Sept. 3, 1951; children: Helen Inez Smith Barrette. BS, Okla. State U., 1943; AM, U. Chgo., 1948; postgrad. Columbia U., 1960. Selector, U.S. Displaced Persons Commn., Washington and Munich, Germany, 1948-51; auditor Phillips Petroleum Co., Caracas, Venezuela, 1951-58; planning analyst Mobil Internat. Oil Co., N.Y.C., 1960, 65-66, Mobil Oil A.G., Deutschland, Hamburg, Germany, 1961-63; asst. to v.p. for Germany, Mobil Inner Europe, Inc., Geneva, 1963-65; asst. prof. No. Ill. U. Sch. Bus., DeKalb, 1966-69, part-time prof. internat. bus., 1970—; owner Westland Publs.; lectr. in field. Author: Federal Land Series, vol. 1, 1972, vol. 2, 1973, vol. 3, 1980, vol. 4, part 1, 1982, vol. 4, part 2, 1986, Encyclopedia of German-American Genealogical Research, American Genealogical Resources in German Archives, 1977, numerous monographs in German-Am., Brit.-Am., French-Am. geneal. research series, German and Central European Emigration Series; contbg. editor Nat. Geog. Soc. Quar., Geneal. jour. (Utah); contbr. articles to profl. jours. Mem. at large exec. com. Friends Com. on Nat. Legis., 1968-75; mem. regional exec. com. Am. Friends Service Com., 1969-76; v.p. Riverside Dem., N.Y.C., 1959-61; precinct committeeman, 1984—; mem. Ariz. State Central Com. of Dem. Party, 1984—; sec. Dem. Cen. Com. of Cochise County. Recipient Distinguished Service medal Ill. Geneal. Soc., 1973, award for outstanding service to sci. genealogy Am. Soc. Genealogists, 1973; court appointed arbitrator for civil cases, 1992. Fellow Geneal. Soc. of Utah; mem. S.R., SAR, Soc. Descs. Colonial Clergy, Soc. Advancement Mgmt., Ill. Genealogic Soc. (dir. 1968-69), Phi Eta Sigma, Beta Alpha Psi, Sigma Iota Epsilon. Mem. Soc. of Friends. Club: American of Hamburg (v.p. 1962-63); contbr. articles to profl. jours. Address: PO Box 117 Mc Neal AZ 85617-0117

SMITH, COLLEEN See SMITH, LEE R.

SMITH, DALE METZ, biological science educator, researcher; b. Portland, Ind., Dec. 23, 1928; s. Homer and Gertrude (Metz) S.; m. Ruth Wyne, Aug. 12, 1950; children: Teresa Lynn Smith Prather, Gayle Marie Smith Seymour. BS, Ind. U., 1950, PhD, 1957; MS, Purdue U., 1952. Instr. U. Ariz., Tucson, 1952-53; from instr. to assoc prof. U. Ky., Lexington, 1955-60; assoc. prof. U. Ill., Champaign, 1960-64, from assoc. prof. to prof. emeritus U. Calif., Santa Barbara, 1964—; cons. Environ. Cons. Firms, Santa Barbara, 1971-80. Author bot. rsch. papers. Recipient Cooley award Am. Soc. Plant Taxonomists, 1963. Fellow Linnean Soc. London; mem. numerous sci. socs. Home: PO Box 106 Deputy IN 47230-0106 Office: U Calif Santa Barbara CA 93106

SMITH, DANA KRUSE, real estate developer; b. Waterloo, Iowa, May 28, 1957; s. Richard Walter and Joanne (Kruse) S.; 1 child, Tara Nicole. AA, Orange Coast Coll., 1976. Dir. comml. devel. Barnett-Range Corp., Stockton, Calif., 1982-86; pres. Dannor Corp., Stockton, 1986-92, Baltic Land Corp., Stockton, 1992—. Mem. Stockton Sailing Club (winner various races), Yosemite Club, Ducks Unltd. Republican. Office: Baltic Land Corp PO Box 7904 Stockton CA 95267-0904

SMITH, DAVID ALAN, systems programmer; b. Williamsburg, Va., Dec. 1, 1949; s. Robert Edward and Anne Katherine (Klein) S.; m. Linda Lark Wasmer, May 28, 1977; children: Amanda Lark, Michael David. BS in Math., U. N.Mex., 1979. Programmer analyst EG&G Energy Measurements, Albuquerque, 1980-83; systems programmer EG&G ENergy Measurements, Albuquerque, 1983-89, sr. systems programmer, 1989-94; sr. systems programmer Allied Signal Aerospace, Albuquerque, 1994-95, sci. specialist, 1995—. Contbr. articles to profl. jours. Sgt. USAF, 1971-75, N.Mex. Air N.G., 1977-81, 83—. Mem. ACM, Am. Def. Preparedness Assn., Nat. Computer Graphics Assn. Home: 12017 Kashmir St NE Albuquerque NM 87111 Office: Allied Signal Aerospace Kirland Ops Sta A PO Box 4339 Albuquerque NM 87196

SMITH, DAVID ALAN, counseling administrator, writer; b. Endicott, N.Y., Aug. 7, 1959; s. Arthur George and Marilyn Joy (Clements) S.; m. Kumiko Oda Smith, June 27, 1993; 1 child, Angelia Ami. BA in Future Studies, Eckerd Coll., 1981; MA in Internat. Rels., Columbia U., 1983; PhD in Polit. Sci., U. Hawaii, 1989. Conf. staff dir. World Future Soc., Bethesda, Md., 1982-84; adminstrv. dir., faculty Friends World Coll.-East Asian Ctr., Kyoto, Japan, 1989-90; acad. advisor U. Hawaii at Manoa, Honolulu, 1990—. Contbg. editor Kyoto Jour., 1989-90; contbr. articles and book revs. to jours. Bd. dirs. Colls. Arts & Scis. Alumni Assn., Honolulu, 1993-95, World Peace U., Kobe, Japan, 1989-90. Fulbright Commn. travel grantee, 1991. Mem. ACA, Nat. Acad. Advisors Assn., Hawaii Counseling Assn. (pres. 1994-95). Mem. Green Party. Buddhist. Office: Univ of Hawaii at Manoa 2500 Campus Rd Honolulu HI 96822-2217

SMITH, DAVID BURNELL, lawyer; b. Charleston, W.Va., Apr. 8, 1941; s. Ernest Dayton and Nellie Dale (Tyler) S.; m. Rita J. Hughes. Sept. 25, 1967. B.A., U. Charleston, 1967; J.D., U. Balt., 1972. Bar: Colo. 1972, Md. 1972, U.S. Supreme Ct. 1980, Ariz. 1983, U.S. Dist. Ct. Md. 1972, U.S. Dist. Ct. Colo. 1972, U.S. Ct. Appeals (4th cir.) 1972, U.S. Ct. Appeals (9th cir.) 1972, U.S. Ct. Appeals (10th cir.) 1983. Sales rep. Gulf Oil, Washington, 1967-72; pvt. practice, Littleton, Colo., 1972-83, Glendale, Ariz., 1983-86, Phoenix, 1986-88, Scottsdale 1988—; pro-tempore judge Wickenburg Mcpl. Ct., 1986—; presiding judge Peoria (Ariz.) Mcpl. Ct., 1987-94. V.p. South Jefferson County Rep., Lakewood, Colo., 1979, pres., 1980. Candidate Dist. 6 for U.S. Congress. Served with USCG, 1959-66. Appeared as actor in movie Deal Girls Don't Tango, 1990. Mem. Nat. Assn. Criminal Lawyers, Am. Judicature Soc., ABA (vice-chmn. family law 1983), Nat. Assn. Criminal Def. Attys., Ariz. Magistrates Assn., Colo. Bar Assn., Ariz. Bar Assn., Md. Bar Assn., Assn. Trial Lawyers Am., Colo. Trial Lawyers Assn., Ariz. Trial Lawyers Assn., Maricopa County Bar Assn. Lodges: Masons, Shriners, Elks. Home: PO Box 5145 36418 N Wildflower Rd Carefree AZ 85377-5145 Office: 4310 N 75th St Scottsdale AZ 85251-3505

SMITH, DAVID ELVIN, physician; b. Bakersfield, Calif., Feb. 7, 1939; s. Elvin W. and Dorothy (McGinnis) S.; m. Millicent Buxton; children: Julia, Suzanne, Christopher Buxton-Smith, Sabree Hill. Intern San Francisco Gen. Hosp., 1965; fellow pharmacology and toxicology U. Calif., San Francisco, 1965-67, assoc. clin. prof. occupational medicine, clin. toxicology, 1967—, dir. psychopharmacology study group, 1966-70; practice medicine specializing in toxicology and addiction San Francisco, 1965—; physician Presbyn. Alcoholic Clinic, 1965-67, Contra Cost Alcoholic Clinic, 1965-67; dir. alcohol and drug abuse screening unit San Francisco Gen. Hosp., 2967-68; co-dir. Calif drug abuse info. project U. Calif Med. Ctr., 1967-72; founder, med. dir. Haight-Ashbury Free Med. Clinic, San Francisco, 1967—; research dir. Merritt Peralta Chem. Dependency Hosp., Oakland, Calif., 1984—; chmn. Nat. Drug Abuse Conf., 1977; mem. Calif. Gov's. Commn. on Narcotics and Drug Abuse, 1977—; nat. health adviser to former U.S. Pres. Jimmy Carter; mem. Pres. Clinton's Health Care Task Force on Addiction and Nat. Health Reform, 1993; dir. Benzodiazepine Research and Tng. Project, Substance Abuse and Sexual Concerns Project, PCP Research and Tng. Project; cons. numerous fed. drug abuse agys. Author: Love Needs Care, 1970, The New Social Drug: Cultural, Medical and Legal Perspectives on Marijuana, 1971, The Free Clnic: Community Approaches to Health Care and Drug Abuse, 1971, Treating the Cocaine Abuser, 1985, The Benzodiazepines: Current Standard Medical Practice, 1986, Physicians' Guide to Drug Abuse, 1987; co-author: It's So Good, Don't Even Try it Once: Heroin in Perspective, 1972, Uppers and Downers, 1973, Drugs in the Classroom, 1973, Barbiturate Use and Abuse, 1977, A Multicultural View of Drug Abuse, 1978, Amphetamine Use, Misuse and Abuse, 1979, PCP: Problems and Prevention, 1981, Sexological Aspects of Substance Use and Abuse, Treatment of the Cocaine Abuser, 1985, The Haight Ashbury Free Medical Clinic: Still Free After All These Years, Drug Free: Alternatives to Drug Abuse, 1987, Treatment of Opiate Dependence, Designer Drugs, 1988, Treatment of Cocaine Dependence, 1988, Treatment of Opiate Dependence, 1988, The New Drugs, 1989, Crack and Ice in the Era of Smokeable Drugs, 1992, others; also drug edn. films; founder, editor Jour. Psychedelic Drugs (now Jour. Psychoactive Drugs), 1967—; contbr. over 300 articles to profl. jours. Pres. Youth Projects, Inc.; founder, chmn. bd., pres. Nat. Free Clin. Council, 1968-72. Recipient Rsch. award Borden Found., 1964, AMA Rsch. award, 1966, Cmty. Svc. award U. Calif.-San Francisco, 1974, Calif. State Drug Abuse Treatment award, 1984, Vernelle Fox Drug Abuse Treatment award, 1985, UCLA Sidney Cohen Addiction Medicine award, 1989, Honor medal U. Calif. Med. Ctr. San Francisco, 1995. Mem. AMA (alt. del.), CMA (alt. del.), APHA, Am. Soc. on Addiction Medicine (bd. dirs., pres.), San Francisco Med. Soc., Calif. Soc. on Addiction Medicine (pres., bd. dirs.), Am. Soc. Addiction Medicine, Sigma Xi, Phi Beta Kappa. Methodist. Home: 289 Frederick St San Francisco CA 94117-4051 Office: 409 Clayton St San Francisco CA 94117-1911

SMITH, DAVID WAYNE, psychologist; b. Ind., Apr. 16, 1927; s. Lowell Wayne and Ruth Elizabeth (Westphal) S.; m. Marcene B. Leever, Oct. 20, 1948; children: David Wayne, Laurreen Lea. B.S., Purdue U., 1949; M.S., Ind. U., 1953, Ph.D., 1955. Prof. rehab., dir. Rehab. Center; asso. dean, later asst. v.p. acad. affairs Ariz. Health Scis. Center, U. Ariz., Tucson, 1955-80; research prof. rehab., adj. prof. medicine, cons. in research S.W. Arthritis Center, Coll. Medicine, 1980-87; prof. rehab. and rheumatology, dept. medicine U. Ariz., 1987—, also dir. disability assessment program; pres. allied health professions sect. Nat. Arthritis Found.; bd. dirs. Nat. Arthritis Found. (S.W. chpt.); nat. vice chmn. bd. dirs.; mem. NIH Nat. Arthritis Adv. Bd., 1977-84; also chmn. subcom. community programs and rehab.; mem. staff Ariz. Legislature Health Welfare, 1972-73; Mem. Gov.'s Council Dept. Econ. Security, 1978-85; pres., bd. dirs. Tucson Assn. for Blind, 1974-86; chmn. Gov.'s Council on Blind and Visually Impaired, 1987—; active Gov.'s Coun. on Arthritis and Musculoskeletal Disease, 1987—. Author: Worksamples; contbr. chpts. to books and articles to profl. jours. Recipient Gov.'s awards for leadership in rehab., 1966, 69, 72, 73; awards for sci. and vol. services Nat. Arthritis Found., 1973, 75; 1st nat. Addie Thomas award Nat. Arthritis Found., 1983, Benson award, 1989, Govt. Affairs award, 1989; Arthritis Found. fellow, 1983. Mem. Am. Psychol. Assn. (div. 17 counseling psychology), Assn. Schs. Allied Health Professions, Nat. Rehab. Assn., Ariz. Psychol. Assn. Home: 5765 N Camino Real Tucson AZ 85718-4213 Office: U Ariz Arizona Health Scis Ctr Tucson AZ 85724

SMITH, DENNIS, professional football player; b. Santa Monica, Calif., Feb. 3, 1959. Student, U. So. Calif. Safety Denver Broncos, 1981-94. Office: Denver Broncos 13655 E Dove Valley Pkwy Englewood CO 80112

SMITH, DIANNE HARRIS, import/export company executive; b. Rock Hill, S.C., July 4, 1942; d. Stanhope Alexander and Dorothy Alma (Ray) Harris; widowed; children: Sandra, Daphne, Rodney. Student, Norwalk Coll., 1980. Clk. Ea. Products, Balt., 1959-60; model Terri Fashions, La Habra, Calif., 1963-64, bookkeeper, 1964-65; acct. Whittier, Calif., 1964-66; sec. Kirk Hill Rubber Co., Brea, Calif., 1968-74; rschr. ESA, Glendora, 1992—. Recipient Presdl. Sports award Sports Assn., 1979. Mem. NAFE, WWF, AnCloc County Santa Soc., United Srs. Assn., Sierra Club, The Colisteali Soc., The Nature Conservancy, Defenders of Wildlife, United Seniors Coalition. Democrat.

SMITH, DICK MARTIN, oil field service company executive-owner; b. Alamosa, Colo., Nov. 20, 1946; s. Jack and Mary (Turnbull) S.; m. Janyce Wood Smith, Jan. 5, 1971 (div. May 1975); 1 child, DAnna Marie; m. Patricia Ann Connors, June 5, 1987; stepchildren: Shawna Parker, Scott Parker. Student, U. Md., 1969-72, U. York, Harrogate, Eng., 1969-72, U. N.Mex., 1975-79. With spl. ops. Nat. Security Agy., U.S. Govt., Ft. Meade, Md., 1969-74; with engring. rsch. U. N.Mex., Albuquerque, 1974-78; engr. fluids Internat. Mineral and Chem. Co., Houston, 1978-82; owner, pres., CEO Corrosions Monitoring Svcs. Inc., Capser, Wyo., 1981—; bd. dirs. Trenching Svcs., Casper, CMS Farms, Alamosa, Colo. With USN, 1964-68. Decorated Navy Unit Citation. Mem. Soc. Petroleum Engrs., Casper Wildcatters, Aircraft Owners Pilots Assn., DAV. Republican. Home: 4471 E 12th St Casper WY 82609-3247 Office: CMS Inc PO Box 9826 Casper WY 82609-0826

SMITH, DONALD E., broadcast engineer, manager; b. Salt Lake City, Sept. 10, 1930; s. Thurman A. and Louise (Cardall) S.; B.A. Columbia Coll., Chgo., 1955; B.S.; U. Utah, 1970; postgrad. U. So. Calif., U. Utah, PhD (hon.) Columbia Coll., 1985; m. Helen B. Lacy, 1978. Engr., Iowa State U., (WOI-TV), 1955-56; asst. chief engr. KLRJ-TV, Las Vegas, 1956-60; studio field engr. ABC, Hollywood, Cal., 1960; chief engr. Teletape, Inc., Salt Lake City, 1961; engring. supr. KUER, U. Utah, Salt Lake City, 1962-74, gen. mgr., 1975-85. Freelance cinematographer, 1950—; cons. radio TV (mgmt. engr. and prodn.), 1965—. Mem. Soc. Motion Pictures and TV Engrs., Lambda Chi Alpha. Home: 963 Hollywood Ave Salt Lake City UT 84105-3347

SMITH, DONALD EVANS, library consultant; b. Shanendoah, Iowa, Dec. 2, 1915; s. William Wesley and Bess Alice (Evans) S.; student Ricks Coll., 1939-40; BA, Hastings Coll., 1946; MLS, U. Wash., 1964. Tchr. English, librarian Tenino (Wash.) High Sch., 1950-51, Rochester (Wash.) High Sch., 1954-59; librarian North Thurston High Sch., Lacey, Wash., 1959-67; head librarian, coord. instructional materials Lakes High Sch., Lakewood Ctr., Wash., 1967-80; library cons., 1980—. Mem. awards com. Wash. Library Commn., 1964-66. With Signal Corps, AUS, 1942-45; to 1st lt., M.I., U.S. Army, 1951-54; to col. Wash. State Guard, 1971-80, now ret. Mem. Wash. Assn. Sch. Librarians (com. chmn.), Clover Park Edn. Assn. (com. chmn. 1970-71), Am. Legion, Phi Delta Kappa (del. nat. confs.). Home and Office: 4530 26th Loop SE Lacey WA 98503-3264

SMITH, DONALD KENDALL, communication educator; b. Portland, Oreg., Aug. 1, 1929; s. Leslie Frederick and Nina Christina (Coffee) S.; m. Faye Gladys Schick, June 25, 1950; children: Donald Vance, Julisa Faye. BS in Biology, U. Oreg., 1951, MS in Gen. Studies, 1952, MA with honors in Journalism, 1967, PhD, 1969. Cert. secondary edn. tchr. Lectr. Evang. Tchr. Tng. Coll., Vryheid, Natal, Union South Africa, 1952-55; dir., pub. Africa Christian Lit. Advance, Johannesburg, Transvaal, Union South Africa, 1956-63; editor-in-chief Our Africa monthly mag., Johannesburg, 1958-63; dir. Daystar Publs., Bulawayo, Zimbabwe, 1964-73; dir. Daystar Comm., Bulawayo, 1969-73, Nairobi, Kenya, 1974-79; founder Daystar U., Nairobi, 1979-81; dir. Inst. Internat. Christian Comm., Portland, Oreg.,

1981—; prof. intercultural comm. Western Sem., Portland, 1981—; rsch. dir. Comm. for Devel. Project, Luth. World Fedn., Sudan, Cameroon, 1979-85; internat. rsch. dir. Living Bibles Internat., Wheaton, Ill., 1971-80. Author: Writing is Thinking - Plbslshd in Rhodesia, 1966, Make Haste Slowly, 1985, Creating Understanding, 1992; editor lit. materials in Ndebele and Shona: Rhodesia Chs. Nat. Lit. Project, 1965-69. NDEA fellow, U. Oreg., 1968. Mem. Internat. Comm. Assn., Am. Soc. Missiology, Evangelical Soc. of Missiology. Baptist. Home: 5235 SE Salmon St Portland OR 97215-2672 Office: Western Bapt Sem 5511 SE Hawthorne Blvd Portland OR 97215-3367

SMITH, DONALD RICHARD, editor, publisher; b. Stockton, Calif., Aug. 20, 1932; s. Robert Gordon and Gertrude (Schweitzer) S.; m. Darlene Ruth Thomas, May 7, 1961; children: Douglas Robert, Deborah Renae. Student, Coll. Pacific, 1951, Delta Coll., 1951-52. Editor, pub. Calif. Odd Fellow & Rebekah, Linden, 1950—; editor Elk Grove (Calif.) Citizen, 1953-55; asst. dir. U.N. Pilgrimage for Youth, N.Y.C., 1956-59; editor, pub. Linden (Calif.) Herald, 1959-86, Lockeford (Calif.)-Clements Post, 1960-62, Internat. Rebekah News, Linden, 1963-86, Internat. Odd Fellow & Rebekah, Linden, 1986—; dir. communications Sovereign Grand Lodge, Linden, 1990-92. Author: From Stagestop to Friendly Community, 1976, Leadership Manual, 1980, The Three Link Fraternity, 1993, Six Links of Fellowship, 1995. Bd. dirs. Odd Fellow-Rebekah Youth Camp, Inc., Long Barn, Calif., 1959-61; chmn. Linden Rep. Com., 1962-66, Linden Centennial Observance, 1963, Linden Mcpl. Council, 1981-90. Recipient Legion of Honor Order of Demolay, 1961, John R. Williams award S.J. Tchrs. Assn., 1963, 87, Golden Key award Stockton Tchrs. Assn., 1971, Achievement award County Bd. Suprs., 1970, Citizen of Yr. award Lions Internat., 1982. Mem. IOOF Internat. Press Assn. (pres. 1962-63), Desktop Pub. Assn., Boston Computer Soc., Berkeley Macintosh Users Assn., Linden Peters C. of C. (pres. 1968-69), S.J. Hist. Soc. (trustee 1986-90). Methodist. Lodges: Lions, Odd Fellows (Calif.) (grand master 1958-59), Odd Fellows Internat. (sovereign grand master 1969-70), Internat. Coun. 100F (sec. 1990—). Home: 5350 Harrison St Linden CA 95236-9630 Office: Linden Publ 19033 E Main PO Box 129 Linden CA 95236-0129

SMITH, DONNA, mayor, small business owner; b. Upper Darby, Pa., July 19, 1954; d. Dave and Theresa (McAleer) Fekay; m. Robert Howard Smith Jr., Dec. 1, 1951; children: Robert H. III, Sean M., Terence J. Grad. high sch., Pomona, Calif., 1970. Mayor City of Pomona, 1987—; owner Pomona Generator Co., 1976—. Pres. Simons Jr. High Sch. PTA, 1983-85; pres., sec. Pomona Youth Sports Com., 1983-85; mem. City Coun. Dist. 3, Pomona, 1985-87; mem. Garey High Sch. Booster Club, 1985—; mem. Hispanic youth task force; mem. econ. and human devel. com. SCAG Community, 1985-87; mem. Pomona Cen. Bus. Dist.; mem. policy com. Rapid Transit Dist.; vice chairperson Tri-City Mental Health; mem. Pomona Valley handicapped and sr. citizens com.; mem. exec. bd. Teen Outreach, ARC; mem. Old Baldy Coun. Boy Scouts Am.; U.S. Olympic torch runner, 1991; mem. U.S. Conf. of Mayors, 1991, chmn. com. disaster preparedness, chair community devel. and housing com., mem. membership com., Lincoln Inst. of Land Policy; mem. adv. bd. Nat. Coalition Against Pornography; mem. U.S. Conf. Mayors; appointed to State of Calif. Rep. Ctrl. Com.; runner U.S. Olympic Torch; hon. chair March of Dimes, Lukemia Soc. Am.; mem. State Rep. Ctrl. Com. Named Women Achiever of 1985, Humanitarian of Yr., 1986, one of Five Outstanding Californians Calif. Jaycees, 1990; recipient PTA Honorary Service award 1985, PTA Honorary Lifetime Service award 1986. Mem. Calif. Elected Women's Assn., Pomona Bus. and Profl. Women's Assn., Pomona Hist. Soc., Pomona C. of C. (legis. action com., edn. com., city affairs com.), Pomona Valley Rep. Women Federated (v.p.), Pomona Jaycees (Disting. Svc. award 1988), Pomona Jaycees (hon. life 1991), Am. Bus. Women's Assn. (hon. life 1991), Nat. League of Cities, League of Calif. Cities (state adminstrv. policy con.), Kiwanis, Fraternal Order of Police, Women of Moose. Mem. Born Again Christian Ch. Office: City of Pomona Office of Mayor 2177 Virginia Ave Pomona CA 91766-6233

SMITH, DORSETT DAVID, pulmonologist; b. N.Y.C., Feb. 2, 1937; s. Harry Dorsett and Kathrin Lowe S.; m. Dorothy Louise Frank, June 12, 1962; children: Talbot St. John, Tiffany Louise, Sarah Carrington. BA, Colgate U., 1959; MD, U. Pa., 1963. Diplomate Am. Bd. Internal Medicine, Am. Bd. Pulmonary Disease. Pres. Most Devel. Inc., Chest Diseases Inc.; pres. N.W. Cardiopulmonary Panel; clin. prof. medicine U. Wash. Contbr. articles to profl. jours. Mem. Med. Disciplinary Bd., State of Wash., 1990-94; pres. Physicians for Moral Responsibility, 1990-92. Fellow ACP, Am. Coll. Chest Physicians. Office: Chest Diseases Inc 4310 Colby Ave Everett WA 98203-2338

SMITH, DOUGLAS G., optometrist; b. North Conway, N.H., Nov. 26, 1948; s. Vernon E. and Rose L. (Zacker) S.; m. Hazel Anne Parker, July 10, 1971; children: Erin Kathleen, Ryan Douglas. BA in Psychology, Colby Coll., 1970; postgrad., Mont. State U., 1974-75; OD, Pacific U. Coll. Optometry, 1979. Lic. optometrist, Oreg., Mont., Calif. Clinic staff Pacific U. Coll. Optometry, 1979; optometrist pvt. practice, Medford, Oreg., 1979—; mem. Oreg. Commn. for Blind; mem. children's svcs. div. citizens adv. com. Oreg. Bd. Optometry, 1991—. Chmn. So. Oreg. State Coll. Learning Disabilities Clinic, Jackson County Juvenile Svcs. Commn.; bd. dirs. Rogue Valley Alcohol Rehab. Ctr., Willaway Ranch for Handicapped; mem. Jackson County Task Force for Pres-sch. Handicapped, Jackson County Head Start Med. Adv. Bd., Oreg. Tchr. Standards and Practices Com. Task Force. Capt. USAF, 1970-74. Recipient William M. Feinbloom Low Vision award, 1979; named Oreg. Optometrist of Yr., 1982, Outstanding Young Men Am., 1978. Mem. AAAS, Am. Pub. Health Assn., Am. Optometric Assn. (low vision sect., Optometric Recognition award 1984)), Oreg. Optometric Assn. (chmn. children's vision sect.), Coll. Optometrists in Vision Devel., Optometric Extension Program, Rotary, Beta Sigma Kappa, Phi Theta Upsilon. Home: 353 Alta PO 253 Ashland OR 97520 Office: 691 Murphy Rd Ste 236 Medford OR 97504-4311

SMITH, DUNBAR WALLACE, retired physician, clergyman; b. Dunbar, Nebr., Oct. 17, 1910; s. Clarence Dunbar and Marie Christine (Eden) S.; m. Kathryn Avis Johnson, May 2, 1935; children: Dunbar Wesley, John Wallace. BSc, La Sierra Coll., Riverside, Calif., 1949; MD, Loma Linda U., 1950; DTM and Hygiene, Sch. of Tropical Med. London U., 1951; MPH, Columbia U., 1967. Diplomate Nat. Bd. Med. Examiners. Pastor 7th-day Adventist Chs., San Diego, Omaha, N.Y., India, Ceylon, 1935-44; med. dir. 7th-Day Adventist Mission Hosps., India, 1951-056; adminstr. Battle Creek (Mich.) Sanitarium, 1957-62; med. dir. Bates Meml. Hosp., Yonkers, N.Y., 1962-67; dep. commr. health Nassau County, N.Y., 1967-69; dir. dept. health for Africa, 7th-day Adventist Ch., 1969-76; dir. dept. health for Far East, 7th-day Adventist Ch., Singapore, 1976-80; adj. asst. prof. internat. health Loma Linda (Calif.) U., 1980-90; pres. Emerald Health and Edn. Found., Loma Linda, 1986-91. Author: Report of CME (now Loma Linda U. Sch. Medicine) Rsch. to Date, 1946, (textbook) Home Health Aide, 1960, Autobiography of Dunbar W. Smith, 1994, (booklet) The Cold Turkey Way to Stop Smoking; contbr. numerous articles to various publs. V.p. Emerald Health and Edn. Found., 1991—. Recipient Honored Alumnus award Loma Linda U. Sch. Medicine, 1975, Golden award La Sierra U. Alumni Soc., 1992. Fellow AMA, SAR, Am. Coll. Nutrition, Royal Soc. Tropical Medicine, Royal Soc. Health, Internat. Med. Assn. (bd. dirs. 1987—); mem. N.Y. Acad. Scis. Republican. Home: 408 Sandalwood Dr Calimesa CA 92320-1507 Office: Emerald Health and Edn Found PO Box 8877 Redlands CA 92375-2077

SMITH, DWIGHT MORRELL, chemistry educator; b. Hudson, N.Y., Oct. 10, 1931; s. Elliott Monroe and Edith Helen (Hall) S.; m. Alice Beverly Bond, Aug. 27, 1955 (dec. 1990); children—Karen Elizabeth, Susan Allison, Jonathan Aaron; m. Elfi Nelson, Dec. 28, 1991. B.A., Central Coll., Pella, Iowa, 1953; Ph.D., Pa. State U., 1957; ScD (hon.), Cen. Coll., 1986; LittD (hon.), U. Denver, 1990. Postdoctoral fellow, instr. Calif. Inst. Tech., 1957-59; sr. chemist Texaco Rsch. Ctr., Beacon, N.Y., 1959-61; asst. prof. chemistry Wesleyan U., Middletown, Conn., 1961-66; assoc. prof. Hope Coll., Holland, Mich., 1966-69, prof., 1969-72; prof. chemistry U. Denver, 1972—, chmn. dept., 1972-83, vice chancellor for acad. affairs, 1983-84, chancellor, 1984-89; pres. Hawaii Loa Coll., Kaneohe, 1990-92; mem. adv. bd. Solar Energy Rsch. Inst., 1989-91; mem. vis. com. Zettlemoyer Ctr. for Surface Studies Lehigh U., 1990—. Editor Revs. on Petroleum Chemistry, 1975-78; contbr. articles to profl. jours.; patentee selective hydrogenation. Chmn. Chs. United for Social Action, Holland, 1968-69; mem. adv. com. Holland Sch. Bd., 1969-70; bd. commrs. Colo. Adv. Tech. Inst., 1984-88, Univ. Senate, United Meth. Ch., Nashville, 1987-88, 91-93; mem. adv. bd. United Way, Inst. Internat. Edn., Japan Am. Soc. Colo., Denver Winter Games Olympics Com.; mem. ch. bds. or consistories Ref. Ch. Am., N.Y., Conn., Mich., United Meth. Ch., Colo. DuPont fellow, 1956-57, NSF fellow Scripps Inst., 1971-72; recipient grants Research Corp., Petroleum Research Fund, NSF, Solar Energy Research Inst. Mem. Am. Chem. Soc. (chmn. Colo. 1976, sec. western Mich. 1970-71, award Colo. sect. 1986), Catalysis Soc., Soc. Applied Spectroscopy, Mile High Club, Pinehurst Country Club, Sigma Xi. Home: 1931 W Sanibel Ct Littleton CO 80120 Office: U Denver Denver CO 80208

SMITH, EILEEN PAZDERKA, dermatologist; b. Fort Belvior, Va., Sept. 17, 1956; d. Robert James and Diane Louis (Lotz) Pazderka; m. Martin James Smith, May 18, 1985; children: Tyler James, Dylan Russell. BS in Med. Tech., U. Nebr., 1978, MS, 1985, MD, 1990. Med. tech. U. Nebr. Med. Ctr., Omaha, 1984-89; intern, resident U. Utah Health Sci. Ctr., Salt Lake City, 1991, fellow divsn. dermatology, 1991-93, resident in dermatology, 1993—; staff urgent care dept. Family Health Plan, Salt Lake City, 1991—. Contbr. chpts. to books and articles to profl. jours. Named one of Outstanding Young Women Am., 1989. Mem. Utah State Med. Soc., AMA (credentials com. 1987, state leadership steering com. 1988, rules com. 1988), Soc. Investigative Dermatology. Democrat. Roman Catholic. Home: 2729 Wilshire Dr Salt Lake City UT 84109-1632 Office: U Utah Health Sci Ctr Divsn Dermatology 50 N Med Dr Salt Lake City UT 84132

SMITH, ELDEN LEROY, recreational vehicle company executive; b. Berwyn, Ill., June 1, 1940; s. Frederick M. and Margaret I. (Larson) S.; B.A. in Bus. Adminstrn., Whittier Coll., 1962; m. Barbara G. Whaley, Apr. 4, 1963; children—Jill Marie, David Elden. Market analyst Autonetics div. N.Am. Aviation, Anaheim, Calif., 1963-66; sales mgr. Pendleton Tool Industries, Los Angeles, 1966-68; plant gen. mgr. Fleetwood Enterprises, Inc., Hancock, Md., 1969-71, v.p. recreational vehicle group, Riverside, Calif., 1972-88, sr. v.p., 1988—. Trustee Whittier (Calif.) Coll., 1991—. Served with USNR, 1962-63. Mem. Recreation Vehicle Industry Assn. (chmn. 1980-82, dir. 1975—). Office: Fleetwood Enterprises Inc 3125 Myers St PO Box 7638 Riverside CA 92503-5544

SMITH, ELDRED GEE, church leader; b. Lehi, Utah, Jan. 9, 1907; s. Hyrum Gibbs and Martha E. (Gee) S.; m. Jeanne A. Ness, Aug. 17, 1932 (dec. June 1977); children: Miriam Smith Skeen, Eldred Gary, Audrey Gay Smith Vance, Gordon Raynor, Sylvia Dawn Smith Isom; m. Hortense H. Child, May 18, 1978; stepchildren: Carol Jane Child Burdette (dec.), Thomas Robert Child. Employed with sales div. Bennett Glass & Paint Co., Salt Lake City, 6 years; mech. design engr. Remington Arms Co., 2 years; design engr., prodn. equipment design Tenn. Eastman Corp., Oak Ridge, Tenn., 3 years; now presiding patriarch Ch. Jesus Christ of Latter-day Saints. Home: 2942 Devonshire Cir Salt Lake City UT 84108-2526 Office: 47 E South Temple Salt Lake City UT 84150-1005

SMITH, ELVIN T., communications executive; b. Aztec, N.M., June 30, 1930; s. Orville V. and E. Avisa (Townsend) S.; m. Elaine C. Andersen, May 21, 1959; children: Eric T., Ellen C. BA, Ft. Lewis Coll., 1956. Sales exec. Sta. KOAT-TV, Albuquerque, 1962-75, sales mgr., 1975—; owner W.A. Group, Albuquerque, 1980-88. Photo dir. TV program Sandia Tram, 1970. Dir. Crime Stoppers, Albuquerque, 1988. Office: Sta KOAT-TV 3801 Carlisle Blvd NE Albuquerque NM 87107-4501

SMITH, FERN M., judge; b. San Francisco, Nov. 7, 1933. AA, Foothill Coll., 1970; BA, Stanford U., 1972, JD, 1975. Bar: Calif. 1975. m. F. Robert Burrows; children: Susan Morgan, Julie. Assoc. firm Bronson, Bronson & McKinnon, San Francisco, 1975-81, ptnr., 1982-86; judge San Francisco County Superior Ct., 1986-88, U.S. Dist. Ct. for Northern Dist. Calif., 1988—; mem. U.S. Jud. Conf., Adv. Com. Rules of Evidence, 1993—; mem. hiring, mgmt. and pers. coms., active recruiting various law schs. Contbr. articles to legal publ. Apptd. by Chief Justice Malcolm Lucas to the Calif. Jud. Coun.'s Adv. Task Force on Gender Bias in the Cts., 1987-89; bd. visitors Law Sch. Stanford U. Mem. ABA, Queen's Bench, Nat. Assn. Women Judges, Calif. Women Lawyers, Women's Forum West/Internat. Women's Forum, Bar Assn. of San Francisco, Fed. Judges Assn., 9th Cir. Dist. Judges Assn., Am. Judicature Soc., Calif. State Fed. Judicial Coun., Phi Beta Kappa.*

SMITH, FREDA L., retired elementary education educator; b. Birds, Ill., Oct. 3, 1923; d. Loney W. and Mattie A. (Perrott) Thomas; m. Lloyd Preston, May 18, 1947 (dec. 1991); 1 child, Thelma. BS, U. Western Ky., 1959. Tchr. Jefferson Sch., Robinson, Ill., 1953-54, Franklin County (Tenn.) Sch., 1954-56, Muhlenberg (Ky.) Pub. Schs., 1956-58, Livingston County Pub. Schs., Salem, Ky., 1958-61, Custer (S.D.) Elem. Sch., 1961-64, Chugwater (Wyo.) Elem. Sch., 1964-87. Vol. Headstart, Wheatland, Wyo., 1991—, Lauback Internat., Kingman, Ariz., 1987-91. With WAVES, 1944-46. Mem. AAUW (pres. 1980-81), NEA, Chugwater Edn. Assn. Episcopalian. Home: PO Box 731 Wheatland WY 82201-0731

SMITH, FREDA M., minister; b. Pocatello, Idaho, Nov. 22, 1935; s. Alfred Avery and Mary V. (Clark) S. BA in Psychology, Calif. State U., Sacramento, 1974, MA in Psychology, 1989; D of Ministry (hon.), Samaritan Theol. Inst., 1990. Ordained to ministry Universal Fellowship Met. Cmty. Chs., 1973. Pastor Cathedral of Promise, Met. Cmty. Chs., Sacramento, 1972—; instr. Samaritan Theol. Inst., L.A., 1974—; dir. evangelism Universal Fellowship Met. Cmty. Chs., worldwide, 1993—, vice-moderator, bd. elders, 1973-93. Author: Dear Dora/Dangerous Derek, 1970; author video series Homosexuality and the Bible, 1993; author audio series Manna for the Journey, 1988. Chair Sacramento LGB Town Coun., 1992-93; co-chair Calif. Com. for Law Reform, 1971-74. Recipient Eleanor Roosevelt Club award, 1975, Woman in History award for courage Sacramento History Ctr., 1991. Mem. Phi Kappa Phi. Home: 6209 Governor Ln Sacramento CA 95828 Office: River City Met Cmty Chs PO Box 245125 Sacramento CA 95824-5125

SMITH, GARY THOMAS, fine arts educator, curator; b. Portland, Oreg., Nov. 25, 1949; s. Bobby H. and Winifred (Kortge) S. BA, Lewis and Clark Coll., 1971; MFA, U. Calif., Santa Barbara, 1975. Instr. Santa Barbara City Coll. Adult Edn., 1974-76; instr. Hartnell Coll., Salinas, Calif., 1976—, gallery dir., 1976—; coord., instr. London semester program Ctrl. Calif. Consortium of C.C., 1989-93, Paris semester program, 1993, London semester program, 1994, Florence semester program, 1995. One-man shows include pvt. galleries in Santa Barbara, San Francisco, Vienna, Austria, N.Y.C., and others. Trustee, chmn. acquisitions com. Monterey (Calif.) Peninsula Mus. Art, 1982—; bd. dirs. Monterey County Culture Coun., 1986-89. Recipient Excellence in Teaching award Harden Found., 1990. Home: 27465 Vista Del Toro Pl Salinas CA 93908-8914 Office: Hartnell Coll Art Dept 156 Homestead Ave Salinas CA 93901-1628

SMITH, GAYNL BEVERLY, hospice director, nurse; b. San Francisco, Nov. 19, 1940; d. Charles Homer and Gladys L. (Harvey) Smith; m. J. Vincent McCann, June 8, 1962 (div. May 1981); children: Kathleen Patricia, Kevin Patrick; m. Paul W. Bachman, Nov. 24, 1989. RN, Johns Hopkins Hosp., 1962; BS, Johns Hopkins U., 1970; MDiv, San Francisco Theol. Sem., 1986. RN, Calif., Md. Asst. dir. nursing Washington Home for Incurables, 1971-73; staff nurse coronary care unit Doctors Hosp., Washington, 1973-74; dir. nursing Washington Home for Incurables, 1974; critical care float Sibley Meml. Hosp., Washington, 1975-82; RN, supr. Hillhaven Victorian Convalescent Hosp., San Francisco, 1984-87; chaplain Hospice, Contra Costa County Health Svcs., Martinez, Calif., 1984-85; nursing dir. and adminstr. Sisters of the Presentation Convent Infirmary, San Francisco, 1987-88; coord. symptom control program Merrithew Meml. Hosp., Martinez, 1988—; mem. Concern for Dying, N.Y.C., 1985—, AIDS Planning Com., Contra Costa County, Martinez, 1988-89, Bereavement Coalition, Contra Costa County, Concord, Calif., 1988—; nursing cons. Sisters of the Presentation Convent Infirmary, San Francisco, 1988—. Vice moderator Golden Gate Assn., United Ch. of Christ, San Francisco, 1986-87, 1st Congl. Ch., San Rafael, Calif., chair pastor search com., 1987-89; active Girl Scouts U.S., San Francisco, 1947—. Mem. Oncology Nursing Soc., Am. Soc. Aging, Nat. Gerontologic Nursing Assn. Democrat. Office: Merrithew Meml Hosp Symptom Control Program 2500 Alhambra Ave Martinez CA 94553-3156

SMITH, GEORGE IRVING, geologist; b. Waterville, Maine, May 20, 1927; s. Joseph Coburn and Ervena (Goodale) S.; m. Patsy Jean Beckstead, Oct. 31, 1954 (div. May 1970); children: Randall G., Laura E.; m. Teruko Kuwada, Aug. 2, 1974; stepchildren: Michele M. Ono, Marla M. Ono, Mireya M. Ono. AB, Colby Coll., Waterville, Maine, 1949; MS, Calif. Inst. Tech., Pasadena, 1951, PhD, 1956. Instr. Occidental Coll., Eagle Rock, Calif., 1951-52; geologist U.S. Geol. Survey, Claremont, Calif., 1952-58, Menlo Park, Calif., 1958-95; geologist emeritus, 1995—. Contbr. articles to profl. jours. With USN, 1945-46. Fulbright sr. rsch. fellow, 1981. Fellow Geol. Soc., Am. Mineral Soc.; mem. Am. Quaternary Assn., Soc. Econ. Geologists, Geochem. Soc., Sigma Xi. Office: US Geol Survey 345 Middlefield Rd # 902 Menlo Park CA 94025-3561

SMITH, GEORGE LARRY, analytical and environmental chemist; b. Beloit, Kans., Oct. 11, 1951; s. Richard Bailey and Vonda Ellene (Cox) S.; m. Charlene Janell Musgrove, Sept. 4, 1973; 1 child, Brian Lawrence. BA, Augustana Coll., 1973. Cert. grade 3 water treatment operator, Calif. Lab. technician Sanitary Dist. of Hammond, Ind., 1973; chemist Federated Metals Corp., Whiting, Ind., 1973-77; rsch. technician Air Pollution Technology, Inc., San Diego, 1978-80, environ. chemist, 1980-81, sr. tech. asst., 1981; staff chemist I Occidental Research Corp., Irvine, Calif., 1981-82, receiving chemist, 1982-84; processing chemist Chem. Waste Mgmt., Inc., Kettleman City, Calif., 1984-87, analytical chemist, 1987-89, wet analytical chemistry group leader, 1989-90, inorganic lab. supr., 1990-94; quality assurance/quality control specialist, 1994—; lab. analyst for published article in environ. sci. and tech., 1981. bd. dirs. Apostolic Christian Missions, Inc., San Diego, 1978-82. Mem. Am. Chem. Soc., Nat. Geographic Soc., Bibl. Archeology Soc., Internat. Union Pure and Applied Chemistry. Home: 205 E Merced St Avenal CA 93204-1251 Office: Chem Waste Mgmt Inc 35251 Old Skyline Rd Kettleman City CA 93239

SMITH, GEORGE VINAL, librarian; b. Chgo., May 14, 1943; s. Earl Wesley and Frances (Kenney) S.; m. Chrystal Jean Stillings, Jan. 29, 1966; children: Rebecca Tyson, Morgen Elizabeth. BA, Whitman Coll., 1965; MA, Wash. State U., 1967; PhD, No. Ill. U., 1974; MS, U. Ill., 1975. Reference libr. Illinet/U. Ill., Urbana, 1975-76; info. svcs. cons. Lincoln Trail Libr. System, Champaign, Ill., 1977-79; circular and network svcs. supr. Oreg. State Libr., Salem, 1979-81; adminstr. of libr. devel. Oreg. State Libr., 1983-85; dir. Canby (Oreg.) Pub. Libr., 1981-82, Woodburn (Oreg.) Pub. Libr., 1982-83; dep. dir. Alaska State Div. of Librs., Archives and Mus., Juneau, 1985—; vol. Peace Corps, Thailand, 1967-69; vis. asst. prof. Grad. Sch. Libr. Sci., U. Ill., 1977-78; instr. Chemekata C.C., Salem, 1980-83, Marylhurst Coll., Lake Oswego, Oreg., 1982; course mentor Grad. Sch. Libr. Sci., U. Ariz., Juneau, Alaska, 1992-94. Author: The Dutch in 17th-Century Thailand, 1977; co-editor and author: Contributions to Asian Studies, 15, 1980. Pres., bd. dirs., coach Juneau Soccer Club, 1992-94; adminstrv. staff Arctic Winter Games/Team Alaska, Fairbanks, 1992—; coach, referee, referee trainer, Juneau Parks and Recreation Dept., 1986—; vol., patron Alaska Folk Festival, 1986—. NDEA fellow No. Ill. U., 1972-73; recipient Gov.'s Mgmt. Recognition award, Gov. Oreg., 1985. Mem. ALA (Libr. fellow to Nat. Libr. Cambodia 1994-95), Pacific N.W. Libr. Assn. (pres., v.p. 1987-89), Alaska Libr. Assn., Oreg. Libr. Assn. (pres., v.p. 1984-85). Home: 124 Behrends Ave Juneau AK 99801-1457 Office: Alaska State Libr/Archives PO Box 110571 Juneau AK 99811

SMITH, GORDON EUGENE, pilot; b. Corpus Christi, Tex., Nov. 22, 1953; s. Orvis Alvin and Helen Lucille (Lockhart) A.; m. Crisanta Lacson Oqueriza, Jan. 5, 1979; children: Pia Marie, Helena Irita. AAS in Electronics, Riverside City Coll., 1985; BSEE, Calif. Polytech., 1987. Electronics technician Lear Siegler, Inc., Ontario, Calif., 1981-86, Rockwell Internat., Palmdale, Calif., 1986-87; pilot Orion Air Inc., Raleigh, N.C., 1987-90; pilot, dir. maintenance, asst. dir. ops. Nat. Air, Riverside, Calif., 1990-93; pilot MGM Grand Air, 1993—. With USAF, 1972-79, with Res. 1979—. Mem. Aircraft Owners and Pilots Assn., Team One (v.p. 1980—). Republican. Dunkard Brethren. Office: MGM Grand Air 1500 Rosecrans Ave Ste 350 Manhattan Beach CA 90266-3721

SMITH, GORDON PAUL, management consulting company executive; b. Salem, Mass., Dec. 25, 1916; s. Gordon and May (Vaughan) S.; m. Daphne Miller, Nov. 23, 1943 (div. 1968); m. Ramona Chamberlain, Sept. 27, 1969; children: Randall B., Roderick F. B.S. in Econs, U. Mass., 1947; M.S. in Govt. Mgmt, U. Denver (Sloan fellow), 1948; postgrad. in polit. sci, NYU, 1948-50; DHL (hon.), Monterey Inst., 1994. Economist Tax Found., Inc., N.Y.C., 1948-50; with Booz, Allen & Hamilton, 1951-70; partner Booz, Allen & Hamilton, San Francisco, 1959-62, v.p., 1962-67, mng. pntr. Western U.S., 1968-70; partner Harrod, Williams and Smith (real estate devel.), San Francisco, 1962-69; state dir. fin. State of Calif., 1967-68; pres. Gordon Paul Smith & Co., Mgmt. Cons., 1968—; pres., chief exec. officer Golconda Corp., 1972-74, chmn. bd., 1974-85; pres. Cermetek Corp., 1978-80; bd. dirs., exec. com. First Calif. Co., 1970-72, Groman Corp., 1976-85; bd. dirs. Madison Venture Capital Corp.; adviser task force def. procurement and contracting Hoover Commn., 1954-55; spl. asst. to pres. Republic Aviation Corp., 1954-55; cons., Hawaii, 1960-61, Alaska, 1963; cons. Wash. Hwy. Adminstrn., 1964, also 10 states and fed. agys., 1951-70, Am. Baseball League and Calif. Angels, 1960-62; bd. dirs. Monterey Coll. Law; chmn. Ft. Ord Econ. Devel. Adv. Group, 1991; chmn. Coalition on Rsch. and Edn., 1993—; bd. dirs. Monterey Bay Futures Project; over 750 TV, radio and speaking appearances on econs., mgmt. and public issues. Author articles on govt., econs. and edn. Mem. 24 bds. and commns. State of Calif., 1967-72; mem. Calif. Select Com. on Master Plan for Edn., 1971-73; mem. alumni council U. Mass., 1950-54, bd. dirs. alumni assn., 1964-70; bd. dirs. Alumni Assn. Mt. Hermon Prep. Sch., 1963; bd. dirs. Stanford Med. Ctr., 1960-62, pres., chmn., 1962-66; chmn. West Coast Cancer Found., 1976-87, Coalition Rsch. and Edn., 1993—; trustee, chmn. Monterey Inst. Internat. Studies, 1978-92; trustee Northfield Mt. Hermon Sch., 1983-93, Robert Louis Stevenson Sch., 1993—; mem. devel. council Community Hosp. of Monterey Peninsula, 1983—; bd. dirs. Friends of the Performing Arts, 1985—; bd. dirs. Monterey County Symphony Orch., 1991—, Monterey Bay Futures Project, 1992—. Served to 1st lt., cav. AUS, 1943-46, ETO. Recipient spl. commendation Hoover Commn., 1955; Alumni of Year award U. Mass., 1963; Trustee of Yr. award Monterey-Peninsula, 1991, Monterey-Peninsula Outstanding Citizen of Yr. award, 1992; Laura Bride Powers Heritage award, 1991; U.S. Congl. award, 1992; Calif. Senate and Assembly Outstanding Citizen award, 1992; Wisdom award of honor Wisdom Soc., 1992; permanent Gordon Paul Smith Disting. Chair for Internat. Study established at Monterey Inst. Internat. Studies; Gordon Paul Smith Scholarship Fund named in his honor Northfield Mt. Hermon Sch.; named to Honorable Order of Ky. Colonels. Mem. Monterey History and Art Assn. (bd. dirs. 1987-92, pres. 1985-87, chmn. 1987-92, hon. lifetime dir. 1992—), The Stanton Ctr. Heritage Ctr. (chmn. 1987-92, chmn. emeritus 1992—), Salvation Army (bd. dirs.) Monterey Peninsula Mus. Art, Carmel Valley (Calif.) Country Club, Monterey Peninsula Country Club, Old Capital Club. Home: 253 Del Mesa Carmel CA 93923

SMITH, GRANT WILLIAM, English language educator, civic fundraiser; b. Bellingham, Wash., July 26, 1937; s. George Whitfield and Hazel (Speirs) S.; m. Lelia Dickinson, June 9, 1961; children: Kathryn, Gavin. BA, Reed Coll., 1964; MA, U. Nev., 1966; PhD, U. Del., 1975. Asst. prof. Eastern Wash. U., Cheney, 1968-76, assoc. prof., 1976-79, prof., 1979—; faculty pres. Eastern Wash. U., Cheney, 1976-77, chair English dept., 1978-84, acting vice provost, 1987-88, coord. humanities, 1979—, dir. cultural outreach, 1995—; host Pub. TV, Here's Shakespeare, 1980, 81. Contbr. articles to profl. jours. and conf. procs. Moderator Cheney United Ch. Christ, 1982-84. With U.S. Army, 1957-60. Grantee U.S. Geol. Survey, State Humanities Commn., NEH, others. Mem. MLA, AAUP, Placename Survey U.S. (chair 1990-96), Connoisseur Concerts Assn. (pres. 1992-95), Am. Dialect Soc. (regional sec. 1982—), Rocky Mountain MLA (program chair 1987), Internat. Coun. Onomastic Scientists, Internat. Soc. Dialectology and Geolinguistics, Am. Name Soc., others. Home: 905 Gary St Cheney WA 99004-1341 Office: Eastern Wash Univ Dept of English MS-25 Cheney WA 99004

SMITH, GREGORY LAURENCE, computer scientist, consultant; b. Youngstown, Ohio, Apr. 15, 1954; s. William Thomas and Joan Duane

(Muir) S.; m. Donna Lois Dickover, Sept. 8, 1983; children: Michael, Michelle. BSEE, Mich. Tech. U., 1978; BS in Computer Sci. magna cum laude, Seattle Pacific U., 1988. Assoc. engr. Boeing Def. and Space Group, Seattle, 1978-79, engr., 1979-81, sr. engr., 1981-83, specialist engr., 1983-85, sr. specialist engr., 1985-89, lead prin. engr., 1989—; prin. engr., cons. Tech. Rsch. Assoc., Renton, Wash., 1986—; invited mem. tech. adv. com. Seattle (Wash.) C.C., 1991—; presenter in field. Author various computer programs; contbr. articles to profl. jours. Mem. IEEE (sr. mem.), Assn. for Computing Machinery, Am. Assn. for Artificial Intelligence, N.W. Artificial Intelligence Forum. Republican. Home: 17952 W Spring Lake Dr SE Renton WA 98058-0610 Office: Boeing Def & Space Group MS-9F-97 PO Box 3999 Seattle WA 98124-2499

SMITH, HARRY MENDELL, JR., science educator; b. Wichita, Kans., Aug. 19, 1943; s. H. Mendell and Sevilla Mae (Cooper) S.; m. Cecile Marie Adams, Sept. 19, 1964; children: Jeff, Shauna, Noelle. AA, Pasadena Coll., 1966; BA, Calif. State U., L.A., 1970; Vocat. Credential, UCLA, 1979. Tchr. Glendora (Calif.) Unified Schs., 1970-80; instr. Citrus Coll., Azusa, Calif., 1978-82; mgr. Christian Chapel, Walnut, Calif., 1980-82; pres. Whitmore Printing, Inc., La Puente, Calif., 1982-85; mgr. Evang. Free Ch., Fullerton, Calif., 1985-87; prof. Mt. San Antonio Coll., Walnut, 1985—, chair divsn. applied sci. and tech., 1993—; dir. Faculty Senate, Mt. San Antonio Coll., 1989-91. Author: Electronic Devices and Circuits Lab Book, 1994. Chancellor's Office Electronic Tech. grantee, 1990. Mem. Nat. Assn. Radio and Telecommunications Engrs., Home Bldrs. Fellowship (pres. 1990-92), Calif. Indsl. Arts and Edn. Assn. Republican. Home: 951 S Idaho St Apt 70 La Habra CA 90631-6649 Office: Mt San Antonio Coll 1100 N Grand Ave Walnut CA 91789-1341

SMITH, HEATHER LYNN, psychotherapist, recreational therapist,; b. Modesto, Calif., May 31, 1956; d. Gary Fremont and Marilyn Rae (Brown) S. BS, Calif. State U., Fresno, 1979; MA, U. San Francisco, 1989. Lic. marriage, family and child counselor, Calif. Recreational therapist Casa Colina Rehab. Hops., Pomona, Calif., 1979-82; evaluator developmentally delayed, coord. family edn. Cath. Charities, Modesto, 1982-87; bereavement counselor Hospice, Modesto, 1983-87; high risk youth counselor Ctr. Human Svcs., Modesto, 1987-90; pvt. practice, family therapist Modesto, 1993—; program dir. chemically dependent treatment program Stanislaus County Juvenile Hall, 1990—. Named Outstanding Young Woman of Stanislaus County, 1986, Citizen of Yr., Civitan, 1986, Outstanding Individual award Stanislaus County, 1992. Mem. Calif. Assn. Marriage and Family Therapists, Kappa Kappa Gamma. Republican. Episcopalian. Home: 806 Claratina Ave Modesto CA 95356-9610 Office: Bldg A Ste 2 250 S Oak Ave Oakdale CA 95361 also: 1015 12th St Ste 8 Modesto CA 95354-0838

SMITH, HELEN DIBELL, executive assistant; b. Ellwood City, Pa., Apr. 9, 1941; d. Nicholas J. and Helen (Pintea) Savu; m. David L. Dibell, July 8, 1961 (div. 1986); children: Marta, Todd, Troy, Mark; m. Gordon H. Smith, Apr. 9, 1991. Student, Geneva Coll., Beaver Falls, 1959-61, U. Ill., 1962. Payroll acct. Babcock & Wilcox Steel Corp., Beaver Falls, Pa., 1960-62; admininstrv. asst. U. Ill., Urbana, 1962-63, Lockheed Missiles & Space Co., Vandenberg AFB, Calif., 1963-64; acct. tng. Vanda Beauty Counselor, N.Y., 1964-78; adminstrv. asst. Okaloosa Walton Jr. Coll., Niceville, Fla., 1977-78; administrv. asst. Tex. Instruments, Va., 1978-79; exec. asst. Allied Signal Bendix Aerospace, Arlington, 1979-89, Orion Group Ltd., Dr. Richard DeLauer and Matra Aerospace Inc., Arlington, 1988-89; asst. to bd. dirs. Fairchild Space and Def. Corp., Germantown, Md., 1989-91; cons. Meridian Strategies, Inc., Fullerton, Calif., 1991-93. Mem. Women Def., Army Assn., Am. Def. Preparedness Assn., Air Force Assn. Republican. Presbyterian. Home and Office: 956 W Rancho Cir Fullerton CA 92635-3337

SMITH, HENRY CHARLES, III, symphony orchestra conductor; b. Phila., Jan. 31, 1931; s. Henry Charles Jr. and Gertrude Ruth (Downs) S.; m. Mary Jane Dressner, Sept. 3, 1955; children—Katherine Anne, Pamela Jane, Henry Charles IV. BA, U. Pa., 1952; artist diploma, Curtis Inst. Music, Phila., 1955. Solo trombonist Phila. Orch., 1955-67; condr. Rochester (Minn.) Symphony Orch., 1967-68; assoc. prof. music Ind. U., Bloomington, 1968-71; resident condr., ednl. dir. Minn. Orch., Mpls., 1971-88; prof. music U. Tex., Austin, 1988-89, Frank C. Erwin Centennial Prof. of Opera, 1988-89; music dir. S.D. Symphony, Sioux Falls, 1989—; prof. Ariz. State U., Tempe, 1989-93, prof. emeritus, 1993—; vis. prof. U. Tex., Austin, 1987-88; founding mem. Phila. Brass Ensemble, 1956—. Composer 5 books of solos for trombone including Solos for the Trombone Player, 1963, Hear Us As We Pray, 1963, First Solos for the Trombone Player, 1972, Easy Duets for Winds, 1972; editor 14 books 20th century symphonies lit. Served to 1st lt. AUS, 1952-54. Recipient 3 Grammy nominations, 1967, 76, 1 Grammy award for best chamber music rec. with Phila. Brass Ensemble, 1969. Mem. Internat. Trombone Assn. (dir.), Am. Symphony Orch. League, Music Educators Nat. Conf., Am. Guild Organists, Am. Fedn. Musicians, Tubist Universal Brotherhood Assn., Acacia Fraternity. Republican. Congregationalist. Home: PO Box 199 Interlochen MI 49643-0199

SMITH, H(OWARD) DUANE, zoology educator; b. Fillmore, Utah, June 25, 1941; s. Howard Martell and Mary Ellen (Mitchell) S.; m. Dahnelle Bower, Dec. 13, 1961; children: Cory, Neichol. BS, Brigham Young U., 1963, MS, 1966; PhD, U. Ill., 1969. From asst. prof. to prof. Brigham Young U., Provo, Utah, 1969—; pvt. practice Orem, Utah, 1973—; dir. Life Sci. Mus. Co-author: Special Publications-Mammalogy, 1994; contbr. articles to profl. jours. Mem. Am. Soc. Mammalogists (sec.-treas. 1987—), Wildlife Soc., Ecol. Soc. Am., Rocky Mountain Elk Found., Sigma Xi (pres.-elect 1994—). Republican. Mormon. Office: Brigham Young Univ 290 MLBM Provo UT 84602-1049

SMITH, HOWARD MCQUEEN, librarian; b. Charlotte, N.C., July 25, 1919; s. Daniel Holt and Pearl Elizabeth (Truitt) S.; m. Elaine Betty Wiefel, June 27, 1949; children: Leslie, Steven Holt. B.A., U. Va., 1941; A.B. in L.S, U. Mich., 1946, M. Pub. Adminstrn., 1947. Reference asst. Enoch Pratt Free Library, Balt., 1947-49; coordinator library activities Richmond (Va.) Area Univ. Center, 1949-50; exec. asst. to dir. Enoch Pratt Free Library, 1950-53, head films dept., 1953-55; personnel officer Free Library Phila., 1955-59; city librarian Richmond Pub. Library, 1959-84. Served to lt. (s.g.) USNR, 1942-46. Mem. ALA.

SMITH, HOWARD NORMAN, JR., educational coordinator, anthropology educator; b. Southgate, Calif., Aug. 26, 1946; s. Howard Norman Smith and Betty Lee (Faust) Jollymour; children: Laurel, Ashley; m. Barbara Lyn Willis, Oct. 8, 1989; stepchildren: Dena, Tiona. AA in Social Sci., Santa Ana Coll., 1971; BA in Anthropology cum laude, Calif. State U., Long Beach, 1972; MA in Anthropology, Ea. N.Mex. U., 1974. Cert. elem. tchr., Calif.; cert. ednl. adminstr., Calif. Ethnic studies instr. Yuba Coll., Marysville, Calif., 1975-77; vets. campus rep. VA, San Francisco, 1974-78; elem. tchr. Page (Ariz.) Unified Sch. Dist., 1979-83; elem. tchr. Sierra Sands Unified Sch. Dist., Ridgecrest, Calif., 1983-84, spl. projects resource, 1984-86, project writer, 1986-90, elem. sch. prin., 1990-93, coord. spl. projects, 1993—; anthropology instr. Cerro Coso C.C., Ridgecrest, Calif., 1992—; co-chairperson Indian Wells Valley Health Start Collaborative, Ridgecrest, 1994—; cons. program quality, rev. trainer, Calif. Dept. Edn., Sacramento, 1985—; bd. dirs. High Desert Child Abuse Prevention Coun., Ridgecrest. Contbr. articles to profl. jours. Chairperson Page (Ariz.) City Libr. Bd., 1982-83. With USCG, 1966-70. Recipient Rsch. grant Ea. N.Mex. U., 1973. Mem. ASCD, Assn. Calif. Sch. Adminstrs., Archaeol. Soc. N.Mex., Calif. Assn. Adminstrs. State and Fed. Edn. Programs, Phi Kappa Phi. Democrat. Home: 200 Michele St Ridgecrest CA 93555-5811 Office: Sierra Sands Unified Sch 113 W Felspar Ave Ridgecrest CA 93555-3520

SMITH, HOWARD RUSSELL, manufacturing company executive; b. Clark County, Ohio, Aug. 15, 1914; s. Lewis Hoskins and Eula (Elder) S.; m. Jeanne Rogers, June 27, 1942; children: Stewart Russell, Douglas Howard, Jeanne Ellen Smith James. A.B., Pomona Coll., 1936. Security analyst Kidder, Peabody & Co., N.Y.C., 1936-37; economist ILO, Geneva, 1937-40; asst. to pres. Blue Diamond Corp., Los Angeles, 1940-46; pres., dir. Avery Dennison Corp., Pasadena, Calif., 1946-75, chmn. bd., 1975-84, chmn. exec. com., 1984—; chmn. bd. Kinsmith Fin. Corp., San Marino, Calif., 1979—. Bd. dirs., past pres., chmn. Los Angeles Philharm. Assn.; chmn. emeritus, bd. trustees Pomona Coll., Claremont, Calif.; past chmn. bd. Children's Hosp. Los Angeles, Community TV of So. Calif. (Sta. KCET), Los Angeles. With USNR, 1943-46. Home: 1458 Hillcrest Ave Pasadena CA 91106-4503 Office: Avery Dennison Corp 150 N Orange Grove Blvd Pasadena CA 91103-3534

SMITH, IRBY JAY, film producer; b. San Antonio, Apr. 17, 1938; s. Irby Jay and Virginia Lee (Algee) S.; m. Elaine Nicholson, June 8, 1956; children: Kimberly, Carrie, Jay. Student, Occidental Coll., 1955-56; BA summa cum laude, U. Calif., Berkeley, 1960. Pub. info. spcialist, tv interview host, writer U.S. Dept. Health, Edn. and Welfare, L.A., 1960-66; writer, dir. CRM/McGraw-Hill Films, L.A., 1969-70; pvt. practice asst. dir., prodn. mgr., prodr., dir., 1966—. Prodr. City Slickers, Rookie of the Year, Angels in the Outfield, Enemies a Love Story, Major League, Young Guns I and II. Recipient ALA award for writing and directing ednl. films, 1970, 2 Cine Golden Eagle awards for writing and directing ednl. films, 1970. Mem. Dirs. Guild Am., Phi Beta Kappa. Democrat.

SMITH, JACK CLIFFORD, journalist, author; b. Long Beach, Calif., Aug. 27, 1916; s. Charles Franklin and Anna Mary (Hughes) S.; m. Denise Bresson, June 17, 1939; children: Curtis Bresson, Douglas Franklin. Student, Bakersfield (Calif.) Coll., 1937-38. Reporter Bakersfield Californian, 1937-38, Honolulu Advertiser, 1941-42, UPI, Sacramento, 1943, Los Angeles Daily News, 1946-49, Los Angeles Herald-Express, 1950-52; reporter Los Angeles Times, 1953-58, columnist, 1958—. Author: Three Coins in the Birdbath, 1965, Smith on Wry, 1970, God and Mr. Gomez, 1974, The Big Orange, 1976, Spend All Your Kisses, Mr. Smith, 1978, Jack Smith's L.A, 1980, How to Win a Pullet Surprise, 1982, Cats, Dogs and Other Strangers at My Door, 1984, Alive in La La Land, 1989. Served with USMC, 1944-45. Club: Sunset. Home: 4251 Camino Real Los Angeles CA 90065-3960 Office: Times Mirror Sq Los Angeles CA 90053

SMITH, JAMES ALEXANDER, metal processing executive; b. Harvey, N.D., Jan. 16, 1926; s. James Kay MacKenzie and Palma Theresa (Johnson) S.; m. Cleo Lorraine, Sept. 1, 1948 (div. 1962); children: Deborah Kay Smith Hooper, Daryl Lynn Smith O'Neill, Darcey Amelia Smith Ryan; m. Louise Mae Hammer, July 21, 1979. BS, U. Minn., 1951. Ptnr., v.p. VIP, Phoenix, 1960-78; founder Therm-O-Low Inc., Phoenix, 1978-84; v.p., gen. mgr., pres. 3XKryogenics, Phoenix, 1984-86; founder, pres. Cryogenics Internat., Inc., Tempe, Ariz., 1987-90; lectr. and speaker on cryogenics. Patentee (U.S. and fgn.) in field. Staff sgt. U.S. Army, 1943-46. Decorated Bronze star, Combat Infantryman Badge with 2 battle stars. Mem. Soc. Mfg. Engrs. (Ariz. chpt. chmn. 1983, chmn. western states zone 1985, Pres.'s award 1984), Cryogenic Soc. Am., Am. Soc. Metals, VFW (life mem.). Republican. Lutheran.

SMITH, JAMES MICHEAL, marketing executive; b. Ft. Carson, Colo., July 14, 1951; s. Richard Allen Smith and Cathrine Clare (Kehl) Ryan; m. Amelia Joann Carr, June 7, 1973; children: Peter Micheal, Lisa Danielle. BS in Basic Scis., USAF Acad., 1973; MA in Bus. Mgmt., Ctrl. Mich. U., 1977. Sr. cons. Strategic Mktg. Group, Inc., Denver, 1986-87; dir. ops. U.S.A. Direct, Inc., Englewood, Colo., 1987; mktg. rep. Martin Marietta Corp., Denver, 1988-90, sr. mktg. rep., 1990-92, mgr. bus. devel., 1992-95; dir. mktg. Hughes Info. Tech. Corp., Aurora, Colo., 1995—. Patroller Nat. Ski Patrol, 1985—; cub scout leader Boy Scouts Am., 1993—. Maj. USAF, 1973-86, lt. col. USAFR. Recipient Purple Merit Star for life saving Nat. Ski Patrol, 1990. Mem. Air Force Assn. (life), Res. Officer Assn. (life), Nat. Security Indsl. Assn. (corp. mem.). Republican. Mem. LDS Ch. Home: 6094 N Ponderosa Way Parker CO 80134-5524 Office: Hughes Info Tech Corp 16800 E CentreTech Pkwy Aurora CO 80011-9046

SMITH, JAMES THOMAS, mathematician; b. Springfield, Ohio, Nov. 8, 1939; s. Earl Gearhart and Betty Mae (McCartney) S.; m. Helen Marie Patteson, Jan. 26, 1963; 1 son, Jedediah. AB, Harvard U., 1961; MA, San Francisco State U., 1964; MS, Stanford U., 1967; PhD, U. Sask., Regina, Can., 1970. Mathematician U.S. Navy, San Francisco, 1962-67; asst. prof. math. San Francisco State U., 1969-72, assoc. prof., 1972-75, prof., 1975—; dir. software devel. Blaise Computing, Berkeley, 1984-85; vis. prof. Mills Coll., Oakland, Calif., 1982-83, U. Alaska-Fairbanks, 1983, Calif. State U.-Hayward, 1984, SUNY, 1988-89. Author tech. reports on mil. ops. analysis, 1963-67. Author: IBM PC/AT Programmer's Guide, 1986, Getting the Most from Turbo Pascal, 1987, Advanced Turbo C, 1989, C++ for Scientists and Engineers, 1991, C++ Applications Guide, 1992; contbr. papers on math. rsch. to profl. publs. Mem. schs. com. Harvard Club, San Francisco, 1978—, v.p. schs., 1989-93. Mem. Am. Math Soc., Math. Assn. Am. (chmn. north Calif. sect. 1992-93), Deutsche Mathematiker-Vereinigung. Home: 1363 27th Ave San Francisco CA 94122-1508 Office: San Francisco State U Math Dept San Francisco CA 98132

SMITH, JAMES WELDON, museum director; b. Richmond, Va., Sept. 7, 1933; s. James Weldon Jr. and Viola Jett (Elliott) S.; m. Nancy Linnaea Lee, July 9, 1955; children: Christian Linnaea, Marshall Taylor. BA, Yale U., 1955; PhD, Northwestern U., 1962. Prof. MacMurray Coll., Jacksonville, Ill., 1962-80, J.F. Kennedy U., Orinda, Calif., 1980-81; dir. Fiberworks, Ctr./Textile Arts, Berkeley, Calif., 1981-87, San Francisco (Calif.) Craft & Folk Art Mus., 1987—; instr. San Francisco (Calif.) Art Inst., 1986; bd. dirs. Calif. Assn. Mus., 1993—; cons. Calif. Arts Coun., Nat. Endowment for the Arts, NEH. Curator exhbns. of African art, various locations, 1980—. Office: San Francisco Craft & Folk Art Mus Fort Mason San Francisco CA 94123

SMITH, JEAN, interior design firm executive; b. Oklahoma City; d. A. H. and Goldy K. (Engle) Hearn; m. W. D. Smith; children: Kaye Smith Hunt, Sidney P. Student Chgo. Sch. Interior Design, 1970. v.p. Billco-Aladdin Wholesale, Albuquerque, 1950-92, v.p. Billco Carpet One of Am, 1970. Pres. Albuquerque Opera, 1979-83, advisor to bd. dirs.; active Civic Chorus, Cen. Meth. Ch.; pres. Inez PTA, 1954-55, life mem.; hon. life mem. Albuquerque Little Theater, bd. dirs. Republican. Clubs: Albuquerque County, Four Hills Country, Daus. of the Nile (soloist Yucca Temple). Home: 1009 Santa Ana Ave SE Albuquerque NM 87123-4232 Office: Billco-Aladdin Wholesale 7617 Menaul Blvd NE Albuquerque NM 87110-4647

SMITH, JEFFREY ALAN, international educational aid administrator; b. Phila., June 30, 1942; s. Richard Somerville and Marguerite Irene (Gebler) S. BS, Yale U., 1965; AM, Harvard U., 1982, EdD, 1983. Field asst. Peabody Mus. and Dept. Anthropology Yale U., U.S., Kenya, Tanzania, Egypt, France, Eng., 1963-65; tchr., coach Webb Sch., Claremont, Calif., 1965-66; tchr. Mass. Correctional Instn., Walpole, 1968-69; founder, dir. Redington Pond Sch., Rangeley, Maine, 1970-76, V-V Ranch Sch., Wardlow, Alta., Can., 1973-75; instr. U. Sci. and Tech., Chengdu, Sichuan, China, 1984; exec. dir. Crisis Ctr., Monterey, Calif., 1985-86, Books to China Found., San Francisco, 1986-87; pres. Bridge to Asia Found., Oakland, Calif., 1987—; math. instr. Wang Labs., Tweksbury, Mass., 1969; tchr. Adult Edn. Ctr., Cambridge, Mass., 1969-70, sr. addiction specialsit Human Svcs. Adminstrn., N.Y.C., 1969-70; instr. Hurricane Island Outward Bound Sch., Rockland, Maine, 1973, Dept. Hosps. and Instns., Santa Fe, 1977; vis. prof. U. Sci. and Tech., Chengdu; vis. libr. Ocean U. Qingdao, Shandong; mem. Nat. Com. on U.S.-China Rels., N.Y. Active San Francisco Shanghai Sister City Com. Mem. Internet Soc. Office: Bridge to Asia 1214 Webster St # F Oakland CA 94612-3919

SMITH, JEFFREY P., supermarket chain executive; b. 1950. Student, Utah State U., 1968-70. With Smith's Food and Drug Ctrs., Salt Lake City, 1970—, pres., COO, 1984-88, chmn., CEO, 1988—, also bd. dirs. Office: Smith's Food & Drug Ctrs Inc 1550 S Redwood Rd Salt Lake City UT 84104-5105

SMITH, JEFFRY ALAN, health administrator, physician, consultant; b. L.A., Dec. 8, 1943; s. Stanley W. and Marjorie E. S.; m. Jo Anne Hague. BA in Philosophy, UCLA, 1967, MPH, 1972; BA in Biology, Calif. State U., Northridge, 1971; MD, UACJ, 1977. Diplomate Am. Bd. Family Practice. Resident in family practice WAH, Takoma Park, Md., NIH, Bethesda, Md., Walter Reed Army Hosp., Washington, Children's Hosp. Nat. Med. Ctr., Washington, 1977-80; occupational physician Nev. Test Site, U.S. Dept. Energy, Las Vegas, 1981-82; dir. occupational medicine and environ. health Pacific Missile Test Ctr., Point Mugu, Calif., 1982-84; dist. health officer State Hawaii Dept. Health, Kauai, 1984-86; asst. dir. health County of Riverside (Calif.) Dept. Health, 1986-87; regional med. dir. Calif. Forensic Med. Group, Monterey, Calif., 1987-94; med. dir. Cmty. Human Svcs., Monterey, Calif., 1987-94, Colstrip (Mont.) Med. Ctr., 1994—. Fellow Am. Acad. Family Physicians; mem. AMA, Am. Occupational Medicine Assn., Flying Physicians, Am. Pub. Health Assn. Home: PO Box 1538 Forsyth MT 59327

SMITH, JERILYNN SUZANNE, educational coordinator; b. Loma Linda, Calif., Aug. 15, 1944; d. Gerald A. and Maxine (McGowan) Smith; m. J. Michael McGinn, July 22, 1966; m. Lynn A. Choate, May 8, 1971; 1 dau., Catherine Anne; m. C. Alen Ritchie, Feb. 17, 1981. BA, U. Redlands (Calif.), 1966, Master of Art in Teaching, 1968; MA in Ed., Calif. State U., San Bernardino, 1980, EdD in Internat. Multicultural Edn., U. San Francisco, 1993. Tchr. elem. sch. Redlands Unified Sch. Dist., 1966-69, tchr. educationally handicapped, 1969-71, tchr. intermediate grades, 1971-74, tchr. bilingual edn., 1975-79, resource specialist, 1979-84, categorical projects resource tchr., 1984-87, dist. tchr. coord. Bilingual/Gate Programs, 1987-89; coord. bi-lingual, ESL programs Fontana Sch. Dist.; supr. student tchrs. Calif. State Coll., 1975; lectr. in field. Bd. dirs. San Bernardino County Mus. Assn. Recipient Hon. Svc. award Lugonia PTA, 1982, Tchrs. Hall of Fame award, 1982, Fontana Hispanic C. of C. award, 1992. Mem. Calif. Assn. Bilingual Edn. (mem. state exec. bd. 1985-92), Nat. Assn. Bilingual Edn. (nat. bd. dirs. 1990-92), Phi Delta Kappa, Pi Lambda Theta. Democrat. Office: Fontana Unified Sch Dist 9680 Citrus Ave Fontana CA 92335-5571

SMITH, JILLAINE SUE, computer services specialist; b. Long Beach, Calif., Jan. 21, 1959; d. John Lincoln and Miriam (Sess) Smith. BA in Comm., U. Calif., San Diego, 1982. Adminstrv. asst. U. Calif.-San Diego, La Jolla, 1982-85; project coord. U.S.-Soviet Space Bridges, La Jolla, 1985-86; pvt. practice computer cons. San Francisco, 1986-89; asst. dir. Ist. for Global Comms. (PeaceNet, EcoNet)., San Francisco, 1989—; coord. On Screen '87: A Celebration of Women in Film/TV film festival, On Screen '88: A Celebration of Women in Film/TV; undergrad. teaching asst. dept. comm. U. Calif., San Diego, 1992. Interviewer for book: Remembering War, 1987; prodn. asst. TV program Moscow Calling San Diego: Children and Film, 1983, Whisper, the Waves, the Wind, 1984. Mem. Bay Area Women in Telecomm., Bay area Nonprofit Computer Consortium, Tech. Resource Consortium (assoc.). Office: Inst for Global Comm 18 De Boom St San Francisco CA 94107-1424

SMITH, JOBAN JONATHAN, security consultant; b. Albuquerque, New Mex., Mar. 7, 1962; s. William Oswalt and Lou Ella (Agan) Hernandez; 1 child, Connor Nigel Smith. Student, Pensacola Christian Coll., 1980-81, Bradley U., 1981-82; BA in Psychology, Fellowship U., 1985; AA in Alcohol and Drug Counseling, SIPI, Albuquerque, 1990. Underwater demolitions trainer Dept. Defense, Pensacola, Fla., 1980-81; courier, escort Dept. Defense, Peoria, Ill., 1982-86, U.S. Consulate, N.Y.C., 1987-88; security cons. Atlantic Record Co., L.A., 1988; recreation therapist Indian Health Svc., Iselta, New Mex., 1990-91, Manor Care Nursing Home, Albuquerque, 1991—; owner Joban Smith & Assocs., Albuquerque, 1990—; cons. S.W. Fun & Lesiure, Albuquerque, 1991—, McGartland & Assocs., 1991—. Mem. NRA, Nat. Assn. Security Cons., New Mex. Activities Assn.

SMITH, JOEY SPAULS, mental health nurse, biofeedback therapist, bodyworker, hypnotist; b. Washington, Oct. 9, 1944; d. Walter Jr. and Marian (Och) Spauls; children: Kelly, Sean. BSN, Med. Coll. Va., 1966; MA in Edn., U. Nebr., Lincoln, 1975. RNC, ANA; cert. psychiat. and mental health nurse; cert. massage practitioner , cert. hypnotist, cert. biofeedback therapist. Staff nurse Booth Meml. Hosp., Omaha, 1969-71; asst. house supr. Nebr. Meth. Hosp., Omaha, 1971-72; head nurse, clin. instr. U. Calif., Davis, 1976-78; staff nurse Atascadero State Hosp., Calif. Dept. Mental Health, 1978-79; nurse instr. psychiat. technician Atascadero State Hosp., 1979-84, insvc. tng. coord., 1984-86; nursing coord. chem. dependency recovery program French Hosp. Med. Ctr., San Luis Obispo, Calif., 1986-87; nurse instr., health svcs. staff devel. coord. Calif. Men's Colony, Dept. Corrections, San Luis Obispo, 1987-92; pvt. practice San Luis Obispo, Calif., 1990—; relief house supr. San Luis Obispo County Gen. Hosp., 1982-88, regional program assoc. statewide nursing program Consortium Calif. State U., 1986-88; clin. instr. nursing div. Cuesta Coll., 1988—. 1st lt. U.S. Army Nurse Corps., 1965-67. Mem. Assn. Applied Psychophysiology and Biofeedback, Am. Holistic Nurses Assn., Consol. Assn. Nurses in Substance Abuse (cert. chem. dependency nurse), Biofeedback Cert. Inst. Am. (cert. biofeedback therapist, cert. stress mgr., stress mgmt. edn.), Alpha Sigma Chi, Phi Delta Gamma. Home: 1321 Cavalier Ln San Luis Obispo CA 93405-4905 Office: PO Box 4823 San Luis Obispo CA 93403-4823

SMITH, JOHN KERWIN, lawyer; b. Oakland, Calif., Oct. 18, 1926; 1 dau., Cynthia. BA, Stanford U.; LLB, Hastings Coll. Law, San Francisco. Ptnr., Haley, Purchio, Sakai & Smith, Hayward, Calif; bd. dirs. Berkeley Asphalt, Mission Valley Ready-Mix; gen. ptnr. Oak Hill Apts., City Ctr. Commercial, Creekwood I and Creekwood II Apts. Road Parks Commn., 1957, mem. city coun., 1959-66, mayor, 1966-70; chmn. Alameda County Mayors Conf., 1968; chmn. revenue taxation com. League Calif. Cities, 1968; vice-chmn. Oakland-Alameda County Coliseum Bd. Dirs.; bd. dirs. Coliseum Found., Mission Valley Rock, Rowell Ranch Rodeo; former pres. Hastings 1066 Found. (Vol. Svc. award 1990), Martin Kauffman 100 Club. Recipient Alumnus of Yr. award Hastings Coll. Law, 1989. Mem. ABA, Calif. Bar Assn., Alameda County Bar Assn., Am. Judicature Soc., Rotary. Office: 22320 Foothill Blvd # 620 Hayward CA 94541-2700

SMITH, KEITH LARUE, research company executive; b. Salida, Colo., Dec. 15, 1917; s. Leroy Holt and Verna Lea (Tunnell) S.; student Marion Coll., 1935-38; A.B. in Math., Ind. U., 1946; postgrad. DePauw U., 1946-47; M.A. in Internat. Affairs, Harvard U., 1955; M.P.A., Calif. State U.-Fullerton, 1979; m. Evelyn May De Bruler, Aug. 29, 1943; 1 son, Eric Douglas. Mil. intelligence research specialist Dept. of Army, Washington, 1951-60; staff engr. Librascope div. Gen. Precision, Inc., Glendale, Cal., 1960-61; sr. operations research analyst Space div. N.Am. Rockwell Corp., Downey, Cal., 1961-71; dir. research Am. Research Corp., Paramount, Calif., 1972—; instr. math. and polit. sci. DePauw U., 1946-47; cons. model bldg. and gaming techniques, 1960—; mgmt. cons., 1970—; instr. math. and sci. Verbum Dei High Sch., 1974-85 . Adult leader Boy Scouts Am., Long Beach, Calif., 1961-75. Treas., UN Council Harvard, 1947-49, Young Democratic Club, Arlington, Mass., 1949-50. Served to capt. USAAF, 1941-46; ETO. Recipient scholarship award Inst. World Affairs, 1947, Outstanding Efficiency award Dept. Army, 1960, Apollo 11 medallion NASA, 1970. Mem. Am. Mus. Natural History, Nat. Geog. Soc., Harvard Alumni Assn., Pi Sigma Alpha. Methodist. Mason. Research on lunar mission cartography, mil. operations research and war game model bldg. Home: 3451 E Curry St Long Beach CA 90805-3815

SMITH, KELLY L., research and development executive; b. 1951. BS in Chem. Engring., Stanford U., 1974, MS in Engring. Sci. and Biomed. Engring., 1974. Chem. engr. Alza Corp., Palo Alto, Calif., 1974-78; dir. controlled release divsn. Bend (Oreg.) Rsch. Inc., 1978—. Office: Bend Research Inc 64550 Research Rd Bend OR 97701-8583*

SMITH, KENNETH JAMES, hematologist; b. White Plains, N.Y., July 19, 1948; s. Henry James and Greta Elizabeth (Olson) S.; m. Catherine Horton, June 25, 1972; children: Patricia, Amy, David. AB, Fordham U., 1970; MD, Cornell U., 1974. Diplomate Am. Bd. Blood Banking, Am. Bd. Internal Medicine, sub-bds. Med. Oncology, Hematology, Am. Bd. Pathology. Intern then resident U. Pitts. Hosp., 1974-77, rsch. fellow in hematology/oncology, 1977-80; asst. prof. pathology and medicine U. N.Mex. Sch. Medicine, Albuquerque, 1980-86, assoc. prof., 1986-90; assoc. med. dir. United Blood Svcs., Albuquerque, 1980-90, med. dir., 1990—; prof. medicine and pathology. Contbr. articles to sci. jours.; patentee blood product, 1988. Mem. Gov.'s AIDS/HIV Task Force, 1990; v.p. Sangre de Oro (N.Mex.) Hemophilia Program. Rsch. fellow U. Wash., 1977-80; rsch. grantee Blood Systems Rsch. Found., Inc., Rorer, Inc., Am. Heart Assn., Bayer, Inc., Baxter Healthcare, Inc. Mem. ACP (councillor N.Mex. chpt. 1990, pres.-elect N.Mex. chpt. 1991, pres. 1992-93), Am. Heart Assn. (vice chmn. rsch. com. N.Mex. affiliate 1991, rsch. grantee), Am. Soc.Hematology, Am. Fedn. Clin. Rsch., Am. Assn. Blood Banks. Democrat. Home: 1522 Wellesley Dr

NE Albuquerque NM 87106-1137 Office: U NMex Sch Medicine Dept Pathology Albuquerque NM 87131

SMITH, KENT ESSAM, real estate developer, flower grower; b. Detroit, Nov. 12, 1953; s. Frank and Aurelia Smith. BS, San Diego State U., 1977. Wine wholesaler Wine Warehouse, L.A., 1979—; pres. Rolling Hills Ranch, San Diego, 1992—. Pres., founder Townspeople, Inc., San Diego, 1984. Democrat. Home: 977 Manor Way San Diego CA 92106-2035 Office: Rolling Hills Ranch 175 La Costa Ave Encinitas CA 92024

SMITH, LE ROI MATTHEW-PIERRE, III, municipal administrator; b. Chgo., Jan. 11, 1946; s. Le Roy Matthew and Norma Buckner (McCamey) S.; 1 son, Le Roi Matthew Pierre. B.A. in Psychology, Idaho State U., 1969; Ph.D. in Psychology, Wash. State U., 1977. Instr. psychology Idaho State U., Pocatello, 1969-70, Wash. State U., Pullman, 1970-71; mem. faculty dept. psychology Evergreen State Coll., Olympia, 1971-81; dir. diversity program Port of Seattle, 1981—; cons. in field. Bd. dirs. Thurston-Mason County Community Mental Health Ctr., Olympia; v.p., Idaho State Human Rights Commn., Bannock County, Idaho, 1968-70. Office Edn. fellow, 1969-70; U.S. Dept. Labor grantee, 1968; NSF grantee, 1972; Lilly Found. fellow, 1980. Mem. Am. Psychol. Assn., Am. Personnel and Guidance Assn., Wash. State Black Econs. and Edn. Conf., Assn. Black Psychologists, Am. Assn. of Affirmative Action Officers, Phi Delta Kappa. Democrat. Roman Catholic. Home: 761 S 45th St Tacoma WA 98408-4962 Office: PO Box 1209 Seattle WA 98111-1209

SMITH, LEE ARTHUR, professional baseball player; b. Jamestown, La., Dec. 4, 1957. Student, Northwestern State U., La. Pitcher Chgo. Cubs, 1975-87, Boston Red Sox, 1987-90, St. Louis Cardinals, 1990-93, N.Y. Yankees, 1993-94; with Balt. Orioles, 1994, Calif. Angels, 1994—. Named Nat. League Fireman of Yr., Sporting News, 1991, 94; holder maj. league record for most consecutive errorless games by pitcher, Nat. League single-season record for most saves; Nat. League Saves Leader, 1983, 91-92; mem. Nat. League All-Star team, 1983, 87, 91-94; named Nat League Co-Fireman of Yr., Sporting News, 1983, 92. Office: Calif Angels 2000 Gene Autry Way Anaheim CA 92806

SMITH, LEE CLARK, apparel company executive; b. Plainfield, N.J., Apr. 13, 1942; s. Harold Irving and Dorothy Taylor (Clark) S.; m. Perry Lea Donovan, Nov. 5, 1966. B.S., Pa. State U., 1964. Mktg. mgmt. trainee Levi Strauss & Co., San Francisco, 1966-72; gen. mgr. Levi Strauss & Co., Thailand, 1972-73, Portugal, 1973-74; mktg. dir. no. Europe div. Levi Strauss & Co., 1974-76, pres., 1976-78, pres. Asia Pacific div., 1978-80, pres. diversified apparel products div., 1980-81, v.p., 1984-85; sr. v.p. Levi Strauss & Co., San Francisco, 1985—. Served to lt. U.S. Army, 1964-66. Home: 117 Hacienda Dr Belvedere Tiburon CA 94920-1103 Office: Levi Strauss Internat 1155 Battery St San Francisco CA 94111-1230

SMITH, LEE L., hotel executive; b. Long Beach, Calif., Oct. 15, 1936; s. Lowell Llake and Violet Margaret (Chrissman) S.; m. Sharon M.C. Lanahan, (div. 1977). AA, Long Beach City Coll., 1958; BA in Music, Chapman Coll., 1965; postgrad., Calif. State U., Long Beach, 1966-67, U. Calif., Santa Barbara, 1974. Cert. tchr. Calif.; lic. ins. agt., Calif. Owner, mgr. Lee's Land Cattle Ranch, Cuyama Valley, Calif., 1960—; tchr. Cuyama Valley Schs., New Cuyama, Calif., 1967-79; owner, mgr. Cuyama Buckhorn Restaurant & Motel, New Cuyama, 1979-83; owner Allstate Ins. Agy., Desert Hot Springs, Calif., 1987-91; owner, mgr. Caravan Resort Spa, Desert Hot Springs, 1983-91; owner S & S Printing, 1990—, Lee's Land Bed & Breakfast, 1992—. Violinist Bakersfield (Calif.) Symphony, 1967—, Brook String Quartet, Palm Springs, Calif., 1984-91; dir. Planning Commn., Desert Hot Springs, 1985-87; chmn. Environ. Rev., Desert Hot Springs, 1986-88; mem. Redevel. Com., Desert Hot Springs, 1983-88; mem. exec. bd. growth and devel. Boys and Girls Club; bd. dirs. Food Now Program, 1988-91. Mem. Am. Fedn. Musicians, Desert Hot Springs C. of C. (Bus. Person Yr. 1987), Breakfast Rotary (pres. 1987-88), Taft Rotary, Elks. Republican. Home: HC 1 Box 185B Maricopa CA 93252-9629 Office: S & S Printing 606 Center St Taft CA 93268

SMITH, LEE R. (COLLEEN SMITH), family therapist, political activist; b. Portland, Oreg., Sept. 6, 1932; d. George A. McClymont and Edna F. (McBride) Lamont; m. William R. Smith, Apr. 16, 1955 (dec. Nov. 1977); children: Mark W. (dec.), Steven R., Stuart J., Leslie Ann, David G. BA in English Lit., U. Calif., Berkeley, 1954; MA in Counseling Psychology, Chapman Coll., 1987. Lic. marriage and family therapist, Oreg. Intern Ctr. for Family Therapy, Costa Mesa, Calif.; pvt. practice Laguna Hills, Calif.; staff therapist Cascase Assocs., Springfield, Oreg.; family therapist Eugene, Oreg. Mem. Am. Counseling Assn., Oreg. Counseling Assn., Nat. Breast Cancer Coalition, Oreg. Breast Cancer Coalition (founder, state coord. 1992, surveillance com. 1993-94). Office: Oreg Breast Cancer Coaltn 1430 Willamette St # 193 Eugene OR 97401-4049

SMITH, LEO GILBERT, hospital administrator; b. Oroville, Calif., July 29, 1929; s. Leo Paul and Laura Mae (Hoffschulte) S.; m. Marcia Elise Ernest, Jan. 26, 1952; children: Matthew Paul, Mara Lee, Bridget Mari, Leo Ernest. B.S.C., U. Santa Clara, 1951; M.P.H., U. Calif., 1958. Adminstrv. resident San Diego County Gen. Hosp., 1958-59; asst. hosp. adminstr. Santa Clara Valley Med. Center, 1959-67, adminstr., 1967-76, dir. planning, 1976-77; health care cons., 1977-80; adminstr. Puget Sound Hosp., 1980-82; mgr. Tacoma Family Medicine dept Multicare Med. Ctr., Tacoma, Wash., 1982-86, dir. clinic services, 1986-91; clinic mgr. Providence Factoria Family Healthcare div. Providence Med. Ctr., Seattle, 1992; ret. Bd. dirs. Children's Home Soc. of Calif., chmn. dist. bd., 1969-70; chmn. br. bd. Children's Home Soc. of Wash., 1985. Served in mil. 1952-54. Mem. Cen. Coast Hosp. Conf. (pres. 1970), Hosp. Coun. No. Calif. (dir. 1970-73), Am. Coll. Hosp. Adminstrs., Med. Group Mgrs. Assn., Tacoma Sunrise Rotary (pres. 1982-83, Dist. 5020 Youth Exch. officer 1991—). Home: 7122 Turquoise Dr SW Tacoma WA 98498-6431

SMITH, LESLIE ROPER, hospital administrator; b. Stockton, Calif., June 20, 1928; s. Austin J. and Helen (Roper) S.; m. Edith Sue Fincher, June 22, 1952; children: Melinda Sue, Leslie Erin, Timothy Brian. A.B., U. Pacific, 1951; M.S. in Pub. Adminstrn, U. So. Calif., 1956. Adminstrv. asst. Ranchos Los Amigos Hosp., Downey, Calif., 1953-57; asst. adminstr. Harbor Gen. Hosp., Torrance, Calif., 1957-65; adminstr. Harbor Gen. Hosp., 1966-71; acting regional dir. Los Angeles County Coastal Health Services Region, 1973; pres. San Pedro Peninsula Hosp., San Pedro, Cal., 1974-86; exec. dir. Los Angeles County/U. So. Calif. Med. Center, 1971-73; adminstr. Long Beach (Calif.) Hosp., 1965-66; asso. clin. prof. community medicine and pub. health, also emergency medicine U. So. Calif., 1968-78; instr. U. So. Calif. (Sch. Pub. Adminstrn.), 1968; preceptor hosp. adminstrn. UCLA Sch. Pub. Health, 1964—; chief exec. officer French Hosp. Med. Ctr. and Health Plan, 1986-87; dir. health care services McCormack & Farrow, 1987—; lectr. in field, 1963—; cons. emergency health services HEW, 1970-73; chmn. com. diaster preparedness Hosp. Council So. Calif., 1966-72, sec., 1971—, pres., 1973; mem. Calif. Assembly Com. on Emergency Med. Services, 1970, Calif. Emergency Med. Adv. Com., 1972-75, Los Angeles County Commn. on Emergency Med. Services, 1975-83, Los Angeles Health Planning and Devel. Agy. Commn., 1980-83; bd. dirs. Blue Cross of So. Calif.; mem. hosp. relations com. Blue Cross of Calif.; mem. adv. com. on emergency health services Calif. Dept. Health, 1974-75; bd. dirs., mem. exec. com. Truck Ins. Exchange of Farmers Ins. Group, 1977-82; bd. dirs. Hosp. Council of So. Calif., 1966-76, 81-86, Health Resources Inst., 1985-86; chmn. Preferred Health Network, 1983-86. Mem. goals com., Torrance, 1968—; pres. Silver Spur Little League, Palos Verdes, 1969-70. Served with AUS, 1946-48. Recipient Silver Knight and Gold Knight award Nat. Mgmt. Assn., 1970, 85, Walker Fellowship award, 1976. Fellow Am. Coll. Health Care Execs. (life); mem. Am., Nat. mgmt. assns., Am. Hosp. Assn. (chmn. com. on community emergency health services 1973), Calif. Hosp. Assn. (chmn. com. emergency services 1965-70, trustee 1973-76, bd. dirs. Calif. Ins. Service Group 1980-82), County Suprs. Assn. Calif. (chmn. joint subcom. on emergency care 1970). Presbyn. (elder, trustee). Home: 27 Marseille Laguna Beach CA 92677-5400

SMITH, LESTER MARTIN, broadcasting executive; b. N.Y.C., Oct. 20, 1919; s. Alexander and Sadie S.; m. Bernice Reitz, Sept. 28, 1962; 1 child, Alexander. B.S. in Bus. Adminstrn, NYU, 1940. Chief exec. officer Alexander Broadcasting Co., radio stas. in, 1954—; gen. partner 700 Investment Co.; past dir. Seattle C. of C.; past chmn. dir. Radio Advt. Bur. Served to maj. U.S. Army, 1942-46. Decorated Bronze Star. Mem. Nat. Assn. Broadcasters (past dir.), Oreg. Assn. Broadcasters (past pres.), Broadcast Pioneers. Clubs: Rotary (Seattle), Rainer (Seattle), Wash. Athletic (Seattle). Address: 700 112th Ave NE Bellevue WA 98004-5106

SMITH, LINDA A., congresswoman, former state legislator; d. Vern Smith; children: Sheri, Robi. Office mgr.; former mem. Wash. State Ho. of Reps.; mem. Wash. State Senate; congresswoman, Wash. 3rd Dist. U.S. House Reps., Washington, D.C., 1995—. Republican. Home: 10009 NW Ridgecrest Ave Vancouver WA 98685-5159 Office: Senate House Legislative Bldg Olympia WA 98504*

SMITH, LOUIS, maintenance engineer; b. Shreveport, La., Nov. 2, 1934; s. Louis and Savannah (Durham) S.; m. Velma Smith, Jan. 1, 1961; 1 child, Gerald W. Student, Rancho Los Amigos, Downey, Calif., 1976. Maintenance engr. L.A. Dept. Water and Power, 1968—; chauffeur Cowboy Limosine Svc., Pasadena, Calif., 1988—; show horseman Com. for Altadena (Calif.) Old Fashioned-Day Parades; leading rider monty police Palm Spring Parade, 1991; 1st pl. Western singleman rider, Lancaster, 1991; featured rider Palm Springs, 1993. Mem. Tournament of Roses Com., Pasadena Coun. Parade of Roses. With U.S. Army, 1957-58. Recipient Trophies, Altadena Town Coun., 1982, Desert Circus, 1985, 86, Palm Springs C. of C., 1981, 87, City of Barstowe (Calif.), 1988, 89, Golden West Parader Assn., 1989, San Bernardino City Coun., 1990. Mem. Internat. Platform Assn., Golden West Parader Assn., Friends of the Friendless, First Travel Club. Democrat. Baptist. Home: 1980 Santa Rosa Ave Pasadena CA 91104-1127

SMITH, MARCIA TAYLOR, special event planning and fundraising consultant; b. Salt Lake City, Jan. 13, 1954; d. John Ralph and Sue (Taylor) S. Student, Chapman Coll., 1973, Middlebury Coll., 1973, Bennington Coll., 1974-75; BA in Humanities, New Coll. of Calif., 1984. Asst. dir. humanities dept. and vis. artist program San Francisco Art Inst., 1980-84; dir. Art Quest New Mus. Contemporary Art, N.Y.C., 1984-86; dir. Stephen Haller Fine Art, N.Y.C., 1987-88; advt. dir. Contemporanea Internat. Art Mag., N.Y.C., 1988-91; spl. events coord./spl. projects mgr. U. Art Mus. and Pacific Film Archive, Berkeley, Calif., 1991-92; acting donor rels. mgr. Exploratorium, San Francisco, 1993; spl. events mgr. San Jose (Calif.) Mus. Art, 1993—; v.p. Ann Bennett & Assocs., San Francisco; spl. projects cons. Bobst Libr., NYU, N.Y.C., 1984-85. Guest curator, coord. Fashion Moda West, 1982 (award 1984); assoc. curator Myth and History at Work, Mus. Hispanic Art, N.Y.C., 1985; contbr. photographs to Appearances mag. Union steward local 3 AFL-CIO, 1982-84. Mem. Nat. Soc. Fundraising Execs., No. Calif. Event Profls., Smart Group (chair 1982-84), Dolphin Club.

SMITH, MARILYN JEAN, administrative analyst; b. Salt Lake City, June 2, 1968; d. Dee Grant and Janet Irene (Smith) Laws; m. Steve Vernon Smith, Dec. 28, 1985; children: Christopher Grant, Daniel Steven. AS, Coll. Ea. Utah, 1988; BS in Polit. Sci., Weber State U., 1990; postgrad., U. Utah. Legis. intern Utah State Legislature, Salt Lake City, 1989; planning intern Layton (Utah) City Corp., 1989-90; rsch. and planning analyst Salt Lake County Commn., Salt Lake City, 1990-92, mgmt. analyst, 1992-95; adminstrv. analyst Davis County Commn., Farmington, Utah, 1995—. Candidate Utah State House Dist. 11, Weber/Davis Counties, 1994; co-chair Caring for Kids Parent Adv. Bd., Salt Lake City, 1991-94; active Roosevelt PTA, Washington Terrace, Utah, 1992—, Citizen Budget Com., Washington Terrace, 1993. Scholar Mt. Am. CU/UPEA, 1992. Mem. Am. Soc. for Pub. Adminstrs., Am. Polit. Sci. Assn., Weber State Alumni Assn. (exec. coun.), Pi Sigma Alpha, Pi Gamma Mu. Democrat. Mormon. Home: 228 E 5000 S Ogden UT 84405-6420 Office: Davis County Courthouse PO Box 618 Farmington UT 84025

SMITH, MARILYN NOELTNER, science educator, consultant; b. Los Angeles, Feb. 14, 1933; d. Clarence Frederick and Gertrude Bertha (Smith) Noeltner; m. Edward Christopher Smith, Sept. 11, 1971. BA, Marymount Coll., 1957; MA, U. Notre Dame, 1966; MS, Boston Coll., 1969. Cert. tchr.; cert. community coll. tchr., Calif.; cert. adminstr., Calif. Tchr., chmn. sci. dept. Marymount High Sch., Santa Barbara, Calif., 1954-57, Los Angeles, 1957-58, 69-79; tchr., chmn. sci. and math. depts. Marymount High Sch., Palos Verdes, Calif., 1959-69; tchr., chmn. math. dept. Corvallis High Sch., Studio City, Calif., 1958-59; instr. tchr. tng. Marymount-Loyola U., Los Angeles, 1965-71, instr. freshman interdisciplinary program, 1970-71; tchr. math. Santa Monica (Calif.) High Sch., 1971-72; instr. math., chemistry, physics Santa Monica Coll., 1971—; tchr. sci. Beverly Vista Sch., Beverly Hills, Calif., 1972—; cons. Calif. State Sci. Framework Revision Com., Los Angeles, 1975; chmn. NASA Youth Sci. Congress, Pasadena, Calif., 1968-69, Hawaii, 1969-70; participant NASA Educators Conf. Jupiter Mission, Ames Research, San Francisco, 1973, NASA Educators Conf. Viking-Mars Ames Project, San Francisco, 1976-77, NASA Landsat Conf., Edward's AFB, Calif., 1978, NASA Uranus Mission, Pasadena, Calif., 1986, NASA Uranus-Voyager Mission, Pasadena, 1989, NASA Neptune-Voyager Mission, Pasadena, 1989; mem. test scoring com. Calif. Learning Assessment System, U. Santa Barbara, 1993, writing com. Trainers Manual, 1993. Author articles, books and computer progs. on space and physics including NASA Voyager-Uranus Sci. Symposium for Educators, 1989, NASA Voyager 2 Neptune Encounter Conf., 1989, others. Sponsor Social Svc. Club, Palos Verdes, 1959-69, moderator, sponsor ARC Youth Svc. Chmn., Beverly Hills, 1974-77, judge L.A. County Sci. Fair, 1969—, mem. blue ribbon com. NATAS, 1971—; bd. dirs. Children First, Beverly Hills, 1990-91; vol. sch. initiative, Beverly Hills, 1989-90; mem. steering com. on tech. Beverly Vista Sch., 1994-95. Recipient Commendation in Teaching cert. Am. Soc. Microbiology, 1962, Salute to Edn. award So. Calif. Industry Edn. Council, 1962, Outstanding Teaching citation Cons. Engrs. Assn. Calif., 1967, Cert. Honor, Silver Plaque Westinghouse Sci. Talent Search, 1963-68, Tchr. award Ford-Future Scientists of Am., 1968, Biomed. award Com. Advance Sci. Tng., 1971, Outstanding Tchr. award Los Angeles County Sci. Fair Com., 1975-76, Contbns. to Youth Service citation ARC, 1976-77, Outstanding Tchr. award Kiwanis Club Beverly Hills, 1987, NAST Pres'. award, 1990, Woman of Yr. award, 1990, cert. appreciation Profl. Leadership and Support for Advancing Sci. Edn. Calif. Dept. Edn., 1992, 93. Mem. We. Assn. Schs. and Colls. (vis. com. 1968, writing com. 1969—), Assn. Advancement Biomed. Edn. (pres. 1970-71), 1st Internat. Sci. Tchrs. Conf. (presider, evaluator 1977), Nat. Sci. Tchrs. Assn. (presider, evaluator 1976, chmn. contributed papers com. 1977-78, presenter 1990), Beverly Hills Edn. Assn.(pres. faculty coun. 1980-81, 85-86, sch. rep. 1990—), Chemist's Club, Calif. Statewide Math. Adv. Com., So. Calif. Industry Edn. Council, Calif. Assn. Chemistry Tchrs. (program chmn. 1960), Calif. Sci. Tchrs. Assn., Am. Chem. Soc., AAAS, South Bay Math. League (sec. 1967-68, pres. 1968-69, 72, 1969-70), Calif. Math. Council, Nat. Assn. Biology Tchrs. Republican. Roman Catholic. Home: 3934 Sapphire Dr Encino CA 91436-3635 Office: Beverly Vista Sch 200 S Elm Dr Beverly Hills CA 90212-4011

SMITH, MARK LEE, architect; b. L.A., Nov. 16, 1957; s. Selma (Moidel) Smith. BA in History of Architecture, UCLA, 1978, MA in Architecture, 1980. Registered architect Calif., Nev., Oreg., Wash., Tenn., Colo. Designer, drafter John B. Ferguson and Assocs., L.A., 1976-83, architect, 1983; pvt. practice architecture L.A., 1984—; mem. Los Angeles County Archtl. Evaluation Bd., 1990—. Contbr. articles to profl. jours. Bd. govs. UCLA John Wooden Ctr., 1978-80. Regents scholar, U. Calif., Berkeley, UCLA, 1975-78; UCLA Grad. Sch. Architecture Rsch. fellow, 1979-80. Mem. AIA (treas. San Fernando Valley chpt. 1986, bd. dirs. 1986—, v.p. 1987, pres. 1988, Design award 1988, 89, 90, 91, chmn. Design awards 1994, bd. dirs. Calif. coun. 1989-94, v.p. 1991-94, chmn. continuing edn. 1991-93, chmn. 1992 conf.), Phi Beta Kappa. Office: 18340 Ventura Blvd Ste 225 Tarzana CA 91356-4234

SMITH, MARTIN BERNHARD, journalist; b. San Francisco, Apr. 20, 1930; s. John Edgar and Anna Sophie (Thorsen) S.; m. Joan Lovat Muller, Apr. 25, 1953; children: Catherine Joan, Karen Anne. AB, U. Calif., Berkeley, 1952, M Journalism, 1968. Reporter, city editor Modesto (Calif.) Bee, 1957-64; reporter, mng. editor Sacramento Bee, 1964-75; polit. editor, columnist McClatchy Newspapers, Sacramento, 1975-92; ret., 1992. Episcopalian.

SMITH, MARTYN THOMAS, toxicology educator; b. Lincoln, U.K., Aug. 17, 1955; came to the U.S., 1982; s. Ronald Vernon and Doris May (Harman) S.; children: Shona Claire, Paul Anthony. BSc in Biology with honors, U. London, 1977, PhD in Biochemistry, 1980. Post-doctoral rschr. Karoliniska Inst., Stockholm, Sweden, 1980-81; tchg. fellow Sch. Pharmacy, U. London, 1981-82; asst. prof. U. Calif., Berkeley, 1982-87, assoc. prof., 1987-92, prof., 1992—, head divsn. environ. health, 1993—; dir. superfund rsch. program U. Calif., Berkeley, 1987—; pvt. practice as cons. in toxicology, Berkeley, 1983-94; staff scientist Lawrence Berkeley Lab., 1988—. Contbr. chpts. to books and articles to profl. jours. Grantee NIH, 1982—. Mem. Soc. Toxicology (councillor 1991-92), Genetic and Environ. Toxicology Assn. (pres. 1989). Democrat. Office: Sch Pub Health Univ Calif Berkeley CA 94720-7360

SMITH, MARVIN ARTELL, biochemistry educator; b. Ogden, Utah, Apr. 8, 1926; s. Ariel Tucker and Mary Josephine (Evans) S; m. Grace Marie Warnick Smith, Aug. 8, 1960; children: Marie, Lynne, Charles, Conrad, Mark, Kyle, Leslie, Matthew. BS, Utah State U., 1969; MS, U. Wis., 1962, PhD, 1964. Post-doctoral fellow chem. dept. NYU Med. Ctr., 1964-66; asst. prof. chem. dept. Brigham Young U., 1966, assoc. prof., 1969; vis. scientist, special fellow, dept. chem. and biophysics U. Calif., Davis, 1972-73, Donald F. Jones rsch. fellow, 1972-73; vis. prof. dept. biochemistry Kuwait U., Kuwait, 1978-80; vis. scientistInst. Plant Physiology Biol. Rsch. Ctr. Hungarian Acad. Scis., Szeged, Hungary, 1986-87; vis. prof.dept. physiology Carlsberg Lab., Copenhagen, Denmark, 1990-91; vis. sci. Institut fü Pflanzen Genetik und Kulturpflanzenforschung, Gatersleben, Germany, 1994-95; prof. of biochemistry Brigham Young U., Provo, 1974—; sci. Union Carbide, Buffalo, N.Y., Summer, 1964; vis. sci. dept. plant genetics Weizman Inst. Scis., Israel, Summer. Contbr. 30 articles to profl. jours. Scoutmaster, explorer, adv., cubmaster Boy Scouts Am., Provo, Utah, 1973-92; chmn. Edgemont Neighborhood, Provo, Utah, 1993, 94. Mem. Am Soc. Biochemistry and Molecular Biology, AAAS, Internat. Soc. Plant Molecular Biology, Sigma Xi. LDS ch. Office: Brigham Young U Dept Chem Provo UT 84602

SMITH, MARY OLIVIA, veterinary medicine educator; b. London, July 10, 1957; came to U.S., 1985; d. Francis William Gruyffyd and Margaret Mary (Sullivan) S. B. Vet. Medicine and Surgery, U. Edinburgh, Scotland, 1980; PhD, U. Calif., Davis, 1992. Diplomate Am. Coll. Veterinary Internal Medicine. Vet. practitioner Eng., 1980-85; resident in vet. neurology U. Calif., Davis, 1985-87, adj. instr. vet. anatomy, 1987-89, postgrad. rschr., 1989-92; asst. prof. Colo. State U., Fort Collins, 1992—. Contbr. articles to Am. Jour. Pathology, Am. Jour. Vet. Rsch. and other sci. jours. Mem. Am. Vet. Med. Assn., Royal Coll. Vet. Surgeons, Brit. Small Animal Vet. Assn., Brit. Goat Vet. Assn. Office: Colo State U Coll Vet Medicine Dept Clin Scis Fort Collins CO 80523

SMITH, MAUREEN MCBRIDE, chemist; b. Santa Monica, Calif., Mar. 4, 1952; d. Clayton Laird McBride and Luella (Sullivan) Boudreau; step-father Henry A Boudreau; m. Gary Howard Cothran, July 27, 1974 (div. Apr. 1982); m. Guy Gordon Smith, Feb. 12, 1983; stepchildren: Keri Lynn, Scott Allen. BS magna cum laude, Calif. State Coll., San Bernardino, 1978, MS, 1993. Analytical chemist Chalco Engring., Edwards AFB, Calif., 1978-79, 82; microbiol. lab. tech. AVEK Water Agy., Quartz Hill, Calif., 1979-81, chemist, lab. mgr., 1982—; instr. Antelope Valley Coll., Lancaster Calif., 1980-82. Mem. AAAS, Am. Chem. Soc. Office: Antelope Valley E Kern Water Agy PO Box 3176 Quartz Hill CA 93586-0176

SMITH, MICHAEL, biochemistry educator; b. Blackpool, Eng., Apr. 26, 1932. BSc, U. Manchester, Eng., 1953, PhD, 1956. Fellow B.C. Rsch. Coun., 1956-60; rsch. assoc. Inst. Enzyme Rsch., U. Wis., 1960-61; head chem. sect. Vancouver Lab. Fisheries Rsch. Bd. Can., 1961-66; med. rsch. assoc. Med. Rsch. Coun. Can., 1966-71, career investigator, 1971—; assoc. prof. biochem. U. B.C., Vancouver, 1966-70, prof., 1970—, u. prof., 1993—, Univ. prof., 1994—, Peter Wall disting. prof. biotech., 1994—;, 1993—. Recipient Gairdner Found. Internat. award, 1986, Nobel Prize in Chemistry, 1993. Fellow Chem Inst. Can., Royal Soc. (London), Royal Soc. Can., Royal Soc. Chemistry; mem. Sigma Xi, Order of British Columbia, Companion of the Order of Can. Home: 303-2466 W 3d Ave, Vancouver, BC Canada V6K 1L8 Office: U BC Biotech Lab, 6174 University Blvd, Vancouver, BC Canada V6T 1Z3

SMITH, MICHAEL C. B., restaurant executive; b. Stanmore, Eng., Feb. 28, 1955; arrived in Can., 1987; s. John Hilary and Isobel Mary (Bowker) S. M in Bus. Edn., Cranfield Bus. Sch., Eng., 1983. Restaurant mgr. Foxy Lady Tavern, Perth, Australia, 1977-78; ptnr. Dinez Chez-Vous, Perth, 1978-79; mgr. Wendy's Restaurants, London, 1980-82; mktg. svc. mgr. Whitbread Retail Div., Luton, Eng., 1983-84; gen. mgr. Quick Hamburger Restaurants, London, 1984-87; v.p. mktg. Beefeater Steak Houses, Dunstable, Eng., 1987; pres., chief exec. officer Keg Restaurants Ltd., Vancouver, B.C., Can., 1987—. Mem. Nat. Restaurant Assn., Can. Restaurant and Foodsvcs. Assn. (bd. dirs. 1988—), Vancouver Bd. Trade. Office: Keg Restaurants Ltd, 150-10760 Shellbridge Way, Richmond, BC Canada V6X 3H1

SMITH, MICHAEL STEVEN, data processing executive; b. San Antonio, May 7, 1956; s. Columbus and Mary Patricia (Leahy) S.; m. Lynda M. Gillen, July 30, 1992. Student, San Bernardino Valley (Calif.) Coll., 1974-76, AS in Computer Scis., 1983; student, L.A. Community Coll., 1978-79, U. Md., 1980-81, City Colls. Chgo., 1980-81. Communications cons. Telephone Products Corp., San Bernardino, 1974-76; student svcs. advisor computer scis. lab. San Bernardino Valley Coll., 1982-83; assoc. programmer Aerojet ElectroSystems Corp., Azusa, Calif., 1983-85; mgr. data processing. Bonita Unified Sch. Dist., San Dimas, Calif., 1985—, dir. computer info. svcs., 1989—; analyst computer mktg. Pentamation Enterprises, Bethelehem, Pa., 1987—; cons. computer systems San Dimas, 1985—. With USN, 1976-82. Mem. Assn. for Computing Machinery, Digital Equipment Computer Users Soc., Calif. Assn. Sch. Bus. Ofcls., Calif. Ednl. Data Processing Assn. Office: 115 W Allen Ave San Dimas CA 91773-1437

SMITH, MILTON JAY, fundraising executive; b. Idaho Falls, ID, June 5, 1949; s. Horace B. Smith and Afton Jane (Cole) Murphy; children: Cami, Lisa, Jennifer. BA in Interpersonal and Mass Comm., Boise State U., 1975; MA in Higher Edn. Adminstrn., Goddard Coll., 1979. Devel. officer Coll. So. Idaho, Twin Falls, 1976-83; pres. The Med. Ctr. Found. Pocatello (Idaho) Regional Med. Ctr., 1983-86; pres. Northbay Healthcare Found., Fairfield, Calif., 1986-92, v.p. pub. affairs, 1987-92; exec. v.p. Mercy Found., Rancho Cordova, Calif., 1992—. Sgt. USMC, 1968-70, Vietnam. Fellow Assn. for Healthcare Philanthropy (regional dir. internat. bd. dirs. 1990); mem. Fairfield C. of C. (bd. dirs. 1990-92). Office: Mercy Found # 160 10540 White Rock Rd Rancho Cordova CA 95670-7984

SMITH, NATHAN MCKAY, library and information sciences educator; b. Wendell, Idaho, Apr. 22, 1935; s. M. Blair and Vaunda H. (Hawkes) S.; m. Joyce A. Carman, July 5, 1953; children: Nathan M., Jeffrey M., Pamela J., Russell A., Kristen E. BS in Secondary Edn., Eastern Oreg. Coll., 1961; MS in Gen. Sci., Oreg. State U., 1965; MLS, Brigham Young U., 1969, PhD in Zoology, 1972. Tchr. sci. Dalles Jr. High Sch., The Dalles, Oreg., 1961-64; asst. sci. librarian Brigham Young U., Provo, Utah, 1968, life sci. librarian, 1970-73; prof. Sch. Library and Info. Sci., Brigham Young U., Provo, Utah, 1973-82, dir., 1982-93, life sci. libr., 1993—; cons. Weber County Library, Ogden, Utah, 1980—; back issues sec. Herpetologists League, 1976-81. Served to sgt. USAF, 1953-57. Yr. scholar NSF Acad., 1964; fellow NDEA Title IV, 1969; recipient research award Assn. Library and Info. Sci. Edn., 1983. Mem. ALA (councilor legis. council), Assn. Library Info. Sci. Edn., Mountain Plains Library Assn., Utah Library Assn. (exec. bd., pres.), N. Am. Soc. Adlerian Psychology, Phi Kappa Phi, Sigma Xi, Beta Phi Mu. Mem. LDS Ch. Home: 1606 Locust Ln Provo UT 84604-2806 Office: Brigham Young U Bean Mus Provo UT 84602

SMITH, NINA MARIA, mental health nurse, administrator, consultant; b. Bethesda, Md., July 15, 1950; d. Albert Henry and Magdalena (Portusach) Geiken; m. Robert John Smith, Nov. 18, 1972; children: Cara Anne, Rachel Marie. ADN, Tarrant County Jr. Coll., 1984; BA in Psychology, U. Md., 1972; MEd, Tex. Christian U., 1990. Charge nurse Psychiat. Inst. Ft. Worth; adolescent program coord. Community Psychiat. Ctr. Oak Bend, Ft. Worth; adminstr. Life Ctrs., Ft. Worth; dir. nursing Community Psychiat.

Ctr. Oak Bend, Ft. Worth; adminstr. Total Home Health Care, Ft. Worth; dir. clin. svcs. Mountain Crest Hosp., Ft. Collins, Colo., 1992-94; nat. dir. psychiat. home svcs. Western Med. Svcs., Ft. Collins, 1994—; mem. psychiat. symposium planning com. U. Tex., Arlington. Mem. Am. Psychiat. Nurses Assn., Am. Assn. Partial Hosps., Partial Hosp. Assn. Colo. (pres. 1994-95). Home: 1430 Hilburn Dr Fort Collins CO 80526-3425

SMITH, OTTO J. M., electrical engineering educator; b. Urbana, Ill., Aug. 6, 1917; s. Otto Mitchell and Mary Catherine (Carr) S.; m. Phyllis P. Sterling, Sept. 3, 1941; children: Candace B., Otto J.A., Sterling M., Stanford D. BS in Chemistry, Okla. State U., 1938; BSEE, U. Okla., 1938; PhDEE, Stanford U., 1941. Registered profl. engr., Calif. Instr. elec. engring. Tufts U., Medford, Mass., 1941-43; asst. prof. elec. engring. Denver U., 1943-44; research engr. Westinghouse Research Labs., Forest Hills, Pa., 1944-46; sr. research fellow econs. Monash U., Melbourne, Australia, 1966-67; prof. elec. engr. U. Calif., Berkeley, 1947—; chief engr. Smith and Sun, Berkeley, 1976—. Author: Feedback Control Systems, 1958; contbr. articles to profl. jours.; patentee in field. Dist. commr. Boy Scouts Am., Berkeley, 1949-53; trustee South Campus Community Ministry, Berkeley, 1968-70, Wesley Found., Berkeley, 1969-72. Guggenheim fellow, 1960. Fellow AAAS, IEEE; mem. Soc. Social Responsibility Engring., Am. Solar Energy Soc., Internat. Solar Energy Soc., Am. Wind Energy Assn., Calif. Writer's Club (bd. dirs.). Democrat. Methodist. Club: Berkeley City Commons (pres. 1963). Home: 612 Euclid Ave Berkeley CA 94708-1332 Office: U Calif Dept Elec Engr & Computer Scis Berkeley CA 94720

SMITH, PATRICIA JACQULINE, marketing executive; b. Orange, N.J., June 13, 1944; d. Michael Joseph and Helen Francis (Costello) S. BS, U. Md., 1967. Field dir. Colgate Palmolive Co., N.Y.C., 1967-71; account exec. Foote Cone & Belding, N.Y.C., 1971-72; dir. regional sales, dir. ARA Services, Inc., Phila., 1973-76; dir. federally funded programs Ogden Food Service, Boston, 1976-79; v.p. Smith Tool Co., Manesquan, N.J., 1979-84; chmn., CEO Hygolet Metro, Inc., New Canaan, Conn., 1984-87; mktg. cons. Smith Mktg. Svcs., La Jolla, Calif., 1988—; bd. dirs. Smith Tool Co., Manesquan, N.J., Shore Precision, Inc., Manesquan, P.J. Smith Interiors, N.Y.C., Hygolet Metro Inc., New Canaan, Conn.; ptnr. La Jolla Playhouse. Bd. dirs., treas. Big Sister League, San Diego; mem. exec. com. Multiple Sclerosis Brunch Soc.; ptnr. La Jolla Playhouse. Mem. Women in Sales, Nat. Assn. Profl. Saleswomen, Bus. and Profl. Women's Club (N.Y.). Republican. Home: 5537 Bellevue Ave La Jolla CA 92037-7627

SMITH, PEGGY ANNE, fundraising executive; b. San Francisco, May 1, 1954; d. Howard Carlton and Margaret Alice (Strauss) S. BA with honors, U. Calif., Santa Cruz, 1976. Bilingual interviewer U. Mich Inst. for Survey Rsch., Ann Arbor, 1976-77; exec. asst. to pres. Nat. Assn. for Hispanic Elderly, L.A., 1978-92; dir. devel. and cmty. rels. Goodwill Industries of So. Calif., L.A., 1992—. Editor: A National Study to Assess the Service Needs of Hispanic Elderly, 1980; co-editor: A National Study of Hispanic Support Systems and the Chronically Ill Older Hispanic, 1982. Mem. Nat. Assn. Fund Raising Execs. (mem. nat. philanthropy day com., bd. dirs., Great L.A. chpt. Pres.'s award 1994), Nat. Notary Assn., Latin Bus. Assn. Roman Catholic. Office: Goodwill Industies So Calif 342 N San Fernando Rd Los Angeles CA 90031

SMITH, PRESTON GIBSON, management consultant, engineering executive; b. Long Beach, Calif., Aug. 4, 1941; s. Preston Gibson and Arlene Frances (Lamar) S.; m. Judy Anne Conkling, Dec. 18, 1966; children: Christina, Marjorie. BSME magna cum laude, U. So. Calif., 1963, MSME, 1964; PhD, Stanford U., 1967. Cert. mgmt. cons. Mem. tech. staff Bell Telephone Labs., Washington, 1967-71; group leader Gen. Motors Rsch. Labs., Warren, Mich., 1971-76; program mgr. Ensco, Inc., Springfield, Va., 1976-80; project leader Inst. for Def. Analysis, Alexandria, Va., 1980-84; mgr. corp. tech. Emhart Corp., Farmington, Conn., 1984-86; pres. New Product Dynamics, Portland, Oreg., 1986—; instr. U. Rochester, 1992—, Portland State U., 1995—. Author: Developing Products in Half the Time; contbr. articles to mags., jours. Mem. ASME, Product Devel. and Mgmt. Assn., Inst. Mgmt. Cons. (pres. New Eng. chpt.), Sigma Xi, Phi Kappa Phi, Tau Beta Pi. Office: New Product Dynamics 3493 NW Thurman St Portland OR 97210-1283

SMITH, RALPH EARL, virologist; b. Yuma, Colo., May 10, 1940; s. Robert C. and Esther C. (Schwarz) S.; m. Sheila L. Kondy, Aug. 29, 1961 (div. 1986); 1 child, Andrea Denise; m. Janet M. Keller, 1988. BS, Colo. State U., 1961; PhD, U. Colo., 1968. Registered microbiologist Am. Soc. Clin. Pathologists. Postdoctoral fellow Duke U. Med. Ctr., Durham, N.C., 1968-70, asst. prof., 1970-74, assoc. prof., 1974-80, prof. virology, 1980-82; prof., head dept. microbiology Colo. State U., Ft. Collins, 1983-88, prof. microbiology, assoc. v.p. rsch., 1989—, interim v.p. rsch., 1990-91, prof. microbiology, assoc. v.p. rsch., 1991—; cons. Bellco Glass Co., Vineland, N.J., 1976-80, Proctor & Gamble Co., Cin., 1985-86, Schering Plough Corp., Bloomfield, N.J., 1987-89. Contbr. articles to profl. jours.; patentee in field. Bd. dirs. Colo. Ctr. for Environ. Mgmt., v.p. for rsch.; mem. pollution prevention adv. bd. Colo. Dept. Pub. Health and Environment; mem. Rocky Mountain U. Consortium on Environ. Restoration, Environ. Inst. Rocky Flats; asst. scoutmaster Boy Scouts Am., Durham, 1972-82, com. mem., Ft. Collins, 1986-91; mem. adminstrv. bd. 1st United Meth. Ch., Ft. Collins. Eleanor Roosevelt fellow Internat. Union Against Cancer 1978-79. Mem. AAAS, Am. Soc. Microbiology, N.Y. Acad. Scis., Am. Soc. Virology, Am. Assn. Immunologists, Am. Assn. Avian Pathologists, Am. Assn. Cancer Rsch., Gamma Sigma Delta. Democrat. Methodist. Home: 2406 Creekwood Dr Fort Collins CO 80525-2034 Office: Colo State U VP Rsch Fort Collins CO 80523

SMITH, RAYMOND EDWARD, health care administrator; b. Freeport, N.Y., June 17, 1932; s. Jerry Edward and Madelyn Holman (Jones) S.; B.S. in Edn., Temple U., 1953; M.H.A., Baylor U., 1966; m. Lena Kathryn Jernigan Hughes, Oct. 28, 1983; children: Douglas, Ronald, Kevin, Doris Jean, Raymond. Commd. 2d lt. U.S. Army, 1953, advanced through grades to lt. col., 1973; helicopter ambulance pilot, 1953-63; comdr. helicopter ambulance units, Korea, 1955, Fed. Republic of Germany, 1961; various hosp. adminstrv. assignments, 1963-73; personnel dir. Valley Forge (Pa.) Gen. Hosp., 1966; adminstr. evacuation hosp., Vietnam, 1967; dep. insp. Walter Reed Gen. Hosp., Washington, 1970; dir. personnel div. Office of Army Surgeon Gen., Washington, 1971-73, ret., 1973; adminstr. Health Care Centers, Phila. Coll. Osteo. Medicine, 1974-76; dir. bur. hosps. Pa. Dept. Health, Harrisburg, 1976-79; contract mgr. Blue Cross of Calif., San Diego, 1979-88, Community Care Network, San Diego, 1989—. Decorated Bronze Star, Legion of Merit. Mem. Am. Hosp. Assn., Am. Legion, Ret. Officers Assn., Kappa Alpha Psi. Episcopalian. Club: Masons. Home: 7630 Lake Adlon Dr San Diego CA 92119-2518 Office: Community Care Network 5251 Viewridge Ct San Diego CA 92123-1646

SMITH, RAYMOND VICTOR, paper products manufacturing executive; b. Vancouver, B.C., Can., Apr. 28, 1926; s. Stanley Victor and Kathryn Stewart (Hunter) S.; m. Marilyn Joyce Meldrum, Oct. 17, 1947; children—Vicki, Kathi, Stan. Student, U. B.C., Banff Sch. Advanced Mgmt.; student Advanced Mgmt. Program, Harvard U. Trumpeter Dal Richards Band, 1942; ptnr. Warren McCuish Mens' Clothiers, 1947; sales rep. Vancouver Paper Box, 1949-54; with Home Oil Distbrs., 1954-57; domestic rep. kraft paper and board sales MacMillan Bloedel Ltd., 1957-67; asst. mgr. Kraft Paper & Board Sales, 1961-65; newsprint rep. Powell River-Alberni Sales Corp., Pasadena, Calif., 1965-67; mgr. Powell River-Alberni Sales Corp., Pasadena, 1967-68; mgr. supply control and sales adminstrn. MacMillan Bloedel Ltd., Vancouver, 1968-70, gen. mgr., 1970-71, v.p. mktg. paper and pulp, 1971-73, v.p., gen. mgr. newsprint, 1973-77, group v.p. pulp and paper, 1977-79, sr. v.p. pulp and paper, 1979-80, chief oper. officer, 1980-83, pres., 1980-90, chief exec. officer, 1983-90, chmn. bd., 1991—; bd. dirs. Can. Imperial Bank of Commerce. Served with Can. Army, 1944. Clubs: Capilano Golf and Country, Vancouver. Office: MacMillan Bloedel Ltd, 925 W Georgia St, Vancouver, BC Canada V6C 3L2

SMITH, RICHARD, construction executive; b. 1927. Exec. v.p., sec., cfo. Pacific Architects Engrs. Inc., L.A., 1970—. Office: Pacific Architects Engrs Inc 1111 W 6th St Bldg 4 Los Angeles CA 90017-1800*

SMITH, RICHARD BOWEN, retired national park superintendent; b. Grandville, Mich., Mar. 8, 1938; s. William Jr. and Mary Elizabeth (Bowen) S.; m. Katherine Theresa Short, Sept. 21, 1980. BA in History, Albion Coll., 1960; MA in English, Mich. State U., 1967. Tchr. Grand Rapids (Mich.) Jr. High Sch., 1960-66; vol. Peace Corps, Asuncion, Paraguay, 1968-70; ranger Nat. Park Service, Yosemite, Calif., 1971-76; ranger. instr. Nat. Park Service, Grand Canyon, Ariz., 1976-78; ranger, legis. specialist Nat. Park Service, Washington, 1978-80; asst. supt. Nat. Park Service, Everglades, Fla., 1980-83; assoc. regional dir. ops. Nat. Park Service, Phila., 1984-86; supt. Nat. Park Service, Carlsbad Caverns, N.Mex., 1986-88; assoc. regional dir. ops. Nat. Park Service, Santa Fe, 1988-89, assoc. regional dir. resources mgmt., 1990-94; cons. on protected area mgmt. in L.Am., 1994—; temporary supt. Yellowstone Nat. Park, 1994—. Recipient Meritorious Svc. award Dept. of Interior, 1992. Home: 2 Roadrunner Trl Placitas NM 87043-9424

SMITH, RICHARD D., supermarkets and drug stores executive; b. 1954. With Smiths Food & Drugs Ctrs. Inc., 1971—, formerly exec. v.p., pres., chief exec. oper. officer. Office: Smith's Mgmt Corp 1550 S Redwood Rd Salt Lake City UT 84104-5105

SMITH, ROBERT BRUCE, former security consultant, retired army officer; b. De Quincy, La., Apr. 22, 1920; s. Malcolm Monard and Jewell (Perkins) S.; m. Gladys Opal Borel, Feb. 22, 1941; children: Susan, Richard, Bruce. B.J., La. State U., 1941; grad., Command and Gen. Staff Coll., 1951-52, Army War Coll., 1958-59. Commd. 2d lt. U.S. Army, 1941, advanced through grades to maj. gen., 1969; plans and ops. officer 83d Div. Arty., Europe, 1943-45; personnel officer Philippine-Ryukyus Command, Manila, 1947-49; prof. mil. sci. and tactics ROTC, Lanier High Sch., Macon, Ga., 1949-51; chief res. officers sect., procurement br. Dept. Army, 1952-55; chief troop info. Office Chief Info., Dept. Army, 1962-63, dep. chief info., 1968-69; comdg. officer 8th F.A. Bn., 25th Inf. Div., Hawaii, 1955-56; G-1 25th Inf. Div. and U.S. Army Hawaii, Hawaii, 1956-58; mem. staff, faculty Command and Gen. Staff Coll., Fort Leavenworth, Kans., 1959-62; chief Alt. Nat. Mil. Command Center, Fort Ritchie, Md., 1963-64; dep. dir. ops. Office Joint Chiefs of Staff, 1964-65; asst. div. comdr. 7th Inf. Div., Korea, 1965-66; dep. comdt. Army War Coll., Carlisle, Pa., 1966-68; dep. comdg. gen. Ryukyus Islands, 1969-72, 6th U.S. Army, Presidio of San Francisco, 1972-73; ret. active duty, 1973; reporter, news editor Lake Charles (La.), 1946-47; region adminstrv. mgr. Burns Security Service, Oakland, Calif., 1974-76; ptnr. constrn. co. Napa, Calif., 1976-77, Burns Security Service, 1978-81; now ret.; dir. 1st Am. Title Co., Napa, Calif., 1988-92. Trustee Queen of Valley Hosp. Found., 1987-89; mem. Nat. coun. Boy Scouts Am., 1969-70; pres. Silverado Property Owners Assn., Inc., 1990-92. Decorated D.S.M. with oak leaf cluster, Legion of Merit with 2 oak leaf clusters, Bronze Star with oak leaf cluster. Club: Silverado Country (Napa, Calif.). Home: 350 St Andrews Dr Napa CA 94558-1544

SMITH, ROBERT HAMIL, author, fund raiser; b. Oak Park, Ill., Nov. 8, 1927; s. Henry Garfield and Mary Ellen (Hamil) S.; student U. Denver, 1946-48, LLB, 1953, JD, 1960; m. Mary Helen Kingsley, Dec. 29, 1948; children: David H., Mark K., Steven H., Rebecca Anne. Dep. clk. County Ct., City and County of Denver, 1948-53; with Colo. Ins. Group, 1953-59; mgr. claims dept. R.H. Smith & Assos., 1959-64; cons. Am. Bapt. Home Mission Soc., 1964-68; assoc. dir. devel. Ill. Wesleyan U., 1968-69; asst. to chancellor U. Calif., San Diego, 1969-77; exec. dir. devel. Scripps Clinic and Research Found., La Jolla, Calif., 1977-82, v.p. devel., 1982-88; pres. Cartographic Enterprises, 1981—; owner C Books, 1981; bd. dirs. Nat. Com. on Planned Giving, 1990-94; fund raising cons. deferred giving. Served with USNR, 1945. Mem. Nat. Soc. Fund Raising Execs., Internat. Yachting Fellowship of Rotarians (San Diego fleet comdr. 1979-81). Baptist. Club: Oceanside Yacht. Author: Guide to Harbors, Anchorages and Marinas So. and No. California edits., 1983, The Physician as a Fundraiser, 1984, Naval Inst. Guide to Maritime Museums in U.S./Canada, 1991, Smith's Guide to Maritime Museums U.S./Canada, 1993; pub. boating cruising guides for no. and so. Calif. and guides to maritime mus. Home: PO Box 2785 Del Mar CA 92014-5785 Office: R H Smith & Assocs PO Box 176 Del Mar CA 92014-0176

SMITH, ROBERT HENRY, economist; b. Detroit, Dec. 16, 1941; s. Henry A. and Patricia (Frolich) S.; m. Martha Eshelman, June 1970 (div. 1978); 1 child, Richard G. BA, Occidental Coll., 1963; PhD, U. Hawaii, 1986. Owner, mgr. RHS & Co., Honolulu, 1976—; mem. faculty U. Hawaii, Honolulu, 1984-86. Author: Balance of Payments in Developing Countries, 1986. 1st lt. U.S. Army, 1966-68. Mem. AAAS, Honolulu Club, Waikiki Yacht Club, Hawaii Yacht Club. Home: 3079 Pacific Heights Rd Honolulu HI 96813-1003 Office: RHS & Co PO Box 22490 Honolulu HI 96823-2490

SMITH, ROBERT LONDON, commissioner, retired air force officer, political scientist, educator; b. Alexandria, La., Oct. 13, 1919; s. Daniel Charleston and Lillie (Roberts) S.; m. Jewel Busch, Feb. 5, 1949; children: Jewel Diane, Robert London, Karl Busch. B.A., Coll. St. Joseph, 1954; M.A., U. Okla., 1955; Ph.D., Am. U., 1964. Commd. 2d lt. USAAF, 1941; advanced through grades to lt. col. USAF, 1961; various assignments in aircraft engring., command and logistics, 1941-60; rsch. logistics Hdqs. Office Aerospace Rsch., 1960-63; project sci., adminstr. postdoctoral rsch. program, asst. dir. NAS, Hdqs. Office Sci. Rsch., 1963-65; ret., 1965; asso. prof. polit. sci., head dept. eve. classes and corr. study U. Alaska, College, 1966-68, dean Coll. Bus., Econs. and Govt., 1968-70, prof., head dept. polit. sci., 1966-84, prof. emeritus, 1984—; commr. Alaska Dept. Health and Social Services, 1983—; mem. govt. panels and planning groups; dir. Arctic 1st Fed. Savs. & Loan Assn.; corporator Mt. McKinley Mut. Savs. Bank. Author: (with others) Squadron Adminstration, 1951; also publs. on nat. security and nat. def.; Contbr. to: (with others) The United Nations Peace University, 1965. Committeeman Western region Boy Scouts Am., 1968-73; mem. exec. bd. Midnight Sun council, 1973-74, committeeman-at-large nat. council, 1968—; mem. Alaska Gov.'s Employment Commn.; pres. United Service Orgn. Council, Fairbanks, Alaska; mem. active corps execs. SBA. Recipient Silver Beaver award Boy Scouts Am.; named Outstanding Prof. U. Alaska, 1975. Mem. Nat. Acad. Econs. and Polit. Sci., AAAS, Air Force Hist. Found., Nat. Inst. Social and Behavioral Scis., Nat. Inst. U.S. in World Affairs, Am. Polit. Sci. Assn., Assn. U.S. Army (bd. dirs. Polar Bear chpt.), Alaska C. of C. (edn. com.), Pi Gamma Mu, Pi Sigma Alpha. Roman Catholic. Club: Rotary. Home: Smithhaven 100 Goldizen Ave Fairbanks AK 99709-3634 also: Smithport 9994 Salcha Dr Salcha AK 99714-9624 also: Smithawaii Nani Kai Hale 73 N Kihei Rd Apt 607 Kihei HI 96753-8827 also: Costa Vida Unit #920-921, KM 4 456 Carr Apdo Postal 186, Puerto Vallarta Jalisco, Mexico

SMITH, ROBERT MICHAEL, lawyer; b. Boston, Nov. 4, 1940; s. Sydney and Minnie (Appel) S.; m. Catherine Kersey, Apr. 14, 1981 (dec. 1983). AB cum laude, Harvard Coll., 1962; diploma, Centro de Estudos de Espanol, Barcelona, 1963; MA in Internat. Affairs, Columbia U., 1964, MS in Journalism with high honors, 1965; JD, Yale U., 1975. Bar: Calif., N.Y., D.C., U.S. Supreme Ct. Intern in econ. devel. UN, Geneva, 1964; corres. Time Mag., N.Y.C., 1965-66, The N.Y. Times, Washington, 1968-72, 75-76; atty. Heller, Ehrman, White & McAuliffe, San Francisco, 1976-78; spl. asst. Office of Atty. Gen. of U.S., Washington, 1979-80; dir. Office Pub. Affairs U.S. Dept. Justice, Washington, 1979-80; mem. U.S. delegation Internat. Ct. of Justice, The Hague, 1980; asst. U.S. atty. No. Dist. Calif., San Francisco, 1981-82; counsel, sr. counsel to sr. litigation counsel Bank of Am. NT & SA, San Francisco, 1982-86; pvt. practice law San Francisco, 1988—; lectr. FBI Acad., Quantico, Va., 1980, Internat. Bankers Assn. Calif., 1994, Cmty. Bankers No. Calif., 1994, 95; judge Golden Medallion Broadcast Media awards State Bar of Calif., 1985; judge pro tem Mcpl. Ct. City and County of San Francisco, 1989—. Bd. editors Yale Law Jour., 1974-75; editor Litigation, jour. ABA litigation sect., 1978-81; mem. editl. adv. bd. Bancroft-Whitney, 1991-94; contbr. articles to profl. jours. Bd. dirs. Neighborhood Legal Assistance Found., San Francisco, 1985-87, Nob Hill Assn., San Francisco, 1985-93; bd. dirs., fin. com. St. Francis Found., San Francisco, 1993-94. 1st lt. inf., USAR, 1965-71. Recipient UPI Award for Newswriting, 1958; Harvard Coll. scholar, 1958-62, Fulbright scholar, 1962-63; Columbia U. Internat. fellow, 1964-65. Mem. ABA (corp. counsel com. 1986—, alternative dispute resolution sect. 1994—), Assn. Atty. Mediators (v.p. No. Calif. chpt. 1995), State Bar of Calif. (pub. affairs com. 1982-85, litigation sect. 1990—), Bar Assn. of San Francisco (bench-bar media com. 1985—, alternative dispute resolution com. 1994—), Assn. Bus. Trial Lawyers No. Calif., Assn. of Former U.S. Attys. No. Dist. Calif., Am. Arbitration Assn. (mem. comml. arbitration panel, No. Calif. adv. coun., mediator Am. Arbitration Ctr. for Mediation), Profl. Atty. Mediators, Cmty. Bds. of San Francisco (conciliator), German-Am. C. of C. West U.S., Harvard Club of San Francisco (bd. dirs. 1986-94, pres. 1992-94), Yale Club of San Francisco (bd. dirs. 1989-94), Soc. Profls. in Dispute Resolution (assoc. mem.), Columbia U. Alumni Club of No. Calif. (exec. com. 1978-92).

SMITH, ROBERT VICTOR, university administrator; b. Glendale, N.Y., Feb. 16, 1942; s. Robert Arthur and Marie Marlene (Florence) S. BS in Pharm. Sci., St. John's U., Jamaica, N.Y., 1963; MS in Pharm. Chemistry, U. Mich., 1964, PhD in Pharm. Chemistry, 1968. Asst. prof., then assoc. prof. U. Iowa, Iowa City, 1968-74; assoc. prof., asst. dir. U. Tex., Austin, 1974-77, area coordinator basic pharmaceutics, 1975-76, assoc. dir. Drug Dynamics Inst., 1977-78, dir. Drug Dynamics Inst., Coll. Pharmacy, 1979-85, James E. Bauerle Centennial prof. Coll. Pharmacy, 1983-85; prof., dean Coll. Pharmacy Wash. State U., Pullman, 1985-86, vice provost for research, dean Grad. Sch., 1987—; cons. E. R. Squibb, New Brunswick, N.J., 1979-82, Upjohn Co., Kalamazoo, Mich., 1982-85; external examiner U. Malaysia, Penang, 1981-82; mem. sci. adv. bd. Biodecision Labs., Pitts., 1985-86; Wash. Biotech. Found., 1989-90; mem. noms. com. Coun. Grad. Schs., Washington, 1990-91; accreditation evaluator Northwest Assn. Schs. and Colls., Seattle, 1991—; mem. exec. com. grad. deans African-Am. Inst., N.Y., 1992—. Author: Textbook of Biopharmaceutic Analysis, 1981, Graduate Research: A Guide for Students in the Sciences, 1990, Development and Management of University Research Groups, 1986. Bd. dirs. Wash. Tech. Ctr., 1990-92. Grantee NIH, 1974-83; fellow Acad. Pharm. Scis., 1981, Am. Assn. Pharm. Scientists, 1987; recipient Disting. Alumnus award Coll. Pharmacy U. Mich., 1990, Outstanding Svc. award Wash. State U., Grad. and Profl. Student Assn., 1993. Mem. Am. Assn. Colls. Pharmacy (chmn. research and grad. affairs com. 1983-84), U.S. Pharmacopeia (revision com. 1985-90), Acad. Pharm. Scis. (chmn., vice chmn. 1983-85, 90, Presdl. citation 1985), Wash. Rsch. Found. (bd. dirs. 1989—). Unitarian. Home: SE 570 Quar Ridge Dr Pullman WA 99163 Office: Grad Sch Wash State U Pullman WA 99164

SMITH, ROGER ALEXANDER, surgeon; b. Smithfield, N.C., Dec. 16, 1922; s. Roger Alexander and Alice (McGee) S,; m. Lillian Willms, Dec. 15, 1952 (div. Sept. 1967); children: Candyce, Frank, Terry, Jerry, Roger; m. Elena Vega Humildad, Oct. 17, 1971. Student, U. N.C., 1945; MD, Washington U., 1945-47. Diplomate Am. Bd. Neuroligical Surgery. Internship Mpls. General Hosp., 1948-49; general surgery residency VA Sawtelle Hosp., L.A., 1949-50; neurosurgery residency U. Ill., 1950-52; pvt. practice neurology & neurosurgery San Bernardino, Calif., 1953-77; asst. clinical prof. neurosurgery Loma Linda U. Medical Ctr., 1966; dir. neurosurgery San Bernardino County Medial Ctr., 1970-89; cons. in neurology Jerry L. Pettis Meml. Vets. Hosp., 1979-89, chief of neurosurgery, 1989-91, cons. in neurosurgery & neurology, 1991—; courtesy staff St. Bernardine's Hosp., 1953, San Bernardino Cmty. Hosp., 1953; instr. of neurosurgery Henry Ford Hosp., Detroit, 1953, instr. anatomy U. Mpls., 1948-49. Contbr. articles to profl. jours. With U.S. Army, 1956-58. Mem. Congress Neurological Surgeons, Calif. Assn. Neurological Surgeons, Western Fedn. of Neurological Surgeons, San Bernardino County Medical Soc., Calif. Medical Soc., Royal Soc. Medicine. Home: 1865 Dale Ln San Bernardino CA 92404-1001 Office: 1384 N Waterman Ave San Bernardino CA 92404-5313

SMITH, SALLYE WRYE, librarian; b. Birmingham, Ala., Nov. 11, 1923; d. William Florin and Margaret (Howard) Wrye; m. Stuart Werner Smith, Sept. 20, 1947 (dec. June 1981); children: Carol Ann, Susan Patricia, Michael Christopher, Julie Lynn, Lori Kathleen. BA, U. Ala., 1945; MA, U. Denver, 1969. Psychometrician U.S. Army, Deshon Gen. Hosp., Butler, Pa., 1945-46, U.S. Vet. Adminstrn. Vocat. Guidance, U. Ala., Tuscaloosa, 1946; clin. psychologist U.S. Army, Walter Reed Gen. Hosp., Washington, 1946-47, U.S. Army, Fitzsimons Gen. Hosp., Denver, 1948, U.S. Vets. Adminstrn., Ft. Logan, Colo., 1948-50; head sci.-engring. libr. U. Denver, Colo., 1969-72; instr., reference libr. Penrose Libr., U. Denver, 1972-80, asst. prof., reference libr., 1980-90, interim dir., 1990-92; vis. prof. U. Denver Grad. Sch. Libr. Info. Mgmt., 1975-77, 83; info. broker Colo. Rschrs., Denver, 1979—; cons., presenter The Indsl. Info. Workshop Inst. de Investigaciones Tecnologicas, Bogota, Colombia, 1979, LIPI-DRI-PDIN workshop on R&D mgmt., Jakarta, Indonesia, 1982; mem. BRS User Adv. Bd., Latham, N.Y., 1983-86. Indexer: Statistical Abstract of Colorado 1976-77, 1977. Recipient Cert. of Recognition, Sigma Xi, U. Denver chpt., 1983. Mem. ALA, Spl. Libr. Assn., Colo. Libr. Assn., Phi Beta Kappa, Beta Phi Mu.

SMITH, SAM CORRY, retired foundation executive, consultant; b. Enid, Okla., July 3, 1922; s. Chester Hubbert and Nelle Kate (Corry) S.; m. Dorothy Jean Bank, Sept. 21, 1945; children: Linda Jean, Nancy Kay, Susan Diane. Student, Phillips U., 1940-43; BS in Chemistry, U. Okla., 1947, MS in Chemistry, 1948; PhD in Biochemistry, U. Wis., 1951. Asst. and assoc. prof. U. Okla., Oklahoma City, 1951-55; assoc. dir. grants Research Corp., N.Y.C., 1957-65, dir., 1965-68, v.p. grants, 1968-75; exec. dir. M.J. Murdock Charitable Trust, Vancouver, Wash., 1975-88; foundation cons., 1988—; pres. Pacific Northwest Grantmakers Forum, 1983-84. Contbr. sci. articles to profl. jours. Trustee Nutrition Found., Washington, 1976-84, Internat. Life Scis. Inst., Washington, 1984-86; bd. councilors U. So. Calif. Med. Sch., L.A., 1977-82; mem. adv. com. Coll. Natural Scis. Colo. State U., 1977-80; pres. Cardiopulmonary Rehab. Programs Oreg., 1990-91; bd. dirs. Clark Coll. Found., 1993—. Named Boss of Yr., Am. Bus. Women's Assn., 1982, Bus. Assoc. of Yr., 1983. Fellow AAAS; mem. Am. Chem. Soc. Home: 5204 Dubois Dr Vancouver WA 98661-6617

SMITH, SAMUEL DAVID, artist, educator; b. Thorndale, Tex., Feb. 11, 1918; s. Otto Frank and Jeanette (Joyce) S.; m. Elizabeth Marie Smith; children: Cezanne, Rembrandt, Michelangelo. Ed. pub. schs. Prof. art U. N.Mex., 1956-84, prof. art emeritus, 1984—. Illustrator: Roots in Adobe, 1967, Cowboy's Christmas Tree, 1956; also: Coronet mag; one man exhbns. include, Corcoran Gallery Art, Washington, 1949, Santa Fe Mus. Art, 1947, Roswell (N.Mex.) Mus. Fine Art, 1953, 64, Goodwell (Okla.) Hist. Mus., 1964, Panhandle Plains Mus., Canyon City, Tex., 1964, Biltmore Galleries, Los Angeles, 1946, First Nat. Bank, Los Alamos, 1968, group exhbns. include, Baker Galleries, Lubbock, Tex., 1964-73, Met. Mus., N.Y.C., 1944, Blue Door Gallery, Taos, N.Mex., 1946-53, Galeria del Sol, Albuquerque, 1968-73, Brandywine Galleries, 1972-73, Watercolor Workshop, Telluride, Colo., 1964; one-man show includes Retrospective Exhbn. U. of N.Mex., Albuquerque, 1986. Served as combat artist AUS, 1942-45. Hon. life mem. N.Mex. Art League. Mem. Artist Equity Assn. (pres. N.Mex. chpt. 1957-58, 66-67, 70-71). Club: Elk. Gallery: PO Box 2006 Telluride CO 81435-2006

SMITH, SAMUEL HOWARD, university president, plant pathologist; b. Salinas, Calif., Feb. 4, 1940; s. Adrian Reed and Elsa (Jacop) S.; m. Patricia Ann Walter, July 8, 1960; children: Samuel Howard, Linda Marie. BS in Plant Pathology, U. Calif., Berkeley, 1961, PhD, 1964; D (hon.), Nihon U., Tokyo, 1989. NATO fellow Glasshouse Crops Research Inst., Sussex, Eng., 1964-65; asst. prof. plant pathology U. Calif., Berkeley, 1965-69; assoc. prof. Pa. State U., Arendtsville, 1969-71; assoc. prof. Pa. State U., University Park, 1971-74, prof., 1974-85, head dept. plant pathology, 1976-81, dean Coll. Agr., dir. Pa. Agrl. Expt. Sta. and Coop. Extension Service, 1981-85; pres. Wash. State U., 1985—; bd. dirs. Assoc. Western Univs., 1993—; adv. com. Wash. Sch. Employees Credit Union, 1993—; exec. adv. com. Tri-Cities Commercialization Partnership, 1993—; mem. adv. com. Battelle Pacific N.W. Lab., 1993—; chair Pacific-10 Conf. CEOs, 1993-94; bd. dirs. All-Nations Alliance for Minority Participation; mem. pres.' commn. NCAA, 1994—, divsn. I chair, 1995—. Bd. dirs. Forward Wash., 1986—, China Rels. Coun.; mem. Wash. Coun. Internat. Trade, Western Interstate Commn. Higher Edn., Am. Coun. on Edn.; bd. dirs. Assn. Western Univs., 1993—; chair divsn. I NCAA Pres. Commn., 1995—; mem. NCAA Pres. Commn., 1994—. Mem. AAAS, Am. Phytopath. Soc., Nat. Assn. State Univs. and Land-Grant Colls. (bd. dirs. 1994—, chair commn. info. tech. 1994—), Gamma Sigma Delta, Alpha Zeta, Epsilon Sigma Phi, Sigma Xi, Omicron Delta Kappa, Golden Key, Phi Kappa Alpha (hon.). Home: 755 NE Campus St Pullman WA 99163-4223 Office: Wash State U French Adminstrn Bldg Pullman WA 99164-1048

SMITH, SELMA MOIDEL, lawyer, composer; b. Warren, Ohio, Apr. 3, 1919; d. Louis and Mary (Oyer) Moidel; 1 child, Mark Lee. Student U. Calif., 1936-39, U. So. Calif., 1939-41; JD, Pacific Coast U., 1942. Bar: Calif. 1943, U.S. Dist. Ct. 1943, U.S. Supreme Ct. 1958. Gen. practice law; mem.

firm Moidel, Moidel, Moidel & Smith. Field dir. civilian adv. com. WAC, 1943; mem. nat. bd. Med. Coll. Pa. (formerly Woman's Med. Coll. Pa.), 1953—, exec. bd., 1976-80, pres., 1980-82, chmn. past pres. com., 1990-92. Decorated La Order del Merito Juan Pablo Duarte (Dominican Republic). Mem. ABA, State Bar Calif. (servicemen's legal com., Disting. Svc. award 1993), L.A. Bar Assn. (psychopathic ct. com., Outstanding Svc. award 1993), L.A. Lawyers Club (pub. defenders com.), Nat. Assn. Women Lawyers (chmn. com. unauthorized practice of law, social commn. UN, regional dir. western states, Hawaii 1949-57, mem. jud. adminstrn. com. 1960, nat. chmn. world peace through law com. 1966-67), League of Ams. (dir.), Inter-Am. Bar Assn., So. Calif. Women Lawyers Assn. (pres. 1947, 48), Women Lawyers Assn. L.A. (chmn. Law Day com. 1966, subject of oral hist. project, 1986), State Bar Conf. Com., Coun. Bar Assns. L.A. County (charter sec. 1950), Calif. Bus. Women's Coun. (dir. 1951), L.A. Bus. Women's Coun. (pres. 1952), Calif. Pres.'s Coun. (1st v.p.), Nat. Assn. Composers U.S.A. (dir. 1974-79, ann. luncheon chmn. 1975), Nat. Fedn. Music Clubs (nat. vice chmn. for Western region, 1973-78), Calif. Fedn. Music Clubs (state chmn. Am. Music 1971-75, state conv. chmn. 1972), Docents of L.A. Philharm. (v.p. 1973-83, chmn. Latin Am. community rels. 1972-75, press and pub. rels. 1972-75, cons. coord. 1973-75), Assn. Learning in Retirement Orgns. in West (pres. 1993-94, exec. com. 1994-95, Disting. Svc. award 1995), Euterpe Opera Club (v.p. 1974-75, chmn. auditions 1972, chmn. awards 1973-75), ASCAP, Iota Tau Tau (dean L.A., supreme treas.), Plato Soc. of UCLA (Toga editor, 1990-93, sec. 1991-92, chmn. colloquium com. 1992-93, discussion leader UCLA Constitution Bicentennial Project, 1985-87, moderator UCLA extension lecture series 1990, Exceptional Leadership award 1994). Composer: Espressivo-Four Piano Pieces (orchestral premiere 1987, performance Nat. Mus. Women in the Arts 1989). Home: 5272 Lindley Ave Encino CA 91316-3518

SMITH, SERAFINA GANGEMI, artist, drug counselor; b. Phila., Sept. 1, 1919; d. Guiseppe I. and Maria Josephine (Meo) Gangemi; widowed, 1988; children: FRancisco Sidney, Guiseppe Scott, Maria Leslie. AA, U. Hawaii Windward Coll., Kaneohe, 1982; BA, U. Hawaii West Oahu, Pearl City, 1985. Ind. art instr. Forrest Heights, Md., 1963-67; stable mgr. Camp Smith Marine Base, Aiea, Hawaii, 1973-74; counselor Rehab. Hosp. of Pacific, Honolulu, 1979; counselor, cons. Hina Mauka Alcohol Rehab. Ctr., Kaneohe, 1980-82; state del. Al-Anon, Honolulu, 1982-84; bd. dirs. Pacific Inst. Chem. Dependency, Honolulu, 1983—; speaker on alcholism and family systems, 1981—; mgr. art gallery Hawaii Maritime Ctr., 1992—; studied with Guido del Corso, Verona, Italy, 1956-60, Lester Cook, Nat. Gallery, Washington, 1963-67, Dr. Chan, Oriental Inst. of Art, Washington, 1964-65, J. Woodward, Washington, 1965-66, Renzetti, Phila. Acad. of Arts, 1966-67, Douglas Walton, La. Tech., 1988—. Exhibited in group shows at Hawaii Watercolor Soc. Exhbn., 1992 (Bank of Hawaii award), 91 (Cresent Bd. award), Water Color Encounter, La. Tech. U., 1990 (Best in Show-Proffecial Judging award); one-women show Hawaii Maritime Mus., 1992. Vol. Hospice Hawaii, Honolulu, 1981-83, Suicide Crisis and Prevention Hotline, Honolulu, 1986-90, Hawaii Maritime Ctr., Honolulu, 1988—. Mem. AAUW (bd. dirs. Hawaii unit 1986-87), Nat. Italian-Am. Found. (coun. mem.), Hawaii Joint Police Assn., U. Hawaii West Oahu Alumni Assn., Assn. Hawaii Artists (publicity chair 1990—), Hawaii Watercolor Soc., Nat. Mus. Women in Arts. Democrat. Roman Catholic.

SMITH, SHANE DALE, cultural organization administrator, consultant; b. Denver, Mar. 2, 1954; d. Dale Donovan and Ann (Mee) S.; m. Paige W. Waldvogel, Aug. 23, 1986; 1 child, Rio. BS in Horticulture, Colo. State U., 1977; postgrad., Harvard U., 1989-90. Dir. Cheyenne (Wyo.) Community Solar Greenhouse, 1977-86, Cheyenne Botanic Garden, 1986—; cons. in field, 1979—; cons. Servicio Desarollo E. Paz, Mex., 1986—; radio host weekly program, 1977—. Author: Bountiful Solar Greenhouse, 1987, Greenhouse Gardener's Companion, 1993; columnist Sunday Tribune-Eagle, Cheyenne, Wyo. Bd. dirs. Needs Inc., Cheyene, 1986-89, Wildflowers for Wyo., Cheyene, 1988—; pres. Wyo. Outdoor Coun., Lander, 1990—, pres., mem. Grand Canyon Visibility Transport Commn., 1993—. Recipient Presdl. Citation, pres. Ronald Reagan, 1986, Point of Light award Pres. George Bush, 1990, Entrepreneurial Leadership award Ptnrs. for Liveable Communities in Assn. with Clinton Whitehouse, 1994. Mem. Am. Community Gardening Assn. (bd. dirs. 1982-86), Am. Horticultural Therapy Assn., Garden Writers Assn. of Am. Office: Cheyenne Botanic Garden 710 S Lions Park Dr Cheyenne WY 82001-7503

SMITH, SHERWOOD PAUL, plastic surgeon; b. Sault St. Marie, Ont., Can., May 25, 1941; came to U.S., 1972; s. Irwin and Sophie Edith (Freeman) S.; m. Judith Ann Gebhard, Jan. 24, 1966; 1 child, Stephen Barclay. MD, U. Toronto, 1965; MSc, McGill U., 1969. Diplomate Am. Bd. Plastic Surgery. Plastic surgeon Olympia (Wash.) Plastic Surgeons Inc. PS, 1972—. Vol. plastic surgeon Gen. Hosp. Columbo, Sri Lanka, 1985—. Fellow ACS, Royal Coll. Physicians and Surgeons of Can.; mem. Olympia Yacht Club, South Sound Sailing Soc. (vice commodore). Office: Olympia Plastic Surg Inc PS 300 Lilly Rd NE # B Olympia WA 98506-5032

SMITH, STANFORD SIDNEY, state treasurer; b. Denver, Oct. 20, 1923; s. Frank Jay and Lelah (Beamer) S.; m. Harriet Holdrege, Feb. 7, 1947; children: Monta Smith Ramirez, Franklin Stanley. Student, Calif. Inst. Tech., 1941-42, Stanford U., 1942-43; BS, U.S. Naval Acad., 1946. Pres. Vebar Livestock Co., Thermopolis, Wyo., 1961-89; mem. Wyo. Senate, 1974-76; pres. Wyo. Wool GrowersAssn., 1976-78; mem. Wyo. Ho. of Reps., Cheyenne, 1978-82; treas. State Wyo., Cheyenne, 1983—; dir. Coun. of State Govts., 1990-92; v.p. Wyo. Wool Growers, dir., 1976-82. County commr. Hot Springs County, Wyo, 1966-74. Lt. USN, 1943-54. Decorated Bronze Star. Mem. Nat. Assn. State Treas. (pres. 1990-91). Republican. Methodist. Office: State of Wyoming State Capital Cheyenne WY 82002

SMITH, STEPHANIE MARIE, lawyer; b. Manhattan, Kans., May 15, 1955; d. William C. and Joyce A. (Davis) S. BS in Fgn. Studies (Economics), Georgetown U., 1977; JD, U. Mich., 1980. Bar: Colo. 1980, U.S. Dist. Ct. Colo. 1980, U.S. Ct. Appeals (10th cir.) 1980, (9th cir.) 1995, Ariz. 1985, Nev. 1985, U.S. Dist. Ct. Nev. 1985. Assoc. Fishman & Geman, Denver, 1980-81, Hart & Trinen, Denver, 1982-85; ptnr. Jolley, Urga, Wirth & Woodbury, Las Vegas, Nev., 1985—; lawyer rep. 9th Cir. Jud. Conf., 1994—, chmn. Nev. delegation, 1995. Mem. ABA, Nev. Bar Assn., Am. Bankruptcy Inst., So. Nev. Bankruptcy Lawyers Assn. Office: Jolley Urga Wirth & Woodbury 300 S 4th St Ste 800 Las Vegas NV 89101-6018

SMITH, STEPHEN RANDOLPH, aerospace executive; b. Des Moines, Apr. 17, 1928; s. Norvin Ellis and Helen (Heberling) S.; m. Margaret Anne Graves, Dec. 20, 1950; children: Stephen Randolph Jr., Susan Canning, Sara Kutler, Anne Barrette, Julia Carroll. BSME, Stanford U., 1951, MSME, 1952; MBA Advanced Mgmt. Program, Harvard U., 1974. Registered profl. engr., Calif. Sr. analyst, preliminary design engr. Northrop & Garrett Corps., L.A. and Hawthorne, Calif., 1952-55; propulsion lead design engr. Northrop Corp., Hawthorne, 1955-59; engring. rep. ea. dist. Northrop Corp., Washington, 1959-60; T-38/F-5/F-20 program mgr. Northrop Corp., Hawthorne, 1960-75; v.p. Iran ops. Northrop Corp., Tehran, 1975-78; v.p. advanced projects Northrop Corp., Hawthorne, 1978-83, v.p. engring. and advanced devel., 1983-86, v.p., program mgr. F-20/YF-23A, 1986-88, corp. v.p., gen. mgr. aircraft divsn., 1988-92; cons. tech. mgmt. Palos Verdes, Calif., 1992—; bd. mem. Quarterdeck Ptnrs., Inc., L.A. and Washington, 1992—, NASA Advanced Aeronautics Com., 1984-86; invited lectr. aircraft design USAF Acad., 1983. Author, designer, patentee in field. Bd. mem. Boy Scouts Am., L.A. coun., 1986—. Sgt. U.S. Army, 1946-48. Recipient Disting. Civilian Svc. medal U.S. Dept. Def., Washington, 1983. Fellow AIAA (chmn. L.A. sect. 1985-86, adv. bd. 1988—, Spl. Citation 1994), Inst. Advancement Engring.; mem. Soc. Automotive Engrs. (chmn. aerotech. 1986-87, honors 1987), Sierra Club, Trailfinders Conservation Coun. (life, coun. chief 1940). Republican. Episcopalian. Home and Office: 2249 Via Guadalana Palos Verdes Estates CA 90274

SMITH, STEVEN SIDNEY, molecular biologist; b. Idaho Falls, Idaho, Feb. 11, 1946; s. Sidney Ervin and Hermie Phyllis (Robertson) S.; m. Nancy Louise Turner, Dec. 20, 1974. BS, U. Idaho, 1968; PhD, UCLA, 1974. Asst. research scientist Beckman Research Inst. City of Hope Nat. Med. Ctr., Duarte, Calif., 1982-84, staff Cancer Ctr., 1983—, asst. research scientist depts. Thoracic Surgery and Molecular Biology, 1985-87, assoc. research scientist, 1987—, dir. dept. cell and tumor biology, 1990—; Wellcome vis. prof. medicine Okla. State U., 1995-96; cons. Molecular Biosystems Inc., San Diego, 1981-84, Am. Inst. Biol. Scis., Washington, 1994. Contbr. articles to profl. jours. Grantee NIH, 1983-93, Coun. for Tobacco Rsch., 1983-92, March of Dimes, 1988-91, Smokeless Tobacco Rsch. Coun., 1992—, Office of Naval Rsch., 1994—; Swiss Nat. Sci. Found. fellow U. Bern, 1974-77, Scripps Clinic and Rsch. Found., La. Jolla, Calif., 1978-82, NIH fellow Scripps Clinic, 1979-81. Mem. Am. Soc. Cell Biology, Am. Assn. Cancer Rsch., Am. Crystallographic Assn., Am. Chem. Soc., Am. Weightlifting Assn., Phi Beta Kappa. Office: City of Hope Nat Med Ctr 1500 Duarte Rd Duarte CA 91010-3012

SMITH, STUART ROBERT, foundation executive; b. South Amboy, N.J., Aug. 14, 1942; s. Stuart Conroy and Elizabeth Beatrice (Keenan) S.; m. Nancy Jo Roberts, Apr. 24, 1965; children: Mark Christopher, Melissa Jo. BA in Psychology, St. Vincent Coll., Latrobe, Pa., 1964; postgrad., Stanford U., 1986. Dist. exec. Raritan coun. Boy Scouts Am., Perth Amboy, N.J., 1965-68, Greater Niagara Frontier Coun., Buffalo, 1968-69; assoc. dir. devel. Canisius Coll., Buffalo, 1969-70; dir. devel. Kenmore (N.Y.) Mercy Hosp., 1971-74; dir. community rels. and devel. United Hosp., Port Chester, N.Y., 1974-77; exec. dir. Shadyside Hosp. Found., Pitts., 1977-79; exec. v.p. Samaritan Med. Found., Phoenix, 1979-87, pres., chief exec. officer, 1988—; cons. fundraising and golf tournaments. Contbr. articles to profl. jours., newsletters. Pres., bd. dirs. Crisis Nursery, Phoenix, 1990-91, v.p., 1987, 88, found. sec.; chmn. Fiesta Bowl Golf Classic, Phoenix, 1988, 89; mem. com. Fiesta Bowl, Phoenix, 1986—; bd. dirs. Palms Clinic & Hosp. Found., Phoenix, Crisis Nursery, 1993, exec. com., v.p.; vol. com. chmn. Super Bowl XXX. Fellow Assn. for Healthcare Philanthropy (nat. v.p. 1977-80, bd. examiners 1986—); mem. Ariz. Assn. Hosp. Devel. (pres. 1990, exec. com. 1989—), Nat. Soc. Fund Raising Execs. (cert. various offices local chpts., Outstanding Fundraising Exec. award Ariz. chpt. 1989), LPGA (sponsors bd., treas. 1988-92), Moon Valley Country Club. Republican. Roman Catholic. Office: The Samaritan Found 1441 N 12th St Phoenix AZ 85006-2837

SMITH, SUSAN BITTER, trade association executive, consultant; b. Phoenix, Aug. 23, 1955; d. Charles R. and Judith (Anderson) Bitter; m. Paul H. Smith, Mar. 10, 1979; 1 child, Prescott R. BS, Ariz. State U., 1977, MBA, 1982. Supr. Inmate Legal Svcs., Phoenix, 1978-80; exec. dir. Ariz. Cable TV Assn., Phoenix, 1980—; cons. Bell Atlantic CTS, Phoenix, 1986—, Sears Sch. Driving, Phoenix, 1987-92. Mem. Rep. Party of Ariz., Phoenix, 1976—; mem. Scottsdale (Ariz.) City Coun., 1988-92; bd. dirs. Morrison Inst. Pub. Policy, Tempe, Ariz., 1986-90, Family Emergency Shelter, Mesa, Ariz., 1990—. Mem. Am. Soc. Assn. Execs. (bd. dirs. 1993-95), Ariz. Soc. Assn. Execs. (pres. 1989-90, Exec. of Yr. 1987, bd. dirs.), Am. Fedn. Bus. and Profl. Women, Valley Leadership Alumni (bd. dirs. 1987-88), Ariz. State U. Coll. Bus. Alumni Assn. (pres. 1976-77), Ariz. State U. Alumni Assn. (bd. dirs. 1985—, pres. 1994-95). Congregationalist. Home: 5806 E Lewis Ave Scottsdale AZ 85257-1926

SMITH, SUSAN KIMSEY, lawyer; b. Phoenix, Jan. 15, 1947; d. William Lewis and Margaret (Bowes) Kimsey; m. Alfred Jon Olsen, Apr. 15, 1979. Student U. Ariz., 1965-66; BA, Principia Coll., 1969; MA, U. Va., 1970; JD, Ariz. State U., 1975. Bar: Ariz. Atty. trust dept. Valley Nat. Bank Ariz., Phoenix, 1976-77; assoc. Lane & Smith, Ltd., Phoenix, 1977-78; mem. Olsen-Smith, Ltd., Phoenix, 1979—, pres., 1979—; mem. Phoenix Tax Workshop, 1976—, Tax Study Group, 1979—, 401 Com., 1982—; chmn. taxation sect. State Bar Ariz., 1985-86, mem. tax. adv. commn.; lectr. profl. confs. and univs., 1977, 80—. Author: Estate Planning Practice Manual, 1984; editorial adv. bd. Practical Tax Lawyer, 1985—; contbr. writings to profl. publs. Bd. dirs. Ariz. Community Found., Samaritan Found. Recipient J.P. Walker Am. History award, Principia Coll., 1969, Ethics award, State Bar Ariz., 1974. Fellow Am. Coll. Trust and Estate Counsel (Ariz. chmn.), Am. Coll. Tax Counsel; mem. ABA (chmn. com. econs. of tax practice 1983-84, chmn. com. liaison with other ABA sects. and coms., sect. econs. of law practice 1983—, selection com. appts. to U.S. Tax Ct., com. mem. sect. taxation 1976—, com. mem. sect. real property probate and trust law 1982—, chmn. taxation task force on family partnerships, editorial bd. Practical Tax Lawyer), Internat. Acad. of Estate and Trust Law, State Bar Ariz. (chmn. taxation sect. 1985—, mem. tax adv. commn.), Maricopa County Bar Assn., Fed. Bar Assn. (vice chmn. estate and gift taxation com., taxation council 1979-80), Valley Estate Planners (pres.), Central Ariz. Estate Planning Council (bd. dirs. 1986-88), The Group, Alpha Lambda Delta, Phi Alpha Eta. Republican. Office: Olsen-Smith Ltd 301 E Virginia Ave Ste 3300 Phoenix AZ 85004-1218

SMITH, TERRY LEE, business owner; b. Eugene, Oreg., July 19, 1954; s. Robert Eugene and Rebecca Anne (Atkinson) S.; m. Kellie Lurline Henry, May 3, 1975. Cert. journeyman, Oreg. Cleanup/delivery man Chase Co., Eugene, Oreg., 1976; apprentice Durbin Heating and Sheet Metal, Eugene, Oreg., 1976-78, Harvey & Price, Eugene, Oreg., 1978-80, Brainard Sheet Metal, Springfield, Oreg., 1980-82; owner Smith Sheet Metal, Inc., Springfield, Oreg., 1983-93, T.K.S., Inc., 1993—; chmn. Area III Sheet Metal Apprenticeship Com., 1987-94. Mem. Am. Soc. Heating, Refrigeration, and Air Conditioning Engrs., Am. Subcontractors Assn., Nat. Roofing Assn., Associated Bldg. Contractors, Construction Specifications Inst., Eugene Builders Exch. (bd. dirs.). Republican. Home: 3905 Hayden Bridge Rd Springfield OR 97477-1860 Office: TKS Inc 3905 Hayden Bridge Rd Springfield OR 97478

SMITH, THEODORE W., construction executive; b. 1927. Pres. Dinwiddie Constrn. Co., San Francisco, 1947—. Office: Dinwiddie Constrn Co Crocker Ctr W Tower 275 Battery St Ste 300 San Francisco CA 94111-3330*

SMITH, THOMAS HARRY, counselor; b. Tonawanda, N.Y., Nov. 17, 1947; s. Richard Sleep and Elsie (Supparritts) S.; m. Linda Sharon Kerr, Nov. 11, 1985 (div. Aug. 1991); children: Nicole Katya, Zachary Thomas. BS, SUNY, Oneonta, 1969. Counselor Upstate Home for Children, Milford, N.Y., 1973; psychometrician Attica (N.Y.) Correctional Facility, 1974-75; tchr. Albion (N.Y.) Head Start, 1975-76, Marion House, Waterport, N.Y., 1976; counselor Otsego County Manpower, Cooperstown, N.Y., 1977-79, Deverenx Found., Santa Barbara, Calif., 1979-81, 89-95, Work Tng. Program, Santa Barbara, 1981-86; nurse asst. channel Cities Nurse Registry, Santa Barbara, 1987-89; bd. dirs. Lake Serene, Santa Barbara. Author: Qim Tunes, 1994. Mem. Am. Union Men (pres. 1983—), Goleta Valley Athletic Club. Home: PO Box 80131 Goleta CA 93117

SMITH, THOMAS JAMES, reference librarian; b. Oceanside, N.Y., Mar. 29, 1963; s. Kenneth Perry and Dorothy Louise (Breidenbach) S. BA in History, U. Nev., Las Vegas, 1985; MLS, Ind. U., 1988. Reference libr. Las Vegas-Clark County Libr., 1988—. Co-editor, compiler: Nevada Funding Directory, 1994. Mem. Phi Kappa Phi, Phi Alpha Theta, Phi Lambda Alpha. Office: Clark County Libr 1401 E Flamingo Rd Las Vegas NV 89119-5256

SMITH, THOMAS KENT, radiologist; b. Bowling Green, Ohio, Aug. 21, 1934; s. Robert O. and Roslyn Smith; m. Jaleh Saidi, Feb. 1, 1974; children: Jeffrey, Todd, Mark, Blake, Tyler. BS with high honors, U. Cin., 1957; MD, Case Western Res. U., 1961. Intern Nat. Naval Med. Ctr., Bethesda, Md., 1961-62; resident in radiology VA Med. Ctr., Long Beach, Calif., 1965-69; dir. radiology Harriman Jones Med. Group, Long Beach, 1969-88; fellow in MRI/CT U. Calif., San Francisco, 1988-89; dir. MRI Orange County MRI, Fountain Valley, Calif., 1989-90; chmn. dept. diagnostic imaging Kaiser Permanente Med. Ctr., Honolulu, 1990—; fellow in radiologic pathology Armed Forces Inst. of Pathology, Washington, 1968; mem. adv. bd. Hawaii Permanente Med. Group, Honolulu, 1990—; bd. dirs. Harriman Jones Med. Group, Harriman Jones Assocs.; assoc. clin. prof. radiology U. Hawaii, Honolulu, 1990—; asst. clin. prof. U. Calif. Irvine, 1970-88; clin. instr. U. Calif. San Francisco, 1988-89, asst. clin. prof., 1989—. Lt. USN, 1961-65. Lt. USN, 1961-65. Mem. Hawaii Radiol. Soc. (pres. 1992-93), Radiol. Soc. N.Am., Am. Coll. Radiology, Soc. Magnetic Resonance, Margulis Soc., Calif. Radiol. Soc., Alpha Omega Alpha. Home: 46-434 Haiku Plantation Dr Kaneohe HI 96744-4207 Office: Kaiser Permanente Med Ctr 3288 Moanalua Rd Honolulu HI 96819

SMITH, THOMAS SHORE, lawyer; b. Rock Springs, Wyo., Dec. 7, 1924; s. Thomas and Anne E. (McTee) S.; m. Jacqueline Emily Krueger, May 25, 1952; children: Carolyn Jane, Karl Thomas, David Shore. BSBA, U. Wyo., 1950, JD, 1959. Bar: U.S. Dist. Ct. Wyo. 1960, U.S. Ct. Appeals (10th cir.) 1960, U.S. Tax Ct. 1969, U.S. Supreme Ct. 1971. Of counsel Smith, Stanfield & Scott, LLC, Laramie, Wyo., 1963—; atty. City of Laramie, 1963-86; instr. mcpl. law U. Wyo., 1987, mem. dean's adv. com. Law Sch.; dir. budget and fin. Govt. of Am. Samoa, 1954-56. Bd. dirs. Bur. Land Mgmt., Rawlins, Wyo., 1984-89, chmn. bd. dirs., 1989; pres. Ivinson Hosp. Found., 1994-95; bd. dirs. U. Wyo. Found., 1991—. Francis Warren scholar, 1958. Mem Wyo. Bar Assn. (pres. 1984-85), Albany County Bar Assn., Western States Bar Conf. (pres. 1985-86), Elks. Republican. Episcopalian. Office: Smith Stanfield & Scott LLC PO Box 971 515 E Ivinson Ave Laramie WY 82070-3157

SMITH, THOMAS WINSTON, cotton marketing executive; b. Crosbyton, Tex., Mar. 16, 1935; s. Lance L. and Willie Mae (Little) S.; m. Patricia Mae Zachary, Dec. 13, 1958; children—Janna Olean, Thomas Mark. B.S., Tex. A&M U., 1957; P.M.D., Harvard U., 1964. Various positions Calcot Ltd., Bakersfield, Calif., 1957-77, exec. v.p., pres., 1977—; v.p. Amcot, Inc., Amcot Internat., Inc., Bakersfield, 1977—, also bd. dirs.; v.p. Nat. Cotton Coun., Memphis; bd. mgrs. N.Y. Cotton Exchange, N.Y.C. Bd. dir. Greater Bakersfield Meml. Hosp.; mem. pres.'s adv. commn. Calif. State Coll., Bakersfield. Mem. Rotary.

SMITH, THORN MCCLELLAN, lawyer; b. Peoria, Ill., Feb. 19, 1958; s. Lester Berry and June Edda (Kopal) S. BS in Fgn. Service, Georgetown U., 1979; JD, Northwestern U., 1982. Bar: Ill. 1982, U.S. Dist. Ct. (ctr. dist.) Ill. 1983, S.C. 1984, U.S. Dist. Ct. S.C. 1985, Calif. 1990, U.S. Dist. Ct. Calif. 1990, U.S. Ct. Appeals (9th cir.) 1990. Assoc. Law Offices of Lester Berry Smith, Peoria, 1982-83, Law Offices of C.R. Dunbar, Spartanburg, S.C., 1983-85; sole practice Spartanburg, 1985—; mem. office of gen. counsel USN, 1987-91; of counsel Tank Protect Engring. No. Calif., Inc., 1992-93. Western field dir. Confederate Lawyer, Western Command, 1993—. Mem. ABA, Spartanburg County Bar Assn., Sons Confederate Vets. Office: 465 California St Ste 521 San Francisco CA 94104-1814

SMITH, VANGY EDITH, accountant, consultant, writer, artist; b. Saskatoon, Sask., Can., Dec. 17, 1937; d. Wilhelm and Anne Ellen (Hartshorne) Gogel: m. Clifford Wilson, May 12, 1958 (de. Dec. 1978); children: Kenneth, Koral, Kevin, Korey, Kyle; m. Terrence Raymond Smith, Dec. 14, 1979. Student, Saskatoon Tech. Collegiate Inst., 1956, BBA, 1958, MBA, 1987, PhD in English with honors, 1988. Prin. Vangy Enterprises, Springfield, Oreg., 1960—; accounts payable clk. Maxwell Labs., Inc., San Diego, 1978; invoice clk. Davies Electric, Saskatoon, 1980-81; office mgr. Ladee Bug Ceramics, Saskatoon, 1981-87, Lazars Investments Corp., Eugene, Oreg., 1987; bookkeeper accounts payable Pop Geer, Eugene, Oreg., 1987; office mgr., bookkeeper Willamette Sports Ctr., Inc., Eugene, Oreg., 1985-89; clk. I Lane C.C., 1992—; self-employed Vangy Enterprises, 1992—; circulation mgr. Nat. WCTU, 1990-92, UN rep. for World WCTUm 1989-91; appointed mem. Parliament for the U. for Peace, Holland, 1991. Contbr. articles to scholarly jours. (recipient doctoral award 1987). Counselor Drug and Rehab. Ctr., Eugene, 1970-88; trustee Children's Farm Home, Corvallis, Oreg., 1989-91, 3d v.p., 1989-90; mem. Found. Christian Living; pres. Oreg. State Christian Temperance Union, 1989-90; mem. pub. safety adv. com. City of Eugene, 1989-90; co-pres. Lane County UN Assn., 1989-90; mem. artist Nat. Bd. Edn., 1989, 90; mem. adv. com. Dept. Pub. Safety for City of Eugene, 1990; exec. dir. H.E.L.P., 1993—; pres. Lane County Coun. of Orgns., 1994—; treas. Cascade/Coast chpt. Alzheimers Assn., 1994. Recipient 3d and 4th place artists' awards Lane County Fair, 1987, 1st and 2d place awards Nat. Writing Contest, 1987, 88, 89, 90, 91. Mem. WCTU (life, pres., state bd. dirs. projection methods circulation 1987-90, Appreciation award 1982, Presdl. award 1985, Lane County Euenge Woman of Yr. 1990), Am. Soc. Writers, Alzheimers Assn. (treas. Cascade/Coast chpt. 1994), Rebekkah Juanita Lodge, Lions (sec. 1994). Democrat.

SMITH, VERNON LOMAX, economist, researcher; b. Wichita, Kans., Jan. 1, 1927; s. Vernon Chessman and Lula Belle (Lomax) S.; m. Joyce Harkleroad, June 6, 1950 (div. Aug. 1975); m. Carol Breckner, Jan. 1, 1980. BSEE, Calif. Inst. Tech., 1949; MA in Econs., U. Kans., 1952; PhD in Econs., Harvard U., 1955; D of Mgmt. (hon.), Purdue U., 1990. Asst. prof. econs. Purdue U., West Lafayette, Ind., 1955-58, assoc. prof., 1958-61, prof., 1961-65, Krannert prof., 1965-67; prof. Brown U., Providence, 1967-68, U. Mass., Amherst, 1968-75; prof. U. Ariz., Tucson, 1975—, Regents' prof.; Contbr. articles to profl. jours. Fellow Ctr. for Advanced Study in Behavioral Scis., Stanford, Calif., 1972-73; Sherman Fairchild Disting. Scholar Calif. Inst. Tech., Pasadena, 1973-74; adj. scholar CATO Inst., Washington, 1983—. Fellow AAAS, Am. Acad. Arts and Scis., Econometric Soc., Am. Econ. Assn. (Disting. fellow); mem. Pvt. Enterprise Edn. Assn. (Adam Smith award). Home: 2122 E Camino El Ganado Tucson AZ 85718-4108 Office: Univ Ariz Dept Economics Tucson AZ 85718

SMITH, VIN, sports editor, business owner, novelist; b. Whittier, Calif., May 19, 1944; s. M. Clifford and Anna Eugenia (Hill) S.; m. Marthea Karen Callaham, May 15, 1969 (div. 1979); children: Jayare Smith, Eric Smith; m. Ginger Hammon, Oct. 20, 1984; children: Amy Michelle, Stacey Erin, Kellie Rae. Student, Columbia Sch. Broadcasting, San Francisco, 1967; AA, Cuesta Coll., 1974; grad., Am. Sch. of Piano Tuning, 1978. Sales mgr. Sta. KTAT, Frederick, Okla., 1967-69; announcer KOCY, Oklahoma City, 1969; owner Melmart Markets, San Luis Obispo, Calif., 1971-73, Am. Direct Sales, Grover City, Calif., 1973-79; instr. piano Valley View Acad., Arroyo Grande, Calif., 1977-78; instr. piano Long Piano Co., San Luis Obispo, 1977-79, piano technician, 1978-79; owner Chocolate Piano, Yreka, Calif., 1979—; instr. piano Makah Indian Tribe, Neah Bay, Wash., 1981-82; sports editor New Words Digest, Bakersfield, Calif., 1988—; cons., stress evaluator seminar Yreka Stress Therapy Clinic, 1986-87. Sports columnist New Words Digest, 1987-91; guest columnist Siskiyou Daily News, 1991-94; nat publicist chamber music concerts So. Oreg. State Coll., 1993—; contbr. articles to profl. jours. Chmn. heart fund Tillman County Okla., 1968; pub. co-chmn. Siskiyou County No-Prop 174, 1973-93; campaign worker Ken Jourdan for sheriff, Yreka, 1986; publicity dir. Gene Breceda for supr., 1993-94. Recipient Cert. of Appreciation, Siskiyou County, 1988, Achievement award, 1988; winner Golden Poet award World of Poetry, 1989. Mem. Nat. Writers Club (chmn. student com. Yreka chpt. 1988), Author's Guild, Inc., Author's League of Am., Mystery Writers Am., Soc. Children's Book Writers, Jr. C. of C. (sgt.-at-arms Frederick chpt. 1967-69), Kiwanis, Moose. Home: 710 Knapp St Yreka CA 96097-2343 Office: Chocolate Piano Svcs PO Box 447 Yreka CA 96097-0447

SMITH, VIRGIL, business education educator. BS in Econs. and Bus. Adminstrn., Portland State U., 1977, MBA, 1979; PhD, Tex. Tech U., 1994. Asst. prof. bus. div. Northwestern Coll., St. Paul, 1985-90; assoc. prof. coll. bus. Biola U., Fullerton, Calif., 1994—; adj. faculty bus., Western Bapt. Coll., Salem, Oreg., 1982-85; active in grant proposals for Northwestern Coll., 1987-90; guest spkr. in field; owner OPUS I, Salem, 1981-85; real estate broker Art Lutz & Co., Portland, 1979-81; pres., gen. mgr. The Rock Industries, Inc., Portland, 1975-79.

SMITH, WALDO GREGORIUS, former government official; b. Bklyn., July 29, 1911; s. John Henry and Margaret (Gregorius) S.; m. Mildred Pearl Prescott, July 30, 1935 (dec. Jan. 1992); 1 dau., Carole Elizabeth Smith Levin. Student CCNY, N.Y., 1928-29; B.S. in Forestry, Cornell U., 1933. Registered prof. engr., Colo. Forester Forest Service, U.S. Dept. Agr., Atlanta, 1933-41, Ala. Div. Forestry, Brewton, 1941-42; engr., civil engring. technician Geol. Survey, U.S. Dept. Interior, 1942-71, cartographic technician, 1972-75; chmn. Public Transp. Council, 1975-89; legislator aide to individuals Colo. State Legis. Internship Program, 1987—. Recipient 40 Yr. Civil Service award pin and scroll; 42 Yr. Govt. Service award plaque. Fellow Am. Congress Surveying and Mapping (life, sec.-treas. Colo. chpt. 1961, program chmn. 1962, reporter 1969, mem. nat. membership devel. com. 1973-74, rep. to Colo. Engring. Council 1976-77); mem. AAAS (emeritus), Denver Fed. Center Profl. Engrs. Group (U.S. Geol. Survey rep. 1973-76, Engr. of Yr. award 1975), Nat. Soc. Profl. Engrs. (pre-coll. guidance com. 1986-91, life 92—), Profl. Engrs. Colo. (chpt. scholarship chmn. 1979—, advt. corr., service award 1983), Cornell U. Alumni Assn. (alumni secondary schs. com. Quadrangle Club), Common Cause, Colo. Engring. Council (chmn. library com. 1970—, spl. rep. Regional Transp. Dist., 1974-75; mem. sci. fair com. 1970-71; rep. ex officio Denver Pub. Library Found.

Bd. Trustees 1975-80, mem. historic agreement with Denver Pub. Libr. 1993, Pres.'s Outstanding Service award 1987), Environ. Concerns (chmn. com. 1988—, treas. 1989-91, mem. site specific adv. bd., restoration adv. bd. Rocky Mountain arsenal cleanup 1994—), Fedn. Am. Scientists, Am. Soc. Engring. Edn., People for Am. Way. Contbr. articles to profl. jours. Home: 3821 W 25th Ave Denver CO 80211-4417

SMITH, WALTER J., engineering consultant; b. Climax, Kans., Feb. 8, 1921; s. Jacob Walter and Thelma Christina (Stark) S.; m. Wanda Jean Sandys, Apr. 20, 1944 (div. 1965); children: Walter Brooke, Judith Jean; m. Evadean Louise Smith, Sept. 21, 1965; stepchildren: Stephen Henslee, Kimberly Ann; 1 adopted child, Nancy Louise. BEE, Cleve. State U., 1948; postgrad., UCLA, 1955-58, Western State U. Law, Anaheim, Calif., 1970-71. Lic. profl. engr., Ohio, Calif. Field tech. rep. to Air Force Jack & Heintz, Inc., Maple Hts., Ohio, 1942-44; rsch. engr. Jack & Heintz, Inc., 1948-50, N. Am. Aviation Inc., Downey, Calif., 1950-54; asst. chief engr. Ala. Engring. & Tool Co., Huntsville, Ala., 1954-55; rsch. specialist to dir. prodn. ops. N. Am. Aviation Inc./Rockwell Internat., Anaheim, 1955-86; engring. mgmt. cons. Anaheim, 1986-93; engring. mgmt. cons., Bermuda Dunes, Calif., 1993—. Contbr. articles to profl. jours. Mem. Anaheim Indsl. Devel. Bd., 1982-86, Anaheim Pub. Utilities Bd., 1987-92; bd. dirs. Rep. Ctrl. Com. of Orange County, 1976-78; pres., bd. dirs. Galerie Homeowners Assn., 1987-93; bd. dirs. Coun. on Environ. Edn. and Econ. Through Devel., Inc., 1974-86, Action Com. to Inform Orange Now, Inc. Mem. Anaheim C. of C. (bd. dirs. 1983-90, pres. 1983-84), Gladhanders Acad. Hospitality Internat. (bd. dirs. 1989-95, Man of Yr. 1989). Republican. Religious Science. Home and Office: 78615 Purple Sagebrush Ave Bermuda Dunes CA 92203-9051

SMITH, WALTER ROGERS, protective services administrator; b. Burlington, Vt., Jan. 20, 1945; s. LeRoy F. and Gertrude (Spurbeck) S.; m. Carolyn S. Snidow, July 11, 1978; 1 child, Nancy C. BA, U. Tex., 1970; MPA, U. Colo., Denver, 1978. Dep. sheriff Denver Sheriff Dept., 1971-77, sgt., 1977-78, lt., 1978-80, capt., 1980-85, major, 1985-90, div. chief, 1990—; mem. curriculum devel. com. detentions Colo. Law Enforcement Tng. Acad., Golden, Colo., 1989-92. Mem. Am. Correctional Assn., Nat. Sheriff Assn., Western Correctional Assn. (pres. 1991), Colo. Correctional Assn. (pres. 1989, Merit award 1986), Am. Jail Assn. (bd. dirs. 1992—), Colo. Jail Assn. (pres. 1987-88), Internat. Assn. Correctional Tng. Personnel (nominating chair 1994). Office: Denver Sheriff Dept PO Box 1108 Denver CO 80201-1108

SMITH, WILLARD GRANT, psychologist; b. Sidney, N.Y., June 29, 1934; s. Frank Charles and Myrtle Belle (Empet) S.; m. Ruth Ann Dissly, Sept. 14, 1957; children—Deborah Sue Henri, Cynthia Lynn Koster, Andrea Kay Richards, John Charles. BS, U. Md., 1976; MS, U. Utah, 1978, PhD, 1981. Lic. psychologist, Utah; cert. sch. psychologist, sch. adminstr., tchr., Utah, nat. cert. sch. psychologist. Rsch. asst. Med. Ctr., U. Utah, 1977, teaching asst. dept. ednl. psychology, 1976-78, rsch. cons. dept. edn., 1977; program evaluator Salt Lake City Sch. Dist.; program evaluator and auditor Utah State Bd. Edn., 1978; sch. psychologist Jordan Sch. Dist., Sandy, Utah, 1978-82, tchr., 1979-80; exec. dir. Utah Ind. Living Ctr., Salt Lake City, 1982-83; spl. edn. cons. Southeastern Edn. Svc. Ctr., 1983-85; sch. psychologist Jordan Sch. Dist., Sandy, 1985—; assoc. psychologist Don W. McBride & Assocs., Bountiful, Utah, 1989-91; pvt. practice Salt Lake City, 1991—. Master sgt. USAF, 1953-76. Decorated Air Force Commendation medal with 2 clusters; recipient U. Md. scholastic achievement award, 1975. Mem. Am. Psychol. Assn., Nat. Assn. Sch. Psychologists, Am. Ednl. Rsch. Assn., Air Force Sgts. Assn., Ret. Enlisted Assn., Phi Kappa Phi, Alpha Sigma Lambda. Home: 6879 Maverick Cir Salt Lake City UT 84121-3301 Office: Jordan Sch Dist 7500 S 1000 E Midvale UT 84047-2910

SMITH, WILLIAM B., research and development executive; b. 1944. BSEE, U. Md., 1962; MS, Princeton U., 1963; PhD, U. Pa., 1968. Exec. dir. comms. svcs. AT&T Bell Labs., Holmdel, N.J.; v.p., gen. tech. dir. ITT Europe, Brussels, 1982-86; sr. v.p. r & d U.S. West Advanced Tech., 1991, now pres. Office: U S West Advanced Tech 4001 Discovery Dr Boulder CO 80303-7813*

SMITH, WILLIAM HUGH, SR., audit manager, consultant; b. Peoria, Ill., Feb. 12, 1920; s. Hugh N. and Catherine Litta (Obrien) S.; m. Betty Lou Uth Smith, June 4, 1941; children: Beverly Ann Clark, William H. Smith Jr., Millie Judkins, Hugh N. Smith, Patrick James Smith. BSBA with honors, U. Dayton. Cert. Fraud Examiner; cert. Fin. Mgr. Mgr. Hugh H. Smith CPA, Chgo., 1946-66; resident mgr. CPA Firms, Chgo., 1966-76; v.p., auditor United of Am. Bank, Chgo., 1976-79; audit mgr. City of Anaheim, Calif., 1979—. Charter Life mem. Rep. Presidential Task Force, Washington, 1982—. Capt. U.S. Army, 1941-46. Mem. Inst. Internal Auditors (bd. govs. Orange County chpt., internat. com. on govt. affairs), Cert. Fraud Examiners. Republican. Roman Catholic. Home: 14415 Baker St Westminster CA 92683-4813 Office: City of Anaheim 200 S Anaheim Blvd Anaheim CA 92805-3820

SMITH, WILLIAM RAY, retired biophysicist, engineer; b. Lyman, Okla., June 26, 1925; s. Harry Wait and Daisy Belle (Hull) S. BA, Bethany Nazarene Coll., 1948; MA, Wichita State U., 1950; postgrad. U. Kans., 1950-51; PhD, UCLA, 1967. Engr., Beech Aircraft Corp., Wichita, Kans., 1951-53; sr. group engr. McDonnell Aircraft Corp., St. Louis, 1953-60; sr. engr. Lockheed Aircraft Corp., Burbank, Calif., 1961-63; sr. engr. scientist McDonnell Douglas Corp., Long Beach, Calif., 1966-71; mem. tech. staff Rockwell Internat., L.A., 1973-86, CDI Corp.-West, Costa Mesa, Calif., 1986-88, McDonnell Douglas Aircraft Corp., Long Beach, 1988-93; ret., 1993. tchr. math. Pasadena Coll. (now Point Loma Coll., San Diego), 1960-62, Glendale Coll., Calif., 1972; asst. prof. math. Mt. St. Mary's Coll., L.A., 1972-73. Recipient Recognition certificate NASA, 1982. Mem. UCLA Chancellor's Assocs., Internat. Visitors Coun. L.A., Town Hall Calif., Yosemite Assocs., Santa Monica Yacht Club, L.A. World Affairs Coun., Sigma Xi, Pi Mu Epsilon. Republican. Presbyterian. Avocations: sailing, photography, teaching Sunday sch. first grade. Home: 2405 Roscomare Rd Los Angeles CA 90077-1839

SMITH, ZACHARY ALDEN, political science and public administration educator; b. Stanford, Calif., Aug. 8, 1953; s. Alden Wallace and Lelia (Anderson) S.; m. Lisa Friel, May 20, 1983. BA, Calif. State U., Fullerton, 1975; MA, U. Calif., Santa Barbara, 1979, PhD, 1984. Adj. lectr. polit. sci. U. Calif., Santa Barbara, 1981-82; asst. prof., dir. Ctr. for Island and Ocean Resources Mgmt. U. Hawaii, Hilo, 1982-87, assoc. prof., 1987-89; assoc. prof. No. Ariz. U., Flagstaff, 1989-93, prof., 1993—. Author: Groundwater and the Future of the Southwest, 1984, Groundwater Policy in the Southwest, 1985, Groundwater in the West, 1989, The Environmental Policy Paradox, 1992, 2d edit., 1995, Hawaii State and Local Government, 1992, Politics and Public Policy in Arizona, 1993, 2d edit., 1995, Environmental Politics and Policy in the West, 1993. Active campaign for various state propositions, 1970, 74, 76; elected to Orange County (Calif.) Dem. Cen. Com., 1976-78. Research grantee U. Calif., Los Alamos (N.Mex.) Sci. Lab., Water Resources Ctr., Davis., Calif. Mem. Am. Water Resources Assn., Am. Polit. Sci. Assn., Southwestern Social Sci. Assn., Western Polit. Sci. Assn., Am. Soc. Pub. Adminstrn., Western Social Sci. Assn. Office: No Ariz U Dept Polit Sci Box 15036 Flagstaff AZ 86011

SMITH-THOMPSON, PATRICIA ANN, public relations consultant, educator; b. Chgo., June 7, 1933; d. Clarence Richard and Ruth Margaret (Jacobson) Nowack; m. Tyler Thompson, Aug. 1, 1992. Student Cornell U., 1951-52; BA, Centenary Coll., Hackettstown, N.J., 1983. Prodn. asst. Your Hit Parade Batten, Barton, Durstine & Osborne, 1953-54; pvt. practice polit. cons., 1954-66; legal sec., asst. Atty. John C. Cushman, 1966-68; field dep. L.A. County Assessor, 1968-69, pub. info. officer L.A. County Probation Dept., 1969-73; dir. consumer rels. Fireman's Fund, San Francisco, 1973-76; pvt. practice pub. rels. cons., 1976-77; spl. projects officer L.A. County Transp. Commn., 1977-78; tchr. Calif. State U.-Dominguez Hills, 1979-86; editor, writer Jet Propulsion Lab., 1979-80; pub. info. dir. L.A. Bd. Pub. Works, 1980-82; pub. info. cons. City of Pasadena, (Calif.), 1982-84; pub. rels. cons., 1983-90, community rels./Worldport L.A., 1990-92. Contbr. articles to profl. jours. Mem. First United Methodist Ch. Commn. on Missions and Social Concerns, 1983-89; bd. dirs. Depot, 1983-87; mem. devel. com. Pasadena Guidance Clinics, 1984-85. Recipient Pro award L.A. Publicity Club, 1978, Outstanding Achievement award Soc. Consumer Affairs Profls. in Bus., 1976, Disting. Alumni award Centenary Coll., 1992. Mem. Pub. Relations Soc. Am. (accredited mem.; award for consumer program 1977, 2 awards 1984, Joseph Roos Community Service award 1985), Nat. Press Women (pub. relations award 1986), Calif. Press Women (awards 1974, 78, 83, 84, 85, community relations 1stplace winner 1986, 87, 88, 89), Nat. Assn. Mental Health Info. Offices (3 regional awards 1986). Republican.

SMITH-WARREN, KATHARINE, art advisor, educator; b. Huntington, N.Y., June 5, 1945; d. James Betts and Mary (McAllister) Smith; m. William Chafee, Mar. 27, 1971 (dec. 1979); 1 child, James Tyler Chafee; m. Peter Warren, May 14, 1982. BFA, Marymount Coll., 1967; MA, Hunter Coll. CCNY, 1970. Asst. dir. admissions Parsons Sch. Design, N.Y.C., 1971-75; instr. dept. art history Colo. Women's Coll., Denver, 1978-82; Colo. editor Artspace mag., Albuquerque; pres. Art Mgmt. and Planning Svcs., Denver, 1979—; adj. prof. U. Denver, 1990—. Contbr. reference book Contemporary Artists, 1983; contbr. articles to art mags. Mem. steering com. Alliance for Contemporary Art, Denver Art Mus., 1981-85; bd. dirs. Urban Design Forum, 1984-86; assoc. Rocky Mountain Women's Inst., Denver, 1977. Colo. Humanities Program grantee, 1978, 82. Mem. Assn. Profl. Art Advisors (pres. 1990-92), City Club (bd. dirs.). Address: Art Mgmt and Planning Svcs Inc 1660 Wynkoop Ste 1060 Denver CO 80206

SMOLAREK, WALDEMAR, artist, printmaker; b. Warsaw, Poland, Sept. 5, 1937; Came to Canada, 1971; Student, Warsaw Sch. Art, 1952-55, Warsaw Acad. Fine Arts, 1955-57. Instr. form and color composition Warsaw Sch. Art, 1957-60; instr. continuing edn. U. B.C., 1972. One-man shows include Warsaw, Poland, 1958-65, Artist Coop. Gallery, San Francisco, 1959, Kunsterhaus Wien, Vienna, Austria, 1961, Selected Artist Gallery, N.Y.C., 1962, Miami (Fla.) Mus. Modern Art, 1962, Gallerie Classigua, Stockholm, 1967, Gallery Herder, Stockholm, 1969, Presentation House, North Vancouver, B.C., Can., 1976, Langton Gallery, London, 1977, Kilakyushu (Japan) City Mus. Art, 1982, Galeria Fernando Vijande, Madrid, 1982, Gallery Silvia Menzel, Berlin, 1984, Galeria Daniel Templon, Paris, 1985, Harrison Galleries, Vancouver, B.C., Can., 1986, Osaka Found. of Culture, Japan, 1991, Montserrat Gallery, N.Y.C., 1992; represented in permanent collections Miami Mus. Modern Art, mus. ModernArt, Stockholm, Nat. Mus., Warsaw. Home and Studio: 807-1424 Nelson St, Vancouver, BC Canada V6G 1L9

SMOLARSKI, DENNIS CHESTER, mathematics educator; b. Harvey, Ill., Sept. 2, 1947; s. Chester Francis and Genevieve Josephine (Pasek) S. BS, Santa Clara U., 1969; MA, U. Calif., Santa Barbara, 1975; MDiv, STM, Jesuit Sch. of Theology, Berkeley, Calif., 1979; PhD, U. Ill., 1982. Instr. math. Santa Clara (Calif.) U., 1975-76, asst. prof., 1982-88, assoc. prof., 1988—; Ordained priest Roman Cath. Ch., 1979; mem. Jesuit Order, 1969—. Author: Eucharistia, 1982, How Not To Say Mass, 1986 (Hon. Mention 1986), Liturgical Literacy, 1990, Sacred Mysteries, 1995; author booklets; contbr. articles to profl. jours. Mem. Math. Assn. Am. (sect. chmn. 1991-92), Am. Math. Soc., Assn. Computing Machinery, Sigma Xi (club pres. 1987-89). Democrat. Home: Jesuit Community Santa Clara Univ Santa Clara CA 95053 Office: Santa Clara Univ Math Dept Santa Clara CA 95053

SMOLENSKY, EUGENE, economics educator; b. Bklyn., Mar. 4, 1932; s. Abraham and Jennie (Miller) S.; m. Natalie Joan Rabinowitz, Aug. 16, 1952; children: Paul, Beth. B.A., Bklyn. Coll., 1952; M.A., Am. U., 1956; Ph.D., U. Pa., 1961. Prof. econs. U. Wis., Madison, 1968-88, chmn. dept., 1978-80, 86-88; dir. Inst. for Research on Poverty, U. Wis., 1980-83; dean Grad. Sch. Pub. Policy U. Calif., Berkeley, 1988—. Author: Public Expenditures, Taxation and the Distribution of Income: The U.S., 1950, 61, 70, 77. Mem. Nat. Acad. Pub. Adminstrn., 1994; mem. com. on child devel. rsch. and pub. policy NAS, Washington, 1982-87, mem. com. on status of women in labor market, 1985-87. With USN, 1952-56. Mem. Am. Econs. Assn. Democrat. Jewish. Home: 669 Woodmont Ave Berkeley CA 94708-1233 Office: U Calif Dept Pub Policy 2607 Hearst Ave Berkeley CA 94709-1005

SMOLKA, JAMES WILLIAM, aerospace research pilot; b. Mt. Clemens, Mich., July 31, 1950; s. Joseph William and Patricia Joan (Righetti) S. BS in Astronautics, USAF Acad., 1972; MS in Aero., Astronautics, MIT, 1980; engineers degree in aero. & astronautics, Stanford U., 1994. Commd. 2d lt. USAF, 1972, advanced through grades to lt. col., 1992; resigned, 1983; served as pilot 3d Tactical Fighter Squadron, Korat RT AFB, Thailand, 1974, 21 Tactical Air Support Squadron, Shaw AFBSC, 1975-77; test pilot 6510 Test Wing, Edwards AFB CA, 1981-83; exptl. test pilot Ft. Worth div. Gen. Dynamics, Edwards AFB, 1984-85; aerospace rsch. pilot N.A.S.A. Dryden FRC, Edwards AFB, 1985—; lt. col. USAFR, 1992—; adj. prof. Calif. State U., Fresno, 1984—. Author: Analysis and Testing of Aircraft Flight Control Systems, 1982. Mem. Soc. Exptl. Test Pilots. Home: PO Box 2123 Lancaster CA 93539-2123 Office: NASA Dryden Flight Rsch Ctr PO Box 273 Edwards CA 93523-0273

SMOLKER, GARY STEVEN, lawyer; b. L.A., Nov. 5, 1945; s. Paul and Shayndy Charolette (Sirott) S.; m. Alice Graham; children: Terra, Judy, Leah. BS, U. Calif.-Berkeley, 1967; MS, Cornell U., 1968; JD cum laude, Loyola U., L.A., 1973. Bar: Calif. 1973, U.S. Dist. Ct. (cen. dist.) Calif. 1973, U.S. Tax Ct. 1973, U.S. Ct. Appeals (9th cir.) 1973, U.S. Supreme Ct. 1978, U.S. Dist. Ct. (so., ea. and no. dists.) Calif. 1981. Guest researcher Lawrence Radiation Lab., U. Calif., 1967; teaching fellow Sch. Chem. Engring., Cornell U.; mem. tech. staff Hughes Aircraft Co., Culver City, Calif., 1968-70; in advanced mktg. and tech. TRW, Redondo Beach, Calif., 1970-72; sole practice, Beverly Hills, Calif., 1973-89, L.A., 1989—; guest lectr. UCLA Extension, 1973-74, Loyola U. Law Sch., 1979; speaker, panelist in field; adv. Loyola U. Law Sch., 1973—. Contbr. articles to profl. jours.; inventor self-destruct aluminum tungstic oxide films, electrolytic anticompromise process. Mem. Nat. Assn. Real Estate Editors, Calif. State Bar Assn., L.A. County Bar Assn., Beverly Hills Bar Assn. (sr. editor jour. 1978-79, contbg. editor jour. 1980-82, 86-90, editor-in-chief 1984-86, pub. Smolker Letter 1985—). Jewish. Lodge: B'nai B'rith (anti-defamation league). Office: 5777 W Century Blvd Ste 1255 Los Angeles CA 90045-5696

SMOLLAN, DAVID LESLIE, retired tax practitioner; b. Middlesbrough, Eng., June 22, 1928; came to U.S., 1948, naturalized, 1954; s. Philip and Sarah (Freedman) S.; BBA, Woodbury Coll., 1950; m. Sheila Joy Glassman, Aug. 5, 1956 (dec.); children: Jeffrey, Debbie. Chief acct. Lucky Plastic Co., Inc., Los Angeles, 1951-64; self-employed tax practitioner, Encino, Northridge, Calif, 1965-84. Named Kiwanian of Yr., Pacoima Kiwanis Club, 1968; enrolled to practice before the IRS, 1967. Mem. Nat. Assn. Enrolled Agts. (pres. 1973-74), Calif. Soc. Enrolled Agts. (dir. 1993-95, v.p. L.A. chpt. 1994-95), Kiwanis (life, pres. Encino 1985-86, treas. 1989-91, sec. 1994—), IRS Practitioners' Forum (L.A. dist. 1991-94).

SMOOT, HAZEL LAMPKIN, retired piano teacher, poet; b. Kamiah, Idaho, Oct. 17, 1916; d. Albert Chuning and Cora Benson (Buckland) Weaver; m. Daniel Joseph Smoot, Feb. 18, 1939 (div. 1960); children: Daniel Jerome, David Reed. AA, Sacramento City Coll., 1937; student, Linfield Coll., 1938. Contbr. poetry to anthologies published by World of Poetry, also to Vantage Press and The Golden Treasury of Great Poems, Great American Poetry Anthology. Scholar Linfield Coll; recipient Golden Poetry awards World of Poetry, 1987, 88, 89.

SMUCKLER, HARVEY GLASGOW, financial consultant; b. Sturgeon Bay, Wis., Aug. 4, 1924; s. Joseph Max and Ruth Mary (Glasgow) S.; m. Harriet Carol Victor, June 28, 1949; children: Alan Lee, David Todd, Joel Jay. BBA, U. Wis., 1949; cert., The Am. Coll., Bryn Mawr, Pa., 1969, The Am. Coll., Bryn Mawr, Pa., 1984. CLU, ChFC; registered investment advisor, SEC and Calif. Asst. mgr. Mut. of N.Y., Chgo., 1955-59; gen. agt. Continental Assurance Co., Milw., 1959-64; pres. Mayflower Life of Wis., Milw., 1964-67; agy. v.p. Bankers Security Life Ins. Soc., Washington, 1967-70, sr. v.p., 1970-74; exec. v.p. Occidental Life Ins. N.C., Raleigh, 1974, pres., 1975-79; CEO Lincoln Am. Life Ins. Co., Memphis, 1979-80; pres., CEO Smuckler Fin., Tarzana, Calif., 1981—; registered rep. Titan Value Equities Group, Tustin, Calif., 1983—; chmn. SS Telecom Inc., Encino, Calif., 1991—. Mem. Am. Arbitration Assn. (panel), San Fernando Valley CLUs and ChFCs, Optimists of Hollywood. Home: 4623 El Caballero Dr Tarzana CA 91356-4812 Office: Smuckler Fin 18801 Ventura Blvd Ste 304 Tarzana CA 91356-3362

SMUKLER, KIM BENNETT, lawyer; b. Aurora, Ill., Oct. 27, 1952; s. Keith Smukler and Loraine (Hallenstein) Reichel. BA in Philosophy, U. Minn., 1980, JD cum laude, 1983. Bar: Calif. 1983, Minn. 1985. Dep. pub. defender Tulare County Pub. Defenders Office, Visalia, Calif., 1984—. Mem. Calif. Pub. Defenders Assn., Porsche Club Am. Office: Tulare County Pub Defenders Office Rm G35 County Civic Ctr Cthouse Visalia CA 93291

SMULDERS, ANTHONY PETER, biology educator; b. Oss, North Brabant, The Netherlands, July 6, 1942; came to U.S., 1963; s. Arnoldus A.P. and Maria A.A. (Horsten) S. T.C. in Edn. and Psychology, St. Stanislaus T.T.C., Tilburg, The Netherlands, 1962; BS in Biology summa cum laude, Loyola U., Los Angeles, 1966; PhD in Physiology with distinction, UCLA, 1970. Joined Bros. of Our Lady Mother of Mercy, Roman Cath. Ch., 1959. Tchr. Loon op Zand (The Netherlands) elem. schs., 1962-63, Santa Clara High Sch., Oxnard, Calif., 1965-67; research physiologist UCLA, 1970—; prof. biology Loyola Marymount U., Los Angeles, 1970—, assoc. dean sci., 1972-94, dir. health professions info. program, 1995—; mem. L.A. County Narcotics and Dangerous Drugs Commn., 1973—, Calif. State Adv. Bd. on Drug Programs, 1982-92. Contbr. articles to profl. jours. Mem. AAUP, AAAS, The Biophys. Soc., Nat. Assn. Advisors for Health Professions (pres. 1978-84), Western Assn. Advisors for Health Professions, Sigma Xi, Sigma Pi Sigma. Democrat. Lodge: KC. Office: Loyola Marymount U 7101 W 80th St Los Angeles CA 90045-2659

SMULLIN, DONALD EVAN, communications company executive; b. Eureka, Calif., July 15, 1947; m. Cecilia Mattana. BS in Fin., U. Calif., Berkeley; student, Harvard U. Engr. KIEM-TV, 1966, Pacific Teletronics, 1968; mgr. So. Cable TV, 1970-73, KOTI-TV, 1973-76; pres. Oreg. Broadcasting Co., 1976-82; ptnr. TV 58, Sacramento, 1984-86; mgr. KSMS-TV, Monterey, Calif., 1987-89; prin. TRC Communications, Corvallis, Oreg., 1982—, Pacific Broadcasting Co, Oreg., 1993—; prin. Cam Internat., Italy, TRC Leasing, Oreg., Cividale, Italy, Internat. Teletronics, Princeton, N.J.; mem. Univision Spanish TV affiliate bd., 1987-89; bd. dirs. affiliates bd. CBS TV Network, 1977; del. to World Conf. Broadcasting Unions, Algiers, 1983, Prague, 1986, Washington, 1989, Internat. Assn. Broadcasters Gen. Assembly, Rio de Janeiro,1 983, Madrid, 1984, Venice, 1986, Montevideo, 1987. Mem. Nat. Assn. Broadcasters (chmn. internat. com. 1987—), Internat. Assn. Broadcasters (pres. bus. com. Madrid 1986-90, bd. dirs. Montevideo, Uruguay 1986-90), Oreg. Assn. Broadcasters (pres. 1979), Broadcast Pioneers Assn. Office: TRC Communications Inc PO Box 731 Corvallis OR 97339-0731

SMYER, MYRNA RUTH, drama educator; b. Albuquerque, June 10, 1946; d. Paul Anthony and Ruth Kelly (Klein) S.; m. Carlton Weaver Canaday, July 5, 1980. BFA, U. N.Mex., 1969; MA, Northwestern U., 1971. Pvt. practice drama instr. Albuquerque, 1974-78; dir. drama Sandia Preparatory Sch., Albuquerque, 1977—, chmn. dept. fine arts, 1980—; dialect coach, dir. Chgo. Acting Ensemble, 1969-71; lectr., performer Albuquerque Pub. Schs. and various civic orgns., Albuquerque, 1974—; writer, dir., performer Arts in the Pks., Albuquerque, 1977-80; performer, crew various indsl. videos, 1981-86; instr. workshops and continuing edn. U. N.Mex. 1977-80. Writer, dir., designer children's plays including May The Best Mammal (Or Whatever) Win, 1977, A Holiday Celebration, 1977, Puppets on Parade, 1978, A Witch's Historical Switches, 1979, Once Upon a Rhyme, 1987—, Little Red Riding Hood, 1987, Goldilocks and The Three Bears, 1988, Cinderella, 1989, Hansel and Gretel, 1990, Rumpelstiltskin, 1991, The Dancing Princesses, 1992, The Three Pigs, 1994; dir. numerous other children and adult plays. Instr., writer, dir. various community theatres including Albuquerque Little Theatre, Corrales Adobe Theatre, Kimo Theatre, Albuquerque Civic Light Opera, Now We Are Theatre; mem. Albuquerque Cable TV Adv. Bd.; mem. task force on the arts for children Albuquerque Little Theatre. Recipient 1st Pl. award for quality in edn. N.Mex. Rsch. and Study Coun., U. N.Mex., 1989-90, Albuquerque Acad. grant (children theatre), 1993. Mem. Am. Alliance for Theatre and Edn., Women in Communications, Four Hills Neighborhood Appreciation. Office: Sandia Preparatory Sch 532 Osuna Rd NE Albuquerque NM 87113-1031

SMYSER, ADAM ALBERT, newspaper editor; b. York, Pa., Dec. 18, 1920; s. Adam Milton and Miriam (Stein) S.; m. Elizabeth Harrison Avery, Dec. 25, 1943 (dec. 1983); children: Heidi, Avery; m. Doris H. Prather, Apr. 24, 1984. B.A., Pa. State U., 1941. Rewrite man Pitts. Press, 1941-42; with Honolulu Star-Bull., 1946—, city editor, 1953-60, mng. editor, 1960-65, editor, 1966-75, editor editorial page, 1975-83, contbg. editor, 1983—; mem. Pulitzer Journalism Awards Jury, 1970. Author: Hawaii's Future in the Pacific: Disaster, Backwater or Future State?, 1988, Hawaii as an East-West Bridge, 1990; past freelance writer McGraw-Hill mags. Chmn. temp. commn. on statewide environ. planning, 1973; bd. dirs. Corp. for Community TV; chmn. steering com. Gov.'s Congress on Hawaii's Internat. Role, 1988; mem. community adv. bd. Tokai U. Pacific Ctr.; Lt. USNR, 1942-46, PTO. Recipient Disting. Alumnus award Pa. State U., 1976, Hawaii's Outstanding Journalist award, 1989, Award for Disting. Contbn. to Hawaii Journalism Honolulu Cmty.-Medic Coun., 1994, award for promotion of U.S.-Asia/Pacific rels. Pacific and Asian Affairs Coun., 1994. Mem. Hawaii Econ. Assn., Honolulu Social Sci. Assn., Honolulu Acad. Arts, Am. Soc. Newspaper Editors, Japan-Am. Soc. Hawaii, Honolulu Cmty.-Media Coun., Honolulu Press Club (named to Hall of Fame 1987), Honolulu Rotary. Home: 1052 Iiwi St Honolulu HI 96816-5111 Office: Honolulu Star-Bull 605 Kapiolani Blvd Honolulu HI 96813-5129

SMYSER, CHARLES ARVIL (SKIP SMYSER), senator, lawyer; b. Caldwell, Idaho, Nov. 14, 1949; s. Samuel H. and Mildred (Skelton) S.; m. Melinda Sloviaczek, Aug. 22, 1981; children: Lincoln, Logan, Landon. BA, Ea. Wash. U., 1972; JD, Gonzaga U., 1977. Bar: Idaho 1977. Dep. pros. atty. Ada County, Boise, Idaho, 1977-79; dep. atty. gen. State of Idaho, Boise, 1979-80; ptnr. Connolly & Smyser, Boise and Parma, Idaho, 1980—; senator State of Idaho, 1982-90. Mem. Idaho Ho. of Reps., Canyon County, 1980-82; bd. dirs. Idaho State Sch. and Hosp., Nampa, Idaho, 1982-88. Capt. Q.M.C., U.S. Army, 1972-74. Named Legis. of Yr. Idaho Prosecuting Atty.'s Assn., one of Outstanding Young Men of Am. U.S. Jaycees, 1977-86. Mem. Idaho State Bar Assn., Parma C. of C. (pres. 1994—), Lions, Masons, Scottish Rite, Shriners. Republican. Presbyterian. Office: Connolly & Smyser 134 S 5th St Boise ID 83702-5949

SMYTH, BERNARD JOHN, retired newspaper editor; b. Renovo, Pa., Nov. 16, 1915; s. John Bernard and Alice C. (Russell) S.; m. Eva Mae Stone, Dec. 31, 1936; children: Constance, Joe, Pamela, Lisa. Grad., Dickinson Jr. Coll., 1935. Machinist helper Pa. R.R. Renovo Shops, 1936-39; mgr. Smyth Bros., Renovo, 1939-45; editor, pub., owner Renovo Daily Record, 1946-53; owner, editor, pub. Del. State News, Dover, 1953-70; chmn. bd. Independent Newspapers Inc., 1970-85; pres. Valley Newspapers Inc., Tempe, Ariz., 1971-85. Served with AUS, 1944-45. Mem. Soc. Profl. Journalists, Ariz. Newspaper Assn., Sigma Delta Chi. Home: 4200 N Miller Rd Apt 422 Scottsdale AZ 85251-3631

SMYTH, DAVID SHANNON, real estate investor, commercial and retail builder and developer; b. Denver, May 13, 1943; s. William James and Constance Ruth (Sherman) S.; student Regis Coll., 1967-69, USAF Acad., 1961-65, U. No. Colo., 1965-67; m. Sharon Kaye Swiderski, Jan. 3, 1980; children—Julia Caitlin, Alexander Jeremiah, Matthew Davis; 1 son by previous marriage, Shannon David. Accountant, Colo. Nat. Bank, 1966-69; bus. analyst Dun & Bradstreet, 1969-70; pres., dir. Georgetown Valley Water & Sanitation Dist., 1973-74, Realists, Inc., 1973-74, Silver Queen Constrn. Co., 1973-74; v.p., sec., dir. Georgetown Assocs., Inc. (Colo.), 1970-74; pres., chief ops. officer Lincoln Cos., Denver, 1975-76; project mgr., sales mgr., prin. Brooks-Morris Homes, Fox Ridge, Colo., 1976-77; project mgr. U.S. West Homes, Denver, 1977-78; pres., dir. Denver Venture Capital, 1978-81; prin., dir., exec. v.p. Shelter Equities, Inc., 1982-87; prin., dir., exec. v.p. Comml. Constrn. Mgmt. Services, Inc., 1987-88, Shelter Equities, Inc., 1984-87; owner, dir., exec. v.p. Maple Leaf Realty Corp.; v.p., dir. Gibraltar Devel. Corp., Dominion Properties Ltd., 1978-82; investment dir. Van Schaack & Co., 1987-91; prin. investor, head devel. The Farkas Group, 1991-92; sr. residential loan officer, Freedom Mortgage Co., 1992-93; sr. loan officer, dir. builder mktg. NVR Mortgage Co., Englewood, Colo., 1994—. Served with USAF, 1961-65. Lic. real estate broker. Home: 8680 S Aberdeen Cir Highlnds Rnch CO 80126-3947 Office: NVR Mortgage Co 7600 E Arapahoe Rd Ste 210 Englewood CO 80112-1262

SNAID, LEON JEFFREY, lawyer; b. Johannesburg, Transvaal, Republic of South Africa, Dec. 24, 1946; came to U.S., 1981; s. Mannie and Hene (Blume) S.; children: Jedd, Nicole. Diploma in Law, U. Witwatersrand, Johannesburg, 1969. Bar: Supreme Ct. Republic South Africa 1971, High Ct. of the Kingdom of Lethoso 1976, Calif. 1982, U.S. Dist. Ct. (so. and cen. dists.) Calif. 1982. Assoc. Reeders, Teeger & Rosettenstein, Johannesburg, 1972; sole practice Johannesburg, 1973-76; ptnr. Snaid & Snaid, Johannesburg, 1976-81; sole practice San Diego, 1982—; lectr. legal edn. seminars, San Diego, 1984—. Author, pub. quar. newsletter Immigration and Internat. Law, The Newcomers Guide to Living in the U.S.A. Mem. ABA, Am. Immigration Lawyers Assn. (past chmn. continuing legal edn. San Diego chpt.), San Diego County Bar Assn. (past chmn. immigration com.). Lodge: Rotary. Home: 5060 Via Papel San Diego CA 92122-3923 Office: 438 Camino Del Rio S Ste 101 San Diego CA 92108-3546

SNARE, CARL LAWRENCE, JR., business executive; b. Chgo., Oct. 25, 1936; s. Carl Lawrence and Lillian Marie (Luoma) S.; B.B.A., Northwestern U., 1968; postgrad. Roosevelt U.; postgrad. in econs. San Francisco State U., 1976-77, Calif. Coast U. Cert. fin. planner. Asst. sec., controller Bache Halsey Stuart & Shields Inc. (now Prudential Bache), Chgo., 1968-73; controller Innisfree Corp. div. Hyatt Corp., Burlingame, Calif., 1973-76; cash mgr. Portland (Oreg.) Gen. Electric Co., 1976-79; chief fin. officer, controller Vistar Fin. Inc., Marina del Rey, Calif., 1979-82; v.p., treas. Carson Estate Co., Rancho Dominguez, Calif., 1988—; pres. Snare Properties Co., Long Beach, Calif., 1984—, Snare Fin. Services Corp., Rialto, Calif., 1985-89, Carl Snare & Assocs., Long Beach. CPA, cert. fin. planner, Calif. Mem. AICPA, Calif. Soc. CPAs. Founder Cash Mgmt. Assn., Portland, Oreg. Home: 3746 Palo Verde Ave Long Beach CA 90808-2221 Office: 18710 S Wilmington Ave Ste 200 Compton CA 90220-5907

SNASDELL, SUSAN KATHLEEN, computer company executive; b. St. Louis, July 17, 1948; d. Russell John and Gertrude Burnett (Gassman) S. BA, So. Nazarene U., 1972. Office adminstr. Lake, Van Dyke & Browne Med. Group, Pasadena, Calif., 1972-83; founder, ptnr., adminstr. ComputerEase, Oxnard, Calif., 1984—. Contbr. articles to profl. jours. Mem. Better Bus. Bur., Oxnard C. of C. Office: ComputerEase 1201 Escalon Dr Oxnard CA 93035-2757

SNAVELY, SHARON MARTIN, interior designer; b. Columbus, Ohio, July 31, 1946; d. John William and Patricia Mary (Mantel) Martin; m. Charles William Isaly, Nov. 5, 1966 (div. May, 1989); children: Jeffrey, Bradley. BA in Liberal Arts, No. Ariz. U., 1967. Interior designer John Martin Construction, Phoenix, 1967-73; v.p., owner Martin Constrn., Missoula, Mont., 1973-80; pres., owner SMI Interiors, Ariz., Mont., and Calif., 1980-92; constrn. adminstr. Trittipo & Assoc., Carlsbad, Calif., 1989-91; owner, ptnr. Design Group, Missoula, 1992—. Adv. bd. Florence Critton, Helena, Mont., 1994—, Missoula Symphony Bd., 1990—; action bd. Young Republicans, Montana, 1994; Extended Families Bd., Missoula, 1994—. Mem. Am. Soc. Interior Designers, Am. Inst. Archs., Gen. Contractors Assn., Art Assocs. (pres.), Women in Art San Francisco, Missoula C. of C. Redcoats, Rotary. Home: 1415 Khanabad Way Missoula MT 59802 Office: Design Group Missoula MT 59802

SNEAD, KATHLEEN MARIE, lawyer; b. Steubenville, Ohio, July 1, 1948; d. Donald Lee and Mary Alice (Hobright) O'Dell; m. John Jones Snead, Oct. 14, 1972; 1 child, Megan Marie. BA, Pa. State U., 1970; JD, U. Denver, 1979. Bar: Colo. 1979, U.S. Ct. Appeals (10th cir.) 1980, U.S. Supreme Ct. 1986. Field examiner NLRB, Pitts., 1970-72; freelance photographer Charleston, W.Va., 1973-74; labor relations examiner U.S. Dept. Labor, Denver, 1974-77, labor relations officer, 1978-79; staff atty. Denver & Rio Grande Western R.R., Denver, 1979-81, asst. gen. atty., 1981-84, gen. atty., 1984-92; gen. atty. Southern Pacific Lines, 1992—. Mem. ABA, Denver Bar Assn., Am. Corp. Counsel Assn., Alliance of Profl. Women, Colo. R.R. Assn. (dir. 1982-84). Republican. Roman Catholic. Home: 233 S Devinney St Golden CO 80401-5316 Office: So Pacific Lines 1860 Lincoln St Ste 601 Denver CO 80295

SNEDKER, CLIVE JOHN, advertising executive; b. London, Dec. 5, 1947; came to U.S., 1979; s. Henry Morris and Iris May (Clapham) S.; m. Judith Ann Stevens, Dec. 5, 1970; children; Sarah Louise, Clare Jane, Karen Ann. Grad., Tollington Grammar Sch., London. Shipping clk. Thomas Meadow & Co., Ltd., London, 1965-67; comml. dir. F.W. Stephens & Co. Ltd., Cuffley, Eng., 1967-77; owner CJs Design, Hoddesdon, Eng., 1977-79; account exec. Process Displays, Hayward, Calif., 1979-87; owner The Freelance Consortium, Tracy, Calif., 1987—. Chmn. fund raising Tracy (Calif.) Tritons Swim Club, 1987-89, M.C. swim meets, 1986-89; artist Tracy High Sch. Water Polo, 1990; mktg. rep. Tracy Arts Commn., 1991; artist, photographer Tracy Drama Club, 1990-92; artist Trouble Inc. Dance Group, 1990. Mem. Internat. Freelance Photographers Orgn. Office: The Freelance Consortium 950 E Grant Line Rd Ste B Tracy CA 95376-2828

SNEE, LAWRENCE WARREN, geologist; b. Grove City, Pa., Dec. 6, 1947; s. William Warren and Ruth Elizabeth (Goehring) S.; m. Karen Ivy Lund, May 27, 1985 (div. Dec. 1994); children: Jens Erik, Torsten Anders. BS in Geology, Chemistry & Biology, Fla. State U., 1974; Ms in Geology, Ohio State U., 1977, PhD in Geology, 1982. Geologist U.S. Geol. Survey, Reston, Va., 1981-83; prof. geology Oreg. State U., Corvallis, 1983-86; rsch. geologist U.S. Geol. Survey, Denver, 1986—; supr. Argon geochronology lab. U.S. Geol. Survey, Denver, 1986—, mem. adv. bd., 1990—, rsch. chief, 1994—. Author/editor: Emeralds of Pakistan, 1989; contbr. articles to profl. jours. Sgt. USMC, 1966-69, Vietnam. Decorated Bronze Star; Rsch. grantee NSF, U.S. Geol. Survey. Mem. Geo. Soc. Am., Am. Geophys. Union, Soc. Econ. Geologists. Office: US Gel Survey Box 25046 MS963 DFC Denver CO 80225

SNEED, GAIL, mortgage company executive. Exec. v.p. Master Fin. Inc., Orange, Calif., 1993—. Office: Master Fin Inc 333 S Anita Dr 150 Orange CA 92668

SNELL, NED COLWELL, financial planner; b. Cowley, Wyo., May 16, 1944; s. Jay Hatton and Freda Hope (Colwell) S.; m. Barbara Anne Frandsen, Apr. 24, 1969; children: Taylor Anthony, Trevor Cameron. BA, U. Utah, 1969; CLU, Am. Coll., 1983, ChFC, 1985. English tchr. Granite Sch. Dist., Salt Lake City, 1969-71; ins. agt. Prudential Ins. Co., Salt Lake City, 1971-76; pres. Snell Fin. Corp., Salt Lake City, 1976—. Bd. dirs. Utah chpt. Arthritis Found., Salt Lake City, 1980-82, pres. 1982-83; missionary Mormon Ch. 1963-66; chmn. voting dist. 2604 Rep. Nominating Convs., 1986, 90. Mem. NALU (Nat. Sales Achievement award 1971-89, Nat. Quality award), Am. Soc. CLU and ChFC (bd. dirs. Utah chpt. 1990-93, treas. 1993-94, v.p. 1994—, Golden Key Soc. Devel. award 1990), Million Dollar Round Table (knight 1988-94), Salt Lake Assn. Life Underwriters (bd. dirs. 1974-76, 80-82). Republican. Home: 1101 S 2000 E Salt Lake City UT 84108-1971 Office: 1800 S West Temple Ste 416 Salt Lake City UT 84115-1874

SNELL, PATRICIA POLDERVAART, librarian, consultant; b. Santa Fe, Apr. 11, 1943; d. Arie and Edna Beryl (Kerchmar) Poldervaart; m. Charles Eliot Snell, June 7, 1966. BA in Edn., U. N.M., 1965; MSLS, U. So. Calif., 1966. Asst. edn. libr. U. So. Calif., L.A., 1966-68; med. libr. Bedford (Mass.) VA Hosp., 1968-69; asst. law libr. U. Miami, Coral Gables, Fla., 1970-71; acquistions libr. U. N.Mex. Law Sch. Libr., Albuquerque, 1971-72; order libr. Los Angeles County Law Libr., 1972-76, cataloger, 1976-90; libr. Parks Coll., Albuquerque, 1990-92; records technician Technadyne Engring. Cons. to Sandia Nat. Labs., 1992-93; instr. libr. sci. program Coll. Edn. U. N.Mex., Albuquerque, 1991—, libr. Tireman Learning Materials Ctr., 1993—. Ch. libr.. Beverly Hills Presbyn. Ch., 1974-90, ch. choir libr., 1976-90. Southwestern Library Assn. scholar 1965. Mem. ALA, N.Mex. Libr. Assn., Pi Lambda Theta. Office: U N Mex Coll Edn EM/LS Program Tireman Libr Albuquerque NM 87131

SNELL, RICHARD, holding company executive; b. Phoenix, Nov. 26, 1930; s. Frank L. and Elizabeth (Berlin) S.; m. Alice Cosette Wiley, Aug. 1, 1954. BA, Stanford U., 1952, JD, 1954. Bar: Ariz. Ptnr. firm Snell & Wilmer, Phoenix, 1956-81; pres., chmn., chief exec. officer Ramada Inc., Phoenix, 1981-89; chmn., chief exec. officer Aztar Corp., 1989-90, chmn., bd. dirs., 1990-92; chmn., chief exec. officer, pres. Pinnacle West Capital Corp., Phoenix, 1990—, bd. dirs. bd. dirs. Bank One Ariz. Corp., Bank One Ariz. NA, Aztar Corp.; bd. dirs., chmn. Ariz. Pub. Svc. Co. Trustee Am. Grad. Sch. Internat. Mgmt., Phoenix; past pres. YMCA Met. Phoenix and Valley of Sun. With U.S. Army, 1954-56. Mem. ABA, Ariz. Bar Assn., Paradise Valley Country Club, Phoenix Country Club. Republican. Lutheran. Office: Pinnacle West Capital Corp 400 E Van Buren St Phoenix AZ 85004 also: Arizona Public Service Co PO Box 53999 # 9960 Phoenix AZ 85072-3999*

SNIDOW, RONALD WAYNE, real estate agent; b. Newport News, Va., Dec. 30, 1941; s. Ralph Woodrow and Dorothy Sue (Ratcliff) S.; m. Marcia Ann Williams, Dec. 22, 1963; children: William Todd, James Evan. BS, U. Oreg., 1963, MS, 1969. Player Washington Redskins, 1963-67, Cleve. Browns, 1968-72; account exec. Ins. Co. N.Am., Washington, 1967-68; account exec. INA/Marketdyne, Internat., Cleve., 1968-71, L.A., 1971-72; indsl. salesman The Seeley Co., Irvine and Anaheim, Calif., 1973-90, Voit Comml. Brokerage, Irvine, 1992-94; pvt. practice, 1994—. Mem. NFL Players Assn., Masons. Republican. Episcopalian.

SNIEZEK, PATRICK WILLIAM, real estate loan officer; b. Zainesville, Ohio, Apr. 25, 1964; s. Richard Anton and Wanda Lee (Sir) S. BSBA in Mktg., U. Ariz., 1987. Customer svc. rep. Great Am. Bank, Tucson, 1983-85, customer svc. rep. II, 1985-87, real estate loan officer, 1987-91; real estate loan officer Waterfield Fin. Corp., Tucson, 1991-93; asst. v.p., br. mgr. Dirs. Mortgage Loan Corp., Tucson, 1993—. Bd. mem. So. Ariz. Kidney Found., Tucson, 1987-88; bus. cons. Jr. Achievement, Tucson, 1987—; treas. Active 20/30 Club, Tucson, 1987-88, sec. 1988-89, bd. dirs., 1989-90. Named Outstanding Young Man of Yr., Outstanding Young Men of Am., Montgomery, Ala., 1988, Future Bus. Leader of Yr., Future Bus. Leaders of Am., Phoenix, 1988. Republican. Roman Catholic. Home: 3725 N Calle Perdiz Tucson AZ 85718-7215 Office: Dirs Mortgage Loan Corp 5255 E Williams Cir # 2080 Tucson AZ 85711

SNIR, SOL BEZALEL, floor covering company executive; b. Wroclaw, Poland, Apr. 29, 1947; came to U.S., 1985; s. Jacob and Lea (Kaplinsky) Kusznir; m. Adit Kalansky, Dec. 29, 1971; children: Inbal, Yaniv, Lilach. BA in Bus. Adminstrn., Bar-Ilan U., Israel, 1982. Chief exec. officer Leo's Stereo Inc., Long Beach, Calif., 1985-91; property mgr. Mercantile Ctr., L.A., 1991-93; v.p. ops. G&O Floor Covering Inc., L.A., 1993—. Lt. col. Israeli Air Force, 1966-85. Mem. IEEE. Home: 4922 Hesperia Ave Encino CA 91316

SNOOK, QUINTON, construction company executive; b. Atlanta, July 15, 1925; s. John Wilson and Charlotte Louise (Clayson) S.; student U. Idaho, 1949-51; m. Lois Mullen, Jan. 19, 1947; children: Lois Ann Snook Matteson, Quinton A., Edward M., Clayson S., Charlotte T. Rancher, Lemhi Valley, Idaho, 1942—; owner, mgr. Snook Constrn., Salmon, Idaho, 1952—; owner Snook Trucking, 1967—, Lemhi Posts and Poles, 1980—. Mem. Lemhi County Commn., Dist. 2, 1980-93. Mem. Am. Quarter Horse Assn., Farm Bur., Nat. Rifleman's Assn., Idaho Assn. Commrs. and Clerks (sec. 1986, v.p. 1987, pres. 1988), Am. Hereford Assn., Idaho Cattlemen's Assn., Elks. Republican. Episcopalian. Home: RR 1 Box 49 Salmon ID 83467-9701

SNOVER, RICHARD LESTER, software engineer; b. Elmira, N.Y., Aug. 5, 1955; s. Richard Platt Snover and Helen Joyce (Glosenger) Kelly; divorced. BS in Liberal Studies, U. State of N.Y./Regents Coll., Albany, 1989; MS in Software Engring., Nat. U., San Diego, 1992. Ocean systems technician-analyst U.S. Navy, various locations, 1976-87; specialist Computer Scis. Corp., San Diego, 1987-90, programmer/analyst, 1990—; chair software reuse com. CSC Navy Systems Support, San Diego, 1994—. Mem. IEEE Computer Soc., Assn. for Computing Machinery, Nat. Rifle Assn., Calif. Rifle and Pistol Assn., Planetary Soc., Nat. Space Soc. Republican.

SNOW, ALAN ALBERT, publisher; b. Van Nuys, Calif., July 20, 1946; s. Perry William and Virginia (Show) S. BA, Pepperdine U., L.A., 1969; MA, Sch. of Theology, Claremont, Calif., 1974; Magister Operae Onerosae (hon.), Inst. Antiquity-Christianity, Claremont, 1972; ThD, Andersonville Bapt. Sem., 1994. bd. dirs. Inst. for Study of Judeo-Christian Origins Calif. State U., Long Beach; mem. Jesus seminar Weststar Inst. Contbg. author to anthologies: The Book Your Church Does Not Want You to Read, 1993; contbr. articles to profl. jours. and newspapers. Mem. Nat. Notary Assn. (ethics com., Cert. Accomplishment), Am. Soc. Notaries, Dead Sea Scroll Rsch. Coun., Bibl. Archaeology Soc. Democrat. Home: 518 S Bay Front Newport Beach CA 92662

SNOW, MARINA SEXTON, reference librarian, playwright; b. Boston, Apr. 9, 1937; d. Charles Ernest Snow and Katherine Alice Townsend; m. Richard DeVere Horton, Aug. 30, 1958 (div. 1968); children: Heather Kertchem, James Horton; m. Charles A. Washburn, Jan. 7, 1978 (div. 1979). BA, U. Iowa, 1958; MA in Speech Pathology, N.Mex. State U., 1967; MA in Librarianship, San Jose State U., 1976; MA in Theatre Arts, Calif. State U., Sacramento, 1979. Cert. clin. competence Am. Speech and Hearing Assn. Tchr. ESL Inst. Colombo-Americano, Cali, Colombia, 1958-59; tchr. Las Cruces (N.Mex.) Pub. Schs., 1964-66; speech therapist Sutter County Schs., Yuba City, Calif., 1967-72; reference libr. Calif. State U. Libr., Sacramento, 1976—. Contbr. articles to profl. jours.; author 2 plays: Apricot Coffee, Alkali Flat. Pres. Alkali Flat Neighborhood Assn., Sacramento, 1987—; mem. Sacramento Old City Assn., 1979—. Mem. Calif. Acad. and Rsch. Librs., Calif. State U. Librs., Theatre Libr. Assn., Music Libr. Assn. Office: Calif State U Libr 2000 Jed Smith Dr Sacramento CA 95819-2640

SNOW, W. STERLING, secondary education educator, sports coach; b. Devils Lake, N.D., Feb. 14, 1947; s. Morgan Williams and Josephine Elizabeth Ann (Erickstad) S.; m. Barbara Kay Jolley, Aug. 29, 1976; 1 child, Michelle Rene. AB, U. Calif., Santa Cruz, 1970; postgrad., U. Calif., Santa Barbara, 1970-71, tchr. credential, 1971; MA, Chapman Coll., 1976. Cert. secondary sch. tchr., Calif., Alaska; cert. adminstrn., Calif. Tchr., coach Monterey (Calif.) Peninsula Unified Sch. Dist., 1972-76; tchr., coach Anchorage (Alaska) Sch. Dist., 1976—, athletic dir., 1987-92, tchr., 1992—; conf. asst. U. Calif., Santa Cruz, 1971-78. Bd. dirs. Dimond Alumni Found., Anchorage, 1987-92. Recipient Merit award for outstanding athletic program Alaska Dept. Edn., 1990. Mem. AAAS, ASCD, Nat. Assn. Biology Tchrs. (life), Nat. Interscholastic Athletic Adminstrs. Assn. (life), Nat. Assn. Basketball Coaches, Alaska Sci. Tchrs. Assn., N.Y. Acad. Scis., Am. Chem. Soc., Nat. Sci. Tchrs. Assn., Alaska Interscholastic Athletic Adminstrs. Assn. (Alaska Athletic Dir. of Yr. 1990). Lutheran.

SNOWHOOK, ANN LAFERTY, social services administrator; b. N.Y.C., May 25, 1929; d. Paul Gause and Anna Gladys (Braun) Laferty; m. John David Snowhook, Sept. 13, 1952; children: Eileen M., Elizabeth J., David P., J. Jordan, Nancy P. BA in Math., UCLA, 1953, postgrad., 1965, 70. Mathematician missiles divsn. The Rand Corp., L.A., 1951-52; substitute tchr. math. Spastic Children's Found., L.A., 1958-60; sec. women's aux. Exceptional Children's Found., L.A., 1960-63; chmn. and treas. parents group, chmn. fundraising, subsitute tchr. Exceptional Children's Class Pacific Palisades, L.A., 1963-73; chmn. area guild, mr. sch. lunch program Corpus Christi Ch., L.A., 1972-74; statistician, rsch. asst. in mental retardation, family therapy and anorexia nervosa Neuropsychiatric Inst. UCLA, 1974-90; mem. program/policy bd. Kennedy Regional Ctr. for Developmentally Disabled, L.A., 1974-78; del. program devel. fund grants review Los Angeles County Area Bd. X, 1978-82; del. We. Regional Ctr. Assn. Regional Ctr. Contracting Agys., L.A., 1981-82; bd. dirs., pres., corp. sec. We. Regional Ctr. for Developmentally Disabled, L.A., 1978-82; bd. dirs., corp. sec., treas. Home Ownership Made Easy, L.A., 1988-91, Found. for Developmentally Disabled, L.A., 1982—; bd. dirs., corp. treas. Marian Homes for Physically Handicapped and Devel. Disabled, L.A., 1992—; rsch. assoc. Family Therapy: An Overview, 1980, Anorexia Nervosa: A Body Image Disturbance, 1978, Autism: A Study for Chromosomal Abnormalities, 1979, Family Therapy Today, Estrogen Therapy in Menopausal Women, 1991; rsch. cons. Estrogen Therapy in Menopausal Women, Family Therapy Today. Mem. Autism Soc. L.A. (v.p., program chair 1993-95, pres. 1995—). Roman Catholic. Home: 901 Iliff St Pacific Palisades CA 90272-3826

SNYDER, ARTHUR KRESS, lawyer, government official; b. Los Angeles, Nov. 10, 1932; s. Arthur and Ella Ruth (Keck) S.; m. Mary Frances Neely, Mar. 5, 1953; children: Neely Arthur, Miles John; m. Michele Maggie Noval, May 14, 1973; 1 child, Erin-Marisol Michele; m. Delia Wu, Apr. 18, 1981. BA, Pepperdine U., 1953; JD, U. So. Calif., 1958; LLD, Union U., 1980. Bar: Calif. 1960, U.S. Supreme Ct. 1982. Sole practice, Los Angeles, 1960-67; founder, pres. Arthur K. Snyder Law Corp., Los Angeles, 1981-94; pres. Snyder & Archuletta, Attys., L.A., 1994—; mem. City Council Los Angeles, 1967-85; pres. Marisol Corp., real estate and fgn. trade, 1978—; pres. land devel. Watt City Ctr., Inc., 1990—; pres. real estate holdings Keck Investment Properties, 1990—; past instr. Los Angeles City Schs. Served to capt. USMC. Decorated La Tizona de El Cid Compeador (Spain), medal Legion of Honor (Mex.), Hwa Chao Zee You medal (Republic of China); numerous other commendations, medals, awards. Mem. Los Angeles County Bar Assn., Calif. Bar Assn., ABA, Internat. Bar Assn., Am. Trial Lawyers Assn. Am. Judicature Soc., Masons. Baptist. Office: 355 S Grand Ave Ste 3788 Los Angeles CA 90071-1597

SNYDER, DAVID MARKEL, marketing executive; b. York, Pa., Aug. 19, 1939; s. Ellis Snyder and Peggy (Myers) Clemensen; m. Linnea Mae Haberland, Aug. 17, 1968; children: David, Greg. BS in Econs., UCLA, 1962. With Hughes Aircraft Co., 1962—, asst. mgr. Hughes Washington D.C., 1969-72, mgr. Boston Dist. Office, 1972-77, assoc. program mgr. Ground System Group, Fullerton, Calif., 1977-80, dir. Hughes Internat., Europe and Middle East, L.A., 1980-85, staff v.p. Hughes Internat. Ops., L.A., 1985-86, v.p., 1986-90, sr. v.p. Hughes Mktg. & Internat., 1987-90; pres. Hughes Aircraft Internat. Svc. Co., Hughes Aircraft Systems Internat., 1980—; also bd. dirs. Internat. scholar Am. Field Svc., 1956. Mem. Assn. U.S. Army, Armed Forces Communications and Electronics Assn., Marine Corps Aviation Assn., Am. Def. Preparedness Assn., Bel-Air Country Club (club champion 1984-86). Republican. Lutheran. Office: Hughes Aircraft Co PO Box 45066 7200 Hughes Terr Los Angeles CA 90045-0066

SNYDER, FRANCINE, psychotherapist, registered nurse, writer; b. Balt., Mar. 13, 1947; d. Jack and Naomi (Rapoport) S. AA, C.C. Balt., 1968; BA in Psychology, Antioch Coll. W, 1973; MA in MFCC, Azusa Pacific Coll., 1975; PhD in Clin. and Ednl. Psychology, Internat. Coll., 1981. RN, Hawaii; Registered marriage, family, and child counselor, Calif.; instr., Calif.; counselor, Calif; cert. instr. in Basic Cardiac Life Support, Am. Heart Assn. Staff & reliefnurse, crisis counselor Midway Hosp., L.A., 1972-77; counselor So. Calif. Counseling Ctr., L.A., 1972-77; counselor, exec. bd. mem., steering com. mem. Healing Ctr. for the Whole Person, Northridge, Calif., 1974-75; counselor The Family Home, North Hollywood, Calif., 1976; pvt. practice Beverly Hills, Calif., 1975-86; counselor St. Johns Mental Health Ctr., Santa Monica, Calif., 1977-79, Calif. Family Study Ctr., Burbank, 1979-80; pvt. practice Kauai, Hawaii, 1986—; clin. dir., therapist Kauai YWCA Sex Abuse Treatment Program, Hawaii, 1989-90; clin. cons. Iniki Ohana Project, Kapaa, Hawaii, 1993; student nurse Johns Hopkins Hosp., Balt., 1965-68; head and relief nurse, team leader, 1966-70; nurse Nix Meml. Hosp., San Antonio, Tex., 1970; staff nurse, team leader Cmty. Hosp, Chandler, Ariz.; cons. Slim Bionics Med. Group, L.A., 1974-75; instr. Pierce Coll., Woodland Hills, Calif., 1977, Saint Johns Med. Ctr., Santa Monica, Calif., 1977-79, Maple Ctr., Beverly Hills, Calif., 1979-80. Speaker in field. Mem. Am. Anorexia Nervosa/Bulimia Assn., Inc., Am. Mental Affiliates for Israel (exec. bd., head of allocations com.), Internat. Platform Assn., Assn. for Humanistic Psychology, Children's Coalition for TV, Ctr. for the Healing Arts, Alliance for Survival, UCLA Alumni Assn.; cons. Help Anorexia, Inc., Performance Design Syss. Home: PO Box 1303 Hanalei HI 96714-1303 Office: Kauai Counseling & Edn Ctr PO Box 1303 Hanalei HI 96714

SNYDER, HENRY LEONARD, history educator, bibliographer; b. Hayward, Calif., Nov. 3, 1929; s. Henry Runyon and Mary (Rosenberg) S.; m. Janette Marie Hannus, July 21, 1961; children: Michael Jesse, Christopher Henry, David Lyle. BA, U. Calif., Berkeley, 1951, MA, 1960, PhD, 1963. Sr. buyer Dohrmann Comml. Co., San Francisco, 1951-59; instr. to prof. U. Kans., Lawrence, 1963-78; assoc. dean to dean research adminstrn. U. Kans., 1967-78; prof. history, dean arts and scis. La. State U., Baton Rouge, 1979-86; prof. history U. Calif., Riverside, 1986—; dir. Ctr. for Bibliog. Studies, 1989—; dean humanities and social scis. U. Calif., Riverside, 1986; vis. lectr. Bedford Coll., U. London, 1965-66; Fulbright lectr., research scholar U. Hamburg, Fed. Republic Germany, 1974; dir. English Short Title Catalogue for N.Am., 1978—. Editor: The Marlborough Godolphin Correspondence, 1975; co-editor: The Scottish Heritage, 1981. Pres. Baton Rouge Opera, 1981-83, Riverside Opera, 1987-90; pres. United Way, Lawrence, 1977; bd. dirs. Arts and Humanities Com., Baton Rouge, 1981-85; Sigmund, Martin, Heller Traveling fellow U. Calif.-Berkeley, 1962-63. Am. Council Learned Soc. sr. fellow, 1969-70. Fellow Royal Hist. Soc. Gt. Brit., Bibliog. Soc. London; mem. Am. Soc. 18th Century Studies (pres. 1980-81), Conf. Brit. Studies (exec. com. 1978-83), Am. Hist. Assn. Republican. Congregationalist. Home: 220 Trinity Ave Kensington CA 94708-1139 Office: U Calif-Riverside Ctr for Bibliog Studies Riverside CA 92521-0154

SNYDER, JOHN DAVID, pediatric gastroenterologist, epidemiologist; b. Bakersfield, Calif., Dec. 2, 1947; s. David Henry and Margaret Louise (Salber) S.; m. Michele Lorraine Mietus, June 21, 1985; children: Michael David, Matthew Alan, Gregory John. AA, Bakersfield Coll., 1968; BS in Chemistry, U. Calif., Santa Barbara, 1970; MD, UCLA, 1975. Diplomate Am. Bd. Pediatrics with subspecialty in pediatric gastroenterology. Pediatric resident Duke U., Durham, N.C., 1975-78; epidemic intelligence svc. staff CDC, Atlanta, 1978-80, med. epidemiologist, 1980-81; fellow in gastroenterology Mass. Gen. Hosp., Boston, 1981-83; instr. pediatrics Harvard Med. Sch., Boston, 1983-85, asst. prof., 1985-91; assoc. prof. pediatrics U. Calif., San Francisco, 1991—; med. epidemiologist WHO, Geneva, 1980—; cons. in field. Author/editor: Common Problems in Pediatric Gastroenterology and Nutrition, 1989; co-editor: Gastroenterology Section: First: Pediatric Medicine, 1993. Lt. comdr. USPHS, 1978-81. UCLA Regent scholar, 1966, U. Calif.-Santa Barbara Regent scholar, 1968. Fellow Am. Acad. Pediatrics; mem. Am. Gastroenterol. Assn., N.Am. Soc. Gastroenterology and Nutrition. Home: 144 Paloma Ave San Francisco CA 94127 Office: Univ of Calif Med Ctr Box 0136 Dept Pediatrics 500 Parnassus Ave San Francisco CA 95413

SNYDER, JOHN HENRY, computer science educator, consultant; b. Wichita, Kans., Mar. 16, 1947; s. Melvin Henry and Cathleen Ann (Collins) S.; m. Patricia Reilly, Mar. 11, 1984; children: Matthew Melvin George, Mark John Joseph. BA, U. Kans., 1970; MS, Nova U., Ft. Lauderdale, Fla., 1984. Cert. tchr. Nev., N.D. Computer sci. tchr. Hyde Park Jr. High Sch., Las Vegas, Nev., 1981-86, Chapparal High sch., Las Vegas, 1986-91, Cimarron Meml. High Sch., Las Vegas, 1991-94; chair dept. sci. & tech. Advanced Tech. Acad., Las Vegas, 1994—; copywriter pub. info. office CCSD, Las Vegas, 1982-84; chmn. gifted children spl. interest group, Am. Mensa, 1984; mem. tech. com. Nev. 2000 Task Force, 1994—, Nev. State Network Internet Com., 1994—; mem. sch. dist. tech. coord. task force, 1994—; cons. Office Supt. Clark County Sch. dist., Las Vegas, 1984, 85, IBM Corp., Atlanta, 1991—; systems analyst Homes & Narver, 1988 (summer); adminstrv. aide EG&G Energy Measurements, Las Vegas, 1989 (summer); adj. instr. computer sci. Nova U., 1984-93, U. Nev. Las Vegas, 1990—, The Meadows Sch., 1991—; bd. dirs. Ctr. for Teaching Resources, The Mazer Corp., N.Y., Akron, Ohio, 1990—. Newsletter editor Nat. State Tchrs. of Yr., 1991—; contbr. articles to profl. jours. Co-chmn. Ednl. Exposition, Las Vegas, 1984; tech. cons. Harry Reid for U.S. Senate, 1986, 92; mem. Nevada 2000 Tech. Subcom., 1994—, Nev. State Network Internet Com., 1993—. Named Tchr. of Yr., State of Nev., 1989-90, U. Nev., Las Vegas, Southland Tchr. of Yr., 1990, Tandy Tech. Scholar, 1991, Nev. Educator of Yr., Milliken Family Found., 1992; recipient Innovative Teaching award Bus. Week Mag., 1990, Mc Caulufffe fellowship, 1994. Mem. NEA (Instrn. and Profl. Devel. chmn. 1979-80), ASCD, KC (sec., v.p., pres., past pres., local lodge newsletter editor), Am. Legion, Phi Delta Kappa (newsletter editor Overall Excellence award 1990). Democrat. Roman Catholic. Office: Advanced Tech Acad 2501 Vegas Dr Las Vegas NV 89106-1607

SNYDER, JOHN JOSEPH, optometrist; b. Wonewoc, Wis., June 30, 1908; s. Burt Frederick and Alta Lavinia (Hearn) S.; A.B., UCLA, 1931, postgrad., 1931-32; postgrad. U. Colo., 1936, 38, 40, 41, U. So. Calif., 1945-46; B.S. in Optometry, Los Angeles Coll. Optometry, 1948, O.D., 1949. Tchr., La Plata County (Colo.) Pub. Schs., 1927-28; supt. Marvel (Colo.) Pub. Schs., 1932-

33; tchr. Durango (Colo.) High Sch., 1933-41; pvt. practice optometry, Los Angeles, 1952-72, Torrance, Calif., 1972-78; now retired. Former bd. dirs. Francia Boys' Club, Los Angeles; former pres. Exchange Club South Los Angeles, also sec. Mem. AAAS, Am. Inst. Biol. Scis., Am., Calif., Los Angeles County Optometric Assn., Internat. Biog. Assn. Republican. Home: 25937 Reynolds St Loma Linda CA 92354-3962

SNYDER, LYNN NELSON, special education educator; b. L.A., Sept. 30, 1951; s. Donald Vernon and Marceline Opal (Nelson) S.; m. Arlene Frances Moon, Oct. 6, 1972; 1 child, Valerie Ann. BS, Christian Heritage Coll., 1980; MA, St. Mary's Coll. Calif., 1992. Cert. tchr. Assn. Christian Schs. Internat. Tchr. Tabernacle Bapt. Sch., Concord, Calif., 1981-87; vice prin. King's Valley Christian Sch., Concord, 1987-91; dir. learning ctr. Berean Christian High Sch., Walnut Creek, Calif., 1991-92; adminstr. New Vistas Christian Sch., Pleasant Hill, Calif., 1992-94, Kings Valley Christian Sch., Concord, Calif., 1994—. Mem. ASCD. Office: Kings Valley Christian Sch 4255 Clayton Rd Concord CA 94521-2711

SNYDER, MARGARET ELIZABETH, assemblywoman, paralegal; b. Elizabethtown, Tenn., Feb. 25, 1940; d. William Clarence Peters and Emma Grace (Elliott) Murphy; m. Melvin Wesley Snyder, Aug. 16, 1968; children: Jonathan L., Jennifer L., David E. Paraglegal cert., Humphreys Coll., 1992. Sec. U.S., Philippines, Germany; assemblywoman State of Calif. Assembly, Sacramento, 1992—. Vol. Family Svc., Philippines, 1962-64, ARC, Germany, 1970-72, bd. dirs., Modesto, Calif., 1981-84; mem. Dem. Ctrl. Com. 1977-86, Stanislaus County Grand Jury, 1978-79; bd. edn. Modesto City Schs., 1985-92; bd. dirs. The Haven, Modesto, 1990-92; mem. Internat. Friendship Com., Modesto, 1988-92. Named Vol. of Yr. Family Svc., Philippines, 1963, ARC, Germany, 1971, Woman of Yr. Stanislaus County Commn. for Women, Modesto, 1992, Woman of Distinction, Soroptimist Internat., Modesto, 1992. Office: 1101 Standiford Ave Ste B5 Modesto CA 95350-0981

SNYDER, MARTIN BRADFORD, mechanical engineering educator; b. Evergreen Park, Ill., Dec. 19, 1942; s. Bernard A. and Helena M. (Piro) S. BS in Physics, MIT, 1964; PhD in Nuclear Engring., Northwestern U., 1972; PhD in Bioengring., U. Mich., 1985. Presdl. intern Argonne Nat. Lab., Chgo., 1972-73; staff engr. Sargent and Lundy Co., Chgo., 1973-74; Parker B. Francis fellow U. Fla., Gainesville, 1979-81; vis. scholar U. Mich., Ann Arbor, 1981-82, asst. rsch. scientist Sch. Medicine, 1984-85; biomed. engr. VA Hosp., Ann Arbor, 1982-84; assoc. prof. dept. mech. engring. U. Nev., Reno, 1985—. Contbr. articles on nuclear engring., physiology and mech. engring. to profl. publs. Sci. tchr. U.S. Peace Corps, India, 1965-67. NSF fellow, 1971; recipient Mark Mills award Am. Nuclear Soc., 1973; NIH trainee, 1975; rsch. fellow Whitaker Found., 1985. Mem. Am. Phys. Soc. Office: U Nev Reno Dept Mech Engring Reno NV 89557

SNYDER, RICHARD GERALD, research scientist, administrator, educator, consultant; b. Northampton, Mass., Feb. 14, 1928; s. Grant B. and Ruth (Putnam) S.; m. Phoebe Jones, Mar. 2, 1949; children: Dorinda, Sherrill, Paul, Jeff, Jon, David. Student Amherst Coll., 1946-48; BA, U. Ariz., 1956, MA, 1957, PhD, 1959. Diplomate Am. Bd. Forensic Anthropology. Teaching asst. dept. anthropology U. Ariz., Tucson, 1957-58, assoc. rsch. engr. Applied Rsch. Lab., Coll. Engring., 1958-60, mem. staff Ariz. Transp. and Traffic Inst., 1959-60, assoc. prof. systems engring., 1960; chief phys. anthropology Civil Aeromed. Rsch. Inst., FAA, Oklahoma City, 1960-66, rsch. pilot, 1962-66, acting chief Protection and Survival Labs., 1963-66; mgr. biomechanics dept. Office of Automotive Safety Rsch., Ford Motor Co., Dearborn, Mich., 1966-68, prin. rsch. scientist, 1968; assoc. prof. anthropology U. Mich., Ann Arbor, 1968-73, prof., 1973-85 , rsch. scientist Hwy. Safety Rsch. Inst., 1968-85, head biomed. dept., 1969-84, dir. NASA Ctr. of Excellence in Man-Vehicle Systems, 1984-85, prof. emeritus, 1985—, rsch. scientist emeritus, 1989—; pres. Biodynamics Internat., Tucson, Ariz., 1986—; pres. George Snively Rsch. Found., 1992—; adj. assoc. prof. U. Okla., 1963; rsch. assoc. Zoller Lab. U. Chgo., 1964-65, rsch. assoc. dept. anthropology, 1965-67; assoc. prof. Mich. State U., East Lansing, 1967-68; cons. USAF Aerospace Med. Rsch. Labs., Nat. Acad. Scis., U.S. Dept. Transp., adv. com. Office Naval Rsch. Dept. Navy, numerous others. Assoc. editor: Jour. of Communication, 1961-63; cons. editor: Jour. of Biomechanics, 1967-81; editorial bd. Product Safety News, 1973—; adv. bd. Aviation Space and Environ. Medicine, 1980-91, 94—; contbr. chpts. to books and numerous articles to profl. jours. Judge, Internat. Sci. Fair, Detroit. 1968; mem. coun. Explorer Scouts, Ann Arbor, 1968-70; dir. Am. Bd. Forensic Anthropology, 1978-84, 85-91; dir. Snell Meml. Found., 1990—; dir. George Snively Rsch. Found., 1992—. 1st lt. USAF, 1949-54, Korea. Recipient Met. Life award, Nat. Safety Coun , 1970; Arch T. Colwell Merit award, Soc. Automotive Engrs., 1973; Award for Profl. Excellence Aerospace Med. Assn., 1978; Admiral Luis de Flores Flight Safety award, Flight Safety Found., 1981; named to Safety and Health Hall of Fame Internat., 1993. Fellow Aerospace Med. Assn. (John Paul Stapp award in aerospace biomechanics 1994), Royal Anthrop. Inst., AAAS, Am. Anthropl. Assn., Am. Acad. Forensic Scis. (T. Dale Stewart award 1992), AIAA (assoc.); mem. Am. Assn. Phys. Anthropologists, Ariz.-Nev. Acad. Sci., Survival and Equipment Assn., Assn. Aviation Psychologists, Soc. Automotive Engrs. (Aerospace Congress award 1982, Tech. contributions to Air Transport Safety), Internat. Soc. Aircraft Safety Investigators, Am. Assn. Automotive Medicine, Aerospace Physiologists Soc., Sigma Xi, Beta Beta Beta. Republican. Congregationalist. Avocations: aviation, aerospace medicine, forensic anthropology. Home: 3720 N Silver Dr Tucson AZ 85749-9709 Office: Biodynamics Internat Tucson AZ 85749

SNYDER, SAM A., oil company executive, lawyer; b. Helen, W.Va., Sept. 11, 1930; s. Russell Brown and Bess Kate (Swim) S.; m. Dorothy Martha Berry, Oct. 26, 1973. Student, Concord Coll., Athens, W.Va., 1947-50; LL.B., So. Meth. U., 1953. Bar: Tex. 1953, Calif. 1962. Landman Union Oil Co., Midland, Tex., 1955-60; atty. Union Oil Co., 1961-69, asst. counsel, 1969-73, asst. gen. counsel, 1973-85; v.p., gen. counsel Unocal Corp., L.A., 1985—. Served with U.S. Army, 1953-55. Mem. ABA, Los Angeles County Bar Assn., Am. Soc. Internat. Law, Fgn. Law Assn., Soc. Mining Law Antiquarians. Republican. Clubs: Petroleum, Jonathan (Los Angeles). Home: 4116 Forest Beach Dr NW Gig Harbor WA 98335-5846 Office: Unocal Corp 1201 W 5th St Los Angeles CA 90051

SNYDER, WILLIAM ARTHUR, JR., lawyer; b. Balt., July 11, 1940; s. William Arthur and Nelda Merle (Bailey) S. BA, Johns Hopkins U., 1960; JD, U. Md., 1964. Bar: Md. 1964, D.C. 1976. Law clk. Ct. Appeals Md., 1964-65; assoc. Ober, Kaler, Grimes & Shriver, Balt., 1965-70, ptnr., 1971-91; mem. faculty Hastings Coll. Advocacy U. Calif., 1987-91. Fellow Am. Coll. Probate Counsel. Mem. ABA, State Bar Calif., Md. Bar Assn., Balt. City Bar Assn.

SNYDER, WILLIAM HARRY, financial advisor; b. Newport, Pa., May 11, 1934; s. William Harry and Mary (Barner) S.; m. Irvil Kear, June, 1956 (div. 1961); 1 child, Geoffrey W.; m. Sandra Elizabeth Wolff, June 25, 1966; 1 child, Tara Elizabeth. BS in Indsl. Engring., Lehigh U., 1956; MS in Applied Stats., Rutgers U., 1961. Cert. fin. planner. Research engr. Johns-Manville Corp., Manville, N.J., 1956-61; indsl. engr., mgr. services and quality control Johns-Manville Corp., Nashua, N.H., 1961-69; mgr. phys. distbn. Johns-Manville Corp., N.Y.C., 1969-72; mgr. div. and corp. planning. Johns-Manville Corp., Denver, 1972-82; dir. corp. devel. Manville Corp. (formerly Johns-Manville Corp.), Denver, 1982-85; prin. Snyder Fin. Services, Littleton, Colo., 1985—; bd. dirs. Manville Employees Fed. Credit Union, Denver, 1985-88; rep. Fin. Network Investment Corp., 1988—; sec., founding mem. Manville Retirees Assn., 1992—; assoc. Fin. Network Adv. Corp., 1993—. Patentee process for making chalkboard; author: (with others) Standard Handbook of Plant Engineering, 1983. Vol. AARP Tax Coun. Program for the Elderly, 1987—. Served as 2d lt. U.S. Army, 1957-58. Mem. Colo. Soc. of Cert. Fin. Planners, Inst. of Cert. Fin. Planners, Pi Kappa Alpha (pres. 1954-55), Tau Beta Pi, Alpha Pi Mu. Republican. Methodist. Lodge: Mason. Home and Office: Snyder Fin Svcs 1952 W Ridge Rd Littleton CO 80120-3139

SNYDER, WILLIAM REGIS, JR., construction company executive; b. Pitts., Mar. 14, 1954; s. William R. Sr. and Laverne V. (Krebs) S.; m. Nancy Mary Meglio, May 31, 1980; children: Sarah Elizabeth, William Joseph, Kathryn Lee. Student, U. Pitts., Pa. State U., McKeesport, Mesa Community Coll. Checker Three Rivers Drafting Co., Pitts., 1973-75; estimator, project mgr. Plasteel Products, Washington, Pa., 1975-77; draftsman Siciliano Interiors, Pitts., 1977-78; engineered inside salesman Steelite, Inc., Pitts., 1978-80; assoc. Ariz. Joist & Deck Co., Scottsdale, 1980-82; sales mgr. George D. Widman, Inc., Gardena, Calif., 1982-83, mgr. Ariz. ops., 1983-84; pres. WRS & Assocs., Inc., Tempe, Ariz., 1984—. Chmn. St. Mary-Basha's Elem. Sch. Bldgs. and Grounds Com. Mem. Constrn. News West. Office: WRS & Assocs Inc PO Box 24664 Tempe AZ 85285-4664

SNYDERS, REBECCA ELAINE, communications specialist; b. Sioux City, Iowa, Feb. 14, 1955; d. Lowell Dean and Betty Elaine (Carpenter) Hill; m. Russell J. Snyders, June 24, 1978; children: Ryan Conrad, Meredith Elaine. BS in Biology, U. Ill., 1977; MS in Biology, Ill. State U., 1979; MA in Journalism, U. Iowa, 1987. News writer health ctr. info. and comm. U. Iowa Coll. Medicine, Iowa City, 1983-86; info. specialist I, facilities mgmt. office U. Wash., 1987-88; media rels. coord. Am. Cancer Soc., Seattle, 1988-90; pub. rels. coord. Gen. Hosp. Med. Ctr., Everett, Wash., 1990-93; comms. and mktg. specialist Valley Gen. Hosp., Monroe, Wash., 1993-94; comm. specialist Monroe Sch. Dist., 1994—. Vol. Healing the Children, 1993—, Am. Cancer Soc., 1990-94. Recipient First Place Pub. Svc. award Wash. Press Assn., 1991, Regional Emmy award Smokeout PSA, 1991, Event Theme Par Excellence award Am. Cancer Soc. Great Am. Smokeout, 1989. Mem. Pub. Rels. Soc. Am. (Puget Sound chpt., Totem award for Smoke-free Comm. Program 1991). Office: 200 E Fremont St Monroe WA 98272

SO, GEORGE J.K., radiologist, researcher; b. Hong Kong, Apr. 22, 1962; s. Peter and Mary (Lee) S. Student, U. Mich., 1984; MS in Engring., U. Calif., Berkeley, 1987; MD, U. Chgo., 1991. Physician Cedars-Sinai Med. Ctr., L.A., UCLA Med. Ctr., L.A. Recipient Franklin Mclean Rsch. award U. Chgo., 1987; Golden Key scholar, 1983; U. Calif. San Francisco fellow, 1987. Mem. Radiol. Soc. N.Am., Am. Roentgen Ray Soc., Soc. Magnetic Resonance, Golden Key, Tau Beta Pi, Eta Kappa Nu. Office: UCLA Med Ctr 10833 LeConte MC 172115 Los Angeles CA 90024

SOBEK, IRVIN GENE, consulting engineer, sales engineer, farmer; b. Cheney, Wash., Apr. 24, 1934; s. Louie and Lena (Schmitt) S.; m. Mary Elizabeth Cottles, Dec. 28, 1958; children: Craig Allen, Julie Ann. BS in Agr., Washington State Coll., 1957; BS in Agrl. Engring., Wash. State U., 1962. Exptl. aide agrl. engring. dept. Wash. State U., Pullman, 1959-61; agrl. engr. Gen. Food Corp., Walla Walla, Wash., 1962-66; plant engr. Gen. Food Corp., Nampa, Wash., 1966-70; plant engr. Gen. Food Corp., Walla Walla, Wash., 1970-73, prodn. supr., 1973-74, corp. project constrn. engr., 1974-75; farmer Edwall, Wash., 1975—; cons. engr. Edwall, 1977—, sales engr., 1988. Mem. alumni bd. Agrl. Coll. Wash. State U., Pullman, 1980-90; bd. dirs., pres. Edwall Grain Growers Inc., 1978-87; bd. dirs. United Grain Grower Inc., Harrington, Wash., 1987-89. With U.S. Army, 1957-59. Mem. Am. Soc. Agrl. Engrs., Washington State Grange, Lions, Alpha Zeta. Methodist. Home: RR 1 Box 7 Edwall WA 99008-9703

SOBEY, EDWIN J. C., museum director, oceanographer, consultant; b. Phila., Apr. 7, 1948; s. Edwin J. and Helen (Chapin) S.; m. Barbara Lee, May 9, 1970; children: Ted Woodall, Andrew Chapin. BS, U. Richmond (Va.), 1969; MS, Oreg. State U., 1974, PhD, 1977. Rsch. scientist Sci. Applications, Inc., Boulder, Colo., 1977-79, div. mgr., 1979-81; exec. dir. Sci. Mus., West Palm Beach, Fla., 1981-88, Mus. Sci. and History, Jacksonville, Fla., 1988, Nat. Invention Ctr., Akron, Ohio, 1989-92, Fresno (Calif.) Met. Mus., 1993-95; exec. prodr. Idea Factory, KFSN-30, Fresno, 1995—. Alumni v.p. Leadership Palm Beach County; expdn. leader Expdn. Tng. Inst., S.E. Alaska, 1980; mem. U.S. Antarctic Research Program, 1974. Author: Complete Circuit Training Guide, 1980; Strength Training Book, 1981; (with others) Aerobic Weight Training Book, 1982, Increasing Your Audience, 1989, Inventing Stuff, 1995; mem. editorial adv. bd. Invent Mag., 1989-92. Founder, bd. dirs. Visually Impaired Sports Program, Boulder, 1978-81; fitness instr. YMCA Boulder, 1977-81; convener 1st Nat. Conf. Sports for the Blind, 1979; bd. dirs. Leadership Palm Beach; vice chmn. County Com. on Artificial Reefs; treas. Leaderdeship Akron Alumni Assn., 1990-91, class pres. Leadership Akron; v.p. Ohio Mus. Assn., 1991-92, pres., 1992-93; co-host Blow the Roof Off Ednl TV show, 1992; bd. dirs. Fla. Mus. Assn., 1988-89; mem. adv. bd. Marine Sci. Inst., 1990—. Lt. USN, 1970-73. Fellow Explorers Club; mem. Marine Tech. Soc. (sect. chmn. 1982-84), Coral Reef Soc. (chpt. pres. 1982-87), Nat. Inventive Thinking Assn. (bd. dirs. 1989—). Home: 8806 N 5th St Fresno CA 93720-1724

SOBH, TAREK MAHMOUD, computer science educator, researcher; b. Giza, Egypt, Feb. 16, 1967; came to U.S., 1988; s. Mahmoud Abd-El-Hakeem Sobh and Nagwa Abd-el-Meguid Reda; m. Nihal Samy Kandil, Sept. 16, 1992; 1 child, Omar Tarek. BSc in Engring. with honors, Alexandria (Egypt) U., 1988; MS in Engring., U. Pa., 1989, PhD in Computer and Info. Sci., 1991. Registered profl. engr., Utah. Postdoctoral rsch. fellow dept. computer and info. sci. Gen. Robotics and Active Sensory Perception Lab. U. Pa., Phila., 1991-92; rsch. asst. prof. dept. computer sci. Coll. Engring., U. Utah, Salt Lake City, 1992—; organizer session discrete event and hybrid sys. internat. conf. Intelligent Robots and Sys., 1994. Author chpts. to books; editor Jour. Robotics and Autonomous Sys., 1994; reviewer for books, jours.; contbr. articles to profl. jours. Grantee NSF, 1993, 94, Def. Advanced Rsch. Projects Agy./Office Navy Rsch., 1993—, Def. Advanced Rsch. Projects Agy., 1993—. Mem. IEEE (chair session on object recognition 1993 2nd CAD-Based Vision Workshop 1994, session chair internat. conf. robotics and automation 1994), IEEE Computer Soc. (mem. tech. com. on pattern analysis and machine intelligence), IEEE Robotics and Automation Soc. (co-chairperson discrete event dynamic sys. tech. com. 1992—), Internat. Soc. Optical Engring., Assn. Computing Machinery, Soc. Indsl. Computing, Tau Beta Pi (advisor Utah chpt.), Phi Beta Delta, Sigma Xi. Office: U Utah Computer Sci Dept 3190 Merrill Engring Bldg Salt Lake City UT 84112

SOBOLEWSKI, JOHN STEPHEN, computer information scientist, director computer services, consultant; b. Krakow, Poland, July 14, 1939; came to U.S., 1966; s. Jan Zygmund and Stefania (Zwolinska) S.; m. Helen Skipper, Dec. 17, 1965 (div. July 1969); m. Carole Straith, Apr. 6, 1974; children: Anne-Marie, Elisa, Martin. BE, U. Adelaide, Adelaide, South Australia, 1962, ME, 1966; PhD in Computer Sci., Wash. State U., 1971. Sci. officer Weapons Research Establishment, Salisbury, South Australia, 1964-66; asst. prof. computer sci. Wash. State U., Pullman, 1966-73; dir. research, assoc. prof. U. Wash., Seattle, 1973-80, dir. computer svcs., 1980-88; assoc. v.p. computing U. N.Mex., Albuquerque, 1988—; cons. govt. and industry, Seattle, 1973—; mem. bd. trustees Fisher Found., Seattle, 1984—. Author: Computers for the Dental Office, 1986; contbr. articles to profl. jours. Served as engr. with Royal Australian Army, 1957-60. Australian govt. scholar, 1954-60, Elec. Res. Bd. scholar CSIRO, Melbourne, Australia, 1961-64. Mem. IEEE, Computer Soc. Roman Catholic. Home: 8501 Northridge Ave NE Albuquerque NM 87111-2107 Office: U NMex CIRT 2701 Campus Ave NE Albuquerque NM 87131

SOCHACKI, ANDRZEJ, mechanical engineer, researcher; b. Warsaw, Poland, July 26, 1948; came to U.S., 1973; s. Jerzy and Halina (Błażejczyk) S. MS, Tech. Acad., Warsaw, 1969; AAS, Maricopa Tech. Coll., Phoenix, 1983. Sr. mech. engr. Roger Bus. Products div. Rogers Corp., Mesa, Ariz., 1986-87; sr. mech. design engr. Parker Aerospace Co., Phoenix, 1987-88; sr. project engr. Micro-Rel Inc., Tempe, Ariz., 1988-90; cons., project engr., pres., owner Design & Fabricating Co., Phoenix, 1985—; founder, pres., chmn. The Vagabond Ctr., Phoenix. Pres. Vagabond Ctr. Found., 1992. Recipient award Medtronic Corp., Phoenix, 1989. Mem. Soc. Mfg. Engrs. (sr.). Roman Catholic. Home and Office: The Vagabond Ctr 3715 E Taylor St Phoenix AZ 85008-6316

SOCWELL, MARGARET GERTRUDE OSBORN HARRIS, reading and language arts educator, consultant; b. Avoca, Iowa, Oct. 7, 1946; d. Fay and Mary Gertrude (Grote) Osborn; m. Richard John Socwell, Mar. 11, 1971 (div. May 1979); 1 child, Benjamin Adam. BS, Ohio State U., Columbus, 1968; MS, U. Wis., 1979. Cert. reading specialist, Spanish and French tchr., Ariz. Tchr. French Mason (Ohio) Pub. Schs., 1969-70; tchr. Spanish and French St. Matthias Cath. Girls High Sch., L.A., 1970-71; tchr. French Whitewater (Wis.) Pub. Schs., 1971-72, tchr. Spanish, 1972-78; reading specialist Chilton (Wis.) Pub. Schs., 1978-79, Tolleson (Ariz.) Elem. Schs., 1979-80; tchr. reading and Spanish Deer Valley Unified Schs., Phoenix, 1980-88; tchr. reading Rio Salado C.C., Phoenix, 1987—, tchr. lang. arts, 1989—, tchr. social studies, 1994—; state forensics judge Whitewater Pub. Schs., 1974—; test designer Deer Valley Reading Curriculum Com., Phoenix, 1986-87, participant lang. arts pilot program Deer Valley Unified Sch. Dist., 1989. Recipient grant Deer Valley Edn. Found., Inc., 1992. Mem. ASCD, Internt. Reading Assn., Internat. Assn. Near-Death Studies. Democrat. Office: Deer Valley Pub Schs #97 20402 N 15th Ave Phoenix AZ 85027-3636

SOEDER, DANIEL JOHN, geologist, hydrologist; b. East Cleveland, Ohio, Sept. 22, 1954; s. Bernard Ernest and Pauline Katherine (Klucher) S.; m. Janice Elizabeth McIntire, Aug. 27, 1976 (div. Mar. 17, 1995); children: Matthew Arnold, Elizabeth Anne, Kathleen Patricia. BS in Geology, Cleve. State U., 1976; MS in Geology, Bowling Green U., 1978. Field geologist Cleveland-Cliffs Iron Co., Morgantown, W.Va., 1978-81; assoc. geologist Inst. Gas Tech., Chgo., 1981-84, staff geologist, 1984-86, lab. supr., 1986-90; lab. scientist Foothill Engring. Cons., Golden, Colo., 1990-91; hydrologist U.S. Geol. Survey, Mercury, Nev., 1991-93, field ops. mgr., 1993—. Mem. Geol. Soc. Am., Am. Geophys. Union, Soc. Core Analysts. Office: US Geol Survey PO Box 327 Mailstop 743 Mercury NV 89023

SOETH, SARAH LAVERNE REEDY MCMILLAN, psychiatric nurse; b. Amory, Miss., Feb. 20, 1925; d. Samuel Thomas and Bessie Lee (Franklin) Reedy; m. Urshel E. McMillan, Jan. 16, 1944 (dec. 1964); children: David Thomas, Joy Laverne McMillan Keys; m. Glenn Eugene Soeth, Nov. 27, 1976 (dec. 1995). Student, Miss. State Coll. Women, 1943-44; LPN, Tupelo Sch. Nursing, 1968; MSN, U. Miss., Jackson, 1972. RN, Miss. Pvt. duty nurse Evart, Mich., 1960-64; staff nurse Aberdeen (Miss.) Monroe County Hosp., 1965-72; lic. psychiat. nurse Hinds Gen. Hosp., Jackson, Miss., 1972-78; charge nurse Tigard (Oreg.) Psychiat. Convalescent Hosp., 1978-79; staff nurse VA Med. Ctr., Reno, 1979-80, Glenn County Hosp., Willows, Calif., 1980-81; staff nurse VA Med. Ctr., Martinez, Calif., 1981-91, Fresno, Calif., 1991-93; ret., 1993; vol. Mental Health Treatment Ctr. Active Diabetes Assn. Mem. Nat. Assn. Ret. Fed. Employees. Presbyterian.

SOFOS, JOHN NIKOLAOS, food science educator; b. Arachneon, Greece, June 14, 1948; came to U.S., 1972; s. Nicholas John and Marina (Paspaliaris) S.; m. Helen Stamatatos, Oct. 21, 1978; children: Marina, Elvera. BS in Agriculture, Aristotelian U., Thessaloniki, Greece, 1971; MS in Animal Sci., U. Minn., 1975, PhD in Food Sci., 1979. Research asst. U. Minn., St. Paul, 1973-78, research assoc., 1978-80; asst. prof. food sci. Colo. State U., Ft. Collins, 1980-84, assoc. prof., 1984-87, prof., 1987—. Contbr. articles to profl. jours. Mem. Am. Soc. Microbiology, Inst. Food Technologists, Rocky Mtn. Inst. Food Tech. (chmn. 1985-86), Am. Soc. Animal Sci., Am. Meat Sci. Assn. (disting. rsch. award 1994), AAAS, Am. Acad. Microbiology Fellow, Sigma Xi, Gamma Sigma Delta, Phi Tau Sigma. Home: 1601 Sagewood Dr Fort Collins CO 80525-2057 Office: Colo State U Dept Animal Sci Fort Collins CO 80523

SOFOS, STEPHANY LOUISE, real estate executive; b. Honolulu, Sept. 16, 1954; d. Thomas A. and Catherine B. (Seros) S. BA in History, U. Hawaii, 1976. Assoc. Chaney Brooks Realty, Inc., Honolulu, 1976-77; supr. property/mgr. shopping ctr. Hawaii Mgmt. Corp., Honolulu, 1977-79; mgr. mktg. and customer relations Kaiser Devel. Co., Honolulu, 1979-82; gen. mgr. Kuhio Mall, Honolulu, 1982-86; pres. SL Sofos and Co., Ltd., Honolulu, 1986—. Mem. Nat. Assn. Realtors, Inst. Real Estate Mgmt. (cert. property mgr., bd. dirs. Hawaii chpt. 1987), Internat. Coun. Shopping Ctrs. (cert. shopping ctr. mgr.), Bldg. Owners and Mgrs. Assn. (real property adminstr.). Greek Orthodox. Clubs: Honolulu, Outrigger Canoe, Oahu Country (Honolulu). Office: 1240 Ala Moana Blvd Ste 305 Honolulu HI 96814-4218

SOGABE, AKIKO, artist; b. Mishima, Japan, June 1, 1945; came to the U.S., 1987; d. Kaoru and Miki (Takahashi) Hirata; m. William Sogabe, Jan. 29, 1971; children: Steve, Sandy. Student, Tokyo Flower Acad., 1970; diploma, Japan Art Inst., 1972. Illustrator: Cinnamon, Mint & Mthballs, 1993, Washington Water Weeks, 1994, The Loyal Cat, 1995, Oregon Trout, 1995. Mem. Guild Am. Paper Cutters, Northcoast Collage Soc., Soc. Children's Book Writers and Illustrators. Home: 3319 170th Ave NE Bellevue WA 98008-2038

SOGNEFEST, PETER WILLIAM, manufacturing company executive; b. Melrose Park, Ill., Feb. 4, 1941; s. Peter and Alvera S.; children from previous marriage: Scott, Brian, Jennifer; m. Donna Stilwell, May 7, 1994. BSEE, U. Ill., 1964, MSEE, 1967. Elec. engr. Magnavox Corp., Urbana, Ill., 1964-67; sr. fellow, mgr. research, United Techs. fellow Mellon Inst., Pitts., 1967-71; gen. mgr. for semicondr. ops. United Techs., Pitts., 1971-77; v.p. indsl. electronics unit Motorola Inc., Schaumburg, Ill., 1977-84; chmn., CEO, bd. dirs. Digital Appliance Controls, Inc., Elgin, Ill., 1984-91; pres., CEO IRT Corp., San Diego, 1991-94, also bd. dirs.; pres. CEO LH Rsch., Inc., Costa Mesa, Calif., 1994—; bd. dirs. Two-Six Inc. Patentee in field. Trustee Humana Hosp., Hoffman Estates, Ill., 1989-92; pres. bd. deacons Presbyn. Ch., 1981-82, elder, 1988—. Mem. IEEE, U. Ill. Elec. Engring. Alumni Assn. (pres. 1986-87, Disting. Alumnus award 1989), Coves Property Owners Assn. (pres. 1982), Chancellor's Assocs. (U. Calif. San Diego), Barrington Hills Country Club, Pacific Golf and Country Club. Republican. Office: LH Rsch Inc 345 Baker St Costa Mesa CA 92626-4518

SOH, CHUNGHEE SARAH, anthropology educator; b. Taegu, Korea, May 1, 1947; came to U.S., 1970; d. Sang Yung and Ock Yun (Choi) S.; m. Jerry Dee Boucher. BA summa cum laude, Sogang U., 1971; postgrad., U. Calif., Berkeley, 1971; MA in Anthropology, U. Hawaii, 1983, PhD in Anthropology, 1987. Staff instr. English Korean Air Lines, Edn. & Tng. Ctr., Seoul, 1978-79; instr. anthropology Ewha Women's U., Seoul, 1985; asst. prof. U. Hawaii, 1990, U. Ariz., 1990-91; asst. prof. anthropology Southwest Tex. State U., San Marcos, 1991-94, San Francisco State U., 1994—; guest lectr. Chaminade U. Honolulu, 1988; vis. asst. prof. anthropology U. Ariz., 1990-91; cons. in field. Author: Women in Korean Politics; contbr. articles to profl. jours. Exec. bd. com. Women in Asian Studies. Fellow Am. Anthrop. Assn.; mem. Am. Ethnological Soc., Soc. Psychol. Anthropology, Assn. Asian Studies, Western Social Sci. Assn., Korean Assn. Women's Studies, Royal Asiatic Soc. Korean Br. Office: San Francisco State U Dept Anthropology 1600 Holloway Ave San Francisco CA 94132-1722

SOHL, NORMAN FREDERICK, program manager; b. Urbana, Ill., Jan. 26, 1954; s. Norman Frederick and Dorothy Martha (Jansen) S.; m. Judith Marie Wickwire; 1 child, Eli Bishop. BA in Music, Hampshire Coll., 1977. Programmer, animator Circ. Studios, Bethesda, Md., 1987-90; engr. Network Tech., Springfield, Va., 1990=91; program mgr. Asymetrix, Bellevue, Wash., 1991-95; program dir. Wiz Bang Software, 1995—; v.p. Non-Sequitur Found., Sante Fe, 1988-94. Office: Asymetrix 110 110th Ave NE Ste 300 Bellevue WA 98004-5840

SOHM, IRENE MAXINE, interior designer; b. Modesto, Calif., Aug. 22, 1949; d. Daniel Winfield and Fern Lea (Streeter) Ingwerson; m. David Sohm, June 17, 1972; children: Sarah, Jill. BA, Occidental Coll., 1971; MA, Calif. State U., Hayward, 1974; design cert., Cañada Coll., 1983. Cert. interior designer, Calif. Subs. tchr. Fremont (Calif.) Unified Sch. Dist., 1971-72, elem. music tchr., 1973-79; designer Kitchen & Bath Assoc., Palo Alto, Calif., 1983-85; pvt. practice Palo Alto, Calif., 1985-92; designer, ptnr. Interiors at the Village, Santa Rosa, Calif., 1992—; instr. Cañada Coll., Redwood City, Calif., 1991-92; interior design adv. com. Santa Rosa Jr. Coll., 1993—. Contbr. photographs to various newspapers and mags. 2d v.p. Santa Rosa Symphony League, 1994—; bd. dirs. Occidental Coll. Bay Area Alumni, San Francisco, 1980-90; active Sonoma Valley Chorale, 1993—. Recipient 1st Place lighting design award Nat. Home Furnishings League, 1983. Mem. Am. Soc. Interior Designers (pres., showhouse chair 1989-90, sec. 1994-95, pres.-elect 1995—), Phi Beta Kappa. Office: Interiors at the Village 4000 Bastoni Ln Santa Rosa CA 95404

SOHNEN-MOE, CHERIE MARILYN, business consultant; b. Tucson, Jan. 2, 1956; d. D. Ralph and Angelina Helen (Spiro) Sohnen; m. James Madison Moe, Jr., May 23, 1981. BA, UCLA, 1977. Rsch. asst. UCLA, 1975-77; ind. cons. L.A., 1978-83; cons. Sohnen-Moe Assocs., Tucson, 1984—. Author: Business Mastery, 1988, 2d edit., 1991; contbr. to Compendium mag., 1987-90, Massage Mag., 1992-94, Am. Massage Therapy

Assn. Jour., 1989—. Vol. Am. Cancer Soc., Tucson, 1984—; mem. Ariz. Sonora Desert Mus., Tucson; pres. Women in Tucson, 1989. Recipient Outstanding Instr. award Desert Inst. of Healing Arts, 1992. Mem. NOW, ASTD (dir. mem. svcs. 1988, Achievement award 1987, Disting. Svc. award 1988), Internat. Assn. Ind. Pubs., Pubs. Mktg. Assn., New Age Pub. and Retailing Alliance, Sierra Club. Office: Sohnen-Moe Assocs 3906 W Ina Rd # 200-348 Tucson AZ 85741-2261

SOKOL, LARRY NIDES, lawyer, educator; b. Dayton, Ohio, Sept. 28, 1946; s. Boris Franklin and Kathryn (Konowitch) S.; m. Beverly Butler, Aug. 3, 1975; children: Addie Teller, Maxwell Philip. BA, U. Pa., 1968; JD, Case Western Res. U., 1971. Bar: Oreg. 1972, U.S. Dist Ct. Oreg. 1972, U.S. Ct. Appeals (9th cir.) 1973, U.S. Supreme Ct. 1980. Law clk. chief judge Oreg. Ct. Appeals, Salem, 1971-72; pvt. practice Portland, Oreg., 1972—; prof. law Lewis and Clark Law Sch., Portland; adj. prof. law sch. environ. litigation Lewis & Clark U., 1984—. Commr. planning City of Lake Oswego, Oreg., 1981-84. Sgt. USAR, 1968-74. Mem. Oreg. State Bar Assn. (chmn. litigation sect. 1983, disciplinary rev. bd. 1982-85), Oreg. Trial Lawyers Assn. Democrat. Jewish. Office: 735 SW 1st Ave Portland OR 97204-3326

SOKOLOFF, NAOMI BERYL, Hebrew language and literature educator; b. Washington, Nov. 15, 1953; d. Leon and Barbara (Snow) S.; m. Douglas H. Berry, May 24, 1981; children: Rachel Berry, Michelle Berry. BA, Swarthmore Coll., 1975; MA, Princeton U., 1979, PhD, 1980. Asst. prof. U. Ariz., Tucson, 1980-82; asst. prof. U. Wash., Seattle, 1985-92, assoc. prof., chair Near Ea. langs. and civilization, 1992—. Author: Imagining the Child in Modern Jewish Fiction, 1992; co-editor: Gender and Text in Modern Hebrew and Yiddish Literature, 1992, Infant Tongues: The Voice of the Child in Literature, 1994; mem. editorial rev. bd. Hebrew Ann. Rev., 1984-87, Hebrew Studies, 1984-85, 88-89. Grantee ACLS, 1987, NEH, 1988, Fulbright-Hayes Found., 1989. Mem. MLA (mem. Hebrew lit. discussion com., exec. com. 1993—), Assn. for Jewish Studies (bd. dirs. 1986-94). Jewish. Office: U Washington 229 B Denny Hall Box 353120 Seattle WA 98195-3120

SOKOLOV, JACQUE JENNING, health care executive, nuclear cardiologist; b. L.A., Sept. 13, 1954; s. Albert I. and Frances (Burgess) S. BA in Medicine magna cum laude, U. So. Calif., 1974, MD with hons., 1978; postgrad., Mayo Clinic, Rochester, Minn., 1978-81, U. Tex., Dallas, 1981-83. Med. diplomate. Cardiologist, nuclear cardiologist Health Sci. Ctr. U. Tex., 1981-84; chief med. officer Baylor Ctr. for Health Promotion Wellness & Lifestyle Corp., Dallas, 1985-87; v.p., dir. health care dept., corp. med. dir. So. Calif. Edison Co., Rosemead, Calif., 1987-92; CEO Advance Health Plans, Inc./Sokolov Strategic Alliance, L.A., 1992—; chmn. bd. Coastal Healthcare Group, Inc., 1994—; cons. Health Care Strategic Planning Southwestern Bell, AT&T, Wang, Rosewood Corp., Dallas, 1985-87; bd. dirs. Calif. Health Decisions. Contbr. articles to profl. jours. Tech. advisor Coun. Social Security; bd. dirs. Washington Bus. Group Health. Grantee NIH, Bethesda, Md., 1983. Office: 900 Sunset Blvd Ste 800 Los Angeles CA 90069

SOKOLOW, MAURICE, physician, educator; b. N.Y.C., May 19, 1911; s. Alexander and Anna (Spiegelman) S.; m. Ethel Schwabacher, June 30, 1941 (dec. 1970); children: Gail Anne, Jane Carol (dec.), Anne May. A.B. cum laude, U. Calif., Berkeley, 1932; M.D., U. Calif., San Francisco, 1936. Intern San Francisco Gen. Hosp., 1935-36; resident U. Calif., San Francisco, 1936-37, research fellow, 1939-40; resident New Eng. Med. Ctr., Boston, 1937-38; research fellow Michael Reese Hosp., Chgo., 1938-39; gen. practice medicine San Francisco, 1946-62; mem. faculty cardiovascular div. Sch. Medicine, U. Calif., San Francisco, 1946—, assoc. prof. medicine, 1952-58, prof., 1958-78, prof. emeritus, 1978—, chief electrocardiograph dept., chief hypertension clinic, 1946-78, chief cardiovascular div., 1954-73; program and founding dir. cardiology tng. grant USPHS, San Francisco, 1960-73; sr. mem. Cardiovascular Rsch. Inst., 1957—; cons. in field. Author: Clinical Cardiology; Contbr. articles to med. jours., texts.; mem. editorial bd.: Jour. Cardiovascular Medicine, 1975—, Western Jour. Medicine, 1946-68. Bd. dirs. Fromm Inst Life Long Learning, U. San Francisco. Served to lt. comdr. M.C. USN, 1942-46. Nat. Heart Inst. grantee, 1950-78; named U Calif. San Francisco Alumnus of Yr., 1986. Fellow Am. Coll. Cardiology (hon.); mem. Am. Fedn. Clin. Research (v.p. 1948-49), Assn. Univ. Cardiologists, Am. Soc. Clin. Investigation, Brit. Cardiac Soc. (corr.), Am. Heart Assn., San Francisco Heart Assn. (pres. 1950-51). Club: Menlo Circus. Home: 3452 Jackson St San Francisco CA 94118-2021 Office: U Calif Sch of Medicine San Francisco CA 94143

SOLANO, NANCY VOGT, chemist; b. Buffalo, Jan. 16, 1958; d. Arthur Charles and Carol (Ford) Vogt; m. Romeo I. Solano, Aug. 7, 1982; children: Dawn M., Ryan R. BS in Chemistry, Baldwin-Wallace Coll., 1980. Toxicologist Cuyahoga County Coroner's Office, Cleve., 1980-84; med. tech. Roche Biomed. Lab., Inc., Highland Heights, Ohio, 1984-86, Cleve. Clinic Found., 1986-89, South Bend Med. Found., 1989-90; devel. scientist Miles, Inc., Elkhart, Ind., 1990-91; mgr. R&D Utak Labs., Inc., Canyon Country, Calif., 1992—. Mem. AAAS, Am. Chem. Soc., Am. Assc. Clin. Chemistry. Home: 27350 Blueridge Dr Valencia CA 91354-1906 Office: Utak Labs Inc 25020 Avenue Tibbitts Valencia CA 91355-3447

SOLARI, R. C., heavy construction company executive; b. 1925; married. With Granite Construction Co., 1946—, formerly pres.; now pres., chief exec. officer, dir. Granite Construction Co., Watsonville, Calif. Office: Granite Constrn Co PO Box 50085 Watsonville CA 95077-5085

SOLDAHL-HERTZOG, NAN, architectural illustrator, artist; b. Redwing, Minn., Aug. 29, 1949; d. Thomas Alan and Florence Lillian (Holm) Soldahl; m. Stephen Paul Hertzog, Nov. 26, 1969; children: Stephanie Marie, Ross Thomas. BA in Fine Arts, Calif. State U., Hayward, 1972. Art studio asst., art educator, artist H.A.R.D. Adobe Art Ctr., Castro Valley, Calif., 1971-73; graphic artist Dahlin (Calif.) Group Architects, 1988; prodn. asst. Forum Publs., Castro Valley, 1991-92; propr. Nan Soldahl Art Svcs., Castro Valley, 1985—. Exhibited in numerous group shows in U.S., Australia, Russia. Vol. local sch. dist.; advocate Family Emergency Shelter Coalition. Mem. Lydia Women's Cir. Democrat. Lutheran. Office: 18392 Center St Castro Valley CA 94546-1608

SOLER, DONA KATHERINE, poet; b. Grand Rapids, Mich., Mar. 7, 1921; d. Melbourne and Katherine Anne (Herbst) Welch; 1 child, Suzette Maria. Grad. Cath. Ctrl., Grand Rapids, Mich. Artist, instr. metaphys. counselor, rschr., animal rights activist, environmentalist. Author: What God Hath Put Together, 1979, Our Heritage From the Angels, 1981, Expose the Dirty Devil, 1984, Treasurey Book of Poetry, 1984, For Love of Henry, 1985, Greyball, 1986, House of Evil Secrets, 1986. Founder, 1st pres. South Coast Art Assn., San Clement, Calif., 1963-65, Orange Coast Cath. Christian Singles, 1970-73, Psychic Exchange, Orange County, 1979; founder, chief Lake Riverside Estates Communicators, Riverside, 1974-79. Recipient First Place Poetry award, 1991-93. Mem. Calif. tax reduction movement campaign Rep. Nat. Com. Mem. Animal Protection Inst. Am., Greenpeace, People for the Ethical Treatment of Animals, Internat. Fund for Animal Welfare, World Wildlife Fund-U.S., Humane Soc. U.S., Am. Soc. Prevention Cruelty Toward Animals, In Def. of Animals., Physicians for Responsible Medicine, Humane Farming Assn.

SOLHEIM, WILHELM GERHARD, II, anthropologist, educator; b. Champaign, Ill., Nov. 19, 1924; s. Wilhelm Gerhard and Ragnhild Risty S.; m. Ludy Montenegro, Sept. 10, 1973; children: Gary, Kristina, Valerie, Lisa, Mei Li, Siri, Edwin. Student, U. Wis., 1943, U. Chgo., 1943-44; BS, U. Wyo., 1947; MA, U. Calif., 1949; PhD, U. Ariz., 1959. Mus. preparator Mus. Anthropology, U. Calif., Berkeley, 1947-49; research assoc. Mus. Archaeology and Ethnology, U. Philippines, 1950-54; lectr. U. East, Manila, 1950-52; provincial public affairs officer USIA, Manila, 1953-54; asst. prof. anthropology Fla. State U., Talahassee, 1960-61; mem. faculty dept. anthropology U. Hawaii, Honolulu, 1961—; prof. U. Hawaii, 1967-91, prof. emeritus, 1992—; asso. archaeologist Social Sci. Research Inst., 1963-67, archaeologist, 1967-70, editor, 1976-87; vis. prof. Inst. Advanced Studies, U. Malaya, Kuala Lumpur, Malaysia, 1979-80; v.p. R&D Transpacific Assocs., Guam, 1992; rsch. in Sarawak, The Philippines, 1983, Ea. Indonesia, 1990; dir. Ctr. for S.E. Asian Studies, U. Hawaii, 1986-89; bd. dirs. Austro-Tai Studies Inst., Guam, 1992—. Author: The Archaeology of Central Philippines, 1964, (with Avelino M. Legaspi and Jaime S. Neri) Archaeological Survey in Southeastern Mindanao, 1979; editor Asian Perspectives, 1957-91, Asian and Pacific Archaeology Series, 1967-91; contbr. articles to profl. jours. Trustee Hawaii Found. for History and Humanities, 1969-74, 1st v.p., 1972, 2d v.p., 1974; bd. dirs. Balik Bahay, Inc., Honolulu, 1976-93, pres., 1977-93; mem. Hawaii Com. Humanities, 1978-79. With USAF, 1943-46. Fulbright grantee, 1958-59, 83, 90; NSF grantee, 1963-66, 69-72; NEH fellow, 1967-68; Ford Found. grantee, 1972, 75-76; Vis. Scholar Exchange Program fellow Com. on Scholarly Communication with Peoples Republic of China, 1986. Fellow Philippine Assn. Advancement Sci. (founding); mem. Siam Soc., Société des Etudes Indochinoises, Royal Asiatic Soc. (Malaysian br.), Burma Research Soc., Assam Sci. Soc., Indian Archaeol. soc., Far-Eastern Prehistory Assn. (pres. 1971-76), Indo-Pacific Prehistory Assn. (pres. 1976-80), Sigma Xi, Phi Kappa Phi, Phi Delta Theta. Office: U Hawaii Dept Anthropology 2424 Maile Way Honolulu HI 96822-2223

SOLINGEN, ETEL, social sciences educator. BA in Polit. Sci. and History, Hebrew U., Jerusalem, 1974, MA with distinction, 1977; MA, UCLA, 1981, PhD, 1987. Instr. dept. internat. rels. Hebrew U., 1974-78; teaching fellow dept. polit. sci. UCLA, 1981-84; rsch. fellow UCLA Ctr. for Internat. and Strategic Affairs, 1987-92; lectr. Sch. Internat. Rels. U. So. Calif., L.A., 1988-89; asst. prof. dept. politics and society U. Calif., Irvine, 1989-95, assoc. prof. dept. politics and society, 1995—. Editor: Scientists and the State: Domestic Structures and the International Context, 1994; contbr. chpts. to books, numerous articles to profl. jours. NSF grantee, 1985, Sloan Found. awardee, 1987-88, UCLA postdoctoral fellow, 1989, ACLS grantee, 1994, NSF/Am. Polit. Sci. Assn. grantee, 1994; recipient rsch. grants from Ctr. for Latin Am. Studies, 1982, UCLA, 1989, Columbia Found., 1989, U. Calif. Inst. on Global Conflict and Cooperation, 1989-90, 93, 94, John D. and Catherine T. Mac Arthur Found. Peace and Internat. Coop. award, 1995-96, others. Mem. Internat. Polit. Sci. Assn. (rsch. com. on sci. and politics, armed forces and soc. com.), Am. Polit. Sci. Assn., Internat. Studies Assn., Soc. for Women in Internat. Polit. Economy, Women's Caucus for Polit. Sci., Acad. Polit. Sci., Am. Acad. Polit. and Social Sci., Latin Am. Studies Assn., Pugwash Confs. on Sci. and World Affairs, Women in Internat. Security, Brazilian Soc. History of Sci. Office: Univ of Calif Dept Politics and Society Irvine CA 92717

SOLINGER, DOROTHY JANE, political scientist, educator; b. Cin., Sept. 20, 1945; d. Nathan and Janet Louise (Weiland) S.; m. Joel Falk, Sept. 2, 1973 (div. 1981); m. Thomas Paul Bernstein, Dec. 23, 1990. BA, U. Chgo., 1967; MA, Stanford U., 1970, PhD, 1975. From asst. prof. to assoc. dir. Asian studies program U. Pitts., 1975-84, adj. assoc. prof. polit. sci., 1975-84; vis. assoc. prof. U. Mich., Ann Arbor, 1985-86; from asst. prof. to prof. U. Calif., Irvine, 1986—; vis. assoc. prof. Stanford (Calif.) U., 1989-90; mem. editorial bd. U. Calif. Press, Berkeley, 1988-93; cons. World Bank, Washington, 1988, 93, 94. Author: Regional Government and Political Integration, 1977, Chinese Business Under Socialism, 1984, From Lathes to Looms: China's Industrial Policy, 1991, China's Transition from Socialism, 1993; editor: Three Visions of Chinese Socialism, 1984; editl. bd. The China Quar., Modern China. Fellow Hoover Instn., 1981, Woodrow Wilson Internat. Ctr. for Scholars, 1985, Com. on Scholarly Communication with the People's Republic of China, 1984, 85, 91-92, Am. Coun. Learned Socs., 1993. Mem. Am. Polit. Sci. Assn., Assn. for Asian Studies (chair China and Inner Asia coun. 1987-89). Democrat. Jewish. Office: U Calif Sch Social Sciences Irvine CA 92717

SOLL, LARRY, pharmaceutical executive; b. South Bend, Ind., Apr. 26, 1942; s. Manuel and Helenjean (Weiss) S.; m. Jean Newman (dec. 1971); m. Nancy Canavan Maron; children: William, Joel, Jonathan. AB, Princeton U., 1964; PhD, Stanford U., 1971. Vis. asst. prof. MIT, Cambridge, Mass., 1973-74; asst. prof. U. Colo., Boulder, 1974-82; pres. Synergen, Inc., Boulder, 1981-89, chief exec. officer, 1984-89, chmn., 1987—. Chmn. Colo. Advanced Tech. Inst., Denver, 1986-87. Office: Synergen Inc 1885 33rd St Boulder CO 80301-2505*

SOLMER, RICHARD, surgeon; b. South Bend, Ind., Feb. 11, 1947. MD, U. Mich., 1972. Diplomate Am. Bd. Plastic Surgery. Surgical intern Hosp. of the U. Pa., Phila., 1972-73; gen. surgical resident Calif. Hosp. Med. Ctr., L.A., 1976-80; plastic surgery resident Allentown (Pa.) Affiliated Hosp., 1980-82; pvt. practice Huntington Beach, Calif., 1982—. Fellow Am. Coll. Surgeons; mem. Am. Soc. Plastic and Reconstructive Surgery. Office: 17742 Beach Blvd Ste 300 Huntington Beach CA 92647-6835

SOLOMON, ARTHUR CHARLES, pharmacist; b. Gary, Ind., May 30, 1947; s. Laurence A. and Dorothy B. (Klippel) S.; m. Janet Evelyn Irak, Aug. 23, 1969; children: Thomas, Michael, Mark, Jill. BS in Pharmacy, Purdue U., 1970, MS in Clin. Pharmacy, 1972; PharmD. Registered pharmacist; cert. nuclear pharmacist. Clin. prof. pharmacy U. Tex., Austin, 1972-75; v.p. Nuclear Pharmacy, Inc., Atlanta, 1975-83; exec. v.p., managed care officer Diagnostek, Inc., Albuquerque, 1983—; pres. Health Care Svcs., Inc., 1990—; adj. prof. U. N.Mex., 1992—. Contbr. articles to profl. jours. Mem. Am. Pharm. Assn., Am. Soc. Hosp. Pharmacy, Nat. Assn. Retail Druggists, Nat. Coun. Prescription Drug Programs, Am. Managed Care Pharmacy Assn. (pres., dir.), Am. Soc. Cons. Pharmacists, Rho Chi, Pi Kappa Phi. Republican. Roman Catholic. Home: 1504 Catron Ave SE Albuquerque NM 87123-4218 Office: Diagnostek Inc 4500 Alexander Blvd NE Albuquerque NM 87107-6805

SOLOMON, EUGENE, JR., executive consultant; b. Detroit, May 29, 1954; s. Eugene Solomon Sr. and Maria Agnes (Rosario) Reynolds; m. Novillelita Denise Bragg, Dec. 3, 1977; children: Danyelle, Alex. BS in Chemistry, Wayne State U., 1976, postgrad., 1977-78. Account exec. IDS, Detroit, 1976-78; v.p. ops. Reynolds Foods, Detroit, 1978-81; maj. account mgr. Xerox, Detroit, 1981-89; dist. v.p. ops. and sales Philip Crosby Assoc., Detroit and Orlando, 1989-91; pres. Solomon & Co., Altadena, Calif., 1991—; v.p. mktg./sales contract Stratus Group, Redland, Calif., 1971-72. Organizer Dem. Party, Detroit, 1972. Mem. Am. Mktg. Assn. Democrat. Roman Catholic. Office: Solomon & Co 257 E Las Flores Dr Altadena CA 91001-4857

SOLOMON, EZRA, economist, educator; b. Rangoon, Burma, Mar. 20, 1920; came to U.S., 1947, naturalized, 1951; s. Ezra and Emily (Rose) S.; m. Janet Lorraine Cameron, May 7, 1949; children—Catherine Shan, Janet Ming, Lorna Cameron. A.B. (hons.), U. Rangoon, 1940; Ph.D., U. Chgo., 1950. Instr. U. Chgo., 1948-51, asst. prof. fin., 1951-55, assoc. prof., 1955-57, prof., 1957-61; Dean Witter prof. fin. Stanford U., 1961-71, 73-90; dir. Internat. Ctr. Mgmt. Edn.; mem. Coun. Econ. Advisers, 1971-73; bd. dirs. Ency. Brit., Benham Capital Funds. Author: The Theory of Financial Management, 1963, Money and Banking, 5th edit, 1968, The Management of Corporate Capital, 1959, Metropolitan Chicago: An Economic Analysis, 1958, The Anxious Economy, 1975, An Introduction to Financial Management, 2d edit, 1980, Beyond the Turning Point, 1981; editor: International Patterns of Inflation— A Study in Contrasts, 1984, Jour. Bus, 1953-57; bd. editors Jour. of Finance, 1965-66, Jour. Bus. Finance, 1969-73, Jour. Quantitative and Financial Analysis, 1969-71. Served as lt., Burma div. Royal Naval Vol. Res., 1942-47. Mem. Am. Econ. Assn., Am. Finance Assn. Home: 775 Santa Ynez St Stanford CA 94305-8478 Office: Stanford Univ Grad School Of Busines Stanford CA 94305

SOLOMON, GEORGE FREEMAN, academic psychiatrist; b. Freeport, N.Y., Nov. 25, 1931; s. Joseph C. and Ruth (Freeman) S.; children: Joshua Ben, Jared Freeman. A.B., Stanford U., 1952, M.D., 1955. Intern, Barnes Hosp., St. Louis, 1955-56; resident in psychiatry Langley Porter Neuropsychiat. Inst., U. Calif. Med. Sch., San Francisco, 1956-59; asst. to asso. prof. psychiatry Stanford U. Med. Sch., 1962-73; dir. med. edn. Fresno County (Calif.) Dept. Health, 1973-83; clin. prof. UCLA Med. Sch., 1974-78; clin. prof. psychiatry U. Calif. Med. Sch., San Francisco, 1976-79, prof., 1980-84, vice-chmn. dept., 1978-83; adj. prof. U. Calif., San Francisco, 1984-90; prof. psychiatry and biobehavioral sci. UCLA, 1984-95, prof. emeritus, 1995—; chief chem. dependency treatment ctr. VA Med. Ctr., Sepulveda, Calif., 1984-89; chief psychoneuroimmunology, 1989-94; chief psychiatry Valley Med. Center, Fresno, 1974-83. Co-author: The Psychology of Strength, 1975; contbr. over 150 papers and articles on psychoneuroimmunology, violence, Vietnam and other topics to profl. jours. and various publs. Capt. USAR, 1959-61. Fellow Internat. Coll. Psychosomatic Medicine, Am. Psychiat. Assn., Acad. of Behavioral Med. Research., Royal Coll. Psychiatrists. Home: 19054 Pacific Coast Hwy Malibu CA 90265-5406 Office: UCLA Sch Med Dean's Office N Cousins Prog Psychoneuro 12-138CHS Los Angeles CA 90025

SOLOMON, JULIUS OSCAR LEE, pharmacist, hypnotherapist; b. N.Y.C., Aug. 14, 1917; s. John and Jeannette (Krieger) S.; student Bklyn. Coll., 1935-36, CCNY, 1936-37; BS in Pharmacy, U. So. Calif., 1949; postgrad. Long Beach State U., 1971-72, Southwestern Colls., 1979, 81-82, San Diego State U., 1994—; PhD, Am. Inst. Hypnotherapy, 1988; postgrad. San Diego State U., 1994—. m. Sylvia Smith, June 26, 1941 (div. Jan. 1975); children: Marc Irwin, Evan Scott, Jeri Lee. Cert. hypnotherapist; cert. hypnoanaesthesia therapist. Dye maker Fred Fear & Co., Bklyn., 1935; apprentice interior decorator Dorothy Draper, 1936; various jobs, N.Y. State Police, 1940-45; rsch. asst. Union Oil Co., 1945; lighting cons. Joe Rosenberg & Co., 1946-49; owner Banner Drug, Lomita, 1949-53, Redondo Beach, Calif., 1953-72, El Prado Pharmacy, Redondo Beach, 1961-65; pres. Banner Drug, Inc., Redondo Beach, 1953-72, Thrifty Drugs, 1972-74, also Guild Drug, Longs Drug, Drug King, 1976-83; pres. Socoma, Inc. doing bus. as Lee & Ana Pharmacy, 1983-86, now Two Hearts Help Clinic, 1986—. Charter commr., founder Redondo Beach Youth Baseball Council; sponsor Little League Baseball, basketball, football, bowling; pres. Redondo Beach Boys Club; v.p. South Bay Children's Health Ctr., 1974, Redondo Beach Coordinating Coun., 1975; bd. dirs. So. Bay Assn. Little Theatres, 1972-75; actor in 8 shows; founder Redondo Beach Community Theater, 1975; actor Man of La Mancha Vangard Theatre, San Diego, 1995; active maj. gift drive YMCA, 1975; mem. SCAG Com. on Criminal Justice, 1974, League Calif. Environ. Quality Com., 1975; mem. Dem. State Cen. Com., Los Angeles County Dem. Cen. Com.; del. Dem. Nat. Conv., 1972; chmn. Redondo Beach Recreation and Parks Commn.; mem. San Diego County Parks Adv. Commn., 1982; mem. San Diego Juvenile Justice Commn., 1986-92; mem. San Diego County Adv. Com. Adult Detention, 1987-92; mem. human resource devel. com., pub. improvement com. Nat. League of Cities; v.p. Redondo Beach Coordinating Coun.; councilman, Redondo Beach, 1961-69, 73-77; treas. 46th Assembly Dist. Coun.; candidate 46 Assembly dist. 1966; nat. chmn. Pharmacists for Humphrey, 1968, 72; pres. bd. dirs. South Bay Exceptional Childrens Soc., Chapel Theatre; bd. dirs. so. div. League Calif. Cities, U.S.-Mex. Sister Cities Assn., Boy's Club Found. San Diego County, Autumn Hills Condominium Assn. (pres.), Calif. Employee Pharmacists Assn. (pres. 1985), Our House, Chula Vista, Calif., 1984-86; mem. South Bay Inter-City Hwy. Com., Redondo Beach Round Table, 1973-77; mem. State Calif. Commn. of Californias (U.S.-Mexico), 1975-78; mem. Chula Vista Safety Commn., 1978, chmn., 1980-81; chmn. San Diego County Juvenile Camp Contract Com., 1982-83; mem. San Diego County Juvenile Delinquency Prevention Commn., 1983-85, 89-91, San Diego County Juvenile Justice Commn., 1986-91, San Diego County Adv. Com. for Adult Detention, 1987-91; spl. participant Calif. Crime and Violence Workshop; mem. Montgomery Planning Commn., 1983-86; mem. Constnl. Observance Com., 1990-93, Troubled Teenagers Hypnosis Treatment Program, 1989—. With USCGR, 1942-45. Recipient Pop Warner Youth award, 1960, 1962, award of merit Calif. Pharm. Assn., 1962, award Am. Assn. Blood Banks, 1982. Diplomate Am. Bd. Diplomates Pharmacy Internat., 1977-81; Fellow Am. Coll. Pharmacists (pres. 1949-57); mem. South Bay Pharm. Assn. (pres.), South Bay Councilman Assn. (founder, pres.), Palos Verdes Peninsula Navy League (charter), Am. Legion, U. So. Calif. Alumni Assn. (life), Assn. Former N.Y. State Troopers (life), AFTRA, Am. Pharm. Assn., Nat. Assn. Retail Druggists, Calif. Pharmacists Assn., Calif. Employee Pharmacist Assn. (bd. dirs. 1980-81), Hon. Dep. Sheriff's Assn., San Ysidro C. of C. (bd. dirs. 1985-87), Fraternal Order of Police, San Diego County Fish and Game Assn., Rho Pi Phi (pres. alumni). Club: Trojan (life). Lodges: Elks (life), Masons (32 deg.; life), Lions (charter mem. North Redondo). Established Lee and Ana Solomon award for varsity athlete witghest scholastic average at 10 L.A. South Bay High Schs. in Los Angeles County and 3 San Diego area South Bay High Schs.

SOLOMON, RHONDA HOPE, school and educational psychologist; b. L.A., Dec. 1, 1962; d. Jerry and Lynn (Cabin) S. BA in Psychology and Child Devel., Calif. State U., Northridge, 1985, MA in Psychology, 1987; PhD in Psychology, Calif. Grad. Inst., 1994. Lic. edni. psychologist, Calif. Play therapist, children's counselor family stress program San Fernando Valley Child Guidance Clinic, Van Nuys, Calif., 1981-84; sch. psychologist, cons., presenter L.A. Unified Sch. Dist., 1987—; pvt. practice ednl. psychology, 1987—. Crisis counselor, helpline worker Haven Hills Shelter for Battered Women, 1983-84. Mem. APA (assoc.), Nat. Assn. Sch. Psychologists, Calif. Assn. Sch. Psychologists, Western Assn. Psychologists, L.A. Assn. Sch. Psychologists, Psi Chi. Home: 6643 Whitaker Ave Van Nuys CA 91406-5519 Office: LA Unified Sch Dist Dept Spl Edn 450 N Grand Ave # G-369 Los Angeles CA 90012-2100

SOLOMON, RUTH, state legislator, teacher; b. Phila., Apr. 16, 1941; d. David and Bella (Azeff) Epstein; m. Arthur Solomon; 1 child, Barry. BA, U. Ariz., 1971. Tchr. Tucson (Ariz.) Unified Sch. Dist., 1971—; mem. Ariz. Legislature; pres. Tucson Edn. Assn., 1983-85; dir. Ariz. Edn. Assn., Phoenix, 1986—. Bd. dirs. Pima County Community Action Agy., Tucson, 1986—, Mayor's Coun. Youth Initiatives, Tucson, 1987—. Mem. Bus. and Profl. Women's Coun., Alpha Delta Kappa, Phi Kappa Phi. Home: 7026 E Kenyon Dr Tucson AZ 85710-4824 Office: Ariz Ho of Reps 1700 W Washington St Phoenix AZ 85007-2812

SOLONE, RAYMOND JOSEPH, advertising executive; b. Chgo., Feb. 6, 1960; s. Arthur Romeo and Florence Marie (Kilgallon) S.; m. Denise Lynn Aaldering, Aug. 20, 1994; children: Caitlin Jean, Mitchell Joseph. BS in Mktg., So. Ill. U., 1982, MS in Orgn. Communications, 1984. Account mgr. Hill & Knowlton, Santa Clara, Calif., 1984-85, Carlson Assocs., Sacramento, Calif., 1985-87; mktg. communications mgr. Intel Corp., Folsom, Calif., 1987-90; v.p., ptnr. Anderson Solone Inc., Sacramento, 1990—. Bd. dirs. NorCal Ctr. on Deafness, Sacramento, 1986-87; pub. rels. cons. United Way Sacramento, 1985-87. Recipient Award of Excellence-Trademark Communication Arts Mag., 1986, Cert. Excellence Strathmore Graphics Galler, 1992, 1st Place Event Mktg. AdWeek, 1993. Mem. Am. Mktg. Assn. (exec., Bronze award 1990), Sacramento Valley Mktg. Assn., Sacramento Ad Club (Gold award direct mail 1986, Silver award newsletter 1986, Silver award advt. 1986, Delta award direct mail 1988, Silver award sales promotion campaigns 1994). Republican. Roman Catholic. Office: Anderson Solone Inc Mktg Comm 3100 Fite Cir Ste 101 Sacramento CA 95827-1805

SOLOW, HERBERT FRANKLIN, film producer, writer; b. N.Y.C., Dec. 14, 1930; s. Morris David and Frances Louise (Burnbrum) S.; m. Maxine Debra Turner, Aug. 6, 1954 (div. 1974); children: Jody, Bonnie, Jamie; m. Yvonne Fern, 1995. AB, Dartmouth Coll., 1953. Agt. William Morris Agy., N.Y.C., 1954-58; dir., exec. NBC, N.Y.C., 1958-59, Los Angeles, 1958-60, CBS, Los Angeles, 1961-63; v.p. Desilu Studios, Los Angeles, 1964-69; v.p. prodn. Paramount TV, Los Angeles, 1969; v.p. worldwide prodn. Metro-Goldwyn-Mayer, Los Angeles, 1969-73; pres. Solow Prodn. Co., Los Angeles, 1976-79; v.p. Sherwood Prodns., Los Angeles, 1980-83; ind. producer, writer Los Angeles, 1984—. Mem. Writers Guild Am., Dirs. Guild Am., Acad. Motion Picture Arts and Scis., Acad. TV Arts and Scis.

SOLT, GAIL ANN, marketing professional, consultant; b. Pitts., Nov. 6, 1951; d. Frank W. and Janet Eighmey (Storey) Stanford; m. Russell E. Solt. BA, Pa. State U., 1973, MPA, 1975; cert. in nutrition, dietetics, Oreg. State U./ U. N.H., 1986. Registered dietician. Head of counseling, Grad. Sch. of Edn. Pepperdine U., L.A., 1975-76; planning, rsch. supr. May Co. Dept. Stores, L.A., 1976-77; mktg. coord. pvt. real estate investments, L.A., Portland, N.H., 1977-93; clin. account mgr. ARA Svcs., Phila., 1988-89; asst. mgr. Seilers' Corp., Waltham, Mass., 1989-92; consulting registered dietician, health care cons. Durango, Colo. and N.H., 1986—; mktg. analyst, cons. Canterbury Creative, Durango, 1992-94. Organizer Mario Cuomo write-in campaign, Concord, N.H., 1992; event planner, organizer Women Owned Network, Manchester, N.H., 1986-88; campaign organizer John Van de Kamp for Dist. Atty., Joseph Keefe for Congress 1st Congl. Dist., Manchester, 1988, 90. Mem. Am. Dietetic Assn., Pa. State Alumni Assn. (bd. dirs., v.p.), Newfoundland Club of New Eng. Democrat. Home: 2593 Arroyo Dr Durango CO 81301-5834

SOLTISIAK, CHRISTINA ANN, management consultant; b. Bridgeport, Conn., Sept. 22, 1945; d. Frank Edward and Ann Georgiana (Pjura) Tomek; m. Aug. 31, 1967 (dec. 1986); 1 child, Scott William Soltisiak; m. Steven Earl Howell, Apr. 25, 1987. AA, Bryant Coll., 1965. Exec. sec. Glass Tite Mfg., Providence, 1965-67; legal sec. Robert D. Moilanen, Atty., Vancouver, Wash., 1974-77; exec. asst., sales and mktg. Devel. Svcs. Corp., Portland, Oreg., 1978-83; mgmt. cons. Exec. Forum, Vancouver, Denver and Phoenix, 1983—; bd. dirs. Columbia Credit Union. Mem. Clark County YWCA, Columbia River Econ. Devel. Coun. Recipient Customer Care award U.S. Army C.E., 1989. Mem. Am. Soc. Tng. and Devel., C. of C., Nat. Speaker Assn. Democrat. Lutheran. Office: Exec Forum 404 E 15th St Ste 7 Vancouver WA 98663-3451

SOMANI, ARUN KUMAR, electrical engineer, educator; b. Beawar, India, July 16, 1951; came to the U.S., 1985; s. Kanwar Lal and Dulari Devi (Mundra) S.; m. Deepa-Toshniwal, Jan. 21, 1976 (dec. 1985); children: Ashutosh, Paritosh; m. Manju-Kankani, July 6, 1987; 1 child, Anju. BS with honors, B.I.T.S., Pilani, India, 1973; MTech, IIT, Delhi, 1979; MSEE, McGill U., 1983, PhD, 1985. Tech. officer Electronics Corp. India, Hyderabad, 1973-74; scientist Dept. Electronics, Delhi, 1974-82; asst. prof. dept. elec. engring. U. Wash., Seattle, 1985-90, assoc. prof. elec. engring. and computer sci. and engring., 1990-95, prof. elec. enring. and computer sci. engring., 1995—. Designer Proteus multi computer system for automated classification of objects; patentee in field; contbr. over 90 articles to profl. jours. and chpts. to books. Mem. IEEE (sr.), Assn. for Computing Machinery, Eta Kappa Nu. Hindu. Home: 16609 126th Ave NE Woodinville WA 98072-7979 Office: U Wash Dept Elec Engring Ft # 10 Seattle WA 98195

SOMMER, TRIPP, radio journalist; b. Peoria, Ill., June 18, 1952; s. Edwin John Jr. and Carol (Moore) S.; m. Carolyn Osborne-Sommer, June 21, 1981; children: Aimee Marie, Thomas Michael. AA, Menlo Coll., 1972; BA, U. Oreg., 1975. News host, reporter Sta. KRXX-AM, Eugene, Oreg., 1984-86; news vol. Sta. KLCC-FM, Eugene, 1981-86, morning news host, 1986-88, news dir., 1988—. Recipient Best Use of Sound award AP, Oreg., 1987. Mem. Pub. Radio News Dirs. Inc. (pres. 1990—, bd. dirs. 1989-90, Best Newscast award 1989, Best News Mag. award 1990), Lane Press Club (bd. dirs. 1986-87, pres. 1987-89). Office: KLCC-FM 4000 E 30th Ave Eugene OR 97405-0640

SOMMERS, ADELE ANN, engineering specialist, technical trainer; b. L.A., Jan. 21, 1955; d. Morris Samuel Sommers and Elizabeth Noreen (Wilson) Bixler. BA in Social Psychology, Antioch U., 1975; MA in Bus. Mgmt., U. Redlands, 1988. Computer operator and programmer TRM Acctg. Svcs., Santa Barbara, Calif., 1979-81; info. systems analyst Raytheon ESD, Goleta, Calif., 1981-84; tech. support and mktg. specialist Archtl. Computer Software, Santa Barbara, 1984-85; tech. support and tng. specialist Softool Corp., Goleta, 1985-86; sr. configuration mgmt. specialist Santa Barbara Rsch. Ctr. (GM-Hughes), Goleta, 1986—; instr. U. Calif., Santa Barbara, 1988—, West Coast U., L.A., 1988—; pres. Open Door Enterprises, tng. publs., Goleta, 1991—. Mem. ASTD, Am. Soc. Quality Control, Nat. Inst. for Performance and Instrn. Office: SBRC GM-Hughes 75 Coromar Dr Santa Barbara CA 93117-3088

SOMMERS, BILL, radio broadcast executive; b. L.A., Sept. 6, 1939; s. Nathan David andLaura (Lifshitz) Hershman; m. Gale Marsha, July 3, 1965 (div. Dec. 1985); children: Michelle Denise, Nicole Danielle; m. Joey Linda Tilley Sommers, Oct. 8, 1988. Student, L.A. City Coll., 1958. Lic. 1st Class FCC Engring Gen. Dee-jay KNJO-FM, Thousand Oaks, Calif., 1963-65, KACY-FM, Oxnard, Calif., 1965-66, KMEN, San Bernadino, Calif., 1966-67; gen. mgr. KMDU-AM-FM, Ventura, Calif., 1967-68; nat. sales mgr./rep. RKO/KHJ Boss Radio, Hollywood, Calif., 1968-73; gen. sales mgr./rep. KLOS-FM, L.A., 1973-78, gen. mgr., 1978-86, pres., 1986—; fund raiser L.A. Foster Children Scholarships, 1990-95; fund raiser dedicated to L.A. Libr. Reconstruction, 1993; funds for shelter L.A. County Food Bank, 1985-95; L.A./KLOS Blood Drive, 1982-95. With U.S. Army, 1958-61. # 1 profit station in Am. Duncan Report, 1991, # 1 profit station in Capital Cities/ABC Capital Cities Annual Report, 1990-94. Mem. So. Calif. Broadcast Assn. (pres. 1989, chmn. 1978—), Hollywood Radio & TV Soc., Arbitron Adv. Coun. (vice chairperson 1985). Jewish. Office: Sta CC/ABC KLOS-FM 3321 S La Cienega Blvd Los Angeles CA 90016-3114

SOMOGYI, LASZLO PETER, food technologist; b. Budapest, Hungary, June 1, 1931; came to U.S., 1957, naturalized, 1962; s. Istvan and Szerena (Wiesel) S.; m. Marika Harmat, June 1, 1951; children—Peter, George. B.S., U. Agrl. Scis., Budapest, 1956; M.S., Rutgers U., 1960, Ph.D., 1962; postdoctoral fellow U. Calif.-David, 1962-64. Jr. research pomologist U. Calif.-Davis, 1962-64; project leader Hunt-Wesson Foods, Fullerton, Calif., 1964-70; tech. dir. VacuDry Co., Emeryville, Calif., 1970-74, Biophys. Research Corp., Hayward, Calif., 1974-75; sr. food scientist Stanford Research Inst., Menlo Park, Calif., 1975-78; v.p. research and devel. Finn-Cal, Inc., San Rafael, Calif., 1978-83; pres. ETEL, Inc., Berkeley, 1983-89; sr. cons. SRI Internat., Menlo Park, 1989—. Fellow Inst. Food Technologists (named No. Calif. sect. Mem. of Yr. 1984); mem. Am. Assn. Cereal Chemists, Am. Oil Chemists Soc. Home: 12 Highgate Ct Kensington CA 94707-1115

SOMORJAI, GABOR ARPAD, chemist, educator; b. Budapest, Hungary, May 4, 1935; came to U.S., 1957, naturalized, 1962; s. Charles and Livia (Ormos) S.; m. Judith Kaldor, Sept. 2, 1957; children: Nicole, John. BS, U. Tech. Scis., Budapest, 1956; PhD, U. Calif., Berkeley, 1960; D (hon.), Tech. U. Budapest, 1989, U. Paris, 1990, Free Univ Brussels, Belgium, 1992. Mem. research staff IBM, Yorktown Heights, N.Y., 1960-64; dir. Surface Sci. and Catalysis Program Lawrence Berkeley Lab., Calif., 1964—; mem. faculty dept. chemistry U. Calif.-Berkeley, 1964—, assoc. prof., 1967-72, prof., 1972—, Miller prof., 1978; Unilever prof. dept. chemistry U. Bristol, Eng., 1972; vis. fellow Emmanuel Coll., Cambridge, Eng., 1989; Baker lectr. Cornell U., Ithaca, N.Y., 1977; mem. editorial bds. Progress in Solid State Chemistry, 1973—, Jour. Solid State Chemistry, 1976-92, Nouveau Jour. de Chemie, 1977—, Colloid and Interface Sci., 1979—, Catalysis Revs., 1981, Jour. Phys. Chemistry, 1981-91, Langmuir, 1985—, Jour. Applied Catalysis, Molecular Physics, 1992—. Author: Principles of Surface Chemistry, 1972, Chemistry in Two Dimensions, 1981, Introduction to Surface Chemistry and Catalysis, 1994; editor-in-chief Catalysis Letters, 1988—; contbr. articles to profl. jours. Recipient Emmett award Am. Catalysis Soc., 1977, Kokes award Johns Hopkins U., 1976, Albert award Precious Metal Inst., 1986, Sr. Disting. Scientist award Alexander von Humboldt Found., 1989, E.W. Mueller award U. Wis.; Guggenheim fellow, 1969. Fellow AAAS, Am. Phys. Soc.; mem. NAS, Am. Acad. Arts and Scis., Am. Chem. Soc. (chmn. colloid and surface chemistry 1981, Surface and Colloid Chemistry award 1981, Peter Debye award 1989, Arthur W. Adamson award 1994), Catalysis Soc. N.Am., Hungarian Acad. Scis. (hon. 1990). Office: U Calif Dept Chemistry D 58 Hildebrand Hall Berkeley CA 94720 Home: 665 San Luis Rd Berkeley CA 94707-1725

SONENBERG, MAYA, writer, educator; b. N.Y.C., Feb. 24, 1960; d. Jack Sonenberg and Phoebe (Rubin) Helman-Sonenberg. BA in English, Wesleyan U., Middletown, Conn., 1982; MA in Creative Writing, Brown U., 1984. Lectr. Sonoma State U., Rohnert Park, Calif., 1986; instr. Chabot Coll., Hayward, Calif., 1989-90; asst. prof. Oreg. State U., Corvallis, 1990-93; asst. prof. dept. English U. Wash., Seattle, 1993—; panelist Artist Trust, Seattle, 1994; editor Calyx Books, Corvallis, 1993—; manuscript reviewer St. Martin's Press, N.Y.C., 1992—. Author: Cartographies, 1989; contbr. stories to Chelsea, Grand Street, Am. Short Fiction. Recipient Drue Heinz Lit. prize U. Pitts. Press, 1989; MacDowell Colony fellow, Peterborough, N.H., 1987; Humanities Ctr. faculty fellow Oreg. State U., 1992-93; U. Wash. grantee, 1994. Mem. MLA, Assoc. Writing Programs, Pacific N.W. Am. Studies Assn. Office: U Wash Dept English GN-30 Seattle WA 98195

SONES, LEON ISAAC, psychiatrist; b. Chelsea, Mass., Jan. 9, 1928; s. Barnet and Rose (Lang) S.; m. Gittelle M. Sones, July 15, 1951; children: Aaron, Daniel, David. AA, UCLA, 1951; BA, U. Calif., Berkeley, 1952; MD, U. Calif., San Francisco, 1955. Diplomate Am. Bd. Psychiatry. Intern Harbor Gen. Hosp., Torrance, Calif., 1955-56; resident in psychiatry UCLA, 1956-59; staff psychiatrist Mental Hygiene Clinic, L.A., 1959-60; pvt. practice Beverly Hills, Calif., 1959—; clin. instr. psychiatry UCLA, 1959-72, asst. clin. prof., 1972—; attending psychiatrist Cedars-Sinai Hosp., L.A., 1962—, founder, dir. Consultation and Liaison Svc., 1966-77, attending chief, 1983-87. Tech. sgt. U.S. Army, 1946-48, Japan. Mem. Am. Psychiat. Assn., So. Calif. Psychiat. Soc. Office: 435 N Bedford Dr Ste 400 Beverly Hills CA 90210-4315

SONNE, MAGGIE LEE, sales executive; b. Pasadena, Calif., July 14, 1958; d. Roscoe Newbold Jr. and Ann Miriam (Vierhus) S.; m. Donald Alan Blackburn, Sept. 8, 1979 (div. 1983). AS, Oreg. Inst. Tech., 1981, BS, 1983. Sales trainee NCR Corp., Dayton, Ohio, 1983-84; sales rep. NCR Corp., Portland, Oreg., 1984-86; account mgr. NCR Corp., Seattle, 1986-87; sr. account mgr. NCR Corp., Portland, 1987-88; sr. account rep. Wang Labs., Portland, 1988-91; account exec. Tandem Computers, Portland, 1991-94; sr. acct. exec. Fin. Svcs., L.A., 1994—. Active Emily's List, Project Vote Smart, Spl. Olympics, Ams. for Change, Presdl. Task Force, Pres. Coun., Tandem Computers, Inc. Mem. Soc. Advancement Mgmt., Costeau Soc., Alpha Chi. Home: PO Box 323 Surfside CA 90743-0323

SONNENFELD, ALBERT, French language and comparative literature educator, food historian; b. Berlin, July 22, 1934; came to U.S. 1938; s. Arthur and Anni (Lichtenstein) S.; m. Portia B. Leys, June 15, 1955 (div. 1986); children: Mark David, Carole Marie Geithner; m. Noel Riley Fitch, Aug. 23, 1987. AB, Oberlin (Ohio) Coll., 1955; AM, Princeton U., 1957, PhD, 1958. Prof. French and comparative lit. Princeton U., 1958-86; M.F. Chevalier prof. French and dept. chmn. U. So. Calif., L.A., 1986—; vis. prof. Dartmouth Coll., UCLA, U. Wis., NYU, CUNY, also others; cons. Linguaphone Inst., London, 1974—; food critic; restaurant cons. Author: L'Oeuvre poetique de Tristan Corbiere, 1961, Crossroads, 1982, Thirty-Six French Poems, 1961; co-author: Temoins de l'Homme, 1965. Fulbright fellow, 1966-67; NEH fellow, 1978-79, 80, 83; recipient Raubenheimer Outstanding Faculty award, U. So. Calif., 1990. Mem. Am. Inst. Wine and Food (bd. dirs.), The Athenaeum (London), Phi Beta Kappa. Home: 11829 Mayfield Ave Apt 303 Los Angeles CA 90049-5791 Office: U So Calif 126 University Pk Los Angeles CA 90089

SONNTAG, VOLKER KARL HEINZ, neurosurgeon, educator; b. Graudenz, Germany, Nov. 23, 1944; came to U.S., 1957, naturalized, 1965; s. Heintz and Gisla Sonntag; m. Lynne Twohig Sonntag, Apr. 24th 1974; children: Alissa, Christopher, Stephen. BA in Chemistry summa cum laude, Ariz. State U., 1967; MD, U. Ariz., 1971. Diplomate Am. Bd. Neurol. Surgery; cert. advanced trauma life support. Intern Ariz. Med. Ctr., U. Ariz., Tucson, 1971-72; resident in neurosurgery Tufts-New Eng. Med. Ctr., Boston, 1972-75, chief resident, 1975-77; pvt. practice, Youngstown, Ohio, 1977-78, Scottsdale, Ariz., 1978-83, Phoenix, 1978—; chmn. spine sect., vice chmn. dept. neurosurgery Barrow Neurol. Inst., Phoenix, 1984—; clin. assoc. prof. surgery U. Ariz., 1985-88, clin. prof., 1989—; numerous presentations in field; invited prof. U. Nev., 1986, Columbia-Presbyn. Neurol. Inst., 1987, U. Ala., Birmingham, 1989, Emory U., Atlanta, 1989, U. Tokyo, 1989, U. Mich., Ann Arbor, 1990, Syracuse (N.Y.) U., 1990, U. Tex. S.W. Med. Ctr., Dallas, 1990, Uniformed Svcs. U. Health Scis., Bethesda, Md., 1991, Chgo. Neurosurg. Ctr., 1991, N.J. Med. Coll., Newark, 1992, SUNY, Buffalo, 1992, U. Chgo., 1993, Johns Hopkins U., Balt., 1993, U. Ark., Little Rock, 1994, numerous others. News editor BNI Quar., 1982-86, sci. editor, 1992—; mem. editl. bd. Jour. Spinal Disorders, 1988-93, Neurosurgery, 1993—, Critical Rev. in Neurosurgery, 1993—; dep. editor Spine, 1993—; contbr. over 200 articles and abstracts to med. jours., numerous chpts. to books. Grantee Ariz. Disease Control Commn., 1987-88, Barrow Neurol. Women's Bd., 1987-88, 90, Barrow Neurol. Inst. and St. Joseph's Hosp., 1987-88, NIH, 1985-90, Ctrs. Disease Control, 1989. Fellow ACS; mem. AMA, Congress Neurol. Surgeons (internat. com. 1987—, exec. com. 1988—, nat. adv. com. 1990—), Soc. for Neurosci., Am. Assn. Neurol. Surgeons, Soc. Neurol. Surgeons (membership com. 1991-94, chmn. 1993-94), Neurosurg. Soc. Am., N.Am. Spine Soc. (bd. dirs. 1993, v.p. 1992-93, pres.-elect 1993-94), Western Neurol. Soc., Rocky Mountain Neurosurg. Soc., Ariz. Med. Assn., Ariz. Soc. for Neurosurgeons, Maricopa County Med. Soc., Alpha Omega Alpha (hon.). Home: 5202 E Exeter Blvd Phoenix AZ 85018-3011 Office: Neurosurg Assocs Ltd Barrow Neurosurg Inst 2910 N 3rd Ave Phoenix AZ 85013-4434

SONS, RAYMOND WILLIAM, journalist; b. Harvey, Ill., Aug. 25, 1926; s. William Henry and Gladys Lydia (Steinko) S.; m. Bettina Dieckmann; children: David, Pamela Sons Clarke, Ronald. B.A., U. Mich., 1950. Reporter, mng. editor Murphysboro (Ill.) Daily Ind. edit. So. Illinoisan newspaper, 1950-52; assoc. news editor Middletown (Ohio) Jour., 1952-53; reporter, asst. city editor, sportswriter, sports editor Chgo. Daily News, 1953-78; sports editor, columnist Chgo. Sun-Times, 1978-92. Served with USAAF, 1945-46. Recipient Best Sports Story in Ill. award U.P.I., 1970, Marshall Field award for outstanding editorial contbn. to Chgo. Daily News, 1972; Best Sports Column award AP Sports Editors, 1979, Best Sports Column award Ill. AP, 1987. Roman Catholic. Home: 4100 Torrington Ct Fort Collins CO 80525-3419

SONTAG, FREDERICK EARL, philosophy educator; b. Long Beach, Calif., Oct. 2, 1924; s. M. Burnett and Cornelia (Nicholson) S.; m. Carol Furth, June 10, 1950; children: Grant Furth, Anne Burnett Karch. BA with great distinction, Stanford U., 1949; MA, Yale U., 1951, PhD, 1952; LLD (hon.), Coll. Idaho, 1971. Instr. Yale U., 1951-52; asst. prof. philosophy Pomona Coll., Claremont, Calif., 1952-55, assoc. prof., 1955-60, prof., 1970—, Robert C. Denison prof. philosophy, 1972—, chmn. dept. philosophy, 1960-67, 76-77, 80-84; chmn. coordinating com. in philosophy Claremont Grad. Sch. and Univ. Ctr., 1962-65; vis. prof. Union Theol. Sem., N.Y.C., 1959-60, Collegio di Sant' Anselmo, Rome, 1966-67, U. Copenhagen, fall 1972; theologian-in-residence Am. Ch. in Paris, fall 1973; Fulbright regional vis. prof., India, East Asia, Pacific areas, 1977-78; mem. nat. adv. council Kent Fellowship Program of Danforth Found., 1963-66. Author numerous books, the most recent being: Love Beyond Pain: Mysticism Within Christianity, 1977; Sun Myung Moon and the Unification Church, 1977, also German, Japanese and Korean transl.; (with John K. Roth) God and America's Future, 1977; What Can God Do?, 1979; A Kierkegaard Handbook, 1979; The Elements of Philosophy, 1984, (with John K. Roth) The Questions of Philosophy, 1988, Emotion, 1989, The Return of the Gods, 1989, Willgenstein and the Mystical, 1995, Uncertain Truth, 1995, The Descent of Women, 1995, The Acts of the Trinity. Pres. bd. dirs. Claremont Family Svc., 1960-64; trustee The Coro Found., Los Angeles and San Francisco, 1967-71; bd. dirs., chmn. ways and means com. Pilgrim Place, Claremont, 1970-77. Served with AUS, 1943-46. Vis. scholar Ctr. for Study Japanese Religions, Kyoto, Japan, spring 1974; vis. fellow East-West Ctr., Honolulu, summer 1974. Wig Disting. Prof. award, 1970, 76; Fulbright regional vis. prof. India, East Asia, Pacific Areas, 1977-78. Mem. Am. Philos. Assn., Metaphys. Soc. Am., Soc. on Religion in Higher Edn. (Kent fellow 1950-52), Am. Acad. Religion, Phi Beta Kappa. Congregationalist. Office: Pomona Coll 551 N College Ave Claremont CA 91711-6355

SOONG, MELVIN KAIPOLEIMANU, circuit court judge; b. Kapaa, Kauai, Hawaii, Aug. 24, 1934; s. Kion and Mary Ann (Wong) S.; m. Barbara Anne Nelson, Oct. 19, 1958; children: Sharon Kaiulani Odom, Michael Kaipoleimanu, Randall Kawelolani, David Kanoa. BA, San Jose State, 1957; JD, Santa Clara U., 1963. Policeman San Jose Police Dept., 1956-57; dep. atty. gen. State of Hawaii, Honolulu, 1963-69, dep. dir. of taxation Gov.'s Cabinet, 1969-74; lawyer Honolulu, 1974-78; asst. U.S. atty. Fed. Dist. Hawaii, Honolulu, 1978-81; dist. ct. judge Hawaii State Judiciary, Honolulu, 1981-90, cir. ct. judge, 1990—; adminstrv. judge Dist. Ct. 1st Cir., Honolulu, 1987-90. 1st lt. U.S. Army, 1957-59; with U.S. Army Res., 1957-87, ret. Mem. Hawaii Judges Assn., ROA, U.S. Army War Coll. Office: Hawaii State Judiciary 777 Punchbowl St Honolulu HI 96813-5018 Home: 422 Iliaina St Kailua HI 96734

SOOT, STEPHEN ERVIN, priest, health facility administrator; b. Maywood, Calif., Apr. 26, 1961; s. Hennok and Rosemary (Richards) S.; m. Mona Lorice Karadsheh, May 29, 1988; children: Nicholas, Katherine, Michael. BA, Pomona Coll., 1983; MDiv, St. Vladimir's Orthodox Sem., Crestwood, N.Y., 1986. Ordained to ministry Ea. Orthodox Ch., 1991. Devel. asst. St. Vladimir's Sem., Crestwood, N.Y., 1985-86, Russ Reid Co., Pasadena, Calif., 1987-88; pastoral asst. St. George Ch., Wichita, Kans., 1986-87; asst. devel. dir. L.A. Mission, 1988-90; devel. dir. Albany (Oreg.) Gen. Hosp., 1990-92, exec. dir., 1992—. Author, editor Health Trust mag., 1991-94; inventor Med-Aware. Parish priest St. Anne Orthodox Mission, Albany, 1992-94; dir. Albany Estate and Gift Planning Forum, 1993-94; loaned exec. United Way of Linn County, Albany, 1992; dir. Stride Cmty. Action Plan, Albany, 1993-94; mem. steering com. Bus.-Sch. Partnership, Albany. Recipient scholarships Am. Field Svc., 1978, Holy Virgin Mary Cathedral, 1983, 84. Mem. Assn. Healthcare Philanthropy, Nat. Soc. Fund Raising Execs., Albany Ministerial Assn., Rotary. Office: Albany Gen Hosp Found 1046 6th Ave SW Albany OR 97321-1916

SORBY, J(OSEPH) RICHARD, artist, educator; b. Duluth, Minn., Dec. 21, 1911; s. Joseph Austin and Lydia A. (Esterly) S.; m. P. Elizabeth Ferguson, Dec. 9, 1950. B.A., U. Northern Colo., 1937, M.A., 1952; post-grad., UCLA, 1953, U. of Americas, 1952, U. Colo., 1954. Instr. art Greeley High Sch., Colo., 1937-41; asst. prof. art U. Nebr., Lincoln, 1941-43; assoc. prof. art U. Denver, 1946-59; prof. design and painting Calif. State U., San Jose, 1959-72, prof. emeritus, 1972—; guest prof. Southern Utah U., Cedar City, June, July 1964; rep. by Spectrum Gallery, Estes Park, Colo.; artist in residence Casa de las Campanas, Rancho Bernardo, Calif., 1989—. Exhibited in numerous nat. competitive exhbns. including Rocky Mountain Nat. Watermedia Exhbn. and various publ. collections. Served with USN, 1943-46, lt. comdr. USNR, ret. Recipient Purchase award Joslyn Art Mus., Omaha, Mid-Am. Annual, Kansas City, Nat. Watercolor Competition, Washington, Denver Art Mus., Mus. N.Mex., Southwestern Artist's Annual; selected for U.S. nat. traveling exhbn. Mem. Fifteen Colo. Artists (pres. 1957-58), Retired officers Assn., Coll. Art Assn. Am., Mil. Order World Wars, East Bay Art Assn. (v.p. 1966-68), Group 21 (pres. Los Gatos, Calif. 1970-71). Home: 18655 W Bernardo Dr San Diego CA 92127-3002 Office: Morningsun Studio 15 N Frk Rd Glen Haven CO 80532-3020

SOREIDE, DAVID CHRISTIEN, physicist; b. Arlington, Va., July 20, 1945; s. Louis Severin and Mae Marie (Barber) S.; divorced. BS, U. Colo., 1967; MS, U. Wash., 1969, PhD, 1978. Prin. engr. Boeing Comml. Airplanes, Seattle, 1977—. Patentee for Laser Doppler Velocimetry; patent pending for Normal Shock Sensing in the Focus of a Laser Beam. Mem. AIAA, Soc. Photo-Optical Instrumentation Engrs., Optical Soc. Am. Office: Boeing Commercial Airplanes PO Box 3707 M/S 17-XH Seattle WA 98124

SOREM, RONALD KEITH, geologist, mineral resources consultant; b. Northfield, Minn., June 18, 1924; s. Melvin L. Sorem; m. Judith Bacon LaFollette, Feb. 21, 1953; children: Kaia, Keith, Sam, Tom. BA, U. Minn., 1946, MS, 1948; PhD, U. Wis., 1958. Strategic minerals advisor U.S. Fgn. Ops. Adminstrn., Philippines, 1953-55; geologist U.S. Geol. Survey, Washington, Maine, Philippines and Cuba, 1948-55; postdoctoral rsch. assoc. U. Wis., Madison, 1957-58; prof. geology Wash. State U., Pullman, 1959-83; cons. geologist Rks Geol. Rsch., Pullman, 1973—; co-chief scientist NOAA-U.S. Geol. Survey Expeditions, Deep Ocean Mining Environ. Studies Project, Pacific Ocean, 1975, 76, 77, observer rsch. vessel Deepsea Miner II, 1978; pres. Rks Geol. Rsch. Svcs., Pullman, 1972; pres. Commn. on Manganese, Internat. Assn. of the Genesis of Ore Deposits, 1986-90; vis. lectr. Japan Soc. for Promotion of Sci. Hokkaido, 1981; fgn. invited scientist USSR Pacific Vinogradov Expdn., 1986. Sr. author: Manganese Nodules, 1979; donor of first extensive deep-sea manganese nodule collection to be archived in the Smithsonian Institution, Washington, 1991; contbr. over 50 articles to profl. jours. and govt. publs. Informal cons. City Coun., NOAA, Wash. State Govt., 1980-90; volcanic ash cons. Mt. St. Helens eruption 1980, Wash. State U. Vis. rsch. fellow in geology Manchester (England) U., 1969, U. Geneva, Switzerland, 1969-70; recipient numerous rsch. grants NSF, U.S. Bur. Mines, others, 1960—. Fellow Mineralogical Soc. of Am., Geol. Soc. of Am., Soc. Econ. Geologists; mem. Sigma Xi. Home: 925 SE Spring St Pullman WA 99163-2245

SOREN, DAVID, archaeology educator, administrator; b. Phila., Oct. 7, 1946; s. Harry Friedman and Erma Elizabeth (Salamon) Soren; m. Noelle Louise Schattyn, Dec. 22, 1967. B.A., Dartmouth Coll., 1968; M.A., Harvard U., 1972, Ph.D., 1973. Cert. Rome Classics Ctr. Curator of coins Fogg Art Mus., Cambridge, Mass., 1972; asst. prof. U. Mo., Columbia, 1972-76, assoc. prof., dept. head, 1976-81; prof. archaeology U. Ariz., Tucson, 1982-83, dept. head, 1984-89; guest curator Am. Mus.. Natural History, N.Y.C., 1983-90, lectr., 1993—; creator/dir. Kourion Excavations, Cyprus, 1982-89, Portugal, 1983-84, Am. Excavations at Lugnano, Italy, 1988-93; pot cons., field dir. Tunisia Excavations, Chgo. Oriental Inst./Smithsonian Instn., 1973-78; bbd. dirs. humanities program U. Ariz., 1992-94; dir. excavations Chianciano Terme, Italy, 1995; subject of The Learning Channel TV program: series "Archaeology", 1995. Author: (books) Unreal Reality, 1978, Rise and Fall of Fantasy Film, 1980, Carthage, 1990, French edit., 1994; co-author: Kourion: Search for a Lost Roman City, 1988, Corpus des Mosaiques de Tunisie, 1972, 3rd rev. edit., 1986, Carthage: A Mosaic of Ancient Tunisia, 1987; editor: Excavations at Kourion I, 1987; producer: (film) Carthage: A Mirage of Antiquity, 1987; creator and guest curator: (internat. traveling exhbn.) Carthage: A Mosaic of Ancient Tunisia, 1987-92; editor, founder Roscius, 1993—; creative cons. TV miniseries Lost Civilizations, 1994; contbr. articles to profl. jours. Subject of National Geographic spl. Archeological Detectives, 1985; work subject of feature articles in Newsweek, Conoisseur, National Geographic and others; recipient Cine Golden Eagle, 1980, Angenieux Film award Industrial Photography mag., 1980, Outstanding American Under 40 award C. Johns Hopkins-Britain's Royal Inst. Internat. Affairs, 1985; named Outstanding American Under 40 Esquire mag., 1985, hon. Italian citizen Lugnano, Italy, 1989; grantee NEH, 1979, 87, Fulbright, Lisbon, 1983. Mem. Nat. Geog. Soc. (project dir. 1983-84), Am. Sch. Oriental Rsch. (dept. rep. 1981-85), Archaeol. Inst. Tucson (pres. 1983-86), Luso-Am. Commn. (citation 1983-84), Explorer's Club. Office: U Ariz Dept Classics 371 MLB Tucson AZ 85721

SORENSEN, CRAIG BURG, county official; b. Salt Lake City, Oct. 17, 1946; s. William Homer and Winona (Burg) S.; m. Aug. 3, 1977; children: Craig Jr., Cameron, Clinton, Crystal, Candice, Carlyn. BS, U. Utah, 1970; postgrad., UCLA, 1970-71. Auditor Peat Marwick Main, Salt Lake City, 1972-74; county auditor Salt Lake County Auditors Office, Salt Lake City, 1978—. Bd. dirs. Salt Lake County Planning Commn., 1986-91, Foothill Western Boys Baseball Assn.; pres. bd. dirs. Work Activity Ctr. for Handicapped Adults, Salt Lake City, 1972-94. Recipient Cert. Achievement for Excellence in Fin. Reporting Govt. Fin. Officers Assn. U.S. and Can., 1988-92. Republican. Mem. Church Latter Day Saints. Home: 1642 Maple Ave Salt Lake City UT 84106-3320 Office: Salt Lake County Auditor 2001 S State St # 2200 Salt Lake City UT 84190

SORENSEN, ELIZABETH JULIA, cultural administrator; b. Kenora, Ont., Can., Nov. 24, 1934; d. John Frederick and Irene Margaret (Dowd) MacKellar; m. O. Leo P. Sorensen, July 7, 1956 (div. 1963); children: Lianne Kim Sorensen Kruger. BA, Lakehead U., 1970; MA, Brigham Young U., 1972; Assoc. Royal Conservatory, U. Toronto, 1978; Assoc., Mt. Royal Coll., Calgary, AB, 1978. Sec. Canadian Med. Assn. Manitoba div., Winnipeg, 1956-59; legal sec. Filmore, Riley & Co., Winnipeg, 1961-63; tchr. Fort Frances (Ont.) High Sch., 1963-70; instr. drama, speech, English Lethbridge (Alta.) Community Coll., 1972-77; tchr. bus. edn. Henderson Coll. Bus., Lethbridge, 1978-80; supr. cultural svcs. City Medicine Hat, Alta., 1980—. Mem. Alta. Mcpl. Assn. for Culture (sec. 1982-87, treas. 1982-90, vice-chair 1990-92, chair 1992—), Can. Conf. Arts, World Leisure and Recreation Assn. Mormon. Office: City of Medicine Hat, 580 1 St SE, Medicine Hat, AB Canada T1A 8E6

SORENSEN, KENNETH CHRIST, church administrator, real estate broker; b. Salt Lake City, Aug. 28, 1941; s. William P. and Marjorie C. (Jorgensen) S.; m. Annette Marie Bowman, June 15, 1964; children: Christina Marie, Clarissa Anne. BS, U. Utah, 1964; MS, Ariz. State U., 1973. Commd. 2d lt. U.S. Army, 1964, advanced through grades to lt. col., 1980, retired, 1985; broker, owner Patriot Realty, El Paso, Tex., 1985—; bus. adminstr. First Presbyn. Ch., El Paso, Tex., 1986-88; bus. mgr. Phoenix House Inc., Dallas, 1990-92; dir. planning and devel. Aliviane, Inc., El Paso, 1992-93; bus. adminstr. St. John's Meth. Ch., Albuquerque, 1993-95. Editor: The Sou'wester, 1982-85. Mem. S.W. Dist. Exch. Clubs (pres. 1985-86, CEO). Republican. Methodist. Home: 1015 Goad St Socorro NM 87801-4471 Office: St Johns United Meth Ch 2626 Arizona St NE Albuquerque NM 87110-3337

SORENSEN, SHEILA, state senator; b. Chgo., Sept. 20, 1947; d. Martin Thomas Moloney and Elizabeth (Koehr) Paulus; m. Wayne B. Slaughter, May, 1969 (div. 1976); 1 child, Wayne Benjamin III; m. Dean E. Sorensen, Feb. 14, 1977; (stepchildren) Michael, Debbie, Kevin, Dean C. BS, Loretto Heights Coll., Denver, 1965; postgrad. pediatric nurse practicioner, U. Colo., Denver, 1969-70. Pediatric nurse practicioner Pub. Health Dept., Denver, 1970-71, Boise, Idaho, 1971-72; pediatric nurse practicioner Boise (Idaho) Pediatric Group, 1972-74, Pediatric Assocs., Boise, 1974-77; mem. Idaho State Ho. Reps., 1987-92; mem. Idaho Senate, 1992—, chair senate health and welfare com., 1992-94, chair senate majority caucus, vice chair state affairs com., 1994—. Precinct committeeman Ada County Rep. Cen. Com., Boise, 1982-86, dist. vice-chair, 1985—; polit. chair Idaho Med. Assn. Aux., 1984-87, Ada County Med. Assocs., 1986-87; bd. dirs. Family Practice Residency Program, 1992—, Univ./Comty. Health Sci. Assn., Bishop Kelly Found., 1993—; chair Senate Majority Caucus, 1995, vice-chair state affairs com. Recipient AMA Nathan Davis award for Outstanding State Legislator, 1994. Mem. Nat. Conf. State Legislators, Nat. Orgn. Women Legislators, Am. Legis. Exch. Coun. Roman Catholic.

SORENSEN, VIBEKE, artist, educator; b. Copenhagen, Feb. 15, 1954; came to U.S., 1957; d. Soren Erik and Doris Sorensen; m. Rand Steiger, Apr. 16, 1989. BFA, Va. Commonwealth U., Copenhagen, 1974; MA in Humanities, SUNY, Buffalo, 1976. Asst. prof. Va. Commonwealth U., Richmond, 1980-83; dir. computer graphics program Art Ctr. Coll. Design, Pasadena, Calif., 1983-85; vis. assoc. computer sci. Calif. Inst. Tech., Pasadena, 1985-89; vis. lectr. Princeton (N.J.) U., 1990, 91, 93; mem. faculty, dir. computer animation lab. Calif. Inst. Arts, Valencia, 1984-94; prof. computer animation U. So. Calif. Sch. Cinema and TV, L.A., 1994—; cons. Jet Propulsion Lab., NASA, Pasadena, 1988-92, San Diego Supercomputer Ctr., 1988-91. Artist (computer graphics) Fish and Chips, 1985, (video installations) Concurrents, 1989, NLoops, 1989, (stereoscopic video) Maya, 1993, Panini Stickers, 1995. Recipient 1st prize Internat. Visual Music Festival, L.A., 1982; rsch. grantee NSF, Washington, 1989. Mem. Coll. Art Assn., Assn. Computing Machinery Spl. Interest Group Graphics. Office: U So Calif Sch Cinema-TV University Park Marcia Lucas Post 201 Los Angeles CA 90021

SORENSON, JAMES LEE, chemical executive; b. 1948. Mgr. LeVoys, Inc.and Excelsius Cosmetics, Salt Lake City, 1969-79; chmn. bd. Datachem Labs., Salt Lake City, 1986—. Office: Datachem Labs 960 Levoy Dr Salt Lake City UT 84123-2500*

SORENSON, SANDRA LOUISE, merchandising manager; b. Santa Monica, Calif., Nov. 30, 1948; d. Edward John and Gordon Dudley (Pollock) S. BA in Telecommunications, BS in Mktg., U. So. Calif., 1970. Merchandiser Montgomery Ward Inc., Los Angeles, 1970-82; sr. fin. planner Plums Co., Los Angeles, 1982-84; mgr. merchandising systems devel. and tng. Millers Outpost, Ontario, Calif., 1984-89; merchandising systems specialist Oshmans Sporting Goods, Santa Ana, Calif., 1989-90; dir. allocations Clothestime, Anahiem, Calif., 1990—. Active Shakespeare Festival Guild, Garden Grove, Calif., 1985—; chairperson membership com. Gem Theatre Guild, Garden Grove, 1986—. Recipient Achievement award Bicentennial Com. Norwalk, Calif., 1976. Mem. Am. Soc. Tng. and Devel. (v.p.), Commerce Assocs., Assn. Retail Technologies, Mensa, Internat. Platform Soc., Casitas de San Jose, Chi Omega, Phi Chi Theta, Alpha Epsilon Rho. Republican. Mem. Reformed Ch. Am. Club: Players of Orange. Home: 76 Carriage Way Pomona CA 91766-6721 Office: Clothestime Inc 5325 E Hunter Ave Anaheim CA 92807-2054

SOROM, TERRY ALLEN, ophthalmic surgeon; b. Lanesboro, Minn., Jan. 9, 1940; s. Martin John and Elvira (Lodahl) S.; m. Suzanne A. Johnson, children: Martin, Jeb, Abraham, Theodore. BS, Luther Coll., 1962; MD, U. Minn.-Mpls., 1966. Diplomate Am. Bd. Ophthalmology. Intern. U. Oreg., Portland, 1967, resident in ophthalmology, 1969-73; ophthalmic surgeon Eye and Ear Clinic, Inc., Wenatchee, Wash., 1973—. Charter trustee Wenatchee Visitor and Conv. Bur., 1980; bd. dirs. Blue Cross Wash., and Alaska; pres. Wenatchee Valley Coll. Found., 1986-88. Capt. M.C., USAF, 1967-69. Mem. AMA, Am. Acad. Ophthalmology, Contact Lens Assn. Ophthalmology, Am. Intraocular Implant Soc., Wash. State Acad. Ophthalmology (trustee 1978-80), Oregon Ophthalmologic Alumni Assn. (pres. 1988—), Greater Wenatchee Found. (bd. dirs.), Chelan-Douglas County Med. Assn., Wash. State Acad. Eye Physicians and Surgeons (pres. elect), Rotary (pres. 1993-94). Republican. Lutheran. Office: Eye & Ear Clinic Wenatchee Inc PS 600 Orondo Ave PO Box 3027 Wenatchee WA 98801

SORRELL, PAUL A., writer; b. Bklyn., Feb. 24, 1937; s. Michael Matthew and Gioconda Patricia (Purinan) Marino; children: Lorena Lehtola, Melinda Marino Bredeck. BA, NYU, 1953; postgrad., DeAnza Coll., 1973-85, San Jose State U., 1982-84. Instr. Kane Acad., Mitchelville, Md., 1964-66; theater dir. City of Cupertino, Calif., 1966-74; columnist, journalist Neighborhood Gazette, Bowie, Md., 1979-81; instr. Langley McCormick Sch., Hyattsville, Md., 1989-91; mem. staff Bush Adminstrn., Washington, 1989-91; liaison Md. U., College Park, 1991-93; reporter, columnist Campbell (Calif.) Express, 1993—. Author: RR2; contbr. column to Cambrian Times, 1992-94, Cupertino Courier, 1992—. Mem. staff Rep. Hdqrs., San Jose, Calif., 1984; pres. Prince George's Opera, Prince George's County, Md., 1988; bd. dirs. Bowie City Coun., 1988; dir., producer City of Cupertino, 1970. Mem. Alliance Francaise.

SORSTOKKE, ELLEN KATHLEEN, marketing executive, educator; b. Seattle, Mar. 31, 1954; d. Harold William and Carrol Jean (Russ) S. MusB with distinction, U. Ariz., 1976; postgrad., UCLA Extension, 1979-83, L.A. Valley Coll., 1984-85, Juilliard Extension, fall 1987, U. Calif. Berkeley Extension, 1992-93, 95—. Pvt. practice music tchr. Music Land, Tucson, 1975-77; music tchr. Eloy (Ariz.) Elem. Schs., 1976-77, Whiteriver (Ariz.) Pub. Schs., 1977-78; svc. writer, acting svc. mgr., asst. svc. mgr. Alfa of Santa Monica, Calif., 1978-79; purchasing agt. Advance Machine Corp., L.A., 1979-80; asst. mgr. Atlantic Nuclear Svcs., Gardena, Calif., 1980-81; mgr. Blue Lady's World Music Ctr., L.A., 1981-83; instrument specialist Baxter-Northup Music Co., Sherman Oaks, Calif., 1983-85; dir. mktg. Mandolin Bros., Ltd., S.I., N.Y., 1985-89; product mgr. Gibson Guitar Corp., Nashville, 1989; sales mgr. Saga Musical Instruments, South San Francisco, Calif., 1990-91, mktg. dir., 1991—; freelance mktg. cons., S.I., 1986-89; freelance music tchr., Tucson, L.A., N.Y.C., 1975-89; music cons. 20th Century Fox, L.A., 1984; freelance music copyist and orchestrator, Tucson, L.A., N.Y.C., 1972-89; freelance graphic designer and advt., Foster City, Calif., 1993—. campaign worker Richard Jones for Supr., Tucson, 1972; mem., program book designer Marina Del Rey-Westchester Symphony Orch., L.A., 1981-83; active Calif. Wind Ensemble, 1992—. Scholar U. Ariz., 1973-76, ASCAP scholar, 1980-81. Mem. Am. Fedn. Musicians, Soc. for the Preservation Film Music, Tucson Flute Club (publicity chmn. 1974-75, v.p. 1975-76). Republican. Office: Saga Musical Instruments 429 Littlefield Ave PO Box 2841 South San Francisco CA 94080

SORSTOKKE, SUSAN EILEEN, systems engineer; b. Seattle, May 2, 1955; d. Harold William and Carrol Jean (Russ) S. BS in Systems Engring., U. Ariz., 1976; MBA, U. Wash., Richland, 1983. Warehouse team mgr. Procter and Gamble Paper Products, Modesto, Calif., 1976-78; quality assurance engr. Westinghouse Hanford Co., Richland, Wash., 1978-80; supr. engring. document ctr. Westinghouse Hanford Co., Richland, 1980-81; mgr. data control and adminstrn. Westinghouse Electric Corp., Madison, Pa., 1981-82, mgr. data control and records mgmt., 1982-84; prin. engr. Westinghouse Elevator Co., Morristown, N.J., 1984-87; region adminstrn. mgr. Westinghouse Elevator Co., Arleta, Calif., 1987-90; ops. rsch. analyst Am. Honda Motor Co. Inc., Torrance, Calif., 1990-95, project leader parts systems, 1995—; adj. prof. U. LaVerne, Calif., 1991-92. Advisor Jr. Achievement, 1982-83; literacy tutor Westmoreland Literacy Coun., 1983-84, host parent EF Found., Saugus, Calif., 1987-88, Am. Edn. Connection, Saugus, 1988-89, 91; instr. Excell, L.A., 1991-92. Mem. Soc. Women Engrs., Am. Inst. Indsl. Engrs., Nat. Coun. Systems Engring., Optimists Charities, Inc. (bd. dirs. Acton, Calif. 1991-94). Republican. Methodist. Home: # 205 2567 Plaza Del Amo Unit 205 Torrance CA 90503-8962 Office: Am Honda Motor Co Inc Dept Parts Quality and Systems 1919 Torrance Blvd Torrance CA 90501-2722

SORTLAND, TRUDITH ANN, speech and language therapist, educator; b. Butte, Mont., Dec. 3, 1940; d. Kenneth Hjalmer Sortland and Sigrid V. (Kotka) Strand. BS, Minot (N.D.) State U., 1965. Tchr. Westby (Mont.) Sch., 1960-61, Glasgow (Mont.) Southside Sch., 1962-65, Glasgow AFB, Mont., 1965-80; tchr., speech and lang. pathologist Mineral County Sch. Dist., Hawthorne, Nev., 1965-68, 78—; kindergarten tchr. Mineral County Sch. Dist., Mina, Nev., 1968-72; elem. tchr. Mineral County Sch. Dist., Mina, 1978-80; speech, language pathologist Mineral County Sch. Dist., Mina, Republic of Korea, 1980—; tchr. Dept. Def., Pusan, Republic of Kores, 1972-73, Illesheim, Fed. Republic Germany, 1973-78; tchr. Mohall (N.D.) Pub. Sch., 1964-65; cons. Mary Kay Cosmetics, tchr. Glasgow AFB, 1965-68. Supt. Sunday sch. Bethany Luth. Ch., Hawthorne, 1987—, sec. Ladies Aid, 1987—. Mem. NEA, Nev. Edn. Assn., AAUW (past sec., pres.), Pair O Dice Square Dance Club (sec. 1989—), Delta Kappa Gamma. Home: PO Box 816 Hawthorne NV 89415-0816 Office: Mineral County Sch Dist A St Hawthorne NV 89415

SOSKIN, STEVE, computer software consultant; b. N.Y.C., Feb. 20, 1947; s. Al and Beatrice (Gordon) Mandel; m. Tobi Eisentein, 1972 (div. 1982); children: Deena Lyn, Sheela Beth; m. Diane Kathie Behling, Mar. 21, 1992. BA, L.I. U., 1969; MA in Psychology, New Sch. for Social Rsch., 1972. Tchr. N.Y.C. Bd. Edn., Bklyn., 1969-76; computer programmer Con Edison, N.Y.C., 1975-79; computer analyst Colgate Palmolive, N.Y.C., 1979-80, Paine Webber, N.Y.C., 1980-81; system analyst Merrill Lynch, N.Y.C., 1981-84; sales engr. Tarkenton Software/Knowledgeware, Atlanta, 1984-87; cons. Interactive Info. Systems, San Francisco, 1987-88; sales engr., tech. mktg. mgr. Micro Focus, Palo Alto, Calif., 1988-91; cons. Interactive Info. and Mgmt. Sys., Santa Cruz, Calif., 1991—; lectr. U. Calif. at Berkeley Ext., San Francisco, 1990-91. Mem. Psi Chi Nat. Honor Soc.

SOTER, NICHOLAS GREGORY, advertising agency executive; b. Great Falls, Mont., Apr. 26, 1947; s. Sam Nick and Bernice (Bennett) S.; m. Kathleen Lyman, Feb. 20, 1970; children: Nichole, Erin, Samuel Scott, Kara, Stephen Andrew, Riley Kyle. BS, Brigham Young U., 1971. With McLean Assocs., Provo, Utah, 1970-75; chmn. bd., CEO Soter Assocs. Inc., Provo, 1975—; founder, pres. RS Corp., 1986-88, Plum C Corp., 1988, Due Respect Corp., 1991; owner, developer Parkside Apts., 1994—; instr. advt. Utah Valley C.C., Orem, 1971-75, Brigham Young U., Provo, 1980-84. Publisher: Journal of Joseph, 1979, Journal of Brigham, 1980, LaVell Edwards, 1980, Amos Wright, 1981, Moments in Motherhood, 1981, What It Means to Know Christ, 1981, Mormon Fortune Builders, 1982, Utah History, 1982; contbr. articles to profl. jours. Active Utah Valley Pub. Communications Coun. for LDS Ch., 1982-87; mem. adv. coun. Monte L. Bean Life Sci. Mus., 1987-89; Rep. dist. chmn.; v.p. exec. com. Am.'s Freedom Festival at Provo, 1990-91; jury chmn. Coun. for Advancement and Support of Edn., 1989; vocalist Ralph Woodward Chorale, 1991—, pres., 1992—; mem. govt. rev. com., Provo, Orem, 1992-95; bd. trustees, v.p. Greek Assn. Family History & Tradition, 1990-95. Recipient N.Y. Art Dir.'s The One Show award, Salt Lake Art Dirs. Communications Assn. of Utah Valley awards. Mem. Utah Advt. Fedn., Pub. Rels. Soc. Am., Communications Assn. Utah Valley (past pres.), Provo C. of C. (bd. dirs.), Innisbrook Network of Advt. Agys. (pres. 1986-87). Home: 1728 S 290 E Orem UT 84058-7928 Office: Soter Assocs Inc 209 N 400 W Provo UT 84601-2746

SOTIRIOU, PETER ELIAS, English language educator, textbook writer; b. San Pedro, Calif., July 24, 1947; s. Elias Panagiotis and Louise (Vengel) S.; m. Vasiliki Zaferis, July 11, 1976; children: Elias Panagiotis, Dimitrios Panagiotis. AB cum laude, UCLA, 1969, MA, 1974; PhD, U. So. Calif., 1991. Secondary sch. tchr. L.A. Unified Sch. Dist., 1969-73, Palos Verdes (Calif.) Unified Sch. Dist., 1974-79; prof. English L.A. C.C. Dist., 1979—. Author: Steps to Reading Proficiency, 4th edit., 1982, Integrating College Study Skills, 4th edit., 1984, Composing Through Reading, 2d edit., 1989; contbg. editor The Writing Instructor, 1993—; contbr. articles to profl. jours. Mem. MLA, Nat. Coun. Tchrs. English, English Coun. Calif. Two Yr. Colls. (2d v.p. 1994—). Democrat. Greek Orthodox. Home: 1154 Lynngrove Dr Manhattan Beach CA 90266-4230 Office: Los Angeles City Coll 855 N Vermont Ave Los Angeles CA 90029-3500

SOTO, SHIRLENE ANN, educator, consultant; b. San Luis Obispo, Calif., Jan. 22, 1950; d. Vernon Ernest and Althea Lorraine S.; m. Walt Elliott, Sept. 1, 1985. BA, San Francisco State U., 1969; MA, U. N.Mex., 1971, PhD, 1977. Instr. U. N.Mex., Albuquerque, 1976-77; asst. prof. Calif. Poly. State U., San Luis Obispo, 1977-80; asst. v.p. Calif. State U., Northridge, 1981-85, prof., 1985—; postdoctoral fellow UCLA, 1985-86; coord. program for gender equality grant Coll. of the Canyons, Valencia, Calif.,1991-94; panelist Fulbright-Hays grants U.S. Dept. Edn., 1993-94. Author: Emergence of the Modern Mexican Woman, 1990; editl. adv. bd. (book) Notable Hispanic Am. Women, 1993; contbr. numerous articles to profl. jours. Mem. Hispanic adv. coun. Calif. Dept. Pks. and Recreation, Sacramento, 1982—; adv. bd. New Horizons project Coll. of the Canyons, Valencia, Calif., 1994—. Adminstrv. fellow Calif. State U. Sys., 1980-81, Ford. Found. fellow Ford Found., 1972-76; Recipient Leadership in Edn. award Atty. Gen. of Calif., 1986. Mem. Mujeres Activas en Letras y Cambio Social (So. Calif. Rep. 1987-88), Western Assn. of Women Historians (chair, Judith Lee Ridge prize 1991-92). Democrat. Roman Catholic. Home: 25025 3/4 Everett Dr Santa Clarita CA 91321 Office: Calif State U 18111 Nordhoff St Northridge CA 91330

SOTO, THOMAS DE, photographer; b. Pomona, Calif., Oct. 30, 1960; s. Eddie and Henrietta (Nunez) S. AA, Palomar Coll., San Marcos, Calif., 1984; student, U. So. Calif., 1987-88. Photojournalist The Citizen Newspaper, Solano Beach, Calif., 1980-82, The Blade Tribune, Oceanside, Calif., 1982-84; dir. photography World Comms. Inc., La Costa, Calif., 1984-87; auteur of photography, fine arts posters Eyes Closed Internat., Solana Beach, 1987—; motion picture camera operator World Wave Pictures, Cardiff, Calif., 1990—; lectr. at schs. and colls. nationwide. Works include documentaries, TV commls., album covers, feature films. Photographer, San Diego Youth and Community Svcs., 1992—, Campaign, Calif., Santa Monica, 1989-90, Performing Arts Theater, Carlsbad, Calif., 1982-86, United Way, AIDS Found., Nat. Wildlife Found., others. Recipient Silver Lone Star award Houston Film Festival, 1990, Van Guard award Am. Women in Radio and TV, 1986, Student Emmy for Gilbert Lost A Tooth, Motion Picture Acad. of Arts, 1987; Polaroid grantee, 1984-86. Mem. Am. Soc. Mag. Photogaphers, Profl. Photographers Am. Inc., Nikon Profl. Svcs. Libertarian.

SOUBERS, RICHARD RODNEY, archivist; b. Yakima, Wash., Feb. 3, 1947; s. Clifford Herbert and Ola Pearl (Ely) S. BA in Polit. Sci., Ctrl. Wash. U., 1972, MA in History, 1974; postgrad., Western Wash. U., 1975. Archivist Eisenhower Presdl. Libr., Abilene, Kans., 1975-85; sr. archivist Civil Archives Divsn. NARA, Washington, 1985-87, Office of Presdl. Librs., NARA, Washington, 1987-88; supervisory archivist Reagan PResdl. Libr., Simi Valley, Calif., 1989—; dir. Kans. State Archival Adv. Bd., Topeka, 1981-85. Bd. dirs. Dickinson County Hist. Soc., Abilene, 1980-85. Sgt. U.S. Army, 1969-71, Vietnam. Decorated Bronze Star, Air medal. Mem. So. Am. Archivists, Soc. Calif. Archivists, Am. Legion, 101st Airborne Assn., Delta Raiders of Vietnam Assn. (sec.-treas. 1986—). Republican. Office: Ronald Reagan Presdl Libr 40 Presidential Dr Simi Valley CA 93065

SOULÉ, MICHAEL ELLMAN, biologist; b. San Diego, May 28, 1936; s. Alan Kenyon Soulé and Berenice Charlotte (Ellman) Bluestone; m. Judith Ann Burgess Bays, Aug. 9, 1965 (div.); children: Aaron, Noah, Ani; m. Joy Ellis McKinney, June 28, 1993. BA, Calif. State U., San Diego, 1959; MA, Stanford U., 1963, PhD, 1965. Lectr. in zoology U. Malawi, Blantyre, Malawi, 1965-67; from asst. prof. to prof. U. Calif., San Diego, 1967-80; dir. Inst. Transcultural Studies, L.A., 1979-83; prof., chair U. Calif., Santa Cruz, 1989—; adj., vis. prof. U. Mich., Ann Arbor, 1984-89; bd. dirs. The Wildlands Project, Portland, Oreg.; mem. sci. adv. com. The Nature Conservancy, 1992—. Author: Conservation and Evolution, 1981; editor: Conservation Biology, 1986, Viable Populations for Conservation, 1987, Reinventing Nature?, Responses to Postmodern Construction, 1995. Fellow Guggenheim Found. Fellow AAAS, N.Y. Zool. Soc.; mem. Nat. Rsch. Coun. (biology bd.), Soc. Conservation Biology (1st pres. 1986-89, Disting. Achievement award 1993). Office: U Calif Dept Environ Studies Dept Biology Santa Cruz CA 95064

SOUTH, MATTHEW TODD, aerospace engineer; b. Sacramento, Dec. 30, 1959; s. Jack Roy and Dorothy (Orr) S.; m. Nancy Ann Fischer, Mar. 26, 1983. BS in Aero. Engring., Calif. Poly. State U., 1983. Aerospace engr. Pacific Missile Test Ctr., Pt. Mugu, Calif., 1983-85; unmanned aerial vehicle br. head Pacific Missile Test Ctr., Pt. Mugu, 1985-87; unmanned aerial vehicle sys. engr. Naval Air Warfare Ctr., Pt. Mugu, 1987-92, dep. for targets test and evaluation, 1992-94, lead test engr. for targets, 1994—. Mem. AIAA, Assn. Unmanned Vehicle Sys. Home: 364 Walnut Dr Ventura CA 93003-2034 Office: Naval Air Warfare Ctr Code 4KLEFOE Bldg 6-1 Point Mugu CA 93042-5001

SOUTHWELL, PHYLLIS ARLENE, medical transcriptionist; b. Havre, Mont., Dec. 29, 1938; d. Edwin G. and Virginia L. (Cross) Brandt; children: Jay M., Lezlie M. AAS, North Seattle C.C., 1974; BA in English Lit., U. Wash., 1983. Med. transcriptionist U. Wash., Seattle, 1986, Providence Med. Ctr., Seattle, 1988—. Author: Love's Shadow, 1990. Mem. Am. Assn. Med. Assts (cert.), Am. Assn. Med. Transcriptionist. Lutheran. Home: 600 7th Ave Apt 304 Seattle WA 98104-1932

SOUTHWICK, CHARLES HENRY, zoologist, educator; b. Wooster, Ohio, Aug. 28, 1928; s. Arthur F. and Faye (Motz) S.; m. Heather Milne Beck, July 12, 1952; children: Steven, Karen. B.A., Coll. Wooster, 1949; M.S., U. Wis., 1951, Ph.D., 1953. NIH fellow, 1951-53; asst. prof. biology Hamilton Coll., 1953-54; NSF fellow Oxford (Eng.) U., 1954-55; faculty Ohio U., 1955-61; assoc. prof. pathobiology Johns Hopkins Sch. Hygiene and Pub. Health, Balt., 1961-68; prof. Johns Hopkins Sch. Hygiene and Pub. Health, 1968-79; assoc. dir. Johns Hopkins Internat. Ctr. for Med. Rsch. and Tng., Calcutta, India, 1964-65; chmn. dept. environ., population and organismic biology U. Colo., Boulder, 1979-82, prof. biology, 1979—, prof. emeritus, 1993—; researcher and author publs. on animal social behavior and population dynamics, influences animal social behavior on demographic characteristic mammal populations, primate ecology and behavior, estuarine ecology and environmental quality; mem. primate adv. com. Nat. Acad. Sci.-NRC, 1963-75, com. primate conservation, 1974-75; mem. Gov.'s Sci. Adv. Com. State of Md., 1975-78; mem. com. on rsch. and exploration Nat. Geog. Soc., 1979—; mem. adv. bd. Caribbean Primate Rsch. Ctr., 1987—, Wis. Primate Rsch. Ctr., 1990—; mem. Integrated Conservation Rsch., 1989—. Editor: Primate Social Behavior, 1963, Animal Aggression, 1970, Nonhuman Primates in Biomedical Research, 1975, Ecology and the Quality of Our Environment, 1976, Global Ecology, 1985; Ecology and Behavior of Food-Enhanced Primate Groups, 1988. Recipient Fulbright Rsch. award India, 1959-60. Fellow AAAS, Acad. Zoology, Animal Behavior Soc.; mem. Am. Soc. Zoologists, Ecol. Soc. Am., Am. Soc. Mammalogists, Am. Soc. Primatology (Disting. Primatologist award 1994), Internat. Primatology Soc., Am. Inst. Biol. Scis., Primatology Soc. Gt. Britain, Internat. Soc. Study Aggression.

SOUTHWORTH, ROD BRAND, computer science educator; b. Binghampton, N.Y., Aug. 24, 1941; s. William Tanner Southworth and Ruth Evelyn (Brabham) Woods; m. Patrice Marie Gapen, Jan. 10, 1978; children: Suzi Lynn, Judi Leigh, Megan Marie, Robin Ashley. BS in Bus., U. Ariz., 1965; MS in Mgmt. Sci. and Info Systems, Colo. State U., 1978. Mktg. rep. IBM, Denver, 1966-69; system analyst Colo. State U., Fort Collins, 1969-73, grad. teaching asst., 1978-79; project mgr. Systems and Computer Tech., Portland, Oreg., 1973-75; asst. dir. Systems and Computer Tech., Fairbanks, Alaska, 1975-77; instr. in computer info. systems Laramie County C.C., Cheyenne, Wyo., 1979—. Author: (software) PC-DOS/MS-DOS Simplified, 1st edit. 1988, 3rd edit. 1992, DOS Complete and Simplified, 1990, DOS Essentials, 1991, DOS 5 Simplified, 1992, DOS 6.2 Simplified, 1994. Mem. Civil Air Patrol, Cheyenne, 1991. Mem. Data Processing Mgmt. Assn. (mem. assoc. level model curriculum 1984-85), Assn. Computing Machinery (mem. assoc. level computer info. processing model curriculum 1991-92). Home: PO Box 5457 Cheyenne WY 82003-5457 Office: Laramie County Comm Coll 1400 E College Dr Cheyenne WY 82007-3204

SOUVEROFF, VERNON WILLIAM, JR., corporate executive, investor, author; b. L.A., Aug. 12, 1934; s. Vernon William Sr. and Aileen (Young) S.; m. Aileen Patricia Robinson; children—Gail Kathleen, Michael William. B.S. in E.E., Stanford U., 1957; postgrad., Ohio State U., 1958-59. With Litton Industries, Beverly Hills, Calif., 1960-75; with ITT Corp., N.Y.C., 1975-87, corp. v.p., 1983-84, sr. v.p., 1984-87; pres. ITT Gilfillan, 1979-83; group exec. ITT Def. Space Group, 1983-84; dir. ITT Telecom and Electronics N.Am., 1984-86; pres., chief exec. officer ITT Def. Tech. Corp., 1986-87; exec. dir. Nat. Ctr. for Career Change, 1990—; mem. U.S. Def. Policy Adv. Com. on Trade, Washington, 1984-88; bd. advisors, investor Venture Resources, Venture Capital, 1988—; prin. Bus. Acquisitions and Investments, 1988—; bd. dirs. Elanix, Inc. Author books on career changes. Served as officer USAF, 1957-60. Recipient Exec. Salute award Los Angeles C. of C., 1981; Ring of Quality ITT Corp., 1983. Mem. IEEE, Nat. Contracts Mgmt. Assn., Electronics Industries Assn., Am. Def. Preparedness Assn. (former dir.), Nat. Security Indsl. Assn., Air Force Assn., Navy League, Assn. U.S. Army, Rancho Mirage Racquet Club (Calif.). Presbyterian.

SOUZA, EDWARD MELVIN, computer science educator; b. Hilo, Hawaii, Oct. 27, 1954; s. Victor Sr. and Genevieve Hazel Souza; m. Joan Ann Mattos, July 7, 1973; children: Shannon C., Genevieve M., Waylen W. Student, Hawaii C.C., U Hawaii-Hilo, 1991—. Officer Humane Edn. Hawaii Island Humane Soc., Keaau, 1975-80; libr. St. Joseph Elem. Sch., Hilo, 1982-87, tchr. computer sci., grant coord., 1987—; grant writer, 1992, after sch. program dir., 1987—. Active Hilo 4-H Club, 1975-80, Hilo chpt. Lehua Jaycees, 1977-80; hosp. pet therapist Hilo Hosp. and Life Care Ctr., 1977-80; v.p. Kaumana Sch. PTG, 1980; CCD tchr., 1980, 90; active Hosp. Ministry, 1990-94, St. Joseph Sch. Country Fair. Home: 726 Waianuenue Ave # A Hilo HI 96720-2016 Office: St Joseph Elem Sch 999 Ululani St Hilo HI 96720-3999

SOVATSKY, STUART CHARLES, psychotherapist; b. Rochester, N.Y., Apr. 14, 1949; s. Jacob J. Sovatsky and Lillian (Kaplan) Sawyer. AB, Princeton U., 1971; MA, Fairleigh Dickinson U., 1975; PhD, Calif. Inst. Integral Studies, San Francisco, 1984. Cert. marriage and family counselor. Probation officer Atlantic County, N.J., 1972-75; dir., asst. dir. Youth Svcs., Atlantic City, N.J., 1975-78; dir. projects Atlantic County Mental Health, Atlantic City, 1978-79; pvt. practice psychotherapy San Francisco, 1980—; asst. prof. Calif. Inst. Integral Studies, 1989—; instr., supr. J.F.K. U., Orinda, Calif., 1988—; clin. dir. Blue Oak and Insight Counseling, Berkeley and San Franciso, 1990—; bd. dirs., Calif. Inst. Integral Studies. Author: Passions of Innocence, 1993, Inner Traditions International, 1992; contbg. author Enlightened Sexuality, 1989; contbr. articles to profl. jours. Scholar Princeton U., 1967-71, Calif. Inst. Integral Studies, 1980-82; N.J. Judiciary Study grantee, 1973-75. Mem. Assn. Transpersonal Psychology, Calif. Marriage-Family Counselor Assn. Home And Office: 3040 Richmond Blvd Oakland CA 94611-5865

SOVISH, RICHARD CHARLES, retired manufacturing executive, consultant; b. Cleve., July 22, 1925; s. Charles and Clara Rita (Spiewak) S.; m. Amelia Martin, Jan. 9, 1954; children: Leslie Jean, Linda Gale, Eric Richard. BS, Ohio U., 1949; MS, Case Western Res. U., 1951, PhD, 1954. Chemist Dow Chem. Co., Midland, Mich., 1954-62; tech. assoc. Lockheed M&S Co., Sunnyvale, Calif., 1962-63; mem. tech. staff Raychem Corp., Menlo Park, Calif., 1963-75; tech. dir. telecom Europe Raychem Corp., Brussels, 1975-78; tech. dir. telecom group Raychem Corp., Menlo Park, 1978-80; tech. dir., U.K., rsch. and devel. Raychem Corp., Swindon, Eng., 1980-83; tech. dir. electronics group Raychem Corp., Menlo Park, 1983-85, dir. corp. rsch. and devel., 1985-89, v.p., corp. tech., 1989-91; ret. Raychem Corp., 1991; cons. R&D mgmt., innovation, 1991—. Patentee in field; contbr. articles to profl. jours. Cpl. U.S. Army, 1943-46, ETO. Mem. Am. Chem. Soc., Soc. Plastic Engrs., Materials Soc., Sigma Xi, Phi Beta Kappa. Home: 1 Ashdown Pl Half Moon Bay CA 94019-2275 Office: Raychem Corp 300 Constitution Dr Menlo Park CA 94025-1140

SOWDER, ROBERT ROBERTSON, architect; b. Kansas City, Kans., Dec. 29, 1928; s. James Robert and Agnes (Robertson) S.; m. Joan Goddard, July 26, 1954; 1 dau., Lisa Robertson Lee. B.A., U. Wash., 1953; B.Arch., U. Va., 1958; grad. diploma in Architecture, Ecole Des Beaux Arts, Fontainebleau, France, 1952. Designer Architects Collaborative, Boston,

1958-59, Peirce & Pierce (architects), Boston, 1959-63; asso. Fred. Bassetti & Co. (architects), Seattle, 1963-67; partner Naramore, Bain, Brady & Johanson (architects), Seattle, 1967-81; pres. NBBJ Internat., 1976-81; architect TRA, Seattle, 1981-83; v.p. Daniel, Mann, Johnson & Mendenhall, San Francisco, 1983-93; prin. RRS Consulting, San Francisco, 1993—; archtl. design critic Boston Archtl. Ctr., 1961-62. Important works include Ridgeway III Dormitories, Bellingham, Wash. (Dept. Housing and Urban Devel. Honor award), Seattle Rapid Transit (HUD Excellence award), Safeco Ins. Co. Home Office Complex, Seattle, King County Stadium, Balt. Conv. Ctr., Oreg. Conv. Ctr., San Francisco (Moscone) Conv. Ctr. Expansion, Honolulu Conv. Ctr., Wilmington (Del.) Conv. Ctr. Served with CIC U.S. Army, 1954-56. Recipient Premier Prix D'Architecture Ecole Des Beaux Arts, Fontainebleau, 1951, 52, Prix D'Remondet Fontainebleau, 1952. Mem. AIA, Internat. Assn. Auditorium Mgrs., Scarab, Sigma Chi. Episcopalian. Clubs: Seattle Tennis, Rainier. Home and Office: 2390 Hyde St San Francisco CA 94109-1505

SOWERWINE, ELBERT ORLA, JR., chemist, chemical engineer; b. Tooele, Utah, Mar. 15, 1915; s. Elbert Orla and Margaret Alice (Evans) S.; BS in Chemistry, Cornell U., 1937, MSChemE, 1938; m. Norma Borge; children: Sue-Ann Sowerwine Jacobson, Sandra Sowerwine Montgomery, Elbert Orla 3d, John Frederick, Avril Ruth Taylor, Albaro Francisco, Octavio Evans, Zaida Margaret. Analytical chemist Raritan Copper Works, Perth Amboy, N.J., summers 1936, 37; rsch. chem. engr. Socony-Vacuum Oil Co., Paulsboro, N.J., 1938-43; prodn. supr. Merck & Co., Elkton, Va., 1943-45; asst. plant mgr. U.S. Indsl. Chems. Co., Newark, 1945-48; project engr. and rsch. dir. Wigton-Abbott Corp., Newark, 1948-50, Cody, Wyo., 1950-55; cons. engring., planning, indsl. and community devel., resource evaluation and mgmt. Wapiti, Wyo., also C.Am., Honduras, 1955—. Commr. N.J., Boy Scouts Am., 1938-43; mem. Wapiti and Park County (Wyo.) Sch. Bds., 1954-58; dir. Mont. State Planning Bd., 1959-61; exec. bd. Mo. Basin Rsch. and Devel. Coun., 1959-61. Fellow Am. Inst. Chemists; mem. Am. Inst. Chem. Engrs., Am. Planning Assn., Nicaraguan Assn. Engrs. and Architects. Libertarian. Mem. Christian Ch. Researcher desulfurization of petroleum products, process control, alternate energy projects; patentee in petroleum and chem. processes and equipment. Home: Broken H Rnch Wapiti WY 82450 Office: Sowerwine Cons Wapiti WY 82450

SOWINSKI, STANISLAUS JOSEPH, artist, retired naval officer; b. Milw., May 7, 1927; s. Francis Anthony and Stefania (Zakszewski) S.; m. R. Jackie Giddens, Oct. 2, 1948; children: Stephanie Ann, Lisa Renée. BA, San Diego State U., 1952; postgrad., Def. Intelligence Sch., 1964-65; cert., San Diego Sch. Arts, 1948-49. Ensign USN, 1952, advanced through grades to comdr., jr. officer, 1952-60; comdg. officer USS Abnaki, Oahu, Hawaii, 1960-62, USS Surfbird, Sasebo, Japan, 1962-64, USN, London, 1965-67; comdr. landing ship squadron USN, San Diego, 1967-69; comdg. officer U.S.S. Fresno, San Diego, 1969-71; ret. USN, 1971, enlisted, 1945-48; painting instr. San Diego Art Inst., 1973-75; painting demonstrator Grumbacher Art Supplies, Inc., N.Y., 1980-85, Inveresk Paper Co., Bath, Eng., 1980-85; instr. painting workshops, San Diego, Rapid City, S.D., 1980-85. One-man shows include Laguna Beach (Calif.) Mus. of Art, 1955, USN,1963, Dept.Def., Washington, 1964, Am. Embassy, London, 1967, San Diego Art Inst. Gallery, 1980, 86, Dahl Fine Art Ctr., Rapid City, S.D., 1982, Wind Gap Gallery of Fine Art, Sacramento, 1983, Art Ctr. Gallery , Rancho Santa Fe, Calif., 1984, Thackeray Gallery of Fine Art, San Diego, 1985, 87, San Diego Mus. of Art, 1985, A. Huney Gallery of Fine Art, San Diego, 1990; artist 23 major icons including Sts. Constantine and Helen Greek Orthodox Ch., 1985-90, Corpus Christi Cath. Ch., 1985-94. Curator major art exhibit Felicita Found. of the Arts, Escondido, Calif., 1985. Mem. Internat. Westerners, The Retired Officers Assn. Republican. Roman Catholic. Home and Office: 13040 Cedilla Pl San Diego CA 92128-1811

SPADA, JAMES, author, publisher; b. S.I., N.Y., Jan. 23, 1950; s. Joseph Vincent and Mary (Ruberto) S. Student, Wagner Coll., 1968-71, Calif. State U., 1979-80. Pres., Spada Pubs, Los Angeles, pub. Barbra Quar., Los Angeles, 1980-83. Mem. Authors Guild, ACLU. Democrat. Author: Barbra: The First Decade-The Films and Career of Barbra Streisand, 1974, The Films of Robert Redford, 1977, The Spada Report, 1979, Streisand-the Woman and the Legend, 1981, Monroe-Her Life in Pictures, 1982, Judy and Liza, 1983, Hepburn: Her Life in Pictures, 1984, The Divine Bette Midler, 1984, Fonda: Her Life in Pictures, 1985, Shirley and Warren, 1985, Grace: The Secret Lives of a Princess, 1987, Peter Lawford: The Man Who Kept the Secrets, 1991, More Than a Woman: An Intimate Biography of Bette Davis, 1993, Streisand: Her Life, 1995; book packager The 1984 Marilyn Monroe Pin-Up Calendar, 1983, The Telephone Book, 1984, Elizabeth Taylor: A Biography in Photographs, 1984, Bette Davis: A Biography in Photographs, 1985, Natalie Wood: A Biography in Photographs, 1986.

SPADE, GEORGE LAWRENCE, scientist; b. Sioux City, Iowa, Dec. 14, 1945; s. Walter Charles and LaVancha May (Green) S.; m. Carol Margaret Deaton, Mar. 14, 1966 (div. June 1985); children: Aaron Michael, Margaret. Mem. earthquake study group for China, U.S. Citizen Amb. Programs, 1989. Contbr. articles to profl. jours. Mem. AAAS, Am. Math. Soc., Math. Assn. Am., N.Y. Acad. Scis., Mensa. Home and Office: PO Box 2260 Columbia Falls MT 59912-2260

SPAFFORD, MICHAEL CHARLES, artist; b. Palm Springs, Calif., Nov. 6, 1935. BA, Pomona Coll., 1959; MA, Harvard U., 1960. One man shows include Seattle Art Mus., 1982, 86, Reed Coll., 1984, Whtcom county Mus., 1987, U. Puget Sound, Tacoma, Wash., 1973, Tacoma Art Mus., 1975, 86, Utah Mus. Fine Arts, Salt Lake City, 1975, Francine Seders Gallery, Seattle, 1965—, Bellevue Art Mus., 1991, Cheney-Cowles Mus., Spokane, Wash., 1994; exhibited in group shows at Wilcox Gallery, Swarthmore Coll., Pa., 1977, Seattle Art Mus., 1977, 80, 84, Am. Acad. and Inst. Arts and Letters, N.Y.C., 1980, 83, 89, Kobe, Japan, 1981, Eastern Wash. U., 1982, Henry Art Gallery, 1982, 86, Bellevue Art Mus., 1987, Cheney Cowles Mus., 1988. Recipient Prix de Rome, 1967-69, award Am. Acad. and Inst. Arts and Letters, 1983; Louis Comfort Tiffany Found. grantee, 1965-66. Home: 2418 E Interlaken Blvd Seattle WA 98112-3029

SPAHR, PETER, agricultural products executive; b. 1955. MBA, Calif. Poly. State U., 1984. With Tulana Farms, Klamath Falls, Oreg., 1979-81; mgr. Sawyer Am., Corcoran, Calif., 1983-85; with River Garden Farms, Inc., Knights Landing, Calif, 1985—. Office: River Garden Farms Co 41758 County Road 112 Knights Landing CA 95645-9500*

SPANDER, ART, sportswriter; b. L.A., Aug. 30, 1938; m. Elizabeth Newman, June 17, 1962; children: Debbie, Wendy. BA in Polit. Sci., UCLA, 1960. With UPI, 1960; joined Santa Monica (Calif.) Evening Outlook, 1963-65, San Francisco Chronicle, 1965-79; columnist San Francisco Examiner, 1979—. Author: Golf: The Passion and the Challenge, 1978, The Art Spander Collection, 1989. Recipient AP Sports Editors awards, Profl. Football Writers Am. awards, 1st place awards San Francisco Press Club, 1st Place Golf Writers Assn. Am. awards, Hayward-Newland Lifetime Achievement award Calif. Golf Writers. Office: San Francisco Examiner 110 5th Ave San Francisco CA 94118-1310

SPANGLER, LYNICE SUE, software engineer; b. Morris, Ill., Oct. 28, 1962; d. Ralph Duain and Vera Jean (Gemmill) S. BS in Computer Sci., Kans. U., 1984; MS in Computer Sci., Portland State U., 1994. System analyst-info. systems Southwestern Bell Telephone Co., St. Louis, Mo., 1984-92; software test engr. Rational Software Corp., Aloha, Oreg., 1993—. Mem. Assn. Computing Machinery. Office: Rational Software Corp 1600 NW Compton Dr Ste 357 Aloha OR 97006-6905

SPANGRUDE, GERALD JOHN, hematologist, researcher; b. Helena, Mont., July 5, 1953; s. George Randolf and Lila Viola (Machulda) S.; m. Paula Elizabeth Braun, Sept. 15, 1984; children: Tegan Elizabeth, Carl Erik. BS in Microbiology, U. Mont., 1979; PhD, U. Utah, 1984. Post doctoral fellow Stanford U., Stanford, Calif., 1984-88; post doctoral fellow Hall Inst., Melbourne, Australia, 1988-89; NIAID investigator NIH, Hamilton, Mont., 1989-94; assoc. prof. U. Utah, Salt Lake City, 1994—; cons. Systemix Inc., Palo Alto, Calif., 1989—; ad hoc advisor NIH, Bethesda, Md., 1994—. Inventor stem cell enrichment, 1988. Post doctoral fellowship Am. Cancer Soc., 1984-86; spl. fellow Leukemia Soc. Am., 1987-90. Mem. AAAS, Am. Soc. Hematology, Internat. Soc. of Exptl. Hematology. Office: Dept Pathology U Utah 50 N Medical Dr Salt Lake City UT 84132-0001

SPANIER, JEROME, mathematics educator; b. St. Paul, June 3, 1930; s. David Howard and Anne (Goldman) S.; m. Bernice Hoffman, Aug. 31, 1952; children: Stephen, Ruth, Adrienne. BA, U. Minn., 1951; MS, U. Chgo., 1952, PhD, 1955. Sr. mathematician and fellow mathematician Bettis Atomic Power Lab., 1955-66, adv. mathematician, 1966-67; mem. tech. staff N. Am. Rockwell Sci. Ctr., 1967-70; group leader math. group N. Am. Rockwell Sci. Ctr., Thousand Oaks, Calif., 1970-71; prof. math., co-dir. math. clinic to dir. math. clinic The Claremont Grad. Sch., 1971—, dean of faculty, 1982-87, v.p. acad. affairs and dean of faculty, 1985-87, v.p. acad. affairs, dean grad. sch., 1987-90; vis. prof. Royal Inst. Tech., Stockholm, 1981, Swiss Fed. Inst. Tech., Zurich, 1981; lectr. in field. Contbr. articles to profl. jours.; editorial bd. Internat. Jour. Math. Modeling, 1979—, Jour. Statis. Physics, 1971—; author: An Atlas of Functions, 1987, The Fractional Calculus, 1974, Monte Carlo Principles and Neutron Transport Problems, 1969. Recipient Westinghouse Disting. Svc. awad, 1963, President's medal Claremont Grad. Sch., 1990; fellow NSF, 1952-55, U. Chgo., 1951-52; grantee U.S. Energy R&D Adminstrn., 1976-80, NSF, 1976-80; Fulbright sr. rsch. scholar Massey U., New Zealand, 1990. Mem. AAAS, Am. Math. Assn., AAUP, Internat. Assn. Math. Modeling, Soc. for Indsl. and Applied Math., Am. Math. Soc., Sigma Xi, Phi Beta Kappa. Office: The Claremont Grad Sch 143 E 10th St Claremont CA 91711-3945

SPANIER, NANCY LOUISE, artistic director, educator, choreographer; b. N.Y.C., Dec. 29, 1942; d. Joseph and Muriel (Terr) S.; m. Paul Stanley Oertel, July 11, 1975. B.A. cum laude, Middlebury Coll., 1964; M.A., Mills Coll., 1969. Artistic dir. Nancy Spanier Dance Theatre, 1974—; prof. dance U. Colo. 1969—; tchr. Nat. Theatre Conservatory, Denver, 1984—. Choreographer including The Balcony, NYU Sch. Arts, over 80 dance, theater creations, 1969—, Le Cabaret de la Passion, 1994; dir. (theater) 1 Man Hamlet, 1986, Fixing a Hole, Copenhagen, 1994, (video) Flesh Chronicles, 1989; movement designer The Traveler, L.A., 1987, On The Sunnyside: Cabaret, Denmark, 1991, The Cutting Edge, Denmark, 1991. Colo. Coun. on Arts grantee, 1974—, Nat. Endowment for Arts grantee, 1975-81, Boulder Arts Commn. grantee, 1979-91. Mem. Colo. Dance Alliance. Office: Nancy Spanier Dance Theatre PO Box 4631 Boulder CO 80306-4631

SPANN, ALAN, business consultant. BA in Acctg., Calif. State U., Fullerton, 1982. Acct. Santa Fe Internat. Corp., Orange, Calif., 1982-84; sr. acct. Nat. Med. Homecare, Orange, 1984-90; divsn. acctg. mgr. Nat. Med. Specialties, Buena Park, Calif., 1984-90, divsn. controller, 1984-90; divsn. controller The Mediscus Group, Buena Park, 1984-90; corp. regional controller MultiVision Cable TV, Anaheim, Calif., 1990-92; owner J.I.L. Fin., Corona, Calif., 1993—.

SPANN, KATHARINE DOYLE, marketing and communications executive; b. Holton, Kans.; d. Edward James and Josephine (Hurla) Doyle; m. Hugh J. Spann; 1 dau., Susan Katharine. BS, Emporia State Coll. V.p. Bozell & Jacobs Advt. (formerly L.C. Cole Co.), San Francisco, 1951-76; pres. Katharine Doyle Spann Assos., 1977—; propr. Kate's Vineyard, Napa Valley, Calif. Bd. dirs. No. Calif. Am. Inst. Wine and Food, Napa Valley Opera House. Named Advt. Woman of Yr., 1962; recipient El Capitan award Peninsula chpt. Pub. Relations Soc. Am., 1962, 66, Am. Silver Anvil award, Pub. Relations Soc. Am., 1962, 66, Excellence award Publicity Club of Bay Area, 1966. Trustee, bd. dirs., mem. exhbn. com., audience devel. com. Fine Arts Mus. San Francisco. Mem. Am. Soc. Enology, Am. Inst. Wine and Food, Napa Valley Women in Wine, Calif. Vintage Wine Soc. (wine com.), Officier Commandeur, Conferie des Chevaliers du Tastevin (events com.), Delta Sigma Epsilon. Club: Metropolitan (San Francisco). Home: 1447 Whitehall Ln Saint Helena CA 94574-9684

SPANOS, ALEXANDER GUS, professional football team executive; b. Stockton, Calif., Sept. 28, 1923; m. Faye Spanos; children: Dean, Dea Spanos Berberian, Alexis Spanos Ruhl, Michael. LLD (hon.), U. Pacific, 1984. Chmn. bd. dirs. A.G. Spanos Constrn. Inc., Stockton, Calif., 1960—; chmn. bd. dirs. A.G. Spanos Properties Inc., Stockton, Calif., 1960—, A.G. Spanos Mgmt. Inc., Stockton, Calif., 1967—, A.G. Spanos Enterprises Inc., Stockton, Calif., 1971—, A.G. Spanos Devel. Inc., Stockton, Calif., 1973—, A.G. Spanos Realty Inc., Stockton, Calif., 1978—, A.G. Spanos Jet Ctr. Inc., Stockton, Calif., 1980—, A.G.S. Fin. Corp., Stockton, Calif., 1980—; pres., chmn. bd. dirs. San Diego Chargers, 1984—; Chmn. bd. dirs. A.G.S. Spanos Land Co., Stockton, Calif., 1982—. Former trustee Children's Hosp., San Francisco, San Francisco Fine Arts Mus.; trustee Eisenhower Med. Ctr., Rancho Mirage, Calif.; hon. regent U. Pacific, Stockton, 1972-82; gov. USO, , Washington, 1982—. Served with USAF, 1942-46. Recipient Albert Gallatin award Zurich-Am. Ins. Co., 1973, Horatio Alger award Horatio Alger Found., 1982, medal of Honor Statue of Liberty-Ellis Islan Found., 1982. Mem. Am. Hellenic Ednl. Progressive Assn., Calif. C. of C. (bd. dirs. 1980-85). Republican. Greek Orthodox. Office: San Diego Chargers Jack Murphy Stadium PO Box 609609 San Diego CA 92160-9609 also: A G Spanos Constrn Co 1341 W Robinhood Dr Stockton CA 95207-5511*

SPARGER, WILLIAM HARRY, gas transmission company executive; b. Durant, Okla., June 13, 1942; s. Alan Jeff Sparger and Ruth S. Strickland Lytton. BSCE, N.Mex. State U., 1965. Registered profl. engr., Tex., La. With Mountain States Tel. & Tel., Santa Fe, N.Mex., 1965-67, Transcontinental Gas Pipeline Corp., Houston, 1967-92; v.p. engring. Colo. Interstate Gas Co., Colorado Springs, 1992—. Mem. ASCE, NSPE, Tex. Soc. Profl. Engrs., La. Soc. Profl. Engrs., Am. Gas Assn. (pipeline rsch. com.), Interstate Natural Gas Assn. of Am. Republican. Office: Colo Interstate Gas Co PO Box 1087 Colorado Springs CO 80901-1087

SPARKS, DALE BOYD, allergist, health facility administrator; b. Springfield, Mo., July 14, 1929; s. Roscoe R. and Ruby V. (Boyd) S.; m. Caroline P. Porter, Aug. 3, 1956; children: Susan L., Laura A., Lisa M., Jennifer G. AB, BS, Southwest Mo. State U., 1951; BS in Medicine, U. Mo., 1953; MD, St. Louis U., 1955. Diplomate Am. Bd. Allergy and Immunology. Intern Kansas City (Mo.) Gen. Hosp. U. Med. Ctr., 1955-56; resident U. Mo. Hosp., 1958-60; fellow in allergy and immunology Northwestern U., 1960-61; mem. courtesy staff Parkview Cmty. Hosp., 1961—; mem. med. staff Riverside (Calif.) Cmty. Hosp., 1961—, dir. respiratory therapy, 1968-85; dir. respiratory therapy and diagnostic svcs. Riverside Gen. Hosp. U. Med. Ctr., 1965—, chmn. dept. medicine, 1978—, chief med. staff, 1990—; acting dir., health officer Riverside Pub. Health Dept., 1991-93; clin. prof. medicine Loma Linda U. Mem. editl. bd. Immunology and Allergy in Practice, 1980—. Lt. USNR. Fellow ACP (coun. subspecialty Socs. 1988—), Am. Coll. Allergy and Immunology (disting., bd. regents 1989-93, pres. 1990-91, chmn. fin. com./treas. 1990-93, recert. com.), Coll. Allergy, Asthma and Immunology; mem. AMA, Am. Soc. Internal Medicine, Am. Lung Assn. (bd. dirs. 1990—), Am. Heart Assn. (bd. dirs. 1964-70, pres. 1966), Joint Coun. Am. Allergy and Immunology (bd. dirs. 1985-90), Calif. Med. Assn., Calif. Soc. Allergy, Inland Soc. Internal Medicine, Riverside County Med. Assn. (bd. councilors 1980—, alt. del. CMA 1988—), Riverside County Found. Med. Care (sec., past pres.). Office: 4500 Brockton Ave Ste 319 Riverside CA 92501

SPARKS, IRVING ALAN, biblical scholar, educator; b. Ft. Wayne, Ind., June 15, 1933; s. James Edwin and Isabelle Mildred S.; A.B., Davidson (N.C.) Coll., 1954; B.D., Union Theol. Sem., Richmond, Va., 1959; S.T.M., Lancaster (Pa.) Theol. Sem., 1970; Ph.D., Claremont (Calif.) Grad. Sch., 1970; m. Helen Daniels, Sept. 3, 1954; children—Lydia Isabelle Sparkswworthy, Leslie Bishop, Robin Alan. Lectr. philosophy and religion LaVerne (Calif.) Coll., 1965-69; asst. prof. religion Claremont Grad. Sch., 1970-74, assoc. dir. Inst. Antiquity and Christianity, 1970-74; mem. faculty San Diego State U., 1974—, prof. religious studies, 1980—, chmn. dept. religious studies, 1983-90, 92—, assoc. dean grad. div. and research, 1974-83; adj. faculty Sch. Theol. Claremont, Calif., 1970-74, 89—; founder/pres. Inst. Bibl. Studies, 1983-85; cons. photog. archival conservation of Dead Sea Scrolls in Jerusalem, 1980; mem adv. bd. Inst. Antiquity and Christianity, 1974—. Trustee, Claremont Collegiate Sch., 1970-75, pres., 1972-74; trustee, mem. exec. com. Ancient Bibl. Manuscript Ctr., 1981—. Fellow Lilly Found., 1964-65, Layne Found., 1965-66; disting. vis. scholar James Madison U., 1982. Mem. Am. Soc. Papyrologists, Soc. Bibl. Lit., Phi Beta Delta. Author: The Pastoral Epistles: Introduction and Commentary, 1981, Exploring World Religions: A Reading and Writing Workbook, 1986, 4th edit., 1991; editor Studies and Documents, 1971-92; contbr. articles on papyrology and bibl. studies to scholarly jours. Office: San Diego State U Dept Religious Studies San Diego CA 92182-0304

SPARKS, JACK NORMAN, college dean; b. Lebanon, Ind., Dec. 3, 1928; s. Oakley and Geraldine Ruth (Edrington) S.; m. Esther Lois Bowen, Apr. 11, 1953; children: Stephen Michael, Robert Norman, Ruth Ann, Jonathan Russell. BS, Purdue U., 1950; MA, U. Iowa, 1951, PhD, 1960. Tchr. math. Leyden Community High Sch., Franklin Park, Ill., 1954-58; rsch. asst. U. Iowa, Iowa City, 1958-60; assoc. prof. applied stats., dir. bur. of rsch. U. No. Colo., Greeley, 1960-65; assoc. prof. ednl. psychology Pa. State U., State Coll., 1965-68; dir. corr. Campus Crusade for Christ, San Bernardino, Calif., 1968-69; dir. Christian World Liberation Front, Berkeley, Calif., 1969-75; pastor, ch. overseer New Covenant Apostolic Order, Berkeley, 1975-77; dean St. Athanasius Acad. Orthodox Theology, Santa Barbara, Calif., 1977-87, St. Athanasius Coll., Santa Barbara, 1987-93, St. Athanasius Acad. of Orthodox Theology, Ben Lomnd, Calif., 1993—; cons. Measurement Rsch. Ctr., Iowa City, 1959-60, Western States Small Schs. Project, Greeley, 1962-65, Colo. Coun. on Edn. Rsch., Denver, 1963-65. Author: Letters to Street Christians, 1971, The Mind Benders, 1977, 79, The Resurrection Letters, 1978, The Preaching of the Apostles, 1987, Victory in the Unseen Warfare, 1993; editor: Apostolic of Fathers; gen. editor The Orthodox Study Bible, 1993, Virtue in the Unseen Warfare, 1995. Trustee Rock Mont Coll., Denver, 1962-77, Thomas Nelson Co., Nashville, 1977-78. 1st lt. U.S. Army, 1952-54. Mem. Am. Scientific Affiliation, Assn. Orthodox Theologians, Conf. on Faith and History, Phi Delta Kappa (Epsilon chpt. pres. 1959-60). Democrat. Orthodox Christian. Home: 9792 Live Oak Ave Ben Lomond CA 95005-9508 Office: St Athanasius Acad Orthodox Theology 9540-2 Central Ave Ben Lomond CA 95005

SPARKS, LARRY LEON, physicist; b. Flagler, Colo., Jan. 11, 1940; s. Lundie Leon Sparks and Ruby Ethyl (Dorsey) Hollenbaugh; m. Patricia Ruth Heid, Aug. 16, 1959; children: Lundy Lane, Jacquelyn Heidi Sparks Fesenmeyer. BS in Engring. Physics, U. Colo., 1962. Physicist Nat. Bur. Standrads (now Nat. Inst. Standards and Tech.), Boulder, Colo., 1961-84, group leader, 1984-88, div. chief, 1988-91, group leader, 1991—; chmn. Internat. Thermal Expansion Symposium, Boulder, 1989; organizer Internat. Thermophys. Properties Conf., Boulder, 1991; chmn. local arrangements Internat. Cryogenic Materials Conf., Colorado Springs, Colo., 1983. Contbg. author: Materials at Low Temperatures, 1983, ASTM Spl. Publ., 1993; contbr. articles to tech. publs.; editor Internat. Jour. Thermophysics, 1991. Chmn. Good Samaritan Found., Longmont, Colo., 1971; moderator United Congl. Ch., Longmont, 1975-76. Recipient cert. of recognition NASA, 1989. Mem. ASTM, ASME, Am. Soc. Metals, Internat. Thermal Expansion Symposium (governing bd. 1988—). Democrat. Office: Nat Inst Standards/Tech 325 Broadway St Boulder CO 80303-3337

SPARKS, ROBERT WILLIAM, publishing executive; b. Seattle, Dec. 30, 1925; s. James Donald and Gladys (Simmons) S. Student, U. Wash., 1947-50; B.A., U. Hawaii, 1954, M.A., 1965. Editor, various pubs., 1947-64; mng. editor U. Hawaii Press, 1964-66, dir., 1967-87; cons. East-West Ctr., Jour. Hawaiian History, Japanese and Chinese book pubs., 1987-92; mem. adv. bd. to pres. Kamehameha Schs. Served with AUS, 1944-46, PTO. Recipient McInerny editorship, 1953; Pacific House citation Pacific and Asian Affairs Council, 1974. Mem. Assn. Am. Univ. Presses, Assn. Am. Publishers, Internat. Assn. Scholarly Publishers, Soc. for Scholarly Pub., Hawaiian Hist. Soc., Hawaii Found. History and Humanities, Honolulu Acad. Arts, Bishop Mus. Assn. Home: 3634 Nihipali Pl Honolulu HI 96816-3307

SPARKS, WALTER CHAPPEL, horticulturist, educator; b. New Castle, Colo., Aug. 22, 1918; s. Lester Elroy and Jean Ivene (Murray) S.; m. Barbara Ferne Gardner, May 31, 1942; children: Robert, Richard, Eugene. Student, Western State Coll., 1936-37; BS, Colo. State U., 1941, MS, 1943; postgrad., U. Minn., 1945, Wash. State U., 1949, 56-57; DSc (hon.), U. Idaho, 1984. Instr., head dept. agr. Pueblo Jr. Coll., 1941; grad. asst. Colo. State U., 1941-43, instr. horticulture, 1943-44, asst. prof., 1944-47, assoc. prof., 1947; assoc. horticulturist U. Idaho, Aberdeen, 1947-57; acting supt. Aberdeen br. Agrl. Expt. Sta., 1951, 57, 65, horticulturist, 1957—, research prof. horticulture, 1968—, prin. liaison coordinator for potato program, 1976—; exchange prof. Research Inst., Kolding, Denmark, 1972-73; adviser and lectr. on potato problems to various fgn. govts.; cons., adv., Israel, 1980, Philippines, 1981, Jamaica, 1988; dir. Postharvest Inst. Perishables, 1980—. Contbr. articles to profl. jours. Recipient 50th Anniversary medal Fed. Land Banks, 1967; Disting. Svc. in Potato Industry award Gov. of Idaho, 1967; named to Hall of Fame Potato Mus. Brussels, 1977, Alumni Svc. award, 1980, Disting. Faculty award Phi Kappa Phi, 1980, Disting. Svc. award rsch. in potato postharvest storage tech., 1987, Cert. of Appreciation Nat. Potato Rsch. Edn. Found., 1986, Agriculture Svc. award N.W. Food Processor Field Reps., 1987; elected Idaho Agrl. Hall of Fame, 1983; Eldred Jenne Rsch. fellow, 1957; named 1 of 100 "People Make the Difference" in Idaho, 1990. Mem. AAAS, Am. Inst. Biol. Scis., Am. Soc. Hort. Sci. (life), European Assn. Potato Research, N.W. Assn. Horticulturists, Entomologists and Plant Pathologists, Idaho Acad. Sci., Nat. Potato Research and Edn. Found. (cert. appraciation seed potato storage tech. 1986), N.W. Food Processors Assn. (Disting. Service award, 1987), N.W. Fieldman's Assn. (Disting. Agrl. Service award, 1987), Potato Assn. Am. (life mem., past pres., dir.), Western Regional Potato Improvement Group (past pres.), C. of C., Scabbard and Blade, Sigma Xi (Outstanding Research Paper award 1974), Gamma Sigma Delta (Outstanding Research Worker award 1977, award of merit 1978), Alpha Zeta, Beta Beta Beta, Epsilon Rho Epsilon. Club: Rotary. Home: 1100 Burnett Dr Apt 513 Nampa ID 83651-7578 Office: U Idaho Rsch & Etension Ctr Aberdeen ID 83210

SPARLING, REBECCA HALL, materials engineer, energy consultant; b. Memphis, June 7, 1910; d. Robert Meredith and Kate Wallace (Sampson) Hall; m. Edwin Kinmonth Smith, Oct. 30, 1935 (div. 1947); 1 child, Douglas Kinmonth; m. Joseph Sparling, July 10, 1948; B.A., Vanderbilt U., 1930, M.S., 1931. Registered profl. engr., Calif. Design specialist Gen. Dynamics, Pomona, Calif., 1951-68, Northrop Aircraft, Hawthorne, Calif., 1944-51; cons. engr., Detroit, 1936-44; tech. writer William H. Baldwin, N.Y.C., 1934-35; metallurgist Lakeside Malleable, Racine, Wis., 1933-34, Am. Cast Iron Pipe, Birmingham, Ala., 1931-32; energy cons., Laguna Hills, Calif., 1973-85. Author; contbr. articles to profl. jours. Officer, leader Fgn. Policy Assn. of Leisure World, Laguna Hills, 1980-84; bd. dirs. AAUW, 1974-84; mem. Air Pollution Control Bd., San Bernardino County, 1973; cons., intervenor Calif. Energy Commn., 1975-82. Recipient Engring. Merit award Orange County Council Engrs. Soc., 1978; named Outstanding Engr. Inst. Advancement of Engring., 1978, Los Angeles Engrs. Week, 1965. Fellow Soc. Woman Engrs. (Achievement award 1957), Inst. Advancement Engring.; mem. Am. Soc. Metals, Am. Soc. Nondestructive Testing, Delta Delta Delta. Republican. Religious Sci. Ch. Address: 650 Harrison Ave Claremont CA 91711-4595

SPARR, DANIEL BEATTIE, federal judge; b. Denver, June 8, 1931; s. Daniel John and Mary Isabel (Beattie) S.; m. Virginia Sue Long Sparr, June 28, 1952; children: Stephen Glenwood, Douglas Lloyd, Michael Christopher. BSBA, U. Denver, 1952, JD, 1966. Bar: Colo. U.S. Dist. Ct. Assoc. White & Steele, Denver, 1966-70; atty. Mountain States Telephone & Telegraph Co., Denver, 1970-71; ptnr. White & Steele, Denver, 1971-74; atty. Wesley H. Doan, Lakewood, Colo., 1974-75; prin. Law Offices of Daniel B. Sparr, Denver, 1975-77; judge 2d dist. Colo. Dist. Ct., Denver, 1977-90; judge U.S. Dist. Ct. Colo., Denver, 1990—. Mem. Denver Bar Assn. (trustee 1975-78), Denver Paralegal Inst. (bd. advs. 1976-88), William E. Doyle's/Am. Inns of Ct., Am. Bd. Trial Advs., ABA, Colo. Bar Assn. Office: US Dist Ct US Courthouse C-540 1929 Stout St Denver CO 80294-2900

SPARREVOHN, FREDERIC REIDTZ, engineering executive; b. L.A., Dec. 2, 1943; s. Frederic D.R. and Dorthy Mae (Utter) S. AA, Mount San Antonio Jr. Coll., 1964; BS, Calif. State U., L.A., 1967. Devel. engr. Communications Mfg. Co., Long Beach, Calif., 1971-77; engr. HTL K West, Santa Ana, Calif., 1975—; owner Sparrevohn Engring., Long Beach, 1975—. Inventor in field. Mem. Heritage Found., Washington, 1987—. Capt.

USAF, 1967-71. Republican. Home and Office: 143 Nieto Ave Apt 1 Long Beach CA 90803-3363

SPARROW, LARRY J., telecommunications executive. With GTE Corp., Thousand Oaks, Calif., 1967—; pres. GTE Northwest Inc., Thousand Oaks, Calif., 1992—; also prin. GTE Calif., Inc., Thousand Oaks, Calif., 1992—. Office: GTE California Inc. One GTE Pl Thousand Oaks CA 91362*

SPATARO, JANIE DEMPSEY WATTS, writer; b. Chattanooga, May 17, 1951; d. Ray Dean and Anne America (Dempsey) Watts; m. Stephen Anthony Spataro, June 18, 1977; children—Anthony Dempsey, Stephen Jackson. B.S. in Journalism, U. Calif.-Berkeley, 1974; M.A. in Broadcast Journalism, U. So. Calif., 1982. Writer, editor McGiffin Newspapers, South Gate, Calif., 1976; news bur. mgr. Loyola Marymount U., Westchester, Calif., 1976; asst. dir. pub. relations Hawthorne (Calif.) Community Hosp. 1977-78; pub. rels. cons. Security Pacific Bank, Los Angeles, 1978-82; writer Cable Card, Inc., Marina del Rey, Calif., 1983; writer Reality Prodns., Huntington Beach, Calif., 1983-86. Writer, producer, editor TV documentary: Who's Minding the Children?, 1983; screenwriter Who's Minding The Children?, Monkey Doll, Fireworks, The Detemer Solution; contbr. articles to mags. and newspapers. Speaker on child care on TV, 1983-84. Beatrice E. Rice scholar U. Calif., 1973-74; Calif. State fellow, 1981-83. Mem. Women in Film, DAR. Home and Office: 2629 Arizona Ave Santa Monica CA 90404-1408

SPAULDING, JOHN PIERSON, public relations executive, marine consultant; b. N.Y.C., June 25, 1917; s. Forrest Brisbine and Genevieve Anderson (Pierson) S.; m. Eleanor Rita Bonner, Aug. 18, 1947; children: Anne Spaulding Balzhiser, John F., Mary T. Spaulding Calvert; m. 2d, Donna Alene Abrescia, May 15, 1966. Student Iowa State Coll., 1935-36, Grinnell Coll., 1936-38, U. Chgo., 1938-39. Reporter, Chgo. City News Bur., UPI, 1939-40; editor Cedar Falls (Iowa) Daily Record, 1940-41; picture editor Des Moines Register & Tribune, 1941-42, 47-50; pub. relations dir. Motor Club Iowa, Davenport, 1950-51; commd. 2d. lt. USAF, 1942, advanced through grades to maj., 1947, recalled, 1951, advanced through grades to lt. col.; ret., 1968; v.p. Vacations Hawaii, Honolulu, 1969-70; dir. pub. relations, mgr. pub. relations services Alexander & Baldwin, Inc., Honolulu, 1970-76; mgr. community relations Matson Navigation Co., Honolulu, 1976-81. Pres., Econ. Devel. Assn., Skagit County, Wash., 1983-85, Fidalgo Island Ednl. Youth Found.; mem. Anacortes (Wash.) Sch. Bd., 1982-88; mem. Gov.'s Tourism Devel. Council, 1983-85; mem. adv. com. State Ferry System, 1982—, productivity coun., 1990—; chmn. Everett chpt. S.C.O.R.E., 1984-86, Bellingham chpt., 1991—. Decorated Air medal. Mem. Pub. Relations Soc. Am. (pres. Hawaii chpt. 1974), Hawaii Communicators (pres. 1973), Nat. Def. Transp. Assn. (pres. Aloha chpt. 1980-81, Disting. Service award 1978-79), Air Force Assn., Can. Inst. Internat. Affairs, Anacortes C. of C., Sigma Delta Chi (life). Clubs: Propeller (pres. Port of Honolulu 1979-80), Honolulu Press, Fidelgo Yacht, Hawaii Yacht, Royal Hawaiian 400 Yacht (comdr. 1977-81), Rotary, Elks. Home: 6002 Sands Way Anacortes WA 98221-4015

SPEACE, OSCAR KIMBROUGH, television producer and director, writer; b. Phila., Mar. 11, 1948; s. Robert St. Clair and Janka (Festinger) S.; m. Janice Joy Noga, Aug. 8, 1981; 1 stepchild, John Nicklas. BA, Fresno State Coll., 1971. Asst. golf pro L.A. Country Club, 1972-73, Phila. Country Club, 1973-76; salesman Sears, Fresno, Calif., 1976-78; newspaper reporter Dinuba (Calif.) Sentinel, 1978-79; videotape libr. Unitel Prodn. Svcs., N.Y.C., 1979-80; freelance dir. Phila. and N.Y.C., 1980-81; producer, dir. Valley Pub. TV, Fresno, 1981—; producer, dir. Valley Press, 1990. Dir. TV documentary film Conquest of My Brother, 1992; screenwriter film scripts The Station, 1985, The Great Marble Shoot, 1987. Phila. Golf Assn. scholar, 1966-71. Mem. Nat. Acad. TV Arts and Scis., Sherwood Golf Club. Republican. Jewish. Home: 1438 Morris Ave Clovis CA 93611-1406

SPEAR, MARGARET C., development officer; b. Wellington, New Zealand, June 20, 1930; d. William Pearsol and Margarita Victoria (Moreno) Cochran; divorced; children: William Aristides, George Joseph, Sarah Spear-Bartlett. Cert., U. Lausanne, Switzerland, 1949; BA, Smith Coll., 1952. Intelligence analyst CIA, Washington, 1952-55; registrar Madeira Sch., Greenway, Va., 1955-56; tchr., mid. sch. coord. Westridge Sch., Pasadena, Calif., 1966-74; freelance writer, 1974-76; devel. assoc. Pacific Oaks Coll., Pasadena, 1976-80; asst. dir. devel. Pacific Asia Mus., Pasadena, 1980-86; dir. found. govt rels. Art Ctr. Coll. Design, Pasadena, 1986-90; major gifts dir. Huntington Libr., San Marino, Calif., 1990—; cons. Pasadena Art Workshops, 1985-86. Mem. task force Kellogg Tng. Program United Way, L.A., 1985-86. Mem. Nat. Soc. Fund Raising Execs. (L.A. chpt., sec. 1992-94, pres.'s award 1994), Sierra Club (leader). Democrat. Home: 1185 Beverly Way Altadena CA 91001-2574 Office: Huntington Libr 1151 Oxford Rd San Marino CA 91108-1218

SPEARS, ALAN ERROL, judicial officer; b. San Bernardino, Calif., Oct. 22, 1948; s. Bertram Lysle Spears and Min (Suesserman) Landau; m. Merry Yin Wong, Feb. 14, 1992. AA, San Bernardino Valley Coll., 1969; JD, Calif. So. Sch. of Law, 1971, U. Calif., Riverside, 1975; DD (hon.), Missionaries of New Truth, 1971. Bar: Calif. 1975, U.S. Dist. Ct. (ctrl. and so. dist.) Calif. 1976, U.S. Ct. Appeals (9th cir.) 1976, U.S. Dist. Ct. (ea. dist.) Calif. 1977, U.S. Supreme Ct. 1979, Nebr. 1984; cert. c.c. law instr. Prof. law Crafton Hills Coll., Yucaipa, Calif., 1973-75; sole practice San Bernardino, Calif., 1975-87; mental health hearing referee L.A. Superior Ct., 1991—; author Paradise Cay Publs., Middletown, Calif., 1994—; lit. agent Alan E. Spears, Esq., Newport Beach, Calif., 1994—. Author: (maritime booklet) Local Knowledge, Newport Harbor, 1993, (maritime legal book) Landfall Legalese, The Pacific, 1994, Landfall Legalese, The Caribbean, 1994. Mem. Pacific Yacht and Balloon Club (commodore, judge advocate 1994), Chula Vista Yacht Club (founding mem., judge advocate 1987—). Office: PO Box 2901 Newport Beach CA 92659-0375

SPEARS, MELVIN STANLEY, lawyer; b. San Bernardino, Calif., Apr. 10, 1927; s. Julius Nathan and Margurite (Blaiss) S.; m. Suzann Pollock Chapman, Aug. 14, 1949; children: Briana London, Eric C. AA, UCLA, 1948; JD, U. So. Calif., 1951. Bar: Calif. 1952, U.S. Dist. Ct. (cen. dist.) Calif. 1952, U.S. Tax Ct. Assoc. Guy E. Ward, Beverly Hills, Calif., 1951-54, Martin H. Webster, L.A., 1954-56; atty. Irving B-J Levine, Beverly Hills, 1956-58; ptnr. Ervin, Cohen & Jessup, Beverly Hills, 1958—. With USN, 1945-46. Mem. ABA, Calif. Bar Assn., L.A. County Bar Assn., Beverly Hills Bar Assn. Office: Ervin Cohen & Jessup 9401 Wilshire Blvd Fl 9 Beverly Hills CA 90212-2928

SPEAS, ROBERT DIXON, aeronautical engineer, aviation company executive; b. Davis County, N.C., Apr. 14, 1916; s. William Paul and Nora Estelle (Dixon) S.; m. Manette Lansing Hollingsworth, Mar. 4, 1944; children: Robert Dixon, Jay Hollingsworth. BS, MIT, 1940; Air Transport Pilot rating, Boeing Sch. Aero., United Air Lines, 1938. Aviation reporter Winston Salem Jour., 1934; sales rep. Trans World Airlines, 1937-38; engr. Am. Airlines, 1940-44, asst. to v.p., 1944-46, dir. maintenance and engring., cargo div., 1946-47, spl. asst. to pres., 1947-50; U.S. rep. A.V. Roe Can., Ltd., 1950-51; pres., chmn. bd. R. Dixon Speas Assocs., Inc (aviation cons.), 1951-76; chmn., chief exec. officer Speas-Harris Airport Devel., Inc., 1974-76; chmn. bd., pres. Aviation Consulting, Inc., 1976-82, chmn. bd., 1982-84; pres. PRC Aviation, 1984—; mem. aeros. and space engring. bd. Nat. Rsch. Coun., 1980-84. Author: Airplane Performance and Operations, 1945, Pilots' Technical Manual, 1946, Airline Operation, 1949, Technical Aspects of Air Transport Management, 1955, Financial Benefits and Intangible Advantages of Business Aircraft Operations, 1989. Recipient 1st award Ann. Nat. Boeing Thesis Competition, 1937, rsch. award Am. Transport Assn., 1942, William A. Downes Airport Operators Coun. Internat. award, 1992; inductee Ariz. Aviation Hall of Fame, 1995. Fellow AIAA (treas. and coun. 1963-64, chmn. ethics com. 1989-92, AIAA-SAE Williams Littenwool lectr. 1994), Royal Aero. Soc., Soc. Automotive Engrs. (v.p. 1955, coun. 1964-66); mem. ASME, Flight Safety Found. (bd. govs. 1958-71, 79-90, exec. com. 1979-90), Inst. Aero Scis. (past treas., coun. 1959-62, exec. com. 1962), Coll. Aeronautics (trustee 1967—), Soc. Aircraft Investigators, Manhasset C. of C. (pres. 1962), Wings Club (pres. 1968-69, coun. 1966-71, 73-90, 92-95, chmn. devel. com. 1989—, Sight lectr. 1992), Skyline Country Club. Home: 4771 E Country Villa Dr Tucson AZ 85718-2640 Office: 6262 N Swan Rd Tucson AZ 85718-3600

SPECK, ROBERT CHARLES, geological engineer; b. Bklyn., June 15, 1944; s. Charles Ernest and Helen Gertrude (York) S.; m. Pia Rey Polanco, July 4, 1971; 1 child, Stephen Ruben. BA, Franklin and Marshal Coll., 1968; BS, U. Missouri, Rolla, 1974, MS, 1975, PhD, 1979. Geologist Peace Corps, Dominican Republic, 1968-70; resident geologist Geokinetics, Inc., Dominican Republic, 1970-72; project geologist Hanson-Rodriguez, S.A., Dominican Republic, 1972-73; staff engr. GAI Cons., Inc., Pitts., 1979-84; prof. U. Alaska, Fairbanks, 1984—. Contbr. articles to profl. jours. Mem. Assn. Engring. Geologists (sect. vice chmn. 1985-89), Soc. Mining Engrs., Am. Inst. Profl. Geologists (lic.), Internat. Soc. for Rock Mechanics, Tau Beta Pi, Sigma Gamma Epsilon. Home: 3030 Forrest Dr Fairbanks AK 99709-5741 Office: U Alaska Dept Mining Geol Engrl Fairbanks AK 99775

SPECKMAN, HERBERT, agricultural products executive. Farmer; pres. Coney Island Farms, Inc., Stockton, Calif., 1975—; ptnr. Herbert Speckman Farms, Stockton, Calif., 1981—. Office: 19500 Clifton Court Rd Stockton CA 95206-9501*

SPECKMAN, JOYCE, agricultural products executive; b. 1943. Sec., treas. Coney Island Farms, Inc., Stockton, Calif., 1975—; ptnr. Herbert Speckman Farms, Stockton, Calif., 1981—. Office: Herbert Speckman Farms 19500 Clifton Court Rd Stockton CA 95206-9501*

SPECTER, RICHARD BRUCE, lawyer; b. Phila., Sept. 6, 1952; s. Jacob E. and Marilyn B. (Kron) S.; m. Jill Ossenfort, May 30, 1981; children: Lauren Elizabeth, Lindsey Anne, Allison Lee. BA cum laude, Washington U., St. Louis, 1974; JD, George Washington U., 1977. Bar: Mo. 1977, U.S. Dist. Ct. (ea. and we. dists.) Mo. 1977, U.S. Ct. Appeals (8th cir.) 1977, Ill. 1978, Pa. 1978, U.S. Dist. Ct. (ea. dist.) Ill. 1979, U.S. Ct. Appeals (7th cir.) 1979, Calif. 1984, U.S. Dist. Ct. (cen. dist.) Calif. 1985, U.S. Ct. Appeals (9th cir.) 1986, U.S. Dist. Ct. (so. dist.) Calif. 1987, U.S. Dist. Ct. (no. dist.) Calif. 1988. Assoc. Coburn, Croft, Shepherd, Herzog & Putzell, St. Louis, 1977-79; ptnr. Herzog, Kral, Burroughs & Specter, St. Louis, 1979-82; exec. v.p. Uniqey Internat., Santa Ana, Calif., 1982-84; pvt. practice law L.A. and Irvine, Calif., 1984-87; ptnr. Corbett & Steelman, Irvine, 1987—; instr. Nat. Law Ctr. George Washington U. 1975. Mem. ABA, Ill. Bar Assn., Mo. Bar Assn., Pa. Bar Assn., Calif. Bar Assn. Jewish. Home: 37 Bull Run Irvine CA 92720-2510 Office: 18200 Von Karman Ave Ste 200 Irvine CA 92715-1029

SPEED, TERENCE PAUL, statistician, educator; b. Victor Harbor, Australia, Mar. 14, 1943; came to the U.S., 1987; s. Harold Hector and Jeanette Elisabeth (Hacklin) S.; m. Freda Elizabeth Pollard, Dec. 22, 1964. BS, Melbourne U., Victoria, Australia, 1965; PhD, Monash U., Victoria, 1969. Tutor Monash U., 1965-67, lectr., 1967-69; lectr. U. Sheffield, United Kingdom, 1969-73; prof. U. Western Australia, 1974-82; chief CSIRO Div. Math. and Statistics, Canberra, Australia, 1983-87; prof. U. Calif., Berkeley, 1987—. Home: 1830 Arch St Berkeley CA 94709-1310 Office: U Calif Dept Statistics Berkeley CA 94720

SPEER, ANDREW KEVIN, art educator; b. Louisville, Dec. 8, 1951; s. Joseph Thomas and Virginia Marie (Anderson) S.; m. Susan Birmingham Garr, May 10, 1970 (div. June 1972); 1 child, Heather; m. Linda Lee Bukszar, Oct. 12, 1974. B Gen. Studies, U. Ky., 1975, MFA in Painting, 1978; postgrad., SUNY, Buffalo, 1976-77. Instr. dept. art U. Ky., Lexington, 1978-79, San Diego State U., 1979-82; instr. studio art Mira Costa (Calif.) Coll., 1981-85; vis. artist Allen R. Hite Art Inst., U. Louisville, 1989, instr., 1990; asst. prof. art Met. State Coll. Denver, 1990—; vis. artist Cornell U., Ithaca, N.Y., 1981. One-man shows include Swanson-Cralle Gallery, Louisville, 1988, Morris B. Belknap Jr. Galleries, U. Louisville, 1990, Auraria Higher Edn. Ctr. Libr., Denver, 1993; exhibited in group shows, 1984—, including Louisville Visual Art Assn., 1987, 88, 89, Mus. Modern Art of Casa de la Cultra, Cuenca, Ecuador, 1990, Headley-Whitney Mus., Lexington, Ky., 1991, Swanson-Cralle Gallery, 1993, Coleman Gallery, Albuquerque, 1994; represented in permanent collection J.B. Speed Art Mus., Louisville. Recipient purchase award J.B. Speed Art Mus., 1977, hon. mention Reader's Digest Artists at Giverny Program, France, 1988, COVision recognition award Colo. Coun. on Arts, 1994; So. Arts Fedn. Regional fellow Nat. Endowment for Arts, 1986, Al Smith fellow Ky. Arts Coun., 1987; grantee Pollock-Krasner Found., 1989, profl. travel grantee Met. State Coll. Denver, 1992. Democrat. Baptist. Office: Met State Coll Denver Art Dept Denver CO 80217

SPEERS, J. ALVIN, editor, publisher, accountant; b. Orangeville, Ont., Can., June 30, 1930; s. Frank A. and Pauline (Albrecht) S.; m. Esther Roth, May 5, 1962; children: Kelly A., Craig J. Student pub. sch., Caledon, Ont., Can.; grad. (corr.), Am. School, Chgo., 1965. Communications installer No. Electric Co. Ltd., Toronto, Ont., Can., 1956-59; owner Small Land Devel., Caledon, Ont., Can., 1959-60; collection mgr. Laurendide Fin. Co., Calgary, Alta., Can., 1960-62; br. mgr. Niagara Fin. Co. Ltd., Calgary, 1962-65; credit and time sales ins. mgr. Stampede Pontiac Buice Ltd., Calgary, 1965-66; mgr. acctg. sect. Alta. Wheat Pool, 1967-69; mgr. surety dept. Morrison & Tait Ins. Ltd., 1969-73; editor, pub., mgr. Aardvark Enterprises div. Speers Investments Ltd., 1973—; pub. Teak Roundup Mag. Author poetry and prose; columnist. Candidate Penticton (B.C., Can.) City Coun., 1983; pack leader Boy Scouts Am., Calgary, 1972; treas. ch., Calgary, 1972; pres. Eugene Coste Home & Sch. Assn., Calgary, 1970-71. With RCAF, 1951-56. Mem. Can. Poetry Assn. Presbyterian. Home and Office: 204 Millbank Dr SW, Calgary, AB Canada T2Y 2H9

SPEISER, BURTON LYLE, radiation oncologist; b. N.Y.C., Jan. 24, 1946; s. Morris and Mollie (Chtive) S.; m. Jeanne Michelle Speiser, Dec. 21, 1968; children: Michael Lawrence, Leonard Robert, Lisa Jennifer. AB in Biology, Queens Coll., 1966; MD, N.J. Coll. Medicine, Newark, 1970; MS in Radiation Biology, U. Rochester, 1977. Diplomate Am. Bd. Radiology, Therapeutic Radiology. Intern Manhattan VA Hosp., N.Y.C., 1970-71; assoc. dir. radiation LDS Hosp., Salt Lake City, 1976-79; resident in radiation oncology U. Rochester, 1971-74; asst. prof. radiation oncology Ind. U., Indpls., 1979-80; dir. radiation oncology St. Joseph's Med. Ctr., Phoenix, 1980—. Pres. Phoenix unit Am. Cancer Soc., 1987. Maj. M.C., USAF, 1974-76. Mem. AMA, Am. Soc. Therapeutic Radiologists and Oncologists, Am. Coll. Radiation Oncology, Am. Brachytherapy Soc., N.Y. Acad. Scis., Sigma Xi. Republican. Office: St Joseph's Med Ctr 350 W Thomas Rd Phoenix AZ 85013-4409

SPEISER, THEODORE WESLEY, astrophysics, planetary and atmospheric sciences educator; b. Del Norte, Colo., Nov. 23, 1934; s. Alfred Theodore and Virginia Melva (Pickens) S.; m. Patricia Jane McCrummen, June 10, 1956; children: Tanya Lee, Kelly Ann, Tertia Ava. BS, Colo. State U., 1956; MS, Calif. Inst. Tech., 1959; PhD, Pa. State U., 1964. Asst. prof. U. Colo., Boulder, 1969-74, assoc. prof., 1974-85, prof. astrophysics, planetary and atmospheric scis., 1985—; cons. NOAA, Boulder, 1970—. Contbr. articles to profl. jours. Served to capt. U.S. Army, 1960-61. Recipient U.S. Sr. Scientist award A.V. Humboldt Found., 1977; Fulbright fellow, 1956. Mem. Am. Geophys. Union (local br. v.p. 1986-87, pres. 1987). Home: 2335 Dartmouth Ave Boulder CO 80303-5209 Office: U Colo Dept of Astrophysics Planetary & Atmospheric Scis C Box 391 Boulder CO 80309

SPELLMAN, DOUGLAS TOBY, advertising executive; b. Bronx, N.Y., May 12, 1942; s. Sydney M. and Leah B. (Rosenberg) S.; BS, Fairleigh Dickinson U., 1964; m. Ronni I. Epstein, Jan. 16, 1966 (div. Mar. 1985); children: Laurel Nicole, Daren Scott; m. Michelle Ward, Dec. 31, 1986, 1 child, Dallas Ward Spellman. Media buyer Doyle, Dane, Bernbach, Inc., N.Y.C., 1964-66, Needham, Harper & Steers, Inc., N.Y.C., 1966; media supr. Ogilvy & Mather, Inc., N.Y.C., 1967-69; media dir. Sinay Advt., L.A., 1969-70; chief ops. officer S.H.H. Creative Mktg., Inc., L.A., 1969—; assoc. media dir. Warren, Mullen, Dolobowsky, Inc., N.Y.C., 1970—; dir. West Coast ops. Ed Libov Assocs., Inc., Los Angeles, 1970-71; media supr. Carson/Roberts Advt. div. Ogilvy & Mather, Inc., L.A., 1971-72; assoc. media dir. Ogilvy & Mather, Inc., L.A., 1972-73; media dir. Vitt Media Internat., Inc., L.A., 1973-74; v.p., dir. West Coast ops. Ind. Media Svcs., Inc., L.A., 1974-75; owner Douglas T. Spellman, Inc., L.A., 1975-77, pres., chmn. bd., 1977-82; pres., chief operating officer Douglas T. Spellman Co. div. Ad Mktg., Inc., L.A., 1982-85; pres., chief exec. officer, chmn. bd. Spellbound Prodns. and Spellman Media divs. Spellbound Communications, Inc., L.A., 1984-86; gen. ptnr. Faso & Spellman, L.A., 1984-86; chief oper. officer, pres. Yacht Mgmt. Internat., Ltd., L.A., 1984-86; v.p. media Snyder, Longino Advt. div. Snyder Advt., L.A., 1985-86; advt./media cons., L.A., 1986-91; gen. mgr. Nucleus Nuance, L.A., 1987-88; gen. ptnr. Convention Photos Unltd, Hawaii, 1988-89; v.p. mktg. Pacific Med. Products, Inc., L.A., 1990-91; media dir., Kennedy-Wilson Inc., L.A., 1991-94; dir. media Goddard & Claussen/First Tuesday, L.A., 1994—; guest lectr. sch. bus UCLA, 1975, U. So. Calif., 1976. Served with U.S. Army Res. N.G., 1964-69. Mem. Aircraft Owners and Pilots Assn., Nat. Rifle Assn., Calif. Pistol and Rifle Assn., Phi Zeta Kappa, Phi Omega Epsilon. Jewish. Clubs: Rolls Royce Owners, Mercedes Benz Am., Aston Martin Owners. Office: Goddard & Claussen/First Tuesday 22917 Pacific Coast Hwy Ste 300 Malibu CA 90265-4934

SPELLMAN, JOHN DAVID, retired electrical engineer; b. Beaver Dam, Wis., July 27, 1935; s. John Joseph and Elsie Marguerite (Schultz) S.; B.S. in Elec. Engring., U. Wis., 1959; m. Kathleen Burns King, May 26, 1972; stepchildren: Kathleen Biegel, Karen Zarling, Kimberly Lyon. Jr. engr., part time, Malleable Iron Range Co., Beaver Dam, 1952-59; mem. tech. staff Rockwell Internat., Anaheim, Calif., 1961-85, lead engr., 1969-78, 81-85; mgr. ground instrumentation ops. unit Rockwell Internat., Vandenberg AFB, 1985-88, mgr. data ops., 1988-91; cons. Data Processing, Santa Maria, Calif., 1965. Served to 1st lt. Signal Corps, AUS, 1959-61. Recipient U.S. Army Accomodation award, 1961, USAF Outstanding Achievement award for Civilian Personnel. Mem. Assn. Computing Machinery, Air Force Assn., Res. Officers Assn. Clubs: Birnam Wood Golf (Montecito, Calif.); Santa Maria Country. Contbr. publs. on minutemen data systems, PCM Telemetry systems. Home: 642 Meadowbrook Dr Santa Maria CA 93455-3604 Office: PO Box 2669 Santa Maria CA 93457-2669

SPELLMAN, WILLIAM JOHN, dentist; b. Long Beach, Calif., Aug. 3, 1936; s. William R. and Lillian May (Ormond) S.; m. Paula Lynn Aselin, Aug. 29, 1964; children: Aselin Spellman Maloney, Dascha Damien. BA, Occidental Coll., 1958; DDS, U. So. Calif., 1962. Dentist USAF, Eielson AFB, Alaska, 1962-64; pvt. practice dentistry Ventura, Calif., 1964-72; owner Woodside Dental Group, Ventura, 1972—; founder, pres. Golden West Dental Plan, Camarillo, Calif., 1972-76, dental dir., 1992—, bd. dirs., 1972—; chmn. rev. form subcom. Calif. Assn. Prepaid Dental Plans, Garden Grove, 1993-94; bd. dirs. Nat. Acad. of Managed Care Dentists. Track & field coach local H.S., 1967—; auction ring chmn. Ventury County Fair Jr. Livestock Auction, 1985—; com. Ventura County Homeless Dental Clinic Project, 1992—. Mem. Assn. Managed Care Providers, Ventura Santa Barbara Dental Soc., Ventura East Rotary (pres. 1973-74). Republican. Office: Golden West Dental & Vision 888 W Ventura Blvd Camarillo CA 93010-8332

SPELTS, RICHARD JOHN, lawyer; b. Yuma, Colo., July 29, 1939; s. Richard Clark and Barbara Eve (Pletcher) S.; children: Melinda, Meghan, Richard John Jr.; m. Gayle Merves, Nov. 14, 1992. BS cum laude, U. Colo., 1961, JD, 1964. Bar: Colo. 1964, U.S. Dist. Ct. Colo. 1964, U.S. Supreme Ct. 1968, U.S. Ct. Appeals (10th cir.) 1970, U.S. Dist. Ct. (ea. dist.) Mich. 1986. With Ford Motor Internat., Cologne, Germany, 1964-65; legis. counsel to U.S. Senator, 89th and 90th Congresses, 1967-68; minority counsel U.S. Senate Subcom., 90th and 91st Congresses, 1968-70; asst. U.S. atty., 1st asst. U.S. atty. Fed. Dist. of Colo., 1970-77; pvt. practice Denver, 1977-89; risk mgr. sheriff's dept. Jefferson County, Golden, Colo., 1990-91; owner Video Prodn. for Lawyers, 1991—. Selected for Leadership Denver, 1977; recipient cert. for outstanding contbns. in drug law enforcement U.S. Drug Enforcement Adminstrn., 1977, spl. commendation for criminal prosecution U.S. Dept. Justice, 1973, spl. commendation for civil prosecution U.S. Dept. Justice, 1976. Mem. Fed. Bar Assn. (chmn. govt. torts seminar 1980), Colo. Bar Assn. (bd. govs. 1976-78), Denver Bar Assn., Colo. Trial Lawyers Assn., Denver Law Club, Order of Coif. Republican. Methodist. Home and Office: 6697 W Hinsdale Ave Littleton CO 80123-4511

SPENCE, A. MICHAEL, economics educator, academic administrator; b. Montclair, N.J., 1943; m. Ann Spence. BA summa cum laude, Princeton U., 1966; MA, Oxford U., 1968; PhD in Econs., Harvard U., 1972. Instr. Harvard U., Cambridge, Mass., 1971-72, prof. econs., 1976-90, prof. bus. adminstrn., 1979-90, chmn. econ. dept., George Gund prof. of econ. and bus. adminstrn., 1983-90, dean faculty arts and scis., 1984-90; assoc. prof. econs. Stanford (Calif.) U., 1973-75, Philip H. Knight prof. econs. and mgmt., 1990—, dean Grad. Sch. Bus., 1990—; bd. dirs. BankAm. Corp., Sun Microsystems, Gen. Mills Inc., VeriFone, Inc., Bay Area Coun.; chmn. Nat. Rsch. Coun. on Sci., Tech. and Econ. Policy; mem. econs. adv. panel, NSF, 1977-79. Author: Market Signaling: Information Transfer in Hiring and Related Screening Processes, 1974; (with R.E. Caves and M.E. Porter) Competition in the Open Economy, 1980; mem. editorial bd. various jours. including Bell Jour. Econs., Jour. Econ. Theory, Pub. Policy. Rhodes scholar, 1966-68; recipient Galbraith Prize for Teaching Excellence, 1978, John Bates Clark Medal, Am. Econ. Assn., 1981. Office: Stanford U Grad Sch Bus Stanford CA 94305

SPENCE, MARY ANNE, geneticist, medical association executive; b. Tulsa, Sept. 8, 1944; married, 1972. BA, Grinnell Coll., 1966; PhD, U. Hawaii, 1969. NIH fellow in human genetics U. N.C., Chapel Hill, 1969-70; asst. prof. to assoc. prof. UCLA, 1970-80; prof. in psychiatry UCLA Sch. Medicine, 1980—; assoc. dean grad. divsn. UCLA, 1988—; mem. Mental Retardation Rsch. Ctr., Neuro-Psychiatric Inst., UCLA, 1974—. Co-editor: Multipoint Mapping & Linkage Based Upon Affected Pedigree Members: Genetic Analysis Workshop 6, 1989. Recipient Woman of Sci. award UCLA, 1979. Am. Soc. Human Genetics, Genetics Soc. Am., Behaviorial & Genetics Assn. Home: 1652 Benedict Canyon Dr Beverly Hills CA 90210*

SPENCER, CAROLINE, library director. Dir. Honolulu br. Hawaii State Libr. Office: HI State Public Lib 478 S King St Honolulu HI 96813-2901

SPENCER, DOROTHY ANN, library director, consultant; b. Yonkers, N.Y., Aug. 31, 1947; d. Joseph Edwin and Lillian (Botz) S. BA, Hope Coll., 1969; MLS, Western Mich. U., 1970; PhD, U. Nebr., 1981. Libr. Rombout Mid. Sch., Beacon, N.Y., 1970-71; chief audio visual svcs. libr., assoc. prof. Med. Coll. Ga., Augusta, 1971-79; logistics mgr. internat. tng. Darwin (Australia) C.C., 1982; libr. dir. Kern Med. Ctr., Bakersfield, Calif., 1985-88; dir. Kauffman libr. Calif. Sch. Profl. Psychology, Fresno, 1988—. Co-author: Biosocial Psychopathology, 1994. Mem. ALA, Med. Libr. Group So. Calif./Ariz., Med. Libr. Assn., Acad. Health Info. Profls. of Med. Libr. Assn. (disting.), Fresno Area Libr. Coun. Office: Calif Sch Profl Psychology 1350 M St Fresno CA 93721-1808

SPENCER, DOUGLAS LLOYD, chemist, manufactuing executive; b. Berkeley, Calif., July 19, 1952; s. Alma Glenn and Anna Lea (Lloyd) S.; m. Connie Jeanette Whitesel, Aug. 23, 1974; children: Jeanette Dawn, Jared Douglas, Jilissa Annette, Janine Marie, Janelle Renee, Jeffrey Brian. AA, Diablo Valley Coll., 1971; BS, Brigham Young U., 1974. Lab. instr. chemistry dept. Brigham Young U., 1973-74; rsch. chemist Dow Chem. Western div., Pittsburg, Calif., 1975-80; pres. Sunset Distbg., Inc., Brentwood, Calif., 1980-82; pres. Maier & Assocs., Inc., Brentwood, 1982-83; pres. Doug Spencer & Assocs., Placerville, 1983—. Mem. Brentwood Planning Commn., 1980-81; missionary, dist. zone leader Eastern States Mission, 1971-73; active Boy Scouts of Am.. Rossmoor residents scholar, 1969-71, Brigham Young U. scholar, 1973-74. Mem. Liahona Club. Republican. Mormon. Avocations: camping, fishing, gardening. Office: 6500 Wagon Loop Placerville CA 95667-8795

SPENCER, FREDERICK GILMAN, newspaper editor in chief; b. Phila., Dec. 8, 1925; s. F. Gilman and Elizabeth (Hetherington) S.; m. Isabel Brannon, July 3, 1965; 1 child, Isabel; children by previous marriage: Amy, Elizabeth Blair, F. Gilman, Jonathan. Student pub. and pvt. schs. Copyboy

Phila. Inquirer, 1947-49; photographer-reporter Chester (Pa.) Times, 1949, 1952-59; photographer, sports editor Mt. Holly (N.J.) Herald, 1949-52; mng. editor Main Line Times, Ardmore, Pa., 1959-63; asst. city editor Phila. Bull., 1963-64; editorial spokesman Sta. WCAU-TV, Phila., 1964-67; editor The Trentonian, Trenton, N.J., 1967-75, Phila. Daily News, 1975-84, N.Y. Daily News, N.Y.C., 1984-89; editor-in-chief Denver Post, 1989-93, columnist, 1993—. With USNR, 1943-46. Recipient Pulitzer prize for editorials, 1974. Mem. Am. Soc. Newspapers Editors, Sigma Delta Chi. Office: Denver Post 1560 Broadway Denver CO 80202-5133

SPENCER, GWYNNE CAROL, writer; b. Abington, Pa., Jan. 2, 1946; d. Harold Winston and Eleanor (Schmidt) S.; m. K. Robert Scholz, Dec. 26, 1971 (div. Oct. 1987); children: Brenna, Matthew. BS, Beaver Coll., 1969. Tchr. Manzano Day Sch., Albuquerque, 1969-73; owner Trespassers William Children's Bookstore, Albuquerque, 1977—. Author: Teach Your Children Well, 1987; columnist Albuquerque Tribune, 1984—; editor Albuquerque Kids, 1993—. Home: 709 Hermosa Dr NE Albuquerque NM 87110-7705

SPENCER, HERBERT WARD, III, air pollution control manufacturing company executive; b. Louisville, June 12, 1945; s. Herbert W. Jr. and Mary (Armstrong) S.; m. Elizabeth Ryan, Sept. 2, 1967 (div. Feb. 1984); children—Andrew Heath, Jennifer Coates; m. Amy R. Soejoto, Aug. 12, 1984. B.A., Vanderbilt U., 1967; M.S., Auburn U., 1969, Ph.D., 1974. Research physicist So. Research Inst., Birmingham, Ala., 1974-76; research engr. Joy Mfg., L.A., 1976-79, mgr. advanced tech., 1979-85, chief devel. engr., 1985-86, mgr. new tech., 1986-87, founder, exec. v.p. EC&C Techs., La Canada, Calif., 1988—; owner HWS Engring. and Rsch. Co., 1989—. Mem. bd. mgrs. Santa Clara Valley YMCA, 1986—. Contbr. articles to profl. publs. NDEA fellow Auburn U., Ala., 1971-73; NSF summer trainee Auburn U., 1969. Mem. Am. Phys. Soc., Air and Waste Mgmt. Assn., Sigma Xi. Republican. Presbyterian. Office: EC&C Techs 4234 Chevy Chase Dr La Canada Flintridge CA 91011-3844

SPENCER, HOWARD DALEE, art museum curator; b. Dayton, Ohio, Mar. 23, 1950; s. Herbert Leo and Nellie Kate (DaLee) S. BS, Ind. State U., 1972, MFA, 1976. Student asst., grad. asst., exhibits preparator Swope Art Mus., Terre Haute, Ind., 1969-78, interim dir., 1978; curator of collections and exhbns. Wichita (Kans.) Art Mus., 1979-89; assoc. curator Butler Inst. Am. Art, Youngstown, Ohio, 1989-90; curator collections and exhbns. Nev. Mus. Art, Reno, 1992—. Office: Nev Mus Art 160 W Liberty St Reno NV 89501-1916

SPENCER, MARY JOSEPHINE, pediatrician; b. Joliet, Ill., Oct. 19, 1936; d. Ray Miller and Marjorie Elizabeth (Tedens) Mason; m. Donald James Spencer, June 3, 1960; children: Kenneth Donald, Marjorie Elizabeth, Katherine Anne, Christine Mary. BA, U. Colo., 1958; MD, UCLA, 1964. Diplomate Am. Bd. Pediatrics; lic. physician, Calif. Intern L.A. County Gen. Hosp., 1964-65; health officer L.A. Count Health Dept., 1965-66; gen. practice Kaiser Permanente Med. Group, West Los Angeles, 1966-69; resident in pediatrics Harbor Gen. Hosp./UCLA, 1969-71; clin. faculty, instr. dept. pediatrics UCLA, 1971-73, fellow in infectious diseases, 1973-75, asst. prof. pediatrics, 1975-82; assoc. clin. prof. pediatrics U. Calif., San Diego, 1983—; pvt. practice pediatrics and infectious diseases San Diego, 1982—; staff ambulatory pediatrics L.A. County Health Dept., 1973; acting dir. Marion Davies Children's Clinic, 1973, chief divsn. ambulatory pediatrics and dir., 1975-81; physician Sex Abuse Team, Children's Hosp., San Diego, 1982-85; med. dir. child abuse program Palomar Med. Ctr., Escondido, Calif., 1985—; cons. and lectr in field; del. Statehouse Conf. on Children and Youth, 1981; cons. pub. adv. com. NIH, 1981; expert witness in ct. child abuse and neglect cases, L.A. Contbr. numerous articles and abstracts to profl. jours., chpts. to books; co-editor: Your Child's Health Care at the UCLA Marion Davies Children's Center, 1982; reviewer Am. Jour. Diseases of Childhood, 1981, Pediatric Infectious Diseases, 1982, 83, 86, Pediatrics, 1986; adv. com. med. World News. Bd. dirs. UCLA Day Care Ctr., Ocean Park Cmty. Ctr., Westside Child Trauma Coun.; mem. L.A. County Task Force on Child Abuse; choir mem. St. Bartholomew's Episcopal Ch., 1990—; mgr., sponsor Rancho Bernardo women's softball teams, 1990-93; coach, mgr. Rancho Bernardo girls' softball, 1987, 88, 90. Grantee NIH, 1974-75, Hoffman LaRoche Labs., 1977, Eli Lilly Co., 1978-80, 80, 81, USPHS, 1977, 78, 80-83, 80-81, 81-84; named Woman of Yr. Santa Monica YWCA, 1982; recipient Woman of Distinction Rancho Bernardo Soroptimist award, 1994, First Ann. Unity award Palomar-Pomerado Health Network. Mem. Am. Acad. Pediatrics, Western Soc. Pediatric Rsch., Ambulatory Pediatric Soc. (region IX co-chmn. 1978-79, vice-chmn. 1979-80, rsch. com. 1979-82), Infectious Disease Soc. Am., Pediatric Infectious Disease Soc. Republican. Home: 18675 Avenida Cordillera San Diego CA 92128-1529 Office: Childrens Med Group 910 E Ohio Ave Ste 103 Escondido CA 92025-3439

SPENCER, MICHAEL, airport terminal executive. BS, Portland State U., 1974. Supr. Consolidated Freightways, Portland, Oreg., 1974-78; plant controller Down River Forest Products, Medford, Oreg., 1978-82; controller C F Arrowhead, Fort Worth, Tex., 1982-86, Oren. Freightways, Medford, Oreg., 1986-88; v.p. fin. Evergreen Aviation Ground Logistic, Mcminnville, Oreg., 1988—. Office: Evergreen Aviation Ground Logistic 3850 Three Mile Ln Mcminnville OR 97128*

SPENCER, NEAL RAYMOND, entomologist; b. Honolulu, Hawaii, July 9, 1936; s. Henry Jackson and Florence Lillian (Evans) S.; m. Patricia Louise Wilbur, Feb. 15, 1965; children: Quentin Reynolds, Nathan Patrick, Lisa Louise, Creighton Reynolds. BS, U. Fla., 1961, postgrad., 1970-77; postgrad., U. Mo., 1965-67. Staff entomologist Govt. of Am.Samoa, Pago Pago, 1963-65, Govt of Guam, Agana, 1968-70; entomologist USDA/ARS, Gainesville, Fla., 1970-77, Rome, Italy, 1977-81, Stoneville, MS, 1981-88, Sidney, Mont., 1988—. Contbr. numerous articles to profl. jours. Scoutmaster, cubmaster, chief exec. officer Boy Scouts of Am. Mem. Entomol. Soc. Am., Weed Sci. Soc. Am. Republican. Office: USDA/ARS PO Box 1109 1500 S Central Ave Sidney MT 59270-5519

SPENCER, RICHARD PRAIL, property management educator, job placement counselor; b. Mar. 1, 1948; s. Richard Victor and Doris Louise (Byington) S.; m. Carol J. Vassar, Apr. 16, 1981; children: Chris, Matthew, Nicholas. Lic. postsecondary tchr., Calif. Real estate assoc. Spencer Realty & Investments, Ukiah, Calif., 1975-81; resort owner Headwater's Inn, Lake Wenatchee, Wash., 1981-83; property mgr. Spencer Property Mgmt., Santa Rosa, Calif., 1983-86; property mgmt. instr., founder Agapé Sch. Property Mgmt., Forestville, Calif., 1986—; spkr., Santa Rosa. Author: Professional Development, 1987; co-author: The Complete Reference Manual for Property Owners and Managers, 1988, The Complete Maintenance Manual for Property Owners and Managers, 1988. Founder Agapé Project for the Homeless, Forestville, Calif., 1989. Recipient SBA award Nat. Bank Score, 1993. Democrat.

SPENCER, ROBERT C., political science educator; b. Chgo., Mar. 28, 1920; m. Edith Maxham McCarthy, Sept. 13, 1941; children: Margaret, Catherine, Anne, Thomas More, David. AB, U. Chgo., 1943, MA, 1952, PhD in Polit. Sci. (Univ. fellow 1952-53), 1955. Instr. polit. sci. and sociology St. Michaels Coll., 1949-51, asst., then assoc. prof. polit. sci., 1953-60, prof. govt., 1960-63, dir. summer sessions, 1960-61, asst. to pres., 1963-65; prof. polit. sci., chmn. dept., dean summer sessions U. R.I., 1965-67; grad. dean U. R.I. (Grad. Sch.), 1967-69; founding pres. Sangamon State U., Springfield, Ill., 1969-78; prof. govt. and public affairs Sangamon State U., 1978-88, prof. emeritus, 1988—; research assoc. Indsl. Relations Center, U. Chgo., 1952-53; extension lectr. N.Y. State Sch. Indsl. and Labor Relations, Cornell U., 1956-57; vice chmn. West Central Ill. Ednl. Telecommunications Consortium, 1975-77, chmn., 1977-78; chmn. task force personnel Vt. Little Hoover Commn., 1957-58; mem. Ill. adv. com. U.S. Commn. on Civil Rights, 1979-87; bd. mgrs. Franklin Life Variable Annuity Funds, 1974—; vis. prof. polit. sci., sr. rsch. assoc. local govt. ctr. Mont. State U., Bozeman, 1985, 89, 90—. Author: (with Robert J. Huckshorn) The Politics of Defeat, 1971. Bd. dirs. City Day Sch., Springfield, 1979-83, Gt. Am. People Show Repertory Co., 1980-90; vice chmn. Petersburg Libr. Bd., 1982-88; chmn. Petersburg Zoning Bd. Appeals, 1984-90; mem. Vt. Senate, 1959-63; faculty fellow Ford Found.'s Nat. Ctr. for Edn. in Politics, rsch. dir. Dem. Nat. Com., 1962-63; mem. adv. bd. Landmark Preservation Coun. Ill., 1986-89; mem., treas. Gallatin County Coun. on Aging, 1993—. Roman Catholic. Home: 2303 S 3rd Ave Bozeman MT 59715-6009

SPENCER, TAMAR LISH, aerospace engineer; b. L.A., July 2, 1963; d. Merrill Arthur and Marganit (Vardi) Lish; m. Todd Steven Spencer, Sept. 2, 1984; children: Shira, Arielle. BA in Econs., UCLA, 1985; BSME, Calif. State U., Long Beach, 1989, MS in Engring., 1991. Mem. tech. staff Space Sys. Divsn. Rockwell Internat., Downey, Calif., 1987-92; math tutor, Huntington Beach, Calif., 1992—. Mem. Huntington Beach Concert Band. Mem. AIAA, Tau Beta Pi.

SPERBER, BURTON S., construction executive; b. 1929. Chmn., pres. Valley Crest Landscape, Inc., Calabasas, Calif., 1949—. Office: Valley Crest Landscape Inc 24121 Ventura Blvd Calabasas CA 91302-1449*

SPERBER, JAMES IRVING, physician, medical educator; b. San Diego, Feb. 23, 1956. BA, Brown U., 1978, MD, 1982. Diplomate Nat. Bd. Med. Examiners, Am. Bd. Internal Medicine. Intern in internal medicine U. Calif. Irvine Med. Ctr., Orange, 1982-83, resident in internal medicine, 1983-85; med. dir. South County Cmty. Clinic, San Juan Capistrano, Calif., 1986-90; pvt. practice San Clemente, Calif., 1990—; chmn. dept. medicine Samaritan Med. Ctr., San Clemente, 1994—; pres. San Clemente Physicians Med. Group, Inc., 1991—; clin. asst. prof. U. Calif., Irvine. Vol. Project Shortstop, Orange County Bar Found., Santa Ana, Calif., 1990—. Mem. Calif. Med. Assn., Orange County Med. Assn. Office: 657 Camino De Los Mares San Clemente CA 92673-2826

SPESER, PHILIP LESTER, social scientist, consultant; b. Buffalo, N.Y., Mar. 17, 1951; s. David and Theodora (Cowen) S.; children: Arendt, Ariel. BA in Polit. Sci. and Journalism, Case Western Res. U., 1973; JD, SUNY, Buffalo, 1980, PhD in Polit. Sci., 1981. Spl. asst. for sci. and tech. Fedn. Am. Scientists, Washington, 1980-81; pres. Foresight Sci. and Tech., Port Townsend, Wash., 1981—; Wash. rep. Soc. Am. Archeology, 1982-89; exec. dir. Nat. Coalition for Sci. and Tech., Washington, 1985-89; session chair Nat. Biotech. Edn. Sharing Conf., Madison, Wis., 1991; cons. Office of Gov. State of N.Y., 1980; adj. prof. dept. anthropology Am. U., Washington, 1988; adv. panelist on univ. small bus. ctrs., NSF, Washington, 1985; steering com. Internat. Biotech. Edn. Leadership Conf., 1992—. Author: The Defense-Space Market, 1985, The Politics of Science, 1987, Technology Transfer Handbook, 1990, The Federal Laser and Optics Market, 1990, Small Business Guide to Federal Research and Development Funding, 1991, Forests In Jefferson County, 1993, others; author, editor numerous reports, articles. Founding chair Glen Echo (Md.) Park Found., 1987-88; bd. dirs. Jefferson County Edn. Found., Port Townsend, 1991—, v.p., 1993—; bd. dirs., exec. com. Jefferson County Econ. Devel. Coun., Port Townsend, 1991-93, v.p., 1992-93; lead lobbyist Small Bus. Innovation Devel. Act of 1982; developer Port Townsend Sch. Dist. Magnet Ctr., 1992; founding pres. Olympic Penninsula Found., 1993; with Woodnet Mfg. Tech. Ctr. Grantee NSF, EPA, USDA, Small Bus. Adminstrn., Dept. Energy, Bullitt Found., U.S. West Found., Archibald Charitable Trust, others. Mem. AAAS, Am. Assn. Artificial Intelligence, Tech. Transfer Soc. (bd. dirs., chair task force on nat. tech. transfer policy 1988-91), Bar Assn. D.C. Democrat. Office: Foresight Sci and Tech 1200 W Sims Way Port Townsend WA 98368-3058 : Foresight Sci & Tech Inc 1200 W Sims Way Ste 201 Port Townsend WA 98368

SPEYER, JASON LEE, engineer, educator; b. Boston, Apr. 30, 1938; s. Joseph Louis and Ruth Sylvia (Steinmetz) S.; m. Barbara Joan Sachs, Sept. 11, 1966; children—Gil, Gavriel, Rakhel, Joseph. B.S., MIT, 1960; M.S., Harvard U., 1964, Ph.D., 1968. Registered profl. engr., Tex. Engr. Boeing Co., Seattle, 1960-61; sr. engr. Raytheon Co.,, Bedford, Mass., 1961-68; sr. analyst Analytical Mechanics Assocs., Inc., Cambridge, Mass., 1968-70; mem. research staff Charles Stark Draper Lab., Cambridge, Mass., 1970-76; Harry H. Power prof. engring. U. Tex., Austin, 1976-90; lectr. MIT, 1971-76; vis. scientist Weizmann Inst. Sci., 1972-73; Lady Davis prof. Technion, Haifa, Israel, 1983; Hunsaker vis. prof. aeros. and astronautics MIT, 1989-90. Recipient Hocott Disting. Engring. Rsch. award Coll. Engring., U. Tex., 1985, Exceptional Civil award USAF, 1991; Raytheon fellow, 1963-67. Fellow IEEE (bd. govs. Control Sys. Soc. 1982—, assoc. editor Transaction on Automatic Control), AIAA (Mechanics and Control of Flight award 1985, Dryden lectureship in rsch. 1995, assoc. editor Jour. Spacecraft and Rockets, Jour. Guidance and Control). Home: 11358 Chalon Rd Los Angeles CA 90049-1721 Office: UCLA Dept Mech Aerospace and Nuclear Engring Los Angeles CA 90024

SPEZZANO, CHARLES LEE, psychologist, writer; b. Schenectady, N.Y., Jan. 2, 1948; s. Peter Spezzano and Katherine (Shelton) Kane; m. Lency K. Abel, Oct. 13, 1984; children: Christopher, J'aime. BA in Psychology and Philosophy, Duquesne U., 1970, MA in Sociology, 1971; PhD in Counseling and Psychology, U.S. Internat. U., 1977. Cert. marriage, family and child counselor; ordained minister, Unity Ch., 1984. Dir. cmty. rels., counselor Bradshear Assoc., Pitts., 1971-72; psychologist, therapy supr., workshop coord. Naval Drug Rehab. Ctr., NAS Miramar, San Diego, 1973-79; sr. trainer ARAS Tng. Corp., San Diego, 1979-80; interim minister Windward Unity Ch., Kailua, Hawaii, 1983-84; pvt. practice marriage, family and child counselor Calif. and Hawaii, 1980-92; founder, seminar leader Break-Through Seminars, Tokyo, 1985; pres., lectr., seminar leader, author Spezzano & Assocs., Ltd., Kaneohe, Hawaii, 1990—; tng. lectr. Spezzano & Assocs. Ltd., Vancouver, B.C., Can., 1980—, Switzerland, 1986, Eng., 1987, France, 1988; therapist, trainer, lectr., Tokyo, Nagoya, Osaka, Mt. Fuji, Fukuoka, and Nagasaki, Japan, 1983—; trainer and lectr., Taiwan, 1991—, Malaysia, 1992—. Author: Awaken the Gods, 1991, 30 Days to Find Your Perfect Mate, 1994. Mem. Assn. for Humanistic Psychology. Office: Spezzano & Assocs Ltd 47-416 Waihee Pl Kaneohe HI 96744-4958

SPICKARD, PAUL R., historian, educator, academic administrator; b. Seattle, June 20, 1950; s. Donald Elliot and Mary Alice (Adkins) S.; m. Rowena Fong, June 9, 1974; children—Naomi, Daniel. Student, U. Wash., 1970-71, Gordon-Conwell Sem., South Hamilton, Mass., 1973; AB, Harvard U., 1973; MA, U. Calif., Berkeley, 1976, PhD, 1983. Instr., Solano Coll., Suisun City, Calif., 1980; acting instr. U. Calif., Berkeley, 1981; lectr. San Francisco State U., 1981; asst. prof. Bethel Coll., St. Paul, 1981-84, assoc. prof., 1984-88; Fulbright sr. lectr., Nankai U., Tianjin, China, 1988-89; asst. prof. Capital U., Columbus, Ohio, 1989-90; assoc. prof. Brigham Young U. at Hawaii, Laie, Hawaii, 1990—, assoc. dean, 1991—, rsch. dir. Inst. Polynesian Studies, 1994—; bd. dirs. Midwest China Ctr., St. Paul, 1982-85. Author: Mixed Blood: Intermarriage and Ethnic Identity in Twentieth-Century America, 1989 (Gustavus Myer Outstanding Book award, 1990), God's Peoples: A Social History of Christians, 1994, Pacific Island Peoples in Hawaii, 1994, Pacific Islander Americans: An Annotated Bibliography, 1995; contbr. articles to profl. jours. Trustee Sunrise Preschool, San Francisco, 1979-81; chmn. Sunset Chinese Bapt. Ch., San Francisco, 1980-81. Recipient Undergrad. Fellowship prize Charles Warren Ctr., Harvard U., 1972, NEH stipend, 1990; McCormack fellow U. Calif., 1978-80, Fulbright-Hays China fellow, 1987, NEH fellow, 1993; grantee Pew Trust Research, 1987, Am. Coun. Learned Socs., 1990. Mem. Orgn. Am. Historians, Am. Hist. Assn., Conf. on Faith and History, Asian Am. Studies Assn., Immigration History Soc., Assn. of Asian Scholars. Democrat. Baptist. Avocations: basketball; running; backpacking. Home: 46-318 Haiku Rd Apt 13 Kaneohe HI 96744-3545 Office: Brigham Young U of Hawaii Divsn Social Scis Laie HI 96762

SPICKLER, JOSEPH WILLIAM, researcher, physician; b. Leaksville, N.C., Nov. 5, 1940; s. Joseph Creath and Helen (Williams) S.; m. Sarah Schneider, June 23, 1962 (div.); 1 child, Scott William Spickler Chesney; m. Delores Papp, Nov. 28, 1969 (div.); 1 child, Nicole Dianna; m. Marilyn Marie Holmes, Jan. 22, 1981. BSEE, Northwestern U., 1962, MSEE, 1964, PhD in Physiology, 1968; MD, Med. Coll. Ohio, 1975. Cert. Nat. Bd. Med. Examiners, 1976, cert. Am. Bd. Internal Medicine, 1978. Head physiology and bio-engring. dept. Cox Heart Inst., Dayton, Ohio, 1968-72; intern internal medicine Presbyn. Med. Ctr., Denver, 1975-76, resident internal medicine, 1976-78; pvt. practice internal medicine Denver, 1978-86; med. dir. Astra Pharm. Products, Westborough, Mass., 1986-89; dir. clin. investigation Syntex Labs., Palo Alto, Calif., 1989-92; v.p., dir. Syntex Rsch., Palo Alto, 1992—; adj. asst. prof. dept. biol. scis. Wright State U., Dayton, 1970-72; presenter in field. Patentee in field; contbr. articles to profl. jours. Mem. ACP. Office: Syntex Devel Rsch M/S A6-209 3401 Hillview Ave Palo Alto CA 94304-1320

SPIEGEL, MARCIA COHN, writer; b. Chgo., Oct. 16, 1927; d. Alfred and Helen (Yankelowitz) Cohn; m. Sidney L. Spiegel; children: Linda Allen, Randi, Judy, Edward, Steven. BA in Psychology, Rockford (Ill.) Coll., 1949; MA in Communal Svc., Hebrew Union Coll., L.A., 1979; Cert. Beyond Classroom, U. So.Calif, L.A., 1980. Instr. U. Judaism, L.A., 1979-91, UCLA Ext., 1980-81; cons. in vol. devel., 1979-92; lectr., workshop facilitator in women's studies and spirituality, 1980—. Co-author: Women Speak to God, Jewish Women's Awareness Guide, 1992, Chemical Dependency: Catholic-Jewish Relfections, 1987; author: The Jewish Woman: A Portrait in Her Own Words, 1978, The Heritage of Noah: Alcoholism in the Jewish Community Today, 1980, Women in the Bible: A Study Course, 1983; contbr. articles to books, mags. and periodicals. Co-founder Jr. Great Books, Palos Verdes, Calif., 1960-75; co-founder, later pres. Alcoholism Coun. South Bay, Torrance, Calif., 1968-80; co-founder, pres. Women Writers West, L.A., 1980; commr. L.A. County Commn. on Alcohol, 1980-83; founder Jewish Arts Assocs., 1981—, Creative Jewish Women's Alliance, 1979, Alcohol/Drug Action Program, 1983—; mem. Bnot Eish Spiritual Cmty., 1981—. Recipient Award of Distinction, Rockford Coll., 1984, Frances Henry award Hebrew Union Coll., L.A., 1978, Alumni of Yr. award, 1994, Cmty. award Jewish Fedn. South Bay, 1992, Achievement award Nat. Fedn. Temple Sisterhoods, 1978. Democrat.

SPIEGEL, RONALD STUART, insurance company executive; b. Chgo., Sept. 12, 1942; s. Arthur I. and Elaine M. (Young); m; Carol J. Lieberthal, July 25, 1964; children: Eric, Elissa. BA, Calif. State U., Los Angeles, 1966. Pres. Newhouse Automotive, Los Angeles, 1966-78; agt. N.Y. Life Ins. Co., Santa Fe Springs, Calif., 1978-82, sales mgr., 1982-86, assoc. gen. mgr., 1986-88, gen. mgr., 1989-91; assoc. gen. mgr. N.Y. Life Ins. Co., Fullerton, Calif., 1991—; v.p. Cerritos Valley Br. Life Underwriters Assn. of Los Angeles, 1984-86, pres., 1987-88. Pres. Temple Shalom, West Covina, Calif., 1975-77, 88-89, 93-94, treas., 1978-83; pres. Temple Ami-Shalom, West Covina, 1994-95, Jewish Fedn. Coun. Ea. Region, L.A., 1986-89, v.p., 1984-85. Mem. Am. Soc. CLUs, Gen. Agts. and Mgrs. Assn., Airline Owners and Pilots Assn., Nat. Assn. Life Underwriters. Democrat. Lodge: Kiwanis. Home: 1720 Orchard Hill Ln Hacienda Heights CA 91745-3843 Office: NY Life Ins Co 3230 E Imperial Hwy Ste 100 Brea CA 92621-6730

SPIEGELBERG, EMMA JO, business education educator; b. Mt. View, Wyo., Nov. 22, 1936; d. Joseph Clyde and Dorcas (Reese) Hatch; BA with honors, U. Wyo., 1958, MEd, 1985; EdD Boston U., 1990; m. James Walter Spiegelberg, June 22, 1957; children: William L., Emory Walter, Joseph John. Tchr. bus. edn. Laramie (Wyo.) High Sch., 1960-61, 65-93, adminstr., 1993—. Bd. dirs. Cathedral Home for Children, Laramie, 1967-70, 72—, pres., 1985-88, Laramie Plains Mus., 1970-79. Author: Branigan's Accounting Simulation, 1986, London & Co. II, 1993; co-author: Glencoe Computerized Accounting, 1993, 2nd edit., 1995, Microcomputer Accounting: Daceasy, 1994, Microcomputer Accounting: Peachtree, 1994, Microcomputer Accounting: Accpac, 1994, Computerized Accounting with Peachtree, 1995, Glencoe Computerized Accounting: Peachtree, 1995. Named Wyo. Bus. Tchr. of Yr., 1982. Mem. Am. Vocat. Assn. (policy com. region V 1984-87, region V Tchr. of Yr. 1986), Wyo. Vocat. Assn. (exec. bd. 1978-80, pres. 1981-82, Outstanding Contbns. to Vocat. Edn. award 1983, Tchr. of Yr. 1985, exec. sec. 1986-89), Nat. Bus. Edn. Assn.(bd. dirs. 1987-88, 1991—, Sec. Tchr. of the Yr. 1991), Mt. Plains Bus. Edn. Assn. (Wyo. rep. to bd. dirs. 1982-85, pres. 1987-88, Sec. Tchr. of the Yr. 1991, Leadership award 1992), Internat. Soc. Bus. Edn., Wyo. Bus. Edn. Assn. (pres. 1979-80), NEA, Wyo. Edn. Assn., Albany County Edn. Assn. (sec. 1970-71), Laramie C. of C. (bd. dirs. 1985-88), U. Wyo. Alumni Assn. (bd. dirs. 1985-90pres. 1988-89), Kappa Delta Pi, Phi Delta Kappa, Alpha Delta Kappa (state pres. 1978-82), Chi Omega, Pi Lambda Theta, Delta Pi Epsilon. Mem. United Ch. of Christ. Club: Zonta. Home: 3301 Grays Gable Rd Laramie WY 82070-5031 Office: Laramie High Sch 1275 N 11th St Laramie WY 82070-2206

SPIEL, ROBERT FREEMAN, distribution services executive; b. South Ruislip, Middlesex, Eng., July 8, 1959; came to U.S., 1959; s. Paul Louie and Elizabeth (Lammers) S.; m. Judene Ray Spiel, Aug. 20, 1981; children: Adam, Craig, Steven, Paul, Heidi. BA in Agrl. Sci. and Mgmt., U. Calif., Davis, 1985; MBA in Fin., Brigham Young U., 1988. Orchard mgr. Deseret Farms of Calif., West Sacramento, 1983-86, West Hills Orchards, Elberta, Utah, 1988-90; fin. analyst Ford Motor Co., Dearborn, Mich., 1990-92; distbn. svcs. mgr. Franklin Quest Co., Salt Lake City, 1992—. Varsity scout leader Boy Scouts Am., Fruit Heights, Utah, 1993-94; gov. Ariz. model legislature Ariz. YMCA, Mesa, 1977; commencement speaker Grad. Sch. Mgmt., Brigham Young U., 1988. Republican. Mem. LDS Ch. Home: 1613 W Phillips St Kaysville UT 84037-9515

SPIER, LUISE EMMA, film editor, director; b. Laramie, Wyo., Aug. 22, 1928; d. Louis Constantine Cames and Vina Jane Cochran; m. John Spier, Sept., 1957 (div. 1962). Student, U. Wyo., 1947, U. Calif., Berkeley, 1948-53. Head news film editor Sta. KRON-TV, San Francisco, 1960-70, film editor, 1980—; freelance film editor, director San Francisco, 1970-80, 83—. Edited and directed numerous news specials and documentaries, including The Lonely Basque, Whaler, The American Way of Eating. Recipient numerous awards for film editing and directing, including Cine Golden Eagle, Best Med. Res. Film award John Muir Med. Found., Chris Statuette, Bronze and Silver Cindy awards Info. Film Producers Am.

SPIES, KAREN BORNEMANN, writer, education consultant; b. Renton, Wash., Sept. 5, 1949; d. William Edward and Aina Jeanette (Johnson) Bornemann; m. Allan Roy Spies, July 18, 1970; children: Karsten, Astrid. BA, Calif. Luth. U., Thousand Oaks, 1970; MEd, U. Wash., 1974. Vice prin., tchr. Lake Washington Sch. Dist., Kirkland, Wash., 1971-79; tchr. various pub. schs. N.J., 1979-82; kindergarten tchr. Mt. Park Sch., Lake Oswego, Oreg., 1982-84; writer, seminar leader, cons. Wash., 1984-87, Oreg., 1984-87, Littleton, Colo., 1987—; lectr. Arapahoe Community Coll., Littleton, 1988—; ski instr. various locations, 1974-87, Copper Mountain Resort, Colo., 1987—; curriculum writer Augsburg-Fortress Pubs.; lectr. in field. Author: Family Activities for the Christmas Season, 1988, Denver, 1988, Raffi: The Children's Voice, 1989, Visiting in the Global Village, Vol. I, 1990, Vol. II, 1991, Vol. III, 1992, Vol. IV, 1993, Vol. V, 1994, Everything You Need to Know About Grieving, 1990, Competitiveness, 1991, Barbara Bush, 1991, George Bush, 1991, Everything You Need to Know About Incest, 1992, Our National Holidays, 1992, Our Money, 1992, The American Family: Can It Survive, 1993, Everything You Need to Know About Diet Fads, 1993, Our Folk Heroes, 1994, Earthquakes, 1994, Our Presidency, 1994, others. Organist Wooden Cross Luth. Ch., 1977-79. Title III grantee, 1974. Mem. AAUW, Soc. Children's Book Writers and Illustrators, Mensa, Profl. Ski Instrs. Am., Pi Lambda Theta. Republican. Lutheran.

SPIKES, ROZELIA KATHERINE, management and leadership consultant; b. Eunice, La.; d. Dominic and Ozelia (Anderson) Simon; m. Isiah Spikes Jr., June 11, 1966 (div. 1985); children: Stacy G., Marcus A. BS in Instn. Mgmt., Grambling State U., 1966; MS, Tex. Women's U., 1977. Pres. RK Spikes Cons., Inc., Houston, 1978-92, R.K. Spikes & Assocs., San Diego, 1992—; prof. bus. mgmt. U. Phoenix, San Diego, 1993—, Nat. U., San Diego, 1993—; human resource devel. specialist Meth. Hosp., Houston, 1985-90; mgr. Baylor Coll. Medicine, Houston, 1981-85; exec. dir. African Am. Heritage Mus., Houston, 1989-90. Bd. advisors Social Movement in Art, San Diego, 1992-94, Land Eagle Project, San Diego, 1992-94; mem. cmty. outreach bd. La Jolla Playhouse, 1994. Mem. Nat. Coalition of 100 Black Women (bd. dirs. 1990, treas. 1988), Toastmasters (v.p. pub. rels. 1993, v.p. edn. Centre City chpt. 1993, Area 14 gov. 1994, pres. Communicators chpt. 1994, Outstanding Mentor Dist. 5 1994). Office: PO Box 124572 San Diego CA 92112-4572

SPILKER, JAMES J., JR., electronics executive; b. 1933. PhD, Stanford U. Mgr. Lockheed Corp., 1958-63; mgr. WDL divsn. Philco Ford, 1963-73; co-founder Stanford Telecommunications, Sunnyvale, Calif., 1973—, now chmn., pres., CEO. Office: Stanford Telecommunications 1221 Crossman Ave Sunnyvale CA 94089-1103

SPILLANE, JOHN MICHAEL, lawyer; b. El Dorado, Ark., Aug. 11, 1956; s. Leo Jerome and Kathryn Francis (Grady) S.; m. Bernadette Marie Smid, Mar. 18, 1978; children: Jonathan, Dominic. BA, Creighton U., 1978; JD, U. Tex., 1981. Bar: Colo. 1981, U.S. Dist. Ct. Colo. 1981, U.S. Ct.

Appeals (10th cir.) 1981. With Grant, McHendrie, Haines & Crouse, Denver, 1981-85, Welborn, Dufford, Brown & Tooley, Denver, 1985-86; ptnr. Deutsch & Sheldon, Englewood, Colo., 1986-91; mem. Deutsch, Spillane & Reutzel, P.C., Englewood, 1991—. Bd. dirs., counsel Beaver Ranch Children's Camp, Conifer, Colo., 1983-92; bd. dirs. Pioneer Jr. Hockey Assn., 1994—. Mem. ABA, Colo. Bar Assn., Denver Bar Assn., Kiwanis (dir. 1983-85, pres. 1985-86). Office: Deutsch Spillane & Reutzel PC 9145 E Kenyon Ave Ste 200 Denver CO 80237-1810

SPILLER, PABLO TOMAS, economics and public utilities educator; b. Montevideo, Uruguay, Apr. 30, 1951; came to U.S., 1976; s. Andres and Elizabeth (Kweksilber) S.; m. Silvia Treibich, June 8, 1972; children: Addy, Elisheba. BA in Econs., Hebrew U., Jerusalem, 1974, MA in Econs., 1976; MA in Econs., U. Chgo., 1978, PhD in Econs., 1980. Asst. prof. econs. U. Pa., Phila., 1980-84; sr. rsch. fellow Hoover Instn., Stanford (Calif.) U., 1984-87; vis. assoc. prof. Stanford (Calif.) U., 1987; William B. McKinley prof. econs. and pub. utilities U. Ill., Champaign, 1987-94; prof. govt. and pub. affairs U. Ill., 1992-94; vis. assoc. prof. U. Calif., Berkeley, 1986, vis. prof. bus. and pub. policy, 1991-92, 93—; vis. prof. Grad. Sch. Bus., U. Chgo., 1989; cons. World Bank, Washington, 1982—, UN, N.Y.C., 1982, 83, FTC, Washington, 1984-89; mem. internat. adv. bd. CERES, Montevideo, 1989—. Assoc. editor Jour. Indsl. Econs., 1992—, Jour. Policy Reform, 1994; co-editor Jour. Law, Econ. and Orgn., Jour. Econ. and Mgmt. Strategy, 1992. Grantee Olin Found., 1977-80, NSF, 1990-91, Bradley Found.; fellow Tinker Found., 1983, Ctr. for Study of Economy and State, U. chgo., 1989, Inst. for Policy Reform, 1992—. Mem. Am. Econ. Assn., Econometric Soc., European Assn. for Ind. Econ. Rsch. Home: 3880 Los Arabis Dr Lafayette CA 94549-2947 Office: U Calif Haas Sch Bus Berkeley CA 94720

SPINDLER, GEORGE DEARBORN, anthropologist, educator, author, editor; b. Stevens Point, Wis., Feb. 28, 1920; s. Frank Nicholas and Winifred (Hatch) S.; m. Louise Schaubel, May 29, 1942; 1 dau., Sue Carol Spindler Coleman. B.S., Central State Tchrs. Coll., Wis., 1940; M.A., U. Wis., 1947; Ph.D., U. Calif. at Los Angeles, 1952. Tchr. sch. in Wis., 1940-42; research asso. Stanford, 1950-51, mem. faculty, 1951—, prof. anthropology and edn., 1960-78, exec. head dept., 1963-67, 84; vis. prof. U. Wis., Madison, 1979, 80, 81, 82, 83, 84, 85; editor Am. Anthropologist, 1962-66; cons. editor Holt, Rinehart & Winston, 1965-91, Harcourt, Brce, 1991—; vis. prof. U. Calif., Santa Barbara, 1986-91. Author: Menomini Acculturation, 1955, (with A. Beals and L. Spindler) Culture in Process, 1967, rev. edit., 1973, Transmission of American Culture, 1959, (with L. Spindler) Dreamers Without Power, 1971, rev. edit., 1984, Burgbach: Urbanization and Identity in a German Village, 1973, (with Louise Spindler) The American Cultural Dialogue and its Transmission, 1990; editor: Education and Anthropology, 1955, (with Louise Spindler) Case Studies in Cultural Anthropology, 1960—, Methods in Cultural Anthropology, 1965—, Case Studies in Education and Culture, 1966—, Basic Units in Anthropology, 1970; editor, contbr.: Education and Culture, 1963, Being An Anthropologist, 1970, Education and Cultural Process, 1974, rev. edit., 1987, The Making of Psychological Anthropology, 1978, 2nd edit., 1994, Doing the Ethnography of Schooling, 1982, Interpretive Ethnography of Schooling at Home and Abroad, 1987, Pathways to Cultural Awareness: Cultural Therapy with Students and Teachers, 1994. Pres. Peninsula Sch. Bd., Menlo Park, Calif., 1954-56. Served with AUS, 1942-45. Recipient Lloyd W. Dinkelspell award Stanford U., 1978, Disting. Svc. award Soc. Internat. Diplomacy and Third World Anthropologists, 1984, Disting. Career Contbn. award Com. on Role and Status of Minorities, Am. Edn. Rsch. Assn., Nat. Acad. Edn., 1994; fellow Ctr. Advanced Study of Behavioral Scis., 1956-57; subject of Vol. 17 Psychoanalytic Study of Soc. essays, 1992. Fellow Am. Anthrop. Assn.; mem. Southwestern Anthrop. Assn. (pres. 1962-63), Coun. for Anthropology and Edn. (pres. 1982, George and Louise Spindler award for outstanding contbns. to ednl. anthropology 1987), Nat. Acad. Edn. Home: 489 Kortum Canyon Rd Calistoga CA 94515-9703 Office: Ethnographics PO Box 38 Calistoga CA 94515-0038

SPINDLER, MICHAEL H., computer company executive; b. 1942. MBA, Rheinische Fachochschule. European mktg. mgr. Apple Computer Inc., 1980-88, pres. Apple Europe divsn., 1988-90, exec. v.p., COO, 1990-91, pres., COO, 1991-93, now pres., CEO, 1993—; also chmn. Claris Corp., Santa Clara, Calif. Office: Apple Computer Inc 20525 Mariani Ave Cupertino CA 95014-6201*

SPINDLER, PAUL, public relations executive; b. Chgo., May 2, 1931; s. Isaac Edward and Sophia (Stein) S.; m. Gail Klynn; children from previous marriage: Kevin, Makayla, Cyd, Jeffrey. BA in Journalism, Temple U., 1952. Reporter Akron Beacon Jour., Akron, Ohio, 1955-58, San Francisco Examiner, 1958-59; editor Santa Clara (Calif.) Daily Jour., 1959-63; dir. pub. affairs Litton Industries, Inc., Beverly Hills, Calif., 1963-68; dir. pub. relations Internat. Industries, Beverly Hills, 1968-70; pres. Paul Spindler & Co., L.A., 1970-75; exec. v.p. Manning Selvage & Lee, Inc., N.Y.C., 1975-85; pres. The Spindler Co., L.A., 1985-87; pres. Western div. GCI Group, L.A., 1987-91; pres. GCI/Spindler, L.A., 1991—; bd. dirs. Phoenix House Calif., Inc.; vis. com. mem. Sch. Bus. Adminstrn. U. So. Calif. Cpl. U.S. Army, 1952-54. Mem. Pub. Relations Soc. Am., Fin. Analysts Fedn., Mountain Gate Country Club (L.A.). Democrat. Jewish. Office: The Spindler Orgn Inc 6100 Wilshire Blvd Ste 804 Los Angeles CA 90048-5115

SPINGOLA, JEANNIE SAUNDRA, college, special education and adult educator; b. San Francisco, June 17; d. Frank and Camella Regina (Mazzaferro) S.; m. Peter William Connolly. BA, San Francisco Coll. Women, 1970; MA, U. San Francisco, 1974; student, Dominican Coll., 1971. Counselor Dept. Store Local 1100, San Francisco; cons. ESL Am. Fgn. Studies, San Francisco; counselor, instr. San Francisco Coll. Dist.; cons. Fgn. Lang. Inst., San Francisco. Composer and vocal performer classical and musical comedy Macy's California. Mem. ASCD, ICF, MEA/OSIA, CABE, Am. Fedn. Tchrs., AMA, CAMP, Nat. Assn. Hist. Preservation, Am. CB Radio Assn., Calif. Psychol. Assn., Friends of J. Paul Libr.

SPINKS, PAUL, retired library director; b. London, Mar. 7, 1922; came to U.S., 1952; m. Clarice Ada Goode, Jan. 27, 1946; 1 child, Philip Andrew. B.A., U. Okla., Norman, 1958; M.L.S., U. Okla., 1959. Catalog asst. Brit. Mus. Library, London, 1939-52; research reports librarian Naval Postgrad. Sch., Monterey, Calif., 1959-61; assoc. librarian Naval Postgrad. Sch., 1961-74, dir. libraries, 1975-93; prof. emeritus, 1993—. Author studies in field. Recipient Civilian Svc. Meritorious award USN, 1993. Mem. ALA, Spl. Libraries Assn., Am. Soc. Info. Sci. Episcopalian. Club: Brit.-Am. (sec. Monterey 1982-85). Home: 855 Capistrano Dr Salinas CA 93901-2420

SPINWEBER, CHERYL LYNN, research psychologist; b. Jersey City, July 26, 1950; d. Stanley A. And Evelyn M. (Pfleger) S.; m. Michael E. Bruich, June 18, 1977; children: Sean Michael Bruich, Gregory Alan Bruich. AB with distinction, Cornell U., 1972; PhD in Exptl. Psychology, Harvard U., 1977. Lic. psychologist, Calif. Asst. prof. psychiatry Tufts U. Sch. Medicine, Medford, Mass., 1977-79; asst. dir. sleep lab. Boston State Hosp., 1973-79; dep. head dept. behavioral psychopharmacology Naval Health Research Ctr., San Diego, 1978-86, head dept. behavioral psychopharmacology, 1986-89; research asst. prof. dept. psychiatry Uniformed Svcs. U. of the Health Scis., Bethesda, Md., 1985—; lectr. workshop instr. U. Calif. San Diego, La Jolla, 1979-81, vis. lectr. 1979-86; assoc. adj. prof. Dept. Psychology, 1989-94, adj. prof., 1994—; courtesy clin. staff oppointee dept. psychiatry Naval Hosp., San Diego, 1984—; clin. dir. Sleep Disorders Ctr. Mercy Hosp., San Diego, 1991—; pediatric sleep specialist Children's Hosp., San Diego, 1992—. Contbr. articles to profl. jours. Scholar Cornell U., Ithaca, N.Y., 1968-72, West Essex Tuition, 1968-72, Cornell U. Fedn. Women, 1917-72, Harvard U., 1972-73, 74-76, NDEA Title IV, 1973-74; postdoctoral associateship Nat. Research Council, 1978-80, Outstanding Tchg. award U. Calif. San Diego, 1994. Fellow Am. Sleep Disorders Assn., Clin. Sleep Soc., We. Psychol. Assn. (sec.-treas. 1986—); mem. Am. Men and Women of Sci., Sleep Rsch. Soc. (exec. com. 1986-89), Calif. Sleep Soc., Sigma Xi. Office: U Calif San Diego Dept Psychology 0109 La Jolla CA 92093

SPIRA, ROBERT SAMUEL, mathematician; b. Detroit, Dec. 12, 1927; s. Adolph and Leta Belle (Hopkins) S.; m. Cyla Siev, Oct. 20, 1946 (div. May 1949); m. Harriett Robena Keeler, Nov. 22, 1953; children: Constance Olivia Simonsen, Bradford Ace Burdick. BA, U. Calif., Berkeley, 1957, PhD, 1962. Asst. prof. Duke U., Durham, N.C., 1962-64, U. Tenn., Knoxville, 1964-67; assoc. prof. Mich. State U., East Lansing, 1967-82; artistic dir. Quartz Theatre, Ashland, Oreg., 1982—; adj. prof. So. Oreg. State Coll., Ashland, Oreg., 1992—; asst. cons. Walter Reed Army Inst., Washington, 1962-64, Armed Forces Inst. of Pathology, Washington, 1962-64. Author: A Course in Playwrighting, 1991; translator: Matthew, 1981; author plays, 1973—; contbr. articles to profl. jours. Ombudsman Linda Vista, Ashland, Oreg., 1992; vol. Crisis Intervention Svcs., Medford, Oreg., 1985-90; bd. dirs. So. Oreg. chpt. Alzheimer's Assn., 1994—. Democrat. Jewish. Office: Quartz Theatre 392 Taylor St Ashland OR 97520-3058

SPIRA-SOLOMON, DARLENE JOY, industrial chemist, researcher, department manager; b. Walnut Creek, Calif., Feb. 7, 1959; d. Erwin Irving and Beverly Sue (Davis) Spira; m. Edward Ira Solomon, Sept. 15, 1984; children: Mitchell Landau, Paige Elana. BS, Stanford U., 1980; PhD, MIT, 1984. Rsch. asst. Beckman Instruments, Palo Alto, Calif., 1978-79; rsch. assoc. MIT, Cambridge, 1980-84; rsch. assoc. Stanford (Calif.) U., 1982-84, asst. in instrn. FT-IR spectroscopy, 1982-83; rsch. scientist Hewlett-Packard Labs., Palo Alto, 1984—. Contbr. numerous articles to profl. jours. Coll. recruiter Hewlett-Packard, 1985—; co-chmn. Hewlett-Packard Tech. Women's Conf., 1988, chmn. adv. bd., 1989-91; workshop coord. Expanding Your Horizons Conf., Humboldt State U., 1987. Fellow chemistry dept. MIT, 1980-82, Stanford U., 1976-80. Mem. Am. Chem. Soc., Sigma Xi, Phi Beta Kappa. Office: Hewlett Packard Labs PO Box 10350 Palo Alto CA 94303-0867

SPIRO, HERBERT TSVI, economist, educator; b. Hattingen, Germany, Feb. 1, 1927; came to U.S., 1947; s. Georg Josef and Antoinette (Kaufmann) S.; m. Helen Goldstein, July 19, 1952; children: Valerie, Carolyn, Neal. BS, U. Pitts., 1952; MS, Carnegie Mellon U., 1953; PhD, UCLA, 1972. Engr. Ford Motor Co., Detroit, 1953-55; sr. analyst Tech. Operation Inc., Ft. Monroe, Va., 1957-58; mgr. Planning Research Corp., L.A., 1958-62, McDonnell Douglas Corp., Santa Monica, Calif., 1962-69; prof. fin. Calif. State U., Northridge, 1969-88; pres. Am. Valuation Group, Woodland Hill, Calif., 1985—. Author: Finance for the Nonfinancial Manager, 4th edit., 1996, Financial Planning for the Independent Professional, 1978; (with others) Automation and the Library of Congress, 1962. With U.S. Army, 1955-57. Mem. Am. Arbitration Assn., Am. Econ. Assn., Am. Soc. Appraisers (sr.). Home: 17516 Lemarsh St Northridge CA 91325-1411 Office: Am Valuation Group 21860 Burbank Blvd Ste 110 Woodland Hills CA 91367-6493

SPIRTOS, NICHOLAS GEORGE, lawyer, financial company executive; b. Youngstown, Ohio, Mar. 19, 1950; s. George Nicholas Spirtos and Tulla (Palaologos) Waldron; m. Andrea Carl DeFrane, Aug. 19, 1979. BA in Physics, Philosophy, UCLA, 1969, MA in Biochemistry, 1974, JD, 1978. Bar: Calif., 1978; cert. rape crisis counselor, Calif. Intelligence analyst, 1969-72; dir. product devel. Adolph's Food Products, Burbank, Calif., 1972-73; asst. to pres. Eckel Research and Devel., San Fernando, Calif., 1973-74; dep. State Public Defender Los Angeles, 1977-82; sole practice Pacific Palisades and Palm Desert, Calif., 1982—; co-founder, Tekni-Query Cons., 1990; appellate lawyer Calif. and U.S. Supreme Ct., 1982; exec. v.p. Gen. Counsel Compensation Strategies Group, Santa Ana, Calif., 1988—; pro bono legal counsel Junipero Serra High Sch., Gardena, Calif., 1987-88; cons. to U.S. Govt., 1982—; mem. bd. dirs. The Myelin Project, Washington. Patentee solubilization of Sodium CMC at room temperature, 1972. Founder, fund raiser Pacific Multiple Sclerosis Research Found., Beverly Hills, Calif., 1982—, coordinator with Reed Neurology Ctr. at UCLA. Westinghouse Sci. scholar, 1965; recipient Gregor Mendell award in genetics, 1962; named Jr. Engr. of Yr. Am. Assn. Aero. Engrs., 1963, Outstanding Speaker U. So. Calif., 1965. Mem. State Bar Calif., Internat. Platform Assn. Republican. Greek Orthodox. Office: 44489 Town Center Way # D-404 Palm Desert CA 92260-2723

SPITALERI, VERNON ROSARIO, newspaper publisher, manufacturing company executive; b. Pelham, N.Y., Aug. 2, 1922; s. Rosario S. and Martha (Landerer) S.; m. Marjorie A. Ferrar, Oct. 14, 1952; children: Marc, Eric, Kris, Lynn. B.S., Carnegie Inst. Tech., 1942. Mgr. mech. dept. Am. Newspaper Pubs. Assn., N.Y.C., 1946-53; research dir., gen. adminstr. Miami Herald and Knight Newspapers (Fla.), 1953-57; chmn. bd., pres. Sta-Hi Corp., Newport Beach, Calif., 1957-74; chmn. bd. Sta-Hi Color Service, Sta-Hi Europe, Brussels, Concrete Floats-Huntington Engring. Corp., Huntington Beach, Calif.; editor, pub. Laguna Beach (Calif.) News-Post, 1967-81; pres. Laguna Pub. Co., Nat. Newspaper Found.; dir. Suburban Newspapers Am.; chmn. bd. Victory Profl. Products, Mango Surfware. Pres., Boys Club, Laguna Beach; mem. citizens adv. com. Laguna Beach; pres. Laguna Beach Library Bd., Laguna Playhouse, Laguna Coordinating Council; bd. dirs. Sta-Hi Found.; dir. Opera Pacific. Served to lt. comdr. USNR, 1942-46. Decorated Purple Heart. Mem. Am. Mgmt. Assn., Nat. Newspaper Assn. (dir.), Calif. Newspaper Pubs. Assn. (dir.), Laguna Beach C. of C. (bd. dir.), Alpha Tau Omega. Republican. Roman Catholic. Club: Dana Point Yacht.

SPITLER, LEE WILLIAM, banker; b. Racine, Wis., Feb. 14, 1919; s. Marion Albert and Agnes Elizabeth (Lowe) S.; m. Helen Deloris Krejci, Mar. 19, 1949; children—Susan D., Lee William, Anne M., James E. B.S., U. Md., 1956; M.B.A., George Washington U., 1962; postgrad. advanced mgmt. program, Harvard U., 1963; grad., U.S. Air Force War Coll., 1959, U.S. Air Force Command and Staff Coll., 1955. Commd. 2d lt. U.S. Air Force, 1943, advanced through grades to col., 1954; chief personnel stats. div. Hdqrs. U.S. Air Force, Washington, 1950-54; asst. dir. statis. services U.S. Air Force, 1958-63; asst. comptroller Hdqrs. U.S. European Command U.S. Air Force, Paris, 1955-58; asst. comptroller Hdqrs. Air Tng. Command U.S. Air Force, Randolph AFB, Tex., 1963-64; ret. U.S. Air Force, 1964; v.p. Computax Corp., El Segundo, Calif., 1965-69; exec. v.p. Irving Bank Corp., N.Y.C., 1969-84; sr. exec. v.p. Irving Trust Co., N.Y.C., 1969-84; ret., 1984; pres. Spitler Fin. Svcs., Monterey, Calif., 1985—; dir. Turkiye Tutunculer Bankasi AS, Izmir, Turkey, 1984-87. mem. nat. adv. bd. Am. Security Council. Decorated Legion of Merit. Mem. Internat. Assn. Fin. Planning, Am. Bankers Assn., Am. Mgmt. Assn., Soc. for Mgmt. Info. Systems, Ret. Officers Assn., Nat. Assn. Uniformed Services, Mil. Order World Wars, Am. Assn. Mil. Comptrollers, Am. Legion, Veterans of Fgn. Wars, Am. Assn. Ret. Personnel, Inst. Cert. Planners, Air War Coll. Alumni Assn., First Fighter Group Assn. Clubs: Harvard, West Point Officers. Home: 200 Glenwood Cir Apt 525 Monterey CA 93940-6747 Office: 200 Glenwood Circle Monterey CA 93940

SPITZER, MARC LEE, lawyer; b. Pitts., Sept. 12, 1957; s. Richard A. and Edith (Brodie) S. BA in History and Polit. Sci. summa cum laude, Dickinson Coll., 1979; JD cum laude, U. Mich., 1982. Bar: Ariz. 1982, U.S. Dist. Ct. Ariz. 1982, U.S. Tax Ct. 1982, U.S. Ct. Appeals (9th cir.) 1985. Ptnr. Fennemore, Craig, Phoenix, 1982—; state sen. dist. 18, chmn. senate fin. com., joint legis. tax com. Bd. dirs. Ariz. Rep. Caucus, Phoenix, 1982—, Ariz. Acad., 1990; mem. devel. com. Dickinson Coll., 1985-86; mem. Soc. for the Arts; vice-chmn. Ariz. 18th Dist., 1986—; alternate del. 1988 Rep. Nat. Conv. GOP; legal counsel Ariz. Rep. Party; apptd. by pres. Ariz. Senate and speaker of house Ariz. Commn. Mcpl. Taxation. Mem. ABA (vice-chmn., tax legis. sect.), State Bar Ariz. (cert. specialist taxation), Ariz. Tax Research Found. (bd. dirs. 1984—), Ariz. Tax Research Assn., Maricopa County Bar Assn., Phi Beta Kappa, Sigma Alpha Epsilon. Jewish. Clubs: Arizona, Phoenix City, Captain's (bd. dirs.). Home: 304 W Orangewood Ave Phoenix AZ 85021-7250

SPITZER, MATTHEW L., retail store executive; b. Pitts., June 20, 1929; s. Martin and Ruth G. S.; student U. Buffalo, 1948-50; children: Mark, Edward, Eric, Joseph. Lic. airline transport pilot. Product line mgr. Gen. Dynamics, Rochester, N.Y., 1962-67; dir. contracts Friden div. Singer, San Leandro, Calif., 1968-69; asst. v.p. Talcott Computer Leasing, San Francisco, 1970-71; pres. Spitzer Music Mgmt. Co., Hayward, Calif., 1972—. chmn. bd. Leo's Audio and Music Techs., Oakland, Calif.; Masons, Mensa. Office: 5447 Telegraph Ave Oakland CA 94609

SPITZER, PETER GEORGE, information systems executive, consultant; b. Oradea, Romania, July 16, 1956; m. Anne Taylor, 1985. BS in Bioelec. Engring., MIT, 1979, MS in Elec. Engring. and Computer Sci., 1980; MD cum laude, Harvard U., 1980; MBA, UCLA, 1986. Sr. systems analyst Nat. Cash Register Co., Los Angeles, 1976-77; dir. pathology diagnosis registry Peter Brigham Hosps., Boston, 1978-80; research analyst Mass. Gen. Hosp., Boston, 1978-80; resident obstetrics and gynecologist UCLA Ctr. for Health Scis., Los Angeles, 1980-81; asst. v.p. Am. Med. Internat., Info. Systems Group, Beverly Hills, Calif., 1981-87; chief info. officer Tex. Children's Hosp., Houston, 1988-90; asst. rsch. prof. pediatrics Baylor Coll. of Medicine, Houston, 1988-90; pres. Spitzer Assocs., 1990—; cons. advanced info. tech., 1990—. Smith-Kline Found. fellow, 1978-80. Fellow Healthcare Info. Mgmt. Systems Soc.; mem. AMA, IEEE, Am. Hosp. Assn., Am. Coll. Physician Execs., Soc. for Info. Mgmt., Am. Soc. Quality Control, Am. Med. Info. Assn., European Community Com. for Standardization (CEN/TC251 - healthcare systems standardization com.), Eta Kappa Nu, Sigma Xi. Office: 11718 Barrington Ct Ste 504 Los Angeles CA 90049-2930

SPIVAK, JACQUE R., bank executive; b. San Francisco, Nov. 5, 1929; d. Robert Morris and Sadonia Clardine Breitstein; m. Herbert Spivak, Aug. 26, 1960; children: Susan, Donald, Joel, Sheri. B.S., U. So. Calif., 1949, M.S., 1950, M.B.A., 1959. Mgr. Internat. Escrow, Inc., Los Angeles, 1960-65, Greater Los Angeles Investment Co., 1965-75; mgr. escrow Transam. Title Ins. Co., Los Angeles, 1975-78; mgr. escrow, asst. v.p. Wells Fargo Bank, Beverly Hills, Calif., 1979-80; adminstr. escrow, v.p. 1st Pacific Bank, Beverly Hills, 1980-85; escrow adminstr. Century City Savs. & Loan Assn., Los Angeles, 1986-87; pres. Producers Escrow Corp., Beverly Hills., 1987—. Recipient awards PTA, Girl Scouts U.S.A., Jewish Fedn. Los Angeles, Hadassah. Mem. Calif. Escrow Assn., Nat. Assn. Bank Women, Inst. Trustees Sales Officers, Hadassah (nat. bd., pres. L.A. chpt.). Republican. Jewish. Office: Producers Escrow Corp P O Box 5771 Beverly Hills CA 90209-5771

SPIVAK, JOEL A., lawyer; b. L.A., Feb. 19, 1958; s. Herbert Alan and Jacque R. (Briet) S. BA in Polit. Sci., UCLA, 1979; JD, Western State U., San Diego, 1981. Bar: Calif. 1982, U.S. Dist. Ct. (cen. dist.) Calif. 1983, U.S. Ct. Appeals (9th cir.) 1983, U.S. Tax Ct. 1984. Lawyer Halperin & Halperin p.c., L.A., 1982-85; pvt. practice L.A., 1985—; corp. counsel Producers Escrow Corp., Beverly Hills, Calif., 1988—; pres., corp. counsel Producers Exchange Corp., Beverly Hills, Calif., 1988—; counsel Victims for Victims, L.A., 1984-86, L.A. Chpt. Hadassah, L.A., 1989-94. Democrat. Jewish. Office: Ste 213 3760 Motor Ave Los Angeles CA 90034-6404

SPIVEY, ROBERTA LEE, paralegal, community counselor; b. Boulder, Colo., July 2, 1940; d. William Elwood Hopkins and Donna Rebecca (Owen) Hopkins Ellis; m. James O. Spivey, Dec. 23, 1961; children: Dawna Jenelle, Michael James. BA in Philosophy, U. Ams., Mex., 1961; postgrad., Ga. State U., 1962-64, Calif. State U., Sacramento, 1992—. Spanish and English tchr. Henrico County Schs., Richmond, Va., 1966-67; legal sec., real estate specialist Gettle & Fraser, Attys., Atlanta, Calif., 1964-75; real estate specialist, closer Merrill Lynch Relocation, Atlanta, Calif., 1975-79; escrow sec. Western Title, Fidelity Title, Sacramento, Calif., 1979-83; exec. sec., legal asst. Evans Fin., Sacramento, Calif., 1983-86; legal sec., asst. Granite Fin., Sacramento, Calif., 1986-88; exec. sec. Infotec/Passar, Sacramento, Calif., 1988-90; real estate paralegal Taylor & Hooper, Attys., Sacramento, Calif., 1990—. Author short stories. Arbitrator auto-line BBB, Sacramento, 1986—. Office: Taylor & Hooper Attys 1435 River Park Dr Ste 300 Sacramento CA 95815-4510

SPIZIZEN, JOHN, microbiologist, b. Winnipeg, Man., Can., Feb. 7, 1917; came to U.S., 1939, naturalized, 1944; s. Nathan and Sarah Spizizen; m. Louise Myers, Apr., 1969; 1 child, Gary. B.A., U. Toronto, 1939; Ph.D., Calif. Inst. Tech., 1942. Assoc. in virus rsch. Merck, Sharp and Dohme, West Point, Pa., 1946-54; assoc. prof. dept. Microbiology Western Res. U., Cleve., 1954-61; prof., head dept. microbiology U. Minn., Mpls., 1961-65; chmn. dept. microbiology Scripps Clinic and Rsch. Found., La Jolla, Calif., 1965-79; prof., head dept. microbiology and immunology U. Ariz., Tucson, 1979-87, prof. emeritus, 1987—; bd. govs. Weizmann Inst. Sci., Israel, 1970-82. bd. sci. advisors La Jolla Cancer Rsch. Found., 1978—; mem. com. for rsch. and tng. NIH, 1962-79, Am. Cancer Soc., 1967—; mem. coms. NASA, 1970-78. Served to capt. U.S. Army, 1943-46. Recipient Career Devel. award NIH, Western Res. U., 1955; rsch. grantee NIH, NSF; fellow NRC; Fulbright scholar U. Lund, Sweden, 1992. Mem. Am. Soc. Microbiology, Am. Soc. Biochem. and Molecular Biology. Home: 2540 E Camino La Zorrela Tucson AZ 85718-3122 Office: U Ariz Sch Medicine Dept Microbiology 1501 N Campbell Ave Tucson AZ 85724-0001

SPLANE, RICHARD BEVERLEY, social work educator; b. Calgary, Alta., Can., Sept. 25, 1916; s. Alfred William and Clara Jane (Allyn) S.; m. Verna Marie Huffman, Feb. 22, 1971. BA, McMaster U., 1940, LLD (hon.), 1990; cert. social sci. and adminstrn., London Sch. Econs., 1947; MA, U. Toronto, 1948, MSW, 1951, PhD, 1961; LLD (hon.), Wilfrid Laurier U., 1988. Exec. dir. Children's Aid Soc., Cornwall, Ont., Can., 1948-50; with Health and Welfare Can., Ottawa, 1952-72; exec. asst. to dep. minister nat. welfare Health and Welfare Can., 1959-60, dir. unemployment assistance, 1960-62, dir. gen. welfare assistance and services, 1960-70, asst. dep. minister social allowances and services, 1970-72; vis. prof. U. Alta., Edmonton, 1972-73; prof. social policy Sch. Social Work, U. B.C., Vancouver, 1973—; cons. Govt. Can., Govt. Alta., UNICEF. Author: The Development of Social Welfare in Ontario, 1965; (with Verna Huffman Splane) Chief Nursing Officers in National Ministries of Health, 1994. Served with RCAF, 1942-45. Recipient Centennial medal Govt. Can., 1967, Charles E. Hendry award U. Toronto, 1981, Commemorative medal for 125th anniversary of Confederation of Canada, 1992. Mem. Can. Assn. Social Workers (Outstanding Nat. Svc. award 1985), Can. Inst. Pub. Adminstrn., Can. Hist. Assn., Can. Coun. on Social Devel. (Lifetime Achievement award 1995), Internat. Assn. Schs. Social Work, Internat. Confs. Social Devel. (pres.), World Federalists of Can. (pres. Vancouver br.), Vancouver Club. Mem. United Ch. Can. Office: Sch Social Work, U BC, Vancouver, BC Canada V6T 1W5

SPOEHEL, JERRI HOSKINS, volunteer agency executive; b. Oak Park, Ill., Mar. 13, 1932; d. George Alex and Myrtle Jean (McBean) Hoskins; BA in English cum laude, Coll. Wooster, 1953; m. Edwin H. Spoehel, Apr. 16, 1955; children: Ronald Ross, Jacqueline Jean. Instr., Success-Plus, 1974; columnist Daily News, San Fernando Valley, Van Nuys, Calif., 1970-85; community rels. dir. Sta. KCSN-FM, Nat. Pub. Radio, Northridge, Calif., 1975-85; exec. dir. Vol. Ctr. of San Fernando Valley, 1985-89; freelance writer, Las Cruces, N.Mex., 1989—; exec. dir. Vol. Ctrs. of So. Calif.; mem. Pres. Assocs. Calif. State U., Northridge; panelist/seminar instr. Nat. Devel. Conf., Corp. Pub. Broadcasting; mem. LWV, Coalition of Conservation Orgns.; pub. rels. contbr. N.Mex. State Mus. Recipient Nat. Abe Lincoln Merit award So. Bapt. Radio and TV Commn.; named Disting. Citizen of Northridge; other awards. Mem. AAUW (pres.), Pub. Rels. Roundtable, Dirs. Vols. in Agys., Dona Ana County Arts Coun., Friends of 4-H, Friends of Internat. Students, Mesilla Valley Writers, Native Plant Soc., Nature Conservancy, Toastmasters Internat., Repub. Women's Club, Welcome Wagon Newcomers Club, Women's Press Club, Soroptimists (pres.), Northridge Cultural Arts Club.

SPOERL, OTTO HEINRICH, psychiatrist, educator; b. Kronach, Germany, Feb. 25, 1933. Student, U. Goettingen Med. Sch., 1951-54, U. Freiburg Med. Sch., 1954-55, U. Heidelberg Med. Sch., 1955, U. Erlangen Med. Sch., 1955-58. Diplomate Am. Bd. Psychiatry and Neurology; lic. Wash., N.C., West Germany. Intern dept. surgery U. Erlangen (Germany) Med. Sch., 1957-58; rotating intern Md. Gen. Hosp., Balt., 1959-60; asst. resident dept. psychiatry Duke U. Med. Ctr., Durham, N.C., 1960-62, resident dept. pschiatry, 1962-63; chief resident dept. psychaitry, asst. in psychiatry U. Wash. Sch. Medicine, Seattle, 1963-64, instr. psychiatry, 1964-68, asst. prof., 1968-70, clin. asst. prof. dept. psychiatry and behavioral scis., 1970—; attending physician psychiatric inpatient svcs. U. Hosp., Seattle, 1964-68; dir. psychiatric inpatient svc. King Country Harborview Hosp., 1968-70; chief mental health svcs. Group Health Eastside Med. Ctr., 1975-78, Group Health Coop., 1980-82; mgr. psychiatric svcs. Cen. Mental Health Svc. Group Health Coop., Seattle, 1989—; cons. Washington State Heart Assn., 1964-74, German Consulate Gen., Seattle, 1964—; coord. student vol. program Psychiatric Inpatient Svc. U. Hosp., 1966-68. Contbr. articles to profl. jours. Med. adv. bd. Seattle Planned Parenthood Ctr., 1967-80; exec. bd. mem. Mental Health Profls. for Human Rights and Responsibilities, 1968-70; med. adv. Stevens Pass Ski area, mem. Nat. Ski Patrol. Fellow Am.

Psychiatric Assn.; mem. Am. Pub. Health Assn., Seattle Psychiatric Soc., U. Dist. Rotary Club. Office: 1730 Minor Ave # 1400 Seattle WA 98101-1448

SPOFFORD, ROBERT HOUSTON, advertising agency executive; b. N.Y.C., Apr. 3, 1941; s. Robert Knowlton and Linda Prieber (Houston) S.; m. Susan Proctor Allerton; children—Margaret, Robert Christopher. B.E.E., Cornell U., 1964. Account exec. Batten, Barton, Durstine & Osborn, Inc., N.Y.C., 1964-71, v.p., 1971-84, sr. v.p., 1984-88, exec. v.p., dir. strategic planning, 1988—. Contbr. articles to advt. and data processing jours. Mem. Westchester County Democratic Com. N.Y. 1974-78; ch. organist. First recipient Founder's medal Batten, Barton, Durstine & Osborn, Inc., 1985. Unitarian. Home: 449 35th St Manhattan Beach CA 90266-3320 Office: BBDO LA 10960 Wilshire Blvd Los Angeles CA 90024-3702

SPOHRER, JAMES HENRY, librarian, consultant; b. Jennings, La., Dec. 18, 1950; s. Henry Stanislaus and Rosalie (Ballard) S.; m. Elisabeth Marie Aurelle, Mar. 20, 1974; 1 child, Bela. BA, La. State U., 1975, MS, 1978; MA, U. Calif., Berkeley, 1983. Pvt. practice translator Freiburg, Germany, 1973-75; test constrn. specialist Louisian Civil Svc. Dept., Baton Rouge, 1975-76; serials libr. U. Nebr., Lincoln, 1978-81; instr. U. Calif., Berkeley, 1981-83, Germanic libr., 1983—, dept. chair, 1992—; cons. linguistics dept. U. Calif., Berkeley, 1989. Author: Guide to Collection Development and Management, 1986; translator: Cajuns de la Louisiane, 1978. Mem. Nebr. Wesleyan Chamber Orch., Lincoln, 1979; bd. dirs. East Bay Suzuki Music Assn., Berkeley, 1981-83. Recipient Nijhoff prize Martinus Nijhoff Internat., The Hague, 1989; Title II-C grantee U.S. Dept. Edn., Washington, 1988-90. Mem. MLA, ALA, Western European Specialist Sect. (chair 1993-94), Medieval Assn. of the Pacific, Beta Phi Mu. Home: 4824 Full Moon Dr El Sobrante CA 94803-2138 Office: Univ Calif 390 Doe Library Berkeley CA 94720

SPOLTER, PARI DOKHT, scientific books writer; b. Teheran, Iran, Jan. 30, 1930; came to U.S., 1957; m. Herbert Spolter, Aug. 16, 1958; children: David, Deborah. Licence chimie biologique, U. Geneva, 1952; PhD in Biochemistry, U. Wis., 1961. Rsch. assoc., instr. Temple U., Phila., 1961-65; researcher U.S. Pub. Health Svc. Hosp., San Francisco, 1965-68; writer Orb Pub. Co., Granada Hills, Calif., 1988—. Mem. AAAS, Am. Math. Soc., N.Y. Acad. Scis. Office: Orb Pub Co 11862 Balboa Blvd # 182 Granada Hills CA 91344-2753

SPONSEL, LESLIE ELMER, anthropologist, ecologist; b. Indpls., Nov. 6, 1943; s. Elmer John and Else Marie (Erhardt) S.; m. Poranee Natadecha, May 1, 1984. BA in Geology, Ind. U., 1965; MA in Anthropology, Cornell U., 1973, PhD, 1981. Vis. lectr. U. Sask., Saskatoon, Can., 1968-70; vis. Fulbright prof. Venezuelan Inst. for Sci. Investigations, Caracas, 1977-78, 81; vis. instr. U. Mass., Amherst, 1978-79; asst. prof. U. Hawaii, Honolulu, 1981-86, assoc. prof., 1986—; Fulbright vis. prof. Prince Songkla U., Pattani, Thailand, 1994-95. Co-editor: The Anthropology of Peace and Nonviolence, 1994, Tropical Deforestation: The Human Dimension, 1995; editor: Indigenous Peoples and the Future of Amazonia: An Ecological Anthropology of An Endangered World, 1995. Mem. Am. Anthrop. Assn. (chair commn. for human rights 1992-95), Siam Soc., Sigma Xi. Office: U Hawaii Dept Anthropology 2424 Maile Way Honolulu HI 96822-2223

SPOOR, JAMES EDWARD, human resouces company executive, entrepreneur; b. Rockford, Ill., Feb. 19, 1936; s. Frank Kendall and Genevieve Eileen (Johnson) S.; B.S. in Psychology, U. Ill., 1958; m. Nancy E. Carlson, Sept. 8, 1962; children—Sybll K., Kendall P., Andrea K., Marcie K. Personnel mgr. Nat. Sugar Refining Co., N.Y.C., 1960-64, Pepsico, Inc., N.Y.C., Auburn, N.Y., 1964-67; mgr. internat. pers. Control Data Corp., Mpls., 1967-75; v.p. personnel and employee rels. Vetco, Inc., Ventura, Calif., 1975-79; v.p. employee rels. Hamilton Bros. Oil Co., Denver, 1979-84; pres., CEO Spectrum Human Resource Systems Corp., 1984—; cons., author, speaker on human resources and entrepreneurism. Mem. adv. bd. Salvation Army, 1978-79; chmn. Spl. Commn. for Ventura County Bd. Suprs., 1978; mem. task force on human resources Colo. Sch. Mines, 1983; state chairperson Coun. Growing Cos., 1991-92, nat. pres., 1992-94; bd. dirs. Breckenridge Outdoor Edn. Ctr. With U.S. Army, 1958-60. Mem. Am. Soc. Pers. Adminstrn. (contbg. author handbook), Assn. for Human Resource Systems Profls., Colo. Soc. Pers. Adminstrn. Republican. Episcopalian. Clubs: Denver, Masons, Shriners. Contbg. author: Am. Soc. Personnel Adminstrn. Personnel and Indsl. Relations Handbook.

SPRADLIN, BYRON LEE, minister; b. Richmond, Calif., Apr. 29, 1949; s. Richard L. and Meathel Spradlin; m. Pamela A. Spradlin, May 11, 1974; children: Sarah Ann, Nathan Lee. BA, U. Calif., Davis, 1971; M in Ch. Music, Western Conservative Bapt. Sem, 1977, MDiv, 1978. Ordained to ministry Bapt. Ch., 1980. Youth pastor 1st Bapt. Ch., Richmond, 1971-73; bd. chmn. Jews for Jesus, San Francisco, Calif., 1973—; founder, exec. dir. Artists in Christian Testimony, Cucamonga, Calif., 1973—; worship pastor Cmty Bapt. Ch., Alta Loma, Calif., 1981-86; founder, exec. dir. Ch. Planting Internat., Cucamonga, 1986—; founder, sr. pastor New Hope Community Ch., Cucamonga, 1986-94; tour dir. Continental Singers, 1968-71; dir. music outreach ministries Western Conservative Bapt. Sem., Portland, Oreg., 1973-78, adj. faculty, 1978-80; mem. World Christian Curriculum Com., Devel. Third World Nations, 1982-84, Campus Crusade for Christ, U. Calif., Davis, 1968-71; mem. all-Am. track NCAA, 1969, 70, 71, cross country, 1970, steeplechase (champion), 1970. Contbr. articles to profl. jours. Named to Athletic Hall of Fame, City of Sacramento, 1970, U. Calif., Davis, 1990. Mem. ASCAP, Nat. Acad. Rec. Arts and Scis., Evang. Theol. Soc., Nat. Assn. Evangelicals, Conservative Bapts. Am., Soc. For Ethno Musicology. Office: Artists in Christian Testimony Box 1002 Rancho Cucamonga CA 91729-1002

SPRAGUE, AMARIS JEANNE, real estate broker; b. Jackson, Mich., Feb. 18, 1935; d. Leslie Markham and Blanche Lorraine (Basnaw) Reed; student Mich. State U., 1952-53; B.S., Colo. State U., 1965; m. John M. Vetterling, Oct. 1985; children by previous marriage—Anthony John, James Stuart. Real estate sales Seibel and Benedict Realty, Ft. Collins, Colo., 1966-69; salesman Realty Brokers Exchange, Ft. Collins, 1969-72; broker, pres. Sprague and Assos., Inc., Realtors, Ft. Collins, 1972-80; broker assoc. Van Schaack & Co., Ft. Collins, 1980-86; broker ptnr. The Group, Inc., 1986—; dir. Univ. Nat. Bank. Mem. bus. adv. council Colo. State U., 1976-84, chmn. 1979-80, mem. adv. council Coll. of Engring., 1981. Cert. real estate broker. Mem. Nat. Assn. Realtors, Colo. Assn. Realtors, Ft. Collins Bd. Realtors, Ft. Collins C. of C. (bd. dirs. 1978-84, pres. 1982-83). Republican. Episcopalian. Home: PO Box 475 Fort Collins CO 80522-0475 Office: 401 W Mulberry St Fort Collins CO 80521-2839

SPRAGUE, PETER JULIAN, semiconductor company executive, lecturer; b. Detroit, Apr. 29, 1939; s. Julian K. and Helene (Coughlin) S.; m. Tjasa Krofta, Dec. 19, 1959; children: Carl, Steven, Kevin, Michael. Student, Yale U., 1961, MIT, 1961, Columbia U., 1962-66. Chmn. bd. dirs. Nat. Semiconductor Corp., Santa Clara, Calif.; chmn. Wave Sys., Inc.; bd. dirs. Software Profls., Inc. Trustee Strang Clinic. Club: Yale. Home: 399 Under Mountain Rd Lenox MA 01240-2036 Office: Wave Sys Corp 540 Madison Ave New York NY 10022-3213 Office: Nat Semiconductor Corp 2900 Semiconductor Dr PO Box 58090 Santa Clara CA 95051*

SPRIGGS, EVERETT LEE, lawyer; b. Safford, Ariz., July 30, 1930; s. Claude E. and Evelyn (Lee) S.; m. Betty Medley, Aug. 22, 1953; children: Claudia Lynn Reynolds, Scott B. BS, Ariz. State U., 1955; JD, U. Ariz., 1958. Bar: Calif. 1960, U.S. Supreme Ct. 1983. City atty. criminal dept. Los Angeles, 1960-61; mem. firm Kinkle & Rodiger, Riverside, Calif., 1961-64; pres. Kinkle, Rodiger & Spriggs (P.C.), Riverside, 1965—; chmn. bd. dirs. Riverside Nat. Bank. With AUS, 1951-52. Mem. ABA, Calif. Bar Assn., Riverside County Bar Assn., L.A. County Bar Assn., Def. Rsch. Inst., So. Calif. Def. Counsel (editorial staff 1970-71), Assn. Trial Lawyers Am., Riverside Downtown Assn., Am. Bd. Trial Advocates, Supreme Ct. Hist. Soc., Def. Orientation Conf. Assn. Home: 1456 Muirfield Rd Riverside CA 92506-5576 also: 1126 E Balboa Blvd Balboa CA 92661-1314 Office: Kinkle Rodiger & Spriggs 3333 14th St Riverside CA 92501-3254 also: 600 N Grand Ave Los Angeles CA 90012-2126 also: 837 N Ross St Santa Ana CA 92701-3451 also: 1620 5th Ave San Diego CA 92101-2795 also: 125 E de la Guerna St Santa Barbara CA 93101-2239

SPRINCZ, KEITH STEVEN, financial services company professional; b. Whitewater, Wis., Mar. 8, 1956; s. Steven B. Sprincz and Mary Lou (Crotte) Zolli; m. Renee Michele Werner, Sept. 11, 1982; children: Nicholas, Cameron. BS in Mktg., Colo. State U., 1978; student, Am. Coll., 1985-86. CLU, ChFC. Agt. Prudential, Denver, 1978-83; ins. broker Nolen/Western, Denver, 1983-88, ptnr., 1988—; tchr. Life Underwriters Tng. Coun., Bethesda, Md., 1991-92. Chmn. bd. elders Bethlehem Luth. Ch., Lakewood, Colo., 1989; campmaster coord. Boy Scouts Am., Denver, 1989—, scoutmaster, 1983—; capt. March of Dimes, Denver, 1981, Big Bros., Denver, 1984; pres. Centennial Assn. Life Underwriters, 1986-87; sch. bd. mem., 1993—, pres., 1995—. Recipient Outstanding Family award Boy Scouts Am., 1986. Office: Nolen Western 5690 Dtc Blvd Ste 140 Englewood CO 80111-3233

SPRING, GLENN ERNEST, composer; b. Hot Springs, Ark., Apr. 19, 1939; s. Glenn Ernest Sr. and Ellen (Maddox) S.; m. Ingrid Kathryn Olesen, Aug. 5, 1962 (dec. Jan. 1973); 1 child, Brian Glenn; m. Kathleen Marie Klein, Dec. 16, 1973; children; Christopher, Heidi. BA, La Sierra U., 1962; M.Mus., Tex. Christian U., 1964; D. Mus. Arts, U. Wash., 1972. Instr. music Otterbein Coll., Westerville, Ohio, 1964-65; prof. music Walla Walla Coll., College Place, Wash., 1965—; concertmaster Walla Walla (Wash.) Symphony, 1965-75, 87-90; sect. violionist (1st) Columbus (Ohio) Symphony, 1964-65; sect. violinist (1st and 2d) Ft. Worth Symphony, 1962-64. Composer: Shapes: A Short Symphony, 1973 (Indpls. Symphony award 1974), (orchestral composition) Perceptions, 1977, Dona nobis pacem for baritone and orch., 1984, Contrasts for organ, 1986, Hold in Your Memory the Land, 1990, many other works; Co-author: Musical Form and Analysis, 1995. Recipient commn. Wash. State Arts Commn., 1973, Musiklager Margess, Switzerland, 1988, 89, Alienor Harpsichord Composition award SE Hist. Keyboard Soc., 1990. Mem. ASCAP (ann. awards 1988-95), Coll. Music Soc. (Burlington-No. award 1991). Office: Walla Walla Coll 204 S College Ave College Place WA 99324-1139

SPRINGER, CHARLES EDWARD, state supreme court justice; b. Reno, Feb. 20, 1928; s. Edwin and Rose Mary Cecelia (Kelly) S.; m. Jacqueline Sirkegian, Mar. 17, 1951; 1 dau., Kelli Ann. BA, U. Nev., Reno, 1950; LLB, Georgetown U., 1953; LLM, U. Va., 1984; student Grad. Program for Am. Judges, Oriel Coll., Oxford (Eng.), 1984. Bar: Nev. 1953, U.S. Dist. Ct. Nev. 1953, D.C. 1954, U.S. Supreme Ct. 1962. Pvt. practice law Reno, 1953-80; atty. gen. State of Nev., 1962, legis. legal adv. to gov., 1958-62; legis. bill drafter Nev. Legislature, 1955-57; mem. faculty Nat. Coll. Juvenile Justice, Reno, 1978—; juvenile master 2d Jud. Dist. Nev., 1973-80; justice Nev. Suprem Ct., Carson City, 1981—; mem. Jud. Selection Commn., 1981—, Nev. Supreme Ct. Gender Bias Task Force, 1981—; trustee Nat. Coun. Juvenile and Family Ct. Judges, 1983—; mem. faculty McGeorge Sch. Law, U. Nev., Reno, 1982—; chmn. Nev. Commn. for women, 1991—. With AUS, 1945-47. Recipient Outstanding Contbn. to Juvenile Justice award Nat. Coun. Juvenile and Family Ct. Judges, 1989, Midby-Byron Disting. Leadership award U. Nev., 1988. Mem. ABA, Am. Judicature Soc., Am. Trial Lawyers Assn., Phi Kappa Phi. Office: Nev Supreme Ct Capitol Complex 201 S Carson St Carson City NV 89701

SPRINGER, FLOYD LADEAN, architect; b. Goodrich, N.D., Feb. 1, 1922; s. George Roy Springer and Louise Baumbach; m. Dorothy Mae Shepard; children: Debra Louise, Tami June. Student, U. Denver, 1948-51; BS in Archtl. Engring., U. Colo., 1952; postgrad., U. Wash., 1953-54, U. Utah, Portland, Oreg., 1980. With Seattle Delta Investment Group, 1984—. Cpl. inf. U.S. Army, 1941-44, PTO. Decorated Silver Star. Presbyterian. Home and Office: 18548 60th Ave NE Seattle WA 98155-4453

SPRINGER, GERALD WILLIAM, sales executive; b. Amherst, Ohio, Nov. 13, 1943; s. Raymond W. and Ione J. (Myers) S.; m. Marilyn F. Gregg, Aug. 28, 1971. BBA, Kent State U., 1966. Dist. sales mgr. Flintkote Co., Kent, Ohio, 1970-72, US Gypson Co., Denver, 1972-75, Ameron Corp., Denver, 1975-79; nat. sales mgr. Blue Bird Internat. Co., Englewood, Colo., 1979-81; sales mgr. Smith & Wesson, Golden, Colo., 1981-85; pres. The West & Assocs., Inc., Golden, 1985—. Served with Ohio N.G., 1963-67. Jeffco Posse Club. Republican. Congregationalist. Office: The West and Assocs Inc 4895 Easley Rd Golden CO 80403-1600

SPRINGER, JEFFREY ALAN, lawyer; b. Denver, Feb. 26, 1950; s. Stanley and Sylvia (Miner) S.; children: Cydney Erin, Samantha Libby. AB, Princeton U., 1972; JD, U. Colo., 1975. Bar: Colo. 1975, U.S. Dist. Ct. Colo. 1975, U.S. Ct. Appeals (10th cir.) 1975, U.S. Supreme Ct. 1978, U.S. Ct. Appeals (8th cir.) 1986. Assoc. Gerash & Springer, Denver, 1975-79; sole practice Denver, 1979-81; pres. Springer and Steinberg, P.C., Denver, 1981—; mem. com. on mcpl. ct. rules Supreme Ct. Colo., 1985-86; mem. standing criminal justice act com. U.S. Dist. Ct., 1994—. Mem. ABA, Assn. Trial Lawyers Am., Colo. Trial Lawyers Assn. (bd. dirs. 1988-90), Colo. Criminal Def. Bar (bd. dirs. 1985-86, 87-88, pres. 1988-89). Office: 1600 Broadway Ste 1500 Denver CO 80202-4915

SPRINGER, SALLY PEARL, university administrator; b. Bklyn., Mar. 19, 1947; d. Nathaniel Margulies and Fanny (Schoen) S.; m. Hakon Hope; children: Erik Jacob Hope, Mollie Liv Hope. BS, Bklyn. Coll., 1967; PhD, Stanford U., 1971. Postdoctoral fellow Stanford U. Med. Sch., Calif., 1971-73; asst. prof. SUNY-Stony Brook, 1973-78, assoc. provost, 1981-85, assoc. prof., 1978-87; exec. asst. to chancellor U. Calif., Davis, 1987-92, asst. chancellor, 1992—. Author (with others): Left Brain, Right Brain, 1981 (Am. Psychol. Found. Disting. Contbr. award 1981), 4th rev. edit., 1993, How to Succeed in College, 1982; contbr. articles to profl. jours. Mem. Internat. Neuropsychol. Soc., Psychonomic Soc. Office: U Calif Office Chancellor Davis CA 95616

SPRINGMEYER, DON, lawyer; b. Miami, Fla., Apr. 11, 1954; s. Archie Eugene Evans and Sally (Springmeyer) Zanjani; m. Pati Parnell Acres, May 31, 1982; children: Parnell Alexander, Wilhelmina Mariah, Shila Susannah. BA cum laude, Yale U., 1976; JD cum laude, U. Wis., 1979. Bar: Nev. 1980, U.S. Dist. Ct. Nev. 1980, U.S. Dist. Ct. (no. dist.) Calif. 1983, U.S. Ct. Appeals (9th cir.) 1983, U.S. Dist. Ct. (cen. dist.) Calif. 1984. Law clk. to sr. judge U.S. Dist. Ct. Nev., Reno, 1980-81; assoc. Lionel, Sawyer & Collins, Reno, 1981, Law Offices Eugene J. Wait Jr., P.C., Reno, 1983-88, Gordon & Silver, Ltd., Reno, 1988-91; pvt. practice Don Springmeyer Ltd., Reno, 1991-94, Springmeyer & Waller, Reno, 1994-95; prifn. Springmeyer Law Frim, Reno and Minder, Nev., 1995—; bd. dirs. Council on Econ. Priorities, N.Y.C., 1984-87. Candidate Springmeyer for Congress Com., Reno, 1981-82; mem. cen. com. Douglas County, Nev., 1981-82, Washoe County, Nev., 1983-85; bd. dirs. Citizen Alert, Reno, 1983-86. Mem. ABA, Washoe County Bar Assn., Assn. Trial Lawyers Am. (bd. govs. 1995—), Nev. Trial Lawyers Assn. (bd. govs. 1993—, treas. 1994—), ACLU (mem. Nev. state bd. 1988-89). Democrat. Office: Springmeyer & Waller 6490 S McCarran Blvd #28 PO Box 21330 Reno NV 89515 also: Box 280 1704 County Rd Ste E Minder NV 89423

SPROUL, JOHN ALLAN, retired public utility executive; b. Oakland, Calif., Mar. 28, 1924; s. Robert Gordon and Ida Amelia (Wittschen) S.; m. Marjorie Ann Hauck, June 20, 1945; children: John Allan, Malcolm J., Richard O., Catherine E. A.B., U. Calif., Berkeley, 1947, LL.B., 1949. Bar: Calif. 1950. Atty. Pacific Gas & Electric Co., San Francisco, 1949-52, 56-62, sr. atty., 1962-70, asst. gen. counsel, 1970-71, v.p. gas supply, 1971-76, sr. v.p., 1976-77, exec. v.p., 1977-89, cons., 1989—; gen. counsel Pacific Gas Transmission Co., 1970-73, v.p., 1973-79, chmn. bd., 1979-89, also bd. dirs.; atty. Johnson & Stanton, San Francisco, 1952-56; bd. dirs. Oreg. Steel Mills, Inc. Bd. dirs. Hastings Coll. of Law. Served to 1st lt. USAAF, 1943-46. Mem. Calif. Bar Assn. (inactive), Pacific Coast Gas Assn., World Trade Club, Pacific-Union Club, Orinda Country Club. Home: 8413 Buckingham Dr El Cerrito CA 94530-2531 Office: Mail Code H17F PO Box 770000 123 Mission St San Francisco CA 94177

SPRUNG, JOHN LEON, film company engineer, cinematographer, auctioneer; b. Chgo., Feb. 26, 1948; s. John George and Loa Ruth (Kemmeter) S. BA in Math., UCLA, 1970, MA in Math., 1971. Lic. auctioneer, Calif. Pvt. practice cinematography, 1974-85; ancillary market post supr. Tri-Star Pictures, Century City, Calif., 1985-86; mgr. engring. Viacom Prodns., Universal City, Calif., 1986—. Inventor News helicopter GPS on-air map. Mem. IEEE (assoc.), Assn. Computing Machinery, Am. Cinema Editors (affiliate), Soc. Motion Picture and TV Engrs. (digital image architecture task force 1992-93), Tech. Coun. Motion Picture/TV Industry (project team leader 1994—), Elysium Inst. Home: 2155 W Paseo Del Mar San Pedro CA 90732-4556

SPUDE, ROBERT LESTER, historian; b. Nampa, Idaho, May 23, 1950; s. Lester E. Simpkins; adopted s. Walter C. and Shirley M. (Powers) S.; m. Katherine M. Birket, June 1971 (div. Apr. 1979); 1 child, Shayne Marie; m. Margaret L. Jensen, Apr. 1981 (div. Feb. 1988); m. Catherine Holder, June 12, 1991; 1 child, Kinsey Anne. AA, Glendale Coll., 1970; BA, Ariz. State U., 1974, MA, 1976; PhD, U. Ill., 1989. Photograph archivist Ariz. Hist. Found., Tempe, 1973-76; teaching asst. U. Ill., Champaign, 1976-78; park historian Nat. Park Svc., Skagway, Alaska, 1978-80; historian Nat. Park Svc., Anchorage, 1980-84, regional historian, 1984-88; chief nat. preservation programs Nat. Park Svc., Denver, 1988-94, dep. chief ecosys. office, 1994-95; external cultural programs chief Santa Fe office Nat. Park Svc., 1995—. Contbr. articles to profl. jours. Recipient LeRoy Hafen award Colo. Hist. Soc., 1993. Mem. Western History Assn., Mining History Assn. (sec. 1990—). Office: Nat Park Svc 12795 W Alameda Pky Lakewood CO 80228-2838

SPURLOCK, CYNTHIA MARIE, government official; b. Phoenix, Apr. 27, 1953; d. Charles Elmer and Edith Marie (Duell) S.; m. Michael C. Schouten. BS in Bus., Ariz. State U., 1977, MBA, 1981. Field examiner NLRB, Phoenix, 1976-88, compliance officer, 1988—. Mem. Ariz. Indsl. Rels. Assn., Soroptomists (officer Phoenix 1990—), East Valley Harley Owners Group (HOG) Assn. Republican. Mem. Community Ch. Office: NLRB 234 N Central Ave Ste 440 Phoenix AZ 85004-2212

SQUARCY, CHARLOTTE VAN HORNE, lawyer; b. Chgo., June 8, 1947; d. Charles Marion and Ruth (Van Horne) S. BA, Smith Coll., 1969; JD, Ind. U., 1977. Bar: Ind. 1977, U.S. Tax Ct. 1977, Mich. 1978, U.S. Supreme Ct. 1980, D.C. 1980, Conn. 1983, Calif. 1986. Law clk. to presiding judge Ind. State Ct., Hammond, 1976-77; dep. atty. gen. State of Ind., 1977-78; mem. legal staff Gen. Motors Corp., Detroit, 1978-81; assoc. counsel Olin Corp., Norwalk, Conn., 1981-85; sr. assoc. Bishop, Barry, Howe & Reid, San Francisco, 1985-87, Carroll, Burdick & McDonough, San Francisco, 1987-90; ptnr. C Van Horne Squarcy & Assocs., San Francisco, 1991—; judge protem Morin County/Superior Ct.; judge pro tem Marin County Supreme Ct. Exec. bd. dirs. U.S.O., No. Calif. Mem. ABA (del. jud. adminstrn. divsn. to ABA competitions com. 1983-87, vice chair cop. counsel com. TIPS 1991-94, judge nat. finals NAAC and client counseling competitions 1983-87), Ind. Bar Assn., Mich. Bar Assn., D.C. Bar Assn., Calif. Bar Assn., San Francisco Bar Assn., Corp. Bar, Knoll Recreation Assn. (v.p. 1990-93), Italian-Am. Bar Assn. San Francisco (v.p. 1993-94), Peacock Gap Golf and Country Club (v.p. 1993-94), Phi Alpha Delta. Methodist. Office: 51 Sulgrave Ln San Rafael CA 94901

SQUILLACE, ALEXANDER PAUL, investment advisor; b. Missoula, Mont., Feb. 25, 1945; s. Dominick Paul and Kathleen Marie S.; m. Miriam Palmer Patterson, June 17, 1967; children: Sandra, Scott, Brian, Susan. BSBA, Ohio State U., 1967. CFA. Investment analyst Nationwide Ins. Cos., Columbus, Ohio, 1967-69; instl. bond rep. Hornblower & Weeks-Hemphill, Noyes, Columbus, 1969-71, mgr. fixed income securities, Indpls., 1971-74; v.p. United Nat. Bank-United Nat. Corp., Sioux Falls, S.D., 1974-79; pres. Investment Mgmt. Group, Sioux Falls, S.D., 1979-85, Farmers State Bank, Stickney, S.D., 1979-88, Bormann Ins. Agy., Stickney, 1979-88, Fin. Svcs. Group Inc., 1984—; chmn. S.D. Investment Coun., Postal Bus. Group Inc., 1986—; bd. dirs. Prairie States Ins. Co., Lemars Mutual Ins. Co., Western Warehouse, Inc., First State Bank, Newcastle, Wyo., Human Resources Devel. Corp., Park County Econ. Devel. Corp.; instr. Am. Inst. Banking. Named hon. citizen of Indpls., 1974. Fellow Fin. Analysts Fedn.; mem. Am. Inst. Banking, S.D. Bankers Assn., S.D. Investment Soc., Twin Cities Soc. Security Analysts, Ohio State Alumni Assn. Home and Office: PO Box 981 Livingston MT 59047-0981

SQUIRES, KATHERINE LANDEY, lawyer; b. N.Y.C., Mar. 28, 1959. BA, Clark U., 1980; JD, U. Dayton, 1982; LLM in Tax, Georgetown U., 1983; MDiv, Biola U., 1994. Bar: D.C. 1983, Calif. 1986. Assoc. Kutak, Rock & Campbell, Washington, 1983-85; pres., chief exec. officer Plan Care, Inc., Irvine, Calif., 1985-88; ptnr. Polack & Landey, Irvine, 1985-86, Finley, Kumble, Wagner et.al., Newport Beach, Calif., 1986-88, Sheppard, Mullin, Richter & Hampton, Newport Beach, 1988-89; prin. Law Office of Katherine L. Squires, Irvine, Calif., 1989-92; pres. LawPrep, Inc., LawPrep Press, Inc., 1989—. Contbr. articles on taxation and comml. law to profl. jours. Rep. candidate for U.S. Senate, 1993-94; commr. Workers' Compensation Appeals Bd., 1994—. Mem. ABA (chmn. internat. law com. of gen. practice sect., 1986—), Orange County Bar Assn., Nat. Assn. Women Lawyers (chmn. bankruptcy com., 1983—), Nat. Assn. Women Execs., Newport Beach (Calif.) C. of C. Republican. Club: Dolphins.

SQUIRES, RICHARD LANE, paleontologist, educator; b. Mexico, Mo., Nov. 19, 1944; s. Carl Standefer and Dorothy (Lane) S.; m. Janet Lee Diskin, Dec. 18, 1976; children: Katherine Marie, Caroline Elizabeth. BS, U. N.Mex., 1966, MS, 1968; PhD, Calif. Inst. Tech., 1973. Postdoctoral assoc. Jet Propulsion Lab., Pasadena, Calif., 1973-74; asst. prof. dept. geol. scis. Calif. State U., Northridge, 1974-78, assoc. prof., 1978-82, prof., 1982—; rsch. assoc. Natural History Mus. Los Angeles County, 1977—. Editor several guidebooks; author monographs and jour. articles. Libr. vol. Emblem Elem. Sch., Santa Clarita, Calif., 1985—. Mem. Paleontological Rsch. Soc., Paleontological Rsch. Instn., Soc. Econ. Paleontologists and Mineralogists, We. Soc. Malacologists, Conchologists of Am., Conchological Club So. Calif. (pres. 1990), Sigma Xi. Democrat. Home: 26800 Espuma Dr Saugus CA 91350-2324 Office: Calif State U Dept Geol Scis 18111 Nordhoff St Northridge CA 91330-0001

SRIDHARAN, NATESA SASTRI, software scientist; b. Madras, India, Oct. 2, 1946; came to U.S., 1967; s. Subrahmanyam N. and Saraswathi; m. Deirdre Higgins, Sept. 4, 1970 (div.); 1 child, Radhika Lily; m. Sheila Foster, Dec. 29, 1988. BTech in Elec. Engring., Indian Inst. Tech., Madras, 1967; MS, SUNY, Stony Brook, 1969, PhD in Computer Sci., 1971. Rsch. assoc. Stanford (Calif.) U., 1971-74; vis. Humboldt scholar Tech. Universitat, Munich, Germany, 1974; assoc. prof. computer sci. Rutgers U., New Brunswick, N.J., 1974-84; div. scientist BBN Labs., Cambridge, Mass., 1984-86; mgr. artificial intelligence FMC Corp., San Jose, Calif., 1986-91; prin. software scientist Intel Corp., Chandler, Ariz., 1991—; sci. advisor French Telecomm. Industry, Lannion, 1982-86. Founding editor book series Rsch. Notes in Artificial Intelligence, 1982; mem. editl. bd. Artificial Intelligence, Machine Intelligence, Jour. Assn. for Computing Machinery, Jour. Intelligent Sys. Mem. Phoenix Environ. Quality Commn., 1992—; bd. dirs. The Phoenix Ctr., 1994. Recipient Siemens medal Indian Inst. Tech., 1967; grantee NSF, NIH, DARPA, others. Mem. IEEE, Assn. for Computing Machinery, Am. Assn. for Artificial Intelligence. Office: Intel Corp MS-C2-23 5000 W Chandler Blvd Chandler AZ 85226-3601

SRINIVASAN, VENKATARAMAN, marketing and management educator; b. Pudukkottai, Tamil Nadu, India, June 5, 1944; came to U.S., 1968; s. Annaswamy and Jambagalakshmi Venkataraman; m. Sitalakshmi Subrahmanyam, June 30, 1972; children: Ramesh, Mahesh. B Tech., Indian Inst. Tech., Madras, India, 1966; MS, Carnegie-Mellon U., 1970, PhD, 1971. Asst. engr. Larsen & Toubro, Bombay, 1966-68; asst. prof. mgmt. and mktg. U. Rochester, N.Y., 1971-73, assoc. prof., 1973-74; assoc. prof. Stanford (Calif.) U., 1974-76, prof., 1976-82, dir. PhD program in bus., 1982-85, Ernest C. Arbuckle prof. mktg. and mgmt. sci., 1982—; mktg. area coord., 1976-78, 88-93; cons. in field. Mem. editorial bd. Jour. Mktg. Rsch., 1988—, Mktg. Sci., 1980—, Mgmt. Sci., 1974-91; contbr. articles to profl. jours. Mem. Am. Mktg. Assn., Inst. Ops. Rsch./Mgmt. Scis. Hindu.

STAAB, JOSEPH RAYMOND, retired federal agency administrator; b. Hays, Kans., Jan. 2, 1932; s. Joseph Leo and Esther Isea (Eaton) S.; m. Joan Annette Schumacher, Nov. 25, 1961; children: Gregory Joseph, William Eric. BSBA, Fort Hays State U., 1958; postgrad., Kans. State U., 1959. Various auditing positions, 1959-67; acct. exec. Dean Witter & Co. Inc., San Marino, Pasadena, Calif., 1967-69; fin. advisor, planner Powell, Johnson & Assocs. Inc., Pasadena, 1969-70; sr. fin. analyst Standard and Poor's Corp., L.A., 1970-71; ind. fin. mgmt. cons. L.A., 1971-74; chief mgmt. systems divsn. FAA N.W. Region, Seattle, 1974-76; dir. ctr. for small bus. Urbana (Ohio) Coll., 1976-77; chief mgmt. info. br. FAA, Washington, 1977-80; mgr. tech. and adminstrv. support staff FAA Transport Airplane Directorate, Seattle, 1980-93; retired, 1993; pres. coop. edn. adv. com., bus. edn. adv. bd. Green River C.C., Auburn, Wash., 1991-94, vice chair gen. coun. adv. com.; freelance fin. mgmt. cons., Federal Way, Wash., 1992—. With USN, 1952-56. Mem. Fraternal Order of Eagles, Sigma Tau Gamma (treas. 1957-58). Republican. Roman Catholic. Home: 3703 SW 319th St Federal Way WA 98023-2154

STACEY, PAMELA, editor, writer; b. Salt Lake City; Mar. 29, 1945; d. Jack Nordvall Freeze and Peggy (Whelan) Sherman; m. Richard C. Murphy, Feb. 22, 1981; stepchildren—Greg, Jeanne. B.A. in English, UCLA, 1968, teaching credential, 1970; M.A. in English, Calif. State U.-Long Beach, 1985. Researcher, Drew Pearson-Journalist, Washington, 1964, 66; adminstr. UNESCO, Paris, 1968-69; Rand Corp., Santa Monica, Calif., 1972-76; editor, writer Cousteau Soc., Los Angeles, 1976—. Author, project dir. (children's book series) To Fly in Freedom, Secret Societies of Dolphins and Whales; editor, creator (mag. for children) Dolphin Log for Cousteau Soc., 1981. Avocations: scuba diving. Office: Cousteau Soc 1933 Cliff Dr Ste 4 Santa Barbara CA 93109-1587

STACK, GEOFFREY LAWRENCE, real estate developer; b. Trinidad, British West Indies, Sept. 16, 1943; s. Gerald Francis and V. Louise (Bell) S.; m. Victoria Hammack, 1970 (div. 1986); 1 child, Kathryn; m. Nancy J. Haarer, Apr. 19, 1987; children: Alexandra, Natalie. BA, Georgetown U., 1965; MBA, U. Pa., 1972. Dir. acquisitions J.H. Snyder Co., L.A., 1972-75; from project mgr. to exec. v.p. Richards West, Newport Beach, Calif., 1975-77; pres. Regis Homes Corp., Newport Beach, 1977-93; mng. dir. Sares-Regis Group, Irvine, Calif., 1993—; bd. dirs. WJS, Inc., Newport Beach, 1988—, Arral & Ptnrs., Hong Kong, 1981—, Calif. Housing Coun., Sacramento, 1986—. Mem. adv. bd. Coro So. Calif., Santa Ana, 1991—; bd. regents Franciscan Sch. of Theology, Berkeley, Calif., 1991—; bd. advisors Grad. Sch. Bus., U. Calif., Irvine, 1992. Capt. USMC, 1967-70. Decorated 2 Bronze Stars, 21 Air medals, Navy Commendation medal, Purple Heart. Mem. Young Pres. Orgn., Big Canyon Country Club, Pacific Club, Ctr. Club. Democrat. Roman Catholic. Office: Sares Regis Group 18802 Bardeen Ave Irvine CA 92715-1521

STACKELBERG, JOHN RODERICK, history educator; b. Munich, May 8, 1935; came to U.S., 1946; s. Curt Freiherr and Ellen (Biddle) von Stackelberg; m. Steffi Heuss, Oct. 10, 1965 (div. Apr. 1983); m. Sally Winkle, Mar. 30, 1991; children: Katherine Ellen, Nicholas Olaf, Emmet Winkle. AB, Harvard U., 1956; MA, U. Vt., 1972; PhD, U. Mass., 1974. Reading instr. Baldridge Reading Svcs., Greenwich, Conn., 1957-62; lang. tchr. Hartnackschule, Berlin, 1963-67; English and social studies tchr. Lake Region Union High Sch., Orleans, Vt., 1967-70; lectr. history San Diego State U., 1974-76; asst. prof. history U. Oreg., Eugene, 1976-77, U. S.D., Vermillion, 1977-78; asst. prof. history Gonzaga U., Spokane, Wash., 1978-81, assoc. prof. history, 1981-88, prof. history, 1988—. Author: Idealism Debased, 1981; contbr. articles to profl. jours. Pres. Spokane chpt. UN Assn., 1986-90. With U.S. Army, 1958-60. Leadership Devel. fellow Ford Found., 1969-70. Home: 9708 E Maringo Dr Spokane WA 99206-4429 Office: Gonzaga U Spokane WA 99258

STACKHOUSE, CHRISTIAN PAUL, computer company executive; b. Lynnwood, Wash., Mar. 24, 1960; s. Paul Sullivan Stackhouse and Trilby Mary (Schultz) Roman; m. MyPhuong Ngoc Le, Sept. 1, 1984; children: Andre Le, Nina Le. BSEE, U. Wash., 1983; MSEE, U. Ariz., 1987. Cert. engr.-in-tng. Elec. engr. IBM, Tucson, 1983-86; software engr. IBM Palo Alto (Calif.) Scientific Ctr., 1986-88, IBM Knowledge Based Systems Lab., Menlo Park, Calif., 1988-90, LaserAccess Corp., Bothell, Wash., 1990-91; mgr. of product devel. LaserAccess Corp., Bothell, 1991-93; mgr. product devel. Network Imaging Systems Corp., Bothell, 1993—. Mem. Amnesty Internat., Nature Conservancy, Sierra Club. Home: 15510 92nd Pl NE Bothell WA 98011-4556 Office: Network Imaging Systems Corp P O Box 3020 Bothell WA 98041-3020

STACY, BILL WAYNE, college president; b. Bristol, Va., July 26, 1938; s. Charles Frank and Louise Nelson (Altwater) S.; m. Sue Varnon; children: Mark, Sara, James. B.S.Ed., S.E. Mo. State U., 1960; M.S., So. Ill. U., 1965, Ph.D., 1968. Tchr. Malden High Sch., Mo., 1960-64; faculty Southeast Mo. State U., Cape Girardeau, 1967-89, dean Grad. Sch., 1976-79, interim pres., 1979, pres., 1980-89; pres. Calif. State U., San Marcos, 1989—; dir. Boatmen's Nat. Bank. Bd. dirs. San Diego United Way. Mem. Am. Assn. State Colls. and Univs. (dir.), Am. Assn. Higher Edn., PIC Policy Bd., San Diego, Rotary. Presbyterian. *

STADLER, CRAIG ROBERT, professional golfer; b. San Diego, June 2, 1953; s. Donald Edwin and Betty M. (Adams) S.; m. Susan Barrett, Jan. 6, 1979; children: Kevin Craig, Christopher Barrett. Student, U. So. Calif. Profl. golfer Palm Beach Gardens, Fla.; winner Hope Classic, 1980, Greater Greensboro Open, 1980, Kemper Open, 1981-82, Tucson Open, 1982, Masters, 1982, World Series of Golf, 1982, 92, Tour Championship, 1991. U.S. amateur champion, 1973; mem. U.S. Walker Cup team, 1975; leading money winner PGA Tour, 1982. Mem. Golf Mag. (Player of Yr. 1982). *

STADLEY, PAT ANNA MAY GOUGH (MRS. JAMES M. STADLEY), author; b. El Paso, Tex., Aug. 31, 1918; d. Thomas and Leona (Plitt) Gough; A.A., Chaffey Jr. Coll., 1936; m. James M. Stadley, Aug. 15, 1936; children—William T., Jerry M. Author books, anthologies, short stories published in over 15 fgn. langs., works include: The Black Leather Barbarians, 1960; Autumn of a Hunter (Edgar Allen Poe spl. award 1970, produced as The Deadly Hunt TV Friday Night Movie Week 1971), 1970; The Deadly Hunt; 1977; The Murder Hunt, 1977; also numerous short stories including The Doe and The Gantlet, 1957, The Waiting Game, 1961, Kurdistan Payload, 1962, Something for the Club, 1963, The Big Measure, 1976, The Tender Trap, 1977, The Stranger, 1980. Democrat. Mem. Christian Ch. Clubs: Calif. Writers (v.p. 1967) (Citrus Heights), Calif. Writers (v.p. 1967—), Mystery Writers Am. Home: 15079 Pinon Rd Magalia CA 95954-9124

STADTMAN, VERNE AUGUST, former foundation executive, editor; b. Carrizoso, N.Mex., Dec. 5, 1926; s. Walter William and Minnie Ethel (Reece) S.; m. Jackolyn Carol Byl, Aug. 26, 1949; children: Kristen Karen, Rand Theodore, Judith Dayna, Todd Alan. A.B., Calif.-Berkeley, 1950. AUS, 1945-47; mng. editor Calif. Monthly, Calif. Alumni Assn., Berkeley, 1950-64; centennial editor U. Calif., Berkeley, 1964-69; assoc. dir., editor Carnegie Commn. on Higher Edn., Berkeley, 1969-73, Carnegie Council on Policy Studies in Higher Edn. Berkeley, 1973-80; v.p. gen. services Carnegie Found. for Advancement Teaching, Princeton, N.J., 1980-89; trustee Editorial Projects Edn., Inc., 1957-91, pres., 1962-63, chmn. bd., 1980-86; guest scholar Hiroshima U., Japan, 1978. Author: California Campus, 1960, University of California, 1868-1968, 1970, Academic Adaptations, 1980; editor: (with David Riesman) Academic Transformation: Seventeen Institutions Under Pressure, 1973 (Book of Yr. award Am. Council Edn.); compiler-editor: Centennial Record of the University of California, 1967. Served with AUS, 1945-47. Recipient Alumnus Service award Calif. Alumni Assn., 1970. Mem. Am. Alumni Council (pres. 1963-64), Edn. Writers Assn., Friends Bancroft Library. Home: 182 St James Dr Sonoma CA 95476-8336

STAEBLER, DAVID LLOYD, materials scientist; b. Ann Arbor, Mich., Apr. 25, 1940; s. Lloyd Albert and Mary Elizabeth S.; m. Betty Jean Craig, Dec. 23, 1961; children: Laurie Elizabeth, Lisa Ann. BSEE, Pa. State U., 1962, MSEE, 1963; MAEE, Princeton U., 1966, PhD, 1970. Tech. staff RCA Labs., Princeton, N.J., 1963-81; head kinescope systems rsch. RCA/Sarnoff Labs., Princeton, N.J., 1981-89; mgr. electron gun lab Thomason Consumer Electronics, Genlis, France, 1989-92; mgr. materials sci. Nat. Renewable Energy Lab., Golden, Colo., 1992—; mem. operating bd. Colo. Advanced Materials Inst., Golden, 1993—; vis. prof. U. Sao Paulo, Sao Carlos, Brazil, 1974-75; vis. staff RCA Labs., Inc., Zurich, Switzerland, 1979-80. Contbr. articles to profl. jours.; patentee in field. Mem. IEEE, Materials Rsch. Soc., Soc. Info. Display. Home: 4387 Witter Gulch Rd Evergreen CO 80439-4514 Office: Nat Renewable Energy Lab 1617 Cole Blvd Golden CO 80401

STAEHELIN, LUCAS ANDREW, cell biology educator; b. Sydney, Australia, Feb. 10, 1939; came to U.S., 1969; s. Lucas Eduard and Isobel (Malloch) S.; m. Margrit Weibel, Sept. 17, 1965; children: Daniel Thomas, Philip Roland, Marcel Felix. Dipl. Natw., Swiss Fed. Inst. Tech., Zurich, 1963, Ph.D. in Biology, 1966. Research scientist N.Z. Dept. Sci. and Indsl. Research, 1966-69; research fellow in cell biology Harvard U., Cambridge, Mass., 1969-70; asst. prof. cell biology U. Colo., Boulder, 1970-73, assoc. prof., 1973-79, prof., 1979—; vis. prof. U. Freiburg, 1978, Swiss Fed. Inst. Tech., 1984, 92; mem. cellular biology and physiology study sect. NIH, Bethesda, Md., 1980-84; mem. DOE panel on rsch. directions for the energy bioscis., 1988, 92; mem. NSF adv. panel for cellular orgn., 1994—. Editor Jour. Cell Biology, 1977-81, European Jour. Cell Biology, 1981-90, Plant Physiology, 1986-92, Plant Jour., 1991—, (with C.J. Antzen) Ency. Plant Physio., Vol. 19, Photosynthesis III, 1986; contbr. numerous articles to sci. jours. Recipient Humboldt award Humboldt Found., 1978, Sci. Tchr. award U. Colo., 1984, NIH research grants, 1971—. Mem. AAAS, Am. Soc. Cell Biology, Am. Soc. Plant Physiology, German Acad. Natural Scis. Leopoldina. Home: 2855 Dover Dr Boulder CO 80303-5305 Office: U Colo Dept Molecular Cell/Devel Biology Campus Box 347 Boulder CO 80309-0347

STAEHLE, ROBERT L., foundation executive; b. Rochester, N.Y., Apr. 22, 1955; s. Henry Carl and Isabel Montgomery S. BS in Aero. and Astronautic Engring., Purdue U., 1977. Prin. investigator Skylab Expt. ED-31 (bacteria aboard Skylab), NASA/Marshall Space Flight Center, Huntsville, Ala., 1972-74; student trainee engring. Skylab Expt. ED-31 (bacteria aboard Skylab), NASA/Marshall Space Flight Center, 1974-77; sci. observation analyst Caltech/Jet Propulsion Lab., Pasadena, Calif., 1977-78; engr. advanced projects group, 1978-83, mem. tech. staff system integration sect. of Space Sta., 1983-87, mem. tech. staff and space sta., user ops. team leader, 1987-88; tech. mgr. Jet Propulsion Lab., Pasadena, Calif., 1988—, mgr. space sta. Freedom support office Pasadena ops., 1990-92, Pluto team leader, 1992-93, mgr. Pluto Express preproject, 1993—; prin. founder, pres. World Space Found., South Pasadena, Calif., 1979—; founding dir. So. Calif. Space Bus. Roundtable, 1987—. Co-author: Project Solar Sail, New Am. Libr., 1990; contbr. articles to profl. jours. Bd. dirs. Caltech Y, 1987-93. Nat. Space Club Goddard scholar, 1977; Charles A. Lindbergh Fund grantee, 1986. Fellow Brit. Interplanetary Soc.; mem. AIAA, Tau Beta Pi, Sigma Gamma Tau. Office: Jet Propulsion Lab 153 Jaxine Dr Altadena CA 91001

STAFFORD, J. FRANCIS, archbishop; b. Balt., July 26, 1932; s. F. Emmett and Mary Dorothy S. Student, Loyola Coll., Balt., 1950-52; B.A., St. Mary's Sem., Balt., 1954; S.T.B., S.T.L., Gregorian U., Rome, 1958; M.S.W., Catholic U., 1964; postgrad., Rutgers U., 1963, U. Wis.-Madison, 1969, St. Mary's Sem. and Univ., Balt., 1973-75. Spiritual moderator Ladies of Charity Ch., Balt., 1966-76; spiritual moderator Soc. St. Vincent de Paul, Balt., 1965-76; urban vicar Archdiocese of Balt., 1966-76, monsignor, 1970, vicar gen., auxiliary bishop, 1976-83; bishop Diocese of Memphis, 1983-86; archbishop Archdiocese of Denver, 1986—; dir. Assn. Cath. Charities, Balt., 1966-76; archdiocesan liaison to Md. Cath. Conf., Balt, 1975-78; Oriental Orthodox/Roman Cath. consultation Nat. Cath. Conf. Bishops, 1977-85, com. on doctrine, 1978-82, chmn. ecumenical and interreligious affairs com., 1987-90; co-chmn. bilateral dialogue Roman Cath./World Meth. Council, 1977-86; co-chmn. U.S. Roman Cath.-Luth. Dialogue, 1986—; chmn. Bishops' com. marriage and family life U.S. Cath. Conf., 1978-84; mem. gen. Synod Bishops, Vatican City, 1980. Contbr. articles to profl. jours. Trustee Good Samaritan Hosp., Balt., 1973-77, Cath. U. Am., 1990—, Blue Cross of Md., Inc., 1973-76, Balt. Urban Coalition, 1970-75; trustee, chmn., St. Thomas Theol. Sem., 1987—; bd. dirs. Sch. Social Work and Planning, U. Md., 1973-76. Recipient Father Kelly Alumni award Loyola High Sch., 1978; Alumni Laureate, Loyola Coll., 1979. Mem. World Meth. Conf. Roman Cath. Dialogue (co-chmn. 1977-86), Oriental Orthodox Roman Cath. Consultation (co-chmn. 1977-85), Nat. Conf. Cath. Bishops, Luth. Roman Cath. Dialogue, Congregation for Doctrine of Faith. Office: 200 Josephine St Denver CO 80206-4710*

STAFFORD, PATRICK PURCELL, poet, writer, management consultant; b. L.A., Mar. 13, 1954; s. Elsan H. Stafford and Ann (Ruelle) Lane; m. Liane Beale Stafford, Jan. 2, 1987; 1 child, David. Student, U.S. Armed Forces Inst., 1971, UCLA, 1980, 81. Head script writer Hollywood (Calif.) Radio Network, 1981-82; mgr. new bus. Harry Koff Agy., Encino, Calif., 1984-85; pres., mgr. Legal Experts, L.A., 1988-94, Creative Adminstrs., L.A., 1994—; office adminstr. Moneymaker & Kelley, L.A., 1989-90; sales rep. Now Messenger Svc., L.A., 1993—; staff mgr. Stafford Resume Svc., L.A., 1990—. Contbr. poems, articles, short stories to profl. publs. Mem. Big Bros. of Greater L.A., 1991. With USMC, 1971-78, Vietnam. Recipient Concept/Essay award L.A. Rtd., 1990, Poetry Contest award Tradition Mag., 1991, Hon. Mention award Iliad Press, 1992, Wash. State Coll., 1990, Winner in Play-Reading Series, Altered Stage Theatre Co., 1991. Mem. The Writer's Exch. (life), Marino's of Beverly Hills (charter), Highlander Club. Conservative. Home and Office: PO Box 826 Grants Pass OR 97526-0070

STAGER, DONALD K., construction company executive. Chmn., CEO, Dillingham Constrn. Corp., Pleasanton, Calif. Office: Dillingham Constrn Corp 5960 Inglewood Dr Pleasanton CA 94588-8535

STAHELI, LYNN TAYLOR, pediatric orthopedist, educator; b. Provo, Utah, Nov. 13, 1933; s. Harvey Roulin and Letha (Taylor) S.; m. Ann Lee Smith, June 4, 1957 (div. 1976); children: Linda Ann, Diane Kay, Todd Kent; m. Lana Ribble, June 11, 1977. BS, Brigham Young U., 1956; MD, U. Utah, 1959. Intern U. Utah, Salt Lake City, 1960; resident in orthopedic surgery U. Wash., 1964-68; dir. rsch. and edn. Children's Hosp., Seattle, 1968-77, dir. dept. orthopedics, 1977-92; prof. dept. orthopedics U. Wash., Seattle, 1968—; mem. med. exec. com. Children's Hosp. and Med. Ctr., Seattle, 1977-92; cons. Fircrest Sch., Seattle, 1968-80, Boyer Children's clinic, Seattle, 1968-80, Seattle Pub. Schs. Spl. Edn. Program, 1968-80; invited speaker for more than 1000 individual presentations in 30 countries, 1960—; founder Duncan Seminar for Cerebral Palsy, 1980. Editor: Jour. Pediatric Orthopedics, 1981—; author: Med. Writing and Speaking, 1986, Fundamentals of Pediatric Orthopedics, 1992; contbr. articles to numerous profl. jours. Founding mem. bd. N.W. Inst. Ethics and Life Scis., Seattle, 1974—; bd. dirs. Rainier Found., Seattle, 1988—; founder Internat. Scholarship for Pediatric Orthopedics, Seattle, 1988-93. Capt. USAF, 1960-63. Mem. Pediatric Orthopedic Soc. N.Am., Am. Acad. Orthopedic Surgeons (pediatric orthopedics com. 1980-86), Am. Acad. Pediatrics (chmn. com. on shoewear 1985—), Am. Acad. Cerebral Palsy and Devel. Medicine (chmn. instrnl. course com. 1982—), Alpha Omega Alpha. Home: 4116 48th Ave NE Seattle WA 98105-5116 Office: Childrens Hosp Dept Orthopedics 4800 Sand Point Way NE Seattle WA 98105-3901

STAHL, GREGORY PHILIP, geologist; b. San Diego, Dec. 17, 1956; s. Philip Wilfred and Dorothy Lucille (Sturdevant) S.; m. Tracy Lynn Suiter, May 5, 1984; children: Eric Gregory, Chelsea Renee, Austin Philip. Student, U. Calif., San Diego, 1975-77; BS in Geology, San Diego State U., 1981; postgrad., Okla. State U., 1990. Registered geologist, Calif. Geophys. technician Rogers Explorations, Inc., Midland, Tex., 1980; wellsite geologist Petrolog, Ventura, Calif., 1981-82; exploration geologist Natura Energy Corp., Midland, 1982-84, Petrom Corp., Midland, 1984-85; sr. geologist Willow Creek Resources, Inc., Midland, 1985-88; prin., geologist Vanguard Primary Resources, Midland, 1988-90; sr. geologist, project mgr. Resna Industries, Inc., Escalon, Calif., 1990-94, tech. dir. scis., 1994-95; ops. mgr. Ground Zero Analysis, Inc., Stockton, Calif., 1995—. Mem. Am. Assn. Petroleum Geologists, Assn. Groundwater Scientists and Engrs., Stanislaus Geol. Soc. (charter mem.). Republican. Lutheran. Home: 1517 Montclair Dr Modesto CA 95350-0560 Office: Ground Zero Analysis, Inc 3422 W Hammer Ln Ste C-294 Stockton CA 95219

STAHL, JACK LELAND, real estate company executive; b. Lincoln, Ill., June 28, 1934; s. Edwin R. and Edna M. (Burns) S.; m. Carol Anne Townsend, June 23, 1956; children: Cheryl, Nancy, Kellea. BS in Edn., U. N.Mex., 1957. Tchr. Albuquerque Public Schs., 1956-59; pres. House Finders, Inc., Albuquerque, 1959-65; v.p. N.Mex. Savs. & Loan Assn., Albuquerque, 1965-67; chmn. bd. Hooten-Stahl, Inc., Albuquerque, 1967-77; mem. N.Mex. Ho. of Reps., 1969-70; pres. The Jack Stahl Co., Albuquerque, 1977—; mem. N.Mex. Senate, 1981-86; lt. gov. State of N.Mex., 1987-90. Mem. N.Mex. Ho. of Reps., 1969-70; mem. exec. bd. Gt. SW coun. Boy Scouts Am., 1982-89; bd. dirs. Better Bus. Bur. N.Mex., 1968-82, pres., 1975-76; trustee Univ. Heights Hosp., 1980-85; vice chmn. N.Mex. Bd. Fin., 1987-90, N.Mex. Community Devel. Coun., 1987-90. Named Realtor of Yr., Albuquerque Bd. Realtors, 1972. Mem. Nat. Assn. Realtors, Nat. Homebuilders Assn., N.Mex. Amigos, 20-30 Club (pres. 1963-64), Rotary. Republican. Methodist. Office: 1911 Wyoming Blvd NE Albuquerque NM 87112-2865

STAHL, RICHARD G. C., journalist, editor; b. Chgo., Feb. 22, 1934; m. Gladys C. Weisbecker; 1 child, Laura Ann. Student, Northwestern U., U. Ill., Chgo. Editor Railway Purchases and Stores Mag., Chgo., 1960-63; editor pub. rels. dept. Sears Roebuck & Co., Chgo., 1963-68; dir pub. rels. dept. St. Joseph's Hosp. Med. Ctr., Phoenix, 1968-72; v.p. pub. rels. Consultation Svcs., Inc., Phoenix, 1972-73; creative dir. Don Jackson and Assoc., Phoenix, 1973; editor, pub. rels. mgr. Maricopa County Med. Soc., Phoenix, 1974-76; mng. editor Ariz. Hwys. mag., Phoenix, 1977—. Regional editor: (travel guides) Budget Travel, 1985, USA, 1986, Arizona, 1986; free-lance writer and editor. Mem. Soc. Profl. Journalists. Office: Ariz Hwys Mag 2039 W Lewis Ave Phoenix AZ 85009-2819

STAHLKE, RICHARD DAVID, human services administrator; b. Waconia, Minn., Dec. 16, 1939; s. Ernst Henry and Clara Ida (Schneider) S.; m. Shirley Mae Anderson, Aug. 22, 1962; children: James Andrew, Karen Andrea. AA, Concordia Jr. Coll., St. Paul, 1959; student, Concordia Sr. Coll., Ft. Wayne, Ind., 1959-60; BA, Augsburg Coll., 1962; MSW, Fla. State U., 1965. Case worker Todd County Welfare Dept., Long Prairie, Minn., 1962-63; social worker Luth. Social Svc. Kans., Wichita, 1965-70; exec. dir. Luth. Social Ministry Ariz., Phoenix, 1970-78; pres. Luth. Social Svcs. No. Calif., San Francisco, 1978—; peer reviewer Coun. on Accreditation, N.Y.C., 1980—; social svc. cons. Evang. Luth. Ch. Am., Chgo., 1986—. Contbr. articles to profl. jours. Mem. Gov.'s Earthquake Preparedness Task Force, Calif., 1982-88; chair disaster preparedness No. Calif. Ecumenical Coun., Calif., 1982-84. Mem. NASW (Calif. Social Worker of Yr. 1992, pres. Calif. chpt. 1984-86), Coalition of Exec. Luth. Agys. (dir. com. 1980—). Lutheran. Office: Luth Social Svcs No Calif 1101 Ofarrell St San Francisco CA 94109-6601

STALEY, JOHN FREDRIC, lawyer; b. Sidney, Ohio, Sept. 26, 1943; s. Harry Virgil and Fredericka May (McMillin) S.; m. Sue Ann Bolin, June 11, 1966; children—Ian McMillin, Erik Bolin. A.B. in History, Fresno State Coll., 1965; postgrad. in pub. adminstrn. Calif. State U.-Hayward, 1967-68; J.D., U. Calif. 1972. Bar: Calif. 1972. Ptnr. Staley, Jobson & Wetherell, Pleasanton, Calif., 1972—; lectr. Hastings Coll. Law, 1973-74; founding mem., Bank of Livermore; bd. dirs. Xscribe Corp. (NASOAQ XSCR)' del. U.S.-China Joint Conf. on Law, Beijing, 1987. Mem. Livermore City Coun., 1975-82, vice mayor, 1978-82; bd. dirs. Alameda County Tng. and Employment Bd., Alameda-Contra Costa Emergency Med. Svcs. Agy., Valley Vol. Ctr. With M.I., U.S. Army, 1966-67. Fellow Am. Acad. Matrimonial Lawyers; mem. ABA, Calif. State Bar, Alameda Bar Assn., Contra Costa Bar Assn., Amador Valley Bar Assn., Calif. Assn. Cert. Family Law Specialists (pres. 1988-89, Hall of Fame award, 1994), Lawyer Friends of Wine. Office: Staley Jobson & Wetherell 5776 Stoneridge Mall Rd Ste 310 Pleasanton CA 94588-2838

STALEY, MARTHA MCCALPIN, dietitian; b. St. Louis, July 24, 1955; d. F. William and Margaret (Wickes) McCalpin; m. Charles A. Staley, Apr. 6, 1991; children: George, Daniel. BS in nutrition & dietetics, U. Mo., 1977; MBA in mktg., Univ. Wash., 1984. Cert. dietitian. Clinical dietitian Jewish Hosp., St. Louis, 1977-78, Barnes Hosp., St. Louis, 1978-79; columnist Dallas Times Herald, 1980-81; asst. instr. U. Tex. Health Sci. Ctr., Dallas, 1979-81; dietetics mgr. Am. Hosp. Supply Corp., Seattle, 1984-86; mkt. mgr. Baxter Healthcare Corp., McGaw Park, Ill., 1986-87; area sales mgr. Baxter Healthcare Corp., Irvine, Calif., 1987-90, region mgr., 1990-91; regional sales dir. ARA Svcs. Inc., Irvine, Calif., 1991-93; teaching asst. U. Washington, 1984. Speaker to cmty. groups U. Tex. Health Sci. Ctr., Dallas., 1979-81. Mem. Am. Dietetic Assn., U. Wash. Alumni Orgn. (life), U. Mo. Alumni Orgn. Roman Catholic.

STALLEY, ROBERT DELMER, retired mathematics educator; b. Mpls., Oct. 25, 1924; s. Francis Charles and Florence Camille (Goode) S.; m. Dorothy Ann Jeffery, Aug. 27, 1950; children: Mark, Jeffery, John, Lorena. BS, Oreg. State U., 1946, MA, 1948; PhD, U. Oreg., 1953. Instr. U. Ariz., Tucson, 1949-51, Fresno (Calif.) State U., 1955-56; instr. Iowa State U., Ames, 1953-54, asst. prof., 1954-55; mathematician Sperry Rand, St. Paul, 1955; mathematician U.S. Naval Ordnance Test Sta., China Lake, Calif., 1956, cons., 1956-60; asst. prof., assoc. prof. math. Oreg. State U., Corvallis, 1956-66, prof., 1966-89, prof. emeritus, 1989—; jour. referee, reviewer; speaker, cons. in field, mem. various sci. panels; dir. Summer Insts. in Math., NSF, 1965-67. Contbr. articles to math. jours. Rsch. grantee NSF, 1967-71. Mem. Am. Math. Soc., Sierra Club, Sigma Xi, Pi Kappa Phi. Home: 1405 NW Forest Dr Corvallis OR 97330-1705 Office: Oreg State U Dept Math Corvallis OR 97331

STALLING, CHARLESETTA, educational consultant, trainer; b. San Diego, June 22, 1944; d. Luther Cecil Stalling and Ruth (Jackson) Howard; m. Gary A. Simpkins, 1969 (div. 1988); children: Gary Simpkins, Ronald Simpkins. AA in English, L.A. City Coll., 1965; BA in Lang. Arts, Calif. State U., L.A., 1969; MEd in Edn., Reading, Harvard U., 1972; EdD in Human Svcs. and Applied Behavioral Sci., U. Mass., 1977. Cert. K-8, Calif., instr., supr. C.C., chief adminstrv. officer. Tchr. Head Start, L.A., 1964-68, Bd. Edn., L.A., 1968-70; dir. therapeutic daycare James Jackson Putnam Children's Ctr., Roxbury, Mass., 1960-71; reading specialist Ed. Co. Reading and Learning Ctr., Cambridge, Mass., 1971-72; dir. Right to Read Bridge Fund, Inc., Boston, 1973-74; asst. dir. rsch. svcs. Chgo. State U., 1974-75; ednl. specialist coord. chpt. 622 State Dept. Edn., Springfield, Mass., 1975-76; dir. teen learning ctr. Juvenile Justice Program, U. Mass., Amherst, 1976-77; coord. vocat. ednl. act program L.A. Trade Tech Coll., 1978-79, asst. dean extended opportunity programs and svcs., 1979-85, asst. dean student svcs., 1985-86; instrnl. svcs. coord., trainer Calif. State U., Sacramento, 1990-91; grant writer, facilitator Grant Joint Union H.S. Dist., Sacramento, 1991-93; pres., owner Stalling Enterprises & Assocs., Sacramento, 1993—; program developer, grant writer Urban League, Sacramento, 1993; model developer Sys. Devel. Corp., Santa Monica, Calif., 1977; instr. Calif. State U., Sacramento, 1990, Nat. U., Sacramento, 1989, U. Mass., Amherst, 1975, Boston Sch. Com., 1974; asst. prof. Westfield, Mass., State Coll., 1976; teaching fellow Grad. Sch. Edn. Harvard U., Cambridge, 1972; cons. State Dept. Edn., Sacramento, Cities in Schs., Sacramento, Evaluation, Mgmt. Tng., Inc., Sacramento, others; cons., trainer Workplace Learning Resource, Sacramento, 1994—. Author: Bridge: A Cross-Cultural Reading Program, 1974, Bridge: Across the Cultural Reading Program, 1977, Effects of the Cultural Context of Language on the Cognitive Performance of Black Students, 1977; contbr. articles to profl. jours. Ptnr. Sacramento 21, 1992-94; pres. Cedar Block Assn., Sacramento, 1994—; co-chair social and civic orgns. United Negro Coll. Fund, Sacramento, 1991, 92; sec., treas. Pacific Foster Care, Sacramento, 1993; sec. Project Chance Job Tng. Partnership Act, Arlington Hgts. Block Club Assn.; vol. trainer Kellogg Tng. Inst.; mem. Coalition for Equity for Minorities, Sacramento, 1992, 93. Mem. ASCD, Toast Masters' Internat. (competent toast master 1993), Sacramento Black Women's Network, Calif. Notary Assn. Mem. Ch. of Christ. Office: Stalling Enterprises & Assocs PO Box 245381 Sacramento CA 95824-5381

STALLKNECHT-ROBERTS, CLOIS FREDA, publisher, publicist; b. Birmingham, Ala., Dec. 31, 1934; d. August and Sadie Bell (Wisener) Anton; m. Randall Scott Roberts; children: Yvonne Denise, April O'dell, Kurt William. Publicist Ms. Clois Presents, L.A., 1968—; advt. Engineered Magic, Advt., Santa Ana, Calif., 1976, 77, 81; pub. Internat. Printing, L.A., 1981—. Editor: Nostradamus, William Bartram, Apuleious, 1990-92. Home: PO Box 165 Inyokern CA 93527-0165 Office: Engineered Magic 510 De La Estrella San Clemente CA 92672

STALNAKER, JOHN HULBERT, physician; b. Portland, Oreg., Aug. 29, 1918; s. William Park II and Helen Caryl (Hulbert) S.; m. Louise Isabel Lucas, Sept. 8, 1946; children: Carol Ann, Janet Lee, Mary Louise, John Park, Laurie Jean, James Mark. Student, Reed Coll., Portland, 1936-38; AB, Willamette U., Salem, Oreg., 1941; MD, Oreg. Health Scis. U., 1945. Diplomate Am. Bd. Internal Medicine. Intern Emanuel Hosp., Portland,

1945-46; resident in internal medicine St. Vincent Hosp., Portland, 1948-51; clin. instr. U. Oreg. Med. Sch., 1951-54, 60-62; staff physician VA Hosp., Vancouver, Wash., 1970-79; cons. in internal medicine, 1951-79. Contbr. articles to profl. jours. Pianist various civic and club meetings, Portland; leader Johnny Stalnaker's Dance Orch., 1936-39. Lt. (j.g.) USNR, 1946-48. Fellow ACP; mem. AMA, Multnomah County Med. Soc., Oreg. State Med. Assn., N.Am. Lily Soc., Am. Rose Soc. Home: 2204 SW Sunset Dr Portland OR 97201-2068

STAMBAUGH, LARRY G., finance executive; b. Topeka, Feb. 1, 1947; s. Merle J. and Eileen M. (Denslow) S.; m. Sallie M. Underwood, Jan. 18, 1969 (div. Oct. 1981); children: Matt, Julie; m. Suzanne Van Slyke, May 14, 1982; children: Todd, Scott, Andy. BBA, Washburn U., 1969. CPA, Kans. Mgr. Peat, Marwick, Mitchell Co., Kansas City, Mo., 1969-76; co-owner Automotive Investment & Devel. Co., Olathe, Kans., 1976-82; chief fin. officer CNB Fin. Corp., Kansas City, Kans., 1983-90; chief fin. officer ABC Labs., Columbia, Mo., 1990, pres., chief exec. officer, 1990-92; chmn., pres., CEO Syntello, Inc., San Diego, Calif., 1993—; dir. City Nat. Bank, Atchison, Kans., 1986-90; chmn. bd. dirs. Advent Enterprises. Pres., dir. Big Bros. and Sisters, Kansas City, 1986-88. Mem. AICPA, Am. Mgmt. Assn., Soc. Environ. Toxicology Edn. Found. (bd. dirs.), Nat. Assn. Corp. Dirs., Columbia C. of C., Rotary Internat. Republican. Presbyterian. Club: Indian Hills Country (Prairie Village, Kans.) (bd. dirs.). Home: 17947 Corazon Pl San Diego CA 92127-1009 Office: Syntello 4350 Executive Dr Ste 310 San Diego CA 92121-2118

STAMES, WILLIAM ALEXANDER, realtor, cost management executive; b. Douglas, Ariz., Mar. 26, 1917; s. Alex Basil and Teresa (Ruis) S.; AA, Long Beach Coll., 1941; postgrad. U. Calif., Berkeley, 1962-64; cert. mgmt. practices Naval Officers CIC Sch., Glenview, Ill., 1955; grad. Real Estate Inst., Calif.; m. Marguerite Winifred Nelson, June 11, 1943; 1 child, Wynn Lorain. Owner, Stames Beverage Co., Brawley, Calif., 1945-50; liaison engr. Lockheed Missiles & Space Co., Sunnyvale, Calif., 1958-60, liaison engr. sr., 1960, adminstr., 1960-62, staff adminstr., 1962-63, liaison engr., sr., design engr. sr., 1965-76; owner, mgr. Cost Reduction Equipment Sales & Tech., Sunnyvale, 1967-76; realtor Cornish & Carey, 1988—. Comdr. USNR, 1941-69, ret., World War II, Korea, Vietnam. Decorated D.F.C., Air medal with two gold stars, Presdl. citation. Mem. Am. Mgmt. Assn., Mountain View Real Estate Bd. (pres.), Calif. Assn. Realtors (bd. dirs.), Tailhook Assn. Clubs: Commonwealth San Francisco, Ret. Officers (past pres. Peninsula chpt.), Lions. Author: Polaris Electrical Subsystems Design History, 1964; Poseidon Subsystem Invention, 1971. Home: 1060 Coronado Ave Coronado CA 92118-2439

STAMNES, KNUT HENRIK, physics educator; b. Rost, Norway, June 30, 1943; s. Alfred Johannes and Petra (Antonsen) S.; m. Anja Elisabeth Moen, Feb. 17, 1984; children: Snorre, Kaja. BS in Physics, U. Oslo, 1969, MS in Physics, 1972; PHD in Astro-Geophysics, U. Colo., 1978. Rsch. assoc. geophysical inst. U. Alaska, Fairbanks, 1978-83; assoc. prof. U. Tromso (Norway), 1983-88; prof. U. Alaska, Fairbanks, 1988—; adj. assoc. prof. U. Alaska, Fairbanks, 1983-88. Contbr. more than 70 articles to profl. jours. Rsch. grantee NSF, NASA, U.S. Dept. Energy, Norwegian Funding Agys. Mem. Am. Geophys. Union, Am. Meteorol. Soc., Norwegian Phys. Soc., European Geophys. Soc., Oceanograph Soc. Office: U Alaska Geophysical Inst Fairbanks AK 99775

STAMPER, MALCOLM THEODORE, aerospace company executive; b. Detroit, Apr. 4, 1925; s. Fred Theodore and Lucille (Cayce) S.; m. Marion Philbin Guinan, Feb. 25, 1946; children: Geoffrey, Kevin, Jamie, David, Mary, Anne. Student, U. Richmond, Va., 1943-44; BEE, Ga. Inst. Tech., 1946; postgrad., U. Mich., 1946-49; DHumanities, Seattle U., 1994. With Gen. Motors Corp., 1949-62; with Boeing Co., Seattle, 1962-90; mgr. electronics ops., v.p., gen. mgr. turbine div. Boeing Co., 1964-66; v.p., gen. mgr. Boeing Co. (747 Airplane program), 1966-69, v.p., gen. mgr. comml. airplane group, 1969-71, corp. sr. v.p. ops., 1971-72; pres. Boeing Co., 1972-85, vice chmn., 1985-90; chief exec. officer Storytellers Ink Pub., Seattle, 1990—, also chmn. bd. dirs.; bd. dirs. Esterline Co., Chrysler Co., Whittaker Corp.; trustee The Conf. Bd., 1988—. Candidate for U.S. Ho. of Reps., Detroit, 1952; trustee, chmn. Seattle Art Mus.; nat. bd. dirs. Smithsonian Assocs. With USNR, 1943-46. Named Industrialist of Year, 1967; recipient Educator's Golden Key award, 1970, Elmer A. Sperry award, 1982, AIEE award, Ga. Inst. Tech. award, Sec. Dept. Health and Human Services award, Silver Beaver award Boy Scouts Am., 1989. Mem. Nat. Alliance Businessmen, Phi Gamma Delta.

STAMPER, NORMAN H., police chief. BS, MS in Criminal Justice Adminstrn., San Diego State U.; PhD in Leadership and Human Behavior, U.S. Internat. U. Chief of police Seattle Police Dept., 1994—; exec. dir. Mayor Pete Wilson's Crime Control Commn.; apptd. (by U.S. Atty. Gen. and Sec. Health and Human Svcs.) Adv. Coun. Violence Against Women; mem. adv. panel on Excessive Force by Police, Police Exec. Rsch. Forum, Major Cities Chiefs; mem. steering com. Seattle Equal Justice Coalition; co-chair Ptnr's. in Pub. Edn's. Urban Scholar's Program; mem. bd. dirs. Leadership Tomorrow; trustee Ctr. for Ethical Leadership. Author: Removing Managerial Barriers to Effective Police Leadership, 1992; tchnical adv. Municipal Police Administration, 1992. Named to Alumni Hall of Fame Boys and Girls Club of Am.; recipient Katharine M. Bullitt award for Leadership Ptnrs. in Pub. Edn. Mem. Internat. Assn. Chiefs of Police. Office: Police Dept 610 3rd Ave Seattle WA 98104-1824*

STAMPER, ROBERT LEWIS, ophthalmologist, educator; b. N.Y.C., July 27, 1939; m. Naomi T. Belson, June 23, 1963; children: Juliet, Marjorie, Alison. BA, Cornell U., 1957-61; MD, SUNY-Downstate, 1965. Diplomate Am. Bd. Ophthalmology (assoc. examiner 1976-92, bd. dirs. 1992—, mem. glaucoma panel 1993—); lic. physician, Calif. Intern Mt. Sinai Hosp., N.Y.C., 1965-66; resident in ophthalmology Washington U.-Barnes Hosp., St. Louis, 1968-71; Nat. Eye Inst.-NIH fellow dept. ophthalmology Washington U., St. Louis, 1971-72, from instr. ophthalmology to asst. prof. dept. ophthalmology, 1971-72; asst. prof. dept. ophthalmology Pacific Presbyn. Med. Ctr., San Francisco, 1972-76, assoc. prof. ophthalmology, 1976-87; chmn. dept. ophthalmology Calif. Pacific Med. Ctr. (formerly Pacific Presbyn. Med. Ctr.), San Francisco, 1987—; asst. ophthalmologist Barnes Hosp., St. Louis, 1971-72, Harkness Hosp., San Francisco, 1973-74; dir. ophthalmic photography and fluorescin angiography, dept. ophthalmology Washington U., St. Louis, 1969-72; dir. resident tng. Pacific Presbyn. Med. Ctr., 1972-89, dir. glaucoma svc., vice-chmn. dept. ophthalmology, 1974-87; chief ophthalmology svc. Highland Hosp., Oakland, Calif., 1974-76; clin. instr. dept. ophthalmology U. Calif., San Francisco, 1974-77; clin. asst. prof. ophthalmology U. Calif., Berkeley, 1974-78, asst. clin. prof. ophthalmology, 1978-85; sr. rsch. assoc. Smith-Kettlewell Inst. Visual Scis., San Francisco, 1972-89; project co-dir. ophthalmic curriculum for med. students Nat. Libr. Medicine, 1973-75; commr. Joint Commn. on Allied Health Pers. in Ophthalmology, 1975-87, bd. dirs., 1978-88, sec., 1980, v.p., 1982-83, pres., 1984-85; provisional asst. chief dept. ophthalmology Mt. Zion Hosp., San Francisco, 1976-87, assoc. chief dept. ophthalmology, 1982-86; ophthalmic cons. Ft. Ord, Calif., 1976—, Oakland (Calif.) Naval Hosp., 1978-83; instr. Stanford (Calif.) U., 1977—; glaucoma cons. U. Calif., Davis, 1978-84; vis. lectr. dept. ophthalmology Hadassah Hebrew U. Med. Ctr., Jerusalem, 1978, Oxford (Eng.) U. Eye Hosp., 1986; ind. med. examiner State of Calif., 1979—; mem. appeals hearing panel Accreditation Coun. for Grad. Med. Edn., 1986-93, mem. residency rev. com. for ophthalmology, 1993—; mem. provisional courtesy staff Peralta Hosp., Oakland, 1988-92; mem. ophthalmic devices adv. panel USFDA, 1989-92; presenter, lectr. in field. Editor Ophthalmology Clinics of North Am., 1988—; mem. editl. adv. com. Ophthalmology, 1982-89, mem. editl. bd., 1983-94; contbr. articles to profl. jours. Chmn. bd. Agy. for Jewish Edn., Oakland, 1986-89; bd. dirs. Jewish Fedn. Greater East Bay, Oakland, 1992-94; bd. dirs. Found. for Glaucoma Rsch.; mem. glaucoma adv. com. Nat. Soc. to Prevent Blindness, 1981—; mem. Am. Diabetes Assn. Surgeon USPHS, 1966-68. Recipient Nat. Soc. for Performance and Instrn. award for self-instrnl. material in ophthalmology, 1975, Honor award Am. Acad. Ophthalmology, 1982, Statesmanship award Joint Commn. on Allied Health Pers. in Ophthalmology, 1989; N.Y. State Regents scholar, 1961, N.Y. State scholar in medicine, 1965; Blalock student fellow UCLA Sch. Medicine, 1961, Fight for Sight student fellow dept. ophthalmology N.Y. Hosp. and Cornell Med. Ctr., 1962, 63, 64. Fellow Am. Acad. Ophthalmology and Otolaryngology (rep. to joint commn. on allied health pers., faculty home study course sect. X, chmn. sect. VIII 1983-85, bd. councilors, editl. adv. com. Opthalmology jour. 1982-89, editl. bd. Ophthalmology jour. 1983-94, and many others), ACS; mem. AMA (Physician's Recognition award 1989), Am. Ophthalmologic Soc., Assn. for Rsch. in Vision and Ophthalmology, Calif. Med. Assn. (asst. sec. sect. ophthalmology, chmn., sci. bd. rep. adv. panel on ophthalmology 1985-91), Nat. Soc. Prevent Blindness (mem. glaucoma adv. com. 1981—, bd. dirs. 1986—), No. Calif. Soc. Prevent Blindness, Calif. Assn. Ophthalmology, Pan Am. Ophthalmological Soc., N.Y. Acad. Scis., Las Vegas Ophthalmological Soc. (hon.). Office: ic Med Ctr 2340 Clay St San Francisco CA 94115-1932

STAMPS, PETER DAVID, manufacturing administrator; b. Dearborn, Mich., June 4, 1963; s. David William and Alice Janette (Travis) S. BSME, USN Acad., 1985. Registered engr.-in-tng. Commd. ensign USN, 1985, advanced through grades to lt., 1992; commd. officer USN, Norfolk, Va., 1988-90; commd. officer Operation Desert Storm USN, 1990-91; current ops. and tng. officer USN, San Diego, 1990-92; lt. commander USNR, 1992—; prodn. supr., quality steering com., quality edn. trainer Cargill Inc., Lynwood, Calif., 1992-93, plant engr., 1993-94; site mgr. McWhorter Techs., Inc. (formerly Resin Products divsn., Cargill Inc.), Lynwood, 1994; western regional quality mgr. McWhorter Techs., Inc. (formerly Resin Products divsn., Cargill Inc.), 1994—. Vol. County Registrar of Voters, San Diego, 1992, store front ops. dir. H. Ross Perot Petition Com., San Diego, 1992; mem. budget and fin. com. Arcada Community Assn., 1993—; econ. devel. com. and scholarship com. Lynwood (Calif.) C. of C., 1994—, mem. bd. dirs. 1995—. Mem. ASME (assoc., pres. student chpt. 1984-85), Am. Soc. Quality Control, UNS Inst. (command liaison 1990—), Am. Soc. Individual Investors, Surface Navy Assn., Am. Mgmt. Assn., Naval Res. Assn., USN Acad. Alumni Assn., Sigma Xi (assoc.), Rotary Internat. (bd. dirs. Lynwood, Calif. chpt. 1995—), Lynwood C. of C. (bd. dirs.-treas. 1995—). Office: McWhorter Techs Inc Lynwood CA 90262

STANBRO, WILLIAM DAVID, physical chemist; b. St. Louis, Nov. 29, 1946; s. William Woodrow and Rosemary Muriel (Conners) S.; m. Helen Frances de Chabert, June 14, 1969; children: Jennifer Margaret, Elizabeth Marie, Patrick William, William Thomas. BS in Chemistry, George Washington U., 1968, PhD in Phys. Chemistry, 1972; MS in Computer Sci., Johns Hopkins U., 1985. NSF presdl. intern Johns Hopkins U. Applied Physics Lab., Laurel, Md., 1972-73; sr. staff chemist Johns Hopkins U. Applied Physics Lab., Laurel, 1973-86; v.p. for rsch. Biotronic Systems Corp., Rockville, Md., 1986-89; staff mem. Los Alamos (N.Mex.) Nat. Lab., 1989—. Contbr. book chpts., articles profl. jours. Fellow Am. Inst. Chemists; mem. Am. Chem. Soc., Inst. Nuclear Material Mgmt., Alpha Chi Sigma. Republican. Roman Catholic.

STANDRING, JAMES DOUGLAS, real estate developer; b. Fresno, Calif., Dec. 2, 1951; s. James Robert Pusey and Jacquelin (Moore); m. Paula Jean Monson, Oct. 27, 1972; children: Craig Douglas, Ryan Scott, Melinda Jean, Kevin Paul. BS, Calif. State U., Fresno, 1975. Pres. Westland Industries, Inc., Portland, Oreg., 1976—; ptnr. Aloha Land and Cattle, Inc., Portland, 1982—; bd. dirs. Homebuilders Assn. Metro Portland, v.p. 1988-90, pres. 1990-91; bd. dirs. Oreg. State Homebuilders Assn., v.p. 1993—; bd. dirs. Nat. Assn. Homebuilders, Washington, Oreg. trustee BUILD-PAC, 1992, exec. com., 1994—. Bd. dirs. Tualitin Valley Econ. Devel. Corp., Portland, 1988—; co-founder, dir. People for Washington County Charities, Beaverton, Oreg., 1985-88. Named Portland Metro. Builder of Yr., 1992, Oregon Builder of Yr., 1992. Mem. Tualitin Valley Econ. Devel. Commn., Multnomah Athletic Club, Portland City Club, Portland Golf Club, 1000 Friends of Oreg., Sierra Club, Elks. Republican. Episcopalian. Home: 5 Nansen Smt Lake Oswego OR 97035-1029 Office: Aloha Land/Cattle Co 17980 SW Kemmer Rd Beaverton OR 97007-6078

STANFILL, SHELTON G., performing arts administrator; m. Brigitte. BA in History and Social Scis., Colo. State U., postgrad. Exec. dir. Hopkins Ctr. Dartmouth Coll.; dir. cultural programs Colo. State U.; dir. Nat. Arts Festival 12th Winter Olympic Games; ptnr. Brown, Stanfill & Brown; pres., CEO Wolf Trap Found. for Performing Arts, Vienna, Va.; pres. Music Ctr. L.A. County, 1994—; chair panels, cons. Nat. Endowment for Arts, Lincoln. Ctr., Bklyn. Acad. Music, UCLA; advisor Telluride Film Festival. Office: Music Ctr LA County 135 N Grand Ave Los Angeles CA 90012-3013

STANFORD, GINNY CROUCH, painter; b. Lamar, Mo., Sept. 3, 1950; d. Howard D. and Mary Elizabeth (Price) Crouch; m. Frank G. Stanford, Oct. 17, 1974 (dec. June 1978). Ind. study, Amsterdam and Brussels, 1972. One-person shows include Landau Gallery, L.A., 1983, San Marco Gallery, Dominican Coll., San Rafael, Calif., 1987, U. Pacific, Stockton, Calif., 1990, Reed Whipple Cultural Ctr., Las Vegas, Nev., 1992; exhibited in group shows at Jan Holloway Gallery, San Francisco, 1988, 90, U. Ariz., Tucson, 1988, Downey (Calif.) Mus. Art, 1988, Angels Gate Cultural Ctr., San Pedro, Calif., 1989, Fla. State U., Tallahassee, 1993; represented in permanent collection Nat. Portrait Gallery, Smithsonian Instn. Recipient 1st Pl. awards Ft. Smith (Ark.) Art Ctr., 1974, 75, 76, 2nd Pl. award Auburn (Calif.) Art Ctr., 1988, Merit awards Ft. Hays State U., Hays, Kans., 1988; Sonoma Found. grantee, 1990, 91. Office: PO Box 2014 Sebastopol CA 95473-2014

STANFORD, JOSEPH BARNEY, medical educator, physician; b. July 9, 1961; s. Kathleen Barnett; children: Matthew Joseph, Jesse Barnett, Hyrum Porter, Caleb Dean. Student, U. Utah, 1978-80; BA magna cum laude, Mankato State U., 1984; MD, U. Minn., 1988. Diplomate Am. Bd. Family Practice. Resident family and cmty. medicine U. Mo.-Columbia, 1988-91, chief resident family and cmty. medicine, 1990-91, academic fellow, clinical instr. dept. family and cmty. medicine, 1991-93; asst. prof. dept. family and preventive medicine U. Utah, Salt Lake City, 1993—; co-coord. Med. Student Rsch. Inst. U. Mo.-Columbia, 1992, 94; part time staff physician Cherchez La Femme Birth Svcs. Ltd., Columbia, Mo., 1991-93; med. cons. U. Utah BirthCare HealthCare, 1994—; physician N.E. Family Health Ctr., Salt Lake Regional Med. Ctr., U. Utah Hosp., Primary Children's Med. Ctr., 1983—; invited observer Pontifical Acad. Scis. Working Group on Natural Fertility Regulation, Vatican, Italy, 1994. Contbr to prof. jours. Mem. Soc. Tchrs. of Family Medicine (mem. group family centered perinatal care 1990—), Am. Acad. Family Physicians, Am. Acad. Natural Family Planning (chairperson sci. and rsch. com. 1993—), Am. Holistic Med. Assn., Am. Soc. Clinical Hypnosis, Collegium Aesculapium, North Am. Primary Care Rsch. Group, Alpha Omega Alpha, Phi Kappa Phi. Office: U Utah Dept Family Preventive Med 50 N Medical Dr Salt Lake City UT 84132-0001

STANG, PETER JOHN, organic chemist; b. Nürnberg, Germany, Nov. 17, 1941; came to U.S., 1956; s. John Stang and Margaret Stang Pollman; m. Christine Schirmer, 1969; children: Antonia, Alexandra. BS, DePaul U., Chicago, 1963; Ph. D., U. California, Berkeley, 1966; hon. degr., Moscow State Lomonossov U., 1992, Russian Academy of Sciences, 1992. Instr. Princeton (N.J.) U., 1967-68; from asst. to assoc. prof. U. Utah, Salt Lake City, 1969-79, prof., 1979-92, Disting. prof. chemistry, 1992—. Co-author: Organic Spectroscopy, 1971; author: (with others) Vincy Cations, 1979; contbr. 300 articles to sci. publs. Humboldt-Forschungspreis, 1977; JSPS Fellowship, 1985; Fulbright-Hays Sr. Scholarship, 1988. Fellow AAAS; mem. Am. Chem. Soc. (assoc. editor Jour. Am. Chem. Soc. 1982—). Office: Univ Utah Dept Chemistry Salt Lake City UT 84112

STANGELAND, ROGER EARL, retail chain store executive; b. Chgo., Oct. 4, 1929; s. Earl and Mae E. (Shaw) S.; m. Lilah Fisher, Dec. 27, 1951; children: Brett, Cyndi Stangeland Meili, Brad. Student, St. Johns Mil. Acad., 1943-47, Carleton Coll., 1947-48; B.S., U. Ill., 1949-51. With Coast to Coast Stores, Mpls., 1960-78, pres., 1972-77; sr. v.p., exec. v.p. Household Merchandising, Chgo., 1978-84; chief exec. officer, chmn. bd. Vons Grocery Co., Los Angeles, 1984-85; past CEO The Vons Cos., Inc., Arcadia, Calif., chmn., 1986—. Chmn. Wauconda (Ill.) Bd. Edn., 1957-60, Hopkins (Minn.) Bd. Edn., 1968-74; bd. fellows Claremont (Calif.) U. Ctr. and Grad. Sch., 1986; bd. dirs. L.A. area Boy Scouts Am.; trustee Hugh O'Brian Youth Found.; mem. CEO bd. advisors U. So. Calif. Sch. Bus. Adminstrn.; trustee St. John's Mil. Acad; bd. visitors Peter F. Drucker Grad. Mgmt. Ctr. Mem. Am. Inst. Wine and Food (bd. dirs.), Food Mktg. Inst. (chmn. bd. dirs.), Food Employers Coun. (exec. com., bd. dirs.), Mchts. & Mfrs. Assn. (bd. dirs.), L.A. Area C. of C. (bd. dirs.), Jonathan Club (L.A.), Calif. Club. Home: 842 Oxford Rd San Marino CA 91108-1214 Office: Vons Cos Inc PO Box 3338 618 Michillinda Ave Arcadia CA 91007-6300*

STANGER, LYNN BETH CARTER, orthopedic nurse; b. Brookfield, Ill., Aug. 4, 1947; d. Richard F. and Patricia Evelyn (Wisecarver) Carter; m. Dean T. Stanger, Aug. 25, 1979; stepchildren: Samantha Stanger Lane, Matthew Stanger. AA, American River Coll., Sacramento, 1968; diploma, St. Luke's Sch. Nursing, San Francisco, 1971; BSN, Carlow Coll., Pitts., 1983. RN, Nev.; cert. orthopaedic nurse; cert. rehab. nurse. Staff nurse Twin Lakes Hosp., Folsom, Calif., 1971-72; staff nurse to nursing mgr. adult orthopedics/neurosurgery Eskaton American River Healthcare Ctr., Carmichael, Calif., 1972-80; asst. head nurse adult orthopedics Forbes Regional Health Ctr., Monroeville, Pa., 1983-84; chmn. nursing and health ARC, Seoul, Korea, 1984-85; coord. exceptional family mem. program U.S. Army 18th Med. Command, Seoul, 1985-86; staff nurse orthopaedic unit Univ. Med. Ctr., Las Vegas, 1986-87; unit. mgr. orthopaedic neurosurg. unit Humana Sunrise Hosp., Las Vegas, 1987-89, charge nurse adult orthopaedics, unit mgr. med.-surg. unit; edn. coord., rehab. Rehabilitation Hosp., Las Vegas, 1993—; adj. faculty health scis. dept. Clark County C.C., Law Vegas, 1988; adj. faculty Mojave C.C., Kingman, Ariz., 1991-93. Mem. ANA, Nat. League Nursing, Nat. Assn. Orthopaedic Nurses (v.p. Las Vegas chpt.), Assn. Rehab. Nurses, So. Nev. Soc. Health Edn. and Tng. Republican. Episcopalian. Office: Rehab Hosp Nev 1250 S Valley View Blvd Las Vegas NV 89102-1855

STANISZEWSKI, JOHN, food products executive; b. 1942. Ranch foreman Lambert-Louck's Ranch, Camarillo, Calif., 1967-71; v.p. Hoson Produce, Inc., Pasadena, 1971—. Office: Hoson Produce Inc 400 W Claremont St Pasadena CA 91103-2414*

STANLEY, BRETT JAMES, chemist; b. Binghamton, N.Y., July 10, 1965; s. Emory R. and Sarah Louise (Dunham) S. BS in Chemistry, U. Pitts., 1987; postgrad. in Chemistry, U. Idaho, 1987-88; PhD in Analytical Chemistry, Utah State U., 1992. Rschr. Utah State U., 1987-92; rschr. divsn. chem. and analytical scis. U. Tenn./Oak Ridge Nat. Lab., Knoxville, 1992-94; asst. prof. analytical chemistry Calif. State U., San Bernardino, 1994—; substitute lectr. quantitative analysis U. Tenn. Presdl. scholar Utah State U., 1990-91. Mem. Am. Chem. Soc., Phi Kappa Phi, Delta Tau Delta (coun. undergrad. rsch.). Office: Calif State U Dept Chemistry 5500 University Pky San Bernardino CA 92407-2318

STANLEY, FORREST EDWIN, fundraiser, university program director; b. Bakersfield, Calif., Sept. 6, 1942; s. James Edwin and Lucile Haworth (Sloan) S.; student U. Calif., Los Angeles, 1960-63, M.S., 1970; B.S., Calif. State U., Northridge, 1969; m. Suzanne Roberts, June 15, 1968 (div. 1984); children—John Forrest, Cheryl Suzanne; m. Virginia Louise Sorenson, Jan. 18, 1987. Sr. clk. So. Calif. Gas Co., 1963-65, programmer analyst, 1965-70; fin. analyst Continental Bldgs. Co., Burbank, Calif., 1970-72; fin. analyst McKinsey & Co., Inc., Los Angeles, 1972-74; analyst Unionamerica Advisors, Beverly Hills, Calif., asst. v.p., asst. treas., 1974-75; dir. alumni and devel. Grad. Sch. Mgmt., UCLA, 1976-80; dir. spl. campaigns U. Calif., Berkeley, 1980-84; dir. devel. U. Colo., Colorado Springs, 1984-86; dir. devel. pub. affairs, Calif. State U., Bakersfield, 1987—, asst. sec., 1989—; v.p. U. Colo. Found., Inc., 1984-86. Mem. Am. Inst. Cert. Computer Profls., Assn. for Computing Machinery, Council for Advancement and Support of Edn., UCLA Mgmt. Alumni Assn. (v.p. 1974, pres. 1975-77), Sons Am. Colonists, Mensa, Lambda Chi Alpha (UCLA alumni chpt. pres. 1974-77, treas. 1977-80). Clubs: North Kern. Office: PO Box 10705 Bakersfield CA 93389-0705

STANLEY, GEORGE DABNEY, JR., geology educator; b. Chattanooga, Jan. 25, 1948; s. George Dabney and Lucille (Proctor) S. B.A., U. Tenn.-Chattanooga, 1970; M.S., Memphis State U., 1972; Ph.D., U. Kans., 1977. Lectr. in geology U. Calif., Davis, 1977-78; geologist, research assoc. Smithsonian Instn., Washington, 1978-81; sr. prof. Fulbright-Hayes, Erlangen, West Germany, 1981-82; assoc. prof. U. Mont., Missoula, 1982-90, prof., 1990—; exch. fellow, Kumamoto, Japan, 1992-93; mem. organizing com. 4th Internat. Com. on Fossil Corals, Washington, 1981-84. Author monograph; editor books; contbr. numerous articles in field to profl. jours. Served to capt. U.S. Army, 1970-72. Grantee NSF, 1976-77, 83—; hon. research assoc. Smithsonian Instn., 1980—; Orgn. for Tropical Studies fellow, 1974, Fulbright-Hayes fellow, 1981-82. Mem. Soc. Sedimentary Geology (metal com. 1990-93), Paleontol. Soc. Washington D.C.(pres. 1980-81, dist. lectr., 1993-94), Internat. Paleontol. Soc., Paleontol. Assn. Gr. Britain, Com. on Coral Reefs (founding mem.).

STANLEY, RICHARD GRAHAM, geologist; b. Berkeley, Calif., Feb. 22, 1951; s. Roger Upson and Ruth Irene (Graham) S.; m. Helen Gibbons, June 22, 1985; children: Sarah Elizabeth, Jenna Louise. BA in Biology with honors, U. Calif., Santa Cruz, 1973, BS in Earth Scis. with honors, 1973, PhD in Earth Scis., 1984; MA in Geology, Rice U., 1976. Geologist Pennzoil Producing Co., Houston, 1975-77, U.S. Geol. Survey, Menlo Park, Calif., 1984—; lectr. U. Calif., Santa Cruz, 1979-81, Calif. State U., Fresno, 1983-84. Author, co-author over 80 reports, articles, maps and abstracts in field. H. L. Doherty fellow, 1973, U. Calif. fellow, 1977. Mem. Am. Assn. Petroleum Geologists (assoc. editor bull. 1993—), Geol. Soc. Am., Soc. for Sedimentary Geology. Office: US Geol Survey 345 Middlefield Rd MS999 Menlo Park CA 94025

STANLEY, SHERYL LYNN, college administrator; b. Moberly, Mo., Oct. 21, 1952; d. James Melvin and Gloria May (Bagby) S. BS, Coll. of the S.W., Hobbs, N.Mex., 1974. Salesman KHOB Radio, Hobbs, 1973-74; adminstrv. asst. Coll. of the S.W., 1974-80, pub. info. officer, 1980-82, dir. pub. info., 1982-84, dir. pub. affairs, 1984, dir. coll. communications, 1988—; community rels. coord. Lea Regional Hosp., Hobbs, 1985-88. Author, editor, photographer numerous univ. publs. Campaign co-chair United Way of Lea County, Hobbs, 1988. Recipient Excellence in Community Svc. award Hosp. Corp. Am., 1986. Mem. N.Mex. Pres Women, Eastern N.Mex. Rose Soc. (treas. 1986-88, sec. 1988-91). Methodist. Office: Coll of the SW 6610 N Lovington Hwy Hobbs NM 88240-9120

STANSKY, PETER DAVID LYMAN, historian; b. N.Y.C., Jan. 18, 1932; s. Lyman and Ruth (Macow) S. B.A., Yale U., 1953, King's Coll., Cambridge (Eng.) U., 1955; M.A., King's Coll., Cambridge (Eng.) U., 1959; Ph.D., Harvard U., 1961; D.L. (hon.), Wittenburg U., 1984. Teaching fellow history and lit. Harvard U., 1957-61, instr., then asst. prof. history, 1961-68; assoc. prof. history Stanford U., 1968-73, prof., 1973-74, Frances and Charles Field prof., 1974—, chmn. dept. history, 1975-78, 79-82, 89-90, assoc. dean humanities and scis., 1985-88; chmn. publs. com. Conf. Brit. Studies, 1970-78; pres. Pacific Coast Conf. Brit. Studies, 1974-76, N. Am. Conf. Brit. Studies, 1983-85; vis. fellow Wesleyan Center Humanities, Middletown, Conn., 1972, All Soul's Coll., Oxford (Eng.) U., 1979, St. Catherine's Coll., Oxford (Eng.) U., 1983. Author: Ambitions and Strategies, 1964, England Since 1867, 1973, Gladstone, 1979, William Morris, 1983, Redesigning the World, 1985; co-author: Journey to the Frontier, 1966, The Unknown Orwell, 1972, Orwell: The Transformation, 1979, London's Burning, 1994. Guggenheim fellow, 1966-67, 73-74; Am. Council Learned Socs. fellow, 1978-79; NEH fellow, 1983, Royal Hist. Soc. fellow Ctr. for Advanced Study Behavioral Scis., 1988-89. Fellow Am. Acad. Arts and Scis. (coun. 1994—); mem. Am. Hist. Assn. (pres. Pacific Coast br. 1988-89), Conf. on Brit. Studies, Victorian Soc., William Morris Soc., AAUP, Century Assn. Home: 375 Pinehill Rd Hillsborough CA 94010-6612 Office: Stanford U Dept History Stanford CA 94305

STANTON, ALAIRE EVELYN, mayor, broadcasting company executive; b. Edmonton, Alta., Can., Oct. 15, 1935; came to U.S., 1941; d. S.A. and Pearl A. (Knutson) Carlson; m. Roland Jaqua Stanton, Sept. 12, 1953; children: Bruce A., Myra J. Stanton Zelensky, Ralph G., Loren K. Student, Linfield Coll., McMinnville, Oreg., 1953, U. Alaska, Ketchikan, 1972-74. Legis. aide Alaska Ho. of Reps., Juneau, 1982-84; mem. coun. City of Ketchikan, 1984-87, 89-91; mayor, 1991—; fin. mgr. Rainbird Broadcasting Corp., 1988—. Mem. Ketchikan-Gateway Brough Sch. Bd., 1971-80, pres., 1972-77; pres. Alaska Assn. Sch. Bds., 1976-78, Pacific region Nat. Sch. Bds. Assn., 1977, S.E. Conf., Juneau, 1993-94; mem. Alaska Bd. Edn., 1980-83, Gov.'s Commn. for Adminstrn. Justice, 1978-80; sec.-treas. Alaska Conf. Mayors, 1992-94, v.p., 1994-95, pres. 1995—. Democrat. Methodist. Office: City of Ketchikan 334 Front St Ketchikan AK 99901-6431

STANTON, CAMPBELL EDGAR, energy consultant; b. Chgo., Nov. 25, 1947; s. Francis Rew and Louise (Parsons) S.; m. Susan Pesses, Mar. 9, 1980; children: Aleta Rose, Corey Elizabeth. BA in Geography, U. Denver, 1970; cert. in Solar Retrofit Tech., Colo. Mt. Coll., 1983; cert. in Energy Auditing, Western Area Power Adminstrn., Glenwood Springs, Colo., 1990. Owner and mgr. Saw-Whet Orchards., Paonia, Colo., 1974—; founder, mgr. KVNF-FM pub. radio, Paonia, 1976-83; station mgr. KVNF-FM pub. radio, Paonia, Colo, 1986-89; sales rep. and installer Sunrise Energy Co., Delta, Colo., 1983-85; ptnr., sales rep., installer Sun Dragon Svcs., Hotchkiss, Colo., 1985-86; energy cons. The Energy Office, Inc., Grand Junction, Colo., 1989—. Home: 503 Reed Mesa Dr Grand Junction CO 81503-1153

STANTON, GRACE PATRICIA, communications executive, consultant; b. Jersey City, Dec. 17, 1951; d. John Joseph and Marjorie Theresa (Nolan) S.; m. Mark Edward Rieger, July 11, 1976; children: Brian Stanton, Colin Mark Stanton, Lauren Elizabeth. Student Wroxton Coll., Oxford U., 1972; B.A., Fairleigh Dickinson U., 1973; M.A., Seton Hall U., 1974; Ph.D., U. Denver, 1979. Reporter Jersey Jour., Jersey City, 1970-73; editorial asst. IBM, Franklin Lakes, N.J., 1973; pub. relations mgr. Fairleigh Dickinson U., 1973-75; editor Kraft, Chgo., 1976-77; mgr. pub. relations IHS, Denver, 1977-78; dir. communications CMC, Denver, 1978-80; v.p. Johnston Group, Denver, 1980-82; pres. Stanton & Assocs., Denver, 1982—. Mem. Leadership Denver Assn., Denver C. of C.; v.p., dir. Arapahoe Mental Health Ctr.; dir. Met. Denver Hospice. Mem. Colo. Press Women (dir., communications award), Internat. Assn. Bus. Communicators (award Chgo. chpt.), Pub. Relations Soc. Am. (Gold Pick award), Speech Communication Assn., Counselor's Acad. Fairleigh Dickinson U. (Pinnacle award). Bd. dirs. U. Denver Alumni, Children's Hospital Cardiac Care Unit. Democrat. Roman Catholic. Home: 1 Killdeer Ln Littleton CO 80127-5773 Office: 1620 Market St Denver CO 80202-1519

STANTON, LEWIS HARRIS, publishing company executive; b. London, Apr. 2, 1954; came to U.S., 1980; s. Gerald and Carole (Harris) S.; m. Victoria Frances Patterson, Sept. 17, 1977; children: Graham, Joshua. BS, U. Birmingham, Eng., 1976. CPA, Calif.; chartered acct., Eng. Sr. mgr. Arthur Andersen & Co., L.A., London, 1976-88; chief fin. officer Data Analysis Inc., L.A., 1988—. Fellow Inst. Chartered Accts.; mem. AICPA, Calif. Soc. CPAs (chmn. mems. in industry com. 1990-94), Assn. Western Securities Mgmt. (pres. 1989). Office: Data Analysis Inc 12655 Beatrice St Los Angeles CA 90066-7300

STANTON, MICHAEL JOHN, newspaper editor; b. New Britain, Conn., Mar. 30, 1944; s. John Martin and Helen (McNally) S.; m. Barbara Ann Mucha, Aug. 27, 1966; 1 child, Sean. A.B. in English, Holy Cross Coll., 1966. Reporter, editor Providence (R.I.) Jour., 1968-72; press sec. Gov. R.I., Providence, 1972-77; asst. news editor St. Louis Globe-Dem., 1977-81; news copy desk chief Detroit Free Press, 1981-83, exec. news editor, 1983-85, asst. to exec. editor, 1985-86; exec. news editor Seattle Times, 1986—. Office: The Seattle Times PO Box 70 Fairview Ave N & John St Seattle WA 98111

STANTON, WILLIAM JOHN, JR., marketing educator, author; b. Chgo., Dec. 15, 1919; s. William John and Winifred (McGann) S.; m. Imma Mair, Sept. 14, 1978; children by previous marriage: Kathleen Louise, William John III. BS, Ill. Inst. Tech., 1940; MBA, Northwestern U., 1941, PhD, 1948. Mgmt. trainee Sears Roebuck & Co., 1940-41; instr. U. Ala., 1941-44; auditor Olan Mills Portrait Studios, Chattanooga, 1944-46; asst. prof., asso. prof. U. Wash., 1948-55; prof. U. Colo., Boulder, 1955-90; prof. emeritus, 1990—; head mktg. dept. U. Colo., 1955-71, acting dean, 1963-64; assoc. dean U. Colo. (Sch. Bus.), 1964-67; vis. prof. summers U. Utah, 1946, 49, U. Calif., Berkeley, 1950, UCLA, 1957; mktg. cons. to various bus. firms and govt. agys., 1950—; lectr. univs. Austria, India, Mex., New Zealand; mem. faculty exec. devel. programs sponsored by Sales and Mktg. Execs. Internat. and by Advanced Mgmt. Rsch., 1963-71. Author: Economic Aspects of Recreation in Alaska, 1953; (with Richard H. Buskirk and Rosann Spiro) Management of a Sales Force, 9th edit., 1995 (also Spanish transl.), (with others) Challenge of Business, 1975, (With M. Etzel and B. Walker) Fundamentals of Marketing, 10th edit., 1994 (also Spanish, Portuguese and Indonesian transls.), (with M.S. Sommers and J.G. Barnes) Can. edit. Fundamentals of Marketing, 7th edit., 1995, (with K. Miller and R. Layton) Australian edit., 3d edit., 1994, (with R. Varalso) Italian edit., 2d edit., 1990, (with others) South African edit., 1992; monographs on Alaska Tourist Industry, 1953-54; contbr. articles to profl. jours. Mem. Am., So., Southwestern, Western mktg. assns., Beta Gamma Sigma. Roman Catholic. Home: 1445 Sierra Dr Boulder CO 80302-7846

STANWAY, PAUL WILLIAM, newspaper editor; b. Manchester, Eng., Apr. 22, 1950; arrived in Canada, 1976; s. William and Gladys (Wright) S.; m. Erina Danyluk, May 5, 1976; children: Scott, Nicole. Reporter Nottingham (Eng.) Post, 1969-72, Express and Star, Wolverhampton, Eng., 1972-76, Free Press, Winnipeg, Can., 1976-77; city editor Edmonton (Can.) Sun, 1978-80, news editor, 1980-81, mng. editor, 1981-84, assoc. editor, columnist, 1988-90; editor Calgary (Can.) Sun, 1988-90; European bureau chief Toronto Sun Pub., London, 1990-92; editor-in-chief Edmonton Sun, 1992—. Office: The Edmonton Sun, 4990 - 92 Ave, Edmonton, AB Canada T6B 3A1

STAPLES, ROBERT EUGENE, nursing educator; b. Roanoke, Va., June 28, 1942; s. John Ambrose and Anna Theresa (Anthony) S. AA, L.A. Valley Coll., Van Nuys, Calif., 1960; AB, Calif. State U., 1963; MA, San Jose State U., 1965; PhD, U. Minn., 1970. Assoc. prof. sociology Howard U., Washington, 1971-73; prof. sociology U. Calif., San Francisco, 1973—. Editor: The Black Family, 1971; author: The Black Woman In America, 1973, Introduction to Black Sociology, 1976, World of Black Singles, 1981, Black Masculinity, 1982, The Urban Plantation, 1987, Black Families Essays, 1991, Black Families at the Crossroads, 1993. Mem. Nat. Coun. on Family Rels., Assn. Black Sociologists, Am. Sociol. Assn. Office: U Calif PO Box 0612 San Francisco CA 94143

STAPLETON, JAMES JAY, agricultural scientist, consultant; b. Santa Monica, Calif.. BS, U. Calif., Davis, 1978, MS, 1981, PhD, 1983. Rsch. plant pathologist USDA Agrl. Rsch. Svc., Beltsville, Md., 1983-85; vis. plant pathologist U. Calif., Davis, 1986-87; area IPM adv. U. Calif., Modesto, 1987-90; integrated pest mgmt. specialist U. Calif., Parlier, 1991—; Collaborator USDA Animal and Plant Health Inspection Svc., Hyattsville, Md., 1986—; agrl. cons., Oakdale, Calif., 1993—; lectr. Calif. State U., Fresno, 1995—. Editor profl. jours. Mem. U. Calif. Methyl Bromide Taskforce, Calif., 1994—. With USN, 1969-70, Vietnam. Host Scientist, Postdoctoral Fellow USA-Israel BARD Found., 1991-92; Fulbright scholar J. Wm. Fulbright Bd., 1995-96; Recipient disting. svc. award U. Calif., 1991, Keynote Address Mediterranean Phytopath. Union, 1994. Mem. Am. Phytopath Soc., Am. Soc. Plasticulture, Soc. Nematologists, Orgn. Nematologists of Tropical Am. Office: U Calif Kearney Agrl Ctr Parlier CA 93648

STAPLETON, JEAN, journalism educator; b. Albuquerque, June 24, 1942; d. James L. and Mary (Behrman) S.; m. John Clegg, Apr. 15, 1965 (dec. Sept. 1972); m. Richard Bright, Jan. 13, 1973 (div. 1985); children: Lynn, Paul. BA, U. N.Mex., 1964; MS in Journalism, Northwestern U., 1968. Reporter Glenview (Ill.) Announcements, 1967-68, Angeles Mesa News Advertiser, L.A., 1968-69, City News Svc., Radio News West, L.A., 1969-71; press sec. polit. campaign, 1972; instr. journalism East L.A. Coll., 1973-75, prof., dept. chair, 1975—. Author: Equal Marriage, 1975, Equal Dating, 1979; co-editor Star, Am. Yankee Assn., 1987-88. Mem. NOW (pres. L.A. chpt. 1973-74), Women in Comm., Soc. Profl. Journalists, L.A. C. of C., Journalism Profs. Assn., Ninety Nines. Democrat. Methodist. Home: 3232 Philo St Los Angeles CA 90064-4719 Office: East LA Coll 1301 Avenida Cesar Chavez Monterey Park CA 91754-6001

STAPLETON, KATHARINE HALL (KATIE STAPLETON), food broadcaster, author; b. Kansas City, Mo., Oct. 29, 1919; d. William Mabin and Katharine (Hall) Foster; m. Benjamin Franklin Stapleton, June 20, 1942; children: Benjamin Franklin, III, Craig Roberts, Katharine Hall. BA, Vassar Coll., 1941. Cookbook reviewer Denver Post, 1974-84; producer, writer, host On the Front Burner, daily radio program Sta. KOA-CBS, Denver, 1976-79, Sta. WGN, Portland, Maine, 1979-81, Cooking with Katie, live one-hour weekly, Sta. KOA, 1979-88; guest broadcaster Geneva Radio, 1974, London Broadcasting Corp., 1981, 82; tour leader culinaries to Britain, France and Switzerland, 1978-85. Eng., 1978. Chmn. women's div. United Fund, 1955-56; founder, chmn. Denver Debutante Ball, 1956, 57; hon. chmn. Nat. Travelers Aid Assn., 1952-56; commr. Denver Centennial Authority, 1958-60; trustee Washington Cathedral, regional v.p., 1967-73; mem. world service council YWCA, 1961-87; trustee, Colo. Women's Coll., 1975-80; sole trustee Harmes C. Fishback Found. Decorated Chevalier de L'Etoile Noire (France); recipient People-to-People citation, 1960, 66, Beautiful Activist award Altrusa Club, 1972, Gran Skillet award Colo./Wyo. Restaurant Assn., 1981, Humanitarian of Yr. award Arthritis Assn., 1995; named Chevalier du Tastevin, 1989. Republican. Episcopalian. Clubs: Denver Country, Denver. Author: Denver Delicious: 150 Past and Present Recipes from the Queen City, 1980, 3d. edit., 1983; High Notes: Favorite Recipes of KOA, 1984. Home: 8 Village Rd Cherry Hills Village CO 80110

STAPLETON, SHIRLEY ANN, retired real estate executive; b. Boise, Idaho, June 17, 1936; d. Charles Edward and Eleanor Lucille (Swiggart) Lee; m. Larry J. Stapleton, July 10, 1954 (div. 1976); children: Terry Michael, William Carroll, Tamara Lee; m. Bruce Frederick Wauters, May 23, 1986. AA, DeAnza Community Coll., Cupertino, Calif., 1976; BS in Bus. Mgmt., Ariz. State U., 1979. Lic. in real estate, Ariz. Exec. sec. Sys. Devel. Corp., Wash., 1961-63; with Cupertino Sch. Dist., Calif., 1968-71; coordinator Women's Opportunity Ctr., DeAnza Coll., Cupertino, 1972-74; owner, mgr. Ariz. Women's Yellow Pages, Inc., 1975-78; realtor assoc. Coldwell Banker Resdl. Real Estate, Scottsdale, Ariz., 1979-82; assoc., ptnr. The Weigelt Corp., Scottsdale, 1982-86; br. mgr., assoc. Carol Vernon & Assocs., Inc., Scottsdale, 1986-88; v.p. real estate sales TransWestern Consolidated Realty, Inc., Scottsdale, 1988-89; assoc., cons. comml. real estate Internat. Ariz. Investments Inc., Scottsdale, 1989—; sec. Ctr. for Environ. Studies, Ariz. State U., 1992—. Bd. dirs. Cupertino Sch. Vol. Bd. Mem. bus. and Profl. Women's Club, Cupertino Fine Arts Assn., NAFE, Women in Comml. Real Estate, Ariz. State U. Alumni Assn., Ariz. State U. Bus. Coll. Alumni Assn. Democrat. Home: 7701 E Palm Ln Scottsdale AZ 85257-2230

STARING, GRAYDON SHAW, lawyer; b. Deansboro, N.Y., Apr. 9, 1923; s. William Luther and Eleanor Mary (Shaw) S.; m. Joyce Lydia Allum-Poon, Sept. 1, 1949; children: Diana Hilary Agnes, Christopher Paul Norman. Student, Colgate U., 1943-44; A.B., Hamilton Coll., 1947; J.D., U. Calif.-Berkeley, 1951. Bar: Calif. 1952, U.S. Supreme Ct. 1958. Atty. Office Gen. Counsel, Navy Dept., San Francisco, 1952-53; atty. admiralty and shipping sect. U.S. Dept. Justice, San Francisco, 1953-60; assoc. Lillick & Charles, San Francisco, 1960-64, ptnr., 1965—; titulary mem. Internat. Maritime Com.; bd. dirs. Marine Exchange at San Francisco, 1984-88, pres. 1986-88; instr. pub. speaking Hamilton Coll., 1947-48. Author: Law of Reinsurance, 1993; assoc. editor Am. Maritime Cases, 1966-92, editor, 1992—; contbr. articles to legal jours. Mem. San Francisco Lawyers Com. for Urban Affairs, 1972-90; bd. dirs. Legal Aid Soc., San Francisco, 1974-90, v.p., 1975-80, pres., 1980-82. With USN, 1943-46, comdr. USNR. Fellow Am. Bar Found., Am. Coll. Trial Lawyers; mem. ABA (chmn. maritime ins. com. 1975-76, mem. standing com. admiralty law 1976-82, 86-90, chmn. 1990, ho. dels. 1986-90), Fed. Bar Assn. (pres. San Francisco chpt. 1968), Bar Assn. San Francisco (sec. 1972, treas. 1973), Calif. Acad. Appellate Lawyers, Maritime Law Assn. U.S. (exec. com. 1977-88, v.p. 1980-84, pres. 1984-86), Brit. Ins. Law Assn., Brit.-Am. C. of C. (bd. dirs. 1987—), World Trade Club San Francisco, Tulane Admiralty Inst. (permanent adv. bd.), Assocs. Maritime Mus. Libr. (dir. 1990-92, pres. 1992-94). Home: 195 San Anselmo Ave San Francisco CA 94127-1513 Office: 2 Embarcadero Ctr Ste 2600 San Francisco CA 94111-3823

STARK, ALLEN LYTTON, psychiatrist, educator; b. McAllen, Tex., Feb. 3, 1949; s. J. Howard and Harriette (Smith) S.; m. Carol Lynn Reynolds, May 14, 1971; children: Elizabeth Kathleen, David Thomas, Michael Christopher. BA, Rice U., 1971; MD, Baylor Coll. Medicine, 1974. Resident in psychiatry Baylor Affiliated Hosp., Houston, 1974-77; pvt. practice in gen. psychiatry, 1977—, pvt. practice psychoanalysis, 1984—; asst. prof. psychiatry Baylor Coll. Medicine, Houston, 1977-88; asst. prof. Oreg. Health Sci. U., 1991—; exec. com. West Br. Ctr., 1986-88; med. dir. adolescent unit Twelve Oaks Hosp., Houston, 1987-88; clin. dir. adolescent treatment program Portland Adventist Med. Ctr., 1988-89; chief profl. staff Pioneer Trail Residential Treatment Ctr., 1989—, med. dir., 1993—; chief med. staff Pacific Gateway Hosp., 1992-94, chmn. med. records and utilization rev., 1992—. Mem. vestry St. John the Evangelist Episcopal Ch., Milw., 1991-93. Mem. Internat. Psychoanalytic Assn., AMA, Am. Psychiat. Assn., Am. Psychoanalytic Assn., Am. Soc. Addiction Medicine, Am. Acad. Psychoanalysis, Am. Soc. Adolescent Psychiatry, Tex. Med. Assn., Oreg. Med. Assn., Oreg. Psychiat. Assn., Oreg. Psychoanalytic Study Group, Houston Psychiat. Soc. (rep. to exec. coun. of Tex. Psychiat. Soc. 1983-85, active numerous coms.), Houston-Glaveston Psychoanalytic Soc., Portland Psychiatrists in Pvt. Practice. Office: 340 Oswego Pointe Dr Ste 205 Lake Oswego OR 97034-3230

STARK, AMY LOUISE, clinical psychologist; b. St. Paul, May 13, 1954; d. Douglas Arvid and Irene Eleanor (Frokjer) S. BA, Gustavus Adolphus Coll., 1976; MA, Calif. Sch. Profl. Psychology, 1979, PhD, 1981. Lic. psychologist, Calif. Psychology intern Juarez-Lincoln Sch., Chula Vista, Calif., 1978-79, Cath. Family Services, San Diego, 1979-80, Southwood Mental Health Ctr., San Diego, 1980-81; clin. psychologist Orange County Children and Youth Services, 1982-84; clin. coordinator Western Youth Services, Tustin, Calif., 1986-88; indsl. psychologist Frederick Capaldi & Assocs., Tustin, 1982—; psychologist Tustin Psychology Ctr., 1985—; cons., presenter in field. Author: Because I Said So, 1992; contbr. articles to L.A. Times. Mem. Am. Psychol. Assn., Orange County Psychol. Assn. Office: 13132 Newport Ave Ste 110 Tustin CA 92680-3425

STARK, DAVID ALBERT, forester; b. Jacksonville, Tex., May 4, 1942; s. Erich Walter and Vera (Wygant) S.;m. Maureen Ann Carroll, June 20, 1969. BS in Forest Mgmt., Purdue U., 1964. Dist. reforestation staff USDA Forest Svc., Walden, Colo., 1964-66; dist. timber staff USDA Forest Svc., Hill City, S.D., 1966-67; dist. recreation staff USDA Forest Svc., Spearfish, S.D., 1967-72; dist. timber staff USDA Forest Svc., Norwood, Colo., 1972-76; forest planning staff USDA Forest Svc., Custer, S.D., 1976-77; forest planner USDA Forest Svc., Cody, Wyo., 1977-79; dist. ranger USDA Forest Svc., Lander, Wyo., 1979-83, Minturn, Colo., 1983-87; recreation planner USDA Forest Svc., Lakewood, Colo., 1987—; first snow ranger, mountain planner Telluride Ski Area, Colo., USDA Forest Svc.,Norwood, 1972-76. Officer USCG Aux., Lakewood, Colo., 1989—. Recipient Meritorious award lifesaving USCG, 1994. Home: 1839 S Union Blvd Lakewood CO 80228-3973

STARK, DENNIS WILLIAM, paralegal, consultant; b. Chgo., Sept. 23, 1952; m. Sharon K. Wells, Feb. 2, 1957; children: Jeremiah, Bart. BS in Criminal Justice, Metro. State Coll., Denver, 1992; postgrad. in Pub. Affairs, U. Colo., Denver, 1993—. Sr. police officer City of Westminster, Colo., 1980-91; ct. clk. 1st Jud. Dist., State of Colo., Golden, 1993; legal tech. Adams County Dept. Social Svcs., Commerce City, Colo., 1994—; criminal justice and law enforcement cons.; mgmt. and adminstrn. specialist. Mem. PTA, Westminster, 1986—. Mem. ASPA, Fraternal Order of Police, Delta Phi Omega, Golden Key Honor Soc. Home: PO Box 686 Wheat Ridge CO 80034-0686 Office: Adams County Social Svcs 7190 Colorado Blvd Commerce City CO 80022-1812

STARK, FORTNEY HILLMAN (PETE STARK), congressman; b. Milw., Nov. 11, 1931; s. Fortney Hillman Sr. and Dorothy M. (Mueller) S.; children: Jeffrey Peter, Beatrice Ann, Thekla Brumder, Sarah Gallup; m. Deborah Roderick. BS, MIT; MBA, U. Calif. Teaching asst. MIT, Cambridge, 1953-54; prin. Skaife & Co., Berkeley, Calif., 1957-61; founder Beacon Savs. & Loan Assn., Antioch, Calif., 1961; pres., founder Security Nat. Bank, Walnut Creek, Calif., 1963-72; mem. 93d-102nd Congresses from 9th Calif. dist., 1973—; chmn. ways and means subcom. on health 93d-103d Congresses from 13th dist. Calif., 1973—; mem., chmn. D.C. com., Ways and Means com., subcom. Health, Select Revenue Measures, joint econ. com. Bd. dirs. ACLU, 1971, Common Cause, 1971, Starr King Sch.; del. Dem. State Cen. Com.; trustee Calif. Dem. Coun. Capt. USAF, 1955-57. Mem. Delta Kappa Epsilon. Office: House of Representatives 239 Cannon Bldg Washington DC 20515-0003

STARK, JACK LEE, college president; b. Urbana, Ind., Sept. 26, 1934; s. Lynn C. and Helen (Haley) S.; m. Jil Carolyn Harris, June 14, 1958; children: Janet, Jeffrey, Jennifer, Jonathan. BA, Claremont McKenna Coll., 1957; hon. degree, Redlands U., LDH, 1973. Asst. to pres. Claremont (Calif.) McKenna Coll., 1961-70, pres., 1970—. Active Pomona Valley Cmty. Hosp.; bd. dirs. Thacher Sch., Ojai, Calif. Capt. USMCR, 1957-60. Mem. Assn. Ind. Calif. Colls. and Univs. (chmn.), Ind. Colls. So. Calif. (bd. dirs.), Western Coll. Assn. (bd. dirs.). Club: California (Los Angeles). Home: 1679 Tulane Rd Claremont CA 91711-3426 Office: Claremont McKenna Coll Office of Pres 500 E 9th St Claremont CA 91711-5903

STARK, JOSEPH P., business owner; b. Phoenix, Mar. 10, 1937; s. Jesse Overton and Loretta Agnes (Kochanowsky) Scott; m. Debra Stark; children: Esther M., Joseph P., Kathryn, Kristina, Julee, Heather, Tanya, Clint, Jennifer, Michael, Ryan. Law student, Phoenix Coll., 1956; grad., Brigham Young U., 1957. Sr. cons., pres. coun. Beneficial Life Ins. Co., Salt Lake City, 1964-74; pres., owner Stark Enterprises, Gilbert, Ariz., 1974—; pvt. investigator, 1987-88. Br. and dist. pres. LDS Ch., Okinawa, 1960, ward and stake Sunday sch. pres., Phoenix, 1965, high councilman and Bishopric, 1967, full-time missionary, 1957-59; scoutmaster Boy Scouts Am., Phoenix, 1991-92, dist. fin. chmn., 1972-73, inst. rep., 1969-70; coach Little League, 1974-75; lt. Maricopa County Sheriff's Exec.Posse. With USAF, 1960-64. Recipient Dist. Leader award Boy Scouts Am., Phoenix, 1970, Nat. Sales Achievement award Nat. Assn. Life Underwriters, 1969-74, others. Republican. Home and Office: Stark Enterprises PO Box 344 Gilbert AZ 85299-0344

STARK, MARY BARBARA, retired educator; b. Boston, Jan. 1, 1920; d. Charles Rathbone and Dorothea Brenton (Burge) S. BA, Whitworth Coll., 1965, MEd, 1968; EdS, U. of the Pacific, 1975; PhD, Southeastern U., New Orleans, 1981. Cert. elem. tchr., jr. high tchr., spl. edn. tchr. Play dir. Spokane (Wash.) Park Dept., 1937-41; tchr. Lanham Act Nursery Sch., Spokane, 1941-45; owner, mgr. Children's Play Room, Spokane, 1945-63; supr. Guild's Sch for Mentally Retarded, Spokane, 1962-66; tchr. primary educable mentally retarded Sacramento City Unified Sch. Dist., 1966-68, tchr. educable kindergarten mentally retarded, 1968-70; kindergarten educator, 1970-87, asst. care of babies of teenage mothers, 1992-94. Moderator United Ch. of Christ, 1992. Recipient 817th Point of Light award Pres.'s Points of Light, 1992. Mem. Calif. Ret. Tchrs. Assn. (pres. State Capital divsn.), Sacramento Bus. and Profl. Women's Club (pres. 1973-74), Assn. Childhood Edn. Internat. (pres. 1983-85, state treas. 1984-86), Delta Kappa Gamma (pres. 1984-86, area legis. chair 1994—), Phi Delta Kappa. Home: 5989 Lake Crest Way Apt 1 Sacramento CA 95822-3302

STARK, MILTON DALE, sports association executive; b. Fellows, Calif., Apr. 28, 1932; s. Ernest Esco and Ruth Hazel (Keeney) S.; m. Katherine Margaret Boyd, Dec. 17, 1955 (div. June 1978); children: Mark Boyd, Kimberly Kay, Matthew Scott, Martin Dean; m. Diana Lynn Mead, July 26, 1980; 1 child, Ryan. AA, Taft Coll., 1956; BA, Whittier Coll., 1958, MEd, 1963. Cert. ednl. adminstr., Calif. Sec. Western Softball Congress, Hollywood, Calif., 1962-70; commr. Internat. Softball Congress, Anaheim Hills, Calif., 1966-75, sec., 1975-83, exec. dir., 1983—; v.p. U.S. Fastpitch Assn., Colorado Springs, Colo., 1993—; mem. coun. Amateur Softball Assn., 1994—; sports cons. Whittier (Calif.) News, 1959-70. Editor-in-chief Softball Illus. mag., 1966-69; columnist The Fastpitch Chronicle, 1993—; contbg. author: FastPitch World, 1993; contbr. articles to softball mags. Served with USAF, 1951-55. Named to Internat. Softball Congress Hall of Fame, 1981, recipient Alumni Achievement award Whittier Coll. Lancer Soc., 1989. Mem. Whittier Coll. Alumni Assn. (bd. dirs. 1989-94). Republican. Home and Office: Internat Softball Congress 6007 E Hillcrest Cir Anaheim CA 92807-3921

STARK, PHILIP HERALD, information company executive; b. Iowa City, Mar. 2, 1936; s. Herald and Helen Annis (Ogelvy) S.; m. Christine K. Baumgartner, Aug. 20, 1981; 1 child, Johnathon Peter. BS in Geology, U. Okla., 1958; MS in Geology, U. Wis., 1960, PhD in Geology, 1962. Exploration geologist Mobil Oil Corp., Wichita, Kans., 1962-65; computer coord. Mobil Oil Corp., Denver, 1965-69; mgr. tech. svcs. Petroleum Info. Corp., Denver, 1969-79, 1979-86, v.p. internat. svcs., 1986-92, v.p. strategic mktg., 1993—; dir. New Ventures. Contbr. articles to profl. jours. Mem. Leadership Denver, 1979; chmn. Alumni Adv. Com., dept. geology, U. Wis., 1991-94. Mem. Assn. Petroleum Geologists, Rocky Mountain Assn. Geologists. Office: Petroleum Info Corp 1675 Broadway Ste # 700 Denver CO 80202

STARK, RAY, motion picture producer. Student, Rutgers U. Publicity agt., lit. agt.; talent agt. Famous Artist Agy., to 1957; co-founder Seven Arts Prodn. Co., 1957; ind. film producer, 1966—. Producer: (films) The World of Suzie Wong, 1960, The Night of the Iguana, 1964, Reflections in a Golden Eye, 1967, Funny Girl, 1968, The Owl and the Pussycat, 1970, Fat City, 1972, The Way We Were, 1973, Funny Lady, 1975, The Sunshine Boys, 1975, Murder By Death, 1976, Smokey and the Bandit, 1977, The Goodbye Girl, 1977, The Cheap Detective, 1978, California Suite, 1978, Chapter Two, 1979, The Electric Horseman, 1979, Seems Like Old Times, 1980, Annie, 1982, Blue Thunder, 1983, Nothing in Common, 1986, Peggy Sue Got Married, 1986, The Secret of My Success, 1987, Biloxi Blues, 1988, Steel Magnolias, 1989, Revenge, 1990, Lost in Yonkers, 1993, Barbarians at the Gate, 1993 (Emmy award Outstanding Made for Television Movie, 1993), Mr. Jones, 1993, Dr. Jekyll and Ms. Hyde, 1995, Mariette in Ecstacy, 1995, To Gillian on Her 37th Birthday, 1995. Recipient Thalberg award Acad. Motion Picture Arts and Scis., 1980. Office: Hepburn Bldg W 10202 W Washington Blvd Culver City CA 90232-3119

STARK, S. DANIEL, JR., convention and visitors bureau executive; b. Port Hueneme, Calif., Mar. 26, 1953; s. S. Daniel and Eloise Marie (Fisher) S.;1 child, Kaitlyn Elizabeth. BS, Calif. Poly. U., Pomona, 1981; cert. in exec. mgmt., Claremont Grad. Sch., 1989, MA in Mgmt., 1992. Driver-guide San Diego Wild Animal Pk., Escondido, Calif., 1974-76; attractions host Disneyland div. The Walt Disney Co., Anaheim, Calif., 1976-80; mgmt. intern Disneyland div. The Walt Disney Co., Anaheim, 1981; supr. ops. Disneyland div. The Walt Disney Co., Anaheim, Calif., 1981-82; area supr. ops., 1982-87; mgmt. cons. S.D. Stark, Jr., Riverside, Calif., 1987-88; dir. mktg. Ramada Express Hotel & Casino, Laughlin, Nev., 1988-89; exec. dir. San Bernardino (Calif.) Conv. and Visitors Bur., 1989—; cons. Sam Houston Bond Ptnrs. Ltd., for Sam Houston Race Park, Houston, Hemmeter Devel. Corp., Honolulu, 1985, Calif. Authority Racing Fairs, Sacramento, 1987-88, USIA for Latvian Ministry Transp., tourism div., 1992, U.S. Bur. Land Mgmt., tourism mgmt. project U. Alaska Sch. Mgmt.; adj. prof. Sch. Bus. and Pub. Adminstrn., Calif. State U., San Bernardino, 1992-93. Bd. dirs. Leadership So. Calif., 1993—, grad. pub. affairs tng., 1993; congl. appointee del. White House Conf. on Travel & Tourism, 1995. Recipient resolution Calif. Assembly, 1989, San Bernardino County Bd. Suprs., 1989, City of San Bernardino Mayor and Coun., 1989, Calif. Senate, 1989; selected as one of 1991 Up and Coming Young Bus. Leaders in San Bernardino County; named one of Inland Empire Bus. All Stars, 1991; recipient World Champion Trail Horse award Am. Jr. Quarter Horse Assn., 1972. Mem. Am. Horse Shows Assn. (life), Am. Quarter Horse Assn (life), Assn. Travel Mktg. Execs., Internat. Assn. Conv. and Visitors Burs. (cert. comm., conv. mktg., tourism mktg.), Pub. Rels. Soc. Am. (bd. dirs. Calif. Inland Empire chpt. 1990—), Meeting Profls. Internat., Travel Industry Assn. Am., Hospitality Sales and Mktg. Assn. Internat., Calif. Travel Industry Assn., Tourism Assn. So. Calif. (bd. dirs. 1990-95, vice chair 1992-95), Western Assn. Convs. and Vis. Bur. (chmn. Calif. coun. 1992-94), Farmhouse Fraternity (internat. bd. dirs. 1986-94, v.p. 1990-92, Snyder Alumni award 1984). Office: San Bernardino Conv and Visitors Bur 201 N E St Ste 103 San Bernardino CA 92401-1520

STARKEY, HARRY CHARLES, geologist; b. Wheeling, W.Va., Dec. 10, 1925; s. Burtice Johannes and Mary Irene (Hilton) S.; BS, W.Va. U., 1950; m. Ruth Woods, May 16, 1964. With U.S. Geol. Survey, 1955-84, geologist specializing in clay mineralogy, Denver, 1958-84. With inf. U.S. Army, 1944-46. Methodist. Research in clay mineralogy, ion-exchange in clay and zeolites, chem. reactions involving clays; contbr. articles to profl. jours. Home: 1636 S Yarrow Ct Denver CO 80232-6754

STARKS, ROSALYN JUNE, physical education and health educator; b. Phoenix, June 17, 1952; d. Ross Owen and Maribel Louise (Barnes) S. BS in

Edn., U. Ariz., 1974; MA in Edn., No. Ariz. U., 1991. Tchr. Phys. Edn. K-12, Ariz. Phys. edn. tchr. Santa Cruz Valley Union High Sch., Eloy, Ariz., 1975-84; phys. edn., health tchr. Phoenix Union High Sch. Dist., 1985—; coach Santa Cruz Valley Union H.S. and So. Mountain H.S., Phoenix, 1975—, facilitator student assistance program, 1987—; Phoenix 5A Metro Region Rep. State Softball Adv. Bd., 1990-94; mem. HIV/AIDS articulation com. Phoenix Union H.S. Dist., 1994—. Named Softball Coach of Yr., A Ctrl. Divsn., 1980. Mem. AAHPERD, NEA, Ariz. Edn. Assn., Ariz. AHPERD, Phoenix Union H.S. Dist. Classroom Tchrs. Assn. Home: 4406 N 111th Dr Phoenix AZ 85037-5333 Office: S Mountain High School 5401 S 7th St Phoenix AZ 85040-3104

STARKWEATHER, FREDERICK THOMAS, data processing executive; b. Sioux City, Iowa, Feb. 24, 1933; s. Fred Ervin and Gertrude Faye (Madden) S.; m. Margot Glassen, Nov. 19, 1959; children: Thomas Frederick, Jerry Russell, Michael Glassen. BA in Math. and Physics, U. Nebr., Omaha, 1955. Mathematician Flight Determination Lab., White Sands Missile Range, N.Mex., 1955-56; supervisory mathematician Analysis & Computation, White Sands Missile Range, 1956-81; chief data scis. div. Nat. Range Ops., White Sands Missile Range, 1981—; Nat. council rep. Am. Def. Preparedness Assn., Washington, 1980—; pres. White Sands Pioneer Group, White Sands Missile Range, 1983-86; bd. dirs. Assn. U.S. Army, Washington. Author hist. and genealog. books; contbr. book reviews and articles to newspapers and mags. Chmn. El Paso (Tex.) City Planning Commn., 1980-84; bd. dirs. El Paso County Hist. Soc., 1983-87; mem. El Paso County Hist. Commn., 1983—. With USAR, 1955-63. Recipient Profl. Secs. Internat. Exec. of Yr. award, 1987, Conquistador award City of El Paso, 1980; named Disting. Alumnus U. Nebr., Omaha, 1985; named to Hon. Order of St. Barbara U.S. Field Arty. Assn., 1988; cited for svcs. to mankind El Paso chpt. Sertoma, 1985. Mem. Fed. Mgrs. Assn. (bd. dirs.), Freedom Found. at Valley Forge (pres. El Paso chpt., George Washington Hon. medal 1982), El Paso C. of C. (assoc. dir. 1984—, bd. dirs.), Toastmasters (dist. gov. 1970-71), Masons, Tau Kappa Epsilon (Hall of Fame 1986). Office: Nat Range Ops Chief Data Scis Div White Sands Missile Range NM 88002

STARR, GRIER FORSYTHE, retired pathologist; b. Jamestown, N.D., Oct. 6, 1926; s. Earl Grier and Grace (Forsythe) S.; m. Virginia Lucille Heidinger, June 25, 1948; children: William Grier, Joan Elizabeth Starr Barton. BS cum laude, Jamestown (N.D.) Coll., 1947; MD, Northwestern U., 1951; MS in Pathology, U. Minn., 1956. Diplomate Nat. Bd. Med. Examiners, 1952, Minn., Mich., Oreg. and Wash. state bds., Am. Bd. Pathology in Clin. Pathology, 1956, and in Pathol. Anatomy, 1957. Intern Evanston (Ill.) Hosp., 1951-52; sr. resident in pathology Henry Ford Hosp., Detroit, 1955-56; fellow in pathology Mayo Clinic, Rochester, Minn., 1952-55, cons. surgical pathology, 1956-59; cons., pathologist Lab. Pathology and Pathology Cons., Eugene, Oreg., 1959-91, pres., 1973-85; mem. staff McKenzie-Willamette Hosp., Springfield, Oreg., 1959-91—; mem. staff Sacred Heart Gen. Hosp., Eugene, Oreg., 1959-91, chief of staff, 1969-71, dir. labs., 1973-86, emeritus staff, 1992—; chmn. bd., chief ops. officer Oreg. Consol. Labs., Eugene, Oreg., 1986-89; bd. dirs. Oreg. Blue Cross-Blue Shield, Portland, 1985-94, Sisters of St. Joseph of Peace Health & Hosp. Svcs., Bellevue, Wash., 1990—; affiliate in pathology Oreg. Health Scis. Ctr., Portland, 1972-88; assoc. prof. U. Oreg., Eugene, 1986. Contbr. articles to profl. jours. Served with USN, 1944-46. Fellow Am. Coll. Pathologists, Am. Soc. Clin. Pathologists; mem. AMA, Lane County Med. Soc. (pres. 1984-85), Am. Soc. Cytology, Internat. Acad. Pathologists, Pacific NW Soc. Pathologists (pres. 1979-80), Oreg. State Soc. Pathologists, Am. Soc. Dermatopathology (chmn. 1984, peer rev. com. 1976-91). Republican. Presbyterian. Home: 2455 S Louis Ln Eugene OR 97405-1026

STARR, ISIDORE, lawyer, educator; b. Bklyn., Nov. 24, 1911. BA, CCNY, 1932; MA, Columbia U., 1939; LLB, St. John's U., Jamaica, N.Y., 1936; JSD, Bklyn. Law Sch., 1942; PhD, New Sch. Social Rsch., 1957. Bar: N.Y. 1937. Tchr. N.Y.C. high schs., 1934-61; assoc. prof., prof. edn. Queens Coll., 1961-75, emeritus, 1975—; dir. Inst. on Law-Related Edn., Lincoln-Filene Ctr., Tufts U., 1963; dir. Law Studies Inst., N.Y.C., 1974; adv. on Our Living Bill of Rights Film Series (6 films) Encyclopedia Britannica Ednl. Corp.; mem. Ariz. Ctr. for Law-Related Edn.; cons. in field. Bd. dirs. Phi Alpha Delta Juvenile Justice Program, 1981—. 1st lt. U.S. Army, 1943-46. John Hay fellow, 1952-53. Recipient Outstanding Citizen award Philip Morris Cos., 1992. Mem. ABA (hon. chair adv. commn. on Youth Edn. for Citizenship, Isidore Starr award for Spl. Achievement in Law Studies, Leon Jaworski award 1989), Am. Judicature Soc., Am. Soc. for Legal History, Am. Legal Studies Assn., Nat. Coun. Social Studies (past pres.), Phi Beta Kappa, Phi Alpha Delta (cert. of appreciation 1981). Author: The Lost Generation of Prince Edward County, 1968, The Gideon Case, 1968, The Feiner Case, 1968, The Mapp Case, 1968, The Supreme Court and Contemporary Issues, 1968, Human Rights in the United States, 1969, The American Judicial System, 1972, The Idea of Libery, 1978, Justice: Due Process of Law, 1981; co-editor Living American Documents, 1971.. Address: 6043 E Harvard St Scottsdale AZ 85257

STARR, MELVIN LEE, education counselor; b. N.Y.C., Mar. 17, 1922; s. Herman and Martha (Aberman) S.; m. Eileen Ferne Kagan, Sept. 7, 1947; children: Marianne, Lisa Caren. BBA, U. Miami, 1947; postgrad. Columbia U., 1949-53, U. Denver, 1955-56, Ariz. State U., 1956-57; MA, U. Ariz., 1950; EdD, Western Colo. U., 1974. Faculty, adminstrn. Tucson Pub. Schs., 1950—; tchr. Doolen Jr. High Sch., 1951-53, counselor high sch., 1953-62, asst. prin. Alice Vail Jr. High Sch., 1962-64, Catalina High Sch., 1964-68; prin. Rincon High Sch., 1968-71, Tucson High Sch., 1971-74; asst. supt. Tucson Pub. Schs., 1974-78, assoc. supt., 1978-82; pvt. practice family counseling. Mem. Tucson Mayor's Com. on Human Relations, 1969—; mem. Ariz. state com. Anti Defamation League, 1971; Ariz. state adv. bd. Good Shepherd Sch. for Girls, 1971; mem. Dem. Cen. Com., Pima City, Ariz., 1968—; bd. dirs., Mobile Meals of Tucson, Pima County Bd. Health, So. Arix. Girl Scouts U.S. Council; chmn. Tucson Community Ctr. Commn.; bd. dirs. Amigos dos los Americanos, AnyTown, Ariz., Lighthouse YMCA, Beacon Found., Big Bros., NCCJ, Jr. Achievement, Tucson Community Center, Pacific Western region Anti-Defamation League, Handmaker Nursing Home Pima County, United Way, CODAC, Planned Parenthood, Girl Scouts Am., Ariz. Mobile Meals, Epilepsy Soc. So. Ariz., Drug Abuse and Alcohol Consortium; adv. bd. Tucson Free Med. Clinic; bd. dirs. Los Ninos Crisis Center. Mem. Ariz. Assn. Student Teaching (state treas.), NEA, Ariz. Interscholastic Assn. (pres. conf. 1971, legis. council), Ariz. Personnel and Guidance Assn., Nat. Assn. Secondary Sch. Prins., Am. Assn. Sch. Adminstrs., Assn. Supervision and Curriculum Devel., Ariz. Sch. Adminstrs., Phi Epislon Pi, Phi Delta Kappa. Home: 7101 E River Canyon Rd Tucson AZ 85715-2111 Office: PO Box 30163 Tucson AZ 85751-0163

STARR, ROBERT IRVING, plant physiologist, chemist; b. Laramie, Wyo., Dec. 11, 1932; s. George Herman and Meriel Louise (Spooner) S.; m. Lavon Fabricius, June 10, 1956; children: Deborah Ann, Kenneth Irving. BS in Chemistry, U. Wyo., 1956, MS in Soil and Biochemistry, 1959, PhD in Plant Physiology and Chemistry, 1972. Ordained deacon and elder Presbyn. Ch. Chemist Shell Chem. Corp., Dominguez, Calif., 1956-57; biochemist Bur. Sport Fisheries and Wildlife, Denver, 1960-63; plant physiologist U.S. Bur. Sport Fisheries and Wildlife, Denver, 1968-74; plant physiologist Colo. State U., Ft. Collins, 1963-64, chemist toxic residue lab., 1965-68; analytical chemist FDA, Denver, 1964-65; environ. scientist coal mining U.S. Geol. Survey, Denver, 1974-77, chief environ. tech. unit, 1977-78; chief biol. and ecol. scis. br. Office of Surface Mining U.S. Dept. Interior, Denver, 1979-81, sr. tech. coord., cons. environ. chemistry, 1984-89; sr. scientist pesticide rsch. Wildlife Rsch. Ctr. USDA, Denver, 1989-93; cons. environ. chemistry Fort Collins, Colo., 1993—; pvt. practice cons. environ. chemistry, 1993—; cons. in environ. chemistry and fin. planning/real estate, 1982-84. Reviewer Jour. Agrl. Food Chemistry, 1970; editor, Reclamation Rev., 1981; contbr. articles to profl. jours. Served to 1st lt., AUS, 1957-64. Fellow Am. Inst. Chemists; mem. Am. Chem. Soc., Ft. Collins Swimming Club, Sigma Xi.

STARR, RUBY, counselor; b. Colonia Dublan, Chihuahua, Mexico, July 25, 1939; came to the U.S., 1957; d. Harvey Ashton and Ruth (McClellen) Longhurst; m. Max Vargas, Nov. 22, 1962 (div. Feb. 1975); children: Michael Kimball, Richard Ryan. BS, So. Ill. U., 1991; MA, Webster U., 1994. Registered counselor, adult tchr., NBCC. Saleswoman Jafra Cosmetics, San Ferdnando, Calif., 1967-72; fiscal sec. Dept. Game and Fish, Santa Fe, 1979-81; med. sec. VA, Albuquerque, 1981-86; sec., tchr. Kirtland AFB, Albuquerque, 1987-91; clk. Social Security Assn., Albuquerque, 1991-92; counselor Displaced Homemakers, Albuquerque, 1985—; support group founder Divorced Women, Albuquerque, 1986-92; rd. com. organizer Edgewood (N.Mex.) Cmty., 1989—;. Founder Woman Free, Albuqueque, 1986-90; adv. Crusaders for Legal Change, Albuqurque, Libertad, Albuquerque; mem. N.Mex. rep. 9-5 Women Work, Washington, 1993—, Making the Connections Intercultural Network, Abuse in the Work Place, 1994. Mem. ACA, Nat. Counseling Cert., Nat. Career Counseling, N.Mex. Career Counseling, Albuquerque Career Network. Home: PO Box 325 Edgewood NM 87015-0325

STARRATT, PATRICIA ELIZABETH, writer, actress, composer; b. Boston, Nov. 7, 1943; d. Alfred Byron and Anna (Mazur) S.; AB, Smith Coll., 1965; grad. prep. dept. Peabody Conservatory Music, 1961. Teaching asst. Harvard U. Grad. Sch. Bus. Aminstrn., 1965-67; mng. dir. INS Assocs., Washington, 1967-68; adminstrv. asst. George Washington U. Hosp., 1970-71; legal asst. Morgan, Lewis & Bockius, Washington, 1971-72; profl. staff energy analyst Nat. Fuels and Energy Policy Study, U.S. Senate Interior Com., 1972-74; cons., exec. asst. energy resource devel. Fed. Energy Adminstrn., Washington, 1974-75; sr. cons. energy policy Atlantic Richfield Co., 1975-76; energy cons., Alaska, 1977-78; govt. affairs assoc. Sohio Alaska Petroleum Co., Anchorage, 1978-85; legal asst. Hughes, Thorsness, Gantz, Powell and Brudin, Anchorage, 1989—; writer, media specialist corp. affairs Alyeska Pipeline Svc., Co., 1990-95; pres. Starratt Monarch Prodns., 1986—; Econ. Devel. Commn., Municipality of Anchorage, 1981; actress/asst. dir. Brattle St. Players, Boston, 1966-67, Washington Theater Club 1967-68, Gene Frankel, Broadway 1968-69; actress Aspen Resident Theater, Colo. 1985-86, Ranyevskya (The Cherry Orchard), Anchorage, 1994, Bonfila (SLAVS!), Anchorage, 1995; writer and assoc. producer Then One Night I Hit Her, 1983; screenwriter, prodr., actress, composer/pianist Invincible Summer, 1995; appeared Off-Broadway in To Be Young, Gifted and Black; performed as Mary in Tennessee, Blanche in A Streetcar Named Desire, Stephanie Dickinson in Cactus Flower, Angela in Papa's Wine, Elizabeth Procter in The Crucible, Candida in Candida, Zeuss in J.B., Martha in Who's Afraid of Virginia Woolf, Amy in Dinny and The Witches, as Columbina in Servant of Two Masters, as Singer in Death of Morris Biederman, as Joan in Joan of Lorraine, as Mado in Amadee, as Mrs. Rowlands in Before Breakfast, as the girl in Hello Out There, as Angela in Bedtime Story, as Hannah in Night of the Iguana, as Lavinia in Androcles and the Lion, as Catherine in Great Catherine, as Julie in Lilliom, as First Nurse in Death of Bessie Smith, as Laura in Tea and Sympathy, as Amelia Earheart in Chamber Music; appeared at Detroit Summer Theatre in Oklahoma, Guys and Dolls, Carousel, Brigadoon, Kiss Me Kate, Finnian's Rainbow; asst. to dir. Broadway plays A Cry Of Players, A Way Of Life, Off-Broadway play To Be Young, Gifted, and Black; screenwriter Challenge in Alaska, 1986, Martin Poll Films; asst. dir. Dustin Hoffman, 1974; contbr. articles on natural gas and Alaskan econ. and environ. to profl. jours. Bd. dirs. Anchorage Community Theatre; industry rep. Alaska Eskimo Whaling Commn.; mem. Alaska New Music Forum. Mem. Actors' Equity. Episcopalian. Avocations: skiing, horseback riding, biking, hiking. Home: 1054 W 20th Ave Apt 4 Anchorage AK 99503-1749

STARRS, ELIZABETH ANNE, lawyer; b. Detroit, Jan. 1, 1954; d. John Richard and Mabel Angeline (Gilchrist) S. BA, U. Mich., 1975; JD, Suffolk U., 1980. Bar: Mass. 1980, U.S. Dist. Ct. Mass. 1980, U.S. Ct. Appeals (1st. cir.) 1980, Colo. 1983, U.S. Dist. Ct. Colo. 1983, U.S. Ct. Appeals (10th cir.) 1983. Assoc. Denner & Benjoya P.C., Boston, 1980-83, Kennedy & Christopher P.C., Denver, 1983-86; ptnr. Kennedy & Christopher P.C. (formerly Cooper & Kelley P.C.), Denver, 1986—, pres., mng. ptnr., 1994—; instr. bus. law Bay State C.C., Boston, 1981-82. Troop leader Girl Scouts U.S., Denver, 1984-85; pres. CWBA Found., 1992-94. Mem. Colo. Bar Assn. (litigation coun. 1989—, chair 1993-94, profl. liability ins. chair 1991-93), Denver Bar Assn., Colo. Women's bar Assn. (bd. dirs. 1984-85, v.p. 1989-90). Roman Catholic. Office: Kennedy & Christopher PC 1660 Wynkoop St Ste 900 Denver CO 80202-1145

STASHOWER, ARTHUR L., lawyer; b. Cleve., Apr. 12, 1930; s. Joseph G. and Tillie (Merlin) S.; m. Joy Schary, Sept. 1, 1957 (div. 1982); children: Keren, Saul, David; m. Barbara Hayden, Jan. 17, 1985. AB, U. Mich., 1951, JD with distinction, 1953. Bar: Ohio 1953, Mich. 1953, Calif. 1957, U.S. Dist. Ct. (mid. dist.) Calif. 1957, U.S. Ct. Appeals (9th cir.) 1962. Assoc. Kaplan Livingston Goodwin & Berkowitz, Beverly Hills, Calif., 1957-64; exec. United Artists Corp., L.A., 1964-65, Artists Agy. Corp., L.A., 1965-67; assoc. Greenberg & Glusker, Beverly Hills, 1967-68; ptnr. Swerdlow Glikbarg & Shimer, Beverly Hills, 1968-71, Sklar Cohen & Stashower, L.A., 1971-84; of counsel Shea & Gould, L.A., 1985-88; ptnr. Chrystie & Berle, L.A., 1988-92, of counsel, 1993—; arbitrator Hughes Aircraft, E.A.S.T. Mem. Anti-Defamation League, 1961-79, exec. com. 1967-73; mem. Assn. Alternative Pub. Schs., L.A., 1973-79. Lt. USCGR, 1953-57. Mem. ABA, Am. Arbitration Assn., L.A. Bar Assn., State Bar Assn. Calif., Beverly Hills Bar Assn., L.A. Copyright Soc. (trustee 1986-90), Fed. Mediation and Conciliation Svc. Democrat. Jewish. Office: Chrystie & Berle 1925 Century Park E Ste 2200 Los Angeles CA 90067-2723

STASTNY, DONALD JOSEPH, architect; b. Klamath Falls, Oreg., May 18, 1943; s. Edwin James and Mariam Francis (Chatham) S.; m. Janet Helen Dalton, June 11, 1966; children—Kimberly, Rory, Joshua. B.S., Oreg. State U., 1965; B.Arch., U. Wash., 1968; M.Arch., M.City Planning, U. Pa., 1969. Registered architect, Oreg., Wash. Designer Roche, Dinkeloo & Assoc., Hamden, Conn., 1969-70; research architect Athens Ctr. of Ekistics, Greece, 1970-71; project architect Bumgardner Architects, Seattle, 1971-73; sr. designer Campbell, Yost, Grube, Portland, Oreg., 1973-75; urban designer Ekistic Cons., Edmonton, Alta., Can., 1973-76; pres. Stastny Architects, Portland, 1975—; founder, chmn. bd. trustees Oreg. Sch. of Design, Portland, 1981—; profl. advisor Beverly Hills Civic Ctr., Calif., 1982. Prin. works include: Columbia World Trade Ctr., 1982; Goose Hollow Village, 1982, Princeton Bldg., 1985. Chmn. central city planning com. City of Portland, 1984-86; mem. planning com. Monterey Design Conf., Calif., 1984-85; panel mem. Oreg. Arts Commn., Salem, 1983; mem. design rev. com. Multnomah County, Oreg., 1977; panel mem. Nat. Endowment for Arts, Washington, 1983-84. Ford Found. fellow, 1970. Mem. AIA, Am. Inst. Cert. Planners, Am. Planning Assn. (State Planning award Oreg. chpt. 1980), Can. Inst. Planners, Inst. Urban Design. Democrat. Office: Stastny Architects PC 813 SW Alder St # 200 Portland OR 97205-3121

STAUB, ANITA (ANITA KILPATRICK), management analyst, educator; b. Oakland, Calif., Dec. 24, 1947; d. Homer Lenel and Martha Bernice Kilpatrick; m. Jay Palmer Eickenhorst, Dec. 9, 1983. BA with honors, U. Calif., Berkeley, 1971, teaching cert., 1974; postgrad., Calif. State U., Hayward, 1972, U. Calif., Berkeley, 1973-74, Calif. Pacific U., 1986—. Cert. secondary tchr., Calif. Substitute tchr. Marin County Schs., San Francisco, 1974—; civil engring. tech. U.S. Army C. E., Sausalito, Calif., 1974-76; substitute tchr. Hendersonville (N.C.) City Schs., 1976-78, Henderson County (N.C.) Schs., 1976-79; park technician Nat. Park Service, Flat Rock, N.C., 1978-81; park technician Nat. Park Service, San Francisco, 1981-83, voucher examiner, 1983-85; mgmt. analyst intern Headquarters 6th U.S. Army, San Francisco, 1985-86; mgmt. analyst Hdqrs. 6th U.S. Army, San Francisco, 1986-89, U.S. Dept. Treasury, San Francisco, 1989—; cons. for interpretive prospectus Golden Gate Nat. Recreation Area, Nat. Park Service, San Francisco, 1981, recording sec. EEO com., 1984-85. Co-designer: Alcatraz Island interpretive display, 1981. Mem. Am. Soc. Mil. Comptrollers. San Francisco Bay Area Fed. Adminstrv. Coun., San Francisco Bay Area Fed. Fin. Mgrs. Coun., Wilderness Soc., Nature Conservancy, Nat. Audubon Soc., Mus. Soc., San Francisco Opera Guild, Stinson Beach Allied Arts Guild, San Francisco Regional Fin. Ctr. Employees Assn. (bd. dirs. sec. 1990, pres. 1991), Marin Conservation League. Home: PO Box 913 Stinson Beach CA 94970-0913 Office: US Treasury Dept Fin Mgmt Svc San Francisco Regional Fin Ctr San Francisco CA 94119-3858

STAUB, SCOTT CHRISTOPHER, fundraiser; b. Henderson, Nev., Mar. 4, 1957. AB, Washington U., St. Louis, 1979; MPA, Golden Gate U., 1984. Cert. fund raising exec. Sr. asst. mgr. Magic Pan Restaurants, St. Louis, 1979-81; admissions counselor Golden Gate U., San Francisco, 1981-85; regional exec. Cmty. Counselling Svc., San Francisco, 1985-93; dir. fund devel. Kapiolani Health Care Found., Honolulu, 1993-94; assoc. v.p. St. Francis Healthcare Found., Honolulu, 1994—. Mem. Nat. Soc. Fund Raising Execs., Assn. Health Care Philanthropy, Rotary Club of Ala Moana (v.p. 1994). Roman Catholic. Office: St Francis Health Care Fdn 2230 Liliha St Honolulu HI 96817-1646

STEAD, TIMOTHY, architect; b. Newark, N.J., July 6, 1958; s. Thomas Eugene and Hilda (Goncalves) S. BA, William Paterson Coll., 1984; BS in Architecture, Cath. U. Am., 1990. Registered architect, D.C., Colo. Project mgr. CDI Design, N.Y.C., 1983-86; project architect Giant Food, Inc., Washington, 1986-89, Martin Reddy Architects, Washington, 1990-93, SEM Architects, Englewood, Colo., 1993—. Architect: (bldgs.) Restoration of Main Lobby, Georgetown U. Hosp., Washington, 1992, Renovation of Gov. Ames Mansion, Boston, 1984, Bildner & Sons, Lenox Square, Ga., 1985, Giant Food Store, Potomac, Md., 1989. Mem. Inst. Store Planners (assoc.), Internat. Assn. Lighting Designers (sr. assoc. 1987-89), AIA, Tau Sigma Delta. Democrat. Roman Catholic. Office: SEM Architects 7935 E Prentice Ave Ste 102 Englewood CO 80111-2711

STEAD LEE, POLLY JAE See LEE, PALI JAE

STEADMAN, LYDIA DUFF, elementary school educator, symphony violinist; b. Hollywood, Calif., Dec. 31, 1934; d. Lewis Marshall and Margaret Seville (Williams) Duff; m. John Gilford Steadman, Apr. 14, 1961 (dec.). Student, Pepperdine U., 1952-55; BA in Music Edn., U. So. Calif., 1957. Cert. spl. secondary music, edn. tchr., Calif. Instrumental music tchr. Lancaster (Calif.) Sch. Dist., 1957-62; instrumental music tchr. Simi Sch. Dist., Simi Valley, Calif., 1962-70, elem. tchr., 1970—; tchr. Polynesian culture, dances, games, 1970—; hist. play write for elem. grades, organizer elem. sch. dance festivals; dir. All Dist. Orch., Lancaster, Simi Valley Schs., 1957-70; compile Japanese Culture Study Unit for elem. grades Ventura County. 1st violinist San Fernando Valley Symphony, Sherman Oaks, Calif., 1962-75, Conejo Valley Symphony, Thousand Oaks, 1975-81, tour concert mistress, 1980; 2d violinist Ventura County Symphony, 1981—. Pres. San Fernando Cmty. Concerts, Van Nuys, Calif., 1982-94; free lancing with pit orch. Cabrillo Music Theatre, Conejo Players Theater; organizer ann. sch. Jump Rope-a-Thon for Am. Heart Assn., Nat. Geog. Geography Bee; bd. dirs. East Ventura County Cmty. Concert Assn. Mem. AAUW, NAFE, Bus. and Profl. Women of Conejo Valley (pres. Golden Triangle chpt. 1988-90, 95-96, issues and mgmt. chair 1990, ways and means chair Coast chpt. 1990, editor Golden Triangle newsletter 1988-90, treas. 1992-93, sec. 1993-94, v.p. 1994—, pres. 1995-96), Sigma Xi-Sci. Rsch. Soc., Pacific Asia Mus., Armand Hammer Mus. Republican. Mem. Ch. of Christ. Home: 32016 Allenby Ct Westlake Village CA 91362

STEADMAN, ROBERT KEMPTON, oral and maxillofacial surgeon; b. Mpls., July 8, 1943; s. Henry Kempton and Helen Vivian (Berg) S.; m. Susan E. Hoffman; children: Andrea Helene, Darcy Joanne, Richard Kempton, Michael Dean. BS, U. Wash., Seattle, 1969, DDS, 1974. Diplomate Am. Bd. Oral and Maxillofacial Surgery. Residency USAF, Elgin AFB, Fla., 1974-75; resident oral and maxillofacial surgery U. Okla., 1977-80, La. State U., Shreveport, 1980-81; pvt. practice Spokane, Wash., 1981—; cons. Group Health Coop., 1989—; mem. adv. bd. Osteoporosis Awareness Resource, 1988—. Select recruiting ptnr. U. Wash. Sch. Dentistry, 1990. Fellow Am. Coll. Oral & Maxillofacial Surgery, Am. Soc. Oral & Maxillofacial Surgery, Acad. Gen. Dentistry; mem. Internat. Soc. Plastic, Aesthetic and Reconstructive Surgery, Delta Sigma Delta (pres. 1987-88). Office: 801 W 5th Ave Ste 212 Spokane WA 99204-2800

STEAR, EDWIN BYRON, corporate executive; b. Peoria, Ill., Dec. 8, 1932; s. Edwin Joseph and Juanita Blanche (Hoffman) S.; married; children—Brian Douglas, Linnea Susan. B.S. in Mech. Engring, Bradley U., 1954; M.S., U. So. Calif., 1956; Ph.D. (Hughes Staff fellow), UCLA, 1961. Mem. tech. staff Hughes Aircraft Co., Culver City, Calif., 1954-59; asst. research engr. U. Calif., Los Angeles, 1959-61; asst. prof. engring. U. Calif., 1964-68, assoc. prof., 1968-69; mgr. guidance and control research lab. Lear Siegler, Inc., Santa Monica, Calif., 1963-64; assoc. prof. elec. engring. U. Calif., Los Angeles and Santa Barbara, 1969-73; prof. U. Calif., 1973-79, chmn. dept., 1975-79; chief scientist USAF, 1979-82; dir. Wash. Technology Ctr., 1983-90; prof. elec. engring. U. Wash., Seattle, 1983-90, assoc. dean research Coll. Engring., 1983-85; corp. v.p. tech. assessment Boeing Co., Seattle, 1990—; mem. sci. adv. bd. USAF, 1971-79, 84-92, vice chmn., 1986-89, chmn., 1989-90; mem. aeros. adv. com. NASA, 1984-90; cons. to industry and govt., 1964-79, 82—; mem. SAE Tech. Stds. Bd., 1994—; industry adv. coun. Accreditation Bd. Engring. and Tech., Inc., 1994—; trustee Analytical Svcs., Inc., 1984-90; mem. guidance and control panel NATO Adv. Group Aerospace R&D, 1981-92, dep. chmn. panel, 1988-90, chmn. 1990-92. Editor: (with A. Kadish) Hormonal Control Systems, 1969; mem. editorial bd. Aircraft jour. AIAA, 1974-77; contbr. articles to profl. lit. Served to 1st lt. USAF, 1961-63. Named Disting. Alumnus Bradley U., 1980; recipient civilian exceptional svc. medals USAF, 1982, 92; Arnold D. Beckman lectr. on rsch. and innovation U. Ill., Urbana, 1993; Mental Health Tng. Program fellow UCLA, 1972-74. Fellow IEEE; mem. AIA, AAAS, Internat. Fedn. Automation Control, Am. Electronics Assn. (sci. and tech. com. 1988-90), Sigma Xi, Eta Kappa Nu, Pi Mu Epsilon, Tau Beta Pi, Phi Eta Sigma, Tau Sigma. Home: 14010 SE 44th Pl Bellevue WA 98006-2331 Office: The Boeing Co PO Box 3707 MS 13-43 Seattle WA 98124-2207

STEBBINS, DENNIS ROBERT, environmental management consultant; b. Evergreen Park, Ill., Mar. 4, 1948; s. Daniel Mathew and Alberta Irene (Schmidt) S.; m. Ida Gattinger, Feb. 14, 1989. AA in Bus. Mgmt./Sci., Mohegan C. C., Norwich, Conn., 1983; BS in Environ. Studies, Chadwick U., 1993, MBA, 1993, MS in Environ. Mgmt., 1994. Enlisted USN, 1966, advanced through grades to commd. chief warrant officer, ret., 1989; pres., CEO Fanciful Notions, Inc., Honolulu, 1989-91; Hawaii state mgr. of field ops. Census '90 U.S. Dept. Commerce/U.S. Bur. of Census, Honolulu, 1990; pres., CEO Stebbins Internat. Ltd., Honolulu; pres. The Global Environ. Mgmt. Devel. Group, Belize, 1993—; dir. project infrastructure devel. in Belize and Venezuela The Global Environ. Mgmt. Devel. Group, 1994; pres., exec. dir. Found. of Earth Resources, Scis. and Techs., Reno and Honolulu, 1994—; instr. Can. Fed. Staff Coll., B.C., 1992; assoc. prof. Chaminade U., Honolulu, 1994—; adj. prof. Chadwick U., Birmingham, Ala., 1994—, Magellan U., Birmingham, Ala., 1995—; spl. advisor UN Environ. Program, 1992—, internat. corp. adv. coun., 1992—; advisor UN Devel. Program, 1994—; mem. faculty Nat. Bus. Inst., Eau Clair, Wis., 1993—, Lincoln Grad. Ctr., San Antonio, 1994—; mem. Law Seminars Internat., Seattle, 1994—, instr., 1995—. Author of one book and co-author four books on environ. sci.; contbr. articles to internat. profl. jours. Advisor, trustee The Tanager Found., Reno, Nev., 1992-93; bd. dirs. Neighborhood Bd., Honolulu, 1992-93, Mayor's Complete County Com., Honolulu, 1990. Mem. ASTD (Hawaii chpt. bd. dirs., pres.-elect 1990-92), UN Assn. U.S. (bd. dirs. 1992-93), Nat. Soc. Environ. Cons. (nat. adv. bd. 1994—), Am. Meteorol. Soc., C. of C. of Hawaii (bd. dirs. small bus. coun. 1990-91), Ret. Officers Assn. (chpt. bd. dirs., pub. rels. dir. 1992-93), N.Am. Environ. Edn. Assn., Nat. Soc. Environ. Cons. Democrat. Home: 1520 Ward Ave Apt 1302 Honolulu HI 96822-3556 Office: Stebbins Internat Ltd The Environ Leadership Consultancy 1750 Kalakaua Ave Ste 3775 Honolulu HI 96826

STEBLAY, CRAIG DOUGLAS, real estate executive, entrepreneur; b. San Bernardino, Calif., Mar. 1, 1948; s. Ralph Edward and Grace J. (Rhody) S.; m. Amina Marie Nickell, Sept. 28, 1968; children: Lavee, Kari Ann, Jennifer. V.p. Phototron Corp., San Bernardino, Calif., 1982—, also dir.; sec., treas. Sunmass Corp., Phoenix, Ariz., 1986—; pres. Sunmass Corp., Phoenix, 1987—. Served with USMC, 1969-71. Lodge: Knights of Malta (named Knight of Honor 1984), Cedam Internat.

STECKBAUER, JAMES J., quality assurance professional; b. Oshkosh, Wis., Jan. 23, 1947; s. William jacob and Mary Catherine (Binder) S. AA in Quality Assurance, Coastline Coll., Fountain Valley, Calif., 1980; BSBA in Mgmt., U. Nev., Las Vegas, 1986. Cert. quality auditor, Am. Soc. Quality Control. Mechanic Oshkosh, Wis., 1965-66; avionics tech. USMC, 1966-70; avionics instr. Naval Air Tech. Tng. Ctr., Millington, Tenn., 1970-72; USMC recruiter Milw., 1972-76; avionics supr. USMC Air Station, Santa Ana, 1976-77; elec. mechanic test tech. US Naval Shipyard, Long Beach, Calif., 1978-79; quality assurance specialist USAF Plant Rep. Office, Redondo Beach, Calif., 1979-80, Fullerton, Calif., 1980-82; with USAF Western Space and Missile Ctr., Vandenberg AFB, Calif., 1982-83; quality assurance specialist U.S. Dept. Energy, Mercury, Nev., 1983-86, U.S. Army Plant Rep. Office,

Mesa, Ariz., 1988-90, U.S. Def. Plant Rep. Office, Mesa, Ariz., 1990—; tng. specialist, instr. U. Nev. Sys., N. Las Vegas, 1987. Ssgt. USMC, 1966-77. Mem. Am. Soc. for Quality Control, Nat. Contract Mgmt. Assn., U. Nev.-Las Vegas Alumni Assn., Fraternal Order of Eagles # 3850, Am. Legion, Harley Owners Group. Roman Catholic. Home: 11431 E Broadway Ave Apache Junction AZ 85220-4729

STECKEL, BARBARA JEAN, city financial officer; b. L.A., Mar. 9, 1939; d. John Herschel and Bernice Evelyn (Selstad) Webb Banta; m. Jimmie Raeburn Lugenbeel, Feb. 16, 1957 (div. 1962); Leanna Virgina, Debra Lynn; m. Dale Robert Steckel, Mar. 16, 1962; 1 child, Richard Alan. AA in Bus., Anchorage Community Coll., 1975; BBA, U. Alaska, Anchorage, 1980. City clk., treas. City of Kotzebue, Alaska, 1973-74, city mgr., treas., 1974-76; grants adminstr. Municipality of Anchorage, Alaska, 1976-79, contr., 1979-82, mcpl. mgr., 1982-84, chief fiscal officer, 1984-87; fin. dir., treas. City of Riverside, Calif., 1988—; bd. dirs. Riverside Cmty. Ventures, Corp., Cmty. Health Corp., chmn. fin. com. Mem. adv. coun. sch. bus. and pub. adminstrn. U. Alaska, Anchorage, 1982-85; bd. dirs. Anchorage Parking Authority, 1984-87, ICMA Retirement Corp., 1985-93, Police and Fire Retirement Sys. Mcpl. of Anchorage, 1982-87, chmn., 1986; devel. com. mem. Am. Heart Assn., Anchorage, 1987. Mem. Govt. Fin. Officers U.S. and Can. (bd. dirs. 1984-87), Mcpl. Fin. Officers Alaska (pres. 1981-82), Nat. Assn. Accts. (bd. dirs. 1986-87), Am. Soc. Women Accts., Calif. Soc. Mcpl. Fin. Officers (chmn. cash mgmt. com. 1989-91, bd. dirs. 1992-95, pres. elect 1995-96), Mcpl. Treas. Assn. (R.E. Phillips award, Svc. award, debt. com. chmn. 1992—), Calif. Mcpl. Treas. Assn., Internat. City Mgrs. Assn., U. Alaska Alumni Assn., Rotary, Elks. Office: City of Riverside 3900 N Main St Riverside CA 92522-0001

STECKLER, CRAIG THEODORE, law enforcement official; b. Scottsfield, Ill., Feb. 3, 1944; s. Albert George and Mary Lorene (Johnston) S.; m. Karen Capellutto, Mar. 11, 1978; children: Theresa, Rachael, Suzanne, Mark. AA, Saddleback Coll., 1973; BA, Calif. State U., L.A., 1975; postgrad., U. Va., 1982, Peace Officer Standards & Tng., Pomona, Calif., 1986. Dist. mgr. Orange County Register, Santa Ana, Calif., 1962-68; police officer, sgt., then lt. City of San Clemente, Calif., 1968-80; police chief City of Piedmont, Calif., 1980-86; dep. police chief City of Fremont, Calif., 1986-92, chief of police, 1992—; instr., Cypress (Calif.) Coll., 1975-77, Los Mondos Coll., Pittsberg, calif., 1982-83. Mem. Am. Mgmt. Assn., Calif. Peace Officers Assn., Calif. Police Chiefs Assn. (bd. dirs.), Command Coll. Grads. (bd. dirs.), Rotary. Republican. Roman Catholic. Office: Fremont Police Dept 39710 Civic Center Dr Fremont CA 94538-2359

STECKLER, LARRY, publisher, editor; b. Bklyn., Nov. 3, 1933; s. Morris and Ida (Beekman) S.; m. Catherine Coccozza, June 6, 1959; children: Gail Denise, Glenn Eric, Kerri Lynn, Adria Lauren. Student, CCNY, 1951. Assoc. editor Radio-Electronics mag., N.Y.C., 1957-62, editor, 1967-85; pub., editor in chief Radio Electronics mag., 1985-92; electronics editor Popular Mechanics mag., N.Y.C., 1962-65; assoc. editor Electronic Products mag., Garden City, N.Y., 1965-67; editorial dir. Merchandising 2-Way Radio mag., N.Y.C., 1975-77; v.p., dir. Gernsback Publs., N.Y.C., 1975-84, pres., dir., 1984—; pub., editorial dir. Spl. Projects mag., 1980-84, Radio-Electronics Ann., 1982-84; pub., editor in chief Hands-On Electronics, 1984-88; Popular Electronics Mag., 1988—, Hobbyists Handbook, 1989—; pub., editor in chief Experimenters Handbook, 1986—; Radio Craft, 1993; pub., editor in chief Computer Digest, 1985-90; pres. Claggk, Inc., 1986—; Silicon Chip, 1993-94; pub., editor in chief The Magic Course, Eating In/Dining Out on Long Island, Modern Short Stories, 1987-90, GIZMO, 1988—, Video/Stereo Digest, 1989-91; pres. Sci. Probe Inc., 1989-93; pub., editor in chief Sci. Probe! mag., 1989-93, StoryMasters, 1989—, Electronics Shopper, 1990—, Electronics Market Ctr., 1991—; mem. electronics adv. bd. Bd. Coop. Ednl. Services, Nassau County, N.Y., 1975-77; pres. Electronics Industry Hall of Fame, 1985—; bd. dirs. Pub. Hall of Fame, 1987-89. Author books, handbooks; pub.; contbr. articles to profl. jours. Bd. dirs. Nassau County council Camp Fire Girls, 1971-72. Served with U.S. Army, 1953-56. Recipient Coop. award Nat. Alliance TV and Electronic Services Assns., 1974, 75; inducted into Electronics Industry Hall of Fame, 1985. Mem. IEEE, Internat. Soc. Cert. Electronic Technicians (chmn. 1974-76, 79-81, 93-95, Chmn.'s award 1985, dir. at large 1991-93, rep. to NESDA bd. 1991-93), Nat. Electronics Sales and Svc. Dealers Assn. (rec. sec. N.Y. state 1976-78, Man of Yr. award 1975, 85, treas. 1991-94, M.L. Finneyberg Excellence award 1994), Am. Mgmt. Assn., Radio Club Am., Internat. Underwater Explorers Soc., Am. Soc. Bus. Press Editors (sr.), Internat. Performing Magicians (exec. dir.), Soc. Profl. Journalists, L.A. Press. Home: 2601 Springridge Dr Las Vegas NV 89134-8848 Office: Gernsback Pub Inc 500B Bi County Blvd Farmingdale NY 11735-3918 also: Claggk Inc 4820 Alpine Pl Ste A101 Las Vegas NV 89107-4065

STEDMAN, WILLIAM PRESTON, music educator; b. Austin, Tex., Feb. 10, 1923; s. Nathan Alexander and Mary Lucille (Sneed) S.; m. Helen Margaret Slessor, Aug. 3, 1946 (div. May 1968); children: Preston Slessor, Alexander Winship; m. Leslie Clark McNeill, June 5, 1970. BA, Tex. Christian U., 1944, MMus, 1948; PhD, U. Rochester, N.Y., 1953. Asst. bus. mgr. Ft. Worth Civic Opera Assn., 1946-47; asst. prof. music Sul Ross State Coll., Alpine, Tex., 1947-51; asst. prin. viola El Paso (Tex.) Symphony Orch., 1948-51; teaching asst. Eastman Sch. Music, Rochester, 1952-53; instr. music Ind. U., Bloomington, 1953-55; music chair, prof. music Tex. A&I U., Kingsville, 1955-66; dean Conservatory of Music U. Pacific, Stockton, Calif., 1966-76; prof. music Calif. State U., Fullerton, 1976—; exec. dir. Pacific Symphony Orch., Fullerton, 1978-79; dir. Western Opera, San Francisco Opera, 1975-78; v.p. exec. bd. Pacific Symphony Orch., Costa Mesa, Calif., 1978-93; examiner Western Assn. Schs./Colls., Oakland, Calif., 1966-92; cons. Calif. Arts Coun., Sacramento, 1968-76; fiscal cons. Calif. Assn. Profl. Music Tchrs. Author: Intro to Stylistic Theory, 3 vols., 1988, The Symphony, Research and Information Guide, 1990, Mexico's Musical Evolution, 1992, The Symphony, 2nd edit., 1993. Lay reader Episcopal Ch., Alpine, Tex., Stockton, Calif., Kingsville, Tex., 1950-76; pres. Kingsville Cmty. Concerts Assn., 1964-66; bd. mem. Fine Arts Commn.,Fullerton, Calif., 1980-84. Lt. (j.g.) USN, 1943-46, PTO. Faculty rsch. grantee Ind. U., Bloomington, 1954, Tex. A&I U., Kingsville, 1963. Mem. Assn. Calif. Symphony Orchestra (bd. mem., v.p. 1988-90), Music Tchrs. Nat. Assn. (chmn. theory composition S.W. divsn. 1958-66). Home: 731 E Avocado Crest Rd La Habra Hgts CA 90631-8132 Office: Calif State U Fullerton CA 92634

STEED, EMMETT D., hotel executive; b. Logan, Utah, July 14, 1950; s. Dale R. and Elizabeth (Emmett) S.; m. Jana Carol Jones, July 31, 1976; 3 children. BA in Journalism, Utah State U., 1974; M in Internat. Mgmt., Am. Grad. Sch., 1975. Asst. contr. Marriott Hotels Camelback Inn, Scottsdale, Ariz., 1975-76, Marriott Hotels Essex Ho., N.Y.C., 1976-78; contr. Marriott Mexicana, Acapulco, Mex., 1978-80, Marriott Hotel, L.A., 1980-82; regional contr. Marriott Hotels, Plantation, Fla., 1982-85; resident mgr. Marriott Hotels, Panama City, Panama, 1985-89, Scottsdale, Ariz., 1985-89; v.p. Red Lion Hotels and Inns, Vancouver, Wash., 1989-92; gen. mgr. Red Lion Hotel/Orange County Airport, 1992—; bd. dirs. South Coast Metro Alliance. Mem. Utah State U. Support Coun., 1992-94; bd. govs. Orange Garde; dir. LDS Ch. Employment, Ft. Lauderdale, 1984-85. Mem. Am. Mgmt. Assn. (treas.), Am. Grad. Sch. of Internat. Mgmt. Alumni Assn., Sigma Chi (life). Republican. Office: Red Lion Hotel Orange County Airport 3050 Bristol Costa Mesa CA 92626

STEEL, CLAUDIA WILLIAMSON, artist; b. Van Nuys, Calif., Mar. 19, 1918; d. James Gordon and Ella (Livingston) Williamson; m. Lowell F. Steel, Aug. 15, 1941; children: Claudia Steel Rosen, Douglas Lowell, roger Conant. BA in Art, U. Calif., Berkeley, 1939, secondary credential, 1940; MFA, Mills Coll., 1967. Tchr. art Greenville Jr./Sr. High Sch., Calif., 1940-42; faculty Calif. State U., Chico, 1967-69; pvt. tchr. art, Chico; one-woman shows include Laboudt Gallery, San Francisco, 1958, Witherspoon Bldg., Phila., 1959, traveling show with Old Bergen Guild to nat. galleries, 1971-84, Redding (Calif.) Mus., 1973, Central Wyo. Mus. Art, Casper, 1976, U. Portland 1976, U. Wis., LaCrosse, 1978, Purdue U., West Lafayette, Ind., 1979, Pratt Inst., Manhatten Gallery, N.Y.C., 1980, Creative Arts Ctr., Chico, Calif., 1980, 84; exhibited in group shows Santa Barbara Art Mus., 1951, San Francisco Arts Festival (award), 1953, Oakland Art Mus., 1954, San Francisco Women Artists juried shows, 1958, 68 (award), 72, 73, 75, 76, Crocker Mus., Sacramento, 1958, 59, 60, 65, 67 (award), 73, Richmond Mus. (Calif.), 1960, DeYoung Mus. Art, San Francisco, 1960, San Francisco Mus. Art, 1959, 61 (award), Legion of Honor Mus., San Francisco, 1960, Mills Coll. Gallery, 1962, 67, 78, Berkeley Art Ctr. Gallery, 1969, San Francisco Art Commn. Gallery, 1972, Brandeis U., Mass., 1973, Ohio State U., Columbus, 1973, Brandt Gallery, Glendale, Calif., 1978, 1987, Chico State U., 1979, 1987, Fisher Gallery, Chico, Walnut Creek Art Gallery and Sonoma State U., 1979, Pratt Inst., Manhattan Gallery, N.Y.C., 1980, 1980, Calif. Soc. Printmakers traveling show, 1981, juried show, Singapore and Switzerland, 1984, Purdue U., 1982, U. Wis.-Eau Claire, 1982, Nat. Gallery, Bangkok, Malmo, Sweden, 1984-86, gallery show, Tokyo, 1985, Pacific Art League Gallery, Palo Alto, Calif., 1986, Tokyo Met. Mus., 1986, U.S.-U.K. Print Connection Barbican Ctr., London, 1989, others. Bd. dirs. Creative Art Ctr., Chico, 1977-81, Omni Arts, Chico, 1979-82. Recipient San Francisco Mus. of Art Serigraphy award, 1961; trustees' scholar Mills Coll., 1935, others. Mem. Calif. Soc. Printmakers (v.p., dir. 1973-77), Los Angeles Printmakers Soc.

STEELE, CHARLES RICHARD, applied mechanics educator; b. Royal, Iowa, Aug. 15, 1933; s. Edwin Silas and Lora Ruth (Walker) S.; m. Marie-Louise Buehler, Dec. 13, 1969; children: Eric, Brett, Jay, Ryan. BS, Tex. A&M U., 1956; PhD, Stanford (Calif.) U., 1960. Engrng. specialist Chance Vought Aircraft, Dallas, 1959-60; rsch. scientist Lockheed Rsch. Lab., Palo Alto, Calif., 1960-66; assoc. prof. Stanford U., 1966-71, prof., 1971—. Editor-in-chief Internat. Jour. Solids and Structures, 1985—; contbr. articles to profl. jours.; inventor bone tissue analyzer. Recipient Claude Pepper award NIH, 1988, Cert. of Recognition NASA, 1987, Humboldt Sr. award 1995. Fellow ASME (chair AMD exec. com. 1983-84, Citation Outstanding Contbn. 1982), Am. Acad. of Mechanics (pres. 1989-90); mem. Acoustical Soc. Am., Am. Soc. for Gravitational Space, Nat. Acad. Engrng. Democrat. Office: Divsn of Applied Mechanics Durand Bldg Stanford CA 94305

STEELE, ELIZABETH MEYER, lawyer; b. San Mateo, Calif., Jan. 12, 1952; d. Bailey Robert and Kathryn Steele (Horrigan) Meyer; m. Gene Dee Fowler, Aug. 9, 1975 (div. Apr. 1985); 1 child, Steele Sternberg. BA, Kirkland Coll., 1974; JD, U. N.Mex., 1977. Counsel U.S. Dept. Energy, Los Alamos, N.Mex., 1977-78; law clk. to judge Howard C. Bratton U.S. Dist. Ct., Albuquerque, 1978-80; assoc. Davis, Graham & Stubbs, Denver, 1980-84, ptnr., 1985-87; v.p., gen. counsel Jones Intercable, Inc., Englewood, Colo., 1987—. Office: Jones Intercable Inc 9697 E Mineral Ave Englewood CO 80112-3408

STEELE, EVELYN JANE, public relations and advertising executive; b. Berkeley, Calif., Feb. 14, 1911; d. Carlos Louis and Jane Catherine (Jensen) de Clairmont; grad. Munson Bus. Coll., San Francisco, 1929-30; m. Donald Dickinson Steele, May 8, 1932; 1 son, Donald de Clairmont. Pvt. sec., 1930-32; engaged in public relations, publicity and advt., 1940—; v.p., dir. Steele Group, San Francisco, 1977—; sec.-treas. Internat. Pub. Relations Co., Ltd., San Francisco; sec.-treas. Internat. Bus. Interface, Inc., Don Steele Advt. Pres. Ladies Aid Retarded Children, San Francisco, 1977-78, bd. dirs., 1978-88. Mem. Fashion Group (regional dir. 1965-67). Republican. Unitarian. Clubs: Metropolitan (dir. 1961-68), Order Rainbow Girls. Office: 703 Market St San Francisco CA 94103-2102

STEELE, FRANK CHANNEL, sales executive; b. N.Y.C., Oct. 1, 1938; s. Ralph E. and Frances (Channell) S.; m. Karon Kay Kennelly, May 22, 1965; children: Darrin, Danielle. BA, U. Rochester, 1960. Sales rep. Scott Paper Co., Salt Lake City, 1964-66; adminstrv. asst. Scott Paper Co., Seattle, 1966-69, asst. dist. mgr., 1969-70; regional sales mgr. Airborne Freight Corp., Phila., 1970-72; regional mgr. Airborne Freight Corp., Boston, 1972-76; regional mgr. N.Y.C., 1976-78, regional mgr., v.p., 1978-80; v.p. sales Seattle, 1980-84, sr. v.p. sales, 1984—. 1st lt. USAF, 1960-63. Office: Airborne Freight Corp 3101 Western Ave Seattle WA 98121-1024

STEELE, JOHN ROY, real estate broker; b. Detroit, Feb. 16, 1945; s. Wallace Lee Roy and Kay F. (Fitzpatrick) S.; m. Beverly Louise Rauh, June 3, 1972; children: Josh Oliver, Matt Edward, Anne Elizabeth. BA, Alma Coll., 1967; MBA, Central Mich. U., 1968 . Pres. Sierra Mercantile, Inc., 1981—; owner/broker Century 21 Steele, Realtors, Jackson, Calif., 1981-95; owner/broker Steele Realtors, 1995—; ptnr./broker Century 21, Lewis-Steele, Realtors, Inc., Jackson and Truckee, Calif., 1975-81; v.p. Century 21 Foothill-Sierra council, 1987-88; dir. Amador Title Co., 1978-83, pres., 1978-79; ptnr. Computer World, Jackson, 1983-85. Writer (newspaper column) Real Estate Corner, 1990-91, (cable TV show) Real Estate Views, 1990; bd. dirs. Century 21 Valley-Lode Coun., 1991, 92, sec.-treas., 1992. Bd. dirs. Trinity Episcopal Ch., Sutter Creek, Calif., 1978-79, 80-83, jr. warden, 1979; trustee Citizens for Progress, 1981-82; chmn. Amador County chpt. Easter Seals Telethon, 1985-88. pres. Amador Swim Team, 1986-87, 87-88, steering com. 1986-89, co-chmn. championship, 1990; coach Mother Lode Youth Soccer League, 1984, 86; coach state finals Odyssey (Olympics) of the Mind, 1986, 87, 91; mem. parent adv. com. Amador High Sch., 1989—, mem. prin. selection com., 1994. Mem. Amador County Bd. Realtors (bd. dirs. 1974-82, 91, 92, profl. standards com. 1988-90, 94—, pres. 1978, grievance comm. 1991-92, budget and fin. com. 1993, nominating com. 1993, 95, chair nominating com. 1993), Calif. Assn. Realtors (dir. 1978), Friends of the Library Club, Toastmasters (charter, Competent Toastmaster). Office: PO Box 610 Jackson CA 95642-0610

STEELE, JULIUS RAYNARD, special education educator; b. Little Rock, Ark., Oct. 18, 1952; s. D. J. Steele and Juanita (Thomas) Gilbert; children: Misty N., Sara M. BS, Northwestern U., Natchitoches, La., 1974; MA, La. Tech. U., 1978; EdS, Point Loma Nazarene Coll., 1992; EdD in Ednl. Leadership, No. Ariz. U., 1992. Cert. tchr. handicapped, severely handicapped, counseling, physical edn., edn. adminstrn, Calif. Tchr. learning handicapped Caddo Parish Schs., Shreveport, La., 1974-81; tchr. severely handicapped Pulaski County Schs., Little Rock, 1988-89, San Diego City Schs., 1989-93; asst. prin. Oxnard Union High Sch. Dist., 1993—; cons. Point Loma Nazarene Coll., San Diego, 1992-93. Mem. adv. bd. San Diego Parks & Recreation Disabled Svcs., 1992-93, adv. com. Lincoln Prep. High Sch., San Diego, 1992-93. Mem. Assn. Calif. Sch. Adminstrs., Omega Psi Phi (treas.). Democrat. Home: PO Box 2765 Oxnard CA 93034-2765

STEELE, MICHAEL RHOADS, humanities and peace studies educator, writer; b. Norfolk, Va., June 8, 1945; s. Harry Eugene and Dorothy Norris (Rhoads) S.; m. Gierianne Gayle Steele, May 31, 1986; children: Erica, Jared, Matthew, Sean. BA in English, U. Notre Dame, 1967; MA in English, Mich. State U., 1971, PhD in English, 1975. Rschr. Brit. Mus., London, 1973; disting. prof. English and humanities Pacific U., Forest Grove, Oreg., 1975—, chmn. peace and conflict studies, 1987—, dir. Humanitarian Ctr., 1993—; pres. Oreg. Holocaust Reource Ctr., 1992—. Author: Knute Rockne: A Bio-Bibliography, 1983, The Fighting Irish Football Enxyclopedia, 1992, Christianity, Tragedy, and Holocaust Literature, 1995. Alumni disting. fellow Mich. State U., 1967; grantee Oreg. Com. for Humanities, 1986, United Ch. of Christ, 1990. Mem. MLA, Nat. Coun. Tchrs. English, U.S. Handball Assn. (nat. commr. 1986-89). Home: 2936 Watercrest Rd Forest Grove OR 97116-1034 Office: Pacific U English Dept 2043 College Way Forest Grove OR 97116-1756

STEELE, SUSAN, art editor; b. Glendale, Calif., Oct. 29, 1944; d. Ralph Arthur and Marjorie E. (Kinzer) Miller; m. Larry L. Steele, Sept. 10, 1966 (div. Sept. 1979); 1 child, Larry Jr. BA, U. Calif., Santa Barbara, 1969. Cert. tchr., Calif. Art editor R/C Modeler, Sierra Madre, Calif., 1970-93, Freshwater and Marine Aquarium Mag., Sierra Madre, Calif., 1993—. Office: Freshwater and Marine Aquar 144 W Sierra Madre Blvd Sierra Madre CA 91024-2435

STEELE, TIMOTHY REID, English language educator, poet; b. Burlington, Vt., Jan. 22, 1948; s. Edward William Steele Jr. and Ruth Bell Reid Gjessing; m. Victoria Lee Erpelding, Jan. 14, 1979. BA, Stanford U., 1970; PhD, Brandeis U., 1977. Jones lectr. in poetry Stanford (Calif.) U., 1975-77; lectr. English UCLA, 1977-83, U. Calif., Santa Barbara, 1986; prof. English Calif. State U., L.A., 1987—. Author: Uncertainties and Rest, 1979, Sapphics Against Anger and Other Poems, 1986, Missing Measures, 1990, The Color Wheel, 1994, Sapphics and Uncertainties: Poems 1970-1986, 1995. Recipient Peter I.B. Lavan award The Acad. Am. Poets, 1986; Guggenheim fellow, 1984-85. Home: 1801 Preuss Rd Los Angeles CA 90035-4313 Office: Calif State Univ Dept of English 5151 State University Dr Los Angeles CA 90032

STEELE, VICTORIA LEE, librarian; b. L.A., Feb. 24, 1952; d. John Wilms and Marjorie (Lee) Erpelding; m. Timothy Reid, Jan. 14, 1979. BA, UCLA, 1974, MLS, 1981; MA, U. So. Calif., 1993. Libr. Belt Libr. of Vinciana UCLA, 1981-82, head history and spl. collections Biomed. Libr., 1983-86, dir. devel. librs., 1986-88; head spl. collections U. So. Calif., L.A., 1988—; fundraising cons. Author: Becoming a Fundraiser, 1992; prodr. film: Every time I See a Patient..., 1994; contbr. articles to profl. publs. Bd. dirs. Oscar Romero Clinic, L.A., 1994—; founder L.A. Preservation Network. U. Calif. rsch. grantee, 1979; Fulbright fellow, (UK), 1995. Mem. ALA (3M/JMRT award 1982). Office: U So Calif Doheny Libr University Park Los Angeles CA 90089-0182

STEELE, WILLIAM ARTHUR, financial analyst, public utilities executive; b. Albuquerque, Dec. 21, 1953; s. William Robert and Lois Ellen (Garvett) S. BSBA, U. No. Colo., 1976; MBA, U. Phoenix, Denver, 1987. Buyer Joslins Dept. Stores, Denver, 1978-79; transp. specialist Colo. Pub. Utilities Commn., Denver, 1979-80, fin. analyst, 1980-83, sr. fin. analyst, 1983-87, prin. fin. analyst, 1987—. Mem. Colo. State Mgr. Assn., Nat. Assn. Regulatory Commn. (staff subcom. on mgmt. analysis). Office: Pub Utilities Commn 1580 Logan St Denver CO 80203-1939

STEEN, EMMA EDITH, dietitian, educator; b. Thayer Junction, Wyo., Aug. 3, 1939; d. Joe and Enrica (Filippi) Profaizer; m. George Henry Steen, Nov. 27, 1965; children: Michelle, David, Michael. BS in Dietetics, Loretto Heights Coll., 1961; student, U. Pavia, Italy, 1964-65. Dietetics intern St. Louis U., 1961-62; nutrition cons. Oreg. Dairy Coun., Portland, 1962-64; registered dietitian Kaiser Permanente Hosp., Portland, 1965-74; instr. Portland C.C./Tektronix, Beaverton, Oreg., 1992—; com. chair St. Thomas More Cath. Sch., Oreg. Campaign worker Oreg. Dem. Com., Portland, 1988. Mem. Am. Dietetic Assn. (registered), Oreg. Dietetic Assn. (chair profl. registration com., chair placement com., chair awards com., chair cookbook com.), Toastmasters Internat. (Competent Toastmaster 1992). Democrat. Roman Catholic. Home and Office: 2304 SW 64th Ave Portland OR 97221-1339

STEEN, PAUL JOSEPH, retired broadcasting executive; b. Williston, N.D., July 4, 1932; s. Ernest B. and Inez (Ingebrigtson) S.; m. Judith Smith; children—Michael M., Melanie. BA, Pacific Luth. U., 1954; MS, Syracuse U., 1957. Producer, dir. Sta. KNTV, San Jose, Calif., 1957-58, Sta. KVIE, Sacramento, 1958-60; asst. prof. telecommunications Pacific Luth. U., Tacoma, 1960-67; dir. ops. Sta. KPBS San Diego State U., 1967-74; gen. mgr., 1974-93, prof. telecommunications and film, 1974-93, dir. univ. telecommunications; co-chmn. Office of New Tech. Initiatives. Dir. (tel. program) Troubled Waters (winner Nat. Ednl. TV award of excellence 1970). With AUS. Named Danforth Assoc. Mem. Pacific Mountain Network (bd. dirs., chmn., bd. of govs. award 1993), NATAS, Assn. Calif. Pub. TV Stas. (pres.), Pi Kappa Delta. Home: 4930 Campanile Dr San Diego CA 92115-2331

STEENHAGEN, ROBERT LEWIS, landscape architect, consultant; b. Grand Rapids, Mich., July 11, 1922; s. Abraham and Rena (Vanden Broek) S.; m. Doris Brisentine, Aug. 2, 1952; children: Deborah, Cynthia, James. A.S., Grand Rapids Jr. Coll., 1942; B.S., Mich. State U., 1949. Chief landscape design Eastern design office Nat. Park Service, Phila., 1963-66; capt. planning team Nat. Park Service, Washington, 1966-70; asst. mgr. N.E. area Design Office Nat. Park Service, Denver, 1971-77, assoc. mgr., 1978-80; cons. landscape architecture Lakewood, Colo., 1980—. Served to sgt. U.S. Army, 1942-45, PTO. Recipient Meritorious Service award Nat. Park Service, 1971; recipient Performance award for Nat. Bicentennial Program, 1976. Fellow Am. Soc. Landscape Architects. Home: 2473 S Carr Ct Denver CO 80227-3104

STEEN OLSON, CHRISTOPHER J., film producer/director, computer consultant; b. Pasadena, Calif., Apr. 10, 1964; s. Ken and Wendy (Treadwell) S. O. Santa Barbara City Coll., 1983, UCLA, 1984-87. Support technician Software Supermarket, L.A., 1983-86; corp. rep. IBM Corp., L.A., 1986-87, Apple Computer, L.A., 1987-88; prodr. Propaganda Films, Hollywood, Calif., 1988-91; head of prodn. Wicked Films, Ltd., London, L.A., 1991-93; prodr., dir. Cave Pictures, L.A., 1994—; owner Prodn. Media Svcs., L.A., 1984—. Mem. AICP. Address: 1902 Hillcrest Rd Los Angeles CA 90068

STEENSGAARD, ANTHONY HARVEY, federal agent; b. Rapid City, S.D., Mar. 21, 1963; s. Harvey Hans and Dorothy Lorraine (Hansen) S. Student, U. Alaska, 1981-83, Anchorage C.C., 1983-84; AAS in Indsl. Security, C.C. Air Force, 1989; BS in Criminal Justice, Wayland U., 1989. Lic. pilot, radio operator. Bookseller B. Dalton Bookseller, Rapid City, S.D., 1978-81, Anchorage, Alaska, 1981-83; warehouseman Sears, Roebuck & Co., Anchorage, 1983-85; security specialist Alaska Air N.G., Anchorage, 1985-88; agt., draftsman, engrng. cons. U.S. Border Patrol, El Centro, Calif., 1988—. Author: Unit Security Manager's Guide Book, 1988. Vol. U.S. Senator George McGovern's Campaign, Rapid City, 1980, Congressman Tom Daschle's Campaign, Rapid City, 1980, Spl. Olympics, Rapid City, 1981; observer CAP, Anchorage, 1981. With USMC, 1981-85, USAFR, 1985-95. Mem. Am. Legion, Air Force Assn., VFW, Rapid City Peace Office Assn., Fraternal Order Eagles. Democrat. Lutheran. Office: US Border Patrol 1111 N Imperial Ave El Centro CA 92243-1739

STEFANICS, ELIZABETH T. (LIZ STEFANICS), state legislator. BA, Eastern Ky. U.; MS, U. Wis.; PhD, U. Minn. Mem. N.Mex. Senate; mem. conservation com., judiciary com., chmn. health and human svcs. com., adminstr. health and human svcs. Democrat. Address: PO Box 10127 Santa Fe NM 87504-6127 Office: N Mex State Senate State Capitol New Mexico State Capitol NM 87503

STEFFEN, THOMAS LEE, state supreme court justice; b. Tremonton, Utah, July 9, 1930; s. Conrad Richard and Jewel (McGuire) S.; m. LaVona Ericksen, Mar. 20, 1953; children—Elizabeth, Catherine, Conrad, John, Jennifer. Student, U. So. Calif., 1955-56; BS, U. Utah, 1957; JD with honors, George Washington U., 1964; LLM, U. Va., 1988. Bar: Nev. 1965, U.S. Dist. Ct. Nev. 1965, U.S. Tax Ct. 1966, U.S. Ct. Appeals 1967, U.S. Supreme Ct. 1977. Contracts negotiator U.S. Bur. Naval Weapons, Washington, 1961-64; private practice Las Vegas, 1965-82; justice Supreme Ct. Nev., Carson City, 1982—, chmn. code of jud. conduct study com., 1991; vice chmn. Nev. State Jud. Edn. Coun., 1983-84; chmn. Nev. State-Fed. Jud. Coun., 1986-91, mem., 1986—. Mem. editorial staff George Washington U. Law Rev., 1963-64; contbr. articles to legal jours. Bd. dirs. So. Nev. chpt. NCCJ, 1974-75; mem. exec. bd. Boulder Dam Area coun. Boy Scouts Am., 1979-83; bd. visitors Brigham Young U., 1985-89. Recipient merit citation Utah State U., 1983. Mem. Nev. Bar Assn. (former chmn. So. Nev. med.-legal screening panel), Nev. Trial Lawyers Assn. (former dir.). Republican. Mem. LDS Ch. Office: Nev Supreme Ct 100 N Carson St Carson City NV 89701-4717*

STEGEMEIER, RICHARD JOSEPH, oil company executive; b. Alton, Ill., Apr. 1, 1928; s. George Henry and Rose Ann (Smola) S.; m. Marjorie Ann Spess, Feb. 9, 1952; children: Richard Michael, David Scott, Laura Ann, Martha Louise. BS in Petroleum Engring., U. Mo., Rolla, 1950, cert. petroleum engr. (hon.), 1981; MS in Petroleum Engring., Tex. A&M U., 1951; D of Engring. (hon.), U. Mo., Rolla, 1990. Registered profl. engr., Calif. Various nat. and internat. mgmt. positions with Unocal Corp. (formerly Union Oil Co.), L.A., 1951—, pres. sci. and tech. div., 1979-80, sr. v.p. corp. devel., 1980-85, pres., COO, 1985-88, CEO, also chmn. bd. dirs., 1988-94; bd. dirs. First Interstate Bancorp, Found. Health Corp., Halliburton Co., Northrop Corp., Outboard Marine Corp. Patentee in field. Bd. dirs. Calif. Econ. Devel. Corp.; bd. govs. Town Hall of Calif., The Music Ctr. of L.A. County; bd. overseers Exec. Coun. on Fgn. Diplomats, Huntington Libr.; chmn. L.A. World Affairs Coun., 1990-94; pres. World Affairs Coun. of Orange County, 1980-82; chmn. Brea (Calif.) Blue Ribbon Com., 1979-80 ; trustee Com. for Econ. Devel., U. So. Calif., Harvey Mudd Coll., Loyola Marymount U.; mem. adv. bds. Northwestern U. Kellogg Grad. Sch. of Mgmt.; bd. vis. UCLA Anderson Grad. Sch. of Mgmt., U. Mo., Rolla;

mem. adv. bd. Calif. State U., Fullerton, adv. coun., Long Beach; bd. dirs. YMCA of L.A., L.A. Philharm. Assn., John Tracy Clinic; chmn. L.A. area coun. Boy Scouts of Am., Calif. C. of C. chmn., 1994; gen. campaign chmn. United Way of Greater L.A., 1990-91; trustee and immediate past pres. Hugh O'Brian Youth Found., 1993-94, L.A. Archidiocese Edn. Found. Recipient Merit award Orange County Engring. Coun., 1980, Outstanding Engr. Merit award Inst. Advancement Engring., 1981, Disting. Achievement medal Tex. A&M U., Hugh O'Brian Youth Found. Albert Schweitzer Leadership award, 1990, Human Rels. award Am. Jewish Com., 1990. Mem. AIChE (Disting. Career award So. Calif. sect. 1989), NAM (bd. dirs.), Nat. Acad. Engring., Am. Petroleum Inst. (bd. dirs.), Soc. Petroleum Engrs. (lectr. 1978), Nat. Petroleum Coun., 25 Yr. Club Petroleum Industry (past pres.), Calif. Bus. Roundtable, Calif. Coun. on Sci. and Tech., Calif. Club. Republican. Roman Catholic. Office: Unocal Corp PO Box 7600 Los Angeles CA 90051-0600*

STEGENGA, DAVID A., mathematics educator; b. Chgo., Aug. 20, 1946; s. Louis A. and Dorothy (Hamater) S.; m. Bridgit Kristen Folstad, Nov. 29, 1972. BS, Purdue U., 1968; MS, U Wis., 1970, PhD, 1973. Teaching asst. U. Wis., Madison, 1968-73; mem. Inst. Adv. Study, Princeton, N.J., 1973-74; asst. prof. math. Ind. U., Bloomington, 1973-80, U. Hawaii, Honolulu, 1980-82; assoc. prof. math. U. Hawaii, 1982-88, prof. math., 1988—; vis. prof. U. N.C., Chapel Hill, 1987, U. Tenn., Knoxville, 1988. Contbr. articles to profl. jours. NSF grantee, 1975-86; Sloan Found. fellow, 1987-88. Mem. Am. Math. Soc., Math. Assn. Am. Office: Univ Hawaii Dept Mathematics Honolulu HI 96822

STEGMAN, CHARLES ALEXANDER (CHUCK ALEXANDER STEGMAN), marketing professional; b. Denver, Apr. 17, 1959; s. Harvey Eugene and Mary Martha (Newell) S. BSEE, U. Colo., 1981. Mktg. rep. Businessland, Oakland, Calif., 1984-86, sr. mktg. rep., 1986; systems engr. instr. Businessland of San Jose, 1986-87; mktg. mgr. of networks Businessland, San Jose, Calif., 1987-88, mgr. mktg. advanced systems div., 1988-90, dir. systems mktg., 1990-91; product mgr. Mail div. Lotus, Mountain View, Calif., 1991-93; prin. analyst Dataquest, San Jose, 1993-94, v.p., group dir. online multimedia and software, 1994—; wordwide lectr. on interactive multimedia, computers and software. Mem. Sigma Phi Epsilon. Home: 700 Grand View Ave San Francisco CA 94114-3510 Office: Dataquest 1290 Ridder Park Dr San Jose CA 95131-2304

STEIN, ALAN L., investment banker; b. Phila., Nov. 21, 1930; s. Harry J. and Minnie (Kohn) S.; m. Ruth Sussman, June 7, 1953; children: Paul, Julie, Jennifer. AB, Columbia Coll., 1952; MBA, Harvard U., 1954. With Goldman Sachs and Co., 1954-68; ptnr. in charge of corp. investment banking activities West Coast Goldman Sachs and Co., San Francisco, 1968-76; dep. dir. dept. econ. and bus. devel. State of Calif., 1978, sec. Bus., Transp. and Housing Agy., 1978-80; assoc. dean exec. edn. Berkeley Sch. Bus. U. Calif., 1981-82; mem. exec. com. Montogomery Securities, 1982—, exec. dir. investment banking, sr. mng. dir. Chmn. bd. dirs. Bridge Housing Corp.; chmn. bd. trustees Am. Conservatory Theater; dir. Bay Area Coun.; trustee, past pres. bd. trustees San Francisco Mus. Modern Art. Mem. Villa Taverna, Calif. Tennis Club, Lake Merced Golf and Country Club. Office: Montgomery Securities 600 Montgomery St San Francisco CA 94111-2702

STEIN, ARTHUR OSCAR, pediatrician; b. Bklyn., Apr. 3, 1932; s. Irving I. and Sadie (Brander) S.; AB, Harvard U., 1953; MD, Tufts U., 1957; postgrad. U. Chgo., 1963-66, San Jose State U., 1995—; m. Judith Lenore Hurwitz, Aug. 27, 1955; children: Susan, Jeffrey, Benjamin. Intern U. Chgo. Hosps., 1957-58, resident, 1958-59; resident N.Y. Hosp.-Cornell U. Med. Center, 1959-61; practice medicine specializing in pediatrics, 1963—; instr. pediatrics U. Chgo., 1963-66, asst. prof. pediatrics, 1966-70; mem. Healthguard Med. Group, San Jose, Calif., 1970-72; mem. Permanente Med. Group, San Jose, 1972-75; ret. 1995; asst. chief pediatrics Santa Teresa Med. Center, 1979-87; clin. instr. Santa Clara Valley Med. Center, Stanford U., 1970-72. Served to capt., M.C., AUS, 1961-63. USPHS Postdoctoral fellow, 1963-66. Fellow Am. Acad. Pediatrics. Jewish (v.p. congregation 1969-70, pres. 1972-73). Clubs: Light and Shadow Camera (pres. 1978-80) (San Jose); Central Coast Counties Camera (v.p. 1980-81, pres. 1981-82), Santa Clara Camera. (pres. 1991). Co-discoverer (with Glyn Dawson) genetic disease Lactosylceramidosis, 1969. Home: 956 Redmond Ave San Jose CA 95120-1831 Office: Kaiser/Permanente Med Group 260 Internat Cir San Jose CA 95119

STEIN, ELLYN BETH, mental health services professional. BS, Ariz. State U., 1988, M in Counseling, 1991. Cert. profl. counselor, Ariz. Rsch. asst. Ariz. State U., Tempe, 1985, 87, practicum, 1990, grad. asst., 1990, 91; residential counselor/supr. Wayland Family Ctrs., Phoenix, Ariz., 1988-91; intern St. Luke's Behavioral Health, Phoenix, 1991, Phoenix Adolescent Recovery, 1991; intake specialist II ComCare, Phoenix, 1991-94; with needs assessment and referral divsn. Charter Behavioral Health, Chandler, Ariz., 1993—; clin. case mgr. Contact, Tempe, 1994—; vol. crisis counselor Terros, Phoenix, 1989—. Active mem. Valley of the Sun 20/30, Phoenix, 1993—. Mem. Am. Counseling Assn., Am. Mental Health Counselors Assn., Phi Beta Kappa (2nd v.p. 1994—).

STEIN, GERALD S., psychiatrist; b. Pueblo, Colo., Oct. 31, 1943; s. Emanuel and Ruth (Dobin) S.; m. Carol A. Maliborski, Mar. 30, 1980; 1 child, Danielle Alexis. BMS, Northwestern U., 1965, MD, 1968. Diplomate Am. Bd. Psychiatry and Neurology; cert. psychoanalyst. Pvt. practice psychaitry and psychoanalysis Colorado Springs, Colo., 1980—; tng. and supervising psychoanalyst, dept. psychiatry Denver Inst. Psychoanalysis/U. Colo. Med. Ctr., 1993-94; presenter in field. Author psychobiographic book on L.L. Dickerson, 1992; contbr. papers to The American Fly-Fisher, 1990, articles to profl. jours. Bd. dirs. Pikes Peak Regional Sci. Fair, Colorado Springs, 1982-85, So. Colo. Med. Practices Assn., Colorado Springs, 1986-88; del. ann. meeting Colo. Med. Assn., Denver, 1987; cons. to paramedics Colorado Springs Fire Dept., 1982-84. Recipient Hoedemaker award Psychoanalytic Soc. Seattle, 1985. Fellow APA, Colo. Soc. for Psychoanalysis and Psychotherapy; mem. Am. Mus. Fly Fishing, Denver Psychoanalytic Soc. (program chmn. 1988-90). Home and Office: 1415 S Cascade Ave Colorado Springs CO 80907

STEIN, JANICE MARIE, interior designer; b. Salinas, Calif., Dec. 4, 1940; d. Albert Ray and Lois May (Dennis) Matheson; m. John Davis, May 11, 1968 (div. May 1975); m. William Douglas Stein, Apr. 11, 1976. BA, U. Calif., Davis, 1965. Cert. secondary tchr., adminstr. Tchr., English dept. chair Del Campo High Sch., Fair Oaks, Calif., 1966-68; tchr. Los Altos (Calif.) High Sch., 1969-83; interior designer, owner Villa Assocs., San Francisco, 1979—; design cons. Landor Assocs., San Francisco, 1983-88, Addison Design, San Francisco, 1989-90; tchr. specialist in lit. and composition, State of Calif., 1967-69; tchr. cons. Bay Area Writing Project, 1973-75. Contbr. design work to various Sunset Books and articles to profl. jours. Bd. dirs. Cmty. Music Ctr., San Francisco, 1988-94, San Francisco Opera Guild, 1989—. Named Outstanding Tchr. of Writing, State of Calif., 1970; Coll. Letters and Sci. fellow U. Calif., Berkeley, summer 1974. Mem. Calif. Coun. Interior Designers, Knights of Order of St. John (dame), San Francisco Garden Club. Republican.

STEIN, KARL N., plastic and reconstructive surgeon; b. Phila., July 1, 1940; s. Jack H. and Lucille Mildred (Somoroff) S.; m. Sandra Diane Segal; children: Laura, Leigh. BA in Chemistry, Temple U., 1962, MD, 1966. Diplomate Am. Bd. Plastic Surgery. Intern U. Pa. Grad. Hosp., 1966-67; resident in surgery Abington Meml. Hosp., 1967-68; resident in surgery SUNY Up-State Med. Ctr., 1970-71, instr. in surgery, 1970—; resident in plastic surgery Hosp. Albert Einstein Coll. Medicine, Bronx Mcpl. Hosp. Ctr., 1971-74, asst. instr. plastic surgery and hand surgery, 1974; pvt. practice in plastic surgery, 1974—; surgeon Sherman Oaks (Calif.) Burn Ctr., 1975—; cons. L.A. Dept. Water and Power. Author (patent) Treatment of Tar Burns, 1980. Capt. USAF, 1969-71. Fellow Am. Coll. Surgeons; mem. AMA, Am. Soc. Plastic and Reconstructive Surgeons, Am. Burn Assn., Am. Assn. Hand Surgery, Am. Soc. Aesthetic Plastic Surgery, Lipolysis Soc. N.Am., Calif. Soc. Plastic Surgeons, Calif. Med. Assn., L.A. Soc. Plastic Surgeons, L.A. County Med. Assn. Office: 4910 Van Nuys Blvd Ste 302 Sherman Oaks CA 91403-1728

STEIN, ROBERT GEORGE, mathematics educator, author; b. N.Y.C., Apr. 16, 1939; s. Ernest and Doris (Blumenthal) S.; m. Veronika Kirschner, Nov. 13, 1970; children: Joseph, Lucy. B.A., Harvard U., 1961; M.A.T., Conn. Wesleyan U., 1962; M.A., Dartmouth Coll., 1967; Ph.D., U. Tex.-Austin, 1975. Math. tchr. Ethical Culture Schs., N.Y.C., 1962-64, Acad. la Castellana, Caracas, Venezuela, 1964-65; mem. faculty Calif. State U., San Bernardino, 1967—, prof., 1982—, chmn. math. dept., 1976-89; mem. coms. Entry Level Math. Test Devel. Com. Author: Mathematics, An Exploratory Approach, 1975; Fundamentals of College Algebra and Trigonometry, 1986, Fundamentals of College Algebra, 1986; also articles; reviewer; reader Advanced Placement Calculus Test. Bd. dirs. Crestline Community Ambulance Assn., Calif., 1979-91; mem. Rim of the World Bd. Edn., 1989—. Fellow Danforth Assn.; mem. San Bernardino County Math. Tchrs. Assn. (founding pres. 1984—), Math. Assn. Am., Nat. Coun. Tchrs. of Math. Republican. Home: PO Box 494 Crestline CA 92325-0494 Office: Calif State U 5500 State University Pky San Bernardino CA 92407

STEIN, STEPHEN, electronics executive; b. N.Y.C., May 5, 1943; s. Solomon and Freda (Nyman) S.; m. Karen M. Rothstein, June 23, 1968; children: Alan, Gabrielle. BA in Physics, Columbia U., 1964, MA in Physics, 1965, PhD in Physics, 1969. Rsch. assoc. SLAC, Stanford, Calif., 1970-74; vis. researcher CERN, Geneva, 1974-77; vis. researcher Coll. De France, Paris, 1976-77, staff physicist, 1977-78; physicist TCI, Mountain View, Calif., 1978-82, mgr. data processing, 1982-84, dir. data processing, 1984-85, dir. advanced systems, 1985-87, v.p. advanced programs, v.p. advanced tech., 1987—. Office: TCI 222 Caspian Dr Sunnyvale CA 94089-1014

STEINBERG, JACK, lawyer; b. Seattle, Jan. 6, 1915; s. Solomon Reuben and Mary (Rashall) S.; widower; children: Roosevelt, Mary Ann Steinberg Shulman, Quentin. BA, U. Wash., 1936, JD, 1938. Bar: Wash. 1938, U.S. Dist. Ct. (we. dist.) Wash. 1938, U.S. Ct. Appeals (9th cir.) 1938. Ptnr. Steinberg & Steinberg, Seattle, 1938—. Former editor and pub. The Washington Examiner; contbr. numerous articles to legal jours. Judge pro tem Seattle Mcpl. Ct., Seattle, 1952; past pres. Emanuel Congregation, Seattle, Seattle chpt. Zionist Orgn. Am. Recipient Scrolls of Honor award (3) The State of Israel. Mem. Assn. Trial Lawyers Am., Am. Judicature Soc., Wash. Bar Assn., Wash. Assn. Trial Lawyers, Seattle-King County Bar Assn. Jewish Orthodox. Office: Steinberg & Steinberg 1210 Vance Bldg Seattle WA 98101

STEINBERG, JOAN EMILY, retired middle school educator; b. San Francisco, Dec. 9, 1932; d. John Emil and Kathleen Helen (Montgomery) S. BA, U. Calif.-Berkeley, 1954; EdD, U. San Francisco, 1981. Tchr., Vallejo (Calif.) Unified Sch. Dist., 1959-61, San Francisco Unified Sch. Dist., 1961-93, tchr. life and phys. sci. jr. high sch., 1978-85, 87-93, sci. cons., 1985-87; lectr. elem. edn. San Francisco State U., 1993-94; ind. sci. edn. cons., 1993—. Contbr. articles to profl. jours. Fulbright scholar U. Sydney (Australia), 1955-56; recipient Calif. Educator award, 1988, Outstanding Educator in Teaching award U. San Francisco Alumni Soc., 1989. Mem. ASCD, San Francisco Zool. Soc., Exploratorium, Astron. Soc. Pacific, Am. Fedn. Tchrs., Calif. Acad. Scis., Calif. Malacozool. Soc., Nat. Sci. Tchrs. Assn., Elem. Sch. Sci. Assn. (sec. 1984-85, pres. 1986-87, newsletter editor 1994—), Calif. Sci. Tchrs. Assn., Sigma Xi. Democrat.

STEINBERG, RUSSELL, composer. BA summa cum laude, UCLA, 1981; MusM with honors, New Eng. Conservatory, Boston, 1983; PhD in Music, Harvard U., 1987. Postdoctoral teaching asst. Harvard U., Cambridge, Mass., 1988-90; orch. dir. Temple Emanuel, Beverly Hills, Calif., 1990-93; composer-in-residence Music Festival Goucher Coll., Balt., 1993; dir. Music Media Lab. and prof. ext. sch. UCLA, 1993, vis. asst. prof. music theory and composition, 1991-93; pres. Five-One Prodns., Ltd., 1995; solo compositions include: Small Rain, Periods of Luminance, Tonal Whispers, Sequoia sonata, Dichroisms, Atonal Variations (all for piano); White Crane Study, Latigo Tides, Canticles, Double Stop Etude (violin); Five Preludes (guitar); duo compositions include Flute Sonata Six Duos for Violin, Fantasy for Flute and Piano, Classic Berlin; trios include Fanfares for Three Trumpets, Rings of Saturn, Piano Trio; quartets include String Quartet, Woodwind Quartet, Change of Heart, others. Film scores include: You Are What You Eat, 1993, Paper Flowers (documentary), 1993, Class (comedy-variety pilot), 1992, Fatal Charm (feature-length psycho-drama), 1991, Dressage Freestyle music, 1991, Amber Waves (documentary), 1990, others; author: (CD-Rom) Richard Strauss: Three Tone Poems, 1992, Microsoft's Multimedia Strauss, 1994; contbr. articles to profl. jours.; commns. include Sheridon Stokes, Flute Sonata, 1993, Endre Granat and Alex Horvath, Violin Duos, 1992, Aspen Ctr. for Advanced Composition, City Strains, 1993, others. Recipient Disting. teaching award Harvard U., 1987, 1st prize New World String Quartet Competition, 1987; Aspen fellow, 1992, 93, MacDowell fellow, 1991, Cummington Cmty. of the Arts fellow, 1985; ASCAP grantee for young composers, 1987. Mem. Musicians Union Local 47, Coll. Music Soc., Am. Music Ctr., Harvard Group for New Music (founding mem.), NuClassix Inc. (founding mem.), Nat. Assn. Composers (2nd prize 1984, 86), Phi Beta Kappa, Phi Kappa Lambda.

STEINBERG, WARREN LINNINGTON, school principal; b. N.Y.C., Jan. 20, 1924; s. John M. and Gertrude (Vogel) S.; student U. So. Calif., 1943-44, UCLA, 1942-43, 46-47, BA, 1949, MEd, 1951, EdD, 1962; m. Beatrice Ruth Blass, June 29, 1947; children: Leigh William, James Robert, Donald Kenneth. Tchr., counselor, coach Jordan High Sch., Watts, Los Angeles, 1951-57; tchr. athletic coordinator Hamilton High Sch., Los Angeles, 1957-62; boys' vice prin. Univ. High Sch., Los Angeles, 1962-67, Crenshaw Hig Sch., Los Angeles, 1967-68; cons. Ctr. for Planned Change, Los Angeles City Sch., 1968-69; instr. edn. UCLA, 1965-71; boys' vice prin. LeConte Jr. High Sch., Los Angeles, 1969-71, sch. prin., 1971-77; adminstrv. cons. integration, 1977-81, adminstr. student to student interaction program, 1981-82; prin. Gage Jr. High Sch., 1982-83, Fairfax High Sch., 1983-90. Pres. Athletic Coordinators Assn., Los Angeles City Schs., 1959-60; v.p. P-3 Enterprises, Inc., Port Washington, N.Y., 1967-77, Century City (Calif.) Enterprises, 1966-88. V.p. B'nai B'rith Anti-Defamation League, 1968-70; mem. adv. com. Los Angeles City Commn. on Human Relations, 1966-71, 72-76, commr., 1976—, also chmn. edn. com.; pres. Los Angeles City Human Relations Commn., 1978-87; mem. del. assembly Community Relations Conf. of So. Calif., 1975-91; mem. citizens adv. com. for student integration Los Angeles Unified Sch. Dist., 1976-79; chmn. So. Calif. Drug Abuse Edn. Month com., 1970. Bd. dirs. DAWN, The Seedling, 1993-95. Served with USMCR, 1943-46. Recipient Beverly Hills B'nai B'rith Presdl. award, 1965, Pres.'s awardCommunity Rels. Conf. So. Calif., 1990; commended Los Angeles City Council, 1968, 88. Mem. West Los Angeles Coordinating Council (chmn. case conf., human relations), Beverly-Fairfax C. of C. (bd. dirs. 1986-88). Lodges: Lions (dir. 1960-62), Kiwanis. Contbr. articles on race relations, youth behavior to profl. jours. and newspapers. Home: 2737 Dunleer Pl Los Angeles CA 90064-4303

STEINBOCK, JOHN T., bishop; b. L.A., July 16, 1937. Student, Los Angeles Diocesan sems. Ordained priest Roman Cath. Ch., 1963. Aux. bishop Diocese of Orange, Calif., 1984-87; bishop Diocese of Santa Rosa, Calif., 1987-91; titular bishop of Midila, 1984; bishop Diocese of Fresno, Calif., 1991—. Office: Diocese of Fresno 1550 N Fresno St Fresno CA 93703-3711

STEINBUCHEL, MAXIMILIAN FREDERICK, contract manager; b. Wichita, Kans., July 1, 1942; s. Maximilian Hubert and Patricia Steinbuchel; m. Toni Kay Smith, Dec. 30, 1966; children: Julie Marie, Kerri Janae. BBA in Acctg., Wichita State U., 1971. Cert. profl. cost estimator, cert. prof. cost analyst, cert. cost estimator/analyst. Cost sys. acct. Cudahy Co., Wichita, 1971-73; gen. acctg. mgr. Roper-Land Corp., Andover, Kans., 1973-74; sr. cost analyst Boeing Inc., Wichita, 1974-76; cost acctg. mgr. Gen. Portland Cement, Wichita, 1976-77; mgr. pricing compliance Boeing Inc., Wichita, 1977-89; contract mgr. Motorola, Inc., Chandler, Ariz., 1989—; nat. v.p. Nat. Estimating Soc., Washington, 1983-85, nat. pres., 1985-87. Vol. fire fighter Derby (Kans.) Fire Dept., 1967-89, adminstr. firemen's relief assn., 1977-89; coun. mem. ward 2 Derby (Kans.) City Coun., 1972-74. With USN, 1960-64. Recipient Estimator of the Yr. Mgmt. awards Nat. Estimating Soc., Wichita, 1983, Washington, 1983, 1987. Mem. Soc. Cost Estimating and Analysis (ednl. conf. chmn. 1993), Internat. Soc. Parametric Analysts. Home: 1927 E Dawn Dr Tempe AZ 85284-3429 Office: Motorola Inc Satellite Comm Divsn 2501 S Price Rd Chandler AZ 85248-2899

STEINER, HERBERT MAX, physics educator; b. Goeppingen, Germany, Dec. 8, 1927; came to U.S., 1939, naturalized, 1944; s. Albert and Martha (Epstein) S. B.S., U. Calif., Berkeley, 1951, Ph.D., 1956. Physicist Lawrence Berkeley Lab., Berkeley, Calif., 1956—; mem. faculty U. Calif., Berkeley, 1958—, prof. physics, 1966—, William H. McAdams prof. physics, chmn. dept., 1992—; vis. scientist European Center Nuclear Research, 1960-61, 64, 68-69, 82-83, Max Planck Inst. Physics and Astrophysics, Munich, 1976-77; vis. prof. Japanese Soc. Promotion Sci., 1978; vis. prof. physics U. Paris, 1989-90. Author articles in field. Served with AUS, 1946-47. Recipient Sr. Am. Scientist award Alexander von Humboldt Found., 1976-77; Guggenheim fellow, 1960-61. Fellow Am. Phys. Soc. Office: U Calif Berkeley Dept Physics Berkeley CA 94720

STEINER, KENNETH DONALD, bishop; b. David City, Nebr., Nov. 25, 1936; s. Lawrence Nicholas and Florine Marie (Pieters) S. B.A., Mt. Angel Sem., 1958; M.Div., St. Thomas Sem., 1962. Ordained priest Roman Catholic Ch., 1962, bishop, 1978; asso. pastor various parishes Portland and Coos Bay, Oreg., 1962-72; pastor Coquille Ch., Myrtle Point, Powers, Oreg., 1972-76, St. Francis Ch., Roy, Oreg., 1976-77; aux. bishop Diocese of Portland, Oreg., 1977—; vicar of worship and ministries and personnel dir. clergy personnel Portland Archdiocese. Democrat. Office: 2838 E Burnside St Portland OR 97214-1830*

STEINER, RICHARD RUSSELL, conglomerate executive; b. Chgo., Feb. 26, 1923; s. Frank Gardner and Ruth (Cowie) S.; m. Colleen M. Kearns, Dec. 6, 1949; children—Robert C., Kevin K., Sheila M. B.A., Dartmouth Coll., 1948. With Steiner Corp., Salt Lake City, 1948—; divisonal dir., v.p. Steiner Corp., 1951-59, pres., 1959—; dir. Am. Uniform Co. Served with USAAF, 1942-46. Decorated D.F.C. Mem. Phi Beta Kappa. Clubs: Alta, Salt Lake Country. Office: 505 E South Temple Salt Lake City UT 84102-1004

STEINER, ROBERTA PEARL, not-for-profit foundation administrator; b. N.Y.C., July 11, 1948; d. Charles and Ethel (Fier) S. BA, U. Calif., Berkeley, 1969, MLS, 1973. Specialist community resources, Sch. Resource Vols. Berkeley Pub. Schs., 1975-77; chief librarian Am. Insts. for Research, Palo Alto, Calif., 1973-77; assoc. in bibliography and instr. library sch. U. Calif., Berkeley, 1975-77; dir. Cen. Pacific Region B'nai B'rith Women, Daly City, Calif., 1977-84; dir. The Foundation Ctr, San Francisco, 1984-94; dir. Found. Ctr. San Francisco office. Bd. dirs. Jewish Vocat. Svcs., 1984-88, San Francisco Jewish Community Ctr., 1984-90, mem. exec. com. Jewish.

STEINER, SHARI YVONNE, publisher, editor; b. Colorado Springs, Colo., Mar. 3, 1941; d. Evan Keith and Blanche Marie (Ketzner) Montgomery; m. Clyde Lionel Steiner, June 24, 1962; children: Vienna Kay, Marco Romano. BA, Adams State Coll., 1962; cert. in sociology, London Sch. Econs., 1978; postgrad., U. Calif., Berkeley, 1988—. Lic. real estate broker, Calif. Freelance journalist various publs., 1964—; owner, mgr. SREI Group, San Francisco, 1985-87; tng. design developer loan div. 1st Nationwide Bank, San Francisco, 1987—; pub., editor Ind. Info. Publs., San Francisco, 1990—; pres. The SREI Group, San Francisco; feature writer Internat. Herald Tribune, Rome, 1964-79; acct. exec. Allen, Ingersol & Weber, Rome, 1970-72; gen. ptnr. Greenhaven Park, Sacramento, 1990—, Port Chicago Indsl., Concord, Calif., 1991—. Author: The Female Factor: A Report on Women in Europe, 1972, 2d edit., 1978, Steiner's Complete How to Move Handbook, 1994; editor The Bottom Line newsletter, 1985—; assoc. editor The Semaphore, 1990—. Coord. urban reforestation Friends of Urban Forest, San Francisco, 1989; co-founder New Sch. for Internat. Elem. Students, Rome, 1970. Recipient internat. journalism award Guida Monaci, 1970, award of merit Lotus Club, N.Y.C., 1975; corr. in archives Am. Heritage Ctr., U. Wyo. Mem. Nat. Assn. Realtors (multiple listing svc. selection com. 1986, 91, investment real estate group 1991), Comml. Real Estate Women (editor, bd. dirs. 1985—), Am. Soc. Journalists and Authors, PEN Internat., Urban Land Inst. (assoc.), Employee Relocation Coun.

STEINFELD, RAY, JR., food products executive; b. Portland, Oreg., Nov. 21, 1946; s. Ray and June Catherine (Cox) S.; m. Janis Bowen, Nov. 11, 1978; children: Erik, Blair. Student, Wheaton Coll., 1964-66, Drew U., 1967; BS in Polit. Sci., Lewis & Clark Coll., 1968. Sales rep. Continental Can Co., L.A., 1969-72; CEO Steinfeld's Products Co., Portland, Oreg., 1972—; chmn. Oreg. Mus. Sci. in Industry, 1992-94. Treas., bd. dirs. Portland Recycling Team, Portland, 1973—; pres. exec. bd. Stop Oreg. Litter and Vandalism, 1973-92, pres., 1976; chmn., exec. com. Oreg. Landmark of Quality, 1985-87; pres. exec. com. William Temple House, 1985-91; vestry mem. Trinity Episcopal Ch., 1987-90; chmn. Oreg. Strategic Plan Agrl. Dept., 1988, World Trade Week, Portland, 1989; mem. Gov. Robert's Task Force, Salem, Oreg., 1991-92; bd. dirs. Oreg. Enterprise Forum, 1992—, chmn., 1995. Mem. Pickle Packers Internat. (mdse. com. chmn.). Democrat. Espiscopalian. also: Oregon Mus of Sci and Industry 1945 SE Water Ave Portland OR 97214-3356

STEINFORT, JAMES RICHARD, university program director; b. Grand Rapids, Mich., Oct. 1, 1941; s. Gerald Gene and Harriett Lois (Stauffer) S.; m. Elizabeth Ann O'Laughlin, Mar. 14, 1964; children: Dawn, Robin, Susan, Troy, Ginger. AA in Computer Sci., San Jacinto Coll., Pasadena, Tex., 1973; BS in Tech. Mgmt. cum laude, Regis Coll., 1987. Chartered cons., Am. Cons. League. Customer engr. Control Data Corp., Mpls., 1964-65; computer engr. GE, Phoenix, 1965-69; tech. analyst Manned Spacecraft Ctr., Houston, 1969-73, systems analyst, 1973-75; tech. support mgr. Ohio Med. Products, Houston, 1975-79; prodn. regional mgr. Johnson & Johnson Co., Denver, 1979-83; prin., internat. cons. J.R. Steinfort & Assocs., Boise, Idaho, 1983-90; dir. TIES (Tech. and Indsl. Ext. Svc.) Boise State U., 1990—. Author: (non-fiction) Conspiracy in Dallas, 1975, rev. edit., 1992; (tech. manuals) Medical/EDP Design Applications, 1985, Factory Quality Audit, 1991; editor newsletter Industry TIES, 1992-94, ISO-9000 Guidelines & Checklist, 1994. Chmn. subcom. Gov.'s Prayer Breakfast Commn., Boise, 1988-92; v.p. Full Gospel Businessman's Internat., Boise, 1990. With USAF, 1960-64. Univ. Ctr. grantee Econ. Devel. Adminstrn., Boise, 1990-92. Mem. Am. Soc. for Quality Control (sr.), Nat. Assn. Mgmt. and Tech. Assistance Ctrs. (bd. dirs. 1990—), Am. Mgmt. Assn., Am. Cons. League (chartered cons.), Idaho Total Quality Inst. (bd. dirs. 1991—), Tech. Transfer Soc. Home: 11934 Ginger Creek Dr Boise ID 83713-3677 Office: Boise State Univ 1910 University Dr Boise ID 83725-0001

STEINHARDT, HENRY, photographer; b. N.Y.C., Nov. 15, 1920; s. Maxwell and Ruth (Davis) S.; m. Elizabeth Smith, 1946 (dec. 1955); children: Elizabeth, Maxwell; m. Helene Fleck, Feb. 1, 1958; 1 child, Henry III. AB, Harvard U., 1942, MArch, 1949. Registered architect. Office mgr. R.H. Cutting, Architect, N.Y.C., 1951-53; ptnr., architect Steinhardt & Thompson, Architects, N.Y.C., 1953-61; architect The Cerny Assocs., St. Paul, 1961-63, John Graham & Co., Seattle, 1963-67, Morse/Kirk, Seattle, 1967-68, N.G. Jacobson & Assocs., Seattle, 1968-69; pvt. practice Mercer Island, Wash., 1969-75; architect USN, Bremerton, Wash., 1975-78; photographer Mercer Island, 1979—. Prin. works exhibited at Washington, Seattle and Andover, Mass.; contbr. articles to fgn. archtl. jours. 1st lt. U.S. Army, 1943-46; capt. USAF, 1950-52. Recipient Design award Progressive Architecture, 1959, Archtl. award Fifth Ave. Assn., 1960. Fellow AIA. Democrat. Home and Office: 7825 SE 63rd Pl Mercer Island WA 98040-4813

STEINHAUSER, JANICE MAUREEN, university administrator, artist; b. Oklahoma City, Okla., Apr. 3, 1935; d. Max Charles and Charlotte (Gold) Glass; m. Stuart Z. Hirschman, Dec. 30, 1954 (div. 1965); children: Shayle, David, Susan; m. Sheldon Steinhauser, May 2, 1965; children: Karen, Lisa Steinhauser Hackel. BFA, U. Colo., Denver, 1972; student, U. Mich., 1953-55. Community affairs adminstr. United Bank Denver, 1973-76; dir. visual arts program Western States Arts Found., Denver, 1976-79; exec. dir. Artreach, Inc., Denver, 1980-82; v.p. mktg. Mammoth Gardens, Denver, 1982-83; dir. pub. rels. Denver Ctr. for Performing Arts, 1983-86; founder, pres. Resource Co., Denver, 1986-88; dir. liberal studies div. Univ. Coll. U. Denver, 1992—. Bd. dirs. Met. Denver Arts Alliance, 1982-85, Denver Internat. Film Festival, 1983-86, Colo. Nat. Abortion Rights Action League, 1991-95. Mem. Women's Forum Colo., Colo. New Music Assn. (bd. dirs.

1987-91), Asian Performing Arts Colo. (bd. dirs. 1989—), Art Students League Denver, Phi Beta Kappa, Kappa Delta Phi. Democrat. Jewish.

STEINHAUSER, JOHN WILLIAM, lawyer; b. Akron, Ohio, June 25, 1924; s. John Hugo and Francis Lillian (Pearson) S.; BSc in Bus. Adminstrn., Ohio State U., 1949; JD, U. Mich., 1950; m. Patricia E. Mooney, Dec. 1, 1956; children: John, Christian, Mark, Sharon. Bar: Colo. 1972, Mich. 1950. With Chrysler Corp., 1950-71, beginning as atty., successively dir. Latin Am., dir. export sales, gen. mgr. Africa-Far East, dir. Chrysler Internat., Geneva, dir. Africa-Far East, 1950-71; corp. atty., Denver, 1971—; founder, pres. Pearson Energy Corp., 1977, Sharon Energy, Ltd., Denver, 1980, also dir., 1971—. Sponsor Platte Valley Pony Club, Denver Symphony; active Colo. Rep. Party; pres. John and Patricia Steinhauser Found. With USNR, 1943-46. Mem. Colo. Bar Assn., Mich. Bar Assn., ABA, Soc. Internat. Law, Rocky Mountain Mineral Law Found., Cherry Hills Country Club, Naples Sailing & Yacht Club, Royal Poinciana Golf Club, Rotary (Denver). Home: 46 Charlou Cir Englewood CO 80111-1103 Office: Sharon Resources Inc Ste 220 5995 Greenwood Plaza Blvd Englewood CO 80111-4714

STEINHAUSER, SHELDON ELI, sociology and gerontology educator; b. N.Y.C., Aug. 11, 1930; s. Charles W. and Helen (Rosenstein) S.; m. Frances Goldfarb, June 28, 1953 (div. 1963); children: Karen, Lisa Steinhauser Hackel; m. Janice M. Glass, May 2, 1965; children: Shayle, David, Susan Hirschman. BS, L.I. U., 1963; DPS (hon.), Regis U., 1994. Community cons. Anti-Defamation League, Columbus, Ohio, 1951-57; regional dir. Anti-Defamation League, Denver, 1957-85, dir. nat. field svcs., 1977-85, dir. nat. community svcs. divsn., 1979-81, western area dir., 1975-85; exec. v.p. Allied Jewish Fedn. of Denver, 1985-91; pres. Sheldon Steinhauser & Assocs., Denver, 1991—; instr. sociology Met. State Coll., Denver, 1969-71, asst. prof. sociology, 1972-94, assoc. prof., 1994—; arbitrator Am. Arbitration Assn., Denver, 1988—; pres. Anti-Defamation League profl. Staff Assn., Agy. Orgn., Denver, 1963; past cons. EEOC. Missions to Egypt and Israel, 1982, 83; staff dir. Mission to Israel, 1986, 87, 90; former mem. Denver Anti-Crime Coun.; chmn. Mountain States Inst. of Judaism, Denver, 1958-59; pres. Adult Edn. Coun. Met. Denver; past mem. cmty. adv. bd. Jr. League Denver, intermittent cons. U.S. Dept. Justice Cmty. Rels. Svc., 1994—; mem. Colo. Martin Luther King Holiday Planning Com., Latin Am. Rsch. and Svc. Agy.; cmty. working group Nat. Civilian Cmty. Corps.; congl. del. White House Conf. on Aging, 1995. Recipient M.L. King Jr. Humanitarian award Colo. M.L. King Commn., Denver, 1986, 1st Ann. Human Rels. award Colo. Civil Rights Commn., Denver, 1965, Humanitarian award NAACP, Denver, 1980, ADL Civil Rights Achievement award, 1989; named to Gallery of Fame, Denver Post, 1979, 80. Mem. Western Social Sci. Assn., Am. Sociol. Assn., Colo. Jewish Reconstructionist Fedn., Am. Soc. on Aging, Sociol. Practice Assn., B'nai B'rith (Columbus v.p., Denver).

STEINKE, BETTINA, artist; b. Biddeford, Maine, June 25, 1913; d. William and Alice Mary (Staples) S.; m. Don Blair, Mar. 21, 1946. Student, Sch. Fine Arts, Newark, 1930, Cooper Union, 1931-33, Phoenix Art Sch., 1934-35. Represented in permanent collections Indpls. Mus., Ft. Worth Mus., Nat. Cowboy Hall of Fame and Western Heritage; artist original drawings of Toscanini, 1938, and Paderewski, 1939 (both now in Smithsonian Inst.); charcoal portraits NBC book on Toscanini and Orch., 1938; many portraits of well known personalities; retrospective shows Palm Springs Desert Mus., Gilcrease Mus., Tulsa, Okla., Nat. Cowboy Hall of Fame, 1995; subject of biography Bettina. Pres. bd. dirs. Harwood Found. U. N.Mex.; exec. bd. Nat. Cowboy Hall of Fame and Western Heritage. Recipient Gold and Silver medals Nat. Cowboy Hall of Fame, Oklahoma City, 1973-89, Gold medal award for Outstanding Contbn. to Painting, 1995, others; scholar Phoenix Art Sch., N.Y.C., 1934-35. Mem. Nat. Acad. Western Artists (Prix de West award, Cowboy Hall of Fame). Home: PO Box 2342 Santa Fe NM 87504-2342

STEINLICHT, STEVEN, astrologer; b. Bloomington, Ill., Mar. 13, 1950; s. Henry Jr. and Mary Elizabeth (Ritter) S.; m. Lynn Alexander, July 1, 1991; 1 child, Marc Doucette. Student, U. Ill., 1968. Shoe stockroom Murray's Shoes, Bloomington, Ill., 1981-86; psychic Rainbow Place, Albuquerque, 1987-89; software mgr. Computer Bazaar, Albuquerque, 1990—; pres., founder Albuqueque Metaphys. Inst., 1993—. Author: Astarunum, The Portable Oracle, 1993. Min. Universal Life Ch., 1972—. Mem. Mensa Internat., Soc. for Creative Anachronism, S.W. Psychic Forum. Home: 422 Girard Blvd SE Albuquerque NM 87106-2234 Office: Computer Bazaar 123 Yale Blvd SE Albuquerque NM 87106-4011

STEINMAN, JOHN FRANCIS, psychiatrist; b. N.Y.C., May 5, 1916; s. David Barnard and Irene Stella (Hoffman) S.; m. Helen G. Meyer (div. 1963); children: James, Judith, Jill; m. Roxane Bear (div. 1972); m. Ellen M. Sears, Nov. 16, 1985. AB with hons., Columbia U., 1936, MD, 1940. Diplomate Am. Bd. Psychiatry and Neurology. Intern Strong Meml. Hosp., Rochester, N.Y. and Cin. Gen. Hosp., 1940-43; resident psychiatry Nebr. Psychiat. Inst., 1948, 58, R.I. Med. Ctr., 1961; psychiatrist, dir. Lincoln (Nebr.) and Lancaster County Child Guidance Ctr., 1948-61; instr. pediatrics, psychiatry and neurology U. Nebr., Lincoln, 1951-52; postdoctoral fellow in psychiatry Yale U., New Haven, Conn., 1962-64; psychiatrist U. Conn., Storrs, 1964-69, Community Mental Health Services, San Francisco, 1971-79; pvt. practice psychiatry San Francisco, 1979—. Delgate, chmn. Nebr. health com. White House Conf. Children and Youth, Washington, 1960. Served to capt. M.C., AUS, 1943-46, PTO. Mem. Am. Psychiat. Assn. (life), Am. Orthopsychiat. Assn., N.Y. Acad. Scis., Phi Beta Kappa. Home and Office: 164 Otsego Ave San Francisco CA 94112-2536

STEINMANN, JOHN COLBURN, architect; b. Monroe, Wis., Oct. 24, 1941; s. John Wilbur and Irene Marie (Steil) S.; m. Susan Koslosky, Aug. 12, 1978 (div. July 1989). BArch., U. Ill., 1964; postgrad. Ill. Inst. Tech., 1970-71; Project designer C.F. Murphy Assocs., Chgo., 1968-71, Steinmann Architects, Monticello, Wis., 1971-73; design chief, chief project architect State of Alaska, Juneau, 1973-78; project designer Mithun Assos., architects, Bellevue, Wash., 1978-80; owner, prin. John C. Steinmann Assos., Architect, Kirkland, Wash., 1980—; bd. dirs. Storytell Internat.; lectr. Ill. Inst. Tech., 1971-72; prin. works include: Grant Park Music Bowl, Chgo., 1971, Menomonee Falls (Wis.) Med. Clinic, 1972, Hidden Valley Office Bldg., Bellevue, 1978, Kezner Office Bldg., Bellevue, 1979, The Pines at Sunriver, Oreg., 1980, also Phase II, 1984, Phase III, 1986, The Pines at Sunriver Lodge Bldg., 1986, 2d and Lenora highrise, Seattle, 1981, Bob Hope Cardiovascular Research Inst. lab. animal facility, Seattle, 1982, Wash. Ct., Bellevue, 1982, Anchorage Bus. Park, 1982, Garden Townhouses, Anchorage, 1983, Vacation Internationale, Ltd. Corp. Hdqrs., Bellevue, 1983, Vallarta Torres III, Puerto Vallarta, Mex., 1987, Torres Mazatlan (Mex.) II, 1988, Canterwood Townhouses, Gig Harbor Wash., 1988, Inn at Ceres (Calif.), 1989, Woodard Creek Inn, Olympia, Wash., 1989, Northgate Corp. Ctr., Seattle, 1990, Icicle Creek Hotel and Restaurant, Leavenworth, Wash., 1990, Bellingham (Wash.) Market Pl., 1990, Boeing Hot Gas Test Facility, Renton, Wash., 1991, Boeing Longacres Customer Svc. Tng. Ctr. Support Facilities, Renton, 1992, also pvt. residences. Served to 1st lt. C.E., USAR, 1964-66; Vietnam. Decorated Bronze Star. Registered architect, Wash., Oreg., Calif., N.Mex., Ariz., Utah, Alaska, Wis., Ill. Mem. AIA, Am. Mgmt. Assn., Nat. Council Archtl. Registration Bds., Alpha Rho Chi. Republican. Roman Catholic. Clubs: U. Wash. Yacht, Columbia Athletic. Address: 4316 106th Pl NE Kirkland WA 98033

STEINMETZ, JOHN CHARLES, geologist, paleontologist; b. St. Paul, Sept. 26, 1947; s. Charles Leonard and Ruth Naomi (Osteraas) S.; m. Sarah Cook Tristán, May 29, 1982; children: Katherine Ruth, Elizabeth Margaret. BS, U. Ill., 1969, MS, 1975; PhD, U. Miami, 1977. Asst. prof. U. South Fla., St. Petersburg, 1977-82; advanced rsch. geologist Marathon Oil Co., Littleton, Colo., 1982-86, sr. geologist, 1986-90, advanced sr. geologist, 1990-94; dir. state geologist Mont. Bur. of Mines and Geology, 1994—. Mem. bd. advisors Micropaleontology Press, N.Y.C., 1986—. Trustee Paleontol. Rsch. Instn., Ithaca, N.Y., 1990—, v.p., 1992-94, pres. 1994—. Mem. Am. Assn. Petroleum Geologists, Geol. Soc. Am., Internat. Nannoplankton Assn. (U.S. treas. 1982-92), Paleontol. Soc., Soc. Econ. Paleontologists and Mineralogists.

STEINMETZ, WAYNE EDWARD, chemistry educator; b. Huron, Ohio, Feb. 16, 1945; s. Ralph Freeman and Helen Louise (Rossman) S. AB, Oberlin Coll., 1967; AM, Harvard U., 1968, PhD, 1973. Asst. prof. chemistry Pomona Coll., Claremont, Calif., 1973-79, assoc. prof., 1979-88; prof. Pomona Coll., Claremont, 1988-91, Carnegie prof., 1991—; akademischer Gast (vis. prof.) Eidgenössische Technische Hochschule, Zurich, Switzerland, 1979-80, 86-87; cons. Abbott Labs., Abbott Park, Ill., 1993-94. Contbr. articles on spectroscopy, molecular modeling and molecular structure to profl. jours. Scoutmaster, Woodbadge course dir. Old Baldy coun. Boy Scouts Am., 1973—. Fellow NSF, Woodrow Wilson Found.; recipient Dist. Merit award Boy Scouts Am., 1978, Silver Beaver award, Boy Scouts Am., 1993. Mem. AAUP, NRA, Am. Chem. Soc., Phi Beta Kappa (local sec.-treas. 1980-89, pres. 1995—). Democrat. Roman Catholic. Home: 1081 W Cascade Pl Claremont CA 91711-2525 Office: Pomona Coll Dept Chemistry 645 N College Ave Claremont CA 91711

STELLMAN, ROBERTA ELISE, psychiatrist; b. N.Y.C., June 30, 1950. MD, SUNY, 1977. Psychiatry resident U. New Mex., Albuquerque, 1977-81; chief inpatient psychiatry VA Med. Ctr., Albuquerque, 1981-83; cons. N.Mex. Dept. Corrections, Santa Fe, 1983-91, Dept. Energy, Albuquerque, 1985-91; pvt. practice Albuquerque, 1983-91; med. dir. mental health Lovelace, Inc., Albuquerque, 1991—. Office: Lovelace Inc 7801 Jefferson St NE Albuquerque NM 87109-4351

STELLWAGEN, ROBERT HARWOOD, biochemistry educator; b. Joliet, Ill., Jan. 6, 1941; s. Harwood John and Alma Dorothy (Handorf) S.; m. Joanne Kovacs, June 15, 1963; children: Robert Harwood, Alise Anne. AB, Harvard U., 1963; PhD, U. Calif.-Berkeley, 1968. Staff fellow NIH, Bethesda, Md., 1968-69; postdoctoral scholar U. Calif.-San Francisco, 1969-70; asst. prof. biochemistry U. So. Calif., L.A., 1970-74, assoc. prof., 1974-80, prof., 1980—, chmn. dept., 1981-86, vice chmn. dept., 1993—; vis. scientist Nat. Inst. for Med. Research, Mill Hill, Eng., 1979. Contbr. articles to profl. jours. Recipient Henderson prize Harvard U., 1963; NSF fellow, 1963-67; NIH grantee, 1971-84. Mem. AAAS, Am. Soc. Biochemistry and Molecular Biology, Sierra Club, Phi Beta Kappa. Democrat. Office: U So Calif 2011 Zonal Ave Los Angeles CA 90033-1034

STELZRIED, CHARLES THOMAS, engineer; b. L.A., Sept. 14, 1928; s. Charles Edward Stelzried and Dorothy Claire (Morgan) Mercer; m. Virginia Stelzried, 1962 (div. Jan. 1974); children: Camile Traci, Charles Thomas; m. Keiko Kawakami, Apr. 4, 1977. BS, UCLA, 1957, MS, 1959; PhD, U. So. Calif., 1969. Program mgr. NASA/Jet Propulsion Lab., Pasadena, Calif., 1953—, team mem. deep space radio sci. Mariner 10, 1967-81, tracking and data sys. mgr. for various deep space missions, 1981-86, advanced sys. dep. program mgr., 1986—. Contbr numerous articles to profl. publs. With USN, 1946-53. Mem. AAAS, Sigma Xi, Tau Beta Pi. Office: Jet Propulsion Lab MS303-402 4800 Oak Grove Dr # Ms303-40 Pasadena CA 91109-8001

STEM, DONALD EDWARD, JR., marketing educator, researcher; b. San Francisco, Dec. 13, 1943; s. Donald Edward and Alma Jewel (Hines) S.; m. Theresa (Deta) Anne Chicoine, Aug. 5, 1972; 1 child, Katherine Ellen. BA in Bus. Econs., U. Calif., Santa Barbara, 1967; MS in Mktg. & Info. Systems, San Diego State U., 1972; PhD in Mktg., U. Wash., 1975. Mgmt. trainee Rohr Corp., Chula Vista, Calif., 1971-72; teaching asst. San Diego State U., 1971-72; asst. prof. Tex. A & M U., College Station, 1975-78; asst. prof. Wash. State U., Pullman, 1978-81, assoc. prof., 1981-86, prof., 1986—, acting dept. chair mktg., 1989-90; vis. prof. Madrid (Spain) Bus. Sch., 1991-92; vis. prof. faculty of psychology dept. methodology U. Santiago de Compostela, Spain, 1992; vis. scholar Ctr. for Survey Methods and Analysis, Mannheim, Germany, 1992; book rev. editor Jour. of Mktg. rsch., Chgo., 1988—; mem. Univ. Minority Mentor program com. Wash. State U., 1991—, Coll. Bus. and Econs. tenure com., 1984—, chair, 1993, chair mktg. dept. behavioral lab. com., 1993—, univ. orgn. and structure com., 1994—, faculty affairs com., 1994—. Mem. editorial rev. bd. Jour. of Bus. Rsch., 1980-85, Jour. of Acad. of Mktg. Sci., Miami, Fla., 1980—, Jour. of Mktg. Rsch., Chgo., 1988—; contbr. articles to Jour. Mktg. Rsch., Jour. Am. Statis. Assn. and others. Capt. U.S. Army Chem. Corps & Infantry, 1967-69. Grantee Gen. Telephone Co., 1979, Washington Water Power, 1982, Bur. Indian Affairs, 1985, 87, The Puyallup Tribe of Indians, 1984-85. Mem. Am. Mktg. Assn., Am. Statis. Assn., Assn. for Consumer Rsch., Acad. Mktg. Sci., Acad. Internat. Bus. Office: Washington State U Dept of Mktg Todd 367 Pullman WA 99164-4730

STEMMER, JAY JOHN, safety engineer, consultant; b. Wilkes-Barre, Pa., Apr. 29, 1939. BSCE, N.J. Inst. Tech., 1962; MBA, Calif. State U., Long Beach, 1969. Registered profl. engr., Calif.; cert. safety profl.; cert. hazard control mgmt. Engr. Factory Mut., N.J., 1973-77; cons. McKay & Assoc., Calif., 1977-81, Index Research, Calif., 1981-83, Fireman's Fund, Calif., 1983-85, AIG Cons., Calif., 1985-87; sr. cons. Argonaut, Calif., 1987—; assoc. prof. Sierra Coll., Los Angeles, 1979-80. Author: Medical Manual of Industrial Toxicology, 1965, Latin America, A Study of Air Transport Development and Potential in the Decade Ahead, 1970. Served to lt. USAF, 1962-65. Mem. NSPE, Calif. Soc. Profl. Engrs., Am. Soc. Safety Engrs., Am. Bd. Motion Pictures and TV Engrs., Screen Actors Guild, Actors Equity Assn., AFTRA. Home: 1935 Alpha Rd Apt 225 Glendale CA 91208-2135

STEMPLE, ALAN DOUGLAS, aerospace engineer; b. Elkins, W.Va., July 19, 1963; s. Stephen Warren and C. Phyllis (Cavalier) S. BS cum laude, Davis and Elkins Coll., 1984; BS in Aero. Engring. cum laude, W.Va. U., 1985; MS, U. Md., 1986, PhD, 1989. Rotorcraft fellow Ctr. for Rotorcraft Edn. and Rsch., U. Md., College Park, 1985-89; structures rsch. engr. McDonnell Douglas Helicopter Co., Mesa, Ariz., 1989—; reviewer tech. papers, 1990—. Contbr. articles to profl. publs. Army Rotorcraft fellow U. Md., 1985-89. Mem. AIAA, Am. Helicopter Soc. (Vertical Flight Found. scholar 1988). Home: 1401 N Hobson St Mesa AZ 85203-3651 Office: McDonnell Douglas Mail Stop 530/B337 5000 E Mcdowell Rd Mesa AZ 85215-9797

STENDER, CHARLES FREDERICK, pilot; b. East Orange, N.J., Nov. 17, 1940; s. Robert Conrad and Ruth Warne (Cobb) S. BSCE, Pa. State U., 1962; MS in Systems Mgmt., U. So. Calif., University Park, Calif., 1982. Commd. ensign USN, 1962; advanced through grades to capt. USNR, 1983, ret., 1991; naval aviator USN, various, 1962-72; test pilot Grumman Aerospace, Point Mugu, Calif., 1972-77; airline pilot TWA, L.A., 1977-80; mgr., test pilot Hughes Aircraft Co., L.A., 1980—. Decorated Disting. Flying Cross (3), Vietnam, Air medal (13), Vietnam, Navy Commendation medal. Mem. Soc. Exptl. Test Pilots (assoc. fellow), Tailhook Assn., Air Line Pilots Assn. Office: Hughes Aircraft Co 16101 Saticoy St Van Nuys CA 91406-2915

STENGER, MARTIN LANE, financial planner; b. Dallas, Jan. 13, 1949; s. Tressie Marie (Merritt) S.; m. Miriam Rose Yant, Mar. 5, 1972; children: Jason Alexander, Michael Lawrence, Amanda Marie. AA, Riverside Community Coll., 1969; BA, Calif. State U., 1972. V.p. United Calif. Bus. & Estate, Riverside, 1975-80; prin. Perkins, Stenger, Baird & Staffieri, San Bernardino, Calif., 1980-83; pres. Consol. Westchester Fin., Riverside, 1983—. Contbr. articles to profl. jours. Bd. dirs. Estate Planning Coun., Riverside, 1983—. Mem. Am. Soc. Pension Actuaries, Internat. Assn. Registered Fin. Planners, Internat. Assn. Fin. Planners, Life Underwriters Assn. (pres. 1981). Republican. Mem. LDS Ch. Office: Consol Westchester Fin 3741 Merced Dr Ste F2 Riverside CA 92503-4956

STENNETT, WILLIAM CLINTON (CLINT STENNETT), radio and television station executive, state legislator; b. Winona, Minn., Oct. 1, 1956; s. William Jessie and Carole Lee (Halsey) S. BA in Journalism, Idaho State U., 1979. Gen. mgr. Wood River Jour., Hailey, Idaho, 1979-85, pres., pub., 1985-87; pres. Sta. KWRV-TV, Ketchum, Idaho, Sta. KSKI-FM, Sun Valley, Idaho; mem. Idaho Ho. of Reps., Boise, 1990-94, state senator, 1995—. Recipient Gen. Excellence award Idaho Newspaper Assn., 1985, 86, 87. Mem. Rotary Internat., Ketchum Sun Valley C. of C. (bd. dirs. 1990-95). Democrat.

STENNIS, WILLIAM, psychiatrist, educator; b. Meridian, Miss., Mar. 5, 1930; s. William Hardy and Amelia Lee (Bell) S.; m. Maria T. Schulcz, Nov. 23, 1968; children: Susan Maria, Jennifer Lee. BA, Vanderbilt U., 1950, MA, 1952; grad., U. Miss. Sch. of Medicine, 1954; MD, Jefferson Med. Coll., 1956. Diplomate Am. Bd. Psychiatry and Neurology (gen. psychiatry, child and adolescent psychiatry). Intern Colo. Gen. Hosp., Denver, 1956-57; resident in gen. psychiatry Norristown (Pa.) State Hosp., 1957-60; resident in child and adolescent psychiatry Ea. Pa. Psychiat. Inst., Phila., 1960-62; pvt. practice Phila., 1962-70, Santa Fe, 1970—; clin. assoc. dept. psychiatry U. N.Mex., Albuquerque, 1972-76, clin. prof. psychiatry, 1981—; cons. Bucks County (Pa.) Schs., 1962-72, Ea. Pa. Psychiat. Inst., 1963-70, Buttonwood Farms Day Camp for Emotionally Disturbed Children, 1960-70, Los Alamos Schs., 1971-80, Brush Ranch Sch., 1970-73; clin. dir. children's svcs., Ea. Pa. Psychiat. Inst., 1963; asst. dir. sect. child psychiatry, Albert Einstein Med. Ctr., Phila., 1964-68; study com. prevention Gov. Coun. Criminal Justice Planning, 19732; chmn. Com. Liaison between Am. Acad. Child and Adolescent Psychiatry and Com. Cert. in Child and Adolescent Psychiatry, Am. Bd. Psychiatry and Neurology, 1974-77; nat. steering com. recertification in psychiatry, 1976-77. Contbr. chpts. to books, articles to profl. jours. Recipient Virgil Lusk Meml. scholarship, N.Mex. Mil. Inst., 1946, 47. Fellow APA, Am. Acad. Child and Adolescent Psychiatry (mem. continuing edn. com. 1974-77); mem. AMA, AAAS, N.Mex. Med. Soc., Psychiat. Med. Assn. N.Mex., Santa Fe County Med. Soc., Regional Coun. Child Psychiatry (pres.-elect 1969-70, pres. 1970), N.Mex. Psychiat. Assn. (pres.-elect 1971-72, pres. 1972-73), Phila. Assn. Psychoanalysis. Home: 116 Tano Rd Santa Fe NM 87501-7024

STENTZ, STEVEN THOMAS, researcher, systems analyst; b. Sidney, Nebr., May 4, 1951; s. Howard William and Orletha Maxine (Gardner) S.; m. Patricia Marie Thompson, Oct. 9, 1971 (div. 1979); 1 child, Carrie Lee; m. Barbara Ann Willie, Dec. 29, 1990. BA magna cum laude, We. Wash. U., 1979; MS, U. Wash., 1982, doctoral postgrad., 1982-85. Counselor Auburn (Wash.) Youth Svcs., 1977-79, Renton (Wash.) Area Youth Svcs., 1980; research analyst Dept. Social & Health Svcs., Olympia, Wash., 1981-82; computer, rsch. cons. U. Wash., Seattle, 1982-85, instr., 1986; instr. We. Wash. U., Bellingham, 1986-88; systems analyst S. Stentz & Assocs., Olympia, 1981—; researcher Wash. Supreme Ct., Olympia, 1986—; Mem. Human Subjecs Rev. Com. U. Wash., Seattle, 1982-85; cons. King County Dept. of Youth Svcs., Seattle, 1984-88, Wash. Assn. Rehab. Psychologists, Seattle, 1983-88, King County Health Planning Coun., Seattle, 1983-84, Children's Home Soc. Wash., Seattle, 1985-86. Contbr. articles to profl. jours.; author software reference manuals. Speaker Assn. Hosp. Adminstrs., 1983-86, Coun. Social Work Edn., Detroit, 1983, Alliance for Children, Youth and Families, Seattle, 1986, Pacific Northwest Assn. Hosp. Adminstrs., 1983-86, Ann. Wash. Jud. Conf., 1987-91, Dist. and Mcpl. Judges Spring Conf., 1988-89, Wash. State Assn. County Clks., 1988-92, 94-95. With U.S. Army, 1971-72.

STEPANEK, JOSEPH EDWARD, industrial development consultant; b. Ellinwood, Kans., Oct. 29, 1917; s. Joseph August and Leona Mae (Wilson) S.; m. Antoinette Farnham, June 10, 1942; children: Joseph F., James B., Antoinette L., Debra L. BSChemE, U. Colo., 1939; DEng in Chem. Engring., Yale U., 1942. Registered profl. engr., Colo. Engr. Stearns-Roger Mfg., Denver, 1939-45; from asst. to assoc. prof. U. Colo., Boulder, 1945-47; from cons. to dir. UN, various countries, 1947-73; cons. internat. indsl devel., U.S.-China bus. relations Boulder, 1973—; bd. dirs. 12 corps., 1973—. Author 3 books on indsl. devel.; contbr. 50 articles to profl. jours. Exec. dir. Boulder Tomorrow, 1965-67. Recipient Yale Engring. award Yale Engring. Assn., 1957, Norlin award U. Colo. 1978, Annual award India League of Am., 1982. Mem. AAAS. Democrat. Unitarian. Home: 1622 High St Boulder CO 80304-4224

STEPHEN, WILLIAM PROCURONOFF, entomologist, educator; b. St. Boniface, Manitoba, Canada, June 6, 1927; s. Steven and Amalia (Hoppe) S.; m. Dorris Jo Williams, June 8, 1952; children: Dana Ann, Jan Marie, Mary Beth, William Thaddeus. BS, U. Manitoba, 1948; postgrad., Iowa State U., 1949-50; PhD, U. Kans., 1952. Asst. assoc. entomologist Canada-Agriculture, Brandon, Ottawa, 1946-53; from asst. prof. to assoc. prof. Oreg. State U., Corvallis, 1953—, prof., 1963—; cons. OAS, Santiago, Chile, 1971-72; program dir. FAO, Buenos Aires, 1973-76; dir. Junto Inc., Corvallis. Contbr. articles to profl. jours. Mem. Entomol. Soc. Am., Kans. Entomol. Soc., Internat. Bee Rsch. Assn., Soc. Study Evolution. Democrat. Office: Oreg State U Corvallis OR 97331

STEPHENS, ALICE ELIZABETH (ALICE WANKE STEPHENS), artist; b. Portland, Oreg., Feb. 2, 1926; d. A.E. and Elfrieda I. (Strauch) Wanke; m. Farrold Franklin Stephens, Feb. 2, 1950; children: Scott, Lynn, Todd. Student, Oreg. State U., 1944-46; BA, Stanford U., Palo Alto, Calif., 1948. bd. dirs., cons. Wanke Cascade, Portland. Exhibited in numerous one-woman shows including Thor Gallery, Louisville, 1971, Unitarian Ch., Portland, 1976, George Fox Coll., Newberg, Oreg., 1987, Beaverton (Oreg.) Arts Commn., 1988, Clackamas C.C., Oreg. City, 1988, World Forestry Ctr., 1989, 94, West Hills Unitarian Fellowship, Portland, 1991, First United Meth. Ch., Portland, 1991, Japanese Garden Pavilion, Portland, 1991, Auditor's Office Portland City Hall, 1990, 95; represented at Rental Sales Gallery, Portland Art Mus. 2d v.p. Portland Womens Union, 1990-91, bd. dirs.; bd. dirs., sec. Park Vista Corp. Mem. Oreg. Soc. Artists, Cap and Gown of Stanford U., City Club Portland, Pi Beta Phi. Democrat. Mem. Disciples of Christ. Home: 2323 SW Park Pl Apt 805 Portland OR 97205-1039

STEPHENS, ELISA, academic administrator. Pres. Acad. Art Coll., San Francisco. Office: Acad Art Coll Office of President 79 New Montgomery St San Francisco CA 94105-3410

STEPHENS, LARRY DEAN, engineer; b. Sterling, Colo., Sept. 1, 1937; s. John Robert and Shirley Berniece (Rudel) S.; m. Carol Ann Wertz, Sept. 1, 1957 (div. May 1975); children: Deborah Lynn, Janell Diane, Dana Larry, Hilary Elizabeth Melton. BS in Engring., Colo. State U., 1960; MBA, U. Colo., 1967. Registered profl. engr., Colo. Engr. Bur. Reclamation, Denver, 1960-90, cons., 1991—; exec. v.p. U.S. Com. on Irrigation and Drainage, Denver, 1971—; exec. dir. U.S. Com. on Large Dams, Denver, 1986—. V.p. Internat. Commn. on Irrigation and Drainage, 1989-92. With USNG, 1961-62. Mem. Am. Soc. Agrl. Engrs., Assn. State Dam Safety Officials, Colo. River Water Users Assn., Coun. on Engring. and Sci. Soc. Execs. Republican. Methodist. Home: 1625 Larimer St Apt 1505 Denver CO 80202-1532 Office: USCID 1616 17th St Ste 483 Denver CO 80202-1277

STEPHENS, LEE AMIEL, business development executive; b. Indpls., Dec. 9, 1962; s. Philip David and Verlee Ester (Foertsch) S.; m. Linda Anne Montrois, Mar. 14, 1986; 1 child, Philip Sterling. Student, Phoenix Coll., 1982, Scottsdale (Ariz.) Community Coll., 1982-83. Supr. automotive testing Lighting Scis., Inc., Scottsdale, Ariz., 1982-88; product design engr. Sylvania div. GTE, Seymour, Ind., 1988-90; bus. development mgr. Lighting Scis., Inc., Scottsdale, Ariz., 1990-91; sales engr. Hoffman Engring. Corp., Phoenix, Ariz., 1992—. Pres. Pepper Ridge Townhomes Homeowner's Assn., Phoenix, 1986-88. Named Explorer of the Yr. Boy Scouts Am., Phoenix, 1981. Mem. Soc. Automotive Engrs., Illuminating Engring. Soc. (edn. chmn. Ariz. sect. 1986-87), Nat. Eagle Scout Assn., Nat. Assn. Outstanding Jr. & Community Coll. Students, Elks. Republican. Methodist. Office: Hoffman Engring Corp 3432 E Utopia St Phoenix AZ 85024

STEPHENS, MICHAEL DEAN, hospital administrator; b. Salt Lake City, May 1, 1942; married. B, Columbia U., 1966, MHA, 1970. Adminstrv. resident Mt. Sinai Med. Ctr., N.Y.C., 1969-70; asst. administr. Greenville (S.C.) Gen. Hosp., 1970-71, assoc. adminstr., 1971-72, adminstr., 1972-75; pres. Hoag Meml. Hosp.-Presbyn., Newport Beach, Calif., 1975—. Mem. Am. Coll. Healthcare Execs. Home: 900 Alder Pl Newport Beach CA 92660-4121 Office: Hoag Meml Hosp Presbyn PO Box 611 Newport Beach CA 92661-0611

STEPHENS, RONALD CARLYLE, retired military officer, academic director; b. L.A., Feb. 25, 1941; s. Ronald Francis Stephens and Martha Virginia (Wright) Hubbard. BA in History, UCLA, 1963; grad., Purdue U., 1964. World wide tour mgr. Laughlin Tours, L.A., 1960-64; commd. ensign USN, 1964, advanced through grades to capt., intelligence officer, 1964-74; sci. and tech. intelligence liaison officer Naval Sea Systems Command, Naval Ship, Port Hueneme, Calif., 1975-85; mil. dir. tech. transfer data base program, reserve liaison officer Office Sec. Def. Def. Tech. Security Adminstrn., Pentagon, Washington, 1985-91; ret. USN, 1991; dir. Coachella Valley Acad. and 29 Palms Acad. Ctrs. Chapman U., Palm Desert, Calif.,

1991—; ops. security cons. Chief of Naval Material, Washington, 1981-85; ops. security officer Naval Sea Systems Command, Washington and Port Hueneme, 1981-85; dir. res. programs trade security policy Office Dep. Undersecretary Def., Pentagon, 1986-91; cons. Def. Dept. Author: course curr. Fleet Operational Intelligence, 1982; author: Shipboard: Over-the-Horizon Targeting Capabilities and Limitations, 1982, 84. Player, coach community sports, L.A., 1975-85; tutor, counselor Oxnard (Calif.) Sch. Systems, 1978-85. Recipient Defense Meritorious Svc. medal, 1987, Defense Superior Svc. medal, 1989. Mem. Naval Res. Assn., Ret. Officers Assn. (life), U.S. Naval Inst., UCLA Alumni Assn. (scholarship com. 1970-82), Blue and Gold Circle, Coachella Valley Industry and Edn. Coun., Palm Desert C. of C. (edn. com.), Assoc. Naval Aviation (life), Assn. Old Crows, Phi Kappa Sigma. Republican. Episcopalian. Home: PO Box 457 Palm Desert CA 92261-0457 Office: Chapman U 42-600 Cook St Ste 134 Palm Desert CA 92211

STEPHENS, TAYLOR LANE, insurance company executive; b. Lawrence, Kans., Apr. 13, 1937; s. George Edward and Helen H. (Houghton) S.; m. Sheila Ruth Tomlin, Aug. 27, 1961; children: Shelley, Taylor. BS, U. Colo., 1959. CLU, CPCU. Claims adjuster Farmers Ins. Group of Cos., Denver, 1960-62; dist. mgr. Farmers Ins. Group of Cos., Aurora, Colo., 1962-90; legis. rep. Colorado Springs, Colo., 1990—. Fellow Life Underwriter Tng. Council; mem. Soc. Chartered Property and Casualty Underwriters (pres. 1983-84), Am. Soc. Chartered Life Underwriters, Nat. Assn. LIfe Underwriters (pres. 1973-74, regional v.p. 1975-76). Republican. Lutheran. Lodge: Optimists (pres. 1968-69), Rotary. Office: Farmers Ins Group Co 3500 N Nevada Ave Colorado Springs CO 80907-5333

STEPHENS, WILLIAM THOMAS, forest products manufacturing company executive; married. BS, U. Ark., 1965, MS, 1966. Various mgmt. positions Manville Forest Products Corp., from 1963; asst. to pres., then sr. v.p., pres. forest products group Manville Corp., Denver, exec. v.p. fin. and adminstrn., from 1984, now pres., chief exec. officer, chmn., bd. dirs. Office: Manville Corp PO Box 5108 Manville Plz Denver CO 80202*

STEPHENSON, BARBERA WERTZ, lawyer; b. Bryan, Ohio, Dec. 10, 1938; d. Emerson D. and Beryl B. (Barber) Wertz; m. Gerard J. Stephenson Jr., June 22, 1960; 1 child, Thomas. Student, Smith Coll., 1956-57; BSEE, MIT, 1961; JD, U. N.Mex., 1981. Bar: N.Mex. 1981. Electronic engr. Digital Equipment Corp., Maynard, Mass., 1960-66; logic analyst Librascope, Glendale, Calif., 1966; electronic engr. Md. Dept. of Def., Ft. Meade, 1966-68; mem. tech. staff Xerox Data Systems, Rockville, Md., 1968; pvt. practice cons., Silver Spring, Md., 1969-78; pvt. practice law, Albuquerque, 1981—. Author: Financing Your Home Purchase in New Mexico, 1992; patentee analog to digital converter, kitchen calculator. Mem. N.Mex. Bar Assn. Office: 4221 Silver Ave SE Albuquerque NM 87108-2720

STEPHENSON, HERMAN HOWARD, banker; b. Wichita, Kans., July 15, 1929; s. Herman Horace and Edith May (Wayland) S.; m. Virginia Anne Ross, Dec. 24, 1950; children: Ross Wayland, Neal Bevan, Jann Edith. BA, U. Mich., 1950; JD with distinction, U. Mo., Kansas City, 1958, LLD (hon.), 1993. Bar: Kans. 1958. With City Nat. Bank, Kansas City, Mo., 1952-54, City Bond & Mortgage Co., Kansas City, 1954-59, Bank of Hawaii, Honolulu, 1959-94; ret., 1994; now chmn. bd., CEO Bancorp Hawaii Inc. and subs. Bank Hawaii, Banque de Tahiti; bd. dirs. Banque de Nouvelle-Caledonie, Pacific Basin Econ. Coun. U.S. Mem. Com, Bancorp Hawaii, Inc., Bank Hawaii, bancorp Hawaii Charitable Found., Bank of Hawaii Internat. Inc., Hawaiian Trust Co. Bd. dirs. Honolulu Symphony, Maunalani Found., Aloha United Way, Pacific Fleet Submarine Meml. Assn., Pacific Basin Econ. Coun. U.S. Mem. Com.; co-chmn. Ellison Onizuka Meml. Scholarship Fund Com.; chmn. bd. regents U. Hawaii. With U.S. Army, 1950-52. Mem. ABA, Am. Bankers Assn. (past chmn. exec. com. housing and real estate fin. div., dir. 1976-77, mem. governing coun. 1976-77, mem. govt. rels. coun. 1986-89), Kans. Bar Assn., Hawaii Bankers Assn. (pres. 1991-92), U.S.-Japan Bus. Coun., Pacific Asia Travel Assn. (Hawaii chpt., assoc.), Navy League of U.S., Hawaii Bus. Roundtable, Pacific Forum/CSIS (bd. govs.), Assn. Res. City Bankers, U.S.-Korea Bus. Coun., Kappa Sigma, Pi Eta Sigma, Oahu Country Club, Pacific Club, Waialae Country Club, Rotary. Office: Bank of Hawaii PO Box 2900 Honolulu HI 96846-0001*

STEPHENSON, IRENE HAMLEN, biorhythm analyst, consultant, editor, educator; b. Chgo., Oct. 7, 1923; d. Charles Martin and Carolyn Hilda (Hilgers) Hamlin; m. Edgar B. Stephenson, Sr., Aug. 16, 1941 (div. 1946); 1 child, Edgar B. Author biorhythm compatibilities column Nat. Singles Register, Norwalk, Calif., 1979-81; instr. biorhythm Learning Tree Open U., Canoga Park, Calif., 1982-83; instr. biorhythm character analysis 1980—; instr. biorhythm compatibility, 1982—; owner, pres. matchmaking svc. Pen Pals Using Biorhythm, Chatsworth, Calif., 1979—; editor newsletter The Truth, 1979-85, Mini Examiner, Chatsworth, 1985—; researcher biorhythm character and compatibility, 1974—, biorhythm columnist Psychic Astrology Horoscope, 1989-94, True Astrology Forecast, 1989-94, Psychic Astrology Predictions, 1990-94; author: Learn Biorhythm Character Analysis, 1980; Do-It-Yourself Biorhythm Compatibilities, 1982; contbr. numerous articles to mags.; frequent guests clubs, radio, TV. Office: PO Box 3893-ww Chatsworth CA 91313

STEPHENSON, LARRY KIRK, strategic planner, management and geography educator; b. Seattle, Sept. 22, 1944; s. Norman Eugene and Virginia Dare (Frost) S.; m. Tamara Leah Ladin, June 24, 1967; children: Mathew Alan, Leah Anela. BS, Ariz. State U., 1966, MA, 1971; PhD, U. Cin., 1973; Manpower research analyst Employment Security Commn. of Ariz., 1969-70; asst. prof. dept. geography U. Hawaii, Hilo, 1973-76, assoc. prof., 1976-78, chmn. dept., 1975-77; vis. lectr. dept. geography Ariz. State U., 1978, adj. assoc. prof., 1979—; planner Ariz. Dept. Health Services, Phoenix, 1978-84; vis. assoc. prof. dept. geography, area devel. and urban planning U. Ariz., 1978; strategic plannner City of Glendale, Ariz., 1984-92; pub. health analyst Gila River Indian Community, 1992—; mem. faculty U. Phoenix, 1979—; adj. prof. Golden Gate U., 1981—; ptnr. Urban Research Assocs., Phoenix, 1981—; adj. prof. Coll. St. Francis, 1982—; mem. faculty Troy State U., 1990—. Mem. Hawaii Island Health Planning Council, 1974-78; mem. Glendale Community Colls. Pres.'s Council, 1986—. Served with U.S. Army, 1966-68. NDEA fellow, 1971-72. Mem. Am. Inst. Cert. Planners, Am. Planning Assn., Assn. Am. Geographers, Ariz. Planning Assn. (pres. 1987—), Southwest Profl. Geog. Assn., Lambda Alpha. Unitarian. Author books in field; contbr. chpts. to textbooks, articles to profl. jours. Home: RR 1 Box 453-f Laveen AZ 85339-9654 Office: PO Box 7 Sacaton AZ 85247-0007

STEPHENSON, NED ELDON, real estate development company executive; b. Salt Lake City, Jan. 15, 1957; s. Robert Eldon and Frances Reeder (Call) S.; m. Lisa Bradley, Dec. 19, 1987; children: David Bradley, Sarah Jane, Bradley Robert, Betsy Jane. BA in Fin., BA in Mgmt., U. Utah, 1982. Lic. real estate agt., Utah. Mgr. Peterson Devel. Co., Salt Lake City, 1978-82, v.p., 1982-89; owner, pres. Stephenson Property Mgmt., Salt Lake City, 1982—, Ned Stephenson Devel., Salt Lake City, 1985-89; v.p. sales and leasing Peterson Devel. Co.; ptnr., pres. Stephenson and Shaw Devel. Co., 1987-89; devel. dir. Woodbury Corp., 1989—. Treas. U. Utah Student Assn., Salt Lake City, 1979-80; del. Rep. Party Salt lake County, 1984-85, 90-91, State of Utah, 1986-87, 92-93. Named one of Outstanding Young Men of Am., U.S. Jaycees, 1980. Mem. Nat. Eagle Scout Assn. Mormon. Home: 3370 Oakledge Rd Salt Lake City UT 84121-5817 Office: Woodbury Corp 2677 Parleys Way Salt Lake City UT 84109-1617

STEPNER, MICHAEL JAY, architect; b. Chgo., Sept. 7, 1940; s. Lester Harry and Florence (Addison) S.; m. Rosemary Reiser, Apr. 2, 1965; children: Rachel, Jessica, Adam, Joshua, Rebekah. Student, U. Minn., 1961-62; BArch, U. Ill., 1964; postgrad., U. Calif., Berkeley, 1971; U.S. Navy Engring. Schs., 1965-66. Registered architect, Calif. Urban designer, planner Crosstown Assocs., Chgo., 1968-71; urban designer, planner planning dept. City of San Diego, 1971-81, asst. planning dir., 1981-88, acting planning dir., 1987-88, city architect, 1988-92, asst. to city mgr., spl. projects coord., 1992-94, city urban design coord., 1994—; vis. critic in urban design U. Ill, Chgo., 1970-71, San Diego State U. Grad. Sch. Planning and Pub. Adminstrn., Urban Design & Site Planning Inst., 1974-85; lectr. Urban Conservation Grad. Sch. History, U. San Diego, 1978, 81, 82, 87; asst. prof., lectr., design critic New Sch. Architecture, San Diego City U., 1980—; faculty assoc. for transp. and land use planning Lincoln Inst. Land Policy, Cambridge, Mass., 1993-95; mem. hist. bldg. code bd. State of Calif.; mem., dir. Community Planning and Design Ctr., San Diego, 1971-74. Bd. dirs. Citizens Coordinate for Century III, 1991—; mem. Regional Urban Design Assistance Team, Seattle, Washington, and Liverpool, Eng.; past bd. dirs. Californians for Preservation Action. Recipient Leadership in Planning award New Sch. Architecture, 1992, Gaslamp Pioneer award San Diego Gaslamp Quarter Found., 1993, Ellen and Roger Revelle award Citizens Coordinate for Century III, 1993. Fellow AIA (co-chair housing assistance team City of Washincton, 1990, bd. dirs. San Diego chpt. 1976-78, mem. nat. urban design com., past mem. Calif. coun., hist. preservation-urban conservation com., urban design commr. San Diego chpt. 1975-76, Spl. award for Excellence in Govt. 1983); mem. Am. Planning Assn. (Disting. Leadership award Calif. chpt. 1991), Am. Inst. Cert. Planners, Inst. for Urban Design, Urban Land Inst., Lambda Alpha. Home: 4260 Hortensia St San Diego CA 92103-1105

STEPP, WILLIAM EDWARD, retired military operations analyst; b. Turtle Creek, Pa., Feb. 23, 1930; s. William George and Emma Jean (McLean) S.; m. Barbara Johanna Barth, Oct. 23, 1965; children: Randal R., Roger W. BS in Physics, Carnegie-Mellon U., 1951; MS in Engring., U. So. Calif., 1977. Physicist Bell Aircraft Co., Buffalo, 1951-53, Convair Aircraft Co., San Diego, 1953-56, Bendix Co., North Hollywood, Calif., 1956-59; ops. analyst ORI, Santa Monica, Calif., 1959-61, Douglas Aircraft Co., Santa Monica, 1961-63; sr. mil. ops. analyst Lockheed Calif. Co., Burbank, 1963-91, ret., 1991.

STERBACH, CHARLES ROBERT, lawyer; b. Nagoya, Japan, June 21, 1955; came to the U.S., 1957; s. Edward Robert and Shizuko (Ishimutsu) S.; m. Kimberly Ann Burke, Sept. 26, 1992; 1 child, Justin Andrew Chard. BA, U. Pa., 1977, 79; JD, Rutgers U., 1983. Bar: Ariz. 1983. Assoc. Streich Lang, P.A., Phoenix, 1983-89; assoc. Gallagher & Kennedy, P.A., Phoenix, 1989-90, ptnr., 1991—; mem. evening faculty Phoenix Coll., 1988-92. Mem. ABA, Ariz. Bar Assn., Ariz. Bankruptcy Bar Assn., Phoenix Adult Hockey League. Office: Gallagher & Kennedy PA 2600 N Central Ave Phoenix AZ 85004-3050

STERBICK, PETER LAWRENCE, lawyer; b. Tacoma, Nov. 12, 1917; s. Anton John and Pearl (Medak) S.; m. Rita J. Morrell, Dec. 26, 1946; children: Marilyn, Lawrence, Thomas, David, Colleen. BBA, U. Wash., 1941, LLB, 1948. Bar: Wash. 1949. Adjuster Gen. Accidenty Ins. Co., Seattle, 1948-49, Farmers Ins. Group, Tacoma, 1949-50; dep. pros. atty. Pierce County, Tacoma, 1950-51; ptnr. Sterbick and Sterbick, Tacoma, 1951-57, Sterbick, Manza, Moceri and Sterbick, Tacoma, 1958-72, Sterbick, Abel and Sterbick, Tacoma, 1972—. 2d lt. USAAF, 1943-45. Mem. Wash. Bar Assn., Tacoma-Pierce County Bar Assn., Kiwanis, KC, Elks. Roman Catholic. Home: 3143 Olympic Blvd W Tacoma WA 98466-1605 Office: Sterbick Abel & Sterbick 15 Oregon Ave Ste 303 Tacoma WA 98409

STERLING, DONALD JUSTUS, JR., retired newspaper editor; b. Portland, Oreg., Sept. 27, 1927; s. Donald Justus and Adelaide (Armstrong) S.; m. Julie Ann Courteol, June 7, 1963; children: Sarah, William, John. A.B., Princeton U., 1948; postgrad. (Nieman fellow), Harvard U., 1955-56. Reporter Denver Post, 1948-52; news staff mem. Oreg. Jour., Portland, 1952-82; editor Oreg. Jour., 1972-82; asst. to pub. The Oregonian, 1982-92, ret., 1992. Pres. Tri-County Community Coun., 1972-73. Recipient Izaak Walton League Golden Beaver award, 1969, Edith Knight Hill award, 1978, Jessie Laird Brodie award Planned Parenthood Assn., 1983, McCall award Women in Communications, 1987, Roger W. Williams Freedom of Info. award Oreg. Newspaper Pubs. Assn., 1989; English-Speaking Union traveling fellow, 1959. Mem. Soc. Nieman Fellows, Oreg. Hist. Soc. (pres. 1977-79), Mazamas, Lang Syne Soc. Clubs: City (Portland) (pres. 1973-74), Multnomah Athletic (Portland); Dial, Elm, Cannon (Princeton). Home: 1718 SW Myrtle St Portland OR 97201-2300

STERLING, DONALD T., professional basketball team executive; b. Chgo.. Lawyer L.A. (formerly San Diego) Clippers, Nat. Basketball Assn., owner, also chmn. bd. Office: care LA Clippers LA Meml Sports Arena 3939 S Figueroa St Los Angeles CA 90037-1207*

STERMER, DUGALD ROBERT, designer, illustrator, writer, consultant; b. Los Angeles, Dec. 17, 1936; s. Robert Newton and Mary (Blue) S.; m. Jeanie Kortum; children: Dugald, Megan, Chris, Colin, Crystal. B.A., UCLA, 1960. Art dir., v.p. Ramparts mag., 1965-70; freelance designer, illustrator, writer, cons. San Francisco, 1970—; founder Pub. Interest Communications, San Francisco, 1974; pres. Frisco Pub Group Ltd.; chmn. illustration dept. Calif. Coll. Arts and Crafts, 1994—; bd. dirs. Am. Inst. Graphic Arts; chair illustration dept. Calif. Coll. Arts and Crafts, 1994—. Cons. editor: Communication Arts mag., 1974-90; designer: Oceans mag., 1976-82; editor: The Environment, 1972, Vanishing Creatures, 1980; author: The Art of Revolution, 1970, Vanishing Creatures, 1980, Vanishing Flora, 1994, Birds and Bees, 1994; designer 1984 Olympic medals; illustration exhbn. Calif. Acad. Scis., 1986. Mem. Grand Jury City and County San Francisco, 1989; bd. dirs. Delancey St. Found., 1990—. Recipient various medals, awards for design and illustration nat. and internat. competitions. Office: 600 The Embarcadero # 204 San Francisco CA 94107

STERN, ANITA ENKEL, English language educator; b. Detroit, July 22, 1941; d. Harry and Ida (Goodman) Enkel; m. Josef Stern, June 25, 1968; children: Tsafrir, Michael. BA magna cum laude, Wayne State U., Detroit, 1963, MA, 1964; MA, Calif. State U., L.A., 1990. Lic. single subject-English and lang. devel. specialist, Calif. Tchr. Highland Park (Mich.) Schs., 1964-65; instr. Bar Ilan U., Ramat Gan, Israel, 1966-68, Tel Aviv (Israel) U., 1965-67; tchr. Tel Aviv Mcpl. H.S., 1968-69, Shein Tchrs. Coll., Petach Tikva, Israel, 1984-85, Levinsky, Tel Aviv, 1981-82, Lynwood (Calif.) Unified Sch. Dist., 1986-90, Baldwin Park (Calif.) Unified Schs., 1990-92, L.A. Unified Schs., 1992—; instr. L.A. S.W. Coll., 1987-88. Author: World Folktales, 1994. Mem. TESOL, Calif. TESOL, Internat. Reading Assn., Authors Guild, Soc. Children's Book Writers and Illustrators, Tex. and Acad. Authors Assn. Home: 344 S Peck Dr Beverly Hills CA 90212-3715 Office: Dorsey HS 3537 Farmdale Ave Los Angeles CA 90016-4707

STERN, ARTHUR PAUL, electronics company executive, electrical engineer; b. Budapest, Hungary, July 20, 1925; came to U.S., 1951, naturalized, 1956; s. Leon and Bertha (Frankfurter) S.; m. Edith M. Samuel; children: Daniel, Claude, Jacqueline. Diploma in Elec. Engring., Swiss Fed. Inst. Tech., Zurich, 1948; MSEE, Syracuse U., 1955. Mgr. electronic devices and applications lab. Gen. Electric Co., Syracuse, N.Y., 1957-61; dir. engring. Martin Marietta Corp., Balt., 1961-64; dir. ops. Bunker Ramo Corp., Canoga Park, Calif., 1964-66; v.p., gen. mgr. advanced products div. Magnavox, Torrance, Calif., 1966-79, pres. Magnavox Advanced Products and Systems Co., Torrance, 1980-90; vice chmn., bd. dirs. Magnavox Govt. and Indsl. Electronics Co., Ft. Wayne, Ind., 1987-90; pres. Ea. Beverly Hills Corp., 1991—; non-resident staff mem. MIT, 1956-59; instr. Gen. Elec. Bus. Mgmt., 1955-57. Chmn. engring. div. United Jewish Appeal, Syracuse, 1955-57; mem. adv. bd. dept. elec. engring. U. Calif., Santa Barbara, 1980-92; mem. Sch. Engring. Adv. and Devel. Council Calif. State U., Long Beach, 1985-90. Co-author: Transistor Circuit Engineering, 1957, Handbook of Automation, Computation and Control, 1961; also articles; U.S., fgn. patentee in field. Fellow AAAS, IEEE (pres. 1975, bd. dirs., officer 1970-77, guest editor spl. issue IEEE Trans. on Circuit Theory 1956, invited guest editor spl. issue Procs. IEEE on Integrated Electronics 1964, Centennial medal 1984). Jewish.

STERN, CLAUDE MICHAEL, lawyer; b. Syracuse, N.Y., Sept. 18, 1955; s. Arthur Paul and Edith Margaret (Samuel) S. BA Philosophy with honors, UCLA, 1977; JD, U. Calif., Hastings, 1980. Bar: Calif. 1980, U.S. Ct. Appeals (9th cir.) 1981, U.S. Dist. Ct. (no., ea. and cen. dists.) Calif. 1982. Law clk. to presiding justice U.S. Ct. Appeals (9th cir.), Seattle, 1980-81; assoc. Morrison & Foerster, San Francisco, 1982-84, Horwich & Warner, San Francisco, 1984-86; ptnr. Horwich & Warner, Seattle, 1987-88, Nossaman, Guthner, Knox & Elliott, San Francisco, 1988—. Editor, Hastings Law Jour., 1979-80. Chmn. regional civil rights com. Anti-Defamation League of B'nai B'rith, San Francisco, 1986-88, regional bd. exec. com., 1988-90. Mem. ABA, San Francisco Bar Assn., Calif. Bar Assn., Am. Telemarketing Assn., Order of Coif, Thurston Honor Soc. Democrat. Office: Nossaman Guthner Knox & Elliott 50 California St Fl 34 San Francisco CA 94111-4712

STERN, DANA LEE, computer company executive, writer, consultant; b. Tulsa, Feb. 26, 1947; s. Charles Daniel and Virginia Rose (Chitwood) S.; m. Mary Beth Hoger Stern, June 22, 1991; 1 child, Dana L. Stern, Jr. Student, L.A. Valley Coll., Glendale Coll. Pres. CompuNet, La Crescenta, Calif., 1991—. Author: Preventing Computer Fraud, 1993.

STERN, DAVID GERALD, philosophy educator; b. London, Sept. 19, 1958; came to U.S., 1979; BA, Oxford (Eng.) U., 1979; MA, U. Pitts., 1980; PhD, U. Calif., Berkeley, 1987. Postdoctoral rschr. U. Alta., Edmonton, Can., 1987-88; asst. prof. philosophy U. Iowa, Iowa City, 1988-93; asst. prof. rhetoric U. Calif., Berkeley, 1993—. Author: Wittgenstein on Mind and Language, 1994; contbr. articles to profl. jours. Killam postdoctoral scholar U. Alta., 1987; May Brodbeck Humanities fellow U. Iowa, 1993. Mem. MLA, Am. Philos. Assn., Philosophy of Sci. Assn. Office: U Calif Berkeley Dept Rhetoric 2125 Dwinelle #2670 Berkeley CA 94720

STERN, JOHN LOUIS, real estate development and management executive; b. L.A., Feb. 11, 1924; s. Harold Melrose and Marion (Levi) S.; m. Eleanor Brill, July 3, 1948; children: Deborah, John B. BS, Calif. Inst. Tech., 1945; MBA, Stanford U., 1948. Real estate appraiser Winter Mortgage Co., L.A., 1948-49; real estate broker, sales mgr. Walter H. Leiment Co., L.A., 1949-51; owner JOhn L. Stern S&M Devel. Co., L.A., 1951—. Mem. Stanford Alumni Exec. bd. 1970s. Served to lt. (j.g.) USN, 1943-45. Mem. Beach Club (Santa Monica, Calif.), Maroon Creek Club (Aspen, Colo.), Cal. Tech Assocs., Stanford Alumni Assn., Riviera Country Club. Democrat. Jewish.

STERN, KINGSLEY ROWLAND, botanist, educator; b. Port Elizabeth, South Africa, Oct. 30, 1927; s. Julius Charles and Vera Grace (Estment) S.; m. Janet Elaine McLeland, June 9, 1956; children: Kevin Douglas, Sharon Maureen. BS, Wheaton (Ill.) Coll., 1949; MA, U. Mich., 1950; PhD, U. Minn., 1959. Instr. botany Hamline U., St. Paul, 1956-57; rsch. fellow in botany U. Minn., Mpls., 1957-58, instr., 1958-59; asst. prof. Chico (Calif.) State Coll., 1959-63, assoc. prof., 1963-68; prof. Calif. State U., Chico, 1968-92, prof. emeritus, 1992—; vis. prof. botany U. Hawaii, Honolulu, 1987; cons. to fed., state and local agys., Calif., 1976—. Author: Introductory Plant Biology, 1978; co-author: Botany, 1995; contbr. articles. to profl. jours. Fellow Conway McMillan Found., 1957-58; NSF grantee, 1963-72. Mem. Botanical Soc. Am., Am. Soc. Plant Taxonomists, Calif. Botanical Soc. (v.p. 1990-92). Office: Calif State U Dept Biolog Scis Chico CA 95929

STERN, LOUIS, gallery owner; b. Casablanca, Morocco, Jan. 7, 1945; s. Frederic and Sultana (Ifergan) S.; m. Karen Anne Honeman, Oct. 12, 1969 (div. 1991); children: Deborah Beth, Daniel William. BA, Calif. State U., Northridge, 1968. Dir. Wally Findlay Galleries, Inc., Beverly Hills, Calif., 1975-78; pres. Wally Findlay Galleries, Inc., 1978-80, Louis Stern Galleries, Inc., 1980-94, Louis Stern Fine Arts, L.A., 1994—. Expert witness L.A. Police Dept., 1984—, L.A. Superior Ct., 1984—. With U.S. Army, 1968-71. U.S. Dept. Def. Joint Commendation medal, 1971. Mem. Art Dealers Assn. Calif. (v.p. 1988—), Am. Arts Coun., Am. Friends of Blerancourt (Paris), Pres. Cir. of L.A. County Mus., L.A. Art Galleries. Office: 9002 Melrose Ave Los Angeles CA 90069-5610

STERN, MATTHEW ARNOLD, technical writer; b. Encino, Calif., July 14, 1961; s. Sheldon Simon and Barbara Jean (Bloom) S.; m. Elizabeth Shawn Newman, Dec. 22, 1990; 1 child, Stephanie Harriet. BA in English, Calif. State U., Northridge, 1985. Pub. rels. rep. EnTech Software, Sun Valley, Calif., 1983-85; freelance writer Reseda, Irvine, Calif., 1984-87; tech. writer Haba/Arrays, Inc., Van Nuys, Calif., 1985-86; sr. tech. writer AST Rsch., Inc., Irvine, 1986-95, Platinum Software, Irvine, Calif., 1995—. Author: (screenplay) Gilmore Field, 1994; columnist: Family Computing, 1988, Run, 1987-88. Recipient Award of Merit Soc. for Tech. Communications, 1989, 90, 93, Award of Achievement, 1991, 94, Disting. Tech. Communication award, 1995. Mem. Irvine Toastmasters Club, Toastmasters Internat. (v.p. pub. rels. 1991—), Soc. Tech. Communications (Orange County chpt.). Home: 27296 Avenida De La Plata Laguna Niguel CA 92656

STERN, MILFORD L., investment company executive; b. 1939. Sales rep. J.B. Hanauer Co., L.A., 1959-62; v.p. Carl M. Hanauer, 1962-64, Taylor & Co., 1964-66; prin. Stern, Brennen & Co., 1966-88; pres. M.L. Stern & Co., Beverly Hills, Calif. Office: 8350 Wilshire Blvd Beverly Hills CA 90211-2327*

STERN, RICHARD DAVID, investment company executive; b. New Rochelle, N.Y., Nov. 5, 1936; s. Leo and Grace Marjorie (Phillips) S.; m. Phyllis Marlene Edelstein, Nov. 20, 1966; children: Marjorie Anne, Andrew Howard. AB, Princeton U., 1958; MBA, Harvard U., 1962. CFA. First v.p. Newburger, Loeb & Co., N.Y.C., 1962-74, also dir., 1969-74; sr. investment officer Central Trust Co., Cin., 1974-76, owner bus. valuation cons. co., 1976-78; v.p. Gt. Western Bank & Trust Co. (now Norwest Bank Ariz. NA), Phoenix, 1978-84; pres. Stern, Ludke & Co. (now Stern Investment Mgmt. Co.), Phoenix, 1984—. Co-author: Air Cushion Vehicles, 1962. Trustee endowment trust Phoenix Chamber Music Soc., 1982-91, v.p., 1986-90, bd.. dirs., 1982-91, 93-94; pres. Ctrl. Ariz. chpt. Arthritis Found., 1982-84, chmn. planned giving com., 1986-91, mem. nat. planned giving com., 1987-89; chmn. endowments and trusts com. Temple Beth Israel, Phoenix, 1980-83; dir., investment com. Endowment Found., Temple Solel, Paradise Valley, 1990—; pres. Am. Jewish Com., Phoenix, 1983-84, bd. dirs., 1980-84, adv. bd., 1985—; bd. dirs. Asian Arts Coun., Phoenix Art Mus., 1987-93, v.p., 1989-90, pres., 1990-92; trustee Ariz. Theatre Co., 1990—, exec. com., 1995—, chair regional nominating com., 1995—. Mem. Phoenix Soc. Fin. Analysts (chmn. profl. conduct com. 1980-83, membership com. 1990-91, bd. dirs.), Anti-Defamation League of B'nai B'rith (dir. Ctrl. Ariz. chpt. 1986—, exec. bd. 1989—, chair nominating com. 1990-94, chair bd. devel. 1993-94, treas. 1994—), Princeton Alumni Assn. No. Ariz. (alumni schs. com. 1992—), Univ Club (Phoenix, bd. dirs. 1990-92, fin. com. 1990-91), Harvard Bus. Sch. Club Ariz. (bd. dirs. 1991—, pres. 1993-95), Assn. for Corp. Growth (Ariz. chpt.). Republican. Home: 6013 E Donna Cir Paradise Vly AZ 85253-1730 Office: 2930 E Camelback Rd Ste 195 Phoenix AZ 85016-4412

STERN, SHERRY ANN, journalist; b. Paterson, N.J., June 27, 1954; d. Richard Norman and Norma (Davidowitz). BA, U. S. Calif., Los Angeles, 1876; MS, Northwestern U., Evanston, 1982. Reporter Ariz. Daily Star, Tucson, 1976-79, TV critic, 1979-81; news editor The Morning Press, Vista, Calif., 1982-83, mng. editor, editor in chief, 1983-84; copy editor The Orange County Register, Calif., 1984-85; asst. features news editor The Orange County Register, Santa Ana, Calif., 1985-86; features news editor Orange County Register, Santa Ana, Calif., 1986—; journalism instr. Mira Costa Coll., Oceanside, 1983-84. Vol. Lit. Vols. of Am., Huntington Beach, 1988—. Named Best Headling Portfolio Orange County Press Club, 1985, Best Student Feature Los Angeles Press Club. Mem. Orange County, Press Club. Democrat. Jewish. Office: The Orange County Register 625 N Grand Ave Santa Ana CA 92701-4347

STERN, STANLEY, psychiatrist; b. N.Y.C., Apr. 5, 1933; s. Frank and Gussie S.; children: Marcus F., David S. BA cum laude, N.Y. U., 1953; MD, SUNY, 1957. Intern Ohio State U. Hosp., Columbus, 1957-58; resident in psychiatry Inst. Living, Hartford, Conn., 1958-60, Austen Riggs Ctr., Stockbridge, Mass., 1960-61; psychoanalytic tng. We. New Eng. Inst. for Psychoanalysis, New Haven, Conn., 1965-73; asst. clin. prof. psychiatry Yale U., New Haven, Conn., 1975-81; assoc. clin. prof. psychiatry U. Calif., San Diego, 1982-84; pvt. practice New Haven, 1965-82, La Jolla, Calif., 1982-84, Phoenix, 1984—; mem. faculty San Diego Psychoanalytic Inst., 1980-84; pres. Ariz. Psychoanalytic Study Group, Phoenix, 1986-88, Phoenix Psychoanalytic Study Group, 1986-88; tng. and supervising analyst So. Calif. Psychoanalytic Inst., 1989; chmn. edn. com. Ariz. Psychoanalytic New Tng. Facility, 1990-91; lectr., presenter, participant seminars and confs. in field. Contbr. article to profl. jours. Trustee, Gesell Inst., New Haven, 1986-88, Ctr. for the Exceptional Patient, New Haven; bd. dirs. ACLU. Capt. USAF, 1961-63. Mem. Am. Coll. Psychoanalysts, Am. Psychoanalytic Assn. (cert.), Am. Psychiatric Assn., Am. Acad. Psychoanalysts, Irene Josselyn Group

Advancement of Psychoanalysis, So. Calif. Psychoanalystic Inst. and Soc. (faculty), San Diego Psychoanalytic Inst., Council for the Advancement of Psychoanalysis (treas. 1972-73, pres.-elect 1973-74, pres. 1974-75, councillor 1975-80), Phi Beta Kappa, Beta Lambda Sigma, Psi Chi. Home and Office: 3352 E Camelback Rd Ste D Phoenix AZ 85018-2312

STERNBERG, BEN KOLLOCK, geophysicist; b. Wausau, Wis., Sept. 11, 1947; s. Lawrence Walter and Jane (Kollock) S.; m. Christine Marie Streiff, Oct. 24, 1970; children: Petra Jane Streiff, Andrew Dennis Kollock, William Lawrence Frederickson. BS in Physics, U. Wis., 1970, MS in Geophysics, 1974, PhD in Geophysics, 1977. Rsch. scientist Conoco Inc., Ponca City, Okla., 1977-79, sr. rsch. scientist, 1980, group leader, 1980-83, supr. elec. methods group, 1979-83; chief geophysicist Barringer Resources, Golden, Colo., 1983-84, mgr. geophysics and computer svcs. dept., 1983-84; mgr. controlled source elec. methods Phoenix Geophysics Inc., Denver, 1984-86; prof., dir. lab. advanced subsurface imaging, dept. head, mining and geol. engr. U. Ariz., Tucson, 1986—. Contbr. articles to profl. jours. Patentee in field. Mem. AIME (Ariz. conf. bd. dirs.), NSGS (pres.), Soc. Exploration Geophysicists, Mining Club of the S.W. Found. (bd. dirs.), European Assn. Exploration Geophysicists, Sigma Xi, Phi Eta Sigma. Presbyterian. Office: U Ariz Dept Mining & Geol Engring Bldg 12 Tucson AZ 85721

STERNS, PATRICIA MARGARET, lawyer, consultant; b. Phoenix, Jan. 30, 1952; d. Lawrence Page and Mildred Dorothy (Barbaras) S. BA, Ariz. State U., 1974; JD, U. Ariz., 1977. Bar: Ariz. bar, 1978, U.S. Dist. Ct. Ariz., 1978, U.S. Supreme Ct. 1986. With Sterns and Tennen, Phoenix, 1978—; judge pro tempore Superior Ct. Ariz., County of Maricopa, 1983—; mem. Domestic Rels. Study Com., 1984-86, judge Jessup Internat. Moot Ct. Competition and semi-finals rounds, 1984—, regional rounds, 1981—; cons. internat. law; lectr. Am. Grad. Sch. Internat. Mgmt., 1982, Princeton U. Space Mfg. Facilities Conf., 1979; participant Internat. Astronautical Fedn., 1978—. Fellow Ariz. Bar Found.; mem. AIAA, ABA (family law, internat. law sects., aerospace law com.), Am. Soc. Internat. Law (space law sect.), Maricopa County Bar Assn. (family law sect.), Internat. Inst. Space Law (bd. dirs., sec., bd. dirs. U.S. membership IISL), Internat. Bar Assn., Internat. Acad. Astronautics (corr.), Firm Mem. Soc., Internat. Astronautics Fedn., Aviation/Space Writers Assn., Ariz. Bar Assn., Profl. Rodeo Cowboys Assn. (assoc.), Am. Quarter Horse Assn. Contbr. articles to profl. publs.; mem. Ariz. Law Rev. Office: 849 N 3d Ave Phoenix AZ 85003-1439

STERRETT, JAMES MELVILLE, accountant, business consultant; b. Chicago, Dec. 25, 1949; s. James McAnlis and Antoinette (Galligan) S.; m. Joyce Mieko Motoda, Sept. 1, 1989; 1 child, Victoria Hanako. BS in Acctg., Chaminade U., Honolulu, 1988; MBA, Chaminade U., 1991. CPA, Hawaii. Cons. Profitability Cons., Honolulu, 1985-87; pres. Sterrett Cons. Group, Honolulu, 1987-88; auditor Deloitte & Touche, Honolulu, 1988-90; acct., cons. pvt. practice, Honolulu, 1990—. Mem. Nat. Soc. Pub. Accts., Nat. Assn. Tax Practitioners, Hawaii Soc. CPA's, Delta Epsilon, Sigma. Office: 1314 S King St Ste 650 Honolulu HI 96814-1941

STERTZER, SIMON HENRY, cardiologist, educator; b. N.Y.C., Feb. 20, 1936; m. Kimberly Watson, Apr. 6, 1991; children: Jessica, Christine, Carolyn. AB, Union Coll., Schenectady, 1957; MD, NYU, 1961. Diplomate Am. Bd. Internal Medicine, Am. Bd. Cardiovasc. Disease, Nat. Bd. Med. Examiners. Intern U. Calif. Hosps., San Francisco, 1961-62; asst. resident in internal medicine NYU, N.Y.C., 1962-64, chief resident, 1964-65; fellow in cardiovasc. disease NYU Hosp., 1965-67; assoc. dir. cardiac catherization divsn. NYU Med. Ctr., N.Y.C., 1967-69; dir. cardiac catheterization lab. Lenox Hill Hosp., N.Y.C., 1969-83; dir. cardiac catheterization lab. Seton Med. Ctr., Daly City, Calif., 1983-94; assoc. clin. prof. medicine U. Calif., San Francisco, 1983-94; clin. prof. medicine, dir. exptl. angioplasty, assoc. dir. internat. med. svcs. Stanford (Calif.) U. Med. Ctr., 1994—. Author: Textbook of Interventional Cardiology, 1990, 2d edit., 1993, Surgical Technology International, 1993, Diagnostic and Therapeutic Cardiac Catheterization, 1989, 2d edit., 1993. Maj. M.C., USAF, 1968-75. Decorated Dato (Malaysia), Knight Comdr. of Merit, Knights of Malta. Fellow ACP, Am. Coll. Cardiology; mem. Am. Heart Assn. (fellow coun. on clin. cardiology). Home: 396 Raymundo Dr Woodside CA 94062-4129 Office: Univ Interventional Assocs 900 Welch Rd Ste 202 Palo Alto CA 94304-1803

STETLER, CHARLES EDWARD, English language educator; b. Pitts., Sept. 12, 1927; s. Charles Edward and Catherine (Seidel) S.; m. Ellen Donovan, June 25, 1956; (div. Jan. 1981); children: Peter, Paul, Casey; m. Kristin Jill Brown, July 17, 1984 (div. 1993); m. Mary Grace Aquino, Aug. 25, 1994. BA, Duquesne U., 1950, MA, 1962; PhD, Tulane U., 1966. Reporter Pitts. Sun Telegraph, 1957-62; instr. in English Rollins Coll., Winter Park, Fla., 1962-63; asst. prof. English Loyola U., New Orleans, 1963-67; prof. English Calif. State U., Long Beach, 1967—; exch. prof. English U. Hull, Eng., fall 1984. Author poetry; contbr. articles to profl. jours. With USN, 1945-46, 50-52. Mem. Honor Soc. for Internat. Scholars, Phi Beta Kappa. Democrat. Home: 5912 Bixby Village Dr Apt 62 Long Beach CA 90803-6314 Office: Calif State U 1250 N Bellflower Blvd Long Beach CA 90840-0006

STEVENS, ANN L. HENSE, art educator, artist; b. Toledo, Nov. 16, 1950; d. Robert Elmer and Helen Louise (Davis) Hense; m. Hobart W. Stevens, June 18, 1988; children: Megan, Parker. BS in Edn., Ohio U., 1972; MS, U. Toledo, 1976; MA, Bowling Green State U., 1981, MFA, 1982. Cert. K-12 art tchr., Ohio, Calif., Colo. Publicity dir. Assoc. Women Students Miami U., 1969; elem. and secondary tchr. art Sylvania (Ohio) Schs., 1972-79; mus. educator Toledo Mus. Art, 1973-88, Kidspace Mus., Pasadena, Calif., 1990-91; instr. art Monroe (Mich.) C.C., 1984-86, Bowling Green (Ohio) State U., 1985-86; secondary tchr. art Springfield (Ohio) Local Schs., 1986-88; elem. tchr. Arcadia (Calif.) Unified Schs., 1989-90; mus. educator Denver Art Mus., 1992-94; chmn. Fibers Alive Competitive Art Exhibit, Toledo, 1984. Docent Pacific Asia Mus., Pasadena, 1988-90. Recipient best of show award Toledo Area Handweavers Guild, 1978; named outstanding tchg. asst. Bowling Green State U., 1983; scholar Miami U., 1979; grantee Denver Art Mus., 1994; recipient 2d Place award State Weaving Competition, Ohio, 1984. Mem. Handweavers Guild Boulder.

STEVENS, CLYDE BENJAMIN, JR., property manager, retired naval officer; b. Denver, Oct. 10, 1908; s. Clyde Benjamin and Maybelle Olive (Boot) S.; m. Lucile Lillian-Louise Kip, May 5, 1933; children: Jane Stevens White, Donald Kip, Patricia Louise Stevens Schley. BS, U.S. Naval Acad., 1930; postgrad., U.S. Naval Postgrad. Sch., Annapolis, Md., 1939, U.S. Naval War Coll., Newport, R.I., 1947. Registered profl. engr. Commd. ensign USN, advanced through grades to rear adm., 1959; comdg. officer USS R-20, S-33 Plaice and Platte, 1950-52; comdr. officer USS Platte 50-52 Destroyer Squad 6, 1954-55; with torpedo prodn. and undersea weapons div. Bur. Ordnance, Washington, 1947-59; with USS Platte, 1950-52, Destroyer squad., 1953-56; program dir. Bur. Ordnance, Washington, 1952-55, 56-59; ret., 1959; product mgr. TRW, Inc., Cleve., 1959-65; rsch. engr. Boeing Co., Seattle, 1965-74, torpedo cons., 1985; apt. owner and mgr. Seattle, 1965—; torpedo cons. Goodyear Aerospace Co., Akron, Ohio, 1965. Patentee automobile generator. Decorated Navy Cross, Silver Star with oak leaf cluster. Mem. Seattle Apt. Assn. (bd. dirs. 1967-91), Army and Navy Club, Rainier Club. Republican. Episcopalian. Home and Office: 2339 Franklin Ave E Seattle WA 98102-3342

STEVENS, DAVID ALEC, medical educator; b. N.Y.C., June 3, 1940; m. Julie Anne Teece, Aug. 15, 1964; children: Joseph John, Emily Beth Stevens Marsh. BA, Cornell U., 1960; MD, U. Rochester, 1965. Diplomate Nat. Bd. Med. Examiners, Am. Bd. Internal Medicine; med. lic. Wis., Calif. Intern, asst. resident dept. medicine U. Wis. Hosps., Madison, 1965-67; rsch. assoc. Nat. Cancer Inst., Bethesda, Md., 1967-69; resident dept. medicine UCLA Med Ctr., 1969-70; fellow divsn. infectious diseases, dept. medicine Stanford (Calif.) U., 1970-72, asst. prof. divsn. infectious diseases dept. medicine, 1972-78; chief divsn. infectious diseases Santa Clara County-Valley Med. Ctr., San Jose, Calif., 1972—, assoc. chief dept. medicine, 1972—, epidemiologist, 1972—; assoc. prof. divsn. infectious diseases, dept. medicine Stanford U., 1978-85, assoc. prof. divsn. geographic medicine, dept. medicine, 1984-85, prof., 1985—; co-dir. microbiology lab. Santa Clara Valley Med. Ctr., 1972—; prin. investigator Infectious Diseases Rsch. Lab., Calif. Inst. Med. Rsch., San Jose, 1973—, bd. regents, 1978-90, 92—, sec.-treas., 1979-81, sci. dir. coun., 1986-88, pres., 1992—; mycology ref. lab. Pub. Health Lab. Svcs. Dept. Microbiology, U. London, 1979; dir. clin. labs. Calif. Inst. Med. Rsch., 1980—; co-dir. AIDS program Santa Clara Valley Med. Ctr., 1986-88, assoc. dir., 1988—. Author: (with others) Coccidioidomycosis, 1980; Contbr. articles to profl. jours; patentee in field. With USPHS, 1967-69. Ian Murray Meml. lectr. British Soc. Mycopathology, Canterbury, Eng., 1985. Fellow ACP, Am. Soc. Microbiology (chair mycology 1992-93), Infectious Diseases Soc. Am.; mem. AMA, AAUP, AAAS, Am. Fedn. Clin. Rsch., Am. Soc. Clin. Investigation, Fedn. Am. Scientists, Med. Mycology Soc. Ams., Calif. Med. Assn., Western Assn. Physicians, Calif. Collaborative Treatment Group, Santa Clara County Med. Soc., Internat. Soc. Human and Animal Mycology (clin. mycology com. 1985-91). Home: 19070 Portos Dr Saratoga CA 95070-5169 Office: Santa Clara Valley Med Ctr 751 S Bascom Ave San Jose CA 95128-2604

STEVENS, DAVID KING, civil engineer, educator; b. Kans. City, Kans., Dec. 17, 1954; s. Arthur David and Patricia (Williams) S.; m. Margaret Marie Cashell, May 18, 1985; children: Michael James, Abby Elizabeth. BSCE, Tufts U., 1976; PhD, U. Wis., 1983. Registered profl. engr., Ohio. Engr. irrigation U.S. Peace Corps, Malacca, Malaysia, 1976-78; rsch. assoc. U. Cin., 1984-86; asst. prof. Utah State U., Logan, 1986-90, assoc. prof., 1990—; cons. Soap and Detergent Assn., N.Y.C., 1982, Peer Cons., Washington, 1987-88, Dynamac Corp., Rockville, Md., 1989—, Am. Petroleum Inst. Contbr. articles to profl. jours. Recipient Cen. States Water Pollution Control Assn. Acad. Excellence award, 1981, Lewis H. Kessler award U. Wis., 1982; grantee EPA, U.S. Geol. Survey, Battelle Meml. Inst., 1984—, Nat. Inst. Environ. Health Scis., Electric Power Rsch. Inst. Mem. ASCE (assoc. editor Jour. Environ. Engring.), Am. Water Works Assn., Internat. Assn. Water Quality, Water Environ. Fedn., Sigma Xi, Phi Kappa Phi, Tau Beta Pi. Office: Utah State U Umc # 4110 Logan UT 84322

STEVENS, ELEANOR SANDRA, professional services executive; b. Oklahoma City, Nov. 1, 1932; d. Benjamin Franklin and Mary Lou (Smith) Williams; children: Fred W., Nathandra, Benjiman, Ola Enaid. AS in medicine, Fresno State U., 1954; student Fresno Adult Edn., Los Angeles Trade Tech., 1972-73. Radio disc jockey, Fresno, Calif., 1954-55; bookkeeper L.A. County Assessor, 1961-69; supervisor Holzman-Begue Real Estate Co., L.A., 1969-73; dist. mgr. United Systems, Inc., L.A., 1973-77; pub. relations cons. Harold G. Simon & Assoc., Vernon, Calif., 1977-81; pres. Stevens Personalized Svcs., L.A., 1982—. Recipient cert. profl. devel. State of Calif., 1983. Mem. NAFE, Van Nuys Women's Referral Svc., D.B. & O. Charity and Social Club, Los Angeles Good Neighbor Council, Order Ea. Star. Methodist. Office: 4350 11th Ave Ste 107 B Los Angeles CA 90008

STEVENS, GEORGE ALEXANDER, realtor; b. Loma, Mont., Nov. 10, 1923; s. Otto Oliver and Josephine (Dale) S.; m. Martha Evie Fultz, Sept. 16, 1944 (div. 1978); children: Gary, Kathleen, Arlene, Tina; m. Arleen Dorothea Largent, Nov. 14, 1978. A in Bus Admisntrn., SUNY, 1992. Prin. George Stevens Farm, Loma, Mont., 1946-93, George Stevens, Realtor, Loma, Mont., 1957-93; pres. George A. Stevens COrp., Loma, 1976-93, Gold and Silver Realty, Inc., Great Falls, Mont., 1993—. Trustee Sch. Dist. # 32, Loma, 1947-50; election judge Precinct # 7, Loma, 1953-88. With USN, 1944-46, PTO. Mem. Nat. Assn. Realtors, VFW (life), Am. Legion (life), Elks (life), Eagles Lodge. Democrat. Lutheran. Home: 810 8th Ave N Great Falls MT 59401-1036

STEVENS, HENRY AUGUST, insurance agent, educator; b. Frankfurt, Main, Germany, July 21, 1921; came to U.S., 1940; m. Rosemary O'Neil, Mar. 23, 1963; children: Michael, Patrick; 1 child from previous marriage, H. Jack Fay. Student, U. Wis., 1943-44; grad., Dale Carnegie Sch., Richland, Wash., 1974. Theatre mgr. Sterling Theatres, Seattle, 1946-54, Alliance Amusement Co., Chgo., 1955-68; ins. agt. N.Y. Life Ins. Co., Richland, 1968—; regional v.p. Washington Assn. Life Underwriters, Richland, 1980; mem. adv. com. Wash. State Ins., Olympia, 1983-89. Chmn. bd. Richland YMCA, 1968; commr. Benton County Dyking Dist., Richland, 1970; chmn. Benton-Franklin Counties Bi-Centennial Commn., Tri-Cities, Wash., 1976; dist. chmn. Rep. Party, Benton County, 1980—. Staff sgt. U.S. Army 1943-46. Recipient Nat. Quality award, Nat. Sales Achievement award. Mem. Tri-Cities Life Underwriters Assn. (pres. 1975, bd. dirs.), Tri-Cities Estate Planning Coun. (pres. 1984), Kiwanis (pres. Chgo. club 1963, Richland club 1986-87, lt. gov. Pacific N.W. dist. 1983, chmn. dist. conv. 1971, 81, 91, sec. Pacific N.W. Found. 1994—). Home: 712 Riverside Dr Richland WA 99352-5216 Office: NY Life Ins Co 8203 W Quinault St Kennewick WA 99336-1093

STEVENS, JEFFREY S., chief of nuclear medicine; b. Newark, Dec. 24, 1942. BA, UCLA, 1965; MD, Stanford U., 1968. Diplomate Am. Bd. Radiology, Am. Bd. Nuclear Medicine. Intern medicine L.A. VA Hosp., 1968-69, resident in radiology, 1971-72; resident in radiology L.A. County Martin Luther King, Jr. Gen. Hosp., 1972-74, fellow nuclear medicine, 1974-75; chief nuclear medicine Portland (Oreg.) Adventist Med. Ctr., 1975-89; chief nuclear medicine Oreg. Health Scis. U., Portland, 1989—, asst. prof. radiology, 1989—. Office: Oreg Health Scis U 3181 SW Sam Jackson Park Rd Portland OR 97201-3011

STEVENS, JOHN GERALD, nuclear engineer; b. Mt. Holly, N.J., Mar. 27, 1965; s. Richard Wilson and Jerry Lee (Aiken) S.; m. Amy Dirks, May 21, 1988. BS in Nuclear Engring., Purdue U., 1988, MS in Nuclear Engring., 1991, PhD, 1995. Undergrad. rsch. asst. Purdue U. Sch. Nuclear Engring., West Lafayette, Ind., 1986-88, U.S. Dept. Energy nuclear engring. fellow, 1989-93; sr. nuclear engr. Studvik of Am., Idaho Falls, Idaho, 1993—; Am. Nuclear Soc. Chgo. sect. bilateral student exch. program participant Commisarit de l'Energie Atomique, Centre d'Etudes Nucleaires Cadarache, St. Paul lez Durance, France, summer 1988. Contbr. articles to profl. jours. Purdue U. Mortar Bd. grad. fellow, 1988. Mem. Am. Nuclear Soc. (Idaho local sect., grad. v.p. 1990-91), Inst. for Ops. Rsch. and Mgmt. Scis., Nature Conservancy, Nat. Wildlife Fedn., Nat. Audubon Soc., Idaho Audubon Soc., Wilderness Soc., Idaho Conservation League, Alpha Nu Sigma. Home: 254 W 19th St Idaho Falls ID 83402-4439 Office: Studsvik of Am 477 Shoup Ave Ste 105 Idaho Falls ID 83402-3658

STEVENS, JOHN JOSEPH, physician; b. Hartford, Conn., Dec. 19, 1929; s. John Joseph and Florence Martha (Wenning) S.; m. Mary Catherine Zeuhlke, Sept. 20, 1956; children: Kathleen, John, Margaret, Erich. BS cum laude, Boston Coll., 1951; MD cum laude, Tufts U., 1955. Diplomate Am. Bd. Internal Medicine, Am. Bd. Allergy and Immunology. Intern U.S. Naval Hosp., Bethesda, Md., 1955-56; resident internal medicine U.S.N. Hosp., Oakland, Calif., 1959-61; fellow allergy Scripps Clinic & Rsch. Found., La Jolla, Calif., 1962-63; asst. chest svc., head allergy clinic Scripps Clinic & Rsch. Found., San Diego, 1963-64; head allergy clinic US Naval Hosp., San Diego, 1964-66; asst. chief medicine US Naval Hosp., Oakland, 1966; staff assoc. divsn. allergy imm. rheumatology Scripps Clinic & Rsch. Found., La Jolla, 1966-67; pvt. practice allergy & clin. immunology La Jolla, San Diego, 1967—; from asst. clin. prof. to clin. prof. medicine and pediatrics U. Calif., San Diego, 1973-1991, clin. prof. medicine and pediatrics, 1991—. Capt. USNR. Fellow Am. Acad. Allergy, Am. Coll. Physicians, Am. Assn. Cert. Allergists; mem. AMA, Calif. Med. Assn. (mem. appeals com. 1973—, adv. panel on allergy 1976-78), San Diego Allergy Soc. (pres. elect 1969, pres. 1970, chmn. ethics and med. review com. 1973, 75, mem. liaison com. with Found. of Med. Care, 1974-84), San Diego County Med. Soc. (mem. med. review com. 1972-90, chair 1983-85, chair loss prevention 1983-90, seminar moderator, mem. profl. conduct com. 1985-90), San Diego Acad. Medicine (treas. 1969, 70, 71, v.p. 1973), The Lung Assn. San DIego and Imperial Counties (mem. bd. dirs. 1972-73, mem. physical conditioning for asthmatics com. 1968-73, chmn. 72-73), San Diego Soc. Internal Medicine (mem. liaison com. with Found. of Med. Care 1974), San Diego Found. for Med. Care (mem. bd. trustees 1993—, mem. com. 1993—), Internat. Assn. Allergology and Clin. Immunology, Alpha Omega Alpha Honor Soc. Roman Catholic. Office: 9610 Granite Ridge Dr Ste B San Diego CA 92123

STEVENS, LINDA TOLLESTRUP, school counselor; b. Salt Lake City, Feb. 7, 1963; d. Garn Alvin and Mary Ann (Cannon) Tollestrup; m. Marshall Le Grand Stevens, Mar. 17, 1982; 1 child, Marli Brynn. BS, U. Utah, 1984, MS, 1989. Cert. sch. counselor, Utah. Tchr. pre-sch. Adventurer's Pre-Sch., Salt Lake City, 1984; adminstr. Headstart program Creative Devel. Ctr., Salt Lake City, 1984-85; vocat. evaluator Utah Div. Rehab. Svcs. Vocat. Evaluation, Salt Lake City, 1985-86; human resource counselor Davis Applied Tech. Ctr., Kaysville, Utah, 1986—; trainee Phoenix Inst., Salt Lake City, 1986, U. No. Colo., Greeley, 1986; instr. Utah State Turning Point, Salt Lake City and Provo, 1992. Mem. Golden Spike Dog Obedience Club, Ogden, Utah, 1986-90, Humane Soc. Utah, 1986—. Mem. NEA, ACA, Am. Vocat. Assn., Am. Bus. Women's Assn. (v.p. 1992), Utah Vocat. Assn. (bldg. fund coord. 1989-90), Utah Fedn. Bus. and Profl. Women (Woman of Achievement award 1991), Golden Key Honor Soc., Delta Soc., Phi Eta Sigma. Mormon. Office: Davis Applied Tech Ctr 550 E 300 St Kaysville UT 84037

STEVENS, MICHAEL KEITH, artist; b. Gilroy, Calif., July 14, 1945; s. Robert Louis and Jane Elizabeth (McCreery) S.; m. Suzanne Adan, Sept. 5, 1970. AA, Am. River Coll., 1965; BA, Calif. State U., Sacramento, 1967; MA, Calif. State U., 1969. Cert. tchr. community coll., secondary edn., Calif. guest artist and lectr. various instns., including Michael Himovitz Gallery, Sacramento, 1993, Oakland Mus., 1992, Humboldt State U., Arcata, Calif., 1991, U. Calif., Davis, 1991, others; curator, panelist in field. One-person shows include Braunstein/Quay Gallery, San Francisco, 1977, 78, 79, 82, 84, 86, 89, 92, 94, Ovsey Gallery, L.A., 1990, Am. River Coll., 1987, Calif. State U., Chico, 1986, Himovitz/Salomon Gallery, Sacramento, 1984, Betsy Rosenfield Gallery, Chgo., 1981, 83, 85, 88, Michael Himovitz Gallery, Sacramento, 1993; group shows include Crocker Art Mus., Sacramento, 1994, Am. Cultural Ctr., Brussels, 1992, Oakland (Calif.) Mus., 1992, 94, Meml. Union Gallery U. Calif., Davis, 1994, Ark. Art Ctr., Little Rock, 1995, numerous others; articles. Recipient James D. Phelan award in art for sculpture, Walnut Creek Civic Arts Gallery, 1982, Pub. Art Commn., Cherry Island Golf Course, Sacramento Met. Arts Commn., 1988.

STEVENS, MURIEL KAUIMAEOLE LEE, elementary educator; b. Hana, Hawaii, May 29, 1942; d. Charles Pohaku and Violet Leimamo (Wahihako) Lee; m. James Gary Stevens, 1964 (div. 1975); 1 child, James Todd (dec.). AS, Ch. Coll. Hawaii, 1962; BS in Edn., Brigham Young U., 1964; postgrad., U. Utah, 1969, LaVerne U., 1972, U. Hawaii, 1974—, U. Ala., 1990. Cert. elem. tchr., Hawaii. 1st grade tchr. Woodstock Elem. Sch., Salt Lake City, 1965-69; kindergarten-1st grade team tchr. Ewa (Hawaii) Elem. Sch., 1971-78; kindergarten tchr. Honowai Elem. Sch., Waipahu, Hawaii, 1978—; aerospace tchr., coord. after sch. improvement program Honowai Elem. Sch., 1991, 95; mem. Citizen Amb. Program, Spokane, 1987-94; participant Tchr. in Space program NASA, 1985-86. Spiritual living tchr. LDS Ch., Kaneohe, 1994, choir mem., 1992-94; amb. People to People Internat., Spokane, Wash., 1987-94. With CAP, 1985-94. Recipient Aerospace Edn. Achievement award Aux. USAF CAP, 1985. Mem. ASCD, Hawaii Parent, Tchr., Student Assn., NEA, Hawaii State Tchrs. Assn., Wilson Ctr. Assocs., Acad. Polit. Sci., World Aerospace Edn. Orgn. Republican. Home: PO Box 658 Wahiawa HI 96786-0658 Office: Honowai Elem Sch 94-600 Honowai St Waipahu HI 96797-1307

STEVENS, ROBERT DAVID, librarian, educator; b. Nashua, N.H., Aug. 11, 1921; s. David Philip and Ruth (Ackley) S.; m. Helen Medora Conrad, Jan. 16, 1943; children: Ruth Wilson Robertson, Hope Conrad. A.B. magna cum laude, Syracuse U., 1942; B.S. in L.S. with honors, Columbia, 1947; M.A., Am. U., 1955, Ph.D., 1965. With Library of Congress, Washington, 1947-64; coordinator pub. law 480 programs Library of Congress, 1962-64; dir. Library East West Center, Honolulu, 1964-65; dean Grad. Sch. Library Studies U. Hawaii, Honolulu, 1966-75; chief cataloging div. Copyright Office, 1975-80, coordinator copyright collections, 1980; lectr. grad. Sch. Library Studies, U. Hawaii, 1981—; chief exec. officer Molesworth Inst. West, Inc., 1984-91, chmn., 1991—; Fulbright lectr. U. Indonesia, 1971; U.S. del. Intergovtl. Conf. Planning Nat. Libraries Infrastructures, 1974. Author: Role of the Library of Congress in International Exchange of Government Publications, 1955, Toshokan Kyoryoku, 1970, Documents of International Organizations, 1974, Japanese and U.S. Research Libraries at the Turning Point, 1977, Short History of the School of Library and Information Studies, 1991; contbr. articles to profl. publs. Served to lt. USNR, 1943-46. Mem. Hawaii Library Assn. (pres. 1966-67), ALA (mem. council 1967-70, mem. U.S.-Japan adv. com. 1972—, chmn. 1974-76, Rlms policy and research com. 1977-81), Assocs. U. Hawaii Library (vice chmn. 1981-84), Japan Library Assn., Hui Dui, Phi Beta Kappa, Pi Sigma Alpha. Club: 15 (Honolulu). Home: 3265 Paty Dr Honolulu HI 96822-1449

STEVENS, RON A., lawyer, public interest organization administrator; b. Indpls., Sept. 4, 1945; s. Granville Thomas and Charlotte May (Wheeler) S.; m. Judy Rohde, June 15, 1968; children: Samuel Thomas, Alison Elizabeth. BA, Okla. State U.; JD with honors, Ill. Inst. Tech., 1976. Bar: Ill. 1976. Staff atty. Legal Assistance Found. Chgo., 1976-79; staff atty., dir. housing agenda Bus. and Profl. People for Pub. Interest, Chgo., 1979-81; chief housing div. Office of Cook County State's Atty., Chgo., 1981-82; campaign coord. north lakefront Washington for Mayor, Chgo., 1982-83; program officer The Joyce Found., Chgo., 1983-86; pres. Citizens for a Better Environment, Chgo., 1986-89; exec. dir. United Way Santa Fe County, 1989—; adv. bd. state support ctr. on environ. hazards Nat. Ctr. for Policy Alternatives, Washington, 1987-89; chair, Local Bd. EFSP, 1989—, chair Santa Fe Affordable Housing Roundtable, 1992—; steer com. Santa Fe Community Needs Assessment, 1990—. Mem. bldg. code enforcement com. Mayor's Transition Team Housing Task Force, Chgo., 1983, steering com. Chgo. Ethics Project, 1986-88; founder, chmn. Progressive Chgo. Area Network, 1981-84; bd. dirs. Uptown Recycling Sta., Chgo., 1987-89; mem. South Ctrl. Regional Coun., United Way of Am. Mem. Chgo. Coun. Lawyers (chmn. housing com. 1978-81, bd. govs. 1981-83, bd. dirs. Fund for Justice, 1986-88), Chgo. Area Runners Assn. (founder, v.p. 1977-81). Home: 739 Gregory Ln Santa Fe NM 87501-4257 Office: United Way Santa Fe County PO Box 261 Santa Fe NM 87504-0261

STEVENS, SERITA DEBORAH MENDELSON, psychiatric nurse, writer; b. Chgo., Jan. 20, 1949; d. Albert Stanley and Frances Zipporah (Rosenberg) Mendelson; m. Raymond Glassenberg, Aug. 29, 1971 (div. 1980); m. Barrie Barr, Oct. 20, 1992 (div. Oct. 15, 1993); 1 stepchild, Shaina Rose Barr; 1 adopted child, Tzipporah Etta Miriam Stevens. BSN, U. Ill., Chgo., 1971; MA in Lit. with honors, Antioch U., London, 1979. Staff nurse Dept. of Psychiatry, 1990—; instr. U. So. Calif., L.A., 1983-84, Loyola U., 1981-82, Santa Monica Calif. City Coll., 1981-82; investigative reporter CBS; writer's digest instr., 1988—; Judge of Hemmett, Edgar and Malice awards. Author: This Bitter Ecstasy, 1981, Tame the Wild Heart, 1983, The Shriekings Shadows of Penporth Island, 1983, A Dream Forever, 19984, Cagney and Lacey, 1985, Bloodstone Inheritance, 1985, A Gathering Storm, 1986, Secrets at Seventeen, 1986, Days of Our Lives, 1986, Champagne for Two, 1986, Buttercup Dreams, 1987, Lighting and Fire, 1987, Daughters of Desire, 1987, Deceptive Desires, 1987, Lilac Dreams, 1986, Unholy Alliance, 1991, Deadly Doses: A Writer's Guide to Poisons, 1991, Red Sea, Dead Sea, 1991, Bagels for Tea, 1993; co-author: Fine Art of Murder, 1994 (Anthony award); numerous short stories; videos: Champagne for Two, Lilac Dreams; contbr. articles to writers' mags. and jours. Recipient Cape Cod Writer's scholarship, Best Synopsis award Dell Publishing. Mem. Soc. Children's Books Writers, Mystery Writers Am. (bd. dirs. S. Calif. chpt. 1987-88), Romance Writers Am. (regional bd. dirs.), HUNA Soc., Sisters in Crime (speakers bur. coord., bd. dirs. 1993-95, Am. Crime Writers, Internat. Crime Writers, Pen Women. Democrat. Jewish. Home: 15004 Vose St Van Nuys CA 91405-2933 Office: PO Box 7908 Mission Hills CA 91346

STEVENS, STEPHEN EDWARD, psychiatrist; b. Phila.; s. Edward and Antonia S.; BA cum laude, LaSalle Coll., 1950; MD, Temple U., Phila., 1954; LLB, Blackstone Sch. Law, 1973; m. Isabelle Helen Gallacher, Dec. 27, 1953. Intern, Frankford Hosp., Phila., 1954-55; resident in psychiatry Phila. State Hosp., 1955-58; practice medicine specializing in psychiatry Woodland Hills, Calif., 1958-63, Santa Barbara, Calif., 1970-77; asst. supt. Camarillo (Calif.) State Hosp., 1963-70; cons. ct. psychiatrist Santa Barbara County, 1974-77; clin. dir. Kailua Mental Health Ctr., Oahu, Hawaii, 1977—. Author: Treating Mental Illness, 1961. Served with M.C., USAAF. Diplomate Am. Bd. Psychiatry and Neurology. Decorated Purple Heart. Fellow Am. Geriatrics Soc. (founding); mem. Am. Acad. Psychiatry and Law, AMA, Am. Psychiat. Assn., Am. Legion, DAV (Oahu chpt. 1), Caledonia Soc., Am. Hypnosis Soc., Am. Soc. Adolescent Psychiatry, Hawaiian Canoe Club, Honolulu Club, Elks, Aloha String Band (founder and pres.). Home: PO Box 26413 Honolulu HI 96825-6413 Office: 2333 Kapiolani Blvd Honolulu HI 96826-4485

STEVENS, THEODORE FULTON, senator; b. Indpls., Nov. 18, 1923; s. George A. and Gertrude (Chancellor) S.; m. Ann Mary Cherrington, Mar. 29, 1952 (dec. 1978); children—Susan B., Elizabeth H., Walter C., Theodore Fulton, Ben A.; m. Catherine Chandler, 1980; 1 dau.; Lily Irene. B.A., U. Calif. at Los Angeles, 1947; LL.B., Harvard U., 1950. Bar: Calif., Alaska, D.C., U.S. Supreme Ct. bars. Pvt. practice Washington, 1950-52, Fairbanks, Alaska, 1953; U.S. atty. Dist. Alaska, 1953-56; legis. counsel, asst. to sec., solicitor Dept. Interior, 1956-60; pvt. practice law Anchorage, 1961-68; mem. Alaska Ho. of Reps., 1965-68, majority leader, speaker pro tem, 1967-68; U.S. senator for Alaska, 1968—, asst. Rep. leader, 1977-85; chmn. Senate Rules Com. Served as 1st lt. USAAF, World War II. Mem. ABA, Alaska Bar Assn., Calif. Bar Assn., D.C. Bar Assn., Am. Legion, VFW. Lodges: Rotary, Pioneers of Alaska, Igloo #4. Home: PO Box 100879 Anchorage AK 99510-0879 Office: US Senate 522 Hart Senate Bldg Washington DC 20510*

STEVENS, THOMAS EDWARD, aerospace engineer; b. Peoria, Ill., Mar. 16, 1965; s. Edward Lee and Dorothy Lorraine (Wozniak) S.; m. Kimberly Marie Scheirer, Sept. 23, 1989; children: Kyle Glen, Kevin Thomas. AAS, Ill. Cen. Coll., 1985; BS in Astronaut. Engring., U. Ill., 1987; MS in Astronaut. Engring., West Coast U., 1991. With engr. profl. program, Western Space and Missile Ctr. USAF, Vandenberg AFB, Calif., 1987-88, telemetry monitoring officer 6595 Test/Evaluation Group, 1988-92, space launch test mgr. Space & Missile Systems Ctr., 1992-95, with Atlas 2 SLC-3E Activation divsn. Space & Missile Systems Ctr., 1995—. Mem. AIAA (chmn. 1994 Lompoc Sci. Fair, treas. Vandenberg sect. 1988-93, chmn. elect 1993-94, chmn. 1994-95). Office: Det 9 SMC/DTP SMC/CLV 1515 Iceland St Ste B Vandenberg AFB CA 93437

STEVENS, TODD OWEN, research microbiologist; b. The Dalles, Oreg., Jan. 27, 1962; s. Albert Edwin and Geraldine Leone (Goggin) S. BS in Microbiology, Oregon State U., 1984; MS in Microbiology, Mich. State U., 1987; PhD in Bacteriology, U. Idaho, 1989. Postdoctoral rsch. assoc. Wash. State U., Richland, 1989-90; staff scientist Battelle Pacific N.W. Lab., Richland, 1990—. Contbr. articles to profl. jours.; inventor; biolog. system for degrading nitro aromatics in soils and waters. Mem. AAAS, Soil Sci. Soc. Am., Am. Soc. Microbiology, N.W. Sci. Assn. Office: Battelle Pacific NW Lab Battelle Blvd M/S P7 54 Richland WA 99352

STEVENS, WILBUR HUNT, accountant; b. Spencer, Ind., June 20, 1918; s. John Vosburgh and Isabelle Jane (Strawser) S.; m. Maxine Dodge Stevens, Sept. 28, 1941; children: Linda Maxine Piffero, Deborah Anne Augello. BS, U. Calif., Berkeley, 1949, MBA, 1949. CPA, Calif. Staff acct. McLaren, Goode, West & Co., San Francisco, 1949-52; mng. ptnr. Wilbur H. Stevens & Co., Salinas, Calif., 1952-70; regional ptnr. Fox & Co., CPAs, Salinas, 1970-73; nat. dir. banking practice Fox & Co., CPAs, Denver, 1973-80; pres., chmn. Wilbur H. Stevens, CPA, PC, Salinas, 1980-94; chmn. Stevens, Sloan & Shah, CPAs, 1994—; adj. prof. acctg. U. Denver, 1975-78; faculty mem. Assemblies for Bank Dirs., So. Meth. U., Dallas, 1976-81, Nat. Banking Sch., U. Va., Charlottesville, 1979-87; chmn., dir. Valley Nat. Bank, 1963-71. Editor Issues in CPA Practice, 1975; contbr. articles to profl. jours. Capt. AUS, 1942-53. Decorated Bronze Star, China War Meml. medal, China Victory medal; Frank G. Drum fellow U. Calif., Berkeley, 1949; Paul Harris fellow Rotary Internat., Evanston, Ill., 1978. Mem. AICPAs (v.p. 1971), Am. Acctg. Assn., Am. Assembly Collegiate Schs. Bus. (accreditation coun. 1975-78, 81-84), Nat. Assn. State Bds. Accountancy (pres. 1976-77), Calif. Soc. CPAs (pres. 1968-69, Disting. Svc. award 1988), Acctg. Rsch. Assn. (pres. 1973-75), Burma Star Assn., CBI Vets. Assn., Acad. Acctg. Historians, Commonwealth Club Calif., Masons (master 1992, grand lodge com. taxation), Knight Templar, 32 deg. Scottish Rite, Nat. Sojourners (v.p. Monterey Bay chpt. 1995), Salinas High Twelve Club (pres. 1995), QCCC London, Rotary (dist. gov. 1983, chmn. internat. fellowship accounts), Phi Beta Kappa, Beta Gamma Sigma (v.p. 1949), Beta Alpha Psi. Republican. Methodist. Home and Office: 38 Santa Ana Dr Salinas CA 93901-4136

STEVENS-ALLEN, DAVID JOSEPH (MARQUESS OF ALN, VISCOUNT OF ST. ETIENNE, BARON OF ST. JOHN AND OF ZELLAN), construction executive; b. Portland, Oreg., Apr. 12, 1925; s. John Raymond and Merle Cleone (Stevens) A. BA, San Diego State U., 1960, MA, 1971; PhD, U. Sarsota, 1972. V.p. Auto Mechanics Inst., L.A., 1965-67; labor rels. specialist Pacific Architects and Engrs., Saigon, Vietnam, 1967-70; edn. cons. Pacific States U., L.A., Paris, 1972-74; labor rels. mgr. Constructeurs Inga/Shaba, Kinshasa, Zaire, 1974-76; exec. v.p. Com. of 50 States, 1994—. Author: The Lexarchy, 1983, Constitution for Kingdom of Hawaii, 1992, Constitution for Alaskan Independence Movement, 1993, Secession and the Rights of the States, 1995, Nullification and the Rights of the States, 1995. Cand. for County Commr., Josephine County, Oreg., 1984, 92; exec. v.p. Com. of 50 States, 1994—. Ensign U.S. Mcht. Marine, 1945, U.S. Army. Decorated Labor medal Republic of South Vietnam, 1969; decorated knight comdr. Merit Order St. John Jerusalem, knight comdr. Order Aztec Crown. Mem. Am. Mcht. Marine Vets., Am. Legion, Josephine County Taxpayers Assn. Home: 442 Honeylynn Ln Grants Pass OR 97527-9013

STEVENSON, JAMES GEOFFREY, pediatrician and cardiologist; b. Long Beach, Calif., Feb. 22, 1945; s. James Terry and Marie Dorothy (Lovell) S.; children: Brittany Jennifer, Emily Andrea. AB, Occidental Coll., L.A., 1966; MD, Baylor Coll. Medicine, Houston, 1970. Diplomate Am. Bd. Pediatrics, Am. Bd. Cardiology. Intern Children's Hosp./U. Wash., Seattle, resident; pediatric cardiologist Naval Regional Med. Ctr., San Diego, 1974-76; asst. prof. pediatrics U. Wash., Seattle, 1976-80, assoc. prof., 1980-85; prof. pediatrics U. Wash., 1985—; hosp.-based practice pediatric cardiology Seattle; staff Children's Hosp. and Med. Ctr., Seattle, U. Wash. Med. Ctr., Seattle, Providence Med. Ctr., Seattle, Swedish Hosp. Med. Ctr. Contbr. numerous articles and abstracts to profl. jours.; lectr. in field. Lt. comdr. USN, 1974-76. Recipient Christian Doppler award in echocardiography Internat. Soc. Intraoperative Cardiovascular Ultrasound, 1992. Fellow Am. Coll. CArdiology; mem. Soc. Pediatric Echo (sec. 1983-85, treas. 1985-87), Am. Soc. Echocardiography (bd. dirs. 1985-88, 90—), Am. Registry Diagnostic Med. Sonographers (bd. dirs. 1990-93), Internat. Cardiac Doppler Soc. (bd. dirs. 1984-92), Am. Heart Assn. (mem. coun. 1987—). Office: Children's Hosp Cardiology CH-11 4800 Sand Point Way NE Seattle WA 98105-3901

STEVENSON, JAMES RALPH, school psychologist, author; b. Kemmerer, Wyo., June 29, 1949; s. Harold Ralph and Dora (Borino) S.; m. Alice M. Paolucci, June 17, 1972; children: Tiffany Jo, Brian Jeffrey. BA, U. No. Colo., 1971, MA, 1974, EdS, 1975. cert. elem. sch. counselor, Colo., nationally cert. sch. psychologist. Sch. psychologist Jefferson County Pub. Schs., Golden, Colo., 1975-87, 89-91, Weld County Sch. Dist. 6, Greeley, Colo., 1987-89, Weld Bd. Coop. Edn. Svcs., LaSalle, Colo., 1991-95; spl. edn. coord. Weld Bd. Coop. Edn. Svcs., LaSalle, 1995—; ltd. pvt. practice sch. psychologist Pathways, Greeley, 1994—. Asst. coach Young Am. Baseball, Greeley, 1989, 90, head coach, 1992, 93; asst. basketball coach Recreation League for 6th-7th Grades, 1992, 93. U. No. Colo. scholar, 1974. Mem. NEA, NASP (alt. del. Colo. chpt. 1975-77, dir. Apple II users group Washington chpt. 1989—), Colo. Soc. Sch. Psychologists (chmn. task force on presch. assessment 1991—), Colo. Edn. Assn., Ft. Lupton Edn. Assn., Jefferson County Psychologists Assn. (sec. 1986-87). Democrat. Roman Catholic. Home: 1937 24th Ave Greeley CO 80631-5027 Office: Weld County BOCES PO Box 578 204 Main St LaSalle CO 80645

STEVENSON, JAMES RICHARD, radiologist, lawyer; b. Ft. Dodge, Iowa, May 30, 1937; s. Lester Lawrence and Esther Irene (Johnson) S.; m. Sara Jean Hayman, Sept. 4, 1958; children: Bradford Allen, Tiffany Ann, Jill Renee, Trevor Ashley. BS, U. N.Mex., 1959; MD, U. Colo., 1963; JD, U. N.Mex. 1987. Diplomate Am. Bd. Radiology, Am. Bd. Nuclear Medicine, Am. Bd. Legal Medicine, 1989; Bar: N.Mex. 1987, U.S. Dist. Ct. N.Mex. 1988. Intern U.S. Gen. Hosp., Tripler, Honolulu, 1963-64; resident in radiology U.S. Gen. Hosp., Brook and San Antonio, Tex., 1964-67; radiologist, ptnr. Van Atta Labs., Albuquerque, 1970-88, Radiology Assocs. of Albuquerque, 1988—, Civerolo, Hansen & Wolf, Albuquerque, 1988-89; adj. asst. prof. radiology U. N.Mex., 1970-71; pres. med. staff AT & SF Meml. Hosp., 1979-80, chief of staff, 1980-81, trustee, 1981-83. Author: District Attorney manual, 1987. Participant breast screening, Am. Cancer Soc., Albuquerque, 1987-88; dir. profl. div. United Way, Albuquerque, 1975. Maj. U.S. Army 1963-70, Vietnam; col. M.C. USAR, 1988—. Decorated Bronze Star. Allergy fellow, 1960. Med.-Legal Tort Scholar award, 1987. Fellow Am. Coll. Radiology (councilor 1980-86, mem. med. legal com. 1990—), Am. Coll. Legal Medicine, Am. Coll. Nuclear Medicine, Radiology Assn. of Albuquerque; mem. AMA (Physicians' Recognition award 1969—), Albuquerque Bar Assn., Am. Coll. Nuclear Physicians (charter), Soc. Nuclear Medicine (v.p. Rocky Mountain chpt. 1975-76), Am. Inst. Ultrasound in Medicine, N.Am. Radiol. Soc. (chmn. med. legal com. 1992—), N.Mex. Radiol. Soc. (pres. 1978-79), N.Mex. Med. Soc. (chmn. grievance com.), Albuquerque-Bernalillo County Med. Soc. (scholar 1959), Nat. Assn. Health Lawyers, ABA (antitrust sect. 1986—), N. Mex. State Bar, Albuquerque Bar Assn., Sigma Chi. Republican. Methodist. Club: Albuquerque Country. Lodges: Elks, Masons, Shriners. Home: 3333 Santa Clara Ave SE Albuquerque NM 87106-1530 Office: Van Atta Imaging Ctr A-6 Med Arts Sq 801 Encino Pl NE Albuquerque NM 87102-2612

STEVENSON, JOHN FRANCIS, beverage company administrator; b. Miami, Fla., Feb. 16, 1959; s. Thomas Charles and Mary Kathryn (Murphy) S.; m. Sharon Louise Keever, Jan. 25, 1986; 1 child, Katherine Reed. BA, DePauw U., 1981; MBA, Pepperdine U., 1989. Account exec. NBI, Inc., Chgo., 1981-83; group sales instr. NBI, Inc., Boulder, Colo., 1983-84; mgr. European sales ops. NBI, Inc., London, 1985-86; br. mgr. NBI, Inc., L.A., 1986-88; v.p., gen. mgr. MGI of Calif., Inc., L.A., 1988-91; mgr. sales ops. and planning Pepsi-Cola Co., L.A., 1991-92; gen. mgr. Denver metro market Pepsi-Cola Co., 1992—. Bd. dirs. Pres.'s Leadership Coun., Colo. State U., Ft. Collins, 1993—. Recipient Thorton F. Bradshaw fellowship Claremont Grad. Sch., 1990. Mem. Colo. Soft Drink Assn. (pres.), Lakewood Country Club. Republican. Roman Catholic. Office: Pepsi Cola Co 3801 Brighton Blvd Denver CO 80216-3625

STEVENSON, MARILYN JOYCE, dietitian; b. Mpls., Mar. 21, 1949; d. William Charles and Joyce (Smith) Steinke; m. H. Eugene Stevenson, May 30, 1970; children: James, John. BS, Iowa State U., 1971. Clin. dietitian Children's Hosp., St. Paul, 1972-74, Columbus, Ohio, 1974-75; nutrition specialist Child Care Food Program, Littleton, Colo., 1983-85; clin. dietitian The Children's Hosp., Denver, 1985—. Mem. Am. Dietetic Assn. (registered), Denver Dietetic Assn., Pediatric Nutrition Practice Group (Colo. chpt. sec. 1992-93, chair 1994—), PEO (recording sec., corres. sec., v.p., 1994—). Home: 16022 E Loyola Dr Aurora CO 80013-2720 Office: The Children's Hosp 1056 E 19th Ave Denver CO 80218-1007

STEVENSON, PATRICE NOEL, rehabilitative medicine physician; b. Puyallup, Wash., Dec. 21, 1955; d. Gerald Hoyt and Alice Vera (Linde) Pilcher; m. Craig Lyle Stevenson, Feb. 26, 1982; children: Collin, Caitlin, Christopher. BS in Biology, Pacific Luth. U., 1978; MD, U. Wash., 1982. Diplomate Am. Bd. Phys. Medicine and Rehab. Staff physiatrist Good Samaritan Rehab. Ctr., Puyallup, 1985—, pediat. rehab. med. dir., 1993—; asst. clin. prof. rehab. medicine U. Wash., Seattle, 1986—; program surveyor Commn. on Accreditation of Rehab. Facilities, Tucson, 1990—. Fellow Am. Acad. Phys. Medicine and Rehab.; mem. AMA, Am. Assn. Electrodiagnostic Medicine (assoc.), Assn. Acad. Physiatrists (diplomate), N.W. Assn. Phys. Medicine and Rehab. (Med. Student award 1980), Wash. State Soc. Phys. Medicine and Rehab. (sec.-treas. 1989—). Wash. State Med. Assn., Pierce County Med. Soc. Home: 4468 185th Ave E Sumner WA 98390-9112 Office: Good Samaritan Rehab Ctr PO Box 190 Puyallup WA 98371-0020

STEVENSON, PATRICIA KENNARD, artist, journalist; b. Pitts., Mar. 15, 1932; d. Ernest Spencer and Alice Ethalinda (Thompson) Kennard; m. Larry Dale Arnhart, Mar. 16, 1949 (div. 1954); 1 child, Tom Ray; m. Donald Andrus Fife, July 9, 1961 (div. 1963), 1 child, Alisa Melita; m. William Arnold Stevenson, Nov. 10, 1964 (dec. Nov. 1991); stepchildren: Kathleen Bates, William Eugene, Carol A. Robbins. Student, Internat. Corr. Sch., Milw., 1954-57. Artist, instr. self-employed, Nampa, Idaho, 1961-65, Lovelock, Nev., 1965-68; reporter Rev.-Miner, Lovelock, 1967-68; reporter, columnist, photographer, advt. Fallon (Nev.) Eagle Standard, 1968-70; pub. rels. dir., editor newsletter Nev. State Edn. Assn., Carson City, 1970-71; founding pub., editor Lahontan Valley News, Fallon, 1971-75; editor Fallon Eagle-Standard, 1978-84; graphic artist, compositor Loganberry Press, Fallon, 1985-89; artist, instr. self-employed, Fallon, 1989—; rural corr. CBS Affiliate, Reno, 1971-75, Reno Newspapers, 1984-86; judge various speech competitions. Author articles; executed mural Scenes in Early Mining Camp, 1990. Charter pres. Rep. Fed. Women's Club, Fallon, 1968. Recipient awards Nev. State Press Assn., 1969, Churchill County Fair, 1989, Best of Show award Walker Lake Art Club, 1993, 1st place-acrylic ElDorado Gallery Miniature Show, 1993. Mem. Nev. Artists Assn. (past bd. dirs., editor newsletter 1991-93), Lahontan Valley Artists Assn. (pres. 1993), Sierra Watercolor Soc. Home: 4020 Reno Hwy Fallon NV 89406-9304

STEVENSON, RICHARD GRAY, III, dentist; b. Long Beach, Calif., July 9, 1958; s. Richard Gray and Carla (Wood) S.; m. Victoria Puthumana, Sept. 15, 1985; 1 child, Richard Gray IV. BS, UCLA, 1982, DDS, 1986. Lic. dentist, Calif. Paramed. vol. Project Nepal, Palo Alto, Calif., 1979-80; dental rschr. Va. Med. Ctr., Sepulveda, Calif., 1980-83; pvt. practice Laguna Niguel, Calif., 1986-94, Santa Ana, Calif., 1987-90; adj. asst. prof. UCLA Sch. Dentistry, 1994—. Active Youth Evolving Solutions, Palo Alto, 1980, Creative Initiative Found., Palo Alto, 1976-82, Students for Global Awareness, UCLA, 1980-82, Beyond War, Palo Alto, 1985—. Fellow Acad. Gen. Dentistry; mem. ADA, Acad. Operative Dentistry, Calif. Dental Assn., Orange County Dental Soc., Orange County Richard V. Tucker Cast Gold Study Club (co-founder, sec. 1991—, pres. 1992), Lions (bd. dirs. 1987-88), Delta Sigma Delta (v.p. 1984-86). Office: UCLA Sch Dentistry Ctr Health Scis 10833 Le Conte Ave Los Angeles CA 90024

STEVENSON, ROBERT MURRELL, music educator; b. Melrose, N.Mex., July 3, 1916; s. Robert Emory and Ada (Ross) S. AB, U. Tex., El Paso, 1936; grad., Juilliard Grad. Sch. Music, 1938; MusM, Yale, 1939; PhD, U. Rochester, 1942; STB cum laude, Harvard U., 1943; BLitt, Oxford (Eng.) U.; Th.M., Princeton U.; DMus honoris causa, Cath. U. Am., 1991; LHD (honoris causa), Ill. Wesleyan U., 1992; Litt honoris causa, Universidade Nova de Lisboa, 1993. Instr. music U. Tex., 1941-43, 46; faculty Westminster Choir Coll., Princeton, N.Y., 1946-49; faculty research lectr. UCLA, 1981, mem. faculty to prof. music, 1949—; vis. asst. prof. Columbia, 1955-56; vis. prof. Ind. U., Bloomington, 1959-60, U. Chile, 1965-66, Northwestern U., Chgo., 1976, U. Granada, 1992; cons. UNESCO, 1977; Louis Charles Elson lectr. Libr. of Congress, Washington, 1969. Author: Music in Mexico, 1952, Patterns of Protestant Church Music, 1953, La musica en la catedral de Sevilla, 1954, 85, Music before the Classic Era, 1955, Shakespeare's Religious Frontier, 1958, The Music of Peru, 1959, Juan Bermudo, 1960, Spanish Music in the Age of Columbus, 1960, Spanish Cathedral Music in the Golden Age, 1961, La musica colonial en Colombia, 1964, Protestant Church Music in America, 1966, Music in Aztec and Inca Territory, 1968, Renaissance and Baroque Musical Sources in the Americas, 1970, Music in El Paso, 1970, Philosophies of American Music History, 1970, Written Sources For Indian Music Until 1882, 1973, Christmas Music from Baroque Mexico, 1974, Foundations of New World Opera, 1973, Seventeenth Century Villancicos, 1974, Latin American Colonial Music Anthology, 1975, Vilancicos Portugueses, 1976, Josquin in the Music of Spain and Portugal, 1977, American Musical Scholarship, Parker to Thayer, 1978, Liszt at Madrid and Lisbon, 1980, Wagner's Latin American Outreach, 1983, Spanish Musical Impact Beyond the Pyrenees, 1250-1500, 1985, La Música en las catedrales españolas del Sigle de Oro, 1993; contbg. editor: Handbook Latin Am. Studies, 1976—; editor: Inter-Am. Music Rev, 1978—; contbr. to: New Grove Dictionary of Music and Musicians, 17 other internat. encys. Served to capt. U.S. Army, 1943-46, 49. Decorated Army Commendation ribbon; fellow Ford Found., 1953-54, Gulbenkian Found., 1966, 81, Guggenheim Found., 1962, NEH, 1974, Comité Conjunto Hispano-Norteamericano (Madrid), 1989; recipient Fulbright rsch. awards, 1958-59, 64, 70-71, 88-89, Carnegie Found. tchg. award, 1955-56, Gabriela Mistral award OAS, 1985, Heitor Villa Lobos Jury award OAS, 1988, OAS medal, 1986, Cert. Merit Mexican Consulate San Bernardino, Calif., 1987, Silver medal Spanish Ministry Culture, 1989, Gold medal Real Conservatorio Superior, 1994. Mem. Am. Musicol. Soc. (hon. life, Pacific SW chpt.), Real Academia de Bellas Artes, Hispanic Soc. Am., Am. Liszt soc. (cons. editor), Heterofonia (cons. editor), Brazilian Musicol. Soc. (hon.), Portuguese Musicol. Soc. (hon.), Argentinian Musicol. Soc. (hon.), Orden Andrés Bello, Primera Clase, Venezuela, 1992. Office: UCLA Dept Music 405 Hilgard Ave Los Angeles CA 90024-1301

STEVENSON, ROBERT W., technologies company executive, financial officer. BA in Econs., Stanford U., 1961; MBA, U. Pa., 1963. Analyst fin. forecasting Boeing Co., 1963, supr. accounts receivable, 1963-64, mgr. fin. statements and planning, 1964-67, project fin. mgr., 1967-68; asst. contr. Criton Techs., 1968, contr., 1968-70, asst. v.p., contr., 1970-72, asst. v.p., sec., 1972-73, asst. v.p., sec. treas., 1973-75, sr. v.p., CFO, 1985-87, exec. v.p., CFO, 1987-89; exec. v.p., CFO Esterline Techs. Corp., Bellevue, Wash., 1987—. Mem. Fin. Execs. Inst. Office: Esterline Techs Corp 10800 NE 8th St Fl 6 Bellevue WA 98004-4429

STEWART, CHERIE ANITA, painter; b. Gadsden, Ala., Sept. 20, 1945; d. Earl Donald Williams and Frances Morgan Bellenger; m. Walter Hurd Stewart, Ap. 2, 1966 (div. Sept. 1988); children: Don Paul, Virginia Elizabeth; m. Charles Frederick Smith, July 21, 1990 (div. Oct. 1991). BS, U. Ala., Tuscaloosa, 1968; BA, U. Ala.-Birmingham, 1983. One-man shows include Barker Gallery, Palm Beach, Fla., 1984, St. Vincent's Gallery, Birmingham, Ala., 1987, Tutwiler Gallery, Birmingham, 1988; exhibited in group shows at Birmingham Frame and Art Gallery, 1984-86, Maralyn Wilson Gallery, Birmingham, 1985—, Abstein Gallery, Atlanta, 1985-91, Gateway Ctr., Newark, 1987, Ariel Gallery, N.Y.C., 1988, Windsors Gallery, Boca Raton, Fl., 1989—, Galerie Jean Lammelim, Paris, 1991, Wildlife Art Gallery, Gatlinburg, Tenn., 1992, World Wildlife Expn., Gatlinburg Conv. Ctr., 1992; contbr. advt. layouts The Stewart Orgn., Birmingham, 1983-84; painter Shippee Gallery, N.Y.C., 1985—, Art South, Inc., Phila., 1987—, Archtl. Arts Co., Dallas. Recipient numerous awards. Mem. Assn. Pour la Promotion du Patrimoine Artistique Français, Birmingham Mus. Art, Birmingham Art Assn., Nat. Mus. Women in the Arts, Knickerbocker Artists N.Y. (assoc.), Allied Artists Am. (assoc.).

STEWART, DAVID WAYNE, marketing educator, psychologist, consultant; b. Baton Rouge, Oct. 23, 1951; s. Wesley A. Stewart and Edith L. (Richhart) Moore; m. Lenora Francois, June 6, 1975; children: Sarah Elizabeth, Rachel Dawn. BA, N.E. La. U., 1972; MA, Baylor U., 1973, PhD, 1974. Rsch. psychologist HHS, La., 1974-76; rsch. mgr. Needham, Harper & Steers Advt., Chgo., 1976-78; assoc. prof. Jacksonville (Ala.) State U., 1978-80; assoc. prof. Vanderbilt U., Nashville, 1980-86, sr. assoc. dean, 1984-86; prof. U. So. Calif., L.A., 1986-90, Ernest W. Hahn prof. mktg., 1990-91, Robert Brooker rsch. prof. mktg., 1991—, chmn. dept. mktg., 1995—; mgmt. cons., 1978—. Author, co-author: Secondary Research: Sources and Methods, Effective Television Advertising: A Study of 1000 Commericals, Consumer Behavior and the Practice of Marketing, Focus Group: Theory and Practice, Attention, Attitude, and Affect in Repsonse to Advertising, Nonverbal Communication and Advertising; contbr. articles to profl. jours.; mem. edtl. bd. Jour. Mktg. Rsch., Jour. Consumer Mktg., Jour. Pub. Policy & Mktg., Jour. Mktg., Jour. Advt., Jour. Promotion Mgmt., Current Issues and Rsch. in Advt., Jour. Internat. Consumer Mktg., Jour. Managerial Issues, Jour. Promotion Mgmt.; past pres. policy bd. Jour. Consumer Rsch., Acad. Mgmt. Fellow APA (coun. rep.), Am. Psychol. Soc. (charter); mem. Soc. for Consumer Psychol. (past pres.), Inst. Mgmt. Scis., Decision Sci. Inst., Am. Mktg. Assn., Assn. Consumer Rsch., Acad. Mgmt., Am. Statis. Assn. Republican. Baptist. Office: U So Calif Sch Bus Adminstrn Dept Mktg Los Angeles CA 90089

STEWART, DONALD EDWIN, association director; b. Modale, Iowa, Aug. 7, 1926; s. Cecil Davis and Ruby Jeanne (Baxter) S.; m. Barbara Joan Swaggerty, Jan. 1, 1977; children: Michael, Kathleen. Student, U. No. Idaho, 1946-47, Coll. of Idaho, 1955-59, Boise State U., 1958-59, Ariz. State U., 1968-70. Ind. bldg. contractor Caldwell, Idaho, 1946-65; owner lumber yard Caldwell, 1958-65; dist./city mgr. ABC Theatres of Ariz., Phoenix, 1966-71; owner DeNovo Stamp & Coin Co., Phoenix, 1972-82, Classic Signs/Western Printer, Phoenix, 1982-90; exec. dir. Key Collectors Internat., Phoenix, 1978—; Author 34 books including Standard Guide to Key Collecting; contbr. articles to profl. jours. Pres. Jaycees, Caldwell, 1955. With USN, 1943-54, World War II, Korea. Named Man of Yr. Caldwell Jaycees, 1955. Home and Office: 902 E Country Gables Dr Phoenix AZ 85022-3713

STEWART, GAIL BENITA, alumni development director, editor; b. Cin., June 19, 1950; d. Charles Arthur Stewart and Ida Bell (McKinney) Tucker. BA, Calif. State U., 1974. Publicity asst. Sta. KCOP Channel 13, L.A., 1975; editor S.W. Regional Lab, L.A., 1975-77; editor, columnist Herald Am. News, Bellflower, Calif., 1977—, columnist, ad rep., 1979-80; researcher, writer asst. Sidney Poitier, Beverly Hills, Calif., 1977-78; pub. info. officer Long Beach (Calif.) Cmty. Svcs., 1982-85; dir. pub. rels. St. Anthony H.S., Long Beach, 1986-91; dir. alumni rels. Long Beach City Coll., 1991—. Contbr. articles to profl. jours. Grantee L.B. Comms., 1983, 84, 85, 86. Home: 1042 Gladys Ave Apt 4 Long Beach CA 90804-6507 Office: Long Beach City Coll 4901 E Carson St Long Beach CA 90808-1706

STEWART, GARY CRAWFORD, oil company executive; b. Pitts., Apr. 5, 1956; s. Donald Eugene and Alma (Crawford) S.; m. Teresa Ann McInturff, Nov. 14, 1958; children: Sara Ann, Jon William. BS, Ariz. State U., 1978; MS in Geology, U. Okla., 1981. Sr. geologist Exxon Co. U.S.A., Denver, 1981-86; v.p. Melange Assocs., Inc., Denver, 1986-94, pres., CEO, 1994—; mem. Pres. Clinton's Energy Team, Washington, 1992—. Author: The Belize Carbonate Complex, 1980, The Influence of tectonics on Modern Carbonate Deposition, 1981. Mem. Am. Assn. Petroleum Geologists, Denver Internat. Petroleum Soc., Future Am. Geologists Soc. (hon. mem.). Office: Melange 821 17th St Ste 600 Denver CO 80202-3004

STEWART, ISAAC DANIEL, JR., state supreme court justice; b. Salt Lake City, Nov. 21, 1932; s. Isaac Daniel and Orabelle (Iverson) S.; m. Elizabeth Bryan, Sept. 10, 1959; children: Elizabeth Ann, Shannon. B.A., U. Utah, 1959, J.D., 1962. Bar: Utah 1962, U.S. Ct. Appeals (4th, 8th, 9th and 10th cirs.) 1965, U.S. Supreme Ct. 1965. Atty. Dept. Justice, 1962-65; asst. prof., then assoc. prof. with tenure U. Utah Coll. Law, 1965-70, chmn. curriculum com., rsch. com., 1967-69, legal adv.; ptnr. firm Jones, Waldo, Holbrook & McDonough, Salt Lake City, 1970-79; justice Utah Supreme Ct., 1979—, assoc. chief justice, 1986-88; presiding judge 2nd dist. Utah Dist. Ct., Ogden, 1988—; lectr. in field; mem. Utah Bd. Oil, Gas and Mining, 1976-78, chmn., 1977-78; Utah rep. Interstate Oil Compact Commn., 1977-78, exec. com. 1978-79; mem. adv. com. rules of procedure Utah Supreme Ct., 1983-87; chmn. com. on bar-press guidelines Utah Bar. Contbr. articles to legal jours. Chmn. subcom. on legal rights and responsibilities of youth Utah Gov's Com. on Youth, 1972; pres. Salt Lake chpt. Coun. Fgn. Rels., 1982; mem. Salt Lake City C. of C., 1974-79, mem. govtl. modernization com., 1976-78; missionary for Mormon Ch. in Fed. Republic Germany, 1953-56; bd. dirs. U. Utah Alumni Assn., 1986-89. Recipient Alumnus of Yr. award U. Utah Coll. Law, 1989. Mem. ABA, Utah Bar Assn. (com. on law and poverty 1967-69, com. on specialization 1977-78, pub. rels. com. 1968-69, chmn. com. on antitrust law 1977-78, com. on civil procedure reform 1968, mem. exec. com. bd. of appellate judges 1990—, Appellate Judge of Yr. 1986), Salt Lake County Bar Assn., Am. Judicature Soc., Order of Coif, Phi Beta Kappa, Phi Kappa Phi, Sigma Chi (Significant Sig award 1987). *

STEWART, JAMES IAN, agricultural water scientist, cropping system developer, consultant; b. San Diego, Jan. 9, 1928; s. Castle Elmore and Myrtle Catherine (Hasty) S.; m. Robbie Nell Oliver, Mar. 23, 1975; children: Virginia Lane Stewart Carton, Ian Castle Stewart, Kevin Scott Overby. BSc, U. Calif., Berkeley, 1950; PhD, U. Calif., Davis, 1972. Farm advisor Agrl. Extension Svc., U. Calif., Stockton and Merced, 1950-61; extension expert Irrigation, Food and Agrl. Orgn. UN, Nicosia, Cyprus, 1962-66; assoc. rsch. water scientist U. Calif., Davis, 1966-77; supervisory soil scientist USDA/Office for Internat. Cooperation and Devel., Nairobi, Kenya, 1977-83; team leader, agrometeorologist USAID/Kenya Mission, 1977-83; founder, pres. Found. for World Hunger Alleviation Through Response Farming (WHARF), Davis, 1984—; cons., agrometeorology AID, USDA, World Bank, FAO/UNDP, 35 countries of Ams., Europe, Asia, Africa, Australia, 1965—; sci. convocations, internat. 14 countries worldwide, 1969—. Author: Response Farming in Rainfed Agriculture, 1988; creator (computer programs) Wharf, Wharfdat, 1990; contbr. numerous articles to profl. jours. Mem. Am. Soc. Agronomy, Crop Sci. Soc. Am., Soil Sci. Soc. Am., Internat. Soil Sci. Soc., World Assn. Soil and Water Conservation, Internat. Com. for

Irrigation and Drainage (life, U.S. com.), Indian Soc. Dryland Agr. (life), Internat. Platform Assn., Sigma Xi, Phi Delta Theta. Home: 640 Portsmouth Ave Davis CA 95616-2738 Office: World Hunger Alleviation Through Response Farming PO Box 1158 Davis CA 95617-1158

STEWART, JAMES M., insurance and securities broker; b. L.A., July 9, 1946; s. Robert Lawrence and Maxine Madeline (Lininger) Stewart; m. Christina Jean Caruso; 4 children. BA, UCLA, 1971, MPH, MBA, 1975. Lic. series 7 securities, probate referee appointment. Dept. head UCLA Med. Ctr., L.A., 1971-77; dir. Children's Hosp., L.A., 1977-80; pres. J.M. Stewart Inc., Beverly Hills, Calif., 1980—; founder First Profl. Bank, Santa Monica, Calif., 1988—. Mem. Calif. Probate Referee Assn. (standards/ethics com., bd. dirs.), Provident Mutual Leaders Assn., St. James's Club. Republican. Office: 9200 W Sunset Blvd Ste 1229 Los Angeles CA 90069-3607

STEWART, JEFFREE ROBERT, environmental planner, artist; b. Concord, N.H., June 20, 1956; s. Robert Davison and Ruth Florence (Olney) S. BA, Evergreen State Coll., Olympia, Wash., 1983; postgrad., U. Wash., 1983-84, Inst. Creative Devel., 1989-91. River guide rafting Rio Bravo, Inc., Durango, Colo., 1981-82; forester, planner Wash. State Parks Commn., Olympia, 1983-84; fisheries biologist U. Wash., Seattle, Alaska and Aleutians, 1984-86; pub. affairs rschr. NOAA, Seattle, 1986; hazardous waste project mgr. Washington Ecology Dept., Olympia, 1987, marine waste disposal project mgr., 1988-92, interagy. liaison, facilitator policy and tech. adv. groups, 1989-90, shorelands planner, 1992—; mem. ecology art com. Ecology Dept., Olympia, 1994; mem. adv. bd. Washington Heritage Conf., Olympia, 1992; exhbns. team coord. Arts Olympia, 1993-94. One man shows include Batdorf & Bronson, Olympia, 1989, 91, 93, 94, Colophon Cafe, Bellingham, Wash., 1987, Dancing Goats, Olympia, 1992, Hungry Moon, LaConner, 1993; exhibited in groups shows at Janet Huston Gallery, LaConner, 1991, 92, 93, Wash. State Capitol Mus., Olympia, 1991, 92, 93, Evergreen State Coll., 1993, Wash. Ctr. Performing Arts, 1992, 93, 94, Valley Mus. N.W. Art, 1994, Tacoma Art Mus., 1995, also pvt. collections. Bd. trustees Evergreen State Coll., Olympia, 1981. Recipient Competent/Able Toastmaster awards Toastmasters Internat., 1989, 91, Oil Painting award of Merit Wash. State Capitol Mus., Olympia, 1993, Wash. Pub. Employees Assn. (bd. dirs. 1992-93), Meridian Toastmasters (pres., v.p. 1989-91). Mem. Arts Olympia (steering group 1994—), Profl. Geographers of Puget Sound, Wash. Planners Assn., Burke Meml. Mus., Mus. N.W. Art, Tacoma Art Mus., Bellevue Art Mus. Home: PO Box 7397 Olympia WA 98507-7397 Office: Wash Ecology Dept PO Box 47609 Olympia WA 98504

STEWART, JOANNE, secondary school educator; b. Vancouver, Wash., Mar. 10, 1944; d. Edward Charles and Claudine Marie (Meilleur) Spencer; m. William Lemley Stewart, Sept. 2, 1966 (dec. June 1983); children: Amy Diane, Nicholas William. BS, Wash. State U., 1966, MA, 1973. Cert. tchr., Mont., Idaho, Wash., Calif. Tchr. foods Seaside High Sch., Monterey, Calif., 1966-67; tchr. home econs. Marysville (Wash.) High Sch., 1967-68, Palouse (Wash.) High Sch., 1968-73, Ennis (Mont.) High Sch., 1973-76, Genesee (Idaho) High Sch., 1976-77; instr. young family Missoula (Mont.) County High Sch., 1983-84; tchr. home econs. Woodman Sch., Lolo, Mont., 1985-86; travel cons. Travel Masters, Missoula, 1984-87; ticketing mgr. Blue Caboose Travel, Missoula, 1987-91; tchr. family and consumer scis. Victor (Mont.) High Sch., 1991—. Co-pres. Lolo PTO, 1980-81; v.p. Lolo Community Ctr., 1981; sec. Lolo Mosquito Control Bd., 1988—; mem. telecommunications com. Conrad Burns & Gov. Racicot. Marysville Edn. Assn. scholar, 1962, Future Homemakers Am. scholar, 1962. Mem. AAUW (sec. 1986, program chmn. 1987), Forestry Triangle (pres. 1981, editor cookbook 1982), Future Homemakers Am. (hon. advisor), Am. Family and Consumer Scis. Assn., Mont. Family and Consumer Scis. Assn. (bylaws chair 1994, pres. 1995-96), Mont. Vocat. Tchrs. Assn. (returning Rookie of Yr. 1992), Am. Federated Tchrs., Mont. Vocat. Family and Consumer Scis. Tchrs. (v.p. 1993-94, pres. 1994-95). Republican. Methodist. Home: 1200 Lakeside Dr Lolo MT 59847-9705 Office: Victor High Sch Home Econs 425 4th Ave Victor MT 59875-9468

STEWART, JOHN WRAY BLACK, college dean; b. Coleraine, Northern Ireland, Jan. 16, 1936; s. John Wray and Margaret Reid (Black) S.; m. Felicity Ann Patricia Poole, Aug. 7, 1965; children: J.W. Matthew, Hannah Louise. BSc with honors, Queen's U., Belfast, Northern Ireland, 1958, B.Agr. with honors, 1959, PhD, 1963, DSc, 1988. Registered profl. agrologist. Sci. officer chem. rsch. div. Ministry of Agr., Belfast, 1959-64; asst. prof. soil sci. dept. U. Sask., Saskatoon, Can., 1966-71, assoc. prof., 1971-76, prof., 1976-81; dir. Sask. Inst. Pedology U. Sask., 1981-89; dean Coll. Agr. U. Sask., Saskatoon, 1989—; tech. expert cons. FAO/IAEA, U.N.D.P., Vienna, Austria, 1971, 1974-75; sec.-gen. Sci. Com. on Problems of Environment, Paris, 1988-92, pres. 1992-95; cons. UNESCO, Paris, 1990; trustee Internat. Inst. Tropical Agr., Nigeria, 1991—; mem. sci. adv. com. Inter-Am. Inst. on Global Change Res., 1994—. Contbr. articles to profl. publs., chpts. to books. Fellow Can. Soc. Soil Sci., Berlin Inst. Advanced Study, Am. Soc. Agronomy, Soil Sci. Soc. Am.; mem. Brit. Soc. Soil Sci., Brazilian Soc. Soil Sci., Internat. Soc. Soil Sci., Agrl. Inst. Can. Office: U Sask, Coll Agr, Saskatoon, SK Canada S7N 0W0

STEWART, KAREN ELAINE, librarian; b. Wyandotte, Mich., Jan. 17, 1951; d. Fred and Helen (Zymboly) Cooksey; m. Richard J. Stewart, Apr. 8, 1978. B, Eastern Mich. U., 1972; MLS, Wayne State U., 1973. Asst. hosp. libr. Detroit-Macomb Hosp. Assn., 1975-78; libr. Colo. Legis. Coun., Denver, 1980—. Mem. Longmont (Colo.) Chorale, 1989—. Mem. ALA, Spl. Librs. Assn. Lutheran. Office: Colo Legis Coun Rm 029 Capitol Bldg Denver CO 80203

STEWART, LARRY RAY, engineer, financial director, quality consultant; b. Rock Springs, Wyo., Mar. 26, 1948; s. Raymond Melvin and Mary Jane (Fillin) S.; m. Della Jean Warren, Aug. 25, 1967; children: Stephanie M., Kara K., Gina R., Laura J. BS in Engring., U. Wyo., 1970, MS in Engring., 1972. Registered profl. engr., Ariz., Colo., Idaho, Mont., N.Mex., Oreg., Tex., Utah, Wyo. Mgr. apt. Willey Enterprises, Laramie, Wyo., 1966-70; grad. asst. U. Wyo., Laramie, 1970-72; systems analyst Dept. Def., Corona, Calif., 1972-73; engr. Mountain Bell, Cheyenne, Wyo., 1973-77; adminstr. Mountain Bell, Denver, 1977-79; mgr. Mountain Bell, Englewood, Colo., 1979-84; dist. mgr. Mountain Bell, Denver, 1985-87; dir. Bell TRICO Services, Englewood, 1984-85, U.S. West CGI, Denver, 1987-92; divsn. mgr. Hamlin Electric Services, Inc., Ft. Morgan, Colo., 1993-94; field engr. Colo. State U., Ft. Collins, 1994—; mem. adv. bd. U. Wyoming Grad. Sch., Laramie, 1970-72; IOF co-chair AT&T/Bell System, Basking Ridge, N.J., 1980-83; curriculum advisor Network Tng., Englewood, 1980-83; fin. advisor Employee Suggestion Plan, Denver, 1984-86. Editor (coll. mag.) Enginews, 1970. Pres. Maplewood Homeowners, Arvada, Colo., 1986; key chair United Way, Denver, 1988. Served with USAF, 1970-76. Mem. IEEE, Nat. Soc. Profl. Engrs. Republican. Lodge: Optimist (lt. gov. of Colo./Wyo. Dist.). Office: NAMTC Colo State Univ PO Box 1460 Arvada CO 80001

STEWART, MARLENE METZGER, financial planner, insurance agent; b. Portland, Oreg., Nov. 1, 1937; d. Eddie Charles and Helen M. (Grant) Metzger; m. Robert W. Stewart, Aug. 1, 1964 (dec. Jan. 1967); m. Melvin N. McBurney, Feb. 14, 1985. BA, U. Oreg., 1959; MA, U. Tex., El Paso, 1971. Exec. dir. Summer 72 Youth Com. Office of Mayor, Portland, 1972; registered rep. Mut. Life Ins. Co. N.Y., Portland, 1973-76, Prudential Life Ins. Co., Portland, 1976-77; ptnr. N.W. Fin. Planning, Portland, 1977-79; pres. Horizons Unltd. Fin. Planning, Portland, 1979-86; prin. EMR Fin. Adv. Svcs., Inc., Portland, 1986-89; registered rep. KMS Fin. Svcs., Inc., Portland, 1979—; owner Stewart Fin. Group, 1991—. Mem.-at-large nat. bd. YMCA's, 1971-73; bd. dirs. Met. YMCA, Portland, 1971-75; bd. dirs. YWCA, Portland, 1989-92, treas., 1990-92, chmn. investment com.; chmn. planned giving com. Arthritis Found., 1984-86. Bill Bottler scholar Portland chpt. CLU and Chartered Fin. Cons., 1981. Mem. Inst. CFP's, Oreg. Soc. Inst. CFP's (treas. 1985-86), Internat. Assn. Fin. Planners (pres. Oreg. chpt. 1987-88), Nat. Assn. Life Underwriters, CLU's and ChFC's (treas. Portland chpt. 1985-86), Assocs. Good Samaritan (steering com., chmn. 1991-92), Rotary. Republican. Presbyterian. Office: 4380 SW Macadam Ave Ste 525 Portland OR 97201-6408

STEWART, PATRICIA ANN, bank executive; b. Phoenix, Nov. 3, 1953; d. Travis Delano and Ann Helen (Lopez) Hill. BS, Ariz. State U., 1975. Programmer, analyst Victor Comptometer Corp., Phoenix, 1975-77, Lewis & Roca, Attys., Phoenix, 1977-79; data processing mgr. Central Mgmt. Corp., Phoenix, 1979-80; corp. systems cons. S.W. Forest Industries, Phoenix, 1981-87; human resources system mgr. Western Savs. and Loan, Phoenix, 1987-90; asst. v.p., loan and deposit systems mgr. Bank of Am., Ariz., 1990-91; application mgr. Data Line S.W. div., 1991-93; v.p. Bank of Am. Ariz., 1993—; ptnr. Abacus Group, 1981-83. Troop leader Ariz. Cactus Pine Coun. Girl Scouts U.S., membership registrar Paradise Vally Neighborhood. Mem. Data Processing Mgmt. Assn. (pres. Phoenix chpt. 1982), Ariz. HP Users Group (mem. dir. 1987). Home: 15849 N 20th Pl Phoenix AZ 85022-3405 Office: Bank of Am Ariz 101 N 1st Ave Phoenix AZ 85003-1902

STEWART, PAUL ANTHONY, II, building association executive, author; b. Oakland, Calif., Apr. 14, 1952; s. Paul Anthony Sr. and Hilda Hensley (Monger) S.; m. Stephanie Anne Pitts, July 8, 1972; children: Jana Lorraine, Robyn Lynne. BA, San Jose (Calif.) State U., 1974, MS, 1975. News editor various pubs., 1974-77; v.p. legis. svcs. Bldg. Industry Assn. of Superior Calif., Sacramento, 1977-82; exec. v.p. So. div. Bldg. Industry Assn. of No. Calif., San Jose, 1982-86; exec. v.p. Bldg. Industry Assn. of San Joaquin Valley, Fresno, Calif., 1986-90; CEO Bldg. Industry Assn. of Cen. Calif., Modesto, 1990-91, Rental Housing Assn. Contra Costa County, Walnut Creek, Calif., 1993—; chmn. Sacramento Regional Legis. Advs. Group, 1977-82. Host (TV show) Stewarts Sports Challenge, 1974 (Emmy nomination 1975); contbr. articles to profl. jours. Chmn. housing element update com. City of Sacramento, 1980, Transp. 2000 Steering LCom., San Jose, 1985-87; transp. commr. County of Santa Clara, Calif., 1986-87; pres. San Joaquin Valley Community Housing Leadership Bd., Fresno, 1988-90. Recipient Community Involvement award Calif. Hwy. Patrol, 1977; named one of Outstanding Young Men of Am., U.S. Jaycees, 1984. Mem. Nat. Assn. Home Bldrs., Calif. Bldg. Industry Assn. (exec. officers coun., pres. 1990-91), Internat. Soc. Poets, Poetry Soc. Am., Calif. Writer's Club, Sigma Delta Chi. Baptist.

STEWART, RENICE ANN, financial analyst, writer; b. Milw., Jan. 2, 1947; d. Fredrick and Lucia (Stewart) Fregin; children: Jennifer Jean, Whitney Susan. BA, U. San Diego, 1988, MA, 1990. Pres. Chubby Bumpkins, Inc., Houston, 1980-82; contracts adminstr. Gulf States Computer Svcs., Houston, 1980-82; pres. RAM Prodns., Houston, 1981-82, Pizza Internat., Inc., Houston, 1982-84; contracts adminstr. First Alliance Corp., Houston, 1982-85; freelance pub. rels. cons. San Diego, 1985—. Tutor U. San Diego Writing Ctr., 1987-89; founder, dir. pub. rels.-tng. Montgomery County (Tex.) Crisis Action Line, Houston, 1979-84; founder, v.p., bd. dirs. Montgomery County Rape Crisis Coalition, 1982-84, speaker, 1982-84; speaker Rape Trauma Coalition, 1982-84; mem. prodn. com. Community Women Together, Montgomery County, 1980-82; pres. Living Arts Coun., Houston, 1980-81. Named Woman of Yr. YWCA, 1981, 82. Mem. Am. Assn. Bus. Women (dir. activities Houston chpt. 1983-84), Bus. Women's Forum (bd. dir. community awareness Houston chpt. 1982-83), Assn. Women Bus. Owners, Lions (hon.), Phi Alpha Delta.

STEWART, SANDRA ITZEL, language educator; b. Lynwood, Calif., Jan. 18, 1964; d. Lynn Meier and Alicia (Moya) Wolf. BA in Hist. and Polit. Sci., UCLA, 1986; MS in Edn. in Bilingual Curriculum and Instrn., U. So. Calif., 1991; EdM in Lang. and Literacy, Harvard U., 1993; postgrad., U. So. Calif. Bilingual cross-cultural gen. subject credential. Spanish tchr., coach Archiodiocese of L.A., Playa Del Rey, Calif., 1987-88; substitute bilingual elem. tchr. L.A. Unified Sch., 1988-89, 92-94; bilingual tchr., 1st grade L.A. Unified Sch. Dist., Wilmington, Calif., 1989-91; bilingual tchr. 5th and 6th grades L.A. Unified Sch. Dist., Wilmington, 1991-92; bilingual math mentor tchr. Mass. Dept. Edn., Boston, 1992-93; rsch. asst. grad. sch. edn. Harvard U., 1992-93; rsch. asst. U. So. Calif., L.A., 1994-95, Rockman et al., San Francisco, 1995; organizer and presenter of writing process staff devel. series at Wilmington Pk. Elem. Sch., 1991-92; presenter Eastman Curriculum Design Project Conf., L.A., 1991, survey bilingual edn. Cambridge Coll., Mass., 1992, Parents without Ptnrs., Calif., 1994, sheltered English methodology and curriculum integration Explorations in Math Project, 1993; spkr. careers in edn. UCLA, 1991; elected faculty rep. office of sec. Wilmington Park Elem. Sch. Local Sch. Leadership Coun., 1991-92; bilingual edn. cons. Merida, Yucatan, Mex., 1994—. Educare scholar Sch. of Edn., U. So. Calif., L.A., 1990; recipient Outstanding Bilingual Tchr. award Accelerated Program, Dept. Edn., U. So. Calif., L.A., 1990; Calif. grad. fellow, 1990-91, title VII fellow U.S. Dept. Edn., 1993—. Mem. TESOL, Nat. Assn. for Bilingual Edn., Edn. Grad. Orgn. of U. So. Calif., Calif. Assn. for Bilingual Edn., Internat. Reading Assn., Am. Ednl. Rsch. Assn., Harvard Alumni Assn., UCLA Alumni Assn., U. So. Calif. Alumni Assn., Phi Delta Kappa. Republican. Roman Catholic.

STEWART, SHARON DIANE, writer; b. Cleveland, Miss., June 16, 1951; d. Elton Stewart and Mary Ruth (Speights) Boyland. BS in Mktg., San Diego State U., 1974; MBA, U. San Diego, 1977; AA in Tech. Writing, Mesa Coll., 1985. Sr. acctg. specialist Motorola Corp., San Diego, 1977-79; supr. acctg. Security Pacific Fin., San Diego, 1979-84; sr. acctg. specialist Sun Savs. and Loan, San Diego, 1984-85; publs. specialist Sundstrand Power Systems, San Diego, 1985-91; sr. analyst/editor MANTECH Advanced Tech., Pasadena, Calif., 1991-92; owner SDS Prodns., San Diego, 1981—; tech. editor Parsons Co., Pasadena, 1992-93; engring. writer Teledyne Laars, Moorpark, Calif., 1994—; instr. Mesa Coll., 1989-91. Contbr. articles to profl. jours. Vol. San Diego Police Dept., 1990-91, Glendale Police Dept., 1991—; vol. COMBO, 1982-83, Sta. KPBS Pub. Radio, 1984-87; chmn. Community Coll. Tech. Writing Coun., 1985-91; pres. Soc. for Technical COmms., 1993-95; mem. bd. dirs., chmn. Simi Valley Cultural Arts Ctr. Commn. & Found., 1994—; mem. Simi Valley Neighbor D Coun., 1993-95. Lt. comdr. USNR, 1985—. Copley Assoc. scholar, 1983, Grocery Industry scholar, 1974; decorated Nat. Def. Svc. medal USNR, 1992. Mem. Naval Res. Assn. (v.p. 1987-90, Diamond in the Rough award 1990), Res. Officers Assn., Soc. Tech. Communicators, San Diego Writers Guild, Nat. Acad. TV Arts (acting chair 1984, cert. 1985), Toastmasters (Toastmaster of Yr. 1983). Republican. Baptist. Home: 78 E Bonita Dr Simi Valley CA 93065-2916 Office: Teledyne Laars 6000 Condor Dr Moorpark CA 93021

STEWART, SUSAN KAY, school administrator; b. Yuba City, Calif., June 3, 1951; d. Leo Max and Velma Claire (Dunlap) Luse; m. Robert Marion Stewart, Dec. 17, 1971; children: Karen, Robert Leo, Bryon. BA in Liberal Studies, Calif. State U., 1976. Substitute tchr. Tehachapi (Calif.) Unified Sch. Dist., 1975-80; tchr./ISP coord. Tehachapi Christian Sch., 1982-85; adminstr. Highland Christian Schs., Tehachapi, 1988—. Field dir. REACT Internat., Chgo., 1980-82; sec., bd. dirs. Tehachapi Crisis Pregnancy Ctr., 1991-93. Recipient Competent Toastmaster Toastmaster Internat., 1980. Mem. Christian Home Educators Assn. Calif. (area contact 1982-84, 90—, mem. svcs. dir. 1993—), Tehachapi Home Educators Group (newsletter editor 1990-93). Republican. Office: Highland Christian Schs PO Box 262 Tehachapi CA 93581-0262

STEWART, THOMAS CLIFFORD, securities company executive; b. Portland, Oreg., Oct. 25, 1950; s. Jack Fry Stewart and Naomi June Gedney Cuyler; m. Susan Elizabeth Sample; children: Cortny, MacKenzie, Tommy, Andrew. Student, U. Gothenburg, Sweden, 1971; BS, U. Oreg., 1974; MBA, UCLA, 1982. Prin. Morgan Stanley & Co., N.Y.C., 1982-90; pres. Cort MacKenzie & Co., Virginia Beach, Va., 1990-92, Cort MacKenzie Securities, Portland, Oreg., 1992—; chmn. Beijing Kang Mei Biol. Products Co., Ltd., 1995—; dir. Acrymed, Lake Oswego, Oreg., 1995—, Morley Fin. Svcs., Lake Oswego, Oreg., 1995—. Contbr. articles to profl. jours. Bd. advisors Coll. Bus., U. Oreg., Eugene, 1990—, Oreg. State Commn. on Higher Bus. Edn., 1992-94; treas. adv. cabinet Oreg. State, 1993-94; adv. bd. sec. of Navy Nat. Naval Res. Policy Bd., Washington, 1987-89; trustee U. Oreg. Found., 1994—. With USN, 1974-80, USNR, 1980-91. Decorated Air medal, Navy Commendation for Valor; Baker scholar, 1981. Mem. Presdl. Roundtable, Naval Res. Assn. (Jr. Officer of Yr. 1988), U.S. Navy League, ROA, Am. Legion, VFW, Beta Gamma Sigma, Beta Alpha Psi, Alpha Mu Alpha, Skull & Dagger. Office: Cort MacKenzie 1000 SW Broadway Portland OR 97205-3035

STEWART, WILLIAM R., artist, painter, educator; b. Waco, Tex., Aug. 18, 1938; s. Joseph Haywood and Era (Orr) S. Student, North Tex. State U., Baylor U.; BFA, U. Tex., 1960, MFA, 1962. Asst. dir., instr. dept. edn. San Francisco Mus. Modern Art, 1963-64; instr. art Baleares Internat. Sch., Palma de Mallorca, Spain, 1966-67, Farleigh Dickinson U., Madison, N.J., 1968-70, CCNY, 1971; instr. dept. edn. Newark Mus., 1973-74; instr. drawing and painting Instituto Allende, San Miguel de Allende, Guanajuato, Mex., 1977-78; vis. artist dept. art and art history U. Iowa, Iowa City, 1981; founder, operator La Cumbre Studio Sch., Ranchos de Taos, N.Mex., 1983; artist in residence Old Jail Mus., Albany, Tex., 1985-86; instr. art Ctr. for Arts No. M.Mex. C.C., Española, 1990-91; art instr. Taos Children's Day Sch., 1991-93, Oo-Oonah Children's Art Ctr., Taos, 1992-93, Taos Edn. Ctr. No. N.Mex. C.C., 1992-93, Taos Inst. Arts, 1993-95, U. N.Mex., Taos, 1993—. One-man shows include Bolles Gallery, San Francisco, 1963, O.K. Harris Gallery, N.Y.C., 1969, Rudolph Zwirner Gallery, Cologne, Germany, 1970, Pergola Gallery, San Miguel de Allende, Guanajuato, Mex., 1978, Regional Mus., Oaxaca, Mex., 1979, Bannafont Gallery, San Francisco, 1979, Old Jail Art Mus., Albany, Tex., 1985, Joseph A. Imhof Room, Harwood Libr. and Mus., Taos, 1988; group shows at U. N.C., 1965, Newark Mus., 1971, Biennale de Paris, 1971, Thomas Moore Chapel Fordham U., Bronx, 1976, Charles Furr Gallery, Sante Fe, 1985, Stewart's Fine Arts, Taos, 1987, R.B. Raven Gallery, Ranchos de Taos, 1990, Bengert Macrae Gallery, Wyckoff, N.J., 1993-94; represented in permanent collections Mus. Modern Art, Vienna, Austria, Fordham U., Fairleigh Dickinson U., Madison, N.J. Home: 5257 NDCBU Taos NM 87511

STEZOSKI-RODRIGUEZ, LORISE ANN, critical care nurse, educator; b. Pitts., July 11, 1963; d. Walter and Pauline (Kurutz) S. ASN, Mt. San Antonio Coll., 1985; BSN, Calif. State U., L.A., 1987, postgrad., 1995. RN, Calif. Part-time mem. faculty Calif. State U., L.A.; staff nurse Huntington Meml. Hosp., Pasadena, Calif.; clin. edn. specialist Hosp. of the Good Samaritan, L.A.; mgr. staff devel. Healthcare Ptnrs. Mem. AACN, AACN, Sigma Theta Tau.

STICKLER, JOHN COBB, publisher, journalist, author; b. Washington, July 18, 1937; s. Joseph Harding and Virginia Murray (Cobb) S.; m. Lucy Han, 1964; children: Stephen Han, Alexander Han. BA with honors, Yale U., 1959; cert. Peace Corps, Pa. State U., 1961. Stringer CBS Radio News, Seoul, Republic of Korea, 1967-76; owner, mgr. S/K Internat. Advt., Seoul, 1966-76; pub., owner Jour. Applied Mgmt., Walnut Creek, Calif., 1978-81; account exec. Cunningham & Walsh, San Francisco, 1981; dir. mktg. Neighborhood Housing Services, Tucson, 1982; dir. pub. relations Sheraton Tucson El Conquistador Resort, 1983-92. Editor, pub.: Advertising in Korea, 1973, 2d revised edit., 1975; (poetry) Growing Up Afraid, 1985; contbr.: Exporting to Mexico, 1992, Berlitz American Southwest, 1993, Fodor's B&B Guide, Southwest, 1994; author: Exporting to the USA, 1992; contbr. numerous articles to mags. Served with U.S. Army, 1962-64. Recipient advt. prize Hotel Sales and Mktg. Assn., 1974, CLIO award, 1975, poetry award Nat. Writers Club, 1977, poetry award World Order Narrative Poets, 1978. Mem. Pub. Rels. Soc. Am. (pres. So. Ariz. chpt. 1991), Am. Soc. Journalists & Authors, Internat. Assn. Bus. Communicators (pres. Tucson chpt. 1985-86), Soc. Southwestern Authors (pres. 1988-90), UNESCO Assn. U.S.A. (bd. dirs. 1981—), Internat. Advt. Assn. (founder Korea chpt. 1967), Internat. Food, Wine and Travel Writers Assn., Soc. Am. Travel Writers, Royal Asiatic Soc. (Korea br.), Tucson Press Club, UN Assn. So. Ariz., Yale Club Tucson (v.p. 1988). Democrat. Office: PO Box 35220 Tucson AZ 85740-5220

STICKLES, BONNIE JEAN, nurse; b. Waukesha, Wis., Nov. 24, 1944; d. Donald William and Betty Jane S.; B.S. in Nursing, U. Wis., 1967; M.S. in Nursing, Midwifery, Columbia U., 1974. Mem. nursing staff Grace Hosp., Detroit, 1970-73; mem. faculty and staff U. Minn. Sch. Nursing and Nurse-Midwifery Svc., Mpls., 1974-76; chief nurse-midwife, clin. instr. St. Paul-Ramsey Med. Ctr., 1976-84; midwifery supr. IHS/PHS Chinle Hosp., 1984-85; program mgr. maternal health sect. N.Mex. Dept. Health and Environ., 1985-90; Lovelace Med. Ctr., 1990-91; St. Vincent's Hosp., 1991-94; NMC Dialysis Divsn., 1994-95; blackjack dealer, 1995—. Mem. FDA Anesthetics, Life Support Adv. Com.; adv. bd. Childbirth Edn. Assn., 1980-85. Served with USNR, 1965-70. Decorated Letter of Commendation. Mem. Am. Coll. Nurse-Midwives (chmn. profl. affairs com. 1975-80), Nurses Assn. Am. Coll. Obstetricians and Gynecologists (charter), Aircraft Owners and Pilots Assn., Gt. Plains Perinatal Orgn., Alpha Tau Delta. Author articles in field; patentee teaching model.

STICKNEY, DOUGLAS HENRY, biostatistician; b. Little Rock, Feb., 21, 1956; s. Henry E. and Delphine D. (Perse). B.S. in Biology, Davidson (N.C.) Coll., 1977; M.S. in Biostats., UCLA, 1980. Statis. cons. Gateways Hyperkinetic Research Clinic, Los Angeles, 1979-81; health care analyst Systemetrics Inc., Santa Barbara, Calif., 1980-81; statis. cons. Ventura (Calif.) County Air Quality Mgmt. Bur., 1982—; biostatistician Am. Edwards Labs., Irvine, Calif., 1980—, now with Quantum Health Resources, Inc. Mem. Am. Statis. Assn. Episcopalian. Contbr. articles to profl. jours. Office: Quantum Health Resources Inc 790 The City Dr S Orange CA 92668-4941

STICKNEY, JESSICA, former state legislator; b. Duluth, Minn., May 16, 1929; d. Ralph Emerson and Claudia Alice (Cox) Page; m. Edwin Levi Stickney, June 17, 1951; children: Claudia, Laura, Jeffrey. BA, Macalester Coll., St. Paul, Minn., 1951; PhD (hon), Rocky Mtn. Coll., Billings, Mont., 1986. Rep. State of Mont., 1989-92; mem. Gov.'s Commn. on Post-Sec. Edn., Mont., 1973-75. Mem. Sch. Bd. Trustees, Miles City, Mont., 1968-74; mem., chmn. zoning bd., Miles City, 1975-89; mem. Govt. Study Commn., Miles City, 1974-76, United Ch. Christ Bd. Homeland Ministries, 1975-81; chmn., conf. moderator United Ch. Christ Bd. Mont.-Northern Wyo. Conf., 1980-82; chmn. Town Meeting on the Arts, Mont., 1980; mem., chmn. Miles Community Coll. Bd., 1975-89, chmn. 1978-80. Mem. Mont. Arts Coun. (chmn. 1982-85), Western States Arts Found. (vice chmn. 1984), Nat. Assembly State Arts Agys. (bd. dirs. 1982-88), AAUW (pres. 1964-66). Democrat.

STICKNEY, PHILIP MICHAEL, accountant, educator; b. Columbus, Ohio, Sept. 9, 1949; s. Palmer Blaine and Esther Milton (Udell) S.; m. Michele Marie Lenihan, June 13, 1970. BS in Math. with high honors, Mich. State U., 1971; postgrad., U. Ariz., 1971-75; M in Acctg., Ohio State U., 1977. CPA, Ariz. Audit supr. Coopers & Lybrand, Tucson, 1977-82; mgr. strategic and fin. planning Burr-Brown Corp., Tucson, 1982-84; contr. P.F. West, Inc. & Lumber Country, Tucson, 1984-86; v.p. fin. Clifton Investment Co., Tucson, 1986-87; contr. Marston's Inc., Tempe, Ariz., 1987-88; acct. in pvt. practice, 1987, 88-89; dir. Community Campus, program coord. Small Bus. Devel. Ctr. Cochise Coll., Douglas and Sierra Vista, Ariz., 1989—. Formerly bd. dirs., treas., chmn. bd. Goodwill Industries of Tucson, Inc.; bd. dirs., v.p. Sierra Vista Econ. Devel. Found.; participant Gov.'s Conf. on Small Bus., 1993, Gov.'s Rural Devel. Conf., 1990-94. Mem. AICPA, Ariz. Soc. CPAs, Phi Kappa Phi, Pi Mu Epsilon, Phi Eta Sigma, Beta Alpha Psi. Home: 5539 S Shawnee Dr Sierra Vista AZ 85635-9639 Office: Cochise Coll 4190 W State Highway 80 Douglas AZ 85607-6100

STIEBER, TAMAR, writer; b. Bklyn., Sept. 15, 1955; d. Alfred and Florence (Spector) S. Student, Rockland C.C., 1972-75, Rockland C.C., 1972-75, West London (Eng.) Coll., 1973-74; BA in Film cum laude, U. Calif., Berkeley, 1985, postgrad., 1985-86; grad. police reserve academycum laude, Napa Valley Coll., 1988. Office mgr., confidential sec. AP, San Francisco, 1981-83; stringer Daily Californian, Berkeley, Calif., 1983-84; film rsch. teaching asst. U. California, Berkeley, 1984-86; libr. and rsch. asst. Pacific Film Archive, Berkeley, 1984-86; intern San Francisco Examiner, 1984; reporter Sonoma (Calif.) Index-Tribune, 1987-88, Vallejo (Calif.) Times Herald, 1988-89, Albuquerque Journal, 1989-94. Recipient Pulitzer prize for specialized reporting, 1990, first place pub. svc. divsn. N.Mex. Press Assn., 1990, pub. svc. award Albuquerque Press Club, 1990; first place newswriting N.Mex. Press Assn., 1991; honorable mention Assn. Press Managing Editors, 1994. Mem. Soc. Profl. Journalists, Investigative Reporters and Editors, N.M. Found. Open Govt., Phi Beta Kappa. Home: PO Box 9835 Santa Fe NM 87504-9835

STIENMIER, RICHARD HAROLD, pathologist; b. Ft. Collins., Colo., June 24, 1936; s. Harold and Agnes M. (Hannah) S.; m. Saundra K. Young, Dec. 20, 1958; children: Richard B., Susan I., Julia T., Laura S. BA cum laude, U. Colo., Boulder, 1958; MD, U. Colo., Denver, 1961. Diplomate Am. Bd. Pathology. Commd. 2d lt. Med. Svcs. Corp. U.S. Army, 1958, advanced through grades to col. Med. Svcs. Corp., ret., 1980; intern U. Cin., 1961-62; resident in pathology Fitzsimmons Army Med. Ctr., Denver, 1964-

68; chief pathology dept. Leonard Wood Hosp., Ft. Leonard Wood, Mo., 1968-69; pathologist Letterman Army Med. Ctr., San Francisco, 1970-72; chief pathology dept. William Beaumont Army Med. Ctr., El Paso, 1972-77; comdr. 10th Med. Lab. U.S. Army, Landstuhl, Germany, 1977-80; chief dept. pathology Ft. Carson Hosp., Colorado Springs, Colo., 1980-82; pathologist St. Francis Hosp., Colorado Springs, Colo., 1982-90, Porter Hosp., Denver, 1990—; cons. in pathology U.S. Army, Heidelburg, Germany, 1977-80. Contbr. articles to profl. jours. Decorated Soldier's medal, Legion of Merit, Meritorious Svc. medal. Fellow Coll. Am. Pathologists (state keyman 1992-94), Am. Soc. Clin. Pathologists; mem. AMA, AAAS, Am. Acad. Forensic Sci., Am. Assn. Blood Banks, Colo. State Med. Soc., Arapaho County Med. Soc., Nat. Assn. Med. Examiners, Assn. Mil. Surgeons of the U.S., Internat. Assn. Pathologists, Colo. Soc. Clin. Pathologists (pres. 1988-89), Flying Physicians Assn. Republican. Episcopalian. Home: 7955 Tangleoak Ln Castle Rock CO 80104-9299 Office: Porter Hosp Pathology Dept 2525 S Downing St Denver CO 80210-5817

STIENMIER, SAUNDRA KAY YOUNG, aviation educator; b. Abilene, Kans., Apr. 27, 1938; d. Bruce Waring and Helen E. (Rutz) Young; m. Richard H. Steinmier, Dec. 20, 1958; children: Richard, Susan, Julia, Laura. AA, Colo. Women's Coll., 1957; student, Temple Buell Coll., U. Colo., 1959, 69; ed., Embre Riddle Aviation U., Ramstein, Germany; student, Harriet-Watt U., Edinborough, Scotland. Cert. FAA pilot. Dir. Beaumont Gallery, El Paso, Tex., 1972-77; mem. grad. studies faculty Embre Riddle Aviation U., 1979-80; mgr. Ramstein Aero Club, USAF, 1977-80, Peterson Aero Club, USAF, Peterson AFB, Colo., 1980—. Named Outstanding S.W. Artist. Mem. AAUW, Order Eastern Star, Scottish Soc. Pikes' Peak, Scots Heritage Soc., Internat. Women Pilots Assn., Beta Sigma Phi, Delta Psi Omega, Aircraft Owners and Pilots Assn., Nat. Pilots Assn., Colo. PilotsAssn., Soc. Arts and Letters, 99's Club. Office: PO Box 14123 Colorado Springs CO 80914-0123

STIFEL, FREDERICK BENTON, pastor, biochemist, nutritionist; b. St. Louis, Jan. 30, 1940; s. Carl Gottfried and Alma J. (Clark) S.; m. Gail Joane Stewart, Aug. 10, 1963; children: Tim, Faith, Seth, Elizabeth. BS, Iowa State U., 1962, PhD, 1967; MDiv., Melodyland Sch. Theol., Anaheim, Calif., 1979. Ordained to ministry Evang. Presbyn. Ch., 1981. Lab. supr., research chemist U.S. Army Med. Research and Nutrition Lab., Denver, 1968-74, Letterman Army Inst. Research, San Francisco, 1974-76; intern pastor Melodyland Christian Ctr., Anaheim, 1979-80; assoc. pastor Faith Presbyn. Ch., Aurora, Colo., 1980—; chmn. care of candidates com. Presbytery of West, Denver, 1985-88, 91-94; bd. dirs., v.p. Love Inc. of Metro Denver, 1987-90; regional coord. Nat. Assn. Single Adult Leaders, 1987-90, coord. Denver area, 1990—; Colo. Pregnancy Ctrs., Inc., 1992-94, Rocky Mountain Prayer Network, 1994—, Christian Family Svcs., 1990—; bd. dirs. St. James Bible Coll., 1995—; mem. faculty St. James Bible Coll., Kiev, Ukraine. Contbr. clin. med. and nutritional articles to profl. jours. Del. Iowa State Rep. Conv., Denver, 1984; mem. parent adv. coun. IMPACT drug intervention team Rangeview High Sch., Aurora, 1985-89, accountability com., 1989—; mem. Friends of the Arts, 1992—; young life leader Hinkley High Sch., Aurora, 1968-74; vice chmn. Young Life Com., Marin County, Calif., 1974-76. Capt. U.S. Army Med. Svc. Corps, 1967-70. Ralston Purina Rsch. fellow, 1962-63; Borden Agrl. scholar, 1962; recipient Sci. Achievement award U.S. Army Sci. Conf., West Point, N.Y., 1968, 70, Parents of the Yr. award Rangeview High Sch., 1992-93. Mem. Am. Inst. Nutrition, Am. Soc. Clin. Nutrition, Am. Sci. Affiliation, Evang. Theol. Soc., Phi Eta Sigma, Phi Kappa Phi, Alpha Zeta, Gamma Sigma Delta, Kappa Sigma, Sigma Xi. Home: 3492 S Blackhawk Way Aurora CO 80014-3909 Office: Faith Presbyn Ch 11373 E Alameda Ave Aurora CO 80012-1023

STIFFLER, DANIEL FRANCIS, biology educator, researcher; b. Los Angeles, Nov. 27, 1942; s. Frank M. and Alice (Holsclaw) S.; m. Gail Helen Clark, June 30, 1967; children—Jason Daniel, Jared Warren, Peter Benjamin. B.A., U. Calif.-Santa Barbara, 1968; M.S., Oreg. State U., 1970, Ph.D., 1972. Instr. zoology Oreg. State U., Corvallis, 1970-72; postdoctoral trainee physiology U. Oreg. Med. Sch., Portland, 1972-74; lectr. physiology U. Calif.-Davis, 1974-75; prof. biology Calif. State Poly. U., Pomona, 1975—, assoc. dean sci., 1983-85. Contbr. articles in field to profl. jours. Served with U.S. Navy, 1960-63. Calif. State Poly. U. Kellogg Unit Found. grantee, 1980; Grantee NSF, 1981, 85, 87, Calif. State U.-Acad. Program Improvement, 1985. Mem. Am. Physiol. Soc., Am. Soc. Zoologists, Canadian Soc. Zoologists, Sigma Xi. Democrat. Office: Biol Scis Dept Calif State Poly Univ Pomona CA 91768

STIGLICH, JACOB JOHN, JR., engineering consultant; b. Milw., Dec. 21, 1938; s. Jacob John Sr. and Augusta (Prezel) S. BSME, Marquette U., 1961; PhD, Northwestern U., 1970. Chief engr. Boride Products, Traverse City, Mich., 1971-74; mgr. ceramic materials Valeron Corp., Madison Heights, Mich., 1974-76; group leader, asst. dir. tech. Eagle Picher, Miami, Okla., 1976-78; program mgr. San Fernando Lab., Pacoima, Calif., 1978-84; tech. specialist Aerojet Ordnance Co., Tustin, Calif., 1984-85; cons. Sierra Madre, Calif., 1985—. Contbr. articles to profl. jours.; patentee in field. Col. USAR, 1961-92. Mem. AIME, Am. Soc. Metals, Am. Ceramic Soc., Mensa, Sigma Xi.

STIGLITZ, JOSEPH EUGENE, economic adviser to President, educator; b. Gary, Ind., Feb. 9, 1943; s. Nathaniel David and Charlotte (Fishman) S.; m. Jane Hannaway, Dec. 23, 1978; children: Siobhan, Michael, Edward, Julia. B.A., Amherst Coll., Mass, 1964; DHL (hon.), Amherst Coll., 1974; Ph.D. in Econs., MIT, 1966; M.A. (hon.), Yale U., 1970; D in Econs. (hon.), U. Leuven, 1994. Prof. econs. Cowles Found., Yale U., New Haven, 1970-74; vis. fellow St. Catherine's Coll., Oxford, Eng., 1973-74; Joan Kenney professorship Stanford U., 1974-76, 88—; Oskar Morgenstern dist. fellow Inst. Advanced Studies Math., Princeton, N.J., 1978-79; Drummond prof. polit. economy Oxford U., Eng., 1976-79; prof. econs. Princeton U., 1979-88; mem. Pres.'s Coun. Econ. Advisers, 1993-95, chmn. council of econ. advisers, 1995—; cons. World Bank, State of Alaska, Seneca Indian Nation, Bell Communications Rsch. Editor Jour. Econ. Perspectives, 1986-93; Am. editor Rev. of Econ. Studies, 1968-76; assoc. editor Am. Econ. Rev., 1968-76, Energy Econs., Managerial and Decision Econs.; mem. editl. bd. World Bank Econ. Rev. Recipient John Bates Clark award Am. Econ. Assn., 1979, Internat. prize Accademia Lincei, 1988, Union des Assurances de Paris prize, 1989; Guggenheim fellow, 1969-70. Fellow Inst. for Policy Rsch. (sr. 1991-93), Brit. Acad. (corr.); mem. Am. Econ. Assn. (exec. com. 1982-84, v.p. 1985), Am. Acad. Arts and Scis., Nat. Acad. Sci., Econometric Soc.

STILLINGS, DENNIS OTTO, research director; b. Valley City, N.D., Oct. 30, 1942; s. Harlow Cecil and Ruth Alice (Wolff) S. BA, U. Minn., 1965. Tchr. Henry (S.D.) Pub. Schs., 1965-66, Darby (Mont.) Pub. Schs., 1966-68; tech. rsch. libr., then mgr. hist. dept. Medtronic, Inc., Mpls., 1968-79; instr. humanities U. Minn., Mpls., 1970-72; founding dir., then curator Bakken Libr., Mpls., 1976-80; ind. antiquarian hist. cons. Mpls., 1979-81; project dir. Archaeus Project, Kamuela, Hawaii, 1981—, v.p., 1989—; cons. Ctr. for Sci. Anomalies Rsch., Ann Arbor, Mich., 1983—; bd. dirs. Dan Carlson Enterprises, Mpls., Hawaii Ctr. Integral Healing. Columnist Med. Progress Through Technology, 1974—; columnist Med. Instrumentation, 1973-76, guest editor, 1975; editor: Cyberphysiology: The Science of Self-Regulation, 1988, Cyberbiological Studies of the Imaginal Component in the UFO Contact Experience, 1989, The Theology of Electricity: On the Encounter and Explanation of Theology and Science in the 17th and 18th Centuries, 1990, Project 2010: On the Current Crisis in Health and Its Implications For the Hospital For the Future, 1992; founding editor: (jours.) Artifex, 1981-93, Archaeus, 1982-84, Healing Island. Bd. dirs. Hawaii Ctr. for Integral Healing. Fellow Am. Inst. Stress; mem. Assn. Sci. Study Anomalous Phenomena, Bioelectromagnetics Soc., Soc. Sci. Exploration.

STILLMAN, GEORGE, artist; b. Laramie, Wyo., Feb. 25, 1921; s. Herman and Estelle (Heimlich) S.; m. Lillian Lucille Blitz, Dec. 1, 1942; children: David, Anthony. Cert. of completion, Calif. Sch. Fine Art, 1949; MFA, Ariz. State U., 1970. Prof. art U. Gudadalajara, Mex., 1950-51; chief map reprodn. Inter Am. Geodetic Survey U.S. Army, Panama C.Z., 1951-58; comm. officer AID, L.Am., 1958-66; prodr. and dir. TV, Ariz. State U., Tempe, 1966-70; chmn. art dept. Columbus (Ga.) Coll., 1970-72; prof., chmn. dept. Ctrl. Wash. U., Ellensburg, 1972-88, prof. emeritus, 1988—. One-man shows include Guild Gallery, San Francisco, 1947, Lucien Labaudt Gallery, San Francisco, 1949, Ariz. State U. Mus., Tempe, 1970, Foster/White Gallery, Seattle, 1986, Ctrl. Wash. U., Ellensburg, 1991; exhibited in group shows at Palace of the Legion of Honor, San Francisco, 1947, San Francisco Mus. Art, 1949, Bklyn. Mus. Art, 1952, Ga. Artists, High Mus., Atlanta, 32d Spokane (Wash.) Ann. Nat., 1980, Art for the Parks, Jackson, Wyo., 1989, 100 Yrs. of Washington Art, Tacoma, Wash., 1990, Art Mus. Santa Cruz, Calif., 1993; represented in permanent collections Met. Mus. Art, N.Y.C., Nat. Mus. Am. Art, Smithsonian, Washington, Oakland (Calif.) Mus. Art, High Mus. Art, Atlanta, Tacoma Mus. Art, Washington State Arts Commn., British Mus. Art, London, Laguna (Calif.) Mus. Art, Worcester (Mass.) Mus. Art. Recipient Bender award Western States Fedn., 1949, Nat. Endowment for Arts, 1990. Mem. Coll. Art Assn. Home: 1127 Franklin St Ellensburg WA 98926-3277

STILLWELL, KATHLEEN ANN SWANGER, healthcare consultant; b. Glendale, Calif., Aug. 12, 1950; d. Robert Dowayne and Irene Margaret (Sawatzky) Swanger; m. Joseph Wayne Stillwell, Nov. 11, 1971; children: Shannon Kristine, Nathan Joseph. AA, Cypress Coll., 1971; AS & diploma, Golden West Coll., 1981; BA in English Lit., Long Beach State U., 1982; MPA, Health Svcs. Adminstrn., U. San Francisco, 1989. RN Calif. Staff nurse Long Beach (Calif.) Meml. Hosp., 1981-84; sr. claims analyst Caronia Corp., Tustin, Calif., 1984-87; dir. quality assurance & risk mgmt. St. Mary Med. Ctr., Long Beach, 1987-89; cons. quality assurance, risk mgmt. Am. Med. Internat., Costa Mesa, Calif., 1989-91; cons. healthcare, 1991—; adj. faculty U. San Francisco; faculty Am. Soc. Healthcare Risk Mgrs. Cert. Program; v.p. Patient Care Assessment Coun., L.A., 1988-89, pres., 1989-90, bd. dirs.; pres. State Bd. Patient Care Coun., 1990-92, past pres., 1992-94; speaker in field. Vol. Calif. Health Decisions, Orange County, 1989—, PTA, Am. Cancer Soc., Patient Care Assessment Coun.; active Constnl. Rights Found.; mem. edn. com. Bus. in Soc. Mem. NLN, Am. Soc. Healthcare Risk Mgmt., Nat. Assn. Healthcare Quality (exec. fin. com. 1993-95), Am. Soc. Quality Control Profls. (sec. healthcare divsn. 1995—, chair membership 1994-95), Am. Soc. Healthcare Risk Mgrs., So. Calif. Assn. Healthcare Risk Mgrs. (sec. 1989-90, mem. chmn. 1989-90), Calif. League for Nurses (bd. dirs. 1993-95), Patient Care Assessment Coun. (v.p. So. Calif. 1988, pres. So. Calif. 1989-90, state bd. pres. 1990-92, state bd. dirs. 1992-94). Democrat. Lutheran. Home and Office: 825 Coastline Dr Seal Beach CA 90740-5810

STILMAN, BORIS, computer science educator, researcher; b. Moscow, Aug. 16, 1950; came to the U.S., 1991.; s. Mikhail and Raisa (Gurevich) S.; m. Zinaida Korenblat, July 11, 1979; 1 child, Michael. MS in Math., Moscow State U., 1972; PhD in Elec. Engring., All-Union Rsch. Inst. Elec. Engring., Moscow, 1984, PhD in Computer Sci., 1984. Sr. engr., mathematician dept. for complex search problems The All-Union Rsch. Inst. for Elec. Engring., Moscow, 1972-75, sr. scientist dept. for complex search problems, 1975-85, sr. scientist/group leader dept. for complex search problems, 1985-88; chief dept. for software design computer tech. divsn. The All-Union Rsch. Geol. Inst. for Oil Devel., Moscow, 1988-90, prin. software designer Inst. Designers Coun., 1988-90; vis. prof. McGill U., Sch. Computer Sci., Montreal, 1990-91; assoc. prof. computer sci. dept. computer sci. and engring. U. Colo., Denver, 1991-94, prof. computer sci. dept. computer sci. and engring., 1994—; sci. sec. The USSR Acad. Scis. All-Union Commn., 1981-88; local divsn. chief, prof. computer sci. The USSR Acad. Scis. Temporary Rsch. Group, Moscow, 1985-89; presenter in field. Author: Programming Within Structured Frame of Algorithmic Language, 1988, Theory of Linguistic Geometry in the Field of Artificial Intelligence; contbr. articles to profl. books and articles to profl. jours.; reviewer Annals of Math. and Artificial Intelligence, IBM Sys. Jour., Jour. of Intelligent Mfg., others. Recipient The USSR Acad. Scis. and Dept. Geology Joint Rsch. grant, 1988, The USSR Acad. Scis. Rsch. grant, 1988, U. Colo. Denver Faculty Grant award, 1993, others. Mem. IEEE Computer Soc., Assn. for Computing Machinery, Am. Assn. for Artificial Intelligence. Office: U Colo Denver Dept Computer Sci & Engring PO Box 109 Denver CO 80210

STILSON, WALTER LESLIE, radiologist, educator; b. Sioux Falls, S.D., Dec. 13, 1908; s. George Warren and Elizabeth Margaret (Zager) S.; m. Grace Beall Bramble, Aug. 15, 1933 (dec. June 1984); children: Carolyn G. Palmieri, Walter E., Judith A. Stirling; m. Lula Ann Birchel, June 30, 1985. BA, Columbia Union Coll., 1929; MD, Loma Linda U., 1934. Diplomate Am. Bd. Radiology, Nat. Bd. Med. Examiners. Intern White Meml. Hosp., Los Angeles, 1933-34; resident radiology Los Angeles County Gen. Hosp., 1934-36; instr. radiology Loma Linda (Calif.) U. Sch. Medicine, 1935-41, asst. prof., 1941-49, exec. sec. radiology, 1945-50, assoc. prof., 1949-55, head dept. radiology, 1950-55, prof. radiology, 1955-83, chmn. dept. radiology, 1955-69, emeritus prof., 1983—; chief radiology service White Meml. Hosp., Los Angeles, 1941-65, Loma Linda U. Med. Ctr., 1966-69; chmn. dept. radiologic tech. Sch. Allied Health Professions, 1966-75, med. dir. dept. radiologic tech., 1975-83. Contbr. articles to health jours. Fellow Am. Coll. Radiology; mem. AAAS, Los Angeles Radiol. Soc. (sec. 1960-61, treas. 1961-62, pres. 1963-64), Radiol. Soc. N.Am., Am. Roentgen Ray Soc., N.Y. Acad. Sci., Inland Radiol. Soc. (pres. 1971), Alpha Omega Alpha. Republican. Adventist. Home: 25045 Crestview Dr Loma Linda CA 92354-3414 Office: Loma Linda Radiol Med Group 11234 Anderson St Loma Linda CA 92354-2804

STINI, WILLIAM ARTHUR, anthropologist, educator; b. Oshkosh, Wis., Oct. 9, 1930; s. Louis Alois and Clara (Larsen) S.; m. Mary Ruth Kalous, Feb. 11, 1950; children—Patricia Laraine, Paulette Ann, Suzanne Kay. B.B.A., U. Wis., 1960, M.S., 1967, Ph.D., 1969. Planner cost acct. Kimberly-Clark Corp., Niagara Falls, N.Y., 1960-62; asst. prof. Cornell U., Ithaca, N.Y., 1968-71, assoc. prof., 1971-73; assoc. prof. U. Kans., Lawrence, 1973-76; prof. anthropology U. Ariz., Tucson, 1976—; head dept. anthropology U. Ariz., 1980-89; panelist anthropology program NSF, 1976-78; cons. NIH, 1974—; mem. Ariz. Cancer Ctr., 1994—; panelist NRC/NSF Grad. Fellowship Program, 1991—. Author: Ecology and Human Adaptation, 1975, Nature, Culture and Human History - A Biocultural Introduction to Anthropology (with Davydd J. Greenwood), 1977, Physiological and Morphological Adaptation and Evolution, 1979 (with Frank E. Poirier and Kathy B. Wreden) In Search of Ourselves: An Introduction to Physical Anthropology, 1990, 5th edit., 1994; field editor phys. anthropology The Am. Anthropologist, 1980-83; editor-in-chief Am. Jour. Phys. Anthropology, 1983-89; assoc. editor Nutrition and Cancer, 1981-95; cons. editor Collegium Antropologicum, 1985—. Mem. Gov.'s Adv. Council on Aging, State of Ariz., 1980-83. Nat. Inst. Dental Rsch. tng. grantee, 1964-68; Clark Found. grantee, Cornell U., 1973; Nat. Dairy Coun. grantee, 1985-88; Wenner-Gren Found. grantee, 1991—; fellow Linacre Coll., Oxford, 1985; vis. fellow U. London, 1991. Fellow AAAS (steering group sect. H 1987-91), Am. Anthrop. Assn., N.Y. Acad. Scis.; mem. Am. Assn. Phys. Anthropologists (exec. com. 1978-81, pres. 1989-91), Soc. for Study Human Biology, Human Biology Coun. (exec. com. 1978-81), Soc. for Study Social Biology, Am. Inst. Nutrition, Am. Soc. on Aging, Sigma Xi. Home: 6240 N Camino Miraval Tucson AZ 85718-3025 Office: U Ariz Dept Anthropology Tucson AZ 85721

STINNETT, LEIA ANN, publisher; b. Woodland, Calif., Oct. 17, 1945; d. Edward Myron and Anna Lois (Dodds) Dryden; m. Douglas Merle Stinnett, Dec. 5, 1992; children: Patric Aaron, Christina Marie. Cert., Integrative Therapy Sch., Sacramento, Calif., 1988-90; DD, Universal Life Ch., Modesto, Calif., 1989. Sec. State of Calif., Sacramento, 1965-74; owner Green's Secretarial Svc., Sacramento, 1974-78, Printing Factory, Sacramento, 1978-86, Sun River Graphics, Sacramento, 1980-88, Integrative Therapy, Sacramento, 1988-91, Crystal Journeys Pub., Sedona, Ariz., 1991—. Author, pub.: (book series for children) Little Angel Books, 1990—, (newsletter) Rainbow Bridge to Light, 1992—, (teaching manual) Circle of Angels Teaching Manual, 1989—; creator spiritual classes for children: Circle of Angels, 1988—. Participant World Clay Stomp, Flagstaff, Ariz., 1993; sponsor Futures & Children Internat., N.Mex., responsibility The Children's Ark and Tibetan Children's Fund, 1992—. Office: Crystal Journeys Pub 3225 White Bear Rd Sedona AZ 86336

STINSON, AVIVA JOCHEBED, psychosocial nurse; b. Jerusalem, Palestine, Mar. 21, 1933; came to U.S., 1957; d. Solomon Isaac and Sarah (Dossik) Ostrovsky; m. Lawrence William Stinson, Jan. 19, 1956; children: Teresa Louise, Lawrence William Jr., John Durant. BS, U. Wash., 1981; MS, U. Alaska, 1987; postgrad., U. Minn., 1990-91. RN, Alaska, Wash., Minn., Ill.; cert. clin. specialist in adult psychiat. and mental health nursing; cert. advanced nurse practitioner. Staff nurse Paxton (Ill.) Gen. Hosp., 1957-58; staff nurse, head nurse Mercy Hosp., Urbana, Ill., 1966-72; staff nurse Guam (Micronesia) Meml. Hosp., 1973-74, Fairbanks (Alaska) Meml. Hosp., 1975-78, Swedish Hosp., Seattle, 1980-81; supr. nurse detox Fairbanks Native Assn., 1981-83; psychosocial nurse, therapist Fairbanks Psychiatric & Neurol. Clinic, Fairbanks, 1985-94; advanced nurse practitioner, psychotherapist Fairbanks, Alaska, 1994—. Bd. dirs. Child Abuse Task Force, Fairbanks, 1982-90, Fairbanks Cmty. Mental Health Ctr., 1985-90, 92-94. Mem. ANA (pres. Dist. IV 1986-89), Alaskan Nurses Assn. Home: 573 Slater Dr Fairbanks AK 99701-3444 Office: 250 Cushman St Ste 5 Fairbanks AK 99701-4640

STIRLING, ISABEL ANN, science librarian; b. San Jose, Calif., Dec. 4, 1948; d. James H. and Betty Stirling. BA, U. Calif., Riverside, 1970; MLS, Western Mich. U., 1977. Head bio-agrl. library U. Calif., Riverside, 1977-82; head sci. libr., prof. U. Oreg., Eugene, 1982—. Author: Self-Paced Library Instruction Workbook for the Sciences, 1981; contbr. articles to jours. Mem. ALA (Libr./Book fellow Ankara, Turkey 1988-89), Assn. Coll. and Rsch. Libr. of ALA (various coms.), Internat. Fedn. Libr. Assn., Oreg. Library Assn. Office: U Oreg Sci Library Eugene OR 97403-5201

STIRM, EUGENE ROBERT, sculptor; b. Portland, Oreg., Jan. 6, 1945; s. Robert Adolf and Matilda Herminia (Niehaus) S.; m. Patricia Dale Button; Feb. 25, 1972; children: Malinda, Daniel, Mark. AA in Fine Arts, West Valley Coll., Campbell, Calif., 1965; postgrad., San Jose State Coll., 1965-66; BA in Comml. Art, N. Am. Coll., 1969; cert., Word of Faith Bible Coll., Dallas, 1983. Ordained minister of the Gospel. Art dir. Joston's Pub. Co., Visalia, Calif., 1972-76; owner, prin. Word Print Shop, Ivanhoe, Calif., 1976-79; freelance artist Orange County, Calif., 1979-85; pastor Christ's Love Fellowship Ch., Corina, Calif., 1980-85; gen. mgr. Menu Printers Inc., Orange, Calif., 1985-87; v.p., ptnr. Stirm/Collins & Assocs., Inc., Anaheim, Calif., 1987-91; gen. mgr. Artco Printers, Anaheim, 1991-95; lectr. in field. Author: Israel, Is Your Fig Tree Budding?, 1978; designer menus Plaza Hotel; executed mural Yorba Linda, Calif., Yorba Linda C. of C., 1991; contbr. art work to profl. jours. Founder, Coarsegold (Calif.) Artist Assn., 1972-74; advisor Yorba Linda (Calif.) Light Opera, 1988-90. Recipient Fine Arts award Bank of Am., 1963, Strathmore Graphics Gallery Gold award, 1989. Mem. Printing Industry Am., Am. Orchid Soc. (editor newsletter 1984). Republican. Presbyterian. Home and Studio: 4665 School St Yorba Linda CA 92686-2441

STIVERS, WILLIAM CHARLES, forest products company executive; b. Modesto, Calif., June 22, 1938; s. William P. and Helen Louise (Cummings) S.; m. Karen L. Gaspar, Aug. 6, 1961; children: William, Gregory, Michael, Kristy, Kelly, John, Jeffrey. BA, Stanford, 1960; MBA, U. So. Calif., 1963; certificate, U. Wash., 1969; grad., Advanced Mgmt. Program, Harvard U., 1977. Asst. cashier, asst. v.p., v.p. First Interstate Bank, San Francisco and Los Angeles, 1962-70; finance mgr. treas. dept. Weyerhaeuser Co., Tacoma, 1970; asst. treas. Weyerhaeuser Co., 1971, treas., 1972—, v.p., 1980-91, sr. v.p., chief fin. officer, 1991—; treas. Weyerhaeuser Real Estate Co., 1970; bd. dirs., exec. com. mem. Protection Mut. Ins. Co., Park Ridge, Ill.; bd. dirs., audit com. mem. 1st Interstate Bank; bd. dirs., pres. S&S Land and Cattle Co.; nat. adv. bd. mem. Chem. Banking Corp. Chmn. bd. trustees St. Francis Community Hosp., Federal Way; bd. dirs. Ctr. Study Banking and Fin. Mkts. U. Wash., Seattle; fin. mgmt. com. mem. Am. Forest and Paper Assn. Mem. Financial Execs. Inst.

STOBER, MASON FREDERICK, JR., retired air traffic control educator; b. Washington, Mar. 8, 1929; s. Mason Frederick and Georgiana Butler (Joyes) S.; m. Dolores Sylvia Determan, Apr. 18, 1950; children: Mason Frederick III, Mary Catherine. BBS, N.H. Coll., 1968. Lic. air traffic controller, FAA. Enlisted USAF, 1947, advanced through grades to major; grad. to 2d lt. Officer Candidate Sch., 1956; navigator, bombardier B-52D USAF, 1956-70, ret., 1970; air traffic controller Boston Air Route Traffic Control Ctr., Nashua, N.H., 1970-87; instr. Seattle Air Rt. Traffic Control Ctr., Auburn, Wash., 1987-94. Decorated DFC, Air medal with nine oak leaf clusters. Mem. Res. Officers Assn. (life, past pres. Nashua chpt.), Nat. Geog. Soc., Alaska Geog. Soc., Am. Legion, VFW, Mil. Order of World Wars, Air Force Assn., Air Force Hist. Soc., U.S. Curling Assn. (Granite Curling Club), AARP, KC (Grand Knight Nashua coun. 5472, 1972-73, 82-83, coun. activity dir. N.H. state coun. 1974-76, state program dir. 1976-78, cmty. activity dir. 1979-81, state program dir. N.H.), Kiwanis (past pres. Greater Fed. Way chpt. 1993-94), Smokey's. Home: 2622 SW 320th Pl Federal Way WA 98023-2268

STOCKDALE, RONALD ALLEN, grocery company executive; b. Aplington, Iowa, Apr. 28, 1934; s. Carl Robert and Mildred Louise (Gerhardt) S.; m. Carol Ann Hermeier, Dec. 23, 1956; children—Bryan Ross, Russell Allen, Paul Roderick. B.S. in Commerce, State U. Iowa, 1958. C.P.A. Auditor Arthur Andersen & Co., Chgo., 1958-63; controller Super Food Services, Bellefontaine, Ohio, 1963-66, Mountain States Wholesale Co., Boise, Idaho, 1966-69; exec. v.p., sec. West Coast Grocery Co., Tacoma, 1969-82, pres., COO, 1982-87, CEO, 1988—; bd. dirs. Profit Sharing Council Am., Chgo., 1977-83. Trustee Humana Hosp.-Tacoma, 1985-87, San Francisco Theol. Sem., 1987—; mem. adv. bd. Sch. Bus. Adminstrn., Pacific Luth. U., 1986—. Served with U.S. Army, 1954-56. Mem. AICPA, Fin. Execs. Inst. Republican. Presbyterian. Home: 2720 Soundview Dr W Tacoma WA 98466-1700 Office: W Coast Grocery Co 1525 E D St Tacoma WA 98421-1609

STOCKING, SHERL DEE, retail executive; b. Boise, Idaho, Aug. 20, 1945; s. Parley Dean and Iola Merrill (Linford) S.; m. Debra Lynn Hunt, Sept. 5, 1982. BS, Brigham Young U., 1968. Automotive specialist Bradshaw Auto Parts, Provo, Utah, 1964-68, J.C. Penney Co., Salt Lake City, 1969-70; store mgr. Uniroyal Tire Co., Salt Lake City, 1970-71; corp. tng. coordinator Uniroyal Tire Co., Houston, 1971, corp. advt. coordinator, 1972; store supr. Uniroyal Tire Co., Norfolk, Va., 1973-76; mgr. automotive dept. K-Mart Corp., Rapid City, S.D., 1976-79; dist. mgr. automotive dept. K-Mart Corp., N.Mex., 1979-80; mgr. Service Mdse. subs. K-Mart Corp., Denver, 1980-88; pres., owner S. & H. Svcs. Inc., Denver, 1988—. Pres. Quail Crossing Homeowner Assn., Denver, 1986—. Mem. Samuel Hall Soc. Mormon. Home: 115 146th St SE Lynnwood WA 98037-6711 Office: 4779 Lincoln St Denver CO 80216-2725

STOCKLAND, ALAN E., microbiology educator; b. Huron, S.D., July 18, 1938; s. C.O. and B.L. (Dawes) S.; m. Pak Moi Lim, Sept. 14, 1968; children: Brian, Tanya. BA/BS, U. Nebr., 1961; MSc, Mich. State U., 1967, PhD, 1970. Tchr. U.S. Peace Corps., Kuantan, Malaysia, 1962-63; prof. Weber State U., Ogden, Utah, 1970—. Office: Weber State U Dept Microbiology Ogden UT 84408

STOCKTON, DAVID KNAPP, professional golfer; b. San Bernardino, Calif., Nov. 2, 1941; s. Gail Rufus and Audrey (Knapp) S.; m. Catherine Fay Hales, Feb. 27, 1965; children—David Bradley, Ronald Edwin. B.S. in Gen. Mgmt., U. So. Calif., 1964. Mem. Golf's All Am. Team, 1974-76. Republican. Roman Catholic. Club: Elk. Office: 32373 Tres Lagos St Mentone CA 92359-9611*

STOCKTON, RODERICK ALAN, chemist; b. Lafayette, La., Jan. 18, 1951; s. Herbert Raymond and Olivet (Smith) S.; m. Pamela Sue Jones, Aug. 1, 1981 (div. 1992). BS, Stephen F. Austin State U., Nacogdoches, Tex., 1974; PhD, Tex. A&M U., College Station, 1985. Rsch. assoc. Tex. A&M U., College Station, 1975-85; sr. chemist Midwest Rsch. Inst., Kansas City, Mo., 1985-87, EG&G Idaho, Idaho Falls, 1987-89; prin. chemist Westinghouse Hanford Co., Richland, Wash., 1989-92; owner SLR Systems, Richland, 1992—; owner Stockton Consulting Svc., Richland, 1990-92. Contbr. articles to profl. jours. Welch Found. fellow. Mem. Am. Chem. Soc. Home: PO Box 1265 Richland WA 99352-1265 Office: SLR Systems 3100 George Washington Way Richland WA 99352-1663

STOCKWELL, SHELLEY LESSIN, writer, hypnotherapist; b. Torrance, Calif., Mar. 7, 1945; d. I. M. Lessin and E. Kapilese. Cert. hypnotist, Hypnosis Inst., Glendale, Calif., 1981, cert. hypnotherapist, 1982; cert. advanced hypnotherapist, Wenatchee Wellness Inst., 1990; DD (hon.), Am. Fellowship Ch., 1989. Cert. transpersonal hypnotherapist. CEO, writer, hypnotherapist, motivational speaker Creativity Unlimited Press, Rancho Palos Verdes, Calif., 1979—, artist, 1989—. Author: Insides Out, 1982, Sex and Other Touchy Subjects, 1991 (Gift of Yr. award 1991), Time Travel: Do-It-Yourself Past Life, 1992, Denial Is Not a River in Egypt: Overcome Depression and Addiction, 1995, Automatic Writing and Hiero-Scripting: How to Tap My Creativity and Guidance, 1995; star: (TV show) The Shelley Show, 1989. Recipient Angel award for Outstanding Cable TV Show, 1990; named Woman of Distinction Soroptimist Internat., 1990. Mem. Nat. Guild Hypnotists, Nat. Speakers Assn., Pubs. Mktg. Assn., Assn. Past Life Therapies, Toastmasters Internat. (pres. 1983—, Toastmaster of Yr. 1983, 84), Assn. Councilors and Therapists. Address: c/o Creativity Unltd 30819 Casilina Rancho Palos Verdes CA 90274

STOCKWELL, SHERWOOD BEACH, architect; b. Winchester, Mass., Nov. 15, 1926; s. Ernest Farnham and Beatrice Burr (Beach) S.; m. Mary Cameron; children: Mary Stockwell Morris, Lisa Stockwell Kessler, Pamela, Sherwood, Kate. BArch, MIT, 1949. With Anderson-Nichols, Boston, 1947-53, Stoner Assocs., Boston, 1953-56, Anshen & Allen, San Francisco, 1956-61; prin. Volkmann & Stockwell, 1961-68, Bull, Volkmann, Stockwell, 1968-90, Bull Stockwell & Allen, San Francisco, 1990-93, Bull Stockwell Allen & Ripley, San Francisco, 1993—; commr. city planning San Francisco, 1967-68; advisor San Francisco Urban Design Study, 1968-69; dir. San Francisco Planning and Urban Renewal, 1968-74; mem. adv. com. State of Calif. Hwy. Commn., 1969; mem. legis. com. on seismic safety State of Calif., 1970-74. Principal works include Ford Motor Co. Office and Parts Depot, Richmond, Calif. (Am. Inst. Steel Constrn. award 1967), Venetian Gardens, Stockton, Calif. (Record Apt. of the Yr. 1977, Bay Area Honor award 1978), McDonald's at Stanford Shopping Ctr., Palo Alto, Calif. (AIA award 1981), Marin County Regional Libr., Fairfax, Calif. (AIA Honor award 1983), Stillwater Cove Resort, Crystal Bay, Nev. (AIA Cedar Shingle Bur. award 1985), Spanish Bay Resort, Pebble Beach, Calif. (AIA Monterey chpt. Honor award 1988), Syntex Evergreen Campus Competition (winner), Kirkwood (Calif.) Meadows Lodge, Keystone Mountain Ski Resort, Colo. Spanish Bay Club, Pebble Beach, Calif., numerous pvt. residencies, others; contbr. numerous articles to profl. jours. Bd. dirs. The Guardsmen, 1962-65; mem. Coun. for the Arts, MIT, 1975-81. Grantee NEA, 1971, 75, Dept. Energy, 1979-80. Fellow AIA (trustee edn. found. San Francisco chpt. 1977-79).

STODDARD, ARTHUR GRANT, pilot; b. Twin Falls, Idaho, Jan. 8, 1947; s. Donald and Merle (Nelson) S.; m. Elfriede Anna Elizabeth Laburda, Apr. 22, 1978; 1 child, Ryan Erich. BS, U. Utah, 1969. Field worker Cornelli Seed Co., Twin Falls, 1963-69; stream guard Dept. Fish and Game, State of Alaska, Anchorage, 1967-69; mill cutter Jackalot Logging Camp, Homer, Alaska, 1969; counselor YWCA Kokokahi, Kailua, Hawaii, 1968; waiter Rustler Lodge, Alta, Utah, 1966-69; pilot Sky Valley Aviation, Minden, Nev., 1970-71, Fairbanks (Alaska) Air Svc., 1972-74, Wien Air Alaska, Anchorage, 1974-84, Hawaiian Air, Honolulu, 1986—. Mem. Airline Pilots Assn. Home: 2825 S King St Apt 601 Honolulu HI 96826-3533

STOEBUCK, WILLIAM BREES, law educator; b. Wichita, Kans., Mar. 18, 1929; s. William Douglas and Donice Beth (Brees) S.; m. Mary Virginia Fields, Dec. 24, 1951; children: Elizabeth, Catherine, Caroline. B.A., Wichita State U., 1951; M.A., Ind. U., 1953; J.D., U. Wash., 1959; S.J.D., Harvard U., 1973. Bar: Wash. 1959, U.S. Supreme Ct. 1967. Pvt. practice, Seattle, 1959-64; asst. prof. law U. Denver, 1964-67; assoc. prof. U. Wash., Seattle, 1967-70, prof., 1970—; of counsel Karr, Tuttle, Campbell, Seattle, 1988—. Author: Washington Real Estate: Property Law, 1995, Washington Real Estate: Transactions, 1995, Basic Property Law, 1989, Law of Property, 1984, 2d edit., 1993; Nontrespassory Takings, 1977; contbr. articles to legal jours. Bd. dirs. Cascade Symphony Orch., 1978-83, Forest Park Libr., 1975-80. Mem. Am. Coll. Real Estate Lawyers, Am. Coll. Mortgage Attys., Wash. State Bar Assn., Assn. Am. Law Schs., Order of Coif, Seattle Yacht Club. 1st lt. USAF, 1951-56. Home: 3515 NE 158th Pl Seattle WA 98155-6649 Office: U Wash Sch Law 1100 NE Campus Pky Seattle WA 98105-6605

STOEN, J. THOMAS, energy company executive, land developer, investor; b. Milw., June 20, 1939; s. Joel A. and Lucile V. (Oliver) S.; m. Sara Peterson (div. 1980); children: Eric Thomas, Erin Kristen. BA, Wheaton (Ill.) Coll., 1961. V.p. Columbia Savs., Denver, 1964-72; pres. Crown Properties, Denver, 1972-74, Columbia Corp., Denver, 1972-74, Cimmaron Corp., Colorado Springs, Colo., 1974-79; chmn. Pacific Energy and Minerals Ltd., Colorado Springs, 1979-87; pres. Remington Oil and Gas Co., 1986—. Served to lt. U.S. Army, 1961-64. Mem. Garden of Gods Club, Broadmoor Golf Club. Clubs: Garden of the Gods, Broadmoor Golf (Colorado Springs). Home: 44 Polo Dr Colorado Springs CO 80906-3144 Office: 2 N Cascade # 580 Holly Sugar Blvd Colorado Springs CO 80903

STOFFEL, KAREN MARIE, nursing coordinator; b. L.A., June 19, 1959; d. John Vincent and Muriel Anita (Rios) Hamman; m. Robert John Stoffel, May 7, 1988. BSN, Calif. State U., 1986. Critical care nurse L.A. County and U.Southern Calif. Med. Ctr., L.A., 1982-88, nurse mgr., 1988-92, nurse coord. info., 1992—. Mem. AACN. Office: LA County Med Ctr 1200 N State St Los Angeles CA 90033-4525

STOGSDILL, ROBIN LYNN, horse trainer, barn manager and owner; b. Springfield, Oreg., Aug. 26, 1961; d. George Lewis and Rhoda Leigh (Harris) Clingan; m. William Carlos Stogsdill, Nov. 9, 1987; children: Destini Shanaé, Cody William, Mikayla Lynne. Student, U. Valencia, Spain, 1978. Cashier, sales clk. Pacific N.W. Bell, Seattle, 1980-81; dance instr. pvt. studio, Albuquerque, 1982-83; model Models Inc, Santa Fe and Albuquerque, 1982-83; cashier K-Mart, Springfield, Oreg., 1983-84; bartender, card rm. mgr. Quarter Deck, Eugene, 1985-86; horse trainer, barn owner Clear Lake Stables, Eugene, 1992—; tchr. aide Irving Elem. Sch., 1993—; vol. horse trainer U. Oreg. Equestrian Team, 1992—. Democrat. Christian. Home: 90161 Lakeview Dr Eugene OR 97402-9424

STOJANIK, KATHRYN ANN, car accounting manager; b. Portland, Oreg., Oct. 24, 1954; d. Alfred Frank and Naomi Rose (Wolf) S. BSBA, Portland State U., 1977. Gen. collections asst. Nat. Assn. Credit Mgmt., Portland, Oreg., 1972-77; jr. acct. Precision Castparts Corp., Milwaukie, Oreg., 1977-86; sr. acct. Greenbrier Leasing Corp., Lake Oswego, Oreg., 1986-89, supr. car hire acctg., 1989-92, mgr. car acctg., 1992—. Democrat. Roman Catholic. Office: Greenbrier Leasing Corp One Centerpointe Dr Ste 200 Lake Oswego OR 97035

STOLLER, CLAUDE, architect; b. N.Y.C., Dec. 2, 1921; s. Max and Esther (Zisblatt) S.; m. Anna Maria Oldenburg, June 5, 1946 (div. Oct. 1972); children: Jacob, Dorothea, Elizabeth; m. Rosemary Raymond Lax, Sept. 22, 1978. Student, Black Mountain Coll., N.C., 1942; M.Arch., Harvard U., 1949. Architect Architects Collaborative, Cambridge, Mass., after 1949, Shepley, Bulfinch, Richardson & Abbot, Boston, 1951; co-founder, partner firm Marquis & Stoller, San Francisco, 1956; pvt. practice architecture N.Y.C. and San Francisco, 1974-78; founder, partner Stoller/Partners, Berkeley, Calif., 1978, Stoller, Knoerr Architects, 1988—; mem. faculty Washington U., St. Louis, 1955-56, U. Calif., Berkeley, 1957-91, prof. architecture, 1968—, acting chmn. dept., 1965-66, chair grad. studies, 1984-91; mem. Berkeley Campus Design Rev. Bd., 1985-91, chmn., 1992-93; commr. Calif. Bd. Archtl. Examiners, 1980-90, mem. exam. com., 1985-88; mem. diocesan commn. architecture Episcopal Diocese Calif., 1961—; vis. architect Nat. Design Inst., Ahmedabad, India, 1963; planning commr. City of Mill Valley, 1961-66; planning commnr. Marin County Planning Commn., 1966-67; mem. pub. adv. panel archtl. services GSA, 1969-71; citizens urban design adv. com. City of Oakland, Calif., 1968; vis. com. nat. archtl. accrediting bd. U. Minn. and U. Wis., Milw., 1971; council Harvard Grad. Sch. Design Assn., 1976—; mem. design rev. com. The Sea Ranch, Calif., 1990—. Prin. works include St. Francis Sq. Coop. Apts., San Francisco, 1961, Pub. Housing for Elderly, San Francisco, 1974, Learning Resources Bldg, U. Calif., Santa Barbara, 1975, Menorah Park Housing for Elderly, San Francisco, 1979, San Jose State U. Student Housing Project, 1984, Delta Airlines Terminal, San Francisco Internat. Airport, 1988. Served with AUS, 1943-46. Recipient numerous awards including AIA Honor awards, 1963, 64, AIA Bay Region Honor award, 1974, Concrete Reinforced Steel Inst. award, 1976, AIA award, 1976, CADA Site I Solar Housing award Sacramento, Calif., 1980, State of Calif. Affordable Housing award, 1981, PG&E Suntherm award, 1981, San Francisco Housing Authority award, 1983, Orchid award City of Oakland, 1989, Citation for achievement and svc. U. Calif. Berkeley, 1991. Fellow AIA. Home: 2816 Derby St Berkeley CA 94705-1325 Office: Stoller Knoerr Architects 1818 Harmon St Berkeley CA 94703-2472

STOLLERY, RODGER GORDON, publisher; b. San Mateo, Calif., Dec. 27, 1936; s. Joseph Gordon and Dorothy Roberta (Crane) S.; m. Linda Louise Hoehn, Aug. 14, 1969 (div. Oct. 1978); 1 child, Michael John; m. Christa Joy Zellerhoff, May 22, 1982; 1 child, Troy Dylan. Student, San Jose State U., 1954-60. Editor Tahoe City (Calif) World, 1963-76; gen. mgr. Lincoln City (Oreg.) News Guard, 1976-81; assoc. pub. Hood River (Oreg.) News, 1983-91; pub. Printer's Northwest Trader, Woodburn, Oreg., 1991—; chmn. Tahoe City Urban Design, 1969-76. Bd. dirs. 20 Miracle Miles C. of C., Lincoln City, 1977-81, Greater North Lake Tahoe C. of C., 1972-76, Meml. Hosp. Hood River, 1986-91; chmn. Tahoe City Pub. Utility Dist. Recreation Commn., 1972-76. Mem. Pacific Printing and Imaging Assn., Portland Club of Lithographers and Printing House Craftsmen, Hood River Rotary (pres. 1989), Stayton Lions (v.p. 1982), Lincoln City Lions (v.p. 1980). Republican. Baptist. Office: Printers Northwest Trader PO Box 450 Woodburn OR 97071-0450

STOLLSTEIMER, JOHN F., food company executive; b. 1932; married. With J.I. Case Co., U.S. Dept. Agr., 1953-61; with econ. research, commodity trading, refinery ops. depts. Beatrice Grocery Group Inc. (subs. Beatrice Cos. Inc.), Fullerton, Calif., from 1962—, v.p. ops. planning logistics distbn., 1969; now exec. v.p. Beatrice/Hunt-Wesson Foods (subs. Beatrice Foods Cos. Inc.), Fullerton; formerly prof. agrl. econs. N.C. State Coll. Office: Beatrice/Hunt-Wesson Foods 1645 W Valencia Dr Fullerton CA 92633-3860

STOLOV, WALTER CHARLES, physician, rehabilitation educator; b. N.Y.C., Jan. 6, 1928; s. Arthur and Rose F. (Gordon) S.; m. Anita Carvel Noodelman, Aug. 9, 1953; children: Nancy, Amy, Lynne. BS in Physics, CCNY, 1948; MA in Physics, U. Minn., 1951, MD, 1956. Diplomate Am. Bd. Phys. Med. and Rehab., Am. Bd. Electrodiagnostic Medicine. Physicist U.S. Naval Gun Factory, Nat. Bur. Stds., Washington, 1948-49; teaching and rsch. asst. U. Minn., Mpls., 1950-54; from instr. to assoc. prof. U. Wash., Seattle, 1960-70, prof., 1970—, also chmn., 1987—; editl. bd. Archives Phys. Medicine and Rehab., 1967-78, Muscle & Nerve, 1983-89, 92—; cons. Social Security Adminstrn., Seattle, 1975—. Co-editor: Handbook of Severe Disability, 1981; contbr. articles to profl. jours. Surgeon USPHS, 1956-57. Recipient Townsend Harris medal CCNY, 1990. Fellow AAAS, Am. Heart Assn.; mem. Am. Acad. Phys. Medicine & Rehab. (Disting. Clinician award 1987), Am. Congress Rehab. Medicine (Essay award 1959), Assn. Acad. Physiatrists, Am. Assn. Electrodiagnostic Medicine (pres. 1987-88), Am. Spinal Cord Injury Assn. Office: U Wash Dept Rehab Medicine RJ-30 1959 NE Pacific St Seattle WA 98195-0004

STOLPE, DANIEL OWEN, artist, printmaking educator; b. L.A., Nov. 14, 1939; s. Andrew Gustave and Mary Magdeleine (Schwind) S.; m. Joyce Anita Berge, Dec. 22, 1960 (div. Sept. 1972); 1 child, Matthew Lloyd; m. Elizabeth Fisher, July 13, 1986 (div. Aug. 1988). AA, Pasadena City Coll., 1960; student, Los Angeles County Art Inst., 1960; studies with, Don La Viere Turner, Glendora, Calif., 1961-62, Joseph Funk, Venice, Calif., 1965-66. Studio worker with Herbert A. Fox Monticeto Press, Sierra Madre, Calif., 1963-69; lithographer with Herbert A. Fox Fox Graphics, Boston, 1972; field worker Swinomish Indian Reservation, La Conner, Wash., 1971-74; artist lithographer with Joe Funk Joseph Graphics, Boston, 1972; founder, dir. Native Images, Inc., Santa Cruz, Calif., 1979—; instr. art Oakes Coll., U. Calif., Santa Cruz, 1978; with CETA and SYEP tng. programs Native Images Print Workshops, Santa Cruz 1979—; instr. artistically gifted and talented program Cultural Coun. Santa Cruz County, Spring 1987; instr. printmaking Inst. Am. Indian Arts, Santa Fe, N.Mex., 1987, Coos Bay (Oreg.) Art Mus., 1987. Artist illustrator Smithsonian Mag., 1972, Atlantic Monthly, Boston, 1972, Houghton-Mifflin Pubs., Boston, 1973, Planet Drum Mag., San Francisco, 1974, Native Am. Series, Am. Indian Studies Ctr., UCLA, 1978, The Best of the Smithsonian...the first decade of Smithsonian Mag., Harmony Books, N.Y.C., 1981, Images & Myths, Coyote Suite I & II (Daniel O. Stolpe), 1982, Renegade Christmas, Poetry by William Everson, 1984, Saturday Rev. Mag., Washington, 1984, Monterey Life Mag., 1987; artist woodcuts plays, poetry; exhbns. include Salt Lake City Art Ctr., 1976, Fort Hall (Idaho) Reservation Ctr.-Shoshone-Bannock Tribe, 1976, McHenry Libr. U. Calif. Santa Cruz, 1978, American West Gallery, Tucson, 1978, U. Utah, 1980, Calif. State U. Hayward, 1981, Mus. Fine Arts, Sante Fe, 1985, Many Horses Gallery, L.A., 1985, Rose Rock Gallery, Carmel, Calif., 1987; juried exhbns. include Okla. Printmakers, Okla. City, 1967, U. N.D. Art Galleries, 1981, Chautauqua (N.Y.) Art Galleries, 1981, Hunterdon (N.J.) Art Ctr., 1982, U. Calif. Santa Cruz, 1987, Monterey (Calif.) Peninsula Mus. Art, 1987, others; represented in permanent collections Smithsonian Mus., Washington, Utah Mus. Fine Arts, Salt Lake City, Portland (Oreg.) Art Mus., Boston Pub. Libr., Huntington Mus. U. Tex., Austin, U. N.Mex., Albequerque, Fogg Art Mus. Harvard, Mass., Everson Mus. Art, Syracuse, many others. Instr. summer job program SYEP , Santa Cruz County, 1982—; supporter Am. Indian Movement, 1980—. Los Angeles County Art Inst. scholar, 1960; Calif. ARts Coun. grantee, 1978, Santa Cruz City Arts Commn. grantee, 1986. Office: Native Images Inc 2539 Mission St Santa Cruz CA 95060-5727

STOLPMAN, THOMAS GERARD, lawyer; b. Cleve., June 2, 1949; s. Joseph Eugene and Katherine Ann (Berry) S.; m. Marilyn Heise, Aug. 17, 1974; children: Jennifer, Peter. BA, UCLA, 1972; JD, Los Angeles, 1976. BAr: Calif. 1976, U.S. Dist. Ct. (ctrl. dist.) Calif. 1976, U.S. Dist. Ct (ea. dist.) Calif. 1985, U.S. Ct. Appeals (9th cir.) 1993, U.S. Supreme Ct. 1994. Ptnr. Stolpman, Krissman, Elber, Mandel & Katzman, Long Beach, CA1971—, 1976—. Editor The Forum, 1978-84; editor-in-chief The Advocate, 1984-87; contbr. articles to profl. jours. Bd. dirs. Miraleste Recreation and Park Dist., Rancho Palos Verdes, Calif., 1982—. Named Trial Lawyer of Yr. So. Calif., Verdictum Juris, 1984. Mem. State Bar of Calif. (bd. govs. 1993—, chair com. client rels. and assistance 1994-95, v.p. 1995-96), L.A. Trial Lawyers Assn. (bd. govs. 1979-93, pres. 1989), Calif. Trial Lawyers Assn. (bd. govs. 1987-90, exec. com. 1989-90), L.A. Coutny Bar Assn. (bd. trustees 1986-87, exec. com. litigation sect. 1990-94), Assn. Trial Lawyers Am., Am. Bd. Trial Advocates, Nat. Bd. Trial Advocacy (cert.), South Bar Bar Assn., Long Beach Bar Assn. Democrat. Roman Catholic. Office: Stoplman Krissman Elber Mandel & Katzman PO Box 1118 111 W Ocean Blvd 19th Fl Long Beach CA 90802

STOLTE, CHARLES ALBERT, company executive; b. Blue Earth, Minn., Apr. 20, 1933; s. Everett L. and Alice Marie (Haase) S.; m. Betty J. Clark, June 13, 1954; children: Daryl, Penny, Susan, David. BSEE, U. Minn., 1955, MSEE, 1958, PhDEE, 1966. Rsch. asst. U. Minn., Mpls., 1955-57, rsch. fellow, 1957-66; mem. tech. staff Hewlett-Packard Co., Palo Alto, Calif., 1966-76, project mgr., 1976-84; R&D sect. mgr. Hewlett-Packard Co., Santa Rosa, Calif., 1984-92, wafer fab mgr., 1992—. Inventor Electrostatic deflection sys. for extended emitter life, 1979. Leader Boy Scouts Am., Los Alto, Calif., 1969-82. Mem. IEEE. Home: 2619 Fir Park Way Santa Rosa CA 95404-1809 Office: Hewlett Packard 1412 Fountaingrove Pky Santa Rosa CA 95403

STOLTZ, ERIC MICHAEL, public relations executive; b. Glendale, Calif., Apr. 13, 1960; s. George Philip and Rosemary (Dunham) S. Student, U. So. Calif., L.A., 1981-83. Account exec. Aaron Cushman & Assocs., L.A., 1985-86; account supr. Aaron Cushman & Assocs., 1986-87, Pollare/Fischer Communications, L.A., 1987-89; account grp. mgr. Pollare/Fischer Communications, 1989-90; communications mgr. Am. Found. for AIDS Rsch., 1991-93; v.p. The Rowland Co., L.A., 1993-94; instr. UCLA, 1994—; sr. v.p. Evans Group, L.A., 1995—; bd. dirs. Urban Fitness Mag.; lectr. and author in field. Mem. mktg. com. L.A. Conservancy, 1988—; steering com. Calif. Preservation Found., Oakland, 1988-89; bd. dirs. L.A. Shanti Found., vice chmn. 1995. Mem. Pub. Rels. Soc. Am. (pres. L.A. chpt., accredited, dir. 1991—, Silver Anvil award 1990, 94, chpt. awards 1986-94), Internat. Assn. Bus. Communicators (chpt. awards of excellence 1987-93), Publicity Club L.A. (Pro awardee 1990, Merit award 1990). Roman Catholic. Home: 401 S Burnside Ave 2F Los Angeles CA 90036 Office: Evans Group Pub Rels Penthouse 1 57570 Wilshire Blvd Los Angeles CA 90036

STOLZ, NEIL N., financial services company executive; b. Ottawa, Kans., June 28, 1935; s. Norbert E. and Vida M. Stolz; m. Patricia L. Stolz, June 22, 1963; children: Sherilyn, Darryl. BS, U. Ariz., 1961. Personnel asst. Am. Savs. and Loan Assn., Whittier, Calif., 1962-66; asst. v.p. personnel Equitable Savs. and Loan Assn. (now Gt. Western Bank), L.A., 1966-68; v.p. adminstrn. Fin. Fedn., Inc. (now Gt. Western Bank), L.A., 1968-83; sr. v.p. corp. planning Gt. Western Bank, Beverly Hills, Calif., 1983-84; exec. v.p., chief adminstrv. officer Fin. Corp. of Am., Irvine, Beverly Hills, 1985—. Mem. adv. bd. U. of Pacific Bus. Sch., Stockton, Calif., 1986—. Mem. Stockton C. of C. (bd. dirs. 1986—), Palos Verdes Golf Club (bd. dirs. 1982-86), Palos Verdes Tennis Club. Republican. Home: 2512 Via Amador Palos Verdes Peninsula CA 90274-2749 Office: Fin Corp Am 18401 Von Karman Ave Irvine CA 92715-1542

STONE, ALEXANDER PAUL, mathematics educator; b. West New York, N.J., June 28, 1928; s. Samuel Bradford and Violet Elizabeth (Schuessler) S.; m. Mary Ann Majeski, July 23, 1960; 1 child, Christopher Bradford. BSEE, Columbia U., 1952; MSEE, Newark Coll. Engring., 1956; PhD, U. Ill., 1965. Field engr. Western Elec./Bell Telephone Labs., Whippany, N.J., 1952-56; instr. in elec. engring. Manhattan Coll., Riverdale, N.Y., 1956-58; asst. prof. physics Dickinson Coll., Carlisle, Pa., 1958-60; asst. prof. math. U. Ill., Chgo., 1965-69; assoc. prof. math. U. Ill., 1969-70, U. N.Mex., Albuquerque, 1970-76; prof. math. U. N.Mex., 1976—, chmn. dept. math. and stats., 1991—; cons. Air Force Weapons Lab., 1984—. Editor: Improperly Posed Boundary Value Problems, 1976; author: Transient Lens Synthesis, 1990; contbr. articles to profl. jours. With USN, 1946-48, 2d lt. U.S. Army, 1951-52. NSF grantee, 1966-70, AFOSR grantee, 1984-85. Mem. Am. Math. Soc., Internat. Union of Radio Sci. (commn. E on electro-magnetic noise and interference). Office: Univ NMex Dept Math And Statisti Albuquerque NM 87131

STONE, ARLENE, writer; b. Phila.. Student, Boston U. Author: (poetry books) The Shule of Jehovah, The Image Maker, Through a Coal Cellar, Darkly, The Women's House, At The Gates of Hell, The Double Pipes of Pan, Son Sonnets.

STONE, DAVID GUY, public relations executive; b. Tualatin, Oreg., June 26, 1957; s. Dale Eugene Stone and Donna Mae (Phelps) Rowles; m. Brenda Lee Pugh, Sept. 3, 1977 (div. Feb. 1990); children: Carlin, Brandon; m. Melanie Anne Anderson, May 25, 1991; 1 stepchild, Ashley Elena. Student, Alaska Meth. U., 1975-76; BS in Geology, U. Alaska, 1979. V.p., dir. consumer affairs Alaska Electric Light & Power Co., Juneau, Alaska, 1980-89; mgr. pub. affairs Echo Bay Mines, Juneau, 1990—. Author: Hard Rock Gold, 1980. Bd. dirs. Alaska Coun. on Econ. Edn., 1991-94; mem. Gov.'s coun. on vocat. edn., 1992—; mem. Gov.'s statewide pvt. industry coun., 1992—, chmn., 1994—; mem. coun. vocat. tech. edn. U. Alaska, 1993—, mem. southeast campus coun., 1993—. Mem. Alaska Miners Assn. (Juneau br., chmn.-bd. dirs. 1989—), Alaska Producers Coun. (vice chair-bd. dirs. 1990—, pres. 1992—, Alaska Mineral Energy Resource Edn. Found. (bd. dirs. 1990—), Juneau C. of C. (bd. dirs. 1989-92), Rotary. Republican. Presbyterian. Home: 9348 Center Ct Juneau AK 99801-9633 Office: Echo Bay Mines 3100 Channel Dr Ste 2 Juneau AK 99801-7814

STONE, DAVID ULRIC, management executive; author; b. Santa Cruz, Calif., Feb. 4, 1927; s. Ernest Marshall and Grace (Stone) S.; student Theol. Ministry Sch., San Jose, Calif., 1945-48; grad. Real Estate Inst., Nat. Inst. Real Estate, 1964; m. Iva Dell Frazier, July 20, 1947; children—Katherine LaVerne, Russell Keith, Susan Marie. With E.M. Stone Realty, San Jose, 1945-48; mgr. Broadway-Hale Co., San Jose, 1948-52; sales mgr. William Perry Co., San Francisco, 1952-56; gen. mgr., ptnr. Stone & Schulte, Inc., San Jose, 1956-66; pres., chmn. bd. dirs. Stone Inst., Los Gatos, Calif., 1966—; pres. Sunchoke Internat., Inc., San Juan Bautista, Calif., 1983-84, chmn. bd. 1985-92; chmn. bd. Custom One Internat. Inc., 1986-90; pres. The Mktg. Forum, Inc., Mpls., 1986-92; dir. Realty Programming Corp. St. Louis. Named Realtor of Yr. Homes for Living Network, 1982. Mem. Nat. Inst. Real Estate Brokers (faculty mem. 1965-82), Nat. Assn. Real Estate Bds. (chmn. joint task force 1966-68), Builder's Mktg. Soc. (founder, chmn. 1985), Calif. Real Estate Assn. (dir.), Nat. Assn. Home Builders (Sales Mgr. of Year award 1960, Bill Molster award, 1990, chmn. joint task force 1966-68, faculty mem. Inst. Residential Mktg. 1982—). Author: How to Operate a Real Estate Trade-In Program, 1962; Training Manual for Real Estate Salesmen, 1966; Guaranteed Sales Plan for Realtors and Builders, 1968 New Home Sales Training Course; The Professional Approach To Selling Real Estate; How To Communicate with Persuasive Power; How to Sell New Homes and Environmental Communities; How to Market and Sell Condominiums; How to Hire, Train and Motivate Real Estate Salespeople, How to Profitably Manage a Real Estate Office, 1977; The Road to Success in Real Estate, 1978; New Horizons in Real Estate, 1980; New Home Sales, 1982, Sales Power: American Sales Masters, 1986, The Gold Series, 1986, New Home Marketing, 1988. Home: 236 Camino del Cerro Los Gatos CA 95032

STONE, DONALD D., investment and sales executive; b. Chgo., June 25, 1924; s. Frank J. and Mary N. (Miller) Diamondstone; student U. Ill., 1942-43; B.S., DePaul U., 1949; m. Catherine Mauro, Dec. 20, 1970; 1 child, Jeffrey. Pres., Poster Bros., Inc., Chgo., 1950-71, Revere Leather Goods, Inc., Chgo., 1953-71; owner Don Stone Enterprises, Chgo., 1954—; v.p. Horton & Hubbard Mfg. Co., Inc. div. Brown Group, Nashua, N.H., 1969-71, Neevel Mfg. Co., Kansas City, Mo., 1969-71. Mem. adv. bd. San Diego Opera; founder Don Diego Meml. Scholarship Fund; mem. bd. overseers U. Calif., San Diego, chancellor's assoc.; mem. exec. bd. Chgo. Area council Boy Scouts of Am. Served with U.S. Army, 1943-45. Clubs: Bryn Mawr Country (Lincolnwood, Ill.) (dir.), Carlton, La Jolla Beach and Tennis, La Jolla Country, Del Mar Thoroughbred. Home: 8240 Caminito Maritimo La Jolla CA 92037-2204

STONE, EDWARD HERMAN, lawyer; b. July 20, 1939; s. Sidney and Ruth S.; m. Pamela G. Gray (dec. 1990); children: Andrew, Matthew. BS in Acctg., U. Ill., 1961; JD, John Marshall Law Sch., 1967. Bar: Ill. 1967, Calif. 1970; cert. specialist Calif. probate, estate planning, and trust law. With IRS, 1963-71; assoc. Eilers, Baranger, Myers & Smith, 1971-72; pvt. practice, Newport Beach, Calif., 1972—; mem. Davis, Samuelson, Goldberg & Blakely (formerly Cohen Stokke & Davis), Santa Ana, Calif., 1984-88; instr. IRS, 1968-69; del. State Bar Conf., 1978—; instr. income and estate taxes Western States U. Sch. Law, 1971-72' mem. CEB Joint Adv. Com., Estate Planning subcom.; judge pro tem, judicial arbitrator Orange County Superior Ct. Contbr. articles to profl. jours. Bd. dirs. Eastbluff Homeowners Community Assn., Newport Beach, 1980-82, pres., 1981-82; pres. Jewish Family Svcs. Orange County, 1975; v.p., bd. dirs. Orange County Jewish Community Found., 1985-92, United Jewish Fedn. of Orange County, 1985-88; bd. dirs. Heritage Points Orange County, 1992-95. Recipient Outstanding award IRS, 1970. Mem. ABA, Am. Arbitration Assn. (panel), Orange County Bar Assn. (vice chmn. estate planning probate and trust law sect. 1976-77, chmn. sect. 1977-78, instr. Probate Clinic 1980, speaker in substantive law; dir. 1977-82; chmn. Profl. Ednl. Council 1980-82, past chmn. profl. edn. coun., chmn. real property and probate sect. for state bar convention 1992—), Phi Alpha Delta (pres. alumni chpt. 1975-76). Successful Estate Planning Ideas and Methods Service; contbr. articles to jour. ABA Young Atty.'s Sect. on Estate Taxes.

STONE, GEORGE ALVIN, protective services official; b. Santa Monica, Calif., Nov. 2, 1956; s. Harvey Earl and Jeanette Lillian (Rogers) S.; m. Marlina Jean Stone, Sept. 14, 1978 (div. 1980); m. Gail Thelma Bozigian, Dec. 4, 1993; children: Jason Allen, Gregory. AA in Social Sci. and Sales, Cerritos C.C., 1988; AS in Emergency Med. Svcs., Mount San Antonio Coll., 1991; postgrad., NYU. Paramedic City of Vernon (Calif.) Fire Dept., 1990—; surg. and emergency room technician Whittier (Calif.) Hosp., 1991—; instr. BLS, ACLS, pediatric ALS Am. Heart Assn., L.A.; paramedic preceptor instr. County of L.A. Team mem. June Lake Search and Rescue, Mono County, Calif., 1988-90. Home: 13270 Brighton Cir Victorville CA 92392-6642 Office: 12505 Lambert Rd Whittier CA 90606-2709

STONE, GREGORY ORVILLE, cognitive psychology educator; b. Chgo., Nov. 7, 1955; s. Orville Joseph and Margaret Elizabeth (Case) S. BA, Harvard U., 1979; PhD, U. Calif., San Diego, 1985. Rsch. psychologist Navy Pers. R&D Ctr., San Diego, 1982; postdoctoral fellow math. dept.

Boston U., 1983-86; asst. prof. psychology dept. Ariz. State U., Tempe, 1986-93, assoc. prof. psychology dept., 1993—. Author: (with others) The Reality of Linguistic Rules, 1994; jr. co-author: Parallel Distributed Processing Vol. I, 1986; contbr. articles to profl. jours. Mem. Psychonomics Soc., Sigma Xi, Sigma Chi (Outstanding tchr. 1991). Office: Ariz State U Psychology Dept Tempe AZ 85287

STONE, JAMES ROBERT, surgeon; b. Greeley, Colo., Jan. 8, 1948; s. Anthony Joseph and Dolores Concetta (Pietrafeso) S.; m. Kaye Janet Friedman, May 16, 1970; children: Jeffrey, Marisa. BA, U. Colo., 1970; MD, U. Guadalajara, Mex., 1976. Diplomate Am. Bd. Surgery, Am. Bd. Surg. Critical Care. Intern Md. Gen. Hosp., Balt., 1978-79; resident in surgery St. Joseph Hosp., Denver, 1979-83; practice medicine specializing in surgery Grand Junction, Colo., 1983-87; staff surgeon, dir. critical care Va. Med. Ctr., Grand Junction, 1987-88; dir. trauma surgery and critical care, chief surgery St. Francis Hosp., Colorado Springs, Colo., 1988-91; pvt. practice Kodiak, Alaska, 1991-92; with South Denver Surg. Cons., Englewood, Colo., 1992-93, Summit Surg. Assocs., 1993—; asst. clin. prof. surgery U. Colo. Health Sci. Ctr., Denver, 1984—; pres. Stone Aire Cons., Grand Junction, 1988—; owner, operator Jjnka Ranch, Flourissant, Colo.; spl. advisor CAP; mem. advisor med. com. unit, 1990-92. Contbr. articles to profl. jours.; inventor in field. Bd. dirs. Mesa County Cancer Soc., 1988-89, Colo. Trauma Inst., 1988-91. Colo. Speaks out on Health grantee, 1988; recipient Bronze medal of Valor Civil Air Patrol. Fellow Denver Acad. Surgery, Southwestern Surg. Congress, Am. Coll. Chest Physicians, Am. Coll. Surgeons (trauma com. Colo. chpt.), Am. Coll. Critical Care; mem. Am. Coll. Physician Execs., Soc. Critical Care (task force 1988—). Roman Catholic.

STONE, JEFFREY THOMAS, musician; b. Topeka, Sept. 27, 1964; s. Thomas Marlin and Christine Ann (Hanson) S. BA in Music cum laude, Calif. Poly., 1992. Cert. tchr., Calif. Freelance profl. musician L.A. area, 1982—; pvt. music tutor. Univ. grantee Calif. Poly., 1988-93; music scholar Calif. Poly., 1988-90. Mem. Am. Fedn. Musicians. Home: 3640 Sumner Ave Apt 103 Pomona CA 91767-1235

STONE, JOHN HELMS, JR., admiralty advisor; b. Andalusia, Ala., Dec. 3, 1927; s. John Helms and Ruth May (Barker) S.;m. Mary Ham, July 24, 1950; children: Malcolm, Mary Ruth, Ronald, John T. Student Ga. Mil. Coll., U.S. Merchant Marine Sch., 1945; student, Tulane U., 1975. Master mariner, USCG. Master capt. Sea-Land Steamship, Port Newark, N.J., 1947-60; Lt. (jg) USNR, 1948-62; sr. pilot Panama Canal Co., Balboa Canal Zone, 1960-73; chief of transit op. Panama Canal Commn., Balboa Canal Zone, 1973-76; chmn. bd. local inspection Panama Canal Commn., Balboa, Republic of Panama, 1976-85; admiralty cons. John H. Stone & Assocs., Boulder, Colo., 1985—, Am. Registry Arbitrators, 1994—; admiralty advisor Phelps-Dunbar, New Orleans, 1958-79, Fowler White, Tampa, Fla., 1984, Terriberry & Assocs., New Orleans, 1992. County treas. Dem. Party, Boulder, 1989. Mem. NRA (v.p. 1970, master pistol and rifle shot), Master, Mates and Pilots Union (v.p. 1970-72). Presbyterian. Home: 3795 Wild Plum Ct Boulder CO 80304-0460

STONE, MICHAEL DAVID, landscape architect; b. Moscow, Idaho, Apr. 11, 1953; s. Frank Seymour Stone and Barbara Lu (Wahl) Stone/Schonthaller; m. Luann Dobaran, Aug. 12, 1978; children: Stephanie Nicole, David Michael. B in Landscape Architecture, U. Idaho, 1976; postgrad., Oreg. State U., 1986, Harvard U., 1990; MA in Orgnl. Leadership, Gonzaga U., 1990. Registered landscape architect, Wash., cert. leisure profl.Nat. Recreation and Park Assn. Landscape designer Robert L. Woerner, ASLA, Spokane, Wash., 1976-77; pk. planner Spokane County Pks. and Recreation, 1977-82; landscape architect City of Spokane Pks. and Recreation, 1982-84, asst. pks. mgr., 1984-86, golf and cmty. devel. mgr., 1986-95, co-dir., 1995—; cons. Lake Chelan (Wash.) Golf Course, 1988. Pres. Sacred Heart Parish Coun., Spokane, 1987-89; v.p. Cataldo Sch. Bd. Dirs., Spokane, 1987-89; pres. South Spokane Jaycees, 1977-86; active Leadership Spokane, 1989, Nat. Exec. Devel Sch., 1993. Named Outstanding Young Man Am., 1980, 85, Outstanding Knight, Intercollegiate Knights, 1972-73, Jaycee of the Yr., South Spokane Jaycees, 1981, Vet. of the Yr., South Spokane Jaycees, 1984-85; recipient Holy Grail award Intercollegiate Knights, 1972-73. Mem. Nat. Recreation and Pk. Assn., Am. Soc. Landscape Architects, Wash. Recreation and Pk. Assn., Nat. Inst. Golf Mgmt. (bd. dirs.), Beta Chi, Delta Tau Delta. Roman Catholic. Home: 2007 E 55th St Spokane WA 99223 Office: City of Spokane 808 W Spokane Falls Blvd Spokane WA 99201-3333

STONE, NORMAN MICHAEL, psychologist; b. Balt., Mar. 23, 1949; s. Forrest Leon and Beverly Iola (Gendason) S.; m. Susan Foster Hoitt, May 18, 1981; children: Shannon, Caroline, Brittany Rain, Forrest. BA, UCLA, 1971; PhD, U. Iowa, 1976. Lic. psychologist, Tex., Calif. Chief youth and family svcs. Abilene (Tex.) Mental Health-Mental Retardation Regional Ctr., 1976-79; coord. family crisis team San Fernando Valley Guidance Clinic, Northridge, Calif., 1980-88, sr. clin. supr., 1989-95; sr. cmty. psychologist L.A. County Dept. Children's Mental Health, Newhall, Calif., 1995—; mem. psychiat. panel of experts on dependency and family law Calif. Superior Ct., 1987—; mem. adj. faculty Hardin-Simmons U., Abilene, 1977-79; vis. prof. UCLA, 1980-81; clin. prof. Fuller Theol. Sem., L.A., 1982—. Contbr. numerous articles on psychology, psychiatry, law and social welfare to internat. profl. jours., books and film. USPHS fellow, 1972-76; Simon Found. rsch. grantee, 1982, 89. Mem. APA, Assn. Family and Conciliation Cts., Am. Profl. Soc. on Abuse of Children, Sojourners. Office: LA County Dept Childrens Mental Health 23504 Lyons Ave Ste 304 Newhall CA 91321-2534

STONE, PATRICK SCAIFE, health science educator, consultant; b. Salt Lake City, May 26, 1942; s. Frank J. and Marie (Moshier) S.; m. Jo Anne Reid, June 9, 1962; children: Joni, Michael, Jennifer, Steven. BS, U. Utah, 1965; MS, Portland State U., 1973; EdD, U. Cin., 1994. Cert. educator of deaf children. Tchr. Denver Pub. Schs., 1965-70; tchr. Tucker-Maxon Oral Sch., Portland, Oreg., 1970-72, supr., 1972-78, dir., 1978—; clin. instr. Oreg. Health Scis. U., Portland, 1991—; pres. A.G. Bell Assn., Washington, 1992-94, Coun. on Edn. of the Deaf, Washington, 1994-96. Author: Developing Conversational Competence, 1988; contbr. articles to profl. jours. Bd. dirs. Portland Ctr. for Hearing and Speech, 1987-93. Recipient Honors of the Assn., Oreg. Speech and Hearing Assn., Svc. to Mankind award Oreg. Sertoma Club, 1986. Mem. Internat. Reading Assn., Coun. for Exceptional Children, Conv. Am. Instrs. of the Deaf, Assn. for Curriculum Devel. Office: Tucker-Maxon Oral Sch 2860 SE Holgate Blvd Portland OR 97202-3658

STONE, RICHARD LEHMAN, chemical engineer, consultant; b. Cleve., Dec. 5, 1916; s. Lawrence Edward and Nina (Lehman) S.; m. Isabelle Stewart, Oct. 24, 1943; children: Richard, Rosalind, Elizabeth, Susan. BSChemE, U. Mich., 1938, MSChemE, 1940; postgrad., Case Western Res. U., 1949-50. Lic. profl. engr. Sr. rsch. engr. Am. Gas Assn. Labs., Cleve., 1946-53; dir. rsch. and engring. Metalbestos Systems, Selkirk Metlabestos div. Household Internat., Belmont, Calif., 1953-85; cons. Selkirk Metalbestos, Los Altos Hills, Calif., 1985-88; pvt. practice cons. Bodega Bay, Calif., 1988—. Contbr. numerous articles to profl. jours. Capt. USAF, 1943-46. Recipient Pioneer Award Fireplace Inst., 1978. Mem. ASHRAE (fuels and combustion com.), Am. Chem. Soc., Am. Soc. Gas Engrs., Nat. Fire Protection Assn. (sectional com. chimneys, fireplaces venting systems). Home: 20205 Osprey Dr Box 940 Bodega Bay CA 94923-0940

STONE, RUBY R., state legislator; b. Portal, Ga., Feb. 6, 1924; d. Eddie Lee and Della (Taylor) Rocker; widowed; children: Dianne Carolyn Stone Milhollin, Raymond Edward Stone. Office mgr., dental asst. to Dr. Richard W. Collins, 1962-68; asst. to mgr. Am. Machine & Foundry Spl. Missile project Vandenberg AFB, 1959-60; aide to Gov. Don Samuelson, 1970-71; mem. Idaho Ho. Reps., 1971-91, chmn. local govt. com., 1991—. Active ARC, and numerous other cmty. projects and cmty. vol. orgns. Recipient Sportsmanship award Idaho State Women's Amateur Golf Tournament, 1980, Plantation Ladies Golf Assn., Outstanding Woman award, 1992; inducted into Idaho Sports Hall of Fame, 1993, Idaho New Agenda Hall of Fame, 1993. Mem. Nat. Orgn. Women Legislators, U.S. Golf Assn. (mem. jr. girls championship com. 1981), Idaho Golf Assn. (bd. dirs. 1975-87), Plantation Golf Club, Gowen Field Officers Club, Gowen Field Officers Wives Club, Daus. of Nile, El Korah Honored Ladies Club, Elks. Republican. Protestant. Home: 6604 Holiday Dr Boise ID 83709-2022

STONE, SUSAN FOSTER, mental health services professional, psychologist; b. Salem, Mass., Mar. 15, 1954; d. Bruce and Carolyn (Foster) Hoitt; m. Norman Michael Stone, May 18, 1981; children: Brittany, Forrest. Student, U. York, Eng., 1974-75; BA in Psychology, Colby Coll., 1976; MS in Clin. Psychology, Abilene Christian U., 1979; PhD in Clin. Psychology, Calif. Sch. Profl. Psychology, 1985. Lic. psychologist, Calif. Mem. emergency response team Simi (Calif.) Dept. Police, 1980-81; cons. Children's Hosp. L.A., 1984-85; postdoctoral fellow Neuropsychiat. Inst. UCLA, 1985-86; clin. dir. Santa Clarita (Calif.) Child and Family Devel. Ctr., 1987-94, dir. tng., 1995—; cons. L.A. County Adoptions, 1985-88; expert witness L.A. Superior Ct., 1987—; clin. asst. prof. Fuller Theol. Sem., Pasadena, Calif., 1989-91, Calif. Sch. Profl. Psychology, L.A., 1991. Author: Bibliography of High-Interest Low-Vocabulary Books for Slow Readers, 1976. Mem. adv. coun. L.A. Foster Parent Assn., 1989-91. Office Juvenile Justice Systems grantee Spl. Children's Ctr., 1990, L.A. Regional Ctr. grantee, 1990. Mem. APA, Assn. Family and Conciliation Cts., Sierra Club, Santa Clarita C. of C. Office: Santa Clarita Child and Family Devel Ctr 21704 Golden Triangle Rd Santa Clarita CA 91350

STONE, WILLIAM GENE, psychiatrist; b. Chgo., May 8, 1931; s. James and Bertha (Freeman) S.; m. Florence Raby, Sept. 4, 1953 (dec. Nov. 1977); children: Janet, Barbara, Lawrence, Robert. BS in Chemistry, Physics, U. Ill., 1952, MS in Physiology, 1954, MD, 1962. Diplomate Am. Bd. Psychiatry and Neurology. Intern Decatur, Macon County Hosp., Ill., 1962-63; resident in psychiatry Mental Health Inst., Independence, Iowa, 1963-68; med. dir. Blackhawk County Mental Health, Waterloo, Iowa, 1968-73; staff psychiatrist St. Francis Hosp., Waterloo, Iowa, 1966-77; chmn. dept. psychiatry St. Francis Hosp., Waterloo, 1975-77; sr. psychiatrist Las. Vegas (Nev.) Mental Health Ctr., 1977. 78. 88; psychiatrist pvt. practice Las Vegas, 1978—; med. staff Valley Hosp., Las Vegsa, Cmty. Hosp., Las Vegas, Desert Springs Hosp., Las Vegas, 1978-94, So. Nev. Meml. Hosp., 1979-84, Monte Vista Hosp., Las Vegas, 1986-94; pres. Redrock Neuropsychiat. Inst., 1980-89; chief psychiat. cons. to substance abuse program, State of Nev., Dept. of Prisons, 1986; chief of staff, Monte Vista Hosp., Las Vegas, 1986; dir. dept. psychiatry Cmty. Hosp., 1988-89; prof. Univ for Humanistic Studies, 1980-85, adj. instr. med. students U. Nev., 1993-94. Author: (book) Does Everybody Need an Analyst?, 1968. Scoutmaster, committeeman Boy Scouts Am., Chgo., 1955-56; bd. dirs. Planned Parenthood of Blackhawk County, Iowa, 1963-66, Unitarian Universalist Soc. of Blackhawk County, 1969-75, pres., 1975; bd. dirs. U. for Humanistic Studies, Adak, Alaska, 1981-85, Nat. Kids Kampus, Las Vegas, 1987. Officer USN, 1954-58. Fellow Am. Psychiat. Assn.; mem. Las Vegas Psychiatric Soc. (sec., treas. 1980-81, pres. 1982-83, v.p. 1994), Nev. Assn. Psychiat. Physicians, (v.p., pres. elect 1989, pres. 1990, dist. rep. to Am. Assn. Psychiat. Physicians). Home: PO Box 12477 Las Vegas NV 89112-0477

STONEHOUSE, JAMES ADAM, lawyer; b. Alameda, Calif., Nov. 10, 1937; s. Maurice Adam and Edna Sigrid (Thuesen) S.; m. Marilyn Jean Kotkas, Aug. 6, 1966; children: Julie Aileen, Stephen Adam. AB, U. Calif., Berkeley, 1961; JD, Hastings Coll. Law, U. Calif., San Francisco, 1965. Bar: Calif. 1966; cert. specialist probate, estate planning & trust law.. Assoc. Hall, Henry, Oliver & McReavy, San Francisco, 1966-71; ptnr. firm Whitney, Hanson & Stonehouse, Alameda, 1971-77; pvt. practice, Alameda, 1977-79; ptnr. firm Stonehouse & Silva, Alameda, 1979—; judge adv. Alameda council Navy League, 1978—. Founding dir. Alameda Clara Barton Found., 1977-80; mem. Oakland (Calif.) Marathon-Exec. Com., 1979; mem. exec. bd. Alameda council Boy Scouts Am., 1979—, pres., 1986-88; mem. Nat. council Boy Scouts Am., 1986—; trustee Golden Gate Scouting, 1986-95, treas. 1988-91, v.p. 1991-92, pres. 1993-95, v.p. area III western region, 1990-95, bd. dirs. western region, 1991—; bd. dirs. Lincoln Child Ctr. Found., 1981-87, 94—, pres., 1983-85; sch. bd. mem. St. Joseph Notre Dame, 1994—. Recipient Lord Baden-Powell Merit award Boy Scouts Am., 1988, Silver Beaver award, 1991; named Boss of Yr. Alameda Jaycees, 1977; Coro Found. fellow in pub. affairs, 1961-62. Mem. ABA, State Bar Calif., Alameda County Bar (vice chmn. com. office econs., 1977-78). Republican. Roman Catholic. Club: Commonwealth. Lodges: Rotary (dir. club 1976-78, trustee Alameda Rotary Found. 1991—, treas., 1994—), Elks (past exalted ruler, all state officer 1975-76, all dist. officer 1975-77, 78-79, Alameda). Home: 2990 Northwood Dr Alameda CA 94501-1606 Office: Stonehouse & Silva 512 Westline Dr Ste 300 Alameda CA 94501-5870

STONER, MICHAEL C., network specialist; b. San Francisco, Oct. 27, 1967; s. William C. and Lani (Bain) S. Grad., A.A. Stagg H.S., Stockton, Calif., 1986. Cert. CNA. Owner CADS, Stockton, 1989-90; v.p. Accelerated Computer Tng., L.A., 1990—. CFO Christopher Street West, L.A., 1994. With USN, 1986-90. IEEE (assoc.). Democrat. Office: Accelerated Computer Tng 3255 Wilshire Blvd Ste 903 Los Angeles CA 90010-1413

STONER, SUE, travel consultant; b. Seminole, Okla., June 8, 1942; d. E.D. and Atha Miriah (Brown) Burkhart; m. George M. Stoner, Jr., Sept. 5, 1964; children—Shelby Lynn, Steven Laird. B.A., Howard Payne Coll., 1964. Pres., Travel World, Inc., Gig Harbor, Wash., 1965—; sec.-treas. Travel Stamps, Inc., Gig Harbor, 1978—. Mem. distributive edn. com. Peninsula Sch. Dist., Gig Harbor. Mem. AAUW, Am. Soc. Travel Agts. (com. chmn.), Inst. Cert. Travel Agts. (cert. travel cons., nat. rep.), Assn. Retail Travel Agts. (com. chmn.), Gig Harbor C. of C. Republican. Baptist. Clubs: Toastmasters (pres. Gig Harbor chpt. 1987) Altrusa. Avocations: reading, travel, painting. Home: 15018 Sherman Dr NW Gig Harbor WA 98332-8723 Office: PO Box 427 Gig Harbor WA 98335-0427

STONEY, RONALD J., vascular surgeon, educator; b. Carmel, Calif., Mar. 4, 1934; s. Ronald Burdette and Gertrude Mathilda (Schram) S.; m. Linda Jean Whaley, Sept. 20, 1972; children: Ronald Mark, David Collis, Steven Lyle, Kathleen Lynn, Jeanette Spencer. BS, U. Santa Clara, Calif., 1955; MD, U. Calif., San Francisco, 1959. Instr. surgery, adminstrv. resident U. Calif., San Francisco, 1965-66, asst. prof. surgery, 1966-73, assoc. prof., 1973-79, prof., 1979-94, dir. Blood Flow Lab., 1981-86, co-chief div. vascular surgery, 1982-87, prof. surgery emeritus, 1994—; dir. Lifeline Found., Manchester, Mass., 1991—; founder, pres. Pacific Vascular Rsch. Found., San Francisco, 1982—. Author: Manual of Vascular Surgery, Vol. I, 1980, Vol. II, 1986, Wylie's Atlas of Vascular Surgery, Vols. I-VI, 1992; mem. editl. bd. Surgery, 1982-93, Jour. Vascular Surgery, 1993—; contbr. articles to profl. jours. 2d lt. M.C., USA, 1966-68. Fellow ACS; mem. AMA, Am. Surgical Assn., Calif. Med. Assn., Soc. for Vascular Surgery, Internat. Soc. Cardiovascular Surgery (pres. N.Am. chpt. 1993), Howard C. Naffziger Surg. Soc. (pres. 1980-81). Democrat. Roman Catholic.

STONG, JOHN ELLIOTT, retail electronics company executive; b. Elkater, Iowa, Sept. 20, 1921; s. Elliott Sheldon and Nora Elizabeth (Daly) S.; m. Olive Miriam Foley, Dec. 11, 1943; children: Mary Myers, Jon, Miriam. Grad. U. Colo., 1943. Salesman, Purucker Music, Medford, Oreg., 1946-48, dept. mgr., 1949-56, store mgr., 1957, partner, 1958-61, owner, 1962-64; pres. Purucker Music Houses, Medford, 1965-67, Music West, Inc., Eugene, Oreg., 1968-70, Magnavox Centers, Medford, 1971—, exec. asst., Consultants Internat., 1972—. Served with USAF, 1943-45. Decorated Air medal. Mem. Nat. Assn. Music Mchts. (dir. 1969-72), Scull Mchts. Rsch. Group (dir., chmn.). Republican. Roman Catholic. Home: 2120 Woodlawn Dr Medford OR 97504-7678 Office: Cons Internat 117 N Central Ave Medford OR 97501-5925

STOOKER, HENDRIK CORNELIS, curator, gallery director; b. Rhenoy, Beesd, The Netherlands, Apr. 22, 1931; came to U.S., 1960; s. Hendrik Cornelis Sr. and Sanderina Maria (Dekker) S. Cert. Tchr. in Art Edn., Art Acad., Arnhem, The Netherlands, 1953; BA in Art History, Calif. State U., L.A., 1972; MA in Art History, U. Calif., L.A., 1976. Gallery dir. Alpha Contemporary Exhibit, L.A., 1983-86; sr. curator, gallery dir. dept. art history and visual arts Occidental Coll., L.A., 1987—. Co-founder Arroyo Arts Collective, L.A., 1989; organizer artists' studios L.A. Open Festival, 1990. Home: 5322 Granada St Los Angeles CA 90042-3312 Office: Occidental Coll Dept Art History 1600 Campus Rd Los Angeles CA 90041-3384

STOOPS, DANIEL J., lawyer; b. Wichita, Kans., May 27, 1934; s. Elmer F. and Margaret J. (Pickrell) S.; m. Kathryn Ann Piepmeier, Aug. 28, 1954; children: Sharon, Janet. BA, Washburn U., 1956, JD, 1958. Bar: Kans. 1958, Ariz. 1959, U.S. Dist. Ct. Kans. 1958, U.S. Dist. Ct. Ariz. 1960, U.S. Ct. Appeals (9th cir.) 1975, U.S. Supreme Ct. 1971. Assoc. Wilson, Compton, & Wilson, Flagstaff, Ariz., 1959-64; ptnr. Wilson, Compton & Stoops, Flagstaff, 1964-67, Mangum, Wall & Stoops, Flagstaff, 1967-77, Mangum, Wall, Stoops & Warden, Flagstaff, 1977. Editor Washburn Law Rev., 1958. Pres. Flagstaff Festival of the Arts, 1988-89, Flagstaff Sch. Bd., 1961-73, Ariz. Sch. Bd. Assn., 1971. Fellow Ariz. Bar Found., Am. Bar Found., Am. Coll. Trial Lawyers (state chmn. 1984-85), Internat. Soc. Barristers; mem. Ariz. Bar Assn. (pres. 1980-81), Masons, Elks. Republican. Methodist. Office: Mangum Wall Stoops & Warden 222 E Birch Ave Flagstaff AZ 86001-5246

STOORZA GILL, GAIL, corporate professional; b. Yoakum, Tex., Aug. 28, 1943; d. Roy Otto and Ruby Pauline (Ray) Blankenship; m. Larry Sttorza, Apr. 27, 1963 (div. 1968); m. Ian M. Gill, Apr. 24, 1981; 1 child, Alexandra Leigh. Student, N. Tex. State U., 1961-63, U. Tex., Arlington, 1963. Stewardess Cen. Airlines, Ft. Worth, 1963; advt. and acctg. exec. Phillips-Ramsey Advt., San Diego, 1963-68; dir. advt. Rancho Bernardo, San Diego, 1968-72; dir. corp. communications Avco Community Developers, San Diego, 1972-74; pres. Gail Stoorza Co., San Diego, 1974—, Stoorza, Ziegaus & Metzger, San Diego, 1974—; CEO Stoorza, Ziegaust, Metzger, Inc., 1993—; chmn. Stoorza/Smith, San Diego, 1984-85, Stoorza Internat., San Diego, 1984-85; CEO ADC Stoorza, San Diego, 1987—, Franklin Stoorza, San Diego, 1993—. Trustee San Diego Art Found.; bd. dirs. San Diego Found. for Performing Arts, San Diego Opera, Sunbelt Nursery Groups, Dallas. Names Small Bus. Person of Yr. Selest Com. on Small Bus., 1984, one of San Diego's Ten Outstanding Young Citizens San Diego Jaycees, 1979; recipient Woman of Achievement award Women in Communications Inc., 1985. Mem. Pubs. Soc. Am., Nat. Assn. Home Builders (residential mktg. com.), COMBO. Methodist. Clubs: Chancellors Assn. U. Calif. (San Diego), Pub. Relations, San Diego Press. Home: PO Box 490 Rancho Santa Fe CA 92067-0490 Office: Franklin Stoorza 225 Broadway Ste 1800 San Diego CA 92101*

STOREK, JAN, hematologist, oncologist, researcher; b. Prague, Czechoslovakia, Aug. 5, 1959; came to U.S., 1989; m. Stepanka Storkova, Mar. 8, 1994. MD, Charles U. Sch. Medicine, 1984. Resident in internal medicine Charles U. Hosp., Prague, 1984-87; scholar Inst. Hematology and Blood Transfusion, Prague, 1987-89; felow in hematology and oncology UCLA, 1989-92; rsch. assoc. Fred Hutchinson Cancer Ctr., Seattle, 1992—. Mem. ACP, AAAS.

STORER, NORMAN WILLIAM, sociology educator; b. Middletown, Conn., May 8, 1930; s. Norman Wyman and Mary Emily (House) S.; m. Ada Joan Van Valkenburg, Aug. 19, 1951; children: Martin Wilson, Thomas Wyman; m. Mary Ashton Pott Hiatt, Mar. 7, 1975. A.B., U. Kans., 1952, M.A., 1956; Ph.D., Cornell U., 1961. Lectr., asst. prof. Harvard U., Cambridge, Mass., 1960-66; staff assoc. Social Sci. Research Council, N.Y.C., 1966-70; prof. sociology CUNY-Baruch Coll., N.Y.C., 1970-88; prof. emeritus CUNY-Baruch Coll., 1989—; dept. chmn. CUNY-Baruch Coll., N.Y.C., 1970-85, chmn. faculty senate, 1981-84. Author: The Social System of Science, 1966, Focus on Society, 1973, 2d edit., 1980, A Leer of Limericks, 1990, (with William Flores) Domestic Violence in Suburban San Diego, 1994; editor: The Sociology of Science, 1973; column editor San Diego Writers' Monthly, 1992-94. Served to sgt. AUS, 1953-55. Mem. AAAS, Phi Beta Kappa, Sigma Xi. Democrat. Home: 1417 Van Buren Ave San Diego CA 92103-2339

STOREY, BRIT ALLAN, historian; b. Boulder, Colo., Dec. 10, 1941; s. Harold Albert and Gladys Roberta (Althouse) S.; m. Carol DeArman, Dec. 19, 1970; 1 child, Christine Roberta. AB, Adams State Coll., Alamosa, Colo., 1963; MA, U. Ky., 1965, PhD, 1968. Instr. history Auburn (Ala.) U., 1967-68, asst. prof., 1968-70; dep. state historian State Hist. Soc. Colo., Denver, 1970-71, acting state historian, 1971-72, rsch. historian, 1972-74; hist. preservation specialist Adv. Coun. on Hist. Preservation, Lakewood, Colo., 1974-88; sr. historian Bur. Reclamation, Lakewood, 1988—. Contbr. articles to profl. publs. Mem. Fed. Preservation Forum (pres. 1990-91), Nat. Coun. Pub. History (sec. 1987, pres.-elect 1990-91, pres. 1991-92), Orgn. Am. Historians (com. 1983-86, chmn. 1985-86), Victorian Soc. Am. (bd. dirs. 1977-79), Western History Assn. (chmn. com. 1982-86), Colo.-Wyo. Assn. Mus. (sec. 1974-76, pres. 1976-77), Cosmos Club (Washington). Home: 7264 W Otero Ave Littleton CO 80123-5639 Office: Bur Reclamation D 5300 Bldg 67 Denver Fed Ctr Denver CO 80225-0007

STOREY, FRANCIS HAROLD, business consultant, retired bank executive; b. Calgary, Alberta, Can., June 20, 1933; s. Bertwyn Morrell and Hilda Josephine (Masters) S.; m. Willomae Saiter, Apr. 25, 1954; children: Daryl, Elizabeth, Brian, Shelley. Student, Gonzaga U., 1953, Pacific Coast Bankers Sch., 1974-76. Designated Certified Profl. Cons. Bank trainee Wash. Trust Bank, Spokane, 1950-56; owner Storey & Storey, Spokane, 1956-64; agt. Bankers Life Nebr., Spokane, 1964-67; sr. v.p. Old Nat. Bank, Spokane, 1967-87, U.S. Bank of Wash., Spokane, 1987-90; pvt. practice cons. Spokane, 1990—; bd. dirs. Alloy Trailers Inc., Output Tech. Corp. Bd. dirs. Spokane Bus. Incubator, United Way of Spokane, 1987-95; bd. dirs., treas., fin. chair, gen. conv. dep. Episcopal Diocese Spokane Dep., 1969—; trustee Spokane Symphony Soc., 1986-93, Spokane Area Econ. Devel. Coun., 1982-89; mem. adv. bd. Intercollegiate Ctr. Nursing Edn. Mem. Acad. Profl. Cons. and Advisors, Spokane Rotary, Spokane Country Club, Spokane Club. Episcopalian. Home: 214 E 13th Ave Spokane WA 99202-1115

STOREY, ISABEL NAGY, writer, television producer; b. Parry Sound, Ont., Can., July 2, 1955; came to U.S., 1961; d. Louis and Denise (Ktorza) N. Diploma in French lang. and lit., Inst. Etrangers, Aix-en-Provence, France, 1976; BA, Calif. State U., Northridge, 1979. Editor Burbank (Calif.) Scene, 1979; reporter Burbank Daily Rev., 1979; mng. editor San Fernando Valley Mag., Studio City, Calif., 1980; writer, producer Sta. KTLA News, L.A., 1980-82, Sta. KCBS News, L.A., 1982-87, Lifetime Med. TV, L.A., 1987-89; writer, producer Channel One Whittle Communications, 1989; segment producer Rescue 911 CBS, 1989-90; segment producer syndicated mag. program Preview TV Program Enterprises, 1990. Writer Stuck in Traffic, Sta. KCET, 1988, The National Driving Test, CBS, 1989, 2d Ann. National Driving Test, 1990, The National Emergency Test, ABC, 1990. Recipient Best Local TV Feature award Odyssey Inst., cert. appreciation Ctr. Improvement Child Caring, 1982. Mem. Writers Guild Am. (outstanding script award 1987), Acad. TV Arts Scis. (Emmy 1982), Internat. Documentary Assn.

STOREY, PHOEBE REED, artist; b. Newton, Mass., Apr. 16, 1945; d. Dale C. and Barbara (Thurman) Reed; m. Roger Alan Storey, Feb. 3, 1967; children: Alan Matthew, Jeffrey Todd, Julia Loraine, Adrienne Reed. BA in Fine Arts, Hollins Coll., 1967. Artist Artistic Touch Gallery, Davis, Calif., 1989—; tchr. Davis (Calif.) Art Ctr., 1993, Munroe Ctr. for the Arts, Lexington, Mass., 1995. Commd. painting U.S. Fish and Wildlife Svc.; work selected for ann. ltd. edit. print Yolo County Arts Coun; exhibited in group show at New Eng. Watercolor Soc., 1994, 95 (hon. mention award, 1995). Bd. mem. LWV, Eureka, Calif., 1970-72, 75-80, Glendale, Calif., 1973-74. Recipient award of merit Calif. State Fair, 1992. Home: 80 Franklin St Arlington MA 02174-3214 Office: Artistic Touch Gallery 205 G St Davis CA 95616-4516

STORIE, EVELYN, public utilities specialist, crisis consultant; b. Arlington, Va.. AD, Clark Coll., Vancouver, Wash., 1986; BS in Bus./Safety/Medicine, Ea. Oreg. State Coll., LaGrand, 1986; MS in Mgmt. Comms., U. Portland, 1988. Hispanic/Native Am. coord. Bonneville Power Adminstrn.-Dept. of Energy, Portland, Oreg., pub. utilities specialist; cons. for earthquake to all fed. agys.; bilingual cons. Med. rsch. dir. lifesaving video When the Neck Breather Stops Breathing, 1993. Recipient numerous EMT awards, 2 internat. Telly awards. Mem. Nat. Assn. Emergency Med. Technicians, Nat. Assn. EMT Instr. Coords., Oreg. State EMT Assn., Wash. EMT/Paramedic Assn., ARC, Am. Cancer Assn. Office: Bonneville Power Adminstrn Dept Energy PO Box 3621 Portland OR 97208-3621

STORK, WILLIAM WILLIS, secondary education educator; b. Toledo, May 25, 1940; s. Willis and Helen (Baldwin) S.; children: Christina, Willis W. III. BA, Yale U., 1962; MAT, Brown U., 1966; MA, Bowdoin Coll., 1969; postgrad., U. So. Calif., L.A. Cert. tchr., Calif., R.I. Dept. head history, instr. Brimmer & May Sch., Chestnut Hill, Mass., 1963-65; asst. dean of students, master St. George's Sch., Newport, R.I., 1965-71; dir.

studies, instr. Marlborough Sch., L.A., 1971-83; dept. head math. Polytechnic Sch., Pasadena, Calif., 1983—, acting head of upper sch., 1985, dir. summer session, 1987; vis. scholar Cambridge (Eng.) U., 1991. Author: Linear Programming and Matrix Games, 1970, Social Change in Rural China, 1980. Pres. Friends of the Pasadena (Calif.) Pub. Libr., 1987; committeeman Pasadena Tournament of Roses, 1973—, mem. cmty. rels. com., 1988-90, mem. float entries com., 1990-92, mem. formation area com., 1992-94. Fulbright scholar, 1978. Mem. Assn. Yale Alumni (sec., bd. govs. 1992—, sec. 1992—, internat. and nat. coord. 1990-92, exec. com. 1990—, among others), Yale Club of So. Calif. (pres. 1987-89). Home: 1586 Oakdale St Pasadena CA 91106-3563

STORM, DONALD JOHN, archaeologist, historian; b. Bradford, Pa., Nov. 20, 1947; s. John Ross and Jean Lamar (Frederick) S. AA, Yuba Coll., 1967; BA, Sacramento State U., 1972; postgrad., Calif. State U., Sacramento, 1972-74, Calif. State U., Chico, 1980, U. Nev., Reno, 1988-89. Instr. Marysville (Calif.) Joint Unified Sch. Dist., 1977-78; state archaeologist Calif. Dept. Parks and Recreation, Sacramento, 1981-84; owner North Yuba Contracting, Oregon House, Calif., 1984-87; archaeologist Elko dist. Nev. Bur. Land Mgmt., Elko, 1988; asst. forest archaeologist Sierra Nat. Forest, Clovis, Calif., 1990-91; archaeol. tech. Tahoe Nat. Forest, Camptonville, Calif., summer 1980; archaeol. cons. Oregon House, 1976-81, 88—; instr. Yuba Coll., Marysville, Calif., 1976-78, 88-93. Activist various conservation/environ. groups; candidate for Yuba County Supr., 1992. With U.S. Army, 1967-70. Mem. Soc. Am. Archaeology, Soc. Hist. Archaeology, Soc. for Calif. Archaeology, Calif. Hist. Soc., Nat. Trust for Historic Preservation, So. Pacific Hist. and Tech. Soc. Home and Office: PO Box 552 Oregon House CA 95962

STORM, JOETTE GETSE, government agency public relations specialist; b. Chgo., Nov. 15, 1946; d. Joseph John and Rose Marie (Reid) G.; m. Eugene Charles Storm, May 2, 1970; 1 child, Nina Erin. BS in Journalism, U. Ill., 1968; postgrad. John Marshall Law Sch., 1968-70. Reporter, Chgo. Tribune, 1968-70, Anchorage Times, 1971-72; pub. relations practitioner Storm Enterprises, 1972-73; pub. affairs specialist Bur. Land Mgmt. U.S. Dept. Interior, Anchorage, 1973-87, pub. affairs officer U.S. Forest Svc., 1989-91, pub. affairs officer, Fed. Aviation Adminstrn., 1991—. mediator, arbitrator, 1981-88. Contbr. articles to profl. jours. Bd. dirs. Susitna council Girl Scouts Am., 1982-88, 88—; mediator Conflict Resolution Ctr., Anchorage, 1982-86; chmn. Anchorage Com. Resource Edn., 1982—; mem. outdoor edn. adv. com. Anchorage Sch. Dist., 1985—; mem. Resource devel. Council; pres. Chugach Optional Sch. Steering Com., 1983; leader, del. Alaska community good will mission to People's Republic China, 1986; adv. bd. chair McAuley Manor Home For Girls, 1993-95. Named Ski Writer of Yr., U.S. Ski Assn., 1973, Outstanding Young Women Am., 1983, Fed. Employee of Yr., Fed. Exec. Assn., 1984, Vol. of Yr., Anchorage Sch. Dist., 1984; recipient Outstanding Performance award Bur. Land Mgmt., 1977, Equal Opportunity award, 1980, Spl. Achievement award for response to Exxon Valdese oil spill U.S. Forest Svc., 1990, Superior Achievement award U.S. Forest Svc., 1991, Superior Accomplishment award FAA, 1992, 94, Environ. Edn. award U.S. Bur. Land Mgmt., 1994; U.S. Dept. Transportation fellow, 1994-95. Mem. Pub. Relations Soc. Am. (bd. dirs. Alaska chpt. 1986—, chpt. pres. 1988), Federally Employed Women, Alaska Press Women, Audubon Soc., Anchorage Ctr. for Environment, Am. Arbitration Anns. (arbitrator 1985-90). Office: Fed Aviation Admin 222 W 7th Ave # 14B Anchorage AK 99513-7504

STORMES, JOHN MAX, instructional systems developer; b. Manila, Oct. 7, 1927; s. Max Clifford and Janet (Heldring) S.; m. Takako Sanae, July 29, 1955; children: Janet Kazuko Stormes-Pepper, Alan Osamu. BS, San Diego State U., 1950; BA, U. So. Calif., 1957, MA, 1967. Cert. secondary and community coll. tchr. Editing supr. Lockheed Propulsion Co., Redlands, Calif., 1957-61; proposals supr. Rockwell Internat., Downey, Calif., 1961-62; publs. dir. Arthur D. Little, Inc., Santa Monica, Calif., 1962-63; publs. coord. Rockwell Internat., Downey, 1963-68; project dir. Gen. Behavioral Systems, Inc., Torrance, Calif., 1969-73; tng. and comm. cons. Media Rsch. Assocs., Santa Cruz, Calif., 1973—; tng. support svc. supr. So. Calif. Gas Co., L.A., 1985—; lectr. Calif. State U., Northridge, 1991—; tng. cons. Nat. Ednl. Media, Chatsworth, Calif., 1966-81, communications cons. Opinion Rsch. Calif., Long Beach, 1974—. Co-author: TV Communications Systems For Business and Industry, 1970. Curriculum adv. bd. communications dept. Calif. State U., Fullerton, 1964-78. Sgt. U.S. Army, 1953-55, Japan. Mem. Soc. Tech. Communication (sr. mem., 2nd v.p. Orange County chpt. 1962-63), Nat. Soc. Performance and Instruction (v.p. L.A. chpt. 1989, pres. 1990). Democrat. Episcopal. Home: 9140 Brookshire Ave Apt 207 Downey CA 90240-2963 Office: So Calif Gas Co 712 T Box 3249 ML 15H0 Los Angeles CA 90051-1249

STORMSHAK, FREDRICK, physiology educator; b. Enumclaw, Wash., July 4, 1936; s. John and Theresa (Vertocnik) S.; m. Alice Mary Burk, June 8, 1963; children: Elizabeth Ann, Laurie Jo. BS, Wash. State U., 1959, MS, 1960; PhD, U. Wis., 1965. Rsch. physiologist USDA, Beltsville, Md., 1965-68; asst. prof. physiology Oreg. State U., Corvallis, 1968-72, assoc. prof., 1972-79, prof., 1979—, Ferguson disting. prof., 1989, affiliate prof. biochemistry, acting assoc. dir. expt. sta., 1985—, interim head dept. animal sci., 1994-95; NIH postdoctoral fellow in biochemistry U. Wis., 1976; mem. study sect. NIH, Bethesda, Md., 1982-86; mem. animal sci. panel USDA, Washington, 1988-90. Sect. editor Jour. Animal Sci., 1975-78, editor-in-chief, 1982-85; mem. editl. bd. Biol. Reproduction, 1978-82, Endocrinology, 1994—, Domestic Animal Endocrinology, 1994—. Mem. Endocrine Soc., Soc. for Study Reproduction (bd. dirs. 1992-95), Soc. for Study Fertility, Am. soc. Animal Sci., Phi Kappa Phi. Office: Oreg State U Dept Animal Sci Corvallis OR 97331-6702

STOROZUM, STEVEN LEE, marketing professional; b. St. Louis, Jan. 14, 1954. AB, Washington U., St. Louis, 1975; MS, Carnegie Mellon U., 1976; postgrad., Va. Poly. U., 1979. Assoc. engr. IITRI-ECAC, Annapolis, Md., 1977; applications engr. ITT, Roanoke, Va., 1977-79; sr. engr. McDonnell Douglas Corp., St. Louis, 1979-82; mgr. LAN systems Am. Photonics, Inc., Brookfield, Conn., 1982-88; product mgr. PCO, Inc., Chatsworth, Calif., 1988-90, Fibermux Corp., Chatsworth, 1990—; cons. Wilton Industries, Ridgefield, Conn., 1988. Lighting designer theatrical prodns., 1978-79, 86-88; contbr. articles to profl. jours. Mem. Am. Phys. Soc., Optical Soc. of Am., Mensa.

STORSTEEN, LINDA LEE, librarian; b. Pasadena, Jan. 26, 1948; d. Oliver Matthew and Susan (Smock) Storsteen. AB cum laude in History, UCLA, 1970, MA in Ancient History, 1972, MLS, 1973. Librarian, L.A. Pub. Library, 1974-79; city librarian Palmdale City Library (Calif.), 1979—. Adv. bd. So. Calif. Inter-Library Loan Network, L.A., 1979-80; commr. So. Calif. Film Circuit, L.A., 1980—; council South State Coop. Library System, 1981—, chmn., 1982-83, 85-86, 87-88, 89-90, 92-93; pres. So. Calif. Film Circuit, 1985-86; rec. sec. So. Antelope Valley Coordinating Council, Palmdale, 1983-84. Mem. ALA, Calif. Library Assn., Pub. Libraries Exec. Assn. So. Calif., Am. Saddle Horse Assn., Pacific Saddlebred Assn., So. Calif. Saddle Bred Horse Assn. (bd. dirs.), Chinese Shar-Pei Club of Am. Home: PO Box 129 Palmdale CA 93590-9971 Office: Palmdale City Libr 700 E Palmdale Blvd Palmdale CA 93550-4742

STORVICK, CLARA AMANDA, nutrition educator emerita; b. Emmons, Minn., Oct. 31, 1906; d. Ole A. and Elise A. (Opdahl) S. AB, St. Olaf Coll., 1929; MS, Iowa State U., 1933; PhD, Cornell U., 1941. Chemistry instr. Augustana Acad., Canton, S.D., 1930-32; rsch. asst. Iowa State U., Ames, 1932-34; nutiritionist Fed. Emergency Relief Adminstrn., Brainerd, Minn., 1934-36; asst. prof. nutrition Okla. State U., Stillwater, 1936-38; rsch. asst. Cornell U., Ithaca, N.Y., 1938-41; asst. prof. nutrition U. Wash., Seattle, 1941-45; assoc. prof. nutrition to prof. Oreg. State U., Corvallis, 1945-72, prof. nutrition and head home econ. rsch., 1955-72, dir. nutrition rsch. inst., 1965-72; ret., 1972. Contbr. over 70 articles to profl. jours. Recipient Borden award Am. Home Econs. Assn., 1952, Disting. Alumni award St. Olaf Coll., 1955, Alumni Achievement award Iowa State U., Ames, 1966. Fellow AAAS, Am. Pub. Health Assn., Am. Inst. Nutrition; mem. N.Y. Acad. Scis., Am. Chem. Soc., Phi Kappa Phi, Sigma Xi., Iota Sigma Pi (nat. pres.), Omicron Nu. Republican. Lutheran. Home: 124 NW 29th St Corvallis OR 97330-5343

STORY, PAUL, food products executive; b. 1947. With Sunkist Growers Inc., 1966-71; mgr., pres. Klink Citrus Assocs., Ivanhoe, Calif., 1971—. Office: Klink Citrus Assoc 32921 Road 159 Ivanhoe CA 93235-1455*

STORZ, DONNA MARIE, clinical dietitian; b. San Mateo, Calif., Nov. 5, 1962; d. Leroy Ernest and Susan A. (Gallier) Friebel; m. Roger Kenneth Storz, Aug. 2, 1992. BS in Dietetics, U. Calif., Davis, 1985; MS in Nutrition Scis., San Jose State U., 1987. Registered dietitian. Clin. dietitian Alexian Bros. Hosp., San Jose, Calif., 1989—. Co-editor newsletter San Jose-Peninsula Dietetic Assn., 1989-90, editor, 1990-91. Mem. Circle of Friends, dept. nutrition and food sci. San Jose State U., 1992—. Named one of Outstanding Young Women of Am., 1987. Mem. Am. Soc. Parenteral and Enteral Nutrition (cert. nutrition support dietitian), Am. Dietetic Assn., Dietitians in Nutrition Support, U. Calif.-Davis Alumni Assn. Office: Alexian Bros Hosp 225 N Jackson Ave San Jose CA 95116

STOSICH, DAVIDJOHN, company executive; b. Idaho Falls, Idaho, May 24, 1938; s. Vaughn T. and Esther (Smith) S.; m. Adeana Marshall, Aug. 28, 1962; children: Jennifer Lynne, Jacquelyn, Bryan, Jill, Jon, Anthony, Vaughndavid, Jelair, Hartman, Jeanne. BS, Brigham Young U., 1964; BPA in Profl. Illustrator, Art Ctr. Coll. Design, L.A., 1967. Graphic support Computer Scis. Corp., El Segundo, Calif., 1967-68; corp. communications staff Geotech, Salt Lake City, 1968-69; asst. to pres. Computer Update, Salt Lake City, 1969-70; corp. communications staff Omnico, Salt Lake City & Tacoma, 1970-71; support staff Big Sky of Mont., Big Sky, Mont., 1972-73; art dir. Artcraft, Bozeman, Mont., 1973-75; owner Stosich Advt., Idaho Falls, 1975-78; pres. Worldwide Achievements, Idaho Falls, 1980-81, Hive Systems, Idaho Falls, 1982-92; pres. Stosich Woodlock, Idaho Falls, 1986-94. Graphic designer Tour Guide to Europe, 1988; sculptor woodlock wood sculptures. Graphic designer Crapo for U.S. Congress, Boise, 1992; active Idaho Falls Arts Coun., Exch. Club Am.; missionary to Switerland LDS Ch., 1958-61. Mem. Art Guild (Pocatello, Idaho). Republican. Home: 2300 S Charlotte Dr Idaho Falls ID 83402-5675

STOTLER, ALICEMARIE HUBER, federal judge; b. Alhambra, Calif., May 29, 1942; d. James R. and Loretta M. Huber; m. James Allen Stotler, Sept. 11, 1971. BA, U. So. Calif., 1964, JD, 1967. Bar: Calif. 1967, U.S. Dist. Ct. (no. dist.) Calif. 1967, U.S. Dist. Ct. (cen. dist.) Calif. 1973, U.S. Supreme Ct., 1976; cert. criminal law specialist. Dep. Orange County Dist. Atty.'s Office, 1967-73; mem. Stotler & Stotler, Santa Ana, Calif., 1973-76, 83-84; judge Orange County Mcpl. Ct., 1976-78, Orange County Superior Ct., 1978-83, U.S. Dist. Ct. (cen. dist.) Calif., L.A., 1984—; assoc. dean Calif. Trial Judges Coll., 1982; lectr., panelist, numerous orgns.; standing com. on rules of practice and procedure U.S. Jud. Conf., 1991—, chair, 1993—; mem. exec. com. 9th Cir. Jud. Conf., 1989-93, Fed. State Jud. Coun., 1989-93, jury com., 1990-92, planning com. for Nat. Conf. on Fed.-State Judicial Relationships, Orlando, 1991-92, planning com for We. Regional Conf. on State-Fed. Judicial Relationships, Stevens, Wash., 1992-93; chair dist. ct. symposium and jury utilization Ctrl. Dist. Calif., 1985, chair atty. liason, 1989-90, chair U.S. Constitution Bicentennial com., 1986-91, chair magistrate judge com., 1992-93; mem. State Adv. Group. on Juvenile Justice and Delinquency Prevention, 1983-84, Bd. Legal Speciliazations Criminal Law Adv. Commn., 1983-84, victim/witness adv. com. Office Criminal Justice Planning, 1980-83, U. So. Calif. Bd. Councilors, 1993—; active team in tng. Leukemia Soc. Am., 1993, 95; legion lex bd. dir. U. So. Calif. Sch. Law Support Group, 1981-83. Winner Hale Moot Ct. Competition, State of Calif., 1967; named Judge of Yr., Orange County Trial Lawyers Assn., 1978, Most Outstanding Judge, Orange County Bus. Litigation Sect., 1990; recipient Franklin G. West award Orange County Bar Assn., 1985. Mem. ABA (jud. adminstrn. divsn.and litigation sect. 1984—, nat. conf. fed. trial judges com. on legis. affairs 1990-91), Am. Law Inst., Am. Judicature Soc., Fed. Judges Assn. (bd. dirs. 1989-92), Nat. Assn. Women Judges, U.S. Supreme Ct. Hist. Soc., Ninth Cir. Dist. Judges Assn., Calif. Supreme Ct. Hist. Soc., Orange County Bar Assn. (mem. numerous coms., Franklin G. West award 1984), Calif. Judges Assn. (mem. com. on judicial coll. 1978-80, com. on civil law and procedure 1980-82, Dean's coll. curriculum commn. 1981), Calif. Judges Found. Office: US Dist Ct PO Box 12339 751 W Santa Ana Blvd Santa Ana CA 92701-4509

STOTT, BRIAN, software company executive; b. Eccles, Eng., Aug. 5, 1941; came to U.S., 1983; s. Harold and Mary (Stephens) S.; m. Patricia Ann Farrar, Dec. 3, 1983. BSc, Manchester U., 1962, MSc, 1963, PhD, 1971. Asst. prof. Middle East Tech. U., Ankara, Turkey, 1965-68; lectr. Inst. Sci. and Tech., U. Manchester (Eng.), 1968-74; assoc. prof. U. Waterloo (Ont., Can.), 1974-76; cons. Electric Energy Rsch. Ctr. Brazil, Rio de Janeiro, 1976-83; prof. Ariz. State U., Tempe, 1983-84; pres. Power Computer Applications Corp., Mesa, Ariz., 1984—; cons. in field. Contbr. numerous articles to rsch. publs. Fellow IEEE. Office: Power Computer Applications 1921 S Alma School Rd Ste 207 Mesa AZ 85210-3038

STOTT, JAMES CHARLES, chemical company executive; b. Portland, Oreg., Sept. 5, 1945; s. Walter Joseph and Rellalee (Gray) S.; m. Caroline Loveriane Barnes, Dec. 7, 1973; children: William Joseph, Maryann Lee. BBA, Portland State U., 1969. Ops. mgr. Pacific States Express, Inc., Portland, 1970-73; bus. mgr. Mogul Corp., Portland, 1974-80; v.p. Market Transport, Ltd., Portland, 1980-85; pres., founder, chmn. bd. dirs. Chem. Corp. Am., Portland, 1985—, also bd. dirs.; chmn. bd. dirs. Carolina Industries, Portland. Mem. TAPPI. Republican. Roman Catholic. Club: University (Portland). Home: 3842 Wellington Ct West Linn OR 97068-3651 Office: Chem Corp Am 2525 SE 9th Ave Portland OR 97202-1048

STOTT, PETER WALTER, forest products company executive; b. Spokane, Wash., May 26, 1944; s. Walter Joseph and Rellalee (Gray) S. Student Portland State U., 1962-63, 65-68, U. Americas, Mexico City, 1964-65. Founder, chmn. bd. dirs. Market Transport Ltd., Portland, Oreg., 1969—; bd. dirs., pres., CEO, prin. Crown Pacific. Bd. dirs. Sunshine divsn. Portland Police Bur. (hon.), Liberty Northwest; assoc. mem. adv. bd. Pacific Crest Outward Bound Sch.; mem. pres.'s adv. bd. for athletics Portland State U. With USAR, 1966-72. Mem. Nat. Football Found. and Hall of Fame, Oreg. Sports Hall Fame (lifetime), Oreg. Trucking Assn., Arlington Club, Astoria Golf and Country, Mazamas Club, Multnomah Athletic Club, Portland Golf Club, Univ. Club. Republican. Roman Catholic. Office: Crown Pacific 121 SW Morrison St Ste 1500 Portland OR 97204-3139

STOTZ, NATALIE HAMER, underwriter; b. Gt. Falls, Mont., Oct. 22, 1921; d. Arthur C. Hamer and Gertrude H. (Kaufmann) Wallace; m. Theodore Philip Stotz, June 9, 1956. Student Great Falls Comml. Coll., 1939. C.L.U. Br. office cashier Occidental Life Ins. Co., Great Falls, 1939-44; sec. to underwriter, San Francisco, 1944-47; head claims dept. Friedman & Co., San Francisco, 1947-62; adminstrv. asst. to underwriter, San Jose, Calif., 1962—. Mem. Am. Soc. C.L.U.s. Sec.-treas. West Bay Opera Guild, Palo Alto, Calif., 1965-67. Republican. Christian Scientist. Avocation: ballet. Home: 988 N California Ave Palo Alto CA 94303-3405 Office: 25 Metro Dr Ste 228 San Jose CA 95110-1338

STOUFER, RUTH HENDRIX, community volunteer; b. Pitts., June 21, 1916; d. Walter Willits and Frances (Ponbeck) Hendrix; m. William Kimball Stoufer, Sept. 8, 1937 (dec.); children: Walter Hendrix, Frances Elizabeth Stoufer Waller. BS, Iowa State U., 1937. Trustee Marcus J. Lawrence Meml. Hosp., 1989—; devel. chairperson Sedona-Verde Valley Am. Heart Assn., 1988-91; mem. adv. bd. L.A. chpt. Freedom's Found., 1965-78; mem. coord. med. adv. bd. U. Ariz., 1986—; founding chairperson Muses of the Mus. No. Ariz., 1984-85, pres., 1986-87, mem. Sinagua Soc., 1983—; bd. dirs. Nat. Charity League, L.A., 1963, Found. for Children, L.A., 1964, 65, 66; pres. Panhellenic adv. bd. U. So. Calif., 1964; key adv. U. So. Calif. chpt. Beta Alpha of Gamma Phi Beta, 1960-63. Named Woman of Yr., Inter-city Coun., Gamma Phi Beta, 1963. Home: 87 Doodlebug Knoll Sedona AZ 86336-6422

STOUT, ADELIA DIANE, therapist; b. Greenville, Mich., Sept. 22, 1956; d. James Robert and Jean Adelia (Sorensen) Stout; 1 child, Jesse Lee. AA, Northwood U., Cedar Hill, Tex., 1975; BA, San Francisco State U., 1993, postgrad., 1993—. Women's dir. Solidarity Fellowship, San Mateo, Calif., 1989-90; piano tchr. Pacifica, Calif., 1987-94, Colton Piano and Organ, San Carlos, Calif., 1986-89; chem. dependency therapist Summit Med. Ctr./MPI/CDTS, Oakland, Calif., 1993—; lectr. San Francisco State U., 1992—; aerobics instr. San Francisco YMCA, Merritt-Peralta Inst. Chem. Dependency Treatment Svcs. Mem. Nat. Assn. Drug and Alcohol Counselors, Suzuki Assn. of Am., Am. Counseling Assn., Calif. Assn. Drug and Alcohol Counselors, Golden Key, Psi Chi. Democrat. Presbyterian. Office: Summit Med Ctr-MPI/CDTS 435 Hawthorne Ave Oakland CA 94609-3031

STOUT, ELIZABETH WEST, administrator; b. San Francisco, Mar. 4, 1917; d. Claudius Wilson and Sarah (Henderson) West; m. Bruce Churchill McDonald, Mar. 19 1944 (dec. 1952); children: Douglas, Anne; m. Charles Holt Stout, Oct. 27, 1958 (dec. 1992); stepchildren: Richard, George (dec.), Martha Stout Gilweit. Student, U. Nev., 1934-37; grad., Imperial Valley Coll., 1990. Cashier, acct. N.Y. Underwriters, San Francisco, 1937-42; sec. supply and accounts USN, San Francisco, 1942-44. Contbr. articles to profl. jours. Mem. adv. bd. Anza-Borrego Desert, 1974-84; founder Stout Paleontology Lab., Borrego Springs, Calif., 1982; found. trustee Desert Rsch. Inst., Reno, 1989—; active Black Rock Desert Project, 1989, Washoe Med. Ctr. League, 1953—, St. Mary's Hosp. Guild, 1953—. Named Disting. Nevadan U. Nev., 1993. Mem. Anza-Borrego Desert Natural History Assn. (dir. emeritus 1984), Soc. Vertebrate Paleontology, De Anza Desert Country Club, Kappa Alpha Theta. Republican. Episcopalian.

STOUT, JAMES TILMAN, minister; b. Pitts., Feb. 20, 1942; s. Randall Stuart and Alice Margaret (Stevenson) S.; m. Leah Ann Hayden, June 24, 1967; children: James T. Jr., John Davis. Student, U. Pitts., 1960-63; BA, Miami U. of Ohio, 1965; MDiv, Gorden Conwell Sem., 1969; DMin, Fuller Sem., 1980. Ordained to ministry Presbyn. Ch., 1969. Assoc. pastor Key Biscayne (Fla.) Presbyn. Ch., 1969-74; pastor First Presbyn. Ch., North Palm Beach, Fla., 1974-81, St. Andrews Presbyn. Ch., Beaumont, Tex., 1981-83, Covenant Presbyn. Ch., Sharon, Pa., 1983-87; assoc. pastor St. Andrews Presbyn. Ch., Newport Beach, Calif., 1987-91; area dir. Gathering of Men, Costa Mesa, Calif., 1992—. Author: Winning Over Depression, 1992. Named Golden Glove Heavyweight Champion, Pitts., 1961. Mem. Exch. Club, Rotary. Office: Gathering of Men 2093 Santa Ana Ave Costa Mesa CA 92627-2140

STOUT, ROGER PAUL, mechanical engineer; b. Phoenix, July 10, 1956; s. Arthur Paul and Marilyn Sue (Munsil) S.; m. Carol Louise Gordon, Mar. 24, 1979; children: Julia Renee, Matthew Paul, Joshua Michael. BSE, Ariz. State U., 1977; MSME, Calif. Inst. Tech., 1979. Registered profl. engr., Ariz. Mem. tech. staff Hughes Aircraft Co., Culver City, Calif., 1977-79; sr. engr. Motorola, Phoenix, 1979-80, staff engr., 1980-82; sr. staff engr. Motorola, Chandler, Ariz., 1982-84, prin. staff engr., 1984-86, mem. tech. staff, 1986-92, sr. mem. tech. staff and mgr. thermal characterization lab., 1992—; guest lectr. Coll. Engring. Ariz. State U., Tempe, 1991. Contbr. articles to profl. jours. Inventor die pick mechanism, voice coil motor with integral capacitor. Lay leader St. Andrews United Meth. Ch., Mesa, Ariz., 1992—, fin. chairperson, 1986-91. Mem. ASME, Soc. Mfg. Engrs. (robotics internat. divsn. 1984), Ariz. Assn. for the Gifted and Talented (treas. exec. bd. dirs. 1992), Tau Beta Pi, Phi Kappa Phi, Pi Tau Sigma, Phi Eta Sigma. Methodist.

STOUT, THOMAS MELVILLE, control system engineer; b. Ann Arbor, Mich., Nov. 26, 1925; s. Melville B. and Laura C. (Meisel) S.; m. Marilyn J. Koebnick, Dec. 27, 1947; children: Martha, Sharon, Carol, James, William, Kathryn. BSEE, Iowa State Coll., 1946; MSE, U. Mich., 1947, PhD, 1954. Registered profl. engr., Calif. Jr. engr. Emerson Electric Co., St. Louis, 1947-48; instr., then asst. prof. U. Wash., Seattle, 1948-54; rsch. engr. Schlumberger Instrument Co., Ridgefield, Conn., 1954-56; dept. mgr. TRW/Bunker-Ramo Corp., Canoga Park, Calif., 1956-65; pres. Profimatics, Inc., Thousand Oaks, Calif., 1965-83; pvt. practice cons. Northridge, Calif., 1984—; active profl. engring. registration and certification. Contbr. articles, revs., papers to profl. publs., chpts. to books. Ens. USN, 1943-46. Fellow, hon. mem. Instrument Soc. Am.; mem. IEEE (sr. mem.), NSPE, Am. Inst. Chem. Engrs., Am. Soc. for Engring. Edn., Calif. Soc. Profl. Engrs. Home and Office: 9927 Hallack Ave Northridge CA 91324-1120

STOVER, MARK EDWIN, librarian; b. Newport News, Va., May 1, 1961; s. Arnold Clinton and Janet Louise (Sheldon) S.; m. Elaine Davis, June 10, 1984; children: Hannah Rose, Malka Gabrielle, Adam Jacob. BA, Biola U., 1983; MA in Religion, Westminster Sem., Phila., 1986; MLS, UCLA, 1988. Theol. libr. Calvin Coll. and Sem., Grand Rapids, Mich., 1988-90; libr. dir. Calif. Family Study Ctr., North Hollywood, Calif., 1990—; cons. St. George's Coll., Jerusalem, 1991-92. Author: (with others) The Reader's Advisor, 1993; editor Libr. Trends, 1992; contbr. articles to profl. jours. Mem. ALA, Calif. Acad. and Rsch. Librs. Office: Calif Family Study Ctr 5433 Laurel Canyon Blvd North Hollywood CA 91607-2114

STOVER, MILES RONALD, manufacturing executive; b. Glendale, Calif., Dec. 23, 1948; s. Robert Miles and Alberta Mae (Walker) S.; m. Cynthia McNeil, Jan. 25, 1975; children: Christopher, Matthew. BS, U. So. Calif., 1974; MBA, Pepperdine U., 1979; D of Bus. Adminstrn., U.S. Internat. U., 1982. V.p., gen. mgr., CFO Johnson Controls Inc., L.A., 1974-82; gen. mgr. MG Products Inc., San Diego, 1982-84; exec. v.p., gen. mgr. ICU Med. Inc., Mission Viejo, 1984-86; v.p., COO B.P. John Inc., Santa Ana, Calif., 1986-88; gen. mgr. MG Products Inc., San Diego, 1988-90; pres. Lucks Co., Kent, Wash., 1991—, also bd. dirs.; cons. Turnaround Mgmt. Assn., Tacoma, 1990. Bd. dirs. Big Bros. Am. With USN, 1967-71. Recipient Gallantry Cross medal USN, 1971, Award for Productivity U.S. Senate, 1978. Republican. Methodist. Home: 2727 41st St SE Puyallup WA 98374

STOWE, NEAL P., architect; b. Odgen, Utah, July 21, 1943; m. Peggy L. Leininger, Aug. 1965; children: Brett Phillip, Amy Lynn, Christopher William. Student, Weber State Coll., 1963-64; BS, U. Utah, 1971, MArch, 1973; cert., Duke U., 1987. Registered architect, Utah. Project mgr. Richardson Assocs. AIA, Salt Lake City, 1974-78, assoc. ptnr., 1978-83, ptnr.-prin., 1983-86; dir. divsn. facilities constrn. and mgmt. State of Utah, Salt Lake City, 1986—; dir. facilities devel. Utah Sports Authority, Salt Lake City; mem. Regional Urban Design Com., Olympia, Wash., 1990; mem. rev. exec. com. Salt Palace Conv. Ctr., 1991—. Voting dist. chmn., county and state del. to polit. convs., 1972, 74, 76; mem. Utah Gov.'s Com. Hist. and Cultural Sites, 1978-86; mem. Ridgecrest Sch. Community Coun., 1988-89; mem. adv. bd. Salt Lake City Downtown Alliance, 1991; officer bd. trustees Assist Inc., 1976-80, pres. bd. trustees, 1980-84. With USAR, 1961-69. Recipient Award for Outstanding Svc., United Way Salt Lake City, 1977, Disting. Achievement award Dixie Coll., 1989, Pub. Svc. award Utah State Dept. Corrections, 1989, Award of Recognition, Air Force Heritage Mus. Found. Utah, 1991; named Hon. Adm., Nebr. State Navy, 1991, Outstanding Constrn. Person of Yr., Intermountain Contractor Mag. and Panel, 1993. Fellow AIA (chmn. united fund dr. Utah soc. 1976-77, chmn. ann. meeting 1985, pres. elect 1985, pres. 1986, v.p., mem. founding com. Salt Lake chpt. 1978, pres. 1979, organizing chmn. ann. meeting western mountain region 1986, chmn. pres. commn. 1986, vice chmn./chmn. elect nat. com. pub. architecture 1990, chmn. 1991, co-chmn. nat. symposium restoration states capitol bldgs. 1991, juror Thomas Jefferson award 1992, Award of Distinction western mountain region 1982); mem. Am. Soc. Pub. Adminstrs., Nat. Assn. State Facilities Adminstrs. (v.p. western states 1989, 90, sr. v.p. 1991, pres. 1992-93, past pres., sr. dir. 1993), Nat. Owners, Contractors, and Designers Adv. Coun. (mem. steering com. 1992), Nat. Com. Design, Nat. Com. Pub. Architecture, Urban Design Com. Office: State of Utah 8819 Hidden Oaks Dr Salt Lake City UT 84121-6330

STOWELL, KENT, ballet director; b. Rexburg, Idaho, Aug. 8, 1939; s. Harold Bowman and Maxine (Hudson) S.; m. Francia Marie Russell, Nov. 19, 1965; children: Christopher, Darren, Ethan. Student, San Francisco Ballet Sch., Sch. Am. Ballet; Lead dancer San Francisco Ballet, 1957-62, N.Y.C. Ballet, 1962-68; ballet dir., ballet master Frankfurt (Fed. Republic Germany) Opera Ballet, 1973-77; artistic dir. Pacific N.W. Ballet, Seattle, 1977—; prof. dance Ind. U., Bloomington, 1969-70; bd. dirs. Dance/USA, Washington, 1986—. Choreographer: Cinderella, Carmina Burana, Coppelia, Time & Ebb, Fauré Requiem, Hail to the Conquering Hero, Firebird, Over the Waves, Nutcracker, The Tragedy of Romeo and Juliet, Delicate Balance, Swan Lake. Bd. dirs. Sch. of Am. Ballet, N.Y.C., 1981—; mem. Goodwill Games Arts Com., Seattle, 1987—; chmn. dance panel NEA, 1981-85. Grantee NEA, 1980, 85; fellow NEA, 1979. Recipient Arts Service award King County Arts Commn., 1985, Outstanding Contbn. to Pacific N.W. Ballet State of Was., 1987, Best Dance Co. award The Weekly Newspaper, Seattle, 1987, Gov. Arts award, 1988. Office: Pacific NW Ballet 301 Mercer St Seattle WA 98109-4600

STOWERS, NELL LOUGENE (GENIE STOWERS), political scientist, educator; b. Huntington, W.Va., May 6, 1957; d. Bernard Lucian and Camille Katherine (Taylor) S. BA in Urban Studies, U. Fla., 1979; MPA in Environ. Growth Mgmt., Fla. Atlantic U., 1980; PhD in Polit. Sci., Fla. State U., 1987. Econ. devel. planning intern Planning Dept., Palm Beach County, Fla., 1980; program analyst HUD, Washington, 1980-81; rsch. assoc. polit. sci. Ariz. State U., 1981-82; rsch. assoc. policy scis. Fla. State U., 1982-86; asst. prof. dept. polit. sci. and pub. affairs U. Ala., Birmingham, 1986-91, dir. Women's Studies Program, 1989-91; asst. prof. pub. adminstrn. San Francisco State U., 1991-93, assoc. prof. pub. adminstrn., 1993—; cons./ expert witness State of Fla., others, 1984—; chair exhibits com. S.E. Conf. Pub. Adminstrn., 1988; spl. cons. San Francisco Urban Inst., 1992—, chair colloquia com., 1993—; active San Francisco Urban Inst. Exec. Com., 1993—, sexual harassment com. Co-author: Big City Governing and Fiscal Choices, Big City Politics Revisited, Administration and Social Work, Research in Micropolitics, Vol. 11; author: Ethnic Groups, Public Budgeting and Finance. Bd. dirs., treas., chair fin. and adminstrv. policies com., WOMAN, Inc., 1992-94; mem. personnel com. Am. Friends Svc. Com., Pacific Mountain Region, 1992—; mem. Revenues Enhancement Working Group, Mayor's Task Force on the Fiscal Crisis, 1993; chief acct. Expert Rating Panel, Jefferson County, Ala. Personnel Bd., 1991; analyst United Way Task Force on AIDS survey of Agy. AIDS Policy Efforts, United Way of Cen. Ala., 1991; numerous other panels and coms. Recipient Faculty Affirmative Action grant, San Francisco State U., 1991-92, 93-94, faculty rsch. grant summer stipend, 1992-93, Am. Polit. Sci. Assn. Rsch. Grant award, 1988, grad. assistantships, Fla. State U., 1982-86; named to Outstanding Young Women of Am., 1979, 86; recipient Hubert Humphrey, Jr. Young Dem. of Yr. Community Svc. award, 1979, others. Mem. Am. Soc. Pub. Adminstrn. (nat. coun. 1994—, bd. mem. Bay area chpt. 1992—), Am. Polit. Sci. Assn., U. Fla. Alumnae Assn., Fla. Atlantic U. Alumnae Assn., Fla. State U. Alumnae Assn., Fla. Blue Key, Omicron Delta Kappa, Gamma Sigma Sigma. Democrat. Mem. Soc. of Friends. Office: San Francisco State U Pub Adminstrn Program 1600 Holloway Ave San Francisco CA 94132-1722

STRACK, STEPHEN NAYLOR, psychologist; b. Rome, N.Y., Nov. 13, 1955; s. Ralph and Grace (Naylor) S.; m. Leni Ferrero. BA, U. Calif., Berkeley, 1978; PhD, U. Miami, Fla., 1983. Psychologist L.A. County Dept. Mental Health, 1984-85; staff psychologist VA Outpatient Clinic, L.A., 1985-92, dir. tng., 1992—; clin. assoc. U. So. Calif., L.A., 1986—; adj. assoc. prof. Calif. Sch. Profl. Psychology, L.A., 1989—; clin. prof. Fuller Grad. Sch. Psychology, Pasadena, 1986—; cons. editor Jour. of Personality Disorder, N.Y.C., 1992—. Author (test): Personality Adjective Check List, 1987; co-author (book): Differentiating Normal and Abnormal Personality, 1994; contbr. articles to profl. jours. U.S. Dept. Vets. Affairs grantee, 1986—. Fellow Soc. for Personality Assessment; mem. APA, Calif. Psychol. Assn., European Assn. of Psychol. Assessment, Soc. for Rsch. in Psychopathology, Western Psychol. Assn., Sigma Xi. Office: VA Outpatient Clinic 351 E Temple St Los Angeles CA 90012-3328

STRACUZZI, DIANE ELIZABETH, marketing director; b. St. Louis, Aug. 8, 1961; d. Robert Louis and Merle Kathleen (Bolin) Stuart; m. James Anthony Stracuzzi, Sept. 6, 1986. BA in Pub. Rels., Bus., San Jose State U., 1984. Asst. mgr. pub. rels. Monterey Bay Aquarium, Monterey, Calif., 1984-88; dir. pub. rels. Pebble Beach (Calif.) Co., 1988-92, dir. mktg., 1992—. Bd. dirs. Jr. League Monterey County, 1991-93. Mem. Pub. Rels. Soc. Am., Golf Writers Assn. Am., Calif. Golf Writers, Soc. Am. Travel Writers. Home: PO Box 683 Pebble Beach CA 93953-0683 Office: Pebble Beach Co. PO Box 567 Pebble Beach CA 93953-0567

STRADLEY, RICHARD LEE, lawyer; b. Chula Vista, Calif. Sept. 10, 1951; s. George R. and Betty J. (Laughman) S.; m. Christine A. Crofts, Sept. 7, 1991. B.A., Coll. Santa Fe, 1972; J.D., U. Miss., 1975. Bar: Miss. 1975, Mont. 1982, U.S. Dist. Ct. (no. dist.) Miss. 1975, U.S. Dist. Ct. (so. dist.) Miss. 1981, U.S. Dist. Ct. (we. dist.) Tenn. 1982, U.S. Dist. Ct. Mont. 1980, U.S. Tax Ct. 1981, U.S. Ct. Appeals (5th and 9th cirs.) 1980, U.S. Ct. Appeals (10th and 11th cirs.) 1981, U.S. Supreme Ct. 1981, U.S. Dist. Ct. (no. dist.) Tex. 1984, Oreg. 1985, U.S. Dist. Ct. Oreg. 1986, U.S. Dist. Ct. Nebr. 1986, Wyo. 1994. Sole practice, 1975—; staff atty. East Miss. Legal Services, Forest, 1979. Mem. Christian Legal Soc., Assn. Trial Lawyers Am. Avocations: chess, computers, woodworking. Office: PO Box 2541 Cody WY 82414-2541

STRAHAN, JULIA CELESTINE, electronics company executive; b. Indpls., Feb. 10, 1938; d. Edgar Paul Pauley and Pauline Barbara (Myers) Shawver; m. Norman Strahan, Oct. 2, 1962 (div. 1982); children: Daniel Keven, Natalie Kay. Grad. high sch., Indpls. With EG&G/Energy Measurements, Inc., Las Vegas, Nev., 1967—; sect. head EG&G Co., 1979-83, mgr. electronics dept., 1984—. Recipient award Am. Legion, 1952, Excellence award, 1986. Mem. NAFE, Am. Nuclear Soc. (models and mentors), Internat. Platform Assn. Home: 5222 Stacey Ave Las Vegas NV 89108-3078 Office: EG&G PO Box 1912 Las Vegas NV 89125-1912

STRAHLER, ARTHUR NEWELL, former geology educator, author; b. Kolhapur, India, Feb. 20, 1918; s. Milton W. and Harriet (Brittan) S.; m. Margaret E. Wanless, Aug. 10, 1940; children: Alan H., Marjorie E. A.B., Coll. Wooster, 1938; A.M., Columbia U., 1940, Ph.D. (Univ. fellow), 1944. Faculty Columbia U., 1941-71, prof. geomorphology, 1958-68, adj. prof. geology, 1968-71, chmn. dept. geology, 1959-62. Author: Physical Geography, rev. edit., 1975, The Earth Sciences, rev. edit., 1971, Introduction to Physical Geography, rev. edit., 1973, Planet Earth, 1971, Environmental Geoscience, 1973, Introduction to Environmental Science, 1974, Elements of Physical Geography, 2d edit., 1979, 3d edit., 1984, 4th edit., 1989, Principles of Earth Science, 1976, Principles of Physical Geology, 1977, Geography and Man's Environment, 1977, Modern Physical Geography, 1978, 4th edit., 1992, Physical Geology, 1981, Science and Earth History—The Evolution/ Creation Controversy, 1987, Investigating Physical Geography, 1989, Understanding Science: An Introduction to Concepts and Issues, 1992. Fellow Geol. Soc. Am., Am. Geog. Soc.; mem. Am. Geophys. Union, Phi Beta Kappa, Sigma Xi. Home: 1039 Cima Linda Ln Santa Barbara CA 93108-1818

STRAIGHT, JAMES WESLEY, secondary education educator; b. Ely, Nev., Jan. 3, 1930; s. James Wesley Sr. and Mary Elizabeth (Hunter) S.; m. Gloria Frances Rosysum, Aug. 22, 1954; children: James W. Jr., Elizabeth Straight Stevenson, Kathryn Straight Hernandez, Douglas Scott. BS in Geol. Engring., U. Nev., Reno, 1954. Cert. secondary tchr., Calif. Geol. engr. Kennecott Copper Corp., McGill, Nev., 1954-57; soil engr. John F. Byerly, Bloomington, Calif., 1967-82; foreman Eagle-Picher, Loverlock, Nev., 1957-61, Kaiser Steel, Fontana, Calif., 1962-67; tchr. indsl. arts Fontana Unified Schs., 1967-92; tchr. prospecting class Rialto (Calif.) Unified Schs., 1969—; tchr. prospecting class U. Calif., Riverside, 1976. Author, pub.: Follow the Drywashers, 1988, vol. 2, 1990, vol. 3, 1993, Magnificent Quest, 1990; contbg. editor mags. Popular Mining, Treas. Found., Western and Ea. Treas., Treas. Gold and Silver. Treas. San Bernadino (Calif.) Area Assn. for the Retarded, 1972. 1st lt. U.S. Army C.E., 1955-57. Mem. Masons. Republican. Episcopalian. Home and Office: 19225 Mesa St Rialto CA 92377-4558

STRAIN, JOHN THOMAS, electronics engineer; b. Raymondville, Mo., Oct. 25, 1939; s. Thomas and Lillie (Merckling) S.; m. Bonnie J. Cline, 1967 (div. 1980); children: Robert Vidmar, Anthony Vidmar. BSEE, U. Mo., Rolla, 1964. Electronics technician Exec. Aircraft Co., Kansas City, Mo., 1960-61; electronic engring. technician Wilcox Electric Co., Kansas City, 1963, sr. electronics technician, 1964-67; sr. electronics technician Exec. Aircraft Co., 1964; electronic engring. tech. Gianni Voltex Co., San Diego, 1967-68; electronic fabricator Bendix Atomic Energy Commn., Kansas City, 1968; electronics engr. Electronic Research Corp., Overland Park, Kans., 1968-69, Monitor Products Co., South Pasadena, Calif., 1969-73, NBC, Burbank, Calif., 1973--. Designed and developed original TV stereo encoder; responsible (with Ron Estes) for first recorded stereo TV program (nominated for Emmy 1983); developer first DIP style crystal controled oscillator for use in computer and areospace industries. With USAF, 1964-65. Home: 6450 Clybourn Ave North Hollywood CA 91606-2728 Office: NBC 3000 W Alameda Ave Burbank CA 91523-0001

STRAIN, JOHN WILLARD, consulting aerospace engineer, landscape artist; b. Ottumwa, Iowa, Dec. 31, 1929; s. John Wells and Agnes Gertrude (Kearns) S.; m. Elizabeth LaVonne Moment, Dec. 27, 1952 (dec.); children: James Anthony, Mary Therese, Michael Douglas, Meagan Kathleen; m. Judith Lee Scott, Feb. 11, 1989. Student Upper Iowa U., 1947-48; B.A., U. No. Iowa, 1952. Supr., aero. rocket power plant engr. White Sands Proving Ground, N.Mex., 1954-55; mgr. Santa Cruz test and Hunters Point, Missile Systems div. Lockheed Missiles & Space Co., Sunnyvale, Calif., 1960-63, mgr. Ea. Test Range support, 1966-73, chief test engr. Aquila RPV/STD Program, 1975-78, factory test mgr. Army RPV Program, 1979-82, qualification and test engring. div. mgr., chief test engr., 1982-84, mgmt. proposal assignment, 1984-89, ret., 1989; owner Indsl. Systems Co. Bd. dirs. San Jose Civic Light Opera, 1971-73, Grants Pass Mus. Art, 1993-95; pres. Josephine County Artists Assn., 1994—; treas. Assn. Unmanned Vehicle Systems, 1982-84. Served with AUS, 1952-54. Recipient Alumni Service award U. No. Iowa, 1981. Assoc. fellow AIAA; mem. Nat. Mgmt. Assn., AAAS, Inst. Environ. Scis. (sr.). Republican. Roman Catholic. Assoc. editor Missile Away mag. Am. Rocket Soc., 1954-55. Office: Industrial Systems Co 4801 Azalea Dr Grants Pass OR 97526-8298

STRAKA, DONALD JOSEPH, technical educator; b. Milw., Apr. 13, 1948; s. Edward Ignatius and Sylvia Genaveise (Wronski) S.; m. Patricia Ann Sowards, Nov. 20, 1971; children: Dawn-Marie, Peggysue-Ann, Cynthia-Marie. Student, Carroll Coll., 1966-68; BSME, Marquette U., 1973. Enlisted USN, 1968, elec. divsn. officer USS Camden, 1974-77, ship's force overhaul mgmt. system officer USS Ranger, 1977-79, instr., tng. support officer, 1979-81, chief engr. officer USS Proteus, 1981-82; asst. supr. tng. Niagara Mohawk Power Corp., 1982-85, supr. ops. tng., 1985-89, assoc. sr. generation specialist, 1989-91; sr. tech. instr. Ariz. Pub. Svc.-Palo Verde Nuclear Generation Sta., Phoenix, 1991—; accreditation peer evaluator Inst. Nuclear Power Operators, Atlanta, 1993. Comdr. USNR, 1982—, Desert Storm. Mem. VFW, Am. Legion, Beer Drinkers Am. Republican. Roman Catholic. Home: 11339 W Primrose Dr Avondale AZ 85323-3414 Office: PVNGS-Ariz Pub Svc MS 7894 PO Box 52034 Phoenix AZ 85072-2034

STRAKA, WILLIAM CHARLES, II, astronomer; b. Phoenix, Oct. 21, 1940; s. William Charles and Martha Nadine (Marshall) S.; m. Barbara Ellen Thayer, Jan. 29, 1966; 1 child, William Charles III. BS, Calif. Inst. Tech., 1962; MA, UCLA, 1965, PhD, 1969. Tchr. Long Beach (Calif.) City Coll., 1966-70; asst. prof. Boston U., 1970-74; prof., dept. head Jackson (Miss.) State U., 1974-84; sr. staff scientist Lockheed Palo Alto (Calif.) Rsch. Lab., 1984—. Contbr. articles to profl. jours. Mem. Am. Astron. Soc., Sigma Xi. Office: Lockheed Palo Alto Rsch Lab 3251 Hanover St Palo Alto CA 94304-1121

STRALING, PHILLIP FRANCIS, bishop; b. San Bernardino, Calif., Apr. 25, 1933; s. Sylvester J. and Florence E. (Robinson) S. BA, U. San Diego, 1963; MS in Child and Family Counseling, San Diego State U., 1971. Ordained priest Roman Catholic Ch., 1959, consecrated bishop, 1978. Mem. faculty St. John Acad., El Cajon, Calif., 1959-60, St. Therese Acad., San Diego, 1960-63; chaplain Newman Club, San Diego State U., 1960-72; mem. faculty St. Francis Sem., San Diego, 1972-76; pastor Holy Rosary Parish, San Bernardino, 1976-78; bishop Diocese of San Bernardino, 1978-95; pub. Inland Cath. newspaper, 1979-95; chmn. USCC/NCCB Com. on Lay Ministry, 1993—; bishop of Reno, Nev., 1995—; bd. dirs. Calif. Assn. Cath. Campus Mins., 1960s; exec. sec. Diocesan Synod II, 1972-76; Episcopal vicar San Bernardino Deanery, 1976-78. Mem. Nat. Cath. Campus Ministries Assn. (bishop rep. 1992—). Office: PO Box 1211 Reno NV 89504-1211

STRAND, CHERYL MARIE, Spanish language, literature educator; b. Viborg, S.D., Aug. 27, 1944; d. Alfred Nicholi and Lillian Evelyn (Wilson) S.; m. Alan Louis Kalter, Feb. 14, 1981; 1 child, Christopher Michael Kalter-Strand. BS, S.D. State U., 1966; MA, Calif. State U., Fresno, 1969; PhD, U. Calif., L.A., 1989. Tchg. asst. Calif. State U., Fresno, 1968-69, U. Calif., L.A., 1969-72, 76; instr. Ohio State U., Columbus, 1976-77; assoc. U. Wash., Seattle, 1979-83, lectr., Spanish coord., 1983-84, 86-89; instr. Shoreline C.C., Seattle, 1985; assoc. prof. Western Oreg. State Coll., Monmouth, 1989—; mem. Latin Am. Exec. Bd., Oreg. State System of Higher Edn., 1989—; chmn. dept. modern langs. Western Oreg. State Coll., Monmouth, 1991-94; mem. Spanish Proficiency Stds. Commn., Chancellor's Office, Oreg. State System Higher Edn., 1993-94; presenter rsch. papers Mid-Am. Conf., Kans., Nebr., 1989, 91. Contbr. articles, reviews to profl. publs. Panelist Office of Fgn. Study Programs, Oreg. State System of Higher Edn., Corvallis, 1992, others. Recipient scholarship for study in Spain, Fulbright, 1972-73, fellowship for doctoral rsch. Del Amo Found., Spain, 1974-75. Mem. MLA, Twentieth Century Spanish Assn. of Am., Confedn. of Oreg. Fgn. Lang. Tchrs., AAUW, AAUP, Phi Sigma Iota, Sigma Delta Pi, Phi Kappa Phi. Office: Dept Modern Langs Western Oreg State Coll Monmouth OR 97361

STRAND, ROGER GORDON, federal judge; b. Peekskill, N.Y., Apr. 28, 1934; s. Ernest Gordon Strand and Lisabeth Laurine (Phin) Steinmetz; m. Joan Williams, Nov. 25, 1961. AB, Hamilton Coll., 1955; LLB, Cornell U., 1961; grad., Nat. Coll. State Trial Judges, 1968. Bar: Ariz. 1961, U.S. Dist. Ct. Ariz. 1961, U.S. Supreme Ct. 1980. Assoc. Fennemore, Craig, Allen & McClennen, Phoenix, 1961-67; judge Ariz. Superior Ct., Phoenix, 1967-85, U.S. Dist. Ct. Ariz., Phoenix, 1985—; assoc. presiding judge Ariz. Superior Ct., 1971-85; lectr. Nat. Jud. Coll., Reno, 1978-87. Past pres. cen. Ariz. chpt. Arthritis Found. Lt. USN, 1955-61. Mem. ABA, Ariz. Bar Assn., Maricopa County Bar Assn., Nat. Conf. Fed. Trial Judges, Phi Delta Phi, Aircraft Owners and Pilots Assn. Lodge: Rotary. Home: 5825 N 3rd Ave Phoenix AZ 85013-1537 Office: US Dist Ct Courthouse and Fed Bldg 230 N 1st Ave Ste 3013 Phoenix AZ 85025-0002

STRANDBERG, LEE R., pharmacist; b. Valley City, N.D., Oct. 12, 1945; s. Merrill H. and Myrtle A. (Olson) S.; m. Rebecca L. Sandal, Aug. 9, 1969; children: Jennifer, Jon. BS in Pharmacy, N.D. State U., 1968, MS in Social Scis., 1970; PhD, U. Colo., 1975. Asst. prof. pharmacy N.D. State U., Fargo, 1968-72; instr. Oreg. State U., Boulder, 1972-75; prof. Oreg. State U., Coll. Pharmacy, Corvallis, 1975—; cons. State Oreg. Medicaid, Salem, 1976-86, Colo. Bus. Coalition on Health, Denver, 1990—, Oreg. Dept. Corrections, Salem, 1989—, Adolph Coors Co., Golden, Colo., 1990—, Teamsters, 1991—; dir. R&D Pharmacists Svc. Group, Salem, Oreg., 1984—, ODS Health Plans, 1993—. Contbr. articles and videos in field. Mem. Am. Pharm. Assn. (chmn. ESAS sect., 1989), Am. Soc. Pharmacy Law, Assn. Health Svcs. Rsch., Oreg. State Pharmacists Assn. Democrat. Lutheran. Office: Oreg State U Coll Pharmacy Corvallis OR 97331-3507

STRANG, SANDRA LEE, airline official; b. Greensboro, N.C., Apr. 22, 1936; d. Charles Edward and Lobelia Mae (Squires) S.; BA in English, U. N.C., 1960; MBA, U. Dallas, 1970. With American Airlines, Inc., 1960—, mgr. career devel. for women, N.Y.C., 1972-73, dir. selection and tng., 1974-75, sr. dir. selection, tng. and affirmative action, 1975-79, sr. dir. compensation and benefits, Dallas/Ft. Worth, Tex., 1979-84, dir. passenger sales tng. and devel., 1984—; regional sales mgr. Rocky Mountain Region, Denver, 1985—; pres. The SLS Group, Inc., (DBAs) Sales Leadership Seminars, Inc., Sr. Leadership Svcs., Inc., Svc. Leadership Seminars, Inc., Speakers, Lectrs., and Seminars, Inc, 1988—. AARP, Mem. Am. Mgmt. Assn., Assn. Advancement of Women into Mgmt., Am. Soc. Tng. and Devel., Am. Compensation Assn., Internat. Platform Assn. Home: 3493 E Euclid Ave Littleton CO 80121-3663

STRATI, TONY J., accountant. BBA in Acctg., U. Notre Dame, MBA in Acctg. CPA, N.Mex. With Peat Marwick Main & Co., Albuquerque, ptnr., 1981—; conductor practice groups on local government and education. Bd. dirs. Greater Albuquerque C. of C. (mem. fin. com., vice-chmn. membership affairs div.), active United Way, Rehabilitation Ctr. Mem. AICPA, N.Mex. Soc. CPAs (past. bd. dirs.), Rotary. Office: Peat Marwick Main & Co 20 First Plaza Ctr NW Albuquerque NM 87102-3347

STRATTON, GREGORY ALEXANDER, computer specialist, administrator, mayor; b. Glendale, Calif., July 31, 1946; s. William Jaspar and Rita Phyllis (Smith) S.; m. Yolanda Margot Soler, 1967 (div. 1974); 1 child, Tiffany; m. Edith Carter, Sept. 27, 1975; stepchildren: John Henkell, Paul Henkell, D'Lorah Henkell. Student, Harvey Mudd Coll., 1964-65; BS in Physics, UCLA, 1968; MBA, Calif. Luth. U., 1977. Elec. engr. Naval Ship Weapon System Engring. Sta., Port Hueneme, Calif., 1968-73; sr. staff mem. Univac, Valencia, Calif., 1973-74; v.p. Digital Applications, Camarillo, Calif., 1974-75; cons. Grumman Aerospace, Point Mugu, Calif., 1975-76; F-14 software mgr. Pacific Missle Test Ctr., Pt. Mugu, 1976-84; software mgr. Teledyne Systems, Northridge, Calif., 1984-92, dir. engring. software dept., 1992-93; dep. dir. software engring. Teledyne Electronic Systems, Northridge, Calif., 1993-94; software mgr. Litton Guidance and Controls, Northridge, Calif., 1995—. Mem. City Coun., City of Simi Valley, Calif., 1979-86, mayor, 1986—; alt. Rep. County Cen. Com., Ventura County, 1986-88; mem. Rep. State Cen. Com., Calif., 1990—; bd. dirs. Simi Valley Hosp., 1987—. Mem. Assn. Ventura County Cities (chair 1990-91), Rotary (Paul Harris award Simi Sunrise chpt. 1989), Jaycees (pres. Simi Valley chpt. 1974-75, nat. bd. dirs. 1975-76, v.p. Calif. state 1976-77). Republican. Lutheran. Home: 254 Goldenwood Cir Simi Valley CA 93065-6771 Office: Office of Mayor 2929 Tapo Canyon Rd Simi Valley CA 93063-2199

STRATTON, JOHN MACLEAN, company executive; b. Rosedale, Kans., Nov. 1, 1916; s. George Weatherworth and Margaret Shearer (Maclean) S.; m. Kathryn McCrea Hines, Dec. 25, 1942 (dec.); children: Laura Kathryn, Mark Hines. BA, U. Kans., 1939; MA, Stanford U., 1940. Mgr. advt. & mktg. Spencer Chem. Co. (now Grace Chem.), 1945-48; v.p., mgr. Rogers & Wmith Advt. Agy., Kansas City, Mo., 1948-49; with Ruthrauff & Ryan ADvt. Agy., N.Y.C., Chgo., Detroit, 1952-54, Ramsey, Stratton, Barley & Brown, 1954-58; owner, chmn. bd. dirs. JAMSCO Enterprises, Inc., L.A., 1958—; chmn. bd. dirs. The Circutone Co., Inc., L.A., 1966—; pres. NAMSCO-Television, Hollywood, Calif. Patentee in field. Maj. USAAC, 1941-45, WWII, lt. col. USAF, 1949-52, Korea. Mem. Nat. 210 Owners Assn. (editor Airletter), Am. Vets. Med. Airlift Svc. (CEO). Home: 931 Flanders Rd La Canada Flintridge CA 91011

STRAUB, RICHARD NEAL, coach; b. Kewaskum, Wis., Dec. 5, 1968; s. Hugo John and Isabelle Laura (Miller) S. BS in Edn. cum laude, U. Wis., Whitewater, 1992; postgrad., Adams State Coll., 1994—. Instr. fitness Bally's Vic Tanny Health Club, Milw., 1991-92; counselor wrestling camp U. Wis., Whitewater, summers 1989-93, Marquette U., Milw., summers 1990-93; tchr. driver edn. Hartford (Wis.) High Sch., 1991, Waterford (Wis.) High Sch., 1992; tchr. English, head wrestling coach Kewaskum (Wis.) Mid. Sch., 1992-93; asst. wrestling coach Adams State Coll., Alamosa, Colo., 1993—. Irving Young scholar, Laura Ferris scholar. Mem. Am. Counseling Assn., Colo. Counseling Assn., Golden Key Honor Soc., Delta Kappa Pi. Home: 102 Ross Ave Alamosa CO 81101-2449

STRAUBEL, JOHN FREDERICK, public relations executive; b. Green Bay, Wis., May 19, 1928; s. Clarence Weise and Ethel (Puchner) S. B.S. in English, Northwestern U., 1950. Dir. pub. relations Hiller Aircraft Corp., Palo Alto, Calif., 1956-64; dir. communications Fairchild Hiller Corp., Washington, 1964-66; owner, pres. Straubel Communications, Portola Valley, Calif., 1966—. Author, editor: Pacific Diary I, 1952; Pacific Diary II, 1953; One Way Up, 1963. Mgr. pub. relations Volunteers for Nixon-Lodge, Washington, 1960. Served to lt. USN, 1950-53; Korea. Mem. Pub. Relations Soc. Am. Presbyterian. Office: Straubel Communications 4370 Alpine Rd Ste 207 Menlo Park CA 94028-7927

STRAUMAN, BRUCE EDWIN, secondary school educator; b. Modesto, Calif., May 2, 1949; s. Edwin Walter and Marjore Marie (Gilbert) S.; m. Nalani Rose Hillar, Aug. 14, 1971; children: Kimberly, Jennifer. BS, U. Oreg., 1972; postgrad. Cert. K-12 health and physical edn.; cert. instr. first aid and CPr, ARC. Tchr. grades 6-8 health, sci., phys. edn., grs. 1-4 phys. edn. St. Alice Cath. Sch., 1972-77; tchr. grades 7, 9 health and phys. edn. Cal Young Jr. H.S., 1977-79; tchr. grades 8, 9 health John F. Kennedy Jr. H.S., 1979-80; tchr. grades 7, 8, 9 health Ashland (Oreg.) Jr. H.S., 1980-84; tchr. health Ashland H.S., 1985—; co-leader, spkr., team leader Seaside Health Conf., 1982—; presenter in field; coach St. Alice Cath. Grade Sch., 1972-77, North Eugene H.S., 1972-74, Marist H.S., 1975-76, Cal Young Jr. H.S., 1977-79, Kennedy Jr. H.S., 1979-80, Ashland Jr. H.S., 1980-84, Ashland H.S., 1986—, YMCA, 1982-89; instr. standard 1st aid adult child baby CPR, ARC, 1990. Subject video, 1990. Eucharistic min. Our Lady of Mountain Cath. Ch., asst. youth min., 1982-85, mem. Mex. mission trip, 1991, 92, mem. youth edn. bd., 1987-90, mem. pastoral coun., 1988-90; dist. coord. Great Am. Smokeout, 1986-87; coord. with Ashland Cmty. Hosp. on project Health Quest Wellness Week, 1986-87; creator Ashland Sch. Dist. health booth for cmty. health fair, 1987. Named Health Tchr. of Yr. for Secondary Edn. by Oreg. Assn. Advancement of Health Edn., 1989; grantee Gibbs Found. Home: 1018 Beswick Way Ashland OR 97520-3576

STRAUS, LEONARD HIRSCH, retail company executive; b. 1914; married. LL.B., Harvard U., 1938. With Thrifty Corp., L.A., 1945—; officer legal dept. Thrifty Corp., Los Angeles, from 1948; chmn., CEO Thrifty Corp., L.A., 1979-90, chmn. emeritus, 1990—; also dir. Thrifty Corp., Los Angeles. Served with USCG, 1943-45. Office: Thrifty Corp Worldway Postal Ctr PO Box 92333 Los Angeles CA 90009-2333*

STRAUSS, HERBERT LEOPOLD, chemistry educator; b. Aachen, Germany, Mar. 26, 1936; came to U.S., 1940, naturalized, 1946; s. Charles and Joan (Goldschmidt) S.; m. Carolyn North Cooper, Apr. 24, 1960; children: Michael Abram, Rebecca Anne, Ethan Edward. A.B., Columbia U., 1957, M.A., 1958, Ph.D., 1960; postgrad, Oxford U., 1960-61. Mem. faculty U. Calif., Berkeley, 1961—, prof. chemistry, 1973—, vice chmn. dept. chemistry, 1975-81, 92-95; asst. dean. Coll. Chemistry Indian Inst. Tech., Kanpur, 1986-92, assoc. dean, 1995—; vis. prof. Indian Inst. Tech., Kanpur, 1968-69, Fudan U., Shanghai, 1982, U. Tokyo, 1982, U. Paris du Nord, 1987; chmn. IUPAC Commn. I.1. Author: Quantum Mechanics, 1968; assoc. editor Ann. Rev. Phys. Chemistry, 1976-85, editor, 1985—. Recipient Bomen-Michaelson award Coblentz Soc., 1994, Ellis Lippincott award Optical Soc. Am., 1994; Alfred P. Sloan fellow, 1966-70. Fellow Am. Phys. Soc., AAAS; mem. Am. Chem. Soc., Sigma Xi, Phi Beta Kappa, Phi Lambda Upsilon. Home: 2447 Prince St Berkeley CA 94705-2021 Office: U Calif Dept Chemistry Berkeley CA 94720-1460

STRAWN, EVELYN RAE, artist; b. Kerman, Calif., Nov. 24, 1921; d. Cloy Ray and Florence Grace (Angell) Hudson; m. Virgil Hollis Strawn, Sept. 19, 1940; children: C.J., Randall, Michael, Reagan. BA, U. Redlands, 1966. Artist freelance Grand Terrace, Calif., 1959—; probation officer San Bernadino (Calif.) County, 1966-89; developed and directed Sch. Based Teen Programs, San Bernardino, 1967-75, Pregnancy Program for Teens to Continue Schooling, 1967-68. Exhibited paintings and sculptures in pvt. collections and galleries. Bd. dirs., pres. Sexual Assault Svcs., San Bernardino, 1980-84; pres. Women in Mgmt., Inland Empire, 1983. Recipient Cert. of Commendation, San Bernardino County Probation Dept., 1989. Mem. Soroptimist Internat. of Riverside (bd. dirs. 1984), DAR.

STREMBITSKY, MICHAEL ALEXANDER, school administrator; b. Smoky Lake, Alta., Can., Mar. 5, 1935; s. Alec and Rose (Fedoretz) S.; m. Victoria Semeniuk, Aug. 12, 1954; children: Michael, William-John. BA, U. Alta., 1955, BEd, 1958; MA, Columbia U., 1968, MEd, 1972, LLD, 1989. With Edmonton (Alta.) pub. schs., now supt. of schs. Mem. Am. Assn. Sch. Adminstrs., Am. Mgmt. Assn., Am. Sch. Bus. Ofls., Assn. for Supr. and Curriculum Devel., Can. Assn. Sch. Adminstrs., Can. Coll. Tchrs., Can. Edn. Assn., Conf. Alta. Sch. Suptds., Alberta Tchr's Assn., Pub. Sch. Admstrs. Assn., Council Edni. Facility Planners Internat., Edmonton C. of C., Edmonton-Harbin (China) Friendship Soc., Edmonton Edn. Soc., U. Alta. Faculty Edn. Alumni Assn., Large City Sch. Supts., Nat. Assn. Ednl. Negotiators, Nat. Assn. Elementary Sch. Prins., Nat. Ukrainian Profl. Bus. Club, World Coun. for Curriculum and Instruction, Phi Delta Kappa. Office: Edmonton Pub Schs, Ctr Edn 1 Kingsway, Edmonton, AB Canada T5H 4G9

STRENA, ROBERT VICTOR, research laboratory manager; b. Seattle, June 28, 1929; s. Robert Lafayette Peel and Mary Oliva (Holmes) S.; m. Rita Mae Brodovsky, Aug. 1957; children: Robert Victor, Adrienne Amelia. AB, Stanford U., 1952. Survey mathematician Hazen Engring., San Jose, Calif., 1952-53; field engr. Menlo Sanitary Dist., Menlo Park, Calif., 1954-55; ind. fin. reporter Los Altos, Calif., 1956-59; asst. dir. Hansen Labs. Stanford U.,

1959-93, asst. dir. emeritus Ginzton Lab., 1993—; ind. fin. cons., Los Altos, 1965—; bd. mem. Rehab. Adv. Bd., Moffett Fed. Airfield, 1994—. Active Edn. System Politics, Los Altos, 1965-80, local Boy Scouts Am., 1968-80; mem. restoration adv. bd. Moffett Fed. Airfield. Maj. USAR, 1948-70. Mem. AAAS, Soc. Rsch. Adminstrs., Mus. Soc., Big X (Los Altos). Republican. Home: 735 Raymundo Ave Los Altos CA 94024-3139 Office: Ginzton Lab Stanford Univ Stanford CA 94305

STRENGER, GEORGE, surgeon; b. N.Y., Sept. 5, 1906; s. Philip and Tillie (Strassman) S.; m. Florence Serxner, June 9, 1931; children: Philip J., Laurence N. BA, Columbia U., 1928, MD, 1931. Diplomate Am. Bd. Surg., 1942. surgeon Bklyn. Jew. Hosp., N.Y., 1934-72, Goldwater Meml. Hosp., N.Y., 1939-53; chief surg. svc. N.Y. regional office VA, 1948-72; surgeon Coney Island Hosp., N.Y., 1953-72; instr. Long Island Med. Coll., N.Y., 1934-36. Mem. Ditmas Pk. Assn. (pres. 1953-54). Comdr. field hosp. U.S. Army, 1942-46, ETO. Recipient commendation Gen. Eisenhower, 1945. Fellow Am. Coll. Surgeons. Home: 31397 E Nine Dr Laguna Niguel CA 92677-2909

STRICHARTZ, JAMES LEONARD, lawyer; b. N.Y.C., Feb. 5, 1951; s. Morris Harvey and Estelle (Flatow) S. BA in Urban Studies, U. Mich., 1973, M in Pub. Policy, 1976, JD, 1977. Bar: Mich., 1977, D.C. 19878, Wash., 1980; diplomate Coll. of Comty. Assn. Lawyers. Law clk. Mich. Ct. Appeals, Detroit, 1977-78; assoc. atty. Weinrich, Gilmore & Adolph, Seattle, 1978-79; gen. counsel The 13th Regional Corp., Seattle, 1979-81; pvt. practice Seattle, 1981—; mem. Senate Jud. Com. Condominium Law Task Force, Seattle, 1986-87, Condominium Act Statutory Revision Com., 1987-91; speaker 22d and 23d nat. confs. Comty. Assn. Inst., Alexandria, Va.; faculty Profl. Mgmt. Devel. Program, 1993. Pres., bd. dirs. Fremont Community Health Clinic, 1982-83, 45th St. Community Health Clinic, 1984-89; gen. counsel, trustee Wash. Trust for Hist. Preservation, 1982-87; mem. Corp. Coun. For The Arts, 1987-88, Coun. for Corp. Responsibility, 1984—; founding mem., founding dir. Shoreline Arts Coun., 1989-92. Mem. Comty. Assn. Inst., Nat. Conf. of Chpts. (vice chmn., N.W. region 1988-89, chmn. 1990-91), Comty. Assns. Inst. Wash. (bd. dirs. 1986-92, v.p. 1987, pres. 1988-90, faculty mem. ops. and mgmt. comty. assns. leadership tng. program 1987, 89, 90, 91, chmn. 1992, 93, faculty profl. mgmt. devel. program 1993—), Comty. Assn. Inst. Rsch. Found. (chmn. symposium on comty. 1990, bd. dirs. 1991—, speaker symposiums 1991, 93, v.p. 1994, treas. 1995). Democrat. Unitarian. Office: 200 W Mercer St # 511 Seattle WA 98119-3958

STRICKLAN, CHARLES LESLIE, JR., advertising executive; b. St. Louis, Apr. 5, 1950; s. Charles Leslie and Helen Marie (Williams) S.; m. Virginia Lea Stoner, Nov. 4, 1972; 1 son, Charles Leslie. AA, Forest Park C. C., 1971; BFA, Washington U., St. Louis, 1973. Art dir. Sta. KPLR-TV, St. Louis, 1968-73; founder, pres., creative dir. Stricklan Studios, St. Louis, 1968—, now SCM Comm., Inc., Phoenix, 1993—; founder, pres. Stricklan Travel Co., 1979; lectr. in field. Founder, pres. SCM Broadcasting, 1990; host, prodr. Saturday AM weekly radio program, Radio Health Club, Celebrity Golf Club, Talk of the Town, Radio Comedy Club. Former advt., pub. rels. chmn. Ctrl. Ariz. Home Builders Assn., Multi-Family Housing Council; bd. dirs. Scottsdale Girls Club, Scottsdale Arts Ctr. Assn.. Recipient Am. Mktg. Assn. Excellence Mktg. award, 1979, Best Brochure (2 yrs.), Best Ad, Best On-Site Graphics, Ctrl. Ariz. Home Builders Assn., Major Achievement in Mktg. Excellence award Nat. Homebuilders Assn., Graphic Arts award of excellence Consolidated Paper, Excellence in Bldr. Advt., Best Direct Mail Target awards. Mem. Scottsdale C. of C., Nat. Assn. Home Builders.Republican. Lutheran. Office: 13845 N Scottsdale Rd Scottsdale AZ 85254-3432

STRICKLAND, JOHN ARTHUR VAN, minister; b. Detroit, Sept. 25, 1952; s. Maurice Alexander and Irma (Surovy) S.; m. Constance Fillmore, Dec. 24, 1976 (div. Aug. 1984); m. Brenda Cecile Bunch, Nov. 23, 1985. BA cum laude, Ga. State U., 1974; ministry program, Unity Ministerial Sch., 1974-76. Ordained to Assn. Unity Chs., 1976. Minister Unity Ch. Christianity, Santa Rosa, Calif., 1976-77, Jacksonville, Fla., 1978-79; dir. prayer ministry Unity Sch. Christianity, Unity Village, Mo., 1979—, mem. task force, 1984-87; mem. adv. council Unity Sch. Christianity, Unity Village, 1987—; trustee Assn. Unity Chs., 1994—, mem. exec. com., 1995—, coord. Internat. Youth of Unity, Unity Village, 1975-76; vol. chaplain Jackson County Jail, Kansas City, 1974-75. Contbr. articles to profl. jours. Trustee, Kans. Children's Mus.; vol. Unity Help Line, Unity Village, 1975-76. Named one of Outstanding Young Men Am., 1982. Mem. Rotary (youth svcs. com., chmn. invocation com. 1988-89, Paul Harris fellow). Home: 1520 Liholiho St Apt 505 Honolulu HI 96822-4093 Office: Unity Ch Hawaii 3608 Diamond Head Cir Honolulu HI 96815-4430

STRICKLAND, N(ANCY) KATHLEEN, lawyer, educator; b. Mobile, Ala., Dec. 12, 1949. Student, U. Vienna, 1969-70; BS, Spring Hill Coll., 1971; JD, U. San Diego, 1974. Bar: Calif. 1975, D.C. 1976, U.S. Dist. Ct. D.C. 1976, U.S. Ct. Appeals (D.C. cir.) 1976, U.S. Dist. Ct. (so. and ctrl. dists.) Calif. 1987, (no. and ea. dists.) Calif. 1988, Tex. 1994. Staff atty., office opinions and rev. FCC, Washington, 1974-76; asst. dist. atty. San Francisco Dist. Atty.'s Office, 1976-84; assoc. Burnhill, Morehouse, Burford, Schofield & Schiller, Walnut Creek, Calif., 1984-86; ptnr. Hassard, Bonnington, Rogers & Huber, San Fransisco, 1987—; adj. prof. Hastings Coll. Law, U. Calif., San Francisco, 1987—; pro tem judge Contra Costa County Superior Ct., Martinez, Calif., 1987—; lectr. U. San Francisco, Harvard U., Stanford U., C.E.B. Basketball coach Lafayette-Moraga Youth Assn., 1986—. Mem. ABA (lectr. environ. law), San Francisco Bar Assn. (bd. dirs. environ. law assn.), Contra Costa Bar Assn., Calif. Women Lawyers. Roman Catholic. Office: Hassard Bonnington Ste 1800 Two Embarcadero Ctr San Francisco CA 94111-3993

STRIMLING, BRUCE SANFORD, pediatrician, educator; b. Chgo., Nov. 21, 1941; s. Nathan and Ruth (Lavine) S.; m. Pamela Stuver, Dec. 28, 1965 (div. Mar. 1991); children: Nathan, Joel; m. Tracy Everton, June 30, 1991. Student, U. Ill., 1959-62, MD, 1966. Diplomate Am. Bd. Pediats., Nat. Bd. Med. Examiners. Intern in pediats. L.A. County-U. So. Calif. Med. Ctr., 1966-67, jr. resident in pediats., 1967-68; sr. resident in pediats. Harbor-UCLA Med. Ctr., L.A., 1970-71; pvt. practice Clinic for Children and Young Adults, Eugene, Oreg., 1971-90; treas. Oreg. Med. Group, Eugene, 1990—, pres., 1995—, also bd. dirs.; clin. asst. prof. pediats. Oreg. Health Scis. U., Portland, 1980-84; assoc. prof. health edn. U. Oreg., Eugene, 1981-82; mem. staff Sacred Heart Med. Ctr., Eugene, 1971—, mem. integrated health care leadership team, 1994, clin. svcs. task force, chief pediats., 1989-92, pharmacy and therapeutics com., emergency dept. com., neonatal/perinatal com. Contbr. articles to profl. jours. Chmn. Gov.'s Adv. Com. on Prevention of Child Abuse and Neglect, 1988-91; chmn. bd. dirs. Birth to Three, 1978-81; mem. adv. bd. Easter Seal Sch.; bd. dirs. Mental Health for Children, Inc., Fanconi Anemia Rsch. Assn., 1989—; mem. adv. bd. Oreg. Infant Watch, Birthways; liaison Action for Children's TV; mem. local coord. com. Children's Miracle TV Network, 1987-91. Maj. U.S. Army M.C., 1968-70. Fellow Am. Acad. Pediatrics (coun. govt. affairs 1985-86, PREP question writers com. 1990-93, coding trainer 1992-94, Outstanding Chpt. award); mem. AMA (diagnostic and therapeutic tech. assessment program), Oreg. Med. Assn. (com. vice-chmn. com. med. care for poor 1982, state medicaid task force 1982, com. chmn. com. care for medically needy 1983, pub. policy com. 1983, 84, 85, welfare adv. com. 1987-89), Oreg. Pediatric Soc. (com. chmn. pediat. practice com., sec.-treas. 1982-84, alt. chmn. 1984-86, pres. 1986-88), Lane County Med. Soc. (chmn. com. on health care for indigent), North Pacific Pediatric Soc., LaLeche League Med. Assn., Lane Ind. Physicians Assns. (mem. cost containment com. 1986-89, mem. medicaide PPO com. 1988-90, bd. dirs. 1993). Office: Oreg Med Group 755 E 11th Ave Eugene OR 97401-3702

STRINGER, JOHN, materials scientist; b. Liverpool, Eng., July 14, 1934; came to U.S., 1977; s. Gerald Hitchen and Isobel (Taylor) S.; m. Audrey Lancaster, Feb. 4, 1957; children: Helen Caroline, Rebecca Elizabeth. BS in Engring., U. Liverpool, 1955, PhD, 1958, D in Engring., 1974. Chartered engr., U.K. Lectr. Univ. Liverpool, Eng., 1957-63; fellow Battelle Columbus (Ohio) Labs., 1963-66; prof. materials sci. Univ. Liverpool, 1966-77; sr. project mgr. Electric Power Rsch. Inst., Palo Alto, Calif., 1977-81; sr. program mgr. Electric Power Rsch. Inst., Palo Alto, 1981-87, dir. tech. support, 1987-91, dir. applied rsch., 1991-95, tech. exec. Applied Sci. and Tech., 1995—; cons. prof. materials sci. and engring. Stanford U., 1977—; chmn. Sci. and Tech. Edn., Merseyside, Liverpool, 1971-74; pres. Corrosion and Protection Assn., London, 1972. Editorial bd.: Oxidation of Metals Jour., 1971—; author: An Introduction to the Electron Theory of Solids, 1967; editor: (book) High Temperature Corrosion of Advanced Materials, 1989, Chlorine in Coal, 1991, Applied Chaos, 1992; contbr. over 300 articles to profl. jours. Recipient U.R. Evans award Inst. Corrosion, U.K., 1993. Fellow AAAS, NACE Internat., AIME, Inst. Energy, Royal Soc. Arts; mem. ASM Internat., Materials Rsch. Soc. Office: Electric Power Rsch Inst 3412 Hillview Ave Palo Alto CA 94304-1395

STRINGER, WILLIAM JEREMY, university official; b. Oakland, Calif., Nov. 8, 1944; s. William Duane and Mildred May (Andrus) S.; BA in English, So. Meth. U., 1966; MA in English, U. Wis., 1968, PhD in Ednl. Adminstrn., 1973; m. Susan Lee Hildebrand; children: Shannon Lee, Kelly Erin, Courtney Elizabeth. Dir. men's housing Southwestern U., Georgetown, Tex., 1968-69; asst. dir. housing U. Wis., Madison, 1969-73; dir. residential life, asso. dean student life, adj. prof. Pacific Luth., Tacoma, 1973-78; dir. residential life U. So. Calif., 1978-79, asst. v.p., 1979-84, asst. prof. higher and post-secondary edn., 1980-84; v.p. student life Seattle U., 1984-89, v.p. student devel., 1989-92, assoc. provost, 1989, assoc. prof. edn., 1990—, chair educational leadership, 1994—. Author: How to Survive as a Single Student, 1972, The Role of the Assistant in Higher Education, 1973. Bd. dirs. N.W. area Luth. Social Services of Wash. and Idaho, pres.-elect, 1989, pres., 1990-91. Danforth Found. grantee, 1976-77. Mem. AAUP, Am. Assn. Higher Edn., Nat. Assn. Student Pers. Adminstrs. (bd. dirs. region V 1985—, mem. editl. bd. Jour. 1995—), Am. Coll. Pers. Assn., Phi Eta Sigma, Sigma Tau Delta, Phi Alpha Theta. Lutheran. Home: 4553 169th Ave SE Issaquah WA 98027-7813 Office: Seattle U Seattle WA 98122

STRISOWER, SUZANNE, clinical hypnotherapist, counselor; b. San Francisco, Oct. 27, 1956; d. Edward Herman and Beverly Gene (Boutell) S. BFA, JFK U., Orinda, Calif., 1988; MA, Pacifica Grad. Inst., 1994. Cert. clin. hypnotherapist; cert. counselor. Wallcovering installer Orinda, Calif., 1974-82; interior designer Lyons, Hill & Ruga Inc., Pleasant Hill, Calif., 1983-85; project mgr. Wayne Ruga Inc., Martinez, Calif., 1985-88; exec. dir. Nat. Symposium for Healthcare Interior Design, Martinez, 1986-88; treatment counselor Youth Homes Inc., Walnut Creek, Calif., 1988-93; clin. hypnotherapist The Inner Journey, Walnut Creek, Calif., 1991—, marriage, family and child counselor, 1994-95; aide and community liaison to supr. Contra Costa County Dist. II, 1995——; tchr. Acalanes Adult Edn. Ctr., Walnut Creek, 1992—; lectr. in field. Child advisor, vice chairperson Contra Costa County Mental Health Commn., 1991-93; pres. Orgn. of Youth Svcs., 1991-94; mem. Juv. Justice Delinquency Prevention Commn. Contra Costa County, 1988-95, mem. family and children's trust com., mem. juv. sys. planning adv. com. Mem. Am. Coun. Hypnotist Examiners. Home: 542 Center Ave # 285 Martinez CA 94553-4600

STROBER, MYRA HOFFENBERG, education educator, consultant; b. N.Y.C., Mar. 28, 1941; d. Julius William Hoffenberg and Regina Scharer; m. Samuel Strober, June 23, 1963 (div. Dec. 1983); children: Jason M., Elizabeth A.; m. Jay M. Jackman, Oct. 21, 1990. BS in Indsl. Rels., Cornell U., 1962; MA in Econs., Tufts U., 1965; PhD in Econs., MIT, 1969. Lectr., asst. prof. dept. econs. U. Md., College Park, 1967-70; lectr. U. Calif., Berkeley, 1970-72; asst. prof. grad. sch. bus. Stanford (Calif.) U., 1972-86, assoc. prof. sch. edn., 1979-90, prof., 1990—, assoc. dean acad. affairs, 1993—; organizer Stanford Bus. Conf. Women Mgmt., 1974; founding dir. ctr. rsch. women Stanford U., 1974-76, 79-84, dir. edn. policy inst., 1984-86, dean alumni coll., 1992, mem. policy and planning bd., 1992-93, chair program edn. adminstrn. and policy analysis, 1991-93, chair provost's com. recruitment and retention women faculty, 1992-93, chair faculty senate com. on coms., 1992-93; mem. adv. bd. State of Calif. Office Econ. Policy Planning and Rsch., 1978-80; mem. Coll. Bd. Com. Develop Advanced Placement Exam. Econs., 1987-88; faculty advisor Rutgers Women's Leadership Program, 1991-93. Author: (with others) Industrial Relations, 1972, Sex, Discrimination and the Division of Labor, 1975, Changing Roles of Men and Women, 1976, Women in the Labor Market, 1979, Educational Policy and Management: Sex Differentials, 1981, Women in the Workplace, 1982, Sex Segregation in the Workplace: Trends, Explanations, Remedies, 1984, The New Palgrave: A Dictionary of Economic Theory and Doctrine, 1987, Computer Chips and Paper Clips: Technology and Women's Employment, Vol. II, 1987, Gender in the Workplace, 1987; editor: (with Francine E. Gordon) Bringing Women Into Management, 1975, (with others) Women and Poverty, 1986, (with Sanford M. Dornbusch) Feminism, Children and the New Families, 1988; mem. bd. editors Signs: Jour. Women Culture and Soc., 1975-89, assoc. editor, 1980-85; mem. bd. editors Sage Ann. Rev. Women and Work, 1984—; mem. editorial adv. bd. U.S.-Japan Women's Jour., 1991—; assoc. editor Jour. Econ. Edn., 1991—; contbr. chpt. to book. Mem. rsch. adv. task force YWCA, 1989—; chair exec. bd. Stanford Hillel, 1990-92; bd. dirs. Resource Ctr. Women, Palo Alto, Calif., 1983-84; pres. bd. dirs. Kaider Found., Mountain View, Calif., 1990—. Fellow Stanford U., 1975-77, Schiff House Resident fellow, 85-87. Mem. NOW (bd. dirs. legal def. and edn. fund 1993—), Am. Econ. Assn. (mem. com. status of women in the profession 1972-75), Am. Ednl. Rsch. Assn., Indsl. Rels. Rsch. Assn. Office: Stanford U School of Education Stanford CA 94305

STROBER, SAMUEL, immunologist, educator; b. N.Y.C., May 8, 1940; s. Julius and Lee (Lander) S.; m. Linda Carol Higgins, July 6, 1991; 1 child, William; children from previous marriage: Jason, Elizabeth. AB in Liberal Arts, Columbia U., 1961; MD magna cum la de, Harvard U., 1966. Intern Mass. Gen. Hosp., Boston, 1966-67; resident in internal medicine Stanford U. Hosp., Calif., 1970-71; research fellow Peter Bent Brigham Hosp., Boston, 1962-63, 65-66, Oxford U., Eng., 1963-64; research assoc. Lab. Cell Biology, Nat. Cancer Inst., NIH, Bethesda, Md., 1967-70; instr. medicine Stanford U., 1971-72, asst. prof., 1972-78, assoc. prof. medicine, 1978-82, prof. medicine, 1982—, Diane Goldstone Meml. lectr., John Putnam Merrill Meml. lectr., chief div. immunology and rheumatology, 1978—; investigator Howard Hughes Med. Inst., Miami, Fla., 1976-81. Assoc. editor Jour. Immunology, 1981-84, Transplantation, 1981-85, Internat. Jour. Immunotherapy, 1985—, Transplant Immunology, 1992—; contbr. articles to profl. jours. bd. dirs. La Jolla Inst. for Allergy and Immunology; founder Activated Cell Therapy, Inc. Served with USPHS, 1967-70. Recipient Leon Reznick Meml. Research prize Harvard U., 1966. Mem. Am. Assn. Immunology, Am. Soc. Clin. Investigation, Am. Rheumatism Assn., Transplantation Soc. (councilor 1986-89), Am. Soc. Transplantation Physicians, Western Soc. Medicine, Am. Assn. Physicians, Clin. Immunology Soc. (pres. elect. 1995), Alpha Omega. Home: 435 Golden Oak Dr Menlo Park CA 94028-7734 Office: Stanford U Sch Medicine 300 Pasteur Dr Palo Alto CA 94304-2203

STROBLE-THOMPSON, COLETTE MARY HOULE, plastering and stucco company executive; b. Manchester, N.H., Aug. 10, 1947; d. George Albert and Mary Agnes (Sala) H.; divorced; children: B.J., Danielle, Alden; m. Dennis W. Thompson. Student, CAP Regional Staff Coll. Tex., 1985, 86. Lic. real estate agt., stucco/plasterer. Switchboard operator Leavitt's Dept. Store, Manchester, N.H., 1965-66, with credit office, 1966-67, merchandizer, advertiser, 1966-69; advt. marketer Ariz. wide K-Mart, Mesa; owner, mgr. Colette's Boutique, Mesa, 1980-82; co-founder, CEO, pres. Stroble Plastering, Gilbert, Ariz., 1977—; cons. area wide constrn. firms, Phoenix, 1979-90; contractor plastering and stucco, Phoenix, 1987-90; realtor personal real estate property, Phoenix, 1988-90. Author, editor Wing Tips, 1985-86; co-inventor, electronic locator transmitter. Maj., squadron leader, fin. officer, personnel officer CAP, Mesa, 1990; active Dept. Disabled/Disadvantaged, Phoenix. Recipient Humanitarian award Dept. Econ. Security, Mesa, 1989, Letters of Appreciation, Leper Colony, Mexico, 1989. Mem. Nat. Assn. Search and Rescue (life), World Wing Kung Fu Assn., Rosicrucian Order Amorc (dep. master, master). Office: Stroble Plastering & Stucco 721 N Monterey St Ste 103 Gilbert AZ 85233-3835

STROCK, ARTHUR VAN ZANDT, architect; b. Los Angeles, Sept. 14, 1945; s. Arthur and Eileen (Cortelyou) S.; m. Hallie vonAmmon, Mar. 22, 1969. BArch, U. Calif., Berkeley, 1971. Registered profl. architect. Asst. dean Sch. Architecture and Fine Arts U. So. Calif., Los Angeles, 1970-71; designer Allied Architects, Long Beach, Calif., 1971-73; architect Langdon and Wilson, Newport Beach, Calif., 1973-77, Lee & Strock Architects, Newport Beach, 1978-82, Strock Architects, Inc., Newport Beach, 1982-91, Pacmar Strock Group, Newport Beach, Calif., 1992—; guest lectr. u. Calif., Irvine; guest speaker Pacific Coast Deisgn Conf., Monterey, Calif. Prin. works include I.R.W.D. Bldg., 1979 (Merit award 1982), Newport/Irvine Ctr., 1980 (Merit award 1982), Bay Corp. Ctr., 1982 (Merit award 1984), Scripps Ctr., 1985, Long Beach Airport Bus. Park, 1986, Orange County Register Hdqrs., 1986. Pres. Beacon Bay Cmty. Assn., Newport Beach, 1985-86; bd. dirs. Nat. History Found. of Orange County, 1982; bd. dirs. Bowers Mus., 1987—, pres., 1988-90, chmn., 1991-92, 93—. Fellow AIA; mem. Urban Land Inst.(internat. coun.), Newport Harbor yacht Club, Sigma Chi, U.S. Sailing (sr. judge). Republican. Home: 23 Beacon Bay Newport Beach CA 92660-7218 Office: Pacmar Strock Group 1111 Bayside Dr Ste 130 Newport Beach CA 92695-3109

STROCK, DAVID RANDOLPH, brokerage house executive; b. Salt Lake City, Jan. 31, 1944; s. Clarence Randolph and Francis (Hornibrook) S.; m. Phyllis A. Tingley, Dec. 13, 1945 (div. June 15, 1982); children: Sarah, Heidi. AA, San Mateo Coll., 1967; BS, San Jose State U., 1970. Investment exec. Paine Webber, San Jose, Calif., 1970-78; corp. trainer Paine Webber, N.Y.C., 1978-79, rsch. coord., 1979-82; br. mgr. Paine Webber, Northbrook, Ill., 1982-84, Palos Verdes, Calif., 1984-89, Napa, Calif., 1989-90; investment exec. Paine Webber, Napa, 1990—. Contbr. articles to profl. jours. Mem. San Jose Jr. C. of C. (chmn. 1977, v.p. 1978), North Napa Rotary (pres.), Moose. Republican. Home: 3324 Homestead Ct Napa CA 94558-4275 Office: Paine Webber 703 Trancas St Napa CA 94558-3014

STROCK, JAMES MARTIN, state agency administrator, lawyer, conservationist; b. Austin, Tex., Aug. 19, 1956; s. James Martin Strock Sr. and Augusta (Tenney) Mullins. AB magna cum laude, Harvard U., 1977, JD, 1981; postgrad, New Coll. Oxford U., 1981-82. Bar: Colo. 1983. Teaching fellow dept. govt. Harvard U., 1980-81; spl. cons. to majority leader U.S. Senate, Washington, 1982-83; spl. asst. to adminstr. EPA, Washington, 1983-85, asst. adminstr. for enforcement, 1989-91; spl. counsel U.S. Senate Com. on Environment and Pub. Works, Washington, 1985-86; environ. atty. Davis, Graham & Stubbs, Denver, 1986-88; acting dir., gen. counsel U.S. Office Pers. Mgmt., Washington, 1988-89; sec. for environ. protection State of Calif., Sacramento, 1991—; mem. bd. advisors CALSTART, 1993—, The Environ. Tech. Export Coun., 1993—, Toxics Law Reporter, 1987-89, Greenwire, 1991—; mem. Intergovtl. Policy Adv. Com., rep. U.S. Trade, 1991—. Contbr. articles to profl. jours.; moderator, producer Lay It On The Line, Sta. WDSU-TV, New Orleans, 1973-74. Bd. dirs. Youth Svc. Am., Washington, 1988-89, Environ. Law Inst., 1992—; nat. chair Bush Campaign Environ. Coalition, 1992. Capt. JAGC USAR, 1987-95. Recipient Retsie Arco Future award, 1992, Ross Essay award ABA, 1985, Environ. Leadership award Calif. Environ. Bus. Coun., 1994; Charles Joseph Bonaparte scholar Harvard U., 1976, Rotary Internat. scholar, 1981-82. Mem. Coun. on Fgn. Rels., University Club (Washington), Phi Beta Kappa. Republican. Office: 555 Capitol Mall Ste 235 Sacramento CA 95814-4503

STROHMEYER, JOHN, writer, former editor; b. Cascade, Wis., June 26, 1924; s. Louis A. and Anna Rose (Saladunas) S.; m. Nancy Jordan, Aug. 20, 1949; children: Mark, John, Sarah. Student, Moravian Coll., 1941-43; A.B., Muhlenberg Coll., 1947; M.A. in Journalism, Columbia, 1948; L.H.D. (hon.), Lehigh U., 1983. With Nazareth Item, 1940-41; night reporter Bethlehem (Pa.) Globe-Times, 1941-43, 45-47; investigative reporter Providence Jour.-Bull., 1949-56; editor Bethlehem Globe-Times, 1956-84, v.p., 1961-84, dir., 1963-84; African-Am. journalism tchr. in Nairobi, Freetown, 1964; Atwood prof. journalism U. Alaska Anchorage, 1987-88, writer-in-residence, 1989—. Author: Crisis in Bethlehem: Big Steel's Struggle to Survive, 1986, Extreme Conditions: Big Oil and The Transformation of Alaska, 1993. Lt. (j.g.) USNR, 1943-45. Pulitzer Traveling fellow, 1948; Nieman fellow, 1952-53; recipient Comenius award Moravian Coll., 1971; Pulitzer prize for editorial writing, 1972; Alicia Patterson Found. fellow, 1984, 85. Mem. Am. Soc. Newspaper Editors, Pa. Soc. Newspaper Editors (pres. 1965-66). Club: Hiawatha Hunting and Fishing (E. Stroudsburg, Pa.). Home: 6633 Lunar Dr Anchorage AK 99504-4550

STROM, MARK ALAN, manufacturing executive; b. Kalamazoo, Mich., Feb. 9, 1962; s. John Rutledge and Marjorie Josephine (Griffin) S.; m. Andrea Logan Thompson, Aug. 2, 1986. BS summa cum laude, Biola U., 1984; MBA, Stanford U., 1990. Material coord. McDonnell Douglas Corp., Long Beach, Calif., 1984-86, sect. mgr., 1986-87, br. mgr., 1987-88, prin. staff specialist, 1990; assoc. Pittiglio, Rabin, Todd & McGrath, Mountain View, Calif., 1990-91, mgr., 1992-93, prin., 1993—. Arjay Miller scholar Stanford U., 1990. Mem. Am. Prodn. & Inventory Soc. Republican. Evangelical Free Christian. Home: 219 Backs Ln Apt A Placentia CA 92670-6011

STROMBERG, G. THOMAS, JR., lawyer; b. San Francisco, Feb. 23, 1955; s. George Thomas and Norma (Clark) S.; m. Lorie Winder Stromberg. Sept. 10, 1982; children: Stephen Winder, Elizabeth Winder. BA, Harvard Coll., 1979; JD, U. Utah, 1982. Bar: Calif., Ill. Atty. Chapman and Cutler, Chgo., 1982-85, Mayer, Brown & Platt, L.A., 1985-88; ptnr. Heller, Ehrman, White & McAuliffe, L.A., 1988—; lectr. in field. Co-editor Calif. Internat. Law Sect. Newsletter; contbr. articles to profl. jours. Named One of 20 Young Lawyers Making a Difference Barrister Mag., 1992. Mem. ABA (sect. of corp. bus. and banking law), Harvard/Radcliffe Club of So. Calif., L.A. County Bar Assn., State Bar of Calif. (exec. com. internat. sect., UCC com. of the bus. sect.). Office: Heller Ehrman White & McAuliffe 601 S Figueroa St Los Angeles CA 90017

STROMBOM, CATHY JEAN, transportation planner, consultant; b. Bremerton, Wash., Nov. 4, 1949; d. Paul D. and Carolyn (Snitman) Powers; m. David Glen Strombom, June 17, 1972; 1 child, Paul Davis. BA summa cum laude, Whitman Coll., 1972; M in City and Regional Planning, Harvard U., 1977; postgrad., U. Wash., 1982-84. Urban planner Harvard Inst. for Internat. Devel., Tehran, Iran, 1977; sr. transp. planner Puget Sound Coun. Govts., Seattle, 1978-84; mgr. transp. planning/prin. profl. assoc. Parsons Brinckerhoff Quade and Douglas, Inc., Seattle, 1984—; v.p. Women's Transp. Seminar, Seattle, 1988-90 (Woman of Yr. 1989). Contbr. articles to profl. jours. Vol. U.S. Peace Corps, Marrakech, Morocco, 1973-75. Mem. Am. Inst. Cert. Planners (cert.), Am. Planning Assn., Inst. Transp. Engrs., Phi Beta Kappa. Home: 2580 W Viewmont Way W Seattle WA 98199-3660 Office: Parsons Brinckerhoff Quade and Douglas Inc 999 3rd Ave Ste 801 Seattle WA 98104-4001

STROMQUIST, DON LEONARD, rheumatologist; b. Salt Lake City, UT, May 26, 1954; s. Donald M. and Jane (Layton) S.; m. Regina E. Rosenthal, May 21, 1989. BA, U. Utah, 1978; MD, Yale U., 1982. Diplomate Am. Bd. Internal Medicine. Resident Boston City Hosp., 1982-86; fellow Boston U. Arthritis Ctr., 1986-88; physician Hitchcock Clinic, Manchester, N.H., 1988-91; physician in pvt. practice pvt. practice, Salt Lake City, 1991—. Bd. trustees Utah Heritage Found., 1993; bd. dirs. Utah chpt. Arthritis Found. Fellow Am. Coll. Rheumatology. Office: 324 10th Ave Ste 250 Salt Lake City UT 84103-2853

STRONG, CAROLYN RAY, electronics company official; b. Pasadena, Calif., Jan. 9, 1951; d. Albert Charles and Juliana (Ray) S. B.A. in Math., Whitworth Coll., 1973; postgrad., DeVry Inst. Tech., 1975-77; MS in Applied Info. Mgmt. U. Oreg., 1992. Math. and aerospace demonstrator Pacific Sci. Ctr., Seattle, 1970, 71; component info. specialist Tektronix, Inc., Beaverton, Oreg., 1973-75, tech. writer, 1975-76, tech. publs. group mgr., 1976-79, tech. communications mgr., 1979-85; tech. publs. and computer tng. mgr., 1985-86, mgr. lab. instruments documentation, 1986-89, mgr. lab. instruments mktg. support, 1989-90, mgr. oscillscope group documentation, 1990-91, mgr. test and measurement customer documentation, 1991-95; dir. worldwide customer comms., 1995—; cons. Portland Community Coll., Chemeketa Community Coll. Bd. dirs. First Tech. Fed. Credit Union, 1984—, sec., 1985-86, vice chmn., 1986-87, chmn. 1987—. Mem. Soc. Tech. Communications (sr. mem., sec. Willamette Valley chpt. 1978, treas. 1979, pres. 1979-80), Assn. Computer Machinery and Sigdoc. Home: 1325 NW 92nd Ave Portland OR 97229-5347 Office: PO Box 500 Beaverton OR 97077-0001

STRONG, GARY EUGENE, librarian; b. Moscow, Idaho, June 26, 1944; s. Authur Dwight and Cleora Anna (Nirk) S.; m. Carolyn Jean Roetker, Mar. 14, 1970; children: Christopher Eric, Jennifer Rebecca. BS in Edn., U.

Idaho, 1966; AMLS, U. Mich., 1967. Adminstrv. and reference asst. U. Idaho, 1963-66; extension librarian Latah County Free Library, Moscow, 1966; head librarian Markeley Residence Library, U. Mich., 1966-67; library dir. Lake Oswego (Oreg.) Public Library, 1967-73, Everett (Wash.) Public Library, 1973-76; asso. dir. services Wash. State Library, Olympia, 1976-79; dep. state librarian Wash. State Library, 1979-80; state librarian Calif. State Library, Sacramento, 1980-94; dir. Queens Borough Pub. Libr., Jamaica, 1994—; dir. emeritus Calif. State Library Found., 1994—; chief exec. Calif. Library Services Bd., 1980-94; founder, bd. dirs. Calif. State Library Found., 1982-94, Calif. Literary Campaign, 1984-94, Calif. Rsch. Bureau, 1992; bd. dirs. No. Regional Library Bd., 1983-94; mem. adv. bd. Ctr. for Book in Libr. of Congress, 1983-86; mem. nat. adv. com. Libr. of Congress, 1987-89; chmn. adv. bd. Calif. Libr. Constrn. and Rennovation Bond Act Bd., 1989-94; vis. lectr. Marylhurst Coll., Oreg., 1968, Oreg. Div. Continuing Edn., 1972, San Jose State U. Sch. Libr. Svc., 1990; lectr. and cons. in field. Host, producer: cable TV Signatures Program, 1974-76, nationwide videoconfs. on illiteracy, censorship, 1985; author: On Reading-in the Year of the Reader, 1987; editor Calif. State Library Found. Bull., 1982-94 (H.W. Wilson Periodical award 1988), Western Americana in the Calif. State Library, 1986, On Reading-In the Year of the Reader, 1987, Chinatown Photographer: Louis J. Stellman, 1989, Local History Genealogical Resources, 1990, Literate America Emerging, 1991; contbr. articles to profl. jours.; editor, designer and pub. of various books. Bd. dirs., v.p. Pacific N.W. Bibliog. Ctr., 1977-80; bd. dirs. Thurston Mason County Mental Health Ctr., 1977-80, pres., 1979-80; bd. dirs. Coop. Library Agy. for Systems and Services, 1980-94, vice chmn., 1981-84; bd. dirs. Sr. Services Snohomish County, 1973-76, HISPANEX (Calif. Spanish lang. database), 1983-86; bd. govs. Snohomish County Hist. Assn., 1974-76; mem. Oreg. Coun. Pub. Broadcasting, 1969-73; mem. psychiat. task force St. Peters Hosp., Olympia, 1979-80; co-founder Calif. Ctr. for the Book, bd. dirs., 1987-94; mem. adv. bd. Calif. State PTA, 1981-86, Gov.'s Tech. Conf., 1993-94; mem. adv. com. Sch. Libr. Sci., UCLA, 1991-94, Sch. Libr. and Info. Studies, U. Calif., Berkeley, 1991-94; mem. Calif. Adult Edn. Steering Com., 1988-94; chmn. collaborative coun. Calif. State Literacy Resource Ctr., 1993-94; bd. dirs. Queens coun. Boy Scouts of Am., 1994—. Recipient Disting. Alumnus award U. Mich., 1984, Disting. Svc. award Calif. Literacy Inc., 1985, Spl. Achievement award Literacy Action, 1988, Assn. Specialized and Coop. Libr. Agys. Exceptional Achievement award, 1992, Gov.'s Award of Achievement Govt. Tech. Conf., 1994, Advancement of Literacy award Pub. Libr. Assn., 1994, John Cotton Dana award Libr. Adminstrn. and Mgmt. Assn., 1994; named Libr. of Yr. Calif. Assn. Libr. Trustees and Commrs., 1994; Oreg. Libr. scholar, 1966. Mem. ALA (legis. com. 1980-82, Commn. on Freedom and Equality of Access to Info. 1983-86), Libr. Adminstrn. and Mgmt. Assn. (dir. 1980-88, pres. 1984-85), N.Y. Libr. Assn., Oreg. Libr. Assn. (hon. life mem., pres. 1970-71), Pacific N.W. Libr. Assn. (hon. life mem., pres. 1978-79), Calif. Libr. Assn. (govt. rels. com. 1980-94), Chief Officers of State Libr. Agys. (pres. 1984-86), Western Coun. State Librs. (pres. 1989-91, Assn. Specialized and Coop. Libr. Agys., Everett Area C. of C. (bd. dirs. 1974-76). Clubs: Book of Calif., Sacramento Book Collectors, Roxburghe, The Book Collectors (L.A.). Office: Queens Borough Pub Libr 89-11 Merrick Blvd Jamaica NY 11432-5200

STRONG, GEORGE GORDON, JR., litigation and management consultant; b. Toledo, Apr. 19, 1947; s. George Gordon and Jean Boyd (McDougall) S.; m. Annsley Palmer Chapman, Nov. 30, 1974; children: George III, Courtney, Meredith, Alexis. BA, Yale U., 1969; MBA, Harvard U., 1971; JD, U. San Diego, 1974. Bar: Calif. 1974, U.S. Dist. Ct. (cen. dist.) Calif. 1974; CPA, Calif., Hawaii, cert. mgmt. cons., U.S. customs house broker. Controller Vitredent Corp., Beverly Hills, Calif., 1974-76; sr. mgr. Price Waterhouse, L.A., 1976-82; ptnr. Price Waterhouse, Los Angeles, 1987-93; mng. ptnr. west region dispute analysis and corp. recovery Price Waterhouse, L.A., 1993—, mem. policy bd., bd. dirs., 1995—; exec. v.p., chief operating officer Internat. Customs Service, Long Beach, Calif., 1982-84; chief fin. officer Uniform Software Systems, Santa Monica, Calif., 1984-85; exec. v.p. and chief operating officer Cipherlink Corp., 1986; pres. Woodleigh Lane, Inc., Flintridge, Calif., 1985-87; ptnr. Price Waterhouse, 1987—. Chmn. bd. trustees Harvard Bus. Sch. Assn. So. Calif. Scholarship Fund. Mem. ABA, AICPA, Calif. State Bar, Calif. Soc. CPAs, So. Calif. Humane Soc. (bd. dirs.), L.A. SPCA, Andover Abbott Alumni So. Calif. (bd. dirs.), Inst. Mgmt. Cons., Harvard Bus. Sch. Assn. So. Calif. (pres. 1988-89), Harvard Club N.Y., Yale Club N.Y., Calif. Club, Jonathan Club, Flint Canyon Tennis Club, Olympic Club, Annandale Golf Club, Coral Beach and Tennis Club, Mid Ocean Golf Club, Royal Bermuda Yacht Club, Palm Valley Coutnry Club. Republican. Presbyterian. Home: 5455 Castle Knoll Rd La Canada Flintridge CA 91011-1319 Office: 400 S Hope St Ste 2200 Los Angeles CA 90071-2823

STRONG, JAMES THOMPSON, financial/management/security consultant, executive search; b. Boca Raton, Fla., Oct. 26, 1945; s. Earl William and Mary Joe (Thompson) S.; m. Lenore Jean Stager, Feb. 2, 1974; 1 child, Daria Nicole. BA in Polit. Sci., U. Calif., Riverside, 1973; MS in Strategic Intelligence, Def. Intelligence Coll., Washington, 1982. Factoring specialist. Commd. USAF, 1968, advaned through grades to maj., ret., 1990; faculty Def. Intelligence Coll., Washington, 1982-86; dir. translations USAF, 1986-88, dir. info. svcs., 1988-90; proprietary security mgr. McDonnell-Douglas Technologies, San Diego, 1990-92; owner/author Delta Cons. and Funding, Poway, Calif., 1992—. Author: The Basic Industrial Counter-Espionage Cookbook, 1993, The Government Contractor's OPSEC Cookbook, 1993; co-author: The Military Intelligence Community, 1985; contbr. articles to profl. jours.; bd. editor Internat. Jour. Intelligence and Counterintelligence, 1986-94. Recipient Disting. EEO award USAF, 1987, Def. Meritorious Svc. medal 1986, Meritorious Svc. medal, 1981, 90, Joint Svc. Commendation medal Def. Intelligence Agy./NATO, 1982, 85. Mem. Nat. Mil. Intelligence Assn. (bd. dirs. 1984—, chpt. pres. 1989, 94), Ops. Security Profls. Soc. (chpt. chair 1993, 94), Nat. Cargo Security Coun., San Diego Roundtable (exec. coord. 1994, 95), Poway C. of C., Assn. Former Intelligence Officers, Am. Soc. for Indsl. Security, Air Force Assn. Republican. Home: 13785 Quinton Rd San Diego CA 92129-3202 Office: Jeffrey Allan Assocs 6060 Cornerstone Ct W S-316 San Diego CA 92121

STRONG, JOHN OLIVER, plastic surgeon, educator; b. Montclair, N.J., Feb. 1, 1930; s. George Joseph and Olivia (LeBrun) S.; m. Helen Louise Vrooman, July 19, 1958 (dec. Mar. 1973); m. Deborah Sperberg, May 20, 1978; children: John Jr., Jean LeB., Andrew D. BS, Yale U., 1952; MD, U. Pa., 1957. Practice medicine specializing in plastic and reconstructive surgery Santa Ana, Calif., 1964—; asst. clin. prof. plastic and reconstructive surgery U. Calif., Irvine, 1970—. Fellow ACS; mem. Calif. Med. Assn. (chmn. sci. adv. panel 1983-89), Calif. Soc. Plastic Surgeons (pres. 1991-92). Republican. Office: 2200 E Fruit St Ste 103 Santa Ana CA 92701-4479

STRONG, MAYDA NEL, psychologist, educator; b. Albuquerque, May 6, 1942; d. Floyd Samuel and Wanda Christmas (Martin) Strong; 1 child, Robert Allen Willingham. BA in Speech-Theatre cum laude, Tex. Western Coll., 1963; EdM, U. Tex., Austin, 1972, PhD in Counseling Psychology, 1978; lic. clin. psychologist, Colo., 1984; cert. alcohol counselor III, Colo., 1987, nat. addiction counselor II, 1991. Asst. instr. in ednl. psychology U. Tex., Austin, 1974-78; instr. psychology Austin Community Coll., 1974-78, Otero Jr. Coll., La Junta, Colo., 1979-89; dir. outpatient and emergency svcs. S.E. Colo. Family Guidance and Mental Health Ctr., Inc., La Junta, 1978-81; pvt. practice psychol. therapy, La Junta, 1981—; exec. dir. Pathfinders Chem. Dependency program, 1985-94; clin. psychologist Inst. for Forensic Psychiatry, Colo. Mental Health Inst., Pueblo, 1989-94; adj. faculty Adams State Coll., 1992; dir. Allstrong Enterprises, Inc., 1992-94. Del. to County Dem. Conv., 1988. Appeared in The Good Doctor, 1980, On Golden Pond, 1981, Chase Me Comrade, 1989, Plaza Suite, 1987; co-dir. The Odd Couple, 1995. AAUW fellow, 1974-76. Mem. Bus. and Profl. People (legis. chairperson 1982-83, chmn. news election svc. 1982-88), Colo. Psychol. Assn. (legis. chmn. for dist.), Am. Contract Bridge League. Contbr. articles in field to profl. publs. Author poems in Chinook: Paths through the Puzzle, Decisions, Passion. Home: 500 Holly Ave PO Box 177 Swink CO 81077-0177 Office: 315 W 3rd St Ste 204 La Junta CO 81050

STRONG, WINIFRED HEKKER, educational counselor, consultant; b. Passaic, N.J., May 16, 1923; d. Frank T. and Wilhelmine (Bohack) Hekker; divorced; 1 child, Frank R. Bush; m. Fred N. Strong, June 21, 1969. BA, Marymount Coll., 1945; MA, NYU, N.Y.C., 1948; postgrad. counseling, Calif. State U., Long Beach, 1958-62, 72, 73. Cert. counselor U.S., Calif. State Bd. Edn. Tchr. Marymount Acad., Tarrytown, N.Y., 1945-46; instr. Fairleigh Dickinson U., Rutherford, N.J., 1950-57; tchr. Long Beach Unified Sch. Dist., 1957-60, sch. counselor, 1960-80, cons. counseling svcs., 1980-90; cons. Calif. Acad. Math. and Sci., Dominguez Hills, 1990-93; pvt. practice Laguna Hills, Calif., 1990—; mem. profl. adv. bd. Learning Disabilities Assn. Calif., San Leandro, 1990—; part-time instr. U. La Verne, Calif., 1991-92; chair profl. devel. com. Calif. Assn. for Counseling and Devel., Fullerton, Calif., 1993—. Author: (elem. career awareness program) Color Me Successful, 1988; contbr. handbook Caution - Crisis Ahead, 1994. Mem. League Women Voters, Long Beach, 1982—. Recipient Counseling Program award Dept. of Edn. Los Angeles County, 1988, Adminstr. Recognition award Calif. Sch. Counselor Assn., 1990, Cmty. Contbn. citation Delta Kappa Gamma, 1990. Mem. AAUW (com. edn. found. 1993—), Am. Assn. Adult Devel. and Aging (exec. coun. 1993—), Am. Counseling Assn., Nat. Learning Disabilities Assn., Learning Disabilities Assn. Calif., Calif. Assn. Counseling & Devel. (Clarion model award 1990), Calif. Assn. for Adult Devel. & Aging (pres. 1991-92), Long Beach C. of C. (bd. dirs. women's coun. 1987-89), Nat. Bd. Cert. Counselors. Home and Office: 5216 Elvira Laguna Beach CA 92653-1817

STROOCK, THOMAS FRANK, business executive; b. N.Y.C., Oct. 10, 1925; s. Samuel and Dorothy (Frank) S.; m. Marta Freyre de Andrade, June 19, 1949; children: Margaret, Sandra, Elizabeth, Anne. BA in Econs., Yale U., 1948; LLB (hon.) U. Wyo., 1995. Landman Stanolind Oil & Gas Co., Tulsa, 1948-52; pres. Stroock Leasing Corp., Casper, Wyo., 1952-89, Alpha Exploration, Inc., 1980-89; ptnr. Stroock, Rogers & Dymond, Casper, 1960-82; dir. Wyo. Bancorp., Cheyenne, First Wyo. Bank, Casper; mem. Wyo. Senate, 1967-69, 71-75, 79-89, chmn. appropriations com. 1983, co-chmn. joint appropriations com., 1983-89, mem. mgmt. and audit com. P; mem. steering com. Edn. Commn. of States; amb. to Guatemala, Govt. of U.S., 1989-92; pres. Alpha Devel. Corp., 1992—; prof. pub. diplomacy U. Wyo., Casper, 1993—. Rep. precinct committeeman, 1950-68; pres. Natrona County Sch. Bd., 1960-69; pres. Wyo. State Sch. Bds. Assn., 1965-66; chmn. Casper Community Recreation, 1955-60; chmn. Natrona County United Fund, 1963-64; chmn. Wyo. State Republican Com., 1975-78, exec. com. 1954-60; delegate Rep. Nat. Convetion, 1956, 76; regional coord. campaign George Bush for pres., 1979-80, 87-88; chmn. Western States Rep. Chmn. Assn., 1977-78; chmn. Wyo. Higher Edn. Commn., 1969-71; mem. Nat. Petroleum Council, 1972-77; chmn. trustees Sierra Madre Found. for Geol. Research, New Haven; chmn. Wyo. Nat. Gas Pipeline Authority 1987-88; bd. dirs. Ucross Found., Denver; mem. Nat. Pub. Lands Adv. Council, 1981-85; chmn. Wyo. Health Reform Commn., 1993-95. Served with USMC, 1943-46. Mem. Rocky Mountain Oil and Gas Assn., Petroleum Assn. Wyo. Republican. Unitarian. Lodge: Kiwanis. Clubs: Casper Country; Casper Petroleum; Denver. Home and Office: PO Box 2875 Casper WY 82602-2875

STROUP, ELIZABETH FAYE, librarian; b. Tulsa, Mar. 25, 1939; d. Milton Earl and Lois (Buhl) S. BA in Philosophy, U. Wash., 1962, MLS, 1964. Intern Libr. of Congress, Washington, 1964-65; asst. dir. North Cen. Regional Libr., Wenatchee, Wash., 1966-69; reference specialist Congl. Reference div. Libr. of Congress, Washington, 1970-71, head nat. collections Div. for the Blind and Physically Handicapped, 1971-73, chief Congl. Reference div., 1973-78, dir. gen. reference, 1978-88; city libr., chief exec. officer Seattle Pub. Libr., 1988—; cons. U.S. Info. Svc., Indonesia, Feb. 1987. Mem. adv. bd. KCTS 9 Pub. TV, Seattle, 1988—; bd. visitors Sch. Librarianship, U. Wash., 1988—; bd. dirs. Wash. Literacy, 1988—. Mem. ALA (pres. reference and adult svcs. div. 1986-87, div. bd. 1985-88), Wash. Libr. Assn., D.C. Libr. Assn. (bd. dirs. 1975-76), City Club, Ranier Club. Office: Seattle Pub Libr 1000 4th Ave Seattle WA 98104-1109*

STROUP, RICHARD LYNDELL, economics educator, writer; b. Sunnyside, Wash., Jan. 3, 1943; s. Edgar Ivan and Inez Louise (Kellet) S.; m. Sandra Lee Price, Sept. 13, 1962 (div. Sept. 1981); children—Michael, Craig; m. Jane Bartlett Steidemann Shaw, Jan. 1, 1985; 1 child, David. Student, MIT, 1961-62; B.A., M.A., U. Wash., 1966, Ph.D. in Econs., 1970. Asst. prof. econs. Mont. State U., Bozeman, 1969-74; assoc. prof. econs. Mont. State U., 1974-78, prof. econs., 1978—; dir. Office Policy Analysis, Dept. Interior, Washington, 1982-84; vis. assoc. prof. Fla. State U., Tallahassee, 1977-78; sr. assoc. Polit. Economy Research Ctr., Bozeman, 1980—/lectr. summer univ., U. Aix (France), 1985—. Co-author: Natural Resources, 1983, Economics: Private and Public Choice, 7th edit., 1995, Basic Economics, 1993, What Everyone Should Know About Economics and Prosperity, 1993; also articles, 1972—; mem. editorial adv. bd. Regulation, 1993—. Adj. scholar Cato Inst., 1993—. Mem. Am. Econ. Assn., Western Econ. Assn. (exec. com. 1985-88), So. Econ. Assn., Mont Pelerin Soc., Phila. Soc., Pub. Choice Soc. Episcopalian. Home: 9 W Arnold St Bozeman MT 59715-6127 Office: Polit Economy Rsch Ctr 502 S 19th Ave Bozeman MT 59715-6827

STRUEVER, STUART MCKEE, archaeologist; b. Peru, Ill., Aug. 4, 1931; s. Carl Chester and Martha McKee (Scobee) S.; m. Alice Ruzzell Melcher, Aug. 21, 1956 (div. June 1983); children: Nathan Chester, Hanna Russell; m. Martha Lee Hopkins, Nov. 12, 1988. AB, Dartmouth Coll., 1953; MA, Northwestern U., 1960; PhD, U. Chgo., 1968. Instr. U. Chgo., 1964-65; from asst. prof. to prof. Northwestern U., Evanston, Ill., 1965-84; pres. Ctr. Am. Archaeology, Evanston, Ill., 1964-84, Crow Canyon Archaeological Ctr., Denver, 1985-92; chair Crow Canyon Ctr., Denver, 1993—; bd. archaeological cons. Tenn. Valley Authority. Knoxville, 1975-88. Author: Koster: Americans in Search of Their Past, 1979; editor: (book series) Studies in Archaeology Series, 1977-92. Recipient Alumni Achievement award U. Chgo., 1976; medal Hist. Preservation Garden Club Am., N.Y.C., 1994; Humanities fellow Ill. Humanities Coun., 1984. Mem. Soc. Am. Archaeology (pres. 1975-76, Disting. Svc. award, 1995), Soc. Profl. Archaeologists (bd. dirs. 1976), Phi Beta Kappa. Office: Crow Canyon Ctr 1777 S Harrison St # H1 Denver CO 80210-3925

STRUHL, STANLEY FREDERICK, real estate developer; b. Bklyn., Oct. 10, 1939; s. Isidore and Yvette (Miller) S.; BS with honors in Engring., UCLA, 1961, MBA in Data Processing, 1963; m. Patricia Joyce Wald, Feb. 26, 1966; children: Marc Howard, Lisa Lynn. Mem. tech. staff Hughes Aircraft Co., Fullerton, Calif., 1963-65; sr. asso. Planning Research Corp., Los Angeles, 1965-70; mgr. corporate info. systems Logicon, Inc., Torrance, Calif., 1970-73; mgr. operations analysis System Devel. Corp., Santa Monica, Calif., 1973-77; gen. partner TST Developers, Canyon Country, Calif., 1977-81; pres. Struhl Enterprises, Inc., Northridge, Calif., 1977-85; owner Struhl Properties, Northridge, 1979—. Mem. planning sub. com. 12th council dist., Los Angeles, 1986—. Lic. real estate broker, Calif. Mem. San Fernando Valley Bd. Realtors, Tau Beta Pi, Beta Gamma Sigma, Alpha Phi Omega. Home: 17074 Knapp St Northridge CA 91325-2637

STRUTZEL, J(OD) C(HRISTOPHER), escrow company executive; b. L.A., Sept. 20, 1947; s. James Rudolph and Charlotte Elizabeth (Weiss) S.; m. Christine Melba Kemp, Dec. 28, 1969; children: Jason James, Jess Warren. BS in Bus. Mgmt., Calif. State U., Long Beach, 1970. Bellman Edgewater Hyatt House Hotel, Long Beach, 1970, night auditor, 1970-71; asst. mgr. Sands Resort Hotel, Palm Springs, Calif., 1971-72; gen. mgr. Sands Resort Hotel, Palm Springs, 1972-73; sales coordinator Bendix Home Systems, Santa Fe Springs, Calif., 1973-74; loan rep. J.E. Wells Fin. Co., L.A., 1974-75; v.p. Express Escrow Co., Huntington Beach, Calif., 1976-78; pres., chmn. bd., bd. dirs. Express Escrow Co., Westminster, Calif., 1978—; pres., chmn. bd., bd. dirs. Elsinore (Calif.) Escrow, Inc., 1977-79; bd. dirs. Sorrel Devel., Redondo Beach, Calif.; expert witness on escrow, litigation and cons., 1982—; chmn. liability reduction com. Fidelity Corp., 1983-84, legis. chmn., 1985-86, 87-90, vice-chmn. bd., 1989-90, 94—, treas., 1992—; bd. dirs., sec. Discovery Escrow Co., 1989—; drafted sections of Calif. Fin. Code, Health and Safety Code, Calif. Adminstrv. Code. Contbr. articles to trade publs. Campaign treas. Californians to Elect Ted Cook, 1982; bd. dirs. publicity chmn. Fountain Valley (Calif.) Youth Baseball, 1986-87; AD HOC com. on Escrow Regulations Dept. Housing and Cmty. Devel., 1980; escrow adv. com. Dept. Corps., 1990-93. Recipient J.E. Wells Meml. award, 1988. Mem. Escrow Agts. Fidelity Corp. (bd. dirs. 1983-90, 91—), Escrow Inst. of Calif. (bd. dirs. 1991), Calif. Manufactured Housing Assn. (treas., bd. dirs. 1984-86), Calif. Manufactured Housing Inst. (bd. dirs. 1986—, treas. 1986-87, legis. chmn. 1993—, Polit. Action Com. Man of Yr. award 1988, Orange County chpt. Man of Yr. award 1988). Republican. Office: Express Escrow Co 14441 Beach Blvd Ste 100 Westminster CA 92683-5342

STRYKER, DENNIS J(AMES), lawyer; b. Canandaigua, N.Y., Aug. 3, 1958; s. Harold E. and Shirley (Hunt) S.; m. Monica Slev, Apr. 12, 1986. BA, Siena Coll., 1980; JD, Calif. Western Sch. Law, 1983; LLM in Taxation, U. San Diego, 1985. Bar: Calif. 1983, U.S. Dist. Ct. (so. dist.) Calif. 1983, U.S. Tax Ct. 1984, U.S. Dist. Ct. (cen. dist.) Calif. 1987, U.S. Dist. Ct. Ariz. 1993. Atty. Fisher-Thurber, San Diego, 1983-87; gen. counsel Rick Engring. Co., San Diego, 1987—. Author various articles in profl. jours. Mem. ABA, Interam. Bar Assn., Calif. Bar Assn., San Diego County Bar Assn., Assn. Trial Lawyers Am. Republican. Roman Catholic. Office: Rick Engring Co 5620 Friars Rd San Diego CA 92110-2513

STUART, BARBARA KATHRYN, real estate broker, consultant, genealogist; b. Havre, Mont., Oct. 21, 1945; d. David Maurice and Sarah Kathryn (Rickman) S.; m. Gerald Lee Trenholm, March 18, 1969 (div. 1971); 1 child, Dawn Bea Rogers. BS in Bus. Adminstrn., Regis Coll., 1990, MBA, 1992; student, U. Denver, 1995; grad. Real Estate, U. Colo., 1978. Leasing dir. Colo. Ctr. I & II, Denver, 1979-81, Environ. Developers, Inc., Aurora, 1981-82; dir. Librian Legacies, Denver, 1986—; pres. Windflower & Co., Denver, 1983—; family history cons. LDS Ch., Denver. Author: (book) Snowball's Gift, 1989, Stuarts From Scotland, 1995, (poetry) The White Rose, 1995; editor: (newsletter) Stu's News, 1994. Vol. chaplain Lutheran Hosp., Wheat Ridge, Colo., 1992—; vol archivist Nat. Archives at Denver Fed. Ctr., 1992—; docent Denver Pub. Library, 1995. Mem. BBB (arbitrator), Nat. Bd. Realtors, Colo. Bd. Realtors, Bd. Realtors Million Dollar Club, Daughters of the Am. Revolution. Office: Windflower & Co PO Box 1324 Wheat Ridge CO 80034

STUART, BRIAN MICHAEL, employee benefits and insurance sales consultant; b. Marin, Calif., Nov. 23, 1961; s. Martin T. and Inez S. S. BA in Econs., Princeton U., 1984; cert. in internat. bus., U. Copenhagen, 1982. Sr. marketer Link-Allen and Assocs., Inc., Foster City, Calif., 1986-92; prin. Stuart Planning Group, San Mateo, Calif., 1992—. Author: Airline Regulation and Deregulation, 1984. Mem. Am. Soc. CLUs, Princeton Club No. Calif. (exec. bd. 1988—, pres. 1995—), San Francisco Estate Palnning Coun., Estate Planning Coun. Penninsula, Ivy League Club San Francisco (v.p. 1986-88, pres. 1988-91, exec. bd. 1992-94), Zeta Psi. Office: Stuart Planning Group 1670 S Amphlett Blvd Ste 304 San Mateo CA 94402-2513

STUART, DAVID EDWARD, anthropologist, author, educator; b. Calhoun County, Ala., Jan. 9, 1945; s. Edward George and Avis Elsie (Densmore) S.; B.A. (Wesleyan Merit scholar 1965-66), W.VA. Wesleyan Coll., 1967; M.A. in Anthropology, U. N.Mex., 1970, Ph.D., 1972, postdoctoral student, 1975-76; m. Cynthia K. Morgan, June 14, 1971. Research assoc. Andean Center, Quito, Ecuador, 1970; continuing edn. instr. anthropology U. N.Mex., 1971, research archeologist Office Contract Archeology, 1974, research coordinator, 1974-77, asst. prof. anthropology, 1975-77, assoc. prof. anthropology, 1984—, asst. v.p. acad. affairs, 1987-95, assoc. v.p. academic affairs, 1995—; asst. prof. Eckerd Coll., St. Petersburg, Fla., 1972-74; cons. archeologist right-of-way div. Pub. Service Co. N.Mex., Albuquerque, 1977-78; cons. anthropologist Bur. Indian Affairs, Albuquerque, 1978, Historic Preservation Bur. N.Mex., Santa Fe, 1978-81, Nat. Park Service, 1980, Albuquerque Mus., 1981; sr. research assoc. Human Systems Research, Inc., 1981-83, Quivira Research Center, Albuquerque, 1984-86; bd. dirs. Table Ind. Scholars, 1979-83, pres., bd. dirs. Rio Grande Heritage Found., Albuquerque and Las Cruces, 1985-87; advisor Human Systems Research, Inc., Tularosa, N.Mex., 1978-80, Albuquerque Commn. on Hist. Preservation, 1984-86. Grantee Eckerd Coll., 1973, Historic Preservation Bur., 1978-80. Essayist award N.Mex. Humanities Council, 1986. Mem. Am. Anthrop. Assn., Royal Anthrop. Inst. Gt. Britain, N.Mex. Archeol. Council, Albuquerque Archeol. Soc. (pres. 1986-88), Descs. Signers Declaration Independence, Sigma Xi, Phi Kappa Phi. Presbyterian. Co-author: Archeological Survey: 4 Corners to Ambrosia, N.Mex., 1976, A Proposed Project Design for the Timber Management Archeological Surveys, 1978, Ethnoarcheological Investigations of Shepherding in the Pueblo of Laguna, 1983; Author: Prehistoric New Mexico, 1981, 2d edit., 1984, 3d edit., 1988, Glimpses of the Ancient Southwest, 1985, The Magic of Bandelier National Monument, 1989, Power and Efficiency in Eastern Anasazi Architecture, 1994, others; columnist New Mexico's Heritage, 1983-87, others. Editor: Archeological Reports, No. 1, 1975, No. 2, 1981. Office: U NMex Rm 263 Student Svcs Ctr Albuquerque NM 87131

STUART, DOROTHY MAE, artist; b. Fresno, Calif., Jan. 8, 1933; d. Robert Wesley Williams and Maria Theresa (Gad) Tressler; m. Reginald Ross Stuart, May 18, 1952; children: Doris Lynne Stuart Willis, Darlene Mae Stuart Cavalletto, Sue Anne Stuart Peters. Student, Calif. State U., Fresno, 1951-52, Fresno City Coll., 1962-64. Artist, art judge, presenter demonstrations at schs., fairs and art orgns. Calif., 1962—. Editor, art dir. Fresno High School Centennial 1889-1989, 1989; art advisor Portrait of Fresno, 1885-1985; contbg. artist Heritage Fresno, 1975; exhibited in group shows, including M.H. De Young Mus., San Francisco, 1971, Charles and Emma Frye Mus., Seattle, 1971, Calif. State U.-Fresno tour of China, 1974. Mem. adv. com. Calif. State Ken Maddy Ctrl. Calif. Conf. on Women, 1989-95, Patrons for Cultural Arts, Fresno, 1987-92, bd. dirs., 1991-92. Recipient 53 art awards, 1966-84; nominated Woman of the Yr., Bus./Profl. of Fresno, 1990. Mem. Soc. Western Artists (bd. dirs. 1968-74, v.p. 1968-70), Fresno Womens Trade Club (bd. dirs. 1986-93, pres. 1988-90), Fresno Art Mus., Fresno Met. Mus., Native Daus. Golden West Fresno. Republican. Home and Office: 326 S Linda Ln Fresno CA 93727-5737

STUART, GERARD WILLIAM, JR., investment company executive, city official; b. Yuba City, Calif., July 28, 1939; s. Gerard William and Geneva Bernice (Stuke) S.; student Yuba Jr. Coll., 1957-59, Chico State Coll., 1959-60; A.B., U. Calif., Davis, 1962; M.L.S., U. Calif., Berkeley, 1963; m. Lenore Frances Loroña, 1981. Rare book librarian Cornell U., 1964-68; bibliographer of scholarly collections Huntington Library, San Marino, Calif., 1968-73, head acquisitions librarian, 1973-75; sec.-treas., dir. Ravenstree Corp., 1969-80, pres., chmn. bd., 1980—; pres., chmn. bd. William Penn Ltd., 1981—. Councilman City of Yuma, 1992—, also dep. mayor; bd. dirs. Ariz. Humanities Coun., 1993—. Lilly fellow Ind. U., 1963-64. Mem. Bibliog. Soc. Am., Phi Beta Kappa, Alpha Gamma Sigma, Phi Kappa Phi. Clubs: Rolls-Royce Owners; Grolier (N.Y.C.); Zamorano (Los Angeles). Office: 204 S Madison Ave Yuma AZ 85364-1421

STUART, WILLIAM ROY, information services executive; b. Redwood City, Calif., June 7, 1972; s. Larry Howard and Happy Helen Francis (Hockabout) S. Mgr. info. svcs. Am. Data Mgmt., Inc., Mountain View, Calif., 1991-93; sr. microcomputer specialist Applied Tech. Assocs., Mountain View, Calif., 1993—. Vol. Tom Nolan for Supr., Redwood City, 1984, Kevin Kelly for Assembly, Belmont, Calif., 1986, Ted Lempert for Assembly, San Mateo, Calif., 1988, PC specialist, 1990. Democrat.

STUBBLEFIELD, JAMES IRVIN, emergency medicine physician, health facility administrator; b. Phila., Aug. 17, 1953; s. James Irvin Sr. and Geri (Harvey) S.; m. Linda Marie Simms, Aug. 12, 1978; children: Lindsay, Shannon. BSEE, MS in Bioengring., U. Pa., 1977; MD, Hahnemann U., Phila., 1982. Diplomate Am. Bd. Emergency Medicine, 1991. Mgr. energy engring. Norcross, Inc., Bryn Mawr, Pa., 1977-78; commd. 2d lt. U.S. Army, 1977, advanced through grades to lt. col., 1993; intern in gen. surgery Letterman Army Med. Ctr., San Francisco, 1982-83; flight surgeon, brigade surgeon 101st Airborne Div., Ft. Campbell, Ky., 1983-87; resident in emergency medicine Madigan Army Med. Ctr., Ft. Lewis, Wash., 1987-90; chief dep. emergency medicine and primary care Silas B. Hays Army Hosp., Ft. Ord, Calif., 1990-94; flight surgeon attack helicopter battalion Operation Desert Storm, Persian Gulf, 1991. Decorated Bronze Star, Air medal. Fellow Am. Coll. Emergency Physicians; mem. AMA, U.S. Army Flight Surgeon Soc., Assn. Mil. Surgeons U.S., Tau Beta Pi, Eta Kappa Nu, Alpha Epsilon Delta. Roman Catholic. Home: 18506 Candace Ln Watsonville CA 95076

STUBBLEFIELD, THOMAS MASON, agricultural economist, educator; b. Taxhoma, Okla., Apr. 16, 1922; s. Temple Roscoe and Martha Lacy (Acree) S.; BS, N.Mex. State U., 1948; MS, A. and M. Coll. Tex., 1951, PhD, 1956; postgrad. U. Ariz., 1954; m. Martha Lee Miller, Mar. 7, 1943; children: Ellen (Mrs. Richard Damron), Paula (Mrs. James T. Culbertson), Thommye (Mrs. Gary D. Zingsheim). Specialist cotton mktg. N.Mex. State U., 1948; extension economist, then asst. agrl. economist U. Ariz., Tucson,

1951-58, from assoc. prof. to prof., 1958-64, prof. and agrl. economist, 1964-83, emeritus prof., 1983—, acting asst. dir. agrl. expt. sta., 1966-68, asst. to dir. sta., 1973-74, chief party Brazil contract, 1968-70. Mem. Pima Council Aging, 1974-77, 80-90; chmn. adv. com. Ret. Sr. Vol. Program, Pima County, 1974-77, 80-90, mem. 1974-95. Chmn. bd. Saguaro Home Found., 1980-85. With AUS, 1942-45. Author bulls. Home: 810 W Calle Milu Tucson AZ 85706-3925

STUBBS, DANIEL GAIE, labor relations consultant; b. Charleston, S.C., Nov. 13, 1940; s. Daniel Hamer and Esther Virginia (Garlow) S.; m. Sherrill Ann Sloan, July 8, 1984; children: Kimberly, Allison, Don; student U. Fla., 1959-60; BA, W.Va. U., 1965; postgrad. Temple U., 1965-67. Tchr., Sch. Dist. of Phila., 1965-67; rep. Am. Fedn. Tchrs., Washington, 1967; exec. sec. Calif. State Coll. Coun., Am. Fedn. Tchrs., AFL-CIO, L.A., 1967-68; rep. Am. Fedn. Tchrs., AFL-CIO, L.A., 1968-69, dir. orgn. Balt. Tchrs. Union, 1969-70; employee relations specialist Calif. Nurses Assn., L.A., 1971-72; exec. dir. United Nurses Assn. Calif., L.A., 1972-74; labor rels. cons. Social Svcs. Union, Svc. Employees Internat. Union, Local 535, AFL-CIO, L.A., 1974-76; exec. dir. Met. Riverside UniServ Unit, Calif. Tchrs. Assn., 1976-79, exec. dir. San Bernardino/Colton Uniserv Unit, 1979-80; gen. svcs. adminstr. Housing Authority, City of L.A., 1980-82; cons. Blanning & Baker Assocs., Tujunga, Calif., 1983-84; asst. exec. dir. adminstrv. svcs. L.A. Housing Authority, 1984-86; labor rels. cons., L.A., 1986—; lectr. in field. With U.S. Army, 1961-62. Recipient W.Va. U. Waitman Barbe Prize for creative writing, 1965. Mem. So. Calif. Indsl. Rels. Rsch. Assn., Orange County Indsl. Relations Research Assn., Indsl. Rels. Rsch. Assn., UCLA Inst. Indsl. Rels. Assn., Soc. of Profls. in Dispute Resolution, Town Hall Club of Calif. Presbyterian. Home: 3200 Fairesta St Apt 11 La Crescenta CA 91214-2681

STUBBS, MARK DARWIN, lawyer; b. Spanish Fork, Utah, Oct. 4, 1950; s. R. Eugene and Joan (Loveless) S.; m. Jan Green, Aug. 28, 1973; children: Julie, Jared, Michael, Melissa, Richard. BA, Brigham Young U., 1974, JD, 1977. Bar: Ariz. 1977, U.S. Dist. Ct. Ariz. 1977, Idaho 1980, U.S. Dist. Ct. Idaho 1980. Assoc. Ryley, Carlock & Ralson, Phoenix, 1976-79; ptnr. Sudweeks, May, Stubbs, Browning & Kershaw (was May & May), Twin Falls, Idaho, 1979—; mem. Idaho Ho. of Reps., Boise, 1990—. Bd. dirs. Lawyers Involved for Idaho, 1986-90; Rep. dist. chmn., Twin Falls, 1982-89. Mem. ABA, Ariz. Bar Assn., Idaho Bar Assn., Idaho Trial Lawyers Assn. (bd. govs., bd. dirs. 1984-87), Greater Twin Falls Area C. of C., Am. Arbitration Assn. (panel of arbitrators 1990—). Republican. Home: 1025 Sawtooth Blvd Twin Falls ID 83301-3583 Office: Sudweeks May Stubbs et al 516 2d St E PO Box 1846 Twin Falls ID 83303

STUCKI, KIM NOLAN, mechanical engineer; b. Logan, Utah, Nov. 17, 1957; s. Nolan David and Marlene (Ward) S.; m. Tammy Gay Cardon Stucki, Aug. 17, 1982; children: Dustin, Zachary, Jaimon, Kaila. A in Engring., Ricks Coll., Rexburg, Idaho, 1978; BS in Mech. Engring., Brigham Young U., Provo, Utah, 1982. Lic. Mech. Engring., Calif. Power prodn. engr. Pacific Gas and electric Co., San Francisco, 1983-88, sr. power prodn. engr., 1988-90, sr. capital projects engr., 1990-91, fin. bus. trainer, 1991-92, site mgr., 1992-93, sr. project engr., 1993—. Recipient Pacific Gas and Electric Co. Recognition awards (6), Community Svc. award,. Home: 3075 Soda Bay Rd Lakeport CA 95453-9749 Office: Pacific Gas & Electric Co PO Box 985 Healdsburg CA 95448-0985

STUDDERT, STEPHEN MARK, investment banker; b. Petaluma, Calif., Nov. 17, 1948; m. Bonnie Jane Beck, June 1, 1968; children: Mark, Christopher, Stephanie, David, Allyson, Michael. BS, Brigham Young U., 1970. Staff asst. to Pres. of U.S. White House, Washington, 1975-77, spl. asst. to Pres. U.S., 1981-85; asst. to Pres. U.S., 1989-90; pres. Maple Hills, Inc., Bountiful, Utah, 1977-81; chmn. and dir. Fed. Home Loan Bank of Seattle, 1987—; founder, dir. Sailors & Mchts. Bank & Trust, Vienna, Va., 1984-87. Chmn. Nat. Mormon Pioneer Hist. Trail Commn., 1987-89; dir. advance Reagan-Bush Campaign, 1980, sr. campaign advisor, 1984; leader Boy Scouts Am., Utah, Va., 1970—; sr. advisor Presdl. Inaugural, Washington, 1981, 85, dir., 1989; stake pres. LDS Ch., Va., 1984-89, Utah, 1992—; chair Utah Statehood Centennial Com., 1992—; co-chair New Am. Revolution, 1994—. Named Outstanding Young Men of Am., 1972-82. Republican. Office: Studdert Cos 60 E South Temple Ste 1225 Salt Lake City UT 84111-1048

STUDEBAKER, IRVING GLEN, engineering educator, researcher; b. Ellensburg, Wash., July 22, 1931; s. Clement Glen and Ruth (Krause) S.; (widowed); children: Ruth, Betty, Raymond, Karl, Donna. BS in Geol. Engring., U. Ariz., 1957, MS in Geology, 1959, PhD in Geol. Engring., 1977. Registered profl. engr., Wash., Nev., Ariz., Colo., Mont. Geophys. engr. Mobil, 1959-61; civil engr. City of Yakima, Wash., 1964-66; instr. Yakima Valley Coll., 1962-67; sr. rsch. geologist Roan Selection Trust, Kalulushi, Zambia, 1967-72; sr. mining engr. Occidental Oil Shale, Grand Junction, Colo., 1974-81; prof. Mont. Coll. Mining Sch., Butte, 1982—; cons. in field. Sgt. U.S. Army, 1951-54, Korea. Mem. N.W. Mining Assn., Geol. Soc. Am., Soc. for Mining and Metall. Engring., Soc. Econ. Geologists, Mont. Mining Assn., Sigma Xi (pres. Mont. tech. chpt. 1990-91). Home: 5 Cedar Lake Dr Butte MT 59701-4337 Office: Mont Tech Mining Dept West Park Butte MT 59701

STUDEMEISTER, PAUL ALEXANDER, geologist; b. Caracas, Venezuela, Mar. 20, 1954; came to U.S., 1966; s. Alexander E. and Marguerite (Preobrajensky) S. BA, U. Calif., Berkeley, 1977; PhD, U. Western Ont., London, Can., 1982. Lic. engring. geologist, Calif.; lic. geologist, Ariz. Geology instr. U. Ottawa, Can., 1982-83; project geologist Dunraine Mines Ltd., Toronto, Can., 1983-84; geology instr. Laurentian U., Sudbury, Can., 1984-85; project geologist Agassiz Resources, Ltd., Toronto, 1985; rsch. petrographer Constrn. Tech. Labs., Skokie, Ill., 1985-90; project geologist Applied GeoSystems, Fremont, Calif., 1990; sr. geologist EVAX Techs., Inc., Scotts Valley, Calif., 1990-93, The Bentley Co., San Francisco, Calif., 1993-94; project mgr. Lee Inc., Sunnyvale, Calif., 1995—. Contbr. 14 articles to profl. jours. Mem. Assn. Engring. Geologists, Groundwater Resources Assn. Calif. Lutheran. Home: 2140 Santa Cruz Ave Apt D105 Menlo Park CA 94025-6343 Office: Lee Inc 1153 Bordeaux Dr #103 Sunnyvale CA 94089

STUDENMUND, ARNOLD HARWOOD, economist, educator; b. Cooperstown, N.Y., Oct. 6, 1944; s. W. R. and Betsy (Harwood) S.; m. Jaynie M. Miller, July 12, 1980; children: Brent, Scott, Connell. AB, Hamilton Coll., 1966; MA, Cornell U., 1969, PhD, 1970. From instr. to Richard W. Millar prof. econs. Occidental Coll., L.A.; various positions Occidental Coll. including dir. core program liberal arts, assoc. dean of faculty, dir. instl. rsch., v.p. student svcs. Author: Using Econometrics, 2d edit., 1992 (best selling econometrics textbook worldwide); contbr. articles to profl. jours. Office: Dept Econs Occidental Coll Los Angeles CA 90041

STUDLEY, HELEN ORMSON, artist, poet, writer, designer; b. Elroy, Wis., Sept. 8, 1937; d. Clarence Ormson and Hilda (Johnson) O.; m. William Frank Studley, Aug. 1965 (div.); 1 son, William Harrison. Owner RJK Original Art, Sherman Oaks, Calif., 1979—; designer Aspen Series custom greeting cards and stationery notes, lithographs Love is All Colors, 1982, Flowers for Ruth (Best of Art Show award). One woman show includes Sherman Oaks, Calif., 1991, Toluca Lake Art Festival, 1991, Art Show for Srs., 1992, Art Show for Youth, 1991; represented in numerous pub. and pvt. collections throughout U.S., Can., Norway, Sweden, Austria, Germany, Eng., France; group exhibits include Art Show for Homeless, L.A., 1990; author poetry Love is Care, Changes, 1988; contbr. poems to publs. Active Luth. Brotherhood, Emmanuel Luth. Ch. Honors include display of lithograph Snow Dreams, Snow Queens at 1980 Winter Olympics, Lake Placid, N.Y., lithograph Summer Dreams, Summer Queens at 1984 Summer Olympics, Los Angeles; named finalist in competition for John Simon Guggenheim fellowship; recipient Golden Poet award World Poetry, 1987-92, Art Show for Youth, 1991, Art Show for Srs., 1992, Art Show at the Park, 1992, Diamond Pin award Carter Hawley Hale, 1991, 92, Outstanding Achievements in Poetry award, 1993, . Mem. Internat. Soc. Poets (publ. in Disting. Poets Am. 1993), Soc. Illustrators, Am. Watercolor Soc., Internat. Soc. Artists, Internat. Platform Assn., Calif. Woman's Art Guild, Sons of Norway Club. Office: RJK Original Art 5020 Hazeltine Ave Sherman Oaks CA 91423-1174

STULZ, DALE WARREN, photographic consultant, appraiser; b. Stamford, Con., Apr. 13, 1951; s. Richard Earl and Harriet Hoffmann S. BA summa cum laude, Princeton (N.J.) U., 1973; postgrad., Inst. Fine Arts N.Y. U., 1973-75. Lic. auctioneer, Calif. Asst. dir. Helios Arts, Inc., N.Y.C., 1974-75; pres. Highland Gallery, Inc., San Francisco, 1975-76; dir. dept. photographs Martin Gordon, Inc., N.Y.C., 1976-77; pres. Argus Ltd., N.Y.C., 1977-78; founding dir. dept. 19th & 20th photographs Christie Manson & Woods Internat., N.Y.C., 1978-83; v.p., auctioneer dir. LIGHT Gallery, Inc., N.Y.C., 1983-84; owner Stulz Cons. and Appraisals, Manhattan Beach, Calif., 1984—; bd. dirs. L.A. Contemporary Exhibitions, chmn., 1989-90, 92-93; adv. bd. mem. L.A. Ctr. for Photographic Studies, 1984—, San Francisco Camerawork, 1986—; founding bd. mem. photography coun. Mus. Contemporary Arts., L.A., 1988—. Author numerous catalogues and photographs in field; contbr. articles and reviews to profl. jours. Patron L.A. Contemporary Exhibitions, The Friends of Photography, Houston Ctr. for Photogrphay. Mem. Royal Photographic Soc. (assoc.), Internat. Coun. of the Arts (trustee emeritus, chmn. 1990-94). Office: Stulz Cons and Appraisals 220 5th St Manhattan Beach CA 90266-5710

STUMBLES, JAMES RUBIDGE WASHINGTON, multinational company executive; b. Harare, Zimbabwe, Aug. 13, 1939; came to U.S., 1980; s. Albert R.W. and Mary Dallas (Atherstone) S.; m. Vyvienne Clare Shaw, Dec. 19, 1964; children: Christopher, Timothy, Jonathan. BA, U. Cape Town, Republic of South Africa, 1960, LLB, 1962. Adv. Supreme Ct. of S. Africa. Mng. dir. Pritchard Services Group of South Africa, Johannesburg, 1972-80; dir. security, pres. subs. Pritchard Svcs. Group Am., Columbus, Ohio, 1980-83; exec. v.p., pres. subs. Mayne Nickless/ Loomis Corp., Seattle, 1984-87; v.p. N.W. Protective Svc. Inc., Seattle, 1987-91, pres., CEO, 1991—; pres., CEO Western Security Svc. Inc., Spokane, 1991—, Northwest Protective Svc. Inc.-Oreg., Portland, 1992—. Sec. Boy Scouts, Johannesburg, 1978-80. Mem. Rand Club, Rainier Club, Rotary, Kiwanis, Round Table (officer 1969-80). Office: NW Protective Svc Inc 2700 Elliott Ave Seattle WA 98121-1109

STUMP, BOB, congressman; b. Phoenix, Apr. 4, 1927; s. Jesse Patrick and Floy Bethany (Fields) S.; children: Karen, Bob, Bruce. B.S. in Agronomy, Ariz. State U., 1951. Mem. Ariz. Ho. of Reps., 1957-67; mem. Ariz. Senate, 1967-76, pres., 1975-76; mem. 95th-104th Congresses from 3rd Dist.Ariz., 1976—; mem. Nat. Security Com. With USN, 1943-46. Mem. Am. Legion, Ariz. Farm Bur. Republican. Seventh-day Adventist. Office: 211 Canon House of Representatives Washington DC 20515-0303 also: 230 N 1st Ave Rm 5001 Phoenix AZ 85025-0230*

STUMP, D. MICHAEL, librarian; b. Santa Monica, Calif., Dec. 22, 1947; s. H. Walter and Margaret June (Stetler) S. B.A. in History, Pasadena Coll., 1971; M.L.S., U. So. Calif., 1977. Library asst. Calif. Inst. Tech., Pasadena, Calif., 1970-74; librarian First Baptist Ch. of Van Nuys, Calif., 1974-81, 1982-87, Laurence/2000, Van Nuys, 1981-82; Van Nuys Christian Coll., 1975-76, Hillcrest Christian Sch., Granada Hills, Calif., 1987—. Asst. scoutmaster San Fernando council Boy Scouts Am., 1970-73. Named to Outstanding Young Men Am. U.S. Jaycees, 1976. Mem. ALA, Am. Assn. Sch. Librs., Evang. Ch. Libr. Assn. (So. Calif. chpt.). Republican. Baptist. Office: Hillcrest Christian Sch 17531 Rinaldi St Granada Hills CA 91344-3319

STUMPF, BERNHARD JOSEF, physicist; b. Neustadt der Weinstrasse, Rhineland, Germany, Sept. 21, 1948; came to U.S., 1981; s. Josef and Katharina (Cervinka) S. Diploma physics, Saarland U., Saarbrucken, West Germany, 1975, Dr.rer.nat., 1981. Rsch. asst. physics dept. Saarland U., Saarbrucken, 1976-81; rsch. assoc. Joint Inst. Lab. Astrophysics, U. Colo., Boulder, 1981-84; instr. physics, physics dept. NYU, N.Y.C., 1984-86, asst. rsch. scientist Atomic Beams Lab., 1984-85, assoc. rsch. scientist Atomic Beams Lab., 1985-86; vis. assoc. prof. physics dept. U. Windsor (Ont., Can.), 1986-88; assoc. prof. physics dept. U. Idaho, Moscow, 1988—; chmn. Conf. on Atomic and Molecular Collisions in Excited States, Moscow, 1990. Contbr. articles to profl. jours. German Sci. Found. postdoctoral fellow U. Colo., 1981-83. Mem. AAUP, German Phys. Soc., Am. Phys. Soc., N.Y. Acad. Scis. Office: U Idaho Dept Physics Moscow ID 83844-2341

STUMPF, MICHAEL HOWARD, psychiatrist; b. Indpls., Aug. 7, 1952; s. Joseph A. and Nettie (Weinberg) S.; m. Sandra Kay Beams, Sept. 2, 1974; 1 child, Amanda Laura. BA in Biology, Ind. U., Bloomington, 1978; MD, Ind. U., Indpls, 1982. Diplomat Am. Bd. Psychiatry and Neurology. Intern, then resident Psych. Residency Trng. Program, Maricopa Med. Ctr., Phoenix, 1982-86; Psychiatrist homeless shelter program Phoenix South Community Mental Health Ctr., 1983-84; psychiatrist Tri-City Behavioral Health Ctr., Mesa, Ariz., 1984; attending psychiatrist County Homeless Alternative Psychiat. Svcs., Phoenix, 1984-86; teaching psychiatrist Maricopa Med. Ctr., Phoenix, 1986-90, chief psychiatrist psychiat. inpatient unit III, 1986-87, attending and chief psychiatrist psychiat. crisis ctr., 1987-88; attending psychiatrist Maricopa County Correctional Health Svcs., Phoenix, 1987-89, 90-92; dir. psychiat. and med. svcs. Cmty. Orgn. for Drug Abuse, Mental Health and Alcoholism, Phoenix, 1989-92; attending psychiatrist Psychist. Outreach Project, Phoenix, 1988-89; instr. SMI program Rio Salado C.C., 1991-93; med. dirs. Superstition Mountain Mental Health Ctr., Apache Junction, Ariz., 1992-95, Rainbows Way Inn, Mesa, Ariz., 1992—. Chmn. com. to rev. other states Ariz. Gov.'s Task Force on Homelesss Chronically Mentally Ill., Phoenix, 1989. Named Psychiat. Attending of Yr. psychiat. nursing svc. Maricopa Med. Ctr., 1987. Fellow Am. Psychiat. Assn.; mem. Am. Assn. Cmty. Psychiatrists, Ariz. Psychiat. Soc. (co-chmn. pub. affairs com. 1987-95, sec. 1991, v.p. 1992, pres. elect. 1993, pres. 1994-95, newsletter editor 1995—, Phoenix Psychiat. Coun. (sec.-treas. 1990-91, v.p. 1992-93, pres. 1994—), Mental Health Assn. Maricopa County (bd. dirs. 1992-95). Jewish. Office: Superstition Mountain Mental Health Ctr PO Box 3160 Apache Junction AZ 85217-3160

STUMPF, PAUL KARL, biochemistry educator emeritus; b. N.Y.C., N.Y., Feb. 23, 1919; s. Karl and Annette (Schreyer) S.; married, June 1947; children: Ann Carol, Kathryn Lee, Margaret Ruth, David Karl, Richard Frederic. AB, Harvard Coll., 1941; PhD, Columbia U., 1945. Instr. pub. health U. Mich., Ann Arbor, 1946-48; faculty U. Calif., Berkeley, 1948-58, prof., 1956-58; prof. U. Calif., Davis, 1958-84, prof. emeritus, 1984—; chief scientist Competitive Rsch. Grants Office USDA, Washington, 1988-91; cons. Palm Oil Rsch. Inst., Kuala Lumpur, Malaysia, 1982-92; mem. sci. adv. bd. Calgene, Inc., Davis, 1990-93; mem. sci. adv. panel Md. Biotech. Inst., 1990-92. Co-author: Outlines of Enzyme Chemistry, 1955, Outlines of Biochemistry, 5th edit., 1987; co-editor-in-chief Biochemistry of Plants, 1980; exec. editor Archives of Biochemistry/Biophysics, 1965-88; contbr. over 250 articles to profl. jours. Mem. planning commn. City of Davis, 1966-68. Guggenheim fellow, 1962, 69; recipient Lipid Chemistry award Am. Oil Chemists Soc., 1974, Sr. Scientist award Alexander von Humboldt Found., 1976, Superior Svc. Group award USDA, 1992. Fellow AAAS; mem. NAS, Royal Danish Acad. Scis., Am. Soc. Plant Physiologists (pres. 1979-80, chmn. bd. trustees 1986-90, Stephen Hales award 1974, Charles Reid Barnes Life Membership award 1992), Yolo Fliers Country Club (Woodland, Calif.). Home: 764 Elmwood Dr Davis CA 95616-3517 Office: Univ of Calif Molecular/Cellular Biology Davis CA 95616

STUPSKI, LAWRENCE J., investment company executive; b. 1945. JD, Yale U., 1970. V.p. Bradford Nat. Corp., N.Y.C., 1971-78; with Western Bradford Tr. Inc., San Francisco, 1978-80; pres., COO, CEO Charles Schwab & Co. Inc. (formerly Charles Schwab Corp.), 1980—, also bd. dirs. Office: Charles Schwab & Co Inc 101 Montgomery St San Francisco CA 94104-4122*

STURE, STEIN, civil engineering educator; b. Oslo, Norway, Nov. 12, 1947; came to U.S., 1970; s. Alf and Gunnvor (Een) S.; m. Karen J. Marley, June 3, 1989. Student, Schous Inst. Tech., Oslo, 1970; BSCE, U. Colo., 1971, MSCE, 1973, PhD, 1976. Asst. prof. Va. Polytechnic Inst., Blacksburg, 1976-80; rsch. scientist Marshall Space Flight Ctr. NASA, Huntsville, Ala., 1979; from asst. prof. to prof. civil engring. U. Colo., Boulder, 1980—, acting chmn. dept. civil engring., 1990-91; chmn. dept. civil engring., 1994—; sr. vis. dept. engring. sci. U. Oxford, Eng., 1985; vis. prof. Norway Inst. Tech., Trondheim, 1985-86. Editor Jour. Engring. Mechanics. Jenkin fellow, 1986. Mem. Am. Soc. Civil Engrs. (pres. Colo. sect. 1990-91, Walter Huber Civil Engring. Rsch. prize 1990), Am. Assn. Advancement Sci., Am. Geophys. Union, Am. Soc. Engring. Edn., NASA Ctr. Space Construction, Internat. Soc. Soil Mech. Found. Engrs., ASTM (affiliate). Home: 1077 Diamond Ct Boulder CO 80303-3244 Office: Univ Colo Dept Civil Engring Boulder CO 80309

STURGEN, WINSTON, photographer, printmaker, artist; b. Harrisburg, Pa., Aug. 27, 1938; s. George Winston and Gladys Erma (Lenker) S.; m. Nancy Kathryn Otto, Jan. 23, 1959 (div. 1981); 1 child, Bruce Eugene Sturgen; m. Jessica Sheldon, Mar. 15, 1988. BS in Forestry, Pa. State U., 1960; postgrad., U. N.H., 1961-62; M of Forestry, Pa. State U., 1964; postgrad., U. Oreg., 1966-68. Cert. profl. photographer. Devel. engr. Weyerhaeuser Co., Longview, Wash., 1964-66; mgr. Wickes Lumber Co., Elkhorn, Wis., 1968-70; dir. ops. Wickes Wanderland, Inc., Delavan, Wis., 1970-72; owner, mgr. Sturgen's Cleaners, Delavan, 1972-80, Images by Sturgen, Delavan, 1980-84; instr. photography continuing edn. dept. Western N.Mex. U., 1988-90; juror numerous orgns., 1982—. One-man shows include Artesia (N.Mex.) Mus. and Art Ctr., 1992, Delavan Art Mus., 1984, Donnell Libr., N.Y.C., 1992; exhibited in group shows at Carlsbad (N.Mex.) Mus., 1992, Sister Kenny Inst., 1992, (3rd Pl.), 93 (1st Pl.), 94, Deming Ctr. for the Arts, N.Mex., 1991, Shellfish Collection, Silver City, N.Mex., 1989, 90, 91, 92, 93, Thompson Gallery, U. N.Mex., 1989, Profl. Photographers Assn. of N.Mex., 1985, 86, 87, 88 (awards), Union Gallery, U. N.Mex., 1987, Gallery Sigala, Taos, N.Mex., 1986, World Trade Ctr., N.Y.C., 1992, 93, 94, Internat. Exposition of Photography, 1983, 84, 85, 87, Beyond Photography Touring Exhibit, 1991-92, An Am. Collection Touring Exhibit, San Francisco, Washington, Brussels, Tokyo, 1993-95, Sapporo (Japan) Internat. Print Biennial, 1993, Very Spl. Arts/N.Mex. Touring Exhibit, 1993-94, Ctr. Contemporary Art, St. Louis, 1994 (Purchase award), many others; pub. poetry, numerous articles in field. Founder, chmn. Winter Arts Festival, Silver City, N.Mex., 1988-90; com. mem. Taos Fall Arts Festival, 1985; com. chair Oktoberfest, Delavan, 1976-80. Residency grant Wurlitzer Found., 1987, 89. Mem. Very Spl. Artists N.Mex., Very Spl. Artists Washington, Enabled Artists United, Fuller Lodge Art Ctr. Home: c/o Gardner 3211 Elm St Harrisburg PA 17109

STURGESS, P. KIM, management executive consultant; b. Ottawa, Ont., Can., Mar. 29, 1955; d. Roy and Sydney Claire (Chamberlain) S. BSc in Engring. Physics, Queen's U., Kingston, 1977; MBA with distinction, U. W. Ont., 1984. Registered profl. engr., Alta. Gas pipelines engr. Nat. Energy Bd., Ottawa, 1977-78; reservoir engr. Esso Resources Can. Ltd., Calgary, Alta., Can., 1978-80, corp. planning analyst, 1980-82; cons. McKinsey and Co., Toronto, Ont., 1984-88; v.p., asst. to pres. Greyhound Lines of Canada, Calgary, 1988-89; v.p. devel. Relax Hotels and Resorts, Calgary, Can., 1989—; mgmt. cons. in pvt. practice Calgary, 1990—; mgr. Nova Corp., Alberta, Calgary, Can., 1990-92; CEO Revolve Techs. Inc., Calgary, Can., 1993—; trustee Queen's U. 1987—, bd. dirs. bookstore 1975-77, mem. univ. council, 1979—; bd. dirs. Alberta Sci. Ctr., 1989—. Mem. Assn. Profl. Engrs., Geologists and Geophysicists Alta, Queen's U. Alumni Assn. (pres. 1980-82). Home: Box 1 Site 32, RR 12, Calgary, AB Canada T3E6W3 Office: Revolve Techs Inc, 300 707 10th Ave SW, Calgary, AB Canada T2R 0B3

STURKEN, MARITA LOUISE, communications educator, writer, critic; b. Plainfield, N.J., Mar. 18, 1957; d. Robert Carl and Marie Jean (Ryan) S. Student, Cornell U., 1977-79; BA in Visual Studies Workshop, Empire State Coll., 1979; PhD, U. Calif., Santa Cruz, 1992. Film/video cataloguer Mus. Modern Art, N.Y.C., 1981-83; prof. San Francisco Art Inst., 1990-91; tchg. fellow U. Calif., Santa Cruz, 1990-91; lectr. dept. comm. U. Calif., San Diego, 1992-94; asst. prof. Annenberg Sch. Comm. U. So. Calif., L.A., 1994—. Author: Circulating Video Library, 1983; co-editor: Electronic Arts Intermix: Video, 1991; contbr. articles to profl. jours. and periodicals. N.Y. State Coun. on the Arts writing grantee, 1982, 83, 85; recipient AAUW dissertation fellowship, 1991. Office: Univ of So Calif Annenberg Sch Comm GFS 344 Los Angeles CA 90089-1694

STURTEVANT, DAVID CHARLES, environmental management consultant; b. Erie, Pa., Nov. 1, 1958; s. Roger Granville and Martha Elizabeth (Bert) S.; m. Susan Rodgers, Dec. 3, 1988; children: Catherine Faye, Summer Anne. BA in Urban Studies, Coll. Wooster, Ohio, 1980. Planner Met. Svc. Dist., Portland, Oreg., 1980-82; cons. Gershman, Brickner, and Bratton, Washington, 1983; project mgr. Govt. Fin. Rsch. Ctr., Washington, 1983-86; dir. bus. devel. CH2M Hill, Bellevue, Wash., 1986—. Co-author: The McGraw Hill Recycling Handbook, 1993; contbr. articles to profl. jours. Mem. Wash. Citizens for Recycling (bd. dirs. 1991-93), Solid Waste Assn. of N.Am. (bd. dirs. 1991—), Overlake G. Country Club, Bellevue Athletic Club. Office: CH2M Hill 777 108th Ave NE Bellevue WA 98004-5118

STUTZ, FREDERICK PAUL, writer, educator; b. Chattanooga, Mar. 14, 1944; s. Albert R. Stutz and Margaret (Groerich) Sneed; m. Pam, July 21, 1974; children: Christa, Tiffany, Derek, Janene, Michelle, Weston. BA, Valparaiso (Ind) U., 1966; MA, Northwestern U., 1968; PhD, Micha. State U., 1970. instr. Northwestern U., Chgo., 1966-68, Mich. State U., Lansing, 1968-70; prof. San Diego State U., 1970—; lectr. Georgetown U., Washington, 1992; cons., researcher CALTRANS (Calif. Dept. Transp.), San DIego, 1988-94. Lutheran. Home: 1824 Shadow Knolls Pl El Cajon CA 92020 Office: San Diego State U San Diego CA 92182

STYLES, BEVERLY, entertainer; b. Richmond, Va., June 6, 1923; d. John Harry Kenealy and Juanita Russell (Robins) Carpenter; m. Wilbur Cox, Mar. 14, 1942 (div.); m. Robert Marascia, Oct. 5, 1951 (div. Apr. 1964). Studies with Ike Carpenter, Hollywood, Calif., 1965—; student, Am. Nat. Theatre Acad., 1968-69; studies with Paula Raymond, Hollywood, 1969-70; diploma, Masterplan Inst., Anaheim, Calif., 1970. Freelance performer, musician, 1947-81; owner Beverly Styles Music, Joshua Tree, Calif., 1971—; v.p. spl. programs Lawrence Program of Calif., Yucca Valley, Calif.; talent coord., co-founder Quiet Place Studio, Yucca Valley, 1994. Composer: Joshua Tree, 1975, I'm Thankful, 1978, Wow, Wow, Wow, 1986, Colour Chords (and Moods), Piano Arrangement, 1990, (with lyricist Betty Curtis) The Whispering, 1994; records include The Perpetual Styles Of Beverly, 1978; albums include The Primitive Styles Of Beverly, 1977; author: A Special Plan To Think Upon, The Truth As Seen By A Composer, 1978, A Special Prayer To Think Upon, 1983. Mem. ASCAP (Gold Pin award), Am. Fedn. Musicians (life, Local 47, Hollywood, Calif.), Internat. Platform Assn. Republican. Office: PO Box 615 Joshua Tree CA 92252-0615

SU, JUDY YA HWA LIN, pharmacologist; b. Hsinchu, Taiwan, Nov. 20, 1938; came to U.S., 1962; d. Ferng Nian and Chiu-Chin (Cheng) Lin; m. Michael W. Su; 1 child, Marvin. BS, Nat. Taiwan U., 1961; MS, U. Kans., 1964; PhD, U. Wash., 1968. Asst. prof. dept. biology U. Ala., Huntsville, 1972-73; rsch. assoc. dept. anesthesiology U. Wash., Seattle, 1976-77, acting asst. prof. dept. anesthesia, 1977-78, rsch. asst. prof., 1978-81, rsch. assoc. prof., 1981-89, rsch. prof., 1989—; mem. surg. anesthesiology & trauma study sect. NIH, 1987-91; vis. scientist Max-Planck Inst. Med. Rsch., Heidelberg, West Germany, 1982-83; vis. prof. dept. anesthesiology Mayo Clinic, Rochester, Minn., Med. Coll. Wis., 1988; editorial bd. cons. Jour. Molecular & Cellular Cardiology, London, 1987—, European Jour. Physiology, Berlin, Germany, Muscle & Nerve, Kyoto, Japan, 1989—, Anesthesiology, Phila., 1987—, Molecular Pharmacology, 1988—, Jour. Biol. Chemistry, 1989—, Am. Jour. Physiology, 1990—; mem. rsch. study com. Am. Heart Assn., 1992-95. Contbr. articles to profl. jours. Grantee Wash. Heart Assn., 1976-77, 1985-87, Pharm. Mfrs. Assn. Found., Inc., 1977, Lilly Rsch. Labs, 1986-88, Anaquest, 1987—, NIH, 1978—; recipient Rsch. Career Devel. award NIH, 1982-87; rsch. fellowship San Diego Heart Assn., 1970-72, Max-Planck Inst., 1982-83. Mem. AAAS, Biophys. Soc., Am. Soc. for Pharmacology and Exptl. Therapeutics, Am. Physiol. Soc., Am. Soc. Anesthesiologists. Home: 13110 NE 33rd St Bellevue WA 98005-1318 Office: U Wash Dept Anesthesiology Box 356540 Seattle WA 98195-6540

SUAREZ-VILLA, LUIS, regional science and economic geography, international development educator; b. Havana, Cuba, July 7, 1947. M in Regional Planning, Cornell U., 1976, PhD, 1981. Asst. prof. social ecology U. Calif., Irvine, 1982-88, assoc. prof., 1988-94, prof., 1994—; mem. selection panels for grad. fellowships NSF; reviewer numerous jour. and grant proposals. Assoc. editor Annals Regional Sci., 1988—; contbr. articles to profl. jours. and books on regional sci., technol. change, internat. devel. and econ.

geography, rsch. focus on invention and tech. innovation, regional econ. devel., internat. rsch. on Brazil, Mex., Korea, Spain, Austria, Sweden, U.S. Orgn. Am. States Rsch. fellow 1977-78, 78-79, Mellon postdoctoral fellow 1982, Fulbright fellow, 1985, 1990-91; numerous grants U. Calif. Mem. AAAS, Regional Sci. Assn. Internat., Western Regional Sci. Assn. (bd. dirs.), Am. Econ. Assn., Assn. Am. Geographers, Soc. for Risk Analysis, Latin Am. Studies Assn. Office: U Calif Sch Social Ecology Irvine CA 92717

SUBACH, JAMES ALAN, infosystems company executive, consultant; b. Lawrence, Mass., Mar. 24, 1948; s. Anthony John and Bernice Ruth (Pekarski) S. m. Marilyn Butler, Feb. 16, 1980. BS with distinction, U. Maine, 1970; MS, U. Ariz., 1975, PhD, 1979. Vis. scientist NASA Johnson Space Ctr., Houston, 1977-79; rsch. assoc. Baylor Coll. Medicine, Houston, 1977-79; pres. Subach Ventures, Inc., San Antonio, 1980-84, JAS & Assocs., Inc., Phoenix, 1984—, C.I.O. Inc., 1987-90; v.p. PTIMS, Inc., Phoenix, 1992—; faculty assoc. Ariz. State U., Tempe, 1992. Assoc. editor Jour. Applied Photog. Engring., 1973-78; author software Gen. Acctg. System, 1987; bus. computing columnist, 1987. Pres. Forest Trails Homeowners Assn., Phoenix, 1987-88. Mem. SPIE, Phoenix C. of C. (Pres.'s Roundtable), Toastmasters (treas. Phoenix chpt. 1984), Ariz. Progress Users Group, Tau Beta Pi, Sigma Pi Sigma. Republican. Office: JAS & Assoc Inc 3625 N 16th St Ste 100 Phoenix AZ 85016-6443

SUBER, ROBIN HALL, former medical/surgical nurse; b. Bethlehem, Pa., Mar. 14, 1952; d. Arthur Albert and Sarah Virginia (Smith) Hall; m. David A. Suber, July 28, 1979; 1 child, Benjamin A. BSN, Ohio State U., 1974. RN, Ariz., Ohio. Formerly staff nurse Desert Samaritan Hosp., Mesa, Ariz. Lt. USN, 1974-80. Mem. ANA, Sigma Theta Tau.

SUBRAMANI, SURESH, biology educator; b. Jabalpur, India, Feb. 21, 1952; came to U.S., 1974; s. Janakiraman and Gomathy S.; m. Feroza Ardeshir, Aug. 15, 1981; children: Anand Subramani, Praveen Subramani. BS in Chemistry, Ferguson Coll., Pune, Maharashtra, 1972; MS in Chemistry, Indian Inst. Tech., Kanpur, India, 1974; PhD in Biochemistry, U. Calif., Berkeley, 1978. Post-doctoral fellow Stanford U., Palo Alto, Calif., 1979-82; asst. prof. U. Calif., San Diego, 1982-87, assoc. prof., 1987-91, prof., 1991—; sci. adv. bd. Viagene, San Diego, 1986-91; cons. Astra, Bangalore, India, 1989—. Contbr. 87 scientific articles in biochemistry, molecular biology and cell biology to profl. jours. Named Nat. Sci. Talent scholar, India, 1969-74; recipient Nat. scholarship, India, 1972, Rsch. Career Devel. award, Nat. Cancer Inst., 1985-90; Searle scholar, 1982-85; Jane Coffin Childs Fund fellow, 1979-81; John Simon Guggenheim fellow, 1993-94; Dr. Narayana Meml. lectr., 1990. Mem. AAAS, Am. Soc. Microbiology, N.Y. Acad. Sci. Office: Dept Biology UCSD 9500 Gilman Dr La Jolla CA 92093-5003

SUBRAMANIAN, SUNDARAM, electronics engineer; b. Emaneswaram, Madras, India, July 9, 1934; came to U.S., 1968; s. Sundaram and Velammal (Subbiah) S.; m. Hemavathy Vadivelu, Feb. 18, 1968; children: Anand Kumar, Malathy. BE, Madras (India) U., 1959; PhD, Glasgow (Scotland) U., 1967; MBA, Roosevelt U., Chgo., 1977. Research engr. Zenith, Inc., Chgo., 1968-75; project engr. Motorola, Inc., Chgo., 1975-77; prof. Chapman Coll., Orange, Calif., 1977-78; cons. MCS, Orange, 1978-80; project engr. Endevco, San Juan Capistrano, Calif., 1980-84; project mgr. Unisys Corp., Mission Viejo, Calif., 1984—; bd. dirs. P.S.B. Inc., Torrance, Calif., 1984-93. Patentee in field. Bd. dirs. Tamil Nadu Found. Inc., Balt. and Washington, 1976-79; pres. S. India Cultural Assn., Villa Park, Calif., 1977-78. Mem. IEEE, Inst. Environ. Sci. (sr.). Office: Unisys Corp 25725 Jeronimo Rd Mission Viejo CA 92691-2711

SUBRAMANYA, SHIVA, aerospace systems engineer; b. Hole-Narasipur, India, Apr. 8, 1933; s. S.T. Srikantaiah and S. Gundamma; m. Lee. S. Silva, Mar. 3, 1967; children: Paul Kailas, Kevin Shankar. BSc, Mysore U., Bangalore, India, 1956; MSc, Karnatak U., Dharwar, India, 1962; postgrad., Clark U., 1963; MBA, Calif. State U., Dominguez Hills, 1973; D in Bus. Adminstrn., PhD in Bus. Adminstrn., Nova Southeastern U., 1986. Sr. scientific officer AEC, Bombay, India, 1961-63; chief engr. TEI, Newport, R.I., 1964-67; prin. engr. Gen. Dynamics Corp., San Diego, 1967-73; asst. project mgr. def. and systems group TRW, Colorado Springs, Colo., 1973-87; asst. project mgr. space and def. group TRW, Redondo Beach, Calif., 1987—. Contbr. over 150 articles to profl. jours. V.p. VHP of Am., Berlin, Conn., 1984-88; pres. IPF of Am., Redondo Beach, 1981-88; appointed by Pres. of India to Atomic Energy Commn., India. Winner of dozens of awards and commendations from U.S. Dept. of Defense and the Aerospace Industry. Mem. Armed Forces Comm. and Electronics Assn. (v.p.-elect Rocky Mountain chpt. 1986—, Meritorious Svc. award 1985, Merit medal 1990), Am. Acad. Mgmt. Hindu. Home: 2115 Shelburne Way Torrance CA 90503-7386 Office: TRW Def and Space Group 1 Space Park Blvd Redondo Beach CA 90278-1001

SUCHENEK, MAREK ANDRZEJ, computer science educator; b. Warsaw, Poland, May 2, 1949; came to U.S., 1986; s. Tadeusz Aleksander and Barbara Krystyna (Zych) S.; m. Ewa Aleksandra Czerny, July 30, 1974 (div. 1991). MSc in Math. Engring., Warsaw Tech. U., 1973, PhD in Tech. Scis. with distinction, 1979. Instr. Warsaw (Poland) Tech. U., 1973-79, asst. prof., 1979-88; vis. asst. prof. Wichita (Kans.) State U., 1986-88; assoc. Nat. Inst. for Aviation Rsch., Wichita, 1987-90; vis. asst. prof. Wichita (Kans.) State U., 1986-88, assoc. prof., 1988-89, assoc. prof., chair, 1989-90; prof. Calif. State U.-Dominguez Hills, Carson, 1990—; mem. organizing com. Internat. Symposium on Methodologies for Intelligent Sys., 1989-90; program com. Ann. Ulam Math. Conf., 1990-91, Internat. Conf. on Computing and Info., 1992—; referee NSF, 1990—, Annals of Math. and Artificial Intelligence, 1992—, Jour. Logic Programming, 1992—; presenter in field. Author: (with Jan Bielecki) ANS FORTRAN, 1980, (with Jan Bielecki) FORTRAN for Advanced Programmers, 1981, 2d edit., 83, 3d edit., 88 (Minister of Sci. Higher Edn. and Techs. prize 1982); reviewer Zentralblatt fur Mathematik, 1980-89, Math. Reviews, 1989-91; mem. editorial bd.: Ulam Quarterly, 1990—; contbr. articles to profl. jours. Recipient rsch. grants Polish Govt., 1974-76, 85-86, FAA, 1988-90. Mem. AAUP, The Assn. for Logic Programming, Computer Soc. IEEE, Assn. for Computing Machinery, Assn. Symbolic Logic, Sigma Xi (chpt. pres.). Home: 830 N Juanita Ave Redondo Beach CA 90277-2229 Office: Calif State Univ Dominguez Hills 1000 E Victoria St Carson CA 90747-0001

SUCKIEL, ELLEN KAPPY, philosophy educator; b. Bklyn., June 15, 1943; d. Jack and Lilyan (Banchefsky) Kappy; m. Joseph Suckiel, June 22, 1973. A.B., Douglass Coll., 1965; M.A. in Philosophy, U. Wis., 1969, Ph.D. in Philosophy, 1972. Lectr. philosophy U. Wis., Madison, 1969-71; asst. prof. philosophy Fla. State U., Tallahassee, 1972-73; asst. prof. philosophy U. Calif., Santa Cruz, 1973-80, assoc. prof., 1980—, provost Kresge Coll., 1983-89. Author: The Pragmatic Philosophy of William James, 1982, also articles. Mem. Am. Philos. Assn., Soc. for Advancement Am. Philosophy. Office: U Calif Cowell Coll Santa Cruz CA 95064

SUDA, TATSUYA, computer science educator; b. Fukushima, Japan, Aug. 20, 1953; came to U.S., 1982; s. Tatsuya and Toshiko (Koshiishi) S.; m. Miyuki Kobayshi, Aug. 20, 1982; children: Kentaro, Shotaro. BS, Kyoto U., 1977, MS, 1979, PhD, 1982. Rsch. assoc. Columbia U., N.Y.C., 1982-84; asst. prof. computer science U. Calif., Irvine, 1984-89, assoc. prof., 1990-94, prof., 1994—. Mem. IEEE, Assn. Computing Machinery. Office: U Calif Dept Computer Sci Irvine CA 92717

SUDARSKY, JERRY M., industrialist; b. Russia, June 12, 1918; s. Selig and Sara (Ars) S.; m. Mildred Axelrod, Aug. 31, 1947; children: Deborah, Donna. Student, U. Iowa, 1936-39; B.S., Poly. U. Bklyn., 1942; D.Sc. (hon.), Poly. U. N.Y., 1976. Founder, chief exec. officer Bioferm Corp., Wasco, Calif., 1946-66; cons. to Govt. of Israel, 1966-67; founder, chmn. Israel Chems., Ltd., Tel Aviv, Israel, 1967-72; chmn. I.C. Internat. Cons., Tel Aviv, 1971-73; vice chmn., bd. dirs. Daylin, Inc., Los Angeles, 1972-76; pres., chmn. J.M.S. Assocs., Los Angeles, 1976-82; vice chmn. bd. Jacobs Engring. Group Inc., Pasadena, Calif., 1982-94; chmn., CEO Health Sci. Properties, Inc., Pasadena, 1994—. Patentee in field of indsl. microbiology. Bd. govs. Hebrew U., Jerusalem; trustee Polytechnic U. N.Y., 1976—; bd. dirs. Arthritis Found., L.A., 1989-94, Mgmt. Edn. Assn., UCLA, 1990—. Served with USNR, 1943-46. Mem. AAAS, Am. Chem. Soc., Sigma Xi. Clubs: Brentwood Country (Los Angeles). Office: Health Sci Properties Inc 251 S Lake Ave Pasadena CA 91101-3003

SUDBECK, RICHARD JAMES, medical imaging engineer; b. Sioux Falls, S.D., Apr. 20, 1957; s. Gorman Francis and Lois Mae (Lawless) S.; m. Margaret Loretta Lochray, Oct. 11, 1986. AAS in Tech. Communication, U. S.D., 1980, AAS in Indsl. Electronics, 1980, BSEET, 1980. With Taylor Oil Co., Worthing, S.D., 1973-76; civil technician S.D. Dept. Transp., Beresford, S.D., 1976; hwy. maint. worker S.D. Dept. Transp., Sioux Falls, 1977; temp. supt. Springfield (S.D.) Water Treatment, 1978, plant operator, 1978-79; tech. writer Sundstrand Aviation Ops., Rockford, Ill., 1980-82; field svc. engr. Gen. Elec. Med. Sys., Des Moines, 1982-86; sr. field svc. engr. InnoServ Techs., Inc., Fresno, Calif., 1986—. Democrat. Roman Catholic. Home: 772 E Vartikian Ave Fresno CA 93710-5435 Office: InnoServ Techs Inc 1611B Pomona Rd Corona CA 91720-6961

SUDDOCK, FRANCES SUTER THORSON, grief educator, writer; b. Estelline, S.D., Oct. 23, 1914; d. William Henry and Anna Mary (Oakland) Suter; m. Carl Edwin Thorson, July 6, 1941 (dec. Apr. 1976); children: Sarah Thorson Little, Mary Frances Thorson; m. Edwin Matthew Suddock, Aug. 7, 1982 (dec. Sept. 1986). BA, Iowa State Tchrs. Coll., 1936; postgrad., Syracuse U., 1940-41, U. Iowa, 1946; MA, Antioch U., San Francisco, 1981. Cert. tchr. Tchr. various high schs., Correctionville and Eagle Grove, Iowa, 1936-38, 38-40, 41-43, 45-47; chief clk. War Price and Rationing Bd., Eagle Grove, 1943-45; instr. (part time) Eagle Grove Jr. Coll., 1953-61; adminstr. Eagle Grove Pub. Library, 1961-77; facilitator Will Schutz Assocs., Muir Beach, Calif., 1987-88. Author: Whither the Widow, 1981. Vol. Nat. Trainer Widowed Persons Svc. Am. Assn. Retired Persons, 1989—, ret. sr. vol. program, Anchorage, 1988—; pres., bd. dirs. Anchorage Widowed Persons Svc., 1992-94; bd. dirs. North Iowa Mental Health Ctr., Mason City, 1959-76, Eagle Grove Cmty. Chest, 1960, Help Line, Inc., Ft. Dodge, Iowa, 1976-77; chmn. Cmty. Mental Health Fund, Eagle Grove, 1966-73; charter pres. Eagle Grove Concerned, Inc., 1973-77; active various civic orgns. Mem. AAUW (charter pres. Eagle Grove br. 1973-75), Am. Soc. on Aging, Alaska Assn. Gerontology (treas. 1992—), Anchorage Woman's Club, P.E.O., Kappa Delta Pi. Home: 333 M St Apt 404 Anchorage AK 99501-1902

SUE, ALAN KWAI KEONG, dentist; b. Honolulu, Apr. 26, 1946; s. Henry Tin Yee and Chiyoko (Ohata) S.; m. Ginger Kazue Fukushima, Mar. 19, 1972; 1 child, Dawn Marie. BS in Chemistry with honors, U. Hawaii, 1968; BS, U. Calif., San Francisco, 1972, DDS, 1972. Film editor, photographer Sta. KHVH-TV ABC, Honolulu, 1964-71; staff dentist Strong-Carter Dental Clinic, Honolulu, 1972-73; dentist Waianae Dental Clinic, Honolulu, 1972-73; pvt. practice Pearl City, Hawaii, 1973—; chief exec. officer Dental Image Specialists, Pearl City, 1975—; dental dir. Hawaii Dental Health Plan, Honolulu, 1987—; dental cons. Calif. Dental Health Plan, Tustin, 1987—, Pacific Group Med. Assn., The Queen's Health Care Plan, Honolulu, 1993—; dental cons. Pacific Group Med. Assn., 1994—; bd. dirs. Kula Bay Tropical Clothing Co.; mem. exec. bd. St. Francis Hosp., Honolulu, 1976-78, chief dept. dentistry, 1976-78; mem. expert med. panel Am. Internat. Claim Svc., 1995—. Mem. adv. bd. Health Svcs. for Sr. Citizens, 1976—; mem. West Honolulu Sub-Area Health Planning Coun., 1981-84; mem. dental task force Hawaii Statewide Health Coordinating Coun., 1980, mem. plan devel. com., 1981-84; vol. oral cancer screening program Am. Cancer Soc.; v.p. Pearl City Shopping Ctr. Merchants Assn., 1975-84, 92-93, pres., 1994—. Regents' scholar U. Calif., San Francisco, 1968-72. Fellow Pierre Fauchard Acad., Acad. Gen. Dentistry; mem. ADA, Acad. Implants and Transplants, Am. Acad. Implant Dentistry, Hawaii Dental Assn. (trustee 1978-80), Honolulu County Dental Soc. (pres. 1982), Am. Acad. and Bd. Head, Facial, Neck Pain and TMJ Orthopedics, Intertel, Internat. Platform Assn., Mensa, Porsche Club, Pantera Owners Club, Mercedes Benz Club. Democrat. Office: Dental Image Specialists 850 Kam Hwy Ste 116 Pearl City HI 96782-2603

SUE, LAWRENCE GENE, statistician; b. Portland, Oreg., Sept. 22, 1939; s. Henry Lock Sue and Dorothy Helen (Wong) Chung. BS in Math., Brigham Young U., 1967, MS in Statistics, 1973. Assoc. engr. Boeing Co., Seattle, 1967-69; math. statistician Ultrasystems Inc., Hill AFB, Utah, 1974-77; mem. tech. staff TRW Systems, Hill AFB, 1977-81; sr. staff engr. Motorola Inc., Phoenix, 1981-84, mgr. engring., 1984-85, statis. engr., 1985—; statis. cons. Motorola Semiconductor Research and Devel. Lab., Phoenix, 1985—; instr. Rio Salado Community Coll., Phoenix, 1984—, Brigham Young U. Extension, Salt Lake City, 1975-81, Highline Coll., Midway, Wash., 1967-69. Voting del. Salt Lake County Rep. Conv., 1973. Mem. Am. Statis. Assn. (2d v.p. Utah chpt., pres. Ariz. chpt. 1988-89), Am. Soc. Quality Control (vice chair Phoenix sect. 1989-90, chair Phoenix sect. 1990-91, editor stats. divsn. newsletter 1994—), Sigma Xi. Home: 2308 W Sagebrush Dr Chandler AZ 85224-2155

SUE, MICHAEL ALVIN, physician; b. L.A., Apr. 15, 1956. MD, U. Chgo., 1980. Diplomate Am. Bd. Internal Medicine, Am. Bd. Allergy and Immunology. Allergist Kaiser Permanente, Panorama City, Calif., 1986—. Fellow Am. Coll. Allergy, Asthma, and Immunology; mem. Am. Acad. Allergy and Immunology. Office: Kaiser Permanente 13652 Cantara St Panorama City CA 91402

SUERMONDT, HENRI JACQUES, research scientist; b. Leiden, The Netherlands, Sept. 2, 1965; s. Rudolf Gerard and Wilhelmina Gustavine (Fabius) S. BS, Stanford U., 1987, MS, 1989, PhD, 1992. Rsch. fellow Stanford (Calif.) U., 1987-92; rsch. scientist Hewlett-Packard Labs., Palo Alto, Calif., 1992—. Contbr. articles to profl. jours. Vol. Children's Hosp. Stanford, Palo Alto, Calif., 1986—, So. Calif. Children's Cancer Soc., L.A., 1986—. Mem. Am. Med. Informatics Assn. (membership com., publs. com., Martin Epstein award 1992), Am. Assn. Artificial Intelligence, Phi Beta Kappa. Home: 2544 Mardell Way Mountain View CA 94043-2716 Office: Hewlett-Packard Labs 3500 Deer Creek Rd Palo Alto CA 94304

SUGGS, PATRICIA ANN, artist; b. Reedley, Calif., Mar. 17, 1936; d. Charles and Dorothy Rema (Prouty) Kofoed; m. Robert Reed Suggs, July 28, 1961; 1 child, Richard William. Student, Leighton Art Acad., San Francisco, 1974-81. judge fine arts Arts Clubs, The Peninsula, No. Calif. and San Joaquin Valley, Calif. county fairs, 1984-93, Santa Clara County, San Jose, 1991, Sonoma County Fair, Santa Rosa, 1990, Alameda County Fair, Pleasanton, 1990. One-woman shows include Group 21, Los Gatos, Calif., 1978, Gt. Western Savs. & Loan, Fremont, Calif., 1982, Rosicrucian Egyptian Museums, San Jose, Calif., 1982, Gadabout Gallery, Los Gatos, Calif., 1986; exhibited in group shows at Pastel Soc. Am., N.Y., 1980, Ashland (Ky.) Gallery, 1990, Pastel Soc. West Coast, Sacramento, 1989-94, Runnings Gallery, Seattle, 1990, Soc. Western Artists Anns., San Francisco, 1976-93, Fremont Art Assn., 1993; also pvt. collections. Recipient Best of show award Fremont (Calif.) Art Assn., 1993. Mem. Pastel Soc. Am. (Best Floral award 1980, Best Pastel Plaque 1993), Pastel Soc. West Coast (adv. bd. 1984-95, award of merit 1991), Soc. Western Artists (bd. trustees 1986-95, 1st Pl. pastels 1993), Allied Artists West (dir. exhbn. 1991-92), Internat. Assoc. of Pastel Soc., (treas. 1994-95), Nat. League Am. Pen Women (Grumbacher award medallion 1993). Home: 4127 Beebe Cir San Jose CA 95135-1010

SUGIKI, SHIGEMI, ophthalmologist, educator; b. Wailuku, Hawaii, May 12, 1936; s. Sentaro and Kameno (Matoba) S.; AB, Washington U., St. Louis, 1957, M.D., 1961; m. Bernice T. Murakami, Dec. 28, 1958; children: Kevin S., Boyd R. Intern St. Luke's Hosp., St. Louis, 1961-62, resident ophthalmology, Washington U., St. Louis, 1962-65; chmn. dept. ophthalmology Straub Clinic, Honolulu, 1965-70, Queen's Med. Ctr., Honolulu, 1970-73, 80-83, 88-90, 93—; assoc. clin. prof. ophthalmology Sch. Medicine, U. Hawaii, 1973—. Served to maj. M.C., AUS, 1968-70. Decorated Hawaiian NG Commendation medal, 1968. Fellow ACS; mem. Am., Hawaii med. assns., Honolulu County Med. Soc., Am. Acad. Ophthalmology, Contact Lens Assn. Opthalmologists, Pacific Coast Oto-Ophthal. Soc., Pan-Pacific Surg. Assn., Am. Soc. Cataract and Refractive Surgery, Am. Glaucoma Soc., Internat. Assn. Ocular Surgeons, Am. Soc. Contemporary Ophthalmology, Washington U. Eye Alumni Assn., Hawaii Ophthal. Soc., Rsch. To Prevent Blindness. Home: 2398 Aina Lani Pl Honolulu HI 96822-2024 Office: 1380 Lusitana St Ste 714 Honolulu HI 96813-2449

SUGRUE, DONAL, food products executive. Various positions Vacu-Dry Co., Sebastopol, Calif., 1963-69, v.p., 1969-82, exec. v.p., 1982-89, pres., CEO, 1989—. Office: Vacu-Dry Co 7765 Healdsburg Ave Sebastopol CA 95472-3309*

SUHRE, E. DOW, internist. BA, U. Colo., 1964; MD, Northwestern U., 1968. Diplomate Am. Bd. Internal Medicine; lic. MD, N.Mex. Internship Jackson Meml. Hosp., Miami, Fla., 1968-69; mil. svc. USNR Med. Corp. 3rd Battalion 1st Marine Divsn., Vietnam, 1969-70, Key West (Fla.) Naval Hosp., 1970-71; residency Wesley Meml. Hosp., Northwestern U., Chgo., 1971-73; chief med. resident Wesley Meml. Hosp., Santa Fe, 1973-74; attending physician St. Vincent Hosp., Santa Fe, 1974—, med. dir. ICU, 1979—, lectr. edn. dept.; clin. assoc. U. N.Mex. Internal Medicine Residency Program, St. Vincent Hosp., Santa Fe, 1979-89, U. N.Mex. Dept. Family, Cmty. and Emergency Medicine, 1984—. Contbr. articles to profl. publs. Inst. for Am. Heart Assn. in BLS and LAS, 1974-92, affiliated faculty, 1982-84; vol. fireman Santa Fe Fire Dept., 1975-88; founder, med. dir. Santa Fe Fire Dept. Rescue Squad, 1977-82. Fellow Coll. Chest Physicians; mem. Am. Coll. Physicians, Soc. Critical Care Medicine, Am. Soc. Internal Medicine. Office: 465 Saint Michaels Dr Ste 105 Santa Fe NM 87505-7621

SUKO, LONNY RAY, judge; b. Spokane, Wash., Oct. 12, 1943; s. Ray R. and Leila B. (Snyder) S.; m. Marcia A. Michaelsen, Aug. 26, 1967; children: Jolynn R., David M. BA, Wash. State U., 1965; JD, U. Idaho, 1968. Bar: Wash. 1968, U.S. Dist. Ct. (ea. dist.) Wash. 1969, U.S. Dist. Ct. (we. dist.) Wash. 1978, U.S. Ct. Appeals (9th cir.) 1978. Law clk. U.S. Dist. Ct. Ea. Dist. Wash., 1968-69; assoc. Lyon, Beaulaurier & Aaron, Yakima, Wash., 1969-72; ptnr. Lyon, Beaulaurier, Weigand, Suko & Gustafson, Yakima, 1972-91, Lyon, Weigand, Suko & Gustafson, P.S., 1991-95; U.S. magistrate judge, Yakima, 1971-91, 95—. Mem. Wash. State Trial Lawyers Assn., Wash. Coun. Sch. Attys., Phi Beta Kappa, Phi Kappa Phi, Phi Eta Sigma. Office: PO Box 2706 Yakima WA 98907-2706

SUKOV, RICHARD JOEL, radiologist; b. Mpls., Nov. 13, 1944; s. Marvin and Annette Sukov; Susan Judith Grossman, Aug. 11, 1968; children: Stacy Faye, Jessica Erin. BA, BS, U. Minn., 1967, MD, 1970; student, U. Calif.-Berkeley, 1962-64. Diplomate Am. Bd. Radiology; lic. physician, Minn., D.C., Calif. Intern pediatrics U. Minn., Mpls., 1970-71; resident radiology UCLA Ctr. for Health Sci., 1973-76; fellow in ultrasound and computed tomography UCLA, 1976-77; staff radiologist Centinela Hosp. Med. Ctr., Inglewood, Calif., 1977-85; staff radiologist Daniel Freeman Meml. Hosp., Inglewood, Calif., 1977—, dir. radiology, 1988-90; asst. clin. prof. radiology UCLA Ctr. for Health Scis., 1977-83; adv. bd. Aerobics and Fitness Assn. Am., 1983—. Contbr. articles to profl. jours. Vol. Venice Family Clinic, 1985—. Lt. comdr. USPHS, 1970-72. U. Minn. fellow, 1964-65, 66, 70. Mem. AMA, Royal Soc. Medicine, Soc. Radiologists in Ultrasound (charter), Minn. Med. Alumni Assn., Los Angeles County Med. Assn., Calif. Med. Assn., Radiol. Soc. N.Am., L.A. Radiol. Soc. (continuing edn. com. 1990—, chmn.), L.A. Ultrasound Soc., Am. Coll. Radiology. Office: Inglewood Radiology 323 N Prairie Ave Ste 160 Inglewood CA 90301-4502

SULLIVAN, CLAIRE FERGUSON, marketing educator; b. Pittsburg, Tex., Sept. 28, 1937; d. Almon Lafayette and Mabel Clara (Williams) Potter; m. Richard Wayne Ferguson, Jan. 31, 1959 (div. Jan. 1980); 1 child, Mark Jeffrey Ferguson; m. David Edward Sullivan, Nov. 2, 1984. BBA, U. Tex., 1958, MBA, 1961; PhD, U. North Tex., 1973; grad., Harvard Inst. Ednl. Mgmt., 1991. Instr. So. Meth. U., Dallas, 1965-70; asst. prof. U. Utah, Salt Lake City, 1972-74; assoc. prof. U. Ark., Little Rock, 1974-77, U. Tex., Arlington, 1977-80, Ill. State U., Normal, 1980-84; prof., chmn. mktg. Bentley Coll., Waltham, Mass., 1984-89; dean sch. bus. Met. State Coll. Denver, 1989-92, prof. mktg., 1992—; cons. Denver Partnership, 1989-90, Gen. Tel. Co., Irving, Tex., 1983, McKnight Pub. Co., Bloomington, Ill., 1983, dental practitioner, Bloomington, 1982-83, Olympic Fed., Berwyn, Ill., 1982, Denver Partnership Econ. Devel. Adv. Coun., 1989-91; mem. African-Am. Leadership Inst. Gov. Bd. Contbr. mktg. articles to profl. jours. Direct Mktg. Inst. fellow, 1981; Ill. State U. rsch. grantee, 1981-83. Mem. Am. Mktg. Assn. (faculty fellow 1984-85), So. Mktg. Assn., Southwestern Mktg. Assn., Denver World Trade Ctr., Denver Partnership (econ. devel. adv. bd.), Rotary, Beta Gamma Sigma. Republican. Methodist. Home: 4715 11th St Greeley CO 80634-2318 Office: Met State Coll Dept Mktg MSCD Box 79 PO Box 173362 Denver CO 80217-3362

SULLIVAN, EDWARD JOSEPH, electrotype company executive; b. Concord, N.H., May 17, 1915; s. Edward J. and Ida (Packard) S.; student St. Anslem's Coll., 1935-36; m. Dorothea M. Ash, Sept. 30, 1944; children: James Ash, Maureen Packard. Treas., Merrimack Electrotyping Corp., 1950-55, pres., 1955—; treas. Sheraton Properties Corp., 1961—; exec. v.p. Blanchard Press Corp., 1968-69; pres. Tridel Housing Devels., 1970—, Ho-Tei Corp., St. Thomas, V.I.; dir. Concord Fed. Savs. Bank; pres. Allied Photo Engraving Corp., 1964. Mem. Concord Hosp. Corp., U.S. Commn. on Civil Rights; chmn. bldg. fund Carmelite Monastery, Concord, 1950, St. Peters Ch. for Bishop Brady High Sch. Bldg. Fund, 1961; citizens com. Concord Housing Authority; commr. Concord Urban Renewal Assn.; v.p., bd. dirs. Diocesan Bur. Housing, Inc., Manchester, N.H., 1975—; bd. dirs. Carpenter Ctr., Inc., Manchester, N.H., Concord chpt. ARC, Concord Hosp.; mem div. labor and industry com. NAACP. Served with USNR, 1942-46. Mem. Internat. Assn. Electrotypers and Stereotypers Union, Internat. Assn. Electrotypers and Stereotypers, Inc., Am. Legion, Aircraft Owners and Pilots Assn., Audubon Soc. N.H., Printing Inst. Am., One Hundred Club N.H. Elk. Republican. Roman Catholic. Club: Serra (v.p.). Kiwanian, K.C. Home and Office: 4025 Terra Granada Dr # 1A Walnut Creek CA 94595-4001

SULLIVAN, EDWARD JOSEPH, lawyer, educator; b. Bklyn., Apr. 24, 1945; s. Edward Joseph and Bridget (Duffy) S.; m. Patte Hancock, Aug. 7, 1982; children: Amy Brase, Molly Elsasser, Mary Christine. BA in Polit. Sci., St. John's U., 1966; JD, Willamette U., 1969; MA, cert. Urban Studies, Portland State U., 1974; LLM, Univ. Coll., London, 1978; diploma in law, Univ. Coll., Oxford, 1984. Bar: Oreg. 1969, D.C. 1978, U.S. Dist. Ct. Oreg. 1970, U.S. Ct. Appeals (9th cir.) 1970, U.S. Supreme Ct. 1972. Counsel Washington County, Hillsboro, Oreg., 1969-75; legal counsel Gov. of Oreg., Salem, 1975-77; ptnr. O'Donnell, Sullivan & Ramis, Portland, Oreg., 1978-84, Sullivan, Josselson, Roberts, Johnson & Kloos, Portland, Salem and Eugene, Oreg., 1984-86, Mitchell, Lang & Smith, Portland, 1986-90, Preston Gates & Ellis, Portland, 1990—; bd. dirs., pres. Oreg. Law Inst. Contbr. numerous articles to profl. jours. Chmn. Capitol Planning Commn., Salem, 1975-77, 78-81. Mem. ABA (local govt. sect., com. on planning and zoning, adminstrv. law sect.) Oreg. State Bar Assn., D.C. Bar Assn., Am. Judicature Soc., Am. Polit. Sci. Assn. Democrat. Roman Catholic. Office: Preston Gates & Ellis 111 SW 5th Ave Ste 3200 Portland OR 97204-3635

SULLIVAN, G. CRAIG, chemical executive; b. 1940. BS, Boston Coll., 1964. With Proctor & Gamble Co., 1964-69, Am. Express Co., 1969-70; regional sales mgr. Clorox Co., Oakland, Calif., 1971-76, v.p. mktg., 1976-78, mgr. food svc. sales devel., mgr. bus. devel., 1978-79, gen. mgr. food svc. products divsn., 1979-81, v.p. food svc. products divsn., 1981, v.p. household products, 1981-89, group v.p. household products, 1989-92, chmn. bd., CEO, 1992—. Office: The Clorox Co 1221 Broadway Oakland CA 94612-1837*

SULLIVAN, JAMES JEROME, lawyer, consultant; b. Fargo, N.D., Feb. 23, 1943; m. Roberta Jean Ranes, Nov. 8, 1980; children: Kristen, Jason, Eric, Amy. PhB, U. N.D., 1966, JD, 1970. Bar: N.D. 1970, Wash. 1982. Atty. Northwestern Nat. Life Ins. Co., Mpls., 1970-73; regional counsel Econ. Devel. Admin. of U.S. Dept. Commerce, Seattle, 1973-90; law pvt. practice Bellevue and Issaquah, Wash., 1986—. Editor, contbr. articles to numerous periodicals. Recipient numerous legal awards. Mem. ABA, Wash. State Bar Assn., Wash. State Trial Lawyers Assn. Home: 11110 NE 38th Pl Bellevue WA 98004-7653 Office: 800 Bellevue Way NE Bellevue WA 98004-4229 Office: 385 Front St N Issaquah WA 98027-2929

SULLIVAN, JAMES KIRK, forest products company executive; b. Greenwood, S.C., Aug. 25, 1935; s. Daniel Jones and Addie (Brown) S.; m. Elizabeth Miller, June 18, 1960; children: Hal N., Kim J. BS in Chemistry, Clemson U., 1957, MS, 1964, PhD, 1966; postgrad. program for sr. execs., MIT, 1975; DSc (hon.), U. Idaho, 1990. Prodn. supr. FMC Corp., South Charleston, W.Va., 1957-62; tech. supt. FMC Corp., Pocatello, Idaho, 1966-

69; mktg. mgr. FMC Corp., N.Y.C., 1969-70; v.p. govtl. and environ. affairs Boise (Idaho) Cascade Corp., 1971—; bd. dirs. Key Bank Idaho, chmn. trust and investment com., 1983-90, exec. com., 1983—; bd. dirs., chmn. audit com. Key Trust Co. of the West; chmn. adv. bd. U. Idaho Coll. Engring., 1966-70, 80-87, centennial campaign, 1987-89, rsch. found., 1980-82; mem. Accreditation Bd. Engring. and Tech., Inc., 1994. Contbr. articles to profl. jours.; patentee in field. Mem. Coll. of Forest and Recreation Resources com. Clemson U., Idaho Found. for Pvt. Enterprise and Econ. Edn., Idaho Rsch. Found., Inc., Idaho Task Force on Higher Edn.; bd. dirs. Idaho Found. for Excellence in Higher Edn., Exptl. Program to Stimulate Competitive Rsch. NSF, N.W. Nazerene Coll., 1988-90, active Len. B. Jordan Pub. Affairs Synposium; trustee Idaho Children's Emergency Fund, 1984—, Bishop Kelly High Sch., chmn. 1987-89; chmn. Bishop Kelly Found., 1972-79, 85-89; chmn. adv. bd. U. Idaho Coll. Engring., Am. Forest and Paper Assn., Govtl. Affairs Com., Environ. Com., Future options Group; pub. affairs com. NAM; active Idaho Found. Pvt. Enterprise and Econ. Edn., 1988—; chmn. centennial campaign U. Idaho, U. Idaho Found., others; mem. environ. com. Future Options Group. 1st lt. U.S. Army, 1958-59. Recipient Presdl. Citation U. Idaho, 1990. Mem. Am. Chem. Soc., Am. Inst. Chem. Engrs., Bus. Week Found. (chmn. Bus. Week 1980), Am. Paper Isnt. (environ. steering com.), Bus. Roundtable (environ. com.), Idaho Assn. Commerce and Industry (chmn. bd. dirs.), C. of C. of U.S. (pub. affairs com.). Republican. Home: 5206 Sorrento Cir Boise ID 83704-2347 Office: Boise Cascade Corp One Jefferson Sq Boise ID 83728

SULLIVAN, JAMES N., fuel company executive; b. San Francisco, 1937. Student, U. Notre Dame, 1959. Formerly v.p. Chevron Corp., until 1988, now vice chmn., dir., 1988—. Office: Chevron Corp 225 Bush St San Francisco CA 94104*

SULLIVAN, JOHN, theater administrator. Mng. dir. Am. Conservatory Theatre, San Francisco. Office: Am Conservatory Theatre 30 Grant Ave Fl 6 San Francisco CA 94108-5800

SULLIVAN, JOHN CHARLES, journalist, editor, publisher; b. Spokane, Wash., Feb. 25, 1946; s. Dalton B. and Helen L. (Schnitzler) S. AB in Journalism, Stanford U., 1968. Pub. rels. dir. Colo. Conv. Bur., Denver, 1968-70; reporter The Bend (Oreg.) Bull., 1970-71, Daily Times Call, Longmont, Colo., 1971; mng. editor Livingston (Mont.) Enterprise, 1972-73, editor, pub., 1973—; pres. The Star Printing Co., Livingston, 1975—; bd. dirs. First State Bank, Newcastle; v.p., dir. Schnitzler Corp., Livingston, 1974—. Trustee Livingston (Mont.) Hosp., 1974-84, Buffalo Bill Mus., Cody, Wyo., 1980—; pres., trustee Livingston (Mont.) Depot Found., 1986—, Livingston (Mont.) Cmty. Trust, 1987—. Mem. Am. Soc. Newspaper Editors, Newspaper Assn. Am., Denver Univ. Club. Office: Livingston Enterprise PO Box 665 401 S Main Livingston MT 59047

SULLIVAN, KEVIN PATRICK, lawyer; b. Waterbury, Conn., June 9, 1953; s. John Holian Sullivan and Frances (McGrath) Coon; m. Peggy Hardy, June 13, 1975 (div. Jan. 1985); m. Jarnine Welker, Feb. 15, 1985; children: S. Craig Lemmon, Michael Scott Lemmon, Lindsay Michelle Lemmon. BS in Polit. Sci., BS in Police Sci. cum laude, Weber State Coll., 1979; JD, Pepperdine U., 1982. Bar: Utah 1982, U.S. Dist. Ct. Utah 1982, U.S. Ct. Appeals (10th cir.) 1986, U.S. Supreme Ct. 1986. Assoc. Farr, Kaufman & Hamilton, Ogden, Utah, 1982-87; ptnr. Farr, Kaufman, Hamilton, Sulivan, Gorman & Perkins, Ogden, 1987-91, Farr, Kaufman, Sullivan, Gorman & Perkins, Ogden, 1991—; judge pro tem Utah 2d Cir. Ct.; city prosecutor of South Ogden, 1990-92. Mem. Eccles Community Art Ctr., Victim's Rights Com. of 2d Jud. Dist. Mem. ABA (criminal justice sect., litigation sect., justice and edn. fund lawyers' coun.), ACLU, ATLA, Utah Bar Assn. (criminal law, young lawyer, litigation sects., unauthorized practice law com.), Utah Trial Lawyers Assn., Utah Assn. Criminal Def. Lawyers, Weber County Bar Assn. (criminal law sect., pres.-elect 1993, pres. 1994), Weber County Pub. Defenders Assn. (assoc. dir. 1987), Weber State Coll. Alumni Assn., Amicus Pepperdine, Elks, Kiwanis, Phi Kappa Phi. Roman Catholic. Home: 2731 E 6425 S Ogden UT 84403-5461 Office: Farr Kaufman Sullivan Gorman & Perkins 205 26th St Ste 34 Ogden UT 84401-3109

SULLIVAN, MARTIN EDWARD, museum director; b. Troy, N.Y., Feb. 9, 1944; s. John Francis and Helen Edna (Lynch) S.; m. Katherine Mary Hostetter, May 9, 1981; children: Abigail, Bethany. BA in History, Siena Coll., 1965; MA in History, U. Notre Dame, 1970, PhD in History, 1974. Exec. dir. Ind. Commn. for Humanities, Indpls., 1972-75; dir. pub. programs NEH, Washington, 1976-81; pres. Inst. on Man and Sci., Rensselaerville, N.Y., 1981-83; dir. N.Y. State Mus., State Edn. Dept., Albany, N.Y., 1983-90, The Heard Mus., Phoenix, 1990—; trustee Am. Indian Ritual Object Repatriation Found., N.Y.C., 1992—; chair U.S. Govt. Cultural Property Adv. Com., 1995—. Author: Museums, Adults and the Humanities, 1981; contbr. articles to profl. jours. Trustee Arizonians for cultural Devel., Phoenix, 1990—, Phoenix Cmty. Alliance, 1991—, Am. Fedn. of Arts, 1994—; mem. Nativ Am. Repatriation Act. Adv. Com., 1992—. With U.S. Army, 1966-68. Mem. Am. Assn. Mus. (v.p. 1990-93, mem. exec. com. internat. com. 1992—). Democrat. Home: 4601 E Solano Dr Phoenix AZ 85018-1280 Office: The Heard Mus 22 E Monte Vista Rd Phoenix AZ 85004-1433

SULLIVAN, MICHAEL EVAN, investment and management company executive; b. Phila., Dec. 30, 1940; s. Albert and Ruth (Liebert) S.; BS, N.Mex. State U., 1966, MA (Ednl. Research Tng. Program fellow), 1967; BS, U. Tex., 1969; MBA, U. Houston, 1974; MS, U. So. Calif., 1976, MPA, 1977, PhD in Adminstrn., 1983; BS in Acctg., U. La Verne, 1981. Sr. adminstrv. and tech. analyst Houston Lighting & Power Co., 1969-74; electronics engr. U.S. Govt., Point Mugu, Calif., 1974-77; mem. tech. staff Hughes Aircraft Co., El Segundo, Calif., 1977-78; staff program adminstr. Ventura div. Northrop Corp., Newbury Park, Calif., 1978-79; div. head engring. div. Navastrogru, Point Mugu, 1979-82; br. head, div. head spl. programs head operational systems integraton office Pacific Missile Test Ctr., Calif., 1983-90, head tech. devel. office, 1993—; CNO, Dir. Rsch., Devel., and Acquisition in the Pentagon, Washington, 1987-88, dir. rsch. devel. test and evaluation and tech. in the Pentagon, 1990-93; pres., chmn. bd. Diversified Mgmt. Systems, Inc., Camarillo, Calif., 1978—. Author: The Management of Research, Development, Test and Evaluation Organizations; Organizational Behavior Characteristics of Supervisors-Public versus Private Sectors, Organizational Behavior Characteristics of Supervisors, Public versus Private Sectors; Self-Actualization in RDT & E Organizations; Self-Actualization in a Health Care Agency; others. V.p., bd. dirs. Ventura County Master Chorale and Opera Assn; bd. dirs. So. Calif. Assn. of Pub. Adminstrn. (also mem. fin. com., programs com., student aid com.). Served with U.S. Army, 1958-62. Ednl. Rsch. Info. Clearing House fellow, 1965-67. Mem. IEEE, Am. Math. Soc., Math. Assn. Am., Am. Statis. Assn., IEEE Engring. Mgmt. Soc., Am. Soc. Pub. Adminstrn., So. Calif. Assn. Pub. Adminstrn. (bd. dirs., various coms.), Am. Pers. and Guidance Assn., Fed. Mgrs. Assn., Am. Assn. Individual Investors, Mcpl. Mgmt. Assts. So. Calif., Acad. Polit. Sci., Internat. Soc. for the Systems Scis., Assn. MBA Execs., Tech. Transfer Soc., Internat. Fedn. for Systems Rsch., Tech. Transfer Soc., Phi Kappa Phi, Pi Gamma Mu. Home: PO Box 273 Port Hueneme CA 93044-0273 Office: PO Box 447 Camarillo CA 93011-0447

SULLIVAN, MICHELLE CORNEJO, lawyer; b. St. Louis, June 29, 1958; m. Dennis Keith Sullivan, May 18, 1985. BS, U. Calif., Berkeley, 1980; JD, U. Santa Clara, 1983. Bar: Calif., 1984; U.S. Dist. Ct. (no. dist.) Calif., 1984, (so. dist.) Calif., 1985; cert. family law specialist. Legal dept. Four-Phase Computers, Cupertino, Calif., 1984; asst. dist. atty. San Benito County, Hollister, Calif., 1984-85; assoc. Walters & Ward, Rancho Bernardo, Calif., 1986-87, Law Offices of Rebecca Prater, Carlsbad, Calif., 1987-88; pvt. practice Escondido, Calif., 1988—. Pres. Women in Networking, San Diego, 1987; western horse show judge Calif. State Horseman's Assn., 1985; adv. com. San diego Regional Conf. on Women (bd. trustees 1993). Recipient Law Faculty scholar U. Santa Clara, 1982-83. Mem. ABA, San Diego Trial Lawyers Assn. (family law sect.), State Bar Assn., San Diego County Bar Assn., No. San Diego County Bar Assn., Rancho Bernardo C. of C. (ambassador 1986-87), Lawyers Club (v.p. 1988—). Office: 127 E 3rd Ave Ste 202 Escondido CA 92025-4201

SULLIVAN, PATRICK ALLEN, strategic management educator; b. Peoria, Ill., Oct. 31, 1932; s. Francis Richard and Carmela Marie (Smith) S.; m. Gwendolyn Jo Herndon, Aug. 25, 1958; children: Richard John, Sharon Louise Little, Patrick Michael, Cecelia Anne, Catherine Marie Markee. BCE, Marquette U., 1955; MBA, San Diego State U., 1975; DBA, U.S. Internat. U., San Diego, 1988. Engr. USMC, 29 Palms, Calif., 1958-63; engr. USN, San Diego, 1963-67, mgmt. analyst, 1967-88; asst. prof. strategic mgmt. U.S. Internat. U., San Diego, 1988-89, assoc. prof. strategic mgmt., 1989-94, prof. strategic mgmr., 1994—; ptnr. Sullivan and Assocs. Mgmt. Cons., San Diego, 1988-89. Pres. St. Pius Ch. Parish Coun., Chula Vista, Calif., 1984. 1st lt. USMC, 1955-58. Mem. ASCE, Acad. Mgmt., Strategic Mgmt. Soc. Planning Forum, K.C., Chi Epsilon, Tau Beta Pi, Sigma Iota Epsilon, Beta Gamma Sigma. Democrat. Roman Catholic. Home: 98 E Emerson St Chula Vista CA 91911-3545

SULLIVAN, PATRICK JAMES, physician, state representative; b. Little Rock, Ark., July 29, 1936; s. Edmond James and Ruth (Morris) S.; m. Dorothy Jane Chapman, June 15, 1963; children: Mary Cathleen, Gayla Anne, Elizabeth Colleen. Grad., Tulane U., 1957; MD, La. State U., 1961. Diplomate Am. Bd. Urology. Asst. prof. urology U. Colo. Med. Sch., Denver, 1968-69; pvt. practice Urology Clinic of Greeley, Colo., 1969—; state rep. Colo. Ho. Reps., Denver, 1991—; caucus chmn. Ho. Reps. Rep. Party, Denver, 1993-94; mem. U. No. Colo. Adv. Bd., Greeley, 1990—. Mem. Greeley Rot Club, 1976—; mem. Dist. Six Sch. Bd., 1983-89, pres. 1989—). Capt. U.S. Army, 1966-68. Recipient Legis. Excellence award Colo. Assn. Sch. Bds., 1993; named Bus. Legislator of Yr. Colo. Assn. Commerce and Industry, 1993, Outstanding Freshman Legislator AP, 1991. Episcopalian. Home: 2411 19th Ave Greeley CO 80631-8123 Office: Colo Ho of Reps State Capital Denver CO 80203

SULLIVAN, ROBERT SCOTT, architect; b. Alexandria, La., Sept. 8, 1955; s. Robert Wallace and Harriette Henri (Fedric) S. BA cum laude, Tulane U., 1979, BArch, 1979. Registered architect, N.Y., Calif., La.; cert. Nat. Coun. of Archtl. Registrations Bds. Staff architect Cavitt, McKnight, Weymouth, Inc., Houston, 1979-81, Hardy, Holzman, Pfeiffer Assocs., N.Y.C., 1981-83; ptnr. Sullivan, Briggs Assocs., N.Y.C., 1983-86; cons. Butler, Rogers, Baskett, N.Y.C., 1985-86; prin. R. Scott Sullivan AIA, Berkeley, Calif., 1986-89; ptnr. Talbott Sullivan Archs., Albany, Calif., 1989-94, Scott Sullivan, Arch., Albany, 1994—; cons. Neometry Graphics, N.Y.C., 1983-86, dir, 1986—; bd. dirs. Middleton/Sullivan Inc., Alexandria, 1981—. Works include specific design projects at N.Y. Hist. Soc. exhibit Grand Cen. Terminal, N.Y.C., 1982, The Houston Sch. of Performing Visual Arts, 1980, The Pingry Sch., Bernards Twp., N.J., 1982, Arts Ctr. at Oak Knoll Sch., Summit, N.J., 1986. Vestry St. Mark's Episc. Ch., Berkeley, 1988-89; bd. dirs. The Parsonage, Episcopal Diocese Calif., 1992-94; cons. Commn. Accessibility, Episcopal Diocese Calif., 1991-93, 95—. Mem. AIA, Calif. Council Architects, Archtl. League N.Y.C., Nat. Trust for Hist. Preservation, Victorian Soc. in Am., Royal Archtl. Inst. of Can. (assoc.), Tau Sigma Delta. Democrat. Episcopalian. Home: 1060 Sterling Ave Berkeley CA 94708-1729 Office: 1323 Solano Ave Albany CA 94706-1829

SULLIVAN, STUART FRANCIS, anesthesiologist, educator; b. Buffalo, July 15, 1928; s. Charles S. and Kathryn (Duggan) S.; m. Dorothy Elizabeth Faytol, Apr. 18, 1959; children: John, Irene, Paul, Kathryn. BS, Canisius Coll., 1950; MD, SUNY, Syracuse, 1955. Diplomate Am. Bd. Anesthesiology. Intern Ohio State Univ. Hosp., Columbus, 1955-56; resident Columbia Presbyn. Med. Ctr., 1958-60; instr. anesthesiology Columbia U. Coll. Physicians and Surgeons, N.Y.C., 1961-62, assoc., 1962-64, asst. prof., 1964-69, assoc. prof., 1969-73; prof. dept. anesthesiology UCLA, 1973-91, vice chair anesthesiology, 1974-77, exec. vice chair, 1977-90, acting chmn., 1983-84, 87-88, 90-91, prof. emeritus, 1991—. Served to capt. M.C., USAR, 1956-58. Fellow NIH, 1960-61; recipient research career devel. award NIH, 1966-69. Mem. Assn. Univ. Anesthetists, Am. Physiol. Soc., Am. Soc. Anesthesiologists. Home: 101 Foxtail Dr Santa Monica CA 90402-2047 Office: UCLA Sch Medicine Dept Anesthesiology Los Angeles CA 90024

SULLIVAN-BOYLE, KATHLEEN MARIE, association administrator; b. Tulsa, Feb. 9, 1958; d. Thomas Anthony and Jeanne Lee (Agnew) Sullivan; m. Thomas C. Boyle. BS in Polit. Sci., Arz. State U., 1980; MA in Govt., Coll. William and Mary, 1982. Sec. Ariz. Rep. Party, Phoenix, 1980-81; rsch. asst. Pete Dunn for U.S. Senate Campaign, Phoenix, 1982; adminstra. sec Ariz. Corp. Commn., Phoenix, 1983-84; pub. relations dir. Epoch Univs. Publ., Phoenix, 1984-86; membership dir. Tempe (Ariz.) C. of C., 1986-93; dir. legis. affairs Ariz. Pharmacy Assn., 1994—. Sec., chmn. publicity Cactus Wren Rep. Women, Phoenix, 1983-89, Fiesta Bowl; bd. dirs Tempe Leadership, Tempe YMCA. Mem. Soroptimist (past pres.), Pub. Rels. Soc. Am., Alpha Phi. (chmn. conv.). Republican. Office: Ariz Pharmacy Assn 1845 E Southern Tempe AZ 85282-5831

SULLWOLD, HAROLD H., geologist; b. St. Paul, Dec. 22, 1916; s. Harold Herman and Emma Cornelia (Sundkvist) S.; m. Mayla Carol Sandbeck, Aug. 31, 1940; children—Eric Verner, Wendy. B.A., UCLA, 1939, M.A., 1940, Ph.D., 1959. Registered profl. engr., Calif.; registered profl. geologist, Calif. Geologist, U.S. Geol. Survey, western states, 1942-44, W.R. Cabeen & Assoc., North Hollywood, Calif., 1944-52, G.H. Roth & Assoc., North Hollywood, 1960-80; tchr. UCLA, 1952-59; ind. geologist, L.A., 1958-60. Carpinteria, Calif., 1980—; adj. prof. U. So. Calif., 1974. Author, publ.: cartoons Andy Cline, 1983. Editor: O & G Fields of L.A. and Ventura, 1958; regional editor: Stratigraphic Oil and Gas, 1972. Contbr. papers to profl. publs. Pres. Concha Loma Improvement Assn., Carpinteria, 1975; chmn. continuing edn. com. Coast Geol. Soc., Ventura, Calif., 1977; chmn. bldg. fund Carpinteria Hist. Soc., 1982—; dir. Carpinteria County Water Dist., 1983-93; geologist pro bono, 1993—; dir. Thomas Dibblee Geol. Found., 1988—. Fellow Geol. Soc. Am.; mem. Am. Assn. Petroleum Geologists (hon. life, v.p. Pacific sect., field trip chmn. 1958, ho. of dels. 1983—), Am. Inst. Profl. Geologists (screening chmn. 1968—). Republican. Presbyterian. Club: Channel City (Santa Barbara, Calif.). Avocations: golf, travel, sketching. Home: 900 Calle De Los Amigos Apt N11 Santa Barbara CA 93105-4436 Office: 910 Linden Ave # A Carpinteria CA 93013-2045

SULTAN, LARRY, photographer. BA, U. Calif., San Francisco, 1968; MFA, San Francisco Art Inst., 1973. One-man shows include Ohio Silver Gallery, L.A., 1972, U. Calif. Gallery, San Francisco, 1974, Ctr. for Creative Photography, Tucson, 1977, Fogg Art Mus., Cambridge, Mass., 1978, Light Gallery, L.A., 1981, Blue Sky Gallery, Portland, Oreg., 1981, Portland (Maine) Sch. Art, 1982, U. Colo. Art Gallery, Boulder, 1982, R.I. Sch. Design, Providence, 1987, Janet Borden, Inc., N.Y.C., 1989, Headlands Ctr. for Arts, Sausalito, Calif., 1989, The Exploratorium, San Francisco, 1990, San Jose (Calif.) Mus. Art, 1992, Stephen Wirtz Gallery, San Francisco, 1992, Mus. Contemporary Art, San Diego, 1994, Chgo. Cultural Ctr., The Corcoran Gallery of Art, Washington, Scottsdale Ctr. Arts, Ariz.; exhibited in group shows at Fogg Art Mus., 1976, La Mamelle Gallery, San Francisco, 1976, San Francisco Mus. Modern Art, 1977, 82, 85, 89, 91, L.A. Inst. of Contemporary Art, 1978, Chgo. Mus. Contemporary Art, 1979, Santa Barbara Mus. Art, 1981, Seibu Mus. Art, Tokyo, 1982, Univ. Art Mus., Berkeley, Calif., 1983, Internat. Ctr. Photography, N.Y.C., 1984, Barbican Art Gallery, London, 1985, Mus. Modern Art, N.Y.C., 1985, 89, 91, U. Colo. Gallery, 1986, Los Angeles County Mus. Art, 1987, Burden Gallery, N.Y.C., 1988, Northlight Gallery, Tempe, Ariz., 1990, Birmingham (Ala.) Mus. Art, 1990, Met. Mus. Art, N.Y.C., 1991, Milw. Art Mus., 1991, Stephen Wirtz Gallery, San Francisco, 1991, List Art Ctr., Providence, 1991, Transamerica Pyramid, San Francisco, Presentation House, Ctr. Visual and Performing Arts, Vancouver, BC, U. ARt Mus. Berkeley, Calif., others; represented in permanent collections at Art Inst. Chgo., Bibliotheque Nationale, Birmingham Mus. Art, Ctr. for Creative Photography, Chase Manhattan Bank, Frods Regional D'Art contemporain, J. Paul Getty Mus., The Mus. Modern Art, Milw. Art Mus., The Met. Mus. Art, The Nat. Mus. Art, San Francisco Mus. Modern Art, U. Ala., U. Colo. Recipient Art in Pub. Places grant Nat. Endowment for the Arts, 1976, Photography fellowship Nat. Endowment for the Arts, 1977, 80, 92, Spl. Projects grant Calif. Arts Coun., 1978, Guggenheim fellowship, 1983, Artists fellowship Marin Arts Coun., 1986, Engelhard award Inst. Contemporary Art, 1988, Fleishhaker Found. Eureka fellowship Calif. Arts Coun., 1989, Pub. Arts award Oakland Cultural Arts, 1990, Louis Comfort Tiffany fellowship, 1991. Office: C O Stephen Wirtz Gallery 49 Geary St San Francisco CA 94108-5705

SUMFEST, JOEL MICHAEL, pediatric urologist; b. Trenton, N.J., Nov. 2, 1959; s. William Abraham and Shirley (Keiner) S.; m. Virginia Maureen Roberts, Oct. 7, 1990; 1 child, Rachel Hannah. BS with highest distinction, Pa. State U., 1980; MD cum laude, Jefferson Med. Coll., 1982. Diplomate Am. Bd. Urology. Commd. U.S. Army Med. Corps, 1977, advanced through grades to lt. col., 1994; staff urologist DDE Army Med. Ctr., Augusta, Ga., 1988-91; pediatric urology fellow Children's Hosp., Seattle, 1991-93; pediatric urologist Tripler Army Med. Ctr., Honolulu, 1993—. Contbr. articles to profl. jours. Mem. Am. Urologists Assn., Am. Assn. Physicians, Hawaiian Urologic Soc., Soc. Govt. Svc. Urologists. Office: Tripler Army Med Ctr Urology Honolulu HI 96859

SUMMER, LYLE C., state agency economist, economics educator; b. Rexburg, Idaho, Apr. 3, 1938; s. Benjamin Earl and Laurene (Christensen) S.; m. Carole Winters, May 25, 1957; children: Jeffery, Serri, Quin, Blake, Holly, Cody. AS, Ricks Coll., 1969; BS, Utah State U., 1972, MS, 1972. Mgr., co-owner Family Farm, Rexburg, 1962-68; economist Soil Conservation Svc., USDA, Salt Lake City, 1968-76; chief economist Utah Divsn. Water Resources, Salt Lake City, 1976—; adj. prof. econ. dept., Utah State U., Logan, 1990—; appraiser, cons. Water Appraisal Svcs. Co., West Jordan, Utah, 1986—. Contbr. articles to profl. jours. Chairperson West Jordan Planning and Zoning Commn., 1980-84; candidate for mayor City of West Jordan, 1988, mem. budget com., 1994. With USMC, 1957-60. Mem. Am. Water Resources Assn. (pres. Utah chpt. 1987). Republican. Mem. LDS Ch. Office: Utah Divsn Water Resources 1636 W North Temple Salt Lake City UT 84116-3156

SUMMERALL, PAT (GEORGE ALLAN SUMMERALL), sportscaster; b. Lake City, Fla., May 10, 1931; m. Katherine Summerall; children: Susan, Jay, Kyle. Degree in Education, U. Ark., M. in Russain History. Football player Detroit Lions, 1952-53, Chgo. Cardinals, 1953-57, N.Y. Giants, 1958-61; played briefly in St. Louis Cardinals baseball orgn.; with CBS Sports, 1962—; dir. sports Sta. WCBS-Radio, N.Y.C., 1964-71; host morning program Sta. WCBS-TV, 1966-67; sportscaster early news Sta. WCBS-TV, N.Y.C.; with CBS Radio Network; sportscaster Sports Time, Predictions, Profiles; host CBS Sports Spectacular.; lead play-by-play announcer NFL Football coverage CBS Sports, anchor golf and tennis coverage; sports commentator, football analyst Fox Network, 1994—. Named Sportscaster of Yr., 1977. Office: care FOX Network PO Box 900 Beverly Hills CA 90213

SUMMERFIELD, JOHN ROBERT, textile curator; b. St. Paul, Feb. 21, 1917; s. Isaac and Irene (Longini) S.; m. Anne Benson, July 14, 1945. S.B. in Mech. Engring., MIT, 1938; M.B.A., U. Calif.-Berkeley, 1947, Ph.D. in Econs., 1954. Asst. prof. Sloan Sch. Mgmtg., MIT, 1952-54; br. chief CIA, Washington, 1954-56; project leader The Rand Corp., Santa Monica, Calif., 1956-62; corp. economist Douglas Aircraft Co., Santa Monica, 1962-66; v.p. econ. planning Western Airlines, Los Angeles, 1966-70; staff v.p. econ. planning Pan Am. Airways, N.Y.C., 1970-71; pres. Summerfield Assocs., Pacific Palisades, Calif., 1972-92; vis. curator Fowler Mus. Cultural History, UCLA, 1993—. Co-curator exhbns. of antique Minangkabau ceremonial textiles from West Sumatra, Textile Mus., Washington, 1990-91, Santa Barbara (Calif.) Mus. Art, 1991, Bellevue (Wash.) Art Mus., 1992, Utah Mus. Fine Art, 1992. Served to lt. USNR, 1942-45.

SUMMERS, CATHLEEN ANN, film producer; b. Chgo.; d. Cecil Paul and Elizabeth Ann S.; m. Patrick Timothy Crowley. BA, U. So. Calif., 1973. Film editor, comml. producer, dir.'s asst. Roman Polanski, Rome, 1972; story editor Albert S. Ruddy Prodns. Paramount Pictures, L.A., 1973-74; exec. asst. Columbia Pictures, Burbank, Calif., 1974; story editor Columbia Pictures, 1974-76; devel. exec., v.p., producer Martin Ransohoff Prodns. Columbia Pictures, 1976; sr. v.p. Tri-Star Pictures, Century City, Calif., 1984-87; motion picture producer Cathleen Summers Prodns., L.A., 1989—; motion picture producer, ptnr. Summers-Kouf Prodns., Burbank, 1986-87; motion picture producer Cathleen Summers Prodns., L.A., 1987, Summers-Quaid Prodns., Century City, Culver City, Calif., 1988—. Producer: (motion picture) Stakeout, 1987, DOA, 1991, Vital Signs, 1990, Mystery Date, 1991, Dogfight, 1991, The Sandlot, 1993, Stakeout II, 1993. Co-founder Diane Thomas Scholarship-UCLA, 1988—. Mem. Am. Film Inst.-3rd Decade Coun. (chair 1993, 94, 95, pres. 1995).

SUMMERS, WILLIAM K., neuropsychiatrist, researcher; b. Jefferson City, Mo., Apr. 14, 1944; s. Joseph S. and Amy Lydia (Koopmans) S.; m. Angela Forbes Taveras, Oct. 2, 1972(div. Apr. 1985); children: Elisabeth Stuart, Wilhelmina Derek. Student, Westminster Coll., Fulton, Mo., 1962-64; BS, U. Mo., 1966; MD, Washington U., St. Louis, 1971. Internal medicine intern Barnes Hosp-Washington U., St. Louis, 1971-72; resident in internal medicine Jewish Hosp., St. Louis, 1972-73; resident in psychiatry Rsch. Hosp., St. Louis, 1973-76; asst. prof. U. Pitts., 1976-78, U. So. Calif., L.A., 1978-82; asst. clin. prof. rsch. UCLA, 1982-88; rschr. Arcadia, Calif., 1988-92, Albuquerque, 1992—. Patentee in field. Mem. AMA, ACP, Am. Psychiat. Assn., Soc. Neurosci., N.Y. Acad. Scis., Am. Fedn. Clin. Rsch. Episcopalian. Office: 3131 Candelaria Rd NE Albuquerque NM 87107-1905

SUMMERS, WYMAN DURAND, pharmacist; b. Kingsley, Iowa, June 3, 1925; s. Russell Raymond and Iona Leila (Clark) S.; m. Loni Johnson, Mar. 7, 1953; children: Rick Eugene, Steven Craig, Jodi Paige. BS, Oreg. State U. Sec.-treas. CentWise Drug Stores, Inc., Lebanon, Oreg., 1950-88; sec. OK Drug Stores, Portland, Oreg., 1956—. With USN, 1943-46, PTO. Republican. Home: 240 Oak Ln Lebanon OR 97355

SUMNER, GORDON, JR., retired military officer; b. Albuquerque, July 23, 1924; s. Gordon and Esstella (Berry) S.; m. Frances Fernandes, May, 1991; children: Ward T., Holly Rose. AS, N.Mex. Mil. Inst., 1943; BA, La. State U., 1955; MA, U. Md., 1963. Commd. 2d. lt. U.S. Army, 1944, advanced through grades to lt. gen., 1975, ret., 1978; founder, chmn. Cypress Internat., 1978-81; chmn. La Mancha Co., Inc., 1981—; cons. U.S. Depts. State and Def; amabassador at large for Latin Am.; spl. ambassador U.S. Dept. State; nat. security advisor Pres.' Bi-Partisan Commn. Cen. Am.; vis. staff mem. Los Alamos Nat. Lab. Contbr. articles to profl. jours. Decorated D.S.M., Silver Star, Legion of Merit with three oak leaf clusters, Disting. Flying Cross with 13 oak leaf clusters, Bronze Star, Army Commendation medal with oak leaf cluster, Purple Heart. Mem. Phi Kappa Phi, Sigma Alpha. Office: La Mancha Co 100 Cienega St Ste D Santa Fe NM 87501-2003

SUMNER, LEO F., II, management consultant; b. San Francisco, Feb. 6, 1949; s. Leo Francis and Elizabeth (Miller) S.; divorced; 1 child, Tara M. BS in Indsl. Tech., So. Ill. U.; MBA, St. Mary's Coll. Bus. devel. mgr. gen. mech. engring. svcs. group western divsn. Babcock and Wilcox Co., 1974-84; regional mktg. mgr. Western states and Pacific Rim Hill Internat., Inc., 1984-86; ind. cons., 1986-87; spl. projects mgr. Western U.S. O'Brien-Kreitzberg and Assocs., Inc., 1987-90; sr. assoc. West Coast divsn. Heery Program Mgmt., Inc., 1990-92; exec. dir., CFO Calif. Constrn. Tech. Transfer, 1992-93; cons. The Sumner Group, San Pedro, 1992—; lectr. Calif. State U., Long Beach, U. Calif., Berkeley, The Bus. Roundtable, The Constrn. Mgmt. Assn. of Am., Western Coun. Constrn. Consumers, Don Todd Assocs., Inc.; program com. chmn. Western Coun. Constrn. Consumers, 1990, 91, program com., membership com., safety and quality com. With USAF, 1967-74. Decorated Airmans medal for Heroism, Air Force Commendation medal for meritorious svc. Mem. ASCE, Soc. Am. Mil. Engrs., Am. Pub. Works Assn., Soc. Mktg. Profl. Svcs., Constrn. Mgmt. Assn. Am. (past pres. No. Calif. chpt., past vice-chmn. regional chpts. com., chmn. nat. pres. coun., Svc. award 1990), County Engrs. Assn. Calif., County Engrs. Assn. Wash., Am. Arbitration Assn. (disputes resolution panelist). Office: The Sumner Group 103 Lora Ct Vallejo CA 94591-4227

SUMRALL, HARRY, journalist; b. Palestine, Tex., Oct. 15, 1950; s. Harry Glenn and Sherea Sue (Selden) S.; m. Leslie Leizear, Dec. 19, 1954; 1 child, Samuel Harry. BA, George Mason U., 1974. Writer, critic The Washington Post, 1978-81; contbg. writer The New Republic, Washington, 1979; assoc. editor Rock Concert Mag., Washington, 1979; music writer San Jose (Calif.) Mercury News/Knight Ridder News Svc., 1982—; advisor New Music Am., Washington, 1983; lectr., guest San Francisco State U., 1991; guest critic Sta. KGO, San Francisco, 1991—. Author: Pioneers of Rock and Roll, 1994; contbg. author: New Grove Dictionary of American Music, 1983; broadcaster: (radio program) Rockology, 1989. Paneslist Chatauquas for Congress, Washington, 1979. Fellow New Music Am., 1980. Office: San Jose Mercury News 750 Ridder Park Dr San Jose CA 95131-2432

SUN, CHARLES CHANGKYUN, minister, college president; b. Seoul, Republic of Korea, Feb. 18, 1931; came to U.S., 1959-61, 65—; s. Chongwhan and Shyin A. (Kim) S.; m. Alice Aiwon Yoon, Apr. 5, 1954; children: Susanna Sun Choi, John H., Mary Sun Roh. BA, Tanbook U., 1955; M of Religious Edn., Conservative Bapt. Theol. Sem., 1966; DD (hon.), U. L.A., 1982. Ordained to ministry Korean Methodist Ch., 1954. Prof. Korean Meth. Theol. Sem., 1961-64; min. Korean Christian Ch., Denver, 1968—; comptr. World of Sleep Mgmt., Inc., Denver, 1970-81; chmn. bd. Korean Sch., Denver, 1972—; owner Korean Christian Book Ctr., 1981—; pres. Bible Correspondence Coll., 1981—, Christian World Mission Coll., 1982—. Contbr. articles to newspapers and mags. Served as chaplain Republic of Korea, 1951-55. Home: PO Box 6715 Denver CO 80206-0715 Office: Korean Christian Ch 1495 S University Blvd Denver CO 80210-2406

SUN, CHIEH, electronics company executive; b. China, Mar. 3, 1943; came to U.S., 1966, naturalized, 1975; s. Chin-Hwa and Jean Y. (Yeh) S.; m. Lin Lynn, June 17, 1967; children—Andrew, Christina. Ph.D., U. So. Calif., 1972. Chmn., Chung-Hwa Picture Ltd., Taiwan, 1969—; pres. Tatung Co. Am., Inc., Long Beach, Calif., 1972—; dir. Am. Asia Bank, San Francisco Chmn. elec. engring. dept. Chinese Culture U., Taiwan, 1979—. Baptist. Office: Tatung Co Am Inc 2850 E El Presidio St Long Beach CA 90810-1119

SUN, COSSETTE TSUNG-HUNG WU, law library director; b. Taipei, Taiwan, July 14, 1937; came to U.S., 1960, naturalized, 1972; d. Lin Tsung and Chiu Ching (Wu) Hsieh; m. Stanley Siann-Shyang Sun, Nov. 23, 1961; children: Carol Sun Crowe, Marina Sheree, Olivia Cossette. LLB, Nat. Taiwan U., Taipei, 1960; MA, U. Houston, 1963; MS, Simmons Coll., Boston, 1965. Asst. prof. law, assoc. libr. St. Louis U., 1965-73; assoc. libr.U. Calif.-Berkeley, 1974-75; br. libr. Alameda County Law Libr., Hayward, Calif., 1975-77, law libr. dir., Oakland, 1978—; chmn. law libr. svcs. to instl. residents, 1979-80; pres. Coun. Calif. County Law Librs., 1982-84. Editor: State Ct. County Law Libraries Newsletter, 1979; contbr. articles to law revs. Mem. Castro Valley Mcpl. Adv. Coun., Castro Valley Libr. Adv. Commn. W.H. Anderson scholar, 1966; Matthew Bender scholar, 1971. Mem. Am. Assn. Law Librs. (cert. 1969), Spl. Librs. Assn., Asian-Pacific Libr. Assn., Alameda County Bar Assn. Office: Alameda County Law Libr Courthouse Rm 200 Oakland CA 94612

SUNDBERG, NORMAN DALE, psychology educator; b. Aurora, Nebr., Sept. 15, 1922; s. Cedric William and Nellie Mae (Akerson) S.; m. Donna Varner, Sept. 25, 1948; children: Kent Alan, Gregory Paul, Scott Donald, Mark William. BA, U. Nebr., 1947; MA, U. Minn., 1949, PhD, 1952. Lic. psychologist, Oreg. Teaching asst, instr. U. Minn., Mpls., 1947-52; from asst. to prof. U. Oreg., Eugene, 1952-88, prof. emeritus, 1988—; vis. prof. U. Calif., Berkeley, 1959-61, LaTrobe U., Melbourne, Australia, 1976, 80, Macquarie U., Sydney, Australia, 1980, U. Hong Kong, 1984; dean Wallace Sch. Cmty. Svc. and Pub. Affairs, U. Oreg., Eugene, 1967-72; cons. VA, 1953-88; dir. clin. and cmty. psychology program U. Oreg., 1977-80, 84-88; lectr., cons. U.S. Ednl. Found., New Delhi, 1965-66, 73; external examiner U. Hong Kong, 1992—. Author: Assessment of Persons, 1977; (with Leona Tyler) Clinical Psychology, 1962; (with Leona Tyler, Julian Taplin) Clinical Psychology, 1973, 83; contbr. articles to profl. jours.; editorial com. Annual Rev. Psychology, 1976-80. Field assessment officer Peace Corps, Oreg., 1963. 1st lt. arty. U.S. Army, 1943-46. Grantee Fulbright-Hays, 1965-66, 73. Fellow Am. Psychol. Assn. (ethics com. 1970-73), Soc. Personality Assessment (Walter Klopfer award 1987); mem. Oreg. Psychol. Assn. (pres. 1962-63), Internat. Coun. Psychologists, Internat. Assn. Cross-Cultural Psychology. Democrat. Office: Univ Oreg Dept Psychology Eugene OR 97403

SUNDEL, HARVEY H., marketing research analyst and consultant; b. Bronx, NY, July 24, 1944; s. Louis and Pauline (Brotman) S. BBA, St. Mary's U., San Antonio, 1969, MBA, 1970; PhD, St. Louis U., 1974. Asst. dir. research Lone Star Brewery, San Antonio, 1970-71; cons. Tri-Mark, Inc., San Antonio, 1972-73; asst. prof. mktg. Lewis and Clark Coll., Godfrey, Ill., 1973-74; asst. prof. mktg. Met. State Coll., Denver, 1974-77, chmn., prof. mktg., 1977-86; pres. Sundel Rsch., Inc., Denver, 1976—; cons. Frederick Ross Co., Denver, 1979-84, U.S. West Direct, Denver, 1986—, Monsanto Chems. Co., St. Louis, 1985—, Mountain Bell, Denver, 1979-88, U.S. West Communications, Denver, 1988—, AT&T, 1986—, Melco Industries, 1987-90, Norwest Banks, 1990—, PACE Membership Warehouse, 1992-93, U.S. Meat Export Fedn., 1992—; expert witness in legal cases. Contbr. papers and proceedings to profl. jours. Com. mem. Mile High United Way, Denver, 1975-80, Allied Jewish Fedn. Cmty. Rels. Action Com., 1994—. Jewish. Home: 1616 Glen Bar Dr Lakewood CO 80215-3014 Office: Sundel Rsch Inc 1150 Delaware St Denver CO 80204-3608

SUNDELL, KENT ALLAN, geologist; b. Olathe, Kans., July 5, 1955; s. Allan R. S. and Joyce H. (Jensen) Bonebright; m. Margaret B. Bertolino, Aug. 31, 1980; children: Jessica Ann, Andrew Kent, Emily Grace. BS in Geology, U. Wyo., 1977, MS, 1980; PhD, U. Calif., Santa Barbara, 1985. Profl. geologist, Wyo. Geologist WGM Inc., Anchorage, 1977; teaching asst. U. Wyo., Laramie, 1978-80, U. Calif., Santa Barbara, 1980-82; pres., owner Ram Oil Co. Inc., Casper, Wyo., 1980—; pres. Absaroka Exploration Co. Inc., Casper, 1986—. Author: Geology of North Fork of Owl Creek, 1982; co-editor: Wyoming Geology Association 1990 Guidebook, 1990; contbr. articles to profl. jours. Mem. Wyo. Geol. Assn. (treas. 1989, chmn. field conf. 1990, Best Paper award 1984, 88, Frank Morgan award 1991), Geol. Soc. Am., Rocky Mountain Assn. Geologists (Best Paper award 1989), Sigma Xi. Office: Absaroka Exploration Co Inc PO Box 1543 Casper WY 82602-1543

SUNDQUIST, LEAH RENATA, physical education specialist; b. El Paso, Tex., July 22, 1963; d. Dominic Joseph and Patricia Ann (Manley) Bernardi; m. David Curtis Sundquist, June 23, 1990. AA, N.Mex. Mil. Inst., 1983; BS, U. Tex., El Paso, 1986. Field exec. Rio Grande Girl Scout Coun., El Paso, 1983-84; customer teller M-Bank, El Paso, 1984-85; soccer coach St. Clements Sch., El Paso, 1985; substitute tchr. El Paso Sch. Dist., 1986; commd. 2nd lt. U.S. Army, 1983, advanced through grades to capt., 1990-91; plans/exercise officer U.S. Army, Ft. Lewis, Wash., 1990; ops. officer U.S. Army, Ft. Lewis, 1990-1991; dir. Childrens World Learning Ctr., Federal Way, Wash., 1992-94; phys. edn. specialist, tchr. K-6 Kent (Wash.) Elem. Sch., Kent, Wash., 1995—; image cons. Beauti-Control Cosmetics, Tacoma, Wash. Coord. Nat. Conf. Christians and Jews, El Paso, 1979-81; v.p. Jr. Achievement, El Paso, 1980-81; adult tng. vol. Girl Scout Coun., (bd. dirs. Pacific Peaks cou n., 1993—; bd. dir. Jr. League Tacoma, 1993, 94. 3rd Res. Officer Tng. Corps scholar, 1981-83, H.P. Saunder scholar, 1982; recipient Humanitarian Svc. medal Great Fires of Yellowstone, U.S. Army, 1988, Gold award Girl Scouts U.S.A., 1981; decorated Nat. Def. Svc. medal Desert Storm. Mem. NEA, Western Edn. Assn., Assn. U.S. Army, Air Def. Artillery Assn., Zeta Tau Alpha (sec. 1983-85, house mgr. 1984-86), Fellowship of Christian Athletes. Republican. Roman Catholic. Home: 2905 N 14th St Tacoma WA 98406-6905

SUNDSTROM, VIRGIL GLENN, petroleum company executive; b. Sask., Can., Mar. 12, 1928; m. Margaret J. Gelder, Sept. 4, 1950; children: Eric, Gail, Katherine, Barbara. V.p. mktg., then group v.p. mfg. and mktg. Pacific Petroleums Ltd., 1972-79; group v.p. mfg. and mktg. Petro Can. Inc., Calgary, Alta., 1979-82; pres. Sundstrom Enterprises Ltd., 1983—; pres. WWC Trading Ltd, 1989—; pres., chief exec. officer Turbo Resources, Ltd., 1990-91.

SUNDT, HARRY WILSON, construction company executive; b. Woodbury, N.J., July 5, 1932; s. Thoralf Mauritz and Elinor (Stout) S.; m. Dorothy Van Gilder, June 26, 1954; children: Thomas D., Perri Lee Sundt Touche, Gerald W. BS in Bus. Adminstrn., U. Ariz., 1954, postgrad., 1957-59. Salesman ins. VanGilder Agys., Denver, 1956-57; apprentice carpenter M.M. Sundt Constrn. Co., Tucson, 1957-58, estimator, 1958-59; adminstrv. asst. M.M. Sundt Constrn. Co., Vandenberg AFB, 1959-62; sr. estimator M.M. Sundt Constrn. Co., Tucson, 1962-64, div. mgr., 1964-65, exec. v.p., gen. mgr., 1965-75, pres., chmn., 1975-79; pres., chmn. Sundt Corp., Tucson, 1980-83, chmn., chief exec. officer, 1983—; bd. dirs. Tucson Electric Power Co., Magma Copper Co., 1987—. Pres. Tucson Airport Authority, 1982; bd. dirs. U. Ariz. Found. 1981. 1st lt. U.S. Army, 1954-56. Recipient Disting. Citizen award U. Ariz., 1982, Centennial Medallion award, 1989. Mem. Tucson Country Club, Old Pueblo Club. Republican. Episcopalian. Home: 6002 E San Leandro Tucson AZ 85715-3014 Office: Sundt Corp PO Box 26685 4101 E Irvington Rd Tucson AZ 85714-2118

SUOZZI, MARY-ANN, engineering executive; b. N.Y.C., Jan. 1, 1955; d. Joseph John Anthony and Alice (Castillo) S.; m. Mark Daniel Tighe, Jan. 7, 1984; children: Nathan Jeremiah, Sarah Ruth. AAS, Bergen C.C., 1976; BS in Indsl. Engring., U. Ariz., 1985, MS in Reliability Engring., 1989. Mgr. quality control dept. Northfield Cheese Co., Northvale, N.J., 1976-78; supr. quality control inspectors Sherwood Med. Products, Tucson, Ariz., 1978-84; engr. Hughes Aircraft Co., Tucson, 1984-92; leader, mgr. quality control engring dept. Mexico ops. C.R. Bard, Bard Urol. Divsn., Nogales, Ariz., 1992—; mem. bus. stats. and rsch. curriculum com., total quality mgmt./svc. curriculum com. U. Phoenix, Tucson; total quality mgmt. curriculum com. Pima C.C., Tucson; instr., facilitator U. Phoenix,Tucson, 1990—, Pima C.C., Tucson, 1989-90. Author: Bard Urol. Divsn., Mexico Ops. Cert. Supplier Manual. Mem. Am. Soc. Quality Control (sr., cert. reliability engr., cert. quality engr.), Am. Soc. Clin. Pathologists. Home: 6649 E Nelson Dr Tucson AZ 85730-1659 Office: Bard Urol 1840 N Industrial Park Dr Nogales AZ 85621

SUPAN, RICHARD MATTHEW, controller; b. Palo Alto, Calif., June 22, 1953; s. James Arthur and Nancy Ann (Rhein) S.; m. Bernadette Joan Bayer, Sept. 8, 1979; children: Raymond, Valerie, Joanna. AA, Foothill Coll., 1973; BSC, Santa Clara U., 1975, MBA, 1979. Cost acctg. supr. Electron Devices div. Litton Industries, San Carlos, Calif., 1975-78; cost acctg. mgr. Microwave Tube div. Varian Assocs., Palo Alto, Calif., 1978-81, ops. controller, 1981-84; dir. acctg. Varian Assocs., Palo Alto, Calif., 1984-85; controller Electron Device & Systems Group, Varian Assocs., Palo Alto, Calif., 1985-89, Oncology Systems, Varian Assocs., Palo Alto, Calif., 1989—. Mem. Beta Gamma Sigma (hon.). Home: 5915 Amapola Dr San Jose CA 95129-3058 Office: Varian Assocs Inc 911 Hansen Way Palo Alto CA 94304-1028

SUPCHAK, PAUL HENRY, business owner, entrepreneur; b. New Brunswick, N.J., Jan. 24, 1958; s. Henry William and Gene (Lack) S.; m. Hilary Ann Rudolph Boyce, Jan. 15, 1981 (div. Apr. 1985); children: Amanda, Melinda; m. Nanci Beth Stone; children: Christopher, Mark. BS in Phys. Sci./Gen. Engring., U.S. Naval Acad., 1980; Hon. Grad Aviation Safety Sch., Naval Postgrad. Sch., 1989. Commd. USMC, advanced through grades to maj., 1993; scheduling officer VT-26 USMC/USN, NAS Chase Field, Beeville, Tex., 1982-84; asst. maintenance officer, asst. ops. officer USMC, Beaufort, S.C., 1984-87; comdg. officer Hqrs. & Svc. Co., 2nd Bn. USMC, Camp Lejeune, N.C., 87-88; future ops. officer, comdg. officer, dir. safety & stds. USMC, Beaufort, S.C., 1988-92; instr. pilot Air Combat U.S.A., Fullerton, Calif., 1992—. Mem. Nat. Eagle Scout Assn., Mensa. Office: Desert Aces 2772 Rancho Rd Las Vegas NV 89103

SUPPES, COURTNEY MERVIN, hazardous waste executive; b. Edmonton, Alta., Can., Mar. 15, 1962; s. Mervin Harold and Joy Carol (Symonds) S.; m. Suzanne Fay Roquemore, May 16, 1987. BA, U. Denver, 1987. Chmn. All West Surveys, Ltd., Edmonton, Alberta, Can., 1972-85; pres. Nat. Indoor Advt. Can., Toronto, 1985-86; project engr., estimator Diamond Back Svcs., Sedalia, Colo., 1986-87; spl. prjects, hazardous waste mgmt. svc. URS Corp., Denver, 1987; asst. dir. Satellite Ops. AMCEE, Ft. Collins, Colo., 1987-88; project supt. Bechtel-Contract Asbestos Mgmt., San Francisco, 1988-89; mgr. of contract svcs. The Brand Co., Inc., Oakland, Calif., 1989-90; pres., prin., dir. Plant Hazardous Svcs., Emeryville, Calif., 1990—. Mem. Am. Hist. Soc. of Germans From Russian, U. Denver Engring. Soc., Nat. Soc. Profl. Engrs., Big Bros. Assn., Young Republicans, The Commonwealth Club of Calif., Nat. Assn. Environ. Profls., Nat. Asbestos. Office: Plant Hazardous Svcs PO Box 8066 Emeryville CA 94662-0066

SUPPES, PATRICK, statistics, education, philosophy and psychology educator; b. Tulsa, Mar. 17, 1922; s. George Biddle and Ann (Costello) S.; m. Joan Farmer, Apr. 16, 1946 (div. 1970); children: Patricia, Deborah, John Biddle; m. Joan Sieber, Mar. 29, 1970 (div. 1973); m. Christine Johnson, May 26, 1979; children: Alexandra Christine, Michael Patrick. B.S., U. Chgo., 1943; Ph.D. (Wendell T. Bush fellow), Columbia U., 1950; LL.D., U. Nijmegen, Netherlands, 1979; Dr. honoris causa, Académie de Paris, U. Paris V, 1982. Instr., Stanford U., 1950-52, asst. prof., 1952-55, assoc. prof., 1955-59, prof. philosophy, statistics, edn. and psychology, 1959-92, prof. emeritus; founder, chief exec. officer Computer Curriculum Corp., 1967-90. Author: Introduction to Logic, 1957, Axiomatic Set Theory, 1960, Sets and Numbers, books 1-6, 1966, Studies in the Methodology and Foundations of Science, 1969, A Probabilistic Theory of Causality, 1970, Logique du Probable, 1981, Probabilistic Metaphysics, 1984, Estudios de Filosofía y Metodologí de la Ciencia, 1988, Language for Humans and Robots, 1991, Models and Methods in the Philosophy of Science, 1993; (with Davidson and Siegel) Decision Making, 1957, (with Richard C. Atkinson) Markov Learning Models for Multiperson Interactions, 1960, (with Shirley Hill) First Course in Mathematical Logic, 1964, (with Edward J. Crothers) Experiments on Second-Language Learning, 1967, (with Max Jerman and Dow Brian) Computer-assisted Instruction, 1965-66, Stanford Arithmetic Program, 1968, (with D. Krantz, R.D. Luce and A. Tversky) Foundations of Measurement, Vol. 1, 1971, (with M. Morningstar) Computer-Assisted Instruction at Stanford, 1966-68, 1972, (with B. Searle and J. Friend) The Radio Mathematics Project: Nicaragua, 1974-75, 1976 (with D. Krantz, R.D. Luce and A. Tversky) Foundations of Measurement, Vol. 2, 1989, Vol. 3, 1990, (with Colleen Crangle) Language and Learning for Robots, 1994. Served to capt. USAAF, 1942-46. Recipient Nicholas Murray Butler Silver medal Columbia, 1965, Disting. Sci. Contbr. award Am. Psychol. Assn., 1972, Tchrs. Coll. medal for disting. service, 1978, Nat. medal Sci. NSF, 1990; Center for Advanced Study Behavioral Scis. fellow, 1955-56; NSF fellow, 1957-58. Fellow AAAS, Am. Psychol. Assn., Am. Acad. Arts and Scis., Assn. Computing Machinery; mem. NAS, Math. Assn. Am., Psychometric Soc., Am. Philos. Assn., Am. Philos. Soc., Assn. Symbolic Logic, Am. Math Soc., Académie Internationale de Philosophie des Scis. (titular), Nat. Acad. Edn. (pres. 1973-77), Am. Psychol. Assn., Internat. Inst. Philosophy, Finnish Acad. Sci. and Letters, Internat. Union History and Philosophy of Sci. (div. logic, methodology and philosophy of sci., pres. 1975-79), Am. Ednl. Research Assn. (pres. 1973-74), Croatian Acad. Scis. (corr.), Russian Acad. Edn. (fgn.), Norwegian Acad. Sci. and Letters (fgn.), European Acad. Scis. and Arts, Chilean Acad. Scis., Sigma Xi.

SURABIAN, ANN, food products executive; b. 1955. Student, Fresno Coll. V.p. Surabian Packing Co., Reedley, Calif., 1979—. Office: Surabian Packing Co Inc 18700 E South Ave Reedley CA 93654-9711*

SURABIAN, DENNIS G., food products executive; b. 1941. With Crocker Bank, San Francisco, 1962-63; various positions Surabian Packing Co., Reedley, Calif., 1963—, now pres. Office: Surabian Packing Co Inc 18700 E South Ave Reedley CA 93654-9711*

SURAWICZ, CHRISTINA MATHILDA, physician; b. Munich, Jan. 4, 1948; d. Borys and Frida (Vanklaveren) S.; m. James Butler Bushyhead. BA, Barnard Coll., 1969; MD, U. Ky., 1973. Resident in medicine U. Wash. Affiliated Hosp., Seattle, 1973-76, asst. prof. medicine, 1981-86, assoc. prof. medicine, 1986—. Contbr. articles to profl. jours. Fellow Am. Coll. Physicians, Am. Coll. Gastroenterology (governor Washington state 1989-93, sec. 1994—). Office: Harborview Med Ctr 325 9th Ave Seattle WA 98104-2420

SURFACE, STEPHEN WALTER, water treatment chemist, environmental protection specialist; b. Dayton, Ohio, Feb. 25, 1943; s. Lorin Wilfred and Virginia (Marsh) S.; m. Suzanne MacDonald, Aug. 29, 1964 (div.); 1 child, Jennifer Nalani; m. Sinfrosa Garay, Sept. 16, 1978; children: Maria Lourdes, Stephanie Alcantara. BS, Otterbein Coll., 1965; MA, U. So. Calif., 1970; postgrad., U. Hawaii, 1971. Tchr. Hawaii State Dept. Edn., Honolulu, 1970-71; staff chemist Del Monte Corp., Honolulu, 1971; head chemist USNPearl Harbor, Honolulu, 1971-76; staff chemist USN Pearl Harbor, Honolulu, 1976-90; chief office installation svcs., environ. protection Def. Logistics Agy., Camp Smith, Hawaii, 1990—. Contbr. articles to profl. jours. Recipient DuPont Teaching award, U. So. Calif., 1966. Fellow Am. Inst. Chemists; mem. Am. Chem. Soc., Am. Def. Preparedness Assn., N.Y. Acad. Scis., Sigma Xeta, Phi Lambda Upsilon. Democrat. Methodist. Home: 94-1139 Noheaiki St Waipahu HI 96797-4138 Office: Def Logistics Agy DPAC-W Camp Smith HI 96861-4110

SURRELL, KEVIN JOEL, insurance company official; b. L.A., Mar. 7, 1966; s. Joe Willis and Marie Louise (Johns) S.; m. Tracey Janelle Urling, Aug. 13, 1988; 1 child, Chantal Miria. BA in Psychology, UCLA, 1989. Field claim rep. Farmers Ins. Group, Glendale, Calif., 1989-91; realtor Internat. Real Estate Group, Walnut, Calif., 1990-92; realtor, CEO, Century 21 Young, West Covina, Calif., 1992-93; claims rep. ICW/Explorer Ins., Burbank, Calif., 1994-95; asst. mgr. Western Gen. Ins., Encino, 1995—. Mem. Am. Tchrs. Martial Arts Assn., Am. Kenpo Karate Assn (1st degree black belt), Mary B. Thorne Scholarship Club. Office: Western Gen Ins 16501 Ventura Blvd Ste 200 Encino CA 91436

SURWILL, BENEDICT JOSEPH, JR., college dean, educator; b. Chgo., Oct. 8, 1925; s. Benedict Joseph and Emily (Zemgolis) S.; m. Frances May Welling, Oct. 16, 1948; children: Thomas, Benedict, Robert, Patricia; m. Charlene R. McClintock, Feb. 17, 1990; 1 child, Michael McClintock. BS in Edn., Ariz. State Coll., 1951, MS in Edn., 1954; EdD, U. Colo., 1962. Elem. tchr. Winnetka (Ill.) Pub. Schs., 1958-61; jr. high sch. prin. Champaign (Ill.) Pub. Schs., 1961-63; dir. Campus Sch. SUNY, Buffalo, 1963-68; dean. Sch. Edn. Ea. Mont. Coll., Billings, 1968-88, asst. to pres., 1988-91, dean Sch. Edn., prof. edn. emeritus, 1991—; chmn. dean's coun. Mont. Univ. System, 1974; mem. Mont. Supts. Adv. Com. on Tchr. Edn. and Cert., 1969-76, chmn., 1972-73; mem. ednl. forum State Supt. Pub. Instrn., 1977-83, Mont. Rural Youth Adv. Coun., Billings, 1979-81; lectr. in field. Editor: A Critical Examination of American Education, 1985; mem. editorial bd., contbg. editor Jour. Creative Behavior, 1966-93. Co-chmn. cancer drive Billings chpt. Am. Cancer Soc., 1988-89, Mont. State Cancer Crusade, 1989. With inf. U.S. Army. Recipient Am. Assn. of Coll. for Tchr. Edn. award, 1972, Presdl. citation Ill. Assn. Sch. Adminstrs., 1973. Mem. Nat. Coun. Accreditation Tchr. Edn. (mem. standards com., mem. multicultural edn. com. 1977, bd. appeals 1980-83, bd. examiners 1988-90), Elks, Yellowstone Country Club, Phi Delta Kappa, Kappa Delta Pi. Home: 5864 Sam Snead Trl Billings MT 59106-1021

SUSICH, ROBERT STEPHENSON, electrical engineer; b. Chgo., Nov. 25, 1931; s. Tripo and Jennie (Vajnovich) S.; m. Doris Arden Schult, Oct. 10, 1952; children: Stephen, Jeffrey, Donna, Kathy, Karen, Amy, Janet. BSEE, U. Ill., Chgo., 1957; MSEE, MIT, 1959. Engr. AT&T, Chgo., 1955-67; sr. engr. Raytheon, Bedford, Mass., 1967-70; project engr. Control Data, Mpls., 1970-79, Motorola, Tempe, Ariz., 1979-81; test dir. GTE, Kwajalein, Marshall Islands, 1981-84; sr. staff engr. TRW, Sunnyvale, Calif., 1984—; adv. programs mgr., Sunnyvale, 1991—. With USAF, 1951-55. Republican. Serbian East Orthodox. Home: 2294 Shade Tree Ln San Jose CA 95131-1952

SUSKI, SHERRIE LEIGH, human resources specialist; b. Clearwater, Fla., June 29, 1960; d. H. Mark and Sandy Ann (Tyler) Sherwood; m. Edward Daniel Suski, Apr. 16, 1988. BS in Psychology cum laude, U. Calif., Irvine, 1982; MS in Psychology, Calif. State U., 1985. Human resources positions including staffing, employee rels., tng. and compensation, benefits Silicon Systems, Tustin, Calif., 1983-93; dir. human resources SmartFlex Systems, Tustin, Calif., 1993—; educator Irvine (Calif.) Valley Coll., 1988-89. Mem. ASTD, Pers. and Indsl. Rels. Assn., Am. Compensation Assn., Phi Beta Kappa, Alpha Lambda Delta. Office: SmartFlex Systems 14312 Franklin Ave Tustin CA 92680-7028

SUSMAN, ALAN HOWARD, lawyer; b. Buffalo, Apr. 7, 1945; m. Jo Ellen Fisher, Aug. 8, 1970; children: Stephanie, Jennifer. BA, Hobart Coll., 1967; JD, SUNY, Buffalo, 1970. Bar: N.Y. 1971, Ariz. 1973, U.S. Dist. Ct. Ariz. 1973, U.S. Ct. Appeals (9th cir.) 1973, U.S. Supreme Ct. 1978. Assoc. Brizdle & Hankin, Buffalo, 1971-72; appellate law clk. Ariz. Ct. Appeals, Phoenix, 1972-73; atty. Maricopa County Atty.'s Office, Phoenix, 1973-75; ptnr. Schwartz & Susman, P.A., Phoenix, 1975-81; asst. atty. gen. State of Ariz., Phoenix, 1981-84; ptnr. Storey & Ross, P.C., Phoenix, 1984-88, Jaburg & Wilk, Phoenix, 1988—; judge pro tem Superior Ct. State of Ariz., Phoenix, 1986—; instr. Phoenix Coll, 1982, 83. Bd. dirs. Phoenix Jewish Community Ctr., 1985-87. Mem. N.Y. Bar Assn., Assn. Trial Lawyers Am., Ariz. Trial Lawyers Assn., Ariz. Bar Assn. (exec. com. young lawyers sect. 1976-77), Maricopa County Bar Assn., Am. Arbitration Assn. (mem. panel arbitrators). Democrat. Office: Jaburg & Wilk PC 3200 N Central Ave Ste 2000 Phoenix AZ 85012-2440

SUSSKIND, CHARLES, engineering educator, author, publishing executive; b. Prague, Czech Republic; came to U.S., 1945, naturalized, 1946; s. Bruno Bronislav and Gertruda (Seger) S.; m. Teresa Gabriel, May 1, 1945; children: Pamela Susskind Pettler, Peter Gabriel, Amanda Frances. Student, City U., London, 1939-40; B.S., Calif. Inst. Tech., 1948; M.Engring., Yale U., 1949, Ph.D., 1951. Research asst. Yale U., 1949-51; research assoc. Stanford U., 1951-55, lectr., asst. dir. Microwave Lab., 1953-55; mem. faculty U. Calif., Berkeley, 1955—; prof. U. Calif., 1964—, asst. dean Coll. Engring., 1964-68, also statewide adminstr., 1969-74; Vis. prof. U. London, 1961-62, U. Geneva, Switzerland, 1968-69; mem., cons. EPA Sci. Adv. Bd., 1982—; cons. electronics industry, govt., publishers; dir. San Francisco Press, Inc. Author: (with M. Chodorow) Fundamentals of Microwave Electronics, 1964, (with L. Schell) Exporting Technical Education, 1968, Understanding Technology, 1973, 74, 85 (transl. into Dutch, French, Italian, Korean, Spanish), Twenty-five Engineers and Inventors, 1976, (with F. Kurylo) Ferdinand Braun, 1981, (with M. E. Rowbottom) Electricity and Medicine: History of their Interaction, 1984, Janáček and Brod, 1985; editor: (with M. Hertz) Heinrich Hertz: Memoirs, Letters, Diaries, bilingual edit., 1977; editor-in-chief: Ency. Electronics, 1962. Served with USAAF, 1942-45. Named to Hon. Order Ky. Cols. Fellow IEEE; mem. AAAS, History of Sci. Soc., Soc. for History of Tech., Instn. Elec. Engrs. (London), Yale Club of N.Y.C., Faculty Club of Berkeley (bd. dirs. 1972-73), Sigma Xi (pres. Berkeley chpt. 1972-73), Tau Beta Pi. Office: U Calif Coll Engring Berkeley CA 94720-1770

SUSSKIND, TERESA GABRIEL, publisher; b. Watford, Eng., came to U.S., 1945, naturalized, 1948; d. Aaron and Betty (Fox) Gabriel; m. Charles Susskind, May 1, 1945; children: Pamela Pettler, Peter Gabriel, Amanda. Ed. U. London, 1938-40. Profl. libr. Calif. Inst. Tech., Pasadena, 1946-48, Yale U., New Haven, Conn., 1948-51, Stanford U., Calif., 1951-52, SRI Internat., Menlo Park, Calif., 1953; founder, pres. San Francisco Press, Inc., 1959—. With Women's Royal Naval Svc., 1943-45. Author: A Room of One's Own Revisited, 1977. Active in cultural affairs; bd. govs. San Francisco Symphony, 1986-89. Mem. Town and Gown Club (Berkeley, Calif., pres. 1984-85). Office: PO Box 426800 San Francisco CA 94142-6800

SUSSMAN, BRIAN JAY, meteorologist, weather broadcaster; b. L.A., Apr. 3, 1956; s. Alan E. and Beverly A. (Carlson) S.; m. Sue Ann Rittenhouse, June 18, 1978; chilren: Elisa, Samuel, Benjamin. BS, U. Mo., 1978. Reporter, anchor Sta. KCBJ-TV, Columbia, Mo., 1977-80; weather anchor Sta. KOLO-TV, Reno, 1980-83; on-air meteorologist Sta. KNTV-TV, San Jose, Calif., 1983-87, Sta. KDKA-TV, Pitts., 1987-89; substitute weatherman CBS This Morning, N.Y.C., 1988—; on-air meteorologist Sta. KPIX-TV, San Francisco, 1989—. Co-author: (textbook) For Spacious Skies, 1987, rev. edit., 1989. Recipient Best Weathercast award Radio-TV News Dirs. Assn., 1987, 90-94, AP, 1989, 92-94, Advancement of Learning Through Broadcasting award NEA, 1989. Mem. Am. Meteorol. Soc. (Seal of Approval cert.). Office: Sta KPIX-TV 855 Battery St San Francisco CA 94111-1503

SUSSMAN, DEBORAH EVELYN, designer, company executive; b. N.Y.C., May 26, 1931; d. Irving and Ruth (Golomb) S.; m. Paul Prejza, June 28, 1972. Student Bard Coll., 1948-50, Inst. Design, Chgo., 1950-53, Black Mountain Coll., 1950, Hochschule für Gestaltung Ulm, Fed. Republic Germany, 1957-58. Art dir. Office of Charles and Ray Eames, Venice, Calif., 1953-57, 61-67; graphic designer Galeries Lafayette, Paris, 1959-60; prin. Deborah Sussman and Co., Santa Monica, Calif., 1968-80; founder, pres. Sussman-Prejza and Co., Inc., Santa Monica, 1980-90, Culver City, Calif., 1990—; speaker, lectr. UCLA Sch. Architecture, Archtl. League N.Y.C., Smithsonian Inst., Stanford Conf. on Design, Am. Inst. Graphic Arts Nat. Conf. at MIT, Design Mgmt. Inst. Conf., Mass.; spl. guest Internat. Design Conf., Aspen, Colo., Fulbright lectr., India, 1976; speaker NEA Adv. Coun.,

1985, Internat. Coun. Shopping Ctrs., 1986, USIA Design in Am. seminar, Budapest, Hungary, 1988, participant exhbn., Moscow, 1989, Walker Art Ctr., Mpls., 1989. Mem. editorial adv. bd. Arts and Architecture Mag., 1981-85, Calif. Mag., Architecture Calif. Fulbright grantee Hochschule für Gestaltung Ulm, 1957-58; recipient numerous awards AIA Nat. Inst. Honors, 1985, 88, Am. Inst. Graphic Arts, Calif. Coun. AIA, Communications Arts Soc., L.A. County Bd. Suprs., Vesta award Women's Bldg. L.A. Fellow Soc. Environ. Graphic Design; mem. AIA (hon.), Am. Inst. Graphic Arts (bd. dirs. 1982-85, founder L.A. chpt., chmn., 1983-84, numerous awards), L.A. Art Dirs. Club (bd. dirs., numerous awards), Alliance Graphique Internat. (elect. mem.), Architects, Designers and Planners Social Responsibility, Calif. Women in Environ. Design (adv. bd.), Trusteeship (affiliate Internat. Women's Forum, chmn.'s circle Town Hall), SEGD. Democrat. Jewish. Avocation: photography. Office: Sussman/Prejza & Co Inc 3960 Ince Blvd Culver City CA 90232-2635

SUSSMAN, MARK ALAN, cell biologist, educator; b. Burbank, Calif., Nov. 14, 1959; s. Paul and Henrietta (Bass) S.; m. Valerie Gaye Marshall, May 29, 1988; children: Eliza, Morgan. BS in Biol. Sci., U. Calif., Davis, 1981; MS in Biology, Calif. State U., Northridge, 1983; PhD in Microbiology, U. So. Calif., 1988. Rsch. asst. U. Calif., Davis, 1980-81; lab. instr. Calif. State. U., Northrdige, 1982-83; postdoctoral fellow Scripps Rsch. Inst., La. Jolla, Calif., 1988-91; grad. asst. U. So. Calif., L.A., 1983-88, rsch. fellow, 1991-93, asst. prof. cell biology, 1993—. Contbr. articles to Devel. Brain Rsch., Circulation Rsch., Exptl. Cell Rsch., others. Am. Heart Assn. grantee, 1993, 94; Muscular Dystrophy Assn. fellow, 1991. Mem. Am. Soc. for Cell Biology, Sigma Xi, Sigma Alpha Mu. Jewish. Office: U So Calif Dept Biochemistry 2025 Zonal Ave Los Angeles CA 90033-4526

SUSSMAN, NEIL A., lawyer; b. N.Y.C., Jan. 26, 1956; s. Herbert and Ruth S.; m. Suzanne R. Thompson, Aug. 31, 1990; 1 child, Annabelle R.T. BS in Econs., U. Pa., 1978; JD, U. Wash., 1982. Bar: Wash. 1982. Atty. pvt. practice, Seattle, 1982—. Mem. Wash. State Bar Assn., King County Bar Assn. Office: 10727 Interlake Ave N Seattle WA 98133-8907

SUSSMAN, WENDY RODRIGUEZ, artist, educator; b. N.Y.C., June 3, 1949. BA, Empire State Coll., 1978; MFA, Bklyn. Coll., 1980. Lectr. Touro Coll., N.Y.C., 1985-86, Pratt Inst., Bklyn., 1987-89; asst. prof. U. Calif., Berkeley, 1989—. One-woman shows include Bowery Gallery, N.Y.C., 1982, 87, D.P. Fong Gallery, San Jose, Calif., 1994; exhibited in group shows in Bowery Gallery, 1980-88, Platt Gallery U. of Judaism, L.A., 1995, Munson-Williams-Proctor Inst. Mus. Art, 1982, 86, Reading (Pa.)(Pub. Mus. and Art Gallery, 1983, Queens Mus., N.Y.C., 1983, Colby Coll. Mus. Art, Waterville, Maine, 1983, Butler Inst. Am. Art, Youngstown, Ohio, 1983, Bklyn. Coll., 1983, Am. Acad. Inst. Arts and Letters, N.Y.C., 1984, Am. Acad. in Rome, 1987, John Berggruen Gallery, San Francisco, 1992, San Francisco Arts Commn. Gallery, 1992, 94, D.P. Fong Gallery, 1994. Rome Prize fellow in painting Am. Acad. in Rome, 1986-87, Visual Arts fellow Nat. Endowment for Arts, 1989; Pollock-Krasner grantee Pollock-Krasner Found., 1988. Office: U Calif Berkeley Dept Art Berkeley CA 94720

SUTCLIFFE, ERIC, lawyer; b. Calif., Jan. 10, 1909; s. Thomas and Annie (Beare) S.; m. Joan Basché, Aug. 7, 1937; children: Victoria, Marcia, Thomas; m. Marie C. Paige, Nov. 1, 1975. AB, U. Calif. at Berkeley, 1929, LLB, 1932. Bar: Calif. 1932. Mem. firm Orrick, Herrington & Sutcliffe, San Francisco, 1943-85, mng. ptnr., 1947-78. Trustee, treas., v.p. San Francisco Law Libr., 1974-88; founding fellow The Oakland Mus. of Calif.; bd. dirs. Merritt Peralta Found., 1988. Fellow Am. Bar Found (life); mem. ABA (chmn state regulation securities com. 1960-65), San Francisco Bar Assn. (chmn. corp. law com., 1964-65), San Francisco C. of C. (past treas., dir.), State Bar Calif., Pacific Union Club, Bohemian Club, Phi Gamma Delta, Phi Delta Phi, Order of Coif. Home: 260 King Ave Oakland CA 94610-1231 Office: Old Fed Reserve Bank Bldg 400 Sansome St San Francisco CA 94111-3308

SUTER, BEN, lawyer; b. Sacramento, Dec. 14, 1954; s. Alexander Frederick and Anne Ida (De Bergen) S.; m. Lizanne Bouchard, Dec. 23, 1979; children: Tycho Benjamin, Hadley Theadora, Miles Kepler, Rex Sebastian. BA in Philosophy, U. Calif., Santa Barbara, 1978; JD, U. Calif., San Francisco, 1982. Bar: Calif. 1982, U.S. Dist. Ct. (cen., ea., no. and so. dists.) Calif. 1982, Ariz. 1983, Hawaii 1984, U.S. Dist. Ct. Ariz. 1990, U.S. Supreme Ct. 1987. Assoc. Keesal, Young & Logan, San Francisco and Long Beach, Calif., 1982-87, ptnr., 1987—. Office: Keesal Young & Logan 4 Embarcadero Ctr San Francisco CA 94111-4106

SUTER, PEGGY JEAN, library director; b. Wilburton, Okla., July 18, 1937; d. Henry Paul and Violet Jessie Eads; m. James William Suter, May 15, 1954; children: Pauline Jeanette Owens, Jo Lavonne Ahlm. Grad., Hartshorne (Okla.) H.S., 1955. Cert. grade I libr., N.Mex. Piano tchr. Lovington, N.Mex., 1968-72, Eunice, N.Mex., 1973-88; kindergarten music tchr. First Meth. Ch., Lovington, 1970-73; substitute sch. tchr. Eunice Pub. Schs., 1978-81; libr. dir. Eunice Pub. Libr., 1981—. Organist First Meth. Ch., Eunice, 1982—. Mem. Am. Libr. Assn., N.Mex. Libr. Assn. (community Svc. award 1992), Lea County Libr. Assn. (v.p. 1982, pres. 1983, treas. 1984). Democrat. Methodist. Office: Eunice Pub Libr Corner of 10th and Ave Eunice NM 88231

SUTHERLAND, BRUCE, composer, pianist; b. Daytona Beach, Fla.; s. Kenneth Francis and Norma (Williams) S.; Mus.B., U. So. Calif., 1957, Mus.M., 1959; studies with Halsey Stevens, Ellis Kohs, Ethel Leginska, Amparo Iturbi. Harpsichord soloist with Telemann Trio in concert tour, 1969-70; tchr. master class for pianists U. Tex., Austin, 1971; dir. Bach festivals Music Tchrs. Assn. Calif., 1972-73, dir. Artists of Tomorrow Music Festivals Music Tchrs. Assn. Calif., 1984—, competitions performed in numerous contemporary music festivals in U.S., 1957—; piano faculty Calif. State U. at Northridge, 1977—; adjudicator music competitions and auditions Nat. Guild Piano Tchrs., others; dir. Brentwood-Westwood Symphony ann. competition for young artists, 1981—; composer: Allegro Fanfara for Orch., world premiere conducted by José Iturbi with Bridgeport Symphony Orch., 1970; Saxophone Quartet, 1971; Quintet for Flute, Strings, Piano, 1972; Notturno for Flute and Guitar, 1973; also string trio, piano and vocal works. Recipient grand prize Internat. Competition Louis Moreau Gottschalk, 1970; Stairway of Stars award Music Arts Soc., Santa Monica, 1973; named one of Los Angeles' Finest Piano Tchrs., New West Mag., 1977; honored as Dist. Tchr. of Anders Martinson, presdl. scholar in arts, 1991; honored by Nat. Found. Advancement Arts 1989, 91, 93. Mem. Nat. Assn. Am. Composers and Condrs., Music Tchrs. Nat. Assn., Music Tchrs. Assn., Calif. Assn. Profl. Music Tchrs., Pi Kappa Lambda.

SUTHERLAND, JOHN CAMPBELL, pathologist, educator; b. Tamingfu, Hopei, People's Republic of China, Oct. 28, 1921; came to U.S., 1926; s. Francis Campbell and Ann Findlay (Bowman) S.; m. Eunice Lucille Kindschi, June 16, 1950; 1 child, John Mark. AB, N.W. Nazarene Coll., 1941; MD, Med. Coll. Wis., 1946. Intern Milw. Hosp., 1946-47; resident in pathology St. Francis Hosp., Wichita, Kans., 1950-52, Barnes Hosp., St. Louis, 1952-54, Stanford (Calif.) Med. Ctr., 1967-68; gen. practitioner Mangum Clinic, Nampa, Idaho, 1949-50; gen. med. officer Raleigh Fitkin Meml. Hosp., Manzini, Swaziland, 1955-56, Ethel Lucas Meml. Hosp., Acornhoek, South Africa, 1956-61, 62-67; acting head biology dept. N.W. Nazarene Coll., Nampa, 1961-62; head rsch. pathology dept. Balt. Cancer Rsch. Ctr., 1968-74; asst. prof. dept. pathology U. Md., Balt., 1974-76, assoc. prof., 1976-84, mem. grad. faculty, 1982-84; vis. assoc. prof. dept. surgery U. Ariz., Tucson, 1984—. Co-author: Guinea Pig Doctors, 1984; contbr. articles to sci. jours. Capt. USAF, 1947-49. Mem. Alumni Assn. of N.W. Nazarene Coll. (Profl. Achievement award 1984), Toastmasters, Gideons. Republican. Mem. Nazarene Ch. Home: 3411 S Camino Seco Unit 337 Tucson AZ 85730-2829 Office: Univ Ariz Dept Surgery 1501 N Campbell Ave Tucson AZ 85724-0001

SUTHERLAND, MICHAEL CRUISE, librarian; b. Morgantown, W.Va., Aug. 29, 1938; s. Charles Fish and Mildred (Haymond) S. BA in English, San Fernando Valley State U., 1967, postgrad., 1968-69; postgrad., UCLA, 1967, MLS, 1970. Office asst., clk. Lindsay & Hall, L.A., 1959-60; libr. asst. I, bindery clk. Biomed. Libr. UCLA, 1961-65; jr. adminstrv. asst. Dept. Pub. Works City of L.A., 1967; intermediate clk. typist San Fernando Valley State U., Northridge, Calif., 1967-69; libr. I, tchg. asst. Grad. Sch. Libr. and Info. Sci. UCLA, 1970; spl. collections libr. Occidental Coll., L.A., 1970—; attendee numerous workshops and seminars; organizer Western Books Exhbn. at various librs. throughout the Western U.S., 1992, 94, judging organizer, 1993. Author numerous exhbn. catalog booklets; author: (with others) Encyclopedia of Library and Information Sciences, 1979, Western Books Exhibition Catalog, 1986, Striking Research Gold: Distinguished Collections in California Independent Academic Libraries, 1988; contbr. articles to profl. jours. Active Neighborhood Watch, AIDS Quilt Program. Mem. ALA (rare books and mag. divsn.), Rounce and Coffin club (sec., treas.). Office: Occidental Coll Mary Clapp Libr 1600 Campus Rd Los Angeles CA 90041-3384

SUTICH, TIMOTHY JAY, small business owner; b. Seattle, Jan. 19, 1955; s. James N. and Barbara M. (Nigro) S.; m. Susan A. Smith, Apr. 4, 1992; 1 child, Griffin Jay. BA in Bus., U. Wash., 1978. V.p. Nigro Optical Labs., Kent, Wash., 1978-85; CEO, pres. Nouveau Vision, Inc., Redmond, Wash., 1986—.

SUTTER, DIANE, radio and television group executive; b. Pitts., Dec. 9, 1950; d. George Edward and Dorothy Ann (Deckard) S.; m. James M. Stuart, Sept. 21, 1974 (div. Nov. 1984). BA in Polit. Sci., Allegheny Coll., 1972; MS in Pub. Rels., Am. U., 1974. Pub. rels. Congressman William S. Conover from 27th Dist. Pa., Washington, 1972; press sec. Congressman Robert P. Hanrahan from 3d Dist. Ill., Washington, 1973; dir. communications D.C. Bicentennial, Washington, 1975; acct. exec. Sta. WPEZ, Pitts., 1975-78, sales mgr., 1978-79; v.p., mgr. Sta. WTKN/WWSW, Pitts., 1979-83, v.p., gen. mgr., 1983-88; corp. v.p., gen. mgr. Sta. WWSW-AM-FM, 1988-89; corp. v.p., gen mgr. Sta. WTVQ-TV (ABC affiliate), Lexington, Ky., 1989-91; exec. v.p. ops. Shamrock Broadcasting, Inc., Burbank, Calif., 1991-93; pres. Shamrock Television, Burbank, Calif., 1994—; chmn. ABC Talk Radio Affiliate Bd., 1983-87. Contbr. articles to various newspapers. Mem. adv. bd. Women's Polit. Caucus, Allegheny County, Pitts., 1979-89; bd. dirs. United Way of Bluegrass, 1990-91, Jr. Achievement of Bluegrass, 1990-91, Support Ctr. for Cancer, 1988-90. Mem. Am. Women in Radio and TV (nat. sec., treas. 1982-84, nat. pres.-elect 1987-88, nat. pres. 1988-89, Nat. Achievement award 1994), Pitts. Radio Orgn. (pres. 1982-83), Pitts. Radio/TV Club (dir. 1979-84), Nat. Assn. Broadcasters (legis. com. 1983—), Pa. Assn. Broadcasters (dir. 1983-87), TV Assn. of Bluegrass (pres. 1989-90), Hollywood Women's Polit. Com. Republican. Methodist. Office: Shamrock Television 4444 W Lakeside Dr Burbank CA 91505-4054

SUTTER, HARVEY MACK, engineer, consultant; b. Jennings, La., Oct. 5, 1906; s. Josiah Harvey and Effie Relief (Murray) S.; AB, U. Wichita, 1932; m. Julia Genevieve Wright, Sept. 19, 1936; children: James Houston, Robert Mack, Julia Ann Boyd, John Norman. Design and prodn. engr. Boeing Aircraft, Wichita, Kans., 1936-38; supr. arts, crafts and coop. activities Bur. Indian Affairs, U.S. Dept. of Interior, 1938-42, chief procurement br. Bur. of Reclamation, Washington, 1946-54, chief div. procurement and property mgmt., 1954-58; asst. to adminstr. Bonneville Power Adminstrn., 1958-61, asst. to chief engr., 1962-66; cons. engr., 1967—; analyst, chief prodn. service WPB, Denver, 1942-44; chief div. supply C.E., Denver, 1944-46. Mem. exec. bd. Portland area Boy Scouts Am. Recipient Silver Beaver award. Presbyterian. Mem. Nat., Western woodcarvers assns., Internat. Wood Collectors Soc., Electric of Oreg. Author or co-author books and articles on woodcarving. Home: 3803 SE Carlton St Portland OR 97202-7635

SUTTERBY, LARRY QUENTIN, internist; b. North Kansas City, Mo., Sept. 11, 1950; s. John Albert and Wilma Elizabeth (Henry) S.; m. Luciana Risos Magpuri, July 5, 1980; children: Leah Lourdes, Liza Bernadette. BA in Chemistry, William Jewell Coll., 1972; MD, U. Mo., Kans. City, 1976. Diplomate Am. Bd. Internal Medicine, Am. Bd. Geriatrics. Resident in internal medicine Mt. Sinai Hosp., Chgo., 1976-79; physician Mojave Desert Health Svc., Barstow, Calif., 1979-86; pvt. practice Barstow, 1986—; med. dir. Mojave Valley Hospice, 1983—, Rimrock Villa Convalescent Hosp., Barstow, VNA Hospice, Optioncare Home Health Svcs. Recipient Loving Care award Vis. Nurse Assn. Inland Counties, 1988. Mem. AMA, ACP, Am. Diabetes Assn., Calif. Med. Assn., San Bernardino County Med. Soc., Am. Soc. Internal Medicine, Am. Geriatric Soc., Acad. Hospice Physicians, Soc. Gen. Internal Medicine, Am. Numismatic Assn., Nat. Hospice Orgn., S.W. Kansas City Clin. Soc., Combined Orgns., Numismatic Error Collectors Am. Democrat. Roman Catholic. Office: 209 N 2nd Ave Barstow CA 92311-2222

SUTTERFIELD, KEVIN JAMES, lawyer, consultant; b. Long Beach, Calif., July 16, 1955; s. George Washington Sutterfield Jr. and Faun (Memmott) Hughes; m. Paula Sowards, May 20, 1987; children: Ashley, Hailey, Nathaniel, Taylor, Morgan. BA, Brigham Young U., 1979, JD, 1982. Bar: Utah 1982, U.S. Dist. Ct. Utah 1982, U.S. Ct. Appeals (10th cir.) 1984. Assoc. Dart & Stegall, Salt Lake City, 1982-83; assoc. Ray G. Martineau, Salt Lake City, 1983-86; mem. Howard, Lewis & Petersen, Provo, Utah, 1987-94; mem., founder Hickinger & Sutterfield, P.C., 1994—. Contbr. articles to profl. jours. Organizer, incorporator, gen. counsel, trustee Nat. Kidney Found. Utah, 1986-88. Mem. ATLA, Utah Trial Lawyers Assn. (bd. dirs. 1992—, editor in chief Utah Trial Jour. 1993—), Utah Bar Assn., Utah Cen. Bar Assn., Cougar Club, Riverside Country Club. Democrat. Mormon. Office: Flickinger & Sutterfield 2750 N University Ave Provo UT 84604

SUTTLES, VIRGINIA GRANT, advertising executive; b. Urbana, Ill., June 13, 1931; d. William Henry and Lenora (Fitzsimmons) Grant; m. John Henry Suttles, Sept. 24, 1977; step-children: Linda Suttles Daniels, Peg Suttles La Croix, Pamela Suttles Diaz, Randall. Grad. pub. schs., Mahomet, Ill. Media estimator and Procter & Gamble budget control Tatham-Laird, Inc., Chgo., 1955-60; media planner, supr. Tracy-Locke Co., Inc., Dallas and Denver, 1961-68; media dir., account exec. Lorie-Lotito, Inc., 1968-72; v.p., media dir. Sam Lusky Assos., Inc., Denver, 1972-86; ind. media buyer, 1984-89; mktg. asst. mktg. dept. Del E. Webb Communities, Inc., Sun City West, Ariz., 1985-88, with telemarketing dept., 1989-90, homeowner coord., 1993—; mktg. coord. asst./media buyer, Del Webb Corp., Phoenix, 1990-93; lectr. sr. journalism class U. Colo., Boulder, 1975-80; condr. class in media seminars Denver Advt. Fedn., 1974, 77; Colo. State U. panelist Broadcast Day, 1978, High Sch. Inst., 1979, 80, 81, 82, 83. Founder, Del E. Webb Meml. Hosp. Found.; patron founder Tree of Life Nat. Kidney Found. of Colo.- Rockies Snow Mountain YMCA Ranch, Winter Park, Colo. Mem. Denver Advt. Fedn. (bd. dir. 1973-75, program chmn. 1974-76, 80-82, exec. bd., v.p. ops. 1980-81, chmn. Alfie awards com. 1980-81, advt. profl. of Yr. 1981-82), Denver Advt. Golf Assn. (v.p. 1976-77, pres. 1977-78), Colo. Broadcasters Assn., Sun City West Bowling Assn. (bd. dirs. 1987-88), Am. Legion Aux., VFW Aux., Air Force Sgt.'s Assn. Aux., Sun City West Women's Social Club. Republican. Congregationalist. Club: Denver Broncos Quarterback. Home: 20002 N Greenview Dr Sun City West AZ 85375-5579 Office: Del Webb Communities Inc 13001 Maker Blvd Sun City West AZ 85375

SUTTON, BARBARA POWDERLY, marketing executive, consultant, author; b. Scranton, Pa., Oct. 29, 1940; d. Eugene Thomas and Kathryn Dorothy (Loftus) Powderly. Student, Miami (Fla.)-Dade Jr. Coll., 1960. Ordained minister, 1992. Asst. controller Oak Ridge, Inc., Hialeah, Fla., 1959-63; v.p., media dir. Harold Gardner Assocs., Inc., Miami Beach, Fla., 1963-67; media dir., adminstrv. asst. Stern, Hays & Lang Advt., Inc., Miami, 1967-69; exec. asst. Los Angeles Times, 1969-71; media dir., adminstrv. asst. Greenman Advt., Inc., Hollywood, Fla., 1971-73; asst. to gen. mgr. Sta. WGMA-FM, Hollywood, 1974; with acctg. and settlement dept. Fed. Res. Bank, Miami, 1974-75; bus. mgr. Impart Pub. Corp., Reno, 1975-76; adminstrv. asst., office mgr. Edn. Advancement Inst., Reno, 1976-78; ind. contractor Du-Bar Internat., Reno, 1979-80; pres. Capital Advt., Reno, 1980-81; dir. media Mktg. Systems Internat., Reno, 1981-82; owner Dolphin Secretarial Service, Reno, 1982-88, Dolphin Services, Reno, 1983-88, Powderly Assocs., Reno, 1982—; pres. Bus.-Promotional Services, Inc., Reno, 1986-89; ptnr. Investigative Rsch. Report Svcs., Sedona, Ariz., 1993-94, B & B Graphics, Sedona, 1991-94, Beyond Belief Metaphysical & Spiritual Resources, Sedona, 1991-94, Megatrends Mktg. Assocs., Sedona, 1991-93, Atkinson Fine Artist's Reps., Sedona, 1992-94; adminstrv. asst. U. Colo., Boulder, 1994—; speaker Mktg. Fedn., Inc., N.Y.C., 1986; seminar developer and presenter Advt. and Mktg. for Small Bus., U. Nev. Small Bus. Ctr., 1987-88; editor non-fiction books Atkinson World Pub., Sedona, Longmont, Colo., 1992-94; writer, researcher non-fiction studies. Bd. dirs. March of Dimes, Reno, 1982; mem. Presdl. Task Force, Washington, 1983-85, Reno Women's Network, 1982-84; appointed commr. Reno Commn. on Status of Women, 1987-88. Named one of 2,000 Women of Achievement, London, 1971. Mem. Entrepreneurial Women of Reno (rec. sec., bd. dirs. 1987-88). Metaphysician.

SUTTON, CHARLES RICHARD, architect, designer; b. Sand Springs, Okla., June 25, 1927; s. Charles A. and Violet L. Sutton; m. Jean Rector, Dec. 18, 1949; children: John Isaac, Adam Franklin. BArch, Okla. State U., 1950; MArch, Cranbrook Acad. Art, Bloomfield Hills, Mich., 1954. Draftsman Parr & Aderhold, Oklahoma City, 1950-53; draftsman/designer Coston, Frankfurt & Short, Oklahoma City, 1954-55; designer I.M. Pei & Assocs., N.Y.C., 1957-62; designer/office dir. John Carl Warnecke & Assocs., Washington, Honolulu, 1962-68; pres. Charles R. Sutton & Assocs. Inc., Honolulu, 1968-85; ptnr. Sutton Candia Ptnrs., Honolulu, 1985—; lectr. in design Columbia U., 1958-62; cons. Honolulu Waterfront Master Plan, 1984; mem. design rev. bd. Kaanapali Resort, Maui, Hawaii, 1985, Kapolei New Town, Oahu, Hawaii, 1991. Archtl. designer East West Ctr., 1961, Hawaii State Capitol, 1962-68; planning designer Honolulu Capitol Dist., 1965-68; architect Aloha Tower Pla,1974-78. Founding mem., v.p. Hist. Hawaii Found.; bd. dirs. Kakaako Improvement Assn., Hawaii, 1990—. Recipient 1st prize Kalakaua Comml. Area Competition (Bishop Estate), 1971; Lloyd Warren fellow Nat. Inst. for Archtl. Edn., N.Y., Paris, 1955-56. Fellow AIA (pres. Hawaii sect. 1973, fellowship 1980); mem. Waikiki Yacht Club (commodore 1984). Mem. Christian Ref. Ch. Home: 3077 Wailani Rd Honolulu HI 96813-1005

SUTTON, MARCELLA FRENCH, interior designer; b. Prague, Czechoslovakia, Sept. 4, 1946; came to U.S., 1952, naturalized, 1956; d. Eugen E. and Frances V. (Pruchovia) French; BS in Profl. Arts, Woodbury U., 1971; m. Michael D. Sutton, Feb. 11, 1978; 1 child, Kevin Christopher. Mgr. design dept. W. & J. Sloane, Beverly Hills, Calif., 1972-76; project dir. Milton I. Swimmer, Beverly Hills, 1977-78; owner, interior designer Marcella French Designs, Woodland Hills and La Crescenta, Calif., 1969-94; owner designer project mgr., constrn. and design Marcella French Designs, 1994—, prin. designer; property mgmt. coord., interior designer Home Savs. and Loan., State of Calif., L.A., 1979-82; regional premises officer, asst. v.p. regional hdqrs. Bank Am., L.A., 1981-86; v.p. M.D. Sutton Ins. Agy.; cons. pvt. residences, comml. bldgs., office and banks. Project mgr., 1st v.p. fundraising Shephard of the Valley Sch., 1989-90, enrichment chmn., 1990-91, mem. enrichment program pub. sch. calendar, 1991; active Young Reps., Vinyard Ch.; treas. West Hills Baseball Aux., 1989-91; arcades coord. Theatre Arts Festival for Youth, Agoura, 1992-94, co-chmn. ways and means RTRWF, 1992-94; treas. Taxpayers United for Fairness, 1994—; co-organizer 9th Grade Parent Network Orgn. & Found., Chaminade, 1994-95. Recipient various scholarships.

SUTTON, ROBERT EDWARD, investment company executive; b. Burlington, Vt., July 3, 1943; s. Rollin Robert and Blanche Margaret (Deforge) S.; m. Julie Robin Levine, Feb. 1, 1975; children: Katherine Vanessa, David Robert. BA in Econs., St. Michaels Coll., 1962-66. V.p. Compretic, Inc., Beverly Hills, Calif., 1967-70; brokerage cons. Conn. Gen. Life Ins. Co., Denver, 1970-74; pres. The Core Corp., Denver, 1975-80; mng. dir. Willshire Investments & Holding Co., Denver, 1981-91; pres., chmn. Gen. Capital, Inc., Denver, 1991-93; pres, CEO WK Capital Advisors, Inc., Denver, 1993—; dir. NAt. Assn. Indep. Contr., Denver. 1991—, Nat. Endowment Trust, Denver, 1990—, Tri Corp, Denver, 1980-89, Nat. Acceptance Corp., L.A., 1991—, Nat. Investment Holdings, L.A., 1990—. Mem. Nat. Rep. Eagles, Washington, 1986-90, Inner Circle, Washington, 1985-90, Denver Ctr. Performing Arts, 1976-86. Mem. Am. Cancer League, Glenmoor Country Club. Home: 57 Glenmoor Cir Cherry Hl Vlg CO 80110-7121 Office: WK Capital Advisors Inc Ste 650 3773 Cherry Creek Dr Denver CO 80209

SUTTON, SAMUEL J., lawyer, educator; b. Chgo., July 21, 1941; s. Samuel J. and Elaine (Blossom) S.; m. Anne V. Sutton, Aug. 28, 1965; children: Paige, Jean, Leah, Jepson. BA in History and Philosophy, U. Ariz., 1964, BSEE, 1967; JD, George Washington U., 1969. Bar: Ariz. 1969, D.C. 1970, U.S. Ct. Appeals (fed. cir.) 1983. Patent atty. Gen. Electric Co., Washington, Phoenix, 1967-70; ptnr. Cahill, Sutton & Thomas, Phoenix, 1970—; prof. law Ariz. State U., Tempe, 1975—; expert witness Fed. Dist. Cts., 1983—; trial cons. to numerous lawyers, 1972—; v.p. engring. Shintech, Inc., 1991—; arbitrator Am. Arbitration Assn., Phoenix, 1971—. Author: Patent Preparation, 1976, Intellectual Property, 1978, Art Law, 1988, Law, Science and Technology, 1991, Licensing Intangible Property, 1994, Commercial Torts, 1995. Chmn. air pollution hearing bd. City of Phoenix, 1970-85. Recipient Patent prize Patent Resources Group, 1979, Publ. award IEEE, 1967, Genematus award U. Ariz., 1964, Disting. Achievement award Ariz. State U., 1980, Construct Sculpture prize, 1989. Office: Cahill Sutton & Thomas 2141 E Highland Ave Ste 155 Phoenix AZ 85016-4737

SUTTON-JONES, SUE, quality systems executive; b. Charlotte, N.C., Aug. 4, 1952; d. Henry Marion and Betty Joane (McKee) Sutton; m. Thomas Buckner Jones, Aug. 3, 1975; children: Anne Buckner, Sara Lynch, Thomas Buckner, Margaret Pearman. BA in Biochemistry, Queens Coll., 1974; student, Temple U., 1985-86, U. Wis., 1991, George Washington U., 1992. Tech. B level Med. Coll. Va., Richmond, 1975-76; sr. tech. Baxter-Travenol Labs., Round Lake, Ill., 1981-82; quality assurance validation supv. Micromedic Sys., Horsham, Pa., 1986-88; quality assurance assoc., mgr. Cintichem, Inc., Tuxedo, N.Y., 1988-90; sr. corporate quality assurance auditor, mgr. quality tech. Pfizer Hosp. Products Group, N.Y., 1990-92; v.p. quality sys. divsn. Biometric Rsch. Inst., Arlington, Va., 1992-94; v.p. regulatory affairs and quality assurance Telectronics Pacing Sys., Denver, 1994—. Mem. Am. Soc. Quality Control (cert. auditor 1989, cert. engr. 1990), Regulatory Affairs Profls. Soc., Parenteral Drug Assn. Republican. Roman Catholic. Office: Telectronics Pacing Sys 7400 S Tucson Way Englewood CO 80112-3938

SUVAL, WILLIAM DAVID, vascular surgeon; b. Jersey City, N.J., June 27, 1949; s. Robert and Rosalie (Grief) S.; m. Mary Julia Boyd, Oct. 5, 1982 (div. May 1994); 1 child, Maggie Boyd; m. Diane Sue Means, July 23, 1994. AB, Rutgers Coll., 1971; student, U. San Francisco, 1973-74; MD, U. Medicine and Dentistry N.J., 1979. Diplomate Am. Bd. Surgery (vascular surgery, surg. critical care). Intern Johns Hopkins U., Balt. City Hosps., 1979-80; resident in gen. surgery U. Medicine and Dentistry N.J., Newark, 1978-85, fellow in vascular surgery, 1985-87, surg. rsch. fellow, 1982-83, jr. surg. oncology fellow, 1983-84, adminstrv. chief resident dept. surgery, 1984-85, clin. instr. II dept. surgery, 1981-87, asst. prof. surgery, 1987-89; pvt. practice Ctrl. Vascular Assocs., Bricktown, N.J., 1988-89; vascular surgeon Redlands (Calif.) Cmty. Hosp., 1993—, St. Mary's Hosp., Apple Valley, Calif., 1993—, Victor Valley Hosp., Victorville, Calif., 1993—, Moreno Valley (Calif.) Community Hosp., 1993—; attending in surgery Ocean County Med. Ctr., Point Pleasant, N.J., 1988-89, East Orange (N.J.) Vet. Hosp., 1987-90, Barstow Cmty. Hosp., 1990—; bd. dirs./trustees Mojave Desert Med. Group, Found. Health Care of San Bernardino; chief of surgery Moreno Valley Med. Ctr., 1994—; conf. speaker. Contbg. author: Vascular Surgery: Principles and Practice, 1993; contbr. articles, abstracts to profl. jours. NIH Biomed. Rsch. Support grantee, 1987-88; recipient Peter B. Samuels award Soc. Clin. Vascular Surgery, 1987. Fellow ACS (N.J. chpt. 2d prize Resident Rsch. award 1984); mem. AMA, Am. Coll. Physician Execs., Soc. Critical Care Medicine, Calif. Med. Assn., Assn. Acad. Surgery, Riverside County Med. Soc., San Bernardino County Med. Soc., Alpha Omega Alpha. Office: William D Suval MD 15201 11th St Ste 300 Victorville CA 92392-3735

SUYETSUGU, GRACE TAMIKO, nurse; b. San Mateo, Calif., Feb. 16, 1957; d. Frank Takiji and Mitsuka (Shimizu) S. BS magna cum laude in Nursing, San Francisco State U., 1979. RN, Calif. Charge nurse med./surg. unit Peninsula Hosp. and Med. Ctr., Burlingame, Calif., 1979-84, staff nurse ICU, 1984-88, charge nurse ICU, 1988-91, staff nurse endoscopy and ICU, 1991-92, staff nurse recovery rm. and same day surgery, 1992—. Mem. AACN, Nat. Nurses Assn., Calif. Nurses Assn., Post Anesthesia Nurses Assn. Calif. Democrat. Buddhist. Avocations: travel, photography, cooking, needlework, sports. Home: 3682 Bobwhite Ter Fremont CA 94555-1524

Office: Peninsula Hosp and Med Ctr 1783 El Camino Real Burlingame CA 94010-3205

SUZUKI, JOHN PATRICK, biochemist; b. Modesto, Calif., Mar. 21, 1952; s. Shigeru and Star (Kaji) S.; m. Belinda T.L. Fong, May 5, 1978; children: Patricia T., Mark D. AS in Chemistry, Modesto Jr. Coll., 1972; BS, U. Calif., Berkeley, 1974. Assoc. rsch. chemist Western Regional Rsch. Lab., Albany, Calif., 1974; rsch. biochemist Chevron Chem. Co., Richmond, Calif., 1974-90, Chevron Rsch. & Tech. Co., Richmond, 1990—; environ. cons. Chevron, Richmond, 1991-94. Patentee in field. Republican. Methodist. Office: Chevron Rsch & Tech Co 100 Chevron Way Richmond CA 94801-2016

SVEE, GARY DUANE, newspaper editor, author, journalist; b. Billings, Mont., Nov. 11, 1943; s. Sigvart Oluf and Beatrice Evelyn (Lund) S.; m. C. Diane Schmidt, June 26, 1966; children—Darren Kirk, Nathan Jared. B.A., U. Mont., 1967. Unit mgr. Midland Bank, Billings, Mont., 1967-69; reporter Billings Gazette, 1969-76, opinion editor, 1982—; pub. Bridger (Mont.) Bonanza, 1976-77; feature editor Missoulian, Missoula, Mont., 1977-81. Author: Spirit Wolf, 1987, Incident at Pishkin Creek, 1989, Sanctuary, 1990 (Best Western novel Western Writers Am. 1990), Single Tree. vestryman St. Luke's Meml. Bd., Billings, 1989, Salvation Army, Missoula, 1980-82; vestryman Holy Spirit Parish, Missoula, 1980-82. Served to lt. USAR, 1966-72. Recipient Business Writing award U. Mo., 1974, Minority Affairs Reporting award N.W. region Sigma Delta Chi, 1980. Mem. Kiwanis (bd. dirs. Billings club 1988-89, 2d v.p. 1989, pres. 1990, 91-92), Theta Chi. Episcopalian. Home: 474 Indian Trl Billings MT 59105-2706 Office: Billings Gazette PO Box 36300 Billings MT 59107-6300

SVETLIK, JOHN ANTHONY, entertainment company executive; b. Appleton, Wis., Apr. 27, 1963; s. Gerald Lawrence and Rita Wilhelmina (Vanden Berk) S. BA in Philosophy, Ariz. State U., 1985; MA in Philosophy, U. Calif., San Diego, 1990. Writer, producer Thistle Prodns., Phoenix, 1992-93; sci. writer ASU Rsch. Mag., Tempe, 1992-95, Intelecom, 1995; prodn. coord. CGI & EFX Walt Disney Future Animation, Glendale, Calif., 1993—; adj. prof. philosophy Maricopa County C.C., Phoenix, 1991-93. Contbr. articles to profl. jours. Grad. fellowship Mellon Fellowships in the Humanities, 1985. Mem. Am. Philos. Assn., Nat. Assn. Sci. Writers, Internat. Documentary Assn. Office: Walt Disney Animation 1420 Flower St Glendale CA 91201-2422

SVIKHART, EDWIN GLADDIN, equipment manufacturing executive; b. Chgo., July 12, 1930; s. Edwin Gabriel and Mildred Charlotte (Slapnicka) S.; m. Joann Barbara Frisk, Aug. 22, 1954; children: David E., Robert E. BA, Beloit (Wis.) Coll., 1952; postgrad., Bradley U., 1957-59. With Caterpillar Tractor Co., Peoria, Ill., 1956-66; chief fin. officer Berglund Inc., Napa, Calif., 1966-71; chief fin. officer, treas. Galion (Ohio) Mfg. Co., 1971-77; chief operating officer constrn. equip. internat. div. Dresser Industries, Inc., Columbus, Ohio, 1977-81; chief operating officer Rocky Mountain Machinery Co., Salt Lake City, 1981-87; chief oper. officer Custom Equipment Corp., Salt Lake City, 1989-92; ptnr. Travis Capital Mkts., Salt Lake City, 1992—. Served to lt. (j.g.) USN, 1952-56. Named an Outstanding Young Man of Am., U.S. C. of C., 1966. Republican.

SWAIM, RUTH CAROLYN, secondary education educator; b. Oklahoma City, May 3, 1940; d. G. Dale and Helen H. (Meister) Arbuckle; children: Stanley Kent, Sharon Gay. BS in Edn., U. Okla., 1963. Cert. secondary edn. tchr., Calif., Okla. Math. substitute tchr. USN Mil. Dependent, Sangley Pt., Philippines, 1961-63; math. tchr. Norman (Okla.) Pub. Schs., 1963, Bartlesville (Okla.) Pub. Schs., 1963-65, Dewey (Okla.) Pub. Schs., 1965-67; math. lab. instr. L.A. City Schs., 1975-83, math. tchr., 1984—; chair All Sch. Tutorial Program Taft High Sch. Instr. first Aid ARC, 1961-67; trustee Woodland Hills Community Ch., 1989—. Recipient Cert. Merit ARC, 1965, hon. svc. award PTA, 1980; named Outstanding Math. Tchr. Tandy, 1989-90. Mem. Nat. Coun. Tchrs. Math., NEA, Calif. Tchrs. Assn., Kappa Delta Pi. Home: 4555 San Feliciano Dr Woodland Hills CA 91364-5037 Office: Taft High Sch 5461 Winnetka Ave Woodland Hills CA 91364-2548

SWAIN, NOLA V., foundation administrator, marketing professional; b. Tacoma, Wash., Mar. 10, 1942; d. Arthur and Viola Mafalda (Sirianni) De Caro; m. Lloyd E. Montgomery, Dec. 8, 1961 (div. 1971); children: Gina N. Montgomery, Melissa R. Montgomery; m. Walter B. Swain, Mar. 11, 1977. Student, U. Puget Sound, 1959-62. First woman cert. real estate appraiser, Wash. Appraiser/assesor Pierce County Assessors Office, Tacoma, 1971-77; chief appraiser Otero Savs. & Loan, Colorado Springs, 1977-78; pvt. fee appraiser, co-owner N.W.S. & Assocs., Colorado Springs, 1978—; pres., designer N.V.S. Enterprises, Colorado Springs, 1980-89; dir. mktg. U S WEST Edn. Found., Seattle, 1990—. Designer numerous gift items. Recipient Women at Work award Council on Working Women, 1985, Pub. Service award Colorado Springs Assn. Life Underwriters, 1985, Salesman With A Purpose Club Booster of Yr. award, 1986. Mem. NAFE, NOW, Urban League, Soc. Real Estate Appraisers (candidate, treas. 1978, bd. dirs. 1982-84), Chi Omega Alumnae. Democrat. Roman Catholic. Avocations: skiing, traveling, crafts. Office: U S WEST Edn Found 720 Olive Way Ste 1725 Seattle WA 98101-1853

SWAIN, PHILIP C., JR., lawyer, mechanical engineer; b. Akron, Ohio, Dec. 10, 1957; s. Philip C. Sr. and Shirley I. (Tessier) S.; m. Roseanne K. Vita, May 5, 1990; children: Kimberly A., Jennifer R. BA and BSME, Tufts U., 1981; JD, Northwestern U., 1984. Bar: Ill. 1984, Mass. 1985, D.C. 1988, Calif. 1990. Acting asst. dean Sch. of Law Northwestern U., Chgo., 1984; law clk. U.S. Ct. Appeals (federal cir.), Washington, 1985-86; from assoc. to ptnr. Kirkland & Ellis, L.A., 1986—. Mem. Federal Cir. Bar Assn. (bd. govs. 1990-93, com. chair 1993—). Home: 1550 Nelson Ave Manhattan Beach CA 90266-7117 Office: Kirkland & Ellis 300 S Grand Ave Bldg 3000 Los Angeles CA 90071-3140

SWAIN, ROBERT EDSON, architect; b. Wareham, Mass., Apr. 19, 1946; s. Albert Hampton and Ellen Nora (Spillane) S. Urban Design Cert., Istituto Univ. di Architettura, Venice, Italy, 1970; BArch, U. Ariz., 1972. Field engr., estimator Eastern Erection Co., Woburn, Mass., 1972-73; project mgr., designer The Architects Collaborative Inc., Cambridge, Mass., 1973-76; architect in pvt. practice Cambridge, 1977-90; real estate prin. various trust properties, Cambridge, 1977—; pilot, prin. SWAIR, Cambridge, 1984-90; pres., prin., architect Swain Assocs. Inc., Cambridge, 1983-90; architect in pvt. practice Seattle, 1990—; trustee Conway (Mass.) Sch. Landscape Design, 1990-94; dir. McKinnon's Neck Conservancy, Argyle, Nova Scotia, Can., 1991—; tchr., guest critic Harvard, MIT, Boston Archtl. Ctr., Boston U., Conway Sch., U. Calif.-Berkeley, 1977—; critic-in-residence U. Nebr. Coll. Architecture, 1986. Prin. archtl. works include residence for Pres. of Boeing Co.; architect more than 350 projects including bldgs., landscapes and interiors, 1977—. Recipient Merit award Am. Sch. and Univ., Rindge, N.H., 1987, Best Office Interior award New Eng. Real Estate Dirs., Boston, 1984, others. Mem. AIA. Home and Office: PO Box 31566 Seattle WA 98103-1566

SWAMINATHAN, VENKATES VADAKANCHERY, electrical engineer, software company executive; b. Bombay, Maharashtra, India, Dec. 31, 1963; came to U.S., 1985; s. Venkateswaran and Radha V. Iyer; m. Debra Kay Ragan, Dec. 20, 1991. B Tech. in Elec. Engring., Indian Inst. Tech., Delhi, India, 1985; MS in Elec. Engring., U. Ill., 1988. Software engr. Teknekron Comm. Systems, Inc., Berkeley, Calif., 1988-91; sr. software engr. Teknekron Comm. Systems, Inc., Berkeley, 1991-92, project mgr., 1992-94, program mgr., 1994—. Designer (computer software) schematic generator, 1985 (Best Project award 1985), chief architect NMS/Core, 1992; sr. architect Carrier Access Billing System, 1994. Bd. dirs. Beacon High Sch., Oakland, Calif., 1992. Recipient fellowship U. Ill., 1985. Mem. Assn. for Computing Machinery, IEEE. Home: 3600 Balfour Ave Oakland CA 94610-1703 Office: Teknekron Comm Systems Inc 2121 Allston Way Berkeley CA 94704-1301

SWAN, ALLAN HOLLISTER, minister; b. Ridgewood, N.J., Oct. 29, 1929; s. Merriam Hollister and Irene Louise (Ferres) S.; m. Janet Louise Peterson, June 6, 1958; children: Jennifer, David, Kimberly, Rebecca. BA, Lafayette Coll., 1951; MDiv, Princeton Sem., 1954; D of Min., San Francisco Theol. Sem., 1975. Ordained to ministry Presbyn. Ch., 1954. Pastor Valmont and Nederland Presbyn. Chs., Boulder, Colo., 1954-57; assoc. pastor 1st Presbyn. Ch., Boulder, 1958-62; pastor Westminster Presbyn. Ch., Ft. Collins, Colo., 1963-70, Lincoln Presbyn. Ch., Stockton, Calif., 1970-80, Covenant Presbyn Ch., Boise, 1981-90; interim pastor Whitworth Presbyn Ch., Spokane, 1990-91, First Presbyn. Ch., Coeur d'Alene, Idaho, 1992-93; interim assoc. pastor Millwood Presbyn. Ch., Spokane, Wash., 1993-94; ret., 1994; bd. dirs. Coun. Evangelism, N.Y.C., 1967-69; bd. dirs., exec. com. Vocation Agy., N.Y.C., 1979-86. Mem. orgn. bd. Larimer County Youth Home, Ft. Collins, 1966-70; bd. dirs. Rotary, Stockton, Calif. and Boise, 1970-90. Mem. Psi Chi, Pi Gamma Mu. Home: 15520 N Meadowglen Ct Spokane WA 99208-8532

SWAN, ANNA, school nurse; b. Albuquerque, Mar. 14, 1953; d. Robert Stutz and Lupita (Lujan) Swan. BSN, U. N.Mex., 1985. Nurse Pres. Hosp., Albuquerque, Children's Psychiat. Hosp./Heights Psychiat. Hosp., Albuquerque; clin. instr. Albuquerque Tech.-Vocat. Inst.; sch. nurse Los Lunas (N.Mex.) Pub. Schs.; rsch. nurse dept. psychiatry U. N.Mex., Albuquerque; pub. health nurse, Albuquerque, dir. health unit/coord. program Albuquerque Tech.-Vocat. Inst.; mem. nursing practice adv. com. for N.Mex. Bd. of Nursing. Camp nurse Girl Scouts U.S., Albuquerque.

SWAN, JAMES ALBERT, environmental psychologist, writer, actor; b. Trenton, Mich., Feb. 25, 1943; s. Donald Miller and Evelyn Ann (Berdan) S.; m. Roberta June Arnett, Dec. 7, 1975; 1 child, Andrew Arnett. BS, U. Mich., 1965, MS, 1967, PhD, 1969. Environ. edn. coord. Ann Arbor (Mich.) Pub. Schs., 1965-69; lectr., rsch. assoc. U. Mich., Ann Arbor, 1969-72; asst. prof. Western Wash. State U., Bellingham, 1972-73; asst. prof., dept. chair U. Ore., Eugene, 1973-76; vis. lectr. U. Wash., Seattle, 1977-78; pres. Life Sys. Edn. Found., Seattle, 1978-82; project dir. Inst. for the Human Environment, San Francisco, 1983-84; assoc. prof. Calif. Inst. Integral Studies, San Francisco, 1988-92; pres. Inst. for Study of Natural Sys., Mill Valley, Calif., 1987-93; published writer in field, 1967—; bd. govs. U. Mich. Sch. Nat. Resources, Ann Arbor, 1993—; adv. bd. Audubon Expedition Inst., N.Y.C., 1981-88; sec. Mich. Natural Areas Coun., Ann Arbor, 1967-72; bd. advisors Internat. Ctr. for Earth Renewal, Vancouver, B.C., Can., 1992—. Author: In Defense of Hunting, 1994; co-author: Bound to the Earth, 1994, Nature as Teacher and Healer, 1992 (award 1993), Sacred Places, 1990, Building Networks, 1985, Environmental Education, 1974; author, editor: The Power of Place, 1991; edtl. adv. bd. Nat. Geog. Jour. of India, 1992—; assoc. editor Jour. of Environment & Behavior, N.Y.C., 1969-74. Mem. SAG, Assn. Songwriters, Composers & Performers, The Author's Guild. Office: PO Box 2460 Mill Valley CA 94942-2460

SWAN, KENNETH CARL, physician, surgeon; b. Kansas City, Mo., Jan. 1, 1912; s. Carl E. and Blanche (Peters) S.; m. Virginia Grone, Feb. 5, 1938; children: Steven Carl, Kenneth, Susan. A.B., U. Oreg., 1933, M.D., 1936. Diplomate: Am. Bd. Ophthalmology (chmn. 1960-61). Intern U. Wis., 1936-37; resident in ophthalmology State U. Iowa, 1937-40; practice medicine specializing in ophthalmology Portland, Oreg., 1945—; staff Good Samaritan Hosp.; asst. prof. ophthalmology State U. Iowa, Iowa City, 1941-44; asso. prof. U. Oreg. Med. Sch., Portland, 1944-45, prof. and head dept. ophthalmology, 1945-78; Chmn. sensory diseases study sect. NIH; mem. adv. council Nat. Eye Inst.; also adv. council Nat. Inst. Neurol. Diseases and Blindness. Contbr. articles on ophthalmic subjects to med. publs. Recipient Proctor Rsch. medal, 1953; Disting. Svc. award U. Oreg., 1963; Meritorious Achievement award U. Oreg. Med. Sch., 1968; Howe Ophthalmology medal, 1977; Aubrey Watzek Pioneer award Lewis and Clark Coll., 1979, Disting. Alumnus award Oreg. Health Scis. U. Alumni Assn., 1988, Disting. Svc. award, 1988; named Oreg. Scientist of Yr. Oreg. Mus. Sci. and Industry, 1959. Mem. Assn. Research in Ophthalmology, Am. Acad. Ophthalmology (v.p. 1978, historian), Soc. Exptl. Biology and Medicine, AAAS, AMA, Am. Ophthal. Soc. (Howe medal for distinguished service 1977), Oreg. Med. Soc., Sigma Xi, Sigma Chi (Significant Sig award 1977). Home: 4645 SW Fairview Blvd Portland OR 97221-2624 Office: Oreg Health Scis U Portland OR 97201

SWAN, PETER ALFRED, systems engineer; b. San Antonio, Apr. 17, 1945; s. Frederic F. and Marion (Marriott) S.; m. Cathy Wood, July 5, 1968. BS in Engring., U.S. Mil. Acad., 1968; MS in Engring., Air Inst. Tech., Dayton, Ohio, 1970; MS in Mgmt., U. So. Calif., 1977; PhD in Engring., UCLA, 1984. Commd. 2d lt. USAF, 1968, advanced through grades to lt. col., 1984; test engr. USAF, Albuquerque, 1970-76; space systems engr. Office Sec. Air Force, L.A., 1976-79, satellite architect, 1984-88; asst. prof. astronautics USAF Acad., Colorado Springs, Colo., 1979-81; cons. Jet Propulsion Lab., Pasadena, Calif., 1982-84; ret., 1988; sr. systems engr. Motorola, Inc. (GEG), Phoenix, 1988-89; mgr. Washington Systems Office, Motorola, Inc. (GEG), McLean, Va., 1989-92; dir. Sunnyvale office Satellite Comms. Motorola Inc., Chandler, Ariz., 1993—. Editor course books; contbr. articles to tech. jours. Bd. dirs. Ctr. for Critical Care, Washington, 1990-91. Assoc. fellow AIAA; fellow Brit. Interplanetary Soc. Home: 5865 E Sanna St Paradise Valley AZ 85253

SWAN, RICHARD ALAN, executive recruiter; b. Hollywood, Calif., May 5, 1944; s. Morris George and Mary Theresa (Fenusz) S.; m. Carol Ann Jacobs, Apr. 15, 1967; children: David Michael, Jennifer Marie, Matthew Richard. BS in Indsl. Mgmt., U. So. Calif., 1966; MS in Health Care Adminstrn., Trinity U., 1970. Adminstrv. resident Tucson (Ariz.) Med. Ctr., 1971; assoc. cons. A.T. Kearney and Co. Inc., Chgo., 1971-72; v.p. Tribrook Group Inc., Oakbrook, Ill., 1972-82; dir. program and spl. studies div. James A. Hamilton Assocs. Inc., Dallas, 1982-83; v.p. corp. devel. Vincentian Health Services, L.A., 1983-88; v.p., dir. healthcare group Boyden Internat., L.A., 1988-89; regional v.p. Kieffer Ford & Assocs., Ltd., Orange, Calif., 1989-92; ptnr. Witt/Kieffer, Ford, Hadelman & Lloyd, Irvine, Calif., 1992—. Contbr. articles to profl. jours. Served to capt. Med. Service Corps, U.S. Army, 1967-69. Fellow Am. Assn. Hosp. Cons., Am. Coll. Healthcare Execs.; mem. Soc. Hosp. Planning and Mktg., So. Calif. Soc. Hosp. Planners (charter), Health Care Execs. of So. Calif., Am. Hosp. Assn. Republican. Roman Catholic. Office: Witt Kieffer Ford Hadelman & Lloyd 2030 Main St Ste 620 Irvine CA 92714-7235

SWANER, PAULA MARGETTS, clinical psychologist; b. Salt Lake City, Nov. 23, 1927; d. Sumner Gray and Pauline (Moyle) M.; m. Leland Scowcroft, May 22, 1951; children: Leland S., Jr., Sumner Margetts, Paula June Swaner-Sargetakis. BA in Eng. Lit., U. Utah, 1949, MA in Eng. Lit., 1972, MS in Ednl. Psychol., 1978, PhD in Clin. Psychology, 1986; postgrad. in Brit. object rels. theory, Washington Sch. Psychiatry, 1991; postgrad., Mill Valley Calif. Acad., 1990. Lic. clin. psychologist, Utah. Psychotherapist Granite Mental Health Ctr., Salt Lake City, 1978-80; postdoctoral intern Mental Health Unit, Juvenile Ct., Salt Lake City, 1984-87; pvt. practice Salt Lake City, 1986—; courtesy mem. profl. staff Western Inst. Neuropsychiatry, Psychiat. Insts. Am., Salt Lake City; mem. Washington Sch. Psychiatry; CEO Evergreen Coalition, 1993—. Lector, All Saints Episcopal Ch., Salt Lake City; chair Leland S. Swaner Meml. Pk. Found., 1993—. Mem. Am. Psychol. Assn., Utah Psychol. Assn., Wasatch Mountain Club. Democrat. Episcopalian. Office: Paula M Swaner 1580 E 3900 S Ste 210 Salt Lake City UT 84124

SWANEY, THOMAS ROBBINS, venture capitalist; b. L.A., Apr. 28, 1952; s. George Robbins and Marian (Smoliga) S.; m. Ines Veronique Szilard, Aug. 31, 1974; children: Elizabeth Marian, Peter Thomas. BA in Econs. and Math., U. Calif., Berkeley, 1974; postgrad., U. Minn., 1974-75. Treasury analyst Fed. Home Loan Bank, San Francisco, 1976-78; fin. analyst Bank of Am., San Francisco, 1978-81; fin. cons. Chase Manhattan Bank, San Francisco, 1981-83, Am. Express, San Francisco, 1984-86; v.p. Bear Stearns, San Francisco, 1986-89; pres. Harwood Capital Inc., Oakland, Calif., 1989—; bd. dirs. West Oakland (Calif.) Devel. Assn., Am. Petroleum Inst., Sacramento. Bd. dirs. Kisha Soc., San Francisco, 1991-93. Mem. Sacramento Petroleum Assn., Calif. Ind. Petroleum Assn., World Affairs Coun. No. Calif., No. Calif. Geol. Soc., No. Calif. Coteneration Assn., World Forum Silicon Valley, U. Calif. Alumni Assn. (bd. dirs.), U. Calif. Berkeley Entrepreneurs Forum, Commonwealth Club. Office: Harwood Capital Inc 6161 Harwood Ave Oakland CA 94618-1339

SWANK, BRADD A, lawyer; b. Normal, Ill., July 8, 1949; s. George Dearborn and Ruth Eileen (Ruggles) S.; m. Nancy McKay (div. 1976); m. Claudia Lynn Howells Williams, Oct. 3, 1987; 1 child, Devon Atticus. BA, Ind. U., Ft. Wayne, 1973; JD, Willamette U., 1976. Bar: Oreg. 1976. Dep. legis. counsel Oreg. Legis. Assembly, Salem, 1976-84; sr. counsel Oreg. Legis. Judiciary Com., Salem, 1984-86; legal/mgmt. analyst Oreg. State Ct. Adminstr., Salem, 1986—; recorder Uniform Trial Ct. Rules Com., Salem, 1987—; mem. staff Oreg. Jud. Conf. Case Disposition Benchmarks Com., Salem, 1991—, Ju. Dept. Uniform Citations Com., Salem, 1991—. Author: Oregon Judicial Department Manual on Garnishments, 1987; author: (with others) Oregon Bar Civil Litigation Manual, 1990; drafter (legis./law) Oreg. Vehicle Code, 1983. Office: Oreg Jud Dept 1163 State St Salem OR 97310-1331

SWANSON, ARTHUR DEAN, lawyer; b. Onida, S.D., Apr. 19, 1934; s. Obert W. and Mary I. (Barnum) S.; m. Paula Swanson, Aug. 22, 1965 (div. Feb. 1984); children: Shelby, Dean, Sherry. BA, Wash. State U., 1956; JD, U. Wash., 1963. Bar: Wash. 1963. Dep. prosecutor King County, Seattle, 1964-65; ct. commr. Renton and Issaquah Dist. Cts., Wash., 1966-68; pvt. practice law Renton, Wash., 1965—; lectr. various orgns.; former counsel Wash. State Law Enforcement Assn., Wash. State Dep. Sheriff's Assn. Served with Fin. Corps, U.S. Army, 1956-58. Named one of Best Lawyers Am., 1991-92, 93-94, 95-96. Fellow Am. Coll. Trial Lawyers; mem. Wash. State Bar Assn. (past sec. trial sect.), Seattle-King County Bar Assn. (bd. trustees 1977-80), Assn. Trial Lawyers Am., Wash. State Trial Lawyers Assn. (past pres.), Am. Bd. Trial Advs. (bd. dirs., pres. Wash. state chpt. 1995-96). Democrat. Office: 4512 Talbot Rd S Renton WA 98055-6216

SWANSON, DAVID PAUL, accountant; b. Everett, Wash., Nov. 27, 1945; s. Lloyd E. and Electa A. (McFarland) S.; m. Barbara J. Clough, Feb. 25, 1968 (div. Sept. 1977); children: Elizabeth, Devin. BA, Western Wash. U., 1968; MBA, City U., Seattle, 1984. CPA, Wash. With Everett Trust Bank, 1968-70, Security Bank, Portland, Oreg., 1970-71; mgr. Herfys, Seattle, 1971-73, Chuckwagon Restaurant, Seattle, Aberdeen, Wash., 1973-74, Yukon Jacks, Seattle, 1974-76; acctg. specialist Data I/O, Bellevue, Wash., 1977-83; acctg. and tax mgr. Balance Sheet Acctg. Svcs. Inc., Lynnwood, Wash., 1983—; pres. Delta Pacific Securites Inc., Everett, Wash., 1989—; instr. City U., 1986-90; treas., bd. dirs. Log C Corp., Everett, 1987—; pres., bd. dirs. Delta Pacific Securities, Everett, 1989—; corp. contbr. Black Mountain Escrow, San Diego, 1990—. Bd. dirs. Everett Drug Abuse Coun., 1984-87, J-Bird Ranch, Everett, 1991—; bd. dirs., pres. Evergreen Manor, 1987—; bd. dirs., treas. Big Bros. and Big Sisters, Everett, 1988-92. Mem. Nat. Fedn. Ind. Bus., Inst. Bus. Appraisers, Wash. State Soc. CPA's, Sons of Norway, South Snohomish County Chamber, Northshore C. of C. Office: Delta Pacific Securities Inc PO Box 2543 Everett WA 98203

SWANSON, DONALD ALAN, geologist; b. Tacoma, July 25, 1938; s. Leonard Walter and Edith Christine (Bowers) S.; m. Barbara Joan White, May 25, 1974. BS in Geology, Wash. State U., 1960; PhD in Geology, Johns Hopkins U., 1964. Geologist U.S. Geol. Survey, Menlo Park, Calif., 1965-68, 71-80, Hawaii National Park, 1968-71; sr. geologist Cascades Volcano Obs. U.S. Geol. Survey, Vancouver, Wash., 1980-90, rsch. scientist-in-charge, 1986-89; sr. geologist U.S. Geol. Survey, Seattle, 1990—; assoc. dir. Volcano Systems Ctr. U. Wash., 1993—; affiliate prof. U. Wash., 1992—; cons. U.S. Dept. Energy, Richland, Wash., 1979-83; volcanologist New Zealand Geol. Survey, Taupo, 1984; advisor Colombian Volcano Obs., Manizales, 1986. Assoc. editor Jour. Volcanolgy and Geothermal Rsch., 1976—, Jour. Geophys. Rsch., 1992-94; editor Bull. of Volcanology, 1985-90; contbr. numerous articles to profl. jours. Recipient Superior Service award U.S. Geol. Survey, 1980, Meritorious Service award U.S. Dept. Interior, 1985; postdoctoral fellow NATO, 1964-65. Fellow Geol. Soc. Am.; mem. AAAS, Am. Geophys. Union, Sigma Xi. Home: 7537 34th Ave NE Seattle WA 98115-4802 Office: U Washington US Geol Survey Geol Scis Box 351310 Seattle WA 98195-1310

SWANSON, E. BURTON, business and information systems educator; b. Fullerton, Calif., Aug. 19, 1939; s. Edwin A. and Fern E. (Anderson) S.; m. Cheryl W. Snell, 1983. BS, San Jose State U., 1962; PhD, U. Calif., Berkeley, 1971. Engr., systems analyst IBM Corp., San Jose, Calif., 1962-72; asst. prof. grad. sch. mgmt. UCLA, 1974-80, assoc. prof., 1980-90, prof., 1990—. Author: Information System Implementation, 1988; co-author: Measurement for Management Decision, 1981, Maintaining Information Systems in Organizations, 1989; editor in chief jour. Info. Systems Rsch., 1987-92. Mem. AAAS, Inst. Mgmt. Scis., Internat. Conf. on Info. Systems (co-founder). Office: UCLA Grad Sch Mgmt Los Angeles CA 90024

SWANSON, EMILY, state legislator; b. Oak Park, Ill., Jan. 12, 1947; m. Tim Swanson; 2 children. BA, Bennington Coll.; MA, U. Calif., Berkeley. Mem. Mont. Ho. of Reps. Home: 15042 Kelly Canyon Rd Bozeman MT 59715-9625 Office: Mont Ho of Reps State Capitol Helena MT 59620

SWANSON, LEE RICHARD, computer security executive; b. Mpls., Apr. 21, 1957; s. Donald Jerome and Wildie (Greenwood) S.; m. Amy Jane Shutkin, Jan. 1, 1980 (div. Apr. 1991). BS, U. Minn., 1983. Owner, prin. Environ. Landforms, Inc., Minnetonka, Minn., 1974-80; v.p. Blomfield-Swanson, Inc., Mpls., 1981-85; contractor Citicorp Card Acceptance Svcs., Seattle, 1986-88; pres., mktg. dir., cons. Room Svcs. Computers, Bellevue, Wash., 1988-91; exec. v.p. First Step Computer Consultants, Inc., Novato, Calif., 1991—. Libertarian. Office: 1001 Bridgeway Ste 238 Sausalito CA 94965-2158

SWANSON, PAUL RUBERT, minister; b. Bakersfield, Calif., May 13, 1943; s. Roland Hilding and Myrtle Isabelle (Magnuson) S.; m. Mary Elizabeth Greene, June 18, 1967; children: Kristen Ann, Karlynn Marie, Jonathan Paul. BA, Pacific Luth. U., 1966; MDiv, Luth. Sch. Theology, 1970. Ordained minister, Luth. Ch. Pastor 1st Luth. Ch., Anaconda, Mont., 1970-76, King of Kings Luth. Ch., Milwaukie, Oreg., 1976-84; asst. to bishop Pacific N.W. Synod-Luth. Ch. in Am., Portland, Oreg., 1984-87; bishop Oreg. Synod-Evang. Luth. Ch. Am., Portland, 1987—; bd. dirs. Legacy Health System, Portland. Regent Pacific Luth. U., Tacoma, 1987—; bd. dirs. Emanuel Hosp., Portland, 1987; chmn. bd. dirs. Hearthstone, Inc., Anaconda, 1973-76; bd. dirs. Ecumenical Ministries Oreg., Portland, 1984—. Recipient Disting. Svc. award Pacific Luth. U., 1993.

SWANSON, RICHARD MARKER, electrical engineering educator; b. Davenport, Iowa, May 13, 1945; s. Carroll A. and Betty M. (Marker) S.; children: Mark G., Craig A. BSEE, Ohio State U., 1969; PhD in Elec. Engring., Stanford U., 1974. Rsch. assoc. Stanford (Calif.) U., 1974-76, asst. prof., 1976-83, assoc. prof., 1983-91; v.p. SunPower Corp., Sunnyvale, Calif., 1989-92, pres., 1993—. Contbr. more than 100 papers to profl. jours. Named fellow NSF, 1970-74. Office: Sunpower Corp 430 Indio Way Sunnyvale CA 94086-4202

SWANSON, RICHARD WILLIAM, statistician; b. Rockford, Ill., July 26, 1934; s. Richard and Erma Marie (Herman) S.; m. Laura Yoko Arai, Dec. 30, 1970. BS, Iowa State U., 1958, MS, 1964. Ops. analyst Stanford Rsch. Inst., Monterey, Calif., 1958-62; statistician ARINC Rsch. Corp., Washington, 1964-65; sr. scientist Booz-Allen Applied Rsch., Vietnam, 1965-67, L.A., 1967-68; sr. ops. analyst Control Data Corp., Honolulu, 1968-70; mgmt. cons., Honolulu, 1970-73; exec. v.p. SEQUEL Corp., Honolulu, 1973-75; bus. cons. Hawaii Dept. Planning and Econ. Devel., Honolulu, 1975-77, tax rsch. and planning officer Dept. Taxation, 1977-82; ops. rsch. analyst U.S. Govt., 1982-89; shipyard statisician U.S. Govt., 1989—. Served with AUS, 1954-56. Mem. Hawaiian Acad. Sci., Sigma Xi. Home: 583 Kamoku St Apt 3505 Honolulu HI 96826-5240 Office: Pearl Harbor Naval Shipyard PO Box 400 Honolulu HI 96809-0400

SWARD, ROBERT STUART, author; b. Chgo., June 23, 1933; s. Irving Michael and Gertrude (Huebsch) S.; children: Cheryl, Barbara, Michael, Hannah, Nicholas. BA with hons., U. Ill., 1956; MA, U. Iowa, 1958; postgrad., U. Bristol (Eng.), 1960-61, Middlebury (Vt.) Coll., 1956-60. Instr. English Conn. Coll., New London, 1958-59; writer-in-residence Cornell U., Ithaca, N.Y., 1962-64, U. Iowa, 1967-68; asst. prof. English/writer-in-residence U. Victoria (B.C.), 1969-73; editor/pubr. Soft Press, Victoria, 1970-79; radio broadcaster Can. Broadcasting Corp., Toronto, Ont., 1979-84; tech. writer Santa Cruz Op. (SCO), Santa Cruz, Calif., 1987-89; writer-in-residence extension program U. Calif., Santa Cruz, 1988—; writer-in-residence Cabrillo Coll., Aptos, Calif., 1988—; vis. poet creative writing program U. Calif.,

Santa Cruz, 1992—; writer in the schs. Ont. Arts Coun., Toronto, 1979-84, Cultural Coun., Santa Cruz, 1984—; cons. to pubs.; book reviewer Toronto Star, others. Author: Uncle Dog and Other Poems, 1962, Autobiography, CAAS, 1991, Poems: New and Selected, 1983, Four Incarnations: New and Selected Poems, 1957-91; (with Charles Atkinson, David Swanger and Tilly Shaw) Family, 1994, A Much-Married Man, A Novel, 1995. Tchr. Oak Bay Sr. Citizens, Victoria, 1973-74; editor, advisor Jazz Press, Poet Santa Cruz Pubs., 1985-87. With USN, 1951-54. Fulbright grantee, 1961, Guggenheim fellow, 1964-65, D.H. Lawrence fellow, U. N.Mex., 1966-67, Yaddo MacDowell Colony grantee, 1959-82; Djerassi Found. grantee, 1990—; recipient Villa Montalvo Lit. Arts award, 1989-90. Mem. League of Can. Poets, Writers Union of Can. (newsletter editor 1983-84), Nat. Writers Union. Democrat. Home: PO Box 7062 Santa Cruz CA 95061-7062 Office: 435 Meder St Santa Cruz CA 95060-2307

SWARNER, JULIA BOYD, nutrition educator; b. Memphis, Sept. 1, 1940; d. Harold Buhalts and Jean Frances (Stewart) Boyd; m. Orville Ward Swarner, Sept. 2, 1962; children: Stephanie, Scott, Stephen. BS, So. Coll., Collegedale, Tenn., 1961; MS in Nutrition, Loma Linda U., 1963, MPH, 1979, DPH, 1979. Coord., dietetic intern Loman Linda (Calif.) U., 1964-65, assoc. prof., 1978-94; therapeutic dietitian White Meml. Hosp., L.A., 1963; instr. nutrition Bapt. Sch. Nursing, Memphis, 1965, 66, Memphis State U., 1967, U. Tenn., Memphis, 1972; lectr. Loma Linda U. Med. Ctr. Cancer Inst., 1993, 94; with Project Eat Bueno, San Bernardino (Calif.) County Health Dept., 1992, 93, Project LEAN, 1993, 94. Author: Wellness-The Inside Story, 1991; contbr. articles to profl. jours. Mem. Am. Dietetic Assn. (registered dietitian). Seventh-day Adventist. Home: 1056 San Jacinto St Redlands CA 92373-6632 Office: Loma Linda U Nichol Hall Loma Linda CA 92350

SWARTWOUT, GLEN MARTIN, optometrist; b. Troy, N.Y., Mar. 25, 1956; s. J. Baxter and Dorothy (Porter) S.; m. Karen Aubrey Niles, Mar. 14, 1987. AB, Dartmouth Coll., 1978; OD, SUNY, N.Y.C., 1982; D of Naturopathy, Clayton Sch., 1989; BD (hon.), Universal Brotherhood, Duluth, Ga., 1990. Vision therapist Swartwout & Lazarus, Latham, N.Y., 1972; dir. Optometric Ctr. Tokyo, 1982-84; clin. dir. Learning Disabilities Assocs., Latham, 1984-89; mem. clinic staff Nat. Coll. Naturopathic Medicine, Portland, Oreg., 1989-90; co-founder Hawaii Ctr. Natural Medicine, Hilo, 1990—; dir. Vision Fitness, Hilo, 1991—; pres. Achievement of Excellence Rsch. Acad. Internat., Hilo, 1990—; cons. Am. Optometric Assn., St. Louis, 1982-84; mem. adv. bd. Pediatric Optometry and Vision Therapy. Author: Electromagnetic Pollution Solutions, 1990, Electromagnetic Health Research Manual, 1990; contbg. editor Jour. N.Y. State Optemetric Assn., 1985—; patentee VDT stress reduction lens, 1990. Cons. Easter Seals Soc., Hilo, 1991—; minister Universal Brotherhood Movement, Hilo, 1991—; bd. dirs. Hawaii Island Environ. Coun., 1991; pres. Holistic Health Network, N.Y., 1985-89, Blackwood Inst. Holistic Studies, N.Y., 1985; pres. Starfire Internat., 1992; co-founder Parents Active for Vision Edn., Hawaii chpt., 1992. Recipient Cert. Appreciation NCAA, 1978. Fellow Coll. Syntonic Optometry (sec., trustee 1987—), Internat. Coll. Applied Nutrition; mem. Coll. Optometrists in Vision Devel., Optometric Extension Program Found., Internat. Soc. Holistic Optometry (state dir. 1984-89, Optometrist of Yr. 1985), Japanese C. of C., Beta Sigma Kappa (chpt. pres. 1981-82). Office: Achievement of Excellence 311 Kalanianaole Ave Hilo HI 96720-4740

SWARTZ, CHARLES S., screenwriter, producer, educator; b. Dallas, Apr. 22, 1939; s. Martin and Jen (Sakowitz) S.; m. Stephanie Rothman, June 16, 1963. BA magna cum laude, Yale U., 1961; postgrad., U. So. Calif., 1961-63. TV prodn. asst. Warner Bros., Inc., Burbank, Calif., 1963-66, assoc. producer, 1966; exec. producer New World Pictures, Inc., Hollywood, Calif., 1969-70; exec. v.p. Dimension Pictures, Inc., Hollywood, 1970-75; freelance writer, producer, 1967-68, 76-83; program mgr., dept. entertainment studies U. Calif. extension, Los Angeles, 1984—. Producer, co-writer: (films) Terminal Island, 1973, Group Marriage, 1972, Sweet Sugar, 1971, The Velvet Vampire, 1971, The Student Nurses, 1970, It's a Bikini World, 1966; producer (film) The Working Girls, 1974. Warner Meml. scholar U. So. Calif. Mem. Writers Guild Am. West, Fin. Adminstrv. and Mgmt. Execs. in Entertainment (co-chair edn. com.), Soc. Motion Picture and TV Engrs. (chair Hollywood chpt. edn. com., nat. edn. com.), Tech. Coun. Motion Picture-TV Industry. Office: U Calif Extension Entertainment Studies 10995 Le Conte Ave Rm 437 Los Angeles CA 90024-2400

SWARTZ, MELVIN JAY, lawyer, author; b. Boston, July 21, 1930; s. Jack M. and Rose (Rosenberg) S.; children: Julianne, Jonathan Samuel. BA, Syracuse U., 1953; LLB, Boston U., 1957. Bar: N.Y. 1959, Ariz. 1961. Assoc., Alfred S. Julian, N.Y.C., 1957-59; ptnr. Finks & Swartz, Youngtown, Sun City, Phoenix, Ariz., 1961-70, Swartz & Jeckel, P.C., Sun City, Youngtown, Scottsdale, Ariz., 1971-82; exec. v.p. APPPRO, Inc., Scottsdale, Ariz. Bd. dirs. Valley of the Sun Sch. for Retarded Children, 1975-79. Mem. ABA, Ariz. Bar Assn., N.Y. Bar Assn., Maricopa County Bar Assn., Scottsdale Bar Assn., Central Ariz. Estate Planning Council. Jewish. Club: Masons (Phoenix). Author: Don't Die Broke, A Guide to Secure Retirement, 1974, Retire Without Fear, 1994, (book and cassettes) Keep What You Own, 1989, rev. edit., 1993, (computer program) Keeping What You Own, 1993, The Realtor's Title Analysis, 1994; columnist News-Sun, Sun City, 1979-83; author column Swartz on Aging. Office: 6619 N Scottsdale Rd Scottsdale AZ 85250-4421

SWARTZ, RAY, data processing executive; b. Glendale, Calif., May 3, 1952; s. Albert and Ethel S. BA, U. Calif., Irvine, 1974; MBA, U. Calif., Berkeley, 1981. Mng. dir. Berkeley Decision Systems, Santa Cruz, Calif., 1981—; adj. lectr. U. Santa Clara, 1982-84; vis. lectr. U. Calif., Santa Cruz, 1984-87, India-sponsored by NIIT, 1988. Author: Doing Business with C, 1989, UNIX Application Development, 1990; editor conf. proc. Modeling and Simulation, 1984; columnist Answers on UNIX, 1989—; creator tng. on video line of C Programming and UNIX system video tng. courses. Coach Cmty. Basketball League, Santa Cruz, 1987, co-facilitator men's group, 1993—; spkr. Santa Cruz AIDS Project, 1993—. Mem. USENIX, Uniforum. Office: Berkeley Decision/Systems 803 Pine St Santa Cruz CA 95062-2444

SWARTZ, ROSLYN HOLT, real estate investment executive; b. Los Angeles, Dec. 9, 1940; d. Abe Jack and Helen (Canter) Holt; m. Allan Joel Swartz, June 2, 1963. AA, Santa Monica (Calif.) Coll., 1970; BA summa cum laude, UCLA, 1975; MA, Pepperdine U., 1976. Cert. community coll. instr., student-personnel worker, Calif. Mgr. pub. relations Leader Holdings, Inc., L.A., 1968-75, pres., 1991—; sec., treas. Leader Holdings, Inc., North Hollywood, Calif., 1975-81, pres., 1981-91; chief exec. officer Beverly Stanley Investments, L.A., 1979—. Condr. An Oral History of the Elderly Jewish Community of Venice, Calif. at Los Angeles County Planning Dept. Library, 1974. Mem. Hadassah (life), Friends of the Hollywood Bowl; bd. dirs. Am. Friends of Haifa Med. Ctr. L.A., L.A. County Mus. Art, West L.A. Symphony; capital patron Simon Wiesenthal Ctr. Fellow Phi Beta Kappa (bicentennial); mem. NAFE, AAUW, Am. Soc. Profl. and Exec. Women, Am. Pub. Health Assn., Am. Pharm. Assn., Women in Comml. Real Estate, L.A. World Affairs Coun., Town Hall (life), Century City C. of C., UCLA Alumni Assn. (life), UCLA Founders Circle, Women's Coun. Women's Guild Cedars-Sinai Med. Ctr., UCLA Prytanean Alumnae Assn., Santa Monica Coll. Alumni Assn. (life), Phrateres Internat., Order of Eastern Star, Phi Alpha Theta, Alpha Gamma Sigma, Alpha Kappa Delta, Phi Delta Kappa, Pi Gamma Mu. Office: PO Box 241784 Los Angeles CA 90024-9584

SWARTZ, TERESA ANNE, marketing educator, researcher, consultant; b. Port Alleghany, Pa., May 3, 1953; d. Robert Wilson and Geraldine Elizabeth (Hess) S. B.S. in Edn., Clarion U., Pa., 1974, M.B.A., 1977; Ph.D. in Bus. Adminstrn., Ohio State U., 1981. Cert. secondary tchr., Pa. High sch. tchr. Bradford Area Schs., Bradford, Pa., 1975-76; grad. asst. Clarion U., Pa., 1976-77; researcher, teaching assoc., Ohio State U., Columbus, 1977-80; lectr. Ariz. State U., Tempe, 1980-81, asst. prof., 1981-86, assoc. prof., 1986-91; prof. mktg. Calif. Poly. U., San Luis Obispo, 1991—; mktg. cons., Tempe, 1981—; vis. prof. Dailey and Assocs., L.A., 1983. Mem. Am. Mktg. Assn. (Phoenix bd. dirs. 1982-85, nat. bd. dirs. 1991—, v.p. elect western region 1985-86, v.p. 1986-87, v.p. elect svcs. mktg. div. 1991-92, v.p. svcs. mktg. divsn. 1992-93), Assn. Consumer Research, Am. Acad. Advt., Acad. Mktg. Sci., Assn. Women in Psychology, Beta Gamma Sigma. Democrat. Avocations: golf, tennis, travel, softball. Office: Calif Poly U Coll Business San Luis Obispo CA 93407

SWASS, MATTHEW J., electrical engineer; b. Paterson, N.J., June 15, 1962; s. John and June (Frey) S. BS in Engring. and Applied Sci., Calif. Inst. Tech., 1984; MS in Elec. Engring., Calif. State U., Northridge, 1988. Mem. tech. staff Hughes Aircraft Radar Systems Group, El Segundo, Calif., 1984—. Founder young adult group Unitarian Cmty. Ch., Santa Monica, Calif., 1994. Mem. IEEE, Robert Andrews Millikan Soc. Home: 1341 E Orange Grove Blvd Apt 2 Pasadena CA 91104-3038

SWEATT, RICHARD ANDREW, computer scientist; b. Fresno, Calif., Nov. 26, 1957; s. Horace Dean and Martha Charlene (Hart) S.; m. Megan Bridget Zale, July 1, 1989. AA in Gen. Edn., Nat. U., San Diego, 1979; AS in Computer Sci., Canada Coll., Redwood City, Calif., 1982; BS in Computer Sci., San Jose State U., 1986. Sys. engr. Comten, Inc., San Mateo, Calif., 1979-81; mktg. analyst NCR Comten, Inc., San Mateo, 1982-84, sr. mktg. analyst, 1984-86; with Vitalink Comms. Inc., 1986-90; product mgr. SynOptics Comms. Inc., Santa Clara, Calif., 1990-92, product line mgr., 1992-94; mgr. LAN arch. Rolm, A Siemens Co., Santa Clara, 1994—; ptnr. Sci. Cons., Livermore, Calif., 1986—; editor Internet Engring. Task Force Bridge MIB, 1989—, ATM Forum LAN Emulation, 1992—. Editor: IEEE 802.1d MAC Bridges, 1993. Sgt. USMC, 1976-80. Mem. IEEE (editor 802.5 1986—). Republican. Baptist. Office: Siemens Rolm Comms Inc MS920 4900 Old Ironsides Dr # Ms920 Santa Clara CA 95054-1811

SWEENEY, CHRISTEE A., public relations executive; b. Eugene, Oreg., June 10, 1950; d. Milton Greer and Rosemarie Walsh Johnson; m. Patrick E. Sweeney, Sept. 22, 1973. BS in Journalism, U. Oreg., 1973. Cons. mktg. communications Pacific N.W. Bell Co., Portland, Oreg., 1972, acting mgr. mktg., 1972-73; editor newsletter Hyster Co., Portland, Oreg., 1973-81, coordinator corp. pub. relations, 1981-83; dir. pub. relations Gerber Advt., Portland, 1983-88; dir. communications Portland Trail Blazers (NBA), 1988—; Bd. dirs. Portland Rose Fest. Assn. Active Friends of Timberline, Portland, 1984—; mem. NBA-Pub. Rels. Adv. Coun.; mem. adv. bd. Oreg. Com. for Prevention of Child Abuse. Mem. Pub. Rels. Soc. Am., Am. Assn. Advt. Agys. Democrat. Roman Catholic. Office: Portland Trail Blazers 700 NE Multnomah St Ste 600 Portland OR 97232-4106

SWEENEY, CHRISTOPHER LEE, applied mathematics engineer; b. Denver, Oct. 14, 1959; s. Roger Lee Sweeney and Beverly Ann (Wagoner) Good; m. Susan Ann Merrell, May 24, 1986. Student, Community Coll. Denver; grad., U. Colo., 1988. Technican Ball Computer Products, Boulder, Colo., 1978-82, devel. engr., 1982-83; devel. engr. Ball Electronic Systems, Westminster, Colo., 1983-88; reliability engr. StorageTek, Louisville, Colo., 1989-94; mem. tech. staff Analysts Internat. Corp., Denver, 1994—. Inventor in field. Mem. Eta Kappa Nu, Tau Beta Pi. Home: 7974 W 108th Ave Broomfield CO 80021-2649 Office: Analysts Internat Corp 7800 E Union Ave Ste 600 Denver CO 80237

SWEENEY, JAMES AUGUSTUS, retired marine engineer; b. Chelsea, Mass., Oct. 5, 1912; s. Michael James and Jane Ann (Goggin) S.; m. Leonora Bixby, Nov. 11, 1939; children: Janet Sweeney Armstrong, Cari Sweeney Damoose, Michelle Sweeney Mellen. BS in Naval Architecture and Marine Engring., MIT, 1934, MS in Naval Architecture and Marine Engring., 1936. Registered profl. engr., N.Y., N.J. Trainee United Shipyards, N.Y.C., 1936-38; structural designer George G. Sharp, Inc., Naval Architect, N.Y.C., 1938-40, freelance rep., 1947-52, constrn. rep., 1972-74; gen. outfitting supt. Ingalls Shipbuilding Corp., Pascagoula, Miss., 1940-47, 52-53; various managerial positions N.Y. Shipbuilding Corp., Camden, N.J., 1953-62; tech. advisor to gen. mgr. L.A. Div. Todd Shipyards Corp., N.Y.C., 1962-63; ind. cons. shipbuilding, 1963-65, 70-72; project engr./mgr. Nat. Steel & Shipbuilding Co., San Diego, 1965-68; mgr. prodn./design support Advanced Marine Tech. div. Litton Systems, El Segundo, Calif., 1968-70; sr. engr. John J. McMullen Assocs., Inc., N.Y.C., 1974-75; naval architect tanker analysis dept.marine and rail equipment div. FMC Corp., Portland, Oreg., 1975-77; cons. James M. Montgomery Internat., Inc., Pasadena, Calif., 1977-78; ret., 1978; instr. warship design MIT, 1934-36. Active various civic and community orgns. Scholarship recipient MIT, 1932-35. Mem. Soc. Naval Architects and Marine Engrs., Am. Soc. Naval Engrs., KC. Republican. Roman Catholic. Home: 16387 Gabarda Rd San Diego CA 92128-3048

SWEENEY, JAMES D., computer engineer; b. Lansing, Mich., June 20, 1949; s. Harold and Margaret Frances (Johnson) S.; m. Sharlene Margaret Kelly, Sept. 5, 1982. BSEE, U. Mich., 1971, MSE, 1972. Computer engr. Unisys, Salt Lake City, 1976—. Capt. USAF, 1972-76. Mem. ACM, IEEE, Wasatch Mountain Club.

SWEENEY, JAMES LEE, engineering and economic systems educator, cons.; b. Waterbury, Conn., Mar. 22, 1944; s. James Wallace and Aletha B. Sweeney; M. Susan L. Van Every, Aug. 21, 1971; children: Erin, Ryan, Regan. BSEE, M.I.T., 1966; PhD in Engring.-Econ. Systems, Stanford U., 1971. Dir. office energy systems, modeling and forecasting U.S. Fed. Energy Adminstrn. Washington, 1974-76; with Stanford U. 1967—, prof. engring.-econ. systems, 1971—, chmn. dept. engring.-econ. systems, 1991—; dir. Energy Modeling Forum, 1978-85, chmn. Inst. Energy Studies, 1981-84, cons. faculty Sch. of Law, 1980-82, mem. steering com. Ctr. Econ. policy Rsch., 1982—, dir., 1984-86; cons. U.S. Dept. Energy, NRC, Exxon, Charles River Assocs. Recipient Disting. Service award Fed. Energy Adminstrn., 1975. Mem. Am. Econ. Assn., Internat. Assn. Energy Econs. (past v.p. for publs.), Eta Kappa Nu, Tau Beta Pi, Rotary (past pres.), Menlo Circus Club. Co-Author: Macroeconomics Impacts of Energy Shocks, 1987, Fuels to Drive Our Future, 1990; editor: Handbook of Natural Resources and Energy Economics, 1985, 93; co-editor: (jour.) Resources and Energy; contbr. numerous publs. in field to profl. jours. Home: 445 El Escarpado Stanford CA 94305 Office: Stanford U Dept Engring-Econ Systems Terman Engring Ctr Rm 312 Stanford CA 94305-4025

SWEENEY, JAMES STEVENS, JR., design engineer; b. Washington, Sept. 10, 1951; s. James Stevens and Phyllis Emely (Johnson) S. BA, U. Calif., Berkeley, 1972. Mgr., analyst, bd. dirs. Unisen, Inc., Tustin, Calif., 1977-88; v.p., bd. dirs. Tectrix Fitness Equipment, Irvine, Calif., 1988—. Holder numerous patents in field. Mem. IEEE Computer Soc., Assn. for Computing Machinery, Sierra Club. Democrat. Office: Tectrix Fitness Equipment 68 Fairbanks Irvine CA 92718-1602

SWEENEY, JOSEPH W., III, investment executive; b. New Rochelle, N.Y., Mar. 8, 1953; s. Joseph W. Jr. and Rita (McCarren) S.; m. Claudia Margaret Campbell, June 5, 1975; children: Joseph IV, Meredith, Peter. BSEE, U.S. Naval Acad., 1975; MS in Aero. Engring., Naval Postgrad. Sch., 1987. Commd. ensign USN, 1975, advanced through grades to lt. comdr., 1984; asst. schedule officer Patrol Squadron Five AV/ARM Divsn. Office, Jacksonville, Fla., 1977-80; enlisted programs officer USN, Albany, N.Y., Orlando, Fla., 1980-83; ops. officer COMDESRON USN, Pearl Harbor, Hawaii, 1983-85; OIC rsch. detachment staff ASWOC Sigonella, 1987-90; mil. instr. aero/astro. engring. dept. Naval Postgrad. Sch., Monterey, Calif., 1990-94; ret. USN, 1994; investment exec./broker Kidder, Peabody & Co., Carmel, Calif., 1994—. Mktg. coord. Big Sur Internat. Marathon, Carmel, 1990-94. Mem. AIAA. Office: Kidder Peabody & Co 26435 Carmel Rancho Blvd Carmel CA 93923-8705

SWEENEY, KATHY A., bank executive; b. Butte, Mont., Sept. 6, 1949; d. Raymond and Gladys (Heino) Miner; m. Michael R. Sweeney, Apr. 28, 1979. Student, Ea. Mont. Coll., 1967-70. Cert. real estate agt., Calif. Servicing officer Met. Service Mortgage, Billings, Mont., 1973-78; br. mgr. Bancshares Mortgage, Billings, 1978-79; asst. personnel dir. Air Base Constructors, Ramon, Israel, 1980-81; visa, real estate mgr. Bechtel Employees Credit Union, San Francisco, 1982-83; br. mgr., asst. v.p. Unified Mortgage, Walnut Creek, Calif., 1983-85; br. mgr., v.p. IMCO Realty Services, Inc., Walnut Creek and San Diego, 1985-87; owner, exec. dir. Kathy Sweeney Promotions, Walnut Creek, 1986—; v.p., retail div. mgr. Monument Mortgage, Inc., Walnut Creek, 1987-89; pres., CEO The SRS Group, Walnut Creek, Calif., 1989—. Author poetry, 1986. Mem. NAFE, Assn. Profl. Mortgage Women, Calif. Assn. Real Estate Lenders (sec. 1987, pres. 1989, editl. bd. Mortgage Originator mag. 1993, 94—), Women's Network Contra Costa County, ToastMasters Internat. (spkr. and workshop leader 1991, 92, 93, 94). Home: 2863 Via Dominguez Walnut Creek CA 94596-2410 Office: SRS Group 1270 Springbrook Rd Ste A Walnut Creek CA 94596-3941

SWEENEY, MICHAEL, state representative; b. Oakland, Calif., 1950. BA, Calif. State U., MA in Polit. Sci. Elected to Hayward City Coun., 1982, reelected, 1986; mayor pro tem City of Hayward, 1983-84, 88-89, mayor, 1990-94; mem. Calif. State Assembly, 1994—; vice chair local govt. com.; mem. edn. com., natural resources com., environ. safety and toxic materialscom.; guest speaker planning action conf. ABAG, 1988, Oceanic Soc., 1988. Chmn. Citizen/Industry Task Force, 1984; established Household Toxics Removal Day with League of Women Voters, 1984; chmn. Hayward Area Shoreline Planning Agy.; pres., city rep. Alameda County Waste Mgmt. Authority, 1992. Recipient Outstanding Svc. award to community Hayward Neighborhood Alert for Crime Prevention, 1985, 86. Office: Calif State Assembly 22320 Foothill Blvd Ste 130 Hayward CA 94541

SWEENEY, NANCY LOUISE, district court clerk; b. Helena, Mont., July 22, 1957; d. Kenneth F. and Elizabeth (Wernsman) Jones; m. Michael R. Sweeney, Aug. 18, 1984; children; Sean T., Jessica L. BS, Mont. State U., 1979. Legal clk. I Office of the Clk. of Dist. Ct., Helena, Mont., 1979; legal clk. II, bailiff Office of the Clk. of Dist. Ct., Helena, 1979-94, clk. dist. ck., 1994—; union pres. Courthouse Unit, Mont. Pub. Employees Assn., 1981-85. Sunday sch. tchr. St. Paul's United Meth. Ch., 1986-90; cubmaster Cub Scouts Am. Pack 214, 1993—. Democrat. Methodist. Home: 538 S Davis St Helena MT 59601-6303 Office: Clk of Dist Ct 228 Broadway Helena MT 59601

SWEENEY, STACIE MUND, critical care nurse; b. Rapid City, S.D., Dec. 17, 1952; d. Edward W. and Ardyse L. (Teskey) Mund; m. Patrick J. Sweeney Jr., Sept. 1, 1973; children: Christopher, Melissa, Dawn, Meagan. LPN with honors, N.H. Vocat.-Tech. Coll., 1983; RN, Tacoma (Wash.) Community Coll., 1986. Cert. ACLS, CCRN. LPN Frisbee Meml. Hosp., Rochester, N.H., 1983; relief charge nurse, neurotrauma ICU St. Joseph's Hosp., Tacoma, 1984—; tchr. critical level I courses. Home: 2214 150th St E Tacoma WA 98445-3415

SWEENEY, WILLIAM ALAN, chemist, researcher; b. Ocean Falls, B.C., Can., Sept. 12, 1926; came to U.S., 1950; s. William Patrick and Florence Harriet (Lewthwaite) S.; m. Sally Lou Grant, Apr. 11, 1953; children: Michael Alan, Peter Grant, Alison Elizabeth. BSChemE, U. B.C., Vancouver, 1949; PhD, U. Wash., 1954; postgrad., U. Calif., Berkeley, 1967-71. Devel. chemist Can. Industries, Ltd., Toronto, Ont., Can., 1949-50; from rsch. chemist to rsch. scientist Chevron Rsch. & Tech. Co., Richmond, Calif., 1954-90; cons. Chevron Rsch., Richmond, Calif., 1976-90, Teltech, Inc., Mpls., 1990—, U.S. Dept. of Energy, Idaho Falls, Idaho, 1990. Contbr. articles to profl. jours.; patentee in field. Pres., bd. dirs. Homeowners Assn., Larkspur, Calif., 1979-82; chmn., dept. lt. comdr. United Way campaign, 1972; mem. PTA. U. B.C. scholar, 1944, 45; U. Wash. fellow, 1952. Mem. Am. Chem. Soc., N.Y. Acad. Scis., Chevron Retirees Club, Sigma Xi. Republican. Home and Office: 27 Corte Del Bayo Larkspur CA 94939-1501

SWEENEY, WILLIAM JAMES, special education educator; b. Grand Rapids, Minn., Oct. 12, 1962; s. William Lawrence and Gail (LeRoux) S. BA, St. John's U., 1985; MS, Moorhead State U., 1989; PhD, The Ohio State U., 1992. Instr. Lake Region Spl. Edn. Coop., Devils Lake, N.D., 1986-87; instr., coord. for severe emotional disorders Fargo (N.D.) Pub. Schs., 1987-88; lead instr., behavioral cons. Cambridge (Minn.)/Isanti Pub. Schs., 1988-89; grad. rsch. fellow The Ohio State U., Columbus, Ohio, 1989-90, grad. rsch. assoc., 1990-93; asst. prof. dept. spl. edn. Gonzaga U., Spokane, 1993—; behavioral cons. Franklin County Bd., Columbus, 1990—, Marburn Acad., Columbus, 1990—, Rum River Spl. Edn. Coop., Cambridge, 1988-89; sec. edn. coord., cons. Fargo Pub. Schs., Fargo, 1987-88. Mem. NEA, Nat. High Sch. Coaches Assn., Minn. Educators of Emotionally and Behaviorally Disordered, Coun. for Exceptional Children, Assn. for Behavior Analysis, Internat. Reading Assn. Roman Catholic. Home: 958 E 39th Ave Spokane WA 99203-3035 Office: Gonzaga U Dept Spl Edn Spokane WA 99258

SWEET, ANDREW ARNOLD, psychologist; b. Mt. Kisco, N.Y., Aug. 26, 1956; s. John Stevens and Deana (Baron) S.; m. Nancy Rainwater, May 19, 1984; 1 child, Adrienne Elizabeth Sweetwater. BS, SUNY, Oneonta, 1978; Psychology D., Denver U., 1982. Lic. psychologist. Asst. prof. U. Colo., Greeley, 1982-83; pvt. practice Assocs. for Change, Denver, Colo., 1982—; clin. supr. Wallace Village for Children, Broomfield, Colo., 1983-84; clin. affiliate sch. profl. psychology U. Denver, 1983—; clin. psychologist Human Performance Inst., Lakewood, Colo., 1985-87. Co-author: Behavior Therapy Outcome, 1986, Anxiety & Stress Disorders, 1987; contbr. articles to profl. jours. Mem. Assn. for Advancement Behavior Therapy, Am. Psychol. Soc. Democrat. Home: 1900 Leyden St Denver CO 80220-1626 Office: 1720 Bellaire St # 808 Denver CO 80220-1049

SWEET, HARVEY, theatric, scenic and lighting designer; b. Detroit, Oct. 27, 1943; s. Sam and Rose Sweet; m. Susan Perrett, Mar. 16, 1964 (div. Mar. 1975); children: Deborah Anne, Rebecca Lynn, Jason Aaron; m. Patricia Ravn, Sept. 9, 1978 (div. July 1987). BS, Ea. Mich. U., 1965; MS, U. Wis., 1967, PhD, 1974. Instr. U. N.D., Grand Forks, 1967-69; asst. prof. Boise (Idaho) State Coll., 1972-73; instr. U. Wis., Madison, 1973-74; prof. of theater arts U. No. Iowa, Cedar Falls, 1974-89; dir. lighting Landmark Entertainment Group, L.A. and Tokyo, 1989-91; cons. Advanced Tech., Tokyo, 1991; cons. in field; owner, operator Sweet Studios Theatrical Equipment, Cedar Falls, 1981-89; dir. theater tech. and design U. No. Iowa, 1974-87; project mgr., sr. designer, Glendale, Calif., 1993—. Author: Graphics for the Performing Arts, 1982, Handbook of Scenery, Properties and Lighting, I and II, 1988, 2nd edit., 1995, The Complete Book of Drawing for the Theatre, 1995; scenic designer Summer Repertory Theatre, 1988, Timberlake Playhouse, 1988-89; lighting designer, scenic designer, tech. dir. various coll. theatrical prodns. Mem. U.S. Inst. for Theatre Tech. (vice commr. 1979-83, mem. graphic standards bd. 1979-86, evaluation commr. 1983-88, mem. publs. com. 1986-89, bd. dirs. 1989). Office: Tru-Roll Inc 622 Sonora Ave Glendale CA 91201-2339

SWEET, MARY FRENCH, artist; b. Cin., Oct. 10, 1937; d. Robert Houston and Dorothy May (Duff) French; m. James Newton Sweet, June 20, 1961; children: Dennis Robert, Nancy Foster, Elizabeth Valerie. AB in Art, Stanford U., 1959, MA in Art, 1960. One-woman shows include Univ. Club, Cin., 1961, Meridian Gallery, Albuquerque, 1979, 80, 81, 83, 85, Gekas-Nicholas Gallery, Tucson, 1983-84, Hummingbird Originals Gallery, Ft. Worth, 1987, Am. Home Furnishings Gallery, Albuquerque, 1995; exhibited in group shows at Weyrich Gallery, Albuquerque, 1985—, Tarbox Gallery, San Diego, 1993, Leon Loard Galleries, Montgomery, Ala., 1993, Laughing Bear Gallery, Placitas, N.Mex., 1993, Blankley Gallery, Albuquerque, 1993, Snowgrass Inst., Cashmere, Wash., 1993, Coll. Santa Fe, 1993, Monothon, Coll. Santa Fe, 1995. Mem. Nat. Mus. of Women in Arts, Escribiente, N.Mex. Watercolor Soc., Albuquerque United Artists. Democrat. Home and Office: PO Box 280 Tijeras NM 87059-0280

SWEET, THOMAS IRA, physician; b. Mpls., Aug. 29, 1958; s. Douglas Morton and Elaine (Solon) S.; m. Lisa Susan Treger, June 5, 1988; children: Jeffrey Aaron, Lauren Melissa. BS, Stanford U., 1980, MS, 1980; MD, U. Minn., 1984. Diplomate Am. Bd. Internal Medicine, Am. Bd. Med. Oncology, Am. Bd. Hematology. Intern U. Calif., San Diego, 1984-85; resident U. Calif. Med. Ctr., San Diego, 1984-87; fellow U. Md. Cancer Ctr., Balt., 1987-90; staff physician So. Calif. Permanente Med. Group, Anaheim, Calif., 1990—. Mem. ACP, Am. Soc. Clin. Oncology, Alpha Omega Alpha. Home: 25 Diamante Irvine CA 92720-1904 Office: 411 N Lakeview Ave Anaheim CA 92807-3028

SWEETWATER, SARAH, art educator; b. Roscoe, Tex., Feb. 18, 1940; d. William Bernard and Opal Pearl (Young) Whisenant; m. Leland Ray Campsey, Nov. 25, 1960 (div. Jan. 1975); children: Keri Opal, Alice Anne, Melissa Lee. BS in Art Edn., West Tex. State U., Canyon, 1965; MEd in Art and Human Rels., U. Utah, 1977. Chmn. dept. art No. Nev. C.C., Elko, 1971—; dir. Ednl. Travel, Elko, 1976—. Artist marble, stone and steel, metals, quilts, bronze. Dir. Pioneer Arts Crafts-Cowboy Poetry, Elko, 1975-85; bd. mem. Nev. State Art Educators, Elko, 1994—; bd. dirs. Crytasia, Elko, 1993—; dir., com. chair Mural Task Force, Elko, 1994-95. Named Woman of Yr. Elko County, Nev., 1979; NEH fellow U. Calif., Berkeley, 1980; recipient Gov. Arts award Nev. State Coun. on Arts, 1981, Excellence in Edn. award NISOD, U. Tex., No. Nev. C.C., 1994. Mem. Nev. State Art Educators (bd. mem., coll. rep. 1994—), Internat. Sculpture Soc. Home: 1375 Oak St Elko NV 89801-3433

SWENSEN, LAIRD S., orthopedic surgeon; b. Provo, Utah, Oct. 5, 1944; s. Russel Brown and Beulah (Strickler) S.; m. Gloria Elaine Matoza, Sept. 23, 1973; children: Lara Ann, Christine, Russel, Tracy, Laird. BA in Chemistry, Brigham Young U., 1968; MD, George Washington U., 1972. Diplomate Am. Bd. Orthopedic Surgery; cert. added qualifications in surgery of hand, 1992. Intern San Francisco Gen. Hosp., 1972-73; resident in orthopedics U. Calif., San Francisco, 1973-77; pvt. practice orthopedic surgery Salt Lake City, 1978—; fellow in hand and microvascular surgery Jack Tupper, 1978; vice chmn. dept. surgery LDS Hosp.; chmn. div. orthopedics LDS Hosp., 1991-92; assoc. clin. prof. dept. orthopedic surgery U. Utah, 1979, asst. clin. prof., 1990—; vol. surgeon Orthopedics Overseas, Nepal, 1988, 90, Bhutan, 1992; med. project advisor Tibetan Resettlement Project, Salt Lake City. Fellow Am. Acad. Orthopedic Surgery; mem. Western Orthopedic Assn. (pres. Utah chpt. 1991), Am. Soc. Surgery of Hand, Utah State Med. Assn. Office: 324 10th Ave Salt Lake City UT 84103-2853

SWENSEN, MARY JEAN HAMILTON, graphic artist; b. Laurens, S.C., June 25, 1910; d. Elvin A. and Della (Brown) Hamilton; m. Oliver Severn Swensen, Mar. 3, 1943 (dec.). BS, Columbia U., 1956, MA, 1960; Cert. Notable, U. Madrid, Spain; postgrad., Ariz. State U., 1974-80. mem. 1st USSA sr. internat. cross-country skiing team. One person shows at Colo. Fed. Savs. and Loan Assn., Denver, 1978, Panoras Gallery, N.Y.C., 1963; exhibited in group shows at Soc. Western Artist, M.H. de Young Mus., San Francisco, 1964, Nat. Art Roundup, Las Vegas, 1965, Fine Arts Bldg., Colo. State Fair, Pueblo, 1965, Duncan Gallery, Paris, 1974, Colo. Fed. Savs. & Loan Assn., Denver, 1978; graphics arts in pub. collections at Met. Mus. Art, N.Y.C., Nat. Graphic Arts Collection, Smithsonian Inst., Laurens (S.C.) Pub. Libr., N.Y.C. Pub. Libr. Recipient Duncan Gallery Prix de Paris, 1974, YWCA of U.S.A. Gold Medal as most admired athlete of the yr., 1977, USSA Nat. Citizens X-Country Racing Team Gold, Silver and Bronze medals for downhill, giant slalom, slalom, and cross country senior citizen and vet. races, 1963-79. Mem. Am. Mensa, Delta Phi Delta.

SWENSON, KATHLEEN SUSAN, music and art educator; b. Reno, Nev., Oct. 23, 1938; d. Harold Ruthaford McNeil and Hollyce Margaret (Scruggs) McNeil Biggs; m. James Michael Phalan, 1956 (div. 1974); children: David Michael, Jeanine Louise Phalan Lawrence, Gregory Shaun; m. Gerald Allen Swensen, Nov. 1976 (div. 1987); stepchildren: Craig Allen, Sarah Ann, Eric Sander. Student, U. Nev., Reno, 1956-58, Foothill Coll., 1966-68; AA, West Valley Coll.; BA, U. Calif., Santa Cruz, 1983. Concert pianist Nev.,Calif, 1950-64; pvt. piano instr. various locations, 1963—, pvt. art instr., 1970—, pvt. astrology instr., 1973—; founder, pres. AAM Triple Arts, Aptos, Calif., 1974—; founder, owner Aptos (Calif.) Acad. Music, 1993—. Producer, instr. art instrn. videos, music instrn. films, books. Mem. Soc Western Artists, Calif. Piano Tchrs. Assn., Los Gatos Art Assn. (pres. 1985-86), Saratoga Contemporary Artists (v.p. 1984-85), Nat. League Am. Pen Women (honorarian 1985), Soroptomists. Republican. Episcopalian. Home and Office: AAM Triple Arts 3000 Wisteria Way Aptos CA 95003-3318 Also: Aptos Acad Music 7000 Soquel Dr Ste 425 Aptos CA 95003

SWENSON, MARY ANN, bishop. Bishop Rocky Mountain Diocese, Denver. Office: Rocky Mountain Diocese 2200 S University Blvd Denver CO 80210-4708*

SWENSON, RICHARD ALLEN, business owner, animal trainer; b. Willmar, Minn., Dec. 1, 1950; s. LeRoy Oswald Boe and Delores G. (Malghist) S.; children: Kristen, Richard Andrew, Kevin. Author: Secrets of Long Distance Sled Dog Racing. Treas. Pride, Alaska, 1993—. Recipient 1st pl. Iditarod, 1977, 79, 80, 81, 91 among others. Office: Denali Sled Dog Tours PO Box 86 Denali National Park AK 99755-0086

SWENSON, ROBERT SANFRED, physician; b. Brooten, Minn., Apr. 19, 1933; s. Silas George and Amy Florence (Everson) S.; m. Carol Jean Conley; children: Cynthia, Dana. BA, U. Minn., 1955; MD, U. Minn., ;, 1958. Intern Mpls. Gen. Hosp., 1958-59; resident U. Calif., San Francisco, 1961-63, Stanford Med. Sch., 1963-65; from asst. prof. to assoc. prof., dir. dialysis Stanford (Calif.) U., Palo Alto (Calif.) VA Med. Ctr., Calif., 1965-89; chief of staff Livermore (Calif.) VA Med. Ctr., 1989-93; assoc. prof., physician Stanford U., 1993—. Lt. USNR, 1959-61. Mem. Am. Soc. Nephrology, Am. Soc. Artificial Internal Organs, No. Calif. Nat. Kidney Found (hon. pres.). Home and Office: 1062 Cathcart Way Stanford CA 94305-1047

SWENSON, SHIRLEY RUTH, elementary education educator; b. Provo, Utah, Dec. 22, 1935; d. Karl Warnick and Ruth Irene (Eldredge) S. BS, Brigham Young U., 1958, MEd, 1972. Cert. tchr. elem. edn., spl. edn., libr., Utah. Tchr. 2d grade Sevier Sch. Dist., Richfield, Utah, 1958-59, Jordan Sch. Dist., Sandy, Utah, 1959-61; tchr. 3d grade Alpine Sch. Dist., American Fork, Utah, 1963-71, resource tchr., 1971-94, team leader Barratt Elem., 1992—. Editor: Swen Swenson Descendants, 1955, Nebeker Family Booke., 1979. Guide, Nauvoo (Ill.) Restoration, 1969-70; missionary LDS Ch., southern states, 1961-63. Mem. DAR, Mayflower Soc., Utah Ednl. Assn. Office: Barratt Elem Sch 168 N 900 E American Fork UT 84003

SWERDA, PATRICIA FINE, artist, author, educator; b. Ft. Worth, Aug. 10, 1916; d. William Emerson and Margaret Ellen (Cull) Fine; B.S. cum laude, Tex. Woman's U., 1941; grad. Ikenobo U., Tokyo, 1965-66, Ikenobo Dojo, Kyoto, Japan, 1976, 77, 81, 83, 85, 87, 91; m. John Swerda, July 7, 1941; children: John Patrick James, Susan Ann Mary Swerda Foss, Margaret Rose Swerda Kownover. Exhibited ikebana in one-woman shows including: Bon Marche, Tacoma, 1966, Seattle, 1967, 85, Gallery Kokoro, Seattle, 1972-78; exhibited in group shows including: Takashimaya Dept. Store, 1965, 76, 77, 83, 85, Matsuzakaya Dept. Store, Tokyo, 1966, Ikenobo Center, Kyoto, 1966, 77, Seattle Art Mus., 1974-80, Sangyo Kaikan, Kyoto, 1976, Burke Mus., U. Wash., ann. Cherry Blossom Festival, Seattle, Bellevue Art Mus., 1984, 85, 87, 89, 90, 91, 92, 93, 94, 95; demonstrations in field for various groups, including Greater Northwest Flower and Garden Show, Milw. Art en Fleurs, Japan Week in Bellevue. Master of Ikebana of Ikenobo Ikebana Soc., Kyoto. Pres. Bellevue Sister Cities Assn. 1985; bd. dirs. Washington State Sister Cities Coord. Com. Named Disting. Alumna class of 1941 Tex. Woman's U., 1991. Mem. N.W. Sakura Chpt. of the Ikenobo Ikebana Soc. (pres. 1960-91), Bonsai Clubs Internat., Puget Sound Bonsai Assn., G.O. Philoptochos (Charitable) Soc. Democrat. Greek Orthodox. Author: Japanese Flower Arranging: Practical and Aesthetic Bases of Ikebana, 1969; Creating Japanese Shoka, 1979; contbr. articles to mags. in field; creator Ikenobo Gardens, Redmond; numerous radio and TV appearances. Home and Office: 9828 NE 4th St Redmond WA 98004

SWETNAM, MONTE NEWTON, petroleum exploration executive; b. Alexandria, La., Oct. 9, 1936; s. Montreville Morris and Margaret Elizabeth (Cullison) S.; m. Elaine Adelia Taylor, Dec. 21, 1957; children: Scott David, Robert Troy. Student, Johns Hopkins, 1955-58; B.S. in Geology, U. Wyo., 1960, M.S. in Geology, 1961; M.B.A. in Bus. Adminstrn, Pepperdine U., 1978. Registered geologist, Calif. Exploration geologist Amerada Petroleum Corp., Durango, Colo., 1961-63; exploration geologist Tenneco Oil Co., Durango, 1963-65; dist. project geologist Tenneco Oil Co., Bakersfield, Calif., 1965-69; div. staff geologist Tenneco Oil Co., Bakersfield, 1969; partner Argonaut Oil & Gas Cons., Denver, 1969-71; internat. exploration mgr. Tesoro Petroleum Corp., San Antonio, 1971-73; v.p. internat. exploration Tesoro Petroleum Corp., 1973-74, sr. v.p. exploration, 1974-82; pres. Tesoro-Bolivia Petroleum Co., 1975-82, Tesoro-Algeria Petroleum Co., 1975-82; sr. v.p. exploration Natural Resource Mgmt. Corp./NRM, Dallas, 1983-86; sr. v.p. exploration and prodn. Harken Energy Corp., 1987-89, exec. v.p., 1991-93; pres. Harken Exploration Co., 1988-91, Harken Bahrain Oil Co., 1989-93; exec. v.p., chief oper. officer Giant Exploration and Prodn. Co., Farmington, N.Mex., 1994—; pres. Canyon Marinas, Inc., San Antonio. Contbr. articles to profl. jours. Mem. Am. Assn. Petroleum Geologists, Geol. Soc. Am., Sigma Xi. Republican. Clubs: Alamo Yacht, Lake Canyon Yacht. Home: 3500 Island Moorings Pky # 231 PO Box 154 Port Aransas TX 78373 Office: PO Box 2810 2200 Bloomfield Hwy Farmington NM 87499-2810

SWETT, DALE EVERETT, physical therapist; b. Eagle River, Wis., June 12, 1937; s. Jess Floyd Swett and Velma O. (Vreeland) Swett-Rozich; children: Jess Scott (dec.), Deanna Marie. BS, Cen. State U., Stevens Point, Wis., 1960; Cert. Phys. Therapy, Northwestern U., Chgo., 1962. Cert. phys. therapist. Commd. USPHS, 1962, advanced through grades to capt., 1983, ret., 1992; staff therapist USPHS, Seattle, 1962-65; chief phys. therapy USPHS/Indian Health Svc., Sitka, Alaska, 1965-70; dep. chief phys. therapy Div. Hosp. and Clinics USPHS, Norfolk, Va., 1970-72; chief phys. therapy USPHS/Indian Health Svc., Gallup, N.Mex., 1972-75; clin. coord. field ops. USPHS/Indian Health Svc., 1975-85; chief, rehab. br. USPHS/Indian Health Svc., Window Rock, Ariz., 1975—; acting sr. clinician USPHS/Indian Health Svc., 1985-88; therapy program dir. Indian Health Svc., Gallup, N.Mex., 1989-92; Indian Health Svc. rep. to Navajo Nation Coun. on Handicapped, Window Rock; cons. in sports medicine Gallup H.S. wrestling team, Gallup Gymnastics Club. Mem. Commd. Officer's Assn., Assn. USPHS (sec. Mt. Edgecumbe chpt. 1968-70, pres. Gallup chpt. 1980-83), Am. Phys. Therapy Assn. (named Therapist of Yr. N.Mex. chpt. 1988, Surgeon Gen.'s Profl. Adv. Com. 1988-92, Meritorious Svcs. medal 1991), Res. Officers Assn. of Uniformed Svcs. of U.S., N.Am. Hunting Club, NRA, others. Presbyterian. Home: Box 116 3410 Tall Timber Tr Trinidad CO 81082

SWIFT, WILLIAM CHARLES, professional baseball player, Olympic athlete; b. Portland, Maine, Oct. 27, 1961. Student, Maine. Mem. U.S. Olympic Baseball Team, 1984; with Seattle Mariners, 1984-91; pitcher San Francisco Giants, 1991-94, Colo. Rockies, 1994—. Office: Colo Rockies 2850 W 20th Ave Denver CO 80211*

SWIG, ROSELYNE CHROMAN, art advisor; b. Chgo., June 8, 1930; m. Richard Swig, Feb. 5, 1950; children—Richard, Jr., Susan, Marjorie, Carol. Student, U. Calif.-Berkeley, UCLA; MFA with honors, San Francisco Art Inst., 1976, DFA (hon.), 1988. Pres. Roselyne C. Swig Artsource, San Francisco, 1977-94; apptd. by pres. as dir. art in embassies program U.S. Dept. of State, 1994—. Mem. bd. trustees San Francisco Mus. Modern Art, U. Art Mus., Berkeley, Calif., Mills Coll., Oakland, Calif., United Jewish Appeal; ex officio bd. mem. Jewish Mus. San Francisco; bd. dirs. San Francisco Opera, Am. Joint Distbn. Com.; pres., bd. dirs. Jewish Community Fedn. San Francisco, the Peninsula, Marin and Sonoma Counties; past commr. San Francisco Pub. Libr.; past bd. dirs. Am. Coun. for Arts, KQED Broadcasting System; mem. Vail, Colo., Art in Pub. Places Bd.; bd. govs. fine arts adv. panel Fed. Res. System; past pres. Calif. State Summer Sch. Arts, San Francisco Art Inst., San Francisco Arts Commission; past nat. v.p. Am./Israel Pub. Affairs Com.

SWIHART, H. GREGG, real estate company executive; b. San Francisco, Sept. 25, 1938; s. Lawson Benjamin and Violet Mary (Watters) S.; B.A., U. Ariz., 1958; postgrad. U. Heidelberg (W.Ger.), 1958-59, Harvard U., 1959-60; M.A., Boston U., 1961; postgrad. U. Freiburg (West Germany), 1961-65; m. Ilse Paula Rambacher, Dec. 24, 1958; children—Tatjana Etta, Brett Marc, Natascha Theda. Stock broker Walston & Co., Tucson, 1966-71; with Solot Co., Tucson, 1971-74; pres. Cienega Properties, Inc., property mgmt. and investment, Tucson, 1975-77; pres. GT Realty Assocs., Ltd., Tucson, 1977—. Mem. Tucson Com. Fgn. Relations, 1973—; pres. Forum for Greater Outdoors, 1977-79; bd. dirs. Tucson Mus. Art, 1968-74, pres. 1969-70; pres. and trustee Canelo Hills Sch., 1977-79. Cert. property mgr. Mem. Tucson Bd. Realtors, Inst. Real Estate Mgmt. (pres. Tucson-So. Ariz. chpt. 1982, mem. nat. governing council 1985-87), Inst. Real Estate Mgmt. (governing council 1985-87, Property Mgr. of Yr. award So. Ariz. chpt. 1988), Realtors Nat. Mktg. Inst. Clubs: Harvard (pres. 1973-74), Active 20-30 (pres. 1969), Downtown Tucson. Home: Tunnel Springd Ranch PO Box 555 Sonoita AZ 85637 Office: 4003 E Speedway Blvd Ste 110 Tucson AZ 85712-4555

SWINDELLS, WILLIAM, JR., lumber and paper company executive; b. Oakland, CA, 1930; married. B.S., Stanford U., 1953. With Willamette Industries, Inc., Portland, Oreg., 1953—; sr. v.p. prodn., mktg. bldg. materials Willamette Industries, Inc., until 1978, exec. v.p., 1978-80, pres. forest products div., 1980-82, pres., chief exec. officer, 1982—, also dir., chmn., 1984—; dir. Oreg. Bank, Portland. Office: Bohemia Inc 1300 SW 5th Ave Portland OR 97201-5667

SWINDLER, DARIS RAY, physical anthropologist, forensic anthropologist; b. Morgantown, W.Va., Aug. 13, 1925; s. George Raymond and Minnie Mildred (McElroy) S.; m. Kathryn Pardo, Nov. 10, 1977; children: Gary, Darece, Linda, Dana, Bruce, Geoffry, Jason. AB, W.Va. U., 1950; MA, U. Pa., 1952, PhD, 1959. Instr. Cornell Med. Sch., N.Y.C., 1956-57, W.Va. Med. Sch., Morgantown, 1957-59; asst. prof. Med. Coll. S.C., Charleston, 1959-64; assoc. prof. Mich. State U., East Lansing, 1964-68; prof. phys. anthropology, comparative primate anatomy, dental anthropology U. Wash., Seattle, 1968-91, prof. emeritus anthropology, 1991—; emeritus curator comparative primate anatomy Burke Mus., Seattle, 1991—; cons. King County Med. Examiner, Seattle, 1968—; vis. sr. scientist U. Frankfurt, Germany, 1982-83, Com. on Scholarly Commns. with Peoples Republic of China, 1987-88; vis. prof. U. Zurich, 1992; field participant Valley of Kings Expdn., Egypt., 1990-93; vis. prof. U. Padua, Italy, 1994. Author: A Racial Study of the West Nakani of New Britain, 1962, Dentition of Living Primates, 1976, Systematics, Evolution and Anatomy, Comparative Primate Biology; (with C.D. Wood) Atlas of Primate Gross Anatomy, 1973 (Gov's. award 1973), (with J. Sirianni) Growth and Development of Pigtailed Macaque, 1985. Served with USN, 1943-46. Recipient Alexander von Humboldt Sr. U.S. Scientist awrd, Germany, 1981. Fellow AAAS, Explorer's Club; mem. Am. Assn. Phys. Anthropologists (v.p. 1976-78), Dental Anthropology Assn. (pres. 1990-92), Internat. Primatology Soc., N.Y. Acad. Sci., Italian Primatol. Assn., Sigma Xi.

SWINDLER, KATHRYN ELIZABETH, writer; b. Seattle, Nov. 8, 1947; d. Joseph Harrison Pardo and Helmi Gloria (Rantala) Dahl; m. Daris R. Swinder, Nov. 10, 1977. Student, U. Wash., 1967-71. Poet various small presses and anthologies various sml. presses, 1974—; freelance tech. writer Seattle, 1974—; mgr. publs. People's Nat. Bank, Seattle, 1978-80, Seattle First Nat. Bank, 1968-78, Seattle Trust and Savs. Bank, 1980-87; mgr. adminstrv. svcs. Key Bank of Wash., Seattle, 1987-93; writer Edmonds, Wash., 1993—; bd. dirs. Highline Community Coll. Tech. Writing Curriculum Com. Seattle; guest moderator Norwescon 15, 1992. Editor: Soc. for Tech. Communications jour., 1977-79; cons. poet, editor: Olympic View Writers Conf., Everett, Wash., 1991; author: (poetry collections) The Dark Man, 1975, The Brickbuilder, 1976 (Capital Hill Arts on Show award); author numerous poems in sml. presses, 1974—. Mem. Med. Ctr. Coun./Group Health Co-op, Seattle, 1987; vol. Puget Sound Transp. Coun., Seattle, 1989, Am. Cancer So., Seattle, 1980. Recipient award of Achievement Soc. for Tech. Communicators, 1980, award of Excellence, 1978. Mem. Sci. Fiction Poetry Assn., Acad. Am. Poets. Home: 1212 8th Ave N Edmonds WA 98020-2603

SWINDLER, STEPHEN FRANCIS, distribution company executive; b. Indpls., Jan. 27, 1942; s. Frank J. and Greta Miskell (Gormley) S.; m. Sally Swindler, Sept. 1, 1970 (div. July, 1985); children: Lori, Scott; m. Carol Ann Obermeier; children: Jeremy, Brndon. Student, Purdue U., 1960-62; BS in Biology, Chemistry, History, Phys. Edn., Ball State U., 1970. Sales rep. Merck & Co., Inc., Janesville, Wis., 1970-72; sales ops. mgr. Merck & Co., Inc., Rahway, N.J., 1972-73; regional sales mgr. Merck & Co., Inc., Chgo., 1973-76; nat. sale mgr. Bayvet Divsn. Cutter Labs., Shawnee Mission, Kans., 1976-80; dir. mktg. svcs. Bayvet Divsn. Miles Labs., Shawnee Mission, 1980-85; gen. mgr. sales and mktg. Mobay (Bayvet) Animal Health Divsn., Shawnee Mission, 1986-92; cons. acquisitions SFS Consulting, Shawnee Mission, 1992; v.p., dir. mktg. and sales WALCO Internat., Inc., Porterville, Calif., 1992-94, COO, 1994—; leader quality process Miles Labs. Shawnee Mission, Kans., 1990-92. Author (manuals) Training a Proactive Rep., 1979, Evaluation for Achievement, 1982. Rep. councilman, Westfield, N.J., 1972-73; coach little league baseball, soccer, basketball, 1977-91. With USN, 1965-70. Mem. VFW, Am. Quarter Horse Assn. (sponsor), Animal Health Inst. (speaker), Nat. Cattlemens Assn., Tex. Cattle Feeders Assn. Roman Catholic. Office: Walco Internat Inc 13 W Putnam Ave Porterville CA 93257-3627

SWING, WILLIAM EDWIN, bishop; b. Huntington, W.Va., Aug. 26, 1936; s. William Lee and Elsie Bell (Holliday) S.; M. Mary Willis Taylor, Oct. 7, 1961; children—Alice Marshall, William Edwin. B.A., Kenyon Coll., Ohio, 1954-58; D.Div. (hon.), Kenyon Coll., 1980; M.A., Va. Theol. Sem., 1958-61, D.Div., 1980. Ordained priest Episcopal Ch. Asst. St. Matthews Ch., Wheeling, W.Va., 1961-63; vicar St. Matthews Ch., Chester, W.Va., 1963-69, St. Thomas Ch., Weirton, W.Va., 1963-69; rector St. Columba's Episcopal Ch., Washington, 1969-79; bishop Episcopal Ch. Calif., San Francisco, 1980—; chmn. bd. Ch. Div. Sch. of the Pacific, 1983-84; founder, chmn. Episcopal Found. for Drama, 1976—. Republican. Home: 2006 Lyon St San Francisco CA 94115-1610 Office: Episcopal Ch Diocesan Office 1055 Taylor St San Francisco CA 94108-2209*

SWISLOCKI, ARTHUR L. M., physician, internist; b. L.A., May 4, 1951; s. Adam and Marie (Spanbock) S.; m. Ann Manheimer, June 16, 1974; children: Pauline, Allison. BA in Zoology, UCLA, 1972, MA in Biology, 1973, MD, 1979; student medicine, Free U. Brussels, Belgium, 1974-75. Diplomate Am. Bd. Internal Medicine, Am. Bd. Endocrinology and Metabolism. Intern in medicine LA County U. So. Calif. Med. Ctr., L.A., 1979-80; resident in medicine U. Calif. Davis Med. Ctr., Sacramento, 1980-82, chief resident in medicine, 1982-83; fellow in endocrinology Stanford (Calif.) U., 1984-86, fellow in clin pharmacology, 1986-88; staff endocrinologist VA Med. Ctr., Martinez, Calif., 1988—; acting chief med. svcs. VA Med. Ctr., Martinez, 1992—; asst. prof. medicine U. Calif., Davis, 1989—. Author: (with others) Endocrine Disorders of Pregnancy, 1989; contbr. articles to profl. jours. Recipient Nat. Rsch. fellowship NIH, 1987. Fellow Am. Coll. Physicians. Office: VA No Calif Sys of Clinics Med Svcs III 150 Muir Rd Martinez CA 94553

SWOFFORD, ROBERT LEE, newspaper editor, journalist; b. Berryville, Ark., Aug. 22, 1949; s. Andrew Madison and Verna Mae (England) S.; m. Karen King, Jan. 24, 1969 (div. 1977); children: Teri, Toby; m. Sandra Dunn, 1978 (div. 1979); m. B. Joanna Rongren, Feb. 14, 1981; 1 child, Tyler. AA, Coll. of the Sequoias, 1969; student, Calif. State U., 1969-71. Photographer, reporter, news editor The Advance-Register, Tulare, Calif., 1965-78; city editor The Record Searchlight, Redding, Calif., 1978-81; suburban editor, Neighbors editor The Sacramento Bee, 1981-86; assoc. metro. editor, community editor The Orange County Register, Santa Ana, Calif., 1986-89; exec. news editor The Press Democrat, Santa Rosa, Calif., 1989-90, mng. editor, 1990—. Mem. Assoc. Press Mng. Editors, Calif. Soc. of Newspaper Editors, Soc. of Newspaper Design. Office: The Press Democrat 427 Mendocino Ave Santa Rosa CA 95401-6313

SYAGE, JACK ALBERT, chemist, physicist; b. Rockville Center, N.Y., Apr. 5, 1954; s. George Jacob and Rose Marie (Shohfi) S.; m. Elizabeth Ann Tallman, Sept. 17, 1983; children: George, Amber. BA, Hamilton Coll., 1976; PhD, Brown U., 1982. Rsch. fellow Calif. Inst. Tech., Pasadena, 1981-84; rsch. scientist The Aerospace Corp., L.A., 1984—. Contbr. articles to Jour. Chem. Physics, Jour. Phys. Chemistry, numerous other profl. publs. Home: 4036 Brighton Cir Cypress CA 90630-2702 Office: Aerospace Corp Mail Stop 754 PO Box 92957 Los Angeles CA 90009

SYDNOR, ROBERT HADLEY, state government geologist; b. Whittier, Calif., July 1, 1947; s. Thurston Edward and Mary Edith (Thompson) S.; divorced; 1 child, Christopher. BA, Whittier Coll., 1969; MS, U. Calif.-Riverside, 1975. Registered geologist, Calif., Alaska, Ariz.; cert. engring. geologist, Calif.; cert. hydrogeologist, Calif. Asst. petroleum geologist Mobil Oil Corp., Anchorage, 1970-71; staff engring. geologist Leighton & Assocs., Irvine, Calif., 1973-77; assoc. engring. geologist Orange County, Laguna Niguel, Calif., 1977-79; sr. engring. geologist VTN Corp., Irvine, 1979; chief engring. geologist R&M Cons., Inc., Irvine, 1979-82; supervising geologist Calif. Div. Mines and Geology, San Francisco, 1982-90, sr. engr. geologist, Sacramento, 1990—; mem. exam. com. Calif. State Bd. of Registration for Geologists and Geophysicists, Sacramento, 1977—, chmn., 1978. Co-editor CDMG spl. publ. on the 1989 Loma Prieta earthquake, 1992 Cape Mendocino earthquake, 1992 Landers earthquake, 1994 Northridge earthquake; contbr. many cons. reports on landslides and seismicity. Mem. alumni scholarship com. U. Calif.-Riverside, 1978-86; mem. City of Los Angeles Grading Appeals Bd., 1979-84; alt. mem. County of Orange Grading Appeals Bd., 1980-84. Donnel Foster Hewett fellow U. Calif., 1972. Mem. Calif. Acad. Sci. (life), Assn. Engring. Geologists (assoc. editor Bull. 1979-86, chmn. So. Calif. sect. 1979-80), Geol. Soc. Am., Seismol. Soc. Am. (life), Am. Assn. Petroleum Geologists, Am. Inst. Profl. Geologists, Nat. Assn. Geology Tchrs., Am. Quarternary Assn., Arctic Inst. N.Am. (life), ASTM, Am. Geophys. Union (life), Sigma Gamma Epsilon (life). Republican. Presbyterian. Home: 4930 Huntridge Ln Fair Oaks CA 95628-4823 Office: Calif Div Mines and Geology 801 K St MS 12-31 Sacramento CA 95814-3531

SYDOR, RICHARD PAUL, social science educator; b. Welland, Ont., Can., Sept. 5, 1947; came to U.S., 1984.; s. Thomas and Olga (Dolishny) S.; m. Linda Joy Evans, Oct. 23, 1971 (div. Apr. 1983); m. Marcia LeDuc, Aug. 24, 1984. BA, Calif. State U., 1988. Distbn. mgr. Toyota Can., Inc., Calgary, Alberta, 1974-80; speech/mtgs. cons. Calgary, 1980-84; social sci. educator Sacramento (Calif.) City Schs., 1984—. Mem. Am. Inst. Parliamentarians, Toastmasters Internat. (dist. gov. 1981-82), Calif. Coun. Social Studies, K. of C. Roman Catholic. Home: 1092 Salmon Dr Roseville CA 95661-4432

SYED, RASHID, protein crystallographer; b. Bombay, India, Jan. 28, 1960; came to U.S., 1983; m. Fehmida, June 1, 1989. BSc, U. Bombay, 1980, MSc, 1982; PhD, U. Toledo, 1987. Rsch. fellow The Scripps Rsch. Inst., San Diego, 1987-94; rsch. scientist Amgen, Inc., Thousand Oaks, Calif., 1994—. NIH fellow, 1991-93. Mem. Am. Crystallography Assn. Office: Amgen Inc M/S 14-2-8 1840 De Havilland Dr Thousand Oaks CA 91320-1789

SYKE, CAMERON JOHN, lawyer; b. Oak Park, Ill., Jan. 29, 1957; s. A. John and Rosemarie (Grasso) S.; m. Susan Royer, Jan. 2, 1982; children: Caroline, Jared. BSBA cum laude, U. Denver, 1977, LLM in Taxation, 1986; JD with honors, DePaul U., 1982. Bar: CPA, Colo. 1983, U.S. Tax Ct. 1985. Acct. Touche, Ross, Chgo., 1978-79, Denver, 1980-83; investment broker Boettcher & Co., Denver, 1983-84; CPA Laventhol & Horwath, Denver, 1984-85; assoc. Roath & Brega, Denver, 1985-87; dir. Hopper and Kanouff, P.C., Denver, 1987—; adj. prof. U. Denver, 1985; instr. Colo. Soc. CPAs, 1986-87; lectr. Nat. Bus. Inst., 1986-87. Candidate councilman City of Denver, 1987. Mem. Colo. Bar Assn., Colo. Soc. CPA's. Republican. Presbyterian. Home: 6942 E Costilla Pl Englewood CO 80112-1110 Office: Hopper & Kanouff 1610 Wynkoop St Ste 200 Denver CO 80202-1135

SYLVESTER, EDWARD JOSEPH, science writer, journalism educator; b. Hackensack, N.J., Oct. 10, 1942; s. Edward Joseph Jr. and Ellen Marian (Hopkins) S.; m. Ginny Ross Gowanloch, Sept. 6, 1969; children: Daniel, Kathleen. AB, Princeton U., 1965; MA, CCNY, 1974. Reporter The Jersey Jour., Jersey City, 1962-63, The Morning Call, Paterson, N.J., 1968-69, The Ariz. Star, Tucson, 1973-76, L.A. Times, 1978-80; rewriteman The Star Ledger, Newark, 1970-72; reporter, editor The Tucson Citizen, 1976-78; prof. Ariz. State U. Walter Cronkite Sch. Journalism, Tempe, 1980—; corr. Wall Street Jour., N.Y.C., 1975-78. Prin. author: The Gene Age, 1983, rev. edit., 1987; author: Target: Cancer, 1986, The Healing Blade: A Tale of Neurosurgery, 1993. With U.S. Army, 1965-67. Recipient teaching award Burlington Resources Found., 1991, Wakonse Teaching Fellow, 1994. Mem. AAAS, Nat. Assn. Sci. Writers, Soc. Profl. Journalists, Investigative Reports and Editors, Assn. for Edn. in Journalism & Mass Communications. Office: Walter Cronkite Sch Journ Ariz State U Tempe AZ 85287

SYLVESTER, RICHARD RUSSELL, economist, management executive; b. Newton, Iowa, Jan. 10, 1938; s. Leslie Gardner and Effie (Williams) S.; BA, UCLA, 1959; MBA, U. So. Calif., 1962; PhD (fellow), UCLA, 1970, postdoctoral scholar in Engring., 1971-74; JD, Loyola U., 1981; m. Irene Elizabeth Lehman, Apr. 17, 1976; children: Bonnie Ann, Vicky Ellis, Juliesta Elaine. Designer corp. offices Gen. Motors Corp., Warren, Mich., 1958; sr. analyst Lockheed Aircraft Corp., Burbank, Calif., 1962-66; sr. planner corp. offices Hughes Aircraft Co., Culver City, Calif., 1966-68; sr. staff economist, staff mgr. TRW, Inc., Redondo Beach, Calif., 1969-70; pres. Def. Rsch. Co., 1970-81, Sylvester Consulting Group, PhD Pub. Co., Sylvester Appraisal Co., 1970—, U.S. Electropower Controls Corp., 1970-71; asst. prof. Calif. State U., 1970-73; mgr. corp. planning Brunswick Def./Celesco, Costa Mesa, Calif., 1973-75; staff specialist strategic planning Gen. Dynamics Corp., 1981-83; strategic analysis specialist Northrop Corp., 1983-89; v.p. Arthur Cons. Group, Inc., 1989-94; cons. econs., engring. and fin., L.A., 1970—; lectr. Northrop U., U. Calif., U. So. Calif., Loyola U., La Verne U., 1961-81; asst. prof. Calif. State U., 1970-73, lectr., 1989—; assoc. prof. Pepperdine U., 1975-76, lectr., 1994—; co-founder Theta Cable TV, L.A., 1966-67. GM scholar, 1953-57, Ford Found. grantee, 1965, U.S. Fed. Govt. rsch. grantee, 1967-70. Mem. Westwood Hills Christian Ch. (bd. dirs. 1978-81, 1991-93), Beta Gamma Sigma, Alpha Kappa Psi. Author: Management Decisions and Actions, 3d edit., 1988; Investment Strategy, 1982; Tax Planning, 4th edit., 1980, Strategic Planning, 6th edit., 1990, Investment Planning and Tax Planning Software, 1983-93, Strategic Financial Planning, 1993, Future Challenge, Financial Strategy and Tax Planning, 1993, International Transfer Pricing, 1994; contbr. tech. reports to profl. lit. Patentee in field. Home: 11606 Charnock Rd Los Angeles CA 90066-2806

SYLVESTER, STEPHEN THOMAS, artist; b. Fairfield, Ohio, Aug. 25, 1945; s. Arthur Clayton and Marjorie May (Preston) S.; m. Christina Lynn Lagomarsino, Apr. 5, 1972; children: Nathan Reade, Marcel Wright. BFA, Brooks Inst. Photography, Santa Barbara, Calif., 1973; student advanced studio art program, Banff Fine Art Centre, Alta., Can., 1973-74; MFA in Perceptual Psychology, Goddard Coll., Plainfield, Vt., 1991; postgrad., San Miguel de Allende Inst., 1994. Calif. State Coll. teaching credential. Artist-in residence Montessori by the Sea, San Buena Ventura, Calif., 1980-81, Ojai (Calif.) Valley Montessori, 1982-83, Krishnamurti Found., Ojai, 1993-94, Happy Valley Found., Ojai, 1984—; photographer Ctr. for Study of Democratic Instns., 1987-88, Christo's Umbrella Project, Japan, 1991; color composition rsch. lectr. Mr. Ed Marcus (Australian) Color Synchromy, 1987; color compositon rsch. seminar Theosophical Video Unit, 1993; rsch. participant Electronic Composer's Symposium, Santa Fe, N.Mex., 1988; fine art chair Fine Art Travel Guide, Happy Valley Found., 1983-94. One-man shows include Ojai Fine Art Centre, 1973, 81, New Media Gallery, San Buena Ventura Coll., 1977, Gilbert Gallery, Ojai, 1986; exhibited in group shows at Ojai Fine Art Centre, 1973-81, Faulkner Gallery, Santa Barbara, 1975, Helen Laufer Gallery, San Buena Ventura, 1979, L.A. Inst. Contemporary Art, 1979, Grayson Gallery, Chgo., 1987-94; represented in permanent collection Stanleys, Sherman Oaks, Calif.; represented by Gilman Gallery, Chgo., 1975-88. Recipient Beatrice Wood Stipend award U.S.-Japan Friendship, Umbrella Project, Japan, 1991, Otis award Otis Coll. Art Design, L.A., 1994. Mem. Coll. Art Assn. Home: 821 Gridley Rd Ojai CA 93023-9620

SYMINGTON, J. FIFE, III, governor; b. N.Y.C., Aug. 12, 1945; s. John Fife Jr. and Martha (Frick) S.; m. Leslie Marion Barker, June 1, 1968 (div. Jan. 1973); childen: Fife IV, Scott; m. Ann Pritzlaff, Feb. 7, 1976; children: Whitney, Richard, Tom. Student, Harvard U., 1968. Ptnr. Lincoln Property Co., Phoenix, 1972-76; chmn. of the bd. The Symington Co., Phoenix, 1976-89; gov. State of Ariz., 1991—. Precinct committeeman Ariz.'s Legis. Dist. 24, Paradise Valley; fin. chmn. State Republican Party, Phoenix, 1982-84; campaign advisor Rep. John Rhodes, Sen. John McCain, Ariz.; chmn. Phoenix Citizens Police Protection Bond Com., 1988; v.p. bd. trustees Heard Mus.; mem. Men's Art Coun., Environ. Quality Commn., 1971-73, Ariz. Children's Found.; dep. sheriff Maricopa County Air Posse; exec. bd. Phoenix Community Alliance. Capt. USAF, 1968-71. Mem. Western Govs.' Assn. (chmn. 1992—). Episcopalian. Office: Govs Office 1700 W Washington St Phoenix AZ 85007-2812*

SYMMES, DANIEL LESLIE, three-dimensional technology executive, producer, director; b. Los Angeles, June 26, 1949; s. Louis Leslie and Mary (Warkentine) S.; m. Joanne Iriye Symmes, June 4, 1988. Student, Columbia Coll., Hollywood, Calif., 1970-71. Co-founder Stereovision Internat., Inc., North Hollywood, Calif., 1971; cons. Dimension 3e, Beverly Hills, Calif., 1975-87; pres., chmn. Spatial Techs. Inc., 3D Video Corp., Hollywood, Calif., 1987—; responsible for comml. 3D TV in U.S. and abroad; known worldwide as Mr. 3D. Author: Amazing 3-D; contbr. numerous articles to profl. jours.; dir. photography local 659 IATSE; patentee 3-D TV; inventor 1st reflex widescreen 3D filming system. Mem. SMPTE.

SYMMONS, CLARE PAYNE, foundation administrator; b. Portland, Oreg., Mar. 3, 1962; d. Roy Alpha and Anna Lee (Bozarth) Payne; m. Michael Laurence Symmons, Oct. 12, 1991. BA in English Lit., Bryn Mawr Coll., 1984. Asst. to dir. mktg. and devel. Portland Opera Assn., 1984-86; asst. found. dir. Holladay Park Med. Ctr. Found., Portland, 1987; dir. fin. devel. YWCA of Ctrl. Jersey, New Brunswick, 1988; cons. Portland, 1990-92; exec. dir. St. John's Luth. Hosp. Found., Libby, Mont., 1992—. Mem. Lincoln County Sustainability Task Force, Libby, Mont., 1993—; chair bd. dirs. Literacy Vols. Am., Lincoln County, 1994; bd. dirs. Mont. Cmty. Found., 1993—; mem. adv. bd. Habitat for Humanity, Lincoln, 1994. Mem. Soc. for Non-Profit Orgns., Western Mont. Fund Raisers Assn., Assn. for Healthcare Philanthropy, Mont. Soc. Mktg. and Cmty. Rels., Rotary. Home: PO Box 464 Libby MT 59923-0464

SYMMS, RICHARD A., vintner; b. 1935. Pres. Symms Fruit Ranch, Inc., Caldwell, Idaho, 1961—; ptnr. Sunny Slope Fruit Co., 1969—. Office: Symms Fruit Ranch Inc 14068 Sunnyslope Rd Caldwell ID 83605-9358*

SYMONDS, NORMAN LESLIE, computer programming specialist; b. Hawthorne, Calif., July 10, 1953; s. Malcolm F. and Nancy J. (Raab) S.; m. Catherine Anne Meades, Jan. 1, 1994. BA in Math., U. Calif., Berkeley, 1978; MBA in Mgmt. Sci., U. So. Calif., 1981. Programmer Burroughs Corp. (Unisys), Pasadena, Calif., 1978-81; sr. systems analyst Sungard Fin. Systems, Canoga Park, Calif., 1981-89; programming project leader Dames & Moore, L.A., 1989—. Home: 19211 Haynes St Apt 4 Reseda CA 91335-5822 Office: Dames & Moore 911 Wilshire Blvd Ste 700 Los Angeles CA 90017-3436

SYMONS, JAMES MARTIN, theater and dance educator; b. Jacksonville, Ill., May 7, 1937; s. James and Pauline (Barton) S.; m. Judith White, Nov. 14, 1959; children: Tracy, Kelly, Carrie. BA, Ill. Coll., 1959; MA, So. Ill. U., 1964; PhD, Cornell U., 1970. Asst. prof. Yankton (S.D.) Coll., 1964-67; assoc. prof. Coll. St. Catherine, St. Paul, 1970-74, SUNY, Albany, 1974-77; prof., chair Trinity U., San Antonio, 1977-84; prof., chair theatre and dance dept. U. Colo., Boulder, 1984—; actor Off-Broadway, N.Y.C., 1959, Mo. Repertory Theatre, Kansas City, 1984; dir., actor Colo. Shakespeare Festival, Boulder, 1985—, producing artistic dir., 1994-95; leader People-to-People Del. of Theater Educators, USSR and Czechoslovakia, 1991. Author: Meyerhold's Theatre of the Grotesque, 1971 (Freedley Meml. award Theatre Libr. Assn. 1971); contbr. articles to scholarly jours. Lt. (j.g.) USN, 1960-63. Mem. Assn. for Theatre in Higher Edn. (pres. 1989-91), Assn. for Communication Adminstrn. (pres. 1990). Democrat. Methodist. Office: U of Colorado Dept Theatre And Dance Boulder CO 80309

SYMONS, ROBERT SPENCER, electronic engineer; b. San Francisco, July 3, 1925; s. Spencer W. and Avesia (Atkins) S.; m. Alice Faye Smith, Dec. 21, 1960; children: Julia Ann, Robert Spencer Jr. BS, Stanford U., 1946, MS, 1948. Engr. Eitel-McCullough, Inc., San Bruno, Calif., 1947, Heinz & Kaufman, South San Francisco, 1948, Pacific Electronics Co., Los Gatos, Calif., 1949; sr. engring. mgr. Varian Assocs., Palo Alto, Calif., 1950-83; tech. dir. Litton Industries, San Carlos, Calif., 1983—. Recipient Charles B. Thornton award for Advanced Technology Achievement, 1991. Patentee in field. Served to 1st lt. AUS, 1950-53. Fellow IEEE (assoc. editor Transactions on Electron Devices jour. 1980-83); mem. Phi Beta Kappa, Tau Beta Pi. Club: Commonwealth of Calif. Home: 290 Surrey Pl Los Altos CA 94022-2146 Office: Litton Industries 960 Industrial Rd San Carlos CA 94070-4116

SYMS, HELEN MAKSYM, educational administrator; b. Wilkes Barre, Pa., Nov. 12, 1918; d. Walter and Anna (Kowalewski) Maksym; m. Louis Harold Syms, Aug. 16, 1947; children: Harold Edward, Robert Louis. BA, Hunter Coll., 1941; MS, Columbia U., 1947; teaching credentials, Calif. State U., Northridge, 1964. Statis. clk. McGraw Hill Pub. Co., N.Y.C., 1941-42; acct. Flexpansion Corp., N.Y.C., 1943-47, Oliver Wellington & Co., N.Y.C., 1947-48, Broadcast Measurement Bur., N.Y.C., 1948-51; tchr. Calif. State U., Northridge, 1964, Burbank (Calif.) Unified Sch. Dist., 1964-79; chmn. bus. edn. dept. Burbank High Sch., 1974-79; docent, acct. arts coun. Calif. State U., Northridge, 1979—; tchr. M.E.N.D. (Meet Each Need with Dignity) Learning Ctr., Pacoima, Calif., 1987-89, assoc. dir., 1989—. Mem. Phi Beta Kappa, Delta Kappa Gamma (pres. 1972-74, treas. Xi chpt. 1982-90, treas. area IX 1975-78). Home: 9219 Whitaker Ave Northridge CA 91343-3538 Office: MEND 13460 Van Nuys Blvd Pacoima CA 91331-3058

SYRING, JAMES JOHN, telecommunications company editor; b. N.Y.C., Oct. 4, 1942; s. John Joseph and Genevieve (Reynolds) S.; m. Virginia Catherine Zemaitis, July 20, 1968. BA in Mass Communications, SUNY, N.Y.C., 1975. Chief editor Sta. KUSA-TV, Denver, 1976-80; news editor Sta. KCNC-TV, Denver, 1980-89; media cons., 1989-93; tech. coord. ABC News, Denver, 1993-94; editor TCI (Telecom. Inc.), Littleton, Colo., 1994—. With USMC, 1961-64. Recipient, Kodak award, Nat. Press Photographers Assn., 1976, Colo. Broadcasters award, Colo. Broadcasters Assn., 1988. Mem. NATAS (Emmy award 1973, regional Emmy, Denver, 1988), Colo. Film and Video Assn. Democrat. Home: 3229 S Forest St Denver CO 80222-7553 Office: TCI 4100 E Dry Creek Rd Littleton CO 80122-3729

SYRMOS, VASSILIS LAMBROS, electrical engineering educator; b. Athens, Greece, Sept. 11, 1964; came to U.S., 1987; s. George Lambros and Aggeliki (Papas) S.; m. Karen Aletta Goelst, Apr. 11, 1992. Diploma in elec. engring., Democritus Univ., 1987; PhDEE, Ga. Inst. of Tech., 1991. Rsch. asst. Ga. Inst. of Tech., Atlanta, 1987-91; asst. prof. U. Hawaii, 1991—. Contbr. articles to profl. jours. Recipient Rsch. Initiation award NSF. Mem. IEEE, Soc. of Indsl. and Applied Math., Sigma Xi (assoc.). Home: 1594 Hoaaina St Honolulu HI 96821-1345 Office: Dept Elec Engring U Hawaii 2540 Dole St # 483 Honolulu HI 96822-2303

SZABO, PETER JOHN, investment company executive, financial planner, mining engineer, lawyer; b. Bklyn., Nov. 22, 1946; s. Paul Simon and Marita Ellen (Coughlin) S.; m. Dorothy Anne Steward, Nov. 14, 1970; children: Peter, David, John Paul Steward. BS in Mining Engring., Columbia U., 1968; LLB, LaSalle Law Sch., 1975; MS in Fin. Planning, Coll. Fin. PLanning, 1994. registered profl. engr., CFP. Mining engr. Halecrest Co., Mt. Hope, N.J., 1973-74; mgr. solid fuels & minerals Ford, Bacon & Davis, N.Y.C., 1974-75; asst. v.p. Mfrs. Hanover Trust Co., N.Y.C., 1975-77, Irving Trust Co., N.Y.C., 1977; v.p. Republic Nat. Bank of Dallas, 1977-80; mgr. bus. devel. AMOCO Minerals, Denver, 1980-84; investment broker B.J. Leonard, Denver, 1984-85; investment exec. Wedbush Nobel Cook, Denver, 1985; regional sr. v.p. Alliance Fund Distbrs., N.Y.C., 1985-92, sr. v.p., 1992—; mining engr. U.S. Bur. Mines, Dallas, 1971-72, IRS, Washington, 1972-73. Treas. Columbia Sch. Engring., 1968—. Lt. USMC, 1969-71, Vietnam, capt. Res. Mem. VFW (post sr. vice comdr. 1993-94, post comdr. 1994-95, all state team post comdrs. 1995, 16th dist. jr. vice comdr. 1995—), Mil. Order of the Cootie (sr. vice-comdr. 1994-95). Republican. Roman Catholic.

SZABO, ZOLTAN, medical science educator, medical institute director; b. Szeged, Hungary, Oct. 5, 1943; came to U.S., 1967; s. Imre and Maria (Szikora) S.; m. Wanda Toy, Dec. 5, 1976; children: Eva, Maria. Student, U. Med. Sch., Szeged, 1962-65; PhD, Columbia Pacific U., 1983. Tech. dir. microsurgery lab. R.K. Davies Med. Ctr., San Francisco, 1972-80; dir. Microsurg. Rsch. Inst., San Francisco, 1980—; assoc. dir. advanced laparoscopic surgery tng. ctr. Sch. Medicine U. Calif., San Francisco, 1992—; rsch. assoc. oral and maxillofacial surgery U. of Pacific, San Francisco, 1980-83, adj. asst. prof., 1983—. Author: Microsurgery Techniques, vol. 1 1974, vol. 2 1984 (1st Place award for excellence in med. writing, 1982); contbr. chpt. books, articles to profl. jours. With U.S. Army, 1969-71. Recipient Cert. of Merit, AMA, 1978, commendation Accreditation Coun. for Continuing Med. Edn., 1984, 90, Spl. Recognition award Sch. Medicine Cen. U. Venezuela, 1988, Sci. Poste Sessions Hon. Mention award Am. Urol. Assn., 1992, 1st prize Roundtable for New Techs. and Innovations we. sect., 1992, James Barrett Brown award Am. Assn. Plastic Surgeons, 1993. Fellow Internat. Coll. Surgeons (Disting. Svc. award 1994); mem. Hungarian Gynecol. Soc. (hon.), Medico-Dental Study Guild Calif., Internat. Microsurg. Soc., Soc. Am. Gastrointestinal Endoscopic Surgeons (hon., 1st prize sci. exhibit 1977, 1st prize Residents and Fellows Rsch. and Sci. Presentation 1992, In-Utero Endoscopic Surgery award 1992), Am. Fertility Soc., Am. Soc. Reconstructive Microsurgery (assoc.), Am. Soc. for Peripheral Nerve. Office: Microsurgery Operative Endoscopy Tng Inst 153 States St San Francisco CA 94114-1403

SZCZERBA, VICTOR BOGDAN, electrical engineer, sales engineer; b. Chgo., Oct. 21, 1966; s. Bogdan and Zosia (Mika) S. BSEE, Marquette U., 1989. Sales engr. New Vision Computers, Milw., 1988-89; mktg. engr. Cypress Semicondr., San Jose, Calif., 1989-91; sales engr. Trinity Tech., Mountainview, Calif., 1991-92, AMD, Santa Clara, Calif., 1992-95; regional svcs. mgr. Nexgen, Milpitas, Calif., 1995—; cons. S3, Santa Clara, 1991-92; tutor Project Read. Mem. Knights of St. Patrick (pres. 1988-89), Sigma Phi Delta (v.p. 1987-88). Republican. Roman Catholic. Home: 825 University Ave Palo Alto CA 94301-2132

SZEGO, CLARA MARIAN, cell biologist, educator; b. Budapest, Hungary, Mar. 23, 1916; came to U.S., 1921, naturalized, 1927; d. Paul S. and Helen (Elek) S.; m. Sidney Roberts, Sept. 14, 1943. A.B., Hunter Coll., 1937; M.S. (Garvan fellow), U. Minn., 1939, Ph.D., 1942. Instr. physiology U. Minn., 1942-43; Minn. Cancer Research Inst. fellow, 1943-44; rsch. assoc. OSRD, Nat. Bur. Standards, 1944-45, Worcester Found. Exptl. Biology, 1945-47; rsch. instr. physiol. chemistry Yale U. Sch. Medicine, 1947-48; mem. faculty UCLA, 1948—, prof. biology, 1960—. Named Woman of Year in Sci. Los Angeles Times, 1957-58; Guggenheim fellow, 1956; named to Hunter Coll. Hall of Fame, 1987. Fellow AAAS; mem. Am. Physiol. Soc., Am. Soc. Cell Biology, Endocrine Soc. (CIBA award 1953), Soc. for Endocrinology (Gt. Britain), Biochem. Soc. (Gt. Britain), Internat. Soc. Rsch. Reprodn., Phi Beta Kappa (pres. UCLA chpt. 1973-74), Sigma Xi (pres. UCLA chpt. 1976-77). Home: 1371 Marinette Rd Pacific Palisades CA 90272-2627 Office: U Calif Dept Biology Los Angeles CA 90024-1606

SZETO, ERIK K., family practice physician; b. Sept. 17, 1949; s. Yat and Siu Fong (Ng) S.; m. Anita Y. Chan; children: Matthew, Eileen, Amanda, Jacob. BA in Chemistry, U. Ore., 1972; MS in Molecular Biophysics, Yale U., 1974; DO, Kirksville Coll. Osteopathic, 1978. Intern Botsford Hosp., Farmington Hills, 1978-79; pvt. family practice Portland, Ore., 1979—; chmn. quality assurance com. Family Care PCO of Oreg., 1991-94, Evergreen PCO of Oreg., 1991-94; chmn. gen. practice dept. Eastmoreland Hosp., Portland, 1985-87; health com. Gov. Roberts transitional team, 1990; com. for appt. diversion program med. dir. State of Oreg., 1992. Chmn., founder, bd. dirs. Chinese Social Svc. Ctr., Portland, 1983—; Chinese Cmty. Devel. Corp., 1991—; mem. leaders round table, Portland, 1992; chmn., exec. com. Asian Am. Coalition, 1992—. Mem. Am. Osteopathic Assn., Osteopathic Physicians and Surgeons of Ore., Ore. Med. Assn. Presbyn. Office: 4130 SE Division St Portland OR 97202-1647

SZETO, HUNG, publisher; b. Hoyping, Canton, People's Republic of China, Sept. 8, 1936; s. Cheong Yee and Sau King(Kwan) S.; m. Sau Hing Chow, Jan. 27, 1962; children: Roland, Lisa, Nancy. B in adminstrn., Tsing Hua Coll., Hong Kong, 1969. Mgr. Far East Trade Ctr., Seattle, 1975-81; editor Seattle Chinese Post, 1982; pres. APC Group, Seattle, 1986—; pub. Chinese Bus. Jour., 1989—. Mem. Asian Am. Journalists Assn., Chinese-Lang. Press. Inst., Northwest Minority Pubs. Assn. Office: Chinese Bus Jour 659 S Weller St Seattle WA 98104-2944

SZETO, PAUL (CHEUK-CHING), religious mission executive; b. Canton, China, July 28, 1940; came to U.S., 1962; s. Fai and Oi-wan (Wong) S.; m. Dorcas Chow, July 8, 1967; children: Tedd, Christine, Melissa. BA, Seattle Pacific U., 1966, MA, 1968; MDiv, Yale U., 1970; D of Missiology, Fuller Theol. Sem., Pasadena, Calif., 1980. Sr. minister Chinese Bapt. Ch., Seattle, 1971-78; dir. ch. planting ABC Pacific N.W., Seattle, 1978-80; gen. dir. Evangelize China Fellowship, Inc., Monterey Park, Calif., 1980—; founding dir. N.Am. of Chinese Evangelicals, 1972; participant Internat. Conf. for Itinerant Evangelists, 1983-86; bd. dirs. Chnese Coordination Centre of West, Hong Kong, 1976-80. Author: Seven Directions of Modern Theology, 1978, Suffering and Hope, 1982; translator: Evangelical Awakening in Eastern Asia, 1981; compiler: The Abundant Life, 1987. Mem. Greater Seattle Asian Am. Coun., 1972; mem. Royal Brougham Found., Seattle, 1974; mem. Campaign for Yale, L.A., 1977. Resident scholar Oxford U., 1991. Mem. Greater L.A. Chinese Ministers Assn. Home: 437 S Garfield Ave Monterey Park CA 91754-3328 Office: Evangelize China Fellowship 437 S Garfield Ave Monterey Park CA 91754-3328

SZILAGYI, MIKLOS (NICHOLAS), electrical and computer engineering educator; b. Budapest, Hungary, Feb. 4, 1936; came to U.S., 1981; s. Karoly and Ilona (Abraham) S.; m. Larissa Dorner, Feb. 23, 1957 (div. July 1970); 1 child, Gabor; m. Julia Levai, May 31, 1975; 1 child, Zoltan Charles. MS in Engring., Physics with honors, Tech. U. Leningrad, USSR, 1960; PhD, Electrotech. U. Leningrad, 1965; D Tech., Tech. U. Budapest, 1965; DSc with exceptional distinction, Hungarian Acad. Scis., 1979. Research asst. phys. electronics Tech. U. Leningrad, 1958-60; research assoc., Inst. Tech. Physics Hungarian Acad. Scis., 1960-66; head electron optics lab. Tech. U. Budapest, 1966-71; prof., head dept. phys. scis. K. Kando Coll. of Elec. Engring., Budapest, 1971-79, pres., 1971-74; cons. Deutsches Elektronen-Synchrotron DESY, Hamburg, Federal Republic of Germany, 1980-81; vis. sr. research assoc., applied and engring. physics Cornell U., 1981-82; prof. elec. and computer engring. U. Ariz., 1982—; sci. adv. Nat. Inst. Neurosurgery, Budapest, 1966-70; vis. prof. Enrico Fermi Inst., U. Chgo., Lawrence Berkeley Lab, U. Calif., Stanford Linear Accelerator Ctr., Stanford U., 1976-77, Inst. Physics, U. Aarhus, Denmark, 1979-81, 88, 89, 90, Delft U. Tech., The Netherlands, 1988-89, U. Heidelberg, Fed. Republic of Germany, Max Planck Inst. Nuclear Physics, Heidelberg, 1984, pres. The Tucson Inst., 1993—. Author eleven books, including Introduction to the Theory of Space-Charge Optics, 1974, Fachlexikon Physik, 1979, Electron and Ion Optics, 1988, How To Save Our Country, 1993; contbr. over 95 articles to profl. jours., also contbr. to internat. confs; editor The New Common Sense. UN Indsl. Devel. Orgn. fellow, 1976. Mem. IEEE (sr.), Am. Phys. Soc., Internat. Soc. Hybrid Microelectronics, European Soc. Stereotactic and Functional Neurosurgery, L. Eotvos Phys. Soc. (Brody prize 1964), J. Neumann Soc. for Computer Sci., Danish Phys. Soc., Danish Engring. Soc. Office: U Ariz Dept Elec And Computer Engring Tucson AZ 85721

SZOSTAK, EDWARD WALTER, JR., pharmaceutical company executive; b. New Brunswick, N.J., Jan. 6, 1957; s. Edward and Matilda Catherine (Seaman) S.; m. Teresa Marie Szostak, Sept. 24, 1988; children: Alexandra Noel, Edward Blake III. BS, Charleston So. U., 1979; MBA in Human Resources, Nat. U., 1987. Med. rep. Geigy Pharms., Sacramento, 1982-83; clin. conf. mgr. Ciba Geigy Pharm., Sacramento, 1983-85; mktg. cons. mgr. Ciba-Geigy Corp., Summit, N.J., 1985-87; nat. account mgr. Ciba Pharms., L.A., 1987-93; dir. strategic planning Ciba Pharms., Summit, 1994—; dir. strategic planning and analysis Ciba Geigy Corp., Basel, Switzerland, 1982, 94, dir. corp. nat. accounts Midwest-West, 1994. Recipient Nat. Best of the Best in Managed Care award Health Internat. Rsch. Corp., 1994. Republican. Roman Catholic. Home: 786 Newbury Way Diamond Bar CA 91765-4625

SZTEINBAUM, SAMUEL, marketing executive, small business owner; b. Barranquilla, Colombia, May 29, 1962; s. Victor and Betty (Braiverman) S.; m. Helen Haim, Mar. 6, 1988; children: Aaron, Raquel. BA in Econs. and Math., U. Calif., Santa Cruz, 1982; MS in Mgmt., Purdue U., 1984. L.Am. fin. analyst Hewlett Packard Co., Palo Alto, Calif., 1984-86; fin. mgr. Hewlett Packard Co., Caracas, Venezuela, 1986-88; product mgr. Hewlett Packard Co., Cupertino, Calif., 1988-89, mkt. devel. mgr., 1989-94; mktg. mgr. Hewlett Packard Co., Santa Clara, Calif., 1991—; chmn. bd., owner Day Care Svc. Jewish. Home: 116 Beach Park Blvd Foster City CA 94404-2708 Office: Hewlett Packard Co MS 54L CC 5301 Stevens Creek Blvd Santa Clara CA 95051-7201

TAAFE, PETER JAMES, financial consultant; b. Youngstown, Ohio, Sept. 26, 1956; s. Francis Edwin and Donna Marie (Halete K) G.; m. Lucretia Laurie Ferch, June 2, 1990. Student, Ohio U., 1975-78. Cert. investment and fin. cons. Prof. Ben Franklin Internat. Sch., Barcelona, Spain, 1986-88; dist. mgr. First Investors Corp., Seattle, 1988-93; sr. mgr., founding mem. Sound Investment Svcs., Seattle, 1993—. Contbr. articles to profl. jours. Vol., supporter Seattle Commons, 1993, 94. Recipient Highest award for Achievement Dale Carnegie, Bellevue, Washington, 1992. Mem. Coll. Club, The Bus. Network Internat. (membership chair 1993), IOOF. Home: 1415 2nd Ave Unit 1408 Seattle WA 98101-2033 Office: Sound Investment Svcs 520 Pike St Ste 2909 Seattle WA 98101-4001

TABAKOFF, BORIS, pharmacologist educator; b. Tien-Tsin, China, Sept. 27, 1942; s. Isaak and Bertha (Neidental) T.; m. Emelia Johnson. BA, U. Colo., 1966, PhD, 1970. Prof. U. Ill., Chgo., 1974-84; dir. Alcohol & Drug Abuse Rsch. and Tng. Ctr., Chgo., 1980-84; sci. dir. Nat. Inst. on Alcohol Abuse & Alcoholism, Bethesda, Md., 1984-90; vis. prof. U. Ill., Rockford, 1984—, Med. Coll. of Va., Richmond, 1989—; faculty fellow Inst. for Behavioral Genetics, Boulder, Colo., 1991—; prof., chmn. U. Colo. Sch. of Medicine, Denver, 1990—; sci. advisor Vt. Alcohol Rsch. Ctr., Colchester, 1988—; cons. in field. Author: Neuropharmacology of Ethanol, New Approaches, 1991, Comprehensive Textbook of Substance Abuse, 1992; contbr. articles to profl. jours. Acting dep. dir. Nat. Inst. on Alcohol Abuse and Alcoholism, Rockville, Md., 1985-86. Recipient Pres. Rank Meritorious Exec. award, 1989, Meritorious award to Disting. Alumnus, Chgo. Med. Sch., 1990, ADAMHA Adminstrv. award for Pub. Svc., 1986, RSA award for Sci. Excellence in Rsch., Am. Rsch. Soc. on Alcoholism, 1988, Jellinek Meml. award for Major and Continuing Contbns. to Alcohol Rsch., 1988. Mem. Rsch. Soc. on Alcholism (pres. 1983-85), Internat. Soc. for Biomed. Rsch. on Alcholism (pres. 1986-90), Am. Coll. of Neuropsychopharmacology, Am. Soc. for Pharmacology & Exptl. Therapeutics. Office: U Colo Sch Medicine Campus Box C236 4200 E 9th Ave Denver CO 80220-3706

TABASCIO, STEFANO ANTONINO, chemical lubricant company executive; b. Toronto, Ont. Can., Sept. 26, 1965; s. Josef Antonino and Helena Ana (Neuhort) T.; m. Linda Ann Wade (div. 1994). Degree in Engring., Karlova U., Prague, Czechoslovakia, 1984; degree in Bus. Adminstrn., Calif. State U., L.A., 1989; degree in Chemistry, U. Nev., Las Vegas, 1991. Automotive engr. Zavodi Crevena Zastava, Knagujevac, Yugoslavia, 1984-85, Yugo Cars, Sun Valley, Calif., 1985; cons. Yugo Am., N.J., 1985-86; automobile dealer Mik Auto Inc./Bertone, North Hollywood, Calif., 1986-89; automotive designer Moretti, Torino, Italy, 1989-90; v.p. engring. Skocar, Markham, Ont., 1990-91; CEO Synlube, Inc. (formerly Pentagram Products), Las Vegas, 1991—. Author: All About Oil, 1989, What You Don't Know About Oil...Will Hurt Your Car", 1993, Q & A of Lubrication, 1994. Mem. Soc. Automotive Engrs., Soc. Tribologists and Lubrication Engrs., Sports Car Club Am. Office: Synlube Inc 2961 Industrial Rd #300 Las Vegas NV 89109-1188

TABET, PAUL MARK, information services executive; b. Belen, N.Mex., Sept. 19, 1963; s. Bonifacio Michael and Eloisa (Griego) T. B in Bus. Adminstrn., N.Mex. State U., Las Cruces, 1986. Programmer analyst General Dynamics, Pomona, Calif., 1986-88; staff cons. Deloitte Haskins and Sells, L.A., 1988-89; sr. cons. Deloitte & Touche, L.A., 1989-92, KPMG Peat Marwick, Costa Mesa, Calif., 1992; di. sys. integration Vans, Inc., Orange, Calif., 1992-93, dir. mgmt. info. svcs., 1993-95; dir. mgmt. info. svcs. Clarion Corp. Am., Gardena, Calif., 1995—; bd. mem. candidate Hope House, Anaheim, Calif. Mem. Lamda Chi Alpha Frat. Republican. Roman Catholic. Home: 26151 Pittsford Lake Forest CA 92630-7282 Office: Clarion Corp Am 661 W Redondo Beach Blvd Gardena CA 90247

TABLER, RONALD DWIGHT, snow and wind engineering consultant; b. Denver, May 18, 1937; s. Dwight Glen and Carol Arline (Turman) T.; m. Alicia Virginia Revollo, May 11, 1964; children: Edward Ronald, Alice Arlene. BS, Colo. State U., 1959, PhD, 1965. Rsch. forester USDA Forest Svc., Laramie, Wyo., 1959-65; rsch. hydrologist, project leader USDA Forest Svc., Laramie, 1965-85; snow and wind engring. cons. Tabler & Assocs., Laramie, 1985-89, Niwot, Colo., 1989—; adj. prof. Dept. Mech. Engring., Univ. Wyo., Laramie, 1986—; rsch. affiliate Geophysical Inst., Univ. Alaska, Fairbanks, 1988—. Author: Design Guidelines for the Control of Blowing and Drifting Snow, 1994; contbr. artilces to profl. jours. Recipient USDA Superior Svc. Honor award USDA, Washington, 1976, D. Grant Mickle award Nat. Acad. Scis., Washington, 1979, Rsch. award for fgn. specialists Japan Sci. & Tech. Agy., Tokyo, 1980-81. Fellow AAAS; mem. Am. Geophysical Union, Internat. Glaciological Soc., Am. Railway Engring. Assn., Am. Water Resources Assn., Western Snow Conf. (life, chmn. N. Cont. area 1980-84). Home: 7505 Estate Cir Longmont CO 80503-7260 Office: Tabler & Assocs PO Box 483 Niwot CO 80544-0483

TABRISKY, JOSEPH, radiologist, educator; b. Boston, June 23, 1931; s. Henry and Gertrude Tabrisky; BA cum laude, Harvard U., 1952; MD cum laude, Tufts U., 1956; m. Phyllis Eleanor Page, Apr. 23, 1955; children: Joseph Page, Elizabeth Ann, William Page. Flexible intern U. Ill. Hosp., 1956-57; resident in radiology Fitzsimons Army Hosp., 1958-60; instr. radiology Tufts U. Med. Sch., 1964-65; cons. radiologist Swedish Med. Center, Denver, 1966-68; chief radiologist Kaiser Found. Hosp., Harbor City, Calif., 1968-72; mem. faculty UCLA Med. Sch., 1972—, prof. radiol. scis., 1975-92, prof emeritus, 1993—, vice chmn. dept., 1976-92 , exec. policy com. radiol. scis.; chmn. radiology dept. Harbor-UCLA Med. Ctr., 1975-92 , pres. faculty soc., 1979-80, exec. dir. MR/CT Imaging Ctr., bd. dirs. Rsch. Ednl. Inst., Harbor Collegium/UCLA Found.; chief exec. officer Vascular Biometrics Inc.; steering com. Harvard U., 1952; cons. L.A. County Dept. Pub. Health; chmn. L.A. County Radiol. Standards Com., 1979. Mem. Harvard-Radcliffe Schs. Com.; chmn., bd. dirs., treas., Harbor-UCLA Med. Found.; chmn. UCLA Coun. for Ednl. Devel. Maj. M.C., U.S. Army, 1957-63. Recipient Silver Knight award Nat, Mgmt, Assn., 1992. Diplomate Am. Bd. Radiology. Fellow Am. Coll. Radiology, Univ. Radcom Assn. (chief exec. officer 1987-89); mem. Radiol. Soc. N. Am., Calif. Med. Assn., Calif. Radiol. Soc., L.A. Med. Assn., L.A. Radiol. Soc., Alpha Omega Alpha. Contbr. articles to med. jours. Office: 1000 W Carson St Torrance CA 90502-2004

TABRISKY, PHYLLIS PAGE, physiatrist, educator; b. Newton, Mass., Aug. 28, 1930; d. Joseph Westley and Alice Florence (Wainwright) Page; m. Joseph Tabrisky, Apr. 23, 1955; children: Joseph Page, Elizabeth Ann, William Page. BS, Douglass Coll., 1952; MD, Tufts U., 1956. Cert. phys. medicine and rehab. Intern U. Ill. Hosp., Chgo., 1956-57; phys. medicine and rehab. residency U. Colo. Sch. Medicine, Denver, 1958-60; gen. med. officer dept. pediatrics and medicine Coco Solo Hosp., Panama Canal Zone, 1961-62; staff physician dept. pediatrics Ft. Hood (Tex.) Army Hosp., 1963; instr. dept. rehab. medicine Boston (Mass.) U. Sch. Medicine, 1964-66; asst. prof. phys. medicine and rehab. U. Colo. Sch. Medicine, Denver, 1966-68; staff physician VA Med. Ctr., Long Beach, Calif., 1968-71; acting chief phys. medicine and rehab. VA Med. Ctr., Long Beach, 1971-73, asst. chief rehab. med. svcs., 1973-91, chief phys. medicine & rehab. svc., 1992—; asst. clin. prof. phys. medicine and rehab. U. Calif. Coll. Medicine, Irvine, 1970-75, assoc. clin. prof., 1975-80, prof., 1980—, vice chair dept. phys. medicine and rehab., 1985—, dir. residency tng., 1982—. Fellow Am. Acad. Phys. Medicine and Rehab. (mem. accreditation coun. grad. med. com., 1993—); mem. Am. Congress Rehab. Medicine, Assn. Acad. Physiatrists, Alpha Omega Alpha. Republican. Episcopalian. Office: VA Med Ctr 5901 E 7th St Long Beach CA 90822-5201

TACAL, JOSE VEGA, JR., public health official, veterinarian; b. Ilocos Sur, Philippines, Sept. 5, 1933; came to U.S., 1969; s. Jose Sr. and Cristina (Vega) T.; m. Lilia Caccam, 1959; children: Joyce, Jasmin, Jose III. DVM, U. Philippines, Quezon City, 1956; diploma, U. Toronto, Ont., Can., 1964. Diplomate Am. Coll. Vet. Preventive Medicine. Provincial veterinarian Philippine Bur. Animal Industry, Manila, 1956-57; instr. vet. medicine U. Philippines, Quezon City, 1957-65, asst. prof., chmn. dept. vet. microbiology, pathology and pub. health, 1966-69; pub. health veterinarian San Bernardino (Calif.) County Dept. Pub. Health, 1970-83, sr. pub. health veterinarian, program mgr., sect. chief, 1984—; zoonotic diseases lectr. Calif. State U., San Bernardino, spring 1984; lectr. U. Calif. Extension, Riverside, spring, 1985; vis. prof. vet. pub. health U. Philippines at Los Banos, Laguna, 1988. Columnist L.A. Free Press, 1991, Pilipinas Times, 1993, Mabuhay Times, 1994-95; contbr. more than 50 articles to profl. jours. Pres. Filipino Assn. of San Bernardino County, Highland, Calif., 1979; charter mem. Greater Inland Empire Filipino Assn., Highland, 1986—; del. First Filipino Media Conf. N.Am., L.A., 1993. Recipient Donald T. Fraser Meml. medal U. Toronto, 1964, Cert. of Merit, Philippine Vet. Med. Assn., 1965, Cert. of Appreciation Calif. State Bd. Examiners in Vet. Medicine, 1979, 84, Cert. of Recognition, Congressman George E. Brown Jr., 42d Congl. Dist. Calif., 1994, Assemblyman Joe Baca, 62d Assembly Dist., Calif. State Legis., 1994, Colombo Plan Study fellow Can./Philippine Govts., 1963-64. Mem. AVMA, Orange Belt Vet. Med. Assn., Western Poultry Disease Conf., Calif. Assn. Filipino Vet. Practitioners, Soc. for the Advancement of Rsch., Phi Kappa Phi, Phi Sigma. Office: San Bernardino County Dept Pub Health 351 N Mountain View Ave San Bernardino CA 92401-1609

TACHA, DEANELL REECE, federal judge; b. Jan. 26, 1946. BA, U. Kans., 1968; JD, U. Mich., 1971. Spl. asst. to U.S. Sec. of Labor, Washington, 1971-72; assoc. Hogan & Hartson, Washington, 1973, Thomas J. Pitner, Concordia, Kans., 1973-74; dir. Douglas County Legal Aid Clinic, Lawrence, Kans., 1974-77; assoc. prof. law U. Kans., Lawrence, 1974-77, prof., 1977-85, assoc. dean, 1977-79, assoc. vice chancellor, 1979-81, vice chancellor, 1981-85; judge U.S. Ct. Appeals (10th cir.), Denver, 1985—. Office: US Ct Appeals 10th Cir 4830 W 15th St Ste 100 Lawrence KS 66049-3846

TACKITT, JAMES WILLIAM, graphic arts/photography educator, genealogical researcher; b. Bell, Calif., Dec. 18, 1935; s. Howard Russell and Ilabess (Hebard) T.; m. Shirley Emma Van Gieson, Jan. 27, 1957; children: Heidi Lynn Tackitt Baker, Pamela Ann Tackitt Thornton, James William II, Eric Russell Iveson, Karen Ellen. BA, Chio State U., 1965, Tchg. Cert., 1966; Vocat. Tchg. Cert., U. Calif., Berkeley, 1980. Vocat. tchr. offset printing/graphics Contra Costa County Regional Occupl. Program, Concord, Calif., 1980-90; tchr. Mt. Diablo Unified Sch. Dist., Concord, Calif., 1966—. Co-compiler: Stafford County, Va., 1800-1850, 1982; compiler (family genealogy) Descendants of Allen J. Tackitt, 1958; editor, pub. Tackett Family Jour., 1963—. City councilman City of Live Oak, Calif., 1963-66; mem. commn. Local Agy. Formation Com., Sutter County, Calif., 1965. Named Ky. Col., Gov. Julian Carroll, 1978. Mem. Ky. Geneal. Soc., Va. Geneal. Soc., Contra Costa County Geneal. Soc. (pres. 1979-80, past editor). Democrat. So. Baptist. Home: 1830 Johnson Dr Concord CA 94520-3917 Office: Mount Diablo HS 2450 Grant St Concord CA 94520-2251

TACKMAN, ARTHUR LESTER, newspaper publisher, management consultant; b. Chgo., July 28, 1916; s. Arthur Lester and Lucy Louise (Gutekunst) T.; m. Mary Lillian Connor, Mar. 31, 1939; children: Arthur Lester III, Laurence Connor, Alan Rhead. BA, Ohio State U., 1938, MPA, 1939. With various depts. U.S. Govt., Washington, 1938-49; staff asst., mem. pers. policy bd. Dept. Def., Washington, 1949; asst. mgr. Savannah river plant AEC, Aiken, S.C., 1950-55; asst. dir. inspection AEC, Washington, 1955-59, dir. pers., 1959-65; dir. pers. HUD, Washington, 1965-70; mgmt. cons. Glenwood, N.Mex., 1970-78; owner, operator Deep Creek Ranch, Inc., Glenwood, 1972—; publisher Catron Co. Pub. Co., Inc., Reserve, N.Mex., 1986-91. Pres. Gila Nat. Forest Permittees, Reserve, 1978-86; mem., treas. N.Mex. Pub. Lands Coun., Albuquerque, 1967-87; coun. mem. Boy Scouts Am., S.C., Washington, 1950-65. Lt. USN, 1943-46. Recipient Man Yr. Award Aiken County C. of C., 1953, Citation for Meritorious Svc. United Def. Fund, 1957. Mem. N.Mex. Press Assn. Democrat. Unitarian. Home: Deep Creek Ranch Glenwood NM 88039

TAEUSCH, H. WILLIAM, pediatrician; b. Cleve., Dec. 4, 1939. AB cum laude, Harvard U., 1961; MD, Case Western Res. U., 1965. Diplomate Am. Bd. Pediatrics, sub-bd. Neonatal/Perinatal Medicine; diplomate Nat. Bd. Med. Examiners. Intern Univ. Hosps., Cleve., 1965-66, resident in pediatrics, 1966-67; sr. resident in pediatrics Johns Hopkins Hosp., Balt., 1967-68; fellow depts. pediatrics and physiology McGill U., Montreal, 1970-72; clin. tng. in neonatology Montreal Children's Hosp./Royal Victoria Hosp., 1970-74; asst. prof. pediatrics McGill U. Sch. Medicine, 1972-74; from asst. prof. to prof. Harvard Med. Sch., 1974-87; prof. pediatrics Charles R. Drew U. Medicine and Sci., also UCLA, 1987-93, U. Calif., San Francisco, 1993—; pediatrician-in-chief Brigham and Women's Hosp., 1980-84; dir. neonatology King/Drew Med. Ctr., co-dir. combined neonatology program Harbor/UCLA-King/Drew Med. Ctr., 1987-93; chief pediatric svc. San Francisco Gen. Hosp., 1993—; vice chair dept. pediatrics U. Calif.-San Francisco. Contbr. numerous articles to med. jours. Served with M.C., U.S. Army, 1968-70. Robert Wood Johnson Found. grantee, 1986; Am. Lung Assn. Calif. grantee, 1988-90; NIH grantee, 1988-95; others. Fellow Am. Acad. Pediatrics; mem. Am. Fedn.Clin. Rsch., Am. Physiol. Soc., Soc. for Pediatric Rsch., Am. Pediatric Soc., Am. Thoracic Soc., Western Soc. for Pediatric Rsch. Home: 52 Ord St San Francisco CA 94114-1415 Office: San Francisco Gen Hosp Pediatrics Svc 1001 Potrero Ave San Francisco CA 94110-3518

TAFOYA, ARTHUR N., bishop; b. Alameda, N.Mex., Mar. 2, 1933; s. Nicholas and Rosita Tafoya. Ed., St. Thomas Sem., Denver, Conception (Mo.) Sem. Ordained priest Roman Cath. Ch., 1962. Asst. pastor Holy Rosary Parish, Albuquerque, 1962-65; pastor Northern N.Mex., from 1965, San Jose Parish, Albuquerque; rector Immaculate Heart of Mary Sem., Santa Fe; ordained bishop of Pueblo Colo., 1980—. Office: 1001 N Grand Ave Pueblo CO 81003-2915*

TAFUR, MARIO HUMBERTO, psychiatrist; b. Libano, Tolima, Colombia, June 22, 1940; came to U.S., 1972; s. Rafael and Clementina (Galvis) T.; m. Clemencia Tafur, Aug. 30, 1969; children: Mario, Joseph, Camilo. MD, U. Javeriana, Bogota, Colombia, 1968. Diplomate Am. Bd. Psychiatry. Psychiat. resident Menninger, Topeka, 1973-76; staff psychiatrist VA Med. Ctr., Topeka, 1976-77, chief acute svcs., 1977-79; mem. faculty Menninger Found., Topeka, 1977—; med. dir. adult svcs. St. Luke's Behavioral Ctr., Phoenix, 1981-87, pres. med. staff, 1984-85; med. dir. Menninger Phoenix, 1987-94; chmn. dept. psychiatry, med. dir. St. Joseph's Hosp. & Med. Ctr., Phoenix, 1988—; med. dir. St. Joseph's Behavioral Health Svcs., Phoenix, 1995—. Mem. AMA, Am. Psychiat. Assn., Am. Acad. Med. Dirs., Menninger Alumni Assn. Office: St Josephs Behavioral Health Svcs 300 W Clarendon Ave Ste 275 Phoenix AZ 85013-3422

TAGGART, PAULETT LONG, architect, educator; b. San Francisco, Sept. 2, 1949; d. Ganson Powers and Paulett (Long) T.; m. William Kenneth Stuit, Sept. 6, 1986. BArch, U. Oreg., 1974; MArch, Harvard U., 1984. Registered architect, Calif. Assoc. Dan Solomon & Assocs., San Francisco, 1977-82; prin. Paulett Taggart Architects, San Francisco, 1986—; adj. prof. Calif. Coll. Arts and Crafts, San Francisco and Oakland, Calif., 1990—. Mem. AIA (Design awards 1982, 88, 89). Unitarian. Office: Paulette Taggart Architects 1831 Powell St San Francisco CA 94133-2809

TAGGART, SONDRA, financial planner, investment advisor; b. N.Y.C., July 22, 1934; d. Louis and Rose (Birnbaum) Hamov; children: Eric, Karen. BA, Hunter Coll., 1955. Cert. fin. planner; registered investment advisor; registered prin. Nat. Assn. Securities Dealers. Founder, dir., officer Copyright Svc. Bur., Ltd., N.Y.C., 1957-69; dir., officer Maclen Music, Inc., N.Y.C., 1964-69, The Beatles Ltd., 1964-69; pres. Westshore, Inc., Mill Valley, Calif., 1969-82; investment advisor, securities broker, chief exec. officer The Taggart Co. Ltd., 1982—. Editor: The Red Tapes: Commentaries on Doing Business With The Russians and East Europeans, 1978. Mem. Internat. Assn. Fin. Planners, Registry Fin. Planning Practitioners. Republican. Club: Bankers. Office: 9720 Wilshire Blvd Ste 205 Beverly Hills CA 90212-2006

TAGGART, TOM, county clerk; b. L.A., July 24, 1953; s. Claude Edward and Patricia Louise (Stark) T.; m. Cynthia L., Oct. 3, 1976; children: Lindsay Allison, Megan Laural. BA in Radio & TV, Calif. State U., Long Beach, 1976. Tax auditor IRS, Carson, Calif., 1977-78, Lewiston, Idaho, 1978-79, Coeur D Alene, Idaho, 1979-84; tax cons. pvt. practice, Coeur D Alene, Idaho, 1984-91; restaurant owner Coeur D Alene, Idaho, 1986-87; clk. of dist. ct. Kootenai County, Coeur D Alene, Idaho, 1991—. Trustee Lakeland Sch. Dist., Rathdrum, Idaho, 1982-88, chair 1984-88; mem. coun. City of Rathdrum, 1989-90. Mem. Am. Soc. Pub. Adminstrn., NAt. Assn. County Recorders & Clks., Idaho Assn. Counties, Idaho Assn. Clks. (chair budget com. 1993-94), The Election Ctr. Democrat. Office: Kootenai County 501 Govt Way Coeur D Alene ID 83814

TAHAN, MARY RIZKALLAH, advertising executive; b. Cairo, Sept. 20, 1960; came to U.S., 1967; d. Rizkallah Naguib and Olga Michele (Karam) T.; m. Kenneth A. Colorado, Nov. 17, 1985. BA in English cum laude, UCLA, 1983, MA in Motion Picture/TV, 1985. Journalist, feature and entertainment reporter Various Newspapers, L.A., 1978-81; TV prodn. intern Alan Landsburg Prodns., Hollywood, Calif., 1980-81; editor, writer The News Cir. Pub. Co., Glendale, Calif., 1980-83; ptnr. Linear Dimensions Graphics, L.A., 1982-87, Colorado & Tahan Advt. Agy., L.A., 1983-87; creative dir. INS Advt., Portland, Oreg., 1987, Brown Dugan & Assocs., Portland, 1988-89, Motivational Design, Portland, 1989; pres., owner Tahan Advt., Portland, 1989—. Playwright, co-producer stage play: Prufrock in the Inferno, 1985; copywriter, producer TV and radio commls. (Silver Microphone award 1988, 94, Telly award 1989, 95); author: (poems) Feminist Broadcast Quarterly, 1992. Judge, Edmonton, Alta., Can. Ace Competition, Portland, 1992. Am.-Arab Ednl. Found. scholar, 1979; recipient News Writing award Detroit News, 1976, Journalist award Am. Newspaper Pubs. Assn., 1979, Rosey award Portland Advt. Fedn., 1989. Home: 1974 SW 5th Ave Portland OR 97201-5224 Office: Tahan Advt Ste 360 1020 S W Taylor St Portland OR 97205

TAHMASSIAN, ARA ZARNEH, university director; b. Tehran, Iran, Apr. 15, 1953; came to U.S., 1981; s. Ohan Zarneh and Nashkoon (Asadourian) T.; m. Linda Khosrof Garabedian, Jan. 7, 1953; children: Levon Zarneh, Ani Verjeen. BSc in Nuclear Engring., London U., 1977; postgrad., Middlesex (Eng.) Poly. U., 1978; MSc in Radiol. Health, Salford (Eng.) U., 1980; PhD in Health Physics, Columbia Pacific U., 1984. Chief field ops. Nat. Safety Cons., Fremont, Calif., 1981-84, v.p. ops., 1987-88; dir. environ. health and safety Vets. Med. Ctr., San Francisco, 1984-87; mgr. radiation safety U. Calif., San Francisco, 1988-93, dir. environ. health and safety, 1993—; cons. various hosps., Calif., 1982—. Co-author papers in field, book chpt. Trustee St. Gregory's Ch., San Francisco, 1991-92; pres. Ararat Armenian Soc., San Francisco, 1991, Armenian Cultural Found., San Francisco, 1989; bd. dirs. Calif. Radioactive Forum, San Francisco, 1993. Mem. Soc. Nuclear Medicine, North Calif. Health Physics Soc. Republican. Armenian Orthodox. Home: 39537 Benavente Ave Fremont CA 94539-3002 Office: U Calif 50 Medical Center Way San Francisco CA 94143-8050

TAI, FRANK, aerospace engineering consultant; b. Omaha, Apr. 10, 1955; s. Shou Nan and May (Chuang) T.; m. Lorraine Mae Fesq, May 14, 1988. BSME, U. Calif., Berkeley, 1977; MS in Automatic Controls Engring., MIT, 1979. Design engr. satellite attitude control systems Ball Aerospace, Boulder, Colo., 1979-84; mgr. satellite attitude control systems TRW, Redondo Beach, Calif., 1984-88; mgr. engring. Microcosm, Inc., Torrance, Calif., 1988-89; pres., engring. cons., founder Tech. Advancements, Inc., Playa del Rey, Calif., 1989—. Contbr. articles to profl. jours. Mem. AIAA, Am. Astronautical Soc., Sigma Xi, Tau Beta Pi, Pi Tau Sigma. Office: Tech Advancements Inc 6738 Esplanade St # 300 Playa Del Rey CA 90293-7525

TAIGMAN, MICHAEL ALLEN, healthcare management development company official; b. Denver, July 4, 1959; s. Leonard George and Joan Bell (Graham) T. Student, Met. State Coll., U. Colo., Denver, Naropa Inst., Boulder, Colo. Cert. paramedic. Paramedic, br. office mgr. Care Ambulance, Castle Rock, Colo., 1974-80; paramedic, field tng. officer Denver Paramedic Div., 1980-88; asst. to med. dir. Pinellas County Emergency Med. Svc., Clearwater, Fla., 1988; mgr. quality improvement Emergency Providers Inc., Kansas City, Mo., 1988-89, Bay Star Med. Svcs., Burlingame, Calif., 1989-92; dir. rsch. and process facilitation Laidlaw Med. Transp. (doing business as MedTrans), San Diego, 1992-94; mng. dir. The Fourth Party: a MedTrans Healthcare Mgmt. Devel. Corp., Oakland, Calif., 1994—; pres., owner Paaramedicine ECR, Oakland, 1983—; mem. affiliate faculty Arapahoe C.C., Littleton, Colo., 1984-85; mem. affiliate faculty Am. Heart Assn., Denver, 1987-89, mem. Colo. affiliate faculty basic trauma life support, Denver, 1989-89; numerous presentations in field, condr. confs., seminars, lectr., 1984—. Mem. editorial bd. EMS Med. Advisor, On Scene, Pulse, EMS Insider, CPR Innovator; contbr. numerous articles to mags.; prodr. audio tapes A Commitment to Excellence in EMS, History Taking; prodr. video tapes Advanced EKG Interpretation. Mem. Colo. Search and Rescue Bd., Littleton, 1975-81; del. to exec. bd. Nat. Assn. Search and Rescue, 1976-77; assoc. mem. bd. dirs. Arapahoe Rescue Patrol, Littleton, 1977-85. Recipient Paramedic of Yr. award Denver Paramedic Div., 1983, Kenny Edwards award, 1985, 87; Paramedic of Yr. award State of Colo., 1987; EMS Responder award AMI St. Lukes, 1987, gold honor award for saving life Colo. EMT Assn., 1988, Buckle of Champions award B.C. Ambulance Svc., 1993. Mem. Nat. Assn. Emergency Med. Svc. Physicians (assoc., clin. standards and practice com.), Am. Soc. Law Enforcement Trainers, Justice System Tng. Assn. Office: The Fourth Party 5711 Hermann St Oakland CA 94609-1705

TAIMUTY, SAMUEL ISAAC, physicist; b. West Newton, Pa., Dec. 20, 1917; s. Elias and Samia (Hawatt) T.; BS, Carnegie Inst. Tech., 1940; PhD, U. So. Calif., 1951; m. Betty Jo Travis, Sept. 12, 1953 (dec.); children: Matthew, Martha; m. Rosalie Richards, Apr. 3, 1976. Physicist, U.S. Naval Shipyard, Phila. and Long Beach, Calif., 1942-46; rsch. asst. U. So. Calif., 1947-51; sr. physicist U.S. Naval Radiol. Def. Lab., 1950-52, SRI Internat., Menlo Park, Calif., 1952-72; sr. staff engr. Lockheed Missiles & Space Co., Sunnyvale, Calif., 1972-89; cons. physicist, 1971—. Mem. Am. Phys. Soc., Sigma Xi. Episcopalian. Contbr. articles to sci. publs. Patentee in field. Home: 3346 Kenneth Dr Palo Alto CA 94303-4217

TAIT, JOHN REID, lawyer; b. Toledo, Ohio, Apr. 7, 1946; s. Paul Reid and Lucy Richardson (Rudderow) T.; m. Christina Ruth Bjornstad, Mar. 12, 1972; children: Gretchen, Mary. BA, Columbia Coll., 1968; JD, Vanderbilt U., 1974. Bar: Idaho 1974, U.S. Dist. Ct. Idaho 1974. Assoc. Keeton & Tait, Lewiston, Idaho, 1974-76, ptnr., 1976-86, 89—, Keeton, Tait & Petrie, 1986-88, Keeton & Tait, 1989—. Chmn. bd. No. Rockies Action Group, Helena, Mont., 1985-86, bd. dirs. 1981-88, Lewiston Hist. Preservation Commn., Idaho, 1975-94, chmn., 1988-94; bd. dirs. Idaho Legal Aid Svcs., Boise, 1975—, Idaho Housing Agy., Boise, 1984-91, St. Joseph Regional Med. Ctr. Found., Inc., 1989-94; Dem. precinct committeeman, 1976-86, state committeeman, 1977-94; co-chmn. Idaho state re-election com. John V. Evans, 1978; Idaho del. Nat. Dem. Conv., N.Y., 1980, standing com. on credentials, N.Y., 1980, San Francisco, 1984; treas. Larry LaRocco for Congress, 1990, 92. Served with U.S. Army, 1968-71. Recipient Pro Bono Svc. award Idaho State Bar 1988, Community Recognition award Lewiston Intergovtl. Coun., 1992, Spl. Recognition award Idaho Legal Aid Svcs., Inc., 1993. Mem. ABA, Assn. Trial Lawyers Am., Idaho Trial Lawyers Assn. (regional dir. 1976-77, 86-88), Clearwater Bar Assn. (sec. 1974-76, pres. 1984-86). Democrat. Office: Keeton & Tait 312 Miller St # E Lewiston ID 83501-1944

TAJON, ENCARNACION FONTECHA (CONNIE TAJON), retired educator, association executive; b. San Narciso, Zambales, Philippines, Mar. 25, 1920; came to U.S., 1948; d. Espiridion Maggay and Gregoria (Labrador) Fontecha; m. Felix B. Tajon, Nov. 17, 1948; children: Ruth F., Edward F. Teacher's cert., Philippine Normal Coll., 1941; BEd, Far Eastern U., Manila, 1947; MEd, Seattle Pacific U., 1976. Cert. tchr., Philippines. Tchr. pub. schs. San Narciso and Manila, 1941-47; coll. educator Union Coll. Manila, 1947-48; tchr. Auburn (Wash.) Sch. Dist., 1956-58, Renton (Wash.) Sch. Dist., 1958-78; owner, operator Manila-Zambales Internat. Grill, Seattle, 1980-81, Connie's Lumpia House Internat. Restaurant, Seattle, 1981-84; founder, pres. Tajon-Fontecha, Inc., Renton, 1980—, United Friends of Filipinos in Am. Found., Renton, 1985—; founder Labrador Fontecha and Baldovi-Tajon Permanent Scholarship Fund of The Philippine Normal U., 1990; bd. mem. World Div. of the Gen. Bd. of Global Ministries of the United Meth. Ch., 1982-84, Ch. Women United Seattle Chapt.; mem. advisory bd Univ. Wash. Burke Mus., 1991—; mem. King TV Asian Am. Adv. Forum, 1993. Editor bull. Renton 1st United Meth. Ch., 1994. Bd. dirs. women's divsn. Gen. Bd. Global Ministries United Meth. Ch., 1982-84, Renton Area Youth Svcs., 1980-85, Girls' Club of Puget Sound, Ethnic Heritage Coun. of Pacific N.W., 1989—; mem. Mcpl. Arts Commn., Renton, 1980—; chair fundraising steering com. Washington State Women's Polit. Caucus, 1985-89; governing mem. nat. steering com. Nat. Women's Polit. Caucus Wash. State Coun., 1990—, mem. vol. action, 1990 Goodwill Games, Seattle, vol. worker Native Am. Urban Ministries, 1990—; adv. bd. Renton Comty. Housing Devel.; comty. adv. bd. U. Wash. Thomas Burke Meml. Mus., 1990—; mem. program com. UN, 1992—, Asian Pacific Task Force of Ch. Coun. Greater Seattle, 1993—; ch. women coord. United Ecumenical World Comty. Day Celebration, 1994; coord. of estabishment and devel. United Filipino-Am. Coll. Fund, Seattle-Renton area, 1995; emeritus bd. mem. Ethnic Heritage Coun. Pacific Northwest, 1993—; co-chmn. Annual Filipino and Filipino Am. Youth Activities Pres.'s Day Spelling Bee of Greater Seattle and vicinity, 1990-94; coord. Ch. Women United Greater Seattle Unit World Cmty. Day Celebration Luncheon, 1994, United Filipino-Am. Coll. Fund, 1995. Recipient spl. cert. of award Project Hope, 1976, U.S. Bicentennial Commn., 1976, UNICEF, 1977, Spirit of Liberty award Ethnic Heritage Coun. Pacific Northwest, 1991; named Parent of Yr. Filipino Community of Seattle, Inc., 1984, One of 500 Seattle Pacific U. Centennial "Alumni of a Growing Vision", 1991. Mem. NEA, Wash. State Edn. Assn. (bd. dirs. 1990-92), Am. Assn. Ret. Persons, Nat. Ret. Tchrs. Assn., Renton Ret. Tchrs. Assn., U. Wash. Alumni Assn. (life), U. Wash. Filipino Alumni Assn. (pres. Wash. state chpt. 1985-87), Renton Hist. Mus. (life), Internat. Platform Assn., United Meth. Women, Pres.'s Forum, Alpha Sigma, Delta Kappa Gamma. Democrat. Home and Office: 2033 Harrington Pl NE Renton WA 98056-2303

TAKAHASHI, GARY WAYNE, internist, hematologist, oncologist; b. Honolulu, Jan. 2, 1959; s. Kenneth Kiyoshi and Grace Setsuko (Ishigure) T. BS in Math. and Biology, Stanford U., 1980; MS in Anatomy/Reproductive Biology, U. Hawaii, 1983; MD, John A. Burns Sch. Medicine, Honolulu, 1984. Diplomate Nat. Bd. Med. Examiners, Am. Bd. Internal Medicine (Hematology, Med. Oncology). Intern, resident Oreg. Health Scis. U., Portland, 1984-87; chief resident St. Vincent Med. Ctr., Portland, 1987-88; fellow hematology/oncology U. Wash., Seattle, 1988-93; physician Hematology Clinic, Seattle, 1993-94, Oreg. Hematology Oncology Assocs., 1994—. Contbr. articles and abstracts to profl. publs. Recipient Achievement Rewards for Coll. Scientists scholarship, 1982, Merck, Sharp & Dohme Acad. award, 1982, Nat. Rsch. Svc. award fellowship NIH, 1990, March of Dimes Rsch. grant, 1993. Mem. Am. Coll. Physicians, Am. Soc. Hematology, Southwestern Oncology Group, Oreg. Med. Assn., Wash. Med. Assn., Oreg. Mycological Soc. Office: Oreg Hematology Oncology Assocs 9155 SW Barnes Rd #530 Portland OR 97225

TAKAHASHI, HIROYASU, computer scientist; b. Morioka, Iwate, Japan, Nov. 23, 1945; came to U.S., 1990; s. Ryozo and Eiko T.; m. Akiko Karino, Apr. 23, 1983; children: Yuta, Kazuma, Yoko. BA, U. Tokyo, Japan, 1969; MA, U. Tokyo, 1971, PhD, 1974. Systems engr. IBM Japan, Tokyo, 1974-78; researcher in Tokyo sci. ctr. IBM Japan, 1978-82, rsch. mgr. in Tokyo rsch. lab., 1982-89; rsch. staff mem. in Almaden rsch. ctr. IBM, San Jose, Calif., 1990-93; sr. technical staff mem. IBM, Japan, 1993—. Mem. Inst. Electronics, Info. and Comm. Engrs., Info. Processing Soc. Japan. Home: 1-18-29 Tachibanadai, Aoba-ku Yokohama Japan Office: IBM Yamato Lab, 1623 Shimotsurama, Yamato Kanagawa 242, Japan

TAKAHASHI, TOMOKO, education educator, writer; b. Ageo, Saitama, Japan, Jan. 25, 1955; came to U.S., 1975; d. Kiyoshi and Sachiko (Takahashi) T.; m. Jitsuro Jason Yamamoto, Oct. 12, 1984. BA magna cum laude, Albertus Magnus Coll., New Haven, Conn., 1977; MA, Columbia U., 1980, MEd, 1981, EdD, 1984. Researcher Columbia U. Tchrs. Coll., N.Y.C., 1984-89; instr. edn. and grad. edn. Coll. New Rochelle, N.Y., 1985-89, asst. prof., 1989-91; textbook writer Redondo Beach, Calif., 1991—; assoc. prof. Soka U. Am., L.A., 1992—, dean grad. sch., 1994—. Author: American English: Changing Culture and Society, 1993, Conversational Strategies, 1990, Oral Communication, 1989, A Study on Lexico-Semantic Transfer, 1984, others; contbr. articles to profl. jours.; translator: Rosa Parks: My Story by Rosa Parks, 1994. Mem. TESOL, MLA, Am. Assn. for Applied Linguistics. Home: 2015A Pullman Ln Redondo Beach CA 90278-4911

TAKASUGI, NAO, state official, business developer; b. Oxnard, Calif., Apr. 5, 1922; s. Shingoro and Yasuye (Hayashi) T.; m. Judith Shigeko Mayeda, Mar. 23, 1952; children—Scott, Russell, Ronald, Tricia, Lea. B.S., Temple U., 1945; M.B.A., U. Pa. Wharton Sch., 1946. Mem. city council City of Oxnard, Calif., 1976-82, mayor, 1982-92; mem. Calif. State Assembly, 1992—; bus. developer, cons. Mem. Oxnard Planning Commn., 1974-76; pres. World Trade Ctr. Assn., Oxnard; apptd. (by Calif. gov.) chmn. UN Anniversary; assemblyman Calif. State Assembly 37th Dist. Decorated Order of Sacred Treasure with Gold Rayette medal Japanese Gov., 1992.

Mem. Ventura County Japanese Am. Citizens League, World Trade Ctr. Assn. (pres. Oxnard chpt.), U.S. Conf. Mayors (mem. nat. adv. bd.), Nat. League of Cities (nat. bd. dirs.), Ventura County Transp. Com., League Calif. Cities (bd. dirs.), South Coast Area Bd. Dirs. (chmn. transp. com.), Assn. Ventura County Cities, Oxnard Housing Authoritry (chmn.), Oxnard Redevel. Agy. (chmn.), Optimists Club (Oxnard). Republican. Methodist. Home: 1221 El Portal Way Oxnard CA 93035-2511 Office: Rm 5158 State Capitol Sacramento CA 95814 also: 221 Daily Dr Ste 7 Camarillo CA 93010-5833

TAKASUGI, ROBERT MITSUHIRO, federal judge; b. Tacoma, Sept. 12, 1930; s. Hidesaburo and Kayo (Otsuki) T.; m. Dorothy O. Takasugi; children: Jon Robert, Lesli Mari. BS, UCLA, Los Angeles, 1953; LLB, JD, U. So. Calif., 1959. Bar: Calif. bar 1960. Practiced law Los Angeles, 1960-73; judge East Los Angeles Municipal Ct., 1973-75, adminstrv. judge, 1974, presiding judge, 1975; judge Superior Ct., County of Los Angeles, 1975-76; U.S. dist. judge U.S. Dist. Ct. (cen. dist.) Calif., 1976—; nat. legal counsel Japanese Am. Citizens League; guest lectr. law seminars Harvard U. Law Sch. Careers Symposium; commencement spkr.; mem. Legion Lex U. So. Calif. Law Ctr.; chmn. Pub. Defs. Indigent Def. & Psychiat. Panel Com.; mem. Affirmative Action Com., Habeas Corpus-Death Penalty Com., Exec. Com., Jury Com., Settlement Rule Com., Adv. Com. on Codes of Conduct of the Jud. Conf. of the U.S., 1988-92, Code of Conduct of Judges. Mem. editorial bd. U. So. Calif. Law Rev., 1959; contbr. articles to profl. jours. Mem. Calif. adv. com. Western Regional Office, U.S. Commn. on Civil Rights; chmn. blue ribbon com. for selection of chancellor L.A. C.C. With U.S. Army, 1953-55. Recipient U.S. Mil. Man of Yr. award for Far East Theater U.S. Army, 1954, Jud. Excellence award Criminal Cts. Bar Assn., cert. of merit Japanese-Am. Bar Assn., Disting. Svc. award Asian Pacific Ctr. and Pacific Clinics, 1994, others; named Judge of Yr. Century City Bar Assn.; Harry J. Bauer scholar, 1959. Mem. U. So. Calif. Law Alumni (dir.), Century City Bar Assn. (judge of yr. 1995). Office: US Dist Ct 312 N Spring St Los Angeles CA 90012-4701

TAKATA, KEVIN KENJI, lawyer; b. Lanai City, Hawaii, Feb. 9, 1956; s. Kengo and Evelyn S. (Ishida) T. BA, U. Hawaii, 1978; JD, Case Western Res. U., 1984. Bar: Hawaii 1984, U.S. Dist. Ct. Hawaii 1984. Assoc. Oliver, Lee, Cuskaden & Ogawa, Honolulu, 1984-87; dep. prosecutor specializing in homicides Dept. of Prosecuting Atty., Honolulu, 1987—. Mem. ABA, Hawaii Bar Assn., Nat. Dist. Attys. Assn., Honolulu C. of C. Office: Dept Prosecuting Atty 1060 Richards St 10th Fl Honolulu HI 96813-2920

TAKEI, TOSHIHISA, otolaryngologist; b. L.A., Apr. 19, 1931; s. Taketomi and Mitsue (Hagihara) T.; m. Emiko Kubota, Jan. 25, 1955; children: H. Thomas, T. Robert. BA, UCLA, 1954; MD, Boston U., 1962. Diplomate, Am. Bd. Otolaryngology. Intern L.A. County Harbor Gen. Hosp., 1962-63; resident in otolaryngology L.A. County/U. So. Calif. Med. Ctr., 1963-67; staff physician Covina (Calif.) Ear, Nose & Throat Med. Group, 1968—; asst. prof. Sch. Medicine, U. So. Calif., L.A., 1968—. 1st lt. U.S. Army, 1955-56, Korea. Fellow Am. Acad. Otolaryngology, Royal Soc. Medicine. Republican. Buddhist. Office: Covina ENT Med Group Inc 236 W College St Covina CA 91723-1902

TAKEOKA, GARY ROBERT, chemist, researcher; b. Culver City, Calif., Nov. 11, 1954; s. George Saburo and Nell Aiko (Iwamiya) T. BS, U. Calif., Davis, 1976, MS, 1979, PhD, 1986. Postdoctoral researcher Nestle, Vers-Chez-Les-Blanc, Switzerland, 1987; postdoctoral fellow Nabisco Brands, East Hanover, N.J., 1988-90, Planters Lifesavers, Winston-Salem, N.C., 1990-91; rsch. chemist USDA, Albany, Calif., 1992—. Editor: Flavor Precursors, 1992; contbr. articles to profl. jours. Mem. Am. Chem. Soc. (chmn. flavor subdivsn.), Inst. Food Technologists. Office: USDA 800 Buchanan St Berkeley CA 94710-1105

TAKUMI, ROY MITSUO, state representative; b. Honolulu, Oct. 13, 1952; m. Wanda A. Kutaka; children: Aisha, Jaron. BA, Friends World Coll., 1991; MPA, U. Hawaii, 1993. Cmty. organizer Osaka, Japan, 1977-83; program dir. Am. Friends Svc. Com., Honolulu, 1984-90; polit. coord. Hawaii State AFL-CIO, Honolulu, 1990-92; rep. Ho. of Reps., Honolulu, 1992—. Office: State Ho of Reps State Capitol Honolulu HI 96813

TALBERT, MELVIN GEORGE, bishop; b. Clinton, La., June 14, 1934; s. Nettles and Florence (George) T.; m. Ethlelou Douglas, June 3, 1961; 1 child, Evangeline. BA, So. U., 1959; MDiv, Interdenominational Theol. Ctr., Gammon Theol. Sem., Atlanta, 1962; DD hon., Huston Tillotson Coll., Austin, 1972; LLD (hon.), U. Puget Sound, Tacoma, 1987. Ordained deacon, Meth. Ch., 1960 , elder, 1962, elected to episcopacy, United Meth. Ch., 1980. Pastor Boyd Chapel, Jefferson City, Tenn., 1960-61, Rising Sun, Sunrise, Tenn., 1960-61, St. John's Ch., L.A., 1961-62, Wesley Ch., L.A., 1962-64, Hamilton Ch., L.A., 1964-67; mem. staff So. Calif.-Ariz. Conf. United Meth. Ch., L.A., 1967-68; dist. supr. Long Beach dist. So. Calif.-Ariz. Conf. United Meth. Ch., 1968-73; gen. sec. Gen. Bd. Discipleship, Nashville, 1973-80; resident bishop Seattle area Pacific N.W. conf. United Meth. Ch., 1980-88, resident bishop San Francisco area Calif.-Nev. Conf., 1988—, sec. coun. bishops, 1988—; mem. exec. com. World Meth. Coun., 1976-81, 84—; mem. governing bd. Nat. Coun. Chs., 1980—; v.p., chmn. funding com. Gen. Commn. on Religion and Race, 1980-84, pres., 1984-88; chmn. Missional Priority Coordinating com. Gen. Coun. Ministries, 1980-84; mem. Gen. Commn. on Christian Unity and Interreligious Concerns, 1984—, African Ch. Growth and Devel. Com., 1981-84; now pres. elect Nat. Coun. Ch. Christ in the U.S.A. Mem. steering com. Student Non-Violent Coordinating com. Atlanta U. Ctr., 1960-61; trustee Gammon Theol. Sem., Atlanta, 1976—, U. Puget Sound, Tacoma, 1980-88 , Sch. Theology at Claremont, Calif., 1981-88, Pacific Sch. Religion, 1988—; bd. dirs. Glide Found., 1988—. Recipient award of merit for outstanding svc. in Christian edn. Gen. Bd. Edn., 1971; recipient Spl. achievement award Nat. Assn. Black Bus. Women, 1971; Nat. Meth. scholar, 1960; Crusade scholar, 1961. Mem. Theta Phi. Democrat. Home: 8735 W Camden Dr Elk Grove CA 95624-3037*

TALBERT, WILLARD LINDLEY, JR., physicist; b. Casper, Wyo., Mar. 8, 1932; s. Willard L. Sr. and Ellen Lunette (Goodlander) T.; m. Mary Alice Williams, Aug. 29, 1952; children: Marc Alan, Kenneth Earl, Linda Sue, Cynthia Lunette. BA cum laude, U. Colo., 1954; PhD, Iowa State U., 1960. Rsch. physicist Ohio Oil Co., Littleton, Colo., 1959-62; prof. physics Iowa State U., Ames, 1962-76; staff mem. Los Alamos Nat. Lab., 1976-93; vis. fellow Nobel Inst., Stockholm, 1970-71; mem. various adv. panels. Editor Procs. of 11th Internat. Conf. on Isotope Separators, 1977; jour. and proposal referee, 1964-93; contbr. numerous articles to profl. jours. NSF fellow, 1956-59. Fellow Am. Phys. Soc.; mem. AAAS, Phi Beta Kappa, Phi Kappa Phi. Home: 1 E Sunrise Dr Santa Fe NM 87501-8513

TALBOTT, GEORGE ROBERT, physicist, mathematician, educator; b. San Diego, Oct. 1, 1925; s. George Fletcher and Mary (Lanz) T.; BA with honors, UCLA, 1960; DSc, Ind. No. U., 1973. Physicist, mem. tech. staff Rockwell Internat. Co., Anaheim, Calif., 1960-85; mem. faculty thermodynamics Pacific States U., 1971-77, prof., 1972-80, chmn. dept. math. studies, 1973-80; lectr. computer sci. Calif. State U., Fullerton, 1979—; cons. physics, computer sci.; disting. guest lectr. Brunel U., London, 1974, 76; spl. guest Forschungsbibliothek, Hannover, W. Ger., 1979; assoc. editor KRONOS jour., Glassboro (N.J.) U., 1978—; chief computer scientist and ednl. videotape dir. Specialized Software, Wilmot, Wis., 1982—; phys. scientist and rsch. assoc. San Diego Mus. Man, 1993—. With M.C., U.S. Army, 1956. Recipient Vis. Scholar's award Western Mich. U., 1979. Mem. Am. Soc. Med. Technologists, Am. Math. Soc., Math. Assn. Am., Am. Soc. Clin. Pathologists (lic. med. lab. technologist). Buddhist. Author: Electronic Thermodynamics, 1973; Philosophy and Unified Science, 1977, Computer Applications, 1989, Sir Arthur and Gravity, 1990, Fermat's Last Theorem, 1991; co-inventor burner. Home: 4031 E Charter Oak Dr Orange CA 92669-2611

TALBOTT, JONATHAN LEE, electrical engineer; b. Denver, May 30, 1952; s. Richard L. and Mary Margaret (Junger) T.; m. Debra K. Gahagen, Jan. 5, 1975 (div. Dec. 18, 1981); m. Donna M. Rodriguez, Apr. 11, 1987; 1 child, Brigette M. BSEE, U. Colo., 1974; MBA, Regis U., 1987. Registered profl. engr. Colo, N.Mex.; engring. and surveying cert. Nat. Coun. Examiners. Summer intern Pub. Svc. of Colo., Boulder, 1973; engr. Stone and Webster, various cities, 1974-76, Ernst/Comstock Elec. Constrn., various cities, 1976-78, Stearns-Roger, Denver, 1978-80, Behrent Engring., Denver, 1980-83; owner, prin., cons. Talbott Co., Denver, 1983-90; project mgr., group leader, sec. treas. The RMH Group, Lakewood, Colo., 1990—; bd. dirs. Colo. Elec. Svc. Network, v.p. and pres. pro-tem, pres. Bd. dirs. City of Thornton (Colo.) Archtl. Rev., 1981-83, City of Westminster (Colo.) Code Bd. of Appeals, 1989—. Mem. IEEE, Soc. Profl. Engrs., Bldg. Owners Mgmt. Assn., Metro North C. of C. Home: 10383 Irving Ct Westminster CO 80030-6704

TALEBZADEH, HOUMAN, financial services executive; b. Tehran, Iran, Sept. 21, 1962; came to U.S., 1978; s. Ghassem and Mina (Seirafi) T. BSEE, Rensselaer Polytech. Inst., 1984; MSEE, U. So. Calif., L.A., 1985, MBA, 1994. Rsch. asst. electrophysics dept. U. So. Calif., L.A., 1984-85, rsch. asst. robotics dept., 1985; mem. tech. staff new products engring. Symbolics, Inc., L.A., 1986-88, sr. mem. tech. staff graphics divsn., 1988-91; v.p. artificial intelligence divsn. Countrywide Funding Corp., Pasadena, Calif., 1991-95; sr. mgr. Andersen Consulting, 1995—; guest spkr. Mortgage Bankers Assn. Am., Washington, 1991-94. Mem. IEEE, Am. Assn. Artificial Intelligence (guest spkr. 1994, Innovative Applications Artificial Intelligence award 1994), Am. Computing Machinery Assn. Home: 28121 Highridge Rd Apt 201 Rancho Palos CA 90275-3453 Office: Andersen Consulting 633 W 5th St Los Angeles CA 90071-2005

TALIAFERRO, ROBERT See BROOKE, TAL

TALIAFERRO, YVON ROCHELLE, accountant, consultant; b. Washington, May 1, 1957; d. Kenneth Wayne and Shirley Yvonne (Dixon) Smith. BS in Acctg., Loma Linda U., 1981. Mgr., personnel cons., acct. K&W Security Patrol, Vallejo, Calif., 1981-85; account exec. Alamo Assocs., Concord, Calif., 1986-88; credit mgr. BTS Group, Oakland, Calif., 1988-91; owner, pres. AAA Notary Svc., Danville, Calif., 1990—; adminstrv. asst. Strategic Fin. Svcs., Walnut Creek, Calif., 1992—; customer svc. rep. Bank of Am., Concord, Calif., 1993—; contracting cons. VIP Bus. Svcs., Danville, Calif., 1990-91; entrepreneur, investor, Walnut Creek, 1991—. Mem. NAFE, Nat. Notary Assn. (notary pub.).

TALLMADGE, DIANE JOYCE, bookstore manager; b. Racine, Wis., May 10, 1934; d. Robert William and LuLu A (Steinike) Sperberg; m. Guy Kasten Tallmadge Jr. Sept. 12, 1957. BA, U. Wis., 1956; MA, 1957; MLS, UCLA, 1962. Ballet instr., choreographer Madison, Wis., 1952-57; tchr. pub. schs. Melbourne, Australia, 1957-58; ballet instr., choreographer Los Angeles, 1959-62; libr./physical sci. cataloger UCLA, 1962-64, Slavic lang. cataloger, 1964-66; docent libr. Stanford U. Mus., 1974—; mgr. Stanford U. Art Gallery Bookshop, 1985-89. Bd. govs. Com. for Art, Stanford, 1985-92; mem. Santa Monica and Westside Jr. Philharmonic, 1964-66. Mem. AAUW (pres. 1970-71), Phi Beta Kappa, Phi Kappa Phi, Beta Phi MU, Chi Omega. Republican. Congregationalist. Home: 446 Guadalupe Dr Los Altos CA 94022-2108

TALLMADGE, GUY KASTEN, research psychologist; b. Milw., Mar. 2, 1932; s. Guy Kasten and Alice (LaBoule) T.; m. Diane Joyce Sperberg, Sept. 12, 1957. AB, Princeton U., 1954; MS, Purdue U., 1956, PhD, 1959. Rsch. scientist Douglas Aircraft Co., Santa Monica, Calif., 1959-61; mgr. behavioral psychology Humetrics div. Thiokol Chem. Corp., L.A., 1961-63; sr. assoc. Planning Rsch. Corp., L.A., 1963-65; dir. instrnl. methods Am. Insts. for Rsch., Palo Alto, Calif., 1965-73; v.p., pres. RMC Rsch. Corp., Mountain View, Calif., 1973-83, sr. v.p., 1987-90; sr. v.p. SRA Techs., Mountain View, 1983-86. Contbr. articles to profl. jours. Fulbright scholar U. Melbourne (Australia), 1957-58; sr. rsch. fellow Am. Insts. for Rsch., Palo Alto, Calif., 1990-92. Mem. Am. Ednl. Rsch. Assn., Nat. Coun. on Measurement in Edn., Am. Evaluation Assn., Los Altos Golf and Country Club, Princeton Club No. Calif.

TALLMAN, CORY ROGER, aerospace engineer; b. Omaha, Mar. 15, 1962; s. Roger Howard and Lauralee (Chadonich) T.; m. Lenka Jean Lee, Dec. 29, 1984; 1 child, Nicole Marie. BS in Aero. Engring., Iowa State U., 1985; MBA, U. Phoenix, 1992. Design engr. Douglas Aircraft Co., Long Beach, Calif., 1985—. Scoutmaster and asst. scoutmaster Boy Scouts Am., Cerritos, Calif., 1986-93. Mem. AIAA. Republican. Presbyterian. Office: Douglas Aircraft Co M/C 801-47 3855 N Lakewood Blvd Long Beach CA 90846-0003

TALLMAN, JOHN GARY, biology educator; b. Sistersville, W.Va., Mar. 20, 1950. AB in Biology, West Liberty State Coll., W.Va., 1971; PhD in Biochem. Genetics, W.Va. U., 1976. Rsch. assoc. Divsn. Biochemistry Kans. State U., 1976-78; asst. prof. biology Pepperdine U., 1978-81, assoc. prof. biology, 1981-88, tenured, 1982—, prof. biology, 1988—; vis. scholar dept. biol. scis., Stanford U., 1986—. Contbr. articles to profl. jours. Grantee NSF, 1988—, Univ. Rsch. Coun., 1985, 89, 90, 92, Ralph M. Parsons Found., 1988-89, John Stauffer Charitable Trust, 1983, 88-89, others; named to Outstanding Young Men of Am., 1982. Mem. AAAS, Am. Genetic Assn., Am. Soc. Plant Physiologists, Coun. Undergrad. Rsch., Chi Beta Phi, Alpha Phi Sigma. Office: Nat Sci Divsn Pepperdine Univ Malibu CA 90263

TALMADGE, PHILIP ALBERT, state senator, lawyer; b. Seattle, Apr. 23, 1952; s. Judson H., Jr., and Jeanne C. T.; m. Darlene L. Nelson, Sept. 6, 1970; children: Adam, Matthew, Jessica, Jonathan, AnnMarie. B.A. magna cum laude with honors in Polit. Sci., Yale U., 1973; J.D., U. Wash., 1976. Bar: Wash. 1976. Pres. Talmadge & Cutler,, 1976—; mem. Wash. Senate, 1978—, ways and means com, children and family svc. com., edn. com.; bd. dirs. Seattle Consumer Credit Counseling Svc. Mem. Wash. State Bar Assn., Seattle-King County Bar Assn. Author: The Nixon Doctrine and the Reaction of Three Asian Nations, 1973; editor Law Rev., U. Wash., 1975-76; contbr. articles to legal publs.

TALMAGE, KENNETH KELLOGG, business executive; b. Morristown, N.J., Jan. 16, 1946; s. Edward Taylor Hunt Talmage Jr. and Dorothy (Rogers) Kaye. BA, Claremont Men's Coll., 1968; MBA, Boston U., Brussels, 1976. Asst. to chmn. fin. com. to Re-elect President Nixon, 1972-73; assoc., Hon. Leonard K. Firestone, L.A., 1973-74; attaché Am. Embassy, Brussels, 1974-77; mgmt. cons. strategic planning and fin. Arthur D. Little, Inc., Cambridge, Mass., 1977-80; sr. v.p. Boston Safe Deposit & Trust Co., 1980-87; pres. Lloyd's Furs, Inc., Denver, Colo., 1987-92; bd. dirs. Monterey Water Co., 1992-95, pres., 1995—; bd. dirs. PureWest Industries, Inc., vice-chmn., 1993-95. Trustee Colo. Outward Bound Sch., 1990—, vice chmn., 1995—. Vols. for Outdoor Colo., 1988-94, Breckenridge Outdoor Edn. Ctr., 1989-92; advisor Hurricane Island Outward Bound Sch., Maine, 1987—, trustee, 1979-87, chmn. bd. trustees, 1980-83; mem. exec. com. Outward Bound, U.S.A., 1980-85. With USNR, 1968-69. Mem. The Country Club (Mass.), Denver Country Club. Home: 458 High St Denver CO 80218-4024 Office: Monterey Water Co 2933 Pebble Falls Ct Stockton CA 95219

TALMI, YOAV, conductor, composer; b. Kibbutz Merhavia, Israel, Apr. 28, 1943; diploma Rubin Acad. Music, Tel Aviv; postgrad. diploma Juilliard Sch. Music; m. Erella Gottesmann; 2 children. Assoc. condr. Louisville Orch., 1968-70; co-condr. Israel Chamber Orch., 1970-72; artistic dir., condr. Gelders Symphony Orch., Arnhem, 1974-80; prin. guest condr. Munich Philharm. Orch., 1979-80; artistic dir., condr. Israel Chamber Orch., 1984-88; music dir. New Israeli Opera, 1985-89, San Diego Symphony Orch., 1990—, Waterloo Festival, N.J., 1994-95; guest condr. Berlin Philharm., Munich Philharm., London Philharm., Philharmonia, Concertgebouw, Rotterdam Philharm., Israel Philharm., Tokyo Symphony, New Japan Philharm., Vienna Symphony, St. Petersburg Philharm., Detroit Symphony, St. Louis Symphony, Houston Symphony, Dallas Symphony, N.Y. Chamber Symphony, L.A. Chamber Orch., Oslo Philharm., Tonhalle Orch. Zurich, others. Composer: Dreams for choir a capella, Music for Flute and Strings; Overture on Mexican Themes (recorded), 3 Monologues for Flute Solo (pub.), Inauguration Fanfare; recs. include: Bruckner 9th Symphony (Oslo Philharm.), Gliére 3rd Symphony, Brahms Sextet/4 Serious Songs, Rachmaninov's Isle of the Dead, Berlioz Overtures Romeo et Juliette (San Diego Symphony), Tchaikowsky/Scoenberg, Bloch/Barber/Grieg/Puccini (Israel Chamber Orch.); (with Erella Talmi) works for flute and piano. Recipient Boskovitch prize for composition, Israel, 1965; Koussevitzky Meml. Conducting prize, Tanglewood, 1969; award Ruppert Found. Condr. competition, London, 1973. Home: PO Box 1384, Kfar Saba 44113, Israel Office: ICM Artists 40 W 57th St New York NY 10019 also: San Diego Symphony Orch 1245 7th Ave San Diego CA 92101-4302

TALTON, CHESTER LOVELLE, bishop; b. El Dorado, Ark., Sept. 22, 1941; s. Chester Talton and Mae Ola (Shells) Henry; m. Karen Louise Warren, Aug. 25, 1963; children: Kathy Louise, Linda Karen, Frederick Douglass, Benjamin Albert. BS, Calif. State U., Hayward, 1967; MDiv, Ch. Divinity Sch. of Pacific, 1970. Ordained to ministry Episcopal Ch., as deacon, 1970, as priest, 1971, as bishop, 1991. Vicar Good Shepherd Episc. Ch., Berkeley, Calif., 1970-71, St. Mathias Mission, Seaside, Calif., 1971-73, Ch. of the Holy Cross, Chgo., 1973-76; curate All Sts. Episc. Ch., Carmel, Calif., 1971-73; rector St. Philips Episc. Ch., St. Paul, 1976-81, St. Philips Ch., N.Y.C., 1985-90; mission officer Parish of Trinity Ch., N.Y.C., 1981-85; suffragan bishop Diocese of L.A., Episc. Ch., 1990—. Pres. Community Svc. Coun. Greater Harlem, N.Y.C., 1985-90, Upper Manhattan Child Devel. Ctr., N.Y.C., 1985-90, Peter Williams Jr. Housing Corp., N.Y.C., 1988-90. Mem. Union of Black Episcopalians. Office: Episc Diocese LA PO Box 2164 1220 W 4th St Los Angeles CA 90017-1412*

TAM, ROLAND FOOK SENG, physician; b. Honolulu, Feb. 19, 1946. BA, U. Hawaii, 1968; MD, U. Wash., 1972. Intern surgery Orange County Med. Ctr., Orange, Calif.; resident otolaryngology U. Calif., San Francisco. Fellow Am. Bd. Otolarngology; mem. AMA, Hi Soc. Otolaryngology, Hawaii Med. Assn., Honolulu County Med. Soc. Episcopalian.

TAMKIN, CURTIS SLOANE, real estate development company executive; b. Boston, Sept. 21, 1936; s. Hayward and Etta (Goldfarb) T.; BA in Econs., Stanford U., 1958; m. Priscilla Martin, Oct. 18, 1975; 1 child, Curtis Sloane. V.p., treas., dir. Hayward Tamkin & Co., Inc., mortgage bankers, L.A., 1963-70; mng. ptnr. Property Devel. Co., L.A., 1970-82; pres. The Tamkin Co., 1982—. Bd. govs. Music Ctr. L.A., 1974—; pres. Los Angeles Master Chorale Assn., 1974-78; mem. vis. com. Stanford U. Libraries, 1982-86; bd. dirs. L.A. Philharm. Assn., 1985—. Served to lt. (j.g.) USNR, 1960-63. Mem. Founders League of L.A. Music Ctr. (pres. 1988—), L.A. Jr. C. of C. (dir. 1968-69). Republican. Clubs: Burlingame Country.

TAMMANY, ALBERT SQUIRE, III, trust and bank executive; b. Paget, Bermuda, Aug. 21, 1946; s. Albert Squire Jr. and Marion Genevieve (Galloway) T.; m. Teresa Reznor, Sept. 8, 1973. BA, Stanford U., 1968; MBA, U. Pa., 1973. Budget and planning officer Tuskegee Univ., Ala., 1973-74; budget analyst contrs. dept. Chase Manhattan Bank, N.Y.C., 1974-75; v.p., div. contr. Wells Fargo Bank, San Francisco, 1975-78, v.p., retail group contr., 1978-79; v.p., contr. Imperial Bank, L.A., 1979-81, sr. v.p. fin., 1981-83; exec. v.p., First Network Savs. Bank, L.A., 1983-87, chief oper. officer, 1987-89, North Am. Trust Co., San Diego, 1990-93, Trustguard, San Diego, 1993-93; sr. trust officer, Exchange Bank, Santa Rosa, Calif., 1993—. cons. Inst. for Svcs. to Edn., Inc., 1973-74. Woodrow Wilson fellow U. Pa. Served with USMC, 1968-71. Wharton Pub. Policy fellow, 1972. Mem. Am. Bankers Assn. (trust ops. com.), Wharton Club, Stanford Club.

TAMORI, DAVID ISAMU, secondary education educator; b. Oakland, Calif., Sept. 20, 1949; s. Shoji Masaharu and Shizu (Akiyama) T.; m. Carolee Jean Zoff, Feb. 14; children: Tina Maria Tamori Riggs, Leanna Gean, Mesha Lynn. AA, Diablo Valley Coll., 1969; BA, Chico State Coll., 1970, secondary teaching credential, 1971. Art tchr., chmn. dept. visual and performing arts Oroville (Calif.) High Sch., 1973—, head coach wrestling, 1973—; staff mem. Calif. Art Project, Calif. State U., Humboldt, Walker Creek and Chico, 1989-93; art panelist Calif. Commn. Tchr. Credentialling, Sacramento, 1990-92; art panelist Ednl. Testing Svc., Princeton, N.J., 1990—; mem. Nat. Bd. for Profl. Teaching Stds./Far West Lab. for Ednl. R&D Art Assessment, 1994—. Devel. team mgr. Sensei Concord/Oroville Judo Club, 1973—, Yodan 4 Degree Black Belt. Mem. Calif. Arts Edn. Assn. (North Area pres., Secondary Art Educator of Yr. 1992-93), Calif. Tchrs. Assn., Oroville Secondary Tchrs. Assn., Calif. Arts Project. Home: 27 Skyline Blvd Oroville CA 95966-9457

TAMURA, CARY KAORU, fundraiser; b. Honolulu, Jan. 9, 1944; s. Akira and Harue (Otake) T.; m. Denise Jeanne Mitts, Oct. 17, 1987; children from previous marriage: Jennifer Joy, Matthew D. Student, U. Hawaii, 1961-63; BA in Philosophy, Nyack Coll., 1966; MA in Theology, Fuller Sem., 1986. Cert. fund-raising exec. Dir. svc. tng. ops. Fin. Adv. Clinic of Hawaii, Honolulu, 1972-76; dir. planned giving The Salvation Army, Honolulu, 1976-78; planned giving cons. InterVarsity Christian Fellowship, Portland, Oreg., 1978-80; account exec. Am. Income Life, Portland, Oreg., 1980-81; dir. planned giving The Salvation Army, Portland, Oreg., 1981-84, L.A., 1984-85; dir. devel., planned giving U. So. Calif., 1985-90; dir. gift planning UniHealth America, Burbank, Calif., 1990-94; pvt. gift planning cons. Brea, Calif., 1995—; bd. dirs. Nat. Com. on Planned Giving, Indpls., 1991-93, sec. exec. com., 1993; mem. adv. com., adj. faculty UCLA Extension; lectr. in field. Bd. dirs. Japanese Evang. Missionary Soc., 1990—, v.p., 1993; bd. deacons Evang. Free Ch., 1992-95. With U.S. Army, 1969-72. Named Profl. Fund Raiser of the Yr., Nat. Philanthropy Day, 1995. Mem. Planned Giving Round Table So. Calif. (pres. 1989-91, Pres.'s award 1992), Nat. Soc. Fund Raising Execs. (Greater L.A. chpt. bd. dirs. 1990—, v.p. 1993, 95, chair FR Day 1994), So. Calif. Assn. Hosp. Developers, Assn. for Healthcare Philanthropy, Asia Pacific Legal Soc. (exec. adv. bd. 1995—). Republican. Home and Office: 1413 N Robert Ct Brea CA 92621-2165

TAMURA, NEAL NOBORU, dentist, consultant; b. Honolulu, May 3, 1953; s. Tony T. and Doris (Fujiki) T.; m. Liana N.N. Pang, May 31, 1980 (div.); 1 child, Randi M.A. BS in Biology with distinction, U. Mo., Kansas City, 1975; DDS, Northwestern U., 1985. Resident asst. in counselling U. Mo., Kansas City, 1974-75; emergency med. technician Pacific Ambulance, Honolulu, 1975-77, mgr. ops., mobile intensive care technician, 1977-79; gen. practice dentistry Honolulu, 1985—; cons. Nuuanu Hale Hosp., Honolulu, 1985—, Hale Nani Hosp., Honolulu, 1990—, Dept. Corrections, State of Hawaii, 1987-89, Job Corps Hawaii, 1989-91, Lilina Healthcare Ctr., 1992—, Program for All Inclusivee Care for the Elderly Maluhia Hosp., 1993—. Vice chair mgmt. area hosps. State of Hawaii Bd. Commrs., Honolulu, 1987, chair, 1989, exec. com., 1989; mem. YMCA, Honolulu, 1987— (svc. award 1972, 73). Mem. ADA, Hawaii Dental Assn., Hawaii Implant Soc., Honolulu County Dental Soc., Papaniho Study Club (founder, sec. 1987-89), Phi Kappa Phi. Democrat. Home: 2016 Metcalf St Honolulu HI 96822-3333 Office: 1600 Kapiolani Blvd Ste 508 Honolulu HI 96814-3802

TAN, ENG MENG, biomedical scientist; b. Seremban, Malaysia, Aug. 26, 1926; came to U.S., 1950; s. Ming Kee and Chooi Eng (Ang) T.; m. Liselotte Filippi, June 30, 1962; children: Philip, Peter. B.A., Johns Hopkins U., 1952, M.D., 1956. Rsch. assoc. Rockefeller U., N.Y.C., 1962-65; asst. prof. Washington U. Sch. Medicine, St. Louis, 1965-67; assoc. mem. Scripps Rsch. Inst., LaJolla, Calif., 1967-70, mem., 1970-77, dir. Autoimmune Disease Ctr., 1982—; prof. U. Colo. Sch. Medicine, Denver, 1977-82; chmn. allergy and immunology rsch. com. NIH, Bethesda, Md., 1982-84; mem. nat. arthritis adv. bd. HHS, Washington, 1981-85. Contbr. chpts. to books, articles to profl. jours. Named to Nat. Lupus Hall Fame, 1984; recipient U.S. Sr. Scientist award Humboldt Found., Fed. Republic Germany, 1986, award Ciba-Geigy-Internat. League Against Rheumatism, 1989, Carol Nachman award Wiesbaden, Fed. Republic Germany, 1989, Paul Klemperer award and medal N.Y. Acad. Medicine, 1993. Fellow AAAS; mem. Arthritis Found. (Lee Howley Sr. award 1989), Am. Coll. Rheumatology (pres. 1984-85, Disting. Investigator award 1991), Assn. Am. Physicians, Am. Soc. Clin. Investigation, Western Assn. Physicians (v.p. 1980-81), Am. Assn. Immunologists, Brazilian Soc. Rheumatology (hon.), Australian Rheumatism Assn. (hon.), Brit. Soc. Rheumatology (hon.). Rsch. on characterization of autoantibodies in autoimmune diseases, systemic lupus erythematosus, scleroderma, Sjogren's syndrome, myositis and mixed connective tissue disease; relationship of autoantibodies to pathogenesis. Home: 8303 Sugarman Dr La Jolla CA 92037-2224 Office: Scripps Rsch Inst 10666 N Torrey Pines Rd La Jolla CA 92037-1027

TAN, JOO SIM, physician consultant; b. Kuala Lumpur, Malaysia, Aug. 8, 1937; came to U.S., 1954; d. Keng Teong T. and Pee Ging (Ding) Khew; children: Stepen S., PEter B., Karen, Clifford. MD, NYU, 1965. Lic. Utah, Ariz., N.Y. Physician pvt. practice, Perry, N.Y., 1970-80; med. dir. FHP-Utah, Salt Lake City, 1980-85, Cigna, San Diego & Dallas, 1985-90,

Travelers, San Diego, 1990-91; cons. pvt. practice, Santa Ysabel, Calif., 1990—. Mem. Am. Coll. Physician Execs. (bd. dirs. 1991-94), Rotary Internat. (bd. dirs. Ramona, Calif. chpt. 1992-94, bd. dirs. La Jolla, Calif. chpt. 1990-92). Home and Office: 25352 Old Julian Hwy Santa Ysabel CA 92070-9761

TAN, WILLIAM LEW, lawyer; b. West Hollywood, Calif., July 25, 1949; s. James Tan Lew and Choon Guey Louie; m. Shelly Mieko Ushio. BA, U. Pa., 1971; JD, U. Calif. Hastings Coll. Law, San Francisco, 1974. Bar: Calif. 1975, U.S. Dist. Ct. (cen. dist.) Calif. 1975, U.S. Ct. Appeals (9th cir.) 1975, U.S. Supreme Ct. 1979. Assoc. Hiram W. Kwan, Los Angeles, 1974-79; ptnr. Mock & Tan, Los Angeles, 1979-80; sole practice Los Angeles, 1980-81; ptnr. Tan & Sakiyama, L.A., 1981-86, 88—, Tan & Sakiyama, P.C., L.A., 1986-88; bd. dirs. Am. Bus. Network, L.A.; pres., bd. dirs. Asian Rsch. Cons., L.A.; mem. adv. bd. Cathay Bank. Co-founder Asian Pacific Am. Roundtable, L.A., 1981; chmn. bd. dirs. Leadership Edn. for Asian-Pacifics, L.A., 1984-87; alt. del. Dem. Nat. Conv., San Francisco, 1984; mem. Calif. State Bd. Pharmacy, Sacramento, 1984-92, v.p., 1988-91, pres., 1991-92; mem. L.A. City and County Crime Crisis Task Force, 1981, L.A. Asian Pacific Heritage Week Com., 1980-85, Asian Pacific Women's Network, L.A., 1981, L.A. City Atty.'s Blue Ribbon Com. of Advisors, 1981, cmty. adv. bd. to Mayor of L.A., 1984, allocations vol. liaison team health and therapy divsn. United Way, L.A., 1986, mem. nominating com. bd. dirs. 1994-95; bd. dirs. Chinatown Svc. Ctr., L.A., 1983; conf. advisor U.S.-Asia, L.A., 1981-83; atty. L.A. City Housing Adv. Com.; mem. Pacific Bell Consumer Product Adv. Panel; vice chair cmty. adv. bd. Sta. KCET-TV, PBA, 1993-94; mem. adv. commn. State of Calif. Com. on State Procurement Practices, 1989-90; mem. L.A. City Attys. Citizens' Task Force on Pvt. Club Discrimination, 1989-90; mem. Calif. Med. Summit, 1993; mem. Mayor's Commn. Children, Youth and Families, 1993—; mem. pub. access subcom. Mayor's Spl. adv. Com. on Tech. Implementation, 1994—. Named one of Outstanding Young Men of Am., 1979. Mem. ABA (mem. numerous coms.), Calif. State Bar Assn. (vice chmn. com. ethnic minority relations 1983-85, chmn. pub. affairs com. 1981-82, mem. others), Los Angeles County Bar Assn. (vice chmn. 1980-82, mem. numerous coms.), So. Calif. Chinese Lawyers Assn. (pres. 1980-81, chmn., 1987-88, mem. various coms.), Minority Bar Assn. (chmn. 1981-82, sec. 1980-81, chmn. adv. bd. 1982-83), Asian Pacific Bar of Calif., Nat. Asian Pacific Am. Bar, Japanese Am. Bar Assn., Assn. Trial Lawyers Am., Bench and Bar Media Council, Calif. Trial Lawyers Assn., Soc. Intercultural Edn. (conf. coordinator, advisor panelist tng. and research com. 1983),. Office: 300 S Grand Ave Ste 2750 Los Angeles CA 90071-3137

TANABE, BARBARA JEAN, communications company executive; b. Tokyo, Jan. 12, 1949; came to U.S., 1955; d. Frank Shinichiro and Setsuko (Onishi) T.; m. Roy H. Kawaguchi, June 18, 1971; children: Bucikas G., Jawagycgu. BA in Comm., U. Washh., 1971; MBA, U. Hawaii, 1983. Anchor, reporter, writer Sta. KOMO-TV, ABC, Seattle, 1970-74; news dir., anchor, prodr. Sta. KHON-TV, NBC, Honolulu, 1974-87; pres., CEO, Hill and Knowlton Hawaii, Inc., Honolulu, 1987—; bd. dirs. Bank of Hawaii, Honolulu; participant oral history project Nat. Press Club, Washington. Prodr., writer documentary The Fence at Minidoka, 1971 (Emmy award 1972). Bd. dirs. Hawaii Visitors Bur., Honolulu, 1991—, chmn. bd., 1994-95; bd. dirs. Conv. Ctr. Authority, Honolulu, 1994-96. Named One of State's Outstanding Women, YWCA, Honolulu, 1987. Mem. Honolulu Japanese C. of C. (bd. dirs. 1989—), Japan-Am. Soc. Hawaii (bd. dirs.). Office: Hill & Knowlton Hawaii Inc 820 Mililani St Ste 400 Honolulu HI 96813-2934

TANAKA, JANICE, artist, educator; b. L.A., Sept. 9, 1940; d. Koto Jack and Lily Yuviko (Yamate) T.; children: Rebecca Eiko Gallardo, David Eitaro Gallardo. Studied with B. Stone and R. Cameron, Stone-Cameron Ballet, 1954-56; studied with R. Lunnon and D. Tempest, Allegro Am. Ballet, 1956-57; student, Conserv. de Musica, Mex., 1962-64; BFA, Sch. of Art Inst. of Chgo., 1978, MFA, 1980. Studio/field prodr. UCLA, 1981-82; lectr. Columbia Coll., Chgo., 1982-83; assoc. prof. U. Colo., Boulder, 1985-89; vis. assoc. prof. visual comm. design UCLA, 1990—; vis. artist Northwestern U., Evanston, Ill., 1983, U. Calif., San Diego, 1982, 85, U. Ill., Chgo., 1983, U. Wis., Madison, 1983, U. Md., Balt., 1984, U. Mich., Mt. Pleasant, 1984, U. Mo., Kansas City, 1984, U. Wis., Stevens Point, 1985, UCLA, 1988, U. Ariz., Tucson, 1989, U. Hawaii, Monoa, 1990, U. Minn., Mpls., 1991, Calif. Inst. Arts, Valencia, 1991, U. Calif., Riverside, 1991, Otis Parsons Sch. Design, L.A., 1992, U. Calif., Irvine, 1992, U. So. Calif., L.A., 1992, Sch. Art Inst. Chgo., 1993. Freelance prodr./dir.; one-woman shows include Mus. Modern Art, N.Y.C., 1991, 93, Wight Art Gallery, L.A., 1992, Whitney Mus. Am. Art, N.Y.C., 1992; exhibited in group shows at L.A. Mcpl. Art Theater, 1994, Vancouver Art Gallery, B.C., Can., 1994, Walter Phillips Gallery, Banff, Alta., Can., 1994, Nat. Mus. Contemporary Art, Korea; represented in permanent collections at Carnegie Mus. Art, Pitts., Japanese Am. Nat. Mus., L.A., Long Beach (Calif.) Mus. Art. Bd. dirs. Ctr. New TV, 1983-85, Film Forum, 1993. NEA Western Regional Media Arts fellow, 1994; Nat. Endowment Art media grantee, 1993; recipient Best Exptl. award Atlanta Film/Video Festival, 1992, James D. Phelan award, 1992, Bronze Appleaward Nat. Edn. Film & Video Festival, 1993, Bronze award WorldFest Houston Internat. Film Festival, 1993, Jurors award Atlanta Film/Video Festival, 1993, Gold Jurors Choice award Charlotte Film and Video Festival, 1993, Bronze Plaque award Film Coun. Greater Columbus, 1993. Home: 1016 Tiverton Ave Apt 101 Los Angeles CA 90024-3003

TANAKA, JEANNIE E., lawyer; b. L.A., Jan. 21, 1942; d. Togo William and Jean M. Tanaka. BA, Internat. Christian U., Tokyo, 1966; MSW, UCLA, 1968; JD, Washington Coll. Law, 1984. Bar: Calif. 1984, U.S. Dist. Ct. (cen. no. dists.) Calif. 1985, U.S. Ct. Appeals (9th cir.) 1985, D.C. 1987. Instr. Aoyama Gakuin, Meiji Gakuin, Sophia U., Tokyo, 1968-75; with program devel. Encyclopedia Britannica Inst., Tokyo, 1976-78; instr. Honda, Mitsubishi, Ricoh Corps., Tokyo, 1975-80; with editorial dept. Simul Internat., Tokyo; assoc. Seki and Jarvis, L.A., 1984-86, Jones, Day, Reavis & Pogue, L.A., 1986-87, Fulbright, Jaworsky and Reavis, McGrath, L.A., 1987-89; asst. counsel Unocal, L.A., 1989-91; pvt. practice, L.A., 1991—; counsel Calif. Dept. Corps., L.A., 1993—. Active Japan-Am. Soc., L.A., 1984—, Japanese-Am. Citizens League, L.A., 1981, 92—, Japanese Am. Cultural and Cmty. Ctr., 1986-89; vol. Asian Pacific Am. Legal Ctr. So. Calif., 1985-86. Mem. Japanese-Am. Bar Assn., Mensa. Democrat. Methodist.

TANAKA, LEILA CHIYAKO, lawyer; b. Honolulu, Mar. 11, 1954; d. Masami and Bernice Kiyoko (Nakamura) T. B Arts and Scis. with distinction in Japanese Lang. and Am. Studies, U. Hawaii, Manoa, 1977; JD, U. Santa Clara, 1980. Bar: Hawaii 1980, U.S. Dist. Ct. Hawaii 1980. Pvt. practice Honolulu, 1980-81; law clk. to judge Hawaii State Cir. Ct. (2d cir.), Wailuku, Maui, 1981-82; spl. dep. atty. gen. Dept. of Atty. Gen., Hawaii, 1983, dep. atty. gen., 1983-88; housing unit supr., 1987-88; eviction hearings trial examiner Hawaii Housing Authority, 1986-88; mgr. departmental liability Dept. Transp., Hawaii, 1988-94; boating regulation officer Dept. of Transp., Hawaii, 1994—. Mem. motor vehicle industry licensing bd. Dept. Commerce and Consumer Affairs, Hawaii, 1991—; mem. bd. Pacific Inst. Chem. Dependency, 1993—. Mem. Am. Judicature Soc., Smithsonian Instn., Hawaii Bar Assn., Soroptimist Internat. (v.p. Honolulu chpt.), Plaza Club, Phi Kappa Phi. Buddhist. Office: Hawaii Dept Transp 79 S Nimitz Hwy Honolulu HI 96813-4805

TANAKA, RICHARD KOICHI, JR., architect, planner; b. San Jose, Calif., Oct. 16, 1931; s. Richard Inoru and Mae Yoshiko (Koga) T.; m. Barbara Hisako Kumagai, Oct. 7, 1961; children: Craig, Todd, Sandra, Trent. BArch, U. Mich., 1954; M in Urban Planning, Calif. State U., San Jose, 1978. Exec. v.p. Steinberg Group, San Jose, L.A., 1954—. Author: American on Trial, 1988. Dir. Human Rels. com., San Jose, 1969-73; dir., pres. Bicentennial Com., San Jose, 1974-77; bd. dirs. Santa Clara County Sch. Bd. Assn., 1980—; pres. Internment of Local Japanese Ams., San Jose, 1984—; past prse., trustee East Side H.S. Dist., San Jose, 1971-72, Japanese Am. Citizens League, San Jose; mem. bd. govs. Boy Scouts Am., San Jose, 1978—, NCCJ, San Jose, 1978—; past pres. Tapestry and Talent, 1976-80; trustee San Jose/Evergreen C.C., 1992—, pres., 1993-94; bd. dirs., v.p. Calif. C.C. Trustees, 1992—. Mem. AIA (pres. 1993-94), Am. Planning Inst., Constrn. Specification Inst., Rotary. Home: 14811 Whipple Ct San Jose CA 95127-2570 Office: 60 Pierce Ave San Jose CA 95110-2819

TANAKA, T., health, medical products executive; b. 1947. BS, Shimane Nat. U., 1973. With Green Cross Corp., 1973-79, Alpha Therapeutic, 1979-84, Green Cross Corp., 1984-88; pres. Oncomembrane, Inc., Seattle, 1988-91. Office: Oncomembrane Inc 1201 3rd Ave Ste 3010 Seattle WA 98101-3000*

TANAKA, TED TOKIO, architect, educator; b. Tokyo, Nov. 27, 1942; came to U.S., 1958, naturalized, 1963. B.Arch., Ariz. State U., 1969. Registered architect, Calif. Designer Gruen Assocs., Los Angeles, 1969-70; ptnr. Environ. Communications, Los Angeles, 1969-76; project designer Flood & Assocs., Los Angeles, 1970-71; dir. design Jenkins Architects, Beverly Hills, Calif., 1971-75; prin. Ted T. Tanaka Architect, Venice, Calif., 1975—; instr. Santa Monica (Calif.) Coll., 1976-78; prin. works include: Hubert Humphrey Comprehensive Health Ctr., Los Angeles, Martin Luther King Service and Supply Bldg., Los Angeles, Hansui Restaurant, Santa Monica, Gilberg Psychiat. Bldg., Sunlight Picture office bldg., Hollywood, Calif., St. Louis Convention Ctr. Contbr. articles to profl. jours. Varney Sexton Seydnor scholar Ariz. State U., 1963. Mem. AIA, Mus. Contemporary Art Los Angeles. Office: Ted Tokio Tanaka Arch AIA 4223 Glencoe Ave # B107 Marina Del Rey CA 90292

TANAKA, TOGO W(ILLIAM), real estate and financial executive; b. Portland, Oreg., Jan. 7, 1916; s. Masaharu and Katsu (Iwatate) T.; m. Jean Miho Wada, Nov. 14, 1940; children: Jeannie, Christine, Wesley. AB cum laude, UCLA, 1936. Editor Calif. Daily News, 1935-36, L.A. Japanese Daily News, 1936-42; documentary historian War Relocation Authority, Manzanar, Calif., 1942; staff mem. Am. Friends Service Com., Chgo., 1943-45; editor to head publs. div. Am. Tech. Soc., 1945-52; pub. Chgo. Pub. Corp., 1952-56; pub. School-Indsl. Press, Inc., L.A., 1956-60; chmn. Gramercy Enterprises, L.A.; dir. T.W. Tanaka Co., Inc.; city commr. Community Redevel. Agy., L.A., 1973-74; dir. L.A. Wholesale Produce Market Devel. Corp., 1979-89, Fed. Res. Bank, San Francisco, 1979-89; mem. adv. bd. Calif. First Bank, L.A., 1976-78, bd. dirs. Meth. Hosp., So. Calif., 1978-93. Author: (with Frank K. Levin) English Composition and Rhetoric, 1948; (with Dr. Jean Bordeaux) How to Talk More Effectively, 1948; (with Alma Meland) Easy Pathways in English, 1949. Mem. citizens mgmt. rev. com. L.A. Unified Sch. Dist., 1976-77; adv. coun. to assessor L.A. County, 1981-84; bd. dirs. Goodwill Industries of So. Calif.; trustee Wilshire United Meth. Ch., 1976-78, Calif. Acad. Decathlon, 1978-81; adv. bd. Visitors and Conv. Bur., 1984-88, Am. Heart Assn., 1984-88, New Bus. Achievement, Inc., YMCA Met. L.A., 1977-91, Boy Scouts Am. Coun., 1980-86; mem. adv. council Calif. World Trade Commn., 1986-87; active Nat. Strategy Info. Ctr. N.Y., Nat. Wellness Community, Western Justice Ctr. Found.; trustee Whittier Coll.; chmn. L.A. chpt. Nat. Safety Coun.; Recipient merit award Soc. Advancement Mgmt., 1950, mag. award Inst. Graphic Arts, 1953, 1st award Internat. Council Indsl. Editors, 1955, UNESCO Literacy award, 1974, L.A. Archbishop's Ecumenical award, 1986, Frances Larkin award ARC, 1993, Spirit of Wellness award, 1995. Mem. L.A. Area C. of C. (dir. 1975-77), Japan Am. Soc. So. Calif. (coun. 1960-78), L.A. Athletic Club, Lincoln Club, Masons, Shriners, Rotary (dir., pres. L.A. club 1983-84), Phi Beta Kappa, Pi Sigma Alpha, Pi Gamma Mu. Home: 949 Malcolm Ave Los Angeles CA 90024-3113 Office: 626 Wilshire Blvd Los Angeles CA 90017-3209

TANCER, SHOSHANA B., lawyer, business educator; b. N.Y.C., May 30, 1935; d. Salo Wittmayer and Jeannette (Meisel) Baron; m. Robert Stephen Tancer, June 10, 1954; children: Sara Tancer Gordon, Manuel, Catherine Lewkowitz, Cynthia. BA, Barnard Coll., 1954; LLB, U. Mich., 1956; PhD, Columbia U., 1970. Researcher Inst. War and Peace Studies Columbia U., 1963-64; rsch. scientist Ctr. for Rsch. in Social Systems Am. U., Washington, 1965-68; with Tancer Law Offices, Ltd., Phoenix, 1976-90; of counsel O'Connor, Cavanagh, Anderson, Westover, Killingsworth, et al, Phoenix, 1992—; assoc. prof. Am. Grad. Sch. Internat. Mgmt., Glendale, Ariz., 1969-70, prof., 1970—; dir. NAFTA Ctr., 1995—; vis. prof. U. Pedro Henriquez Urena, Santo Domingo, Dominican Republic, 1968-69; bd. dirs. The Finova Group, Inc., Xantel Corp. Contbr. articles to profl. jours. Mem. adv. bd. U. Ariz. Coll. Bus. and Pub. Adminstrn., 1984—, bd. visitors Law Sch., 1982-85; founding mem. Phoenix Com. on Fgn. Rels., 1978—, mem. exec. com., 1990—; founder mem. Charter 100, treas., mem. exec. com., 1980—; trustee Phoenix Country Day Sch., 1976—; bd. dirs. Ariz. Theater Co., 1994—; active Ariz. Acad., 1978—; bd. visitors Stanford U. Librs., 1990-92; bd. dirs. United Way, v.p., 1976-82; also others. Mem. Assn. for Corp. Growth (bd. dirs. Ariz. chpt. 1994—), Internat. Studies Assn., Ariz. Bar Assn. (various coms.), Bar Assn. D.C., Strategic Mgmt. Assn., Maricopa County Bar Assn., Internat. Indsl. Rels. Assn., Acad. Internat. Bus. Office: O Connor Cavanagh Anderson Westover Killingsworth et al E Camelback Rd Ste 1100 Phoenix AZ 85012-1656

TANENBAUM, BASIL SAMUEL, engineering educator; b. Providence, R.I., Dec. 1, 1934; s. Harry Milton and Rena Ada (Herr) T.; m. Carol Binder, Aug. 26, 1956; children: Laurie, Stephen, David. B.S. summa cum laude, Brown U., 1956; M.S. (NSF fellow, 1956-60), Yale U., 1957, Ph.D. in Physics, 1960. Staff physicist Raytheon Co., Waltham, Mass., 1960-63; prof. engrng. Case Western Res. U., Cleve., 1963-75; dean of faculty Harvey Mudd Coll., Claremont, Calif., 1975-93, prof. engring., 1975—; vis. scientist Cornell U., Arecibo (P.R.) Obs., 1968-69; vis. asso. prof. Northwestern U., Evanston, Ill., 1970; vis. scholar U.C. Irvine Beckman Laser Inst., 1993-94; sci. adv. com. Nat. Astronomy and Ionosphere Center, 1972-77, Calif. Poly. Inst., Pomona, 1976-87; engrng. and sci. adv. com. Calif. State U., Fullerton, 1976-87; mem. nat. adv. com. Rowan Coll., Glassboro, N.J., 1993—; Eisenhower adv. com. Cal. Postsec. Edn. Com., 1993—; bd. dirs. University Circle, Inc., 1973-75; dir. Minority Engrs. Indsl. Opportunity Program, 1973-75; dir. summer sci. program Thacher Sch., Ojai, Calif., 1977-82; cons. various corps., univ. labs., govt. agencies. Author: Plasma Physics, 1967. Woods Hole Oceanog. Inst. fellow, 1959; sr. Sterling fellow, 1959; recipient Wittke teaching award, 1974. Mem. AAAS, Am. Phys. Soc., Am. Soc. for Engrng. Edn., IEEE, AAUP, Sigma Xi (research award 1969). Home: 611 W Delaware Dr Claremont CA 91711-3458 Office: Harvey Mudd Coll 301 E 12th St Claremont CA 91711-5901

TANG, PAUL CHI LUNG, philosophy educator; b. Vancouver, B.C., Can., Jan. 23, 1944; came to U.S., 1971; s. Pei-Sung and Violet (Wong) T. BSc with high distinction, U. B.C., 1966; MA in Edn., Simon Fraser U., Vancouver, 1971; MA, Washington U., St. Louis, 1975, PhD, 1982; cert. Inst. Ethics, Georgetown U., 1983; diploma in piano, U. Toronto, 1962. Teaching asst. philosophy of edn. Simon Fraser U., 1969-71; instr. philosophy St. Louis C.C. at Meramec, Kirkwood, Mo., 1975-82; instr., lectr. philosophy Washington U., 1972-76; adj. asst. prof. Harris-Stowe State Coll., St. Louis, 1980-82; asst. prof. philosophy Grinnell (Iowa) Coll., 1982-85; asst. prof. to assoc. prof. to prof. dept. philosophy Calif. State U., Long Beach, 1985—, chmn. dept. philosophy, 1988-94. Contbr. numerous articles and revs. to profl. publs.; editor Philosophy of Sci. Assn. Newsletter, 1985-90; asst. editor Philosophy of Sci. acad. jour., 1972-75. Senator Internat. Parliament for Safety and Peace, Palermo, Italy. Washington U. fellow, 1971, Summer Rsch. fellow Calif. State U., Long Beach, 1988, NEH fellow Harvard U., 1988, NEH Summer Seminar fellow, 1968; Internat. scholar Phi Beta Delta, Interdisciplinary scholar Phi Kappa Phi, 1993; grantee Vis. Philosophers Program, Coun. for Philos. Studies, 1987, 91, 92, Disting. Vis. Scholars and Artists Fund, Calif. State U., Long Beach, 1988, 89; recipient Cert. of Merit, Student Philosophy Assn., 1988, 89, 90, 93, 94; named Faculty Mem. of Yr., 1991; recipient Meritorious Performance award, 1986, 88, 90, Associated Students' Faculty advisor of Yr. award, 1987, 90, 91, 95, award for internationalizing the curriculum Calif. State Univ., Long Beach, 1993, Univ. Disting. Faculty Tchg. award, 1994-95, Outstanding Grad. Prof. award, 1995, Coll. Liberal Arts Most Valuable Prof. award, 1995, Univ. Scholarly and Creative Activity award, 1995. Fellow World Literary Acad. (Cambridge, Eng.); mem. Am. Philos. Soc., Philosophy of Sci. Assn., History of Sci. Soc., Kennedy Inst. Ethics, Hastings Ctr., Iowa, Philos. Soc. (pres. 1985-86), Internat. Platform Assn., Brit. Soc. Philosophy of Sci., Soc. Philosophy and Psychology, Templar ORder of Jerusalem (knight), Order of Holy Cross of Jerusalem (knight), Lofsenic Ursinius Order (knight comdr.), Chevalier Grand Croix de la Milice du Saint Sepulcre, Maison Internat. des Intellectuels de l'Académie Francaise, Internat. Order of Merit (Eng.), numerous others. Home: 5050 E Garford St Apt 228 Long Beach CA 90815-2859 Office: Calif State U Dept Philosophy 1250 N Bellflower Blvd Long Beach CA 90840-0006

TANG, WING TSANG, chemical researcher; b. Kowloon, Hong Kong, July 16, 1958; came to U.S., 1977; s. Pak Chiu and Pui Tsang (Chan) T.; m. Wai-Chun Wong, Aug. 11, 1984; children: Ming-Yun, Tin-Yun. AA, Vincennes (Ind.) U., 1978; BA, Hamilton Coll., 1981; MS, Stanford U., 1985, PhD, 1987. Vis. scientist IBM, San Jose, Calif., 1987-88, staff scientist, 1988-92; R&D project engr. Komag Inc., Milpitas, Calif., 1992-93; product devel. mgr. Conner Peripherals, San Jose, Calif., 1993—; rsch. asst. Stanford (Calif.) U., 1981-86. Patentee ferroelectric liquid crystal, a novel thin film disk lubricant. Recipient Root fellowship in sci., 1981. Mem. Material Rsch. Soc. Home: 1451 Mount Diablo Ave #C206 Milpitas CA 95035 Office: Conner Peripherals 195 S Milpitas Blvd Milpitas CA 95035-5425

TANIGUCHI, RAYMOND MASAYUKI, neurosurgeon; b. Waipahu, Hawaii, May 14, 1934; s. James Takeo and Yoshiko (Yamaguchi) T.; m. (div.); 1 child, Stacy. Student, U. Hawaii, 1952-54; BA, Washington U., St. Louis, 1956; MD, Tulane U., 1960. Diplomate Am. Bd. Neurological Surgery, 1973. Rotating internship McLeod Infirmary, Florence, S.C., 1960-61; resident, gen. pathology and neuropath Duke Med. Ctr., 1961-62; resident in gen. surgery N.C. Baptist Hosp., 1962-63; resident in neurology Duke Med. Ctr., 1963-64; resident in clin. neurosurgery N.C. Baptist Hosp., 1964-65, Duke Med. Ctr., 1965-66, 68-70; clin. assoc. prof. U. Hawaii Sch. of Med., Honolulu, 1980—; pvt. practice, neurosurgeon Honolulu, to date; cons. in neurosurgery, Tripler Army Med. Ctr., Kaiser Found. Hosp., spl. physician cons. on spinal cord injury and trauma, Hawaii Med. Assn., Emergency Med. Svcs. Program, ADHOC com. on trauma, State of Hawaii, 1981-82. Contbr. articles to profl. jours. Capt. U.S. Army Med. Corps, 1966-68, Vietnam, Japan. Fellow ACS (chmn. credential com.); mem. Am. Assn. Neurol. Surgeons, Pan Pacific Surg. Assn. (past chmn. bd. trustees), Congress of Neurol. Surgeons. Office: 1380 Lusitana St Ste 415 Honolulu HI 96813-2440

TANIGUCHI, TOKUSO, surgeon; b. Eleele, Kauai, Hawaii, June 26, 1915; s. Tokuichi and Sana (Omaye) T.; BA, U. Hawaii, 1941; MD, Tulane U., 1946; 1 son, Jan Tokuichi. Intern Knoxville (Tenn.) Gen. Hosp., 1946-47; resident in surgery St. Joseph Hosp., also Marquette Med. Sch., Milw., 1947-52; practice medicine, specializing in surgery, Hilo, Hawaii, 1955—; chief surgery Hilo Hosp.; teaching fellow Marquette Med. Sch., 1947-49; v.p., dir. Hawaii Hardware Co., Ltd. Capt. M.C., AUS, 1952-55. Diplomate Am. Bd. Surgery. Fellow Internat., Am. colls. surgeons; mem. Am., Hawaii med. assns., Hawaii County Med. Soc., Pan-Pacific Surg. Assn., Phi Kappa Phi. Contbr. articles in field to profl. jours. Patentee automated catheter. Home: 277 Kaiulani St Hilo HI 96720-2530

TANIMOTO, GEORGE, agricultural executive, farmer; b. Gridley, Calif., Feb. 10, 1926; s. Hikoichi and Rewa Tanimoto; m. Hanami Yamasaki, Dec. 19, 1946; 1 child, Patricia. Grad., Coyne Electric Sch., Chgo., 1950. Elec. technician, 1951, owner peach and prune orchards, 1952; founder Kiwifruit Nursery, Calif., 1965; pres. Tanimoto Bros., Gridley, Calif., 1977—, Tanimoto Enterprises, Inc., Gridley, 1979—; bd. dirs. Blue Anchor, Inc., Sacramento; chmn. Calif. Fruit Exchange, Inc.; U.S. rep. Internat. Kiwifruit Orgn., Lake Tahoe, Calif., 1985, Rome, 1986, Biarritz, France, 1987, Hong Kong, 1988, chmn. Orgn.,Rome, 1986; dir. Butte County Agrl. Adv. Commn., Oroville, Calif.; founder, chmn. Calif. Kiwifruit Commn., 1980-84, 1988-89, vice chmn. 1985-87. Pres. South Shore Assn., Bucks Lake, Calif., 1989. Mem. Kiwifruit Growers Calif. (founder, bd. dirs., pres. 1973-80), Kiwifruit Mktg. Assn. Calif. (founder, chmn. 1989-95), Gridley Sportsman Club (founder, pres. 1975-78). Republican. Buddhist. Home: 948 River Ave Gridley CA 95948-9774

TANK, HIMAT G., pediatrician; b. Kalana, India, Aug. 1, 1951; came to U.S., 1976; s. Gangdas V. and Maniben G. (Chotala) T.; m. Mina H.; children: Sumi, Pinki, Niki, Rikin. MD, Meghji Pethraj Shah Med. Coll., Jamnagar, India, 1975; FAAP (hon.), Am. Acad. Pediatrics, 1985. Resident in pediatrics N.Y.C., 1976-79, pvt. practice in pediatrics, 1979-81; pvt. practice in pediatrics Santa Maria, 1981—. Fellow Am. Acad. Pediatrics; chmn. Child Health and Disability Prevention Program adv. bd., Santa Barbara County, 1992-93. Office: 1414 S Miller St Ste 10 Santa Maria CA 93454-6916

TANKELEVICH, ROMAN LVOVICH, computer scientist; b. Odessa, USSR, Apr. 25, 1941; came to U.S., 1990; s. Lev Faivel and Irina Rudolph (Novak) T.; m. Raye Ja. Sapiro, Jan. 28, 1961; children: Alex, Kate. BS in Physics, Moscow Phys. Engring. Inst., 1963, MS in Physics, 1965; PhD in Computer Sci., Moscow State U., 1968. Rscher., head rsch. lab. Moscow Rsch. Inst. for Computing Tech., 1965-74; prof. Moscow Tech. Inst., 1974-81; dir. rsch. lab. Moscow Comml. Inst., 1981-89; dir. R & D Micrel, Inc., Denver, 1990; v.p. R & D System 6, Inc., Denver, 1989-94; dir. software devel. Logixx, Inc., Denver, 1994—. Author: Simulation of Physical Fields, 1968, Analog Systems for Simulation, 1974, Microprocessor Systems, 1979; tech. writer, translator All-Union Inst. for Sci. and Tech. Info., Moscow, 1963-85; patentee in field. Mem. Scientists for Polit. Freedoms Com., Moscow, 1981-86. Recipient Gold Medal Int. Exhbn., Moscow, 1987. Mem. Soc. Computer Stimulation, N.Y. Acad. Scis. Jewish. Office: Logixx Inc 433 Park Point Dr Ste 200 Golden CO 80401-5752

TANNEN, RICHARD LAURENCE, medical educator, nephrologist; b. N.Y.C., Aug. 31, 1937; s. Harold and Fannie (Rosenberg) T.; m. Elizabeth Whitney Harriman, Aug. 8, 1964 (div. Apr. 1990); m. Vivien Baraban, Nov. 17, 1990; children: Bradford, Whitney, Jennifer, Alison, Julie. Student, Vanderbilt U., 1957; MD, U. Tenn., Memphis, 1960. Rsch. internist Walter Reed Inst. Rsch., Washington, 1966-69; assoc. prof., co-dir. nephrology unit U. Vermont, Burlington, 1969-78; prof., chief nephrology divsn. U. Mich., Ann Arbor, 1978-88; prof., chmn. dept. medicine U. So. Calif., L.A., 1988—; established investigator Am. Heart Assn., 1971-76. Co-editor: Fluids and Electrolytes, 1986, 2d edit., 1990; mem. editorial bd. Am. Jour. Medicine, Am. Jour. Nephrology, Seminars in Nephrology; contbr. over 130 sci. articles to profl. jours. Maj. U.S. Army, 1966-69. Recipient Merit award NIH, 1986-94, Disting. Alumnus award U. Tenn., 1991. Fellow ACP; mem. Am. Soc. Nephrology (pres. 1991-92), Am. Soc. Clin. Investigation, Assn. Am. Physicians, Nat. Kidney Found. (regional v.p. 1984-87, Pres.'s award 1986). Jewish. Office: U So Calif Dept Medicine 2020 Zonal Ave # 220 Los Angeles CA 90033-1080

TANNER, DAVID EARL, education educator; b. Lethbridge, Alberta, Canada, July 31, 1948; s. Earl Pingree and Betty (Bridge) T.; m. Susan Elizabeth Bodell, Aug. 21, 1972; children: Dylan, David, Gillian, John, Suzanna. BA, Brigham Young U., 1973, MA, 1977; PhD, Tex. A&M U., 1984. Tchr. Jordan Sch. Dist., Sandy, Utah, 1977-81; lectr. Tex. A&M U., College Station, 1981-84; asst. prof. U. Tex., Tyler, 1984-85; asst. prof. Calif. State U., Fresno, 1985-87, assoc. prof., 1987-90, prof., 1990—, chmn. dept. ednl. rsch., adminstrn. and founds., 1990—; cons. Calif. Dept. Edn., 1985-86; coord. spl. projects div. grad. studies Calif. State U., Fresno, 1989-90. Editor: The Network Journal, 1986-89; contbr. articles to profl. jours. Mem. Am. Ednl. Rsch. Assn. Mem. Latter-day Saints. Office: Calif State U Fresno Ms # 2 Fresno CA 93740

TANNER, DEE BOSHARD, lawyer; b. Provo, Utah, Jan. 16, 1913; s. Myron Clark and Marie (Boshard) T.; m. Jane Barwick, Dec. 26, 1936 (div. Aug. 1962); children: Barry, Diane McDowell; m. Reeta Walker, Dec. 6, 1981. BA, U. Utah, 1935; LLB, Pacific Coast U., 1940; postgrad., Harvard U., 1936, Loyola U., L.A., 1937. Bar: Calif. 1943, U.S. Dist. Ct. (so. dist.) Calif. 1944, U.S. Ct. Appeals (9th cir.) 1947, ICC 1964, U.S. Dist. Ct. (ea. dist.) Calif. 1969, U.S. Supreme Ct. 1971. Assoc. Spray, Davis & Gould, L.A., 1943-44; pvt. practice L.A., 1944; assoc. Tanner and Sievers, L.A., 1944-47, Tanner and Thornton, L.A., 1947-54, Tanner, Hanson, Meyers, L.A., 1954-64; ptnr. Tanner and Van Dyke, L.A., 1964-65, Gallagher and Tanner, L.A., 1965-70; pvt. practice Pasadena, Calif., 1970-95; retired, 1995. Mem. L.A. Bar Assn., World Affairs Assn., Harvard Law Sch. Assn., Lawyers' Club L.A. Home and Office: 1720 Lombardy Rd Pasadena CA 91106-4127

TANNER, GLORIA GERALDINE, state legislator; b. Atlanta, July 16, 1935; d. Marcellus and Blanche Arnold Travis; m. Theodore Ralph Tanner, 1955 (dec.); children: Terrance Ralph, Tanvis Renee, Tracey Lynne. BA, Met. State Coll., 1974; MUA, U. Colo., 1976. Office mgr. Great Western Mfg. Co., Denver, 1965-67; writer Rage mag., 1969-70; reporter, feature writer Denver Weekly News, 1970-75; dir. East Denver Cmty. Office, 1974—; also real estate agt.; mem. Colo. Ho. of Reps., 1985—; minority caucus chairwoman; mem. appropriations, bus. affairs, labor coms. Dist. capt. Denver Dem. Com., Colo., 1973-75; chairwoman Senatorial Dist. 3 Dem. Com., 1974-82; adminstrv. aide Colo. State Senator Regis Groff, Denver, 1974-82; alt. del. Dem. Nat. Conv., 1976, del., 1980; commr. Colo. Status of Women, 1977—; chairwoman Colo. Black Women for Polit. Action, 1977—; exec. asst. to Lt. Gov., 1978-79; mem. adv. bd. United Negro Coll. Fund, Colo. State Treas. Served USAF, 1952-55. Recipient Outstanding Cmty. Leadership award Scott's Meth. Ch., 1974, Tribute to Black Women award, 1980; named Woman of Yr., Colo. Black Women Caucus, 1974. Mem. Colo. Black Media Assn. (pub. dir. 1972—), Reginas' Civic Club (founder, first pres. 1959—, Outstanding Woman of Yr. 1975), Nat. Assn. Real Estate Brokers. Roman Catholic. Democrat. Home: 2150 Monaco Pky Denver CO 80207-3951 Office: Colo Ho of Reps State Capital Denver CO 80203

TANNER, JOHN D., real estate developer, contractor; b. Calgary, Alta., Can., Feb. 2, 1939; came to U.S., 1956; s. Earl Pingree and Betty (Bridge) T.; m. Barbara Steed, Dec. 27, 1965; children: Jeffrey, Scott, Daniel, David, William, Joanna, Trisha. BS, Brigham Young U., 1965. Constrn. engr. Tide Water Oil Co., Sacramento, Calif., 1965-67; regional constrn. engr. Phillips Petroleum Co., Inc., San Francisco, 1967-69; mgr., v.p. Staiger Constrn. Co., Inc., Sacramento, 1969-71, owner, pres., 1971-76; owner, pres. Tanner Industries, Inc., Roseville, Calif., 1972—, Western Single Ply. Nev., Inc., Las Vegas, 1987—, Western Single Ply. Calif. Inc., Loomis, 1981—. Pres. sch. bd. dirs. Eureka Sch. Dist., Granite Bay, Calif., 1987—. Mem. Granite Bay Golf Club (founding mem.). Republican. Mem. LDS Ch. Home: 7150 J Bar B Dr Granite Bay CA 95746-9453

TANNER, JOHN DOUGLAS, JR., history educator, writer; b. Quantico, Va., Oct. 2, 1943; s. John Douglas and Dorothy Lucille (Walker) T.; m. Jo Ann Boyd, Jan. 1964 (div. Aug. 1966); 1 child, Lorena Desiree; m. Laurel Jean Selfridge, Dec. 19, 1967 (div. Oct. 1987); children: John DouglasIII, Stephen Douglas, Elizabeth Jane; m. Karen M. Olson, Apr. 16, 1988. BA, Pomona Coll., 1966; MA, Claremont Calif. Grad. Sch., 1968; postgrad., U. Calif., Riverside, 1976, 84-86, U. Calif., San Diego, 1984-87, U. Pacific, 1993. Cert. tchr., Calif. Asst. swimming, water polo coach Pomona Coll., 1966-69; rsch. asst. history dept. Claremont Grad. Sch., 1967-69; assoc. prof. history Palomar Coll., San Marcos, Calif., 1969—, pres. faculty, 1970-71, v.p. faculty senate, 1971-72. Author: Olaf Swenson and his Siberian Imports jour., 1978 (Dog Writers Assn. Am. Best Series award 1979), Campaign for Los Angeles, 1846-47, 69; co-editor: Don Juan Forster, 1970, Alaskan Trails, Siberian Dogs, 1994; contbr. articles to profl. jours. Mem. citizens com. Fallbrook (Calif.) San. Dist., 1980; merit badge counselor Boy Scouts Am., 1975-85; Martin County Hist. Soc., Morgan County Hist. Soc., Fallbrook Hist. Soc., San Diego Opera Guild, San Diego Classical Music Soc., Opera Pacific Guild. Chautauqua fellow NSF, 1979. Mem. Custer Battlefield Hist. and Mus. Assn. (life), The Westerners, Siberian Husky Assn. Am. (bd. dirs. 1974-78, 1st v.p. 1978-79), So. Calif. Siberian Husky Assn. (pres. 1972-79), U.S. Shooting Team (Inner Circle), Sons of the Rep. of Tex. Republican. Episcopalian. Home: 2308 Willow Glen Rd Fallbrook CA 92028-9752 Office: Palomar Coll 1140 W Mission Rd San Marcos CA 92069-1415

TANNER, JOHN SEARS, English language educator, academic administrator; m. Susan Winder, Sept. 3, 1974; children: Jonathan, Barbara, Rebecca, Elizabeth, MaryAnne. BA in English magna cum laude, Brigham Young U., 1974; PhD in English, U. Calif., Berkeley, 1980. Instr. honors program Brigham Young U., summer 1973, 74; vis. instr. LDS Inst. Religion, Berkeley, 1977-78; tchg. assoc. dept. English U. Calif., Berkeley, 1978-80; asst. prof. English Fla. State U., 1980-82, Brigham Young U., Provo, Utah, 1982-86; assoc. prof. English Brigham Young U., Provo, 1987, prof. English, 1993—, assoc. acad. v.p., 1992—; bd. mem. Assn. for Mormon Letters, 1985-89, pres., 1986-88; asst. coord., co-founder Medieval and Renaissance Studies Group, 1985—; cons. The HarperCollins World Reader, 1992; active various coms. Brigham Young U., Provo, 1982—; meeting chair various profl. assns.; presenter and lectr. in field. Author: Anxiety in Eden: A Kierkegaardian Reading of Paradise Lost, 1992; editor, exec. officer: Jour. of the Rocky Mountain and Medieval Renaissance Assn., 1990-93; editorial bd.: Literature and Belief, 1983-86, Letras: Revista do Instituto de Letras, 1991—; author of poetry and essays; contbr. articles to profl. jours. mem. strategic planning com. Canyon Crest Elem. Sch.; missionary, Brazil, 1969-71; elders quorum pres., counselor, ward exec. sec. Brigham Young U., 1971-74; counselor to Bishop, Tallahassee, Fla. and Berkeley, Calif., 1979-81; Gospel Doctrine tchr. Salt Lake City, 1982-84; bishop Brigham Young U. 111th Ward, 1984-87; asst. scoutmaster, Provo, 1987; others. Recipient Alcuin Gen. Edn. Tchg. award, 1986-91; grantee Brigham Young U. and Fla. State U., 1981-87, Wilbur Found., Ctr. for the Study of Christian Values in Lit., 1990-91; Hinckley fellow Brigham Young U., 1973, fellow Bay Area Writing Project, U. Calif., Berkeley, 1979, fellow NEH Summer Inst. on Paradise Lost, Ctr. for Medieval and Renaissance Studies, Ariz. State U., Tempe, 1985; Fulbright scholar, Campinas, Brazil, 1991, others. Mem. Milton Soc. Am., Friends of Milton's Cottage, Modern Lang. Assn., Rocky Mountain Modern Lang. Assn., Rocky Mountain Medieval and Renaissance Assn., Assn. for Mormon Letters, Internat. Comparative Lit. Assn., Medieval and Renaissance Studies Group. Office: Brigham Young Univ D-380 ASB Provo UT 84602

TANNER, LYNN, actress; b. N.Y.C., Mar. 22, 1953; d. Harry J. and Barbara Sylvia (Hirschman) Maurer; m. Allen Barry Witz, Aug. 31, 1975. BS, NYU, 1975; JD, DePaul U., 1980. Bar: Ill. 1980. Actress various, 1980—. Appeared in (film) Human Error, 1987, Another Time, Another Place, 1988, Twisted, 1995; (theatre) Pack of Lies, Back at the Blue Dolphin Saloon, Toyer. Mem. SAG, AFTRA, Actors Equity Assn., Women in Film, Women in Theatre.

TANNER, WILLIAM COATS, JR., business owner; b. Magna, Utah, Oct. 22, 1920; s. William Coats and Clara (Sutton) T.; m. Athelia Sears, Feb. 14, 1942; children: Roberta Graham, Athelia Woolley, Terri Mitchell, William Coats Tanner III, John Sears Tanner, Richard Sears Tanner, Mark Sears Tanner, Claralyn Palfreyman, Kaye Whitworth, Daken Sears Tanner, Scott Sears Tanner, Janet Perry, Bryan Sears Tanner. BS, U. Utah, 1943; MA, U. Minn., 1948; PhD, U. Utah, 1952. Lic. psychologist, Calif. Instr. Ea. Montana Coll. Edn., Billings, 1952; rsch./statis. assoc. Ednl. Testing Svc., L.A., 1952-54; prin. Tanner Thought Dynamics, L.A., 1954—, PAR ASK, Salt Lake City, 1992—; instr. U. So. Calif., L.A., 1972-76; therapist, therapists trainer; lecturer. Author in field. Pres. Mormons Ill. Chgo. Mission, Oakbrook, 1986-89. 1st lt. arty. U.S. Army, 1943-46. Mem. Rotary Club, Phi Kappa Phi. Republican. Home: 5055 Holladay Blvd Salt Lake City UT 84117-6307

TANNO, RONALD LOUIS, dentist; b. San Jose, Calif., Dec. 17, 1937; s. George Anthony and Rose Marie (Manghisi) T. BS magna cum laude, Santa Clara U., 1959; DDS, U. of Pacific, 1963. Dentist Santa Clara County Health Dept., San Martin, Calif., 1965-67, Alameda County Health Dept., Oakland, Calif., 1965-67; pvt. practice San Jose, 1966—; dental cons. Found. Med. Care, San. Jose, 1977-81, Dental Ins. Cons., Saratoga, Calif., 1980-88, Santa Clara County Sch. Dists. Dental Plan, San Jose, 1983—; cons. quality rev. Delta Dental Plan Calif., San Francisco, 1983—; mem. dental staff Los Gatos (Calif.) Community Hosp., 1978-94, chief dental dept., 1983, 84. Capt. USAF, 1963-65. Mem. ADA, Calif. Dental Assn., Santa Clara County Dental Soc., Elks, Lions, Xi Psi Phi, Omicron Kappa Upsilon. Office: 1610 Westwood Dr Ste 3 San Jose CA 95125-5110

TANOUS, MICHAEL ALLAN, consulting company executive; b. Hettinger, N.D., Dec. 11, 1939; s. Alfred George and Wilma Verna (Potter) T.; m. Jean Marie Maercklein, Aug. 22, 1960; (div. Dec. 1974); children: Stephen, David, Carl, Jennifer, Elizabeth; m. Valerie Ann Pokoyski, June 6, 1986. B in Philosophy, U. N.D., 1961; postgrad., U. Calif., L.A., 1970-72. Mathematician System Devel. Corp., Grand Forks, N.D., 1961-63; systems analyst System Devel. Corp., Santa Monica, Calif., 1963-68; group mgr. System Devel. Corp., Santa Monica, 1968-75; program mgr. Gen. Electric Co., Valley Forge, Pa., 1976-77; v.p. Sci. Applications Internat. Corp., Colorado Springs, Colo., 1978-86; v.p., ptnr. Booz, Allen & Hamilton, Inc., Colorado Springs, 1986-89; pres. The Matrix Group, Colorado Springs, 1990-92; v.p. Nat. Systems & Rsch. Co., Colorado Springs, 1992—; Contbr. articles to profl. jours. Mem. engring. adv. com. U. Colo., 1987—; bd. dirs. Multiple Sclerosis Soc., Colorado Springs, 1986—. Mem. IEEE, AIAA, Tau Kappa Epsilon. Republican. Office: Nat Systems & Rsch Co 5475 Mark Dabling Blvd Colorado Springs CO 80918-3846

TANOUYE, MARIAN NATSUKO, accountant; b. Honolulu, July 30, 1965; d. Masao and Hanayo T. BS in Math., U. Hawaii, 1987; AS in acctg., Leeward C.C., Pearl City, Hawaii, 1988. Bookkeeper Enterprise Realty, Honolulu, 1985-87; acctg. clk. Wayne Choo, CPA, Honolulu, 1988-89; secondary mktg. clk. Am. Savs. Bank, Honolulu, 1989-90, acct., 1990-91, sr. acct., 1991—. Office: Am Savs Bank 915 Fort Street Mall Honolulu HI 96813-5602

TANOUYE, ROYCE TSUZUKI, religious foundation administrator; b. Johnson Air Base, Japan, June 30, 1959; parents Am. citizens; s. Roy Shigeo and Frances Toyoko (Akita) T.; m. Sherylyn Yukie Kimta, June 18, 1988; children: Kayla, Jana. MusB, Coe Coll., 1981; MA, U. Hawaii, 1983. Cert. tchr. music edn. K-12, Iowa, secondary music edn., Hawaii. Tchr. spl. edn. Waipahu (Hawaii) Intermediate Sch., 1983-84; band dir. McKinley H.S., Honolulu, 1984-87; band dir. elem. sch. Honolulu dist. Dept. Edn., 1987-88; coord. spl. projects Word of Life Christian Ctr., Honolulu, 1988—; ind. distbr. Quorum Internat., 1994—. Mem. Nat. Assn. Desktop Pubs., Hawaii Macintosh Users Group. Republican. Office: Word of Life Christian Ctr 544 Queen St Honolulu HI 96813-5016

TAN WONG, LILY, textile executive; b. Medan, Sumatra, Indonesia, Aug. 10, 1947; came to U.S., 1968; d. Eng Chuan and Sor Choo (Peh) T.; m. Wilson Wong, Feb. 16, 1990. BA, I.K.I.P., Medan, 1967, Gustavus Adolphus Coll., St. Peter, Minn., 1972; MM, U. So. Calif., L.A., 1974. Adminstrn. officer Lloyds Bank, Los Angeles, 1974-80; v.p. Comml. Flooring Assn., Marina Del Rey, Calif., 1981-83; contract mgr. Harbinger Co., L.A., 1983-86; v.p. regional sales Princeton Techs., Ltd., L.A., 1986-87; v.p. export Bentley Mills, Inc., City of Industry, Calif., 1987-90, Evergreen (Colo.) Internat., 1990-92; pres. Marina Pacific Trading, 1992—. Mem. Network Exec. Women in Hospitality, Indonesian Bus. Soc. Office: Marina Pacific Trading Co Inc 13082 Mindanao Way Apt 31 Marina Del Rey CA 90292

TANZI, CAROL ANNE, interior designer; b. San Francisco, Apr. 9, 1942; d. Raymond Edward and Anne Marie Giorgi. BA, U. San Jose, Calif., 1966. Teaching credential, Calif.; cert. interior designer, Calif. Home furnishings coord. R.H. Macy's, San Francisco, 1966-72; owner, pres. Carol A. Tanzi & Assocs., Burlingame, Calif., 1972—; instr. interior design Recreational Ctrs., Burlingame/Foster City, Calif., 1972-85; design cons. Am. Cancer Soc., San Mateo, Calif., 1994-95; mem. adv. com. for interior design students Coll. San Mateo, 1984-87; head designer San Mateo Battered Women's Shelter Pro Bono, 1993. Interior designer mags. Sunset, 1982, House Beautiful, 1992, 1001 Home Ideas, 1983; monthly cable TV program Interior Design by Tanzi, 1994. Pres. Aux. to Mission Hospice, Burlingame, 1988-89, Hist. Soc. Burlingame, 1992-93; v.p. Cmty. for Edn., Burlingame, 1993-94; mem. adv. com. Breast Ctr./Mills Peninsula Hosp., 1994-95; mem. Oaks. Hist. Adv. Bd., 1993—; commr., pres. San Mateo County Commn. on the Status of Women, 1990—. Recipient Recogniton of Outstanding Performance Rotary Club of Burlingame, 1988—, Congl. Recognition U.S.A., Burlingame, 1994, Commendation Bd. Suprs., County of San Mateo, 1994, Recognition Calif. Legis. Assembly, Burlingame, 1994; named Superior Interior Designer Bay Area San Francisco Examiner, 1991, Woman of Distinction Soroptimist Internat., Burlingame/San Mateo, 1994. Mem. Am. Soc. Interior Designers (v.p. 1988, Presdl. citation for disting. svc. 1986, 87, 88, Calif. Peninsula Chpt. Design award 1995), Burlingame C. of C. Women's Forum (chair 1986—), Rotary Club of Burlingame (sec. 1988—). Home: 1528 Columbus Ave Burlingame CA 94010-5512 Office: Carol A Tanzi & Assocs PO Box 117281 Burlingame CA 94011-7281

TANZI, RONALD THOMAS, artist, educator; b. Brookline, Mass., Mar. 3, 1949; s. Henry Francis and Jennie (Vicenza) T.; m. Patricia Marie Morrill, Mar. 16, 1974 (div. Apr. 1990); children: Jenni Grace, Jacob Thomas. Student, Chapman Coll., Orange, Calif., 1968-70, Ea. Wash. U., Cheney, 1970-72; BFA magna cum laude, U. Wash., 1984; MFA, U. Cin., 1986. Artist self-employed, Spokane, Boston, Seattle, 1970—; art editor Contbr.'s Copy Quar., Spokane, 1970-73; instr., lectr. U. Cin., 1984-86; instr. U. Wash., Seattle, 1986-87, North Seattle C.C., 1987—, Edmonds (Wash.) C.C., 1992—, Bellevue (Wash.) C.C., 1993—; dir. R's Studio Gallery, Cheney, 1971-73; visual advisor Masque Theater Co., Everett, Wash., 1987-88; lectr. Seattle Art Mus., 1991, Seattle Art League, 1992, Bellevue Art Mus., 1995. Exhibited paintings in shows including Spokane City Arts, 1971, Pacific Northwest Annual, 1976, N.W. Traditions: A Retrosepctive, 1987, King County Arts Commn., 1988; artist, pub. commn. Metro Bus Shelter Mural Program, 1991, Harborview Med. Ctr. Mural, 1995; represented in pvt. collections in U.S., Japan, Germany, Finland. Instr. City Arts Program, Lynnwood, Wash., 1987-93, Pike Place Sr. Ctr., Seattle, 1992-94, S.E. Seattle Sr. Ctr., 1993-94, Creative Retirement Ctr., Seattle, 1993-94. Sgt. USAF, 1966-70, Vietnam. U. Cin. Grad. scholar, 1984, 85, 86. Mem. Coll. Art Assn., Am. Fedn. Tchrs., Wash. State Fedn. Tchrs., Seattle Art Mus., Phi Beta Kappa. Office: 540 1st Ave S # 203A Seattle WA 98104-2804

TAO, CHIA-LIN PAO, humanities educator; b. Soochow, Kiangsu, China, July 7, 1939; came to U.S., 1961; d. Tsung-han and Hoi-chin Pao; m. Jing-shen Tao, Aug. 22, 1964; children: Rosalind, Jeanne, Sandy. BA, Nat. Taiwan U., Taipei, 1961; MA, Ind. U., 1963, PhD, 1971. Assoc. prof. Nat. Taiwan U., Taipei, 1969-76, 78-79; vis. assoc. prof. U. Ariz., Tucson, 1976-78, 79-85, assoc. prof., 1989—; v.p. Hist. Soc. for the Study of 20th Century in N.Am., 1992-93, pres., 1993-94. Editor, author: (3 vols.) Studies in Chinese Women's History, 1979-93. Mem. Tucson-Taichung Sister-City Com., Tucson, 1984—; sec. Ariz. Asian Am. Assn., Phoenix, 1989, dir., 1989-93. Rsch. grantee Nat. Sci. Coun., Taipei, 1971-72, 73-74, Harvard-Yenching Inst., Cambridge, Mass., 1972-74, Pacific Cultural Found., Taipei, 1984-85. Mem. AAUP, Assn. for Asian Studies (pres. Western conf. 1994), Am. Assn. for Chinese Studies, Chinese-Am. Profl. Soc., Hist. Soc. for Gender Studies. Democrat. Office: Dept East Asian Studies Univ Ariz Tucson AZ 85721

TAPIA, JOHN REYNA, foreign language educator; b. Ajo, Ariz., Jan. 29, 1922; s. Genaro Villa-Gomez and Guillerma (Reyna) T.; m. Bertha Velasco Cervantes, Sept. 21, 1942. BA, W.Va. State Coll., 1960; LLB, Blackstone Sch. of Law, 1960, JD, 1961; MA, U. Utah, 1966, PhD, 1969. Asst. prof. Western Mich. U., Kalamazoo, 1969-70, So. Ill. U., Edwardsville, 1970-71; prof., chmn. Ft. Lewis Coll., Durango, Colo., 1971-84, prof. emeritus, 1984—; part-time prof. Yavapai Coll., Prescott, Ariz., 1981—. Author: Alecia En Flowerland, 1970, Tierra Comprometida, 1980, Indian in Spanish-American Novel, 1981; author poetry. Mem. exec. com. Ariz. Rep. Party, Phoenix, 1989—; commr. Prescott Preservation Commn., 1986-89; chmn. Yavapai County Rep. Party, 1989-91. Decorated 3 Bronze Stars, 7 Purple Hearts; named to Hon. Order of Ky. Cols. Mem. Nat. Assn. Civilian Conservation Corp Alumni, Internat. Acad. Poets (vice chancellor 1982—), Ret. Officers Assn. (life), Mil. Order of the Purple Heart Hall of Honor, Rocky Mountain MLA, Vets of the Battle of the Bulge, 70th Tank Btn. Assn. (pres. 1994-95), Order Don Quijote, Phi Kappa Phi. Home: 326 S Mt Vernon Ave Prescott AZ 86303-4349

TAPPAN, JANICE RUTH VOGEL, animal behavior researcher; b. Pasadena, Mar. 13, 1948; d. Robert Samuel and Etta (Berry) Vogel; m. David Stanton Tappan IV, Dec. 20, 1970; children: Stacey, Christina, Danny. BA in Anthropology, U. Calif., Berkeley, 1970. Rsch. asst. L.A. Zoo, 1982—; owner Fiddlers Crossing, Pasadena, 1989—. Calif. Arts Coun. folklore grantee, 1989-90. Mem. Scottish Fiddling Revival (v.p. 1986—, judge fiddling 1989—), Scottish Fiddlers of Calif. (v.p. 1986—), Calif. Traditional Music Soc. (devel. dir. 1990-94, v.p. 1994—), Scottish Fiddlers of L.A. (music dir. 1990—), Phi Beta Kappa. Democrat. Soc. of Friends. Home: 1938 Rose Villa St Pasadena CA 91107-5046

TAPPER, DAVID, pediatric surgeon; b. Balt., Aug. 26, 1945; s. Herman A. and Sylvia Phyllis (Golomb) T.; m. Susan Irene Wagner, June 25, 1968; children: Joellen, Erica, Jacalyn, Aaron. BS, U. Md., College Park, 1966; MD, U. Md., Balt., 1970. Surg. intern and resident U. Calif. San Francisco Med. Ctr., 1970-73; pediatric surg. rsch. fellow Boston Children's Hosp., 1973-75; sr. and chief surg. resident U. Calif., San Francisco, 1975-77; sr. and chief pediatric surg. fellow Children's Hosp., Boston, 1977-79; asst. prof. surgery Harvard Med. Sch., Boston, 1979-83; surgeon-in-chief Children's Hosp. Med. Ctr., Seattle, 1983—; prof. surgery and pediatrics U. Wash., Seattle, 1983—, vice chmn. dept. surgery, 1986—; bd. dirs. Am. Bd. Surgery, Phila., 1991—. Served to maj. USAR, 1971-82. Fellow ACS; mem. Am. Surg Assn., Am. Pediatric Surgery Assn. (bd. govs. 1993—), Soc. Univ. Surgeons, Pacific Coast Surg. Soc. Republican. Jewish. Office: Children's Hosp Med Ctr 4800 Sand Point Way NE Seattle WA 98105-3901

TAPPER, JOAN JUDITH, magazine editor; b. Chgo., June 12, 1947; d. Samuel Jack and Anna (Swoiskin) T.; m. Steven Richard Siegel, Oct. 15, 1971. BA, U. Chgo., 1968; MA, Harvard U., 1969. Editor manuscripts Chelsea House, N.Y.C., 1969-71, Scribners, N.Y.C., 1971; editor books Nat. Acad. Scis., Washington, 1972-73; assoc. editor Praeger Pubs., Washington, 1973-74; editor New Rep. Books, Washington, 1974-79; mng. editor spl. pubs. Nat. Geog. Soc., Washington, 1979-83; editor Nat. Geog. Traveler, Washington, 1984-88; editor-in-chief Islands (internat. mag.), Santa Barbara, Calif., 1989—. Recipient Pacific Asia Travel Assn. Journalist of the Yr. award, 1995. Mem. Am. Soc. Mag. Editors, Soc. Am. Travel Writers (editors' coun.), Channel City Club. Democrat. Jewish. Home: 603 Island View Dr Santa Barbara CA 93109-1508 Office: Islands Mag 3886 State St Santa Barbara CA 93105-3112

TAPPER, LANCE HOWARD, secondary education educator; b. Encino, Calif., Apr. 11, 1961; s. Lloyd Edward and Dorothy Charlotte (Silvers) T. BA in History, UCLA, 1983. Lic. tchr., Calif.; lic. Hazzan Commn., Cantors Assembly, N.Y. Cantor Verdugo Hills Hebrew Ctr., Tujunga, Calif., 1979-81, Temple Ner Tamid, Simi Valley, Calif., 1981-82; Hazzan Hazzan, Downey, Calif., 1983—; tchr. Birmingham High Sch., Van Nuys, Calif., 1984-90, Taft High Sch., Woodland Hills, Calif., 1990—. Madelyn Hunter teaching fellow Grad. Sch. Edn., UCLA, 1985; recipient Outstanding Secondary Student Teaching award Grad. Sch. Edn., UCLA, 1985. Mem. United Tchrs. L.A. (mem.-at-large 1986-87), Cantors Assembly (western region chair 1992-94, nat. exec. coun. 1993—), Guild Temple Musicians, L.A. Sertoma Club (freedom award in gen. edn. 1994). Democrat. Jewish. Office: Taft High Sch 5461 Winnetka Ave Woodland Hills CA 91364-2548

TARANIK, JAMES VLADIMIR, geologist, educator; b. Los Angeles, Apr. 23, 1940; s. Vladimir James and Jeanette Downing (Smith) T.; m. Colleen Sue Glessner, Dec. 4, 1971; children: Debra Lynn, Danny Lee. B.Sc. in Geology, Stanford U., 1964; Ph.D., Colo. Sch. Mines, 1974. Chief remote sensing Iowa Geol. Survey, Iowa City, 1971-74; prin. remote sensing scientist Earth Resources Observation Systems Data Ctr., U.S. Geol. Survey, Sioux Falls, S.D., 1975-79; chief non-renewable resources br., resource observation div. Office of Space and Terrestrial Applications, NASA Hdqrs., Washington, 1979-82; dean mines Mackay Sch. Mines U. Nev., Reno, 1982-87, prof. of geology and geophysics, 1982—; pres. Desert Research Inst., Univ. and Community Coll. System Nev., 1987—; adj. prof. geology U. Iowa, 1971-79; vis. prof. civil engring. Iowa State U., 1972-74; adj. prof. earth sci. U. S.D., 1976-79; program scientist for space shuttle large format camera expt. for heat capacity mapping mission, liaison Geol. Scis. Bd., Nat. Acad. Scis., 1981-82; dir. NOAA Coop. Inst. Aerospace Sci. & Terrestrial Applications, 1986-94; program dir. NASA Space Grant consortium Univ. and Community Coll. System Nev., Reno, 1991—; team mem. Shuttle Imaging Radar-B Sci. Team NASA, 1983-88, mem. space applications adv. com. 1986-88; chmn. remote sensing subcom. SAAC, 1986-88; chmn. working group on civil space commercialization U.S. Dept. Commerce, 1982-84, mem. civil operational remote sensing satellite com., 1983-84; bd. dirs. Newmont Gold Co.; mem. NASA Space Sci. and Applications adv. com., 1988—, Nat. Def. Exec. Res., 1986—, AF Studies Bd., Com. on Strategic Relocatable Targets, 1989-91; mem. NASA Pre-Launch Rev. Bd., Space Radar Lab., 1993-94; mem. NASA Fed. Lab. Rev. Task Force, 1994—; prin. investigator Japanese Earth Resources Satellite, 1991—; mem. eviron. task force, MEDEA Mitre Corp., McLean Va., 1993—; cons. Jet Propulsion Lab. Calif. Tech. Inst., Hughes Aircraft Corp., Lockheed-Marietta Corp., Mitre Corp., TRW; developer remote sensing program and remote sensing lab. for State of Iowa, ednl. program in remote sensing for Iowa univs. and U. Nev., Reno; Office Space and Terrestrial Applications program scientist for 2d space shuttle flight; terrestrial geol. applications program NASA, 1981—. Contbr. to profl. jours. Served with C.E. U.S. Army, 1965-67; mil. intellegence officer Res. Decorated Bronze Star medal; recipient Spl. Achievement award U.S. Geol. Survey, 1978, Exceptional Sci. Achievement medal NASA, 1982, NASA Group Achievement award Shuttle imaging radar, 1990, NASA Johnson Space Ctr. Group Achievement award for large format camera, 1985; NASA prin. investigator, 1973, 83-88, prin. investigator French Spot-1 Program to Evaluate Spot 1986-88; NDEA fellow, 1968-71. Fellow AAAS, Explorers Club, Geol. Soc. Am.; mem. Am. Assn. Petroleum Geologists (charter, mem. energy minerals divsn., divsn. environ. geoscis.), Soc. Mining Engrs., Am. Inst. Profl. Geologists (certified, pres. Nev. sect. 1985-87), AIAA (sr. mem.), Am. Astronautical Soc. (sr. mem., engring. scis. sect. 1994—), Internat. Acad. Astronautics (corr. mem. 1986-84), Soc. Exploration Geophysicists, Geosci. and Remote Sensing Soc. of IEEE (bd. dirs., geosat. com. 1983-84), Am. Soc. Photogrammetry and Remote Sensing (dep. dir. for remote sensing cert., conf. chmn. annual meeting Reno 1994, Merit award 1994), Internat. Soc. Photogrammetry and Remote Sensing (pres. working group II/4 1976-80, working group VII-5 non-renewable resources 1980-88, working group VII-4 geology and mineral resources applications 1992—, U.S. corr. commn. VII, 1994—), nev. Quality and Productivity Inst. (chmn. bd. 1989-94), Nev. Industry Sci., Engring., and Tech. Task Force, Grand Canyon Visibility Commn. (pub. adv. com. 1992—), Bohemian Club of San Francisco, Sigma Xi, Phi Kappa Phi (life). Home: PO Box 7175 Reno NV 89510-7175 also: 2108 Calle De Espana Las Vegas NV 89102-4013 Office: Univ and Community Coll Sys Nev Desert Rsch I NV 89512

TARBELL, JIM, printer, publishing executive, writer; b. Spokane, Wash., Dec. 11, 1949; s. Harry and Polly (Gallagher) T.; m. Judy Widmer, July 3, 1979; children: Rebecca, Shamli, Crescent. BA in Econs., Am. U., 1972. Mem. staff Congressman Wendell Wyatt Ho. of Reps., Washington, 1968-72; economist Peace Corps, Quito, Ecuador, 1973-75; carpenter Annapolis, Calif., 1975-79; bilingual instr. Horicon Sch. Dist., Annapolis, Calif., 1979-81; owner Black Bear Press, Medicino, Calif., 1981-85, Caspar, Calif., 1990-94; owner, pub. Ridge Times Press, Mendicino and Caspar, Calif., 1981—. Editor, pub. (quar. mag.) Ridge Rev., 1981—, (cmty, newsletter) An Apple Press, 1976-84; author: I Came Not Alone, 1994. Democrat. Home: 15168 Caspar Rd Caspar CA 95420-0132 Office: Black Bear Press 14951 Caspar Rd Caspar CA 95420-9603

TARBI, WILLIAM RHEINLANDER, secondary education educator, curriculum consultant, educational technology researcher; b. San Bernardino, Calif., Feb. 23, 1949; s. William Metro and Sue (Rheinlander) T.; m. Jenny Workman, Apr. 10, 1980 (div. 1985); m. Michele Hastings, July 4, 1990; children: Amy, Melissa. AA, Santa Barbara City Coll., 1969; BA in History, U. Calif., Santa Barbara, 1976; MA, U. Redlands, 1992. Cert. secondary edn. social studies tchr., Calif. Reporter AP, Santa Barbara, Calif., 1976-80, UPI, Seattle, 1980-85, Golden West Radio Network, Seattle, 1980-85; tchr. Redlands (Calif.) Unified Sch. Dist., 1988—; cons. IMCOM, Redlands, 1985—. Mrm. E Clampus Vitus, Phi Delta Kappa.

TARBUCK, BARBARA JOAN, actor; b. Detroit, Jan. 15, 1942; d. George and Ruth Erma (Fillmore) T.; m. James Denis Connolly, May 17, 1980; 1 child, Jennifer Lane. B of Philosophy, Wayne State U., 1963; MA, U. Mich., 1965; postgrad., Ind. U., 1965-66. Author: (children's play) Who Am I?, 1972; author/actor: They Call Me Dr. Greer, 1994; guest star: (TV shows) Picket Fences, Civil Wars, Golden Girls, L.A. Law, Cagney & Lacey, others; feature films include Curly Sue, Short Circuit, Police Squad, others; Broadway shows include Brighton Beach Memoirs, Water Engine, Landscape and Silence; nat. tours: Broadway Bound, America Hurrah!. Fulbright grantee, 1966-67; recipient L.A. Drama Critics award, 1985. Mem. Zeta Phi Eta. Democrat.

TARDIO, THOMAS A., public relations executive; b. Pa., Jan. 26, 1952. V.p. strategic planning and other positions Columbia Pictures Industries, 1979-88; CFO, v.p. adminstrn. Rogers & Cowan, Inc., L.A., 1988-89, exec. v.p. entertainment sect., 1989-91, pres., CEO, 1991—. Mem. Pub.

Rels. Soc. Am., Nat. Acad. Recording Arts and Scis., Acad. Motion Picture Arts and Scis. Offcie: Rogers & Cowan Inc 10000 Santa Monica Blvd Ste 400 Los Angeles CA 90067-7007

TARGOW, JEANETTE GOLDFIELD, clinical social worker; b. Chgo., May 21, 1910; d. Isadore and Rebecca Covici Goldfield; children—Patricia Skinner, Richard Targow. Ph.B., U. Chgo., 1930; M.S.W., UCLA, 1953. Social worker U. So. Calif. Psychology Clinic, Los Angeles, 1953-55; clin. social worker Psychol. Service Center, Los Angeles, 1955-60; pvt. practice clin. social work, Los Angeles, 1960—; instr. Calif. Sch. Profl. Psychology; mem. faculty dept. psychology Loyola-Marymount Coll., 1981-83; supr. Didi Hirsch Mental Health Center, Culver City, Calif., 1977-81. Fellow Am. Group Psychotherapy Assn. (chmn. task force on womens' issues 1983-86), Group Psychotherapy Found. (bd. dirs.), Soc. for Clin. Social Work; mem. Los Angeles Group Psychotherapy Soc., Nat. Assn. Social Workers, Nat. Acad. Practice in Social Work, ACLU. Democrat. Jewish. Home: 1835 N Doheny Dr West Hollywood CA 90069-1150 Office: 648 N Doheny Dr Los Angeles CA 90069

TARIN, WILLIAM MICHAEL, publications engineer; b. San Antonio, July 15, 1942; s. Joseph Walter and Dorothy Mae (Perry) T.; m. Elizabeth Ann Scout, Feb. 1, 1969; children: Dorothy Elizabeth, William Michael, Joseph Clement. BS in Info. Systems, Nat. Coll., 1988. Communications analyst USAF, Ft. Meade, Md., 1961-81; tech. writer Docu-Data Corp., Millersville, Md., 1981-83; document control mgr. Ford Aerospace & Communications Corp., Hanover, Md., 1983; data processing mgr. Dept. Def., Ft. Meade, 1983-84; tech. writer Intercon Systems Corp., Aurora, Colo., 1984-87; sr. publ. engr. Lockheed Missiles & Space Co., Aurora, 1987—; cons. in field. Recipient Air Force Commendation Medal Air Force, 1967, 1979, 1981, Commendation Cert. Nat. Security Agy., 1977. Mem. Am. Legion (Elizabeth, Colo.). Democrat. Methodist. Office: Lockheed Missiles & Space 16000 E Lockheed Dr Aurora CO 80011-9028

TARKINGTON, DICKEY EDWARD, artist, educator; b. Russellville, Ark., Nov. 16, 1937; s. William Edward and Dessie Odell (Hallmark) T.; m. Patricia Ann Lincoln, May 2, 1960 (div.); children: D. Edward, Kimberly Dawn. Student, East L.A. Coll., 1962-64, Cerritos Coll., 1973-78, Rio Hondo Coll., 1978-83, Citrus Coll., 1984—. Printer Omaha Nat. Bank, 1958-59; press operator Western Electric, Omaha, 1959-60; systems analyst Bus. Systems Inc., L.A., 1960-64; comml. artist Compton (Calif.) Press, 1964-65; gen. clk. P and A Carloading Co., L.A., 1965-69; freight ops. supr. P.I.E. Trucking Co., L.A., 1969-74; owner, operator Tarkington/Harman, Bassett, Calif., 1974-79, Tarkington Ltd., Rosemead, Calif., 1978-84; freelance woodcarver, 1981—; tchr. Tri-Communities Adult Edn., West Covina, Calif., 1989—. Exhbns. include Fiesta de Artes, 1980 (Best of Show award), Calif. Ceramics and Craft Assn., 1983 (Best of Show award, 1st place award, Spl. Merit award, Best of Class award), Great Am. Irish Fair, 1990 (2nd place overall award). With USAF, 1955-58. Mem. East Valley Art Assn. (show chmn. 1992—), Mid Valley Art Assn., Calif. Carving Guild. Democrat. Home: 1054 W Hollyvale St Azusa CA 91702-3356

TARKOWSKI, LARRY MICHAEL, municipal official; b. Flint, Mich., May 15, 1952; s. Lavern Joseph and Barbara Ann (Wade) T.; m. Nancy Susan Ostapuk, May 7, 1983; children: Jonathon, Logan. B in Gen. Studies, U. Mich., Ann Arbor, 1974. Supt. Warren Smith Contracting, Flagstaff, Ariz., 1979-89; dir. pub. works Town of Prescott Valley, Ariz., 1989—. Co-chmn. No. Ariz. Coun. Govt. Transp. Bd., Flagstaff, 1990—. Named Profl. Man of Yr., Prescott Valley Rotary Club, 1993. Mem. Am. Pub. Works Assn. (pres. No. Ariz. br. 1995), Ctrl. Yavapai Transp. Planning Orgn., Prescott Valley C. of C., Lions (pres.1994), Yavapai Soccer Club (coord. 1992—).

TARLSON, NICK GLENN, financial advisor; b. Anchorage, May 31, 1955; s. Glenn Robert and Popi (Zafiri) T.; m. Mauna Anne Arnzen, Aug. 16, 1980; children: Claire, Diana, George. BBA, Seattle U., 1976. CPA, Calif., Wash., La. Mgr. Ernst & Whinney, San Francisco, 1976-83; v.p., sec., treas. Brayer Elec. Co., San Francisco, 1983-86; owner, mgr. Tarlson & Assoc., San Francisco, 1986—; bd. dirs. Brayer Electric Co., Brayer Lighting Co., San Francisco; pres.Jupiter Group, 1986-87, bd. dirs.; treas. Galacar & Co., 1987—, bd. dirs. Treas., trustee Opera West Found., San Francisco, 1986—, Patriarch Athenagoras Orthodox Inst. Republican. Greek Orthodox. Home: 73 Orange Ave Larkspur CA 94939-1953 Office: Tarlson & Assoc 22 Battery St Ste 1100 San Francisco CA 94111-5525

TARN, NATHANIEL, poet, translator, educator; b. Paris, June 30, 1928; s. Marcel and Yvonne (Suchar) T.; children : Andrea, Marc. BA with honors, Cambridge (Eng.) U., 1948, MA, 1952; postgrad., U. Sorbonne, U. Paris, 1949-51; MA, U. Chgo., 1952, PhD, 1957; postgrad., London Sch. Econs., 1953-58. Anthropologist Guatemala, Burma, Alaska, and other locations, 1952—; prof. comparative lit. Rutgers U., 1970-85; vis. prof. SUNY, Buffalo and Princeton, 1969-70. Author: Old Savage/Young City, 1964, Where Babylon Ends, 1968, The Beautiful Contradictions, 1969, October, 1969, A Nowhere for Vallejo, 1971, Lyrics for the Bride of God: Section: The Artemision, 1972, The Persephones, 1974, Lyrics for the Bride of God, 1975, The House of Leaves, 1976, Birdscapes, with Seaside, 1978, The Desert Mothers, 1985, At the Western Gates, 1985, Palenque, 1986, Seeing America First, 1989, Flying the Body, 1993, Multitude of One, 1995, Views from the Weaving Mountain: Selected Essays in Poetics and Anthropology, 1991; co-author: (with Janet Rodney) The Forest, 1978, Atitlan/Alashka, 1979, The Ground of Our Great Admiration of Nature, 1978; contbg. author: Penguin Modern Poets No. Seven: Richard Murphy, Jon Silkin, Nathaniel Tarn, 1965, A.P.E.N. Anthology of Contemporary Poetry, 1966, The Penguin Book of Modern Verse Translation, 1966, Poems Addressed to Hugh MacDiarmid, 1967, Music and Sweet Poetry: A Verse Anthology, 1968, Frontier of Going: Anthology of Space Poetry, 1969, Shaking the Pumpkin, 1972, America: A Prophecy, 1973, Open Poetry, 1973, Active Anthology, 1974, Symposium of the Whole, 1983, Random House Book of Twentieth Century French Poetry, 1983, Beneath a Single Moon: Buddhism in American Poetry, 1991, American Poetry since 1950: Innovators and Outsiders, 1993; translator: The Heights of Macchu Picchu (Pablo Neruda), 1966, Stelae (Victor Segalen), 1969, Zapotec Struggles, 1993; editor, co-translator: Con Cuba: An Anthology of Cuban Poetry of the Last Sixty Years, 1969, Selected Poems (Pablo Neruda), 1970; editor Cape Edits. and founder-dir. Cape Goliard Press, J. Cape Ltd., 1967-69. Recipient Guinness prize for poetry, 1963. Office: PO Box 8187 Santa Fe NM 87504-8187

TARSON, HERBERT HARVEY, university administrator emeritus; b. N.Y.C., Aug. 28, 1910; s. Harry and Elizabeth (Miller) T.; m. Lynne Barnett, June 27, 1941; 1 son, Stephen. Grad., Army Command Gen. Staff Coll., 1942, Armed Forces Staff Coll., 1951, Adavnced Mgmt. Sch. Sr. Air Force Comdrs., George Washington U., 1954; B.A., U. Calif., Los Angeles, 1949; Ph.D., U.S. Internat. U., 1972. Entered U.S. Army as pvt., 1933, advanced through grades to maj., 1942; transfered to U.S. Air Force, 1947, advanced through grades to lt. col., 1949; adj. exec. officer Ft. Snelling, Minn., 1940-42; asst. adj. gen. 91st Inf. Div., 1942-43; chief of personnel, advance sec. Comd. Zone, ETO, 1944-45; dir. personnel services 8th Air Force, 1946-47; dep. dir. dept. info. and edn. Armed Forces Info. Sch., 1949-51; dir. personnel services Japan Air Def. Force, 1951-53, Continental Air Command, 1953-62; dir. adminstrv. services, spl. asst. to Comdr. 6th Air Force Res. Region, 1962-64; ret., 1964; asst. to chancellor L.I. U., Brookville, 1964-69; dean admissions Tex. State Tech. Inst., San Diego Indsl. Center, 1970-72; v.p. acad. affairs Nat. U., San Diego, 1972-75, sr. v.p., 1975-88, founding sr. v.p. emeritus, 1988—. Decorated Bronze Star medal with oak leaf cluster, Air Force Commendation medal with 2 oak leaf clusters. Fellow Bio-Med Research Inst.; mem. Doctoral Soc. U.S. Internat. U., Am. Soc. Tng., Devel., World Affairs Council, Air Force Assn., Navy League U.S., Pres.'s Assos. of Nat. U. (presidential life). Home: 4611 Denwood Rd La Mesa CA 91941-4803

TARTER, BLODWEN, marketing and information technology executive; b. Sacramento, Dec. 2, 1954; d. Bill and Blodwen Edwards (Coburn) Tarter; m. Alan May, Aug. 6, 1983. BA, MA, Stanford U., 1976; MBA, U. Chgo., 1978; PhD, Golden Gate U., 1991. Mgr. mkt. rsch. Mead Products, Dayton, Ohio, 1978-79; assoc. mktg. mgr. Mead Products, 1979-80; mgr. mktg. svcs. Mead Paperboard Products, 1980-81; mgr. mktg. planning Mead Data Cen., N.Y.C., 1981-82; v.p. mktg. Info. Access Co., Belmont, Calif., 1982-86; dir. mktg. Channelmark Corp., San Mateo, Calif., 1986-87; v.p. mktg. Ins. Equities Corp., Palo Alto, Calif., 1987-89; dir. product mgmt. Charles Schwab & Co., Inc., San Francisco, 1989-91, v.p. applications devel. and info. systems divsn., 1991-93, v.p. telecom., 1993-94, v.p. customer tech. and info. (mktg.), 1994—. Fundraiser Stanford Keystone campaign, 1988-91; vol. AIDS Meml. Grove. Mem. Stanford Profl. Women. Office: Charles Schwab & Co Inc 101 Montgomery St San Francisco CA 94104-4122

TARULLI, MICHAEL GENE, military officer; b. Dover, Ohio, July 2, 1952; s. Pat and Madeline Eleanor (Galanga) T.; m. Rita Faye Espenschied, Jan. 12, 1973; children: Saundra Tarulli Davis, Jason Todd. BA in Pub. Adminstrn., Upper Iowa U., 1978; MS in Acquisition Logistics, Air Force Inst. Tech., Wright-Patterson AFB, Ohio, 1982. Advanced profl. designation in logistics mgmt. Enlisted USAF, 1973, advanced through grades to maj., 1990; automatic flight control sys. specialist (AFSC 32570) MAC, 436th Avionics Maintenance Squadron, Dover AFB, Del., 1973-77; avionics technician AFSC, 4950th Test Wing, Andrews AFB, Md., 1977-79; officer trainee ATC, Lackland AFB, Tex., 1979; logistics contr. SAC, Hdqs. 8th Air Force, Barksdale AFB, La., 1979-81; avionics intermediate, computer resources mgr. AFALD (AFLC) F-16 Sys. Program Office, Wright-Patterson AFB, 1982-83; chief manned space-flight logistics space transp. sys. test team, dep. test dir. of operational suitability AFOTEC OL-DD, Johnson Space Ctr., Houston, 1983-85; chief logistics evaluation br. space ops. ctr. Air Force Operational Test and Evaluation Ctr. Consol., Falcon AFB, Colo., 1985-88; chief logistics plans br. 6171 Air Base Squadron, Kwang Ju Air Base, Republic of Korea, 1988-89; dir. fitness testing and evaluation divsn., dept. of athletics USAF Acad., Colo. Springs, 1989-91, asst. athletic dir., dept. of athletics, 1991-92; dep. test dir. and dep. for logistics, Global Positioning Sys. test team USAF, Colo. Springs, 1992, test dir. Global Positioning System test team, 1993—. Mem. Internat. Test and Evaluation Assn. (v.p. Rocky Mountain chpt. 1993). Home: 5045 Willowbrook Rd Colorado Springs CO 80917-1132 Office: Air Force Operational Test and Evaluation Ctr 4146 E Bijou St Colorado Springs CO 80909-6824

TASHIMA, ATSUSHI WALLACE, federal judge; b. Santa Maria, Calif., June 24, 1934; s. Yasutaro and Aya (Sasaki) T.; m. Nora Kiyo Inadomi, Jan. 27, 1957; children: Catherine Y., Christopher I., Jonathan I. A.B. in Polit. Sci., UCLA, 1958; LL.B., Harvard U., 1961. Bar: Calif. 1962. Dep. atty. gen. State of Calif., 1962-67; atty. Spreckels Sugar div. Amstar Corp., 1968-72, v.p., gen. atty., 1972-77; partner Morrison & Foerster, Los Angeles, 1977-80; judge U.S. Dist. Ct. Central Dist. Calif., Los Angeles, 1980—; mem. Calif. Com. Bar Examiners, 1978-80. Served with USMC, 1953-55. Mem. ABA, State Bar Calif., Los Angeles County Bar Assn. Democrat. Office: US Dist Ct 312 N Spring St Los Angeles CA 90012-4701*

TASHJIAN, LEVON DONALD, psychiatrist; b. Phila., Aug. 18, 1934; s. Levon O. and Anna L. (Mahmarian) T.; m. Stefanie M. Halus, June 17, 1961; children: Audrey, Paul, Peter. BA magna cum laude, Harvard Coll., 1952-56; MD, U. Pa., 1956-60. Diplomate Am. Bd. Neurology and Psychiatry; med. lic., Pa. Rotating intern Pa. Hosp., Phila., 1960-61; neurology resident Jefferson Med. Coll. Hosp., 1961; psychiatry resident Hosp. U. Pa., 1963-66; Sol Ginsberg fellow Group for the Advancement of Psychiatry, 1965-67; clin. psychiatry instr. U. Pa., 1966-68, assoc., 1968-72, asst. prof., 1972-84; clin. assoc. prof. Temple U., 1989—, 1984—; attending psychiatrist The Inst. of Pa. Hosp., 1968-90, assoc. dir. adolescent treatment ctr., 1968-74, dir. young adult unit and program, 1973-80, sr. attending psychiatrist, 1990-93; cons. adolescent psychiatry, Phila. Child Guidance Ctr., 1971-78; dir. adult unit and program, attending psychiatrist The Horsham Clin, Ambler, Pa., 1980-84, med. dir., 1984-88; med. dir. The Consultation Ctr., Phila., 1982-83; chmn. dept. psychiatry Mt. Sinai Hosp., Phila, 1988-89; med. dir. continuum care svcs. Editor: (newsletter) Am. Soc. Adolescent Psychiatry, 1983-85; editorial bd. mem. Child and Adolescent Mental Health Care, 1991—; author: (with Harold Rashkis) Understanding Your Parents, 1978; presenter in field; contbr. articles to profl. jours. Named One of Best Physicians of Phila., Phila. Mag., 1979, 91. Fellow Coll. of Physicians of Phila.; mem. Phila. soc. Adolescent Psychiatry (pres.-elect 1972-73, pres. 1973-74), Pa. Psychiatric Soc., Phila. Psychiatric Soc. (program chmn. 1971, 83). Home: 644 Canyon Rd Ste 12 Santa Fe NM 87501-2769 Office: 200 W DeVargas St Ste 4 Santa Fe NM 87501

TATA, GIOVANNI, publishing executive; b. Taranto, Italy, Apr. 26, 1954; came to U.S., 1974, naturalized, 1982; s. Vito and Angela (Colucci) T.; m. Brenda Susan Smith, Feb. 14, 1978; children: Elizabeth Ariana, Katherine Allison, Margaret Anne, Michael Anthony. BS cum laude (scholar), Brigham Young U., 1977, MA, 1980; grad. cert. area studies U. Utah, 1980; PhD, 1986; postgrad. U. Turin (Italy), 1980-81. Archaeologist, Utah State Hist. Soc., Salt Lake City, 1979; instr. dept. langs. U. Utah, Salt Lake City, 1983-85; Mediterranean specialist Soc. Early Hist. Archaeology, Provo, Utah, 1978-91; mus. curator Pioneer Trail State Park, Salt Lake City, 1982-83; instr. dept. art Brigham Young U., Provo, 1982-84; research fellow Direzione Generale per la Cooperazione Scientifica Culturale e Technica, Rome, 1980-81; research curator Utah Mus. Fine Arts, Salt Lake City, 1985-87; chmn. 35th Ann. Symposium on the Archaeology of the Scriptures, 1986; pres. Transoft Internat., Inc., 1988—, Mus. Info. Systems, 1987-93; chmn. Taras Devel. Corp., 1994—. Republican. Mem. Ch. Jesus Christ of Latter-day Saints. Mem. Am. Assn. Museums, Internat. Coun. Museums, Utah State Hist. Soc. Home: PO Box 2194 Provo UT 84603-2194 Office: Taras Devel Corp 117 250 W Center St Provo UT 84603

TATARSKII, VALERIAN IL'ICH, physics researcher; b. Kharkov, USSR, Oct. 13, 1929; s. Il'ya A. and Elizabeth A. (Lapis) T.; m. Maia S. Granovskaia, Dec. 22, 1955; 1 child, Viatcheslav V. MS, Moscow State U., 1952; PhD, Acoustical Inst. Acad. Scis., 1957; DSc, Gorky State U., 1962. Scientific rschr. Geophys. Inst. Acad. Sci. USSR, Moscow, 1953-56; scientific rschr. Inst. Atmospheric Physics, Acad. Sci. USSR, Moscow, 1956-59, sr. scientific rschr., 1959-78, head lab., 1978-90; head dept. Lebedev. Phys. Inst. Acad. Sci., Moscow, 1990-91; sr. rsch. assoc. U. Colo. Coop. Inst. for Rsch. in Environ. Sci., Boulder, 1991—, NOAA/ERL. Environ. Tech. Lab., Boulder. Author: Wave Propagation in a Turbulent Medium, 1961, 67, The Effect of the Turbulent Atmosphere on Wave Propagation, 1971, Principles of Statistical Radiophysics, 1989; contbr. articles to profl. jours. Recipient USSR State prize, 1990, Max Born award Optical Soc. of Am., 1994. Fellow Optical Soc. Am. (Max Born award 1994); mem. Russian Acad. Sci., U.S.A. Nat. Acad. Engring. (fgn. assoc.), N.Y. Acad. Sci. Office: NOAA/ERL/ETL 325 Broadway St Boulder CO 80303-3337

TATE, STAN DAVIS, priest, clinical bioethicist; b. Boise, Idaho, Dec. 5, 1932; s. John P. and Marjorie (Davis) T.; m. Lynn Campbell, June 10, 1955; children: Teri McColly, Scott, Phil. BA, U. Idaho, 1955; MDiv, Princeton (N.J.) Sem., 1958; DMin, San Francisco Theol. Sem., Berkeley, Calif., 1988. Ordained priest Episcopalian Ch., 1962. Chaplain Smokejumpers USFS, McCall, Idaho, 1953-63, N.J. Prison, Trenton, 1957-58; pastor Presbyn. Ch., Hysham, Mont., 1958-61; vicar Episc. Ch., McCall, 1961-70; probate judge Valley County, Cascade, Idaho, 1965-70; instr. Boise State Coll., 1970-74; dir. Youth Alternatives, Boise, 1974-78; chaplain Oreg. State U., Corvallis, 1978-81; rector St. Mark's Episc. Ch., Moscow, Idaho, 1981-88; clin. bioethicist Gritman Med. Ctr., Moscow, 1989—. Author: Pastoral Bioethics, 1989. Active Idaho Commn. on Juvenile Justice, Boise, 1989—. Home: 1423 Alpowa St Moscow ID 83843-2401 Office: Gritman Med Ctr 2000 S Main St Moscow ID 83843-8970

TATHAM, WILLIAM R., vintner; b. 1934. Pres., chmn. bd. Consol Industries, Inc., Clovis, Calif., 1962—. Office: Consol Industries Inc 2148 E Copper Ave Clovis CA 93611-9128*

TATOMER, WILLIAM REEVES, psychiatrist; b. Apr. 29, 1945; s. Harry Nicholas and Norma Ethyl (Reeves) T.; m. Mary Catherine Hourican, Sept. 9, 1978; children: Deirdre Catherine, Meghan Norma, Andrew Hourican. BA in Biology, U. Va., 1967, MD, 1971. Diplomate Am. Bd. of Psychiatry and Neurology; lic. Va., Calif. Intern Greenwich Community Hosp., Conn. and Mary's Help Hosp., 1971-72; resident San Mateo (Calif.) County Mental Health Svcs., 1971-74; pvt. practice San Mateo, 1974—; mem. adv. com. dept. psychiatry Peninsula Hosp. and Med. Ctr., 1981-86, suicide review com. chair 1981-92; supr. residents San Mateo County Mental Health, 1985; lectr. clin. case confs., 1985. Trustee Suicide Prevention and Crisis Ctr., 1980-90, v.p., 1985-87, profl. rels. com., 1980-90, chair, 1985-87; citizens adv. com. State Parks and Beaches in San Mateo County, 1972-82, chair, 1975, 77; cubmaster pack 12 Boy Scouts Am., 1994—; trustee Health Care Found. San Mateo County, 1984—, mem. exec. com., 1985—, sec./treas., 1985-87, v.p., 1987-89, pres. 1989-91, immediate past pres., 1991—, mem. numerous coms. Fellow Am. Psychiatric Assn.; mem. AMA, Calif. Med. Assn., San Mateo County Med. Assn. (bd. dirs. ex officio 1989-91, long term care com. 1982-85, fee and ins. mediation com. 1983-88, profl. rels. com. 1987-88, 93—, chair physician well being com. 1993—, pres. elect 1994—), Calif. Psychiatric Assn. (polit. action exec. com. 1987-93), No. Calif. Psychiatric Soc. (bd. dirs. coun. 1985-91, budget and fin. com. 1985-88, nominating com. 1985086, pvt. practice com. 1985-91, managed care com. 1994—), San Mateo Individual Practice Assn. (chair psychiat. subcom. 1985—, psychiat. peer reviewer 1985-92), Calif. Found. Med. Care (bd. dirs. 1991—). Office: 101 S San Mateo Dr Ste 300 San Mateo CA 94401-3844

TATUM, RONALD WINSTON, physician, endocrinologist; b. Joplin, Mo., Apr. 29, 1935; s. Dorothy Elizabeth (Messick) T.; m. Phyllis Wainman, June 25 (div. May 1974); children: Jeffrey, Stacey; m. Ruby Germaine Trujillo, Aug. 21, 1983 (div. Sept. 1993); children: Tracea, Susan; m. Yvonne Marie Laug, Oct. 8, 1994. AB, Harvard U., 1957; MD, U. Rochester, 1961. Intern Strong Meml. Hosp., Rochester, N.Y., 1961-62; resident U. Rochester, 1962-64, fellow, 1964-66; clin. endocrinologist in pvt. practice Albuquerque, 1966—; active staff Presbyn. Hosp. and St. Joseph Hosp., Albuquerque, 1966—; med. dir. Cottonwood Treatment Ctr., Albuquerque, 1985-90, N.Mex. Monitored Treatment Program, Albuquerque, 1990—; clin. endocrine cons. Charter Hosp. and Heights Psychiat. Hosp., Albuquerque, 1985—. Contbr. articles to profl. jours. Mem. med. adv. com. Hospice Home Health Care, Albuquerque, 1991—. Mem. Am. Assn. Clin. Endocrinologists (charter), Am. Assn. Internal Medicine, Am. Diabetes Assn. (pres. N.Mex. chpt. 1970, 74), Am. Soc. Addiction Medicine, Assn. for Med. Rsch. in Substance Abuse. Home: 842 Southeast Cir NW Albuquerque NM 87104-1967 Office: 8008 Constitution Pl NE Albuquerque NM 87110-7628

TATUM, THOMAS DESKINS, film and television producer, director; b. Pineville, Ky., Feb. 16, 1946; s. Clinton Turner and Gaynelle (Deskins) T.; m. Laura Ann Smith, Aug. 15, 1968 (div. 1974); m. Suzanne Pettit, Sept. 29, 1983; children: Rhett Cowden, Walker Edwin. BA, Vanderbilt U., 1968; JD, Emory U., 1974. Bar: Ga. 1974, D.C. 1980. Spl. asst. City of Atlanta, 1974-76; dep. dir. fed. relations Fed. Relations Nat. League of Cities, Washington, 1977-78; dir. communications Office of Conservation and Solar Energy, Washington, 1979-80; chmn. exec. producer Tatum Communications., Inc., Telluride, and Burbank, Calif., 1981—; chmn., pres. Western Film & Video, Inc., Telluride, 1987—; mem. adv. bd. Electric Light Fund, Washington, 1990—; apptd. chief operating officer Planet TV, L.A., 1995—. Prodr. feature film Winners Take All, 1987; prodr., dir. documentaries Double High, 1982 (award), Maui Windsurf, 1983, home videos Greenpeace in Action, Girls of Winter/Skiing mag., Am. Ultra Sports with Prime Network, 1989--94, various TV, cable and home video sports programs, 1982—. Dep. campaign mgr. Maynard Jackson, 1973, Jimmy Carter campaign, 1976, staff conf. Dem. Mayors, 1974-75, media cons. Greepeace, 1988; bd. dirs. Atlanta Ballet, v.p., 1975; nat. urban affairs coord. Carter Mondale campaign 1976, mem. Carter Mondale transition team 1976-77; mem. adv. bd. Solar Electric Light Fund, Washington, 1990-93. Mem. Ga. Bar Assn., Washington Bar Assn., Hollywood Film and TV Soc., L.A. Tennis Club. Presbyterian. Home: PO Box 944 Telluride CO 81435-0944 Office: Tatum Comm Inc 2219 W Olive Ave Ste 173 Burbank CA 91506-2648

TAUB, ABRAHAM HASKEL, mathematician; b. Chgo., Feb. 1, 1911; s. Joseph Haskell and Mary (Sherman) T.; m. Cecilia Vaslow, Dec. 26, 1933; children: Mara, Nadine, Haskell Joseph. B.S., U. Chgo., 1931; Ph.D., Princeton U., 1935. Asst. Inst. Advanced Study, Princeton, 1935-36; from instr. to prof. U. Wash., 1936-48; research prof. applied math. U. Ill. at Urbana, 1948-64, head digital computer lab., 1961-64; prof. math. U. Calif., Berkeley, 1964-78, prof. emeritus, 1978—; dir. computer center, 1964-68; mem. Inst. Advanced Study, 1940-41, 47-48, 62-63; vis. prof. Coll. de France, Paris, 1967, 75, 76; mem. theoretical physicist div. 2 Nat. Def. Research Com., 1942-45; mem. adv. panel applied math. Nat. Bur. Standards, 1951-60. Editor: Collected Works of John von Neumann, 1961-63, (with S. Fernbach) Computers and Their Role in the Physical Sciences, 1971, Studies in Applied Mathematics, 1972; editorial bd.: Communications in Mathematical Physics, 1965-74. Recipient Pres.'s Cert. of Merit, 1946, medal City of Lille, France, 1969, Berkeley citation, 1978; Guggenheim fellow 1947-48, 58. Fellow Am. Acad. Arts and Scis., AAAS (v.p. sect. A 1968-69), Am. Phys. Soc.; mem. Soc. Indsl. and Applied Math. (past trustee), Am. Math. Soc. (past trustee), Math. Assn. Am. Home: 1526 Arch St Berkeley CA 94708-1850

TAUBE, HENRY, chemistry educator; b. Sask., Can., Nov. 30, 1915; came to U.S., 1937, naturalized, 1942; s. Samuel and Albertina (Tiledetski) T.; m. Mary Alice Wesche, Nov. 27, 1952; children: Linda, Marianna, Heinrich, Karl. BS, U. Sask., 1935, MS, 1937, LLD, 1973; PhD, U. Calif., 1940; PhD (hon.), Hebrew U. of Jerusalem, 1979; DSc (hon.), U. Chgo., 1983, Poly. Inst., N.Y., 1984, SUNY, 1985, U. Guelph, 1987; DSc honoris causa, Seton Hall U., 1988; Lajos Kossuth U. of Debrecen, Hungary, 1988; DSc, Northwestern U., 1990; hon. degree, U. Athens, 1993. Instr. U. Calif., 1940-41; instr., asst. prof. Cornell U., 1941-46; faculty U. Chgo., 1946-62, prof., 1952-62, chmn. dept. chemistry, 1955-59; prof. chemistry Stanford U., 1962—, Marguerite Blake Wilbur prof., 1976, chmn. dept., 1971-74; Baker lectr. Cornell U., 1965. Hon. mem. Hungarian Acad., Scis., 1988. Guggenheim fellow, 1949, 55; recipient Harrison Howe award, 1961, Chandler medal Columbia U., 1964, F. P. Dwyer medal U. NSW, Australia, 1973, Nat. medal of Sci., 1976, 77, Allied Chem. award for Excellence in Grad. Tchg. and Innovative Sci., 1979, Nobel prize in Chemistry, 1983, Bailar medal U. Ill., 1983, Robert A. Welch Found. award in Chemistry, 1983, Disting. Achievement award Internat. Precious Metals Inst., 1986, Brazilian Order of Sci. Merit award, 1994. Fellow Royal Soc. Chemistry (hon.), Indian Chem. Soc. (hon.); mem. NAS (award in chem. scis. 1983), Am. Acad. Arts and Scis., Am. Chem. Soc. (Kirkwood award New Haven sect. 1965, award for nuclear applications in chemistry 1955, Nichols medal N.Y. sect. 1971, Willard Gibbs medal Chgo. sect. 1971, Disting. Svc. in Advancement Inorganic Chemistry award 1967, T.W. Richards medal NE sect. 1980, Monsanto Co. award in inorganic chemistry 1981, Linus Pauling award Puget Sound sect. 1981, Priestley medal 1985, Oesper award Cin. sect. 1986, G.M. Kosolapoff award Auburn sect. 1990), Royal Physiographical Soc. of Lund (fgn. mem.), Am. Philos. Soc., Finnish Acad. Sci. and Letters, Royal Danish Acad. Scis. and Letters, Coll. Chemists of Catalonia and Beleares (hon.), Can. Soc. Chemistry (hon.), Hungarian Acad. Scis. (hon. mem.), Royal Soc. (fgn. mem.), Brazilian Acad. Scis. (corr.), Engring. Acad. Japan (fgn. assoc.), Australian Acad. Scis. (corr.), Chem. Soc. Japan (hon. mem. 1993), Phi Beta Kappa, Sigma Xi, Phi Lambda Upsilon (hon.). Office: Stanford U Dept Chemistry Stanford CA 94305

TAUCK, DAVID LAWRENCE, neurobiologist; b. Dearborn, Mich., June 7, 1956; s. William Howard and Helen Jean Tauck. AB, Middlebury (Vt.) Coll., 1977; PhD, Duke U., 1983. Postdoctoral fellow Stanford (Calif.) U., 1983-85, Harvard U.-Children's Hosp., Boston, 1985-87; asst. prof. biology Santa Clara (Calif.) U., 1987-93, assoc. prof., 1993—; ad hoc reviewer Benjamin Cummings Pub. Co., Redwood City, Calif., 1991—; reviewer NSF Aviation, Space and Environ. Medicine, Neurosci., Wadsworth Pub. Co., Belmont, Calif. Contbr. articles to profl. jours. Recipient Nat. Rsch. Svc. award Pub. Health Svc., 1978, 85; Pilot Rsch. grantee Alzheimer's Assn., 1990. Mem. AAAS, Soc. Neurosci., Internat. Brain Rsch. Orgn., N.Y. Acad. Sci., Phi Beta Kappa. Office: Santa Clara U Biology Dept Santa Clara CA 95053

TAUER, PAUL E., mayor, educator; b. 1935; m. Katherine Eldredge, Sept. 1, 1956; children: Paul E. Jr., Edward, Roch, Eugene, Kathryn, Tammie, Andrew, Timothy. BA in Historyand Edn., Regis Coll., 1961; MA in Edn. Adminstrn., U. No. Colo., 1964. Tchr. Denver Pub. Schs., 1961-92; ret., 1992. Mayor City of Aurora, Colo., 1987—, mem. Aurora City Coun., 1979-1987; mem. Adams County Coordinating Com., Gov.'s Met. Transp. Roundtable; active Aurora airport coms. Mem. Noise. Office: Office of Mayor 1470 S Havana St Aurora CO 80012-4014

TAULBEE, AMY LOUISE, college administrator; b. Washington, Feb. 2, 1963; d. John Earl and Sylvia Ida (Beer) T. BA, Stanford U., 1985; MDiv, Fuller Theol. Sem., Pasadena, Calif., 1992. Coll. asst. Menlo Park (Calif.) Presbyn. Ch., 1985-88; pres. student govt. Sch. of Theol. Fuller Theol. Sem., Pasadena, Calif., 1989-90, dir. academic advising, 1990-93; dir. found. and corp. rels. Pomona Coll., Claremont, Calif., 1993—. Recipient Pres.'s award Fuller Theol. Sem., 1992. Mem. Coun. for Advancement and Support of Edn., L.A. Jr. C. of C. Presbyterian. Office: Pomona Coll 550 N College Ave Claremont CA 91711

TAUNTON, KATHRYN JAYNE, accountant; b. Thomaston, Ga., Nov. 3, 1953; d. Mack Doudal and Martha Jayne (Goolsby) T. AA, Cypress Coll., 1973; BA in Accounting, Calif. State U., 1977. Circulation clk. Buena Park Library Dist., Buena Park, Calif., 1973-76; account supr. ORCO State Employees Credit Union, Santa Ana, Calif., 1977-78, Santa Ana City Credit Union, 1978-79; self employed Reliable Credit Union Service, Buena Park, 1979—.

TAUSIG, MICHAEL ROBERT, college administrator, higher education planning consultant; b. L.A., May 3, 1948; s. Maurice James and Georgia Ann (Bullgreen) T.; m. Cheryl Irvin, Jan. 30, 1972; children: Michael Robert Jr., Matthew Paul. BA in Music, Whittier Coll., 1971; MA, Calif. State U., Sacramento, 1973; ABD, Nova U., 1987. Dir. summer music programs Anaheim (Calif.) Arts Dept., 1968-73; tchr. music Borrego Springs (Calif.) High Sch., 1973-75; div. chmn., asst. to v.p. instrn. Napa (Calif.) Valley Coll., 1975-88; v.p. planning and devel. Mt. San Jacinto (Calif.) Coll., 1988-92; v.p. student svcs., 1994—; Calif. chief Student Svcs. Officers; dir. C.C.'s Facilities Coalition. Author: Fundamentals of Music, 1985. Chmn., pres. Napa County Arts Coun., 1985; chmn. spl. issues San Jacinto Planning Commn., 1990-91; elder Presbyn. Ch., Napa, 1985-87. Mem. Nat. Coun. Rsch. and Planning, Rsch. and Planning Group for Calif., C.C., Kiwanis (bd. dirs. Hemet, Calif. 1990—, pres.-elect 1993—, pres. 1994-95). Republican. Office: Mt San Jacinto Coll 1499 N State St San Jacinto CA 92583-2325

TAUSSIG, H. ARTHUR, film analyst, film and photography educator; b. L.A.; s. Ervin and Elsie (Elsner) T. BA, U. Calif. Berkeley, 1963; MS, UCLA, 1971; PhD, 1972. Prof. Orange Coast Coll., Costa Mesa, Calif., 1973—; adjunct curator film Newport Harbor Art Mus., Newport Beach, Calif., 1991—. Editor The Film Analyst Jour.; contbr. articles to profl. jours. Fellow NEA, 1975. Mem. Assn. Psychol. Types, Mensa. Home: 2404 Narbonne Way Costa Mesa CA 92627-1424 Office: Orange Coast College 2701 Fairview Rd Costa Mesa CA 92626-5563

TAUSSIG, ROBERT TRIMBLE, engineering executive; b. St. Louis, Apr. 26, 1938; s. Joseph Bondi and Frances Shackleford (McConnell) T.; m. Judith Ann Pryor, July 13, 1963; 1 child, Emily Barr. BA, Harvard Coll., 1960; MA, Columbia U., 1963, PhD, 1965. Rsch. assoc. Columbia U., N.Y.C., 1965-66, Inst. for Plasma Physics, Nagoya, Japan, 1966-67; lectr. Harvard U., Cambridge, Mass., 1968-69; assoc. prof. Sch. of Engring. Columbia U., 1969-75; v.p. Spectra Tech., Inc., Bellevue, Wash., 1975-90; bus. devel. mgr. Bechtel Rsch. and Devel., San Francisco, 1990-92, mgr. applied physics, 1992—; cons. Allerton Press, N.Y.C., 1974-76, Edison Electric Inst., N.Y.C., 1974-75; bd. dirs. Spectra Tech., Inc., Bellevue. Contbg. author: Efficient Electricity Use, 1976; referee and assoc. editor: Energy jour., 1978. Intern sponsor Seattle (Wash.) Sch. System, 1980-88. Recipient award for Acad. Excellence, Harvard Coll., 1957-58. Mem. IEEE, ASME, ANS. Democrat. Presbyterian. Office: The Bechtel Corp 50 Beale St San Francisco CA 94105-1813

TAVEGGIA, THOMAS CHARLES, management educator, management consultant; b. Oak Lawn, Ill., June 15, 1943; s. Thomas Angelo and Eunice Louise (Harriss) T.; m. Brigitte I. Adams, Jan. 23, 1965; children—Michaela, Francesca. BS, Ill. Inst. Tech., 1965; MA, U. Oreg., 1968, PhD, 1971. Prof., U. Oreg., Eugene, 1970, U. B.C. (Can.), Vancouver, 1970-73, U. Calif.-Irvine, 1973-74, Ill. Inst. Tech., Chgo., 1974-77; mgmt. cons. Towers, Perrin, Forster & Crosby, Chgo., 1977-80; ptnr. Manplan Cons., Chgo., 1980-81; ptnr. Coopers & Lybrand, San Francisco, 1981-86; ptnr. Touche Ross, San Francisco, 1986-88; prof. Calif. Sch. Profl. Psychology, Berkeley, 1988—. NDEA Title IV fellow, 1967-71; U. B.C. faculty research grantee, 1970, 71, 73. Faculty Rsch. grantee Calif. Sch. Profl. Psychology, 1993-94. Mem. Acad. Mgmt. Soc., Am. Sociol. Assn., Nat. Bur. Profl. Mgmt. Cons., Human Resource Mgmt. Soc., Inst. Mgmt. Cons. Presbyterian. Author: (with R. Dubin and R. Arends) From Family and School To Work, 1967; (with Dubin) The Teaching-Learning Paradox: A Comparative Analysis of College Teaching Methods, 1968; (with Dubin and R.A. Hedley) The Medium May Be Related to the Message: College Instruction by TV, 1969; contbr. numerous articles to books and profl. jours. Home: 2188 Lariat Ln Walnut Creek CA 94596-6515 Office: Calif Sch Profl Psychology 1005 Atlantic Ave Alameda CA 94501-1148

TAVENNER, PATRICIA MAY, artist, printmaker; b. Doster, Mich.; d. Raymond Paul and Ruth Viola T. BA, Mich. State U.; MFA, Calif. Coll. Arts and Crafts. Mem. faculty art U. Calif., Berkeley Extention, 1967—; asst. prof. art and painting U. Calif., Davis, 1987; lectr. in field. Solo show U. Calif., Berkeley, 1985, 89, 92; participant exhbns. Mus. Contemporary Crafts, N.Y.C., 1971, First Environ., Paris, 1974, Site Sculpture, Mills. Coll., Oakland, Calif., 1982, OHS Parsens, L.A., 1982, Atkins Mus. Fine Arts, Kansas City, Mo., Mus. Fine Arts, Budapest, Hungary, Atlanta Coll. of Art, 1988, Davidson Art Gallery, Seattle, 1989, 93, Mus. Modern Kunst, Weddle, Germany, 1989; commns. include facade Mus. Contemporary Crafts, N.Y.C., 1971, sect. of wall Can. Nat. Rsch. Libr., Ottawa, Ont., 1973; works represented San Francisco Mus. Modern Art., Royal Mus. Fine Art, Antwerp, Belgium, Mus. of Modern Art, N.Y.C., Cornell U., Ithica, N.Y.; contbr. to publs. including Art et Communication Marginale, 1974, Art: A Womans Sensibility, 1975, Rubber Stamp Art, 1978, California Artists Cook Book, Correspondence Art, 1985, Art in the San Francisco Bay Area, 1985, U. Calif. Press, Timbres des Artists French Postal Mus., Paris, France, 1994, Collage Techniques, 1994, Women Artists' News, 1989. Mem. Women's Caucus for Art, Pro Arts, Internat. Sculpture Ctr, Coll. Art Assn. Office: 55 Laguna St San Francisco CA 94102-6232

TAVERNA, RODNEY ELWARD, financial services company executive; b. Springfield, Ill., Aug. 8, 1947; s. Jerome Thomas and Virginia (Holcomb) T.; m. Cheryl Ann Walters, Sept. 4, 1968 (div. 1983); children: Lara Lyn, Melinda Marie, Ryan Thomas; m. Caroline Whiffen, Apr. 1985. BA, U. Mo., 1969; MBA in Fin., Nat. U., 1988. Commd. 2d lt., supply officer USMC, 1969, advanced through grades to maj., 1979; supply officer Central Svcs. Agy., Danang, Vietnam, 1970-71, Marine Air Control Squadron, Futenma, Okinawa, 1977-78; logistics officer Hdqrs. Marine Corps Recruit Depot, Paris Island, S.C., 1972-75; support officer Marine Barracks, Treasure Island, San Francisco, 1975-77; regimental supply officer 1st Marine Div., Camp Pendleton, Calif., 1978-79; brigade supply officer 1st Marine Brigade, Kaneohe Bay, Hawaii, 1980-82; exec. officer 1st Maintenance Bn., Camp Pendleton, 1982-85; asst div. supply officer 1st Marine Div., 1985-88; pres. Freedom Fin. Group, 1991—; br. mgr. WMA Securities, Inc., 1991—; owner, mgr. Opportunities Unltd., Oceanside, Calif., 1985-91; cons. Incentive Leasing Corp., San Diego, 1985-86, The Profit Ctr., Santa Ana, Calif., 1991; founding mgr. Meditrend Internat., San Diego, 1987-88; founding dir. Am. 3-D Corp., Cathedral City, Calif., 1990-91. Republican. Home and Office: 1632 Avenida Andante Oceanside CA 92056-6905

TAVOULARIS, MARJORIE OSTERWISE, psychiatrist; b. Mt. Pleasant, Pa., May 28, 1938; d. Robert Russell and Violet Jane (Watson) Osterwise; m. James Harry Tavoularis, May 23, 1962 (div. 1987); children: Laura, Suzanne, Diana, Patricia. BS, U. Pitts., 1961; MD, Pitts. Pschomalytic Inst., 1966; postgrad., Pitts. Psychiat. Inst., 1976-85, So. Calif. Psychomalytic Inst., 1986—. Rotating intern St. Francis Gen. Hosp., 1966-67; resident in psychiatry U. Pitts. Western Psychiat. Inst., 1967-70; staff psychiatrist St. Frances Med. Ctr., Pitts., 1972-85, Kern Med. Ctr., Bakersfield, Calif., 1986-89; sr. psychiatrist Calif. Correctional Inst., Teachapi, 1989-91, Calif. Parole Office, Bakersfield, 1991—; psychiatrist pvt. practice, Pitts. & Bakersfield, 1972—. Mem. Am. Psychiat. Assn., Ctrl. Calif. Psychiat. Soc., Kern County Med. Soc., Pa. Psychiat. Soc. (pres. 1984-85), Pitts. Psychiat. Soc. (pres. 1981-82). Office: Bakersfield Parole Office 1128 Truxtun Ave Bakersfield CA 93301-4618

TAYLOR, BARRY LLEWELLYN, microbiologist, educator; b. Sydney, Australia, May 7, 1937; came to U.S., 1967; s. Fredrick Llewelyn and Vera Lavina (Clarke) T.; m. Desmyrna Ruth Tolhurst, Jan. 4, 1961; children: Lyndon, Nerida, Darrin. BA, Avondale Coll., Cooranbong, New South Wales, 1959; BSc with honors, U. New South Wales, Sydney, 1966; PhD, Case Western Res. U., 1973; postgrad., U. Calif., Berkeley, 1973-75. Vis. postdoctoral fellow Australian Nat. U., Canberra, 1975-76; asst. prof. biochemistry Loma Linda (Calif.) U., 1976-78, assoc. prof. biochemistry, 1978-83, prof. biochemistry, 1983—, prof., chmn. dept. microbiology, 1988—, interim dir. Ctr. for Molecular Biology, 1989-94. Contbr. articles to profl. publs. Rsch. grantee Am. Heart Assn., 1978-85, NIH, 1981—. Mem. Am. Soc. Microbiology, Am. Soc. Biochemistry and Molecular Biology. Office: Loma Linda U Dept Microbiology Loma Linda CA 92350

TAYLOR, BRUCE, agricultural products executive; b. 1956. BS, UC Berkeley; MBA, Harvard U. Pres. Freshco Internat. Corp., Salinas, CA, 1979—; co-Chmn. Bd. Fresh Internat. Corp., Salinas, CA, 1981—. Office: Fresh Internat Corp 1020 Merrill St Salinas CA 93901*

TAYLOR, CARROLL STRIBLING, lawyer; b. Port Chester, N.Y., Jan. 14, 1944; s. William H. Jr. and Anna P. (Stribling) T.; m. Nancy S. Tyson, Apr. 7, 1968; children: Heather, Kimberly, Tori, Tiffany, Tacy. AB, Yale U., 1965; JD, U. Calif., Berkeley, 1968. Bar: Hawaii 1969, Calif. 1969, U.S. Dist. Ct. Hawaii 1969, U.S. Dist. Ct. (cen. dist.) Calif. 1975, U.S. Ct. Appeals (9th cir.) 1975. Researcher Legis. Reference Bur., Honolulu, 1968-70; reporter Jud. Coun. Probate Code Revision Project, Honolulu, 1970-71; assoc. Chun, Kerr & Dodd, Honolulu, 1971-75; ptnr. Hamilton & Taylor, Honolulu, 1975-80; officer, dir. Char, Hamilton, Taylor & Thom, Honolulu, 1980-82, Carroll S. Taylor Atty. at Law, A Law Corp., Honolulu, 1982-86; ptnr. Taylor & Leong, Honolulu, 1986-91, Taylor, Leong & Chee, Honolulu, 1991—; adj. prof. Richardson Sch. Law U. Hawaii, Honolulu, 1981-86, 88-90; mem. Disciplinary bd. of Supreme Ct. of Hawaii, 1994—. Fellow Am. Coll. Trust and Estate Counsel; mem. ABA, Calif. Bar Assn., Hawaii Bar Assn., Hawaii Inst. Continuing Legal Edn. (pres. 1986-88), Pla. Club (Honolulu). Episcopalian. Home: 46-429 Hololio St Kaneohe HI 96744-4225 Office: 737 Bishop St Ste 2060 Honolulu HI 96813-3211

TAYLOR, CHARLES E., biologist; b. Chgo., Sept. 9, 1945; s. Stewart Ferguson and Barbara (Ellett) T.; m. Minna Glushiens, June 22, 1969. AB, U. Calif., 1968; PhD, SUNY, Stony Brook, 1973. Prof. U. Calif., Riverside, 1974-80, UCLA, 1980—; expert witness in genetic fingerprinting, 1989—. Mem. Santa Fe Inst. Office: Dept Biology UCLA 405 Hilgard Ave Los Angeles CA 90024-1301

TAYLOR, CYNTHIA HINKEL, English literature educator; b. Lovell, Wyo., Dec. 23, 1954; s. Robert Harold Hinkel and Sandra Tippetts Dodds; m. Ted Michael Taylor, Dec. 31, 1977. B of English, U. Idaho, 1977, M of English, 1979; Phd in English, U. Minn., 1993. Instrnl. asst. U. Idaho, Moscow, 1977-79; teaching asst. U. Minn., Mpls., 1979-89, adminstrv. fellow, 1987-89; asst. prof. English U. So. Colo., Pueblo, 1989—. Mem. MLA, Rocky Mountain MLA (pres. we. lit. sect. 1991), We. Lit. Assn., Nat. Women's Studies Assn., Phi Beta Kappa, Sigma Tau Delta. Democrat. Home: 18 Arrowsmith Dr Pueblo CO 81008-1849 Office: U So Colo Pueblo CO 81001

TAYLOR, DARLA JEAN, nurse; b. L.A., Feb. 21, 1959; d. Samuel and Darlene Taylor. AS, Compton Community Coll., 1983. Pediatric nurse Harbor UCLA Med. Ctr., Torrance, Calif., 1983-86; pediatric nurse U. So. Calif., L.A., 1986-89, recovery rm. nurse, 1989-91, health facilities evaluator I, 1991—. Author, editor: (video) Living With Illness as a Teenager, 1985. author: (manuel) Medications Policy and Procedures, 1986. Mem. Black Nurses Assn. Office: 600 S Commonwealth Ave Ste 800 Los Angeles CA 90005-4018

TAYLOR, DENNIS MERRILL, state official; b. Richmond, Calif., July 8, 1946; s. Merrill Edward and Bettey (Orthman) T.; m. Joan South, Oct. 25, 1974; children—Morgan Clare, Merrill South. B.A., U. Kans., 1968; postgrad. U. Mont., 1976-82. Vista vol. ACTION, Helena, Mont., 1972-74; health planner Dept. Health and Environ. Scis., Helena, 1974-76; research Mont. Legis. Council, Helena, 1974-80; dir. Dept. Budget and Adminstrn., Helena, 1980-81; dir. Mont. State Personnel Div., Helena, 1981-85, dir. Mont. Devel. Disabilities Div., Helena, 1985-90, dep. dir. dept. family svcs., Helena, 1990—; chief adminstrv. officer City of Missoula, Mont., 1990-93; dep. dir., chief of staff Mont. dept. justice, Helena, 1993—; chmn. Mgmt. Devel. Council, Helena, 1983-85; chmn. State Employees Group Benefits Council, 1981-91; mem. Gov.'s adv. council on Health Care Cost Containment, Mont., 1985-88. Chmn. Lewis and Clark City-County Bd. Health, 1979-83, Helena Citizens Council, 1975-77, 84-89; chmn. bd. trustees Broad Valley Library Fedn., 1985-88; del. Democratic Nat. Conv., San Francisco, 1984, 88; precinct committeeman Lewis and Clark County Dem. Central Com., Helena, 1975-85, chmn. 1985-87, state committeeman 1987-89, state rules com., 1984—; trustee Lewis & Clark Library Bd., 1985—, vice chmn., 1987-88; commr. Helena Reg. Airport Authority, 1994—;mem. bd. dirs. Mont. Spl. Olympics, 1987-93; pres. Mont. Coun. for Families, Inc., 1991-94, mem. bd. dirs. 1991—; mem. bd. dirs. Mont. Youth Homes, Inc., 1994—; trustee Helena Sch. Dist. # 1, 1990-91. Served to 1st lt. USMC, 1968-71, Vietnam. Recipient Disting. Community Service award Helena Jaycees, 1981; named Employee of Yr. Helena area C. of C., 1983. Mem. Sigma Alpha Epsilon, Omicron Delta Kappa. Lodge: Rotary. Home: 2607 Gold Rush Ave Helena MT 59601-5622 Office: Dept Justice PO Box 201401 215 N Sanders St Helena MT 59601-4522

TAYLOR, FREDERICK WILLIAM, JR., lawyer; b. Cleve., Oct. 21, 1933; s. Frederick William Sr. and Marguerite Elizabeth (Kistler) T.; m Mary Phyllis Osborne, June 1, 1985. BA in History, U. Fla., 1957; MA in Near East Studies, U. Mich., 1959; JD cum laude, NYU, 1967. Bar: N.Y. 1968, Calif. 1969, U.S. Dist. Ct. (cen. dist.) Calif. 1969. Govt. rels. rep. Arabian Am. Oil Co., Dhahran, Saudi Arabia, 1959-63; oil supply coord. Arabian Am. Oil Co., N.Y.C., 1963-68; sr. counsel Arabian Am. Oil Co., Dhahran, 1969-71, gen. mgr. govt. rels. orgn., 1971-74, v.p. indsl. rels., 1974-78; assoc. O'Melveny & Myers, L.A., 1968-69; ptnr. Burt & Taylor, Marblehead, Mass., 1978-80; pres., chief exec. officer nat. med. enterprises Internat. Group, L.A., 1980-82; counsel Chadbourne, Parke & Afridi, United Arab Emirates, 1982-84; ptnr. Sidley & Austin, Cairo, 1984-87, Singapore, 1987-93; spl. counsel Heller Ehrman White & McAuliffe, L.A. and Singapore, 1993-95; legal advisor AT&T Internat. (Saudi Arabia), Riyadh, Saudi Arabia, 1995—. Contbr. articles to profl. jours. Mem. ABA, Calif. Bar Assn., Order of Coif, Singapore Cricket Club, Tanglin Club, Chanqi Sailinq Club, American Club. Home: Box 6942 Taos NM 87571 Office: AT&T Internat, PO Box 4945 al Mutlaq Bldg Sitteen St, Riyadh 11412, Saudi Arabia

TAYLOR, GARY L., federal judge; b. 1938. AB, UCLA, 1960, JD, 1963. Assoc. Wenke, Taylor, Evans & Ikola, 1965-86; judge Orange County Superior Ct., 1986-90, U.S. Dist. Ct. (ctrl. dist.) Calif., Santa Ana, 1990—. With U.S. Army, 1964-66. Mem. Am. Coll. Trial Lawyers, State Bar Calif., Orange County Bar Assn. (bd. dirs. 1980-82, founder, chmn. bus. litigation com., Disting. Svc. award 1983). *

TAYLOR, GEORGE ALLEN, advertising agency executive; b. Lake City, Iowa, Oct. 26, 1906; s. Bertrand Franklin and Mabel (Minard) T.; m. Regina Helen Wickland, July 3, 1938 (div. 1956). PhB in Fine Arts, Northwestern U., 1947, MEd, 1951, postgrad., 1951-54; art edn. diploma, U. No. Iowa, 1926. Art supr. pub. schs. Indianola, Iowa, 1926-29; instr. art Simpson Coll., Indianola, 1926-29; designer Modern Art Studios, Chgo., 1929-30; display designer W.J. Rankin Corp., Chgo., 1930-35; creative dir. Arthur Meyerhoff Assocs., Inc., Milw., 1935-38; br. mgr. Arthur Meyerhoff Assocs., Inc., L.A., 1938-42; account exec. Arthur Meyerhoff Assocs., Inc., Chgo., 1942-59, account supr., 1959-61, v.p. adminstrn., 1961-65, vice chmn., 1965-80; pres. GATA Ltd.; lectr. semantics Ill. Inst. Tech., Chgo., 1947-50, Northwestern U. Sch. Commerce, 1948. Lyricist popular songs. Reader Recs. for Blind, Inc., 1956-94, CRIS Radio, 1981-85; mem. Chgo. Architecture Found., Landmarks Preservation Coun. Ill. Recipient 1st place awards in copy and layout L.A. Advt. Club, 1940. Mem. AAAS, Friends of Downtown, Art Inst. Chgo. Home (summer): 1212 N Lake Shore Dr Apt 29a-s Chicago IL 60610-2371 Home (winter): 1212 N Lake Shore Dr Apt 29as Chicago IL 60610-2375

TAYLOR, GEORGE FREDERICK, newspaper publisher, editor; b. Portland, Oreg., Feb. 28, 1928; s. George Noble and Ida Louise (Dixon) T.; m. Georga Bray, Oct. 6, 1951; children—Amelia Ruth, Ross Noble. B.S., U. Oreg., 1950. Reporter Astoria (Oreg.) Budget, 1950-52, Portland Oregonian, 1952-54; copy reader Wall St. Jour., 1954-55, reporter, 1957-59, Detroit Bur. chief, 1959-64, Washington corr., 1964-68; asst. mng. editor Wall St. Jour., San Francisco, 1968-69; mng. editor Wall St. Jour., N.Y.C., 1970-77, exec. editor, 1977-86; pub. North Bend (Oreg.) News, 1986—, Prime Time, 1987—, Coquille Valley Sentinel, 1989—. Served to lt. USAF, 1955-57. Office: 1 Bartons Aly Coquille OR 97423-1270

TAYLOR, GREGORY HOBBS, publisher; b. Joplin, Mo., Jan. 27, 1946; s. George Vincent and Beverly (Sharp) T.; m. Sarah Hughes, Mar. 9, 1968; children: Gregory Hughes, Matthew Sharp. BS in Marketing, U. Mo., 1970. Mktg. rep. Internat. Paper Sales Co., Chgo., 1970-72; asst. to gen. mgr. Joplin (Mo.) Globe, 1973-77; gen. mgr. The Joplin (Mo.) Globe, 1979-86; asst. to pub. The News Times, Danbury, Conn., 1977-79; pub. Sharon (Pa.) Herald, 1986-93, Allied News, Grove City, Pa., 1986-93; pres., pub. Mail Tribune, Medford, Oreg., 1993—; ptnr. C&T Land Co., 1988—. Chmn. Sharon chpt. United Way, 1992, bd. dirs., 1995—; vice chmn. Indsl. Devel. Authority, Sharon, 1990; bd. dirs. So. Oreg. State Coll. Found., 1995—, Providence Hosp., 1995—. With U.S. Army, 1963-67. Mem. Mo. Pub. Assn. (bd. dirs. 1984—), Pa. Newspaper Pub. Assn. (bd. dirs.), Oreg. Newspaper Pub. Assn. (bd. dirs.), Am. Newspaper Pub. Assn., Sharon Social Fishing Club, Subscribers Encouraging Econ. Devel. (vice chmn. 1989—), Twin Hills Country Club (pres. 1985), Univ. Club of Medford, Rogue Valley Country Club. Republican. Home: 1278 Gardner Way Medford OR 97504-9300 Office: Mail Tribune 111 N Fir St Medford OR 97501-2772

TAYLOR, GUY WATSON, symphonic conductor; b. Anniston, Ala., Dec. 25, 1919; s. Stokely Brackston and Ola Mae (Shaw) T.; m. Renee Lifton, Oct. 19, 1947; children: Eric Anthony, Ellen Jane. Diploma, Birmingham Conservatory of Music, 1941, Juilliard Sch. Music, 1948; pvt. studies and workshops with, Dimitri Mitropoulos, 1941-42, L'Ecole Monteux, 1949, Eugene Ormandy, 1953, George Szell, 1956. Conductor Springfield (Ohio) Symphony Orch., 1948-51, Nashville Symphony Orch., 1951-59, Phoenix Symphony Orch., 1959-69, Fresno Philharmonic Orch., 1969-84; guest conductor, U.S., Gt. Britain, Philippines, P.R., Can. and Mexico City; musical commentator Springfield News & Sun, 1948-51, Ariz. Republic, 1959-61, Fresno Bee, 1970-76. Has appeared on, BBC Radio, CBS-TV. Served with AUS, 1942-45. Recipient Conductor Recognition award Am. Symphony Orch. League, 1960, Alice M. Ditson Orch. award, 1961, citation for adventuresome programming of contemporary music ASCAP, 1977. Mem. Am. Symphony Orch. League, Phi Mu Alpha Sinfonia.

TAYLOR, HENRY STUART, financial consultant; b. Syracuse, N.Y., Oct. 21, 1931; s. Stuart Baldwin and Margurite (Brown) T.; m. Mira Takla, Aug. 14, 1970 (div. Sept 1989); children: Karima Ashley, Sharifa Naima. BA, Colgate U., 1957; MA, London Sch. Econs., 1960; MBA, Stanford U., 1959. Asst. to chmn. IBM Corp., 1950-52; assoc. Stewart, Dougall & Assocs., 1960-62; sr. mktg. cons. Economist Intelligence Unit Ltd., London, 1962-64; chmn., founder Taylor, Nelson Group, Ltd., Ewell, Eng., 1964-76; cons., advisor NISR Enterprises Ltd., London, 1976-82; spl. advisor to ptnrs. Karifa Capital Corp., Geneva, Switzerland, 1983—. Served in U.S. Army, 1952-54. Home: PO Box 256 Menlo Park CA 94026-0256

TAYLOR, HOURIE LEE, law enforcement official; b. L.A., July 3, 1946; s. Edward Lee and Mariah (Matthews) T.; m. Elouise Webb, March 11, 1967 (div. July 1977); children: Kimberly Michelle, Chonna Rachelle; m. Yolanda McCarty, May 30, 1987; 1 child, Lashawn Nichelle. AA in Police Sci., Compton C.C., 1972; cert. Teaching and Supervisory Techniques, El Camino Coll., Gardena; BS in Criminal Justice, Calif. State U., Long Beach, 1979; cert. in Acctg. and Computers, Cerritos Coll. Police officer Compton Police Dept., Calif., 1969-74, police sgt., 1974-88, police lt., 1988-90, police comdr., 1990-91, acting police chief, 1992-93, police chief, 1993—; cons. Calif. Dept. Justice, Sacramento, 1988-90, FBI, Va., 1990—, DEA, Va., 1990—; lectr. various agencies and instutions such as DEA, FBI, State of Calif. Dept. Justice, Calif. District Atty's Assn., Calif. Gang Investigators Assn, State of Alaska, State of N. Mex. and numerous others. Named Law Enforcement Officer of the Yr. Internat. Footprints Assn., 1990; recipient Calif. Youth Authority commendation, 1992, L.A. County Dist. Atty. Office commendation, 1992. Mem. NAACP, Nat. Orgn. Black Law Enforcement Execs., Southeast Police Chiefs Assn. (pres. 1994), L.A. County Police Chiefs Assn., Police Officers Assn. L.A. County, Compton Police Officers Assn. (bd. dirs, pres. 1969—). Democrat. Baptist.

TAYLOR, HUGH PETTINGILL, JR., geologist, educator; b. Holbrook, Ariz., Dec. 27, 1932; s. Hugh Pettingill and Genevieve (Fillerup) T.; m. Candis E. Hoffman, 1982. B.S., Calif. Inst. Tech., 1954; A.M., Harvard U., 1955; Ph.D., Calif. Inst. Tech., 1959. Asst. prof. geochemistry Pa. State U., 1960-62; mem. faculty div. geol. and planetary scis. Calif. Inst. Tech., 1962—, now prof. geology, Robert P. Sharp prof., 1981; Crosby vis. prof. M.I.T., 1978; vis. prof. Stanford U., 1981; William Smith lectr. Geol. Soc. London, 1976; Hofmann lectr. Harvard U., 1980; Cloos lectr. Johns Hopkins U., 1986; with U.S. Geol. Survey, Saudi Arabia, 1980-81. Author: The Oxygen Isotope Geochemistry of Igneous Rocks, 1968, Stable Isotopes in High Temperature Geological Processes, 1986, Stable Isotope Geochemistry, 1991; assoc. editor Bull. Geol. Soc. Am, 1969-71, Geochimica Cosmochimica Acta, 1971-76; editor Chem. Geology, 1985-91. Recipient Day medal Geol. Soc. Am., Vrey medal European Assn. Geochem., 1995. Fellow NAS, Soc. Econ. Geol., Geol. Soc. Am., Am. Geophys. Union, Mineral. Soc. Am. (councillor), Am. Acad. Arts and Scis.; mem. Geochem. Soc. (councillor). Republican.

TAYLOR, IRVING, mechanical engineer, consultant; b. Schenectady, N.Y., Oct. 25, 1912; s. John Bellamy and Marcia Estabrook (Jones) T.; m. Shirley Ann Milker, Dec. 22, 1943; children: Bronwen D., Marcia L., John I., Jerome E. BME, Cornell U., 1934. Registered profl. engr., N.Y., Mass., Calif. Test engr. Gen. Electric Co., Lynn, Mass., 1934-37; asst. mech. engr. M.W. Kellogg Co., N.Y.C., 1937-39; sect. head engring. dept. The Lummus Co., N.Y.C., 1939-57; research engr. Gilbert and Barker, West Springfield, Mass., 1957-58, Marquardt Corp., Ogden, Utah, 1958-60, Bechtel, Inc., San Francisco, 1960-77; cons. engr. Berkeley, Calif., 1977-91; adj. prof. Columbia U., 1950-60, NYU, 1950-60. Contbr. articles to profl. jours. Fellow ASME (life, Henry R. worthington medal 1990); mem. Pacific Energy Assn., Soaring Soc. Am. (life), Sigma Xi (assoc.). Unitarian. Home: 300 Deer Valley Rd Apt 2P San Rafael CA 94903-5514

TAYLOR, JACQUELINE SELF, state legislator; b. Thomas, Okla., Feb. 16, 1935; d. MArtin Richard and Bertha Inez (Murray) Self; m. Nelson Edwin Taylor, May 17, 1952; children: Lucinda Susan Shannon, Robin Melinda. BA in Social Work, Boise State U., 1971. Lic. social worker Idaho. Dir. vol. svcs. Idaho Dept. of Health & Welfare, Caldwell, 1971-77; dir. Clatsop County Assn. REtarded Citizens, Astoria, Oreg., 1980-81; ptnr., owner Johnson Drug Store, Warrenton, Oreg., 1984-92; state rep. Legis. Assembly State of Oreg., 1991-93. Bd. dirs. Pioneer House, Warrenton, 1992, Astoria C. of C., 1988-91, treas., 1988-91; civil svc. com. City of Astoria, 1988-91; mem. North Coast Women's Polit. Caucus, 1988 (named Outstanding Woman 1988), Oreg. Women's Polit. Caucus. Democrat. Home: 1324 Miller Ln Astoria OR 97103-3947 Office: Oreg State Legis State Capitol Salem OR 97310

TAYLOR, JAMES WALTER, marketing educator; b. St. Cloud, Minn., Feb. 15, 1933; s. James T. and Nina C. Taylor; m. Joanne Syktte, Feb. 3, 1956; children: Theodore James, Samuel Bennett, Christopher John. BBA, U. Minn., 1957; MBA, NYU, 1960; DBA, U. So. Calif., 1975. Mgr. research div. Atlantic Refining, Phila., 1960-65; dir. new product devel. Hunt-Wesson Foods, Fullerton, Calif., 1965-72; prof. mktg. Calif. State U., Fullerton, 1972—; cons. Smithkline Beecham Corp., Tokyo, Govt. of Portugal, Lisbon, Sealand Svcs., Seattle, KF Fackhandel, Stockholm. Author: Profitable New Product Strategies, 1984, How To Create A Winning Business Plan, 1986, Competitive Marketing Strategies, 1986, The 101 Best Performing Companies In America, 1987, How to Write A Successful Advertising Plan, 1988,

The Complete Manual for Developing Winning Strategic Plans, 1988, Every Manager's Survival Guide, 1989, Developing Winning Strategic Plans, 1990, How to Develop Successful Advertising Plans, 1993. Fulbright scholar Ministry of Industry, Lisbon, Portugal, 1986-87, U. We. Sydney, Australia, 1989-90; recipient Merit award Calif. State U., 1986-90. Mem. The Planning Forum, Am. Mktg. Assn., Strategic Mgmt. Assn., Assn. for Consumer Rsch., Acad. Mktg. Sci. Home: 3190 Mountain View Dr Laguna Beach CA 92651-2056 Office: Calif State U Dept of Mktg Nutwood at State College Fullerton CA 92634

TAYLOR, JANICE LARUE, elementary education educator; b. Salina, Utah, Nov. 15, 1946; d. Wallace Gustave and Arnelda (Murphy) Poulson; m. Roger Eldon Elkins, Aug. 26, 1967 (wid. Feb. 1990); children: Bobbi Jan, Becki LaRue, Brendi Mae, Wesly Eldon; m. Richard Don Taylor, Jan. 2, 1992; stepchildren: Jared, Renerah. BS, Brigham Young U., 1990; MA, U. Phoenix, 1993. ESL aide Plano (Tex.) Ind. Sch. Dist., 1983-87; tchr. second grade Alpine Sch. dist., Orem, Utah, 1989-90; tchr. sixth grade Provo (Utah) Sch. Dist., 1990—; arts specialist Maeser Elem., Provo, 1992—; profl. devel. com. Bonniville Uniserve, Provo, 1994; K-12 curriculum com. Provo Sch. Dist., 1994; P.E.A. rep. Provo Edn. Assn., 1994—. Co-author: Student Organizer, 1993-94. Artists-in-residence grantee Utah Arts Coun., Provo, 1994-95; career edn. grantee Provo Sch. dist., 1994-95. Mem. NEA, Utah Edn. Assn., Provo C. of C. (mem. bus. and edn. partnership com. 1994). Home: 1928 N 230 E Orem UT 84057-2255 Office: Maeser Elem 1505 500 E Provo UT 84606

TAYLOR, JEREMY MICHAEL GEORGE, statistician, educator; b. Newbury, Eng., Dec. 25, 1956; came to U.S., 1979; s. Arthur Eric and Ruth Mary (Elliott) T.; m. Elizabeth Pennywitt Korns, Dec. 27, 1986; children: Evan George, Graham Patrick. BA, Cambridge (Eng.) Coll., 1978, diploma in stats., 1979, MA, 1981; PhD in Stats., U. Calif., Berkeley, 1983. Asst. prof., dept. biostats, radiation oncology UCLA, 1983-89, assoc. prof., dept. biostats, 1989-93, prof., dept. biostats, 1993—. Contbr. articles to statistics and medical jours. Grantee NIH, Am. Found. for AIDS Rsch., U. Calif. AIDS Rsch. Program. Mem. Royal Stats. Soc., Am. Stats. Assn., Radiation Rsch. Soc., Inst. of Math. Stats., Bernoulli Soc. Office: Dept Biostats UCLA Sch of Pub Health Los Angeles CA 90095 Home: 13025 Bloomfield St Studio City CA 91604-1404

TAYLOR, JOHN LOCKHART, city official; b. N.Y.C., Nov. 4, 1927; s. Floyd and Marian (Lockhart) T.; m. Barbara Becker, July 19, 1952; children: Catherine, Robert, William, Susan. A.B., Middlebury Coll., 1952; M.Govtl. Adminstrn., U. Pa., 1956. Reporter Providence Jour.-Bull., 1952-54; adminstrv. intern City of Xenia, Ohio, 1955-56; mcpl. mgr. Borough of Narberth, Pa., 1956-60, Twp. of Lakewood, N.J., 1960-64; asst. city mgr. Fresno, Calif., 1964-65; city mgr., 1965-68, Kansas City, Mo., 1968-74, Berkeley, Calif., 1974-76; lectr. U. Pa., 1957-58, Golden Gate U., 1977; sr. urban mgmt. specialist Stanford Research Inst., 1977-80; dir. Internat. Devel. Center, 1980-82; clk. of bd. suprs. City of San Francisco, 1982—; pres. Calif. Clks. Bd. Suprs. Assn., 1988-89. Served with USN, 1945-48. Mem. Internat. City Mgrs. Assn., Am. Soc. Pub. Adminstrn., Mcpl. Execs. Assn. (pres. 1991-93). Home: 2133 Stockton St San Francisco CA 94133-2067 Office: City Hall 401 Van Ness Ave San Francisco CA 94102-4522

TAYLOR, JOHN O'MARA, engineer; b. Birmingham, U.K., Aug. 11, 1953; came to U.S., 1990; s. Dennis O. and Renee (Franklin) T. BSc, U. Aston, Birmingham, 1975; PhD, U. Birmingham, Birmingham, 1983. Registered profl. engr., England. Core metallurgist Rolls Royce & Assocs., Derby, U.K., 1979-80; section mgr. GKN Tech. Ltd., Wolverhampton, U.K., 1980-90; tech. cons. Rohr Inc., Chula Vista, Calif., 1990—. Author (patent application) Crack Detecting Apparatus, 1989. Mem. British Inst. of NDT, Acoustic Emission Working Group. Home: 5290 Vickie Dr San Diego CA 92109-1332

TAYLOR, JUDITH ANN, sales executive; b. Sheridan, Wyo., July 9, 1944; d. Milo G. and Eleanor M. (Wood) Rinker; m. George I. Taylor, Sept. 15, 1962; children: Monte G., Bret A. Fashion dept. mgr. Montgomery Ward, Sheridan, 1968-73; pers. mgr., asst. mgr. Dan's Ranchwear, Sheridan, 1973-80; sales/prodn. coord. KWYO Radio, Sheridan, 1981-83; sales mgr., promotions coord. KROE Radio, Sheridan, 1984—; mng. editor BOUNTY Publ., 1993—; notary pub. State of Wyo., 1985—; lectr., instr. BSA Merit U.; lectr. acad. achievement LVA Adv. Bd., 1993—, instr. Tongue River Middle Sch. Academic Enrichmen t Program, 1994-95; S.C. Ambs., 1980—, pres., 1995—. mng. editor BOUNTY Publ., 1993—. Sec.-treas. Sheridan County Centennial Com., 1986-89; local sec.-treas. Wyo. Centennial Com., Sheridan, 1986-90; exec. dir. Sheridan-Wyo. Rodeo Bd., 1983—; bd. dirs. Sheridan County Fair Bd., 1991—, treas., 1995—; bd. dirs. "Christmas in April" Sheridan County, 1992—; mem. WJTP Coun., Cheyenne, 1990-92; mem. adv. coun. Tutor-Literacy Vols. of Am., 1993—; Mrs. Santa Claus for local groups; vol. coord. AIDS Quilt. Mem. Wyo. Assn. Broadcasters, S.C. C. of C. (dir. 1988—, pres. 1989-91), UMWA Aux. (pres. 1982-89), Kiwanis (v.p. 1992—, pres.-elect 1993, pres. 1994). Democrat. Christian Ch. Home: 98 Decker Rd Sheridan WY 82801-9612 Office: KROE AM PO Box 5086 Sheridan WY 82801-1386

TAYLOR, KENDRICK JAY, microbiologist; b. Manhattan, Mont., Mar. 17, 1914; s. William Henry and Rose (Carney) T.; BS, Mont. State U., 1938; postgrad. (fellow) U. Wash., 1938-41, U. Calif. at Berkeley, 1952, Drama Studio of London, 1985; m. Hazel Marguerite Griffith, July 28, 1945; children: Stanley, Paul, Richard. Rsch. microbiologist Cutter Labs., Berkeley, Calif., 1945-74; microbiologist Berkeley Biologicals, 1975-86. Committeeman Mount Diablo coun. Boy Scouts Am., 1955, dist. vice-chmn., 1960-61, dist. chmn., 1962-65, cubmaster, 1957, scoutmaster, 1966; active Contact Ministries, 1977-80; bd. dirs. Santa Clara Community Players, 1980-84; vol. instr. English as a Second Lang., 1979-80; vol. ARC Blood Ctr., VA Hosp., San Jose; life mem. PTA; census taker, 1980; mem. Berkely Jr. C. of C., 1946-49. Served with AUS, 1941-46, lt. col. Res., ret. Recipient Scout's Wood badge Boy Scouts Am., 1962; recipient Golden Diploma Mont. State U., 1988. Mem. Am. Soc. Microbiology (chmn. local com. 1953, v.p. No. Calif. br. 1963-65, pres. 1965-67), Sons and Daus. Mont. Pioneers, Mont. State Univ. Alumni Assn., Mont. Hist. Soc., Gallatin County Hist. Soc., Headwaters-Heritage Hist. Soc., Am. Legion Post 89, Parent-Tchrs. Assn. Calif. (life). Presbyterian (trustee 1951-53, elder 1954—). Home: 550 S 13th St San Jose CA 95112-2361

TAYLOR, LEE ROGER, JR., English language educator; b. Long Beach, Calif., Apr. 15, 1944; s. Lee Roger and Penny (Woody) T.; m. Gaye Diane Elliott, Aug. 20, 1968; children: Patrick Andrew, Jacqueline Yvonne. AB in English, East Carolina U., 1970, MA in English, 1972. English and reading specialist Beaufort C.C., Washington, N.C., 1973-76; asst. prof. Brevard (N.C.) Coll., 1976-78; assoc. prof. English, Western Wyo. Coll., Rock Springs, 1978—; columnist, film reviewer Casper (Wyo.) Star-Tribune, 1991—. Author: English Grammar Made Difficult, 1975; also articles. Mem. Wyo. Coun. for Humanities, Laramie, 1980-84, Rock Springs Downtown Adv. Com., 1991—. With USAF, 1962-65. Grantee NEH, 1986, NSF, 1991; Fulbright scholar, 1987. Office: Western Wyo Coll 2500 College Dr Rock Springs WY 82901-5802

TAYLOR, LESLIE GEORGE, mining and financial company executive; b. London, Oct. 8, 1922; came to U.S., 1925; s. Charles Henry and Florence Louisa (Renouf) T.; m. Monique S. Schuster, May, 1964 (div. 1974); children: Leslie G. Anthony II, Sandra J. Mira, Linda S. Marshall; m. Wendy Ann Ward, July 4, 1979. BBA, U. Buffalo, 1952. Asst. to pres. Kelsey Co., 1952-60; pres. Aluminum Industries and Glen Alden Co., Cin. and N.Y.C., 1960-63; pres., chmn. bd. dirs. DC Internat. (and European subs.), Denver, 1963-68, prin. Taylor Energy Enterprises, Denver, 1968—, Taylor Mining Enterprises, Denver, 1968—, Leslie G. Taylor and Co., Denver, 1968—; cons. Lucky Break Gold Inc., Vancouver, B.C.; bd dirs. Amrion Inc., Boulder, Colo.; del. Internat. Astronautical Soc., Stockholm, 1968, London, 1969, Speditur Conv., 1976. Mem. USCG Aux. Mem. Soc. Automotive Engrs., Denver Country Club, Shriners, Masons, Scottish Rites. Republican. Episcopalian. Office: 5031 S Ulster St Ste 200 Denver CO 80237-2810

TAYLOR, LESTER DEAN, economics educator, consultant; b. Toledo, Iowa, Mar. 8, 1938; s. Samuel George and Willa Emma (Brown) T.; m. Carol Austin, Aug. 13, 1966 (div. May 1980); children: James, Rebecca. B.A., U. Iowa, 1960; Ph.D., Harvard U., 1963. Instr., Harvard U., Cambridge, Mas., 1963, asst. prof. econs., 1964-68; staff economist Council Econ. Advisers, Washington, 1964-65; adviser Harvard Inst. Internat. Devel., Bogotá, Colombia, 1967-68; assoc. prof. econs. U. Mich., Ann Arbor, 1969-74; prof. U. Ariz., Tucson, 1974—. Author: (with H.S. Houthakker) Consumer Demand in the U.S., 1966, 2d, rev. edit., 1970; Telecommunications Demand in Theory and Practice, 1980, 2d edit., 1994. Woodrow Wilson fellow Harvard U., 1960-62. Mem. Am. Econ. Assn., Econometric Soc., Royal Econ. Soc., Phi Beta Kappa. Avocations: golf, numismatics. Home: 1997 E Campbell Ter Tucson AZ 85718-5951

TAYLOR, LOUIS HENRY, laboratory geologist; b. Albion, Pa., Feb. 2, 1944; s. Stanley Mearl and Doris Aleen (Redfoot) T.; m. Mary Jean Soine, Dec. 21, 1971; 1 child, Taito Clayton. BS, Edinboro State Coll., 1965; MA, No. Ariz. U., 1971; MS, U. Ariz., 1977, PhD, 1984. Tchr. NW High Sch., Albion, 1965-71; instr. Cen. Ariz. Coll., Coolidge, Ariz., 1971-74; lab. geologist Texaco Inc., Midland, Tex., 1981-84, Denver, 1984-92; pres. Standard Geol. Svcs., Inc., Englewood, Colo., 1992—. Contbr. articles to profl. jours. Mem. Soc. Econ. Paleontologists and Mineralogists (sec. Permian Basin Sect. 1983), Western Interior Paleontological Soc. (pres. 1988), Am. Assn. Petroleum Geologists, Paleontology Soc., Soc. Vertebrate Paleontology, Rocky Mountain Assn. Geologists. Democrat. Home: 4931 W Rowland Ave Littleton CO 80123-6419 Office: Standard Geol Svcs 6920 S Jordan Rd Englewood CO 80112-4248

TAYLOR, MARY ELIZABETH, dietitian, educator; b. Medina, N.Y., Dec. 10, 1933; d. Glenn Aaron and Viola Hazel (Lansill) Grimes; m. Wilbur Alvin Fredlund, Apr. 12, 1952 (div. Jan. 1980); 1 child, Wilbur Jr.; m. Frederick Herbert Taylor, Mar. 15, 1981; children: Martha Dayton, Jean Grout, Beth Stern, Cindy Hey, Carol McLellan, Cheryl, Robert. BS in Food and Nutrition, SUCB, Buffalo, 1973; MEd in Health Sci. Edn. and Evaluation, SUNY, 1978. Registered dietitian, 1977. Diet cook Niagara Sanitorium, Lockport, N.Y., 1953-56; cook Mount View Hosp., Lockport, N.Y., 1956-60, asst. dietitian, 1960-73, dietitian, food svc. dir., 1973-79, cons. dietitian, 1979-81; instr. Erie Community Coll., Williamsville, N.Y., 1979-81; sch. lunch coord. Nye County Sch. Dist., Tonopah, Nev., 1970-93; retired Nye County Sch. Dist., 1993; food svc. mgmt. cons., fin. mgmt. advisor pvt. practice, 1994—; activity dir. Preferred Equity Corp. Recreation Vehicle Resort, Pahrump, Nev., 1993—; cons. dietitian Nye Gen. Hosp., Tonopah, 1983-88; adj. instr. Erie Community Coll., Williamsville, 1978-79; nutrition instr. for coop. extension Clark County Community Coll., 1990—; cons. Group Purchasing Western N.Y. Hosp. Adminstrs., Buffalo, 1975-79, vice-chmn. adv. com., 1976-78; cons. BOCES, Lockport, 1979-81. Nutrition counselor Migrant Workers Clinic, Lockports, 1974-80; mem. Western N.Y. Soc. for Hosp. Food Svc. Adminstrn., 1974-81; nutritionist Niagara County Nutrition Adv. Com., 1977-81. Recipient Outstanding Woman of the Yr., YWCA-UAW Lockport, 1981, Disting. Health Care Food Adminstrn. Recognition award Am. Soc. for Hosp. Food Svc. Adminstrs., 1979, USDA award Outstanding Lunch Program in Nev. and Western Region, 1986, 91. Mem. Am. Assn. Ret. Persons, Am. Sch. Food Svc. Assn. (bd. dirs. 1987, 92-93, cert. dir. II 1987, 5-yr. planning com. 1990, mem. ann. confs. 1988-93), Am. Dietetic Assn. (nat. referral system for registered dietitians 1992-93), So. Nev. Dietetic Assn. (pres. 1985-86), Nev. Food Svc. Assn. (participant ann. meetings 1990-93), Nutrition Today Soc., Nev. Sch. Food Svcs. Assn. (dietary guidelines com. 1991-93). Republican. Baptist. Home: 481 N Murphy PO Box 656 Pahrump NV 89041-0656

TAYLOR, MINNA, lawyer; b. Washington, Jan. 25, 1947; d. Morris P. and Anne (Williams) Glushien; m. Charles Ellett Taylor, June 22, 1969; 1 child, Amy Caroline. BA, SUNY, Stony Brook, 1969; MA, SUNY, 1973; JD, U. So. Calif., 1977. Bar: Calif. 1977, U.S. Dist. Ct. (cen. dist.) Calif. 1978. Extern to presiding justice Calif. Supreme Ct., 1977; field atty. NLRB, L.A., 1977-82; dir. employee rels., legal svcs. Paramount Pictures Corp., L.A., 1982-85, v.p. employee rels. legal svcs., 1985-89; dir. bus. and legal affairs Wilshire Ct. Prodns., L.A., 1989-91; sr. counsel Fox Broadcasting Co., L.A., 1991-92, v.p. legal affairs, 1992—. Editor notes and articles: U. So. Calif. Law Rev., 1976-77. Mentor MOSTE, L.A., 1986-87, 88-89; pres. Beverly Hills chpt. ACLU, L.A., 1985. Fellow ABA, Calif. State Bar (mem. copyright subcom. 1994—), L.A. County Bar Assn.; mem. Beverly Hills Bar Assn., L.A. Bead Soc. (membership sec. 1992-94, mem. bd. dirs. 1994—), Order of Coif. Office: Fox Broadcasting Co 10201 W Pico Blvd Los Angeles CA 90064-2606

TAYLOR, NATHANIEL HUTCHINS, real estate executive; b. Boston, Sept. 15, 1945; s. Frederick Daylies and Lex (Huckel) T.; m. Susan Lee Anderson, May 4, 1974; children: Eric Benson, Emily Jane, Elizabeth Anderson. BA in English Lit., Columbia U., 1968; M of City Planning, U. R.I., 1973. Social worker divsn. children Mass. Dept. Pub. Welfare, Boston, 1968-70; city planner San Francisco Dept. City Planning, 1973-80; Mayor's Office, San Francisco, 1980; v.p. devel. Grosvenor Properties, Ltd., San Francisco, 1980-83; exec. v.p. devel. Grosvenor Developmental Corp., San Francisco, 1983-87; v.p. real estate S. H. Cowell Found., San Francisco, 1988—. Commr. Orinda (Calif.) City Planning Commn., 1992—; treas. Golden Gate Luth. Ch., San Francisco, 1985-87; exec. bd. dirs. Coalition for Better Housing, San Francisco, 1983-86; mem. San Franciscans Seeking Consensus, San Francisco, 1990-91; regent JFK U., 1995—. Mem. Urban Land Inst.

TAYLOR, NIGEL BRIAN, financial planner; b. Winchester, June 17, 1953. Grad., Coll. Fin. Planning, Denver, 1993. Cert. fin. planner; NASD Series 6, 7, 24 lics.; registered principle. Owner Family Trust Planners, domestic and internat. retirement, estate planning, asset protection, L.A. and Santa Monica, Calif., 1988—. Mem. Santa Monica Bar (assoc.), Inst. CFPs (registered practitioner). Office: 1011 4th St Apt 209 Santa Monica CA 90403-3843

TAYLOR, PETER VAN VOORHEES, advertising and public relations consultant; b. Montclair, N.J., Aug. 25, 1934; s. John Coard and Mildred (McLaughlin) T.; m. Janet Kristine Kirkebo, Nov. 4, 1978; 1 son, John Coard III. BA in English, Duke U., 1956. Announcer Sta. WQAM, Miami, 1956; announcer, program dir. Sta. KHVH, Honolulu, 1959-61; promotion mgr. Sta. KPEN, San Francisco, 1962; with Kaiser Broadcasting, 1962-74, GE Broadcasting Co., 1974-78; program/ops. mgr. Sta. KFOG, San Francisco, 1962-66; mgr. Sta. WXHR AM/FM, Cambridge, Mass., 1966-67; gen. mgr. Sta. WJIB, Boston, 1967-70; v.p., mgr. FM div. Kaiser Broadcasting, 1969-72; v.p., gen. mgr. Sta. KFOG, San Francisco, 1970-78; pres. Taylor Communications, 1978-90, Baggott & Taylor, Inc., 1990-91, Taylor Advt. & Pub. Rels., 1991—, Broadcast Skills Bank, 1975-76, Roast Host, 1993—. Trustee, WDBS, Inc., Duke U., 1974-80; bd. dirs. San Francisco BBB, 1976-78, 89-94, San Francisco Boys & Girls Club, 1991-93, Coast Guard Found., 1991—, Leukemia Soc., San Francisco, 1992-93, San Francisco Found., 1994—, Duke Devel. Coun., 1992—. Mem. No. Calif. Broadcasters Assn. (pres. 1975-77, bd. dirs. 1984-86), Nat., Internat. Radio Clubs, Mus. Assn., San Francisco Symphony, Bay Area Publicity Club, Worldwide TV/FM Dx Assn., Advt. Tennis Assn. (pres. 1975-77), Olympic Club, Golden Gate Breakfast Club (v.p. 1995—), The Family Club, Rotary (San Francisco - bd. dirs. 1988-93, 1st v.p. 1990-91, pres. 1991-92, dist. 5150 - pub. rels. chmn. 1986-89, conf. chmn. 1990, area rep. 1992-93, bd. dirs. 1994-95, dist. governor nom., 1995—). Lt. USCGR, 1957-63. Home and Office: 2614 Jackson St San Francisco CA 94115-1123

TAYLOR, R. ERVIN, JR., archaeologist; b. Los Angeles, Jan. 15, 1938; s. Royal Ervin and Francys Ellen (McMurtry) T.; m. Marilynn Julia Lampley, Aug. 22, 1959; children: Gregory Michael, Karen Louane. BA, Pacific Union Coll., 1960; MA, UCLA, 1965, PhD, 1969. Asst. prof. Calif. State U., Northridge, 1967-70; from assoc. prof. to prof. anthropology, chair dept. anthropology U. Calif., Riverside, 1970—. Author: Radiocarbon Dating, 1987; editor: Chronologies in New World Archaeology, 1978, Advances in Obsidian Glass Studies, 1980; co-editor: Radiocarbon After Four Decades, 1992. Grantee NSF, 1978—. Fellow AAAS, Am. Anthropol. Assn.; mem. Southwestern Anthropol. Assn. (pres. 1975-76), Soc. Archaeol. Scis. (pres. 1982, gen. sec. 1982—). Home: 25155 Crestview Dr Loma Linda CA 92354-3508 Office: U Calif Radiocarbon Lab Riverside CA 92521

TAYLOR, RICHARD EDWARD, physicist, educator; b. Medicine Hat, Alta., Can., Nov. 2, 1929; came to U.S., 1952; s. Clarence Richard and Delia Alena (Brunsdale) T.; m. Rita Jean Bonneau, Aug. 25, 1951; 1 child, Norman Edward. B.S., U. Alta., 1950, M.S., 1952; Ph.D., Stanford U., 1962; Docteur honoris causa, U. Paris-Sud, 1980; DSc, U. Alta., 1991; LLD (hon.), U. Calgary, Alta., 1993; DSc (hon.), U. Lethbridge, Alta., 1993, U. Victoria, B.C., Can., 1994. Boursier Lab. de l'Accelerateur Lineaire, Orsay, France, 1958-61; physicist Lawrence Berkeley Lab., Berkeley, Calif., 1961-62; staff mem. Stanford (Calif.) Linear Accelerator Ctr., 1962-68, assoc. dir., 1982-86, prof., 1968—. Fellow Guggenheim Found., 1971-72, von Humboldt Found., 1982; recipient Nobel prize in physics, 1990. Fellow AAAS, Am. Acad. Arts and Scis., Am. Phys. Soc. (W.K.H. Panofsky prize div. particles and fields 1989), Royal Soc. Can.; mem. Can. Assn. Physicists, Nat. Acad. Scis. (fgn. assoc.). Office: Stanford Linear Accelerator Ctr PO Box 4349, M/S 96 Stanford CA 94309

TAYLOR, RICHARD W., public relations executive. V.p. spl. projects ICPR, 1975-80; with Rogers & Cowan, 1980—, v.p. corp. div., 1980-81, sr. v.p. corp. div., 1981, pres. corp. div., 1982—, pres., chief exec. officer, 1986—. Office: Hill & Knowlton 5900 Wilshire Blvd Ste 1200 Los Angeles CA 90036-5012

TAYLOR, ROWAN SHAW, music educator, composer, conductor; b. Ogden, Utah, June 1, 1927; s. Hugh Taylor and Lucille (Olsen) Gaenger; m. Dorothy Foulger, June 26, 1946 (div. 1953); children: Kathleen, Scott; m. Priscilla Pulliam, Aug. 29, 1957; children: Mark, Dianne, Paul, Eric, Brent, Charlotte. BA, Brigham Young U., 1952, MA, 1957. Tchr. San Juan Sch. Dist., Blanding, Utah, 1948-50; with C.F. Braun Engring. Firm, 1950-58; tchr. L.A. Unified Dist., 1958-64; from instr. to prof. L.A. Community Coll., Woodland Hills, Calif., 1964—. Conductor, composer 146 symphonies and numerous musical works, 1994—. With U.S. Army, 1955-56, Korea. Republican. Mem. Ch. Jesus Christ of LDS. Home: 22544 Tiara St Woodland Hills CA 91367-3335

TAYLOR, RUTH ANNE, lawyer; b. Honolulu, Feb. 18, 1961; d. Gerald Lou and Charlotte Anne (Nelson) Allison; m. Thomas Scott Taylor, Dec. 28, 1985; children: Kyle Thomas, Kelly Gerald. BA in Journalism, U. So. Calif., 1984; JD, N.Y. Law Sch., 1987. Bar: Calif. 1987, U.S. Dist. Ct. (so. dist.) Calif., U.S. Ct. Appeals (9th cir.). Assoc. Carlsmith, Wichman, Case Mukai & Ichiki, L.A., L.A., 1987-89, Christensen, White, Miller, Fink & Jacobs, L.A., 1989-93; sr. counsel Warner Bros. Records, Inc., 1993—. Mem. Los Angeles County Bar Assn., Beverly Hills Bar Assn. Republican.

TAYLOR, SANDRA ORTIZ, artist, educator; b. L.A., Apr. 27, 1936; d. John Santry and Juanita Loretta (Shrode) T. BA in Art, UCLA, 1958; MA in Art, State U. Iowa, 1962. Instr. art State U. Iowa, Iowa City, 1961-62, Indian Valley Colls, Marin County, Calif., 1973-74, San Francisco C.C., 1966—; seminar guest speaker Nat. Book Conf., 1991; chair all-media nat exhibit Fine Arts Gallery Broward C.C., Davie, Fla., 1994, Humanities Art Gallery Palm Beach C.C. Exhibited in group shows Calif. Mus. Art, Santa Rosa, 1991, 92, 93, Falkirk Ctr., San Rafael, Calif., 1992, 93, Gallery Route One, Point Reyes Station, Calif., 1993, San Jose (Calif.) Inst. Contemporary Art, 1993-94, San Francisco Airport Com. & Corp. of Fine Arts Mus. of San Francisco, 1994, San Mateo County Arts Coun., Belmont, Calif., San Francisco Women Artists Gallery, San Jose Contemporary Art & Performance Gallery; commd. for grad. program Chicano and Latino studies U. Calif., Irvine, 1992; work reviewed in various publs. Recipient jurors award Calif. Mus. Art, 1992; scholar Anderson Ranch Art Ctr., Snow Mass, Colo., 1991. Home and Office: Ephemera Studio 2854 Harrison St San Francisco CA 94110-4117

TAYLOR, STEVEN BRUCE, agriculture company executive; b. Salinas, Calif., Dec. 29, 1954; s. Edward Horton and Joanne (Church) T.; m. Kathryn Hagler, Dec. 17, 1978; children: Meghan Jean, Kyle Hagler, Christian Steven. BA, U. Calif., Berkeley, 1978; MBA, Harvard U., 1985. Pres. Fresh Concepts, San Marino, Calif., 1985-87; mktg. staff Bruce Church, Inc., Salinas, Calif., 1987-91; pres. Fresh Express Retail Mktg., Salinas, 1991—, Fresh Internat., Salinas, 1991—; v.p. Salinas Valley Lettuce Co-op, Salinas, 1990—; bd. dirs. Produce for Better Health, Del., 1991—. Bd. Elders First Presbyn. Ch., Salinas, 1989-92, personnel com. 1989-94, bldg. com. 1990—; founding mem. Lincoln Club of Monterey County, Salinas, 1990. Home: 515 Santa Paula Dr Salinas CA 93901-1517 Office: Fresh Internat 1020 Merrill St Salinas CA 93901-4409*

TAYLOR, T. RABER, lawyer; b. Colorado Springs, Colo., Dec. 31, 1910; s. Ralph Franklin and Mary Catherine (Burns) T.; m. Josephine Loretto Reddin, Sept. 20, 1938; children: Mary Therese, Carol Anne, Margaret Claire, Josephine R., Rae Marie, Kathleen Mae, Anne Marie. BA magna cum laude, Regis Coll., 1933; JD, Harvard U., 1937. Bar: Colo. 1937, U.S. Dist. Ct. Colo. 1937, U.S. Tax Ct. 1938, U.S. Ct. Appeals (10th cir.) 1940, U.S. Supreme Ct. 1950. Pvt. practice law Denver, 1937—. Bd. dirs. Denver Cath. Charities, 1946-71; v.p. Nat. Conf. Cath. Charities, 1956-57, 69-75; mem. gov.'s com., White House Conf. on Children and Youth, 1971. Lt. comdr. USNR, 1943-45, NATOUSA, ETO. Knight Order St. Gregory, 1971, Equestrian Order of Holy Sepulchre of Jerusalem, 1973; recipient St. Vincent de Paul medal St. John's U., Jamaica, N.Y., 1971, St. Thomas More award Cath. Lawyers Guild Denver, 1981. Fellow Am. Coll. Probate Counsel; mem. ABA, Colo. Bar Assn., Denver Bar Assn., Denver Estate Planning Coun. (pres. 1962-63), Greater Denver Tax Counsel Assn., Serra Club Denver, Denver Athletic Club. Home: 790 Fillmore St Denver CO 80206-3848 Office: 250 Century Bank Pla 3300 E 1st Ave Denver CO 80206-5810

TAYLOR, TIMOTHY KEVIN, business owner; b. Raymond, Wash., May 22, 1944; s. John Hunt Taylor and Helen Lenor (Howdeshell) Johnson; 1 child, Derrick Kevin. Student, Sitka (Alaska) C.C., 1973. Comml. fisherman S.E. Alaska, 1959-69; superintendent mainenance Sitka Sch Dist., 1970-76; owner M.H.P., Sitka, 1972-79, South Bend, Wash., 1977-86; owner Mini Mall, South Bend, 1979-81, Peppertree West Motor Inn, Centralia, Wash., 1985—; owner restaurant Peppermill Inc. Ltd., Centralia, 1987—; owner Mobile Home Park, Othello, Wash., 1994—. Mem. City Coun., South Bend, 1979; mem. Planning and Zoning Com., Sitka, 1975. Mem. Masons, Shriners. Home: 1208 Alder St Centralia WA 98531-1017 Office: Peppermill Inc Ltd 1208 Alder St Centralia WA 98531-1017

TAYLOR, W. O. (BILL TAYLOR), state legislator, business consultant; b. Zanesville, Ohio, July 29, 1932; s. Henry Ray and Lorena Louise (Winkler) T.; m. Shirley Ann Jacobs, Mar. 11, 1951; children: Bill, Larry, Sallie, Charles, Richard, Julie. AA in Bus. Adminstrn., Jacksonville (Fla.) U., 1957; B of Sci. Edn., Midwestern State U., Wichita Falls, Tex., 1968, MEd, 1972. Advanced secondary cert., Idaho. Acct. Swift & Co., Jacksonville, 1955-58; v.p. Taylor Bros. Inc., Baton Rouge, 1958-60; pres. Carter Paint Co., Inc., Wichita Falls, 1960-68; tchr. econs. Wichita Falls Pub. Sch., 1968-78; pres. Taylor Enterprises, Inc., Nampa, Idaho, 1978—; mem. Ho. of Reps, State of Idaho, Boise, 1986—, chmn. bus. com., 1994. Bishop Ch. of Jesus Christ of Latterday Saints, Wichita Falls, 1964-69. Served to sgt. USMC, 1950-53, Korea. Named Republican of Yr., Canyon County Rep. Ctrl. Com., 1987. Mem. DAV, Sertoma (life, pres. 1965, Sertoman of Yr. award 1964). Republican. Home: 8367 Track Rd Nampa ID 83686-9424 Office: Idaho Ho of Reps State Capitol Boise ID 83720

TAYLOR, WALTER WALLACE, lawyer; b. Newton, Iowa, Sept. 18, 1925; s. Carrol W. and Eva (Greenly) T.; A.A., Yuba Coll., 1948, A.B., 1950, M.A., U. Calif., 1955, J.D., McGeorge Coll. Law, 1962; m. Mavis A. Harvey, Oct. 9, 1948; children—Joshua Michael (dec. 1980), Kevin Eileen, Kristin Lisa, Jeremy Walter, Margaret Jane, Melissa E., Amy M. Adminstrv. analyst USAF, Sacramento, 1951-53; personnel, research analyst Calif. Personnel Bd., Sacramento, 1954-56; civil service, personnel analyst, chief counsel, gen. mgr. Calif. Employees Assn., Sacramento, 1956-75; staff counsel, chief profl. standards Calif. Commn. Tchr. Credentialing, 1975-88, ret. 1988; staff counsel State Office Real Estate appraiser Licensing and Certification, 1992—; tchr. discipline civil service, personnel cons. Served USCGR, 1943-46. Mem. Calif. State Bar, Am., Sacramento County bar assns. Democrat. Author: Know Your Rights, 1963-64. Home: 4572 Fair Oaks Blvd Sacramento CA 95864-5336

TAYLOR, WILLIAM AL, judge; b. Lusk, Wyo., Nov. 2, 1928; m. Jane Y.; 3 children. BA, U. Wyo., 1951, LLB, 1959. Bar: Wyo. 1959. Teacher Lusk, 1950-51,54-55, pvt. practice, 1959-78; city atty. Town of Lusk, 1962-74; atty. Niobrara County, Wyo., 1964-77; judge Wyo. Dist. Ct. (8th dist.), Cheyenne, 1980—; justice Wyoming Supreme Ct., 1993—; Exec. dir. Wyo. State Bar, 1977-80. Staff sgt. U.S. Army, 1951-53. Mem. Wyo. State Bar (Civil Rules com.), Wyo. Judicial Conf. (chmn. 1984-85),Tenth Cir. Bar Assn., Nat. Trial Judges, Am. Legion, Sigma Alpha Epsilon. Office: Wyo Supreme Ct PO Box 66 Cheyenne WY 82003-0066

TAYLOR, WILLIAM MALCOLM, environmental science educator; b. South Hiram, Maine, June 18, 1933; s. William Myers and Gladys Marie (Weldy) T.; stepson: Edna (Tyson) T.; m. Carrie Mae Fiedler, Aug. 31, 1957 (div. Sept. 1980); children: William Stephan, Alyson Marie, Eric Fiedler; m. Elizabeth Van Horn, June 18, 1983. Student, George Sch., 1948-50; BA in Liberal Arts, Pa. State U., 1956. Cert. secondary sch. tchr. Instr. ESL Anatolia Coll., Am. Lang. Ctr., Thessaloniki, Greece, 1956-58; tchr. biology-chemistry Coral Shores H.S., Tavernier, Fla., 1961-62; pk. naturalist Everglades Nat. Pk., Fla., 1962-65; tech. editor Nat. Pk. Svc., Washington, 1965-67; chief naturalist Canyonlands Nat. Pk., Utah, 1967-71; environ. edn. specialist western regional office Nat. Pk. Svc., Calif., 1971-77; dir. program devel. Living History Ctr., Novato, Calif., 1981-83; exec. recruiter, ptnr. Van Horn, Taylor & Assocs., Santa Cruz, Calif., 1983-95. Author: The Strands Walk, Exercises in Guided Inquiry for Children; originator (ednl. program) Environ. Living Program, 1973 (Calif. Bicentennial Commn. award 1974, Don Perryman award Calif. Social Studies Coun., 1975, Nat. Bicentennial Adminstrn. sponsorship 1976). Bd. dirs. Novato Environ. Quality Com., 1973-76; mem. Calif. Conservation Com., 1973-76. Mem. Lighthawk/Environ. Air Force, Flying Samaritans, Mensa. Home: 30714 Ty Valley Rd Lebanon OR 97355-9262

TAYLOR-GRIGSBY, QUEENIE DELORES, minister, consultant; b. Oklahoma City, Aug. 21, 1948; d. Barnett C., Sr. and Bedell (Boles) Taylor; m. Walter Thomas White II, Nov. 26, 1966 (div. June 1976); children: Walter Thomas III, Robin Orlando; m. James O. Grigsby, Oct. 19, 1976 (dec. Dec. 1976); 1 child, James Tumaané. BS, Howard U., 1970. Ordained to ministry Ray Deliverance Found., 1989. Assoc. cons. Trust Inc., Richmond, Va., 1974-80, Orgnl. Devel. Cons., Richmond, 1980-82; cons., pres. Taylor & Co., Phoenix, 1974—; min. Man Child Ministries, Phoenix, 1988—; cons. MARTA Atlanta, 1980-82, Fredrick County, Md., 1974, Richond Pub. Sch. System, 1977, Black Police Officers, Tulsa, 1986. Author poetess. Advocate child welfare Dept. of Corrections, Phoenix, 1990, advocate tchr. rights, 1991; active tchr. rights Phoenix Pub. Sch. System, 1992; supr. elections County Election Bd., Maricopa County, Ariz., 1987. Lucille McMahn scholar, 1965, Nellie Green scholar, 1965; recipient Danforth Leadership award, 1965, Golden Poet award, 1991. Mem. Soc. Tng. and Devel. (cert. housing specialist), Housing Specialist Inst. Republican. Office: Taylor & Co PO Box 9605 Phoenix AZ 85068-9605

TEAGUE, LAVETTE COX, JR., systems educator, consultant; b. Birmingham, Ala., Oct. 8, 1934; s. Lavette Cox and Caroline Green (Stokes) T.; student Auburn U., 1951-54; B.Arch., MIT, 1957, M.S.C.E., 1965, Ph.D., 1968; MDiv with distinction Ch. Div. Sch. Pacific, 1979. Cert. computer profl. Inst. Cert. of Computer Profls. Archtl. designer Carroll C. Harmon, Birmingham, 1957, Fred Renneker, Jr., Birmingham, 1958-59; architect Rust Engring. Co., Birmingham, 1959-62, Synergetics, Inc., Raleigh, N.C., 1962-64, Rust Engring. Co., Birmingham, 1964-68; research asst., inst., research assoc. MIT, Cambridge, 1964-68; dir. computer services Skidmore, Owings & Merrill, San Francisco, Chgo., 1968-74; postdoctoral fellow UCLA, 1972; adj. assoc. prof. architecture and civil engring. Carnegie-Mellon U., Pitts., 1973-74; archtl. systems cons., Chgo., 1974-75, Berkeley, Calif., 1975-80, Pasadena, Calif., 1980-82, Altadena, Calif., 1982—; lectr. info. systems Calif. State Poly. U., Pomona, 1980-81, prof., 1981—, asst. chair, 1990-91, chair, 1991-93. Fulbright lectr., Uruguay, 1985. Co-author: Structured Analysis Methods for Computer Information Systems, 1985. Recipient Tucker-Voss award M.I.T., 1967; Fulbright scholar, 1985. Mem. AIA (Arnold W. Brunner scholar 1966), Assn. Computing Machinery, Sigma Xi, Phi Eta Sigma, Scarab, Scabbard and Blade, Tau Beta Pi, Chi Epsilon. Episcopalian. Home: 1696 N Altadena Dr Altadena CA 91001-3623 Office: 3801 W Temple Ave Pomona CA 91768-2557

TEAL, DONALD F., physician, surgeon; b. N.Y.C., Oct. 9, 1939; s. Gordon Kidd and Lyda (Smith) T.; m. Judith Horton, July 19, 1969; children: Randall Frasier, Brent Christopher. BA in History, Rice U., 1961; MD, U. Texas, Dallas, 1965. Diplomate Am. Bd. Gen. Surgery, Am. Bd. Plastic and Reconstructive Surgery. Pvt. practice Eugene, Oreg., 1975-95; assoc. prof. surgery Health Sci. Ctr. U. Oreg., Portland, 1975-95. Visiting plastic surgeon, Oaxaca, Mex. Lt. USNR, 1966-68, Vietnam. Fellow: ACS; mem. Am. Soc. Surgery of Hand, Am. Soc. Reconstructive Microsurgery (founder), Internat. Soc. Reconstructive Microsurgery (founder), Am. Assn. Hand Surgery, Am. Soc. Plastic and Reconstructive Surgery. Office: 1200 Hilyard St Ste S 550 Eugene OR 97401-8122

TEAL, GILBERT EARLE, II, lawyer, coast guard officer; b. Lafayette, Ind., May 1, 1959; s. Gilbert Earle and Evangeline Maxine (Piper) T.; m. Mary Anne Liwoch, Oct. 3, 1987. AS, Western Conn. State U., 1979; BS, USCG Acad., 1983; MPA, George Mason U., 1988; JD, Coll. William and Mary, 1991. Bar: Va. 1991, U.S. Mil. Ct. Appeals 1991, U.S. Ct. Appeals (4th cir.) 1991, D.C. 1992, U.S. Ct. Claims 1992, U.S. Ct. Appeals (fed. cir.) 1992. Commd. ensign USCG, 1983, advanced through grades to lt. comdr., 1993; assigned to USCG Cutter Vigorous (WMEC 627), New London, Conn., 1983-85; intelligence officer COMDT (G-OIS-3) Hdqs. USCG, Washington, 1985-88; law clk. to chief trial judge Capt. Thomas Snook, USCG, N.Y.C., 1989; law clk. USCG RTC Yorktown, 1990; staff atty. Maintenance and Logistics Command Atlantic, Governors Island, N.Y., 1991-94; legal officer USCG Support Ctr., Kodiak, Alaska, 1994—. Mem. ABA, FBA, Va. State Bar, Va. Bar Assn., D.C. Bar, Jud. Advs. Assn. (life), U.S. Naval Inst. (life), Nat. Eagle Scout Assn. (life), Army and Navy Club (Washington), Army-Navy Country Club (Arlington, Va.), Rotary Internat., Phi Delta Phi (life), Phi Delta Kappa. Home: 100 Albatross Ave # A Kodiak AK 99615-6804 Office: USCG Support Ctr PO Box 195005 Kodiak AK 99619-5005

TEAMAN, RICHARD ALAN, accountant; b. Fairfield, Calif., Aug. 19, 1960; s. Glenn Richard and Dorothy Teaman; m. Lisa A. Turner, June 22, 1985 (div. Nov. 1990); 1 child, Grace Ann; m. Sally Thomas, July 5, 1991; 1 child, Stephanie Kathline. AA, Riverside (Calif.) City Coll., 1981; BS, Calif. State U., San Bernardino, 1983. CPA, Calif. Staff acct. Thomas, Byrne & Smith, Riverside, 1983-85, sr. acct., 1985-88, mgr., 1988-92, ptnr., 1992; ptnr. Thomas, Bigbie & Smith (formerly Thomas, Byrne & Smith), Riverside, 1993—. Mem. AICPA, Calif. Soc. CPAs, Assn. Govt. Accts., Govt. Fin. Officers Assn., Calif. Soc. Mcpl. Fin. Officers. Home: 11503 Chaucer St Moreno Valley CA 92557-8318 Office: Thomas Bigbie & Smith 4201 Brockton Ave Ste 100 Riverside CA 92501-3431

TECHNER, MARC, information systems manager; b. Phila., Aug. 8, 1958; s. Joseph and Dolores Edith (MacLachlan); m. Norma Oseda De La Peña, Jan. 1, 1988; 1 child, José Marc. BA in Journalism and Latin Am. Studies, Pa. State U., 1980; MA in Latin Am. Studies, U. Tex., 1984. Cert. Banyan engr.; cert. Novell adminstr. News anchor WDFM-FM, University Park, Pa., 1977; freelance corr. The Phila. (Pa.) Inquirer, 1978; reporter, editorial writer, columnist, copy editor The Daily Collegian, University Park, 1977-80; translator, relief worker Cuban-Haitian Refugee Task Force, 1980; wire editor The Daily Texan, Austin, 1982; tech. support editor Univ. Presses of Fla., Gainesville, 1987-88; microcomputer coord., editor Computer Econs., Inc., Carlsbad, Calif., 1989; wide area network mgr. ct. info. sys. Superior Ct. of Calif., County of San Diego, 1989-95; network mgr. dept. info. svcs. County of San Diego, 1995—; policy cons. Ctrl. Am. Refugee Policy/LBJ Sch. Pub. Affairs Policy Rsch. Project, U. Tex., Austin, 1983-84; editorial and typographical cons. U. Fla., 1986. Contbr. articles to profl. jours. vol., Vols. in Svc. to Am., Legal Svcs. Greater Miami (Fla.), Inc., 1981-82. Recipient cert. of merit U.S. Dept. of the Army, Ft. Indiantown Gap, Pa., 1980. Mem. Assn. Banyan Users Internat. Office: County of San Diego Dept Info Svcs 1600 Pacific Hwy San Diego CA 92101

TECK, RONALD JAY, county assessor; b. Pueblo, Colo., Sept. 22, 1947; s. John Alan Teck and Chloie Beatrice (Barnett) Morris; m. Beverly Merline Smith Kanda, Sept. 9, 1978 (div. 1987); m. Patricia Kay Artz, Nov. 6, 1989; children: Michael Alan, John Franklin. BA in Chemistry, U. Colo., 1970. Chemist Nat. Ctr. Atmosphere Rsch., Boulder, Colo., 1970-74; cons. Dames & Moore, Park Ridge, Ill., 1974-75, Ambient Analysis Inc., Boulder, 1975; sales rep. Sargent-Welch Scientific, Denver, 1975-77; program analyst Bendix Field Engring., Grand Junction, Colo., 1977-83; realtor Gale & Co., others, Grand Junction, 1983-92; assesor Mesa County Govt., Grand Junction, 1992—. Contbr. articles to profl. jours. Mem. legis. com. Grand Junction Bd. of Realtos, 1988-92, pres. 1986-87. Named Realtor of Yr. Grand Junction Bd. of Realtors, 1988-92. Mem. Colo. Assessors Assn., Grand Junction C. of C. (govtl. affairs). Republican. Office: Mesa County Assessor Mesa County Courthouse Grand Junction CO 81501

TEDESCO, STEVEN ANTHONY, oil company executive; b. Lansing, Mich., Nov. 14, 1955; s. Paul Herbert and Eleanor (Hollis) T.; m. Christine Tunkey; children: Trevor, Caitlin, Cassie. BS in Geology, Northeastern U., Boston, 1977; MS in Geology, So. Ill. U., 1980. Geologist Weston Geophys., Westboro, Mass., 1977-78, project geologist, 1981-83; exploration geologist Mobil Oil Corp., Denver, 1980-81; exploration mgr. Stanley Energy, Denver, 1983-85; owner Atoka Esploration Corp., Denver, 1989—, CST Oil & Gas Corp., Denver, 1985—. Author: Surface Geochemistry in Petroleum Exploration, 1994. Coach Spartans Baseball Youth League, Aurora, Colo., 1993-94. Mem. Am. Assn. Petroleum Geologists, Assn. Petroleum Geochem. Explorationists (treas. 1990-91). Home: 16746 E Prentice Cir Aurora CO 80015-4130 Office: CST Oil and Gas Corp 103 Inverness Dr E # 160 Englewood CO 80112

TEDFORD, CHARLES FRANKLIN, biophysicist; b. Lawton, Okla., June 26, 1928; s. Charles E. and Loula B. (Waters) T.; m. Julie Reme Sauret, Sept. 15, 1951; children: Gary Franklin, Mark Charles, Philip John. BS with distinction in Chemistry, S.W. Tex. State U., 1950, MS, 1954; postgrad. in radiobiology Reed Coll., 1957, in biophysics U. Calif., Berkeley, 1961-63. Enlisted USN, 1945-47, commd. ensign, 1950, advanced through grades to capt., 1968; biochemist U.S. Naval Hosp., San Diego, 1953-54, U.S. Naval Biol. Lab., Oakland, Calif., 1954-56; sr. instr., radiation safety officer Nuclear, Biol. and Chem. Warfare Def. Sch., Treasure Island, Calif., 1956-61; asst. chief nuclear medicine div. Navy Med. Sch., Bethesda, Md., 1963-66; adminstrv. program mgr. radiation safety br. Bur. Medicine and Surgery, Washington, 1966-72; dir. radiation safety and health physics program Navy Regional Med. Center, San Diego, 1972-74; mgr. Navy Regional Med. Clinic, Seattle, 1974-78, ret., 1978; dir. radiation health unit Ga. Dept. Human Resources, Atlanta, 1978-79; dir. Ariz. Radiation Regulatory Agy., Tempe, 1979-91; chief, Radiological Health Prog., Juneau, Alaska, 1991-93, ret. 1993; cons. 1993—. elected chmn. Conf. Radiation Program Dirs., 1987; named Ariz. Southwestern Low Level Radioactive Waste Compact Commr., 1990. Recipient Ariz. Adminstr. of Yr. award Ariz. Adminstrs. Assn., 1988; decorated Legion of Merit, Meritorious Service medal. Mem. Health Physics Soc., Am. Nuclear Soc. Contbr. articles on radiation safety to profl. publs.

TEDFORD, JACK NOWLAN, III, construction executive, small business owner; b. Reno, Jan. 1, 1943; s. Jack Nowlan Jr. and Elizabeth (Kolhoss) T.; m. Nancy Joanne Stiles, Feb. 27, 1971; children: Jack Nowlan IV, James Nathan. BS, U. Nev., 1966, MBA, 1969. Bus. mgr. Los Angeles Bapt. Coll., Newhall, Calif., 1969-71; v.p. Jack N. Tedford, Inc., Fallon, Nev., 1971—; owner/broker Tedford Realty, Fallon, 1974-94; owner/mgr. Tedford Bus. Systems, Fallon, 1978-94; pres. JNT, Inc., Fallon, 1994—; bd. dirs. Masters Coll., Newhall, Calif., 1972—. Author numerous computer programs. Mem. Selective Svc. Local Bd., Fallon, 1971-76; chmn. City of Fallon Bd. Adjustment, 1975—, Churchill Co. Reps., Fallon, 1976-80; mem. ctrl. com. Nev. Reps., 1976—; del. Nat. Conv., Detroit, 1980, Dallas, 1984; coun. ofcls. Western Nev. Devel. Dist.; treas. Lahontan Valley Environ. Alliance. Mem. Assn. Gen. Contractors (treas. Nev. chpt.), Nat., State and Fallon Bd. Realtors, CEDA Bus. Coun. (bd. dirs.), Nev. Motor Transport Assn., NAt. Asphalt Pavement Assn., Am. Trucking Assn., Rotary (bd. dirs. 1969-71). Republican. Baptist. Home: 115 N Bailey St Fallon NV 89406-2720 Office: 235 E Williams Ave Fallon NV 89406-3027

TEERLINK, J(OSEPH) LELAND, real estate developer; b. Salt Lake City, July 16, 1935; s. Nicholas John and Mary Luella (Love) T.; student U. Utah, 1953-55; m. Leslie Dowdle, Nov. 5, 1975; children: Steven, David, Andrew, Suzanne, Benjamin. Sales rep. Eastman Kodak Co., Salt Lake City, 1960-69; founder Graphic Systems, Inc., Salt Lake City, 1969-82, pres., 1969-79, chmn. bd., 1979-82; founder Graphic Ink Co., Salt Lake City, 1973, pres., 1975-79, chmn. bd., 1979-82; founder G.S.I. Leasing Co., Salt Lake City, 1975, pres., 1975-82; chmn. bd. Graphic Systems Holding Co., Inc., Salt Lake City, 1978-82; dir. leasing and acquisitions Terra Industries, Inc., real estate developers, 1982-86, ptnr., 1986—; bd. dirs. ARC, Salt Lake City, 1979-82; co-founder, dir. Hope Living Ctr. Found. for Mothers and Children, 1993—; vice consulate of the Netherlands for Utah, 1977-92; mem. active corps of execs., SBA, 1979-83; mem. adv. bd. House of Hope Mothers and Children Utah Alcoholism Found., 1992-94. Recipient Masters award Salt Lake Bd. Realtors, 1993; named Small Businessman of the Yr. for Utah, SBA, 1978. Mem. Graphic Arts Equipment and Supply Dealers of Am. (dir. 1978-82), Printing Industry of Am., Nat. Assn. Indsl. and Office Parks (pres. Utah chpt., 1986-87), Nat. Fedn. Ind. Businessmen, Million Dollar Club (life). Republican. Mormon. Home: 2984 Thackeray Pl Salt Lake City UT 84108-2517 Office: 6925 Union Park Ctr Midvale UT 84047-4142

TEETS, JOHN WILLIAM, diversifed company executive; b. Elgin, Ill., Sept. 15, 1933; s. John William and Maudie T.; m. Nancy Kerchenfaut, June 25, 1965; children: Jerri, Valerie Sue, Heide Jane, Suzanne. Student, U. Ill.; LLD (hon.), Trinity Coll., 1982; DBA in Foodsvc. Mgmt. (hon.), Johnson and Wales U., 1991; D in Comml. Sci. (hon.), Western Internat. U., 1992. Pres., ptnr. Winter Garden Restaurant, Inc., Carpenterville, Ill., 1957-63; v.p. Greyhound Food Mgmt. Co.; pres. Post Houses, Inc., and Horne's Enterprises, Chgo., 1964-68; pres., chief operating officer John R. Thompson Co., Chgo., 1968-71; pres., corp. v.p. pub. restaurant divsn. Canteen Corp., Chgo., 1971-75; divsn. pres. Jacques Restaurant Group, 1975; exec. v.p., CEO Bonanza Internat. Co., Dallas, 1975; group v.p. food svcs., pres. Greyhound Food Mgmt., Inc (now named Restaura), Phoenix, 1975; vice chmn. The Greyhound Corp., Phoenix, 1980; chmn., CEO Greyhound Corp. (now The Dial Corp), Phoenix, 1981—; now chmn., pres., CEO The Dial Corp, Phoenix; vice chmn. Pres.' Conf. on Foodservice Industry. Recipient Silver Plate award, Golden Plate award Internat. Foodsvc. Mgrs. Assn., 1980, Order of the Crown Kingdom of Belgium, 1990, Bus. Leadership award Harvard Bus. Sch. Club Ariz., 1985, Ellis Island medal of honor Nat. Ethnic Coalition of Orgns. Found., 1995; named Top Bus. Spkr. of Yr. Forbes Mag., 1990, Capt. of Achievement Acad. of Achievement, 1992, CEO of Yr. Leaders Mag., 1986. Mem. Nat. Inst. Foodsvc. Industry (trustee), Am. Mgmt. Assn., Christian Businessmen's Assn. (chmn. steering com. 1977). Office: The Dial Corp 1850 N Central Ave Phoenix AZ 85077-0001

TEH, CHO HUAK, computer scientist; b. Singapore, May 18, 1955; came to U.S., 1982; s. Siong Keong and Kah Ching (Tan) T.; m. Thin-Fong Tsuei, Aug. 22, 1982; children: Audris Yunlin Teh, Alec Yongjie Teh. BSEE with honors, Nat. U. Singapore, 1980, MSEE, 1983; PhD in Elec. Engring., U. Wis., 1988. Teaching and rsch. asst. Nat. U. Singapore, 1980-82, asst. prof., 1988-89; teaching and rsch. asst. U. Wis., Madison, 1982-88, vis. scientist, 1989-90; staff scientist Innovision Inc., Madison, 1990; sr. vision engr. Electroglas, Santa Clara, Calif., 1990-93; sr. mem. tech. staff Photo Dynamics, Milpitas, Calif., 1993-94; sr. machine vision scientist Therma-Wave, Fremont, Calif., 1994—. Recipient Overseas Grad. scholarship Nat. U. Singapore, 1982, Singapore PSC merit scholarship Nat. U. Singapore, 1976. Mem. IEEE, Chinese Software Profl. Assn., The Photonics Soc. of Chinese-Americans, Chinese-Am. Semiconductor Profl. Assocs. Home: 639 Dorset Way Sunnyvale CA 94087-3437

TEHRANI, FLEUR TAHER, electrical engineer, educator, researcher; b. Tehran, Feb. 16, 1956; came to U.S., 1984; d. Hassan and Pourandokht (Monfared) T. BS in Elec. Engring., Sharif U. of Tech., Tehran, 1975; DIC in Comm. Engring., Imperial Coll. Sci. and Tech., London, 1977; MSc in Comm. Engring., U. London, 1977, PhD in Elec. Engring., 1981. Registered profl. engr., Calif. Comm. engr. Planning Orgn. of Iran, Tehran, 1977-78; lectr. A elec. engring. Robert Gordon's Inst. Tech., Aberdeen, U.K., 1982-83; lectr. II elec. engring. South Bank U., London, 1984; asst. prof. elec. engring. Calif. State U., Fullerton, 1985-91, assoc. prof. elec. engring., 1991-94, prof. elec. engring., 1994—; vis. assoc. prof. elec. engring. Drexel U., Phila., 1987-88; sys. cons. Telebit Corp., Cupertino. Calif., 1985; engring. cons. PRD, Inc., Dresher, Pa., 1989-92; mem. NASA/Am. Soc. Engring. Edn. summer faculty Jet Propulsion Lab., Calif. Inst. Tech., Pasadena, 1995. Contbr. articles to profl. jours.; patentee in field. Recipient Best Ann. Rsch. Manuscript award Assn. for the Advancement of Med. Instrumentation, 1993, Outstanding Excellence in Rsch. Faculty award Calif. State U., 1993. Mem. IEEE, Women in Sci. and Engring. (chair Calif. State U. chpt. 1990-91), Assn. Profs. and Scholars of Iranian Heritage (pres. 1991-92), Sigma Delta Epsilon. Office: Calif State U Dept Elec Engring 800 N State College Blvd Fullerton CA 92631-3547

TEICHROB, CAROL, Canadian provincial official; b. Sask., Can., Aug. 27, 1939; d. J. Delbert and Elizabeth (Spenst) Sproxton; m. Donald P. Teichrob, Mar. 1, 1958; children: Lori, Sharon, James. Sr. matriculation, Notre Dame Convent, Morinville, Alta., Can. Cert. profl. ct. reporter, exec. mem. Can. and Saskatchewan Fedns. Agriculture, 1976-81; chmn. Can. Turkey Mktg. Agy., 1980-81, Plains Poultry Wynyard, Sask., 1981-88; founding ptnr. Primrose Books, Saskatoon, Sask., 1988—. Reeve, Rural Municipality of Corman Park, Saskatoon, Sask., 1981-91; active U. Sask. Senate, 1981-86; mem. legis. assembly N.D.P. Caucus. Recipient Golden WHeel award Sask. Rotary, 1990; named Woman of Yr. in Bus., Saskatoon YWCA, 1981. Mem. Saskatoon C. of C. Office: MLA Saskatoon Meewasin, Legis Bldg Rm 105, Regina, SK Canada S4S OB3

TEIRSTEIN, PAUL SHEPHERD, physician, health facility administrator; b. N.Y.C., July 5, 1955; s. Alvin Stanley and Alice Teirstein. BA in Biology, Vassar Coll., 1976; MD, CUNY, 1980. Diplomate Am. Bd. Internal Medicine and Cardiovascular Diseases. With Lab. of Vision Rsch. NIH, Bethesda, Md., 1977-79; intern and resident Brigham & Women's Hosp., Boston, 1980-83; fellow in cardiology Stanford (Calif.) U., 1983-86; fellow in advanced coronary angioplasty Mid-Am. Heart Inst., Kansas City, Mo., 1986-87; fellow in stents, artherectomy and lasers NIH, Bethesda, 1987; dir. interventional cardiology Scripps Clinic and Rsch. Found., La Jolla, Calif., 1987—; presenter at Am. Coll. Cardiology, 1987-94, Am. Heart Assn., 1990-93, The French Hosp., San Luis Obispo, Calif., 1989, St. Luke's Med. Ctr., Phoenix, 1989, Cardiology for the Cons., Rancho Santa Fe, 1989, U. Calif., Irvine, 1989, ACP, Scottsdale, Ariz., 1989, Presbyn. Hosp., Whittier, Calif, 1989, St. Jude Med. Ctr., Fullerton, Calif., 1990, Oscala Med. Ctr., Osaka, Japan, 1992, Cedars-Sinai Med. Ctr., L.A., 1993, European Congress of Cardiology, Nice, France, 1993, Tokyo U., 1993, Lenox Hill Hosp., N.Y., 1993, Japanese Soc. Internat. Cardiology, 1994, Nat. Hindu Hosp., Bombay, 1994, G.B. Pant Hosp., Delhi, India, 1994, Escort's Hosp., 1994, B.M. Birla Hosp., Calcutta, 1994, Shaare Zedek Med. Ctr., Jerusalem, 1994, XV Gongresso da Sociedad de Cardiology de Sao Paulo, Ribeirao Preto, Brazil, 1994, and others. Grantee NSF, 1975. Fellow Am. Coll. Cardiology, Assn. for Rsch. in Vision and Ophthalmology, Beta Beta Beta, Alpha Omega Alpha. Office: Scripps Clinic & Rsch Found 10666 N Torrey Pines Rd La Jolla CA 92037-1027

TEIWES, HELGA, photographer; b. Meerbusch, Germany, Jan. 19, 1930; came to U.S., 1960; d. Reinhold and Gertrud (Zaepke) Kulbe. MA, Handwerks Kammer, Dusseldorf, Germany, 1957; BA in Art History, U. Ariz., 1978. Photographic apprentice Hehmke-Winterer Studio, Dusseldorf, 1950-53, studio photographer, 1953-57; staff photographer Bagel Printing Co., Dusseldorf, 1957-60; freelance photographer N.Y.C., 1960-61; photographer Cartier Jeweler, N.Y.C., 1961-62; transparency retoucher Creative Color Svc., N.Y.C., 1962-64; staff photographer Ariz. State Mus., Tucson, 1965-93; photographer, rschr. O'odham, Hopi, Navajo, Apache, Ariz. Indian Tribes, 1965—; photographer Mission San Xavier del Bac Restoration Projects, Tucson, 1968-69, 79, 93, 94, 95. Author, photographer: Kachina Dolls, 1991; photographer: Navajo, 1991; designer, photographer posters S.W. Pottery and Cultural Material, 1980. Recipient Spur award Western Writers Am., 1982, Grand prize World Photography Soc., Calif., 1983, 2nd prize for photography Sangre de Cristo Art Ctr., Pueblo, Colo., 1986, 88, 90; Ariz. Humanities Coun. grantee, Phoenix, 1992. Home: 2611 N Teresa Ln Tucson AZ 85745

TELEGDY, MARYLL ILONA, librarian, archaeologist; b. Budapest, Hungary, Aug. 16, 1932; d. Andrew and Susan V. (Lenkey) T.; m. Istvan Telegdy, Oct. 2, 1971; 1 stepchild, Zsolt Telegdy. PhD in Museology & Archaeology, Eötvös Lòrànd U., Budapest, Hungary, 1955; MA in Classics, Yale U., 1958; MLS, U. Calif., Berkeley, 1960. Curator intern Hungarian Nat. Mus., Budapest, Hungary, 1954-55; curator Hist. Mus. of Budapest, Hungary, 1955-56; descriptive cataloging asst. Yale U. Libr., New Haven, Conn., 1958-59; bibliographer in Humanities and Western Lang. U. Calif. Libr., Berkeley, 1960-63; vis. prof. in Mediterranean Archaeology Stanford (Calif.) U., 1963; cataloger in Humanities and Western Lang. Calif. State U., Hayward, 1963-65; vis. prof. in Mediterranean Archeology and Humanities Calif. State U., San Francisco, 1964-65; head ref., head acquisitions U. Calif., Irvine, 1965-71; ESL teaching cons. Budapest, Hungary, 1971-86; head tech. svcs. Napa (Calif.) City-County Libr., 1986—. James Sutton fellow U. Calif., Berkeley, 1959-60; Boies fellowship Yale U., New Haven, Conn., 1957-58. Mem. Calif. Libr. Assn. Democrat. Roman Catholic. Home: 779-K S Freeway Dr Napa CA 94558 Office: Napa City-County Library 580 Coombs St Napa CA 94559

TELLEM, SUSAN MARY, public relations executive; b. N.Y.C, May 23, 1945; d. John F. and Rita C. (Lietz) Cain; m. Marshall R.B.. Thompson; children: Tori, John, Daniel. BS, Mt. St. Mary's Coll., L.A., 1967. Cert. pub. health nurse; RN. Pres. Tellem Pub. Rels. Agy., Marina del Rey, Calif., 1977-80, Rowland Grody Tellem, L.A., 1980-90; chmn. The Rowland Co., L.A., 1990—; pres., CEO Tellem, Inc., L.A., 1992-93; instr. UCLA Extension, 1983—; speaker numerous seminars and confs. on pub. rels. Editor: Sports Medicine for the '80's, Sports Medicine Digest, 1982-84. Bd. dirs. Marymount High Sch., 1984-87, pres., 1984-86; bd. dirs. L.A. Police Dept. Booster Assn., 1984-87; mem. Cath. Press Coun.; mem. pres.'s coun. Mus. Sci. and Industry. Mem. Am. Soc. Hosp. Mktg. and Pub. Rels., Healthcare Mktg. and Pub. Rels. Assn., Pub. Rels. Soc. Am. (bd. dirs. 1994—), L.A. Counselors, PETA, Am. Lung Assn. (chair comm. com. L.A. chpt.) Soc. for Prevention of Cruelty to Animals (chair PetSet), Sports Club (L.A.). Roman Catholic. Office: Tellem Inc Museum Sq 5757 Wilshire Blvd Ste 655 Los Angeles CA 90036-3686

TELLINGTON, WENTWORTH JORDAN, engineer; b. Gorham, N.H., Oct. 11, 1916; s. Jesse James and Myrtle Myneleh (Jordan) T.; m. Elizabeth Haman-Ashley, Apr. 29, 1939 (div. 1956); children: Wentworth J. Jr., Joan Elizabeth Gabert. AB, Columbia U., 1940. Instr. U.S. Mil. Acad., West Point, N.Y., 1941-45; field supr. Century Geophys. Corp., Tulsa, 1946-48; chief geophysicist Pacific Petroleums Ltd., Calgary, Alberta, Can., 1949-51; exec. v.p. Overland Inds. Ltd., Edmonton, Alberta, Can., 1952-55; head math. dept. Chadwick Sch., Rolling Hills, Calif., 1956-60; proprietor PAcific Coast Equestrian Rsch. Farm, Badger, Calif., 1961-70, Whitehurst Products Co., San Francisco, 1970-75, Deep Moon Gold Mine, Downieville, 1982-92; chmn. Airdock Enterprise Inc., Phoenix, 1994; adj. prof. Prescott (Ariz.) Coll., 1972-75. Engr. ethics com. Soc. Profl. Engrs., Can., 1953-54; bd. govs. Western States Trail Assn., Auburn, Calif., 1962-80. Mem. Am. Assn. Petroleum Geologists. Republican. Congregationalist. Office: Airdock Enterprise PO Box 68291 Tucson AZ 85737

TEMA, WILLIAM JOHN, librarian; b. June 23, 1937; married; 1 son. BS in Edn., U. Minn., 1959, MA, 1961. Lic. real estate broker. Reference libr. Cedar Rapids (Iowa) Pub. Libr., 1961-63; page supr., reference libr. Pasadena (Calif.) Pub. Libr., 1963-67; adult libr. La Pintoresca br. Pasadena Pub. Libr., 1967-69; br. libr. Allendale br. Pasadena Pub. Libr., 1969-70, Hastings br. Pasadena Pub. Libr., 1970-73; dist. libr. Altadena (Calif.) Libr. Dist., 1973—; pres. Pub. Libr. Film Circuit, 1976-77; v.p. Met. Coop. Libr. System, 1984, pres., 1985-86, exec. com. 1994-96; v.p./pres.-elect Pub. Libr. Video Circuit, 1988-89, pres., 1989-90. Pres. Pasadena Am. Sr. Little League, 1981; bd. dirs. Altadena Sr. Ctr., 1982-85. With U.S. Army Res., 1959-69. Mem. Am. Libr. Assn. (membership bd. mem. Pub. Libr. Assn. 1976-78), Calif. Libr. Assn. (nominating com. 1981, govt. rels. com. 1988-91), Pasadena Mcpl. Employee Assn. (dir. 1968), Pasadena Pub. Libr. Assn. (pres. 1970-71), Pub. Libr. Execs. Soc. Calif. (pres. 1977), Altadena Kiwanis

Club (pres. 1976-77), Altadena Kiwanis Club (pres. 1976-77, disting. pres., sec. 1978—), Altadena C. of C. (2d v.p. 1978, v.p. 1979, pres. 1980, co-chmn. Altadena's Old Fashioned Days 1981, 95), Calif. Assn. Realtors, Nat. Bd. Realtors, Pasadena Bd. Realtors. Home: 1115 Sierra Madre Villa Ave Pasadena CA 91107-1528 Office: Altadena Libr Dist 600 E Mariposa St Altadena CA 91001-2211

TEMES, GABOR CHARLES, electrical engineering educator; b. Budapest, Hungary, Oct. 14, 1929; s. Erno and Rozsa (Angyal) Wohl-Temes; m. Ibi Kutasi-Temes, Feb. 6, 1954; children: Roy Thomas, Carla Andrea. Dipl.Ing., Tech. U. Budapest, 1952, DSc (hon.), 1991; Dipl. Phys., Eotvos U., Budapest, 1954; Ph.D., U. Ottawa, Ont., Can., 1961. Asst. prof. Tech. U. Budapest, 1952-56; project engr. Measurement Engring. Ltd., 1956-59; dept. head No. Electric Co. Ltd., 1959-64; group leader Stanford Linear Accelerator Center, 1964-66; corp. cons. Ampex Corp., 1966-69; prof. elec. engring. UCLA, 1969-90, chmn. dept., 1975-80; dept. head Oreg. State U., Corvallis, 1990—; cons. Xerox Corp., ANT GmbH. Author: (with others) Introduction to Circuit Synthesis and Design, 1977, Analog MOS Integrated Circuits for Signal Processing, 1986; assoc. editor: (with others) Jour. Franklin Inst, 1971-82; co-editor, contbg. author: (with others) Modern Filter Theory and Design, 1973, Oversampling Delta-Sigma Data Converters, 1991. Recipient Western Electric Fund award Am. Soc. Engring. Edn., 1982, Humboldt Sr. Rsch. award, 1991; NSF grantee, 1970—. Fellow IEEE (editor Transactions on Circuit Theory 1969-71 Best Paper award 1969, 81, 85, Centennial medal 1984, Edn. award 1987, Tech. Achievement award 1989). Home: 7100 NW Grandview Dr Corvallis OR 97330-2708 Office: Oreg State U Corvallis OR 97330

TEMKO, ALLAN BERNARD, writer; b. N.Y.C., Feb. 4, 1924; s. Emanuel and Betty (Alderman) T.; m. Elizabeth Ostroff, July 1, 1950; children: Susannah, Alexander. AB, Columbia U., 1947; postgrad. U. Calif., Berkeley, 1949-51, Sorbonne, 1948-49, 51-52. Lectr. Sorbonne, 1953-54, Ecole des Arts et Metiers, Paris, 1954-55; asst. prof. journalism U. Calif., Berkeley, 1956-62, lectr. in city planning and social scis., 1966-70, lectr. Grad. Sch. Journalism, 1991; prof. art Calif. State U., Hayward, 1971-80; lectr. art Stanford U., 1981, 82; architecture critic San Francisco Chronicle, 1961-93, art editor, 1979-82; archtl. planning cons.; chmn. Yosemite Falls Design Workshop, 1992; Pulitzer Prize juror, 1991-92. Author: Notre Dame of Paris, 1955, Eero Saarinen, 1962, No Way To Build a Ballpark and Other Irreverent Essays on Architecture, 1993; contbr. articles to U.S. and fgn. mags. and newspapers; West Coast editor, Archtl. Forum, 1959-62. Served with USNR, 1943-46. Recipient Gold medal Commonwealth Club Calif., 1956, Silver medal, 1994, Journalism award AIA, 1961, Silver Spur award San Francisco Planning and Urban Renewal Assn., 1985, AIA Inst. Honor award, 1991, Nathaniel A. Owings award AIA Calif. Coun., 1995, 1st prize in archtl. criticism Mfrs. Hanover/Art World, 1986, Critic's award Mfrs. Hanover/Art World, 1987, Profl. Achievement award Soc. Profl. Journalists, 1988, Pulitzer Prize for criticism, 1990; grantee Rockefeller Found., 1962-63, 20th Century Fund, 1963-66, NEA, 1988, Graham Found., 1990; Guggenheim fellow, 1956-57. Home: 1015 Fresno Ave Berkeley CA 94707-2517

TEMPELMAN, STEVEN CARLOS, lawyer; b. Caracas, Venezuela, Mar. 22, 1967; came to U.S., 1967; s. Russell Neil and Hannelore (Keck) T. B of Individualized Studies, U. Minn., 1990. Air ops. mgr. UPS, Mpls., 1985-87; self-employed, 1987-90; human resources exec. Northwest Transp. Svc., Denver, 1990-91; pvt. practice law Denver, 1992—. Recipient Pres'. Student Leadership and Svc. award, 1988. Mem. Sigma Alpha Epsilon (pres. 1988-89, Merill Cragun award 1989). Address: 2545 S Lafayette St Denver CO 80210-5120

TEMPLIN, JOHN ALTON, historical theology educator, minister; b. Hoehne, Colo., Sept. 27, 1927; s. John Wesley and Stella Mable (Canterbury) T.; m. Dorothy Jean Lear, Dec. 31, 1952; children: Kayla Jean, Ann Revae, Bryce Alton. BA, U. Denver, 1950; ThM, The Iliff Sch. Theology, 1953, ThD, 1956; PhD, Harvard U., 1966. Ordained United Meth. Ch., 1951. Asst. prof. Southwestern Coll., Winfield, Kans., 1954-57; min. Meth. Ch., Mass., 1957-66; asst. prof. U. S.D., Vermillion, 1966-67; asst. to full prof. The Iliff Sch. Theology, Denver, 1967—. Editor: The United Methodist, Evangelical and United Brethren Churches in the Rockies, 1977; author: Ideology on a Frontier: The Theological Foundation of Afrikaner Nationalism, 1652-1910, 1984; author, editor: An Intellectual History of the Iliff School of Theology: A Centennial Tribute, 1892-1992, 1992. Cpl. USAF, 1945-47. Named Alumnus of Yr., The Iliff Sch. Theology, Denver, 1989. Mem. Am. Soc. Ch. History, Am. Soc. Reformation History, Am. Hist. Assn., Sixteenth Century Study Conf. Democrat. Office: The Iliff Sch Theology 2201 S University Blvd Denver CO 80210-4707

TENCER, ALLAN FRED, mechanical engineer, medical educator; b. Montreal, Aug. 23, 1949; came to U.S., 1981; m. Signe Steinbach; 1 child, Holly. BEng, McGill U., 1971, MEng, 1973, PhD in Mech. Engring., 1981. Registered profl. engr., Que., Tex. Asst. prof. bioengring. U. Tex., Arlington, 1981-84; asst. prof. orthopedics U. Tex. Med. Br., Galveston, 1984-88; assoc. prof. orthopedics, adj. prof. bioengring. U. Wash., Seattle, 1988—. Author: Biomechanics in Orthopedic Trauma, 1994; contbr. numerous articles to profl. jours.; co-inventor fracture brace, spinal implant. Grantee NSF, 1982, NIH, 1987, VA, 1993, Ctrs. Disease Control, 1993, 94. Mem. ASME, Orthopedic Rsch. Soc., Soc. for Biomaterials. Office: Harborview Med Ctr 325 9th Ave # 48 Seattle WA 98104-2420

TENNANT, HOWARD EDWARD, academic administrator; b. Lethbridge, Alberta, Can., May 13, 1941; s. Rex. Joseph and Jean Sylvia (Engle) T.; m. Sharon Lea Buckley, Sept. 7, 1963; children: Carmen, Patricia, Daniel. BBA cum laude, Gonzaga U., 1963; MBA, U. Oreg., 1964, PhD, 1970. Asst. prof. U. Saskatchewan, Saskatoon, Can., 1966-70, assoc. prof., 1970-74, prof. mgmt., head dept. mgmt. and mktg., 1972-77, assoc. dean grad. studies, prof. mgmt., 1977-84, dean grad. studies, assoc. v.p. rsch., 1984-87; pres., vice-chancellor U. Lethbridge, 1987—; chmn. bd. dirs. SED Systems Inc., Saskatoon, 1980-90; bd. dirs. Assn. Univ. & Colls. Can., Ottawa, Ontario, 1987—, chmn., 1995—; chmn. Univs. Coordinating Coun., Edmonton, Alberta, 1989-91, 95; bd. dirs. Alberta Rsch. Coun., Edmonton, 1990—; instr. Banff Sch. Advanced Mgmt., 1970-87; labor mediator U. Saskatchewan, 1989; vis. scholar U. Wash. Grad. Sch. Bus., Seattle, 1974-75. Dir. Saskatchewan Rsch. Coun., Saskatoon, 1984-87; bd. dirs. Can. Plains Rsch. Ctr., Regina, Saskatchewan, 1984—, Saskatchewan Expo 86 Corp., Regina., 1985-86. Named adopted son and chief Bull Horn Soc., 1987, 90, Kainai Chief by Blood Indians, 1991; decorated 125th Can. medal Gov. Gen., 1992. Mem. Rotary, Beta Gamma Sigma. Roman Catholic. Home: 61 Ridgewood Cres W, Lethbridge, AB Canada T1K 6C3 Office: Univ Lethbridge, Pres Office, Lethbridge, AB Canada T1K 3M4

TENNANT, MARY JO, secondary education educator; b. Tacoma, Jan. 6, 1938; d. Glenn Everett and Adelia Maurine (Converse) Sigler; m. Charles Edward Tennant, June 27, 1959; children: Stephen Victor, Catherine J. Tennant Mc Guire, Susan M. Tennant Swenson, William G. AB, Cornell U., 1959; MT, U. Ariz., 1976. Tchr. Yuma (Ariz.) Dist. 1, 1975-77, Children's Way Sch., Fairfax, Va., 1977-78, St. Michael Sch., Annandale, Va., 1978-84; substitute tchr. Conejo Valley Unified Dist., Thousand Oaks, Calif., 1985; tchr. English Newbury Park High Sch., 1986-87, Redwood Intermediate Sch., Thousand Oaks, 1987—, chmn. dept. English, 1989—; mem. Dist. Secondary Curriculum adv. com.; mem. Dist. Writing Assessment com.; mem. Dist. Writing Portfolio assessment com.; mem. Tri-Dist. Celebration of Learning com.; mem. Cornell Club of Washington, 1979-84, Cornell Club So. Calif., 1984—; area chmn. Cornell Alumnae Amb., 1994—, area v.p. class of 1959, 1995—; v.p. sch. bd. Am. Sch. Vientiane, Laos, 1973-74, sec. sch. bd., 1972-73. Neighborhood chmn. Ariz. Cactus-Pine council Girl Scouts U.S., 1974-77, bd. dirs., 1976-77; mem. apostolic commn. St. Jude's Ch., Westlake Village. Recipient Service award Lao Mil. Wives, 1974. Mem. NEA, Calif. Tchrs. Assn., Alpha Phi (dist. alumnae chmn. 1985-89, ho. corp. bd. Calstate Northridge, 1995—). Republican. Roman Catholic. Avocations: reading, sewing, walking. Home: 1317 Breckford Ct Westlake Vlg CA 91361-1707 Office: Redwood Intermediate Sch 233 W Gainsborough Rd Thousand Oaks CA 91360-3442

TENNANT, SAMUEL MCKIBBEN, aerospace systems company executive; b. Feb. 1, 1928; s. Richard Grenville and Margaret Louise (McKibben) T.; m. June Ann Fleischer, June 20, 1953; children: Samuel McKibben Jr., Ann Tennant Boehler, Catherine Tennant Jacobi. BME, MIT, 1950; MME, Purdue U., 1951. Vibration engr. Change Vought Aircraft Corp., Dallas, 1951-52; group engr. dynamics and computations Temco Aircraft Corp., Dallas, 1952-58; sr. staff engr. Titan Space Tech. Labs., Redondo Beach, Calif., 1958-61; assoc. group dir. advanced planning Aerospace Corp., El Segundo, Calif., 1961-66, group dir. engring. manned orbiting lab., 1966-69, v.p., gen. mgr. advanced orbital systems div., 1969-84, group v.p. programs, 1984-87, pres., chief exec. officer, 1987—; cons. Los Alamos (N.Mex.) Nat. Lab. Patentee total knee prosthesis. Mem. sci. adv. bd. USAF, 1984-88; mem. sci. adv. group Air Force Logistics Ctr.; mem,. Def. Sci. Bd., 1988—. Mem. AIAA. Office: Aerospace Corp 2350 E El Segundo Blvd El Segundo CA 90245-4609

TENNENT, VALENTINE LESLIE, accountant; b. Apia, Western Samoa, Apr. 5, 1919; came to U.S., 1922; s. Hugh Cowper and Madge Grace (Cook) T.; m. Jeanne Marie Elder, Dec. 10, 1941; children: Madeline Jeanne Walls, Hugh Cowper II, Michael Waller, Val Leslie, Paul Anthony. Student, U. Calif., Berkeley, 1938-40. CPA, Hawaii, La. Mgr. Tennent & Greaney, CPAs, Hilo, Hawaii, 1945-50; ptnr. Cameron, Tennent & Dunn, CPAs, Honolulu, 1950-56; ptnr. KPMG Peat Marwick LLP, Honolulu, 1956-79, cons., 1979-84; ind. rschr. pub. fin. and banking, politico-econ. sci., San Diego, 1984—. Founding trustee, pres., treas. Tennent Art Found., Honolulu, 1955-77; trustee, treas. Watumull Found., Honolulu, 1963-90 (G.J. Watumull award for disting. achievement 1982); bd. dirs. Iolani Sch., Inst. for Human Svcs., Honolulu, Lyman Mus., Hilo. Capt. USAF, 1941-45. Recipient G.J. Watumull award for Disting. Achievement, 1982, Bishop's Cross for Disting. Svc. Protestant Episcopal Ch., Dist. of Hawaii, 1965. Mem. AICPA (governing coun. 1961-64), Hawaii Soc. CPAs (pres. 1960). Episcopalian. Home and Office: 700 Front St Apt 1607 San Diego CA 92101-6011

TENNEY, ROBERT NELSON, finance company executive; b. Detroit, Jan. 14, 1942; s. Elmer L. and Marguerite E. (Proper) T. BS, Ferris State Coll., 1965. Asst. v.p. Congress Fin. Corp., N.Y.C., 1970-76; sr. v.p. Congress Fin. Corp., L.A., 1984-88; v.p. A.J. Armstrong Corp., L.A., 1976-81, Chase Comml. Corp., L.A., 1981-84; pres. Fremont Fin. Corp., Santa Monica, Calif., 1989—. Pres. Park Kenwood Homeowners Assn., Glendale, Calif., 1983-84, Ridge Homeowners Assn., 1990-92. Mem. Comml. Fin. Conf. Calif. (bd. dirs. 1981—, chmn. bd. dirs. 1985-87, pres. 1983-85), Nat. Comml. Fin. Assn. (mem. Far Western edn. com. 1983—, mem. program com. 1985, bd. dirs. 1989—, mem. exec. com. 1991—), Nat. Edn. Found. (bd. dirs.), Jonathan Club, St. James Club, Tau Kappa Epsilon (chmn. bd. trustees Calif. Poly. State U. Pomona chpt. 1984—). Office: Fremont Fin Corp 2020 Santa Monica Blvd Santa Monica CA 90404-2023

TENNEY, WILLIAM FRANK, pediatrician; b. Shreveport, La., June 5, 1946; s. William Bonds and Pat (Patton) T.; m. Elizabeth Carter Steadman, Oct. 4, 1973; children: Amy Karen, William Allen. BA, Vanderbilt U., 1968; MD, La. State U., New Orleans, 1972. Diplomate Am. Bd. Pediatrics, sub-Bd. Pediatric Nephrology. Intern Grady Meml. Hosp., Atlanta, 1972-73; resident in pediatrics Emory U. Affiliated Hosps., Atlanta, 1973-74, fellow in pediatric nephrology and inorganic metabolism, 1974-76; practice medicine specializing in pediatric nephrology St. Helens, Oreg., 1976-79, Shreveport, 1979-85, Seattle, 1985—; mem. staff Children's Orthopedic Hosp. and Med. Ctr., Seattle; chief dept. pediatrics Swedish Hosp. Med. Ctr., Seattle, 1987-90, 95—; clin. asst. prof. pediatrics La. State U. Sch. Medicine, 1979-85, U. Wash. Sch. Medicine, Seattle, 1985—; chmn. Renal com. Schumpert Med. Ctr., Shreveport, 1982, co-chmn. 1979-81, mem. 1983-84, co-dir. Renal Dialysis Unit, 1979-84, mem. renal transplantation com., 1984; cons. pediatric nephrology Shriner's Hosp. Crippled Children, Shreveport, 1979-84, Shreveport Regional Dialysis Ctr., 1979-84, Bossier Dialysis Ctr., Bossier City, La., 1983-84, Natchitoches (La.) Dialysis Facility, 1984. Author: (with others) Pediatric Case Studies, 1985; contbr. articles to profl. jours. Mem. Union Concerned Scientists, Cambridge, Mass., 1986—, Internat. Physicians for Prevention of Nuclear War, Boston, 1986—. Fellow Am. Acad. Pediatrics; mem. Am. Soc. Pediatric Nephrology, North Pacific Pediatric Soc., AMA, Wash. State Med. Assn., Internat. Soc. Peritoneal Dialysis, Empirical Soc. Emory U., King County Med. Soc., AAAS, Northwest Renal Soc., Southwest Pediatric Nephrology (mem. study group 1981-84). Home: 23915 SE 42nd Ct Issaquah WA 98027-7521 Office: 1221 Madison St Seattle WA 98104-1360

TENNISON, WILLIAM RAY, JR., financial planner, stockbroker, recreational facility executive; b. Deming, N.Mex., July 22, 1941; s. William Ray and Mildred Rose (Frei) T., m. Mary Kay Reid, Jan. 27, 1963; children: William Ervin, Bradley Joseph, Stephanie Kay (dec.). BS in Indsl. Mgmt., Ariz. State U., 1963; MBA in Econs., U. Ariz., 1966. Indsl. engr. USAF, 1963-71; from account exec. to br. office mgr., stockbroker E. F. Hutton & Co., Mesa, Ariz., 1971-88, first v.p., also mem. Dirs. Adv. Coun.; sr. v.p., stockbroker Kemper Security Group, Mesa, Ariz., 1988-92, sr. v.p. Boettcher divsn., also Kemper Exec. Coun.; exec. v.p. D.E. Frey, Mesa, Ariz., 1992—; pres. Tennison and Assocs., Inc., Mesa, Ariz., 1992—; owner Crystal Meadows Ranch, Inc., Somerset, Colo.; speaker in field at sales confs. and conventions. Author: (book/tng. program) Bill Tennison Master Class, 1990.; featured in Registered Representative Mag., 1989, Rsch. Mag., 1992, 93, Arizona Business Mag., 1993; contbr. articles to profl. jours; presenter weekly radio show. Mem. East Valley Sr. Found., 1986-91. Mem. Paonia (Colo.) Rotary Club. Republican. Mem. Christian Ch. Home: 1735 N Val Vista Dr Mesa AZ 85213-3223 Office: DE Frey & Co 40 N Center Ste 100 Mesa AZ 85201-7300

TENORIO, VICTOR, community college official, researcher; b. Trinidad, Colo., Dec. 30, 1937; s. Felix and Porfiria (Montoya) T.; divorced; children: Victor Jr., Yvonne Rene, Mark Anthony. BS in History, Psychology and Edn., So. Colo. State Coll. (now U. So. Colo.), 1971. Neighborhood aide So. Colo. State Coll. (name now U. So. Colo.), Pueblo, 1971-72, admissions and records counselor, 1972-74; asst. dir. fin. aide Adams State Coll., Alamosa, Colo., 1974-75; asst. dir. admissions So. Colo. State U. (now U. So. Colo.), Pueblo, 1975-78, asst. dir. fin. aid, 1975-79; dir. student svcs. Pueblo Community Coll., 1979—, dir. admissions, fin. aid and vet. affairs, 1979-83, coord. instrnl. support, 1983-85, coord. student employment, 1985—; owner Joe's Miffler & Brake Ctr., Pueblo, Colo.; organizer, mem. Community Referral System, Canon City, Colo., 1985, Employer Svc. System (for Disabled), Pueblo, 1985—. With USMC, 1956-59. Recipient Outstanding Staff Svc. award U. So. Colo., 1979. Mem. Latin Am. Rsch. and Svcs. Agy, Colo. Ednl. Svcs. and Devel. Assn. Democrat. Roman Catholic. Office: Vic's Muffler & Brake Ctr 2114 S Prairie Ave Bldg C Pueblo CO 81005-2432

TERAMURA, ALAN HIROSHI, science educator; b. L.A., Dec. 26, 1948; s. Kuniyoshi and Mineko (Nakamura) T.; m. Karen Lee McKnight, Sept. 10, 1974; 1 child. BA, Calif. State U., 1971, MA, 1973; PhD, Duke U., 1978. Asst. prof. botany U. Md., College Park, 1979-82, assoc. prof. botany, 1982-88, prof. botany, 1988-93; dean coll. natural scis. U. Hawaii, Honolulu, 1994—; guest prof. Botanishes Inst., Karlsruhe, Germany, 1982-83; chmn. sci. adv. bd. Ctr. Global Change, College Park, 1989-93; cons. USDA, EPA, Nat. Acad. Sci., Washington, 1982—. Contbr. chpts. to 12 books and 80 articles to profl. jours. Grantee NSF, 1977, U.S. EPA, 1980-90, USDA, 1989-93. Mem. Am. Soc. Plant Physiologists, Botanical Soc. Am., Ecol. Soc. Am., Sigma Xi. Office: U Hawaii Office Dean Coll Natural Scis 102 Bilger Honolulu HI 96822

TERAWAKI, DEREK KUNIO, engineer; b. Honolulu, Mar. 29, 1970; s. Kenneth Haruto and Evie Hanae (Tokeshi) T. BSEE, Santa Clara U., 1992. Project engineer Adtech, Inc., Honolulu, 1992—. Home: 336 N Kuakini St Apt 421 Honolulu HI 96817-2353

TERENCE, FRANK, financial executive; b. Panama, Mar. 9, 1959. BS in Fin., Internat. Bus., Spanish Lit., Fla. State U., 1981; M in Internat. Bus., U. S.C., 1983. Cert. mgmt. acct. Planning analyst, pricing analyst, mktg. planning analyst NCR Corp., Dayton, Ohio, 1983-86; capital investment analyst, info. system ctr. Rockwell Internat., Seal Beach, Calif., 1986-88; sr. ops. systems analyst to acctg. supr. franchise acctg. Taco Bell divsn. PepsiCo, Inc., Irvine, Calif., 1988-90; mgr. fin., contr. Ashton-Tate, Torrance, Calif., 1990-91; contr. Borland Internat., Scotts Valley, Calif., 1991-94; gen. mgr. Latin Am. Borland Internat., 1994; dir. internat. fin. Ingram Micro Inc., Santa Ana, Calif., 1994—. Mem. Inst. Mgmt. Accts. Office: Ingram Micro Inc 1600 E St Andrew Pl Santa Ana CA 92799

TERESI, JOSEPH, publishing executive; b. Mpls., Mar. 13, 1941; s. Cliff I.A. and Helen Ione (Leslie) T.; divorced; 1 child, Nicholas. Chief exec. officer Jammer Cycle Products Inc., Burbank, Calif., 1968-80, Paisano Pubs. Inc., Agoura Hills, Calif., 1970—. Pub. (mags.) Easyriders, 1971—, In the Wind, 1974—, Biker Lifestyle, 1986—, Tatoo, 1986—, Am. Rodder, 1987, Womens Enterprise, 1987-89, Eagles Eye, 1989—, Tattoo Flash, 1993—, Tattoo Savage, 1993—, VQ, 1994—, Earlyriders, 1994—, Quick Throttle, 1995—, Roadware, 1995—. Office: Paisano Pubs Inc PO Box 3000 Agoura Hills CA 91376-3000

TERMINI, OLGA ASCHER, music educator; b. Hamburg, Germany, May 19, 1930; came to U.S., 1952; d. Viktor and Martha M. (Schuett) Ascher; married, Nov. 20, 1955 (dec. July 1979). MusB, U. So. Calif., 1954, MusM, 1957, PhD, 1970. Instr. music Stevenson Jr. H.S., L.A., 1954-57, Fairfax H.S., L.A., 1957-72; asst. prof. music Calif. State U., L.A., 1972-76, assoc.prof. music, 1976-81, prof. music, 1981—; instr. voice classes L.A. City Coll., 1957-64; instr. music history and theory Pasadena (Calif.) City Coll., 1973-76; vis. prof. musicology Claremont (Calif.) Grad. Sch., 1986,95. Contbr. articles to music revs. and profl. publs.; translator various German-English articles for profl. jours. Mem. edit. bd. Jour. of the Arnold Schoenberg Inst., 1974-81; bd. dirs. Glendale (Calif.) Chamber Orch., 1985-89; mem. philharmonic women's com. L.A. Philharmonic Women's Assn., 1985-86; assoc. dir. Pacific Contemporary Music Ctr., 1987—, newsletter editor, 1988—; substitute soloist 1st Ch. Christian Scientist, Alhambra, Calif., 1990—. Music scholar Ebell Club, 1953-54, Fulbright grantee, Venice, Italy, 1966-67, Calif. State U. Instnl. grantee, 1974-75, 75-76. Mem. NEA, Am. Musicol. Soc. (Pacific S.W. chpt. sec. 1981-83, v.p. 1984-86, pres. 1986-88, elective counselor 1990-92), Coll. Music Soc. (life), N.Am. Vivaldo Assn. (charter), Western Soc. 18th Century Studies, Calif. Music Tchrs. Assn., Am. Handel Soc., Music Tchrs. Assn. Calif. (scholarship com. Pasadena br.), Phi Beta Delta, Phi Kappa Phi, Pi Kappa Lambda. Democrat. Home: 4278 Sea View Ln Los Angeles CA 90065-3350 Office: Calif State U dept Music 5151 State University Dr Los Angeles CA 90032-4221

TERRANOVA, PATRICIA HELEN, treasurer; b. Tacoma, Mar. 25, 1952; d. Donald John and Alicia Katherine (Rose) Marcan; m. Richard James McDonald, Aug. 28, 1971 (div. 1974); 1 child, Christopher Ryan; m. Anthony James Terranova, July 3, 1986. A.Acctg., Ft. Steilacoom Coll., Tacoma, 1974. Contract adminstr. Titan Pacific Corp., Ft. Lewis, Wash., 1974-77; office mgr. Sequoia Supply, Tacoma, 1977-78; treas., chief fin. officer Woodworth & Co., Inc., Tacoma, 1978—. Active PTA, Tacoma, 1978—; sec.-treas. Adelaine Acres Homeowners' Assn. Mem. Nat. Assn. Credit Mgrs., Credit Execs. of Puget Sound, Women in Constrn. Republican. Roman Catholic. Office: Woodworth & Co Inc 1200 E D St Tacoma WA 98421-1710

TERRAS, AUDREY ANNE, mathematics educator; b. Washington, Sept. 10, 1942; d. Stephen Decatur and Maude Mae (Murphy) Bowdoin. BS with high honors in Math., U. Md., 1964; MA, Yale U, 1966, PhD, 1970. Instr. U. Ill., Urbana, 1968-70; asst. prof. U. P.R., Mayaguez, 1970-71; asst. prof. Bklyn. Coll., CUNY, 1971-72; asst. prof. math. U. Calif.-San Diego, La Jolla, 1972-76, assoc. prof., 1976-83, prof., 1983—, vis. positions MIT, fall 1977, 83, U. Bonn (W.Ger.), spring 1977, Inst. Mittag-Leffler, Stockholm, winter, 1978, Inst. Advanced Study, spring 1984, Math. Scis. Rsch. Inst., Berkeley, Calif., winter 1992, spring 1995; dir. West Coast Number Theory Conf., U. Calif.-San Diego, 1976, AMS joint summer rsch. conf., 1984; lectr. in field. Author: Harmonic Analysis on Symmetric Spaces and Applications, Vol. I, 1985, Vol. II, 1988. Contbr. articles and chpts. to profl. publs. Woodrow Wilson fellow, 1964; NSF fellow, 1964-68; NSF grantee Summer Inst. in Number Theory, Ann Arbor, Mich., 1973; prin. investigator NSF, 1974-88. Fellow AAAS; mem. AAAS (nominating com. math. sect. project 2061), Am. Math. Soc. (com. employment and ednl. policy com. on coms., council, transactions editor, com. for the yr. 2000), Math. Assn. Am. (program com. for nat. meeting 1988-90, chair joint com. Am. Math. Soc. and Math. Assn. Am. 1991), Soc. Indsl. and Applied Math., Assn. for Women in Math., Assn. for Women in Sci. Research in harmonic analysis on symmetric spaces and number theory. Office: U Calif San Diego Dept Math La Jolla CA 92093-0112

TERRAS, RITA, German language educator; b. Bremen, Germany, July 31, 1927; came to U.S., 1952; d. Richard and Marie Schubert; m. Victor Terras, 1951; 1 child, Alexander. BA, U. Ill., 1961, MA, 1966; PhD, U. Wis., 1969. Lectr. in German U. Wis., 1969-70; asst. prof. U. R.I., 1971-72; prof. of German Conn. Coll., New London, 1972-88, prof. of German emerita, 1988—; freelance writer, 1988—; editor Trans-Lit, 1992—. Author: Wilhelm Heinses Aesthetik, 1972, Unterwegs 1981, Informative Definitionen, 1989; editor Symposium on Romanticism, 1975; contbr. articles to profl. jours. Recipient travel grant Am. Philos. Soc., 1970, rsch. grant Deutsche Forschungsgemeinschaft, 1976, vis. faculty fellowship Yale U., 1978-79, vis. professorship Brown U., 1983. Mem. MLA, Am. Assn. Tchrs. German (pres. Conn. chpt. 1970s), German Studies Assn., Goethe Soc. N.Am. (co-founder), Internat. Herder Soc. (co-founder), Nat. Mus. Women in Arts (co-founder), Soc. for German-Am. Studies, Lessing Soc., Soc. Contempory Am. Lit. in German (pres. 1992—). Home: 128 Maple Ave Little Compton RI 02837-1714

TERRELL, A. JOHN, university telecommunications director; b. Pasadena, Calif., Dec. 27, 1927; s. Harry Evans and Elizabeth (Eaton) T.; m. Elizabeth Schalk, June 6, 1949; children—Patricia Elyse, Marilee Diane, John Scott. Student, Chaffey Coll., 1947-48; B.B.A., U. N. Mex., 1952. Communications cons. Mountain States Tel. & Tel., Albuquerque, 1951-56; mgr. office and communications services A.C.F. Industries, Inc., Albuquerque, 1956-62; mgr. communications and services Norton Simon Industries, Inc., Fullerton, Ca., 1962-68; v.p. gen. mgr. Wells Fargo Security Guard Service Div. Baker Industries, Fullerton, Ca., 1968-71; adminstrv. mgr., budget adminstr. Hyland div. Baxter-Trevenol Labs. Inc., Costa Mesa, CA, 1971-77; exec. v.p. Am. Tel. Mgmt. Inst Inc., Newport Beach, Calif., 1977-78; telecommunications dir. UCLA, 1978-89, retired, 1989. Contbr. articles to profl. jours. Republican. candidate for state rep., Albuquerque, 1960; precinct chmn. and mem. Bernalillo County Rep. Central Com., 1961-62; Rep. candidate for N. Mex. State Bd. Edn., 2nd Jud. Dist., 1962; colonial aide-de-camp Gov. N. Mex., Santa Fe, 1968. Served with U.S. Mcht. Marine, 1944-45, U.S. Army, 1946-47, USAR, 1947-50. Mem. Nat. Assn. Accts. (dir. 1967-77) (Most Valuable mem. 1974-75), Telecommunications Assn., Am. Legion, Am. Legion Yacht Club , VFW. Episcopalian. Lodges: Greater Irvine Lions (charter pres. 1975-76), Albuquerque Jaycees (v.p., treas. 1956-62). Home: 1725 Port Charles Pl Newport Beach CA 92660-5319

TERRELL, HOWARD BRUCE, psychiatrist; b. Cleveland, Calif., Feb. 19, 1952. BS magna cum laude, Calif. State U., Hayward, 1974; MD, U. Calif., San Diego, 1980. Diplomate Am. Bd. Psychiatry and Neurology. Intern. Kaiser Found. Hosp., Oakland, Calif., 1980-81; resident in psychiatry U. Calif., San Francisco/Fresno, 1982-85; staff psychiatrist Kings View Corp., Reedley, Calif., 1985-87, sr. staff psychiatrist, 1987-88, dir. outpatient psychiatry, 1988-89; dir. dual diagnosis and affective disorders programs Sierra Gateway Hosp., Clovis, Calif., 1989-91. Contbr. articles to profl. jours. Fellow Am. Coll. Forensic Psychiatry, Am. Bd. Forensic Examiners (diplomate); mem. Am. Acad. Psychiatry and the Law, Am. Psychiat. Assn., U. Calif.-San Francisco-Fresno Psychiat. Residency Program (alumni pres. 1985—). Office: 3100 Willow Ave Ste 102 Clovis CA 93612-4741

TERRELL, PAUL L., social work educator, university administrator; b. Bronx, N.Y., Sept. 25, 1942; s. Herbert Terrell; m. Kathy Terrell; children: Joshua, Benjamin; 1 stepson, Sean Bartmasser. BA, U. Calif., Berkeley, 1964, MA, 1965, MSW, 1967, DSW, 1975. Planner Kaplan, Gans & Kahn, San Francisco, 1967-69; social worker San Francisco Child Svcs., 1970-71; assoc. dir. Regional Rsch. Inst. U. So. Calif., L.A., 1974-76; instr. San Diego State U., 1976-79; tchr., adminstr. Sch. of Social Welfare U. Calif., Berkeley, 1979—. Co-author: Dimensions of Social Welfare Policy, 1993; also other books, articles, chpts., reports. Office: University of California School of Social Welfare Berkeley CA 94720

TERRELL, W(ILLIAM) GLENN, university president emeritus; b. Tallahassee, May 24, 1920; s. William Glenn and Esther (Collins) T.; m. Gail Strandberg Terrell; children by previous marriage: Francine Elizabeth, William Glenn III. BA, Davidson Coll., 1942, LLD (hon.), 1969; MS, Fla. State U., 1948; PhD, State U. Iowa, 1952; LLD (hon.), Gonzaga U., 1984, Seattle U., 1985. Instr., then asst. prof. Fla. State U., Tallahassee, 1948-55; asst. prof., then assoc. prof., chmn. dept. psychology U. Colo., Boulder, 1955-59, assoc., acting dean Coll Arts and Scis., 1959-63; prof. psychology, dean Coll. Liberal Arts and Scis., U. Ill. at Chgo. Circle, 1963-65, dean faculties, 1965-67; pres. Wash. State U., Pullman, 1967-85, pres. emeritus, 1985—; Pres. Nat. Assn. State Univs. and Land-Grant Colls., 1977-78; cons. The Pacific Inst., Seattle, 1987—. Contbr. articles to profl. jours. Served to capt. inf. U.S. Army, 1942-46, ETO. Recipient Disting. Alumnus award U. Iowa, 1985. Fellow APA, Soc. Rsch. in Child Devel.; mem. AAAS, Sigma Xi, Phi Kappa Phi. Home: 2438 36th Ave W Seattle WA 98199-3704 Office: The Pacific Inst 1011 Western Ave Seattle WA 98104-1040

TERRILL, DAVID PHILIP, fair industry executive; b. Escalon, Calif., Oct. 17, 1955; s. William Dean Terrill and Shirley Ann (Hall) Barnett; ;m. Karen Sue Bonds, Jan. 2, 1950. BA in Journalism, Calif. State U., Fresno, 1978. Publicity dir. 21st Dist. Agrl. Assn., Fresno, 1977-78, exhibit supr., 1978-83, sec.-mgr., 1983; sec.-mgr. 19th Dist. Agrl. Assn., Santa Barbara, Calif., 1984-86; fairs mgmt. cons. State of Calif., Sacramento, 1986-91; pres. Calif. Fair Svcs. Authority, Sacramento, 1991-94, mgr. mgmt. svcs., 1991-93, asst. exec. dir. svcs., 1993-94; prin. Affordable Bus. Concepts, Gold River, Calif., 1994—. Mem. Am. Mgmt. Assn., Western Fairs Assn. (profl. devel. com. 1986—, agr. and edn. com. 1990—, 5 Achievement awards 1977-82). Office: Affordable Bus Concepts Ste 310-16 11230 Gold Express Dr Gold River CA 95670-4400

TERRILL, KAREN STAPLETON, retired medical planning consultant; b. Milw., Mar. 21, 1939; d. Thomas John and Olive Patrea (Thorbjornsen) Stapleton; m. Max Kurt Winkler, Dec. 18, 1965 (dec. June 1976); m. Richard Terrill, Jan. 23, 1991 (dec. May 1991). BS in Nursing, U. Mich., 1961; MBA, U. Nev., 1974. RN, Calif. Project nurse Langley Porter N.P.I., San Francisco, 1962-64; asst. dir. nursing Milw. County Mental Health Ctr., 1964-66; instr. Fond du Lac (Wis.) Sch. Dist., 1966-67; sch. nurse Inglewood (Calif.) Sch. Dist., 1968-69; instr. nursing U. Nev., Reno, 1969-74; health planner manpower State of Nev. Comp B. Agy., Carson City, 1974-75; planning analyst St. Mary's Hosp., Reno, 1974-76; sr. system analyst U. Calif., San Francisco, 1976-79; med. planning cons. Stone Marraccini & Patterson, San Francisco, 1979-93. Mem. citizen's adv. group City of Richmond, Calif., 1987-88; founding dir. of B.O.A.T. non-profit corp. to promote ferry transit on San Francisco Bay. Mountain State Regional Planning Commn. grantee, 1973-74. Home: 1308 Mallard Dr Richmond CA 94801-4113

TERRILL, W(ALLACE) ANDREW, international security analyst; b. Pasadena, Calif., Aug. 15, 1954; s. Wallace and Gloria (Acheson) T. BA in Polit. Sci., Calif. State Poly. U., 1975; MA in Polit. Sci., U. Calif., Riverside, 1976; PhD in Internat. Rels., The Claremont Grad. Sch., 1983. Rsch. asst. Analytical Assessments Corp., L.A., 1978-80, rsch. assoc., 1980-87; part-time instr. Calif. State Poly. U., Pomona, 1987-89; asst. prof. polit. sci. Old Dominion U., Norfolk, Va., 1989-93; internat. security analyst Proliferation Assessments Divsn. Lawrence Livermore Nat. Lab., Livermore, Calif., 1993—; cons. Sys. Rsch. and Devel. Corp., L.A., 1987-89; adj. asst. prof. Occidental Coll., L.A., 1988-89; workshop leader; interviewed on TV, radio and in print media on Mid. Eastern and nonproliferation issues. Contbr. numerous book revs., articles and rsch. to acad. jours. Served with USAR, 1976—, maj., 1990—. Recipient Haynes Found. dissertation fellowship, 2 Claremont Grad. Sch. full-tuition fellowships.

TERRIS, DAVID JAMES, head and neck surgeon, research scientist; b. Rome, N.Y., May 12, 1962; s. Frederick Morton and Elaine Marie (Crimmins) T.; m. Martha Bernice Kennedy, Dec. 28, 1987; children: Trevor, Garrett. BA, Cornell U., 1984; MD, Duke U., 1988. Diplomate Am. Bd. Otolaryngology. Intern in surgery Stanford (Calif.) U. Med. Ctr., 1988-89, resident in surgery, 1989-93, fellow in head and neck oncologic surgery, 1993-94, asst. prof. surgery, 1994—. Author: (with others) Manual of Surgical Procedures, 1994; contbr. articles to profl. jours. Mem. AMA, Am. Acad. Otolaryngology, Am. Assn. Facial Plastic and Reconstructive Surgery, Phi Beta Kappa, Alpha Omega Alpha. Republican. Home: 1000 Border Rd Los Altos CA 94024 Office: Stanford U Med Ctr R-135 Edwards Bldg Stanford CA 94305-5328

TERRY, DARRELL MERLE, sociology educator, consultant; b. Council Bluffs, Iowa, Nov. 11, 1933; s. Riley Merle and Sara Blanche (Grove) T.; m. Alice Rebecca Beams, Dec. 27, 1957 (div. 1975); children: Crescent Lynn, Angela Anne. BA, Lincoln (Ill.) Christian Coll., 1956; MDiv, Lincon Christian Sem., 1963; BA in Sociology, Whittier (Calif.) Coll., 1968, MA in Sociology, 1969; PhD in Human Behavior, U.S. Internat. U., San Diego, 1975. Founding min. First Christian Ch., La Mirada, Calif., 1961-64; founder, dir. Project Challenge, Inc., Avalon, Calif., 1963-71; prof. Cypress (Calif.) Coll., 1971-80, chmn. dept. human svcs., 1981-88, prof. human svcs., 1988—; dir. DM Terry Cons., Long Beach, Calif., 1980—; bd. dirs. U.S. Div. of Toc-H, London, City of Refuge, Tijuana, Mex., Resource Inst., Long Beach. Bd. dirs. LAOS, Inc., El Toro, Calif., 1975—; creator Eagles Nest Self Esteem program. Mem. Calif. Assn. Drug and Alcohol Educators (v.p. bd. dirs. Mission Viejo, Calif. chpt. 1984—), Lincoln Christian Coll. Alumni Assn. (Restoration award 1968, Alumni of Yr.), Alpha Kappa Delta. Mem. Christian Ch. Home: 5796 Campo Walk Long Beach CA 90803-5035 Office: Cypress Coll 9200 Valley View St Cypress CA 90630-5805

TERRY, DAVID LEE, enlisted air force officer; b. Mpls., Sept. 30, 1966; s. Kenneth Lee and Grace Dorothea (Kornmann) T.; m. Kimberly Anne McNeal, Apr. 29, 1989; children: Gretchen Marie, Samantha Morgan. AS in Intelligence Collection, C.C. of the Air Force, Maxwell AFB, Ala., 1991. Desk clk. Spring Mill Inn, Mitchell, Ind., 1984-85; signals intelligence ops. specialist Detachment 2, 6994th Electronic Security Squadron, USAF, Ft. Meade, Md., 1986-89; chief ops. tng. Detachment 1, 4th Space Surveillance Squadron, USAF, San Vito Air Station, Italy, 1987-92; ops. stds. non-commd. officer (sgt.) 73D Ops. Support Squqadron, USAF, Falcon AFB, Colo., 1992—, non-commd. officer in charge low altitude space sys. devel., 1994. Vol. Rick McIntyre Congl. Campaign, Bedford, 1984. Decorated Air Force Commendation medal. Mem. Air Force Sgts. Assn. Home: 507B McChord St Colorado Springs CO 80915

TERRY, FRANK JEFFREY, bishop. Bishop Diocese of Spokane, Wash., 1991—. Office: Diocese of Spokane 245 E 13th Ave Spokane WA 99202-1114*

TERRY, PATRICIA A., literature educator; b. Hartford, Conn., Feb. 13, 1929; d. William Samuel and Sarah Harriet (Press) Blech; m. Robert Davis Terry, June 27, 1952; 1 child, Nicolas S. Terry. BA, Wellesley U., 1950; PhD, Columbia U., 1958. adj. prof. French Lit., Barnard Coll., N.Y.C., 1958-84, U. Calif. San Diego, La Jolla, Calif., 1984-91. Translator: (books) Poems of Jules LaForgue, 1958, reprinted 1986, Lays of Courtly Love, 1965, The Song of Roland, 1969, 2d edit. 1992, Modern European Poetry, 1966, Poems of the Vikings, 1969, 2d edit., 1992, Modern French Poetry, 1981, Roof Slates and Other Poems of Pierre reverdy (with Mary Ann Caws), 1981, The Romance of Renard, 1983, reprinted 1992, Pierre Reverdy, Selected Poems, 1991, The Romance of the Rose or Guillaume de Dole, 1993, others. Grantee Nat. Endowment for the Humanities, 1982. Home: 14868 High Valley Rd Poway CA 92064-2714

TERRY, RICHARD FRANK, data transcriber; b. Ogden, Utah, July 19, 1949; s. Frank Nebeker and Gertrude Angeline (Berghout) T. BA, Weber State Coll., 1979. Data transcriber IRS, Marriott, Utah, 1976—. Mem. Ch. of Jesus Christ of Latter Day Saints.

TERRY, ROBERT DAVIS, neuropathologist, educator; b. Hartford, Conn., Jan. 13, 1924; m. Patricia Ann Blech, June 27, 1952; 1 son, Nicolas Saul. AB, Williams Coll., 1946, DSc (hon.), 1991; MD, Albany (N.Y.) Med. Coll., 1950. Diplomate: Am. Bd. Pathology, Am. Bd. Neuropathology. Postdoctoral tng. St. Francis Hosp., Hartford, 1950, Bellevue Hosp., N.Y.C., 1951, Montefiore Hosp., N.Y.C., 1952-53, 54-55, Inst. Recherches sur le Cancer, Paris, France, 1953-54; sr. postdoctoral fellow Inst. Recherches sur le Cancer, 1965-66; asst. pathologist Montefiore Hosp., 1955-59; assoc. prof. dept. pathology Einstein Coll. Medicine, Bronx, N.Y., 1959-64; prof. Einstein Coll. Medicine, 1964-84, acting chmn. dept. pathology, 1969-70, chmn., 1970-84; prof. depts. neuroscis. and pathology U. Calif.-San Diego, 1984-94, prof. emeritus, 1994—; mem. study sect. pathology NIH, 1964-68; study sects. Nat. Multiple Sclerosis Soc., 1964-72, 74-78; mem. bd. sci. counselors Nat. Inst. Neurol. and Communicative Disorders and Stroke, NIH, 1976-80, chmn., 1977-80; mem. nat. sci. coun. Huntington's Disease Assn., 1978-81; mem. med. and sci. adv. bd. Alzheimer Assn., 1978-88; mem. sci. adv. bd. Max Planck Inst., Martinsried, 1990—. Mem. editorial adv. bd. Jour. Neuropathology and Exptl. Neurology, 1963-83, 85-88, Lab. Investigation, 1967-77, Revue Neurologique, 1977-87, Annals of Neurology, 1978-82, Ultrastructural Pathology, 1978-86, Am. Jour. Pathology, 1985-89. Served with AUS, 1943-46. Recipient Potamkin prize for Alzheimer Rsch., 1988, Met. Life Found. award, 1991. Fellow AAAS; mem. Am. Assn. Neuropathologists (pres. 1969-70, Meritorious Contbn. award 1989), N.Y. Path. Soc. (v.p. 1969-70, pres. 1971-73), Am. Assn. Pathologists, Am. Neurol. Assn., Am. Acad. Neurologists. Office: U Calif San Diego Dept Neuroscis La Jolla CA 92093

TERRY, STEPHEN, gynecologist/obstetrician; b. N.Y.C., Jan. 3, 1936; s. James Hendrick and Theodosia Ruggels Hatch T.; m. Barbara Anne Brown, Sept. 3, 1960; children: Stephen Wilson, Andrew Brock, Sarah Elizabeth. BA in Chemistry cum laude, U. Ariz., 1957, BA in Zoology cum laude, 1957; MD, Columbia U., 1961. Diplomate Am. Bd. Ob/Gyn. Intern in medicine, surgery Bellevue Hosp., N.Y.C., 1961-62; resident in ob-gyn N.Y. Lying-In Hosp., 1962-65; ob-gyn U.S. Army Med. Corps, Nuremberg, Germany, 1965-68, Okla. City Clinic, 1968-69; fellow in gynecology/oncology M.D. Anderson Hosp., Houston, 1969-70; pvt. practice ob/gyn Tucson, 1970—; clin. asst. Cornell Med. Sch., N.Y.C., 1963-65, U. Okla. Med. Sch., Oklahoma City, 1968-69; co-chief ob-gyn Pima County Hosp., Tucson, 1970; bd. dirs. Gaslight Enterprises, Tuscon; lect. U. Ariz. Med. Sch., Tuscon, 1992—; rsch. cons., investigator Argus Rsch., Tucson, 1993—. Recipient commendation medal U.S. Army, 1968, certificate of achievement, 1967. Fellow Am. Coll. Obstetricians & Gynecologists, Am. Fertility Soc., Am. Urogynecol. Soc.; mem. Southwest Obstetrical/Gynecol. Soc. (coun. 1989, pres. 1994), Med. Soc. U.S. & Mexico, Am. Soc. Colposcopy, Am. Assn. Gynecol. Laparascopists, Am. Gynecol. Laser Soc., Tucson Obstet. and Gynecol. Soc. (pres. 1982), Social Register Assn., Knights of the Vine (social chmn., scholarship chmn.), Delta Sigma Phi (social chmn., scholarship chmn.), Phi Beta Kappa, Phi Lambda Upsilon, Beta Beta Beta. Home: 6121 E San Marino Tucson AZ 85715-3017 Office: 5295 E Knight Dr Tucson AZ 85712-2147

TERRY, STEVEN SPENCER, mathematics educator, consultant; b. Hoodriver, Oreg., July 9, 1942; s. Steven Bliss and Kathryn (Spencer) T.; m. Vivian Hickman, Aug. 20, 1964; children: Yvette, Kathryn, S. Matthew, Spencer, Stuart, Heather. BS, Utah State U., 1964, MS, 1967. Tchr. math Clayton Jr. High, Salt Lake City, 1964-67, 29 Palms (Calif.) High Sch., 1967-68; tchr. math, coach Yucca Valley (Calif.) High Sch., 1968-76; prof. math. Ricks Coll., Rexburg, Idaho, 1976—; chmn. dept. Author: (textbook) Elementary Teachers' Math, 1985. Pres. Yucca Valley City Coun., 1972-76, mem. water bd., fire and streets bd., lighting bd., recreation bd.; judge Young Woman of Yr. contests, Idaho; officer Madison County (Idaho) Baseball Assn.; mem. Rexburg Airport Bd. Recipient Outstanding Tchrs. award San Bernardino and Riverside Counties, Calif., 1976, Outstanding Secondary Educator, 1974, 75. Mem. Am. Math. Assn. Two-Yr. Colls. (v.p. 1980-86, dir. Summer Inst., Outstanding Contbn. award 1982, 94, 96, co-chair Summer Inst. at Ricks Coll., co-chair 1988 conv.), Nat. Coun. Tchrs. Math., NEA (life), Phi Delta Kappa (life, sec. 1974-76, Outstanding Contbn. award 1984). Republican. Mormon. Home: 221 S 2nd E # D Rexburg ID 83440-2202 Office: Ricks Coll Rexburg ID 83460-0515

TERRY, WARD EDGAR, JR., lawyer; b. Denver, Aug. 1, 1943; s. Ward E. and Peggy Helen Louise (Smith) T.; m. Juliann Dire, Apr. 8, 1967; children: Seth S., Nicole E. BA, U. Colo., 1965, JD, 1968; LLM in Taxation, U. Denver, 1976. Bar: Colo. 1968, U.S. Dist. Ct. Colo. 1968, U.S. Tax Ct. 1980. Assoc. McMartin & Burk, Englewood, Colo., 1968-70, Modesitt & Shaw, Denver, 1970-71, Gorsuch, Kirgis, Campbell, Walker & Grover, Denver, 1971-72, Hopper and Kanouff, Denver, 1976-78; sec., dir. Ward Terry and Co., Denver, 1972-76; ptnr. Hopper, Kanouff, Smith, Peryam & Terry, Denver, 1979-91; shareholder Hopper and Kanouff, P.C., Denver, 1991—, also bd. dirs.; gen. ptnr. PSW Investments Ltd., Denver, 1984—. Trustee Denver Country Day Sch., Englewood, 1969-70; campaign chair Roseanne Ball Election Com., Denver, 1974. Mem. ABA (bus. law sect., real estate and probate sect., taxation sect., antitrust sect.), Colo. Bar Assn. (bus. law and taxation sect.), Denver Bar Assn., Denver Gyro Club (pres. 1994-95, v.p. 1993-94, membership chmn. 1991-92), Phi Alpha Delta. Republican. Presbyterian. Office: Hopper and Kanouff PC 1610 Wynkoop St Ste 200 Denver CO 80202-1196

TERWILLIGER, CYNTHIA LOU, software designer; b. Cherry Pt., N.C., May 28, 1955; d. James Alexander and Shirley Mae (Zent) Marks; m. Paul Wayne Terwilliger Jr., Sept. 23, 1978; children: Bryce Ashley, Natalie Cadence. BA, U. Redlands, Redlands, 1977; MA, U. Calif., Riverside, 1980; EdD, U.S. Internat. U., 1987. Classroom tchr. Yucaipa (Calif.) Joint Unified Sch. Dist., 1977-83; edn. therapist Learning Devel. Svcs., San Diego, 1983-88; instrnl. designer Perspective Instrnl. Communication, San Diego, 1984, ISSCO, San Diego, 1985, Jostens Learning Corp., San Diego, 1986-94; v.p. edn. and sch. programs Futurekids, Inc., L.A., 1994—. Designer of software including Elementary Math Curricula, 1987, Take Home Computer, 1990, Home Learning System, 1990, TEAMS & TAAS Inventory, 1988-90, Tapestry, 1991-92. Swim instr. ARC, Redlands, 1973-84; fundraiser Am. Heart Assn., Yucaipa, 1982. Mem. Learning Disabilities Assn., Phi Delta Kappa. Republican. Home: 4636 Serenata Pl San Diego CA 92130-2462 Office: Futurekids Inc 5777 W Century Blvd Ste 1555 Los Angeles CA 90045-5678

TERZ, JOSE JUAN, physician, surgical educator; b. Buenos Aires, Apr. 18, 1929; came to U.S., 1954; s. Barbar and Eva (Alem) T.; m. Rosa Basilia Tomsich, Apr. 7, 1954; children: Roxanna, Joseph, David. BA, Sarmiento Coll., 1946; MD, U. Buenos Aires, 1952. Diplomate Am. Bd. Surgery. Intern Lincoln Hosp., 1954-55, resident in surgery, 1955-56; resident in surgery Mt. Sinai Hosp., 1956-59, Meml. Hosp. for Cancer and Allied Diseases and James Ewing Hosp., 1959-62; rsch. fellow Sloan-Kettering Inst. for Cancer Rsch., 1964-66; dir. dept. gen. and oncologic surgery City of Hope Med. Ctr., Duarte, Calif., 1980-91, chmn. div. surgery, 1988-91; prof. clin. surgery U. So. Calif., L.A., 1993—; mem. cancer clin. investigation review com. Nat. Cancer Inst., 1988-91; mem. Pacificare of Calif. Tech. Assessment Com., 1992-93; cons. Santa Teresita Hosp., Duarte, Calif., 1991-93, Meth. Hosp., Arcadia, Calif., 1991-93, Inter-Community Med. Ctr., Covina, Calif., 1991-93, Pomona (Calif.) Valley Hosp. Med. Ctr., 1991—, Queen of the Valley Hosp., West Covina, Calif., 1991—, Hosp. of Good Samaritan, L.A., 1991—, Kenneth Norris Jr. Cancer Hosp., L.A., 1993—, U. So. Calif. Univ. Hosp., L.A., 1993—, LAC/USC Med. Ctr., L.A., 1993—. Author, contbr. numerous chpts. and books; reviewer editl. bd. Jour. Surg. Oncology, 1989—, Cancer, 1992—; contbr. over 100 articles to profl. jours. Mem. AAAS, AMA, Am. Assn. for Cancer Rsch., Am. Coll. Surgeons, Am. Soc. Clin. Oncology, Internat. Soc. Surgery, Pacific Coast Surg. Assn., Soc. for Surgery of Alimentary Tract, Soc. Head and Neck Surgeons, Soc. Surg. Oncology, L.A. Surg. Soc., So. Calif. Acad. Clin. Oncology. Home: 700 S Lake Ave Apt 206 Pasadena CA 91106-3943 Office: Univ So Calif Med Ctr 1510 San Pablo St # 514 Los Angeles CA 90033-4586

TESH, JOHN, television talk show host; b. Garden City, N.Y., 1953; s. John and Mildred Tesh; m. Connie Sellecca, Apr. 4, 1992; children: Gib, Prima. Co-host Entertainment Tonight, 1986—; host One-On-One with John Tesh, 1991; co-host John and Leeza from Hollywood, 1993. Television appearances include: The U.S. Open Tennis Championship, 1985, Macy's Thanksgiving Day Parade, 1987, Wimbledon, 1991; film appearances include Shocker, 1989, Soapdish, 1991; albums include Tour de France, 1988, The Early Years, 1990, Ironman, 1992, The Games, 1992, Monterey Nights, 1993, A Romantic Christmas, 1993; composers theme music Bobby's World, 1990, The Knife and Gun Club, 1990, One on One, 1991, NFL Live. Recipient 4 Emmy awards for composing, 2 Emmy awards for reporting. Office: Paramount TV 5555 Melrose Ave Los Angeles CA 90038-3149

TESLOW, PAUL ANDRE, retired health executive; b. Chgo., May 12, 1934; s. Reuben Clayton and Eva Valborg (Oefstedal) T.; m. Marilyn Renée Lund, Aug. 28, 1955; children: Lori, Linda Teslow Gerlach, Sandra Teslow Wagner. BA, Concordia Coll., 1956; MHA, U. Minn., 1959. Adminstrv. staff asst. Immanuel Hosp., Mankato, Minn., 1956-57; adminstrv. resident San Jose (Calif.) Hosp., 1958-59; adminstr. Good Samaritan Hosp., Puyallup, Wash., 1959-70; pres., CEO Northridge (Calif.) Hosp., 1970-79, HealthWest Found., Chatsworth, Calif., 1979-88; pres., CEO UniHealth Am., Burbank, Calif., 1988-92, pres. emeritus, bd. dirs., 1993—. Mem. editl. bd. Managed Care Quar. Mem. adv. bd. health svcs. adminstrn. U. So. Calif.; mem. cabinet L.A. Music Ctr. Campaign, 1992; bd. dirs. PacifiCare NASDAQ, 1988-93, Nat. Fund for Med. Edn. Recipient VICA award for corporate excellence, 1987. Fellow Am. Coll. Healthcare Execs.; mem. Am. Hosp. Assn., Am. Healthcare Syss. (bd. dirs., exec. com.), Calif. Assn. Hosps. and Health Sys. (trustee, Walker fellow 1986), Hosp. Coun. So. Calif. (bd. dirs. 1973-75, mem. exec. com. 1975-82, chmn. 1982-83), Indian Wells Country Club. Home: 615 Bayside Dr Newport Beach CA 92660

TESS, ROY WILLIAM HENRY, chemist; b. Chgo., Apr. 25, 1915; s. Reinhold W. and Augusta (Detl) T.; m. Marjorie Kohler, Feb. 19, 1944; children: Roxanne, Steven. BS in Chemistry, U. Ill., 1939; PhD, U. Minn., 1944. Rsch. chemist, group leader Shell Devel. Co., Emeryville, Calif., 1944—, rsch. supr., 1959-61, 63-66; rsch. supr. Royal Dutch/Shell Plastics Lab., Delft, The Netherlands, 1962-63; tech. planning supr. Shell Chem. Co., N.Y.C., 1967-70; tech. mgr. solvents Shell Chem. Co., Houston, 1970-77, cons., 1977-79; ind. cons. Fallbrook, Calif., 1979—; pres. Paint Rsch. Inst., Phila., 1973-76. Editor, organizer: Solvents Theory and Practice, 1973; (with others) Applied Polymer Science, 1975, Applied Polymer Science, 2d edit., 1985. Pres. Assn. Indsl. Scientists, Berkeley, Calif., 1948-50, Minerinda Property Owners Assn., Orinda, Calif., 1965-67, Houston Camellia Soc., 1973-74. Fellow Am. Inst. Chemists; mem. Nat. Paint and Coatings Assn. (air quality com. 1967-79), Fedn. Socs. Coatings Tech. (bd. dirs. 1973-76, Roon award 1957, Heckel award 1978), Am. Chem. Soc. (divsn. polymeric materials chmn. 1978, exec. com. 1977—, Disting. Svc. award 1993). Home and Office: 1615 Chandelle Ln Fallbrook CA 92028-1707

TESSIER-LAVIGNE, MARC TREVOR, neurobiologist, researcher; b. Trenton, Ont., Can., Dec. 18, 1959; came to U.S., 1987; s. Yves Jacques and Sheila Christine (Midgley) Tessier-L.; m. Mary Alanna Hynes, Feb. 4, 1989; children: Christian, Kyle. BSc, McGill U., 1980; BA, Oxford U., 1982; PhD, U. London, 1986. Exec. dir. Can. Student Pugwash Orgn., Ottawa, Ont., 1982-83; rsch. fellow devel. neurobiology unit Med. Rsch. Coun., London, 1986-87; rsch. fellow Ctr. for Neurobiology, Columbia U., N.Y.C., 1987-91; asst. prof. dept. anatomy U. Calif., San Francisco, 1991—; asst. investigator Howard Hughes Med. Inst., 1994—. Contbr. articles on neurobiology to profl. jours. Recipient McKnight Investigation award, 1994, Charles Judson Herrick award Am. Assn. Anatomists, 1994; Rhodes scholar, 1980, Commonwealth scholar, 1983, Markey scholar, 1989, Searle scholar, 1991, McKnight scholar, 1991; Klingenstein fellow, 1992. Home: 1000 Chenery St San Francisco CA 94131-2923 Office: U Calif Dept Anatomy San Francisco CA 94143-0452

TESTA, STEPHEN MICHAEL, geologist, consultant; b. Fitchburg, Mass., July 17, 1951; s. Guiseppe Alfredo and Angelina Mary (Pettito) T.; m. Lydia Mae Payne, July 26, 1986; 1 child, Brant Ethan Gage. AA, Los Angeles Valley Jr. Coll., Van Nuys, 1971; BS in Geology, Calif. State U., Northridge, 1976, MS in Geology, 1978. Registered geologist, Calif., Oreg.; cert. profl. geol. scientist., Idaho, Alaska; cert. engrng. geologist, Calif.; registered environ. asessor, Calif. Engrng. geologist R.T. Frankian & Assocs., Burbank, Calif., 1976-78, Bechtel, Norwalk, Calif., 1978-80, Converse Cons., Seattle, 1980-82; sr. hydrogeologist Ecology Environment, Seattle, 1982-83; sr. geologist Dames & Moore, Seattle, 1983-86; v.p. Engrng. Enterprises, Long Beach, Calif., 1986-89; CEO Applied Environ. Svcs., San Juan Capistrano, Calif., 1990-94; pres. Testa Environ. Corp., San Juan Capistrano, Calif., 1994—. Author: Restoration of Petroleum Contaminated Aquifiers, 1990, Principles of Technical Consulting and Project Management, 1991, Geological Aspects of Hazardous Waste Management, 1994, Reuse and Recycling of Contaminated Soil, 1995; editor Geologic Field Guide to the Salton Basin, 1988, Environmental Concerns in the Petroleum Industry, 1989; contbr. over 60 articles to profl. jours. a preface and chpts. to books. Mem. AAAS, Am. Inst. Profl. Geologists (profl. devel. com. 1986, continuing edn. com. program chmn., 1988—, Presidential Cert. of Merit, 1987 and 1994, Nat screening bd. mem. 1992-94, chmn. 1995—, exec. bd. del. 1993, nat. v.p. 1994, bd. trustees 1995—), L.A. Basin Geol. Soc. (pres. 1991-92), Geol. Soc. Am., Am. Assn. Petroleum Geologists (Pacific sect. environ. com., co-chmn. 1993—), Am. Mineralogical Soc., South Coast Geol. Soc., Assn. Ground Water Scientists and Engrs., Assn. Engrng. Geologists, Assn. Mil. Engrs., Environ. Assessment Assn., Mineral Soc. Can., Hazardous Materials Rsch. Inst., Calif. Water Pollution Control Assn., Sigma Xi. Republican. Roman Catholic. Home: 31232 Belford Dr San Juan Capistrano CA 92675-1833 Office: Testa Environ Corp 31831 Camino Capistrano Ste 100 San Juan Capistrano CA 92675

TETHER, ANTHONY JOHN, aerospace executive; b. Middletown, N.Y., Nov. 28, 1941; s. John Arthur and Antoinette Rose (Gesualdo) T.; m. Nancy Engle Pierson, Dec. 27, 1963 (div. July 1971); 1 child, Jennifer; m. Carol Suzanne Dunbar, Mar. 3, 1973; 1 child, Michael. AAS, Orange County C.C., N.Y., 1961; BS, Rensselaer Poly Inst., 1963; MSEE, Stanford (Calif.) U., 1965, PhD, 1969. V.p., gen. mgr. Sys. Control Inc., Palo Alto, Calif., 1968-78; dir. nat. intelligence Office Sec. of Def., Washington, 1978-82; dir. strategic tech. DARPA, Washington, 1982-86; corp. v.p. Ford Aerospace, Newport Beach, Calif., 1986-90, LORAL, Newport Beach, 1990-92; corp. v.p., gen. mgr. Sci. Application Internat., Inc., San Diego, 1992-94; CEO Dynamics Tech. Inc., Torrance, Calif., 1994—; chmn., bd. dirs. Condyne Tech., Inc., Orlando, Fla., 1990-92; dir. Orincon, La Jolla, Calif. Contbr. articles to profl. jours. Recipient Nat. Intelligence medal DCI, 1986, Civilian Meritorious medal U.S. Sec. Def., 1986. Mem. IEEE, Cosmos Club, Sigma Xi, Eta Kappa Nu, Tau Beta Pi. Home: 4518 Roxbury Rd Corona Del Mar CA 92625-3125

TETLOW, WILLIAM LLOYD, computer consultant; b. Phila., July 2, 1938; s. William Lloyd and Mary Eleanor (Ferris) T.; m. Amber Jane Riederer, June 13, 1964; children: Jennifer Kay, Rebecca Dawn, Derek William. Student, Cornell U., 1956-60; B in Gen. Edn., U. Omaha, 1961; MA, Cornell U., 1965, PhD, 1973. Dir. instl. research Cornell U., Ithaca, N.Y., 1965-70; dir. planning U. B.C., Vancouver, Can., 1970-82; dir. NCHEMS Mgmt. Products, Boulder, Colo., 1982-85; pres., dir. Vantage Info. Products, Inc., Boulder, 1985-87; pres., propr. Vantage Computer Svcs., Boulder, 1986—; cons. various univs. U.S., Can. and Australia, 1970—. Editor/author: Using Microcomputers for Planning and Decision Support, 1984; contbr. numerous articles to profl. jours. Mem. Mt. Calvary Luth. Ch. Coun., 1985-86, 89—, pres., 1991-92. Served to 1st lt. AUS, 1961-63. Recipient U. Colo. medal, 1987. Mem. Assn. Inst. Research (sec. 1973-75, v.p. 1980-81, pres. 1981-82). Republican. Lodges: Concordia, Kiwanis. Home: 3650 Smuggler Way Boulder CO 80303-7224

TETREAULT, MARK DAVID, nuclear engineer and financial planner; b. Torrington, Conn., June 12, 1959; s. David Ronald and Audrey Bernice (Mierzwa) T.; m. Linda Jean Tetreault, July 11, 1981. BS, New Sch. for Social Rsch., 1985. Lic. gen. securities rep., Hawaii; lic. ins. solicitor, Hawaii. Nuclear engr. Pearl Harbor (Hawaii) Naval Shipyard, 1988—; fin. planner E.A. Buck Co., Honolulu, 1993—; stock trader, 1983—. With USN, 1980-88. Mem. Am. Nuclear Soc., Am. Legion, Nat. Assn. Securities Dealers (registered rep.), Mus. of Natural History. Home: 1296 Kahili St Kailua HI 96734-4058

TETTEGAH, SHARON YVONNE, education educator; b. Wichita Falls, Tex., Jan. 14, 1956; d. Lawrence Guice and Doris Jean (Leak) Oliver; 1 child, Tandra Ainsworth; m. Joseph Miller Zangai, Dec. 22, 1978 (div. 1983); 1 child, Tonia Manjay Zengai; m. George Tettegah, Apr. 28, 1989; 1 child, Nicole Jennifer Tettegah. AA, Coll. Alameda, 1985; BA, U. Calif., Davis, 1988, teaching cert., 1989, MA, 1991; postgrad., U. Calif., Santa Barbara. Cert. elem. tchr., Calif. Clk. II Alameda County Mcpl. Ct., Oakland, Calif.,

1976-77; acct. clk. Alameda County Social Svcs., Oakland, 1977-78, eligibility technician, 1978-82; supervising clk. Alameda County Health Care Svcs., Oakland, 1982-84; tchr. Davis (Calif.) Joint Unified Sch. Dist., 1988-89, L.A. Unified Schs., L.A., 1990-92; tchr. Oakland Unified Sch. Dist., Oakland, 1992—, tchr. sci. mentor, 1993—; teaching asst. U. Calif., Santa Barbara, 1993-94; adminstrv. intern Oxnard Unified Sch. Dist., 1994, U. Calif. Cultural Awareness Program, Santa Barbara, 1994—; rsch. cons. to vice chancellor students affairs U. Calif., Santa Barbara, 1995—; cons. U. Calif., Davis, 1988-89, multicultural cons. Davis Unified Sch. Dist., 1988-89; edn. cons. Ednl. Testing Svc., Emeryville, Calif., 1994; chair diversity com. of Santa Barbara Village Charter Sch.; mem. academic senate com. undergrad. enrollment and admissions U. Calif. Santa Barbara, 1995, tchr. cross-cultural interctions course, summer 1995. Mem. U. Calif. Santa Barbara Acad. Senate Bd. Undergraduate Admissions and Records; co-chair Diversity Com. Montecito-Santa Barbara Charter Sch.; pres. African-Am. Grad. and Profl. Students Orgn., Davis, 1988-89. Recipient Charlene Richardson Acad. Honors award Coll. Alameda, 1985; Calif. State Acad. fellow, 1989-91, Grad. Opportunity Acad. Excellence fellow, 1994—. Mem. Am. Ednl. Researchers Assn., Calif. Sci. Tchrs. Assn., Calif. Advocacy for Math and Sci., Calif. Tchrs. Assn., Calif. Media Libr. Educators Assn., PTA, Multicultural Curriculum Assn., Supervision and Curriculum Leadership Assn., Bay Area Sci. and Tech. Educators Corsortium, Pan-African Students Assn.. Address: PO Box 1782 Santa Barbara CA 93116-1782 Office: U Calif Santa Barbara Sch Edn/Ednl Psychology Santa Barbara CA 93106

TEVIS, BARRY LEE, television producer, marketing executive; b. Pasadena, Calif., Feb. 5, 1956; s. John Larry Tevis and Renee Lydia Clement; m. Julie Marie Knauss, Mar. 31, 1990; children: Ben, Ann Marie, Hilary, Andrew. Student, Bates Vocat. Tech. Inst., Tacoma, 1973-75. Master control operator KTBN-TV, Santa Ana, Calif., 1975-76; producer, dir. KOTI-TV, Klamath Falls, Oreg., 1976-77, KPAZ-TV, Phoenix, Ariz., 1977-78; prodn. mgr., dir. advt. and promotion KTVL-TV, Medford, Oreg., 1978—. Sound dir. Rogue Valley Fellowship Ch., Medford. Recipient various broadcast awards. Mem. Promax Internat. (award of merit 1990). Republican. Office: KTVL-TV 1440 Rossanley Dr Medford OR 97501-1751

TEVRIZIAN, DICKRAN M., JR., federal judge; b. Los Angeles, Aug. 4, 1940; s. Dickran and Rose Tevrizian; m. Geraldine Tevrizian, Aug. 22, 1964; children: Allyson Tracy, Leslie Sara. BS, U. So. Calif., 1962, JD, 1965. Tax acct. Arthur Andersen and Co., Los Angeles, 1965-66; atty., ptnr. Kirtland and Packard, Los Angeles, 1966-72; judge Los Angeles Mcpl. Ct., Los Angeles, 1972-78, State of Calif. Superior Ct., Los Angeles, 1978-82; ptnr. Manatt, Phelps, Rothenberg & Tunney, Los Angeles, 1982-85, Lewis, D'Amato, Brisbois & Bisgaard, Los Angeles, 1985-86; judge U.S. Dist. Ct., Los Angeles, 1986—. Mem. Calif. Trial Lawyer's Assn. (trial judge of yr. 1987), L.A. County Bar Assn. (trial judge of yr. 1994-95). Office: US Dist Ct Royal Federal Bldg 255 E Temple St Los Angeles CA 90012-3334

TEXTOR, ROBERT BAYARD, cultural anthropology writer, consultant, educator; b. Cloquet, Minn., Mar. 13, 1923; s. Clinton Kenney and Lillian (Nickles) T.; divorced; children: Alexander Robertson, Marisa Elizabeth. Student, Lafayette Coll., 1940-41, Antioch Coll., 1941-43; B.A. in Asian Studies, U. Mich., 1945; Ph.D. in Cultural Anthropology, Cornell U., 1960. Civil info. and edn. officer Mil. Govt., Kyoto-Wakayama, Japan, 1946-48; rsch. fellow anthropology and S.E. Asia studies Yale U., 1959-60, assoc., 1960-61; rsch. fellow in stats. Harvard U., 1962-64; assoc. prof. edn. and anthropology Stanford U., 1964-68, prof. edn. and anthropology, 1968-86, prof. anthropology, 1986-90, prof. anthropology emeritus, 1990—; vis. prof. U. Saar, Saarbrücken, Germany, 1984-85; cons. Motorola U., 1991—; mem. S.E. Asia Coun., 1974-77; cons. cultural anthropology to govt. agys., 1957-58, 61-62. Author: (most recent) Roster of the Gods: An Ethnography of The Supernatural in a Thai Village, 6 vols., 1973, Austria 2005: Projected Sociocultural Effects of the Microelectronic Revolution, 1983, Anticipatory Anthropology, 1985, (with Sippanondha Ketudat) The Middle Path for the Future of Thailand, 1990; assoc. editor Jour. Conflict Resolution, 1965-70; mem. editorial bd. Human orgn., 1966-71, Jour. Cultural Futures, 1979-87; adv. editor Behavior Sci. Rsch., 1974-86. Bd. dirs. Vols. in Asia, Stanford, Calif., 1968-73; mem. Metro Portland Future Vision Commn., 1993-95. Served with U.S. Army, 1943-46. Fellow Rockefeller Found., 1951-52, fgn. area tng. fellow Ford Found., Thailand 1955-58, Carnegie fellow, 1958-59, Fulbright West Europe rsch. fellow, 1984-85, East-West Ctr. fellow, 1988-90; NSF grantee, Thailand, U.S., 1969-73, Volkswagen Found. grantee, Thailand and Germany, 1984. Fellow Am. Anthrop. Assn. (life mem.); mem. Siam Soc. (life mem.), Assn. Asian Studies (life mem.), Council on Anthropology and Edn. (pres. 1974-75), AAUP (pres. Stanford chpt. 1975-76), Phi Kappa Phi.

TEYLER, SHARON MARIE, secondary educator; b. Lynwood, Calif., Oct. 27, 1951; d. Fred George and Norma Francis (Tredo) Mann; m. Joseph Charles Cherocci, Feb., 1979 (div. 1991); children: Casey, Rebecca; m. Robert Wayne Teyler, Mar. 21, 1992. AA, Fullerton Coll., 1975; BA in Social Studies, Calif. Poly. U., 1987. Cert. tchr., Calif., Oreg. Presch. tchr. City of Duarte, Calif., 1980-82, Christ Luth. Sch., West Covina, Calif., 1982-84; tchr. Baldwin Park (Calif.) Sch. Dist., 1984-92; life in Am. tchr. E.F. for Fgn. Study, Brighton, England, 1984-87, Mass., 1988, N.Y.C., 1989-91; edn. specialist Alternative Youth Activities, Coos Bay, Oreg., 1993-94; social studies tchr. Marshfield High Sch., Coos Bay, 1994—; cheerleader dir. Baldwin Park High Sch., 1985, dir. Operation Big Switch, 1990-92, sr. class advisor, 1990-91; cheerleader dir. Christ Luth. Sch., 1982-84. Active Baldwin Park Hist. Soc., 1986-87; pageant dir. Baldwin Park City, 1967, 69, 70, 80-84; Coos Bay Parks commr., 1995—; Oreg. Assn. for Alternatives in Edn. rep., 1994-95; chairperson Coos Bay Fun Festival Parade, 1995. Named Jr. Miss Baldwin Park, 1966, Miss Baldwin Park, 1969, Miss San Gabriel Valley, 1970, Club Woman of Yr. Baldwin Park Woman's Club, 1980; recipient achievement awards U.S. Congressman Esteban Torres, 1990-91. Mem. Hist. Preservation Soc. Republican. Home: 1453 Cedar Ave Coos Bay OR 97420-1867 Office: Marshfield High Sch 10th and Ingersoll Coos Bay OR 97420

THACKER, GARY WILLIAM, agricultural extension agent; b. Yuma, Ariz., Sept. 18, 1953; s. William Hubert and Betty (Nelson) T.; m. Linda Speer, Oct. 6, 1979; 1 child, Robert. BS in Agrl. Econ., U. Ariz., 1975, MS in Agronomy, 1979, MBA, 1993. Cotton farmer Thacker Farms, Yuma, 1979-82; mng. ptnr., grower Yuma Farming Co., 1982-85; agrl. ext. agt. U. Ariz., Tucson, 1985—; pres., CEO Pegasus Machinery Co., Tucson, 1993—; chmn. peer review com. U. Ariz. Coop. Ext., Tucson, 1994. inventor stalk and root embedding apparatus, self-aligning herbicide sprayer. Advisor Pima Natural Resource Conservation Dist., Tucson, 1986-92. Recipient First place award 1992 Bus. Plans Competition, Karl Eller Grad. Sch. Mgmt. Coll. of Bus. and Pub. Adminstrn., U. Ariz. Mem. Soil and Water Conservation Soc. (sec. Ariz. chpt. 1991), Soc. for Range Mgmt., Ariz. county Agts. Assn. (Achievement award 1991). Presbyterian. Home: 5255 N Avenida Largo Tucson AZ 85745-9498 Office: Pima County Coop Ext 4210 N Campbell Ave Tucson AZ 85719-2361

THACKER, NETHA LYNN, editor; b. Sanger, Calif., Aug. 21, 1945; d. Derrel Wilbur and Ruth Marion (Henning) Houdashelt; m. Gerald William Thacker, Nov. 21, 1964; children: Cynthia Ann, Laura Ellen, Deborah Lynn. BA, San Jose State U., 1984. Editor Bus. Woman Mag., San Jose, Calif., 1984-86, CTB/McGraw Hill, Monterey, Calif., 1986-87, The Villager, San Jose, 1987-89, ETR Assocs., Santa Cruz, Calif., 1989-94; cons. editor ETR Assocs., 1994—; cons. in field, bd. dirs. Future Families. Home: 620 Breckenridge Ln Soquel CA 95073

THAGARD, SHIRLEY STAFFORD, sales and marketing executive; b. Detroit, Nov. 29, 1940; d. Walter Jay Stafford and Marjorie Gertrude Stafford Goode; children: Grayson Jay, Devon Charles. Assoc. Bus., Webber Coll., 1961; cert. Pierce Coll., 1973, UCLA, 1989. Dir. pub. relations Miami Herald, Fla., 1963-67; pres. Thagard Enterprises, Woodland Hills, Calif., 1980—; v.p. mktg. R.T. Durable Med. Products, Inc., Miami, also Woodland Hills, 1983-85; investment cons., 1985-86; v.p. real estate investments, M.W. Palmer and Assocs., 1986-87, with real estate sales dept. Country Club West Realtors, 1987-89; owner Property Mgmt. North Idaho, 1991—; ind. lectr. women's issues and children's health care, 1980—. Editor, pub. Pediatric Network, 1980-85. Contbr. articles to various jours. Creator Med. Moppets healthcare teaching tools, 1983. Chairperson L.A. County Mental Health (Expressing Feelings), 1985-87. Avocations: travel, water and snow skiing, writing. Office: PO Box 8396 Calabasas CA 91372-8396

THALL, RICHARD VINCENT, education program director; b. San Francisco, Sept. 12, 1940; s. Albert Vincent and Alice Stella (O'Brien) T.; m. Ellyn Marie Wisherop, June 15, 1963; children: Kristen Ellyn, Richard Vincent Jr. AA, City Coll. San Francisco, 1961; BA, San Francisco State Coll., 1964; MA, San Francisco State U., 1971. Cert. elem. tchr., Calif.; cert. secondary tchr., Calif.; cert. community coll. tchr., Calif. Tchr. biology San Francisco Unified Sch. Dist., 1965-66; tchr. biology Mt. Diablo Unified Sch. Dist., Concord, Calif., 1966-79, coord. water environ. studies program, 1979—; ranger/naturalist State of Calif., Brannan Island, 1973-78; naturalist Adventure Internat., Oakland, Calif., 1979-81; lectr. Princess Cruise Lines, 1982-84, Sea Goddess, 1986—, Sun Lines, 1987, Sitmar Lines, 1989, RCCL, 1991-94; spkr. commencements U. Calif., Berkeley, 1989. Author: Ecological Sampling of the Sacramento-San Joaquin Delta, 1976; Water Environment Studies Program, 1986; co-author: Project MER Laboratory Manual, 1982. Mem. Contra Costa County (Calif.) Natural Resources Commn., 1975-78, vice-chmn., 1977-78; active Save Mt. Diablo, Concord, 1969-76, v.p., 1974-75; mem. citizens com. Assn. Bay Area Govt. Water Quality, 1979-82, vice-chmn., 1980-82; active John Marsh Home Restoration Com., Martinez, Calif., 1977-78; mem. edn. adv. com. Marine World/Africa USAd, Vallejo, Calif., 1988—; troop com. chmn. Boy Scouts Am., Concord, 1984-86, asst. scoutmaster, 1985-87. Recipient Recognition and Excellence cert. Assn. Calif. Sch. Adminstrs., 1984, Wood Badge award Boy Scouts Am., 1986; grantee State Calif., 1982, 84, San Francisco Estuary Project, 1992, EPA, 1992, Shell Oil Co., 1993. Mem. AAAS, Nat. Assn. Biology Tchrs., Nat., Audubon Soc., Am. Mus. Natural Hist., Nat. Geog. Soc., Smithsonian Instn. (assoc.). Republican. Roman Catholic. Home: 1712 Lindenwood Dr Concord CA 94521-1109 Office: Mt Diablo Unif Sch Dist 1936 Carlotta Dr Concord CA 94519-1358

THAMES, CARROLL THOMAS, financial consultant; b. Webbers Falls, Okla., Sept. 26, 1938; s. Carroll Hilton and Opal (Gillespie) T.; m. Ramona Pepin, Dec. 16, 1961 (div. July 1980); children: Kimberly Ann, Gavin Thomas. BA, Coll. of Notre Dame, Belmont, Calif., 1972; MBA, U. Santa Clara, 1974. CLU, chartered fin. cons.; cert. fin. planner. Chief industr. engr. Kaiser Aluminum Chem. Corp., Oakland, Calif., 1966-83; registered prin. Anchor Nat. Fin. Svcs. Inc., Phoenix, 1980—; pres. Capital Mgmt. Network, Inc., Woodbridge, Calif., 1985—; lectr. U. Calif., Santa Cruz, 1986, Golden Gate U., Monterey, Calif., 1984-85, Hartnell Coll., Salinas, Calif., 1986-87. Contbr. fin. planning articles to profl. jours. Bd. dirs. YMCA, Salinas, 1986-87. Mem. Internat. Assn. for Fin. Planning Inc. (pres.-chmn. Monterey Bay chpt. 1985-88), Am. Soc. CLU & Chartered Fin. Consultants (pres. Monterey Bay chpt. 1984-85), Calif. Assn. for Fin. Planning (sec. 1986-87), Inst. Cert. Fin. Planners, Internat. Bd. Cert. Fin. Planners, Alpha Gamma Sigma. Republican. Office: PO Box 1024 Woodbridge CA 95258-1024

THAPA, MUKUND NARAIN-DHAMI, software company executive; b. Bombay, India, Apr. 13, 1954; came to U.S., 1976; s. Narain Singh and Devi (Jhangiani) Thapa; m. Radhika Hegde. BTech, Indian Inst. of Tech., Bombay, 1976; MS in Ops. Rsch., Stanford (Calif.) U., 1979, PhD in Ops. Rsch., 1981. Sr. analyst Applied Decisions Analysis, Inc., Menlo Park, Calif., 1980-83; pres. Stanford Bus. Software, Inc., Mountain View, Calif., 1984—. Office: Stanford Bus Software Inc 2680 Bayshore Pkwy Mountain View CA 94043

THATCHER, CAROL JEAN, sociology and psychology educator, writer; b. Bell, Calif., Sept. 11, 1937; d. Lloyd Thatcher and Nadine (Crismon) T.; m. Donald E. Ross, June 7, 1955 (div. 1969); children: Dawn Ross, Jeffrey Ross, Jannette Ross, Christopher Ross; m. Charles R. Waistell, Mar. 26, 1993. MA in Social Sci., Calif. State U., Chico, 1992. mem. speakers bur. Calif. State U., Chico, 1992—. Owner, mgr. Pan Gallery, 1972-74, Body & Bath, 1976-80; mktg. dir. Olives Inc., 1980-82; contractors office mgr. Bob Burleson, 1983-87; maintenance and utilities supr. Chico Area Recreation/Parks Dist., 1988-90; adminstrv. asst., intern, counselor Family Svc. Assn., 1990-91; instr., writer, pub. speaker Calif. State U., Chico, 1993—. Author: Female Body Modification Practices, 1992; actress, singer. Treas. Chico Art Ctr., 1991; minister 1st Spiritual Sci. Ch., Chico, 190—; active United We Stand, Chico, Pub. Citizens, 1989—, Chico Peace Ctr., 1980, Clergy and Laity Concerned, 1990. Mem. AAUW, Bus. and Profl. Women (legis. chair 1978-80), Chico Jazz Soc. (co-founder 1981), Chico Dem. Club. Office: Calif State U Chico CA 95928

THAYER, SHELLEY L, marketing professional; b. 1952. MI, No. Mich. U., 1973; BS in Edn., Ctrl. Mich. U., 1975. Tchr. East Jordan (Mich.) Pub. Schs., 1975-80; v.p. Multi Mktg., Irvine, Calif., 1980-88; with Supermktg. Inc., Irvine, 1988—. Office: Supermarketing Inc 15375 Barranca Pky Irvine CA 92718-2217*

THEIS, JOAN C., accountant; b. Flushing, N.Y., Feb. 22, 1948; d. Phillip Martin and Juanita Elizabeth (Weigelt) Brown; m. John H. Theis, Jr., Mar. 24, 1979; children: Mathew, Jacqueline. BA, U. Denver, 1970; MA, U. Colo., 1978; BS summa cum laude, Met. State Coll., Denver, 1984. CPA, Colo.; cert. master tchr., Colo. Tchr. Englewood (Colo.) Pub. Schs., 1976-82; acct. Diane D. Blackman, CPA, Denver, 1984-88, Pester & Co., CPAs, P.C., Denver, 1989-91; ptnr. Grubb, Theis & Assocs. PC CPAs, 1991—. Pres. Englewood Educators, 1981-82. Mem. AICPA, Colo. Soc. CPAs, Toastmasters (v.p. 1992—), Colo. Women C. of C. (bd. dirs. 1994—), Phi Beta Kappa. Office: Grubb Theis & Assocs PC CPAs 1660 S Albion St Ste 403 Denver CO 80222-4020

THEISEN, LEE SCOTT, foundation director; b. Baldwin, Wis., July 3, 1943; s. Harvey L. and Evelyn (Scott) T.; children: Elizabeth, Scott, Andrew. BA, U. Iowa, 1963, MA, 1966; PhD, U. Ariz., 1973. Archivist, historian Nat. Archives, Washington, 1973-74, asst. editor, 1974-75, exhibits officer, 1975-77; asst. dir. Ariz. Hist. Soc., Phoenix, 1977-80; dir. Cen. Ariz. Mus., Phoenix, 1980-83; exec. dir. Ind. State Mus. and Hist. Sites, Indpls., 1983-89, AHS Found., Phoenix, 1989-95, Portland State U. Fdn., 1995—; adj. prof. Ariz. State U., 1978-83, Ind. U., Indpls., 1987-89. Author: The Written Word Endures, 1976. Legis. asst. to Congressman Fred Schwengel, 1962-65. Fellow Royal Geog. Soc.; mem. Central Ariz. Mus. Assn. (pres. 1978-80), Am. Assn. State and Local History, Am. Assn. Mus., Lambda Chi Alpha, Phi Alpha Theta. Home: 1727 NE Schuyler Portland OR 97212 Office: Portland State U Fdn PO Box 243 Portland OR 97207

THELEN, MAX, JR., foundation executive, lawyer; b. Berkeley, Calif., Aug. 18, 1919; s. Max and Ora Emily (Muir) T.; m. Phyllis J. Barnhill, Mar. 8, 1952; children—Nancy B. Thelen Rehkopf, Jane M. Thelen Greene, Max, III, William B. A.B. with highest honors, U. Calif., Berkeley, 1940; J.D. cum laude, Harvard U., 1946. Bar: Calif. 1946. Ptnr. Thelen, Marrin, Johnson & Bridges, San Francisco, 1946-87; v.p., dir. S.H. Cowell Found., 1970—. Trustee World Affairs Council. Served to lt. USNR, 1942-46. Mem. State Bar Calif., Am. Coll. Trial Lawyers, Com. Fgn. Rels., Commonwealth Club, World Trade Club, Marines Meml. Club. Home: 199 Mountain View Ave San Rafael CA 94901-1347 Office: 2 Embarcadero Ctr Ste 2100 San Francisco CA 94111

THENELL, ARTHUR LEE, retail supermarket executive; b. Eugene, Oreg., June 24, 1940; s. Edward J. and Rose Ann (Nairz) T.; m. Sharon E. Efteland, Feb. 28, 1964 (div. Nov. 1984); children: Andra L., Daniel E., Jennifer L., Matthew A.; m. Janice Marcoux Tafte, Dec. 1, 1988. BBA, U. Oreg., 1969. Asst. produce mgr. Mayfair Mkts., Eugene, 1960-62; asst. store mgr. Marks Mkts., Roseburg, Oreg., 1962-64; mktg. rep. Del Monte Corp., San Francisco, 1964-67; ptnr. L.D. Pierce Brokerage Co., Eugene, 1968-76; CEO Arcly Stores, Inc., Sisters, Oreg., 1976—; pres. Sentry Stores, Inc., Portland, Oreg., 1983. Oreg. dist. gov. Active 20-30 Internat., Sacramento, Calif., 1976; chmn. Sisters Sch. Dist. Bd. of Edn., 1983; dir. Ctrl. Oreg. Econ. Devel. Coun., Bend, 1989-91. Mem. United Grocers Inc. (dir. 1984-86, chmn. bd. 1992), Oreg. Food Industries (dir. 1986-89).

THEOBALD, GILLIAN LEE, artist; b. La Jolla, Calif., Nov. 17, 1944; d. John Richmond and Mary Lee (Nugent) T.; m. Yuris Zeltins, July 20, 1974 (div. 1985); m. L.A. Heberlein, Mar. 15, 1992; 1 stepdaughter, Elaine Elizabeth. BA, San Diego State U., 1968, MA, 1971. One-woman shows incude Cirrus Gallery, L.A., 1983, 86, 88, 89, 90, 93, 94, Patty Aande Gallery, San Diego, 1987, Boehm Gallery, San Marcos, Calif., 1988, Occidental Coll., L.A., 1990, Mark Quint Gallery, La. Jolla, 1993; exhibited in group shows in L.A. County Mus. of Art, 1995, Fitchburg (Mass.) Mus., Contemporary Arts, 1993, David Lewinson Gallery, Del Mar, Calif., 1992, Biota Gallery, L.A., 1991, Rose Art Mus. Brandeis U., Waltham, Mass., 1991, many others. Home: 9610 7th Ave NE Seattle WA 98115-2115

THEODOSAKIS, JASON J., physician; b. Chgo., Feb. 17, 1963; s. John C. and Helen Theodosakis. BA in Chemistry and Biology with honors, Fla. Internat. U., 1985; MD, Univ. Health Scis./Chgo. Med. Sch., 1989; M in Exercise Physiology summa cum laude, U. Ariz., 1991, MPH summa cum laude, 1994. Diplomate Am. Bd. Preventive Medicine and Pub. Health, Nat. Bd. Med. Examiners. Intern in internal medicine Tucson Hosp., 1989-90; resident in preventive medicine U. Ariz. Health Scis. Ctr., Tucson, 1990-92, chief resident, 1992, fellow in faculty devel. program, 1992-93, fellow in clin. sports medicine, 1992-93, asst. clin. prof., 1995—; staff physician Canyon Ranch Med. Dept., Tucson, 1992—; team physician Tucson Area High Sch. Football, 1992—; designer, mfr., tester exercise/rehab. equipment; tchr., rschr. in field. Acad. scholar Fla. Internat. U., 1981-85. Mem. AMA, Am. Coll. Sports Medicine (cert. team physician), Am. Coll. Preventive Medicine, Am. Profl. Practice Assn., Assn. of Tchrs. of Preventive Medicine. Nat. Osteoporosis Found.

THEURER, ALAN CLARK, information management specialist; b. Tucson, Jan. 16, 1966; s. Clark Brent and Cheri Laurel (Peterson) T.; m. Julie Ann Coleman, Nov. 13, 1993. Degree infor. mgmt., Brigham Young U., 1991. Sr. support operator WordPerfect Corp., Orem, Utah, 1988-91; sr. cons. Andersen Cons., Phoenix, 1991-93; edn. product devel. mgr. Novell, Orem, 1993—. Republican. Mem. LDS Ch. Office: Novell Inc 1555 N Technology Way Orem UT 84057

THEURER, BYRON W., business owner, aerospace engineer; b. Glendale, Calif., July 1, 1939; s. William Louis and Roberta Cecelia (Sturgis) T.; m. Sue Ann McKay, Sept. 15, 1962 (div. 1980); children: Karen Marie, William Thomas, Alison Lee. BS in Engring. Sci., USAF Acad., 1961; MS in Aero. Sci., U. Calif., Berkeley, 1965; MBA, U. Redlands, 1991. Commd. USAF, 1961, advanced through grades to lt. col., ret. 1978; project officer Space Shuttle Devel. Prog., Houston, 1971-76; chief of test F-15 Systems Prog. Office Wright Patterson AFB, Ohio, 1976-78; sr. engr. Veda, Inc., Dayton, 1979-81, Logicon Inc., Dayton, 1981-83; project mgr. Support Systems Assocs., Inc., Dayton, 1983-84, CTA Inc., Ridgecrest, Calif., 1985-89; owner, operator The Princeton Rev. of Ctrl. Calif., Ridgecrest, 1989-92, San Luis Obispo, 1993—; cons. in field. Decorated Silver Star, D.F.C., Air Medals (16); named Officer of the Yr., Air Force Flight Test Ctr., Edwards AFB, 1970. Mem. Air Force Assn., Assn. Old Crows, USAF Acad. Assn. Grads. (nat. bd. dirs. 1972-75, chpt. pres. 1981-83). Republican. Episcopalian. Home: PO Box 697 Cayucos CA 93430-0697

THIEL, ARTHUR WARREN, journalist; b. Hot Springs, Mont., Nov. 27, 1952; s. Robert Harry and Mary (Previs) T.; m. Julia Claire Akoury, July 16, 1988. BA, Pacific Luth. U., 1975. Reporter News Tribune, Tacoma, 1972-76; reporter, asst. sports editor Jour. Am., Bellevue, Wash., 1976-80; reporter, columnist Post-Intelligencer, Seattle, 1980—; commentator, analyst Sta. KIRO, Seattle, 1989—; commentator Sta. KZOK-FM, Seattle, 1991—. Bd. dirs. Alzheimers Assn. Western and Ctrl Wash., Seattle, 1990—. Named State Sportswriter of Yr., Nat. Sportswriter & Sportscasters Assn., 1990, 92, Disting. Alumnus, Pacific Luth. U., 1991. Office: Seattle Post-Intelligencer 101 Elliott Ave W Seattle WA 98119-4220

THIELGES, BART ARTHUR, university adminstrator; b. Chgo., June 16, 1938; s. Bart Herbert and Norma Ethel (Ohlin) T.; m. Mary Judith McMullen, June 4, 1960; children: Bart, Jon S., Patrick A. BS, So. Ill. U., 1963; M of Forestry, Yale Sch., 1964; MPhil, Yale U., 1967, PhD, 1968. Rsch. fellow Yale U., New Haven, 1964-67; asst. prof. Ohio State U., Wooster, 1967-71; assoc. prof. La. State U., Baton Rouge, 1971-76; prin. geneticist USDA-Forest Svc., New Orleans, 1976-77; prof., chmn. U. Ky., Lexington, 1977-90; assoc. dean Oreg. State U., Corvallis, 1990—; vis. prof. U. Oxford, Eng., 1983-84; program mgr. USDA Competitive Grants, Washington, 1985-86. Editor: Forest Tree Improvement, 1975, Cottonwood and Related Species, 1977. Mem. Soc. of Am. Foresters, Forest Products Soc., Sigma Xi. Office: Coll of Forestry Oreg State U Peavy Hall # 150 Corvallis OR 97331-8566

THIERS, EUGENE ANDRES, mineral economist, educator; b. Santiago, Chile, Aug. 25, 1941; came to U.S., 1962, naturalized, 1976; s. Eugenio A. and Elena (Lillo) T.; m. Marie H. Stuart, Dec. 23, 1965 (div. 1979); children: Ximena, Eugene, Alexander; m. Patricia Van Metre, Jan. 29, 1983. B.S., U. Chile, 1962; M.S., Columbia U., 1965, D.Eng.Sc., 1970. Mgr.-tech. Minbanco Corp., N.Y.C., 1966-70; dir. iron info. Battelle Inst., Columbus, Ohio, 1970-75; minerals economist SRI Internat., Menlo Park, Calif., 1975-79, dir.-minerals and metals, 1979-83, sr. cons., 1983-86; bus. mgr. inorganics, 1986—; vis. prof. mineral econs. Stanford U., Calif., 1983—; bd. dirs Small Mines Internat. Contbr. articles, chpts. to profl. pubs. Campbell and Krumb fellow Columbia U., 1965-67. Fellow AAAS; mem. AIME (chmn. Columbus sect. of Ohio chpt. 1973-75, chmn. Bay Area chpt. of metall. sect. 1979-80), AIME (San Francisco sect.). Home: 426 27th Ave San Mateo CA 94403-2402 Office: SRI Internat 333 Ravenswood Ave Menlo Park CA 94025-3453

THIESEN, GREGORY ALAN, accountant; b. Denver, Apr. 24, 1958; s. Gene Duane and Virginia Ruth (Haas) T.; m. Karen Elise McGrew, Aug. 17, 1984; children: Jeffrey Richard, Jeremy Eugene. BS in Bus., U. Colo., 1980. CPA, Colo. Sr. mgr. Ernst & Whinney, Denver, 1980-89; chief fin. officer, chief info. officer Monfort, Inc., Greeley, 1989-95, CFO, CIO ConAgra Refrigerated Products, 1995—. Mem. student adv. coun. U. No. Colo.; mem. exec. com. Pvt. Industry Coun. Weld County; active Weld County Retirement Bd. Mem. MIT Enterprise Forum Colo. (mem. exec. com. 1987-89), Greeley Country Club, No. Colo. Acctg. Club. Office: MonFort Inc PO Box G Greeley CO 80632-0350

THIESSEN, BETTY JEAN, special education educator; b. Jordan, Mont., Oct. 30, 1930; d. Elmer Theodore and Adaline Marie (Barrett) Brink; m. MacLeod Chris Thiessen, June 23, 1962; children: Mark Owen, Scott David. B of Edn., U. No. Colo., 1957; MA in Edn., Calif. Poly. U., 1992. Cert. resource specialist, learning handicapped tchr. Tchr. elem. schs. N.Mex. and Mont., 1948-61; tchr. 3d grade Alhambra (Calif.) Sch. Dist., 1961-63; substitute tchr. Hacienda La Puente Unified Sch. Dist., Hacienda Heights, Calif., 1967-87, tchr. learning handicapped, 1987—. Bd. dirs. Hacienda Heights Improvement Assn., 1987-91; mem. Colima Rep. Women's Club, Hacienda Heights, 1985—. Recipient Contbns. to Learning Disabled award Pomona Valley chpt. Learning Disabilities Assn. Calif., 1993, Feddersohn Svc. award Los Altos PTA, 1985, Disting. Svc. award Los Robles PTA, 1993, Wailer award for Svc. Above and Beyond the Call of Duty, Bear Mt. Nat. Ski Patrol, 1986. Mem. San Gabriel Assn. Reading Tchrs., Alpha Kappa Gamma (mem. legis. com. 1993—), Phi Kappa Phi. Home: 15730 Agosta Dr Hacienda Heights CA 91745 Office: Los Robles Elem Sch 1530 Ridgley Ave Hacienda Heights CA 91745

THIROUX, EMILY LOFTON, English educator, theater director; b. Porterville, Calif., July 26, 1949; d. Thomas Orville and Hazel Marie (Ketcham) Lofton; m. Jacques Thiroux, Apr. 8, 1984; children: Jason Ragle, Abigale Ragle. AA, Mesa Coll., 1971, AS, 1975; BA, Calif. State U., Bakersfield, 1985, MA, 1988. Instr. Bakersfield (Calif.) Coll., 1986-92; staff developer Pacific Regency Care Ctr., Bakersfield, 1986-94; lectr. English composition Calif. State U., Bakersfield, 1987—; dir., designer Bakersfield (Calif.) Civic Light Opera, 1992—; cons. Pacific Regency Care Ctr., Bakersfield, 1994—. Author: Cultures: Diversity in Reading and Writing, 1993. Vol. Bakersfield (Calif.) Cmty. Theatre, 1985—; commr. Kern County (Calif.) Commn. on Self Esteem and Personal and Social Responsibility, 1991—. Mem. AAUW (past. pres., bd. mem. 1986—, state com. mem. 1994-95, Barbara Leask award), Sigma Tau Delta. Democrat.

THISSELL, CHARLES WILLIAM, lawyer; b. Sioux Falls, S.D., Nov. 23, 1931; s. Oscar H. and Bernice Grace Janet (Olbertson) T.; m. Leila Amoret Rossner; Jan. 24, 1959; children—Amoret Gates, William Richards. B.A., Augustana Coll., Sioux Falls, 1953; J.D., U. Calif.-Berkeley, 1959. Bar: Calif. 1960, U.S. Dist. Ct. (no. and ea. dists.) Calif. 1960, Ct. Appeals (9th cir.) 1966, U.S. Claims Ct. 1974, U.S. Ct. Appeals (D.C., 5th cirs.) 1985, U.S. Supreme Ct. 1985. Cert.in trial advocacy Nat. Bd. Trial Advocacy. Trial counsel Calif. Dept. Transp. San Francisco, 1959-66; asst. gen. counsel law dept. Pacific Gas and Electric Co., San Francisco, 1966-91; ptnr. Morris, Taylor & Hill (formerly Morris, Taylor, Hays & Higaki), San Francisco, 1991-93; pvt. practice law, 1993—; instr. San Francisco Law Sch., 1962-63; arbitrator Superior Cts. San Francisco and Marin County, 1979—. Vice chmn. Marin County Rep. Cen. Com., 1983-84; pres. Marin County Rep. Coun., 1981-82; chancellor, vestry mem. St. Luke's Episcopal Ch., San Francisco, 1979-82. Lt. (j.g.) USNR, 1953-56; comdr., Ret. Mem. ABA, San Francisco Bar Assn. (chmn. trial lawyers sect. 1974). Clubs: Commonwealth of Calif. (chmn. environ. energy sect. 1981-83), Marines Meml. Home: 652 Koula Pl Diamondhead MS 39525-3818 Office: Charles William Thissell Atty at Law 1 Bush St Ste 200 San Francisco CA 94104-4425

THISSELL, JAMES DENNIS, physicist; b. Lincoln County, S.D., June 1, 1935; s. Oscar H. and Bernice G.J. (Olbertson) T. BA cum laude, Augustana Coll., 1957; MS, U. Iowa, 1963. Rsch. physicist U. Iowa, Iowa City, 1958-64; engr. McDonnell Douglas, St. Louis, 1965-66; scientist E.G. & G., Inc., Las Vegas, Nev., 1967-68; engr. Bendix Field Engring. Corp. Ames Rsch. Ctr., Moffett Field, Calif., 1970-77, Lockheed Missiles & Space Co., Sunnyvale, Calif., 1978-95, Lockheed Martin Tech. Ops., Sunnyvale, 1995—. Mem. AIAA, IEEE, Am. Phys. Soc., Am. Geophys. Soc., Sigma Xi. Republican. Lutheran. Home: 38475 Jacaranda Dr Newark CA 94560-4727 Office: Lockheed Corp 0/23-20 B-100 FAC 1 PO Box 61687 Sunnyvale CA 94088-1687

THISTEL, CYNTHIA GRELLE, nursing educator, nurse epidemiologist; b. Pitts., June 2, 1955; d. Albert Charles and Mary Jane (Hol) Grelle; m. James N. Thistel, Sept. 22, 1985. BSN, U. Fla., 1978; MSN, U. Md., 1985. Nurse epidemiologist Washington Adventist Hosp., Takoma Park, Md., 1986-89, Malcolm Grow Med. Ctr., Andrews AFB, Md., 1989, Porter Meml. Hosp., Denver, 1989—. Mem. Assn. for Practitioners in Infection Control, Sigma Theta Tau.

THISTLE, HAROLD WILLIAM, JR., physical scientist; b. New Haven, July 29, 1958; s. Harold William and Myrta Lenore (Irwin) T.; m. Gay Ellen Schlichting, Jan. 14, 1984; children: Andrew Gregory, Brian Harold. BA in Geography, U. Conn., 1980, PhD in Forest Meteorology, 1988; MS in Climatology, U. Del., 1983. Cert. cons. meteorologist, Am. Meteorol. Soc. Rsch. assoc. U. Conn., Storrs, 1988; sr. scientist TRC Environ. Co., Windsor, Conn., 1988-92; project leader tech. and devel. USDA Forest Svc., Washington, Mont., 1992—; coop. observer NOAA, Coventry, Conn., 1983-88. Co-author: Environmental Modeling, Vol. II, 1994; contbr. articles to profl. jours. Active Univ. Congl. Ch., Missoula, Mont. Fellow Ctr. for Environ. Health, 1987, U. Conn., 1985, 87; recipient Cert. Merit USDA, 1994. Mem. AAAS, ASCE, ASCE (affiliate), Am. Meteorol. Soc., Air and Waste Mgmt. Assn., Am. Geophys. Union. Office: Missoula Tech and Devel Fort Missoula Rd # 1 Missoula MT 59801-7203

THISTLETHWAITE, DAVID RICHARD, architect; b. Burlington, Iowa, Aug. 24, 1947; s. Robert and Nona (Binder) T.; m. Carol Anne Armstrong, Aug. 22, 1970. BArch, Iowa State U., 1971. Registered arch., Calif., Minn.; registered Nat. Coun. Archtl. Registration Bds. Designer Morrison Architects, St. Paul, 1971-73, Times Architects, Mpls., 1973-74; project architect Bentz/Thompson Assocs., Mpls., 1974-77; project mgr. Setter Leach Lindstrom, Mpls., 1977-78; project architect Wurster Bernardi Emmons, San Francisco, 1978-79, Strotz & Assocs., Tiburon, Calif., 1979-81, Hood Miller Assoc., San Francisco, 1981-84; prin., ptnr. R S T Architects, San Francisco, 1984-88; prin. Thistlethwaite Archtl. Group, San Francisco, 1988—. Contbr. articles to profl. jours. Mem. AIA (nat. profl. devel. com. 1983-86, treas. San Francisco chpt. 1985-86, chmn. Calif. coun. health facilities com. 1994—, chmn. design com. Acad. Architecture for Health 1994—), Am. Soc. Hosp. Engrs. Office: 250 Sutter St San Francisco CA 94108-4403

THOENI, MARY IRENE, business consultant; b. Miami, Fla., Jan. 15, 1950; d. Joseph Daniel Sr. and Mary Irene (Flieschman) Kinney; m. David Leigh Parker, Sept. 16, 1969 (div. Jan. 1975); m. Kenneth D. Theoni, Aug. 8, 1975; David Leigh, Lisa Marie, Emma Catherine. BS in Health Sci., Charter Oak Coll., 1989; MBA, Cardinal Stritch Coll., 1991. With budget and fin. dept. USDA, Ketchikan, Alaska, 1978-81; with purchasing dept. Naval Regional Med. Ctr., Charleston, S.C., 1981-82; with acctg. dept. Charleston Naval Shipyard, 1982-87, U.S. VA, Milw., 1987-88; founder, pres. Bus. Solutions, Etc., Milw., 1988-93; founder, owner Bus. Solutions, Anchorage, 1994—; with Dept Def.-Def. Fin. & Acctg. Svc., Ft. Richardson, Alaska, 1994—. Mem. racial discrimination task force NOW, Milw., 1989-91. Recipient Take Charge award Clairol Found., 1989. Mem. NAFE, Nat. Soc. Pub. Accts. Home: 2900 Boniface Pky # 476 Anchorage AK 99504-3195

THOLE, MARY ELIZABETH, insurance company executive; b. Salt Lake City, July 29, 1950; d. John Bernard and Emily Josephine T. BA, U. Hawaii, Hilo, 1984, paralegal cert. cum laude, 1989; postgrad.in bus. administrn., U. Hawaii, Manoa, 1985-86. Lic. ins. agt. Hawaii, Calif., Fla., N.C. Regional rep. Lightolier, Inc., Salt Lake City, 1978-80; group sales rep. FHP/Utah, Salt Lake City, 1980-81; health net rep. Blue Cross Corp., L.A., 1981-82; v.p. fin. Bus. Support Systems, Hilo, 1983-89; rep. Prudential Ins. and Fin. Svcs., Honolulu, 1989—; registered rep. Pruco Securities Corp., 1989—. Docent Lyman House, 1984-85, L.A. County Mus. of Art, 1980-81, S.L.C. Art Mus., 1970-80; bd. dirs. YWCA, Hawaii Island, 1980-91, 1st v.p., 1988. Recipient Nat. Quality award 1991, 92, 93, 94, Nat. Sales Achievement award 1992, 93; named YWCA Vol. of Yr., 1991. Fellow Life Underwriters Tng. Coun.; mem. AAUW (fundraiser chair Kona chpt. 1992, bd. dirs. Hilo chpt. 1987-89, cmty. area rep. 1989), Am. Bus. Women's Assn. (pres. Nani O Hilo chpt. 1995—, cmty. svc. chair 1993-95, audit com. chair Kanoelani chpt. 1992, program chair Hilo chpt. 1985, expansion com. Hilo Lehua chpt. 1985, Steven Bufton grantee 1985, ways and means com. 1984, memberships chair Lehua chpt. 1983), Nat. Assn. Life Underwriters (legis. rep. West Hawaii 1989—), Million Dollar Round Table (qualifying mem. 1992, 93, 94, 95). Roman Catholic. Home: Prudential Ins Co Am PO Box 4638 Hilo HI 96720

THOLLANDER, EARL GUSTAVE, artist, author; b. Kingsburg, Calif., Apr. 13, 1922; s. Gus Alfred and Helen Marie (Peterson) T.; m. Janet Marie Behr, May 31, 1947; children: Kristie, Wesley. BA, U. Calif., Berkeley, 1944. Staff artist Patterson and Hall, San Francisco, 1946-47, San Francisco Examiner, 1947-57, Landphere and Assocs., 1957-60; free-lance artist, writer, 1960—. Author: Back Roads of California, 1971, revised 1988; Back Roads of New England, 1974, Barns of California, 1974, Back Roads of Arizona, 1978 (now called Arizona's Scenic Byways), revised 1992, Back Roads of Oregon, 1979, revised 1993, Back Roads of Texas, 1980, Back Roads of Washington, 1981, revised 1993, Earl Thollander's Back Roads of California, 1983, revised 1994, Back Roads of the Carolinas, 1985, Earl Thollander's San Francisco, 1994. Served to lt. (j.g.) USN, 1942-45, PTO. Democrat. Unitarian. Home and Studio: 19210 Hwy 128 Calistoga CA 94515-9502

THOMAN, JOHN EVERETT, architect, mediator; b. Dixon, Ill., Aug. 6, 1925; s. George Dewey and Agnes Katherine (Fane) T.; m. Paula Ann Finnegan, Oct. 31, 1953; children: Shawn Michael, Brian Gerard, Kevin Charles, Trace Marie, Patricia Ann, Ronan Patrick, Caron Lynn. AA, UCLA, 1948; BArch cum laude, U. So. Calif., 1955. Registered architect and gen. contractor, Calif. Project dir. A. Quincy Jones & Frederick E. Emmons, L.A., 1956-57, assoc., 1958, dir. constrn., 1958-73; dir. specifications A. Quincy Jones, FAIA & Assocs., L.A., 1973-77; dir. specifications Albert C. Martin and Assocs., L.A., 1977-79, dir. constrn. and industry rels., 1979—, assoc., 1979-90, sr. assoc., 1990—, prin., 1991—; gen. contractor Martin of Calif., L.A., 1984—, v.p., 1985—; guest lectr. U. So. Calif. Lusk Sch. Real Estate, UCLA Grad. Sch., also various student, trade and tech. groups. Mem., vice chmn. Culver City (Calif.) Planning Commn., 1959; mem. Calif. Gov.'s Housing Commn., L.A., 1960, Community Redevel. Agy., Culver City, 1992—. With U.S. Army, 1943-45, USAF, 1950-51. Mem. AIA (chmn. design awards com. L.A. 1960), Constrn. Specifications Inst. (bd. dirs. 1977-80, guest lectr.), Phi Eta Sigma, Tau Sigma Delta. Office: Albert C Martin and Assocs 811 W 7th St Los Angeles CA 90017-3408

THOMAN, MARY E., rancher, vocational and secondary educator; b. Kemmerer, Wyo., Sept. 14, 1949; d. William J. and Mary A. (Ferentchak) T. AA, Western Wyo. C.C., Rock Springs, 1970; BS in Bus., U. Wyo., 1972; MEd in Mktg., Colo. State U., 1978, PhD in Vocat./Secondary Adminstrn., 1981. Profl. Teaching Cert., Wyo. Bus. edn. Green River (Wyo.) High Sch., 1972-75; part time bus. and mktg. instr. Western Wyo. C.C., Green River, 1972-77, Rock Springs, Wyo., 1972-80, Kemmerer, Wyo., 1983—; mktg. and coop. educator Green River (Wyo.) High Sch., 1975-77; asst. dir. Nev. St. Coun. on Vocat. Edn., Carson City, Nev., 1977; exec. dir. Mont. St. Coun. on Vocat. Edn., Helena, Mont., 1981-82; cattle/sheep rancher Kemmerer, 1981—; sr. sales dir. Mary Kay Cosmetics, Kemmerer, Wyo., 1988—; ednl. cons. past chair Wyo. St. Coun. on Vocat. Edn., Cheyenne, 1984-93; bus. cons. Western Wyo. Coll., Rock Springs, 1983—; sch.-to-work, S.W. Wyo. Collaborative Team; edn. cons. Kemmerer Sch. Dist., 1993—, chair voc/tech prep bus. curriculum com.; mem. Wyo. Agr. in Classroom, 1992-94. Active western range issues; testifier on Range Reform Hearings; mem. Cumberland Allotment Coordinated Resource Mgmt. Team Bur. Land Mgmt.; mem. S.W. Wyo. Resource Rendezvous Steering Com. Ednl./Profl. Devel. Act fellow, 1977-78, Grad. Leadership Devel. awardee, 1978-81. Mem. Kemmerer C. of C. (edn. com., bd. dirs. 1992—). Roman Catholic. Home: PO Box 146 Green River WY 82935-0146

THOMAS, BOB, public relations executive; b. San Diego. Sports editor, automotive writer, columnist L.A. Times; pres. Bob Thomas & Assocs., 1972-92, chmn. Office: Bob Thomas & Assos Inc Pub Rels 340 Main St Venice CA 90291-2524

THOMAS, BRIAN CHESTER, state legislator, engineer; b. Tacoma, Wash., May 19, 1939; s. Ralph R. and Katheryne (Chester) T.; m. Judith Lynn Adams, Feb. 20, 1965; children: Jeffrey, Kyle, Cheryl. BS in Indsl. Engring., Oreg. State U., 1961; postgrad., U. Wash., 1968-70; MBA, Pacific Luth. U., 1979. Civil engr. U.S. Coast Guard, Seattle, 1962-63; ops. officer U.S. Coast Guard, Astoria, Oreg., 1964-65; sr. sales engr. Puget Sound Power & Light Co., Bellevue, Wash., 1965-70, mgr. market rsch., 1971-80, rsch. adminstr., 1981-89, prin. engr., 1989—; mem. Wash. Ho. of Reps., Olympia, 1993—, chmn. joint select com. on edn. restructuring, 1991—, chmn. fin., edn., natural resources coms., 1991—; chair EEI Rsch. Mgmt. Com., Washington, 1988-89, EPRI Renewable Com., Palo Alto, Calif., 1989-90; adv. bd. Nat. Renewable Energy Lab., Golden, Colo., 1990-92; mem. adv. bd. sch. elec. engring. Oreg. State U., Corvallis, 1991-93; dep. dir. region 10 U.S. Dept. Transp. Emergency Orgn., Seattle, 1989-93. Bd. dirs. Issaquah (Wash.), Sch. Dist., 1989-93. Capt. USCGR, 1961-84. Mem. Issaquah Rotary (pres. 1982-83), Rainier Club. Republican. Home: 14715 182nd Pl SE Renton WA 98059-8028 Office: Wash Ho Reps PO Box 40610 Olympia WA 98504-0610 Office: Puget Sound Power & Light PO Box 97034 Bellevue WA 98009-9734

THOMAS, BRIAN GORDON, municipal finance executive; b. Pasadena, Calif., July 23, 1954. BS in Biology, BS in Econs., Calif. State Poly. U., 1977; MA in Econs., U. Calif., Riverside, 1981, PhD in Econs., 1986, cert. in exec. mgmt., 1992. Lectr. econs. Riverside City Coll., 1980-81, Calif. State U., Fullerton, 1985-89, Calif. State Poly. U., Pomona, 1988-91; assoc. in econs. Calif. State U., Riverside, 1982-83, rsch. asst. dept. econs., 1980-83; engr. power resource planning Dept. Pub. Utilities City of Anaheim, Calif., 1983-85, mgr. fin. requirements, 1985-88; with utilities acctg., mgr. fin. Dept. Utilities City of Riverside, 1988-89, asst. dir. utilities, fin./adminstrn. Dept. Utilities, 1989-93; asst. dir. fin. Met. Water Dist. So. Calif., L.A., 1993-94, asst. chief planning divsn., 1994—. Contbr. articles to profl. jours. Regents fellow U. Calif., 1981. Mem. Am. Econs. Assn., Western Econ. Assn., Am. Water Works Assn.

THOMAS, CHRISTOPHER ROBERT, food products company executive; b. San Diego, Dec. 5, 1948; m. Christina Q. Thomas, Apr. 16, 1979. BSBA, U. So. Calif., 1977. CPA, Calif. Auditor Arthur Andersen & Co., Calif., 1977-84; v.p. fin., chief fin. officer Collins Foods Internat. Inc., L.A., 1984—. Sgt. USMC, 1967-70. Mem. AICPA, Calif. Soc. CPA's, Fin. Acctg. Found., Fin. Execs. Inst. Office: Collins Foods Internat Inc 12665 W Jefferson Blvd Los Angeles CA 90066-7008

THOMAS, CLAUDEWELL SIDNEY, psychiatry educator; b. N.Y.C., Oct. 5, 1932; s. Humphrey Sidney and Frances Elizabeth (Collins) T.; m. Carolyn Pauline Rozansky, Sept. 6, 1958; children: Jeffrey Evan, Julie-Anne Elizabeth, Jessica Edith. BA, Columbia U., 1952; MD, SUNY, Downstate Med. Ctr., 1956; MPH, Yale U., 1964. Diplomate Nat. Bd. Med. Examiners, Am. Bd. Psychiatry. From instr. to assoc. prof. Yale U., New Haven, 1963-68, dir. Yale tng. program in social community psychiatry, 1967-70; dir. div. mental health service programs NIMH, Washington, 1970-73; chmn. dept. psychiatry U.M.D.N.J., Newark, 1973-83; prof. dept. psychiatry Drew Med. Sch., 1983—, chmn. dept. psychiatry, 1983-93; prof. dept. psychiatry UCLA, 1983-94, vice chmn. dept. psychiatry, 1983-93, prof. emeritus dept. psychiatry, 1994—; cons. A.K. Rice Inst., Washington, 1978-80, SAMSA/PHS Cons., 1991—; mem. L.A. County Superior Ct. Psych. Panel, 1991—. Author: (with B. Bergen) Issues and Problems in Contemporary Society, 1966; editor (with R. Bryce LaPorte) Alienation in Contemporary Society, 1976, (with J. Lindenthal) Psychiatry and Mental Health Science Handbook; mem. editorial bd. Internat. Jour. Mental Health, Adminstrn. In Mental Health. Served to capt. USAF, 1959-61. Fellow APHA, Am. Psychoanalytic Assn. (hon.), Am. Psychiat. Assn. (life), Royal Soc. Health, N.Y. Acad. Sci., N.Y. Acad. Medicine; mem. Am. Sociol. Assn. Home and Office: 30676 Palos Verdes Dr W Palos Verdes Peninsula CA 90274

THOMAS, CRAIG, senator; b. Cody, Wyo., Feb. 17, 1933; s. Craig E. and Marge Oweta (Lynn) T.; m. Susan Roberts; children: Peter, Paul, Patrick, Alexis. BS, U. Wyo., 1955. Exec. v.p. Wyo. Farm Bur., Laramie, 1960-66; asst. legis. dir. Am. Farm Bur., Wash., 1966-71; dir. nat. resource Am. Farm Bur., Chgo., 1971-75; gen. mgr. Wyo. Rural Elec. Assn., 1975-89; mem. Wyo. Ho. of Reps., 1985-1989, 101st-103rd Congresses from Wyo., Washington, D.C., 1989-95; senator State Wyo., Washington, 1995—. Former chmn. Natrona County (Wyo.) Rep. Com.; state rep. Natrona County Dist.; del. Rep. Nat. Conv., 1980. Capt. USMC. Mem. Am. Soc. Trade Execs., Masons. Methodist. Office: US Senate Washington DC 20510

THOMAS, DALTON, food products executive; b. 1942. Degree, U. Wash., 1965. Fruit inspector State of Wash., Wenatchee, 1965-66; with Oneonta Trading Co., Wenatchee, 1966—; pres. Custom Apple Packers, Inc., Brewster, Wash. Office: Custom Apple Packers Inc 824 Grange Rd Brewster WA 98812*

THOMAS, DANIEL FOLEY, telecommunications company executive; b. Washington, Aug. 24, 1950; s. Richard Kenneth and Margaret (Foley) T.; m. Barbara Jane Clark, June 30, 1973; 1 child, Alison Clark. BS in Acctg., Mt. St. Mary's Coll., 1972. CPA, Va. Auditor Deloitte, Haskins and Sells, Washington, 1972-74; various fin. positions Communications Satellite Corp., Washington, 1974-78, asst. treas., 1984-85, treas., 1986-87, controller, 1987-89; controller Comsat Telesystems, Washington, 1978-79; mgr. acctg. and taxes Satellite Bus. Systems, McLean, Va., 1979-81, treas., 1981-84; v.p. fin. Comsat Tech. Products, Inc., Washington, 1985-86, Comsat Video Enterprises, Inc., Washington, 1989-90; v.p. Leasetec Corp., Boulder, Colo., 1990—. Named One of Outstanding Young Men Am., 1981. Mem. AICPA, Va. Jaycees (life), Great Falls Jaycees (pres. 1978). Roman Catholic. Home: 1299 S Teal Ct Boulder CO 80303-1480 Office: Leasetec Corp 1401 Pearl St Boulder CO 80302-5319

THOMAS, DARRELL DENMAN, lawyer; b. Lake Cormorant, Miss., Sept. 10, 1931; s. Darrell Dane and Maggie Adele (McKay) T.; m. Dora Ann Bailey, Feb. 12, 1957 (div. 1988). BS, Memphis State U., 1957; JD, U. Denver, 1960. Bar: Colo. 1960, U.S. Dist. Ct. Colo. 1960, U.S. Supreme Ct. 1967, U.S. Ct. Appeals (10th cir.) 1971. Law clk. to presiding justice U.S. Dist. Ct., Colo., 1960-61; ptnr. Mills & Thomas, Colorado Springs, Colo., 1961-65; pvt. practice Colorado Springs, 1965—; U.S. commr. U.S. Dist. Ct., 1961-71, U.S. magistrate, 1971-91. Pres. Colorado Springs Symphony, 1979-82; v.p. Colorado Springs Symphony Orch. Found. With U.S. Army, 1952-54. Mem. ABA, Colo. Bar Assn., El Paso County Bar Assn., El Paso Club (dir. 1985-88), Broadmoor Golf Club, Garden of the Gods Club, Masons, Shriner. Republican. Office: 115 E Vermijo Ave Colorado Springs CO 80903-2004

THOMAS, DAVID SNOW, plastic surgeon; b. Chgo., Feb. 7, 1951; s. Allan Perry and Verna Bea (Snow) T.; m. Becky Williams Thomas, Aug. 25, 1973; children: Nathan David, Abigail, Elizabeth. BA, U. Utah, 1974, MD, 1978. Diplomate Am. Bd. Plastic Surgery, Am. Bd. Surgery. Resident surgery UCLA, 1978-83, resident plastic surgery, 1983-85, fellow craniofacial surgery, 1985; pvt. practice Salt Lake City, 1986—; chief plastic surgery Primary Childrens Med. Ctr., Salt Lake City, 1988-90, Los Hosp., 1993—; clin. asst. prof. U. Utah Plastic Surgeons, Salt Lake City, 1986-89, assoc. prof. surgery, 1990-93, clin. assoc. prof., 1993—. Bd. Dirs. AMICUS, Salt Lake City, Utah, 1990-92. Fellow Am Coll. Surgeons; mem. Am. Soc. Plastic & Reconstructive Surgery, Am. Soc. Maxillofacial Surgery, Am. Cleft Palate Craniofacial Assn., Am. Soc. Aesthetic Plastic Surgery, Interplast (pres. Salt Lake City, 1992—, bd. dirs. Palo Alto, Calif., 1992—), The Country Club (Salt Lake City). Office: 370 9th Ave Ste 200 Salt Lake City UT 84103-2877

THOMAS, DAVID STANLEY, sales executive; b. Malad, Idaho, July 4, 1946; s. Stanley and Erma (Peterson) T.; m. Rochelle Skinner, Sept. 27, 1974; children: Aaron, Adam, Amanda. BS in Acctg., Brigham Young U., 1969. Ptnr. Emporium Gift Shop and Union Block Inc., Provo, Utah, 1971-73; prin. Keith Warshaw & Co., Salt Lake City, 1973-79; regional sales mgr. Eddie Parker Sales, Dallas, 1979-84; v.p. mktg. Country Cozy's Inc., Buena Park, Calif., 1984—. Bd. dirs. AYSO Soccer. Mem. Am. Legion. Republican. Mem. LDS Ch. Home: 13126 San Felipe St La Mirada CA 90638-3450 Office: Country Cozy's Inc 8011 Orangethorpe Ave Buena Park CA 90621-3801

THOMAS, DAVID TIMOTHY, marketing professional; b. Circleville, Ohio, Jan. 2, 1946; s. Verneal Marshall and Lucile Frances (May) Y.; m. Nancy Sue Bradford Thomas, July 5, 1969 (div. 1984); m. Susan Rae Alreck Thomas, June 23, 1984; 1 child, Jennifer Sue. BA, Otterbein Coll., Westerville, Ohio, 1969. News dir. KSIR-AM, Estes Park, Colo., 1975-77; owner, mgr. The Oxen Yoke and Covered Wagon Crafts, Estes Park, Colo., 1976-80; news editor Estes Park Trail-Gazette, Estes Park, Colo., 1979-80; owner De Nada Prodns., Estes Park, Colo., 1978-82; station mgr. KSIR-AM, Estes Park, Colo., 1982-84; dir. comms. YMCA of the Rockies, Estes Park, Colo., 1984—. Author: PR: The Proof of the Pudding, 1982; contbr. articles to profl. jours. Dist. capt., mem. County Ctrl. Com. Larimer County Dem. Party, Colo., 1980-84; mem. Estes Park Planning Commn. Recipient 2nd Place Best Program Colo. Broadcasters Assn., 1975, 1st Place, 1976, Pub. Svc. Announcement, 1st Place, 1976, Best Promotion for a Client 2nd Place, 1976, Best Topical News Series, 1st Place, 1982, Best Spot News Coverage, 1st Place, 1982, Best Spot News Coverage United Press Internat. 1st Place, 1982, Best Program, 1st Place, 1983, Slide presentation 2nd Place Colo. Ednl. Media Assn., 1978, 1st Place, 1979. Mem. Internat. Assn. Conf. Ctr. Adminstrs., Estes Park Conf. Assn. (pres.), Soc. Govt. Meeting Planners, Pub. Rels. Soc. Am., Assn. Profl. Dirs. YMCAs (past chpt. pres.), Christian Camping Internat. U.S.A., Rooftop Riders Horse Club. Democrat. United Methodist. Home: PO Box 4448 1560 Axminster Ln Estes Park CO 80517-4448 Office: YMCA of the Rockies 2515 Tunnel Rd Estes Park CO 80511

THOMAS, DUNCAN WINTON, botanist, consultant; b. Hastings, Sussex, Eng., Feb. 27, 1950; came to U.S., 1973; s. James Andrew Thomas and Kathleen Margaret (King) Gobbett; m. Jane Anne McCauley, May 5, 1973; children: Rhiannon, Emily. BS, U. Wales, 1971, PhD in Botany, 1977. Asst. curator Mo. Bot. Garden, St. Louis, 1983-88; assoc. prof. Oreg. State U., Corvallis, 1992—; botanist Duncan & Jane Thomas Environ. Consultants, Corvallis, 1989—; biodiversity cons. for Ctrl. Africa/Cameroon Nat. Cancer Inst., Bethesda, Md., 1991—, World Bank, Washington, 1992, 93, Overseas Devel. Adminstrn., London, 1992-94. Discoverer, namer new plant species Ancistrocladus korupensis, 1987 (source of anti-HIV alkaloid Nat. Cancer Inst. 1993). Mem. Assn. for Tropical Biology, Soc. for Econ. Botany, Soc. of Wetland Scientists. Home: 2060 NW Dogwood Dr Corvallis OR 97330-1102 Office: Oreg State Univ Office Internat Rsch/Devel Dept Botany Corvallis OR 97331

THOMAS, EDWARD DONNALL, physician, researcher; b. Mart, Tex., Mar. 15, 1920; married; 3 children. BA, U. Tex., 1941, MA, 1943; MD, Harvard U., 1946; MD (hon.), U. Cagliari, Sardinia, 1981, U. Verona, Italy, 1991, U. Parma, Italy, 1992, U. Barcelona, Spain, 1994. Lic. physician Mass., N.Y., Wash.; diplomate Am. Bd. Internal Medicine. Intern in medicine Peter Bent Brigham Hosp., Boston, 1946-47, rsch. fellow hematology, 1947-48; NRC postdoctoral fellow in medicine dept. biology MIT, Cambridge, 1950-51; chief med. resident, sr. asst. resident Peter Bent Brigham Hosp., 1951-53, hematologist, 1953-55; instr. medicine Harvard Med. Sch., Boston, 1953-55; rsch. assoc. Cancer Rsch. Found. Children's Med. Ctr., Boston, 1953-55; physician-in-chief Mary Imogene Bassett Hosp., Cooperstown, N.Y., 1955-63; assoc. clin. prof. medicine Coll. Physicians and Surgeons Columbia U., N.Y.C., 1955-63; attending physician U. Wash. Hosp., Seattle, 1963-90; prof. medicine Sch. Medicine U. Wash., Seattle, 1963-90, head divsn. oncology Sch. Medicine, 1963-85, prof. emeritus medicine Sch. Medicine, 1990—; dir. med. oncology Fred Hutchinson Cancer Rsch. Ctr., Seattle, 1974-89, assoc. dir. clin. rsch. programs, 1982-89, mem., 1974—; mem. hematology study sect. NIH, 1965-69; mem. bd. trustees and med. sci. adv. com. Leukemia Soc. Am., Inc., 1969-73; mem. clin. cancer investigation review com. Nat. Cancer Inst., 1970-74; 1st ann. Eugene C. Eppinger lectr. Peter Bent Brigham Hosp. and Harvard Med. Sch., 1974; Lilly lectr. Royal Coll. Physicians, London, 1977; Stratton lectr. Internation Soc. Hematology, 1982; Paul Aggeler lectr. U. Calif., San Francisco, 1982; 65th Mellon lectr. U. Pitts. Sch. Medicine, 1984; Stanley Wright Meml. lectr. Western Soc. Pediatric Rsch., 1985; Adolfo Ferrata lectr. Italian Soc. Hematology, Verona, Italy, 1991. Mem. editl. bd. Blood, 1962-75, 77-82, Transplantation, 1970-76, Proc. of Soc. for Exptl. Biology and Medicine, 1974-81, Leukemia Rsch., 1977-87, Hematological Oncology, 1982-87, Jour. Clin. Immunology, 1982-87, Am. Jour. Hematology, 1985—, Bone Marrow Transplantation, 1986—. With U.S. Army, 1948-50. Recipient A. Ross McIntyre award U. Nebr. Med. Ctr., 1975, Philip Levine award Am. Soc. Clin. Pathologists, 1979, Disting. Svc. in Basic Rsch. award Am. Cancer Soc., 1980, Kettering prize Gen. Motors Cancer Rsch. Found., 1981, Spl. Keynote Address award Am. Soc. Therapeutic Radiologists, 1981, Robert Roesler de Villiers award Leukemia Soc. Am., 1983, Karl Landsteiner Meml. award Am. Assn. Blood Banks, 1987, Terry Fox award Can., 1990, Internat. award Gairdner Found., 1990, N.Am. Med. Assn. Hong Kong prize, 1990, Nobel prize in medicine, 1990, Presdl. medal of sci. NSF, 1990,. Mem. NAS, Am. Assn. Cancer Rsch., Am. Assn. Physicians (Kober medal 1992), Am. Fedn. Clin. Rsch., Am. Soc. Clin. Oncology (David A. Karnoksky Meml. lectr. 1983), Am. Soc. Clin. Investigation, Am. Soc. Hematology (pres. 1987-88, Henry M. Stratton lectr. 1975), Internat. Soc. Exptl. Hematology, Internat. Soc. Hematology, Academie Royale de Medicine de Belgique (corresponding mem.), Swedish Soc. Hematology (hon.), Swiss Soc. Hematology, Royal Coll. Physicians and Surgeons Can. (hon.), Western Assn. Physicians, Soc. Exptl. Biology and Medicine, Transplantation Soc., Nat. Acad. Medicine (hon.). Office: Fred Hutchinson Cancer Ctr 1124 Columbia St Seattle WA 98104-2015

THOMAS, ESTHER MERLENE, elementary education educator; b. San Diego, Oct. 16, 1945; d. Merton Alfred and Nellie Lida (Von Pilz) T. AA with honors, Grossmont Coll., 1966; BA with honors, San Diego State U., 1969; MA, U. Redlands, 1977. Cert. elem. and adult edn. tchr. Tchr. Cajon Valley Union Sch. Dist., El Cajon, 1969—; sci. fair coord. Flying Hills Sch.; tchr. Hopi and Navajo Native Americans, Ariz, Calif., Utah, 1964-74, Goose and Gander Nursery School, Lakeside, Calif., 1964-66; dir., supt. Bible and Sunday schs. various chs., Lakeside, 1961-87; mem. sci. com., math coun. Cajon Valley Union Sch. Dist., 1990-91. Author: Individualized Curriculum in the Affective Domain; contbg. author: Campbell County, The Treasured Years, 1990, Legends of Lakeside; contbr. articles to profl. jours. and newspapers. Tem. U.S. Senatorial Club, Washington, 1984—, Conservative Caucus, Inc., Washington, 1988—, Ronald Reagan Presdl. Found., Ronald

Reagan Rep. Ctr., 1988, Rep. Presdl. Citizen's Adv. Commn., 1989—, Rep. Platform Planning Com., Calif., 1992, at-large del. representing dist. #45, Lakeside, Calif., 1992, 1995—, Am. Security Coun., Washington, 1994, Congressman Hunter's Off Road Adv. Coun., El Cajon, Calif., 1994, Century Club, San Diego Rep. Century Club, 1995; mem. health articulation com. project AIDS, Cajon Valley Union Sch. Dist., 1988—, Concerned Women Am., Washington, Recruit Depot Hist. Mus., San Diego, 1989, Citizen's Drug Free Am., Calif., 1989—, The Heritage Found., 1988—; charter mem. Marine Corps; mem. Lakeside Centennial Com., 1985-86; hon. mem. Rep. Presdl. Task Force, Washington, 1986; del. Calif. Rep. Senatorial Mid-Term Conv., Washington, 1994; mus. curator Lakeside Hist. Soc., 1992-93. Recipient Outstanding Svc. award PTA, 1972-74; recognized for various contbns. Commdg. Post Gen., San Diego Bd. Edn., 1989. Mem. Tchrs. Assn., Calif. Tchrs. Assn., Nat. Trust for Hist. Preservation, Cajon Valley Educators Assn. (faculty advisor, rep. 1980-82, 84-86, 87-88), Christian Bus. and Profl. Women, Lakeside Hist. Soc. (mus. curator 1992), Capitol Hill Women's Club, Am. Ctr. for Law and Justice, Internat. Christian Women's Club (Christian amb. to Taiwan, Korea, 1974). Republican. Home: 13594 Highway 8 Business Apt 3 Lakeside CA 92040-5235 Office: Flying Hills Elem Sch 1251 Finch St El Cajon CA 92020-1433

THOMAS, ETHEL COLVIN NICHOLS (MRS. LEWIS VICTOR THOMAS), counselor, educator; b. Cranston, R.I., Mar. 31, 1913; d. Charles Russell and Mabel Maria (Colvin) Nichols; Ph.B., Pembroke Coll. in Brown U., 1934; M.A., Brown U., 1938; Ed.D., Rutgers U., 1979; m. Lewis Victor Thomas, July 26, 1945 (dec. Oct. 1965); 1 child, Glenn Nichols. Tchr. English, Cranston High Sch., 1934-39; social dir. and adviser to freshmen, Fox Hall, Boston U., 1939-40; instr. to asst. prof. English Am. Coll. for Girls, Istanbul, Turkey, 1940-44; dean freshman, dir. admission Women's Coll. of Middlebury, Vt., 1944-45; tchr. English, Robert Coll., Istanbul, 1945-46; instr. English, Rider Coll., Trenton, N.J., 1950-51; tchr. English, Princeton (N.J.) High Sch., 1951-61, counselor, 1960-62, 72-83, coll. counselor, 1962-72, sr. peer counselor, 1986—. Mem. NEA, AAUW, Nat. Assn. Women Deans Adminstrs. and Counselors, Am. Assn. Counseling and Devel., Bus. and Profl. Women's Club (named Woman of Yr., Princeton chpt. 1977), Met. Mus. Art, Phi Delta Kappa, Kappa Delta Pi. Presbyn. Clubs: Brown University (N.Y.C.); Nassau.

THOMAS, FRANK JOSEPH, nuclear engineer; b. Pocatello, Idaho, Apr. 15, 1930; s. Emil C. and Jean (Jones) T.; m. Carol Jones, Feb. 4, 1949; children: Dale, Wayne, Keith. BSEE, U. Idaho, 1952; MS, U. Calif., Berkeley, 1957. Registered profl. mech. engr., Calif. Engr. Sandia Corp., Albuquerque, 1952-56; mgr. engring. div. Aerojet Gen., San Ramon, Calif., 1957-64; dir. nuclear program Office Sec. Defense, Washington, 1964-67; sr. scientist Rand Corp., Santa Monica, Calif., 1967-71; chmn. Pacific-Sierra Rsch. Corp., L.A., 1971—; lectr. U. Calif., Berkeley, 1956-58; chmn. treaty evaluation panel Def. Advanced Rsch. Projects Agy., Washington, 1969-71; clear sky panel USAF, Washington, 1967-73. Author: Evasive Foreign Nuclear Testing, 1971, Blackjack Strategy, 1961; contbr. articles to profl. jours. including Nature, Physics Letters. Recipient Master Design award Product Engring. Mag., 1963. Mem. AAAS, Am. Inst. Aeronautics and Astro. Office: Pacific Sierra Rsch Corp 2901 28th St Santa Monica CA 90405-2938

THOMAS, GARETH, metallurgy educator; b. Maesteg, U.K., Aug. 9, 1932; came to U.S., 1960, naturalized, 1977; s. David Bassett and Edith May (Gregory) T.; 1 child, Julian Guy David. B.Sc., U. Wales, 1952; Ph.D., Cambridge U., 1955, Sc.D., 1969. I.C.I. fellow Cambridge U., 1956-59; asst. prof. U. Calif., Berkeley, 1960-63; asso. prof. U. Calif., 1963-67, prof. metallurgy, 1967—, assoc. dean grad. div., 1968-69, asst. chancellor, acting vice chancellor for acad. affairs, 1969-72; founder, sci. dir. Nat. Ctr. Electron Microscopy, 1982-93; cons. to industry. Author: Transmission Electron Microscopy of Metals, 1962, Electron Micoscopy and Strength of Crystals, 1963, (with O. Johari) Stereographic Projection and Applications, 1969, Transmission Electron Microscopy of Materials, 1980; contbr. articles to profl. jours. Recipient Curtis McGraw Rsch. award Am. Soc. Engring. Edn., 1966, E.O. Lawrence award Dept. Energy, 1978, I-R 100 award R & D mag., 1987, Henry Clifton Sorby award Internat. Metallographic Soc., 1987, Albert Sauveur Achievement award, 1991; Guggenheim fellow, 1972. Fellow Am. Soc. Metals (Bradley Stoughton Young Tchrs. award 1965, Grossman Publ. award 1966), Am. Inst. Mining, Metall. and Petroleum Engrs.; mem. Electron Microscopy Soc. Am. (prize 1965, pres. 1976), Am. Phys. Soc., Nat. Acad. Scis., Nat. Acad. Engring., Brit. Inst. Metals (Rosenheim medal 1977), Internat. Fedn. Electron Microscopy Socs. (pres. 1986-90), Brit. Iron and Steel Inst. Club: Marylebone Cricket (Eng.). Office: U Calif Dept Materials Sci/Engring 561 Evans Hall Berkeley CA 94720-1760

THOMAS, HAROLD WILLIAM, avionics systems engineer, flight instructor; b. Cle Elum, Wash., Sept. 29, 1941; s. Albert John and Margaret Jenny (Micheletto) T.; children: Gregg Wallace, Lisa Michele. BS, U. Wash., 1964; M of Engring., U. Fla., 1968. Sci. programmer Aerojet Gen. Corp., Sacramento, Calif., 1964-65; systems analyst GE Co., Daytona Beach, Fla., 1965-69; systems engr. GE Co., Phoenix, 1969-70; sr. software engr. Sperry Flight Systems, Phoenix, 1970-77; sr. systems engr. Honeywell, Inc., Phoenix, 1977-80; engr. section head Sperry Flight Systems, Phoenix, 1980-87; free lance flight instr., 1981—; staff engr. Honeywell, Inc., Phoenix, 1987—; designated engring. rep. Fed. Aviation Adminstrn., Long Beach, 1987—. Mem. AIAA, SAE Internat. Internat. Soc. Air Safety Investigators, Am. Mensa Ltd. Home: 2514 W Pershing Ave Phoenix AZ 85029-1445 Office: Honeywell INc 21111 N 19th Ave Phoenix AZ 85027-2708

THOMAS, HAYWARD, manufacturing company executive; b. Los Angeles, Aug. 9, 1921; s. Charles Sparks and Julia (Hayward) T.; m. Phyllis Mary Wilson, July 1, 1943; children: H. David, Steven T. BS, U. Calif., Berkeley, 1943. Registered profl. engr. Staff engr. Joshua Hendy Corp., Los Angeles, 1946-50; prodn. mgr. Byron Jackson Co., Los Angeles, 1950-55; mgr. mfg. Frigidaire div. Gen. Motors Corp., Dayton, Ohio, 1955-70; group v.p. White Motor Corp., Cleve., 1971-73; sr. v.p. Broan Mfg. Co., Hartford, Wis., 1973-85; pres. Jensen Industries, Los Angeles, 1985-87; retired, 1987. Served to lt. USNR, 1943-46. Mem. Soc. Mfg. Engrs. (chmn. mfg. mgmt. council 1984-86). Republican. Episcopalian. Home: 1320 Granvia Altamira Palos Verdes Peninsula CA 90274-2006

THOMAS, HOWARD PAUL, civil engineer, consultant; b. Cambridge, Mass., Aug. 20, 1942; s. Charles Calvin and Helen Elizabeth (Hook) T.; m. Ingrid Nybo, Jan. 4, 1969; children: Kent Michael, Lisa Karen, Karina Michelle. BS in Engring., U. Mich., 1965, MS in Engring., 1966. Registered profl. engr., Alaska, Calif. Engr. Ove Arup & Ptnrs., London, 1966-67; project engr. Woodward-Clyde Cons., San Francisco, 1967-73; assoc. Woodward-Clyde Cons., Anchorage, 1975-89; spl. cons. Cowiconsult Cons., Copenhagen, 1973-75; prin. engr. Harding-Lawson Assocs., Anchorage, 1989-90; v.p., chief engr. EMCON Alaska, Inc., Anchorage, 1991-94; gen. mgr. Internat. Tech. Corp., Anchorage, 1994—; chmn. Nat. Tech. Coun. Cold Regions Engring., 1982-84, chmn. com. program and publs., 1988-89; chmn. 4th Internat. Conf. Cold Regions Engring., Anchorage, 1986; liaison Nat. Acad. Sci./Nat. Rsch. Coun. Polar Commn., 1989-93. Contbr. articles to profl. jours. Named Alaskan Engr. Yr., 1986. Fellow ASCE (pres. Anchorage chpt. 1985-86, mem. mgmt. group A. 1994—); mem. Internat. Soc. Soil Mechs. and Found. Engring., Soc. Am. Mil. Engrs., Cons. Engrs. Coun. Alaska (pres. 1989-90), Am. Cons. Engrs. Coun. (nat. dir. 1990-91), Project Mgmt. Inst. (v.p. Alaska chpt. 1991-95), Toastmasters (pres. Anchorage club 1984), Sons of Norway. Lutheran. Home: 2611 Brittany Dr Anchorage AK 99504-3332

THOMAS, JACK E., utility company executive. Exec. v.p., chief operating officer San Diego Gas & Electric Co. Office: San Diego Gas & Electric Co 101 Ash St San Diego CA 92101-3017

THOMAS, JACK G., water quality manager; b. Sheridan, Mont., July 17, 1956; s. Alve J. and Charlotte (Romee) T.; m. Vicki V. Thomas, July 11, 1981; children: Shane, Amy. BS, U. Mont., 1979. Range conservationist USDI Bur. of Land Mgmt., Malta, Mont., 1979, USDA Forest Svc., Townsend, Mont., 1980; resource programs specialist Dept. Natural Resources and Conservation, Helena, Mont., 1981-88; water quality program mgr. Water Quality Bur./Dept. Health and Environ. Scis., Helena, 1988—; prin., owner Hydrotech Water Resource Cons., Helena, 1989—. Mem. Blackfoot Tour Unltd. (dir. 1988-94). Home: 2031 E 6th Ave Helena MT 59601-4863 Office: Mont Dept Health/Environ Sc 1400 E Broadway St Helena MT 59601-5231

THOMAS, JANET VERLINE, counselor; b. Caldwell, Idaho, June 14, 1936; d. Lougene and Josephine Connaway (Hill) Andersen; m. Carol Lloyd Thomas, May 10, 1956 (div. 1965); children: Gary Lee, Michael Louis. BA, Coll. Idaho, 1958, MEd, 1968; EdD, U. Nev., 1994. Cert. counselor; lic. profl. counselor, cert. sch. counselor, Idaho. Tchr. Wilder (Idaho) Elem. Sch., 1958-59, Matteson Sch. Dist, Park Forest, Ill., 1960-67; counselor Marsing (Idaho) Schs., 1968-72; career guidance specialist Canyon-Owyhee Sch. Svc. Agy., Caldwell, Idaho, 1972-74; elem. sch. counselor Boise Schs., 1974—; grad. asst. instr. U. Nev., Reno, 1991-93; spl. lectr. Boise State U., 1978—; adj. faculty Albertson Coll. Idaho, Caldwell, 1988—. Contbr. articles and columns to profl. newsletters and jours. Mem. N.Am. Soc. Adlerian Psychologists, Idaho Soc. Individual Psychology (Significant Adlerian Contbr. 1987, pres. 1982-83, Am. Counseling Assn. (APGA senator 1979-82, Outstanding Svc. award 1982), Idaho Counseling Assn. (pres. 1977-78, Disting. Svc. award 1979), Am. Sch. Counselors Assn. (regional elem. coord. 1976-77), Idaho Sch. Counselor Assn. (pres. 1975-76), Internat. Assn. Marriage and Family Counselors, Idaho Career Devel. Assn., Idaho Mental Health Counselors Assn., Idaho Assn. Counselor Educators and Suprs., Phi Delta Kappa, Phi Kappa Phi. Home: 4007 Northbridge Way Boise ID 83706-5941 Office: Boise Ind Sch Dist 1207 W Fort St Boise ID 83702-5314

THOMAS, JEANETTE MAE, accountant; b. Winona, Minn., Dec. 19, 1946; d. Herbert and Arline (Shank) Harmon; m. Gerald F. Thomas, Aug. 9, 1969; children: Bradley, Christopher. BS, Winona State U., 1968; postgrad., Colo. State U.; CFP, Coll. for Fin. Planning, Denver, 1985. Enrolled agt.; cert. fin. planner; registered rep. NASD; registered investment advisor; accredited tax advisor. Tchr. pub. schs. systems Colo., N.Mex., Mich., 1968-72; adminstrv. asst. Bus. Men's Svcs., Ft. Collins, Colo., 1974-75; tax cons. Tax Corp. Am., Ft. Collins, Colo., 1972-80; chief acct. Jayland Electric, La Porte, Colo., 1981-90; pres., CEO Thomas Fin. Svcs. Inc., Ft. Collins, 1980—. Contbr. articles to newspapers and profl. newsletters. Bd. dirs. local PTO, 1984-85; treas. Boy Scouts Am., 1985-88; master food safety advisor coop. ext. Colo. State U., 1988—; spkr., mem. steering com. AARP Women's Fin. Info. Program, 1988—; chair adv. bd. Larimer County Coop. Ext., Colo. State U.; mem. quality rev. com. Poudre R-1 Schs. Mem. Internat. Assn. Fin. Planning (past officer), Am. Soc. Women Accts. (bd. dirs. 1984-86), Pvt. Industry Coun. (chair 1994-95), Nat. Soc. Pub. Accts., Inst. CFPs, Am. Notary Assn., Ft. Collins C. of C. (red carpet com. bus. assistance coun. 1989—). Home: PO Box 370 Laporte CO 80535-0370 Office: 400 S Howes St Ste 2 Fort Collins CO 80521-2802

THOMAS, JIM, professional basketball team executive. Mng. gen. ptnr. Sacramento Kings. Office: Sacramento Kings 1 Sports Pky Sacramento CA 95834-2300*

THOMAS, JOSEPH EDWARD, lawyer; b. Atlantic City, N.J., June 4, 1955; s. George Lewis and Annabelle (Murphy) T.; m. Susan Marie Rutten, Oct. 2, 1982. BA, Lehigh U., 1977; LLB, Pepperdine U., 1981. Bar: Calif. 1981, U.S. Dist. Ct. (cen. dist.) Calif. 1981, U.S. Ct. Appeals (9th cir.) 1982. Jud. extern U.S. Dist. Ct. (cen. dist.), Los Angeles, 1980; assoc. Lawler, Felix & Hall, Los Angeles, 1981-85; ptnr. Pettit & Martin, Newport Beach, Calif., 1985-91, Brobeck, Phleger & Harrison, Newport Beach, 1991—; gen. counsel Thomas Co., Atlantic City, 1981—. Mem. ABA, Calif. Bar Assn., Orange County Bar Assn., Los Angeles County Bar Assn. Republican. Roman Catholic. Clubs: Lincoln (Orange County); Town Hall (Los Angeles). Home: 455 Panorama Dr Laguna Beach CA 92651-1225 Office: Brobeck Phleger & Harrison 4675 Macarthur Ct Ste 1000 Newport Beach CA 92660-1846

THOMAS, JOSEPH FLESHMAN, architect; b. Oak Hill, W.Va., Mar. 23, 1915; s. Robert Russel and Effie (Fleshman) T.; m. Margaret Ruth Lively, Feb. 28, 1939 (dec.); children: Anita Carol, Joseph Stephen; m. Dorothy Francene Root, Apr. 29, 1967 (div.); m. Bonnie Abbott Buckley, June 15, 1991. Student, Duke, 1931-32; B.Arch., Carnegie-Mellon U., 1938. Practice architecture various firms W. Va., Va., Tenn., Calif., 1938-49; staff architect Calif. Div. Architecture, Los Angeles, 1949-52; prin. Joseph F. Thomas, architect, Pasadena, Calif., 1952-53; pres. Neptune & Thomas (architects-engrs.), Pasadena and San Diego, 1953-78; Mem. Pasadena Planning Commn., 1956-64, chmn., 1963-64; pres. Citizens Coun. for Planning, Pasadena, 1966-67; mem. steering com. Pasadena NOW, 1970-74; mem. Pasadena Design Com., 1979-86; mem. adv. bd. Calif. Office Architecture and Constrn., 1970-72; mem. archtl. adv. com. Calif. State U. System, 1981-84; mem. adv. coun. Sch. Environ. Design Calif. Poly. Inst., 1983—; mem. outreach for architecture com. Carnegie Mellon U., 1989—, pres.'s devel. com., 1991—. Prin. works include Meth. Hosp, Arcadia, Calif., Foothill Presbyn. Hosp, Glendora, Calif., master plans and bldgs., Citrus Coll., Azusa, Calif., Riverside (Calif.) Coll., Westmont Coll., Monticeto, Calif., Northrop Inst. Tech., Inglewood, Calif., Indian Valley Coll., Marin County, Calif.; other coll. bldgs. Pacific Telephone Co, Pasadena, Los Angeles County Superior Ct. Bldg, U.S. Naval Hosp, San Diego. Trustee Almansor Edn. Ctr., 1986-92; bd. dirs., co-founder Syncor Internat., 1973-83; founding dir. Bank of Pasadena, 1962-65. Lt. (j.g.) USNR, 1943-46. Recipient Service award City of Pasadena, 1964; Disting. Service award Calif. Dept. Gen. Services, 1972; Gold Crown award Pasadena Arts Council, 1981. Fellow AIA (4 awards honor, 13 awards merit 1957-78, dir. Calif. coun. 1966-68, exec. com. 1974-77, pres. Pasadena chpt. 1967, chmn. Calif. sch. facilities com. 1970-72, mem. nat. jud. bd. 1973-74, nat. dir. 1974-77, treas. 1977-79, exec. com., planning com., chmn. finance com.); mem. Breakfast Forum (chmn. 1983), Annandale Golf Club, Pi Kappa Alpha. Republican. Methodist. Home: 330 San Miguel Rd Pasadena CA 91105-1446

THOMAS, KEITH VERN, bank executive; b. Provo, Utah, Oct. 21, 1946; s. Vern R. and Lois (Doran) T.; m. Sherrie Hunter, Oct. 7, 1969; children: Genevieve, Joshua, Rachel, William, Rebecca. AA, Dixie Coll., 1969; BS, Brigham Young U., 1971; MBA, St. Mary's Coll., 1980. Examiner Fed. Home Loan Bank Bd., San Francisco, 1971-79, field mgr., 1979-84, asst. dir., 1984-85; sr. v.p., dir. exams. and supervision Fed. Home Loan Bank, Seattle, 1985-88; exec. v.p. and COO Frontier Savings Assn., Las Vegas, Nev., 1988-89, pres., CEO, dir., 1989-90; sr. v.p. Am. Fed. Savs. Bank, Las Vegas, 1991—; bd. dirs., chmn. Nev. Cmty. Reinvestment Corp.; bd. dirs. So. Nev. Housing Corp. Editor: Real Estate Textbook, 1983-84. Trustee Nev. Sch. of Arts; mem. fin. com. North Las Vegas Neighborhood Housing Svcs.; mem. cmty. reinvestment and housing com. Western League of Savs. Instns.; bd. dirs., scoutmaster Boulder Dam Area coun. Boy Scouts Am.; active Leadership Las Vegas; bd. dirs. Nev. Cmty. Found., Local Initiatives Support Coun.; contract com. mem. United Way; mem. Leadership Las Vegas Alumni Assn. Named Outstanding Instr., Inst. Fin. Edn. 1984. Mem. Nev. Clearing House Assn. (v.p., bd. dirs.), Nat. Assn. Rev. Appraisers and Mortgage Underwriters, Brigham Young Mgmt. Soc., So. Nev. Exec. Coun. (bd. dirs., past pres.), Las Vegas C. of C., Nev. Devel. Authority, So. Nev. Home Builders Assn., Las Vegas S.W. Rotary. Republican. Mormon. Office: Am FSB 2887 S Maryland Pky Las Vegas NV 89109-1511

THOMAS, KENT SWENSON, sales executive; b. Logan, Ut., Jan. 8, 1955; s. Don Wylie and Merla (Swenson) T.; m. Laurie Belle Jackson, Dec. 17, 1976; children: Joel, Jared, Katie, Jacob, Hollie. BS in Mktg. and Distribut, Utah State U., Logan, 1982. Mktg. Mgr. Metroshare Inc., Salt Lake City, Utah, 1982-83; nat. and internat. sales mgr. Wescor Inc., Logan, Utah, 1983-. Republican. Mormon. Office: Wescor Inc 459 S Main St Logan UT 84321-5207

THOMAS, LAURA FALER, nutrition educator; b. Wallace, Idaho, Mar. 6, 1961; d. Roy Lee and Kaarlene (Anderson) Faler; m. James Alan Thomas, Sept. 1, 1984; children: Matthew Faler, Michael Robert. BS in Home Econs., Food and Nutrition, U. Idaho, 1983, MEd in Vocat./Adult Edn., 1995. Therapeutic dietitian Idaho State Sch. and Hosp., Nampa, 1983-85; nutrition edn. cons. Idaho Dairy Coun., Boise, 1985-86, dir. nutrition edn., 1986—; instr. food svc. course Idaho State Dept. Edn./Boise (Idaho) State U., 1986; steering com. mem. Idaho's Ptnrs. in Health Through Nutrition, Boise, 1990—. Co-author, co-editor: Body Walk Resource Manual, 1989; contbr. articles to profl. jours. Mem. Am. Dietetic Assn. (registered dietitian, Young Registered Dietitian of Yr. 1987), Idaho Dietetic Assn., Am. Assn. Family and Consumer Sci. (New Achiever award 1989), Idaho Assn. Family and Consumer Sci., Soc. for Nutrition Edn. (Young Nutrition Educator Yr. 1992),. Roman Catholic. Office: Idaho Dairy Coun 1365 N Orchard #203 Boise ID 83706

THOMAS, LAURA MARLENE, artist, private antique dealer; b. Chico, Calif., Apr. 29, 1936; d. Boyd Stanley Beck and Lois Velma (Behrke) Lyons; m. Charles Rex Thomas; children: Tracy Loraine, Jeffory Norris. AA in Fine Arts, Sacramento City Coll., 1978; BA in Fine Arts, Calif. State U., 1981. Tchrs. asst. Hanford Elem. Sch., Hanford, Calif., 1963-68; asst. dir. RSVP: Retired Sr. Vol. Program, Hanford, 1971-74; dir. of Art Bank Sacramento City Coll., Sacramento, 1976-78; pub. asst. Student Activities Calif. State Univ., Sacramento, 1978-81; antique dealer pvt. practice, Sacramento, 1981--, arts and crafts bus., 1976--; social worker Cath. Social Svcs., Sacramento, 1985--. Artist: weaving, Double Image, 1977, 2nd Place 1977; ceramic sculptor, Bird. Charter mem. YWCA, Sacramento, 1972, Folsum Hist. Soc., 1988. Cert. of appreciation, Carmellia City Ctr. Adv. Council, Sacramento, 1986. Mem. Statue of Liberty-Ellis Island Found., 1985, North Shore Animal League (Benefactors award 1985), Calif. State U. Alumni Assn., Hanford Sportsman Club (v.p. 1963-68). Republican. Protestant. Home: 2719 I St Apt 4 Sacramento CA 95816-4354

THOMAS, LINDA MARRI GANDY, administrative assistant; b. Salt Lake City, Oct. 7, 1951; d. Rupert Kennedy and Marilyn Irma (Murdock) Gandy; m. Norman Clark Thomas, Feb. 23, 1968; children: Tina Sue, Tonya Marie, Norman Clark II. BS in Computer Sci., Westminster Coll., 1994. Supr. pers. lines underwriting Northwestern Nat. Ins. Co., Salt Lake City, 1976-85; sr. agy. mktg. rep. Aetna Life and Casualty, Salt Lake City, 1985-86; comml. lines customer rep. Affiliated Ins. Agy., Salt Lake City, 1987-89; adminstrv. asst. Westminster Coll., Salt Lake City, 1989-95; programmer analyst Huish Detergents, Salt Lake City, 1995—. Home: 4355 Alice Way West Valley City UT 84119-5867 Office: Huish Detergents 3540 West 1987 South Salt Lake City UT 84125

THOMAS, LOWELL, JR., author, lecturer, former lieutenant governor, former state senator; b. London, Oct. 6, 1923; s. Lowell Jackson and Frances (Ryan) T.; m. Mary Taylor Pryor, May 20, 1950; children: Anne Frazier, David Lowell. Student, Taft Sch., 1942; B.A., Dartmouth Coll., 1948; postgrad., Princeton Sch. Pub. and Internat. Affairs, 1952. Asst. cameraman Fox Movietone News, S.Am., 1939, Bradford Washburn Alaskan mountaineering expdn., 1940; illustrated lecturer, 1946—; asst. economist, photographer with Max Weston Thornburg, Turkey, 1947, Iran, 1948; film prodn. Iran, 1949; Tibet expdn. with Lowell Thomas, Sr., 1949; field work Cinerama, S.Am., Africa, Asia, 1951-52; travels by small airplane with wife, writing and filming Europe, Africa, Middle East, 1954-55; mem. Rockwell Polar Flight, first flight around the world over both poles, Nov., 1965; mem. Alaska State Senate, 1967-74; lt. gov. State of Alaska, 1974-79; owner Talkeetna Air Taxi, Inc., air contract carrier, Anchorage, Alaska, 1980-94. Producer series of films Flight to Adventure, NBC-TV, 1956; producer, writer TV series High Adventure, 1957-59; producer documentary film Adaq, King of Alaskan Seas, 1960; producer two films on Alaska, 1962, 63, film on U. Alaska, 1964, South Pacific travel documentary, 1965, film on Arctic oil exploration, Atlantic-Richfield Co., 1969. Author: Out of this World, A Journey to Tibet, 1950, (with Mrs. Lowell Thomas, Jr.) Our Flight to Adventure, 1956, The Silent War in Tibet, 1959, The Dalai Lama, 1961, The Trail of Ninety-Eight, 1962, (with Lowell Thomas Sr.) More Great True Adventures, 1963, Famous First Flights that Changed History, 1968. Past pres. Western Alaska council Boy Scouts Am.; bd. dirs. Anchorage unit Salvation Army, Alaska Conservation Fund. Served 1st lt. USAAF, 1943-45. Mem. Nat. Parks and Conservation Assn. (bd. dirs.), Alaska C. of C., Aircraft Owners and Pilots Assn. Clubs: Explorers, Marco Polo, Dutch Treat (N.Y.C.); Rotary, (Anchorage), Press (Anchorage); Dartmouth Outing; American Alpine. Address: 10800 Hideaway Lake Dr Anchorage AK 99516-1145

THOMAS, MITCHELL, JR., aerospace company executive; b. Terre Haute, Ind., Nov. 25, 1936; s. Mitchell and Carolyn Amalia (Wolff) T.; m. Helen Steimle, June 28, 1970; children: Sheri Helen, Deborah Michal, Mitchell III. AB cum laude, Harvard U., 1958; MS, U. Ill., 1959; PhD, Calif. Inst. Tech., 1964. With McDonnell Douglas, Santa Monica, Calif., 1959-64, group leader launch vehicles, 1964-65, sect. chief ablation and applied research sect., 1965-67; br. chief thermophysics lab. McDonnell Douglas, Huntington Beach, Calif., 1969-75; dir. research and devel. L'Garde Inc., Newport Beach, Calif., 1975-76, pres., 1976—; mem. adv. com. on Gossamer structures NASA, 1981. Contbr. articles to profl. jours. Mem. AAAS, AIAA (assoc. fellow thermophysics com., tech. program chmn. for 8th thermophysics conf.). Home: 5000 Old Shepard Pl Apt 1028 Plano TX 75093-4405 Office: L'Garde Inc 15181 Woodlawn Ave Tustin CA 92680-6419

THOMAS, PATRICK A., civil engineer; b. Costa Mesa, Calif., Sept. 27, 1962; s. Harold James and Nancy Louise (Cherry) T.; m. Mary Johanna Langenhorst, Aug. 22, 1987; 1 child, Johanna Leigh. BS in Civil & Environ. Engring., Wash. State U., 1984; MPA, Calif. State U., Long Beach, 1991. Registered profl. engr., Calif. Project engr. The Ceco Corp., Seattle, 1984-87; sr. engr. City of Irvine, Calif., 1987-91; dep. dir. pub. works/asst. city engr. City of Escondido, Calif., 1991—; mem. regional GIS adv. commn., San Diego, 1993-94. Mem. ASCE, Am. Pub. Works Assn. (local chpt. del. 1991-94), City Engr. Assn. (dir.), Urban & Regional Info. Sys. Assn., Toastmasters, St. Michael's Men's Club. Republican. Roman Catholic. Home: 15880 Cumberland Dr Poway CA 92064-2345 Office: City of Escondido 201 N Broadway Escondido CA 92025-2709

THOMAS, PETER M., real estate developer; b. Las Vegas, Nev., Feb. 6, 1950; s. E. Parry and Peggy (Chatterton) T.; m. Nancy Paxman, June 12, 1972; children: David P., Megan, Lindsey, Adam. BS, U . Utah, 1972. V.p. Valley Bank of Nev., Las Vegas, 1977-79, exec. v.p., 1979-82, pres., 1982-92; pres. Bank of Am., Nev., 1992-95, pres., coo, 1992-95; mng. dir. Thomas and Mack Co., 1995—. Mem. long range planning com. United Way, 1982-84; bd. dirs. Friends of Channel 10, 1982-85; mem. Las Vegas Conv. and Visitor's Authority, 1984-88, sec./treas., 1985-86, treas./v.p., 1987-88; chmn. Las Vegas Met. Police Dept. Com. Fiscal Affairs, 1994—, Citizen's Adv. Com. on Downtown Redevel., 1986—, Nev. Bankers Legislative Com., Nev. Devel. Authority, (mem. exec. com. 1986—, trustee 1986-90, chmn.-elect 1992—); mem. Downtown Progresss Assn., 1986-90, Nev. Nuclear Projects Commn., 1993—, Am. Bankers Assn. Govt. Rels. and Adminstrv. Coms., Las Vegas Mayor's Multi-jurisdictional Cmty. Empowerment Commn.; mem. vision project exec. coun. U. Nev., 1988-90, Pres.'s Assn., 1988—; bd. trustees U. Nev. Las Vegas Found., 1994—. Mem. Nev. Bar Assn., Utah Bar Assn., D.C. Bar Assn., Las Vegas C. of C., Nev. Bankers Assn. (pres. 1987-89, chmn. legis. com. 1988—), Am. Bankers Assn. (govt. rels. coun. mgmt. com. 1988—), Young Pres.'s Orgn. Office: Thomas and Mack Co 2300 W Sahara Box 1 Las Vegas NV 89102

THOMAS, ROGER PARRY, interior designer, art consultant; b. Salt Lake City, Nov. 4, 1951; s. E. Parry and Peggy Chatterton T.; m. Marilyn Harris Hite, Nov. 21, 1976 (div. Apr. 1979); m. H. Andrea Wahn, Nov. 20, 1982; 1 child, Andrew Chatterton. Student, Interlochen Arts Acad., 1969; BFA, Tufts U., 1973. Pres. Miller-Thomas, Inc., Las Vegas, Nev., 1973-76; v.p. Yates-Silverman, Inc., Las Vegas, 1976-81; v.p. design Atlandia Design a Mirage Resorts Inc. Co., Las Vegas, 1981—. Mem. Nev. State Coun. on the Arts, McCarren Arts Adv. Bd.; vice chmn. McCarren Arts. Mem. Country Club (Las Vegas). Republican. Mem. LDS Ch. Office: Atlandia Design 3260 Industrial Rd Las Vegas NV 89109-1132

THOMAS, SEAN, insurance company president; b. San Juan, P.R., Jan. 14, 1944; s. John Parzych and Catalina (Alicea) T. BS, U. Md., 1966; MBA, George Washington U., 1970. CLU. Dir. personnel Schwartz Bros., Inc., Washington, 1968-72; dir. indsl. rels. Fairchild Industries, L.A., 1972-78; v.p. human resources Gillespie Furniture, L.A., 1978-88, Ibis Systems, Inc., West Lake Village, Calif., 1988-92; pres. T.L. Ins. Svcs., L.A., 1992—; chmn. Isla Verde Enterprises, L.A., El Patio del Viejo San Juan; pres. T.L. Ins. Svcs., L.A., 1991—. Author: The Sentence, 1982, The Microwave Generation, 1992, Ploughshares or Swords?, 1974. Mem. Pres.'s Com. on Handicapped, Washington, 1993, Estado 51/P.R., San Juan, 1993, Nat. Trust for Hist.

Preservation, Washington, 1994; bd. dirs. Calif. Coun. of the Blind, L.A., 1994; mem. AIDS Project/ L.A., 1989—. Mem. Save the Am. Rep. (pres. 1992—), Personnel and Indsl. Rels. Assn., L.A. C. of C., NAACP. Democrat. Office: TL Ins Svcs PO Box 411616 Los Angeles CA 90041-8616

THOMAS, SHIRLEY, author, educator, business executive; b. Glendale, Calif.; d. Oscar Miller and Ruby (Thomas) Annis; m. W. White, Feb. 22, 1949 (div. June 1952); m. William C. Perkins, Oct. 24, 1969. BA in Modern Lit., U. Sussex, Eng., 1960, PhD in Comm., 1967; diploma, Russian Fedn. Cosmonautics, 1995. Actress, writer, producer, dir. numerous radio and TV stas., 1942-46; v.p. Commodore Prodns., Hollywood, Calif., 1946-52; pres. Annis & Thomas, Inc., Hollywood, 1952—; prof. technical writing U. So. Calif., L.A., 1975—; Hollywood corr. NBC, 1952-56; editor motion pictures CBS, Hollywood, 1956-58; corr. Voice of Am., 1958-59; now free lance writer; cons. biol. scis. communication project George Washington U., 1965-66; cons. Stanford Rsch. Inst., 1967-68, Jet Propulsion Lab., 1969-70. Author: Men of Space vols. 1-8, 1960-68, Spanish trans., 1961, Italian, 1962; Space Tracking Facilities, 1963, Computers: Their History, Present Applications and Future, 1965; The Book of Diets, 1974. Organizer, chmn. City of L.A. Space Adv. Com., 1964-73, Women's Space Symposia, 1962-73; foudner, chmn. aerospace hist. com. Calif. Mus. Sci. and Industry; chmn. Theodore von Karman Postage Stamp Com., 1965—, stamp issued 1992. Recipient Aerospace Excellence award Calif. Mus. Found. 1991, Nat. Medal Honor DAR, 1992, Yuri Gagarin Medal Honor, 1995. Fellow Brit. Interplanetary Soc.; mem. AIAA, AAAS, Internat. Soc. Aviation Writers, Air Force Assn. (Airpower Arts and Letters award 1961), Internat. Acad. Astronautics, Nat. Aero. Assn., Nat. Asn. Sci. Writers, Soc. for Tech. Communications, Am. Astronautical Soc., Nat. Geog. Soc., Am. Soc. Pub. Adminstrn. (sci. and tech. in govt. com. 1972—), Achievement Awards for Coll. Scientists, Muses of Calif., Theta Sigma Phi, Phi Beta. Home: 8027 Hollywood Blvd Los Angeles CA 90046-2510 Office: U So Calif Profl Writing Program University Park Waite-Phillips Hall 404 Los Angeles CA 90089-4034

THOMAS, STEPHEN CECIL, Chinese politics educator, university official; b. Columbus, Ohio, Nov. 8, 1944; s. Cecil Albert and Frances Catherine (Smith) T.; m. Carol Isabel Dreselly, Aug. 25, 1982; children: Michael and Nicolas (twins), Matthew. BA in Polit. Sci., San Jose State U., 1967; MA in East Asian Studies, Stanford U., 1972, PhD in Polit. Sci., 1979. Mem. faculty U. Colo., Denver, 1976—, prof. Chinese politics, chmn. dept. polit. sci., 1984-90, co-dir. Internat. Affairs Office, 1987-92, dir. Office Internat. Edn., 1992-94, Fei Yi-Ming prof. comparative politics Hopking-Nangjing program, 1994—; sec.-treas. Nat. Com. Internat. Studies and Programs Adminstrs., 1991-92. Bd. dirs. Nat. Com. on U.S.-China Rels., N.Y.C., 1972-74, Am. Friends Svc. Co., Phila., 1972-76. Grantee USIA, 1987-90, U.S. Dept. Edn., 1987-89, 90-92, NEH, 1992-95. Mem. Am. Polit. Sci. Assn., Internat. Studies Assn. Mem. Soc. of Friends. Home: 541 Arapahoe Ave Boulder CO 80302-5826 Office: U Colo Office Internat Edn Campus Box 185 Denver CO 80217

THOMAS, STEVE D., infosystem specialist; b. Butte, Mont., Aug. 8, 1951; s. William James and Catherine (Murphy) T.; m. Kathy Ann McCarthy, Aug. 22, 1971; children: Shawn, Heather. Programmer analyst Anaconda Co., Butte, 1973-81, systems analyst, 1981-82; systems programmer ARCO Metals, Columbia Falls, Mont., 1982-83, supr. ops. and tech. support, 1983-85; supt. of mgmt. info. systems Columbia Falls Aluminum Co., Columbia Falls, 1985—. Office: CFAC 2000 Aluminum Dr Columbia Falls MT 59912-9424

THOMAS, SYLVIA ANN, community college dean; b. Hanford, Calif., Jan. 16, 1947; d. Antonio R. and Esperanza R. (Gonzales) Vallejo; m. Francis Thomas, June 28, 1970; 1 child, Aric Vincent. BA, UCLA, 1968; teaching degree, Fresno State U., 1970; MA, Pepperdine U., 1973, postgrad., 1992. Cert. tchr., elem. K-9, jr. coll. and adminstrn. Tchr. Colton (Ill.) Sch. Dist., 1970-83; dean instruction, 1994—; dean instrnl. support svcs. Moreno Valley Campus of Riverside C.C., 1993-94, dean instrn. Mem. Jr. League of Riverside, 1985—. Mem. Akita Club Am. (sec., nat. liaison), Kin Ken Akita Club (newsletter editor), Inland Empire Akita Club (newsletter editor), Lake Mathews Kennel Club (treas.), Channel Islands Akita Club, Orange Empire Dog Club, Lake Mathews Kennel Club, Samoyed Club Am. Democrat. Roman Catholic. Home: 2155 Hackamore Pl Riverside CA 92506-4616

THOMAS, TERESA ANN, microbiologist, educator; b. Wilkes-Barre, Pa., Oct. 17, 1939; d. Sam Charles and Edna Grace T. BS cum laude, Coll. Misericordia, 1961; MS in Biology, Am. U. Beirut, 1965; MS in Microbiology, U. So. Calif., 1973. Tchr., sci. supr., curriculum coord. Meyers High Sch., Wilkes-Barre, 1962-64, Wilkes-Barre Area Public Schs., 1961-66; rsch. assoc. Proctor Found. for Rsch. in Ophthalmology U. Calif. Med. Ctr., San Francisco, 1966-68; instr. Robert Coll. of Istanbul (Turkey), 1968-71, Am. Edn. in Luxembourg, 1971-72, Bosco Tech. Inst., Rosemead, Calif., 1973-74, San Diego Community Coll. Dist., 1974-80; prof. math., sci. and engring. div. Southwestern Coll., Chula Vista, Calif., 1980—, pres. acad. senate, 1984-85, del., 1986-89; chmn., coord., steering com. project Cultural Rsch. Educational and Trade Exchange, 1991—, Southwestern Coll.-Shanghai Inst. Fgn. Trade; coord. Southwestern Coll. Great Teaching Seminar, 1987, 88, 89, coord. scholars program, 1988-90; mem. exec. com. Acad. Senate for Calif. C.Cs., 1985-86, Chancellor of Calif. C.Cs. Adv. and Rev. Council Fund for Instrnl. Improvement, 1984-86; co-project dir. statewide, coord. So. Calif. Biotech Edn. Consortium, 1993—; adj. asst. prof. Chapman Coll., San Diego, 1974-83; asst. prof. San Diego State U., 1977-79; chmn. Am. Colls. Istanbul Sci. Week, 1969-71; mem. adv. bd. Chapman Coll. Community Center, 1979-80; cons. sci. curriculum Calif. Dept. Edn., 1986—; pres. Internat. Relations Club 1959-61; mem. San Francisco World Affairs Coun., 1966-68, San Diego World Affairs Coun., 1992—; v.p. Palomar Palace Estates Home Owners Assn., 1983-85, pres. 1994—. mem. editorial rev. bd. Jour. of Coll. Sci. Teaching, NSTA, 1988-92; bd. dirs. San Diego-Leon Sister Cities Soc., 1991-94. Mem. Chula Vista Nature Interpretive Ctr. (life), Internat. Friendship Commn., Chula Vista, 1985—, vice chmn. 1989-90, chmn. 1990-92, Chula Vista, Calif., 1987—; mem. U.S.-Mex. Sister Cities Assn., nat. bd. dirs., 1992-94, gen. chair 30th nat. conv., 1993. NSF fellow, 1965; USPHS fellow, 1972-73; recipient Nat. Teaching Excellence award Nat. Inst. Staff and Orgnl. Devel., 1989; recognized at Internat. Conf. Teaching Excellence, Austin, 1989; Pa. Heart Assn. research grantee, 1962; named Southwestern Coll. Woman of Distinction, 1987. Mem. Am. Soc. Microbiology, Nat. Sci. Tchrs. Assn. (life, internat. com., coord. internat. honors exchange lectr. competition sponsored with Assn. Sci Educators Great Britain, 1986), Nat. Assn. Biology Tchrs. (life), Soc. Coll. Sci. Tchrs. (life), S.D. Zool. Soc., Calif. Tchrs. Assn., NEA, Am. Assn. Community and Jr. Colls., Giraffes, Am.-Lebanese Assn. San Diego (chmn. scholarship com., pres. 1988-93), Am. U. of Beirut Alumni and Friends of San Diego (1st v.p. 1984-91), Lions Internat. (pres. SW San Diego County chpt. 1994-95, bull. editor 1991-93, best bull. award 1992, 93, 2nd v.p. 1992-93, 1st v.p. 1993-94, editor Roaring Times Newsletter 1993-94, pres. 1994-95, chmn. dist. internat. rels. and cooperations com. 1993-95), Kappa Gamma Pi (pres. Wilkes-Barre chpt. 1963-64, San Francisco chpt. 1967-68), Sigma Phi Sigma, Phi Theta Kappa (hon. mem. 1994—), Alpha Pi Epsilon (advisor Southwestern Coll. chpt. 1989-90, Am. Lebanese Syrian Ladies Club (pres. 1982-83). Office: Southwestern Coll 900 Otay Lakes Rd Chula Vista CA 91910-7223

THOMAS, VERNEDA ESTELLA, perfusionist; b. Chgo., June 21, 1936; d. Russel Huston and Verneda (Williams) T. BS, Graceland Coll., Lamoni, Iowa, 1973. Cardiovascualr technician Michael Reese Hosp., Chgo., 1962; cardiopulmonary technician Chgo. State Tuberculosis Sanitorium, Chgo., 1962-66, Loyola U. Sch. Medicine, Maywood, Ill., 1966-68; physiology technician Loyola U. Sch. Medicine, 1968-69; med. technologist Cook County Hosp., Chgo., 1969-71; rsch. assoc. Queen's Med. Ctr., Honolulu, 1973-78; intra aortic balloon pump technician Queen's Med. Ctr., 1973—; perfusionist for pvt. med. practice Honolulu, 1978-82; perfusionist Mid Pacific Perfusion, Honolulu, 1982-88, Psicor, Inc., Honolulu, 1988—; referee, U.S. Volleyball Assn., 1978. Contbr. articles to med. publs. Mem. U.S. Pan-Am. high jump team, Mex., 1955; mem. U.S. Olympic volleyball team, Tokyo, 1964. Mem. Am. Soc. Cardiopulmonary Technology, Am. Bd. Cardiovascular Perfusion. Baptist. Home: 217 Prospect St Apt D7 Honolulu HI 96813-1755 Office: Psicor Inc 16818 Via Del Campo Ct San Diego CA 92127-1714

THOMAS, VIOLETA DE LOS ANGELES, real estate broker; b. Buenos Aires, Dec. 21, 1941; came to U.S., 1962; d. Angel and Lola (Andino) de Rios; m. Jess Thomas, Dec. 23, 1974; 1 child, Victor Justin. Student, Harvard U. and U. Buenos Aires, 1967-73. Mgr. book div. Time-Life, N.Y.C., 1967-73; real estate broker First Marin Realty, Inc., Mill Valley, Calif., 1985—; mem. bd. dirs. Alliance Francaise, Saint Louis, 1995—. Bd. dirs. City of Tiburon, Calif., 1987-93, Art and Heritage Commn., Tiburon, Allianuse Francaise, St. Louis. Named Woman of Yr., City of Buenos Aires, 1977, Agt. of Yr., Marin County and San Francisco, 1987-92. Home: PO Box 6608 Chesterfield MO 63006

THOMAS, WILLIAM GERAINT, museum administrator; b. Columbo, Sri Lanka, June 27, 1931; came to U.S., 1941; s. Cecil James and Iris Katharine (Evans) T.; m. Maria Alcalde, Jan. 2, 1976; 1 child, Laura. BA, U. Calif., Berkeley, 1952. Reporter, editor San Francisco Chronicle, 1952-64; asst. to mayor City of San Francisco, 1964-66; chief cons. majority caucus Calif. State Assembly, Sacramento, 1966-68; adminstrv. asst. U.S. Congressman Phillip Burson, Washington, 1968-70; cons. interior com. U.S. Ho. of Reps., Washington, 1972-78; ptnr. Thomas & Iovino, San Francisco, 1972-78; asst. regional dir. Nat. Park Svc., San Francisco, 1978-89; supt. San Francisco Maritime NHP, 1989—. Mem. Nat. Dem. Club; bd. dirs. Nat. Libery Ship Meml., 1978-80. Sgt. U.S. Army, 1952-54, Korea. Mem. Nat. Maritime Mus. Assn., Nat. Maritime Hist. Soc., Press Club of San Francisco (pres. 1973-74, Best News Story 1963). Episcopalian. Office: San Francisco Maritime Bldg 201 Ft Mason San Francisco CA 94123

THOMAS, WILLIAM MARSHALL, congressman; b. Wallace, Idaho, Dec. 6, 1941; s. Virgil and Gertrude Thomas; m. Sharon Lynn Hamilton, Jan. 1968; children: Christopher, Amelia. B.A., San Francisco State U., 1963, M.A., 1965. Mem. faculty dept. Am. govt. Bakersfield (Calif.) Coll., 1965-74, prof., 1965-74; mem. Calif. State Assembly, 1974-78, 96th-104th Congress from 18th, now 21st Calif. Dist., 1979—; vice chmn. of House Task Force on Campaign Fin. Reform; mem. Ho. of Reps. Ways and Means Com.; chmn. Com. on House Oversight, Ways & Means Health Subcom.; mem. Ways & Means subcom on Trade; mem. del. to Soviet Union, by Am. Council Young Polit. Leaders, 1977; chmn. Kern County Republican Central Com., 1972-74; mem. Calif. Rep. Com., 1972-80; del. Republican Party Nat. Conv., 1980, 84, 88; mem. Rep. Leader's Task Force on Health Care Reform. Office: Ho of Reps 2208 Rayburn Ho Office Bldg Washington DC 20515

THOMAS-COTE, NANCY DENECE, office products manufacturing company executive; b. Long Beach, Calif., Feb. 20, 1959; d. Alan and Barbara Jean (Rush) Tuthill; m. Gary Cote, Sept. 1, 1988; children: Liana Barbara, Wyatt Thomas. V.p. BTE, Inc., Long Beach, 1978-88; gen. mgr. BTE, Inc., Huntington Beach, Calif., 1982-88, pres., 1988—; pres. Omni Label, Inc., Huntington Beach, 1985-90; co-owner LeMac Leasing, La Canada, Calif., 1985-90; owner Dayspring Wedding Cons., Long Beach, 1991-93. V.p. Long Beach Spl. Charities, Inc., 1987; pres. Long Beach Spl. Charities, Inc., 1988. Mem. NAFE, Am. Health Info. Mgmt. Assn., Office Products Mfg. Assn., Wholesale Stationers Assn., Calif. Health Info. Assn., Bus. Products Industry Assn. Office: BTE Inc 5672 Bolsa Ave Huntington Beach CA 92649-1113

THOMASON, PHILLIP BRIAN, Spanish language educator; b. Shawmut, Ala., Dec. 12, 1949; s. Earl Marchel and Margaret Evelyn (Wall) T.; m. Cathy Lea Ray, Aug. 19, 1972; 1 child, Brian Michael. AB, U. Montevallo, 1972; M of Hispanic Studies, Auburn U., 1975; PhD, U. Ky., 1987. Cert. tchr. Spanish tchr. Kendrick High Sch. Muscogee County Schs., Columbus, Ga., 1972-74; grad. teaching asst., instr. Auburn (Ala.) U., 1974-75, 82; instr. econs. and Spanish Marion (Ala.) Mil. Inst., 1975-81; grad. teaching asst., dir. Spanish House U. Ala., Tuscaloosa, 1981; grad. teaching asst. U. Ky., Lexington, 1982-86; instr. Spanish Asbury Coll., Wilmore, Ky., 1986; assoc. prof. Spanish Pepperdine U., Malibu, Calif., 1986—, lang. divsn. coord., 1992-95; adv. coun. Ctrl. States Conf. on Lang. Teaching, 1991, Fgn. Lang. Alliance of So. Calif.; dir. lang. program Madrid; presenter in field. Author and translator articles to profl. jours. Deacon Ch. of Christ, Thousand Oaks, Calif., 1988-92. Fellow Ministry of Spain, 1985. Mem. Am. Assn. Tchrs. Spanish and Portuguese, Modern Lang. Assn. (grant for profl. devel.), Southwest Conf. on Lang. Teaching (adv. coun. 1989-91), Calif. Fgn. Lang. Tchrs. Assn., Soc. of Seven Sages, Adult Children of Alcoholics, Sigma Delta Pi. Home: 76 W Avenida De Las Flores Thousand Oaks CA 91360-3109 Office: Pepperdine U 24255 Pacific Coast Hwy Malibu CA 90263-0001

THOME, DENNIS WESLEY, lawyer; b. Yakima, Wash., Feb. 1, 1939; s. Walter John and Vareta Lucille (Voris) T.; m. Penelope Lee Freeman, Aug. 27, 1961; children: Christopher, Geoffrey. BSBA, U. Denver, 1961, JD, 1967. Bar: Colo. 1967, U.S. Dist. Ct. Colo. 1967, Calif. 1971, U.S. Dist. Ct. (cen. dist.) Calif. 1971, U.S. Supreme Ct. 1971, U.S. Ct. Appeals (9th cir.) 1972. Assoc. Pehr & Newman, Westminster, Colo., 1967-69, Juggert, VaVerka & Wayman, Costa Mesa, Calif., 1975-77; house counsel Wycliffe Bible Translators, Inc., Huntington Beach, Calif., 1969-73; pvt. practice Newport Beach, Calif., 1973-75, Denver, 1977—; bd. dirs. First Fruit, Inc., Newport Beach, MOPS Internat., Inc., Denver, Reach Internat., Inc., Denver; mem. Centennial Estate Planning Coun., 1977—. Treas. Gibson for Mayor Com., Denver, 1967; bd. dirs. Christian Eye Ministry, Inc., San Diego, 1983-91, World Eye Care, Inc., 1990-91, Christian Legal Soc. Metro Denver, Inc., 1994—; chmn. Arvada (Colo.) Covenant Ch., 1993-94. Mem. ABA, Colo. Bar Assn. (Bill of Rights com. 1977-90, 92—), State Bar Calif., Omicron Delta Kappa. Office: 7400 W 20th Ave Lakewood CO 80215-2001

THOMPSON, ANNA BLANCHE, retired educator; b. Ft. Worth, Oct. 8, 1914; d. George Lewis and Gula Gertrude (Cook) Turnbow; m. Jess Lee, May 27, 1939; children: Jess Lee II, Mary Ann Thompson Archbold. BA in Edn., Ariz. State U., Tempe, 1935; postgrad., U. Ariz., 1940, U. Hawaii, 1964, Pepperdine U., 1967. Tchr. Parke (Ariz.) Elem. Sch., 1935-40; tchr. music Parker High Sch., 1940-42; tchr. Scottsdale (Ariz.) Elem. Sch., 1948-71; tchr. U. Hawaii, Laie, 1971-72; tchr. U. Hawaii, 1972-79, ret., 1979. Mem. edn. bd. Phoenix Women's Club, 1983-84; pres. Ariz. Res. Officers Ladies, Phoenix, 1982-84, state pres., 1986-87; pres. Ladies of the Ribbon, Phoenix, 1987-90, Tempe Garden Club, 1987-88. Recipient Mus. plaque Phoenix Symphony Symphonette, 1982-83, Cert. of Appreciation, St. Luke's Hosp. Aux., 1985, Cert. of Appreciation, Mil. Order of World Wars, 1989. Mem. Ariz. Res. Officers Ladies (state sec. 1990—), Tri-City Angels of Ariz. (pres. 1984—), Collectors Club Am. (nat. pres. 1987—), Ikebana Internat., AAUW (historian Tempe chpt. 1987-90), Delta Kappa Gamma (pres. Phoenix chpt. 1974-76, 88-90, parliamentarian 1990—). Home: 533 E Fairmont Dr Tempe AZ 85282-3722

THOMPSON, ANNE MARIE, newspaper publisher; b. Des Moines, Feb. 7, 1920; d. George Horace and Esther Mayer Sheely; m. J. Ross Thompson, July 31, 1949; children: Annette McCracken, James Ross. BA, U. Iowa, 1940; postgrad. U. Colo., 1971. Co-pub. Baca County Banner, Springfield, Colo., 1951-54, Rocky Ford (Colo.) Daily Gazette, 1954-82, pub., 1982—. Editor Toastmasters, 1983-94. Mem. Otero Jr. Coll. Coun., 1987-93, Colo. Ho. of Reps., 1957-61; Colo. presdl. elector, 1972; chmn. Colo. adv. com. SBA, 1979-81. Recipient Community Service award Rocky Ford C. of C., 1975; named Colo. Woman of Achievement in Journalism, 1959, Colo. Bus. Person of Yr., Future Bus. Leaders of Am., 1981; elected to Colo. Community Journalism Hall of Fame, 1981. Mem. Nat. Fedn. Press Women (dir. 1971-81), Nat. Newspaper Assn. (Emma C. McKinney award 1984), Colo. Press Assn. (dir. 1981-83, Golden Make-Up award 1991) , Colo. Press Women, PEO, Bus. and Profl. Women's Club. Republican. Methodist.

THOMPSON, ARLENE RITA, nursing educator; b. Yakima, Wash., May 17, 1933; d. Paul James and Esther Margaret (Danroth) T. BS in Nursing, U. Wash., 1966, Masters in Nursing, 1970, postgrad., 1982—. Staff nurse Univ. Teaching Hosp., Seattle, 1966-69; mem. nursing faculty U. Wash. Sch. Nurses, Seattle, 1971-73; critical care nurse Virginia Mason Hosp., Seattle, 1973—; educator Seattle Pacific U. Sch. Nursing, 1981—; nurse legal cons. nursing edn., critical care nurse. Contbr. articles to profl. jours. USPHS grantee, 1969; nursing scholar Virginia Mason Hosp., 1965. Mem. Am. Assn. Critical Care Nurses (cert.), Am. Nurses Assn., Am. Heart Assn., Nat. League Nursing, Sigma Theta Tau, Alpha Tau Omega. Republican. Presbyterian. Home: 2320 W Newton St Seattle WA 98199-4115 Office: Seattle Pacific U 3307 3rd Ave W Seattle WA 98119-1940

THOMPSON, ARTHUR KIMBAL, architect; b. Dixon, Ill., Mar. 4, 1947; s. Arthur Kile and Mary (Strobel) T.; m. Nicki Ann Sertich, Apr. 15, 1989; 1 child, Taylor Kaile. Student, Chapman Coll., 1967, Frank Lloyd Wright Sch. Architecture, Scottsdale, Ariz., 1967-68; BFA in Architecture, U. Hawaii, 1972, postgrad., 1973. Cert. comml. interior designer. Chmn. bd. dirs. oceanic archtl. design Toad, Ltd., Honolulu, 1979-86; chief exec. officer Kimbal Thompson & Assocs., Ltd., Honolulu, 1978-79, Arthur Kimbal Thompson & Assocs., Ltd., Honolulu & Kailua, 1986—; instr. U. Hawaii, 1989; ptnr. Waimea (Hawaii) Devel. Group, 1985—. Editor Hawaii-Pacific Architecture, 1994—. Exec. intern Gov. State of Hawaii, Honolulu, 1970; dir. Taliesin Fellows, 1993-94; pres. Maumawili Estates Cmty. Assn., 1994. Recipient lighting design award Illuminating Engrs. Soc. Kaiser Mililani Clinic, 1983, Kaiser Hawaii Kai Clinic, 1984, Village Coral Shop, 1987. Mem. AIA (design award of merit Honolulu Clinic), Constrn. Specificatins Inst., Outrigger Canoe Club, Waikiki Yacht Club, Am. Arbitration Assn. (arbitrator), U. Hawaii Sch. Architecture Alumni Assn. (dir. 1992—). Unitarian. Office: AKTA Ltd 146 Hekili St Ste 104 Kailua HI 96734-2835

THOMPSON, BETTY JANE, small business owner; b. Ladysmith, Wis., Nov. 18, 1923; d. Edward Thomas and Mayme Selma (Kratwell) Potter; m. Frederick Sturdee Thompson, Apr. 19, 1945 (div. Apr. 1973); children: Denise Alana, Kent Marshall; m. J.R. Critchfield, Feb. 14, 1977 (div. 1989). Student, Jamestown (N.D.) Coll., 1946-47, U. Calif., Long Beach, 1964-69; AA, Orange Coast Coll., 1976; postgrad., Monterey Peninsula Coll., 1979-80; SBA Cert., Hartnell Coll., 1982. Cert. fashion cons. Owner, mgr., buyer Goodview (Minn.) Food Mart, 1947-50; dist. mgr. Beauty Counselor of Minn., Winona County, 1951-61; Boy Scout liaison J.C. Penney Co., Newport Beach, Calif., 1969-72; dept. mgr. and buyer boyswear At Ease, Newport Beach, 1972-77; mgr. Top Notch Boys Wear, Carmel, Calif., 1977-83, buyer, 1984-88; owner, mgr. Top Notch Watch, Sun City, Ariz., 1989—; v.p., chmn. Don Loper Fashion Show, 1967, pres., 1968, bd. dirs., 1969. Co-editor Aux. Antics mag., 1965. Vol. fundraising leadership Family Svc. Assn., Orange County, Calif., 1962-68, other orgns.; chmn. publicity, study group, Sunday sch. tchr., Congl. Ch., Winona, Minn., 1956-58, fellowship pres., Santa Ana, Calif., 1963-65; pres. Goodview Civic Club, 1948. Recipient Athena award Panhellenic Assn. Orange City, Calif., 1968, El Camino Real Dist. Svc. award Orange Empire coun. Boy Scouts Am., Baden-Powell award, Outstanding Leadership award, El Camino Real Dist., Calif., 1972J. Ringling North award, 1949; named Outstanding Svc. Vol. Family Svc. Assn., 1969. Mem. Carmel Bus. Assn. Home and Office: 10048 W Hawthorn Dr Sun City AZ 85351-2829

THOMPSON, BILLY DEAN, accountant; b. Boise City, Okla., Sept. 12, 1944; s. James Larmen and Nora Lee (Risley) T.; m. Linda Kay Bearden, Aug. 21, 1965 (div. June 1976); children: Deana Kay, Lance Dean. BS, BA, Okla. Panhandle State U., 1969. CPA, Calif., Okla., Tex. Tax acct., prin. Thompson Acctg., Boise City, 1968-69; tax acct. Gaskill & Pharis, Dalhart, Tex., 1969-72; tax mgr. Arthur Andersen & Co., Oklahoma City, 1972-77; v.p.-tax Landmark Land Co., Inc., Carmel, Calif., 1977-93, mem. bd. adv., pres., 1993—; owner bdt Advisors, 1993—. Mem. Am. Inst. CPAs, Calif. Soc. CPAs (taxation com.), Okla. Soc. CPAs, Tex. Soc. CPAs, Nat. Assn. Accts. Democrat. Methodist. Home and Office: 26135 Zdan Rd Carmel Valley CA 93924-9205

THOMPSON, CARYN ELIZABETH, banker; b. Palo Alto, Calif., Mar. 22, 1954; d. Robert Louis and Harriet Elizabeth (Jeffs) Hildebrand; m. Terence William Thompson, Aug. 30, 1975; children: Cory Elizabeth, Christopher William. Student, U. Ariz., 1972-75; BS, Ariz. State U., 1979, MBA, 1984. Asst. treas. Great Western Bank, Phoenix, 1984-85; asst. v.p. Citibank (Ariz.), Phoenix, 1985-87; v.p. Nat. Processing Co., Phoenix, 1987—. Dem. precinct committee-person, dist. 26, Phoenix, 1983; registrar Ariz. State Govt., 1980. Mem. Nat. Assn. Female Execs., Nat. Assn. Banking Women (bd. dirs. 1985), Ariz. Bank Assn. (bank rep.), Delta Gamma. Democrat. Home: 202 W Lawrence Rd Phoenix AZ 85013-1226 Office: Nat Processing Co 16402 N 28th Ave Phoenix AZ 85023-7534

THOMPSON, CHARLES EDWARD, electronics company executive; b. Seattle, July 30, 1929; s. Edward Oliver and Mae (Green) T.; m. Jean Thompson (div. 1974); children: Lynn, David; m. Wanda Laverne Wallace, Nov. 15, 1974; children: Richard, Russell, Steven. BS in Math., U. Wash., 1951. With software devel. dept. Hanford div. GE, Richland, Wash., 1951-61; product planning mgr. computer div. Hanford div. GE, Phoenix, 1961-64, div. mktg. mgr., 1965-69; dir. mgmt. info. systems Motorola Semicondr. Prodn. Sector, Phoenix, 1969-75, dir. mktg., 1975-79, v.p., dir. worldwide mktg., 1980—. Bd. dirs. Mesa (Ariz.) Luth. Hosp., 1979-81. Mem. Phoenix C. of C., Phi Beta Kappa, Mesa Country Club, White Mountain Country Club (Pinetop, Ariz.). Home: 3750 E Minton Pl Mesa AZ 85215-1700 Office: Motorola Semicondr 56th St Thomas Ave Phoenix AZ 85008

THOMPSON, CLAIRE LOUISA, medical-surgical nurse; b. Columbus, Ohio, Sept. 29, 1938; d. Harry Edgar and Clara Etta (Brackenbusch) McKeever; m. Roger Lee Thompson, Dec. 20, 1958 (div. 1988); children: Jeffrey, Michael. Diploma, Bethesda Hosp. Sch. Nursing, Cin., 1959; student, Ball State, 1970, Ind. U., 1981, Purdue U., 1982-83. RN, Ohio, Ind., Calif.; cert. ins. rehab. specialist, 1985, case mgr., 1994. Staff nurse Greene Meml. Hosp., Xenia, Ohio, 1959-60; med.-surg. nurse, charge nurse Bethesda Hosp., 1960-64; med.-surg. nurse Porter Meml. Hosp., Valparaiso, Ind., 1965-66; staff and charge nurse Mercy Hosp., Elwood, Ind., 1968-74; gen. practice nurse W. A. Scea, MD, Elwood, 1970-74; exec. dir. Vis. Nurse Assn., Elwood, 1974-78; analyst Blue Cross/Blue Shield of Indpls., 1978-79; supr. Meth. Hosp. Clinic, Indpls., 1980; dir. nursing Upjohn Health Care, Indpls., 1980-81; instr. health occups. Washington Twp. Schs., Indpls., 1981-84; br. mgr. health & rehab. Crawford & Co., Indpls., 1984-88; regional med. svcs. advisor western region Crawford & Co., San Francisco, 1988-92; br. mgr. Crawford & Co. Health Care Mgmt., Modesto, Calif., 1992-94; ret., 1994; pioneer in devel. case mgmt. nursing svcs., 1984-94. Founder Meals on Wheels, Elwood, 1975, Visiting Nurses Assn., Elwood, 1976. Mem. Nat. League for Nursing, Assn. Rehab. Nurses (pres. Ind. chpt. 1987-88), Nat. Ins. Womens Assn., Case Mgmt. Soc. Am., San Francisco Ins. Womens Assn., Rehab. Ins. Nurses Group. Roman Catholic. Home: 37097 Denning Ter Apt 196 Fremont CA 94536-1971

THOMPSON, CRAIG SNOVER, corporate communications executive; b. Bklyn., May 24, 1932; s. Craig F. and Edith (Williams) T.; m. Masae Sugizaki, Feb. 21, 1957; children: Lee Anne, Jane Laura. Grad., Valley Forge Mil. Acad., 1951; B.A., Johns Hopkins U., 1954. Newspaper and radio reporter Easton (Pa.) Express, 1954-55, 57-59, Wall St. Jour., 1959-60; account exec. Moore, Meldrum & Assocs., 1960; mgr. pub. relations Cen. Nat. Bank of Cleve., 1961-62; account exec. Edward Howard & Co., Cleve., 1962-67; v.p. Edward Howard & Co., 1967-69, sr. v.p., 1969-71; dir. pub. relations White Motor Corp., Cleve., 1971-76; v.p. pub. relations No. Telecom Inc., Nashville, 1976-77, White Motor Corp., Farmington Hills, Mich., 1977-80; v.p. corp. communications White Motor Corp., 1980-81; dir. exec. communications Rockwell Internat. Corp., Pitts., 1981-86, El Segundo, Calif., 1986-91, Seal Beach, Calif., 1992—. Bd. dirs. Shaker Lakes Regional Nature Center, 1970-73. Served to 1st lt., inf. U.S. Army, 1955-57. Mem. Pub. Rels. Soc. Am. (accredited), Alumni Assn. Valley Forge Mil. Acad. (bd. dirs. 1988-94). Office: Rockwell Internat Corp 2201 Seal Beach Blvd Seal Beach CA 90740-5603

THOMPSON, DANIEL EMERSON, vending machine service company; b. Fairbanks, Alaska, Jan. 24, 1947; s. George Edmond and Emma Jean (Burns) T.; m. Yvette Clarice Brazeau, Aug. 16, 1980. Student, U. Notre Dame, 1965-67. Vice-pres. Music Inc., Fairbanks, 1965-67; pres. Music Inc. (doing bus. as Alaska Music Co.), Fairbanks, 1967-81; sec.-treas. Music Inc. (doing bus. as Alaska Music Co. and TLC Vend), Anchorage, 1981-84; sec. Music Inc. (doing bus. as Vend Alaska-Fairbanks), Fairbanks, 1984-87, pres., 1987—; pres. Vend Inc. (doing bus. as Vend Alaska-Anchorage), Anchorage, 1984—; bd. dirs. Music Inc., Fairbanks, Vend Inc., Anchorage, Denali State Bank, Fairbanks; ptnr. Thompson Investment Co., Fairbanks, 1976—. Trustee Hi Pow, Fairbanks, 1972—; pres. Fairbanks Downtown Assn., 1987-88, bd. dirs., 1984-94; bd. dirs. Alaska State Devel. Corp., Juneau, 1971-82, Monroe Found., Fairbanks, 1991—. Mem. Amusement Music Operators Am., Nat. Automatic Merchandising Assn., Northwest Automatic Vending Assn. (bd. govs. 1983—), Rotary, Fairbanks C. of C.

(co-chmn. local govt. com. 1988-90). Roman Catholic. Office: Vend Alaska 1890 Marika Rd Fairbanks AK 99709-5520

THOMPSON, DAVID ALFRED, industrial engineer; b. Chgo., Sept. 9, 1929; s. Clifford James and Christobel Eliza (Sawin) T.; children: Nancy, Brooke, Lynda, Diane, Kristy. B.M.E., U. Va., 1951; B.S. in Indsl. Engring. U. Fla., 1955, M.S. in Engring, 1956; Ph.D., Stanford U., 1961. Registered profl. engr., Calif; cert. profl. ergonomist. Research asst. U. Fla. Engring. and Industries Exptl. Sta., Gainesville, 1955-56; instr. indsl. engring. Stanford U., 1956-58, acting asst. prof., 1958-61, asst. prof., 1961-64, asso. prof., 1964-72, prof., 1972-83, prof., asso. chmn. dept. indsl. engring., 1972-73, prof. emeritus, 1983—; mem. clin. faculty occupational medicine U. Calif. Med. Sch., San Francisco, 1985—; pres., chief scientist Portola Assocs., Palo Alto, Calif., 1965—; prin. investigator NASA Ames Research Center, Moffatt Field, Calif., 1974-77; cons. Dept. State, Fed. EEO Commn., maj. U.S. and fgn. cos.; cons. emergency communications ctr. design Santa Clara County Criminal Justice Bd., 1974, Bay Area Rapid Transit Control Ctr., 1977, Govt. of Mex., 1978, Amadahl Corp., 1978-79, Kerr-McGee Corp., 1979, Chase Manhattan Bank, 1980, St. Regis Paper Co., 1980-82, Pacific Gas & Electric, 1983-85, Pacific Bell, 1984-86, 89-93, IBM, 1988-91, Hewlett-Packard, 1990-91, Reuter's News Svc., 1990-92, Safeway Corp., 1992—, New United Motors Mfg., 1993—; mem. com. for office computers Calif. OSHA. Dir., editor: documentary film Rapid Answers for Rapid Transit, Dept. Transp., 1974; mem. editorial adv. bd. Computers and Graphics, 1970-85; reviewer Indsl. Engring. and IEEE Transactions, 1972-86; contbr. articles to profl. jours. Served to lt. USNR, 1951-54. HEW grantee, 1967-70. Mem. Am. Inst. Indsl. Engrs., Human Factors Soc., IEEE, Am. Soc. Safety Engrs., World Safety Orgn., Internat. Assn. Indsl. Ergonomics and Safety Rsch. Home: 121 Peter Coutts Cir Stanford CA 94305-2519 Office: Portola Assocs 2600 El Camino Real Ste 414 Palo Alto CA 94306-1705

THOMPSON, DAVID CHARLES, SR., management executive; b. Oneonta, N.Y., Jan. 27, 1942; s. Gordon George and Evelyn Beatrice (Michaels) T.; m. Carol Anne Peele, Dec. 24, 1976; children: David Charles Jr., Robert Edward. BS in Mgmt., U. La Verne, 1989, MS in Mgmt., 1991. Mgr. Hughes, West Covina, Calif., 1968-93, CH2M Hill, Santa Ana, Calif., 1993—; bd. dirs. Honeywell West Coast Fed. Credit Union, Azusa, Calif. Officer Glendora (Calif.) Police Aux., 1972-74; agt. South Pasadena Police Res., 1978-82; active Foothill Apt. Owners Assn., Pasadena, Calif., 1979—. Served with USN, 1960-68. Mem. Soc. Logistics Engrs., Soc. Tech. Communication, Assn. Proposal Mgmt. Profls., NRA, Rogues Club (chief Arcadia, Calif. chpt. 1987-88), Elks. Republican. Home: 6792 N Country Club Dr La Verne CA 91750-1347 Office: CH2M Hill 2510 Red Hill Ave Santa Ana CA 92705-5542

THOMPSON, DAVID RENWICK, federal judge. BS in Bus., U. So. Calif., 1952, LLB, 1955. Pvt. practice law with Thompson & Thompson (and predecessor firms), 1957-85; judge U.S. Ct. Appeals (9th cir.), 1985—. Served with USN, 1955-57. Mem. ABA, San Diego County Bar Assn., Am. Bd. Trial Lawyers (sec. San Diego chpt. 1983, v.p. 1984, pres. 1985). Office: US Ct Appeals 940 Front St San Diego CA 92101-8994*

THOMPSON, DENNIS PETERS, plastic surgeon; b. Chgo., Mar. 18, 1937; s. David John and Ruth Dorothy (Peters) T.; m. Virginia Louise Williams, June 17, 1961; children: Laura Faye, Victoria Ruth, Elizabeth Jan. BS, U. Ill., 1957, BS in Medicine, 1959, MS in Physiology, MD, 1961. Diplomate Am. Bd. Surgery, Am. Bd. Plastic Surgery. Intern Presbyn.-St. Lukes Hosp., Chgo., 1961-62; resident in gen. surgery Mayo Clinic, Rochester, Minn., 1964-66, fellow in gen. surgery, 1964-66; resident in gen. surgery Harbor Gen. Hosp., Los Angeles, 1968-70; resident in plastic surgery UCLA, 1971-73, clin. instr. plastic surgery, 1975-82, asst. clin. prof. surgery, 1982—; practice medicine specializing in plastic and reconstructive surgery, Los Angeles, 1974-78, Santa Monica, Calif., 1978—; chmn. plastic surgery sect. St. John's Hosp., 1986-91; mem. staff Santa Monica Hosp., UCLA Ctr. Health Scis.; chmn. dept. surgery Beverly Glen Hosp., 1978-79; pres. Coop. of Am. Physicians Credit Union, 1978-80, bd. dirs., 1980—, chmn. membership devel. com., 1983—, treas., 1985—. Contbr. articles to med. jours. Moderator Congl. Ch. of Northridge (Calif.), 1975-76, chmn. bd. trustees, 1973-74, 80-82; bd. dirs. L.A. Bus. Coun., 1987-90. Am. Tobacco Inst. research grantee, 1959-60. Fellow ACS; mem. AMA (Physicians Recognition award 1971, 74, 77, 81, 84, 87, 90, 93), Calif. Med. Assn., Los Angeles County Med. Assn. (chmn. bylaws com. 1979-80, chmn. ethics com. 1980-81, sec.-treas. dist. 5 1982-83, program chmn. 1983-84, pres. 1985-86, councilor 1988—), Pan-Pacific Surgical Assn., Am. Soc. Plastic and Reconstructive Surgeons, Calif. Soc. Plastic Surgeons (chmn. bylaws com. 1982-83, chmn. liability com. 1983-85, councilor 1988-91, sec. 1993-95, v.p. 1995—), Los Angeles Soc. Plastic Surgeons (sec. 1980-82, pres. 1982—), Lipoplasty Soc. N.Am., UCLA Plastic Surgery Soc. (treas. 1983-84), Am. Soc. Aesthetic Plastic Surgery, Western Los Angeles Regional C. of C. (bd. dirs. 1981-84, 86-89, chmn. legis. action com. 1978-80), Phi Beta Kappa, Alpha Omega Alpha, Nu Sigma Nu, Phi Kappa Phi, Delta Sigma Delta, Omega Beta Pi, Phi Eta Sigma. Republican. Office: 2001 Santa Monica Blvd Santa Monica CA 90404-2102

THOMPSON, DWIGHT ALAN, vocational rehabilitation expert; b. Monterey Park, Calif., Mar. 2, 1955; s. Irvin Edward and Lydia (Busch) T.; m. Irene Anita Arden, June 18, 1977; children: Dwight Christopher, Meredith Irene, Hilda Arden. BA in Social Welfare, U. Wash., 1978, MSW, 1980. Registered vocat. rehab. counselor, Wash., Oreg.; cert. social worker, Wash., case mgr.; diplomate Am. Bd. Clin. Examiners in Social Work; cert. Ins. Rehab. Specialist Commn. Houseparent Parkview Home for Exceptional Children, Seattle, 1976-77; rsch. analyst Wash. State Ho. Reps., Olympia, 1979-81; v.p. The James L. Groves Co., Everett, Wash., 1982-86; exec. dir. Evaluation & Tng. Assocs., Seattle, 1984-86; pres., owner Rehab. & Evaluation Svcs. Inc., Seattle, 1986—; social work officer 50th Gen. Army Res. Hosp., Seattle, 1982-87, 91-93; med. adminstrv. officer Operation Desert Storm, Riyadh, Saudi Arabia, 1990-91; aide-de-camp 2d Hosp. Ctr., San Francisco, 1987-88, pub. affairs officer, 1988-90; acting commdr. 1972 MED DET-Combat Stress Control, 1993, exec. officer, 1994—. Co-author Correction Study Report, 1981. Registered lobbyist Wash. State, 1983-87; conf. pres. St. Vincent de Paul Soc., 1975-78; lt. Thurston County Fire Dist #6, East Olympia, Wash., 1980-83; alumni rep. COS Track Com. U. Wash., 1984-87; primary candidate Dem. Primary for State Rep., Renton, Wash., 1984; mem. Wash. Vocat. Rehab. adv. com. Dept. Labor Indusrires, 1992—; pres. Sheridan Beacy Cmty. Club, Inc., 1994-95; chair human svcs. commn. City Lake Forest Park, Wash, 1995—; candidate city coun., 1995. Maj. USAR, 1982—, Persian Gulf. Fellow Am. Acad. Pain Mgmt. (cert.); Mem. NASW (cert.), Nat. Assn. Rehab. Profls. (pvt. sector, Wash. legis. chair), Acad. Cert. Social Workers, Wash. Self-Insurers Assn. (mem. legis. com.), Assn. Mil. Surgeons U.S., Res. Officers Assn., Nat. Eagle Scout Assn., Am. Bd. Forensic Examiners, Case Mgmt. Soc. Am., Boy Scouts Am., Theta Xi (pres. 1975-77). Roman Catholic. Home: 16136 41st Ave NE Lk Forest Park WA 98155-6726 Office: Rehab and Evaluation Svcs 226 Summit Ave E Seattle WA 98102-5619

THOMPSON, EDGAR JOSEPH, musician, educator. BS, MS in Physics and Math., Brigham Young U.; MA in Music, Calif. State U., Long Beach; PhD in Choral Music Edn., U. Utah; studies with Frank Pooler, Newell B. Weight. Asst. dir. Choral Activities Calif. State U., Long Beach; mem. faculty U. Utah, Salt Lake City, 1978, chmn. Music dept., conductor Univ. A Cappella Choir, 1979—; mus. dir. Utah Symphony Chorus, 1982—; conductor clinics, guest conductor in field. Producer film on new choral literature and techniques, 1972; developer computer program to teach fundamental music skills. Mem. Music Educators Nat. Conf., Utah Music Educators Assn., Am. Choral Dirs. Assn. (past state pres.). Office: U Utah Music Dept 204 Gardner Hall Salt Lake City UT 84112

THOMPSON, ELBERT ORSON, retired dentist, consultant; b. Salt Lake City, Aug. 31, 1910; s. Orson David and Lillian (Greenwood) T.; m. Gayle Larsen, Sept. 12, 1935; children: Ronald Elbert, Karen Thompson Toone, Edward David, Gay Lynne. Student, U. Utah, 1928-30, 33-35; DDS, Northwestern U., 1939; hon. degree, Am. Coll. Dentistry, Miami, Fla., 1958, Internat. Coll. Dentistry, San Francisco, 1962. Pvt. practice dentistry Salt Lake City, 1939-78; ret., 1978; inventor, developer and internat. lectr. postgrad./undergrad. courses various dental schs. and study groups, 1953-83; developer, tchr. Euthenics Dentistry Concept; cons. in field. Contbr. numerous dental articles to profl. jours. Life mem. Rep. Presdl. Task Force, Washington, 1985—. Recipient Merit Honor award U. Utah, 1985; named Dentist of the Yr. Utah Acad. Gen. Dentistry, 1991, Father of Modern Dentistry, 1991. Mem. ADA (life), Utah Dental Assn. (life, sec. 1948-49, Disting. Svc. award 1980), Salt Lake City Dental Soc. (life, pres. 1945-46), Utah Dental Hygiene Soc. (hon.), Am. Acad. Dental Practice Adminstrn. (life, pres. 1965-66), Internat. Coll. Dentists, Am. Coll. Dentists, Sons of Utah Pioneers (life), Dinorators Club (charter), Northwestern U. Alumni Assn. (Merit award 1961), Omicron Kappa Upsilon. Mormons. Home: 5672 S 960 E South Ogden UT 84405-4964

THOMPSON, FLOYD HENRY, cytogenetic oncologist; b. Blue Earth, Minn., Aug. 18, 1951; s. Ansel Clinton and Dorothy June Thompson. BA, So. Ill. U., 1972; MS, U. Ill., Chgo., 1981. Cytogenetic technician Cook County Hosp., Chgo., 1972-73; cytogenetics lab. mgr. U. Ill. Med. Ctr., Chgo., 1973-81; cytogenetic oncology lab. mgr. Ariz. Cancer Ctr., Tucson, 1981-90, dir. cytogenetic oncology lab., 1990—; cons. U.S. Congress, Washington, 1974-76; lectr. So. Ill. U. Sch. Medicine, Carbondale, 1973-77; organizer, coord. internat. workshops on chromosomes in solid tumors, 1985-95. Author: (with others) Association of Cytogenetic Techonogists Lab Manual, 2d edit., 1991; mem. editorial staff Applied Cytogenetics, 1986—; contbr. articles to profl. jours. Mem. AAAS, Am. Soc. Human Genetics, Found. for Sci and Disability, Assn. Cytogenic Technologists. Office: Ariz Cancer Ctr 1515 N Campbell Ave Tucson AZ 85724-0001

THOMPSON, GARY W., public relations executive; b. Berkeley, Calif., July 15, 1947. BA, Northwestern U., England, 1969—. Acct. exec. Allen & Doward Advt., 1971-74; acct. exec. Hoefer-Amedei Assocs., 1978-81, acct. supr., 1978, v.p., 1978-81; v.p., assoc. dir. Ketchum, 1981-82, sr. v.p., dir., 1982-84, exec. v.p., 1984-87, exec. v.p., dir. we. region, 1987-89, exec. v.p., dir. U.S.A., 1989-90; pres., CEO Hi-Tech Comm., 1990—. Mem. Pub. Rels. Soc. Am. (counselors acad., membership chmn. San Francisco chpt. 1983, placement, newsletter chmn. 1985), Internat. Assn. Bus. Communicators,. Office: Hi-Tech Comm 101 Howard St San Francisco CA 94105-1629

THOMPSON, GEORGE FREDERICK, JR., public management educator; b. Anderson, Ind., Oct. 29, 1942; s. George Frederick and Ellen Leah (Reuter) T.; m. Sharon O'Rand, Sept. 8, 1968 (div. Nov. 1978); children: MacKendree and Kyrie' O'Rand; m. Ruth Ann Crowley, June 20, 1980; 1 child, Jonathan Crowley. BA, Pomona Coll., 1964; PhD, Claremont Grad. Sch., 1972. Asst. to sr. analyst Dept. Fin. State of Calif., Sacramento, 1972-75; asoc. dep. dir. for fin. and capital outlay planning Calif. Postsecondary Edn. Commn., Sacramento, 1975-76; vis. asst./assoc. prof. U. British Columbia faculty commerce and bus. adminstrn., 1976-77; sr. rsch economist Econ. Coun. Can., Ottawa, Ont., 1978-79; vis. assoc. prof., acting chmn. Grad. Sch. Mgmt. Pub. and Not for Profit Mgmt. Group UCLA, 1981; assoc. prof. Columbia U. Sch. Internat. and Pub. Affairs MPA Program, N.Y.C., 1980-85; Grace and Elmer Goudy Prof. Pub. Mgmt. and Policy Analysis Atkinson Grad. Sch. Mgmt. Willamette U., Salem, Oreg., 1985—; mem. task force on state budgeting Nat. Ctr. for Higher edn. Mgmt. Systems, Boulder, Colo., 1975-76, adv. com. Calif. State Senate Judiciary Com. subcom. on Consumr Affairs, 1980-81, Gov.'s Task Force on Sch. Fin. Reform, Oreg., 1988-89, adv. com. on Tax Reform, Oreg., 1990, Govt. Standards and Practices Commn., Oreg., 1995—; cons. House of Commons Can., on Regulatory Reform, Pub. Svcs. Commn. N.Y. Atty. Gen.'s Office of Consumer Affairs, Defense Sec.'s Commn. on Base Realignment and Closure, Senate Armed Svcs. subcom. on mil. constrn., others. Co-author: (with W.T. Stanbury) Regulatory Reform in Canada, 1982, (with L.R. Jones) Regulatory Power and Practices: Regulating Power and Regulating Laws, 1982; translator (with Ruth Crowley): F. Scharpf's Crisis and Choice in Europen Social Democrcy, 1991; editor: Regulatory Regimes in Conflict, 1984; co-editor: (with LeRoy Gramer) Reforming Social Regulation, 1982, (with W.T. Stanbury) Managing Public Enterprises, 1982; contbr. numerous articles, notes, essays, bookr reviews to profl. jours. Mem. acad. adv. bd. Cascade Policy Inst. Recipient Clara Ihrig Linhardt Traveling fellowship, Mexico, Cen. Am., 1970-71, Mayr Found. Essay award, Lincoln Inst. Pub. Fin., Claremont Grad. Sch., 1973; nominated for Koopman prize of ORSA spl. interest group of defense analysis, 1987. Mem. Assn. for Pub. Policy and Mgmt., Am. Soc. for Pub. Adminstrn. (exec. coun. sect. on pub. budgeting and fin. 1991-94), Pub. Choice Soc., Western Polit. Sci.Assn., Midwest Polit. Sci. Assn., The Inst. Mgmt. Scis., Oreg. Acad. Scis.. Home: 540 Tillman Ave SE Salem OR 97302-3786 Office: Willamette Univ Atkinson Grad Sch Mgmt Salem OR 97301

THOMPSON, GEORGIA BETH, university department administrator; b. Milford, Utah, Jan. 25, 1940; d. George E. and Berniece (Miller) Smith; m. Richard A. Thompson, July 22, 1972; children: Richelle Lynne Thompson. BS, Utah State U., 1962; MA, The Am. Univ., 1967. Copy editor, reader Utah State U., Logan, 1962-63, asst. info. specialist, 1963-65; staff writer Larry Hogan Assocs., Washington, 1966; dean of women, instr. Southern Utah State Coll., Cedar City, 1967-72, adj. instr., 1976-78; office mgr., case worker Congressman Wayne Owens, Cedar City, 1973-75; dir. ednl. opportunity programs So. Utah State U., Cedar City, 1986-89; asst. v.p. student svcs. Southern Utah State Coll., Cedar City, 1989-92, assoc. v.p. student svcs., 1992—. Co-editor (jour.) Western Anasazi Reports, 1976-85; bibliography editor Archeolog. jours., 1986; contbr. articles to Womens Exponent II., 1979. Chmn. Cedar City Planning Commn., 1979-86; mem., vice chair Cedar Dist. Adv. Bd., Bur. Land Mgmt., 1985-91; coord. Dem. County campaigns, Iron County, Utah, 1974—; mem. Women's Resource Com., Southern Utah U., Cedar City, 1993—; bd. dirs. Cedar City Housing Authority, 1991—, Women's Domestic Violence Shelter, Cedar City, 1994—. Mem. LWV (pres. local chpt.), Utah Consortium of Women in Higher Edn. Mem. LDS Ch. Office: Southern Utah U Student Svcs Dept Cedar City UT 84720

THOMPSON, GORDON, JR., federal judge; b. San Diego, Dec. 28, 1929; s. Gordon and Garnet (Meese) T.; m. Jean Peters, Mar. 17, 1951; children—John M., Peter Renwick, Gordon III. Grad., U. So. Calif., 1951, Southwestern U. Sch. Law, Los Angeles, 1956. Bar: Calif. 1956. With Dist. Atty.'s Office, County of San Diego, 1957-60; partner firm Thompson & Thompson, San Diego, 1960-70; U.S. dist. judge So. Dist. Calif., San Diego, 1970—, chief judge, 1984-91, sr. judge, 1994—. Bd. dirs. Sharp Meml. Hosp. Mem. Am. Bd. Trial Advocates, ABA, San Diego County Bar Assn. (v.p. 1970), Delta Chi. Club: San Diego Yacht. Office: US Dist Ct 940 Front St San Diego CA 92101-8994

THOMPSON, HENRY NAINOA, hospital administrator; b. Honolulu, July 15, 1921; s. Henry Nainoa Sr. and Irmgard Luukia (Harbottle) T.; m. Pearl Elvina Mary Barbel, Nov. 16, 1946; children: Scott Henry Nainoa, Noni Nora Glynnis Bridget Skeffington Thompson, Kirk Leopold Kumulani. Student, U. Wash., 1940-42, Columbia U., 1942-44; BA in Phys. Therapy, Columbia U., 1946, MA in Corrective Phys. Edn. & Rehab., 1950; cert. poliomyelitis, U. So. Calif., L.A., 1950; cert. adminstr. phys. therapy, Stanford U., 1950; cert. adminstrn. rehab., Inst. Phys. Medicine & Rehab., 1953; cert. adminstrn. pers., U. Hawaii, 1956; cert. job sampling testing, Ins. for Crippled and Disabled, 1958; cert. analysis fin. statements, U. Hawaii, 1960. Phys. therapist VA Regional Office, N.Y.C., 1946; chief phys. therapy Nat. Soc. for Crippled Children and Adults, Honolulu, 1948-49, Kauikeolani Children's Hosp., Honolulu, 1950-53; asst. dir. Rehab. Ctr. Hawaii, Honolulu, 1953-68; adminstr. Wahiawa (Hawaii) Gen. Hosp., 1968-71; hosp. adminstr. The Queen's Med. Ctr., Honolulu, 1971-74; dir. arthritis ctr. U. Hawaii Sch. Medicine, Honolulu, 1974-75; dep. dir. county state hosps. Dept. of Health, State of Hawaii, Honolulu, 1975-82; adminstr. Hawaii State Health Planning and Devel. Agy, State of Hawaii, Honolulu, 1982—; past dir. Family Medicine, Inc., Honolulu. Past pres. Hawaii Kai Comty. Assn.; past pres., dir. Abilities Unltd. With AUS, 1946-48. Named one of 12 Nat. Phys. Fitness Leaders of Am., Pres.'s Johnson's Program for Phys. Fitness, 1965. Fellow Am. Coll. Hosp. Adminstrs.; mem. APHA, Am. Health Planning Assn., Hosp. Assn. Hawaii (assoc.), Am. Hosp. Assn. (assoc.), Koko Head Athletic Club (past pres.), Hawaii State Health Coun. (past pres.), Nat. Rehab. Assn. (past dir. Hawaii chpt.), Am. Assn. Phys. Therapy (past pres. Hawaii chpt.), Elks. Home and Office: 6815 Niumalu Loop Honolulu HI 96825

THOMPSON, HERBERT ERNEST, tool and die company executive; b. Jamaica, N.Y., Sept. 8, 1923; s. Walter and Louise (Joly) T.; student Stevens Inst. Tech., 1949-51; m. Patricia Elaine Osborn, Aug. 2, 1968; children: Robert Steven, Debra Lynn. Foreman, Conner Tool Co., 1961-62, Eason & Waller Grinding Corp., 1962-63; owner Endco Machined Products, 1966-67, Thompson Enterprises, 1974—; pres. Method Machined Products, Phoenix, 1967; pres., owner Quality Tool, Inc., 1967—. Served to capt. USAAF, 1942-46. Decorated D.F.C., Air medal with cluster. Home: 14009 N 42nd Ave Phoenix AZ 85023-5306 Office: 4223 W Clarendon Ave Phoenix AZ 85019-3618

THOMPSON, JAMES AVERY, JR., legal intern; b. Whiteville, N.C., Oct. 3, 1947; s. James Avery and Mary Elizabeth (Davis) T.; m. Julia Lee Stephens Thompson, June 7, 1969 (div. July 1979); 1 child, Marlee Amanda Elizabeth Thompson; m. Susannah Elizabeth Rupp Thompson, May 16, 1987; 1 child, Sarah Mary Elizabeth Thompson. AA (hon.), Marion (Ala.) Mil. Inst., 1967; BA, U. Ala., Tuscaloosa, 1969; MLS, 1973; MBA, So. Calif. Inst., Claremont, 1988; JD, Am. Coll. of Law, 1988. Mus. curator U. Ala., Birmingham, 1972-73, med. libr., 1973-82; asst. law libr. U. Laverne (Calif.) Law Sch., 1985-86; ref. libr. Western State U. Sch. Law, Fullerton, Calif., 1986-88; prof., instr. Am. Coll. Law, Brea, Calif., 1988-89; dir., instr. U. West L.A. Law Libr., 1988-90; legal intern Law Office Frank Phillips, Yorba Linda, Calif., 1990-91, Law Office Susannah Thompson, Temecula, Calif., 1991—. Author numerous periodicals in field. Campaign chmn. Med. Libr. United Way, Birmingham, Ala., 1979-80; mem. Lions Club, Tarrant, Ala., 1975-77; dir., spon. Tennis Assn. Pleasant Grove, Ala., 1980-82. Recipient Eagle Scout award, Order of Arrow Boy Scouts Am., 1963; named pres. Student Bar Assn., Am. Coll. Law, Brea, Calif., 1987-88, editor Law Review Am. Coll. Law, Brea, Calif., 1988. Mem. Royal Numismatic Soc. Can., Royal Philatelic Soc. Can., U.S. Tennis Assn., Am. Numismatic Assn., Delta Theta Phi, Alpha Sigma Phi. Democrat. Methodist.

THOMPSON, JAMES WILLIAM, lawyer; b. Dallas, Oct. 22, 1936; s. John Charles and Frances (Van Slyke) T.; BS, U. Mont., 1958, JD, 1962; m. Marie Hertz, June 26, 1965 (dec. 1995); children: Elizabeth, Margaret, John. Acct., Arthur Young & Co., N.Y.C., summer 1959; instr. bus. adminstrn. Eastern Mont. Coll., Billings, 1959-60, U. Mont., Missoula, 1960-61; admitted to Mont. bar, 1962; assoc. Cooke, Moulton, Bellingham & Longo, Billings, 1962-64, James R. Felt, Billings, 1964-65; asst. atty. City of Billings, 1963-64, atty., 1964-66; ptnr. Felt, Speare & Thompson, Billings, 1966-72, McNamer, Thompson & Cashmore, 1973-86, McNamer & Thompson Law Firm PC, 1986-89, McNamer, Thompson, Werner & Stanley, P.C., 1990-93, McNamer Thompson Law Firm PC, 1993—; bd. dirs. Associated Employers of Mont., Inc., 1989—. Mem. Billings Zoning Commn., 1966-69; v.p. Billings Community Action Program (now Dist. 7 Human Resources Devel. Council), 1968-70, pres., 1970-75, trustee, 1975—; mem. Yellowstone County Legal Services Bd., 1969-70; City-County Air Pollution Control Bd., 1969-70; pres. Billings Symphony Soc., 1970-71; bd. dirs. Billings Studio Theatre, 1967-73, Mont. Inst. of Arts Found., 1986-89, Downtown Billings Assn., 1986-90, Billings Area Bus. Incubator, Inc., 1991-94, Found. of Mont. State U., Billings, 1992—; mem. Diocesan exec. council, 1972-75; mem. Billings Transit Commn., 1971-73; mem. City Devel. Agy., 1972-73; bd. dirs. United Way, Billings, 1973-81. CPA, Mont. Mem. ABA, Am. Acad. Estate Planning Attys., Nat. Acad. Elder Law Attys., State Bar Mont., Yellowstone County Bar Assn. (bd. dirs. 1983-87, pres. 1985-86), C. of C., Elks, Kiwanis (pres. Yellowstone chpt. 1974-75), Sigma Chi (pres. Billings alumni assn. 1963-65). Episcopalian. Home: 123 Lewis Ave Billings MT 59101-6034 Office: 300 First Bank Bldg Billings MT 59101

THOMPSON, JEREMIAH BEISEKER, international medical business executive; b. Harvey, N.D., July 20, 1927; s. Linden Brown and Ferne Althea (Beiseker) T.; m. Paula Maria Ketchum, Feb. 5, 1960; children: Cole, Per, Gover, Susannah. BS, U. Minn., 1949, MD, 1953. Rsch. assoc. U. Colo. Med. Sch., Denver, 1956-57, U. Calif. Med. Sch., San Francisco, 1957-59; applications rsch. scientist Beckman/Spinco Co., Palo Alto, Calif., 1959-61; mgr. Asia and Africa Hewlett Packard Co., Palo Alto, 1965-71; med. cons. Alyeska Pipeline Co., Anchorage, 1973-76; mgr. Asia, Africa, Australasia Corometrics Med. Systems, Wallingford, Conn., 1976-82; dir. internat. ops. Oximetrix (Abbott), Mountain View, Calif., 1982-84, Novametrix Med. Systems, Wallingford, 1984-88; ptnr. TMC Internat., Tokyo and Concord, Calif., 1988—; advisor, cons. Yokogawa-Hewlett Packard, Tokyo, 1966-70; cons. Kupat Holim, Tel Aviv, Israel, 1967-87, Itochu, Tokyo, 1984-90, Nat. Heart-Lung Inst., Beijing, China, 1984-94. Project dir. Comparative Study of Western and Japanese Medicine in Taisho and Showa Eras, 1991—. With USN, 1945-46; PTO. Founding fellow Brit. Interplanetary Soc.; assoc. Japan Found., Assn. Asian Studies; mem. Kokusai Bunka Kaikan, Tokyo, World Affairs Coun., Mechanics Inst. Republican. Home and Office: TMC Internat 3718 Barrington Dr Concord CA 94518-1614

THOMPSON, JOHN REED, librarian; b. Atlanta, Jan. 22, 1948; s. Edgar Allen and Ruth Lorraine (Maguire) T.; m. Rebecca Ann Williams, June 18, 1975 (div. June 1982); m. Elaine Faye Beeninga, Apr. 11, 1992. BA, Purdue U., 1970; MSLS, U. So. Calif., L.A., 1973, PhD, 1986. Libr. Citrus Coll., Glendora, Calif., 1973-80, tech. svcs. libr., 1980-86, coll. libr., 1986—. Mem. Covina Concert Band, 1982—. Office: Citrus College Libr 1000 W Foothill Blvd Glendora CA 91741-1885

THOMPSON, JOHN WILLIAM, international management consultant; b. Hurricane, Utah, Oct. 14, 1945; s. Thomas Thurman and Lula (Brinkerhoff) T.; m. Pamela Ruth Williams, Sept. 14, 1991. BSEE, Utah State U., 1969, MBA, 1972; PhD, U. Oreg., 1978. Rsch. asst. Utah State U., Logan, Utah, 1967-69, tching. asst., 1971-72; elec. engr. Collins Radio, Newport Beach, Calif., 1969-72; tching. fellow U. Oreg., Eugene, 1972-78; tng. dir. Lifespring Inc., San Rafael, Calif., 1978-80; pres., CEO Human Factors Inc., San Rafael, Calif., 1980—; chmn. bd. Acumen Internat., San Rafael, Calif., 1985—. Author: The Human Factor: An Inquiry into Communication and Consciousness, 1983, Leadership in the 21st Century in New Traditions in Business, 1992, The Renaissance of Learning in Learning Organizations: Developing Cultures for Tomorrow's Workplace, 1994; author of software based management assessment programs, system theory based management development courses, 1980-92. Rockefeller Found. grantee, 1971. Office: Human Factors Inc 4000 Civic Center Dr Ste 500 San Rafael CA 94903

THOMPSON, JOSIE, nursing administrator; b. Ark., Apr. 16, 1949; d. James Andrew and Oneda Fay (Watson) Rhoads; m. Mark O. Thompson, Feb. 14, 1980. Diploma, Lake View Sch. Nursing, 1970; student, Danville Community Coll., 1974-75, St. Petersburg Jr. Coll., 1979. RN, Ill., Wyo. Staff nurse St. Elizabeth Hosp., Danville, Ill., 1970-78, Osteopathic Hosp., St. Petersburg, Fla., 1980-81, Wyo. State Hosp., Evanston, 1981-83; staff nurse Wyo. Home Health Care, Rock Springs, 1984—, adminstr., 1986—; pres. Home Health Care Alliance Wyo., 1991-92. Mem. nursing program adv. bd. Western Wyo. Community Coll.; mem. Coalition for the Elderly, Spl. Needs Com. Sweetwater County, 1992-93. Home: PO Box 1154 1207 McCabe Rock Springs WY 82902

THOMPSON, JUDITH KASTRUP, nursing researcher; b. Marstal, Denmark, Oct. 1, 1933; came to the U.S., 1951; d. Edward Kastrup and Anna Hansa (Knudsen) Pedersen; m. Richard Frederick Thompson, May 22, 1960; children: Kathryn Marr, Elizabeth Kastrup, Virginia St. Claire. BS, RN, U. Oreg., 1958, MSN, 1963. RN, Calif., Oreg. Staff nurse U. Oreg. Med. Sch., Eugene, 1957-58; staff nurse U. Oreg. Med. Sch., Portland, 1958-61, head staff nurse, 1960-61; instr. psychiat. nursing U. Oreg. Sch. Nursing, Portland, 1963-64; rsch. asst. U. Oreg. Med. Sch., Portland, 1964-65, U. Calif., Irvine, 1971-72; rsch. assoc. Stanford (Calif.) U., 1982-87; rsch. asst. Harvard U., Cambridge, Mass., 1973-74; rsch. assoc. U. So. Calif., L.A., 1987—. Contbg. author: Behavioral Control and Role of Sensory Biofeedback, 1976; contbr. articles to profl. jours. Treas. LWV, Newport Beach, Calif., 1970-74; scout leader Girl Scouts Am., Newport Beach, 1970-78. Named Citizen of Yr. State of Oreg., 1966. Mem. Soc. for Neurosci., Am. Psychol. Soc. (charter), ANA, Oreg. Nurses Assn. Republican. Lutheran. Home: 28 Sky Sail Dr Corona Del Mar CA 92625-1436 Office: U So Calif University Park Los Angeles CA 90089-2520

THOMPSON, LEIGH LASSITER, psychologist, educator; b. Houston, Jan. 13, 1960; d. Don Raines and Ann Janet (Visintin) Thompson; m. Robert Warner Weeks, June 20, 1992. BS, Northwestern U., 1982, PhD,

1988; MA, U. Calif., Santa Barbara, 1984. Asst. prof. psychology U. Wash., Seattle, 1988-92, assoc. prof., 1992-95; prof. J.L. Kellogg Disting. chair organ. behavior NorthWestern U., Evanston, Ill., 1995—; fellow Ctr. for Advanced Study in the Behavioral Scis., 1994-95. Edtl. bd. Orgnl. Behavior & Human Decision Processes, Internat. Jour. Conflict Mgt., Jour. Exptl. Social Psychology, 1990—; assoc. editor Group Decision Making and Negotiations; contbr. articles to profl. jours. Recipient Presdl. Young Investigator award NSF, 1991, Grad. Rsch. award Sigma Xi Found., 1987; grantee NSF, 1991, 89—, Nat. Inst. Dispute Resolution, 1987, APA, 1989; fellow Ctr. for Advanced Study Behavioral Sci. Mem. APA (S. Rains Wallace Dissertation award 1989), Am. Psychol. Soc., Acad. Mgmt. Office: Northwestern U Psychology Box 35-1525 Evanston WA 98195-1525

THOMPSON, LINDA LEE, educational consultant; b. Ottumwa, Iowa, Sept. 21, 1940; d. Clarence Adelbert and Ollie Mae (Easley) Andrews; m. Richard Bruce Thompson, Aug. 13, 1961 (div. Nov. 1986); children: Bruce Edward, Curtis Lowell. BA, U. No. Iowa, 1961; postgrad., U. Wis., 1962-66, U. Ariz., 1967-68. Cert. tchr. Math. tchr. Franklin Jr. High Sch., 1961-63; tchr., head math. dept. LaFollette High Sch., Madison, Wis., 1963-67; cons., editor, writer, 1968—; cons. Ariz. State Dept. Edn., Phoenix, 1981. Author: General Mathematics, 1977; co-author: Consumer Mathematics, 2d edit., 1986, McGraw-Hill Mathematics, 1987, You, The Consumer, 1987, Business Mathematics, 988, Pre-Algebra, 1991, Prentice Hall Mathematics; Explorations and Applications, 1995; also articles. Chmn. bd. dirs. Tucson Jr. Strings, 1981-84; com. mem. Rincon-Univ. H.S. Drug Impact Group, Tucson, 1986-90, co-chmn., 1989-90; mem. Univ. H.S. Parents Bd., co-chmn., 1989-90; mem. Clatsop Cmty. Action Bd., 1993—, chmn., 1994—; mem. Surf Pines Homeowners' Bd., 1993—, pres., 1994-95; mem. Pioneer House bd., 1994—, chmn., 1995—. Mem. Nat. Coun. Tchrs. Math. Home and Office: 2370 Manion Dr Warrenton OR 97146-9783

THOMPSON, LOIS JEAN HEIDKE ORE, industrial psychologist; b. Chgo., Feb. 22, 1933; d. Harold William and Ethel Rose (Neumann) Heidke; m. Henry Thomas Ore, Aug. 28, 1954 (div. May 1972); children: Christopher, Douglas; m. Joseph Lippard Thompson, Aug. 3, 1972; children: Scott, Les, Melanie. BA, Cornell Coll., Mt. Vernon, Iowa, 1955; MA, Idaho State U., 1964, EdD, 1981. Lic. psychologist, N.Mex. Tchr. pub. schs. various locations, 1956-67; tchr., instr. Idaho State U., Pocatello, 1967-72; employee/orgn. devel. specialist Los Alamos (N.Mex.) Nat. Lab., 1981-84, tng. specialist, 1984-89, sect. leader, 1989-93; pvt. practice Los Alamos, 1988—; sec. Cornell Coll. Alumni Office, 1954-55, also other orgns.; bd. dirs. Parent Edn. Ctr., Idaho State U., 1980; counselor, Los Alamos, 1981-88. Editor newsletter LWV, Laramie, Wyo., 1957; contbr. articles to profl. jours. Pres. Newcomers Club, Pocatello, 1967, Faculty Womens Club, Pocatello, 1968; chmn. edn. com. AAUW, Pocatello, 1969. Mem. APA, ACA, N.Mex. Psychol. Assn. (bd. dirs. div. II, 1990, sec. 1988-90, chmn. 1990), N.Am. Soc. Adlerian Psychology, N.Mex. Soc. Adlerian Psychology (pres. 1990, treas. 1991-94), Soc. Indsl. and Orgnl. Psychology, Nat. Career Counseling Assn. Mem. LDS Ch. Home: 340 Aragon Ave Los Alamos NM 87544-3505 Office: Thompson Counseling & Cons 340 Aragon Ave Los Alamos NM 87544-3505

THOMPSON, LYLE EUGENE, electrical engineer; b. Pocatello, Idaho, May 16, 1956; s. Clyde Eugene and Doris (Pratt) T.; m. Barbara Mae Dickerson, Dec. 31, 1986. Grad. high sch. Sr. diagnostic engr. Calma/GE, Santa Clara, Calif., 1978-83; mem. tech. staff Telecommunications Tech., Inc., Milpitas, Calif., 1983-84; proprietor/cons. Lyle Thompson Cons., Fremont, Calif., 1984-87; sys. analyst Raynet Corp., Menlo Park, Calif., 1987-88; proprietor/cons. Lyle Thompson Cons., Hayward, Calif., 1988-89; mgr. sys. design Raylan Corp., Menlo Park, Calif., 1989-90; dir. system design Raylan Corp., Menlo Park, 1990-91; pvt. practice cons. San Lorenzo, Calif., 1991—; cons. in field. Patentee in field. Mem. ACM, IEEE. Home: 664 Paseo Grande San Lorenzo CA 94580-2364

THOMPSON, MARI HILDENBRAND, medical staff services operations coordinator; b. Washington, Apr. 26, 1951; d. Emil John Christopher Hildenbrand and Ada Lythe (Conklin) Hildenbrand-Kammer; m. R. Marshall Thompson, Sept. 27, 1970 (div. June 1981); 1 child, Jeremy Marshall. BA in Secondary Edn., Am. U., 1976, BA in Performing Arts, 1976. Cert. med. staff coord. Employment interviewer Scripps Meml. Hosp., La Jolla, Calif., 1977-81; office mgr. Jacksina & Freedman Press Office, N.Y.C., 1982-83; staffing coord., med. staff asst. Am. Med. Internat. Clairemont Hosp., San Diego, 1983-85; adminstrv. asst. Am. Med. Internat. Valley Med. Ctr., El Cajon, Calif., 1985-88; med. staff coord. Sharp Meml. Hosp., San Diego, 1988-92; adminstrv. asst. Grossmont Hosp., La Mesa, Calif., 1992-93, coord. Sharp family practice residency program, 1993-94; ops. coord. Sharp Meml. Hosp. med. staff svcs., San Diego, 1994—; wardrobe mistress various community theatres, San Diego, 1978-79, actress, San Diego, 1979-81. Appeared N.Y.C. (N.Y.) Playreaders Group, 1981-83, N.J. Shakespeare Theatre, Madison, 1982, Good Humor Improv Co., N.Y.C., 1982-83; contbg. writer to Poetry Revival: An Anthology, 1994. Mem. NOW, 1995, World Wildlife Fedn., Calif., 1991, Greenpeace, Calif., 1991, Sierra Club, Calif., 1991, 92, Audubon Soc., Calif., 1991, 92, Internat. Wildlife Fedn., 1992, Smithsonian, 1993, 94. Included in Outstanding Young Women of Am., 1986. Mem. NAFE, AFTRA, Nat. Assn. Med. Staff Svcs., Calif. Assn. Med. Staff Svcs., San Diego Assn. Med. Staff, Nat. Assn. Health Care Quality, Assn. Family Practice Adminstrs. Democrat. Home: 7951 Beaver Lake Dr San Diego CA 92119-2610

THOMPSON, (GERRY) MAXINE LEAK, supply manager, inventory director; b. Brigham, Utah, Nov. 25, 1938; d. Gerald L. and Luetta Grace (Peterson) Leak; m. Gordon Wise Thompson, Sept. 27, 1957; children: Kellee, Kris, Kasey. A in Bus. Adminstrn., GTE, 1992, A in Mktg., 1992; BS in Bus. Adminstrn. and Mgmt., U. Phoenix, 1992. Cert. real estate agent, Utah. Plant clk. Contel, Tremonton, Utah, 1977-78, warehouse person, 1978-82, storekeeper, 1982-89, Utah state purchasing/supply agt., 1989-91; Utah state purchasing/supply agt. GTE, Tremonton, 1992—. Editor: T-P Times, 1970-74. Active LDS Primary Orgn., LDS Mutual Improvement Assn. Orgn., Thatcher-Penrose, Utah, 1960-80; exhibit chmn. Box Elder County Fair, 1969, 74. Recipient award LDS Ch., 1981. Home: 266 S Tremont Tremonton UT 84337-9201

THOMPSON, OLIVER MAURICE, protective services official; b. Mar. 20, 1942; married; 4 children. BS in Police Adminstrn., Calif. State U., L.A., 1970; MPA, U. So. Calif., 1973, PhD in Pub. Adminstrn., 1988. Cert. basic peace officer acad. instr.; cert. c.c. instr. Sgt. Riverside (Calif.) County Sheriff's Dept., 1972-73, lt. Indo Sta., 1973-75, lt. Banning Rehab. and Counseling Ctr., 1975-79, capt. Lake Elsinore Sta., 1980-86, chief dep. Riverside Sta. Ops., 1986-91, chief dep. Corrections divsn., 1991-92; asst. dir. adminstrn. of justice Riverside (Calif.) C.C., 1979-80; chief of police Inglewood (Calif.) Police Dept., 1992—; mem. adj. faculty Riverside C.C., 1971—, UCLA, Riverside campuses, 1979—, U. Redlands, Calif., 1979-81, 89—; supervisory staff person Basic Peace Officer Tng. Acad., 1973-74; instr. jail mgmt. Calif. Poly U., Pomona, Calif., 1984—; adj. faculty, lectr. Calif. State U., San Bernardino, 1988—; instr. pers. mgmt. and supervision August Vollmer U., Santa Ana, Calif., 1988—. Bd. dirs. Inglewood YMCA, Inglewood Drug/Violence Prevention Coalition; active NAACP, Coalition for Alternatives to Domestic Violence, Riverside County, Urban League, Vine Life Christian Fellowship, Riverside County Cmty. Action Agy., Riverside County Blue Ribbon Select Com., Bible Enrichment Fellowship, Boys & Girls Club of Inglewood. Mem. ASPA, Am. Soc. Criminology, Acad. Criminal Justice Scis., Assn. Criminal Justice Rsch., Calif. Assn. Adminstrn. Justice Educators, Calif. Peace Officer's Assn. (vice chmn. region 6 1988-90), Inland Empire Peace Officers Assn., L.A. County Police Chief's Assn., Nat. Orgn. Black Law Enforcement Execs. (v.p. region 6 1991-93, nat. v.p. 1994, nat. pres. 1995), Peace Officers Rsch. Assn. Calif., South Bay Police Chief's Assn. (chmn. 1995), So. Calif. Assn. Pub. Adminstr. Praetors, Riverside C. of C., Inglewood C. of C., Inglewood Kiwanis, Inglewood Mins. Assn., South Bay Criminal Justice Adminstrn. Assn. Office: Inglewood Police Dept One Manchester Blvd Inglewood CA 90301-1750*

THOMPSON, PAUL HAROLD, university president; b. Ogden, Utah, Nov. 28, 1938; s. Harold Merwin and Elda (Skeen) T.; m. Carolyn Lee Nelson, Mar. 9, 1961; children: Loralyn, Kristyn, Shannyn, Robbyn, Daylyn, Nathan. BS, U. Utah, 1964; MBA, Harvard U., 1966, D Bus. Adminstrn., 1969. Rsch. assoc. Harvard U., Cambridge, Mass., 1966-69; asst. prof. Harvard U., Cambridge, 1969-73; assoc. prof. bus. Brigham Young U., Provo, Utah, 1973-78, prof., 1978-84, asst. dean, 1978-81, dean, 1984-89, v.p., 1989-90; pres. Weber State U., Ogden, Utah, 1990—; cons. Goodyear, Hughes Aircraft, Portland GE, Esso Resources Ltd., GE. Co-author: Organization and People: Readings, Cases, and Exercises in Organizational Behavior, 1976, Novations: Strategies for Career Management, 1986; also articles. Named Outstanding Prof. of Yr., Brigham Young U., 1981; Baker scholar Harvard U., 1966. Mem. Am. Assn. State Colls. and Univs. (com. 1991—), Ogden C. of C. (exec. com. 1990—), Rotary (prograam com. Ogden 1991—, Harris fellow 1992—), Phi Beta Kappa. Office: Weber State U 3750 Harrison Blvd Ogden UT 84408-0001*

THOMPSON, PETER L. H., golf course architect; b. Modesto, Calif., Apr. 26, 1939. BS in East Asian Studies, U. Oreg., 1962, B in Landscape Architecture, 1971, M in Urban Planning, 1971; postgrad., U. Calif., Berkeley, 1975, Nat. U. Registered landscape arch., Calif., Oreg., Wash., Nev. With Oreg. Planning Commn., Lane County, 1965-70; commr. Oreg. Planning Commn., Eugene, 1981-83; sr. assoc. Ruff, Cameron, Lacoss, Eugene, Oreg., 1971-75; prin. Peter L. H. Thompson & Assocs., Eugene, 1975-82, John H. Midby & Assocs., Las Vegas, 1982-86, Thompson-Wihlborg, Ltd., Corte Madera, Calif., 1982-89, Thompson Planning Group, Ltd., San Raphael, Calif., 1989—; with Oreg. Planning Commn., commr., 1981-83, Novato, Calif. Planning Commn., commr. 1989-93, pres. 1989-93; spkr. Oreg. Home Builders Conf., 1980, Pacific Coast Builders Conf., 1984, Tacoma Country Club Pro-Pres. Tournament, 1991, Madrona Links Men's Golf Club, 1991, Twin Lakes Country Club Pro-Pres. Tournament, 1992, Golf Expo, Palm Springs, Calif., 1993, 95, Golf Expo, Nashville, 1993, Golf Expo, Monterey, Calif., 1994, others. Contbr. articles to mags. Mem. citizen's adv. bd. City of Eugene, Oreg., City of Las Vegas. Mem. USGA, Am. Soc. Landscape Archs., Am. Assn. Planners, Nat. Golf Found., Urban Land Inst., Rotary Internat. Office: Thompson Planning Gp Ltd 2175 Francisco Blvd E Ste A San Rafael CA 94901-5524

THOMPSON, RICHARD CRAIG, artist; b. McMinnville, Oreg., 1945. Student, Oreg. State U., 1963-64, U. N.Mex., 1967; BFA, MA in Painting, U. N.Mex., 1972. artist in residence U. Md., Balt., 1969, Living Arts Ctr., Corsicana, Tex., 1979, Roswell (N.Mex.) Mus. and Art Ctr., 1981, Gippsland Inst., Victoria and the Visual Arts Bd., Australia, 1982, Pacific N.W. Coll. Art, Portland, 1983. One-man shows include Whitney Mus., N.Y., 1975, 81, Monique Knowlton, N.Y., 1981, 82, 84, Spau Gallery, L.A., 1980-84, William Campbell Contemporary Art, Ft. Worth, 1986, 90, 93, Harris Gallery, Houston, 1985, 87, 90, 94, Art Base, Singapore, 1989, Robischon Gallery, Denver, 1991, others; exhibited in groups shows at Blue Star Art Space, San Antonio, 1988, Whitney Mus., N.Y., 1975, 81, Groninger (Netherlands) Mus., 1988, Robischon Gallery, 1990, Palm Desert Mus., Calif., 1990, Nat. Portrait Gallery, D.C., 1993, others; represented in permanent collections including Edunburg Mus. Modern Art, Scotland, Roswell (N.Mex.) Mus., Mus. Albuquerque, N.Mex., Modern Art Mus., Ft. Worth, Tex., Barrett Collection, Dallas, others. Recipient Alfred Morang award N.Mex. Bienniel, Mus. N.Mex., 1975, Mid-Am. Arts Alliance award-painting fellowship, 1986; individual fellow Nat. Endowment for the Arts, 1978; guest artist Printmaking, Anderson Ranch, Colo., 1994. Office: Robischon Gallery 1740 Wazee St Denver CO 80202-1232

THOMPSON, RICHARD DICKSON, lawyer; b. Lexington, Ky., Aug. 14, 1955; s. Lawrence Sidney and Algernon Smith (Dickson) T.; m. Bobbi Dale Magidoff, Aug. 3, 1980; children: Anne Katherine, Harrison Asher. AB, Harvard U., 1977; JD, Stanford U., 1980. Bar: Calif. 1980, U.S. Dist. Ct. (so. dist.) Calif. 1980. Assoc. Rosenfeld Meyer & Susman, Beverly Hills, Calif., 1980-83, Silverberg Rosen Leon & Behr, L.A., 1983-86; ptnr. Silverberg Rosen Leon & Behr, 1986-89; assoc., then ptnr. Silverberg Katz Thompson & Braun, L.A., 1989—. Bd. trustees L.A. Copyright Soc. Mem. Order of the Coif, Phi beta Kappa. Office: Bloom De Kom Hergott & Cook 150 S Rodeo Ste # 300 Beverly Hills CA 90212

THOMPSON, ROBERT CHARLES, lawyer; b. Council, Idaho, Apr. 20, 1942; s. Ernest Lavelle and Evangeline Montgomery (Carlson) T.; m. Marilyn Ann Wilcox, Jan. 17, 1960 (dec. Mar. 1962); m. Patricia Joan Price, June 1, 1963 (div. 1969); m. Jan Nesbitt, June 29, 1973; 1 child, Tanya. AB, Harvard U., 1963, LLB, 1967. Bar: Mass. 1967, Calif. 1983, U.S. Dist. Ct. (ea. dist.) Mass. 1975, U.S. Ct. Appeals (1st cir.) 1976, U.S. Ct. Appeals (9th cir.) 1984, U.S. Dist. Ct. (no. dist.) Calif. 1983. Assoc. Choate, Hall & Stewart, Boston, 1967-73; asst. regional counsel EPA, Boston, 1973-75, regional counsel, 1975-82, assoc. gen. counsel, 1979-82; regional counsel EPA, San Francisco, 1982-84; ptnr. Graham & James, San Francisco, 1984-91, LeBoeuf, Lamb, Greene & MacRae, San Francisco, 1992—. Contbr. articles to profl. jours. Bd. dirs. Peninsula Indsl. and Bus. Assn., Palo Alto, Calif., 1986—; chmn. Cambridge (Mass.) Conservation Commn., 1972-74; co-chmn. The Clift Confs. on Environ. Law, 1983-95. John Russell Shaw traveling fellow Harvard Coll., 1963-64; recipient Regional Adminstrs. Bronze medal EPA, 1976, 84. Mem. ABA (natural resources sect., com. on native Am. natural resources law, spl. com. on mktg.), Natural Resources Def. Coun., Sierra Club, Commonwealth Club, Phi Beta Kappa. Democrat. Episcopalian. Office: LeBoeuf Lamb Greene & MacRae One Embarcadero Ctr San Francisco CA 94111

THOMPSON, ROBERT RANDALL (ROBBY THOMPSON), professional baseball player; b. West Palm Beach, Fla., May 10, 1962. Student, Palm Beach Jr. Coll., Fla. State U. With San Francisco Giants, 1983—; mem. Nat. League All-Star Team, 1988, 93. Named Sporting News Rookie Player of Yr., 1986, Nat. League Leader in Triples, 1989, Nat. League Gold Glove 1993, Silver Slugger Team 1993; named to Sporting News All-Star Team, 1988, 93. Office: San Francisco Giants Candlestick Park San Francisco CA 94124*

THOMPSON, RONALD EDWARD, lawyer; b. Bremerton, Wash., May 24, 1931; s. Melville Herbert and Clara Mildred (Griggs) T.; m. Marilyn Christine Woods, Dec. 15, 1956; children—Donald Jeffery, Karen, Susan, Nancy, Sally, Claire. B.A., U. Wash., 1953, J.D., 1958. Bar: Wash. 1959. Asst. city atty. City of Tacoma, 1960-61; pres. firm Thompson, Krilich, LaPorte, Tucci & West, P.S., Tacoma, 1961—; judge pro tem Mcpl. Ct., City of Tacoma, Pierce County Dist., 1972—, Pierce County Superior Ct., 1972—. Chmn. housing and social welfare com. City of Tacoma, 1965-69; mem. Tacoma Bd. Adjustment, 1967-71, chmn., 1968; mem. Tacoma Com. Future Devel., 1961-64, Tacoma Planning Commn., 1971-72; bd. dirs., pres. Mcpl. League Tacoma; bd. dirs. Pres. Tacoma Rescue Mission, Tacoma Pierce County Cancer Soc., Tacoma-Pierce County Heart Assn., Tacoma-Pierce County Council for Arts, Econ. Devel. Council Puget Sound, Tacoma Youth Symphony, Kleiner Group Home, Tacoma Community Coll. Found., Pierce County Econ. Devel. Corp., Wash. Transp. Policy Inst.; Coalition to Keep Wash. Moving, precinct committeeman Republican party, 1969-73. Served with AUS, 1953-55; col. Res. Recipient Internat. Community Service award Optimist Club, 1970, Patriotism award Am. Fedn. Police, 1974, citation for community service HUD, 1974, Disting. Citizen award Mcpl. League Tacoma-Pierce County, 1985; named Lawyer of the Yr. Pierce County Legal Secs. Assn., 1992. Mem. Am. Arbitration Assn. (panel of arbitrators), ABA, Wash. State Bar Assn., Tacoma-Pierce County Bar Assn. (sec. 1964, pres. 1979, mem. cts. and judiciary com. 1981-82), Assn. Trial Lawyers Am., Wash. State Trial Lawyers Assn., Tacoma-Pierce County C. of C. (bd. dirs., exec. com., v.p., chmn.), Downtown Tacoma Assn. (com. chmn., bd. dirs. exec. com., chmn.), Phi Delta Phi, Sigma Nu. Roman Catholic. Clubs: Variety (Seattle); Lawn Tennis, Tacoma, Optimist (Tacoma, Internat. Pres. 1973-74). Home: 3101 E Bay Dr NW Gig Harbor WA 98335-7610 Office: 524 Tacoma Ave S Tacoma WA 98402-5416

THOMPSON, RONALD MACKINNON, family physician, artist, writer; b. N.Y.C., Oct. 19, 1916; s. George Harold and Pearl Anita (Hatfield) T.; m. Ethel Joyce Chastant, June 30, 1950; children: Phyllis Anita, Walter MacKinnon, Charles Chastant, Richard Douglas. BS, U. Chgo., 1947, MS, 1948, MD, 1949. Diplomate Am. Bd. Family Practice. Intern U. Mich., Ann Arbor, 1950-51; resident in psychiatry U. Tex., Galveston, 1951-52; pvt. practice, family and internal medicine South Dixie Med. Ctr., West Palm Beach, Fla., 1952-85; instr. Anatomy, U. Chgo., 1946-47, Pharmacology, 1948-49. Contbr. articles to profl. jours.; exhibited in 7 one-man shows (over 30 awards for painting in regional and nat. shows); represented in permanent collections at 5 mus. Mem. Civitan Club W. Palm Beach, Fla., 1951; former bd. dirs. Norton Gallery Mus. of Art, West Palm Beach. Mem. Fla. Nat. Guard, 1936-40; cadet Army Air Force, 1943-44. Over thirty awards for painting in juried regional and nat. shows. Fellow Am. Acad. Family Physicians; mem. AMA, Fla. Med. Assn., Fla. Acad. of Family Physicians, Palm Beach County Med. Soc., Nat. Watercolor Soc., Ariz. Watercolor Soc. Republican. Episcopalian. Home: 308 Leisure World Mesa AZ 85206-3142

THOMPSON, TERENCE WILLIAM, lawyer; b. Moberly, Mo., July 3, 1952; s. Donald Gene and Carolyn (Stringer) T.; m. Caryn Elizabeth Hildebrand, Aug. 30, 1975; children: Cory Elizabeth, Christopher William, Tyler Madison. BA in Govt. with honors and high distinction, U. Ariz., 1974; JD, Harvard U., 1977. Bar: Ariz. 1977, U.S. Dist. Ct. Ariz. 1977, U.S. Tax Ct. 1979. Assoc. Brown & Bain P.A., Phoenix, 1977-83, ptnr., 1983-92; ptnr. Gallagher and Kennedy, P.A., Phoenix, 1992—; legis. aide Rep. Richard Burgess, Ariz. Ho. of Reps., 1974; mem. bus. adv. bd. Citibank Ariz. (formerly Great Western Bank & Trust, Phoenix), 1985-86. Mem. staff Harvard Law Record, 1974-75; rsch. editor Harvard Internat. Law Jour. , 1976; contbr. articles to profl. jours. Mem. Phoenix Mayor's Youth Adv. Bd. 1968-70, Phoenix Internat.; active 20-30 Club, 1978-81, sec. 1978-80, Valley Leadership, Phoenix, 1983-84, citizens task force future financing needs City of Phoenix, 1985-86; exec. coun. Boys and Girls Clubs of Met. Phoenix, 1990—; bd. dirs. Phoenix Bach Choir, 1992-94; deacon Shepherd of Hills Congl. Ch., Phoenix, 1984-85; pres. Maricopa County Young Dems., 1982-83, Ariz. Young Dems., 1983-84, sec. 1981-82, v.p. 1982-83; exec. dir. Young Dems. Am., 1985, exec. com. 1983-85; others. Fellow Ariz. Bar Found.; mem. ABA, State Bar Ariz. (vice chmn. internat. law sect. 1978, sec. securities law sect. 1990-91, vice chmn. sect. 1991-92, chmn.-elect 1992-93, chmn. 1993-94, exec. coun. 1988—, sec. bus. law sect. 1992-93, vice chmn. 1993-94, chmn. 1994-95), Maricopa County Bar Assn., Nat. Assn. Bond Lawyers, Am. Acad. Hosp. Attys., Nat. Health Lawyers, Blue Key, Phi Beta Kappa, Phi Kappa Phi, Phi Eta Sigma. Home: 202 W Lawrence Rd Phoenix AZ 85013-1226 Office: Gallagher & Kennedy PA 2600 N Central Ave Phoenix AZ 85004-3050

THOMPSON, TINA LEWIS CHRYAR, publisher; b. Houston, Dec. 31, 1929; d. Joshua and Mary Christine (Brown) Thompson; m. Joseph Chryar, May 25, 1943; 1 child, Joseph Jr. Cosmetologist, Franklin Coll., Houston, 1950; student, Crenshaw Coll., L.A., 1961. Pubr., composer, author B.M.I., N.Y.C., 1964-74; pubr. ASCAP, N.Y.C., 1974-86, The Fox Agy., N.Y.C., 1986—, Tech. World, L.A., 1990—; v.p. music Asset Records, L.A., 1978—; music dir., v.p. Roach Records, L.A., 1968; music dir. Rendezvous Records, Hollywood, 1950; v.p. Assoc. Internat., L.A., 1973; bd. govs. ABI, Inc., 1994; pres. Cling Music Pub., Soprano Music; pub. processor music catalogs Broadcast Music Inc. Author: Soprano Poems, 1985; creator/designer Baby Napin brand form-fitting, no-leak, no pins baby diaper, 1967, Saver Belt, 1993; patentee/pub. Letter's Tech in Word, used by TV stas. to advertise, 1972. Recipient recognition award IBC, Cambridge, Eng., 1991, cert. of proclamation Internat. Woman of Yr., 1991-92, Merit award Pres. Ronald Reagan, 1986; named Most Admired Woman of Decade, ABI, 1993. Mem. AAUW, NARAS, NOW, ABI (bd. govs. 1994), Am. Soc. Authors and Composers, Nat. Mus. Pubs. Assn., Songwriters Guild Am. (Cert. of Ranks of Composers and Lyracists 1991), Am. Fedn. Label Co. Unions, Am. Theatre Assn. Broadcast Music Inc. (pres. Soprano Music Publ. 1968), Rec. Acad. Country Music Acad., Internat. Platform Assn., L.A. Women in Music. Home: PO Box 7731 Beverly Hills CA 90212-7731

THOMPSON, VIRGINIA LOU, agricultural products supplier and importer; b. Malcolm, Iowa, July 15, 1928; d. Isaac Cleveland and Viola (Montgomery) Griffin; m. Alfred Thompson, Mar. 1, 1946 (dec. March 1992); children: Michael Duane, Cathryn Lynn, Steven Curtis, Laura Lue; m. David Hartman Rud, Sept. 5, 1993. Student Phoenix Coll., 1962, Phoenix-Scottsdale Jr. Coll., 1973-74. With sales dept. Trend House, Phoenix, 1962-67; importer World Wide Imports, Ft. Collins, Colo., 1974-79; owner, mgr. Windsor Elevator Inc. (Colo.), 1979-89; participant in trade shows, seminars. Pres. Am. Luth. Ch. Women, 1973-74. Mem. Nat. Grain and Feed Assn., Colo. Grain and Feed Assn., Rocky Mountain Bean Dealers, Colo. Cattle Feeders Assn., Western U.S. Agrl. Assn., Rice Millers Assn. Democrat. Lutheran. Clubs: Christian Women (Greeley, Colo.); Order of Eastern Star (Iowa). Home: 3331 Riva Ridge Dr Fort Collins CO 80526-2887

THOMPSON, WILLIAM BENBOW, JR., obstetrician/gynecologist, educator; b. Detroit, July 26, 1923; s. William Benbow and Ruth Wood (Locke) T.; m. Constance Carter, July 30, 1947 (div. Feb. 1958); 1 child, William Benbow IV; m. Jane Gilliland, Mar. 12, 1958; children: Reese Ellison, Belinda Day. AB, U. So. Calif., 1947, MD, 1951. Diplomate Am. Bd. Ob-Gyn. Resident Gallinger Mun. Hosp., Washington, 1952-53; resident George Washington U. Hosp., Washington, 1953-55; asst. ob-gyn. La. State U., 1955-56; asst. clinical prof. UCLA, 1957-64; assoc. prof. U. Calif.-Irvine Sch. Med., Orange, Calif., 1964-92; dir. gynecology U. Calif.-Irvine Sch. Med., 1977-92; prof. emeritus U. Calif.-Irvine Sch. Med., Orange, 1993—; vice chmn. ob-gyn. U. Calif.-Irvine Sch. Med., 1978-89; assoc. dean U. Calif.-Irvine Coll. Med., Irvine, 1969-73. Inventor: Thompson Retractor, 1976; Thompson Manipulator, 1977. Bd. dirs. Monarch Bay Assn. Laguna Niguel, Calif. 1969-77, Monarch Summitt II A ssn. 1981-83. With U.S. Army, 1942-44, PTO. Fellow ACS, Am. Coll. Ob-Gyn. (life), L.A. Ob-Gyn. Soc. (life); mem. Orange County Gynecology and Obstetrics Soc. (hon.), Am. Soc. Law and Medicine, Capistrano Bay Yacht Club (commodore 1975), Internat. Order Blue Gavel. Office: UCI Med Ctr OB/GYN 101 City Blvd W Orange CA 92668-2901

THOMPSON-JURICH, SUSAN KAYE, therapist, addictions consultant; b. Pueblo, Colo., Feb. 20, 1953; d. Everett Frederick and Lila Lee (Faust) Thompson; m. Peter L. Jurich, Oct. 13, 1982 9div. Mar. 1985); children: Andrew Merek Starfinder, Michelle Sunshine Raven. BA in Sociology magna cum laude, Seattle Pacific U., 1989; MA in Ednl. Counseling, Seattle U., 1982-94; doct. student, U. Wash., 1994—. Founder, dir. Homeskills Workshop, Bellingham, Wash., 1976-85; owner, mgr. Harvest Yarns, Seattle, 1985-89; probation counselor King County Dist. Ct., Seattle, 1987-93; co-founder, co-dir., therapist N.W. Network for Christian Recovery, Lynnwood, Wash., 1989-93; co-dir. Sonora Ctr., Lynnwood, Wash., 1993—; cons. Shoreline Family Care, Seattle, 1989—, Bethesda House Shelter, Seattle, 1989-90; trainer King County Probation Dept., Seattle, 1991; dir. SMART, Seattle, 1989—. Author tng. manuals. Mem. AACD, Christian Assn. for Psychol. Studies, Am. Assn. for Christian Counselors, Nat. Assn. for Christian Recovery (N.W. regional rep. 1991—, co-chair N.W. Regional Conf., vice chair nat. bd.). Home: 3233 180th Pl SW Lynnwood WA 98037-3935 Office: Sonora Ctr 20016 Cedar Valley Rd Ste 104 Lynnwood WA 98036-6332

THOMS, BONNIE ANNE, elementary school educator; b. Vancouver, B.C., Can., Dec. 6, 1952; d. Arthur and Irna T. AA, Flathead Valley Community Coll, Kalispell, Mont., 1973; BS, Dickinson State U., 1975; MA, Lesley Coll., 1986; postgrad., Walden U., 1993—. Cert. phys. fitness specialist, helath promotion dir. Coach, instr. Bozeman (Mont.) Sch. Dist.; instr. health, phys. edn., driver's edn. Campbell County Sch. Dist., Gillette, Wyo.; tchr. gifted & talented Campbell County Sch. Dist., Gillette; active in TESA, Wellness, & Curriculum programs; cons. tech. & wellness. State and regional volleyball ofcl., 1986-94; local coord. United Blood Svc. Drive; bd. dirs. ARC, Am. Heart Assn. Recipient Wyo. Gov.'s Innovative grant 1991-92; nat. finalist Profl. Best 1990 Educator; named Young Educator of Yr., Jaycees, 1990. Mem. AAHPERD, NEA, AHA, ASA, Wyo. Edn. Assn., Nat. Coaches Assn., Campbell County Edn. Assn., NAESP, Epsilon Sigma Alpha, Alpha Sigma Alpha. Home: 916 Fairway Dr Gillette WY 82718-7608

THOMSON, GRACE MARIE, nurse, minister; b. Pecos, Tex., Mar. 30, 1932; d. William McKinley and Elzora (Wilson) Olliff; m. Radford Chaplin, Nov. 3, 1952; children: Deborah C., William Earnest. Assoc. Applied Sci., Odessa Coll., 1965; extension student U. Pa. Sch. Nursing, U. Calif., Irvine, Golden West Coll. RN, Calif., Okla., Ariz., Md., Tex. Dir. nursing Grays Nursing Home, Odessa, Tex., 1965; supr. nursing Med. Hill, Oakland, Calif.; charge nurse pediatrics Med. Ctr., Odessa; dir. nursing Elmwood Extended Care, Berkeley, Calif.; surg. nurse Childrens Hosp., Berkeley; med./surg. charge nurse Merritt Hosp., Oakland, Calif.; adminstr. Grace and Assocs.; advocate for emotionally abused children; active Watchtower and Bible Tract Soc.; evangelist for Jehovah's Witnesses, 1954—.

THOMSON, JOHN ANSEL ARMSTRONG, biochemist; b. Detroit, Nov. 23, 1911; s. John Russell and Florence (Antisdel) T.; m. June Anna Mae Hummel, June 24, 1938; children: Sheryll Linn, Patrisha Diane, Robert Royce. AA, Pasadena (Calif.) City Coll., 1935; AB cum laude, U. So. Calif., 1957; BGS (hon.), Calif. Poly. State U., 1961; MA, PhD, Columbia Pacific U., 1978, 79; DA, Internat. Inst. Advanced Studies, Clayton, Mo., 1979. Cert. secondary tchr., Calif. Chemist J.A. Thomson Bio-Organic Chemist, L.A., 1938, Vitamin Inst. (formerly J.A. Thomson Bio-Organic Chemist), L.A. and North Hollywood, Calif., 1939—; vocat. edn. instr. U.S. War Manpower Commn., 1943-44; chmn. activities coun. World Coun. of Youth, L.A., 1932; pres. Coun. of Young Men's Divs. Athletic Commns., YMCA Pasadena area, 1931, chmn. exec. coun., 1932; dist. officer Boy Scouts Am., San Fernando Valley coun., 1954-64, del. to nat. conf., 1959, and others. Author: (booklets) Whose Are the Myths?, 1949, Open Eyes, Illegalize Agency Abuses, 1968, Non-toxic Vitamins-hormones Answers to Environmental, Public Problems, 1972, Lobby Interest Goals to Sequester Nutrients Among Those Rarely Educated in Them, 1973, Support of Pressures to Homeostasis, Normality, 1990, Minimization of Toxics in Agriculture, 1991; contbr. articles to jours. Prog. leader United Meth. Men Quadrennial Conf., Lafayette, Ind., 1982, instr. United Methodist Ch. nat. seminar for profls., Nashville, Tenn., 1983, pres. United Meth. Men, 1979-80, mem. adminstv. bd., 1952—, chmn. commn. ch. and soc., 1986—, First United Meth. Ch., North Hollywood; mem. Rep. county ctrl. Com. L.A. County, 1941-50, chmn. 63d assembly dist., 1948-50, Rep. state ctrl. com., Calif. 1948-50. Recipient Sci. and Industry award San Francisco Internat. Expn., 1940, various scouting leadership awards Boy Scouts Am., Civic Svc. award State of Calif., 1949, others. Mem. AAAS (life), Am. Inst. Biol. Scis., Soc. Nutrition Edn., N.Y. Acad. Scis., Am. Horticultural Soc., Am. Chem. Soc. (So. Calif. sect.), Internat. Acad. Nutrition and Preventive Medicine, Western Gerontol. Assn., Am. Forestry Assn., Am. Assn. Nurserymen, Garden Writers Assn. Am., Profl. Grounds Mgmt. Soc., Soc. Am. Florists and Ornamental Horticulturists, Internat. Soc. Hort. Sci., Nat. Coun. Improved Health, Nat. Recreation and Parks Assn., Nat. Landscape Assn., Nat. Nutritional Foods Assn. (Pioneer Svc. award 1970), Nat. Health Fedn. (life), Nat. Assn. Mfrs., Nat. Resources Def. Coun., Nat. Lawn and Garden Distbrs. Assn., Universal City-North Hollywood C. of C., Sierra Club, Soc. Colonial Wars (life), Kiwanis (projects panelist internat. confs. 1987, 91), Friends of the Earth, Negative Population Growth, Amnesty Internat. Republican. Office: Vitamin Inst PO Box 230 5411 Satsuma Ave North Hollywood CA 91601-2838

THOMSON, JOHN RANKIN, city manager; b. Oakland, Calif., Nov. 1, 1935; s. John Stalker and Mary Josephine (Estes) T.; m. Loretta Earlene Edwards, Aug. 13, 1960 (div. June 1982); children: John Christopher, Deborah Ann. AB, San Diego State U., 1960, MPA, 1973. Budget analyst City of San Diego, 1960-62, adminstrv. analyst, 1962-64, asst. sanitation supt., 1964-67, asst. utilities supt., 1967-68; asst. city mgr. City of Chula Vista, Calif., 1968-70; city mgr. City of Chula Vista, 1970-75, City of Lawton, Okla., 1975-76, City of Medford, Oreg., 1976-87, City of Covina, Calif., 1987-94; bd. dirs. Covina Irrigating Co., 1990-92; city clk. City of Covina, 1990-92, redevel. exec. dir., 1987-94; redevel. exec. dir. City of Chula Vista, 1973-75; grad. instr. San Diego State U., 1973-74, U. Nev., Las Vegas, 1995. Author: manual Municipal Budgeting for Smaller Cities, 1973. With USMC, 1954-56. Recipient ASPA Community Svc. award, 1976. Mem. Internat. City Mgmt. Assn., MENSA. Democrat. Roman Catholic. Home: 8253 Bermuda Beach Dr Las Vegas NV 89128-7441

THOMSON, THYRA GODFREY, former state official; b. Florence, Colo., July 30, 1916; d. John and Rosalie (Altman) Godfrey; m. Keith Thomson, Aug. 6, 1939 (dec. Dec. 1960); children—William John, Bruce Godfrey, Keith Coffey. B.A. cum laude, U. Wyo., 1939. With dept. agronomy and agrl. econs. U. Wyo., 1938-39; writer weekly column Watching Washington pub. in 14 papers, Wyo., 1955-60; planning chmn. Nat. Fedn. Republican Women, Washington, 1961; sec. state Wyo. Cheyenne, 1962-86; mem. Marshall Scholarships Com. for Pacific region, 1964-68; del. 72d Wilton Park Conf., Eng., 1965; mem. youth commn. UNESCO, 1970-71, Allied Health Professions Council HEW, 1971-72; del. U.S.-Republic of China Trade Conf., Taipei, Taiwan, 1983; mem. lt. gov.'s trade and fact-finding mission to Saudi Arabia, Jordan, and Egypt, 1985. Bd. dirs. Buffalo Bill Mus., Cody, Wyo., 1987—; adv. bd. Coll. Arts and Scis., U. Wyo., 1989, Cheyenne Symphony Orch. Found., 1990—. Recipient Disting. Alumni award U. Wyo., 1969, Disting. U. Wyo. Arts and Scis. Alumna award, 1987; named Internat. Woman of Distinction, Alpha Delta Kappa; recipient citation Omicron Delta Epsilon, 1965, citation Beta Gamma Sigma, 1968, citation Delta Kappa Gamma, 1973, citation Wyo. Commn. Women, 1986. Mem. N.Am. Securities Adminstrs. (pres. 1973-74), Nat. Assn. Secs. of State, Council State Govts. (chmn. natural resources com. Western states 1966-68), Nat. Conf. Lt. Govs. (exec. com. 1976-79). Home: 3102 Sunrise Rd Cheyenne WY 82001-6136

THOR, LINDA MARIA, college president; b. L.A., Feb. 21, 1950; d. Karl Gustav and Mildred Dorrine (Hofius) T.; m. Robert Paul Huntsinger, Nov. 22, 1974; children: Erik, Marie. BA, Pepperdine U., 1971, EdD, 1986; MPA, Calif. State U., Los Angeles, 1980. Dir. pub. info. Pepperdine U., Los Angeles, 1971-73; pub. info. officer L.A. C.C. Dist., 1974-75, dir. comm., 1975-81, dir. edn. svcs., 1981-82, dir. high tech., 1982-83, sr. dir. occupl. and tech. edn., 1983-86; pres. West Los Angeles Coll., Culver City, Calif., 1986-90, Rio Salado C.C., Phoenix, 1990—; bd. dirs. Coun. for Adult and Experiential Learning, 1990—, Tech. Exch. Ctr., 1986—, Greater Phoenix Econ. Coun., 1994—. Editor: Curriculum Design and Development for Effective Learning, 1973; author: (with others) Effective Media Relations, 1982, Performance Contracting, 1987; contbr. articles to profl. jours. Active Am. Assn. Cmty. Coll. Commn. Acad. and Student Devel., 1995—, Publs./Pub. Rels. Commn., 1993—, Continuous Quality Improvement Network for Cmty. Colls., 1991—, Am. Coun. Edn. Commn. on Leadership Devel., 1995—; mem. Ariz. Gov.'s Adv. Coun. on Quality, 1992; pres. Ariz. Cmty. Coll. Pres.'s Coun., 1995—. Recipient Delores award Pepperdine U., 1986, Alumni Medal of Honor, 1987, Outstanding Achievement award Women's Bus. Network, 1989; named Woman of the Yr., Culver City Bus. and Profl. Women, 1988. Office: 640 N 1st Ave Phoenix AZ 85003-1515

THOR, PAUL VIETS, software engineer, consultant, educator; b. Schenectady, N.Y., Mar. 10, 1946; s. Donald D. and Eleanor B. (Viets) T.; m. Barbara K. Nelson, Mar. 27, 1982 (div. Dec. 1993). BSME, U. Denver, 1968; MS in Engring. Mgmt., UCLA, 1976; MS in Computer Sci., George Mason U., 1993. Engr. Martin Marietta Corp., Denver, 1968-69; commd. 2d lt. USAF, 1969, advanced through grades to maj., 1982; pilot trainee USAF-Williams AFB, Phoenix, Ariz., 1970-71; pilot C141A 15 MAS-Norton AFB, San Bernardino, Calif., 1971-75, pilot C141B, 1981-84; communications and computer officer 2044 CG-Pentagon, Washington, 1977-81; air field mgr. 18TFW-Kadena AB, Okinawa, Japan, 1984-86; pilot C12 1402 MAS-Andrews AFB, Washington, 1986-87; communications and computer officer 7 Communications Group-Pentagon, Washington, 1987-89; cons. George Mason U., Fairfax, Va., 1990-93; ind. cons. Colorado Springs, Colo., 1993—; wing flight examiner 63 MAW-Norton AFB, San Bernardino, 1981-84; acquisitions officer 7th Communications Group-Pentagon, 1987-89; adj. assoc. prof. computer sci. Colo. Tech. U., Colorado Springs, 1993—. Mem. Computer Soc. of IEEE, Assn. Computer Machinery, Air Force Assn. (life), Ret. Officers Assn. Home and Office: 5330 Slickrock Dr Colorado Springs CO 80918-7646

THORDARSON, WILLIAM, retired hydrogeologist, volunteer; b. N.Y.C., Mar. 14, 1929; s. William and Lillian (Hirsch) T. BA, Columbia U., 1950; postgrad., U. Kans., Lawrence, 1953-55; MA, U. Colo., 1987. Hydrogeologist U.S. Geol. Survey, Denver, 1955-94, vol., 1994—. Author: Perched Groundwater, Nevada, 1965, Hydrogeology of Test Wells, 1975, Hydrogeology of South-Central Great Basin, 1983, Hydrogeologic Monitoring, Nevada, 1985, Hydrogeology of Anhydrite, 1989. Served with U.S. Army, 1950-52. Mem. Geol. Soc. Am., Am. Assn. Petroleum Geologists, Am. Geophys. Union, Am. Inst. Profl. Geologists (cert.), Am. Inst. Hydrology (cert.), Assn. Engring. Geologists, Geol. Soc. Wash., Am. Geol. Inst., Nat. Geographic Soc., Am. Mus. Nat. History, Denver Mus. Nat. History, others.

THOREN-PEDEN, DEBORAH SUZANNE, lawyer; b. Rockford, Ill., Mar. 28, 1958; d. Robert Roy and Marguerite Natalie (Geoghegan) Thoren; m. Steven E. Peden, Aug. 10, 1985. BA in Philosophy, Polit. Sci./Psychology, U. Mich., 1978; JD, U. So. Calif., 1982. Bar: Calif. 1982. Assoc. Bushkin, Gaines & Gaims, L.A., 1982-84, Rutan & Tucker, Costa Mesa, Calif., 1984-86; counsel First Interstate Bancorp, L.A., 1986—; lectr. on Bank Secrecy Act and Ethics. Supervising editor U. So. Calif. Entertainment Law Jour., 1982-83, Entertainment Publishing and the Arts Handbook, 1983-84. Mem. ABA (retail investment task force, regulatory compliance com.), Calif. Bankers Assn. (regulatory compliance com., co-chair regulatory compliance conf., ex-officio mem state govt. rels. com.). Office: First Interstate Bancorp 633 W 5th St # T7 10 Los Angeles CA 90071-2005

THORN, NORMAN ROBERT, software development company executive; b. Buffalo, Apr. 14, 1950; s. Norman Henry and Athalee Nadine (Stinde) T. BS in Bus. Mgmt., Calif. Poly. U., 1976. Mgr. Xanax Industries, Chino, Calif., 1974-77, Nat. Semiconductor Corp., Sunnyvale, Calif., 1977-81; cons. Boole & Babbage, Inc., Sunnyvale, 1981-86; pres. NOROC Tech., Brea, Calif., 1981—. Disaster vol. ARC, 1986—. Mem. Kiwanis Club of Brea (Kiwanian of Yr. 1993-94, pres.-elect 1994-95). Office: NOROC Tech 615 N Berry Ste C Brea CA 92621-3016

THORNDAL, JOHN LAFLEUR, lawyer; b. Ironwood, Mich., June 13, 1936; s. Herbert Ladegard and Lucille (LaFleur) T.; m. Loretta Ann Vendramin, June 8, 1968; children: Daniel Leyton, Debra Louise, Jason Andrew. BS, U. N.D., 1958; JD, U. Denver, 1965. Bar: Colo. 1965, U.S. Dist. Ct. Colo. 1966, Nev. 1967, U.S. Dist. Ct. Nev. 1967, U.S. Supreme Ct. 1971, U.S. Ct. Appeals (9th cir.) 1972. Law clerk Law Office Morton Galane, Las Vegas, 1965-67; asst. legal counsel Reynolds Elec. and Engring. Co., Inc., Las Vegas, 1967-69; asst. U.S. atty. U.S. Dept. Justice, Las Vegas, 1969-70; asst. pub. defender Clark County Pub. Defender, Las Vegas, 1970; ptnr. Austin & Thorndal, Las Vegas, 1970-72, Austin, Thorndal & Liles, Ltd., Las Vegas, 1972-75, Thorndal & Liles, Las Vegas, 1975-78, Thorndal, Backus, Maupin & Armstrong, Las Vegas, 1978-93, Thorndal, Backus, Armstrong & Balkenbush, Las Vegas, 1993—; spl. asst. U.S. atty. U.S. Dept. Justice, Las Vegas, 1978-79, contract atty., 1981-83; lawyer del. 9th Cir. Judicial Conf., Las Vegas, 1984-87, chmn., lawyer del., 1986-87; treas. Clark County Bar Assn., Las Vegas, 1972-74, v.p., 1974-75, pres., 1976. Note editor: Denver Law jour., 1964-65. Bd. trustees Cath. Community Svc. Nev., 1980-92, pres., 1985-87 (Community Individual Svc. award 1991). Lt. Col. USAF Res., 1958-62. Mem. Am. Bd. Trial Advocates (assoc.), Nev. Am. Inns of Ct. (master). Roman Catholic. Office: Thorndal Backus Armstrong & Balkenbush 1100 Bridger Ave Las Vegas NV 89101-5315

THORNE, BARRIE, sociologist, educator; b. Logan, Utah, May 22, 1942; d. David Wynne and Alison (Comish) T.; m. Peter Lyman, Nov. 17, 1970; children: Andrew L. Thorne-Lyman, Abigail L. Thorne-Lyman. BA in Anthropology, Stanford U., 1964; MA in Sociology, Brandeis U., 1967, PhD in Sociology, 1971. From asst. prof. to prof. sociology Mich. State U., East Lansing, 1971-87; Streisand prof. sociology and gender studies U. So. Calif., L.A., 1987-95; prof. sociology and women's studies U. Calif., Berkeley, 1995—; cons. AAUW, Washington, 1993—. Author: Gender Play: Girls and Boys in School, 1993; co-editor: Language, Gender and Society, 1983, Rethinking the Family, 1992; mem. editl. bd. Signs: Jour. of Women in Culture and Soc., 1983—; assoc. editor Contemporary Sociology, 1994—; contbg. editor Theory and Society, 1990—; contbr. articles to profl. publs. Recipient Rsch. Network on Mid. Childhood award MacArthur Found., 1994—. Mem. NOW, Am. Sociol. Assn. (v.p. 1993-94), Soc. for Study of Social Problems (bd. dirs. 1987-90), Sociologists for Women in Soc. (chair social issues 1973-76, Outstanding Mentor 1993), Nat. Women's Studies Assn., Internat. Sociol. Assn., Sociol. Rsch. Assn., Women's Internat. League for Peace and Freedom. Democrat. Office: U Calif Dept Sociology Berkeley CA 94720

THORNE, KATE RULAND, writer, publisher; b. Del Norte, Colo., Dec. 15, 1937; d. Joseph Lydian Norman and Avis Frances Kiemsteadt; m. Edwin G. Ruland, Aug. 20, 1960 (div. 1984); children: Gregory, Jeanie, Rebecca. BA, So. Meth. U., 1976. Speech pathologist Shady Brook Sch., Dallas, 1960-61, Hillside Rehab., Grand Junction, Colo., 1962-72; pub. Thorne Enterprises Pub. Inc., Sedona, Ariz., 1989—; editor, pub. Thorne/Swiftwind Pub., Sedona, 1993—; lectr. in field. Author: (books) Lion of Redstone, 1980, Experience Sedona: Legends and Legacies, 1990; (screenplay) Blood Oath; author, editor: Experience Jerome and the Verde Valley: Legends and Legacies, 1992, The Yavapai: People of the Red Rocks, 1993; editor, columnist Sedona Mag., 1986-87; columnist Art Talk, Directions Mag.; contbr. numerous articles to mags. and newspapers; 1st woman editor Sedona Red Rock News, 1987-88. Founder, pres., Ariz. Indian Living Treasures, 1990-91; founding mem., sec. Western Am. Week, 1990-94. Mem. Ariz. Small Pub. Assn. (founding mem.), Sedona Hist. Soc. (pres.). Home and Office: 149 Gambel Ln Sedona AZ 86336-7119

THORNE, LINDA MARIE, elementary education educator; b. Watertown, S.D., Oct. 27, 1963; d. Charles Edward Thorne and Billie Joyce (White) Bymers. BS in Edn., No. State U., 1981; MA in Edn., Chadron State Coll., 1994. Grades K-3 rural sch. tchr. Haakon Sch. dist., Philip, S.D., 1985-86; grades 5-6 combination tchr. Henry (S.D.) Sch. Dist., 1986-87; 1st grade tchr. Edgemont (S.D.) Sch. Dist., 1987-89, Big Horn Sch. Dist. #1, Cowley, Wyo., 1989—; treas.-sec. U.S. #1 Tchrs. Orgn., Cowley, 1992-93. Outstanding Educator of the Yr. Lovell Area C. of C., 1994-95. Mem. NEA, S.D. Edn. Assn., Am. Sch. Counseling Assn., Am. Counseling Assn., Wyo. Counseling Assn., Delta Kappa Gamma Soc. Democrat. Methodist. Home: PO Box 173 Deaver WY 82421-0173 Office: Big Horn Sch Dist #1 PO Box 38 Cowley WY 82420-0038

THORNE, OAKLEIGH BLAKEMAN, publishing company executive; b. Santa Barbara, Calif., 1932. BA, Harvard U., 1954. With First Nat. City Bank N.Y., 1954-62; chmn., dir. Ct Corp. Systems; with Commerce Clearing House, Inc., Deerfield, Ill., 1959—; chmn., pres. legal info. Commerce Clearing House, Inc., Deerfield, 1975—. Office: Commerce Clearing House Inc 2700 Lake Cook Rd Deerfield IL 60015-3867 Office: CCH Computax Inc 21250 Hawthorne Blvd Torrance CA 90503-5506

THORNE, RICHARD PAGE, software engineer, consultant; b. Greeneville, Tenn., Dec. 13, 1957; s. Victor Page and Jeanne Rita (Parent) T.; m. Diane Patricia Henry, Feb. 26, 1987; children: Yllys, Nichoel. BSEE, La. Tech. U., 1985. Enlisted USAF, 1980; missile analyst, staff sgt. USAF, Barksdale AFB, Okla., 1980-85; advanced through grades to capt. USAF, 1985; software engr. USAF, Tinker AFB, Okla., 1985-90; sr. data sys. engr. Lockheed Missiles & Space Co., Sunnyvale, Calif., 1990—, mem. software test working group, 1993—, mem. comm. mgmt. working group, 1994—. Inventor ednl. software MathQuiz. Mem. IEEE, Tau Beta Pi. Home: 427 Leigh Ave San Jose CA 95128-2325 Office: Lockheed Missles & Space Co 1111 Lockheed Way Sunnyvale CA 94089-1212

THORNSLEY, RANDALL G., management consultant; b. Cleve., Apr. 20, 1954; s. Ronald N. and Evelyn Jean (Adams) T.; divorced; children: Calista Marie, Adam Garrett. Owner Capri-Consol. Industries, Anchorage, Alaska, 1974-87; CEO Silver Screen Mgmt. Corp., Anchorage, 1987—.

THORNTON, CAMERON MITCHELL, financial planner; b. L.A., Sept. 30, 1954; s. H. Walter and Naomi L. (Brown) T.; m. Jane Kubasak, June 18, 1978; children: Mitchell, Kathryn, Andrew. BA, U. So. Calif., L.A., 1976; MBA, U. La Verne, 1983. CFP. Planner Lockheed Calif. Co., Burbank, 1980-84; adv. assoc. Fin. Network Adv. Corp., Burbank, 1983—; fin. cons. Fin. Network Investment Corp., Burbank, 1983—; prin. Cameron Thornton Assocs., Burbank, 1982—; lic. charitable gift planner Renaissance Inc., 1992—. Author: (manual) Computer Aided Planning System, 1982-83. Mem., vice chair St. Joseph Med. Ctr. Found., 1988-92, chmn. planned giving dept., 1991-92; mem., chair Burbank Police Commn., 1981-85, Burbank Planning Commn., 1989-93; with ARC, Burbank, 1984-88, chmn. 1985-87. Lt. comdr. USN/USNR, 1976-88. Named Friend of Campfire, Camp Fire Coun., Pasadena, Calif., 1989, 92. Mem. Nat. Assn. Renaissance Advisors, Inst. CFP's, Internat. Assn. for Fin. Planning, Cert. Fin. Planner Bd. Standards, Burbank C. of C. Republican. Roman Catholic. Office: Cameron Thornton Assocs 290 E Verdugo Ave Ste 205 Burbank CA 91502-1342

THORNTON, IVAL CRANDALL, interior architect; b. American Falls, Idaho, Apr. 28, 1932; s. Crandall Dunn and Enid Rosalie (Walker) T.; m. Bonnie Jean Larson, June 10, 1951 (div. May 1961); children: Blake, Brek; m. Cheryl Lynn Bader, July 13, 1974; 1 child, Anne Bader. Student, Weber State Coll., 1956-58, Colo. Inst. Art, 1959-60, Art Ctr. Sch. of Design, L.A., 1963-64. Artist Richard Daly Art Studio, Salt Lake City; illustrator Victor Gruen & Assocs., L.A., Carlos Diniz Assocs., L.A.; sr. assoc. Arthur Gensler Assocs., San Francisco, 1972-75. Prin. works include Investment Mortgage Internat., San Francisco (design award 1984), Mountain Bell Tng. Ctr., Denver (design award), Denver Sporting House Interior (1st pl.), Caesar's Palace Forum Shops and Gateway, Internat. Cruise Ships and Corp. Aircraft Interiors, including SS U.S. Cruise Vessel, Elitch's Amusement Pk., Denver, Princess Cruises Grand Princess 97, Prince Fahd's Summer Palace interior, Saudi Arabia, Hall of Fame Colo. Inst. Art, 1995, painted murals in Salt Lake Temple, 1962. With USMC. Republican. Mem. LDS Ch.

THORNTON, J. DUKE, lawyer; b. Murray, Ky., July 11, 1944; s. Arthur Lee and Ruth Maxine (Billings) T.; m. Carol Caceres, Dec. 26, 1966 (dec.); children: Jennifer, Carey. BBA, U. N.Mex., Albuquerque, 1966, JD, 1969. Bar: N.Mex. 1969, U.S. Ct. Appeals (10th cir.) 1969, N.Y. 1985, U.S. Supreme Ct. 1992. With Butt, Thornton & Baehr, P.C., Albuquerque, 1971—; legal counsel N.Mex. Jaycees, 1972; clk. N.Mex. Supreme Ct., Santa Fe, 1969; mem. com. N.Mex. Uniform Jury Instructions, 1987-88. Author: Trial Handbook for New Mexico Lawyers, 1992. Bd. dirs. N.Mex. Bd. of Dentistry, Santa Fe, 1987-88; commr. N.Mex. Racing Commn., Albuquerque, 1988—. Mem. ABA, Assn. Coll. and Univ. Counsel, Internat. Assn. Ins. Counsel, Am. Bd. Trial Advs., Albuquerque Bar Assn. (bd. dirs. 1978-79), Nat. Collegiate Athletic Assn. (agt.). Office: Butt Thornton & Baehr PC 2500 Louisiana Blvd NE Albuquerque NM 87110-4319

THORNTON, JOHN S., IV, bishop. Bishop Diocese of Idaho, Boise, 1990—. Office: Diocese of Idaho Box 936 510 W Washington St Boise ID 83702-5953*

THORNTON, LAURIE ANNE, veterinarian; b. Kansas City, Mo., Sept. 20, 1962; d. William Clements and Marianne (MacMain) T.; m. Ernest Daniel Stefely, Oct. 28, 1989. BS, Coll. of William and Mary, 1984; DVM, Colo. State U., 1989. Assoc. veterinarian Hermosa Vet. Clinic, Denver, 1989-91, Deer Creek Animal Hosp., Littleton, Colo., 1991—. Mem. Am. Vet. Med. Assn., Colo. Vet. Med. Assn., Denver Area Vet. Med. Soc., Am. Animal Hosp. Assn. Home: 8010 Garrison Ct # A Arvada CO 80005-2264 Office: Deer Creek Animal Hosp 10148 W Chatfield Ave Littleton CO 80127-4225

THORP, EDWARD OAKLEY, investment management company executive; b. Chgo., Aug. 14, 1932; s. Oakley Glenn and Josephine (Gebert) T.; B.A. in Physics, UCLA, 1953, M.A., 1955, Ph.D. in Math., 1958; m. Vivian Sinetar, Jan. 28, 1956; children: Raun, Karen, Jeffrey. Instr., UCLA, 1956-59, C.L.E. Moore instr. MIT, Cambridge, Mass., 1959-61; asst. prof. N.Mex. State U., 1961-63, assoc. prof. math., 1963-65, U. Calif., Irvine, 1965-67, prof. math., 1967-82, adj. prof. fin., 1982-87; regents lectr. U. Calif., Irvine, 1992-93; vis. prof. UCLA, 1991; chmn. Oakley Sutton Mgmt. Corp., Newport Beach, Calif., 1972-91; mng. gen. ptnr. Princeton/Newport Ptnrs., Newport Beach, 1969-91, OSM Ptnrs., MIDAS Advisors, Newport Beach, 1986-89; gen. ptnr. Edward O. Thorp & Assocs., L.P., Newport Beach, 1989—; portfolio mgr., cons. Glenwood Investment Corp., Chgo., 1992-94; prin., cons. Grosvenor Capital Mgmt., Chgo., 1992-93; pres. Noesis Corp., 1994—. Grantee NSF, 1954-55, 62-64, Air Force Office Sci. Research, 1964-73. Fellow NSF, Inst. Math. Stats.; mem. Phi Beta Kappa, Sigma Xi. Author: Beat The Dealer: A Winning Strategy for the Game of Twenty-One, 1962, rev. edit., 1966, Elementary Probability, 1966, The Mathematics of Gambling 1984; co-author: Beat The Market, 1967; The Gambling Times Guide to Blackjack, 1984; columnist Gambling Times, 1979-84. Avocations: astronomy, distance running.

THORPE, CALVIN E., lawyer, legal educator, legal journalist; b. Springville, Utah, May 22, 1938; s. Ronald Eaton and Lillian (Thorn) T.; m. Patricia Warren, Feb. 2, 1961; children: Amber, Jill, Marc, Linda, Michael. BS in Physics, Brigham Young U., 1962; MS in Engring., U. Pa., 1963; JD, Seton Hall U., 1969. Bar: N.J. 1969, Tex. 1971, Utah, 1974, U.S. Dist. Ct. Utah 1974, U.S. Ct. Customs and Patent Appeals 1975, U.S. Ct. Appeals (10th cir.) 1980. Assoc. Law Offices Giles C. Clegg, Dallas, 1971-73; ptnr. Thorpe, North & Western, Sandy, Utah, 1973—; adj. prof. U. Utah, Salt Lake City, 1975—; lectr. Brigham Young U., Provo, 1983-88. Chmn., mem. Sandy City Planning Commn., 1975-84; mem. Sandy City Bd. Adjustment, 1980-81, Utah Citizen's Coun. on Alcoholic Beverage Control, 1991-93; chmn. Sandy Econ. Devel. Council, 1984-88; bd. dirs. Salt Lake City Metro Water Dist., 1990—. Editor-in-chief, Utah Bar Journal, 1987—. Mem. Am. Planning Assn. (Utah chpt., Citizen Planner award 1985), Utah C. of C. (Total Citizen award 1986), Sandy Area C. of C. (chmn. 1985), Am. intellectual Property Law Assn., Sigma Pi Sigma. Mormon. Office: Thorpe North & Western 9035 S 700 E Sandy UT 84070-2418

THORPE, GARY STEPHEN, chemistry educator; b. Los Angeles, Mar. 9, 1951; s. David Winston and Jeanette M. (Harris) T.; m. Patricia Marion Eison, Apr. 13, 1949; children: Kristin Anne, Erin Michelle. BS, U. Redlands, 1973; MS, Calif. State U., Northridge, 1975. Tchr. L.A. Schs., 1975-80, L.A. Community Colls., 1976-81, Beverly Hills (Calif.) High Sch., 1980—; instr. chemistry Coll of the Canyons, Santa Clarita, Calif., 1994—; gen. ptnr. High 5 AP Test Pres. Svc., Beverly Hills, Calif., 1994—. Author: AP Chemistry Study Guide, 1993. Res. police officer L.A. Police Dept., 1991. Recipient Commendation, L.A. County Bd. Supers., 1983, 84, Commendation Beverly Hills City Council, 1983, 84, Resolution of Commendation, State of Calif. Senate and Assembly, 1983, 84, Cert. Appreciation, L.A. County Bd. Edn., 1984-85, Cert. Appreciation, Gov. George Deukmejian, Sacramento, 1984-85. Mem. Am. Chem. Soc. (Selected as Outstanding Chemistry Tchr. of So. Calif. 1989, 92), NEA, Calif. Tchrs. Assn., Phi Delta Kappa. Republican. Lutheran. Lodge: Masons. Home: 6127 Balcom Ave Encino CA 91316-7207

THORPE, JAMES, humanities scholar; b. Aiken, S.C., Aug. 17, 1915; s. J. Ernest and Ruby (Holloway) T.; m. Elizabeth McLean Daniells, July 19, 1941; children: John D., Sally Jans-Thorpe. A.B., The Citadel, 1936, LL.D., 1971; M.A., U. N.C., 1937; Ph.D., Harvard U., 1941; Litt.D., Occidental Coll., 1968; L.H.D., Claremont Grad. Sch., 1968; H.H.D., U. Toledo, 1977. Instr. to prof. English Princeton, 1946-66; dir. Huntington Libr., Art Gallery and Bot. Gardens, San Marino, Calif., 1966-83; sr. research assoc. Huntington Libr., San Marino, Calif., 1966—. Author: Bibliography of the Writings of George Lyman Kittredge, 1948, Milton Criticism, 1950, Rochester's Poems on Several Occasions, 1950, Poems of Sir George Etherege, 1963, Aims and Methods of Scholarship, 1963, 70, Literary Scholarship, 1964, Relations of Literary Study, 1967, Bunyan's Grace Abounding and Pilgrim's Progress, 1969, Principles of Textual Criticism, 1972, 2d edit., 1979, Use of Manuscripts in Literary Research, 1974, 2d edit., 1979, Gifts of Genius, 1980, A Word to the Wise, 1982, John Milton: The Inner Life, 1983, The Sense of Style: Reading English Prose, 1987, Henry Edwards Huntington: A Biography, 1994. Served to col. USAAF, 1941-46. Decorated Bronze Star medal.; Guggenheim fellow, 1949-50, 65-66. Fellow Am. Acad. Arts and Scis., Am. Philos. Soc.; mem. MLA, Am. Antiquarian Soc., Soc. for Textual Scholarship. Democrat. Episcopalian. Clubs: Zamorano, Twilight. Home: 1199 Arden Rd Pasadena CA 91106-4143 Office: Huntington Libr San Marino CA 91108

THORPE, JAMES ALFRED, retired utilities executive; b. Fall River, Mass., Apr. 19, 1929; s. James and Charlotte Ann (Brearley) T.; m. Maxine Elva Thompson, Mar. 4, 1950; children: James Alfred, Peter R., David T., Carol L., Mark W. B.S., Northeastern U., 1951. Asst. supt. prodn. Fall River Gas Co., 1951-55; chief engr. Lake Shore Gas Co., Ashtabula, Ohio, 1955-57; cons. Stone & Webster Mgmt. Corp., 1958-67; pres. Wash. Natural Gas Co., Seattle, 1972; chmn., chief exec. officer Wash. Natural Gas Co., 1980-94; also chmn., chief exec. officer, dir. Wash. Energy Co.; dir. Sea First Corp. Bd. dirs. Salvation Army. Mem. Am. Gas Assn., Pacific Coast Gas Assn. (pres. 1977-78), Rainier Club (Seattle). Methodist. Home: 11160 SE 59th St Bellevue WA 98006-2606

THORPE, OTIS HENRY, professional basketball player; b. Boynton Beach, Fla., Aug. 5, 1962. Student, U. Providence. Basketball player

Kansas City Kings, 1984-85, Sacramento Kings (formerly Kansas City), 1985-88, Houston Rockets, 1988-94, Portland Trail Blazers, 1994—. Mem. NBA championship team 1994. Office: Portland Trail Blazers Port of Portland Bldg 700 NE Multnomah St Ste 600 Portland OR 97232

THORSEN, JAMES HUGH, aviation director, airport manager; b. Evanston, Ill., Feb. 5, 1943; s. Chester A. and Mary Jane (Currie) T.; m. Nancy Dain, May 30, 1980. BA, Ripon Coll., 1965. FAA cert. comml. pilot, flight instr. airplanes and instruments. Asst. dean of admissions Ripon (Wis.) Coll., 1965-69: adminstrv. asst. Greater Rockford (Ill.) Airport Authority, 1969-70; airport mgr. Bowman Field, Louisville, 1970-71; asst. dir. St. Louis Met. Airport Authority, 1971-80; dir. aviation, airport mgr. City of Idaho Falls (Idaho), 1980—. Named Hon. Citizen, State of Ill. Legislature, 1976, Ky. Col., Flying Col. Delta Airlines; recipient Contbns. to Aviation Safety award FAA, 1994. Mem. Am. Assn. Airport Execs. (accredited airport exec.), Idaho Airport Mgmt. Assn. (pres. 1991—), Internat. NW Aviation Council, Greater Idaho Falls C. of C. (bd. dir. 1986-89), Mensa, Quiet Birdmen Club, Sigma Alpha Epsilon. Home: 1270 1st St Idaho Falls ID 83401-4175 Office: Mcpl Airport Idaho Falls ID 83401

THREADGILL, MAE ELLEN, educational administrator; b. Stroud, Okla., Apr. 25, 1938; d. Edward Allen Cupp and Lucy Mae (Burns) Cupp Pickens; m. John Douglas Threadgill, Dec. 2, 1958 (div. 1969); children: Naudja Mijanou, John Arthur, John Allen. BA in Elem. Edn., San Francisco State U., 1961, MA in Elem. Sch. ADminstrn., 1966. Tchr. Redding Sch. and Twin Peaks Annex, San Francisco, 1961-66; community tchr. various schs., San Francisco, 1966-67; coord. San Francisco Unified Sch. Dist. Berkeley Program, 1967-68; asst. prin. various schs., San Francisco, 1968-74; prin. Bret Harte Sch. and Fairmount Sch., San Francisco, 1974-84, El Dorado Sch., San Francisco, 1985—. Mem. exec. com. San Francisco chpt. Am. Heart Assn., 1991-92, bd. dirs., 1990-92, chmn. Heart in Black Comty., 1990-94; participant Coro Found. City Focus Leadership Tng. program, 1992-93. Recipient Educator award Top Ladies of Distinction, San Francisco, 1991, Outstanding Svc. award Am. Heart Assn., 1992. Mem. United Adminstrs. San Francisco, Delta Sigma Theta. Democrat. African Methodist Episcopal. Office: El Dorado Elem Sch 70 Delta St San Francisco CA 94134-2145

THRELKELD, STEVEN WAYNE, transportation/civil engineer; b. La Jolla, Calif., Feb. 22, 1956; s. Willard Wayne and Sylvia Eileen (Daugherety) T.; m. Sheree Leslie Chabot, Nov. 17, 1984; children: Tristan David, Kayla Lee. BS in Geol. Scis., San Diego State U., 1985. Geophys. trainee Western Geophys., Bakersfield, Calif., 1985; civil engr. Dee Jaspar & Assocs., Bakersfield, 1986, Bement, Dainwood & Sturgeon, Lemon Grove, Calif., 1987, Calif. Dept. Transp., San Diego, 1988—; comml. scuba diver, San Diego, 1987-88. Photo editor Montezuma Life Mag., San Diego, 1981; portrait photographer Coast Prodns., San Diego, 1975. Mem. ASCE Transp. Study Group, Profl. Engrs. in Calif. Govt. (San Diego chpt.), Common Cause, nat. Parks and Conservation Assn., World Wildlife Fund, CARE. Home: 4262 Bancroft Dr La Mesa CA 91941-6744

THREN, ROBERT, science executive; b. 1946. MA, Calif. State U., Northridge, 1976. With L.A. Unified Sch. Dist., 1968-76; audit mgr. Arthur Anderson & Co., L.A., 1976-83; CFO Bell Enterprises, Rancho Santa Fe, Calif., 1983-88; v.p. fin. Twyford Internat., Inc., Santa Paula, Calif., 1988—. Office: Twyford Internat Inc 15245 W Telegraph Rd Santa Paula CA 93060-3039*

THRO, BROYDRICK (ELAINE THRO), educator; b. Boston, Feb. 19, 1945; d. Fredrick and Mary Frances (Goggin) Broydrick; m. A. Brooker Thro, June 19, 1965. Student, Conn. Coll., 1963-65; BA, U. Calif., Berkeley, 1969; MA, UCLA, 1970, PhD, 1990. Tchg. asst. dept. philosophy UCLA, 1974-77, tchg. assoc. dept. philosophy, 1977-80; vis. scholar dept. psychology Ctr. Human Info. Processing U. Calif. San Diego, La Jolla, 1991-92, 92-93; rsch. scholar Ctr. for Medieval and Renaissance Studies, UCLA, 1994—; assoc. Behavioral and Brain Scis.: An Internat. Jour. Current Rsch. and Theory, Princeton, N.J., 1987—. Contbr. articles to profl. jours. Mem. Am. Philos. Assn. Home: 4771A La Villa Marina Marina Del Rey CA 90292

THROCKMORTON, REX DENTON, lawyer; b. Lima, Ohio, June 4, 1941; s. Francis and Jane (Corwin) T.; m. Barbara Catherine Poore, July 21, 1962; children: Scott, John. BS, Denison U., 1963; JD, Ohio State U., 1965. Bar: Ohio 1966, N. Mex. 1971, U.S. Dist. Ct. N. Mex. 1971, U.S. Ct. Appeals (10th cir.) 1973. Assoc. Squire, Sanders & Dempsey, Cleve., 1965-66; shareholder, bd. dirs. Rodey, Dickason, Sloan, Akin & Robb, P.A., Albuquerque, 1971—, chmn. comml. litigation dept., 1985–. Editor Ohio State Law Jour., 1965. Pres. Albuquerque Civic Light Opera Assn., 1985. Capt. JAGC, USAF, 1966-71. Mem. ABA, N.Mex. Bar Assn. (bd. of bar commrs. 1990—, sec.-treas. 1994, v.p. 1995). Republican. Home: 9109 Luna De Oro Rd NE Albuquerque NM 87111-1640 Office: Rodey Dickason Sloan Akin & Robb PO Box 1888 Albuquerque NM 87103-1888

THRONDSON, EDWARD WARNER, residential association administrator; b. Woodland, Calif., May 22, 1938; s. Edward J. and Arden Warner (Law) T.; m. Marjorie Jean Waite, June 25, 1960 (div. 1993); children: Mark Edward, Kimberly Anne, Sulin Marget; m. Mary Jo Riddell Law, Jan. 13, 1994. BS, Stanford U., 1960; MBA, Harvard U., 1962. Profl. Community Assn. Mgr., Community Assn. Inst. Asst. br. mgr. Pacific Delta Gas, Santa Rosa, Calif., 1962-65; corp. staff asst. Pacific Delta Gas, San Jose, Calif., 1965-72; regional mgr. Pargas, San Jose, 1972-86; gen. mgr., COO The Villages Golf and Country Club, San Jose, 1986-93; sr. v.p. West Coast Community Assocs., Campbell, Calif., 1994—. Mem. Cmty. Assns. Inst. (com. chair 1991—, Pres.'s Appreciation award 1991), Calif. Assn. Cmty. Mgrs. (cert., founding mem., com. chair 1992—, author course 1992, 94). Office: West Coast Community Assocs 145 Dillon Ave Ste D Campbell CA 95008-3020

THUESON, DAVID OREL, pharmaceutical executive, researcher, educator, writer; b. Twin Falls, Idaho, May 9, 1947; s. Orel Grover and Shirley Jean (Archer) T.; m. Sherrie Linn Lowe, June 14, 1969; children: Sean, Kirsten, Eric, Ryan, Todd. BS, Brigham Young U., 1971; PhD, U. Utah, 1976. Postdoctoral fellow U. Tex. Med. Br., Galveston, 1976-77, asst. prof., 1977-82; sr. rsch. assoc. Parke-Davis Pharms., Ann Arbor, Mich., 1982-88; dir. pharmacology Immunetech Pharms., San Diego, 1988-90; dir. immunopharmacology Tanabe Rsch. Labs., San Diego, 1990-92; v.p. discovery Cosmederm Techs., San Diego, 1992—. Contbr. articles to profl. jours.; patentee in field. Scout leader Boy Scouts Am., Mich., Tex. and Calif., 1979—. NIH grantee, 1978-81. Mem. Am. Acad. Allergy and Clin. Immunology, Am. Assn. Immunologists, Am. Thoracic Soc. Republican. Mormon. Home: 12740 Boxwood Ct Poway CA 92064-2643 Office: Cosmederm Techs 3252 Holiday Ct Ste 226 San Diego CA 92037

THUMS, CHARLES WILLIAM, designer, consultant; b. Manitowoc, Wis., Sept. 5, 1945; s. Earl Oscar and Helen Margaret (Rusch) T. B. in Arch., Ariz. State U., 1972. Ptnr., Grafic, Tempe, Ariz., 1967-70; founder, prin. I-Squared Environ. Cons., Tempe, Ariz., 1970-78; designer and cons. design morphology, procedural programming and algorithms, 1978—. Author: (with Jonathan Craig Thums) Tempe's Grand Hotel, 1973, The Rossen House, 1975; (with Daniel Peter Aiello) Shelter and Culture, 1976; contbg. author: Tombstone Planning Guide, 5 vols., 1974. Office: PO Box 3126 Tempe AZ 85280-3126

THUNDER, SPENCER K, retired elementary school principal; b. Longview, Wash., Dec. 5, 1939; s. Maynard King and Aarah Avona (Hearn) T.; m. Joyce Marie Sjogren, June 22, 1959 (div. June 1972); children: Scott, Mark, Karen; m. Jeanine Louise Pratt. BA, Cen. Wash. U., 1962; MEd, U. Wash., 1975. Cert. elem. educator, prin., reality therapist. Tchr. jr. and sr. high Yakima (Wash.) Sch. Dist., 1962-66; tchr. elem. Olympia (Wash.) Sch. Dist., 1966-67; tchr. high sch. Edmonds (Wash.) Sch. Dist., 1967-71, program mgr., high sch. spl. edn., 1971-76; prin. Maplewood Handicapped Children's Ctr., Edmonds, 1976-87, Mountlake Terrace (Wash.) Elem. Sch., 1987—; adj. prof. Seattle Pacific U., 1991—; instr. Edmonds Community Coll., 1978-79; vis. faculty Cen. Wash. U., Ellensberg, 1976; instr. Olympia Vocat. Tech, 1966-67, Yakima Valley Coll., 1964-66. Author: (pamphlet) Work Evil in Schools, 1975; contbr. articles to profl. jours. Bd. dirs. Smithwright Estates Group Home, Edmonds, Wash., 1980-91. Sgt. Wash. Nat. Guard, 1955-63. Home: 708 Hoyt Ave Everett WA 98201-1320

THURBER, HOWARD L., management consultant, writer; b. Pawtucket, R.I., Oct. 28, 1938; s. Howard L. Thurber and Mary E. (Flynn) Kemper; m. Jacquelyn Thurber, Feb. 18, 1970; 1 child, Anthony. Cert. purchasing mgr., NAPM. Prodn. control mgr. GenCable Corp., Westminster, Colo., 1973-74; mktg. analyst ITT Cannon Electric, Fountain Valley, Calif., 1965-70; sr. buyer Wilkerson Corp., Englewood, Colo., 1975-78; purchasing mgr. Amphemol-Cadre, Longmont, Colo., 1974-75, Storagetek, Louisville, Colo., 1978-91; commodity mgr. Storage Tech. Corp., Louisville, Colo., 1992-93; pres. TBS Consulting, Broomfield, Colo., 1994—; exec. com. Electrnics Group NAPM, Tempe, Ariz., 1990-93. With U.S. Army, 1961-63. Named Cert. Purchasing Mgr. Nat. Assn. Purchasing Mgmt., Tempe, Ariz., 1983. Mem. Nat. Assn. Purchasing Mgmt., Am. Mgmt. Assn., Inst. Mgmt. Consultants. Office: TBS Consulting 3961 W 134th Pl Ste B Broomfield CO 80020-5501

THURLOW, SCOTT A., computer company executive; b. Van Nuys, Calif., Feb. 21, 1966; s. Virgil S. and Joan K. (Kincheloe) T.; m. Carrie A. Gorringe, June 24, 1989. BSc Trinity Coll., U. Toronto, 1988; MBA, George Mason U., 1995. Programmer Va. Thoroughbred Assoc., Warrenton, 1985; dir. mktg. Unicus Corp., Toronto, Can., 1986-88; systems designer ICL, Dallas, 1988-93; programme mgr. Microsoft Corp., Redmond, Wash., 1993—. Contbr. article to jour. in field. Mem. Assoc. for Computing Machinery.

THURMOND, AMY SUZANNE, physician, radiologist, educator; b. Santa Monica, Calif., May 14, 1956; d. Robert Lee Thurmond and Nancy Lou (Reganall) Ross; m. Richard Michael Scanlan, Apr. 3, 1982; children: Charles, Meredith, William. BA, Wellesley Coll., 1978; MD, UCLA, 1982. Diplomate Am. Bd. Radiology. Intern gen. surgery Oreg. Health Scis. U., 1982; resident in radiology Oreg. Health Scis. U., Portland, 1984-87; rsch. asst. Wellesley (Mass.) Coll., 1975, U. Calif., Berkeley, 1977, Harvard U., Cambridge, Mass.; asst. prof. Oreg. Health Scis. U., Portland, 1988-90, assoc. prof., 1991—; cons. Conceptus, Inc., San Carlos, Calif., 1991—; lectr. Riverdale Elem. Sch., Portland, 1992, 93. Editor: Women's Imaging, 1995; contbr. articles to profl. jours.; patentee in field. Parent participant 4-H Club, Wilsonville, Oreg., 1994; basketball coach Lake Oswego, Oreg., 1994-95. Rsch. grantee Oreg. Health Scis. U., 1990; grantee Zimmerman Found., 1977. Mem. Soc. Uroradiology, Am. Coll. Radiology (expert panel on women's imaging 1993—), Radiol. Soc. N.Am. (reviewer 1990—, Editor's Distinction award 1991, 92, 93, Magna Cum Laude Sci. Exhibit com. award 1988), Am. Fertility Soc., Oreg. Med. Assn., Alpha Omega Alpha. Office: Oreg Health Scis U UHN-70 3181 SW Sam Jackson Park Rd Portland OR 97201-3011

THURSTON, JACQUELINE BEVERLY, art educator; b. Cin., Jan. 27, 1939; d. John O. and Frances Beverly Thurston; children: Mark, Beverly Thurston-Baller. BFA in Painting, Carnegie-Mellon U., 1961; MA in Painting, Stanford U., 1962. Prof. art San Jose (Calif.) State U., 1965—. Co-author: Optical Illusions, 1965; one woman shows include Susan Spiritus Gallery, 1995. Fellow Nat. Endowment for the Arts, 1976, 78. Office: San Jose State U Sch of Art and Design One Washington Sq San Jose CA 95112

THURSTON, WILLIAM RICHARDSON, oil and gas industry executive, geologist; b. New Haven, Sept. 20, 1920; s. Edward S. and Florence (Holbrooke) T.; m. Ruth A. Nelson, Apr. 30, 1944 (div. 1966); children: Karin R., Amy R., Ruth A.; m. Beatrice Furnas, Sept. 11, 1971; children: Mark P., Stephen P., Douglas P., Jennifer P. AB in Geol. Sci. with honors, Harvard U., 1942. Registered profl. engr., Colo. Field geologist Sun Oil Co., Corpus Christi, Tex., 1946-47; asst. to div. geologist Sun Oil Co., Dallas, 1947-50; chief geologist The Kimbark Co., Denver, 1952-59; head exploration dept. Kimbark Exploration Co., Denver, 1959-66; co-owner Kimbark Exploration Ltd., Denver, 1966-67, Kimbark Assocs., Denver, 1967-76, Hardscrabble Assocs., Denver, 1976-80; pres. Weaselskin Corp., Durango, Colo., 1980—. Bd. dirs. Denver Bot. Gardens, 1972—, Crow Canyon Ctr. for Archaeology, Cortez, Colo., 1980-92. Comdr. USNR, World War II, Korea. Decorated D.F.C. (with 3 stars). Mem. Am. Assn. Petroleum Geologists, Denver Assn. Petroleum Landmen, Rocky Mountain Assn. Petroleum Geologists, Four Corners Geol. Soc. Republican. Office: Weaselskin Corp 12995 Highway 550 Durango CO 81301-6674

THYDEN, JAMES ESKEL, professional society administrator, former diplomat, educator; b. L.A., Apr. 10, 1939; s. Eskel A. and Mildred Aileene (Rock) T.; m. Patricia Irene Kelsey, Dec. 15, 1959; children: Teresa Lynn, Janice Kay, James Blaine. BA in Biology, Pepperdine U., 1961; MA in Scandinavian Area Studies, U. Wash., 1992. Cert. secondary tchr., Calif., Wash. Tchr. Gompers Jr. High Sch., L.A., 1962-64; fgn. svc. officer U.S. Dept. State, Washington, 1964-90; rschr. U. Wash., Seattle, 1991-93; now exec. dir. Seattle chpt. UN Assn.; travel lectr. Cunard Lines, Royal Viking Sun, 1995. Editor govt. report, ann. human rights report, 1983-86; author, editor in-house govt. reports, documents. Dir. Office Human Rights, 1983-86; counselor Embassy for Polit. Affairs, Am. Embassy, Oslo, Norway, 1986-90. Named Outstanding Young Man Am., 1969, Alumnus of Yr., Pepperdine U., 1984. Mem. Am. Fgn. Svc. Assn., World Affairs Coun. Seattle. Home: 5631 153rd Pl SW Edmonds WA 98026-4239

THYGERSON, ALTON LUIE, health sciences educator; b. Pampa, Tex., Apr. 23, 1940; s. Luie S. and Callie N. (Spradlin) T.; m. Ardith Moss, Dec. 26, 1964; children: Scott, Michael, Steven, Whitney, Matthew, Justin. BrighamYoung U., 1962; M Health Edn., 1965, EdD, 1969. Tchr. Blackford High Sch., San Jose, Calif., 1963-65; instr. Chabot Coll., Hayward, Calif., 1965-67; prof. health scis. Brigham Young U., Provo, 1967—; cons. Wyo., Utah and Nebr. depts. edn., also Nat. Safety Coun., Chgo. Author 30 books on first aid, health and safety; contbr. 60 articles to Emergency: Jour. Emergency Svcs., also other jours.; contbr. more than 800 weekly newspaper columns; author, design Nat. Safety Coun. First Aid CPR tng. program. Recipient safety award Sta. KSL-AM-TV, 1972. Mem. AAHPERD (various offices), Presdl. Citation 1983, scholar award 1984, S.W. dist. Health Educator of Yr. award 1991), Am. Acad. Safety Edn. (various offices), Wilderness Med. Soc., Nat. Safety Coun., Phi Kappa Phi. Mem. LDS Ch. Home: 3300 Mohican Ln Provo UT 84604-4831 Office: Brigham Young U 229-J RB Provo UT 84602

TIANO, ANTHONY STEVEN, television producer, book publishing executive; b. Santa Fe, Mar. 27, 1941; s. Joseph A. and Marian (Adlesperger) T.; m. Kathleen O'Brien, Dec. 29, 1972; children: Mark A., A. Steven. BA, U. N.Mex., 1969, MA, 1971; LittD (hon.), Calif. Sch. Profl. Psychology, 1985. Dir. programming Sta. KNME-TV U. N.Mex., Albuquerque, 1968-72; sta. mgr. Sta. WHA-TV U. Wis., Madison, 1972-76; exec. dir. Sta. KETC-TV, St. Louis, 1976-78; pres., CEO KQED, Inc., San Francisco, 1978-93; chmn., CEO Santa Fe Ventures, Inc., San Francisco, 1993—. Vice-chair bd. dirs. Calif. Sch. Profl. Psychology, San Francisco, 1985-90. Mem. Nat. Assn. Pub. TV Stas. (vice chair bd. dirs. 1986). Office: Santa Fe Ventures 582 Market St Ste 1300 San Francisco CA 94104

TICE, ELIZABETH, counseling educator, corporate trainer, educational administrator, consultant; b. Logan, Utah, Sept. 11, 1957; d. Charles Delmer Jr. and Hazel Dianne (Coray) Tate; m. Jeffery Scott Tice, May 15, 1980; children: Emily L., Caleb J., Samantha D., Alexander C. BS in Recreation Mgmt., Brigham Young U., 1981, MEd in Edn. Psychology-Counseling, 1984; cert., S.W. Gestalt Ctr., 1994. Student svcs. counselor U. Phoenix, Salt Lake City, 1984-85, faculty mem., 1985—, dir. of assessment; corp. trainer, cons. Phoenix, 1987—; psychometric diagnostician Ednl. Support Sys., Salt Lake City, 1985-86; recruiter Ctr. Bilingual Studies, Cuernavaca, Mex., 1993—; curriculum developer. Editor: Golf Etiquette, 1994. Mem. ACA, ASTD, Friends of Jung.

TICE, ROBERT GALEN, paralegal, computer training consultant; b. Lincoln, Nebr., June 8, 1956; s. Wayne Kilmer and Jean Louise (Bell) T. Student, Tex. Christian U., 1976; BS in Fin., Samford U., 1978; MBA in Fin., Rockhurst Coll., 1984; Litigation Specialist with hons., U. So. Calif., 1994. Asst. debate coach Samford U., Birmingham, Ala., 1978-79; asst. mgr. Barclay's Am. Credit, Birmingham, 1978-82; credit analyst Home State Bank, Kansas City, Kans., 1982-83; asst. cashier, loan officer Landmark K.C.I. Bank, Kansas City, Mo., 1983-85; dir. bus. devel. Centerre Bank Northland, North Kansas City, Mo., 1985-87; loan brokerage and investment cons. The Provo Group, Kansas City, Mo., 1987-88; bus. banking officer Nev. Nat. BAnk, Las Vegas, 1987-88; pres. Fin. Services Co., Las Vegas, 1988—; v.p. sales Prime Merchant Svcs., Inc., Las Vegas, 1988-90; sales mgr. Sta. KJUL, Las Vegas, 1990—; bd. dirs. Indsl. Devel. Com., Platte County, Mo., Clay County Indsl. Devel. Com., Ambassadors Com.; v.p. sales Prime Mcht. Svcs., Inc., Genre Mag., Christopher Street West Gay Pride and Parade Program; adminstr. Centry Bus. Coll., 1992-93; JTPA adminstrs./instr. word processing. Mem. race rels. com., issue selection & edn. com. Kansas City (Mo.) Consensus, 1986, pub. improvements adv. com. City of Kansas City, 1986, issue selection com. and mail-in ballot task force; key gifts chmn. Boy Scouts of Am., Kansas City, 1985; Platte County chmn. ; media coord. Nat. Coming Out Day; bd. dirs. Citizens for Equal Justice & Gay Pride; Las Vegas coord. Human Rights Campaign Fund; active Shanti Found., L.A., Lesbian & Gay Acad. Union, Aid for AIDS of L.A., Las Vegas (Nev.) Met. Community Ch., The Experience; vol. publicity coord. AIDS Project L.A., 1993-94, Labor Day L.A., 1993. Mem. Suburban Bankers Assn. (bd. dirs. 1985-86), United Ostomy Assn. (bd. dirs. treas. 1984-86), Bus. and Profl. Assn. of Platte County (legis. action com., pub. rels. com. 1985-86), Gay and Lesbian Community Svcs. Ctr., Citizens Assn. of Kansas City, Greater Kansas City C. of C. (co-host Bus. After Hours 1985-86), Northland C. of C. (legis. com., Look North com. 1985-86), Rotary (Las Vegas chpt.). Presbyterian. Lodges: Rotary (local bd. dirs. 1986), Lions (bd. dirs. 1984-85). Home: 10456 Riverside Dr Toluca Lake CA 91602-2432

TICKELL, WILLIAM EARL, architect, educator; b. San Pedro, Calif., May 2, 1935; s. William Earl Sr. and Maybelle Annabelle (Lee) T.; m. Laurie Monroe, 1976 (div. 1988); m. Judith Allen, 1967 (div. 1969); children: Shawn Rice, William Earl III. BS in Archtl. Engring., Calif. Poly. U., 1964, BArch, 1969. Registered architect, Calif. Draftsman designer Charles Warren Callister, Tiburon, Calif., 1955-60; designer, planner B.A. Berkus, L.A., 1961-62; prin. William Earl Tickell Architect, San Luis Obispo, Calif., 1967—. Prin. works include Stuart Condominium, Signal Hill, Calif. (Design Excellence award 1974). Bd. dirs. Mission Coll. Preparatory Acad., San Luis Obispo, 1993-94. With USN, 1953-55. Home: 3233 Davis Canyon Rd San Luis Obispo CA 93405-8051

TIDWELL, ENID EUGENIE, sculptor, advocate; b. Farmington, N.Mex., Sept. 20, 1944; d. James Eugene and Eleanor Pynchon (Davenport) MacDonald; m. Thomas Russell Walker, May 12, 1963 (div. 1968); 1 child, Thomas Shawn; m. Roy Mc Tidwell, June 19, 1969; 1 child, Michael Eric. BA in English, Teaching cum laude, U. Ala., Huntsville, 1975. Sec. U. N.Mex., Albuquerque, 1964-66, Sandia Labs., Albuquerque, 1966-69; office mgr. Stanford Rsch. Inst., Kuwait, 1977-78; artist Calif., Va., 1978—; chmn., treas. Gallery House, Palo Alto, Calif., 1979-80. Exhibited in one person shows including Stanford U. Faculty Club, Palo Alto, Calif., 1979, Dominican Coll. Gallery, San Rafael, Calif., 1980; group shows include Quadrangle Devel. Corp., Washington, 1990, Artists Equity 3d Annual Memberhip Awards Exhibit, Washington, 1988, Allied Artists Am. 74th Annual Exhbn., N.Y.C., 1987, Hudson Valley '86, Poughkeepsie, N.Y., 1986, Washington Women's Art Ctr. Sculpture Show, 1982, 85, 86, Allied Artists Am. 71st Annual Exbn., N.Y.C., 1984, City Art 1981, Washington, 4th Annual Open Juried Non-Member Exbn. The Salmagundi Club, N.Y., 1981, Nat. Small Sculpture and Drawing Open Juried Competition Westwood Ctr. the Arts, L.A., 1981, numerous others; represented in permanent collections including Ingersoll & Block, Walker Wire, Centennial Devel. Corp., Signet Bank, Fisher Group, others. Mem. Fairfax County (Va.) Cultural Facility Task Force, 1989-90; treas. Bluffs of Wolftrap Homeowners Assn., Vienna, Va., 1985-88; pres. Monte Sano Homeowners Assn., Huntsville, Ala., 1975-76; bd. dirs. Monte Sano Elem. PTA, Huntsville, 1970-72; active PTA, Ala., Calif., Va., 1969-89, Boy Scouts Am., Ala., Va., 1971-89. Mem. AAUW (pres. McLean br. 1988-90, Ednl. Found. grantee 1986, 91, program v.p. N.Mex. chpt. 1994—), Allied Artists Am., Sigma Tau Delta. Home and Office: 5 E Sunflower Cir Santa Fe NM 87501-8523

TIDWELL, JOSEPH PAUL, JR., technical specialist research and engineering; b. Tuscaloosa, Ala., Oct. 29, 1943; s. Joseph Paul and Jeanette (Steinwinder) T.; m. Susan Kay White, Oct. 3, 1970; children: Joseph Paul III, James Boland, Heather Loran, Shawn Damon. A.S., NYU, 1978, BS, 1984; postgrad. Murray (Ky.) State U., 1984-85; MBA Embry Riddle Aero. U., 1991. Lic. pilot rotorcraft, cert. safety mgr., safety exec. Commd. aviation ops. officer U.S. Army, 1976, advanced through grades to maj., 1985; aviation safety officer Ft. Campbell, Ky., 1982-85, Chun Chon, Korea, 1981-82; chief aviation and product safety/flight safety parts programs McDonnell Douglas Helicopter, Co., Mesa, Ariz., 1985-89, dept. mgr., supplier evaluation and requirements Quality Control div., 1989-91, sr. systems safety engr. Advanced Devel. and Tech. div., 1991-93; rsch., engring. tech. specialist (aviation and product safety) advanced devel. and engring. divsn. McDonnell Douglas Corp., 1993—. Adj. instr. Embry Riddle Aero. Univ.; developer safety engring., safety cons., safety instr. Webelos den leader Clarksville council Cub Scouts Am., Tenn., 1983-85; asst. scout master Clarksville council Boy Scouts Am., 1983-85, scoutmaster Mesa council, 1985—; bd. dirs., vice-chairperson External Affairs S.W. Health and Safety Congress, 1985-86. Decorated Purple Heart, Meritorious Service medal, recipient Den Leaders Tng. Key Middle Tenn. council Boy Scouts Am., 1985, Woodbadge Beads Middle Tenn. Council Boy Scouts Am., 1985. Named Scoutmaster of Yr., Mesa Dist., Theodore Roosevelt Council Boy Scouts Am., 1986, award of merit Mesa Dist. 1988.. Mem. Am. Soc. Safety Engrs. (profl.; Safety Officer of Month award 1985, chmn. awards and elections Ariz. chpt. 1985-87), System Safety Soc. (leader Ariz. chpt.), Army Aviation Assn. Am. (air assault chpt. exec. treas. 1983-85, Aviation Safety Officer of Yr. award 1984), U.S. Army Warrant Officer's Assn. (Ky.-Tenn. chpt. pres. 1984-85, Disting. Service plaque 1984, Cert. of Merit for Disting. Achievement in Youth Leadership Devel. Men of Achievement, Cambridge, Eng., 1987. World Safety Orgn. (affiliate), Internat. Soc. Air Safety Investigators, S.W. Safety Congress and Exposition (bd. govs., conv. and advt. dir.), Aviation Edn. Coun. of Ariz. (bd. govs.), System Safety Soc. (organizer Ariz. chpt. 1993). Republican. Roman Catholic. Lodge: WIPALA WIKI, Order of Arrow. Avocations: golfing, camping, cycling. Home: 2338 W Lindner Ave Apt 10 Mesa AZ 85202-6430 Office: McDonnell Douglas Helicopter Co 5000 E Mcdowell Rd Mesa AZ 85215-9797

TIEKOTTER, KENNETH LOUIS, electron microscopist; b. Montgomery, Ala., Jan. 23, 1955; s. Kenneth Heil and Elaine June (Krause) T.; m. Kathryn Parks, July 29, 1978. BS, Portland State U., 1983. Cert. electron microscopy technologist. Histology technician U. Nebr. Sch. Dentistry, Lincoln, 1978-80; rsch. assoc. neurology rsch. VA Med. Ctr., Portland, Oreg., 1980-84; electron microscopy coord., dir. dept. ophthalmology Good Samaritan Hosp. and Med. Ctr., Portland, 1984—; adj. prof. U. Portland; electron microscopy cons. neurology rsch. VA Med. Ctr., Portland, 1984—, Portland State U., Pacific U., Forest Grove, 1992—. Contbr. articles to profl. jours. Recipient awards Polaroid Corp., 1984, 89, Nikon Corp., 1989, 90. Mem. Am. Soc. Parasitologists, Am. Microscopical Soc., Electron Microscopical Soc. Am., Helminthological Soc. Wash., B.C. Parasitologists, N.Y. Acad. Scis., Sigma Xi. Home: 2920 NE 25th Ave Portland OR 97212-3459 Office: Good Samaritan Hosp N320 1015 NW 22nd Ave Portland OR 97210-3025

TIEMAN, NANCY LEE, mental health counselor; b. Vancouver, B.C., Can., Mar. 5, 1952; came to U.S., 1986; d. Fredrick James and Janet Alma (Ormandy) Marshall; m. Michael L. Tieman, Jun. 16, 1972; children: Heather Anne, Katherine Jane. Diploma in dental hygiene, Ohio State U., 1973; BS in Psychology, Portland State U., 1990, MS in Counseling, 1994. Cert. counselor Nat. Bd. Cert. Counselors, Inc. Dental hygienist numerous dentists, Can. and Oreg., 1977-88, Oreg. State U. Dental Sch., Portland, 1988-93; counselor Good Samaritan Ministries, Beaverton, Oreg., 1993—. Mem. Save the Arts, Lake Oswego, Oreg., 1994-95. Mem. Am. Counseling Assn., Am. Mental Health Counseling Assn., Chi Sigma Iota (co-chair mentorship com. 1993). Office: Good Samaritan Ministries 7929 SW Cirrus Dr Beaverton OR 97005

TIEN, CHANG-LIN, chancellor; b. Wuhan, China, July 24, 1935; came to U.S., 1956, naturalized, 1969; s. Yun Chien and Yun Di (Lee) T.; m. Di-Hwa

Liu, July 25, 1959; children: Norman Chihnan, Phyllis Chihping, Christine Chihyih. BS, Nat. Taiwan U., 1955; MME, U. Louisville, 1957; MA, PhD, Princeton U., 1959. Acting asst. prof. dept. mech. engring. U. Calif., Berkeley, 1959-60, asst. prof., 1960-64, assoc. prof., 1964-68, prof., 1968-88, 90—, A. Martin Berlin prof., 1987-88, 90—, dept. chmn., 1974-81, also vice chancellor for research, 1983-85; exec. vice chancellor U. Calif., Irvine, 1988-90; chancellor U. Calif., Berkeley, 1990—; tech. cons. Lockheed Missiles and Space Co., GE; trustee Princeton (N.J.) U., 1991—; bd. dirs. Wells Fargo Bank. Contbr. articles to profl jours. Guggenheim fellow, 1965; recipient Heat Transfer Meml. award, 1974, Larson Meml. award, 1975. Fellow AAAS, ASME (hon., AIChE/ASME Max Jakob Meml. award 1981), AIAA (Thermophysics award 1977); mem. NAE. Office: U Calif Berkeley Chancellor's Office 200 Calif Hall 1500 Berkeley CA 94720-1500

TIEN, JONATHON, engineer; b. Henan, China, 1959; s. Yu-he T. and Hanzhan Liu; m. Diane Barrett, May, 1991; 1 child, Connor Gao-Wei. BS in Math., U. Sci. & Tech. China, 1982; MA in Math., Queens Coll. N.Y., 1986; MS in Computer Sci., CCNY, 1986; PhD in Applied Math., CUNY, 1991. Instr. math. Hunter Coll., N.Y.C., 1984-86; mem. tech. staff AT&T Bell Labs., Naperville, Ill., 1986-88; sr. software engr. WANG Labs., Inc., Lowell, Mass., 1988-91; staff engr. SpaceLabs Med. Inc., Redmond, Wash., 1991—. Office: P O Box 6037 Crossroad Sta Bellevue WA 98008-0037

TIETZ, WILLIAM JOHN, JR., research institute executive, university president emeritus; b. Chgo., Mar. 6, 1927; s. William John and Irma (Neuman) T.; children: Karyn Elizabeth, William John, Julia Wells. BA, Swarthmore Coll., 1950; MS, U. Wis., 1952; DVM, Colo. State U., 1957; PhD, Purdue U., 1961, DSc, 1982; fellow, Va. Poly. and State U., 1991. Rsch. assoc. Baxter Labs., Morton Grove, Ill., 1952-53; instr., then assoc. prof. Purdue U., 1957-64; faculty Colo. State U., 1964-77, prof., chmn. physiology and biophysics, 1967-70, v.p. student and univ. relations, 1970-71, dean Coll. Vet. Medicine and Biomed. Scis/, 1971-77, assoc. dir. Agrl. Expt. Sta., 1975-77; pres. Mont. State U., Bozeman, 1977-90; pres., COO Deaconess Rsch. Inst., Billings, Mont., 1992—; mem. Gov.'s Com. on Econ. Devel., 1984-87; mem. Mont. Sci. and Tech. Alliance, 1985-87; chmn. bd. Intermountain Community Learning and Info. Svc., 1987-89, N.W. Commn. of Schs. and Colls., Commn. on Colls., 1982-89. Bd. dirs. Children's House, Montessori Sch., 1966-70, chmn., 1968-70; bd. dirs. Colo. State U. Found., 1970-71, Colo. chpt. Am. Cancer Soc., 1976-79; mem. rsch. bd. Denver Zool. Soc., 1975-77; treas. Mont. Energy Rsch. and Devel. Inst., 1977-78, v.p. 1978-80, pres., 1981-83; bd. dirs. Greater Mont. Foun., 1979-91, 93—; mem. Mont. Com. for Humanities, 1980-83; mem. div. rsch. resources adv. coun. NIH, 1979-82; trustee Yellowstone Pk. Found., 1981-93, chmn., 1989-92. Recipient Svc. award Colo. Vet. Med. Assn., 1976; named Honor Alumnus Colo. State U., 1977, Coll. Vet. Medicine, 1979; recipient Blue and Gold award Mont. State U., 1993. Mem. Larimer County Vet. Med. Assn. (pres. 1968-69), Am. Assn. Vet. Physiologists and Pharmacologists (pres. 1971-72), Am. Physiol. Soc., Sigma Xi, Phi Zeta (sec.-treas. 1970-71), Assn. Am. Colls. Vet. Medicine (chmn. council of deans 1975-76), Phi Kappa Phi, Phi Sigma Kappa, Omicron Delta Kappa, Beta Beta Beta. Home and Office: 10030 Cottonwood Rd Bozeman MT 59715-8968

TIFFANY, SANDRA L., state legislator; b. Spokane, Wash., June 30, 1949; m. Ross M. Tonkens; 1 child, Courtney. Student, U. Calif. Mem. Nev. Assembly, 1993—. Mem. Nev. Rep. Women's Club, Green Valley Cmty. Assn. Home: 75 Quail Run Rd Henderson NV 89014-2151 Office: Nev Assembly State Capitol Carson City NV 89710

TIGER, PAUL, import-export company executive, consultant; b. Houston, Jan. 2, 1958; s. Paul McCollum and Judith Ellen (Sawyer) T.; m. Dorothy Patricia Moller, Apr. 11, 1982; children: Tara Louise. Student, Humboldt State U., 1978-81. Acct. mgr. Seapac Svcs., Oakland, Calif., 1982-83; sr. acct. exec. Hanjin Container Lines, Oakland, Calif., 1983-85; nat. acct. exec. CF Export Import, San Francisco, 1985-86; regional mgr. CF Ocean Svc., San Francisco, 1986-88; mgr. internat. sales Con-Way Western Express, Santa Fe Springs, Calif., 1988-90; regional sales mgr. Fritz Cos., San Francisco, 1990-92; owner, mng. gen. ptnr. Tara Imports, Vallejo, Calif., 1992—. Author: Introduction of Emu Leather as Exotic Leather to U.S. Markets, 1994. Mem. World Affairs Coun., San Francisco Ballet, San Francisco De Young Mus. Office: 636 Valle Vista Ave Vallejo CA 94590-3456

TILES, JAMES EDWARD, philosophy educator; b. Racine, Wis., Jan. 16, 1944; s. Paul Rudolph and Mary Lois (Millar) T.; m. Mary Elizabeth Tollyfield, June 5, 1969. B.A., Carleton Coll., 1966; B.A., Bristol U. (Eng.), 1968, M.Sc., 1970; D.Phil., Oxford U., 1978. Lectr. Reading U., Eng., 1974-89; prof. philosophy U. Hawaii, Manoa, 1989—. Author: Dewey, 1988, 2 other books; contbr. articles to profl. jours. Served with U.S. Army, 1969-71. Marshall scholar Marshall Aid Commemoration Commn., 1966. Home: 555 University Ave Apt 1100 Honolulu HI 96826-5025 Office: U Hawaii Dept Philosophy 2530 Dole St Honolulu HI 96822-2303

TILLERY, BILL W., physics educator; b. Muskogee, Okla., Sept. 15, 1938; s. William Earnest and Bessie C. (Smith) Freeman; m. Patricia Weeks Northrop, Aug. 1, 1981; 1 child, Elizabeth Fielding; children by previous marriage: Tonya Lynn, Lisa Gail. BS, Northeastern U., 1960; MA, U. No. Colo., 1965, EdD, 1967. Tchr. Guthrie Pub. Schs., Okla., 1960-62; tchr. Jefferson County schs., Colo., 1962-64; teaching asst. U. No. Colo., 1965-67; asst. prof. Fla. State U., 1967-69; assoc. prof. U. Wyo., 1969-73, dir. sci. and math. teaching ctr., 1969-73; assoc. prof. dept. physics Ariz. State U., Tempe, 1973-75, prof., 1976—; cons. in field. Author: (with Ploutz) Basic Physical Science, 1964; (with Sund and Trowbridge) Elementary Science Activities, 1967, Elementary Biological Science, 1970, Elementary Physical Science, 1970, Elementary Earth Science, 1970, Investigate and Discover, 1975; Space, Time, Energy and Matter: Activity Books, 1976; (with Bartholomew) Heath Earth Science, 1984; (with Bartholomew and Gary) Heath Earth Science Activities, 1984, 2d edit. 1987, Heath Earth Science Teacher Resource Book, 1987, Heath Earth Science Laboratory Activity, 1987, Physical Science, 1991, 2d edit. 1993, Physical Science Laboratory Manual, 1991, 2d edit. 1993, Physical Science Instructor's Manual, 1991, 2d edit. 1993, Physical Science Laboratory Manual Instructor's Manual, 1991, 2d edit. 1993, (with Grant) Physical Science Student Study Guide, 1991, 2d edit. (with Claassen) 1993, Introduction to Physics and Chemistry: Foundations of Physical Science, 1992, Laboratory Manual in Conceptual Physics, 1992, Physics, 1993, Chemistry, 1993, Astronomy, 1993, Earth Science, 1993; editor: Ariz. Sci. Tchrs. Jour., 1975-85, Ariz. Energy Edn., 1978-84. Fellow AAAS; mem. Nat. Sci. Tchrs. Assn., Ariz. Sci. Tchrs. Assn., Assn. Edn. of Tchrs. in Sci., Nat. Assn. Research in Sci. Teaching. Republican. Episcopalian. Home: 8986 S Forest Ave Tempe AZ 85284-3142 Office: Ariz State U Dept Physics Tempe AZ 85287-1504

TILLEY, DENNIS LANE, research engineer; b. Presque Isle, Maine, Aug. 27, 1964; s. Alva George and Bonita Beth (Boykin) T.; m. Danielle Renay Osier, July 28, 1990; 1 child Alexandra Elisabeth. BS, U. Wash., 1986, MS in Aeronautics and Astronautics, 1988; MS in Mech. and Aerospace Engring., Princeton U., 1991. Rsch. engr. Air Force Phillips Lab., Edwards AFB, Calif., 1991—. Contbr. articles to profl. jours. Recipient Rockwell Space Design award U. Wash., 1986; Guggenheim Merit scholar Princeton U., 1988. Mem. AIAA (electric propulsion tech. com. 1993—, Outstanding Tech. Paper award, 1993), Tau Beta Pi. Office: Phillips Lab OL-AC PL/RKCO 4 Draco Dr Edwards CA 93524

TILLMAN, HENRY BARRETT, author; b. Pendleton, Oreg., Dec. 24, 1948; s. John Henry and Beverly Jean (Barrett) T. BS in Journalism, U. Oreg., 1971. Freelance author Athena, Oreg., 1972-82, 1989—; pub. Champlin Mus. Press, Mesa, Ariz., 1982-86; mng. editor The Hook Mag., Bonita, Calif., 1986-89. Author: (nonfiction) Wildcat: F4F in WW II, 1983, reprint 1990, MiG Master, 1980, reprint 1990, (novel) Warriors, 1990, The Sixth Battle, 1992, Dauntless, 1992; co-author: (nonfiction) On Yankee Station, 1987. Pres. C. of C., Athena, 1976-77, Caledonian Games, Athena, 1978-79; commr. County Planning Commn., Umatilla County, Oreg., 1976-79; councilor City Coun., Athena, 1990, commr. police, parks, libr. Recipient Contbrs. award Am. Aviation Hist. Soc., L.A., 1978, Writing award USAF Hist. Found., Washington, 1981, Writing award N.Am. Oceanographic Soc., 1987, Writing award Naval Order of the U.S., 1993, Adm. Arthur Radford award, 1994. Mem. U.S. Naval Inst., NRA, Tailhook Assn. (all life). Republican. Baptist. Home: 3536 E Camino Cir Mesa AZ 85213-7033

TILLMAN, JOSEPH NATHANIEL, engineering executive; b. Augusta, Ga., Aug. 1, 1926; s. Leroy and Canarie (Kelly) T.; m. Alice Lavonia Walton, Sept. 5, 1950 (dec. 1983); children: Alice Lavonia, Robert Bertram; m. Areerat Usahaviriyakit, Nov. 24, 1986. BA magna cum laude, Paine Coll., 1948; MS, Northrop U., 1975, MBA, 1976; DBA, Nova U., 1989. Dir. Rockwell Internat., Anaheim, Calif., 1958-84; pres. Tillman Enterprises, Corona, Calif., 1985—; guest lectr. UCLA, 1980-85. Contbr. articles to profl. jours. Capt. USAF, 1948-57, Korea. Recipient Presdl. Citation Nat. Assn. for Equal Opportunity in Higher Edn., 1986. Mem. Acad. Mgmt. (chmn. 1985-86), Soc. Logistics Engrs. (pres. 1985-86), Paine Coll. Alumni Assn. (v.p. 1976—), NAACP (pres. 1984-88). Office: Tillman Enterprises 1550 Rimpau Ave Trlr 45 Corona CA 91719-3206

TILLMAN, PEGGY LOUISE (PEGGY LOUISE LARSON), human factors company executive; b. Baldwin, Wis., Nov. 1, 1943; d. Richard Louis and Dorothy (Baland) Larson; m. Barry William Tillman, Mar. 3, 1967. Student, Ch. Coll. Hawaii, Laie, 1962-63; BA in Psychology, Sonoma State Coll., Rohnert Park, Calif., 1967; std. Calif. teaching credential, San Jose State Coll., 1971. Photographer, lab. mgr. Sonoma State Coll., Rohnert Park, 1964-66; tchr. Union Sch. Dist., Los Gatos, Calif., 1967-79; pres. Tillman Ergonomics Co. Inc., Fox Island, Calif., 1983—. Author: Human Factors Essentials; co-author: Human Factors Design Handbook, 2nd edit.; contbg. author: (std.) Man-System Integration Standards (NASA-STD-3000); contbr. articles to profl. jours. Founder, dir. Synchronized Swimming Team, Wheeler AFB, Hawaii, 1961-62; developer Water Babies Swim Course, San Jose, Calif., 1968; founder Concerned Citizens, Cachagua, Calif., 1987-89; bd. dirs. Hist. Soc., Fox Island, Wash., 1992; mem. Pierce County Air Quality Bd., Tacoma, Wash., 1993; vol. tchr. Franke Tobey Jones Retirement Estates, Tacoma, 1994. Recipient Disting. Presentation Soc. Automotive Engrs., San Francisco, 1988. Mem. AIAA, Human Factors Soc. Home and Office: PO Box 165 Fox Island WA 98333

TILLQUIST, JOHN, information technology researcher; b. Denver, Oct. 4, 1958. BA in Psychology, U. Colo., 1983; MS in Info. and Computer Sci., U. Calif., Irvine, 1994, postgrad., 1994—. Staff specialist US West, Inc., Denver, 1980-87; tech. project leader Telic Corp., Chgo., 1987-88; sr. engr. GTE Data Svcs., Tampa, Fla., 1988-90; mng. editor Info. Sys. Rsch., Irvine, 1993—. U. Calif. Grad. Studies fellow, 1992-93; grantee NSF, 1994—. Mem. Assn. Computing Machinery, Acad Mgmt., Decision Scis. Inst., Inst. Mgmt. Sci., U. South Fla. Doctoral Fellows (officer, treas. 1991-92), Phi Kappa Phi.

TILSON THOMAS, MICHAEL, symphony conductor; b. L.A., 1944; s. Ted and Roberta T. Studies with, Ingolf Dahl, U. So. Calif., others; student conducting, Berkshire Music Festival, Tanglewood, Mass.; student conducting (Koussevitsky prize 1968); LL.D., Hamilton Coll.; L.H.D. (hon.), D'Youville Coll., 1976. Asst. condr. Boston Symphony Orch., 1969, assoc. condr., 1970-72, prin. guest condr., 1972-74; also Berkshire Music Festival, summer 1970, 74; music dir., condr. Buffalo Philharmonic Orch., 1971-79; music dir., prin. condr. Great Woods Ctr. for Performing Arts, 1985-88; prin. condr. London Symphony Orch., 1988—; artistic dir. New World Symphony, Fla., 1988—. Condr., dir., N.Y. Philharmonic Young People's Concerts, CBS-TV, 1971-77; vis. condr. numerous orchs., U.S., Europe, Japan; chief condr. Ojai Festival, 1967, dir., 1972-77; opera debut, Cin., 1975; condr.: Am. premiere Lulu (Alban Berg), Santa Fe Opera, summer 1979; prin. guest condr., L.A. Philharm., 1981-85, Am. premiere Desert Music (Steve Reich), 1984; prin. condr. Gershwin festival London Symphony Orch., Barbcan Ctr., 1987; composer: Grace (A Song for Leonard Bernstein), 1988, Street Song (for Empire Brass Quintet), 1988, From the Diary of Anne Frank (for orchestra and narrator Audrey Hepburn and New World Symphony), 1990; commd. by UNICEF for Concerts for Life's European premiere, 1991; recording artist Sony Classical/CBS Masterworks, 1973—; co-artistic dir. Pacific Music Festival, 1990—, with Leonard Bernstein 1st ann. Pacific Music Festival, Sapporo, Japan, 1990; co-artistic dir. 2d ann. Pacific Music festival, 1991, Salzburg Festival, 1991; conducted Mozart Requiem. Named Musician of Year, Musical Am. 1970; recipient Koussevitsky prize, 1968, Grammy award for Carmina Burana with Cleve. Orch., 1976, for Gershwin Live with Los Angeles Philharm., 1983, Grammy nomination, Best Classical Album - Debussy: Le Martyre de Saint Sebastien (with the London Symphony Orchestra), 1994. Office: 888 7th Ave Fl 37 New York NY 10106-3799 Office: San Francisco Symphony Davies Symphony Hall San Francisco CA 94102

TILTON, GEORGE ROBERT, geochemistry educator; b. Danville, Ill., June 3, 1923; s. Edgar Josiah and Caroline Lenore (Burkmeyer) T.; m. Elizabeth Jane Foster, Feb. 7, 1948; children—Linda Ruth, Helen Elizabeth, Elaine Lee, David Foster, John Robert. Student, Blackburn Coll., 1940-42; B.S., U. Ill., 1947; Ph.D., U. Chgo., 1951; D.Sc. (hon.), Swiss Fed. Inst. Tech., Zurich, 1984. Phys. chemist Carnegie Instn., Washington, 1951-65; prof. geochemistry U. Calif.-Santa Barbara, 1965-91, emeritus, 1991—, chmn. dept. geol. scis., 1973-77; guest prof. Swiss Fed. Inst., Zurich, 1971-72; prin. investigator NSF research grant, 1965—; mem. earth scis. panel NSF, 1966-69, 82-85. Assoc. editor Jour. Geophys. Research, 1962-65, Geochimica et Cosmochimica Acta, 1973—; contbr. articles to profl. jours. Served with AUS, 1942-45. Decorated Purple Heart; recipient Sr. Scientist award Alexander von Humboldt Found., 1989. Fellow AAAS, Am. Geophys. Union, Geol. Soc. Am.; mem. Nat. Acad. Scis., Geochem. Soc. (pres. 1981), Sigma Xi. Episcopalian. Home: 3425 Madrona Dr Santa Barbara CA 93105-2652 Office: U Calif Dept Geol Scis Santa Barbara CA 93106

TILTON, JOHN ELVIN, mineral economics educator; b. Brownsville, Pa., Sept. 16, 1939; s. John Elvin Sr. and Margaret Julia (Renn) T.; m. Elizabeth Martha Meier, June 18, 1966; children: Margaret Ann, John Christian. AB, Princeton U., 1961; PhD in Econs., Yale U., 1965. Staff analyst Office of Sec. of Def., Washington, 1965-67; rsch. assoc. Brookings Inst., Washington, 1967-70; asst. prof. econs. U. Md., College Park, 1970-72; assoc. prof. mineral econs. Pa. State U., University Park, 1972-75, prof., 1975-85; Coulter prof. Colo. Sch. Mines, Golden, 1985-94, dir. Divsn. Econs. and Bus., 1994—; officer econ. affairs commodities divsn. UN Conf. on Trade and Devel., Geneva, 1977; leader rsch. Internat. Inst. Applied Systems Analysis, Laxenburg, Austria, 1982-84; joint dir. mineral econs. and policy Program of Resources for Future, Colo. Sch. Mines, Washington, 1982—; vice chmn. bd. mineral and energy resources NRC, Washington, 1980-83, mem. nat. materials adv. bd., 1987-89. Author: International Diffusion of Technology, 1971, The Future of Nonfuel Minerals, 1977; editor: Material Substitution, 1983, World Metal Demand, 1990, Mineral Wealth and Economic Development, 1992; co-editor: Economics of Mineral Exploration, 1987, Competitiveness in Metals, 1992. Capt. U.S. Army, 1965-67. Fulbright scholar Ecole Nat. Supérieure des Mines de Paris, 1992. Mem. Am. Econ. Assn., Am. Inst. Mining Metall. and Petroleum Engrs. (Mineral Econs. award 1985), Mineral Econs. and Mgmt. Soc. (pres. 1993-94), Mining and Metall. Soc. Am. Office: Colo Sch Mines Divsn Econs and Bus Golden CO 80401

TILTON, KATHLEEN JOAN, English language educator; b. Denver, Feb. 14, 1953; d. Warren deBlois and Virginia (Haught) T. BA, Adams State Coll., 1974; MA, Colo. State U., 1982. Elem. tchr. various schs., 1974-88; instr. Colo. State U., Ft. Collins., 1982-83, Regis Coll., Denver, 1983-85, Aurora (Colo.) Community Coll., 1985-87, L.A. Pierce Community Coll., 1990, Mission Community Coll., Santa Clara, Calif., 1990—, West Valley Community Coll., Saratoga, Calif., 1990—, Skyline Coll., San Mateo, Calif.; owner Tilton Typesetting Co., Denver, 1985-89; mgr. Graphic Concepts, Denver, 1990; office mgr. Lovewell, Palo Alto, Calif., 1990—. Asst. editor Colo. State Review, 1980-82; editor: Genesis Adams State Coll., 1973, Tilton House; contbr. numerous poems and short stories to literary mags. and jours. Mem. Jr. League. Mem. AAUW. Republican.

TILTON, RONALD WILLIAM, naval officer; b. Brookline, Mass., Dec. 28, 1944; s. John Walter and Audrey Muriel (Rice) T.; m. Thuy-Nhi Tran, Jan. 2, 1993. BA in Mgmt., Jacksonville U., 1967; cert., Naval War Coll., 1979, Air U., 1985; MS in Systems Mgmt., U. Southern Calif., 1985. Commd. ens. USN, 1967, advanced through grades to comdr., 1982; sr. pilot evaluator of Atlantic fleet patrol squadrons Patrol Squadron Thirty, Jacksonville, Fla., 1975-78; patrol plane comdr., maintenance officer Patrol Squadron 17, Barbers Point, Hawaii, 1980-82; ops. and plans officer Commander in Chief Pacific, Camp H.M. Smith, Hawaii, 1982-84; comptroller Naval Air Sta., Barbers Point, 1984-86; exec. officer, chief test pilot NAVPRO, Lockheed Aero. Systems Co., Burbank, Calif., 1986-90; pilot UPS, Louisville, 1990—. Loaned exec. United Way, Jacksonville, 1975. Mem. Naval Air Exec. Inst., Order of Daedalians, Phi Delta Theta. Home: 24660A Brighton Dr Santa Clarita CA 91355-2057

TIMM, JERRY ROGER, fiberglass manufacturing company executive; b. Nampa, Idaho, Apr. 16, 1942; s. Sheldon A. and Beulah M. (Bell) T.; children: Bryan Lee, Michelle Ann; m. Marcy Marrs, Oct. 18, 1991. B.S. in Acctg, U. Idaho, 1965; student, Stanford Fin. Mgmt. Program, 1986. C.P.A., Idaho. With Touche Ross & Co. (C.P.A.), 1965-73; mgr. Touche Ross & Co. (C.P.A.), Boise, Idaho, 1973; asst. controller to controller corp. div. Albertson's, Inc., Boise, 1973-76; controller Albertson's, Inc., 1976-81, v.p. and controller, 1981-89; v.p., chief fin., adminstrv. officer Fiberglass Systems, Inc., Boise, 1990—; pres., dir. Albertson's Fed. Credit Union, 1976-84; past chmn. Idaho Bd. Accountancy. Bd. dirs. Boise Family YMCA, 1978-81; chmn., dir. Boise chpt. ARC, 1986-90; campaign chmn. United Way of ADA Countk Inc., 1985, pres. elect 1986, pres. 1987; bd. dirs. Associated Taxpayers of Idaho, Inc., 1983-89. Mem. AICPA, Nat. Assn. Accts. (past pres. Boise chpt.), Idaho Soc. CPAs, Boise Capital Lions (pres. 1970-83), Boise Sunrise Rotary (pres. 1984—). Office: Fiberglass Systems Inc 4545 Enterprise St Boise ID 83705-5425

TIMMER, ROBERT SCOTT, geologist; b. Danville, Ill., July 19, 1949; s. George William and Dorthey Ann (Henderson) T.; m. Margaret Holle Young, July 12, 1975 (div. Apr. 1983); children: Jessica Ann, Christopher Scott. BS in Geology, U. Alaska, 1971; MS in Geology, U. N.Mex., 1976. Registered geologist, Calif. Exploration geologist Earth Resources Co., Cuba, N.Mex., 1973-75; exploration geologist Mobil Oil/Uranium, Denver, 1975-78, geol. supr., 1978-83; geol. supr. Mobil Oil, Houston, 1983-85; geol. supr., advisor Mobil Oil, Midland, Tex., 1985-90; geol. advisor Mobil Oil, Bakersfield, Calif., 1990—. Contbr. articles, map to profl. publs. Recipient Coenosystis Timmeri award Stremple, Allison & Kline, 1971. Mem. Am. Assn. Petroleum Geologists, San Joaquin Well Logging Soc. (v.p. 1994-95, 95—), Soc. Petroleum Engrs. Home: 6004 Lindbrook Way Bakersfield CA 93309-3646 Office: Mobil Oil Co 10000 Ming Ave Bakersfield CA 93311-1301

TIMMERMANN, SANDRA, educational gerontologist, communications specialist; b. Orange, N.J., Mar. 25, 1941; d. Bernhard and Matilda (Schaaf) T.; m. George W. Bonham. BA with honors, U. Colo., 1963; MA, Columbia U., 1967; EdD, 1979. Account exec. Rowland Co., N.Y.C., 1964-67; dir. pub. info. The N.Y. TV Network. SUNY, N.Y.C., 1967-72; asso. Hoefer/Amidei Pub. Relations/Mktg., 1972-74; asso. dean Inst. Lifetime Learning, Am. Assn. Ret. Persons, Washington, 1974-76, dir. Inst., 1976-84, dir. geriatric edn., 1984-86 ; exec. dir. Peninsula Ctr. for the Blind, Palo Alto, Calif., 1986-88; dir. western states region Am. Found. for the Blind, San Francisco, 1988—; bd. dirs. Calif. Council of Gerontology and Geriatrics, 1988-90; edn. and tng. cons. Am. Soc. on Aging; mem. tng. com. Nat. Ctr. for Black Aged; mgr. older adults sect. HEW Lifelong Learning Project; cons. Brookdale Ctr. on Aging, Hunter Coll.; cons. to bus. and industry; adv. com. nat. project on counseling older people Am. Personnel and Guidance Assn.; nat. adv. com. vocat. edn. and older adults U.S. Dept. Edn. Trustee, chmn. adv. com. on later years Am. Found. for the Blind. Kellogg fellow. Chmn. Youth and Edn. Community United Meth. Ch., Half Moon Bay, Conn. Mem. Am. Soc. on Aging (dir. edn., tng. San Francisco chpt.), Am. Assn. Adult and Continuing Edn. (editor Edn. and Aging newsletter, chmn. commn. on aging, bd. dirs.), Coalition Adult Edn. Orgns. (dir., pres. 1984-85), Pi Beta Phi, Pi Lambda Theta, Kappa Delta Pi, Phi Delta Kappa. Club: Capital Speakers. Contbr. articles to profl. jours. and newspapers. Home: 371 Cypress Point Rd Half Moon Bay CA 94019-2242

TIMMERMANN, THOMAS JOSEPH, journalist; b. Encino, Calif., June 23, 1962; s. Henry Vernon and Jeanne Emily (Hitchcock) T.; m. Carol Ann Needham, July 23, 1994. BA in Econs., BA in Comm. Studies, UCLA, 1984. Staff writer L.A. Herald Examiner, 1985-89; staff writer L.A. Daily News, 1989-93, asst. sports editor, 1993—. Author (jour.) Soccer America, 1993. Pastoral adv. bd. mem. Univ. Cath. Ctr., L.A., 1993—. Mem. AP Sports Editor (2nd place newswriting award 1990), U.S. Basketball Writers Assn., L.A. Conservancy. Democrat. Roman Catholic. Office: Los Angeles Daily News 21221 Oxnard St Woodland Hills CA 91367-5015

TIMMINS, EDWARD PATRICK, lawyer; b. Denver, June 8, 1955; s. M. Edward and Elizabeth Jean (Imhoff) T.; m. Mary Joanne Deziel, Dec. 27, 1985; children: Edward Patrick Jr., Joan Deziel. BA with honors, Harvard U., 1977; JD magna cum laude, U. Mich., 1980. Bar: Colo. 1981, U.S. Ct. Appeals (D.C. and 9th cirs.) 1982, U.S. Dist. Ct. Colo. 1984, U.S. Ct. Appeals (10th cir.) 1984. Law clk. to cir. justice U.S. Ct. Appeals (7th cir.), Chgo., 1980-81; trial atty. U.S. Dept. Justice, Washington, 1981-84; asst. U.S. atty. Denver, 1984-88; dir. Otten, Johnson, Robinson, Neff & Ragonetti P.C., Denver, 1985—. Sr. editor U. Mich. Law Rev., 1979-80. Dir., vice chair Colo. Easter Seals; bd. dirs., chmn. career exploring com. Boy Scouts Am. Harvard Nat. scholar, 1976. Harvard Nat. scholar, 1976. Mem. ABA, Colo. Bar Assn. (exec. coun. jud. sect.), Denver Bar Assn., Order of Coif, Friends of Harvard Rowing. Office: Otten Johnson Robinson Neff & Ragonetti 950 17th St Ste 1600 Denver CO 80202-2828

TIMMINS, JAMES DONALD, venture capitalist; b. Hamilton, Ont., Can., Oct. 3, 1955; came to U.S., 1979; s. Donald G. and Myrna L. (Seymour) T. BA, U. Toronto, 1977; law degree, Queen's U., 1979; MBA, Stanford U., 1981. Investment banker Wood Gundy, Toronto, 1980, Salomon Bros., San Francisco, 1981-84; mng. dir. and chief exec. officer McKewon & Timmins, San Diego, 1984-87; ptnr. Hambrecht & Quist, San Francisco, 1987-90, Glenwood Capital, Menlo Park, 1991—; bd. dirs. Artios Corp., Irvine. Mem. Olympic Club of San Francisco. Home: 735 Laurelwood Dr San Mateo CA 94403-4058 Office: Redwood Ptnrs 3000 Sand Hill Rd Ste 230 Menlo Park CA 94025-7116

TIMMONS, CLARA ELIZABETH, chemist, educator; b. Columbia, Mo., Apr. 18, 1926; d. Elbert M. and Carla Gertrude (Walker) Gallemore; m. Richard Dean Abernathy Timmons, Aug. 14, 1954 (div. Dec. 1960); children: Beth, Pamela Kay. BS in chem. & music, Central Mo. State Coll., 1946; MS in chem., U. Okla., 1948. Analytical chemist Haver Glover Labs., Kansas City, Mo., 1948-49; sr. analyst Pacific Coast Borax Co., Boron, Calif., 1950-55; chemist, co-owner Agri-Lab, Inc., Kearney, Nebr., 1956-60; chief chemist dairy foods Iowa Dept. Agriculture, Des Moines, 1961-62; chemist Kaiser Chemical Co., Wendover, Utah, 1969-71, Nat. Lead, Salt Lake City, 1973-74, Rocky Mountain Arsenal, Commerce City, Colo., 1977, Hill Air Force Base, Ogden, Utah, 1977-93; bd. dirs. U-Vest, Salt Lake City, 1972-73. Mem. Am. Chem. Soc., Am. Assn. Univ. Profs., AAUW.

TIMMONS, EVELYN DEERING, pharmacist; b. Durango, Colo., Sept. 29, 1926; d. Claude Elliot and Evelyn Allen (Gooch) Deering; m. Richard Palmer Timmons, Oct. 4, 1952 (div. 1968); children: Roderick Deering, Steven Palmer. BS in Chemistry and Pharmacy cum laude, U. Colo., 1948. Chief pharmacist Meml. Hosp., Phoenix, 1950-54; med. lit. rsch. librarian Hoffman-LaRoche, Inc., Nutley, N.J., 1956-57; staff pharmacist St. Joseph's Hosp., Phoenix, 1958-60; relief mgr. various ind. apothecaries, Phoenix, 1960-68; asst. then mgr. Profl. Pharmacies, Inc., Phoenix, 1968-72; mgr. then owner Mt. View Pharmacy, Phoenix and Paradise Valley, Ariz., 1972—; pres. Ariz. Apothecaries, Ltd., Phoenix, 1976—; mem. profl. adv. bd., bereavement counselor Hospice of Valley, 1983—; mem. profl. adv. bd. Upjohn Health Care and Svcs., Phoenix, 1984-86; bd. dirs. Am. Council on Pharm. Edn., Chgo., 1986-92, v.p. 1988, 89, treas., 1990-91. Author poetry; contbr. articles to profl. jours. Mem. Scottsdale (Ariz.) Fedn. Rep. Women, 1963; various other offices Rep. Fedn.; mem. platform com. State of Ariz., Nat. Rep. Conv., 1964; asst. sec. Young Rep. Nat. Fedn., 1963-65; active county and state Rep. coms.; fin. chmn. Internat. Leadership Symposium:Woman in Pharmacy, London, 1987; treas. Leadership Internat. Women Pharmacy, 1991—. Named Outstanding Young Rep. of Yr., Nat. Fedn. Young Reps., 1965, Preceptor of Yr., U. Ariz./Syntex, 1984; recipient Disting. Public Svc. award Maricopa County Med. Soc., 1962, Disting. Alumni award Wasatch Acad., 1982, Career Achievement award, 1983, Leadership and Achievement award Upjohn Labs., 1985-86, Outstanding Achievement in Profession award Merck, Sharp & Dohme, 1986, award of Merit, 1988, Disting. Coloradoan award U. Colo., 1989, Vanguard award, 1991. Fellow Am. Coll. of Apothecaries (v.p. 1982-83, pres. 1984-85; chmn. bd. dirs. 1985-86, adv. council 1986—, Chmn. of Yr. 1980-81 Victor H. Morganroth award 1985, J. Leon Lascoff award 1990); mem. Ariz. Soc. of Hosp. Pharmacists, Am. Pharm. Assn. (Daniel B. Smith award 1990), Ariz. Pharmacy Assn. (Svc. to Pharmacy award 1976, Pharmacist of Yr. 1981, Bowl of Hygeia 1989, 1st Innovative Pharmacy award 1994), Maricopa County Pharmacy Assn. (pres. 1977, Svc. to Pharmacy award 1977), Am. Soc. of Hosp. Pharmacists, Aux. to County Med. Soc. (pres. 1967-68), Am. Aircraft Owners and Pilots Assn., Air Safety Found., Nat. Assn. of Registered Parliamentarians, Kappa Epsilon (recipient Career Achievement award 1986, Vanguard award 1991, Unicorn award 1993). Lodge: Civinettes (pres. Scottsdale chpt. 1960-61). Avocations: flying, skiing, swimming, backpacking, hiking. Office: Mt View Pharmacy 10565 N Tatum Blvd Ste B-118 Paradise Valley AZ 85253

TIMMONS, TERRY LEE, photographer, educator; b. Santa Paula, Calif., Mar. 13, 1946; s. Alvin Odell and Patricia Cristel (Henry) T. AA, Venture Coll., 1966; BPA, Brooks Inst., 1973. Cert. C.C. tchr., Calif. Owner, operator Gallery Photographic Svc., Ventura, Calif., 1974-80; instr. photographic scis. Ventura Coll., 1975—; forensic specialist State of Calif. and local police agys., 1974—. Exhibited in shows at Buena Ventura Art Assn., 1974, Camarillo Art Assn.; author: Introduction into the Photographic Process, 1993. Tribal healer Cherokee and Chumash Nation, Okla., Ariz., Calif.; candidate trustee Ventura C.C. Dist., 1991. Mem. SAG, Am. Fedn. Tchrs. (negotiator), Brooks Alumni Assn. Home: 406 Sespe Ave Fillmore CA 93015-2024

TIMMONS, WILLIAM MILTON, producer, freelance writer, retired cinema arts educator, publisher, film maker; b. Houston, Apr. 21, 1933; s. Carter Charles and Gertrude Monte (Lee) T.; m. Pamela Cadorette, Dec. 24, 1975 (div. 1977). BS, U. Houston, 1958; MA, UCLA, 1961; PhD, U. So. Calif., 1975. Child actor Houston Jr. Theater, 1945-46; staff announcer Sta. KMCO, Conroe, Tex., 1951-52; prodn. asst. Sta. KUHT-TV, Houston, 1953-54, 56-57; teaching fellow UCLA, 1960-61; ops. asst. CBS-TV, Hollywood, Calif., 1961-62; prof. speech and drama Sam Houston State U., Huntsville, Tex., 1963-67; chmn. dept. cinema Los Angeles Valley Coll., Van Nuys, Calif., 1970-91, ret., 1992; producer Sta. KPFK, Los Angeles, 1959-60, 1983—; pub. Acad. Assocs., L.A., 1976—; proofreader, cons. Focal Press Pub. Co., N.Y.C., 1983—. Author: Orientation to Cinema, 1986; contbr. articles to mags.; prodr., dir.: (radio programs) Campus Comments, 1963-67, numerous ednl. films, 1963—; prodr. ednl. series for cable TV, 1993—. With USNR, 1954-56. Named Hon. Tex. Ranger, State of Tex., Austin, 1946; U. Houston scholar, 1957. Mem. Soc. for Scholarly Pub., Mensa, U. So. Calif. Cinema-TV Alumni Assn., Red Masque Players, Secular Humanists L.A., Alpha Epsilon Rho, Delta Kappa Alpha. Democrat.

TIMMRECK, THOMAS C., health sciences and health administration educator; b. Montpelier, Idaho, June 15, 1946; s. Archie Carl and Janone (Jensen) T.; m. Ellen Prusse, Jan. 27, 1971; children: Chad Thomas, Benjamin Brian, Julie Anne. AA, Ricks Coll., 1968; BS, Brigham Young U., 1971; MEd, Oreg. State U., 1972; MA, No. Ariz. U., 1981; PhD, U. Utah, 1976. Program dir. Cache County Aging Program, Logan, Utah, 1972-73; asst. prof. div. health edn. Tex. Tech U., Lubbock, 1976-77; asst. prof. dept. health care adminstrn. Idaho State U., Pocatello, 1977-78; program dir., asst. prof. health services program No. Ariz. U., Flagstaff, 1978-84; cons., dir. grants Beth Israel Hosp., Denver, 1985; assoc. prof. dept. health scis. and human ecology, coordinator grad. studies, coordinator health adminstrn. and planning Calif. State U., San Bernardino, 1985—; pres. Health Care Mgmt. Assocs., 1985—; presenter at nat. confs.; mem. faculty Loretto Heights Coll., Denver, Dept. Mgmt. U. Denver, Dept. Mgmt. and Health Adminstrn. U. Colo., Denver. Author: Dictionary of Health Services Management, rev. 2d. edit., 1987, An Introduction to Epidemiology, 1994, Handbook of Planning and Program Development for Health and Social Services, 1994; mem. editl. bd. Jour. Health Values, 1986—, Introduction to Epidemiology; contbr. numerous articles on health care adminstrn., behavioral health, gerontology and health edn. to profl. jours. Chmn., bd. dirs. Inland Counties Health System Agy.; bd. dirs. health svc. orgns. Served with U.S. Army, 1966-72, Vietnam. Mem. Assn. Advancement of Health Edn., Am. Acad. Mgmt., Assn. Univ. Programs in Health Care Adminstrn., Healthcare Forum. Republican. Mormon. Office: Calif State U Dept Health Scis and Human Ecology San Bernardino CA 92407

TIMMS, EUGENE DALE, wholesale business owner, state senator; b. Burns, Oreg., May 15, 1932; s. Morgan Oscar and Dorothy Vera (Payne) T.; m. Edna May Evans, Aug. 24, 1953; children: Tobi Eugene, Trina Maria. BA, Willamette U., 1954. Sen. State of Oreg., 1982, 84, 88, 92; pres. Harney City C. of C.; bd. trustees Assoc. Oreg. Industries; chmn. Parks & Recreation Dist. Bd.; mem. Harney City Hosp. Bd. Mem. SBA, Jaycees (state v.p.), Elk Lodge, Masonic Lodge, Al Kader Harney City Shrine Club. Presbyterian. Home: 1049 N Court Ave Burns OR 97720-1016

TINDALL, ROBERT EMMETT, lawyer, educator; b. N.Y.C., Jan. 2, 1934; s. Robert E. and Alice (McGonigle) T.; BS in Marine Engring., SUNY, 1955; postgrad. Georgetown U. Law Sch., 1960-61; LLB, U. Ariz., 1963; LLM, N.Y.U., 1967; PhD, City U., London, 1975; children: Robert Emmett IV, Elizabeth. Mgmt. trainee Gen. Electric Co., Schenectady, N.Y., Lynn, Mass., Glen Falls, N.Y., 1955-56, 58-60; law clk. firm Haight, Gardner, Poor and Havens, N.Y.C., 1961; admitted to Ariz. bar, 1963; prin., mem. firm Robert Emmett Tindall & Assocs., Tucson, 1963—; asso. prof. mgmt. U. Ariz., Tucson, 1969—; vis. prof. Grad. Sch. of Law, Soochow U., Republic of China, 1972, Grad. Bus. Centre, London, 1974, NYU, 1991—; dir. MBA program U. Ariz., Tucson, 1975-81; investment cons. Kingdom of Saudi Arabia, 1981—; dir. entrepreneurship program, U. Ariz., Tucson, 1984-86; lectr. USIA in Eng., India, Middle East, 1974; lectr. bus. orgn. and regulatory laws Southwestern Legal Found., Acad. Am. and Internat. Law, 1976-80. Actor community theatres of Schenectady, 1955-56, Harrisburgh, Pa., 1957-58, Tucson, 1961-71; appeared in films Rage, 1971, Showdown at OK Corral, 1971, Lost Horizon, 1972; appeared in TV programs Gunsmoke, 1972, Petrocelli, 1974. Served to lt. USN, 1956-58. Ford Found. fellow, 1965-67; Asia Found. grantee, 1972-73. Mem. Strategic Mgmt. Soc., State Bar of Ariz., Acad. Internat. Bus., Screen Actors Guild, Honourable Soc. of Middle Temple (London), Phi Delta Phi, Beta Gamma Sigma, Assoc. for Corp. Growth. Clubs: Royal Overseas League (London). Author: Multinational Enterprises, 1975; contbr. articles on domestic and internat. bus. to profl. jours. Home: 2020 E Elm St Tucson AZ 85719-4328 Office: Coll Bus and Public Adminstrn U Ariz Dept Mgmt and Policy Tucson AZ 85721

TING, ALBERT CHIA, bioengineering researcher; b. Hong Kong, Sept. 7, 1950; came to U.S., 1957; s. William Su and Katherine Sung (Bao) T.; m. Shirley Roung Wang, July 30, 1988. BA, UCLA, 1973; MS, Calif. State U., L.A., 1975, Calif. Inst. Tech., 1977; PhD, U. Calif., San Diego, 1983. Rsch. asst. Calif. Inst. Tech., Pasadena, 1975-77, U. Calif., San Diego, 1982-83; sr. staff engr. R&D Am. Med. Optics, Irvine, Calif., 1983-86; project engr., rsch. Allergan Med. Optics, Irvine, Calif., 1987-89; sr. project engr., rsch., 1989-92, sr. project engr., engring., 1993-94. Inventor med. and optical devices, recipient patent awards 1988, 89, 91, 92, 93; contbr. articles to sci. jours. Mem. AAAS, Biomed. Engring. Soc., Assn. for Rsch. in Vision and Ophthalmology, Biomed. Optics Soc.

TING, CHIHYUAN CHARLES, chemist; b. Qingdao, China, Feb. 1, 1947; came to U.S., 1971, naturalized, 1979; s. Shu-Ren and Shu-Yin (Yin) T.; m. Margaret An, Aug. 6, 1971; children: Michelle, Michael. BS, Fu-Jen U., Taipei, Taiwan, 1970; MS, Wilkes U., 1973; PhD, Pa. State U., 1978. Sr. rsch. specialist Monsanto, St. Louis, 1977-88. Patentee in field. Mem. Am. Chem. Soc., Sigma Xi. Avocations: Reading, music, sports. Office: Sequus Pharm Inc 1050 Hamilton Ct Menlo Park CA 94025

TING, PANG-HSIN, linguistics educator; b. Ju-Kao, Chiang-Su, China, Oct. 15, 1937; came to U.S., 1989; s. Ting-I and Sou-Yu (Li) T.; m. Chi Chen, Nov. 11, 1963; children: Tsuo-Wen, Tsuo-Chi, Tsuo-Li. BA, Nat. Taiwan U., 1959, MA, 1963; PhD, U. Wash., 1972. Rsch. asst. Academia Sinica, Taipei, Taiwan, 1963-64, from asst. rsch. fellow to assoc. rsch. fellow, 1964-75, rsch. fellow, 1975-89; from assoc. prof. to prof. Nat. Taiwan U., Taipei, 1972-89; prof. Chinese linguistics U. Calif., Berkeley, 1989-94, Agassiz prof., 1994—; chmn. linguistics sect. Inst History & Philology, Academia Sinica, Taipei, 1973-81, dir., 1981-89; dir. Chao Yuen Ren Ctr. for Chinese Linguistics, U. Calif., Berkeley, 1993—. Author: Chinese Phonology of the Wei-Chin Period--Reconstruction of the Finals as Reflected in Poetry, 1975 (award 1977), The Tan-chou Ts'un-hua Dialect, 1986; translator: A Grammar of Spoken Chinese, 1980. 2d lt. Taiwanese Army, 1959-61. Recipient Outstanding Scholar award NSF, 1985-89. Mem. Internat. Assn. Chinese Linguistics (v.p. 1992-93, pres. 1993-94), Chinese Lang. Tchrs. Assn. Office: U Calif Dept East Asian Langs Berkeley CA 94720

TING, SHAO KUANG, artist, educator; b. Beijing, Oct. 7, 1939; came to U.S., 1980; s. Jun Sheng and Shiang Jun (Lee) T.; m. Daxi Zhang, Oct. 8, 1968 (div. Oct. 1987); children: Angelina, Li. B degree, Ctrl. Acad. Arts & Design, Beijing, 1962. Prof. Yunnan Inst. Arts, Kunming, Peoples Republic of China, 1962-80; lectr. dept. visual arts UCLA, 1983; profl. artist Beverly Hills, Calif., 1980—; prof. Ctrl. Acad. Arts & Design, Beijing, 1992—, U. Shanghai (People's Republic of China), Sch. Fine Arts, 1992—, U. Shan Xi, Taiyuan, People's Republic of China, 1992—, Yunan Inst. Arts, 1992—. One-man shows include Ginza Art Mus., Tokyo, 1988, Studio 47 Gallery, N.Y.C., 1989, Bernheim Gallerr, Paris, 1990, Historical Mus., Beijing, 1992; exhibited in group shows at Internat. Art Expo, 1986-94, Floriade Artist, Amsterdam, The Netherlands, 1991, Exhbn. by Chinese Artists in USA, Taipei, Taiwan, 1994; prin. works include mural The Great Hall of the People, People's Republic of China, 1989-90, Mus. Shanghai, Mus. Beijing, Matsuzakaya Gallery, Nagoya, Japan. Artist World Fedn. of UN, 1993, 94, 95; artist, donator UNICEF Charity Art Bazar, Tokyo, 1990, Midwest Inundation, L.A., 1993. Recipient Best of Show award U. So. Calif., 1984; recipient Outstanding Chinese Am. Role Model award Chinese Cultural Club Orange County, 1993, Pan Pacific Performing Arts, Internat., 1993; Ting Shao Kuang Day proclaimed by Mayor of Sante Fe, 1993; recipient Golden Image award Transpacific, Face and XO mags., 1994. Mem. Chinese Artists Assn. (pres. 1992—), Pang Xunqin Art Mus. (hon. curator 1992—). Home: 707 N Alpine Dr Beverly Hills CA 90210-3305

TINGLEY, WALTER WATSON, computer systems manager; b. Portland, Maine, July 24, 1946; s. Edward Allen Tingley and Ruth Annie (Howard) Tuttle; m. Elizabeth A. Fletcher, May 1970 (div. 1975). BS, U. Md., 1974. Programmer analyst U.S. Ry. Assn., Washington, 1974-80, Digital Equipment Corp., Maynard, Mass., 1980-81, Interactive Mgmt. Systems, Belmont, Mass., 1981; systems designer Martin Marietta Data Systems, Greenbelt, Md., 1982-84; mgr. computer ops. Genex, Rockville, Md., 1984; system mgr. Applied Rsch. Corp., Landover, Md., 1985; programmer analyst Input/Output Computer Svcs., Washington, 1986-87, Lockheed Engring. and Scis., Las Vegas, Nev., 1987-91, Computer Profls., Inc., Los Alamos, N.Mex., 1992—. Author tech. book revs., software revs. With USAF, 1964-68. Mem. IEEE Computer Soc., Assn. Computing Machinery. Home: PO Box 429 Los Alamos NM 87544-0429

TINKER, IRENE, city and regional planning educator, women's studies educator; b. Milw., Mar. 8, 1927; d. John Marlin and Irene Laverty (Casto) T.; m. Millidge P. Walker, Febr. 2, 1952; children: Stuart Tjipto, Janet Shakuntala, Jennifer Njoro. AB magna cum laude, Radcliff/Harvard Colls., 1949; PhD, London Sch. Econs. and Polit. Sci., 1954. Rsch. polit. sci. U. Calif., Berkeley, 1954-57; asst. prof. govt. Howard U., 1961-67; asst. provost for curriculum devel., prof. Fed. City Coll., 1967-71; dir. Ednl. Policy Ctr., 1971-73; founding dir. office of internat. sci. AAAS, 1973-77; asst. dir., dir. office policy and planning U.S. Agy. for Vol. Svc., 1977-78; founder, dir. Equity Policy Ctr., Washington, 1978-89; prof., chair women's studies U. Calif., Berkeley, 1989—; adj. prof. Sch. Internat. Studies Johns Hopkins U., 1966-67; vis. prof. Internat. Devel. Program The Am. U., Washington, 1985-89. Author: (books) The Organization for Development and Support of Street Food Vendors in the City of Minia: Model For Empowering the Working Poor, 1993; co-editor: Leadership and Political Institutions in India, 1959, rev. edit., 1968, Culture and Population Change, 1974, rev. edit., 1976, Population: Dynamics, Ethics and Policy, 1975, The Many Factes of Human Settlements: Science and Society, 1977; editor: Persistent Inequalities: Women and World Development, 1990; contbr. chpts. to books, articles to profl. jours. Convenor numerous confs.; mem. adv. bd. Ency. of Third World Women, 1993—, Ctr. for Women Policy Studies, 1985—, Inst. for Women's Policy Rsch., 1987-95; mem. internat. coun. adv. Healthy Cities Found., 1994—; various com. assignments UN; candidate for Md. Assembly, 1966. Recipient Fulbright Regional award Nepal and Sri Lanka, 1987-88; grantee Am. Inst. Indian Studies, U. India, 1964-65; Ford Found. Area and AAUW fellow, Indonesia, 1957-59. Fellow AAAS; mem. Nat. Coun. Rsch. on Women, Internat. Studies Assn., Rural Sociological Assn. (hon. life), Assn. for Women in Devel., Assn. Asian Studies, Assn. Collegiate Schs. of Planning. Home: 7515 Claremont Ave Berkeley CA 94705 Office: Dept City & Regional Planning U Calif Berkeley CA 94720-1850

TINKER, JUDY MARIE, nutritionist, musician; b. Albuquerque, Oct. 13, 1955; d. Robert Ellsworth and Marian La Verne (Hughes) Northrop; m. Richard Roy Tinker, July 30, 1978 (div. 1989); children: Roy Timothy, Ray Nathanael. BMus, Pacific Union Coll., Angwin, Calif., 1978; BS in Nutrition and Dietetics, Loma Linda (Calif.) U., 1992. Computer typesetter Adventist Media Ctr., Newbury Park, Calif., 1981-82; with Concerned Comms., Arroyo Grande, Calif., 1982; piano tchr. Newbury Park/Yucaipa, Calif., 1980—; organist St. Alban's Episcopal Ch., Yucaipa, 1988—; nutritionist County of San Bernardino Pub. Health Dept., Ontario, 1992—. Recipient Fgn. Langs. Achievement award Bank of Am., 1974, Achievement award for outstanding accomplishment and performance in piano Dept. of Music, Pacific Union Coll., 1978; Ruth Little Nelson scholar, 1991, Am. Dietetic Assn. Corps Tested Advt. Techniques scholar, 1991; Soroptimist Internat. scholar, 1992. Mem. Am. Dietetic Assn. (registered), Calif. Dietetic Assn., Inland Dist. Dietetic Assn. SDA. Office: San Bernardino Pub Health WIC Program 320 East D St Ontario CA 91764

TINKER, ROBERT EUGENE, minister, educational consultant; b. Lincoln, Kans., June 10, 1915; s. Eugene F. and Mildred Adelaide (Brown) T.; A.B., Am. U., 1937; M.Div., Garrett Theol. Sem., 1942; postgrad. Northwestern U., 1942-46; m. Anne Elizabeth Hall, June 13, 1942; children—Anne Terrill, Robert Bruce, MaryBeth. Ordained to ministry Methodist Ch., 1942, Congregational Ch., 1947-77, United Ch. Christ; minister Oxen Hill, Md., Tuxedo, Md., 1934-37, Evergreen Park, Ill., 1940-41; assoc. minister 1st Presbyterian Ch., Evanston, Ill., 1942-44; minister Glenview Meth. Ch. (Ill.), 1944-46, Broadway Meth. Ch., Chgo., 1946-47; with Chgo. Theol. Sem., 1947-58, asst. sec., asst. treas., bd. dirs., 1947-58, asst. bus. mgr., 1947-50, bus. mgr., 1951-55, dir. devel., 1953-55, v.p. charge devel., 1955-58; assoc. Gonser and Gerber, 1958-64; ptnr. Gonser Gerber Tinker Stuhr, ednl. cons. in devel. and public relations, Chgo., 1964-82, cons., 1982—; pres. Tabco Corp., Chgo., 1983-85; lectr. Creighton U., Omaha, summers 1978-80. N.J. State scholar, 1933; Larry Foster scholar, 1933; Wanamaker scholar Lingnon U., Canton, Republic of China, 1935-36; Howes Meml. scholar, 1939-42. Bd. dirs. Hyde Park YMCA, Chgo., Hyde Park Union Ch., Porter Found., U. Chgo., 1947-58, Bryn Mawr Cmty. Ch., Habitat for Humanity, Tucson, 1992—, Phi Sigma Kappa, Phi Beta Zeta, Pi Gamma Mu. Republican. Contbr. articles to profl. books and jours. Mem. Oro Valley Townhouses Improvement Assn. (bd. dirs. 1993-94). Home: 63 W Oro Pl Oro Valley AZ 85737-7625

TINKLENBERG, JARED RAY, psychiatrist, researcher; b. Madison, S.D., Nov. 25, 1939; s. Richard John and Frances (DeBruyn) T.; m. Mae Van Der Weerd, Aug. 8, 1964; children: Karla Jean, Julie Ann. BA with highest distinction, U. Iowa, 1962, MD, 1965. Intern Yale New Haven Med. Ctr., 1965-66; resident in psychiatry Stanford U. Sch. Medicine, 1966-69, from instr. to assoc. prof. psychiatry, 1969-84, prof. psychiatry and behavioral scis., 1984—; chief clin. svcs., psychiatry svc. VA Med. Ctr., Palo Alto, Calif., 1984-87, chief geriatric psychiatry, 1987—; dir. Stanford/VA Alzheimer's Disease Ctr., Palo Alto, 1989—. Editor: Marijuana and Health Hazards, 1975; contbr. articles to profl. jours. Served to cpl. U.S. Army, 1958-59. Fellow Psychiat. Assn., Am. Coll. Neuropsychopharmacology; mem. Phi Beta Kappa, Alpha Omega Alpha. Office: Palo Alt Vets Med Affairs 3801 Miranda Ave # A3 Palo Alto CA 94304-1207

TINNIN, THOMAS PECK, real estate professional; b. Albuquerque, May 15, 1948; s. Robert Priest and Frances (Ferree) T.; m. Jamie Tinnin Garrett, Dec. 12, 1986; children: Megan Ashley, Courtney Nicole, Robert Garrett. Student, U. Md., 1969-72; BA, U. N.Mex., 1973. Ins. agt. Occidental Life of Calif., Albuquerque, 1972—; gen. agt. Transamerica-Occidental Life, Albuquerque, 1978—; pres. Tinnin Investments, Albuquerque, 1978—, Tinnin Enterprises, Albuquerque, 1978—, Tinnin Real Estate & Devel., Albuquerque, 1989—; mem. N.Mex. State Bd. Fin., Santa Fe., 1985-87, 90—, sec. 1990-92; del. White House Conf. on Small Bus., Washington, 1986; bd. dirs. Albuquerque Econ. Devel., 1987-88. Bd. dirs. Albuquerque Conv. and Visitor's Bureau, 1982-84, St. Joseph's Hosp, Better Bus. Bur., 1983, Albuquerque, 1984-86, N.Mex. Jr. Livestock Found., pres. 1988, Presbyn. Heart Inst., 1989—, N.Mex. First Confs., 1992; chmn. Manzano Dist. Boy Scouts Am., 1981-82; chmn. Manzano Dist. Finance, 1983; del. White House Conf. Small Bus., 1986; pres. N.Mex. Jr. Livestock Investment Found., Albuquerque, 1988—; trustee N.Mex. Performing Arts Coun., 1989-90. Mem. NALU, N.Mex. Life Leaders Assn., Nat. Assn. Real Estate Appraisers, Albuquerqye Armed Forces Adv. Assn., Albuquerque C. of C. (bd. dirs. 1978-84, chmn. ambassador's com. 1983), N.Mex. Life Underwriters Assn., Albuquerque Country Club. Republican. Presbyterian. Home: 2312 Calle Del Estavan NW Albuquerque NM 87104-3072 Office: Tinnin Enterprises 20 First Plaza Ctr NW Ste 518 Albuquerque NM 87102-3352

TINSLEY, BARBARA SHER, historian, educator, writer; b. Gloversville, N.Y., Apr. 29, 1938; d. Max and Ruth Ida (Shpritzer) Sher; m. William Earl Tinsley, Dec. 30, 1959; children: Claire Jennifer, Yve Hillary. BA, U. Wis., Milw., 1959; MA, U. Calif., Berkeley, 1960; PhD, Stanford U., 1983. Instr. English and French Stephens Coll., Columbia, Mo., 1963-64; instr. European history San Jose (Calif.) State U., 1969-71; prof. European history Foothill Coll., Los Altos Hills, Calif., 1974—; lectr. in English Santa Clara (Calif.) Univ., 1977-79; lectr. in western culture Stanford (Calif.) U., 1985, vis. scholar, 1989-94. Author: History and Polemics in the French Reformation: Florimond de Raemond Defender of the Church, 1992, (with Lewis S. Spitz) Johann Sturm and Education, 1995; contbr. articles to profl. jours. Woodrow Wilson fellow U. Calif.-Berkeley, 1959-60; NDEA fellow Mich. State U. and Emory U., 1961, 63; Jessie Speyer fellow Stanford U., 1965-67; Fulbright fellow U. Strasbourg, 1983-84; NEH fellow Duke U., 1988, Princeton, 1995. Mem. Am. Hist. Assn., Sixteenth Century Studies Conf., YMCA. Democrat. Home: 15550 Glen Una Dr Los Gatos CA 95030-2936

TINSLEY, WALTON EUGENE, lawyer; b. Vanceburg, Ky., Jan. 22, 1921; s. Wilbur Walton and Sarah Edith (Frizzell) T.; m. Joy Mae Matthews, Aug. 31, 1952; children—Merry Walton Tinsley Moore, Troy Eugene, Paul Richard. E.E., U. Cin., 1943; M.S. in Aero. Engring, NYU, 1947; J.D., U. So. Calif., 1953. Bar: Calif. 1954, U.S. Supreme Ct. 1971. Practiced in Los Angeles, 1954—; mem. firm Harris, Wallen, MacDermott & Tinsley, 1958—. Author: (book) Tasmania: Stamps and Postal History, 1986. Pres. World Philatelic Exhbn., Pacific 97 Inc. Signatory Roll of Disting. Philatelists, 1983. Fellow Royal Philatelic Soc. London; mem. IEEE (assoc.), AIAA, ABA, L.A. County Bar Assn., Am. Philatelic Soc. (v.p. 1965-69, Luff award 1986), S.R., English Speaking Union (dir. L.A. br.), Mensa. Presbyterian (elder, trustee, chmn. trustees 1972). Home: 2210 Moreno Dr Los Angeles CA 90039-3044 Office: Harris Wallen MacDermott Tinsley 650 S Grand Ave Los Angeles CA 90017-3809

TIPTON, GARY LEE, retired services company executive; b. Salem, Oreg., July 3, 1941; s. James Rains and Dorothy Velma (Dierks) T. BS, Oreg. Coll. Edn., 1964. Credit rep. Standard Oil Co. Calif., Portland, Oreg., 1964-67; credit mgr. Uniroyal Inc., Dallas, 1967-68; ptnr., mgr. bus. Tipton Barbers, Portland, 1968-94; ret., 1994. Mem. Rep. Nat. Com., 1980—, Sen. Howard Baker's Presdl. Steering Com., 1980; dep. dir. gen. Internat. Biog. Ctr., Cambridge, Eng., 1987—; mem. U.S. Congl. adv. bd. Am. Security Coun., 1984-93; mem. steering com. Coun. on Fgn. Rels. Portland Com., 1983-84, chmn. 1984-86, mem. exec. com., 1988-90, bd. dirs., 1990-91. Recipient World Culture prize Accademia Italia, 1984, Presdl. Achievement award, 1982, cert. Disting. Contbn. Sunset High Sch. Dad's Club, 1972, 73, Cert. of Perfection award Tualatin Valley Fire and Rescue Dist., 1994. Fellow Internat. Biog. Assn. (life, Key award 1983, U.K.); mem. Sunset Mchts. Assn. (co-founder, treas. 1974-79, pres. 1982-83), Internat. Platform Assn., Smithsonian Assocs., UN Assn. (steering com. UN day 1985), World Affairs Coun. of Oreg., City Club of Portland.

TIPTON, HARRY BASIL, JR., state legislator, physician; b. Salida, Colo., Mar. 14, 1927; s. Harry Basil Sr. and Nina Belle (Hailey) T.; m. Dorothy Joan Alexander, Sept. 16, 1950; children: Leslie Louise, Harry Basil III, Robert Alexander. BA, U. Colo., 1950, MD, 1953. Diplomate Am. Bd. Family Practice. Postgrad. med. tng. Good Samaritan Hosp., Phoenix., Ariz., Maricopa County Hosp., Phoenix; ptnr., dir. Lander (Wyo.) Med. Clinic, 1954—; mem. Wyo. Ho. Reps., Cheyenne, 1981—, chmn. judiciary com., 1986—; cons. Indian Health Svc., Ft. Washakie, Wyo., 1968—; dir NOWCAP Family Planning, Worland, Wyo., 1975-90. Mem., pres. Fremont County Sch. Dist. # 1, Lander, 1958-78. With USMC, 1945-46, capt. USNR Med. Corps, 1950-87. Named Capt. Med. Corps. USNR, 1974. Fellow Am. Coll. Ob.-Gyn., Am. Assn. Family Practice (charter); mem. Wyo. Med. Soc. (Physician of Yr. 1989), Rotary (pres. 1960-61), Elks. Republican. Office: Lander Med Clin PC 745 Buena Vista Dr Lander WY 82520-3431

TIRMAN, VALENTIN WOLDEMAR, JR., engineering executive and educator; b. Tallinn, Estonia, Sept. 15, 1940; came to U.S., 1949; s. Valentin Woldemar and Natalie (Barchow) T.; children: Valentin III, Grigori, Mark, Mike. BSEE, Ariz. State U., 1963; MS in Sys. Mgmt., U. So. Calif., L.A., 1969. Commd. lt. USAF, 1962, advanced through grades to lt. col., 1978; sys. software engr. Ford Aerospace, Colorado Springs, Colo., 1982-88; v.p. Productive DAta Sys., Englewood, Colo., 1988—; adj. prof. Webster U., Colorado Springs, 1984—; assoc. prof. USAF Acad., Colorado Springs, 1973-82. Mem. ACM, IEEE, Assn. Old Crows. Home: 3250 Parade Cir E Colorado Springs CO 80917-2927 Office: Productive Data Sys Inc 2110 Vickers Dr # 100 Colorado Springs CO 80918-8129

TISCHLER, DAVID WILLIAM, music educator; b. Sacramento, Dec. 16, 1935; s. William and Myrta Holland (Smith) T. Diploma, U. Paris, 1956; BA, U. Calif., Berkeley, 1958. Tchr. Loomis (Calif.) High Sch., 1960-61, John F. Kennedy Sch., Berlin, Fed. Republic of Germany, 1962-64; pvt. studio, piano tchr. Cypress, Calif. Performer: (piano concerts) Bridges Hall of Music, Pomona Coll., 1978, UCLA, 1978. With U.S. Army, 1958-60, 61-62. Mem. Music Tchrs. Assn. of Calif., Mensa. Home: 8801 Walker St Apt 57 Cypress CA 90630-5920

TISDALE, DOUGLAS MICHAEL, lawyer; b. Detroit, May 3, 1949; s. Charles Walker and Violet Lucille (Battani) T.; m. Patricia Claire Brennan, Dec. 29, 1972; children: Douglas Michael, Jr., Sara Elizabeth, Margaret Patricia, Victoria Claire. BA in Psychology with honors, U. Mich., 1971, JD, 1975. Bar: Colo. 1975, U.S. Dist. Ct. Colo. 1975, U.S. Ct. Appeals (10th cir.) 1976, U.S. Supreme Ct. 1979. Law clk. to chief judge U.S. Dist. Ct. Colo., Denver, 1975-76; assoc. Brownstein Hyatt Farber & Madden, P.C. ; ptnr., dir. Brownstein Hyatt Farber & Strickland, P.C., 1976-92; shareholder Popham, Haik, Schnobrich & Kaufman, Ltd., 1992—, dir. 1995—. lectr. Law Seminars, Inc., 1984-92, Continuing Legal Edn. in Colo., Inc., 1984-93, Nat. Bus. Insts., 1985—, ABA Nat. Insts. 1988-92; Colo. Law-Related Edn. Coord., 1982-88; bd. dirs. Vail Valley Med. Ctr., 1992—. Mem. ABA (mem. litigation sect. trial evidence com. 1981—, vice chmn. real property sect. com. on enforcement of creditors rights and bankruptcy 1984-90, vice chmn. real property sect. com. on pub. edn. concerning the lawyers role 1984-87, chmn. 1987-90, chmn. real property sect. sub-com. on foreclosures in bankruptcy 1982-90), Colo. Bar Assn. (conv. com. 1979-88), Denver Bar Assn. (jud. adminstrn. com. 1978-89), Am. Judicature Soc., Assn. Trial Lawyers Am., Colo. Trial Lawyers Assn., Law Club of Denver (sec. 1984-85, v.p. 1990-91), Phi Alpha Delta, Phi Beta Kappa. Democrat. Roman Catholic. Home: 4662 S Elizabeth Ct Cherry Hills Village CO 80110 Office: Popham Haik Schnobrich & Kaufman Ltd 1200 17th St Ste 2400 Denver CO 80202-5824

TISS, GEORGE JOHN, pediatrician, educator; b. Weiser, Idaho, Aug. 24, 1925; s. George Joseph and Mildred Gwendolyn (Barham) T.; m. Catherine Cassady, June 6, 1968; children: Randy, Carolyn, Danny, Mary, Andy. BS, U. Oreg., 1950, MD, 1954. Diplomate Am. Bd. Pediatrics. Intern U. Oreg. Hosps. and Clinics, Portland, 1954-55, resident in pediatrics, 1955-57; practice medicine specializing in pediatrics Visalia (Calif.) Med. Clinic, 1957—, chmn. bd., 1959-70; specialist Care Medico, Malaysia, 1969, Indonesia, 1976;

specialist Managua, Nicaragua, 1979; med. dir. Free Good News Clinic, 1991—; cons. Keweah Delta Dist. Hosp., Visalia, Tulare (Calif.) Dist. Hosp., Tulare County Hosp.; chmn. 1st Rubella mass immunization program in U.S., Tulare, 1960; chmn. Visalia Comprehensive Health Planning Bd., 1973-74; mem. bd. consortium San Joaquin Valley, 1975—; co-chmn. Calif. Immunization adv. com., 1973-76, chmn., 1976-77, chmn. Toddler Immunization adv. com., Calif., 1983—; assoc. clin. prof. pediatrics U. Calif., San Francisco. Mem. sch. bd. Liberty Sch., 1980—. Served with USAAF, 1945-46. Fellow Am. Bd. Allergy and Immunology, 1987; recipient Lyda M. Smiley award, Calif. Assn. Sch. Nurses, 1981; named Man of Yr. Kaweah Delta Hosp., 1992. Mem. AMA, Calif. Med. Assn, (Lessner award 1994), Am. Acad. Pediat. (bd. dirs. 1992—, Marty Gershwin award 1995), Tulare County Med. Soc. (pres. 1969-70), West Coast Allergy Soc., L.A. Pediat. Soc., Calif. Thoracic Soc., Am. Coll. Allergy, Christina Med. Soc. (missions to Mex. 1987, 90, Dominican Republic 1988, Ecuador 1992), Am. Legion. Office: 5400 W Hillsdale Ave Visalia CA 93291-8222

TITUS, ALICE CESTANDINA (DINA TITUS), state legislator; b. Thomasville, Ga., May 23, 1950. AB, Coll. William and Mary, 1970; MA, U. Ga., 1973; PhD, Fla. State U., 1976. Prof. polit. sci. U. Nev., Las Vegas; mem. Nev. Senate, 1989—; alt. mem. legis. commn., 1989-91, mem., 1991-93; minority floor leader, 1993—; chmn. Nev. Humanities Com., 1984-86; mem. Eldorado Basin adv. group to Colo. River Commn.; active Gov. Commn. Bicentennial of U.S. Constn.; former mem. Gov. Commn. on Aging. Author: Bombs in the Backyard: Atomic Testing and American Politics, 1986, Battle Born: Federal-State Relations in Nevada during the 20th Century, 1989. Mem. Western Polit. Sci. Assn., Clark County Women's Dem. Club. Greek Orthodox. Home: 1637 Travois Cir Las Vegas NV 89119-6283 Office: Nev State Senate State Capitol Carson City NV 89710*

TITUS, EDWARD DEPUE, psychiatrist, administrator; b. N.Y.C., May 24, 1931; s. Edward Kleinhans and Mary (Brown) Chadbourne; m. Virginia Van Den Steenhoven, Mar. 24, 1963 (div.); m. Catherine Brown, Apr. 22, 1990. BA, Occidental Coll., 1953; MS, U. Wis., 1955; MD, Stanford U., 1962; PhD, So. Calif. Psychoanalytic Inst., 1977. Mng. ptnr. Hacker Clinic Assn., Lynwood, Calif., 1968-90; chief psychiatrist parole outpatient clinic region III Calif. Dept. Corrections, L.A., 1991—; asst. clin. prof. psychiatry U. So. Calif., 1993—; chmn. dept. psychiatry St. Francis Hosp., Lynwood, 1979-80. Fellow Am. Psychiat. Assn.; mem. Calif. Med. Assn. (ho. of dels. 1983-95), So. Calif. Psychiat. Soc. (sec. 1984-85), Los Angeles County Med. Assn. (dist. pres. 1980-81, pres. sect. psychiatry 1990-92). Office: Parole Outpatient Clinic 307 W 4th St Los Angeles CA 90013-1104

TOADVINE, JOANNE ELIZABETH, physical therapy foundation executive; b. Covington, Ky., Nov. 29, 1933; d. Ralph and Myrtle (Wasson) Bailer; children: Daniel, Michael, Patrick, Michell, Joseph. Student, St. Benedict Coll. Bus. Sch., 1948; PhD, U. for Humanistic Studies, Las Vegas, Nev., 1986. Cert. rehab. technician in functional elec. stimulation, Nev. Founder, pres. Help Them Walk Again Found., Inc., Las Vegas, 1976—. Contbr. articles to profl. jours. Mem. State of Nev. Dem. Cen. Com., Clark Clunty (Nev.) Dem. Cen. Com. Recipient Humanitarian award Chiropractic Assn. of Ariz., Channel 3 Spirit award, Humanitarian award Dr. Otto Kestler, Spl. Congl. recognition, 1992; named to Honorable Order Ky. Cols., Mother of Yr. Clark County, 1988, Disting. Women of So. Nev., 1989, 90, 91, 92, 93, 94; recognized in The Congl. Recorder, 1980. Mem. Am. Acad. of Neurol. Orthopedic Surgeons (nat. coordinating council on spinal cord injury), Nat. Coordinating Coun. on Spinal Cord Injury, Las Vegas C. of C. (Women's Achievement award in health care), VFW, NAFE, The Pilot Club Internat. Office: Help Them Walk Again Found 5300 W Charleston Blvd Las Vegas NV 89102-1307

TOBER, MARK ROBERT, investment representative, stockbroker; b. Arcadia, Calif., Sept. 15, 1959; s. Robert and Joanne Marie (Leuschner) T.; m. Carol Lynne Weeshoff, Apr. 4, 1987; children: William Robert, Christian Michael. BA, U. So. Calif., 1981; JD, Western State U., Fullerton, Calif., 1992. CFP. Ins. broker Rossmore Property & Casualty, L.A., 1981-84, Aetna Life & Casualty, Orange, Calif., 1984-86, Elmco Ins., Inc., Santa Ana, Calif., 1986-91; investment rep. Edward D. Jones & Co., San Clemente, Calif., 1991-94; fin. advisor Linsco/Private Ledger, San Clemente, 1994—. Recipient Am. Jurisprudence award for legal writing & criminal law Am. Jurisprudence, 1988, 89. Fellow Internat. Bd. CFPs, San Clemente C. of C., Kiwanis, Sigma Alpha Epsilon (pres. 1980-81). Republican. Office: LINSCO/Private Ledger De Los Mares #105 San Clemente CA 92673

TOBIAS, CHRISTOPHER ORD, software company executive; b. Phila., Aug. 17, 1962; s. Joel Allen Tobias and Lucy Cresap (Beebe) T. Student, Reed Coll., 1980-82. Mgr. DaVinci Personal Tech., Portland, Oreg., 1982-84, Computer One, Portland, 1984-85; ptnr. PC Profls., Portland, 1985-87; devel. mgr. Somex, Lake Oswego, Oreg., 1987-91; owner Tobias Cons., 1992-93; sr. systems specialist PC Support Inc., Portland, 1993—; bd. dirs. Oreg. Computer Cons., Portland, 1986-87. Contbr. articles to profl. jours. Mem. Am. Seed Trade Assn. Office: PC Support Inc 3323 SW Harbor Dr Portland OR 97201

TOBIAS, SHEILA, writer, educator; b. N.Y., Apr. 26, 1935; d. Paul Jay and Rose (Steinberger) Tobias; m. Carlos Stern, Oct. 11, 1970 (div. 1982); m. Carl T. Tomizuka, Dec. 16, 1987. BA, Harvard Radcliffe U., 1957; MA, Columbia U., 1961, MPhil, 1974; PhD (hon.), Drury Coll., 1994, Wheelock Coll., 1995. Journalist W. Germany, U.S. and Fed. Republic Germany, 1957-65; lect. in history C.C.N.Y., N.Y.C., 1965-67; univ. adminstr. Cornell U., Wesleyan U., 1967-78; lect. in women's studies U. Calif., San Diego, 1985-92; lect. in war, peace studies U. So. Calif., 1985-88. Author: Overcoming Math Anxiety, 1978, rev. edit., 1994, Succeed with Math, 1987, Revitalizing Undergraduate Science: Why Some Things Work and Most Don't, 1992, Science as a Career: Perceptions and Realities, 1995; co-author: The People's Guide to National Defense, 1982, Women, Militarism and War, 1987, They're Not Dumb, They're Different, 1990, (with Carl T. Tomizuka) Breaking the Science Barrier, 1992. Chmn. bd. dirs. The Clarion newspaper. Mem. Am. Assn. Higher Edn. (bd. dirs. 1993—), Coll. Sci. Tchrs. Assn., Nat. Women's Studies Assn., Phi Beta Kappa.

TOBIASON, FREDERICK LEE, chemistry educator; b. Pe Ell, Wash., Sept. 15, 1936; s. Joseph Oliver and Beatrice Olivia (Olaveson) T.; m. Dorothy Anne Puotinen, Sept. 3, 1961; children: Laura Anne Riddle, Anne Marie Bessette, Joseph Daniel. BA, Pacific Luth. U., 1958; PhD, Mich. State U., 1963. Rsch. assoc. Emory U., Atlanta, 1963-64; rsch. chemist E.I. du Pont de Nemours, Waynesboro, Va., 1964-66; from asst. prof. chemistry to assoc. prof. chemistry Pacific Luth. U., Tacoma, 1966-72, prof., 1973-91; regency prof., 1975; prof. emeritus Pacific Luth. U., Tacoma, 1992—; cons. Reichold Chems., Inc., Tacoma, 1967-87; vis. prof. Chengdu U. of Sci. & Tech., Sichuan, China, 1989-91; vis. rsch. prof. U. Sci. & Tech., Lille, France, 1992-93; vis. scholar Dnepropetrovsk Chem. Inst., Ukraine, 1991, 92. Contbr. book chpt.: Handbook of Adhesives, 1989; contbr. articles to profl. jours., sci. papers, manuals and book chpts. Mem. stream restoration com. Clover Creek Coun., Tacoma, 1988—; bd. dirs. Tahoma Land Conservancy, 1993—; assoc. Danforth Found., 1978-85; mem. Danforth N.W., Pacific N.W. region, 1986—. Recipient faculty teaching award Burlington No. Found., 1989. Mem. Am. Chem. Soc., Tahoma Audubon Soc. (pres., bd. dirs.). Lutheran. Office: Pacific Luth U Tacoma WA 98447

TOBIN, JAMES MICHAEL, lawyer; b. Santa Monica, Calif., Sept. 27, 1948; s. James Joseph and Glada Marie (Meisner) T.; m. Kathleen Marie Espy, Sept. 14, 1985. BA with honors, U. Calif., Riverside, 1970; JD, Georgetown U., 1974. Bar: Calif. 1974, Mich. 1987. From atty. to gen. atty. So. Pacific Co., San Francisco, 1975-82; v.p. regulatory affairs So. Pacific Communications Co., Washington, 1982-83; v.p., gen. counsel Lexitel Corp., Washington, 1983-85; v.p., gen. counsel, sec. ALC Communications Corp., Birmingham, Mich., 1985-87, sr. v.p., gen. counsel, sec., 1987-88; of counsel Morrison & Foerster, San Francisco, 1988-90, ptnr., 1990—. Mem. ABA, Calif. Bar Assn., Mich. Bar Assn., Fed. Communications Bar Assn. Republican. Unitarian. Home: 2739 Octavia St San Francisco CA 94123-4303 Office: Morrison & Foerster 345 California St San Francisco CA 94104-2635

TOBIN, ROBERT MANFORD, JR., karate instructor; b. Idaho Falls, Idaho, Feb. 17, 1958; s. Robert Manford and Marilyn Hilma (Harju) T. BS in Fin. and Acctg., U. Colo., 1979. Asst. instr. taekwon-do U. Colo., Boulder, 1977-85, instr. basketball team, 1985-88, head instr., 1985—; fin. mgr. Tobin Engrs. & Constructors, Longmont, Colo., 1979-80, gen. mgr., 1981-82; gen. mgr. Roofguard of Colo., Longmont, 1981-83; oximetry rschr. Bioximetry Tech., Inc.-Ohmeda Boulder, Boulder and Louisville, Colo., 1984—; instr. Sereff Taekwon-Do, Broomfield, Colo., 1984-85. Contbr. articles to various publs. Del. Colo. Dem. Com., 1980, Boulder County Dem. Com., 1984. Mem. U.S. Taekwon-Do Fedn. (mem. test bd. 1985—, bd. dirs. 1986—, nat. referee trainer 1995), Internat. Taekwon-Do Fedn. (1st through 6th degree black belts). Democrat. Presbyterian. Home: 1365 Brown Cir Boulder CO 80303-6724 Office: Ohmeda 1315 W Century Dr Louisville CO 80027-9560

TOBIN, WILLIAM JOSEPH, newspaper editor; b. Joplin, Mo., July 28, 1927; s. John J. and Lucy T. (Shoppach) T.; m. Marjorie Stuhldreher, Apr. 26, 1952; children—Michael Gerard, David Joseph, James Patrick. BJ, Butler U., 1948. Staff writer AP, Indpls., 1947-52, news feature writer, N.Y.C., 1952-54, regional membership exec., Louisville, 1954-56, corr., Juneau, Alaska, 1956-60, asst. chief of bur., Balt., 1960-61, chief of bur., Helena, Mont., 1961-63; mng. editor Anchorage Times, 1963-73, assoc. editor, 1973-85, gen. mgr., 1974-85, v.p., editor-in-chief, 1985-89, editor editorial page, 1990, asst. pub., 1991, senior editor Voice of the Times, 1991—; bd. dirs. Enstar Corp., 1982-84. Mem. devel. com. Anchorage Winter Olympics, 1984-91, bd. dirs. Anchorage organizing com., 1985-91; bd. dirs. Alaska Coun. on Econ. Edn., 1978-84, Boys Clubs Alaska, 1979-83, Anchorage Symphony Orch., 1986-87, Blue Cross Wash. and Alaska, 1987—, chmn. 1990-91; chmn. Premera Corp., 1994—; mem. adv. bd. Providence Hosp., Anchorage, 1974-91, chmn., 1980-85. Served to sgt. AUS, 1950-52. Mem. Alaska AP Mems. Assn. (pres. 1964), Anchorage C. of C. (bd. dirs. 1969-74, pres. 1972-73), Alaska World Affairs Council (pres. 1967-68), Phi Delta Theta. Clubs: Alaska Press (pres. 1968-69), Commonwealth North (Anchorage). Home: 2130 Lord Baranof Dr Anchorage AK 99517-1257 Office: Anchorage Times PO Box 100040 Anchorage AK 99510-0040

TODARO, MICHAEL JOSEPH, JR., military officer; b. Darby, Pa., Aug. 31, 1969; s. Michael Joseph and Judith Francis (Meehan) T. BS in Aerospace Engring., U. So. Calif., 1991. Engring. intern Teledyne Ryan Aero., San Diego, summer 1988, 89, Morton Internat., Ogden, Utah, 1991-92; commd. 2d lt. USAF, 1991; advanced through grades to 1st lt., 1993; asst. flight chief, peacekeeper missile mech. flight USAF, Cheyenne, Wyo., 1992-93, chief missile mech. flight, 1993, chief team tng. flight, 1993-94; promoted to capt., 1995; assigned 2d Space Ops. Squadron, Falcon AFB, Colo., 1995—. Mem. AIAA, Co. Grade Officers Assn., Air Force Assn. Roman Catholic.

TODD, FRANCES EILEEN, pediatrics nurse; b. Hawthorne, Calif., Aug. 20, 1950; d. James Clark and Jean Eleanor (McGinty) Nailen; m. Steven Charles Todd, Oct. 25, 1975; 1 child, Amanda Kathryn. ASN, El Camino Jr. Coll., 1974; BSN, Calif. State Coll., Long Beach, 1982, postgrad. RN, Calif.; cert. nurse practitioner, pub. health nurse, Calif.; cert. pediatric nurse practitioner; cert. pediatric advanced life support Am. Heart Assn. Nursing attendant St. Earne's Nursing Home, Inglewood, Calif., 1973; clinic nurse I Harbor-UCLA Med. Ctr., Torrance, Calif., 1974-77, evening shift relief charge nurse, clinic nurse II, 1977-85, pediatric liaison nurse, 1984-90, pediatric nurse practitioner, 1985—; steward Local Union 660, 1995—; tutor Compton (Calif.) C.C., 1988, clin. instr., 1987-88; lectr. faculty dept. pediatrics UCLA Sch. Medicine, 1980—; lectr. in field. Contbr. articles to profl. jours. Co-chair parent support group Sherrie's Schs., Lomita, Calif. Mem. Nat. Assn. Pediatric Nurse Assocs. and Practitioners, L.A. Pediatric Soc., Emergency Nurses Assn., Local 660 (shop steward), Svc. Employees Int. Union, local 660 (union steward), Peruvian Paso Horse Registry N.Am. (co-chair judge's accreditation com. 1989—, judge's Andalusian horses). Office: Harbor UCLA Med Ctr 1000 W Carson St PO Box 14-7W Torrance CA 90509

TODD, HAROLD WADE, retired air force officer, consultant; b. Chgo., Jan. 17, 1938; s. Harold Wade and Jeanne (Fayal) T.; m. Wendy Yvonne Kendrick, July 12, 1981; children by previous marriage: Hellen J. Wilson, Kenneth J., Stephen D., Joseph M., Michelle M. Adams, Mark A.; stepchildren: Jamie Y. White, James K. Mills, Timothy S. Emerson. B.S., U.S. Air Force Acad., 1959; grad., Nat. War Coll., 1975. Commd. 2d lt. U.S. Air Force, 1959, advanced through grades to maj. gen., 1982; aide to comdr. (2d Air Force (SAC)), Barksdale AFB, La., 1970-71; exec. aide to comdr.-in-chief U.S. Air Forces Europe, Germany, 1971-74; spl. asst. chief of staff USAF, 1975-76; chief Concept Devel. Div., 1976-77, chief Readiness and NATO Staff Group, Hdqrs. USAF, 1977-78; exec. asst. to chmn. Joint Chiefs Staff Washington, 1978-80; comdr. 25th region N. Am. Aerospace Def. Command McChord AFB, Wash., 1980-82; chief staff 4th Allied Tactical Air Force Heidelberg, 1982-85; commandant Air War Coll., 1985-89; vice comdr. Air U., 1985-89, ret., 1989; ind. cons. Colorado Springs, Colo., 1989—. Founder, pres. Bossier City (La.) chpt. Nat. Assn. for Children with Learning Disabilities, 1970-71. Decorated Def. D.S.M., Air Force D.S.M. (2), Legion of Merit (2), D.F.C., Air medal (8), Air Force Commendation medal. Mem. Air Force Assn., USAF Acad. Assn. Grads., Nat. War Coll. Alumni Assn. Home: 1250 Big Valley Dr Colorado Springs CO 80919-1015

TODD, JAMES HIRAM, II, management consultant; b. Oklahoma City, Nov. 2, 1942; s. Prentiss Oliver and Itillious Vener (Jackson) T.; m. Unzerlo Verginia General, June 19, 1963; 1 child, Mark A. BA, U. Okla., 1972, MA, 1986; PhD, Western Inst. Social Rsch., Berkeley, Calif., 1990. Health adminstr. Mary Mahoney Health Ctr., Spencer, Okla., 1973-76; spl. project dir. North Tulsa Ambulatory Care System, 1976-78; clin. nurse Bapt. Med. Ctr., Oklahoma City, 1979-83; pres., CEO Ednl. Resource Devel. Group, Oklahoma City, 1983-94; regional mgr. STAT Nursing Svcs., Oakland, Calif., 1986-88; rsch. prof. San Francisco State U., 1988—; adv. com. San Francisco Unified Sch. Dist., 1989-94; White House Conferee, 1975. Author: Our Home is Not the Ghetto, 1995. Fin. com. United Way, Oklahoma City, 1973-76; scout master Boy Scouts Am., Norman, Okla., 1970-72; v.p. Nat. Black Child Devel. Inst., San Francisco, 1990—; bd. dirs., congrl. cons. Nat. Assn. Cmty. Health Ctrs., Washington, 1973-78; bd. dirs. Emergency Med. Svcs. Auth., Tulsa, 1976-78. With U.S. Army, 1960. Recipient Cert. Commendation, City of Tulsa, 1978, Cert. Appreciation, U.S. Dept. Edn., 1991, proclamation award Mayor San Francisco, 1990. Mem. AAUP, Nat. Assn. Black Sch. Educators, Calif. Commonwealth, Calif. Acad. Sci., World Future Soc., Ernest W. Lyons Lodge. Democrat. Office: San Francisco State U 8 Tapia Dr San Francisco CA 94132-1717

TODD, LINDA MARIE, air traffic-weather advisor, financial consultant; b. L.A., Mar. 30, 1948; d. Ithel Everette and Janet Marie (Zito) Fredricks; m. William MacKenzie Cook, Jan. 11, 1982 (div. Oct. 1989); m. Robert Oswald Todd, Apr. 8, 1990; 1 child, Jesse MacKenzie Todd. BA in Psychology and Sociology, U. Colo., 1969; student Psychology Grad. work, U. No. Colo., 1970. Pilot lic., weather cert., FCC lic., Calif. life ins. lic., coll. teaching credential; registered with Nat. Assn. Securities Dealers. Counselor Jeffco Juvenile Detention Ctr., Golden, Colo., 1969-71; communications Elan Vital, Denver, 1971-81; legal sec. Fredman, Silverberg & Lewis, San Diego, 1980-82; escrow supr. Performance Mktg. Concepts, Olympic Valley, Calif., 1982-85; mgmt. commn. instr. Sierra Coll., Truckee, Calif., 1986-87; regional mgr. Primerica Fin. Svcs., Reno, 1987-91; air traffic, weather advisor Truckee (Calif.) Tahoe Airport Dist., 1986—; student tour leader, air show organizer Truckee (Calif.) Tahoe Airport; fin. cons. Primerica Fin. Svcs., Truckee, Calif., 1987-91; gen. agt. TTS Fin., 1992—. Editor: (newsletter) Communications, 1975. Sec. gen. High Sch. Model UN, Arapahoe, Littleton, Colo., 1965; del. State Model UN, Colo., 1966; conv. del. Elan Vital, The Ninety-Nines, Inc. Recipient Univ. scholarship Littleton (Colo.) Edn. Assn., 1966, flight scholarship The Ninety-Nines Inc., Reno, 1990; named Recruiter of Month, Al Williams Primerica, Reno, 1987. Mem. Plane Talkers, The Ninety Nines, Elan Vital, Planetary Soc. Home and Office: PO Box 1303 Truckee CA 96160-1303

TODD, PAUL WILSON, biophysicist, educator; b. Bangor, Maine, June 15, 1936; s. Albert Clayton and Sylvia May (Preble) T.; m. Judith Stow Blackmer, June 16, 1957; children: Kevin, Dana, Trevor, Andrea. BA, Bowdoin Coll., Brunswick, Maine, 1959; BS, Mass. Inst. Tech., 1959; MS, U. Rochester, 1960; PhD, U. Calif., Berkeley, 1964. Lectr. U. Calif., Berkeley, 1964-66; asst. prof. Pa. State U., University Park, 1966-72; assoc. prof. Pa. State U., 1972-77, chmn. genetics program, 1974-79, prof., 1977-86; dir. Bioprocessing & Pharm. Rsch. Ctr., Phila., 1984-87; physicist Nat. Inst. Stds. and Tech., Boulder, Colo., 1988-91; adj. prof. U. Colo., Boulder, 1990-91, rsch. prof., 1991—, assoc. dir. BioServe Space Tech. Rsch. Ctr., 1994—. Co-editor: Space Radiation Biology, 1973, Frontiers in Bioprocessing, 1989, Gravity and the Cell, 1991, Frontiers in Bioprocessing II, 1991, Cell Separation Science and Technology, 1991; inventor in field; contbr. articles to profl. jours. Radiol. Physics fellow AEC, 1959, Eleanor Roosevelt fellow Am. Cancer Soc., 1967, Fogarty Internat. fellow NIH, Moscow, 1979, Yamagiwa-Yoshida fellow Internat. Union Against Cancer, Sweden, 1979, R & D 100 award, 1990. Mem. AAAS, AIAA, AIChE, Am. Chem. Soc., Electrophoresis Soc. (assoc. editor 1986-92), Cell Kinetics Soc., Radiation Rsch. Soc. (assoc. editor 1975-79), Soc. for Analytical Cytology (assoc. editor 1979-88), Am. Soc. for Gravational and Space Biology (coun. 1988-91, editl. bd. 1992—), Tissue Culture Assn., Am. Soc. Engring. Edn., Com. on Space Rsch. Home: 2595 Vassar Dr Boulder CO 80303-5730 Office: U Colo Dept Chem Engring Campus Box 424 Boulder CO 80309-0424

TODD, STEVEN DAVIS, fine art consultant, agent, company owner; b. Chgo., Sept. 3, 1948; s. Irving Davis and Osna (Rubin) Proskaner; 1 child, Lindsey Channah Todd. AA, Wright Coll., 1973; BA, Northeastern Ill. U., 1975. Nat. dir. Budget Furniture, Santa Monica, Calif., 1983-85; sales rep. eastern div. Collectors Editions, Canoga Park, Calif., 1988-93; western mgr. London Contemporary Art, 1993; owner Fine Art Acquisitions, Simi Valley, Calif., 1993—; cons. in field. Vol. Spl. Olympics, 1988, 89, Beverly Hills Arts Coun., 1993. With USMC, 1968-70. Performed in Hallmark of Fame. Mem. Screen Actors Guild. Jewish. Home: 1142 Tivoli Ln Apt 162 Simi Valley CA 93065-1971

TODD, WILLIAM MICHAEL, counselor, educator; b. Dayton, Ohio, Jan. 4, 1957; s. J.T. and Bessie Kate (Lowe) T.; m. Kim Kristine Todd, Oct. 14, 1994; children: Lukas, Leigh. BA in Psychology, Ottawa U., 1993, MA in Profl. Counseling, 1994. Cert. cmty. coll. tchr., 1995. Counselor Arrowstar Counseling, Phoenix, 1992—; prof. psychology Glendale (Ariz.) C.C., 1994; bus. owner Antique Market, MT Constrn., Arrowstar Cons., Phoenix, 1983—. Assoc. pastor Nazarene Ch., Phoenix, 1991-93, youth min., 1993; counselor Boys and Girls Club, Phoenix, 1993-94. Mem. Am. Counselors Assn., Am. Clin. Mental Health Assn., Marriage and Family Counseling Assn., Phi Theta Kappa. Home: 3507 E Windsor Ave Phoenix AZ 85008 Office: Arrowstar Counseling 3520 E Indian School Rd Phoenix AZ 85018-5115

TODSEN, THOMAS KAMP, botanist; b. Pittsfield, Mass., Oct. 21, 1918; s. Lorenz and Ellen Paula (Christensen) T.; m. Margaret Cumming Dorsey, Aug. 4, 1939 (dec. 1988); children: Thomas A., William L. BS, U. Fla., 1939, MS, 1942, PhD, 1950. Instr. N.Mex. Coll. of A & MA, State College, 1950-51; chief chemist White Sands Proving Ground, N.Mex., 1951-53; chief warheads and spl. projects White Sands Proving Ground, 1953-57; chief sci. adv. office White Sands Missile Range, 1957-59, chief surf-to-surf project, 1959-65, dir. test ops., 1965-68, chief land combat project, 1968-72, tech. dir. Army test and evaluation, 1972-78; asst. prof. botany N.Mex. State U., Las Cruces, 1978—; chmn. Joint AEC-DOD subcom., Washington, 1953-62; cons. in field. Contbr. articles to profl. jours., chpts. to books; co-editor: Rare and Endemic Plants of New Mexico; asst. editor the Heliograph Jour.; author: New Mexico Territorial Postmarks; editor La Posta jour., 1974-76. Elder First Presbyn. Ch., Las Cruces, 1960—; dir. Rio Grande Hist. Collections, Inc., Las Cruces, 1975-85; wildflower chmn. N.Mex. Garden Clubs, Inc., Albuquerque, 1987-91. Tenn. Corp. rsch. fellow, Atlanta, 1949. Fellow Ariz.-Nev. Acad. Scis.; mem. Am. Chem. Soc. (emeritus), Am. Soc. Mag. Photographers (emeritus), AAAS, Am. Soc. Plant Taxonomists, Assn. for Tropical Biology, Sigma Xi.

TOEPPE, WILLIAM JOSEPH, JR., retired aerospace engineer; b. Buffton, Ohio, Feb. 27, 1931; s. William Joseph Sr. and Ruth May (Hipple) T. BSEE, Rose-Hulman Inst. Tech., Terre Haute, Ind., 1953. Engr. Electronics divsn. Ralph M. Parsons Co., Pasadena, Calif., 1953-55; pvt. practice cons. Orange, Calif., 1961-62; engring. supr. Lockheed Electronics Co., City of Commerce, Calif., 1962-64; staff engr. Interstate Electronics Corp., Anaheim, Calif., 1957-61; engring. supr. Interstate Electronics Corp., Anaheim, 1964-89, ret., 1989. Author: Finding Your German Village, 1990, Gazetteers and Maps of France for Genealogical Research, 1990, GGSA Library User's Guide, 1995. Pres. Golden Cir. Home Owners' Assn., Orange, 1989-95. With U. S. Army, 1955-57. Mem. Ohio Geneal. Soc. (life), Geneal. Soc. Pa., So. Calif. Geneal. Soc., German Geneal. Soc. Am. (bd. dirs. 1993—). Home: 700 E Taft Ave Unit 19 Orange CA 92665-4400

TOFF, HOWARD DAVID, psychiatrist; b. Phila., July 26, 1947; s. Fred and Evelyn (Gross) T.; m. Carol Hope Saturansky, July 4, 1976; children: Stephen Andrew, Benjamin Jacob. BS, Pa. State U., 1968; MD, Jefferson Med. Coll., Phila., 1970; PhD, So. Calif. Psychoanalytic Inst, L.A., 1992. Asst. dir. outpatient clinic, tng. dir. child psychiatry Cedars Sinai Med. Ctr., L.A., 1978-84; pvt. practice L.A. and Tucson, Ariz., 1978—; tng. dir. child psychiatry U. Ariz., Tucson, 1990-92; cons. ACCM, Tucson, 1992—. Lt. USPHS, 1971-73. Mem. Am. Psychiat. Assn., Am. Psychoanalytic Assn., Am. Acad. Child & Adolescent Psychiatry, Ariz. Psychiat. Soc. Democrat. Jewish. Office: 1050 E River Rd Ste 202 Tucson AZ 85718-5736

TOFFLER, WILLIAM LOUIS, medical educator; b. Ft. Knox, Ky., Feb. 9, 1949; s. Alan R. and Rosemary (Jacobs) T.; m. Marlene Toffler, Aug. 11, 1973; children: Emily, Elizabeth, Adrienne, Christopher, Alan, Susan, Mark. BS in Aerospace Engring. cum laude, U. Notre Dame, 1971; postgrad., Georgetown U., 1972; MD, U. Va., 1976. Diplomate Nat. Bd. Med. Examiners; lic. physician, Calif., Oreg., Va. Resident in family medicine dept. family practice Med. U. S.C., Charleston, 1976-79, clin. instr. dept. family practice, 1979; family physician Sweet Home (Oreg.) Family Practice, M.D., P.C., 1979-85; clin. asst. prof. dept. family medicine Oreg. Health Scis. U., Portland, 1981-85, asst. prof., dir. patient care dept. family medicine, 1985-88, asst. prof., dir. predoctoral edn. dept. family medicine, 1988-91, assoc. prof., dir. edn. sect. and predoctoral edn., 1991—; med. staff Lebanon Community Hosp., 1979-85, sec. med. staff, 1981-83, chmn. hosp. infection control com., 1983-84; mem. adv. com. pub. health grant Oreg. Health Scis. U., 1985-86, mumerous offices and coms., 1990-91; physician, cons. Portland Sports Medicine Assocs., 1986-91; mem. Gov.'s Task Force on Field Burning, 1988-89; med. advisor Crisis Pregnancy Ctr., Beaverton, Oreg., 1987-89; physician, med. dir. Rosemont Adolescent Treatment Ctr., Portland, 1986—; vis. nurse Assn. Med. Adv. Bd., Portland, Oreg., 1986-93; faculty sponsor Am. Heart Assn. Fellowship, 1991-92, 92-93, Am. Cancer Soc. Rsch. Fellowship, 1987-88; aviation med. examiner FAA; presenter in field. Peer reviewer: Family Practice Rsch. Jour., 1990—, Family Medicine, 1992—, Acad. Medicine, 1992—, Am. Family Physician, 1994—, others; mem. editl. bd. Jour. Family Practice, 1993—. With U.S. Army, 1971; capt. USAR, 1971-79. Mem. AMA, Am. Running and Fitness Assn., Am. Acad. Family Physicians, Am. Coll. Sports Medicine, Oreg. D.O.C., Oreg. Acad. Family Physicians (del. 1981—, chmn. rsch. com. 1985-88, chmn. student activities com. 1988-91, com. for advancement of family medicine), Oreg. Med. Assn. (com. on med. aspects of sch. sports 1979—, pub. edn. com. 1986—, ho. dels. reference com. 1992), Portland Regional Acad. Family Practice (treas. 1990—), Multnomah County Med. Soc. (sch. sports com. 1986-93, del. 1991—). Office: Oreg Health Scis U Dept Family Medicine 3181 SW Sam Jackson Park Rd Portland OR 97201-3011

TOFTNESS, CECIL GILLMAN, lawyer, consultant; b. Glasgow, Mont., Sept. 13, 1920; s. Anton Bernt and Nettie (Pedersen) T.; m. Chloe Catherine Vincent, Sept. 8, 1951. AA, San Diego Jr. Coll., 1943; student Purdue U., Northwestern U.; BS, UCLA, 1947; JD cum laude, Southwestern U., 1953. Bar: Calif. 1954, U.S. Dist. Ct. (so. dist.) Calif. 1954, U.S. Tax Ct. 1974, U.S. Supreme Ct. 1979. Sole practice, Palos Verdes Estates, Calif., 1954—; dir., pres., chmn. bd. Fisherman & Mchts. Bank, San Pedro, Calif., 1963-67; dir., v.p. Palos Verdes Estates Bd. Realtors, 1964-65. Chmn. Capital Campaign Fund, Richstone Charity, Hawthorne, Calif., 1983. Served to lt. (j.g.) USN, 1938-46, ETO, PTO. Decorated Silver Star; named Man of Yr., Glasgow, 1984. Mem. South Bay Bar Assn., Southwestern Law Sch. Alumni Assn. (class rep. 1980—), Internat. Physicians for the Prevention of Nuclear War (del. 7th World Congress, 1987), Themis Soc.-Southwestern Law Sch., Schumacher Founder's Circle-Southwestern Law Sch. (charter). Democrat. Lutheran. Lodges: Kiwanis (sec.-treas. 1955-83, v.p., pres., bd. dirs.), Masons, K.T. Participant Soc. Expedition thur the N.W. Passage. Home:

2229 Via Acalones Palos Verdes Estates CA 90274 Office: 2516 Via Tejon Pls Vrds Est CA 90274-6802

TOGNETTI, GENE, protective services official, consultant; b. Watsonville, Calif., July 3, 1940; s. John Louis and Mary Louise (Viglieca) T. AA, City Coll. San Francisco, 1962; student, U. Calif., San Francisco, 1977; BA cum laude, Golden Gate U., 1977, MPA, 1980. Cert. BLS, Calif. Mgr. Majectic Plastics, San Francisco, 1973; plastics mgr. Thomas Swan Sign Co., San Francisco, 1973-75; police officer Colma (Calif.) Police Dept., 1975-78; detective sgt. Hillsborough (Calif.) Police Dept., 1981-85, comdr. adminstrn. and svcs. divsn., 1986-92; interim fire chief Point Montara Fire Protection Dist., Moss Beach, Calif., 1992-93; res. police officer San Francisco Police Dept., 1969-70; police officer Broadmoor Police Dept., Colma, 1970-75; owner, cons. Epoch Enterprises, San Francisco; cons. IBM Corp., Armonk, N.H., Viking Freight Sys., Inc., San Jose, Calif., Pfizer, Inc., N.Y.C., Liberty House of Calif., San Francisco, J.C. Penney Inc., San Bruno, Calif.; chief moderator Western State Crime Seminar, 1990-94, asst. chief moderator, 1988, state coord., 1984-87. Mem. Internat. Assn. Chiefs of Police, Calif. Burglary and Theft Investigators Assn. (pres. 1986, chmn. by-laws com. 1983-89), No. Calif. Safe and Burglary Investigators Assn. (pres. 1982), Calif. Peace Officers Assn., Peninsula Police Officers Assn., Calif. State Firefighters' Assn., Am. Soc. for Indsl. Security. Office: Epoch Enterprises 906 Edinburgh St San Francisco CA 94112-3818

TOGO, YUKIYASU, automotive executive; b. Yokohama, Kanagawa, Japan, Nov. 13, 1924; came to U.S., 1983; s. Kinji Togo and Nobuko Watanabe; m. Misako Mineta, Apr. 2, 1948; children: Yukinori, Yumi. Gen. mgr. Toyota Motor Sales, Tokyo, Japan, 1976-78, assoc. dir., 78-79, dir., 1979-80; pres. Toyota Can. Inc., Ontario, Can., 1980-82; dir. Toyota Motor Corp., Aichi, Japan, 1982, mng. dir., 1982-83; pres. Can. Auto Parts Toyota Inc., B.C., Can., 1983—; pres., chief exec. officer Toyota Motor Sales U.S.A. Inc., Torrance, Calif., 1983—; pres. Toyota Motor Credit Corp., Torrance, Calif., 1989—, Toyota Motor Ins. Svcs., Torrance, Calif., 1989—, Toyota Aviation USA Inc., Torrance, Calif., 1989—. Bd. dirs. Los Angeles World Affairs Coun., 1989. Office: Toyota Motor Sales USA Inc 19001 S Western Ave Ste 2991 Torrance CA 90501-1106*

TOHILL, BRUCE OWEN, geologist; b. Chgo., Oct. 21, 1941; s. Kenneth Fay and Jane Fayette (Dickinson) T.; Mary Alice (Wieber) Tohill; children—Damon, Kevin, Brian. B.S., U. Nebr., 1964, M.S., 1965. Geologist, Humble Oil & Refining Co., Kingsville, Tex., 1965-67, Amoco Prodn. Co., Denver, 1967-72, Pubco Petroleum Corp., Denver, 1972-73; ptnr. Peppard & Assocs., Denver, 1973-83, Basin Analysis Cons., Denver, 1983-92, Tohill & Assocs., Inc., 1992—; mem. adv. bd. dept. geology U. Nebr., 1981-85. Contbr. articles to profl. jours. Recipient Disting. Svc. award dept. geology U. Nebr. Rocky Mountain Assn. Geologists. Mem. Calif. Explorationists Group (founder), Rocky Mountain Assn. Geologists, Am. Assn. Petroleum Geologists (chmn. ho. of dels. 1983-84), Soc. Econ. Paleontologists and Mineralogists (pres. sect. 1975), Am. Inst. Profl. Geologists (bd. dirs. 1977, v.p. 1979), U. Nebr. Alumni Club (pres. 1976), Masons, Shriners. Republican. Methodist. Home: 12546 Rivera St Broomfield CO 80020-7930

TOKÉ, ARUN NARAYAN, editor, educator, electrical engineer; b. Indore, India, July 2, 1949; came to U.S., 1971; s. Narayan Ganesh and Laxmibai (Chinchalkar) T. BSEE, U. Indore, 1971; postgrad., U. Vt., 1974-75, U. Notre Dame, 1974; MSEE, U. Wis., Milw., 1974. Cert. energy auditor, Vt. Energy auditor State of Vt., Morrisville, 1979; design engr. N.C.R. Corp., Columbia, S.C., 1978-79; asst. prof. Vt. Tech. Coll., Randolph, 1980-84; rsch. asst. Ctr. for Sci. and Environment, New Delhi, India, 1986; editor, publs. mgr. Approvecho Inst., Cottage Grove, Oreg., 1987-89; exec. editor, founder Skipping Stones, multi-cultural mag. for young people, Eugene, Oreg., 1989—; also bd. dirs. Skippings Stones mag., Eugene, Oreg. Author: Song of Winter Wonderland, 1982; co-author: Energy, Economics and the Environment, 1984; contbr. articles to various mags. and newspapers. Organizer Ctrl. Am. Peacewalk, Ctrl. Am., 1984. Recipient Disting. Achievement award Ednl. Press Assn. Am., 1993, Golden Shoestring award, 1995. Office: Skipping Stones Mag PO Box 3939 Eugene OR 97403-0939

TOKMAKOFF, GEORGE, history educator; b. Tientsin, Hopei, China, July 9, 1928; s. Vasili and Claudia (Kalinin) T.; m. Erika Berzewski, Aug. 30, 1959 (dec. 1988); children: Andrei, Larisa. BA, U. Wash., 1952, MA, 1957; PhD, U. London, 1963. Instr. U. Md., London, 1959-61; asst. prof. history U. Wis., Milw., 1962-63; prof. history Calif. State U., Sacramento, 1963-93, prof. emeritus of History, 1993—. Author: Stolypin and the Third Duma, 1981; contbr. articles to profl. jours. With USAF, 1951-54. Named Faculty of the Yr., Calif. State U., Sacramento, 1964; NEH grantee, 1971; recipient Outstanding Faculty award, Phi Kappa Phi, 1975. Mem. Am. Assn. for Advancement of Slavic Studies. Democrat. Orthodox Ch. Home: 4837 Foster Way Carmichael CA 95608-2912

TOKOFSKY, JERRY HERBERT, film producer; b. N.Y.C., Apr. 14, 1936; s. Julius H. and Rose (Trager) T.; m. Myrna Weinstein, Feb. 21, 1968 (div.); children: David, Peter; m. Fiammetta Bettuzzi, 1970 (div.); 1 child, Tatianna; m. Karen Oliver, Oct. 4, 1981. BS in Journalism, NYU, 1957, LLD, 1959. Talent agt. William Morris Agy., N.Y.C., 1953-59; v.p. William Morris Agy., L.A., 1959-64; exec. v.p. Columbia Pictures, L.A., 1964-69; v.p. Paramount Pictures, London, 1970; exec. v.p. MGM, London, 1971; pres. Jerry Tokofsky Prodns., L.A., 1972-82; exec. v.p. Zupnik Enterprises, L.A., 1982-92; pres. Jerry Tokofsky Entertainment, Encino, Calif., 1992—; prof. Sch. TV and Film U. So. Calif. Prodr. films Where's Poppa, 1971, Born To Win, 1972, Dreamscape, 1985, Fear City, 1986, Wildfire, 1988, Glengarry Glen Ross, 1992, The Grass Harp, 1994, Indubious Battle, 1995, American Buffalo, 1995, Double Down, 1995. With U.S. Army, 1959, res. 1959-63. Named Man of Yr. B'nai B'rith, 1981; recipient L.A. Resolution City of L.A., 1981. Mem. Variety Club Internat.

TOLAN, VICKI IRVENA, physical education educator; b. Vancouver, B.C., Can., Apr. 8, 1949; d. James R. and Adah St. C. (Holmes) Butchart; m. John C. Tolan, Mar. 26, 1988; children: Shauna, Jeffrey, Julie, Kelcie. BA in Edn., Western Wash. U., 1971, postgrad., 1972; M of Sports Sci., U.S. Sports Acad., 1988. Cert. tchr., Wash., Calif. Tchr. Pt. Garden Mid. Sch., Everett, Wash., 1971-74; tchr. phys. edn. Deaconnes Children's Home, Everett, 1972; tchr. phys. edn., health, social studies Mid. Sch., Everett, 1971-74; subs. tchr. Everett and Marysville, Wash., 1974-76, Lakewood, Wash., 1976-77; tchr. ESL Pt. Angeles (Calif.) Sch. Dist., 1983-86, tchr. photography, swimming, health, phys. edn., aerobics, 1986-87, phys. edn. and health specialist, 1987-89; tchr. Alta Loma (Calif.) Sch. Dist., 1989—; student tchr. phys. edn., Lynnwood, Wash., 1971, Bellingham, Wash., 1971; soccer coach youth teams. Pt. Angeles Sch. Dist., 1972—, mem. AIDS/drugs curriculum com., 1986—; cheerleader advisor, 1988, 89, tchr. elem. summer sch., 1986, 87; owner Kits Camera, Pt. Angeles, 1974-83; dist. chair phys. edn. dept. Alta Loma Jr. High Sch., 1989—, chmn. phys. edn. dept., 1992-93. Instr. swimming, Kenmore, 1965-72; founder, coord., pres. Olympic Peninsula Women's Soccer League, 1979-86; bd. dirs. Womanfest, 1985, 86; coord. Jump Rope for Heart, Pt. Angeles, 1989. Named Mother of Yr. Pt. Angeles, 1983, 84, Sports Woman of Yr. Pt. Angeles, 1986; recipient State Phys. Fitness award Pres.'s Challenge, 1988, Nat. Phys. Fitness award Pres.'s Challenge, 1988. Mem. AAHPERD, AAUW, Internat. Pageant Assn., Calif. Assn. Health, Phys. Edn., Recreation and Dance, Delta Kappa Gamma. Republican. Roman Catholic. Office: Alta Loma Jr High Sch 9000 Lemon Ave Alta Loma CA 91701-3357

TOLANEY, MURLI, environmental engineering executive; b. 1941. BS in Civil Engring., U. Kans., MS in Environ. Engring. Jr. engr. Coun. Sci. and Indsl. Resources, New Delhi, 1963-66; project engr. L.A. County Sanitary Dist., 1966-70; with Montgomery Watson Assn., Pasadena, Calif., 1970—, now pres., CEO. Office: Montgomery Watson Ams 300 N Lake Ave # 1200 Pasadena CA 91101-4106*

TOLENTINO, CASIMIRO URBANO, lawyer; b. Manila, May 18, 1949; came to U.S., 1959; s. Lucio Rubio and Florence (Jose) T.; m. Jennifer Masculino, June 5, 1982; 2 children: Casimiro Masculino, Cristina Cecelia Masculino. BA in Zoology, UCLA, 1972, JD, 1975. Bar: Calif. 1976. Gen. counsel civil rights div. HEW, Washington, 1975-76; regional atty. Agrl. Labor Relations Bd., Fresno, Calif., 1976-78; regional dir. Sacramento and San Diego, 1978-81; regional atty. Pub. Employment Relations Bd., Los Angeles, 1981; counsel, west div. Writers Guild Am., Los Angeles, 1982-84; dir. legal affairs Embassy TV, Los Angeles, 1984-86; sole practice Los Angeles, 1986-87; mediator Ctr. Dispute Resolution, Santa Monica, Calif., 1986-87; asst. chief counsel Dept. of Fair Employment and Housing, State of Calif., 1986-92; adminstrv. law judge dept. social svcs., 1992—. Editor: Letters in Exile, 1976; contbr. articles and revs. to Amerasia Jour. Chmn. adv. bd. UCLA Asian Am. Studies Ctr., 1983—; chmn. bd. Asian Pacific Legal Ctr., L.A., 1983-93 (Decade award); pres. bd. civil svc. commrs. City of L.A., 1984-85, 90-93; bd. dirs. met. region United Way,; bd. dirs. Rebuild L.A., 1992—; mem. Asian-Pacific Am. adv. coun. L.A. Police Commn. Mem. State Bar Calif. (exec. com. labor law sect. 1985-88), Los Angeles County Bar Assn., Minority Bar Assn. (sec. 1984-85), Philippine Lawyers of So. Calif. (pres. 1984—, Award of Merit 1982). Democrat. Roman Catholic.

TOLIVER, HAROLD EARL, language professional, English; b. McMinnville, Oreg., Feb. 16, 1932; s. Marion E. and Mable A. (Mallery) T.; m. Mary Bennette, June 20, 1954; children: Tricia, Brooks. BA, U. Oreg., 1954; MA, Johns Hopkins U., 1958; PhD, U. Wash., 1961. Asst. prof. Ohio State U., Columbus, 1961-64, UCLA, 1965-66; asst. prof., prof. U. Calif., Irvine, 1966—. Author: Marvell's Ironic Vision, 1965, Pastoral Forms and Attitudes, 1971, Animate Illusions, 1974, Lyric Provinces, 1985, The Past That Poets Make, 1981, Transported Styles, 1989, Herbert's Christian Narrative, 1993. Pvt. first class, U.S. Army, 1954-56. Recipient Guggenheim fellowship, 1964, 76. Home: 1405 Skyline Dr Laguna Beach CA 92651-1942 Office: U of Calif Dept Of English Irvine CA 92717

TOLIVER, LEE, mechanical engineer; b. Wildhorse, Okla., Oct. 3, 1921; s. Clinton Leslie and Mary (O'Neall) T.; m. Barbara Anne O'Reilly, Jan. 24, 1942; children: Margaret Anne, Michael Edward. BSME, U. Okla., 1942. Registered profl. engr., Ohio. Engr. Douglas Aircraft Co., Santa Monica, Calif., 1942, Oklahoma City, 1942-44; engr. Los Alamos (N.Mex.) Sci. Lab., 1946; instr. mech. engring. Ohio State U., Columbus, 1946-47; engr. Sandia Nat. Labs., Albuquerque, 1947-82; instr. computer sci. and math. U. N.Mex., Valencia County, 1982-84; number theory researcher Belen, N.Mex., 1982—. Co-author: (computer manuals with G. Carli, A.F. Schkade, L. Toliver) Experiences with an Intelligent Remote Batch Terminal, 1972, (with C.R. Borgman, T.I. Ristine) Transmitting Data from the PDP-10 to Precision Graphics, 1973, (with C.R. Borgman, T.I. Ristine) Data Transmission-PDP-10/Sykes/Precision Graphics, 1975. With Manhattan Project (Atomic Bomb) U.S. Army, 1944-46. Mem. Math. Assn. Am., Am. Math. Soc., Am. Mensa Ltd. Home: 206 Howell St Belen NM 87002-6225

TOLLETT, GLENNA BELLE, accountant, mobile home park operator; b. Graham, Ariz., Dec. 17, 1913; d. Charles Harry and Myrtle (Stapley) Spafford; m. John W. Tollett, Nov. 28, 1928; 1 child, Jackie J., 1 adopted child, Beverly Mae Malgren. Bus. cert., Lamson Coll. Office mgr. Hurley Meat Packing Co., Phoenix, 1938-42; co-owner, sec., treas. A.B.C. Enterprises, Inc., Seattle, 1942—; ptnr. Bella Investment Co., Seattle, 1962—, Four Square Investment Co., Seattle, 1969—, Warehouses Ltd., Seattle, 1970—, Tri State Partnership, Wash., Idaho, Tex., 1972—; pres. Halycon Mobile Home Park, Inc., Seattle, 1979—; co-owner, operator Martha Lake Mobile Home Park, Lynwood, Wash., 1962-73. Mem. com. Wash. Planning and Community Affairs Agy., Olympia, 1981-82, Wash. Mfg. Housing Assn. Relations Com., Olympia, 1980-84; appointed by Gov. Wash. to Mobile Home and RV Adv. Bd., 1973-79. Named to RV/Mobile Home Hall of Fame, 1980. Mem. Wash. Mobile Park Owners Assn. (legisl. chmn., lobbyist 1976-85, cons. 1984, pres. 1978-79, exec. dir. 1976-84, This is Your Life award 1979), Wash. Soc. of Assn. Execs. (Exec. Dir. Service award 1983), Mobile Home Old Timers Assn., Mobile Home Owners of Am. (sec. 1972-76, Appreciation award 1976), Nat Fire Protection Assn. (com. 1979-86), Aurora Pkwy. North C. of C.)sec. 1976-80), Fremont C. of C. Republican. Mormon. Home: 18261 Springdale Ct NW Seattle WA 98177-3228 Office: ABC Enterprises Inc 3524 Stone Way N Seattle WA 98103-8924

TOLLIVER, JAMES DAVID, JR., aerospace engineer; b. Long Branch, N.J., Dec. 27, 1938; s. James David and Daisy E. (Brabham) T.; m. Evelyn C. Davis, Jan. 16, 1965 (div. 1982); children: Yvette, James D. III; m. Rachel Evelyn Thornton, June 14, 1986. BS in Law, Glendale U., 1974; postgrad., UCLA, 1965-72, cert. numerical analysis, 1968. Mem. staff Cambridge (Mass.) electron accelerator div. Harvard U. and MIT, 1963-64; mem. staff Cyclotron lab. UCLA, 1964-73; elec. engr., 1973-77; system engr. Honeywell Systems Co., West Covina, Calif., 1977-80, Magnavox Systems Co., Torrance, Calif., 1980-86, Teledyne Systems Co., Northridge, Calif., 1986—; speaker at profl. seminars. With USMC, 1958-62. Mem. Am. Math. Soc., Bioelectromagnets Soc., Elec. Discharge and Elec. Over Stress Soc., Toastmasters Internat. (pres. Magnavox Toastmasters, Torrance, 1985-86). Home: PO Box 67426 Los Angeles CA 90067-0426

TOLLIVER-PALMA, CALVIN EUGENE, violist, instructor, performer; b. Corpus Christi, Tex., Sept. 24, 1950; s. Jack Terrell Tolliver and Sara Lee (Palma) Denmon. MusB, Baylor U., 1973; MusD, U. Colo., 1981; studied with Mary Ellen Proudfit, Waco, Tex., 1969-71; studied with Wayne Crouse, Houston, 1971-72. Violist Corpus Christi (Tex.) Symphony, 1967-69, Waco (Tex.) Symphony, 1970-73, Tucson Symphony, 1971; union musician Denver and Boulder (Colo.) Locals, 1973-88; violist, violinist Boulder Philharmonic, 1974-88; pvt. music instr., performer Boulder, 1973—. Home: 664 Manhattan Dr Apt 3A Boulder CO 80303-4020

TOLMAN, RICHARD ROBINS, zoology educator; b. Ogden, Utah, Dec. 1, 1937; s. Dale Richards and Dorothy (Robins) T.; m. Bonnie Bjornn, Aug. 18, 1964; children: David, Alicia, Brett, Matthew. BS, U. Utah, 1963, MSEd, 1964; PhD, Oreg. State U., 1969. Tchr. sci. Davis County Sch. Dist., Bountiful, Utah, 1964-66; instr. Mt. Hood C.C., Gresham, Oreg., 1968-69; staff assoc., project dir. Biol. Scis. Curriculum Study, Boulder, Colo., 1969-82; prof. zoology, chair zoology dept. Brigham Young U., Provo, Utah, 1982—, chair dept. of zoology, 1994—. Contbr. articles to profl. jours. Scoutmaster Boy Scouts Am., Orem, Utah, 1992. With USAF, 1956-63. Alcuin fellow Brigham Young U., 1991. Mem. Nat. Sci. Tchrs. Assn., Utah Sci. Tchrs. Assn. (exec. sec. 1991—), Nat. Assn. for Rsch. in Sci. Teaching, Nat. Assn. of Biology Tchrs. Mem. Ch. of LDS. Home: 174 E 1825 S Orem UT 84058-7836 Office: Dept Zoology Brigham Young U Provo UT 84602

TOLMAN, RUTH, personal care industry executive; b. Salt Lake City, July 20, 1919; d. James Albert and Evelyn (Roberts) Miller; m. Morton Stanley Male, Sept. 20, 1956 (dec. May 1979); children: Chad, Radon, Kim, James, Rari Lee. Owner John Robert Powers Modeling Sch., Salt Lake City, Denver, 1950-59, World Modeling Assn., N.Y.C., 1961—. Author: A Woman's Guide to Business and Social Success, Personally Yours, Success Insurance, Call Me Mister, Guide to Fashion Merchandise Knowledge, Fashion Marketing and Merchandising, Photo Modeling and Posing, European Looks for Portfolios. Mem. World Modeling Assn. (chmn. 1980-94). Democrat. Unitarian. Office: World Modeling Assn 4401 San Pedro Dr NE Apt 801 Albuquerque NM 87109-2608

TOM, CLARENCE YUNG CHEN, retired city and county official; b. Honolulu, Jan. 25, 1927; s. John Chong and Dorothy Oi Fook (Ing) T.; m. Vivian Kam Oi Lum, July 19, 1969; children: Claire-Anne, Karen-Anne, Patricia-Anne. BS in Chem. Engring., Purdue U., 1947, MS in Chem. Engring., 1957; M City Planning, Harvard U., 1959. Chem. engr. Libby, McNeill & Libby, Honolulu, 1947-50, 52-54; planner City and County Honolulu, 1958-89, chief environ. and plans assessment br. dept. gen. planning, 1960-88; mem. Hawaii Census Tract Com., 1960-89. Jr. warden St. Mary's Ch., Honolulu, 1970-82; vestryman Ch. Holy Nativity, Honolulu, 1984-86. Served with U.S. Army, 1950-52, Korea. Mem. Hawaii Govt. Employees Assn. (steward 1971-72, 81-82, alt. steward 1988). Democrat. Home: 2911A Koali Rd Honolulu HI 96826-1805

TOM, CREIGHTON HARVEY, aerospace engineer, consultant; b. Oakland, Calif., Mar. 29, 1944; s. Harvey and Katherine (Lew) T. BS in Forestry, U. Calif., Berkeley, 1966; MS in Stats., Colo. State U., 1972, PhD in Computer Sci., 1978. Sr. environ. analyst HRB-Singer, Inc., Ft. Collins, Colo., 1977-78; staff scientist Sci. Applications, Golden, Colo., 1979-80; cons. Golden, 1981; scientist, specialist ConTel Info. Systems, Littleton, Colo., 1981-84; sr. staff engr. Hughes Aircraft Co., Aurora, Colo., 1984-91; shuttle astronaut cand. NASA, Houston, 1980; cons. to companies and schs. Contbr. articles to profl. jours. Adviser CAP, Golden, 1981—; mem. YMCA. Served to maj. U.S. Army, 1966-67, with Res. 1967—. Decorated Bronze Star and Air medals, U.S. Army, 1967. Mem. Am. Soc. Photogrammetry, AAAS, NRA, Mensa, Intertel, Sigma Xi, Xi Sigma Pi, Phi Kappa Phi. Republican. Methodist. Home: 7951 S Cedar St Littleton CO 80120-4432 Office: C&H Enterprises 7951 S Cedar St Littleton CO 80120-4432

TOM, LAWRENCE, engineering executive; b. L.A., Jan. 21, 1950; BS Harvey Mudd Coll., 1972; JD Western State U., San Diego, 1978; spl. diploma U. Calif., San Diego, 1991. Design engr. Rockwell Internat., L.A., 1972-73; design engr. Rohr Industries, Inc., Chula Vista, Calif., 1973-76, sr. design engr., 1980, computer graphics engring. specialist, 1980-83, chief engring. svs., 1989-91, chief engring. quality, 1991-93, project engr. 1993—; sr. engr. Rohr Marine, Inc., Chula Vista, 1977-79; chief exec. officer Computer Aided Tech. Svcs., San Diego, 1983-87; software cons. Small Systems Software, San Diego, 1984-85; computer graphics engring. specialist TOM & ROMAN, San Diego, 1986-88; dir. Computervision Users Group, 1986-88, vice chmn. 1988-91, pres., 1991-93, exec. chmn., 1992-94; bd. dirs. Exec. Program for Scientists and Engrs.-Alumni Assn. U. Calif., San Diego, 1991—; pres. Art to Art, San Diego, 1994—. cons. in field. George H. Mayr Found. scholar, 1971, Bates Found. Aero. Edn. scholar, 1970-72. Mem. Aircraft Owners and Pilots Assn., Infiniti Club. Office: 7770 Regents Rd Ste 113-190 San Diego CA 92122-1937

TOMA, KYLE TAKEYOSHI, recreational therapist; b. Honokaa, Hawaii, Aug. 30, 1953; s. Takeo and Kikue (Ishiki) T. BA in Sociology, U. Hawaii, 1976, BS in Recreation, 1978, student, 1992—. Recreation dir., dormitory coun. Mid-Pacific Inst., Honolulu, 1985—; display specialist Shirokiya Dept. Store, Honolulu, 1986-88; fitness specialist Hickam (Hawaii) AFB, 1988-90; aerobics instr. Manoa Recreation Ctr., Honolulu, 1990—, Kaiser Permanente, Honolulu, 1990—; recreation therapist III State Dept. of Health, Honolulu, 1990—; aerobics instr. U. Hawaii, 1991—. Mem. YMCA, Am. Alliance Health, Physical Edn., Recreation, and Dance, Hawaii Assn. for Health, Physical Edn., Recreation, and Dance, Internat. Dance Exercise Assn., Reebpk Profl. Instr. Alliance. Democrat. Home: 2445 Kaala St Honolulu HI 96822-2204

TOMA, RAMSES BARSOUM, food science and nutrition educator; b. Cairo, Nov. 9, 1938; came to U.S., 1968; s. Barsoum Toma Khalil and Fieka (Ibrahim) Gabriel; m. Rosette Toma; children: Narmer, Kamy. BS in Agr., Ain Shams U., Cairo, 1959, MS in Food Tech., 1965; PhD in Food Sci., La. State U., 1971; MPH, U. Minn., 1980. Food inspector Ministry of Food Supplies, Egypt, 1960-67; chemist Crystal Foods, New Orleans, 1968; from asst. prof. to prof. U. N.D., Grand Fork, 1972-84; prof. Calif. State U., Long Beach, 1984—; mem. trade mission to Mid. East countries for N.D., 1976; cons. to food industries, Long Beach, 1984—; vis. prof. Cairo U., Manseira U.; mem. bd. dirs. Internat. Cmty. Coun. Contbr. numerous rsch. articles to profl. and sci. jours. Mem. Rep. Com., Orange County, Calif., 1984; mem. St. George Ch. Fellow Am. Inst. Chemists; mem. Am. Dietitian Assn., Am. Chem. Soc., Inst. Food Tech., Am. Assn. Cereal Chemists, Am. Home Economists Assn., Am. Inst. Nutrition, Internat. Cmty. Coun., Egypt Am. Scholars, Sigma Xi, Phi Kappa Phi, Phi Beta Delta. Republican. Mem. Christian Ch. Office: Calif State U 1250 N Bellflower Blvd Long Beach CA 90840-0006

TOMASI, DONALD CHARLES, architect; b. Sacramento, Calif., Oct. 24, 1956; s. Thomas M. and Anita (Migliavacca) T.; m. Loretta Elaine Goveia, Feb. 1, 1986; children: Jeffrey, Genna, Michael. AB in Architecture with honors, U. Calif., Berkeley, 1979; MArch, U. Wash., 1982. Registered architect, Calif. Project mgr. Robert Wells and Assocs., Seattle, 1982-84, Milbrandt Architects, Seattle, 1984, T.M. Tomasi Architects, Santa Rosa, Calif., 1984-86; prin. Tomasi Architects, Santa Rosa, 1986-93, Tomasi Lawry Coker De Silva Architecture, Santa Rosa, 1993—. Grad. Leadership Santa Rosa, 1992; mem. design rev. com. Sonoma County, 1988-90; chmn. Santa Rosa Design Rev. Bd., 1990—. Recipient Honor award Coalition for Adequate Sch. Housing, 1991, 93, Merit award, 1991. Mem. AIA (chpt. bd. dirs. 1990-91, Merit award 1986).

TOMBES, AVERETT SNEAD, academic administrator; b. Easton, Md., Sept. 13, 1932; s. Thomas N. and Susie (Broaddus) T.; m. Jane R. Gill, June 15, 1957; children: Thomas, Robert, Jonathan, Susan. BA, U. Richmond, 1954; MS, Va. Poly. Inst., 1956; PhD, Rutgers U., 1961. Asst. prof., assoc. prof., then prof. Clemson (S.C.) U., 1961-77; chmn. dept. biology George Mason U., Fairfax, Va., 1977-81, dean Grad. Sch., 1981-86; v.p. grad. studies and rsch. Wichita (Kans.) State U., 1986-88; v.p. rsch., econ. devel. N.Mex. State U., Las Cruces, 1988—; cons. NSF, Washington, 1968-69, Oconee (S.C.) Hosp., 1972-73, Fairfax Hosp., 1978-80. Author textbook; contbr. chpts. to books, articles to profl. jours. Capt. U.S. Army, 1956-58. A.I. DuPont fellow U. Richmond, 1953-54; Thomas Headlee fellow Rutgers U., 1958-61; Am. Coun. Edn. fellow U. Del., U. Md., 1980-81. Fellow AAAS (counselor 1971-74); mem. Am. Soc. Cell Biology, Soc. Rsch. Adminstrs., Am. Physiol. Soc., Am. Soc. Zoologists, Soc. Gen. Physiologists, Sigma Xi, Phi Kappa Phi. Presbyterian. Home: 6621 Vista Hermosa Las Cruces NM 88005-4958 Office: NMex State U Las Cruces NM 88003

TOMBRELLO, THOMAS ANTHONY, JR., physics educator, consultant; b. Austin, Tex., Sept. 20, 1936; s. Thomas Anthony and Jeanette Lilian (Marcuse) T.; m. Esther Ann Hall, May 30, 1957 (div. Jan. 1976); children: Christopher Thomas, Susan Elaine, Karen Elizabeth; m. Stephanie Carhart Merton, Jan. 15, 1977; 1 stepchild, Kerstin Arusha. B.A. in Physics, Rice U., 1958, M.A., 1960, Ph.D., 1961. Research fellow in physics Calif. Inst. Tech., Pasadena, 1961-62, 64-65, asst. prof. physics, 1965-67, assoc. prof., 1967-71, prof., 1971—; asst. prof. Yale U., New Haven, 1963; cons. in field; disting. vis. prof. U. Calif.-Davis, 1984; v.p., dir. rsch. Schlumberger-Doll Rsch., Ridgefield, Conn., 1987-89; mem. U.S. V.P.'s Space Policy Adv. Bd., 1992. Assoc. editor Nuclear Physics, 1971-91, Applications of Nuclear Physics, 1980—, Radiation Effects, 1985-88, Nuclear Instruments and Methods B, 1993—. Recipient Alexander von Humboldt award von Humboldt Stiftung, U. Frankfurt, Federal Republic of Germany, 1984-85; NSF fellow Calif. Inst. Tech. 1961-62; A.P. Sloan fellow, 1971-73. Fellow Am. Phys. Soc.; mem. AAAS, Materials Rsch. Soc., Phi Beta Kappa, Sigma Xi, Delta Phi Alpha. Avocations: reading, jogging. Democrat. Office: Calif Inst Tech Dept Physics Mail Code 91125 Pasadena CA 91125

TOMCZYK, THEODORE CLAYTON, secondary education educator; b. Flint, Mich., Nov. 10, 1962; s. Stanley Anthony and Doris Lorraine (Erickson) T.; m. Laurie Ann Burke, Oct. 21, 1989; children: Kristen, Clayton. BS, Mich. State U., 1985; MS, Purdue U., 1987. Geophysicist Chevron Oil Co. USA, Houston, 1987-91; H.S. tchr. Denver (Colo.) County, 1992—, Jefferson County, Golden, Colo., 1994—; rschr. Hughes Rsch. for Tchrs., Ft. Collins, 1993, Boulder, 1994. Grantee Pub. Edn. Coalition, Denver, 1993, Cub Foods, Denver, 1993—, Rsch. for Tchrs. grantee Hughes Found., Ft. Collins, 1993. Home: 9436 W Geddes Pl Littleton CO 80123-4116 Office: D'Evelyn HS 13200 W 32nd Ave Golden CO 80401-1614

TOMICH, LILLIAN, lawyer; b. L.A., Mar. 28, 1935; d. Peter S. and Yovanka P. (Ivanovic) T. AA, Pasadena City Coll., 1954; BA in Polit. Sci., UCLA, 1956, cert. secondary teaching, 1957, MA, 1958; JD, U. So. Calif., 1961. Bar: Calif. Sole practice, 1961-66; house counsel Mfrs. Bank, Los Angeles, 1966; assoc. Hurley, Shaw & Tomich, San Marino, Calif., 1968-76; assoc. Driscoll & Tomich, San Marino, 1976—; dir. Continental Culture Specialists Inc., Glendale, Calif. Trustee, St. Sava Serbian Orthodox Ch., San Gabriel, Calif. Charles Fletcher Scott fellow, 1957; U. So. Calif. Law Sch. scholar, 1958. Mem. ABA, Calif. Bar Assn., Los Angeles County Bar Assn., Women Lawyers Assn., San Marino C. of C., UCLA Alumni Assn., Town Hall and World Affairs Council, Order Mast and Dagger, Iota Tau Tau, Alpha Gamma Sigma. Office: 2460 Huntington Dr San Marino CA 91108-2643

TOMISKA, CORA LORENA, civic worker; b. Fontana, Calif., July 30, 1928; d. Riley Royston and Winifred Lillian (Humphry) Green; m. Joseph Frank Tomiska, June 19, 1950; children: Jo Ann, William Joseph, Robert Royston, Charity Lillianne, Angelina Kathleen. AA, Chaffey Jr. Coll., 1948; BA, Calif. State Coll., San Bernardino, 1976, postgrad., 1976—. Owner Tomiska Aviaries, Fontana, 1963—. Pres. Redwood PTA, 1976, Sequoia Jr.

High PTA, 1969-70, Fontana Council PTA, 1972-74; mem. exec. bd. 5th Dist. PTA, 1972-83, historian, 1976-79, v.p., dir. health, 1979-81, v.p., dir. parent edn., 1981-83; mem. Redwood PTA; sec. consol. projects adv. com. Fontana Unified Sch. Dist., 1972-81, sec. family life edn. project, 1982-86; mem. Mayoral Candidacy Com., 1978: counselor jr. gardening Fontana Redwood Blue Jays, 1964-83; pres. Fontana Garden Club, 1974-77; vol. Fontana Youth Svc. Ctr., Am. Heart Fund, Am. Cancer Soc., Christian Youth Edn., Valley Bible Ch., Fontana United Way; scholarship chmn. San Bernardino Valley dist. Calif. Garden Clubs, 1974-83; sec.-treas. Fontana Family Svc. Agy., 1976-79, pres., 1980-82; mem. Arthritis Found., Westside Bapt. Ch., tchr. trainer, 1991; mem., personal care provider, estate mgr. Fellowship of the Living Water, 1984-88; vol. Literacy Vol. Am., Inc., 1992—. Recipient 1st place award Calif. Jr. Flower Shows, 1969-73. Mem. AAUW (edn. chmn. 1981-82), ARC, San Bernardino County Mus. Assn., Fontana Hist. Soc. Address: 8365 Redwood Ave Fontana CA 92335-8059

TOMOEDA, CHERYL KUNIKO, academic researcher; b. Honolulu, Sept. 24, 1958; d. Charles Kunio and Doris Masue (Takehara) T. BS, U. Hawaii, 1980; MS, U. Ariz., 1982. Cert. speech-lang. pathology. Speech pathologist Amphitheater Pub. Schs., Tucson, 1983-84; rsch. asst. U. Ariz., Tucson, 1982-83, rsch. asst. II, 1984-86, rsch. coord., 1985-91, sr. rsch. specialist, 1991—. Author: (test) Ariz. Battery for Comm. Disorders of Dementia, 1991, The Functional Linguistic Communication Inventory, 1994, (book) The ABC's of Dementia, 1993; prodr. videoconf. series Telerounds. Mem. Acad. Neurologic Communication Disorders and Scis. (acting sec. 1991, sec. 1992-93), Internat. Neuropsychol. Soc., Am. Speech-Lang.-Hearing Assn. Office: U Ariz Nat Ctr Neurogenic Comm Disorders Dept Speech & Hearing Scis Tucson AZ 85721

TOMPKINS, CYNTHIA MARGARITA, women's studies educator; b. Alta Gracia, Cordoba, Argentina, Jan. 30, 1958; came to U.S., 1982; d. Harold Stanley Albert and Ines Leonor (Hawkins) T. Prof. English Lang. and Lit., Nat. U. Cordoba, 1979, Lic. in Modern Langs., 1981; MA in Comparative Lit., Pa. State U., 1985, PhD in Comparative Lit., 1989. Teaching asst. in Spanish and comparative lit. Pa. State U., University Park, 1983-88; instr. Spanish Dickinson Coll., Carlisle, Pa., 1988-89; asst. prof. Spanish U. Wis.-Parkside, Kenosha, 1989-92; asst. prof. women's studies Ariz. State U. West, Phoenix, 1992—. Editor, contbg. author: Utopias, ojos, azules, bocas suicidas la narrativa de Alina Diaconu, 1993; contbr. articles to profl. jours.; editor: Confluencia: Revista Hispanica de Cultura y Literature, 1994—; reviewer: World Literature Today, 1989—. Mem. steering com. Sisters of Color Internat., 1991—. Fulbright fellow, Pa. State U., 1982, E. Sparks fellow Coll. Liberal Arts, 1982-83. Mem. MLA, Am. Comparative Lit. Assn. Office: Ariz State U PO Box 37100 4701 W Thunderbird Rd Phoenix AZ 85069-7100

TOMPKINS, NICK, agricultural products executive; b. 1955. Farmer, 1976—; v.p., sec. APIO Inc., Guadalupe, Calif., 1979—. Office: APIO Inc 4575 W Main St Guadalupe CA 93434-1659*

TOMS, KATHLEEN MOORE, nurse; b. San Francisco, Dec. 31, 1943; d. William Moore and Phyllis Josephine (Barry) Stewart. RN, AA, City Coll. San Francisco, 1963; BPS in Nursing Edn., Elizabethtown (Pa.) Coll., 1973; MS in Edn., Temple U., 1977; MS in Nursing, Gwynedd Mercy Coll. 1988; m. Benjamin Peskoff; children from previous marriage: Kathleen Marie Toms Myers, Kelly Terese Toms. Med.-surg. nurse St. Joseph Hosp., Fairbanks, Alaska, 1963-65; emergency room nurse St. Joseph Hosp., Lancaster, Pa., 1965-69, blood, plasm and components nurse, 1969-71; pres. F.E. Barry Co., Lancaster, 1971—; dir. inservice edn. Lancaster Osteo. Hosp., 1971-75; coord. practical nursing program Vocat. Tech. Sch., Coatesville, Pa., 1976-77; dir. nursing Pocopson Home, West Chester, Pa., 1978-80, Riverside Hosp., Wilmington, Del., 1980-83; assoc. Coatesville VA Hosp., 1983-89; chief Nurse, 1984-89; with VA Cen. Office; supr. psychiat. nursing Martinez (Calif.) VA Med. Ctr., 1989-94; assoc. chief nursing svc. edn. VA No. Calif. Sys. Clinics, Pleasant Hill, Calif., 1994—; trainee assoc. chief Nursing Home Care Unit, Washington; mem. Pa. Gov.'s Council on Alcoholism and Drug Abuse, 1974-76; mem. Del. Health Council Med.-Surg. Task Force, 1981-83; dir. Lancaster Community Health Ctr., 1973-76; lectr. in field. Col. Nurse Corps, USAR. Decorated Army Commendation medals (5), Meritorious Svc. medal XI; recipient Community Service award Citizens United for Better Public Relations, 1974; award Sertoma, Lancaster, 1974; Outstanding Citizen award Sta. WGAL-TV, 1975; U.S. Army Achievement award, 1983. Mem. Elizabethtown, Temple U. Alumni Assns., Pa. Nurses' Assn. (dir.), Sigma Theta Tau, Beta Gamma. Inventor auto-infuser for blood or blood components, 1971. Home: 208 Sea Mist Dr Vallejo CA 94591-7748 Office: VA No Calif System of Clinics 2350 Contra Costa Blvd Pleasant Hill CA 94523-3930

TOMSKY, JUDY, fundraiser and event planner, importer; b. Oklahoma City, Nov. 28, 1959; d. Mervin and Helen (Broude) T. Student, Hebrew U. of Jerusalem, 1979-80; BA in Liberal Studies, Sonoma State U., 1981. Internat. tour group dir. Kibbutz Yahel, Israel, 1981-83; telemktg. supr., mktg. and advt. coord. The Sharper Image, San Francisco, 1983-85; br. mgr., acct. exec. advt. Marin Express Ltd., Corte Madera, Calif., 1986; spl. events coord., fundraiser Sausalito, Calif., 1987; Pacific N.W. regional dir. Jewish Nat. Fund, San Francisco, 1987-90; event mgmt., mktg. and promotion specialist, 1990-93; devel. dir. Insight Meditation West, Woodacre, Calif., 1993-94; proprietor import/wholesale bus. San Anselmo, Calif., 1994—. Office: PO Box 855 San Anselmo CA 94979-0855

TONELLO-STUART, ENRICA MARIA, political economist; b. Monza, Italy; d. Alessandro P. and Maddalena M. (Marangoni) Tonello; m. Albert E. Smith; m. Charles L. Stuart. BA in Internat. Affairs, Econs., U. Colo., 1961; MA, Claremont Grad. Sch., 1966, PhD, 1971. Sales mgr. Met. Life Ins. Co., 1974-79; pres. E.T.S. Rsch. and Devel., Inc., 1977—; dean internat. studies program Union U., L.A. and Tokyo; lectr. internat. affairs and mktg. UCLA Ext., Union U.; CEO, ETS Internat. Investments and ETS Publs., Inc., 1986—. Pub., editor Tomorrow Outline Jour., 1963—, The Monitor, 1988; pub. World Regionalism-An Ecological Analysis, 1971, A Proposal for the Reorganization of the United Nations, 1966, The Persuasion Technocracy, Its Forms, Techniques and Potentials, 1966, The Role of the Multinationals in the Emerging Globalism, 1978; developed the theory of social ecology and econsociometry. Organized first family assistance program Langley AFB Tactical Air Command Commandation, 1956-58. Recipient vol. svc. award VA, 1956-58, ARC svc. award, 1950-58. Mem. Corp. Planners Assn. (treas. 1974-79), Investigative Reporters and Editors, World Future Soc. (pres. 1974—), U.S.-China Journalists Fellowship Assn., Asian Bus. League, Chinese Am. Assn. (life), Japan Am. Assn., L.A. World Trade Ctr., Palos Verdes C. of C. (legis. com.), L.A. Press Club (bd. dirs.), L.A. World Trade Ctr., Zonta (chmn. internat. com. South Bay), Pi Sigma Alpha.

TONEY, W. ALAN, battery manufacturing company executive; b. Culver City, Calif., July 10, 1955; s. Warren Larrimore Toney and Betty Ruth (Juroske) Thomas; m. Jeanine Marie Laslett, Feb. 16, 1974; children: Timothy John, Karina Marie. Grad., Agoura (Calif.) H.S., 1973. Restaurant mgr. Colony Coffee Shop, Malibu, Calif., 1974-75; ops. mgr. Automated Vending Corp., Arleta, Calif., 1975-81; dir. vending svcs. West Coast Food Svc., L.A., 1981-85; svc. mgr. Sunrise Ford, Tujunga, Calif., 1985-86; sales rep. Mighty Distbg., Palmdale, Calif., 1986-87; account exec. Exxon Co. U.S.a., Houston, 1987-92; sales mgr. GNB Battery Techs., North Hollywood, Calif., 1992—. Author newsletter News to Use, 1987-92. Mem. Automotive Svc. Coun., Ground Support Equipment Coun. Mem. Jehovah's Witnesses. Office: GNB Battery Techs PO Box 903055 Palmdale CA 93590-3055

TONG, RICHARD DARE, anesthesiologist; b. Chgo., Oct. 20, 1930; s. George Dare and June (Jung) T.; student U. Calif., Berkeley, 1949-52; MD, U. Calif., Irvine, 1956. m. Diane Helene Davies, Apr. 12, 1970; children: Erin, Jason; m. Deanna Johnson, Jan. 5, 1993; stepchildren: Jeffery John, Ryan Johnson. Intern, Phoenix Gen. Hosp., 1956-57; resident in anesthesiology UCLA, 1965-67; pvt. practice, Lakewood, Calif., 1967—; clin. instr. UCLA Sch. Medicine, 1968—. Dep. sheriff reserve med. emergency team, L.A. County. With USNR, 1947-53. Diplomate Am. Bd. Anesthesiology. Fellow Am. Coll. Anesthesiology; mem. Am. Soc. Anesthesiologists, AMA, Calif. Med. Assn., L.A. County Med. Assns. Office: PO Box 1131 Lakewood CA 90714-1131

TONG, SIU WING, computer programmer; b. Hong Kong, May 20, 1950; came to U.S., 1968; BA, U. Calif., Berkeley, 1972; PhD, Harvard U., 1979; MS, U. Lowell, 1984. Research assoc. Brookhaven Nat. Lab., Upton, N.Y., 1979-83; software engr. Honeywell Info. Systems, Billerica, Mass., 1984-85; sr. programmer, analyst Hui Computer Cons., Berkeley, Calif., 1985-88; sr. v.p. devel., chief fin. officer Surgicenter Info. Systems, Inc., Orinda, Calif., 1989-94; sr. sys. specialist Info. Sys. Divsn. Contra Costa County Health Svcs., MArtinez, Calif., 1995—. Vol. tchr. Boston Chinatown Saturday Adult Edn. Program of Tufts Med. Sch., 1977-79. Muscular Dystrophy Assn. fellow, 1980-82. Mem. AAAS, IEEE, Assn. Computing Machinery, N.Y. Acad. Scis. Home: 17 Beaconsfield Ct Orinda CA 94563-4203 Office: Contra Costa County Health Svcs 595 Center Ave Ste 210 Martinez CA 94553

TONINI, LEON RICHARD, sales professional; b. Pittsfield, Mass., May 16, 1931; s. John Richard and Mabel Grayce (Rushbrook) T.; B.A. in Mgmt., U. Md., 1951; m. Helen Jo, Aug. 15, 1966; 1 son, John Richard, II. Enlisted in U.S. Army, 1947, advanced through grades to master sgt., 1968; service in W.Ger., Vietnam; ret., 1974; dir. vets. employment and assistance Non-Commd. Officers Assn., San Antonio, 1974-75; supr. security Pinkerton's Inc., Dallas, 1975-78; gen. mgr. civic center Travelodge Motor Hotel and Restaurant, San Francisco, 1978-85; sales representative Vernon Co., 1985—. Chmn. San Francisco Vets. Employment Com., 1981. Served as sgt. maj. Calif. N.G., res. Decorated Bronze Star; Republic Vietnam Honor medal 2d class. Mem. San Francisco Hotel Assn. (dir.), Non-Commd. Officers Assn. (dir. Calif. chpt.), Am. Legion, Regular Vets. Assn. (nat. sr. vice comdr.), Amvets, Patrons of Husbandry. Republican. Baptist. Club: Masons. Home and Office: 205 Collins St Apt 9 San Francisco CA 94118-3429

TONJES, MARIAN JEANNETTE BENTON, education educator; b. Rockville Center, N.Y., Feb. 16, 1929; d. Millard Warren and Felicia E. (Tyler) Benton; m. Charles F. Tonjes (div. 1965); children: Jeffrey Charles, Kenneth Warren. BA, U. N.Mex., 1951, cert., 1966, MA, 1969; EdD, U. Miami, 1975. Dir. recreation Stuyvesant Town Housing Project, N.Y.C., 1951-53; tchr. music., phys. edn. Sunset Mesa Day Sch., Albuquerque, 1953-54; tchr. remedial reading Zia Elem. Sch., Albuquerque, 1965-67; tchr. secondary devel. reading Rio Grande High Sch., Albuquerque, 1967-69; rsch. asst. reading Southwestern Coop. Ednl. Lab., Albuquerque, 1969-71; assoc. dir., vis. instr. Fla. Ctr. Tchr. Tng. Materials U. Miami, 1971-72; asst. prof. U.S. Internat. U., San Diego, 1972-75; prof. edn. Western Wash. U., Bellingham, 1975-94, prof. emerita, 1994—, dir. summer study at Oxford (Eng.) U., 1975-94; vis. prof. adult edn. Palomar (Calif.) Jr. Coll., 1974; reading supr. Manzanita Ctr. U. N.Mex., Albuquerque, 1968; vis. prof. U. Guam, Mangilao, 1989-90; speaker, cons. in field; invited guest Russian Reading Assn., Moscow, 1992. Author: (with Miles V. Zintz) Teaching Reading/Thinking Study Skills in Content Classrooms, 3d edit., 1992, Secondary Reading, Writing and Learning, 1991; contbr. articles to profl. jours. Tng. Tchr. Trainers grantee, 1975; NDEA fellow Okla. State U., 1969. Mem. Am. Reading Forum (chmn. bd. dirs. 1983-85), Adult and Adolescent Literacy Confs. (spkr. 1991—), Internat. Reading Assn. (mem. travel, interchange and study tours com. 1984-86, mem. non-print media and reading com. 1980-83, workshop dir. S.W. regional conf. 1982, mem. com. internat. devel. N.Am. 1991—, Outstanding Tchr. Educator 1988-90), U.K. Reading Assn. (spkr. 1977-93), European Conf. in Reading (Berlin 1989, Edinburgh 1991, Malmo 1993, Budapest 1995 spkr.), European Coun. Internat. Schs. (The Hague, spkr. 1993), World Congress in Reading Buenos Aires (spkr. 1994), PEO (past chpt. pres.), Phi Delta Kappa, Delta Delta Delta.

TONKIN, THOMAS ELDEN, health foundation executive; b. McCloud, Calif., Oct. 27, 1925; s. Elden Alvah and Marie Agnes (Curneen) T.; m. Florence Kate Karstadt, Dec. 29, 1955; children: Jane, Martha, Andrew, Emily. B of Pub. Health, U. Calif., Berkeley, 1949, MHA, 1951. Asst. to dir. Nat. Comm. Fin. Hosp. Care, Chgo., 1951-53; adminstr. Cowell Meml. Hosp., Berkeley, 1953-55; adminstr. Community Hosp. Monterey (Calif.) Peninsula, 1955-73, pres., 1973-90; pres. Cmty. Hosp. Found., 1990—; asst. to statewide dir. Environ. Safety and Student Health, Berkeley, 1953-55; cons. Eisenhower Med. Ctr., Rancho Mirage, 1968-69. Chmn. profl. gifts Monterey United Way, 1972; mem., com. chmn. Monterey County Grand Jury, 1971; dir. World Appreciation Fund (for the environment), 1990-94. Served with USNR, 1944-46. Mem. AIA, Am. Coll. Health Care Execs., Assn. Western Hosps. (chmn., trustee 1971-78), Am. Hosp. Assn. (chmn. hosp. design and constrn. com. 1972-75), Calif. Assn. Hosps. and Health Systems (trustee, chmn. bd. trustees), Calif. Hosp. Assn. Ins. Services (founding dir., com. chmn. 1975-89, Harry Walker fellow 1966), Vis. Nurse Assn. (dir. 1968), Monterey County Heart Assn. (pres. 1970). Clubs: Beach (Pebble Beach, Calif.); Carmel Valley (Calif.) Golf and Country; Old Capital (Monterey). Lodge: Rotary (pres. 1969-70). Office: Community Hosp Monterey PO Box HH Monterey CA 93942-1085

TONN, ELVERNE MERYL, pediatric dentist, dental insurance consultant; b. Stockton, Calif., Dec. 10, 1929; s. Emanuel M. and Lorna Darlene (Bryant) T.; m. Ann G. Richardson, Oct. 28, 1951; children: James Edward, Susan Elaine Tonn Yee. AA, La Sierra U., Riverside, Calif., 1949; DDS, U. So. Calif., 1955; BS, Regents Coll., U. State N.Y., 1984. Lic. dentist; cert. tchr., Calif., dental ins. cons. Pediatric dentist, assoc. Walker Dental Group, Long Beach, Calif., 1957-59, Children's Dental Clinic, Sunnyvale, Calif., 1959-61; pediatric dentist in pvt. practice Mountain View, Calif., 1961-72; from clin. instr. to assoc. prof. U. Pacific, San Francisco, 1964-84; pediatric dentist, ptnr. Pediatric Dentistry Assocs., Los Altos, Calif., 1972-83; assoc. prof. U. Calif., San Francisco, 1984-86; pediatric dentist, ptnr. Valley Oak Dental Group, Manteca, Calif., 1987—; ; pediatric dental cons. Delta Dental Plan, San Francisco, 1985—; chief dental staff El Camino Hosp., Mountain View, 1964-65, 84-85; lectr. in field. Weekly columnist Manteca Bull., 1987-92; producer 2 teaching videos, 1986; contbr. articles to profl. jours. Lectr. to elem. students on dental health Manteca Unified Sch. Dist., 1982-92; dental health screener Elem. Schs., San Joaquin County Pub. Health, 1989-92; dental cons. Interplast program Stanford U. Sch. Medicine. Capt. U.S. Army, 1955-57. Fellow Internat. Coll. Dentistry, Internat. Assn. Dental Rsch., Fedn. Dentaire Internationale, Am. Acad. Pediat. Dentistry, Am. Coll. Dentists, Royal Soc. Health (Eng.), Acad. of Dentistry for Handicapped, Pierre Fauchard Acad., Acad. Dental Materials; mem. ADA, Am. Assn. Dentists Children, Am. Assn. Dental Cons., Calif. Dental Assn., Calif. Soc. Dentistry for Children (pres. 1968), Calif. Soc. Pediat. Dentists, N.Y. Acad. Sci., Calif. Acad. Sci., Am. Bd. Quality Assurance & Utilization Rev. Physicians (diplomate), Nat. Assn. for Healthcare Quality, Rotary Internat. Republican. Home: 374 Laurelwood Cir Manteca CA 95336-7122 Office: Valley Oak Dental Group Inc 1507 W Yosemite Ave Manteca CA 95337

TONSO, CHERYL JACKSON, retired secondary education educator; b. Denver, Jan. 12, 1934; d. James Homer and Virginia Isabelle (Anderson) Jackson; m. Jerome Peter Tonso, Mar. 2, 1957 (dec. May 1977); children: Tawlys Grace Tonso Kaufman, Trynis Marie Tonso Bradley. AA, Cottey Coll., 1954; BA, U. Colo., 1956. Classroom tchr. Mesa Valley Schs., Grand Junction, Colo., 1956-58; classroom tchr. Boulder (Colo.) Valley Pub. Schs., 1965-77, 80-87, organizational specialist, 1977-80, dean of students, 1987-92; pvt. bus. owner; real estate, property devel. specialist Colo., 1992—; cons. Denver Pub. Schs., 1979-80, Elizabeth (Colo.) Pub. Sch., 1979-80, St. Vrain Valley Pub. Sch., 1979-80. Collaborative author: Organization Development, 1977-90, Boulder Schools English Curriculum, 1987-89, Boulder Schools Junior High School Curriculum, 1969-73. Active Denver Mus. Natural History, Women of West Mus. Mem. NEA, POK, PED, AAUW (pres. 1969-71), Colo. Edn. Assn., Boulder Valley Edn. Assn. (several offices), Colo. North Ctrl. Assn. (state com. 1981-95, chmn. 1990-91), Western History Assn., Delta Kappa Gamma (pres. 1977-79), Phi Delta Kappa. Democrat. Home: 1690 Dogwood Ln Boulder CO 80304-1525

TOOHEY, CYNTHIA D., state legislator; b. N.Y.C., Apr. 16, 1934; widowed; children: Camden, Sean, Kate. ADN, U. Alaska-Anchorage C.C., 1974. Co-owner, operator Crow Creek Mine, 1970—; mem. Alaska House of Reps., Anchorage, 1992—. Trustee Alaska Regional Hosp.; bd. dirs. Anchorage Conv. & Visitors Bur.; past mem. Girdwood Bd. Suprs. Office: The House of Representatives 2642 Forest Park Dr Anchorage AK 99517-1326

TOOKEY, ROBERT CLARENCE, consulting actuary; b. Santa Monica, Calif., Mar. 21, 1925; s. Clarence Hall and Minerva Maconachie (Anderson) T.; BS, Calif. Inst. Tech., 1945; MS, U. Mich., 1947; m. Marcia Louise Hickman, Sept. 15, 1956; children: John Hall, Jennifer Louise, Thomas Anderson. With Prudential Ins. Co. Am., Newark, 1947-49; assoc. actuary in group Pacific Mut. Life Ins. Co., Los Angeles, 1949-55; asst. v.p. in charge reins. sales and service for 17 western states Lincoln Nat. Life Ins. Co., Ft. Wayne, Ind., 1955-61; dir. actuarial services Peat, Marwick, Mitchell & Co., Chgo., 1961-63; mng. partner So. Calif. office Milliman & Robertson, cons. actuaries, Pasadena, 1963-76; pres. Robert Tookey Assos., Inc., 1977—. Committeeman troop 501 Boy Scouts Am., 1969-72. Served to lt. (j.g.) USNR, 1943-45, 51-52. Fellow Soc. Actuaries, Conf. Consulting Actuaries; mem. Am. Acad. Actuaries, Pacific States Actuarial Club, Pacific Ins. Conf., Rotary Club (Pasadena), Union League Club (Chgo.). Home and Office: 3950 San Augustine Dr Glendale CA 91206-1232 also: PO Box 646 La Canada Flintridge CA 91012-0646

TOOL, MARCUS REED, economics educator, author, editor; b. Murdock, Nebr., Aug. 3, 1921; s. Harold Warren and Edna Mina (Goehry) T.; m. Lillian Mae Redington, Dec. 12, 1943; children: Laurence Alan, Marilyn Louise. BS in Commerce, U. Denver, 1943, MA, 1950; PhD in Econs., U. Colo., Boulder, 1953. Instr. social sci. U. Denver, 1947-50; asst. prof. econs. U. Colo., Boulder, 1952-53, San Diego State Coll., 1953-55; asst. prof. to prof. econs. Calif. State U., Sacramento, 1955-83, prof. emeritus, 1984—. Author: Philosophy of Neoinstitutionalism, 1953; California State Colleges Under Master Plan, 1966; The Discretionary Economy, 1979, 2d edit., 1985, Essays in Social Value Theory, 1986, Pricing, Valuation and Systems, 1995; editor: Institutionalist Guide to Economic Theory and Policy, 1984, Evolutionary Economics, I & II, 1988, Institutional Economics: Theory, Method, Policy, 1993; co-editor: The Elgar Companion to Institutional and Evolutionary Economics, 1994; contbr. articles to profl. jours.; editor Jour. Econ. Issues, 1981-91. 1st lt. U.S. Army, 1943-46, ETO. Recipient Outstanding Faculty award Phi Kappa Phi, Calif. State U., 1982, Veblen-Commons award Assn. for Evolutionary Economics, 1988. Mem. Assn. for Evolutionary Econs. (pres. 1992), European Assn. Evolutionary Polit. Economy, Assn. Instl. Thought (pres. 1979-80), Am. Econs. Assn. Democrat. Unitarian. Home: 5708 Mcadoo Ave Sacramento CA 95819-2516

TOOLE, FLOYD EDWARD, manufacturing company executive; b. Moncton, N.B., Can., June 19, 1938; s. Harold Osman and Arilla Adeltha (Allen) T.; m. Noreen Beckie, June 31, 1961. BSc in EE, U. N.B., Fredericton, 1961; PhD in EE, U. London, 1965. Sr. rsch. officer NRC Can., Ottawa, Ont., 1965-91; v.p. engring. Harman Internat. Industries Inc., Northridge, Calif., 1991—. Contbr. articles to profl. jours. Fellow Audio Engring. Soc. (pres. 1992-93, Publs. award 1988, 90); mem. Acoustical Soc. Am. Office: Harman Internat Industries 8500 Balboa Blvd Northridge CA 91329-0001

TOOLE, LEE K., telecommunications company executive; b. 1936. BSBA, U. Tenn., 1961. With AT&T Long Lines, 1961-76, dep. dir. internat.; with GTE Hawaiian Tel. Co., Inc., Honolulu, 1976-83, 85—, v.p., also chief oper. officer, 1985, then v.p., chief oper. officer, mgr., v.p. nat. accounts mktg. and nat. sales, 1983-85, now pres., also bd. dirs. With U.S. Army, 1956-59. Office: GTE-Hawaiian Tel Co PO Box 2200 Honolulu HI 96841-0001

TOOLEY, CHARLES FREDERICK, communications executive, consultant; b. Seattle, Sept. 29, 1947; s. Creath Athol and Catherine Ella (Wainman) T.; m. Valerie Adele Gose, Mar. 7, 1981 (dec. Feb. 1991); children: Paige Arlene Chytka, Marni Higdon Tooley. BA, Lynchburg Coll., 1968. Producer, stage mgr., tech. dir. various theatre cos. and performing arts orgns., Ala., Fla., Va., N.Y., Ariz., 1965-74; field underwriter N.Y. Life Ins. Co., Billings, Mont., 1974-77; market adminstr. Mountain Bell Telephone Co., Butte and Billings, Mont., 1978-83; pres. BCC Inc., Billings, Mont., 1983—. Mem. Mont. Arts Coun., 1982-92; active Billings/Yellowstone County Centennial, 1981-82; mem. steering com. Mont. Cultureal Advocacy, 1982-92; bd. dirs. Yellowstone 89ers, 1987-89, Christian Chs. in Mont., 1983—; elder Ctrl. Christian Ch., Billings, chmn. trustees, 1983-85; mem. Mont. Dem. Exec. Bd.; 1982-87; mem. adv. bd. Salvation Army, Billings, 1984—; del. Dem. Nat. Conv., 1980; Dem. candidate Mont. Ho. of Reps., 1986; mem. Billings City Coun., 1988-94, mayor pro tem, 1992-94; mayor City of Billings, 1996—. Sgt. U.S. Army, 1969-72, Vietnam. Mem. Billings Coun. Fgn. Rels., Toastmasters (Div. Gov.'s Cup 1978), Kiwanis (bd. dirs. 1981-88), Masons, Shriners, Elks. Mem. Disciples of Christ. Home: 502 Alderson Ave Billings MT 59101-5920 Office: BCC Inc PO Box 555 Billings MT 59103-0555

TOON, OWEN BRIAN, earth scientist; b. Bethesda, Md., May 26, 1947; s. Owen Russell and Adrienne Joan (Van Burk) T.; m. Teresa Eileen Hand, Sept. 6, 1968; 1 child, Christopher Russell. AB, U. Calif., Berkeley, 1969; PhD, Cornell U., 1975. Nat. Rsch. Coun. fellow, Ames Rsch. Ctr. Nat. Acad. Sci., Mountain View, Calif., 1975-78; sr. scientist, Ames Rsch. Ctr. NASA, Moffett Field, Calif., 1978—. Contbr. 150 articles to profl. jours. Recipient Leo Spilard award for physics in pub. interest Am. Phys. Soc., 1986. Fellow Calif. Acad. Sci., Am. Geophys. Union, Am. Meterol. Soc. Office: Earth System Sci Divsn NASA Ames Rsch Ctr Moffett Field CA 94035

TOPE, DWIGHT HAROLD, retired management consultant; b. Grand Junction, Colo., Aug. 29, 1918; s. Richard E. and Elizabeth (Jones) T.; m. Carolyn Stagg, Apr. 29, 1949; children: Stephen R., Chris L. AS, Mesa Coll., 1940; student, George Washington U. With Fgn. Funds Control, a Div. of U.S. Treasury Dept.; staff adjuster Fire Cos. Adjustment Bur., Denver, Albuquerque, 1946-48; br. mgr. Gen. Adjustment Bur., Deming, N.Mex., 1948-50; spl. agt. Cliff Kealey State Agy., Albuquerque, 1950-56; pres. Dwight Tope State Agy., Inc., Albuquerque, 1956-84, also chmn. bd., sr. cons., 1985-87. Mem. adv. bd. Salvation Army, Albuquerque, 1974—, Meals on Wheels, 1987—; past chmn. bd., pres. Presbyn. Heart Inst., Albuquerque, 1977—. Maj. Coast Arty. Anti-Aircraft, 1941-45. Mem. N.Mex. Ins. Assn. (past chmn.), Ins. Info. Inst. (past chmn.), N.Mex. Surplus Lines Assn. (past pres.), Air Force Assn., Assn. of U.S. Army, Am. Legion, Albuquerque C. of C. (mil. rels. com.), Rotary, Masons, Shriners, Albuquerque Country Club, Petroleum Club. Republican. Home: 1812 Stanford Dr NE Albuquerque NM 87106-2538 Office: 8100 Mountain Rd NE Ste 204E Albuquerque NM 87110-7833

TOPHAM, DOUGLAS WILLIAM, writer, consultant; b. Hollywood, Calif.; s. Ollie Austin and Harriet Winifred (Scott) T. BS, Stanford U., 1964, AM, 1965. Cert. secondary tchr., Calif. Tchr. The Principia, St. Louis, 1969-72; instr. Can. Coll., Redwood City, Calif., 1973-74; writer Varian Assocs., Palo Alto, Calif., 1977, Four-Phase Systems Inc., Cupertino, Calif., 1977-80, MicroPro Internat., San Rafael, Calif., 1980-81, Zentec Corp., Santa Clara, Calif., 1981-85; contract writer various cos., 1985—, TeleVideo Systems Inc., Sunnyvale, Calif., 1988-89; freelance writer, cons. Santa Clara, 1989—; cons. ABC-TV, Burbank, Calif., 1974. Author: WordStar Training Guide, 1981, UNIX and XENIX, 1985 (Small Computer Club Book of Month 1985), Using WordStar, 1988, WordPerfect 5.0 with 5.1 Extensions, 1990, A DOS User's Guide to UNIX, 1990, First Book of UNIX, 1990 (Small Computer Club Book of Month 1992), A System V Guide to UNIX and XENIX, 1990, Up and Running with Q & A, 1991, Portable UNIX, 1992 (Small Computer Club Book of Month 1993). Bd. dirs. Las Brisas Condominium Assn., 1988-89, Christian Sci. Ch., 1988-89. Capt. USAF, 1965-69. Acad. scholar Stanford U., 1960-64. Mem. Authors Guild, Writers Connection, Nat. Writers Union.

TOPIK, STEVEN CURTIS, history educator; b. Montebello, Calif., Aug. 6, 1949; s. Kurt and Gertrude Irene (Kriszanich) T.; m. Martha Jane Marcy, Feb. 3, 1979; children: Julia, Natalia. BA, U. Calif., San Diego, 1971; MA, U. Tex., 1973, PhD, 1978. Asst. prof. Universidade Fed. Fluminense, Rio de Janeiro, 1978-81, vis. prof., 1984; asst. prof. Colgate U., Hamilton, N.Y., 1981-84; vis. prof. Univ. Ibero Americana, Mexico City, 1982; prof. U. Calif., Irvine, 1984—; vis. prof. Ecols des Hautes Etudes en Sci. Social, Paris, 1990; cons. in field; mem. editorial com. U. Calif. Press, Berkeley, 1987-89. Author: The Political Economy of the Brazilian State, 1987, Trade and Gunboats, The United State and Brazil in the Age of Empire, 1995; contbr. articles, revs. to profl. publs. Mem. Mayor's Adv. Bd. on Sister Cities, Irvine, 1989-90; mem. adv. bd. Orange County (Calif.) Com. on Latin Am.,

1989-90. Fellow NEH, 1987, 89-90, Rockefeller Found., 1977, Social Sci. Rsch. Coun. Mexico City, 1982-83, Fulbright-Hayes Found., 1978-79, 84, U. Calif., 1988-89. Mem. Latin Am. Studies Assn., Am. Hist. Assn., Conf. Latin Am. History (com. on hist. statistics, com. on projects and publs., chair Brazilian studies com. 1988-90), Pacific Coast Coun. on Latin Am. Studies (bd. govs. 1987-90).

TOPILOW, CARL S., symphony conductor; b. Jersey City, N.J., Mar. 14, 1947; s. Jacob Topilow and Pearl (Roth) Topilow Josephs; 1 child, Jenny Michelle. B.Mus., Manhattan Sch. of Mus., 1968, M.Mus., 1969. Exxon/Arts Endowment Condr. Denver Symphony Orch., 1976-79, asst. condr., 1979-80; mus. dir. Denver Chamber Orch., 1976-81, Denver Youth Orch., 1977-80, Grand Junction Symphony, Colo., 1977-80, Nat. Repertory Orch., Keystone, Colo., 1978—; dir. orchs. Cleve. Inst. Mus., 1981—, condr. Summit Brass 1986—. Recipient Conducting fellowship Nat. Orch. Assn., N.Y.C., 1972-75, Aspen Mus. Festival, Colo., 1976; winner 1st place Balt. Symphony Conducting Competition, Md., 1976.*

TOPJON, ANN JOHNSON, librarian; b. Los Angeles, Dec. 2, 1940; d. Carl Burdett and Margaret Elizabeth (Tildesley) Johnson; m. Gary M. Topjon, 1963; children: Gregory Eric and Cynthia Elizabeth (twins); m. Philip M. O'Brien, 1990. BA, Occidental Coll., 1962; MLS, UCLA, 1963. Reference asst. Whittier (Calif.) Pub. Library, 1973-78; pub. services and reference librarian Whittier Coll., 1981—. Author, bibliography: Carl Larsson. Faculty rsch. grantee Whittier Coll., 1987-88, 91-92, grantee The Am.-Scandinavian Found., N.Y., 1991. Mem. Calif. Acad. and Rsch. Librs. (liaison at Whittier Coll. 1990—), AAUW (Whittier br. 1968-77, Brea-La Habra br., Calif. 1977—, chmn. lit. group, 1977—, chmn. scholarship fund raising 1988-89). Office: Whittier Coll Wardman Libr 7031 Founders Rd Whittier CA 90608

TOPP, ALPHONSO AXEL, JR., environmental scientist, consultant; b. Indpls., Oct. 15, 1920; s. Alphonso Axel and Emilia (Karlsson) T.; m. Mary Catherine Virtue, July 7, 1942; children: Karen, Susan, Linda, Sylvia, Peter, Astrid, Heidi, Eric, Megan, Katrina. BS in Chem. Engring., Purdue U., 1942; MS, UCLA, 1948. Commd. 2d lt. U.S. Army, 1942, advanced through grades to col., 1966, ret., 1970; environ. scientist Radiation Protection Sect., State of N.Mex., Santa Fe, 1970, program mgr., licensing and registration sect., 1978, chief radiation protection bur., 1981-83; cons., 1984—. Decorated Legion of Merit, Bronze Star with 2 oak leaf clusters. Mem. Health Physics Soc., Sigma Xi, Rotary. Republican. Presbyterian. Home and Office: 872 Highland Dr Los Osos CA 93402-3902

TORBERT, GEORGE KENNETH, elementary educator; b. Canal Zone, Panama, June 16, 1949; parents U.S. citizens; s. Lynn Elwood Torbert and Daisy Oderay Whalen; m. Arlene Mary Urias, Aug. 27, 1983; 1 child, Lynn Kristine. BA in History, U. Wyo., 1973, BA in Secondary Edn., 1979, BA in Elem. Edn., 1983; MA in Bilingual Crosscultural Edn., Calif. State U., Dominguez Hills, 1988. Coach, social studies tchr. Sioux County, Harrison, Nebr., 1979-80; bilingual elem. tchr. Pasadena (Calif.) Unified Sch. Dist., 1983-85, Lynwood (Calif.) Sch. Dist., 1985-87, Santa Maria (Calif.)-Bonita Sch. Dist., 1987—; cons. on lang. tests Santa Maria-Bonita Sch. Dist., 1987—, on migrant program Santa Barbara County, 1991-93; bilingual dist. action com. Santa Maria-Bonita Sch. Dist., 1992—; action team Santa-Maria Bilingual Office, 1992-94. Served in USAF, 1972-74, Southeast Asia, USAR, 1980—. Recipient achievement medal USAR, 1988, 93, Vietnam support medal USAF, 1973, Vietnam combat support medal, 1973. Mem. NEA, VFW, Calif. Tchrs. Assn., Calif. Assn. Bilingual Edn., Nat. Assn. Bilingual Edn. Democrat. Roman Catholic. Home: 4348 Whitefield Ct Santa Maria CA 93455-3551 Office: Miller Sch 410 E Camino Colegio Santa Maria CA 93454-6752

TORBERT, MEG BIRCH, artist, design and color consultant; b. Faribault, Minn., Sept. 30, 1912; d. William Alfred and Lucille Birch; m. Arnnold Clair, Aug. 30, 1937 (dec.); m. Donald Torbert, Aug. 12, 1940 (dec. 1985); 1 child, Stephanie B. BA, U. Minn., 1934; MA, U. Iowa, 1938. Prof. Kans. Wesleyan U., Salina, 1934-35, U. Mont., Dillon, 1937-38; assoc. prof. U. Minn., Mpls., 1939-49; curator, editor Walker Art Ctr., Mpls., 1950-63; film dir. NSF, Mpls., 1963-68; freelance color cons., Mpls., 1968-78. Editor Design Quar., 1950-63; dir. (films): Vectors, 1967, Equidecomposable Polygons, 1968; one-woman shows: Hutchins Gallery, Cambria, Calif., 1986, 88, 90, Elizabeth Fortner, Santa Barbara, Calif., 1987, 88, 90, 91, Santa Barbara Art Co., 1992. Carnegie fellow U. Iowa, 1935-37. Home and Studio: 2643 State St Apt 1 Santa Barbara CA 93105-5514

TORBET, LAURA, graphic designer, author; b. Paterson, N.J., Aug. 23, 1942; d. Earl Buchanan and Ruth Claire (Ehlers) Robbins; B.A., B.F.A., Ohio Wesleyan U., 1964; m. Bruce J. Torbet, Sept. 9, 1967 (div. 1971); m. Peter H. Morrison, June 19, 1983 (dec. Nov. 1988). Mng. editor Suburban Life mag., East Orange, N.J., 1964-65; asst. public relations dir. United Funds N.J., Newark, 1965-67; art dir. Alitalia Airlines, N.Y.C., 1967-69; propr. Laura Torbet Studio, N.Y.C., 1969-84; author: Macrame You Can Wear, 1972, Clothing Liberation, 1973, Leathercraft You Can Wear, 1975, The T-Shirt Book, 1976, The Complete Book of Skateboarding, 1976, How To Do Everything With Markers, 1977; (with Doug McLaggan) Squash: How to Play, How to Win, 1977; The Complete Book of Mopeds, 1978; (with Luree Nicholson) How to Fight Fair With Your Kids...and Win!, 1980; editor: Helena Rubenstein's Book of the Sun, 1979, The Encyclopedia of Crafts, 1980, (with George Bach) The Inner Enemy, 1982, A Time for Caring, 1982; (with Hap Hatton) Helpful Hints for Hard Times, 1982, The Virgin Homeowners Handbook, 1984, Helpful Hints for Better Living, 1984, (with James Braly) Dr. Braly's Optimum Health Program, 1985; (with Bernard Gittelson) Intangible Evidence, 1987; (with Harville Hendrix) Keeping the Love You Find, 1992, The Couples Companion, 1994; editor, ghost writer, co-author books. Bd. dirs. The Living/Dying Project. Mem. Boss Ladies. Home and Office: 1111 Butterfield Rd San Anselmo CA 94960-1181

TOREN, ROBERT, photojournalist; b. Grand Rapids, Mich., Oct. 9, 1915; s. Clarence J. and Helen (Holcomb) T.; student Winona Sch. Profl. Photography, 1957, West Coast Sch. Photography, 1959-62; m. Miriam Jeanette Smith, July 17, 1940. Photographer, Harris and Ewing, Washington, 1938-39, Versluis Studios, Grand Rapids, Mich., 1939-43, prodn. mgr., 1940-43; owner, photographer Toren Galleries, San Francisco, 1946-70; photographer Combat Tribes of World, Rich Lee Orgn., 1978-84, Darien jungle expdn. Am. Motors, 1979; feature writer Auburn (Calif.) Jour., El Dorado Gazette, 1983-87, Georgetown Gazette, 1983-93. One man shows various univs.; prints in permanent collections: Photog. Hall of Fame, Coyote Point Mus., San Mateo County Hist. Mus.; photog. column San Mateo Times, Georgetown Gazette; lectr. Am. Pres. Lines, Coll. San Mateo, Peninsula Art Assn., Mendicino Art Ctr. Historian City of Foster City; vice chmn. Art Commn. Foster City. Trustee, West Coast Sch.; bd. dirs. Foster City Art League, Hillbarn Theatre, San Mateo County Arts Council; mem. art com. San Mateo County Fair, 1979-87; coord., dir. Georgetown (Calif.) Mountain Mus., 1982-88; founding pres. Music on The Divide, 1989; pres. El Dorado County Arts Coun. Served from pvt. to staff sgt. AUS, 1943-46. Mem. Calif. Writers (br. pres.), Profl. Photographers Am. Presbyn. Author: Peninsula Wilderness. Illustrator: The Tainted Tree, 1963. Editor: The Evolution of Portraiture, 1965; The Western Way of Portraiture, 1965, Conquest of the Darien, 1984. Home: 3140 Cascade Trl Cool CA 95614-2615

TORKILDSON, RAYMOND MAYNARD, lawyer; b. Lake City, S.D., Nov. 19, 1917; s. Gustav Adolph and Agnes (Opitz) T.; m. Sharman Elizabeth Vaughn, Sept. 8, 1956; children—Stephen, Thomas. S.B., U. S.D., 1946; J.D., Harvard U., 1948. Bar: Calif. 1949, Hawaii 1950. Assoc. James P. Blaisdell, Honolulu, 1949-52; ptnr. Moore, Torkildson & Rice and successors, Honolulu, 1955-64; exec. v.p. Hawaii Employers Council, Honolulu, 1964-67; ptnr. Torkildson, Katz, Jossem, Fonseca, Jaffe, Moore & Hetherington and predecessors, Honolulu, 1967-72, sr. ptnr., 1972-92, of counsel, 1993—. Mem. mgmt. com. Armed Forces YMCA, Honolulu, 1971; treas. Hawaii Republican Com. 1977-83. Served with U.S. Army, 1941-46; lt. col. Res. ret. Mem. ABA, Hawaii Bar Assn. Roman Catholic. Clubs: Oahu Country, Pacific (Honolulu).

TORLAKSON, JAMES DANIEL, artist; b. San Francisco, Feb. 19, 1951; s. Allen Daniel and Catherine Agnus (Leary) T.; 1 child, Elizabeth. BA with high distinction, Calif. Coll. Arts and Crafts, Oakland, 1973; MA, San Francisco State U., 1974. Fine artist/painter, printmaker, filmmaker Pacifica, Calif., 1971—; prof. of art Skyline Coll., San Bruno, Calif., 1982—, Coll. of San Mateo, Calif., 1986—, Calif. Coll. Arts and Crafts, 1978-85. Solo exhibits include Horvath Gallery, Sacramento, Calif., 1993, Cudahy's Gallery, Inc., N.Y.C., 1992, John Berggruen Gallery, San Francisco, 1974, 78, 80, 83, 86, 88, 91, Concept Art Gallery, Pitts., 1987, Dubins Gallery, L.A., 1984, Mus. of Art, Carnegie Inst., Pitts., 1982, Getler/Pall, N.Y.C., 1981, others; mus. collections include San Francisco Mus. of Art, Oakland Mus., Achenbach Foun. for Graphic Arts/Calif. Palace of Legion of Honor, San Francisco, Bklyn. Mus., others.; contbr. to publs. Home: 433 Rockaway Beach Ave Pacifica CA 94044-3226

TORME, MARGARET ANNE, public relations executive, communications consultant; b. Indpls., Apr. 5, 1943; d. Ira G. and Margaret Joy (Wright) Barker; children—Karen Anne, Leah Vanessa. Student Coll. San Mateo, 1961-65. Pub. rels. mgr. Hoefer, Dieterich & Brown (now Chiat-Day), San Francisco, 1964-73; v.p., co-founder, creative dir. Lowry & Ptnrs., San Francisco, 1975-83; pres., founder Torme & Co. (now Torme & Kenney), San Francisco, 1983—; cons. in communications. Mem. Pub. Rels. Soc. Am., San Francisco Advt. Club, North Bay Advt. Club, San Francisco C. of C. (outstanding achievement award for women entrepreneurs 1987), Jr. League (adv. bd.) Office: 545 Sansome St San Francisco CA 94111-2908

TORNSTROM, ROBERT ERNEST, lawyer, oil company executive; b. St. Paul, Jan. 17, 1946; s. Clifford H. and Janet (Hale) T.; m. Betty Jane Hermann, Aug. 5, 1978; children: Carter, Gunnar, Katherine. BA, U. Colo., 1968, JD, 1974; diploma grad. sch. mgmt. exec. program, UCLA, 1990. Bar: Colo. 1974, U.S. Dist. Ct. Colo. 1974, Calif. 1975, U.S. Dist. Ct. (cen. dist.) Calif. 1975. Atty. Union Oil Co. of Calif., Los Angeles, 1974-76, counsel internat. div., 1977-78; regional counsel Union Oil Co. of Calif., Singapore, 1976-77; sr. atty. Occidental Internat. Exploration and Prodn. Co., Bakersfield, Calif., 1978-81, mng. counsel, 1981-85, v.p., assoc. gen. counsel, 1985-88, v.p., regional ops. mgr., 1988-91; pres. Occidental Argentina, Buenos Aires, 1991-93, Occidental of Russia, Moscow, 1993-94; dir. comml. negotiations Occidental Internat., 1994—; bd. dirs., chmn. bd. Parmaneft Joint Venture, Vanyogannef JV, Moscow; bd. dirs. Calif. Land and Cattle Co., King City, 602 Operating Corp., Bakersfield; legal cons. Island Creek Coal Co., Lexington, Ky. Served to capt. U.S. Army, 1968-71, Vietnam. Decorated Bronze Star. Recipient Am. Jurisprudence award Bancroft-Whitney Co., 1974; named Eagle Scout, Boy Scouts Am. Mem. Am. Soc. Internat. Law, Am. Corp. Counsel Assn., Soc. Mayflower Descendants, Moscow Country Club, Stockdale Country Club. Republican. Episcopalian. Home: 310 Mt Lowe Dr Bakersfield CA 93309 Office: 1200 Discovery Way Bakersfield CA 93309 also: PO Box 12021 Bakersfield CA 93389-2021

TORRACA, LOUIS A., JR., public relations executive; b. New Haven, May 13, 1935; s. Louis Anthony Sr. and Mary Elizabeth (Pyle) T.; m. Beryl Joyce Collins, Mar. 15, 1963. BS in Comm./Pub. Rels., Boston U.; MA in Journalism/Mass Comm., U. Okla. Commd. 2d lt. USAF, 1958, advanced through grades to Col., retired, 1983; pres. Internat. Pub. Rels. Ltd., Honolulu, 1983-89; assoc. fin. investment divsn. United Way, Honolulu, 1984-85; dir. Mayor's Office of Info. and Complaint, Honolulu, 1985-87; dir. comm. Dept. Edn., Honolulu, 1987-90; spl. asst. to the pres. Bishop Mus. Corp., Honolulu, 1991—; mem. comm. faculty Chaminade U. Honolulu, 1991—. Mem., sub-com. chair Gov.'s Traffic Safety Task Force; dir. Pkwy. Cmty. Assn.; mem. Armed Svcs. Bd. Mgmt.; bd. trustees Honolulu Theatre for Youth; bd. dirs. Play it Safe Internat.; mem. adv. com. Hawaii Criminal Justice Commn. Recipient Dept. Def. Superior Svc. medal, Legion of Merit, Bronze star, Meritorious Svc. medal with 1 oak leaf cluster, Air Force commendation with 3 oak leaf clusters. Mem. Pub. Rels. Soc. Am. (accredited, pres. Hawaii chpt. 1995—), Soc. Profl. Journalists, Internat. Assn. Bus. Communicators, Honolulu Press Club, Kappa Sigma, Tau Mu Epsilon, Kappa Tau Alpha. Episcopalian. Home: 184 Aikahi Loop Kailua HI 96734-1642 Office: Spl Asst to Pres Bishop Mus 1525 Bernice St Honolulu HI 96817-0916

TORRANCE, ROBERT MITCHELL, comparative literature educator; b. Washington, May 9, 1939; s. Charles Mitchell and Ayma Jean (Sharpe) T.; m. Mildred D. Fischer, June 14, 1963 (div. July 1991); children: Benjamin Henry, Nicholas Aaron; m. Donna K. Reed, Aug. 24, 1991; stepchildren: Benjamin Reed-Lunn, Rebecca Reed-Lunn. BA Classics and English summa cum laude, Harvard U., 1961; MA in Comparative Lit., U. Calif., Berkeley, 1963; PhD in Comparative Lit., Harvard U., 1970. Asst. prof. comparative lit. Harvard U., Cambridge, 1971-75; assoc. prof. comparative lit. CUNY, Bklyn., 1975-76; prof. comparative lit. U. Calif., Davis, 1976—. Author: The Comic Hero, 1978, Ideal and Spleen, 1987, The Spiritual Quest, 1994; translator: Sophocles, The Women of Trachis and Philoctetes, 1966. Jr. fellow Soc. of Fellows, Harvard U., 1966-69, Humanities Inst. fellow U. Calif., Davis, 1990. Home: 2800 Corona Dr Davis CA 95616-0116 Office: U Calif Comparative Lit Program Davis CA 95616

TORRES, ESTEBAN EDWARD, congressman, business executive; b. Miami, Ariz., Jan. 27, 1930; s. Esteban Torres and Rena Baron (Gomez) T.; m. Arcy Sanchez, Jan. 22, 1955; children: Carmen D'Arcy, Rena Denise, Camille Bianca, Selina Andre, Esteban Adrian. Student, East Los Angeles Coll., 1960, Calif. State U., Los Angeles, 1963, U. Md., 1965, Am. U., 1966; PhD (hon.), Nat. U., 1987. Chief steward United Auto Workers, local 230, 1954-63, dir. polit. com., 1963; organizer, internat. rep. United Auto Workers (local 230), Washington, 1964; asst. dir. Internat. Affairs Dept., 1975-77; dir. Inter-Am. Bureau for Latin Am., Caribbean, 1965-67; exec. dir. E. Los Angeles Community Union (TELACU), 1967-74; US ambassador to UNESCO, Paris, 1977-79; chmn. Geneva Grp., 1977-78; chmn. U.S. del. Gen. Conf., 1978; spl. asst. to pres. U.S., dir. White House Office Hispanic Affairs, 1979-81; mem. 98th-103rd Congresses from 34th Dist. Calif., 1983—, mem. appropriations com., subcom. fgn. ops., subcom. military constrn.; campaign coordinator Jerry Brown for Gov., 1974; Hispanic coordinator Los Angeles County campaign Jimmy Carter for Pres., 1976; mem. Sec. of State Adv. Group, 1979-81; v.p. Nat. Congress Community Econ. Devel., 1973-74; pres. Congress Mex.-Am. Unity, 1970-71, Los Angeles Plaza de la Raza Cultural Center, 1974; dir. Nat. Com. on Citizens Broadcasting, 1977; cons. U.S. Congress office of tech. assessment, 1976-77; del to U.S. Congress European Parliament meetings, 1984—; ofcl. congl. observer Geneva Arms Control Talks; chmn. Congl. Hispanic Caucus, 1987; speaker Wrights Del. to USSR, 1987; Dem. dep. Whip, 1990. Contbr. numerous articles to profl. jours. Co-chmn. Nat. Hispanic Dems., 1988—; chmn. Japan-Hispanic Inst. Inc.; bd. visitors Sch. Architecture U. Calif. at Los Angeles, 1971-73; bd. dirs. Los Angeles County Econ. Devel. Com., 1972-75, Internat. Devel. Conf., 1976-78. Served in AUS, 1949-53, ETO. Recipient various awards for public service. Mem. Americans for Dem. Action (exec. bd. 1975-77), VFW Post 6315, Pico Rivera, Calif., Am. Legion Post 0272, Montebello, Calif. Office: House of Representatives Rayburn Bldg Rm 2368 Washington DC 20515-0005

TORREY, JAMES D., communications executive, consultant; b. Drayton, N.D., July 16, 1940; s. Howard J. Torrey and Gertrude (Carpenter) Steenson; m. Katherine Joann Kowal, Sept. 2, 1958; children: Tamara, Timonthy (dec.), Teresa, Todd. Student, U. Oreg. Mgr. Waldport (Oreg.) Food Market, 1959-67; dist. mgr. Obie Outdoor Advt., Aberdeen, Wash., 1967-68; dir. sales Obie Media Corp., Eugene, Oreg., 1968-71, exec. v.p., 1971-78, pres., CEO, 1980-88; pres., CEO Total Comm., Inc., Eugene, Oreg., 1989—; N.W. area market mgr. 3M Nat. Advt., Eugene, Oreg., 1978-80; dir. mktg. State Accident Ins. Fund, Salem, Oreg., 1988-89; mem. exec. com. affiliate bd. Mut. Broadcasting, 1981-87. Pres. Waldport City Coun., 1962-67; coach Eugene Kidsports, 1968-92, Am. Softball Assn. Girls Softball Team, 1988; mem. adv. com. 4 J Sch. Dist., 1988-90; bd. dirs. Lane County United Way, 1983-86, dir., 1992, Lane County Goodwill Industries, 1989-90; mem. Eugene City Budget Com., 1992-94, Eugene City Coun., 1994—. Named JCI senator, Oreg. State Jaycees, 1966, Citizen of Yr., City of Waldport, 1967, Outstanding Vol., City of Eugene, 1991. Mem. Oreg. Outdoor Advt. Assn. (pres. 1971-80), Oreg. Assn. Broadcasters (dir. 1984-87), Eugene C. of C. (bd. dirs., pres. 1991-92), Eugene Rotary (dir., pres. 1984, Paul Harris fellow 1985). Republican. Roman Catholic. Home: 2545 Chuckanut St Eugene OR 97408-4766 Office: Station KUGN-AM & FM 2545 Chestnut St Eugene OR 97401

TORREZ, NAOMI ELIZABETH, copyright review editor, librarian; b. Scranton, Pa., July 3, 1939; d. Sterling E. and Naomi (Reynolds) Hess; m. Lupe F. Torrez, Dec. 23, 1961; children: Sterling Edward, Stanley Marshall. BA, U. Ariz., 1961; MA, U. Calif., Berkeley, 1964, MLS, 1970; DRE, Golden State Sch. Theology, Oakland, Calif., 1988; cert. in travel industry, Vista C.C., 1993. Libr. asst. Oakland Pub. Libr., 1966-67, U. Calif. Libr., Berkeley, 1967-70; tutor-couns. Sonoma State Hosp., Eldridge, Calif., 1973-77, libr. tech. asst., 1977-79; health scis. libr. Kaiser Hosp., Vallejo, Calif., 1979-87; copyright rev. editor Kaiser Dept. Med. Editing, Oakland, 1987—; participant Statewide Latino Congress, 1994. Author: Not in My Pew, 1990, GSST Research Manual, 1990; contbr. to Co-op Low Cost Cookbook, 1965. Active Albany 75th Anniversary Com., 1983, Women's Health Initiative, 1995—; officer Ariz. Fedn. of the Blind, Calif. Coun. of the Blind, 1959-66. Woodrow Wilson fellow, 1961; winner Nat. Spelling Bee, 1953; Nat. Merit scholar, 1957-61. Mem. Kaiser Permanente Latino Assn., Kaiser Affirmative Action Com., Kaiser Health Edn. Com., K.P. Regional Libr.'s Group (chair 1988), Internat. Platform Assn., Phi Beta Kappa, Phi Kappa Phi. Baptist. Home: 829 Jackson St Albany CA 94706-1504 Office: Kaiser Dept Med Editing 1800 Harrison St Fl 16 Oakland CA 94612-3429

TORRIANNI, DIANE LOUISE, acquisitions specialist; b. Whittier, Calif., Sept. 5, 1954; d. Harvey Nels and Betty Carol (Fulton) Olson; m. Mark Wilfred Torrianni, Apr. 5, 1975 (div. Apr. 1981); children: Jeana Marie, Paul Joseph; m. Thomas Edwin Greer, July 2, 1989. Student, Azusa Pacific U., 1972-73, Calif. State U., Fullerton, 1974-75, U. Calif., Irvine, 1987—. Admisntr. procurement systems Fluor Engrs., Inc., Irvine, 1981-84; exec. asst. Coldwell Banker Corp. Hqrs., Newport Beach, Calif., 1984-85; dir. mktg. Ernst & Whinney, Newport Beach, Calif., 1985-86; paralegal Legal Network, Inc., Irvine, 1986-89; acquisitions rep. Chevron Land & Devel. Co., Irvine, 1989-92; sr. project analyst acquisitions Chevron Land & Devel. Co., Newport Beach, 1993—. Bd. dirs. Orange County chpt. City of Hope, 1987-92; western region coord. White House Conf. Small Bus., 1986; polit. coord. Congressman ed. Szchau Campaign Com.; polit. coord. Orange County Office of Protocol, 1986, Senator John Seymour Campaign Com. With USNR, 1993—. Mem. Orange County Bldg. Industry Alliance (bd. dirs. 1993, Riverside legis. affairs com. 1993, bd. dirs., Baldy View govtl. affairs com. 1993). Republican. Office: Chevron Land & Devel Co 23 Corporate Plaza Dr Ste 250 Newport Beach CA 92660-7922

TORTEN, MICHAEL, microbiologist, educator; b. Haifa, Israel, Sept. 25, 1935; came to U.S. 1956; s. Joseph and Fella (Vierny) T.; m. Judith Ann Keller, Aug. 25, 1959; children: Dina, Dan, Ron. BSc, U. Calif., Davis, 1959, DVM, 1963; PhD, Hebrew U., Jerusalem, 1968. Prof. microbiology Israel U. Bio Rsch., Ness Ziona, 1965-90, Tel-Aviv U. Sch. Medicine, 1970—; prof. immunology and surg. oncology UCLA, 1981-83; vis. prof. vet. medicine U. Calif., Davis, 1988-90, rsch. virologist, 1991—; dir. WHO/FAD Leptospirosis Lab., Ness Ziona, 1965-90. Editor-in-chief: Israel Jour. Vet. Medicine, 1985-88; co-editor 2 handbooks on diseases common to humans and animals, 1980, 94; contbr. more than 100 articles to sci. publs. Recipient Zur award Israel Ministry of Agr., 1975; Hon. Diplomate Am. Vet. Epidemiology Soc., 1985. Mem. Internat. Immunology Soc., Internat. Microbiology Soc., Internat. Vet. Soc., Rotary (chpt. pres. 1975-76). Office: Univ of Calif Sch Vet Medicine Davis CA 95616

TOSTI, DONALD THOMAS, psychologist, consultant; b. Kansas City, Mo., Dec. 6, 1935; s. Joseph T. Tosti and Elizabeth M. (Parsons) Tosti Addison; m. Carol J. Curless, Jan. 31, 1957 (dec. 1980); children: Rene, Alicia, Roxanna, Brett, Tabitha, Todd Marcus; m. Annette Brewer, Dec. 29, 1989. B.S. in Elec. Engring., U. N. Mex., 1957, M.S. in Psychology, 1962, Ph.D. in Psychology, 1967. Chief editor Teaching Machines Inc., Albuquerque, 1960-64; div. mgr. Westinghouse Learning Corp., Albuquerque, 1964-70; founder, sr. v.p. Ind. Learning Systems, San Raphael, Calif., 1970-74, pres., 1974-76; chmn. bd. Omega Performance, San Francisco, 1976-77; pres. Operants Inc., San Rafael, 1978-81; v.p. Forum corp., San Rafael, 1981-83; mng. ptnr. Vanguard Cons. Group, San Francisco, 1983—. Author: TMI Programmed Arithmetic Series, 1960-63; Behavior Technology, 1970; A Guide to Child Development; Tactics of Communication; co-author: Learning Is Getting Easier, 1973; Introductory Psychology, 1981, Performance Based Management, Positive Leadership, 1986, Strategic Alliances, 1990. Mem. APA, Soc. Performance and Instrn. (v.p. research 1983-85; outstanding mem. award 1984, life membership award 1984, outstanding product award 1974). Home: 41 Marinita Ave San Rafael CA 94901-3443

TOTH, ELIZABETH LEVAY, retired educational organization executive, lawyer; b. Woodbridge Twp., N.J.; d. Nicholas and Elizabeth (Nagy) Levay; m. Frederick Louis Toth; children: Frederick Albert, Thomas Franklin. BA, Rutgers U., 1970; JD, Seton Hall U., 1973; LLM, NYU, 1980. Bar: N.J. 1973. Mgr., dispatcher, prin. Tri-R-Bus Svc., Inc., Metuchen, N.J., 1959-71; arbitration atty. Robert J. Casulli, East Orange, N.J., 1973; mediator, hearing officer N.J. Pub. Employment Relations Commn., Trenton, 1974-75; assoc. dir. employee relations Woodbridge (N.J.) Twp. Pub. Schs., 1975-81; dir. govt. and community relations Ariz. Sch. Bd. Assn., Phoenix, 1981-85; exec. dir. Greater Phoenix Ednl. Mgmt. Coun., 1985-92; ret., 1992; completed Insts. for Orgnl. Mgmt., San Jose (Calif.) State U. and Stanford U., Calif., 1985-90. Mem. community adv. bd. Sta. KAET-TV, Ariz. State U., Tempe, 1985-91; bd. dirs. North Community Behavioral Health Ctr. (merged into Terros Community Mental Health Orgn. 1988), Phoenix, 1984-88, Ariz. Partnership, 1988-92, Ariz. Alliance Sci., Math. & Tech., 1989-92; sr. arbitrator Better Bus. Bur., Phoenix, 1987—; judge Acad. Decathlon, 1988-92. Recipient plaque and pub. recognition North Community Behavioral Health Ctr., 1987. Mem. Am. Arbitration Assn. (arbitrator), Nat. Panel Mediators, Am. Soc. Assn. Execs., Ariz. Soc. Assn. Execs. (life, bd. dirs. 1987-88, Exec. of Yr. 1987), Soc. Profls. in Dispute Resolution), Pub. Affairs Profls. Ariz., Rutgers U. Alumni Club (pres. 1992-93), Ariz. State U. West Alumni Assn. (sec. 1990-92), Phi Alpha Delta, Alpha Sigma Lambda. Home: 1825 W Ray Rd Apt 1123 Chandler AZ 85224-4091

TOTMAN, PATRICK STEVEN, lawyer, retail executive; b. Stockton, Calif., Sept. 29, 1944; s. Mervyn Willis and Margaret Elizabeth (McDow) T.; m. Rosemarie Bachle, Aug. 27, 1966 (div. Jan. 1989); children—Michael, Jarrod; m. Nancy Choate, July 15, 1991; 1 stepson, Jason. A.B., U. San Francisco, 1966, J.D., 1969. Bar: Calif. 1969. Atty. Safeway, Inc., Oakland, Calif., 1969-72, asst. v.p., 1973-79, v.p., 1979-83, sr. v.p. treasury, 1983—; bd. dirs. Goodwill Industries; seminar leader NYU, 1983-84. Mem. ABA, Calif. Bar Assn., Nat. Assn. Corp. Retail Execs., Internat. Council Shopping Ctrs. Roman Catholic. Office: Safeway Inc 201 4th St Oakland CA 94607-4311

TOTTINO, LESLIE, food products executive; b. 1956. Ptnr. Castroville (Calif.) Laundromat, 1969—, Ralph's Hardware, Castroville, 1969-93, Calif. Artichoke, Castroville, 1977—. Office: Calif Artichoke 11500 Del Monte Ave Castroville CA 95012-3155*

TOUCH, JOSEPH DEAN, computer scientist, educator; b. Bristol, Pa., Apr. 20, 1963; s. Ralph Benjamin and Filomena (Cianfrani) T. BS in Biophysics and Computer Sci., U. Scranton, 1985; MS in Computer Sci., Cornell U., 1987; PhD in Computer Sci., U. Pa., 1992. Cons., indsl. undergrad. rsch. participation program student GTE Labs., Inc., Waltham, Mass., 1983-85; cons. The Software Enging. Inst., Pitts., 1986; rsch. asst. Cornell U., Ithaca, N.Y., 1985-87; cons. Bell Comm. Rsch., Morristown, N.J., 1987-88; grad. rsch. fellow, AT&T Bell Labs. Rsch. assistantship U. Pa., Phila., 1988-92; cons. NASA Goddard Space Flight Ctr., Greenbelt, Md., 1992; computer scientist U. So. Calif. Info. Scis. Inst., Marina del Rey, Calif., 1992—; rsch. asst. prof. U. So. Calif., L.A., 1994—; mem. U. Scranton Acad. Computing Adv. Coun., 1983-85; univ. coun. com. on comm. U. Pa., 1989-90, com. on rsch. policy, 1990-91, acad. planning and budget com., 1990-91; reviewer various jours.; lectr. in field. Contbr. articles to profl. jours.; patentee in field. Mem. IEEE, Assn. for Computing Machinery (chpt. pres. 1984-85), IEEE Comm. Soc. (tech. program com. 1993), U. Scranton Phila. Alumni Soc. (v.p. 1990-91), Sigma Xi, Alpha Sigma Nu, Sigma Pi Sigma, Upsilon Pi Epsilon. Democrat. Roman Catholic. Home: 14005 Palawan Way Ph 23 Marina Del Rey CA 90292 Office: USC Info Scis Inst 4676 Admiralty Way Marina Del Rey CA 90292

TOUPIN, EDWARD BERNARD, engineer, mathematician and computer scientist; b. Houma, La., Mar. 2, 1964; s. Bernard Ovid and Edna Mae

(Pennison) T. AAS, North Harris County Coll., Houston, 1986; BS in Math. and Computer Sci., Met. State Coll. of Denver, 1992. Bench tech. R&D Instrument Svcs., Inc., Houston, 1984-85; owner, technician Hi Res. Technologies, Houston, 1985-88; programmer/analyst Johnson & Higgins of Tex., Houston, 1988-89; programmer/analyst cons. Edward B. Toupin, Houston and Denver, 1989—; automation engr. Texaco Trading and Transp., Inc., Denver, 1990—; tech. editor, author Prentice Hall/QUE, Denver, 1993—; condr. seminars in field; designer/developer comms. classes various software packages. Author and tech. editor publs.; inventor distbd. real time CLNS proto, 1993; patentee in field. Purchse toys for Denver Children's Hosp. With USAF. Met. State Coll. Colo. Scholars awardee, 1991, 92. Mem. ACM, Microsoft Developers Network, AI-CD Network, Am. Assn. Artificial Intelligence, Colo. Advanced Software Inst., U.S. Powerlifting Fedn., Gulf Coast Sailing Assn., Gulf Coast Cycling Assn., Golden Key. Roman Catholic.

TOUR, ROBERT LOUIS, ophthalmologist; b. Sheffield, Ala., Dec. 30, 1918; s. R.S. and Marguerite (Meyer) T.; m. Mona Marie Elien, Oct. 3, 1992. Chem.E., U. Cin., 1942, M.D., 1950. Intern, U. Chgo. Clinics, 1950-51; resident U. Calif. Med. Center-San Francisco, 1951-54; practice medicine, specializing in ophthalmology, occupational medicine and plasmapheresis, San Francisco, 1954-76, Fairbanks, Alaska, 1976-79, Phoenix, 1979—; clin. prof. ophthalmology U. Calif.-San Francisco, 1974-76. Maj. AUS, 1942-45. Diplomate Am. Bd. Ophthalmology. Fellow ACS, Am. Acad. Ophthalmology; mem. AMA, MENSA, Ariz. Ophthal. Soc., Phoenix Ophthal. Soc., Calif. Assn. Ophthalmology, Contact Lens Assn. Ophthalmologists, Pacific Coast Oto-Ophthal. Soc., Ariz. Med. Assn., Maricopa County Med. Soc. , F.C. Cordes Eye Soc., Masons, K.T., Lions, Shriners, Sigma Xi, Nu Sigma Nu, Alpha Tau Omega, Tau Beta Pi, Alpha Omega Alpha, Phi Lambda Upsilon, Omicron Delta Kappa, Kappa Kappa Psi. Home: 2201 E Palmaire Ave Phoenix AZ 85020-5633

TOVAR, CAROLE L., real estate management administrator; b. Toppenish, Wash., May 19, 1940; d. Harold Max and Gertrude Louisa (Spicer) Smith; m. Duane E. Clark, Aug. 1959 (div. 1963); 1 child, David Allen; m. Vance William Gribble, May 19, 1966 (div. 1989), m. Conrad T. Tovar, June 25, 1992. Student, Seattle Pacific Coll. With B.F. Shearer, Seattle, 1959-60, Standard Oil, Seattle, 1960-62, Seattle Platen Co., 1962-70; ptnr. West Coast Platen, Los Angeles, 1970-87, Waldorf Towers Apts., Seattle, 1970—, Cascade Golf Course, North Bend, Wash., 1970-88; co-owner Pacific Wholesale Office Equipment, Seattle and L.A., 1972-87; owner Pacific Wholesale Office Equip., Seattle, L.A. and San Pablo, Calif., 1988-92, Pac Electronic Service Ctr., Commerce and San Pablo, Calif., 1988-90, Waldorf Mgmt. Co. dba Tovar Mgmt. Co., 1988—; Tovar Properties, 1993—. Mem. Nat. Ctr. Housing Mgmt. (cert. occupancy specialist), Assisted Housing Mgmt. Assn. (nat. cert., Wash. bd. dirs.). Methodist. Office: 706 Pike St Seattle WA 98101-2301

TOVAR, NICHOLAS MARIO, mechanical engineer; b. Ogden, Utah, Jan. 18, 1960; s. Gerdo and Alice (Martinez) T.; m. Suzanne Oxborrow, Sept. 17, 1982; children: Ashley, Nicholas Brock, Clinton Gregory, Lance Edward, Marshall Prescott. BSME in Logistics Engring., Weber State U., 1986; BSME in Mech. Engring. and Mfg., Nat. U., 1990. Warehouseman R.C. Willey & Son Co., Syracuse, Utah, 1982-85; logistics contr. Utah-Idaho Supply Co., Salt Lake City, 1985-86; assoc. engr. Aerojet TechSystems Co., Sacramento, 1986-87, engr., 1988-89; mech. engr. Aerojet Solid Propulsion, Sacramento, 1990; sr. mech. engr. Aerojet Propulsion div. GenCorp, Sacramento, 1991-93, BP Chems. Adv. Materials Divsn., Stockton, 1993-94; NDE engr. indsl. testing, dir. quality engring. Internat. Akleinfelder Divsn., 1994—. Republican. Mormon. Home: 2360 Cobbleoak Ct Rancho Cordova CA 95670-4230 Office: Indsl Testing Internat divsn Kleinfelder Corp 2100 Flightline Dr Ste 4 Lincoln CA 95648-9443

TOWE, THOMAS EDWARD, lawyer; b. Cherokee, Iowa, June 25, 1937; s. Edward and Florence (Tow) T.; m. Ruth James, Aug. 21, 1960; children: James Thomas, Kristofer Edward. Student, U. Paris, 1956; BA, Earlham Coll., 1959; LLB, U. Mont., 1962; LLM, Georgetown U., 1965. Ptnr. Towe, Ball, Enright, Mackey & Sommerfeld, Billings, Mont., 1967—; legislator Mont. House of Rep., Billings, 1971-75, Mont. State Senate, Billings, 1975-87, 91-94; served on various coms. Mont. Senate, 1975-87, 91-94. Contbr. articles to law revs. Pres. Alternatives, Inc., Halfway House, Billings, 1985-86, mem. 1977—; mem. adv. com. Mont. Crime Control Bd. 1973-78, Youth Justice coun., 1981-83; mem. State Dem. Exec. com., 1969-71, Yellowstone County Dem. Exec. Com., 1969-73, candidate for congress, 1976; bd. dirs. Mont. Consumer Affairs Coun., Regl. Community Svcs. for the Devel. Disabled, 1975-77, Rimrock Guidance Found., 1975-80, Vols. of Am., Billings, 1984-89, Youth Dynamics Inc., 1989—, Zoo Mont., 1985—. Capt. U.S. Army, 1962-65. Mem. Mont. Bar Assn., Yellowstone County Bar Assn., Am. Hereford Assn., Billings C. of C. Mem. Soc. of Friends. Home: 2739 Gregory Dr S Billings MT 59102-0509 Office: 2525 6th Ave N Billings MT 59101-1338

TOWERS, GORDON THOMAS, province official; b. Red Deer, Alta., Can., July 5, 1919; s. Thomas Henry and Janet (Morrison) T.; m. Doris Roberta, Dec. 27, 1940; children: Thomas Robert, Gary Lee, Lynda Marie, Ross Gordon, Leona. LLD, U. Alta., 1992. Farmer; M.P. Ho. of Commons, 1972, re-elected, 1974, 78, 80, 84; Parliament Sec. to Solicitor Gen., Parliament Sec. to Min. of State; Lt. Gov. Province of Alta., Edmonton, Can., 1991—; appted. Dep. Critic of Veterans Affairs, 1984; del. U.N. Gen. Assembly, 1978. Past pres. Red Deer 4-H Coun. Mem. Can.-Brit. Commonwealth Parliamentary Assn. (del. Westminster 29th Parliament 1980); Red Deer Exhbn. Assn. (past pres.), Prairy Fairs Assn, River Glen Home and Sch. Assn., Masons (Grand Master Red. Deer dist.), Alta. Order of Excellence (chancellor), Knights of St. J., Rotary Internat. (Paul Harris fellow), Red Deer C. of C. (Citizen of the Year 1990). Presbyterian. Office: Legis Bldg 3rd Fl, Edmonton, AB Canada T5K 2B6

TOWERSAP, MARC ERROL, nuclear engineer; b. Pocatello, Idaho, July 21, 1965; s. LeRoy and Zelphia Myra (Pokibro) T. BA in Physics, The Colo. Coll., 1987; postgrad., U. Idaho, 1990—. Engr. II Westinghouse Idaho Nuclear Co., Inc., Idaho Falls, 1988-90, assoc. engr., 1990—; presenter in field. Mem. Am. Ind. Sci. and Engring. Soc. Home: PO Box 830 Fort Hall ID 83203-0830 Office: Westinghouse Idaho Nuclear Box 4000 MS 3210 Idaho Falls ID 83415

TOWNER, HOWARD FROST, biologist, educator; b. Los Angeles, Aug. 10, 1943; s. Leonard Wimberley and Caroline Warren (Frost) T.; m. Linda Lorraine Pardee, Aug. 25, 1978; children: Mary, Elizabeth. AB, U. Calif., Riverside, 1965; PhD, Stanford U., 1970. Prof. biology Loyola Marymount U., Los Angeles, 1972—. Bd. dirs. Friends of Ballona Wetlands, Los Angeles, 1977—. Mem. Ecol. Soc. Am., Calif. Bot. Soc., Phi Beta Kappa, Sigma Xi. Home: 8114 Westlawn Ave Los Angeles CA 90045-2753 Office: Loyola Marymount U Dept Biology 7101 W 80th St Los Angeles CA 90045-2659

TOWNER, LARRY EDWIN, consulting company executive; b. Gallup, N.Mex., Sept. 27, 1937; s. Edwin Robert and Esther Kathryn (Kern) T.; m. D. Yvonne Turner, Mar. 12, 1966; children: Kristina Kay, Jennifer Kate. BS in Tech. Mgmt., Am. U., Washington, 1976. Project mgr. Wolf Research, Houston, 1965-66, Gulton SRG, Arlington, Va., 1966-67; dep. for database devel. USN, Washington, 1967-79; mgr., BTP teleprocessing RCA, Cherry Hill, N.J., 1979-80; mgr., data base adminstrn., solid state div. RCA, Somerville, N.J., 1980-82; mgr., systems devel. Hughes Aircraft, El Segundo, Calif., 1982-89; pres. TCSI, Richland, Wash., 1989—. Author: Ads/Online Cookbook, 1986, A Professionals Guide, 1989, Case: Concepts and Implementation, 1989, Oracle: The Professionals Reference, 1991; contbr. articles to profl. jours. Treas. Va. Hills Recreation Assn., Alexandria, 1970-72, pres. 1975-77; active Civil Air Patrol, Alexandria, 1968-79; bd. dirs. Northwest Citizens Radio Emergency Service, Spokane, Wash., 1960-63. Recipient Meritorious Service award Civil Air Patrol, 1976. Mem. IDMS User Assn. (bd. dirs., Outstanding Svc. award 1984), Hughes Mgmt. Club, Amateur Radio Relay League, Assn. for Systems Mgmt. (v.p. Columbia chpt. 1993, pres. 1994), Richland Rotary Club. Methodist. Home and Office: TCSI 266 Adair Dr Richland WA 99352-9453

TOWNES, CHARLES HARD, physics educator; b. Greenville, S.C., July 28, 1915; s. Henry Keith and Ellen Sumter (Hard) T.; m. Frances H. Brown, May 4, 1941; children: Linda Lewis, Ellen Screven, Carla Keith, Holly Robinson. B.A., B.S., Furman U., 1935; M.A., Duke U., 1937; Ph.D., Calif. Inst. Tech., 1939. Mem. tech. staff Bell Telephone Lab., 1939-47; assoc. prof. physics Columbia U., 1948-50, prof. physics, 1950-61; exec. dir. Columbia Radiation Lab., 1950-52, chmn. physics dept., 1952-55; provost and prof. physics MIT, 1961-66, Inst. prof., 1966-67; v.p., dir. research Inst. Def. Analyses, Washington, 1959-61; prof. physics U. Calif., Berkeley, 1967-86, 94, prof. physics emeritus, 1986-94, prof. grad. sch., 1994—; Guggenheim fellow, 1955-56; Fulbright lectr. U. Paris, 1955-56, U. Tokyo, 1956; lectr., 1955, 60; dir. Enrico Fermi Internat. Sch. Physics, 1963; Richtmeyer lectr. Am. Phys. Soc., 1959; Scott lectr. U. Cambridge, 1963; Centennial lectr. U. Toronto, 1967; Lincoln lectr., 1972-73, Halley lectr., 1976, Krishman lectr., 1992, Nishina lectr., 1992; dir. Gen. Motors Corp., 1973-86; mem. Pres.'s Sci. Adv. Com., 1966-69, vice chmn., 1967-69; chmn. sci. and tech. adv. com. for manned space flight NASA, 1964-69; mem. Pres.'s Com. on Sci. and Tech., 1976; researcher on nuclear and molecular structure, quantum electronics, interstellar molecules, radio and infrared astrophysics. Author: (with A.L. Schawlow) Microwave Spectroscopy, 1955; author, co-editor: Quantum Electronics, 1960, Quantum Electronics and Coherent Light, 1964; editorial bd.; Rev. Sci. Instruments, 1950-52, Phys. Rev., 1951-53, Jour. Molecular Spectroscopy, 1957-60, Procs. Nat. Acad. Scis., 1978-84; contbr. articles to sci. publs.; patentee masers and lasers. Trustee Calif. Inst. Tech., Carnegie Instn. of Washington, Grad. Theol. Union, Calif. Acad. Scis.; mem. corp. Woods Hole Oceanographic Instn. Decorated officier Légion d'Honneur (France); recipient numerous hon. degrees and awards including Nobel prize for physics, 1964; Stuart Ballantine medal Franklin Inst., 1959, 62; Thomas Young medal and prize Inst. Physics and Phys. Soc., Eng., 1963; Disting. Public Service medal NASA, 1969; Wilhelm Exner award Austria, 1970; Niels Bohr Internat. Gold medal, 1979; Nat. Sci. medal, 1983, Berkeley citation U. Calif., 1986; named to Nat. Inventors Hall of Fame, 1976, Engring. and Sci. Hall of Fame, 1983; recipient Common Wealth award, 1993. Fellow IEEE (life, medal of honor 1967) Am. Phys. Soc. (pres. 1967, Plyler prize 1977), Optical Soc. Am. (hon., Mees medal 1968), Indian Nat. Sci. Acad., Calif. Acad. Scis.; mem. NAS (coun. 1968-72, 78-81, chmn. space sci. bd. 1970-73, Comstock award 1959), Am. Philos. Soc., Am. Astron. Soc., Am. Acad. Arts and Scis., Royal Soc. (fgn. mem.), Russian Acad. Scis. (fgn. mem.), Pontifical Acad. Scis., Max-Planck Inst. for Physics and Astrophysics (fgn. mem.). Office: U Calif Dept Physics Berkeley CA 94720

TOWNLEY, CHARLES THOMAS, librarian, educator; b. Oklahoma City, Okla., Feb. 7, 1946; s. Max Henry and Helen Betty (Hawk) T.; m. Joyce Wiedler Nissley, May 22, 1988. BA, U. Okla., 1968, MLS, 1969; MA, U. Calif., Santa Barbara, 1975; PhD, U. Mich., 1983. Asst. libr. U. Calif., Santa Barbara, 1969-72; asst. project dir., dir. Nat. Indian Edn. Assn. Libr. Project, Mpls., 1972-75; lectr. U. Mich., Ann Arbor, 1976-78; head libr. Pa. State U., Middletown, 1979-90; dean New Mex. State U., Las Cruces, 1990—; cons. Dept. Interior Libr., Washington, 1976-80; team mem. Mid. States Assn., Phila., 1989—. Author: Human Relations in Library Network Development, 1988; contbr. articles to profl. jours. Rackham fellow U. Mich., 1975-79; grantee Dept. Edn., 1988. Mem. ALA (chair, councilor 1972-76, Disting. Svc. award 1976), Internat. Fedn. Libr. Assns. (sect. chair 1991-93), N.Mex. Consortium of Acad. Librs. (pres. 1994—), Rotary (comm. chair 1993—), Beta Phi Mu. Democrat. Episcopalian. Home: 1766 Vista Montana Las Cruces NM 88005-6264 Office: NMex State U Box 300006 Dept 3475 Las Cruces NM 88003

TOWNSEND, GREG, professional football player; b. Los Angeles, Calif., Nov. 3, 1961. Student, Long Beach City Coll., Tex. Christian U. Defensive end L.A. Raiders, 1983—. Named defensive end The Sporting News NFL All-Pro team, 1990. Office: L A Raiders 332 Center St El Segundo CA 90245-4047*

TOWNSEND, RUSSELL HENRY, lawyer; b. Ft. Lewis, Wash., Dec. 27, 1949; s. Peter Lee and Irma Matilda (Greisberger) T.; m. Patricia Susan Parks, Feb. 9, 1985; children: Alexander Peter, Jennifer Sabrina. BS, Calif. Maritime Acad., 1971; JD, Lincoln U., San Francisco, 1979. Bar: Calif., U.S. Dist. Ct. (no. and ea. dists.) Calif. Title examiner Western Title Ins. Co., Oakland, Calif., 1971-74; clk. Garrison, Townsend, Hall and predecessor, San Francisco, 1974-79; ptnr. Amberg & Townsend, San Francisco, 1980-83, Townsend and Bardellini, San Francisco, 1983-87, Townsend, Bardellini, Townsend and Wechsler, San Francisco, 1988-92. Lt.j.g. USNR, 1971-75. Mem. ABA, State Bar Calif., Marin County Bar Assn. Republican. Home: 5 Mae Ct Novato CA 94947-1961 Office: Townsend Law Offices 2169 Francisco Blvd E Ste D San Rafael CA 94901-5531

TOWNSEND, SANDRA LYNNETTE, nurse; b. Boise, Idaho, Nov. 16, 1957; d. Edward Elmo and Betty Jean (Maus) Letney; m. Richard Wayne Townsend, Apr. 2, 1982; 1 child, Mallory Jean. BSN, Boise State U., 1992. CNA. From claims approver to internal auditor, asst. supr. John Hancock Ins. Co., 1978-88; RN III on oncology/BMT unit. Singer-dancer Mayors and Minors, Nampa, Idaho, 1988. Mem. Nat. Student Nurses Assn. (treas. 1991-92, western dir. 1991-92), Idaho Nurses Assn. (membership dir. 1993, treas. 1994—). Republican. Home: 11101 Hummingbird Dr Boise ID 83709-1371

TOWNSEND, STORM DIANA, sculptor; b. London, Aug. 31, 1937; came to U.S., 1963; d. Douglas Arthur and Winnifred Lilian (Collinson) T. BFA, London U., 1955, MFA, nat. diploma in design, 1962. Cert. art tchr. Instr. basic sculpture and ceramics Marlebone Inst., England, 1962; tech. asst. Nambe Mills Bronze Foundry, Santa Fe, 1968-70, Shidoni Bronze Foundry, Santa Fe, 1970-74; instr. sculpture Coll. Santa Fe, 1974-75; instr. sculpture U. Albuquerque, 1976-78, instr. basic design 2 and 3 dimensional, 1979-83; instr. adult beginning drawing Albuquerque Arts Ctr., 1977-78; instr. pvt. studio classes, 1977-78; instr. adult beginning and intermediate sculpture U. N.Mex. Community Coll., 1979-83; contractor to mold and cast dinosaur, fossil, and skeleton's for N.Mex. Mus. Natural History, 1986, 87, 88, 91. One-woman shows include Joya de Taos Gallery, Taos, N.Mex., 1965, Maitland-Stokes Gallery, Santa Fe, 1966, West Gallery, Santa Fe, 1970, Gallery Marquis, Denver, 1972, Discovery Gallery, Santa Fe, 1975, Gallery Eleven, Lubbock, Tex., 1976, Kimo Gallery, Albuquerque, 1984, Am. Inst. Architects, N. Mex., 1991; exhibited in group shows at Fine Arts Mus. N.Mex., Santa Fe, 1972, 1976, Atlanta Arts Mus., 1982, Salmagundi Club, N.Y.C., 1984, Gallery 16 East, N.Y.C., 1986, N.M.S.F. Fine Arts Gallery, Albuquerque, N.Mex., 1987, Coll. of Santa Fe, N.Mex., 1988, Gov. Gallery State Capital, Santa Fe, N.Mex., 1989, Rio Grande Outdoor Sculpture Show, N.Mex., 1991 and others; represented in permanent collections Genesse County Mus., Rochester, N.Y., 1983, City of Albuquerque, N.Mex., 1983, Sunwest Bank, N.Mex., 1988. Recipient First Prize Sculpture award N.Mex. Art League Exhibition, 1966; Resident fellow Jajasan Siswa Lokantara of Indonesia, 1960-61, Huntington Hartford Found., 1963, Helen Wurlitzer Found., 1964; grantee London County Coun., 1959. Home: PO Box 1165 Corrales NM 87048-1165

TOWNSEND, SUSAN LOUISE, elementary school administrator; b. Denver, Apr. 16, 1951; d. Calvin William and Roselyn Louise (Wilder) Scheidler; m. John Richard Townsend, July 28, 1973; children: Jeffrey, Kristen. BA in Elem. Edn., U. No. Colo., 1973, MA in Edni. Adminstrn., 1990. Cert. tchr. elem. edn., adminstr., Colo. Tchr. Arlington Elem. Sch., Greeley, Colo., 1973-75, Meeker Elem. Sch., Greeley, 1975-77; adminstr. Child Devel. Ctr., Billings, Mont., 1982-84; tchr. Cameron Elem. Sch., Greeley, 1984-88; tchr. Scott Elem. Sch., Greeley, 1988-89, spl. adminstrv. assignment, 1989-91, adminstr., 1991-94; curriculum coord. Weld Sch. Dist. 6, 1994—; cons. Weld Sch. Dist. 6, Greeley, 1988—; presenter on edn. and classroom mgmt., Greeley, 1988—. Author: (learning programs) Jump Start, 1989—, Fast Track, 1990—, Read, Write and Launch, 1991—, Parent Power Plus, 1991 (Gov.'s Creativity Initiative award 1991). Named United Meth. Woman of Yr. United Meth. Ch., 1982; nominated for Colo. Excellence in Edn. award, 1993, Phi Delta Kappa Outstanding Educator award, 1994. Fellow Danforth Assn.; mem. NEA, ASCD, Colo. Assn. Sch. Execs., Colo. Edn. Assn., Greeley Educators Assn., Phi Delta Kappa, Alpha Delta Kappa (sec. 1976—). Office: Weld Sch Dist 6 Ednl Svcs Bldg Greeley CO 80631-4304

TOYER, RICHARD HENRY, accountant; b. Snohomish, Wash., Aug. 6, 1944; s. Henry James Toyer and Bertha Maud (Darrow) Gilmore; m. Jean Ann Moore, July 1, 1966; 1 child, David K. BS in Acctg., Cen. Wash. U., 1973. CPA. Staff acct. Moss, Adams and Co., Everett, Wash., 1973-74, sr. staff acct., 1975-77; prin. Toyer and Assocs., CPAs Inc., PS, Everett, Wash., 1977—. Mayor City of Lake Stevens, Wash., 1983-91, city councilman, 1977-83; state treas. Wash. Jaycees, 1975-76; pres. Snohomish Jaycees, 1974-75; mem. Snohomish County Estate Planning Coun.; chmn. Snohomish County Subregional Coun., 1981-82; exec. bd. Puget Sound regional coun., 1981-83; chmn. City of Everett Navy Review Task Force, 1987-88, Snohomish County HUD policy adv. bd., 1982-91; chmn. Snohomish County Cities and Towns, 1983-84, Snohomish County Transp. Authority, 1987-89, Snohomish County Dept. Emergency Mgmt., 1981-91, Snohomish County Tomorrow Steering Com., 1989-91; treas. Lake Stevens Aquafest, 1983-84; sponsor Miss Lake Stevens Pageant, 1983-84; bd. dirs., treas. Josephine Sunset Home, 1993-94. Served as Sgt. U.S. Army, 1965-67, Vietnam. Mem. AICPA, Wash. Soc. CPAs, Everett C. of C. (treas. 1990-94), Marysville C. of C., Lake Stevens C. of C. (charter), Rotary (charter). Lutheran. Home: 15128 76th St SE Snohomish WA 98290-6150 Office: 3201 Broadway Ste C Everett WA 98201-4470

TRABITZ, EUGENE LEONARD, aerospace company executive; b. Cleve., Aug. 13, 1937; s. Emanuel and Anna (Berman) T.; m. Caryl Lee Rine, Dec. 22, 1963 (div. Aug. 1981); children: Claire Marie, Honey Caryl; m. Kathryn Lynn Bates, Sept. 24, 1983; 1 stepchild, Paul Francis Rager. BA, Ohio State U., 1965. Enlisted USAF, 1954, advanced through grades to maj.; served as crew commdr. 91st Stragetic Missile Div., Minot, S.D., 1968-70; intelligence officer Fgn. Tech. Div., Dayton, Ohio, 1970-73; dir. external affairs Aero Systems Div., Dayton, 1973-75; program mgr. Air Force Armament Div., Valparaiso, Fla., 1975-80; dir. ship ops. Air Force Ea. Test Range, Satellite Beach, Fla., 1980-83; dep. program mgr. Air Force Satellite Text Ctr., Sunnyvale, Calif., 1983-84; ret., 1984; sr. staff engr. Ultrasystems Inc., 1984-86; pres. TAWD Systems Inc., Palo Alto, Calif., 1986-92, Am. Telenetics Co., San Mateo, Calif., 1992—; cons. Space Applications Corp., Sunnyvale, 1986-87, Litton Computer Svcs., Mountain View, Calif., 1987-91, Battelle Meml. Inst., Columbus, 1993-95. V.p. Bd. County Mental Health Clinic, Ft. Walton Beach, Fla., 1973-75. Decorated Bronze Star. Mem. DAV (life), World Affairs Coun., U.S. Space Found. (charter), Air Force Assn. (life), Assn. Old Crows, Nat. Sojourners, Commonwealth Club Calif., Masons (32 degree). Home: 425 Anchor Rd Apt 317 San Mateo CA 94404-1058

TRACY, EMILY ANNE MILLER, social services administrator; b. N.Y.C., June 5, 1947; d. James Edward and Margaret Howard (Kinsey) Miller; m. Jack Herbert Tracy, June 7, 1969 (div. 1986); children: Christopher Ryan, Neil Brendan. BA, U. Colo., 1969, MPA, 1983. Writer, reporter Fremont County SUN Newspapers, Canon City, Colo., 1981-83; quality control compliance reviewer Colo. Dept. Social Svcs., Colo. Springs, 1983-85; child protection caseworker Fremont County Dept. Social Svcs., 1985-90; foster care reviewer, team leader Colo. Dept. Human Svcs., Denver, 1990—. Mem. Canon City City Coun., 1983-92; mem. Jud. Performance Commn. 11th Jud. Dist. Colo., Gt. Outdoors Colo.; bd. dirs. Fremont County Econ. Devel. Corp., 1985-91, Main Street U.S.A., Canon City, 1987-89. Mem. Nat. Assn. Counsel for Children, Colo. State Mgr.'s Assn., Phi Beta Kappa, Pi Alpha Alpha. Democrat. Home: 612 N 11th St Canon City CO 81212-3049

TRACY, JAMES JARED, JR., law firm administrator; b. Cleve., Jan. 17, 1929; s. James Jared and Florence (Comey) T.; m. Elizabeth Jane Bourne, June 30, 1953 (div. 1988); children: Jane Mackintosh, Elizabeth Boyd, James Jared IV, Margaret Gardiner; m. Judith Anne Cooper, Feb. 18, 1989. AB, Harvard U., 1950, MBA, 1953. CPA, Ohio. Acct., mgr. Price Waterhouse & Co., Cleve., 1953-65; treas., CFO Clevite Corp., Cleve., 1965-69; asst. treas. Republic Steel Corp., Cleve., 1969-70, treas., 1970-75; v.p., treas. Johns-Manville Corp., Denver, 1976-81; v.p., treas., CFO I. T. Corp., L.A., 1981-82; exec. dir. Hufstedler, Miller, Carlson & Beardsley, L.A., 1983-84, Shank, Irwin & Conant, Dallas, 1984-85, Pachter, Gold & Schaffer, L.A., 1985-86; v.p., sr. cons. Right Assocs., L.A., 1987-91; dir. adminstrn. Larson & Burnham, Oakland, Calif., 1991—; trustee and v.p. Miss Hall's Sch., Pittsfield, Mass., 1970-78; dir. Union Commerce Bank, Cleve., 1971-76; adv. bd. mem. Arkwright-Boston Ins. Co., Boston, 1976-81. Trustee and v.p. Cleve. Soc. for Blind, 1965-76; trustee Western Res. Hist. Soc., Cleve., 1972-76; treas. St. Peters by the Sea Presbyn. Ch., Palos Verdes, Calif., 1981-91. Recipient Alumni award Harvard U., Denver, 1981. Mem. AICPA, Ohio Soc. CPAs, Assn. Legal Adminstrs., Nat. Assn. Realtors, Piedmont Montclair Rotary Club (pres.), Harvard Club of San Francisco, Harvard Bus. Sch. Club No. Calif. Home: 180 Lombardy Ln Orinda CA 94563-1126 Office: Larson & Burnham 1901 Harrison St Fl 11 Oakland CA 94612-3574

TRACY, ROBERT (EDWARD), English language educator, poetry translator; b. Woburn, Mass., Nov. 23, 1928; s. Hubert William and Vera Mary (Hurley) T.; m. Rebecca Garrison, Aug. 26, 1956; children: Jessica Janes, Hugh Garrison, Dominick O'Donovan. AB in Greek with honors, Boston Coll., 1950; MA, Harvard U., 1954, PhD, 1960. Teaching fellow Harvard U., Cambridge, Mass., 1954-58; instr. Carleton Coll., Northfield, Minn., 1958-60; from asst. prof. English, to assoc. prof., then prof. U. Calif., Berkeley, 1960-89, prof. English and Celtic Studies, 1989-94, assoc. dir. Dickens Project, 1994—; vis. prof., Bruern fellow in Am. studies, U. Leeds, England, 1965-66; vis. prof., Leverhulme fellow Trinity Coll., Dublin, 1971-72; vis. Kathryn W. Davis prof. slavic studies Wellesley (Mass.) Coll., 1979; Charles Mills Gayley lectr. U. Calif., Berkeley, 1989-90; vis. prof. Ango-Irish lit. Trinity Coll., Dublin, Ireland, 1995—. Author: Trollope's Later Novels, 1978; translator (poems by Osip Mandelstam): Stone, 1981, 2d edit., 1991; editor J.M Synge's The Aran Islands, 1962, The Way We Live Now (Anthony Trollope), 1974, The Macdermots of Ballycloran (Anthony Trollope), 1989, Nina Balatka and Linda Tressel (Anthony Trollope), 1991, In A Glass Darkly (Sheridan Le Fanu) 1993, Rhapsody in Stephen's Green (Flann O'Brien), 1994; adv. editor The Recorder, 1985—, LIT (Lit., Interpretation, Theory), 1989—; contbr. articles and revs. to numerous jours. including Shakespeare Quarterly, So. Rev., Nineteenth-Century Fiction, Eire-Ireland, Irish Literary Supplement, others; poetry translations in New Orleans Rev., Poetry, N.Y. Rev. of Books, others. Appointed mem. cultural panel San Francisco-Cork Sister City Com. Fulbright travel grantee, 1965-66; recipient humanities research fellowships U. Calif., Berkeley, 1962, 69, 78, 81, 86 , 92; Guggenheim fellow, 1981-82. Mem. MLA, Philol. Assn. Pacific Coast, Am. Conf. for Irish Studies, Internat. Assn. for Study of Anglo-Irish Lit. Office: U Calif Dept English Berkeley CA 94720

TRAFTON, STEPHEN J., banking executive; b. Mt. Vernon, Wash., Sept. 17, 1946; m. Diane Trafton; children: John, Roland. BS in Zoology, Wash. State U., 1968. V.p., mgr. dept. money market Seattle-First Nat. Bank, 1968-79; v.p., mgr. bank consulting group Donaldson Lufkin Jennrette, N.Y.C., 1980; exec. v.p., treas. Gibraltar Savings Bank, L.A., 1980-84; banking cons., 1984-86; v.p., treas. Hibernia Bank, San Francisco, 1986-88; sr. v.p., treas. Goldome Bank, Buffalo, N.Y., 1988-90; sr. exec. v.p., CFO Glenfed Inc., 1990-91, vice chmn., CFO, 1991—, pres., 1992—; sr. exec. v.p., CFO Glendale Fed. Bank, 1990-91, vice chmn., CFO, 1991, pres., COO, 1991-92, chmn. bd., pres., CEO, 1992—, also bd. dirs. Mem. Phi Eta Sigma. Office: Glendale Fed Bank 700 N Brand Blvd Glendale CA 91209*

TRAGER, RUSSELL HARLAN, advertising consultant; b. Cambridge, Mass., Sept. 26, 1945; s. Nathan Allan and Shirley (Gibbs) T.; m. V. Jan Adams, Aug. 19, 1968 (div. July 1975); 1 child, Eric Todd; m. Edna Marie Sanchez, Feb. 16, 1980; children: Felice Rosanne, Justin Tomas. AA, Newton Jr. Coll., 1965; BS, U. Miami, 1968; postgrad., Harvard U., 1968-69. Account rep. Hervic Corp., Sherman Oaks, Calif., 1972-75, Canon USA, Lake Success, N.Y., 1975-78; key account sales rep. Yashica Inc., Glendale, Calif., 1978-79; sales rep. Region I United Pubs. Corp., Beverly Hills, Calif., 1979-81, sales mgr., 1981-83; regional pres. United Pubs. Corp., Carson, Calif., 1983-86, region v.p., 1986-88; v.p. sales United Pubs. Corp. divsn. of Nynex Co., El Segundo, Calif., 1988-91; dir. sales Yelex Corp., L.A., 1991-92; sales mgr. Trader Pub. Co., L.A., 1992-93; cons. Russ Trager & Assocs., Manhattan Beach, Calif., 1994—. Home and Office: Russ Trager & Assocs 1201 11th St Manhattan Beach CA 90266-6025

TRAHAN, ELLEN VAUNEIL, nonprofit association executive, public administrator; b. Rosie, Ark., June 30, 1941; d. Jess James Ross and Ellen Alabama (Spears) Massey; m. Terrance Dale Trahan, June 9, 1961; children:

Ginny-Marie, Anthony Scott, Julie Jeanette. BA in Home Econs., Magic Valley Christian Coll., Albion, Idaho, 1962; BA in Psychology, Pepperdine U., 1966; postgrad., Willamette U., 1983-84; MBA, Chaminade U., Honolulu, 1985. Social worker Los Angeles Dept. Social Service, 1966-70; adminstr. Socialization Ctr. Marion County Mental Health Clinic, Salem, Oreg., 1973; social service worker Fairview Hosp. and Tng. Ctr., Salem, 1973-85; exec. dir. Autistic Vocat. Edn. Ctr., Honolulu, 1986-89; supr. adult clin. svcs. community mental health Cen. Oahu Community Mental Health, Mental Health Div. Hawaii, Pearl City, 1989—. Mem. bus. adv. com. Supported Employment Task Force, Goodwill Corp, 1986-87; orgn. cons. Fairview Parents Club, Salem, 1977-85; advisor Honolulu Dept. Health Community Service to Developmentally Disabled, 1986-91. Mem. NAFE, ACLU, NOW, Nat. Soc. Autistic Citizens, Assn. Retarded Citizens, Nat. Alliance for the Mentally Ill. Home: 250 Ohua Ave Apt 8D Honolulu HI 96815-3634 Office: Dept Health Hawaii Cen Oahu Community Mental Health 860 Fourth St Pearl City HI 96782-3312

TRAHANT, MARK NEIL, newspaper editor; b. Pocatello, Idaho, Aug. 13, 1957; s. Neil Walter Trahant and Sharon Dianne (Murray) Empey; m. Lenora Ann Begay, Nov. 2, 1991; 1 child, Marvin Sam. Student, Idaho State U., 1975. Editor Sho-Ban News, Ft. Hall, Ind., 1977-79; pub. info. officer U.S. Bur. Indian Affairs, Washington, 1979-80; freelance writer Washington, 1980-83; pub. Navajo Times Today, Widow Rock, Ariz., 1983-87; reporter Ariz. Republic, Phoenix, 1989-91; pres., pub. Navajo Nation Today, Window Rock, 1991-92; exec. news editor Salt Lake Tribune, Salt Lake City, 1992—; bd. dirs. Robert C. Maynard Inst. for Journalism Edn.; mem. nat. adv. bd. Poynter Inst. for Media Studies; vis. scholar Freedom Forum's First Amendment Ctr., Vanderbilt U. Contbg. author: A Circle of Nations. Founding bd. dirs. UNITY '94. Mem. Native Am. Journalists Assn. (past pres.), Am. Soc. Newspaper Editors. Office: Salt Lake Tribune 143 S Main St Salt Lake City UT 84111-1917

TRAM, KENNETH KHAI KT, internist; b. Saigon, Vietnam, Oct. 29, 1961; came to U.S., 1978; s. Felix Ngan and Lisa Hong (Pham) T.; m. Christine Tram-Hong Tran, June 19, 1993. BS summa cum laude, U. Calif., Irvine, 1984; MD, UCLA, 1988. Diplomate Am. Bd. Internal Medicine, Am. Bd. Geriatric Medicine. Resident in internal medicine UCLA-San Fernandy Valley, 1988-91; geriatric medicine fellow UCLA Sch. Medicine, 1992-94; clin. instr./assoc. investigator Sepulveda (Calif.) VA Med. Ctr., 1991-94, acting med. dir., 1994; internist Facey Med. Group, Sepulveda, 1994—. Contbr. articles to profl. jours. Mem. CPAG/CHOMS, Calif., 1991—. Recipient Solomon Scholars Resident award UCLA Sch. Medicine, 1991, Nat. Kidney Found. Fellowship award, 1991-92, VA Rsch. and Devel. Career Devel. award, 1992-94. Mem. ACP, AAAS, AMA, Am. Soc. for Bone and Mineral Rsch., U.S. Table Tennis Assn., Nat. Geog. Soc., Mus. Heritage Soc. Home: 6 Malaga Irvine CA 92714-7304 Office: Facey Medical Group Inc 11211 Sepulveda Blvd Mission Hills CA 91345-1115

TRAMIEL, JACK, computer game company executive. Founder, pres. Commodore Internat. Ltd., 1958-84; chmn., chief exec. officer Atari Corp., Sunnyvale, Calif., from 1984, now chmn. Office: Atari Inc 1196 Borregas Ave Sunnyvale CA 94089-1302

TRAMIEL, SAM, microcomputer and video game company executive; b. 1950. With Commodore Internat. Ltd., 1974-84, Atari Corp., 1984—; now pres., chief exec. officer. Office: Atari Corp 1196 Borregas Ave Sunnyvale CA 94089-1302

TRAMMELL, MARTIN GIL, humanities educator; b. Seattle, Apr. 13, 1959; s. Charles and Joyce (Reeves) T.; m. Linda Elaine Markwood, Aug. 28, 1982; children: Justin, Christopher, Joshua. BS, We. Oreg. State U., 1982, MA, 1986; BEd, We. Bapt. Coll., 1983, ThB, 1985. Rte. coord. Stovers, Seattle, 1982; dir. of field edn. We. Bapt. Coll., Salem, Oreg., 1983, instr., 1982-84; asst. prof. We. Bapt. Coll., Salem, 1985-86, assoc. prof., 1986—; pastor of youth and family Valley Bapt. Ch., Perrydale, Oreg., 1982-91; CEO, SpeakWrite Cons., 1995; seminar spkr. Western Baptist Coll., 1982—. Asst. dir. Salem-Willamette Area Teens, Salem, 1987—. Mem. Internat. Soc. for Gen. Semantics. Office: Western Bapt Coll 5000 Deer Park Dr SE Salem OR 97301-9330

TRAMPOSCH, WILLIAM JOSEPH, museum director, consultant; b. Bridgeport, Conn., Dec. 14, 1948; s. Emil J. and Alice Catherine Tramposch; m. Margaret Simpson, May 4, 1976; children: Emma, Molly. AB, U. Calif., Berkeley, 1970; MA, Coll. William and Mary, 1982, EdD, 1986. Coord. interpretation Old Sturbridge Village, Mass., 1976-79; dir. interpretation Colonial Williamsburg, Va., 1979-89; dir. Oreg. Hist. Soc., Portland, Oreg., 1989—. Sgt. USAFR, 1970-76. Fulbright scholar, New Zealand, 1986, 88. Mem. Am. Assn. for State and Local History (coun. 1987-91), Am. Assn. Mus., Internat. Coun. Mus. (bd. dirs. 1986, participant Moscow meeting 1986), Phi Beta Kappa. Mem. Soc. of Friends. Home: 65 SW Custer St Portland OR 97219-2953 Office: Oreg Hist Soc 1230 SW Park Ave Portland OR 97205-2441

TRAN, HAI PHUOC, purchasing executive, manufacturing engineer; b. Tay-Ninh, Vietnam, Dec. 7, 1953; came to U.S., 1975; s. Du P. and Bich T. (Lam) T.; m. Hoa L. Tang, Jan. 7, 1959; children: Hainam P., Haiviet P. BA in Bus. Mgmt., Minh-Duc U., Saigon, Vietnam, 1975; BSEE, Calif. State U., Northridge, 1985. R & D technician Data Products Corp., Woodland Hills, Calif., 1978-84; sr. R & D technician Litton Industries, Woodland Hills, 1984-85; mem. tech. staff Hughes Aircraft Co., Canoga Park, Calif., 1985-86; staff engr. Amerasia Tech. Inc., Westlake Village, Calif., 1986-94; dir. purchasing Display Tech. Industries, Westlake Village, 1994—. Home: 20650 Valerio St Canoga Park CA 91306-2748 Office: Display Tech Industries 2248 Townsgate Rd Westlake Village CA 91361-2412

TRAN, JACK NHUAN NGOC, gas and oil reservoir engineer; b. Quang Binh, Vietnam, Sept. 21, 1933; came to U.S., 1975; s. Dieu Ngoc and Ly Thi (Nguyen) T.; m. Tamie Nguyen, July 25, 1990; children: Andy Nguyen, Quoc Dung, Ann Nga Huyen, Ephram Anh Dung, John Hung Dung. BS, U. San Francisco, 1977, MBA, 1978. With Republic of Vietnam Mil., 1952-67; cadet Rep. Vietnam Mil. Acad., Dalat, 1952-53; 1st lt., co. comdr. 1st Republic of Vietnam Bn., South Vietnam, 1953-54; editor-in-chief Republic of Vietnam Revs., Saigon, 1955-57; commandant Republic of Vietnam Aerial Photo Ctr., Saigon, 1958-61, Republic of Vietnam Mil. Intelligence Sch., Caymai and Saigon, 1962-67; mem. Republic of Vietnam Senate, 1967-73; v.p. The Meteco Corp., Saigon, Vietnam, 1971-72; pres., chmn. bd. Meteco-Vinageco Co., Saigon, 1972-75; air photo analyst Std. Oil Co., San Francisco, 1975-79; gas and oil engr. Chevron Oil Co., San Francisco, 1980—; col. U.S. Intelligence, Calif., 1980-90. Author: Flower in the Battle Field, 1956, Geological Survey of the Kndu, CA, 1982, Beluga River Oil Development, 1984, The Military Life, 1992; editor-in-chief Chien-Si Quoc-Gia Mag. Recipient Honorary Key of the City, City of Omaha, Nebr., 1989, Honorary Citizen City of Fayettville, N.C., 1969. Mem. The U. of San Francisco Alumni Assn., Rotary Internat. Roman Catholic. Home: 1418 Lundy Ave San Jose CA 95131-3310

TRAN, JEAN-MARIE, electrical engineer; b. Saigon, Vietnam, Dec. 28, 1962; s. Tran Quoc Phong and Françoise (Bodet); m. Sophie Yvonne Dayot, June 5, 1987; 1 child, Benjamin. Diplome D'Ingenieur, Ecole Nat. Superieure Tech. Avancees, Paris, 1985; MS, U. Calif., San Diego, 1988, PhD, 1990. Rsch. asst. Marine Phys. Lab., San Diego, 1986-90; postdoctoral researcher Scripps Inst. Oceanography, San Diego, 1990-91; systems engr. Dassault Electronique, Paris, 1991-92; chief scientist ThermoTrex Corp., San Diego, 1993—. Contbr. articles to profl. jours. Recipient Fellowship, Henri Kummerman Found., 1986. Mem. IEEE, Acoustical Soc. Am. Office: Thermotrex Corp 9550 Distribution Ave San Diego CA 92121-2306

TRANER, NORMAN, food products executive. Grower Organo Farms, Orange County, Calif., 1961-74; sec., treas. Eco Farms Avocados, Inc., Temecula, Calif., 1974—. Office: Eco Farms Avocados Inc 28790 Las Haciendas St Temecula CA 92590-2614*

TRAPP, GERALD BERNARD, journalist; b. St. Paul, May 7, 1932; s. Bernard Edward and Lauretta (Mueller) T.; m. Bente Joan Moe, Jan. 29, 1954; children—Eric Gerald, Lise Joan, Alex Harold. B.A., Macalester Coll., St. Paul, 1954. Editor Mankato (Minn.) Free Press, 1954-57; with AP, 1957-80; nat. broadcast exec. charge sales AP, East of Miss., 1966-68; gen. broadcast news editor AP, N.Y.C., 1968-79; dep. dir. broadcast services AP, 1979-80, liaison broadcast networks, 1968-80; v.p., gen. mgr. Intermountain Network, Salt Lake City, 1980-87; v.p., dir. mktg. Travel Motivation, Inc., Salt Lake City, 1987-88; ops./program mgr. Mountain Cable Network, Inc., Salt Lake City, 1988-89; sr. v.p. Travel Motivation, Inc., Salt Lake City, 1990-92; mktg. specialist Morris Travel, 1992-95, pricing analyst, 1995—. Bd. dirs. Westminster Coll. Found. Mem. Radio TV News Dirs. Assn., Oratorio Soc. Utah (bd. dirs.), Pro Musica, Sigma Delta Chi. Mem. United Ch. Christ. Home: 785 Three Fountains Cir # 17 Salt Lake City UT 84107-5085 Office: 240 E Morris Ave Salt Lake City UT 84115-3200

TRASK, LINDA ANN, sales executive; b. Cambria Heights, N.Y., Oct. 13, 1956; d. Lewis Volkert and Ethel May (Sheid) T. Cert. Transp., Delta Coll., 1985. Office mgr. Roofers Supply, Modesto, Calif., 1978-80; terminal mgr. Prouty Trucking, Modesto, 1980-82; mgr. Cert. Transpn., Modesto, 1982-86; mgr. regional sales Provisioners Express, Modesto, 1987-91; mktg. mgr. Willis Shaw Express, Modesto, Calif., 1991—; Mem. Cen. Valley Transpn., Modesto, 1987—.

TRASK, ROBERT CHAUNCEY RILEY, author, lecturer, foundation executive; b. Albuquerque, Jan. 2, 1939; s. Edward Almon Trask and Florence Jane (White) Jones; m. Katie Lucille Bitters (div. 1981); m. Mary Jo Chiarottino, Dec. 1, 1984; 1 child, Chauncey Anne. Student pub. schs., San Diego. Lic. master sea capt. Entertainer, singer, comedian, 1964–; founder, pres. Nat. Health & Safety Svcs., San Francisco, 1968-71, ARAS Found., Issaquah, Wash., 1978—; capt., dive master San Diego Dive Charters, 1972-75; sr. capt., dive master Pacific Sport Diving Corp., Long Beach, Calif., 1975-77; lectr., bus. cons., 1978—; cons., tng. developer Nissan, Gen. Dynamics, AT&T, religious orgns., also other corps., 1978–. Author: (manual) Tulip, 1971, Living Free, 1982, God's Phone Number, 1987, (video program for adolescents) Breaking Free, also seminar manuals. Mem. SAG. Office: ARAS Found # 93 3020 Issaquah Pine Lk Rd SE Issaquah WA 98029

TRASK, TALLMAN HARLOW, III, university administrator; b. L.A., Dec. 1, 1947; s. Tallman Harlow Jr. and Nancy Lou (Hargrave) T.; m. Marcy Muchmore, Mar. 15, 1986; children: Tallman IV, Merrill Kathryn. AB in History, Occidental Coll., 1969; MBA, Northwestern U., 1971; PhD, UCLA, 1974. Spl. cons. Calif. State Dept. Fin., Sacramento, 1973; asst. to pres. Occidental Coll., L.A., 1973-76; asst. to exec. vice chancellor UCLA, 1976-78, asst. exec. vice chancellor, asst. to chancellor, 1978-84, vice chancellor for acad. adminstrn., 1984-86; v.p. for fin. and adminstrn. U. Wash., Seattle, 1986-87, exec. v.p., 1987-95; exec. v.p. Duke U., Durham, N.C., 1995—; affiliate assoc. prof. coll. of edn. U. Wash., 1987—. Office: Duke U Allen Bldg Durham NC 27708

TRATT, DAVID MICHAEL, physicist; b. Southampton, Hampshire, U.K., July 3, 1955; came to U.S. 1986; s. Alfred Oliver and Margaret Aline (Harding) T. BSc in Physics, U. Wales, 1976; MSc in Physics, Heriot-Watt U., Edinburgh, 1981; PhD in Physics, Heriot-Watt U., 1984. Chartered physicist, U.K. Exptl. officer Heriot-Watt U., Edinburgh, 1976-86; rsch. assoc. Jet Propulsion Lab., Pasadena, 1986-88; exptl. officer Heriot-Watt U., 1988-89; mem. tech. staff Jet Propulsion Lab., Pasadena, 1989—. Contbr. articles to profl. jours. Fellow Brit. Interplanetary Soc.; mem. IEEE, IEEE Lasers and Electro-Optics Soc., Optics Soc. Am., Inst. Physics (U.K.), Am. Geophys. Union. Home: 355 S Los Robles Ave Apt 107 Pasadena CA 91101-3283 Office: Jet Propulsion Lab 4800 Oak Grove Dr Pasadena CA 91109-8001

TRAVERS, JUDITH LYNNETTE, human resources executive; b. Buffalo, Feb. 25, 1950; d. Harold Elwin and Dorothy (Helsel) Howes; m. David Jon Travers, Oct. 21, 1972; 1 child, Heather Lynne. BA in Psychology, Barrington Coll., 1972; cert. in paralegal course, St. Mary's Coll., Moraga, Calif., 1983; postgrad., Southland U., 1982-84. Exec. sec. Sherman C. Weeks, P.A., Derry, N.H., 1973-75; legal asst. Mason-McDuffie Co., Berkeley, Calif., 1975-82; paralegal asst. Blum, Kay, Merkle & Kauftheil, Oakland, Calif., 1982-83; CEO, bd. dirs. Dela Pers. Svcs. Inc., Concord, Calif., 1983—; pres. All Ages Sitters Agy., Concord, 1986—; CEO Guardian Security Agy., 1992—; bd. dirs. Guardian Security Agy., Concord, Calif. Vocalist record album The Loved Ones, 1978. vol. local Congl. campaign, 1980, Circle of Friends, Children's Hosp. No. Calif., Oakland, 1987—; mem. Alameda County Sheriff's Mounted Posse, 1989, Contra Costa Child Abuse Prevention Coun., 1989; employer adv. coun. Ctrl. Contra Costa County, 1993—. Mem. NAFE, Am. Assn. Respiratory Therapy, Soc. for Human Resource Mgmt., Am. Mgmt. Assn., Gospel Music Assn., Palomino Horse Breeders Am., DAR, Barrington Oratorio Soc., Commonwealth Club Calif., Nat. Trust Hist. Preservation, Alpha Theta Sigma. Republican. Baptist. Home: 3900 Brown Rd Oakley CA 94561-2664 Office: Delta Pers Svcs Inc 1820 Galindo St Ste 3 Concord CA 94520-2447

TRAVIS, JOHN RICHARD, nuclear and mechanical engineer; b. Billings, Mont., Sept. 3, 1942; s. Lynn E. and Dorothy (Howard) T.; m. Carole M. Lahti, Aug. 1, 1963 (div. 1980); children: Kristi Ann, Patti Sue. BSME with hons., U. Wyo., 1965; MS, Purdue U., 1969, PhD, 1971. Registered profl. engr., N.Mex. Instr. engring. sci. U. Wyo., Laramie, 1965-66; instr. fluid mechanics Purdue U., Lafayette, Ind., 1970-71; staff Argonne (Ill.) Nat. Lab., 1971-73, Los Alamos (N.Mex.) Nat. Lab., 1973-90; sr. scientist Sci. Applications Internat. Corp., Albuquerque, 1990-94; pres. Enring. and Scientific Software, Inc., Albuquerque, 1994—; summer staff Argonne Nat. Lab., Idaho Falls, Idaho, 1965, Battelle Meml. Inst., Columbus, Ohio, 1966; cons. in field; official U.S. Cons. to Internat. Atomic Energy Agy. on nuclear reactor safety issues, Vienna, 1984—; official U.S. Del. to Fed. Republic of Germany on nuclear reactor safety issues, 1989—. Contbr. articles to profl. jours. Nat. Ctr. Atmospheric Rsch. fellow, 1970. Mem. ASME, Am. Nuclear Soc., Los Alamos Ski Club, Sigma Xi, Sigma Pi Sigma, Sigma Tau, Elks. Home: 5422 Avenida Cuesta NE Albuquerque NM 87111-6719 Office: Engring & Sci Software Inc 8500 Merrimac Court NE Albuquerque NM 87109

TRAYLOR, WILLIAM ROBERT, publisher; b. Texarkana, Ark., May 21, 1921; s. Clarence Edington and Seba Ann (Talley) T.; m. Elvirez Sigler, Oct. 9, 1945; children: Kenneth Warren, Gary Robert, Mark Daniel, Timothy Ryan. Student, U. Houston, 1945-46, U. Omaha, 1947-48. Div. mgr. Lily-Tulip Cup Corp., N.Y.C., 1948-61; asst. to pres. Johnson & Johnson, New Brunswick, N.J., 1961-63; mgr. western region Rexall Drug & Chem. subs. Dart Industries, L.A., 1963-67; pres. Prudential Pub. Co., Diamonds Springs, Calif., 1967—; cons. to printing industry, 1976—; syndicated writer (under pseudonym)s. Bill Friday's Bus. Bull., 1989—. Author: Instant Printing, 1976 (transl. into Japanese), Successful Management, 1979, Quick Printing Encyclopedia, 1982, 7th edit., 1988, How to Sell Your Product Through (Not to) Wholesalers, 1980; pubr. Professional Estimator and Management Software for Printing Industry, 1992, Small Press Printing Encyclopedia, 1994. With USCG, 1942-45. Named Man of Yr. Quick Printing Mag., 1987. Mem. Nat. Assn. Quick Printers (hon. lifetime), C. of C., Kiwanis, Toastmasters. Democrat. Office: Prudential Pub Co 7089 Crystal Blvd El Dorado CA 95623

TRAYNOR, J. MICHAEL, lawyer; b. Oakland, Calif., Oct. 25, 1934; s. Roger J. and Madeleine (Lackmann) T.; m. Shirley Williams, Feb. 11, 1956; children: Kathleen Traynor Millard, Elizabeth Traynor Fowler, Thomas. B.A., U. Calif., Berkeley, 1955; J.D., Harvard U., 1960. Bar: Calif. 1961, U.S. Supreme Ct. 1966. Dep. atty. gen. State of Calif., San Francisco, 1961-63; spl. counsel Calif. Senate Com. on Local Govt., Sacramento, 1963; assoc. firm Cooley Godward Castro Huddleson & Tatum, San Francisco, 1963-69, ptnr., 1969—; adviser 3d Restatement of Unfair Competition, 3d Restatement of Torts: Product D Liability, 1992—, Apportionment, 1994—, 1988 Revs. 2d Restatement of Conflict Laws, 2d Restatement of Restitution, 1981-85; lectr. U. Calif. Boalt Hall Sch. Law, Berkely, 1982-89; chmn. Sierra Club Legal Def. Fund, 1989-91, pres., 1991-92, trustee. Mem. bd. overseers Inst. for Civil Justice The RAND Corp., 1991—; bd. dirs. Environ. Law Inst., 1992—. Served to 1st lt. USMC, 1955-57. Fellow Am. Bar Found. (life); mem. Am. Law Inst. (coun. 1985—, 2d v.p. 1993—), Bar Assn. San Francisco (pres. 1973). Home: 3131 Eton Ave Berkeley CA 94705-2713 Office: Cooley Godward Castro Huddleson & Tatum 1 Maritime Plz Ste 2000 San Francisco CA 94111-3510

TRAYNOR-KAPLAN, ALEXIS ELAINE, biomedical researcher; b. Chgo., Aug. 22, 1952; d. Gerald Edmund and Ruth Eleanor (Fritsche) Traynor; m. Richard Jay Kaplan. BS, U. Mich., 1974; PhD, U. Calif., San Diego, 1979. Postdoctoral fellow The Salk Inst., San Diego, 1979-83; rsch. assoc. The Scripps Rsch. Inst., La Jolla, Calif., 1984-88; asst. rsch. biochemist U. Calif., San Diego, 1989-90, asst. prof., 1990—. Contbr. articles to profl. jours., chpts. to books. Recipient Miles and Shirley Fiterman Basic Rsch. award AGA Found., 1994; grantee NIH, Washington, 1994. Mem. Internat. Soc. Immunomodulation (charter mem.), Internat. Soc. Neurochemistry, Am. Soc. for Biochemistry and Molecular Biology, Gastroenterology Rsch. Group. Office: U Calif San Diego 200 W Arbor Dr San Diego CA 92103-1911

TREANOR, WALTER JOHN, physician; b. County Tyrone, No. Ireland, May 14, 1922; came to U.S., 1949, naturalized, 1954; s. Hugh and Marion (deVine) T.; M.D., Nat. U. Ireland, 1947; Diplomate Am. Bd. Phys. Medicine & Rehab.; m. Mary Stewart, Dec. 29, 1971; children: James P., Wanden, Dona, June. Intern, St. Mary's Hosp., San Francisco, 1949-52; resident Mayo Found., Rochester, Minn.; practice medicine specializing in rehab. medicine, Santa Rosa, Calif.; emeritus prof. medicine U. Nev., Reno, 1979—. Served to capt., M.C., U.S. Army, 1953-55. Fellow ACP, Royal Soc. Medicine; mem. Am. Acad. Neurology, Internat. Med. Soc. Paraplegia, Am. Acad. Phys. & Rehab. Medicine. Republican. Contbr. articles to profl. jours. Home: 1370 Spring St Santa Rosa CA 95404-3656

TREAS, JUDITH KAY, sociology educator; b. Phoenix, Jan. 2, 1947; d. John Joseph and Hope Catherine (Thomas) Jennings; m. Benjamin C. Treas II, May 14, 1969; children: Stella, Evan. BA, Pitzer Coll., Claremont, Calif., 1969; MA, UCLA, 1972, PhD, 1976. Instr. U. So. Calif., L.A., 1974-75, asst. prof., 1975-81, assoc. prof., 1981-87, dept. chair, 1984-89, prof., 1987-89; prof. U. Calif., Irvine, 1989, dept. chair, 1989-94; bd. overseers Gen. Social Survey, 1986-88; cons. social sci. and population study sect. NIH, 1989-92. Contbr. articles to profl. jours. Trustee Pitzer Coll., 1977-79. Recipient Rsch. award NSF, 1978-81, 84-91, NIH, 1979-81; Univ. scholar U. So. Calif., 1982-83. Fellow Gerontological Assn. Am.; mem. Golden Key (hon.), Am. Sociol. Assn., Population Assn. Am., Internat. Union for Sci. Study Population. Office: U Calif-Irvine Dept Sociology Irvine CA 92717

TREASTER, MELBA MAUCK, educational consultant; b. Langdon, Kans., Dec. 10, 1929; d. Phillip Alvis and Bessie F. (Holmes) Mauck; m. W. Arlen Treaster, Dec.16, 1950 (dec. Nov. 1985); children: Paul Arlen, Andrew Philip. BA in Edn., Sterling (Kans.) Coll., 1951; MS in Psychology, Emporia State U., 1964. Cert. elem. tchr., reading endorsement, Colo. Elem. tchr. Union Five Sch., Reno County, Kans., 1951-52, Sterling (Kans.) Pub. Schs., 1952-53; kindergarten tchr. sub Lucas (Kans.) Pub. Schs., 1956-61; elem. tchr. Sunny Grove Sch., Atchison County, Kans., 1963-64; H.S. tchr. English/social studies Atchison County Cmty. H.S., Effingham, Kans., 1964-67; chpt. I tchr./supr. Poudre Sch. Dist., Ft. Collins, Colo., 1967-90; ednl. cons. Ft. Collins, 1990—; developer, demonstrator Prior Project Nat. Diffusion Network, 1979-81; presentor nat., regional profl. confs. Internat. Reading Assn., 1983-92. Co-author: (videos) Reading Aloud to Children, 1989, Listening to Children Read, 1990. Elder Westminster Presbyn. Ch., Ft. Collins, 1989-91. Recipient Recognition award Chpt. I/Title I, U.S. Dept. Edn., Washington, 1990. Mem. ASCD, Internat. Reading Assn. (local pres., chair Colo. Commn., 1965—), Nat. Dissemination Assn. Home: 3414 Seneca B Fort Collins CO 80526

TREAT, JAMES MICHAEL, secondary education educator; b. Ft. Hood, Tex., June 16, 1951; s. Charles Joseph and Lariene Amelia (Moffett) T.; m. Trudi Anne Hostetler, Aug. 12, 1978 (div. May 1989); children: Erin Kathleen, Colin James. BS in Physics Edn., U. Ariz., 1978, MEd in Ednl. Adminstrn., 1987. Sci. tchr. Bel Air High Sch., El Paso, 1978-80; math. and sci. tchr. Apollo Jr. High Sch., Tucson, 1980-85; physics tchr. Desert View High Sch., Tucson, 1985—. Rsch. Corp. fellow U. Ariz., 1988. Mem. NEA, ASCD, Nat. Sci. Tchrs. Assn., Ariz. Archaeol. and Hist. Soc. Home: 9341 N Eagle Dancer Dr Tucson AZ 85741-9477 Office: Desert View High Sch 4101 E Valencia Rd Tucson AZ 85706

TREBEK, ALEX, television game show host; b. Sudbury, Ont., Can., July 22, 1940; came to U.S., 1973; s. George Edward and Lucille (Lagace) T.; m. Elaine Callei (div. 1981); m. Jean Currivan, Apr. 30, 1990; 2 children. BA and PhB, U. Ottawa, Ont., 1961. Staff announcer CBC, Toronto, Ont., 1961-73; game show host Wizard of Odds for NBC, Calif., 1973-74, High Rollers for NBC, Calif., 1974-79, Stars on Ice for Can. TV, 1974-77, $128, 000 Question for Global TV, Can., 1976-77, Double Dare for CBS, Calif., 1977-78, Battle Stars for NBC, Calif., 1981-82; game show host, producer Jeopardy!, Calif., 1984-87, game show host, 1987—; game show host Classic Concentration, Calif., 1987-90, To Tell the Truth, 1991. film appearances include: Short Cuts, 1993. Mem. Screen Actors Guild, AFTRA, Assn. Can. TV and Radio Artists. Roman Catholic. Office: Jeopardy! 1020 W Washington Blvd Culver City CA 90232

TREECE, JAMES LYLE, lawyer; b. Colorado Springs, Colo., Feb. 6, 1925; s. Lee Oren and Ruth Ida (Smith) T.; m. Ruth Julie Treece, Aug. 7, 1949 (div. 1984); children—James (dec.), Karen Peterson, Teryl Wait, Jamilyn Smyser, Carol Crowder. Student Colo. State U., 1943, Colo. U., 1943, U.S. Naval Acad., 1944-46; B.S., Mesa Coll., 1946; J.D., U. Colo., 1950; postgrad. U. N.C., 1976-77. Bar: Colo. 1952, U.S. Dist. Ct. Colo. 1952, U.S. Ct. Appeals (10th cir.) 1952, U.S. Supreme Ct. 1967. Assoc., Yegge, Hall, Treece & Evans and predecessors, 1951-59, ptnr., 1959-69; U.S. atty., Colo., 1969-77; pres. Treece & Bahr and predecessor firms, Littleton, Colo., 1977-91; mcpl. judge, 1967-68; mem. faculty Nat. Trial Advocacy Inst., 1973-76, Law-Sci. Acad., 1964. Chmn. Colo. Dept. Pub. Welfare, 1963-68; chmn. Colo. Dept. Social Services, 1968-69; mem. Littleton Bd. Edn., 1977-81. Served with USNR, 1944-46. Recipient awards Colo. Assn. Sch. Bds., 1981, IRS, 1977, FBI, 1977, DEA, 1977, Fed. Exec. Bd., 1977. Mem. Fed. Bar Assn. (pres. Colo. 1975), Colo. Bar Assn. (bd. govs.), Denver Bar Assn. (v.p., trustee). Republican. Episcopalian. Home: 12651 N Pebble Beach Dr Sun City AZ 85351-3327

TREECE, JOSEPH CHARLES, insurance broker; b. Loma Linda, Calif., Sept. 1, 1934; s. Roy G. and Jeane L. (Reade) T.; children: Debbie, Mike, David. BA, Chapman Coll., 1956. Cert. Ins. Counselor, Assoc. in Risk Mgmt. Comml. banker Security Pacific Nat. Bank, Hemet, Calif., 1959-72; ins. broker H.I.S./Kent & Hamilton, Hemet, 1972-89, Russell & Kaufmann, Hemet, 1989—. Dir. YMCA, Hemet. Lt. USN, 1956-59. Recipient Associate Achievement award Am. Assn. Mng. Gen. Agts., 1991, Disting. Svc. award Cert. Profl. Ins. Agents Soc., 1995. Mem. Ramona Pageant Assn. (life, chmn.-supr. 1962—), Profl. Ins. Assn. (state dir. 1988-91), Profl. Ins. Agts. (pres. Riverside and San Bernardino, Calif. 1989-90), Joint Ins. Assn. (pres. Riverside and San Bernardino 1991), Ind. Ins. Agts. (pres.), Cert. Profl. Ins. Agts. (nat. pres. 1992, Disting. Svc. award 1995), Hemet C. of C. (pres. 1970), Kiwanis Club (life, Hemet chpt. pres. 1971, lt. gov. divsn. 6 Cal-Na-Ha 1972). Home: PO Box 1731 San Jacinto CA 92581-1731 Office: Russell & Kaufmann Ins Agts 400 S State St Hemet CA 92543-5956

TREFNY, JOHN ULRIC, physics educator; b. Greenwich, Conn., Jan. 28, 1942; s. Ulric John and Mary Elizabeth (Leech) T.; m. Sharon Livingston, 1992; 1 child from previous marriage, Benjamin Robin. BS, Fordham U., 1963; PhD, Rutgers U., 1968. Rsch. assoc. Cornell U., Ithaca, N.Y., 1967-69; asst. prof. physics Wesleyan U., Middletown, Conn., 1969-77; asst. prof. physics Colo. Sch. Mines, Golden, 1977-79, assoc. prof., 1979-85, prof. 1985—, dir. Amorphous Materials Ctr., 1986—, assoc. dean rsch., 1988-90, head physics dept., 1990—; cons. Solar Energy Rsch. Inst., Golden, Energy Conversion Devices, Troy, Mich., various other cos. Contbr. articles to profl. jours. Recipient Teaching award AMOCO Found., 1984, Friend of Sci. Edn. award, 1990. Mem. Am. Ceramic Soc., Am. Phys. Soc., Am. Assn. Physics Tchrs., Colo. Assn. Sci. Tchrs. (bd. dirs. 1986-88), Sigma Xi, Sigma Pi Sigma. Avocations: golfing, traveling, whiskey. Home: 14268 W 1st Ave Golden CO 80401-5354

TRELOAR, HARRIETTE ELLEN, lawyer; b. Mpls., Feb. 21, 1950; d. Alan Edward and Dorothy Elizabeth (Buchanan) T. BA, Oberlin Coll., 1972; JD, U. Calif., Davis, 1976. Bar: Calif. 1977. Legis. rsch. asst. U.S. Senate (John V. Tunney), Washington, 1971-73; law clk. Yolo County Superior Ct., Woodland, Calif., 1975-77; asst. regional counsel U.S. Dept. Health and Human Svcs., San Francisco, 1978—. Author, editor: (book) University of California, Law Review, 1974-75, 75-76. Chair adv. bd. Volunteers-in-Parole, San Francisco, 1989—. Recipient Exemplary Svc. award U.S. Surgeon Gen., 1993. Mem. Calif. Women Lawyers (bd. gov. 1994—), Queen's Bench (bd. dirs. 1994—). Democrat.

TREMBLAY, WILLIAM ANDREW, English language educator; b. Southbridge, Mass., June 9, 1940; s. Arthur Achille and Irene (Fontaine) T.; m. Cynthia Ann Crooks, Sept. 28, 1962; children: William Crooks, Benjamin Philip, John Fontaine. BA, Clark U., 1962, MA, 1969; MFA in Poetry, U. Mass., 1972. English tchr. Southbridge (Mass.) High Sch., 1962-63, Sutton (Mass.) High Sch., 1963-65, Tantasqua Regional High Sch., Sturbridge, Mass., 1965-67; asst. prof. Leicester (Mass.) Jr. Coll., 1967-70; teaching asst. U. Mass., Amherst, 1970-72; instr. Springfield (Mass.) Coll., 1972-73; prof. English Colo. State U., Fort Collins, 1973—; Fulbright-Hays lectureship, Lisbon, Portugal, 1979, NEH summer program, 1981; mem. program dirs. coun. Associated Writing Programs, Norfolk, Va., 1984-86. Author: The June Rise: The Apocryphal Letters of Antoine Janis, 1994, (poetry) Duhamel: Ideas of Order in Little Canada, 1986, other books; editor-in-chief: Colo. Rev., 1983-91. Active High Plains Arts Ctr., Fort Collins, 1979-83; past pres. Fort Collins Gifted and Talented Parents Support Group, 1979. Summer writing fellow Corp. of Yaddo, 1989, Creative Writing fellow Nat. Endowment for Arts, 1985; recipient Pushcart prize Pushcart Prize Anthology, 1987. Mem. Puerto del Sol (bd. advisors). Home: 3412 Lancaster Dr Fort Collins CO 80525-2817 Office: Colo State U Dept English Fort Collins CO 80523

TREMBLY, CRISTY, television executive; b. Oakland, Md., July 11, 1958; d. Charles Dee and Mary Louise (Cassidy) T. BA in Russian, German and Linguistics cum laude, W.Va. U., 1978, BS in Journalism, 1978, MS in Broadcast Journalism, 1979; advanced cert. travel, West L.A. Coll., 1982; advanced cert. recording engring., Soundmaster Schs., North Hollywood, Calif., 1985. Videotape engr. Sta. WWVU-TV, Morgantown, W.Va., 1976-80; announcer, engr. Sta. WVVW Radio, Grafton, W.Va., 1979; tech. dir., videotape supr. Sta. KMEX-TV, L.A., 1980-85; broadcast supr. Sta. KADY-TV, Oxnard, Calif., 1988-89; news tech. dir. Sta. KVEA-TV, Glendale, Calif., 1985-89; asst. editor, videotape technician CBS TV Network, Hollywood, Calif., 1989-90; videotape supr. Sta. KCBS-TV, Hollywood, 1990-91, mgr. electronic news gathering ops., 1991-92; studio mgr., engr.-in-charge CBS TV Network, Hollywood, 1992—; radio operator KJ6BX Malibu Disaster Comm., 1987—. Producer (TV show) The Mountain Scene, 1976-78. Sr. orgn. pres. Children of the Am. Revolution, Malibu, Calif., 1992—; chmn. adminstrv. coun. Malibu United Meth. Ch., 1994-96; sec., mem. adv. com. Tamassee (S.C.) Sch., 1992—; vol. Ch. Coun., L.A. Riot Rebldg., Homeless shelter work, VA Hosps., Mus. docent; sponsor 3 overseas foster children. Recipient Outstanding Young Woman of Am., 1988, Asst. editor Emmy award Young and the Restless, 1989-90, Golden Mike award Radio/TV News assn., 1991, 92. Mem. DAR (state chmn. jr. membership 1987-88, state chmn. scholarships 1992-94, state chmn. jr. contest 1994-96, others, Malibu chpt. regent 1991, state chmn. motion pictures radio and TV Calif. 1988-90, Mex. 1990—, Nat. Outstanding Jr. 1993, nat. vice chmn. broadcast media 1995—), Am. Women in Radio and TV (so. Calif. bd. 1984-85, 93-95, pres.-elect 1995-96), Soc. Profl. Journalists, Women in Comms., Travelers Century Club (program chair 1987—), Mensa (life), Beta Sigma Phi. Democrat. Methodist. Home: 2901 Searidge St Malibu CA 90265-2969 Office: CBS TV City 7800 Beverly Blvd Los Angeles CA 90036-2165

TRENARY, RALPH HIRAM, III, federal agency administrator, human resources manager; b. Hardtner, Kans., June 20, 1961; s. Ralph Hiram Trenary Jr. and Ardath Ann (Bruner) Mayer; m. Molly Ann Hershman, June 15, 1985; 1 child, Caroline. BA, U. No. Colo., 1985. Exec. adminstrv. asst. Mortgage Plus, Inc., Denver, 1989-90; adminstrv. officer Colo. Nat. Guard, Fed. Civil Svc., Aurora, Colo. Springs, 1990-93; capt. nat. guard artillery battery comdr. Colo. Nat. Guard, Fed. Civil Svc., Englewood, 1993—, artillery battery comdr., 1992-95. 1st lt. U.S. Army, 1985-89. Democrat. Home: 1390 Masthead Way Monument CO 80132-9005 Office: Dept Mil Affairs ATTN HRO 6848 S Revere Pky Englewood CO 80112

TRENBERTH, KEVIN EDWARD, atmospheric scientist; b. Christchurch, New Zealand, Nov. 8, 1944; came to U.S., 1977; s. Edward Maurice and Ngaira Ivy (Eyre) T.; m. Gail Neville Thompson, Mar. 21, 1970; children: Annika Gail, Angela Dawn. BSc with honors, U. Canterbury, Christchurch, 1966; ScD, MIT, 1972. Meteorologist New Zealand Meteorol. Service, Wellington, 1966-76, supt. dynamic meteorology, 1976-77; assoc. prof. meteorology U. Ill., Urbana, 1977-82, prof., 1982-84; scientist Nat. Ctr. Atmospheric Research, Boulder, Colo., 1984-86, sr. scientist, 1986—, leader empirical studies group, 1987, head sect. climate analysis, 1987—; dep. dir. climate and global dynamics divsn. Nat. Ctr. Atmospheric Rsch., Boulder, Colo., 1991—; mem. joint sci. com. for world climate programme, com. climate changes and the ocean Tropical Oceans Global Atmosphere Program Sci. Steering Group, 1990-94; mem. Climate Variability and Predictability Sci. Steering Group, 1995—. Editor: Climate System Modeling, 1992; contbr. articles to profl. jours. Grantee NSF, NOAA, NASA. Fellow Am. Meteorol. Soc. (editor sci. jour. 1981-86, com. chmn. 1985-87, editor's award 1989), AAAS (coun. del. sect. atmosphere and hydrosphere sci. 1993—); mem. NAS (earth scis. com. 1982-85, tropical oceans global atmosphere adv. panel 1984-87, polar rsch. bd. 1986-90, climate rsch. com. 1987-90, global oceans atmosphere land sys. panel 1994—), Atmosphere Obs. Panel of Globe Climate Observing Sys., Royal Soc. New Zealand, Meteorol. Soc. New Zealand. Home: 1445 Landis Ct Boulder CO 80303-1122 Office: Nat Ctr Atmospheric Research PO Box 3000 Boulder CO 80307-3000

TRENNERT, ROBERT ANTHONY, JR., historian, educator; b. South Gate, Calif., Dec. 15, 1937; s. Robert Anthony Sr. and Mabel Valentine (Chesnut) T.; m. Linda Lee Griffith, July 31, 1965; children: Robert Anthony III, Kristina M. BA, Occidental Coll., 1961; MA, L.A. State Coll., 1963; Phd, U. Calif., Santa Barbara, 1969. Asst. prof. Temple U., Phila., 1967-74; Asst. prof. Ariz. State U., Tempe, 1974-76, assoc. prof., 1976-81, prof. history, 1981--, chmn. dept. history, 1986-92; chmn. Ariz. Hist. Sites Rev. Com., 1989-91. Author: Alternative to Extinction, 1975, Indian Traders on Middle Border, 1981, Phoenix Indian Sch., 1988. Bd. dirs. Ariz. Hist. Found. Mem. Orgn. of Am. Historians. Home: 3581 W Golden Ln Chandler AZ 85226-1347 Office: Ariz State U Dept Of History Tempe AZ 85287

TRENT-OTA, JANE SUZANNE, elementary school educator; b. Long Beach, Calif., June 10, 1935; d. George Lionel and Jennie Bolton (Rundio) Heap; children from previous marriage; Katharine Trent, Cecily Finegan; m. William T. Ota, Sept. 27, 1991; stepchildren: William N. Ota, Douglas W. Ota. BA, Mary Washington Coll., Fredericsburg, Va., 1957; MA in Edn., Azua-Pacific U., 1978; student, Calif. Western-USIU, San Diego, 1970. Cert. elem. tchr. K-8, Calif., Level I Orff-Schulwerk nat. cert; cert. in master gardening, Calif. Tchr. 5th and 6th grades Chula Vista (Calif.) Elem. Sch. Dist., kindergarten tchr., ret., 1991; cons. bargaining team Chula Vista Edn. Assn. Vol. with U. Calif. Cooperative Extension/U.S. Dept. Agr. Vol. numerous civic orgns. Recipient Instruction grant, ORFF Instrumentarium, We Honor Ours award San Diego county svc. ctr. coun. Calif. Tchrs. Assn., 1991. Mem. Calif. Ret. Tchrs. Assn., NSF Math. Inst. Univ. Calif. San Diego, Am. ORFF-Schulwerk Assn. (bd. sec. San Diego chpt. 1991-93), Delta Kappa Gamma (chpt. exec. bd., chmn. scholarship). Home: 620 1st St Coronado CA 92118-1202

TREVITHICK, RONALD JAMES, underwriter; b. Portland, Oreg., Sept. 13, 1944; s. Clifford Vincent and Amy Lois (Turner) T.; m. Delberta Russell, Sept. 11, 1965; children: Pamela, Carmen, Marla, Sheryl. BBA U. Wash., 1966. CLU, CPA, ChFC. Mem. audit staff Ernst & Ernst, Anchorage, 1966, 68-70; pvt. practice acctg., Fairbanks, Alaska, 1970-73; with Touche Ross & Co., Anchorage, 1973-78, audit ptnr., 1976-78; exec. v.p., treas., bd. dirs. Veco Internat., Inc., 1978-82; pres., bd. dirs. Petroleum Contractors Ltd., 1980-82; bd. dirs. P.S. Contractors A/S, Norcon, Inc., OFC of Alaska, Inc., V.E. Systems Svcs., Inc., Veco Turbo Services, Inc., Veco Drilling, Inc., Vemar, Inc., 1978-82; with Coopers & Lybrand, Anchorage, 1982-85; field underwriter, registered rep. New York Life Ins., 1985—; instr. acctg. U. Alaska, 1971-72; lectr. acctg. and taxation The Am. Coll., 1972, instr. adv. sales Life Underwriters Tng. Coun., 1988-89; bd. dirs. Ahtna Devel. Corp., 1985-86. Div. chmn. United Way, 1975-76, YMCA, 1979; bd. dirs., fin. chmn. Anchorage Arts Coun., 1975-78, Am. Diabetes Assn., Alaska affiliate, 1985-91, chmn. bd. 1988-89, chmn. hon. bd. 1992—, Am. Heart Assn., Alaska affiliate, 1986-87, Anchorage dist. com. Alaska State Youth Soccer Assn, 1994—. With U.S. Army, 1967-68. Mem. Fin. Execs. Inst. (pres. Alaska chpt. 1981-83), Am. Soc. CLUs & ChFCs (v.p. Alaska chpt. 1993-94, pres. 1994—), Alaska Assn. Life Underwriters (sec., treas. 1987-90), Beta Alpha Psi. Clubs: Alaska Goldstrikers Soccer (pres. 1992-93). Home: 4421 Huffman Rd Anchorage AK 99516-2211 Office: 1400 W Benson Blvd Anchorage AK 99503-3660

TREYBIG, JAMES G., computer company executive; b. Clarendon, TX, 1940. BS, Rice U., 1963; MBA, Stanford, 1968. Mkgt. mgr. Hewlett-Packard Co., 1968-72; with Kleiner and Perkins, 1972-74; with Tandem Computer Inc., Cupertino, Calif., 1974—, now pres., chief exec. officer, dir. Office: Tandem Computers Inc 19333 Vallco Pky Cupertino CA 95014-2506*

TRIBBETT, JAMES VERNON, federal agency administrator; b. Logansport, Ind., Feb. 22, 1941; s. Gerald Herbert and Mary Catherine Tribbett. BS in Chemistry, Purdue U., 1963; MS, U. So. Miss., Hattiesburg, 1976; postgrad., U. So. Ill. Commd. USAF, 1963, advanced through grades to col., ret., 1984; tech. mgr. Jet Propulsion Lab., Pasadena, Calif. Author: Security Requirements, 1990. Mem. IEEE, VFW, Am. Inst. Aero. and Astro., Air Force Assn., Soc. Logistics Engrs., Am. Legion. Republican. Baptist. Home: 5525 E Virginia Ave Phoenix AZ 85008-1707 Office: Jet Propulsion Lab 4800 Oak Grove Dr Pasadena CA 91109-8001

TRIBBLE, ALAN CHARLES, physicist; b. Little Rock, Aug. 11, 1961; s. George Alan and Barbara Jean (Stocks) T.; m. Elizabeth Ellen Gunion, July 30, 1988; 1 child, Matthew Alan. BS, U. Ark., 1983; MS, U. Iowa, 1986, PhD, 1988. Physicist Rockwell Internat., Downey, Calif., 1988—; instr. U. So. Calif.; U.S. rep. to Internat. Standards Orgn. Author: The Space Environment: Implications for Spacecraft Design. Grad. Student Rschr. Program fellowship NASA, 1987. Mem. AIAA, Am. Geophys. Union, Am. Phys. Soc.

TRIBBLE, DAVID HENRY, software engineer; b. Frederick, Md., Aug. 6, 1965; s. Henry Rawlings and Lois Marie (Whitmore) T. BS in Computer Sci., U. Md., 1988. Coop., programmer MITRE, McLean, Va., 1986-89; software engr. Sci. Applications Internat. Corp., McLean, 1989-91, I-NET, Bethesda, Md., 1991-93, Inter-National Rsch. Inst., Mililani, Hawaii, 1993—. Mem. Assn. for Computing Machinery. Office: Inter-National Rsch Inst 300 Kahelu Ave Ste 5 Mililani HI 96789-3911

TRIBBLE, RICHARD WALTER, brokerage executive; b. San Diego, Oct. 19, 1948; s. Walter Perrin and Catherine Janet (Miller) T.; m. Joan Catherine Sliter, June 26, 1980. BS, U. Ala., Tuscaloosa, 1968; student, Gulf Coast Sch. Drilling Practices, U. Southwestern La., 1977. Stockbroker Shearson, Am. Express, Washington, 1971-76; ind. oil and gas investment sales, Falls Church, Va., 1976-77; pres. Monroe & Keusink, Inc., Falls Church and Columbus, Ohio, 1977-87; instnl. investment officer FCA Asset Mgmt., 1983-85; fin. cons. Merrill Lynch Pierce, Fenner & Smith, Inc., Phoenix, 1987—, cert. fin. mgr., 1989—, sr. fin. cons., 1992—, asst. v.p., 1993—. Served with USMC, 1969-70. Republican. Methodist. Office: 2525 E Camelback Rd Phoenix AZ 85016-4219

TRIBUS, MYRON, management consultant, engineer, educator; b. San Francisco, Oct. 30, 1921; s. Edward and Marie D. (Kramer) T.; m. Sue Davis, Aug. 30, 1945; children—Louanne, Kamala. B.S in Chemistry, U. Calif. at Berkeley, 1942; Ph.D. in Engring, U. Calif. at Los Angeles, 1949; D.Sc. (hon.), Rockford (Ill.) Coll., 1965, Oakland (Mich.) U., 1971. Registered profl. engr., Mass. Instr. to prof. engring. U. Calif. at Los Angeles, 1946-61; dir. aircraft icing research U. Mich., 1951-54; dean engring. Thayer Sch. Engring., Dartmouth Coll., 1961-69; asst. sec. sci. and tech. Dept. Commerce, Washington, 1969-70; sr. v.p. tech. and engring. info. tech. group Xerox Corp., Rochester, N.Y., 1970-74; dir. Center for Advanced Engring. Study, Mass. Inst. Tech., Cambridge, 1974-86; cons. in quality mgmt., 1986—; dir. rsch. Exergy, Inc., Hayward, Calif., 1987—; cons. heat transfer Gen. Electric Co., 1950; cons. Fed. Office Saline Water; tech. adv. bd. Dept. Commerce; adviser to NATO, 1953; mem. Nat. Adv. Com. Oceans and Atmosphere, 1971-72; bd. dirs. Exergy, Inc., Hayward, Calif. Author: Thermostatics and Thermodynamics, 1961, Rational Descriptions, Decisions and Designs, 1969; Contbr. articles to profl. jours. Bd. govs. Technion, Haifa, Israel, 1973-84. Served to capt. USAAF, 1942-46. Recipient Thurman H. Bane award Inst. Aero. Scis., 1945; Wright Bros. medal Soc. Automotive Engrs., 1945; Alfred Noble prize Engring. Socs., 1952; named U. Calif. at Los Angeles Alumnus Year, 1972. Mem. Am. Soc. M.E., IEEE, Am. Soc. for Engring. Edn., Nat. Soc. Profl. Engrs. Home: 350 Britto Ter Fremont CA 94539-3824 Office: Exergy Inc 22320 Foothill Blvd Hayward CA 94541-2700

TRICK, ROGER LEE, national park ranger; b. Port Clinton, Ohio, Aug. 28, 1950; s. Carl Franklin and Marilyn Mae (Kemp) T.; m. Terri Ann Jacob, Aug. 8, 1977; children: Randy, Hillary, Brian. BA, U. Pa., 1972; MA, U. Ariz., 1975. Park technician Grand Canyon (Ariz.) Nat. Park, 1975-77; park ranger Mesa Verde (Colo.) Nat. Park, 1977-79; area mgr. Hovenweep Nat. Monument, Cortez, Colo., 1979-83; chief ranger Whitman Mission Nat. Historic Site, Walla Walla, Wash., 1983—; instr. in vegetation mgmt. Nat. Park Svc., Washington, 1990—; instr. Oreg. Trail seminar Whitman Mission Nat. Historic Site, 1991—. Editor: Hovenweep Trail Guide, 1981; contbr. chpts. to books. Bd. dirs. Little Theatre Walla Walla, 1985-89; cubmaster Walla Walla area Boy Scouts Am., 1989—. Mem. Nat. Assn. Interpreters, Assn. Nat. Park Rangers, Kiwanis Club Walla Walla (bd. dirs. 1985-87). Home: 2141 Leonard Dr Walla Walla WA 99362-4427 Office: Whitman Mission Nat Historic Site RR 2 Box 247 Walla Walla WA 99362-9699

TRICOLES, GUS PETER, electromagnetics engineer, physicist, consultant; b. San Francisco, Oct. 18, 1931; s. Constantine Peter and Eugenia (Elias) T.; m. Beverly Mildred Ralsky, Dec. 20, 1953 (dec. Dec. 1974); children: Rosanne, Robin; m. Aileen Irma Aronson, Apr. 1, 1980 (div. June 1980). BA in Physics, UCLA, 1955; MS in Applied Math., San Diego State U., 1958; MS in Applied Physics, U. Calif., San Diego, 1962, PhD in Applied Physics, 1971. Engr. Convair div. Gen. Dynamics, San Diego, 1955-59, engr. Electronics div., 1962-75, engring. mgr. Electronics div., 1975-89, sr. engring. staff specialist, 1989-92; sr. engring. staff specialist GDE Systems Inc., 1992—; engr. Smyth Rsch. Assn., San Diego, 1959-61; rsch. asst. Scripps Instn. Oceanography, La Jolla, Calif., 1961-62; sr. engring. staff specialist G.D.E. Systems, Inc., San Diego, 1992—; cons. Ga. Inst. Tech., Atlanta, 1972, 79-80, Transco Industries, L.A., 1973, Aero Geo Industries, San Antonio, 1980-82, Vantage Assocs., San Diego, 1988; rsch. reviewer NRC, NAS, Boulder, Colo., 1986-88. Author: (with others) Radome Engineering Handbook, 1970, Antenna Handbook, 1988; contbr. articles to profl. jours.; holder 18 patents. With USN, 1952-53. Fellow IEEE (antenna standards com. 1980—, advancement com. 1988), Optical Soc. Am. (local sect. v.p. 1966); mem. N.Y. Acad. Scis., Am. Geophys. Union. Home: 4633 Euclid Ave San Diego CA 92115-3226 Office: GDE Sys Inc PO Box 92150 San Diego CA 92150-9009

TRIEWEILER, TERRY NICHOLAS, lawyer; b. Dubuque, Iowa, Mar. 21, 1948; s. George Nicholas and Anne Marie (Oastern) T.; m. Carol M. Jacobson, Aug. 11, 1972; children: Kathryn Anne, Christina Marie, Anna Theresa. BA, Drake U., 1970, JD, 1972. Bar: Iowa 1973, Wash. 1973, U.S. Dist. Ct. (so. dist.) Iowa 1973, U.S. Dist. Ct. (we. dist.) Wash. 1973, Mont. 1975, U.S. Dist. Ct. Mont. 1977. Staff atty. Polk County Legal Services, Des Moines, 1973; assoc. Hullin, Roberts, Mines, Fite & Riveland, Seattle, 1973-75, Morrison & Hedman, Whitefish, Mont., 1975-77; sole practice, Whitefish; now justice Mont. Supreme Ct., Helena; lectr. U. Mont. Law Sch., 1981—; mem. com. to amend civil proc. rules Mont. Supreme Ct., Helena, 1984, commn. to draft pattern jury instrns., 1985; mem. Gov.'s Adv. Com. on Amendment to Work Compensation Act, adv. com. Mont. Work Compensation Ct. Mem. ABA, Mont. Bar Assn. (pres. 1986-87), Wash. Bar Assn., Iowa Bar Assn., Assn. Trial Lawyers Am., Mont. Trial Lawyers Assn. (dir., pres.). Democrat. Roman Catholic. Home: 1615 Virginia Dale St Helena MT 59601-5823 Office: Mont Supreme Ct Justice Bldg 215 N Sanders St Rm 323 Helena MT 59620

TRIGG, DOUGLAS A., marketing and business development executive; b. Durby, Va.; s. Louie and Vera B. (Barker) T. BA in Internat. Mktg. Mgmt., Calif. State U., San Francisco, 1973; M in Internat. Mktg. Mgmt., Am. Grad. Sch. Internat. Mgmt., 1976. Account exec. Compton Advt., San Juan, P.R., 1976-78; sr. account exec. N W Ayer ABH Internat. Advt., N.Y., 1978-81; account dir. Latin Am. region McCann-Erickson Worldwide Advt., 1981-82; account supr. Benton & Bowles Advt., L.A., N.Y., 1982-85, Cohen/Johnson Advt., L.A., 1985-86; dir. mktg. and bus. devel. Sansum Med. Clinic, Santa Barbara, Calif., 1986—; adj. prof. mktg., mktg. rsch., advt. Calif. State U., Northridge, U. Calif., Santa Barbara. Contbr. articles to profl. publs. Leader United Way, Santa Barbara. Capt. U.S. Army, 1966-69. Mem. Med. Group Mgmt. Assn., Am. Mktg. Assn. (Presdl. citation 1992). Home: 257 Cloydon Cir Montecito CA 93108-1050 Office: Sansum Med Clinic Inc PO Box 1239 Santa Barbara CA 93102-1239

TRIGIANO, LUCIEN LEWIS, physician; b. Easton, Pa., Feb. 9, 1926; s. Nicholas and Angeline (Lewis) T.; children: Lynn Anita, Glenn Larry, Robert Nicholas. Student Tex. Christian U., 1944-45, Ohio U., 1943-44, 46-47, Milligan Coll., 1944, Northwestern U., 1945, Temple U., 1948-52. Intern, Meml. Hosp., Johnstown, Pa., 1952-53; resident Lee Hosp., Johnstown, 1953-54; gen. practice, Johnstown, 1953-59; med. dir. Pa. Rehab. Center, Johnstown, 1959-62, chief phys. medicine and rehab., 1964-70; fellow phys. medicine and rehab. N.Y. Inst. Phys. Medicine and Rehab., 1962-64; dir. rehab. medicine Lee Hosp., 1964-71, Ralph K. Davies Med. Center, San Francisco, 1973-75, St. Joseph's Hosp., San Francisco, 1975-78, St. Francis Meml. Hosp., San Francisco, 1978-83; asst. prof. phys. medicine and rehab. Temple U. Sch. Medicine; founder Disability Alert. Served with USNR, 1944-46. Diplomate Am. Bd. Phys. Medicine and Rehab. Mem. AMA, A.C.P., Pa., San Francisco County Med. socs., Am. Acad. Phys. Medicine and Rehab., Am. Congress Phys. Medicine, Calif. Acad. Phys. Medicine, Nat. Rehab. Assn., Babcock Surg. Soc. Author various med. articles. Home: 1050 North Point St San Francisco CA 94109-8302 Office: 1150 Bush St Ste 4B San Francisco CA 94109-5920

TRIMBLE, PAUL JOSEPH, lawyer; b. Springfield, Mass., Oct. 9, 1930; s. Peter Paul and Bernnese (Myrick) T.; m. Suzanne Hrudka; children: Troy, Derrick, Andrew. B.A., Am. Internat. U., Springfield, Mass., 1952; LL.B., U. Tex., Austin, 1955. Bar: Calif., Tex., Ill., Alaska. Counsel Mobil Oil Corp., Joliet, Ill., 1964-72; assoc. counsel Fluor Corp., Irvine, Calif., 1972-73, corp. counsel, 1973-74, sr. corp. counsel, 1974, asst. gen. counsel, 1974-80, gen. counsel, 1980-82, sr. v.p., gen. counsel, 1982—, sr. v.p. law, gen. counsel, 1984—, corp. sec., 1992—. Mem. ABA, Calif. Bar Assn., Tex. Bar Assn., Ill. Bar Assn., Alaska Bar Assn. Republican.

TRINKL, FRANK HERMAN, economist, educator; b. Cudahy, Wis., July 3, 1928; s. Frank and Celia (Damhazel) T.; m. Barbara Ruth Henry, June 9, 1951; children: Peter, Garth, Alison. MA in Econs., U. Mich., PhD in Econs.; MS in Statistics, Stanford U. Staff scientist Ramo-Wooldridge Corp., L.A., 1956-57; staff mem. RAND Corp., Santa Monica, Calif., 1957-61; spl. asst. to asst. sec. def. U.S. DOD, Washington, 1961-65; cons. various orgns., 1966-70, 74-79; sr. lectr. grad. sch. pub. policy U. Calif., Berkeley, 1970-74; pres., dir. for planning and econ. analysis Ctr. for Policy Studies, Inc., Berkeley, 1979-83; prin. cons. Calif. Legislature, Sacramento, 1983-85; dir. pub. law rsch. inst., adj. prof. U. Calif. Hastings Coll. Law, San Francisco, 1986-93, ret. Contbr. articles to profl. jours. Fellow AAAS; mem. Am. Econ. Assn., Ops. Rsch. Soc. Am.

TRIPLETT, RAYMOND FRANCIS, insurance underwriter; b. Detroit Lakes, Minn., Oct. 14, 1921; s. Raymond LeRoy Triplett and Barbara A. (Wambach) Van Der Wey; m. Shirley J. Koenig, Feb. 14, 1942; children: Kathleen, Barbara, Joan, Therese, Raymond J. CLU. Mgr. western sales Minn. & Ont. Paper Co., Calif., 1950-53; life underwriter N.Y. Life Ins. Co., San Jose, Calif., 1953—; faculty 2nd annual Inst. Estate Planning, Law Ctr. U. Miami, 1968, Inst. Fed. Taxation, Law Ctr. U. So. Calif., 1971. Author: Voyage of Commitment, 1983. Mem. personnel bd. Santa Clara County, 1965-66; mem. Jud. Selection Adv. Bd., San Jose, 1976-74; bd. dirs. O'Connor Hosp. Found., bd. fellows Santa Clara U. Lt. USMS, 1942-44. Recipient Circumnavigators award Cruising Club Am. Mem. Santa Clara County Estate Planning Coun. (pres. 1958), San Jose Life Underwriters Assn., CLU (pres. Santa Jose chpt. 1964), N.Y. Life Ins. Co. (pres. coun. 1964), Am. Soc. CLU and ChFC (nat. pres. 1972-73), Am. Coll. Life Underwriters (trustee), Cath. Layman's Retreat Assn. Home: 16203 Hillvale Ave Monte Sereno CA 95030-4159 Office: 25 Metro Dr Ste 228 San Jose CA 95110-1338

TRIPOLI, MASUMI HIROYASU, financial consultant and diplomat; b. Fukuyama, Japan, Apr. 23, 1956; d. Yoshimi and Suzuko Hiroyasu; 1 child, Mona Lisa Tripoli. BA cum laude, U. Wash., 1978; MA, Sophia U., Tokyo, 1981; MBA, Ecole des Hautes Etudes Comml, Jouy-en-Josas, France, 1983. Cert. fin. planner, chartered fin. cons. Corp. planning mgr. Kowa Corp., Osaka, Japan, 1983-85; internat. bond trader Banque Baribas, Tokyo, 1985-86, Westpac Bank, Tokyo, 1987-88; fin. cons. CIGNA Fin. Advisors, Glendale, Calif., 1989—, Masumi Tripoli & Assocs., Glendale, Calif., 1989—; anchor newscaster United TV, L.A., 1989-92; bd. dirs. Sunny Side Properties, Altadena; condr. seminars in field. Contbr. articles to profl. jours. Grantee Sophia U., 1979, H.E.C., 1983. Mem. Internat. Bd. Cert. Fin. Planners, Ritz-Carlton Fitness Club. Office: Masumi Tripoli and Assocs 100 W Broadway Ste 1200 Glendale CA 91210-1202

TRIPPE, ANTHONY PHILIP, business consultant, technology manager, electronics company executive; b. Buffalo, Aug. 30, 1943; s. Anthony John and Carolyn Agnes (Peschio) T.; m. Dorothy Ann Fazzina, June 26, 1965; children: Anthony Joseph, Michael Anthony, Madonna Marie. BS in Chemistry, Rochester Inst. Tech., 1966; MS in Math., Fairleigh Dickinson U., 1972; DBA, U.S. Internat. U., 1982. Registered profl. engr., N.Y., profl. chem. engr., Calif. Co-op student/analytical Eastman Kodak Co., Rochester, N.Y., 1963-66; organic chemist Smith, Kline & French, Phila., 1966-67; chem. engr. U.S. Army-Picatinny, Dover, N.J., 1967-72; sys. analyst Calspan Corp., Buffalo, 1972-77; program mgr. IRT Corp., San Diego, 1977-82, v.p. govt. programs, 1982-87; bus. devel. mgr. Maxwell Labs., San Diego, 1987-93, v.p. sales and mktg., 1993-95; bus. cons. Coastal Pacific Consulting, San Diego, 1995—. Contbr. numerous papers to conf. procs., articles to profl. jours. Corp. leader United Way of San Diego County, 1988, 89, 92; project bus. cons. Jr. Achievement, San Diego, 1986, 90. Mem. IEEE, Am. Chem. Soc., Am. Def. Preparedness Assn., Armed Forces Comm. and Electronics Assn., Nat. Assn. Radio and Telecomm. Engrs. (cert. electromagnetic compatibility engr.), Internat. Soc. Optical Engring., Soc. Automotive Engrs. (cert. of appreciation 1991, 92), Assn. Old Crows. Republican. Roman Catholic. Office: Coastal Pacific Consulting PO Box 420007 San Diego CA 92142-0007

TRISKA, JAN FRANCIS, retired political science educator; b. Prague, Czechoslovakia, Jan. 26, 1922; came to U.S., 1948, naturalized, 1955; s. Jan and Bozena (Kubiznak) T.; m. Carmel Lena Burastero, Aug. 26, 1951; children: Mark Lawrence, John William. J.U.D., Charles U., Prague, 1948; LL.M., Yale U., 1950, J.S.D., 1952; Ph.D., Harvard U., 1957. Co-dir. Soviet treaties Hoover Instn., Stanford, Calif., 1956-58; lectr. dept. polit. sci. U. Calif.-Berkeley, 1957-58; asst. prof. Cornell U., Ithaca, N.Y., 1958-60; assoc. prof. Stanford U., Calif., 1960-65, prof. polit. sci., 1965-89, assoc. chmn. dept., 1965-66, 68-69, 71-72, 74-75, emeritus prof. polit. sci., 1990—. Coauthor: (with Slusser) The Theory, Law and Policy of Soviet Treaties, 1962, (with Finley) Soviet Foreign Policy, 1968, (with Cocks) Political Development and Political Change in Eastern Europe, 1977, (with Ike, North) The World of Superpowers, 1981, (with Gati) Blue Collar Workers in Eastern Europe, 1981, Dominant Powers and Subordinate States, 1986; bd. editors: East European Quar. Comparative Politics, Internat. Jour. Sociology, Jour. Comparative Politics, Studies in Comparative Communism, Soviet Statutes and Decisions, Documents in Communist Affairs. Recipient Rsch. award Ford Found., 1963-68, Josef Hlavka Commemorative medal Czechoslovak Acad. Scis., 1992, M.A. Comenius 1592-1992 Meml. medal Czechoslovak Pedagogical Mus., Prague, 1991; fellow NSF, 1971-72, Sen. Fulbright fellow,

1973-74, Woodrow Wilson fellow Internat. Ctr. for Scholars, 1980-81. Mem. Am. Polit. Sci. Assn. (sec. pres. conf. on communist studies 1970-76), Assn. Advancement Slavic Studies (bd. dirs. 1975-83), Am. Soc. Internat. Law (exec. coun. 1964-67), Czechoslovak Soc. Arts and Scis. (pres. 1978-80, 90-92), Inst. for Human Scis. Vienna (acting for Commn. European Communities, Brussels, com. experts on transformation of nat. higher edn. and rsch. system in Ctrl. Europe, Brussels 1991—). Democrat. Club: Fly Fishers (Palo Alto, Calif.). Home: 720 Vine St Menlo Park CA 94025-6154 Office: Stanford U Dept Polit Sci Stanford CA 94305

TRIVEDI, NARENDRA SHANTILAL, physician, educator, researcher; b. Jalia, Gujarat, India, June 24, 1955; came to U.S., 1982; s. Shantilal P. and Sushilaben S. (Mehta) T.; m. Trupti N. Trivedi, Feb. 1, 1983; children: Akash, Nikunj. MB, BS, NHL Mcpl. Med. Coll., Ahmedabad, India, 1979. Diplomate Am. Bd. Anesthesiology, Am. Bd. Pain Mgmt. Resident in orthopedic surgery KM Sch. of PG Medicine, Ahmedabad, 1978-80; house officer orthopedic surgery Kitwe (Zambia) Ctrl. Hosp., 1980-82; med. asst. allergy Jefferson Med. Ctr., Pitts., 1982-84; house physician surgery Brookdale Med. Ctr., Bklyn., 1984-85; resident in surgery Mt. Sinai Med. Sch., N.Y.C., 1985-87; resident in anesthesiology Maimonides Med. Ctr., Bklyn., 1987-90; fellow cardiac anesthesiology Cleve. Clin. Found., 1990; asst. clin. prof. U. Calif., Irvine, 1991-94, assoc. clin. prof., 1994—; lectr. in field, 1991—. Author: (chpt.) Textbook of Critical Care, 1989, Textbook of Thoracoscopic Surgery; edtl. bd. Clin. Anesthesia Jour., 1992—; contbr. articles to profl. jours. Mem. Am. Soc. Indian Anesthesiologists (bd. dirs. 1993—), Am. Soc. Anesthesiologists, Internat. Anesthesia Rsch. Soc., Soc. Cardiovascular Anesthesia, Calif. Soc. Anesthesiologists, Orange County Soc. Anesthesiologists. Hindu. Home: 1011 S Mountcrest Ct Anaheim CA 92808-2127 Office: Univ Calif 101 The City Dr S Orange CA 92668-3201

TROAN, GORDON TRYGVE, accountant, financial planner, entrepreneur; b. Mpls., Mar. 1, 1960; s. John Trygve and Janet Lillian (Cook) T.; m. Stefanie Louise Mock, July 15, 1989. BS in Acctg., Ariz. State U., 1982, MBA, 1985. CPA, CFP, Ariz. Pres., CFO Five Star Enterprises, Inc., Phoenix, 1982-90, CEO, 1990—, also bd. dirs.; cons. St. Andrew's Found., Phoenix, 1988—. Precinct commiteeman Ariz. Dems., Phoenix, 1982; mem. coun. of deacons St. Andrew Luth. Ch., Phoenix, 1982-84. Mem. Ariz. Soc. CPAs, North Valley C. of C., Son's of Norway (sec. fin. com. 1986—). Office: Five Star Enterprises Inc 5927 W Bell Rd Glendale AZ 85308-3711

TROSPER, ROBERT THOMAS, software engineer; b. Salt Lake City, July 29, 1952; s. Alfred Benjamin and Josephine Theresa (Henson) T.; m. Mary Sue Robison, Dec. 22, 1978; children: Brendan Thomas, Benjamin Joseph. BS in English, U. Utah, 1976, BSEE, 1985. Tchr. St. Brigid's Sch., San Francisco, 1978; software engr. Cericor, Salt Lake City, 1985, Hewlett-Packard Co., Salt Lake City, 1985-89, Evans & Sutherland, Salt Lake City, 1989-90, VZ Corp., Salt Lake City, 1990-91, Global Integrated Sys., Orem, Utah, 1992, Word Perfect Corp., Orem, 1992-93; software engr. Novell, Inc., Salt Lake City, 1993, mgr. software engring., 1993—. Co-op tchr. Eastwood Elem., Salt Lake City, 1993—. Mem. IEEE, ACM. Office: Novell Inc 4001 S 700 E Ste 380 Salt Lake City UT 84107-2178

TROST, BARRY MARTIN, chemist, educator; b. Phila., June 13, 1941; s. Joseph and Esther T.; m. Susan Paula Shapiro, Nov. 25, 1967; children: Aaron David, Carey Daniel. B.A. cum laude, U. Pa., 1962; Ph.D., MIT, 1965; D (hon.), U. Claude Bernard, Lyons, France, 1994. Mem. faculty U. Wis., Madison, 1965—, prof., chemistry, 1969—, Evan P. and Marion Helfaer prof. chemistry, from 1976; Vilas rsch. prof. chemistry U. Wis.; prof. chemistry Stanford U., 1987—, Tamaki prof. humanities and scis., 1990; cons. Merck, Sharp & Dohme, E.I. duPont de Nemours.; Chem. Soc. centenary lectr., 1982. Author: Problems in Spectroscopy, 1967, Sulfur Ylides, 1975; editor-in-chief Comprehensive Organic Synthesis, 1991—, Chem-Tracts/Organic Chemistry, 1993—; editor: Structure and Reactivity Concepts in Organic Chemistry series, 1972—; assoc. editor Jour. Am. Chem. Soc., 1974-80; mem. editorial bd. Organic Reactions Series, 1971—; contbr. numerous articles to profl. jours. Recipient Dreyfus Found. Tech.-Scholar award, 1970, 77, Creative Work in Synthetic Organic Chemistry award, 1981, Baekland medal, 1981, Alexander von Humboldt award, 1984, Guenther award, 1990, Janssen prize, 1990, Roger Adams award 1995; named Chem. Pioneer, Am. Inst. Chemists, 1983; NSF fellow, 1963-65, Sloan Found. fellow, 1967-69, Am. Swiss Found. fellow, 1975—; Cope scholar, 1989. Mem. AAAS, Am. Chem. Soc. (award in pure chemistry 1977, Roger Adams award 1995), Nat. Acad. Scis., Am. Acad. Arts and Scis., Chem. Soc. London. Office: Stanford U Dept Chemistry Stanford CA 94305

TROTT, STEPHEN SPANGLER, federal judge, musician; b. Glen Ridge, N.J., Dec. 12, 1939; s. David Herman and Virginia (Spangler) T.; divorced; children: Christina, Shelley. B.A., Wesleyan U., 1962; LL.B., Harvard U., 1965; LLD (hon.), Santa Clara U., 1992. Bar: Calif. 1966, U.S. Dist. Ct. (cen. dist.) Calif. 1966, U.S. Ct. Appeals (9th cir.) 1983, U.S. Supreme Ct. 1984. Guitarist, mem. The Highwaymen, 1958—; dep. dist. atty. Los Angeles County Dist. Atty.'s Office, Los Angeles, 1966-75; chief dep. dist. atty. Los Angeles County Dist. Atty.'s Office, 1975-79; U.S. dist. atty. Central Dist. Calif., Los Angeles, 1981-83; asst. atty. gen. criminal div. Dept. Justice, Washington, 1983-86; mem. faculty Nat. Coll. Dist. Attys., Houston, 1973—; chmn. central dist. Calif. Law Enforcement Coordinating Com., Houston, 1981-83; coordinator Los Angeles-Nev. Drug Enforcement Task Force, 1982-83; assoc. atty. gen. Justice Dept., Washington, 1986-88; chmn. U.S. Interpol, 1986-88; judge U.S. Ct. of Appeals 9th Cir., Boise, Idaho, 1988—; chmn. U.S. Interpol. Trustee Wesleyan U., 1984-87; bd. dirs. Children's Home Soc., Idaho, 1990—, Boise Philharm. Assn., 1995—. Recipient Gold record as singer-guitarist for Michael Row the Boat Ashore, 1961, Disting. Faculty award Nat. Coll. Dist. Attys., 1977. Mem. Am. Coll. Trial Lawyers, Wilderness Fly Fishers Club (pres. 1975-77), Brentwood Racing Pigeon Club (pres. 1977-82), Magic Castle, Internat. Brotherhood Magicians, Idaho Classic Guitar Soc. (founder, pres. 1989—). Republican. Office: US Ct Appeals for 9th Cir 550 W Fort St Boise ID 83724-0101

TROTTER, F(REDERICK) THOMAS, retired university president; b. L.A., Apr. 17, 1926; s. Fred B. and Hazel (Thomas) T.; m. Gania Demaree, June 27, 1953; children—Ruth Elizabeth, Paula Anne (dec.), Tania, Mary. AB, Occidental Coll., 1950, DD, 1968; STB, Boston U., 1953, PhD, 1958; LHD, Ill. Wesleyan U., 1974, Cornell Coll., 1985, Westmar Coll., 1987; LLD, U. Pacific, 1978, Wesleyan Coll., 1981; EdD, Columbia Coll., 1984; LittD, Alaska Pacific U., 1987. Exec. sec. Boston U. Student Christian Assn., 1951-54; ordained elder Calif.-Pacific, Methodist Ch., 1953; pastor Montclair (Calif.) Meth. Ch., 1956-59; lectr. So. Calif. Sch. Theology at Claremont, 1957-59, instr., 1959-60, asst. prof., 1960-63, assoc. prof., 1963-66, prof., 1966, dean, 1961; prof. religion and arts, dean Sch. Theology Claremont, 1961-73; mem. Bd. Higher Edn. and Ministry, United Meth. Ch., 1972-73, gen. sec., 1973-87; pres. Alaska Pacific U., Anchorage, 1988-95; ret., 1995; dir. Inst. for Antiquity and Christianity at Claremont. Author: Jesus and the Historian, 1968, Loving God with One's Mind, 1987, weekly column local newspapers; editor-at-large: Christian Century, 1969-84. Trustee Dillard U. Served with USAAF, 1944-46. Kent fellow Soc. for Values in Higher Edn., 1954; Dempster fellow Meth. Ch., 1954. Mem. Rotary Internat. (Anchorage Downtown), Commonwealth North. Home: 75-136 Kiowa Dr Indian Wells CA 92210

TROUNSTINE, PHILIP J., editor, journalist; b. Cin., July 30, 1949; s. Henry P. and Amy May (Joseph) Trounstine; children: Jessica, David; m. Deborah Williams, May 1, 1993; children: Amy, Ryan, Patrick Wilkes. Student, U. Vt., 1967-68, Stanford U., 1968-70; BA in Journalism, San Jose State U., 1975. Graphic artist Eric Printing, San Jose, Calif., 1972-75; reporter Indpls. Star, Ind., 1975-78; reporter San Jose Mercury News, Calif., 1978-83, editoral writer, 1983-86, political editor, 1986—. Co-author: Movers & Shakers: The Study of Community Power, 1981. Creator, writer SPJ Gridiron Show, San Jose, 1981-91. Pulliam fellow, 1975, Duke U., 1991, J.S. Knight Stanford U., 1993-94. Mem. Soc. Profl. Journalist (mem. nat. ethics com. 1993—). Jewish. Home: 960 Asbury St San Jose CA 95126-1805 Office: San Jose Mercury News 750 Ridder Park Dr San Jose CA 95131-2432

TROUSDALE, STEPHEN RICHARD, newspaper editor; b. L.A., May 29, 1963; s. Richard Gardner Trousdale and Geraldine Barbara Wisdom. AB, Stanford U., 1985. News editor L.A. Daily Commerce, 1986-87; edit. page editor L.A. Daily Jour., 1987-89, mng. editor, 1989—. Mem. Soc. Profl. Journalists, Calif. Soc. Newspaper Editors, Soc. Newspaper Design. Home: 10933 Huston St Apt 203 North Hollywood CA 91601-5135 Office: LA Daily Jour 915 E 1st St Los Angeles CA 90012-4050

TROUTWINE, GAYLE LEONE, lawyer; b. Kansas City, Mo., Feb. 26, 1952. BS, N.W. Mo. State U., 1973; JD with honors, U. Mo., 1978. Bar: Mo. 1978, Oreg. 1983, U.S. Dist. Ct. (we. dist.) Mo., Wash. 1984, U.S. Ct. Appeals (9th cir.), U.S. Dist. Ct. (we. dist.) Wash., U.S. Supreme Ct., Hawaii 1995. Ptnr. Williams & Troutwine, P.C., Portland, Oreg., 1986—; speaker in field. Contbr. articles to profl. jours. Steering com. mem. Breast Implant Litigation, 1992—, Tobacco Litigation; bd. mem. Portland Area Women's Polit. Caucus, 1992—; mem. Jud. Steering com., 1994. Mem. Assn. Trial Lawyers Am. (bd. govs.), Mo. Bar, Oreg. State Bar (exec. bd. litigation sect. 1984—, chmn. 1987-88, procedure and practice com. 1985-88, bd. govs. 1990-93), Wash. State Bar, Oreg. Trial Lawyers Assn. (bd. govs. 1987-91), Calif. Trial Lawyers Assn., Hawaii Trial Lawyers Assn., Wash. Trial Lawyers Assn., Women Lawyers Assn., Greater Kansas City (sec. 1981-82), Western Trial Lawyers Assn. (bd. govs. 1992—). Democrat. Office: Williams and Troutwine PC 1900 Security Pacific Plz 1001 SW 5th Ave Ste 1900 Portland OR 97204-1135

TROVER, ELLEN LLOYD, lawyer; b. Richmond, Va., Nov. 23, 1947; d. Robert Van Buren and Hazel (Urban) Lloyd; m. Denis William Trover, June 12, 1971; 1 dau., Florence Emma. AB, Vassar Coll., 1969; JD, Coll. William and Mary, 1972. Asst. editor Bancroft-Whitney, San Francisco, 1973-74; owner Ellen Lloyd Trover Atty.-at-Law, Thousand Oaks, Calif., 1974-82; ptnr. Trover & Fisher, Thousand Oaks, 1982-89; pvt. practice law, Thousand Oaks, 1989—. Editor: Handbooks of State Chronologies, 1972. Trustee, Conejo Future Found., Thousand Oaks, 1978-91, trustee emeritus, 1992—, vice chmn., 1982-84, chmn., 1984-88; pres. Zonta Club Conejo Valley Area, 1978-79; trustee Hydro Help for the Handicapped, 1980-85, Atlantis Found., 1994—. Mem. State Bar Calif., Va. State Bar, World Affairs Coun., Phi Alpha Delta. Democrat. Presbyterian. Home: 11355 Presilla Rd Camarillo CA 93012-9230 Office: 1107E E Thousand Oaks Blvd Thousand Oaks CA 91362-2816

TROWBRIDGE, DALE BRIAN, educator; b. Glendale, Calif., May 17, 1940; s. Dale Beverly and Alison Amelia (Goldsborough) T.; m. Helen Elaine Turner, July 2, 1966; children: Katelin Elizabeth, David Brian. BA, Whittier Coll., 1961; MS, U. Calif., Berkeley, 1964, PhD, 1970. Chemist Aerojet Gen., Azusa, Calif., 1961-62; chemistry tchr. Berkeley (Calif.) High Sch., 1964-66; prof., chemistry dept. chmn. Sonoma State U., Rohnert Park, Calif., 1969—; vis. prof. chemistry U. Calif., Berkeley, 1970-74, 88. Contbr. articles to profl. jours. Mem. Am. Chem. Soc., AAAS, Internat. Platform Assn., Sigma Xi. Home: 6039 Elsa Ave Rohnert Park CA 94928-2246 Office: Sonoma State U 1801 E Cotati Ave Rohnert Park CA 94928-3613

TROWBRIDGE, THOMAS, JR., mortgage banking company executive; b. Troy, N.Y., June 28, 1938; s. of Thomas and Elberta (Wood) T.; m. Delinda Bryan, July 3, 1965; children: Elisabeth Tacy, Wendy Bryan. BA, Yale U., 1960; MBA, Harvard U., 1965. V.p. James W. Rouse & Co., Balt., 1965-66, Washington, 1966-68, San Francisco, 1968-73, 76-78; pres. Rouse Investing Co., Columbia, Md., 1973-76, Trowbridge, Kieselhorst & Co., San Francisco, 1978—. Bd. dirs. Columbia Assn., 1975-76; trustee, treas. The Head-Royce Sch., Oakland, Calif., 1980-84; trustee, pres. Gen. Alumni Assn. Phillips Exeter Acad., 1984-90. Lt. USNR, 1960-63. Mem. Urban Land Inst., Calif. Mortgage Bankers Assn. (bd. dirs. 1991—), Mortgage Bankers Assn. Am. (bd. govs. 1993—), Olympic Club, Pacific Union Club, Lambda Alpha Internat. Republican. Presbyterian. Home: 4 Ridge Ln Orinda CA 94563-1318 Office: Trowbridge Kieselhorst & Co 555 California St Ste 2850 San Francisco CA 94104-1604

TROXEL, JOHN MILTON, physician; b. Missoula, Mont., Jan. 14, 1960; s. George Owen and Christina M. (Long) T.; m. Sarah C. Burrell, Jan. 14, 1989. BS, Stanford (Calif.) U., 1982, MD, 1986. Intern in surgery U. Calif., San Francisco, 1986-87; resident in otolaryngology Stanford Med. Ctr., 1987-90, chief resident in otolaryngology, 1990-91, resident plastic surgery, 1991-92; chief resident plastic surgery, 1993-94. Mem. AMA, N.Y. Acad. Scis., Alaska Med. Assn. Office: 950 Bogard Rd Ste 203 Wasilla AK 99654-7172

TROXELL, LUCY DAVIS, consulting firm executive; b. Cambridge, Mass., Apr. 25, 1932; d. Ellsworth and Mildred (Enneking) Davis; m. Charles DeGroat Bader, June 13, 1952 (div. Aug. 1974); children: Christie P. Walker, Mary Ellsworth Bader, Charles D. Bader Jr., Davis Bradford Bader; m. Victor Daniel Shirer Troxell, Aug. 1974. BA, Smith Coll., Northampton, Mass., 1952. Cert. paralegal, employee benefit specialist, assoc. in risk mgmt. Paralegal O'Melveny & Myers, L.A., 1976-77; account exec. Olanie Hurst & Hemrich, L.A., 1977-78; asst. to trustee Oxford Ins. Mgmt., L.A., 1978-80; dir. corp. svcs., asst. corp. sec. Consolidated Elec. Distbrs., Inc., Westlake Village, Calif., 1980-93; pres. MONMAK LDT, Westlake Village, 1993—. Sustaining mem., bd. dirs. Jr. League, Hartford, Conn., L.A., 1952—; clk. St. Mathew's Parish Vestry, Pacific Palisades, Calif., 1988, sr. warden, 1989-90; bd. dirs. Smith Coll. Club, Hartford, L.A., 1952—, Nat. Charity League, L.A., 1964-68; lic. lay eucharistic minister Episcopal Ch. Sophia Smith scholar. Fellow Internat. Soc. Cert. Employee Benefit Specialists (charter mem., bd. dirs., sec., treas. 1988-89, pres. 1989-90, edn. chmn. 1986-88 L.A. chpt.), Risk and Ins. Mgmt. Soc. (program chmn. L.A. chpt. 1985-86), Theatre Palisades (bd. dirs. 1960-74). Republican. Home: 450 Puerto Del Mar Pacific Palisades CA 90272-4233 Office: MONMAK LDT 31220 La Baya Dr # 319 Westlake Village CA 91362-4008

TROXELL-GURKA, MARY THERESA (TERRY TROXELL-GURKA), geriatrics services professional; b. Syracuse, N.Y., Aug. 29, 1950; d. Henry and Mary (McDermott) Flynn; m. Richard Gurka, Apr. 2, 1994; 1 child, Melissa Lee. BSN, U. Pa., 1971. Cert. quality improvement specialist; cert. gerontol. nurse specialist; cert. case mgr. Supr. neonatal ICU St. Joe's, Syracuse, 1976-79; dir. nursing Hillhaven, Phoenix, 1979-81; quality assurance nurse long term care Maricopa County, Phoenix, 1981-83; dir. nursing Desert Haven Nursing Home, Phoenix, 1983-84; team leader, surveyor health care licensure State of Ariz., Phoenix, 1985-87, program mgr. long term care licensure and certification, 1987-89, program mgr. enforcement and compliance licensure and cert., 1989-91; dir. profl. svcs. SunQuest Healthcare, Phoenix, 1991-94, v.p. clin. ops., 1994—. Author: (manuals) Licensure Procedures, 1990, Quality Improvement, Restorative Nursing: A Key to Quality, 1992, Director of Nursing Manual, 1993. Developer legislation for adult care homes, health care licensure laws State of Ariz., 1990. Mem. Ariz. Health Care Assn. (chair legis. com. 1992-94, chair devel./revision nursing facility laws 1992-94), Am. Health Care Assn. (nat. facility stds. com. 1992-95, nat. multifacility com. 1993-95, LTC nurses coun. 1995), Quality Improvement Nurses Assn., Gerontol. Nurses Assn. Home: 3608 E Woodland Dr Phoenix AZ 85044-7330 Office: Sunquest Health Care 7272 E Indian School Rd Ste 214 Scottsdale AZ 85251-3948

TRUAX, DONALD ROBERT, mathematics educator; b. Mpls., Aug. 29, 1927; s. William Raymond and Hermina Wilhelmina (Sobolick) T.; m. Barbara June Eckton, Sept. 16, 1950; children: Mary, Catherine, Patricia, Gail. BS in Math., U. Wash., 1951, MS in Math., 1953; PhD in Statistics, Stanford U., 1955. Rsch. fellow Calif. Inst. Tech., Pasadena, 1955-56; asst. prof. math. U. Kans., Lawrence, 1956-59, U. Oreg., Eugene, 1959-62; assoc. prof. math. U. Oreg., 1962-69, prof. math., 1969—. Mng. editor Inst. Math. Statistics, 1975-81; contbr. articles to profl. jours. With USN, 1945-47. Fellow Inst. Math. Statistics; mem. Am. Statis. Assn. Home: 2323 University St Eugene OR 97403-1547 Office: University of Oregon Dept Of Mathematics Eugene OR 97403

TRUBNER, HENRY, museum curator; b. Munich, Ger., June 10, 1920; s. Jorg and Gertrude T.; m. Ruth Trubner, July 10, 1948; children: Susan, Karen. BA, Harvard U., 1942, MA, 1944; postgrad., Fogg Art Mus., 1942-47. Curator Oriental art L.A. County Mus. Art, 1947-58; curator Far Eastern dept. Royal Ont. Mus., Toronto, 1958-68; curator Asian art Seattle Art Mus., 1968-87, assoc. dir. and curator Asian Art, 1976-87, sr. curator emeritus, 1987—; dir. Son of Heaven Exhbn. Imperial Arts of China, Seattle, 1988; mem. art adv. com. The Asia Soc., Japan Soc. Gallery, China Inst. in Am., Inc.; mem. Am. adv. com. The Japan Found., Tokyo, 1978-80. Contbr. articles to profl. jours. Recipient Fujio Koyama Meml. prize, Idemitsu Mus. Art, Tokyo, 1988. Mem. Am. Assn. Mus., Oriental Ceramic Soc. London, The Asia Soc. N.Y., The Japan Soc. N.Y., China Inst. in Am., Acad. Laquer Rsch. Tokyo, Soc. for Japanese Arts. Home: 9341 Vineyard Cres Bellevue WA 98004-4028

TRUCKER, ALBERT, plastic surgeon; b. St. Joseph, Mich., Aug. 5, 1924; s. Albert and Louise (Goebel) T. BA, Johns Hopkins U., 1951; MD, U. Md., 1956. Diplomate Am. Bd. Plastic Surgery. Intern in gen. surgery U. Calif., San Francisco, 1956-59; resident in plastic surgery Mayo Clinic, Rochester, Minn., 1959-62; pvt. practice Santa Rosa, Calif., 1962—. Mem. Am. Soc. Plastic Surgery, Calif. Soc. Plastic Surgery. Office: 200 Montgomery Dr Santa Rosa CA 95404-6633

TRUDEL, JOHN DAVIS, management consultant; b. Trenton, N.J., Aug. 1, 1942; s. Leroy and Elizabeth (Reading) T. BEE cum laude, Ga. Inst. Tech., 1964; MSEE, Kans. State U., 1966. Cert. profl. cons.; cert. mgmt. cons. Engr. Collins Radio, Richardson, Tex., 1966-67, sr. engr., 1969-70; sr. engr. Sanders Assoc., Nashua, N.H., 1967-68, LTV E-Systems, Inc., Greenville, Tex., 1968-69, F&M Systems, Inc., Dallas, 1970; pres. Sci. System Tech., Inc., Dallas, 1970-74; mgr. mktg. Tektronix, Inc., Beaverton, Oreg., 1974-83, mgr. bus. devel., 1983-89; v.p. mktg. Cable Bus. Systems Corp., Beaverton, 1981-83; owner, mng. dir. The Trudel Group, Scappoose, Oreg., 1988—; v.p. TCI, Portland, Oreg., 1992-94; adj. prof. Oreg. Grad. Inst., 1994. Author: (software) MAGIC CAE, (book) High Tech with Low Risk, 1990; writer regular columns for Upside and Electronic Design mags.; inventor Waveform Storage, 1984. Aviation com. mem., OMSI, Portland, 1986-87. Mem. Am. Mgmt. Assn., Inst. Mgmt. Cons., Acad. Profl. Cons. and Advisors, Am. Electronics Assn., Nat. Avionics Soc., IEEE, Product Devel. and Mgmt. Assn., Assn. Old Crows, Aircraft Owners and Pilots Assn. Office: The Trudel Group 33470 SW Chinook Plz Scappoose OR 97056-3726

TRUE, LELAND BEYER, civil engineer, consultant; b. Cheyenne, Wyo., Aug. 20, 1921; s. James Beaman and Mary Laura (Beyer) T.; m. Janet R. Hill (dec. Aug. 1976); 1 child, Patricia Ann; m. Alef Collins, May 8, 1977. BSCE, U. Wyo., 1943. Hydrographic field asst. U.S. Geol. Survey, Cheyenne and Laramie, Wyo., 1942-43; engr. P.1 Boysen Dam U.S. Bur. Reclamation, Thermopolis, Wyo., 1946-52; with Morrison-Knudsen Co., Inc., 1952-70, 77-86; project mgr. Greer's Ferry Dam Morrison-Knudsen Co., Inc., Heber Springs, Ark., 1961-63; project mgr. Blue Ridge Dam Morrison-Knudsen Co., Inc., Payson, Ariz., 1963-65; project mgr., estimator home office Morrison-Knudsen Co., Inc., Boise, Idaho, 1965-69; project mgr. Toa Vaca Dam Morrison-Knudsen Co., Inc., Villalba, P.R., 1969-70; resident area engr. metro subway A.A. Mathews, Inc., Washington, 1970-77; asst. chief engr. Morrison-Knudsen Co., Inc., Boise, 1977-86; pvt. practice constrn. cons. Boise, 1986—. Staff sgt. U.S. Army Corps Engrs., 1943-46. Mem. ASCE (life). Home and Office: 1143 Santa Maria Dr Boise ID 83712-6526

TRUE, VIRGIL, retired government official, consultant; b. Richview, Ill., July 21, 1925; s.Robert Thurman and Beulah Hazel (Wilson) T.; m. Ruth Louise Hotle, Oct. 7, 1949; children: Kenneth Allen, Virgil David. BSEE, Washington U., St. Louis, 1950. Electronic scientist Naval Rsch. Lab., Washington, 1950-54; supervisory electronic scientist Naval Rsch. Lab., Port Huenene, Calif., 1954-58; br. head Navy Missile Test Ctr., Point Mugu, Calif., 1958-61; sta. dir. Navy Missile Range, Kauai, Hawaii, 1961-65; sta. dir. NASA Network, Kauai, 1965-78, White Sands, N.Mex., 1978-89; cons. NASA, Las Cruces, N.Mex., 1990—. Chmn. Kauai Econ. Devel. Com., 1974-76. With USMCR, 1943-46, PTO. Recipient Exceptional Svc. medal NASA, 1984, 89. Home: 701 Frank Maes Ave Las Cruces NM 88005-1230 Office: NASA Sta Facility PO Drawer GSC Las Cruces NM 88004

TRUEBLOOD, PAUL GRAHAM, retired English educator, author, editor; b. Macksburg, Iowa, Oct. 21, 1905; s. Charles E. and Adele (Graham) T.; m. Helen Churchill, Aug. 19, 1931; children—Anne Williams, Susan Stuart. BA, Willamette U., 1928; MA, Duke U., 1930, Ph.D., 1935; Litt.D. (hon.), Willamette U., 1984. Instr. Friends U., 1931-34; English master Mohonk Sch. Boys, Lake Mohonk, N.Y., 1935-37; instr. U. Idaho, 1937-40; asso. prof. Stockton Coll., 1940-46; asst. prof. U. Wash., 1947-52; vis. prof. U. Oreg., 1954-55; prof. English, head dept. Willamette U., 1955-70, prof. emeritus, 1971—; vis. lectr. U. B.C., summer 1963. Author: The Flowering of Byron's Genius, 2d edit, 1962, Lord Byron, 2d edit, 1977; Editor: Byron's Political and Cultural Influence in Nineteenth-Century Europe: A Symposium, 1981; Contbr. to charter issues Keats-Shelley Jour, 1952, Byron Jour, 1973. Pendle Hill fellow, 1934-35; fellow Am. Council Learned Socs., 1952-53; recipient Disting. Alumni citation Willamette U., 1975. Mem. MLA, Keats-Shelley Assn. Am., Philol. Assn. Pacific Coast (exec. com. 1964-65), Byron Soc. (founding mem. Am. com. 1973, bd. dirs. 1975, delivered lecture to Byron Soc. in Ho. of Lords 1975). Home: Capitol Manor 1955 Dallas Hwy NW Apt 903 Salem OR 97304-4496

TRUETT, HAROLD JOSEPH, III (TIM TRUETT), lawyer; b. Alameda, Calif., Feb. 13, 1946; s. Harold Joseph and Lois Lucille (Mellin) T.; 1 child, Harold Joseph IV; m. Anna V. Billante, Oct. 1, 1983; 1 child, James S. Carstensen. BA, U. San Francisco, 1968, JD, 1975. Bar: Calif. 1975, Hawaii 1987, U.S. Dist. Ct. (ea., so., no., and cen. dists.) Calif. 1976, Hawaii 1987, U.S. Ct. Appeals (9th cir.) 1980, U.S. Supreme Ct. 1988, U.S. Ct. Fed. Claims, 1995. Assoc. Hoberg, Finger et al, San Francisco, 1975-78, Bledsoe, Smith et al, San Francisco, 1979-80, Abramson & Bianco, San Francisco, 1980-83; mem. Ingram & Truett, San Rafael, 1983-90; prin. Law Office of H.J. Tim Truett, San Francisco, 1991-93, Winchell & Truett, San Francisco, 1994—; lectr. trial practice Am. Coll. Legal Medicine, 1989, 90, Calif. Continuing Edn. of the Bar. Bd. dirs. Shining Star Found. 1991—, Marin County, Calif.; mem. Marin Dem. Coun., San Rafael, 1983-90. Lt., aviator USN, 1967-74. Mem. ABA, Hawaii Bar Assn., Assn. Trial Lawyers Am., Calif. Bar Assn. (com. for adminstrn. of justice, conf. of dels.), San Francisco Bar Assn., Calif. Trial Lawyers Assn., Lawyers Pilots Assn. Roman Catholic. Home: 2622 Leavenworth St San Francisco CA 94133-1614

TRUFFAUT, MICHELLE, film director; b. San Francisco, Nov. 17, 1942; d. Louis and Eve (Schefski) Mardecich. Student, U. Calif., Berkeley, 1964-65; MFA, Am. Film Inst., 1990. Freelance performer U.S., Eng. and France, 1965-72; pub. rels. asst. Am. Conservatory Theatre, San Francisco, 1972-74; producing and artistic dir. San Francisco Repertory Theatre, San Francisco, 1974-87; artistic dir. San Francisco Shakespeare Festival, 1986-87; freelance filmmaker, dir. L.A., 1987—; mem. adv. bd. Theatre Communications Bay Area, San Francisco, 1983-86. Dir. in field; dir., adapter (play) Animal Farm Orwell, 1984, Lulu-Wedekind, 1985 (Best Prodn. and Best Directing awards Dramalogue 1993); writer, dir. (screenplay) Ralph's Arm, 1988, Willie Won't Dance, 1992. Recipient Best Directing and Best Prodn. Achievement award Bay Area Critics Circle, 1984, 86, Outstanding Best Directing and Best Prodn. Achievement award Bay Area Critics, 1986, Best Directing award Dramalogue, 1984. Democrat. Jewish.

TRUHLAR, DORIS BROADDUS, lawyer; b. Oklahoma City, Sept. 18, 1946; d. Elbridge Sidney and Doris Mary (Prock) Broaddus; div.; children: Samara Taryle, Brett Taryle (dec.); m. Robert John Truhlar, June 234, 1978; children: Ivy, Holly. B in journalism, U. Mo., 1967; MA, U. Denver, 1976, JD, 1980. Bar: Colo. 1981, U.S. Dist. Ct. Colo. 1981, U.S. Ct. Appeals (10th cir.) 1981. Law clk. to Hon. Robert H. McWilliams, Jr. U.S. Ct. Appeals (10th cir.), Denver, 1980-81; assoc. Holme, Roberts & Owen, Denver; corp. sec., gen. counsel Hart Exploration and Prodn. Co., Englewood, Colo.; ptnr. Truhlar & Truhlar, Littleton, Colo., 1985—; adj. prof. U. Denver Coll. Law, 1986-88, 90-91, mem. adv. com. advocacy skills program, 1990; speaker Continuing Legal Edn. Programs; expert witness regarding attys. fees; bd. dirs. Colo. Foster Care Tng. Inst., 1991-93. Trainer attys. and vols. who work with abused and neglected children; active various vol. programs; mem. vestry bd. Good Shepherd Episcopal Ch., 1992—. Recipient Woman of Achievement, Entreprneur of Yr. award Met. YWCA of Denver, 1993, Denver Gridiron award, 1st pl. Editorial Writing award Nat. Edn. Writers Assn., also several Mo. Press Assn. awards and newspaper writing awards. Mem: ABA, Am. Trial Lawyers Assn., Denver Bar Assn. (Vol. Atty. of Yr. award), Colo. Bar Assn. (organizer, tchr. pro se div. clinics, ethics com. 1984-91, calling com.), Colo. Trial Lawyers Assn. (chmn. Torts Involving Children 1990), Arapahoe County Bar Assn. (Community Svc.

award, Pro Bono Atty. 1992). Office: 1901 W Littleton Blvd Littleton CO 80120-2058

TRUJILLO, LORENZO A., lawyer; b. Denver, Aug. 10, 1951; s. Filbert G. and Marie O. (Duran) T.; children: Javier Antonio, Lorenzo Feliciano. BA, U. Colo., 1972, MA, 1974, postgrad.; EdD, U. San Francisco, 1979; JD, U. Colo., 1993. Bar: Colo. 1994, U.S. Dist. Ct. Colo. 1994, U.S. Ct. Appeals (10th cir.) 1994; cert. edn. tchr., prin., supt., Colo., Calif. Exec. assoc. Inter-Am. Rsch. Assocs., Rosslyn, Va., 1980-82; exec. dir. humanities Jefferson County Pub. Schs., Golden, Colo., 1982—; pvt. practice edn. cons. Lakewood, Colo., 1992-93; gen. corp. counsel Am. Achievement Schs., Inc., Lakewood, Colo., 1994—; atty. Frie, Arndt & Trujillo Law Firm, Arvada, Colo., 1994-95, ptnr., 1995—; co-chair Mellon fellowships The Coll. Bd., N.Y.C., 1987-93; cons. U.S.I.A. Fulbright Tchr. Exch. Program, Washington, 1987-93; editorial advisor Harcourt, Brace, Jovanovich Pub., Orlando, Fla., 1988-93. Contbr. numerous articles to profl. jours. Mem. panel of arbitrators Am. Arbitration Assn., 1994. Recipient Legal Aid Clinic Acad. award Colo. Bar Assn., 1993, Pro Bono award, 1993, Loyola U. Acad. award, 1993. Mem. Colo. chpt. Am. Assn. Tchrs. of Spanish and Portuguese (pres. 1985-88), Am. Immigration Lawyers Assn., Nat. Sch. Bds. Coun. Sch. Attys., Nat. Assn. Judiciary Interpreters and Translators, Colo. Bar Assn. (family law sect., probate and trust sect.), Colo. Lawyers Com. on Sch. Discipline, Interdisciplinary Com. on Child Custody, Soc. Security Benefits Panel, U. San Francisco Alumni Assn. (founder, pres. 1987-90), Phi Delta Kappa (chair internat. edn. com. 1988-89), Phi Alpha Delta. Home: 1556 S Van Dyke Way Lakewood CO 80228-3917 Office: Frie Arndt & Trujillo Ste 201 7400 Wadsworth Blvd Arvada CO 80003

TRUJILLO, LUCY ANN, elementary education counselor; b. Trinidad, Colo., July 9, 1965; d. Robert Anthony James and Rose Helen DeCarolis; m. Michael Rafael Trujillo, June 20, 1992. BS in Elem. Edn., U. So. Colo., 1987; postgrad., Adams State Coll., 1993—. Cert. elem. tchr., Colo. Kindergarten tchr. Trinidad (Colo.) Sch. Dist. #1, 1987-94, elem. counselor, 1994—. Mem. ACA, Am. Fedn. Tchrs.

TRUMAN, EDWARD CRANE, real estate manager, consultant, composer; b. Des Moines, Dec. 28, 1915; s. Wright Edward and Annie Louise (Cate) T.; m. Maxine LeVon Hemping, June 28, 1947 (dec. Apr. 1983); 1 child, Robert E.C. Student, UCLA, 1966, 72; BA in English, Immaculate Heart Coll., 1978; MA in Psychology, U. Redlands, 1980. Asst. program dir. Cowles Broadcasting, Des Moines, 1938-44; pub. rels. writer Armed Forces Radio Svcs., Hollywood, Calif., 1944-46; staff musician Don Lee Mut. Radio, Hollywood, Calif., 1946-48, ABC-TV, Hollywood, Calif., 1948-53; music dir., composer TV series NBC-TV, Burbank, Calif., 1955-60; freelance organist, composer Hollywood, 1960—, real estate property mgr., owner, 1974—; bd. dirs. Gen. Affiliates U. Calif. Santa Barbara, chair scholarship com., 1988—; founder Artasia Seminars, L.A., 1972-75. Composer: Matinee, 1956, Broadcast Mood Music, Bowie Knife, 1958, Songs for Builders, 1960. Endowment grantor in religious studies U. Calif., Santa Barbara, 1984—, Drake U., Des Moines, 1994—. Sgt. Signal Corps, U.S. Army, 1944-46. Recipient citation Dept. Edn., 1976, commendation City Atty. Office, L.A., 1993. Mem. Nat. Acad. TV Arts and Scis. (Emory panels, music br.), Pacific Pioneer Broadcasters (bd. dirs. 1988-91, Golden Circle award 1991), Musicians Union (asst. to pres. Local 47 1966-77). Democrat. Episcopalian. Home: 1826 Jewett Dr Los Angeles CA 90046-7702 Office: Compass-Am Prodns Inc 1826 Jewett Dr Los Angeles CA 90046

TRUMBLE, ROBERT JASPER, fishery biologist; b. Whitmire, S.C., Apr. 21, 1943; s. Robert E. and Jessie (Abrams) T.; m. Cynthia Wright, Sept. 6, 1969. BS, U. Wash., 1965, MS, 1973, PhD, 1979. Oceanographer Naval Oceanographic Office, Washington, 1966-71; fishery biologist Wash. Dept. Fisheries, Seattle, 1975-86, Internat. Pacific Halibut Commn., Seattle, 1986—; mem. Herring plan team Pacific Fishery Mgmt. Coun., Portland, Oreg., 1980-82, Sci. and stats. commn., 1984-86; mem. groundfish plan team North Pacific Fishery Mgmt. Coun., Anchorage, 1986-90. Contbr. articles to profl. jours. Mem. Am. Fisheries Soc., Sigma Xi. Office: Internat Pacific Halibut Commn PO Box 95009 Seattle WA 98145-2009

TRUSSELL, R(OBERT) RHODES, environmental engineer; b. National City, Calif; s. Robert L. and Margaret (Kessing) T.; m. Elizabeth Shane, Nov. 26, 1969; children: Robert Shane, Charles Bryan. BSCE, U. Calif.-Berkeley, 1966, MS, 1967, PhD, 1972. With Montgomery Watson, Inc. (formerly J.M. Montgomery Cons. Engrs.), Pasadena, Calif., 1972—, v.p., 1977, sr. v.p., 1986, dir. applied tech., 1988-92, sr. v.p., dir. of corp. devel., 1992— Mem. com. on water treatment chems. Nat. Acad. Sci., 1980-82, mem. com. 3d part cert., 1982-83, com. on irrigation-induced water quality problems, 1985-88, Am. Water Work Commn. on mixing of water treatment chems., 1988-90; mem. U.S./German research com. on corrosion of water systems, 1984-85; mem. U.S./Dutch research com. on organics in water, 1982-83; mem. U.S./USSR rsch. com. on water treatment, 1985-88, U.S./E.C. Com. Corrosion in Water, 1992-94. Mem. joint editorial bd. Standards Methods for Examination of Water and Wastewater, 1980-89; mem. editorial adv. bd. Environ. and Sci. and Tech., 1977-83; contbr. articles to profl. publs. Mem. AIChE, NAE, Water Works Assn. (mem. editorial adv. bd. jour. 1987-94, EPA sci. adv. bd. com. on drinking water 1988-91, 94—, cons. radon disinfectant by products 1993, cons. on disinfecate and disinfection 1994), Internat. Water Supply Assn. (U.S. rep. to standing com. on water quality and treatment 1990-94, chmn. com. on disinfection and mem. tech. exec. com. 1994—), Water Pollution Control Fedn., Internat. Water Pollution Rsch. Assn., Am. Chem. Soc., Nat. Assn. Corrosion Engrs., Sigma Xi.

TRUTA, MARIANNE PATRICIA, oral and maxillofacial surgeon, educator, author; b. N.Y.C., Apr. 28, 1951; d. John J. and Helen Patricia (Donnelly) T.; m. William Christopher Donlon, May 28, 1983; 1 child Sean Liam Riobard Donlon. BS, St. John's U., 1974; DMD, SUNY, Stonybrook, 1977. Intern The Mt. Sinai Med. Ctr., N.Y.C., 1977-78, resident, 1978-80, chief resident, 1980-81; asst. prof. U. of the Pacific, San Francisco, 1983-85, clin. asst. prof., 1985—; asst. dir. Facial Pain Rsch. Ctr., San Francisco, 1986-92; pvt. practice oral and maxillofacial surgery Peninsula Maxillofacial Surgery, South San Francisco, Calif., 1985—, Burlingame, Calif., 1988—, Redwood City, Calif., 1990-95, San Carlos, Calif., 1995—. Contbr. articles to profl. jours., chpts. to textbooks. Mem. Am. Assn. Oral Maxillofacial Surgeons, Am. Dental Soc. Anesthesiology, Am. Soc. Cosmetic Surgery, Am. Assn. Women Dentists, Western Soc. Oral Maxillofacial Surgeons, No. Calif. Soc. Oral Maxillofacial Surgeons, San Mateo County Dental Soc. (bd. dirs. 1995). Office: Peninsula Maxillofacial Surgery 1860 El Camino Real Ste 300 Burlingame CA 94010-3114

TRYBUS, RAYMOND J., higher education executive, psychologist; b. Chgo., Jan. 9, 1944; s. Fred and Cecilia (Liszka) T.; m. Sandra A. Noone, Aug. 19, 1967; children: David, Nicole. BS, St. Louis U., 1965, MS, 1970, PhD, 1971. Lic. psychologist, Md., D.C., Calif. Clin. psychologist Jewish Vocat. Svc., St. Louis, 1968-71; clin. psychologist Gallaudet U., Washington, 1971-72, rsch. psychologist, 1972-74, dir. demographic studies, 1974-78, dean grad. studies and rsch., 1978-88; provost, prof. psychology Calif. Sch. of Profl. Psychology, 1988—, chancellor, 1992—; dir. Rehab. Rsch. and Tng. Ctr., 1994—; mem. Sci. Rev. Bd. Dept. Vets. Affairs Rehab. Rsch. and Devel. Program, 1991—; cons. Mental Health Ctr. for Deaf, Lanham, Md., 1982-88, Congl. Rsch. Svc., 1982-84, McGill U. Nat. Study Hearing Impairment in Can., 1984-88. Contbg. author: The Future of Mental Health Services for the Deaf, 1978, Hearing-impaired Children and Youth with Devel. Disabilities, 1985; editor Jour. Am. Deafness and Rehab. Assn., 1988-91. Grantee NIMH, Nat. Inst. Disability and Rehab. Rsch., Spencer Found., Tex. Edn. Agy., W.K. Kellogg Found. Mem. APA, Am. Assn. Univ. Adminstrs., Calif. Psychol. Assn. (pres. div. edn. and tng. 1990-92), San Diego Psychol. Assn., Am. Coun. Edn., Am. Deafness and Rehab. Assn., Am. Assn. Higher Edn., Am. Psychol. Soc. Roman Catholic. Home: 6342 Cibola Rd San Diego CA 92120-2124 Office: 6212 Ferris Sq San Diego CA 92121-3250

TRYTHALL, ROBERT C., athletic director; b. Salt Lake City, Apr. 8, 1951; s. Francis Turner Trythall and Inez Christensen; m. Debra Lynn Nessen, Apr. 19, 1974; children: Tom, Jim, Valerie, Blake. BS, Brigham Young U., 1975, MA, 1977. Park supr. Ingelwood (Calif.) Park & Recreation, 1966-69; intramural GTA Brigham Young U. Intramurals, Provo, UT, 1972-77; dir. activity ctr. Snow Coll., Ephraim, UT, 1977—, physical edn. divsn. chmn., 1981—, athletic dir., 1990—; city recreation dir. Ephraim City, UT, 1980—. Tchr. of Yr. Snow Coll., 1983. Home: 305 N 550 E 23-6 Ephraim UT 84627 Office: Intermountain Collegiate Athletic Snow College 150 College Ave Ephraim UT 84627

TRZYNA, THOMAS NICHOLAS, college dean; b. Evanston, Ill., Nov. 30, 1946; s. Thaddeus and Irene (Giese) T.; m. Martha Hannah Deutsch, Sept. 13, 1969; children: Alexander, Margaret. BA, U. Calif., Berkeley, 1968; PhD, U. Wash., 1977. Asst. prof. Ohio State U., Columbus, 1978-80; from asst. prof. to prof. Seattle Pacific U., 1980—, dean Sch. Humanities, 1987-94, dean Coll of Arts and Sci, 1994—; editor Aquaseed Press, Seattle, 1989—, Calif. Inst. Pub. Affairs, Claremont, 1979. Author: Writing for Technical Professionals, 1987, also poems and textbooks in field; contbr. articles to profl. publs. Episcopalian. Office: Seattle Pacific U 3307 3rd Ave W Seattle WA 98119-1940

TSAI, MICHAEL MING-PING, psychiatrist; b. Chiayi, Taiwan, Mar. 28, 1939; came to U.S., 1966; s. Yang-Ming and Hsien (Wang) T.; m. Pi-Zu Tsai, Apr. 27, 1968; 1 child, Patricia. MD, Kaohsiung Med. Coll., Taiwan, 1965. Diplomate Am. Bd. Psychiatry and Neurology. Intern Meth. Hosp., Bklyn., 1966-67; resident in psychiatry Phila. State Hosp., Phila., 1968-69, VA Hosp., N.Y.C., 1969-71; fellow in child & adolescent psychiatry Hillside Hosp., Glen Oaks, N.Y., 1971-72; clin. psychiatrist N.J. Neuro-psychiatric Inst., Princeton, 1972-75; staff psychiatrist Met. State Hosp., Norwalk, Calif., 1978—. Office: 1878 Calle La Paz Rowland Heights CA 91748

TSAKIRIS, THEODORA LYDIA, mathematics educator; b. Chgo., Jan. 14, 1926; d. George Theodore and Angeline (Sellas) Tselos; m. Paul Louis Tsakiris, DEc. 26, 1949; children; Lee, Dimitri, Philip. M in Secondary Edn., Ariz. State U., 1947. Instr. Gate Way C.C., Phoenix, 1975—. Auditor Ladis Soc., Phoenix, 1973-93. Mem. Am. Math. Assn., Nat. Devel. Edn., S.W. Devel. Edn., Tchrs. of Maths. of 2 Yr. Coll. Democrat. Greek Orthodox. Office: Gate Way CC 108 N 40th St Phoenix AZ 85034-1704

TSCHACHER, DARELL RAY, mortgage banking executive; b. Wendell, Idaho, Oct. 17, 1945; s. Lewis Edward and Erma Irene (Parmely) T.; m. Judith Allyn Evers, Dec. 30, 1966; children: Kendall Ray, Kristin Allyn. Grad. high sch. Cert. bus. counselor; lic. real estate broker, Calif., Idaho. Ptnr. KD Air Svc., Apple Valley, Calif., 1967-68; real estate broker Calif., 1968-73; v.p., dir. mktg. Chism Homes, Inc., Las Vegas, Nev., 1973-78; self-employed real estate, fin., bus. cons., 1978-87; reg. v.p. br. ops. Nat. First Mortgage Co., 1987-88; sr. v.p., western reg. mgr. Nat. First Mortgage Co., Rancho Cordova, Calif., 1988-91; v.p., div. mgr. Ryland Mortgage Co., Rancho Cordova, 1991-94; v.p., regional mgr. Ryland Mortgage Co., Woodland Hills, Calif.; pres. Premier Escrow Co., Woodland Hills, Calif. Bd. dirs. Tomorrow's Hope, Boise, Idaho, 1985; exec. com. MDA of No. Calif., Sacramento, 1991. With USAF, 1963-67. Mem. Homebuilders of S.W. Idaho (bd. dirs. 1976-78), Idaho Home Owners Warranty Coun. (bd. dirs. 1977), Treasure Valley Exchangors (bd. dirs. 1980-84, Exchangor of the Yr. 1982), Soc. Exchange Counselors. Republican. Home: 3123 E Hillcrest Dr Thousand Oaks CA 91362

TSCHANG, TAI-PO, pathologist; b. Taipei, Taiwan, Republic of China, Feb. 14, 1947; came to U.S., 1965; s. Hsi-Lin and Ping (Ching) T.; m. Pui-Suen Wong (dec. 1984); children: Chi-Chu, Chi-Young, Chi-Jia; m. Grace C. Huang. BA, So. Ill. U., 1969; MD, Duke U., 1972. Diplomate Am. Bd. Anatomic and Clin. Pathology. Pathologist St. Elizabeth Hosp., Beaumont, Tex., 1977-86; dir. pathology St. Agnes Med. Ctr., Fresno, Calif., 1986—. Contbr. articles to profl. jours. Fellow Coll. Am. Pathologists, Am. Soc. Clin. Pathology; mem. Am. Assn. Blood Banks. Office: St Agnes Med Ctr 1303 E Herndon Ave Fresno CA 93720-3309

TSCHERNISCH, SERGEI P., academic administrator. BA, San Francisco State U.; MFA in Theatre, Stanford U.; student, San Francisco Actors' Workshop, Stanford Repertory Theatre. Founding mem. Calif. Inst. of Arts, 1969, mem. faculty, assoc. dean Sch. Theatre, dir., 1969-80; prof. dept. theatre U. Md., College Park, 1980-82; dir. divsn. performing and visual arts Northeastern U., Boston, 1982-92; dean Coll. of Comm. and Fine Arts Loyola Marymount U., L.A., 1992-94; pres. Cornish Coll. of Arts, Seattle, 1994—; advisor NEA; mem. com. USIA; cons. to many festivals. Office: Cornish Coll of Arts 710 East Roy Seattle WA 98102*

TSENG, FELIX HING-FAI, accountant; b. Kowloon, Hong Kong, May 11, 1964; s. Hin-Pei and Selena Suk-Ching (Young) T.; m. Rachel Wai-Chu Woo, Feb. 16, 1992; children: Walter Fan-Kong, Riley Fan-Wei. BS, Pepperdine U., 1985, MBA, 1989. CPA. Acct. Ronald A. Stein CPA, Woodland Hills, Calif., 1989—; contr. Benebase Investment Inc., Monterey Park, Calif., 1991—; also bd. dirs. Benebase Investment Inc., Monterey Park, Calif., Hong Kong; bd. dirs. YTT Corp., Monterey Park. Editor (newsletter) El Toro, 1993—. Mem. AICPA, Inst. Mgmt. Accts. (v.p. comm. 1994-95, pres. 1995—), Calif. Soc. CPA, So. Calif. Soc. CMAs, Assn. MBA Execs. Office: Benebase Investments Inc 108 N Ynez Ave Ste 209 Monterey Park CA 91754-1680

TSINIGINE, ALLEN, educator; b. Tuba City, Ariz., Feb. 25, 1952; s. Claw and Desbah (Martin) T.; 1 child, Ryan Allen. BS in Elem. Edn., No. Ariz. U., 1974. Cert. tchr., Ariz. Tchr. Page (Ariz.) Unified Sch. Dist. # 8, 1974-85; instr., curriculum coord. LeChee Vocat. Edn. Program, Page, 1987-93; instr. Coconino County C.C., Page, 1992—. Mem. gov. bd. dirs. Page Unified Sch. dist. # 8, 1987-93, pres., 1988-90, 91-92, clk., 1990-91, 92-93; sec.-treas. LeChee chpt. Navajo Nation, 1979-87; mem. Navajo Way, Inc., Window Rock, Ariz., 1987-92. Mem. Nat. Sch. Bds. Assn., Nat. Ind. Edn. Assn. (pres. elect), Ariz. Sch. Bds. Assn., Navajo Nation Pub. Sch. Bds. Assn. Home: PO Box 292 Page AZ 86040-0292

TSIROS, JOHN ANDREAS, accountant; b. Boston, Oct. 2, 1963; s. Constantine Louis and Martha Sophia (Pappas) T. BA, Boston U., 1985; MBA, U. So. Calif., 1990. CPA, Calif. Acct. Golden/Goldberg Acctg. Corp., L.A., 1990-94, Kellogg & Anderson Acctg. Corp., Sherman Oaks, Calif., 1994—. Greek Orthodox. Office: Kellogg & Anderson Acctg Corp 14724 Ventura Blvd Sherman Oaks CA 91304

TSU, VIVIEN DAVIS, epidemiologist, educator; b. Havre de Grace, Md., Dec. 1, 1947. BA with honors, Wellesley Coll., 1969; MA, U. Calif., Berkeley, 1971; MPH, UCLA, 1977; PhD, U. Wash., 1991. Rsch. asst. Internat. Agy. for Rsch. on Cancer, Nairobi, Kenya, 1972-73, Stanford (Calif.) U., 1974-76; healthcare cons. Calif. and Wash., 1978-83; program officer PATH, Seattle, 1984-86, dep. dir., 1986-89, sr. program officer, 1989-90, dir., 1992—, v.p., 1994—; affiliate asst. prof. dept. epidemiology U. Wash., Seattle, 1991—. Author monograph; contbr. articles to profl. jours. Mem. citizens adv. group City Health Dept. Family Planning Program, Seattle, 1982-85. Spl. Career fellow U. Calif. Berkeley, 1969-71; Fulbright fellow, 1989-90. Mem. APHA, NOW (bd. dirs. 1977-81). Home: 2532 11th Ave W Seattle WA 98119-2505 Office: PATH 4 Nickerson St Seattle WA 98109-1651

TSUKIJI, RICHARD ISAO, international marketing and financial services consultant; b. Salt Lake City, Jan. 31, 1946; s. Isamu and Mitsuie (Hayashi) T.; children: Angela Jo, Richard Michael. Grad. Sacramento City Coll., 1966; AA, U. Pacific, McGeorge Sch. Law, 1970-72. Grocery mgr. Food Mart, Inc., Sacramento, 1963-65; agy. supr. Takehara Ins. Agy., Sacramento, 1965-68; sales rep. Kraft Foods Co., Sacramento, 1969-71; sales mgr. Olivetti Corp., Sacramento, 1972-73; co-founder Mktg. Devel. and Mgmt. Coll., Sacramento, 1973, pres., 1973-74; pres. Richard Tsukiji Corp., Sacramento, 1974-77; chief exec. officer, chmn. bd. Assocs. Investment Group, Sacramento, 1978-82 ; chmn. bd. RichColor Corp. Sacramento, 1978-83, E.J. Sub Factories, Inc., Elk Grove, Calif., 1978-81; gen. agt. Comml. Bankers Life Ins. Co., 1974-82; chmn. bd. Phoenix Industries, Inc., Carson City, Nev., 1981-84, Databank, Inc., Roseburg, Oreg., 1982-83; pres. Computers, Etc. Corp., Carson City, 1982-84; regional v.p. U.S. BankCard Group, Salem, Oreg., 1993-95; pres. Richard Tsukiji Comm., Inc., Sacramento, 1993—; bd. dirs. Michton, Inc., Pontiac, Mich., Hunt & Johnson, Inc., Phoenix Group, Melbourne, A.N.D. Corp., New Orleans, ET World Travel, Salt Lake City, Utah, Bonaventure Group, Inc., Wilmington, Del., Royal Am. Bank, Cayman Islands; exec. v.p. Edco Corp., Glide, Oreg., 1982—; chmn. bd. Computer Edn. Resource Ctr., 1983-90, Bonaventure, Inc., Roseburg, 1984-91; editor ST World, Melrose, Oreg., 1985-88, publisher, 1988-91; editor ST World Reseller, 1988-91. Mem. Yolo County Oral Rev. Bd., 1975-76; bd. dirs. Valley Area Constrn. Opportunity Program, 1972-76, chmn., 1976-77; bd. dirs. Douglas County Citizens Community Involvement, 1980-82; bd. dirs. Computer Edn. Found., Sacramento, 1983-93, Access Sacramento Cable Television, 1993, Heart to Heart Found., 1993; chmn. pub. rels. Sacramento Asian Pacific C. of C., 1993—; bd. dirs. Chinese Am. Coun. Sacramento, 1994—; mem. Asian Cmty. Ctr., 1994—, Sacramento Chinese Cmty. Svc. Ctr., 1994—; bd. dirs. ARC Sacramento-Sierra chpt., 1995—, No. Calif. Asian Peace Officers Assn., 1995—, Sacramento Chinese Cmty. Svc. Ctr., 1995—, Japanese Am. Citizens League, 1995—; democratic precinct committeeman, Melrose, Oreg., 1982-86. Served with U.S. Army, 1962-63. Recipient Commendation, Calif. Senate, 1978. Mem. Internat. Assn. Fin. Planners, Associated Gen. Contractors, VIC-20 Users Group (pres. Roseburg 1983-84), Atari Computer Enthusiasts (pres. Sacramento 1983-85), U.S. Commodore Council (pres. Natl. 1984-85), Sacramento Jaycees (dir. 1977-78), Asian Alliance, Japanese Am. Citizens League, Sacramento Urban League. Democrat. Roman Catholic. Office: 9 Heathfield Rd Unit #1, Coolum Beach 4573, Queensland Australia also: 1530-16th St Sacramento CA 95814

TSUO, ANNE LI, database specialist; b. Taipei, Taiwan, Republic of China, June 5, 1950; d. Bing-Ching Benn and Chong-Jye (Liang) Lee; m. Yuan-Huai Simon Tsuo, Apr. 7, 1974; children: Lee Kirjohn, Leo Kirtie. M in Computer Info. Sci., U. Denver, 1989; postgrad., NYU. Therapeutic dietitian Coney Island Hosp., Bklyn., 1974-75; dietitian Carlton Nursing Home, Bklyn., 1975-76; therapeutic dietitian Flatbush Gen. Hosp., Bklyn., 1976-78; clin. dietitian Johnston-Willis Hosp., Richmond, Va., 1978-79, Mercy Med. Ctr., Denver, 1982-87; cons. nutritionist ALT Nutrition Cons. Svc., Golden, Colo., 1982—; data analyst Colo. Found. for Med. Care, Denver, 1989-90, tech. program coord., 1990-92; database specialist Nat. Renewable Energy Lab., Golden, 1992—; speaker for health and nutrition subjects The Rocky Mountain Engrng. and Sci. Coun., Denver, 1989-92. Contbr. articles to profl. jours. Bd. dirs. The Colo. Chinese Club, Denver, 1991-93; record custodian The Boy Scout of Am., Troop 166, Lakewood, Colo., 1992—. Fellow The Am. Dietetic Assn.; mem. The Colo. Dietetic Assn., The Denver Dietetic Assn., The Data Processing Mgmt. Assn. Democrat. Roman Catholic. Home: 2850 Joyce St Golden CO 80401-1323

TSUTAKAWA, EDWARD MASAO, management consultant; b. Seattle, May 15, 1921; s. Jin and Michiko (Oka) T.; student U. Wash., 1941, Wash. State U., 1949; m. Hide Kunugi, Aug. 11, 1949; children: Nancy Joyce Tsutakawa Seigel, Margaret Ann Langston, Mark Edward. Free-lance comml. artist, Spokane, 1943-47; artist Maag & Porter Comml. Printers, Spokane, 1947-54; organizer Litho Art Printers, Inc., Spokane, 1954—, gen. mgr., pres., 1965-80; charter organizer, dir. Am. Comml. Bank, 1965-80; prin. E. M. Tsutakawa Co., bus. cons. and dir., 1980—; v.p., operation officer, dir. Mukogawa Ft. Wright Inst. Pres. emeritus Spokane-Nishinomiya Sister City Soc., Sister Cities Assn. of Spokane; mem Eastern Wash. State Hist. Soc.; bd. dirs., chmn. Skokane Area Trade Assistance Ctr., Intercollegiate Nursing Edn., Leadership Spokane. Recipient Disting. Svc. medal Boy Scouts of Japan, 1967, Cultural medal in Edn., Japan, 1985, Disting. Svc. award City of Nishinomiya, 1971, Disting. Svc. to Expo '74 State of Wash., 1974, Book of Golden Deeds award Exchange Club, 1978, Disting. Community Scv. award UN Assn., 1979, Whitworth Coll., 1987, Svc. to Youth award Spokane YMCA, 1988; decorated Order of Sacred Treasure medal Govt. of Japan, 1984. Mem. Japanese Am. Citizens League. Methodist. Clubs: Kiwanis (Spokane). Home: 4116 S Madelia St Spokane WA 99203-4229

TSVANKIN, ILYA DANIEL, geophysics educator; b. Moscow, Apr. 6, 1956; came to U.S., 1990; s. Daniel and Maya (Slonimskaya) T.; m. Olga Dashevskaya, July 27, 1985; 1 child, Edward. MS in Geophys. Exploration, Moscow State U., 1978, PhD in Geophysics, 1982. Rsch. scientist Inst. Phys. of the Earth, Moscow, 1978-86, dep. chief of lab., 1986-89; cons. Rsch. Ctr. Amoco Prodn. Co., Tulsa, 1990-92; assoc. rsch. prof. Colo. Sch. Mines, Golden, 1992—; co-leader Ctr. for Wave Phenomena rsch. project. Contbr. articles to profl. publs.; patentee in field. Recipient Gold medal in Geophysics for Young Scientists, Soviet Acad. Scientists, 1988. Mem. Am. Geophys. Union, Denver Geophys. Soc., Soc. Exploration Geophysicists (translation com. 1990—), European Assn. Exploration Geophysists. Office: Colo Sch Mines 1500 Illinois St Golden CO 80401-1887

TSZTOO, DAVID FONG, civil engineer; b. Hollister, Calif., Oct. 13, 1952; s. John and Jean (Woo) T.; m. Evelyn Yang, July 31, 1982; children: Michaela Gabrielle, Shawn Michael. BS, Calif. Poly. State U., 1974; MS in Engrng., U. Calif., 1976. Registered profl. civil engr., Calif. Engr., dispatcher Conlec Corp., Hollister, Calif., 1972-73; rsch. asst. U. Calif. Engrng. Dept., Berkeley, 1975-76; jr. civil engr. Contra Costa County Pub. Works, Martinez, Calif., 1977-78, asst. civil engr., 1978-81, civil engr. III, 1981-83; assoc. civil engr. East Bay Mucpl. Util. Dist., Oakland, Calif., 1983-88; sr. civil engr. East Bay Mucpl. Util. Distbr., Oakland, Calif., 1988—; chpt. chmn. We. Coun. Engrs., Martinez, Calif., 1977-82; mem. Nat. Soc. Profl. Engrs., Martinez, Calif., 1977-82. Co-author: Energy Absorbing Devices in Structures, 1977, EQ Testing of Stepping Frame with Devices, 1977, Development of Energy-Absorbing Devices, 1978. Sponsor Sing & Bring Children's Club, Oakland, San Lorenzo, Calif., 1982-90; v.p. Sun Country Homeowners, Martinez, Calif., 1977-82. Recipient Presdl. Design Achievement award Nat. Endowment for the Arts, Washington, 1984. Mem. Am. Soc. Civil Engrs., Tau Beta Pi, Phi Kappa Phi. Republican. Baptist. Office: E Bay Mcpl Util Dist 375-11th St Oakland CA 94607

TU, ANTHONY TSUCHIEN, biochemistry and molecular biology educator; b. Taipei, Taiwan, Aug. 12, 1930; came to U.S., 1954; s. Tsungming and Songsui (Lin) T.; married; children: Marcia, Janice, Caroline, Kenneth, Alan. BS, Nat. Taiwan U., Taipei, 1953; MS, U. Notre Dame, 1956; PhD, Stanford (Calif.) U., 1961. Postdoctoral fellow Stanford U., 1960-61, Yale U., New Haven, Conn., 1961-62; asst. prof. biochemistry Utah State U., Logan, 1962-67; assoc. prof. Colo. State U., Ft. Collins, 1967-70, prof., 1970—. Author: Venoms: Chemistry and Molecular Biology, 1977, Raman Spectroscopy, 1982; editor: Handbook of Natural Toxins (8 vols.), 1982, Jour. of Natural Toxins, Toxin Review; assoc. editor Applied Spectroscopy. Recipient career devel. award NIH, 1969, merit award, 1987. Mem. Am. Chem. Soc., Applied Spectroscopy, Am. Soc. Biol. Chemistry, Sigma Xi. Home: 2619 Silver Creek Dr Fort Collins CO 80525-2338 Office: Colo State U Dept Biochem & Mol Biol Fort Collins CO 80523

TU, SAMSON W., computer science researcher; b. Taipei, Taiwan, Jan. 31, 1954; came to U.S., 1972; s. Grant T. and Lillian L. T.; m. Polly Lien, Feb. 20, 1987 (div. July 1992). AB in Math., Harvard U., 1977; MS in Computer Engrng., Stanford U., 1985. Mem. tech. staff Sytek, Inc., Mountain View, Calif., 1982-83; rsch. scientist Stanford (Calif.) U., 1985—. Group coord. Amnesty Internat. U.S.A., Palo Alto, Calif., 1994. Mem. Am. Assn. Artificial Intelligence, Assn. Computing Machinery.

TUAZON, JESUS OCAMPO, electrical engineer, educator, consultant; b. Manila, Jan. 2, 1940; came to U.S., 1963; s. Filomeno and Patrocino (Ocampo) T.; m. Norma Mamangun, Oct. 12, 1963; children: Maria, Noel, Norman, Mary, Michelle. BSEE, Mapua Inst., Manila, 1962; MSEE, Iowa State U., 1965, PhD, 1969. Elec. prof. Calif. State U., Fullerton, Calif., 1969—; scientist Jet Propulsion Lab., Pasadena, Calif., 1984—; computer cons. Hughes Aircraft, Fullerton, 1977, Gen. Dynamic, Pomona, Calif., 1983, U.S. Naval Weapon Sta., Seal Beach, Calif., 1978-83. Author of papers for profl. confs. Mem. IEEE, Am. Assn. Engring Educators. Democrat. Roman Catholic. Home: 816 S Verona St Anaheim CA 92804-4035 Office: Calif State Univ 800 N State College Blvd Fullerton CA 92631-3547 also: Jet Propulsion Lab 4800 Oak Grove Dr Pasadena CA 91109-8001

TUBBS, JANET CAROLYN, educational consultant; b. Mineola, N.Y.; d. Gale Huntington and Janet McKinnon (Sloan) Rice; children: Linda, John, Robert, Debra. Founder Arcadia Press; founder, ednl. cons. Children's Resource Ctr., Scottsdale, Ariz., 1988—; condr. workshops in field; lectr. in field. Author: Don't Worry, They'll grow Up - A Parent's Survival Guide, If You Can't Pronounce It, Don't Eat It, All Children Are Special; developer: The Phrenogarten Method of Education, 1991; contbr. numerous articles in

Can. Writer's Jour., L.I. Parent's News, Family ABC's, Ariz. Parenting, Parents' Guide to Preventing Substance Abuse, Springfield Parent, A Family Affair. Bd. dirs. Very Spl. Arts; exhibit chair World Congress, 1992. Mem. Nat. Assn. for Edn. Young Children, World Orgn. for Early Childhood Edn. (exhibit chmn.). Office: Children's Resource Ctr PO Box 8697 Scottsdale AZ 85252-8697

TUBLITZ, NATHAN J., neurobiologist; b. Newark, Aug. 16, 1952; s. Ramon and Mindele (Chipkiewicz) T.; m. Tasker L. Houston, June 18, 1978; children: Rachel, Rebecca, Lucas. BA, Reed Coll., 1974; postgrad., Princeton U., 1976-77; PhD, U. Washington, 1983. Research asst. Neurol. Sci. Inst., Portland, Oreg., 1974-75; lab instr. Reed Coll., Portland, 1977-79; reseach assoc. U. Washington, Seattle, 1983-84; research fellow dept. zoology U. Cambridge, Eng., 1984-86; asst. prof. biology U. Oreg., 1986-92, assoc. prof., 1992—. Contbr. articles to profl. jours. NSF fellow, 1979-82, Welcome Rsch. fellow, 1988, Sloan rsch. fellow, 1988-90, Fogarty Sr. Internat. fellow, 1993-94, Achievement rewards for collegiate sci. fellow, 1983, Brit.-Am. Rsch. fellow Am. Heart Assn., 1984-86; recipient Rsch. Career Devel. award NIH, 1988-93. Mem. AAAS, Soc. Neurosci., Am. Soc. Zoologists. Office: U Oreg Inst Neuroscience Eugene OR 97403

TUBMAN, WILLIAM CHARLES, lawyer; b. N.Y.C., Mar. 16, 1932; s. William Thomas and Ellen Veronica (Griffin) T.; m. Dorothy Rita Krug, Aug. 15, 1964; children: William Charles Jr., Thomas Davison, Matthew Griffin. BS, Fordham U., 1953, JD, 1960; postdoctoral, NYU Sch. Law, 1960-61. Bar: N.Y. 1960, U.S. Ct. Appeals (2d cir.) 1966, U.S. Supreme Ct. 1967, U.S. Ct. Customs and Patent Appeals 1971. Auditor Peat, Marwick Mitchell & Co., N.Y.C., 1956-60; sr. counsel Kennecott Corp., N.Y.C., 1960-82; sr. counsel Phelps Dodge Corp., N.Y.C., 1982-85, sec., 1985-87, v.p., 1987—; pres. Phelps Dodge Found., Phoenix, 1988—. Author: Legal Status of Minerals Beyond the Continental Shelf, 1966. Mem. scholarship adv. coun. U. Ariz., 1990-92; active Big Bros., Inc., N.Y.C., 1963-73; trustee Phoenix Art Mus., 1989-94; chmn. bd. dirs. St. Joseph Hosp. Found., 1994-95; bd. dirs. The Phoenix Symphony. Recipient Cert. Disting. Service, Big Brothers Inc., 1968. Mem. ABA, N.Y. State Bar Assn., Maricopa County Bar Assn. Democrat. Roman Catholic. Office: Phelps Dodge Corp 2600 N Central Ave Phoenix AZ 85004-3050

TUCCIO, SAM ANTHONY, aerospace executive, physicist; b. Rochester, N.Y., Jan. 15, 1939; s. Manuel Joseph and Phillis (Cannizzo) T.; m. Jenney Laprell Elvington, May 1, 1982; children: David Samuel, Karen Ann, Rebecca Jean, Ashley Lauren. BS, U. Rochester, 1965. Research physicist Eastman Kodak Co., Rochester, 1965-72; program mgr. Lawrence Livermore (Calif.) Labs., 1972-75; sr. physicist Allied Corp., Morristown, N.J., 1975-81; gen. mgr. Allied Laser Products Div., Westlake Village, Calif., 1981-84; sr. bus. mgr. Northrop Corp., Hawthorne, Calif., 1984-89; dir. space bus. Loral Corp., Pasadena, Calif., 1989-92; dir. bus. devel. ThermoTrex Corp., San Diego, 1992—. Patentee in field; contbr. numerous articles to profl. jours. Recipient IR 100 award Indsl. Rsch. Assn., 1971. Republican. Methodist. Home: 3662 Barham Blvd # 219 Los Angeles CA 90068-1150 Office: ThermoTrex Corp 9550 Distribution Ave San Diego CA 92121-2306

TUCH, RICHARD HOWARD, psychoanalyst, psychiatrist; b. L.A., Apr. 14, 1949; s. Irving and Shirley Josephine (Edelstein) T.; m. Sunnye Louise Jaffe, Oct. 31, 1952; children: Alexander, Zachary. BA, U. Calif., Santa Barbara, 1971; MD, U. So. Calif., 1975. Diplomate Am. Bd Psychiatry and Neurology. Intern Children's Hosp., L.A., 1975-76; resident Neuropsychiat. Inst. UCLA, 1976-79; v.p. med. staff Van Nuys (Calif.) Psychiat. Hosp., 1981-82; med. dir. Treatment Ctrs. of Am., San Fernando Valley, 1984-87; clin. dir. adult program Westwood Hosp., 1988-93; pvt. practice L.A., 1979—; asst. clin. prof. psychiatry Neuro-Psychiat. Inst., UCLA, mem. faculty Grad. Ctr. for Child Devel. and Psychotherapy; mem. sr. faculty L.A. Psychoanalytic Soc. and Inst., 1992—; presenter in field. Contbr. articles to profl. jours. Past bd. dirs. Family Svcs. L.A. Mem. Am. Psychiat. Assn., So. Calif. Psychiat. Soc. (program com. 1981-84, co-chair program 1986-87, treas. elect 1990, treas., 1991), Am. Psychoanalytic Assn., L.A. Med. Assn., Calif. Med. Assn. Office: 1800 Fairburn Ave Ste 206 Los Angeles CA 90025-4968

TUCK, EDWARD FENTON, business consultant, venture capitalist; b. Memphis, July 5, 1931; s. Edward Fenton and Jane Florence (Lewis) T.; m. Janet Allene Barber, July 6, 1957; children: Jean, Ann. BSEE, Mo. Sch. Mines, 1953; elec. engr. (hon.), U. Mo., 1980. Registered profl. engr., Calif., Mo., Ala. Various engring. and mfg. mgmt. positions Lenkurt Elec. Co. div. GTE, San Carlos, Calif., 1957-62; v.p., co-founder Kebby Microwave Corp., San Carlos, 1962-64; v.p., tech. dir. ITT Telecommunications, N.Y.C., 1965-72; gen. mgr., pres. Tel-Tone Corp., Kirkland, Wash., 1972-74; v.p. mktg. and engring. Am. Telecommunications Corp., El Monte, Calif., 1975-79; pres. Edward Tuck & Co., Inc., West Covina, Calif., 1979-86; gen. ptnr. The Boundary Fund, West Covina, 1986-95; dir. Peninsula Wireless, Inc., San Carlos, Calif., Applied Digital Access, San Diego, Tri Quiet Semiconductors, Beaverton, Oreg.; chmn. Endgate Corp., Sunnyvale, Calif.; vice-chmn. Teledesic Corp., Kirkland, Wash. Contbr. articles to profl. jours. Trustee U. Mo., Rolla. Served with U.S. Army, 1954-56. Named mem. Acad. Elec. Engring. U. Mo. Fellow Instn. Radio, Elec. and Electronic Engrs. Australia; mem. IEEE (sr., 1st prize for article 1962), Assn. Profl. Cons. (pres., bd. dirs. 1979-86), AAAS. Democrat. Office: Kinship Partners II Ste 200 1900 W Garvey S West Covina CA 91790

TUCK, MICHAEL RAY, technical services executive; b. Pocatello, Idaho, Aug. 9, 1941; s. Amos R. and Phyllis (Day) T.; m. Heather K. Fowler, Oct. 22, 1962; children: Lisa M., Jennifer A., M. Mark. BS in Math., Idaho State U., 1964; MS in Math., U. Idaho, 1971. Programmer analyst Argonne Nat. Labs., Idaho Falls, Idaho, 1964-69; computer scientist Argonne Nat. Labs., Idaho Falls, 1969-76; engr., mgr. computer div. Montana Energy Inst., Butte, Mont., 1976-81; v.p. MultiTech Inc. div. MSE Inc., Butte, 1981-82, pres., 1982-83, v.p., 1983-87; sr. v.p., COO MSE Inc., Butte, 1987-94, pres., COO, 1994—, also bd. dirs.; cons. TMA Assocs., Butte, 1982-83. Mem. Exchange Club. Methodist. Office: MSE Inc PO Box 4078 Butte MT 59702-4078

TUCKER, ANNABELLE DORIS, medical company executive; b. Whittier, Calif., Jan. 11, 1922; d. Raymond Kleeman and Violet N. (Arnold) Covington; m. John Warren Tucker, Aug. 29, 1948; children: Richard Warren, Brian Lee. Degree in Nursing, Bishop Johnson Coll. Nursing, L.A., 1946. RN, Calif. Maternal and child health nurse Foster Mem. Hosp., Ventura, Calif., 1946; med. and cardioly ward Birmingham Vets. Hosp., Van Nuys, Calif., 1946-47; maternal and child health nurse Hosp. Good Samaritan, L.A., 1947-50; nurse various drs. offices, 1950-73; maternal and child health nurse Tarzana (Calif.) Regional Med. Ctr., 1973-87; pres. RN/MDs, Sherman Oaks, Calif., 1992—; cons. in field. Contbr. articles to profl. jours.; patentee in field. Mem. Assn. Practitioners in Infection Control, Hosp. Good Samaritan Alumni Assn. Republican. Episcopalian. Home and Office: 4480 Sherman Oaks Cir Sherman Oaks CA 91403-3823

TUCKER, CHARLES CYRIL, information systems consultant; b. N.Y.C., Mar. 7, 1942; s. Bernard Anthony and Charlotte Yvonne (Carron) T.; children: Michele, Christine. BS in Mech. Engring., U. Santa Clara, 1964, MBA, 1968. Mktg. rep. IBM, L.A., 1968-72; sr. assoc. McKinsey & Co., L.A., 1972-76; v.p. planning and info. services 20th Century-Fox, L.A., 1977-81; v.p. planning and corp. devel. MSI Data Corp., Costa Mesa, Calif., 1981-83; sr. v.p. planning and control 1st Interstate Services Co., Torrance, Calif., 1983-88; sr. mgr. Nolan, Norton & Co., L.A., 1988-90; pres. Tucker & Assocs., Rancho Palos Verdes, Calif., 1990—; mem. product adv. bd. Teradata Corp., L.A., 1980-83; chmn. computers and info. systems adv. bd. Grad. Sch. Mgmt. UCLA, 1984-85. Served to 1st lt., U.S. Army, 1964-66, Korea. Mem. Soc. for Info. Mgmt. Roman Catholic. Home and office: Tucker & Assocs 3200 La Rotonda Dr Unit 108 Palos Verdes Peninsula CA 90275-6147

TUCKER, CONNIE, legal assistant, insurance consultant; b. Richmond, Calif., Mar. 20, 1956; d. Ray Field Braxton and Maudrie (Harding) Wimbley; m. Keith Dwayne Tucker, Dec. 29, 1974; 1 child, Dwayne B. Student, Merritt Coll., 1982. Lic. life and disability, variable annuity, lic. securities. Claims specialist Aetna Life & Casualty, San Francisco, 1973-78; claims rep. Calif. Casualty, San Mateo, 1978-90; legal asst./owner Tucker Claims Assistance, Suisun City, Calif., 1990—. Mem. Life Assn. of Life Underwriters. Office: Tucker Claims Assistance PO Box 144 Suisun City CA 94585-0144

TUCKER, JAMES RAYMOND, elementary educator; b. Pueblo, Colo., Apr. 18, 1944; s. James George and Pauline F. (Sena) T.; m. Kathie Owens; 1 child, Brittany. BA, U. So. Colo., 1966; MA, U. No. Colo., 1990, post-grad., 1991. Tchr. Sinclair Mid. Sch., Englewood, Colo., 1971-93, Denver Pub. Schs., 1993—; co-dir. Nick Bolleteri Tennis Acad., Boulder, Colo., 1986; head tennis coach Englewood High Sch., 1971—. Sgt. U.S. Army, 1967-70. Mem. NEA, U.S. Profl. Tennis Assn., U.S. Profl. Tennis Registry, Internat. Platform Assn., Colo. Edn. Assn., Meadow Creek Tennis and Fitness, Colo. H.S. Coaches Assn. (Achievement award 1989, 92, Tchr. of Yr. 1973, 78, 86, Coach of Yr. 1986, 87, 90, 93, Franklin award 1988, 89). Home: 2316 S Harlan Ct Denver CO 80227-3962

TUCKER, JOEL LAWRENCE, aviation company executive; b. Berkeley, Calif., Feb. 23, 1932; s. Lawrence Otis Tucker and Edythe Lauretta (Pye) Connolly; m. Constance Nadine Finnick, Oct. 19, 1951 (div. Sept. 1975); 1 child, John Lawrence; m. Cristeta Gozarin, Feb. 15, 1992. BS, U. Wash., 1953. Statistician Bell Telephone System, Seattle, 1953-6l, AID, Washington, 196l-64; dir. sales Boeing Comml. Airplanes, Seattle, 1965-87; pres. J.E.T. Cons. Ltd., Kirkland, Wash., 1987—; mng. dir. Lorad Boeing Ltd., Hamilton, Bermuda, 1988-89. Chmn. Citizens Sch. Adv. Coun., Bellevue, Wash., 1969-7l. With U.S. Army, 1954-56. Republican. Presbyterian.

TUCKER, MARCUS OTHELLO, judge; b. Santa Monica, Calif., Nov. 12, 1934; s. Marcus Othello Sr. and Essie Louvonia (McLendon) T.; m. Indira Hale, May 29, 1965; 1 child, Angelique. BA, U. So. Calif., 1956; JD, Howard U., 1960. Bar: Calif. 1962, U.S. Dist. Ct. (cen. dist.) Calif. 1962, U.S. Ct. Appeals (9th cir.) 1965, U.S. Ct. Internat. Trade 1970, U.S. Supreme Ct. 1971. Pvt. practice, Santa Monica, 1962-63, 67-74; dep. atty. City of Santa Monica, 1963-65; asst. atty. U.S. Dist. Ct. (Cen. Dist.) Calif., 1965-67; commr. L.A. Superior Ct., 1974-76; judge mcpl. ct. Long Beach (Calif.) Jud. Dist., 1976-85; judge superior ct. L.A. Jud. Dist., 1985—; supervising judge L.A. County Dependency Ct. L.A. Superior Ct., 1991-92, presiding judge Juvenile divsn., 1993—; asst. prof. law Pacific U., Long Beach, 1984, 86; justice pro tem U.S. Ct. Appeals (2d cir.), 1981; exec. com. Superior Ct. of L.A. County, 1995—. Mem. editorial staff Howard U. Law Sch. Jour., 1959-60. Pres. Community Rehab. Industries Found., Long Beach, 1983-86, Legal Aid Found., L.A., 1976-77; bd. dirs. Long Beach coun. Boy Scouts Am., 1978-92. With U.S. Army, 1960-66. Named Judge of Yr. Juvenile Cts. Bar Assn., 1986, Disting. Jurist Long Beach Trial Trauma Coun., 1987, Honoree in Law Handy Community Ctr., L.A., 1987, Bernard S. Jefferson Jurist of Yr. John M. Langston Bar Assn. Black Lawyers, 1990, Judge of Yr. Long Beach Bar Assn., 1993; recipient award for Law-Related Edn. Constl. Rights Found./L.A. County Bar Assn., 1992. Mem. ABA, Calif. Judges Assn. (chmn. juvenile law com. 1986-87), Langston Bar Assn. (pres. bd. dirs. 1972, 73), Calif. Assn. Black Lawyers, Santa Monica Bay Dist. Bar Assn. (treas. 1969-71), Am. Inns of Ct., Selden Soc. Office: 201 Centre Plaza Dr Ste 3 Monterey Park CA 91754-2142

TUCKER, MARY LINDA, management educator, consultant; b. Andalusia, Ala., Dec. 7, 1945; d. Bennett D. and Pearl (Nelson) T.; children: Mandi Shayne Tucker, Matthew Little. BS, Nicholls State U., Thibodaux, La., 1984; MEd summa cum laude, Nicholls State U., Thibodeau, La., 1985; PhD in Ednl. Leadership and Founds., U. New Orleans, 1990. Tchrs. aide St. Clements Episc. Sch., El Paso, 1975-76; co-owner sporting goods store, Marianna, Fla., 1976-82; prof. Nicholls State U., 1984-93; prof. dept. mgmt. Colo. State U., Ft. Collins, 1993—; cons. to banks, La., 1984-93. Contbr. chpts. to books, articles and book revs. to bus. jours. and newspapers; presenter at confs. Mem. Rep. Nat. Com., Ft. Collins, 1993-94; friend New Orleans Ctr. for Creative Arts, 1984-93; del. La. Gov.'s Conf. on Women, 1992-93. Mem. The Acad. of Mgmt. (Ocis divsn. exec. bd., membership chair 1993-94, Best Paper award 1994), Assn. Bus. Comms. (reviewer), Ft. Collins C. of C., Phi Kappa Phi (sec. 1991, pres. 192-93), Delta Sigma Pi, Delta Kappa Gamma, Alpha Kappa Si (faculty mem.). Episcopalian. Office: Colo State U Dept Mgmt B272 Clark Bldg Fort Collins CO 80523

TUCKER, WALTER RAYFORD, III, congressman, lawyer, former mayor; b. Compton, Calif., 1957; s. Walter Rayford Jr. and Martha H. Tucker; m. Robin Tucker; children: Walter Rayford IV, Autumn Monet. BA in Polit. Sci. cum laude, U. So. Calif., 1978; JD, Georgetown U., 1981. Ordained Christian minister. Staff Segrue, Rothwell, McPeak, Washington; dep. dist. atty. County of Los Angeles, 1984-86; pvt. practice Compton, 1986—; mayor City of Compton, Calif., 1991-92; mem. 103rd-104th Congresses from 37th Calif. dist., 1993—; mem. transp. and infrastructure com., mem. small bus. com. Active Compton Juvenile Delinquency Panel; Sunday Sch. teacher. Mem. NAACP (life), Calif. Bar Assn., South Ctrl. Bar Assn., L.A. Bar Assn., Langston Bar Assn., Kiwanis Club of Compton. Democrat. Office: US Ho of Reps 419 Cannon Office Of Ho Mems Washington DC 20515-0531*

TUDDENHAM, W(ILLIAM) MARVIN, chemist, metallurgist, consultant; b. Salt Lake City, July 8, 1924; s. William Calder and Laura (Pack) T.; m. Dorothy Evelyn Snelgrove, May 1, 1945; children: William Marvin Jr. (dec.), Mary Alice, Evelyn, Laurie. BA in Chemistry, U. Utah, 1947, MS in Chemistry, 1948, PhD in Fuels, 1954, teaching cert., 1984. Rsch. chemist Eastman Kodak Co., Rochester, N.Y., 1948-50; dept. mgr. Kennecott Rsch., Salt Lake City, 1953-83; v.p., gen. mgr. Master Travel, Salt Lake City, 1984-91; pres. Mining & Metall. Assocs., Salt Lake City, 1991—. Editor: Sampling and Analysis Copper, 1983; contbr. articles to tech. jours. and encys., chpts. to books; patentee in electrowinning and refining field. Chmn. Salt Lake City Adv. Com. on Waste Disposal, 1981, Salt Lake City Pub. Utilities Adv. Bd., 1983-90; mem. Salt Lake City Mayor's Budget Adv. Com., 1985-90. Ensign USNR, 1944-46, PTO. Recipient Silver Beaver award Gt. Salt lake coun. Boy Scouts Am., 1978. Mem. AIME (sr.), Metall. Soc. of AIME (past chmn. nat. electrolytic process com.), Am. Chem. Soc. (emeritus, chmn. nat. membership affairs com. 1980-82, various offices 1953—, Utah award Salt Lake-Cen. Utah sects. 1973), Sigma Xi, Alpha Chi Sigma. Republican. Mem. LDS Ch. Office: 1828 Lincoln St Salt Lake City UT 84105-3308

TUDMAN, CATHI GRAVES, elementary education educator, music director; b. Fresno, Calif., June 24, 1953; d. Robert Eugene and Bettyelou (Seagraves) Graves; divorced; children: Colleen Melissa, Andrew James. BA in Music cum laude, Calif. State U., Fresno, 1978, MA in Communication, 1991. Gen. elem., English, music and gen. sci. teaching credentials, Calif. Founder, coord. Lake Sequoia Symphonic Music Camp, Miramonte, Calif., 1985—; asst. lectr. communications speech dept. Calif. State U., 1988-91, instr. reading ednl. opportunity program summer bridge, 1990, instr. writing ednl. opportunity program summer bridge, 1991, coach, judge Peach Blossom Festival, 1988-91; band dir. Yosemite Mid. Sch., 1991-93, Mayfair Elem. Sch., 1991—, Hidalgo Elem. Sch., 1991-92, Balderas Elem., 1992-93, Turner Elem., 1993, Burroughs Annex Elem. Sch., 1993—; instr. comms. dynamics Phillips Coll., Fresno, 1989-90; rsch. assoc. Renshaw Assocs., Fresno, 1989-91; flutist, piccoloist Fresno Philharm. Orch., 1981—, libr., 1985, pers. mgr., 1984-85; flute clinician Selmer Corp., Ind., 1988-93; festivals chmn. cen. sect. Calif. Music Educators, 1972-82, publicity chmn., 1992-93; pvt. tutor in math., music and social studies; chmn. Fresno Unified Showcase Mid. Sch. Massed Band, 1993. Flute clinician Fresno County Schs., 1980—; founder San Joaquin Valley Instrument Fund, 1984; bd. dirs. Community Concert Series, Fresno County, 1986-88; liaison com. bd. dirs. Fresno Philharm. Orch., 1992-94; asst. chair FMCMEA Hon. Band, 1992-93; bd. dirs. Cen. Valley YMCA, 1994-95. Rsch. grantee Calif. State U., 1991; recipient Outstanding Teaching award Internat. Communication Assn., 1991. Mem. Western States Communication Assn., Fresno-Madera Music Educators Assn., Fresno Tchrs. Assn., Calif. Tchrs. Assn., Fresno Mus. Club (social chmn. 1992-95, Calif. Music Educators (festival chmn. cen. sect. 1972-82), Calif. State U.-Fresno Alumnae Assn. (sec. 1982-83, nat. friendship chmn. 1979-81), Blue Key, Phi Kappa Phi, Mu Phi Epsilon (pres., v.p. Phi Chi chpt.). Home: 5467 E Saginaw Way Fresno CA 93727-7536 Office: Yosemite Mid Sch 1292 N 9th St Fresno CA 93703-4229

TUELL, JACK MARVIN, retired bishop; b. Tacoma, Nov. 14, 1923; s. Frank Harry and Anne Helen (Bertelson) T.; m. Marjorie Ida Beadles, June 17, 1946; children—Jacqueline, Cynthia, James. B.S., U. Wash., 1947, LL.B., 1948; S.T.B., Boston U., 1955; M.A., U. Puget Sound, 1961, DHS, 1990; D.D., Pacific Sch. Religion, 1966; LLD, Alaska Pacific U., 1980. Bar: Wash. 1948; ordained to ministry Meth. Ch., 1955. Practice law with firm Holte & Tuell, Edmonds, Wash., 1948-50; pastor Grace Meth. Ch., Everett, Wash., 1950-52, South Tewksbury Meth. Ch., Tewksbury, Mass., 1952-55, Lakewood Meth. Ch., Tacoma, 1955-61; dist. supt. Puget Sound dist. Meth. Ch., Everett, 1961-67; pastor 1st United Meth. Ch., Vancouver, Wash., 1967-72; bishop United Meth. Ch., Portland, Oreg., 1972-80, Calif.-Pacific Conf., United Meth. Ch., L.A., 1980-92; interim sr. pastor First United Meth. Ch., Boise, Idaho, 1995; Mem. gen. conf. United Meth. Ch., 1964, 66, 68, 70, 72; pres. coun. of Bishops United Meth. Ch., 1989-90. Author: The Organization of the United Methodist Church, 1970, 7th edit. 1993. Pres. Tacoma U.S.O., 1959-61, Vancouver YMCA, 1968; v.p. Ft. Vancouver Seamens Cnt., 1969-72; vice chmn. Vancouver Human Rels. Commn., 1970-72; pres. Oreg. Coun. Alcohol Problems, 1972-76; trustee U. Puget Sound, 1961-73, Vancouver Meml. Hosp., 1967-72, Alaska Meth. U., Anchorage, 1972-80, Willamette U., Salem, Oreg., 1972-80, Willamette View Manor, Portland, 1972-80, Rogue Valley Manor, Medford, Oreg., 1972-76, Sch. Theology at Claremont, Calif., 1980-92, Methodist Hosp., Arcadia, Calif., 1983-92; pres. nat. div. bd. global ministries United Meth. Ch., 1972-76, pres. ecumenical and interreligious concerns div., 1976-80, Commn. on Christian Unity and interreligious concerns, 1980-84, Gen. Bd. of Pensions,1984-92, Calif. Coun. Alcohol Problems, 1985-88. Jacob Sleeper fellow, 1955. Mem. Lions. Home and Office: 2697 S North Bluff Rd Greenbank WA 98253-9713

TUFTS, ROBERT B., academic administrator; b. Cleve., Nov. 5, 1940; s. Robert L. and Dora Mae (Yingling) T.; m. Nancy Intihar, June 22, 1968 (div. Feb. 1990); children: Therese, Kevin R. BA cum laude, Cleve. State U., 1967; MA, Case Western Res. U., 1972; postgrad., U. Akron, 1973-76. Admissions counselor Cleve. State U., 1967-69, asst. registrar, 1969-70; asst. registrar Youngstown (Ohio) State U., 1970-73; asst. registrar U. Akron (Ohio), 1973-75, assoc. registrar, 1975-78; registrar Portland (Oreg.) State U., 1978—; com. mem. Park Recreation Adv. Bd., W. Linn., Oreg., 1981-84; presenter on fraudulent credentials, 1987—. Contbr. articles to profl. jours. With U.S. Army, 1959-62, Korea. Mem. Oreg. Assn. Registrars and Admissions Officers (sec.-treas. 1988-90), Pacific Assn. Collegiate Registrars and Admissions Officers (mem. program com. 1986-87, exec. bd., chair local arrangement 64th Ann. Mtg., Portland 1990), Am. Assn. Collegiate Registrars and Admissions Officers (local arrangements com., chair pub. com. 82nd Ann. Mtg., Reno, 1996, mem. facilities planning mgmt. com. 1975-78, chmn. of com. 1977-78), Nat. Assn. Coll. and Univ. Bus. Officers, Theta Rho. Democrat. Mem. Unitarian Ch. Home: 4981 Prospect St West Linn OR 97068-3116 Office: Portland State U PO Box 751 Portland OR 97207-0751

TUGENDER, RONALD, software executive; b. N.Y.C., July 22, 1948; s. Robert and Lily (Klein) T.; m. Jeannette Louise Christensen, Aug. 20, 1977 (div. Dec. 1981). BS, SUNY, Stony Brook, 1971; MS, Carnegie Mellon U., 1978. Sr. rsch. assoc. Info. Scis. Inst., Marina del Rey, Calif., 1974-79; program mgr. Logicon, Inc., Woodland Hills, Calif., 1979-82; dept. mgr. Transaction Tech. Inc., Santa Monica, Calif., 1982-83; dir. knowledge engring. svcs. Teknowledge, Inc., Palo Alto, Calif., 1983-86; gen. mgr. Rental Pro, Mountain View, Calif., 1986-87; sr. mgr. Price Waterhouse, Menlo Park, Calif., 1987-88; sr. cons. Corp. Solutions, Mountain View, 1988-93; mgr. applications group Blyth Software, Foster City, Calif., 1993-94; dir. applications product group Quintus Corp., Mountain View, 1994—; cons. Amdahl Corp., Sunnyvale, Calif., 1989-91. Editor: Metamorphosis: Transformation in Action, 1993. Pres. Quaint Villa Junction Homeowners Assn., Mountain View, 1990—; comm. chief South Bay Nation of Men, San Jose, Calif., 1992-93. Mem. IEEE, Software Entrepreneurs Forum, Internat. Interactive Comm. Soc., San Francisco Multimedia Devel. Group, Assn. for Computing Machinery. Home: 2149 Junction Ave Apt 11 Mountain View CA 94043-2850

TUKEY, HAROLD BRADFORD, JR., horticulture educator; b. Geneva, N.Y., May 29, 1934; s. Harold Bradford and Ruth (Schweigert) T.; m. Helen Dunbar Parker, June 25, 1955; children: Ruth Thurbon, Carol Tukey Schwartz, Harold Bradford. B.S., Mich. State U., 1955, M.S., 1956, Ph.D., 1958. Research asst. South Haven Expt. Sta., Mich., 1955; AEC grad. research asst. Mich. State U., 1955-58; NSF fellow Calif. Inst. Tech, 1958-59; asst. prof. dept. floriculture and ornamental horticulture Cornell U., Ithaca, N.Y., 1959-64, assoc. prof., 1964-70, prof., 1970-80; prof. urban horticulture U. Wash., Seattle, 1980—, dir. Arboreta, 1980-92, dir. Ctr. Urban Horticulture, 1980-92; cons. Internat. Bonsai mag., Electric Power Rsch. Inst., P.R. Nuclear Ctr., 1965-66; lectr. in field; mem. adv. com. Seattle-U. Wash. Arboretum and Bot. Garden, 1980-92, vice chmn., 1982, chmn., 1986-89; vis. scholar U. Nebr., 1982; vis. prof. U. Calif.-Davis, 1973; lectr. U. Western Sydney and Victoria Coll. of Agriculture, Australia; Hill Disting. vis. prof. U. Minn., 1996; mem. various coms. Nat. Acad. Scis.-NRC; bd. dirs. Arbor Fund Bloedel Res., 1980-92, pres., 1983-84. Mem. editorial bd. Jour. Environ. Horticulture, Arboretum Bull. Mem. nat. adv. com. USDA, 1990—; pres. Ithaca PTA; troop advisor Boy Scouts Am., Ithaca. Lt. U.S. Army, 1958. Recipient B.Y. Morrison award USDA, 1987; NSF fellow, 1958-59; named to Lansing (Mich.) Sports Hall of Fame, 1987; grantee NSF, 1962, 75, Bot. Soc. Am., 1964; hon. dr. Portuguese Soc. Hort., 1985. Fellow Am. Soc. Hort. Sci. (pres. 1970-71); mem. Internat. Soc. Hort. Sci. (U.S. del. to coun. 1971-90, chmn. commn. for amateur horticulture 1974-83, exec. com. 1974-90, v.p. 1978-82, pres. 1982-86, past pres. 1986-90, chmn. commn. Urban Horticulture 1990—, hon. mem. 1994), Wash. State Nursery and Landscape Assn. (hon. mem. 1995), Internat. Plant Propagators Soc. (hon., eastern region dir. 1969-71, v.p. 1972, pres. 1973, internat. pres. 1976), Am. Hort. Soc. (dir. 1972-81, exec. com. 1974-81, v.p. 1978-80, citation of merit 1981), Royal Hort. Soc. (London) (v.p. hon. 1993—), Bot. Soc. Am., N.W. Horticulutre Soc. (dir. 1980-92), Arboretum Found. (dir. 1980-92), Rotary, Sigma Xi, Alpha Zeta, Phi Kappa Phi, Pi Alpha Xi, Xi Sigma Pi. Presbyterian. Home: 3300 E St Andrews Way Seattle WA 98112-3750 Office: U Wash Ctr Urban Horticulture Ctr Frst #Gf-15 Seattle WA 98195

TULK, STEVEN ANTHONY, director information systems; b. Santa Monica, Calif., Apr. 22, 1967; s. William Frederick and Daisy (McDonald) T.; m. Yafit N.A. Gat, Aug. 1, 1993. BSBA, U. Calif., 1990. Owner Tulk & Assocs., Riverside, Calif., 1985-90; sr. tech. specialist The J. Paul Getty Trust, Santa Monica, Calif., 1990-92; micro computer info. systems dir. Pharmacia Ophthalmics, Monrovia, Calif., 1992-94; v.p. tech. devel. PB Adminstrs., Inc., L.A., 1994—; dir. info. systems Pacific Casino Mgmt., L.A., 1994—; cons. The J. Paul Getty Trust, Santa Moncia, 1993—, The Kennedy Found., Washington, 1994—. Cons. Matt Fong for Treas., Industry, Calif.; mem. Heal the Bay Found., Santa Monica, 1992. Mem. Ind. Computer Cons. Assn., Phi Delta Theta Alumni (pres. 1987). Office: PBA Adminstrs Inc 1990 S Bundy Ste 600 Los Angeles CA 90025

TULLOCH-REID, ELMA DEEN, nurse, consultant; b. Erie, Pa., June 27, 1938; d. Theodore and Roberta (Hicks) Carlisle; B.S., N.C. Agrl. and Tech. State U., 1960; M.A., Calif. State U., 1977; Ed.D., Nova U., 1981; children: Robynne and Stacey (twins). Staff nurse Michael Reese Hosp., Chgo., 1960-62; instr. Cook County Sch. Nursing, Chgo., 1962-64; tchr. St. Joseph Convent, Trinidad, West Indies, 1964-66; med./surg. coordinator St. Vincent Coll. Nursing, L.A., 1966-68, med./surg. coord., 1968-69; charge nurse Century City Hosp., L.A., 1971-72; tchr. L.A. Unified Schs., 1972-75; instr. inservice dept. St. Vincent Med. Center, Los Angeles, 1972-75; dir. edn. and tng. Imperial Hosp., Inglewood, Calif., 1977-79; pres. Elma Tulloch-Reid Assocs., L.A., 1981—; asst. prof. dept. continuing edn. Calif. State U., Long Beach, 1977-81, asso. prof., 1982—; instr. Pilot Program in Health Occupations, Culver City Unified Sch. Dist., 1985—; mem. Citizen Amb. Program to Republic China, 1995; DON edn. and rsch. King Drew Med. Ctr., L.A., 1991—; clin. performance examiner Regent's Coll. NYU; provider Advanced Life Support in Cardiopulmonary Resuscitation, Am. Heart Assn., 1982-84. Cmty. instr. certified basic life support L.A. Cardio-Pulmonary Resuscitation Consortium, 1981-82. Recipient commendation City of Los Angeles XXIII Olympiad, 1984. Mem. Nat. Orgn. Mothers of Twins, NAFE, Am. Nurses Found., Am. Coll. Healthcare Execs., N.C. Agrl. and Tech. State U. Alumni Assn., AAUW, Assn. for Psychological Type, Nat. Nursing Staff Devel. Orgn., Phi Kappa Phi. Club: Westside Mothers Twins (pres. 1971-73) (Los Angeles). Home: 1056 S Cochran Ave Los Angeles CA 90019-2857 Office: 5350 Wilshire Blvd Los Angeles CA 90036-4212

TULLY, SUSAN BALSLEY, pediatrician, educator; b. San Francisco, July 12, 1941; d. Gerard E. Balsley Sr. and Norma Lilla (Hand) Carey; m. William P. Tully, June 19, 1965; children: Michael William, Stephen Gerard. BA in Premed. Studies, UCLA, 1963, MD, 1966. Diplomate Am. Bd. Pediatrics, Am. Bd. Pediatric Emergency Medicine. Intern L.A. County-U. So. Calif. Med. Ctr., 1966-67, jr. resident pediatrics, 1967-68; staff pediatrician, part-time Permanente Med. Group, Oakland, Calif., 1968; sr. resident pediatrics Kaiser Found. Hosp., Oakland, 1968-69; sr. resident pediatrics Bernalillo County Med. Ctr., Albuquerque, 1969-70, chief resident pediatric outpatient dept., 1970; instr. pediatrics, asst. dir. outpatient dept. U. N.Mex. Sch. Medicine, 1971-72; asst. prof. pediatrics, dir. (ambulatory pediatrics) U. Calif., Irvine, 1972-76, asst. prof. clin. pediatrics, vice chair med. edn., 1977-79; staff pediatrician Ross-Loos Med. Group, Buena Park, Calif., 1976-77; assoc. prof. clin. pediatrics and emergency medicine U. So. Calif. Sch. Medicine, 1979-86; dir. pediatric emergency dept. L.A. County/U. So. Calif. Med. Ctr., 1979-87; prof. clin. pediatrics and emergency medicine U. So. Calif. Sch. Medicine, 1986-89; dir. ambulatory pediatrics L.A. County/U. So. Calif. Med. Ctr., 1987-89, L.A. County-Olive View/UCLA Med. Ctr., 1989—; clin. prof. pediatrics U. Calif., L.A., 1989-93, prof. clin. pediatrics, 1993—; pediatric toxicology cons. L.A. County Regional Poison Control Ctr. Med. Adv. Bd., 1981—; faculty exec. com., clin. faculty rep. UCLA Sch. Medicine, 1992-93, strategic planning action com. subcom. on ednl. structure, 1992-93, dept. pediatrics alliance-wide rev. and appraisal com., 1992-93, steering com., 1993—; pediatric liaison dept. emergency medicine Olive View/UCLA Med. Ctr., 1989—, dir. lead poisoning clinic, 1993—, L.A. County Dept. Health Svcs., 1990—; mem. quality assurance com. L.A. County Community Health Plan, 1986-89; mem. survey team pediatric emergency svcs. L.A. Pediatric Soc., 1984-86; mem. adv. bd. preventive health project U. Affiliated Program Children's Hosp. L.A., 1981-83; active numerous coms. Author: (with K.E. Zenk) Pediatric Nurse Practitioner Formulary, 1979; (with W.A. Wingert) Pediatric Emergency Medicine: Concepts and Clinical Practice, 1992; (with others) Educational Guidelines for Ambulatory/General Pediatrics Fellowship Training, 1992, Physician's Resource Guide for Water Safety Education, 1994; reviewer Pediatrics, 1985-89; editorial cons. Advanced Pediatric Life Support Course and Manual, 1988-89; dept. editor Pediatric Pearls Jour. Am. Acad. Physician Assts., 1989-94; tech. cons., reviewer Healthlink TV Am. Acad. Pediatrics, 1991; reviewer Pediatric Emergency Care, 1992—; question writer sub-bd. pediatric emergency medicine Am. Bd. Pediatrics, 1993—; cons. to lay media NBC Nightly News, Woman's Day, Sesame Street Parents, Parenting, Los Angeles Times; author numerous abstracts; contbr. articles to profl. jours. cons. spl. edn. programs Orange County Bd. Edn., 1972-79; mem. Orange County Health Planning Coun., 1973-79; co-chairperson Orange County Child Health and Disability Prevention Program Bd., 1975-76; mem. Orange County Child Abuse Consultation Team, 1977-79; mem. project adv. bd. Family Focussed "Buckle Up" Project, Safety Belt Safe, U.S.A., 1989—. Fellow Am. Acad. Pediatrics (life, active numerous sects. and coms., active Calif. chpt.); mem. APHA, Ambulatory Pediatric Assn., L.A. Pediatric Soc. (life), L.A. Area Child Passenger Safety Assn. Democrat. Office: Olive View UCLA Med Ctr Pediatrics 3A108 14445 Olive View Dr Sylmar CA 91342-1495

TULSKY, FREDRIC NEAL, journalist; b. Chgo., Sept. 30, 1950; s. George and Helen (Mailick) T.; m. Kim Rennard, June 20, 1971; children: Eric George, Elizabeth Rose. B.J., U. Mo., 1972; J.D. cum laude, Temple U., Phila., 1984. Bar: Pa. 1984. Reporter Saginaw News, Mich., 1973-74, Port Huron Times Herald, Mich., 1974-75, Jackson Clarion-Ledger, Miss., 1975-78, Los Angeles Herald Examiner, 1978-79, Phila. Inquirer, 1979-93; mng. editor Ctr. for Investigative Reporting, San Francisco, 1993-94, exec. dir., 1994; reporter L.A. Times, 1995—; adj. prof. urban studies U. Pa., 1990-93. Recipient nat. awards including Robert F. Kennedy Found. award, 1979, Heywood Broun award Newspaper Guild, 1978, Disting. Svc. medal Sigma Delta Chi, 1978, Pub. Svc. award AP Mng. Editors, 1978, Silver Gavel award ABA, 1979, 87, Pulitzer prize for investigative reporting, 1987, Pub. Svc. award Nat. Headliners Club, 1987; Nieman fellow Harvard U., 1989. Mem. Investigative Reporters and Editors (pres. 1988-91, chair 1991-93), Reporters Com. for Freedom of Press, Kappa Tau Alpha. Office: LA Times 388 Market St Fl 12 San Francisco CA 94111-5311

TUMELSON, BETSY MARTIN, consulting and training company executive; b. Paris, Tenn., July 29, 1943; d. Frank and Bassie Destine (Moore) Martin; m. Ronald Adrian Tumelson, Dec. 14, 1963; children: Arlene Dawn Dettler, Gretchen Loraine, Ronald Adrian, Karen Destine. BS in Human Relations Orgn. Behavior, U. San Francisco, 1982; MS in Human Resource Mgmt. Devel., Chapman U., 1984. Cert. orgn. cons. Cons. to city mgr. Heidelberg Am. Community, Fed. Republic Germany, 1979-80; cons., trainer U.S. Army Organizational Effectiveness Ctr. and Sch., Ford Ord, Calif., 1980-84; instr. Hartnell Coll., Salinas, Calif., 1985-87; expert community leader Dept. of Def., Washington, 1983—; pres. Betsy Tumelson, Cons., Monterey, Calif., 1980-84, Systems Excellence, Monterey, 1984—; adj. prof. U. San Francisco; pres. Mgmt. Inst. Monterey, 1986-94; cons. Smith/Trahern Mansion, Clarksville, Tenn., 1986—; sec. bd. dirs. Monterey Fed. Credit Union, 1991; bd. dirs. Nat. Coalition Bldg. Inst., 1993—. Author: Moving In and Moving Up, 1982, Managerial Competencies, 1982, Volunteer Motivational Index, 1981. Founder Leaderspirit, 1990. Named one of Outstanding Women in Leadership, County of Monterey (Calif.), 1990. Mem. Am. Mgmt. Assn. (speaker Pres.'s Assn.), Leadership Salinas Valley, German-Am. Club (Heidelberg, chmn. protocol and hospitality), Am. Women's Club (Heidelberg). Home: 54 Castro Rd Monterey CA 93940-4932 Office: Systems Excellence SYSTEX 177 Webster St Ste 3784A Monterey CA 93940-3119

TUNE, SUELYN CHING, secondary education educator; b. Palo Alto, Calif., June 7, 1944; d. Hung Leong and Mabel Chun Kiam (Tom) Ching; m. Gerald Robert Tune, Aug. 9, 1968; 1 child, Padraic Man Ching Tune. BA in Comparative Lit., Occidental Coll., 1965; MA in Ednl. Psychology, NYU, 1966; Profl. Diploma, Calif. State Coll., 1967. Cert. secondary educator, Calif.; cert. elem. educator, Hawaii. Tchr. L.A. City Schs., 1967-70, Hawaii State Dept. of Edn., Honolulu, 1970-71, Kamehameha Schs. Bishop Estate, Honolulu, 1971—. Co-author: (book) Made in Hawaii, 1983; author: (book) How Maui Slowed the Sun, 1988, Maui and the Secret of Fire, 1991, (booklet) Hawai'i in 1819: The Breakdown of the Kapu System, 1985, (booklet) Furs, Sandalwood, and Whales, 1989, (booklet) Liholiho, Kamehameha II, 1991. Mem. ASCD, Internat. Reading Assn., Honolulu Acad. Arts, Bishop Mus. Office: Kamehameha Schs Bishop Estate 1887 Makuakane St Honolulu HI 96817-1800

TUNG, PRABHAS, plastic surgeon; b. Ubol, Thailand, Apr. 3, 1944; s. Sathee and Sene (Ngium) T.; m. Patarin C. Sinjin; children: Tony, Tommy. MD, Mahidol U., Bangkok, 1968. Diplomate Am. Bd. Plastic Surgery. Plastic surgeon pvt. practice, Flint, Mich., 1980-82, Sacramento, Calif., 1982—. Office: 2801 K St Ste 200 Sacramento CA 95816-5118

TUNG, ROSALIE LAM, business educator, consultant; b. Shanghai, China, Dec. 2, 1948; came to U.S., 1975; d. Andrew Yan-Fu and Pauline Wai-Kam (Cheung) Lam. BA (Univ. scholar), York U., 1972; MBA, U. B.C., 1974, PhD in Bus. Adminstrn. (Univ. fellow, Seagram Bus. fellow, H.R. MacMillan Family fellow), 1977; m. Byron Poon-Yan Tung, June 17, 1972; 1 child, Michele Christine. Lectr. diploma div. U. B.C., 1975, lectr. exec. devel. program, 1975; asst. prof. mgmt. grad. sch. mgmt. U. Oreg., Eugene, 1977-80; assoc. prof. U. Pa., Phila. 1981-86; prof., dir. internat. bus. ctr. U. Wis., Milw., 1986-90; endowed chaired prof. Simon Fraser U., 1991—; vis. scholar U. Manchester (Eng.) Inst. Sci. and Tech., 1980; vis. prof. UCLA, 1981, Harvard U., 1988; Wis. disting. prof. U. Wis. System, 1988-90, Ming and Stella Wong chair in internat. bus., 1991—. Mem. Acad. Internat. Bus. (mem. exec. bd., treas. 1985-86), Acad. Mgmt. (bd. govs. 1987-89), Internat. Assn. Applied Psychology, Am. Arbitration Assn. (comml. panel arbitrators). Author: Management Practices in China, 1980, U.S.-China Trade Negotiations, 1982, Chinese Industrial Society After Mao, 1982, Business Negotiations with the Japanese, 1984, Key to Japan's Economic Strength: Human Power, 1984, The New Expatriates: Managing Human Resources Abroad, 1988; editor: Strategic Management in the U.S. and Japan, 1987, International Management in International Library of Business and Management Series, 1994. Oppenheimer Bros. Found. fellow, 1973-74, U. B.C. fellow, 1974-75, H.R. MacMillan Found. fellow, 1975-77; named Wis. Disting. Prof., 1988, Ming and Stella Wong Prof., 1991. Roman Catholic; recipient Leonore Rowe Williams award U. Pa., 1990, U. B.C. Alumni 75th Anniversary award, 1990. Avocation: creative writing. Office: Simon Fraser U, Faculty Bus Adminstrn, Burnaby, BC Canada V5A 1S6

TUNISON, ELIZABETH LAMB, education educator; b. Belfast, Northern Ireland, Jan. 7, 1922; came to U.S., 1923; d. Richard Ernest and Ruby (Hill) Lamb; m. Ralph W. Tunison, Jan. 24, 1947 (dec. Apr. 1984); children: Eric Arthur, Christine Wait, Dana Paul. BA, Whittier Coll., 1943, MEd, 1963. Tchr. East Whittier (Calif.) Schs., 1943-59; tchr. T.V. Stas. TV Channels 13 and 28, So. Calif. Counties, 1960-75; dir. curriculum Bassett (Calif.) Schs., 1962-65; elem. sch. prin. Rowland Unified Schs., Rowland Heights, Calif., 1965-68; assoc. prof. edn. Calif. State Poly. U., Pomona, 1968-71; prof. Whittier Coll., 1968-88, prof. emerita, 1988—. Bd. dirs. Presbyn. Intercommunity Hosp. Found. Recipient Whittier Coll. Alumni Achievement award 1975; Helen Hefernan scholar 1963. Mem. AAUP, Assn. Calif. Sch. Adminstrs. (state bd., chmn. higher edn. com. 1983-86, region pres. 1981-83, Wilson Grace award 1983), PEO (pres. 1990-92), Assistance League of Whittier (v.p. 1994—), Delta Kappa Gamma. Home: 5636 Ben Alder Ave Whittier CA 90601-2111

TUPIN, JOE PAUL, psychiatry educator; b. Comanche, Tex., Feb. 17, 1934; m. Betty Thompson, June 19, 1955; children: Paul, Rebecca, John. BS in Pharmacy, U. Tex., 1955, postgrad., 1955; MD, U. Tex., Galveston, 1959, Wash. Sch. Psychiatry, 1962, NIH Grad. Sch., 1962-64. Lic. psychiatrist, Tex., Calif. Intern U. Calif. Hosps., San Francisco, 1959-60; resident U. Tex. Med. br., Galveston, 1960-62, asst. prof. psychiatry, 1964-68, mem. staff John Sealy Hosp., 1964-69, dir. psychiatric consultation service, 1965-66, dir. psychiatric research, 1965-69, asst. dean medicine, 1967-68, assoc. prof., 1968-69, assoc. dean, 1968-69; resident NIMH div NIH, 1963-64; assoc. prof. psychiatry U. Calif., Davis, 1969-71, mem. staff Davis Med. Ctr., 1969—, vice-chmn. dept. psychiatry, 1970-76, prof., 1971-93, prof. emeritus, 1993, acting chmn. dept. psychiatry, 1977, acting dir. admissions sch. medicine, 1977-78, chmn. dept. psychiatry, 1977-84; med. dir. U. Calif. Davis Med. Ctr., 1984-93; cons. staff St. Mary's Infirmary, Galveston, 1967-69, Moody House Retirement Home for the Aged, Galveston, 1967-69, VA Hosp., Martinez, 1977-82, Yolo Gen. Hosp., 1980-81; dir. psychiatric consultation service U. Calif., Davis, 1969-74, co-director 1974-77; vis. prof. King's Coll. Med. Sch., London, 1974; acting dir. admissions sch. medicine, U. Calif., Davis, 1977-78; chief div. mental health U. Calif. Davis Med. Ctr., 1977-84, also mem. quality care com., 1979-85, chmn. com., 1981-85; med. dir. and assoc. dir. Hosp. and Clinics U. Calif., Davis, 1984-93; cons. U. Calif., Davis, 1993. Referee and book reviewer numerous publs.; mem. sci. editorial bd. Am. Jour. Forensic Psychiatry, 1985-88, Jour. Clin. Psychopharmacology, 1981—, Psychiatry, 1985, Tex. Reports on Biology and Medicine, 1965-67, 68-69; Western Jour. Medicine, 1979-89; contbr. numerous articles to profl. jours. Mem. Academically Talented Child com. Galveston City Sch. Bd., 1966-67; chmn. bd. dirs. William Temple Found., Galveston, 1967-68; bd. dirs. Citizens for Advancement of Pub. Edn., Galveston, 1967-69, pres., 1968-69, Moody House Retirement Home for the Aged, 1968, Cal Aggie Athletic Assn., 1978-82; mem. Davis Master Plan com., 1971. Served to lt. commdr. USPHS, 1962-64, with Res. 1964-80. Recipient Career Teaching award NIMH, 1964-66; named to Friars Soc. U. Tex., 1954; Mosby scholar U. Tex., Ginsberg fellow Group for Advancement of Psychiatry, 1960-62, Nat. Found. Infantile Paralysis fellow, 1957; grantee U. Tex. Med. br., 1964-69, NIMH, 1965-68. Fellow Am. Psychiat. Assn., Am. Coll. Psychiatrists (mem. com., editorial com.); mem. AMA, Yolo County Med. Assn. (chmn. credentials com. 1974-75, nominating com. 1980-84), Calif. Med. Assn. (sec. psychiatry sect. 1977-78, 78-79, sci. adv. panel on psychiatry 1975-80, psychiatry adv. sect. 1977-80, sci. adv. bd. 1978-80), Titus Harris Soc., Cen. Calif. Psychiat. Soc. (chmn. mem. com. 1970-73, pres. 1976), AAAS, Soc. Health and Human Values (exec. council 1970-73), Am. Acad. Psychiatry and the Law, AAUP, West Coast Coll. Biol. Psychiatries Com., Sigma Xi, Rho Chi, Alpha Omega Alpha. Home: 108 Kent Dr Davis CA 95616 Office: U Calif Davis Med Ctr Office of Med Scis 2315 Stockton Blvd Sacramento CA 95817-2201

TURCO, RONALD NICHOLAS, psychiatrist, educator; b. Phila., Apr. 11, 1940; s. Luigi A. and Antonetta Luci (Tucci) T.; m. Joanne L. Labezius, June 8, 1966; children: Annyce, Diana. BS, Pa. State U., 1962; MD, Jefferson Med. Coll., Phila., 1966. Diplomate Am. Bd. Psychiatry and Neurology, Am. Bd. Med. Examiners. Surg. intern Bryn Mawr (Pa.) Hosp., 1966-67; resident in psychiatry U. N.C., Chapel Hill, 1967-68, U. Oreg. Health Sci. Ctr., Portland, 1968-70; staff psychiatrist Brooklane Psychiat. Ctr., Hagerstown, Md., 1973-74; dir. psychiatry Cedar Hills Psychiat. Hosp., Portland, 1974-75; pvt. practice psychiatry Portland, 1974—; assoc. clin. prof. Oreg. Health Scs. U., Portland, 1974—; cons. Newberg and Portland Police Depts., 1974—, Circuit, Dist. and Fed. Cts., Portland, 1974—, Reed Coll., Portland, 1974—. Contbr. articles to profl. jours. Tchr. First Presbyn. Ch., Portland, 1981—, Portland Film Study Ctr., 1985—; campaign chmn. Jim Davis for Mayor Com., Portland, 1990; sponsor Futures for Childre, Albuquerque, 1990—. Maj. USAF, 1970-73. Recipient Milton Erickson award Am. Soc. Clin. Hypnosis, 1990, commendation for community svc. Newberg Police Dept., 1991. Mem. Am. Acad. Psychoanalysis (transcultural com.), Portland Psychiatrists in Pvt. Practice (pres. 1985), Am. Acad. Psychoanalytic Physicians, Am. Acad. Psychoanalysis (transcultural com.), Def. for Chldren Interant., Oreg. Med. Assn., Internat. Assn. Chiefs of Police. Home and Office: 1220 SW Morrison St Ste 805 Portland OR 97205-2227

TURGEL, STUART CHARLES, hospital administrator; b. Boston, June 15, 1948; m. Lynn Greenberg, Mar. 28, 1976; children: Mindy Sue, Ariel David, Sarah Ruth. Student, Marietta Coll., N.E. Broadcasting Sch., U.S. Def. Dept. Schs. Journalism and Broadcasting, U. Denver. Music dir. Sta. WCMO-FM, Marietta, Ohio, 1966-67; news dir., chief announcer Armed Forces Radio and TV Network, Johnston Island, 1968-70; external media liaison, sr. info. officer Fitzsimons Gen. Hosp., Denver, 1970-71; pub. rels. asst. Nat. Jewish Hosp. and Rsch. Ctr., Denver, 1971-72, devel. assoc., 1972-73, area dir. fin. devel., 1973-74, asst. dir. fin. devel., 1974-78; exec. dir. Menorah Med. Ctr. Found., Kansas City, Mo., 1978-80; exec. v.p. The Children's Hosp. Found., Denver, 1980-87; pres. The Sheridan (Wyo.) Inn, 1985-87; sr. v.p. external affairs, exec. dir. Children's Hosp. Found. Children's Hosp. and Health Ctr., San Diego, 1987-93; sr. v.p. mktg. and external affairs Lucile Salter Packard Children's Hosp. Stanford, Palo Alto, Calif., 1993—. Active LEAD San Diego, 1991; past pres. Congregation Beth Am, Solana Beach, Calif.; former trustee Rocky Mountain Philanthropy Fund, Osmond Found.; bd. dirs. Congregation Kol Emeth, Palo Alto, Calif. Recipient Presdl. letter of commendation, 1969, McEachern award, 1970, Gold Pick award Pub. Rels. Soc. Am., 1983, regional Emmy award, 1984. Mem. Am. Soc. Health Care Mktg. and Pub. Rels. of Am. Hosp. Assn., Acad. Health Svcs. Mktg. of Am. Mktg. Assn., Nat. Assn. Children's Hosps. and Related Instns. (mem. child health policy coun.), Assn. Healthcare Philanthropy, Colo. Assn. Fund Raisers (past pres.), Knights of Pythias. Address: 2938 Waverley St Palo Alto CA 94306-2440 Office: Lucile Salter Packard Children's Hosp Stanford 725 Welch Rd Palo Alto CA 94304-1601

TURK, RUDY HENRY, artist, retired museum director; b. Sheboygan, Wis., June 24, 1927; s. Rudolph Anton and Mary Gertrude (Stanisha) T.; m. Wanda Lee Borders, Aug. 4, 1956; children: Tracy Lynn, Maria Teresa, Andrew Borders, Jennifer Wells. BS in Edn., U. Wis., 1949; MA in History, U. Tenn., 1951; postgrad., Ind. U., 1952-56. Instr. art history, gallery dir. U. Mont., Missoula, 1957-60; dir. Richmond (Calif.) Art Ctr., 1960-65; asst. dir. San Diego Mus. Art, 1965-67; dir. Ariz. State U. Art Mus., 1967-92; from assoc. prof. to prof. art Ariz. State U., 1967-77. Painter, paintings exhibited in solo and group exhbns.; mus. cons., juror, art cons., art lectr; author: (with Cross and Lamm) The Search for Personal Freedom, 2 vols., 1972, 76, 80, 85, Merrill Mahaffey: Monumental Landscapes, 1979, (with others) Scholder, 1983, also commentaries and critiques. Bd. dirs. Chandler Arts Com., 1983-86, Friends of Mex. Art, Ariz., 1986—, pres. 1988-90; mem. Tempe Arts Com., 1987-89, Ariz. Living Treasures Com., 1988-93; bd. dirs. Ariz. Mus. for Youth, 1993—. Recipient merit award Calif. Coll. Arts and Crafts, 1965, Senator's Cultural award State of Ariz., 1987, Golden Crate award Western Assn. Art Mus., 1974, Ariz. Gov.'s Art award, 1992; named Hon. Ariz. Designer Craftsman, 1975; named dir. emeritus Ariz. State U. Art Mus., 1992, Rudy Turk Gallery at Ariz. State U. Art Mus. named in his honor, 1992; Fulbright scholar U. Paris, 1956-57; hon. fellow Am. Craft Coun., 1988. Mem. Nat. Coun. Edn. Ceramic Arts (hon. mem. coun. 1991), Phi Alpha Theta, Phi Kappa Phi. Democrat. Home: 760 E Courtney Ln Tempe AZ 85284-4003 Office: Ariz State U U Art Museum Tempe AZ 85287-2911

TURKS, VICTOR LEONARD, English language educator; b. Lübeck, Germany, Feb. 18, 1946; came to U.S., 1950; s. John Leonard and Helena (Ruskulis) T.; m. Laurie Jane Larson, June 8, 1968 (div. 1988); m. Michiko Adachi, June 8, 1988; children: Aaron, Terence. AA, San Francisco City Coll., 1965; BA, San Francisco State U., 1968, MA, 1969. Cert. lifetime jr. coll. lang. arts and lit. tchr., Calif. Instr. English Sprach-Inst. Cologne, Hamburg, Germany, 1970-72; instr. English and composition San Francisco C.C.-City Coll. San Francisco, 1973—; instr. English lang. San Francisco State U.-Am. Lang. Inst., summer 1980; instr. English composition and lit. Eugene J. McAteer H.S., San Francisco, 1987-92; instr. English Nagoya (Japan) Sch. Bus., 1985; adminstr. in charge evening-Saturday-summer programs Mission Comty Coll. Ctr., San Fancisco, 1977, 78, 79. Contbr. poetry to anthologies, articles to profl. jours. Democrat. Home: 775 23rd Ave San Francisco CA 94121-3736 Office: City Coll San Francisco 50 Phelan Ave San Francisco CA 94112-1821

TURLEY-MOORE, SUSAN GWEN, minister; b. Boston, June 19, 1952; d. Calvin Earl and Marilyn (Anderson) Turley; m. Clifford Jesse Moore, Jr., Jan. 7, 1978; 1 child, Keith Jesse. BA in Sociology, Urbana (Ohio) U.; MEd, Suffolk U. Lic. cert. social worker, Mass.; ordained to ministry Swedenborgian Ch. Pvt. practice as pastoral psychotherapist Turley and Assocs., Newton, Mass., 1979-81; pastor Swedenborgian Ch., Portland, Maine, 1981-84; pastor on ministerial team Wayfarer's Chapel, L.A., 1984-87; founder, dir. Swedenborigan Social Action Concerns Com., 1987-92; guidance counselor Fairbanks Elem. Sch., Sacramento, Calif., 1987-89; interim assoc. pastor Swedenborgian Ch., San Francisco, 1989-90; chaplain and pastoral staff New Ch. Youth League West Coast, 1990-92; founding exec. dir. of living waters HIV ministry Swedenborgian Ch., San Francisco, 1992—. Mem. ACA, Nat. Coun. of Chs. (counseling com. 1977—),. Office: Swedenborgian Ch Living Waters PO Box 460388 San Francisco CA 94146-0388

TURNAGE, JEAN A., state supreme court chief justice; b. St. Ignatius, Mont., Mar. 10, 1926. JD, Mont. State U., 1951, LLD, 1995. Bar: Mont. 1951, U.S. Supreme Ct. 1963. Formerly ptnr. Turnage, McNeil & Mercer, Polson, Mont.; formerly Mont. State senator from 13th Dist.; pres. Mont. State Senate, 1981-83; chief justice Supreme Ct. Mont., 1985—. Mem. Mont. State Bar Assn., Nat. Conf. Chief Justices (past pres.), Nat. Ctr. State Courts (past chair). Office: Mont Supreme Ct 215 N Sanders St Helena MT 59601-4522

TURNBOW, JEFFERY THEODORE, radio news director; b. Kellogg, Idaho, June 19, 1961; s. Gerald Glenn and Corrine Marcella (Hermunstad) T. AA, Columbia Basin Coll., 1992. Air talent KIZN Radio, Boise, Idaho, 1983; music dir. KDUK Radio, Eugene, Oreg., 1983-84; air talent KBOL Radio, Boulder, Colo., 1984-85, KHOW Radio, Denver, 1985-86; ops. mgr. KRXK Radio, Rexburg, Idaho, 1986-87; news dir. KORD Radio, Pasco, Wash., 1987—; bd. dirs. Products Indsl. Exposition. Adult literacy tutor Columbia Basin Coll., Pasco, 1992—. Mem. Soc. Profl. Journalists. Office: KORD Radio 2621 W A St Pasco WA 99301-4702

TURNBULL, DOREEN JOYCE, electronic data processing consultant; b. Evanston, Ill., Jan. 10, 1938; d. Dale M. and Juliet L. (Van Buskirk) T. B.S. in Bus. Mgmt., Calif. State Poly., Pomona, 1969; M.A. in Mgmt., Claremont Grad. Sch., 1984. Sr. systems analyst Sunkist Growers Inc., Sherman Oaks, Calif., 1968-74; EDP systems analyst Ralphs Grocery Co., Compton, Calif., 1974-77; propr. DJT Cons., 1977-80; project mgr., sr. systems analyst, Xerox Corp., Pasadena, Calif., 1980-84; project mgr. DHL Corp., San Bruno, Calif., 1984-86; propr. DJT Cons., 1986; computer security analyst Westinghouse Marine div., Sunnyvale Calif., 1986-92. Mem. NAFE, Data Processing Mgmt. Assn. (past. chpt. dir., sec.), Am. Mgmt. Assn., Women in Mgmt., IS/DP Alumni Assn. (past dir.). Club: Altrusa (past treas., past sec.) (Arcadia, Calif.). Home and Office: 760 Edgemar Ave Pacifica CA 94044-2319

TURNBULL, WILLIAM, JR., architect; b. N.Y.C., Apr. 1, 1935; s. William and Elizabeth (Howe) T. A.B., Princeton U., 1956, M.F.A. in Architecture, 1959; student, Ecole des Beaux Arts Fontainebleau, 1956. With Skidmore, Owings & Merrill, San Francisco, 1960-63; founding ptnr. Moore, Lyndon, Turnbull, Whitaker, 1962; partner-in-charge Moore, Turnbull (San Francisco office), 1965-69; mem. design group Pres.'s Adv. Coun. Pennsylvania Ave., 1963; lectr. U. Calif.-Berkeley, 1965-69; vis. prof. U. Oreg., 1966-68; dir. MLTW/Turnbull Assocs., 1970-83; dir. William Turnbull Assocs., 1983—; lectr. Stanford U., 1974-77; vis. design critic MIT, 1975, U. Calif., Berkeley, 1977-81, 95; Mobil vis. design critic Yale U., 1982, Bishop vis. prof. archtl. design, 1986; Hyde prof. excellence U. Nebr. 1994; design cons. Formica Corp., 1978-85, World Savs. and Loan, 1976—; mem. design rev. bd. U. Calif., San Diego, 1988-93, City of Sausalito, Calif., 1976-77. Author: Global Architecture Series: Moore, Lyndon, Turnbull & Whitaker: The Sea Ranch, The Sea Ranch Details, The Poetics of Gardens, 1988; illustrator: The Place of Houses; prin. works include Sea Ranch Condominium I, 1965, Sea Ranch Swim Tennis Club, 1966, Lovejoy Fountain Plaza, Portland (assoc. architect), Faculty Club at U. Calif.-Santa Barbara, Kresge Coll. at U. Calif.-Santa Cruz, Biloxi (Miss.) Library, Am. Club, Hong Kong, Ariz. State U. Sonora Ctr., Tempe, Foothill Student Housing, U. Calif., Berkeley, Mountain View City Hall and Community Theater, Calif.; mem. editorial adv. bd. Architecture California, 1986-92. Mem. tech. adv. com. Calif. Legislature Joint Com. Open Space Lands, 1968-71; mem. regional honor awards (90) jury AIA, 1968—, nat. honor awards jury, 1969, chmn. jury, 1977, 1988; chmn. jury C.E. honor award, 1973, 79; mem. Progressive Architecture Honor Awards Jury, 1975, Pres.'s Jury for Nat. Design Excellence, 1984; bd. dirs. Pub. Sculpture Pub. Places, 1981-85. Served with AUS, 1959-60. Recipient Calif. Gov. award planned communities, 1966; citation Progressive Architecture Design awards, 1962-66, 68-70, 81; 1st honor award, 1971, 74; First honor award Homes for Better Living, 1963; Merit award, 1966; Honor award Western Home awards, 1961-62, 62, 63, 66-67, 88, 89; Merit award, 1966-67; House of Year award Archtl. Record, 1961, 67, 69, 70, 72, 83; award of Honor San Francisco Art Commn., 1982; Am. Wood Council Design award, 1984, Honor award, 1985, 89, 92, 94, 95; Firm of the Yr. award Calif. Council AIA, 1986, Maybeck award 1993, cited for continuous distinctive practice of architecture in Calif. by an individual; Am. Wood Coun. Merit award, 1991; Honor award San Francisco AIA, 1991. Fellow AIA (dir. chpt. 1981, Nat. Honor award 1967, 68, 73, 79, 90, 95, award of merit, bay region honor awards 1963, 67, 74, 78, 82, Nat. 25 Yr. Honor award 1991), Am. Acad. in Rome. Office: William Turnbull Assocs Pier 1 1/2 The Embarcadero San Francisco CA 94111

TURNER, BONESE COLLINS, artist, educator; b. Abilene, Kans.; d. Paul Edwin and Ruby (Seybold) Collins; m. Glenn E. Turner; 1 child, Craig Collins. BS in Edn., U. Idaho, MEd; MA, Calif. State U., Northridge, 1974. Instr. art L.A. Pierce Coll., Woodland Hills, Calif., 1964—; prof. art Calif. State U., Northridge, 1986-87; art instr. L.A. Valley Coll., Van Nuys, 1987-89, Moorpark (Calif.) Coll., 1988—; advisor Coll. Art and Architecture U. Idaho, 1988—; juror for numerous art exhibitions including Nat. Watercolor Soc., 1980, 91, San Diego Art Inst., Brand Nat. Watermedia Exhibition prin. gallery Orlando Gallery, Sherman Oaks, Calif. Prin. works exhibited in The White House, 1984, 85, Smithsonian Inst., 1984, 85, Olympic Arts Festival, L.A., 1984; one woman shows include Angel's Gate Gallery, San Pedro, Calif., 1989, Art Store Gallery, Studio City, Calif., 1988, L.A. Pierce Coll. Gallery, 1988, Brand Art Gallery, Glendale, Calif., 1988, 93, Coos (Oreg.) Art Mus., 1988, U. Nev., 1987, Orlando Gallery, Sherman Oaks, Calif., 1993, others; prin. works represented in pub. collections including Smithsonian Inst., Hartung Performing Arts Ctr., Moscow, Idaho, Home Savs. and Loan, San Bernardino Sun Telegram Newspapers, Oreg. Coun. for the Arts, Newport, Nebr. Pub. Librs., Lincoln (Nebr.) Indsl. Tile Corp. Recipient awards Springfield (Mo.) Art Mus., 1989, Butler Art Inst., 1989. Mem. Nat. Mortar Bd. Soc., Nat. Watercolor Soc. (life, past pres., Purchase prize 1979), Watercolor U.S.A. Honor Soc. (award), Watercolor West.

TURNER, CLYDE T., service executive; b. Las Vegas, Nev., July 18, 1937; s. Benjamin Joseph and Ruby (Denny) T.; m. Vivian Lee (div.); children: Gregory Einor, Blair Alexander, Susan Irene Keefe; m. Vera M., June 16,

1963. BS, U. Nev., Reno, 1960. Gaming commr. Nev. State Gaming commn., 1970-73; bd. dirs., mng. ptnr. Kafoury, Armstrong, Turner & Co. CPAs, Las Vegas, Nev., 1966-79; exec. v.p., chief fin. officer, treas. Golden Nugget Inc., Las Vegas, 1979—; chmn., pres. CEO Circus Circus Enterprises, Inc., Las Vegas, NV, Now; bd. dirs. Golden Nugget subs., Las Vegas. Mem. Am. Bd. CPAs. Home: 3035 Ashby Ave Las Vegas NV 89102-1948 Office: Circus Circus Enterprises 2880 Las Vegas Blvd S Las Vegas NV 89109-1138

TURNER, DAVID WINBURN, aerospace engineer; b. Havre, Mont., Sept. 12, 1946; s. David Henry and Mary Fay (Winburn) T.; m. Irene McLean Miller, Sept. 12, 1986. BS in Physics, Mont. State U., 1968; MS in Systems Engring., Calif. State U., Fullerton, 1971; PhD in Engring., U. Calif., Irvine, 1979; M Engring. in Aeronautics, Calif. Poly. Inst., Pomona, 1989. Mem. tech. staff Autonetics, Anaheim, Calif., 1968-79, Lear Siegler Astronics, Santa Monica, Calif., 1979-83; sr. tech. specialist Northrop Aircraft Co., Hawthorne, Calif., 1983—. Contbr. articles to profl. publs. Mem. AIAA, IEEE. Office: Northrop Aircraft Co 1 Northrop Ave # 710 90 Hawthorne CA 90250-3236

TURNER, DEE STONE, adult nurse practitioner, diabetes researcher; b. Seattle, Mar. 27, 1934; d. George Harrison and Dulyce Ione (Follette) Stone; m. James W. Turner, June 29, 1955; children: James Harrison, Kenneth Winslow, Gary Stephen, Jonathan Addison. Diploma in nursing, U. Wash., 1954; AA, Golden West Coll., 1978; BSN, Calif. State U., Long Beach, 1980, MSN, 1988. RN, Calif.; cert. pub. health nurse, nurse practitioner, Calif.; CCRN; cert. adult nurse practitioner. Staff nurse Virginia Mason Hosp., Seattle, 1955; staff nurse respiratory ICU, Los Angeles County-U. So. Calif. Med. Ctr., L.A., 1967-69; critical care nurse Lescoulie Nurses Registry, Newport Beach, Calif., 1970-82; adult nurse practitioner, rsch. coord. U. Calif., Irvine, 1987—. Contbr. numerous articles on diabetes rsch. to profl. jours. Mem. Am. Diabetes Assn. (profl. sect.), Am. Assn. Diabetes Educators (cert.), Calif. Nurses Assn. (profl. practice commn. 1988-92), Calif. Coalition Nurse Practitioners (founding sec. Orange County chpt. 1988-89), Sigma Theta Tau, Phi Delta Gamma, Phi Kappa Phi. Home: 409 Bayside Dr Newport Beach CA 92660-7212 Office: U Calif UCI Med Plz Irvine CA 92717

TURNER, DENNIS M. J., pharmaceutical executive. Pres., CEO, dir. Pharm. Mktg. Svc., Scottsdale, Ariz. Office: Pharm Mktg Svcs Inc 2394 E Camelback Rd Phoenix AZ 85016*

TURNER, FLORENCE FRANCES, ceramist; b. Detroit, Mar. 9, 1926; d. Paul Pokrywka and Catherine Gagal; m. Dwight Robert Turner, Oct. 23, 1948; children: Thomas Michael, Nancy Louise, Richard Scott, Garry Robert. Student, Oakland C.C., Royal Oak, Mich., 1975-85, U. Ariz., Yuma, 1985, U. Las Vegas, 1989—. Pres., founder Nev. Clay Guild, Henderson, 1990-94, mem. adv. bd., 1994—; workshop leader Greenfield Village, Dearborn, Mich., 1977-78, Plymouth (Mich.) Hist. Soc., 1979, Las Vegas Sch. System, 1989-90, Detroit Met. area, 1977-85. Bd. dirs. Las Vegas Art Mus., 1987-91; corr. sec. So. Nev. Creative Art Ctr., Las Vegas, 1990-94. Mem. Las Vegas Gem Club, Nev. Camera Club, Golden Key, Phi Kappa Phi. Office: Nev Clay Guild PO Box 50004 Henderson NV 89016-0004

TURNER, GARRISON F., lawyer; b. Modesto, Calif., Nov. 8, 1947; s. Paul William and Raylene F. (Smith) T.; m. Pamela Ann Burkholder, Oct. 11, 1981; 1 child, Abigail. BA, U. Calif., Berkeley, 1969; JD, U. Calif., San Francisco, 1972. Bar: Calif. 1972, Oreg. 1985. Dep. pub. defender San Joaquin County, Calif., 1973-80; assoc. Freeman, Rishwain & Hall, Stockton, 1981-82; ptnr. Freeman, Hall, Turner & Brown, Stockton, 1982-85; assoc. Frohnmayer, Deatherage, deSchweinitz, Pratt & Jamieson, Medford, Oreg., 1985-88; ptnr. Frohnmayer, Deatherge, Pratt, Jamieson & Turner, Medford, 1988-94; sole practice Ashland, Oreg., 1994—; instr. Humphreys Coll. Law, Stockton, 1974-75. Capt. U.S. Army, 1969-77. Mem. State Bar Calif., State Bar Oreg., Jackson County Bar Assn., Oreg. Assn. Def. Counsel. Democrat. Office: 108 N 2nd St Ashland OR 97520-1935

TURNER, HAL WESLEY, state agency administrator; b. Winchester, Mass., Nov. 18, 1932; s. Wesley Francis and Anna Louise (Hodgkins) T.; children: Julie, Karen. BA, Sioux Falls (S.D.) Coll., 1955. Cert. Govtl. Fin. Mgr. Mem. tech. and mgmt. staff Boeing Computer Svcs., Seattle, 1958-69; mgr. prodn. systems Kennecott Copper Corp., Salt Lake City, 1970-71; dir. MIS State of Idaho, Boise, 1971-74, adminstr. of budget, 1974-77; sales assoc. White Riedel Realtors, Boise, 1978-81; chief dep. Idaho State Controller's Office, Boise, 1981—; pres., Student Loan Fund Idaho, Inc., Fruitland, 1978—. Mem. Boise State U. Profl. Tng. Devel. Coun. Exec. Com., Boise Samaritan Village Health Facility Adv. Bd., Idaho Com. for Employer Support of Guard and Reserve. With U.S. Army, 1955-57. Mem. Nat. Assn. State Auditor's Comptr. and Treas., Nat. Assn. Govtl. Accts., Elks, Broadmore Country Club. Democrat. Methodist. Home: 3512 S Brookshore Pl Boise ID 83706-5582 Office: State Contrs Office PO Box 83720 Boise ID 83720-0002

TURNER, LILLIAN ERNA, nurse; b. Coalmont, Colo., Apr. 22, 1918; d. Harvey Oliver and Erna Lena (Wackwitz) T. BS, Colo. State U., 1940, Columbia U., 1945; cert. physician asst., U. Utah, 1978. Commd. 2d lt. Nurse Corps, U.S. Army, 1945; advanced through grades to lt. comdr. USPHS, 1964; 1st lt. U.S. Army, 1945-46; U.S. Pub. Health Svc., 1964-69; dean of women U. Alaska, Fairbanks, 1948-50; head nurse Group Health Hosp., Seattle, 1950-53; adviser to chief nurse Hosp. Am. Samoa, Pago Pago, 1954-60; head nurse Meml. Hosp., Twin Falls, Idaho, 1960-61; shift supr. Hosp. Lago Oil and Transport, Siero Colorado, Aruba, 1961-63; nurse adv. Province Hosp., Danang, South Vietnam, 1964-69, Cho Quan Hosp., South Vietnam, 1970-72; chief nurse, advisor Truk Hosp., Moen, Ea. Caroline Islands, 1972-74; nurse advisor Children's Med. Relief Internat., South Vietnam, 1975; physician's asst. U. Utah, 1976-78, Wagon Circle Med. Clinic, Rawlins, Wyo., 1978-89, Energy Basin Clinic Carbon County Meml. Hosp., Hanna, Wyo., 1989—. Named Nat. Humanitarian Pa. of Yr., 1993, Wyo. Pa. of Yr., 1992. Mem. Wyo. Acad. Physician Assts. (bd. dirs. 1982-83), Am. Acad. Physician Assts., Nat. Assn. Physician Assts. Home: PO Box 337 Hanna WY 82327-0337

TURNER, MAUREEN BARBARA, mathematics educator, researcher; b. Washington, July 20, 1936; d. Max and Florence Estelle (Tanenbaum) T. AB, Cornell U., 1956; postgrad., Johns Hopkin's U., 1960; MA, Columbia U., 1961; postgrad., U. Calif., Berkeley, 1965. Teaching asst. in maths. Columbia U., N.Y.C., 1960-61, U. Calif., Berkely, 1962, 63; instr. in maths. Reed Coll., Portland, Oreg., 1965-66; prof. maths. Calif. State U., Long Beach, 1966—. Bd. reviewers Col. Maths. Jour.; contbr. articles to profl. jours. Mem. Phi Beta Kappa, Phi Kappa Phi, Alpha Epsilon Delta. Office: Calif State U Math Dept 1250 N Bellflower Blvd Long Beach CA 90840-0006

TURNER, MORTIMER DARLING, research geologist; b. Greeley, Colo., Oct. 24, 1920; s. Clarence Earnest and Satia May (Darling) T.; m. Laura Mercedes Perez-Mendez, Jan. 25, 1945 (dec. Mar. 1965); children: Satia Elisa, Ylla Sofia, Robert Stuart; m. Joanne Kay Church, Dec. 5, 1965; 1 stepchild, Christopher Scott Dort. BS, U. Calif., Berkeley, 1943; student, Va. Polytechnic Inst., 1943-44; MS, U. Calif., Berkeley, 1954; PhD, U. Kans., 1972. Registered geologist and engring. geologist, Calif. Asst. mining geologist Calif. Div. Mines and Geology, San Francisco, 1949-54; state geologist P.R. Econ. Devel. Adminstrn., Santurce, 1954-59; phys. sci. adminstr. NSF, Washington, 1959-61, program mgr. polar earth scis., 1965-85; rsch. assoc. U. Kans., Lawrence, 1962-65, Tex. Tech U., Lubbock, 1985; sr. rsch. assoc. emeritus U. Colo., Boulder, 1988—; cons., ptnr. JCT Enterprises, Boulder, 1977—; assoc. professorial lectr. George Washington U., Washington, 1972-88, U. Colo., Denver, 1990—; adj. prof. Quaternary studies U. Maine, Orono, 1985-94; chmn. sci. coun. Ctr. for Study of First Ams., Orono, 1989-91, Corvallis, Oreg., 1991—; lectr. Antarctica Expdn. Cruises, Seattle, 1990. Editor: Clays and Clay Technology, 1957, Geology of Central Transantarctic Mountains, 1987; contbr. articles to profl. jours. With U.S. Army, 1943-46. Recipient Presdl. award for mgmt. improvement, White House, 1975; Fellow Shell Oil, 1964. Fellow Geol. Soc. Am.; mem. Internat. Geol. Congress (v.p. 1956), Antarctican Soc. (dir., pres. 1959-68), numerous other sci. and engring. socs. Democrat. Home: 701 Crescent Dr Boulder CO 80303-2712 Office: Univ Colo INSTARR Campus Box 450 Boulder CO 80309-0450

TURNER, NANCY ELIZABETH, artist, designer; b. Cumberland Mountains, Ky.; d. Earl K. and Mary Lee (Jones) T.; m. Peter Alvet, Mar. 31, 1989. BA in Liberal Arts, U. Southwestern La.; Master Painter and Restorer, Yelland Acad. Fine Art, Calif.; cert. completion, Interior Decorators Inst. of L.A., 1990. Owner, chmn. The Turner Studio, Los Angeles; head artist/designer The Art Connection, Beverly Hills, Calif. Work includes fine paintings, artwork and decorative svcs. for residential and comml. interiors, trompe l'oeil murals, huge comml. fine art murals and signs, creator fine arts naturalism-natural looking flowers and foliage painted on walls and buildings, hand painted furniture and standing screens; creator bestselling collector's plates Michael's Miracio, 1982, Susan's World, 1983, illustrations appearing in the L.A. Times. Leader nat. multi-ch. religious freedom crusade, 1985-86. Winner Lithograph of Yr. award, 1982. Mem. Am. Inst. Fine Arts, Am. Soc. Interior Designers (accessorizing cons.). Address: PO Box 9223 Glendale CA 91226

TURNER, NORRIS, marketing professional; b. Angelina, Tex., May 3, 1934; s. Ezra and Frankie Turner; m. Katherine Fields, Aug. 16, 1962; 1 child, Tammie Diatrice. BS, Fisk U., 1968. Cert. real estate appraiser; lic. notary pub., ins. agt. Admission officer West Point N.Y., L.A., 1971; dir. vets. programs, profl. recorder, in-sch. coord. L.A. Urban League, 1983; loan officer Empire of Am., Inglewood, Calif., 1983-86; account exec. Imperial Thrift & Loan, Burbank, Calif., 1986-88; v.p., dir. The Mortgage Acad., Ventura, Calif., 1988—; instr. Compton (Calif.) Coll., 1977-78. Author: A Balance Approach to Career Training, 1992. HAC mem. Century Freeway, State of Calif., 1982; chairperson L.A. City Vets. Svcs., 1980-81; treas. reelection svc. L.A. Calif. Reps., 1983; pres. Luth. Day-Care Sch., 1988-89; mem., vol. L.A. Urban League, 1990-92; v.p. local dist. Rep. party, 1987-88. With U.S. Army, 1956-58. Recipient awards L.A. City Coun., 1980, Pres. U.S.A., 1978-79, Cert. of Appreciation U.S. Mil. Acad., 1980, Hon. Admissions Officer award U.S. Mil. Acad., 1980, award L.A. Urban League, 1981-82. Mem. Am. Banking Assn. (treas. 1980-81). Lutheran. Home: 8813 S 4th Ave Inglewood CA 90305-2811

TURNER, RICHARD ARLEN, financial executive; b. Lynchburg, Ohio, Feb. 5, 1934; s. Issac Hamilton and Cleo (Wood) T.; m. Marilyn June Rose, Aug. 30, 1959; children: Kimberly Ann, David Arlen. BS, Miami U., 1960, postgrad., 1962-63. CPA, Ohio, Calif. Mgr. Deloitte Haskins & Sells, Dayton, Ohio, San Francisco and Caracas, Venezuela, 1960-73; sec.-treas. Grihalva Chevrolet, San Diego, 1973-74; cons. various cos., San Diego and Phoenix, 1975-76; v.p. fin. Pepper Industries, San Diego, 1976-80; v.p. fin. Ernst Enterprises, Inc., Dayton, Ohio, 1980-86; pres. H.R. Large & Assocs., Inc., San Diego, 1986-88; v.p. fin. Sail Am. Found. (name changed to Am.'s Cup Organizing Com., 1988—; ptnr., co-founder Corp. Mgmt. Specialists, San Diego, 1988—; chief fin officer High Ground Assocs., San Diego, 1988-90; v.p. fin. Am's. Cup Svcs., 1990-91; co-founder, stockholder, CFO Coral Information Systems, Inc., San Diego, 1993; bd dirs. Dolly Toy Co., Tipp City, Ohio, R & R Constrn. Co., Union, Ohio; fin. cons. Kuhns Tool Co., Brookville, Ohio, 1983-86. Bd. dirs. Grace Brethern Community Ch., Union, 1984-86. Served with USAF, 1952-56. Mem. AICPA, Nat. Ready Mixed Concrete Assn. (fin. mgmt. com.), Ohio Ready Mixed Concrete Assn. (treas. 1984-86), Rotary, Optimist (treas. 1974-75). Republican. Home: 803 Concerto Gln Escondido CA 92025-7922 Office: Corp Mgmt Specialists 16935 W Bernadino Dr Ste 110 San Diego CA 92127 also: Sail America Found 1660 Hotel Circle N San Diego CA 92108

TURNER, ROBERT EUGENE, retail executive; b. Pittsburgh, Kans., Jan. 16, 1952; s. Roy and Anne Turner; m. Susan Alexander. Owner Bizarre Guitar & Drum, Phoenix, 1975—; guitar/drum retailer, vintage guitar historian, cons., appraiser. Contbr.: (book) The Guitar Book; contbr. articles to profl. jours. and books. Named Best Guitar Dealer in Phoenix, Readers Choice, Guitar Mag. Mem. Nat. Assn. Music Merchants, Train Collectors Assn., Toy Trains Operators Soc., Ferrari Club of N.A. Office: Bizarre Guitar & Drum 749 W Camelback Rd Phoenix AZ 85013-2206

TURNER, STEPHEN WAYNE, library director; b. Sacramento, Calif., July 31, 1945; s. George Rodgers and Louise Betty (Baumgart) T.; m. Patricia Ann Robison, June 25, 1972; children: Dorothy L., Elizabeth N., Peter E., Emily Jane. BA, U. Rochester, 1967; MA, U. Calif., Irvine, 1969; MLS, U. Denver, 1972. Head reference Lake Oswego (Oreg.) Pub. Libr., 1972-82, libr. dir., 1982-90; libr. dir. Wilsonville (Oreg.) Pub. Libr., 1990—. Author: Tracing Your Ancestors: A Guide to Research, 1978. Mem. Oreg. Libr. Assn. Office: Wilsonville Pub Libr 8200 SW Wilsonville Rd Wilsonville OR 97070

TURNER, TAMARA ADELE, medical librarian; b. Seattle, Mar. 27, 1940; d. Fredrick Patrick and Florence Elfreda (Puntenney) T. BA, U. Wash., 1972, MLS, 1974. Staff libr. Rainier Sch., Wash. State Libr., Buckley, 1974-77; dir. med. libr. Children's Hosp. and Med. Ctr., Seattle, 1977—. U.S. Dept. Edn. fellow, 1973-74. Mem. Wash. Med. Librs. Assn., Seattle Area Hosp. Libr. Consortium (pres. 1980-81), Med. Libr. Assn., Am. Soc. Info. Sci. (pres. Pacific northwest chpt. 1987-88). Home: 1931 E Calhoun St Seattle WA 98112-2644 Office: Childrens Hosp and Med Ctr PO Box 5371 Seattle WA 98105-0371

TURNER, TAMARA MICHELE, child and family therapist; b. Kennewick, Wash., Sept. 30, 1969; d. Richard Harvey and Linda Marie (Jacky) T. BS in Psychology, Wash. State U., 1991; MS in Counseling, Lewis and Clark Coll., 1994. Child counselor Western Psychiatric Inst., Pitts., 1991; officer basic course USAR, Aberdeen Proving Grounds, Md., 1991-92; preschool tchr. Little Tykes, Pullman, Wash., 1992; daily living asst. United Cerebal Palsy, Seattle, 1992; kindergarten supr. YMCA, Portland, 1992-93; milieu therapist Parry Ctr. for Children, Portland, 1993-94; child and famlily therapist intern Edgefield Children's Ctr., Portland, 1994—. Contbr. article to profl. jour. 1st lt. USAR, 1991—. Recipient Leadership award Assoc. Students of WSU, 1991; scholar US Army, 1987. Mem. ACA, Reserve Officers Assn., Psi Chi Psychology Honors Club. Democrat. Home: 108 Mount Adams Rd Trout Lake WA 98650-9723

TURNER, WALLACE L., reporter; b. Titusville, Fla., Mar. 15, 1921; s. Clyde H. and Ina B. (Wallace) T.; m. Pearl Burk, June 12, 1943; children: Kathleen Turner, Elizabeth Turner Everett. B.J., U. Mo., 1943; postgrad. (Nieman fellow), Harvard U., 1958-59. Reporter Springfield (Mo.) Daily News, 1943, Portland Oregonian, 1943-59; news dir. Sta. KPTV, Portland, 1959-61; asst. sec. HEW, Washington, 1961-62; reporter N.Y. Times, San Francisco, 1962—; bur. chief N.Y. Times, 1970-85, Seattle bur. chief, 1985-88. Author: Gamblers Money, 1965, The Morman Establishment, 1967. Recipient Heywood Broun award for reporting, 1952, 56; Pulitzer Prize for reporting, 1957. Office: Box 99269 Magnolia Sta Seattle WA 98199-4260

TURNER, WARREN AUSTIN, state legislator; b. Berkeley, Calif., Dec. 21, 1926; s. Warren Mortimer and Rebecca Oline (Noer) T.; m. Beverly Daune Mackay, Mar. 29, 1952; children: Daune Scott, Warren Adair, Alan Corey. BA, U. Calif., Berkeley, 1950, BS, 1952, MPH, 1958. Pub. acct. Price Waterhouse, San Francisco, 1951-52, AW Blackman, Las Vegas, Nev., 1952-56; asst. adminstr. Marin Gen. Hosp., San Rafael, Calif., 1958-60; assoc. dir. UCLA Hosp., 1960-68; founding adminstr. Walter O. Boswell Meml. Hosp., Sun City, Ariz., 1968-81; pres. Sun Health Corp., 1981-89; mem. Ariz. Senate, Phoenix, 1993—, chmn. rules com., vice chair health com., mem. appropriations, family svcs. and transp. com., 1995—; chmn. appropriation subcom. K-12, C.C.'s and natural resources. With USN, 1944-46. Mem Ariz. Acad., Rotary Internat. Republican. Home: 18432 W Glendale Ave Waddell AZ 85355-9737 Office: Ariz State Senate Capital Complex Phoenix AZ 85007

TURNER, WILLIAM COCHRANE, international management consultant; b. Red Oak, Iowa, May 27, 1929; s. James Lyman and Josephine (Cochrane) T.; m. Cynthia Dunbar, July 16, 1955; children: Scott Christopher, Craig Dunbar, Douglas Gordon. BS, Northwestern U., 1952, LLD (hon.), Am. Grad. Sch. Internat. Mgmt., 1993. Pres., chmn. bd. dirs. Western Mgmt. Cons., Inc., Phoenix, 1955-74, Western Mgmt. Cons. Europe, S.A., Brussels, 1968-74; U.S. amb., permanent rep. OECD, Paris, 1974-77, vice chmn. exec. com., 1976-77, U.S. rep. Energy Policy Com., 1976-77, mem. U.S. dels. internat. meetings, 1974-77; mem. western internat. trade group U.S. Dept. Commerce, 1972-74; chmn., CEO Argyle Atlantic Corp., Phoenix, 1977—; chmn. European adv. coun., 1981-88, Asia Pacific adv. coun. AT&T Internat., 1981-88; bd. dirs Microtest, Inc., Phoenix; founding mem. Pacific Coun. Internat. Policy, L.A., 1995—; mem. U.S.-Japan Bus. Coun., Washington, 1987-93, European adv. coun. IBM World Trade Europe/Mid. East/Africa Corp., 1977-80; mem. Asia Pacific adv. coun. Am. Can Co., Greenwich, Conn., 1981-85, GE of Brazil adv. coun. GE Co., Coral Gables, Fla., 1979-81, Caterpillar of Brazil adv. coun. Caterpillar Tractor Co., Peoria, Ill., 1979-84, Caterpillar Asia Pacific Adv. Coun., 1984-90, U.S. adv. com. Trade Negotiations, 1982-84; bd. dirs. Goodyear Tire & Rubber Co., Akron, Ohio, 1978—, Rural/Metro Corp., 1993—, Microtest, Inc., Phoenix, 1995—; chmn. internat. adv. coun. Avon Products, Inc., N.Y.C., 1985—; mem. Spencer Stuart adv. coun. Spencer Stuart and Assocs., N.Y.C., 1984-90; chmn., mem. internat. adv. coun. Advanced Semiconductor Materials Internat. NV., Bilthoven, The Netherlands, 1985-88; bd. dirs. The Atlantic Coun. of U.S., Washington, 1977-92; co-chmn. internat. adv. bd. Univ. of Nations, Kona, Hawaii, 1985—; bd. dirs. World Wildlife Fund/U.S., 1983-85, World Wildlife Fund/The Conservation Found., 1985-89, Nat. Coun., 1989—; bd. govs. Joseph H. Lauder Inst. Mgmt. and Internat. Studies, U. Pa., 1983—; trustee Heard Mus., Phoenix, 1983-86, mem. nat. adv. bd., 1986-93; trustee Am. Grad. Sch. Internat. Mgmt., 1972—, chmn. bd. trustees, 1987-89; bd. govs. Atlantic Inst. Internat. Affairs, Paris, 1977-88; adv. bd. Ctr. Strategic and Internat. Studies, Georgetown U., 1977-81; dir. Atlantic Inst. Found., Inc., N.Y.C., 1984-90; mem. European Cmty.-U.S. Businessmen's Coun., 1978-79; bd. govs. Am. Hosp. of Paris, 1974-77; trustee Nat. Symphony Orch. Assn., Washington, 1973-83, Am. Sch., Paris, 1976-77, Orme Sch., Mayer, Ariz., 1970-74, Phoenix Country Day Sch., 1971-74; mem. nat. coun. Salk Inst., 1978-82; mem. U.S. Adv. Com. Internat. Edn. and Cultural Affairs, 1969-74; nat. rev. bd. Ctr. Cultural and Tech. Interchange between East and West, 1970-74; mem. vestry Am. Cathedral, Paris, 1976-77; pres., bd. dirs. Phoenix Symphony Assn., 1969-70; chmn. Ariz. Joint Econ. Devel. Com., 1967-68; exec. com., bd. dirs. Ariz. Dept. Econ. Planning and Devel., 1968-70; chmn. bd. Ariz. Crippled Children's Services, 1964-65; treas. Ariz. Rep. Com., 1956-57; chmn. Ariz. Young Rep. League, 1955-56; chmn. bd. Mercy Ships Internat., Inc., A Ministry of Youth With A Mission, Lindale, Tex., 1985—; mem. trade and environment com. Nat. Adv. Coun. for Environ. Policy and Tech.-U.S. EPA, Washington, 1991—; dir. exec. com., chmn. internat. com. Ariz. Econ. Coun., Phoenix, 1989-93; dir. exec. com. Orgn. for Free Trade and Devel., Phoenix, 1991-93; chmn. Internat. Adv. Coun. Plasma Tech., Inc., Sante Fe, 1992—. Recipient East-West Ctr. Disting. Svc. award, 1977. Mem. U.S. Coun. Internat. Bus. (trustee, exec. com.), Coun. Fgn. Rels., Coun. of Am. Ambs. (vice chmn. bd.), Nat. Adv. Coun. on Bus. Edn., Coun. Internat. Edn. Exchange, Greater Phoenix Leadership, Govs. Strategic Partnership Econ. Devel., Phoenix, 1992—, Met. Club, Links Club (N.Y.C.), Plaza Club (Phoenix), Paradise Valley (Ariz.) Country Club. Episcopalian. Office: 4350 E Camelback Rd Ste 240B Phoenix AZ 85018-2722

TURNER, WILLIAM WEYAND, author; b. Buffalo, N.Y., Apr. 14, 1927; s. William Peter and Magdalen (Weyand) T.; m. Margaret Peiffer, Sept. 12, 1964; children: Mark Peter, Lori Ann. BS, Canisius Coll., 1949. Spl. agt. in various field offices FBI, 1951-61; free-lance writer Calif., 1963—; sr. editor Ramparts Mag., San Francisco, 1967—; investigator and cons. Nat. Wiretap Commn., 1975. Author: The Police Establishment, 1968, Invisible Witness: The Use and Abuse of the New Technology of Crime Investigation, 1968, Hoover's F.B.I.: The Men and the Myth, 1970, Power on the Right, 1971, (with Warren Hinckle and Eliot Asinof) The Ten Second Jailbreak, 1973, (with John Christian) The Assassination of Robert F. Kennedy, 1978, (with Warren Hinckle) The Fish is Red: The Story of the Secret War Against Castro, 1981, updated, expanded, retitled as Deadly Secrets: The CIA-Mafia War Against Castro and the Assassination of JFK, 1992; contbg. author: Investigating the FBI, 1973; contbr. articles to popular mags. Dem. candidate for U.S. Congress, 1968. Served with USN, 1945-46. Mem. Authors Guild, Internat. Platform Assn., Press Club of San Francisco. Roman Catholic. Home and Office: 163 Mark Twain Ave San Rafael CA 94903-2820

TURNEY, STEVEN CRAIG, architect; b. Lima, Ohio, Sept. 18, 1958; s. Paul Raymond and Barbra Jean (Metzger) T.; m. Mary Hollis Von Dach, July 24, 1991. AS, Boise State U., 1982; BArch, U. Idaho, 1990. Iron worker, welder Hartman Mfg., Boise, Idaho, 1976-80; crew chief T.W. Blasingame & Assocs., Boise, 1982-86; intern architect Walter H. Miller AIA, Clarkston, Wash., 1989-90; project mgr. Hosford & Larson AIA, Boise, 1990-91; project architect Zabala Giltzow Albanese, Boise, 1991—. Mem. Local Govt. Com., Boise, 1992. Mem. AIA, NCARB, Constrn. Specifications Inst. (v.p. Idaho chpt. 1995), Boise C. of C., Golden Key, Tau Sigma Delta. Home: 23838 Old Highway 30 Caldwell ID 83605-7786 Office: 815 Park Blvd Ste 350 Boise ID 83712-7740

TURNIPSEED, PAMELA JEAN, insurance company executive; b. Lake Arrowhead, Calif., Mar. 28, 1947; d. Robert Earl and Dean Ann (Pitcher) T. BA, U. Calif., Santa Barbara, 1970. Claims adjuster Allstate Ins. Co., Los Angeles, 1970-74; claims mgr. Allstate Ins. Co., Honolulu, 1974-78, Tucson, 1978-79, Las Vegas, 1979-81, San Diego, 1981-83, Santa Ana, Calif., 1983-86; pres., chief exec. officer Creative Settlements, Honolulu, 1986—; mgmt. cons. Peak Performance Systems, HonoluLu, 1986—. Mem. NAFE, Nat. Assn. Life Underwriters, Am. Bus. Women's Assn. Office: Creative Settlements 201 Merchant St # 1610 Honolulu HI 96813

TURNIPSEED, VICTORIA LEE, foundation administrator, public relations executive; b. Yakima, Wash., Jan. 13, 1951; d. Kenneth Ray and Shirley Ann (Dexter) T. BA, Okla. State U., 1973; MSW, U. Okla., 1975. Dir. med. social svcs. Espanola (N.Mex.) Hosp./S.W. Community Health Svcs., 1975-82; assoc. dir. devel. S.W. Community Health Svcs., Albuquerque, 1982-83; exec. dir. found. and pub. rels. Swedish Health Systems, Englewood, Colo., 1983-86; assoc. dir. resource devel. Scripps Meml. Hosp. Found., La Jolla, Calif., 1986-90; v.p. major gifts/found. rels. Sharp Hosps. Found., San Diego, 1990—; devel. cons. Child Abuse Prevention Found., San Diego, 1990, Internat. Aerospace Hall of Fame, San Diego, 1990, Assn. Western Hosps., San Francisco, 1983; program devel. cons. El Centro de Vida Nueva, Espanola, N.Mex. Contbr. articles to profl. jours. Mem. mktg. and spl. events com. LEAD San Diego, Inc., 1990—; vol. Planned Parenthood. Recipient Golden Leaflet award Colo. Hosp. Assn., 1985; named one of Outstanding Young Women of Am., 1983. Mem. Assn. for Healthcare Philanthropy (cert., nat. nominating com. 1990, sec. Region 9/regional conf. 1982-83, pub. rels. com. 1983, pub. rels. chmn. Regions 10 and 11/regional confs. 1988), Women's Inst. for Fin. Edn. (pub. rels. coord. 1988-90), Jr. League of San Diego (nominating com. 1991-92, project and com. chmn. 1987-90, endowment com. 1991-93), City Club of San Diego. Home: 1075 Klish Way Del Mar CA 92014-2647 Office: Sharp Health Care Found 8525 Gibbs Dr Ste 302 San Diego CA 92123-1755

TUROCI, MARSHA MAY, county official; b. East Chicago, Ind., Mar. 21, 1940; d. Marshall W. and Georgia May Burrell; m. Les Turoci, Aug. 6, 1960 (div. 1994). Field rep. San Bernardino (Calif.) County, mem. bd. suprs., 1988—; chmn. Victor Valley Econ. Devel. Authority; active Mojave Desert Air Quality Control Bd., Southwestern Low Level Radiation Waste Commn. Active Calif. State Rep. Ctrl. Com. Recipient Law Enforcement award Optimists Club, 1985, Disting. Citizen award Boy Scouts Am., 1993; named Hesperian of Yr., Hesperia C. of C., 1981, Woman of Achievement, Victor Valley Bus. and Profl. Women, 1989. Mem. Nat. Assn. Counties (mem. pub. lands com.), So. Calif. Regional Assn. County Suprs., So. Calif. Associated Govts., Calif. State Assn. Counties, Calif. Elected Women's Assn. for Edn. and Rsch. Office: San Bernardino County Bd Suprs 385 N Arrowhead Ave San Bernardino CA 92415-1002

TUROFF, MARSHALL ARNOLD, consulting company executive; b. Chgo., July 9, 1927; s. Nat and Bertha (Leavitt) T.; m. Gloria Auerbach, May 6, 1951 (div. Apr. 1983); children: Sara Ann, Barbara, Charles; m. Barbara Phillips, Apr. 18, 1983. BSc, Roosevelt Coll., 1950; MBA, U. Chgo., 1954. Asst. mgr. mktg. research Signode Steel Strapping Co., Chgo., 1951-55; mgr., mktg. research Precision Scientific Co., Chgo., 1955-56; dir., mktg. research Ohmite Corp., Skokie, Ill., 1956-57; cons. Booz, Allen & Hamilton, Chgo., 1957-60; pres., chief executive officer Turoff Industries,

Ltd., Chgo., 1960-78, Jomar Warehousing Co., Chgo., 1966-78; pres. Photonic Environmental Corp., Chgo., 1972-78, Turoff Consulting Svcs., Chgo., 1978—. Treas. Jewish Vocational Service, Chgo., 1978-79, sec. 1979-80, v.p. 1980-81); pres. North Cen. Home Owners Assn., Skokie, Ill., 1963-65; mem. Bd. Zoning, Skokie, 1961-63. With U.S. Army Air Corps, 1945-46. Mem. Am. Soc. Profl. Cons. (pres. Midwest div. 1980-83), Am. Statistical Assn., Am. Mktg. Assn., Packaging Inst., USA (Chmn. and Excellence awards 1982). Republican. Jewish. Office: Turoff Consulting Svcs Inc PO Box 5740 Scottsdale AZ 85261-5740

TURPEN, LOUIS A., airport terminal executive. Dir. San Francisco Internat. Airport; dir., San Francisco Airports Commn. Office: San Francisco Intl Airport PO Box 8097 San Francisco CA 94128*

TURPIN, JOSEPH OVILA, psychologist, educator; b. Rockford, Ill., July 11, 1943; s. D. John and Mona Belle (Albright) T.; m. Hester R. Thompson, June 26, 1969; children: Matthew, Michael. AB in Sociology, Ind. U., 1965, MS in Mental Retardation, 1966, postgrad., 1966-67; PhD in Rehab. Psychology, U. Wis., 1986. Rsch. assoc. Ind. U., Bloomington, 1966-67; instr. U. Wis. Parkside Extension, Kenosha, 1967-71; tchr. Kenosha Unified Sch. Dist., 1967-71; coord. Racine area Gov.'s Com. on Spl. Learning State of Wis. Dept. Adminstrn., 1971-73; dir. Racine County Comprehensive Mental Health, Mental Retardation, Alcohol and Other Drug Abuse Svcs. Bd, 1973-78; vocat. cons., counselor supr. Industrial Injury Clinic, Neenah, Wis., 1978-83; owner, vocat. expert Vocat. Counseling Svc., Inc., Madison, Wis., 1983-88; teaching intern, counseling supr., student tchr. supr. U. Wis., Madison, 1983-86; asst. prof. rehab. counselor edn. Ohio U., Athens, 1986-89; assoc. prof. rehab. counseling program Calif. State U., San Bernardino, 1989-94, prof. rehab. counseling program, 1994—, coord. rehab. counseling program, 1990-94; mem. sch. psychologist exam. com. Dept. Edn. State of Ohio, 1989; rschr., presenter, cons. in field. Contbr. articles to profl. publs. Bd. dirs. United Cerebral Palsy of Racine County, 1969-73, Children's House, Inc., Racine, 1971-73, Ctrl. Ohio Regional Coun. on Alcoholism, 1987-89, Inland Caregivers Resource Ctr., 1993—, Health and Hosp. Planning Com. of Racine County, 1976; treas. Cub Scout Pack # 68, Boy Scouts Am., Neenah, 1981-83, Whitcomb Village Assn., Inc., 1984; bd. dirs. Aquinas H.S., 1992-94, pres. 1994; H.S. liaison West Point Parents Club of Inland Empire, 1992-94; budget rev. com. United Fund Racine County, 1975. Grantee Rehab. Svcs. Adminstrn., 1985-88, Ohio U., 1987-88, Ohio U. Coll. Osteo. Medicine and Coll. Edn., 1989, Office Spl. Edn. and Rehab., 1989-92, Calif. State U.-San Bernardino and Calif. Dept. Rehab., 1994. Mem. ACA (pub. policy and legis. com. 1992-94, various subcoms.), APA, San Bernardino Area Mental Health Assn. (bd. dirs. 1990—), Am. Rehab. Counseling Assn. (exec. coun. 1992—, ethics com. 1990-91, chair coun. on profl. preparation and stds. 1992—), Nat. Rehab Counseling Assn. (bd. dirs. 1993-94, chmn. grievance com. Office: Calif State U 5500 University Pky San Bernardino CA 92407-2318

TURPIN, RICHARD HAROLD, electrical engineering educator; b. Manning, Iowa, July 30, 1939; s. Harold Bell and Esther (Christian) T.; m. Sylvia Sue Strong, Aug. 21, 1960; children: Timothy Richard, Mark Allan, Rebecca Sue. BSEE, BS in Math., Iowa State U., 1962; MSEE, U. So. Calif., 1964; PhD, Ohio State U., 1969. Technician Hercules Powder Co., Salt Lake City, 1961; elec. engr. Hughes Aircraft Co., Fullerton, Calif., 1962-64; rsch. assoc. electro-sci. lab. Ohio State U., Columbus, 1964-69; from asst. prof. to prof. sch. engring. and tech. Purdue U., Indpls., 1969-84; prof. U. Pacific, Stockton, Calif., 1984-90, chair elec. engring. dept., 1990—; cons. Internat. Energy Mgmt., Indpls., 1976-79, Processor Interface, Inc., Indpls., 1976-77, 84, Bell Telephone Lab., Indpls., 1980-81, Union Carbide, Indpls., 1980-81. Patentee in field. Mem. IEEE, Am. Soc. Engr. Edn., Phi Eta Sigma, Eta Kappa Nu, Tau Beta Pi, Sigma Xi. Office: U Pacific 3601 Pacific Cir Stockton CA 95211-0110

TURRELL, EUGENE SNOW, psychiatrist; b. Hyattsville, Md., Feb. 27, 1919; m. Denise Deuprey, Dec. 26, 1942 (div. Jan. 1976); children: David Hillyer, Gregory Sherman (dec.); m. Zenobia A. Hopper, Apr. 16, 1988; stepchildren: Elizabeth Ann Crofoot, Mary Jane Cooper. BS, Ind. U., 1939, MD, 1947. Diplomate Am. Bd. Psychiatry and Neurology. Intern Peter Bent Brigham Hosp., Boston, 1947-48; resident physician Kandakee (Ill.) State Hosp., 1948-49; clin. asst. psychiatry U. Calif., San Francisco, 1949-51; asst. prof. Ind. U. Sch. Medicine, 1952-53, assoc. prof., 1953-58; prof., chmn. dept. psychiatry Marquette U. Sch. Medicine, 1958-63, clin. prof. psychiatry, 1963-69; lectr. U. Calif., San Francisco, 1969-75; assoc. prof. Ind. U., 1975-80, prof., 1980-89, prof. emeritus, 1989—; staff psychiatrist San Diego County Psychiat. Hosp., 1990—; assoc. clin. prof. U. Calif., San Diego, 1991—; mem., bd. dirs. Community Addictions Svcs. Agy, Indpls., 1975-79, pres. bd., 1976-77. Contr. articles to profl. jours. Lt. USNR, 1950-52. Recipient Certs. of Appreciation Office Sci. Rsch. and Devel., 1945, VA, 1964, Ind. U. Found., 1966. Fellow Am. Psychiat. Assn. (life); mem. AMA (Physician's Recognition award 1978-94), AAAS, Calif. State Med. Assn., Calif. State Psychiatric Assn., San Diego County Med. Soc., San Diego County Soc. Psychiat. Physicians, Sigma Xi, Alpha Omega Alpha. Democrat. Episcopalian. Office: San Diego County Psychiat Hosp 3851 Rosecrans St San Diego CA 92110-3115

TURRENTINE, HOWARD BOYD, federal judge; b. Escondido, Calif., Jan. 22, 1914; s. Howard and Veda Lillian (Maxfield) T.; m. Virginia Jacobsen, May 13, 1965 (dec.); children: Howard Robert, Terry Beverly; m. Marlene Lipsey, Nov. 1, 1992. A.B., San Diego State Coll., 1936; LL.B., U. So. Calif., 1939. Bar: Calif. 1939. Practiced in San Diego, 1939-68; judge Superior Ct. County of San Diego, 1968-70, U.S. Dist. Ct. (so. dist.) Calif., Calif.; sr. judge U.S. Dist. Ct. (so. dist.) Calif., San Diego, 1970—. Served with USNR, 1941-45. Mem. ABA, Fed. Bar Assn., Am. Judicature Soc. Office: US Dist Ct 940 Front St San Diego CA 92101-8994

TUSHER, THOMAS WILLIAM, apparel company executive; b. Oakland, Calif., Apr. 5, 1941; s. William C. and Betty J. (Brown) T.; m. Pauline B. Kensett, Jan. 1, 1967; children: Gregory Malcolm, Michael Scott. B.A., U. Calif., Berkeley, 1963; M.B.A., Stanford U., 1965. Asst. to v.p. internat. Colgate Palmolive Co., N.Y.C., 1965-67; product mgr. Colgate-Palmolive P.R., 1967-68; supt. corp. planning Levi Strauss & Co., San Francisco, 1969; pres. Levi Strauss Internat., 1977-84; sr. v.p. Levi Straus & Co., before 1984, exec. v.p., chief operating officer, dir., from 1984, now pres., chief oper. officer; regional gen. mgr., Australia/N.Z., Levi Strauss Australia, 1970-74; area gen. mgr. Levi Strauss No. Europe, London, 1974-75; pres. European div. Levi Strauss Internat., San Francisco, 1976; dir. various subs's. Levi Strauss Internat.; dir. Gt. Western Garment Co., Can. Bd. dirs. Calif. Council Internat. Trade, 1977—, U. Calif. Grad. Bus. Sch. Served with Intelligence Corps. USAR, 1966-67. Mem. San Francisco C. of C. (dir.). Republican. Presbyterian. Clubs: World Trade, Bay. Office: Levi Strauss & Co 1155 Battery St San Francisco CA 94111-1230*

TUSO, JOSEPH FREDERICK, English language educator, academic dean emeritus; b. Oak Park, Ill., Nov. 2, 1933; s. Joseph Salvator and Agnes Louise (Berge) T.; m. Mildred Jean Werthmuller, Aug. 30, 1958; children: Ann, Mary, Lisa, Kathleen, Jody. BA, Don Bosco Coll., 1955; MA, U. Ariz., 1964; MSA, Ga. Coll., 1981; PhD, U. Ariz., 1966. Commd. 2d lt. USAF, 1957, advanced through grades to lt. col., 1973, ret., 1976; from asst. prof. to prof. of English U.S. Air Force Acad., Colorado Springs, 1964-76; chmn. English dept. Ga. Coll., Milledgeville, 1976-79; head, English dept. N.Mex. State U., Las Cruces, 1979-82; chmn. English dept. U. of Sci. and Arts of Okla., Chickasha, 1982-84, chmn. Div. Arts & Humanities, 1984-87; acad. dean N.Mex. Mil. Inst., Roswell, 1987-93, prof. English, dean emeritus, 1993—. Editor: Beowulf, A Critical Edition, 1975; author: Singing the Vietnam Blues, 1990. Decorated Meritorious Svc. medal USAF, Disting. Flying Cross, USAF, Bronze Star, USAF, Air medal with 12 oak leaf clusters, USAF, Vietnamese Cross of Gallantry, Republic of Vietnam. Mem. Phi Beta Kappa. Roman Catholic. Home: 200 W College Blvd Roswell NM 88201-5164 Office: New Mexico Mil Inst 101 W College Blvd Roswell NM 88201-5174

TUTASHINDA, ABD KARIM KWELI (BRIAN P. ALTHEIMER), chiropractic physician, educator; b. Wynne, Ark., May 14, 1956; s. Joe Porché and Lura Ella (Darden) Altheimer; divorced; 1 child, Chinyere R.; m. Leonor Quiñonez, June 13, 1987; children Xihuanel, Rukiya, Jomoké. BA in Philosophy magna cum laude, U. Ark., 1978; D of Chiropractic cum laude, Life Chiropractic Coll. West, San Lorenzo, Calif., 1989. Tchr. English Oakland (Calif.) Pub. Schs., 1984-86; tchr. spl. programs U. Calif., Berkeley, 1984-92, 94—; instr. phys. diagnosis & chiropractic tech. Life Chiropractic Coll. West, San Lorenzo, Calif., 1989—; pvt. practice chiropractic physician Oakland, Berkeley, 1990—; owner Imhotep Chiropractic & Wellness Clinic; dir. Imhotep Wellness Workshops & Seminars. Editor, pub. Foresight Mag., 1982-84; author, pub. Toward a Holistic Worldview, 1985. Recipient 1st degree Black Belt Tae Kwon Do, 1976. Mem. Assn. Chiropractic History. Mem. Sufi Order of the West, Naqshbandi Sufi Order. Islam. Office: 3358 Adeline St Berkeley CA 94703-2737

TUTT, MARGARET HONNEN, retail store owner; b. Garden City, Kans., Oct. 11, 1951; d. Russell Thayer and Louise (Honnen) T.; m. Frank John Steinegger, Sept. 7, 1974 (div. Aug. 1981); children: John F. Steinegger, Elisabeth Sophia Tutt Steinegger. BA, U. Denver, 1974. Owner Foster & Son-The Gift Collection, Denver, 1992—. Chmn. fundraising Newborn Hope, Inc., Denver, 1990; bd. dirs. Hist. Denver, Inc., 1986-92, Hist. Denver Guild, Colo. Preservation, Inc.; docent Denver Zoo Assocs., 1976-81, chair, 1979-80. Mem. Jr. League of Denver (lectr. on volunteering for cmty. orgns. 1991, 92), Glenmoor Country Club, Centennial Club (chair 1989-90). Republican. Episcopalian. Home: 5925 E Princeton Cir Cherry Hl Vlg CO 80111-1038 Office: Foster & Son The Gift Collection 235 Steele St Denver CO 80206-5208

TUTT, RUSSELL THAYER, investment company executive; b. Coronado, Calif., July 27, 1913; s. Charles Leaming and Eleanor (Armit) T.; m. Margaret Louise Honnen, Aug. 12, 1950 (dec. Nov. 1974); children: Margaret Honnen Tutt Steinegger, Russell Thayer. B.S. in Engring., Princeton U., 1935. With buying dept. Halsey, Stuart & Co., Inc., N.Y.C., 1935-40; v.p., gen. mgr. Garden City (Kans.) Co., 1946-56; pres. S.W. Kans. Power, Inc., Garden City, 1946-56; v.p. El Pomar Investment Co., Colorado Springs, Colo., 1956-61; pres. El Pomar Investment Co., 1961-82; chmn. El Pomar Investment Co., Colo. Springs, 1982-86, now pres.; chmn. bd. Holly Sugar Corp., 1977-81; chmn. exec. com. Affiliated Bank Shares of Colo., Inc., 1970-84, CENTEL Corp.; pres. Garden City Co., 1956-92; pres. Broadmoor Hotel, Inc., 1977-82, chmn., 1982-91; chmn. bd. First Nat. Bank Colorado Springs., 1975-84. Trustee Cheyenne Mountain Mus. and Zool. Soc., 1956—, pres., 1963-74, chmn. bd., 1974-80, hon. chmn. bd., 1980—; chmn., trustee El Pomar Found., 1982-89, chmn. exec. com. 1989-92; trustee Colo. Coll., 1957—, chmn., 1966-84; life trustee Fountain Valley Sch. of Colo., Nat. Recreation Found., N.Y.C. Maj. AUS, 1940-45. Decorated Bronze Star. Republican. Episcopalian. Clubs: Cheyenne Mountain Country (Colorado Springs), Broadmoor Golf (Colorado Springs), El Paso (Colorado Springs), Country of Colo. (Colorado Springs), Cooking (Colorado Springs). Home: 8 Broadmoor Ave Colorado Springs CO 80906-3636 Office: El Pomar Bldg 10 Lake Cir Colorado Springs CO 80906-4201*

TUTTLE, FRANK DOUGLAS, marketing executive; b. Peterborough, N.H., Sept. 30, 1957; s. Robert Perry and Marion Laura (Edoy) T.; m. Valerie Marie Ogrodski, July 29, 1989; children: Lauren Elizabeth, Rebecca Marie. BS in Electrical Engring., Vanderbilt U., 1979; MBA, Pepperdine U., 1983; postgrad., Calif. Coast U. Project engr. Hughes Aircraft Co., Fullerton, Calif., 1979-91; secondary mktg. Renet Fin. Co., Anaheim, Calif., 1991—. Mentor Big Brothers of Am., Fullerton, 1981-85. Home: 20756 Ivy Cir Yorba Linda CA 92687-3323

TUUL, JOHANNES, physics educator, researcher; b. Tarvastu, Viljandi, Estonia, May 23, 1922; came to U.S., 1956, naturalized, 1962; s. Johan and Emilie (Tulf) T.; m. Marjatta Murtoniemi, July 14, 1957 (div. Aug. 1971); children—Melinda, Melissa; m. Sonia Esmeralda Manosalva, Sept. 15, 1976; 1 son, Johannes. B.S., U. Stockholm, 1955, M.A., 1956; Sc.M., Brown U., 1957, Ph.D., 1960. Research physicist Am. Cyanamid Co., Stamford, Conn., 1960-62; sr. research physicist Bell & Howell Research Center, Pasadena, Calif., 1962-65; asst. prof., assoc. prof. Calif. State Poly. U., Pomona, 1965-68; vis. prof. Pahlavi U., Shiraz, Iran, 1968-70; chmn. phys. earth sci. Calif. State Poly. U., Pomona, 1971-75, prof. physics, 1975-91, prof. emeritus, 1992—; cons. Bell & Howell Research Center, Pasadena, Calif., 1965, Teledyne Co., Pasadena, 1968; guest researcher Naval Weapons Center, China Lake, Calif., 1967, 72; resident dir., Calif. State U. Internat. Programs in Sweden and Denmark, 1977-78. Author: Physics Made Easy, 1974; contbr. articles in field to profl. jours. Pres. Group Against Smoking Pollution, Pomona Valley, Calif., 1976; foster parent Foster Parents Plan, Inc., Warwick, R.I., 1964—; block capt. Neighborhood Watch, West Covina, Calif., 1982-84. Brown U. fellow, 1957-58; U. Namur (Belgium) research grantee, 1978; Centre Nat. de la Recherche Scientifique research grantee, France, 1979; recipient Humanitarian Fellowship award Save the Children Fedn., 1968. Mem. Am. Phys. Soc., AAAS (life), Am. Assn. Physics Tchrs., N.Y. Acad. Scis. Republican. Roman Catholic. Research in energy conservation and new energy technologies. Office: Calif State Poly U 3801 W Temple Ave Pomona CA 91768-2557

TWA, CRAIGHTON OLIVER, power company executive; b. Drumheller, Alta., Can., Oct. 15, 1937; s. Joe Philander and Freda Alice (Fowler) T.; m. Irene Adam, May 7, 1960; children: Tracy, Robert, Carey. BSEE, U. Alta., Edmonton, 1959. Registered profl. engr., Alta. Engr. Can. Utilities Ltd., Edmonton, 1959-80; v.p. customer svcs. Alta Power Ltd., Edmonton, 1980-85, sr. v.p., gen. mgr., 1985-86, pres., 1986-93; pres. CU Power div. Can. Utilities Ltd., Edmonton, 1988-93; exec. v.p. Can. Utilities Ltd., Edmonton, 1994—, Can. Utilities Ltd. and ATCO Ltd. Office of the Chmn., 1995—; bd. dirs. Alta. Power ltd., CU Power Internat. Ltd., Northland Utilitiess Enterprises Ltd., The Yukon Elec. Co. Ltd., Thames Power Ltd., Frontec Logistics Corp., Can. Western Natural Gas Co. Ltd., Northwestern Utilities Ltd. Mem. Assn. Profl. Engrs., Geologists and Geophysicists Alta. Office: Can Utilities Ltd, 10035-105th St, Edmonton, AB Canada T5J 2V6

TWEDDLE, JENNIFER LYNNE, academic mental health counselor; b. Toronto, Ont., July 15, 1963; d. Allan Stanley Tweddle and Beth Margaret (Gerry) Smith. Student, U. London, 1983; BA, Calif. State U., Hayward, 1986; MA, Gallaudet U., 1988. Lifeguard Sierra Madre (Calif.) Aquatic Program, 1979-85, instr. water safety, 1980-85, asst. mgr., 1982-85, dir. adapted aquatics, 1984-86; info. asst. Nat. Info. Ctr. on Deafness, Washington, 1986-87; rsch. asst. Gallaudet Rsch. Inst., Washington, 1987; mental health counselor Phoenix Day Sch. for Deaf, 1988-93; counselor Calif. Sch. for Deaf, Riverside, 1993—; speaker, guest Minn. Found. for Better Speech and Hearing, Mpls., 1988; speaker Breakout Conf., Washington, 1992, Calif. Edn. Conf., Sacramento, 1994; conf. coord. Drug Free Schs. Ariz. State U., 1993. Mem. ACD, Am. Sch. Counselor Assn. (speaker 1990), Kappa Delta Pi (speaker, guest 1987). Episcopalian. Office: Calif Sch for Deaf 3044 Horace St Riverside CA 92506-4420

TWEEDIE, RICHARD LEWIS, statistics educator, consultant; b. Leeton, NSW, Australia, Aug. 22, 1947; came to U.S., 1991; s. Lewis Chabaud and Nel (Dahlenburg) T.; m. Catherine Robertson, Sept. 13, 1971; 1 child, Marianne Louise Robertson. BA, Australian Nat. U., Canberra, 1968, MA, 1969, DSc, 1986; PhD, Cambridge (Eng.) U., 1972. Sr. rsch. scientist Commonwealth Sci. and Indsl. Rsch. Orgn., Canberra, 1974-77; prin. rsch. scientist Commonwealth Sci. and Indsl. Rsch. Orgn., Melbourne, Australia, 1979-81; assoc. prof. U. Western Australia, Perth, 1978; gen. mgr. Siromath Pty. Ltd., Sydney, Australia, 1981-83, mng. dir., 1983-87; prof., dean Bond U., Gold Coast, Australia, 1987-91; prof. stats. Colo. State U., Ft. Collins, 1991—, chair dept. stats., 1992—. Author: Markov Chains and Stochastic Stability, 1993; also over 80 articles. Fellow Inst. Math. Stats., Internat. Statis. Inst.; mem. Statis. Soc. Australia (pres. 1984-85). Office: Colo State U Dept Stats Fort Collins CO 80523-1877

TWENEY, GEORGE HARRISON, aeronautical engineer; b. Moosejaw, Sask., Can., Sept. 16, 1915; s. Charles Rank and Mary Elizabeth (Peirce) T.; m. Maxine Calvert, July 11, 1955; 1 child, Craig Peirce. B Aero. Engring., U. Detroit, 1938, profl. degree in Aero. Engring., 1942; MS, U. Mich., 1942. Test engr. Pan Am. World Airways, N.Y.C., 1938-41; Aero. Engr. U. Detroit and Wayne State U., Detroit, 1941-54; staff engr. in charge tech. Sci. Rsch. Labs., Boeing Co., Seattle, 1955-73; pvt. practice cons. in field.; vis. sr. prof. engring. Trinity Coll., Dublin, Ireland, 1985. Author: American Student Flyer, 1942, Jack London - A Bibliography, 1966, 2d edit., 1973, The Washington 89, 1989 (Rounce and Coffin award 1990), ; editor BSRL Sci. Rev., 1964-70, Univ. Rsch. Newsletter, 1964—; contbr. articles to profl. jours. Chmn. Wash. State Nat. Libr. Week, 1968; chmn. Wash. State Lewis and Clark Com., 1973—; trustee U. Mich. Clements Libr., 1965-72; life mem., past pres. bd. trustees Seattle Pub. Libr.; bd. dirs. Lewis and Clark Trail Heritage Found. Fellow AIAA (assoc.); mem. Am. Antiquarian Soc., Am. Soc. Engring. Edn. (chmn. aeros divsn. 1978), Grolier Club, Monday Club. Home: 16660 Marine View Dr SW Seattle WA 98166-3210

TWIGG-SMITH, THURSTON, newspaper publisher; b. Honolulu, Aug. 17, 1921; s. William and Margaret Carter (Thurston) Twigg-S.; m. Bessie Bell, June 9, 1942 (div. Feb. 1983); children: Elizabeth, Thurston, William, Margaret, Evelyn; m. Laila Roster, Feb. 22, 1983 (div. Dec. 1994). B.Engring., Yale U., 1942. With Honolulu Advertiser, 1946—, mng. editor, 1954-60, asst. bus. mgr., 1960-61, pub., 1961-86; pres., dir., chief exec. officer Honolulu Advertiser, Inc., 1962-93, chmn., 1993—; chmn., dir., CEO Persis Corp.; bd. dirs. Atalanta/Sosnoff Capital Corp., N.Y. Trustee Punahou Sch., Old Sturbridge Inc., Honolulu Acad. Arts, The Contemporary Mus., Hawaii, Mus. Contemporary Art, L.A., The Skowhegan Sch., Maine, Yale Art Gallery, New Haven, Philatelic Found., N.Y., Whitney Mus. Am. Art, N.Y. Maj. AUS, 1942-46. Mem. Honolulu C. of C., Waialae Country Club, Pacific Club, Oaho Country Club, Outrigger Canoe Club. Office: Persis Corp PO Box 3110 96802 605 Kapiolani Blvd Honolulu HI 96813

TWIST, ROBERT LANPHIER, farmer, rancher, cattle feeder; b. Memphis, Dec. 27, 1926; s. Clarence C. and Edith G. Twist; student Springfield (Ill.) Jr. Coll., 1943; B.S. in Agr., U. Ill., 1950; postgrad. U. Edinburgh (Scotland); 1 dau., Marilyn Edith. Owner, operator farm lands, Twist, Ark., 1949—, Bow Fiddle Ranch, Laramie, Wyo., 1961—, Lost Creek Ranch, Masters, Colo., 1963, Rolling T Ranch, Ft. Morgan, Colo., 1965—, R.L. Twist Ranches Cattle Feeding Enterprises, Greeley, Colo. and Ft. Morgan, 1974—; prin. R.L. Twist Land & Investments, Paradise Valley, Ariz., 1974—; Rocker M Ranch, Douglas, Ariz., 1981—, Circle J Ranch, Gunnison, Colo., 1993; cons. agrl. mgmt. Justice of Peace, Twist, Ark., 1954. Served with USAAF, 1944-46. Mem. Colo. Farm Bur., Wyo. Farm Bur., Nat. Cattlemen's Assn. (charter). Republican. Presbyterian. Home: 4612 E Sparkling Ln Paradise Valley AZ 85253

TWITCHELL, CLEVELAND EDWARDS, journalist, writer; b. N.Y.C., May 8, 1937; s. Hanford Mead and Virginia (Sterry) T.; m. Linda Elaine Johnson, Aug. 20, 1977; children: Peter, Wendy, Richard, Kathryn. Grad., Phillips Exeter Acad., 1955. Editor, pub. Bay Window, San Francisco, 1957-59; asst. city editor Post Advocate, Alhambra, Calif., 1959-61; regional editor Mail Tribune, Medford, Oreg., 1961-64, news editor, 1964-83, lifestyles editor, 1983—. Author: The UFO Saga, 1966, Living & Other Good Ideas, 1977, Daytrips, 1992, Dining Out in Southern Oregon, 1994. Mem. Soc. Profl. Journalists (treas. So. Oreg. chpt. 1976-78), Soc. of Mayflower Descendants (dep. gov. Cascade County chpt. 1992—). Office: Mail Tribune 111 N Fir St Medford OR 97501-2772

TWITCHELL, KENT, mural artist; b. Lansing, Mich., Aug. 17, 1942; s. Robert Edward and Wilma Doris (Berry) T.; m. Susan Catherine Fessler, Dec. 27, 1975 (div. 1986); m. Pandora Seaton, Feb. 23, 1990; children: Rory, Artie. AA, East L.A. Coll., 1969; BA, Calif. State U., 1972; MFA, Otis Art Inst., 1977; DA (hon.), Biola U., 1989. Display artist J.C. Penney Co., Atlanta, 1965-66; abstract artist, painter L.A., 1968=70, mural artist, 1971—; instr. L.A. County High Sch. for the Arts, L.A., 1987-90, Otis/Parsons Art Inst., L.A., 1980-83; cons. Olympic Murals Program, L.A., 1983-84. Executed exterior murals at Union at 12th St. (Steve McQueen monument), L.A., 1971, Hollywood Fwy. (The Freeway Lady), L.A., 1974, Hill St. at Olympic (Edward Ruscha monument), 1987, 405 Fwy. (La Marathon mural), Inglewood, Calif., 1987, 1420 Locust St. (Dr J monument), 1989, Harbor Fwy. (La Chamber Orch.), L.A., 1991-93; one-man shows include: L.A. Mcpl. Art Gallery, 1980, Thinking Eye Gallery, L.A., 1986, Valparaiso (Ind.) U. Art Mus., 1987, Westmont Coll. Art Gallery, Santa Barbara, Calif., 1987, Biola U. Art Gallery, La Mirada, Calif., 1987, Vincent Price Gallery-East L.A. Coll., 1990, Lizardi-Harp Gallery, Pasadena, Calif., 1991; exhibited in group shows at L.A. Mcpl. Art Gallery, 1977, 81, 94, Calif. Polytech. U., Pomona, Calif., 1978, Santa Monica Coll., 1978, L.A.C.E. Gallery, L.A., 1981, Otis/Parsons Art Inst., L.A., 1987, Mayer Schwarz Gallery, Beverly Hills, 1988, 90, Principia Coll., Elsah, Ill., 1989, Koplin Gallery, Danta Monica, 1992, L.A. County Mus. Art, 1992, Robert Berman Gallery, Santa Monica, 1995. mem. adv. bd. Artists Equity Assn., 1980-95, Mural Conservancy of L.A., 1988-95. Grantee Calif. Arts Coun., 1978, Nat. Endowment for Arts, 1986. Studio: 6480 Lyons Rd Lakeport CA 95453-6410

TWITCHELL, THEODORE GRANT, music educator and composer; b. Melrose, Kans., Jan. 26, 1928; s. Curtis and Sarah Frances (Lane) T.; m. Rebecca Janis Goldsmith, Nov. 18, 1989; stepchildren: Ralph Norman, Russell Norman, Dawn Jiricek. AA in Music, L.A. City Coll., 1949; BA in Social Studies, Calif. State U., L.A., 1951, MA in Secondary Edn., 1955; EdD in Secondary and Higher Edn., U. So. Calif., L.A., 1964. Tchr. Barstow (Calif.) Union High Sch., 1952, Burbank (Calif.) Unified Sch. Dist., 1954-66; dean instrn., dir. evening divsn., dir. summer sessions, 1966-69; pres. Palo Verde Coll., Blythe, Calif., 1969-70; adult tchr. L.A. Unified Sch. Dist., 1977-78; faculty Columbia West U., L.A., 1993—; pvt. English tutor, 1979—. Composer: The Gettysburg Address, Tidewater, The Pride of Monticello, Labor Day March, Valley Forge, Normandy Prayer, Christmas in L.A., L.A., Overture to Tidewater, The Joy of Snow, Walt Whitman and Friends, over 90 others; contbr. articles to profl. jours.; author: Dear Mr. President, 1982, Courage, Conflict and Love, 1988, The Magnificent Odyssey of Michael Young, 1992. With U.S. Army, 1952-53. Recipient Coll. Faculty Senate Award for Achievements for the coll., Palo Verde Coll., Student Body award. Mem. Cmty. Coll. Pres.'s Assn., Am. Assn. Composers, Authors and Pubs., Calif. PTA (hon. life mem.), Rho Delta Chi. Republican. Methodist. Home: 2737 Montrose Ave Apt 10 Montrose CA 91020-1318

TWOGOOD, RICHARD EDWARD, electrical engineer; b. National City, Calif., May 29, 1951; s. Frederick John and Gladys Ruth (Belttary) T.; m. Beth Ellen Norman, June 11, 1972; children: Kate, Sara, Richard. BS, U. Calif., Davis, 1972, MS, 1973, PhD, 1977. Engr. Lawrence Livermore (Calif.) Nat. Lab., 1972-79, group leader, 1979-83, div. leader, 1983-88, prog. leader, 1988—. Contbr. articles to profl. jours. Mem. IEEE. Office: Lawrence Livermore Labs PO Box 808 Livermore CA 94551-0808

TWOMLEY, BRUCE CLARKE, commissioner, lawyer; b. Selma, Ala., Jan. 23, 1945; s. Robert Clarke and Eleanor Jane (Wood) Anderson T.; m. Sara Jane Minton, June 13, 1979; children: Christopher Mario, Jonathan Marion. BA in Philosophy, Northwestern U., 1967; LLM, U. Calif., San Francisco, 1970; postgrad. Nat. Jud. Coll., Reno, Nev., 1983, 88. Bar: Calif. 1972, Alaska 1973, U.S. Dist. Ct. Alaska, 1973, U.S. Ct. Appeals (9th cir.) 1982. VISTA vol., Anchorage, 1972-73; lawyer Alaska Legal Services Corp., Anchorage, 1973-82; commr. Alaska Comml. Fisheries Entry Commn., Juneau, 1982-83, chmn., 1983—; mem. Gov.'s Fisheries Cabinet, 1983—, Child Support Enforcement Divsn. Rural Task Force, 1985—, Alaska Fedn. of Natives Task Force on IRS and Alaska Native Fishermen, 1994; cons. IRS, Sta. WNED-TV, Buffalo, 1988; presenter in field. Contbr.: Limited Access Management: A Guidebook to Conservation, 1993. Recipient Alaska Legal Services Disting. Service award, 1983, 92. Mem. Britol Bay Native Assn. (mem. blue ribbon commn. on ltd. entry 1994—), Juneau Racquet Club (adv. bd. 1989—), Kappa Sigma (pres. interfraternity council 1966-67). Home: PO Box 20972 Juneau AK 99802-0972 Office: Alaska Comml Fisheries Entry Commn 8800 Glacier Hwy Ste 109 Juneau AK 99801-8079

TYKESON, DONALD ERWIN, broadcasting executive; b. Portland, Oreg., Apr. 11, 1927; s. O. Ansel and Hillie Martha (Haveman) T.; m. Rilda Margaret Steigleder, July 1, 1950; children: Ellen, Amy, Eric. BS, U. Oreg., 1951. V.p., dir. Liberty Communications, Inc., Eugene, Oreg., 1963-67, pres., chief exec. officer, dir., 1967-83; pres. Bend Cable Communications, Inc., 1983—; chmn. bd. Telecomm Systems, Inc., 1983—, Telecomm Svcs. Inc., 1988—; Ctrl. Oreg. Cable Advt., Inc., 1992—; pres. Northwest TV Inc., 1985—. Bd. dirs. Nat. Coalition Rsch. in Neurol. and Communicative Disorders, 1984-89, Sacred Heart Med. Ctr. Found., 1995—; chmn. Nat. Coalition in Rsch. pub. and govt. info. com., 1986-89, C-SPAN, 1980-89; mem. bus. U. Oreg. Coll. Bus. Adminstrn., 1973—; vice-chmn. we. area Nat. Multiple Sclerosis Soc., 1983—, dir., mem. rsch. and med. programs com., 1986—; trustee Eugene Art Found., 1980-85, Oreg. Health Scis. U. Found.,

1988-91, mem. investment com., 1992—; mem. Oreg. Investment Coun. State of Oreg., vice chmn., 1988-92. Mem. Nat. Assn. Broadcasters, Nat. Cable TV Assn. (dir. 1976-83), Chief Execs. Orgn., Vintage Club (pres. Custom Lot Assn. 1992—), Country Club Eugene (dir. 1975-77, sec. 1976—, v.p. 1977), Multnomah Athletic Club, Arlington Club, Rotary, Elks. Home: 447 Spyglass Dr Eugene OR 97401-2091 Office: PO Box 70006 Eugene OR 97401-0101

TYLER, DARLENE JASMER, dietitian; b. Watford City, N.D., Jan. 26, 1939; d. Edwin Arthur and Leola Irene (Walker) Jasmer; BS, Oreg. State U., 1961; m. Richard G. Tyler, Aug. 26, 1977 (dec.); children: Ronald, Eric, Scott. Clin. dietitian Salem (Oreg.) Hosp., 1965-73; sales supr. Sysco Northwest, Tigard, Oreg., 1975-77; clin. dietitian Physicians & Surgeons Hosp., Portland, Oreg., 1977-79; food svc. dir. Meridian Park Hosp., Tualatin, Oreg., 1979—. Registered dietitian. Mem. Am. Dietetic Assn., Oreg. Dietetic Assn., Portland Dietetic Assn., Am. Soc. Hosp. Food Svc. Adminstrs. Episcopalian. Home: 9472 SW Hume Ct Tualatin OR 97062-9039 Office: 19300 SW 65th St Tualatin OR 97062

TYLER, GAIL MADELEINE, nurse; b. Dhahran, Saudi Arabia, Nov. 21, 1953 (parents Am. citizens); d. Louis Rogers and Nona Jean (Henderson) Tyler; m. Alan J. Moore, Sept. 29, 1990; 1 child, Sean James. AS, Front Range Community Coll., Westminster, Colo., 1979; BS in Nursing, U. Wyo., 1989. RN. Ward sec. Valley View Hosp., Thornton, Colo., 1975-79; nurse Scott and White Hosp., Temple, Tex., 1979-83, Meml. Hosp. Laramie County, Cheyenne, Wyo., 1983-89; dir. DePaul Home Health, 1989-91; field staff nurse Poudre Valley Hosp. Home Care, 1991—. Avocations: collecting internat. dolls, sewing, reading, travel.

TYLER, JOANN, ultrasonographer; b. Balt., Mar. 15, 1950; d. Eslie and Kathleen (Riley) Knox. Student, C.C. Balt., 1970-73, Foothill Coll., 1991-93; cert., St. Agnes Sch. Radiology, 1975. ARRT, CRT, RDMS. Clk. Social Security Adminstrn., Balt., 1970-73; radiologic technician St. Agnes Hosp., Balt., 1976-85; ultrasonographer Summit Med. Ctr., Oakland, Calif., 1986—. Mem. Am. Inst. Ultrasound in Medicine, Calif. Soc. Radiologic Tech.

TYLER, RICHARD R., marketing executive; b. Denver, June 27, 1935; s. George Franklin and Josephine (Grassi) T.; m. Marcella Leonetti, Nov. 12, 1960; children: Marcella, Mark, Scott, Christine. BA, Calif. State U., San Jose, 1957. Reporter Daily News, L.A.; pub. rels. rep. Ford Motor Co., L.A.; account exec. Carl Byoir & Assocs., L.A.; west coast pub. rels. dir. Am. Airlines, L.A. and other cities; dir. corp. pub. rels. Six Flags Corp., L.A.; regional v.p. N.W. Ayer Pub. Rels., L.A., 1984-87; mktg. v.p. Triple Check Cos., L.A., 1987—. Pub. rels. adv. L.A. City Fire Chief, 1988—. Fellow Pub. Rels. Soc. Am. (Disting. Profl. 1987); mem. Pub. Rels. Soc. Am. L.A. (pres. 1986), L.A. Press Club (bd. mem. 1993-95), San Fernando Valley Press Club (pres. 1966), San Fernando Valley Press Club (pres. 1966), Soc. Profl. Journalists. Home: 15400 Valley Vista Blvd Sherman Oaks CA 91403-3812 Office: Triple Check Cos 727 S Main St Burbank CA 91506-2528

TYLER, STEVEN ANTHONY, aerospace engineer; b. Chgo., July 8, 1964; s. Edwin Chester and Lillian Josephine (Mierzwinski) Drzymkowski; m. Debra Jean Gaetke, June 15, 1991. BSME, U. Ill., 1986; MSME, Stanford U., 1992. Registered profl. engr., Calif. Design engr. Argonne (Ill.) Nat. Lab., 1986-87; flight test engr. Lockheed - Missiles div., Sunnyvale, Calif., 1987-88; optical phenomenologist Lockheed - Rsch. & Devel., Palo Alto, Calif., 1988—. Mem. NSPE, ASME, AIAA. Democrat.

TYLER-PARKER, SYDNEY BILLIG, publishing executive, author, consultant; b. L.A., May 11, 1938; d. Harvey Ellsworth Jr. and Sidney Roberta (Woolslair) Billig; m. Thomas True Tyler, July 11, 1969 (div. 1986); 1 child, Lee Harris Tyler Argabrite; m. Minot Harold Parker, Dec. 30, 1988. BA in English Lit., Coll. William and Mary, 1960; MSC in Sci. Edn., U. So. Calif., 1968; post masters, Tavistock Inst. Human Rels., London, 1975. cert. elem. and secondary tchr., U.S., U.K., West Germany, Canada. Tchr. math., social studies Torrance (Calif.) Unified Sch. Dist., 1966-68; math rsch. assoc. southwest Reg. Fed. Lab., Inglewood, Calif., 1967-68; tchr. Am. lit., Latin, great issues of man Palos Verdes USD, Rolling Hills, Calif., 1968-69; tchr. math. Mayfield Comprehensive Sch., London, 1970; tchr. AFCENT NATO Internat. Sch., Brunssum, The Netherlands, 1970-75; internat. primary coord., rsch. head, 1972-74; tchr., program dir. RAF Alcombury (U.K.) U.S. Air Force Schs., 1975-81; pres. Thomas Geale Pubs., Inc., Montara, Calif., 1982—; gifted and talented cons., tchr. Cabrillo Unified Sch. Dist., Half Moon Bay, Calif., 1991—; cons., counselor U.S. Air Force Offices of Social Actions, Alconbury, 1976-79; project dir. The Think Bridge, Inc. Author: Young Think, 1980—, Just Think, 1980—, Stretch Think, 1982—, Think Quest, 1990—; editorial adv., article contbr. THINK Magazine, San Antonio, Tex., 1990—. Recipient 200 Women of Achievement in England award United Kingdom Soc., 1970, Outstanding World-wide Social Actions Cons. Counselor award U.S. Air Force, Alconbury, 1978. Mem. NEA, Overseas Edn. Assn., Phi Delta Kappa (U.K. chpt. treas. 1978-81). Home and Office: PO Box 370540 Montara CA 94037-0540

TYRAN, GARRY KEITH, banker; b. Washington, D.C., Feb. 25, 1953; s. Benjamin and Jeanne Marie (Deckman) T.; children: Keith West, Charlotte Lyles. BA, Stanford U., 1975; MBA, UCLA, 1982. Rep. Fahran Overseas, Ltd., Burlingame, Calif., 1976-77; with Tarfa Comml. and Indsl. Co., Riyadh, Saudi Arabia, 1977-79; mgmt. asst. Fahran Overseas, Ltd., Ashland, Ore., 1979-80; economist Dept. Energy, Washington, 1980; v.p. Bank Am., Houston, 1982-90; v.p., mgr. Bank Am., Pleasant Hill, Calif., 1990—. Mem. Kappa Sigma, Stanford Alumni Assn. Methodist. Home: 1846 Shirley Dr Benicia CA 94510-2668 Office: Bank Am 300 Ellinwood Way Ste 160 Pleasant Hill CA 94523-4811

TYTLER, LINDA JEAN, communications and public affairs executive; b. Rochester, N.Y., Aug. 31, 1947; d. Frederick Easton and Marian Elizabeth (Allen) T.; m. George Stephen Dragnich, May 2, 1970 (div. July 1976); m. James Douglas Fisher, Oct. 7, 1994. AS, So. Sem., Buena Vista, Va., 1967; student U. Va., 1973; student in pub. adminstrn. U. N. Mex., 1981-82. Spl. asst. to Congressman John Buchanan, Washington, 1971-75; legis. analyst U.S. Senator Robert Griffin, Washington, 1975-77; ops. supr. Pres. Ford Com., Washington, 1976; office mgr. U.S. Senator Pete Domenici Re-election, Albuquerque, 1977; pub. info. officer S.W. Community Health Service, Albuquerque, 1978-83; cons. pub. relations and mktg., Albuquerque, 1983-84; account exec. Rick Johnson & Co., Inc., Albuquerque, 1983-84; dir. mktg. and communications St. Joseph Healthcare Corp., 1984-88; mktg. and bus. devel. cons., 1987-90; mgr. communications and pub. affairs Def. Avionics Systems div., Honeywell Inc., 1990—; sgt. N.Mex. Mounted Patrol, 1993—; mem. N.Mex. Ho. of Reps., Santa Fe, 1983-95, ret. 1995, vice chmn. appropriations and fin. com., 1985-86, interim com. on children and youth, 1985-86, mem. consumer and pub. affairs com., transp. com., 1992-95; chmn. Rep. Caucus, 1985-88; chmn. legis. campaign com. Rep. Com.; del. to Republic of China, Am. Council of Young Polit. Leaders, 1988. Bd. dirs. N. Mex. chpt. ARC, Albuquerque, 1984. Recipient award N.Mex. Advt. Fedn., Albuquerque, 1981, 82, 85, 86, 87. Mem. Am. Soc. Hosp. Pub. Rels. (cert.), Nat. Advt. Fedn., Soc. Hosp. Planning and Mktg., Am. Mktg. Assn., N.Mex. Assn. Commerce and Industry (bd. dirs.), Republican. Baptist.

TYTLER, MORTON MAYNARD, lawyer, retired state assistant attorney general; b. Poulsbo, Wash., Dec. 30, 1932; s. George Fitzroy and Annie (Hokonson) T.; m. Sylvia Virginia Komedal, May 29, 1957; children: Ian Morton, Karen Marie. BA, U. Wash., 1954, JD, 1961. Bar: Wash. 1961. Pvt. practice Tonasket, Wash., 1961-62; asst. atty. gen. State of Wash., Olympia, 1962-93; pvt. practice Olympia, 1994—; Bd. trustees Thurston County Legal Svcs. Assn., Olympia, 1969-73; mem. planning com. Pacific Coast Labor Law Conf., Seattle, 1980-83; liaison to state bar assn. Govt. Lawyers Bar Assn., Olympia, 1990-93. Author: Enforcement of Law Governing Public Drinking Water in Washington, 1985; contbr. chpt. to book. Mem. Constl. Revision Commn., Olympia, 1968-69. With U.S. Army, 1955-58. Democrat. Home and Office: 3303 Fairfield Rd SE Olympia WA 98501

UBEROI, MAHINDER SINGH, aerospace engineering educator; b. Delhi, India, Mar. 13, 1924; came to U.S., 1945, naturalized, 1960; s. Kirpal Singh and Sulaksha (Kosher) U. B.S., Punjab U., Lahore, India, 1944; M.S., Calif. Inst. Tech., 1946; D.Eng., Johns Hopkins U., 1952. Registered profl. engr. Mem. faculty U. Mich., Ann Arbor, 1953-63, prof. aeros., 1959-63, vis. prof., 1963-64; prof. aerospace engring. U. Colo., Boulder, 1963—, chmn. dept. aerospace engring., 1963-75; fellow F. Joint Inst. for Lab. Astrophysics, Boulder, 1963-74; hon. research fellow Harvard U., 1975-76; invited prof. U. Que., Can., 1972-74. Author numerous rsch. publs. on dynamics of ionized and neutral gases and liquids with and without chem. reactions, gravity and electromagnetic fields; editor Cosmic Gas Dynamics, 1974. Council mem. Ednl. TV Channel 6, Inc., Denver, 1963-66. Guggenheim fellow Royal Inst. Tech., Stockholm, Sweden, 1958; exchange scientist U.S. Nat. Acad. Scis.; exchange scientist Soviet Acad. Scis., 1966. Mem. Am. Phys. Soc., Tau Beta Pi. Home: 819 6th St Boulder CO 80302-7418

UBERSTINE, MITCHELL NEIL, bank executive; b. N.Y.C., Apr. 27, 1956; s. Elliott and Barbara Marilyn (Wernick) U.; m. Janice Diane Wemple, Dec. 26, 1987; children: Jeffrey Aaron, Andrew Louis. AA, Pierce Coll., Woodland Hills, Calif., 1975. Purchasing agt. Workshop West, Inc., Beverly Hills, Calif., 1975-78, Allianz Ins., L.A., 1978-79, Allstate Savs., Glendale, Calif., 1979-80; gen. svc. supr. First Fed. Bank Calif., Santa Monica, 1980-83, asst. v.p., 1983-86, v.p., 1986-93, sr. v.p., 1994—. Contbr. articles to profl. jours. Bd. dirs., v.p. Jewish Family Svc., Santa Monica, 1991—; bd. dirs. Santa Monica region NCCJ. Mem. Purchasing Mgmt. Assn. L.A. Republican. Jewish. Office: First Fed Bank Calif 401 Wilshire Blvd Ste 220 Santa Monica CA 90401-1430

UCHIMOTO, EIJIRO, physicist, educator; b. Tokyo, Oct. 28, 1955; came to the U.S., 1974; s. Heihachiro and Kiyo (Ichikawa) U.; m. Yoshiko Kawasato, Sept. 20, 1983; children: Mari Lisa, Kentaro Jim. BS in Physics and Astrophysics, U. Minn., 1978; MS in Physics, U. Wis., 1981, PhD, 1988. Teaching asst. U. Wis., Madison, 1979-80, rsch. asst., 1980-88; assoc. rsch. scientist Courant Inst. NYU, N.Y.C., 1988-90; asst. prof. dept. physics and astronomy U. Mont., Missoula, 1990—, summer acting chair, 1991, faculty senator, 1993—. Contbr. articles and abstracts to profl. jours. Hon. fellow U. Wis., 1992-94. Mem. Am. Astron. Soc., Am. Phys. Soc. (STEP travel grantee 1984), Am. Assn. Physics Tchrs., Sigma Xi, Phi Beta Kappa, Tau Beta Pi, Phi Kappa Phi. Home: 3380 Jack Dr Missoula MT 59803-2754 Office: U Mont Dept Physics Astron Missoula MT 59812

UDALL, SHARYN R., art historian, writer, curator; b. Pitts.; d. Ralph F. and Irene J. (Larson) Rohlfsen; m. Kimball Udall, Aug. 27, 1966; 1 child, Dana Michelle. BA, Colo. Women's Coll., 1966; MA, Ariz. State U., 1969; PhD, U. N.Mex., 1981. Curatorial asst. Mus. of Navaho Cermonial Art, Santa Fe, 1971-74; art history and humanities instr. Santa Fe C.C., 1983-89; humanities lectr. Coll. of Santa Fe, 1986-90; woment studies and art history lectr. U. N.Mex., Albuquerque, 1989-90, art history adj. lectr., 1991—; art edn. instr. San Juan Pueblo, 1973-74; hist. preservation project cons. Picuris Pueblo, N.Mex., 1980; N.Mex. area cons. Archives of Am. Art, Smithsonian Inst., 1983-85; participant NEH seminar for coll. tchrs. Brown U., 1986, Paris, 1989; mem. nat. selection panel for art history fellows NWH, Washington, 1988. Author: Modernist Painting in New Mexico, 1984, Victor Higgins in New Mexico, 1984, Spud Johnson & Laughing Horse, 1994, Inside Looking Out: Art of Gina Knee, 1994; mem. editl. collective and visual arts editor Frontiers: A Jour. of Women Studies, 1990—; contbr. articles to profl. jours.

UDINK, JOHNNY RAY, printing company executive; b. Alhambra, Calif., Oct. 15, 1947; s. William Robert and Peggy Jo (McDowell) U.; m. Linda Joyce Dietz, Feb. 3, 1968 (div. Oct. 1975); 1 child, Brian John; m. Margaret Mary Michaud, May 20, 1978; children: Kevin William, Kimberly Allison. AA, Mount San Antonio Coll., 1972; BA, U. Redlands, 1979. Fin. control planner Jeffries Banknote, L.A., 1973-76; v.p. sales Pandick Press, L.A., 1976-80; v.p. sales and mktg. Gore Graphics, L.A., 1980-84, Frye & Smith, Costa Mesa, Calif., 1984—. With USCG, 1966-70. Decorated Nat. Def. medal USCG, 1966, Good Conduct medal USCG, 1970, Coast Guard Achievement medal USCG, 1971. Mem. Advt. Prodn. Assn. So. Calif., Advt. Prodn. Assn. Orange County, Printing Inst. Am. (So. Calif. sales club). Republican. Roman Catholic. Home: 21101 Cantebury Ln Lake Forest CA 92630-5876 Office: Frye & Smith 150 Baker St E Costa Mesa CA 92626-4503

UDWADIA, FIRDAUS ERACH, engineering educator, consultant; b. Bombay, Aug. 28, 1947; came to U.S., 1968.; s. Erach Rustam and Perin P. (Lentin) U.; m. Farida Gagrat, Jan. 6, 1977; children: Shanaira, Zubin. BS, Indian Inst. Tech., Bombay, 1968; MS, Calif. Inst. Tech., 1969, PhD, 1972; MBA, U. So. Calif., 1985. Mem. faculty Calif. Inst. Tech., Pasadena, 1972-74; asst. prof. engring. U. So. Calif., Los Angeles, 1974-77, assoc. prof., 1977-83, prof. mech. engring., civil engring. and bus. adminstrn., 1983-86; prof. engring, bus. adminstrn. U. So. Calif., 1986—; also bd. dirs. Structural Identification Computing Facility U. So. Calif.; cons. Jet Propulsion Lab., Pasadena, Calif., 1978—, Argonne Nat. Lab., Chgo., 1982-83, Air Force Rocket Lab., Edwards AFB, Calif., 1984—, vis. prof. of Applied Mechanics and Mech. Engring., Calif. Inst. Tech., 1993. Assoc. editor: Applied Mathematics and Computation, Jour. Optimization Theory and Applications, Jour. Franklin Inst., Nonlinear Digest, Jour. of Mathematical Analysis and Applications, Jour. Mathematical Problems in Engineering; mem. adv. bd. Internat. Jour. Tech. Forecasting and Social Change; mem. publs. com. Jour. Aerospace Engring.; contbr. articles to profl. jours. Bd. dirs. Crisis Mgmt. Ctr., U. So. Calif. NSF grantee, 1976—; recipient Golden Poet award, 1990. Mem. AIAA, ASCE, Am. Acad. Mechanics, Soc. Indsl. and Applied Math., Seismological Soc. Am., Sigma Xi (Earthquake Engring. Research Inst., 1971, 74, 84). Home: 2100 S Santa Anita Ave Arcadia CA 91006-4611 Office: U So Calif 430K Olin Hall University Park Los Angeles CA 90007

UEDA, ISSAKU, medical educator, researcher; b. Tokyo, Mar. 24, 1924; came to U.S., 1968; s. Ichiro and Yoshiko (Uchiyama) U.; m. Setsuko Hirama, Dec. 8, 1955; children—Shunsaku, Marie A. M.D., Keio U., Tokyo, 1948, Ph.D. in Biochemistry, 1960. Diplomate Am. Bd. Anesthesiology. Intern, Keio Univ. Hosp., Tokyo, 1948-49; resident U. Utah Coll. Medicine affiliated hosps., 1957-60; chief Nat. Cancer Ctr., Tokyo, 1962-66; assoc. prof. Osaka U. Med. Sch. (Japan), 1966-68; assoc. prof. U. Utah, Salt Lake City, 1972-74, prof. dept. anesthesia, 1978—; prof. U. Kans., Kansas City, 1974-78. Contbr. research articles on anesthesia to med. jours. Mem. Am. Soc. Anesthesiologists, AMA, Am. Chem. Soc. Home: 1447 Ambassador Way E Salt Lake City UT 84108-2858 Office: U Utah Sch Medicine Dept Anesthesia Salt Lake City UT 84132

UFFNER, BETH MARILYN, television and film agent; b. N.Y.C., Sept. 30, 1942; d. George and Lillian Elizabeth (Becker) U.; 1 child, Darlene. BA, NYU, 1964. Asst. producer Tony Awards, N.Y.C., 1967-69; assoc. producer Emmy Awards, Los Angeles, 1969-74; casting dir. Barney Miller, Hollywood, Calif., 1974-76; casting exec. NBC-TV, Burbank, Calif., 1977; dir. comedy devel. Warner Bros. TV, Burbank, 1977-79; agt., exec. Internat. Creative Mgmt., Los Angeles, 1979-82; v.p. MTM Enterprises, Studio City, Calif., 1982-85; pres. Beth Uffner & Assocs., Studio City, 1985-88; ptnr. Broder, Kurland Webb Uffner, 1988—. Office: Broder Kurland Webb & Uffner 9242 Beverly Blvd # 200 Beverly Hills CA 90210-3710

UFIMTSEV, PYOTR YAKOVLEVICH, physicist, electrical engineer, educator; b. Ust'-Charyshskaya Pristan, Altai Region, Russia, July 8, 1931; s. Yakov Fedorovich and Vasilisa Vasil'evna (Toropchina) U.; m. Vera M. Umnova, 1958 (div. 1968); 1 child, Galina; m. Tatiana Vladimirovna Sinelschikova, May 3, 1986; children: Ivan, Vladimir. Grad., Odessa State U., USSR, 1954; PhD, Cen. Rsch. Inst. of Radio Industry, Moscow, 1959; DSc, St. Petersburg State U., Russia, 1970. Engr., sr. engr., sr. scientist Cen. Rsch. Inst. of Radio Industry, Moscow, 1954-73; sr. scientist Inst. Radio Engring. & Electronics Acad. Scis., Moscow, 1973-90; vis. prof., adj. prof. UCLA, 1990—; mem. Sci. Bd. of Radio Waves, Acad. Scis., Moscow, 1960-90. Author: Method of Edge Waves in the Physical Theory of Diffraction, 1962; contbr. articles to profl. jours. Recipient USSR State Prize, Moscow, 1990, Leroy Randle Grumman medal for outstanding sci. achievement, N.Y.C., 1991. Mem. AIAA, IEEE, Electromagnetics Acad. (U.S.), A.S. Popov Sci. Tech. Soc. Radio Engring., Electronics & Telecommunication (Russia). Office: UCLA Dept Elec Engring 405 Hilgard Ave Los Angeles CA 90024-1301

UHALLEY, STEPHEN, JR., history educator; b. Akron, Ohio, Sept. 22, 1930; s. Stephen and Julia Clara (Kovac) U.; m. Allene Mable Lyons (dec. May 1959); children: Kathryn Allene, Stephen III; m. Joan Carol Mooney, Nov. 7, 1964; children: Mark Christopher, Dawn Therese, David Alexander. AA, San Bernardino Valley Coll., 1954; BA, U. Calif., Riverside, 1956; MA, Claremont Grad. Sch., 1957; PhD, U. Calif., Berkeley, 1967. Program officer, asst. rep. The Asia Found., San Francisco, 1960-67; asst. prof. U. Ariz., Tucson, 1967-68; assoc. prof. Duke U., Durham, N.C., 1968-70; sr. fellow East-West Ctr., Honolulu, 1970-71; prof., chmn. U. Hawaii, Honolulu, 1972-77; faculty assoc. Am. Univs. Field Staff, 1977-78; scholar in residence The Asia Soc., N.Y.C., 1978; dir., prof. U. Hawaii, Honolulu, 1980-85, prof., 1985—, chair, 1991—; vis. prof. Peking U., Beijing, 1993, internat. hon. rsch. fellow, 1993—. Author: Critical Biography of Mao Tsetung, 1975, History of the Chinese Communist Party, 1988; editor: Sino-Soviet Documents 1989, 1993, (jour.) Hong Kong Br. Royal Asiatic Soc., 1965-66; contbr. articles to profl. jours. Bd. mem. Pacific and Asian Affairs Coun., Honolulu, 1975-85, pres., 1976-77. Sgt. USMC, 1949-52, Korea. Woodrow Wilson fellow Woodrow Wilson Found., Claremont Grad. Sch., 1957-58. Mem. Am. Assn. for Chinese Studies (bd. mem. 1990—), Assn. for Asian Studies, Phi Beta Kappa. Office: U Hawaii Dept History 2350 Dole St Honolulu HI 96822-2410

UHDE, LARRY JACKSON, joint apprentice administrator; b. Marshalltown, Iowa, June 2, 1939; s. Harold Clarence and Rexine Elizabeth (Clemens) U.; m. Linda-Lee Betty Best, Nov. 19, 1960; children: Mark Harold, Brian Raymon. Student, Sacramento City Coll., 1966, Am. River Coll., Sacramento, 1975. Equipment supr. Granite Constrn., Sacramento, 1962-69; truck driver Iowa Wholesale, Marshalltown, Iowa, 1969-70; mgr. Reedy & Essex, Inc., Sacramento, 1970-71; dispatcher Operating Engrs. Local Union 3, Sacramento, 1971-73; tng. coord. Operating Engrs. Joint Apprenticeship Com., Sacramento, 1973-83, apprenticeship div. mgr., 1983-87, adminstr., 1987-95; ret., 1995; chmn. First Women in Apprenticeship Seminar, 1972, Calif. Apprentice Coun., 1992, Blue Ribbon com.; com. mem. Sacramento Gen. Jount Apprenticeship Com., 1973-74; rep. Sacramento Sierra's Bldg. and Constrn. Trades Coun., 1973-75; com. mem. Valley Area Constrn. Opportunity Program, 1974-77; commr. State of Calif. Dept. Indsl. Rels., Calif. Apprenticeship Coun; mem. Apprenticeship Adv. Com. Internat. Union of Oper. Engrs. Contbr. articles to trade papers. Mgr., v.p. Little League, 1971-75; co-chmn. Fall Festival St. Roberts Ch., 1973-75; v.p. Navy League Youth Program, 1978-81; instr. ARC, 1978-87; counselor United Way 1980—; bd. mem. County CETA Bd., 1981-82; coun. mem. Calif. Balance of State Pvt. Industry Coun., 1982-83, Sacramento Pvt. Industry Coun., 1982-83; coord. Acholic Recovery Program, 1984—. With USN, 1956-60. Mem. Western Apprenticeship Coords. Assn. (statewide dir. 1987—), U.S. Apprenticeship Assn., Sacramento Valley Apprenticeship Tng. Coords. Assn. (rep.), Rancho Murieta County, U.S. Golf Assn., Bing Maloney Golf Club. Democrat. Roman Catholic. Office: Operating Engrs Apprentice 7388 Murieta Dr Sloughhouse CA 95683-9725

UHL, PHILIP EDWARD, marine artist; b. Toledo, Aug. 19, 1949; s. Philip Edward and Betty Jean (Mayes) U. Student, Dayton Art Inst., 1967-68, Art Students League, 1974. Creative dir. Ctr. for Civic Initiative, Milw., 1969-71; VISTA vol. Office Econ. Opportunity, 1969-71; art dir. Artco Advt. Agy., Honolulu, 1972-73; artist, photographer Assn. Honolulu Artists, 1974-77; pres. Uhl Enterprises div. Makai Photography, Honolulu, 1977—, Videoscapes div. Channel Sea TV, Honolulu, 1977—; cons. Pan Am. Airways, N.Y.C., Honolulu, 1979-84, ITTC Travel Ctr., Honolulu, 1982-83, Royal Hawaiian Ocean Racing Club, Honolulu, 1984—, Sail Am.-Am's Cup Challenge, Honolulu, 1985-86, Am. 3 Found., Am. Cup Def., San Diego, 1991-92, Am. 3 Found. Womens Team, 1994-95. Co-producer video documentary White on Water, 1984 (Emmy 1984), Racing the Winds of Paradise (Golden Monitor award Internat. TV Assn. 1989); producer: Joy of Life (Golden Monitor award Internat. TV Assn. 1988), Sailors on the Sea, 1990, Teamwork, Talent, Technology (Tele award 1993); cameraman: Pan Am. Clipper Cup, 1980, 82, 84, and Kenwood Cup, 1986, 88, 90, 92, 94 (2 Tele awards 1994), ESPN Kenwood Cup, 1990, 92, 94, ESPN Am.'s Cup, 1991-92, 94-95, Transpac, 1991, 93, 95, (video documentary) Rocking the Boat, 1994-95, Dateline NBC Setting Sail, 1994-95, numerous spls., reports on ABC-TV, NBC-TV, CBS-TV, PBS, NHK, BBL, TFI, FL, TVNZ, and numerous other major worldwide broadcast networks; photographer: (book) Nautical Quar. (Soc. Pub. Designer award 1984); contbr. numerous articles, photos to yachting publs. Mem. Am. Film Inst., Internat. Platform Assn., Soc. Internat. Nautical Scribes, Am. Soc. Media Photographers, U.S. Sailing Assn., Royal Hawaiian Ocean Racing Club, Tutukaka S. Pacific Yacht Club, Waikiki Yacht Club. Office: UHL Enterprises 1750 Kalakaua Century Ctr Ste 3-757 Honolulu HI 96826

UHLANER, JULIUS EARL, psychologist, educator; b. Vienna, Apr. 22, 1917; came to U.S., 1928; naturalized 1928; s. Benjamin and Ethel Uhlaner; m. Vera Kolar, Sept. 3, 1949; children: Carole Jean, Lorraine Uhlaner-Hendrickson, Robert Theodore. BS, CUNY, 1938; MS, Iowa State U., 1941; PhD, NYU, 1947. Indsl. psychology asst. Ford Motor Co., Dearborn, Mich., 1940-41; rsch. asst. Iowa State U., Ames, 1940-41; rsch. assoc. NYU, 1941-42; asst. dir. tng. N.Y. State div. Vets. Affairs, N.Y.C., 1946-49; with U.S. Army Rsch. Inst., Washington, 1947-78, tech. dir., 1964-78; chief psychologist U.S. Army, Washington, 1964-78; adj. prof. psychology George Washington U., 1971—; v.p. Perceptronics, Inc., Woodland Hills, Calif., 1978-81; pres. Uhlaner Cons., Inc., Encino, Calif., 1981—. Author: Psychological Research in National Defense Today, 1964; cons. editor Jour. Applied Psychology, 1970—; contbr. articles to profl. jours. Served with USAF, 1944-46. Recipient Presdl. Mgmt. Improvement award, 1978. Fellow Am. Psychol. Assn. (pres. div. mil. psychology 1969-70), Human Factors Soc., Washington Acad. Scis., Iowa Acad. Scis., Ops. Rsch. Soc. Am.; mem. Cosmos Club, Psi Chi. Home and Office: 4258 Bonavita Dr Encino CA 91436-3525

UHM, KEN KWANG-HEUM, trading company executive; b. Seoul, Republic of Korea, June 2, 1954; came to U.S., 1988; s. Jae-Han and In-Rak (Lee) U.; m. Nam-Hyun Cho, Apr. 19, 1985; children: John, James. B in Commerce, Myung-Ji U., Seoul, 1977. Asst. mgr. Hyundai Engring. & Constrn. Co., Seoul, 1977-85; mgr. Hyundai Precision and Ind. Co., Seoul, 1985-88; gen. mgr. Hyundai Golf Cars, U.S.A., L.A., 1988-91; v.p. Utility cars Internat., Fullerton, Calif., 1991-92; gen. mgr. K. Young Inc., L.A., 1992—. Home: 18559 Dancy St Rowland Hghts CA 91748-4757 Office: K Young Inc 3701 Wilshire Blvd Ste 1050 Los Angeles CA 90010-2817

UHRICH, RICHARD BECKLEY, hospital executive, physician; b. Pitts., June 11, 1932; s. Leroy Earl and Mabel Hoffer (Beckley) U.; m. Susan Kay Manning, May 25, 1985; children by previous marriage—Mark, Karen, Kimberly. B.S., Allegheny Coll., 1954; M.D., U. Pa., 1958; M.P.H., U. Calif.-Berkeley, 1966. Diplomate: Am. Bd. Preventive Medicine. Intern Lancaster Gen. Hosp., (Pa.), 1958-59; commd. asst. surg. USPHS, 1959, advanced through grades to med. dir., 1967; resident U. Calif., 1965-66; various adminstrv. positions regional and service unit levels Indian Health Services, until 1971; dir. div. programs ops. Indian Health Service, Health Services Adminstrn. USPHS, Washington, 1971-73; assoc. dir. div. profl. resources Office Internat. Health, Office Asst. Sec. for Health, HEW, Washington, 1973-74; assoc. dir. for program devel. and coordination Office Internat. Health, 1974-78; dir. Phoenix Indian Med. Ctr. and Phoenix Services Unit, 1978-81, ret., 1982; sr. adminstr. Good Samaritan Med Ctr., Phoenix, 1981-82, chief exec. officer, 1982-89; v.p. for managed care programs Samaritan Health Svcs., Phoenix, 1989-90; cons. health care systems Phoenix, 1990-93; dir. S.E. Asia, internat. dir. Med. Ambs. Internat., Modesto, Calif., 1993—; mem. Phoenix Regional Hosp. Coun., 1981-88, pres., 1982-83; bd. dirs. Med. Ctr. Redevel. Corp., Phoenix; v.p. Samaritan Redevel. Corp., 1983-88. Bd. dirs. Phoenix Symphony Orch., 1984-89, Ariz. Sr. Olympics Bd., 1985-89. Recipient Meritorious Service medal USPHS, 1973; recipient citation USPHS, 1973, Commd. Officers award, 1981. Mem. Ariz. Hosp. Assn. (bd. dirs. 1980-86, chmn. council on planning 1980-81, council on human resources 1982-83, council on patient care 1983-84, fin. com. 1984-86), Am. Coll. Health Care Adminstrs., Am. Pub. Health Assn., Christian Med. Soc.

UITERMARK, HELEN JOAN, computing services executive; b. Zandvoort, Netherlands, May 4, 1941; came to U.S., 1968, naturalized, 1977; d. Peter Theodore and Maria Francisca (Castien) U.; ed. London, Ont., Can.

With Drug Trading Co., London, 1957-59, Richard-Wilcox, London, 1959-62, Friden Bus. Machines, Toronto, Ont., 1962-68, Permatex, West Palm Beach, Fla., 1968-70, Singer Bus. Machines, London, Ont., Can., 1970-72, Los Angeles, 1972-74; with Safariland Leather Co., Monrovia, Calif., 1974-81, v.p. adminstrn., 1975-81; ind. systems analyst, Los Angeles, 1981-83; owner Timor Computing Services, Azusa, Calif., 1983—; exec. dir. Forum Internat., 1976-91.

ULAM, FRANÇOISE, freelance writer, editor; b. Paris, Mar. 8, 1918; came to U.S., 1938, naturalized, 1945; d. Pierre and Madeleine (Carcassonne) Aron; m. Stanislaw M. Ulam, Aug. 19, 1941 (dec. May 1984); 1 child, Claire Anne. BA, Mills Coll., 1939; MA, Mt. Holyoke Coll., 1941. Data analyst Los Alamos (N.Mex.) Sci. Lab., 1946-67; freelance writer book revs., profiles, feature stories, 1965—. Editor: Adventures of a Mathematician (Stanislaw M. Ulam), Analogies Between Analogies (Stanislaw M. Ulam). Bd. dirs. Santa Fe Women's Health Com., 1982-95.

ULIN, SAMUEL ALEXANDER, computer systems developer; b. Nov. 8, 1955; s. Webster Beattie Ulin and Ann (Fletcher) Rainier; m. Lida Ohan, May 30, 1992. Student, U. Del., 1973-78. Systems design cons. Alpha Ro Inc., Wilmington, Del., 1982-83, Command Computer Svcs., N.Y.C., 1983-84; systems designer DBS Films, Inc., Malvern, Pa., 1984-86; dir. engring. Flight Safety Inc., ISD, Malvern, 1986-87, Irving, Tex., 1987-89; sr. system designer Litigation Scis., Culver City, Calif., 1989—. Designer software for interactive tng. on aircraft sys., 1983, one of first interactive ct. evidence presentation systems used in fed. ct., 1987. Home: Ste K 449 E Providencia Ave Apt K Burbank CA 91501-2916 Office: Graphic Evidence 200 Corporate Pointe # 300 Culver City CA 90230

ULLIMAN, JOSEPH JAMES, forester, educator; b. Springfield, Ohio, July 19, 1935; s. Joseph James Sr. and Iola Mae (Roth) U.; m. Barbara Blessing Gish, Apr. 29, 1961; children: Kathryn Nicole, Barbara Anne, Mark Joseph. BA in English, U. Dayton, 1958; MF in Forest Mgmt., U. Minn., 1968, PhD in Forest Mgmt., 1971. Research asst. U. Minn., Mpls., 1966-68, from instr. to asst. prof., 1968-74; mem. staff land use planning Willamette Nat. Forest, Eugene, Oreg., 1973; from assoc. prof. to prof. U. Idaho, Moscow, 1974-79; dir. U. Idaho FWR Remote Sensing Ctr.; co-dir. U. Idaho Remote Sensing Rsch. Unit, assoc. dean 1988-89, dept. head of forest resources, 1989—; cons. USAID, 1979—. Contbr. numerous articles on forestry and remote sensing to profl. jours. and books. Chmn. Natural Resources Com., Moscow, 1980-81, Environ. Commn., South St. Paul, Minn., 1972-74; pres. Moscow Swim Team Parents Assn., 1976. Recipient Phi Kappa Phi Disting. Faculty award, 1985, German Acad. Exchange Program award, 1985. Mem. Am. Soc. Photogrammetry and Remote Sensing (pres. Minn. chpt. 1974, dep. dir. 1983-85, Ford Bartlett award 1981), Soc. Am. Foresters (counselor 1981-84, chmn. remote sensing working group 1982-84), Internat. Soc. Photogrammetry (chmn. working group 1981-84). Democrat. Roman Catholic. Home: 2226 Weymouth St Moscow ID 83843-9618 Office: U Idaho Coll of Forestry Moscow ID 83844-1133

ULLMAN, DANA GREGORY, educational administrator, publisher, author; b. L.A., Dec. 22, 1951; s. Sanford and Estelle Nancy (Pulvers) U.; m. Clare Francis Schlicting, Oct. 14, 1989. BA, U. Calif., Berkeley, 1975, MPH, 1978. Dir. Homeopathic Ednl. Services, Berkeley, Calif., 1975—; co-pub. North Atlantic Books, Berkeley, 1979—; pres., founder Found. for Homeopathic Edn. & Rsch., 1986—; conf. organizer U. Calif. Berkeley Ext., 1981; formulator and product spokesperson for Medicine from Nature Line of Homeopathic Medicines. Author: Discovering Homeopathy: Medicine for the 21st Century, 1988, The One-Minute (or so) Healer, 1991, Homeopathic Medicine for Children and Infants, 1992; co-author: Everybody's Guide to Homeopathic Medicine, 1984 (Med. Self-Care Book award 1985); co-pub.: numerous titles of homeopathic medicine. Fellow San Francisco Found., 1977-78, grantmaker, 1977-78; bd. dirs. Elmwood Inst., Berkeley, 1993-94. Mem. Soc. Pub. Health Edn., Nat. Ctr. Homeopathy (bd. dirs. 1985—, organizer ann. conf.), Assn. for Humanistic Psychology (exec. bd. dirs. 1986-88), Calif. Bd. Med. Quality Assurance (cons. 1980-81). Office: Homeopathic Ednl Svcs 2124 Kittredge St Berkeley CA 94704-1414

ULLMAN, EDWIN FISHER, research chemist; b. Chgo., July 19, 1930; s. Harold P. and Jane F. Ullman; m. Elizabeth J. Finlay, June 26, 1954; children—Becky L., Linda J. BA, Reed Coll., 1952; MA, Harvard U., 1954, PhD, 1956. Research chemist Lederle Labs., Am. Cyanamid, Pearl River, N.Y., 1955-60; group leader central research div. Am. Cyanamid, Stamford, Conn., 1960-66; sci. dir. Synvar Research Inst., Palo Alto, Calif., 1966-70; v.p., dir. research Syva Co., Palo Alto, 1970-95; v.p., dir. rsch. Behring Diagnostics Inc., Palo Alto, 1995—; mem. sci. adv. bd. EnSys Inc., Research Triangle Park, N.C., 1992—; mem. adv. bd. San Francisco State U. Coll. of Sci. and Engring., 1994—. Edit. bd.: Jour. Organic Chemistry, 1969-74, Jour. Immunoassay, 1979—, Jour. Clin. Lab., Analysis, 1986-87; contbr. articles to sci. jours. Patentee in field. NSF predoctoral fellow, 1952-53; U.S. Rubber Co. fellow, 1954-55. Recipient Clin. Ligand Assay Soc. Mallinckrodt award, 1981, Can. Soc. Clin. Chemists Health Group award, 1982, Inventor of Yr. award Peninsula Patent Law Assn., 1987. Fellow AAAS; mem. Am. Chem. Soc., Am. Assn. Clin. Chemists (Van Slyke award N.Y. sect. 1984, No. Calif. sect. award 1991), Am. Soc. Biol. Chemists, Clin. Ligand Assay Soc., Phi Beta Kappa. Office: Behring Diagnostics Inc PO Box 49013 San Jose CA 95161-9013

ULLMAN, MYRON EDWARD, III, retail executive; b. Youngstown, Ohio, Nov. 26, 1946; s. Myron Edward Jr. and June (Cunningham) U.; m. Cathy Emmons, June 20, 1969; children: Myron Cayce, Denver Tryan, Peter Brynt, Benjamin Kyrk, Kathryn Kwynn. BS in Indsl. Mgmt., U. Cin., 1969; postgrad. Inst. Ednl. Mgmt., Harvard U., 1977. Internat. account mgr. IBM Corp., Cin., 1969-76; v.p. bus. affairs U. Cin., 1976-81; White House fellow The White House, Washington, 1981-82; exec. v.p. Sanger Harris div. Federated Stores, Dallas, 1982-86; mgr. dir., chief oper. officer Wharf Holdings Ltd., Hong Kong, 1986-88; chmn., CEO, dir. R.H. Macy & Co. Inc., N.Y.C., 1986-95; dir. Federated Dept. Stores, Inc.; chmn., CEO, dir. DFS Group Ltd., San Francisco, 1995—; mng. dir. Lane Crawford Ltd., Hong Kong, 1986-88; bd. advisors Gt. Traditions Corp., Cin.; dep. chmn. Omni Hotels, Hampton, N.H., 1988; vice chmn. bd. dirs. Mercy Ships Internat. Internat. v.p. U. Cin. Alumni Assn., 1980—; bd. dirs. Nat. Multiple Sclerosis Soc., N.Y.C.; bd. dirs. Brunswick Sch., Greenwich, Conn., U. Cin. Found., Lincoln Ctr. Devel. Mem. White House Fellow Alumni Assn., Econ. Club N.Y.C. (bd. dirs., exec. com. 1993—), Nat. Retail Fedn. (vice chmn., bd. dirs., exec. com. 1993—), Delta Tau Delta (treas. 1967-68). Republican.

ULLMAN, PATRICIA, secondary education educator; b. Norfolk, Va., Nov. 27, 1953; d. Cyril Alfred and Beatrice (Halpert) U.; 1 child, Nicole Ullman-Rose. AB, U. So. Calif., 1975; MS, Purdue U., 1983, PhD, 1986. Teaching and rsch. asst. Purdue U., West Lafayette, Ind., 1980-86; NIMH postdoctoral fellow UCLA, 1986-88; staff rsch. assoc. U. Calif., Riverside, 1989; tchr. sci. Mountain View Jr. High Sch., Beaumont, Calif., 1989—; cons. Found. for Advancement Sci. Edn., L.A., 1986-87. Traveling scholar U. Chgo., 1985-86; David Ross fellow Purdue U., 1985; math. and sci. grantee GTE, 1991-92. Mem. NSTA, Hastings Ctr. Office: Mountain View Jr High Sch PO Box 187 Beaumont CA 92223-0187

ULLRICH, DONALD WILLIAM, JR., lawyer, real estate broker; b. Pasadena, Calif., Sept. 26, 1952; s. Donald William Ullrich and Laura Elizabeth (Holsinger) McNicol; m. Diane Elizabeth Natale, May 1, 1980 (div. 1983); 1 child, Anthony Fitzdonald; m. Cynthia Louise Cooke, Nov. 26, 1983; children: Brittany Louise, Austin-Cooke Alexander, Evan Nathaniel. BA in Polit. Sci., U. Calif., Santa Barbara, 1974; JD, U. Pacific, 1984, LLM in Bus. and Tax Law, 1989; postgrad., U. Calif., Davis, 1994—. Bar: Calif. 1985, U.S. Dist. Ct. (so. dist.) Calif. 1985, U.S. Dist.Ct. (ea. dist.) Calif. 1986, U.S. Dist. Ct. (no. dist.) Calif. 1990; lic. real estate broker, Calif. Commd. 2d lt. USMC, 1977, advanced through grades to capt., 1982; served various assignments with JAGC USMC, Camp Pendleton, Calif., 1984-88; resigned USMC, 1988; assoc. atty. Desmond, Miller & Desmond, 1989-93; pvt. practice Rancho Murieta, Calif., 1993—. Maj. USMCR, 1988—. Mem. Calif. State Bar (bus. law real property and tax sect.), Sacramento County Bar Assn., Federalist Soc., Calif. Assn. Realtors, Los Altos Bd. Realtors, San Jose Real Estate Bd. Republican. Home: 15112 Reynosa Dr Rancho Murieta CA 95683 Office: PO Box 371 3331 Sloughhouse Ln Sloughhouse CA 95683-0740

ULMER, FRAN, state official; m. Bill Council; children: Amy, Louis. B in Econs. and Polit. Sci., U. Wis.; JD with honors, Wis. Sch. Law. Polit. advisor Gov. Jay Hammond, Alaska, 1973-83; former mayor City of Juneau, Alaska; mem. 4 terms, minority leader Alaska Ho. Reps.; lt. gov. State of Alaska, 1995—. Home: 1700 Angus Way Juneau AK 99801-1411 Office: State Capitol PO Box 110015 Juneau AK 99811

ULMER, HARRIET GLASS, health services adminstrator; b. St. Louis, June 7, 1940; d. Melvin Gabriel and Deenie Joy (Laskowitz) Shcolnik; m. Allen L. Glass, Sept. 4, 1956 (div.); children—Bonnie Nielson, Bernard J., Laura Yeager; m. 2d, Raymond A. Ulmer, Feb. 26, 1980 (div.). B.A. in English, UCLA, 1976; M.P.A. in Health Services Adminstrn., U. So. Calif., 1980. Regional project coordinator Kaiser Found. Health Plan, Los Angeles, 1977-80; dir. planning and mktg. Hosp. of Good Samaritan, Los Angeles, 1981, v.p. mktg. and bus. devel., 1981-86; cons. healthcare Laventhol & Horwath, Los Angeles, 1986-87; Western regional dir. PPO Provider Svcs., Provident Life and Accident Ins. Co., Los Angeles, 1987-88; exec. dir., chief exec. officer Med. Research Found., Ventura, Calif., 1988-90; regional dir. Hosp. Coun. of So. Calif., L.A., 1990—, adv. bd. L.A. Reg. Drug and Poison Ctl. Ctr., 1992—; cons. Humana Corp., Los Angeles Health Planning and Devel. Agy. Mem. Coro Assocs.; mem. Los Angeles Area Planning Com. Mem. Am. Hosp. Assn., Am. Coll. Healthcare Execs., Women in Health Adminstrn. (charter), Healthcare Execs. of So. Calif., So. Calif. Soc. for Hosp. Planners, Am. Soc. Assn. Execs., Am. Soc. Hosp. Planning, Am. Mktg. Assn. (founder, pres. health care div. So. Calif. chpt. 1984-85), Am. Heart Assn. (chmn. pub. policy edn. com. Greater Los Angeles affiliate 1982-84), Acad. Health Services Mktg. (nominating com. 1985, award coordinator and presentation com. 1987), U. So. Calif. Health Services Adminstrn. Alumni Assn. (treas. 1983-84, v.p. 1984-85).

ULMISHEK, GREGORY FINEAS, geologist; b. Moscow, Nov. 5, 1934; came to U.S., 1980; s. Fineas G. and Polina B. (Karp) U.; m. Valeria F. Likhacheva, July 5, 1969; 1 child, Marina. MS, Moscow Petroleum Inst., 1957; PhD, Inst. Geology and Exploration, Moscow, 1971. Geologist S.E. Karakum Expdn., Turkmenistn, 1957-59; scientist Inst. Geology Fgn. Countries USSR Ministry of Geology, Moscow, 1959-69; sr. scientist Inst. Onceanology Acad. Scis. USSR, Moscow, 1969-79; scientist Argonne (Ill.) Nat. Lab., 1980-87; geologist U.S. Geol. Survey, Denver, 1987—. Contbr. 60 articles to profl. jours. Mem. Am. Assn. Petroleum Geologists (lectr.). Office: US Geol Survey Denver Fed Ctr Box 25046 MS 940 Denver CO 80225

ULRICH, DELMONT MARION, physician; b. Connell, Wash., Jan. 22, 1919; s. Otto Carl and Hannah M. (Zimmerman) U.; m. Doris Pauline Swanson, Mar. 25, 1946; children: Beverly, James, Dean. Student, U. Wash., 1937-40; BS, U. Minn., 1941, MD, 1944. Diplomate Am. Bd. Internal Medicine. Intern Milw. County Hosp., 1944, resident internal medicine, 1944-46; practice medicine specializing in internal medicine Seattle, 1949—; assoc. clin. prof. medicine U. Wash., Seattle, 1950—; pres. med. staff Providence Hosp., Seattle, 1968-69. Served to capt. AUS, 1946-48. Mem. AMA, Seattle Acad. Medicine, NW Soc. Clin. Research, Wash. State Soc. Internat. Medicine (pres. 1956-57), Theta Chi, Phi Rho Sigma. Republican. Episcopalian. Club: Seattle Yacht. Home: 5017 NE Laurelcrest Ln Seattle WA 98105-5245

ULRICH, JOHN AUGUST, microbiology educator; b. St. Paul, May 15, 1915; s. Robert Ernst and Mary Agnes (Farrell) U.; m. Mary Margaret Nash, June 6, 1940 (dec. May 1985); children: Jean Anne, John Joseph, Robert Charles, Karl James, Mary Ellen, Lenore Alice; m. Mary Matkovich, July 19, 1986. BS, St. Thomas Coll., 1938; PhD, U. Minn., 1947. Instr. De La Salle High Sch., Mpls., 1938-41; rsch. asst. U. Minn., Mpls., 1941-45, 49, Hormel Inst., U. Minn., Austin, 1945-49; instr. Mayo Clinic, U. Minn., Rochester, 1949-55; asst. prof. Mayo Found., U. Minn., Rochester, 1955-66; assoc. prof. U. Minn., Mpls., 1966-69; prof. U. N.Mex., Albuquerque, 1969-82, prof. emeritus, 1982—; chmn. Bacteriology & Mycology Study Sect., NIH, Washington, 1961-64, Communicable Diseases Study Sect., Atlanta, 1968-69; rsch. chmn. in field. Chmn. Zumbry Valley Exec. Bd., Boy Scouts Am., Rochester, 1953-55; mem. Gamehaven Exec. Bd., Boy Scouts Am., Rochester, 1952-62, Dem. Com., Olmsted County, Minn., 1964-69. Recipient Silver Beaver award Boy Scouts Am., 1962, Bishop's award Winona Diocese, 1962, Katahli award U. N.Mex., 1980. Mem. Am. Soc. Microbiology, Am. Chem. Soc., Am. Bd. Med. Mycology, Am. Acad. Microbiology, Am. Acad. Dermatology (affiliate) Elks. Democrat. Roman Catholic. Home: 3807 Columbia Dr Longmont CO 80503-2122

ULRICH, JOHN ROSS GERALD, aerospace engineer; b. Kalispell, Mont., Nov. 25, 1929; s. Alva Austin and Hattie Lenora (Kingston) U.; m. Virginia Jean Breinholt, June 19, 1954; children: Virginia, John, Annette, Lenora, James. BS in Engring., Northrup U., 1952. Registered profl. engr., Colo. Engr. Lockheed Aircraft, Burbank, Calif., 1952-54, Radioplane, Van Nuys, Calif., 1956-57; sect. head Aerojet-Gen., Sacramento, 1957-65; chmn. of SCUT Martin Marietta, Denver, 1965-92. Lectr. Arapahoe County Pub. Schs. With U.S. Army, 1954-56. Mem. AIAA. Home: 3435 E Arapahoe Littleton CO 80122

ULRICH, MARYBETH PETERSON, air force officer, political science educator; b. Oak Lawn, Ill., Nov. 2, 1962; d. John Mansfield and Virginia (Dunne) Peterson; m. Mark Alan Ulrich, Mar. 26, 1994. BS, USAF Acad., 1984; MA, U. Ill., 1992, postgrad., 1994—. Commd. ensign USAF, 1980, advanced through grades to capt., 1988; navigator, instr. 9th Strategic Reconnaissance Wing USAF, Beale AFB, Calif., 1985-90; instr. dept. polit. sci. USAF Acad., Colorado Springs, Colo., 1993-94, instr. navigator 50th Airmanship Tng. Squadron, 1993—. Author: (book chpt.) Encyclopedia of Policy Studies, 1994; contbr. articles to profl. jours. Coach cadet women's fast pitch softball club USAF Acad., Colorado Springs, 1993-94, adviser cadet forum on pub. affairs, 1993-94. Rsch. grantee Inst. Nat. Security Studies, 1993, 95. Mem. Am. Assn. Advancement of Slavic Studies, Internat. Studies Assn., Am. Polit. Sci. Assn., Women Military Aviators. Democrat. Roman Catholic. Home: 15555 Holbein Dr Colorado Springs CO 80921-2519

ULRICH, PAUL GRAHAM, lawyer, author, publisher, editor; b. Spokane, Wash., Nov. 29, 1938; s. Donald Gunn and Kathryn (Vandercook) U.; m. Kathleen Nelson Smith, July 30, 1982; children—Kathleen Elizabeth, Marilee Rae, Michael Graham. B.A. with high honors, U. Mont., 1961; J.D., Stanford U., 1964. Bar: Calif. 1965, Ariz. 1966, U.S. Supreme Ct. 1969, U.S. Ct. Appeals (9th cir.) 1965, U.S. Ct. Appeals (5th cir.) 1981. Law clk. judge U.S. Ct. Appeals, 9th Circuit, San Francisco, 1964-65; assoc. firm Lewis and Roca, Phoenix, 1965-70; ptnr. Lewis and Roca, 1970-85; pres. Paul G. Ulrich PC, Phoenix, 1985-92, Ulrich, Thompson & Kessler, P.C., 1992-95; ptnr. Ulrich, Kessler & Anger, P.C., Phoenix, 1995—; pres. Ulrich & Kessler, P.C., 1994-95, Ulrich, Kessler & Anger, P.C., 1995—; owner Pathway Enterprises, 1985-91; judge pro tem Div. 1, Ariz. Ct. Appeals, Phoenix, 1986; instr. Thunderbird Grad. Sch. Internat. Mgmt., 1968-69, Ariz. State U. Coll. Law, 1970-73, 78, Scottsdale Community Coll., 1975-77, also continuing legal edn. seminars. Author and pub.: Applying Management and Motivation Concepts to Law Offices, 1985; editor, contbr.: Arizona Appellate Handbook, 1978—; Working with Legal Assistants, 1980, 81, Future Directions for Law Office Management, 1982, People in the Law Office, 1985-886; co-author and pub.: Arizona Healthcare Professional Liability Handbook, 1992, supplement, 1994, Arizona Healthcare Professional Liability Defense Manual, 1995, Arizona Healthcare Professional Liability Update Newsletter, 1992—; co-author: Federal Appellate Practice Guide: Ninth Circuit, 1994; contbg. editor Law Office Economics and Management, 1984—; contbr. articles to profl. jours. Mem. Ariz. Supreme Ct. Task Force on Ct. Orgn. and Adminstrn., 1988-89; mem. com. on appellate cts. Ariz. Supreme Ct., 1990-91; bd. visitors Stanford U. Law Sch., 1974-77; adv. com. legal assisting program Phoenix Coll., 1985-95. With U.S. Army, 1956. Recipient continuing legal edn. award State Bar Ariz., 1978, 86, 90, Harrison Tweed spl. merit award Am. Law Inst./ABA, 1987. Fellow Ariz. Bar Found. (founding 1985—); mem. ABA (chmn. selection and utilization of staff personnel com., econs. of law sect. 1979-81, mem. standing com. legal assts. 1982-86, co-chmn. joint project on appellate handbooks 1983-85, co-chmn. fed. appellate handbook project 1985-88, chmn. com. on liaison with non-lawyer orgns. Econs. of Law Practice sect. 1985-86), Am. Acad. Appellate Lawyers, Am. Law Inst., Am. Judicature Soc. (Spl. Merit Citation 1987), Ariz. Bar Assn. (chmn. econs. of law practice com. 1980-81, co-chmn. lower ct. improvement com. 1982-85, co-chmn. Ariz. appellate handbook project 1976—), Coll. Law Practice Mgmt., Maricopa County Bar Assn. (bd. dirs. 1994—), Calif. Bar Assn., Phi Kappa Phi, Phi Alpha Delta, Sigma Phi Epsilon. Republican. Presbyterian. Home: 6536 N 10th Pl Phoenix AZ 85014 Office: 3030 N Central Ave Ste 1000 Phoenix AZ 85012-2717

UMAN, STEPHEN JONAS, physician; b. Jersey City, Jan. 26, 1947; m. Gwen C. Uman, 1971; 1 child, Russell Eli. Student, Palm Beach Jr. Coll., 1963-64, U. Fla., 1965; MD, Tulane U., 1969. Diplomate Am. Bd. Internal Medicine, Am. Bd. Infectious Disease. Intern Charity Hosp. of La., New Orleans, 1969-70; resident in medicine, chief resident Cedars-Sinai Med. Ctr., L.A., 1972-73; fellow in infectious disease U. Wis., 1973-75; past chmn. infectious disease com. Cedars-Sinai Med. Ctr., L.A., 1977-84, chief of staff, 1994—, mem. med. adv. com., 1978—, mem. med. exec. com., bd. dirs. profl. programs, co-chair geriatrics task force for strategic planning com.; pvt. practice L.A., 1975—; attending physician Midway Hosp. Med. Ctr., past chmn. infectious diseases com., 1981-85; past mem. internal medicine com.; cons. Century City Hosp., past mem. pharmacy and therapeutics com.; assoc. clin. prof. medicine UCLA Med. Ctr. Author: (with others) Medical Management of the Cardiac Surgical Patient, 1990; contbr. articles to profl. jours. Mem. AMA, Am. Soc. for Microbiology, Infectious Disease Soc. Am., Calif. Med. Assn., L.A. County Med. Assn. (past pres. Beverly Hills, Calif. dist.).

UMEK, ANTHONY MATTHEW, engineering development company administrator, school system administrator; b. New Kensington, Pa., Apr. 17, 1947; s. Anthony Jr. and Veronica Dorothy (Yugovich) U.; m. Kristy Sue Kocher, July 9, 1977; 1 child, Janelle Kristine. B.S. in Mech. Engring., Carnegie Mellon U., 1969; M.B.A., U. Pitts., 1971. Engr., Westinghouse Hanford Co., Madison, Pa., 1970-74, mgr. engring. div., Richland, Wash., 1974-88, administrator Westinghouse Idaho Nuclear Co., Idaho Falls, Idaho, 1988-94, dir. engring. Westinghouse Hanford Co., Richland, Wash., 1994—. pres./dir. Tri City Estates Water Dist., Richland, 1979-88. Contbr. research articles on non lethal weapons to profl. jours.; inventor thermocouple device for nuclear reactor, 1975; appointed mem. tech. team to evaluate impacts of Chernobyl accident on specific US Reactor type. Vol. YMCA, Richland, 1982—; loaned exec. United Way, Richland, 1983—. Recipient scholarship Croation Fraternal Union, Pitts., 1965. Mem. ASME (engring. div., chmn. pub. nuclear issues com. 1984-86, mem. nuclear engring. exec. com.), Am. Nuclear Soc., Am. Mgmt. Assn., Alpha Tau Omega (house mgr. 1968-69). Roman Catholic. Lodge: Croation Fraternal Union. Home: 3590 East Lake Dr Richland WA 99352 Office: Westinghouse Hanford Co PO Box 1970 Richland WA 99352

UNDERWOOD, B. JOANN, paralegal; b. Akron, Ohio; children: Maridel, Melisa, Thomas. AA, Panama Canal Zone Coll., Balboa, Panama; BS, Tenn. Tech. U.; cert. with honors, Roosevelt U., 1985. Paralegal Mut. Security Life Ins. Co., Ft. Wayne, Ind., 1986-87, Parkinson, Wolf, Lazar & Leo, L.A., 1988-89, Kornblum, Ferry & Frye, L.A., 1989-91, Joseph E. DiLoreto, Downey, Calif., 1992—. Vol. pro bono rsch. Citizens for Term Limits, Downey, 1993. Mem. L.A. Paralegal Assn., L.A. Trial Lawyers Assn., Panama Canal Soc. So. Calif.

UNDERWOOD, JERRY LAWRENCE, nonprofit corporation executive, writer; b. Clearfield, Pa., Oct. 19, 1941; s. Howard Broughton and Mildred Ethel (Bauman) U.; m. June Oechler, Oct. 8, 1963; 1 child, Jan. BA in English, Pa. State U., 1963; MA in English, U. Wyo., 1969; PhD in English, SUNY, Stony Brook, 1974. Instr. English U. Wyo., Laramie, 1972-75; reporter, editor The Emporia (Kans.) Gazette, 1978-88; exec. dir. Vestibular Disorders Assn., Portland, Oreg., 1989—. Editor On the Level newsletter, 1989—. Mem. Phi Kappa Phi. Office: Vestibular Disorders Assn PO Box 4467 Portland OR 97208-4467

UNDERWOOD, RALPH EDWARD, computer systems engineer; b. Houston, Sept. 26, 1947; s. Harry Anson and Ethel Jackson Underwood; m. Linda Sue Merkel, Apr. 10, 1976. BS in Biology, Baker U., 1969; JD, Washburn U., 1973; MS in Computer Sci., Kans. U., 1984. Bar: Kans. 1973. Free-lance stock and options trader Prairie Village, Kans., 1974-79; mem. staff BDM Corp., Leavenworth, Kans., 1982-84; sr. research and devel. engr. Ford Aerospace and Communications Corp., Colorado Springs, Colo., 1984-87, subcontract adminstr., 1987-89; sr. engr., program mgr. CTA Inc., Colorado Springs, 1989-93; sr. staff system engring. MCI Telecomms. Corp., Colorado Springs, 1993—. Patentee in field. Mem. IEEE, Info. System Security Assn., Armed Forces Communications and Electronics Assn., Kans. Bar Assn., Upsilon Pi Epsilon, Sigma Phi Epsilon (social chmn. 1968, asst. house mgr. 1968, sec./treas. sr. coun. 1969), Phi Alpha Delta. Office: MCI Telecomm Corp 2424 Garden Of The Gods Rd Colorado Springs CO 80919-3172

UNDERWOOD, THOMAS WOODBROOK, communications company executive; b. Royal Oak, Mich., Nov. 29, 1930; s. Elmer and Della Marie (Zimmer) U.; m. Louise Virginia, May 24, 1953 (dec. Feb. 1979); children: Ann Marie Underwood Shuman, Dan and Dave (twins). BAS in Elec. Engring., Milw. Sch. Engring., 1957. Service analyst, writer ITT Gillfillan, Los Angeles, 1958-60; sr. tech. editor, writer Smithkline Beckman, Fullerton, Calif., 1960-78; tech. com. mgr. Smithkline Beckman, Brea, Calif., 1978-85; pres. Tranwood Communications, Santa Ana, Calif., 1985—. Tech. editor, writer manuals for manned space flights to Mars and the moon. Served to staff sgt. USAF, 1950-54, Korea. Mem. Soc. Tech. Communications (Orange County chpt., sr., pres. 1992, 93, treas. 1966, 88), Am. Med. Writers Assn, U.S. C. of C., Santa Ana C. of C. Democrat. Office: Tranwood Communications PO Box 5578 Buena Park CA 90622-5578

UNDERWOOD, VERNON O., JR., grocery stores executive; b. 1940. With Youngs Market Co., L.A., pres., from 1976, chmn. bd., 1989—, also chief exec. officer. Office: Young's Market Co 500 S Central Ave Los Angeles CA 90013-1715

UNGAR, LISA ELAINE, school counselor, education educator; b. Youngstown, Ohio, Apr. 13, 1951; d. Herbert Leonard and Selma (Deitchman) U. MEd in Ednl. Psychology, U. Ariz., 1975, MEd in Counseling and Guidance, 1976. Tchr. Cin. Pub. Schs., 1972-74; religious sch. tchr. Congregation Chaverim, Tucson, 1976-85, Congregation Anshei Israel, Tucson, 1985-89; sch. counselor Tucson Unified Sch. Dist., 1977—; mem. edn. faculty U. Phoenix, Tucson; ednl. counselor, Tucson, 1988-92; mem. Ariz. State Sch. Counselor Cadre, Dept. Edn., Phoenix, 1990-93. Editor/co-editor resource manuals, including Remediation Counseling Manual, 1982, Developmental Counseling Resource Manual, 1986-87, Sex Role Stereotyping Implementation Manual. Chair women's div. Jewish Fedn. So. Ariz., Tucson, 1987-89, now solicitation trainer, div. chair; bd. dirs. Tucson Jewish Cmty. Ctr., 1984-87; vol., com. mem. United Way, Tucson, 1993-94. Named Young Woman of Yr., Jewish Fedn. So. Ariz., 1984, recipient Meritorious Svc. award, 1989; named to Outstanding Young Women of Am., 1984. Mem. ASCD, ACA, Ariz. Counselors Assn. (past v.p. mid. sch. counselors), Nat. Mid. Sch. Assn., Nat. Bd. Cert. Counselors. Democrat. Home: 1601 W Caspian Dr Tucson AZ 85704-1914

UNGER, ARLENE KLEIN, medical company executive, counselor, consultant; b. Bklyn., May 12, 1952; d. Eli and Harriet Barbara (Shapiro) Klein; m. Stefan Howard Unger, Aug. 19, 1979; children: Max Elias, Elana Rose. BS with distinction, Emerson Coll., 1974; MS, So. Conn. State Coll., 1976, Calif. State U., Hayward, 1981; PhD, Western Grad. Sch. Psychology, Palo Alto, Calif., 1991. Site adminstr., teaching specialist Severely Delayed Langs. Program Santa Clara (Calif.) County, 1976-81; language-movement counselor Peninsula Children's Ctr., Palo Alto, 1981-83; marriage, family and child counselor Woodside (Calif.) Psychol. Services, 1983-84; dir. tng. and sales Human Resource Services Employee Assistance Program, Sunnyvale, Calif., 1984-86; pvt. practice psychol. counseling Palo Alto, 1984-86; regional Employee Assistance mgr. Occupational Health Services, Sunnyvale, 1986-91; pvt. practice Counseling and Cons. Resources, Palo Alto, 1991—; founder, CEO Allied Health Svcs., A Med. Corp., 1992—; mental health counselor, instr. Foothill Coll., Los Altos, Calif., 1984-85; exec. dir. Sunnyvale Children's Arts and Movement Program, 1979-81, Cafe Motek, 1976-81; vol. instr. in music and movement Ohlone Sch., Palo Alto, 1986—;

founder, pres. Boutique Supply, Palo Alto, 1985; founder Let's Talk Program, Western Athletic Clubs, 1991—; speaker to various groups and orgns. Active Palo Alto Docent. Mem. ACA, Assn. Labor Mgmt. Administrs. and Cons. on Alcoholism (conf. chair Santa Clara chpt. 1987—), Calif. Assn. Marriage and Family Counselors, Calif. Psychol. Assn., Assn. Tng. and Devel., Am. Dance Therapy Assn., Palo Alto Run, Santa Clara Decathlon. Home: 2250 Webster St Palo Alto CA 94301-4053

UNIS, RICHARD L., state supreme court justice; b. Portland, Oreg., June 11, 1928. Grad., U. Va., U. Oreg. Bar: Oreg. 1954, U.S. Dist. Ct. Oreg. 1957, U.S. Ct. Appeals (9th cir.) 1960, U.S. Supreme Ct. 1965. Judge Portland Mcpl. Ct., 1968-71; judge Multnomah County Dist. Ct., 1972-76, presiding judge, 1972-74; former judge Oreg. Cir. Ct. 4th Judicial Dist., 1977; former sr. dep. city atty. City of Portland; adj. prof. of local govt. law and evidence Lewis & Clark Coll. Northwestern Sch. Law, 1969-76, 77—; faculty mem. The Nat. Judicial Coll., 1971—; former faculty mem. Am. Acad. Judicial Edn. Author: Procedure and Instructions in Traffic Court Cases, 1970, 101 Questions and Answers on Preliminary Hearings, 1974. Bd. dirs. Oreg. Free from Drug Abuse; mem. Oreg. Adv. Com. on Evidence Law Revision, chmn. subcom., 1974-79. Maj. USAFR, JAGC, ret. Recipient Meritorius Svc.award U. Oregon sch. Law, 1988; named Legal Citizen of Yr. Oreg. Law Related Edn., 1987; inducted into The Nat. Judicial Coll. Hall of Honor, 1988. Mem. Am. Judicature Soc. (bd. dirs. 1975), Am. Judges Assn., Multnomah Bar Found., Oregon Judicial Conf. (chmn. Oreg. Judicial Coll. 1973-80, legis. com. 1976—, exec. com. of judicial edn. com., judicial conduct com.), N.Am. Judges Assn. (tenure, selection and compensation judges com.), Dist. Ct. Judges of Oreg. (v.p., chmn. edn. com.), Nat. Conf. Spl. Ct. Judges (exec. com.), Oreg. State Bar (judicial adminstrn. com., sec. local govt. com., com. on continuing certification, uniform jury instrn. com., exec. com. criminal law sect., trial practice sect. standards and certification com., past chmn., among others), Oreg. Trial Lawyers Assn. (named Judge of Yr. 1984). Office: Oreg Supreme Ct Supreme Ct Bldg Salem OR 97310*

UNRUH, LEON DALE, newspaper editor; b. Larned, Kans., Dec. 26, 1956; s. Elgie Larey Unruh and Anita Faye Byers; m. Margaret E. Jones, Apr. 30, 1988. BS in Journalism, U. Kans., 1979. Copy editor Austin (Tex.) Am.-Statesman, 1979-83; copy desk chief Wichita (Kans.) Eagle-Beacon, 1983-86; asst. news editor Dallas Morning News, 1986-90; travel editor Anchorage Daily News, 1990—; freelance coll. textbook editor Harcourt Brace & Co., The Dryden Press, 1989—. Vol. Dallas Soc. Visually Impaired Children, 1986-90; active Alaska Photographic Ctr. Mem. Soc. Newspaper Design (Excellence award 1982). Office: Anchorage Daily News 1001 Northway Dr Anchorage AK 99508-2030

UNSER, AL, professional auto racer; b. Albuquerque, May 29, 1939; s. Jerry H. and Mary C. (Craven) U.; m. Wanda Jesperson, Apr. 22, 1958 (div.); children: Mary Linda, Debra Ann, Alfred; m. Karen Barnes, Nov. 22, 1977 (div.). Auto racer U.S. Auto Club, Speedway, Ind., 1964-94. Home: 7625 Central Ave NW Albuquerque NM 87121-2115

UPHAM, STEADMAN, anthropology educator, university dean, academic administrator; b. Denver, Apr. 4, 1949; s. Albert Tyler and Jane Catherine (Steadman) U; m. Margaret Anne Cooper, Aug. 21, 1971; children: Erin Cooper, Nathan Steadman. BA, U. Redlands, 1971; MA, Ariz. State U., 1977, PhD, 1980. Dist. sales mgr. Ind. News Co. Inc., Los Angeles, 1971-72; regional sales mgr. Petersen Pub. Co, Los Angeles, 1972-74; archeologist, researcher Bur. Land Mgmt., Phoenix, 1979; research asst. Ariz. State U., Tempe, 1979-80; chief archeologist Soil Sytems Inc., Phoenix, 1980-81; chief archeologist N.Mex. State U., Las Cruces, N.Mex., 1981-85, asst. prof. to assoc. prof., 1982-87, assoc. dean, 1987-90; prof. anthropology, vice provost for rsch., grad. dean U. Oreg., Eugene, 1990—; interim dir. Cultural Resources Mgmt. div, N.Mex. State U., Las Cruces, 1988. Author: Polities and Power, 1982, A Hopi Social History, 1992; editor: Computer Graphics in Archaeology, 1979, Mogollon Variability, 1986, The Sociopolitical Structure of Prehistoric Southwest Societies, 1989, The Evolution of Political Systems, 1990; also articles. Advanced seminar grantee Sch. of Am. Research, 1987, research grantee NSF, 1979, 1984-85, Hist. Preservation grantee State of N.Mex., 1982-84, 1991, 92, Ford Found. 1991-92, U.S. Dept. Edn. 1991-93. Mem. Nat. Phys. Sci. Consortium (pres. 1992-95), We. Assn. Grad. Schs. (pres. 1994-95). Office: U Oreg Office Acad Affairs 207 Johnson Hall Eugene OR 97403

UPP, ROBERT DEAN, lawyer; b. Allerton, Ill., Feb. 6, 1916; s. Dean Foreman Upp and Ruby (Armstrong) Upp Mason; m. Margaret Bernice Thiel, July 1, 1939 (div. June 1951); children: Dolores Dean Upp Boutin, Robert Rexford; m. Jane McIntosh Dinneen, Dec. 26, 1953. BS in Journalism, U. Ill., 1937; JD, U. So. Calif., 1948, MA in Social Sci., 1948, MS in Edn., 1949. Bar: Calif., U.S. Supreme Ct. Commd. 2d lt. U.S. Army, 1941, advanced through grades to Maj., 1951; asst. mgr. W.T. Grant Co., 1939-41; pvt. practice L.A., 1948—; prof. law L.A. City Coll., 1949-79. Contbr. articles to profl. jours. Pres. Hollywood (Calif.) Dem. Club, 1957-58. Brigadier gen. JAGC, USAR, 1970-76. Decorated Bronze Star with V oak leaf cluster, Legion of Merit. Mem. VFW (life), Res. Officers Assn. U.S. (pres. 1972-73, Calif. state pres. 1960), Interallied Confederation Res. Officers/NATO (past v.p.), Am. Legion (life), Retired Officers Assn., U.S. Army Assn., Mil. Order of World Wars, Judge Advocate's Assn., Inter-Am. Bar, San Diego Bar Assn., U. So. Calif., Alumni Assn., U. Ill. Alumni Assn. Democrat. Home and Office: 341 Pacific Ave Solana Beach CA 92075-1147

UPTON, DELL, historian, educator; b. Ft. Monmouth, N.J., June 24, 1949; s. Wentney B. and Carley A. (White) U. BA, Colgate U., 1970; MA, Brown U., 1975, PhD, 1980. Archtl. historian Va. Historic Landmarks Commn., Richmond, 1974-79; asst. prof. Am. studies Case Western Reserve U., Cleve., 1982-83; prof. archtl. history U. Calif., Berkeley, 1983—. Author: Holy Things and Profane: Anglican Parish Churches in Colonial Virginia, 1986 (Alice Davis Hitchcock Book award 1987, John Hope Franklin Book award 1987, Abbott Lowell Cummings Book award 1987), Madaline: Love and Survival in Antebellum New Orleans, 1995; editor: Common Places: Readings in American Vernacular Architecture, 1986, America's Architectural Roots: Ethnic Groups That Built America, 1986. Guggenheim fellow, 1990, NEH Rsch. fellow, 1981-82, Getty Sr. Rsch. grantee in art history, 1990. Mem. Am. Studies Assn., Am. Hist. Assn., Orgn. Am. Historians (bd. dirs. 1985-88), Vernacular Archtl. Forum (founder, editor 1979-89). Office: U Calif Dept Architecture Berkeley CA 94720-1800

URBANOWSKI, JOHN RICHARD, lighting systems company official; b. Jamaica, N.Y., May 31, 1947; s. John Casimir and Alfreda (Dabrowski) U.; m. Linda Holmes, Dec. 17, 1967 (div. June 1973); 1 child, Richard. BA, U. South Fla., 1968. Ptnr. Freeman Assocs., Ft. Lauderdale, Fla., 1972-76; sales engr. Holophane Lighting Co., Portland, Oreg., 1977—. Author computer program Microlux, 1984. With USN, 1969-72. Mem. Illuminating Engring. Soc. (bd. dirs. 1981-86, pres. 1983-84), Holophane Lighting Co. Dir.'s Club, Founder's Club. Unitarian. Office: Holophane Lighting Co 34 NW 1st Ave Ste 203 Portland OR 97209-4015

URCIA, INGEBORG, English language educator; b. Nurnberg, Germany, Apr. 6, 1934; came to U.S., 1952; d. Werner Edward and Ilse (Lebermann) O.; m. Jose Urcia, July 25, 1958; children: Benjamin Urcia, Gwendolyn Urcia. BA in English, U. Wash., 1955, MA in English, 1956, PhD in English, 1960. Instr. Yakima Valley Coll., Yakima, Wash., 1962-63; asst. prof. U. Nev., Las Vegas, 1963-65, Calif. Poly. U., Pomona, 1965-68; assoc. prof. Eastern Wash. U., Cheney, 1969-83, prof., 1983—; book reviewer and critical adv. Eastern Wash. Book Review Coun., Spokane Sch. Dists., 1983—. Author: All About Rex Cats, 1983, This is the Russian Blue, 1984, For the Love of Cats, 1985, The American Shorthair Cat, 1992, The Russian Blue Cat, 1992, Big Sky Country, 1994. Bd. dirs. Spokanimal Humane Soc., 1985-88; editor Spokanimal newsletter, 1985-88; adv. and judge Spokane area 4-H clubs. Mem. Nat. Conf. Tchrs. and Educators, Modern Lang. Assn., Phi Beta Kappa, Cat Writers of Am. Lutheran. Home: PO Box 36 Cheney WA 99004-0036 Office: Ea Wash U Dept English Cheney WA 99004

UREEL, PATRICIA LOIS, retired manufacturing company executive; b. Detroit, Nov. 29, 1923; d. Peter Walter and Ethel Estelle (Stewart) Murphy; grad. Detroit Bus. Inst., 1941; student Wayne State U., 1942, U. Detroit, 1943, U. Miami, 1945-46; m. Joseph Ralph Ureel, Jan. 4, 1947; children—Mary Patricia, Ronald Joseph. Exec. sec. to chmn. bd. and pres. Detroit Ball Bearing Co. of Mich., 1965-67; exec. sec. to partner charge Mich. dist. Ernst & Ernst, Detroit, 1967-71, Clubs of Inverrary, Lauderhill, Fla., 1971-72, partner charge of group Coopers & Lybrand, Miami, Fla., 1972-74; corp. sec., personnel mgr. Sanford Industries, Inc. and 4 subsidiaries, Pompano Beach, Fla., 1974-81; corp. sec., asso. Asphalt Assos., Ft. Lauderdale, 1982-86. Named Sec. of Yr. for City of Detroit, 1966; cert. profl. sec. Mem. Nat. Secs. Assn., Women's Econ. Club Detroit, Moose, Zeta Tau Alpha Sorority (Gamma Alpha chpt). Republican. Roman Catholic. Home: 19737 Suncrest Dr West Linn OR 97068

URENA-ALEXIADES, JOSE LUIS, electrical engineer; b. Madrid, Spain, Sept. 5, 1949; s. Jose L. and Maria (Alexiades Christodulakis) Urena y Pon. MSEE, U. Madrid, Spain, 1976; MS in Computer Science, UCLA, 1978. Rsch. asst. UCLA, 1978; systems analyst Honeywell Info. Systems, L.A., 1978-80; mem. tech. staff Jet Propulsion Lab., Pasadena, Calif., 1980-91; exec. dir. Empresa Nacional de Innovacion S.A., L.A., 1991—. Contbr. various articles to profl. jours. Two times recipient NASA Group Achievement award. Mem. IEEE, IEEE Computer Soc., IEEE Communications Soc., Assn. for Computer Machinery, World Federalist Assn., Spanish Profl. Am. Inc. Roman Catholic. Home: 904 Dickson St Marina Dl Rey CA 90292-5513 Office: Empresa Nacional Innovacion SA 2049 Century Park E Ste 2770 Los Angeles CA 90067-3202

URI, GEORGE WOLFSOHN, accountant; b. San Francisco, Dec. 8, 1920; s. George Washington and Ruby (Wolfsohn) U.; m. Pamela O'Keefe, May 15, 1961. A.B., Stanford U., 1941, I.A., 1943, M.B.A., 1946; postgrad., U. Leeds, Eng., 1945. CPA, Calif.; chartered fin. cons.; CFP; accredited estate planner, Nat. Assn. Estate Planning Coun. Mem. acctg., econs. and stats. depts. Shell Oil Co., Inc., San Francisco, 1946-48; ptnr. Irelan, Uri, Mayer & Sheppie, San Francisco; pres. F. Uri & Co., Inc.; instr. acctg. and econs. Golden Gate Coll., 1949-50. Contbr. articles to profl. jours. Chmn. San Rafael Redevel. Adv. Com., 1977-78, mem., 1978-91, mem. emeritus, 1991—; bd. dirs. San Francisco Planning and Urban Renewal Assn., 1958-60. Served with AUS, 1942-46, to col. Res. (ret.). Recipient Key Man award San Francisco Jr. C. of C.; Meritorious Service medal Sec. of Army, 1978. Mem. AICPA (hon. 1991), Inst. Mgmt. Scis. (treas. No. Calif. chpt. 1961-62), Calif. Soc. CPAs (sec.-treas. San Francisco chpt. 1956-57, dir. 1961-63, state dir. 1964-66, mem. Forbes medal com. 1968-69, chmn. 1969-71, hon. 1991), Am. Econs. Assn., Inst. Mgmt. Accts., San Francisco Estate Planning Coun. (dir. 1965-68), Am. Soc. Mil. Comptrollers, Execs. Assn. San Francisco (pres. 1965-66), Inst. Cert. Mgmt. Accts. (cert. mgmt. acctg., Disting. Performance cert. 1978), Inst. Cert. Fin. Planners, Am. Soc. CLUs and Chartered Fin. Cons. Clubs: World Trade (San Francisco), Commonwealth (quar. chmn. 1971), Stanford (dir. 1990—); Army and Navy (Washington). Home: 11 McNear Dr San Rafael CA 94901-1545 Office: 160 Pine St Ste 710 San Francisco CA 94111-5530

URIBE, JENNIE ANN, elementary school educator; b. National City, Calif., Apr. 17, 1958; d. Robert and Alice (Packard) U. BA, San Diego State U., 1981, cert. teacher, 1982. Tchr. Langdon Ave. Sch., L.A. Unified Sch. Dist., Sepulveda, Calif., 1984-94, tchr. potentially gifted students class, 1987-94; tchr. Spreckels Elem. Sch., San Diego City Schs., 1994—; tchr./advisor for student govt., 1987-93. Mem. adv. coun. Sch. Site, 1992—. Home: 2259 Peach Tree Ln Spring Valley CA 91977 Office: Spreckels Elem Sch 6033 Stadium St San Diego CA 92122-3307

URISTA, JUAN, computer scientist; b. L.A., July 3, 1957; s. Pablo and Teresa (Franco) U.; m. Laura White, July 31, 1983; children: Timothy James, Tawny Joy. AS, Don Bosco Tech. Inst., Rosemead, Calif., 1976; BS, Calif. State U., L.A., 1990. Software engr. Deep Space Network Jet Propulsion Labs/NASA, Pasadena, Calif., 1982-90, design engr. advanced info. systems, 1990—; mem. speaker's bur. Jet Propulsion Lab., Pasadena, 1992. Author: (design documents) Software Design of Antenna Pointing, 1985. Mem. Pasadena Speech Club (pres. 1991-92, v.p. 1988-89). Home: 707 Charter Oak St South Pasadena CA 91030-2305 Office: Jet Propulsion Lab 4800 Oak Grove Dr Pasadena CA 91109-8001

URMER, DIANE HEDDA, management firm executive, financial officer; b. Bklyn., Dec. 15, 1934; d. Leo and Helen Sarah (Perlman) Leverant; m. Albert Heinz Urmer, Sept. 2, 1952; children: Michelle, Cynthia, Carl. Student U. Tex., 1951-52, Washington U., St. Louis, 1962-63; BA in Psychology, Calif. State U.-Northridge, 1969. Asst. auditor Tex. State Bank, Austin, 1952-55; v.p., contr. Enki Corp., Sepulveda, Calif., 1966-70, also dir., 1987—; v.p., fin. Cambia Way Hosp., Walnut Creek, Calif., 1973-78; v.p., contr. Enki Health & Rsch. Sys., Inc., Reseda, Calif., 1978—, also dir. Contbr. articles to profl. jours. Pres. Northridge PTA, 1971; chmn. Northridge Citizens Adv. Council, 1972-73. Mem. Women in Mgmt. Club: Tex. Execs. Avocations: bowling, sailing, handcrafts, golf. Office: Enki Health and Rsch Systems Inc 21601 Devonshire St Chatsworth CA 91311-2946

USHER, RONALD LEE, government health care consultant, retired county official; b. Wenatchee, Wash., Sept. 14, 1935; s. Harlan King and Lida Marie (Hall) U.; m. Nancy Jean Mallon, Dec. 30, 1961; children: Bradley, Eric, Craig, Michael. BBA, U. Puget Sound, 1957; M in Govtl. Adminstrn., U. Pa., 1959; PhD in Pub. Adminstrn., Golden Gate U., 1980. Adminstrv. intern City of Vallejo (Calif.), 1958-59, asst. city mgr. and personnel dir., 1962-65; adminstrv. analyst Sonoma County, Santa Rosa, Calif., 1959-62; town mgr. Town of Corte Madera (Calif.), 1965-70; city and borough mgr. City and Borough of Juneau (Alaska), 1970-74; city mgr. City of Mill Valley (Calif.), 1974-75; dir. health and human svcs. Marin County, San Rafael, Calif., 1975-78; dir. health Sacramento County, Sacramento, 1978-92; adj. prof. Golden Gate U., San Francisco and Sacramento, 1977—; asst. prof. Calif. State U., Sacramento, 1978-88; asst. clin. prof. U. So. Calif., Sacramento, 1983-84, 90; cons. Placer County Grand Jury, Auburn, Calif., 1981, County of Sacramento, 1992-93, Health For All, Inc., 1992-94, Sacramento Cmty. Clinics Assn., 1994-95. Contbr. articles to profl. jours. Bd. dirs. Community Svcs. Planning Coun., Sacramento, 1978-92, Parent Support Program, Sacramento, 1984-87, Golden Empire Hypertension Coun., 1987-90, Cities in Schs., Sacramento, 1989-92; exec. couple Sacramento Marriage Encounter, 1988-90. Recipient Exceptional Svc. in Pub. Health award Taxpayers League Sacramento County, 1988. Mem. ASPA (chpt. pres. 1972-73, 86-87, Outstanding Pub. Adminstr. award Sacramento 1991), Calif. Conf. Local Mental Health Dirs. (exec. bd. 1981-86), County Health Execs. Calif. (exec. bd. 1988-92).

USHIJIMA, JOHN TAKEJI, state senator, lawyer; b. Hilo, Hawaii, Mar. 13, 1924; s. Buhachi and Sano (Nitahara) U.; m. Margaret Kunishige, June 6, 1954. B.A., Grinnell Coll., 1950; J.D., George Washington U., 1952. Bar: Hawaii, 1953. Ptnr. Pence & Ushijima, Hilo, 1953-61, Ushijima & Nakamoto, Hilo, 1961-69; mem. Hawaii Senate, 1959—, pres. pro tem, 1974—; bd. dirs. Cyanotech Corp., Woodinville, Wash. Bd. dirs. Waiakea Settlement YMCA. With AUS, 1943-46, ETO. Mem. Am. Bar Assn., Phi Delta Phi. Democrat. Home: 114 Melani St Hilo HI 96720-2766 Office: 192 Kapiolani St Hilo HI 96720-2687

USINGER, MARTHA PUTNAM, counselor, educator; b. Pitts., Dec. 10, 1912; d. Milo Boone and Christiana (Haberstroh) Putnam; m. Robert Leslie Usinger, June 24, 1938 (dec. Oct. 1968); children: Roberta Christine, Richard Putnam. AB cum laude, U. Calif., Berkeley, 1934; postgrad., Oreg. State U., 1935, U. Ghana, 1970, Coll. Nairobi, 1970. Tchr. Oakland (Calif.) Pub. Schs., 1936-38; tchr. Berkeley (Calif.) Pub. Schs., 1954-57, dean West Campus, counselor, 1957-78; lectr., photographer in field. Author: Ration Books and Christmas Crackers, 1989. Mem. adv. coun. Lifespan Alta Bates Hosp. Mem. DAR, Berkeley Ret. Tchrs., U. Calif. Emeriti Assn., U. Calif. Alumnae Assn., Prytanean Alumnae Assn. (pres. 1952-54), Mortar Bd., Delta Kappa Gamma. Congregationalist.

USITALO, IRENE JOANN, vocational school educator, small business owner; b. Seattle, June 6, 1921; d. Edwin A. and Vivien I. (Rice) Walton; m. Richard R. Usitalo, Jan. 15, 1940; children: Richard E., Carol Usitalo Donaldson, Clinton D. Grad., Met. Bus. Coll., Seattle, 1940; student, Western Wash. U., 1958-59, Tacoma Community Coll., 1983; AA in Humanities, Highline Coll., Midway, Wash., 1976. Cert. vocat. tchr., Wash. Tchr. Clover Park Vocat. Coll., Tacoma, 1984—; exec. sec. Puyallup (Wash.) Sch. Dist., 1972-86; adminstrv. sec. Auburn (Wash.) Sch. Dist., 1965-72; exec. sec. U. Wis., Milw., 1964-65; adminstrv. sec. Seattle Sch. Dist., 1961-64; bookkeeper McBeath Glass Co., Bellingham, 1960-62, Bellingham Flying Svc., 1959-60, Silverdale (Wash.) Fuel and Transfer, 1947-49; adminstrv. asst. to dietitian Western Wash. U., Bellingham, 1950-53; adminstrv. sec., office mgr. Bellingham (Wash.) High Sch., 1953-58; instr. Highline Community Coll., 1976-84, South Sound Community Coll., Yelm, Wash., 1987; owner, mgr., presenter profl. workshops IJ Usitalo & Assocs., Federal Way, Wash., 1985—; advisor com. for office occupation Tacoma Community, Pierce Community, Highline Community Colls., Federal Way High Sch., 1975-88. Contbr. articles to newsletters and mags. Mem. Wash. Women United, 1984—, Women for Choice, 1989—. Recipient Spl. Dir.'s award Puyallup Sch. Dist., 1984. Mem. NAFE (networking com. 1986), Nat. Assn. Ednl. Office Pers. (life, cert. ednl. office employee award of distinction 1981, advisor profl. standards program 1985-91, chmn. vocat.-adult edn. coun. 1989-91, editor/pub./contbr. Nat. Ednl. Sec. mag. and Crossroads newsletter), Am. Bus. Womens Assn. (chpt. pres. 1986), NW Adult Edn. Assn., Am. Mgmt. Assn., Wash. Assn. Ednl. Office Pers. (life, past pres., Employee of Yr. award 1982, editor/pub./contbr. newsletter), Wash. Assn. Maintenance and Ops. Adminstrs. (editor/pub./contbr. newsletter), Past Pres. Assn. (treas, pres.), Order Ea. Star (life). Home: 3025 SW 300th Pl Federal Way WA 98023-2373

USUI, LESLIE RAYMOND, clothing executive; b. Wahiawa, Hawaii, Feb. 2, 1946; s. Raymond Isao and Joyce Mitsuyo (Muramoto) U.; m. Annie On Nor Hom, Oct. 23, 1980; 1 child, Atisha. BA in Zool., U. Hawaii, 1969, MA in Edn., 1972. Cert. tchr., Hawaii. Flight steward United Airlines, Honolulu, 1970; spl. tutor Dept. Edn., 1971-73; v.p. Satyuga, Inc., Honolulu, 1974-80; pres. Satyuga, Inc., 1980—; also bd. dirs.; cons. Hawaii Fashion Guild, 1978-79. Composer: Song to Chenrayzee, Song to Karmapa. Cofounder, bd. dirs. Kagyu Thegchen Ling Meditation Ctr., 1974—, Maitreya Inst., 1983-86; bd. dirs. Palpung Found., 1984—; mem. U.S. Senatorial Bus. Adv. Bd., Washington, 1988; charter mem. Citizens Against Govt. Waste, 1988—, Citizens for Sound Economy, 1987-91, Nat. Tax Limitation Com., 1988-89. Mem. Nat. Fedn. Ind. Bus., Am. Biog. Inst. (life, bd. govs. 1990), Hawaii Bus. League, Internat. Biog. Centre (life), Internat. Platform Assn., World Inst. Achievement (life), Cousteau Soc., Nature Conservancy, Honolulu Zool. Soc., Waikiki Aquarium. Republican. Buddhist. Home: 1417 Laamia Pl Honolulu HI 96821-1403 Office: Satyuga Inc 248 Mokauea St Honolulu HI 96819-3110

UTAIN, MARSHA, marriage family child counselor, author, lecturer; b. Phila., Oct. 16, 1947; d. Charles and Diana Green; m. Arthur Melville, May 28, 1978. BA in English, Beaver Coll., 1969; MS in Counseling, Calif. State U., Long Beach, 1979. Lic. marriage family child counselor, Calif.; cert. high sch. and jr. coll. tchg., Calif. Tchr. Neshaminy (Pa.) Sr. H.S., 1969-71, spl. project tchr. Sch. Without Walls, 1971-72; chair dept. English-Reading Garden Gate Alternative H.S., L.A., 1976-79; co-tchr., spl. clin. supr. Calif. State U., Long Beach, 1979-81, co-tchr. Sch. Nursing Continuing Edn., 1980-81; co-host mental health mag. KFOX Radio, L.A., 1987-89; pvt. practice Long Beach, 1980—; cons. Orange County Dept. Mental Health, Laguna, Calif., 1983, Long Beach Psychiat. Clinic for Children, 1985; lectr./trainer U.S. Jour. Tng., Inc., Deerfield Beach, Fla., 1989-91; presenter Calif. Consortium for Prevention of Child Abuse, 1992; clin. dir. So. Calif. Youth Offender Recovery Program, 1991—. Author: (pamphlet) Stepping Out of Chaos, 1989; co-author: The Healing Relationship, 1989; contbg. author: The Partnership Way, 1990. Charter mem. Orange County Task Force on Organized Abuse of Children, Costa Mesa, Calif., 1991-93. Mem. ACA (clin. mem.), Calif. Assn. Marriage Family Therapists (clin. mem.), Phi Kappa Phi, Phi Delta Kappa, Kappa Delta Pi, Phi Alpha Theta (past sec.). Office: 5520 E 2nd St Ste K Long Beach CA 90803-3957

UTLEY, DONNA LAVELLE, healthcare human resources administrator; b. Tulare, Calif., June 30, 1948; d. Donald Raymond and Vivian Lee (Baber) Rogers; married, July 23, 1970. BS, Calif. State U., Fresno, 1970; MPA, U. So. Calif., 1985. Resources and devel. asst. Concentrated Employment Program, Fresno, Calif., 1970-72; pers. analyst Fresno County Pers. Dept., 1972-74; pers. mgr. Fresno County Health Dept., 1974-79; pers. dir. Merced (Calif.) Community Med. Ctr., 1979-81; dir. H.R., Bay Area Hosp., Coos Bay, Oreg., 1981-85; asst. adminstr. H.R., St. Elizabeth Med. Ctr., Yakima, Wash., 1985-90; dir. H.R., Washoe Med. Ctr., Reno, 1990-92, Mercy Am. River/Mercy San Juan Hosp, Carmichael, Calif., 1992—; bd. dirs. Enterprise for Progress in the Community, 1986-90, sec., 1989-90, chair pers. com., 1987, 88, 89, 90. Mem. Am. Soc. Healthcare H.R. Adminstrn., Soc. for Human Resources Mgmt., Healthcare H.R. Mgmt. Assn. Calif. Republican. Methodist. Office: 6501 Coyle Ave Carmichael CA 95608

UTNE, JOHN RICHARD, retired radiation oncologist; b. Fergus Falls, Minn., Oct. 2, 1924; s. John Arndt and Dagney Louise (Thyse) U.; m. Bernice Gertrude Kiefer, June 19, 1948; children: John Stephen, Susan Elizabeth, Barbara Ellen, Linda Louise. Student, Marquette U., 1943; BS, U. Ill., Chgo., 1946, MD, 1948; MS, U. Minn., 1955. Diplomate Am. Bd. Radiology. Intern Mpls. Gen. Hosp., 1948-49; pvt. practice, Mpls., 1948-50, Northfield, Minn., 1951-52; resident in radiology Mayo Clinic, Rochester, Minn., 1953-55; radiologist, chief staff St. John's Mercy Hosp., Mason City, Iowa, 1956-74; radiologist Scripps Meml. Hosp., La Jolla, Calif., 1974-85; locum tenens radiologist, 1985—. Former mem. Mason City Sch. Bd.; former dist. pres. Boy Scouts Am., Mason City; radiologist Project Hope, Managua, Nicaragua, 1965, Tunis, Tunisia, 1969. Lt. M.C., USN, 1951-53, Korea. Named Man of Yr., Sertoma Club, Mason City, 1968. Fellow Am. Coll. Radiology; mem. Radiol. Soc. N.Am. (emeritus). Republican. Lutheran. Home: 220 Coast Blvd La Jolla CA 92037-4617

UTTAL, WILLIAM R(EICHENSTEIN), psychology and engineering educator, research scientist; b. Mineola, N.Y., Mar. 24, 1931; s. Joseph and Claire (Reichenstein) U.; m. Michiye Nishimura, Dec. 20, 1954; children: Taneil, Lynet, Lisa. Student, Miami U. Oxford, Ohio, 1947-48; B.S. in Physics, U. Cin., 1951; Ph.D. in Exptl. Psychology and Biophysics, Ohio State U., 1957. Staff Psychologist, mgr. behavioral sci. group IBM Research Center, Yorktown Heights, N.Y., 1957-63; assoc. prof. U. Mich., Ann Arbor, 1963-68, prof. psychology, 1968-86, research scientist, 1963-86, prof. emeritus, 1986—; grad. affiliate faculty dept. psychology U. Hawaii, 1986—; research scientist Naval Ocean Systems Ctr.-Hawaii Lab., Kailua, 1985-88; prof., chmn. dept. psychology Ariz. State U., Tempe, 1988-92, prof. dept. indsl. and mgmt. systems engring., 1992—, affiliated prof., Dept. of Computer Sci. and Engring., 1993—; vis. prof. Kyoto (Japan) Prefectural Med. U., 1965-66, Sensory Sci. Lab., U. Hawaii, 1968, 73, U. Western Australia, 1970-71, U. Hawaii, 1978-79, 80-81; pres. Nat. Conf. on On-Line Uses Computers in Psychology, 1974. Author: Real Time Computers: Techniques and Applications in the Psychological Sciences, 1968, Generative Computer Assisted Instruction in Analytic Geometry, 1972, The Psychobiology of Sensory Coding, 1973, Cellular Neurophysiology and Integration: An Interpretive Introductin, 1975, An Autocorrelation Theory of Visual Form Detection, 1975, The Psychobiology of Mind, 1978, A Taxonomy of Visual Processes, 1981, Visual Form Detection in Three Dimensional Space, 1983, Principles of Psychobiology, 1983, The Detection of Nonplanar Surfaces in Visual Space, 1985, The Perception of Dotted Forms, 1987, On Seeing Forms, 1988, The Swimmer: A Computational Model of a Perceptual Motor System, 1992; also numerous articles; editor: Readings in Sensory Coding, 1972; assoc. editor Behavioral Research Method and Instrn., 1968-90, Computing: Archives for Electronic Computing, 1963-75, Jour. Exptl. Psychology: Perception and Performance, 1974-79; cons. editor Jour. Exptl. Psychology: Applied, 1994—. Served to 2d lt. USAF, 1951-53. USPHS spl. postdoctoral fellow, 1965-66; NIMH research scientist award, 1971-76. Charter fellow Am. Psychol. Soc.; fellow AAAS, Soc. Exptl. Psychologists; mem. Psychonomics Soc. Office: Ariz State U Dept Indsl and Mgmt Systems Engring Tempe AZ 85287-1104

UTTER, ROBERT FRENCH, state supreme court justice; b. Seattle, June 19, 1930; s. John and Besse (French) U.; m. Elizabeth J. Stevenson, Dec. 28, 1953; children: Kimberly, Kirk, John. BS, U. Wash., 1952; LLB, 1954. Bar: Wash. 1954. Pros. atty. King County, Wash., 1955-57; individual practice law Seattle, 1957-59; ct. commr. King County Superior Ct., 1959-64, judge, 1964-69; judge Wash. State Ct. Appeals, 1969-71; judge Wash. State Supreme Ct., 1971—, chief justice, 1979-81; lectr. in field; leader comparative law tour Peoples Republic of China, 1986, 87, 88, 91, USSR, 1989; adj. prof. constl. law U. Puget Sound, 1987, 88, 89, 90, 91, 92, 93, 94; cons. CEELI, 1991, 93—, USIA, 1992; visitor to Kazakhstand and Kyrgystan Judiciary,

1993, 94; lectr. to Albanian Judiciary, 1994. Editor books on real property and appellate practice. Pres., founder Big Brother Assn., Seattle, 1955-67; pres., founder Job Therapy Inc., 1963-71; mem. exec. com. Conf. of Chief Justices, 1979-80, 81-86; pres. Thurston County Big Bros./Big Sisters, 1984; lectr. Soviet Acad. Moscow, 1991; USIA visitor to comment on jud. system, Latvia, 1992, Kazakstan, 1993-94,. Named Alumnus of Yr., Linfield Coll., 1973, Disting. Jud. Scholar, U. Ind., 1987, Judge of Yr., Wash. State Trial Lawyers, 1989, Outstanding Judge, Wash. State Bar Assn., 1990, Outstanding Judge, Seattle-King County Bar Assn., 1992, Conder-Faulkner lectr. U. Wash. Sch. Law, 1995. Mem. ABA (commentator on proposed constns. of Albania, Bulgaria, Romania, Russia, Lithuania, Azerbaijan, Uzbekistan, Byelarus, Kazakhstan & Ukraine), Am. Judicature Soc. (Herbert Harley award 1983, sec. 1987—, chmn. bd. dirs., mem. exec. com.), Order of Coif. Baptist. Office: Wash Supreme Ct Temple of Justice (AV-11) Olympia WA 98504*

UWAKAH, ONYEBUCHI TIMOTHY, export company executive; b. Akoli-Imenyi, Abia, Nigeria, Aug. 25, 1942; came to U.S., 1981; s. Timothy Ikeocha and Rebecca Nwayinnaya (Ejimele) U.; m. ugonma Onyebuchi Nwankwo, Aug. 31, 1986; children: Obinna, Uzoma, Ikenna. BA, Golden Gate U., 1983, MPA, 1984, PhD, 1991. Officer Dept. of Agr., Owerri, Nigeria, 1977-81; asst. to pres. N.W. Equity Corp., San Francisco, 1985-87; pres. Manuman, Ltd., San Francisco, 1990—; examiner State Employment Devel. Dept., Oakland, Calif., 1993—. Vol. ops. analyst City of Oakland, 1991-92; mem. Mayor Jordan's Transit Team, San Francisco, 1991, San Francisco State U. Ctr. Profl. Devel., 1992—; bd. dirs. Loren Miller Homes, Inc., San Francisco, 1992—. Capt. Biafra Army, 1968-70. Mem. Am. Soc. Pub. Adminstrn., Agrl. Soc. Nigeria, Golden Gate U. Justice Club (sec. 1982-83). Methodist. Home: 954 Buchanan St San Francisco CA 94102-4117

UYEHARA, CATHERINE FAY TAKAKO (YAMAUCHI), physiologist, educator, pharmacologist; b. Honolulu, Dec. 20, 1959; d. Thomas Takashi and Eiko (Haraguchi) Uyehara; m. Alan Hisao Yamauchi, Feb. 17, 1990. BS, Yale U., 1981; PhD in Physiology, U. Hawaii, Honolulu, 1987; postgrad., U. Hawaii, 1994—. Postdoctoral fellow SmithKline Beecham Pharms., King of Prussia, Pa., 1987-89; asst. prof. in pediatrics U. Hawaii John Burns Sch. Medicine, Honolulu; rsch. pharmacologist Kapiolani Med. Ctr. for Women and Children, Honolulu, 1989—; statis. cons. dept. clin. investigation Tripler Army Med. Ctr., Honolulu, 1984-87, 89—, chief rsch. pharmacology sect., 1991—, dir. coop. rsch. and devel. projects, 1995—; asst. prof. pharmacology U. Hawaii John A. Burns Sch. Medicine, grad. faculty Interdisciplinary Biomed. Sci. program. Contbr. articles to profl. jours. Mem. Am. Fedn. Clin. Rsch., Am. Physiol. Soc., Soc. Uniformed Endocrinologists, Endocrine Soc., We. Soc. Pediatric Rsch., We. Soc. Pediatric Rsch., N.Y. Acad. Scis. Democrat. Mem. Christian Ch. Office: Tripler Army Med Ctr Dept Clin Investigation 1 Jarrett White Rd Honolulu HI 96859-5000

UYEHARA, OTTO ARTHUR, mechanical engineering educator emeritus, consultant; b. Hanford, Calif., Sept. 9, 1916; s. Rikichi and Umi (Nakayama) U.; m. Chisako Suda, Aug. 12, 1945; children: Otto Kenneth, Susan Joy Uyehara Schultheiss, Emi Ryu Uyehara-Stewart. BS, U. Wis., 1942, MS, 1943, PhD, 1946. Postdoctoral fellow U. Wis., Madison, 1945-46, rsch. assoc., 1946-47, asst. prof., then assoc. prof., 1949-57, prof., 1957-82, prof. emeritus, 1982—; pvt. practice cons. Anaheim, Calif., 1985—; mem. sci. adv. com. Eclin Corp., Branford, Conn., 1980—. Recipient Sci. Achievement awrd Japan Soc. Automotive Engrs. FEllow Soc. Automotive Engrs.; mem. ASME (internal combustion divsn., Internal Combustion award 1994), Japan Soc. Mech. Engrs. (hon.). Home: 544 S Bond St Anaheim CA 92805-4823

UYENO, LANI AKEMI, education educator; b. Wahiawa, Hawaii, Apr. 4, 1954; d. Gilbert Kenichi and Tomoyo (Imura) Yuruki; m. Kenneth Akira Uyeno, May 6, 1978; children: Julie Masako, Joy Hiromi. BEd, U. Hawaii, 1976, MEd, 1977. Cert. tchr., Hawaii. Tchr. Kapiolani C.C., Honolulu, 1977-85; asst. prof. Leeward C.C., Pearl City, Hawaii, 1977—; mem. adv. bd. Hawaii Writing Project, Honolulu, 1991—, co-dir., 1991. Contbr. articles, short stories to profl. publs. Buddhist. Office: Leeward CC 96-045 Ala Ike St Pearl City HI 96782-3366

UZILEVSKY, MARCUS, artist; b. Bklyn., Apr. 10, 1937; s. Chaim and Sarah (Zucker) U.; divorced; children: Boni Scott, Daniel. Grad. high sch., N.Y.C. Artist, fine art pub. Oaksprings Impressions, Woodacre, Calif., 1980—. Recipient Purchase award 19th Bradley Nat. Print Exhbn., 1988, Alexandra Mus., 1988, Design Excellence award Print Mag., 1988. Home: PO Box 166 Woodacre CA 94973-0166

VACCARINO, ROBIN, artist; b. Seattle; m. Maurice Vaccarino; 1 child, Donna. BFA, MFA, Otis Art Inst. Drawing and printmaking faculty Calif. State U., Northridge, 1970-72; painting faculty Otis Art Inst., L.A., 1972-93, Parsons Sch. Design, Paris, 1981-92. Maestra grantee Calif. Arts Coun., 1978, Individual Artist grantee NEA, Washington, 1980.

VACCARO, CHRISTOPHER MARK, lawyer; b. Phoenix, Mar. 24, 1959; s. San Eugene and Denise (Darroch) V. BA, U. Redlands, Calif., 1982; JD, Whittier Coll., 1985. Bar: Calif. 1986, U.S. Dist. Ct. (cen. dist.) Calif. 1986, U.S. Ct. Appeals (9th cir.) 1987. Mgr. legal dept. Marlin Industries, Beverly Hills, Calif., 1985-86; assoc. Katsky & Hunt, Los Angeles, 1986-89; assoc. Curtis & Vaccaro, Newport Beach, Calif., 1989-90, ptnr., 1990—. Mem. ABA, Bus. and Profl. Assn. (sec./treas. 1986-89, bd. dirs. 1987-89), Lawyers for Human Rights, Sigma Delta Pi. Office: Curtis & Vaccaro 5120 Birch St 150 Newport Beach CA 92660-2120

VACHON, ROGATIEN ROSAIRE (ROGIE VACHON), professional hockey team executive; b. Palmarolle, Que., Can., Sept. 8, 1945; m. Nicole Vachon; children: Nicholas, Jade, Mary Joy. Goaltender Montreal (Que.) Canadiens, NHL, 1966-72, Los Angeles Kings, NHL, 1972-78, Detroit Red Wings, NHL, 1978-80, Boston Bruins, 1980-82; asst. coach Los Angeles Kings, 1982-84, gen. mgr., 1984—, alt. gov., now asst. to chmn. Co-recipient Vezina Trophy, 1968. Office: care Los Angeles Kings PO Box 17013 3900 W Manchester Blvd Inglewood CA 90306*

VAGHJIANI, GHANSHYAM L., research chemist; b. Mbale, Uganda, Jan. 6, 1960; s. Lalji Natha and Prembai Lalji Vaghjiani; m. Manjula Ghanshyam Pindolia, Dec. 7, 1985; 1 child, Raj. BSc, U. London, 1982, PhD, 1985. Postdoctoral rsch. assoc. Coop. Inst. Rsch. in Environ. Scis. U. Colo., Boulder, 1986-90; rsch. chemist U. Dayton Rsch. Inst., Edwards AFB, Calif., 1990-93, Hughes STX, Edwards AFB, 1993—; presenter in field. Contbr. articles to profl. jours. Recipient Disting. Authorship award U.S. Dept. Commerce, 1993. Mem. Am. Chem. Soc., Am. Geophys. Union, Combustion Inst. Office: Hughes STX Phillips Lab PL/RKFA 10 E Saturn Rd Edwards CA 93524

VAIL, CHRISTIAN BYRON, software engineer; b. Orlando, Fla., Aug. 26, 1959; s. Lewis Allen and Claudia Joy (Groth) V.; m. Barbara Joyce Stone. BS in computer and info. sci., U. Calif., 1985; MS in computer engr., Santa Clara U., 1994. Salesman The Bank Store, San Jose, Calif., 1979; mgr. The Hip Pocket, San Jose, Calif., 1980; sr. salesman Hardy Shoe Store, San Jose, Calif., 1980; computing opr. Intel Corp., Santa Cruz, Calif., 1980-85; computing analyst McDonnell Douglas, Huntington Beach, Calif., 1985-87; artificial intelligence engr. GTE Gov. Systems Corp., Mt. View, Calif., 1987-88; test & integration engr. Mirage Systems, Inc., Sunnyvale, Calif., 1988-90; engr. specialist Stanford telecommunications, Sunnyvale, Calif., 1990-94; sr. software engr. Digital Link Corp., Sunnyvale, Calif., 1994—. Mem. IEEE. Democrat. Office: Digital Link Corp 217 Humboldt Ct Sunnyvale CA 94089-1300

VAIL, MARY BARBARA, museum consultant; b. Kingsville, Tex., Apr. 24, 1956; d. Fred G. and Nora J. (Smith) Leon; m. David L. Vail, Mar. 30, 1980; children: Sean Kristofer, Ashley Noel. Student, Tex. A&I U.; BS, U. Hawaii, 1982; postgrad., Hawaii Pacific U., 1991—. Display specialist Linda's, Kingsville, 1986-87; membership dir. Malibu (Calif.) Riding and Tennis Club, 1990-91; mktg. dir. Pacific Aerospace Mus., Honolulu, 1991-93; pres. Vail Media, Inc. (Scarlett Mktg. & Promotions), Aiea, Hawaii, 1993—. Vol. fundraiser AOWC, Point Mugu, Calif., 1990-91; vol. Laguna Vista Elem. Sch., Camarillo, Calif., 1990, Barbers Point (Hawaii) Elem. Sch., 1992—; vol., mil. liaison 1st Night Honolulu, 1991; co-chmn. Aloha Family Festival, Pearl Harbor, Hawaii, 1991, Fly Thru Time, 1992, 93, 94, Mugu Air Show, Chinese C. of C. Fashion Show, 1994, Narcissus Festival; Ho'Okipa Aloha, HIA Hospitality Tng. Coun. Mem. Pub. Rels. Soc. Am., Pub. Rels. Soc. Hawaii, CINCPAC Fleet Officers Wives Club, U. Hawaii Alumni Assn., Food Science and Numan Nutrition Alumni Assn. Home and Office: 15 Honu St PO Box 998 Aiea HI 96701

VAIL, MICHAEL GEORGE, academic director; b. Fullerton, Calif., Oct. 3, 1950; s. Harold Ford and Mabel (Williams) V.; m. Laura Marie Yeoman, Mar. 31, 1973. AA, Fullerton Coll., 1970; BA, Calif. State U., Fullerton, 1973. Planner City of Irvine, Calif., 1980-83; dir. facilities planning Capistrano Unified Sch. Dist., San Juan Capistrano, Calif., 1983-89; sr. dir. facilities Santa Ana (Calif.) Unified Sch. Dist., 1989—. State chair Calif. for Schs., Sacramento, 1988, Coalition for Adequate Sch. Housing, Sacramento, 1991-92; mem. State Supt's Sch. Facilities Adv. Com., Sacramento, 1989-92, State Treas.'s Sch. Facilities Task Force, Sacramento, 1990-92; pres. Coun. Ednl. Facility Planners, S.W. region Calif., 1990-91; treas. Nat. Com. for Adequate Sch. Housing, Washington, 1994—. Democrat. Office: Santa Ana Unified Sch Dist 1405 French St Santa Ana CA 92701-2414

VAIL, PATRICK JOSEPH, physicist; b. Miami Beach, Fla., Nov. 24, 1943; s. John Francis and Josephine Genevive (Goding) V.; m. Bridget Ann Fahy, July 4, 1970. BS in Physics and in Nuclear Sci., U. Mass., Lowell, 1965, PhD in Physics, 1969; CAS in Humanities, Harvard U., 1980; MA in Philosophy, U. N.Mex., 1987. Physicist GS-9 USAF, Hanscom AFB, Mass., 1965-68, physicist GS-14, 1977-85; physicist GS-13 USAF, Kirtland AFB, N.Mex., 1969-77, physicist GS-15, 1985—; U.S. rep. NATO RSG-1 Com., Brussels, Belgium, 1990-94, Four-Powers Sr. Nat. Reps. HPM Panel, Gramat, France, 1990-94. Contbr. over 50 articles to profl. jours. Sec. N.Mex. Coun. of Ind. Coll. and Univs., Santa Fe, 1991—. Capt. USAF, 1969-73. Mem. IEEE, Am. Phys. Soc.; sr. mem. AIAA; companion mem. Brothers of the Good Shepherd. Roman Catholic. Home: 5001 Calle De Carino NE Albuquerque NM 87111-2966 Office: Phillips Lab 3550 Aberdeen Ave SE Kirtland AFB NM 87117-5748

VALA, ROBERT (DONALD ROBERT MANN), artist; b. Berkeley, Calif., Apr. 19, 1930; s. Robert H. and Nell (Curry) Mann. Student, Coll. Arts & Crafts, Oakland, Calif., 1947, Art Student League, N.Y.C., 1950; BA, U. Calif.-Berkeley, 1951. Designer Ballet Russe, Europe, 1952, San Francisco Opera, 1953-56, San Francisco Ballet, 1953-56, Spanish Dance Co., Santa Cruz, Calif., 1986—, Patri Nader Co., Santa Cruz, Calif., 1986—; artist-in-residence, tchr. Calif. State U., Sacramento, 1987. Multi-media one-man shows include: Art Dirs. Gallery, N.Y.C., 1963, Galeries Raymond Duncan, Paris, 1963, Madison Gallery, N.Y.C., 1964; group shows include: UN Bldg., N.Y.C., 1970, Bohman Gallery, Stockholm, 1965, Arlene Lind Gallery, San Francisco, 1987, Will Stone Gallery, San Francisco, 1987; represented in comml. installations and numerous pvt. collections. Recipient Prix de Paris, L'Art Modern Mus., 1962, 1st prize Salon 50 States, N.Y.C., 1963. Home: 3109 Vista Sandia Santa Fe NM 87501-8528

VALDES, ALFONSO J., research engineer; b. Habana, Cuba, Mar. 9, 1956; came to U.S., 1961; s. Alfonso A. and Volga L. (Gatria) V.; m. KAthryn A. Kottmeier, July 3, 1977; 1 child, Dyan G. AB in Math., U. Calif., Berkeley, 1978; MS in Engring., Stanford U., 1983. Sr. analyst SRI Internat., Menlo Park, Calif., 1978—. Mem. parks and recreation commn. City of San Carlos (Calif.), 1994; bd. dirs. San Carlos Children's Theater, 1991-93.

VALDEZ, ARNOLD, dentist; b. Mojave, Calif., June 27, 1954; s. Stephen Monarez Jr. and Mary Lou (Esparza) V.; m. Brandy Radovich, Dec. 31, 1994; 1 child, Bayleigh. BS in Biol. Sci., Calif. State U., Hayward, 1976; BS in Dental Sci. and DDS, U. Calif., San Francisco, 1982; MBA, Calif. State Poly. U., 1985; BS and JD, Pacific West Coll. Law, 1995. Cert. ind. med. examiner, qualified med. examiner, Calif. Pvt. practice specializing in temporomandibular joint and Myofascial Pain Dysfunction Disorders Pomona, Calif., 1982, Claremont, Calif., 1982—; CEO Valcom, 1994—; CEO Valcom-A Telecom. Corp.; mem. adv. com. dental assisting program Chaffey Coll., Rancho Cucamonga, Calif., 1982—; mem. staff Pomona Valley Hosp. Med. Ctr. vol. dentist San Antonio Hosp. Dental Clinic, Rancho Cucamonga, 1984—, Pomona Valley Assistance League Dental Clinic, 1986—; bd. dirs. Pacific West Coll. Law, 1993—. Fellow Acad. Gen. Dentistry (master 1994); mem. ADA, Calif. Dental Assn., Tri-County Dental Soc. (co-chmn. mktg. 1986, chmn. sch. screening 1987, Golden Grin award), Acad. Gen. Dentistry, U. Calif.-San Francisco Alumni Assn., U. So. Calif. Sch. Dentistry Golden Century Club, Psi Omega, Delta Theta Phi. Democrat. Roman Catholic. Home: 515 Seaward Rd Corona Del Mar CA 92625 Office: 410 W Baseline Rd Claremont CA 91711-1607

VALDEZ, HORACIO, food products executive. With R C Farms, Salinas, Calif., 1979-89; ptnr. Buena Vista Packing, Soledad, Calif., 1989—. Office: Buena Vista Packing 155 Kidder St Ste C Soledad CA 93960-3021*

VALDEZ, JAMES GERALD, automotive aftermarket executive; b. Vallejo, Calif., Jan. 26, 1945; s. Charles Arthur and Margaret Ellen (Chavez) V.; m. Cathy Evelyn Gudliesuski, Oct. 9, 1970; children: Mitchell Charles, Jason Garrett. BS in Engring. Tech., Calif. Poly. U., 1967; MBA in Mktg., Pepperdine U., 1975. Sales engr. Shell Oil Co., L.A., 1969-70; regional mgr. Ethyl Corp., L.A., 1970-76; dir. product engring. Pennzoil Co., Houston, 1976-84; owner, operator Valco Enterprises, L.A., 1984-86; sr. v.p. mktg. Analysis, Inc., L.A., 1986-88; dir. sales and mktg. Castrol Inc., L.A., 1988-93; v.p., gen. mgr. CSF, Inc., L.A., 1993—, also dir.; cons. in field, 1984-86. Major USAR, 1967-80. Decorated Commendation medal. Mem. SAE (chmn. various coms., gen. materials coun. 1980), Am. Petroleum Inst. (chmn. lubricants com. 1980-84). Republican. Home: 5850 E Trapper Anaheim CA 92807

VALDEZ, JESSE NAJERA, psychologist; b. La Pryor, Tex., Nov. 17, 1944; s. Jose Cordova and Margarita (Najera) V.; m. Gloria Mary Ruiz, Sept. 27, 1969; children: Richard Kenneth, James Roderick, David Joseph. AA, Southwest Tex. Jr. Coll., 1966; BA, Southwest Tex. State U., 1969; MEd, Sul Ross State U., 1972; PhD, U. Wis., 1985. H.S. tchr. Uvalde (Tex.) Sch. Dist., 1969-76; counselor Developmental Edn. Svcs., Uvalde, 1976-79; asst. prof. dept. psychology Colo. State U., Ft. Collins, 1984-88; psychologist U. Calif., Santa Barbara, 1988-95; asst. prof. counseling psychology dept. U. Denver, 1995—; lectr. U. Wis., Madison, 1983; cons. Psychotherapy Svcs., Ft. Collins; psychotherapist Cmty. Mental Health, Loveland, Colo. Cubmaster Boy Scouts Am., Madison, 1980-81. Mem. APA, Soc. for Psychol. Study of Ethnic Minority Issues, Pi Lambda Theta, Sigma Delta Pi. Home: 544 Sussex Ct Goleta CA 93117-1614 Office: U Calif Counseling & Career Svcs Santa Barbara CA 93106-1740 Also: Counseling Psychology Dept Univ Denver Denver CO 80208

VALDEZ, JOSEPH VINCENT, II, state government information management executive; b. Oakland, Calif., Aug. 13, 1955; s. Joseph Vincent and Joann Marinda (Dunn) V.; m. Teresa Ann Casaus, Apr. 9, 1984; children: Joseph Vincent III, Kristi Amber. AA with honors, Merritt Coll., Oakland, 1980; BA in History, U. Calif., Berkeley, 1982. Asst. mgr., caterer Soup Pot/Party Makers, Oakland, 1981-82; client svc. agt. Social Svc. div. N.Mex. Human Svcs., Santa Fe, 1983-85; ctrl. office unit records mgr. N.Mex. Corrections Dept., Santa Fe, 1985-86, parole records mgr., 1986-88, asst. substance abuse program dir., 1988-89; city records mgr. City of Santa Fe, 1989—; mem. records task force City of Santa Fe, 1994—. Author: La Iglesia de Santa Ana: Celebra Cinquenta Anos de Gloria, 1992, (booklet) City of Santa Fe: A Centennial Publication, 1991. Chmn. fiesta float com. N.Mex. Green Party, Santa Fe, 1994. Recipient Cert. of Honor/Councilor's award Merritt Coll., 1980, Silver Plaque, La Entrada Alternative Sch. Bd., 1985, Olsten award for excellence in records mgmt., 1990; named col., aide-de-camp Gov.'s Office, N.Mex., 1976, 80, 84, 91. Mem. Assn. Records Mgrs. and Adminstrs. (chmn. legis. com. No. N.Mex. chpt. 1990-91, historian 1990-92, bd. dirs. 1990-91, 93—, pres. 1993-94), Nat. Assn. Govt. Archives and Records Adminstrs., Eagles (v.p. 1993-94). Democrat. Roman Catholic. Office: City of Santa Fe 200 Lincoln Ave PO Box 909 Santa Fe NM 87504

VALDEZ, STEPHEN KENNETH, music educator, researcher, consultant; b. Los Alamos, N.Mex., Sept. 12, 1954; s. Daniel Carlos Sr. and Maria de Jesus (Garibay) V.; m. Cherese Dee Cartlidge, July 6, 1985; children: Olivia Katherine, Thomas Michael. B of Music Edn., N.Mex. State U., Las Cruces, 1977, MMus, 1984; D of Musical Arts, U. Oreg., 1992. Grad. teaching fellow U. Oreg. Sch. Music, Eugene, 1985-92, instr., 1992-93, asst. prof. music, 1993—; cons., book reviewer Prentice-Hall Inc., Englewood Cliffs, N.J., 1992—. Mem. Am. Musicological Soc., Internat. Assn. for Study of Popular Music, Coll. Musci Soc. Office: Sch of Music 1225 U of Oreg Eugene OR 97403

VALENTE, MICHAEL F., philosopher, consultant; b. Albany, N.Y., Nov. 4, 1937; s. Abel A. and Anna Elizabeth Valente. BA in Philosophy, Stonehill Coll., 1959; MS in Math., Notre Dame U., 1961, MA in Theology, 1962; PhD in Religion, Columbia U., 1968; MSL in Law, Yale U., 1974. Mem. faculty dept. religious studies Seton Hall U., South Orange, N.J., 1967-81, chmn. dept. religious studies, 1968-71; cons. TCIM Consulting Svcs., Beverly Hills, Calif., 1981—. Office: TCIM Consulting Svcs 9201 Wilshire Blvd Beverly Hills CA 90210-5529

VALENTI, JOANN MYER, environmental and mass communications researcher, educator; b. Miami, Fla., Apr. 6, 1945; d. Isaac William and Myra Cecile (Chawluk) Myer; m. Henry Vincent Valenti, Jr., Aug. 24, 1976; children: John Henry, Sarita Jo. BS in Journalism, U. Fla., 1967, MA in Mass Communication, 1969; PhD in Natural Resources, U. Mich., 1983. With pub. rels. dept. ENJAY Chem. Co., N.Y.C., 1967-68, Corn Products Co. Internat., N.Y.C., 1968-69; dir. tourism Brevard County, Cocoa Beach, Fla., 1969-70; exec. dir. Fla. Defenders of Environ., 1970-73; teaching fellow U. Mich., Ann Arbor, 1973-76; dir. community rels. Tampa (Fla.) Gen. Hosp., 1977-79; prof. journalism and communications U. Tampa, 1980-87; prof. journalism and mass communication U. Fla., Gainesville, 1987-92; prof. communications Brigham Young U., Provo, Utah, 1992—. Contbr. numerous articles to profl. jours. and media publs., also chpts. to books; producer TV talk show and documentaries. Rackham fellow, 1975, Rockefeller Bros. Found. fellow, 1975-76. Mem. AAAS, Pub. Rels. Soc. Am., Assn. Educators in Journalism and Mass Comm., Soc. Environ Journalists, Women in Comm., Inc. Home: 1531 Dawn Dr Salt Lake City UT 84121-2819 Office: Brigham Young U Dept Communications Hfac # 509 Provo UT 84602-1026

VALENTINE, CAROL ANN, educational program director, consultant; b. Mt. Clemens, Mich., Dec. 5, 1942; d. Joseph Eldon and Erna Fredericka (Brandt) V.; married; children: Christopher, David. BA, U. Mich., 1964, MA, 1965; PhD, Pa. State U., 1971. Tchr. Oak Park (Ill.)-River Forest High Sch., 1965-67; research assoc. U. Md., College Park, 1967; dir. grants Pa. State U., State College, 1967-78; asst. prof. Oreg. State U., Corvallis, 1970-74; vis. prof. U. Oreg., Eugene, 1974-75; assoc. prof. Ariz. State U., Tempe, 1975-85, assoc. dir. women's studies, 1975—; cons. Tempe, 1975—. Author: First Impressions, 1980, Women and Communicative Power, 1988. Bd. dirs. Tempe Pub. Library, 1984—. Named Outstanding Woman of Phoenix, 1987. Mem. Zeta Phi Eta. Democrat. Presbyterian. Home: 2607 S Forest Ave Tempe AZ 85282-3520 Office: Ariz State U Stauffer Hall 412 Tempe AZ 85287

VALENTINE, GENE C., securities dealer; b. Washington, Pa., June 19, 1950; s. John N. and Jane S. Valentine. BS in Psychology, Bethany Coll., 1972; student, U. Vienna, Austria, 1971-72. Commd. ensign USN, 1972, advanced through grades to lt., 1987, hon. discharged, 1978; owner Horizon Realty, San Francisco, 1978-82; dir. land acquisitions Windfarms Ltd. subs. Chevron, U.S.A., San Francisco, 1980-82; v.p. mktg. Christopher Weil & Co., Sherman Oaks, Calif., 1982-85; co-chmn., CEO Pacific Asset Group Inc. (name now Fin. West Group, Inc.), Pasadena, Calif., 1985—; Bd. dirs. Fin. West Group, Inc., Paradox Holdings, Kennsington Holdings. Mem. Rep. Party, L.A. Mem. Internat. Assn. Fin. Planning (bd. dirs. L.A. chpt. 1982—). Episcopalian. Office: Fin West Group Inc 600 Hampshire Rd Ste 200 Westlake Village CA 91361-2500

VALENTINE, GREGORY ALLEN, geologist; b. Alva, Okla., Apr. 18, 1962; s. Allen Monroe and Judith Anne (Glisan) V.; m. Mary Suzanne Foster, Aug. 4, 1984; children: Jeremy Allen, Patrick Richard, Suzanne Clare, Rebekah Christine. BS in Geol. Engring. & Geology, N.Mex. Inst. Mining and Tech., 1984; PhD in Geol. Scis., U. Calif., Santa Barbara, 1988. Grad. rsch. asst. geology, geochemistry group Los Alamos Nat. Lab., 1984; rsch. asst. dept. geol. scis. U. Calif., Santa Barbara, 1984-86, teaching asst. dept. geol. scis., 1986-87; staff rsch. asst. Geoanalysis group Los Alamos (N.Mex.) Nat. Lab., 1987-88, tech. staff mem., 1989—; adj. prof. dept. geology Ariz. State U., 1991-93; presenter in field. Editor-in-chief Jour. Volcanology and Geothermal Rsch., 1993—, assoc. editor, 199-92; contbr. articles to profl. jours. Inst. Geophys. and Planetary Physics grantee, 1992-93, Geol. Soc. Am. Rsch. grantee, 1986, U. Calif. Acad. Sentat Patent Fund grantee, 1985, 86; Los Alamos Nat. Lab. Postdoctoral fellow, 1988-89; Regents scholar N.Mex. Inst. Mining and Tech. Mem. Am. Geophys. Union, Internat. Assn. Volcanology and Chemistry of Earth's Interior, Sigma Xi. Democrat. Methodist. Office: Los Alamos Nat Lab MS F665 Los Alamos NM 87545

VALENTINE, JAMES WILLIAM, paleobiology, educator, author; b. Los Angeles, Nov. 10, 1926; s. Adelbert Cuthbert and Isabel (Davis) V.; m. Grace Evelyn Whysner, Dec. 21, 1957 (div. 1972); children—Anita, Ian; m. Cathryn Alice Campbell, Sept. 10, 1978 (div. 1986); 1 child, Geoffrey; m. Diane Mondragon, Mar. 16, 1987. B.A., Phillips U., 1951; M.A., UCLA, 1954, Ph.D., 1958. From asst. prof. to assoc. prof. U. Mo., Columbia, 1958-64; from assoc. prof. to prof. U. Calif., Davis, 1964-77; prof. geol. scis. U. Calif., Santa Barbara, 1977-90; prof. integrative biology U. Calif., Berkeley, 1990—. Author: Evolutionary Paleoecology of the Marine Biosphere, 1973; editor: Phanerozoic Diversity, 1985; co-author: Evolution, 1977, Evolving, 1979, also numerous articles, 1954—. Served with USNR, 1944-46; PTO. Fulbright research scholar, Australia, 1962-63; Guggenheim fellow Yale U., Oxford U., Eng., 1968-69; Rockefeller Found. scholar in residence, Bellagio, Italy, summer 1974; grantee NSF, NASA. Fellow Am. Acad. Arts and Scis., AAAS, Geol. Soc. Am.; mem. Nat. Acad. Scis., Paleontol. Soc. (pres. 1974-75). Home: 1351 Glendale Ave Berkeley CA 94708-2025 Office: U Calif Dept Integrative Biolo Berkeley CA 94720

VALENTINE, JANE LEE, environmental health sciences educator; b. Nashville, July 29, 1945; d. Ollie Carter and Lillian Bernice (Scruggs) V.; 1 child, Catherine Elizabeth Sweetser. BS in Chemistry, Tenn. State U., 1967; MS in Water Chemistry, U. Wis., 1970; PhD in Environ. Health, Pub. Health, U. Tex., 1973. Postdoctoral fellow in preventive medicine, program of environ. toxicology N.J. Coll. Medicine and Dentistry, Newark, 1973-74; from asst. prof. to assoc. prof. pub. health, divsn. environ. and nutritional scis. Sch. Pub. Health UCLA, 1974-83, assoc. prof. pub. health Dept. Environ. Health Scis., Sch. Pub. Health, 1983—; mem. Calif. State Sanitarian Registration Adv. Com., 1984—, pub. health subcom. San Joaquin Valley Drainage Program U.S. Bur. Reclamation, 1986-90, pub. health strategic planning environ. health panel County of L.A. Dept. Health Svcs., 1987-88, pub. health assessment work group San Joaquin Valley Post-Drainage Programs, 1992—; cons. in field; presenter papers in field. Reviewer profl. jours.; contbr. chpts. to books, articles to profl. jours. Mem. AAAS, Internat. Soc. Trace Element Rsch. in Humans (founding mem.), Am. Pub. Health Assn., Am. Water Resources Assn., Internat. Soc. Environ. Epidemiology, Delta Omega, Sigma Xi. Democrat. Roman Catholic. Home: 1721 Las Lunas St Pasadena CA 91106-1304 Office: UCLA Sch Pub Health 10833 Le Conte Ave Los Angeles CA 90024

VALENTINE, JOHN LESTER, state legislator, lawyer; b. Fullerton, Calif., Apr. 26, 1949; s. Robert Lester and Pauline C. (Glood) V.; m. Karen Marie Thorpe, June 1, 1972; children: John Robert, Jeremy Reid, Staci Marie, Jeffrey Mark., David Emerson, Patricia Ann. BS in Acctg. and Econs., Brigham Young U., 1973, JD, 1976. Bar: Utah 1976, U.S. Dist. Ct. Utah, U.S. Ct. Appeals (10th cir.), U.S. Tax Ct.; CPA. Atty. Howard, Lewis & Petersen, Provo, Utah, 1976—; mem. Utah Ho. Reps., 1988—; instr. probate and estates Utah Valley State Coll.; instr. fin. planning., adj. prof. law Brigham Young U.; mem. exec offices, cts., corrections and legis. appropriations subcom., 1988-90, capital facilities subcom., 1988-90, retirement com., 1988-90, judiciary com., 1988—, strategic planning steering com., 1988-90, interim appropriations com., 1988—, tax. review commn., 1988-92, ethics com., 1990-92, human svcs. and health appropriations subcom., 1990-92, revenue and taxation com., 1988—, vice chmn. 1990-92; vice chmn. exec. appropriations., 1990-92, chmn. 1992—; chmn. exec. appropriations com., 1992-94, chmn. rules com., 1994, higher edn. appropriations com. 1994; bd. dirs. Utah Corrections Industries. Mem. adv. bd. Internat. Sr. Games, 1988—; active Blue Ribbon Task Force on Local Govt. Funding, Utah League Cities and Towns, 1990—, Criminal Sentencing Guidelines Task Force, Utah Judicial Coun., 1990-92, Access to Health Care Task Force, 1990-92, Utah County Sheriff Search and Rescue, Orem Met. Water Bd., Alpine Sch. Dist. Boundary Line Com., Boy Scouts Am.; bd. regents Legis. Adv. Com. UVCC.; mem. exec. bd. Utah Nat. Parks Coun.; mem. adv. coun. Orchard Elem. Sch., Mountainlands Com. an Aging; bd. trustees Utah Opera Co.; judge nat. and local competitions Moot Ct.; voting dist. chmn.; state, county del.; lt. incident command sys. Utah County Sheriff. Recipient Silver Beaver award Boy Scouts Am., Taxpayer Advocate award Utah Taxpayer Assn. Mem. ABA (tax sect.), Utah State Bar, CPA Com., Tax Sect. Specialization Com., Bicentennial Com. Republican. Mormon. Office: Howard Lewis & Petersen 120 E 300 N Provo UT 84606-2907

VALENTINE, WILLIAM EDSON, architect; b. Winston-Salem, N.C., Sept. 3, 1937; s. Howard Leon and Sally (Cunningham) V.; m. Jane Dorward, Aug. 13, 1939; children: Anne, Karen, William. BArch, N.C. State U., 1960; MArch, Harvard U., 1962. Prin. Hellmuth, Obata & Kassabaum Inc., San Francisco, 1962—; chmn. Hellmuth, Obata & Kassabaum Design Bd., also bd. dirs. Served to 1st lt. U.S. Army, 1960-61. Fellow AIA. Club: Harvard. Office: Hellmuth Obata & Kassabaum Inc 71 Stevenson St Ste 2200 San Francisco CA 94105-2934

VALENTINO, STEPHEN ERIC, production and entertainment company executive, actor, singer; b. N.Y.C., Apr. 2, 1954; s. Joseph and Ina Mae (Diamond) V. Student, Hofstra U., N.Y.C., 1972-74, San Francisco Conservatory Music, 1974-78, Am. Inst. Mus. Studies, Graz, Austria, 1982. Gen. dir., chmn. bd. Mastic Community Theatre, Mastic Beach, N.Y., 1971-74; dir. advt. Marin Opera Co., San Rafael, Calif., 1979-80, Marin Ctr., San Rafael, 1983-85; pres., chief exec. officer Valentino & Assocs., Novato, Calif., 1978—; pres., CEO, co-founder Celebrity Events Internat., 1992—. Contbg. author: Come Barefoot Eating Sensuous Things, 1979; appeared in Firestorm, 1992, La Boheme, Daughter of the Regiment, (world premier) Calisto and Melibea, U. Calif., Davis, La Cenerentola, Le Nozze de Figaro, The Merry Widow, La Traviata, The Bartered Bride, The TwelfthNight, Barber of Seville, Carmen, Die Fledermaus, Gianni Schicchi, I Pagliacci, Hansel and Gretel, The Magic Flute, Old Maid and the Thief, The Mikado, The Merry Wives of Windsor, (comml.) Ind. Life Ins. Corp. Am., (play) Feuerbach. Celebrity coord. Kids Say No To Drugs, 1987, MADD, 1987, ARC, San Jose, Calif., 1989; entertainment coord. Earthquake Relief Fund, San Francisco, 1989, Christmas Tree Program for the Needy, San Francisco, 1986, San Francisco Grand Prix BMW Polo Classic, Marin Suicide Prevention Ctr., 1987, Calif. Health Rsch. Found., 1988, UNICEF San Francisco, 1985, Little Sisters of The Poor, 1985, San Francisco Child Abuse Coun., 1988, 92; fundraiser Easter Seals, Marin County, Calif., 1988, Toys for Tots, Bay Area, Calif., 1987—, Global Youth Resource Orgn., Sunnyvale, Calif., 1989-90; mem. Dem. Nat. Com., 1988-90; commr. Bus. Ins. Adv. Commn., 1989; dir. celebrity basketball game Special Olympics, 1992, celebrity basketball game Easter Seals Soc., 1993; entertainer Shelters for the Homeless of L.A. Earthquake, 1994. Recipient Cert. of Honor, Bd. Suprs., City and County San Francisco, 1986, Awards of Appreciation Easter Seals Soc., 1988, Spl. Olympics, 1992. Mem. AFTRA, SAG. Home and Office: Valentino and Assocs 428 Bloom Ln Novato CA 94947-4202

VALENZUELA, MANUEL ANTHONY, JR., lawyer; b. L.A., Dec. 4, 1955; s. Manuel and Artimesa B. (Ruiz) V.; m. Guadalupe Roa, Nov. 8, 1980; children: Manuel Anthony III, Nancy Christine. BA in Polit. Sci., UCLA, 1978; MPA, U. So. Calif., 1982; JD, Southwestern U., L.A., 1987. Bar: Calif. 1987, U.S. Dist. Ct. (cen. dist.) Calif. 1987, U.S. Ct. Appeals (9th cir.) 1988, U.S. Supreme Ct. 1991. Legis. analyst L.A. City Coun., 1981-88; legal extern ACLU, L.A., 1985; assoc. county counsel County of Los Angeles, 1988-89, sr. assoc county counsel, 1989-90, dep. county counsel, 1990-94; sr. dep. county counsel, 1994—. Vol. Papal visit Cath. Archdiocese L.A., 1987; coord. WalkAmerica campaign March of Dimes, 1988; vol. Larryann Willis for Congress com., Oreg. and L.A., 1982. Mem. L.A. County Bar Assn. (exec. com. govtl. law sect. 1990-91, sec. govtl. law sect. 1991-92, 2d vice chair govtl. law sect. 1992-93, 1st vice chair govtl. law sect. 1993-94, chair govtl. law sect. 1994-95, bd. trustees 1995-96), Mexican Am. Bar Assn. (bd. dirs. 1990, 91), L.A. County Counsel Assn. (bd. dirs. 1989—), UCLA Latino Alumni Assn. (founder, bd. dirs. 1989-90). Democrat. Roman Catholic. Home: 9647 Val St Temple City CA 91780-1438 Office: Office of County Counsel 648 Hall of Adminstrn 500 W Temple St Los Angeles CA 90012-2713

VALENZUELA, RICARDO, investment banker, rancher; b. Hermasillo, Mex., Dec. 23, 1945; came to U.S., 1979; s. Ricardo and Celia (Torres) V.; m. Zuzette Hanessian, Mar. 14, 1970 (div. Jan. 1987); children: Zuzette, Verkine, Satenik. 010BBA, Inst. Tech. de Monterrey, Mex., 1967; MBA, U. Nacional Autonoma, Mexico City, 1971; student, U. Calif. Berkeley, 1967-68, Inst. Pan-Am., Mexico City, 1985. Bank br. mgr. Banco de Comercio, Mexico City, 1969-71; pres., CEO Banco Ganadero y Agricola, Hermosillo, 1971-77, Banpacifico, Guadalajara, Mex., 1977-79; sr. ptnr. for internat. bus. rels. Corbec-Westar, Tucson, 1979-88; operator, mgr. Las Calaveras Ranch, Sonora, Mex., 1985—; pres., CEO INTERMEX, Tucson, 1988—; bd. dirs. Cattlemen's Assn. Sonora, 1984-85; ptnr., bd. dirs. Big Tower Produce Co., Nogales, Ariz., Ariz. Cattle Importers, Tucson. Roman Catholic. Office: Intermex 6303 E Tanque Verde Rd Tucson AZ 85715-3857

VALESCO, FRANCES KAY, artist, educator; b. L.A., Aug. 3, 1941; parents Adolph and Ethel Valesco; 1 child, David. BA, UCLA, 1963; post-grad., Sacramento State U., 1964-65; MA, Calif. State U., Long Beach, 1972. Artist in residence Calif. State Arts Coun., San Francisco, 1980-85; instr. U. Calif. Extension, Santa Barbara, 1968-69, Irvine, Riverside, 1970-72; instr. U. Calif., Berkeley, 1975-76, 79, Somoma State U., Rohnert Park, Calif., 1977-80; owner, dir. Big Ink, L.A. and San Francisco, 1969—; instr. Haystack Mountain Sch. Crafts, Maine, 1992; instr. Acad. Art Coll., San Francisco, 1982—, San Francisco Art Inst., 1993-95, San Francisco State U., 1993-94; artist San Francisco Neighborhood Arts Commn., 1975-80; cons. HUD, Hartford, Conn., 1978; mem. San Francisco Mural Adv. Bd., 1981—. One-person shows include Hatley Martin Gallery, 1989, Mus. Conceptual Art, 1993; exhibited in group shows at Tokyo Met. Mus., 1986, Bronx Mus., 1987, Computer Mus., Boston, 1989, Triton Mus., 1994; represented in permanent collections N.Y. City Pub. Libr., Fine Arts Mus., San Francisco, Oakland Mus. Recipient Cert. Honor, City of San Francisco, 1987, 93; Mural grant Neighborhood Initiated Improvement Program, City of San Francisco, HUD, 1981-82, 86, 93, NEA and N.Y. State Coun. for Arts grant, Lexington, N.Y., 1989-90, 92. Mem. YLEM, Am. Print Alliance (bd. dirs. 1994—, v.p. 1995—), Calif. Soc. Printmakers (v.p. 1993-94, pres. 1994—, historian 1980-82, organizing com. Pratt Print Ctr. exhibit 1979).

VALLA, ROBERT, aeronautical engineer, aerodynamicist; b. Milan, Italy, Mar. 11, 1967; came to U.S., 1983; s. Gian Edoardo and Lucilla (Petrazzini) V.; m. Kristi Lynette Loenser, June 6, 1992. BS in Aerospace Engring., Northrop U., L.A., 1989; MS in Aeronautical Engring., Stanford U., 1990. Physics lab. instr. Northrop U., 1986-87; asst. design engr. Downs Crane & Hoist Co., L.A., 1987-88; aerodynamicist McDonnell Douglas Aerospace, Long Beach, Calif., 1991—. John K. Northrop scholar, 1985-89. Mem. AIAA, Soc. Automotive Engrs., Tau Beta Pi, Sigma Gamma Tau. Office: McDonnell Douglas Aerospace 1510 Hughes Way # 71 35 Long Beach CA 90810-1864

VALLBONA-RAYNER, MARISA, public relations counselor; b. Houston, Tex., Jan. 2, 1964; d. Carlos and Rima (Rothe) Vallbona; m. Don R. Rayner Jr., July 12, 1986; children: Donald R. Rayner III, Timothy Carlos Rayner. Student, U. Colo.; BS in Journalism, U. Tex. Account exec. Jae Stefan & Assocs., Austin, Tex., 1987-88; media rels. asst. America's Cup XXVII, 1988; sr. account exec. pub. rels. Berkman & Daniels, 1988-90; prin. Rayner & Vallbona Inc. Advt. & Pub. Rels., San Diego, 1990—. Editor: Flowering Inferno, 1994, Soldiers Cry By Night, 1994, Assumed Name, 1994, People on the Prowl, 1995; contbr. articles to profl. jours. Pub. rels. chair, bd. dirs. Women of St. James Episc. Ch., 1994, 1st v.p., 1995; mem. pub. affairs disaster task force ARC, 1993—; pub. rels. chair Sunkist Am. Cancer Soc. Cup Regatta, 1989; mem. elections mktg. task force City of San Diego, 1989. Mem. Pub. Rels. Soc. Am. (accredited; San Diego chpt. chair accreditation com. 1994, dir.-at-large 1995), Am. Soc. Health Care Mktg. and Pub. Rels., Health Care Communicators San Diego (v.p. bd. dir. 1994, sec. 1993, numerous awards), Pub. Rels. Club San Diego (exec. bd. dirs. 1991-92, various awards), Jr. League San Diego. Office: Rayner & Vallbona Inc 6961 Petit St San Diego CA 92111-3303

VALLEE, JACQUES FABRICE, venture capitalist; b. Pontoise, France, Sept. 24, 1939; came to U.S., 1962; s. Gabriel and Madeleine (Passavant) V.; m. Janine M. Saley, Oct. 19, 1960; children: Olivier, Catherine. BS in Math., U. Paris Sorbonne, 1959; MS in Astrophysics, U. Lille, France, 1961; PhD in Computer Sci., Northwestern U., 1967. Sr. software specialist RCA Corp., Cherry Hill, N.J., 1969-70; mgr. infosystems Stanford U., Palo Alto, Calif., 1970-71; rsch. engr. SRI Internat., Menlo Park, Calif., 1971-72; sr. rsch. fellow Inst. for Future, Menlo Park, 1972-76; chmn. Infomedia Corp., Palo Alto, 1976-81; v.p. Sofinnova, Inc., San Francisco, 1982-86; pres. Eurolink Internat., San Francisco, 1987—; bd. dirs. Accuray Inc., Sunnyvale, IXYS Inc., San Jose, Diametrix Detectors, San Diego, Ubique Inc., San Francisco. Author: Computer Message Systems, 1984, Dimensions, 1988, Confrontations, 1990, Revelations, 1991, Forbidden Science, 1992. Recipient Jules Verne prize, Paris, 1961. Mem. Coun. Soc. for Sci. Exploration. Office: Eurolink Internat 657 Mission St Ste 601 San Francisco CA 94105-4120

VALLERAND, PHILIPPE GEORGES, sales executive; b. Montreal, Que., Can., June 12, 1954; came to U.S., 1982; s. Louis Philippe and Beatrice (Goupil) V.; m. Laura Jean Frombach, Sept. 25, 1979; children: Harmonie May, Jeremy Thomas, Emilie Rose. Student, U. Montreal, 1974, U. Sherbrooke, 1975, U. Que., 1976, White Mgmt. Sch., London, 1981. Dir. resort Club Mediterranee Inc., Bahamas, Switzerland,, Africa,, Guadelupe, West Indies, 1978-80; v.p. Franglo/Sunsaver Inc., London and Hyeres, France, 1980-82; v.p. sales Source Northwest, Inc., Woodinville, Wash., 1982-93; pres. Prime Resource Group, Prime Source, Inc. Sr. comdr. Royal Rangers Boys Club, Monroe, Wash., 1988—; bd. mem. Christian Faith Ctr., Monroe, 1988-94; mem. Rep. Nat. Com. Named to 500 Inc. Mag., 1983, 89, Registry of Global Bus. Leaders; recipient Disting. Sales & Mktg. Exec. award Internat. Orgn. Sales & Mktg. Execs., 1993. Mem. Am. Mktg. Assn. (new mem. adv. bd.).

VALNER, RUDY, lawyer; b. Mexico City, Dec. 23, 1960; came to U.S., 1979; s. Benito and Lia (Sod) V.; m. Marci Lynn Zweben, June 22, 1985; children: Danielle Kasey, Alexander Jason, Gabriela Bryn. BA in Polit. Sci. cum laude, UCLA, 1983; JD, Loyola U., L.A., 1987. Bar: Calif. 1989. Assoc. Smylie & Leven, L.A., 1989-90, Warren & Marks, Calabasas, Calif., 1990-92; pvt. practice L.A., 1992—; cons. Mex.-U.S. bus. and real estate devel., transactions, investments, gen. bus.; spkr. on NAFTA opportunities and needs. Contbr. articles to profl. jours. Mem. ABA (real property, bus. and internat. law sects.), L.A. County Bar Assn. (real property, bus. and internat. law sects.), State Bar Calif. Office: Law Offices of Rudy Valner 10100 Santa Monica Blvd Ste 945 Los Angeles CA 90067-4013

VALOT, DANIEL L., oil industry executive; b. 1944. Student, Ecol Nationale d'Administration, Paris. Mng. dir., head corp. planning divsn. Total Petroleum South East Asia, 1981—; chmn. bd., pres., CEO Total Petroleum, Inc., Denver, 1992—; chmn. Total Petroleum N.Am. Ltd. Office: Total Petroleum Inc 900 19th St Ste 2201 Denver CO 80202-2518

VAMPOLA, ALFRED LUDVIK, aerospace consultant; b. Dwight, Nebr., July 10, 1934; s. Ludwig Anton and Pauline Christine (Trousil) V.; m. Karen Agnes Kirkwood, Apr. 7, 1956; children: Joseph, John, Elaine, Mary, Mark, Robert, James, Donald. BS, Creighton U., 1956; MS, St. Louis U., 1958, PhD, 1961. Sr. physicist Convair, San Diego, 1961-62; sr. staff scientist Aerospace Corp., El Segundo, Calif., 1962-90; cons. Space Environ. Effects, Torrance, Calif., 1990—; vis. fellow Otago U., Dunedin, New Zealand, 1986-87; guest rsch. fellow Max Planck Inst. for Aeronomie, Lin Dau, Germany, 1991. Assoc. editor Jour. Spacecraft and Rockets, 1984—; contbr. articles to profl. jours. Fellow AIAA (assoc.); mem. Am. Geophys. Union. Office: Space Environ Effects PO Box 10225 Torrance CA 90505-1025

VAN ALLEN, PHILIP ANDREW, multimedia production company executive, educator; b. Santa Monica, Calif., Jan. 15, 1958; s. William Allen and Dorothy (Wright) van A. BA in Exptl. Psychology highest honors, U. Calif., Santa Cruz, 1988. Freelance audio engr. L.A., 1975-81; programmer analyst Santa Monica Coll., 1981-83; sr. mktg. support analyst Prime Computer, Culver City, Calif., 1983-85; software developer PVA Rsch., Santa Cruz, 1985-88; sr. software engr., mgr. tech. design Philips Interactive Media, L.A., 1988-91, sr. producer, 1991-93; pres., founder Commotion New Media, Santa Monica, 1993—; adj. prof. McGill U., Montreal, 1994—. Producer CD-ROM and On-line titles. Mem. Phi BEta Kappa. Democrat. Unitarian. Office: Commotion New Media 1424 4th St Ste 604 Santa Monica CA 90401-3413

VAN AMRINGE, JOHN HOWARD, retired oil industry executive, geologist; b. L.A., Oct. 11, 1932; s. Edwin Verne and Viola (Hail) Van A.; m. Mary Jane Lothras, Jan. 29, 1955; children: Kathryn Jean Van Amringe Ball, Kenneth Edwin. AA, Pasadena City Coll., 1954; BA, UCLA, 1956, MA, 1957. Geologist Unocal Corp., Santa Maria, Calif., 1957-58, Santa Fe Springs, Calif., 1958-64, New Orleans, 1964-66; dist. geologist Unocal Corp., Lafayette, La., 1966-68, dist. exploration mgr., 1968-79; exploration mgr. western region Unocal Corp., Pasadena, Calif., 1979-88; v.p. exploration Unocal Corp., L.A., 1988-92. Editor: Typical Offshore Oil and Gas Fields, 1973; author profl. paper. Bd. dirs. Pasadena City Coll. Found., 1986—, treas., 1992-95; pres. Pasadena Cmty. Orch., 1990-94. With U.S. Army, 1949-52, Korea. Named Geologist of Yr., Lafayette chpt. Am. Inst. Profl. Geologists, 1972. Mem. Am. Assn. Petroleum Geologists (del. 1972-73), Pacific Sect. of Am. Assn. Petroleum Geologists (editor 1961-63), Lafayette Geological Soc. (pres. 1971-72), Petroleum Club L.A., Jonathan Club. Republican. Home: 1455 Old House Rd Pasadena CA 91107-1518

VAN ARSDALE, DICK, professional basketball team executive; b. Indpls., Feb. 22, 1943; m. Barbara V.; children: Jill, Jason. AB in economics, Indiana U., 1965. Player New York Knicks (Nat. Basketball Assn.), N.Y.C., 1965-68; with Phoenix Suns, Phoenix, Ariz., 1968-77; color commentator, TV broadcasts Phoenix Suns, from 1977, interim mgr., 1987, from v.p., player personnel. Named "Mr. Basketball" of Indiana during high school, NCAA All-American, Indiana U. Office: care Phoenix Suns 201 E Jefferson St Phoenix AZ 85004-2412*

VANARSDEL, ROSEMARY THORSTENSON, English studies educator; b. Seattle, Sept. 1, 1926; d. Odin and Helen Catherine (McGregor) Thorstenson; m. Paul P. VanArsdel Jr., July 7, 1950 (dec. Jan. 1994); children: Mary M., Andrew P. BA, U. Wash., 1947, MA, 1948; PhD, Columbia U., 1961. Grad. tchg. asst. Columbia U., N.Y.C., 1948-50; acting instr. U. Wash., Seattle, 1961-63; asst. prof. U. Puget Sound, Tacoma, Wash., 1967-69; assoc. prof. U. Puget Sound, Tacoma, 1970-77, prof. English, 1977-87, disting. prof. emeritus, 1987—, dir. Writing Inst., 1976-86, dir. semester abroad, 1977, dir. Legal English program Sch. Law, 1973-77; vis. prof. Gonzaga U., Pacific Luth. U., Whitman Coll., Willamette U., 1977. Author: Victorian Periodicals: A Guide to Research, Vol. I, 1978, Vol. II, 1989, George Eliot: A Centenary Tribune, 1982, Victorian Periodicals and Victorian Society, 1994; mem. editl. bd. Wellesley Index for Victorian Periodicals, 1968-89; contbr. articles to profl. jours. Recipient Doris Bronson Morrill award Kappa Kappa Gamma, 1982, Disting. Alumnae award Broadway H.S., Seattle, 1991. Mem. MLA, Royal Soc. Lit., Oxford Bibliog. Soc., Nat. Coun. Tchrs. English (Achievement awards, dir. 1974-77), Rsch. Soc. for Victorian Periodicals (pres. 1981-83). Home: 4702 NE 39th St Seattle WA 98105-5205

VAN ASPEREN, MORRIS EARL, banker; b. Wessington, S.D., Oct. 5, 1943; s. Andrew and Alyce May (Flagg) Van A.; m. Anne Virginia Merritt, July 2, 1966; 1 child, David Eric. BS in Math., U. Okla., 1966; MBA, Pepperdine U., 1979. Mgr. western dist. Svc. Rev. Inc., Northbrook, Ill., 1970-77; v.p. Hooper Info. Systems Inc., Tustin, Calif., 1977-78; v.p., chief fin. officer ATE Assocs. Inc., Westlake Village, Calif., 1978-84; mgmt. cons. Thousand Oaks, Calif., 1984—; sr. v.p. Nat. Bank Calif., L.A., 1986—; chmn. liaison com. region IX SBA, 1990-94. Nat. advocate fin. svcs. SBA, 1989. Lt. USN, 1966-70. Mem. Nat. Assn. Govt. Guaranteed Lenders (bd. dirs. 1990-93), Robert Morris Assocs., Nat. Assn. Credit Mgmt., The Am. Legion Post 339 (bd. dirs. 1995—). Office: Nat Bank Calif 145 S Fairfax Ave Los Angeles CA 90036-2166

VANATTA, MERRY JANICE, accountant; b. Mpls., July 18, 1938; d. Lief Erick and Lucille Evelyn (Tucker) Larson; m. Larry Lee VanAtta, Oct. 12, 1956 (div. Dec. 1981); children: Jan Luell, Lori Lee, Erick Donald. Student, Linn Benton Community Coll., 1973-78. Lic. tax cons., Oreg. With various acctg. firms, Lebanon, Oreg., 1956-64, Sharp, Young et al CPAs, Lebanon, Oreg., 1964-72; sole propr. M.J. VanAtta, Acct., Lebanon, Oreg., 1972—. Treas. Oreg. Fedn. Women's Clubs, 1972-74; sec. Lebanon Rural Fire Protection Dist., Lebanon, 1978-87. Mem. Nat. Soc. Pub. Accts. (state dir. 1988-92), Oreg. Assn. Ind. Accts. (pres. 1988-89, 1st v.p. 1987-88, 2d v.p. 1986-87, sec. 1985-86, Martin Fitzgerald award 1988-89, William Blair award 1986-87).

VAN BAAK, ANTHONY EDWARD, resort executive, accountant; b. Shanghai, China, Mar. 26, 1949; came to U.S., 1949; s. Edward Anthony and Frances Ruth (Ribbens) Van B.; BA in History, Calvin Coll., 1970; postgrad. Western Mich. U., 1970-71; m. Arlene Florence Dewey, Aug. 7, 1982; children: Edward Anthony, Florence Ribbens, Rachel Dewey. Pres., stockholder The Entertainment Store, Inc., Steamboat Springs, Colo., 1976-83; asst. controller LTV Corp., 1971-76, Utah Internat., Craig, Colo., 1976-77; controller Mountain Resorts, Steamboat Springs, 1978-80, Steamboat Resorts, 1980-89 ; owner Resort Group Ltd., Inc., 1983—. Republican. Mem. Christian Reformed Ch. Home: PO Box 1809 65 Park Ave Steamboat Springs CO 80477

VAN BARSELAAR, LESLIE FRANCES, private school director; b. Boston, Jan. 23, 1952; d. Arie and Edith Grace (Leslie) van den Barselaar; m. David Randolph Kallgren, Nov. 10, 1976. B in Individual Concentration, U. Mass., 1973. Field instr. Wyo. and Wash. Nat. Outdoor Leadership Sch., Lander, Wyo., 1973-79; Kenya br. co-dir. Nat. Outdoor Leadership Sch., Lander, 1979-82, field instr. Alaska and Baja, 1982-86, Mexico br. co-dir., 1986—. Mem. Am. Birding Assn., Wyo. Carriage Club. Office: Nat Outdoor Leadership Sch 288 W Main St Lander WY 82520-3128

VAN BRUNT, EDMUND EWING, physician; b. Oakland, Calif., Apr. 28, 1926; s. Adrian W. and Kathryn Anne (Shattuck) Van B.; m. Claire Monod, Feb. 28, 1949; children: Karin, Deryk, Jahn. BA in Biophysics, U. Calif., Berkeley, 1952; MD, U. Calif., San Francisco, 1959; ScD, U. Toulouse, France, 1978. Postdoctoral fellow NIH, 1961-63; rsch. assoc. U. Calif., San Francisco, 1963-67; staff physician Kaiser Permanente Med. Ctr., San Francisco, 1964-91; dir. div. rsch. Kaiser Permanente Med. Program, Oakland, Calif., 1979-91; assoc. dir. Kaiser Found. Rsch. Inst., Oakland, 1985-91, sr. cons., 1991—; adj. prof. U. Calif., San Francisco, 1975-92; chmn. instnl. rev. bd. Kaiser Found. Rsch. Inst., 1986—; pres. bd. trustees French Found. Med. Rsch. and Edn., San Francisco, 1992—. Contbr. articles to profl. books and jours. With U.S. Army, 1944-46. Fellow ACP, Am. Coll. Med. Informatics; mem. AAAS, Calif. Med. Assn., U. Calif. Emeritus Faculty Assn., Sigma Xi. Office: 131 Tamalpais Rd Berkeley CA 94708

VAN BUSKIRK, EDMUND MICHAEL, ophthalmologist; b. Lafayette, Ind., July 13, 1941; s. Edmund Linford and Dorothey Elizabeth (Deming) Van B.; m. Bette Jo Lueck, June 19, 1965; children: Audrey Elizabeth, Sarah Lynn, Amy Louise. AB cum laude, Harvard U., 1963, AM in Anthropology, 1964; MD, Boston U., 1968. Diplomate Am. Bd. Ophthalmology. Intern Santa Barbara (Calif.) Cottage-Gen. Hosp., 1968-69; resident in ophthalmology Boston U. Med. Ctr., 1969-72; fellowship Mass. Eye and Ear Infirmary, Harvard Med. Sch., 1972-74; asst. prof. ophthalmology Milton S. Hershey Med. Ctr., Pa. State U., 1974-79; assoc. prof. ophthalmology Oreg. Health Scis. U., Portland, 1979-84, prof. ophthalmology, 1984—, vice chmn. ophthalmology, 1984-94; chmn. dept. ophthalmology Devers Eye Inst., Good Samaritan Hosp. and Med. Ctr., Portland, 1990—, Richard G. Chenoweth chair, 1990—; assoc. examiner Am. Acad. Bd. of Ophthalmology, 1986, 88, 89, 91; mem. visual scis. study sect. NIH, 1986-89; glaucoma adv. bd. Nat. Soc. to Prevent Blindness, 1987—; glaucoma rsch. rev. bd. Am. Health Assistance Found.; chief dept. ophthalmology Legacy Portland Hosps., 1992—; lectr. in field. Author: Clinical Atlas of Glaucoma, 1986, A Color Atlas of Ophthalmic Surgery: Surgery, 1991; founding editor, editor-in-chief Jour. of Glaucoma, 1991—; editl. bd. Am. Jour. Ophthalmology, 1985-91, modules program, 1986-89, Glaucoma Forum, 1989—, Focus on Glaucoma, 1990—; contbr. chpts. to books and articles to profl. jours. Capt. U.S. Army Res. Spl. fellowship NIH, Nat. Eye Inst., 1972-74, Mass. Lions Club, EB Dunphy Eye rsch. fellowship Mass. Eye and Ear Infirmary, 1973-74; Rsch. Career Devel. award Nat. Eye Inst., 1976-81, Faculty Excellence award Oreg. Health Scis. U., 1986, Achievement award Alcon Rsch. Inst., 1988. Fellow ACS, Am. Acad. of Ophthalmology (com. ethics 1987, dir. spl. focus course on glaucoma surgery, 1986, 88, chmn. regional update program 1988-92, Honor award 1986), Coll. of Physicans of Phila.; mem. AMA, Am. Glaucoma Soc. (sec. 1992—), Assn. for Rsch. in Vision and Ophthalmology (mem. program planning com. 1986, 88, chmn. glaucoma sect. 1987-88), Chandler Grant Soc., Internat. Glaucoma Soc., Mass. Eye and Ear Infirmary Alumni Assn., Oreg. Acad. of Ophthalmology, Am. Ophthalmol. Soc. Office: Devers Eye Assocs PC 1040 NW 22nd Ave Portland OR 97210-3057

VAN CAMP, BRIAN RALPH, lawyer; b. Halstead, Kans., Aug. 23, 1940; s. Ralph A. and Mary Margaret (Bragg) Van C.; m. Diane D. Miller, 1992; children: Megan M., Laurie E. A.B., U. Calif., Berkeley, 1962, LL.B., 1965. Bar: Calif. 1966. Dep. atty. gen. State Calif., 1965-67; agy. atty. Redevel. Agy., City of Sacramento, 1967-70; asst./acting sec. Bus. and Transp. Agy., State Calif., 1970-71; commr. of corps. State of Calif., Sacramento, 1971-74; partner firm Diepenbrock, Wulff, Plant & Hannegan, Sacramento, 1975-77, Van Camp & Johnson, Sacramento, 1978-90; sr. ptnr. Downey, Brand, Seymour & Rohwer, 1990—; lectr. Continuing Edn. Bar, Practicing Law Inst., Calif. CPA Soc., others; mem. adv. bd. UCLA Securities Law Inst., 1978. Contbr. articles to profl. jours. Rep. State Ctrl. Com. Calif., 1974-78; pres. Sacramento Area Commerce and Trade Orgn., 1986-87; mem. electoral coll. Presdl. Elector for State of Calif., 1976, Calif. Health Facilities Fin. Authority, 1985-89, Capital Area Devel. Authority, 1989—, chmn., 1990—; bd. dirs. Sacramento Symphony Assn., 1973-85, 92-94, Rep. Assocs. Sacramento County, 1975-79, Sacramento Valley Venture Capital Forum, 1986-90, League to Save Lake Tahoe, 1988—, Valley Vision, Inc., 1993—; leder Fremont Presbyn. Ch., 1968—. Recipient Sumner-Mering Meml. award Sacramento U. of Calif. Alumni Assn., 1962, Thos. Jefferson award Am. Inst. Pub. Svc., 1994; named Outstanding Young Man of Yr. Sacramento Jaycees, 1970, Internat. Young Man of Yr. Active 20-30 Club Internat., 1973. Mem. ABA, Calif. State Bar (mem. com. on corps. 1977-80, partnerships and unincorporated bus. assns. 1983-87), Sacramento County Bar Assn., Calif. C. of C. (chmn. statewide energy task force 1979-85, bd. dirs. 1982—, chmn. edn. com. 1988-90), Sacramento Met. C. of C. (co-chmn. econ. devel. com. 1979, bd. dirs. 1986-88), Boalt Hall Alumni Assn. (bd. dirs. 1991-94), Lincoln Club of Sacramento Valley (bd. dirs., pres. 1984-86), U. Calif. Men's Club (pres. 1968), Sutter Club, Kandahar Ski Club, Rotary Club of Sacramento (pres. 1993-94). Republican. Presbyterian. Office: 555 Capitol Mall 10th Fl Sacramento CA 95814

VAN DAM, HEIMAN, psychoanalyst; b. Leiden, The Netherlands, Feb. 5, 1920; s. Machiel and Rika (Knorringa) van D.; m. Barbara C. Strona, Oct. 6, 1945; children: Machiel, Claire Ilena, Rika Rosemary. A.B., U. So. Calif., 1942, M.D., 1945. Fellowship child psychiatry Pasadena (Calif.) Child Guidance Clinic, 1950; gen. practice psychiatry and psychoanalysis Los Angeles, 1951—; instr. Los Angeles Psychoanalytic Inst., 1959—, co-chmn. com. on child psychoanalysis, 1960-67, tng. and supervising psychoanalyst, 1972—; supr. child and adolescent psychoanalysis So. Calif. Psychoanalytic Inst., 1986—; cons. Reiss Davis Child Study Center, 1955-76, Neighborhood Youth Assn., Los Angeles, 1964-69; asso. clin. prof. psychiatry UCLA Sch. Medicine, 1960—, asso. clin. prof. pediatrics, 1980—; vis. supr. child psychoanalysis San Francisco Psychoanalytic Inst., 1969-79, Denver Psychoanalytic Inst., 1972-74; mem. adv. bd. Western State U. Coll. Law, Fullerton, Calif., 1965-83. Corr. editor Arbeits Hefte Kinderanalyse, 1985—;

contbr. articles to profl. jours. Trustee, mem. edn. com. Center for Early Edn., 1964-92, v.p., 1978-79; bd. dirs. Child Devel. and Psychotherapy Tng. Program, Los Angeles, 1975-80, pres., 1975-77; bd. dirs. Los Angeles Child Devel. Center, 1977-86, treas., 1978-80; mem. cult clinic Jewish Family Service, Los Angeles, 1978-86; bd. dirs. Lake Arrowhead Crest Estates, 1990—. Served to capt. M.C. AUS, 1946-48. Mem. Am. Psychoanalytic Assn. (com. on ethics 1977-80), Assn. Child Psychoanalysis (councillor 1966-69, sec. 1972-74, mem. nominating com. 1978-84, membership com. 1988—), Internat. Assn. Infant Psychiatry (co-chmn. program com. 1980-83), Internat. Soc. Adolescent Psychiatry (sci. adv. com. 1988—), Phi Beta Kappa. Office: 1100 Glendon Ave Ste 941 Los Angeles CA 90024-3513

VAN DE KAMP, JOHN KALAR, lawyer; b. Pasadena, Calif., Feb. 7, 1936; s. Harry and Georgie (Kalar) Van de K.; m. Andrea Fisher, Mar. 11, 1978; 1 child, Diana. BA, Dartmouth Coll., 1956; JD, Stanford U., 1959. Bar: Calif. 1960. Asst. U.S. atty. L.A., 1960-66, U.S. atty., 1966-67; dep. dir. Exec. Office for U.S. Attys., Washington, 1967-68, dir., 1968-69; spl. asst. Pres.'s Commn. on Campus Unrest, 1970; fed. pub. defender L.A., 1971-75; dist. atty. Los Angeles County, 1975-83; atty. gen. State of Calif., 1983-91; ptnr., chmn. litigation dept. Dewey Ballantine, L.A., 1991—; bd. dirs. United Airlines. Mem. Calif. Dist. Attys. Assn. (pres. 1975-83), Nat. Dist. Attys. Assn. (v.p. 1975-83), Peace Officers Assn. L.A. County (past pres.), Nat. Assn. Attys. Gen. (exec. com. 1983-91), Conf. Western Attys. Gen. (pres. 1986). Office: Dewey Ballantine 333 S Hope St Ste 3000 Los Angeles CA 90071-3039

VANDENBERG, PETER RAY, magazine publisher; b. Geneva, Ill., Sept. 8, 1939; s. Don George and Isabel (Frank) V.; m. Kathryn Stock, June 1973 (div. Apr. 1977). BBA, Miami U., 1962. Creative adminstr. E.F. McDonald Incentive Co., Dayton, Ohio, 1966-73; mfrs.' rep. Denver, 1974-75; mgr. Homestake Condominiums, Vail, Colo., 1975-76; desk clk. Vail Run Resort, 1976-77; sales rep. Colo. West Advt., Vail, 1977-79, pres., 1980-83; pres. Colo. West Publ., Vail, 1983—. With U.S. Army, 1963-66. Mem. Sigma Chi.

VAN DEN BERGHE, PIERRE LOUIS, sociologist, anthropologist; b. Lubumbashi, Zaire, Jan. 30, 1933; s. Louis and Denise (Caullery) van den B.; m. Irmgard C. Niehuis, Jan. 21, 1956; children—Eric, Oliver, Marc. B.A., Stanford U., 1952, M.A., 1953; Ph.D., Harvard U., 1960. Asst. prof. sociology Wesleyan U., Middletown, Conn., 1962-63; asso. prof. sociology SUNY, Buffalo, 1963-65; prof. sociology and anthropology U. Wash., Seattle, 1965—; vis. prof. U. Natal, South Africa, 1960-61, Sorbonne, Paris, 1962, U. Nairobi, Kenya, 1967-68, U. Ibadan, Nigeria, 1968-69, U. Haifa, Israel, 1976, U. New South Wales, Australia, 1982, U. Strasbourg, France, 1985, U. Tuebingen, Fed. Republic Germany, 1986, Tel Aviv U., 1988, U. Cape Town, South Africa, 1989; fellow Advanced Study in Behavioral Scis., Stanford, Calif., 1984-85. Author: 22 books including South Africa, A Study in Conflict, 1965, Race and Racism, 1967, Academic Gamesmanship, 1970, Man in Society, 1978, Human Family Systems, 1979, The Ethnic Phenomenon, 1981, Stranger in Their Midst, 1989, State Violence and Ethnicity, 1990, The Quest for the Other, 1994. Served with M.C. U.S. Army, 1954-56. Mem. Am. Sociol. Assn., Am. Anthrop. Assn., Sociol. Research Assn., Human Behavior and Evolution Soc. Home: 2006 19th Ave E Seattle WA 98112-2902 Office: U Wash Dept Sociology DK-40 Seattle WA 98195

VANDENBERGHE, RONALD GUSTAVE, accountant, real estate developer; b. Oakland, Calif., July 1, 1937; s. Anselm Henri and Margaret B. (Bygum) V.; B.A. with honors, San Jose State Coll., 1959; postgrad. U. Calif. at Berkeley Extension, 1959-60, Golden Gate Coll., 1961-63; CPA, Calif.; m. Patricia W. Dufour, Aug. 18, 1957; children: Camille, Mark, Matthew. Real estate investor, pres. VandenBerghe Fin. Corp., Pleasanton, Calif., 1964—. Instr. accounting U. Cal., Berkeley, 1963-70; CPA, Pleasanton, 1963—. Served with USAF. Mem. Calif. Soc. CPAs. Republican. Presbyterian. Mason (Shriner). Home: PO Box 803 Danville CA 94526-0803 Office: 20 Happy Valley Rd Pleasanton CA 94566

VANDEN HEUVEL, MICHAEL JOHN, literature educator; b. Madison, Wis., Feb. 18, 1956; s. Norbert Anthony and Joan Marie (Sandman) V.; m. Tracy Lee Wolenec, July 11, 1992. BA in English, U. Wis., 1979; MA, U. Chgo., 1981; PhD, U. Wis., 1988. With Ariz. State U., Tempe. Author: Performing Drama/Dramatizing Performance, 1991, ELmer Rice: A Research and Production Sourcebook, 1995; contbr. articles to profl. jours. Am. Coun. Learned Soc. fellow, 1993. Office: Ariz State U Dept English Box 870302 Tempe AZ 85287-0302

VANDERBILT, KERMIT, English language educator; b. Decorah, Iowa, Sept. 1, 1925; s. Lester and Ella (Qualley) V.; m. Vivian Osmundson, Nov. 15, 1947; 1 dau., Karen Paige. B.A., Luther Coll., Decorah, 1947, Litt. D. (hon.), 1977; M.A., U. Minn., 1949, Ph.D., 1956. Instr. English U. Minn., 1954-57; instr. U. Wash., 1958-60, asst. prof. English, 1960-62; asst. prof. San Diego State U., 1962-65, assoc. prof., 1965-68, prof., 1968-90, prof. emeritus, 1990—; vis. prof. Am. lit. U. B.C., Can., Vancouver, summer 1963; vis. prof. U. Oreg., summer 1968. Author: Charles Eliot Norton: Apostle of Culture in a Democracy, 1959, The Achievement of William Dean Howells: A Reinterpretation, 1968, American Literature and the Academy: The Roots, Growth and Maturity of a Profession, 1986 (Choice award for outstanding acad. books), Theodore Roethke in A Literary History of the American West, 1987; editor: (with others) American Social Thought, 1972, April Hopes (W.D. Howells), 1975, The Rise of Silas Lapham, 1983, spl. issue Am. Literary Realism, winter 1989, La Litterature Americaine, 1991, 2nd edit., 1994; mem. edit. bd. U. Wash. Press, 1960-62, Twentieth Century Lit., 1969—; contbr. numerous articles to profl. jours. Served with USNR, 1943-46. Outstanding Prof. San Diego State U., 1976; Guggenheim fellow, 1978-79; Huntington Library fellow, 1980; Am. Philos. Soc. grantee, 1964, Am. Council Learned Socs. grantee, 1972, Nat. Endowment for Humanities grantee, 1986. Mem. Am. Studies Assn. (exec. council 1968-69), So. Calif. Am. Studies Assn. (pres. 1968-69), Philol. Assn. Pacific Coast (chmn. sect. Am. lit. 1968), MLA, Internat. Mark Twain Soc. (hon.), United Profs. of Calif. (Disting. prof. 1978). Home: 6937 Coleshill Dr San Diego CA 92119-1920

VANDER DUSSEN, SHERI TULLEY, city official; b. Inglewood, Calif., Mar. 21, 1959; d. Harry Alexander Tulley and Dorothy Ann (Herder) Pagenstecher; m. Nicholas Paul Vander Dussen, June 20, 1981; children: David Nicholas, Matthew John. BA in Social Ecology, U. Calif., Irvine, 1980. Assoc. planner City of Newport Beach, 1980-85; sr. planner City of Norwalk, 1985-86; sr. planner City of Irvine, 1986-89, prin. planner, 1989-90, mgr. devel. svcs., 1990-93, mgr. planning and devel. svcs., 1993—; devel. cons. Faith Reformed Ch., Norwalk, 1991; spkr. Am. Planning Assn., Newport Beach, 1990; guest lectr. U. Calif., Irvine, 1992. Mem. task force Orange County Affordable Housing, Santa Ana, Calif., 1992; coord. ann. drive, United Way, Irvine, 1991; mem. Bellflower (Calif.) Christian Sch. Soc., 1989—; mem. Orange County Forum, 1994—. Mem. Am. Inst. Cert. Planners, Am. Planning Assn., Nat. Assn. Housing and Redevel. Ofcls. Office: City of Irvine PO Box 19575 Irvine CA 92713-9575

VANDERGRIFF, JERRY DODSON, computer store executive; b. Ft. Leonard Wood, Mo., Nov. 6, 1943; s. Oliver Wyatt Vandergriff and Mary Ella (Perkins) Myers; m. Donna Jean Niehof, Aug. 14, 1976 (div. Nov. 1987); children: Robert Lee II, William Oliver. BS in Bus., Emporia State U., 1974. Customer svc. mgr. Pictures, Inc., Anchorage, 1975-83, v.p., gen. mgr., 1983-87; gen. mgr. Pictures-The Computer Store, Anchorage, 1987—. Bd. dirs. Community Schs. Coun., Anchorage, 1986-87; mem. Gov.'s Coun. on Edn., 1989-90; bd. dirs. Romig Jr. High Sch., 1989-90, pres. PTSA, 1990-92; mem. exec. bd. Alaska's Youth Ready for Work, 1989-92. Mem. VFW, Moose. Republican. Home: 3831 Balchen Dr Anchorage AK 99517-2446 Office: The Computer Store 601 W 36th Ave Ste 19 Anchorage AK 99503-5849

VANDERHEIDEN, RICHARD THOMAS, government official, lawyer; b. Omaha, Nov. 10, 1947; s. Frederick Joseph and Margaret (Burke) V.; m. Mary Margaret Schuster, June 1, 1969; children: Brian, Paul. BS, U. Nebr., 1970, JD, 1973. Bar: Nebr. 1974. Dep. county atty. Merrick County, Central City, Nebr., 1974-75; ptnr. Phares Torpin Vanderheiden & Mesner, Central City, 1976-87; v.p. Founders Bank of Ariz., Scottsdale, 1987-88, Chase Trust Co. of Ariz., Scottsdale, 1988-91; pub. fiduciary Maricopa County, Phoenix, 1991—; jud. nominating commn. 21st Jud. Dist., Nebr., 1984-86; bd. dirs. Merrick County Mental Health Ctr., 1975-82, Maricopa County Justice Com., 1991—, exec. team, 1991; vice chmn. Maricopa County Deferred Compensation Bd., 1994—, NaCo Deferred Compensation Adminstrv. Com., 1995—. Pres. Bd. Edn., Central City, 1975-82; chpt. chmn. ARC, Central City, 1976-80; co-chair United Way Campaign, Maricopa County; chmn. cert. com. Nat. Guardianship Assn. Mem. ABA, Nat. Guardianship Assn. (bd. dirs. 1992—, v.p. 1995), Scottsdale Bar Assn., Valley Estate Planners (pres. 1990-91), Ariz. Bankers Assn. (trust com. 1989-91), Sertoma Internat. (pres. 1979), Central City C. of C. (bd. dirs. 1980-84). Democrat. Roman Catholic. Office: First Am Title Bldg 111 W Monroe St Fl 5 Phoenix AZ 85003-1728

VANDERHOEF, LARRY NEIL, university administrator; b. Perham, Minn., Mar. 20, 1941; s. Wilmar James and Ida Lucille (Wothe) V.; m. Rosalie Suzanne Slifka, Aug. 31, 1963; children: Susan Marie, Jonathan Lee. B.S., U. Wis., Milw., 1964, M.S., 1965; Ph.D., Purdue U., 1969. Postdoctorate U. Wis., Madison, 1969-70; research assoc. U. Wis., summers 1970-72; asst. prof. biology U. Ill., Urbana, 1970-74; assoc. prof. U. Ill., 1974-77, prof., 1977—, head dept. plant biology, 1977-80; provost Agrl. and Life Scis., U. Md., College Park, 1980-84; exec. vice chancellor U. Calif., Davis, 1984-91, exec. vice chancellor, provost, 1991-94; chancellor, 1994—; vis. investigator Carnegie Inst., 1976-77, Edinburgh (Scotland) U., 1978; cons. in field. NRC postdoctoral fellow, 1969-70, Eisenhower fellow, 1987; Dimond travel grantee, 1975, NSF grantee, 1972, 74, 76, 77, 78, 79, NATO grantee, 1980. Mem. AAAS, Am. Soc. Plant Physiology (bd. editors Plant Physiology 1977-82, trustee, mem. exec. com., treas. 1982-88, chmn. bd. trustees 1994—), Nat. Assn. State Univ. and Land Grant Colls. Home: 615 Francisco Pl Davis CA 95616-0210 Office: U Calif Davis Office Chancellor Davis CA 95616

VANDERLINDEN, CAMILLA DENICE DUNN, telecommunications industry manager; b. Dayton, July 21, 1950; d. Joseph Stanley and Virginia Danley (Martin) Dunn; m. David Henry VanderLinden; Oct. 10, 1980; 1 child, Michael Christopher. Student, U. de Valencia, Spain, 1969; BA in Spanish and Secondary Edn. cum laude, U. Utah, 1972, MS in Human Resource Econs., 1985. Asst. dir. Davis County Community Action Program, Farmington, Utah, 1973-76; dir. South County Community Action, Midvale, Utah, 1976-79; supr. customer service Ideal Nat. Life Ins. Co., Salt Lake City, 1979-80; mgr. customer service Utah Farm Bur. Mutual Ins., Salt Lake City, 1980-82; quality assurance analyst Am. Express Co., Salt Lake City, 1983-86, quality assurance and human resource specialist, 1986-88; mgr. quality assurance and engring. Am. Express Co., Denver, 1988-91; mgr. customer svc. Tel. Express Co., Colorado Springs, Colo., 1991—; mem. adj. faculty Westminster Coll., Salt Lake City, 1987-88. mem. adj. faculty, mem. quality adv. bd. Red Rocks Community Coll., 1990-91. Vol. translator Latin Am. community; vol. naturalist Roxborough State Park; internat. exch. coord. EF Fgn. Exch. Program. Christian. Home: 10857 W Snow Cloud Trl Littleton CO 80125-9210

VANDERLINDEN, CARL RENE, consulting company executive; b. Pella, Iowa, Sept. 26, 1923; s. Marinus and Julia (Fennema) V.; m. Shirley A. Beatty, Mar. 8, 1945; children: Patricia, David. Student, Central Coll., 1941-43; BS in Chem. Engring., U. Wash., 1944; PhD in Chem. Engring., Iowa State U., 1950. Registered profl. engr., Iowa. Rsch. sect. chief Johns-Manville, Manville, N.J., 1953-61, rsch. dept. mgr., 1961-69, dir. R&D, 1969-73, Denver, 1972-75, v.p. dir., R&D, 1975-81; staff v.p. dir. R&D, Manville Sales Corp., Denver, 1981-86; pres. VanderLinden & Assocs., Littleton, Colo., 1987—; treas. Chem. cons. of Colo., 1988—. Pres. Columbine Valley Homewoners Assn., 1986-88, treas., 1988-91; mem. U.S. Dept. of Energy Advanced Indsl. Materials Guidance and Evaluation Bd., 1986—, chmn., 1989-90. Ensign USN, 1943-46. Recipient Profl. Achievement Citation in Engring. Iowa State U., 1982. Fellow Am. Inst. Chem. Engrs. (dir. 1979-81); mem. Am. Chem. Soc., Nat. Inst. Bldg. Scis., Bldg. Futures Council (operating com. 1979-87), Perlite Inst. (pres. 1974-76, Lewis Lloyd award, 1983), Bldg. Thermal Envelope Coordinating Com. (bd. dirs. 1985-88). Republican. Presbyterian. Club: Columbine Country. Office: Vander-Linden & Assocs 5 Brassie Way Littleton CO 80123-6608

VANDERLIP, ELIN BREKKE, professional society executive; b. Oslo, Norway, June 7, 1919; came to U.S., 1944; m. Kelvin Cox, Nov., 1946 (dec. 1956); children: Kelvin Jr., Narcissa, Henrik and Katrina (twins). With Norwegian Embassy, Norway, Norwegian Fng. Ministry, London, 1941-44, Red Cross, Calcutta, India, Norwegian Embassy, Norway; pres. Friends of French Art, Portuguese Bend, Calif.; tour guide garden tours Friends of French Art in April; tour guide to Ile de France, Anjou, Bordelais, Provence-Cote d'Azur, Alsace, Dordogne, Lyonnais-Isere, Brittany, Burgundy, Normandy, Languedoc, Loire, Gascony, Le Nord, Charente, Provence and Champagne, 1978—. Decorated comdr. Order of Arts and Letters (France). Home and Office: 100 Vanderlip Dr Rancho Palos Verdes CA 90275

VAN DER MEULEN, JOSEPH PIERRE, neurologist; b. Boston, Aug. 22, 1929; s. Edward Lawrence and Sarah Jane (Robertson) VanDer M.; m. Ann Irene Yadeno, June 18, 1960; children—Elisabeth, Suzanne, Janet. A.B., Boston Coll., 1950; M.D., Boston U., 1954. Diplomate: Am. Bd. Psychiatry and Neurology. Intern Cornell Med. div. Bellevue Hosp., N.Y.C., 1954-55; resident Cornell Med. div. Bellevue Hosp., 1955-56; resident Harvard U., Boston City Hosp., 1958-60, instr., fellow, 1962-66; assoc. Case Western Res. U., Cleve., 1966-67; asst. prof. Case Western Res. U., 1967-69, assoc. prof. neurology and biomed. engring., 1969-71; prof. neurology U. So. Calif., L.A., 1971—; also dir. dept. neurology Los Angeles County/U. So. Calif. Med. Center; chmn. dept. U. So. Calif., 1971-78, v.p. for health affairs, 1977—, dean Sch. Medicine, 1985-86, dir. Allied Health Scis., 1991—; vis. prof. Autonomous U. Guadalajara, Mex., 1974; pres. Norris Cancer Hosp. and Research Inst., 1983—. Contbr. articles to profl. jours. Mem. med. adv. bd. Calif. chpt. Myasthenia Gravis Found., 1971-75, chmn., 1974-75, 77-78; med. adv. bd. Amyotrophic Lateral Sclerosis Found., Calif., 1973-75, chmn., 1974-75; mem. Com. to Combat Huntington's Disease, 1973—; bd. dirs. Calif. Hosp. Med. Ctr., Good Hope Med. Found., Doheny Eye Hosp., House Ear Inst., L.A. Hosp. Good Samaritan, Children's Hosp. of L.A., Barlow Respiratory Hosp., USC U. Hosp., chmn., 1991—; bd. govs. Thomas Aquinas Coll.; bd. dirs. Assn. Acad. Health Ctrs., chmn., 1991-92; pres. Scott Newman Ctr., 1987-89; pres., bd. dirs. Kenneth Norris Cancer Hosp & Rsch. Inst. Served to lt. M.C. USNR, 1956-58. Nobel Inst. fellow Karolinska Inst., Stockholm, 1960-62; NIH grantee, 1968-71. Mem. AMA, Am. Neurol. Assn., Am. Acad. Neurology, L.A. Soc. Neurology and Psychiatry (pres. 1977-78), L.A. Med. Assn., Mass. Med. Soc., Ohio Med. Soc., Calif. Med. Soc., L.A. Acad. Medicine, Alpha Omega Alpha (councillor 1992—), Phi Kappa Phi. Home: 39 Club View Ln Palos Verdes Peninsula CA 90274-4208 Office: U So Calif 1540 Alcazar St Los Angeles CA 90033-1058

VANDERSPEK, PETER GEORGE, management consultant, writer; b. The Hague, Netherlands, Dec. 15, 1925; came to U.S., 1945; s. Pieter and Catherine Johanna (Rolf) V.; m. Charlotte Louise Branch, Aug. 18, 1957. Student, Tilburg (Netherlands) U., 1944; MA in Econs., Fordham U., 1950, PhD in Econs., 1954; postgrad., George Washington U., 1967-68. Internat. economist Mobil Oil Corp., N.Y.C., 1956-59; mgr. internat. market rsch. Celanese Corp., N.Y.C., 1959-63; internat. economist Bethlehem (Pa.) Steel Corp., 1964-65; sr. tech. adviser Battelle Meml. Inst., Washington, 1965-66; indsl. adviser Inter-Am. Devel. Bank, Washington, 1967-69; economist Fed. Res. Bank, N.Y.C., 1970-72; mgr. internat. market rsch. Brunswick Corp., Skokie, Ill., 1973-76; mgr. advanced planning Sverdrup Corp., St. Louis, 1979-87; cons. Sverdrup Corp., 1988-90; pres. OBEX, Inc., San Luis Obispo, Calif., 1988—. Author: Planning for Factory Automation, 1993; contbr. to profl. jours. Thomas J. Watson fellow, IBM-Fordham U., 1945-49. Mem. Nat. Assn. Bus. Economists, Mensa. Home and Office: 1314 Vega Way San Luis Obispo CA 93405-4815

VANDERTUIN, VICTORIA ELVA, book seller; b. New Bedford, Mass., Oct. 16, 1933; d. Harry Robinson and Elva Gladys (Ramsay) Belot; m. David Kent Roy, Dec. 13, 1983 (div.); children: Lowell Ramsay, Jewell Pauline. Book seller New Age World Svcs. & Books, Joshua Tree, Calif.; min. Internat. Evangelism Crusades, 1964, Inst. Mentalphysics, 1982. Editor/pub. New Age World Polaris newsletter, 1994.

VAN DERVEER, TARA, university athletic coach; b. Niagara Falls, N.Y., 1954. Grad., Indiana U., 1975. Coach women's basketball Stanford U. Cardinals, 1985—, U.S. Nat. Women's Team, 1995—. Office: c/o Stanford Univ Stanford CA 94305*

VANDER VORSTE, JAMES LEROY, architect; b. Bismark, N.D., Mar. 4, 1947; s. Martin and Marjorie (Jones) Vander V.; m. Joanne Marie Carlson, June 23, 1967; 1 dau., Gwyn. B.Arch. with honors, N.D. State U., 1970. Tech. asst. Elken, Geston & Hanson, Moorhead, Minn., 1968-70; designer Foss, Engelstad, Foss, Fargo, N.D., 1970; architect Hobart D. Wagener, Assocs., Boulder, Colo., 1970-78; ptnr. Wagener/Vander Vorste, Boulder, 1978—. Mem. AIA, Constrn. Specifications Inst., Kappa Tau Delta, Tau Beta Pi, Phi Kappa Phi. Methodist. Office: Wagener Vander Vorste Architects 3515 Smuggler Cir Boulder CO 80303-7220

VAN DER WERFF, TERRY JAY, management consultant, professional speaker; b. Hammond, Ind., May 16, 1944; s. Sidney and Johanna (Oostman) van der W.; m. Renee Marie Leet, Mar. 2, 1968; children: Anne Cathleen, Valerie Kay, David Edward, Michele Renée, Julia Leigh. SB and SM, MIT, 1968; DPhil, Oxford (Eng.) U., 1972. Registered profl. engr., Colo., South Africa; profl. biomed. engr., South Africa. Staff engr. ARO, Inc., Tullahoma, Tenn., 1968; asst. prof. mech. engring., physiology and biophysics Colo. State U., Ft. Collins, 1970-73; vis. asst. prof. medicine U. Colo., Denver, 1973-74; head biomed. engring. U. Cape Town/Groote Schuur Hosp., Cape Town, South Africa, 1974-80; dean of sci. and engring. Seattle U., 1981-90; exec. v.p. for acad. affairs St. Joseph's U., Phila., 1990-91; pres. van der Werff Assoc., Inc., Seattle, 1991—. Co-author: Mathematical Models of the Dynamics of the Human Eye; author 100 book revs., monthly newspaper and mag. columns; contbr. over 40 articles to profl. jours. Recipient Ralph R. Teetor award Soc. Automotive Engrs., Detroit, 1972. Fellow Royal Soc. South Africa, Biomed. Engring. Soc. South Africa; mem. AAAS, Am. Phys. Soc., Nat. Spkrs. Assn., Inst. Mgmt. Cons., Planning Forum, Sigma Xi. Republican. Roman Catholic. Home: 2410 NE 123rd St Seattle WA 98125-5241

VAN DER WESTHUIZEN, BRIAN IVAN, business educator; b. Mafeking, Cape, South Africa, Jan. 23, 1939; came to U.S., 1990; m. Moyra P. Morhen, May 6, 1961 (dec. May 1986); children: Susan, Gillian; m. Rosemary Emily Grant, Jan. 24, 1987. BCom, U. South Africa, Pretoria, 1982; MBA, U. Witwatersrand, Johannesburg, 1985; DCom, U. Pretoria, 1991. Sales mgr. Stanley Porter, Cape Town, South Africa, 1966-68; asst. sales mgr. Cargo Motor Corp., Johannesburg, 1969-71; gen. mktg. mgr. Malcomess-Scania, Isando, South Africa, 1972-75; br. mgr. Internat. Harvester, Isando, 1976; sales mgr. Barlows, Oshkosh Div., Isando, 1977-78; gen. mktg. mgr. Dresser South Africa, Germiston, 1979-82; mktg. mgr. Barclay's Western Bank, Johannesburg, 1983-87; sr. lectr. U. of the Witwatersrand, Johannesburg, 1988-89; prof. Calif. State U., Northridge, 1990—; dir. acad. devel. Inst. Mktg. Mgmt., Johannesburg, 1980-89. Co-author: Sales Management, 1989; contbg. author: Marketing Communications, 1987. Inst. Mktg. Mgmt. fellow. Fellow Acad. Mktg. Sci.; mem. Chartered Inst. Mkgt., Western Mktg. Educators Assn. (bd. dirs. 1991-93). Baptist. Home: 9542 Swinton Ave North Hills CA 91343-1926 Office: Calif State U 18111 Nordhoff St Northridge CA 91330-8245

VANDERWOOD, PAUL JOSEPH, history educator; b. Bklyn., June 3, 1929; s. Joseph and Mildred (Horstmann) V. BA, Bethany Coll., 1950; MA, Memphis State U., 1956; PhD, U. Tex., 1970. Reporter Scripps-Howard Newspapers, Memphis, 1956-64; prof. San Diego State U., 1969—. Author: Night Riders of Reelfoot Lake, 1970, Disorder and Progress, 1981, Border Fury, 1988, War Scare on the Rio Grande, 1992. 1st lt. U.S. Army, 1951-53. Recipient Hubert Herring awards Pacific Coast Coun. Latin-Am. studies, 1981, 82, Southwest Book award Regional Libr. Assn., 1989. Mem. Conf. Latin Am. Studies, Historians Film Com., Pacific Coast Coun. Latin Am. Studies (pres. 1970—). Democrat. Home: 8705 Jefferson Ave La Mesa CA 91941-5145 Office: San Diego State U History Dept San Diego CA 92182

VANDERZANDEN, DANA KATHLEEN, public relations professional; b. Portland, Oreg., Oct. 13, 1965; d. Gordon and Carol Ann (Day) VanderZ. BA in Journalism, Comms. cum laude, Linfield Coll., 1987. Mktg. specialist Good Samaritan Hosp., Portland, Oreg., 1987-89; pub. rels. mgr. Payless Drug Stores, Wilsonville, Oreg., 1989—. Tutor Oreg. Literacy Program, Portland, 1993-94. Mem. Pub. Rels. Soc. Am. (accredited pub. rels. profl., Merit award 1992).

VANDIVER, LINTON MITCHELL, II, publisher; b. Rome, Ga., Sept. 7, 1937; s. Edmund Marshall and Mary Betty (Bradshaw) V.; m. Gail Hemmeter, Aug. 13, 1975 (div. Nov. 1985); children: Leslie, Linton Mitchell III. BSc, Georgetown U., 1960. Editorial dir. Butterworth, Inc., Washington, 1961-65; assoc. dir., sr. editor The Pa. State U. Press, University Park, 1966-72; pres., CEO University Park Press, Balt., 1967-85; exec. v.p., COO College Hill Press, San Diego, 1985-88; exec. v.p. First Liberty Bancorp, Inc., Washington, 1988-90; pub., COO Singular Pub. Group, Inc., San Diego, 1990-92; pres., pub., dir., CEO Index Pub. Group, Inc, San Diego, 1992—; bd. dirs. First Liberty Bancorp, Inc., Washington; bd. dirs., treas. Singular Pub. Group, Inc., San Diego. Home: 6755 Mission Gorge Rd Apt 6 San Diego CA 92120-2459 Office: Index Pub Group Inc 3368 Governor Dr Ste 273 San Diego CA 92122-2936

VANDIVER, ROBERT SANFORD, civic association executive; b. Barksdale Field, La., Apr. 2, 1937; s. William Marion and Mattie Katherine (Tiller) V.; m. Patricia Gail Kelly, Feb. 10, 1956; children: Cynthia Ann, Kathleen. AA, U. Md., 1973; BA, SUNY, Albany, 1975; MS, Golden Gate U., 1985, MPA, 1986. Enlisted U.S. Army, 1955, commd. lt., 1967, advanced through grades to maj., 1978; materiel mgr. Pima County Sheriff Dept., Tucson, 1979-81; task leader Computer Scis. Corp., Sierra Vista, Ariz., 1981-83, Mandex, Inc., Sierra Vista, 1983-86; project mgr. Planning Rsch. Corp., Sierra Vista, 1986-90; Boy Scout exec. Catalina Coun., Tucson, 1990—; adj. faculty Cochise Coll., Sierra Vista, 1987-90, Golden Gate U., San Francisco, 1988-92; instr. Sch. Pub. Adminstrn., Ariz. State U., Tucson, 1988-92. Co-editor, South Vietnam Boy Scout Handbook, 1965. Vol. leader Boy Scouts Am., various locations, 1956-90. Decorated Legion of Merit, Bronze Star medal, Soldier's medal; recipient Silver Beaver award, Boy Scouts Am., 1977. Mem. Nat. Property Mgmt. Assn., Soc. Logistics Engrs., Am. Soc. Pub. Adminstrn., Co. Mil. Historians. Lutheran. Home: 8345 E Cypress Point Ln Tucson AZ 85710-7164 Office: Catalina Coun Boy Scouts Am 5049 E Broadway Blvd Ste 200 Tucson AZ 85711-3636

VAN DORP, JOHAN JACOBUS, oil company engineer; b. Velsen, The Netherlands, Aug. 28, 1954; came to U.S., 1992; s. Adriaan and Baukje (Brijker) van D.; m. Ingrid Zeggelink, Nov. 7, 1981; children: Remco J., Rutger D. M in Exptl. Physics, Math., Bus. Econs., U. Utrecht, The Netherlands, 1980. Drilling engr. Shell Expro-U.K., Eng., 1982-85; sr. reservoir engr. Dutch Petroleum Co., The Netherlands, 1986-91; staff reservoir engr. Shell Western EP Inc., Calif., 1992—. 1st lt. Dutch Army, 1980-81. Mem. IEEE, Soc. Petroleum Engrs., Astron. Soc. Office: Shell Western EP Inc 5060 California Ave Bakersfield CA 93309-1682

VAN DYKE, ELIZABETH ARTEMIS, management executive and consultant; b. Cin., Jan. 9, 1953; m. Morgan Van Dyke, Aug. 8, 1986. AA, U. Cin., 1973, BS cum laude, 1975; PhD in Comms. and Orgnl. Effectiveness, Union Inst., Cin., 1991. Internat. tour control agent Am. Airlines, Cin., 1978-85; orgnl. analyst GE Aircraft Engines, Cin., 1985-88; tng. and orgnl. effectiveness mgr. Procter & Gamble Co., Cin., 1988-91; pres., CEO Van Dyke & Assocs., San Mateo, Calif., 1988—; trainer, lectr., and cons. various high tech. corps. Contbr. articles to profl. jours. Co-founder Ohio Women's Archives; lectr. Incest Survivors, Productivity, Mgmt., Leadership, Strategic Planning, Communications, Organizational Effectiveness, Tng.; speaker numerous profl., vol. and civic groups. Mem. ASTD (bd. dirs., v.p. membership com. Silicon Valley chpt. 1993—), Am. Mgmt. Assn., Am. Soc. for Pers. Adminstrn., Human Resource Planning Soc., Nat. Soc. for Performance and Instrn., Orgnl. Devel. Network, Soc. Am. Archivists, Soc. for Tech. Comms., Women in Comms., Bay Area Career Women, San Jose Met. C. of C. Office: Van Dyke & Assocs 1700 De Anza Blvd Apt 111 San Mateo CA 94403-3967

VANE, SYLVIA BRAKKE, anthropologist, cultural resource management company executive; b. Fillmore County, Minn., Feb. 28, 1918; d. John T. and Hulda Christina (Marburger) Brakke; m. Arthur Bayard Vane, May 17, 1942; children: Ronald Arthur, Linda, Laura Vane Ames. AA, Rochester Jr. Coll., 1937; BS with distinction, U. Minn., 1939; postgrad., Radcliffe U., 1944; MA, Calif. State U., Hayward, 1975. Med. technologist Dr. Frost and Hodapp, Willmar, Minn., 1939-41; head labs. Corvallis Gen. Hosp., Oreg., 1941-42; dir. lab. Cambridge Gen. Hosp., Mass., 1942-43, Peninsula Clinic, Redwood City, Calif., 1947-49; v.p. Cultural Systems Rsch., Inc., Menlo Park, Calif., 1978—; pres. Ballena Press, Menlo Park, 1981—; cons. cultural resource mgmt. So. Calif. Edison Co., Rosemead, 1978-81, San Diego Gas and Elec. Co., 1980-83, Pacific Gas and Elec. Co., San Francisco, 1982-83, Wender, Murase & White, Washington, 1983-87, Yosemite Indians, Mariposa, Calif., 1982-91, San Luis Rey Band of Mission Indians, Escondido, Calif., 1986-89, U.S. Ecology, Newport Beach, Calif., 1986-89, Riverside County Flood Control and Water Conservation Dist., 1985-95, Infotec, Inc., 1989-91, Alexander & Karshmer, Berkeley, Calif., 1989-92, Desert Water Agy., Palm Springs, Calif., 1989-90, Metropolitan Water Dist., Nat. Park Svc., 1992—. Author: (with L.J. Bean), California Indians, Primary Resources, 1977, rev. edit., 1990, The Cahuilla and the Santa Rosa Mountains, 1981, The Cahuilla Landscape, 1991; contbr. chpts. to several books. Bd. dirs. Sequoia Area coun. Girl Scouts U.S., 1954-61; bd. dirs., v.p., pres. LWV, S. San Mateo County, Calif., 1960-65. Fellow Soc. Applied Anthropology, Am. Anthropology Assn.; mem. Southwestern Anthrop. Assn. (program chmn. 1976-78, newsletter editor 1976-79), Soc. for Am. Archaeology. Mem. United Ch. of Christ. Office: Ballena Press 823 Valparaiso Ave Menlo Park CA 94025-4206

VANESS, MARGARET HELEN, artist, consultant; b. Seattle; d. Paul Edward and Alma Magdalena Lauch; B.F.A., U. Wash., Seattle, 1970, 71, M.F.A., 1973; cert. bus. Drexel U., Phila., 1975; m. Gerard Vaness; children—Bette, Bruce, Barbara, Helen-Cathleen. Teaching asst. Sch. Art, U. Wash., 1971-73; illustrator DuPont Co., Wilmington, Del., 1973-74, Boeing Vertol Co., Phila., 1974-75; illustrator, program mgr. Boeing Co., Seattle, 1978-84; judge art shows, 1969—; executed mural for Dr. L. Mellon-Boeing Vertol Med. Ctr., 1974; commd. by USIA, 1973; zone dir. Bellevue Art Mus., 1994—. Mem. Coll. Art Assn., Soc. for Tech. Communication, Photog. Soc. Am. (area rep. 1985-88, dist. rep. 1988—), Seattle Photographic Soc. (editor official bulletin Cable Releases 1985-89, bd. dirs. 1986-88), U. Wash. Alumni Assn. (life), U. Wash. Arboretum Found. (unit pres. 1981-83), Nat. Mus. of Women in the Arts (charter mem.), N.W. Coun. Camera Clubs (bd. dirs. 1991-94, assoc. editor newsletter 1991-94), Lambda Rho (past pres.). Address: 17128 2nd Ave SW Seattle WA 98166-3521

VAN HALDEREN, LAUREL LYNN, dietitian; b. Milw., June 27, 1951; d. Vern LeRoy and Elizabeth (Siegel) Johnson; m. Robert John Van Halderen, Aug. 7, 1971; children: Nickolas James, Christine Kate. BS, U. Ariz., 1973. Registered dietitian, Ariz. Intern Houston VA Med. Ctr., 1973-74; clin. dietitian Miami (Fla.) VA Med. Ctr., 1974-76; ambulatory care dietitian Tucson VA Med. Ctr., 1976-78; chief clin. dietetic sect. Battle Creek (Mich.) VA Med. Ctr., 1978-79, chief adminstrv. dietetic sect., 1979-81; chief dietetic svc. Am. Lake VA Med. Ctr., Tacoma, Wash., 1981-84, Phoenix VA Med. Ctr., 1984—; chairperson VA Dietetic Decentralized Hosp. Computer Program Expert Panel, 1987—; vice chair VA Nat. Adv. Group for Info. Security Officers, 1994—. Mem. Am. Dietetic Assn., Ariz. Dietetic Assn. (bd. dirs. 1994—), Am. Soc. for Hosp. Food Svc. Adminstrs. Office: VA Medical Center 650 E Indian School Rd Phoenix AZ 85012-1839

VAN HASSEL, HENRY JOHN, dentist, educator, university dean; b. Paterson, N.J., May 2, 1933; s. William Cornelius and Ina (Sturr) Van H.; m. Ann Newell Wiley, Dec. 28, 1960. BA, Maryville Coll., Tenn., 1954; DDS, U. Md., 1963; MSD, U. Wash., 1967, PhD, 1969. Diplomate Am.Bd. Endodontics. Dental dir. USPHS, Seattle, 1965-81; prof., chmn. dept. endodontics U. Md., Balt., 1981-84; dean dental sch. Oreg. Health Scis. U., Portland, 1984—, v.p. instl. affairs, 1989-91. Recipient Schlack award Assn. Mil. Surgeons U.S., 1976, Borrish award Acad. Gen. Dentistry, 1989. Mem. Am. Assn. Endodontists (pres. 1981-82, Grossman Gold medal 1984), Oreg. Dental Assn. (pres. 1990). Office: Oreg Health Scis U Dental Sch 611 SW Campus Dr Portland OR 97201-3001

VAN HOOMISSEN, GEORGE ALBERT, state supreme court justice; b. Portland, Oreg., Mar. 7, 1930; s. Fred J. and Helen F. (Flanagan) Van H.; m. Ruth Madeleine Niedermeyer, June 4, 1960; children: Geroge T., Ruth Anne, Madeleine, Matthew. BBA, U. Portland, 1951; JD, Georgetown U., 1955, LLM in Labor Law, 1957; LLM in Jud. Adminstrn., U. Va., 1986. Bar: D.C. 1955, Oreg. 1956, Tex. 1971, U.S. Dist. Ct. Oreg. 1956, U.S. Ct. Mil. Appeals 1955, U.S. Ct. Customs and Patent Appeals 1955, U.S. Ct. Claims 1955, U.S. Ct. Appeals (9th cir.) 1956, U.S. Ct. Appeals (D.C. cir.) 1955, U.S. Supreme Ct. 1960. Law clk. for Chief Justice Harold J. Warner Oreg. Supreme Ct., 1955-56; Keigwin teaching fellow Georgetown Law Sch., 1956-57; dep. dist. atty. Multnomah County, Portland, 1957-59; pvt. practice Portland, 1959-62; dist. atty. Multnomah County, 1962-71; dean nat. coll. dist. attys. U. Houston, 1971-73; judge Cir. Ct., Portland, 1973-81, Oreg. Ct. Appeals, Salem, 1981-88; assoc. justice Oreg. Supreme Ct., Salem, 1988—. Mem. Oreg. Ho. of Reps., Salem, 1959-62, chmn. house jud. com. With USMC, 1951-53; col. USMCR (ret.). Recipient Disting. Alumnus award U. Portland, 1972. Mem. ABA, Oreg. State Bar, Tex. Bar Assn., Arlington Club, Multnomah Athletic Club, Univ. Club. Roman Catholic. Office: Oreg Supreme Ct 1163 State St Salem OR 97310-1331

VAN HORN, O. FRANK, counselor, consultant; b. Grand Junction, Colo., Apr. 16, 1926; s. Oertel F. and Alta Maude (Lynch) Van H.; m. Dixie Jeanne MacGregor, Feb. 1, 1947 (dec. Nov. 1994); children: Evelyn, Dorothy. AA, Mesa Coll., 1961; BA, Western State Colo., 1963; MEd, Oreg. State U., 1969. Counselor, mgr. State of Oreg.-Employment, Portland and St. Helens, 1964-88; pvt. practice counselor and cons. St. Helens, 1988—; chair Task Force on Aging, Columbia County, 1977-79; advisor Western Interstate Commn. on Higher Edn., Portland, 1971, Concentrated Employment and Tng., St. Helens, 1977, County Planning Bd., Columbia County, Oreg., 1977-80, City Planning Bd., St. Helens, 1978, Youth Employment Coun., St. Helens, 1978, Task Force on Disadvantaged Youth, St. Helens, 1980; counselor Career Mgmt. Specialists Internat.; instr. Portland C.C. Mem. ACA, Oreg. Counseling Assn., Internat. Assn. Pers. in Employment Svc. (Outstanding Achievement award 1975), Nat. Employment Counselors Assn. Democrat. Home: 1111 St Helens St Saint Helens OR 97051

VAN HORSSEN, ARDEN DARRELL, retired manufacturing executive; b. Cottonwood County, Minn., June 14, 1917; s. Charles and Mabel Rosina (Schaffer) Van H.; m. Margaret Eleanor Ellingsen, Nov. 29, 1941; children: Charles A., Ronald D. Student, U. Minn., 1935-38, DePauw U., 1938-40, Lawson Sch. Engring., Chgo., 1941. Trainer Nunn Mfg., Evanston, Ill., 1941-42; dept. supr. Mpls. Moline Mfg., Mpls., 1942-44; plant mgr. Indsl. Tool & Die, Mpls., 1944-47; part owner Tonka Toys, Minnetonka, Minn., 1947-49; plant supt. Woodmark Industries, St. Louis Park, Minn., 1949-51; owner Nu-Line Industries, Mpls., 1951-65; pres. Cinch Nu-Line divsn. United Carr, Mpls., 1965-67; cons. mgmt. and engring., 1968-73. Patentee in field. Home: 10015 Royal Oak Rd Apt 150 Sun City AZ 85351

VAN HORSSEN, CHARLES ARDEN, manufacturing executive; b. Mpls., June 28, 1944; s. Arden Darrel and Margaret E. (Ellingsen) V H.; m. Mary Katherine Van Kempen, Sept. 11, 1967 (div. 1975); children: Lisa, Jackie; m. Mary Ann Pashuta, Aug. 11, 1983; children: Vanessa, Garrett. BSEE, U. Minn., 1966. Design engr. Sperry Univac, Mpls., 1966-68; sr. project engr. Sperry Univac, Salt Lake City, 1975-80; systems engr. EMR Computer, Mpls., 1968-75; pres. A&B Industries Inc., Phoenix, 1980—. Patentee in field. Mem. Ariz. Tooling and Machining Assn. (bd. dirs., v.p. 1987-89, pres. 1989-91). Republican. Episcopalian. Office: A&B Industries Inc 9233 N 12th Ave Phoenix AZ 85021-3018

VAN HOUTEN, ADRIAN JAMES, auditor, controller; b. Artesia, Calif., May 15, 1948; s. John Andrew and Fem Ida (Dekker) Van H.; m. Valerie Diane Weidert, Mar. 20, 1976; children: Alison, Chad, Janna, Lindsey. AA, Modesto Jr. Coll., 1969; BA, Calif. State U., Turlock, 1972, MBA, 1982. Acct. auditor San Joaquin County, Stockton, Calif., 1974-83, div. chief, 1983-87, asst. auditor contr., 1987-90, auditor-contr., 1990—. Bd. dirs. United Way, Stockton, 1988-94, treas., 1993-94. Republican. Christian Reformed. Office: San Joaquin County 24 S Hunter St Rm 103 Stockton CA 95202-3225

VANIDES, ALEXIA, marketing consulting executive; b. L.A., Mar. 11, 1951; d. Thanos Demitrious and Constance (Trigonis) V. BA in English cum laude, Calif. State U., Long Beach, 1973; MBA, Pepperdine U., 1980. Vice pres., creative dir. Thanos Vanides & Co., West L.A., 1973-75, Chgo., 1975-77; mktg. comm. mgr. Tubular group Hydril Co., L.A., 1977; mktg. comm. specialist Hughes Helicopters, L.A., 1977-79; advt. mgr. Electron Device group Varian Assos., Palo Alto, Calif., 1979-85; pres. Vanides Mktg. Comm., Belmont, Calif., 1985—; part-time prof. Coll. Notre Dame, Belmont, Calif. Recipient 1st Pl. award Nat. Agrl. Advertisers Assn., 1978. Mem. Bus./Profl. Advt. Assn. (sec. bd. dirs. 1978-79, 2d v.p. bd. dirs. L.A. chpt. 1979-80; sec. bd. dirs. No. Calif. chpt. 1980-81, v.p. programs 1981-82, dir. 1982-83, chpt. pres. 1983-84), Am. Mktg. Assn., Am. Helicopter Assn. Writer award-winning ads for indsl. cos., 1977-79, 80-81. Home and Office: 1506 Winding Way Belmont CA 94002-1944

VAN KARNES, KATHLEEN WALKER, realtor; b. Providence, June 17, 1944; d. Robert Edward Walker and Mary Antoinette (Brouillard) Holl; m. Eugene Sergei Tolegian, Dec. 3, 1966 (div. 1987); children: Elisabeth Ani, Aram Eugene; m. Karl Robert Van Karnes, Mar. 31, 1990. Student, East L.A. Coll., 1970-71, Pan Am. Coll., 1962-63. Sec. 3M Co., Los Angeles, 1963-68; office adminstr. Imperial Clin. Lab., Inc., Lynwood, Calif., 1978-80, v.p., chief fin. officer, 1980-87; realtor Bliss Keeler, Inc., San Marino, Calif., 1986-90, Fred Sands Realtors, San Marino, 1990—. Co-chmn. program Los Angeles chpt. Foothill affiliate Am. Diabetes Assn., 1987. Mem. White Ho. Confederacy Mus. (founding), Nat. Assn. Realtors, Calif. Assn. Realtors, Braille Aux. Pasadena (pres. 1991-93). Republican. Presbyterian. Office: Fred Sands Realtors 2101 Huntington Dr San Marino CA 91108-2643

VAN KILSDONK, CECELIA ANN, retired nursing administrator, volunteer; b. Beaver Dam, Wis., Sept. 28, 1930; d. Walter and Pauline (Yagodzinski) Klapinski; (div.); children: Dan, Greg, Paula, Steve. Diploma, Mercy Hosp. Sch. Nursing, 1951; BS, Coll. of St. Frances, Peoria, Ill., 1983. Clin. nurse Divsn. of Ambulatory Care, Phoenix, 1965-70, clin. charge nurse, 1970-82, regional nursing supr., 1982-87, nurse adminstr., 1987-92; mgr. nursing svc. Maricopa County Health Dept. Svcs., Phoenix. Mem. Continuing Edn. review Com., 1989—; vol. Primary Care Ctr.; disaster nurse ARC. Mem. ANA, Ariz. Nurse's Assn., Nat. League for Nursing, Phi Theta Kappa. Home: 2502 E Minnezona Ave Phoenix AZ 85016-4927

VAN KIRK, JOHN ELLSWORTH, cardiologist; b. Dayton, Ohio, Jan. 13, 1942; s. Herman Corwin and Dorothy Louise (Shafer) Van K.; m. Patricia L. Davis, June 19, 1966 (div. Dec. 1982); 1 child, Linnea Gray. BA cum laude, DePauw U., Greencastle, Ind., 1963; BS, Northwestern U., Chgo., 1964, MD with distinction, 1967. Diplomate Am. Bd. Internal Medicine, Am. Bd. Internal Medicine subspecialty in cardiovascular disease; cert. Nat. Bd. Med. Examiners. Intern Evanston (Ill.) Hosp., 1967-68; staff assoc. Nat. Inst. of Allergy & Infectious Diseases., Bethesda, Md., 1968-70; resident internal medicine U. Mich. Med. Ctr., Ann Arbor, 1970-72, fellow in cardiology, 1972-74, instr. internal medicine, 1973-74; staff cardiologist Mills Meml. Hosp., San Mateo, Calif., 1974—, vice-chief medicine, 1977-78, dir. critical care, 1978—, critical care utilizaton rev., 1988—, dir. pacemaker clinic, 1976—; mem. active staff Peninsula Hosp. and Med. Ctr.; mem. courtesy staff Sequoia Hosp. Contbr. rsch. articles to profl. jours. Recipient 1st prize in landscaping Residential Estates, State of Calif., 1977, Physician's Recognition award AMA, 1968, 72, 75, 77, 80, 82, 85, 87, 89, 93. Fellow Am. Coll. Cardiology; mem. AMA, Calif. Med. Assn., San Mateo County Med. Soc., Am. Heart Assn., San Mateo County Heart Assn. (bd. dirs. 1975-78, bay area rsch. com. 1975-76, edn. com. 1975-77, pres. elect 1976-77, pres. 1977-79), Alpha Omega Alpha. Republican. United Brethren. Office: Unified Med Clinics of Peninsula 50 S San Mateo Dr Ste 270 San Mateo CA 94401-3859

VAN LEER, ROBERT ROY, editor, publisher; b. St. Louis, Aug. 28, 1927; m. Betty Lee Templeton; four daughters. BA, Washington U., 1950; BJ, U. Mo., 1951. Retail advt. sales The Courier and Press, Evansville, Ind., 1951-52; with The Daily Gazette, Sterling, Ill., 1952-55, The Humboldt Times and Standard, Eureka, Calif., 1955-56; editor, pub. Curry County Reporter, Gold Beach, Oreg., 1956—; dir., sec. Nat. Newspaper Found., Washington, 1987-88; mem. work fellowship com., study mission com. Nat. Newspaper Assn. Campaign mgr. Congressman Charles O. Proter, 1960; precinct committeeman Curry County Dem. Precinct 12, 1966-74; active Curry County Fair Bd., 1966-75, Curry County Mounted Sheriff's Posse, 1966-78, City of Golf Beach Promotion Com., 1982-86, Gov.'s Task Force on Land Use, 1982; mem. adv. bd. Coos Bay U.S. Dept. Land. Mgmt. Dist. 19, Siskiyou Nat. Forest-Western Oreg. Health Sys. Agy., Facilities Rev. Com.; past pres., elected dir. Curry Health Dist., 1983-93. Wuth USN, 1945-46, USNR, 1946-49. Ruhl fellow U. Oreg., 1986-87. Mem. Oreg. Newspaper Pubs. Assn. (bd. dirs., freedom of info. com., ins. com., govt. affairs com., nominating com., hall of fame com., tech. com., membership task force, Wendell Webb project), Gold Beach Rotary Club, Gold Beach and Brookings Elks Lodges, Gold Beach Masonic Lodge, Nature Conservancy, Friends of Cape Blanco, Agness Cmty. Coun., Curry Anadromous, NRA. Democrat. Home: Box 766 510 N Ellensburg Gold Beach OR 97444

VAN LEEUWEN, KATO, psychiatrist; b. Rotterdam, The Netherlands, June 23, 1917; came to U.S., 1940; d. Henry Bernard and Evalina (van Zwanenberg) van L.; m. Sydney Lawrence Pomer, Mar. 6, 1948; children: Judith, Karen, Lisa. Student, U. Leiden Med. Sch., 1935-40; MD, Johns Hopkins U., 1943. Intern in pediat. Strong Meml. Hosp., Rochester, N.Y., 1943-44; intern in psychiatry Bellevue Hosp., N.Y.C., 1944; staff pediat. Permanente Hosp., Vancouver, Wash., 1944-45, Oakland, Calif., 1945; resident psychiatrist Mt. Zion Hosp., San Francisco, 1946-48; mental health program organizer Oakland City Health Dept., 1948-49; tng. and supervising analyst in adult and child analysis So. Calif. Psychoanalytic Inst., L.A., 1953—, former chair child and adolescent analysis sect.; staff UCLA Med. Sch., 1958—. Former bd. dirs. Little Village Nursery Sch., San Fernando Valley Child Guidance Clinic. Grantee NIMH, 1947-48, 1960s. Home: 430 S Bundy Dr Los Angeles CA 90049-4032 Office: 10444 Santa Monica Blvd Los Angeles CA 90025-5057

VANLEEUWEN, LIZ SUSAN (ELIZABETH VANLEEUWEN), state legislator, farmer; b. Lakeview, Oreg., Nov. 5, 1925; d. Charles Arthur and Mary Delphia (Hartzog) Nelson; B.S., Oreg. State U., 1947; m. George VanLeeuwen, June 15, 1947; children—Charles, Mary, James, Timothy. Secondary sch. and adult tchr., 1947-70; news reporter, feature writer The Times, Brownsville, Oreg., 1949—; co-mgr. VanLeeuwen Farm, Halsey, Oreg.; mem. Oreg. Ho. of Reps., 1981—; mem. Western States Forestry Legis. Task Force, Pacific Northwest Econ. Region; weekly radio commentator, 1973-81. Mem. E.R. Jackman Found., PTA, sch. adv. com.; precinct committeewoman; founder, apptd. spl. advs. Linn County Ct.; mem. regional strategies bd. Linn County Commn. on Children and Families. Recipient Outstanding Service award Oreg. Farm Bur., 1975, Oreg. Farm Family of Yr. award, 1983; Chevron Agrl. Spokesman of Yr. award, 1975. Mem. Oreg. Women for Agr. (pres.), Oreg. Women for Timber, Linn-Benton Women for Agr. (pres.), Linn County Farm Bur., Am. Legion (aux.), Linn County Econ. Devel. Com., Grange, Am. Agri-Women. Republican. Office: H-291 Capitol Bldg Salem OR 97310

VAN LEUNEN, ALICE LOUISE, artist, educator; b. Evansville, Ind., Feb. 7, 1943; d. Robert Arthur and Margaret (Frank) V. B.A., Smith Coll., 1965, student Ind. U., 1965-67. Exhbn. asst. Contemporary Crafts Assn., Portland, Oreg., 1978-79; lectr. dept. art and architecture Portland State U., 1980-91; mem. collaborative design team Nexus, Portland, 1976—. Prin. works include Weavings Oreg. Dept. Revenue Bldg., Salem, Oreg., 1981, Mt. Hood Community Hosp., Gresham, Oreg., 1985, Kodiak (Alaska) Auditorium, 1986, P.T. Mulia Bank Tower, Djakarta, 1993, (sculpture) Nat. High Magnetic Field Lab., FSU, (with Walter Gordinier) Tallahassee and PCC Library, Portland, 1995; represented in collections at Atlantic County Office Bldg., N.J., Seattle City Light Portable Works, Gen. Motors Corp., N.Y.C., City Hall, Lake Oswego, Oreg.; represented in 2 yr. traveling solo exhibit through Northwest, U. Oreg. Mus. Art Visual Arts Resources 1977-79. Juror, Met. Arts Commn., Portland, 1982, Oreg. Arts Commn., Salem, 1983. Recipient Individual Artist fellow Oreg. Arts Commn., 1994. Mem. Artists Equity (bd. dirs. Oreg. chpt. 1977-78). Scientologist. Office: PO Box 408 Lake Oswego OR 97034-0408

VAN LOUCKS, MARK LOUIS, venture capitalist, business advisor; b. Tampa, Fla., June 19, 1946; s. Charles Perry and Lenn (Bragg) Van L.; m. Eva Marianne Forsell, June 10, 1986; children: Brandon, Charlie. BA in Comm. and Pub. Policy, U. Calif., Berkeley, 1969. Sr. v.p. mktg., programming and corp. devel. United Cable TV Corp., Denver, Colo., 1970-81, advisor, 1983-89; sr. v.p., office of chmn. Rockefeller Ctr. TV Corp., N.Y.C., 1981-83; advisor United Artists Commun. Corp., Englewood, 1989-91; investor, business advisor in pvt. practice Englewood, 1983—; founder, prin. owner Glory Hole Saloon & Gaming Hall, Central City, Colo., 1990—, Harrah's Casino, Black Hawk, Colo., 1990—; chmn., CEO Bask Internat., Englewood, 1990—; bd. dirs. Wild West Devel. Corp., Denver; sr. v.p., bd. dirs. GSI Cable TV Assocs., Inc., San Francisco, 1984-90; guest lectr. on cable TV bus., 1985-91; cons. Telecommunications, Inc., Denver, 1989-93. Producer HBO spl. Green Chili Showdown, 1985; producer TV spl. 3 Days for Earth, 1987; producer, commd. artist nuclear war armament pieces; contbr. articles to profl. jours. Chmn. Cops in Crisis, Denver, 1990—; bd. dirs. The NOAH Found., Denver, 1976—; founding dir. Project for Responsible Advt., Denver, 1991-92; chmn. mayor's mktg. adv. bd., Central City, Colo. Named hon. capt. Denver Police Dept., 1991—, fin. advisor L. Rose Co., 1995—. Mem. Casino Owners Assn. (founding dir. 1989—), Colo. Gaming Assn. (dir. 1990—), recipient S'nnaeel Evol award, 1995), Glenmoor Country Club, The Village Club. Republican. Jewish. Office: MLVL Inc 333 W Hampden Ave Ste 1005 Englewood CO 80110-2340

VAN MAERSSEN, OTTO L., aerospace engineer, consulting firm executive; b. Amsterdam, The Netherlands, Mar. 2, 1919; came to U.S., 1946; s. Adolph L. and Maria Wilhelmina (Edelmann) Van M.; m. Hortensia Maria Velasquez, Jan. 7, 1956; children: Maria, Patricia, Veronica, Otto, Robert. BS in Chem. Engring., U. Mo., Rolla, 1949. Registered profl. engr., Tex., Mo. Petroleum engr. Mobil Oil, Caracas, Venezuela, 1949-51; sr. reservoir engr. Gulf Oil, Ft. Worth and San Tome, Venezuela, 1952-59; acting dept. mgr. Sedco of Argentina, Comodoro Rivadavia, 1960-61; export planning engr. LTV Aerospace and Def., Dallas, 1962-69, R & D adminstr. ground transp. div., 1970-74, engr. specialist new bus. programs, 1975-80; mgr. cost and estimating San Franciso and Alaska, 1981-84; owner OLVM Cons. Engrs., Walnut Creek, Calif., 1984—; cons. LTV Aerospace and Def., Dallas, 1984—. Served with Brit. Army. Intelligence, 1945, Germany. Mem. Soc. Petroleum Engrs. (sr.), Toastmasters (sec.-tres. Dallas chpt. 1963-64), Pennywise Club (treas. Dallas chpt. 1964-67). Democrat. Roman Catholic. Home and Office: OLVM Cons Engrs 1649 Arbutus Dr Walnut Creek CA 94595-1705

VAN MECHELEN, RODERICK DANIEL, publisher; b. Seattle, June 9, 1953; s. Daniel L. and Bernice E. (Benson) Van M. AA, Highline C.C., 1978; BA, U. Wash., 1981. Contract adminstr. Microsoft Corp., Redmond, Wash., 1988-91; pub. New Chivalry Press, Bellevue, Wash., 1993—; mag. pub. The Eqalitarian, 1994, The Backlash!, 1993—. Author: What Every Man Should Know About Feminist Issues, 1992, What Every Man Should Know About Sexual Harassment, 1993. Co-founder Movement to Establish Real Gender Equality, Seattle, 1993; founding mem. Native Ams. at Microsoft, Redmond, 1991. Office: New Chivalry Press/ Shameless Men Press PO Box 70524 Bellevue WA 98007-0524

VAN MOLS, BRIAN, publishing executive; b. L.A., July 1, 1931; s. Pierre Matthias and Frieda Caryll (MacArthur) M.; m. Barbara Jane Rose, Oct. 1, 1953 (dec. 1968); children—Cynthia Lee, Matthew Howard, Brian; m. Nancy Joan Martell, June 11, 1977; children—Thomas Bentley, Cynthia Bentley, Kristi. A.B. in English, Miami U., Oxford, Ohio, 1953. Media supr. McCann-Erickson Inc., 1955-58; salesman Kelly Smith Co., 1959; with sales Million Market Newspaper Inc., 1959-63; sales mgr. Autoproducts Mag., 1964; sr. salesman True Mag., 1965-68, Look Mag., 1969-70; regional advt. dir. Petersen Pub. Co., Los Angeles, 1971-74; pub. Motor Trend, 1982-84; nat. automotive mktg. mgr. Playboy Enterprises, Inc., N.Y.C., 1984-85, nat. sales mgr., 1985—; western advt. dir. Playboy mag., 1985-86; assoc. pub., advt. dir. Cycle World CBS, Inc., Newport Beach, Calif., 1974-81, pub., 1981; v.p., advt. dir. Four Wheeler Mag., Canoga Pk., Calif., 1986-88; v.p., dir. advt. western div. Gen. Media, Inc., 1988-91; v.p., dir. new bus. devel. Paisano Pub., Inc., Agoura Hills, Calif., 1991-92; dir. mktg. Crown Publs., 1993-94; exec. v.p. Voice Mktg. Inc., Thousand Oaks, Calif., 1994, DMR The Reis Co., Thousand Oaks, Calif., 1995—. Served with U.S. Army, 1953-55. Mem. Los Angeles Advt. Club, Adcraft Club Detroit, Advt. Sportsmen of N.Y. Republican. Episcopalian. Home and Office: 1453 Valecroft Ave Thousand Oaks CA 91361

VANNATTER, MICHAEL STEVEN, art director; b. Pomona, Calif., May 13, 1954; s. Robert Lee and Avis May (Whitlock) V.; m. Betty Ann Woolley, Sept. 19, 1981; 1 child, Lauren Avis. Student, DeAnza C.C., Cupertino, Calif., 1976-77, Art Ctr. Coll. of Design, Pasadena, Calif., 1978-79. Art dir. Foote, Cone & Belding Advt., L.A., 1979-80; assoc. art dir. Orange Coast Mag., Irvine, Calif., 1980-81; assoc. art dir., registered rep. Newport Beach, Calif., 1981-84; art dir. Calif. Bus., L.A., 1985-86, Petersen's Fishing, L.A., 1988-94, Petersen' Bowhunting, L.A., 1988-94, Guns and Ammo mag., L.A., 1994—. Office: Petersen Pub Co Inc 6420 Wilshire Blvd Los Angeles CA 90048-5502

VAN NESS, JOHN RALPH, university foundation administrator; b. Columbus, Ohio, Oct. 22, 1939; s. Ralph Taylor and Norma Gertrude (Thorp) Van N.; children: Heather Thorpe, Hilary Clark. BA, The Colo. Coll., Colo. Springs, 1965; MA, U. Pa., 1969, PhD, 1979. Instr. West Chester (Pa.) U., 1969-70, Knox Coll., Galesburg, Ill., 1970-73, Fort Lewis Coll., Durango, Colo., 1974-76; cons. fund raising pvt. practice Phila., 1977-79; capital campaign con. John F. Rich Co., Phila., 1979-84; v.p. for coll. relations, adjunct prof. Anthropology Ursinus Coll., Collegeville, Pa., 1984-89; exec. v.p., prof. Moore Coll. Art and Design, Phila., 1989-90, pres., 1990-92; pres. Mus. N.Mex. Found., Santa Fe, 1992-93, N.Mex. State U. Found., 1995—; bd. dirs. Ctr. for Land Grant Studies, Santa Fe, 1978-94; editl. bd. Jour. of the West, Manhattan, Kans., 1980-88. Co-author: Cañones: Values, Crisis and Survival in a Northern New Mexico Village, 1981; author: Hispanos in Northern New Mexico, 1991; co-editor: Spanish and Mexican Land Grants in New Mexico and Colorado, 1980, Land, Water and Culture, 1987; editor: New Mexico Land Grant Series, vols. 1-5, 1983, 84, 87, 89, 94. Recipient Teaching Fellowship U. Pa.; grantee Ford Found., Nat. Sci. Found. Mem. Am. Anthrop. Assn., Am. Assn. Museums, Coun. for Advance and Support Edn., Nat. Soc. Fund Raising Execs., Pi Gamma Mu. Democrat.

VAN NESS, LOTTYE GRAY, author, genealogist; b. Clarksville, Tenn., Nov. 14, 1925; d. Charles Robert and Willie (Murphy) Gray; m. Robert Parmelee Van Ness, Jan. 3, 1947; 1 child, Marc Robert. Student, Austin Peay State U., 1946, Murray State U., 1963. Civilian sec. U.S. Army, 1944-48; mgr. Associated Underwriters, Inc., Louisville, 1948-51; exec. sec. to the pricing dir. Reynolds Metals Co., Louisville, 1951-53; instr. classes on genealogy, Paducah, Ky., 1962-64, Louisville, 1970. Author: The Van Ness Heritage and Allied Genealogies, 1960, The Cookie Connection, 13th rev. edition, 1992; newspaper poetry columnist, 1947-48. Cookbook judge various orgns., Louisville, 1986. Named to hon. Ky. Col., 1978. Mem. Nat. Soc. So. Dames of Am., Northfield Garden Club (v.p. 1976-77, various chairmanships), Filson Hist. Club, United Daus. of Confederacy, Beta Sigma Phi. Republican. Episcopalian. Home: 6644 Foxdale Cir Colorado Springs CO 80919-1778

VANNIX, C(ECIL) ROBERT, programmer, systems analyst; b. Glendale, Calif., June 14, 1953; s. Cecil H. Jr. and Gloria Jenny (Zappia) V.; married, 1980; 1 child, Robert Jeremy. AS in Plant Mgmt., BS in Indsl. Arts, Loma Linda U., 1977; AS in Info. Systems, Ventura City Coll., 1985. Instr. indsl. arts Duarte (Calif.) High Sch., 1977-79, Oxnard (Calif.) High Sch., 1979-81; computer cons. Litton Data Comand Systems, Agoura, Calif., 1976-81, sr. engr. instr., 1981-85; computer cons. McLaughlin Research Corp., Camarillo, Calif., 1976-77, sr. program analyst, 1985-88; sr. program analyst Computer Software Analysts, Camarillo, Calif., 1988-90; sr. systems analyst, mgr. S/W systems devel. V.C. Systems, 1990—. Recipient Spl. Achievement award One Way Singers, Glendale, 1975. Mem. Apple PI Computer Club, Litton Computer Club (pres. 1975-76), West Valley Xbase Users Group.

Republican. Adventist. Home and Office: 407 Appletree Ave Camarillo CA 93012-5125

VAN NOY, TERRY WILLARD, insurance company executive; b. Alhambra, Calif., Aug. 31, 1947; s. Barney Willard and Cora Ellen (Simms) V.; m. Betsy Helen Pothen, Dec. 27, 1968; children: Bryan, Mark. BS in Bus. Mgmt., Calif. State Poly. U., 1970; MBA, Pepperdine U., 1991. CLU. Group sales rep. Mutual of Omaha, Atlanta, 1970-74, dist. mgr., 1974-77; regional mgr. Mutual of Omaha, Dallas, 1977-82; nat. sales mgr. Mutual of Omaha, Omaha, Neb., 1982-83; v.p. group mktg. Mutual of Omaha, Omaha, 1983-87; div. dir. Mutual of Omaha, Orange, Calif., 1987—. Presenter in field. Vice chmn. Morning Star Luth. Ch., Omaha, 1987; mem. adv. bd. Chapman U. Sch. Bus.; mem. exc. com. ABL Orgn. Mem. Am. Soc. CLU, Orange County Employee Benefit Coun., We. Pension and Benefits Conf. Republican. Home: 381 S Smokeridge Ter Anaheim CA 92807-3711 Office: Mut of Omaha PO Box 11018 Orange CA 92668-8118

VAN ORDEN, HARRIS OLSON, retired chemistry educator, researcher; b. Smithfield, Utah, Oct. 6, 1917; s. Harris Olonzo Van Orden and Ingra (Pearson) Olson; m. Eleanor Young, Oct. 16, 1948; 1 child, Peter Lee. BS, Utah State U., 1938; MS, Wash. State U., 1942; PhD, MIT, 1951; postgrad., U. Utah, 1953-54, U. Calif., Berkeley, 1962-63. Asst. prof. chemistry Utah State U., Logan, 1946-47, assoc. prof., 1950-59, acting dept. head, 1958-59, prof., 1959-83, emeritus prof., 1983—; dir. Summer Inst. for High Sch. Tchrs. Chemistry, Logan, 1957, 58. Co-author textbooks on gen. chemistry, 1960-73; also articles. Maj. AUS, 1942-46, PTO. Univ. fellow MIT, 1947-49, fellow NIH U. Utah, 1953. Fellow AAAS, Am. Chem. Soc., Sigma Xi, Phi Lambda Upsilon. Republican. Mem. LDS Ch. Home: 281 E 8th N Logan UT 84321-3329

VAN PELT, MEREDITH ALDEN, general and vascular surgeon; b. Lake Preston, S.D., June 22, 1923; s. Herman Earl and Pearl Glenn (Williams) Van P.; m. Margaret E. Springs, Nov. 9, 1947 (div. Feb. 1969); children: Gregory Alden, Sharman Louise Van Pelt Halloran, Susan Lee Van Pelt Lockett, Stephanie Lane Van Pelt Stemmark; m. Sheila Mae Kimball, July 19, 1969; 1 child, Stephen. BA, U. Iowa, 1943, MD, 1946; postgrad., U. Vienna, 1948. Diplomate Am. Bd. Surgery. Intern Good Samaritan Hosp., Cin., 1946-47; resident in surgery Swedish Med. Ctr., Seattle, 1949-53; asst. chief surgery VA Hosp., Fresno, Calif., 1953-55; pvt. practice gen. and vascular surgery San Rafael, Calif., 1955-92; surgeon, cons. San Quentin State Prison, San Rafael, 1989—; chief of surgery San Rafael Gen. Hosp., 1962-65, Terra Linda Valley Hosp., San Rafael, 1962-68; chief of gen. surgery Ross (Calif.) Gen. Hosp., 1987-88, Marin Gen. Hosp., San Rafael, 1964-65; commr. Calif. State Bd. Med. Examiners 1992—; instr. vascular surg. clinic U. Calif., San Francisco, 1957-69; civilian cons. in surgery U.S. Air Force, Hamilton Field, Calif., 1960-65. Capt. M.C., U.S. Army, 1947-49. Fellow ACS, Am. Coll. Angiology, Internat. Coll. Angiology; mem. AMA, Calif. Med. Assn., Marin Med. Soc., San Francisco Yacht Club (life). Episcopalian. Home: 14 Eucalyptus Rd Belvedere CA 94920-2436

VAN REMMEN, ROGER, management consultant; b. Los Angeles, Sept. 30, 1950; s. Thomas J. and Elizabeth (Vincent) V.; B.S. in Bus., U. So. Calif., 1972. Account mgr. BBDO, Los Angeles, 1972-78; account mgr. Dailey & Assocs. Advt., L.A., 1978—, v.p., mgmt. supr., 1980-84, sr. v.p., 1985-90; dir. Aux. Aids Inc., Richstone Family Ctr; dir. mktg. communications, Teradata, 1990-91, ptnr. Brown, Bernardy, Van Remmen Exec. Search, L.A., 1991—. Chmn. adv. bd. El Segundo (Calif.) First Nat. Bank; bd. dirs. Advt. Emergency Relief Fund., Richstone Family Ctr. Mem. Univ. So. Calif. Alumni Assn., Advt. Club of Los Angeles. Roman Catholic. Office: Brown Bernardy Van Remmen 12100 Wilshire Blvd Ste 40M Los Angeles CA 90025-7120

VAN RIPER, KENNETH ALAN, astrophysicist and researcher; b. New Brunswick, N.J., Feb. 7, 1949; s. Raymond Walsh Van Riper and Beulah Mae Higgins Scheer. AB, Cornell U., 1970; PhD, U. Pa., 1976. Rsch. assoc. U. Chgo., 1976, U. Ill., Urbana, 1978-81; mem. tech. staff Los Alamos (N.Mex.) Nat. Lab., 1981—. Editor: Isolated Pulsars, 1993; contbr. articles to profl. jours. Mem. Am. Astron. Soc., Am. Phys. Soc., Internat. Astron. Union, New Eng. Sonett Club. Office: Los Alamos Nat Lab X-6 MSB226 PO Box 1663 # 226 Los Alamos NM 87544-0600

VAN SEVENTER, A., accountant; b. Amsterdam, The Netherlands, Sept. 25, 1913; came to U.S., 1940; s. A. and Maria (van Dijk) van S.; m. Ruth E. Smith, Nov. 5, 1949; children: Antony, Ronald E. AB, U. Amsterdam, 1934; MBA, Stanford U., 1949; PhD, U. Mich., 1966. Acct. C.A. Gall and Co., N.Y.C., 1940-41, Credit Suisse, N.Y.C., 1941, Haskins and Sells, San Francisco, 1949, Philip A. Hershey, San Francisco, 1949, O.M. Beaver CPA, Anchorage, 1950, Beaver and van Seventer CPAs, Anchorage, 1950-62; pvt. practice acctg. Anchorage and Palo Alto, Calif., 1957-62; instr. acctg. Cleary (Mich.) Coll., 1963; instr., lectr. acctg. U. Mich., Ann Arbor, 1963-66; asst. and assoc. prof. acctg. San Jose (Calif.) State U., 1966-76; prof. acctg. San Francisco State U., 1976-84; pres. Bay Books Publishing, Palo Alto, Calif., 1976—; vis. lectr. taxation Ea. Mich. U., Ypsilanti, 1963; instr. acctg. Anchorage Community Coll., 1954-62. Author: The History of Accountancy - translation, 1976, 2nd edit., 1986, Intermediate Accounting Problems, 1973, 3rd edit. 1981; editor: Accounting Bibliography, 1986; contbr. articles to profl. jours., chpt. to book. Sec. Alaska Bd. Pub. Accountancy, 1953-57. With USAAF, 1942-45. Lybrand fellow, 1965; decorated French Medal of Honor in Bronze. Mem. AICPA, Am. Acctg. Assn., Acad. Acctg. Historians (Hourglass award 1977), Calif. Soc. CPAs, Peninsula Symphony, Phi Beta Kappa (pres. No. Calif. chpt. 1980-81), Rotary (Anchorage chpt.).

VAN SICKLE, FREDERICK L., federal judge; b. 1943; m. Jane Bloomquist. BS, U. Wis., 1965; JD, U. Wash., 1968. Ptnr. Clark & Van Sickle, 1970-75; prosecuting atty. Douglas County, Waterville, Wash., 1971-75; judge State of Wash. Superior Ct., Grant and Douglas counties, 1975-79, Chelan and Douglas Counties, 1979-91; judge U.S. Dist. Ct. (ea. dist.) Wash., Spokane, 1991—; co-chair rural ct. com. Nat. Conf. State Trial Judges, 1987-91. 1st lt. U.S. Army, 1968-70. Mem. ABA (nat. conf. state trial judges jud. adminstrn.), Am. Adjudicature Soc., Wash. State Bar Assn., Masons (pres. badger mountain lodge 1982-84), Scottish Rite, Spokane Rotary. Office: US Dist Cts US Courthouse 920 W Riverside Ave Rm 914 Spokane WA 99201-1008

VAN STEKELENBURG, MARK, food service executive. Pres., CEO G.V.A., The Netherlands; pres., CEO, also bd. dirs. Rykoff-Sexton Inc., L.A. Office: Rykoff-Sexton Inc 761 Terminal St Los Angeles CA 90021-1112*

VAN VELZER, VERNA JEAN, retired research librarian; b. State College, Pa., Jan. 22, 1929; d. Harry Leland and Golda Lillian (Cline) Van V. BS in Library Sci., U. Ill., 1950; MLS, Syracuse U., 1957. Head librarian Orton Library, Ohio State U., Columbus, 1952-54; serials assoc. Syracuse (N.Y.) U. Library, 1954-57; head cataolger SRI Internat., Menlo Park, Calif., 1957-58; head librarian GE Microwave Lab., Palo Alto, Calif., 1958-64, Fairchild Rsch. and Devel. Lab., Palo Alto, 1964-65, Sylvania Intelligence Library, Mountain View, Calif., 1965-66; rsch. librarian ESL Inc. subs. TRW, Sunnyvale, Calif., 1966-92; cons. in field. Vol. Lantos Re-election Campaign, San Mateo, Calif., 1972—, Wildlife Rescue, Palo Alto, 1980—; mem. Barron Park Assn., Palo Alto, 1975—; mem. Calif. Polit. Action Com. for Animals, San Francisco, 1986—. Recipient Commemorative medal of Honor, Am. Biographical Inst., 1946, Paul Revere Cup, Santa Clara Camellia Soc., 1968, Internat. Cultural Diploma of Honor, Am. Biographical Inst., 1988. Mem. Spl. Librs. Assn., IEEE, AIAA, Calif. Holistic Vet. Assn., Internat. Primate Protection League, People for Ethical Treatment of Animals, Assn. Old Crows, In Def. of Animals, Primarily Primates, Sierra Club, World Wildlife Club, Greenpeace. Home: 4048 Laguna Way Palo Alto CA 94306-3122

VAN VOORHIES, WAYNE ALAN, biologist; b. Plainfield, N.J., Apr. 4, 1956; s. Robert Leon and Dolores E. (Schiffel) Van V.; m. Laurie Abbott, Nov. 1992. BA, Prescott Coll., 1978; MS, U. Ariz., 1988, PhD, 1993. Rsch. specialist U. Ill., Antarctica, 1978-81; instr. Outward Bound, Portland, Oreg., 1981-84; river guide Expeditions, Grand Canyon, Ariz., 1984; grad. teaching asst. U. Ariz., Tucson, 1985—; foreign fishers observer Nat. Marine Fisheries, Alaska, 1989. Contbr. article on sci. discovery to Nature mag. Recipient Teagle scholarship Exxon Found., 1986, grad. fellowship grant U. Ariz., 1991, NSF Tng. grant, 1992. Home: 1125 N Olsen Ave Tucson AZ 85719-4718 Office: U Ariz Dept Molecular/ Cellular Biology Dept Ecology & Evol Biology Tucson AZ 85721

VAN WAGNER, ELLEN, lawyer, educator; b. Chgo., Dec. 10, 1942; d. Paul David and Eleanor (Sullivan) Van W.; m. Burton Neal Genda, Mar. 27, 1964 (div.); children: Kevin Paul, Kelly Elan. BA, U. Ariz., 1964; MA, Calif. State U., L.A., 1971; JD, U. La Verne, 1984. Bar: Calif. 1984, U.S. Dist. Ct. (cen. dist.) Calif. 1985, U.S. Ct. Appeals (9th cir.) 1985. Tchr., adminstr. Baldwin Park (Calif.) Sch. Dist., 1965-81; ptnr. Rose, Klein & Marias, Pomona, Calif., 1985-94; prof. U. La Verne (Calif.) Coll. Law, 1987—. Writer, asst. editor U. La Verne Law Rev., 1981-83, editor-in-chief, 1983-84. Chmn. youth activities commn. City of Baldwin Park, 1971-81. Recipient Humanitarian and Svc. awards L.A. Human Rels. Commn., 1976, 77. Mem. Calif. Bar Assn., L.A. County Bar Assn., Ea. County Bar Assn., Phi Delta Theta. Home: PO Box 351 Blue Jay CA 92317-0351 Office: Law Offices Ellen Van Wagner 12490 Central Ave Ste 104 Chino CA 91710-2664

VAN WHY, REBECCA RIVERA, guidance counselor; b. Casa Blanca, N.Mex., Sept. 14, 1932; d. Charles and Doris (Thompson) Rivera; m. Raymond Richard Van Why, Aug. 27, 1955; children: Raymond R., Ronald R., Randall R. BS, U. N.Mex., 1959. Tchr. Bur. of Indian Affairs, Albuquerque, 1960-62, guidance counselor, 1969-94, tchr., supr., 1973-74, acting dir. student life, 1987, ret., 1994; head tchr. Laguna (N.Mex.) Headstart OEO, 1967-69, acting dir., 1969. Appt. N.Mex. Youth Conservation Corps Commn., 1992-95. Recipient Cert. of Recognition, Sec. of Interior, 1975, Cert. of Appreciation, State of N.Mex., 1986, N.Mex. Commn. on the Status of Women, 1993; named honoree Internat. Women's Day, U. N.Mex., 1987. Republican. Home: 14417 Central Ave NW Albuquerque NM 87121-7756

VAN WINKLE, WESLEY ANDREW, lawyer, educator; b. Kansas City, Mo., Sept. 22, 1952; s. Willard and Cleone Verlee (O'Dell) Van W.; m. Ruth Kay Shelby, Apr. 10, 1984. B, U. Nebr., 1972; JD, San Francisco Law Sch., 1987. Bar: Calif. 1987, U.S. Dist. Ct. (no. dist.) Calif. 1987, U.S. Supreme Ct. 1994. Atty. Bagetelos & Fadem, San Francisco, 1987-91; pvt. practice Berkeley, Calif., 1991—; prof. law San Francisco Law Sch., 1990—. Editor (legal newspaper/rev.) Res Ipsa Loquitur, 1986. Mem. Calif. Attys. for Criminal Justice, Calif. Appellate Def. Counsel (v.p.), San Francisco Law Sch. Alumni Assn., Delta Theta Phi. Democrat. Office: PO Box 5216 Berkeley CA 94705-0216

VANYO, JAMES PATRICK, engineering educator; b. Wheeling, W.Va., Jan. 29, 1928; s. John Andrew and Thelma Rose (Barrett) V. BSME, W.Va. U., 1952; JD, Chase Law Coll., 1959; MA in Astronomy, UCLA, 1966, PhD in Engring., 1969. Bar: Ohio 1959, U.S. Patent Office 1959, Calif. 1961. Asst. traffic supr. AT&T, N.Y.C., 1952-53; engr./designer Van Industries, Dayton, Ohio, 1953-59; engr. mgr. Remanco, Inc., Santa Monica, Calif., 1959-61; proposal/contracts staff Marquardt Corp., Van Nuys, Calif., 1961-63; researcher UCLA, 1963-69; long range planning specialist Litton Industries, Woodland Hills, Calif., 1969-70; prof. U. Calif., Santa Barbara, 1970—; reviewer grants NSAS, NSF, USN, others, 1972—; cons. Ford Aerospace, 1980—, ERNO Raumfahrttechnik, Bremen, 1991—. Author: Rotating Fluids in Engineering and Science, 1993; editorial bd. Jour. Environ. Systems, 1972—; reviewer articles sci. and engring. jours., 1972—, books tech. book pubs., 1972—; contbr. articles to profl. jours. Mem. Harbor Commn., Santa Barbara, 1980-84; mem. exec. com. Sierra Club, Santa Barbara, 1988-90. Doctoral fellow NASA, 1966-69; grantee NASA, NSF, and others, 1975—. Mem. Calif. Bar Assn., Ohio Bar Assn., Am. Geophysical Union, Am. Phys. Soc., Tau Beta Pi, Sigma Xi. Office: U Calif Mech & Environ Engring Santa Barbara CA 93106

VANZI, MAX BRUNO, editor; b. Ferrara, Italy, Sept. 24, 1934; s. Lambert S. Vanzi and Helen (Larimer) Hughes; m. Lynn A. D'Costa; children: Linda, Victor. A.B. in Journalism, U. Calif., Berkeley, 1959. Reporter Oroville (Calif.) Mercury, 1959-60; reporter UPI, Seattle, 1960-62, San Francisco, 1962-64, Japan, India, Pakistan, 1964-67; editor, correspondent UPI, Hong Kong, 1967-68; mgr. Southeast Asia UPI, Singapore, 1969-75; editor for Tex. UPI, Dallas, 1975-77; editor for Calif. UPI, San Francisco, 1977-81, gen. editor for Pacific div., 1981-84; editor L.A. Times, Washington Post News Service, L.A., 1984-86; asst. met. editor L.A. Times, 1986—; news editor Los Angeles Times, Sacramento Bureau, Sacramento, 1990—. Co-author: Revolution in the Philippines: The United States in a Hall of Cracked Mirrors, 1984. Served with USAF, 1953-55. Am. Press Inst. fellow Reston, Va., 1980; recipient cert. excellence Overseas Press Club. Am., N.Y.C., 1983. Office: LA Times Times Mirror Sq Los Angeles CA 90053-3816

VARADARAJAN, KALATHOOR, educator, researcher; b. Bezwada, India, Apr. 13, 1935; parents Kalathoor Soundara and Parimalavalli (Parimalavalli) Rajan; m. Pattu Varadarajan, June 22, 1961; children: Suchitra, Srinivasan. BA with honors, Loyola Coll., Madras, India, 1955; PhD, Columbia U., 1960. Rsch. fellow Tata Inst. Fundamental Rsch., Bombay, 1960-61, fellow, 1961-67; vis. assoc. prof. U. Ill., Urbana, 1967-69; reader Tata Inst. Fundamental Rsch., Bombay, 1969-71; assoc. prof. U. Calgary, Alta., Can., 1971-73, prof., 1973—; nat. bd. vis. prof. Nat. Bd. Higher Math, India, 1986, 91; vis. prof. Univ. Sydney, Australia, 1984. Author: The Finiteness Obstruction of C.T.C. Wall, 1989; contbr. over 76 articles to profl. jours. Home: 5944 Dalridge Hill NW, Calgary, AB Canada T3A1L9 Office: U Calgary, Dept Math 2500 Univ Dr NW, Calgary, AB Canada T2N1N4

VARALLO, FRANCIS VINCENT, security executive, consultant; b. Chgo., June 28, 1935; s. Frank vincent and Winifred Eileen (Durkin) V.; m. Merrilyn Susan Hire, June 26, 1970; children: Valerie, Sean, Cara. Bs in Humanities, Loyola U., Chgo., 1953-58. From second lt. to col. U.S. Army, 1958-74, attache, 1974-75, plans & policy intelligence officer, def. intelligence agy., 1975-78, installation commdr., 1978-79, duty dir. for intelligence, def. intelligence agy., 1979-81; sr. intelligence officer U.S. Forces, Japan, 1981-84; dir. intelligence and security, def. nuclear agy. U.S. Army, 1985-88; regional security mgr. Unisys Corp., Salt Lake City, 1988-90; pres. Unicorn Assocs., Las Vegas, Nev., 1990—. Col. U.S. Army, 1958-88. Mem. Am. Soc. Indsl. Security, Am. Mgmt. Assn., Nat. Assn. of Chiefs of Police, Assn. of Former Intelligence Officers, Rotary Internat., K. of C., Am. Legion, Retired Officers Assn. Roman Catholic. Home: 2900 S Valley View Blvd Las Vegas NV 89102-5922

VARGA, STEVEN CARL, reinsurance company official; b. Columbus, Ohio, Jan. 19, 1952; s. Stephen Thomas and Eva Jeney V.; BA in Psychology and Philosophy magna cum laude, Carthage Coll., 1977, MSA with honors Cen. Mich. U., 1986; m. Michelle L. Auld, Nov. 17, 1973; children: Zachary Steven, Joshua Lewis. Svc. mgr. Chem-Lawn Corp., Columbus, 1972-75; respiratory therapist St. Catherine's Hosp., Kenosha, Wis., 1975-77; policy analyst Nationwide Ins. Cos., Columbus, 1978-79, asst. mgr. Corp. Tng. Ctr., 1979-86; dir. ednl. tng. Sullivan Payne Co., Seattle, 1986-88, asst. v.p. human resource devel., 1989-93; v.p. Reinsurance Solutions, Inc., Seattle, 1994—. Mem. civic action program com., 1979-86, Nat. Mental Health Assn., 1972-79; mem. occupational adv. coun. Bellevue Community Coll., 1989—; v.p. Kenosha County chpt., 1975-77; mem. Franklin County (Ohio) Mental Health Assn., 1978-86. Rhodes scholar, 1976-77. Mem. Am. Soc. Tng. and Devel., Soc. Broadcast Engrs., Ins. Inst. Am. (contbg. author Principles of Reinsurance, vol. I and II, nat. advisory com. assoc. in reinsurance program), Brokers and Reinsurers Markets Assn. (edn. and tng. co-chair), Am. Psychol. Assn., Am. Mgmt. Assn., Soc. of Ins. Trainers and Educators (chmn. regional area planning com.), Carthage Coll. Alumni Assn., Phi Beta Kappa, Psi Chi. Home: 15586 Sandy Hook Rd NE Poulsbo WA 98370-7823 Office: Sedgwick Payne Co 1501 4th Ave Seattle WA 98101-1662

VARGAS, AL GARCIA, building contractor; b. Fresno, Calif., Apr. 21, 1943; s. Aurelio Villegas and Anita (Garcia) V.; m. Luci Guerrero Cruz, Sept. 22, 1968; children: Sylvia, Al Jr., George. AA, Fresno City Coll., 1974; BS in Bus. Adminstrn., Calif. State U., Fresno, 1977. Acctg. clerk Anderson/Clayton, Fresno, 1968-70; constrn. salesman Wilson Constrn., Fresno, 1974-76; bldg. contractor Vargas Homes, Fresno, 1981-82; mktg. exec. Econ. Opportunity Commns. Fresno County, 1983-90; bldg. contractor Sequoia Homes, Fresno, 1990—. Recipient Ambassador award Calif.-Nev. Weatherization Bd., Sacramento, 1985, Superior Performance award, Fresno County Econs. Opportunity Commns. Weatherization Project, 1985. Republican. Mem. Assemby of God Ch. Home: 6643 Latonia PO Box 751 Laton CA 93242-0751 Office: Vargas & Assocs 1900 Mariposa Mall Ste 100 Fresno CA 93721-2525

VARGO, GEORGE JAMES, JR., health physicist; b. Pitts., July 3, 1956; s. George James and Lois Irene (Sammer) V.; m. Mary Elizabeth Malesky, Aug. 26, 1978 (div. 1993). BS, Duquesne U., 1978; MS, Ga. Inst. Tech., 1988; PhD, Columbia Pacific U., 1989. Diplomate Soc. Radiol. Protection, Am. Bd. Health Physics (comprehensive and power reactor splty.), Nat. Registry Radiation Protection Technologists; cert. hazart control mgmt., hazardous materials mgr. Sr. health physicist Radiation Svc. Orgn., Laurel, Md., 1978-79; instr. tng. N.Y. Power Authority, Lycoming, 1979-80, shift tech. advisor, 1980-8l, radiol. tng. supr., 198l-84; lead radiol. specialist N.Y. Power Authority, White Plains, 1984-85; radiol. engring. gen. supr. N.Y. Power Authority, Lycoming, 1985-89; radiol. and environ. svcs. mgr. N.Y. Power Authority, Lycoming, 1989-91; staff scientist Battelle-Pacific N.W. labs., Richland, Wash., 1991—; adj. asst. prof. nuclear engring. and engring. physics Rensselaer Poly. Inst., 1990-94; adjuct assoc. prof. nuclear engring. and engring. Physics Rensselaer Poly Tech. Inst., 1994—. Editorial bd. Health Physics jour., 1993—, software editor, 1993—; author conf. papers; inventor directional radiation probe. Mem. ASTM (chair subcom. E10.04 radiation protection methodology 1993—), Health Physics Soc. (admissions com. 1989-92, manpower and profl. edn. com. 1992-93, continuing edn. com. 1993), Am. Nuclear Soc., Am. Indsl. Hygiene Assn., Soc. Radiol. Protection (U.K.), N.Y. Acad. Scis., Am. Bd. Health Physics (power reactor splty panel of examiners 1987-91, panel chair 1991, bd. dirs. 1993-95), Can. Radiation Protection Assn. Home: PO Box 338 Richland WA 99352-0338 Office: Battelle-Pacific NW Labs Health Protection Dept K3-56 PO Box 999 # 56 Richland WA 99352-0999

VARMUS, HAROLD ELIOT, government health institutes administrator, educator; b. Oceanside, N.Y., Dec. 18, 1939; s. Frank and Beatrice (Barasch) V.; m. Constance Louise Casey, Oct. 25, 1969; children: Jacob Carey, Christopher Isaac. AB, Amherst Coll., 1961, DSc (hon.), 1984; MA, Literature, Harvard U., 1962; MD, Columbia U. Med. Sch., 1966. Lic. physician, Calif. Intern, resident Presbyterian Hosp., N.Y.C ., 1966-68; clin. assoc. NIH, Bethesda, Md., 1968-70; lectr. dept. microbiology U. Calif.-San Francisco, 1970-72; asst. prof., depts. microbiology and immunology, biochemistry and biophysics U. Calif., San Francisco, 1972-74; assoc. prof. U. Calif., San Franisco, 1974-79; prof. U. Calif., San Francisco, 1979-83, Am. Cancer Soc. research prof., 1984-93; dir. NIH, Bethesda, Md., 1993—; chmn. bd. on biology NRC. Editor: Molecular Biology of Tumor Viruses, 1982, 85; Readings in Tumor Virology, 1983; assoc. editor Genes and Development Jour., Cell Jour.; mem. editorial bd. Cancer Surveys. Named Calif. Acad. Sci. Scientist of Yr., 1982; co-recipient Lasker Found. award, 1982, Passano Found. award, 1983, Armand Hammer Cancer prize, 1984, GM Alfred Sloan award 1984, Shubitz Cancer prize, 1985, Nobel Prize in Physiology or Medicine, 1989. Mem. AAAS, NAS, Inst. Medicine of NAS, Am. Soc. Virology, Am. Soc. Microbiology, Am. Acad. Arts and Scis. Democrat. Office: NIH Bldg 1 Rm 126 1 Center Dr MSC 0148 Bethesda MD 20892-0148*

VARNEY, PETER JUSTIN, international geology consultant; b. San Diego, Oct. 26, 1942; s. Newell Foster Varney and Mary Lillian (Norris) Dennis; m. Sara Carol Yaple, Feb. 28, 1967 (div. 1980); children: Darcy Gwen, Jonathan Glenn; m. Patricia Gail Evans, Apr. 1, 1983. BA, U. Colo., 1966; MS, U. Utah, 1972. Cert. profl. geologist, Am. Inst. Profl. Geologists. Exploration mgr. Wise Oil Co., Denver, 1975-78; chief geologist Impel Energy Corp., Denver, 1978-81; v.p. exploration J.M. Resources, Inc., Denver, 1981-84; sr. geologist Tex. Gas Exploration Co., Denver, 1984-86; exec. v.p. TerraSciences, Denver, 1988-90; ind. cons. petroleum and computer geology Denver, 1986-88, 90—; instr. geology Denver Free U., 1975-76, Colo. Women's Coll., Denver, 1982. Contbg. editor Petro Sys. World, 1993—; contbr. articles on computer geology to sci. publs. Pres. Denver Concert Band, Inc., 1979-81; bd. dirs. Littleton (Colo.) Chamber Orch., 1990-93, Great West Rocky Mountain Brass Band, Silverton, Colo., 1989—. 1st lt. U.S. Army, 1967-69. Named Man of Yr., Mile High Desk and Derrick Club, Denver, 1982. Mem. Am. Assn. Petroleum Geologists (computer applications com. 1990—), Computer Oriented Geol. Soc., Rocky Mountain Assn. Geologists (editor Mountain Geologist 1986, treas. 1992, 2d v.p. 1995). Home: 5903 S Fairfield St Littleton CO 80120-2821

VARO, MARTON-GEZA, sculptor; b. Szekelyudvarhely, Hungary, Mar. 15, 1943; came to U.S., 1989; s. Gyorgy and Viola (Tomori) V.; 1 child, Kata; m. Ilona Magdolna Kalmar, Sept. 25, 1979; children: Marton, Ilona. Diploma in Fine Arts, Ion Andreescu U., Cluj, Romania, 1966. Sculptor in limestone and marble. Works include sculptures at Conv. Ctr. Budapest, 1984, Breaking Free, Brea, Calif., 1990, Peace Meml., Palm Desert, Calif., 1992, Dallas Plaza of the Americas, 1992, marble sculpture at Volos, Greece, 1988. Recipient award Studio of Young Artists, Hungary, 1976, Munkacsy prize Ministry of Culture, Hungary, 1984; Derkovits grantee Ministry of Culture, 1972-75; Fulbright scholar, 1989-91. Home: 2 Charity Dr Irvine CA 92715

VASILEV, STEVEN ANATOL, gynecologic oncologist, educator; b. San Francisco, July 17, 1954; s. Anatol and Katherina (Welbitzky) V.; m. Kathryn Joanne Shaw, Jan. 13, 1985; children: Alexander, Andrei. BS in Biol. Scis., U. So. Calif., 1979, BA in Slavic Langs. and Lits., 1979, MD, 1984. Diplomate Am. Bd. Ob.-Gyn. and Gynecologic Oncology. Intern/resident L.A. County USC Med. Ctr.; fellow in gynecologic oncology U. So. Calif., L.A., 1988-90; staff surgeon City of Hope Nat. Med. Ctr., Duarte, Calif., 1990—; asst. prof. in residence U. Calif., Irvine, 1991—; dir. dept. gynecology City of Hope Nat. Med. Ctr., 1992—. Contbr. articles and abstracts to profl. jours. and chpts. to books. Chmn. Calif. State Cervical Adv. Coalition Com., 1992; chmn. pub. edn. com. Am. Cancer Soc., Coastal Cities Unit, Calif., 1977-84. Recipient Outstanding Achievement award Am. Cancer Soc., 1980. Fellow Am. Coll. Ob.-Gyn., Am. Coll. Surgeons; mem. Am. Soc. Clin. Oncologists, Soc. Gynecologic Oncologists, AMA, Calif. Med. Assn., Soc. Critical Care Medicine, Sigma Xi, Alpha Omega Alpha. Republican. Russian Orthodox. Office: City of Hope Nat Med Ctr 1500 Duarte Rd Duarte CA 91010-3012

VASSALLI, SHORTY See COLLINGS, CELESTE LOUISE

VASUDEVAN, RAMASWAMI, engineering consultant; b. Trichi, Tamil Nad, India, Nov. 28, 1947; came to U.S. 1970; s. Rajagopal and Jembakalakshmi; m. Padmini Vasudevan, Mar. 20, 1980 (div. 1992); m. Suryaprabha, June 11, 1993. BE, Madras U., India, 1970; MS, UCLA, 1972. Registered profl. engr., Calif.; cert. plant engr., Calif. Project engr. Anco Engrs., Culver City, Calif., 1971-77; mgr. Wyle Labs., Norco, Calif., 1977-78, EDAC, Palo Alto, Calif., 1978-82; project mgr. Los Alamos (N.Mex.) Tech. Assocs., 1982-85; assoc. EQE Inc., Irvine, Calif., 1985-87; pres. Sidhi Cons., Inc., Santa Ana, Calif., 1987—. Contbr. articles to profl. jours. Mem. ASME, IEEE (stds. com. 1982-84), EERI, NFPA, EPRI-EQAG, Am. Inst. Plant Engrs. Republican. Office: Sidhi Cons Inc 4642 E Chapman Ave # 210 Orange CA 92669-4111

VATH, RAYMOND EUGENE, psychiatrist, educator; b. Butte, Mont., Aug. 2, 1931; s. Gustave Henry and Clara Wilhelmina (Meyers) V.; m. Joanne Vath, June 7, 1952; children: Connie, Christy, Brian. BS, Coll. Great Falls, 1952; MD, U. Wash., 1965. Diplomate Nat. Bd. Med. Examiners; lic. physician, lic. surgeon, Wash. Meteorologist USAF, 1952-61; intern Madigan Gen. Hosp., Tacoma, 1965-66; lectr. family counseling Seattle Pacific U., 1969-80; prof. counseling Seattle br. Fuller Theo. Sem., 1971-74; rsch. asst. dept. psychiatry U. Wash., Seattle, 1962-65, resident in psychiatry, 1966-69, clin. instr. psychiatry and preventive medicine, 1965-82, clin. asst. prof. psychiatry, 1982—; cons. King County Pub. Health Nurses, 1969-72, MEDEX/U. Wash. and Wash. State Med. Assn., 1969-72, Cath. Children's Svcs., 1969-79, Teen Challenge Drug Program, 1970-80, Youth With a Mission, 1974-85, Neighbors Who Care program area ch., 1974-87; condr. seminars Marrying for Life, 1980, 81; active Student Rsch. Soc., Sch. Medicine U. Wash. Author: Counseling Those with Eating Disorders, 1986, (with D. O'Neill) Marrying for Life, 1982; contbr. chpt. to: Eating Disorders: Nutritional Therapy in the Recovery Process, 1992; contbr. articles to profl. publs.; guest appearances various radio and TV programs, including Seattle

Today, 1981, Regis Philbin Show, NBC, 1982, others. Chmn. bd. dirs. Mercy Corps, Internat., 1981—, N.W. Found. for Eating Disorders, 1981-85. Capt. USAF, 1952-61, capt. M.C. U.S. Army, 1965-66. Mem. AMA, Wash. State Med. Soc., Am. Psychiat. Assn., Wash. State Psychiat. Assn., King County Med. Soc., Kappa Pi Lambda. Home: 5009 134th Pl NE Bellevue WA 98005-1019 Office: 2661 Bel Red Rd Ste 195 Bellevue WA 98008-2200

VATTER, HAROLD GOODHUE, economics educator; b. Glen Rock, N.J., Dec. 18, 1910; s. George C. and Della Goodhue V.; children: Marguerita, Theresa, Marc. B.A., U. Wis.-Madison, 1936; M.A., Columbia U., 1938; Ph.D., U. Calif.-Berkeley, 1950. Assoc. prof. econs. Oreg. State U., Corvallis, 1948-56, U. Mass., Amherst, 1956-58; assoc. prof. Carleton Coll., Northfield, Minn., 1958-64; prof. econs. Portland State U., Oreg., 1965-79, prof. econs. emeritus, 1980—. Author: U.S. Economy in the 1950s, 1960, Drive to Industrial Maturity, 1975, U.S. Economy in World War II, 1985, (with John Walker) The Inevitability of Government Growth, 1990. Lilly fellow, U. Chgo., 1964. Mem. Am. Econ. Assn., Econ. History Assn., Assn. Evolutionary Econs. Home: 3041 NE 25th Ave Portland OR 97212-3462 Office: Portland State U PO Box 751 Portland OR 97207-0751

VAUGHAN, MARK BASS, naval officer; b. Norfolk, Va., Oct. 9, 1958; s. Edgar III and Patricia (Bass) V.; m. Donna Ruth Hallberg; children: Anna, Nathan, Rachel. BS in Aerospace Engrng., U.S. Naval Acad., 1980. Commd. ensign USN, 1980, advanced through grades to lt. comdr.; divsn. officer Naval Air Test Ctr., Patuxent River, Md., 1980; flight instr. Tng. Squadron 3, Milton, Fla., 1981-83; leadership instr. Naval Tech. Tng. Ctr., San Francisco, 1983-86; ops. officer Naval Air Facility, Washington, 1986-87; maintenance officer Support Squadron 48, Washington, 1987-89; ops. officer Support Squadron 59, Dallas, 1989-92; tng. officer Logistics Support Wing, Dallas, 1992-93; officer in charge Logistics Support Squadron 57, San Diego, 1993—; master tng. specialist USN, San Francisco, 1986, transport aircraft comdr., 1987-94; airline transport pilot FAA, Dallas, 1992. Asst. coach Tierra Santa Little League, San Diego, 1994. Mem. SAR, Jamestowne Soc., Soc. Mayflower Descendants, Huguenot Soc. Presbyterian. Home: 12321 Calle Albara Apt 8 El Cajon CA 92019-4836 Office: VR 57 PO Box 357108 NAS NI San Diego CA 92135

VAUGHAN, ROBERT OREN, lawyer; b. Elko, Nev., Mar. 19, 1925; m. Barbara Schreiner, 1950; children: Meg, Brad. BA, U. Nev., Reno, 1950; JD cum laude, U. Denver, 1952. Bar: Nev. 1952, U.S. Dist. Nev. 1955, U.S. Supreme Ct. 1961, U.S. Ct. Appeals (9th cir.) 1973. Ptnr. Vaughan & Hull, Ltd. and predecessor firms, Elko, 1953—; mem. Nev. State Assembly, 1955-58, minority floor leader, 1958; city atty. City of Wells, Nev., 1957-75; dep. city atty. City of Elko, 1962-82; gen. counsel Wells Rural Electric Co., 1958—, Mt. Wheeler Power, Inc., 1963-92, Nev. Rural Electric Assn., 1974; mem. Nev. Jud. Selection Commn., 1981-89; ptnr. AAA Self Storage, Western Enterprises; owner Vaughan Ranch, Ruby Valley, Nev., 1958-95. Bd. editors U. Denver Law Rev., 1952. Trustee Elko County Libr. Bd., 1959-63; bd. dirs. Elko Knife and Fork Club, 1962; dir. Heart Fund, 1957-85; active youth sports; trustee No. Nev. C.C. Found., 1981—, mem. exec. com., planned giving com., 1991—, chmn. spkrs. bur., 1989-90, chmn. major gifts com., 1991—; mem. devel. com. No. Nev. C.C., 1992—; deacon, ruling elder 1st Presbyn. Ch. of Elko. 1st lt. USAF, 1943-47; with Nev. N.A.G., 1948-50. Mem. ABA, Nev. State Bar Assn. (adminstrv. com. 1956-66, adminstrv. com. 1961-66, probate and property practice com., unauthorized practice of law com., fee dispute com.), Elko County Bar Assn. (pres. 1963-64), Elko C. of C. (past bd. dirs., treas.), Rotary (pres. 1964-65), Masons, Royal and Select Masters, Royal Arch, K.T., Shriners, Ea. Star. Republican. Home: 1065 Dotta Dr Elko NV 89801-2707 Office: Vaughan & Hull Ltd 530 Idaho St PO Box 1420 Elko NV 89803

VAUGHAN, SANDRA JEAN, real estate asset manager; b. Fullerton, Calif., July 27, 1961; d. Lewis Albert and Mary Katherine (Fisher) Wallace; m. Jim Alan Vaughan, Nov. 8, 1986. BA in Bus. Adminstrn., Calif. State U., Fullerton, 1984. Facilities mgr. Builders Emporium, Irvine, Calif., 1984-85; asst. property mgr. Santa Fe Pacific Realty, Brea, Calif., 1985-86; project acct. Santa Fe Pacific Realty, Brea, 1986-88; project coord. Catellus Devel., Anaheim, Calif., 1988-90; asset mgr. Catellus Devel., Anaheim, 1990—; active mem. Inst. Real Estate Mgmt., Orange County, Calif., 1993—. Player, coach Am. Girls Softball Assn., 1970-80; mem. Young Adult Ministry Adv. Com., 1981-84; vol. Orange County Juvenile Detention Ctr., Orange, 1982; spkr., presenter Cath. Engaged Encounter, Orange County, 1989—, conv. coord., Irvine, 1994, unit coord., 1994—. Roman Catholic. Home: 1615 Juniper Ave Pomona CA 91766 Office: Catellus Devel Corp 1065 N Pacificenter Dr Ste 200 Anaheim CA 92806-2131

VAUGHAN, SUZANNE LOWE, professional speaker, consultant; b. Casper, Wyo., May 19, 1947; d. Charles Stanley and Reva (Lowe) Rippon; m. Douglas Charles Vaughan, June 12, 1967; children: Jeffrey, Richard, Rebecca, Valerie. BS in Edn., Utah State U., Logan, 1970. Cert. tchr., Colo. Clk.-typist IRS, Salt Lake City, 1965-66, U.S. Forest Svc., Logan, 1967-68; lectr. Weight Watchers, Inc., Denver, 1971-80; substitute tchr. Aurora (Colo.) Pub. Schs., 1981-86; instr. Platte Coll., Aurora, 1986-88; speaker-trainer Vaughan & Assocs., Aurora, 1988-92; cons. H.B. Zachry, Stearns-Rogers, Denver, 1991; contract instr. Arapahoe Community Coll., Denver, 1986-91, Nat. Vets. Tng. Inst., Denver, 1989-90, Area Health Edn. Ctrs., Greeley and Pueblo, Colo., 1989-92. Featured in news and mag. articles. Pres., Middle Sch. Parent Orgn., Aurora, 1984, Ch. Women's Orgn., Aurora, 1989-91. Mem. Nat. Spkrs. Assn. (v.p. Colo. chpt. 1988-89, Chpt. Mem. of Yr. 1990, liaison 1992-93, 94-96, Colo. chpt. pres.-elect 1990-91, Colo. chpt. pres. 1991-92). Republican. Mormon. Home and Office: 16566 E Girard Ave Aurora CO 80013-2005

VAUGHN, JAMES ENGLISH, JR., neurobiologist; b. Kansas City, Mo., Sept. 17, 1939; s. James English and Sue Katherine (Vaughn); m. Christine Singleton, June 18, 1961; children: Stephanie, Stacey. B.A., Westminster Coll., 1961; Ph.D., UCLA, 1965. Postdoctoral rsch. fellow in brain rsch. U. Edinburgh (Scotland), 1965-66; asst. prof. Boston U. Sch. Medicine, 1966-70; head sect. of molecular neuromorphology Beckman Rsch. Inst. of City of Hope, Duarte, Calif., 1970—, pres. rsch. staff, 1986, chmn. div. neuroscience, 1987—. Fellow Neuroscience Rsch. Program, 1969; Rsch. grantee NIH, 1969—, NSF, 1983-87. Mem. AAAS, Am. Soc. Cell Biology, Am. Assn. Anatomists, Soc. for Neuroscience (chmn. short course 1977), Internat. Brain Rsch. Orgn., N.Y. Acad. Scis., Sigma Xi. Achievements include original immunoelectron microscopic demonstration of a neurotransmiter synthesizing enzyme in brain synaptic terminals; original proposal and evidence of synaptotropic modulation of dendritic development in the central nervous system; discovered that genetically-associated changes in neuronal migration correlate with altered patterns of synaptic connectivity in the brain; discovered that all neurons of a major brain relay station use GABA as their neurotransmitter; discovered previously unknown cholinergic neurons in the brain and spinal cord; discovered unique migratory patterns of preganglionic sympathetic neurons in developing spinal cord; first immunocytochemical evidence of a role gamma aminobutyric acid (GABA) neurons in focal epilepsy; first demonstration of lesion-induced synaptic plasticity of GABA neurons; contbr. articles to profl. jours.; assoc. editor Jour. Neurocytology, 1978-86; mem. editorial bd. Synapse, 1986—; reviewer for Jour. Comparative Neurology, 1974—, Brain Research, 1976—. Office: Beckman Research Inst 1450 Duarte Rd Duarte CA 91010-3011

VAUX, DORA LOUISE, sperm bank official, consultant; b. White Pine, Mont., Aug. 8, 1922; d. Martin Tinus and Edna Ruth (Pyatt) Palmlund; m. Robert Glenn Vaux, Oct. 25, 1941; children: Jacqueline, Cheryl, Richard, Jeanette. Grad. high sch., Bothell, Wash. Photographer Busco-Nestor Studios, San Diego, 1961-68; owner, mgr. Vaux Floors & Interiors, San Diego, 1968-82; cons., mgr. Repository for Germinal Choice, Escondido, Calif., 1983-91; adminstr. Found. for the Continuity of Mankind, Spokane, 1991— Republican. Home: 605 S Liberty Lake Rd Liberty Lake WA 99019-9739 Office: Found Continuity of Mankind 1209 W 1st Ave Spokane WA 99204-0601

VAWTER, DONALD, retired personnel management consultant; b. Spokane, Wash., May 19, 1920; s. Edgar F. and Lina M. Vawter; m. Margaret Schroeder, May 5, 1950; children: Charlotte, Sara. Student in Polit. Sci., Wash. State U., 1946-49. Supr. employer svcs. Wash. State Employment Svc., Seattle, 1950-58; employment mgr. Sundstrand Data Control, Redmond, Wash., 1958-72; profl. recruiter DBA Bellevue Employment Agy., Bellevue, Wash., 1972-73; pers. mgr., workers compensation adminstr. Crown Zellerbach, Omak, Wash., 1973-82; bd. dirs. Pacific N.W. Pers. Mgmt. Assn. 1974-78; apptd. Gov's. Svcs. Coun., 1977-83. Served with USCGR, 1942-46, 50-53, comdr. Res. ret., 1968. Mem. Am. Soc. Pers. Adminstrn. (accredited pers. mgr.). Home: PO Box 296 Tonasket WA 98855-0296

VAZSONYI, ANDREW, computer and management scientist; b. Budapest, Hungary, Nov. 4, 1916; came to U.S.,, naturalized, 1945; s. Maximilian and Hermine V.; m. Laura Thalia Saparoff, Jan. 16, 1943; 1 dau., Beatrice Ann. Ph.D., U. Budapest, 1938; S.M., Harvard U., 1942. Teaching fellow Harvard U., 1942-44; engr. Elliott Co., Jeanette, Pa., 1944-45; supr. N. Am. Aviation, Los Angeles, 1945-46; div. head Naval Ordnance Test Sta., Pasadena, Calif., 1947-51, Hughes Aircraft Co., Culver City, Calif., 1951-54; div. mgr. TRW, Los Angeles, 1954-58; partner Alderson Assos., Phila., 1959-60; div. dir. TRW, 1960-61; sci. adv. Rockwell Internat., Los Angeles, 1961-69; prof. computer sci. U. So. Calif., 1969-72; prof. computer and mgmt. sci. U. Rochester, 1972-79; Emil C.E. Jurica prof. computer mgmt. St. Mary's U., San Antonio, 1979-88; prof. psychology Sonoma State U., Rohnert Park, Calif., 1988-89; prof. mgmt. U. San Francisco, 1989—. Author: Scientific Programming in Business and Industry, 1958, Problem Solving by Digital Computers with PL/I Programming, 1970, Finite Mathematics, 1977, Introduction to Electronic Data Processing, 1977, 3d edit., 1980, Quantitative Methods of Management, 1982, Raise Your Productivity with an IBM PC, 1985; former asso. editor: Interfaces; contbr. numerous articles to profl. jours. Fellow Am. Inst. Decision Scis., AAAS; mem. Inst. Mgmt. Scis. (chmn. 1953-54), Ops. Research Soc. Am., Assn. Computing Machinery. Office: U San Francisco San Francisco CA 94117

VEA, HENRY WALTER, radiologist, nuclear medicine specialist; b. Henderson, Nev., May 22, 1953; s. Matthew Johnson and Ethelyne Elvira (Hendrickson) V.; m. Julia Allen Grothaus, June 14, 1980; children: Kathleen Arvilla, Hollister Charles. BS in Nuclear Engrng. cum laude, Rensselaer Poly. Inst., 1975, M in Engring., 1976, BS in Physics, 1976; MD, U. Wash., 1980. Diplomate Am. Bd. Internal Medicine, Am. Bd. Nuclear Medicine, Am. Bd. Radiology. Resident in internal medicine U. Wash., Seattle, 1980-83, resident in nuclear medicine, 1983-84, chief resident in nuclear medicine, 1984-85; resident in diagnostic radiology Oreg. Health Scis. U., Portland, 1985-88; staff radiologist Good Samaritan Hosp./Med. Ctr., Portland, 1988—. Contbr. articles to profl. jours. NSF grad. fellow, 1975-76. Mem. AMA, Soc. Nuclear Medicine, Radiol. Soc. N.Am., Am. Coll. Radiology, Am. Coll. Nuclear Physicians, Oreg. Med. Assn., Tau Beta Pi, Alpha Omega Alpha. Presbyterian. Office: Good Samaritan Hosp Med Ctr 1015 NW 22nd Ave Portland OR 97210-3025

VECCI, RAYMOND JOSEPH, airline executive; b. N.Y.C., Jan. 22, 1943; s. Romeo John and Mary (Fabretti) V.; m. Helen Cecelia Clampett, Sept. 3, 1967; children: Brian John, Damon Jay. BBA, CCNY, 1965; MBA, NYU, 1967. Adminstrv. asst. Internat. Air Transport Assn., N.Y.C., 1961-66; econ. analyst United Airlines, Chgo., 1967-74; asst. v.p. planning and regulatory affairs Alaska Airlines Inc., Seattle, 1975-76, staff v.p. planning and regulatory affairs, 1976-79, staff v.p. planning, 1979, v.p. planning, 1979-85, exec. v.p., chief operating officer, 1986-90, pres., chief exec. officer, 1990—; chmn., dir. Alaska Airlines Inc., 1991—; also chmn., pres., chief exec. officer, dir. Alaska Air Group Inc. Served with U.S. Army, 1968-69, Vietnam. Decorated Bronze Star. Roman Catholic. Office: Alaska Airlines Inc PO Box 68900 19300 Pacific Hwy S Seattle WA 98168-5303*

VEGA, BENJAMIN URBIZO, retired judge; b. La Ceiba, Honduras, Jan. 18, 1916; m. Janie Lou Smith, Oct. 12, 1989; AB, U. So. Calif., 1938, postgrad., 1939-40; LLB, Pacific Coast U. Law, 1941. Bar: Calif. 1947, U.S. Dist. Ct. (so. dist.) Calif. 1947, U.S. Supreme Ct. 1958. Assoc. Anderson, McPharlin & Connors, L.A., 1947-48, Newman & Newman, L.A., 1948-51; dep. dist. atty. County of L.A., 1951-66; judge L.A., County Mcpl. Ct., East L.A. Jud. Dist., 1966-86, retired, 1986; leader faculty seminar Calif. Jud. Coll. at Earl Warren Legal Inst., U. Calif-Berkeley, 1978. Mem. Calif. Gov.'s Adv. Com. on Children and Youth, 1968; del. Commn. of the Califs., 1978; bd. dirs. Los Angeles-Mexico City Sister City Com.; pres. Argentine Cultural Found., 1983. Recipient award for outstanding services from Mayor of L.A., 1973, City of Commerce, City of Montebello, Calif. Assembly, Southwestern Sch. Law, Disting. Pub. Service award Dist. Atty. L.A. Mem. Conf. Calif. Judges, Mcpl. Ct. Judges' Assn. (award for Outstanding Services), Beverly Hills Bar Assn., Navy League, L.A. County, Am. Judicature Soc., World Affairs Council, Pi Sigma Alpha. Home: 101 California Ave Apt 1207 Santa Monica CA 90403-3525

VEGA, JOSE GUADALUPE, psychologist, clinical director; b. San Benito, Tex., June 4, 1953; s. Jose Guadalupe and Bertha (Saenz) V.; m. Beth Susan Brimmer, Aug. 20, 1979 (div. 1986); children: Lilian Anna, Jose Guadalupe III; m. Andrea M. Arnold, Mar. 23, 1988 (div. 1989); m. Alberta L. Valdez, Oct. 5, 1990. BA, Pan. Am. U., Edinburg, Tex., 1975; MA, U. Denver, 1976, PhD, 1979. Lic. psychologist, Colo., 1983, profl. counselor, Tex., 1982; diplomate Am. Bd. Med. Psychotherapists, Am. Bd. Vocat. Neuropsychology, Am. Bd. Profl. Disability Cons.; cert. adminstrn. Halstead-Reitan Neuropsychology test batteries. With Oasis of Chandala, Denver, 1978-79, Maytag-Emrick Clinic, Aurora, Colo., 1979; psychologist Spanish Peaks Mental Health Ctr., Pueblo, Colo., 1980-85; pvt. practice Assocs. for Psychotherapy and Edn., Inc., 1985-86; co-owner Affiliates in Counseling, Psychol. Assessment and Consultation, Inc., Pueblo, 1986-87; psychologist Parkview Psychol. Testing Clinic, Pueblo, 1987-93, Colo. Dept. Corrections, 1994—; pvt. practice, Pueblo, 1993—; mem. state grievance bd. Psychology Augment Panel, 1988-95. Active Colo. Inst. Chicano Mental Health Community Youth Orgn., Boys Club Pueblo. Mem. Am. Psychol. Assn., Nat. Acad. Neuropsychology, Internat. Neuropsychol. Soc., Colo. Neuropsychol. Soc., Am. Assn. for Counseling and Devel., Health and Human Services Com. City of Pueblo, Colo. Psychol. Assn. (bd. mem. non-metro rep. 1995—), Nat. Hispanic Psychol. Assn., Hispanic Neuropsychological Soc., Phi Delta Kappa, Kappa Delta Pi. Democrat. Roman Catholic. Office: 2705 N Elizabeth St Pueblo CO 81003-3643

VEIT, WILLIAM ARTHUR, financial planner; b. Altadena, Calif., July 10, 1947; s. Richard Earl and Sally Nell (Brown) V.; m. Maureen Alice Connors, Sept. 13, 1969; children: Stephen, Shereen. BS, Ariz. State U., 1969. Cert. fin. planner. Assoc. v.p. Prudential-Bache, Phoenix, 1983-88; asst. v.p. Kidder, Peabody & Co., Phoenix, 1988-90; v.p. fin. planner Cushman Ramras Cornelius & Crowe, Scottsdale, Ariz., 1990-91; dir., sr. cons. Anasazi Investment Group Inc., Phoenix, 1991—. Coach Little League, Scottsdale, 1979-83, Pop Warner Football, Scottsdale, 1979-82. Mem. Internat. Bd. Cert. Fin. Planners (Phoenix chpt.). Republican. Roman Catholic. Office: Anasazi Investment Group Inc 11801 N Tatum Blvd Ste 240 Phoenix AZ 85028-1613

VEITH, RICHARD CHARLES, geriatric psychiatrist, educator; b. Seattle, May 23, 1947; s. Michael C. Veith and Barbara E. (Maguire) Seaman; m. Marcella Pascualy, Sept. 9, 1988; children: Ryan, Carly, David. BA, Western Wash. U., 1969; MD, U. Wash., 1973. Diplomate Nat. Bd. Med. Examiners, Am. Bd. Psychiatry and Neurology (mem. examination com. 1989-93), Am. Bd. Geriatric Psychiatry. Intern in internal medicine Sch. Medicine, U. Wash., Seattle, 1973-74, resident in psychiatry, 1974-77; chief psychiat. consultation and liaison sect. psychiat. svc. Seattle VA Med. Ctr., 1977-79, staff rsch. psychiatrist, geriatric rsch., edn. and clin. ctr., 1977-87, dir., 1987—, fellowship dir. geriatric psychiatry fellowship program, 1991—; instr. dept. psychiatry and behavioural scis. Sch. Medicine U. Wash., 1977-80, asst. prof., 1980-83, assoc. prof., 1983-89, prof., 1989—, head divsn. gerontology and geriatric psychiatry, 1991—; active Nat. Inst. on Aging Task Force on Reversible Causes of Dementia, 1978-80; rsch. program specialist in psychiatry dept. medicine and surgery med. rsch. svc. Dept. VA, Washington, 1989-92, mem. rev. com. geriatric psychiatry fellowship program tng. sites, 1990, mem. regional geriatric psychiatry working group region 4, 1990; study sect. reviewer biochem. endocrinology study sect. Nat. Inst. Aging-NIH, Bethesda, Md., 1990; mem. adv. bd. U. Wash. Alzheimer's Disease Rsch. Ctr., 1988—, chair, 1991—; grant investigator in field; presenter in field. Mem. editl. bd. Geriatric Cons., 1984—; ad hoc rev. numerous jours.; contbr. articles to profl. jours. Bd. dirs. Norwest Day Care Ctr., Seattle, 1978-82, pres., 1980;. Fellow Am. Psychiat. Assn. (mem. psychopharmacology subcom. Psychiat. Knowledge and Skills Self-Assessment Program 1983-84); mem. Am. Geriatrics Soc. (mem. editl. bd. Jour. Am. Geriatric Soc. 1989-91, Internat. Jour. Geriatric Psychiatry 1990—), Am. Assm. Geriatric Psychiatry, Gerontol. Soc., Psychiat. Rsch. Soc., Soc. Neurosci., Soc. Biol. Psychiatry. Office: Geriatric Rsch Edn and Clinic Ctr VA Med Ctr 1660 S Columbian Way Seattle WA 98108-1532

VELASQUEZ, THOMAS AQUINAS, English language educator; b. Trinidad, Colo., June 23, 1935; s. Thomas Aquinas and Josephine (Sandoval) V.; m. Ruth Laura Lind, Aug. 14, 1957; children: Laura Lind Velasquez-Murray, Donna Lind Velasquez-Lee. BA, San Francisco State U., 1969, MA, 1970. Hwy. engr.-technician State of Calif. Div. of Hwys., San Francisco, 1954-60, materials engr., surveyor, 1960-68; dir. SB164 program City Coll. San Francisco, 1970-71, prof. English, 1970-91, prof. emeritus, 1992—; staff devel. dir. City Coll. San Francisco, 1986-87; dir. First Stage Reading Co., Daly City, Calif. Author: The Passport - How to Study Program, 1994; (reading program) 1st Stage Reading, 1974-91; editor (monthly mag.) Scootourist, 1964-68; editor: Redwood Church Messenger, 1995. Bd. dirs. Com. for Better Informed Citizens, San Mateo County, Calif., 1974-78; poetry judge Daly City San Mateo County Fair, 1993-95. Mem. Internat. Reading Assn., Internat. Soc. Semantics, Am. Fedn. Tchrs. (exec. v.p. City Coll. San Francisco 1981-83, Bay Area Epson Salts (pres., editor 1988-95). Home: 703 Higate Dr Daly City CA 94015-4215

VELTFORT, THEODORE ERNST, electrical engineer, physicist; b. Cambridge, Mass., Feb. 23, 1915; s. Theodore Ernst and Helen (Gaston) V.; m. Helene Rank, Oct. 27, 1941 (div. Jan. 1952); children: Ruhama Danielle, Susan Marlene; m. Leonore Valeton, Oct. 14, 1954; children: Anna Cornelia, Kevin Daniel. BA in Econ., Columbia U., 1940; MS in Physics, Stanford U., 1947. Registered profl. engr., Calif. Chief devel. engr. Shand and Jurs Co., Berkeley, Calif., 1955-58; sr. project engr. Lynch Comm. Systems, San Francisco, 1958-59; chief electronics engr. Shockley Unit Clevite Corp, Stanford, Calif., 1960-61; sr. cons. engr. Sierra Electronics Corp., Menlo Park, Calif., 1961; prof. physics, dir. dept. solid state physics U. Havana, Cuba, 1962-68; chief engr. Bioelectric Instruments, Inc., Yonkers, N.Y., 1968-70; electronics systems engr. Mt. Sinai Med. Ctr., N.Y.C., 1970-80; cons. engr. Veltek, Oakland, Calif., 1981—; adj. prof., course advisor CCNY, 1971-78. Ambulance driver Cuerpo Sanitario de la Republica Espanola, 1937-38. Sgt. Signal Corps U.S. Army, 1942-45. Mem. IEEE (life), AAAS, Vets. the Abraham Lincoln Brigade (exec. sec. San Francisco chpt. 1983-84, fgn. corres. sec. 1985—), Sigma Xi (assoc.). Home and Office: 6534 Whitney St Oakland CA 94609-1028

VENEMA, JON ROGER, pastor, educator; b. Modesto, Calif., Apr. 11, 1953; s. Roger Edwin and Marilyn Ailene (Johnson) V.; m. Shelley Elizabeth, Mar. 29, 1974; children: Jordan Christopher Wilder, Susanna Lee. AA, Modesto (Calif.) Jr. Coll., 1974; BA magna cum laude, Simpson Coll., 1976; MDiv, Mennonite Brethren Bibl. Sem., 1980; postgrad., Golden Gate Bapt. Theol. Sem., 1990—. Instr. bibl. and religious studies Fresno Pacific Coll., Modesto, 1980-84; sr. pastor 1st Bapt. Ch., So. San Francisco, 1984-94; adj. faculty Fresno Pacific Coll., 1984-87, Simpson Coll., San Francisco, 1987-88; instr. St. James Coll., Pacifica, Calif., 1987-90; adj. prof. Golden Gate Bapt. Theol. Sem., Marin, Calif., 1992, mem. faculty Highland Christian Coll. San Bruno, Calif., 1992-93, We. Conservative Baptist Theol. Sem., 1994—; dir. Sacramento Teaching Site, 1994—. Mem. Soc. Bibl. Lit., Delta Epsilon Chi. Republican. Home: 2228 Canadian Cir Modesto CA 95356-2700 Office: We Conservative Baptist Sem 2924 Becerra Way Sacramento CA 95821-3939

VENKATESH, ALAGIRISWAMI, cardiologist; b. Madras, Tamilnadu, India, July 4, 1946; came to U.S., 1972; s. Alwar Naicker and Hamsa (Alagarsingari) Alagiriswami; m. Nagammal Sampath, July 15, 1970; 1 child, Sujatha. P.U.C., Madras U., 1962. Intern Jewish Hosp. Bklyn., 1972-73, resident, 1973-75; cardiology fellow U. Wis. Hosps., Madison, 1975-77, U. Iowa Hosps., Iowa City, 1977-78; asst. prof. medicine U. Okla., Oklahoma City, 1978-79; pvt. practice cardiology Encino, Calif., 1979—; asst. clin. prof. medicine UCLA, 1980—. Fellow Am. Coll. Cardiology, Coun. on Geriatric Cardiology (founder). Office: 16133 Ventura Blvd Ste 1015 Encino CA 91436-2414

VENNESLAND, BIRGIT, biochemistry educator; b. Kristiansand, Norway, Nov. 17, 1913; came to U.S, 1917; d. Gunnuf Olav and Sigrid Kristine (Brandsborg) V. BS in Biochemistry, U. Chgo., 1934, PhD in Biochemistry, 1938; D.Sc. (hon.), Mt. Holyoke Coll., 1960. Asst. biochemistry U. Chgo., 1938-39; fellow biochemistry Harvard Med. Sch., Boston, 1939-41; instr. biochemistry U. Chgo., 1941-44, asst. prof. biochemistry, 1944-48, assoc. prof. biochemistry, 1948-57, prof. biochemistry, 1957-68; dir. Max-Planck Inst. for Cell Physiology, Berlin, 1968-70; leader Forschungsstelle Vennesland, Berlin, 1970-81; adj. prof. biochemistry and biophysics U. Hawaii, Honolulu, 1986—. Editor: Cyanide in Biology, 1981; contbr. rsch. papers and rev. articles to sci. jours. Study sec. mem. NSF, USPHS, Washington, 1954-63; mem. Wooldridge Com., Washington, 1964. kRecipient Hales award Am. Soc. Plant Physiology, 1950. Fellow AAAS, N.Y. Acad. Scis.; mem. Am. Chem. Soc. (Garvan medal 1964), Am. Soc. Biol. Chemistry, Am. Soc. Plant Physiology. Home: 1206 Mokapu Blvd Kailua HI 96734-1847

VENNUM, WALT, geology educator; b. Seattle, May 10, 1941; s. Francis Lorenzo and Myrle Marie (Paisley) V.; m. Barbara Louise Young, June 9, 1964 (div. Sept. 1990). BA in Geology with honors, U. Mont., 1964; PhD in Geology, Stanford U., 1971. Smoke jumper Bur. Land Mgmt., Fairbanks, Alaska, 1962-66; rsch. asst. Found. for Glacier Rsch., Juneau, Alaska, 1967; geologist U.S. Geol. Survey, Denver and Menlo Park, Calif., 1971-89; teaching asst., acting instr. geology Stanford (Calif.) U., 1967-71; prof. geology Sonoma State U., Rohnert Park, Calif., 1971—; participant 5 expeditions unexplored area in Antarctica, geological mapping Alaskan wilderness area, 1971, 72, 74; igneous petrologist on 2 cruises on deep sea drilling ship The Glomar Challenger, 1974, 76; vis. prof. geology U. Mont., Missoula, 1978; geology lectr., naturalist Seaquest Quark & Clipper Cruise Lines, Antarctica, Alaska, New Zealand, and Russian Far East; mountain climbing guide Palisades Sch. Mountaineering, Lone Pine, Calif., 1968-69, 78-79; dir. gold exploration project, Saudi Arabia, 1988. Contbr. papers to sci. jours. With USAF, 1965. Recipient Antarctic Svc. medal, 1978; Penrose grantee Geol. Soc. Am., 1969, Small Coll. Sci. Equipment grantee NSF, 1988; geographic feature in Antarctica named Mt. Vennum. Mem. Am. Alpine Club, Geol. Hon. Soc., Sigma Gamma Epsilon. Presbyterian. Home: 3925 Kim Ct Sebastopol CA 95472 Office: Sonoma State U Dept Geology 1801 E Cotati Ave Rohnert Park CA 94928-3613

VENN-WATSON, PATRICIA, psychiatrist; b. L.A., Aug. 14, 1944; d. Joseph Harry and Yetta (Margarick) Bernhard; 1 child, Eric Joseph. BA, UCLA, 1966; MD, U. Calif., Irvine, 1970. Intern U. N.Mex., Albuquerque, 1970-71, resident in psychiatry, 1971-75; cons. Cath. Family Svcs., San Diego, 1975-78; pvt. practice psychiatry San Diego, 1975—. Fellow Am. Psychiat. Assn.; mem. Am. Women's Med. Soc., Calif. Psychiat. Assn., San Diego County Med. Soc., San Diego Soc. Psychiat. Physicians (rep. 1993—), San Diego Soc. Adolescent Psychiatry (pres., treas. 1985-93). Office: 15644 Pomerado Rd Ste Gse Poway CA 92064-2418

VENTURINI, DONALD JOSEPH, special education educator; b. San Francisco, Feb. 7, 1930; s. Mansueto Giuseppe and Josephine (Ingrassia) V. BA, U. San Francisco, 1954; cert., San Francisco State Coll., 1960, San Francisco State Coll., 1965. Tchr. orthpaedically handicapped Sonoma (Calif.) State Hosp., 1965-83, ret., 1983 Author: Poems of Love and the Sea, 1989, Alexander Glazounov, 1992, Off Balance, A Collection of Short Stories, 1994, (documentary) A Personal Vision - The Seascapes of Donald J. Venturini, 1994; freelance sleeve writer for compact discs. Mem. Glazounov Soc. (pres.). Home: 17320 Park Ave Sonoma CA 95476-3447

VENUTI, STEPHEN, advertising executive. Pres., CEO Lai, Venuti & Lai, Santa Clara, Calif. Office: Lai Venuti & Lai Ste 1000 3945 Freedom Cir Santa Clara CA 95054

VENZKE, RAY FRANK, psychotherapist; b. Wood County, Wis., Sept. 7, 1933; s. Herman A. and Christina (Sojka) V.; m. Dawn Woltman, June 14, 1953 (div. Feb. 1972); 1 child, Diane W. Doersch; m. Joy Leadbetter, June

21, 1972 (div. Nov. 1985); m. DeMaris Hafner Unruh, May 31, 1986. BA in Ednl. Psychology, Wartburg Coll., 1955; MDiv, Trinity Sem., Columbus, Ohio, 1959; MA in Psychology, U. N.D., 1974. Lic. clin. profl. counselor, Mont. Pastor Bearlake Luth. Parish, Twin Lakes, Minn., 1959-63; missionary Thailand Luth. Mission, 1963-64; pastor First Luth. Parish, Washburn, N.D., 1965-67; addiction counselor Heartview Found., Mandan, N.D., 1971-74; therapist, program evaluator Badlands Human Svc. Ctr., Dickinson, N.D., 1975-85; psychotherapist Dickinson, N.D., 1985-87, Chyrsalis Counseling Svcs., Helena, Mont., 1988—; cons. Lewis and Clark County Law Enforcement Chaplains, Helena, 1988—. Narrator Mont. Libr. for the Blind, Helena, 1990—; chair task force CISM Mont. Dept. Disaster, 1994—; mem. Mont. Gov.'s Task Force on Mental Health Medicaid, Helena, 1993—. Mem. Am. Counselors Assn., Am. Mental Health Counselors, Mont. Clin. Mental Health Counselors (treas. 1992-94), Mont. Counselors Assn., Lions (Dist. Gov. 5NW award 1983), Am. Philatelic Soc. Home: 2019 Missoula Ave Helena MT 59601-3245 Office: Chyrsalis Counseling Svc 3117 Cooney Dr Apt 201 Helena MT 59601-0200

VEOMETT, COLLEEN MICHELLE, librarian; b. Ft. Monmouth, N.J., June 17, 1957; d. Willis K. and Norma G. (Mulcahy) V. BA, Oreg. Coll. Edn., 1979; MLS, U. Hawaii, 1982. Head libr. Yakama Indian Nation Libr., Toppenish, Wash., 1987—. Active Amnesty Internat. Mem. ALA. Democrat. Roman Catholic. Office: Yakama Indian Nation Libr PO Box 151 Toppenish WA 98948-0151

VERDUIN, CLAIRE LEONE, publishing company executive; b. Chgo., Mar. 23, 1932; d. David R. and Helen (Vande Velde) Ellman; m. J. Richard Verduin, Aug. 25, 1956 (Mar. 1979); children: Pamela A., Paul D., Beth L. Verduin Bacher. BBA, U. Wis., 1954. Editorial asst. Brooks/Cole Pub. Co., Pacific Grove and Monterey, Calif., 1973, project devel. editor, 1974-78, editor, 1978-85, mng. editor, 1985-91; pub., 1991—. Treas. Am. Field Service, Pacific Grove, 1978; mem. Pacific Grove Sch. Bd., 1983. Mem. ACA, AAUW, Nat. Assn. Human Svc. Educators, Nat. Assn. Devel. Edn., Coun. Social Work Edn., Audubon Soc. Office: Brooks/Cole Pub Co 511 Forest Ave Pacific Grove CA 93950-4202

VERGER, MORRIS DAVID, architect, planner; b. Ft. Worth, Mar. 25, 1915; s. Joseph and Dora (Bunyan) V.; m. Florence Brown, June 21, 1939; children: Paul, Alice. B.Arch., U. Calif., Berkeley, 1943. Naval architect U.S. Navy Bur. Ships, San Pedro, Calif., 1943-45; draftsman various archtl. firms So. Calif., 1946-50; pvt. practice as architect and planner Los Angeles, 1951—; lectr. architecture UCLA Extension; vis. critic Calif. State U., San Luis Obispo; leader Seminar on Interactive Planning, San Francisco; cons. to legal profession, tech. witness. Works include program for City of Hope, Duarte, Calif., 1972, Terman Engring. Ctr., Stanford U., 1974, and design of Huntington Dr. Sch., L.A., 1975, Flax Artist Materials Bldg., L.A., 1976, Frank D. Lanterman H.S., L.A., 1978, exec. offices S.E. Rykoff & Co., L.A., 1982, condominiums, Stoneman Corp., L.A., 1988, 91; developed DiscoveryBased Planning, 1994. Recipient design awards Westwood C. of C., 1974, 75. Fellow AIA (pres. So. Calif. chpt. 1975, v.p. environ. affairs Calif. council 1976, v.p. Calif. council 1979-80, pres. Calif. council 1980). Home: 1362 Comstock Ave Los Angeles CA 90024-5315 Office: 10801 National Blvd Los Angeles CA 90064-4126

VERHEY, JOSEPH WILLIAM, psychiatrist, educator; b. Oakland, Calif., Sept. 28, 1928; s. Joseph Bernard and Anne (Hanken) V.; BS summa cum laude, Seattle U., 1954; MD, U. Wash., 1958; m. Darlene Helen Seiler, July 21, 1956. Intern, King County Hosp., Seattle, 1958-59; resident Payne Whitney Psychiatric Clinic, N.Y. Hosp., Cornell Med. Center, N.Y.C., 1959-62, U. Wash. Hosp., Seattle, 1962-63; pvt. practice, Seattle, 1963-78; mem. staff U. Providence Hosp., 1963-78, Fairfax Hosp., 1963-78, VA Med. Center, Tacoma, 1978-83, chief inpatient psychiatry sect., 1983—; clin. instr. psychiatry U. Wash. Med. Sch., 1963-68, clin. asst. prof. psychiatry, 1968-82, clin. assoc. prof., 1982—; cons. psychiatry U.S. Dept. Def., Wash. State Bur. Juvenile Rehab.; examiner Am. Bd. Psychiatry and Neurology. Diplomate Am. Bd. Psychiatry and Neurology. Fellow N. Pacific Soc. Psychiatry and Neurology, Am. Psychiat. Assn.; mem. AMA, Am. Fedn. Clin. Rsch., World Fedn. Mental Health, Soc. Mil. Surgeons of U.S., Wash. Athletic Club, Swedish Club (life). Home: 1100 University St Seattle WA 98101 Office: VA Med Ctr Tacoma WA 98493

VERLOT, FRANK OSCAR, aerospace executive; b. Ghent, Belgium, Oct. 18, 1941; came to U.S., 1946; s. Max Gustave and Eva Emily (Danilevits) V.; m. Marian Elizabeth Berkner, June 24, 1967; children: Nancy Elizabeth, Susanne Marie. BSME, MIT, 1963; MSME, Stanford U., 1964. Thermodynamics engr. Grumman Aircraft, Bethpage, N.Y., 1962-65; sr. thermodynamics engr. Lockheed Missiles & Space Co., Sunnyvale, Calif., 1966-68; project engr. program mgmt. United Tech. Ctr. divsn. of United Aircraft, Sunnyvale, 1968-72, mgr. procurement liaison engring., 1972-76; mgr. procurement liaison engring. Chem. Systems divsn. United Techs., Sunnyvale, 1976-82; dir. strategic and bus. planning Chem. Systems divsn. United Techs., San Jose, Calif., 1982-94; dir. strategic bus. planning Pratt & Whitney Space Propulsion Ops., San Jose, 1994—. Planning commr. City of Los Altos, 1978-82, mem. city coun., 1982-89, mayor, 1983-84; chmn. Santa Clara County (Calif.) Rep. Com., 1971, 72; state precinct chmn. Calif. Rep. Party, 1973-74. Mem. AIAA (state transp. tech. com. 1994—). Roman Catholic. Home: 634 S Springer Rd Los Altos CA 94024-4105 Office: United Tech Pratt & Whitney Space Propulsion Ops P O Box 49028 San Jose CA 95161-9028

VERNIERO, JOAN EVANS, special education educator; b. Wilkes-Barre, Pa., Nov. 30, 1937; d. Raymond Roth and Cary Hazel (Casano) Evans; m. Daniel Eugene Verniero Jr., Jan. 7, 1956; children: Daniel Eugene III, Raymond Evans. BA, Kean Coll., 1971; MS in Edn. Adminstrn., Monmouth Coll., West Long Branch, N.J., 1974; postgrad., Calif. Coast U., 1986-92. Cert. elem. sch. tchr., spl. edn. tchr., sch. adminstr., N.J., N.Mex., Colo.; nat. registered emergency med. technician. Tchr. Children's Psychiat. Ctr., Eatontown, N.J., 1965-69; tchr. Arthur Brisbane Child Treatment Ctr., Farmingdale, N.J., 1969-71, prin., 1971-75; prin. S.A. Wilson Ctr., Colorado Springs, Colo., 1976-82; tchr. pub. schs. Aurora, Colo., 1982-93; retired, 1993; edn. rep. Aurora Pub. Schs. Crew leader Black Forest (Colo.) Rescue Squad 1979-85, treas., bd. dirs. Fire Protection Dist., 1980-85; evaluator Arson divsn. Aurora (Colo.) Fire Dept., 1993—. Mem. Phi Delta Kappa. Republican. Presbyterian. Home: 671 S Paris St Aurora CO 80012-2315

VERNON, DAVID PAUL, computer scientist; b. N.Y.C., July 31, 1948; s. Chester Millman and Lillian (Rosenfeld) V.; m. Joan Phyllis Satow, Oct. 22, 1988. BS, Pa. State U., 1969; MA, Calif. State U., L.A., 1975; MS, Ind. State U., 1983, PhD, 1984. Tech. writer DPAI, Inc., Beachwood, Ohio, 1985; instr. Sawyer Coll. Bus., Cleveland Heights, Ohio, 1986; sr. analyst Bell Tech. Ops., Tucson, 1987-88; systems analyst Comcon, Inc., Sierra Vista, Ariz., 1989; systems engr. Telos Corp., Sierra Vista, Ariz., 1990-93; computer scientist Mevatec Corp., Ft. Huachuca, Ariz., 1993—. Author: The Guide to Natural Area Inventory, 1982. Mem. choir Temple Emanuel, Cleve., 1985-86, Temple Emanu-El, Tucson, 1987-90. Ind. State U. fellow, 1979-84. Mem. Sigma Xi. Office: Mevatec Corp PO Box 375 Fort Huachuca AZ 85613-0375

VERNON, LEO PRESTON, biochemist, educator; b. Roosevelt, Utah, Oct. 10, 1925; s. William M. and Roseltha (Bingham) V.; m. Marion Fern Trunkey, Sept. 5, 1946; children: Richard Leo, Marion Elise, Martin Preston, Jillaine, Eric Eugene. A.B. in Chemistry, Brigham Young U., 1948; Ph.D., Iowa State U., 1951. Research asso. Washington U., St. Louis, 1952-54; prof. chemistry dept. Brigham Young U., Provo, Utah, 1954-61, 80—; asst. acad. v.p. research Brigham Young U., 1970-80; dir. Charles F. Kettering Research Lab., Yellow Springs, Ohio, 1961-70; prof. chemistry Antioch Coll., Yellow Springs, 1962-70; prof. botany dept. Ohio State U., Columbus, 1962- 70; Research fellow Nobel Inst., Stockholm, 1960. Author: (with H. Guest, A. San Pietro) Bacterial Photosynthesis, 1963, (with G. Seely) The Chlorophylls, 1966, (with R. Sanadi) Current Topics in Bioenergetics, Vol. 8; assoc. editor Bioenergetics, 1969-80, Photochemistry and Photobiology, 1970-76; contbr. numerous articles to sci. jours. Served with AUS, 1944-46. Mem. Am. Soc. Photobiology, Am. Soc. Plant Physiologists, Am. Soc. Biol. Chemists. Home: 1680 N 1550 E Provo UT 84604-5772

VERRONE, PATRIC MILLER, lawyer, writer; b. Glendale, N.Y.C., Sept. 29, 1959; s. Pat and Edna (Miller) V.; m. Margaret Maiya Williams, 1989; 1 child, Patric Carroll Williams. BA, Harvard U., 1981; JD, Boston Coll., 1984. Bar: Fla. 1984, U.S. Dist. Ct. (mid. dist.) Fla. 1984, Calif. 1988. Assoc. Allen, Knudsen, Swartz, DeBoest, Rhoads & Edwards, Ft. Myers, Fla., 1984-86; writer The Tonight Show, Burbank, Calif., 1987-90; temp. judge L.A. Mcpl. Ct., 1995—. Dir., producer, writer The Civil War-The Lost Episode, 1991; writer The Larry Sanders Show, 1992-94, The Critic, 1993-95; producer, writer The Simpsons, 1994-95; editor Harvard Lampoon, 1978-84, Boston Coll. Law Rev., 1983-84, Fla. Bar Jour., 1987-88, L.A. Lawyer, 1994—; contbr. articles to profl. jours. including Elysian Fields Quarterly, 1994, Baseball and the American Legal Mind, 1995. Bd. dirs. Calif. Confedn. of Arts, Mus. Contemporary Art. Mem. ABA (vice chair arts, entertainment, and sports law com.), Calif. Bar, Calif. Lawyers for Arts, L.A. County Bar Assn. (sec. barristers exec. com., chair artiest and the law com., mem. steering com. homeless shelter project, mem. intellectual property and entertainment law sect., legis. activity com.), Fla. Bar Assn., Writers Guild Am. West (contracts com. animation writers caucus), Harbard Club Lee County (v.p. 1985-86), Harvard Club of So. Calif. Republican. Roman Catholic. Home and Office: 6466 Odin St Los Angeles CA 90068-2730

VER STEEG, DONNA LORRAINE FRANK, nurse, sociologist, educator; b. Minot, N.D., Sept. 23, 1929; d. John Jonas and Pearl H. (Denlinger) Frank; m. Richard W. Ver Steeg, Nov. 22, 1950; children: Juliana, Anne, Richard B. BSN, Stanford, 1951; MSN, U. Calif., San Francisco, 1967; MA in Sociology, UCLA, 1969, PhD in Sociology, 1973. Clin. instr. U. N.D. Sch. Nursing, 1962-63; USPHS nurse rsch. fellow UCLA, 1969-72; spl. cons., adv. com. on physicians' assts. and nurse practitioner programs Calif. State Bd. Med. Examiners, 1972-73; asst. prof. UCLA Sch. Nursing, 1973-79, assoc. prof., 1979-94, asst. dean, 1981-83, chmn. primary ambulatory care, 1976-87, assoc. dean, 1983-86, prof. emeritus/recalled, 1994—, chair primary care, 1994—; co-prin. investigator PRIMEX Project, Family Nurse Practitioners, UCLA Extension, 1974-76; assoc. cons. Calif. Postsecondary Edn. Commn., 1975-76; spl. cons. Calif. Dept. Consumer Affairs, 1978; accredited visitor Western Assn. Schs. and Colls., 1985; mem. Calif. State Legis. Health Policy Forum, 1980-81. Contbr. chpts. to profl. books. Recipient Leadership award Calif. Area Health Edn. Ctr. System, 1989, Commendation award Calif. State Assembly, 1994; named Outstanding Faculty Mem. UCLA Sch. Nursing, 1982. Fellow Am. Acad. Nursing; mem. AAAS, ANA, APHA, Am. Soc. Law and Medicine, Nat. League Nursing, Calif. League Nursing, N.Am. Nursing Diagnosis Assn., Am. Assn. History Nursing, Assn. Health Svcs. Rsch., Calif. Nurse Assn. (pres. 1979-81, Jean Sullivan award 1992), Am. Sociol. Assn., Profl. Nurses Network, Stanford Nurses Club, Sigma Theta Tau (Gamma Tau chpt. Leadership award 1994), Sigma Xi. Home: 708 Swarthmore Ave Pacific Palisades CA 90272-4353 Office: UCLA Sch Nursing 10833 Le Conte Ave Los Angeles CA 90024

VERTS, LITA JEANNE, university administrator; b. Jonesboro, Ark., Apr. 13, 1935; d. William Gus and Lolita Josephine (Peeler) Nash; m. B. J. Verts, Aug. 29, 1954 (div. 1975); 1 child, William Trigg. BA, Oreg. State U., 1973; MA in Lingustics, U. Oreg., 1974; postgrad., U. Hawaii, 1977. Librarian Forest Research Lab., Corvallis, Oreg., 1966-69; instr. English Lang. Inst., Corvallis, 1974-80; dir. spl. svcs. Oreg. State U., Corvallis, 1980—, faculty senator, 1988—. Editor ann. book: Trio Achievers, 1986, 87, 88; contbr. articles to profl. jours. Precinct com. Rep. Party, Corvallis, 1977-80; adminstrv. bd. 1st United Meth. Ch., Corvallis, 1987-89, mem. fin. com., 1987-93, tchr. Bible, 1978—; bd. dirs. Westminster Ho., United Campus Ministries, 1994-95; adv. coun. Disabilities Svc., Linn, Benton, Lincoln Counties, 1990—, vice-chmn., 1992-93, chmn. 1993-94. Mem. N.W. Assn. Spl. Programs (pres. 1985-86), Nat. Coun. Ednl. Opportunities Assn. (bd. dirs. 1984-87), Nat. Gardening Assn., Alpha Phi (mem. corp. bd. Beta Upsilon chpt. 1990—). Republican. Methodist. Home: 530 SE Mayberry Ave Corvallis OR 97333-1866 Office: Spl Svcs Project Waldo 337 OSU Corvallis OR 97331

VESELACK, MARILYN SUE, musician, silversmith, massage therapist; b. Rushville, Ill., Dec. 25, 1936; d. Mack Arlington and Edith May (Day) Warren; m. Ronald Lee Veselack, June 9, 1957; children: Mark Roy, Joan Marie. B of Music Edn., Ill. Wesleyan U., 1959; MS in Music, Ill. State U., 1969; ArtsD, Ball State U., 1979. Cert. massage therapist. Tchr. San Jose (Ill.) Pub. Schs., 1959-60, Mesa Jr. Coll., Grand Junction, Colo., 1965-67, Mesa County Sch. Dist. # 51, Grand Junction, 1960-69; botany scientist Ball State U./Rico Reed Co., Muncie, Ind., 1972-86; supr. libr. circulation Ball State U., Muncie, 1981-85; clerical ops. Ea. Ind. Libr. Svc. Authority, Muncie, 1987-92; silversmith Silver Sensations, Muncie, 1987—; massage therapist, Muncie, 1972-86, 91-92, Grand Junction and Palisade, Colo., 1992—; lectr., instr. clarinet Mesa State Coll., Grand Junction, 1993—; lectr. Internat. Double Reed Soc. Conv., Occidental Coll., 1978, cellular studies of Arundo donax L.; presenter 94th, 95th, 96th ann. meeting Ind. Acad. Sci., Anderson U., 1978, 79, 80 comparative studies of reeds; Am. panelist Internat. Reed seminar Internat. Clarinet Soc., La Cité Université, Pariss, 1981. Clarinetist, exec. sec. Am.'s Hometown Band, Muncie, 1982-92; clarinetist Bloomington-Normal (Ill.) Symphony, 1953-59, Mesa Coll. Civic Symphony, Grand Junction, 1961-68, Muncie Civic Theater, 1986-91, Sinfonietta-Chamber Orch., Muncie, 1990-91, Grand Junction Symphony Orch., 1992—, Centennial Band, Grand Junction, 1992—. Mem. Am. Massage Therapy Assn., Internat. Clarinet Soc., Pfrimmer Deep Muscle Assn. (nat. cert. in therapeutic massage and bodywork), Phi Kappa Lambda, Sigma Alpha Iota (v.p. 1974-75, 88-90, pres. 1975-76, 90-92, Sword of Honor 1976, Rose of Honor, clarinetist chamber trio internat. conv. 1974).

VEST, ROSEMARIE LYNN TORRES, secondary educator; b. Pueblo, Colo., Jan. 16, 1958; d. Onesimo Bernabe and Maria Bersabe (Lucero) Torres; m. Donald R. Vest, May 1, 1982. BA, U. So. Colo., 1979, BS, 1991; cert. travel agt., Travel Trade Sch., Pueblo, 1986. Cert. secondary tchr., Colo.; cert. travel agt., Colo. Tutor U. So. Colo., Pueblo, 1977-79; sales rep. Intermountain Prodns., Colorado Springs, Colo., 1979-80; tutor, Pueblo, 1980-82, 84-85; travel agt. So. Colo. Travel, Pueblo, 1986-88; children's program facilitator El Mesias Family Support Program, Pueblo, 1987-88; substitute tchr. social studies Sch. Dist. 60, Pueblo, 1990—, Freed Mid. Sch., Pueblo, 1991, 92; Chpt. 1 Summer Reading Program, 1992, 93, 94, 95; instr. Travel and Tourism Dept. Pueblo C.C., 1994-95. Tchr. Sunday sch., chairperson adminstrv. bd. cert. lay spkr., lay rep. to ann. conf. Ch. Evangelism, co-chmn. Trinity United Meth. Ch., Pueblo, 1989-94, parish coun. rep. to Trinity/Bethel Coop. Parish; sponsor United Meth. Youth United Meth. Ch.; tchr. Sunday Sch., co-coord. vacation Bible sch., pastoral asst., edn. chairperson, 1994—, cert. lay spkr., ministerial program asst., lay leader Bethel United Meth. Ch., 1994—; craft facilitator Integrated Health Svcs., Pueblo, 1991—; spiritual devotions/worship leader Pueblo Manor Nursing Home, 1993—; vol. resident svcs. Pueblo County Bd. for Developmental Disabilities, 1989—; mem. conf. leadership team, parliamentarian Rocky Mountain Conf. United Meth. Ch., 1995; ministerial candidate United Meth. Ch. Recipient Excellence in Tchg. award Freed Mid. Sch., 1992, Vol. of Yr. award IHS of Pueblo, 1995. Mem. Assn. Am. Geographers, Nat. Oceanog. Soc., Nat. Geog. Soc. Democrat. Home: 1106 Berkley Ave Apt 1 Pueblo CO 81004-2802

VETTO, JOHN TYSON, surgeon, educator; b. Cin., May 11, 1956; s. R. Mark and Marianne (Tyson) V.; m. Irene Perez, Jan. 11, 1992. BS in Biology with highest honors, Portland State U., 1978; MD summa cum laude, Oreg. Health Scis. U., 1982. Intern, jr. resident Brigham and Women's Hosp., Boston, 1982-84; fellow Nat. Cancer Inst., Bethesda, Md., 1984-86; resident UCLA, L.A., 1986-89; fellow Meml. Sloan-Kettering Cancer Ctr., N.Y.C., 1989-91; asst. prof. surgery Oreg. Health Scis. U., Portland, 1991—; chief sect. of surg. oncology Portland VA Med. Ctr., 1991—; co-chmn. Oreg. Breast & Cervical Cancer Coalition, Portland, 1993—. Recipient Lange award Lange Publs., 1981, Mosby award Mosby Publs., 1982. Fellow ACS (liaison commn. on cancer 1992—), Soc. Surg. Oncology, Am. Bd. Surgery; m. Assn. Acad. Surgery, Soc. Head & Neck Surgeons (assoc.), North Pacific Surg. Assn.

VEVERKA, MICHAEL J., diagnostic radiologist; b. Mitchell, S.D., May 5, 1947; s. Joe and Dorothy (Schiltz) V.; m. Kathleen Sullivan, Sept. 26, 1970; children: David, Marie. BS cum laude, St. John's U., 1969; MD, U. Minn., 1975. Diplomate Am. Bd. Radiology. Intern in surgery Oreg. Health Scis. U., Portland, 1976-77, resident in diagnostic radiology, 1977-80, instr. in radiology, 1980; radiologist Legacy Portland Hosp., 1981—; chmn. dept. imaging Northwest Magnetic Imaging, 1992—; radiologist Meridian Park Hosp., Tualatin, Oreg., 1981—; consulting radiologist Northwest Magnetic Imaging, Portland, 1984—; med. advisor Portland C.C., 1992—; clin. asst. prof. dept. diagnostic radiology Oreg. Health Scis. U., 1986—. Mem. AMA, Am. Coll. Radiology, Soc. Breast Imaging, Radiol. Soc. N.Am., Oreg. Radiol. Soc. (pres. 1993-94), Oreg. Med. Assn. Office: Meridian Imaging Ctr 6464 SW Borland Rd Tualatin OR 97062-9749

VEZOLLES, JANET LEE, newspaper publisher; b. Evansville, Ind., June 13, 1953. BA in English, Fresno State U., 1990. Commd. USMC, 1977, electronic calibrator, 1977-81; with air ops. USAF, Fresno, Calif., 1982-85; pub., contbr. The Fresno County Sun, Fresno, 1986—; also pub. The San Joaquin Valley Bus. & Industry News; pres. Sunnyside Bus. Assn., Fresno, 1991-92; owner Cross Country Equestrian Acad. Pres. Patrons for Cultural Arts, Fresno, 1988-90. Mem. MENSA (internat.), U.S. Trotting Assn., Jr. League Fresno. Office: Suter News Group 1060 Fulton Mall # 315 Fresno CA 93721

VICK, AUSTIN LAFAYETTE, civil engineer; b. Cedervale, N.Mex., Jan. 28, 1929; s. Louis Lafayette and Mota Imon (Austin) V.; BSCE, N.Mex. State U., 1950, MSCE, 1961; m. Norine E. Melton, July 18, 1948; children: Larry A., Margaret J., David A. Commd. 2d lt. USAF, 1950, advanced through grades to capt., 1959, ret., 1970; ordnance engr. Ballistics Rsch. Lab., White Sands Proving Ground, Las Cruces, N.Mex., 1950-51, civil engr., 1951-55, gen. engr. White Sands Missile Range, 1957-73, phys. scientist adminstr., 1955-57, supr. gen. engr., 73-84; owner A.V. Constrn., Las Cruces, 1979-93; realtor Campbell Agy., Las Cruces, 1979-84; cons. test and evaluation, instrumentation systems, ops. maintenance and mgmt. to Dept. of Def., major comml. firms, 1984—; pres., treas. Survey Tech., Inc., 1985—; cons. in field, Las Cruces, 1984—. Mem. outstanding alumni awards com. N.Mex. State U., 1980. Recipient Outstanding Performance award Dept. Army, White Sands Missile Range, 1972, Spl. Act awards, 1967, 71, 75. Mem. Mil. Ops. Research Soc. (chmn. logistics group 1968-69), Am. Def. Preparedness Assn. (pres. 1970-72), Assn. U.S. Army (v.p. 1970-71), Am. Soc. Photogrametry, Am. Astronautical Soc. (sr. mem.), N.Mex. State U. Acad. Civil Engring. Contbr. articles to profl. jours. Home and Office: 4568 Spanish Dagger Las Cruces NM 88011-9635

VICKER, RAY, writer; b. Wis., Aug. 27, 1917; s. Joseph John and Mary (Young) V.; m. Margaret Ella Leach, Feb. 23, 1944. Student, Wis. State U., Stevens Point, 1934, Los Angeles City Coll., 1940-41, U.S. Mcht. Marine Officers' Sch., 1944, Northwestern U., 1947-49. With Chgo. Jour. Commerce, 1946-50, automobile editor, 1947-50; mem. staff Wall St. Jour., 1950-83; European editor Wall St. Jour., London, Eng., 1960-75. Author: How an Election Was Won, 1962, Those Swiss Money Men, 1973, Kingdom of Oil, 1974, Realms of Gold, 1975, This Hungry World, 1976, Dow Jones Guide to Retirement Planning, 1985, The Informed Investor, 1990; also numerous articles. Served with U.S. Merchant Marine, 1942-46. Recipient Outstanding Reporting Abroad award Chgo. Newspaper Guild, 1959; Best Bus. Reporting Abroad award E. W. Fairchild, 1963, 67; hon. mention, 1965; Bob Considine award, 1979; ICMA Journalism award, 1983. Mem. Soc. Profl. Journalists, Authors Guild. Roman Catholic. Clubs: Overseas Press (Reporting award 1963, 67) (N.Y.C.); Press (Chgo.). Home and Office: 4131 E Pontatoc Canyon Dr Tucson AZ 85718-5227

VICKERMAN, SARA ELIZABETH, ecology organization executive; b. Aspen, Colo., Sept. 20, 1949; d. Harry Edwin and Sarah Elizabeth (Forbes) V.; m. Charles Polenick, Feb. 5, 1972 (div. Feb. 1982). AA, Fullerton (Calif.) Jr. Coll., 1969; BS in Anthropology, Calif. State U., Fullerton, 1972; MS in Biology Geography Edn., So. Oreg. State Coll., 1974. Tchr. Medford (Oreg.) Sch. Dist., 1974-78; N.W. field rep. Defenders of Wildlife, Salem, Oreg., 1978-82; legis. dir. Defenders of Wildlife, Washington, 1982-84; dir. state conservation programs Defenders of Wildlife, Washington, Portland (Oreg.), 1984—; mem. Oreg. State Parks and Recreation Commn., 1992—. Bd. dirs. Oreg. League Conservation Voters. Recipient awards for Oreg. Resource Conservation Trust Fund, Oreg. Parks Assn., 1989, Natural Resource Coun. Am., 1990, Disting. Achievement award Soc. Conservation Biology, 1991, Nat. Wildlife Program, Nat. Conf. Com., 1992. Mem. Soc. for Conservation Biology, Nat. Audubon Soc., The Nature Conservancy. Democrat. Office: Defenders of Wildlife 1637 Laurel St Lake Oswego OR 97034-4755

VICKERS, LAURICE SAMUEL, laboratory administrator, medical examiner; b. San Mateo, Calif., May 27, 1939; s. Samuel Edward and Helen Hazel (Sisk) V.; m. Elizabeth Starr Cooper, Aug. 9, 1964 (div. Oct. 1975); m. Dana Erin Africa, Feb. 14, 1981; children: Aja, Catlyn, Sierra. Student, Stanford U., 1957-62; MD, U. Calif., San Francisco, 1967. Lic. physician, Oreg., Wash., Calif.; cert. in anatomic and clin. pathology, med. microbiology and forensic pathology. Intern, resident in anatomic pathology U. Calif. Sch. Medicine, San Francisco, 1967-69, resident in clin. pathology, 1971-73; co-dir. Olympic Meml. Hosp. Lab., Pt. Angeles, Wash., 1973-86, chief med. staff, 1981; med. dir. Sequim Diagnostic Svcs., 1981-85, McKenzie Willamette Hosp. Lab., Springfield, Oreg., 1986—; chmn. lab., blood transfusion and infection control coms. McKenzie Willamette Hosp., Springfield, 1988-91, chief med. clin. svcs., 1992; med. examiner Lane County, 1986—. Maj. U.S. Army, 1969-71. Mem. AMA, Am. Soc. Clin. Pathologists, Nat. Assn. Med. Examiners, Am. Acad. Forensic Scis., Coll. Am. Pathologists, Oreg. Med. Assn., Oreg. Pathology Assn., Lane County Med. Soc., Clallam County Med. Soc. (pres. 1985), Pacific NW Soc. of Pathologists, Alpha Omega Alpha. Office: Path Cons PO Box 369 Eugene OR 97440-0369

VICKERS, THOMAS EUGENE, finance company executive; b. Panama Canal Zone, Jan. 11, 1949. BBA, U. Iowa, 1971; MBA, U. Chgo., 1973. V.p. institutional sales Goldman Sachs & Co., Chgo., 1973-82; v.p. pvt. client svcs. Goldman Sachs & Co., San Francisco, 1982-92; founder, dir. Pro-Conscience Funds, Inc., San Francisco, 1993—, Horus Investment Mgmt., San Francisco, 1992—; founder, dir. Wave Elec., Denver, founder, chmn., dir. The Isis Found., San Francisco; dir. The Ch. of Revelation and Astral Physics Sch., Hilo, Hawaii. Mem. Social Investment Forum, Bus. for Soc. Responsibility. Office: Horus Investment Mgmt 850 Montgomery St # 100 San Francisco CA 94133-5118 Home: 2423 Massachusetts Ave Redwood City CA 94061-3268

VICKERY, BYRDEAN EYVONNE HUGHES (MRS. CHARLES EVERETT VICKERY, JR.), retired library services administrator; b. Belleview, Mo., Apr. 18, 1928; d. Roy Franklin and Margaret Cordelia (Wood) Hughes; m. Charles Everett Vickery, Jr., Nov. 5, 1948; 1 child, Camille. Student, Flat River (Mo.) Jr. Coll., 1946-48; BS in Edn., S.E. Mo. State Coll., 1954; MLS, U. Wash., 1964; postgrad. Wash. State U., 1969-70. Tchr. Ironton (Mo.) Pub. Schs., 1948-56; elem. tchr. Pasco (Wash.) Sch. Dist. 1, 1956-61, jr. high sch. libr., 1961-68, coord. librs., 1968-69; asst. libr. Columbia Basin Community Coll., Pasco, 1969-70, head libr., dir. Instructional Resources Ctr., 1970-78, dir. libr. svcs., 1979-87, assoc. dean libr. svcs., 1987-90, ret., 1990; owner Vickery Search & Research, 1990—; chmn. S.E. Wash. Libr. Svc. Area, 1977-78, 88-90. Bd. dirs. Pasco-Kennewick Community Concerts, 1977-88, pres., 1980-81, 87-88, Pasco-Kennewick Community Concerts, treas., 1991—; bd. dirs. Mid-Columbia Symphony Orch., 1983-89; trustee Wash. Commn. Humanities, 1982-85; bd. mem. Arts Coun. Mid-Columbia Region, 1991-93. Author, editor: Library and Research Skills Curriculum Guides for the Pasco School District, 1967; author (with Jean Thompson), also editor Learning Resources Handbook for Teachers, 1969. Recipient Woman of Achievement award Pasco Bus. and Profl. Women's Club, 1976. Mem. ALA, AAUW (2d v.p. 1966-68, corr. sec. 1969), Wash. Dept. Audio-Visual Instrn., Wash. Libr. Assn., Am. Assn. Higher Edn., Wash. Assn. Higher Edn., Wash. State Assn. Sch. Librs. (state conf. chmn. 1971-72), Tri-Cities Librs. Assn., Wash. Libr. Media Assn. (community coll. levels chmn. 1986-87), Am. Assn. Rsch. Libr., Soroptimist Internat. Assn. (rec. sec. Pasco-Kennewick chpt. 1971-72, treas. 1973-74, pres. 1978-80, v.p. 1989-90, treas. 1991), Columbia Basin Coll. Adminstrs. Assn. (sec.-treas. 1973-74), Pacific N.W. Assn. Ch. Libr., Women in Communications, Pasco Bus. and Profl. Women's Club, PEO, Beta Sigma Phi, Delta Kappa Gamma, Phi Delta Kappa (sec. 1981-82, Outstanding Educator award 1983). Home: 3521 S Fisher Ct Kennewick WA 99337-2559

VIDAL, ALEJANDRO LEGASPI, architect; b. Kawit, Cavite, The Philippines, May 3, 1934; s. Antonio and Patrocinia (Legaspi) V.; m. Fe Del Rosario, Aug. 16, 1962; 1 child, Alex Anthony. BS in Architecture, Mapua Inst. Tech., 1962. Registered arch., The Philippines. Prin. A.L. Vidal Arch., Manila, The Philippines, 1962-63; staff arch. Vinnell Wall & Green, Agana, Guam, 1963-64; project engr. Dillingham Corp. of Nevada, Hawaii and Guam, 1964-74; sr. project mgr., preconstrn. svc. mgr. Fletcher-Pacific Constrn. Co. Ltd., Honolulu, 1974—. Designer, builder first application of integrated aluminum forming sys. for high rise concrete construction; co-inventor building sys. Active Rep. Presdl. Task Force, Washington, 1980-88, Rep. Senatorial Com., Washington, 1980-88. With USN, 1954-58, Korea. Mem. Am. Concrete Inst., Am. Mgmt. Assn., Soc. Am. Mil. Engrs., Am. Legion, U. Hawaii Found., Chancellor's Club, Disabled Am. Vets., Comdrs. Club, Oxford Club. Roman Catholic. Home: 1051 Kaluanui Rd Honolulu HI 96825-1321

VIDAL, DELIA, medical/surgical and oncological nurse; b. Nogales, Ariz., June 27, 1936; d. Jesus V. and Maria (Escoto) Lopez; m. Richard B. Vidal, July 28, 1956; children: Richard, Raymond, Raul, Rosanne, Rachel, Rosella, Robert, Rebecca. Diploma, St. Mary's Nursing Sch., Tucson, 1956; student, U. Ariz. Cert. med.-surg. nurse. Staff nurse St. Mary's Hosp. Vol., ARC; active United Way. Recipient Excellence in Nursing Svcs. award Ariz. Hosp. Assn., 1989. Mem. ANA, Am. Urol. Assn. Allied (urology com.), Ariz. Nurses Assn. (Nurse of Yr. Excellence in Nursing Clin. Practice dist. 2 1993), Oncology Nursing Soc., Nat. Cancer Inst., Tucson Assn. Hispanic Nurses (charter, treas.). Home: 3301 S Naco Vis Tucson AZ 85713-6543

VIDGEN, RICK, food products executive; b. 1941. With Arnotts Biscuits P/L, Sydney, Australia, 1962-83, Ram Group, Inc., Oakland, Calif., 1983-86; with Macadamia Farms of Hawaii, Inc., Captain Cook, 1986—, now pres. Office: Mac Farms of Hawaii Inc Honomalino District Captain Cook HI 96704*

VIELEHR, WILLIAM RALPH, sculptor, business executive; b. Chgo., Jan. 6, 1945; s. Charles Conrad and Jane (Kingsly) V.; m. Pauline Marie Bustamante, Nov. 1976 (div.); 1 child, William Nathan Bustamante Vielehr; m. Teresa Stolsenberg, 1989; 1 child, Caylon Kingsly Vielehr. BFA, Colo. State U., 1969. Free lance artist, Boulder, Colo., 1969—; curator, coordinator form sculpture exhibits Denver Botanical Gardens, 1983, Fiddlers Green, Denver, 1984, Central Park, Boulder, Colo., 1986, Sculpture in the Park, 1978-88, Colo. Coll., Colo. Springs, Colo., 1987, Warren Place, Tulsa, 1991; dir. Form Sculpture, Boulder. Works include sculpture: Wall Figure, 1983; commns. include: Environ. Refection, Mace Rich, 1983, Wall Treatment, Cherry Creek Plaza, Denver, 1983, Freestanding Wall, Prudential Bache, 1983, Metal Sketch, Digital, 1986, Interaction, Boulder Reservoir, 1986. Bd. dirs. Boulder Ctr. Visual Arts, 1978-80. Recipient Purchase award Colo. Designer Craftsman, 1972; sculpture grantee City of Boulder, 1980. Mem. Bully Boys Beer Coop. Club (pres. Boulder 1984—). Office: Form Sculpture 2888 Bluff St # 447 Boulder CO 80301-1200

VIERHELLER, TODD, software engineering consultant; b. Winter Park, Fla., June 22, 1958; s. Irvin Theodore and Jeanne Marie (Zeller) V.; m. Susan Lindhe Watts, Dec. 22, 1984; children: Renate Jeanne, Clark, Lindhe Marie, Kent. BS in Computer Sci., U. Mo., Rolla, 1980; MA in Bibl. Studies, Multnomah Sch. Bible, Portland, Oreg., 1986. Tech. writer, software engr. Tektronix, Beaverton, Oreg., 1981-86, software engrng. mgr., 1988-89; software engr., supr. Intel Corp., Hillsboro, Oreg., 1986-88; software engrng. mgr. Summation, 1989-90; software cons. Quality First, Lynnwood, Wash., 1990—; software engrng. cons. Digital Equipment Corp., Bellevue, Wash., 1990-91, GTE, Bothell, Wash., 1990-91, Frank Russell Co., Tacoma, Wash., 1992-93, InterConnections, Inc., Bellevue, Wash., 1993, Novell, San Jose, Calif., 1993; software engrng. mgmt. cons. Weyerhauser, Federal Way, Wash., 1991-92, Frank Russell, Tacoma, Wash., 1994, ConnectSoft, Inc., Bellevue, Wash., 1994. Mem. IEEE, Washington Software Assn., Upsilon Pi Epsilon, Kappa Mu Epsilon. Republican. Mem. Evang. Christian Ch. Home: 22810 25th Ave W Lynnwood WA 98036-8303 Office: Quality First PO Box 6212 Lynnwood WA 98036-0212

VIERLING, JOHN MOORE, physician; b. Bellflower, Calif., Nov. 20, 1945; s. Lester Howard and Ruth Ann (Moore) V.; m. Gayle Aileen Vandermast, June 30, 1968 (div. 1984); children: Jeffrey M., Janet A.; m. Donna Marie Sheps, May 4, 1985; children: Matthew R., Mark L. AB in Biology with great distinction, Stanford U., 1967, MD, 1972. Intern then resident Strong Meml. Hosp. U. Rochester, N.Y., 1972-74; clin. assoc. liver unit NIH, Bethesda, Md., 1974-77; gastroenterology fellow U. Calif., San Francisco, 1977-78, instr. medicine, 1978-79; from asst. to assoc. U. Colo. Sch. Medicine, Denver, 1979-90; dir. hepatology, med dir. liver transplantation Cedars-Sinai Med. Ctr., L.A., 1990—; assoc. prof. medicine UCLA, 1990—; lectr. Schering Corp., Kenilworth, N.J., 1990—. Assoc. editor: Prinicples and Practice of Gastroenterology and Hepatology, 1992; editorial bd. Hepatology, 1985-90, Gastroenterology, 1993—; co-patentee in hybridization assay for hepatitis virus, 1992. With USPHS, 1974-77. Fellow ACP; mem. Am. Assn. Study Liver Diseases, Am. Gastroenterolog. Assn., Internat. Assn. for Study Liver, European Assn. for Study Liver, Am. Liver Found. (chmn. bd. dirs. 1994—). Office: Cedars-Sinai Med Ctr Hepatology Dept 8700 Beverly Blvd Los Angeles CA 90048-1804

VIGDOR, JAMES SCOTT, distribution executive; b. Bklyn., Oct. 12, 1953; s. Irving and Betty Jean (Wolkenbrod) V.; m. Mindy Sue Neirs, May 30, 1982; 1 child, Rachel Dyan. BA, Ohio State U., 1975. Regional distbn. mgr. Gestetner Corp., L.A., 1979-83; asst. ops. mgr. Wall-Pride, Inc., Van Nuys, Calif., 1983-88; ops. mgr. Opportunities for Learning, Inc., Chatsworth, Calif., 1988-89; dir. ops. Image Entertainment, Chatsworth, 1989-91; ops mgr. Cal-Abco and Legend Computer Products, Woodland Hills, Calif., 1991—. Office: Cal-Abco 6041 Variel Ave Woodland Hills CA 91367-3720

VIGIL, CHARLES S., lawyer; b. Trinidad, Colo., June 9, 1912; s. J.U. and Andreita (Maes) V.; m. Kathleen A. Liebert, Jan. 2, 1943; children: David Charles Edward, Marcia Kathleen. LL.B., U. Colo., 1936. Bar: Colo. 1936. Dep. dist. atty. 3d Jud. Dist. Colo., 1937-42, asst. dist. atty., 1946-51; U.S. atty. Dist. Colo., 1951-53; pvt. practice law Denver.; Dir., sec. Las Animas Co. (Colo); ARC. Author: Saga of Casimiro Barela. Bd. dirs. Family and Children's Svc. Denver, Colo. Humane Soc., Animal Rescue Soc., Auraria Community Ctr.; mem. Bishop's com. on housing; Dem. candidate for U.S. Congress, 1988. Lt. USCG, 1942-46. Recipient award of civil merit Spain, 1960, award of civil merit Colo. Centennial Expn. Bd., 1976; award Colo. Chicano Bar Assn., 1979. Mem. Internat. Law Assn., ABA, Fed. Bar Assn., Colo. Bar Assn. (bd. govs.), So. Colo. Bar Assn., Hispanic Bar Colo. (bd. dirs.), Am. Judicature Soc., Internat. Bar Assn., Inter-Am. Bar, V.F.W. (comdr.), Am. Legion (comdr.), Nat. Assn. Def. Lawyers, Assn. Trial Lawyers Am., Lambda Chi Alpha, Elks, Eagles, Cootie. Home: 1085 Sherman St Denver CO 80203-2880 Office: 1715 Colo State Bank 1600 Broadway Denver CO 80202-4927

VIGIL, DANIEL AGUSTIN, academic administrator; b. Denver, Feb. 13, 1947; s. Agustin and Rachel (Naranjo) V.; m. Claudia Cartier. BA in History, U. Colo., Denver, 1978, JD, 1982. Bar: Colo. 1982, U.S. Dist. Ct. Colo. 1983. Project mgr. Mathematics Policy Rsch., Denver, 1978; law clk. Denver Dist. Ct., 1982-83; ptnr. Vigil and Bley, Denver, 1983-85; asst. dean sch. law U. Colo., Boulder, 1983-89; assoc. dean sch. law U. Colo., 1989—; apptd. by chief justice of Colo. Supreme Ct. to serve on Colo. Supreme Ct. Ad Hoc Com. on miniority participation in legal profession; adj. prof. U. Colo. Sch. Law; bd. dirs. Continuing Legal Edn. in Colo., Inc.; mem. Gov. Colo. Lottery Commn. Editor (newsletter) Class Action, 1987-88; co-editor (ethics com. column) Colo. Lawyer. Bd. dirs. Legal Aid Soc. Met. Denver, 1986—; past v.p. Colo. Minority Scholarhip Consortium, pres. 1990-91; mem. Task Force on Community Race Rels., Boulder, 1989-94; past mem. jud. nomination rev. com. U.S. Senator Tim Wirth. Mem. Colo. Bar Assn. (mem. legal edn. and admissions com. 1989-94, chmn. 1989-91, bd. govs. 1991), Hispanic Nat. Bar Assn. (chmn. scholarship com. 1990-95), Colo Hispanic Bar Assn. (bd. dirs. 1985-89, pres. 1990), Denver Bar Assn. (joint com. on minorities in the legal profession), Boulder County Bar Assn. (ex-officio mem., trustee), Phi Delta Phi (faculty sponsor). Roman Catholic. Home: 4415 Laguna Pl Apt 209 Boulder CO 80303-3784 Office: U Colo Sch Law PO Box 401 Boulder CO 80303

VIGIL, DOUGLAS ELLIOTT, lawyer; b. Denver, Jan. 19, 1953; s. Joseph M. and Sally A. (Roberts) V.; m Gloria M. Kephart, May 30, 1981; 1 child, Aislinn Elizabeth. BFA, Utah State U., 1977; AD in Radiol. Sci., U. N.Mex., 1981, BSN, 1984, JD, 1989. Bar: N.Mex. 1989, U.S. Ct. Appeals N.Mex. 1991, U.S. Ct. Appeals (10th cir.) 1991. Self employed ceramic potter Logan, Utah, 1975-79, San Jose, Calif., 1975-79; radiol. tech. Albuquerque, 1981-84; staff nurse trauma ICU U. N.Mex. Hosp., Albuquerque, 1984-89; staff nurse St. Josephs Hosp. Intensive Care Unit, Albuquerque, 1984-85; atty. Simon, Cuddy & Friedman, Santa Fe, 1989-90, Branch Law Firm, Albuquerque, 1990—. Mem. ABA, N.Mex. Trial Lawyers. Home: 9709 Fostoria Rd NE Albuquerque NM 87111-1251 Office: Branch Law Firm 2025 Rio Grande Blvd NW Albuquerque NM 87104-2525

VIGIL, KAREN LAVERNE, reporter; b. Walsenburg, Colo.; d. Ben and Cordelia Guadalupe (Pacheco) V. BS, U. So. Colo., Pueblo, 1977. Asst. to pub. info. officer City of Pueblo, 1977-84, pub. info. officer, 1984-88; reporter The Pueblo Chieftain, 1988—. Recipient Reporting award Mothers Against Drunk Driving, Pueblo, 1990. Office: The Pueblo Chieftain 825 W 6th St Pueblo CO 81003-2313

VIGIL, ROBERT E., state government official; b. El Pueblo, N.Mex., Oct. 26, 1953; s. Antonio and Felicita Vigil; m. Viola Baca, Sept. 8, 1973; children: Roberta, Robin. BA, N.Mex. Highlands U., 1982. CPA. Govt. employee State of N.Mex., Las Vegas, 1977-91; state auditor State of N.Mex., Santa Fe, 1991—. Mem. N.Mex. Border Authority, Santa Fe, N.Mex. Commn. Pub. Records, Santa Fe, Exec. Com. of S.W. Inter-Govtl. Audit Forum, Santa Fe. Named Citizen of Yr. Las Vegas Hispano C. of C., Outstanding Young Am. N.Mex. Jaycees. Mem. AICPA, N.Mex. Soc. CPAs, N.Mex. Assn. Hispanic CPAs, Inst. Internal Auditors, Nat. Assn. State Auditors, Nat. Assn. Latino Elected Ofcls. Democrat. Home: 410 Diego Dr Las Vegas NM 87701-4845 Office: State Auditor's Office PERA Bldg Rm 302 Santa Fe NM 87503

VIGLIONE, EUGENE LAWRENCE, automotive executive; b. Paterson, N.J., Nov. 23, 1931; s. Fred and Caroline (Cantilina) V.; m. Vera Yonkens, June 12, 1954 (div. June 1976), m. Evila (Billie) Larez Viglione, Sept. 19, 1976; children: Victoria, David, Valerie, Vanessa, Francine, Margaret, Robert. Student, Cooper Union, N.Y., 1950-51. Sales mgr. Village Ford, Ridgewood, N.J., 1953-66, Carlton Motors, Frankfurt, Germany, 1966-67, Jones Minto Ford, Burlingame, Calif., 1967-72, Terry Ford, Pompano Beach, Fla., 1974-75; gen. mgr. Kohlenberg Ford, Burlingame, 1975-76; v.p. Morris Landy Ford, Alameda, Calif., 1976-80, Burlingame Ford, 1980-85; emeritus chmn. bd. Valley Isle Motors, Wailuku, Hawaii, 1985—; pres. Marriott Luau, Lahaina, Hawaii; pres. Maui Auto Dealers Assn., Wailuku, 1986-87. Del. Rep. State Conv., Honolulu, 1988, State House of Rep.'s, 1992; v.p. Rep. Party Precinct, Lahaina, Hawaii, 1988, trustee Rep. Presdl. Task Force, Washington, 1983-88, pres. Maui County Rep. Party, 1993; pres. Big Bros./Big Sisters, 1993; exec. dir.'s Light Bringers; bd. dirs. Following Maui Symphony, Lahaina Action Com., Maui United Way, Homeless Resource Ctr. Named Top 250 Exec. Hawaii Bus. Mag., 1986-92. Mem. Nat. Auto Dealers Assn., Internat. Auto Dealers Assn., Nat. Fed. of Ind. Bus., Maui Rotary, Lahaina Yacht Club, Maui Country Club, Gideons, Maui C. of C. Home: 2481 Kaanapali Pky Lahaina HI 96761-1910 Office: Valley Isle Motors 2026 Main St Wailuku HI 96793-1647

VIGNAPIANO, LOUIS JOHN, municipal official; b. Bklyn., Aug. 7, 1952; s. Emilio Anthony and Lillian (De Santo) V.; m. Jeanne Elizabeth Zultowksi, July 19, 1975 (div. June 1993). AS in Fin., Grossmont Coll., 1987; BSBA in Mgmt., San Diego State U., 1994. Computer programmer Bank of Tokyo, N.Y.C., 1972-77; mgr. systems and programming Calif. First Bank, San Diego, 1977-88; mgr. end user computing Union Bank, San Diego and L.A., 1988-90; dir. mgmt. svcs. City of Chula Vista, Calif., 1990—; cons. in field. Mem. Mcpl. Info. Systems Assn. Calif. Republican. Roman Catholic. Home: PO Box 1087 Chula Vista CA 91912-1087 Office: City of Chula Vista 276 4th Ave Chula Vista CA 91910-2631

VIGNE, JEAN-LOUIS, biochemist; b. Pertuis, Vaucluse, France, Nov. 8, 1945; came to U.S., 1976; s. Francis Fortuné and Denise (Sube) V.; m. Josefina Maria Naya, Sept. 8, 1976; 1 child, Carole. D in Specialité, U. d'Aix-Marseille I, France, 1972; D in Phys. Scis., U. d'Aix-Marseille II, France, 1981. Postdoctoral fellow U. Calif., San Francisco, 1976-78; attaché de recherches Institut National de la Santé et de la Recherche Medicale, Marseille, 1978-81; charge de recherches INSERM, Marseille, 1981-84; scientist project leader Calif. Biotech. Inc., Mountain View, Calif., 1984-88; vis. asst. endocrinologist U. Calif., San Francisco, 1988-90, co-dir. analytical lab., 1990—; vis. asst. prof. Fed. U., Rio de Janeiro, 1973-76; vis. scientist Cardiovascular Rsch. Inst., San Francisco, 1982-84. Contbr. articles to profl. jours.; inventor pharmaceutical microemulsions and mature apoA1 protein production. Fellow Brazilian Nat. Rsch. Coun., 1972-76, French Fgn. Affairs, 1976-78, NATO, 1982-83, Phillipe Found., 1982-83; grantee HHS, 1986. Mem. N.Y. Acad. Scis., Endocrine Soc. Home: 201 Dellbrook Ave San Francisco CA 94131-1210

VIGNES, MICHELLE MARIE, photographer, educator; b. Reims, France, May 13, 1926; came to U.S., 1961; d. Jacques and Helene (Charbonneaux) V. Picture editor Magnum Photo Agy., Paris, 1953-57, UNESCO, Paris, 1957-61; pub. rels. for photographers covering UN, 1962-66; free-lance photographer, 1967—; tchr. documentary photography U. Calif., San Francisco, 1978—; tchr. ethnology and photography Coll. of Acad. of Arts, San Francisco, 1989—; tchr. photography and ethnology Paris U., 1989. Exhibited in shows at Oakland Mus., 1971, 73, Indian Mus., Mpls., 1975, Librarie des Arts, Reims, 1976, Whiteside Gallery, San Francisco, 1978, Ecology Ctr., San Francisco, 1978, Joseph Dee Mus., San Francisco, 1983, Santa Fe Ctr. for Photography, 1983, Cultural Ctr., Nevada City, 1984, D.V.S. Taos, 1985, Ctr. for Photography, Geneva, 1987, 90, Alliance Francaise, San Francisco, 1987, Gallerie Agathe Gaillard, Paris, 1989, Eye Gallery, San Francisco, 1989, Galeries FNAC, Paris, 1990, Vision Gallery, San Francisco, 1990, Musee Carnavalet, Paris, 1992, others; contbr. photographs to profl. jours. Home: 654 28th St San Francisco CA 94131-2116

VIHSTADT, ROBERT FRANCIS, real estate broker; b. Rochester, Minn., Oct. 6, 1941; s. Francis A. and Catherine P. (Condon) V.; m. Kathleen A. McGuire, Sept. 14, 1963 (div. Oct. 1976); children: Maureen T., Michael R., Mark T.; m. Leslie P. Teutsch, Mar. 16, 1979 (div. Jan. 1988). BA, Mankato State Coll., 1962. Employment counselor Minn. Dept. Employment Security, St. Paul, 1963-64; mktg. adminstr. IBM Corp., St. Paul, 1964-65; dir. mktg. administrn. Control Data Corp., Albuquerque, Los Angeles, and Bloomington, Minn., 1965-70; mgr. Ackerman-Grant, Inc., Realtors, Albuquerque, 1970-74; pres. Key Realty, Albuquerque, 1974—; dir. mktg. Stewart Title Co., Albuquerque, 1984-86; exec. v.p. Am. Property Tax Co., 1988-93. Active Ronald McDonald House, John Baker PTA, Mile-High Little League. Mem. Nat. Assn. Realtors, Realtors Assn. N.Mex., Albuquerque Bd. Realtors (cert. residential specialist, bd. dirs., com. chmn.). Democratic. Roman Catholic. Lodge: Lions. Office: Key Realty PO Box 11771 Albuquerque NM 87192-0771

VIKING, NANCY LEE, special events management and marketing consultant; b. St. Paul, Nov. 2, 1943; d. Clarence Lee and Helen Voila (Olson) Law; m. Don Stuart Johnson, Aug. 1, 1963 (div. 1967); 1 child, Eric Don; m. Robert Edward Viking, Dec. 31, 1985. Student, U. Minn., 1961-62. cert. Festival Exec. degree, Purdue, 1986. Adminstrv. asst. St. Paul Winter Carnival Assn., 1966-67, First Bank St. Paul, 1967-69; festival mgr. Mpls. Aquatennial Assn., 1969-86; adminstrv. coordinator Internat. Festivals Assn., Mpls., 1970-83; parade coordinator City of Santa Ana (Calif.) Community Events Ctr., 1986-87; pres. Times Orange County Holiday Parade, 1988-93. Pub relations dir. Minn. Little Gophers Baseball Team, Mpls., 1983-86. Mem. Internat. Festivals Assn. (bd. dirs. 1986-87), Minn. Press Club, Pub. Relations Soc. Am., Mpls. Chinese Am. Assn. of Minn., Exec. Women in Tourism, Mpls./Iberaki (Japan) Sister City Assn. Republican. Lutheran. Lodge: Zonta.

VILARDI, AGNES FRANCINE, real estate broker; b. Monson, Mass., Sept. 29, 1918; d. Paul and Adelina (Mastrioanni) Vetti; m. Frank S. Vilardi, Dec. 2, 1939; children: Valerie, Paul. Cert. of dental assisting Pasadena Jr. Coll., 1954. Lic. real estate broker. Real estate broker, owner Vilardi Realty, Yorba Linda, Calif., Placentia, Calif., Fullerton, Calif., 1968—; cons. in property mgmt. Mem. Am. Dental Asst. Assn., North Orange County Bd. Realtors (sec./treas. 1972), Yorba Linda Country Club, Desert Princess Country Club. Home and Office: 18982 Villa Ter Yorba Linda CA 92686-2610

VILLA, JACQUELINE I., newspaper editor; b. N.Y.C., Oct. 30, 1917; d. Thomas Charles and Ada Louise (Clementi) V. BA, Hofstra U. Reporter Newsday, Hempstead, N.Y., 1942, editor, 1942-47; editor L.I. Press, Jamaica, N.Y., 1951-58, night city editor, 1958-67, editl. editor, 1967-77; travel and food editor The Ariz. Daily Star, Tucson, 1977—. Mem. Ariz. Press Women (bd. dirs., sec., chairwoman So. chpt.). Office: The Ariz Daily Star PO Box 26807 4850 S Park Ave Tucson AZ 85726-6807

VILLA, THEODORE B., artist, educator; b. Santa Barbara, Calif., Sept. 28, 1936; s. Theodore G. Villa and Josephine Melendez Willette; m. Judith Ann McConnell Villa, Aug. 21, 1963; children: Rebecca Lynn, Paul Andrew. BA, U. Calif., Santa Barbara, 1963, MFA, 1974. Cert. tchr. secondary and cmty. coll. Art instr. U. Calif., Santa Barbara, Santa Barbara City Coll., Sun Valley Ctr. for the Arts; One man shows at U. Calif. Art Mus., Santa Barbara, 1974, Esther Bear Gallery, Santa Barbara, 1975, 77, Jodi Scully Gallery, L.A., 1977, Mekler Gallery, L.A., 1980, Niles Gallery, Santa Barbara, 1981, 82, Sun Valley Ctr. for Arts and Humanities, 1982, 83, Kneeland Gallery, Sun Valley, Idaho, 1984, 85, 86, 87, 88, 89, Bridgitte Schluger Gallery, Denver, 1988, Anne Reed Gallery, Ketchum, Idaho, 1989, 90, 91, 92, Broschofsky Gallery, Ketchum, 1992, 93, many others. Exhibited in numerous group shows including L.A. County Mus. Art, 1975, 77, 78, 80, 81, 82, M. Shore and Sons Gallery, Santa Barbara, 1980, Sacred Circles Gallery, Seattle, 1982, 83, 85, Palais de Nations, Geneva, Switzerland, 1984, Nimbus Gallery, Dallas, 1985, Harcus Gallery, Boston, 1987, Munson Gallery, Santa Fe, N.Mex., 1987, 88, Lakota Gallery, Santa Monica, Calif., 1988, 89, Brigitte Schluger Gallery, Denver, 1990, Gallery 10, Santa Fe, 1991, Ctr. for Cont. Art, Seattle, 1992, Heard Mus., Phoenix, 1991, Mus. No. Ariz., Flagstaff, Ariz., 1995, Heard Mus., Phoenix, 1993, many others; one man shows include Centro Washington Irving, Madrid, 1993, ,Millicent Rogers Mus., Taos, N.Mex., 1990. Bd. dirs. Contemporary Art Forum, 1987-94; dir. Atkinson Gallery, Santa Barbara City Coll., 1986-87, coord., 1979-83, dir. smallimages exhbn., 1979-83; lectr. in field.

VILLABLANCA, JAIME ROLANDO, medical scientist, educator; b. Chillàn, Chile, Feb. 29, 1929; came to U.S., 1971; naturalized, 1985; s. Ernesto and Teresa (Hernàndez) V.; m. Guillermina Nieto, Dec. 3, 1955; children: Amparo C., Jaime G., Pablo J., Francis X., Claudio I. Bachelor in Biology, Nat. Inst. Chile, 1946; licentiate medicine, U. Chile, 1953, MD, 1954. Cert. neurophysiology. Rockefeller Found. postdoctoral fellow in physiology John Hopkins and Harvard Med. Schs., 1959-61; Fogarty internat. rsch. fellow in anatomy UCLA, 1966-68, assoc. research anatomist and psychiatrist, 1971-72, assoc. prof. psychiatry and biobehavioral scis., 1972-76, prof. psychiatry and biobehavioral scis., 1976—, prof. anatomy and cell biology, 1977—; mem. faculty U. Chile Sch. Medicine, 1954-71, prof. exptl. medicine, 1970-71; vis. prof. neurobiology Cath. U. Chile Sch. Medicine, 1974; cons. in field. Author over 200 rsch. papers, book chpts., abstracts; chief regional editor Developmental Brain Dysfunction, 1988—. Decorated Order Francisco de Miranda (Venezuela); recipient Premio Reina Sofia, Madrid, 1990, Fgn. Scientist Traveling grant Tokyo (Japan) Met. Govt., 1995; fellow Rockefeller Found., 1959-61, Fogarty Internat. Rsch. fellow NIH, 1966-68; grantee USAF Office Sci. Rsch., 1962-65, Found. Fund Rsch. Psychiatry, 1969-72, USPHS-Nat. Inst. Child Human Devel., 1972—, USPHS-Nat. Inst. Drug Abuse, 1981-85, USPHS-Nat. Inst. Neurol. Disorders and Stroke, 1988-92. Mem. AAAS, AAUP, AVEPANE (internat. sic. com., Caracas, Venezuela), Am. Assn. Anatomists, Mental Retardation Rsch. Ctr., Brain Rsch. Inst., Internat. Brain Rsch. Orgn., Am. Physiol. Soc., Soc. Neurosci., Assn. Venezolana Padres de Niños Exepcionales, Sci. Coun. Internat. Inst. Rsch. and Advice in Mental Deficiency (Madrid), Sigma Xi. Home: 200 Surfview Dr Pacific Palisades CA 90272-2911 Office: UCLA Dept Psychiatry & Biobehavioral Scis Los Angeles CA 90024

VILLANUEVA, DONNA-MAE, English educator; b. S.I., N.Y., May 20, 1964; d. E. Gary and Imelda (Garcia) V. BS in English/Biology magna cum laude, CUNY, Bklyn., 1987; MS in English, NYU, 1989; postgrad., Claremont (Calif.) Grad. Sch. Prof. English Calif. State U., Northridge, 1990-94, Calif. Inst. of Arts, Valencia, 1991—, L.A. Trade Tech. Coll., 1991—; asst. copy editor/cons. Blue Panther, S.I., 1988-91; tchr. Bishop Alemany H.S., Mission Hills, Calif., 1990; basic skills cons. Sylvan Learning Ctr., Valencia, 1989-91; instr. English Antelope Valley Coll., Lancaster, Calif., 1990-91, Coll. of Canyons, Valencia, 1989-91, L.A. Mission Coll., Mission Hills, 1989-91; pub. rels. intern, jr. adminstr. Barbara Martz & Assocs., N.Y.C., 1988; mktg. assoc. Home Box Office, N.Y.C., 1987-88; rsch. inst. Inst. Basic Rsch., S.I., 1985-86. Contbr. articles to profl. jours. Claremont Grad. Sch. fellow, 1994—. Mem. MLA, Nat. Coun. Tchrs. English, Assn. for Asian Am. Studies, Philippine Jr. Sci. League in Am., Asian Am. Journalists Assn. Home: 17454 Keswick St Northridge CA 91325-4514 Office: LA Trade Tech Coll 400 W Washington Blvd Los Angeles CA 90015-4108

VILLEGAS, RICHARD JUNIPERO, artist; b. Santa Monica, Calif., Apr. 19, 1938; s. Robert Narciso and Jessie (Rodrigues) V. Student, Art Students League, N.Y.C., 1965-66. Artist Joseph Sarosi Inc., N.Y.C., 1961-62, Vozzo & Binetti, N.Y.C., 1962-64, Siegman-Ambro, N.Y.C., 1964-77; chief artist Greenbaum Bros., Paterson, N.J., 1978-89; owner The Villegas Art Studio, Thousand Oaks, Calif., 1989—. Mem. Westlake Village (Calif.) C. of C., C.G. Jung Found., Am. Mus. Natural History, Nat. Geog. Soc., Nat. Trust for Hist. Preservation, Gold Coast Bus. and Profl. Alliance. Home and Studio: 980 Camino Flores Thousand Oaks CA 91360-2367

VILLEPONTEAU, BRYANT RICHARD, biochemist, molecular biologist; b. Camden, N.J., Dec. 19, 1944; s. Bryant Marion and Lena Ann (Baticore) V.; m. Junli Feng, Aug. 2, 1989. BA, UCLA, 1967, MS, 1969, PhD, 1977. Postdoctoral fellow UCLA, 1978-80, asst. rsch. chemist, 1981-86; asst. prof. U. Mich., Ann Arbor, 1986-92; program leader telomerase therapy Geron Corp., Menlo Park, Calif., 1993—. Mem. editorial bd. Jour. of Gerontology, 1991-94. Recipient Am. Fedn. of Aging award, 1990; Am. Cancer Soc. grantee, 1988-91; NIA sr. fellow, 1990-91; NSF grantee, 1991-95. Mem. AAAS, Am. Soc. for Microbiology, Am. Soc. for Biochemistry and Molecular Biology. Office: Geron Corp 200 Constitution Dr Menlo Park CA 94025-1130

VILNROTTER, VICTOR ALPÀR, research engineer; b. Kunhegyes, Hungary, Nov. 8, 1944; came to U.S., 1957; s. Nicholas and Aranka (Vidovits) V.; m. Felicia D'Auria, Jan. 20, 1974; children: Katherine, Brian. BSEE, NYU, 1971; MS, MIT, 1974; PhD in EE, U. So. Calif., L.A., 1978. Teaching asst. MIT, Cambridge, Mass., 1972-74; rsch. engr. Jet Propulsion Lab., Pasadena, Calif., 1979—. Contbr. articles to profl. jours.; patentee in field. Mem. IEEE (referee in communications soc. 1980—), N.Y. Acad. Scis., Sigma Xi, Eta Kappa Nu. Home: 1334 Greenbriar Rd Glendale CA 91207-1254

VINCENT, CLAUDIA GOTTSCHALL, English and German educator; b. Nuremberg, Germany, May 18, 1962; came to U.S., 1986; d. Rudolf Konrad and Ingeborg (Schöffel) Gottschall; m. Wayne Elliott Vincent, May 29, 1994. BA, U. Würzburg, Germany, 1983, MA, 1986; PhD, U. Oreg., 1993. Tchg. asst. U. N.Mex., Albuquerque, 1987-88; grad. tchg. fellow U. Oreg., Eugene, 1988-93, postgrad. instr., 1993; instr. Umpqua C.C., Roseburg, Oreg., 1992—, Lane C.C., Eugene, Oreg., 1993—. Home: 26414 Perkins Rd Veneta OR 97487-9513

VINCENT, DAVID RIDGELY, management consulting executive; b. Detroit, Aug. 9, 1941; s. Charles Ridgely and Charlotte Jane (McCarroll) V.; m. Margaret Helen Anderson, Aug. 25, 1962 (div. 1973); children: Sandra Lee, Cheryl Ann; m. Judith Ann Gomez, July 2, 1978; 1 child, Amber; stepchildren: Michael Jr., Jesse Joseph Flores. BS, BA, Calif. State U.-Sacramento, 1964; MBA, Calif. State U.-Hayward, 1971; PhD Somerset U, 1991. Cert. Mgmt. Cons. 1994. Sr. ops. analyst Aerojet Gen. Corp., Sacramento, 1960-66; contr. Hexcel Corp., Dublin, Calif., 1966-70; mng. dir. Memorex, Austria, 1970-74; sales mgr. Ampex World Ops., Switzerland, 1974-76; dir. product mgmt. NCR, Sunnyvale, Calif., 1976-79; v.p. Boole & Babbage Inc., gen. mgr. Inst. Info. Mgmt., Sunnyvale, Calif., 1979-85; pres. The Info.

Group, Inc., Santa Clara, Calif., 1985—. Deacon Union Ch., Cupertino, Calif.; USSF soccer referee. Author: Perspectives in Information Management, Information Economics, 1983, Handbook of Information Resource Management, 1987, The Information-Based Corporation: stakeholder economics and the technology investment, 1990, Reengineering Fundamentals: Business Processes and the Global Economy, 1994; contbr. monographs and papers to profl. jours. Home: 2803 Kalliam Dr Santa Clara CA 95051-6838 Office: PO Box Q Santa Clara CA 95055-3756

VINCENT, EDWARD, mayor; b. Steubenvill, Ohio, 1934. Student, State U. Iowa; BA in Corrections and Social Welfare, Calif. State U. With L.A. County Probation Dept. Mcpl. and Superior Cts.; mayor City of Inglewood, Calif., 1983—. Bd. dirs. Inglewood Neighbors, Inglewood Neighborhood Housing Svcs., Inc.; mem. Urban League, New Frontier Dem. Club, Inglewood Dem. Club, Morningside High Sch. PTA, Monroe Jr. High Sch. PTA, Kew-Bennett PTA; pres. Morningside High Sch. Dad's Club. With U.A. Army, 1957-1959. Mem. NAACP, Calif. Probation Parole Corrections Assn., Black Probation Officers Assn., Calif. Narcotic Officers Assn., Mexican-Am. Corrections Assn., S.W, Horseman, Assn., Imperial Village Blck Club, Inglewood Block Club (chmn. human affairs). Office: 1 W Manchester Blvd Inglewood CA 90301-1750*

VINCENT, JOHN GRAHAM, administrator; b. Rustington, Sussex, England, Sept. 17, 1935; came to U.S., 1965; s. Leroy Michael and Ethel Maude (Pascoe) V. BA in Bldg., Worthing Coll., 1957; MA in Archtl. Design, Brighton Coll., 1960. Asst. mng. dir. Vincent Bros., England, 1959-61; mktg. dir. Mktg. Assocs. Internat., England, 1960-62; trade show officer Am. Embassy Depts. Agrl. and Commerce, England, 1962-65; acct. exec. United Expn. Svcs., Chgo., 1965-71; resort owner Casa Grand, Portugal, 1971-76; v.p., dir. nat. sales Greyhound Corp., San Francisco, 1976-81, Washington, 1976-81; gen. mgr. Freeman Decoration Co., Atlanta, 1981-83; dir. trade shows Nat. Assn. Music Mchts., Carlsbad, Calif., 1984—. Mem. Internat. Assn. Expn. Mgmt. (bd. dirs. So. Calif. chpt. 1984-94, pres. 1991). Home: 1904 Carter Mill Way Brookeville MD 20833-2200 Office: Nat Assn Music Merchants 438-4051 Avenida Encinas Carlsbad CA 92008

VINCENT, MARK KENT, lawyer; b. Murray, Utah, May 10, 1959; s. Kent Bryan and Edith Theone (Paxton) V. BA, Brigham Young U., 1984; JD, Pepperdine U., 1987. Corp. sec. Vincent Drug Co. Inc., Midvale, Utah, 1980-87; dep. dist. atty. Office of Dist. Atty. County of Ventura, Calif., 1987-89; asst. U.S. atty. U.S. Dept. of Justice, Salt Lake City, 1989—; law clk. Utah State Supreme Ct., Salt Lake City, 1986; v.p. Barrister's Bar Orgn., Ventura, 1988-89. Margaret Martin Brock scholar Pepperdine U., 1986-87. Mem. Calif. Bar Assn., Utah Bar Assn. Mormon. Office: US Attys Office 350 S Main St # 476 Salt Lake City UT 84101-2106

VINCENT, STEVE, environmental engineer; b. 1951. BS in Oceanography, U. Wash., 1974. With Weyerhaeuser, Tacoma, 1974-85; with Columbia Analytical Svcs., Kelso, Wash., 1986—, now pres. Office: Columbia Analytical Svc 1317 S 13th Ave Kelso WA 98626-2845*

VINCENTI, SHELDON ARNOLD, law educator, lawyer; b. Ogden, Utah, Sept. 4, 1938; s. Arnold Joseph and Mae (Burch) V.; m. Elaine Cathryn Wacker, June 18, 1964; children: Matthew Lewis, Amanda Jo. AB, Harvard U., 1960, JD, 1963. Bar: Utah 1963. Sole practice law, Ogden, 1966-67; ptnr. Lowe and Vincenti, Ogden, 1968-70; legis. asst. to U.S. Rep. Gunn McKay, Washington, 1971-72, adminstrv. asst., 1973; prof., assoc. dean U. of Idaho Coll. of Law, Moscow, Idaho, 1973-83, dean, prof. law, 1983-95, prof. law, 1995—. Home: 2480 W Twin Rd Moscow ID 83843-9114 Office: U Idaho Coll Law 6th & Rayburn St Moscow ID 83843

VINCENTI-BROWN, CRISPIN RUFUS WILLIAM, engineering executive; b. Epsom, Surrey, England, Sept. 20, 1951; came to U.S., 1989; s. Douglas Hector and Joan Margaret Patricia (Lowe) Brown; m. Terry Doreen Bennett, May 20, 1978 (dec. Oct. 1992); children: Genevieve Louise, Juliette Alexandra; m. Margaret Anna Vincenti, Feb. 13, 1993. BSc in Engring. Prodn., U. Birmingham, 1974. Mgr. Soc. M.O.M, Grans, France, 1975; prin. cons. Ingersoll Engrs. Inc., Rugby, England, 1975-79; pres., dir. Ingersoll Engrs. SA, Annecy, France, 1979-89; sr. ptnr. Ingersoll Engrs. Inc., Los Altos, Calif., 1989—; v.p. Groupe de Talloires, Geneva, 1987-89; bd. dirs. Ops. Mgmt. Assn., Waco, Tex. Fellow Inst. Elec. Engrs. (chartered engr.). Home: 1098 Eastwood Ct Los Altos CA 94024-5015 Office: Ingersoll Engrs 5100 E State St Ste 4 Rockford IL 61108-2398

VINCENZI, FRANK FOSTER, pharmacology educator; b. Seattle, Mar. 14, 1938; s. Frank Vincenzi and Thelma C. (McAllister) Olson; m. Judith I. Heimbigner, Aug. 27, 1960; children: Ann Marie, Franklin R., Joseph P. BS in Pharmacy, U. Wash., 1960, MS in Pharmacology, 1962, PhD in Pharmacology, 1965. NSF postdoct. fellow U. Bern, Switzerland, 1965-67; asst. prof. U. Wash., Seattle, 1967-72, assoc. prof., 1972-80, acting chair, pharmacology, 1975-77, prof., 1980—. Contbr. articles to profl. jours. Mem. Am. Med. Informatics Assn., Am. Soc. of Hypertension, Am. Soc. for Pharmacology Exptl. Therapeutics, Biophys. Soc., Oxygen Soc., Western Pharmacology Soc. (pres. 1988-89). Office: Univ Wash Pharmacology Box 357280 Seattle WA 98195-7280

VINES, HENRY ELLSWORTH, III, financial executive, wood product executive, computer and tax consultant; b. Chgo., Apr. 17, 1950; s. Henry Ellsworth and Verle (Low) V.; m. Ethel Melton (div. 1977); 1 child, Tiffany Layne; m. Cindy Lou Rich, Jan. 5, 1985; 1 child, Sasha Teresa Root. BS, Menlo Sch. Bus. Adminstrn., 1972; MBA, Golden Gate Grad. Sch., 1985; CFP, Coll. Fin. Planning, Denver, 1987; JD, William F. Taft Law Sch., 1994. CPA. Asst. contr. Legallet Tanning, San Francisco, 1973-79; auditor Martin Schoonover & Paddock, Orange, Calif., 1980-82; tax mgr. Helsley Mulcahy & Fesler, Santa Ana, Calif., 1982-85; v.p. fin. Catalina Furniture Co., Fullerton, Calif., 1985-94; CFO Precision Concepts, Anaheim, Calif., 1987-93; pvt. practice in tax preparation Orange, Calif., 1985—, pvt. practice in computer consulting, 1985—; CFO M.E. Woodworking, Riverside, Calif., 1989-93, Textured Design Furniture, Anaheim, 1994—. Contbr. articles in field. Mem. Am. Inst. CPA's, Calif. Inst. CPA's, Foster City Tennis Club (pres. 1977), San Mateo Tennis Club (pres. 1978). Republican. Home and Office: 30720 N Singingwood St Orange CA 92669

VINSON, CONNIE SUE, aerospace engineer; b. Gardner, Kans., May 3, 1956; d. Vernon L. and Beatrice Marie (McCann) Messer; m. John Willliam Vinson, Jan. 24, 1987; children: Kyla Marie, Richard Glenn. BS in Physics, Baker U., Baldwin City, Kans., 1977; MS, Trinity U., San Antonio, 1979; MBA, Harvard U., 1983. Engr. Armstrong Machine Works, New Braunfels, Tex., 1979-81; asst. to v.p. Barnes and Jones, Newton, Mass., 1982; engr. Boise Cascade Corp., DeRidder, La., 1983-84; ops. mgr. Geneva Group Inc., Woburn, Mass., 1984-87; product mgr. TLB, Inc., Findlay, Ohio, 1987-88; tech. staff Rocketdyne div. Rockwell Internat. Corp., Canoga Park, Calif., 1990—; mem. adv. bd. Geneva Group, 1986-88. Recipient Leadership award Rocketdyne and YWCA of L.A., 1994. Mem. Harvard Bus. Sch. Assn. So. Calif. Republican. Presbyterian. Home: 2666 Velarde Dr Thousand Oaks CA 91360-1337 Office: Rocketdyne 6633 Canoga Ave Canoga Park CA 91301

VINSON, JOHN WILLIAM, aerospace engineer; b. Champaign, Ill., Feb. 3, 1955; s. William Glenn and Virginia Grace (Marsh) V.; m. Connie Sue Messer, Jan. 24, 1987; children: Richard Glenn, Kyla Marie. BS in Aero. and Astronautical Engring., U. Ill., 1977; MS in Aerospace Engring., U. Cin., 1982. Engr. GE Aircraft Engines, Cin., 1977-84; mgr. combustor design GE Aircraft Engines, Lynn, Mass., 1984-86, mgr. augmentor design, 1986-87; mgr. NASP propulsion module design GE Aircraft Engines, Cin., 1987-88, mgr. demonstrator engine cycle design, 1988-89; mem. tech. staff hypersonic and combined cycle Rocketdyne div. Rockwell Internat., Canoga Park, Calif., 1989—. Co-patentee gas turbine engine carburetor, bimodal swirler injector for gas turbine carburetor. Mem. AIAA, Nat. Mgmt. Assn. Home: 2666 Velarde Dr Thousand Oaks CA 91360-1337 Office: Rocketdyne Divsn Rockwell Internat 6633 Canoga Ave # 45 Canoga Park CA 91303-2790

VINTAS, GUSTAVO HORACIO, actor, psychiatrist; b. Buenos Aires, Argentina, Nov. 27, 1948; came to U.S., 1976; s. Mauricio and Zelmira (Silbert) V. BS, U. Poitiers, France, 1967; MD, U. Buenos Aires, 1973. Resident in psychiatry McGill U., Montreal, 1976; fellow in child psychiatry Cornell U., N.Y.C., 1978; instr. psychiatry N.Y. Hosp.-Cornell U., N.Y.C., 1978-84; assoc. psychiatrist Cedars-Sinai Med. Ctr., L.A., 1986—; Diplomate in psychiatry and child psychiatry Am. Bd. Psychiatry and Neurology, Royal Coll. Physicians and Surgeons of Canada. Appeared in films including Lethal Weapon, Mickie and Maude, Vampire at Midnight, The Journey Inside, Midnight, Fair Game; TV appearances include Drug Wars, Tales From the Crypt, Beauty and the Beast, Mistress, Murder She Wrote, (Madonna video) Express Yourself; preformer one-man show Merci Maurice, Evoking the Memory of Maurice Chevalier. Mem. Royal Coll. Physicians and Surgeons, Am. Psychiat. Assn. Office: 9000 Cynthia St Apt 401 Los Angeles CA 90069-4845

VINTON, ALICE HELEN, real estate company executive; b. McMinnville, Oreg., Jan. 10, 1942; d. Gale B. and Saima Helen (Pekkola) V. Student, Portland State Coll., Northwestern Sch. Commerce. Lic. real estate broker, Hawaii. Owner, prin. broker Vinton Realty, Honolulu, 1988—. Founder, bd. dirs. Kekuaanaui, Hawaii Big Sisters, 1972-76; former vol. Child and Family Svc., women's divsn. Halawa Prison; bd. dirs. Kindergarten and Children's Aid Assn., 1977-88, advisor, mem. long-range planning com. 1988-90; former mem. tuition aid com., chmn. nominating com. and capital improvements com. Laura Morgan Pre-Sch.; bd. dirs. Hawaii Theatre Ctr., 1985-86; mem. Lyon Arboretum Assn. Recipient proclamation Hawaii Ho. of Reps., cert. of merit for disting. svc. to community, Dictionary of Internat. Biography, Vol. XXI, 1990. Mem. Nat. Assn. Realtors, Hawaii Assn. Realtors, Honolulu Bd. Realtors, Honolulu C. of C., Downtown Improvement Assn., Acad. Arts, Bishop Mus. Assn., Wildlife Fedn., Neighborhood Justice Ctr. Honolulu, Friends of Iolani Palace, Smithsonian Inst., Hawaii Polo Club, Honolulu Press Club (membership chmn. 1988-90), Rainbow Girls Club (life), Hawaii Humane Soc., Sierra Club, Hist. Hawaii, Cen. Bus. Club Honolulu, Nature Conservancy Hawaii, Women's Healthsource, YWCA, Cousteau Soc., Wolf Haven, Honolulu Polo Club, Orchid Soc. Manoa, North Shore Animal League, Nat. Pks. and Conservation Assn., Wilderness Soc. Republican. Episcopalian. Office: 650 Ala Moana Blvd Ste 211 Honolulu HI 96813-4907

VIOLET, WOODROW WILSON, JR., retired chiropractor; b. Columbus, Ohio, Sept. 19, 1937; s. Woodrow Wilson and Alice Katherine (Woods) V.; student Ventura Coll., 1961-62; grad. L.A. Coll. Chiropractic, 1966; m. Judith Jane Thatcher, June 15, 1963; children: Woodina Lonize, Leslie Alice. Pvt. practice chiropractic medicine, Santa Barbara, Calif., 1966-73, London, 1973-74, Carpinteria, Calif., 1974-84; past mem. coun. roentgenology Am. Chiropractic Assn. Former mem. Parker Chiropractic Rsch. Found., Ft. Worth. Served with USAF, 1955-63. Recipient award merit Calif. Chiropractic Colls., Inc., 1975, cert. of appreciation Nat. Chiropractic Anti-trust Com., 1977. Mem. Nat. Geog. Soc., L.A. Coll. Chiropractic Alumni Assn., Ctr. Scis. in Pub. Interest, Delta Sigma. Patentee surg. instrument.

VIOLETTE, GLENN PHILLIP, construction engineer; b. Hartford, Conn., Nov. 15, 1950; s. Reginald Joseph and Marielle Theresa (Bernier) B.; m. Susan Linda Begam, May 15, 1988. BSCE, Colo. State U., 1982. Registered profl. engr., Colo. Engring. aide Colo. State Hwy. Dept., Glenwood Springs, Colo., 1974-79, hwy. engr., 1980-82; hwy. engr. Colo. State Hwy. Dept., Loveland, Colo., 1979-80; project engr. Colo. State Hwy. Dept., Glenwood Canyon, Colo., 1983—; guest speaker in field. Contbg. editor, author, photographer publs. in field. Recipient scholarship Fed. Hwy Adminstrn., 1978. Mem. ASCE, Amnesty Internat., Nat. Rifle Assn., Internat. Platform Assn., Siera Club, Audubon Soc., Nature Conservancy, World Wildlife Fund, Cousteau Soc., Chi Epsilon. Office: Colo Dept Transp 202 Centennial Dr Glenwood Springs CO 81601-2845

VISCOVICH, ANDREW JOHN, educational management consultant; b. Oakland, Calif., Sept. 25, 1925; s. Peter Andrew and Lucy Pauline (Razovich) V.; m. Roen Shirley Mulvana, Apr. 19, 1952 (div. Feb. 1985); children: Randal Peter, Andra Clair; m. Elena Beth Wong, Apr. 28, 1993; 1 child, Alison Wong. BA, U. Calif., Berkeley, 1949; MA, San Francisco State U., 1960; EdD, U. Calif., Berkeley, 1973; cert. labor dispute resolution, Golden Gate U., 1976. Supt. Palm Springs (Calif.) Unified Sch. Dist., 1976-79, Garvey Sch. Dist., Rosemead, Calif., 1979-88, Berkeley Unified Sch. Dist., 1988-900; pres. Ctr. for Ednl. Rsch. in Adminstrn., Stockton, Calif., 1990—; state adminstr. Coachella Unified Sch. Dist., Sacramento, Calif., 1992; adj. prof. U. Calif., Berkeley, 1965-67, Calif. State U., Hayward, 1970-76, L.A., 1971-88; exec. dir. Marcus Foster Edn. Found., Oakland, 1975-76; cons. Spanish Ministry Edn., 1987—, Republic of China Ministry Edn., Taipei, Taiwan, 1986-89, Croatian Ministry Edn., Zagreb, 1993—, Morriott Sch. Svcs, 1992—, CSHQH, Idaho; pre-sch. dir. Oakland Unified Sch. Dist., 1974-76; asst. dir. Bay Area Bilingual Edn. League, 1971-75; dir. Bay Area Tchr. Ctr., 1974, asst. dir. Far West Ednl. Lab., 1974; adj. assoc. prof. Calif. State U. at L.A.and Hayward, U. South Fla., U. Oreg., Coll. of Holy Names; exec. dir. ANRO Cons., Inc., 1973-82. Author: Language Programs for the Disadvantaged, 1965, R.E.S. Plus, 1978; contbr. The School Principal, 1978. Chair United Way, Pasadena, Calif., 1985; pres. Croation Scholarship Found., San Ramon, Calif., 1993-94. Served to Lt. USNR, 1959-64. Recipient award for innovations in alternative schools Behavioral Rsch. Lab., San Francisco, 1973; named Knight of Civil Order of Merit King Juan Carlos of Spain, 1990. Mem. Am. Mgmt. Assn., Am. Assn. Sch. Adminstrs., Assn. Calif. Sch. Adminstrs., Calif. City Sch. Supts., Calif. Tchrs. Assn. (John Swett award 1978). Home: 3754 Fort Donelson Dr Stockton CA 95219

VISLOSKY, FRANK MICHAEL, nursing educator; b. Pueblo, Colo., Sept. 29, 1957; s. Frank and Frances Eleanor (Kochevar) V. Dipoma, Mass. Gen. Hosp. Sch. Nursing, 1978; BS in Physiology, MIT, 1985; student, Harvard Med. Sch., 1987. Registered cardiovascular technologist. Staff nurse surg. ICU Boston City Hosp., 1978-79; staff nurse Mass. Gen. Hosp., Boston, 1979-80, 85-87, tchr. nursing, 1980-82, clin. rsch. nurse, 1982-84, head nurse, unit tchr., 1984-85, hemodynamic monitoring specialist, 1987-89, cons. critical care, staff nurse, 1989-90; head nurse cardiovascular ICU St. Mary-Corwin Regional Med. Ctr., Pueblo, Colo., 1990-91, head nurse cardiovascular svcs., 1991, educator nursing, cardiac clinician, 1991—. Contbr. articles to profl. jours. Mem. AACN, Am. Assn. Oper. Rm. Nurses, Am. Heart Assn., Emergency Nurses Assn. Roman Catholic. Home: 1425 Claremont Ave Pueblo CO 81004-3009 Office: St Mary Corwin Hosp 1008 Minnequa Ave Pueblo CO 81004-3733

VISSOTZKY, DAVID ANTHONY, army officer, aviator; b. Houston, Mar. 15, 1958; s. Henry Joeseph and Wilma June (Parker) V.; m. Andrea Julia Leach, Oct. 25, 1986; 1 child, Alexander Joseph. BS in Phys. Sci., Wash. State U., 1980. Commd. 2d lt. U.S. Army, 1980, advanced through grades to maj.; platoon leader 1st Cavalry Divsn., Ft. Hood, Tex., 1981-84; battalion ops. officer 224th ATK HEL BN, Aberdeen Proving Ground, Md., 1985-89; asst. brigade ops. officer 17th Aviation Brigade, Korea, 1989-90, comdr. attack helicopter co., 1990-91; chief aircraft devel. br. Directorate Combat Devel., Ft. Rucker, Ala., 1991-93; chief aviation asst. team dep. comdr. U.S. Army Readiness Group Pacific, Ft. Shafter, Hawaii, 1993-94; battalion ops. officer 1/25th ATK HEL BN, Schofield Barracks, Hawaii, 1994—. Mem. Army Aviation Assn. Am. (treas. 1987-89). Office: 1/25th ATK HEL BN 25th Infantry Divsn (LT) Schofield Barracks HI 96857-6000

VISTICA, JERROLD FRANCIS, publishing executive; b. Stockton, Calif., Jan. 16, 1925; s. Louis and Mary Theresa (McCarty) V.; m. Lorraine Louise Miller, May 3, 1957 (dec. Nov. 1961); children: Victoria Vistica Palmieri, Mary Theresa II. AA, Yuba Coll., 1951; postgrad., U. Calif., Berkeley, 1952; BS, U. San Francisco, 1963; postgrad., Golden Gate U., 1983-84. Lic. real estate broker Calif. Ranch mgr. L. Vistica & Son Ranch, Live Oak, Calif., 1953; pres. Louis Vistica Nurseries, Yuba City, Calif., 1954-59; real estate sales Trevor & Co., San Francisco, 1960, Andre F. Bosc, San Francisco, 1961; real estate broker pvt. practice, San Francisco, 1962-89; mng. dir., auctioneer Asset Disposal Svcs., San Francisco, 1989-93; mng. editor The Common Good Press, San Francisco, 1994—; environ. cons. O.E. Griffin & Assocs., San Francisco, 1971-80; security cons., San Francisco, 1980-89. Author: Common Sense Self Protection Primer, 1993; editor: (newsletter) Self Protection Letter, 1994. Pres. Bella Vita Soc., San Francisco, 1974; mem. Fine Arts Mus., 1960—. Mem. Calif. Acad. Scis. (life), Mechanics Inst., Commonwealth Club Calif., Calif. Alumni Assn., U. San Francisco Alumni Assn., Alpha Gamma Sigma. Office: The Common Good Press PO Box 193002 San Francisco CA 94119-3002

VISTNES, LARS M., plastic surgeon; b. Stavanger, Norway, 1927. MD, U. Man., Can., 1957. Intern Winnipeg (Man., Can.) Gen. Hosp., 1956-57; resident in surgery St. Luke's Hosp., 1962-65; resident in plastic surgery St. Francis Meml. Hosp., San Francisco, 1965-68; plastic surgeon Stanford (Calif.) U. Hosps., 1971—. Fellow ACS, Royal Coll. Surgeons Can., Am. Assn. Plastic Surgery. Office: Stanford U Med Ctr Divsn Plastic Surgery NC 104 Palo Alto CA 94305*

VITULLI, MARIE ANGELA, mathematician; b. Mineola, N.Y., Nov. 19, 1949; d. Vito Nunzio and Marie Georgiana (Mangoni) V. BA, U. Rochester, N.Y., 1971; MA, U. Pa., 1973, PhD, 1976. Asst. prof. math. U. Oreg., Eugene, 1976-82; assoc. prof. math. U. Oreg., 1982-91, prof. math, 1991—. Contbr. articles to profl. jours. Chmn. Com. on Status Women, Eugene, 1989-92; violist Emerald Chamber Orch., 1988—. NSF traineeship, 1972-73; U. Pa. fellow, 1975; Stoddard Prize in Math., U. Rochester, 1969. Mem. Am. Math. Soc., Am. Assn. U. Profs., Math. Assn. Am., Assn. for Women in Math., Phi Beta Kappa. Home: 4427 Fox Hollow Rd Apt 16 Eugene OR 97405-4575 Office: Univ of Oregon Dept Math Eugene OR 97403

VIVIAN, LINDA BRADT, sales and public relations executive; b. Elmira, N.Y., Nov. 22, 1945; d. Lorenz Claude and Muriel (Dolan) Bradt; m. Robert W. Vivian, Apr. 5, 1968 (div. Sept. 1977). Student, Andrews U., 1963-66. Adminstrv. asst. Star-Gazette, Elmira, 1966-68; editor Guide, staff writer Palm Springs (Calif.) Life mag., 1970-75; dir. sales and pub. rels. Palm Springs Aerial Tramway, 1975—; sec. Hospitality and Bus. Industry Coun. Palm Springs Desert Resorts, 1989-91, vice-chmn. 1991-94, chmn., 1994-95. Mem. Hotel Sales and Mktg. Assn. (allied nominating chmn. Palm Springs chpt. 1986-88), Am. Soc. Assn. Execs., Travel Industry Assn., Hospitality Industry and Bus. Coun. of Palm Springs Resorts (sec. 1989-91, vice-chmn. 1991-94, chmn. 1994-95), Nat. Tour Assn. (co-chair Team Calif. promotions com. 1993—), Calif. Travel Industry Assn., Palm Springs C. of C. (bd. dirs. 1984-85). Republican. Office: Palm Springs Aerial Tramway One Tramway Rd Palm Springs CA 92262

VIVIANI, KIMBERLY JEAN, software programmer; b. San Francisco, Mar. 2, 1969; d. Ben and Diane Marie (Debono) V. BA in Math., U. Calif., Santa Cruz, 1991. Bioanalyst Syntex, Palo Alto, Calif., 1992-94; authorware programmer Acad. Systems Corp., Mountain View, Calif., 1994—. Mem. Phi Beta Kappa. Democrat. Roman Catholic.

VIZCAINO, HENRY P., mining engineer, consultant; b. Hurley, N.Mex., Aug. 28, 1918; s. Emilio D. and Petra (Perea) V.; m. Esther B. Lopez, Sept. 16, 1941; children: Maria Elena, Rick, Arthur, Carlos. BS in Engring., Nat. U., Mexico City, 1941; geology student, U. N.Mex., 1951-54. Registered profl. engr. With Financiera Minera S.A., Mexico City, 1942-47; gen. mgr. Minas Mexicanas S.A., Torreon, Mex., 1947-51; exploration engr. Kerr McGee Corp., Okla., 1955-69; cons. Albuquerque, 1969-75, 84—; regional geologist Bendix Field Engring., Austin, Tex., 1976-79; staff geo-scientist Bendix Field Engring., Grand Junction, Colo., 1979-81; sr. geologist Hunt Oil Co., Dallas, 1981-84. Contbr. articles to profl. publs. Mem. AIME, Internat. Platform Assn., Aircraft Owners and Pilots Assn., Rotary, Elks. Republican. Congregationalist. Home and Office: 20 Canoncito Vista Rd Tijeras NM 87059-7833

VLASAK, WALTER RAYMOND, state official, management development consultant; b. Hartsgrove, Ohio, Aug. 31, 1938; s. Raymond Frank and Ethel (Chilan) V.; m. Julia Andrews, Feb. 25, 1966; children: Marc Andrew, Tanya Ethel. BSBA, Kent State U., 1963; MA, U. Akron, 1975. Commd. 2d lt. U.S. Army, 1963; platoon leader, anti-tank platoon leader and battalion adjutant 82d Airborne Div., 1963-65; combat duty Viet Nam, 1965-66, 68-69; exec. officer, co. comdr. and hdqrs. commandant of the cadre and troops U.S. Army Sch. Europe, Oberammergau, Fed. Republic Germany, 1966-68; asst. prof. Mil. Sci. Kent (Ohio) State U., 1970-74; infantry battalion exec. officer 9th Infantry Div., Ft. Lewis, Wash., 1976-77, orgnl. effectiveness cons. to commanding gen., 1977-79, brigade exec. officer, 1980-82; orgnl. effectiveness cons. to commanding gen. 8th U.S. Army, U.S. Forces, Korea, 1979-80; advanced through ranks to lt. col. U.S. Army, 1980, ret., 1984; pres. Comsult, Inc., Tacoma, 1984—; mgr. employee devel. tng. dept. social and health svcs. State of Wash., Tacoma, 1985—. Decorated Legion of Merit, Bronze Star with V device and two oak leaf clusters, Air medal, Purple Heart, Vietnamese Cross of Gallantry with Silver Star. Mem. Am. Soc. for Tng. and Devel., Assn. U.S. Army (bd. dirs. Tacoma 1984—). Home: 10602 Hill Terrace Rd SW Tacoma WA 98498-4337 Office: State of Wash Dept Social and Health Svcs 8425 27th St W Tacoma WA 98466-2722

VLOSKY, MARK ALAN, psychologist; b. N.Y.C., Dec. 23, 1944; s. Victor Victoroff and Margery (Weintraub) Vlosky; m. Bertha Dinger, Aug. 25, 1968 (div. Jan. 1987); children: Robin, Karen; m. Louise Benson, July 25, 1987; 1 child, Eric Blosky. BA, NYU, 1967; MA, New Sch. for Social Rsch., 1977, PhD, 1979. Lic. psychologist, N.Y., Colo. Clin. dir. Wyo. Mental Health Ctr., Douglas, 1980-83; staff psychologist Kaiser-Permanente, Denver, 1983-86, Family Psychology Assocs., Longmont, Colo., 1989—; pvt. practice Broomfield, Colo., 1984—; clin. assoc. U. Denver, 1986—; cons. Parents of Murdered Children, Denver, 1986-90. Inventor (game for child therapists) Our Game, 1986. Cons. City of Broomfield, 1988. Recipient Values in Wyo. award Wyo. Coun. for Humanities, Cheyenne, 1981; Hiram Halle fellow New Sch. for Social Rsch., N.Y.C., 1979. Mem. APA, Colo. Psychol. Assn. (dist. coord.), Boulder Interdisciplinary Com. Office: 80 Garden Ctr # 6 Broomfield CO 80020-1735

VO, HUU DINH, pediatrician, educator; b. Hue, Vietnam, Apr. 29, 1950; came to U.S., 1975; s. Chanh Dinh and Dong Thi (Pham) V.; m. Que Phuong Tonnu, Mar. 22, 1984; children: Katherine Hoa-An, Karyn Bao-An. MD, U. Saigon, 1975. Diplomate Am. Bd. Pediatrics. Adminstr. bilingual vocat. tng. Community Care and Devel. Svc., L.A., 1976-77; resident in pediatrics Univ. Hosp., Jacksonville, Fla., 1977-80; physician, surgeon, chief med. officer Lanterman Devel. Ctr., Pomona, Calif., 1980-92, chief med. staff, 1984-88, coord. med. ancillary svc., 1984-88, 91—; physician Pomona Valley Community Hosp., 1988-90; asst. clin. prof. Loma Linda (Calif.) Med. Sch., 1985-92; chief med. officer So. Reception Ctr.and Clinic., Norwalk, Calif., 1992—; bd. dirs. Pomona Med. Clinic Inc. Pres. Vietnamese Cmty. Ponoma Valley, 1983-85, 87—, chmn., 1993—; nat. co-chair mem. Vietnamese Am. Cmty. in USA, 1993—; bd. dirs. YMCA, Pomona, 1988—, Sch.-Cmty. Partnership, Ponoma, 1988—. Mem. AMA (Physician recognition award 1989, 1992), L.A. Pediatrics Soc., Vietnamese-Am. Physicians Assn. La. and Orange County (founding mem., sec. 1982-84, bd. dirs. 1987-90). Republican. Buddhist. Home: 654 E Lennox Ct Brea CA 92621-7302 Office: So Reception Ctr and Clinic 13200 Bloomfield Ave Norwalk CA 90650-3253

VOBEJDA, WILLIAM FRANK, aerospace engineer; b. Lodgepole, S.D., Dec. 5, 1918; s. Robert and Lydia (Stefek) V.; m. Virginia Parker, Oct. 24, 1942; children—William N., Margaret, Mary Joan, Barbara, Lori. B.C.E., S.D. Sch. Mines and Tech., 1942. Registered profl. engr., Colo. Stress analyst Curtiss Wright Corp., Columbus, Ohio, 1942-45; civil/hydraulic engr. Bur. Reclamation, Denver, 1945-54; mech. supr. Stearns Roger Corp., Denver, 1954-62; mgr. Martin Marietta Corp., Denver, 1962-86, mgr. engring. M-X Program, 1978-86; pres. BV Engring., Inc., Englewood, Colo., 1986-89. Active Boy Scouts Am. Recipient Silver Beaver award. Mem. Englewood City Council 1984-87, Englewood Water and Sewer Bd., 1990—. Mem. AIAA. Democrat. Roman Catholic. Clubs: St. Louis Men's, K.C., Martin Marietta Chess, Lions Internat. (sec.).

VOELKER, MARGARET IRENE (MEG VOELKER), gerontology, medical/surgical nurse; b. Bitburg, Germany, Dec. 31, 1955; d. Lewis R. and Patricia Irene (Schaffner) Miller; 1 child, Christopher Douglas. Diploma, Clover Park Vocat.-Tech., Tacoma, 1975, diploma in practical nursing, 1984; ASN, Tacoma (Wash.) C.C., 1988; postgrad., U. Washington Tacoma, Tacoma, 1992-95. Cert. ACLS. Nursing asst. Jackson County Hosp., Altus, Okla., 1976-77; receptionist Western Clinic, Tacoma, 1983; LPN, Tacoma Gen. Hosp., 1984-88, clin. geriatric nurse, 1988-90, clin. nurse post anesthesia care unit perioperative svcs., 1990—, mem. staff nurse coun., 1990-91.

Recipient G. Corydon Wagner endowment fund scholarship. Mem. Post Anesthesia Nurses Assn., Phi Theta Kappa.

VOGEL, RICHARD WIEDEMANN, business owner, ichthyodynamicist; b. N.Y.C., Apr. 12, 1950; s. Jack and Edna Jeanne (Wiedemann) V.; m. Pamela Jane Gordon, Aug. 7, 1974; children: Amy Jane, Katy Lynn, Gina Marie, Krista Jeanne. Grad. high sch., Calif. Owner, operator ichthyol. rsch. and comml. fishing vessel Santa Barbara, Calif., 1973-88; designer advanced hydrodynamic curvature Clark Foam Factory, Laguna Beach, Calif., 1994—; lectr. Surfrider Found. Conf., U. Calif., San Diego, 1994. Inventor in field. Episcopalian. Office: Ichthyodynamics PO Box 1167 Hanalei HI 96714-1167

VOGEL, RONALD BRUCE, food products executive; b. Vancouver, Wash., Feb. 16, 1934; s. Joseph John and Thelma Mae (Karker) V.; m. Donita Dawn Schneider, Aug. 8, 1970 (dec. June 1974); 1 child, Cynthia Dawn; m. Karen Vogel, Feb. 14, 1992. BS in Chemistry, U. Wash., 1959. Glass maker Peuberthy Instrument Co., Seattle, 1959-60; lab. technician Gt. Western Malting Co., Vancouver, 1960-62, chief chemist, 1962-67, mgr. corp. quality control, 1967-72, mgr. customer svcs., 1972-77, v.p. customer svcs., 1977-79, v.p. sales, 1979-84, gen. mgr., 1984-89, pres., CEO, 1989—; chmn. bd. dirs. R&K Bus. Mgmt. Cons., Vancouver. Contbr. articles to profl. jours. Chmn. bd. dirs. Columbia Empire Jr. Achievement, Portland, Oreg., 1991-92. With U.S. Army, 1954-56. Recipient numerous awards. Mem. Master Brewers Assn. Am. Home: 11500 NE 76th St # A3-151 Vancouver WA 98662-3939

VOGELSANG, PHILIP JOHN, pathologist; b. Oakland, Calif., Sept. 3, 1954; s. Otto C. and Margaret Vogelsang; m. Kathleen Fischer, Oct. 14, 1979; children; Kirsten, Emily, Laura. AB in Zoology, Humboldt State U., 1978; MD, U. Calif., San Diego, 1984; PhD in Comparative Pathology, U. calif., Davis, 1993. Diplomate Am. Bd. Pathology with subspecialty in anatomic and clin. pathology, qualfications in cytopathology. Intern U. Calif. Affiliate Cmty. Hosp., Santa Rosa, 1984-85; resident clin. pathology U. Calif., Davis, 1985-90, Dean's scholar, 1986-88; hon. clin. fellow in cytopathology U. Alberta, Edmonton, Can., 1990-91; staff pathologist Mad River Cmty. Hosp., Arcata, Calif., 1991—.

VOGLER, JAMES WAYLAN, physicist, consultant; b. Barrington, Ill., June 4, 1948; s. Richard D. and Shirlee (Gardner) V. BS in Physics, MIT, 1971; MA in Physics, U. Ill., Chgo., 1978; PhD in Physics, U. Calif., Berkeley, 1988. Engr. Hewlett-Packard, Palo Alto, Calif., 1971-76; staff engr. Motorola, Schaumburg, Ill., 1976-83; staff engr., cons. Omni Spectra div. M/A Co., Tempe, Ariz., 1983-86; sr. ptnr. Mirage/KLM Communs., Morgan HIll, Calif., 1989—; ptnr., v.p. R&D, sr. scientist Atlantis Fiberoptics, Scottsdale, Ariz., 1988—; pwner, sr. cons. JV Assocs., Phoenix, 1986—; cons. Rockwell Internat., Cedar Rapids, Iowa, 1987-89, Teledyne, Culver City, Calif., 1989—, Hughes Aircraft Co., L.A., 1987—. Contbr. articles to profl. jours.; patentee in field. NSF fellow U. Cambridge, Eng., 1970; recipient John T. Chambers Meml. award Ctrl. States VHF Soc., 1991. Mem. IEEE, Am. Inst. Physics. Office: JV Assocs 2540 E Heatherbrae Dr Phoenix AZ 85016-5668

VOGT, EVON ZARTMAN, III, merchant banker; b. Chgo., Aug. 29, 1946; s. Evon Zartman Jr. and Catherine C. (Hiller) V.; m. Mary Hewit Anschuetz, Sept. 26, 1970; 1 child, Elizabeth Christine. AB, Harvard U., 1968; MBA, U. Colo., 1976. Vol., then staff mem. U.S. Peace Corps, Brazil, 1968-72; asst. dir. Stanford Program Indian Demography, Mex., 1973; v.p. Wells Fargo Bank, Sao Paulo, Brazil, 1977-81; mng. dir. Wells Fargo Internat. Ltd., Grand Cayman, 1982-84; mgr. global funding Wells Fargo Bank, San Francisco, 1984-86; mng. dir. Arbi Transnational, Inc., San Francisco, 1986—, also bd. dirs.; bd. dirs. Magtech Recreational Products, Inc., San Antonio, 1990—. Bd. dirs. Internat. Diplomacy Coun., San Francisco, 1990—, pres. 1995%; active No. Calif. C.A.R.E. Found., 1993—, The Mex. Mus., 1994—. Mem. Brazil Soc. No. Calif. (pres. 1989-94), Pan Am. Soc. Calif. (bd. dirs., pres. 1991-94). Office: Arbi Transnational Inc 600 Montgomery St Ste 350 San Francisco CA 94111-2702

VOIGHT, JOAN, publisher; b. Calif., Nov. 16, 1953. AA in Journalism, San Jose State U., 1974; BA in English, U. Santa Clara, 1975; postgrad., U. Calif., Berkeley, 1992. News editor Santa Rosa (Calif.) News Herald, 1981-86; editor Lesher Communications, Walnut Creek, Calif., 1986-88; asst. bus. editor Santa Rosa Press Dem., 1988-90; editor No. Calif. Publs., Santa Rosa, 1990-91; publisher Diablo Publs., Walnut Creek, 1991-94; bureau chief Adweek N.Y., 1994—. Recipient San Francisco Press Club award Best Feature, 1984.

VOIGT, DONALD BERNARD, tool designer; b. St. Cloud, Minn., Jan. 24, 1947; s. Roman Edward and Alma Mary (Weber) V.; m. Delphine B. (Schmitz) Kliber, Aug. 25, 1990; stepchildren: Ross Louis Kliber, Jason Gilbert Kliber, Shawn Eugene Kliber, Kurt Gerald Kliber, Karl Raphael Kliber. Student, St. Cloud Area Voc. Tech. Inst. Machinist Nat. Bushing and Parts, St. Cloud, 1966-67, Am. Machine and Tool, Mpls., 1967-72; tool maker, designer Columbia Gear, Avon, Minn., 1972-89; machinist U.S. Mint, Denver, 1989—; cons. Joseph Kenning, St. Cloud, 1985-90. Author: Effects of Electromagnetic Fields on Biological Systems, Magnets in Your Future, Vol. 3, No. 4, April, 1988. Mem. AAAS, N.Y. Acad. Scis. Roman Catholic. Home: 7611 Shrine Rd Larkspur CO 80118-8701 Office: US Mint 320 W Colfax Ave Denver CO 80204-2605

VOIGT, JOHN LOUIS, advertising and marketing executive; b. Appleton, Wis., June 1, 1935; s. John Louis and Anne (Strommen) V.; m. Beverley Jean Hilleque, June 16, 1957; children: Cynthia Anne Voigt Scanland, John Louis III. BBA in Mktg., U. Wis., 1957; postgrad., Lake Forest Coll., 1967-70. Mktg. rsch. analyst Smith Kline and French Labs., Phila., 1957; mktg. specialist Abbott Labs., North Chicago, Ill., 1969; dir. mktg. Hycel, Inc., Houston, 1973-77; account supr. Baxter, Gurian and Mazzei, Inc., L.A., 1977-81; exec. v.p. Reavis Comms., Inc., Cardiff by the Sea, Calif., 1981-87, Beach Internat., Inc., San Diego, 1987-90; v.p. mktg. Forsythe Marcelli Johnson Advt., Inc., Newport Beach, Calif., 1990-93; pres. Medmar Comms., Inc., Carlsbad, Calif., 1993—. Capt. U.S. Army, 1958-61. Mem. Med. Mktg. Assn., Biomed. Mktg. Assn., Mktg. Rsch. Assn. Office: Medmar Comms Inc 2638 Unicornio St Carlsbad CA 92009-5333

VOIGT, LYNDA FAY, cancer researcher; b. Longview, Wash., Feb. 6, 1945; d. Leseray and Bessie Edna (Steadman) Norris; m. George Q. Voigt Jr., Dec. 25, 1966 (div. Dec. 1988); children: Cathleen Marie, Barbara Jean; m. Michael Rolland Turner, Sept. 8, 1991. BSN, U. Wash., 1967; BS, Seattle Pacific U., 1967; MSN, Emory U., 1969; PhD, U. Wash., 1990. Pub. health nurse Seattle-King County Dept. Health, Seattle, 1967-68, Atlanta Comprehensive Health Ctr., 1969-70; staff nurse neonatal unit Presbyn. Hosp., Dallas, 1970-71; pub. health nurse Vis. Nurse Svcs., Seattle, 1977-83; teaching asst. epidemiology and biostats. U. Wash., Seattle, 1982-83; rsch. asst. Fred Hutchinson Cancer Rsch. Ctr., Seattle, 1983, statis. rsch. assoc., 1984-92, sr. staff scientist, 1992—. Author: (book chpt.) Epidemiology of Endometrial Cancer, 1989; editl. cons. Am. Jour. Epidemiology; contbr. articles to med. jours. Sunday sch. tchr. Bapt. and Episcopal Ch., 1964—; vol., bd. dirs. student activities PTA, Renton, Wash., 1975-92; foster parent Dept. Social Svcs., Bellevue, Wash., 1985-88; vol. leader, day camp worker Camp Fire Girls, Renton, 1977-83; vol. Humane Soc., Bellevue, 1994; mem. Nature Conservancy, Habitat for Humanity, ASPCA. Weyerhaeuser scholar, 1963. Mem. Soc. Epidemiologic Rsch., Eastside Astronomical Soc., Issaquah Alps Trail Club. Office: Fred Hutchinson Cancer Ctr 1124 Columbia St # P381 Seattle WA 98104-2015

VOIGT, MILTON, English language educator; b. Milw., Mar. 19, 1924; s. Arthur and Esther Johanna (Bartelt) V.; m. Leta Jean Slack, July 27, 1947 (div. 1969); children: John Gregory, James Lewis, Andrew Charles. Ph.B., U. Wis., 1948; MA, U. Calif., Berkeley, 1950; PhD, U. Minn., Mpls., 1960. Assoc. U. Calif., Berkeley, 1949-50; instr. English U. Idaho, Moscow, 1952-55, U. Ky., Lexington, 1956-60; asst. prof. U. Utah, Salt Lake City, 1960-64, assoc. prof., 1964-68, prof., 1968-92, assoc. dean Coll. of Letters and Sci., 1965-66, acting dean, 1966-67, dean, 1967-70, chair English dept., 1971-75, prof. emeritus, 1992—. Author: Swift & the 20th Century, 1964; contbr. articles to profl. jours. Sec. ACLU, Salt Lake City, 1979-83, Chamber Music Soc., Salt Lake City, 1982-86. 2d lt. USAAF, 1943-45. John R. Park fellow U. Utah, 1970. Mem. MLA, Am. Soc. 18th Century Studies. Episcopalian. Home: 1376 Princeton Ave Salt Lake City UT 84105-1921 Office: U Utah Dept English Salt Lake City UT 84112

VOJTA, PAUL ALAN, mathematics educator; b. Mpls., Sept. 30, 1957; s. Francis J. and Margaret L. V. B in Math., U. Minn., 1978; MA, Harvard U., 1980, PhD, 1983. Instr. Yale U., New Haven, 1983-86; postdoctoral fellow Math. Scis. Rsch. Inst., Berkeley, Calif., 1986-87; fellow Miller Inst. for Basic Rsch., Berkeley, 1987-89; assoc. prof. U. Calif., Berkeley, 1989-92, prof., 1992—; mem. Inst. for Advanced Study, Princeton, 1989-90. Author: Diophantine Approximations and Value Distribution Theory, 1987. Recipient perfect score Internat. Math. Olympiad, 1975. Mem. Am. Math. Soc. (Frank Nelson Cole Number Theory prize 1992), Math. Assn. Am., Phi Beta Kappa, Tau Beta Pi. Office: Univ Calif Dept of Math Berkeley CA 94720

VOKT, ERIC STEPHEN, hydrogeological engineer; b. Shenandoah, Iowa, Nov. 28, 1969; s. Danny Lee and Susanne Marie (Gibson) V. BS in Geol. Engring., Mont. Coll. Mineral Sci./Tech., 1992. Hydrogeologist/environ. engr. Cortez Gold Mines - Placer Dome, U.S., Inc., Beowawe, Nev., 1992—. Editor Northeastern Nev. AutoCad Users Group, Elko, Nev., 1993—; co-author: Open File Report -- Curent Geological and Geophysical Studies in Montana, 1990; co-author map: Landslide Map of Montana, 1990. Recipient Chester H. Steele award Mont. Coll. Mineral Sci. and Tech., 1992. Fellow AIME (co. rep. No. Nev. chpt. 1994), Northeastern AutoCad Group; mem. Nat. Ground Water Assn., Soc. Mining Metallurgy and Exploration, Am. Assn. Petroleum Geologists, Tau beta Pi. Republican. Roman Catholic. Home: 677 Maple St Elko NV 89801-3259 Office: Cortez Gold Mines Placer Dome US Inc Star Rt HC66-50 Beowawe NV 89821

VOLGY, THOMAS JOHN, political science educator, organization official; b. Budapest, Hungary, Mar. 19, 1946; m. Susan Dubow, Feb. 1987. BA magna cum laude, Oakland U., 1967; MA, U. Minn., 1969, PhD, 1972. Prof. polit. sci. U. Ariz., Tucson; dir. Univ. Teaching Ctr.; mayor City of Tucson, 1987-91; exec. dir. Internat. Studies Assn., 1995—; chmn. telecom. com. U. Conf. Mayors, 1988—; cons. H.S. curriculum project Ind. U.; bd. dirs. Nat. League of Cities, 1989-91. Co-author: The Forgotten Americans, 1992; editor: Exploring Relationships Between Mass Media and Political Culture: The Impact of Television and Music on American Society, 1976; contbr. numerous articles to profl. jours.; producer two TV documentaries for PBS affiliate. Mem. Nat. Women's Polit. Caucus Conv., 1983, U.S. Senate Fin. Com., 1985, U.S. Ho. of Reps. Telecommunications Com., 1988—, Polit. Sci. Adminstrn. Com., 1986, Gov.'s Task Force on Women and Poverty, 1986, United Way, 1985-87; bd. dirs. Honors Program, 1981—, U. Teaching Ctr., 1988—, Tucson Urban League, 1981, Ododo Theatre, 1984, So. Ariz. Mental Health Care Ctr., 1987, Nat. Fedn. Local Cable TV Programmers; chmn. Internat. Rels. Caucus, 1981, 86—, Transp. and Telecommunications Com. Nat. League Cities, 1986, 88, 89-91. Recipient NDEA scholarship, 1964-76, NDEA fellowship, 1967-70, Oasis award for oustanding prodn. of local affairs TV programming; named Outstanding Young Am., 1981, Outstanding Naturalized Citizen of Yr., 1980; faculty research grantee U. Ariz., 1972-73, 73-74, 74-75, 77-78. Mem. Pima Assn. Govts., Nat. Fedn. Local Cable Programmers. Democrat. Jewish. Office: U Ariz Polit Dept Sci Tucson AZ 85721

VOLIN, JOHN JOSEPH, lawyer; b. Elgin, Ill., June 9, 1956. BA, Western Ill. U., 1978; JD, So. Ill. U., 1982. Bar: Ill 1982, Ariz. 1984, U.S. Dist. Ct. Ariz. 1986. Assoc. Tyler, Solomon & Hughes, Aurora, Ill., 1983-84, Jacoby & Myers, Phoenix, 1984-85, Lawrence Slater, P.C., Mesa, Ariz., 1985-86; pvt. practice law Mesa, 1986—. Mem. ATLA, Ariz. Bar Assn., Ariz. Trial Lawyers Assn., Maricopa County Bar Assn., Ariz. State Bar Bankruptcy Sect. (consumer bankruptcy com.), Mesa Jaycees (legal counsel 1986-87, v.p. membership 1987-88). Office: 1811 S Alma School Rd Ste 220 Mesa AZ 85210-3004

VOLK, ROBERT HARKINS, aviations company executive; b. East Orange, N.J., Nov. 27, 1932; s. Harry Joseph and Marion (Waters) V.; m. Barbara June Klint, Sept. 10, 1954; children: Christopher G., William W., Laura L., Elisabeth M. BA, Stanford U., 1954, LLB, 1958. Bar: Calif. 1959. Assoc. Adams Duque & Hazeltine, L.A., 1959-62; ptnr. Adams Duque & Hazelyine, L.A., 1962-67; commr. of corps. State of Calif., Sacramento, 1967-69; pres. Union Bancorp, L.A., 1969-73; pres., chmn. Union Am., L.A., 1973-79; owner, chief exec. officer Martin Aviation Inc., Santa Ana, Calif., 1980-90, Media Aviation L.P. Burbank, 1984—. Sgt. USAF, 1955-57. Mem. Calif. Bar Assn. Republican. Episcopalian. Home: 332 Conway Ave Los Angeles CA 90024-2604 Office: Media Aviation LP 3000 N Clybourn Ave Burbank CA 91505-1012

VOLKMANN, DANIEL GEORGE, JR., architect; b. San Francisco, June 3, 1924; s. Daniel George and Beatrice (Simpson) V.; m. Marvin Johnson, Sept. 1, 1949 (dec. 1991); children: Daniel G., William R., David R., Wendy. BA, Yale U., 1945, U. Calif., Berkeley, 1950; MA, U. Calif., Berkeley, 1951. Practice architecture San Francisco, 1952—; prin. emeritus Bull, Volkmann, Stockwell, Architects, 1969-91; ltd. ptnr. Dean Witter & Co., San Francisco, 1967-69; bd. dirs. St. Francis Hosp Found., Gleeson Libr. Assoc., San Francisco Libr. Found. Mem. coun. Friends Bancroft Libr. U. Calif., Berkeley, 1976-82; trustee San Francisco Mus. Art, 1970-81, Marin Country Day Sch., 1972-77, San Francisco Conservatory Music, 1982-90, Cypress Lawn Cemetery, 1979—; pres., bd. dirs. Cypress Lawn Cemetery, 1993—; mem. Art Commn. City and County San Francisco, 1975—; bd. dirs. Pacific Enterprises, 1967-93. With USNR, 1944-46. Mem. AIA (numerous awards in design), San Francisco Planning and Urban Renewal Assn., Cow Hollow Improvement Assn. (bd. dirs., pres. 1970), Bohemian Club, Olympic Club, McCloud Fly Fishing Club, Pacific Union (San Francisco), Grolier Club (N.Y.C.). Home: 2616 Union St San Francisco CA 94123-3817

VOLLACK, ANTHONY F., state supreme court justice; b. Cheyenne, Wyo., Aug. 7, 1929; s. Luke and Opal Vollack; m. D. Imojean; children: Leah, Kirk. Bar: Colo. 1956. Pvt. practice law Colo., from 1956; formerly state senator; judge Colo. Dist. Ct. (1st jud. dist.), 1977-85; justice Colo. Supreme Ct., 1986—. Office: Colo Supreme Ct 2 E 14th Ave Denver CO 80203-2115*

VOLLHARDT, KURT PETER CHRISTIAN, chemistry educator; b. Madrid, Mar. 7, 1946; came to U.S., 1972; Vordiplom, U. Munich, 1967; PhD, U. Coll., London, 1972. Postdoctoral fellow Calif. Inst. Tech., Pasadena, 1972-74; asst. prof. chemistry U. Calif., Berkeley, 1974-78, assoc. prof., 1978-82, prof., 1982—; prin. investigator Lawrence Berkeley Lab., 1975—; cons. Monsanto Corp., St. Louis, Exxon Corp., Annandale, N.J., Maruzen Corp., Tokyo; vis. prof. U. Paris-Orsay, 1979, U. Bordeaux, 1985, U. Lyon, 1987, U. Rennes, 1991, U. Paris VI, 1992, Tech. U. Munich, 1992. Author: Organic Chemistry, 1987, 2d edit., 1994; co-author: Aromatizität, 1972; assoc. editor: Synthesis, 1984-89; editor Synlett, 1989; contbr. articles to profl. jours.; patentee in field. Sloan fellow, 1976-90; Camille and Henry Dreyfus scholar, 1978-83; recipient Adolf Windaus medal, 1983, Humboldt Sr. Scientist award, 1985, 92, Otto Bayer prize, 1990, A.C. Cope Scholar award, 1991, Japan Soc. for Promotion of Sci. award, 1995; named one of Am.'s 100 Brightest Scientists Under 40, Sci. Digest, 1984. Mem. Am. Chem. Soc. (Organometallic Chemistry award 1987), German Chem. Soc., Chem. Soc. of London, Internat. Union Pure & Applied Chemistry (organic chemistry div. com.). Office: U Calif Berkeley Dept of Chemistry Berkeley CA 94720

VOLLMER, TIMOTHY LEE, medical center executive, educator; b. Lusk, Wyo., Nov. 15, 1954; s. Milton Robert and Dorothy Mae (Canfield) V.; m. Debra Marie Orth; children: Norrina, Katrina, Briana, Brandi. BA, U. Wyo., 1977; MD, Stanford U., 1982. Intern Yale New Haven (Conn.) Hosp., 1982-83; resident in neurology Stanford (Calif.) U. Hosp., 1983-85, asst. prof. neurology, 1987-93; postdoctorate fellow dept. neurology Stanford U., 1985-86; dir. neuroimmunology lab. Yale Sch. Medicine, New Haven, 1987-93; staff neurologist West Haven (Conn.) VA Hosp., 1993; dir. clin. rsch. program Rocky Mountain MS Ctr., Englewood, Colo., 1993—; assoc. clin. prof. dept. neurology Colo. U. Sch. Medicine, Denver, 1994—; dir. N.Am. Consortium on MS, 1994—. Author: (with others) Neurology, 1991, Neurologic Emergencies, 1992; author numerous abstracts; contbr. articles to profl. jours.; ad hoc reviewer: Annals of Neurology, Jour. of Immunology, Neurology, Paralyzed Vets. of Am., Jour. Neurosci. Stanford U. scholar, 1979, Dean's fellow, 1975, 81; recipient honors scholarship U. Wyo., 1973. Mem. AAAS, Am. Acad. Neurology, Am. Assn. Immunology, N.Y. Acad. Scis., Clin. Investigation Soc., Soc. Neurosci. Home: 23 Golden Eagle Ln Littleton CO 80127 Office: Rocky Mountain MS Ctr 701 E Hampden Ave Englewood CO 80110

VOLPE, ELLEN MARIE, middle school educator; b. Bronx, N.Y., Aug. 2, 1949; d. George Thomas and Mary (Popadinecz) Soloweyko; m. Ronald Edward Volpe, May 22, 1971; children: Keith, Daniel, Christopher, Stephanie. BBA, Pace U., 1971; MA in Teaching, Sacred Heart U., 1986. Tchr. Conn. Bus. Inst., Stratford, 1979-80, Katherine Gibbs Sch., Norwalk, Conn., 1980-89; adj. instr. So. Cen. Community Coll., New Haven, 1986-87, Salt Lake C. C., Phillips Jr. Coll., Salt Lake City, 1992-93; instr. Bryman Sch., Salt Lake City, 1990-92; tchr. Indian Hills Mid. Sch., Sandy, Utah, 1993—; mem. reaccreditation and tech. coms. Indian Hills Mid. Sch.; mem. curriculum rev. com. Katharine Gibbs Sch., 1989-90. Mem. ASCD, NEA, Am. Vocat. Assn., Nat. Bus. Edn. Assn., Western Bus. Edn. Assn. Home: 8390 Sublette Cir Sandy UT 84093-1164

VOLPE, RICHARD GERARD, insurance accounts executive, consultant; b. Swickley, Pa., Apr. 10, 1950; s. Ralph Carl and Louise P. (Cosentino) V.; m. Janet Lynn Henne, May 10, 1986; 1 child, John Ralph. BA, Vanderbilt U., 1972. CPCU. Trainee, asst. mgr. Hartford (Conn.) Ins. Group, 1973-74; v.p. sales Roy E. Barker Co., Franklin, Tenn., 1975-80; asst. v.p., product mgr. comml. ins. Nat. Farmers Union Ins., Denver, 1980-82; prin. R.G. Volpe & Assocs, Denver, 1982-85; account exec. Millers Mut. Ins., Aurora, Colo., 1985-89; pres, chief exec. officer AccuSure, Inc., Arvada, Colo., 1989—; account exec. J.R. Misken, Inc., Denver, 1990-92, The Prudential, Colorado Springs, 1992—; edn. chmn. Insurors Tenn., Nashville, 1978-79; new candidate chmn. Mid-Tenn. chpt. CPCU, Nashville, 1979-80; cons. Bennett Nat. Bank Colo., mktg. mgr., 1989-90; cons. Plains Ins., Inc., 1987-90. Contbr. articles to profl. jours. Dem. chmn. Williamson County, Tenn., 1979; campaign mgr. legis., Franklin, 1979. Named Hon. Col. Gov. Tenn., 1979. Mem. Soc. Property and Casualty Underwriters, South Metro Denver C. of C. Roman Catholic. Home: 10908 W Snow Cloud Trl Littleton CO 80125-9083 Office: The Prudential 5225 N Academy Blvd Ste 310 Colorado Springs CO 80918-4084

VON BERG, HORST RÜDIGER, computer company executive; b. Gotenhafen, Germany, Nov. 20, 1941; came to U.S., 1988; s. Alexander Nicolai and Kira (Tahv) von B.; m. Montserrat R. Torres, May 9, 1968 (div. Sept. 1987); children: Nathalie, Alexandre; m. Micheline T. Verhaegen, Mar. 19, 1988. Lic. in linguistics, U. Antwerp, 1967; postgrad., Inst. Catholique Hautes Études Commerciales, Brussels, 1970. Freelance translator Brussels, 1967-69; with Redirack, Nivelles, Belgium, 1969-70; sales mgr. Desmed & Meynaert, Brussels, 1970-71, Metal Profil, Liege, Belgium, 1972-73; br. mgr. Applicon Inc., Brussels and Paris, 1973-81; mktg. exec. Computervision Corp., Hayes, Eng., 1981-83; mng. dir. Computervision Corp., Brussels, 1983-87; v.p. internat. sales Prime Computer Corp. div. Computervision Corp., Bedford, Mass., 1988-89, v.p. European ops., 1989-93; v.p. internat Formtek (Lockheed), Sunnyvale, Calif., 1993-94; v.p., co-founder Integration Ptnrs., Inc., San Diego, 1994—. Mem. Am. Mgmt. Assn., Mgmt. Ctr. Europe.

VONDERHEID, ARDA ELIZABETH, nursing administrator; b. Pitts., June 19, 1925; d. Louis Adolf and Hilda Barbara (Gerstacker) V.; diploma Allegheny Gen. Hosp. Sch. Nursing, 1946; B.S. in Nursing Edn., Coll. Holy Names, Oakland, Calif., 1956; M.S. in Nursing Adminstrn., UCLA, 1960. Head nurse Allegheny Gen. Hosp., Pitts., 1946-48; staff nurse Highland-Alameda County Hosp., Oakland, Calif., 1948-51, staff nurse poliomyelitis units, 1953-55; pvt. duty nurse Directory Registered Nurses Alameda County, Oakland, 1951-53; adminstrv. supervising nurse Poliomyelitis Respiratory and Rehab. Center, Fairmont, Alameda County Hosp., Oakland, 1955-58; night supr., relief asst. dir. nursing Peninsula Hosp., Burlingame, Calif., 1960, adminstrv. supr., 1961-62, inservice educator, 1963-69; staff nurse San Francisco Gen. Hosp., 1969, asst. dir. nurses, 1969-72; mem. faculty continuing edn. U. Calif., San Francisco, 1969-71; dir. nursing services Kaiser Permanente Med. Center, South San Francisco, 1973-1982, asst. adminstr. Med. Center Nursing Services, 1982-85; asst. adminstr. Kaiser Hosp., San Francisco, 1985-87; ret. 1987. Chmn. edn. com. San Mateo County (Calif.) Cancer Soc., 1962-69; bd. dirs. San Mateo County Heart Assn., 1968-71; mem., foreman pro tem San Mateo County Civil Grand Jury, 1982-83; mem. San Mateo County Health Council, 1982-85, vice chmn., 1984; mem. all ch. coms., lay leader Honolua United Meth. Ch. Cert. advanced nursing adminstrn. Mem. San Mateo County (dir. 1964-69, pres. elect 1967-68, pres. 1968-70), Golden Gate (1st v.p. 1974-78, dir. 1974-78), Calif., Am. nurses assns., Nat. League Nursing, Soc. for Nursing Service Adminstrs., State Practice and Edn. Council, AAUW, Maui Hospice Assn. (vol.), San Mateo County Grand Jury Assn., Calif. Grand Jury Assn., Sigma Theta Tau. Republican. Club: Kai-Perm. Contbr. articles in field to profl. jours. Home: 150 Puukolii Rd Apt 47 Lahaina HI 96761-1961

VON DOEPP, CHRISTIAN ERNEST, psychiatrist; came to U.S., 1949; s. Philip and Elizabeth von Doepp; m. Janet Carol Brown, Jan. 2, 1994; children: Heidi Louise von Doepp Lemon, Peter Anders, Niels Christian. Student, U. Heidelberg, Germany, 1955; BA, DePauw U., 1957; MD, Stanford U., 1961; intern, Boston City Hosp., Tufts U., 1962. Diplomate Am. Bd. Psychiatry and Neurology, Nat. Bd. Med. Examiners. Resident psychiatry Langley Porter Psychiat. Inst. U. Calif., San Francisco, 1968; house call physician Permanente Med. Group, San Francisco, 1966-68; consulting psychiatrist Somerville (Mass.) Child Guidance Ctr., 1969; brig psychiatrist and cons. to correctional program Boston Naval Sta., 1968-69; lectr. and preceptor Calif. Dept. Health, Health Tng. Resource Ctr., Berkeley, Calif., 1970-77; dir. day hosp. and aftercare programs San Mateo (Calif.) Ctrl. County Psychiat. Svcs., 1970-87; sr. psychiatrist San Mateo County Mental Health Divsn., 1987—; cons. psychiatrist Calif. Med. Facility,CDC, Vacaville, 1995—; fellow Inst. Pathology, U. Freiberg, Germany, 1960, Lab. Cmty. Psychiatry, Harvard Med. Sch., Boston, 1969; supr., coord. cmty. psychiatry rotation for residents U.S. Naval Hosp., Oakland, Calif., 1970-81; med. examiner State of Calif., 1971-78; cons. Counseling and Assistance Ctr., U.S. Naval Sta., Treasure Island, Calif., 1974-76; asst. clin. prof. dept. psychiatry U. Calif., San Francisco, 1971—; chmn. or mem. numerous coms. San Mateo County Mental Health Div., 1970—. Bd. dirs. Tahoma Meadows Homeowners Assn., 1986-92, pres., 1980-81; pres. Tahoma Mut. Water Co., 1978-80. With M.C., USN, 1962-65; capt. USNR, 1965—. Mem. Am. Psychiat. Assn., No. Calif. Psychiat. Soc., San Mateo County Psychiat. Soc. (sec.-treas. 1987-89, bd. dirs. 1987-93), Calif. Med. Assn., San Mateo County Med. Assn., Faculty-Alumni Assn. Dept. Psychiatry U. Calif. San Francisco (bd. dirs. 1985-90). Office: 19 W 39th Ave Ste 4 San Mateo CA 94403

VONDRAK, ROBERT RICHARD, environmental engineer; b. Chgo., Jan. 4, 1949; s. Henry Francis and Mary Ann Vondrak. BS in Chemistry, Loyola U., Chgo., 1972; MS in Chemistry, Ariz. State U., Tempe, 1977. Grad. teaching assoc. chemistry dept. Ariz. State U., Tempe, 1972-77; chemist Ariz. Dept. Health Svcs., Phoenix, 1978-79; environ. engring. specialist Ariz. Dept. Environ. Quality, Phoenix, 1979-87, environ. program supr., 1987-88; utilities cons. Ariz. Corp. Commn., Phoenix, 1988-90. Mem. Soc. Applied Spectroscopy. Republican. Roman Catholic. Home: 343 E Garfield St Tempe AZ 85281-1014

VON FLOTOW, ANDREAS HUBERTUS, university educator, consultant; b. St. Thomas, Ontario, Can., Dec. 18, 1955; came to U.S., 1980; s. Andreas Hans and Hildegard (Keunecke) von F.; m. Lucia Laura Alviano, Sept. 26, 1984; children: Andreas Luigi, Friedrich Leopold, Claudia Maria, Maurizio Auguste. BA in Sci., U. Toronto, 1977, MA in Sci., 1979; PhD, Stanford U., 1984. Rsch. scientist Univ. Toronto, 1979-80, Stanford Univ., 1984, Deutshe Forshungs und Versuchs Anstalt Für Luft und Raumfahrt, Munich, 1984-85; prof. MIT, Cambridge, Mass., 1985-92; pres. Flotow & Assoc., Hood River, Oreg., 1989—; pres. Hood Tech. Corp., 1993—; v.p. Mide Tech. Corp., Cambridge, Mass., 1991-93; adj. prof. U. Wash., 1992—. Patentee in field; contbr. numberous tech. articles to profl. jours. and books. With Can. Army, 1973-74. Recipient NATO Post Doctoral fellowship, Germany, 1984-85; Alexander von Humboldt fellowship A.V. Humboldt Found., Germany, 1984-85. Mem. AIAA, ASME.

VON HERRMANN, BRUCE ANTHONY, marketing professional; b. San Francisco, June 19, 1954; s. Alan and Dorothy Mae (Brasil) von Herrmann. BS in Acctg., San Francisco State U., 1983, MBA in Mktg., 1990. Divsn. supr. Bechtel Power Bechtel Corp., San Francisco, 1973-79; v.p., mgr. systems engring. Bank of Am., San Francisco, 1981-86; mgr. telecom. Syntex Corp., Palo Alto, Calif., 1986-89; v.p., dir. data processing West Am. Bank, Novato, Calif., 1988-89; info. tech. mgr. Hewlett-Packard Co., Santa Clara, Calif., 1989-92; product line mgr. Hewlett-Packard Co., Mountain View, Calif., 1992—; cons. Saint Francis Meml. Hosp., San Francisco, 1986, Dome Constrn. Co., San Francisco, 1987. Recipient Disting. Achievement award San Francisco State U., 1990. Mem. Assn. for Systems Mgmt., Beta Gamma Sigma. Home: PO Box 7165 San Carlos CA 94070-7165

VON KALINOWSKI, JULIAN ONESIME, lawyer; b. St. Louis, May 19, 1916; s. Walter E. and Maybelle (Michaud) von K.; m. Penelope Jayne Dyer, June 29, 1980; children by previous marriage: Julian Onesime, Wendy Jean von Kalinowski. BA, Miss. Coll., 1937; JD with honors, U. Va., 1940. Bar: Va. 1940, Calif. 1946. Assoc. Gibson, Dunn and Crutcher, L.A., 1946-52, ptnr., 1953-62, mem. exec. com., 1962-82, adv. ptnr., 1985—; CEO, chmn. Litigation Scis., Inc., Culver City, Calif., 1991-94, chmn. emeritus, 1994—; bd. dirs., mem. exec. com. W.M. Keck Found.; mem. faculty Practising Law Inst., 1971, 76, 78, 79, 80; instr. in spl. course on antitrust litigation Columbia U. Law Sch., N.Y.C., 1981; mem. lawyers dels. com. to 9th Cir. Jud. Conf., 1953-73; UN expert Mission to People's Republic China, 1982. Contbr. articles to legal jours.; author: Antitrust Laws and Trade Regulation, 1969, desk edit., 1981; gen. editor: World Law of Competition, 1978, Antitrust Counseling and Litigation Techniques, 1984. With USN, 1941-46, capt. Res. ret. Fellow Am. Bar Found., Am. Coll. Trial Lawyers (chmn. complex litigation com. 1984-87); mem. ABA (mem. ho. dels. 1970, chmn. antitrust law sect. 1972-73), State Bar of Calif., L.A. Bar Assn., U. Va. Law Sch. Alumni Assn., Calif. Club, L.A. Country Club, La Jolla Beach and Tennis Club, N.Y. Athletic Club, Regency Club, The Sky Club (N.Y.C.), Phi Kappa Psi, Phi Alpha Delta. Republican. Episcopalian. Home: 12320 Ridge Cir Los Angeles CA 90049-1151 Office: Litigation Scis Inc 200 Corporate Pointe Ste 300 Culver City CA 90230-7633

VON KRENNER, WALTHER G., artist, writer, art consultant and appraiser; b. W. Ger., June 26, 1940; s. Frederick and Anna-Marie (von Wolfrath) von K.; m. Hana Renate Geue, 1960; children—Michael P., Karen P. Privately educated by Swiss and English tutors; student Asian studies, Japan, 1965-68; student of Southeast Asia studies, Buddhist U., Bankok, Thailand, Cambodia. Curator, v.p. Gallery Lahaina, Maui, Hawaii; pres. Internat. Valuation Honolulu, 1980—; owner Al Hilal Arabians; instr. aikido, 1962-81; founder, dir. Sandokan Aikido Schs. Mem. Am. Soc. Appraisers (sr. mem.; pres., dir.). Author books on Oriental art. Home: PO Box 1338 Kalispell MT 59903-1338

VON LINSOWE, MARINA DOROTHY, information systems consultant; b. Indpls., July 21, 1952; d. Carl Victor and Dorothy Mae (Quinn) von Linsowe; m. Clayton Albert Wilson IV, Aug. 11, 1990; 1 dau., Kira Christina von Linsowe. Student Am. River Coll., Portland State U. Verbal operator Credit Bur. Metro, San Jose, Calif. and Portland, Oreg., 1970-72; computer clk. Security Pacific Bank, San Jose, 1972-73; proof operator Crocker Bank, Seaside, Calif., 1973-74; proof supr. Great Western Bank, Portland, 1974-75; bookkeeper The Clothes Horse, Portland, 1976-78; computer operator Harsh Investment Co., Portland, 1978-79; data processing mgr. Portland Fish Co., 1979-81; data processing mgr. J & W Sci. Inc., Rancho Cordova, Calif., 1981-83; search and recruit specialist, data processing mgr. Re:Search Exec. Recruiters, Sacramento, Calif., 1983; sr. systems analyst Unisys Corp. (formerly Burroughs), 1983-91; sr. systems cons. FileNet Corp., Portland, Oreg., 1991-92; owner Optimal System Svcs., Portland, Oreg., 1992—; mfg. specialist, computer conversion cons., Portland. First violinist Am. River Orch. Recipient Bank of Am. Music award, 1970. Mem. NAFE, Am. Prodn. and Inventory Control Soc., Am. Mgrs. Assn., MENSA, Data Processing Mgmt. Assn. Republican. Lutheran.

VON PASSENHEIM, JOHN B., lawyer; b. Calif., Nov. 25, 1964; s. Burr Charles and Kathryn E. (Kirkland) Passenheim. BA in English with honors, U. Calif.-Santa Barbara, 1986; JD, U. Calif., Hastings, 1989. Bar: Calif. 1989, U.S. Dist. Ct. (so. dist.) Calif. 1991. Pvt. practice law Law Office J. B. Von Passenheim, San Diego, 1990—; organizer Rock The Vote, San Diego, 1992; primary atty. Calif. Lawyers for the Arts, San Diego; panelist Independent Music Seminar, 1992, 93, 94; gen. counsel HYPNO mag., Poptones Records, STV. Contbg. staff DICTA mag., 1990-94; editor (legal column) It's the Law, 1990-93. Exec. counsel San Diego chpt. Surfrider Found., 1991-95; vol. atty. San Diego Vol. Lawyer Program, 1990-93. Office: 4425 Bayard St Ste 240 San Diego CA 92109-4089

VON STUDNITZ, GILBERT ALFRED, state official; b. Hamburg, Germany, Nov. 24, 1950; came to U.S., 1954; s. Helfrid and Rosemarie Sofie (Kreiten) von S.; m. Erica Lynn Hoot, May 26, 1990. BA, Calif. State U., L.A., 1972. Adminstrv. hearing officer State of Calif., Montebello, 1987-91; mgr. III driver control policy unit Dept. Motor Vehicles State of Calif., Sacramento, 1991-93; ops. mgr. Driver Safety Review, 1993—. Author: Aristocracy in America, 1989; editor publs. on German nobility in U.S., 1986—. Active L.A. Conservancy, West Adams Heritage Assn., dir., 1989-91. Mem. Calif. State Mgrs. Assn., Assn. German Nobility in N.Am. (pres. 1985—), Driver Improvement Assn. Calif. (v.p. 1992—), Benicia Hist. Soc., Sierra Club, Intertel, Mensa, Phi Sigma Kappa (v.p. chpt. 1978). Roman Catholic. Home: 1101 W 2nd St Benicia CA 94510-3125

VON TILSIT, HEIDEMARIE, information management specialist; b. Heinrichswalde, Germany, Sept. 26, 1944; came to U.S., 1967; d. Heinz and Kaethe Krink; m. Leonard Wierzba, May 14, 1969 (div. 1980). Buchhandel, Dt. Buchh. Schule, Kiel, Germany, 1965; profl. cert., Coll. of Further Edn., Oxford, Eng., 1966; BA, Calif. State U., Fullerton, 1979. Library asst. Allergan, Inc., Irvine, Calif., 1975-76; info. analyst Allergan Pharms., Irvine, Calif., 1976-79, library supr., 1979-81, mgr. corp. info. ctr., 1982—; cons. in field, Irvine, 1980—; owner, pres. Unitran, Corona, Calif., 1980—; mem. adv. bd. CB&S Career Cons., Orange, Calif., 1987—; mem. adv. bd. for univ.-industry rsch. and tech. U. Calif., Irvine, 1992—. Editor/writer articles sci. and information mgmt. Bd. dirs. Nat. Woman's Polit. Caucus, Irvine, 1984-85; vol. AIDS Svcs. Found., 1994—. Mem. Indsl. Tech. Info. Mgmt. Group (steering com. 1984-86, acting pres. 1986), Am. Soc. Info. Sci., Spl. Librs. Assn., Pharm. Mfg. Assn. (com. info. mgmt. sect. 1985—), Monterey Village Homeowners Assn. (pres. 1992—). Democrat. Home: 1543 San Rafael Dr Corona CA 91720-3795 Office: Allergan Inc 2525 Dupont Dr Irvine CA 92715-1531

VOORHEES, JOHN LLOYD, columnist; b. DeWitt, Iowa, Aug. 30, 1925; s. Lloyd William and Elsie Irene (Bousselot) V. BA in History, U. Iowa, 1951; BA in Journalism, U. Wash., 1953. Tchr. Oelwein (Iowa) High Sch., 1951-52; columnist Seattle Post-Intelligencer, 1953-71; columnist, critic Seattle Times, 1971—. With U.S. Army, 1946-48. Democrat. Office: The Seattle Times Fairview Ave N & John St Seattle WA 98111

VOORHEES, LORRAINE ISOBEL, college dean; b. Pitts., Sept. 23, 1947; d. Glenn and Helen L. (Urban) V. OD, So. Calif. Coll. Optometry, Fullerton, 1971; MS, Calif. State U., Fullerton, 1986. Asst. prof. So. Calif. Coll. Optometry, 1972-80, dir. admissions and records, 1980-86, dir. student affairs, 1986-90, dean student affairs, 1990—. Office: So Calif Coll Optometry 2575 E Yorba Linda Blvd Fullerton CA 92631-1615

VORHIES, CARL BRAD, dentist; b. Indpls., Jan. 21, 1949; s. Jack Mckim and Georgia Thelma (Reese) V.; m. Catherine Isabel Leitch, Aug. 30, 1975; children: Michael, Colin, Jeffrey. BA, Ind. U., 1971, DDS, 1975. Practice dentistry Beaverton, Oreg., 1975—; team dentist Portland Winterhawks Hockey Team, 1979—. Vol. Dental Aid for Children, Washington County, Oreg. Named Dentist of Yr. Oreg. Acad. Gen. Dentistry, 1990; Paul Harris fellow, 1985. Fellow Am. Coll. Dentists, Internat. Coll. Dentists; mem. ADA, Acad. Gen. Dentistry (master 1986, bd. dirs. 1987-91, bd. trustees 1991-93, treas. 1992—), Oreg. Acad. Gen. Dentistry (pres. 1985-86), Oreg. Dental Assn. (sec.-treas. 1980-82), Rotary Club. Home: 5240 SW Humphrey Blvd Portland OR 97221-2315 Office: 12755 SW 2nd St Beaverton OR 97005-2765

VORIS, WILLIAM, educational administrator; b. Neoga, Ill., Mar. 20, 1924; s. Louis K. and Faye (Hancock) V.; m. Mavis Marie Myre, Mar. 20, 1949; children: Charles William II, Michael K. BS, U. So. Calif., 1947, MBA, 1948; PhD, Ohio State U., 1951; LLD, Sung Kyun Kwan U. (Korea), 1972, Eastern Ill. U., 1976. Teaching asst. Ohio State U., Columbus, 1948-50; prof. mgmt. Wash. State U., Pullman, 1950-52; prof., head dept. mgmt. Los Angeles State Coll., 1952-58, 60-63; dean Coll. Bus. and Pub. Adminstrn., U. Ariz., Tucson, 1963-71; pres. Am. Grad. Sch. Internat. Mgmt., Glendale, Ariz., 1971-89, pres. emeritus, 1989—, adj. prof., 1994—. Ford Found. research grantee Los Angeles State Coll., 1956; prof. U. Tehran (Iran), 1958-59; Ford Found. fellow Carnegie Inst. Tech., Pitts., 1961; prof. Am. U., Beirut, Lebanon, 1961, 62; cons. Hughes Aircraft Co., Los Angeles, Rheem Mfg. Co., Los Angeles, Northrop Aircraft Co., Palmdale, Calif., Harwood Co., Alhambra, Calif., ICA, Govt. Iran. Served with USNR, 1942-45. Fellow Acad. Mgmt.; mem. Ariz. Acad., Beta Gamma Sigma, Alpha Kappa Psi, Phi Delta Theta. Author: Production Control, Text and Cases, 1956, 3d edit., 1966; Management of Production, 1960. Research in indsl. future of Iran, mgmt. devel. in Middle East. Home: Thunderbird Campus Glendale AZ 85306

VORLICK, ROBERT JERRY, construction consultant; b. Stamford, Conn., Oct. 12, 1943; s. Jerry Nichols and Mae (Marsh) V.; m. Yuri Sasaki, Mar. 4, 1974; children: Darian, Klayton. BS, U. Tampa, 1969; MA, U. Tokyo, 1974; PhD, Pacific Western U., 1990. Sr. rep. Tremco, Inc.-USA, 1974-84; product mgr., sr. cons. Fosroc/Tremco - Far West Ops., Hong Kong; pres., sr. cons. RJ Cons. Internat., Inc., Diamond Bar, Calif., 1984—; presenter, lectr. in field. Author: Evolution of Protective Systems, 1989; contbr. articles to profl. publs. With USAF, 1964-74. Mem. AIA, Am. Inst. Plant Engrs., Constrn. Specifications Inst., Am. Arbitration Assn. Home: 21121 E Snow Creek Dr Walnut CA 91789-1285 Office: RJ Cons Internat 23441 Golden Springs Dr Ste 147 Diamond Bar CA 91765-2030

VORPAGEL, WILBUR CHARLES, historical consultant; b. Milw., Feb. 26, 1926; s. Arthur Fred and Emma (Hintz) V.; Betty J. Hoch, June 19, 1952; stepchildren: Jerry L., Sharon Belveal Sullenberger. Student Army specialized tng. program, U. Ill., 1943-44; BBA, U. Wis., 1949; MBA, U. Denver, 1953. Cert. tchr., Colo. Instr. Montezuma County High Sch., Cortez, Colo., 1949-51; coord. bus. edn. Pueblo (Colo.) Pub. Schs., 1951-56; pvt. practice bus. cons. Pueblo and Denver, 1956—; tchr. bus. edn. Emily Griffith Opportunity Sch., Denver, 1959-69; various positions with Denver & Rio Grande Western R.R. Co., Denver, 1959-88; cons. in field. Bd. dirs. Colo. Ret. Sch. Employees Assn., Denver, 1988—; rep. Custer Battlefield Hist. & Mus. Assn. Sgt. U.S. Army, 1944-46, ETO. Mem. Augustan Soc., St. John Vol. Corp., S.E. Colo. Geneal. Soc., Rio Grande Vets. Club (bd. dirs. Pueblo chpt.), Biblical Archaeol. Soc. (contbg. writer), Nat. Huguenot Soc., Colo. Huguenot Soc. (organizing pres. 1979-95), 70th Inf. Divsn. Assn., Shriners, Masons. Republican. Mem. Christian Ch. Home and Office: 335 Davis Ave Pueblo CO 81004-1019

VOS, HUBERT DANIEL, private investor; b. Paris, Aug. 2, 1933; s. Marius and Aline (Porge) V.; m. Susan Hill, Apr. 18, 1958; children: Wendy, James. BA, Institut d'Etudes Politiques, U. Paris, 1954; M in Pub. Adminstrn., Princeton U., 1956. Internal auditor Internat. Packers Ltd., 1957-61, dir. fin., 1962-64; asst. to contr. Monsanto Co., 1964-66, contr. internat. div., 1966-69; v.p. planning and fin. Smith Kline Corp., 1969-72; sr. v.p. fin. Comml. Credit Co., Balt., 1972-74; sr. v.p. fin. and adminstrn., dir. Norton Simon Inc., N.Y.C., 1974-79; sr. v.p. fin., dir. Becton Dickinson and Co., Paramus, N.J., 1979-83; pres. Stonington Capital Corp., Santa Barbara, Calif., 1984—; bd. dirs. Rowe Price New Era Fund Inc., New Horizons Fund Inc., Equity Income Fund Inc., Capital Appreciation Fund, Inc., Sci. and Tech. Fund, Inc., Small Capital Appreciation Fund, Inc., Balanced Fund, Inc., Monarch Health Systems Inc. Bd. dirs. Surg. Eye Expdns. Internat. Mem. Am. Mgmt. Assn. (gen. mgmt. coun.), La Cumbre Golf and Country Club. Home: 800 Via Hierba Santa Barbara CA 93110-2222 Office: 1114 State St Ste 247 Santa Barbara CA 93101-2716

VOS, ROBERT A., nurse, health care facility executive; b. Des Moines, July 4, 1957; s. John M. and Marie J. (Branderhorst) V.; m. Mary Jane Vos, July 5, 1986; children: Jonathan Joseph, Elaine Marie, Robert Alan II. Diploma, Iowa Luth. Hosp., Des Moines, 1978; BSN, Loretto Hts. Coll., Denver, 1981; MS, Calif. State U., L.A., 1987. Charge nurse Swedish Med. Ctr., Englewood, Colo.; adminstrv. supr. Children's Hosp., L.A.; br. mgr. N.S.I. Svcs., Long Beach, Calif.; mgr. nursing unit UCLA Med. Ctr.; dir. nursing Pleasant Valley Hosp., Camarillo, Calif.; dir. oncology svcs. Huntington Meml. Hosp., Pasadena, Calif. Mem. Am. Orgn. Nurse Exec's. (Nat. and Calif. chpts.).

VOSBECK, ROBERT RANDALL, architect; b. Mankato, Minn., May 18, 1930; s. William Frederick and Gladys (Anderson) V.; m. Phoebe Macklin, June 21, 1953; children: Gretchen, Randy, Heidi, Macklin. BArch, U. Minn., 1954. Various archtl. positions, 1956-62; ptnr. Vosbeck-Vosbeck & Assocs., Alexandria, Va., 1962-66, VVKR Partnership, Alexandria, 1966-79; exec. v.p. VVKR Inc., 1979-82, pres., 1982-88; prin. Vosbeck/DMJM, Washington and Alexandria, Va., 1989-94; archtl. cons., 1994—; mem. Nat. Capital Planning Commn., 1976-81, U.S./USSR Joint Group on Bldg. Design and Constrn., 1974-79; mem. Nat. Park System Adv. Bd., 1983-88. Archtl. works include Pub. Safety Ctr., Alexandria, Va., 1987, Yorktown (Va.) Visitors Ctr, 1976, Frank Reeves Mcpl. Office Bldg., Washington, 1986, Fed. Bldg., NOrfolk, Va., 1979, Jeff Davis Assocs. Office Complex, Arlington, Va., 1991, Westminster Continued Care Retirement Community, Lake Ridge, Va., 1993. Served as engr. officer USMC, 1954-56. Recipient Plaque of Honor Fedn. Colegios Architects (Republic of Mexico); named Acadamecian, Internt. Acad. Architecture, hon. fellow Royal Architects of Can., Soc. Architects of Mexico; recipient hons. Collegios Architects Spain, Union Bulgarian Architects. Fellow AIA (bd. dirs. 1976-78, v.p. 1979-80, pres. 1981); mem. Internat. Union Architects (coun. 1981-87), Nat. Trust Hist. Preservation, Alexandria C. of C. (pres. 1974-75). Presbyterian. Home and Office: Unit A 770 Potato Patch Dr Vail CO 81657-4441

VOSTIAR, JOHN, telecommunications industry executive; b. Newark, Mar. 2, 1949; s. Peter and Anna (Glogoski) V. AS in Edn., Essex County Coll., 1970; BA in Psychology, William Patterson Coll., 1976; M of Spl. Studies in Applied Comm., U. Denver, 1991. Test desk tech. N.J. Bell, Newark, 1972-78, Mountain Bell, Denver, 1978-80; comm. tech. AT&T Long Line, Denver, 1980-82; supr. engr. AT&T Transmission Systems, San Francisco, 1982-83; comm. tech. AT&T, Denver, 1983—; union steward Comm. Worker Am., Denver, 1981-83. Editor: Comm. Worker Am. paper, 1982-83. Mem. Colo. Tai Chi Soc., U. Denver Alumni Assn. Home: 13211 W Alaska Pl Lakewood CO 80228-2421 Office: AT&T Internat 2535 E 40th Ave Rm D32 Denver CO 80205

VOTH, ALDEN H., political science educator; b. Goessel, Kans., May 4, 1926; s. John F. and Helena (Hildebrandt) V.; m. Norma E. Jost, Aug. 18, 1956; children: Susan, Thomas. BA, Bethel Coll., 1950; MS in Econs., Iowa State U., Ames, 1953; PhD in Internat. Rels., U. Chgo., 1959. Assoc. prof. polit. sci. Upland (Calif.) Coll., 1960-63; prof. polit. sci. San Jose (Calif.) State U., 1963-65, 67-91, prof. emeritus, 1991—; vis. prof. polit. sci. Am. U. in Cairo, 1965-67. Author: Moscow Abandons Israel, 1980, (with others) The Kissinger Legacy, 1984. Trustee Pomona (Calif.) Valley Am. Assn. UN, 1963. Am. U. in Cairo Rsch. grantee, 1966; Nat. Coun. on U.S.-Arab Rels. fellow, 1990—. Home: 1385 Kimberly Dr San Jose CA 95118-1426 Office: San Jose State U One Washington Sq San Jose CA 95192

VREDENBURGH, MARK DE, chemical engineer; b. Long Beach, Calif., Aug. 13, 1957; s. David Gowen and Gloria Jean (Knapp) V. BSChemE, Calif. Poly. U., Pomona, 1981. Refinery engr. Chevron U.S.A., El Segundo, Calif., 1981-83; project engr. M.C. Gill Corp., El Monte, Calif., 1984-85; chief engr. Space-Flex Co. div. M.C. Gill Corp., L.A., 1985-90; project engr. Arrowhead Products, Los Alamitos, Calif., 1990-94; gen. mgr. Flexible Composite Svcs., Inc., Fredonia, Ariz., 1994—. Mem. Soc. for Advancement of Material and Process Engring., Belmont Shore Sailing Assn. (commodore 1988), Morgan Plus 4 Club (pres. 1988). Office: Flexible Composite Svcs Inc P O Box 250 E Fredonia AZ 86022

VREE, DALE, editor; b. L.A., Feb. 25, 1944; s. Henry and Marion (Wyma) V.; m. Elena Maria Reyes, June 18, 1965; children: Maria, Pieter, Magdalena, Pilar. BA, U. Calif., Berkeley, 1965, MA, 1967, PhD, 1972; student, Humboldt U., East Berlin, Germany, 1966. Editor New Oxford Rev., Berkeley, 1977—. Contbg. editor: National Catholic Register, Encino, Calif., 1980—; author: (books) On Synthesizing Marxism and Christianity, 1976, From Berkeley to East Berlin and Back, 1985. Rockefeller Found. Humanities fellow Inst. Internat. Studies, U. Calif., Berkeley, 1975-76, Nat. Endowment for Humanities fellow, Hoover Instn., Stanford (Calif.) U., 1976-77. Roman Catholic.

VREELAND, ROBERT WILDER, electronics engineer; b. Glen Ridge, N.J., Mar. 4, 1923; s. Frederick King and Elizabeth Lenora (Wilder) V.; m. Jean Gay Fullerton, Jan. 21, 1967; 1 son, Robert Wilder. BS, U. Calif., Berkeley, 1947. Electronics engr. Litton Industries, San Carlos, Calif., 1948-55; sr. devel. electronics engr. U. Calif. Med. Ctr., San Francisco, 1955-89; ret.; cons. electrical engring; speaker 8th Internat. Symposium Biotelemetry, Dubrovnik, Yugoslavia, 1984, RF Expo, Anaheim, Calif., 1985, 86, 87. Contbr. articles to profl. jours., also to internat. meetings and symposiums; patentee in field. Recipient Chancellor's award U. Calif., San Francisco, 1979; cert. appreciation for 25 years' service U. Calif., San Francisco, 1980. Mem. Nat. Bd. Examiners Clin. Engring. (cert. clin. engr.), IEEE, Assn. Advancement Med. Instrumentation (bd. examiner), Am. Radio Relay League (pub. service award 1962). Home: 45 Maywood Dr San Francisco CA 94127-2007 Office: U Calif Med Ctr 4th and Parnassus Sts San Francisco CA 94143

VU, DUNG QUOC, systems analyst; b. Vungtau, Vietnam, Sept. 12, 1963; came to U.S., 1980; s. Tu Duy and Ha Chieu (Phan) V. BS in Math./Computer Sci., UCLA, 1986; MS in Computer Sci., Calif. State U., Fullerton, 1992. Sys. analyst L.A. County Sanitation Dists., 1985—; cons. VNI, Inc., Westminster, Calif., 1987—; pvt. tutor, Huntington Beach, Calif., 1982-83; writer, Anaheim, Calif., 1988—. Chmn. Vietnamese New Year Festival com., Santa Ana, Calif., 1989. Recipient Community Svc. award UCLA Community Svc. Commn., 1985. Mem. IEEE, Assn. for Computing Machinery, N.Y. Acad. Scis., Ice Skating Inst. Am., Union Vietnamese Student Assns. So. Calif. (internal regulation com.). Republican.

VUCANOVICH, BARBARA FARRELL, congresswoman; b. Fort Dix, N.J., June 22, 1921; d. Thomas F. and Ynez (White) Farrell; m. Ken Dillon, Mar. 8, 1950 (div. 1964); children: Patty Dillon Cafferata, Mike, Ken, Tom, Susan Dillon Stoddard; m. George Vucanovich, June 19, 1965. Student, Manhattanville Coll. of Sacred Heart, 1938-39. Owner, operator Welcome Aboard Travel, Reno, 1968-74; Nev. rep. for Senator Paul Laxalt, 1974-82; mem. 98th-104th Congresses from 2d Nev. dist., 1983—; chmn. appropriations subcom. on military construction. Pres. Nev. Fedn. Republican Women, Reno, 1955-56; former pres. St. Mary's Hosp. Guild, Lawyer's Wives. Roman Catholic. Club: Hidden Valley Country (Reno). Office: US Ho of Reps 2202 Rayburn Washington DC 20515*

VUCKOVIC, GOJKO MILOS, public administration scholar; b. Belgrade, Yugoslavia, Feb. 27, 1952; came to U.S., 1989; s. Milos Boza and Zorka Milan (Cubra) V.; m. Ivana Vojin Ognjanovic, July 5, 1986; children: Ivan, Milosh. BA, U. Belgrade, 1976; MSM, Arthur D. Little Mgmt. Inst., 1990; MPA, Harvard U., 1991; PhD, U. So. Calif., 1995. Mgr. export-import Rudnap Inc., Belgrade, 1977; counselor Fed. Secretariat for Fgn. Econ. Rels., Belgrade, 1977-89; fellow UN Indsl. Devel. Orgn., Cambridge, Mass., 1989-90; cons. Compex Internat. Inc., Cambridge, 1991-92; project coord. Coro So. Calif., L.A., 1992-93; fellow Inst. for Study of World Politics, L.A. and Washington, 1994-95; affiliated scholar Ctr. for Multiethnic and Transnat. Studies, U. So. Calif., L.A., 1994—. Mem. Am. Soc. for Pub. Adminstrn., Am. Polit. Sci. Assn., Acad. Polit. Sci., Minza de Gunzberg Ctr. for European Studies, Pi Sigma Alpha, Pi Alpha Alpha. Home: 3144 S Canfield Ave Apt 107 Los Angeles CA 90034-4302 Office: U So Calif Ctr Multiethnic & Transnational Studies Los Angeles CA 90089

VURICH, JOHN DAVID, electronics company executive, engineer; b. Detroit, Mar. 13, 1946; s. Joseph Peter and Elisebeth (Vahlberg) V.; m. Sandra Ann Burris, July 12, 1968 (div. Aug. 1975); 1 child, Daniel John; m. Mary Sharman Summers, Sept. 8, 1985. BSEE, Ariz. State U., 1968. Engr. Motorola Inc., Tempe, Ariz., 1968-75; chief engr. Mirco Inc., Phoenix, 1975-76; mgr. product mktg. Nat. Semicondr., Santa Clara, Calif., 1976-77; mgr. product planning Atari Inc., Sunnyvale, Calif., 1977-79; pres., founder Axlon Inc., Sunnyvale, 1980-85; mgr. advanced products Plantronics Inc., Santa Cruz, Calif., 1986-87, v.p. Advanced Transducer Devices, Sunnyvale, 1987-89; pres., founder BFM Products, Los Gatos, Calif., 1989—; cons. ACS Inc., Scotts Valley, Calif., 1988-89. Inventor 1st computer pinball Spirit of '76 (best design award 1975), smallest computer terminal Datalink 1000, cordless headset telephone (best design award 1987). Pres. Lunar Landowners Assn., Los Gatos, 1989. Home: 876 Brookside Dr Felton CA 95018-9109 Office: BFM Products 876 Brookside Dr Felton CA 95018-9109

VYAS, GIRISH NARMADASHANKAR, virologist, immunohematologist; b. Aglod, India, June 11, 1933; came to U.S., 1965, naturalized, 1973; s. Narmadashankar P. and Rukshmani A. (Joshi) V.; m. Devi Ratilal Trivedi, Apr. 3, 1962; children: Jay, Shrikrishna. B.Sc., U. Bombay, 1954, M.Sc., 1956, Ph.D., 1964. Postdoctoral fellow Western Res. U., 1965-66; mem. faculty U. Calif., San Francisco, 1967—, chief blood bank, 1969-88; prof. lab. medicine U. Calif., 1977—; dir. transfusion rsch. program, 1985—; WHO cons., S.E. Asia, 1980; cons. in field; mem. com. viral hepatitis NRC, 1974-76; mem. task force blood processing Nat. Heart and Lung Inst., 1972-73; sci. program com. Am. Assn. Blood Banks, 1971-76; com. immunoglobulin allotypes WHO, 1974—; mem. U.S. del. immunologists to Romania and Hungary, 1980; mem. FDA com. on blood and blood products, 1987-92; cons. to VA on med. rsch., 1985, UN Devel. Program in India, 1986; and others; chmn. Transmed Biotech Inc., South San Francisco, 1989-95. Author: Hepatitis and Blood Transfusion, 1972, Laboratory Diagnosis of Immunological Disorders, 1975, Membrane Structure and Function of Human Blood Cells, 1976, Viral Hepatitis, 1978, Viral Hepatitis and Liver Disease, 1984, Use and Standardization of Chemically Defined Antigens, 1986; also research papers. Recipient Julliard prize Internat. Soc. Blood Transfusion, 1969; named Outstanding Immigrant in Bay Area Communities Mayor of Oakland, Calif., 1969; Fulbright scholar France, 1980. Mem. AAAS, Am. Soc. Hematology (chmn. com. on transfusion medicine 1989-90), Am. Assn. Immunologists, Am. Soc. Clin. Pathologists, Internat. Assn. for Biol. Standarization (coun. 1992—). Democrat. Hindu. Office: U Calif Lab Med S-555 San Francisco CA 94143-0134

WACHBRIT, JILL BARRETT, accountant, tax specialist; b. Ventura, Calif., May 27, 1955; d. Preston Everett Barrett and Lois JoAnne (Fondersmith) Batchelder; m. Michael Ian Wachbrit, June 21, 1981; children: Michelle, Tracy. AA, Santa Monica City Coll., 1975; BS, Calif. State U., Northridge, 1979; M in Bus. Taxation, U. So. Calif., 1985. CPA. Supervising sr. tax acct. Peat, Marwick, Mitchell & Co., Century City, Calif., 1979-82; sr. tax analyst Avery Internat., Pasadena, Calif., 1982-83; tax mgr., asst. v.p. First Interstate Leasing, Pasadena, 1983-88, Gibraltar Savs., 1988, Security Pacific Corp., L.A., 1988-92; tax mgr., acct. El Camino Resources Ltd., Woodland Hills, Calif., 1992-95. Republican. Jewish.

WACHS, MARTIN, urban planning educator, author, consultant; b. N.Y.C., June 8, 1941; s. Robert and Doris (Margolis) W.; m. Helen Pollner, Aug. 18, 1963; children: Faye Linda, Steven Brett. B.C.E., CUNY, 1963; M.S., Northwestern U., 1965, Ph.D., 1967. Asst. prof. U. Ill.-Chgo., 1967-69, Northwestern U., Evanston, Ill., 1969-71; assoc. prof. urban planning UCLA, 1971-76, prof., 1976—; dir. UCLA Inst. Tranp. Studies, 1993—; vis. disting. prof. Rutgers U., New Brunswick, N.J., 1983-84; mem. exec. com. Transp. Rsch. Bd., 1995—. Author: Transportation for the Elderly: Changing Lifestyles, Changing Needs, 1979, The Clean Air Act in Court: New Demands on Transportation Planning, 1995; also numerous articles; editor: Ethics in Planning, 1984, The Car and the City, 1992. Mem. steering com. Los Angeles Parking Mgmt. Study, 1976-78; bd. dirs. Los Angeles Commuter Computer, 1978—. Served to capt. Ordnance Corps, U.S. Army, 1967-69. Recipient Pike Johnson award Transp. Research Bd., 1976, Disting. Teaching award UCLA Alumni Assn., 1986, Disting. Planning Educator award Calif. Planners Found., 1986, vis. fellow Oxford U. (Eng.), 1976-77; Guggenheim fellow, 1977; Rockefeller Found. humanities fellow, 1980. Fellow Am. Coun. Edn.; mem. Am. Planning Assn., Am. Inst. Cert. Planners, Architects, Designers, Planners for Social Responsibility. Jewish.

Home: 1088 N Kenter Ave Los Angeles CA 90049-1336 Office: UCLA Dept Urban Planning 1118A Perloff Hall Los Angeles CA 90024

WADA, DAVID RUSSELL, biomedical engineer, researcher; b. Pasadena, Calif., Nov. 28, 1961; s. Ben Kazuho and Agnes Reiko (Yamada) W.; m. Inhwa Choi, Dec. 18, 1987; 1 child, Jules Russell. BS in Engring. Physics, U. Calif., Berkeley, 1983, MSEE, 1984; PhDEE, UCLA, 1991. Mem. tech. staff, engr. TRW, Redondo Beach, Calif., 1983-84, Hughes Aircraft, El Segundo, Calif., 1985-86; cons. Minimed, Sylmar, Calif., 1991-92; postdoctoral fellow Stanford (Calif.) U., 1992-93, rsch. assoc. dept. anesthesiology, 1994—; cons. Siemens, Sylmar, 1992-93. Contbr. articles to profl. jours. Mem. IEEE Control Sys. Soc., IEE Biomed. Engring. Soc., Am. Assn. Pharm. Scientists. Office: Stanford U Anesthesiology Dept 300 Pasteur Dr Palo Alto CA 94304-2203

WADDELL, EMILIE JEAN MCCARTNEY, mental health counselor; b. Oakland, Calif., Mar. 14, 1950; d. Harry Hollis McCartney and Alma Ethal (Collins) McCartney York; m. James Richard Waddell, Aug. 1, 1970; children: Nathan James, Benjamin Isaac, Aaron Luke. BA in Social Sci. and Psychology, Marylhurst (Oreg.) Coll., 1991; MA in Counseling Psychology, Lewis and Clark Coll., 1993. Registered counselor, Wash.; nat. cert. counselor. Spl. edn. tchrs. asst. Portland (Oreg.) Pub. Schs., 1987-90; counselor Metro Crisis Intervention Svc., Portland, 1989-91; vol. counselor YWCA Counseling Ctr., Portland, Oreg., 1991-92; counselor, intern Dammasch State Hosp., Wilsonville, Oreg., 1992-93, Catholic. Cmty. Svcs., Vancouver, Wash., 1992-93; asst. instr. Marylhurst Coll., 1993, psychology instr., 1994; mental health therapist, counselor Mt. Hood Mid County Family Svc. Ctr., Portland, 1993—. Mem. editorial staff The Citizens Companion, 1994—; contbr. articles to profl. jours. Vol. publicist N.E. YMCA, Portland, 1985-86; den leader, com. sec. Boy Scouts Am., Portland, 1985-87; vol. tchrs. aide Portland Pub. Schs., 1985-89, chmn. local sch. adv. com., 1986-89. Leslie S. Parker Meml. scholar, 1991-93. Mem. ACA, APA, Am. Mental Health Counselors Assn., Oreg. Counseling Assn., N.W. Civil War Coun., 1st Oreg. Vol. Infantry (historian, rschr. 1992—), Aurora Colony Hist. Soc. (mem. steering com. Stauffer-Will Farm). Office: Mt Hood Mid County Family Svc Ctr 131 NE 102d Ave Portland OR 97220

WADDELL, JOHN HENRY, sculptor; b. Des Moines, Feb. 14, 1921; s. William Wilder and Isabel Catherine (McGee) W.; m. Leslie Owen, 1942 (div. 1948); children—Sean, Seamus, Seanchan; m. Ruth Holland, Mar. 24, 1949; children—Lindsey, William, Amy. BFA, Art Inst. Chgo., 1948; B in Art Edn., 1949, MFA, 1949, M in Art Edn., 1951; DFA (hon.), Nat. Coll. Edn., 1979. Instr. Nat. Coll. Edn., Evanston, Ill., 1949-55; asst. prof. Ill. Inst. Tech., Chgo., 1955-57; prof. Ariz. State U., Tempe, 1957-64; head Waddell Sculpture Fellowship, Cornville, Ariz., 1971—. Executed sculpture Dance, Phoenix Civic Ctr., 1974, The Family, Maricopa County, Phoenix, 1967, That Which Might Have Been, Birmingham, 1963, Unitarian Ch., Paradise Valley, Ariz., 1964, Dance Mother, Kenyon Coll., Gambier, Ohio, 1969, Seated Flutist and Relief Dancers, Nat. Coll. Edn., Evanston, Ill., 1979, Backwalkover, Phoenix Sports Medicine Ctr., 1985, Apogee and Momentum, USTA Nat. Tennis Ctr., Flushing Meadows, N.Y., 1988, Seated Harpist, Ravinia, Highland Park, Ill., 1990, Touchstone, Boswell Meml. Hosp., Sun City, Ariz., 1994, Life's Celebration, 1985-95; represented Scottsdale (Ariz.) Ctr. For the Arts, 1984, others. Served with AUS, 1943-45. Grantee Valley Beautiful Commn., Phoenix, 1965, Nat. Endowment Arts/Commn. Arts and Humanities, 1969-74, Nat. Endowment Arts, 1978; recipient Gov. Artist award, 1995. Unitarian. Home: 10050 E Waddell Rd Cornville AZ 86325-6010

WADDINGHAM, JOHN ALFRED, artist, journalist; b. London, Eng., July 9, 1915; came to U.S., 1927, naturalized, 1943; s. Charles Alfred and Mary Elizabeth (Coles) W.; m. Joan Lee Larson, May 3, 1952; children: Mary Kathryn, Thomas Richard. Student, Coronado (Calif.) Sch. Fine Arts, 1953-54, Portland Art Mus., 1940-65, U. Portland, 1946-47; pupil, Rex Brandt, Eliot Ohara, George Post. Promotion art dir. Oreg. Jour., Portland, 1946-59; with The Oregonian, Portland, 1959-81; editorial art dir. The Oregonian, 1959-81; tchr. watercolor Ore. Soc. Artists, 1954-56; tchr. art Oreg. Sch. Arts and Crafts, 1981—, Portland Community Coll.; represented by several galleries, Oreg. and Wash. One man show includes Art in the Gov.'s Office Ore State Capitol, 1991; rep. mus. rental collections, Portland Art Mus., Bush House, Salem, Ore., U. Oreg. Mus., Vincent Price collection, Ford Times collection, also, Am. Watercolor Soc. Travelling Show; judge art events, 1946—, over 50 one-man shows; ofcl. artist, Kiwanis Internat. Conv., 1966; designed, dir. constrn. cast: concrete mural Genesis, St. Barnabas Episcopal Ch., Portland, 1960; spl. work drawings old Portland landmarks and houses; propr. John Waddingham Hand Prints, fine arts serigraphs and silk screen drawings, 1965—; featured artist: Am. Artist mag., May 1967, June 1990, published in numerous mags. Served with USAAF, 1942-46. Recipient gold medal Salone Internazionale dell' Umorismo, Italy, 1974, 76, 80; honored with a 45 yr. retrospective Assignment: The Artist as Journalist Oreg. Hist. Soc., 1991. Artist mem. Portland Art Mus.; mem. Portland Art Dirs. Club (past pres.), N.W. Watercolor Soc., Watercolor Soc. Oreg., Oreg. Soc. Artists (watercolor tchr.), Multnomah Athletic Club, Jewish Community Ctr., Univ. Oreg. Med. Sch., Art in the Mounts., Oreg. Old Time Fiddlers, Clan Macleay Bagpipe Band. Home and Studio: 955 SW Westwood Dr Portland OR 97201-2744

WADDINGTON, RAYMOND BRUCE, JR., English language educator; b. Santa Barbara, Calif., Sept. 27, 1935; s. Raymond Bruce and Marjorie Gladys (Waddell) W.; m. Linda Gayle Jones, Sept. 7, 1957 (div.); children: Raymond Bruce, Edward Jackson; m. Kathleen Martha Ward, Oct. 11, 1985. B.A., Stanford U., 1957; Ph.D., Rice U., 1963; postdoctoral (Univ. fellow in Humanities), Johns Hopkins U., 1965-66. Instr. English U. Houston, 1961-62; instr. U. Kans., 1962-63; asst. prof., 1963-65; asst. prof. English lit. U. Wis., Madison, 1966-68; asso. prof. U. Wis., 1968-74, prof., 1974-82; prof. English lit. U. Calif., Davis, 1982—. Author: The Mind's Empire, 1974; co-editor: The Rhetoric of Renaissance Poetry, 1974, The Age of Milton, 1980, The Expulsion of the Jews, 1994; mem. editl. bd. The Medal, 1991; sr. editor: Sixteenth Century Jour.; editor: Garland Studies in the Renaissance. Huntington Library fellow, 1967, 75; Inst. Research in Humanities fellow, 1971-72; Guggenheim fellow, 1972-73; NEH fellow, 1977, 83; Newberry Library fellow, 1978; Am. Philos. Soc. grantee, 1965. Mem. Renaissance Soc. Am., Milton Soc. Am., 16th Century Studies Conf. (pres. 1985). Club: Logos. Home: 39 Pershing Ave Woodland CA 95695-2845 Office: U Calif Dept English Davis CA 95616

WADE, LEROY GROVER, JR., chemistry educator; b. Jacksonville, Fla. Oct. 8, 1947; s. Leroy Grover and Margaret Lena (Stevens) W.; children: Christine Elizabeth, Jennifer Diane. BA summa cum laude, Rice U., 1969; AM, Harvard U., 1970, PhD, 1974. Resident research fellow Du Pont Corp., Wilmington, Del., 1969; teaching fellow in chemistry Harvard U., Cambridge, Mass., 1969-74, sr. adviser to freshmen, 1971-74; resident sci. tutor Radcliffe Coll., Cambridge, 1970-74; asst. prof. chemistry Colo. State U., Ft. Collins, 1974-80, assoc. prof., 1980-89; prof. chemistry Whitman Coll., Walla Walla, Wash., 1989—. Author: Annual Reports in Organic Synthesis, 1975-82, 8 vols., Compendium of Organic Synthetic Methods, Vols. III, IV, V, 1977, 80, 84, Organic Chemistry, 1987, 3d edit., 1995; contbr. articles to sci. jours.; reviewer profl. jours., papers. Mem. Am. Chem. Soc., AAAS, Catgut Acoustical Soc., Am. Acad. Forensic Scis., Phi Beta Kappa (pres. Colo. State U. chpt. 1983-84), Sigma Xi. Office: Whitman Coll Chemistry Dept Walla Walla WA 99362

WADE, MICHAEL ROBERT ALEXANDER, marketing specialist; b. N.Y.C., June 29, 1945; s. Burton Jean and Celia (Handleman) W.; student U. Rennes, France, 1964; AB, U. Chgo., 1967; postgrad. in pub. adminstrn., Am. U., 1967-71; MBA in Fin., N.Y. U., 1975; m. Carole Kay West, Aug. 25, 1974. Program analyst, mgmt. intern HUD, 1967-71; dep. dir. Mgmt. Communications and Briefing Center, U.S. Price Commn., 1972; asst. exec. sec. policy coordination U.S. Cost of Living Council, 1973-74; asso. dir. U.S. Indochina Refugee Program, 1975-76; pres. China Trade Devel. Corp. of Chgo., 1977—; participant with W.R. Grace & Co. in Okla. oil and gas prodn. Recipient Meritorious Service award Exec. Office of the Pres., 1972, Disting. Service award U.S. Cost of Living Council, 1974. Mem. Soc. Contemporary Art, Internat. Bus. Council MidAm. (bd. dirs.). Office: China Trade Devel Corp 2049 Century Park E Ste 480 Los Angeles CA 90067-3106

WADE, MICHAEL STEPHEN, management consultant; b. Mesa, Ariz., Sept. 13, 1948; s. William Conrad and Geraldine (Pomeroy) W.; m. Mary Ann Kraynick, Aug. 30, 1971; children: Jonathan, Hilary. BA, U. Ariz., 1970, JD, 1973. Command equal opportunity officer U.S. Army Criminal Investigation Command, Washington, 1974-76; EEO investigative specialist City of Phoenix, 1977-79, EEO adminstr., 1979-84; cons. Phoenix, 1984—; instr. Ariz. Govtl. Tng. Service. Author: The Bitter Issue: The Right to Work Law in Arizona, 1976. Active Ch. of the Beatitudes, Ariz. Rep. Caucus. With U.S. Army, 1974-76. Recipient Phoenix Mayor's Com. on Employment of Handicapped award, 1984, Cert. Appreciation award Phoenix Fire Dept. Mem. Nat. Assn. Pub. Sector EEO Officers (founding pres. 1984-85, Pres.'s award 1989), Am. Soc. Equal Opportunity Profls. (v.p.), North Ctrl. Phoenix Homeowners Assn. Home: 7032 N 3rd Ave Phoenix AZ 85021-8704 Office: PO Box 34598 Phoenix AZ 85067-4598

WADE, RODGER GRANT, financial systems analyst; b. Littlefield, Tex., June 25, 1945; s. George and Jimmie Frank (Grant) W.; m. Karla Kay Morrison, Dec. 18, 1966 (div. 1974); children: Eric Shawn, Shannon Annelle, Shelby Elaine; m. Carol Ruth Manning, Mar. 28, 1981. BA in Sociology, Tex. Tech. U., 1971. Programmer First Nat. Bank, Lubbock, Tex., 1971-73, Nat. Sharedata Corp., Odessa, Tex., 1973; asst. dir. computing ctr. Odessa Community Coll., 1973-74; programmer/analyst Med. Sci. Ctr., Tex. Tech U., Lubbock, 1974-76; sys. mgr. Hosp. Info. Sys., Addison, Tex., 1976-78; programmer, analyst Harris Corp., Grapevine, Tex., 1978-80, Joy Petroleum, Waxahachie, Tex., 1980-82; owner R&C Bus. Sys./Requerdos de Santa Fe, N.Mex., 1982-84; fin. sys. analyst Los Alamos (N.Mex.) Tech. Assocs., 1984—; owner El Rancho Herbs, Santa Fe, 1988-91, Wade Gallery, Santa Fe, 1990-91, Wade Systems, Santa Fe, 1992—. Vol. programmer Los Alamos Arts Coun., 1987-88; mem. regulations task force N.Mex. Gov.'s Health Policy Adv. Com.; vol. systems support Amigos Unidos of Taos, 1990—. Republican. Home: 3336 La Avenida De San Marc Santa Fe NM 87505-9209 Office: Los Alamos Tech Assocs 1650 Trinity Dr Los Alamos NM 87544-3044

WADE, WILLIAM EDWARD, JR., oil company executive; b. Memphis, Aug. 3, 1942; s. William Edward and Martha (Moulder) W.; m. Noel Lynn Galloway; 1 child, William Galen. BS in Chem. Engring., U. Tenn., Knoxville, 1965; MS, MIT, 1968. Mgr. resource planning Atlantic Richfield, Los Angeles, 1975-76, mgr. Anaconda planning, 1976-79; mgr. oil, gas planning Atlantic Richfield, Dallas, 1979-81, v.p. fin. Arco Exploration, 1981-82, v.p. land acquisitions, mgmt. Arco Exploration, 1982-85; v.p. corp. planning Atlantic Richfield, Los Angeles, 1985-87, now sr. v.p.; pres. ARCO Alaska, Inc., Anchorage, 1987—. Bd. dirs. Los Angeles Theater Ctr. of the Arts, 1985—. Office: ARCO Alaska Inc Anchorage Tower 700 G St Anchorage AK 99501-3439 Other: Atlantic Richfield Co 515 S Flower St Los Angeles CA 90071-2201

WADIA, MANECK SORABJI, management consultant, writer; b. Bombay, Oct. 22, 1931; came to U.S., 1953.; s. Sorabji Rattanji and Manijeh M. (Pocha) W.; m. Harriet F. Schilit, Nov. 22, 1962; children: Sara Wadia Fascetti, Mark Sorab. MBA, Ind. U., 1958, PhD, 1957. Mem. faculty Ind. U., Bloomington, 1958-60; Ford Found. fellow U. Pitts., 1960-61; prof. Stanford U., Palo Alto, Calif., 1961-65; mgmt. and personal cons., pres. Wadia Assoc., Del Mar, Calif., 1965—; cons., lectr. presenter in field. Author: The Nature and Scope of Management, 1966, Management and the Behavioral Sciences, 1968, Cases in International Business, 1970, Holistic Management: A Behavioral Philosophy of Successful Leadership, 1990; co-author: (with Harper W. Boyd, Jr.) Cases from Emerging Countries, 1977; contbr. articles to profl. publs. Fellow Soc. Applied Anthropology; mem. Soc. Advancement Mgmt., Acad. Mgmt., Ind. Acad. Sci. (pres. anthropology sect.), Sigma Xi (assoc.), Sigma Iota Epsilon. Home and Office: 1660 Luneta Dr Del Mar CA 92014-2435

WADLEY, M. RICHARD, consumer products executive; b. Lehi, Utah; s. Merlyn R. and Verla Ann (Bali); m. Nancy Zwiers; children: Lisa Kathleen, Staci Lin, Eric Richard, Nicole Marie. BS, Brigham Young U., 1967; MBA, Northwestern U., 1968. Brand asst. packaged soap and detergent div. Procter & Gamble Co., Cin., 1968-69, asst. brand mgr. packaged soap and detergent div., 1970-71, brand mgr. Dawn detergent, 1972-73, copy supr. packaged soap and detergent div., 1974-75, brand mgr. Tide detergent, 1975-77, assoc. advt. mgr. packaged soap and detergent div., 1977-81; corp. product dir. Hallmark Cards, Inc., Kansas City, Mo., 1982-83, corp. product dir. Ambassador Cards div., 1983-85; v.p., gen. mgr. feminine protection div. Tambrands Inc., Lake Success, N.Y., 1986-88; sr. v.p. Bongrain, Inc., N.Y.C., 1988-89; pres., CEO Alta-Dena Inc., Divsn. of Bongrain, Inc., 1989-91; pres. The Summit Group, 1991—; chmn., CEO T-Chem Products Inc., 1993—, also bd. dirs.; mgmt. bd. Bongrain N.A., 1988-91; bd. dirs. Calif. Dairy Inst., 1989-90, Nat. Milk Assn., 1990-91, Alta Dena, Inc., 1989-91, Creative Nail Design, 1992—. Bd. dirs. Long Beach Opera, 1991-95, L.I. Friends of the Arts, 1986-88; mem. adv. bd. Bus. Sch. Calif. State U., Long Beach, 1991-93.

WADLOW, JOAN KRUEGER, university chancellor; b. LeMars, Iowa, Aug. 21, 1932; d. R. John and Norma I. (IhLe) Krueger; m. Richard R. Wadlow, July 27, 1958; children: Dawn, Kit. B.A., U. Nebr., Lincoln, 1953; M.A. (Seacrest Journalism fellow 1953-54), Fletcher Sch. Law and Diplomacy, 1956; Ph.D. (Rotary fellow 1956-57), U. Nebr., Lincoln, 1963; cert., Grad. Inst. Internat. Studies, Geneva, 1957. Mem. faculty U. Nebr., Lincoln, 1966-79; prof. polit. scis. U. Nebr., 1964-79, assoc. dean Coll. Arts and Scis., 1972-79; prof. polit. scis., dean Coll. Arts and Scis., U. Wyo., Laramie, 1979-84, v.p. acad. affairs, 1984-86; prof. polit. sci., provost U. Okla., Norman, 1986-91; chancellor U. Alaska, Fairbanks, 1991—; cons. on fed. grants; bd. dirs. Key Bank Alaska; mem. Commn. Colls. N.W. Assn. Author articles in field. Bd. dirs. Nat. Merit Scholarship Corp., Lincoln United Way, 1976-77, Bryan Hosp., Lincoln, 1978-79, Washington Ctr., 1986—, Key Bank of Alaska; v.p., exec. commr. North Cen. Assn., pres., 1991; pres. adv. bd. Lincoln YWCA, 1970-71; mem. def. adv. com. Women in the Svcs., 1987-89; mem. community adv. bd. Alaska Airlines. Recipient Mortar Board Teaching award, 1976, Disting. Teaching award U. Nebr., Lincoln, 1979; fellow Conf. Coop. Man, Lund, Sweden, 1956. Mem. Internat. Studies Assn. (co-editor Internat. Studies Notes 1978-91), Nat. Assn. State Univs. and Land-Grant Colls. (exec. com. coun. acad. affairs 1989-91), Western Assn. Africanists (pres. 1980-82), Assn. Western Univs. (pres.-elect 1993—), Coun. Colls. Arts and Scis. (pres. 1983-84), Greater Fairbanks C. of C., Gamma Phi Beta. Republican. Congregationalist. Home and Office: PO Box 900147 Fairbanks AK 99775

WADMAN, WILLIAM WOOD, III, technical research executive, consulting company executive; b. Oakland, Calif., Nov. 13, 1936; s. William Wood, Jr., and Lula Fay (Raisner) W.; children: Roxanne Alyce Wadman Hubbling, Raymond Alan (dec.), Theresa Hope Wadman Boudreaux; m. Barbara Jean Wadman; stepchildren: Denise Ellen Varine Skrypkar, Brian Ronald Varine. M.A., U. Calif., Irvine, 1978. Cert. program mgr. tng. Radiation safety specialist, accelerator health physicist U. Calif. Lawrence Berkeley Lab., 1957-68; campus radiation safety officer U. Calif., Irvine, 1968-79; dir. ops., radiation safety officer Radiation Sterilizers, Inc., Tustin, Calif., 1979-80; prin., pres. Wm. Wadman & Assocs. Inc., 1980—; mem. operational review team Princeton U. Rsch. Campus TOKOMAK Fusion Test Facility, 1993-94; technical project mgr. Los Alamos Nat. Lab. for Upgrades Projects. mem. team No. 1, health physics appraisal program NRC, 1980-81; cons. health physicist to industry; lectr. sch. social ecology, 1974-79, dept. community and environ. medicine U. Calif., Irvine, 1979-80, instr. in environ. health and safety, 1968-79, Orange Coast Coll., in radiation exposure reduction design engring. Iowa Electric Light & Power; trainer Mason & Hanger-Silas Mason Co., Los Alamos Nat. Lab., instr. in medium energy cyclotron radiation safety UCLBL, lectr. in accelerator health physics, 1966, 67; curriculum developer in field; subject matter expert Los Alamos Nat. Lab., Earth and Environ. Scis., Tech. Support Office. Active Cub Scouts; chief umpire Mission Viejo Little League, 1973. Served with USNR, 1955-63. Recipient award for profl. achievement U. Calif. Alumni Assn., 1972, Outstanding Performance award U. Calif., Irvine, 1973. Mem. Health Physics Soc. (treas. 1979-81, edittor proc. 11th symposium, pres. So. Calif. chpt. 1977, Professionalism award 1975), Internat. Radiation Protection Assn. (U.S. del. 4th Congress 1977, 8th Congress 1992), Am. Nuclear Soc., Am. Public Health Assn. (chmn. program 1978, chmn. radiol. health sect. 1979-80), Campus Radiation Safety Officers (chmn. 1975, editor proc. 5th conf. 1975), ASTM. Club: UCI Univ. (dir. 1976, sec. 1977, treas. 1978). Contbr. articles to tech. jours. Achievements include research in radiation protection and environmental sciences; Avocations: sailing, Tae Kwon Do, wood working, numesmantics. Home: 3687 Red Cedar Way Lake Oswego OR 97035-3525 Office: 675 Fairview Dr Ste 246 Carson City NV 89701-5468

WAETJEN, HERMAN CHARLES, theologian, educator; b. Bremen, Germany, June 16, 1929; Arrived in U.S., Sept., 1931.; s. Henry and Anna (Ruschmeyer) W.; m. Mary Suzanne Struyk, July 15, 1960; children: Thomas (dec.), Thembisa, Elaine, David. BA, Concordia Sem., St. Louis, 1950, BD, 1953; Dr. Theol., Tuebingen U., Fed. Republic Germany, 1958; postgrad., Hebrew U., Jerusalem, 1955. Instr. Concordia Sem., 1957; asst. prof. U. So. Calif., L.A., 1959-62; assoc. prof. San Francisco Theol. Sem., San Anselmo, Calif., 1962-70, prof., 1970-74, Robert S. Dollar prof. of New Testament, 1974—; vis. prof. U. Nairobi, Kenya, 1973-74, Fed. Theol. Sem., Republic South Africa, 1979-80, U. Zimbabwe, 1986-87, U. Namibia, 1993-94. Author: Origin and Destiny of Humanness, 1976, 78, A Reordering of Power, 1989, (with others) Reading from this Place: Social Location and Biblical Interpretation; contbr. chpts. to texts. mem. Soc. Biblical Lit., Pacific Coast Theol. Soc., Pacific Coast Theol. Soc. Democrat. Presbyterian. Home: 83 Jordan Ave San Francisco CA 94118-2502 Office: San Francisco Theol Sem 2 Kensington Rd San Anselmo CA 94960-2905

WAGEMAKER, DAVID ISAAC, human resources development executive; b. Grand Rapids, Mich., Feb. 10, 1949; s. Raymond Ogden and Inez Loraine W. BA in Philosophy, Grand Valley State U., 1971. Owner Edn. Ctr., Grand Rapids, 1970-72; cons. Am. Leadership Coll., Washington, 1972-78, Wagemaker Co., Honolulu, 1978-80; edn. cons. Batten, Batten, Hudson & Swab, Inc., San Diego, 1980-81, mgr., 1981; securities broker, ins. agt. The Equitable Assurance Co., San Diego, 1982; assoc. cons. Pacific S.W. Airlines, San Diego, 1982-83; project mgr. GM Hughes Electroncis, Westchester, Calif., 1983—; v.p. Wagemaker, Inc., Grand Rapids, 1984—; sr. cons. Nat. Mgmt. Isnt., Flower Mound, Tex., 1985—; mgmt. cons. Mgmt. Devel. Ctr., San Diego State U., 1980—. Co-author: Build A Better You Starting Now, 1982; author: (cassette program) Effective Time Management, 1979, (with others) How To Organize Yourself To Win, 1988; featured in tng. film Managing Diversity, 1991. Mem. Acad. Mgmt., Hughes Mgmt. Club, Hughes Golf Club, Sigma Chi, Zeta Nu. Republican. Congregationalist. Home: 2227F Robinson St # A Redondo Beach CA 90278-2019

WAGEMAN, LYNETTE MENA, librarian; b. Trinidad, West Indies, Aug. 18, 1934; came to U.S., 1955.; d. Hubert and Alma (Sampath) Jagbandhansingh. BA in Modern Fgn. Langs., Park Coll., Parkville, Mo., 1959; MLS, U. Hawaii, 1966, MA in Asian Studies, 1976. Serials asst. East-West Ctr. Libr., Honolulu, 1962-66; catalog libr. U. Hawaii, Honolulu, 1966-71, South Asia specialist, 1971-93, acting head Asia collection, 1991-93, head, 1993—, collection devel. mgr. Asia collection, pub. svc. head rep., 1991—; exec. com. Ctr. South Asian Studies, 1973-75, 77-79, 81-83, 85-86, 87-90, acting dir., 1988, 90, 92. Mem. Hawaii Libr. Assn. (mem. bd. 1990-92, co-editor newsletter 1990-92), Assn. Asian Studies (exec. bd. com. on South Asian Librs. and Documentation 1983-85, 90—, chairperson 1992—, exec. com. Asian Libr. Liaison com. 1991—, adv. com. Bibliography Asian Studies 1992—), Internat. Assn. Orientalist Librs., South Asian Lit. Assn., Com. on Women in Asian Studies. Office: U Hawaii Asia Collection Hamilton Libr 2550 The Mall Honolulu HI 96822-2233

WAGEMANN, DOUGLAS GERALD, banker; b. Oshawa, Ont., Can., Oct. 5, 1954; s. Edward and Sylvia Ella Wagemann; m. Rita Viola Hillock, Dec. 27, 1973; children: Shawna Lynn, Christine Renee, Douglas Gerald II. BS in Bus. magna cum laude, Calif. State Poly. U., 1984; MBA, Calif. State U., San Bernardino, 1987. Adminstrv. trainee Pomona (Calif.) First Fed., 1984-85, asst. br. mgr., 1985-87, corp. rsch. analyst, 1987-90, v.p. rsch. planning mgr., 1990-93, v.p. mktg./planning dir., 1993—; lectr. Calif. State Poly U., 1992—, La Sierra U., Riverside, Calif., 1995. Dir., v.p. Inland Hospice Assn., Claremont, Calif., 1991; lectr. Jr. Achievement, Anaheim, Calif., 1990. Named Vol. of Yr. Jr. Achievement, 1990. Mem. Internat. Soc. Strategic Mgmt. and Planning, Am. Mktg. Assn., Bank Mktg. Assn., Fin. Inst. Mktg. Assn., Calif. League of Savs. Inst. (pub. affairs com. 1993—), Phi Kappa Phi, Delta Mu Delta. Office: Pomona First Fed 350 S Garey Ave Pomona CA 91766-1722

WAGENER, HOBART D., retired architect; b. Sioux Falls, S.D., May 10, 1921; s. Frank Samuel and Beatrice (Hobart) W.; m. Violet LaVaughn, Dec. 16, 1944; children: Diane Kay Wagener Welch, Jeffrey Scott, Shaw Bradley. BArch, U. Mich., 1944. Registered architect, Colo. Draftsman Eggers & Higgins, Architects, N.Y.C., 1946-47, Pietro Belluschi, Architect, Portland, Oreg., 1947-50; designer James Hunter, Architect, Boulder, Colo., 1950-53; prin. Hobart D. Wagener Assocs., Boulder, 1953-77; prin. ptnr. Wagener VanderVorste, Architects, Boulder, 1977-86; ret., 1986; mem. selection com. Colo. Supreme Ct., Denver, 1968-72. Co-author: The School Library, 1962; work pub. in Archtl. Record, Sunset mag., N.Y. Times, House Beautiful, 25 Years of Record Houses. Chmn. Boulder Planning Commn., 1966; pres. Boulder C. of C., 1971. Lt. (j.g.) USN, 1944-46, PTO. Named Outstanding Designer for past 50 yrs. Hist. Boulder, 1983; also numerous nat. and regional design awards. Fellow AIA (pres. Colo. 1973, Colo. Architect of Yr. award 1985), Lions (pres. Boulder 1965). Address: 1730 Avenida Del Mundo Apt 1607 Coronado CA 92118-3028

WAGENER, ROBERT JOHN, bioethicist, mediator; b. Buffalo, N.Y., Mar. 6, 1946; s. Philip John and June Augusta (Bartels) W. BA, SUNY, Buffalo; MDiv, McCormick Theol. Sem., Chgo.; MA, Canisius Coll. Co-founder, pres. Ctr. for Med. Ethics and Mediation, San Diego, 1992—; mediation coord. Am. Arbitration Assn., 1993—; cons. U. Calif. San Diego Ethics Consultation Svc., 1985—; lectr., mediator, mentor, trainer in field. Contbr. articles to profl. jours. Bd. dirs. Hospice Buffalo, Victim Offender Reconciliation Program, San Diego, UCSD Med. Ctr. Ethics Com.; cons. San Diego Hospice Chaplaincy Project; vice chair Hotel Dieu Hosp. Hospice, New Orleans; v.p. Sudden Infant Death Found. Western N.Y. Mem. Am. Soc. Law, Medicine and Ethics, Soc. Profls. in Dispute Resolution, So. Calif. Mediation Assn., Internat. Bioethics Inst., Hastings Ctr. for Bioethics. Office: Ctr for Med Ethics & Mediation 1081 Camino del Rio S Ste 217 San Diego CA 92108

WAGGENER, MELISSA, public relations executive; b. 1954. With Tektronix Inc., Beaverton, Oreg., 1975-80, Regis McKenna, Portland, 1980-83; with Waggener Edstrom, Inc., 1983—, now pres. Office: Waggener Edstrom Inc 6915 SW Macadam Ave Portland OR 97219*

WAGGENER, THERYN LEE, law enforcement professional; b. Cedar Rapids, Iowa, Sept. 7, 1941; s. Hollis Angisa (Fowler) Hogan; m. Zoetta Jean Hamilton, May 30, 1967; 1 child, Drugh Kincade. BBA, Nat. U., 1977, MBA, 1979; JD, Western State Coll. Law, 1980. Traffic officer Calif. Hwy. Patrol, San Diego, 1966-72; owner, operator Am. Nat. Chem., San Diego, 1972-82; chief investigator N.Mex. Real Estate Commn., Albuquerque, 1983-86, Nev. Real Estate Div., Carson City, 1986-89; lt., shift comdr. Nev. Dept. Prisons, Ely, 1989—; prof., Sierra Nev. Coll., Incline Village, 1988-89, Western Nev. Community Coll., Carson City, 1987-89; No. Nev. C.C., 1992—. Mem. Washoe County (Nev.) Rep. Cen. Com., 1989. With USN, 1960-65. Mem. Nat. Assn. Real Estate Lic. Law Ofcls. (enforcement and investigative com. 1987-89), Toastmasters, Rotary, Lions, Masons, Shriners, Nu Beta Epsilon.

WAGGONER, DAVID CARL, college administrator; b. Boise, Idaho, Jan. 17, 1953; s. J. Earl and Pauline Ann (Vocu) W.; m. Lorette Diane Koenig, June 18, 1977; 1 child, Bethany. BA, Northwest Christian Coll., 1976; MDiv, Tex. Christian U., 1979; MA, U. Oreg., 1981, postgrad., 1994—. Ordained to ministry Disciples of Christ Ch., 1979. Minister of youth Rosemont Christian Ch., Dallas, 1977-79; assoc. minister First Christian Ch., Eugene, Oreg., 1980-82; v.p., dean student affairs Northwest Christian Coll., Eugene, 1982—; coord. Willamette Valley Collegiate Drug and Alcohol Consortium, 1991-93; chair Oreg. Higher Edn. Alcohol and Drug Coordinating Com., 1993—; mem. Commn. on Ministry, Christian Ch. Oreg. Recipient 1st Pl. Speech Contest Toastmasters Internat. Oreg. Cen. Div., 1985, 89; Consortium grantee Fund for the Improvement Post-Secondary Edn., 1991. Mem. Assn. Christians in Student Devel. (N.W. regional dir.

1989-93), Nat. Assn. Student Pers. Adminstrs., Western Assn. Student Employment Adminstrs., N.W. Coll. Pers. Assn., Pacific Northwest Assn. Instnl. Rsch. and Planning, Eugene Lunch Bunch Toastmasters (pres. 1991). Republican. Office: Northwest Christian Coll 828 E 11th Ave Eugene OR 97401-3727

WAGMAN, DAVID S., computer company executive; b. 1951. BBA, Armstrong State Coll., 1973. With Nixdorf Computer, 1973-75, Computer Software Inc., 1975-79, Transaction Tech. Inc., 1979-80; with Merisel Internat., 1980—, chmn. bd., from 1980, co-chmn. bd., 1985—. Office: Merisel Internat 200 Continental Blvd El Segundo CA 90245-4526

WAGNER, BRUCE DIETER, environmental engineer; b. Vancouver, B.C., Can., Mar. 13, 1957; came to U.S., 1960; s. Kurt and Wiltrud Wagner; m. Nancy Gwen Wade, Feb. 27, 1957; children: Jennifer, Jeffrey. BA in Geotechnical Engring., U. Colo., 1988; MS in Environ. Engring., Colo. Sch. Mines, 1993. Environ. technician Marathon Oil Co., Denver, 1986-89; waste mgmt. engr. Wastren Inc., Denver, 1990-91; environ. coord. Total Petroleum, Denver, 1991-93, environ. mgr. mktg. svcs., 1994—; adv. com. underground storage tank fund Colo. Dept. Pub. Health & Environ., Denver, 1994—. Office: Total Petroleum Inc 900 19th St Ste 2201 Denver CO 80202-2518

WAGNER, CHRISTIAN NIKOLAUS JOHANN, materials engineering educator; b. Saarbrucken-Dudweiler, Germany, Mar. 6, 1927; came to U.S., 1959, naturalized, 1969; s. Christian Jakob and Regina (Bungert) W.; m. Rosemarie Anna Mayer, Apr. 5, 1952; children—Thomas Martin, Karla Regine, Petra Susanne. Student, U. Poitiers, France, 1948-49; Licence es Sci., U. Saar, Ger., 1951, Diplom-Ingenieur, 1954, Dr.rer.nat., 1957. Research asst. Inst. fur Metallforschung, Saarbrucken, 1953-54; vis. fellow M.I.T., 1955-56; research asso. Inst. fur Metallforschung, 1957-58; teaching, research asst. U. Saarbrucken, 1959; asst. prof. Yale U., New Haven, Conn., 1959-62; assoc. prof. Yale U., 1962-70; prof. dept. materials engring. UCLA, 1970-91, prof. emeritus, 1991—, chmn. dept., 1974-79, asst. dean undergrad. studies Sch. Engring. and Applied Sci., 1982-85, acting chmn., 1990-91; vis. prof. Tech. U., Berlin, 1969, U. Saarbrücken, 1979-80. Contbr. articles to profl. jours. Recipient U.S. Sci. Humboldt award U. Saarbrucken, 1989-90, 92. Fellow Am. Soc. Metals Internat.; mem. Am. Phys. Soc., Am. Crystallographic Assn., Minerals, Metals and Materials Soc., Materials Rsch. Soc., Sigma Xi. Home: 20407 Seaboard Rd Malibu CA 90265-5349 Office: UCLA 5731 Boelter Hall 6532 Boelter Hall Los Angeles CA 90024-1595

WAGNER, DAVID JAMES, lawyer; b. Cleve., Feb. 7, 1946; m. Martha Wilson, June 22, 1979; 1 child, Diana Jane. BS, USAF Acad., 1969; JD, Georgetown U., 1973. Bar: Colo. 1973, U.S. Supreme Ct. 1975, U.S. Dist. Ct. of Colo. 1973, U.S. Tax Ct. 1974. Asst. assoc. gen. counsel Presdl. Clemency Bd., Washington, 1974-75; sec., gen. counsel Cablecomm-Gen. Inc., Denver, 1975-77; adj. prof. law Metro. State Coll., Denver, 1975-80; atty., mng. prin. Wagner & Waller, P.C., Denver, 1977-84; chmn. bd. GILA Comm., Inc., Denver, 1987; pvt. practice David Wagner & Assocs., P.C., Englewood, Colo., 1984—. Editor Am. Criminal Law Rev., Georgetown U. Law Sch., 1972-73. Trustee Kent Denver Sch., Cherry Hills Village, Colo., 1990-96, treas., 1992, pres., 1992-96; treas., dir. Denver Chamber Orch., 1979-81; dir. Leadership Denver Assn., 1978-80. Capt. USAF, 1973-75. Republican. Episcopalian. Office: David Wagner & Assocs PC Penthouse 8400 E Prentice Ave Englewood CO 80111-2912

WAGNER, DIANE MASTERS, newspaper editor; b. Corvallis, Oreg., May 7, 1938; d. Donald William and Marjorie Irene (Masters) Wagner; widowed; children: Victoria D. Masters, Dana L. Herbert, Benjamin D. Herbert. BA in Comms., Wash. State U., Pullman, 1961. Newspaper reporter Bellingham (Wash.) Herald, 1961-63; pub. info., vol. program dir. Douglas County Health Dept., Roseburg, Oreg., 1978-80; exec. dir. Umpqua Cmty. Action Coun., Roseburg, 1980-85; prodn. mgr. Pry Pub., Portland, Oreg., 1985-90; comms. coord. City of Vancouver, Wash., 1990—. Mem. SW Washington Writers, Oreg. Writers Colony (bd. dirs. 1993-94, newsletter editor 1994—). Office: City of Vancouver PO Box 1995 210 E 13th St Vancouver WA 98668

WAGNER, GERALDINE MARIE, nursing educator; b. Renton, Wash., Apr. 12, 1948; d. Ernest F. and Vera P. (Temiraeff) W. AA, Pasadena City Coll., 1970; BA cum laude, Calif. State U., Northridge, 1977; BSN, Calif. State U., L.A., 1982; MEd, Azusa Pacific U., 1993. Cert. pub. health nurse, Calif. Dept. Health Svcs. In utilization mgmt. Blue Cross, Woodland Hills, Calif., 1987-88, Healthmarc, Pasadena, Calif., 1988-90; nursing educator, asst. dir. vocat. nursing program Casa Loma Coll., L.A., 1991-92; dir. program planning and devel., and coord. continuing edn. Casa Loma Coll., Lake View Terrace, 1992-93; dir. vocat. nursing program Glendale (Calif.) Career Coll., 1994—. Capt. Nurse Corp, U.S. Army, 1979-84. Mem. Am. Nursing Informatics Assn., Computer Using Educators, Nat. League for Nursing, Orgn. of Nurse Leaders, So. Calif. Dirs. Vocat. Nursing Programs, Calif. Orgn. Nurse Execs., Calif. Soc. Hosp. Pharmacists, Nat. Honor and Profl. Assn. Edn., Pi Lambda Theta. Roman Catholic.

WAGNER, HAZEL EDITH, medical/surgical and neurological nurse; b. San Jose, Calif., Aug. 26, 1931; d. LaRena Beall; m. Raymond Wagner, May 20, 1951; children: Randel Ray, Wes Lee. BSN, Wash. State U., 1984, M of Nursing, 1992. Staff nurse Deaconess Rehab. Inst. (formerly St. Luke's Meml. Hosp.), Spokane, Wash., 1985-87, charge nurse, 1987-89, adminstrv. supr., 1989-94, also coord. quality assurance, 1992-93; clin. mgr. St. Joseph Care Ctr., 1994—; mgr. health care Waterford on South Hill, 1992-94, clin. instr. Intercollegiate Ctr. for Nursing Edn., 1994. Mem. Wash. League Nursing (sec.), Assn. Rehab. Nurses, Sigma Theta Tau.

WAGNER, HERMAN, JR., research laboratory official; b. Jacksonville, Fla., May 1, 1959; s. Herman and Beatrice Luretta (Gillen) W.; m. Wanda Lynette Sapp, Oct. 23, 1982; children: Divon D. Sapp, Herman L., Antonio H., Monica L. BS in Econs., Tuskegee U., 1982; postgrad., Clark-Atlanta U., 1982-85, 88-89. Grad. rsch. asst. econs. dept. Clark-Atlanta U., 1982-85; buyer II, Jet Propulsion Lab., Pasadena, Calif., 1985-87, assoc. contract negotiator, 1987-91, contract negotiator, 1991—; fin. advisor A.L. Williams Co., Pasadena, 1986-89. Author: How To Calculate and Improve Your Salary, 1994. Mem. United Way, Arcadia, Calif., 1987, United Negro Coll. Fund, N.Y.C., 1988. Mem. Nat. Econ. Assn., Alpha Assn., Jet Propulsion Lab. Multicultural Profl. Orgn., Jet Propulsion Lab. Writer's Club, I Kare Club. Democrat. Home: 6825 Rosemead Blvd San Gabriel CA 91775-1567 Office: Jet Propulsion Lab 4800 Oak Grove Dr Pasadena CA 91109-8001

WAGNER, JUDITH BUCK, investment firm executive; b. Altoona, Pa. Sept. 25, 1943; d. Harry Bud and Mary Elizabeth (Rhodes) B.; m. Joseph E. Wagner, Mar. 15, 1980; 1 child, Elizabeth. BA in History, U. Wash., 1965; grad. N.Y. Inst. Fin., 1968. Registered Am. Stock Exch., N.Y. Stock Exch., investment advisor. Security analyst Morgan, Olmstead, Kennedy & Gardner, L.A., 1968-71; security analyst Boettcher & Co., Denver, 1972-75; pres. Wagner Investment Mgmt., Denver, 1975—; chmn., bd. dirs. The Women's Bank, N.A., Denver, 1977-94, organizational group pres., 1975-77; chmn. Equitable Bankshares Colo., Inc., Denver, 1980-94; bd. dirs. Equitable Bank of Littleton, 1983-88, pres., 1985; bd. dirs. Colo. Growth Capital, 1979-82; lectr. Denver U., Metro State, 1975-80. Author: Woman and Money series Colo. Woman Mag., 1976; moderator 'Catch 2' Sta. KWGN-TV, 1978-79. Pres. Big Sisters Colo., Denver, 1977-82, bd. dirs., 1973-83; bd. fellows U. Denver, 1985-90; bd. dirs. Red Cross, 1980, Assn. Children's Hosp., 1985, Colo. Health Facilities Authority, 1978-84, Jr. League Community Adv. Com., 1979-92, Brother's Redevel., Inc., 1979-80; mem. Hist. Paramount Found., 1984, Denver Pub. Sch. Career Edn. Project, 1972; mem. investment com. YWCA, 1976-88; mem. adv. com. Girl Scouts U.S.; mem. agy. rels. com. Mile High United Way, 1978-81, chmn. United Way Venture Grant com., 1980-81; fin. chmn. Schoettler for State Treas., 1986; bd. dirs. Downtown Denver Inc., 1988-95; bd. dirs., v.p., treas. The Women's Found. Colo., 1987-91; treas., trustee, v.p., Graland Country Day Sch., 1990-94, pres. 1994—; trustee Denver Rotary Found., 1990-95; trustee Hunt Alternatives Fund, 1992—. Recipient Making It award Cosmopolitan Mag., 1977, Women on the Go award, Savvy mag., 1983, Minouri Yasoui award, 1986, Salute Spl. Honoree award, Big Sisters, 1987; named one of the Outstanding Young Women in Am., 1979; recipient Woman Who Makes A Difference award Internat. Women's Forum, 1987. Fellow Assn. Investment Mgmt. and Rsch.; mem. Women's Forum of Colo. (pres. 1979), Women's Found. [illegible] Inc. (bd. dirs. 1986-91), Denver Soc. Security Analysts (bd. dirs. 1976-83, v.p. 1980-81, pres. 1981-82), Colo. Investment Advisors Assn., Rotary (treas. Denver chpt. found., pres. 1993-94), Leadership Denver (Outstanding Alumna award 1987), Pi Beta Phi (pres. U. Wash. chpt. 1964-65). Office: Wagner Investment Mgmt Inc 3200 Cherry Creek S Dr Ste 240 Denver CO 80209

WAGNER, ORVIN EDSON, physicist, research facility administrator; b. L.A., Jan. 23, 1930; s. Edward Benjamin and Mary Esther (May) W.; m. Doris Joan Byram, Aug. 23, 1953 (div. Aug. 1976); children: Dianne, Darrell, Susan, Sharon; m. Claudia May Eells, Aug. 12, 1977; children: Raymond, Michael, Kimberly. BA, Walla Walla Coll., 1953, BS, 1959; MS, Ariz. State U., 1963; PhD, U. Tenn., 1968. Registered profl. engr., Calif. Scientist Lockheed Rsch. Labs., Palo Alto, Calif., 1961-62; physics instr. Walla Walla Coll., College Pl., Wash., 1962-64; asst. prof. Calif. State Poly. U., San Luis Obispo, 1969-74; pres. Wagner Rsch. Lab., Rogue River, Oreg., 1976—; cons. Wagner Electronic Products, Rogue River, 1969—. Author: W-Waves and A Wave Universe; contbr. articles to profl. jours.; patentee in field. With U.S. Army, 1955-57. Fellow NIH, 1964-68, AEC, 1968-69. Mem. Am. Physical Soc., Sigma Xi, Sigma Pi Sigma. Republican. Home: 2500 Sykes Creek Rd Rogue River OR 97537-9703 Office: Wagner Rsch Lab 2645 Sykes Creek Rd Rogue River OR 97537-9703

WAGNER, RAY DAVID, historian, educator, consultant; b. Phila., Feb. 29, 1924; s. James D. and Ethel S. (Schreiber) W.; m. Beatrice Walsh, Apr. 1952 (div. Nov. 1965); 1 child, Roger Ray; m. Mary Kathleen Davidson, Nov. 17, 1967; children: Wendy Lynne, David Frederick. BS, U. Pa., 1953, MS in Edn., 1955; postgrad., San Diego State U., 1958-65. Tchr. Crawford High Sch., San Diego, 1957-84; instr. City Colls. USN/PACE, 1985; archivist San Diego Aerospace Mus., 1985—. Author: American Combat Planes, 1960, 68, 82, North American Sabre, 1963, German Combat Planes, 1970, Mustang Designer, 1990; editor: The Soviet Air Force in World War II, 1973, Guide for Teaching World History, 1974. Air Force Hist. Ctr. grantee, 1988. Mem. Am. Aviation Hist. Soc. (v.p. 1973-76), Air Force Hist. Found. Home: 5865 Estelle St San Diego CA 92115-5432 Office: San Diego Aerospace Mus 2001 Pan American Plz San Diego CA 92101-1636

WAGNER, RICHARD, business executive, former baseball team executive; b. Central City, Nebr., Oct. 19, 1927; s. John Howard and Esther Marie (Wolken) W.; m. Gloria Jean Larsen, May 10, 1950; children—Randolph G., Cynthia Kaye. Student, pub. schs., Central City. Gen. mgr. Lincoln (Nebr.) Baseball Club, 1955-58; mgr. Pershing Mcpl. Auditorium, Lincoln, 1958-61; exec. staff Ice Capades, Inc., Hollywood, Calif., 1961-63; gen. mgr. Sta. KSAL, Salina, Kans., 1963-65; dir. promotion and sales St. Louis Nat. Baseball Club, 1965-66; gen. mgr. Forum, Inglewood, Calif., 1966-67; asst. to exec. v.p. Cin. Reds, 1967-70, asst. to pres., 1970-74, v.p. adminstrn., 1975, exec. v.p., 1975-78, gen. mgr., 1977-83, pres., 1978-83; pres. Houston Astros Baseball Club, 1985-87; spl. asst. Office of Baseball Commr., 1988-93; asst. to chmn. Major League Exec. Coun., 1993-94; pres. RGW Enterprises, Inc., Phoenix, 1978—. Served with USNR, 1945-47, 50-52. Named Exec. of Yr., Minor League Baseball, Sporting News, 1958. Mem. Internat. Assn. Auditorium Mgrs. Republican. Methodist.

WAGNER, RICHARD, artist; b. Trotwood, Ohio. BFA, U. Colo., 1950, MFA, 1952. Instr. Mansfield Art Ctr., Steamboat Springs, Colo., Castle Hill Art Ctr., Ipswich, Mass., U. Colo., 1950-53, Dartmouth Coll., 1953-66. One-man shows include Grand Central Galleries, N.Y.C., Shore Gallery, Boston, Dartmouth Coll., DeCordova Mus., Lincoln, Mass., Fairleigh Dickinson U., N.J., Middlebury Coll., Telluride Gallery Fine Art, Colo., El Prado Art Galleries, Santa Fe, Sedona, Ariz., Western Colo. Ctr. Arts, Mus. Modern Art, Pa. Acad. Fine Arts, Joslyn Art Mus., Libr. Congress, Madison Square Gardens, Butler Art Inst. and numerous others; contbr. articles to profl. jours.; represented in private collections. Recipient Colo. Springs Fine Arts Guild Juror's award, 1989, Pinon Arts Show First Pl., 1992, Naples Fla. Art Assn. First Pl., and others. Home: 13980 County Road 29 Dolores CO 81323-9356

WAGNER, STEVE, social service program director; b. Colfax, Wash., Feb. 20, 1949; s. George David and Trudy Adella (Vowell) W.; m. Catherine Huhndorf, Feb. 24, 1970 (div. Dec. 1971); m. Beth Golladay, Oct. 21, 1978; 1 child, Heather. Paralegal cert., City Coll., 1987. Coord. Echo Landlord/Tenant Program, Hayward, Calif., 1987-90; program dir. Echo Housing, Inc., Oakland, Calif., 1990—; bd. dirs. Emergency Svc. Network, Oakland. Editor (newsletter) S.E.T. Free the Newsletter Against Television. Organizer Lake Merritt Neighbors Organized for Peace, Oakland, 1991. Recipient Vol. Mediator Cert. Victim-Offender Reconciliation Program, 1990. Mem. Soc. for the Eradication of TV (bd. dirs. 1986—). Democrat. Home: PO Box 10491 Oakland CA 94610-0491

WAGNER, SUE ELLEN, state official; b. Portland, Maine, Jan. 6, 1940; d. Raymond A. and Kathryn (Hooper) Pooler; m. Peter B. Wagner, 1964 (dec.); children: Kirk, Kristina. B.A. in Polit. Sci., U. Ariz., 1962; M.A. in History, Northwestern U., 1964. Asst. dean women Ohio State U., 1963-64; tchr. history and Am. govt. Catalina High Sch., Tucson, 1964-65; reporter Tucson Daily Citizen, 1965-68; mem. Nev. Assembly, 1975-83; mem. Nev. Senate from 3d dist.; elected lt. gov. of Nev., 1990-94. Author: Diary of a Candidate, On People and Things, 1974. Mem. Reno Mayor's Adv. Com., 1973-84; chmn. Blue Ribbon Task Force on Housing, 1974-75; mem. Washoe County Republican Central Com., 1974-84, Nev. State Rep. Central Com., 1975-84; mem. Nev. Legis. Commn., 1976-77; del. social service com. Council State Govts.; v.p. Am. Field Service, 1973, family liaison, 1974, mem.-at-large, 1975. Kappa Alpha Theta Nat. Grad. scholar, also Phelps-Dodge postgrad. fellow, 1962; named Outstanding Legislator, Nev. Young Republicans, 1976. Mem. AAUW (legis. chmn. 1974), Bus. and Profl. Women, Kappa Alpha Theta. Episcopalian. Home: 845 Tamarack Dr Reno NV 89509-3640 Office: Office of Lt Gov Capitol Complex Carson City NV 89710*

WAGNER, WILLIAM GERARD, university dean, physicist, consultant, information scientist, investment manager; b. St. Cloud, Minn., Aug. 22, 1936; s. Gerard C. and Mary V. (Cloone) W.; m. Janet Agatha Rowe, Jan. 30, 1968 (div. 1978); children: Mary, Robert, David, Anne; m. Christiane LeGuen, Feb. 21, 1985 (div. 1989). B.S., Calif. Inst. Tech., 1958, Ph.D. (NSF fellow, Howard Hughes fellow), 1962. Cons. Rand Corp., Santa Monica, Calif., 1960-65; sr. staff physicist Hughes Research Lab., Malibu, Calif., 1960-69; lectr. physics Calif. Inst. Tech., Pasadena, 1963-65; asst. prof. physics U. Calif. at Irvine, 1965-66; assoc. prof. physics and elec. engring. U. So. Calif., L.A., 1966-69, prof. depts. physics and elec. engring., 1969—, dean div. natural scis. and math. Coll. Letters, Arts and Scis., 1973-87, dean interdisciplinary studies and developmental activities, 1987-89, spl. asst. automated record services, 1975-81; founder program in neural, informational & behavioral scis., 1982—; chmn. bd. Malibu Securities Corp., L.A., 1971—; cons. Janus Mgmt. Corp., L.A., 1970-71, Croesus Capital Corp., L.A., 1971-74, Fin. Horizons Inc., Beverly Hills, Calif., 1974—; allied mem. Pacific Stock Exch., 1974-82; fin. and computer cons. Hollywood Reporter, 1979-81; mem. adv. coun. for emerging engring. techs. NSF, 1987—. Contbr. articles on physics to sci. publs. Richard Chase Tolman postdoctoral fellow, 1962-65. Mem. Am. Phys. Soc., Nat. Assn. Security Dealers, Sigma Xi. Home: 2828 Patricia Ave Los Angeles CA 90064-4425 Office: U So Calif Hedco Neurosci Bldg Los Angeles CA 90089

WAGNER, WILLIS HARCOURT, vascular surgeon; b. Long Beach, Calif., May 13, 1955; s. William Franklin and Caroline (Willis) W.; m. Diane Elaine Benkert, Sept. 14, 1982; children: Daniel, Samuel, Alison, Matthew. BS in Biol. Sci., Stanford U., 1977; MD, U. So. Calif., L.A., 1981. Intern U. So. Calif. Med. Ctr., L.A., 1981-82, resident, 1982-86; instr. in surgery U. So. Calif., 1986-87; fellow in vascular surgery U. N.C., Chapel Hill, 1987-88; vascular surgeon Cedars Sinai Med. Ctr., L.A., 1988—, chief div. vascular surgery, 1994—; clin. asst. prof. surgery U. So. Calif., 1988—. Author chpts. to books; contbr. articles to profl. jours. Mem. So. Calif. Vascular Surgery Soc., So. Assn. for Vascular Surgery (Pres. award 1988), Western Vascular Soc., Peripheral Vascular Surg. Soc., Internat. Soc. Vascular Surgery, Alpha Omega Alpha. Office: 8631 W 3rd St Ste 615-e Los Angeles CA 90048-5901

WAGONER, DAVID EVERETT, lawyer; b. Pottstown, Pa., May 16, 1928; s. Claude Brower and Mary Kathryn (Groff) W.; children: Paul R., Colin H., Elon D., Peter B.; m. Jean Morton Saunders; children: Dana F., Constance A., Jennifer L., Melissa J. B.A., Yale U., 1950; LL.B., U. Pa., 1953. Bar: D.C. 1953, Pa. 1953, Wash. 1953. Law clk. U.S. Ct. Appeals (3d cir.), Pa., 1955-56; law clk. U.S. Supreme Ct., Washington, 1956-57; ptnr. Perkins & Coie, Seattle, 1957—; panel me. of arbitration forum worldwide including Republic of China, British Columbia Internat. Comml. Arbitration Ctr., Hong Kong Internat. Arbitration Centre, Asian/Pacific Ctr. for Resolution of Internat. Bus. Disputes and the Ctr. for Internat. Dispute Resolution for Asian/Pacific Region. Mem. sch. com. Mcpl. League Seattle and King County, 1958—, chmn., 1962-65; mem. Seattle schs. citizens coms. on equal ednl. opportunity and adult vocat. edn., 1963-64; mem. Nat. Com. Support Pub. Schs.; mem. adv. com. on community colls., to 1965, legislature interim com. on edn., 1964-65; mem. community coll. adv. com. to state supt. pub. instrn., 1965; chmn. edn. com. Forward Thrust, 1968; mem. Univ. Congl. Ch. Council Seattle, 1968-70; bd. dirs. Met. YMCA Seattle, 1968; bd. dirs. Seattle Pub. Schs., 1965-73, v.p., 1966-67, 72-73, pres., 1968, 73; trustee Evergreen State Coll. Found., chmn. 1986-87, capitol campaign planning chmn.; trustee Pacific NW Ballet, v.p. 1986. Served to 1st lt. M.C., AUS, 1953-55. Fellow Am. Coll. Trial Lawyers (mem. ethics com., legal ethics com.), Chartered Inst. Arbitrators, Singapore Inst. Arbitrators; mem. ABA (mem. standing com. fed. judicial imprisonment, chmn. appellate advocacy com.), Wash. State Bar Assn., Seattle-King County Bar Assn., British Acad. Experts, Swiss Arbitration Assn., Comml. Bar Assn. London, Nat. Sch. Bds. Assn. (bd. dirs., chmn. coun. Big City bds. edn. 1971-72), English-Speaking Union (v.p. Seattle chpt. 1961-62), Chi Phi. Office: Perkins Coie 1201 3rd Ave Fl 40 Seattle WA 98101-3000

WAGSTAFF, ROBERT HALL, lawyer; b. Kansas City, Mo., Nov. 5, 1941; s. Robert Wilson and Katherine Motter (Hall) W. A.B., Dartmouth Coll., 1963; J.D., U. Kans., 1966. Bar: Kans., Alaska, U.S. Ct. Appeals (9th cir.), U.S. Supreme Ct. Asst. atty. gen. State of Kans., 1966-67; asst. dist. atty. Fairbanks (Alaska), 1967-69; ptnr. Boyko & Walton, Anchorage, 1969-70; sr. ptnr. Wagstaff et. al., Anchorage, 1970—. Pres. U.S. Aerobatic Found., Oshkosh, Wis., 1986—. Mem. Alaska Bar Assn. (bd. govs. 1985-88, pres. 1987-88), Lawyer-Pilots Bar Assn. (regional v.p.), ACLU (nat. bd. dirs. 1972-78), Nat. Transp. Safety Bd. Assn. Office: 425 G St Ste 610 Anchorage AK 99501-2137

WAHL, FLOYD MICHAEL, geologist; b. Hebron, Ind., July 7, 1931; s. Floyd Milford and Ann Pearl (DeCook) W.; m. Dorothy W. Daniel, July 4, 1953; children: Timothy, David, Jeffrey, Kathryn. A.B., DePauw U., 1953; M.S., U. Ill., 1957, Ph.D., 1958. Cert. profl. geologist. Prof. geology U. Fla., Gainesville, 1969-82, assoc. dean Grad. Sch., 1974-80, acting dean, 1980-81; exec. dir. Geol Soc Am., Boulder, Colo., 1982-94; ret., 1994. Contbr. articles to profl. jours. Served to cpl. U.S. Army, 1953-55. Recipient Outstanding Tchr. award U. Ill., 1967. Fellow Geol. Soc. Am.; mem. Mineral Soc. Am., Am. Inst. Profl. Geologists (chpt. pres.), Sigma Xi.

WAHL, MICHAEL FREDERICK, insurance underwriter; b. Inglewood, Calif., June 9, 1951; s. Frederick E. and Hazel Marie (Carroll) W.; m. Rita Marie Dennis, June 26, 1976; children: Kathleen, Andrew. BA in English, Loyola U., 1974. Claims examiner Transport Indemnity Co., L.A., 1976-79, claims supr., 1979-83; underwriter Physicians & Surgeons Underwriter Corp., Pasadena, Calif., 1983, The Doctors Co., Santa Monica, Calif., 1983-85; underwriting mgr. Warschaw Ins. Agency, L.A., 1985-89, Profl. Underwriters Liability Ins. Corp., L.A., 1989-92, Pacific Profl. Ins., L.A., 1992—. Office: Pacific Profl Ins Inc 101 S Robertson Blvd Ste 207 Los Angeles CA 90048

WAHLER, DENNIS DANIEL, business studies educator, administrator; b. Freeport, Ill., Oct. 20, 1938; s. Robert Richard and Elizabeth A. (Schubert) W.; m. Beverly A. Davis, June 30, 1961 (div. 1972); children: Richard, Rene; m. Maryam Behbod, June 30, 1978; 1 child, Yusuf Ali. BS in Gen. Engring., Met. Colgate Inst., London, 1968; MBA, U. Phoenix, San Jose, Calif., 1984; D Bus. Adminstrn., So. Calif. U., 1995. Project engr. Hughes Aircraft, L.A., 1974-76, Iran Electronics, Shiraz, Iran, 1976-78; owner, pres. Delta Design, San Jose, 1976-80, D.D. Wahler Design Group Ltd., San Jose, 1980—; prof. bus. studies San Jose City Coll., 1982—, dir. internat. bus. studies, 1993—. Co-author: Drafting for Electronics, 1985, 93, The Small Business Challenge, 1992, Mechanical Design, 1994, International Business Terrorism and Personal Security, 1994. Mem. Am. Inst. Bldg. Designers, San Jose Met. C. of C. Office: San Jose City Coll 2100 Moorpark Ave San Jose CA 95128-2723

WAHLKE, JOHN CHARLES, political science educator; b. Cin., Oct. 29, 1917; s. Albert B.C. and Clara J. (Ernst) W.; m. Virginia Joan Higgins, Dec. 1, 1943; children: Janet Parmely, Dale. A.B., Harvard U., 1939, M.A., 1947, Ph.D., 1952. Instr., asst. prof. polit. sci. Amherst (Mass.) Coll., 1949-53; assoc. prof. polit. sci. Vanderbilt U., Nashville, Tenn., 1953-63; prof. polit. sci. SUNY, Buffalo, 1963-66, U. Iowa, 1966-71, SUNY, Stony Brook, 1971-72, U. Iowa, Iowa City, 1972-79; prof. polit. sci. U. Ariz., Tucson, 1979-87, prof. emeritus, 1987—. Author: (with others) The Legislative System, 1962, Government and Politics, 1966, The Politics of Representation, 1978; editor: Causes of the American Revolution, 1950, Loyalty in a Democratic State, 1952; co-editor: Legislative Behavior, 1959, The American Political System, 1967, Comparative Legislative Behavior, 1973. Served to capt., F.A. AUS, 1942-46. Decorated Air medal with 2 oak leaf clusters. Mem. AAAS, Am. Polit. Sci. Assn. (past pres.), Internat. Polit. Sci. Assn., So. Polit. Sci. Assn., Midwest Polit. Sci. Assn. (past pres.), Western Polit. Sci. Assn., Southwestern Polit. Sci. Assn., Assn. Politics and the Life Scis. Home: 5462 N Entrada Catorce Tucson AZ 85718-4851 Office: U Ariz Dept Polit Sci Tucson AZ 85721

WAIDE, LLOYD A(RNOLD), protective services official; b. Pueblo, Colo., July 14, 1955; s. Allen and Alice (Freeman) W.; m. Susan J. Hull, Feb. 11, 1976; children: Michael, Laura, Brandi. Student, Ctrl. Ariz. Coll., 1981-82, Otero Jr. Coll., La Junta, Colo., 1990-91; grad., Colo. Correctional Acad., 1988. Cert. peace officer; cert. law enforcement officer, Ariz.; accredited in law enforcement, Colo. Patrolman Rawlins (Wyo.) Police Dept., 1978-81; patrolman/canine handler Casa Grande (Ariz.) Police Dept., 1981-86; patrol sgt. Monte Vista (Colo.) Police Dept., 1986-87; patrol. lt. Rio Grande County Sheriff's Dept., Del Norte, Colo., 1987-88; correctional officer Colo. Dept. Corrections, Buena Vista, 1988-89; correctional technician/sgt. Colo. Dept. Corrections, Ordway, 1989-90, correctional specialist/lt., 1990-91; correctional supr./capt. Colo. Dept. Corrections, Limon, 1991—; instr. OSHA, 1993—. With USAF, 1973-77. Trophy recipient Police K-9 Trials, Modesto (Calif.) Police Dept., 1984. Mem. Colo. Assn. Pub. Employees, Am. Percheron Horse Assn., Elks. Republican. Office: Limon Correctional Facility PO Box 10000 Limon CO 80828

WAINESS, MARCIA WATSON, legal management consultant; b. Bklyn., Dec. 17, 1949; d. Stanley and Seena (Klein) Watson; m. Steven Richard Wainess, Aug. 7, 1975. Student, UCLA, 1967-71, 80-81, Grad. Sch. Mgmt. Exec. Program, 1987-88, grad. Grad. Sch. Mgmt. Exec. Program, 1988. Office mgr., paralegal Lewis, Marenstein & Kadar, L.A., 1977-81; office mgr. Rosenfeld, Meyer & Susman, Beverly Hills, Calif., 1981-83; adminstr. Rudin, Richman & Appel, Beverly Hills, 1983; dir. adminstrn. Kadison, Pfaelzer, L.A., 1983-87; exec. dir. Richards, Watson and Gershon, L.A., 1987-93; legal mgmt. cons. L.A., 1993—; faculty mem. UCLA Legal Mgmt. & Adminstrn. Program, 1983, U. So. Calif. Paralegal Program, L.A., 1985; mem. adv. bd. atty. asst. tng. program, UCLA, 1984-88. Mem. ABA (chair Displaywrite Users Group 1986, legal tech. adv. coun. litig. support working group 1986-87), San Fernando Valley Bar Assn., Profl. Liability Underwriting Soc., Assn. Legal Adminstrs. (bd. dirs. 1990-92, asst. regional v.p. Calif. 1987-88, regional v.p. 1988-89, pres. Beverly Hills chpt. 1985-86, membership chair 1984-85, chair new adminstrn. sect. 1982-84, mktg. mgmt. sect. com. 1989-90, internat. conf. com.), Internat. Platform Assn., Calif. Women Bus. Owners. Office: 78 Coolwater Rd Canoga Park CA 91307-1005

WAINIO, MARK ERNEST, insurance company consultant; b. Virginia, Minn., Apr. 18, 1953. BA, Gustavus Adolphus Coll., 1975. Cert. safety profl., assoc. loss control mgmt., assoc. risk mgmt., assoc. claims, CPCU. Carpenter ABI Contracting Inc., Virginia, 1975-77; co-owner Mesabi Builders, Albuquerque and Eveleth, Minn., 1977-79; sr. engring. rep. Aetna Life & Casualty, Albuquerque, 1979-86; loss control specialist CNA Ins. Cos., Albuquerque, 1986-91, loss control cons., 1991-94, mgr. loss control svcs., 1994—; owner MEW Safety and Risk Mgmt., 1989—; pres. MW

Enterprises, 1990—. Mem. Am. Soc. Safety Engrs., CPCU. Office: CNA Ins Cos 8500 Menaul Blvd NE Albuquerque NM 87112-2298

WAINIONPAA, JOHN WILLIAM, systems engineer; b. Quincy, Mass., July 13, 1946; s. Frank Jacob and Jennie Sofia (Kaukola) W.; m. S. Linda Rapo, Oct. 18, 1969; children: Heidi Liisa, Erik David, Sinikka Lin. BSEE, U. N.Mex., 1972; MS in Aero. Engring., Naval Postgrad. Sch., 1981. Engr.-in-tng., Colo. Enlisted USN, 1968, commd. ens., 1972, advanced through grades to lt. comdr., 1982; flight instr. Tng. Squadron 27, Corpus Christi, Tex., 1973-75; aircraft, mission comdr. Patrol Squadron 49, Jacksonville, Fla., 1976-79; ops. officer Anti-Submarine Warfare Ops. Ctr., Kadena, Okinawa, Japan, 1982-84; launch and control systems officer Naval Space Command, Dahlgren, Va., 1984-86; naval space systems ops. officer U.S. Space Command, Colorado Springs, 1986-88; ret. USN, 1988; systems engr. CTA INC., Colorado Springs, 1988-93, tng. coord., 1993-94, profl. devel. orgn. mgr., 1994—. Merit badge counselor Boy Scouts Am., Colorado Springs, 1986—. Mem. AIAA (sr.), IEEE, U.S. Naval Inst., Sigma Tau, Eta Kappa Nu. Office: CTA Inc 7150 Campus Dr Ste 100 Colorado Springs CO 80920-3178

WAITE, JOANNE LISCHER, systems analyst; b. N.Y.C., July 17, 1938; d. Carl Fredrick and Blanche Edna (Hestwood) Lischer; m. William McCastline Waite, June 18, 1960; 1 child, William Frederick. AB, Oberlin Coll., 1960; MSEE, U. Colo., 1970. Systems analyst Mut. of N.Y., N.Y.C., 1960-65, U. Sydney, Australia, 1965-66; sr. network analyst U. Colo., Boulder, 1974—. Mem. Assn. for Computing Machinery, Eta Kappa Nu (bd. dirs. 1979-81, v.p. 1984-85, pres. 1985-86). Office: U Colo at Boulder Computing and Network Svcs Box 455 Boulder CO 80309-0455

WAKEFIELD, HOWARD, medical representative; b. Chgo., Dec. 19, 1936; s. Howard and Thelma Elizabeth (Roach) W.; m. Laura Collier, Jan. 1, 1957 (div. June 1976); children: Kimberly, Howard III, Anthony. BA in Econs., U. Ariz., 1959. Sales rep. N.Y. Life, Tucson, 1959-63; sr. med. rep. Pfizer Pharm., Ventura County, Calif., 1963—. Fund raiser Am. Heart Assn., Ventura, Calif., 1983—; mgr. Pleasant Valley Boys Baseball, Camarillo, Calif., 1968-82; vol. Arthritis Found. Mem. Am. Heart Assn. (bd. dirs. Ventura County chpt.), Ventura County Pharm. Assn. (v.p.). Republican. Home: PO Box 626 Somis CA 93066-0626 Office: Pfizer Pharm 16700 Red Hill Ave Irvine CA 92714-4802

WAKS, DENNIS STANFORD, lawyer; b. Decatur, Ill., Apr. 2, 1949; s. Paul and Regina (Geisler) W.; m. Jaclyn Hoyle, Nov. 29, 1985; 1 child, Kelly. BA, U. Wis., 1971; JD, U. Miss., 1973; LLM, U. Mo., Kansas City, 1975. Bar: Miss. 1973, Ill. 1975, U.S. Dist. Ct. (no. dist.) Miss. 1973, U.S. Dist. Ct. (so. dist.) Ill. 1975, U.S. Dist. Ct. (ea. dist.) Calif. 1988, U.S. Ct. Apeals (9th cir.) 1989, Calif. 1989. Dir. prison legal svcs. project So. Ill. U. Sch. Law, Carbondale, Ill., 1976-77; asst. pub. defender Jackson County Pub. Defenders Office, Murphysboro, Ill., 1977-80, chief pub. defender, 1980-85; spl. prosecutor Perry County States Atty. Office, Pinckneyville, Ill., 1985; prof. dept. law enforcement So. Ill. U., Carbondale, 1978-87; pvt. practice Murphysboro, 1985-87; asst. atty. Fed. Pub. Defenders Office Ea. Dist. Calif., Sacramento, 1988—, supervising sr. atty., 1990—; faculty Ill. Defender Program, Chgo., 1982-86, bd. dirs.; faculty masters thesis and doctoral com. So. Ill. U., Carbondale, 1978-87. Editor Miss. Law Rev., 1973. Organizer Paul Simon for Senator, Carbondale, 1984; bd. dirs. Hill Ho. Resdl. Ctr. for Substance Abuse, Carbondale, 1981-87, v.p. 1984-87. Named Outstanding Young Man of Am., 1985. Mem. ABA, Nat. Assn. Criminal Def. Attys., Ill. Pub. Defender Project, Ill. Pub. Defenders Assn., Calif. Attys. for Criminal Justice, Calif. Pub. Defenders Assn. Democrat. Jewish. Home: 4700 Lake Dr Carmichael CA 95608-3138 Office: Fed Defenders Office 801 K St Ste 1024 Sacramento CA 95814-3518

WALASEK, OTTO FRANK, chemical engineer, biochemist, photographer; b. Park Falls, Wis., Mar. 11, 1919; s. Frank Otto and Mary (Swoboda) W.; m. Annie May Stockton (div. Nov. 1959); 1 child, Richard A.; m. Joan Constance Ashton, Sept. 18, 1965; children: Arthur, Carl. BS in Chem. Engring., U. Wis., 1946; MS in Biochemistry, U. Ill., 1968; postgrad., Loyola U., 1968-72. Penicillin processing product engr. I Abbott Labs., North Chgo., Ill., 1946-49; antibiotic process rsch. and devel. Abbott Labs., North Chgo., 1950-55, biochemical rsch., 1956-68, sr. biochemist, 1968-77, staff Leukemia project, 1978-80; pvt. photographer Sonora, Calif., 1981—. Patentee in field; contbr. articles to profl. jours. Recipient Excellence award Fedn. Internat. of Art Photographic, Switzerland, 1972; named Hon. Master of Profl. Photography, Profl. Photographic Assns., Taiwan, 1990. Mem. Photographic Soc. Am. (associateship), Royal Photographic Soc., Nat. Stereoscopic Soc., Internat. Stereoscopic Union. Democrat. Office: 10165 Us Highway 49 Sonora CA 95370-9456

WALCH, DAVID BEAN, librarian, university official; b. La Grande, Oreg., May 19, 1936; s. Charles Lloyd and Lila (Bean) W.; m. Phyllis Collins, June 23, 1959; children—Shane, Shawna, Sherece, Curt, Shaleen. B.S., Eastern Oreg. Coll., 1960; M.S. in L.S, U. Ill., 1962, cert. advanced studies, 1969; Ph.D., U. Utah, 1973. Tchr. LaGrande, 1960-61; asso. librarian Ch. Coll. of Hawaii, Laie, 1962-64; dir. library services Ch. Coll. of Hawaii, 1965-67; asst. prof. library sci. U. Utah, Salt Lake City, 1967-74; dean acad. services SUNY, Buffalo, 1974-80; univ. librarian Calif. Polytech. State U., San Luis Obispo, 1980—; cons. library orgn. C&W Library Cons., 1969—. Katherine Sharp fellow, 1960-61. Mem. ALA, Calif. Library Assn. Home: 597 Jeffrey Dr San Luis Obispo CA 93405-1003 Office: Calif Polytech State U Robert E Kennedy Libr Dept Of Science Engine San Luis Obispo CA 93407

WALD, ROBERT DAVID, psychiatrist; b. Cleve., Dec. 8, 1924; s. Herman and Dorothy (Sherower) W.; m. Martha Jan Fuller, Oct. 15, 1947 (div. Feb. 1963); children: Jean, Malie, M. Daniel, Shanti, Rebecca; m. Nicole diPadua, Feb. 8, 1981. Student, U. Calif., Berkeley, 1950-52; MD, Wash. U., 1956. Diplomate Am. Bd. Psychiatry & Neurology. Intern U. Calif., 1957; resident Langley Porter Neurologist, 1957-59, fellow, 1959-61; assoc. prof. U. Calif. Sch. Medicine, San Francisco, 1961-93; med. dir. outpatient divsn. Charter North Hosp., Anchorage, Alaska, 1993—. Office: Charter No Counseling Ctr 240 E Tudor Rd Anchorage AK 99503-7228

WALD, ROBERT GRAY, electro-optical engineer; b. Kansas City, Mo., Nov. 9, 1963; s. Robert Irwin and Helen Jane (Gray) W. BS in Elec. Engring., Kans. State U., 1986; MS in Optical and Elec. Engring., U. Colo., Boulder, 1990. Power engr. Burns & McDonnel Engring., Kansas City, Mo., 1984; control engr. Black & Veatch Engring., Overland Park, Kans., 1985, Kansas City, 1986; artificial intelligence researcher Boeing/Kans. State U., Manhattan, 1986-87; optical artificial intelligence computing researcher NSF, Boulder, 1987-88; laser power energy engr. Nat. Inst. Standards and Tech., U.S. Dept. Commerce, Boulder, 1988-90; cons. in photonics, electronics and software applications Boulder, 1991—; telcom. project mgr. U. Colo., Boulder, 1993; mgr. advanced product mktg. McDATA Corp., Broomfield, Colo., 1994—. Contbr. articles to profl. jours. Mem. IEEE, Nat. Soc. Profl. Engrs. (v.p. 1985-86), Lasers and Electro-Optical Soc. of IEEE, Am. Assn. Artificial Intelligence, Soc. for Photo-Instrumentation Engrs. Roman Catholic. Home: 437 University Ave Boulder CO 80302-5805

WALDEN, RICHARD KEITH, agri-business executive; b. Santa Paula, Calif., July 4, 1913; s. Arthur Frisbie and Eva Juanita (Southwick) W.; m. Barbara Eldredge Culbertson, Sept. 25, 1938 (div.); 1 son, Richard Sheffield; m. 2d, Dorothy Dayton Beck, July 5, 1967. B.A., Pomona Coll., 1936; postgrad. UCLA, 1934, 39. With Limoneira Ranch Co., Santa Paula, 1936-40; mgr. Ford-Craig Ranch Co., San Fernando, Calif., 1940-46; founder, chmn. bd. Farmers Investment Co., Calif., Ariz. and Fla., 1946—; dir. Ariz. Feeds Co., 1950-74, 1st Interstate Bank, 1962-84, Cotton, Inc., 1961-73; cons. Ford Found., Pakistan, 1969; dir. agr. adv. com. Stanford Research Inst., 1960-66; chmn. Pima County Agr. and Stblzn. Com., 1956-61. Bd. trustees Pomona Coll., 1978-81, Continental Sch. Bd., 1950-67; bd. advisors U. Ariz. Coll. Bus., 1983-88; bd. dirs. Tucson C. of C.; chmn. Ariz. Oil and Gas Comm., 1960-66, Green Valley Community Health Ctr., 1981—; mem. Gov.'s Emergency Resources Planning Com., 1964. Recipient Disting. Citizen award U. Ariz. Alumni Assn., 1973, Outstanding Citizen award Ariz. State Farm Bur., 1988; named Citizen of Yr., Rotary Club, 1980, Agrl. of the Year, U. Ariz., 1994. Mem. Nat. Pecan Council, Ariz. Cotton Growers, Nat. Cotton Council (dir. 1960), Western Pecan Growers Assn. (dir. 1972-82), Ariz. Cattle Growers Assn. (dir. 1954-60), U. Ariz. Pres.'s Club, Cotton Council Internat. (chmn., pres. 1961-66), Town Hall Ariz., Balboa Club (Mazatlan, Sinaloa, Mex.), Old Pueblo Club (Tucson), Plaza Club (Phoenix), Green Valley (Ariz.) Country Club, Mountain Oyster Club. Republican. Home: 635 W Twin Buttes Rd PO Box 504 Green Valley AZ 85622-0504 Office: PO Box 7 Sahuarita AZ 85629-0007

WALDHAUER, FRED DONALD, health care executive; b. Bklyn., Dec. 6, 1927; s. Fred G. and Elsie L. (Haybach) W.; B.E.E., Cornell U., 1948; M.S.E.E., Columbia U., 1960; m. Ruth Irene Waina, Feb. 12, 1955; children—Neil, Amy, Ann, Alice, Kim. Engr. RCA, Camden, N.J., 1948-55, patent agt., Princeton, N.J., 1953-55; mem. tech. staff Bell Telephone Labs., Holmdel, N.J., 1956-87, supr. transmission tech. lab., 1963-87; with venture start-up in hearing health care Resound Corp., Redwood City, Calif., 1987—; sec., dir. Expts. in Art and Tech., Inc. Fellow IEEE (mem. solid state circuits council 1974-78, mem. steering com. on lightwave tech. 1982); mem. Audio Engring. Soc. Author: Feedback, 1982. Patentee in field; contbr. articles to profl. jours. Home: 22296 Skyline Blvd La Honda CA 94020

WALDMAN, JERALD PAUL, orthopedic surgeon; b. Newark, N.J., Apr. 9, 1946; s. Samuel and Estelle (Lefkowitz); m. Patricia Maite, Sept. 8, 1973; children: Genevieve, Dawn, Jacqueline, Aimee, Olivia. BA in Biology, U. Rochester, 1968; MD, U. Md., 1972. Diplomate Am. Bd. Surgeons. Surg. intern Harbor Cen./UCLA, Torrance, Calif., 1973, orthopedic resident, 1977; orthopedic surgeon Community Orthopedic Med. Group, Mission Viejo, Calif., 1977—; bd. dirs. Mission Quality IPA, Mission Viejo; clin. faculty UCI Med. Sch., Orange, Calif., 1978—; chmn. interdisciplinary coms. Mission Hosp. Regional Med. Ctr., Mission Viejo, 1992-93, mem. vis. com., 1988—, others. Bd. dirs. Laguna Beach (Calif.) School Power, 1990-92. Fellow Am. Acad. Orthopedic Surgeons, Am. Coll. Surgeons, Internat. Coll. Surgeons; mem. Calif. Med. Assn., Orange County Med. Assn., Undersea Med. Soc. Office: Community Orthopedic Med 27800 Medical Center Rd Mission Viejo CA 92691-6410

WALDMANN, CHRISTOPHER HAWTHORNE, psychotherapist; b. San Francisco, Mar. 30, 1954; s. Robert Paul and Ruth Anne (Hawthorne) W.; m. Peggy Malm, Aug. 18, 1972; children: Kelly, Kim, J. Chris. BA in Psychology, U. Pacific, 1978; MA in Counseling, U. Colo., 1983. Lic. profl. counselor, Colo. Psychotherapist Evergreen Cons. in Human Behavior, 1983—; lectr. Evergreen (Colo.) Cons., 1983—; lectr. nationwide, 1985—. Author: Don't Touch My Heart, 1994. Foster parent Attachment Ctr. of Evergreen, 1986—. Office: Evergreen Cons 28000 Meadow Dr # 206 Evergreen CO 80439-8341

WALDO, BURTON CORLETT, lawyer; b. Seattle, Aug. 11, 1920; s. William Earl and Ruth Ernestine (Corlett) W.; m. Margaret Jane Hoar, Aug. 24, 1946; children: James Chandler, Bruce Corlett. BA, U. Wash., 1941, JD, 1948. Bar: Wash. 1949. Assoc. Vedova, Horswill & Yeomans, Seattle, 1949-50, Kahin, Carmody & Horswill, Seattle, 1950-54; ptnr. Keller Rohrback & predecessor firms, Seattle, 1954-86; mng. ptnr. Keller Rohrback & predecessor firms, 1978-83, sr. ptnr., 1983—. Mem. Seattle Bd. Theater Suprs., 1958-61, Mcpl. League of Seattle/King County, 1949—. Capt. U.S. Army, 1942-46; ETO. Mem. ABA, Internat. Assn. Def. Counsel, Fedn. Ins. and Corp. Counsel, Wash. Bar Assn., Wash. Def. Trial Lawyers Assn., Seattle-King County Bar Assn. (trustee 1965-68), Fedn. Fly Fishers (life), S.R., Puget Sound Civil War Roundtable, Rainier Club, Wash. Athletic Club, The Steamboaters, Flyfishers Club Oreg., Hope Island King-50 Club, Delta Tau Delta, Phi Delta Phi, Alpha Kappa Psi.

WALDRON, VANIS ROY, artist, educator; b. Parkersburg, W.Va., Sept. 19, 1936; s. James Michael and Edna Marie (Caplinger) W. Diploma, Oakland (Calif.) Art Inst., 1970, Bongart Sch. Art, L.A., 1979; teaching credential, U. Calif., Berkeley, 1981. Pvt. tchr. art, San Leandro, Calif., 1970-80; tchr. San Leandro Unified Sch. Dist., 1980—; art judge numerous orgns. countrywide, 1985—. One man shows include Jack London Sq., Oakland, Calif., 1988, 89, 90, 91, 95; group shows include Casa Peralta, San Leandro, Calif., 1985, 86, 87, 88, 89, 90, 91, Cheek Gallery, Tacos, N.Mex., 1992—, Who's Who in Art, Monterey, Calif., 1989, 90, 91, 92, 93, 94, Collectors Gallery, Carmel, 1994, Pennfield Fine Arts, San Ramone, Calif., 1991—, The Gallery, Burlingame, Calif., 1994—. With U.S. Army, 1960-66. Recipient over 300 art awards from numerous nat. orgns., 1975—. Home: 240 Bristol Blvd San Leandro CA 94577-1611 Office: San Leandro Unified Sch Dist 2000 Bancroft Ave San Leandro CA 94577-6112

WALEN, JAMES ROBERT, engineering specialist; b. N.Y.C., Nov. 23, 1947; s. John Nicholas and Carol Susan (Rannbury) W.; m. Lisa L. Burdick, Sept. 27, 1993; children from previous marriage: Heather Renee, Aaron James. Grad., Citrus Coll., 1966, Orange Coast Coll., 1970. Assoc. engr. Hughes Aircraft Co., Irvine, Calif., 1966-78; ptnr., chief engr. D&L Engring., Irvine, 1978-80; design supr. Interconics, Irvine, 1980-85; engring. specialist Packard-Hughes Interconnect, Irvine, 1985—; instr. Inst. for Interconnecting & Pkg. Electronic Circuits, 1979, 82. Inventor, patentee in field. Mem. Rep. Nat. Com., 1981—, Nat. Rep. Congl. Com., 1988—, Ronald Reagan Presdl. Found., 1989—; vol. Friendship Home of Laguna Beach, Calif., 1992—. With U.S. Army, 1968. Mem. San Onofre Surfing Club (bd. dirs. 1985-88). Office: Packard-Hughes Interconnect 17150 Von Karman Ave Irvine CA 92714-4927

WALENDOWSKI, GEORGE JERRY, business analyst, accounting educator; b. Han-Minden, Germany, Mar. 25, 1947; came to U.S., 1949; s. Stefan (dec.) and Eugenia (Lewandowska) W. AA, L.A. City Coll., 1968; BS, Calif. State U., L.A., 1970, MBA, 1972. Cert. community coll. instr. acctg. and mgmt., Calif. Acct. Unocal (formerly Union Oil Co. Calif.), L.A., 1972-76, data control supr., 1976-78, acctg. analyst, 1978-79; sr. fin. analyst Hughes Aircraft Co., El Segundo, Calif., 1979-83, fin. planning specialist, 1983-86; instr. bus. math. L.A. City Coll., 1976-80, instr. acctg., 1980—, mem. acctg. adv. com., 1984, 87, 89; bus. mgmt. specialist, 1986-93; bus. analyst, 1993—. Contbr. articles to profl. jours. Mem. commn. Rep. Pres. Task Force, 1986; softball co-organizer Precious Blood Ch., L.A., 1979. Recipient Medal of Merit, Rep. Presdl. Task Force, 1984, cert. of merit, named registered life mem. commn., 1986, named Honor Roll life mem., 1989; recipient Vice-Presdl. Cert. of Commendation, Rep. Nat. Hall of Honor, 1992, Rep. Congl. cert. of Appreciation, 1993, Rep. Congl. Order of Freedom award Nat. Rep. Congl. Com., 1995. Mem. Acad. Mgmt. (reviewer social issues in mgmt. divsn. 1991, review panelist bus. policy and strategy divsn. 1994), Inst. Mgmt. Accts. (author's cir. L.A. chpt. 1980, Robert Half Author's trophy 1980, cert. of appreciation 1980, 83), Am. Acctg. Assn., Nat. Assn. Mgmt., Planning Forum (recognition award L.A. chpt. 1983), Am. Econ. Assn., Am. Fin. Assn., Fin. Mgmt. Assn., Strategic Mgmt. Soc., U.S. Chess Fedn., Beta Gamma Sigma. Republican. Roman Catholic. Home: 426 N Citrus Ave Los Angeles CA 90036-2632 Office: Hughes Aircraft Co HSC Bldg S24 M/S D543 PO Box 92919 Los Angeles CA 90009-2919

WALES, HUGH GREGORY, marketing educator, business executive; b. Topeka, Feb. 28, 1910; s. Raymond Otis and Nola V. (Chestnut) W.; m. Alice Fulkerson, June 11, 1938. A.B., Washburn Coll., 1932; M.B.A., Harvard U., 1934; Ph.D., Northwestern U., 1944; D.Sc., Washburn Municipal U., 1968. Dean men N.W. Mo. State Tchrs. Coll., 1935-38, dean students, head dept. econs., 1938-39; dean students, dir. summer sch., vets. bur., head dept. econs. Washburn U., 1939-46; assoc. prof. marketing U. Ill., 1946-53, prof., 1953-70, prof. emeritus, dir. micro-precision projects, 1970—; prof. marketing and mgmt., head dept. Roosevelt U., 1970-75; pres. Decisions, Evaluations & Learning, Internat. Assocs.; vis. prof. marketing U. South Africa, Pretoria, 1962; lectr. U. Stellenbosch, South Africa, 1973, 75, 76; cons. South African Govt., Pretoria, 1974; participant internat. confs.; bus., marketing research cons.; internat. pres. Micro-precision Miniaturization Inst., 1970—, dir., program chmn., Chgo., 1970—. Author: Changing Perspectives in Marketing, 1951, Marketing Research, 1952, 4th edit., 1974, Marketing Research-Selected Literature, 1952, Cases and Problems in Marketing Research, 1953, (with Robert Ferber) Basic Bibliography in Marketing Research, 1956, 3d edit., 1974, Motivation and Market Behavior, (with Ferber), 1958, Advertising Copy, Layout, and Typography, (with Gentry and M. Wales), 1958, (with R. Ferber) The Champaign-Urbana Metropolitan Area, (with Engel and Warshaw) Promotional Strategy, 1967, 3d edit., 1975, (with Dik Twedt and Lyndon Dawson) Personality Theory in Marketing Research: A Basic Bibliography, 1976, (with Sharon Abrams) English as a Second Language in Business, 1978, (with Luck, Taylor and Rubin) Marketing Research, 1978; numerous others, works transl. several langs.; Contbr. (with Luck, Taylor and Rubin) articles to profl. jours. Pres. Civic Symphony Soc., 1964-65. Mem. Am. Econ. Assn., Am. Marketing Assn. (sec., acad. v.p.), Am. Watchmakers Inst. (dir. research and edn. 1963-66), Nat. Assn. Watch and Clock Collectors (chpt. pres. 1981, 83), Arizonans for Nat. Security (chmn. visual aids com. 1979—), Internat. Alliance Theatrical Stage Employees and Moving Picture Machine Operators, Internat. Platform Assn., Internat. TV Assn., Assn. Edn. Internat. Bus., Soc. Internat. Devel., Am. Statis. Assn., Nat. Assn. for Mgmt. Educators., Acad. Mgmt.

WALHA, SANTOKH SINGH, physician; b. Jhansi, India, Mar. 16, 1959; came to U.S., 1986; s. Gurdial Singh and Surinder Kaur (Panjhatha) W.; m. Sandeep Kaur Randhawa; 1 child, Gurtej. MBBS, Dayanand Med. Coll., 1983. Resident, 1989-93; internist Carl Albert Indian Hosp., Ada, Okla., 1993; emergency rm. physician VA Hosp., Murfreesboro, Tenn., 1993; primary care physician VA Hosp., Hot Springs, S.D., 1993—; internist Yuma (Ariz.) Regional Hosp., 1993-94; physician Ceres Med. Office, Stanislaus (Calif.) Med. Ctr., 1994. Mem. AMA.

WALIZE, REUBEN THOMPSON, III, health research administrator; b. Williamsport, Pa., May 28, 1950; s. Reuben Thompson Jr. and Marion Marie (Smith) W.; m. Kathleen Anne Smith, Aug. 13, 1979; children: Heather, Amanda, Reuben IV. BS, Pa. State U., 1972; MPH magna cum laude, U. Tenn., 1975; cert. exec. mgmt., Boston U., 1978. Manpower planner North ctrl. Pa. Area Health Edn. Sys. The Inst. for Med. Edn. and Rsch. Geisinger Med. Ctr., Danville, Pa., 1975-76; asst. dir. Northcentral Pa. Area Health Edn. System, Danville, 1976, exec. dir., 1976-78; health mgr. Seda-Cog, Timberhaven, Pa., 1978; exec. asst. VA Med. Ctr., Erie, Pa., 1978-81; trainee VA Med. Ctr., Little Rock, 1981; adminstrv. officer rsch. svc. VA Med. Ctr., White River Junction, Vt., 1981-88; mgmt. analyst Dept. Vets. Affairs Med. Ctr., Roseburg, Oreg., 1988-90, health systems specialist, 1990-92; adminstrv. officer rsch. Vets. Affairs Med. Ctr. Am. Lake, Tacoma, 1992-95; EEO investigator, 1995—; mem. Pa. Coun. Health Profls., 1975-77, Ctrl. Pa. Health Sys. Agy. Manpower Com., 1975-77; mem. Interagy. Coun. Geisinger Med. Ctr., Danville, 1976-78; liaison for rsch. Dartmouth Med. Sch., Hanover, N.H., 1981-88; mem. instnl. rev. bd. Madigan Army Med. Ctr., 1994—; EEO investigator; cons. in field. Recipient Man of Achievement award Queens Coll., Eng., 1978, Student Am. Med. Assn. Found. award, 1975; 1st pl. Douglas County Lamb Cooking Contest, 1992. Mem. APHA, AAAS, N.Y. Acad. Scis., Soc. Rsch. Adminstrs., Assn. Hosps., Pa. State Alumni Assn., Nat. Audubon Soc., Steamboaters, Nat. Wildlife Fedn., Record Catch Club, VIP Club. Home: 1103 25th Ave SE Puyallup WA 98374-1362

WALKER, BURTON LEITH, engineering writer, psychotherapist; b. Mt. Morris Twp., Mich., Oct. 23, 1927; s. Dalton Hugh and Muriel Joyce (Black) W.; m. Norva Jean Trochman, June 28, 1949; children: Paul, Cynthia Halverson, Mark; m. Carol Jean D'Andrea, July 31, 1981. Cert. psychology. tchr., lic. psychotherapist, hypnotherapist, Calif. A.A., Allan Hancock Coll., 1971; B.A., Chapman Coll., 1974, M.A., 1975. Contract estimator Ryan Aeronaut., San Diego, 1949-59; logistics rep. GD/A, San Diego, 1960-62; systems engr., cons. fgn. svc. Ralph M. Parsons, L.A., 1962-68; lead engring. writer, sr. analyst Fed. Electric, Vandenberg AFB, Calif., 1969-86; psychotherapist Access, Vandenberg Village, Family Guidance Svc., Santa Ynez, Calif.; ret.; part time prof. Allan Hancock Coll., Santa Maria, Calif., 1974-93, small bus. owner 1974-86. Active Santa Ynez Valley Presbyn. Ch.; mem. Republican Nat. Com. Served with USN, 1946-48. Mem. Am. Assn. Christian Counselors, Nat. Mgmt. Assn. (Outstanding Svc. award 1982), Calif. Assn. Marriage and Family Therapists, Assn. Advancement Ret. People. Republican. Home: 3149 E Hwy 246 Santa Ynez CA 93460-9634

WALKER, CAROLYN LOUISE, nursing researcher, educator; b. Ft. George, Wash., Apr. 4, 1947; d. Marvin John and Louise Olive (Billings) W.; m. Simon I. Zemel, Apr. 6, 1968 (div. 1981); children: Michelle, Brent Zemel. AA, Fullerton (Calif.) Coll., 1968; BSN, Calif. State U., Fullerton, 1976; MSN, Calif. State U., L.A., 1979; PhD in Nursing, U. Utah, 1986. RN, Calif. Staff nurse Children's Hosp. Orange (Calif.) County, 1969-71; instr. nursing Cypress (Calif.) Coll., 1978-81, 81-82, Saddleback Coll., Mission Viejo, Calif., 1979-80; nurse oncology Children's Hosp. Orange County, 1980-81; asst. prof. U. Utah, Salt Lake City, 1984-85; asst. prof. San Diego State U., 1986-90, assoc. prof., 1990-94, prof., 1994—. Mem. editorial rev. bd. Am. Jour. Continuing Edn. in Nursing, 1987-90, Oncology Nursing Forum, 1988-91, Jour. Pediatric Oncology Nursing, 1991—. Mem. children's com. Am. Cancer Soc., San Diego, 1988—. Mem. ANA, Assn. Pediatric Oncology Nurses (chair rsch. 1988-91, exec. bd. dirs. 1992-94, pres.-elect 1994), Oncology Nursing Soc. Democrat. Episcopalian. Office: San Diego State U Sch Nursing San Diego CA 92182

WALKER, CAROLYN PEYTON, English language educator; b. Charlottesville, Va., Sept. 15, 1942; d. Clay M. and Ruth Peyton. BA in Am. History and Lit., Sweet Briar Coll., 1965; cert. in French, Alliance Francaise, Paris, 1966; EdM, Tufts U., 1970; MA in English and Am. Lit., Stanford U., 1974, PhD in English Edn., Stanford U., 1977. Tchr. Elem. and jr. high schs. in Switzerland, 1967-69; tchr. elem. grades Boston Sch. System, 1966-67, 69-70; Newark (Calif.) Unified Sch. System, 1970-72; instr. div. humanities Canada Coll., Redwood City, Calif., 1973, 76-78; instr. Sch. Bus., U. San Francisco, 1973-74; evaluation cons. Inst. Profl. Devel., San Jose, Calif., 1975-76; asst. dir. Learning Assistance Ctr., Stanford U., Calif., 1972-77, dir., 1977-84, lectr. Sch. Edn., 1975-84, dept. English, 1977-84, supr. counselors, tutors and tchrs., 1972-84; assoc. prof. dept. English, San Jose State U., Calif., 1984—; dir. English dept. Writing Ctr., 1986—, Steinbeck Rsch. Ctr., 1986-87; pres. Waverley Edn., Inc., Ednl. Cons., 1983-91; head cons. to pres. to evaluate coll.'s writing program, San Jose City Coll., 1985-87; cons. U. Tex., Dallas, 1984, Stanford U., 1984, 1977-78, CCNY, 1979, U. Wis., 1980, numerous testing programs; cons. to pres. San Diego State U., 1982, Ednl. Testing Svc., 1985-88, also to numerous univs. and colls.; condr. reading and writing workshops, 1972—; reviewer Random House Books, 1978—, Rsch. in the Teaching of English, 1983—, Course Tech., Inc., 1990—; cons. Basic Skills Task Force, U.S. Office Edn., 1977-79, Right to Read, Calif. State Dept. Edn., 1977-82, Program for Gifted and Talented, Fremont (Calif.) Unified Sch. Dist., 1981-82; bd. dirs. high tech. sci. ctr., San Jose, 1983-84; speaker numerous profl. confs. Author: (with Patricia Killen) Handbook for Teaching Assistants at Stanford University, 1977, Learning Center Courses for Faculty and Staff: Reading, Writing, and Time Management, 1981, How to Succeed as a New Teacher: A Handbook for Teaching Assistants, 1978, ESL Courses for Faculty & Staff: An Additional Opportunity to Serve the Campus Community, 1983, (with Karen Wilson) Tutor Handbook for the Writing Center at San Jose State University, 1989, (with others) Academic Tutoring at the Learning Assistance Center, 1980, Writing Conference Talk: Factors Associated with High and Low Rated Writing Conferences, 1987, Lifeline Mac: A Handbook for Instructors in the Macintosh Computer Classrooms, 1989, Communications with the Faculty: Vital Links for the Success of Writing Centers, 1991, Coming to America, 1993, Teacher Dominance in the Writing Conference, 1992, Instant Curriculum: Just Add Tutors and Students, 1993; contbr. chpts. to Black American Literature Forum, 1991; contbr. articles to profl. jours. Vol. fundraiser Peninsula Ctr. for the Blind, Palo Alto, Calif., 1982—, The Resource Ctr. for Women, Palo Alto, 1975-76. Recipient Award for Outstanding Contbns., U.S. HEW, 1979, award ASPIRE (federally funded program), 1985, two awards Student Affirmative Action, 1986, award Western Coll. Reading & Learning Assn., 1984; numerous other awards and grants. Mem. MLA, Coll. Reading & Learning Assn. (treas. 1982-84, bd. dirs. 1982-84), Nat. Coun. Tchrs. English, No. Calif. Coll. Reading Assn. (sec.-treas. 1976-78), Am. Assn. U. Profs., Jr. League Palo Alto (bd. dirs. 1977-78, 83-84). Home: 2350 Waverley St Palo Alto CA 94301-4143 Office: San Jose State U English Dept San Jose CA 95192

WALKER, DANIEL DAVID, JR., lime company executive; b. Decatur, Ala., Sept. 29, 1923; s. Daniel D. and Altie (Humphries) W.; m. Vernea Greer, Jan. 2, 1951; children: Joan, David, Daniel III, Deborah. BA, Brigham Young U., 1949. Chemist U.S. Lime, Henderson, Nev., 1952-87; v.p. tech. svc. Chemstar Lime, Henderson, 1987-93, cons., 1993—. Inventor in field. 1st lt. U.S. Army, 1943-46, PTO. Recipient Merit award ASTM.

Office: Chem Lime Co BMI Complex PO Box 127 8000 W Lake Mead Henderson NV 89015

WALKER, DEWARD EDGAR, JR., anthropologist, educator; b. Johnson City, Tenn., Aug. 3, 1935; s. Deward Edgar and Matilda Jane (Clark) W.; m. Candace A. Walker; children: Alice, Deward Edgar III, Mary Jane, Sarah, Daniel, Joseph Benjamin. Student, Ea. Oreg. Coll., 1953-54, 56-58, Mexico City Coll., 1958; BA in Anthropology with honors, U. Oreg., 1960-61, PhD in Anthropology, 1964; postgrad., Wash. State U., 1962. Asst. prof. anthropology George Washington U., Washington, 1964-65; asst. prof. anthropology Wash. State U., Pullman, 1965-67, research collaborator, 1967-69; assoc. prof., chmn. dept. Sociology/Anthropology, lab. dir. U. Idaho, Moscow, 1967-69; prof. U. Colo., Boulder, 1969—, research assoc. in population processes program of inst. behavioral sci., 1969-73, assoc. dean Grad. Sch., 1973-76; affiliate faculty U. Idaho, 1971—; presenter in field. Founder, co-editor Northwest Anthropol. Rsch. Notes, 1966—; editor, Plateau Vol.: Handbook of North American Indians, 1971—; author, co-author of fifteen books, 125 conf. reports on the Northern Plains; contbr. articles to profl. jours. Mem. tech/ steering panel Hanford Environ. Dose Reconstrn. Project; advisor on Native Am. affairs Smithsonian Inst. With U.S. Army, 1954-62. Fellow NSF, 1961, NDEA, 1961-64. Fellow Am. Anthropol. Assn. (assoc. editor Am. Anthropologist 1973-74), Soc. Applied Anthropology (hon. life, exec. com. 1970-79, treas. 1976-79, chmn. 1980-95, cons., expert witness tribes of N.W., editor Human Orgn. 1970-76, rsch. over 65 separate projects); mem. AAAS, Am. Acad. Polit. Social Scis., Northwest Anthropol. Conf. Home: PO Box 4147 Boulder CO 80306-4147 Office: U Colo PO Box 233 Boulder CO 80309-0233

WALKER, DUNCAN EDWARD, military officer; b. Washington, Aug. 2, 1942; s. Edward John and Katherine Edith (Duncan) W. BA in Indsl. Psychology, N.Mex. State U., 1965; MS in Systems Mgmt., U. So. Calif., 1978; MPA, Golden Gate U., 1980. Commd. 2d lt. USAF, 1965, advanced through grades to lt. col., 1981; grad. Squadron Officers Sch., 1973, Air Command and Staff Coll., 1974, Indsl. Coll. Armed Forces, 1977; chief devel. and deployment br. ICBM requirements SAC, Offutt AFB, Nebr., 1981-84; dep. for ICBM ops. and evaluation Air Force Operational Test and Evaluation Ctr., Vandenberg AFB, Calif., 1984-88; program engr. Fed. Svcs. Corp., Western Space and Missile Ctr., Vandenberg AFB, Calif., 1988-92; pvt. practice cons., 1993—. Mission coun. exec. Boy Scouts of Am. Decorated Bronze Star, Meritorious Service medal with two oak leaf cluster, Air Force Commendation medal with three oak leaf clusters. Mem. AIAA, Order Pour Le Merite, Internat. Test and Evaluation Assn., Air Force Assn., Mil. Order of World Wars, Am. Legion, Elks (past exalted ruler), Order Moose. Republican. Methodist. Home: 113 N Y St Lompoc CA 93436-5514

WALKER, E. JERRY, retired clergyman; b. Seattle, May 31, 1918; s. Septimus and Mae Ruth (Roys) W.; m. Holly Rae Harding, Nov. 10, 1941; children: Jerrianne, Dale Harding, Barbara Rae. AB, Seattle Pacific U., 1940; MDiv, Garrett Theol. Sch., 1945; DD, Wiley Coll., 1958, Northland Coll., 1971. Ordained to ministry United Meth. Ch. Teaching fellow State Coll. Wash., 1940-41; dir. edn. Prairie Farmer Sta. WLS, Chgo., 1942-45; dir. radio Internat. Coun. Religious Edn., 1945-48; freelance writer, dir. radio and TV Sta. WBKB-TV, Chgo., 1948-53; pastor St. James Meth. Ch., Chgo., 1953-62, First United Meth. Ch., Duluth, 1962-74; freelance daily commentary Sta. KDAL-TV, Duluth, Minn., 1964-76; exec. dir. Ctr. for Family Studies, Duluth, 1972-82; ptnr. SoundVideo Prodns., Tahuya, Wash., 1987—; cons. environ. grants, 1987—; project dir. Hood Canal Wetlands Interp Ctr., 1988—; bd. dirs. Pacific N.W. WRiters Conf., Wash., 1983-88; mem. gen. bd. Nat. Coun. Chs., 1954-66. Author: Five Minute Stories from the Bible, 1948, Stories from the Bible, 1955, Seeking a Faith of Your Own, 1961, Sinner's Parish, 1963, (plays) Checkerboard, Kyrie, The Unpainted Wall; also numerous articles. Bd. dirs. Chgo. chpt. NCCJ, 1955-62, nat. bd. trustees, 1974-76; mem. Kenwood-Ellis Cmty. Renewal Commn., 1957-62, Gov. Ill.'s Adv. Commn. on Aged, 1958-62, S.E. Chgo. Commn., 1958-62, United Fund Survey Com., 1968-70; co-chmn. Duluth Citizens Com. Secondary Edn., 1963-64; bd. dirs. Mary E. Theler Cmty. Ctr., Belfair, Wash., 1988-91; cons. Mason County United Way, 1990-94, co-chmn. needs assessment com., 1992-94; cons. Bremerton Hist. Ships Assn., 1994—. Recipient Human Rels. award Chgo. Commn. Human Rels., 1954, Friend of Youth award Southside Community Com., 1955, Disting. Citizen award Com. of One Hundred, 1962, Achievement award Freedom Found., 1963-65, Broadcast Journalism award Minn. Coun. Chs., 1971, Appreciation award North Mason Sch. Dist., 1990, Environ. Pride award Pacific Northwest Mag., 1992; named Chicagoan of Yr. Chgo. Jaycees, 1962. Mem. Internat. Platform Assn., Seattle Free Lances, Kiwanis. Democrat. Home: 18341 E State Highway 106 Belfair WA 98528-9588 Office: North Mason Sch Dist PO Box 167 Belfair WA 98528-0167

WALKER, EDWARD DONALD (RUSTY WALKER), artist, educator; b. Danville, Ill., Oct. 31, 1946; s. Edward Glennen and Hazel Mary (Castledine) W.; children: Melody Robin, Courtney Elizabeth, Hunter Nicholas. BA in Illustration, Queensland Inst. Tech., Brisbane, Australia, 1966; MFA in Studio Art, Greenwich U., Hilo, Hawaii, 1990, PhD in Art Edn., 1992. Art dir. SAC Hdqs., Offutt AFB, Nebr., 1967-71; artist, illustrator Walker Studio, San Francisco, 1971-89; assoc. prof. Al Collins Graphic Design Sch., Tempe, Ariz., 1989—; awards juror Calif. State Fair, Sacramento, 1979; condr. Hewitt Painting Workshops, San Miguel de Allende, Mex., 1982, Asilomar Watercolor Workshops, Monterey, Calif., 1977-79. One-man show Jalisco Mus., Guadalajara, Mex., 1974, Scott Gallery, Orinda, Calif., 1977-81, John Pence Gallery, San Francisco, 1981; exhibited in group shows C.G. Rein Galleries, Scottsdale, Ariz., Mpls., Denver, Houston, 1985-94; represented in permanent collection San Francisco Mus. Modern Art; author: Writer's Digest Transparent Watercolor, 1985, Classroom Companion, 1993; portrait commd. John Steinbeck Found., 1974, also others. Recipient Emily Lowe award Am. Watercolor Soc., 1977, Tchr. of Yr., Career Coll. Assn., 1990.

WALKER, ELJANA M. DU VALL, civic worker; b. France, Jan. 18, 1924; came to U.S., 1948; naturalized, 1954; student Med. Inst., U. Paris, 1942-47; m. John S. Walker, Jr., Dec. 31, 1947; children—John, Peter, Barbara. Pres., Loyola Sch. PTA, 1958-59; bd. dirs. Santa Claus shop, 1959-73; treas. Archdiocese Denver Catholic Women, 1962-64; rep. Cath. Parent-Tchr League, 1962-65; pres. Aux. Denver Gen. Hosp., 1966-69; precinct committeewoman Arapahoe County Republican Women's Com., 1973-74; mem. re-election com. Arapahoe County Rep. Party, 1973-78, Reagan election com., 1980; block worker Arapahoe County March of Dimes, Heart Assn., Hemophilia Drive, Muscular Dystrophy and Multiple Sclerosis Drive, 1978-81; cen. city asst. Guild Debutante Charities, Inc. Recipient Distinguished Service award Am.-by-choice, 1966; named to Honor Roll, ARC, 1971. Mem. Cherry Hills Symphony, Lyric Opera Guild, Alliance Francaise (life mem.), ARC, Civic Ballet Guild (life mem.), Needlework Guild Am. (v.p. 1980-82), Kidney Found. (life), Denver Art Mus., U. Denver Art and Conservation Assns. (chmn. 1980-82), U. Denver Women's Library Assn., Chancellors Soc, Passage Inc., Friends of the Fine Arts Found. (life), CHildren's Diabetes Found. (life). Roman Catholic. Clubs: Union (Chgo.); Denver Athletic, 26 (Denver); Welcome to Colo. Internat. Address: 2301 Green Oaks Dr Littleton CO 80121-1562

WALKER, ERNEST K., engineer, educator; b. L.A., Jan. 13, 1927; s. Ernest Kenneth and Margaret Josephine (Holmberg) W.; m. Annie Lee Power, Apr. 9, 1954; children: Colleen Ann Walker Lydick, Michael Kenneth. AA, Glendale (Calif.) Coll., 1948; BSCE, U. So. Calif., 1952, MSCE, 1956. Profl. engr., Calif. Civil engr. L.A. Dept. Water & Power, 1952-54; instr. engring. U. So. Calif., L.A., 1954-56; asst. prof. engring. U. Hawaii, Honolulu, 1956-62; rsch. engr. Northrop, Hawthorne, Calif., 1963-66; sr. staff engr. Lockheed, Burbank, Calif., 1966-86, engr. dept. advanced structures & techs., 1986-87; cons. engr. EK Walker Engring., Fillmore, Calif., 1989—; mem. adv. com. fracture control NASA, 1971, 73; instr. workshops and short courses in field. Author, originator Walker Equation for Stress Ratios. Mem. gen. aviation adv. com. County of Ventura, Calif., 1971; mem. gov.'s task force Tsunami Evaluation Zones, Honolulu, 1960, 61; mem. city planning commn. City of Fillmore, 1969, 70. Served with USNR, 1944-46. Mem. ASTM (chmn. com. fracture applications 1971, 75, mem.-at-large exec. com. on fatigue 1972-76), AIAA (structure com. 1982, 87, chmn. fatigue [illegible]). Office: EK Walker Engring PO Box 855 Fillmore CA 93016-0855

WALKER, FRANCIS JOSEPH, lawyer; b. Tacoma, Aug. 5, 1922; s. John McSweeney and Sarah Veronica (Meechan) W.; m. Julia Corinne O'Brien, Jan. 27, 1951; children: Vincent Paul, Monica Irene Hylton, Jill Marie Nudell, John Michael, Michael Joseph, Thomas More. B.A., St. Martin's Coll., 1947; J.D., U. Wash., 1950. Bar: Wash. Asst. atty. gen. State of Wash., 1950-51; pvt. practice law, Olympia, Wash., 1951—; gen. counsel Wash. Cath. Conf., 1967-76. Lt. (j.g.) USNR, 1943-46; PTO. Home and Office: 2723 Hillside Dr SE Olympia WA 98501-3460

WALKER, GAIL JUANICE, electrologist; b. Bosque County, Tex., Sept. 3, 1937; d. Hiram Otis and Hazel Ruth (Carmichael) Gunter; cert. Shults Inst. Electrolysis, 1971; children—Lillian Ruth, Deborah Lynn. In quality control Johnson & Johnson, San Angelo, Tex., 1962-70; owner, pres., electrologist Ariz. Inst. Electrolysis, Scottsdale, 1979—; ednl. cons. Gail Walker's Internat. Sch. Electrolysis, Tokyo, 1980; area corr. Hair Route mag., 1981; co-founder Gailshay Worldwide Bio-Tonique and Epluche Skin Care Products. participant continuing edn. program in electrology Shelby State Coll., 1981. Editor Electrolysis World. Cert., Pvt. Bus. and Tech. Schs., State of Ariz. Mem. Ariz. Assn. Electrologists (pres. 1980—), Am. Electrolysis Assn., Internat. Guild Profl. Electrologists, Nat. Fedn. Ind. Businessmen, Ariz. Assn. Electrologists (organizer 1980). Republican. Baptist. Club: Order of Eastern Star.

WALKER, JOHN SUMPTER, JR., lawyer; b. Richmond, Ark., Oct. 13, 1921; s. John Sumpter, Martha (Wilson) W.; m. Eljana M. duVall, Dec. 31, 1947; children: John Stephen, Barbara Monika Ann, Peter Mark Gregory. BA, Tulane U., 1942; MS, U. Denver, 1952, JD, 1960; diploma Nat. Def. U., 1981. Bar: Colo. 1960, U.S. Dist. Ct. Colo. 1960, U.S. Supreme Ct., 1968, U.S. Ct. Appeals (10th cir.) 1960, U.S. Tax. Ct., 1981. With Denver & Rio Grande Western R.R. Co., 1951-61, gen. solicitor, 1961-89 ; pres. Denver Union Terminal Ry. Co. Apptd. gen. counsel Moffat Tunnel Commn., 1991; life mem. Children's Diabetes Found. With U.S. Army, 1942-46. Decorated Bronze Star. Mem. Colo. Bar Assn., Arapahoe County Bar Assn., Alliance Francaise (life), Order of St. Ives, U. Denver Chancellors' Soc., Cath. Lawyers Guild. Republican. Roman Catholic. Club: Denver Athletic.

WALKER, JOSEPH ROBERT, neurosurgeon; b. Atlantic City, N.J., Mar. 2, 1942; s. Joseph West and Helen (Mendte) W.; m. Mary Cynthia Long, Aug. 23, 1968; children: Joseph West II, Scott Robert, Heather Elizabeth. BS, St. Josephs Coll., 1964; MD, Creighton U., 1968. Diplomate Am. Bd. Neurol. Surgery. Intern Atlantic City (N.J.) Hosp., 1968-69; resident surgery Jefferson Med. Coll. Hosp., Phila, 1969-70; resident neurosurgery U. N.C., Chapel Hill, 1972-76, fellow, instr. neurosurgery, 1976-77; chief neurosurgery Washoe Med. Ctr., Reno, Nev., 1982, St. Mary's Hosp., Reno, 1982; vice-chief neurosurgery Washoe Med. Ctr., Reno, 1989, St. Mary's Hosp., Reno, 1989; clin. prof. neurosurgery U. Nev. Med. Sch., Reno. Served as lt. comdr. USN, 1970-72. Office: 850 Mill St Fl 3 Reno NV 89502-1413

WALKER, JOYCE MARIE, secondary school educator; b. Kansas City, Kans., Jan. 24, 1948; d. Frank Cornelius and Inez (Pennington) W.; divorced; 1 child, Kevin Cornelius. BS, U. Ark., Pine Bluff, 1972. Cert. ch. adminstr. Bus. tchr. U.S. Trade Sch., Kansas City, 1972-74; exec. sec. Kansas City Mo. Sch. Dist., 1974-77; tchr. vocat. bus. Aurora (Colo.) Pub. Sch., 1977—; vocat. bus. tchr. Pioneer Community Coll., 1975-77. Mem. Aurora Human Rels. Martin Luther King Jr. Com., 1986—; asst. sec. Sunday sch. Macedonia Bapt. Ch., 1985—, evangelism counselor, 1992—; 2d v.p. E.L. Witchfield Missionary Soc., 1989; chmn. We. States Fgn. Mission, 1990. Mem. Nat. Coun. Negro Women, Nat. Assn. Bus. Educators, NAACP (Aurora br. 1990—), Delta Sigma Theta. Home: 12948 E 48th Ave Denver CO 80239-4408 Office: Aurora Pub Schs 11700 E 11th Ave Aurora CO 80010-3758

WALKER, KEITH ALLEN, plant genetics company executive; b. Cleve., Oct. 17, 1948; s. Joseph Fordun and Audrey Marie (Brindley) W.; m. Marguerite Joyce Ming, Aug. 29, 1970; children: Kenneth Alec, Andrew Fordun. BA, Coll. of Wooster, 1970; PhD, Yale U., 1974. Sr. rsch. biologist Monsanto Chem. Co., St. Louis, 1974-76, rsch. group leader, 1976-79, sr. rsch. group leader, 1979-81; dir. product devel. Plant Genetics, Inc., Davis, Calif., 1981-82, v.p. rsch., dir., 1982-89; dir. devel. and licensing Agrigenetics Co., Davis, Calif., 1989-93; dir. planning and licensing Mycogen Corp., San Diego, 1993, exec. dir. biotechnology rsch., 1993—; vice chair Gordon Rsch. Conf. in Plant Cell and Tissue Culture, 1985, chair, 1987. Assoc. editor: Plant Cell, Tissue & Organ Culture, 1988; contbr. articles to tech. jours., chpts. to books. Mem. Am. Soc. Plant Physiologists, Am. Soc. Agronomy, Crop Sci. Soc. Am., Am. Oil Chem. Soc., Sigma Xi. Office: Mycogen Corp 4980 Carroll Canyon Rd San Diego CA 92121-1736

WALKER, KENT PITT, veterinarian; b. Glendale, Calif., Feb. 18, 1950; s. Pitt Arthur and Myrthe (Conerly) W.; m. Patricia Ann Meek, June 1969 (div. Jan. 1981); children: Jason, Taylor; m. Joyce Elizabeth Beck, May 6, 1981; 1 child, Holland. BS in Agr., Okla. State U., 1974, DVM, 1976. Intern Newport Ctr. Animal Hosp., Newport Beach, Calif., 1976-77, staff vet., mgr., 1977-79; mgr., vet. Orange County Emergency Pet Clinic, Garden Grove, Calif., 1979-80, East Fullerton (Calif.) Pet Clinic, 1980-81, Walnut Village Vet. Hosp., Irvine, Calif., 1981-82; owner North Shore Animal Hosp., Big Bear City, Calif., 1982-94; prin. Relief Vet. Svc., 1994—. Mem. Am. Vet. Med. Assn., Calif. Vet. Med. Assn., Greenpeace, Nat. Wildlife Assn. Home: 33420 Pauba Rd Temecula CA 92592

WALKER, LARRY GILBERT, computer scientist; b. Astoria, Oreg., June 17, 1949; s. Gilbert L. and Arlene E. (Hanson) W.; children: Amanda G., Grant L. BS in Indsl. Mgmt., U. Wyo., 1978, MS in Indsl. Mgmt., 1982. Logistics analyst Gen. Dynamics/Convair, San Diego, 1978-81, divsn. systems mgr., 1982-84; sr. indsl. engr. Paccar, Inc., Kansas City, Mo., 1982-83. With U.S. Army, 1970-73. Mem. Am. Mgmt. Assn. Home: 1726 Kennington Rd Encinitas CA 92024-1025

WALKER, LISA LEE, interior designer, artist; b. Columbus, Nebr., Oct. 31, 1954; d. Jerry Burke and Ramona (Esty) Worsencroft; divorced; children: Andrew, Ben. BA, Brigham Young Univ., 1975. Owner Park Ave. Design, Park City, Utah, 1980-83; design dir. Clark Learning Inc., Salt Lake City, 1978-80, MHT Arch., Salt Lake City, 1983-87, DMJM Internat., Phoenix, 1987-91; owner Lisa Walker Design, Scottsdale, Ariz., 1991—. Vol. Women's Shelter, Phoenix, 1992. Named one of Best Designers of S.W., Phoenix Consumer Guide Mag., 1994. Mem. Am. Soc. Interior Designers (art cons. graffiti project 1994, treas. Intermountain chpt. 1986-87, Best Office Over 3000 1st pl. award 1992, Best Health Care Design 1st pl. award 1992, Best Comml. Design over 20,000 1st pl. award 1992). Office: Lisa Walker Design 4130 N Marshall Way # A Scottsdale AZ 85251-3810

WALKER, MARGARET SMITH, real estate company executive; b. Lancashire, Eng., Oct. 14, 1943; came to U.S., 1964; d. Arthur Edward and Doris Audrey (Dawson) Smith; m. James E. Walker, Feb. 6, 1992. Lic. real estate agt., Hawaii. Broker Lawson-Worrall Inc. (now Worrall-McCarter), Honolulu, 1974-81; pres. Maggie Parkes & Assocs., Inc., Honolulu, 1981—. Bd. dirs. Hawaii Combined Tng. Assn., Honolulu, 1985—; dist. commr. Lio Lii Pony Club, Honolulu, 1980; com. chmn. Hist. Hawaii Found., Honolulu, 1990. Mem. Am. Horse Shows Assn., Hawaii Horse Shows Assn., Outrigger Canoe Club. Episcopalian. Office: PO Box 25083 Honolulu HI 96825-0083

WALKER, MARY CHRISTINE, community services facilitator, educator; b. Great Bend, Kans., Dec. 25, 1949; d. George William and Thelma Julia (Jacobson) W.; 1 child, Yvette Denice. BA, Met. State Coll., Denver, 1976; MA, U. Colo., Denver, 1985. Head tutor Home Tutoring Svc., Denver, 1990—; pres. Black Transplants Action Com., Denver, 1990—; cmty. liaison Accelerated Schs. Scholarship Program, Denver, 1990—. Author: From Here to There to Anywhere - A Curriculum Guide for Preschool/Kindergarten, 1993. Recipient Vol. award Transplant Coun. of Rockies, 1991, Profl. Svc. award Black Student Alliance, 1994. Fellow Black Bookwriters Network. Home and Office: 3241 Newport St Denver CO 80207-2221

WALKER, MOIRA KAYE, sales executive; b. Riverside, Calif., Aug. 2, 1940; d. Frank Leroy and Arline Rufina (Roach) Porter; m. Timothy P. Walker, Aug. 30, 1958 (div. 1964); children: Brian A., Benjamin D., Blair K., Beth E. Student, Riverside City Coll., 1973. With Bank of Am., Riverside, 1965-68, Abitibi Corp., Cucamonga, Calif., 1968-70; with Lily div. Owens-Illinois, Riverside, 1970-73; salesperson Lily div. Owens-Illinois, Houston, 1973-77; salesperson Kent H. Landsberg div. Sunclipse, Montebello, Calif., 1977-83, sales mgr., 1983-85; v.p., sales mgr. Kent H. Landsberg div. Sunclipse, Riverside, 1985—. Mem. NAFE, Women in Paper (treas. 1978-84), Kent H. Landsberg President's Club. Lutheran. Office: Kent H Landsberg Div Sunclipse 1180 W Spring St Riverside CA 92507-1327

WALKER, RAYMOND FRANCIS, business and financial consulting company executive; b. Medicine Lake, Mont., Nov. 9, 1914; s. Dennis Owen and Rose (Long) W.; m. Patricia K. Blakey, May 15, 1951; children: Richard A., Mark D., Maxie R. Forest, Victoria L. Le Huray, Suzanne J. Buhl, Tracy Walker Stampanoni. Grad. pub. schs.; student, Edison Vocat. Sch., 1935-39. Truck mgr. Pacific Food Products, Seattle, 1939-42; machinist Todd Shipyard, Seattle, 1943-45; owner Delbridge Auto Sales, Seattle, 1945-48; pres. Pacific Coast Acceptance Corp., 1949-60; v.p. West Coast Mortgage, Seattle, 1960-67, United Equities Corp., Seattle, 1965-69; pres. Income Mgmt. Corp., Seattle, 1970-90; v.p. Internat. Mint and Foundry, Redmond, Wash., 1983-87; pvt. practice bus. and fin. cons. Sequim, Wash., 1987—; cons. Life Ins. Co. Am., Bellevue, Wash., 1982-87, Consumer Loan Svc., Lynwood Wash., 1980-92; dir., cons., v.p. fin. Am. Campgrounds, Bellevue, 1971-79; cons., bd. dirs. Straits Forest Products, Inc. , Port Angeles, Wash.; dir., cons. Synergy Techs., Inc., Sequim, 1990—, co-founder, dir. Sequim Tech., Inc., 1994—. Mem. Nat. Assn. Security Dealers. Methodist. Lodge: Elks. Home: 3347 W Sequim Bay Rd Sequim WA 98382-9031

WALKER, RICHARD ALLEN, multimedia computing executive, consultant; b. Flushing, N.Y., Sept. 24, 1935; s. John Randall and Estella Viola (Stephenson) W.; m. Jauhree Ann Sparks, July 14, 1973. BA in Econs. and History, U.S. Internat. U., 1963, MS in Mgmt. Sci., 1968; PhD in Instructional Sci., Brigham Young U., 1978. Commd. ensign USN, 1958, advanced through grades to comdr., ret., 1976; sr. instructional psychologist Courseware, Inc., 1978-82, mgr. electronics pub. group, 1982-83; founder, pres., acting v.p. instrnl. devel. Interactive Tech. Corp., 1983-86, chmn., 1986; pvt. practice, 1986-87; dir. tng. svcs. WICAT Systems, Inc., 1987-90; group dir. Jostens Learning Corp., 1990-92; pres. Multimedia Group, Coronado, Calif., 1992—. Mem. Soc. for Applied Learning Tech. (sr.), Am. Ednl. Rsch. Assn., Assn. Aviation Psychologists, Eagle Scout Assn., Arlberg Ski Club (silver medal), Crown Club (v.p. 1985). Republican. Presbyterian. Home: 740 Olive Ave Coronado CA 92118-2136 Office: Multimedia Group 740 Olive Ave Coronado CA 92118-2136

WALKER, RICHARD HUGH, orthopaedic surgeon; b. Elgin, Ill., Jan. 29, 1951; m. Wendy Allen; children: Ashley Elizabeth, Blake Allen, Emily Paige. AB cum laude, Occidental Coll., 1973; MD, U. Chgo., 1977. Diplomate Nat. Bd. Med. Examiners, Am. Bd. Orthopaedic Surgery. Resident I in surgery UCLA, 1977-78, resident II in surgery, 1978-79; jr. resident in orthopaedic surgery Stanford (Calif.) U., 1979-81, sr. resident, 1981-82, chief resident, 1982-83; clin. mem. divsn. orthopaedic surgery, sect. lower extremity reconstructive surgery Scripps Clinic and Rsch. Found., La Jolla, Calif., 1983—, co-dir. lower extremity reconstructive surgery fellowship, divsn. orthopaedic surgery, 1989—, assoc. head. divsn. orthopaedic surgery, 1990—; staff physician dept. surgery Green Hosp. of Scripps Clinic, La Jolla, 1983—, chief of staff, 1995—; staff physician Pomerado Hosp., Poway, Calif., 1983-92; team physician San Diego Padres, 1983-86, 95—; clin. instr. divsn. orthopaedics and rehab. U. Calif., San Diego, 1983-92, asst. clin. prof., 1992—; bd. dirs., trustee Scripps Clinic Med. Group, La Jolla; mem. bd. govs. Scripps Clin. and Rsch. Found., 1992—, mem. joint exec. bd., 1992-93; presenter, lectr. in field. Mem. manuscript rev. bd. Clin. Orthopaedics and Related Rsch., 1989—, Jour. Bone and Joint Surgery, 1994—; contbr. articles to profl. jours. Mem. AMA, Am. Acad. Orthopaedic Surgeons, We. Orthopaedic Assn. (program chmn. San Diego chpt. 1994-95, treas. 1995-96, Resident Paper award 1983), Calif. Orthopaedic Assn., Assn. Arthritic Hip and Knee Surgery (charter mem. 1991). Office: Scripps Clinic and Rsch Found Divsn Orthopaedic Surgery 10666 N Torrey Pines Rd La Jolla CA 92037-1027 also: Scripps Clinic and Rsch Found 15025 Innovation Dr San Diego CA 92128-3409

WALKER, ROGER ALFRED, lawyer; b. Norman, Okla., Feb. 9, 1958; s. John Adams and Norma Jean (English) W.; m. Amy Bess Rupprecht, Aug. 9, 1980; children: Marie Elizabeth, Caitlin Ruth, John Alfred. BS in Secondary Edn. with honors, U. Ill., 1980, JD cum laude, 1989. Bar: N.Mex. 1989, U.S. Dist. Ct. N.Mex. 1991. Assoc. Modrall, Sperling, Roehl, Harris & Sisk, P.A., Albuquerque, 1989—; tchr. jr. high lang. arts and social studies Comty. Christian Sch., Savoy, Ill., 1981-83. Contbr. articles to profl. jours. Primary Sunday sch. tchr. Trinity Ch., Albuquerque, 1993—; bd. dirs. Little Shepherd Child Care, Albuquerque, 1990-93; vol. Men's Winter Emergency Shelter, Champaign, Ill., 1978-84, Mercy Hosp. Hospice Care, Urbana, Ill., 1980-83. Office: Modrall Law Firm 500 4th St NW Ste 700 Albuquerque NM 87102-2183

WALKER, RUBYLEE FRANCE, counselor; b. American Falls, Idaho, Mar. 15, 1942; d. Dan Wesley and Marie (McLean) France; m. Dennis L. Walker, Apr. 1, 1963; 1 child, Randy Alan. BS, Idaho State U., 1965, M Phys. Edn., 1971, M of Counseling, 1993. Cert. edn. counselor, K-12, Idaho. Tchr., coach Snake River High Sch., Blackfoot, Idaho, 1966-70, 71-72, counselor, 1994—; grad. tchg. asst. Idaho State U., Pocatello, 1970-71; tchr., coach Blackfoot High Sch., 1972-89; elem. counselor Blackfoot Dist. 55, 1994—; mem. state phys. edn. com. State Planning com., Boise, 1984, high sch. activities bd. Assn. Bd. for Women's Athletics, Boise, 1981-90; mem. Idaho State U. Counseling Bd., Pocatello, 1993—. 4-H Leaders Blackfoot, Idaho, 1990—. Named Phys. Edn. Educator of Yr., State Phys. Edn. Assn., 1989, Winningest Girls Basketball Coach of Idaho, USA Today, 1985, 86, named to New Agenda Hall of Fame, Idaho, 1989. Mem. Blackfoot Edn. Assn., Idhao Edn. Assn., NEA, Am. Counseling Assn., Idaho Counseling Assn., Delta Kappa Gamma.

WALKER, SALLY C., fundraising executive. BA cum laude with honors, Stetson U., Deland, Fla., 1971; grad., Grantsmanship Ctr. Tng. Program, 1980, Mgmt. Fund Raisers Program, 1987. Devel. dir. Direct Relief Found., Santa Barbara, Calif., 1977-82; prin., cons. Walker & Assocs., Santa Barbara, 1982—; endowment dir. United Way Santa Barbara, 1982—; mem. steering com., del. Nat. Conf. Planned Giving, 1987-88, Nat. Editorial Bur. chief, 1989; faculty mem. Nat. Acad. Voluntarism, Washington. Contbg. editor: The Endowment Builder. Co-founder, pres. Planned Giving Roundtable Santa Barbara County, Calif., 1986-88, v.p., 1984-86. Mem. Nat. Soc. Fund-Raising Execs. (chair endowment com. 1989-90), Santa Barbara Audubon Soc. (bd. dirs. 1989—, pres. 1992-93, v.p. 1993—). Office: 1423 W Valerio St Santa Barbara CA 93101-4954

WALKER, SALLY WARDEN, state legislator; b. Wilmette, Ill., Feb. 5, 1929; d. Sydney C. and Florence (Collins) Warden; m. O.B. Walker, Dec. 28, 1948; children: Richard, Christine, Nancy, Catherine, Sara. Student, William Jewell Coll., 1947-48. Commr., chmn. Univ. Pl. Parks and Recreation Bd., Tacoma, 1979-85; mem. Wash. Ho. of Reps., 1985—, environ. affairs, edn., and commerce and labor coms., transp. com. Formerly vol. dir. Pierce County Rep. Party, del. Pierce County Conv., precint committeewoman 28th dist., 1978—; past bd. dirs. Town Hall Lecture Series; former dir. Christian Edn., mem. vestry St. Mary's Episc. Ch. Recipient Woman of Community award Inter-Chpt. Council Am. Bus. Women's Assn., 1986, Achievement award Puget Sound Inter-Chpt., Golden Acorn award PTA. Mem. Tacoma/Pierce County C. of C., Lakewood C. of C., LWV. Clubs: 28th Dist. Rep., Lakewood Rep. Women's. Home: 4617 Bellview St W Tacoma WA 98466-1013 Office: Office County Coun County-City Bldg Rm 1046 930 Tacoma Ave S Tacoma WA 98402-2102

WALKER, THEODORE DELBERT, landscape architect; b. Tremonton, Utah, Feb. 17, 1933; s. Delbert Stevenson and Geneve (Cutler) W.; m. Doris Jenkins, June 1, 1957; children: Steven, Alan, Dahn, Jayne. BS, Utah State U., 1957; M Landscape Architecture, U. Ill., 1967. Registered landscape architect, Ariz. Assoc. landscape architect Office of Leon Frehner, Salt Lake City, 1957-60; site planner Brigham Young U., Provo, Utah, 1960-66; prof. Purdue U., West Lafayette, Ind., 1967-82; pres. Walker Harris Assocs. Inc., West Lafayette and Mesa, Ariz., 1973-84, PDA Pubs. Corp., West Lafayette, Ind. and Mesa, Ariz., 1971-88; adj. prof. Ariz. State U., Tempe, 1985—;

pres. The Walker Design Group, Mesa, 1988—; cons. Browning Day Mullins Dierdorf, Indpls., 1969—, Van Nostrand Reinhold, N.Y.C., 1988—. Author 9 books including Plan Graphics, 3d edit., 1985, Site Design and Construction Detailing, 3d edit., 1991, Perspective Sketches, 5th edit., 1989, Plan Graphics, 4th edit., 1990. Mem. Design Rev. Advisory Bd., City of Mesa, Ariz., 1986-88. Recipient cert. of special recognition for contbns. to landscape archtl. edn. Coun. Educators in Landscape Architecture, 1980. Fellow Am. Soc. Landscape Architects (trustee 1972-80). Mem. LDS Ch. Office: Arizona State U Dept Planning Tempe AZ 85287

WALKER, VAUGHN R., federal judge; b. Watseka, Ill., Feb. 27, 1944; s. Vaughn Rosenworth and Catharine (Miles) W. AB, U. Mich., 1966; JD, Stanford U., 1970. Intern economist SEC, Washington, 1966, 68; law clk. to the Hon. Robert J. Kelleher U.S. Dist. Ct. Calif., L.A., 1971-72; assoc. atty. Pillsbury Madison & Sutro, San Francisco, 1972-77, ptnr., 1978-90; judge U.S. Dist. Ct. (no. dist.) Calif., San Francisco, 1990—; mem. Calif. Law Revision Commn., Palo Alto, 1986-89. Dir. Jr. Achievement of Bay Area, San Francisco, 1979-83, St. Francis Found., San Francisco, 1991—. Woodrow Wilson Found. fellow U. Calif., Berkeley, 1966-67. Fellow Am. Bar Found.; mem. ABA (jud. rep., antitrust sect. 1991—), Lawyers' Club (pres. 1985-86), Am. Law Inst., Am. Saddlebred Horse Assn., San Francisco Mus. Modern Art, Bokemian Club. Office: US Dist Ct 16700 Valley View Ave Ste 300 La Mirada CA 90638-5841

WALKER, WALTER HERBERT, III, lawyer, writer; b. Quincy, Mass., Sept. 12, 1949; s. Walter H. Jr. and Irene M. (Horn) W.; m. Anne M. DiScuillo, June 17, 1982; children: Brett Daniel, Jeffrey St. John. BA, U. Pa., 1971; JD, U. Calif., San Francisco, 1974. Bar: Calif. 1974, Mass. 1981. Appellate atty. ICC, Washington, 1975-77; trial atty. Handler, Baker, Greene & Taylor, San Francisco, 1977-80; ptnr. Sterns and Walker and predecessor firm Sterns, Smith, Walker & Grell, San Francisco, 1981-88; ptnr. firm Walker & Durham, San Francisco, 1988—. Author: A Dime to Dance By, 1983 (Best 1st Novel by Calif. Author), The Two Dude Defense, 1985, Rules of The Knife Fight, 1986, The Immediate Prospect of Being Hanged, 1989, The Appearance of Impropriety, 1992. Mem. Assn. Trial Lawyers Am., Calif. Trial Lawyers Assn., San Francisco Trial Lawyers Assn., Mystery Writers Am. Democrat. Club: Hastings Rugby. Home: 211 Meda Ln Mill Valley CA 94941-4907 Office: 50 Francisco St Ste 160 San Francisco CA 94133-2108

WALKUP, HUGH ROBERT, education adminstrator; b. Harlingen, Tex., Nov. 9, 1943; s. Robert Hugh and Berniece Janet (Neurenschwader) W. BA magna cum laude, Harvard U., 1965; MEd, U. Wash., 1975, PhD, 1986. Dir. Summerhill Secondary, Seattle, 1969-73; head resident U. Wash., Seattle, 1973-76; rschr. Seattle Sch. Dist., 1976-78; dir. Seattle Vets. Action Ctr., 1978-82, Adminstrn. Human Resources, Seattle, 1982-86; mgr. data analysis Social and Health Svcs., Olympia, Wash., 1986-88; assoc. dir. Higher Edn. Coordinating Bd., Olympia, 1988-94; dir. Washington Goals Zooo, Olympia, 1994—. 1st lt. U.S. Army, 1966-68, Vietnam. Office: Goals Zooo/OSPI MS-47200 Old Capitol Bldg Olympia WA 98504-7200

WALKUP, KATHLEEN ANN, English language educator; b. Portland, Calif., Apr. 10, 1946; d. Lowell Edward and Dorothy Olive (Tyrrell) W.; m. Walter L. Martin, Dec. 15, 1978; children: Owen Lowell, Nora Lennox, Clare Elizabeth. BA, Temple U, 1967. Founder, ptnr. Hovey Street Press, Cambridge, Mass., 1971-72; prodn. coord. Jupiter Thermographers, San Francisco, 1972-76; founder, ptnr. Five Trees Press, Printers and Pubs., San Francisco, 1973-79, Peartree Printers, Commissioned Printers, San Francisco, 1976-79; lectr. Mills Coll., Oakland, Calif., 1978-83, program coord. grad. book arts, 1983-89, asst. prof. in English, 1993—; founder, owner Matrix Press, Printer and Pub., Palo Alto, Calif., 1979—; vis. asst. prof. in fine arts and letters, Mills Coll., 1983-93; vis. lectr. Calif. Coll. of Arts and Crafts, Oakland, 1978-79. Book/presses exhibits include Bay Area Bookmaking: Art and Craft Tradition, Oakland, 1991, Eighty from the Eighties, N.Y. Pub. Libr., 1990-91, The Arts of the Book, The Univ. of the Arts, Phila., 1988, Forwarding the Book in Calif., Victoria and Albert Mus., London, 1988, Literate Letterpress, Ctr. for Book Arts, N.Y., 1987, Oxford Polytechnic, eng., 1986, numerous others; curator and cons. numerous book arts exhbns.; contbr. to profl. jours. and publs. Adv. coun. Menlo-Atherton Sch. dist., 1992—; pres. site coun., Menlo Park Pub. Sch. Dist., 1992-93; bd. dirs. Friends of the Palo Alto Children's Theatre, 1992-93; trustee Keys Sch., Palo Alto, 1987-89; vol. Ecumenical Hunger Program, East Palo Alto. Recipient fellowship Ctr. for Book at the Brit. Libr., 1993, faculty devel. grant Mills Coll., 1987, 90, 91, 93, Book design award Bookbuilders West, San Francisco, 1984, award of merit for book design Western Books, L.A., 1984, others. Mem. Pacific Ctr. for the Book Arts (founding dir.), Roxburghe Club (San Francisco), Am. Printing History Assn., Ctr. for Book Arts/N.Y. Office: Mills Coll 5000 Macarthur Blvd Oakland CA 94613-1301

WALL, BRIAN RAYMOND, forest economist, policy analyst, business consultant, telemarketing sales, researcher; b. Tacoma, Wash., Jan. 26, 1940; s. Raymond Perry and Mildred Beryl (Pickert) W.; m. Joan Marie Nero, Sept. 1, 1962 (div. Aug. 1990) children: Torden Erik, Kirsten Noel. BS, U. Wash., 1962; MF, Yale U., 1964. Forestry asst. Weyerhaeuser Timber Co., Klamath Falls, Oreg., 1960; inventory forester West Tacoma Newsprint, 1961-62; timber sale compliance forester Dept. Nat. Resources, Kelso, Wash., 1963; rsch. forest economist Pacific N.W. Rsch. Sta., USDA Forest Svc., Portland, Oreg., 1964-88, cons. 1989—; co-founder, bd. dirs. Cordero Youth Care Ctr., 1970-81; owner Brian R. Wall Images and Communications, Sage Mentors Bus. Cons.; owner Sage Mentors Consultancy; cons. to govt. agys., Congress univs., industry, small bus.; freelance photographer. Co-author: An Analysis of the Timber Situation in the United States, 1982; contbr. articles, reports to profl. publs., newspapers. Interviewed and cited by nat. and regional news media. Recipient Cert. of Merit U.S. Dept. Agr. Forest Service, 1982. Mem. Soc. Am. Foresters (chmn. Portland chpt. 1973, Forester of Yr. 1975), Conf. of Western Forest Economists Inc. (founder, bd. dirs. 1988-91, treas. 1982-87), Portland Photographic Forum, Common Cause, Oregon Economists Assn., Nat. Audubon Soc., Zeta Psi. Home and Office: Sage Mentors Consultancy 16810 S Creekside Ct Oregon City OR 97045-9206

WALL, DAVID ELLIOTT, substance abuse specialist; b. Evanston, Wyo., Aug. 27, 1965; s. Max Melvin and Wilma Ann (Slover) W.; m. Barbara Joy Webster, Sept. 30, 1964; children: David Lewis, Alexandria Elizabeth. BS, U. Utah, 1987. Sales mgr. Tinder Box, Inc., Salt Lake City, 1985-88; sr. rsch. tech. Gull Lab., Inc., Salt Lake City, 1988-92; from chemist to confirmation analyst ARUP, Salt Lake City, 1992—; lab. tech. Bioremediation Tech., Inc., Salt Lake City, 1991; instr. biology Salt Lake C.C., 1991-92. Mem. AAAS, Associated Regional and Univ. Pathologists, Masons, Shriners, Scottish Rite. Republican. Presbyterian. Home: 4353 Larson Way Salt Lake City UT 84124-2717

WALL, FRED WILLARD, agricultural products supplier; b. 1923. With Porterville (Calif.) Drug Co., 1946-49; with Walco Internat. Inc., 1950—, now pres., chmn. bd., CEO. With USN, 1946. Office: Walco Internat Inc 15 W Putnam Ave Fl 2 Porterville CA 93257-3627

WALL, JANET E., assessment and testing professional; b. Chgo., Dec. 15, 1946; d. Al Evans and Josephine (Evinskas) Simpson; m. Robert G. Gard Jr., July 26, 1984. BS, No. Ill. U., 1968; MEd, Tex. A & M U., 1970; EdS, U. Ga., 1973; EdD, Nova U., 1979. State specialist testing and evaluation Del. Dept. Pub. Instrn., Dover, 1975-79; coord. rsch. and evaluation Dept of Defense Dependents Schs., Alexandria, Va., 1979-81; dir. rsch. adminstrn. Naval Postgrad. Sch., Monterey, Calif., 1981-84; vis. prof. Johns Hopkins U., Sch. Adv. Internat. Studies, Bologna, Italy, 1984-87; dep. div. dir. Sci. Applications Internat. Corp., Monterey, 1987-89; mgr. Dept. of Defense student testing program Def. Manpower Data Ctr., Monterey, 1989—. Developer: (assessment program) Delaware Objective Referenced Testing Program, 1979, (career guidance program) Armed Svcs. Vocat. Aptitude Battery Career Exploration Program, 1992, ASVAB Career Exploration System, 1995, The Interest Finder, 1995. Mem. ACA, Assn. for Assessment in Counseling (com. chair), Nat. Career Devel. Assn., Sch. Sci. and Math. (officer), Armed Svcs. Voc. Aptitude Battery Career Exploration System, Phi Delta Kappa (officer). Home: 3053 Forest Way Pebble Beach CA 93953-2904 Office: Def Manpower Data Ctr DOD Ctr Monterey Bay 400 Gigline Rd Seaside CA 93955-6771

WALL, LLOYD L., geological engineer; b. Jerome, Idaho, Feb. 2, 1936; s. Lloyd and Ola (Buck) W.; m. Myrna Bradshaw, Aug. 25, 1954; children: Jeffrey B., Julie, Neil S., Charlene, Gail, Matthew W., Suzzane, Michael L., Connie. AS in Chemistry, Coll. Eastern Utah, 1956; BS in Geology, Brigham Young U., 1958. Pres., owner Cons. Geologist, Salt Lake City and Brigham City, 1958—; plant mgr. Thiokol, Brigham City, Utah, 1958-66; mgr. ops. Sealcraft, Salt Lake City, 1966-68; mgr. programs Eaton-Kenway, Bountiful, Utah, 1968-76; pres., owner HydraPak, Inc., Salt Lake City, 1976-86; pres. Kolt Mining Co., Salt Lake City, 1979—; owner Lloyd L. Wall & Assocs., Salt Lake City, 1986—. Author: Seal Technology, 1993; developer largest rocket motor vacuum casting system in free world, only high pressure water reclamation system for solid propellant rocket motors in free world, only acceptable seal mfg. process for NASA Space Shuttle rocket motor. Vol. tchr. Alta Acad., Salt Lake City, 1983—. Served as sgt. N.G., 1954-62. Mem. Geol. Soc. Am., Utah Geol. Assn. Republican. Mormon. Home: 2180 Claybourne Ave Salt Lake City UT 84109-1727

WALL, SONJA ELOISE, nurse, administrator; b. Santa Cruz, Calif., Mar. 28, 1938; d. Ray Theothornton and Reva Mattie (Wingo) W.; m. Edward Gleason Holmes, Aug. 1959 (div. Jan. 1968); children: Deborah Lynn, Lance Edward; m. John Aspesi, Sept. 1969 (div. 1977); children: Sabrina Jean, Daniel John; m. Kenneth Talbot LaBoube, Nov. 1, 1978 (div. 1989); 1 child, Tiffany Amber. BA, San Jose Jr. Coll., 1959; BS, Madonna Coll., 1967; student, U. Mich., 1968-70; postgrad., Wayne State U. RN, Calif., Mich., Colo. Staff nurse Santa Clara Valley Med. Ctr., San Jose, Calif., 1959-67, U. Mich. Hosp., Ann Arbor, 1967-73, Porter and Swedish Med. Hosp., Denver, 1973-77, Laurel Grove Hosp., Castro Valley, Calif., 1977-79, Advent Hosp., Ukiah, Calif., 1984-86; motel owner LaBoube Enterprises, Fairfield, Point Arena, Willits, Calif., 1979—; staff nurse Northridge Hosp., L.A., 1986-87, Folsom State Prison, Calif., 1987; co-owner, mgr. nursing registry Around the Clock Nursing Svc., Ukiah, 1985—; critical care staff nurse Kaiser Permanente Hosp., Sacramento, 1986-89; nurse Snowline Hospice, Sacramento, 1989-92; carepoint home care and travel nurse Hosp. Staffing Svcs. Inc., Placerville, Calif., 1992-94, interim home health nurse, 1994-95; owner Sunshire Manor Resdl. Care Home, Placerville, Calif., 1995—; owner Royal Plantation Petites Miniature Horse Farm. Contbr. articles to various publs. Leader Coloma 4-H, 1987-91; mem. mounted divsn. El Dorado County Search and Rescue, 1991-93; docent Calif. Marshall Gold Discovery State Hist. Park, Coloma, Calif. Mem. AACN, NAFE, Soc. Critical Care Medicine, Am. Heart Assn. (CPR trainer, recipient awards), Calif. Bd. RNs, Calif. Nursing Rev., Calif. Critical Care Nurses, Soc. Critical Care Nurses, Am. Motel Assn. (beautification and remodeling award 1985), Nat. Hospice Nurses Assn., Soroptimist Internat. Calif., Am. Miniature Horse Assn. (winner nat. grand championship 1981-82, 83, 85, 89), DAR (Jobs Daus. hon. mem.), Cameron Park Country Club. Republican. Episcopalian. Home and Office: Around the Clock Nursing Svc PO Box 559 Coloma CA 95613-0559

WALL, WILLIAM E., lawyer, former utility executive; b. 1928. BS, U. Wash., 1951, LLB, 1954. Asst. atty. gen. State of Wash., 1956-59; chief examiner Pub. Svc. Commn., 1959; sec., house counsel Cascade Natural Gas Corp., 1959-64; pres. United Cities Gas Co., 1964-65; exec. v.p. Cascade Natural Gas Corp., 1965-67; spl. asst. to chmn. bd. Consol. Edison Co., N.Y.C., 1967-68, v.p., 1968-70, sr. v.p. gas ops., 1970-71, exec. v.p. div. ops., 1971-73; gen. mgr. pub. affairs Standard Oil Co., 1973-74; exec. v.p. Kans. Power and Light Co., Topeka, 1974-75, pres., 1975-85, chief exec. officer, 1976-88, chmn., 1979-88; of counsel Siderius, Lonergan & Crowley, Seattle, 1988—. Served with AUS, 1954-56. Office: Siderius Lonergan & Crowley 847 Logan Bldg Seattle WA 98101*

WALLACE, ELAINE WENDY, lawyer; b. Worcester, Mass., Feb. 16, 1949; d. Louis S. and Ida (Zeiper) W. BA, Yeshiva U., 1971; JD, John F. Kennedy Sch. Law, 1976. Sole practice Oakland, Calif. Home: 2430 Palmetto St # 1 Oakland CA 94602-2923 Office: 2430 Palmetto St # 2 Oakland CA 94602-2923

WALLACE, HELEN MARGARET, physician, educator; b. Hoosick Falls, N.Y., Feb. 18, 1913; d. Jonas and Ray (Schweizer) W. AB, Wellesley Coll., 1933; MD, Columbia U., 1937; MPH cum laude, Harvard U., 1943. Diplomate Am. Bd. Pediatrics, Am. Bd. Preventive Medicine. Intern Bellevue Hosp., N.Y.C., 1938-40; child hygiene physician Conn. Health Dept., 1941-42; successively jr. health officer, health officer, chief maternity and new born div., dir. bur. for handicapped children N.Y.C. Health Dept., 1943-55; prof., dir. dept. pub. health N.Y. Med. Coll., 1955-56; prof. maternal and child health U. Minn. Sch. Pub. Health, 1956-59; chief prof. tng. U.S. Children's Bur., 1959-60, chief child health studies, 1961-62; prof. maternal and child health U. Calif. Sch. Pub. Health, Berkeley, 1962-80; prof., head divsn. maternal and child health Sch. Pub. Health San Diego State U., 1980—; Univ. Research lectr. San Diego State U., 1985—; cons. WHO numerous locations, including Uganda, The Philippines, Turkey, India, Geneva, Iran, Burma, Sri Lanka, East Africa, Australia, Indonesia, China, Taiwan, 1961—, traveling fellow, 1989—; cons. Hahnemann U., Phila., 1993, Ford Found., Colombia, 1971; UN cons. to Health Bur., Beijing, China, 1987; fellow Aiiku Inst. on Maternal and Child Health, Tokyo, and NIH Inst. Child Health and Human Devel., 1994; dir. Family Planning Project, Zimbabwe, 1984-87. Author, editor 10 textbooks; contbr. 325 articles to profl. jours. Mem. coun. on Disabled Children to Media, 1991; dir. San Diego County Infant Mortality Study, 1989—, San Diego Study of Prenatal Care, 1991. Recipient Alumnae Achievement award Wellesley Coll., 1982, U. Minn. award, 1985; Ford Found. study grantee, 1986, 87, 88; fellow World Rehab. Fund, India, 1991-92, Fulbright Found., 1992—, NIH Inst. Child Health and Human Devel., 1994, Aiiku Inst. of Maternal-Child Health, Tokyo, 1994. Fellow APHA (officer sect., Martha May Eliot award 1978), Am. Acad. Pediatrics (Job Smith award 1980, award 1989); mem. AMA, Assn. Tchrs. Maternal and Child Health, Am. Acad. Cerebral Palsy, Ambulatory Pediatric Assn., Am. Sch. Preventive Medicine. Home: 850 State St San Diego CA 92101-6046

WALLACE, J. CLIFFORD, federal judge; b. San Diego, Dec. 11, 1928; s. John Franklin and Lillie Isabel (Overing) W.; m. Virginia Lee Schlosser, Apr. 8, 1957; children: Paige, Laurie, Teri, John. B.A., San Diego State U., 1952; LL.B., U. Calif., Berkeley, 1955. Bar: Calif. 1955. With firm Gray, Cary, Ames & Frye, San Diego, 1955-70; judge U.S. Dist. Ct. (so. dist.) Calif., 1970-72; judge U.S. Ct. Appeals (9th cir.), 1972-91, chief judge, 1991—. Contbr. articles to profl. jours. Served with USN, 1946-49. Mem. Am. Bd. Trial Advocates, Inst. Jud. Adminstrn. Mem. LDS Ch. (stake pres. San Diego East 1962-67, regional rep. 1967-74, 77-79). Office: US Ct Appeals 9th Cir 940 Front St Ste 4192 San Diego CA 92101-8918

WALLACE, JEANNETTE OWENS, state legislator; b. Scottsdale, Ariz., Jan. 16, 1934; d. Albert and Velma (Whinery) Owens; m. Terry Charles Wallace Sr., May 21, 1955; children: Terry C. Jr., Randall J., Timothy A., Sheryl L., Janice M. BS, Ariz. State U., 1955. Mem. Los Alamos (N.Mex.) County Coun., 1981-82; cons. County of Los Alamos, 1983-84; chmn., vice chmn. Los Alamos County Coun., 1985-88; cons. County of Los Alamos, Los Alamos Schs., 1989-90; rep. N.Mex. State Legislature, 1991—; mem. appropriations & fin. govt. and urban affairs, N.Mex., 1991—, legis. fin. com., Indian affairs; co-chmn. Los Alamos County's Dept. Energy Negotiating Com., 1987-88; mem. legis. policy com. Mcpl. League, N.Mex., 1986-88. Bd. dirs. Tri-Area Econ. Devel., Pojoaque, N.Mex., 1987-92, Los Alamos Econ. Devel., 1988-94, Crime Stoppers, Los Alamos, 1988-92, Los Alamos Citizens Against Substance Abuse, 1989-94; mem. N.Mex. First, Albuquerque, 1989-93; legis. chmn. LWV, 1990; mem. Los Alamos Rep. Women, pres., 1989-90. Mem. Los Alamos Bus. & Profl. Women (legis. chmn. 1990), Los Alamos C. of C., Mana del Norte, Kiwanis. Methodist. Home: 146 Monte Rey Dr S Los Alamos NM 87544-3826

WALLACE, JOHN BARRY, lawyer; b. N.Y.C., June 14, 1954; s. Bert H. and Carol (Lomnitz) W. BA, SUNY, Stony Brook, 1975; JD, U. So. Calif., 1980. Bar: Calif. 1980, U.S. Dist. Ct. (ctrl. dist.) Calif. 1980, U.S. Ct. Appeal (9th cir.) 1985. Assoc. Egerman, Brown & Rosen, Beverly Hills, Calif., 1980-81, Mazlrow, Forer, Lawrence, Cunningham & Giden, Inc., Century City, Calif., 1981-82, Bronson, Bronson & McKinnon, L.A., 1983-85, Kircher & Nakazato, L.A., 1985-86, Contos & Bunch, Woodland Hills, Calif., 1986-91, Matthew B.F. Biren & Assocs., L.A., 1991-92; pvt. practice Agoura Hills, Calif., 1992—. Author: Attorney's Calendar Reference, 1982-83; contbr. articles to law rev. Mock trial coach Constnl. Rights Found., 1991—; vol., fundraiser L.A. Bar Assn. Lawyer Referral Svc. Mem. Sierra Club (life).

WALLACE, KENNETH ALAN, investor; b. Gallup, N.Mex., Feb. 23, 1938; s. Charles Garrett and Elizabeth Eleanor (Jones) W. A.B. in Philosophy, Cornell U., 1960; postgrad. U. N.Mex., 1960-61; m. Rebecca Marie Odell, July 11, 1980; children: Andrew McMillan, Aaron Blue, Susanna Garrett, Megan Elizabeth, Glen Eric. Comml. loan officer Bank of N.Mex., Albuquerque, 1961-64; asst. cashier Ariz. Bank, Phoenix, 1964-67; comml. loan officer Valley Nat. Bank, Phoenix, 1967-70; pres. WWW, Inc., Houston, 1970-72; v.p. fin. Hometels of Am., Phoenix, 1972-77, Precision Mech. Co., Inc., 1972-77; ptnr. Schroeder-Wallace, 1977-93; chmn. Shalako Corp., Phoenix; mng. ptnr., pres. Blackhawk, Inc., Phoenix, 1977—, also, bd. dirs.; pres., chmn. bd. AlphaSat Corp., Phoenix, 1990—; pres. chmn. bd. dirs. AlphaVision, Inc., Las Vegas; gen. ptnr. Wallco Enterprises, Ltd., Mobile, Ala.; mng. gen. ptnr. The Village at University Heights, Flagstaff. Loaned exec. Phoenix United Way, 1966, Tucson United Way, 1967; mem. Valley Big Bros., 1970—; bd. dirs. Phoenix Big Sisters, 1985-87; mem. Alhambra Village Planning Com.; fin. dir. Ret. Sr. Vol. Program, 1973-76; mem. Phoenix Men's Arts Coun., 1968—, dir., 1974-75; mem. Phoenix Symphony Coun. Campaign committeeman Rep. gubernatorial race, N.Mex., 1964; treas. Phoenix Young Reps., 1966; bd. dirs. Devel. Authority for Tucson, 1967. Mem. Soaring Soc. Am. (Silver badge), Am. Rifle Assn. (life), Nat. Mktg. Assn. (Mktg. Performance of Year award 1966), Nat. Assn. Skin Diving Schs., Pima County Jr. C. of C. (bd. dir. 1967), Phoenix Little Theatre, Phoenix Musical Theatre, S.W. Ensemble Theatre (bd. dir.), Wheelmen of Am., Masons, Shriners, Kona Kai Club (San Diego), Paradise Valley Country Club, Alpha Tau Omega. Office: The Wallace Group of Cos PO Box 7703 Phoenix AZ 85011-7703

WALLACE, MARK RAYMOND, physician; b. Seattle, Feb. 22, 1955; s. George Warren and Grace Joann (Balch) W.; m. Kathleen Cornell, Jan. 19, 1985; 1 child, Luke Randall. BA in Chemistry, Whitman Coll., Walla Walla, Wash., 1977; MD, St. Louis U., 1981. Diplomate Am. Bd. Internal Medicine, sub-bd. Infectious Diseases. Intern Med. Ctr. Hosp. of Vt., Burlington, 1981-82; resident U. Wash., Seattle, 1982-84; staff physician Naval Hosp., Long Beach, Calif., 1984-85, head internal medicine dept., 1986-87; fellow in infectious diseases Naval Hosp., San Diego, 1987-89, staff physician, 1989-90, head HIV unit, 1990-93, dir. infectious disease fellowship, 1993—. Author/co-author 75 jour. articles and 50 abstracts. Served to comdr. USN, 1984—. Decorated Navy Commendation medal, Meritorious Svc. medal; Nat. Merit scholar, 1973. Fellow ACP, Infectious Disease Soc. Am.; mem. AMA, Am. Soc. Microbiology, Physicians Assn. for AIDS Care, Phi Beta Kappa, Alpha Omega Alpha. Office: Naval Med Ctr San Diego CA 92134

WALLACE, MATTHEW WALKER, entrepreneur; b. Salt Lake City, Jan. 7, 1924; s. John McChrystal and Glenn (Walker) W.; m. Constance Cone, June 22, 1954 (dec. May 1980); children—Matthew, Anne; m. Susan Struggles, July 11, 1981. B.A., Stanford U., 1947; M.C.P., MIT, 1950. Prin. planner Boston City Planning Bd., 1950-53; v.p. Nat. Planning and Research, Inc., Boston, 1953-55; pres. Wallace-McConaughy Corp., Salt Lake City, 1955-69; pres. Ariz. Ranch & Metals Co., Salt Lake City, 1969-84; chmn. Wallace Assocs., Inc., Salt Lake City, 1969—; dir. 1st Interstate Bank, Salt Lake City, 1956—, dir. Arnold Machinery Co., 1988—, dir. Roosevelt Hot Springs Corp., 1978—; mem. adv. bd. Mountain Bell Telephone Co., Salt Lake City, 1975-85. Pres., Downtown Planning Assn., Salt Lake City, 1970; chmn. Utah State Arts Coun., Salt Lake City, 1977; mem. Humanities and Scis. Coun., Stanford U., also mem. athletic bd., bd. vis. sch. law; mem. nat. adv. bd. Coll. Bus., U. Utah; lifetime dir. Utah Symphony Orch.; chmn. arts adv. coun. Westminster Coll. Lt. (j.g.) USN, 1944-46; PTO. Recipient Contbn. award Downtown Planning Assn., 1977, Govs. Award in the Arts, 1991, Utah Nat. Guard Minuteman award, 1994. Mem. Am. Inst. Cert. Planners (charter), Am. Arts Alliance (bd. dirs. 1991), Alta Club (dir.), Cottonwood Club (pres. 1959-63), Salt Lake Country Club (dir.), Flat Rock Club (Island Pk., Idaho pres. 1994-95), Phi Kappa Phi. Home: 2510 Walker Ln Salt Lake City UT 84117-7729 Office: Wallace Assocs Inc 165 S Main St Salt Lake City UT 84111-1918

WALLACE, ROBERT EARL, geologist; b. N.Y.C., July 16, 1916; s. Clarence Earl and Harriet (Wheeler) W.; m. Gertrude Kivela, Mar. 19, 1945; 1 child: Alan R. BS, Northwestern U., 1938; MS, Calif. Inst. Tech., 1940, PhD, 1946. Registered geologist, Calif., engring. geologist, Calif. Geologist U.S. Geol. Survey, various locations, 1942—; regional geologist U.S. Geol. Survey, Menlo Park, Calif., 1970-74; chief scientist Office of Earthquakes, Volcanoes and Engring. U.S. Geol. Survey, Menlo Park, 1974-87, emeritus, 1987—; asst. and assoc. prof. Wash. State Coll., Pullman, 1946-51; mem. adv. panel Nat. Earthquake Prediction Evaluation Coun., 1980-90, Stanford U. Sch. Earth Sci., 1972-82; mem. engring. criteria rev. bd. San Francisco Bay Conservation and Devel. Commn., chmn. 1981-92. Contbr. articles to profl. jours. Recipient Alfred E. Alquist award Calif. Earthquake Safety Found., 1995. Fellow AAAS, Geol. Soc. Am. (chair cordillidan sect. 1967-68), Earthquake Engring. Rsch. Inst., Calif. Acad. Scis. (hon. 1991); mem. Seismol. Soc. Am. (medalist 1989). Office: US Geol Survey MS-977 345 Middlefield Rd Menlo Park CA 94025-3561

WALLACE, TED, wholesale goods distribution executive; b. 1948. BA, Muskingum Coll., 1971. Store mgr. Fazio Foods, 1971-77; warehouse mgr. Price Co., San Diego, 1977-82, sr. warehouse mgr., 1982-83, v.p. ops., 1983-84, exec. v.p. ops., 1984—. Office: Price Co 4649 Morena Blvd San Diego CA 92117-3650

WALLACE, WESLEY KENT, geology educator; b. Staten Island, N.Y., Aug. 30, 1950; s. Sidney Arthur and Jacqueline (Theis) W.; m. Catherine Leigh Hanks, Oct. 8, 1983; children: Theresa Anne, Joanna Verree. BA, Rice U., 1972; MSc, U. Wash., 1976, PhD, 1981. Teaching asst. U. Wash., Seattle, 1973-77; geologist Shannon & Wilson, Seattle, 1978, BP Alaska Exploration, Anchorage, 1979, ARCO Alaska, Inc., Anchorage, 1981-85; asst. prof. U. Alaska, Fairbanks, 1985-91, assoc. prof., 1991-95; prof., 1995—; group leader tectonics and sedimentation rsch. group Geophys. Inst. U. Alaska, Fairbanks, 1991—; collaborative rschr. U.S. Geolog. Survey, Menlo Park, Calif., 1990—, Russian Acad. Scis., Yakutsk, Russia, 1993—. Contbr. articles to profl. jours., chpts. to books. Recipient Fulbright scholarship U. Helsinki, Finland, 1972-73; grantee various petroleum cos., 1986—, NSF, 1993-95. Mem. Geolog. Soc. Am., Alaska Geolog. Soc., Am. Geophys. Union. Office: Univ Alaska Dept Geology & Geophysics Fairbanks AK 99775-5780

WALLACE, WILLIAM ARTHUR, JR., environmental engineering executive; b. N.Y.C., Dec. 6, 1942; s. William Arthur and Helene Marie (Hoene) W.; m. Diane Marie Guillot, July 11, 1964; children: Kathleen Marie, Jane Coventry. BSChemE, Clarkson U., 1964; MS in Mgmt., Rensselaer Poly. Inst., 1971; advanced mgmt. program course, Harvard U., 1989. Chief plans and programs U.S. Naval Ammunition Depot, Hawthorne, Nev., 1973-75; chief hazardous waste enforcement EPA, Washington, 1975-78; chief enforcement br. U.S. Dept. Interior, Washington, 1978-79; v.p. Fred C. Hart Assocs., N.Y.C., 1979-81; engring. exec. mktg. and strategic planning CH2M Hill, Bellevue, Wash., 1981—; testified Overview of Superfund Cleanup Techs. U.S. Ho. Reps., Washington, 1985, Overview of Superfund, 1988, 91, Soil Contaminants: PCB, 1988, U.S. Senate inquirey into environ. tech., 1993. Bd. dirs. Hazardous Waste Action Coalition, 1986—, treas., 1990-91, pres.-elect, 1995—; invited panel mem. Office of Tech. Assesment Nuclear Waste Remediation Workshop, Washington, 1990; mem. sci. adv. com. Western Regional Hazardous Substance Rsch. Ctr. Stanford U., 1989—; mem. panel ad hoc criteria group environ. tech., We. Govs.' Assn., 1993. Recipient George A. Hogaboom award Am. Electroplaters Soc., 1968, Bronze Medal award EPA, 1978, Outstanding Citizenship award Met. Law Enforcement Assn., Denver, 1980. Mem. Planning Forum, Bellevue Athletic Club, Lakes Club. Office: CH2M Hill 6060 S Willow Dr Englewood CO 80111

WALLACH, LESLIE ROTHAUS, architect; b. Pitts., Feb. 4, 1944; s. Albert and Sara F. (Rothaus) W.; m. Susan Rose Berger, June 15, 1969; 1 child, Aaron. BS in Mining Engring., U. Ariz., 1967, BArch, 1974. Registered architect, Ariz.; registered contractor, Ariz. Prin. Line and Space

Tucson, 1978—. Representative projects include Ariz. Sonora Desert Mus. Restaurant Complex, Tucson Ariz., Elgin Elem. Sch., Ariz., Hillel Student Ctr. U. Ariz., Tucson, Boyce Thompson Southwestern Arboretum Vis. Ctr., Superior, Ariz., San Pedro Riparian Ctr., Sierra Vista, Ariz.; contbr. to Sunset Mag., Architecture Mag. and Fine Homebuilding; exhibited at U. Ariz., AIA Nat. Convention, Wash., D.C. Bd. dirs Tucson Regional Plan, Inc. Recipient Roy P. Drachman Design award, 1982, 85, 93, Electric League Ariz. Design award, 1987, 88, Gov. Solar Energy award, 1989, Desert Living awards Citation, 1991, Ariz. Architect's medal, 1989. Fellow AIA (Ariz. Honor award 1989, 92, AIA/ACSA Nat. Design award 1991, Western Mountain region Design award 1992, CA AIA/Phoenix Homes and Gardens Home of the Yr. Honor award 1992); mem. SAC AIA (past pres., Design award 1985, 88, 90). Office: Line and Space 627 E Speedway Blvd Tucson AZ 85705-7433

WALLACH, PAUL, publishing executive, author; b. L.A., May 23, 1925; s. Charles Wallach and Carolyn (Agate) Bak; m. Merle Wallach, Apr. 19, 1945 (div. 1974); children: Stuart Lane, Brad Paul. Student, Calif. State U., Long Beach, 1977. Freelance writer, 1960—; pres., chief exec. officer Wallach Co., Anaheim, Calif., 1960-74, Paul Wallach Inc., Glendale, Calif., 1974—; author Travel Guides Inc., Burbank, Calif., 1971—; columnist Westways mag., L.A., 1972—, Guide Publs., L.A., 1974-90. With USNR, 1942-45, PTO. Knighted Chevalier L' Odre des Coteaux de Champagune Govt. France, 1988; named Conferie de Vignorons da St Vincent, 1988, Man of Yr., Pub. Rels. Inst., 1970; recipient Lifetime Achievement award City of Hope, Commendation City of L.A., 1984, County of L.A., 1985. Home: 712 E Angeleno Ave Burbank CA 91501-2213

WALLER, EDMUND KEMP, oncologist, researcher, educator; b. Chgo., July 12, 1957; s. Frederick O. and Nancy (Ames) W.; m. Chiara Stella, Jan. 17, 1983; children: Anthony F., Alessia V., Giacomo C. AB, Harvard U., 1978; PhD, Rockefeller U., 1984; MD, Cornell U., 1985. Diplomate internal medicine and med. oncology. Med. resident Stanford (Calif.) U., 1985-88, oncology fellow, 1988-91, pathology rsch. fellow, 1990-93, clin. asst. prof., 1993—; attending physician Palo Alto (Calif.) Vets. Hosp., 1993—; sr. rsch. fellow Becton Dickinson, San Jose, Calif., 1993—; cons. in fibrinolysis Monsanto Co., St. Louis, 1984-86; cons. in immunology Palo Alto (Calif.) Vets. Hosp., 1990-91. Contbr. articles to profl. jours. McDonnell Found. scholar McDonnell Found., St. Louis, 1990-93; grantee NIH, Bethesda, Md., 1993—. Mem. ACP. Democrat. Unitarian. Home: 890 Los Angeles Ave NE Atlanta GA 30306-3602 Office: Becton Dickinson 2350 Qume Dr San Jose CA 95131-1812

WALLER, JOHN JAMES, lawyer; b. Red Cloud, Nebr., May 14, 1924; s. James Emery and Gail Fern (Perry) W.; m. Norma Louise Kunz, June 19, 1949; children: Diane Leslie, John James Jr, William Scott. Student, Rhode Island State Coll., Kingston, 1943-44, Biarritz Am. U., France, 1945-46; BA magna cum laude, Harvard U., 1947, JD, 1950. Bar: Calif. 1951, U.S. Dist. (cen. dist.), 1951, U.S. Ct. Appeals (9th cir.) 1959, U.S. Tax Ct. 1959, U.S. Supreme Ct. 1976. Assoc. Gibson, Dunn & Crutcher, L.A., 1950-62; ptnr. Flint & MacKay, L.A., 1962-67; with Law Offices of Max Fink, Beverly Hills, Calif., 1968-73; pvt. practice Santa Ana, Tustin, Calif., 1973-83, Buena Park, Calif., 1984—; spl. counsel Fluor Corp., Irvine, Calif., 1983-84; judge pro-tem Orange County (Calif.) Superior Ct., 1992—. Chmn. unification com. Buena Park Sch. Dist., 1969-70; pres., sec., dir. Bellehurst Comty. Assn., 1970; chmn., mem. City of Buena Park Airport Commn., 1969-74, City Buena Park Transp. Com., 1975-77; dist. vice chmn. Boy Scouts Am., 1970-72. Sgt. U.S. Army, 1943-46, ETO. Recipient Merit award Boy Scouts Am.. Mem. ABA, State Bar Calif., L.A. County Bar Assn., Orange County Bar Assn. (del. 1984), Am. Judicature Soc., Banyard Am. Inn of Ct. Democrat. Office: 5591 Monticello Ave Buena Park CA 90621-1543

WALLER, KIRSTEN ORLETTE, epidemiologist; b. Mpls., Dec. 1, 1958; m. Kai John Hagen. BA, St. Olaf Coll., 1980; MD, U. Minn., 1985, MPH, 1988. Diplomate Am. Bd. Preventive Medicine. Epidemic intelligence svc. officer Ctrs. Disease Control, Atlanta, 1988-90; pub. health med. officer Calif. Dept. Health Svcs., Berkeley, 1990—. Lt. commdr. USPHS, 1988-90. Home: 7450 Terrace Dr El Cerrito CA 94530 Office: Environ Health Invest Annex 11 Fl 5 2151 Berkeley Way Berkeley CA 94702-1011

WALLER, LARRY GENE, mortgage banking executive; b. Corpus Christi, Tex., Nov. 18, 1948; s. Paul Hobson and Marie (Armellini) W.; m. Mary Sandra Cupp, Dec. 27, 1969 (div. 1987); children: Stacey Ann, Jaime Lynn; m. Sharon Elizabeth Falls, Jan. 28, 1988; 1 child, Lisa Suzanne Cantello. AA, Bakersfield Jr. Coll., 1970. Lic. real estate broker, Calif. Asst. v.p. Bank of Am., Stockton, Calif., 1970-78, Wells Fargo Mortgage Co., Sacramento, 1978-81; regional v.p. Weyerhaeuser Mortgage Co., Sacramento, 1981-89; sr. v.p. Koll Realty Advisors, Sacramento, 1989-91; pres. L. G. Waller Co., 1991-93; pres., CFO Waller, Kaufman & Sutter of Nev., Sacramento, 1991—; pres., chief fin. officer Waller, Kaufman & Sutter of Nev., Reno, 1995—. Mem. Nat. Assn. Indsl. and Office Parks (bd. dirs. Sacramento chpt.), Mortgage Bankers Assn. (income property com.), Calif. Mortgage Bankers Assn. Home: 2134 Campton Cir Gold River CA 95670-8306 Office: 2277 Fair Oaks Blvd Ste 400 Sacramento CA 95825-5533

WALLER, PETER WILLIAM, public affairs executive; b. Kewanee, Ill., Oct. 1, 1926; s. Ellis Julian and Barodel (Gould) W.; m. Anne-Marie Appelius van Hoboken, Nov. 10, 1950; children: Catherine, Hans. BA with hons., Princeton U., 1949; MA with hons., San Jose State U., 1978. Bur. chief Fairchild Publs., San Francisco, 1953-55; freelance writer Mountain View, Calif., 1956-57; pub. relations coord. Lockheed Missiles and Space, Sunnyvale, Calif., 1957-64; Pioneer info. mgr. for 1st mission to Jupiter, Saturn and NASA Ames Rsch. Ctr., Mountain View, 1964-83, mgr. pub. info., 1983-95; ret., 1995; speechwriter for pres. Lockheed Missiles and Space, 1960-64. Producer (documentary) Jupiter Odyssey, 1974 (Golden Eagle, 1974); producer, writer NASA Aero. program, 1984; contbr. articles to profl. jours, encyclopedias. Cons. on preservation of Lake Tahoe, Calif. Resources Agy., Sacramento, 1984. Mem. No. Calif. Sci. Writers Assn., Sierra Club. Democrat. Congregationalist. Home: 3655 La Calle Ct Palo Alto CA 94306-2619 Office: NASA Ames Rsch Ctr Moffett Field CA 94035

WALLER, ROBERT CARL, chiropractor; b. Chgo., Aug. 1, 1931; s. Morton Sam and Linea Matilda (Anderson) W.; children by previous marriage—Wendy, Jeff. B.S., U. Ill., 1957; D.Chiropractic, Los Angeles Coll. Chiropractic, 1979; postgrad. UCLA, 1968-74. Staff pharmacist Savon Drugs, Granada Hills, Calif., 1968-70; mgr. pharmacy Hy-Lo Drug Co., Sepulveda, Calif., 1970-79; practice chiropractic medicine, Santa Monica, Calif., 1980-89, Culver City, 1989-93, Westlake Village, 1993—. With USNR, 1949-50. Mem. Am. Pharm. Assn., Am. Chiropractic Assn., Calif. Chiropractic Assn., UCLA Alumni Assn., Mensa. Democrat. Home and Office: 2141 Hillsbury Rd Westlake Village CA 91362

WALLERICH, PETER KENNETH, banker; b. Tacoma, Mar. 4, 1931; s. Clarence W. and Ellen (Hansen) W.; m. Marylu Ann Oakland, July 9, 1954; children—Karen, Kristen, Karla, Kaari. B.A.A., U. Wash., 1953. Investment officer N.Pacific Bank, Tacoma, 1956-59, exec. v.p., 1959-71, chmn. bd., 1971-73, pres., 1973—; gen. mgr. Soutn Tacoma Motor Co., 1959-68, pres., 1968-71; dir. North Pacific Bank, Western Fin. Co., Mountain View Devel. Co. Pres. Design for Progress, 1970-71; bd. dirs. Goodwill Industries, Wash. Research Council; trustee, treas. U. Puget Sound.; chmn. bd. trustees Mary Bridge Children's Hosp; trustee Lakewood Gen. Hosp.; bd. visitors Sch. Law U. Puget Soun.; gen. chmn. Tacoma Pierce County United Way, 1981. Mem. Wash. Bankers Assn. (dir., treas.), Am. Bankers Assn. (nat. exec. planning com.), C. of C. (dir.), Mensa, Beta Gamma Sigma (chpt. award 1980). Home: 12111 Gravelly Lake Dr SW Tacoma WA 98499-1415 Office: N Pacific Bank 5448 S Tacoma Way Tacoma WA 98409-4313

WALLERSTEIN, BRUCE LEE, psychologist; b. Boston, May 23, 1943; s. Michael and Mildred (Cohen) W. AB, Boston U., 1965; MS, PhD, U. Pa., 1968. Cons. Met. State Hosp., Norwalk, Calif., 1968-70; assoc. prof. U. So. Calif., L.A., 1970-72; pvt. practice Long Beach, Calif., 1969—. Author: A Place to Live Not to Die: A Practical Guide to Nursing Homes, 1975. Fellow Am. Orthopsychiat. Assn., Group Psychotherapy Assn. So. Calif. (pres. 1975-77), Calif. Assn. Health Facilities (assoc.), Long Beach Yacht Club, Naples Bus. Assn., Long Beach C. of C. Office: Naples Counseling Ctr 5855 E Naples Plz Ste 308 Long Beach CA 90803-5091

WALLERSTEIN, RALPH OLIVER, physician; b. Dusseldorf, Germany, Mar. 7, 1922; came to U.S., 1938, naturalized, 1944; s. Otto R. and Ilse (Hollander) W.; m. Betty Ane Christensen, June 21, 1952; children: Ralph Jr., Richard, Ann. A.B., U. Calif., Berkeley, 1943; M.D., U. Calif., San Francisco, 1945. Diplomate: Am. Bd. Internal Medicine. Intern San Francisco Hosp., 1945-46, resident, 1948-49; resident U. Calif. Hosp., San Francisco, 1949-50; research fellow Thorndike Meml. Lab., Boston City Hosp., 1950-52; chief clin. hematology San Francisco Gen. Hosp., 1953-87; faculty U. Calif., San Francisco, 1952—; clin. prof. medicine U. Calif., 1969—. Served to capt. M.C. AUS, 1946-48. Mem. AMA, ACP (gov. 1977-87, chmn. bd. govs. 1980-81, regent 1981-87, pres. 1988-89), Am. Soc. Hematology (pres. 1978), San Francisco Med. Soc., Am. Clin. and Climatol. Assn., Am. Fedn. Clin. Rsch., Am. Soc. Internal Medicine, Am. Bd. Internal Medicine (bd. govs. 1975-83, chmn. 1982-83), Am. Assn. Blood Banks, Inst. Medicine, Calif. Acad. Medicine, Internat. Soc. Hematology, Western Soc. Clin. Rsch., Western Assn. Physicians, Gold Headed Cane Soc. Republican. Home: 3447 Clay St San Francisco CA 94118-2008 Office: 3838 California St Rm 707 San Francisco CA 94118-1509

WALLERSTEIN, ROBERT SOLOMON, psychiatrist; b. Berlin, Jan. 28, 1921; s. Lazar and Sarah (Guensberg) W.; m. Judith Hannah Saretsky, Jan. 26, 1947; children—Michael Jonathan, Nina Beth, Amy Lisa. B.A., Columbia, 1941, M.D., 1944; postgrad., Topeka Inst. Psychoanalysis, 1951-58. Assoc. dir., then dir. rsch. Menninger Found., Topeka, 1954-66; chief psychiatry Mt. Zion Hosp., San Francisco, 1966-78; tng. and supervising analyst San Francisco Psychoanalytic Inst., 1966—; clin. prof. U. Calif. Sch. Medicine, Langley-Porter Neuropsychiat. Inst., 1967-75, prof., chmn. dept. psychiatry, also dir. inst., 1975-85, prof. dept. psychiatry, 1985-91, prof. emeritus, 1991—; vis. prof. psychiatry La. State U. Sch. Medicine, also New Orleans Psychoanalytic Inst., 1972-73, Pahlavi U., Shiraz, Iran, 1977, Fed. U. Rio Grande do Sul, Porto Alegre, Brasil, 1980; mem., chmn. rsch. scientist career devel. com. NIMH, 1966-70; fellow Ctr. Advanced Study Behavioral Scis., Stanford, Calif., 1964-65, 81-82, Rockefeller Found. Study Ctr., Bellagio, Italy, 1992. Author 14 books and monographs; mem. editl. bd. 19 profl. jours; contbr. over 200 articles to profl. jours. Served with AUS, 1946-48. Recipient Heinz Hartmann award N.Y. Psychoanalytic Inst., 1968, Disting. Alumnus award Menninger Sch. Psychiatry, 1972, J. Elliott Royer award U. Calif., San Francisco, 1973, Outstanding Achievement award No. Calif. Psychiat. Soc., 1987, Mt. Airy gold medal, 1990, Mary Singleton Sigourney award, 1991. Fellow ACP, Am. Psychiat. Assn., Am. Orthopsychiat. Assn.; mem. Am. Psychoanlytic Assn. (pres. 1971-72), Internat. Psychoanalytic Assn. (v.p. 1977-85, pres. 1985-89), Group for Advancement Psychiatry, Brit. Psycho-Analytical Soc. (hon.), Phi Beta Kappa, Alpha Omega Alpha. Home: 290 Beach Rd Belvedere Tiburon CA 94920-2472 Office: 655 Redwood Hwy Ste 261 Mill Valley CA 94941-3011

WALLMANN, JEFFREY MINER, author; b. Seattle, Dec. 5, 1941; s. George Rudolph and Elizabeth (Biggs) W.; B.S., Portland State U., 1962. Pvt. investigator Dale Systems, N.Y.C., 1962-63; asst. buyer, mgr. pub. money bidder Dohrmann Co., San Francisco, 1964-66; mfrs. rep. electronics industry, San Francisco, 1966-69; dir. pub. rels. London Films, Cinelux-Universal and Trans-European Publs., 1970-75; editor-in-chief Riviera Life mag., 1975-77; cons. Mktg. Svcs. Internat., 1978—; instr. U. Nev., Reno, 1990—; books include: The Spiral Web, 1969, Judas Cross, 1974, Clean Sweep, 1976, Jamaica, 1977, Deathtrek, 1980, Blood and Passion, 1980; Brand of the Damned, 1981; The Manipulator, 1982; Return to Conta Lupe, 1983; The Celluloid Kid, 1984; Business Basic for Bunglers, 1984, Guide to Applications Basic, 1984; (under pseudonym Leon DaSilva) Green Hell, 1976, Breakout in Angola, 1977; (pseudonym Nick Carter) Hour of the Wolf, 1973, Ice Trap Terror, 1974; (pseudonym Margaret Maitland) The Trial, 1974, Come Slowly, Eden, 1974, How Deep My Cup, 1975; (pseudonym Amanda Hart Douglass) First Rapture, 1972, Jamacia!, 1978; (pseudonym Grant Roberts) The Reluctant Couple, 1969, Wayward Wives, 1970; (pseudonym Gregory St. Germain) Resistance #1: Night and Fog, 1982, Resistance #2: Maygar Massacre, 1983; (pseudonym Wesley Ellis) Lonestar on the Treachery Trail, 1982, numerous others in the Lonestar series; (pseudonym Tabor Evans) Longarm and the Lonestar Showdown, 1986; (psyeudonym Jon Sharpe) Trailsman 58: Slaughter Express, 1986, numerous others in Trailsman series; also many other pseudonyms and titles; contbr. articles and short stories to Argosy, Ellery Queen's Mystery Mag., Alfred Hitchcock's Mystery Mag., Mike Shayne's Mystery Mag., Zane Grey Western, Venture, Oui, TV Guide; also (under pseudonym William Jeffrey in collaboration with Bill Pronzini) Dual at Gold Buttes, 1980, Border Fever, 1982, Day of the Moon, 1983. Mem. Mystery Writers of Am., Sci. Fiction Writers Am., Western Writers Am., Nat. Coun. Tchrs. English, Crime Writers Assn., Nev. State Coun. Tchrs. English, Esperanto League N.Am., Western Literature Assn., Internacia Societo De Amikeco Kaj Bonvolo, Science Fiction Rsch. Assn., Internat. Assn. of the Fantastic in the Arts, Nat. Assn. Sci. Tech. & Sci., Soc. Internat. d'Amitié et Bonne Volonté, Nat. Coun. Tchrs. English, Western Lit. Assn. Office: Jabberwocky Lit Agy 41-16 47th Ave # 2D Sunnyside NY 11104-3040

WALLS, JOSEPH PATRICK, orthopaedic surgeon; b. Phila., Nov. 3, 1955; s. Thomas Francis and Margaret Mary Walls; m. Ellen Vera Eliassen, July 29, 1989. BA in Biology summa cum laude, Temple U., 1978; MD, Thomas Jefferson Med. Coll., 1982. Diplomate Am. Acad. Orthopaedic Surgeons. Resident in orthpaedic surgery Med. Coll. of Va., Richmond, 1982-87; attending orthpaedic surgeon, maj. Luke AFB, Glendale, Ariz., 1987-91; orthopaedic surgeon with 363rd Tactical Fighter Wing USAF, Middle East, 1990-91; fellowship in sports medicine Penn State U., Hershey, Pa., 1991-92; pvt. practice orthopaedic surgeon Carson-Douglas Orthopaedic and Sports Medicine Ctr., Carson City, Nev., 1992—. Contbr. articles to profl. jours. Mem. AMA, Am. Acad. Orthopaedic Surgeons, Carson City Rotary (bd. dirs. 1994—). Office: Carson-Douglas Orthopaedics and Sports Medicine Ctr 1000 N Division St Carson City NV 89703-3929

WALLSTRÖM, WESLEY DONALD, bank executive; b. Turlock, Calif., Oct. 4, 1929; s. Emil Reinhold and Edith Katherine (Lindberg) W.; student Modesto Jr. Coll., 1955-64; certificate Pacific Coast Banking Sch., U. Wash., 1974; m. Marilyn Irene Hallmark, May 12, 1951; children: Marc Gordon, Wendy Diane. Bookkeeper, teller First Nat. Bank, Turlock, 1947-50; v.p. Gordon Hallmark, Inc., Turlock, 1950-53; asst. cashier United Calif. Bank, Turlock, 1953-68, regional v.p., Fresno, 1968-72, v.p., mgr., Turlock, 1972-76; founding pres., dir. Golden Valley Bank, Turlock, 1976-84; pres. Wallström & Co., 1985—. Campaign chmn. United Crusade, Turlock, 1971; chmn., founding dir. Covenant Village, retirement home, Turlock, 1973-94, treas. Covenant Retirement Communities West; founding pres. Turlock Regional Arts Coun., 1974, dir., 1975-76. Served with U.S. N.G., 1948-56. Mem. Nat. Soc. Accts. for Coops., Ind. Bankers No. Calif., Am. Bankers Assn., U.S. Yacht Racing Union, No. Calif. Golf Assn., Turlock C. of C. (dir. 1973-75), Stanislaus Sailing Soc. (commodore 1980-81), Pacific Inter-Club Yacht Assn. (bd. dirs. 1994—, regatta chmn.), Turlock Golf and Country Club (pres. 1975-76, v.p., 1977, dir. 1977, 83), Stockton Sailing Club, Grindstone Joe Assn., Masons, Rotary. Republican. Mem. Covenant Ch. Home: 1720 Hammond Dr Turlock CA 95382-2850 Office: Wallstrom & Co 2925 Niagra St Turlock CA 95382-1056

WALRAD, CHARLENE CHUCK, software and total quality management consultant; b. Palm Beach, Fla., Feb. 21, 1946; d. Jack Maynard and Marian (Davenport) W.; m. Larry Starr, Oct. 1, 1972 (div. 1980). BA, Ariz. State U., 1967, MA, 1969; MS, U. Calif., San Diego, 1971. Linguist LATSEC, Inc., La Jolla, Calif., 1971-75, sr. linguist, 1975-84; v.p. World Translation Ctr., La Jolla, 1981-84; dir. mktg. Automated Lang. Processing Systems, Provo, Utah, 1984-85; dir. R & D, WICAT Systems, Orem, Utah, 1985-86; dir. quality mgmt. Ingres, Alameda, Calif., 1986-87; software engrng. cons. San Francisco, 1987—; cons. Xerox Corp., Webster, N.Y., 1983-84, Sci. Applications, Inc., La Jolla, 1984, Dept. Commerce, 1988, CIA, 1989, NAS, 1989, Control Data Corp., 1989, Word Star, 1990, Ford Motor Co., 1990-91, Dialog/Knight-Ridder, 1991, IBM, 1991-94, Esprit de Corps, 1992-93, Calif. State Automobile Assn., 1994, So. Pacific R.R., 1994, Frame Tech., 1994—; presenter in field. Co-author: Introduction to Luiseno, 1972. Bd. dirs. Shelter Ridge Assn., Mill Valley, Calif., 1988-90, v.p., 1989-90, pres., 1990; mem. Mill Valley Bus. Task Force, 1990-91; bd. dirs. Marin Mus. of Am. Indian; chmn. Bus. Advocacy Ctr., Mill Valley, 1992-93; bd. dirs. Mill Valley Fall Arts Festival, 1994—. Mem. Ariz. State U. Alumni Assn. (pres. San Diego chpt. 1982-83, Utah chpt. 1985-86), Mensa. Home: 12 Brooke Cir Mill Valley CA 94941-4604

WALRATH, HARRY RIENZI, minister; b. Alameda, Calif., Mar. 7, 1926; s. Frank Rienzi and Cathren (Michlar) W.; A.A., City Coll. San Francisco, 1950; B.A., U. Calif. at Berkeley, 1952; M.Div., Ch. Div. Sch. of Pacific, 1959; m. Dorothy M. Baxter, June 24, 1961; 1 son, Gregory Rienzi. Dist. exec. San Mateo area council Boy Scouts Am., 1952-55; ordained deacon Episcopal Ch., 1959, priest, 1960; curate All Souls Parish, Berkeley, Calif., 1959-61; vicar St. Luke's, Atascadero, Calif., 1961-63, St. Andrew's, Garberville, Calif., 1963-64; asso. rector St. Luke's Ch., Los Gatos, 1964-65, Holy Spirit Parish, Missoula, Mont., 1965-67; vicar St. Peter's Ch., also headmaster St. Peter's Schs., Litchfield Park, Ariz., 1967-69; chaplain U. Mont., 1965-67; asst. rector Trinity Parish, Reno, 1969-72; coordinator counciling services Washoe County Council Alcoholism, Reno, 1972-74; adminstr. Cons. Assistance Services, Inc., Reno, 1974-76; pastoral counselor, contract chaplain Nev. Mental Health Inst., 1976-78; contract mental health chaplain VA Hosp., Reno, 1976-78; mental health chaplain VA Med. Ctr., 1978-83, staff chaplain, 1983-85, chief, chaplain service, 1985-91, also triage coord. for mental health, ret., 1991; per diem chaplain Washoe Med. Ctr., Reno, 1993; assoc. priest Mountain Ministries, Susanville, Calif., 1995; dir. youth Paso Robles Presbytery; chmn. Diocesan Commn. on Alcoholism; cons. teen-age problems Berkeley Presbytery; mem. clergy team Episcopal Marriage Encounter, 1979-85, also Episc. Engaged Encounter. Mem. at large Washoe dist. Nev. area council Boy Scouts Am., scoutmaster troop 73, 1976, troop 585, 1979-82, asst. scoutmaster troop 35, 1982-92, assoc. adviser area 3 Western region, 1987-89, regional com. Western Region, 1989-90; lodge adviser Tannu Lodge 346, Order of Arrow, 1982-87; docent coun. Nev. Hist. Soc., 1992; South Humboldt County chmn. Am. Cancer Soc. Trustee Community Youth Ctr., Reno. Served with USNR, 1944-46. Decorated Pacific Theater medal with star, Am. Theater medal, Victory medal, Fleet Unit Commendation medal; recipient dist. award of merit Boy Scouts Am., St. George award Episc. Ch.-Boy Scouts Am., Silver Beaver award Boy Scouts Am., 1986, Founders' award Order of the Arrow, Boy Scouts Am., 1985; performance awards VA-VA Med. Ctr., 1983, 84; named Arrowman of Yr., Order of Arrow, Boy Scouts Am. Cert. substance abuse counselor, Nev. Mem. Ch. Hist. Soc., U. Calif. Alumni Assn., Nat. Model R.R. Assn. (life), Sierra Club Calif., Missoula Council Chs. (pres.), Alpha Phi Omega. Democrat. Club: Rotary. Home: 580 E Huffaker Ln Reno NV 89511-1203

WALSER, MILTON WESLEY (BUDDY WALSER), systems engineer; b. Orlando, Fla., Dec. 2, 1958; s. Milton Wesley and Carolyn Wenona (Blake) W.; m. Zoe Dimassis (div.); m. Tammy Jo Beil, Mar. 5, 1994. BS in Ecology and Evolutionary Biology, U. Ariz., 1980, MS in Sys. Engring., 1983. Teaching asst. U. Ariz., Tucson, 1981-83; project engr. Hughes Aircraft Co., Tucson, 1983-89; sys. engr. The Mitre Corp., Ft. Huachuca, Ariz., 1989-91; group leader The Mitre Corp., San Antonio, 1992-93; site leader The Mitre Corp., Sacramento, Calif., 1993—; oceanographer USNR, 1986—. Vol. instr. Rendokan Dojo, Tucson, 1986-91, Calif. Muscle Dojo, Sacramento, 1993—. Named Jr. Officer of Yr. San Diego area Reserve Officer's Assn. Mem. Am. Soc. Quality Control, Am. Geophys. Union, U.S Judo Assn. (life). Home: 305 Withington Ave Rio Linda CA 95673 Office: The Mitre Corp 5050 Dudley Blvd Ste 3 Mcclellan AFB CA 95652-1385

WALSH, BERNARD LAWRENCE, JR., physicist; b. Detroit, Jan. 11, 1932; s. Bernard Lawrence Sr. and Catherine Bridget (McCarthy) W.; m. Margaret Barbara Milko, Feb. 16, 1957; children: Bernard Lawrence III, Catherine Teresa. AB, U. Detroit, 1954. With Hughes Aircraft Co., L.A., 1954—, sr. scientist, 1968-75, chief scientist, 1975—. Contbr. articles to profl. jours.; patentee in field. Mem. IEEE, Am. Phys. Soc., ASM Internat., Profl. Group Electron Devices, Profl. Group Microwave Theory and Techniques. Home: 9609 Wystone Ave Northridge CA 91324-1858 Office: Hughes Aircraft Co PO Box 92919 Los Angeles CA 90009-2919

WALSH, DANIEL FRANCIS, bishop; b. San Francisco, Oct. 2, 1937. Grad., St. Joseph Sem., St. Patrick Sem., Catholic U. Am. Ordained priest, Roman Catholic Ch., 1963. Ordained titular bishop of Tigia, 1981; aux. bishop of San Francisco, 1981-87, bishop of Reno-Las Vegas, 1987—. Home: 2809 Cameo Cir Las Vegas NV 89107-3213 Office: Diocese of Reno-Las Vegas Office of Bishop PO Box 18316 Las Vegas NV 89114-8316*

WALSH, DENNY JAY, reporter; b. Omaha, Nov. 23, 1935; s. Gerald Jerome and Muriel (Morton) W.; m. Peggy Marie Moore, Feb. 12, 1966; children by previous marriage—Catherine Camille, Colleen Cecile; 1 son, Sean Joseph. B.J., U. Mo., 1962. Staff writer St. Louis Globe-Democrat, 1961-68; asst. editor Life mag., N.Y.C., 1968-70; assoc. editor Life mag., 1970-73; reporter N.Y. Times, 1973-74, Sacramento Bee, 1974—. Served with USMC, 1954-58. Recipient Con Lee Kelliher award St. Louis chpt. Sigma Delta Chi, 1962; award Am. Polit. Sci. Assn., 1963; award Sigma Delta Chi, 1968; Pulitzer prize spl. local reporting, 1969; 1st prize San Francisco Press Club, 1977. Office: Sacramento Bee 21st and Q Sts Sacramento CA 95813

WALSH, DOLORES ANN GONCZO, special education educator; b. Detroit, Sept. 3, 1933; d. Joseph John and Dolores (Carey) Gonczo; m. Bernard Waldrup, Aug. 23, 1958 (div. 1980); children: Elizabeth, Carey, Leslie, Bernard III; m. Deleon Walsh, Sept. 3, 1982 (dec. 1990). Student, Barat Coll., 1951-52; PhB, U. Detroit, 1955; MPS, Manhattanville Coll., 1978. Tchr. 2d grade East Detroit (Mich.) Pub. Schs., 1955-58; tchr. 4th grade Birmingham (Ala.) Schs., 1958-59, St. Francis Xavier Sch., Birmingham, 1959-62; homebound tchr. Greenburg Cen. #7, Hartsdale, N.Y., 1969-73; tchr. spl. edn. Greenburg Cen. 7, Hartsdale, N.Y., 1973-91; ret., 1991. Dist. leader Dem. Party Greenburgh, 1981-89; sec. Greenburgh Health Cen. Bd., Greenburgh, N.Y., 1986-89. Roman Catholic.

WALSH, EDWARD JOSEPH, toiletries and food company executive; b. Mt. Vernon, N.Y., Mar. 18, 1932; s. Edward Aloysius and Charlotte Cecilia (Borup) W.; m. Patricia Ann Farrell, Sept. 16, 1961; children: Edward Joseph, Megan Simpson, John, Robert. BBA, Iona Coll., 1953; MBA, NYU, 1958. Sales rep. M & R Dietetic Labs., Columbus, Ohio, 1955-60; with Armour & Co., 1961-71, Greyhound Corp., 1971-87; v.p. toiletries div. Armour Dial Co., Phoenix, 1973-74; exec. v.p. Armour Dial Co., 1975-77; pres. Armour Internat. Co., Phoenix, 1978-84; pres. The Dial Corp. (formerly Armour-Dial Co.), Phoenix, 1984-87, chief exec. officer, 1984-87; pres., chief exec. officer Purex Corp., 1985; chmn., chief exec. officer The Sparta Group Ltd., Scottsdale, Ariz., 1988—; bd. dirs. Phillips Ramsey Advt., San Diego, Phoenix, Guest Supply Inc., New Brunswick, N.J., WD-40 Co., San Diego, Nortrust Ariz. Holding Corp., Phoenix, Ariz., No. Trust Bank of Ariz., N.A., Executive Services Corps. of Ariz., Inc. Bd. trustees Scottsdale Meml. Health Found.; pres. Mt. Vernon Fire Dept. Mems. Assn., 1960-61. Served with U.S. Army, 1953-55, Germany. Mem. Am. Mgmt. Assn., Nat. Meat Canner Assn. (pres. 1971-72), Cosmetic, Toiletries and Fragrance Assn. (bd. dirs. 1985—), Nat. Food Processors Assn. (bd. dirs.). Republican. Roman Catholic. Office: The Sparta Group Ltd 6623 N Scottsdale Rd Scottsdale AZ 85250-4421

WALSH, JOHN, JR., museum director; b. Mason City, Wash., Dec. 9, 1937; s. John J. and Eleanor (Wilson) W.; m. Virginia Alys Galston, Feb. 17, 1962; children: Peter Wilson, Anne Galston, Frederick Matthiessen. B.A., Yale U., 1961; postgrad., U. Leyden, Netherlands, 1965-66; MA, Columbia U., 1965, PhD, 1971. Lectr., rsch. asst. Frick Collection, N.Y.C., 1966-68; assoc. higher edn. Met. Mus. Art, N.Y.C., 1968-71; assoc. curator European paintings Met. Mus. Art, 1970-72, curator dept. European paintings, 1972-74, vice-chmn., 1974-75; adj. assoc. prof. art history Columbia U., N.Y.C., 1969-72; adj. prof. Columbia U., 1972-75; prof. art history Barnard Coll., Columbia U., N.Y.C., 1975-77; Mrs. Russell W. Baker curator paintings Mus. Fine Arts, Boston, 1977-83; dir. J. Paul Getty Mus., Malibu, Calif., 1983—; vis. prof. fine arts Harvard U., 1979; mem. governing bd. Yale U. Art Gallery, 1975—, Smithsonian Coun., 1990—. Contbr. articles to profl. jours. Mem. Dem. County Com., N.Y.C., 1968-71; mem. vis. com. Fogg Mus., Harvard U., 1982-87; bd. fellows Claremont U. Ctr. and Grad. Sch., 1988—. With USNR, 1957-63. Fulbright grad. fellow The Netherlands, 1965-66. Mem. Coll. Art Assn., Am. Assn. Mus., Archaeol. Inst. Am., Am. Antiquarian Soc., Assn. Art Mus. Dirs. (trustee 1986—, pres. 1989-90), Century Assn. N.Y.C. Office: J Paul Getty Museum PO Box 2112 Santa Monica CA 90406

WALSH, JOHN BREFFNI, aerospace consultant; b. Bklyn., Aug. 20, 1927; s. George and Margaret Mary (Rigney) W.; m. Marie Louise Leclerc, June

18, 1955; children: George Breffni, John Leclerc, Darina Louise. B.E.E., Manhattan Coll., 1948; M.S., Columbia U., 1950; postgrad., NYU, 1954-62. Asst., instr. Columbia U., N.Y.C., 1948-51, asst. prof., asst. dir. Electronics Research Labs., 1953-66; various positions through tech. dir. Intelligence and Reconnaissance Div., Rome Air Devel. Center, N.Y., 1951-53; dep. for research to asst. sec. Air Force, 1966-71; sr. staff mem. Nat. Security Council, 1971-72, asst. to Pres.'s sci. advisor, 1971-72; dep. dir. Def. Research and Engring., 1972-77; asst. sec. gen. for def. support NATO, 1977-80; holder chair in systems acquisition mgmt., dean exec. inst. Def. Systems Mgmt. Coll., Ft. Belvoir, Va., 1981-82; prof. emeritus Def. Systems Mgmt. Coll., Ft. Belvoir, 1982—; v.p., chief scientist Boeing Mil. Airplane Co., Wichita, Kans., 1982-89; v.p. rsch. and engring. programs Boeing Aerospace and Electronics div., Seattle, 1990-92; v.p. strategic analysis Boeing Defense and Space Group, Seattle, 1992-93; prin. John B. Walsh Assocs., 1993—; mem. aeros. adv. com. NASA; mem. Congl. Adv. Com. on Aeros., 1984-85; assoc. Def. Sci. Bd.; mem. indsl. adv. bd. Wichita State U. Coll. Engring., adj. prof. elec. engring., 1989-90; chmn. tech. working group Defense Trade Adv. Group Dept. State, 1992—. Author: Electromagnetic Theory and Engineering Applications, 1960, (with K.S. Miller) Introductory Electric Circuits, 1960, Elementary and Advanced Trigonometry, 1977; contbr. tech. papers to publs.; patentee in field. Mem. planning bd., Cresskill, N.J., 1964-66; commr. Kans. Advanced Tech. Commn., 1985-86; bd. dirs. Kans. Inc., 1986-90; mem. math. scis. edn. bd. NRC, 1989-92. Served with U.S. Army, 1946-47. Recipient Air Force Exceptional Civilian Service award, 1969; recipient Dept. Def. Meritorious Civilian Service award, 1971, Disting. Civilian Service award, 1977, Air Force Assn. citation of honor as outstanding Air Force civilian employee of year, 1971, Theodore von Karman award Air Force Assn., 1977. Fellow IEEE (life), AIAA (v.p. tech. 1987-89); mem. N.Y. Acad. Scis., GPS Internat. Assn., Electromagnetics Acad., Sigma Xi, Eta Kappa Nu. Roman Catholic. Office: John B Walsh Assocs 13822 NE 37th Pl Bellevue WA 98005-1420

WALSH, MARIE LECLERC, nurse; b. Providence, Sept. 11, 1928; d. Walter Normand and Anna Mary (Ryan) Leclerc; m. John Breffni Walsh, June 18, 1955; children: George Breffni, John Leclerc, Darina Louise. Grad., Waterbury Hosp. Sch. Nursing, Conn., 1951; BS, Columbia U., 1954, MA, 1955. Team leader Hartford (Conn.) Hosp., 1951-53; pvt. duty nurse St. Luke's Hosp., N.Y.C., 1953-57; sch. nurse tchr. Agnes Russel Ctr., Tchrs. Coll. Columbia U., N.Y.C., 1955-56; clin. nursing instr. St. Luke's Hosp., N.Y.C., 1957-58; chmn. disaster nursing ARC Fairfax County, Va., 1975; course coord. occupational health nursing U. Va. Sch. Continuing Edn., Falls Church, 1975-77; mem. disaster steering com. No. Va. C.C., Annandale, 1976; adj. faculty U. Va. Sch. Continuing Edn., Falls Church, 1981; disaster svcs. nurse ARC, Wichita, Kans., 1985-90; disaster svcs. nurse Seattle-King County chpt. ARC, Seattle, 1990—; rsch. and statis. analyst U. Va. Sch. Continuing Edn. Nursing, Falls Church, 1975; rsch. libr. Olive Garvey Ctr. for Improvement Human Functioning, Inc., Wichita, 1985. Sec. Dem. party, Cresskill, N.J., 1964-66; county committeewoman, Bergen County, N.J., 1965-66; pres., v.p., Internat. Staff Wives, NATO, Brussels, Belgium, 1978-80; election officer, supr. Election Bd., Wichita, 1987, 88. Mem. AAAS, AAUW, N.Y. Acad. Sci., Pi Lambda Theta, Sigma Theta Tau. Home: 13822 NE 37th Pl Bellevue WA 98005-1420

WALSH, MASON, retired newspaperman; b. Dallas, Nov. 27, 1912; s. Herbert C. and Margaret (Hayes) W.; m. Margaret Anne Calhoun, Mar. 7, 1947; children: Margaret Anne (Mrs. James G. Dunn), Timothy Mason, Kevin Calhoun. B.A. in Polit. Sci., So. Meth. U., 1934. Staff Dallas Evening Jour., 1929-37; staff Dallas Dispatch-Jour. (later Dallas Jour.), 1938-42; editor Austin (Tex.) Tribune, 1942; dir. employee relations N.Am. Aviation, Dallas, 1942-45; with Dallas Times-Herald, 1945-60, mng. editor, 1952-60; mng. editor Phoenix Gazette, 1960-66; gen. mgr. Phoenix Newspapers, Inc., 1966-75, asst. pub., 1975-78; pub. Ariz. Republic and Phoenix Gazette, 1978-80, pub. emeritus, 1980—. Profl. musician, 1929-35. Chmn. Ariz. Dept. Econ. Planning and Devel. Bd., 1968-71; bd. dirs., v.p. Goodwill Industries Central Ariz., 1978-84, v.p., 1982-83; bd. dirs. Western Newspaper Found., 1974-81; trustee Desert Found., Scottsdale, 1982-85; mem. Nat. Def. Exec. Res., 1964-80. Mem. A.P. Mng. Editors Assn. (dir. 1956-63, pres. 1963), A.P. Assn. Calif., Ariz., Hawaii and Nev. (pres. 1976-77), Ariz. Acad. (dir. 1973-81, v.p. 1980-81), Valley Forward Assn. (dir. 1970-87), Newcomen Soc., Phoenix 40, Sigma Delta Chi. Episcopalian. Clubs: University, Arizona. Home: 4102 N 64th Pl Scottsdale AZ 85251-3110

WALSH, ROBERTA ANNETTE, conservation biologist; b. Bellingham, Wash., Dec. 11, 1938; d. Robert Davis and Freida Caroline (Hirschkorn) Blake; m. James Anthony Walsh, Sept. 17, 1957; children: Jennifer Margaret, Robert Adam. Student, Stanford U., 1956-57; BS, U. Wash., 1960; postgrad., Iowa State U., 1968-70; MS, U. Mont., 1992. Sr. ptnr. Evaluation Rsch. Assocs., Missoula, Mont., 1964—; cons. Casey Family Program, Seattle, 1981-88, Gov.'s Office of Budget and Program Planning, Helena, Mont., 1980-81. Co-author: Quality Care for Tough Kids, 1990; contbr. articles to profl. jours. Scholar Nat. Merit Scholarship Corp., 1956-60. Mem. Soc. Conservation Biology, Sigma Xi (nat. sci. hon.). Democrat. Home: 2340 55th St Apt 15 Missoula MT 59803-3155 Office: Evaluation Rsch Assocs 2340 55th St Apt 15 Missoula MT 59803-3155

WALSH, THOMAS GEORGE, information services industry executive; b. Carroll, Iowa, Aug. 28, 1945; s. Raphael Edward and Helen Esther (Lawler) W.; m. Barbara Ellen Stoffel, Aug. 16, 1969; children: Meghan M., Molly A., Michaela E., Thomas P., Timothy R., Mary Colleen, Michael F., Brighid C., Daniel X., Emily M. BSBA, Creighton U., 1967. Customer svc. mgr. Mid-Am. Bankcard Assn., Omaha, Nebr., 1969-71; customer svc. dir. First Data Resources, Omaha, 1971-74; customer svc. dir. SE region First Data Resources, Atlanta, 1975-77; v.p. mktg. First Data Resources, Omaha, 1978-88; v.p. client svcs. Am. Express Integrated Payment Sys., Englewood, Colo., 1989-91, sr. v.p. mktg., 1991-92; exec. v.p. integrated svcs. divsn. First Data Corp., Englewood, 1992—; mem. exec. com. FDC Colo. Open Golf Tournament, Englewood, 1992—. Sec., treas., bd. dirs. Travis Hukil Fund, Englewood, 1989—; mem. Boys Hope-Denver, St. Louis, 1994—; pres. bd. dirs. Boys Town Booster Club, 1984-92. With U.S. Army, 1967-68. Mem. KC (Family of Yr. 1988), Ducks Unltd. (Littleton chpt.), N.Am. Fishing Club(life), Douglas County Soccer Assn. (bd. dirs. 1991-93). Roman Catholic. Office: First Data Corp 6200 S Quebec St Englewood CO 80111-4750

WALSH, TIMOTHY JOHN, geologist; b. L.A., Aug. 9, 1952; s. Edward Francis and Lenore (Beerli) W.; m. Pamela Jeanne Shaffer, Sept. 10, 1977; children: Maureen Elizabeth, Brigid Eileen. BS, UCLA, 1976, MS, 1979. Staff geologist Dept. Natural Resources, Divsn. Geology and Earth Resources, Olympia, Wash., 1980-88; chief geologist, environ. sect. Dept. Natural Resources, Divsn. Geology and Earth Resources, 1988—. Contbr. numerous articles to profl. jours. Recipient Honor by Resolution, Wash. State Ho. of Reps., 1988, Disting. Lectr., N.W. Petroleum Assn., 1990. Mem. Am. Geophys. Union (sec. Pacific N.W. Br. 1986-87, pres. 1987-88), Am. Assn. Petroleum Geologists, Soc. Econ. Paleontologists and Mineralogists (Pacific sect.), Assn. Engring. Geologists. Office: Wash Dept Natural Resources PO Box 47007 Olympia WA 98504-7007

WALSH, WILLIAM, former football coach; b. Los Angeles, Nov. 30, 1931. Student, San Mateo Jr. Coll.; BA, San Jose State U., 1954, MA in Edn., 1959. Asst. coach Monterey Peninsula Coll., 1955, San Jose State U., 1956; head coach Washington Union High Sch., Fremont, Calif., 1957-59; asst. coach U. Calif., Berkeley, 1960-62, Stanford U., 1963-65, Oakland Raiders, Am. Football League, 1966-67, Cin. Bengals, 1968-75, San Diego Chargers, Nat. Football League, 1976; head coach Stanford U., 1977-78; head coach, gen. mgr. San Francisco 49ers, NFL, 1979-89, exec. v.p., 1989; broadcaster NBC Sports, 1989-91; head coach Stanford U., 1992-95. Named NFL Coach of Yr., Sporting News, 1981; coached Stanford U. winning team Sun Bowl, 1977, Bluebonnet Bowl, 1978, Blockbuster Bowl, 1993, San Francisco 49ers to Super Bowl championships, 1981, 84, 88; elected to Pro Football Hall of Fame, 1993. Office: c/o Stanford U Gary Migdol Sports Info Office Dept Athletics Stanford CA 94305-1684*

WALSH, WILLIAM DESMOND, investor; b. N.Y.C., Aug. 4, 1930; s. William J. and Catherine Grace (Desmond) W.; m. Mary Jane Gordon, Apr. 5, 1951; children: Deborah, Caroline, Michael, Suzanne, Tara Jane, Peter. JD, Fordham U., 1951; LL.B., Harvard, 1955. Bar: N.Y. State bar 1955. Asst. U.S. atty. So. dist. N.Y., N.Y.C., 1955-58; counsel N.Y. Commn. Investigation, N.Y.C., 1958-61; mgmt. cons. McKinsey & Co., N.Y.C., 1961-67; sr. v.p. Arcata Corp., Menlo Park, Calif., 1967-82; gen. ptnr. Sequoia Assocs., 1982—; pres., chief exec. officer Atacra Liquidating Trust, 1982-88; chmn. bd. dirs. Deanco, Inc., Ithaca, N.Y., Newell Indsl. Crop, Lowell, Mich., Champion Rd. Machinery Ltd., Goderick, Ont.; bd. dirs. URS Inc., San Francisco, Newcourt Credit Group, Inc., Toronto, Basic Vegetable Products, King City, Calif., Consolidated Freightways, Inc., Palo Alto, Calif., Nat. Edn. Corp. of Irvine, Calif. Mem. bd. visitors Sch. Bus. U. So. Calif., Harvard Law Sch., vis. com. on univ. resources. Mem. N.Y. State Bar Assn., Harvard Club (N.Y.C. and San Francisco), Knights of Malta. Home: 279 Park Ln Menlo Park CA 94027-5448 Office: 3000 Sand Hill Rd Bldg 2 Ste 140 Menlo Park CA 94025-7116

WALSTON, RICK LYLE JOSH, clergyman, seminary executive, educator; b. Longview, Wash., Sept. 3, 1954; s. Lyle Basil and Harriet Marion (Salhus) W.; m. Susan Elizabeth Insel, Oct. 29, 1988. AS in Practical Theology, Christ for the Nations Inst., 1980; BA, Warner Pacific Coll., 1982, MREL magna cum laude, 1987; STD summa cum laude, Bethany Theol. Sem., 1988; PhD, Greenwich U., 1991. Ordained minster. Assoc. pastor Christian Life Ctr. Assemblies of God Ch., Longview, 1977-82; tchr., registrar Berean Coll. Extension Sch., Longview, 1980-82; sr. pastor Praise Song Assemblies of God Ch., Longview, 1982-86; registrars asst. Warner Pacific Coll., Portland, Oreg., 1986-87; sr. pastor Home Fellowship Assembly Ch., Longview, 1988; ednl. cons., owner Coll. Degree Cons. Svcs., Longview, 1989-92; sr. pastor Christian Assembly, Longview, 1992—; pres. Faraston Theol. Sem., Longview, 1990—; co-founder Clackamas (Oreg.) Bible Inst., Clackamas Christian Ctr., 1987; co-dir. edn. dept. Kelso (Wash.) First Assembly of God Ch., 1989-92. Author: Divorce and Remarriage, 1991, (with John Bear) Walston & Bear's Guide to Earning Religious Degrees Non-Traditionally, 1993; contbr. articles to profl. jours. Coord. religious events Christian Life Ministerial Assn., Longview, 1979-82; retirement home minister Praise Song Assembly of God Ch., 1982-86, hosp. minister, 1982-86. Recipient Cert. of Recognition, Christ for the Nations Inst., 1980, Full Gospel Fellowship Internat., 1980. Fellow Faraston Theol. Rsch. Fellowship (pres. 1990-92, Rsch. Fellow of Yr. 1990); mem. Oreg. Assn. for Psychol. Type, Evang. Theol. Soc., Evang. Philos. Soc., Assn. Christian Continuing Edn. Schs. and Sems. Republican. Office: Faraston Theol Sem PO Box 847 Longview WA 98632-7521

WALSTON, RODERICK EUGENE, state attorney general; b. Gooding, Idaho, Dec. 15, 1935; s. Loren R. and Iva M. (Boyer) W.; m. Margaret D. Grandey; children: Gregory Scott W., Valerie Lynne W. A.A., Boise Jr. Coll., 1956; B.A. cum laude, Columbia Coll., 1958; LL.B. scholar, Stanford U., 1961. Bar: Calif. 1961, U.S. Supreme Ct. 1973. Law clk to judge U.S. Ct. Appeals 9th Cir., 1961-62; dep. atty. gen State of Calif., San Francisco, 1963-91, head natural resources sect, 1969-91, chief asst. atty. gen. pub. rights div., 1991—; spl. dep counsel Kings County, Calif., 1975-76; mem. environ. and natural resources adv. coun. Stanford (Calif.) Law Sch. Contbr. articles to profl. jours.; bd. editors: Stanford Law Rev., 1959-61, Western Natural Resources Litigation Digest, Calif. Water Law and Policy Reporter; spl. editor Jour. of the West. Co-chmn. Idaho campaign against Right-to-Work initiative, 1958; Calif. rep. Western States Water Coun., 1986—; environ. and natural resources adv. coun., Stanford Law Sch. Nat. Essay Contest winner Nat. Assn. Internat. Rels. Clubs, 1956, Stanford Law Rev. prize, 1961; Astor Found. scholar, 1956-58. Mem. ABA (chmn. water resources com., 1988-90, vice chmn. and conf. chmn., 1985-88, 90—), Contra Costa County Bar Assn., U.S. Supreme Ct. Hist. Soc., World Affairs Coun. No. Calif. Office: Calif Atty Gen's Office 1515 K St Fl 6 Sacramento CA 95814-4017

WALTER, FREDERICK JOHN, motel executive; b. East Orange, N.J., Jan. 26, 1944; s. Fred Gottlieb and Emily (Mast) W.; m. Jane Elizabeth Schackner, Aug. 20, 1966; children: Emily Jane, Meredith Waite. BA, N.C. State U., 1966; MBA, Ga. State U., 1968. Exec. Intercontinental Diversified Corp., Freeport, Bahamas, 1969-76; mng. ptnr. Best Western-Nellis Motor Inn, Las Vegas, Nev., 1977-87, Best Western-Lake Mead Motel, Henderson, Nev., 1984-87, Best Western-McCarran Inn, Las Vegas, 1986—; hotel-motel cons., sales rep. Helen Naugle & Assocs., Las Vegas, 1982—; regional gov. Best Western Internat., Inc., Phoenix, 1977-91, bd. dirs., 1991—. Bd. dirs. Boys and Girls Clubs, Las Vegas, 1982—, Las Vegas Conv. and Visitors Authority, 1988-91; chmn. Taxicab Authority of Nev., 1989-93, So. Nev. Civilian Mil. Coun., Las Vegas, 1983—. With USMC, 1963-65. Mem. Nev. Hotel and Motel Assn. (bd. dirs., pres. 1981—), Greater Las Vegas C. of C. (bd. dirs. 1990-91), Am. Hotel and Motel Assn. (cert. hotel adminstr.), Air Force Assn., Rotary. Lutheran. Office: Best Western McCarran Inn 4970 Paradise Rd Las Vegas NV 89119-1206

WALTER, MICHAEL CHARLES, lawyer; b. Oklahoma City, Nov. 25, 1956; s. Donald Wayne and Viola Helen (Heffelfinger) W. BA in Polit. Sci., BJ, U. Wash., 1980; JD, Univ. Puget Sound, 1983. Bar: Wash. 1985, U.S. Dist. Ct. (9th cir. 1985). Shareholder Keating, Bucklin & McCormack, Seattle, 1985—; instr. Bellevue (Wash.) C.C., 1983—. Mem. ABA, ACLU, Internat. Assn. Bus. Communicators, Wash. State Bar Assn., Reporters Com. for Freedom of Press, Seattle-King County Bar Assn., Wash. Assn. Def. Counsel, Seattle Claims Adjustors Assn., Wash. Assn. Mcpl. Attys. Home: 11920 27th Pl SW Burien WA 98146-2438 Office: Keating Bucklin & McCormack 4141 SeaFirst 5th Ave Pla Seattle WA 98104

WALTER, PATRICIA ANN, graphic designer; b. Oshkosh, Wis., Nov. 17, 1948; d. Edgar Harvey and Jeanne Ann (Schermerhorn) W. BS in Secondray Edn., U. Wis., Oshkosh, 1970, postgrad., 1970-71. Graphic artist I and II, U. Wis., 1973-74, 78-80; with DDM & Assocs., advt. publs., Madison, Wis., 1974-76; designer Baxandall Co./Work Force Publs., Oshkosh, 1976-78; freelance graphic artist, Breckenridge, Colo., 1980-83; art dir. Cope Daley McCrea, advt. agy., Breckenridge, 1983-84, Hesdorfer Assocs., advt. agy., Denver, 1987-88, The Clifton Group, Denver, 1988-89; owner, designer The Art Dept., Breckenridge, 1984-87; exec. art dir. Wiesner Pub., Englewood, Colo., 1990-91; owner, mgr. Pat Walter Art & Design, Englewood, 1991—. Office: 4137 S Hazel Ct Englewood CO 80110-4327

WALTER-ROBINSON, CAROL SUE, investment executive; b. Joliet, Ill., Dec. 24, 1942; d. Loren John Sr. and Myrtle F. (Sistler) Walter; adopted d. Lillian M. Winnett; m. Patrick Allen Robinson, Apr. 17, 1991; adopted children: Teresa, Christopher, Ellen, Melissa, Catrina, Elizabeth, Sherlene. Student, Waubonsee Jr. Coll., Aurora, Ill., 1963-65, Aurora Coll., 1967-71, Hypnosis Motivation Inst., 1992, U. Metaphysics, 1992. Lic.. cosmetologist, paralegal; cert. hypnotherapist. Office mgr., bookkeeper Edward M. Kyser Appraiser, Aurora, 1961-66; legal sec., aide Hon. Paul Schnake, Aurora, 1961-66; pers. mgr. H.W. Gossard Co., Batavia, Ill., 1966-68; pers. recruiter Dresser Industries, Franklin Park, Ill., 1968-71; exec. sec., pres. Am. Picture Co., Anaheim, Calif., 1972-75; contract mgr. state operators incorp. divsn. Mobil Oil Corp., Orange County, Calif., 1975-81; owner Inland Tele-Sec., Riverside, Calif., 1982-84; pvt. practice investment mgr. Riverside, 1984—; sec. Legal Sec.-Fox Valley, Aurora, 1964-66. Author: Capital Punishment—Pro and Con, 1970; editor (newsletter) Humane News, 1964-68. Pres./founder The Fosterkids Alliance, Riverside, 1988-91; exec. sec. Fox Valley Animal Welfare, Aurora, 1963-68; historian Am. Cancer Soc., Aurora, 1964; exec. sec. pub. rels. Humane Soc. U.S., Garden Grove, Calif., 1972; community liaison El Centro Hispano Americano, Aurora, 1970; coun. No. Ill. Pers. Assn., Chgo., 1966-68; com. chair-advisor Employee Personnel Testing, Melrose Park, Ill., 1965; arbitration moderator I.G.W.U., Chgo., 1969. Democrat. Unity. Home: 845 Spruce St Riverside CA 92507-2525 Office: TFA PO Box 52092 Riverside CA 92517-3092

WALTERS, BRUCE ALLEN, special effects designer; b. Tacoma, Wash., Mar. 9, 1948; s. Joel Lavern and Betty Katherine (Bush) W.; m. Ginny Lee Gordon, July 10, 1972; children: Jon, Berry. Graphic artist, illustrator Denver and Seattle, 1967-78; spl. effect designer Trickfilm, Seattle, 1978-83; effects designer, dept. head Indsl. Light and Magic, San Rafael, Calif., 1983-93; owner X.O. Digital Arts, Mill Valley, Calif., 1994—. Recipient Brit. Acad. award Baftra, London, 1987, Emmy hon., 1992-93. Mem. I.A.T.S.E.. Office: XO Digital Arts 48 Morning Sun Ave Mill Valley CA 94941

WALTERS, DANIEL RAYMOND, political columnist; b. Hutchinson, Kans., Oct. 10, 1943; s. Howard Duke and Glenna Lucille (Hesse) W.; m. Diana Lee Flak, July 8, 1963 (div.); children: Danielle, Staci. Mng. editor Hanford (Calif.) Sentinel, 1966-69, Herald News, Klamath Falls, Oreg., 1969-71, Times-Standard, Eureka, Calif., 1971-73; polit. writer and columnist Sacramento (Calif.) Union, 1973-84; polit. columnist Sacramento Bee, 1984—. Author: The New California: Facing the 21st Century, 1986; founding editor Calif. Polit. Almanac, 1989. Office: The Sacramento Bee 925 L St Ste 1404 Sacramento CA 95814-3704

WALTERS, DENNIS H., lawyer; b. Rochelle, Ill., Mar. 2, 1950; s. Harold R. and Helen M. (Eshbaugh) W.; m. Marilyn E. Hoban, Jan. 1, 1984. BA, Ill. Wesleyan U., 1972; MS in Bus. Adminstrn., Boston U., 1975; JD, Harvard U., 1979. Bar: Wash. 1979, Alaska, 1985, U.S. Ct. Appeals (9th cir.) 1991, U.S. Supreme Ct. 1991; lic. comml. pilot, flight instr. Assoc. Karr Tuttle Campbell, Seattle, 1979, shareholder, 1987—, head of appellate practice, 1991—. Trustee, pres. Vision Svcs., Seattle, 1980-86; trustee Literacy Coun. of Kitsap, 1993—. With U.S. Army, 1972-76. Named Citizen of Day, Sta. KIXI, Seattle, 1985. Mem. ABA, Seattle-King County Bar Assn. (chmn. aviation sect. 1984-85), Lawyer-Pilots Bar Assn., N.W. Environ. Claims Assn., Wing Point Golf and Country Club. Home: 25853 W Canyon Rd NW Poulsbo WA 98370-9503

WALTERS, EDWARD ALBERT, chemistry educator; b. Whitefish, Mont., Jan. 2, 1940; s. Eric Albert and Katie W. (Kuehn) W.; m. Susan Elaine Dally, June 27, 1964; children: Eric Nash, Gregory Edward, Elaine Mee Sun. BS, Pacific Luth. U., 1962; PhD, U. Minn., 1966. Research assoc. Cornell U., Ithaca, N.Y., 1966-68; asst. prof. U. N.Mex., Albuquerque, 1968-74, assoc. prof., 1974-85, prof. chemistry, 1985—; facilitator interactions with fed. labs., industry and univs. U. N.Mex., 1994—; vis. staff mem. Los Alamos (N.Mex.) Nat. Lab., 1970—; rsch. collaborator Brookhaven Nat. Lab., Upton, N.Y., 1980—, Sandia Nat. Lab., USAF Weapons Lab., Kirkland AFB. Author: Contemporary Chemistry, 1974. Mem. AAAS, Am. Chem. Soc. (councillor), Am. Vacuum Soc., Royal Soc. Chemistry. Lutheran. Home: 8109 Harwood Ave NE Albuquerque NM 87110-1515 Office: U N Mex Dept Chemistry Albuquerque NM 87131

WALTERS, FREDERICK K., JR., judge; b. Chgo., May 17, 1934; s. F.K. Sr. and Violet I. Walters; children from previous marriage: Wendy Roxanne, Frederick Kevin. BS, Ariz. State U., 1957. Civilian employee Dept. Army Dept. of Def., White Sands Missle Range, 1957-89; mcpl. judge Village of Cloudcroft, N.Mex., 1982—. Trustee Village of Cloudcroft, 1976-78, vol. fireman, 1976-86; apptd. rep. Jud. Automation Commn. N.Mex., 1993—. Mem. Nat. Judges Assn. (bd. dirs., editor newsletter), N.Mex. Mcpl. Judges Assn. (bd. dis. 1985—, scholarship chmn. 1992-95). Democrat. Home: 536 Balsam Cir Cloudcroft NM 88317-0097 Office: Village of Cloudcroft Mcpl Ct PO Box 317 Cloudcroft NM 88317-0317

WALTERS, JESSE RAYMOND, JR., judge; b. Rexburg, Idaho, Dec. 26, 1938; s. Jesse Raymond and Thelma Rachael (Hodgson) W.; m. Harriet Payne, May 11, 1959; children—Craig T., Robyn, J. Scott. Student Ricks Coll., 1957-58; B.A. in Polit. Sci., U. Idaho, 1961, J.D., 1963; postgrad. U. Washington, 1962; LLM U. Va., 1990. Bar: Idaho 1963, U.S. Dist. Ct. Idaho 1964, U.S. Ct. Appeals (9th cir.) 1970. Law clk. to chief justice Idaho Supreme Ct., 1963-64; sole practice, Boise, Idaho, 1964-77; atty. Idaho senate, Boise, 1965; dist. judge 4th Jud. Dist., Idaho, Boise, 1977-82, adminstrv. dist. judge, 1981-82; chief judge Idaho Ct. Appeals, Boise, 1982—; chmn. magistrate's commn. 4th jud. dist.; chmn. Supreme Ct. mem. services; chmn. Criminal Pattern Jury Instrn. Com.; mem. Civil Pattern Jury Instrn. Com; Republican committeeman, Boise, 1975-77; mem. Ada County Rep. Central Com., 1975-77. Mem. Idaho Bar Assn. (bankruptcy com.), Idaho Adminstrv. Judges Assn., ABA, Am. Judicature Soc., Assn. Trial Lawyers Am. Idaho Trial Lawyers Assn., Council Chief Judges Ct. Appeals, Boise Estate Planning Council, Jaycees (nat. dir. 1969-70, pres. Boise chpt. 1966-67). Mormon. Lodges: Lions, Elks, Eagles. Office: State Idaho Ct Appeals 537 W Bannock St Boise ID 83702-5968

WALTERS, PAUL, protective services official; b. Reading, Eng., 1945; (parents Am. citizens); m. Linda; children: Gary, Michael. Attended, Orange Coast Coll.; BA in Criminal Justice, Calif. State U., Fullerton; MPA, U. So. Calif.; JD, Am. Coll. of law; grad., Calif. Command Coll., 1986, Police Exec. Rsch. Forum, Sr. Mgmt. Inst., Harvard U. From patrol officer to capt. City of Santa Ana (Calif.) Police Dept., 1971-88, chief of police, 1988—. Sgt. USAF. Recipient Appreciation cert. Orange County Bar Assn., 1990, Commendation cert. Orange County Human Rels. Commn., 1990, Orange County Cmty. Policing award, 1994. Mem. Orange County Chiefs of Police and Sheriff's Assn. (mem. exec. com., past pres.). Office: Santa Ana Police Dept PO Box 1988 Santa Ana CA 92702*

WALTERS, RAYMOND L., private investigator, association executive, educator; b. Highland Park, Mich., June 6, 1943; s. Raymond E. and Peggy J. W.; m. Linda L. Hochwalt, Jan. 29, 1964; children: Amy L., Wendy L., Heather L., Summer L. BS, Mich. State U., 1970, MS, 1977; EdS, Temple U., 1986. Lic. pvt. investigator, Mont. Instr. Lansing Community Coll., East Lansing, Mich., 1973-74; supr. jail tng. Mich. Dept. Corrections, East Lansing, 1972-74; prison warden Detroit House Corrections, Plymouth, Mich., 1974; supr. advanced police tng. Mich. State Police, East Lansing, 1974-77; asst. prof. West Chester (Pa.) State U., 1977-82; assoc. prof. Coll. Gt. Falls, Mont., 1982-86; instr. Park Coll., Gt. Falls, 1988—; pres. Mont. Security Works/Walters' Investigative Svcs., Gt. Falls, 1986—, USA-Korean Karate Assn., Gt. Falls, 1981—; adminstr. Cascade County Regional Youth Svcs. Ctr., Gt. Falls, 1994—; owner Jade Dragon Martial Arts Acad., Gt. Falls, 1988—; pub. info. officer Cascade County Sheriff Dept., Gt. Falls, 1989—. Contbr. articles to edn. and martial arts publs. Bd. dirs. Pre-Release Ctr., Gt. Falls, 1983-84, Demolay Youth Ctr., Gt. Falls, 1985. With USNR, 1961-65. Recipient Spl. award Am. Soc. Tng. and Devel., 1973; named Outstanding Instr. Martial Arts Hall of Fame, 1989. Mem. Mont. Assn. Pvt. Investigators, Mont. Assn. Law Enforcement Profls. (pres. 1983-84). Democrat. Office: Cascade County Regional Youth Svcs Ctr 1600 26th St S Great Falls MT 59405

WALTHER, DAVID LOUIS, lawyer; b. Stevens Point, Wis., Oct. 31, 1936; children: Christopher, Elizabeth, Jonathan, Jennifer, Mark, Gretchen. BS, Marquette U., 1958, JD cum laude, 1961. Bar: Wis. 1961, U.S. Dist. Ct. (ea. and we. dists.) Wis. 1961, U.S. Ct. Appeals (7th cir.) 1974, U.S. Supreme Ct. 1979, N.Mex. 1986; diplomate Am. Coll. Family Trial Lawyers. Legal asst. Wis. Supreme Ct., Madison, 1961-63; asst. legal counsel to Gov. John W. Reynolds, Madison, 1963; assoc. Brady, Tyrell & Bruce, Milw., 1963-64; pvt. practice Milw., 1964-66; ptnr. Walther & Burns, Milw., 1966-70, Walther & Halling, S.C., Milw., 1970-86, Walther & Walther, S.C., Milw., 1986-89; pvt. practice Santa Fe, 1989—; adj. prof. Marquette U. Sch. Law, Milw., U. N.Mex. Sch. Law. Author: Wisconsin Appellate Practice, 1965, 2d rev. edition, 1986. Mem. Pres.'s Coun., Marquette U., Milw. Fellow Am. Acad. Matrimonial Lawyers (at-large mem. bd. govs.); mem. N.Mex. Bar (mem. bd. of bar comm.), Wis. Bar Assn., Milw. Bar Assn., Woolsack Soc., University Club. Home: 1875 Forest Cir Santa Fe NM 87505-4506 Office: 1640 Old Pecos Trl Ste E Santa Fe NM 87505-4768

WALTI, RANDAL FRED, management consultant; b. Chgo., Apr. 10, 1939; s. Fred Henry and Alice Ann (Steger) W.; m. Judith Ann Hodson, Jan. 31, 1960; children: Lee, Rod, Lynn. BSME, Purdue U., 1961. Program mgr. Aerojet Gen., El Monte, Calif., 1961-66; applications mgr. TRW Systems, Redondo Beach, Calif., 1966-70; br. mgr. A.B. Dick Co., Long Beach, Calif., 1970-71; pres. Randal Data Systems, Inc., Torrance, Calif., 1971-79, The Oaktree Consulting Group, Torrance, Calif., 1980—; chmn. chief exec. officer Oaktree Publ. Inc., Torrance, Calif., 1993—; founder, bd. dirs. Software Coun. So. Calif., Torrance; bd. dirs. Silver Cloud Travel, Inc., Torrance; chmn. The Exec. Com., La Jolla, Calif., 1986-88. Chmn. So. Calif. Leadership Coun., Christian Businessmen's Com., Santa Ana, Calif., 1991—. Republican. Mem. Covenant Ch. Home: 1806 Mount Shasta Dr San Pedro CA 90732-1527 Office: Oaktree Consulting Group 21041 S Western Ave Ste 160 Torrance CA 90501-1727

WALTON, BRIAN, lawyer, union negotiator; b. London, Dec. 24, 1947; came to U.S., 1966; s. Frank William and Irene Mary (Thornton) W.; m. Pamela Abegg Nemelka (div.); children: Robert, Sarah. BA with honors, Brigham Young U., 1969, MA in Polit. Sci., 1971; JD, U. Utah, 1974. Bar: Calif. 1974, U.S. Dist. Ct. (ctrl., so. and no. dists.) Calif. 1974. Law clk. to

Hon. J. Allan Crockett Utah Supreme Ct., 1974; assoc. Reavis & McGrath and predecessor firms, L.A., 1974-82; ptnr. Selvin and Weiner, L.A., 1982-85; exec. dir. Writers Guild Am., West, Inc., L.A., 1985—; teaching asst. Coll. Law, Utah U., 1973, asst. to v.p. of spl. projects, 1971-73, rsch. asst. Coll. Law, 1972-74, tchr., dir. legal skills seminar Coll. Law, 1974. Contbr. articles to law jours. Edwin S. Hinckley scholar. Mem. ABA (antitrust sect.), L.A. County Bar Assn. (antitrust sect., intellectual property and unfair competition sect.), Assn. Bus. Trial Lawyers, Internation Assn. des Avocats du Droit d'Auteur. Office: Writers Guild Am West Inc 8955 Beverly Blvd Los Angeles CA 90048-2420*

WALTON, (DELVY) CRAIG, philosopher, educator; b. L.A., Dec. 6, 1934; s. Delvy Thomas and Florence (Higgins) W.; m. Nancy Young, June 6, 1965 (div. May 1977); children: Richard, Kerry; m. Vera Allerton, Aug. 30, 1980; children: Matthew, Ruth, Peter, Benjamin. BA, Pomona Coll., 1961; PhD, Claremont Grad. Sch., 1965. Asst. prof. U. So. Calif., L.A., 1964-68; asst. prof. No. Ill. U., DeKalb, 1968-71, assoc. prof., 1971-72; assoc. prof. U. Nev., Las Vegas, 1972-75, prof., 1975—, chmn. dept. philosophy, 1986-89, dir. Inst. for Ethics and Policy Studies, 1986—; bd. dirs. Jour. History of Philosophy. Author: De la recherche du Bien, 1972, Philosophy & the Civilizing Arts, 1975, Hobbe's Science of Natural Justice, 1987; translator: (intro.) Treatise on Ethics (Malebranche), 1992; mem. editorial bd. Studies in Early Modern Philosophy, 1986—; contbr. articles to profl. jours. V.p. Nev. Faculty Alliance, 1984-86, pres. 95—; mem. Clark County Sch. Dist. Task Force on Ethics in schs., 1987. 1st lt. USAF, 1956-59. Recipient NDEA Title IV fellowship Claremont Grad. Sch., 1961-64, rsch. sabbaticals U. Nev., 1978, 85, 92; named Barrick Disting. scholar U. Nev., 1988. Mem. AAUP (pres. Nev. chpt. 1983-84), Internat. Hume Soc. (exec. com. 1979-81), Am. Philos. Assn., Soc. for Study History of Philosophy (founder and mem. exec. com. 1974-91), Internat. Hobbes Soc., Phi Beta Kappa. Democrat. Home: 6140 Eisner Dr Las Vegas NV 89131-2303 Office: U Nev Inst Ethics Policy Studies 4505 S Maryland Pky Las Vegas NV 89154-9900

WALTON, DEBORAH GAIL, advertising agency executive; b. L.A., June 22, 1950; d. Philip Hall and Virginia Mary (Schreiber) W.; m. Timothy Alan Schaible, Sept. 12, 1987; children: Adam, Melissa, Amanda, Jennifer (dec.). BA in English, Russell Sage Coll., 1972. Copywriter STA-Power Industries, San Rafael, Calif., 1972-73; asst. advt. mgr. Albany (N.Y.) Pub. Markets, 1973-75; dir. pub. relations Sta. WMHT-TV, Schenectady, N.Y., 1975-78; creative dir. LUYK Advt., Albany, 1978-81; freelance pub. relations cons. Albany, 1981-85; creative dir. H. Linn Cushing Co., Albany, 1985-87; pres. Genus Group, Inc., Santa Rosa, Calif., 1987—. Bd. dirs. Sonoma County Pvt. Industry Coun., 1988-89, Sonoma County World Affairs Coun., 1988-89, Home Hospice of Sonoma County, 1994—, Jenn Lioy Edn. Found., 1991—; grad. Leadership Santa Rosa, 1990. Recipient cert. excellence No. Calif. Addy awards, 1989. Mem. Am. Mktg. Assn., Am. Assn. Advt. Agys., San Francisco Ad Club, Sonoma County Ad Club, Santa Rosa C. of C. Office: Genus Group Inc 375 E St # 200 Santa Rosa CA 95404-4427

WALTON, JAMES STEPHEN, research scientist; b. Kingston-upon-Thames, Eng., Nov. 27, 1946; came to U.S., 1968, permanent resident, 1975; s. Ronald Walter and Jean Edna (Hudson) W.; m. Dorcas Ann Graham, July 20, 1974; children: Kirstyn Amy, Lars Timothy. Diploma in Phys. Edn., Leeds U., 1968; MA in Exercise Physiology, Mich. State U., 1970; MS in Applied Mechanics, Stanford U., 1976; PhD in Biomechanics, Pa. State U., 1981. Cert. tchr., Eng. Research asst. Stanford (Calif.) U., 1974-76; tchr. Gaynesford High Sch., Carshalton, Eng., 1969-70; dir. engring. Computerized Biomech. Analysis Inc., Amherst, Mass., 1979; sr. biomed. research scientist Gen. Motors Research Labs., Warren, Mich., 1979-85; applications engring. and product planning mgr. Motion Analysis Corp., Santa Rosa, Calif., 1985-87, v.p. applications engring., 1987-88; pres. 4D Video, Sebastopol, Calif., 1988—; cons. Sci. mag., 1982, 83, Mich. State U., 1984-85; trampoline coach several gymnastics clubs and univ. teams, 1968—. Contbr. articles to profl jours. Mem. Nat. Boy's Club Gt. Britain, London, 1964—. Recipient Research award Nat. Collegiate Gymnastics Assn., 1968-69. Fellow Brit. Assn. Phys. Tng. (hon.); mem. AAAS, Internat. Soc. Biomechanics, Internat. Soc. Biomechanics in Sports, Am. Acad. Forensic Scis., Am. Coll. Sports Medicine, Am. Soc. Biomechanics, Am. Soc. Photogrammetry and Remote Sensing (cert. photogrammetrist), Human Factors Soc., N.Y. Acad. Scis., Soc. Photo-Optical Instrumentation Engrs. (chmn. high speed photography working group, 1994—), Digital Equipment Computer Users' Soc., Sun Users' Group, Mensa, U.S. Gymnastics Fedn., Brit. Trampoline Fedn., Stanford Alumni Club, Sigma Xi. Home and Office: 4D Video 3136 Pauline Dr Sebastopol CA 95472-9741

WALTON, PAUL TALMAGE, petroleum geologist; b. Salt Lake City, Feb. 4, 1914; s. Paul and Margaret Lenore (Watts) W.; m. Dorothy Woolley, May 29, 1942 (div. Nov. 1943); 1 child, Holly Lenore; m. Helen Elizabeth Baer, July 3, 1944; children: Paul Talmage Jr., Ann Elizabeth. BS in Geol. Engring., U. Utah, 1935, MS in Geology, 1940; PhD in Geology, MIT, 1942. Cert. petroleum geologist. Engr. soil conservation svc. S.C.S. U.S. Dept. Agr., Price, Utah, 1935-38; geophysicist St. Oil Calif., Dahran, Saudi Arabia, 1938-39; geologist Texaco, Denver, 1942-44, Getty Oil Interest, Casper, Wyo., 1944-49; geologist, ptnr. Morgan Walton Oils, Salt Lake City, 1949-54, Walton Kearns, Salt Lake City, 1954-69, Paul T. Walton & Assocs., Salt Lake City, 1970—; pres. Am. Geol. Enterprises, Salt Lake City, 1972—. Author: Prospect to Prosperity, 1994. Mem. AAPG, AIPG. Republican. Home: Box 325 Star Rt Jackson WY 83001 Office: Paul T Walton & Assoc 175 S Main St Salt Lake City UT 84111-1916

WALTON, ROGER ALAN, public relations executive, mediator, writer; b. Denver, June 25, 1941; s. Lyle R. and Velda V. (Nicholson) W.; m. Helen Anderson. Attended, U. Colo., 1960-63. Govt. rep. Continental Airlines, Denver, 1964-72; dir. pub. affairs Regional Transp. Dist., Denver, 1972-77; pub. affairs cons. Denver, 1977—; res. pub. info. officer Fed. Emergency Mgmt. Agy., 1995—; pres. Colo. Times Pub. Co.; res. pub. info. officer FEMA, 1995. Author: Colorado-A Practical Guide to its Government and Politics, 1973, 6th rev. edit., 1990, Colorado Gambling - A Guide, 1991; columnist The Denver Post newspaper, 1983—, The Rocky Mountain Jour., 1977-81. Mem. U.S. Presdl. Electoral Coll., Washington, 1968; commr. U.S. Bicentennial Revolution Commn., Colo., 1972-76, U.S. Commn. on the Bicentennial of U.S. Constn., Denver, 1985-90, pres.; trustee Arapahoe County (Colo.) Libr. Bd., 1982-86; chmn. lobbyist ethics com. Colo. Gen. Assembly, 1990-91. Republican. Home and Office: 12550 W 2nd Dr Lakewood CO 80228-5012

WALTZ, MARCUS ERNEST, retired prosthodontist; b. Brownsville, Oreg., July 29, 1921; s. Roswell Starr and Eva Ione (Cherrington) W.; m. Constance Jean Elwood, May 31, 1952 (div. Nov. 1973); children: Melody Ann, Martha Louise, Kathryn Jean, Holly Jay, Joy Evalyn, Ross Elwood; m. Shelby Annette Schwab, June 10, 1975. AB, Willamette U., 1942; DMD, U. Oreg., 1945. Cert. Nev. State Bd. Dental Examiners. Practice dentistry specializing in prosthodontics Forest Grove, Oreg., 1946-52; practice dentistry specializing in prosthodontics Reno, 1954-95, ret., 1995; councillor Pacific Coast Dental Conf.; pres. Pacific Coast Soc. of Prosthodontics, 1983. Mem. State of Nev. Selective Svc. Appeals Bd., 1970-76, pres., 1974-76. Lt. USN, 1945-46, 52-54, Korea. Decorated Combat Medics award, Battle Stars (oak leaf cluster). Fellow Internat. Coll. Dentistry, Acad. Dentistry Internat.; mem. ADA, Northern Nev. Dental Soc. (pres. 1959), Nev. Dental Assn., Nev. Acad. Gen. Dentistry (pres. 1974), Sigma Chi, Omicron Kappa Upsilon. Democrat. Methodist. Club: Reno Exec. (dir. 1960-66, pres. 1964-65). Lodges: Sigma Tau (pres. 1941-42), Masons (32 degree), Shriners. Home: 715 Manor Dr Reno NV 89509-1944

WALUCONIS, CARL JOSEPH, English language educator, humanities educator; b. Balt., Oct. 27, 1946; s. George Jospeh and Alberta Mary (Romouski) W.; m. Susan M. Beardsley, Aug. 30, 1970 (div. June 1975); m. Joan Leslie McBride, June 2, 1979; children: Gabriel, Lilian, Jacob. BA, Towson State U., 1968; MA, Western Wash. State U., 1970. Adj. faculty humanities Bellevue (Wash.) C.C., 1970-75, 83-87; prof. humanities Seattle (Wash.) Ctrl. C.C., 1988—; workshop presenter. Author: (novel) Whispers of Heavenly Death, 1980; contbr. chpts. to books on learning in higher edn. Recipient award of excellence Wash. Fedn. Tchrs., 1992, Exemplary Status award Wash. C.C. Humanities Assn., 1992. Mem. Am. Assn. Higher Edn., [illegible] Undergrad. Edn., Nat. Coun. Tchrs. English, Am. Gen. Liberal Studies. Democrat. Home: 6536 102nd Ave NE Kirkland WA 98033-6922 Office: Seattle Ctrl CC BE 4128 1701 Broadway Seattle WA 98122-2413

WAMBOLT, THOMAS EUGENE, financial consultant; b. Scottsbluff, Nebr., Aug. 9, 1938; s. Andrew, Jr. and Anne (Altergott) W.; B.S., Met. State Coll., Denver, 1976; cert. Total Quality Mgmt. m. Linda E. Shifflett, Oct. 31, 1967; 1 son, Richard Duane King. Pres. Universal Imports Co., Westminster, Colo., 1967-71; printer Rocky Mountain News, Denver, 1967-78; propr., accountant Thomas E. Wambolt Co., Arvada, Colo., 1974-77, fin. cons., 1977—. Baptist. Address: 6035 Garrison St Arvada CO 80004-5345

WAN, YU-JUI YVONNE, educator, scientist; b. Taipei, Taiwan, Sept. 8, 1956; came to U.S., 1979; d. Shin-Chang and Yat-Gen (Shiu) W.; m. Tsung-Chieh Jackson Wu, Feb. 21, 1982; children: Joshua Wu, Julia Wu. BS, Taipei Medical Coll., Taipei, Taiwan, 1979; MSc in pathology, Hahnemann U., 1981, PhD in pathology, 1983. Rsch. asst. electron microscopy and immunochemistry Hahnemann U., Phila., 1980-82; postdoctoral fellow, lab. devel. and molecular immunity NICHD, NIH, Bethesda, Md., 1984-86, staff and sr. staff fellow sect. on cellular differentiation, 1986-89; assoc. morphology core dir. Population Rsch. Ctr. Harbor-UCLA Med. Ctr., Torrance, Calif., 1989-91; co-dir. molecular biology diagnostic lab. Harbor UCLA Med. Ctr., Torrance, Calif., 1989-95; asst. prof. dept. pathology UCLA Sch. Medicine, L.A., 1989-95, assoc. prof dept. pathology, 1995—; instr. U. Calif. Riverside; cons. NIH, 1992—. Contbr. numerous articles to profl. jours.; expert in retinoic acid, cancer and devel. Adminstrn. policies com. Rsch. & Edn. Inst., Inc., 1991—; exec. com. Population Rsch. Ctr., 1989-92. Recipient Upjohn scholarship award Hahnemann U., 1980-82, Purvis Martin M D award, 1992, numerous rsch. grants. Mem. The Endocrine Soc., Am. Assn. Cancer Rsch., Am. Soc. Microbiology, Am. Assn. Advancement Sci., Soc. Chinese Bioscientists in Am. Office: Harbor UCLA Medical Ctr Dept Pathology 1000 W Carson St Torrance CA 90502-2004

WANDS, JOHN MILLAR, English language educator, researcher; b. Buffalo, Jan. 18, 1946; s. John and Mildred Carmella (Denall) W.; m. Frances Terpak, June 22, 1974; 1 child, Ann. BA, Canisius Coll., 1968; MA, U. Chgo., 1970; PhD, Pa. State U., 1976. Instr. English Pa. State U., University Park, 1974, European divsn. U. Md., Heidelberg, Germany, 1974-75; asst. prof. Yale U., New Haven, 1976-78, Carnegie-Mellon U., Pitts., 1978-84; head English dept. Marlborough Sch., L.A., 1984—; fellow Calhoun Coll., Yale U., 1977-78; test cons. Ednl. Testing Svc., Princeton, N.J., 1979-80; reader Advanced Placement Ednl. Testing Svc., Princeton, 1987-91, table leader, 1992—. Contbr. articles to profl. jours. Mem. Friends of UCLA Libr. NEH grantee, 1981, A. Whitney Griswold grantee Yale U., 1977-78, Falk Found. grantee, 1979, Elizabethan Club grantee, 1981; Exxon Found. fellow Newberry Libr., 1982, Coun. Basic Edn./NEH fellow, 1987. Mem. MLA, Nat. Coun. Tchrs. of English, Renaissance Soc. Am., Calif. Assn. Ind. Schs. (profl. svcs. com.). Democrat. Home: 11817 Bellagio Rd Los Angeles CA 90049-2116 Office: Marlborough Sch 250 S Rossmore Ave Los Angeles CA 90004-3739

WANDS, ROBERT JAMES, art educator; b. Denver, June 24, 1939; s. Alfred James and Dorothy L. (Payne) W.; m. Carol Louise Longgrear, Aug. 12, 1966; children; Kirby Lynn Marquez, Cassandra Leann Dickey. BFA, Denver U., 1961, MA, 1962-63; postgrad., Western Res. U., 1961-62, Cleve. Art Inst., 1961-62. Instr. Denver U., 1962-63; art prof. U. So. Colo., Pueblo, 1963—; artist in residence YMCA Ctr., Estes Park, Colo., 1972-77; dir. Wands Art Studio and Gallery, Estes Park, 1978—. One-man shows include Western Colo. Ctr. for Arts, Grand Junction, 1974, El Pueblo Mus., Pueblo, 1976, Off Broadway Art Galleries, Pueblo, 1986, The Colo. Gallery, Pueblo, 1994, and others; group shows include Colo. State Fair Exhibition, Pueblo, 1986, 93, Perry Coldwell Gallery, Ft. Worth, Tex., 1986, Colo. Art Educators Exhibit, Pueblo, 1988, 1989, Colo. Tchrs. Exhibition, Manitou Springs, 1989, Estes Park Art Ctr., 1990, and others; represented in permanent collections U. Denver, Colo. Women's Coll., We. Colo. Ctr. for Arts, U. So. Colo., Dain Bosworth, United Bank, Intrawest Bank, Colo. Nat. Bank, Pueblo Bank & Trust, Pueblo Tchrs. Credit Union. Bd. dirs. Sangre de Cristo Art Ctr., Pueblo, 1981-87. Home: 1306 W Abriendo Ave Pueblo CO 81004-1006

WANERMAN, LEON RALPH, psychiatrist; b. Phila., July 12, 1935, s. Charles and Marion Wanerman; m. Nancy Rosenblum, Sept. 22, 1991; children: Brian, Todd, Laura; stepchildren: Leah Maxwell, Sarah Maxwell. AB, U. Chgo., 1954; postgrad., L.I. U., 1954-55, U. Geneva, Switzerland, 1955-56; MD, Albany Med. Coll., 1960. Intern Mount Zion Hosp. and Med. Ctr., San Francisco, 1960-61, resident child psychiatry, 1963-65; resident psychiatry Langley-Porter Psychiat. Inst., San Francisco, 1961-63; cons. outpatient dept. Adolescent Clinic Mount Zion Hosp. and Med. Ctr., San Francisco, 1964-69, dir. consultation svcs. dept. psychiatry, 1970-73; staff psychiatrist Cmty. Mental Health Svcs., Marin County, Calif., 1965-67; dep. dir., chief children's svcs. Cmty. Mental Health Svcs., Marin County, 1967-69, dir., 1969-70; pvt. practice psychiatry San Francisco/Mill Valley, Calif., 1965-91; assoc. clin. prof. health U. Calif., Berkeley, 1973-80, assoc. clin. prof. psychiatry, 1977-84; clin. prof. psychiatry U. Calif., San Francisco, 1984—; dep. med. dir., dir. consultation svcs. U.S. Behavioral Health, Emeryville, Calif., 1990—; mem. teaching staff Mt. Zion Hosp. Med. Ctr., San Francisco, 1965-84; guest instr. divsn. maternal and child health U.Calif., Berkeley, 1966-73, vis. lectr. helath and med. scis., 1980-83; cons. for planning and devel., coord. children's svcs. Westside Cmty. Mental Health Ctr., San Francisco, 1969; coord. planning project Doctor of Mental Health Program, San Francisco, 1971-75; cons. Alameda County Mental Health Svcs., Residency Tng. Program, Oakland, Calif., 1975-77; dir. Doctor of Mental Health Program, U. Calif., Berkeley, San Francisco, 1975-80; cons. The Poplar Ctr., San Mateo, Calif., 1980-87; chief mental health dept. Rockridge Health Care Plan, Oakland, 1980-84, Rockridge Practitioners Assn., 1984-86, v.p. ops., treas., 1986-87; med. dir. mental health svcs. children Dept. Health Svcs., Contra Costa County, Calif., 1987-90. Contbr. articles to profl. jours. Mt. Zion Hosp. rep. bd. dirs., Westside Cmty. Mental Health Ctr., San Francisco, 1970-73, v.p. bd. dirs., 1972-73, chairperson children's svcs. com., 1971-73; chairperson bd. dirs. The Beginning Sch., Marin County, 1971-72; awards adv. commn. Dept. Mental Health Commonwealth Mass., 1974; mem. Proposition 9 Contingency Planning Commn., Cmty. Mental Health Svcs., San Francisco, 1980; bd. dirs. Mountain Play Assn., Marin County, 1980-82, pres. bd. dirs., 1981-82; others. With USPHS, 1962-65. Fellow Am. Coll. Mental Health Adminstrn., Am. Orthopsychiat. Assn. (bd. dirs. 1994—); mem. Am. Acad. Child Psychiatry, Am. Psychiat. Assn. (no. Calif.), No. Calif. Regional Orgn. Child and Adolescent Psychiatry. Office: US Behavioral Health 2000 Powell St Ste 1180 Emeryville CA 94608-1804

WANG, ARTHUR C., law educator, lawyer; b. Boston, Feb. 4, 1949; s. Kung Shou and Lucy (Chow) W.; m. Wendy F. Hamai, May 22, 1976 (div. 1981); m. Nancy J. Norton, Sept. 1, 1985; children: Alexander Xinglin, Sierra Xinan. BA, Franconia Coll., 1970; JD, U. Puget Sound, 1984. Bar: Wash. 1984. Printer Carmel Valley (Calif.) Outlook, 1970-73; project coord. Tacoma (Wash.) Community House, 1973-76; rsch. analyst Wash. Ho. of Reps., Olympia, Wash., 1977-80, mem., 1981-94; of counsel Davies Pearson, P.C., Tacoma, 1984-94; adj. prof. U. Puget Sound Law Sch., Tacoma, 1987-93, Seattle U. Law Sch., Tacoma, 1995—; chmn House Capital Budget Com., 1993-94, Revenue Com., 1989-92, Commerce and Labor Com., 1985-88; mem. Wash. Pers. Appeals Bd., Olympia, 1994—. Assoc. editor U. Puget Sound Law Review, 1983-84. Vista vol. Tacoma Urban League, 1973-74; del. Dem. Nat. Conv., 1976. Named Chinese Am. Man of Yr., Seattle Chinese Post, 1991, Legislator of Yr., Wash. Health Care Assn., 1992. Democrat. Home: 3319 N Union Ave Tacoma WA 98407-6043 Office: Wash Pers Appt Bd PO Box 40911 Olympia WA 98504

WANG, CHANGLIN, microbiologist, researcher; b. Chao County, Anhui, Peoples Republic of China, Dec. 11, 1949; came to U.S., 1990; s. Anrong and Anyun (Ma) W.; m. Shizhen Gu, Oct. 30, 1978; 1 child, Peter Haiming. BS, Wuan-Nan Agrl. Coll., Anhui, 1977; PhD, China Agrl. U., Wuhan, Peoples Republic of China, 1987. Rsch. asst. Anhui Acad. Agrl. Scis., 1977-81; rsch. scientist Inst. of Plant Physiology, Acad. of China, Shanghai, 1988-90; postdoctoral rsch. assoc. U. Ill., Urbana, 1990-91, U. Idaho, Moscow, 1992—. Editor: Research Advances in Life and Soil Science, 1993; patentee in field; author rsch. reports. Mem. AAAS, Chinese Soc. Genetics. Office: MMBB U Idaho Moscow ID 83843

WANG, CHARLES PING, scientist; b. Shanghai, Republic of China, Apr. 25, 1937; came to U.S., 1962; s. Kuan-Ying and Ping-Lu (Ming) W.; m. Lily L. Lee, June 29, 1963. BS, Taiwan U., Republic of China, 1959; MS, Tsinghua U., Singchu, Republic of China, 1961; PhD, Calif. Inst. Tech., 1967. Mem. tech. staff Bellcomm, Washington, 1967-69; research engr. U. San Diego, 1969-74; sr. scientist Aerspace Corp., Los Angeles, 1976-86; pres. Optodyne, Inc., Compton, Calif., 1986—; adj. prof. U. Calif., San Diego, 1979-90; pres. Chinese-Am. Engr. and Scientists Assn. So. Calif., Los Angeles, 1979-81; program chmn. Internation Conf. of Lasers, Shanghai, 1979-80; organizer and session chmn. Lasers Conf., Los Angeles, 1981-84, program chmn., Las Vegas, 1985. Editor in chief Series in Laser Tech., 1983-91; contbr. articles to profl. jours.; inventor discharge excimer laser. Calif. Inst. Tech. scholar, 1965. Fellow Am. Optical Soc., AIAA (assoc., jour. editor 1981-83). Office: Optodyne Inc 1180 W Mahalo Pl Compton CA 90220-5443

WANG, CHEN CHI, electronics company executive, real estate executive, finance company executive, investments services executive, international trade executive; b. Taipei, Taiwan, Aug. 10, 1932; came to U.S., 1959, naturalized, 1970; s. Chin-Ting and Chen-Kim Wang; m. Victoria Rebisoff, Mar. 5, 1965; children: Katherine Kim, Gregory Chen, John Christopher, Michael Edward. B.A. in Econs., Nat. Taiwan U., 1955; B.S.E.E., San Jose State U., 1965; M.B.A., U. Calif., Berkeley, 1961. With IBM Corp., San Jose, Calif., 1965-72; founder, chief exec. officer Electronics Internat. Co., Santa Clara, Calif., 1968-72, owner, gen. mgr., 1972-81, reorganized as EIC Group, 1982, now chmn. bd., chief exec. officer; dir. Systek Electronics Corp., Santa Clara, 1970-73; founder, sr. ptnr. Wang Enterprises (name changed to Chen Kim Entrprises 1982), Santa Clara, 1974—; founder, sr. ptnr. Hanson & Wang Devel. Co., Woodside, Calif., 1977-85; chmn. bd. Golden Alpha Enterprises, San Mateo, Calif., 1979—; mng. ptnr. Woodside Acres-Las Pulgas Estate, Woodside, 1980-85; founder, sr. ptnr. DeVine & Wang, Oakland, Calif., 1977-83; Van Heal & Wang, West Village, Calif., 1981-82; founder, chmn. bd. EIC Fin. Corp., Redwood City, Calif., 1985—; chmn. bd. Maritek Corp., Corpus Christi, Tex., 1988-89; chmn. EIC Internat. Trade Corp., Lancaster, Calif., 1989—, EIC Capital Corp., Redwood City, 1990—. Served to 2d lt., Nationalist Chinese Army, 1955-56. Mem. Internat. Platform Assn., Tau Beta Pi. Mem. Christian Ch. Author: Monetary and Banking System of Taiwan, 1955, The Small Car Market in the U.S., 1961. Home: 195 Brookwood Rd Woodside CA 94062-2302 Office: EIC Group Head Office Bldg 2055-2075 Woodside Rd Redwood City CA 94061-2095

WANG, HUAI-LIANG WILLIAM, mechanical engineer; b. Hsinchu, Taiwan, Republic of China, Apr. 4, 1959; came to U.S., 1984; s. Feng-Chi and Hu-Mei (Chou) W.; m. Wen-Pei Chen, June 28, 1986; 1 child, James. BSME, Tatung Inst. of Tech., Taipei, Taiwan, 1981; MSME, Okla. State U., 1985. Asst. engr. Teco Electric and Machinery Corp., Taipei, Taiwan, 1984; electro-mech. engr. Microsci. Internat. Corp., Sunnyvale, Calif., 1987-89; engr. Lockheed Engring. and Scis. Co., Houston, 1989-91, sr. engr., 1991-92; mgr. mech. engring. Orbiter Tech. Co., Fremont, Calif., 1992; sr. engr. Avatar Sys. Corp., Milpitas, Calif., 1993, Quantum Corp., Milpitas, 1994—. Mem. IEEE. Office: Quantum Corp 500 Mccarthy Blvd Milpitas CA 95035-7908

WANG, I-TUNG, atmospheric scientist; b. Peking, People's Republic of China, Feb. 16, 1933; came to U.S., 1958; s. Shen and Wei-Yun (Wen) W.; m. Amy Hung Kong; children: Cynthia P., Clifford T. BS in Physics, Nat. Taiwan U., 1955; MA in Physics, U. Toronto, 1957; PhD in Physics, Columbia U., 1965. Rsch. physicist Carnegie-Mellon U., Pitts., 1965-67, asst. prof., 1967-70; environ. systems engr. Argonne (Ill.) Nat. Lab., 1970-76; mem. tech. staff Environ. Monitoring and Svcs. Ctr. Rockwell Internat., Creve Coeur, Mo., 1976-80, Newbury Park, Calif., 1980-84; sr. scientist, combustion engr. Environ. Monitoring and Svcs. Inc., Newbury Park, Camarillo, 1984-88; sr. scientist ENSR Corp (formerly ERT), 1988; pres. EMA Co., Thosand Oaks, Calif., 1989—; tech. advisor Bur. of Environ. Protection, Republic of China, 1985; environ. cons. ABB Environ., 1989-92, ARCO, 1990-91, Du Pont (SAFER Systems Divsn.), 1992-93, So. Calif. Edison, 1993—. Contbr. papers to profl jours. First violin Conejo Symphony Orch., Thousand Oaks, Calif., 1981-83. Grantee Bureau of Environ. Protection, Taiwan, 1985. Mem. N.Y. Acad. of Scis., Air and Waste Mgmt. Assn., Sigma Xi. Office: EMA Co Ste 435 2219 E Thousand Oaks Blvd Thousand Oaks CA 91362-2905

WANG, JIAN CHUAN-QIU, artist; b. Dalian, China, Sept. 26, 1958; came to U.S., 1986; s. Shoulun and Jing (Xu) W.; m. Xiutao Zhu, Oct. 2, 1983; 1 child, Shuya. BS in Engring., Dalian (China) Railway Inst., 1982; MA in Fine Art, Calif. State U., Sacramento, 1994. Chmn. Dalian (China) Coll. Student Arts Assn., 1979-82; bd. dirs. Dalian (China) Painting and Calligraphy Assn., 1982-86; artist self-employed Carmichael, Calif., 1986—. Exhibited in one-man shows at Aaron Gallery, 1994, Artists Contemporary Gallery, 1988-94, Gump's Gallery, 1992-94, Karl Walburg Gallery, 1993-94, Ray and Joyce Witt Galery, 1992-94, Sunbird Gallery, 1994; works represented in Owl-57 Gallery, N.Y., Kurtz Bingham Gallery, Memphis, Fay Gold Gallery, Atlanta, Contemporary Realist Gallery, San Francisco, Winfield Gallery, Carmel, Watezman Gallery, London; represented in pvt. and pub. institutions. Recipient Roberson fellowship Calif. State U. Sacramento, 1992. Home and Office: 2641 Riverpine Ct Carmichael CA 95608-5321

WANG, JOSEPH, education educator, scientist; b. Haifa, Israel, Jan. 8, 1948; came to U.S., 1978; s. Moshe and Elka Wang; m. Ruth Wang, Mar. 2, 1976; 1 child, Sharon. BSc, Technion, Israel, 1972, MS, 1974, DSc, 1978. Rsch. assoc. U. Wis., Madison, 1978-80; asst. prof. N.Mex. State U., Las Cruces, 1980-84, assoc. prof., 1984-88, prof., 1988—. Author 4 books and 350 papers in field; chief editor Electroanalysis, 11988—; mem. editl. bd. 6 jours. Office: NMex State U Dept Chem Las Cruces NM 88003

WANG, LIN, physicist, computer science educator, computer software consultant; b. Dandong, China, June 11, 1929; came to U.S., 1961, naturalized, 1972; s. Lu-Ting and Shou-Jean (Sun) W.; m. Ingrid Ling-Fen Tsow, July 8 1961; children: W. Larry, Ben. BS in Physics, Taiwan U., 1956; MS in Physics, Okla. State U., 1965, PhD in Physics, 1972. Mem. physics faculty Cheng Kung U., Tainan, China, 1957-61; asst. prof. physics Southwestern Okla. State U., Weatherford, 1965-72; prof., chmn. physics dept. N.E. Coll. Arts and Sci., Maiduguri, Nigeria, 1973-75; mem. tech. staff Pacific Engring. Corp., Bellevue, Wash., 1976-78; sr. software engr., Far East cons. Electro-Sci. Industries, Inc., Portland, Oreg., 1979-82; mem. sr. computer sci. faculty South Seattle C.C., 1983—. Mem. Assn. for Computing Machinery, Am. Phys. Soc., AAUP. Home: 9322 168th Pl NE Redmond WA 98052

WANG, ROBERT CHING-HUEI, engineer; b. Taipei, Taiwan, Aug. 6, 1957; s. Ping-Huang and Chin-Chih (Lo) W.; m. Glori Chu-shu Lee, Dec. 28, 1981; children: Terrence, Edward. BS in Indsl. Engring., Tsing Hwa U., Hsin-Chu, Taiwan, 1979; ME in Indsl. Engring., Rochester Inst. of Tech., 1983; MS in Computer Sci., SUNY, Buffalo, 1985, PhD in Computer Sci., 1988. Engr. Boeing, Seattle, 1988—. Patentee in field. Mem. Soc. of Chinese Engrs. of Seattle (chmn. bd. dirs. 1992—, pres. 1991, v.p. 1990), Am. Assn. of Computing Machinery. Home: 4207 170th Ct NE Redmond WA 98052-5494 Office: Boeing PO Box MS 3E-33 Seattle WA 98124-2499

WANG, SHENG-YONG, cardiologist and research physiologist; b. Zhijiang, Hubei, China, Dec. 25, 1956; s. Chang-Fan and Jin-Zhi (Xie) W.; m. Ling Dong, Sept. 13, 1983; 1 child, Qing. MD, Hubei Med. U., 1982, M. of Medicine, 1985; PhD, U. Bonn, Germany, 1992. Physician Hubei Med. U., 1985-87, physician-in-chg., 1987-89; sci. asst. U. Bonn, 1989-92; postdoctoral fellow UCLA, 1992-94. Contbr. articles to profl. jours. Freidrich-Nauman Found. scholar, 1990-91; Am. Heart Assn. postdoctoral fellow, 1992-94. Office: UCLA Sch of Medicine MRL Bldg Rm 3645 675 Circle Dr S Los Angeles CA 90024-8322

WANG, TONY KAR-HUNG, automotive and aerospace company executive; b. Shanghai, People's Republic of China, Apr. 28, 1952; came to U.S., 1970; s. Kuo-Tung and Chien-Wen (Chu) W.; m. Vivian Wei-Pie, May 25, 1980;

children: Stephen, Jason. BSE in Materials and Metall. Engring., U. Mich., 1973, MSE in Materials, 1975. Materials engr. Burroughs Corp., Detroit, 1976-78; sr. project engr. Gen. Motors Corp., Warren, Mich., 1978-85; staff engr. Hughes Aircraft Co., El Segundo, Calif., 1985; staff engr. Gen. Motors-Hughes Electronics Corp., El Segundo, 1986-87, mgr. program, staff engr., 1987-89, sr. staff engr., 1989-93; exec. v.p. Xenon Group USA, 1993—. Contbr. articles to profl. jours. Goodrich scholar, U. Mich., Ann Arbor, 1974. Mem. Soc. Advanced Materials and Process Engring. Republican.

WANGER, OLIVER WINSTON, federal judge, educator; b. L.A., Nov. 27, 1940; m. Lorrie A. Reinhart; children: Guy A., Christopher L., Andrew G., W. Derek, Oliver Winston II. Student, Colo. Sch. Mines, 1958-60; BS, U. So. Calif., 1963; LLB, U. Calif., Berkeley, 1966. Bar: Calif. 1967, U.S. Dist. Ct. (ea. dist.) Calif. 1969, U.S. Tax Ct. 1969, U.S. Dist. Ct. (cen. dist.) Calif. 1975, U.S. Dist. Ct. (so. dist.) Calif. 1977, U.S. Dist. Ct. (no. dist.) Calif. 1989, U.S. Ct. Appeals (9th cir.) 1989. Dep. dist. atty. Fresno (Calif.) County Dist. Atty., 1967-69; ptnr. Gallagher, Baker & Manock, Fresno, 1969-74; sr. ptnr. McCormick, Barstow, Sheppard, Wayte & Carruth, Fresno, 1974-91; judge U.S. Dist. Ct. (ea. dist.) Calif., Fresno, 1991—; adj. prof. law Humphreys Coll. Law, Fresno, 1968-70; adj. prof. law San Joaquin Coll. Law, Fresno, 1970-94, dean Law Sch., 1980-82, pres., chmn. bd. dirs., 1982-94. Fellow Am. Coll. Trial Lawyers, Internat. Acad. Trial Lawyers; mem. Am. Bd. Trial Advs. (pres. San Joaquin Valley chpt. 1987-89, nat. bd. dirs. 1989-91), Am. Bd. Profl. Liability Attys. (founder, diplomate), Calif. State Bar (mem. exec. com. litigation sect. 1989-92, mem. com. on fed. cts. 1989-90), San Joaquin Valley Am. Inn of Ct. (pres. 1992-93), Beta Gamma Sigma. Office: US Dist Ct 5104 US Courthouse 1130 O St Fresno CA 93721-2201

WARD, ALBERT EUGENE, research center executive, archaeologist, ethnohistorian; b. Carlinville, Ill., Aug. 20, 1940; s. Albert Alan and Eileen (Boston) W.; m. Gladys Anena Lea, Apr. 26, 1961 (div. Apr. 4, 1974); children—Scott Bradley, Brian Todd; m. Stefanie Helen Tschaikowsky, Apr. 24, 1982. AA, Bethany Luth. Jr. Coll., Mankato, Minn., 1961; BS, No. Ariz. U., 1968; MA, U. Ariz., 1972. Lab. asst., asst. archeologist Mus. No. Ariz., Flagstaff, 1965-67; research archeologist Desert Research Inst., U. Nev., Las Vegas, 1968; research archeologist Archeol. Survey, Prescott Coll., Ariz., 1969-71, research assoc., 1971-73; research archeologist Ariz. Archeol. Ctr., Nat. Park Service, Tucson, 1972-73, research collaborator Chaco Ctr., Albuquerque, 1975; founder, dir. archaeol. research program Mus. Albuquerque, 1975-76; founder, dir., 1976-79 pres. bd. dirs. Ctr. Anthrop. Studies, Albuquerque, 1976—; lectr. U. N.Mex. C.C., 1974-77, others; contract archaeol. salvage and research projects in N.Mex. and Ariz. Editorial adv. bd. Hist. Archeology, 1978-80; editor publs. Ctr. Anthrop. Studies, 1978—. Contbr. articles to scholarly jours. Grantee Mus. No. Ariz., 1972, S.W. Monuments Assn., 1973, CETA, 1975-79, Nat. Park Service, 1978-79. Mem. Soc. Am. Archeology, Soc. Hist. Archeology, No. Ariz. Soc. Sci. and Art, Ariz. Archeol. and Hist. Soc., Archeol. Soc. N.Mex., Albuquerque Archeol. Soc., Am. Anthrop. Assn., S.W. Mission Research Ctr., Am. Soc. Conservation Archeology, Soc. Archeol. Scis., Southwestern Anthrop. Assn., N.Mex. Archeol. Council, Living Hist. Farms and Agrl. Mus. Assn. Republican. Lutheran.

WARD, ANTHONY JOHN, lawyer; b. L.A., Sept. 25, 1931; s. John P. and Helen C. (Harris) W.; A.B., U. So. Calif., 1953; LL.B., U. Calif. at Berkeley, 1956; m. Marianne Edle von Graeve, Feb. 20, 1960 (div. 1977); 1 son, Mark Joachim; m. 2d, Julia Norby Credell, Nov. 4, 1978. Admitted to Calif. bar, 1957; asso. firm Ives, Kirwan & Dibble, Los Angeles, 1958-61; partner firm Marapese and Ward, Hawthorne, Calif., 1961-69; individual practice law, Torrance, Calif., 1969-76; partner firm Ward, Gaunt & Raskin, 1976—. Served to 1st lt. USAF, 1956-58. Mem. ABA, Blue Key, Calif. Trial Lawyers Assn., Lambda Chi Alpha. Democrat. Home: 4477 Wilshire Blvd Apt 209 Los Angeles CA 90010-3727 Office: Pavilion A 21525 Hawthorne Blvd Torrance CA 90503-6605

WARD, BARRY JOHN, historian; b. West Covina, Calif., Nov. 25, 1964; s. Bobby Joe Ward and Eileen June (McCormick) Allred. BA, U. Pacific, 1988. Loan officer Fin. Ctr. Bank, Stockton, Calif., 1986-88; asst. curator Haggin Mus., Stockton, 1988-91, devel. officer, 1991, spl. projects archivist, 1993—; analyst-underwriter Trillium Mortgage Bank, Lake Oswego, Oreg., 1992-93; hist. cons. Duraflame, Inc., Stockton, 1993—; featured speaker Mystic (Conn.) Seaport Mus., 1991, St. Francis Yacht Club, San Francisco, 1992, Nat. Maritime Mus., San Francisco, 1993, Seattle Yacht Club, 1995. Feature writer: The Cen. Valley Harvester, 1994. Bd. dirs. Historic Records Commn., San Joaquin County, Calif., 1992, Cultural Heritage Bd., Stockton, 1994; mem. bd. trustees Land Utilization Trust, 1995. Republican. Home: 1523 Cameron Way Stockton CA 95207-2413

WARD, CARL EDWARD, research chemist; b. Albuquerque, Oct. 16, 1948; s. Joe E. and Loris E. (Wenk) W.; m. Bertha R. Schloer, June 9, 1970. BS in Chemistry, N.Mex. Inst. Mining and Tech., 1970; MS in Chemistry, Oreg. Grad. Ctr., 1972; PhD in Chemistry, Stanford U., 1977. Research chemist Union Carbide Corp., Charleston, W.Va., 1977-79, Dynapol Corp., Palo Alto, Calif., 1979-80; research chemist Chevron Chem. Co., Richmond, Calif., 1980-85, sr. research chemist, 1986-88; apptd. supr. chemical synthesis Chevron Chem. Co., Richmond, 1988-90; sr. rsch. assoc. Chevron Rsch. & Tech. Co., Richmond, 1990-91, staff scientist, 1991—. Referee Jour. Organic Chemistry, 1983—; patentee in field; contbr. articles to profl. jours. Recipient NSF traineeship, Stanford U., 1972-73; Upjohn fellow, Stanford U., 1976-77. Mem. AAAS, Soc. Tribologists and Lubrication Engrs., Am. Chem. Soc., Calif. Acad. Sci., N.Mex. Inst. Mining and Tech. Pres. Club (Socorro), Stanford Alumni Assn. Democrat. Home: 1355 Nisich Dr San Jose CA 95122-3061 Office: Chevron Rsch & Tech Co PO Box 1627 Richmond CA 94802-1796

WARD, DAVID CHARLES, police chief; b. Glendive, Mont., Aug. 12, 1948; s. Charles Maxwell and Harriet Cora (Oellermann) W.; m. Valerie Jean Remfert Ward, Mar. 20, 1971; children: Kimberlee, Kyla, Kelley. BA in gen. bus., Mont. State U., 1970. Police officer Billings (Mont.) Police Dept., 1972-79, patrol sergant, 1979-84, detective sergant, 1984-89, patrol lt., 1989-92, asst. chief, 1992-94, police chief, 1994—; cmty. policing task force Mont. Bd. of Crime Control, 1994; criminal hist. improvement task force, 1995. Bd. mem. Rimrock Credit Union, Billings, Mont., 1987—; mem. Mont. PTSA, Billings. Chief Warrant Officer USAR. Mem. U.S. Army Warrant Officers Assn., Internat. Assn. Chiefs of Police, FBI Nat. Acad. Assn., Mont. Assn. Chiefs of Police (v.p. 1993-95, pres. 1995—), Billings Police Protective Assn. (pres., v.p., sec.), Lions Club Internat. (v.p., dir.), Bd. of Private Investigators, Helena, Mont., Atty. Gen. Law Enforcement Adv. Com., Helena, Mont., Police Cmty. Adv. Com., Billings, Mont.; bd. mem. Eastern Coal County DARE. Mem. Evangelical Ch. of N.Am. Office: Billings Police Dept 220 N 27th St Billings MT 59101

WARD, DENNIS FRANCIS, librarian; b. Redwood City, Calif., Dec. 13, 1946; s. Thomas Francis and Dorothy Blanche (Coates) W.; m. Anne Marie Pierce, Feb. 12, 1977; children: Lisa Anne, Matthew Thomas, Patrick Timothy. BA in History cum laude, Santa Clara U., 1969; MLS, U. Calif., Berkeley, 1973. Libr. Kratter Law Libr. U. San Diego, 1973-74; libr. Calif. State Law Libr., Sacramento, 1974-78; sr. libr. Sierra Conservation Ctr., Jamestown, Calif., 1978—; legal ref. instr. Calif. Dept. Corrections, Sacramento, 1989—. Catechist, rite of Christian initiation of adults St. Patrick's Ch., Sonora, Calif., 1983—. With U.S. Army, 1970-72. Edwin Brown fellow U. Santa Clara, 1969-70. Mem. Ctrl. Assn. Librs. (vice chair, chair elect 1984-85, chmn. 1985, 91). Office: Sierra Conservation Ctr 5100 O'Byrnes Ferry Rd Jamestown CA 95327

WARD, DIANE KOROSY, lawyer; b. Cleve., Oct. 17, 1939; d. Theodore Louis and Edith (Bogar) Korosy; m. S. Mortimer Ward IV, July 2, 1960 (div. 1978); children: Christopher LaBruce, Samantha Martha; m. R. Michael Walters, June 30, 1979. AB, Heidelberg Coll., 1961; JD, U. San Diego, 1975. Bar: Calif. 1977, U.S. Dist. Ct. (so. dist.) Calif. 1977. Ptnr. Ward & Howell, San Diego, 1978-79, Walters, Ward & Howell, A.P.C., San Diego, 1979-81; mng. ptnr. Walters & Ward, A.P.C., San Diego, 1981—; dir., v.p. Oak Broadcasting Systems, Inc., 1982-83; dir. Elisabeth Kubler-Ross Ctr., Inc., 1983-85; sheriff Ranchos del Norte Corral of Westerners, 1985-87; trustee San Diego Community Defenders, Inc., 1986-88; dir. Calif. State U. Found., San Marcos, 1990—. Pres. bd. dirs. Green Valley Civic Assn., 1979-80; dir. Poway Ctr. for the Performing Arts, 1990-93; trustee Palomar-Pomerado Hosp. Found., 1985-89; v.p. Endowment Devel., 1989-91; bd. dirs. Clean Found.; trustee Episc. Diocese of San Diego. Recipient Dove award Assn. Retarded Citizens, 1992. Mem. ABA, Rancho Bernardo Bar Assn. (chmn. 1982-83), Lawyers Club San Diego, Profl. and Exec. Women of the Ranch (founder, pres. 1982—), San Diego Golden Eagle Club, Soroptimist Internat. (pres. chpt. 1979-80, Woman of Distinction 1992), Phi Delta Phi. Republican. Episcopalian. Home: 16503 Avenida Florencia Poway CA 92064-1807 Office: Walters & Ward 11665 Avena Pl Ste 203 San Diego CA 92128-2428

WARD, FRANK ALAN, natural resource economist, educator; b. San Francisco, Oct. 8, 1948; s. John Martin and Jane (Ingley) W.; 1 child, Ryan David. BS, Colo. State U., 1970, MS, 1975, PhD, 1978. Asst. prof. resource econs. N.Mex. State U., Las Cruces, 1978-82; assoc. prof. N.Mex. State U., 1982-88, prof., 1988—. Assoc. editor Water Resources Rsch., 1991—; contbr. articles to sci. jours. Recipient Best pub. paper award Water Resources Bull, 1990/. Mem. Am. Econ. Assn., Assn. for Environ. and Resource Economists, Am. Agrl. Econs. Assn. (nat. outstanding PhD Dissertation award 1978). Office: NMex State U PO Box 3169 Las Cruces NM 88003-3169

WARD, JAMES HUBERT, dean, social work educator, researcher, consultant; b. Lawndale, N.C., Apr. 8, 1937; s. Frank A. and Helen (Wray) W.; m. Jacqueline Ferman Ward, Dec. 29, 1966; children—Dawn Alese, Audran Maria, James H., Christopher F. B.S., N.C. A&T State U., 1960; M.S.W., U. Md., 1968; Ph.D., Ohio State U., 1974. Tchr., counselor Ohio Youth Commn., Columbus, 1962-66, dep. dir., 1971-73; adj. instr. social work dept. sociology and anthropology, U. Dayton (Ohio), 1968-69; exec. dir. Montgomery County Community Action Agy., Dayton, 1969-71; asst. prof. sociology and anthropology, Central State U., Wilberforce, Ohio, 1973; asst. prof., sr. research assoc. Sch. Applied Social Scis., Case Western Res. U., Cleve., 1975-76, asst. prof., assoc. dean, 1976-79, assoc. prof., assoc. dean, 1979-81; dean, prof. Sch. Social Work, U. Ala., Tuscaloosa, 1981-88; prof., dean, Grad. Sch. Social Work, Portland State U., Portland, Oreg., 1988—; cons. in field; mem. Ala. Juvenile Justice Adv. Com., 1983—; mem. adv. council on social work edn. Ala. Commn. on Higher Edn., 1982—; mem. ho. of dels. Council on Social Work Edn., 1981-87; mem. Coun. Social Work Edn. Accreditation Commn., 1987-93; mem. annual program planning com. Council on Social Work Edn., 1984-85; chmn. bd. dirs. United Way of Columbia-Willamette, 1988—, mem. exec. com., mem. community orgn. and planning com., chair agency rels. com., mem. strategic planning com.; bd. dirs. Urban League, Portland, 1988-89; bd. dirs. Mt. Hood Community Mental Health Ctr., 1988-91; mem. govs. panel on ecclesia, 1988-89; mem adv. coun. mental health edn. planning Dept. Human Resources, Mental Health Divsn., Salem, Oreg., 1988-91; mem. Portland City Club, 1988—; mem. task force on licensing for social work practice, Ala. State Bd. Social Work Examiners, 1985; mem.local human resources bd. Tuscaloosa County Dept. Pensions and Security, 1982-87, mem. external central adminstrv. rev. panel, 1985. Bd. dirs. Greater Tuscaloosa chpt. ARC, 1982-87; pres. Eastwood Middle Sch. PTA, Tuscaloosa Bd. Edn., 1983-84; hon. mem. bd. Parents Anonymous of Ala. State Bd., 1982; mem. W. Ala. Nat. Issues Forum, 1984-86; bd. dirs., chmn. fin. com. Tuscaloosa County Mental Health Assn., 1984-87. Served to capt. U.S. Army, 1960-68. Recipient Pace Setters award for disting. achievement Coll. Adminstrv. Sci., Ohio State U., 1974; named Outstanding Profl. in Human Services, Acad. Human Services, 1974. Mem. Acad. Cert. Social Workers (cert), Council on Social Work Edn., Internat. Assn. Schs. Social Work, Internat. Council on Social Welfare, Nat. Assn. Social Workers (mem.-at-large, bd. dirs. Ala. Chpt. 1985, v.p. Oreg. chpt. 1991—, edit. bd. jour. Social Work 1990-93), Am. Assn. Deans and Dirs. of Grad. Schs. of Social Work (chair deans group S.E. region 1985-87), Ala. Conf. of Social Work (chmn. program com.), Greater Tuscaloosa C. of C. Contbr. numerous articles to various profl. jours., also chpts. to books. Office: Portland State Univ Grad Sch Social Work PO Box 751 Portland OR 97207-0751

WARD, JOHN J., bishop; b. Los Angeles, 1920. Student, St. John's Sem., Camarillo, Calif., Catholic U. Am. Ordained priest, Roman Catholic Ch., 1946. Apptd. titular bishop of Bria, aux. bishop Diocese of Los Angels Roman Cath. Ch., 1963—; vicar gen. Roman Cath. Ch., Los Angeles., 1963—. Office: 10425 W Pico Blvd Los Angeles CA 90064-2307*

WARD, LESLIE ALLYSON, journalist, editor; b. L.A., June 3, 1946; d. Harold Gordon and Marilyn Lucille (Dahlstead) W.; m. Robert L. Biggs, 1971 (div. 1977); m. Colman Robert Andrews, May 26, 1979 (div. 1988). AA, Coll. San Mateo, 1966; BA, UCLA, 1968, MJ, 1971. Reporter, researcher L.A. Bur. Life mag., 1971-72; reporter, news asst. L.A. bur. N.Y. Times, 1973-76; sr. editor New West mag., L.A., 1976-78, 79-80; L.A. bur. chief US mag., 1978-79; Sunday style editor L.A. Herald Examiner, 1981-82, editor-in-chief Sunday mags., 1982-83, Olympics editor, 1984, sports editor, 1985-86, sr. writer, 1986; sr. editor L.A. Times Mag., 1988-90; travel editor L.A. Times, 1990—. Democrat. Office: LA Times Times Mirror Sq Los Angeles CA 90053

WARD, LESTER LOWE, JR., arts association executive, lawyer; b. Pueblo, Colo., Dec. 21, 1930; s. Lester Lowe and Alysmai (Pfeffer) W.; m. Rosalind H. Felps, Apr. 18, 1964; children: Ann Marie, Alison, Lester Lowe. AB cum laude, Harvard U., 1952, LLB, 1955. Bar: Colo. 1955. Pvt. practice Pueblo, 1957-89; ptnr. Predovich, Ward & Banner, Pueblo, 1974-89; pres., chief oper. officer Denver Ctr. for the Performing Arts, 1989—. Trustee, Thatcher Found., Frank I. Lamb Found., Helen G. Bonfils Found.; pres. bd. trustees Pueblo Pub. Library, 1960-66; trustee St. Mary-Corwin Hosp., 1972-80, pres., 1979-80. With U.S. Army, 1955-57. Named Outstanding Young Man of Yr., Pueblo Jaycees, 1964. Fellow Am. Coll. Trust and Estate Counsel; mem. ABA (ho. of dels. 1986-88), Colo. Bar Assn. (bd. govs. 1977-79, 82-88, pres. 1983-84), Pueblo County Bar Assn. (Outstanding Young Lawyer award 1965, 67, pres. 1976-77), Denver Metro C. of C. (bd. dirs.), Denver Civic Ventures, Harvard Law Sch. Assn. Colo. (pres. 1972), Kiwanis (pres. 1969). Democrat. Roman Catholic. Home: 1551 Larimer St Apt 2601 Denver CO 80202-1638 Office: Denver Ctr Performing Arts 1050 13th St Denver CO 80204-2157

WARD, RICHARD ALAN, lawyer; b. Oneonta, N.Y., Nov. 27, 1960; s. Eurfryn L. and Sandra L. (Cook) W. BA magna cum laude, Claremont McKenna Coll., 1982; JD, UCLA, 1993. Bar: Calif. Systems analyst Great Western Bank, Northridge, Calif., 1984-86; sr. systems analyst Valley Fed. Savs., Van Nuys, Calif., 1986-89; assoc. atty. Arnold & Porter, L.A., 1993—. Mem. ABA, L.A. County Bar Assn. (vol. hospice/AIDS project 1993—), Order of Coif. Office: Arnold & Porter 777 S Figueroa St Fl 44 Los Angeles CA 90017-5800

WARD, ROBERT EDWARD, retired political science educator and university administrator; b. San Francisco, Jan. 29, 1916; s. Edward Butler and Claire Catherine (Unger) W.; m. Constance Regina Barnett, Oct. 31, 1942; children: Erica Anne, Katherine Elizabeth. B.A., Stanford U., 1936; M.A., U. Calif.-Berkeley, 1938, Ph.D., 1948. Instr. in polit. sci. U. Mich., 1948-50, asst. prof. polit. sci., 1950-54, assoc. prof., 1954-58, prof., 1958-73; prof. Stanford U., 1973-87, dir. Center for Research in Internat. Studies, 1973-87; cons. in field; advisor Center for Strategic and Internat. Studies, Washington, 1968-87. Author: Modern Political Systems: Asia, 1963, Political Modernization in Japan and Turkey, 1964. Mem. nat. council Nat. Endowment for Humanities, Washington, 1968-73; mem. Pres.'s Commn. on Fgn. Lang.-Internat. Studies, 1978-79; chmn. Japan-U.S. Friendship Commn., 1980-83; mem. Dept. Def. Univ. Forum, 1982-87. Served to lt. (j.g.) USN, 1942-45. Recipient Japan Found. award Tokyo, 1976; recipient Order of Sacred Treasure 2d class (Japan), 1983. Fellow Am. Acad. Arts and Scis.; mem. Am. Polit. Sci. Assn. (pres. 1972-73), Assn. Asian Studies (pres. 1972-73), Social Sci. Research Council (chmn. 1969-71), Am. Philos. Soc. Home: Box 8129 501 Portola Rd Portola Valley CA 94028

WARD, R(OBERT) SCOTT, physical therapist; b. Boston, Dec. 17, 1955; s. John Robert and Norma (Harris) W.; m. Diane McVey, Dec. 19, 1983; children: Kristin Anne, Sarah McVey. BA in Phys. Therapy magna cum laude, U. Utah, 1980, PhD in Physiology, 1994. Lic. phys. therapist, Utah. Phys. therapist dept. phys. medicine and rehab. U. Utah Med. Ctr., Salt Lake City, 1980-81, phys. therapist, assoc. dir. burn therapy dept., 1981-84; pres., co-owner Continuing Edn. Assocs., 1982-83; phys. therapist Lewis-Hamblin Health Care, Salt Lake City, 1982-85; clin. instr. Weber State Coll., Ogden, Utah, 1983-84; clin. instr. divsn. phys. therapy U. Utah, 1982-84; phys. therapist Mountain States Hemophilia Ctr. U. Utah Health Scis. Ctr., Salt Lake City, 1987—, staff phys. therapist Intermountain Burn Ctr., 1986—; co-dir. divsn. phys. therapy Coll. Health U. Utah, Salt Lake City, 1990—, asst. prof., 1987—; vis. asst. prof. divsn. phys. therapy Coll. Health, U. Utah, 1984-87; Am. Phys. Therapy Assn. liaison to Am. Burn Assn., 1993—; mem. med. adv. bd. Utah chpt. Nat. Hemophilia Found., 1988—; cons. Hemophilia and AIDS/HIV Network for Dissemination of Info., Nat. Hemophilia Found., 1992—; cons., physiology lab. coord. U. Utah Sch. Medicine, Salt Lake City, 1988—. Abstracter, book reviewer Phys. Therapy; contbr. articles to profl. jours., chpts. to books. Grantee Cutter Biol., 1991, Dumke Found., 1992, J-Tech, 1993, Internat. Assn. Fire Fighters, 1993. Mem. Am. Phys. Therapy Assn. (del. ho. of reps. 1993, chief del. 1994, mem. Task Force on Americans With Disabilities Act 1992-94), Am. Burn Assn. (trustee 1994—), Nat. Hemophilia Found. (edn. com. 1992—, regional rep. Mountain States region phys. therapy com., 1989—), Soc. Neurosci., Internat. Soc. Burn Injuries. Office: U Utah Phys Therapy Annex Building # 1130 Salt Lake City UT 84112-1116

WARD, ROGER WILSON, corporate executive, physicist; b. Paris, Tex., Dec. 2, 1944; s. Alvin Lavell Ward and Anna Muriel (Miller) Anderson; m. Patricia Ann Lambright, Aug. 20, 1967 (div. 1979); m. Kimberley Elaine Lohman, May 4, 1979; children: Tara D., Eric N.D. BA in Physics, McMurry Coll., 1967; MS in Physics, Purdue U., 1969. With Hewlett Packard Co., Palo Alto, Calif., 1969-75; product mgr. Litronix, Cupertino, Calif., 1975-77; design engr. Statek, Orange, Calif., 1977-79; v.p. Colo. Crystal Corp, Loveland, 1979-81; engring mgr. Motorola Corp., Ft. Lauderdale, Fla., 1981-83; v.p., co-owner Quartztronics, Inc., Salt Lake City, 1983-90; pres., co-owner QuartzDyne, Inc., Salt Lake City, 1990—; chmn. bd. QuartzDyne. Inventee in field; contbr. articles to profl. jours. Mem. IEEE (sr.), Instrument Soc. of Am. (sr.), Sigma Pi Sigma. Office: QuartzDyne Inc 1020 Atherton Dr Bldg C Salt Lake City UT 84123-3402

WARD, RON, food products executive; b. 1943. With Growers Credit, Wenatchee, Wash., 1968-84, Seattle 1st Nat. Bank, Wenatchee, Wash., 1984-92; CFO, sec. Chief Wenatchee, 1992—. Office: Chief Wenatchee 1705 N Miller St Wenatchee WA 98801-1585*

WARDELL, JOE RUSSELL, JR., pharmacologist; b. Omaha, Nov. 11, 1929; s. Joe Russell and Marie Hamilton (Waugh) W.; m. Leta Harris, July 14, 1952 (div. Oct. 1981); children: Michael R., Susan E., John D.; m. Doris Erway, Aug. 27, 1983. BS in Pharmacy, Creighton U., 1951; MS in Pharmacology, U. Nebr., Omaha, 1959, PhD in Pharmacology, 1962. Lic. pharmacist Nebr. Pharmacist Osco Drug, Waterloo, Iowa, 1953-56; grad. asst. Coll. of Medicine U. Nebr., Omaha, 1956-62; sr. pharmacologist Smith Kline & French Labs., Phila., 1962-64, advanced to assoc. dir. biol. rsch., 1974-78; dir. R & D compound acquistions R&D, 1978-86; pres. Wardell Assocs., Park City, Utah, 1986—. Author: more than 40 articles in profl. pubs.; inventor/co-inventor 4 patents respiratory and cardiovascular drugs. Asst. scoutmaster, Boy Scouts of Am., N.J., 1969-75. Recipient Merck Award Creighton U., 1951. Mem. Soc. of Parmacology & Experimental Therapeutics, Am. Acad. of Pharmaceutical Scis., Am. Chem. Soc., Licensing Exec. Soc., Exptl. Aircraft Assn. Home and Office: Wardell Assocs 55 Thaynes Canyon Dr Park City UT 84060-6713

WARD III-OLSON, JAMES DAY (EDÄH HÖE), retired career officer; b. San Luis Obispo, Calif., July 8, 1943; s. Burnell D. Ward and Grutrude Amey Olson; m. Nancy Ann Jacobson, Nov. 22, 1967 (div. Jan. 1986); children: James L. Olson, Jeffery F. Olson, Cynthia K. Olson; m. Vicki C. Biederman, Aug. 19, 1989; children: Jared R.B.W. Olson, Gabrielle. BS, U. Wash., 1971; BSME, U. Md., 1966; MSME, U. N.Y., 1980; BA, Mt. Hood C.C., Gresham, Oreg., 1984; PhD, MIT, 1985. With USCG, 1961, ret., 1981; pvt. practice as cons. Portland, 1990—; cons. Wagner Mining Corp. R&D, Portland, 1983-84, N.W. Marine & Iron Workers, Portland, 1984-86, Am. Wood Dryers, Inc., Clackamas, Oreg., 1986-88, Quillutte Indian Reservation, Wash., 1988-90. Col. USAF. Mem. VFW (life) Mobile Riverine Force Assn., Coast Guard Combat Vet. Assn., Disabled Vets. Assn., Vietnam Vets. of Am., Game Wardens Assn. Vietnam, Optimist Internat., Elks, Moose. Republican. Home and Office: c/o General Delivery Index WA 98256

WARDINSKY, TERRANCE DAVID, physician; b. Great Falls, Mont., Aug. 22, 1943. BS in Gen. Studies, Mont. State U., 1965; MD, St. Louis U., 1969. Diplomate Am. Bd. Pediats., Mont. State Bd. Med. Examiners. Intern Wilford Hall Med. Ctr. USAF, Lackland AFB, Tex., 1969-70, resident, 1970-73; lt. col., chief dept. pediats. USAF Hosp., Malmstrom AFB, Mont., 1973-76; asst. chmn., chief ambulatory pediats., staff pediatrician David Grant USAF Med. Ctr., Travis AFB, Calif., 1976-84, congenital defects and inheritable disease cons. pediats., 1989—; chief dept. pediats. USAF Regional Hosp., Elmendorf AFB, Alaska, 1984-87; fellow in congenital birth defects and clin. genetics Children's Hosp. and Med. Ctr., Seattle, 1987-89; asst. clin. prof. pediats. Uniformed Svcs. U. of the Health Scis., Bethesda, Md., 1977-84, clin. asst. prof., 1980—; asst. clin. prof. pediats. U. Calif., Davis, 1989—; cons. pediats. Mont. State U., 1975-76, Surgeon Gen. in Child Abuse, 1980—, Am. Acad. Pediats., 1993—; presenter papers in field. Contbr. articles to profl. jours. Bd. dirs. Early Intervention Local Planning, Solano County, 1990—, United Cerebral Palsy of the North Bay, 1990—, Redwood Home Health Care, 1992—; pediat. rep. Solano County Death Rev. Com.; participant Anchorage (Alaska) Pediat. Grand Round Group. Recipient Outstanding Recognition award, Regional Ctr. for Developmental Disabilities, 1979-84, Genetics Rsch. award, Soc. of Perinatal Obstetrics, 1989. Fellow Am. Acad. Pediats. (mil. sect., chpt. West), Am. Acad. for Cerebral Palsy and Developmental Medicine; mem. Am. Soc. Human Genetics, Air Force Soc. Physicians, Assn. Mil. Surgeons of the U.S., N.W. Soc. for Developmental and Behavioral Pediats., N.W. Genetic Exch., Teratology Club, Phi Beta Kappa. Office: David Grant Med Ctr Congenital Defects Travis AFB CA 94535

WARD-SHAW, SHEILA THERESA, nurse; b. N.Y.C., June 20, 1951; d. Arthur and Cynthia Melba (Mapp) Jenkins; m. Howard J. Ward, Nov. 1977 (div. 1981); m. Thomas N. Shaw, Sept. 1988; children: Tanyatta, Barbara, Thomas. Student, Rockland Community Coll., 1973, U. Nev., Las Vegas, 1984, San Jose State U., 1994—. Charge nurse Hillcrest (N.Y.) Nursing Home, 1973-74; infirmary nurse St. Agatha's Home for Children, Nanuet, N.Y., 1974-75; temp. bldg. charge nurse Letchworth Village, Thiells, N.Y., 1976; charge nurse New Paltz (N.Y.) Nursing Home, 1977; non secure detention, foster bdg. parent St. Agatha's Home for Children, Nanuet, 1977-79; asst. nursing supr., inservice coord., infection control nurse So Nev. Mental Retardation, Las Vegas, 1979-84; psychiat. nurse II evening duty officer Harbor View Devel. Ctr., Valdez, Alaska, 1987-89; infection control, employee health nurse, unit coord. North Star Hosp., Anchorage, 1989-92; psychiat. nurse, infection control Oak Creek Hosp., San Jose, Calif., 1992-93, writer, producer OSHA precaution tng. staff video, 1993; psychiat. nurse VA Hosp. Menlo Park Divsn., Palo Alto, 1992—. Campaign worker Nev. Gov. Bryan Dem. Candidate, Las Vegas, 1983-84, Pearson for County Commn. Race, Las Vegas, 1984; pres. Clark County Health Educators, 1983; mem. APIC., 1980-85. Mem. Assn. for Practioners of Infection Control. Roman Catholic. Office: VA Hosp Palo Alto MPD 3801 Miranda Ave Palo Alto CA 94304-1207

WARE, JAMES EDMAN, human resources consultant; b. Nampa, Idaho, Jan. 19, 1937; s. Allden Edman and Ruby Lillian (Bachman) W.; m. Judith Lee Druxman, July 17, 1959; children: Bradford James, Heather Lee. BBA, U. Wash., 1959. Mgr. employee tng. Transamerican Ins. Co., Los Angeles, 1959-66; regional personnel mgr. Allstate Ins. Co., Pasadena, Calif., 1966-69, Salem, Oreg., 1969-70, Seattle, 1970-72; v.p. adminstrv. services Intermountain Gas Co., Boise, Idaho, 1972-92. bd. dirs. Stemilt Growers, Idaho St. Personnel Com., Boise, 1988, Ada County Civil Service Com., Boise, 1978-88. Named Profl. of the Year 1985, Human Resources Assn. of Treasure Valley, Boise, ID. Mem. Am. Soc. Personnel Adminstrn., Soc. Human Resource Mgmt. (past nat. chmn.). Office: IEC Mgmt Resource Group PO Box 7186 Boise ID 83707-1186

WARE, JAMES W., federal judge; b. 1946. BA, Calif. Luth. U., 1969; JD, Stanford U., 1972. Assoc. Blase, Valentine & Klein, Palo Alto, Calif., 1972-77, ptnr., 1977; judge Santa Clara County Superior Ct., U.S. Dist. Ct. (no. dist.) Calif., 1990—; pro bono East Palo Alto Law Project. Active Am. Leadership Forum; mem. bd. visitors Stanford Law Sch.; active Martin Luther King Papers Project. 2nd lt. USAR, 1969-86. Office: US Dist Cts 280 S 1st St Rm 2112 San Jose CA 95113-3002*

WARE, ROGER B., insurance company executive; b. 1934. With Reliance Ins. Co., Phila., 1967-83, Guaranty Nat. Ins. Co., Englewood, Colo., Landmark Am. Ins. Co., Englewood, Colo.; pres., CEO Guaranty Nat. Ins. Co. Office: Guaranty Nat Corp 100 Inverness Ter E Englewood CO 80112-5313

WARICK, LAWRENCE HERBERT, psychiatrist; b. Warsaw, Poland, May 2, 1936; came to U.S., 1949, naturalized, 1954; s. Joseph and Marsha (Beck) W.; m. Elaine Ruth Christensen, Feb. 24, 1963; children: Catherine Ann, David Mark. BS, CCNY, 1956; MD, Albert Einstein Coll. Medicine, 1960; PhD, So. Calif. Psychoanalytic Inst, 1980. Diplomate Am. Bd. Psychiatry and Neurology. Rotating intern L.A. County Gen. Hosp., 1960-61; resident neurology U. So. Calif. Sch. Medicine, L.A. County Gen. Hosp., 1961-62, resident psychiatry, 1962-65; clin. assoc. So. Calif. Psychoanalytic Inst., L.A., 1973-80, instr., 1981—; pvt. practice L.A., 1980—; asst. clin. prof. psychiatry UCLA Sch. Medicine, 1967—; instr. faculty Psychoanalytic Inst. So. Calif., L.A., 1980—; Contbr. articles to profl. jours., chpts. to books. Contbr. articles to profl. jours., chpt. to book. Capt. USAF, 1962-68. Mem. Am. Psychiat. Assn., Am. Acad. Psychiatry and Law, So. Calif. Psychiatry Soc., So. Calif. Psychoanalytic Soc., Phi Beta Kappa. Home: 2443 Pesquera Dr Los Angeles CA 90049-1224 Office: 2444 Wilshire Blvd Ste 418 Santa Monica CA 90403-5808

WARING, REBECCA LYNN, magazine editor, freelance writer; b. Phila., May 1, 1957; d. Philip Brooks Waring and Charlotte Snowden (Rockey) Bell. SB in Civil Engring., MIT, 1979, SM in Mgmt., 1983. Environ. engr. U.S. EPA, Ann Arbor, Mich., 1979-80; rsch. asst. MIT, Cambridge, 1983-88; sr. editor MacWeek Mag., San Francisco, 1988-91; exec. editor New Media mag., San Mateo, Calif., 1991—; exec. dir. Macintosh Group, Boston Computer Soc., 1985-88. Contbr. freelance articles to mags. Edn. counselor MIT Alumni Assn., 1984-95. Recipient Maggie for Best Buyers Guide, Western Mag. Assn., 1994. Mem. Computer Press Assn., Sys. Dynamics Soc., Boston Computer Soc. (life). Democrat. Episcopalian. Office: New Media Mag 901 Mariners Island Blvd San Mateo CA 94404-1592

WARK, ROBERT RODGER, art curator; b. Edmonton, Can., Oct. 7, 1924; came to U.S., 1948, naturalized, 1970; s. Joseph Henry and Louise (Rodger) W. B.A., U. Alta., 1944, M.A., 1946, LLD (hon.), 1986; A.M., Harvard, 1949, Ph.D., 1952. Instr. art Harvard U., 1952-54; instr. history art Yale U., 1954-56; curator art Henry E. Huntington Library and Art Gallery, San Marino, Calif., 1956-90; lectr. art Calif. Inst. Tech., 1960-91, UCLA, 1966-80. Author: Sculpture in the Huntington Collection, 1959, French Decorative Art in the Huntington Collection, 1961, Rowlandson's Drawings for a Tour in a Post Chaise, 1963, Rowlandson's Drawings for the English Dance of Death, 1966, Isaac Cruikshank's Drawings for Drolls, 1968, Early British Drawings in the Huntington Collection 1600-1750, 1969, Drawings by John Flaxman, 1970, Ten British Pictures 1740-1840, 1971, Meet the Ladies: Personalities in Huntington Portraits, 1972, Drawings from the Turner Shakespeare, 1973, Drawings by Thomas Rowlandson in the Huntington Collection, 1975, British Silver in the Huntington Collection, 1978; editor: Sir Joshua Reynolds: Discourses on Art, 1959. Served with RCAF, 1944-45; Served with RCNVR, 1945. Mem. Coll. Art Assn. Home: 1330 Lombardy Rd Pasadena CA 91106-4120 Office: Huntington Library San Marino CA 91108

WARNAS, JOSEPH JOHN, municipal official; b. Boston, Aug. 31, 1933; s. Augustas and Nellie (Pipiras) W.; m. Bernice Gearlene Sarver (dec. July 1983); children: Robert John, Kimberly Joanne; m. Ruth Ellen Haaker, Jan. 12, 1985. BS in Mgmt., Boston Coll., 1955; MBA in Mgmt., Ariz. State U., 1971. Adminstr. subcontract Gen. Motors, Oak Creek, Wis., 1958-65; mgr. purchasing Sperry Rand Corp., Phoenix, 1965-70; dir. material mgmt. dept. Maricopa County, Phoenix, 1971-93; Mem. Joint Fed., State and local Govt. Adv. Bd GSA, Washington, 1974; mem. exptl. tech. adv. com. Nat. Inst. Govt. Purchasing & GSA, Washington, 1975; guest lectr. Ariz. State U., Tempe, Glendale Community Coll.; instr. seminars Nat. Inst. Govt. Purchasing, Washington. Assoc. editor Aljian's Purchasers Handbook, 4th rev. edit., 1982; contbr. articles to profl. jours. Mem. State Ariz. Purchasing Rev. Bd., Phoenix, 1980, Men's Zoo Aux., Phoenix, 1976—. Served as 1st lt. U.S. Army, 1956-58. Mem. Nat. Inst. Govtl. Purchasing (pres. 1971, bd. dirs. 1972—, sr. del. to Internat. Fedn. Purchasing and Mgmt. 1983), Ariz. State Capitol Chpt. Nat. Inst. Govtl. Purchasing Inc. (founder, pres. 1977), Purchasing Mgmt. Assn. Ariz. (pres. 1973), Sigma Iota Epsilon. Republican. Roman Catholic. Home: 12511 N 76th Pl Scottsdale AZ 85260-4839

WARNATH, MAXINE AMMER, organizational psychologist, mediator; b. N.Y.C., Dec. 3, 1928; d. Philip and Jeanette Ammer; m. Charles Frederick Warnath, Aug. 20, 1952; children: Stephen Charles, Cindy Ruth. BA, Bklyn. Coll., 1949; MA, Columbia U., 1951, EdD, 1982. Lic. psychologist, Oreg. Various profl. positions Hunter Coll., U. Minn., U. Nebr., U. Oreg., 1951-62; asst. prof. psychology Oreg. Coll. Edn., Monmouth, 1962-77; assoc. prof. psychology, chmn. dept. psychology and spl. edn. Western Oreg. St. Coll., Monmouth, 1978-83, prof. 1986—, dir. organizational psychology program 1983—; pres. Profl. Perspectives Internat., Salem, Oreg., 1987—; cons., dir. Orgn. R & D, Salem, Oreg., 1983-87, seminar leader Endeavors for Excellence program. Author: Power Dynamism, 1987. Mem. APA (com. pre-coll. psychology 1970-74), ASTD, N.Y. Acad. Sci., Oreg. Acad. Sci., Oreg. Psychol. Assn. (pres. 1980-81, pres.-elect 1979-80, legis. liaison 1977-78), Western Psychol. Assn. Office: Profl Perspectives Internat PO Box 2265 Salem OR 97308-2265

WARNE, WILLIAM ELMO, irrigationist; b. nr. Seafield, Ind., Sept. 2, 1905; s. William Rufus and Nettie Jane (Williams) W.; m. Edith Margaret Peterson, July 19, 1929; children: Jane Ingrid (Mrs. David C. Beeder), William Robert, Margaret Edith (Mrs. John W. Monroe). AB, U. Calif., 1927; DEcons (hon.), Yonsei U., Seoul, 1959; LLD, Seoul Nat. U., 1959. Reporter San Francisco Bull. and Oakland (Calif.) Post-Enquirer, 1925-27; news editor Brawley (Calif.) News, 1927, Calexico (Calif.) Chronicle, 1927-28; editor, night mgr. L.A. bur. AP, 1928-31, corr. San Diego bur., 1931-33, Washington corr., 1933-35; editor, bur. reclamation Dept. Interior, 1935-37; on staff Third World Power Conf., 1936; assoc. to reviewing com. Nat. Resources Com. on preparation Drainage Basin Problems and Programs, 1936, mem. editorial com. for revision, 1937; chief of information Bur. Reclamation, 1937-42; co-dir. (with Harlan H. Barrows) Columbia Basin Joint Investigations, 1939-42; chief of staff, war prodn. drive WPB, 1942; asst. dir. div. power Dept. Interior, 1942-43, dept. dir. information, 1943; asst. commr. Bur. Reclamation, 1943-47; apptd. asst. sec. Dept. Interior, 1947, asst. sec. Water and Power Devel., 1950-51; U.S. minister charge tech. cooperation Iran, 1951-55, Brazil, 1955-56; U.S. minister and econ. coord. for Korea, 1956-59; dir. Cal. Dept. Fish and Game, 1959-60, Dept. Agr., 1960-61, Dept. Water Resources, 1961-67; v.p. water resources Devel. and Resources Corp., 1967-69; resources cons., 1969—; pres. Warne & Blanton Pubs. Inc., 1985-90, Warne Walnut Wrancho, Inc., 1979—; Disting. Practitioner in Residence Sch. Pub. Adminstrn., U. So. Calif. at Sacramento, 1976-78; adminstr. Resources Agy. of Calif., 1961-63; Chmn. Pres.'s Com. on San Diego Water Supply, 1944-46; chmn. Fed. Inter-Agy. River Basin Com., 1948, Fed. Com. on Alaskan Devel., 1948; pres. Group Health Assn., Inc., 1947-51; chmn. U.S. delegation 2d Inter-Am. Conf. Indian Life, Cuzco, Peru, 1949; U.S. del. 4th World Power Conf., London, Eng., 1950; mem. Calif. Water Pollution Control Bd., 1959-67; vice chmn. 1960-62; mem. water pollution control adv. bd. Dept. Health, Edn. and Welfare, 1962-65, cons., 1966-67; chmn. Calif. delegation Western States Water Council, 1965-67. Author: Mission for Peace-Point 4 in Iran, 1956, The Bureau of Reclamation, 1973, How the Colorado River Was Spent, 1975, The Need to Institutionalize Desalting, 1978; prin. author: The California Experience with Mass Transfers of Water over Long Distances, 1978; editor Geothermal Report, 1985-90. Served as 2d lt. O.R.C., 1927-37. Recipient Disting. Svc. award Dept. Interior, 1951, Disting. Pub. Svc. Honor award FOA, 1955, Order of [illegible] Svc. citation UN Command Korea, 1959, Order of Indsl. Sv. Merit Bronze Star, Korea, 1991. Fellow Nat. Acad. Pub. Adminstrn. (sr., chmn. standing com. on environ. and resources mgmt. 1971-78); mem. Nat. Water Supply Improvement Assn. (pres. 1978-80, Lifetime Achievement award 1984), Internat. Desalination Assn. (founding mem., Lifetime Disting. Service award 1991), Soc. Profl. Journalists, Sutter Club, Nat. Press Club (Washington), Lambda Chi Alpha. Home and Office: 1570 Madrono Ave Palo Alto CA 94306-1015

WARNER, FRANK SHRAKE, lawyer; b. Ogden, Utah, Dec. 14, 1940; s. Frank D. and Emma (Sorensen) W.; m. Sherry Lynn Clary; 1 child, Sheri. JD U. Utah 1964. Bar: Utah 1964. Assoc. Young, Thatcher, Glasmann & Warner, and predecessor, Ogden, 1964-67, ptnr., 1967-72; chmn. Pub. Svc. Commn. Utah, Salt Lake City, 1972-76; ptnr. Warner & Wikstrom, Ogden, 1976-79, Warner, Marquardt & Hasenyager, Ogden, 1979-82; pvt. practice, Ogden, 1982—. Mem. Utah Gov.'s Com. on Exec. Reorgn., 1978-80. Mem. Utah Bar Assn. (ethics and discipline com. 1981-90), Ogden Gun Club (past pres.). Office: 505 27th St Ogden UT 84403-0101

WARNER, JANET CLAIRE, software design engineer; b. Portland, Oreg., May 2, 1964; d. W. J. and Wendelyn A. (Twombly) W. Student, Clackamas Community Coll., 1982-85; BS in Computer Sci., U. Portland, 1987, MSEE, 1992. Systems asst. U. Portland, 1986-87, programmer Applied Rsch. Ctr., 1987; software design engr. Photon Kinetics, Inc., Beaverton, Oreg., 1987-92; software engr. FLIR Sys., Inc., Portland, 1993; ind. software cons., 1993—. Mem. IEEE, Assn. Computing Machinery (chmn. U. Portland chpt. 1986-87), Soc. Women Engrs. (treas. Oreg. sect. 1988-89), U. Portland Alumni Assn. (Portland programming bd. 1993—), Portland Rose Soc., Eta Kappa Nu (treas. chpt. 1991-92).

WARNER, LEE MICHAEL, food products executive; b. Cleve., Oct. 10, 1917; s. Ray I. and Ann (Goldber) W.; m. Janet Hoffman, Aug. 3, 1941 (dec. 1961); m. Hope Landis, Mar. 1, 1963; 1 child, Christopher Arthur. BSc, Ohio State U., 1939. Pres., chief executive officer Laurbank Sales Corp., L.A., 1947-53, Pacific Fruit Processing, Beverly Hills, Calif., 1960-78, CENSA, Beverly Hills, 1967-78, Santa Fe Driscoll, Beverly Hills, 1952-78; chmn. Pacific Fruit Processing Inc., South Gate, Calif., 1978—; chmn. State of Calif. Strawberry Adv. Bd., Sacramento, 1963-65; pres. Warner Investment Co., Santa Monica. Bd. mem. Andrus Sch. Gerentology, L.A., 1987—. Capt. U.S. Army, 1942-46. Office: Warner Investment Co 2850 Ocean Park Blvd Ste 292 Santa Monica CA 90405-6200

WARNER, MICHAEL D., museum director; b. Salt Lake City, Nov. 1, 1949; s. Reed H. and Alma (Henline) W.; m. Ilene G. Reflow, Nov. 9, 1973; children: Ryan D., Joshua T. Student, Met. State Coll., 1969-71. Dist. mktg. mgr. Frontier Airlines, Inc., Denver, 1970-80; gen. mgr. Frontier Airlines, Inc., Colorado Springs, Colo., 1980-85; exec. dir. ProRodeo Hall of Fame, Colorado Springs, 1985—. Editor: (mag.) Roundup. Dir. Pikes Peak Sertoma, Colorado Springs, 1990, Tax Adv. Com., Colorado Springs, 1985-89; pres. Conv. and Vis. Bur., Colorado Springs, 1984. Republican. Office: PRO Rodeo Hall Fame & Mus Am Cowboy 101 Pro Rodeo Dr Colorado Springs CO 80919-2301

WARNER, PAUL WELLMAN, film and theater director, educator; b. Pt. Jefferson, N.Y., Apr. 1, 1962; s. Wellman Joel and Ida Mastri Warner. BA, Harvard U., 1984; MFA, Am. Film Inst., 1992. Artistic assoc. Second Stage Theatre, N.Y.C., 1986-88; instr. acting and directing, artistic cons. L.A. County H.S. for Arts, L.A., 1991—, co-chair film dept., 1995—; film dir. Am. Film Inst., L.A., 1991-92; stage dir. L.A. Theatre Festival, 1993; dir. film Live Entertainment, L.A., 1993-94; lectr. Gail Abbot Enterprises, 1991—; mem. adv. bd. Cornerstone Theatre, L.A., 1991—; artistic cons. Opera-At-The Acad., N.Y.C., 1988-89. ,ir. films In the Name of the Father, 1992, FallTime, 1995; dir stage play Chinese Cabaret 1993; asst. dir. film Glory 1989 (Acad. award 1990). Bd. dirs. L.A. H.S. for the Arts, 1991—; vol. AIDS Project L.A., 1991—, Comty. Works, L.A., 1993—. Recipinet Gold Hugo awrd Chgo. Film Festival, 1993, Gold awrd Houston Film Festival, 1993, Sundance Internat. Film Festival, 1993, Brit. Internat. Film and Video Festival. Mem. Dirs. Guild Am., Harvard-Radcliffe Club. Democrat. Home: 734 S Sycamore Ave Los Angeles CA 90036 Office: Urost/Chaplain Mgmt 9911 W Pico Blvd # Phi Los Angeles CA 90035-2703

WARNER, ROLLIN MILES, JR., economics educator, financial planner, real estate broker; b. Evanston, Ill., Dec. 25, 1930; s. Rollin Miles Warner Sr. and Julia Herndon (Polk) Clarkson. BA, Yale U., 1953; cert. in law, Harvard U., 1956; MBA, Stanford U., 1960; cert. in edn. adminstrn., U. San Francisco, 1974. Lic. real estate broker, Calif.; registered investment advisor. Asst. to v.p. fin. Stanford U., 1960-63; instr. history Town Sch., San Francisco, 1963-70; instr. econs. and math., dean Town Sch., 1975—; prin. Mt. Tamalpais, Ross, Calif., 1972-74; dir. devel. Katharine Branson Sch., Ross, 1974-75, instr. econs./math., outdoor edn., computer-aided design; cons. Nat. Ctr. for Fin. Edn., San Francisco, 1986—. Author: America, 1986, Europe, 1986, Africa, Asia, Russia, 1986, Greece, Rome, 1981, Free Enterprise at Work, 1986. Scoutmaster to dist. commr. Boy Scouts Am., San Francisco, 1956—. Recipient Silver Beaver award Boy Scouts Am., 1986, Town Sch. medal. Mem. Am. Econs. Assn., Inst. CFPs, Math. Assn. Am., Manteca Bd. Realtors, Real Estate Cert. Inst., Grolier Club N.Y., Univ. Club San Francisco, San Francisco Yacht Club, Old Oundelian Club London. Office: Town Sch 2750 Jackson St San Francisco CA 94115-1144

WARNER, VINCENT W., bishop. Bishop Diocese of Olympia, Seattle, 1990—. Office: Diocese of Olympia PO Box 12126 1551 10th Ave E Seattle WA 98102-4298*

WARNER, WALTER DUKE, corporate executive; b. Davenport, Iowa, Feb. 26, 1952; s. Robert Martin and Opal Louise (Gibbons) W.; m. Susan Dee Hafferkamp, Nov. 15, 1975 (div. 1982); 1 child, Natalie. BS, Drake U., 1975. Ops. officer Iowa-Des Moines Nat. Bank, 1975-78; from asst. v.p. to v.p. ops., to v.p. corp. rsch. and devel., to v.p. and dir. mktg. and pub. rels. Cen. Savs. and Loan Assn., San Diego, Calif., 1978-84; pres. The Lomas Santa Fe Cos., Solana Beach, Calif., 1985-91; pres. Ebert Composites Corp., San Diego, 1991—, also bd. dirs.; bd. dirs. Torrey Pines Bank, Solana Beach, Lomas Group Inc., Del Mar, Calif., Madison Valley Properties, Inc., La Jolla, Calif., Nature Preserved of Am. Inc., San Clemente, Calif.; pres., bd. dirs. Regents Pk. Comml. Asns., La Jolla. Bd. dirs. Inst. of the Ams., La Jolla, 1986—, mem. internat. council, 1986—; chmn. bd. dirs., pres. San Diego chpt. Arthritis Found., 1985-87; dir., pres. Gildred Found., Solana Beach, 1986—; founding dir., treas. Golden Triangle Arts Found. Mem. The Exec. Com., Calif. League of Savs. and Loans (mem. mktg. and ops. com. 1982-84), Internat. Forum for Corp. Dirs., Iowa Club of San Diego (founding dir. 1984-85). Republican. Protestant.

WARREN, CHRISTOPHER CHARLES, electronics executive; b. Helena, Mont., July 27, 1949; s. William Louis and Myrtle Estelle (Moren) W.; m. Danette Marie Geordge, Apr. 21, 1972; 1 child, Jeffrey Scott. Grad. high sch., Helena, 1967. Electrician Supreme Electronics, Helena, 1972-81; v.p., svc. technician Capital Music Inc., Helena, 1981—; state exec. Amusement & Music Operators Assn. Coun. of Affiliated States, Chgo., 1990-92, bd. dirs., 1992—. Sgt. USAF, 1968-72, Vietnam. Mem. Internat. Flipper Pinball Assn. (sec./treas. 1991-92, pres. 1993-94), Mont. Coin Machine Operators Assn. (pres. 1989-91), Mont. Coin Machine Operators State 8-Ball (chmn.), Valley Nat. 8 Ball Assn. (charter), Amusement and Music Operators Assn. (bd. dirs. 1992—), Ducks Unltd., Eagles, Moose, Rocky Mountain Elk Found. Home: 8473 Green Meadow Dr Helena MT 59601-9379 Office: Capital Music Inc 3108 Broadwater Ave Helena MT 59601-9201

WARREN, DAVID LESLIE, lawyer; b. Seattle; s. Charles Alexander and Alice Marietta (Leslie) W. BA in Polit. Sci., U. Wash., 1973, JD, 1976. Bar: Wash. 1976. Atty. Spokane (Wash.) Legal Svcs., 1977-79, Office of Hearings and Appeals, Portland, Oreg., 1980—. Mem. Wash. State Bar Assocs., Phi Beta Kappa.

WARREN, DWIGHT WILLIAM, III, physiology educator; b. L.A., Dec. 21, 1942; s. Dwight William Jr. and Edna (Rainen) W.; m. Grace Anita Sturm, Nov. 24, 1965; 1 child, Jennifer Anne. AB, U. Calif., Berkeley, 1964; PhD, U. So. Calif., L.A., 1972. Asst. prof. U. So. Calif., L.A., 1972-78, assoc. prof., 1978-88, prof. dept. physiology and biophysics, 1988—, prof. and acting chmn., dept. Pharmacology and Nutrition, 1992-94; prof. dept. cell and neurobiology Univ. So. Calif., L.A., 1994—, prof. dept. ophthalmology, 1993—, assoc. dean for curriculum, 1994—. Mem. editl. bd. Reproductive Scis., 1989-93, Biology of Reproduction, 1989-95; contbr. articles to profl. jours. Nat. rsch. svc. sr. fellow USPHS, 1980-81; Fulbright scholar USIA, Finland, 1990. Mem. AAAS, Endocrine Soc., Soc. Study Reproduction, Am. Soc. Andrology, N.Y. Acad. Scis., Assn. Rsch. in Vision and Ophthalmology. Office: Univ So Calif 1333 San Pablo St Los Angeles CA 90033-1026

WARREN, EUGENE HOWARD, JR., economic consultant; b. Oak Park, Ill., Jan. 1, 1943; s. Eugene H. and Lorene Winifred (Long) W.; m. Linda Lou Glascock, Mar. 1, 1964; children: Kristen Lynn, Brooke Anne. AB, Ind. U., 1967; MS, Purdue U., 1969, PhD, 1975. Instr. econs. Western Mich. U., Kalamazoo, 1971-73; asst. prof. U. Tenn., Chattanooga, 1973-74; asst. prof. U. Calgary, Alta., Can., 1974-76, assoc. prof., 1976-78; sr. economist Jet Propulsion Lab., Pasadena, Calif., 1978-82; pvt. practice econ. cons. Claremont, Calif., 1982-87; assoc. prof. econs. and mgmt. sci. Chapman U., Orange, Calif., 1987-93; mng. gen. ptnr. Thomas, Warren & Assocs., Claremont, Calif., 1993—; panel mem. Office Tech. Assessment, Washington, 1981; area coord. faculty of mgmt. U. Calgary, 1974; mem. tech. evaluation bd. Jet Propulsion Lab., 1978. Co-author: The Solar Alternative: An Economic Perspective, 1981; also articles to profl. jours. Treas. Mount Baldy Aquatics, Claremont, 1982-85; deacon Claremont Presbyn. Ch., 1982-85. Krannert Research fellow Purdue U., West Lafayette, Ind., 1971-72. Mem. AAAS, Am. Econ. Assn. Republican. Home: 691 E Clarion Pl Claremont CA 91711-2930 Office: Thomas Warren & Assocs 2058 N Mills Ave Ste 454 Claremont CA 91711-2812

WARREN, GERALD LEE, newspaper editor; b. Hastings, Nebr., Aug. 17, 1930; s. Hie Elias and Linnie (Williamson) W.; m. Euphemia Florence Brownell, Nov. 20, 1965 (div.); children: Gerald Benjamin, Euphemia Brownell; m. Viviane M. Pratt, Apr. 27, 1986. A.B., U. Nebr., 1952. Reporter Lincoln Star, Nebr., 1951-52; reporter, asst. city editor San Diego Union, 1956-61; bus. rep. Copley News Service, 1961-63; city editor San Diego Union, 1963-68, asst. mng. editor, 1968-69, editor, 1975-92; editor San Diego Union-Tribune, 1992-95, editor at large, 1995—; dep. press sec. to Pres. Richard Nixon, 1969-74, Pres. Gerald Ford, 1974-75. Lt. (j.g.) USNR, 1952-56. Mem. Am. Soc. Newspaper Editors, Coun. Fgn. Rels., Sigma Delta Chi, Sigma Nu. Republican. Episcopalian. Office: Copley Press Inc 350 Camino De La Reina San Diego CA 92108-3003

WARREN, JAMES RONALD, retired museum director, author, columnist; b. Goldendale, Wash., May 25, 1925; stepson H.S. W.; m. Gwen Davis, June 25, 1949; children: Gail, Jeffrey. B.A., Wash. State U., 1949; M.A., U. Wash., 1953, Ph.D., 1963. Adminstrv. v.p. Seattle Community Coll., 1965-69; pres. Edmonds Community Coll., Lynnwood, Wash., 1969-79; dir. Mus. of History and Industry, Seattle, 1979-89; lectr. in field. Author history books; columnist Seattle Post Intelligencer, 1979-92, Seattle Times, 1992—. Served with U.S. Army, 1943-45, ETO, prisoner-of-war, Germany. Mem. VFW, Am. Ex-POW Assn., 42d (Rainbow) Div. Vets., others. Lodge: Rotary (Seattle). Home and Office: 3235 99th Ave NE Bellevue WA 98004-1803

WARREN, LARRY MICHAEL, clergyman; b. Bonne Terre, Mo., Nov. 25, 1946; s. Orson Wesley and Ruth Margaret (Stine) W.; m. Bonnie Jean Monk Chandler, Apr. 9, 1983; children: Samantha Chandler, John, Abigail Chandler, Anne, Meredith. BA cum laude, Lincoln U., 1969; MDiv with honors, St. Paul Sch. Theology, Kansas City, Mo., 1976; D of Ministry, San Francisco Theol. Sem., 1987. Ordained elder United Meth. Ch., 1978. Pastor Cainsville (Mo.) United Meth. Ch., 1975-76, Lakelands Parish, Rathdrum, Idaho, 1976-78; assoc. pastor Audubon Park United Meth. Ch., Spokane, Wash., 1978-83; pastor Faith United Meth. Ch., Everett, Wash., 1983-90, Tacoma First United Meth. Ch., 1990-95; co-pastor Renton First United Meth. Ch., 1995—; adviser Kairos Prison Ministry Wash., Monroe, 1984-92; conf. rep. grad. bd. St. Paul Sch. Theology, Kansas City, 1984, 94—. Contbr. to col. Dialogue Everett Herald, 1984-88. Adviser DeMolay, Spokane, 1979-81; team mem. Night-Walk, inner-city ministry, Spokane, 1979-82; coord. Ch. Relief Overseas Project Hunger Walk, Spokane and Everett, 1981, 85; vol. chaplain Gen. Hosp. Everett, 1983-90; trustee Deaconess Children's Svcs., Everett, 1983-88. Recipient Legion of Honor DeMolay Internat., 1982. Mem. Fellowship of Reconciliation, North Snohomish County Assn. Chs. (v.p. 1985-89), Pacific N.W. Ann. Conf. Bd. Global Ministries (sec. 1988-92, pres. 1993—). Democrat. Home: 121 Monterey Pl NE Renton WA 98056 Office: Renton First United Meth Ch 2201 NE 4th St Renton WA 98056

WARREN, RICHARD WAYNE, obstetrician and gynecologist; b. Puxico, Mo., Nov. 26, 1935; s. Martin R. and Sarah E. (Crump) W.; m. Rosalie J. Franzola, Aug. 16, 1959; children: Lani Marie, Richard W., Paul D. BA, U. Calif., Berkeley, 1957; MD, Stanford U., 1961. Intern, Oakland (Calif.) Naval Hosp., 1961-62; resident in ob-gyn Stanford (Calif.) Med. Ctr., 1964-67; practice medicine specializing in ob-gyn, Mountain View, Calif., 1967—; mem. staff Stanford and El Camino hosps.; pres. Richard W. Warren M.D., Inc.; assoc. clin. prof. ob-gyn Stanford Sch. Medicine. Served with USN, 1961-64. Diplomate Am. Bd. Ob-Gyn. Fellow Am. Coll. Ob-Gyn; mem. AMA, Am. Fertility Soc., Am. Assn. Gynecologic Laparoscopists, Calif. Med. Assn., San Francisco Gynecol. Soc., Peninsula Gynecol. Soc., Assn. Profs. Gynecology and Obstetrics, Royal Soc. Medicine, Shufelt Gynecol. Soc. Santa Clara Valley. Contbr. articles to profl. jours. Home: 102 Atherton Ave Menlo Park CA 94027-4021 Office: 2500 Hospital Dr Mountain View CA 94040-4106

WARREN, SANDRA LYN, quality assurance professional; b. Castro Valley, Calif., Oct. 30, 1958; d. Harold J. and Anneliese (Ohlwerther) W. BS in Phys. Sci., Calif. State U., Hayward, 1993. Supr. escrow dept. Union Bank, Oakland, Calif., 1978-80; mgr. quality assurance Aerotest Ops., Inc., San Ramon, Calif., 1980—. Mem. Am. Nuclear Soc., Am. Soc. for Non-Destructive Testing (level III), Horsemen's Benevolent and Protective Assn., Calif. Thoroughbred Breeders Assn. Republican. Office: Aerotest Ops Inc 3455 Fostoria Way San Ramon CA 94583-1317

WARREN, THOMAS HENRY, philosophy educator; b. San Antonio, June 24, 1939; s. Joe Tom and Avalon Elizabeth (Rines) W.; children: Mark, Tyler. BA in Polit. Sci., U. Calif., Berkeley, 1961; PhD in Polit. Philosophy, U. Calif., Santa Barbara, 1973. Social studies tchr. Laguna Beach (Calif.) Schs., 1966-69; asst. prof. polit. theory SUNY, Oswego, 1973-76; instr. in philosophy Solano Coll., Suisun, Calif., 1976—. 1st lt. U.S. Army, 1963-65. NDEA fellow U.S. Govt., 1970-72. Mem. Am. Philos. Assn. Home: 7052 Gibson Canyon Rd Vacaville CA 95688-9708

WARSCHAUER, DOUGLAS MARVIN, physicist; b. Haverstraw, N.Y., Sept. 3, 1925; s. Frederic and Lillian Phyllis (Falk) W.; m. Susan Yvonne Idstein, June 18, 1950 (div. June 1975); children: Lynn A., Karen A. Warschauer Brooks, Jeffrey F. BA, Drew U., 1946; PhD, U. Pa., 1951. Solid state rsch. physicist, mgr. Lincoln Lab./MIT, Harvard, Raytheon, Mass., 1951-67; chief electronics components lab. NASA Electronics Rsch. Lab., Cambridge, Mass., 1967-70; rsch. physicist Naval Weapons Ctr./Meret Corp., L.A. and China Lake, Calif., 1972-75; program mgr. photovoltaics U.S. Dept. Energy, Washington, 1975-79; retailer Et Cetera & Rocs, Santa Maria, Calif., 1981—; part time prof. Calif. Poly. Inst., San Luis Obispo, 1981—; cons. Meret Corp., China Lake and L.A., Calif.; part time prof. Northeastern U., Boston, Rutgers U., New Brunswick, N.J., 1947-67. Patentee in field; author text: Semiconductors and Transistors, 1959; author rsch. papers in field; co-editor monograph Solids Under Pressure, 1963. Vol. China Lake Mountain Rescue Group, 1973-76. Mem. AAAS. Home and Office: 918 Felicia Way San Luis Obispo CA 93401-7626

WARTHEN, JOHN EDWARD, construction, leasing and finance executive; b. Cedar City, Utah, May 8, 1922; s. Mark Tew and Emma (Simkins) W.; student Branch Agrl. Coll. So. Utah, Cedar City, 1940-41; m. Norma Jane Hansen, June 22, 1943; children—Russel Edward, John Merrill, Judith Lally, Linda Fahringer, Carla Jean Thompson, Lauri Janette Sherratt. Pres., mgr. St. George Service, Inc. (Utah), 1945-61, Warthen Constrn. Co., Las Vegas, 1961—, Warthen Buick, 1961—; pres., gen. mgr. Diversified Investment &

Leasing Corp., Las Vegas. Councilman, City of St. George, 1950-54. Past trustee, treas. Latter Day Saint Br. Geneal. Library, Las Vegas, 1964-76 ; co-founder Ctr. for Internat. Security Studies; past dist. dir. Freeman Inst.; past nat. dir. Liberty Amendment Com.; past chmn. Citizens for Pvt. Enterprise, Las Vegas; mem. Coun. Inter-Am. Security, Americanism Ednl. League; past fin. chmn. Boy Scouts Am.; past state chmn. Nev. Dealer Election Action Com.; mem. Nev. Devel. Authority. Mem. Ludwig Von Misses Inst. Econs. (charter), SAR (Good Citizenship award nat. soc.). Mormon (bishop 1957-61). Clubs: Rotary, Kiwanis. Home: 2475 E Viking Rd Las Vegas NV 89121-4109 Office: 3025 E Sahara Ave Las Vegas NV 89104-4315

WARWICK, MAL, publisher, consultant, author. BA with distinction, U. Mich., 1963; postgrad. in Latin Am. Affairs, Columbia U., 1963-65. Vol. Peace Corps, Ecuador, 1965-69; freelance writer Calif., 1969-76; exec. editor, co-founder Alternative Features Service, Berkeley, Calif., 1971-73; campaign mgr., coordinator Berkeley Citizens Action, 1976-80; chmn., founder Mal Warwick & Assocs., Inc., Berkeley, 1979—; chmn., co-founder The Progressive Group, Inc., Northampton, Mass., 1985-95; vice-chmn., co-founder Share Group, Inc. (merger The Progressive Group and Share Sys., Inc.), Somerville, Mass., 1995—; chief fundraiser Jesse Jackson for Pres. campaign, 1987-88; pres., founder Response Mgmt. Techs., Inc., Berkeley, Calif., 1986—, Changing Am. Inc., Berkeley, 1986—; founder, pub. Strathenoor Press, Inc., Berkeley, 1989—; co-founder, chair exec. com. Berkeley Cmty. Fund, 1992—; organizing com. Cmty. Bank of the Bay, 1993-94; bd. dirs., v.p. Berkeley Symphony Orch., 1991—; bd. dirs., treas. Inst. for Studies in Environment, Devel. and Security, 1991—; sponsor Berkeley Peace Prize, 1985-92; co-founder, bd. dirs., exec. com. Bus. for Social Responsibility, 1993-94; mem. Social Venture Network, 1991—. Author: Raising Money by Mail, 1995, How to Write Successful Fundraising Letters, 1994, Technology and the Future of Fundraising, 1994, 999 Tips, Trends and Guidelines for Successful Direct Mail and Telephone Fundraising, 1993, You Don't Always Get What You Ask For: Using Direct Mail Tests to Raise More Money for Your Organization, 1992, Revolution in the Mailbox, 1990; editor: Type & Layout: How Typography and Design Can Get Your Message Across-or Get in the Way (Colin Wheildon), 1995; editor: (newsletter) Successful Direct Mail and Telephone Fundraising, 1993—; columnist for The Non-Profit Times, 1990—. Mem. Com. for Ronald V. Dellums Campaign, 1979—; mem. exec. bd. Calif. Dems., 1982-86, co-founder Environ. Caucus, 1984; mem. bd. Berkeley Support Svcs., 1980-82; chmn. Berkeley Citizens' Commn. Automatic Data Processing Ops., 1981-82. Mem. Nat. Soc. Fund Raising Execs. (bd. dirs. 1986—), Assn. Direct Response Fundraising Counsel (pres. 1993-95). Office: Mal Warwick & Assocs Inc 2550 9th St Ste 103 Berkeley CA 94710-2516

WASCHER, DANIEL CHARLES, orthopaedic surgeon; b. Elmer, N.J., Mar. 6, 1959; s. William and Rachel (Roudebush) W.; m. Kelly Berenson, Sept. 3, 1989. BS in Biochemistry, Northwestern U., 1980; MD, St. Louis U., 1984. Diplomate Am. Bd. Orthopaedic Surgeons. Resident in internal medicine Loyola U., 1984-85, resident in gen. surgery, 1985-86; resident in orthopaedic surgery U. Rochester, 1986-89; fellowship in sports medicine UCLA Divsn. of Orthopaedics, 1989-91; asst. prof. dept. of orthopaedics U. N.Mex. Sch. of Medicine, 1991—, chief divsn. of sports medicine, 1991—; team physician varsity athletics U. N.Mex.; cons. reviewer Clin. Orthopaedics and Related Rsch., 1990; presenter in field. Contbr. articles to profl. jours. Mem. N.Mex. Ortho. Assn. (bd. dirs. 1993—). Home: 445 Live Oak Loop NE Albuquerque NM 87122-1406 Office: Dept Ortho Surgery U NMex Sch Medicine 2211 Lomas Blvd NE Albuquerque NM 87106-2745

WASDEN, WINIFRED SAWAYA, English language educator, writer; b. Kemmerer, Wyo., Apr. 15, 1938; d. George Sabeh and Letta Louise (Gerken) Sawaya; m. John Frederic Wasden, Dec. 20, 1960; children: Frederic Keith, Carol Elizabeth. BA with honors, U. Wyo., 1960, MA, 1961. Emergency instr. U. Wyo., Laramie, 1960-61; tchr. English Worland (Wyo.) High Sch., 1963; instr. NW Community Coll., Powell, Wyo., 1964-91, prof., 1991—, English coord., 1990-93. Contbr. articles to pubs.; author numerous poems. Mem. Powell Bd. Adjustments, 1974-86; chmn., bd. dirs. Civic Orch. and Chorus, Powell, 1981-88; mem. Wyo. Coun. for the Humanities, 1978-79, coord. Big Horn Basin Project, 1980-85. Mem. Wyo. Oral History and Folklore Assn. (v.p. 1984-85, bd. dirs. 1985-86), Wyo. Assn. Tchrs. English, N.W. Community Coll. Faculty Assn. (pres. 1977-78), AAAUW, Oral History Assn., Am. Folklore Soc., Northwest Oral History Assn., Delta Kappa Gamma (pres. Powell chpt. 1978-80), Phi Rho Pi (hon.). Republican. Roman Catholic. Office: NW CC Powell WY 82435

WASHBURN, JERRY MARTIN, accountant, corporate executive; b. Powell, Wyo., Dec. 31, 1943; s. Roland and Lavon (Martin) W.; divorced; children: Garth, Gavin, Kristina. BS in Acctg. Brigham Young U., 1969. CPA, Wash., Idaho, Oreg. Staff acct. Arthur Andersen & Co., Seattle, 1969-70, sr. auditor, Boise, Idaho, 1971-73, audit mgr., 1974-75, Boise and Portland, Oreg., 1976-79; v.p. contr. Washburn Musicland, Inc., Phoenix, 1980-82; mgr., ptnr. Washburn Enterprises, Phoenix, 1977-90; pres. Total Info. Systems, Inc., Phoenix, 1984-90; v.p. KJ Mktg., Inc., 1990-91; dir. mktg. IPRO, Inc., 1991-94; assoc. Perfect Strategies, Inc., 1994—; v.p., CFO Global Indsl. Products, Inc., Scottsdale, Ariz., 1995—; founding dir. Internat. and Commerce Bank, Phoenix, 1985-86. Mem. Inst. Internal Auditors (pres. Boise chpt. 1974, bd. dirs. Boise and Portland chpts. 1975-77), Am. Mgmt. Soc., Am. Inst. CPAs, Wash. Soc. CPAs, Idaho Soc. CPAs. Republican. Office: Global Indsl Products, Inc 7898 E Acoma Dr Scottsdale AZ 85260

WASHBURN, LAWRENCE ROBERT, manufacturing executive; b. Jackson, Mich., Aug. 5, 1941; s. Lawrence Merton and Elvina Marie (Morgan) W.; m. Kay Frances Wieczerzak, Nov. 21, 1970; children: Lawrence Robert II, Alexa Kay. BA in History, Govt., So. Calif. Coll., 1974. Supr., engr. Tool Rsch. & Engring., Inc., Santa Ana, Calif., 1968-77; ops. mgr. Knudsen Systems, Inc., Anaheim, Calif., 1977-86; plant mgr. Flourcarbon, Anaheim, Calif., 1986-88; dir. engring. Ricoh Electronics, Inc., Tustin, Calif., 1988-92; chmn., CEO Teqcom Industries, Santa Ana, 1992—. Dist. commr. Boy Scouts Am., Orange County, Calif., 1982-90; exec. dir. Immanuel Luth. Ch. & Sch., 1987-92; bd. dirs. Luth. High Sch. Orange County, 1990—. With USN, 1966-68. Decorated Navy Achievement medal; recipient Scouter medal Boy Scouts Am., 1986, Award of Merit, 1988. Mem. Am. Soc. Mech. Engrs., Soc. Mfg. Engrs., Air Traffic Control Assn., Ridgeline Country Club. Republican. Office: Teqcom Industries 1712 Newport Cir Ste O Santa Ana CA 92705-5118

WASHINGTON, JAMES WINSTON, JR., artist, sculptor; b. Gloster, Miss., Nov. 10, 1909; s. James and Lizie (Howard) W.; m. Janie R. Miller, Mar. 29, 1943. Student, Nat. Landscape Inst., 1944-47; D.F.A., Center Urban-Black Studies, 1975. tchr. summer class N.W. Theol. Union Seattle U., 1988. One man shows U.S.O. Gallery, Little Rock, 1943, Foster-White Gallery, Seattle, 1974, 78, 80, 83, 89 (also at Bellevue Art Mus., 89), Charles and Emma Frye Art Mus., Seattle, 1980, 95, Mus. History and Industry, Seattle, 1981; exhibited in group shows Willard Gallery, N.Y.C., 1960-64, Feingarten Galleries, San Francisco, 1958-59, Grosvenor Gallery, London, Eng., 1964, Lee Nordness Gallery, N.Y.C., 1962, Woodside Gallery, Seattle, 1962-65, Foster-White Gallery, Seattle, 1974, 76, 89, Smithsonian Instn., 1974, San Diego, 1977, Foster/White Gallery, Seattle, 1992, others; retrospective exhbn. Bellevue Art Mus., Washington, 1989; represented in permanent collections Seattle, San Francisco, Oakland art museums, Seattle First Nat. Bank, Seattle Pub. Library YWCA, Seattle, Meany Jr. High Sch., Seattle World's Fair, Expo 70 Osaka, Japan., Whitney Mus. Am. Art, N.Y.C.; commd. sculpture: Bird With Covey, Wash. State Capitol Mus., Olympia, 1983, Obelisk with Phoenix and Esoteric Symbols of Nature in granite, Sheraton Hotel Seattle, 1982, Life Surrounding the Astral Alter, In Matrix, owner T.M. Rosenblume, Charles Z. Smith & Assocs., Seattle, 1986, The Oracle of Truth (6 1/2 ton sculpture at M. Zion Bapt. Ch., Seattle, 1987, commd. sculptures King County Arts Commn., 1989, Bailey Gatzent Elem. Sch., Seattle, 1991, Twin Eaglets of the Cosmic Cycle (Quincy Jones), 1993, Fountain of Triumph (Bangasser Assocs. Inc.), 1992-93, Seattle, 1994-95. Passover leader Mt. Zion Baptist Ch., Seattle, 1974-87. Recipient Spl. Commendation award for many contbns. to artistic heritage of state Gov., 1973, plaque City of Seattle, 1973, plaque Benefit Guild, Inc., 1973, arts service award King County Arts Commn., 1984, cert. of recognition Gov. of Wash., 1984, Editor's Choice award Outstanding Achievement in Poetry Nat. Libr. Poetry, 1993; named to Wash. State Centennial Hall of Honor, Wash. State Hist. Soc., 1984; home and studio designated historic landmark (city and state), 1991. Mem. Internat. Platform Assn., Internat. Soc. Poets (life, awards 1993), Profl. Artists Phila., Masons (33 degree Prince Hall Lodge #67). Home: 1816 26th Ave Seattle WA 98122-3110

WASHINGTON, NAPOLEON, JR., insurance agent, clergyman; b. Ft. Baker, Calif., Apr. 12, 1948; s. Napoleon and Annie D. (Carter) W.; m. Nadine Reed, Nov. 6, 1968; children: Gregory D., Kimberlee N., Geoffrey N. AA, Merced Coll., 1976; student Stanislaus State Coll., 1976-77; grad. Billy Graham Sch. Evangelism, 1987; BA in Social Sci., Chapman U., 1994, postgrad., 1994—. Ordained Baptist Gospel minister, 1989. Agt., Met. Life Ins. Co., Merced, Calif., 1970-72, sr. sales rep., 1972-83; broker Gen. Ins. Brokers, Merced, 1973—; owner Washington Assocs. Fin. Services; tchr. salesmanship Merced Coll., 1979—; assoc. pastor, bd. dirs. Christian Life Ctr., Merced, Calif., 1993. Chmn. bd. trustees St. Matthew Baptist Ch., 1978-84, ordained deacon, lic. minister, assoc. minister, 1982-91; pastor New Canaan Bapt. Ch., Los Banos, Calif., 1991-92; vice-chmn. Merced County Pvt. Industries Coun., 1981-83; mem. ins. adv. coun. City of Merced Schs.; vocat. mgr. New Hope Found., Dos Palos, Calif., 1984-85; trustee Matthew Bapt. Ch., 1978-84; pastor New Canaan Bapt. Ch., 1991-92. Served with U.S. Army, 1968-70. Recipient Nat. Quality award Nat. Assn. Life Underwriters, 1979, Nat. Sales Achievement award, 1979, Health Ins. Quality award, 1977; mem. Million Dollar Round Table, 1973-78; teaching cert. Calif. community colls.; Life Underwriting Coun. fellow, 1987. Mem. Nat. Assn. Life Underwriters, Calif. Assn. Life Underwriters (dir. 1975-76), Merced County Assn. Life Underwriters (pres. 1976-77), Merced County Estate Planning Council (dir.), Merced County Pvt. Industries Council, NAACP, Rotary (dir. 1974-76), Phi Beta Lambda. Democrat. Home: 1960 Cedar Crest Dr Merced CA 95340-2729 Office: 935 W 18th St Merced CA 95340-4502

WASHINGTON, REGINALD LOUIS, pediatric cardiologist; b. Colorado Springs, Colo., Dec. 31, 1949; s. Lucius Louis and Brenette Y. (Wheeler) W.; m. Billye Faye Ned, Aug. 18, 1973; children: Danielle Larae, Reginald Quinn. BS in Zoology, Colo. State U., 1971; MD, U. Colo., 1975. Diplomate Nat. Bd. Med. Examiners, Am. Bd. Pediatrics, Pediatric Cardiology. Intern in pediatrics U. Colo. Med. Ctr., Denver, 1975-76, resident in pediatrics, 1976-78, chief resident, instr., 1978-79, fellow in pediatric cardiology, 1979-81, asst. prof. pediatrics, 1982-1988, assoc. prof. pediatrics, 1988-90, assoc. clin. prof. pediatrics, 1990—; staff cardiologist Children's Hosp., Denver, 1981-90; v.p. Rocky Mountain Pediatric Cardiology, Denver, 1990—; mem. admissions com. U. Colo. Sch. Medicine, Denver, 1985-89; chmn., bd. dirs. Coop. Health Care Agreements, 1994—. Cons. editor Your Patient and Fitness, 1989-92. Chmn. Coop. Health Care Agreements Bd. State of Colo., 1994—; adv. bd. dirs. Equitable Bank of Littleton, Colo, 1984-86; bd. dirs. Ctrl. City Opera, 1989—, Cleo Parker Robinson Dance Co., 1992-94, Rocky Mountain Heart Fund for Children, 1984-89, Raindo Ironkids, 1989—; nat. bd. dirs. Am. Heart Assn., 1992—; bd. dirs. Nat. Coun. Patient Info. and Edn., 1992—, Children's Heart Alliance, 1993-94, Regis U., Denver, 1994—, Colo. State U. Devel. Coun., 1994—; trustee Denver Ctr. Performing Arts, 1994—; mem. Gov.'s coun. Phys. fitness, 1990-91. Named Salute Vol. of Yr. Big Sisters of Colo., 1990; honoree NCCJ, 1994, Physician of Yr., Nat. Am. Heart Assn., 1995. Fellow Am. Acad. Pediatrics (cardiology subsect.), Am. Coll. Cardiology, Am. Heart Assn. (coun. on cardiovascular disease in the young, exec. com. 1988-91, nat. devel. program com. 1990-94, vol. of yr. 1989, pres. Colo. chpt. 1989-90, Torch of Hope 1987, Gold Heart award Colo. chpt. 1990, bd. dirs. Colo. chpt., exec. com. Colo. chpt. 1987—, grantee Colo. chpt. 1983-84, mem. editorial bd. Pediatric Exercise Scis. 1988—, Nat. Physician of the Yr., 1995), Soc. Critical Care Medicine; mem. Am. Acad. Pediatrics/Perinatology, N.Am. Soc. Pediatric Exercise Medicine (pres. 1986-87), Colo. Med. Soc. (chmn. sports medicine coun. 1993-94), Leadership Denver 1990, Denver Athletic Club, Met. Club, Glenmoor Golf Club. Democrat. Roman Catholic. Home: 7423 Berkeley Cir Castle Rock CO 80104-9278 Office: Rocky Mountain Pediatric Cardiology 1601 E 19th Ave Ste 5600 Denver CO 80218-1216

WASHINGTON-KNIGHT, BARBARA J., military officer, nurse; b. Chgo., July 13, 1948; d. Lewis and Carrie Mae (Randolph) Washington; m. William S. Knight, Aug. 23, 1986; children: Carlton, Carrie. Diploma, St. Elizabeth's Hosp., Chgo., 1971; B in Health Scis., Chapman Coll., 1979, postgrad. CCRN; cert. instr., advanced cardiac life support provider and instr. Commd. lt. USAF, 1972, advanced through grades to lt. col.; asst. head nurse med. unit USAF, Fairfield, Calif., 1976-78, asst. head nurse orthopedic unit, 1978-79; asst. head nurse spl. care unit USAF, Montgomery, Ala., 1979-80, head nurse spl. care unit, 1980-82; head nurse spl. care unit USAF, Riverside, Calif., 1982-85; head nurse surg. ICU USAF, San Antonio, 1985-87, clin. supr. dept. of critical care, 1987-88; head nurse spl. care unit USAF, Riverside, Calif., 1988-91, coord. quality improvement, 1990-92; asst. chief nurse, clin. nurse specialist inpatient svcs. USAF, Tinker AFB, Oklahoma City, 1992-93; clin. nurse post critical care unit Moreno Valley (Calif.) Cmty. Hosp., 1993—. Mem. Soc. Retired Air Force Nurses, Am. Assn. Critical Care Nurses, Air Force Assn., Air War Coll. Assn., Women's Meml. Found.

WASKELL, LUCY ANN, anesthesiologist, researcher; b. Radford, Va., Feb. 1, 1942; d. Ernest and Suzanne (Hosage) W. B.S., Pa. State U., 1963; M.D., Columbia U., 1967; Ph.D., U. Calif.-Berkeley, 1974. Diplomate Am. Bd. Anesthesiology. Intern San Francisco Gen. Hosp., 1967-68; resident Stanford U. Hosp., Palo Alto, Calif., 1973-74; prof. U. Calif.-San Francisco, 1979—. Office: VA Hosp 43rd and Clement St San Francisco CA 94121

WASON, BETTY (ELIZABETH WASON), author; b. Delphi, Ind., Mar. 6, 1912; d. James Paddock and Susan Una (Edson) W.; divorced; 1 child, Ela Bannick; 1 stepson, Lance Hall. BS, Purdue U., 1933. Cert. home economist. Radio cooking sch. hostess WLAP Radio, Lexington, N.Y., 1934; asst. women's editor McCall's mag., 1935; publicist R. C. Mayer, 1936-38; roving corr. Transradio Press, 1938-40; war corr. CBS, Stockholm, spring 1940, Athens, 1940-41; stringer Newsweek, 1940-41; spl. corr. PM Newspaper, N.Y., 1940-41; editor Voice of Am., 1942-43; talk show moderator WINX Radio, 1945-46; prodn. mgr. Am. Forum Mutual Broadcasting of Air, 1947; women's editor Voice of Am., 1948-52; editor food booklets Gen. Foods Corp., 1954; asst. food editor Women's Home Companion, 1955-56; publicist Spanish olive oil Selvage & Lee, N.Y., 1956-68; author, freelance writer, 1968—. Author: Miracle in Hellas, 1943, Cooking Without Cans, 1944, Dinners That Wait, 1954, Language of Cookery, 1956, Travel Fair, 1960, Cooks, Gluttons & Gourmets, 1962, It Takes Jack to Build a House, 1963, Bride in the Kitchen, 1964, Hair Today, Gone Tomorrow, 1964, Art of Vegetarian Cookery, 1965, A Salute to Cheese, 1966, Art of German Cooking, 1967, Mediterranean Cook Book, 1969, Betty Wason's Greek Cook Book, 1969, Cooking to Please Kids, 1969, Everything Cook Book, 1970, Low Calorie Hors d'Oeuvres, 1970, Giving Cheese & Wine Party, 1974, High Fiber Cookbook, 1975, Remodelling For Pleasure & Profit, 1976, Ellen, A Mother's Story, 1976, (with Pamela Hall) Heads You Lose, 1971; author, editor: F-Plan Diet, 1982. Mem. Nat. Press Club (mem. libr. com., travel com., new club com., arts com., hon. life mem.), Seattle Freelancers, English Speaking Union, C. S. Jung Soc. Democrat. Episcopalian. Home: 3011 NW 56th St Apt 3 Seattle WA 98107-4249

WASSER, SAMUEL K., medical educator, conservation center executive; b. Detroit, Aug. 27, 1953; s. Frank Irving and Ethel Wasser; m. Lauren Montgomery Marra, July 28, 1985; children: Jenna Liana, Noah Bruce. BS in Zoology, Mich. State U., 1974; MS in Zoology, U. Wis., Milw., 1975; PhD in Psychology, U. Wash., 1981. Grad. teaching asst. dept. zoology U. Wis., Milw., 1975-76; grad. teaching asst., lectr. dept. psychology U. Wash., Seattle, 1977-81, rsch. assoc., lectr. dept. psychology, 1981-89, rsch. assoc. ob/gyn and Wash. Regional Primate Rsch. Ctr., 1981-89, asst. prof. ob/gyn Med. Sch., 1993—; sr. rsch. fellow Smithsonian INstn., Washington, 1989-93; assoc. producer IVth Internat. Conf. on World's Cats and Sociobiology of Carnivores, Seattle, 1977; mem. workshop NIMH/NICHD, 1990; dir. Animal Behavior Rsch. Unit, Mikumi Nat. Park, Tanzania, 1985—; collaborator Africa Bur., USAID, 1992—; mem. primate specialists group Internat. Union for Conservation of Nature and Natural Resources, 1986—; sci. dir. Ctr. for Wildlife Conservation, Seattle, 1993—. Mem. editorial bd. Am. Jour. Primatology, 1988—; assoc. editor Human Nature, 1989—; contbr. numerous articles to profl. publs. Grantee Guggenheim Found., 1982-84, 90-91, Nat. Geog. Soc., 1986-87, 90, World Wildlife Fund, 1986-87, NSF, 1986-88, L.S.B. Leakey Found., 1989, Wenner-Gren Found., 1989, NIMH, 1990-92, USAID, 1991-93, Smithsonian Instn., 1991-92, 92, 92-93, 92-94; recipient Career Devel. award H.F. Guggenheim Found., 1984-87, Rsch. Devel. award Nat. Zool. Park, Smithsonian Instn., 1989-91. Mem. Tanzania Wildlife Fund (pres. 1993—). Home: 11702 Durland Ave NE Seattle WA 98125-5901 Office: Ctr Wildlife Conservation 5500 Phinney Ave N Seattle WA 98103-5865 also: U Wash Sch Medicine Divsn Reproductive Endocrinology XD-44 Seattle WA 98195

WASSERBURG, GERALD JOSEPH, geology and geophysics educator; b. New Brunswick, N.J., Mar. 25, 1927; s. Charles and Sarah (Levine) W.; m. Naomi Z. Orlick, Dec. 21, 1951; children: Charles David, Daniel Morris. Student, Rutgers U.; BS in Physics, U. Chgo., 1951, MSc in Geology, 1952, PhD, 1954, DSc (hon.), 1992; Dr. Hon. Causa, Brussels U., 1985, U. Paris, 1986; DSc (hon.), Ariz. State U., 1987. Research assoc. Inst. Nuclear Studies, U. Chgo., 1954-55; asst. prof. Calif. Inst. Tech., Pasadena, 1955-59, assoc. prof., 1959-62, prof. geology and geophysics, 1962-82, John D. MacArthur prof. geology and geophysics, 1982—; served on Juneau Ice Field Research Project, 1950; cons. Argonne Nat. Lab., Lamont, Ill., 1952-55; former mem. U.S. Nat. Com. for Geochem., com. for Planetary Exploration Study, NRC, adv. council Petroleum Research Fund, Am. Chem. Soc.; mem. lunar sample analysis planning team (LSAPT) Manned Spacecraft Ctr., NASA, Houston , 1968-71, chmn.,1970; lunar sample rev. bd. 1970-72; mem. Facilities Working Group LSAPT, Johnson Space Ctr., 1972-82; mem. sci. working panel for Apollo missions, Johnson Space Ctr., 1971-73; advisor NASA, 1968-88, physical scis. com., 1971-75, mem. lunar base steering com., 1984; chmn. com. for planetary and lunar exploration, mem. space sci. bd. NAS, 1975-78; chmn. div. Geol. and Planetary Scis., Calif. Inst. Tech., 1987-89; vis. prof. U. Kiel, Fed. Republic of Germany, 1960, Harvard U., 1962, U. Bern, Switzerland, 1966, Swiss Fed. Tech. Inst., 1967, Max Planck Inst., Mainz and Heidelberg, Fed. Republic of Germany, 1985; invited lectr., Vinton Hayes Sr. Fellow, Harvard U., 1980, Jaeger-Hales lectr., Australian Nat. U., 1980, Harold Jeffreys lectr. Royal Astron. Soc., 1981, Ernst Cloos lectr., Johns Hopkins U., 1984, H.L. Welsh Disting. lectr. U. Toronto, Can. 1986., Danz lectr. U. Washington, 1989; Goldschmidt Centennial lectr. Norwegian Acad. Sci. and Letters, 1989; Green vis. prof. U. B.C. 1982; 60th Anniversary Symposium speaker, Hebrew U., Jerusalem, 1985. Served with U.S. Army, 1944-46. Decorated Combat Inf. badge. Recipient Group Achievement award, NASA, 1969, Exceptional Sci. Achievement award, NASA, 1970, Disting. Pub. Service medal, NASA, 1973, J.F. Kemp medal Columbia U., 1973, Profl. Achievement award U. Chgo. Alumni Assn., 1978, Disting. Pub. Service medal with cluster, NASA, 1978, Wollaston medal Geol. Soc. London, 1985, Sr. Scientist award, Alexander von Humboldt-Stiftung, 1985, Crafoord prize Royal Swedish Acad. Scis., 1986. Gold medal Royal Astron. Soc., 1991; named Hon. Fgn. Fellow European Union Geoscis., 1983, recipient Holmes medal 1987; Rgents fellow Smithsonian Inst. Fellow Geol. Soc. London (hon.), AAAS, Am. Geophys. Union (planetology sect., Harry H. Hess medal 1985), Geol. Soc. Am. (life, Arthur L. Day medal 1970), Meteoritical Soc. (pres. 1987-88, Leonard medal 1975); mem. Geochem. Soc. (Goldschmidt medal 1978), Nat. Acad. Scis. (Arthur L. Day prize and lectureship 1981, J. Lawrence Smith medal 1985), Norwegian Acad. Sci. and Letters, Am. Phil. Soc. Office: Calif Inst of Tech Divsn Geol & Planetary Scis Pasadena CA 91125

WASSERMAN, BARRY L(EE), architect; b. Cambridge, Mass., May 25, 1935; s. Theodore and Adelaide (Levin) W.; m. Wilma Louise Greenfield, June 21, 1957 (div. 1971); children: Tim Andrew, Andrew Glenn; m. Judith Ella Michaelowski, Apr. 22, 1979. B.A., Harvard U., 1957, M. Arch., 1960. Registered architect, Calif. Assoc. John S. Bolles Assocs., San Francisco, 1960-69; prin. Wasserman-Herman Assocs., San Francisco, 1969-72; prin., dir. Office Lawrence Halprin U Assocs., San Francisco, 1972-76; dep. state architect State of Calif., Sacramento, 1976-78, state architect, 1978-83; prof. dept. architecture, dir. Inst. Environ. Design, Sch. Environ. Design Calif. State Poly. U., Pomona, 1983-87, chair dept. architecture, Coll. Environ. Design, 1988—; cons. architecture, Sacramento, 1983—; program advisor Fla. A&M U., Tallahassee, 1981-83. Architect Wasserman House, San Rafael, Calif., 1963 ((AIA-Sunset Mag. award of Merit) 1965-66), Anna Waden Library, San Francisco, 1969 ((AIA award of Merit 1970)), Capitol Area Plan, Sacramento, 1977 (Central Valley chpt. AIA Honor award 1979). Recipient Awards citation Progressive Architecture 26th awards Program, 1979. Fellow AIA chmn. architecture in govt. com. (1979). Democrat. Jewish. Home: 6456 Fordham Way Sacramento CA 95831-2218

WASSERMAN, BRUCE ARLEN, dentist, mail order company executive; b. San Mateo, Calif., June 7, 1954; s. Albert and Dunia (Frydman) W.; m. Pamela Carole Ward, June 8, 1972; children:Rachael, Rebecca, Meir, Keren. BA in Mass Communications, Winona State U., 1981; DDS, U. Pacific, 1985. Apprentice blacksmith Reuben Syhre Blacksmith Shop, Pine River, Minn., 1973-74; blacksmith Walden Forge, Pine River, 1974-79; founding dir. Team Redeemed, San Mateo, 1984-92; pvt. practice dentistry San Mateo, 1985—; pres. Manx USA, San Mateo, 1987-92. Editor: (quar. jour.) Cycle Lines, 1983-85, Good News, 1984-92, No. Calif. Reporter, 1987-90; assoc. editor: Internat. Communicator, 1988-89, editor, 1990; editor: (mo. jour.) The Mouthpiece, 1986-89; author: A Manual of Uniforming. Cubmaster Boy Scouts Am., San Mateo, 1986-87; fund raiser Am. Lung Assn., San Mateo County, 1986-90, bd. dirs., 1989-94, chmn. Bike Trek, 1989, fund devel. com., 1989-90, membership com., 1991; chmn. Sofitel Bastille Tour, 1992-93. Recipient Disting. Young Alumni award Winona State U., 1988; Mosby scholar Tau Kappa Omega, 1985. Fellow Am. Acad. Dentistry Internat. (editor 1990, mem. bylaws com. 1990), Am. Coll. Dentists, Royal Soc. Health, Pierre Fauchard Acad. (chmn. No. Calif. sect. 1992-95); mem. ADA (cert. recognition 1987, 89, 90), Calif. Dental Assn. (Disting. Svc. award 1987), San Mateo County Dental Soc. (exec. bd. 1986-89, editor 1986-89, Pres. award 1989, Bd. Dirs. award 1987, bd. dirs. 1991-92), Acad. Gen. Dentistry, Christian Classic Bikers Assn. (Calif. rep. 1983-94), Order Ky. Cols., 78th Fraser's Highlanders Regiment (lt./capt., recruiting officer 1993-94, maj. O.C. 77th Montgomery Highlanders Regiment Headquarters Garrison), Pacific Road Riders (pres., editor 1983-85). Office: 410 N San Mateo Dr San Mateo CA 94401-2418

WASSERMAN, MARTIN STEPHEN, psychiatrist, psychoanalyst, child psychiatrist; b. N.Y.C., Jan. 19, 1938; s. Sol and Frances (Levine) W.; m. Ann Beckett, June 8, 1963 (div. June 1976); children: Gregory, Eric; m. Francine B. Heller, June, 1976. AB, Columbia Coll., 1959; sr. elective student, Trinity Coll., Dublin, Ireland, 1963; MD, SUNY, Bklyn., 1963. Diplomate Am. Bd. Psychiatry and Neurology (psychiatry, child psychiatry), Nat. Bd. Examiners. Intern Albany (N.Y.) Med. Ctr., 1963-64; resident in psychiatry Kings County Med. Ctr. Hosp., Bklyn., 1964-67, fellow in child psychiatry, 1966-67; fellow in child psychiatry U. Mich. Med. Ctr., Children's Psychiat. Hosp., Ann Arbor, 1969-70; instr. psychiatry SUNY, Bklyn., 1966-67; asst. prof. psychology L.I. U., Southampton, N.Y., 1966-68; asst. prof. psychiatry, asst. dir. student psychiat. svcs. U. So. Calif. Sch. Medicine, L.A., 1970-75, assoc. clin. prof. psychiatry and child psychiatry, 1975—; faculty L.A. Psychoanalytic Soc. and Inst., 1977-88, sr. faculty, 1989—; staff psychiatrist Sisters of Mercy Orphanage, Bklyn., 1965-67, Little Flower House of Providence, Ctr. Forensic Psychiatry, Ypsilanti, Mich., 1969-70; cons. Operation Head Start, San Diego, 1967-69, Oceanside (Calif.) Union Sch. Dist., 1967-69; consulting psychiatrist Ingham County Mental Health Ctr., Lansing, Mich., 1969-70, U.S. Pub. Health Svc., Milan, Mich., 1969-70; field supr. St. John's Seminary, Plymouth, Mass., 1969-70; attending psychiatrist L.A. County Hosp., 1970—; dir. postgrad. edn. L.A. Psychoanalytic Soc. and Inst., 1975-78, sec. bd. dirs., 1977-78, candidates evaluation com., 1990—; dir. rotating six internship U. So. Calif., L.A., 1970-72; profl. staff C.P.C. Westwood Hosp., L.A., 1975-92; examiner Am. Bd. Psychiatry and Neurology, 1977-82, sr. examiner, 1982; cons. MGM Film Corp., Columbia Pictures, 20th Century Fox Films, Carolco Pictures, Jaffe-Lansing Prodns., Indie Prodns., The Landsburg Co., 1975—. Bd. dirs. Anna Freud Found., L.A., 1975-78. Lt. comdr. M.C., USNR, 1967-69. NIMH psychiat. rsch. fellow, 1962; recipient Career Tchr. award NIMH, 1972. Fellow APA; mem. Am. Psychoanalytic Assn., L.A. Psychoanalytic Soc. and Inst., So. Calif. Psychiat. Soc. (chmn. continuing edn. com., program com. 1970-73, counselor 1974-77), Am. Coll. Psychiatrists, Am. Acad. Child Psychiatry, Am. Assn. Psychiatry Clinic for Children, AAUP, Med. Com. for Human Rights. Office: 510 E Channel Rd Santa Monica CA 90402-1342

WASSERMAN, STEPHEN IRA, physician, educator; b. Los Angeles, Dec. 17, 1942; m. Linda Morgan; children: Matthew, Zachary. BA, Stanford U., 1964; MD, UCLA, 1968. Diplomate Am. Bd. Allergy & Immunology. Intern, resident Peter B. Brigham Hosp., Boston, 1968-70; fellow in allergy, immunology Robert B. Brigham Hosp., Boston, 1972-75; asst. prof. medicine Harvard U., Boston, 1975-79, assoc. prof., 1979; assoc. prof. U. Calif.-San Diego, La Jolla, 1979-85, prof., 1985—, chief allergy tng. program Sch. Medicine, 1979-85, chief allergy div. Sch. Medicine, 1985-93, acting chmn. dept. medicine, 1986-88, chmn. dept. medicine, 1988—, Helen M. Ranney prof., 1992—; co-dir. allergy sect. Robert B. and Peter B. Brigham Hosps., 1977-79; dir. Am. Bd. Allergy and Immunology, Am. Bd. Internal Medicine. Contbr. articles to profl. jours. Served to lt. comdr. USPHS, 1970-72, San Francisco. Fellow Am. Acad. Allergy and Immunology; mem. Am. Soc. Clin. Investigation, Assn. Am. Physicians, Am. Assn. Immunologists, Collegium INternationale Allergologicum, Phi Beta Kappa, Alpha Omega Alpha. Office: U Calif Med Ctr 402 Dickinson St Ste 380 San Diego CA 92103-6902

WASSERMANN, FRANZ WALTHER, physician; b. Munich, Sept. 11, 1920; arrived in U.S., 1938; s. Friedrich and Margarete (Schmidgall) W.; m. Sarah Hortense Webster, Jan. 4, 1945; children: Paul F., Margaret Marie Wassermann Bone. BS, U. Chgo., 1941, MD, 1943. Diplomate Am. Bd. Psychiatry and Neurology. Staff psychiatrist VA Hosp., Palo Alto, Calif., 1948-49; psychiatrist Piedmont Psychiatric Clinic, Oakland, Calif., 1949-51, Walnut Creek, Calif., 1951—; staff psychiatrist Agnew (Calif.) State Hosp., 1951-52; staff psychiatrist Contra Costa County Mental Health Svcs., Martinez, Calif., 1952-93, program chief, 1959-65; chief, east county mental health Contra Costa County Mental Health Svcs., Pittsburg, Calif., 1965-89, med. dir., east county mental health, 1989-93. Co-founder Many Hands, Inc., Pittsburg, 1970. Capt. Army M.C., 1944-46, ETO. Fellow APA; mem. No. Calif. Psychiat. Soc. (v.p. 1982-83), East Bay Psychiat. Assn. (pres. 1977-78), Contra Costa Coun. Alcoholism (chmn. 1969-71), Contra Costa County Mental Health Assn. (v.p. 1958), Concord Mount Diablo Trail Ride Assn., AMA. Democrat. Home: 58 Terrace Rd Walnut Creek CA 94596-3462 Office: 177 La Casa Via Ste 2 Walnut Creek CA 94598-3009

WASSON, JAMES WALTER, aircraft manufacturing company executive; b. Pitts., Dec. 9, 1951; s. George Fredrick and Dolores Helen (Weurl) W.; m. Evelyn Fay Gonzales, Dec. 28, 1974; children: Robert, Brian. AST, Pitts. Inst. Aeronautics, 1972; BSET, Northrop U., Inglewood, Calif., 1981; MBA, U. Phoenix, 1988, govt. contracts mgmt. cert., 1989. Avionics technician various cos., 1972-74; electronics prodn. mgr. Ostgaard Industries, Gardena, Calif., 1974-75; sr. avionics design engr. Allied Signal Garrett Airesearch Aviation Co., L.A., 1975-81; v.p. engring., co-founder Avionics Engring. Svcs., Inc., Tucson, 1980-81; sr. tech. specialist Northrop Aircraft Div., Hawthorne, Calif., 1981-84; prog. mgr. McDonnell Douglas Helicopter Co., Mesa, Ariz., 1984-86; tech. devel. mgr. McDonnell Douglas Helicopter Co., 1986-93; exec. v.p., co-founder Leading Edge Technologies, Inc., Mesa, 1991-95; mgr. bus. devel. McDonnell Douglas Helicopter Sys., Mesa, 1993-95; dir. tech. mktg. Smiths Aerospace, Grand Rapids, Mich., 1995—; adj. prof. govt. contract mgmt., program mgmt., proposal devel., strategic mgmt., tech. mgmt., rsch. projects U. Phoenix, 1990—; cons. in field. Author: Avionics Systems Operation and Maintenance, 1993, Business Opportunities in Artificial Intelligence, 1988; contbr. articles to profl. jours. Inventor in field. Com. chmn. industry adv. bd. Northrop U., 1981; chmn. bd. dirs., pres. Alta Mesa Community Assn., 1989; organizer Boy Scouts Am., Mesa, 1988. Named Engr. of Yr., Northrop U., 1980; recipient Disting. Alumnus award Pitts. Inst. Aeronautics, 1981; named to Hall of Fame, Career Colls. Assn., 1991. Mem. IEEE, NSPE, Assn. Avionics Educators, Soc. Automotive Engrs., Army Aviation Assn. (chpt. sr. v.p. 1988-91, treas. 1993—), Am. Def. Preparedness Assn., Am. Helicopter Soc. (chmn. avionics com. 1990). Republican. Roman Catholic.

WASTERLAIN, CLAUDE GUY, neurologist; b. Courcelles, Belgium, Apr. 15, 1935; s. Desire and Simone (De Taeve) W.; m. Anne Marguerite Thomsin, Feb. 28, 1967; 1 child, Jean Michel. Cand. Sci., U. Liege, 1957, MD, 1961; LS in Molecular Biology, U. Brussels, 1969. Resident Cornell U. Med. Coll., N.Y.C., 1964-67, instr. neurology, 1969-70, asst. prof., 1970-75, assoc. prof., 1975-76; assoc. prof. UCLA Sch. Medicine, 1976-79, prof., 1979—, vice chair dept. neurology, 1976—; chief neurology svc. VA Med. Ctr., Sepulveda, Calif., 1976—; cons. neurologist Olive View Med. Ctr., Sylmar, Calif., 1976—; attending neurologist UCLA Ctr. Health Scis., 1976—. Author, editor: Status Epilepticus, 1984, Neonatal Seizures, 1990, Molecular Neurobiology and Epilepsy, 1992; contbr. articles to med. jours. William Evans fellow, U. Auckland, New Zealand, 1984; recipient N.Y. Neurol. Soc. Young Investigator award, 1965, Rsch. Career Devel. award NIH, 1973-76, Worldwide AES award, 1992. Fellow Am. Acad. Neurology; mem. Am. Neurol. Assn., Am. Soc. Neurochemsitry (coun. mem. 1991—), Internat. Neurochemistry, Am. Epilepsy Soc., Royal Soc. Medicine. Office: VA Med Ctr 1611 Plummer St Sepulveda CA 91343

WATANABE, HIROSHI, film production company executive; b. Sappro, Hokkaido, Japan, Jan. 12, 1951; came to U.S., 1976; s. Tetsuo and Sachiko (Kotani) W.; m. Ellen G. McLaughlin, Feb. 15, 1977 (div. Dec. 31, 1988); children: Aya Nicole, Mika Linette; m. Eiko Fukuhara, Sept. 2, 1989. BA, Nihon U., Tokyo, 1976; postgrad. in Bus. Adminstrn., UCLA, 1993. Prodn. mgr. Creative Enterprises Internat., L.A., 1976-80; producer Chapman & Olson Film Co., L.A., 1980-82; pres. Sunny Side Up, Inc., L.A., 1983—. Mem. Japan-US Producers Assn. (chmn. 1991). Office: Sunny Side Up Inc 8810 Melrose Ave West Hollywood CA 90069-5604

WATANABE, LARRY GEO, biomaterials scientist; b. Fresno, Calif., May 7, 1950; s. George and Hanayo (Yokota) W.; m. Janice Elaine Lee, Nov. 1, 1980; 1 child, Lauren Elisabeth. AA, Fresno City Coll., 1970; BA in Indsl. Arts, Fresno State U., 1972; cert., San Francisco City Coll., 1974. Mgr. crown and bridge dept. McLaughlin Dental Lab., Oakland, Calif., 1975-76; sr. rsch. technician USPHS Hosp., San Francisco, 1976-83; coord. biomaterials rsch. testing, mgr. U. Calif., San Francisco, 1983—; presenter in field. Contbr. articles and abstracts to profl. jours. Bd. dirs. Wah Mei Presch. Mem. Internat. Assn. Dental Rsch., Am. Assn. Dental Rsch., ASTM, Acad. Dental Materials, San Francisco Amateur Golf Assn., U. Calif. Golf Sports Club, Epsilon Pi Tau. Buddhist. Home: 1963 12th Ave San Francisco CA 94116-1305

WATANABE, NATHAN K., military officer, helicopter pilot; b. Hilo, Hawaii, Sept. 11, 1966; s. Herbert S. and Ellen T. Watanabe. BS, USAF Acad., 1988. Lic. aviator. Commd. 2d lt. U.S. Army, 1988, advanced through grades to capt., 1992; infantry platoon leader Co. C., 1st Bn., 506th Infantry Regiment, Camp Greaves, Korea, 1989-90; co. exec. officer Co. A, U.S. Jungle Ops. Tng. Bn., Ft. Sherman, Panama, 1990-91; aviation platoon leader Co. C, 4th Bn., 123d Aviation Regiment, Ft. Wainwright, Alaska, 1992-93, aviation co. comdr., 1993-94; asst. ops. officer 6th Aviation Brigade, 6th Infantry Div., Ft. Wainwright, 1993; aviation liaison officer 4th Bn., 123d Aviation Regiment, Ft. Wainwright, 1994. Jr. asst. scoutmaster Troop 60, Boy Scouts Am., Hilo, 1983-84; Kendo instr. Hilo Koubu Kan Kendo Club, Hilo, 1982-85, USAF Acad., Colorado Springs, Colo., 1985-88. Mem. Assn. of U.S. Army, Army Aviation Assn. Am.

WATANABE, RICHARD MEGUMI, medical research assistant; b. San Fernando, Calif., Sept. 7, 1962; s. Takashi and Toshiko (Yamane) W. BS, U. So. Calif., L.A., 1986; MS, U. So. Calif., 1989, PhD, 1995. Lab. asst. U. So. Calif. Sch. Medicine, L.A., 1985-87; data entry clk. L.A. County/U. So. Calif. Med. Ctr. Women's Hosp., 1985-89; rsch. asst. U. So. Calif. Sch. Medicine, L.A., 1987—; statis. cons. U. So. Calif. Sch. Medicine, 1988, dir. kinetic core, 1992—. Recipient Pacific Coast Fertility Soc. 1st prize in-tng. award, 1990, Student award for meritorious rsch. Am. Fedn. for Clin. Rsch. 1990—, Michaela Modan Meml. award Am. Diabetes Assn., 1995. Mem. AAAS, Am. Diabetes Assn., Am. Physiol. Soc., European Assn. Study of Diabetes. Office: 1333 San Pablo St # 620 Los Angeles CA 90033-1026

WATANABE, TAKEO, psychology educator; b. Tokyo, Apr. 3, 1957; came to U.S., 1989; s. Gyo and Miyako (Hiroho) W.; m. Keiko Omo, Dec. 5, 1983; 1 child, Louis Patrick Watanabe. BA, U. Tokyo, 1983, MA, 1985, PhD, 1989. Asst. prof. U. Tokyo, 1988; rsch. assoc. Harvard U., 1989-92; asst. prof. Ariz. State U. West, Phoenix, 1992—; affiliate prof. Ariz. State U., Phoenix, 1992—. Contbr. articles to profl. jours. Mem. U.S.-Japan Assocs. in Phoenix, 1992-94. Mem. Assn. for Rsch. in Vision and Opthalmology, Psychonomic Soc., Japanese Psychol. Assn., Tokyo. Office: Ariz State U West Campus 4701 W Thunderbird St Phoenix AZ 85069

WATARI, SHINICHIRO, holding company executive. Chmn. bd. dirs. Cornes USA Ltd., San Diego; with Cornes and Co., Ltd., Tokyo. Office: Cornes USA Ltd 9010 Miramar Rd 100 San Diego CA 92126

WATARU, WESTON YASUO, civil engineer; b. Honolulu, Mar. 30, 1957; s. Ralph Mitsuo and Anna Setsuko (Ogami) W.; m. Celine Jacqueline Teasdale, Nov. 1, 1986; children: Maile, Hope, Amber, Adam. BS, U. Hawaii, 1980. Registered profl. engr., Hawaii. Asst. engr. Dames and Moore, Honolulu, 1980-82; civil engr. I City and County of Honolulu Dept. Pub. Works, 1982-84, civil engr. IV, 1985-87, civil engr. V, 1987-89, svc. engr., civil engr. VI, 1989—; Mem. City and County of Honolulu Utilities Coordinating Com., 1989—. Mem. ASCE, NSPE, Am. Pub. Works Assn., Hawaii Govt. Employees Assn. Office: City and County of Honolulu Dept Pub Works 650 S King St Honolulu HI 96813-3017

WATERHOUSE, BLAKE E., health facility administrator; b. 1936. Physician Jackson Clinic, Madison, Wis., 1965-87, Physicians Plus Med. Group, Madison, 1987-90; with Straub Clinic Hosp. Inc., Honolulu, 1990—, pres., CEO. Office: Straub Clinic Hosp Inc 888 S King St Honolulu HI 96813-3009

WATERMAN, MIGNON REDFIELD, public relations executive, state legislator; b. Billings, Mont., Oct. 13, 1944; d. Zell Ashley and Mable Erma (Young) Redfield; m. Ronald Fredrick Waterman, Sept. 11, 1965; children: Briar, Kyle. Student, U. Mont., 1963-66. Lobbyist Mont. Assn. Chs., Helena, 1986-90; senator State of Mont., Helena, 1990—; with pub. rels. dept. Mont. Coun. Tchrs. Math., Helena, 1991—; mem. human svc. subcom., fin. and claims commn. Mont. Senate; chair interim com. on job tng. partnership act, 1991-92. Sch. trustee Helena (Mont.) Sch. Dist. 1, 1978-90; bd. dirs. Mont. Hunger Coalition, 1985—; pres. Mont. Sch. Bds. Assn., 1989-90; active Mont. Alliance for Mentally Ill (Mon Ami award 1991). Recipient Marvin Heintz award Mont. Sch. Bds. Assn., 1987, Friends of Edn. award Mont. Assn. Elem. and Middle Sch. Prins., 1989, Child Advocacy award Mont. PTA, 1991, award Mont. Alliance for Mentally Ill, 1991. Mem. Mont. Sch. Bds. Assn. (Marvin Heintz award 1988, pres.1989-90), Mont. Elem. Sch. Prins., Mont. Parent, Teacher, Student Assn. (child advocacy award 1991). Democrat. Methodist. Home and Office: 530 Hazelgreen Ct Helena MT 59601-5410 Office: Mt State Senate State Capitol Helena MT 59620

WATERS, GEORGE GARY, financial service executive; b. Garyville, La., June 3, 1928; s. Elisha McCLendon and Lena Mae (Anderson) W.; m. Genevieve Corley, Aug. 15, 1952; children: Gary, George D., Gina, Glenda, Genevieve J., Grant. BA, U. Nebr., 1963; MBA, Nat. U., San Diego, 1979. Lic. ins. agt., securities aft., tax advisor, enrolled agent lic. to practice before IRS. Enlisted USAF, 1951, advanced through grades to lt. col.; stationed at Keesler AFB Biloxi, Miss., 1958-59; detachment comdr. Encampment, Wyo, 1959-61, AFTAC 415, Chiengmai, Thailand, 1962-65, AFTAC Det 333, Teheran, Iran, 1970-72; plans officer HQ USAF, Washington, 1966-69; sr. air force advisor 162 Mobile Command, Sacramento, Calif., 1976-78; systems analyst Planning Rsch. Corp., Camp Pendleton, Calif., 1979-80; tax practitioner, pres. Palomar Tax Svc. Inc., San Marcos, Calif., 1979—; speaker in field. Pub. Palomar Tax Svc. newsletter. Alt. del. Calif. Reps., 1992. Fellow Nat. Tax Practice Inst.; mem. Inland Soc. Tax Cons. (founding pres. No. San Diego 1985-86, past pres. 1987), Calif. Assn. Independent Accts. (pres.-elect, pres. 1993-94), Nat. Soc. Pub. Accts. (del. to conv. 1990-93), Nat. Soc. Enrolled Agts., Calif. Soc. Enrolled Agts., San Marcos C. of C. Republican. Roman Catholic. Office: Palomar Tax Svc Inc 470 S Rancho Santa Fe Rd San Marcos CA 92069-3621

WATERS, J. KEVIN, university administrator, educator; b. Seattle, June 24, 1933; s. Thomas and Eleanor (Hynes) W. BA in Classics, Gonzaga U., Spokane, Wash., 1957; MA in Philosophy, Gonzaga U., 1958; MA Theology, Santa Clara (Calif.) U., 1963; BA in Music, U. Wash., 1964, D of Music Arts, 1970. Asst. prof. Seattle U., 1969-74; vis. prof. Gonzaga-in-Florence, Italy, 1971; assoc. prof. Seattle U., 1974-81, prof. fine arts, 1981-83; prof. music Gonzaga, 1983—, dean arts and scis., 1983—; sec., trustee Seattle U., 1971-73, presiding officer, bd. dirs., 1975-77; pres. Seattle Archdiocesan Music Com., 1978-80; chmn. Jesuit Inst. For Arts, Washington, 1980—; panelist Nat. Endowment Arts, 1991—. Composer various musical compositions; commn. work Hearst Found. The Mask of Hiroshima, 1970, Job: A Play with Music, 1971, Solemn Liturgy, 1973, Dear Ignatius, Dear Isabel, 1978, Edith Stein, 1987, Psalm 150, 1991, A Child's Psalm of Creation, 1993, In Dulci Jubilo, 1994. Mem. Am. Guild Organists. Home: 502E E Boone Ave Spokane WA 99202-1713 Office: Sch Arts & Scis Gonzaga U Spokane WA 99258

WATERS, JONATHON HALE, anesthesiologist; b. Cin., July 21, 1959; s. Robert Charles and Frances Elyse (Reynolds) W.; m. Janet Frances Robinson, Aug. 16, 1990; 1 child, Samuel. BS, U. Mo., 1981; MD, George Washington U., 1986. Diplomate Nat. Bd. Med. Examiners, Am. Bd. Anesthesiology. Intern Roanoke (Va.) Meml. Hosp., 1987; resident NYU, Bellevue Hosp. Ctr., N.Y.C., 1987-90; staff anesthesiologist Naval Hosp., San Diego, 1990-94, dir. obstetrical anesthesia, 1990-94, coord. dept. rsch., 1990-94; asst. clin. prof. U. Calif., Irvine, 1994—; presenter in field. Contbr. articles to profl. jours. Lt. comdr. USN, 1983—. Decorated Navy Commendation medal. Mem. Internat. Anesthesia Rsch. Soc., Am. Soc. Anesthesiology, Calif. Soc. Anesthesiology, Soc. Obstet. Anesthesia and Perinatology. Office: U Calif Irvine Dept Anesthesiology 101 City Dr S Rte 81A Orange CA 92668

WATERS, LAUGHLIN EDWARD, federal judge; b. L.A., Aug. 16, 1914; s. Frank J. and Ida (Bauman) W.; m. Voula Davanis, Aug. 22, 1953; children: Laughlin Edward, Maura Kathleen, Deirdre Mary, Megan Ann, Eileen Brigid. A.B., UCLA, 1939; J.D., U. So. Calif., 1946. Bar: Calif. 1946. Dep. atty. gen. Calif., Los Angeles, 1946-47; individual practice law Los Angeles, 1947-53; sr. ptnr. Nossaman, Waters, Krueger & Marsh, 1961-76; U.S. atty. So. Dist. Calif., 1953-61; judge U.S. Dist. Ct. (cen. dist.) Calif., 1976—; cons. U.S. Dept. State in London, 1970; mem. U.S. Del. to Conf. Environ. Problems in Prague, 1971, White House Conf. on Aging, 1970-71; sr. dist. judge rep. Jud. Conf.; judge Atty Gen.'s Adv. Inst. Mem. Calif. Legislature, 1946-53; vice chmn. Rep. State Ctrl. Com., 1950-51, chmn., 1952-53; bd. dirs. Legal Aid Found., 1954-60; past pres. Cath. Big Brothers. Served as capt. U.S. Army, 1942-46. Decorated Bronze Star with oak leaf cluster, Purple Heart with oak leaf cluster, Combat Inf. badge. Fellow Am. Bar Found., Am. Coll. Trial Lawyers; mem. ABA (chmn. com. on housing and urban devel. 1977-79), Am. Judicature Soc., Assn. Bus. Trial Lawyers, U. So. Calif., UCLA Law Assn., Am. Legion, U. So. Calif. Legion Lex, Order Blue Shield, Town Hall, Polish Order Merit Cross with Swords, Hon. Citizen of Chambois, Trun, France, 10th Polish Dragons (hon.), Soc. Friendly Sons St. Patrick (past pres., Medallion of Merit award), Knights of Malta, Anchor Club, Calif. Club. Roman Catholic. Office: US Dist Ct 255 E Temple St Los Angeles CA 90012-3334

WATERS, M. BRUCE, engineering technician; b. Houston, Apr. 17, 1950; s. Wayland O. and Snellah G. (Holt) W.; m. Jean H. Sudduth, June 26, 1971; 1 child, Tegan Joy. Student, La. State U., 1968-69, '70-74, U. Houston, 1969, San Jacinto Jr. Coll., Deer Park, Tex., 1969. Engring. aide I La. Dept. Highways, Baton Rouge, 1971-73, engring. aide II, 1973-74; sta. mgr. Cliff Brice Gas Stas., Boulder, Colo., 1975; mill worker Red Dale Coach, Longmont, Colo., 1975; engring. aide B Colo. Dept. Highways, Boulder, 1975-76, engring. aide C, 1976-91, engring tech. I, 1991—. Blood donor Belle Bonfils, Boulder, Colo., 1975—; mem. and crew leader Vols. for Outdoor Colo.; sec. Boulder County Libertarian Party, 1991-93. Mem. Nat. Inst. Cert. Engring. Techs., Chpt. C Freewheelers, Am. Motorcyclist Assn., Soc. for Preservation and Encouragement of Barbershop Quartet Singing in Am. Office: Colo Dept Transp 1050 Lee Hill Dr Boulder CO 80302-9404

WATERS, MAXINE, congresswoman; b. St. Louis, Aug. 15, 1938; d. Remus and Velma (Moore) Carr; m. Sidney Williams, July 23, 1977; children: Edward, Karen. Grad. in sociology Calif. State U., L.A.; hon. doctorates, Spelman Coll., N.C. Agrl. & Tech. State U., Morgan State U. Former tchr. Head Start; mem. Calif. Assembly from dist. 48, 1976-91, Dem. caucus chair, 1984; mem. 102nd-104th Congresses from Dist. 35, Calif., 1991—; mem. Banking, Fin., Urban Affairs com., Ho. subcom. on banking, capitol subcom. on banking, employment and tng. subcom. on vets., veterans affairs com. Mem. Dem. Nat. Com., Dem. Congrl. Campaign com.; del. Dem. Nat. Conv., 1972, 76, 80, 84, 88, 92, mem. rules com. 1984; mem. Nat. Adv. Com. for Women, 1978—; bd. dirs. TransAfrica Found., Nat. Women's Polit. Caucus, Ctr. Nat. Policy, Clara Elizabeth Jackson Carter Found. Spellman Coll., Nat. Minority AIDS Project, Women for a Meaningful Summit, Nat. Coun. Negro Women, Black Women's Agenda; founder Black Women's Forum. Office: US Ho of Reps 330 Cannon HOB Washington DC 20515*

WATERS, NOEL SCOTT, county district attorney, lawyer; b. Portland, Oreg., Oct. 3, 1948; s. Leon Syxton and Sammy E. Rhea (Davis) W.; m. Celia Carter Nase, Sept. 19, 1967 (div. 1971); 1 child, Kristin; m. Bonnie Kathleen Morris Waters, July 16, 1983; children: Ian, Scott, Sarah. BA, U. Nev., 1977; JD, U. of the Pacific McGeorge Sch. of Law, Sacramento, Calif., 1981. Bar: State Bar Nev. 1981. Judicial law clk. 1st Judicial Dist. Ct., Carson City, Nev., 1981; deputy dist. attorney City of Carson City (Nev.), 1981-85, dist. attorney, 1985—; fire suppression technician U.S. Dept. of Interior Bur. Land Mgmt., 1969-75; adv. bd. mem. Nev. Criminal Justice Info. Sys., Carson City, Nev., 1986—, Uniform Crime Reporting, Carson City, Nev., 1993—; pres. Nev. Dist. Attorney's Assn., Nev., 1989, 93. Mem. Sch. Master Plan Com. PTA, Carson City, Nev., 1994. With USAF, 1967-69, Korea. Outstanding Journalism Intern Reno Gazette Journal Newspapers, 1975. Republican. Office: Carson City Dist Atty's Office 333 N Curry St Carson City NV 89703

WATIA, TARMO, artist; b. Detroit, May 11, 1938; s. Oiva and Mildred (Saari) W.; divorced; 1 child, Talvi Oiva. BS inDesign, U. Mich., 1960, MFA, 1962. Prof. Minot (N.D.) State Coll., 1964, Montana State U., Bozeman, 1965, So. Oreg. Coll., Ashland, 1965-69, Boise (Idaho) State U., 1969-86; artist Boise, Idaho, 1986—. One-man exhibitions include Raven Gallery, Detroit, AAA Gallery, Detroit, Rackham Galleries, Ann Arbor, Mich., White Chapel Gallery, Bozeman, Rogue Valley Art Assn., Medford, Oreg.; exhibited in numerous group shows including The Art Studio Gallery, Birmingham, Mich., U. Oreg. Art Mus., Eugene, Am. Relief Prints, Pitts., Image Gallery, Portland, Oreg., Redwood Show, Eureka, Calif.; selected juried exhibitions at Art Mus. Show, Coos Bay, Oreg., Rock Springs (Wyo.) Nat. Art Exhibit, 5th Annual Nat. Art Exhibition Soumi Coll., Hancock, Mich., 15th Annual Watercolor Exhibition Wayne State U., Detroit, Graphics 71 Nat. Print and Drawing Exhibition, Silver City, N.Mex., among others. Home: 1015 N 10th St Boise ID 83702-4132

WATKINS, CHARLES REYNOLDS, medical equipment company executive; b. San Diego, Oct. 28, 1951; s. Charles R. and Edith A. (Muff) W.; children: Charles Devin, Gregory Michael. BS, Lewis and Clark Coll., 1974; postgrad., U. Portland, 1976. Internat. salesman Hyster Co., Portland, Oreg., 1975-80, Hinds Internat. Corp., Portland, 1980-83; mgr. internat. sales Wade Mfg. Co., Tualatin, Oreg., 1983-84; regional sales mgr. U.S. Surg., Inc., Norwalk, Conn., 1984-86; nat. sales mgr. NeuroCom Internat., Inc., Clackamas, Oreg., 1986-87; pres. Wave Form Systems, Inc., Portland, 1987—; bd. dirs. U.S. Internat., Inc., Portland, Clearfield Med., Minorax, Inc. Bd. dirs. Portland World Affairs Coun., 1980. Mem. Am. Soc. Laser Medicine and Surgery, Am. Fertility Soc., Am. Assn. Gynecol. Laparoscopists, Portland City Club. Republican. Office: Wave Form Systems Inc PO Box 3195 Portland OR 97208-3195

WATKINS, EUGENE LEONARD, surgeon, educator; b. Worcester, Mass., Jan. 4, 1918; s. George Joseph and Marcella Katherine (Akels) W.; A.B. with honors in biology, Clark U., 1940; M.D. (Hood scholar), Harvard U., 1943; m. Victoria Peake, Sept. 23, 1944; children—Roswell Peake, Priscilla Avery. Intern, Roosevelt Hosp., N.Y.C., 1944; resident in surgery, 1944-46, sr. asst. resident in surgery, 1948-49, resident surgery, 1949-50; fellow in surgery, clin. research fellow, Mass. Gen. Hosp., Boston, 1947-48; practice medicine specializing in surgery, N.Y.C., 1950-56, Morristown, N.J., 1950—, Denville, N.J., 1956-85, Boonton, N.J., 1961-85; mem. staff Morristown Meml. Hosp., 1950, vice chmn. dept. surgery, 1974-77, chmn., 1959-61, mem. corp.; cons. surgeon St. Clare's Hosp., Denville, N.J., Riverside Hosp., Boonton, N.J., Community Med. Center, Morristown; courtesy surg. staff St. Luke's-Roosevelt Hosp. Center, N.Y.C.; asst. clin. prof. surgery Rutgers U. Coll. Medicine and Dentistry, New Brunswick, N.J., 1972-85; asst. clin. prof. surgery Columbia Coll. Phys. and Surg., 1985—; v.p. chmn. fin. com. Morristown Bd. Health, 1954-56. Served to 1st lt., AUS, 1946. Diplomate Am. Bd. Surgery. Fellow ACS (chmn. N.J. Adv. Com. 1965-77, chmn. N.J. State com. Trauma, 1960); mem. N.J., Morris County med. socs., AMA, Soc. Surgeons N.J. (1st v.p. 1982, pres. 1983), Am. Thoracic Soc., AAAS, Harvard Med. Soc. N.Y. (pres. 1960-61), West Side Med. Soc., Roosevelt Hosp. Alumni Assn. Republican. Presbyterian. Clubs: Harvard (N.Y.C.), Morristown, Morristown Field. Development spring-loop surg. suture holder. Home: PO Box 1037 Buffalo WY 82834-1037

WATKINS, JOHN GOODRICH, psychologist, educator; b. Salmon, Idaho, Mar. 17, 1913; s. John Thomas and Ethel (Goodrich) W.; m. Evelyn Elizabeth Browne, Aug. 21, 1932; m. Doris Wade Tomlinson, June 8, 1946; m. Helen Verner Huth, Dec. 28, 1971; children: John Dean, Jonette Alison, Richard Douglas, Gregory Keith, Rodney Philip, Karen Stroobants, Marvin R. Huth. Student, Coll. Idaho, 1929-30, 31-32; BS, U. Idaho, 1933, MS, 1936; PhD, Columbia U., 1941. Instr. high sch. Idaho, 1933-39; faculty Ithaca Coll., 1940-41, Auburn U., 1941-43; assoc. prof. Wash. State Coll., 1946-49; chief clin. psychologist U.S. Army Welch Hosp., 1945-46; clin. psychologist VA Hosp., American Lake, Wash., 1949-50; chief clin. psychologist VA Mental Hygiene Clinic, Chgo., 1950-53, VA Hosp., Portland, Oreg., 1953-64; prof. psychology U. Mont., Missoula, 1964-84; prof. emeritus U. Mont., 1984—, dir. clin. tng., 1964-80; lectr. numerous univs.; clin. asso. U. Oreg. Med. Sch., 1957; pres. Am. Bd. Examiners in Psychol. Hypnosis, 1960-62. Author: Objective Measurement of Instrumental Performance, 1942, Hypnotherapy of War Neuroses, 1949, General Psychotherapy, 1960, The Therapeutic Self, 1978, (with others) We, The Divided Self, 1982, Hypnotherapeutic Techniques, 1987, Hypnoanalytic Techniques, 1992; contbr. articles to profl. jours. Mem. Internat. Soc. Clin. and Exptl. Hypnosis (co-founder, pres. 1965-67, recipient awards 1960-65), Soc. Clin. and Exptl. Hypnosis (pres. 1969-71, Morton Prince award), Am. Psychol. Assn. (pres. divsn. 30 1975-76, recipient award 1993), Sigma Xi, Phi Delta Kappa. Home and Office: 413 Evans Ave Missoula MT 59801-5827

WATKINS, JUDITH ANN, nurse; b. Chgo., Mar. 11, 1942; d. Russell and Louise Bernadine (Aloy) Keim; m. Thomas H. Watkins III, Dec. 24, 1961; children: Tamara Sue, Randall Scott. Grad. in nursing, Knapp Coll. Nursing, Santa Barbara, Calif., 1963; BSN, Pacific Union Coll., 1991, PHN cert., 1991; MHA, LaVerne U., 1995. Cert. CPR instr., vocat. edn. instr. Obstetrics supr. Bowling Green (Ky.) Warren County Hosp., 1963-67; clin. staff nurse Chula Vista (Calif.) Med. Clinic, 1967-69; nurse aide instr. Sawyers Coll., Ventura, Calif., 1972; ob-gyn. supr. Westlake (Calif.) Community Hosp., 1972-77; RN acute patient care Medical Personnel Pool, Bakersfield, Calif., 1984; med. asst. instr., dir. of allied health San Joaquin Valley Coll., Bakersfield, 1984-88; dir. nurses Bakersfield Family Med. Ctr., 1988—, asst. adminstr., 1992-94, asst. adminstr. clin. svcs., 1994—. Named Mother of the Yr., Frazier Pk. (Calif.) Community Ch., 1979, Instr. of the Yr., 1986. Mem. Kern County RN Soc., Kern County Trade Club, Pine Mt. Golf Club (founder Lilac Festival 1982, Lady of the Yr. 1983) Sundale Country Club, Seven Oaks Country Club, Toastmasters Internat. Home: 9513 Steinbeck Ln Bakersfield CA 93311-1445 Office: Bakersfield Family Med Ctr 4580 California Ave Bakersfield CA 93309-1104

WATKINS, KAREN J., librarian; b. Albuquerque, July 5, 1947; d. Clifford Ray and Glenys Bell (Frevert) Jurgensen; m. William Gray Watkins, May 15, 1976. BA magna cum laude, St. John's Coll., Santa Fe, 1967; MA, U. Denver, 1972; postgrad., U. Calif., Berkeley, 1980-82. Libr. Santa Fe Pub. Schs., 1972-78; libr. cons. N.Mex. State Libr., Santa Fe, 1978-84, adminstr., 1984-89, dir., 1989—. Mem. AAUW (pres. Santa Fe chpt. 1991), N.Mex. Libr. Assn. (pres. 1988-89), N.Mex. Libr. Found. (bd. dirs. 1994), Rotary (bd. dirs. 1994). Office: N Mex State Libr 325 Don Gaspar Ave Santa Fe NM 87501-2745

WATKINS, WILLIAM HENRY, education educator; b. N.Y.C., Oct. 19, 1946; s. William Alfred Watkins and Katherine (Terrill) Campbell; m. Audrey Panchita DeShields, Oct. 19, 1970 (div. Mar. 1990); 1 child, William Josef; m. Shirley Ann Hutchinson (div. Apr. 1995). AA, L.A. City Coll., 1968; BA, Calif. State U., L.A., 1970; MEd, U. Ill., Chgo., 1979, PhD, 1986. Mgr. Lazar Constrn. Corp., Bklyn., 1971-75; instr. City Colls. Chgo., 1975-86; asst. prof. edn. U. Utah, Salt Lake City, 1986-92, assoc. prof., 1992—. Contbr. articles to profl. jours., entries to encys. Abraham Lincoln grad. fellow, 1985-86. Mem. Soc. for Study of Curriculum History (past pres.), Am. Ednl. Rsch. Assn., Profs. of Curriculum. Home: 7742 S Bennett Chicago IL 60649 Office: Coll of Edn U Ill Chicago IL 60607

WATKINS, WILLIAM SHEPARD See SIVADAS, IRAJA

WATKINSON, PATRICIA GRIEVE, museum director; b. Merton, Surrey, Eng., Mar. 28, 1946; came to U.S., 1972; d. Thomas Wardle and Kathleen (Bredl) Grieve. BA in Art History and Langs. with honors, Bristol U., Eng., 1968. Sec. Mayfair Fine Arts and The Mayfair Gallery, London, 1969-71; adminstr. Bernard Jacobson, Print Pub., London, 1971-73; freelance exhbn. work, writer Kilkenny Design Ctr., Davis Gallery, Irish Arts Council in Dublin, Ireland, 1975-76; curator of art Mus. Art, Wash. State U., Pullman, 1978-83, dir., 1984—; asst. prof. art history Wash. State U., Pullman, 1978. Co-author, co-editor: Gaylen Hansen: The Paintings of a Decade, 1985. Mem. Assn. Coll. & Univ. Museums and Galleries (western regional rep. 1987-89), Art. Mus. Assn. Am. (Wash. state rep. 1986-87), Internat. Council Museums (modern art com. 1986-89), Wash. Mus. Assn. (bd. dirs. 1984-87), Am. Fedn. Arts (western region rep. 1987-89). Office: Wash State U Mus Art Pullman WA 99164-7460

WATKINSON, W. GRANT, distribution company executive; b. Seattle, Oct. 17, 1941; s. Percy John and Betty Lou (Grant) W.; m. Diane Weiblen, June 25, 1966; children: Brett, Tara. BS, Oreg. State U., 1964; MBA, U. Oreg., 1966, PhD, 1971. Asst. prof. Pacific Luth. U., Tacoma, 1970-72; v.p. fin. Stiles Enterprises, Portland, Oreg., 1972-76, Discount Fabrics, Portland, 1976; pres. Paulsen & Roles Labs., Portland, 1977—; bd. dirs. Internat. Sanitary Supply Assn., Chgo.; pres. Preferred Distbrs., Inc., San Antonio, 1988-89. Office: Paulsen & Roles Labs 1836 NE 7th Ave Portland OR 97212-3904

WATRING, WATSON GLENN, gynecologic oncologist, educator; b. St. Albans, W.Va., June 2, 1936; m. Roberta Tawell. BS, Washington & Lee U., 1958; MD, W.Va. U., 1962. Diplomate Am. Bd. Ob-Gyn, Am. Bd. Gynecol. Oncology. Intern The Toledo Hosp., 1963; resident in ob-gyn Ind. U., Indpls., 1964-66, Tripler Gen. Hosp., Honolulu, 1968-70; resident in gen. and oncologic surgery City of Hope Nat. Med. Ctr., Duarte, Calif., 1970-71, assoc. dir. gynecol. oncology, sr. surgeon, 1973-77; fellow in gynecol. oncology City of Hope Nat. Med. Ctr. and UCLA Med. Ctr., 1972-74; asst. prof. ob-gyn UCLA Med. Ctr., 1972-77; assoc. prof., sr. gynecologist, sr. surgeon Tufts New Eng. Med. Ctr. Hosp., Boston, 1977-80, asst. prof. radiation therapy, 1978-80; practice medicine specializing in ob-gyn Boston, 1980-82; assoc. prof. ob-gyn U. Mass., Worcester, 1982; regional dir. gynecol. oncology So. Calif. Permanente Med. Group, Los Angeles, 1982—, asst. dir. residency tng., 1985—; dir. gynecol. oncology St. Margarets Hosp. for Women, Dorchester, Mass., 1977-80; clin. prof. ob-gyn U. Calif., Irvine, 1982—. Contbr. articles to profl. jours. Mem. ch. council Luth. Ch. of the Foothills, 1973-75. Served to lt. col. M.C., U.S. Army, 1965-71. Fellow Am. Coll. Ob-Gyn, Los Angeles Obstet. and Gynecol. Soc.; mem. AAAS, ACS (Calif. and Mass. chpts.), Boston Surg. Soc., AMA, Mass. Med. Soc., Mass. Suffolk Dist. Med. Soc., Internat. Soc. Gynecol. Pathologists, Western Soc. Gynecologists and Obstetricians, Am. Soc. Clin. Oncology, Soc. Gynecol. Oncologists, Western Assn. Gynecol. Oncologists (sec.-treas. 1976-81, program chmn. 1984, pres. 1985—), New Eng. Assn. Gynecol. Oncologists (chmn. charter com.), New Eng. Obstet. and Gynecol. Soc., Obstet. Soc. Boston, Am. Radium Soc., Soc. Study Breast Disease, New Eng. Cancer Soc., Internat. Gynecol. Cancer Soc., Daniel Morton Soc., Sigma Xi. Republican. Office: So Calif Permanente Med Group 4950 W Sunset Blvd Los Angeles CA 90027-5822

WATSON, DAVID COLQUITT, electrical engineer, educator b. Linden, Tex., Feb. 9, 1936; s. Colvin Colquitt and Nelena Gertrude (Keasler) W.; m. Flora Janet Thayn, Nov. 10, 1959; children: Flora Janeen, Melanie Beth, Lorrie Gaylene, Cheralyn Gail, Nathan David, Amy Melissa, Brian Colvin. BSEE, U. Utah, 1964, PhD in Elec. Engring. (NASA fellow), 1968. Electronic technician Hercules Powder Co., Magna, Utah, 1961-62; rsch. fellow U. Utah, 1964-65, rsch. asst. microwave devices and phys. electronics lab., 1964-68; sr. mem. tech. staff ESL, Inc., Sunnyvale, Calif., 1968-78, head dept. Communications, 1969-70; sr. engring. specialist Probe Systems, Inc., Sunnyvale, 1978-79; sr. mem. tech. staff ARGO Systems, Inc., Sunnyvale, 1979-90; sr. mem. tech. staff GTE Govt. Systems Corp., Mountain View, Calif., 1990-91; sr. cons. Watson Cons. Svcs., 1991-92; sr. staff engr. ESL, Inc., 1992—; mem. faculty U. Santa Clara, 1978-81, 1992—, San Jose State U., 1981—, Coll. Notre Dame, 1992—, Chapman U., 1993—. Contbr. articles to IEEE Transactions, 1965-79; co-inventor cyclotron-wave rectifier; inventor gradient descrambler. Served with USAF, 1956-60. Mem. IEEE, Phi Kappa Phi, Tau Beta Pi, Eta Kappa Nu. Mem. LDS Ch. Office: ESL/TRW 495 Java Dr Sunnyvale CA 94089-1125

WATSON, DAVID LOCKE, psychology educator; b. Nashville, Jan. 20, 1934; s. Manly A. and Faye (Givens) W.; m. Joyce Frank, Sept. 13, 1957 (div. Nov. 1987); children: Daniel, Malia. BA, Vanderbilt U., 1959; PhD, Yale U., 1963. Prof., chair undergrad. program U. Hawaii, Honolulu. Author: Self-directed Behavior, 1972, 6th edit., 1992, Psychology, 1993. Served with U.S. Army, 1955-56. Fellow APS (charter). Home: 769 N Kainalu Dr Kailua HI 96734-2022 Office: Univ Hawaii Dept Psychology 2430 Campus Rd Honolulu HI 96822-2216

WATSON, DENNIS MICHAEL, career development and strategy firm executive; b. Buffalo, Aug. 9, 1951; s. George and Betty (Therrien) W.; m. Darlene Hall, Mar. 21, 1970 (div. Sept. 1981); 1 child, Dennis M. AAS, Nat. U., San Diego, 1975, BBA, 1978, MBA, 1983. Office mgr. U.S. Civil Svc., San Diego, 1974-76; mktg. rep. IBM Corp., San Diego, 1976-80; account exec. Paine, Webber, San Diego, 1980-81; regional sales mgr. InterBank Fin., Inc., Carlsbad, Calif., 1981-84; brokerage mgr. CNA Ins. Cos., San Diego, 1984-86; regional sales mgr. Am. Health Care, San Diego, 1986-89; pres. DMW & Assocs., Inc., Carlsbad, 1989—; cons. U.S. Dept. Edn. and Tng., Washington, 1992-94, U.S. Dept. Labor, Washington, 1993-94, USN, San Diego, 1994—. Author: (tape program and learning manual) Career Success and Strategies, 1993. Advisor Unity of Escondido, Calif., 1976-89; instr., trainer San Diego Minority Purchasing Coun., 1977-80. Served with USN, 1970-74, Vietnam. Burcin Found. grantee, 1993. Mem. VFW (chaplain 1982-83). Republican. Roman Catholic.

WATSON, DIANE EDITH, state legislator; b. L.A., Nov. 12, 1933; d. William Allen Louis and Dorothy Elizabeth (O'Neal) Watson. A.A., L.A. City Coll., 1954, B.A., UCLA, 1956; M.S., Calif. State U., Los Angeles, PhD Claremont Grad. Sch., 1987. Tchr., sch. psychologist L.A. Unified Sch. Dist., 1960-69, 73-74; assoc. prof. Calif. State U., L.A., 1969-71; health occupations specialist Bur. Indsl. Edn., Calif. Dept. Edn., 1971-73; mem. L.A. Unified Sch. Bd., 1975-78; mem. Calif. Senate from dist. 28, 1978—, chairperson health and human svcs. com.; Legis. Black Caucus, mem. edn. com., budget and fiscal rev. com., criminal procedure com., housing and land use com.; del. Calif. Democratic Party; mem. exec. com. Nat. Conf. State Legislators. Author: Health Occupations Instructional Units-Secondary Schools, 1975; Planning Guide for Health Occupations, 1975; co-author; Introduction to Health Care, 1976. Del. Democratic Nat. Conv., 1980. Recipient Mary Church Terrell award, 1976, Brotherhood Crusade award, 1981, Black Woman of Achievement award NAACP Legal Def. Fund, 1988; named Alumnus of Yr., UCLA, 1980, 82. Mem. Calif. Assn. Sch. Psychologists, Los Angeles Urban League, Calif. Tchrs. Assn., Calif. Commn. on Status Women. Roman Catholic. Office: 4401 Crenshaw Blvd # 300 Los Angeles CA 90043-1200

WATSON, GEORGE WILLIAM, oil company executive; b. Leamington, Ont., Can., May 31, 1947; s. Grant Watson and Janke (de Jong) W.; m. Sheila Kathleen Smith, Apr. 29, 1972; children—Eric, Tara, Scott. B.Sc. in Engring., Queen's U., Ont., Can., 1970; M.B.A., Queen's U., 1972. Br. mgr. Can. Import Bank of Commerce, Ont., 1972-74; with fin. project Can. Import Bank of Commerce, Toronto, Ont., 1974-79; mgr. corp. banking Can. Import Bank of Commerce, Calgary, Alta., Can., 1979-80; asst. gen. mgr. oil and gas div. Can. Import Bank of Commerce, 1980-81; dir. fin. Dome Petroleum Ltd., Calgary, 1981-82; v.p. fin. Dome Petroleum Ltd., 1982—. Clubs: Calgary Petroleum, Calgary Winter. Home: 3364 Varna Ct, Calgary, AB Canada T3A 0E6 Office: Dome Petroleum Ltd, 333 7th Ave SW, Calgary, AB Canada T2P 2Z1

WATSON, HAROLD GEORGE, ordnance company executive, mechanical engineer; b. Phoenix, Oct. 19, 1931; s. Clarence Elmer and Eunice A. (Record) W.; m. Ruth May Thomas, Aug. 30, 1951 (dec.); children: Patricia Ruth, Linda Darlene, Harold George; m. Katherina Anna Kish, Sept. 22, 1990. B.S., U. Ariz., 1954. Engr. Shell Oil Co., L.A., 1954; project engr. Talco Engring. Co., Hamden Conn., 1956, area mgr., Mesa, Ariz., 1956-57, chief engr. Rocket Power, 1958-61, dir. engring., 1961-64; dir. engring. Space Ordnance Systems, El Segundo, Calif., 1964-68; dir. engring. Universal Propulsion Co., Riverside, Calif., 1968-70, gen. mgr., v.p. engring., Tempe, Ariz., 1970-76, v.p., mgr., 1976-77, pres., gen. mgr., Phoenix, 1977—. Patentee in field. 1st lt. USAR, 1954-56. Mem. Am. Mgmt. Assn., SAFE Assn. (past pres.), AIAA, Air Force Assn., Internat. Pyronetics Soc., Am. Def. Preparedness Assn. Office: Universal Propulsion Co Inc 25401 N Central Ave Phoenix AZ 85027-7837

WATSON, JOHN FRANCIS, software engineer, consultant; b. Glendive, Mont., Jan. 23, 1962; s. Harry Lawrence and Marian Francis (McNulty) W.; m. Crystal Lee Flanders, May 1, 1986; children: Chester Lawrence, Quinton John. BSEE, U. Utah, 1985. Software engr. Dept. Air Force, Hill AFB, Utah, 1985—; cons. in field. Mem. Golden Key, Tau Beta Pi, Eta Kappa Nu.

WATSON, JULIA, women's studies and liberal studies educator; b. Detroit, Jan. 4, 1945; d. Walter J. and Florence M. (Ryan) W.; 1 child, Evan Orion. BA, Western Mich. U., 1967; MA, U. Calif., Irvine, 1971, PhD, 1979. Assoc. in English U. Calif., Irvine, 1972-73; instr. U. Mass., Amherst, 1974-75; asst. prof. English Hobart & William Smith Colls., Geneva, N.Y., 1979-86; sr. assoc. Lutz Assocs., Inc., Detroit, 1986-87; assoc. prof. English Elizabethtown (Pa.) Coll., 1987-88; assoc. prof. liberal studies, dir. women's studies U. Mont., Missoula, 1988—; sr. lectr. Fulbright Assn., Dakar, Senegal, 1992-93. Co-editor: Getting a Life, 1995, (with Sidonie Smith) Decolonizing the Subject, 1995; mem. edit. bd. Auto/Biography Studies, 1990—. NEH grantee, 1979, 83, 87, 88, 92, 95; DAAD fellow German Acad. Exch. Assn., 1973-74. Mem. MLA (regional del. 1993—, exec. bd. autobiography divsn. 1988-92), Autobiographical Soc. (editorial bd. 1990—), Soc. for Study of Narrative Lit., Am. Comparative LIt. Assn., Nat. Women's Studies Assn. Office: U Mont Women's Studies Program Missoula MT 59812-1045

WATSON, KENNETH FREDERICK, molecular biologist, consultant; b. Pasco, Wash., Feb. 17, 1942; s. Walter Irvin and Isabel Danforth (Frost) W.; m. Janice Pauline Wilson, June 6, 1964; children: Heidi Michelle, Julie Monique. A.B., N.W. Nazarene Coll., 1964; Ph.D., Oreg. State U., 1969. Postdoctoral fellow Columbia U., N.Y.C., 1969-71, instr. human genetics, 1971-72; research fellow Internat. Agy. for Cancer Research, Berlin, 1972-73; from asst. prof. to prof. U. Mont., Missoula, 1973-83; head Lab. Viral Genetics, Abbott Labs, Abbott Park, Ill., 1983-85; v.p. academic affairs Northwest Nazarene Coll., 1985-87; asst. to pres. and prof. biochemistry, 1989—; cons. Abbott Labs., North Chicago, 1981-83; cons. Life Scis. Inc., St. Petersburg, Fla., 1976-83, Molecular Genetic Resources, Tampa, Fla., 1983—. Achievements include patent in Transferase Enzymes which Modify the 3'-Termini of Ribonucleic Acids and Methods. Bd. regents N.W. Nazarene Coll., 1980-83. Faculty research award Am. Cancer Soc., 1976-81; research grantee USPHS, 1973-83, Am. Cancer Soc., 1976-82. Mem. Am. Soc. Microbiology, N.W. Nazarene Coll. Alumni Assn. (bd. dirs. 1973-83, pres. 1980-83), Sigma Xi. Avocations: fly fishing, skiing, jogging. Home: 3600 S Midland Blvd Nampa ID 83686-8215 Office: NW Nazarene Coll 623 Holly St Nampa ID 83686-5897

WATSON, KENNETH MARSHALL, physics educator; b. Des Moines, Sept. 7, 1921; s. Louis Erwin and Irene Nellie (Marshall) W.; m. Elaine Carol Miller, Mar. 30, 1946; children: Ronald M., Mark Louis. B.S., Iowa State U., 1943; Ph.D., U. Iowa, 1948; Sc.D. (hon.), U. Ind., 1976. Rsch. engr. Naval Rsch. Lab., Washington, 1943-46; mem. staff Inst. Advanced Study Princeton (N.J.) U., 1948-49; rsch. fellow Lawrence Berkeley (Calif.) Lab., 1949-52, mem. staff, 1957-81; asst. prof. physics U. Ind., Bloomington, 1952-54; asso. prof. physics U. Wis., Madison, 1954-57; prof. physics U. Calif., Berkeley, 1957-81; prof. oceanography, dir. marine physics lab. U. Calif., San Diego, 1981-93; cons. Mitre Corp., Sci. Application Corp.; mem. U.S. Pres.'s Sci. Adv. Com. Panels, 1962-71; adviser Nat. Security Coun., 1972-75; bd. dirs. Ctr. for Studies of Dynamics, 1979-88; mem. JASON Adv. Panel; mem. sci. adv. bd. George C. Marshall Inst., 1989—. Author: (with M.L. Goldberger) Collision Theory, 1964, (with J. Welch and J. Bond) Atomic Theory of Gas Dynamics, 1966, (with J. Nutall) Topics in Several Particle Dynamics, 1970, (with Flatté, Munk, Dashen) Sound Transmission Through a Fluctuating Ocean, 1979. Mem. Nat. Acad. Scis. Home: PO Box 9726 Rancho Santa Fe CA 92067-4726 Office: U Calif Marine Physics Lab La Jolla CA 92093

WATSON, MARY ANN, psychologist, educator; b. St. Clairsville, Ohio, Jan. 27, 1944; d. William Glenn and Jeanette (Shannon) W.; m. Robert Montgomery (div. 1974); m. Dennis A. Whitlock, Oct. 6, 1978; children: Suzanne, Matthew Montgomery. BA, Grove City (Pa.) Coll., 1966; PhD, U. Pitts., 1969; postgrad., Johns Hopkins U., Balt., 1972-73. Lic. psychologist, Colo. Rsch. assoc. dept. biophysics and genetics/psychiatry U. Colo. Med. Ctr., Denver, 1973-77; prof. psychology Met. State Coll., Denver, 1974—, U. Colo., Denver, 1979-82; pvt. practice clin. psychology, 1975—; clin. psychologist Pub. Health Svc., Navajo and Hopi Reservations, Ariz., 1970-72; asst. prof. psychology Community Coll. of Phila., 1969-70; lectr. in field; cons. in field; mem. State Bd. Psychologist Examiners, 1979-85, chmn., 1981-83. Contbr. articles to profl. jours.; author: Breaking the Bonds, 1981; editor: Reading in Sexology, 1986, 2d edit. 1991. Home: 6840 Richthofen Pky Denver CO 80220-4848 Office: Met State Coll Denver Dept Psychology Campus Box 54 PO Box 173362 Denver CO 80217-3362

WATSON, MILTON RUSSELL, surgeon; b. Silverton, Oreg., July 14, 1934; s. Milton R. and Alice Violet (Sommers) W.; m. Shirley Ilene Kiel, June 20, 1958; children: Mark R., Tamara Faye. BA in Biology, Whitman Coll., Walla Walla, 1956; MD, U. Wash., 1960. Intern, then resident Santa Clara County Medical Ctr., San Jose, Calif., 1960-65; pvt. practice Walla Walla Clinic, 1969--. Contbr. articles to profl. jours. Capt. U.S. Army, 1965-69. Paul Harris fellow Rotary, 1980. Fellow ACS; mem. AMA, North Pacific Surg. Soc., Soc. Clin. Vascular Surgery, Internat. Cardiovascular Soc., Christian Med. Soc. (del. 1989). Presbyterian. Home: 545 Edgewood Dr Silverton OR 97381-2278 Office: 324 Fairview St Silverton OR 97381-1917

WATSON, NOEL G., construction executive; b. 1936. BSChemE, U. N.D., 1958; postgrad., Colo. Sch. Mines, 1958-60. With Jacobs Engring., 1960-62, AMAX Inc., 1962-65; pres., COO Jacobs Engring. Group Inc., Pasadena, Calif., 1965-92, pres., CEO, 1992—. Office: Jacobs Engring Group Inc 251 S Lake Ave Pasadena CA 91101-3003*

WATSON, OLIVER LEE, III, aerospace engineering manager; b. Lubbock, Tex., Sept. 18, 1938; s. Oliver Lee Jr. and Sallie Gertrude (Hale) W.; m. Judith Valeria Horvath, June 13, 1964; 1 child, Clarke Stanford. BSEE, U. Tex., 1961; MSEE, Stanford U., 1963; MBA, Calif. State U., Fullerton, 1972; cert., U. So. Calif., 1980. Mgr. ballistic analysis Rockwell Internat. Autonetics Div., Anaheim, Calif., 1973-78, mgr. minuteman systems, 1978-83, mgr. preliminary engring., 1983-84, mgr. analysis group, 1984-85; mgr. aircraft systems Rockwell Internat. Autonetics Dept., Anaheim, Calif., 1985-93; deputy dir. Integrated Product Devel. N.Am. Aircraft Modification Divsn., 1993-94; dep. dir. engring. N. Am. Aircraft Modification Divsn., Anaheim, 1994—; lectr. engring. Calif. State U., Fullerton, 1981-90, mem. indsl. adv. bd., 1994—. Co-author Digital Computing Using Fortran IV, 1982; Fortran 77, A Complete Primer, 1986. Bd. dirs. Olive Little League, Orange, 1980; vol. Stanford U. Engring. Fund, Orange County, Calif., 1983, regional chmn. 1984-86, So. Calif. chmn. 1986-91; mem. Stanford Assocs., 1988—. N.Am. Aviation Sci.-Engring. fellow, L.A., 1962, 63, Inst. Advancement Engring. fellow, L.A., 1976. Mem. IEEE (sr., sec. v.p. 1974-75, sect. chmn. 1975-76), Jaycees (v.p. Orange chpt. 1973-74), Rockwell-Calif. State Univ. Alumni Club (v.p. 1993, pres. 1993-94). Republican. Club: Lido Sailing. Office: Rockwell Internat 3370 E Miraloma Ave # 031-df62 Anaheim CA 92806-1911

WATSON, RAYMOND LESLIE, architect; b. Seattle, Oct. 4, 1926; s. Leslie Alexander and Olive (Lorentzen) W.; m. Elsa Constance Coito, Sept. 18, 1954; children: Kathy Ann, Bryan Frederich, Lisa Marie, David John. B.A., U. Calif.-Berkeley, 1951, M.A., 1953. Architect firm Donald Haines & Assocs., San Francisco, 1955-60; mgr. planning The Irvine Co., Newport Beach, Calif., 1960-64, v.p. planning, 1964-66, sr. v.p. land devel., 1966-70, exec. v.p., 1970-73, pres., 1973-77; pres., partner Newport Devel. Co., 1977-83; chmn. bd. The Walt Disney Co., 1983-84, chmn. exec. com., 1984—; vice chmn. bd. The Irvine Co., 1986—; vice chmn. The Irvine Co., 1986—; dir. Disney Corp., Mitchell Energy and Devel. Co., Pacific Mut. Life Ins. Co., The Irvine Co.; Regent's prof. U. Calif.-Irvine, 1985-86. Served with USAAF, 1944-45. Fellow AIA. Home: 2501 Alta Vista Dr Newport Beach CA 92660-4101 Office: The Walt Disney Co 500 S Buena Vista St Burbank CA 91521-0001 also: The Irvine Co 9th Fl 550 Newport Center Dr Fl 9 Newport Beach CA 92660-7011

WATSON, SHARON GITIN, psychologist, executive; b. N.Y.C., Oct. 21, 1943; d. Louis Leonard and Miriam (Myers) Gitin; m. Eric Watson, Oct. 31, 1969; 1 child, Carrie Dunbar. B.A. cum laude, Cornell U., 1965; M.A., U. Ill., 1968, Ph.D., 1971. Psychologist City N.Y. Prison Mental Health, Riker's Island, 1973-74; psychologist Youth Services Ctr., Los Angeles County Dept. Pub. Social Services, Los Angeles, 1975-77, dir. clin. services, 1978, dir. Youth Services Ctr., 1978-80; exec. dir. Crittenton Ctr. for Young Women and Infants, Los Angeles, 1980-89, Assn. Children's Svcs. Agys. of So. Calif., L.A., 1989-92, L.A. County Children's Planning Coun., 1992—. Contbr. articles to profl. jours. Mem. Commn. for Children's Svcs. Family Preservation Policy Com., Mayor's Com. on Children, Youth and Families, L.A. Learning Ctrs. Design Team, Interagy. Coun. Child Abuse and Neglect Policy Com.; bd. dirs. L.A. Roundtable for Children, 1988-94, Adolescent Pregnancy Childwatch, 1985-89; trustee L.A. Ednl. Alliance for Restructuring Now; co-chmn. Los Angeles County Drug and Alcohol Abuse Task Force, 1990; mem. planning coun. Dept. Children's Svcs., 1986-88; mem. steering com. western region Child Welfare League Am., 1985-87. Mem. APA, Calif. Assn. Svcs. for Children (sec.-treas. 1983-84, pres. elect 1985-86, pres. 1986-87), Assn. Children's Svcs. Agys. So. Calif. (sec. 1981-83, pres. elect 1983-84, pres. 1984-85), Town Hall Calif., U.S. Figure Skating Assn. (bd. dirs., chair sanctions and eligibility com.), Inter-Club Assn. of Figure Skating Clubs (vice chair 1989-91, chair 1991-93), Pasadena Figure Skating Club (bd. dirs., pres. 1985-87, 89-90). Home: 4056 Camino Real Los Angeles CA 90065-3928 Office: LA County Children's Planning Coun 500 W Temple St Rm B-26 Los Angeles CA 90012-2713

WATSON, WILLIAM RANDY, marketing executive; b. Roswell, N.Mex., July 13, 1950; s. William Floyd and Billie Dean (Mathews) W.; m. Dorothy Elinor Connole, Feb. 28, 1987; children: Matthew Scott, Amy Suzanne, Chadd William, Tyler William; 1 stepdaughter, Nicole Maloney. AAS, N.Mex. Jr. Coll., 1970; BBA, Ea. N.Mex. U., 1972. Telecommunications specialist Electronic Data Systems, Dallas, 1973-78; regional product specialist Storage Tek, Dallas, 1978-82; hdqr. product specialist Storage Tek, Louisville, Colo., 1982-84, disk mktg. product mgr., 1984-85; dir. tech mktg. Aweida Systems, Boulder, Colo., 1985-86; owner, pres. Tech. Mktg. Cons., Boulder, 1986—; pres. Midrange Performance Group, Boulder, 1989—. Election judge Boulder County, 1988, 94. Home: 445 Poplar Ave Boulder CO 80304-1059 Office: Tech Mktg Cons 445 Poplar Ave Boulder CO 80304-1059

WATSON-FRANKE, MARIA-BARBARA, womens studies anthropologist; b. Adorf, Germany, Sept. 14, 1938; came to U.S., 1967; d. Herwig Ortwin and Gudrun Maria (Haberkorn) Franke. MA, Goethe U., Frankfurt, Fed. Republic Germany, 1967; PhD, U. Vienna, 1970. Research assoc., Latin Am. Ctr. UCLA, 1971-78; prof. women's studies San Diego State U., 1974—, chair dept. women's studies, 1983-86; field work with Guajiro Indians, Venezuela, 1967-68, 72, 75, 77, 78, 87; with women's carnival socs., Fed. Republic Germany, 1983. Co-author: Interpreting Life Histories, 1985; contbr. chpt. to book, articles to profl. jours. Research grantee Latin Am. Ctr., 1972, German Research Council, 1972-74, German Acad. Exchange Service, 1967-68. Fellow Am. Anthropol. Assn., Soc. Applied Anthropology; mem. Current Anthropology (assoc.), Nat. Women's Studies Assn. Office: San Diego State U Dept Womens Studies San Diego CA 92182

WATT, DIANA LYNN, social worker; b. Leon, Iowa, Mar. 21, 1956; d. Charles Edward Sr. and Nora Eunice (Dickerson) W. BSW, Graceland Coll., 1980; postgrad., U. Kans., 1981-83. Social work intern St. Michael's (Ariz.) Sch., 1979, Father Benedict Justice Sch. and Seton Ctr., Kansas City, Mo., 1980, Mattie Rhodes Ctr., Kansas City, Mo., 1982-83; child care worker Gillis Home for Boys, Kansas City, 1980-84; community work experience program worker Social and Rehab. Svcs. State of Kans., Kansas City, 1983-84; contractual assignee Reorganized Ch. of Jesus Christ of Latter-day Saints, San Jose, Calif., 1984-87; counselor II summer youth NOVA/Summer Youth Employment Program, 1987; tchr. ESL Wilson Adult Edn. Ctr., 1987-88, Overfelt Adult Edn. Ctr., 1987—; eligibility worker II East Valley Social Svcs., Santa Clara County, Calif., 1992-94; eligibility worker AFDC, Medi-Cal, Foodstamps, Santa Clara, Calif., 1992-94; family support officer Santa Clara County, 1994—; Occupational Tng. Inst. Job Tng. Partnership Act Intake specialist for GAIN, JTPA, NOVA, 1987—; instr. DTAC Serra Residential Ctr., Fremont, Calif., ESL instr. Overfelt Adult Edn. Program, 1990—. Counselor in tng. for camps and bible schs. Reorganized Ch. Jesus Christ Latter-day Saints, Iowa, 1969-73, counselor children's camp, San Jose, 1985, mem. ethnic community program com., East San Jose, 1984-87. Honored for Community Outreach in Ethnic Ministries, Reorganized Ch. Jesus Christ Latter-day Saints, 1985-87. Mem. Nat. Assn. Soc. Workers (cert.). Club: Intercultural (Lamoni, Iowa) (activity chmn. 1977-79).

WATTENBERG, FRANK ARVEY, mathematician; b. N.Y.C., May 16, 1943; s. William W. and Jean A. Wattenberg; m. Julie Cheryl Miles, Sept. 1, 1964; children: Martin, Alina; m. Margo Lynn Mankus, Aug. 28, 1993. BS, Wayne State U., Detroit, 1964; MS, U. Wis., Madison, 1965, PhD, 1968. Asst. prof. Harvard U., Cambridge, Mass., 1968-71; prof. U. Mass., Amherst, 1971-94; prof. math. dept. Weber State U., Ogden, Utah, 1994—. Mem. Am. Math. Soc. Office: Weber State U Math Dept Ogden UT 84408-1702

WATTERS, JOHN KENNETH, social scientist, educator; b. Feb. 23, 1948; s. James Albert and Myrtle Ann (Stienmetz) W.; 1 child, James Toru. AB in Psychology and Sociology cum laude, Boston U., 1975; EdM, Harvard U., 1975; AM in Psychology, The U. Mich., 1978, PhD in Psychology, 1986. Various to dir. planning and devel. Seven-Thirty-Five, Inc., Melrose, Mass., 1974-75; dean of devel. Franconia (N.H.) Coll., 1975-76; rsch. dir. MRC Mental Health Ctr., Southfield, Mich., 1977-78; pub. health analyst treatment rsch. br. Nat. Inst. on Drug and Alcohol Abuse, USPHS, Rockville, Md., 1979-81; dep. dir. Dept. Pub. Health, City and County of San Francisco, San Francisco, 1982, dir. rsch. community substance abuse svcs., 1983-85; dir. The Urban Health Study Inst. Health Policy Studies/Sch. Medicine, U. Calif., San Francisco, 1985—; asst. prof. dept. family and community medicine Sch. Medicine, U. Calif., San Francisco, 1988-92, assoc. prof., 1993—; prin. investigator in field; attending psychologist San Francisco Gen. Hosp., 1992-93; guest lectr. Sch. Pub. Health, U. Calif., Berkeley, 1991, 88-90, others. Asst. editor: Jour. of Drug Issues, 1989—; contbg. editor: Internat. Jour. of the Addictions, 1990-91; reviewer various jours. in field; contbr. articles to profl. jours. Mem. AAAS, APA, Am. Psychol. Soc., Am. Pub. Health Assn., Am. Soc. Epidemiol. Rsch., Internat. AIDS Soc.

WATTS, CHRISTOPHER JOHN, artist, educator; b. London, Oct. 12, 1947; s. Victor George and Maureen (Olver) W.; m. Karen Denise Larson. Student, Plymouth Coll. Art, 1964-66; BFA in Art, U. London, 1969; MFA with honors, Ohio U. Grad. asst. Ohio U., Athens, 1969-71; instr. in sculpture and drawing U. R.I., Kingston, 1971-73; lectr. Trent Pol...

tingham, Eng., 1973-74; chair art dept., gallery dir. Cornish Inst., Seattle, 1978-84; chair art dept. Mid. Tenn. State U., Murfreesboro, 1984-88; chair fine arts dept. Wash. State U., Pullman, 1988—; speaker, lectr. in field; vis. artist Trent Poly., 1974-78, Gloucester (Eng.) Coll. of Art, 1973-74, Dartington (Eng.) Coll. of Arts, 1974, U. Reading, Eng., 1975-76, Slade Sch. Fine Art, London, 1975-78; art dir., coord., mem. adv. bd. Gov.'s Sch. for Arts of Tenn., 1986-88; external assessor rev. dept. fine arts Weber State U., 1990; mem. various panels in field; bd. advisors And/Or Gallery, Seattle, 1980; mem. Contemporary Arts Coun., Seattle, 1981-82. Exhibited in numerous one person shows, including Cornish Inst., Seattle, 1979, Traver Gallery, Seattle, 1980, Mus. Art, Carnegie Inst., Pitts., 1981, Seattle Pacific U., 1982, 86, Traver/Sutton Gallery, 1981, 83, Seattle Ctr., 1983, Mid. Tenn. State U., 1984, Cumberland Gallery, 1985, 86, 90, in many group shows, including Wash. State U., 1989, Linda Farris Gallery, Seattle, 1989, Cumberland Gallery, 1987, 88, 89, 90, 92, U. Idaho, Moscow, 1991, Seattle Pacific U., 1993, others; represented in permanent collections U.S. and Europe including 1st Nat. Bank, Providence, R.I., Seattle 1st Nat. Bank, Honeywell, Inc., Seattle, Carnegie Mus., Pitts., Arts Coun. Great Britain, Seattle Arts Commn., Hartt Sch. Music Libr., Hartford, Conn., H.C.A., Nashville, 3d Nat. Bank, Nashville, Endata, Nashville, No. Telecom, Nashville, J.D. Nichols Assoc., Atlanta, Bass, Berry, Conners & Sims, Nashville, Wash. State Arts Commn., Ea. Wash. U./Spokane Ctr. Office: Wash State U Dept Fine Arts Pullman WA 99164

WATTS, CYNTHIA GAY, lawyer; b. Indpls., Aug. 20, 1962; d. Leslie J and Nell (Jackson) W. BA magna cum laude, Yale U., 1984; JD cum laude, Harvard U., 1988. Bar: Calif. 1988. Assoc. Paul, Hastings, Janofsky & Walker, L.A., L.A., 1988-93; v.p., gen. counsel, sec. Leslie's Poolmart, Chatsworth, Calif., 1993—. Mem. ABA, Calif. State Bar Assn., L.A. County Bar Assn. Episcopalian. Home: 1017 Berkeley St Santa Monica CA 90403-2309 Office: Leslie's Poolmart 20222 Plummer St Chatsworth CA 91311-5449

WATTS, DAVID H., construction company executive; b. Newark, 1938. Grad., Cornell U., 1960. Pres., CEO Granite Constrn. Inc., Watsonville, Calif. Office: Granite Constrn Co 585 W Beach St Watsonville CA 95076-5125*

WATTS, JAMES HARRISON, architect; b. Cleve., Apr. 28, 1951; s. Gregory Dean and Bubbles Joan (Browning) W.; m. Janice Fahey, Aug. 28, 1976; children: Jane, Molly. BArch, R.I. Sch. Design, 1974. Registered architect, Calif. Urban designer, film maker State of R.I., Providence, 1976-77; project mgr. Thomas Williamson Architect, San Diego, 1979-82; prin. Williamson & Watts Architects, San Diego, 1982-88, Fahey-Watts Architects, San Diego, 1988—; asst. architect San Diego Unified Sch. Dist., 1989—. Vol. architect U.S. Peace Corps, Nuku Alofa Tonga, 1977-79; chmn. San Diego Noise Abatement and Control Bd., 1988—. Mem. AIA, Am. Arbitration Assn., San Diego Yacht Club. Home: 3619 Front St San Diego CA 92103-4005

WATTS, JILL MARIE, history educator; b. Pomona, Calif., May 28, 1958; d. Thomas H. and Doris Ruth (Hohlfeld) W. BA, U. Calif., San Diego, 1981; MA, UCLA, 1983, PhD, 1989. Asst. prof. Weber State U., Ogden, Utah, 1989-91; asst. prof. Calif. State U., San Marcos, 1991-94, assoc. prof., 1994—, dir. history program, 1994—. Author: God, Harlem USA: The Father Divine Story, 1992; contbr. articles to profl. publs. (Theodore Salautos award). Carey McWilliams fellow, 1986-87, Rosecrans fellow, 1986-87, Inst. for Am. Cultures fellow, 1986-87, Cornell U. Soc. for Humanities fellow, 1994-95. Mem. Am. Hist. Assn., Orgn. Am. Historians, Am. Studies Assn., Western Assn. Women Historians, Oral History Assn. Office: Calif State U History Program San Marcos CA 92096

WATTS, MICHAEL ARTHUR, materials engineer; b. San Pedro, Calif., Nov. 18, 1955; s. Melvin A. Watts and Arlene P. Ault; m. Susan J. Reis, Dec., 1973 (div. Apr., 1983); m. Ann E. Winkelman, July 21, 1988; children: Arthur, Andy, Erin Winkelman, Heather Winkelman. BS in Materials Engring., N.Mex. Inst. Mining & Tech., 1988. Radar technician western svc. div. Raytheon, Fountain Valley, Calif., 1978-80; sr. engr. analyst Bournes Instruments, Riverside, Calif., 1980-82; mem. tech. staff Monolithic Microsystems, Santa Cruz, Calif., 1982-83; student rsch. asst. N.Mex. Inst. Mining and Tech., Socorro, 1983-88; corrosion engr. Arco Alaska, Achorage, 1989—. With USAF, 1974-78. Mem. Nat. Assn. Corrosion Engrs., Am. Soc. Metallurgy, Tau Beta Pi (pres. 1987-88). Home: 13670 Karen St Anchorage AK 99515-4106 Office: Arco Alaska PO Box 196105 NSK 39 Anchorage AK 99519-6105

WATTS, OLIVER EDWARD, engineering consultancy company executive; b. Hayden, Colo., Sept. 22, 1939; s. Oliver Easton and Vera Irene (Hockett) W.; m. Charla Ann French, Aug. 12, 1962; children—Erik Sean, Oliver Eron, Sherilyn. BS, Colo. State U., 1962. Registered profl. engr., Colo., Calif.; profl. hand surveyor, Colo. Crew chief Colo. State U. Rsch. Found., Ft. Collins, 1962; with Calif. Dept. Water Resources, Gustine and Castaic, 1964-70; land and water engr. CF&I Steel Corp., Pueblo, Colo., 1970-71; engring. dir. United Western Engrs., Colorado Springs., Colo., 1971-76; ptnr. United Planning and Engring Co., Colorado Springs, 1976-79; owner Oliver E. Watts, Cons. Engr., Colorado Springs, 1979—. Dir. edn. local Ch. of Christ, 1969-71, deacon, 1977-87, elder, 1987—. 1st lt. C.E., AUS, 1962-64. Recipient Individual Achievement award Colo. State U. Coll. Engring., 1981. Fellow ASCE (v.p. Colorado Springs br. 1975, pres. 1978); mem. NSPE (pres. Pike's Peak chpt. 1975, sec. Colo. sect. 1976, v.p. 1977, pres. 1978-79, Young Engr. award 1976, Pres.'s award 1979), Cons. Engrs. Coun. Colo. (bd. dirs. 1981-83), Am. Cons. Engrs. Coun., Profl. Land Surveyors Colo., Colo. Engrs. Coun. (del. 1980—), Colo. State U. Alumni Assn. (v.p., dir. Pike's Peak chpt. 1972-76), Lancers, Lambda Chi Alpha. Home: 7195 Dark Horse Pl Colorado Springs CO 80919-1442 Office: 614 Elkton Dr Colorado Springs CO 80907-3514

WATTS, VAN, retired career navy officer; b. Mooers, N.Y., Aug. 26, 1920; s. Bert and Margaret (Baker) W.; m. Lilie Remoreras, 1971; children: Michelle Remie, Philip, Charlotte, Britt, Lance, Douglas. With USN, 1937-62. prodr. TV and radio navy-slanted shows, Norfolk, Va., 1952-54. Decorated battle stars Nat. Def. Svc., Am. Def. Svc., Am. Campaign, Asiatic-Pacific Campaign, WWII Victory, Navy Occupl., Navy Occupl. Svc. (Europe), Armed Forces Expeditionary (Lebanon), Guadal Canal and New Guinea; recipient letter of commendation Nat. Trust for Hist. Preservation, 1975. Mem. VFW, Am. Legion, U.S. Naval Inst., USS Albany CA123 Assn., USS Enterprise CV6 Assn., USS Fremont APA44 Assn., USS Sierra AD18 Assn., Nat. Chief Petty Officers Assn., Tin Can Sailors Assn., Surface Navy Assn. (San Diego chpt.), Guadalcanal Campaign Vets. Assn., Naval Hist. Found., Navy Supply Corps Assn., Fleet Res. Assn., Botsford Family Hist. Assn., N.H. Hist. Soc., Brattleboro (Vt.) Hist. Soc., Chesterfield (N.H.) Hist. Soc., Burbank (Calif.) Hist. Soc., Hollywood Coun. Navy League (life).

WATZ, MARTIN CHARLES, brewery executive; b. St. Louis, Oct. 31, 1938; s. George Michael and Caroline Theresa (Doggendorf) W.; m. Deborah Jurgan; children: Pamela, Kathlene, Karen. BS in Chemistry and Microbiology, SE Mo. State U., 1961; postgrad. Washington U., 1966-67. Safety engr. McDonnell-Douglas, 1962-64; sr. brewing chemist Anheuser-Busch, Inc., St. Louis, 1965-68, asst. brewmaster, Columbus, Ohio, 1968-79, sr. asst. brewmaster, St. Louis, 1979-82, resident brewmaster, Baldwinsville, N.Y., 1982-84, Williamsburg, Va., 1984-87; v.p. Anheuser-Busch Indsl. Products Corp., St. Louis, 1987-88, dir. brewing ops., 1988-89; resident brewmaster Anheuser-Busch, Ft. Collins, Colo., 1989—. Patentee in field. With USAF, 1962-65. Mem. Master Brewers Assn. Am. (pres., nat. bd. govs.), Am. Soc. Brewing Chemists, Internat. Food Tech. Assocs., Aircraft Owners and Pilots Assn., U.S. Pilots Assn. Avocation: flying. Home: 1417 N County Line Rd # 3 Fort Collins CO 80524-9312 Office: Anheuser-Busch Ft Collins Brewery 2351 Busch Dr Fort Collins CO 80524-9400

WAUGH, KATHLEEN MARY, archivist; b. Bellingham, Wash., Feb. 2, 1952; d. Robert Burton and Shirley Kathleen (Stewart) W.; m. David Warren Hastings, Aug. 23, 1975; children: Rebecca, Ian. BA in History, Western Wash. U., 1973, BA in Anthrop., 1976; BS in Geology, Evergreen State Coll., 1983. Surveyor hist. records Wash. State Hist. Records Survey, Olympia, 1977-79; archival clk. Wash. State Archives, Olympia, 1979—. Author, editor: (catalogs) Index to Mining Surveys, 1985, Roll On, Columbia, 1987, Galloping Gertie, 1993, Guide to Records of Dixie Lee Ray, 1994. Mem. Mason County Heritage Bd., Shelton, Wash, 1993.

WAUTERS, SHIRLEY STAPLETON, retired real estate executive; b. Boise, Idaho, June 17, 1936; d. Charles Edward Lee and Eleanor L. (Swiggart) Noble; m. Bruce F. Wauters, May 23, 1986. AA in Liberal Arts summa cum laude, DeAnza Coll., Cupertino, Calif., 1975; BS in Bus. Mgmt., Ariz. State U., 1979. Lic. realtor assoc. Founder, dir. Women's Opportunity Ctr., Cupertino, 1970-73; owner, pub. Ariz. Women's Yellow Pages, Inc., Scottsdale, Ariz., 1973-80; pvt. practice cons. Cupertino, 1967-73, Scottsdale, Ariz., 1973-83; ptnr. The Weigelt Co., Inc., Phoenix, 1973-87; br. mgr. B. Rich, Inc., Tempe, Ariz., 1987, R. Richard Vick, Inc., Scottsdale, 1987-88; v.p. real estate sales TransWestern Consol. Realty, Inc., Phoenix, 1988-89; assoc. Internat. Ariz. Investments, Inc., Scottsdale, 1989-91; sec. Ariz. State U. Ctr. Environ. Studies, Tempe, 1992—; comml. real estate cons., Scottsdale. Mem. Ariz. State U. Alumni.

WAXMAN, HENRY ARNOLD, congressman; b. Los Angeles, Sept. 12, 1939; s. Louis and Esther (Silverman) W.; m. Janet Kessler, Oct. 17, 1971; children: Carol Lynn, Michael David. B.A. in Polit. Sci, UCLA, 1961, J.D., 1964. Bar: Calif. 1965. Mem. Calif. State Assembly, 1969-74, chmn. com. on health, until 1974; mem. 94th-104th Congresses from 24th (now 29th) Calif. dist., 1975—, ranking minority mem. house subcom. on health and environment, 1979—; mem. govt. reform & oversight com. Pres. Calif. Fedn. Young Democrats, 1965-67. Mem. Calif. Bar Assn., Guardians Jewish Home for Aged, Am. Jewish Congress, Sierra Club, B'nai B'rith, Phi Sigma Alpha. Office: US Ho of Reps 2408 Rayburn HOB Washington DC 20515*

WAY, JACOB EDSON, III, museum director; b. Chgo., May 18, 1947; s. Jacob Edson Jr. and Amelia (Evans) W.; m. Jean Ellwood Chappell, Sept. 6, 1969; children: Sarah Chappell, Rebecca Stoddard, Jacob Edson IV. BA, Beloit Coll., 1968; MA, U. Toronto, 1971, PhD, 1978. Instr. Beloit (Wis.) Coll., 1972-73, asst. prof., 1973-80, assoc. prof., 1980-85; dir. Logan Mus. Anthropology, Beloit, 1980-85, Wheelwright Mus. Am. Indian, Santa Fe, 1985-89; interim dir. N.Mex. Mus. Natural History, Albuquerque, 1990-91; exec. dir. Space Ctr. Internat. Space Hall of Fame, Alamogorgo, N.Mex., 1991-94; dir. N.Mex. Farm and Ranch Heritage Mus., 1994—; evaluator Nat. Park Service, Denver, 1986. Contbr. articles to profl. jours. Mem. Nuke Watch, Beloit, 1983-84. Research grants Wis. Humanities Com., 1984, NSF, 1981; grantee Cullister Found., 1978-84; fellow U. Toronto, 1971. Mem. Am. Assn. Mus., Am. Assn. Phys. Anthropology, Can. Assn. for Phys. Anthropology, N.Mex. Assn. Mus. (pres. 1994-96), Soc. Am. Archaeology, Wis. Fedn. Mus. (adv. bd. 1982-85). Mem. Soc. Friends. Office: N Mex Farm & Ranch Heritage Mus P O Drawer BB Las Cruces NM 88004

WAYBURN, EDGAR, internist, environmentalist; b. Macon, Ga., Sept. 17, 1906; s. Emanuel and Marian (Voorsanger) W.; m. Cornelia Elliott, Sept. 12, 1947; children: Cynthia, William, Diana, Laurie. AB magna cum laude, U. Ga., 1926; MD cum laude, Harvard U., 1930. Hosp. tng. Columbia-Presbyn. Hosp., N.Y.C., 1931-33; assoc. clin. prof. Stanford (Calif.) U., 1933-65, U. Calif., San Francisco, 1960-76; practice medicine specializing in internal medicine San Francisco, 1933-1985; mem. staff Pacific Presbyn. Med. Ctr., San Francisco, 1959-86, chief endocrine clinic, 1959-72, vice chief staff, 1961-63, hon. staff, 1986—. Editor: Man Medicine and Ecology, 1970; contbr. articles to profl. and environ. jours. Mem. Sec. of Interior's Adv. Bd. on Nat. Park System, 1979-83, commn. on nat. parks and protected areas Internat. Union for Conservation Nature and Natural Resources; leader nat. campaigns Alaska Nat. Interest Lands Conservation Act; trustee Pacific Presbyn. Med. Ctr., 1978-86; chmn. People For a Golden Gate Nat. Recreation Area, 1971—; mem. citizens' adv. commn. Golden Gate Nat. Recreation Area, San Francisco, 1974—, leader nat. campaigns, 1978-86; prin. citizen advocate Redwood Nat. Park; dir. The Antarctica Project; mem. adv. bd. Pacific Forest Trust; hon. chmn. Tuolumne River Preservation Trust; bd. dirs. Garden Sullivan Hosp., 1965-78. Maj. USAF, 1942-46. Recipient Douglas award Nat. Pks. and Conservation Assn., 1987, Leopold award Calif. Nature Conservancy, 1988, Fred Packard award Internat. Union Conservation Nature, 1994, Laureate of Global 500 Roll of Honour award U.N. Environment Programme, 1994, 1st Conservation award Eco-trust, 1994, Albert Schweitzer prize, 1995. Fellow ACP; mem. AMA, Am. Soc. Internal Medicine, Calif. Med. Assn. (del. 1958-83, Recognition award 1986, Leadership and Quality awards 1986), San Francisco Med. Soc. (pres. 1965, Resolution of Congratulations 1986), Sierra Club (pres. 1961-64, 67-69, John Muir award 1972, hon. pres. 1993), Fedn. Western Outdoor Clubs (pres. 1953-55). Home: 314 30th Ave San Francisco CA 94121-1705

WAYBURN, LAURIE ANDREA, environmental and wildlife foundation administrator, conservationist; b. San Francisco, Sept. 27, 1954; d. Edgar A. and Cornelia (Elliott) W. BA, Harvard U., 1977. Program mgr. UN Environment Program, Nairobi, Kenya, 1978-81; program cons. UNESCO, Paris and Montevideo, Uruguay, 1983-86; cons. BBC, London, 1986-87; exec. dir. Point Reyes Bird Obs., Stinson Beach, Calif., 1987—; speaker numerous confs., 1987—; coord. Cen. Calif. Coast Biosphere Res., 1988—; com. mem. U.S. Nat. Program Man and Biosphere, Washington, 1989—; bd. dirs. UN Assn. Panel, San Francisco, People for A GGNRA, San Francisco, 1989—; del. Internat. Coun. Bird Preservation, Washington, 1989—. Contbr. articles to profl. jours. Advisor Switzer Found., San Francisco, 1990—. Home: PO Box 858 Boonville CA 95415-0858

WAYBURN, PEGGY (CORNELIA E. WAYBURN), author, editor; b. N.Y.C., Sept. 2, 1917; d. Thomas Ketchin and Cornelia (Ligon) E.; m. Edgar Wayburn Sept. 12, 1947; children: Cynthia, William, Diana, Laurie. BA cum laude, Barnard, 1942. Copywriter Vogue Mag., N.Y.C., 1943-45, J. Walter Thompson, San Francisco, 1945-47; self employed freelance writer, San Francisco, 1948—; Author: Adventuring in the San Francisco Bay Area, Adventuring in Alaska; (audio visual series) Circle of Life; contbr. articles to profl. jours. Mem. bd. advisors Am. Youth Hostels; trustee Sierra Club Found. Recipient annual award Calif. Conservation Assn., 1966. Mem. Sierra Club (spl. svc. award 1967, women's award 1989), Phi Beta Kappa. Home: 314 30th Ave San Francisco CA 94121-1705

WAYLAND, NEWTON HART, conductor; b. Santa Barbara, Calif., Nov. 5, 1940; s. L.C. Newton and Helen Bertha (Hart) W.; m. Judith Anne Curtis, July 3, 1969 (div. 1986). MusB, New Eng. Conservatory Music, 1964, MusM, 1966. Host, composer, performer Sta. WGBH-TV, Boston, 1963-82; pianist, harpsichordist Boston Symphony Orch., 1964-71; music dir. Charles Playhouse, 1965-67; pianist, guest condr., arranger Boston Pops Orch., 1971-74; resident Pops condr. Midwest Pops Orch., South Bend, Ind., 1979-91, Oakland Symphony Orch., Calif., 1980-85, Houston Symphony Orch., 1986-93; prin. Pops condr. Denver Symphony Orch., 1987-89, Vancouver (B.C.) Symphony Orch., 1993—; guest condr. numerous orchs. U.S. and Canada, 1977—. Recs. include: Music for Zoom (PBS Emmy-winning TV show), 1971-78, Music for Nova (award-winning PBS-TV show), 1972-78, America Swings, 1987, Gershwin Plays Gershwin, 1987, Pop Go the Beatles, 1987, Classical Jukebox, 1988, Stompin' at the Savoy, 1988, Sophisticated Ladies, 1988, A Touch of Fiedler, 1989, Prime Time, 1989; arranger, performer: Jazz Loves Bach, 1968, Fiedler in Rags, 1974; arranger, condr.: Berlin to Broadway with Kurt Weill, 1972; condr. Oedipus Tex (Grammy award 1991); arranger, composer, performer (songs A&M Records) Come On and Zoom, Zoom Tunes. Recipient highest honors New Eng. Conservatory Music, 1974, Chadwick Disting. Achievement medal New Eng. Conservatory Music, 1966. Home and Office: 2970 Hidden Valley Ln Santa Barbara CA 93108-1619

WAYMAN, COOPER HARRY, environmental legal counsel; b. Trenton, N.J., Jan. 29, 1927; s. Cooper Ott and Helen Viola (Unverzagt) W.; m. Ruth Treier, June 16, 1951; children: Carol Beth Withers, Andrea Lee Daschbach. BS, Rutgers U., 1951; MS, U. Pitts., 1954; PhD, Mich. State U., 1959; JD, U. Denver, 1967. Bar: Colo. 1969, Tex. 1972; registered profl. engr., Colo.; cert. real estate broker, Colo. Rsch. chemist U.S. Geol. Survey, Lakewood, Colo., 1960-65; assoc. prof. chemistry Colo. Sch. Mines, Golden, 1965-70; asst. to regional adminstr. EPA, Denver, 1971-74, regional counsel, 1974-83; exec. asst. to mayor City of Denver, 1981-85; dir. environment compliance Cord Labs., Inc., Broomfield, Colo., 1986-88; environ. and permits mgr. Chem. Waste Mgmt. Inc., Port Arthur, Tex., 1988-92; regional regulatory mgr. Chem. Waste Mgmt., Inc., Houston, 1992-94; compliance branch mgr. Adv. Scis., Inc., Carlsbad, N.Mex., 1994-95; area office legal counsel Waste Isolation Project, Dept. Energy, Carlsbad, N.Mex., 1995—; dir. energy office EPA, Denver, 1974-78; adj. prof. law U. Denver, 1981-84; mem. State of Colo. Air Pollution Commn., Denver, 1969-70. Author: Detergents and Environment, 1965, Permits Handbook, 1981; contbr. articles to profl. jours. V.p. WE Lockwood Civic Assn., Lakewood, 1985-86. With USNR, 1945-46. Grantee U.S. Fish and Wildlife Svc., 1967; fellow, rsch. assoc. MIT, 1956-58. Fellow Am. Inst. Chemists, 1993. Home: 1408-A W Church St Carlsbad NM 88220 Office: US Dept Energy Carlsbad Area Office PO Box 3090 Carlsbad NM 88221

WAYMIRE, EVAN SAGE, automotive engineer; b. Portland, Oreg., July 25, 1960; s. John Franklin and Nona Jane (Sage) W. BSME, Oreg. State U., 1984. Registered profl. engr., Oreg. Test engr. I, Freightliner Corp., Portland, 1985-87, test engr. II, 1987-90, sr. design engr., 1990-91, automotive devel. engr., 1991—; cons. engr. Waymire Engring., Portland, 1990—. Mem. ASME, Soc. Automotive Engrs. (vice chmn. adminstrn. Oreg. sect. 1985—), Sports Car Club Am., Cascade Sports Car Club. Office: Freightliner Corp 4747 N Channel Ave Portland OR 97217-7613

WAYNE, KYRA PETROVSKAYA, writer; b. Crimea, USSR, Dec. 31, 1918; came to U.S., 1948, naturalized, 1951; d. Prince Vasily Sergeyevich and Baroness Zinaida Fedorovna (Fon-Haffenberg) Obolensky; m. George J. Wayne, Apr. 21, 1961; 1 child, Ronald George. B.A., Leningrad Inst. Theatre Arts, 1939, M.A., 1940. Actress, concert singer, USSR, 1939-46; actress, U.S., 1948-51; enrichment lectr. Royal Viking Line cruises, Alaska-Can., Greek Islands-Black Sea, Russia/Europe, 1978-79, 81-82, 83-84, 86-87, 88. Author: Kyra, 1959; Kyra's Secrets of Russian Cooking, 1960, 93; The Quest for the Golden Fleece, 1962; Shurik, 1971; The Awakening, 1972; The Witches of Barguzin, 1975; Max, The Dog That Refused to Die, 1979 (Best Fiction award Dog Writers Assn. Am. 1980); Rekindle the Dreams, 1979, Quest for Empire, 1986, Li'l Ol' Charlie, 1989. Founder, pres. Clean Air Program, Los Angeles County, 1971-72; mem. women's council KCET-Ednl. TV; mem. Monterey County Symphony Guild, 1989-91, Monterey Bay Aquarium, Monterey Peninsula Mus. Art, Friends of La Mirada. Served to lt. Russian Army, 1941-43. Decorated Red Star, numerous other decorations USSR; recipient award Crusade for Freedom, 1955-56; award Los Angeles County, 1972, Merit award Am. Lung Assn. L.A. County, 1988. Mem. Soc. Children's Book Writers, Authors Guild, P.E.N., UCLA Med. Faculty Wives (pres. 1970-71, dir. 1971-75) UCLA Affiliates (life), Los Angeles Lung Assn. (life), Friends of the Lung Assn. (pres. 1988), Carmel Music Soc. (bd. dirs. 1992-94), Idyllwild Sch. Music, Art and Theatre Assn. (trustee 1987), Los Angelenos Club (life). Home: 25031 Hidden Mesa Ct Monterey CA 93940-6633

WAYNE, VALERIE, English language educator; b. Chgo., Aug. 2, 1945; d. Robert August and Eleanor Margaret (Kalow) W.; m. David Lee Callies, June 18, 1966 (div. Mar. 1986); 1 child, Sarah Anne. BA in Philosophy cum laude, DePauw U., 1966; MA in English, U. Ill., Chgo., 1972; PhD in English, U. Chgo., 1978. Tchg. asst. in humanities U. Chgo., 1973-74; lectr. in composition Chgo. State U., 1974; lectr. U. Ill., Chgo., 1976-78; from vis. asst. prof. to assoc. prof. English U. Hawaii at Manoa, Honolulu, 1978-93, prof. English, 1993—, dir. grad. program English, 1994—; vis. lectr. U. Liverpool, U.K., 1988. Editor: The Matter of Difference: Materialist Feminist Criticism of Shakespeare, 1991, The Flower of Friendship: A Renaissance Dialogue Contesting Marriage, 1992, A Trick to Catch the Old One in the Collected Works of Thomas Middleton; contbr. articles and poetry to profl. jours. and anthologies. Mem. Shakespeare Assn. Am., Modern Lang. Assn., Early Modern Women, Renaissance Eng. Text Soc. Home: 2406 Oahu Ave # A Honolulu HI 96822-1967 Office: Univ Hawaii English Dept 1733 Donaghho Rd Honolulu HI 96822-2315

WEARING, J.P., English language educator; b. Birmingham, Eng., Mar. 1, 1945; s. Jhn and Joan (Hall) W. BA with honors, U. Wales, Swansea, 1967, PhD, 1971; MA, U. Sask., Can., 1968. Lectr. U. Alta., Edmonton, 1971-74, asst. prof. English U. Ariz., Tucson, 1974-77, assoc. prof., 1977-84, prof. English, 1984—; cons. NEH, Washington, 1978—. Author: The Collected Letters of Sir Arthur Pinero, 1974, The London Stage 1890-1959: A Calendar of Plays and Players, 16 vols., 1976-93, English Drama and Theatre, 1800-1900, 1978, American and British Theatrical Biography: A Directory, 1979, G.B. Shaw: An Annotated Bibliography of Writings About Him: Vol. I· 1871-1930, 1986, many others; editor: 19th Century Theatre Rsch., 1972-86; adv. editor English Literature in Transition, 1976—, 19th Century Theatre, 1986—; contbr. articles to profl. jours. Killam Found. fellow, 1971-73, Guggenheim Found. fellow, 1978-79; NEH grantee, 1987-91. Mem. Soc. for Theatre Rsch. (Eng.). Office: U Ariz Dept English Tucson AZ 85721

WEARLY, WILLIAM LEVI, business executive; b. Warren, Ind., Dec. 5, 1915; s. Purvis Gardner and Ethel Ada (Jones) W.; m. Mary Jane Riddle, Mar. 8, 1941; children: Patricia Ann, Susan, William Levi, Elizabeth. B.S., Purdue U., 1937, Dr. Engring. (hon.), 1959. Student career engr. C.A. Dunham Co., Michigan City, Ind., 1936; mem. elec. design staff Joy Mfg. Co., Franklin, Pa., 1937-39; v.p., gen. sales mgr. Joy Mfg. Co., 1952-56, exec. v.p., 1956-57, pres., dir., 1957-62; v.p., dir. Ingersoll-Rand Co., 1964-66, exec. v.p., 1966-67, chmn., chief exec. officer, 1967-80, chmn. exec. com., 1981-85; dir. ASA Ltd., Med. Care Am.; trustee LMI; speaker engring. groups. Author tech. pubs. relating to mining. Bd. dirs. Boys Clubs Am. Mem. NAE, IEEE, AIME, Nat. Acad. of Engring., C. of C., Sky Club N.Y.C., Blind Brook Golf Club, Desert Forest Golf Club, Ariz. Club, Masons, Shriners, Eta Kappa Nu, Tau Beta Pi, Beta Theta Pi. Republican. Methodist. Home: One Milbank IIF Greenwich CT 06830 also: PO Box 1072 Carefree AZ 85377-1072

WEATHERFORD, ALAN MANN, business educator; b. Lake Charles, La., Feb. 6, 1947; s. Clester Mann and Nell (Birdsong) W.; m. Elizabeth A. Weatherford (div. Dec. 1991); children: William B., Victoria L. BA, La. State U., 1969; MBA, U. Dallas, 1981; PhD, U. Tex., Richardson, 1986. Claims adjuster Royal Globe Ins. Cos., San Antonio, 1969-71; staff nurse Univ. Hosp., Augusta, Ga., 1977, Garland (Tex.) Community Hosp., 1978-79; mem. staff Baylor Med. Ctr., Grapevine, Tex., 1982-85; rsch. asst. U. Tex., 1983-85; assoc. prof. bus. Calif. Poly. State U., San Luis Obispo, 1986—. Editor: Econ. Rev., 1991-93; contbr. articles to profl. jours. Dir. Small Bus. Inst., San Luis Obispo, 1991—. 1st lt. USAF, 1973-76. Mem. Fin. Mgmt. Assn., Am. Fin. Assn., S.W. Fin. Assn., Mensa. Office: Calif Poly State U Sch Bus San Luis Obispo CA 93407

WEATHERHEAD, ANDREW KINGSLEY, educator; b. Manchester, Eng., Oct. 8, 1923; came to U.S., 1951; s. Leslie Dixon and Evelyn (Triggs) W.; m. Ingrid Antonie Lien, Aug. 28, 1952; children: Lyn Kristin, Leslie Richard, Andrea Kathryn. BA, U. Cambridge, Eng., 1944, MA, 1947; MA, U. Edinburgh, Scotland, 1950; PhD, U. Wash., Seattle, 1958. Assoc. prof. La. State U., New Orleans, 1958-60; with U. Oreg., Eugene, 1960—, assoc. prof., 1962-68, prof., 1968-89, prof. emeritus, 1989—. Author: A Reading of Henry Green, 1961, The Edge of the Image, 1967, Stephen Spender and the Thirties, 1975, Leslie Weatherhead: A Personal Potrait, 1975, The British Dissonance, 1983; contbr. articles to profl. jours. Home: 2698 Fairmount Blvd Eugene OR 97403-1758 Office: U Oreg English Dept 118 PLC Eugene OR 97403-4152

WEATHERHEAD, LESLIE R., lawyer; b. Tacoma, Sept. 28, 1956; s. A. Kingsley and Ingrid A. (Lien) W.; m. Anali C. Torrado, June 24, 1985; children: Spencer, Madeleine. BA, U. Oreg., 1977; JD, U. Wash., 1980. Bar: Wash. 1980, U.S. Ct. Appeals (9th cir.) 1981, U.S. Dist. Ct. (ea. dist.) Wash. 1984, U.S. Ct. Internat. Trade 1984, Hawaii 1987, U.S. Dist. Ct. (we. dist.) Wash. 1989, Idaho 1989, U.S. Dist. Ct. Idaho 1989, U.S. Supreme Ct. 1994, Colville Tribal Ct. 1993. Asst. terr. prosecutor Territory of Guam, Agana, 1980-83; spl. asst. U.S. Atty. Dist. of Guam and No. Marianas, Agana, 1982-83; atty. Witherspoon, Kelley, Davenport & Toole, Spokane, 1984—; lawyer-rep. 9th cir. jud. conf., 1989-95; adj. faculty Gonzaga U. Sch. of Law, 1994—. Contbr. articles on Indian law and adminstrv. investigations to profl. jours. Bd. dirs. Spokane Uptown Opera, 1989—, pres., 1992-94. Mem. ABA, Hawaii Bar Assn., Idaho Bar Assn., Wash. State Bar Assn. Office: Witherspoon Kelley Davenport & Toole 428 W Riverside Ave Spokane WA 99201-0301

WEATHERMON, SIDNEY EARL, elementary school educator; b. Abilene, Tex., Jan. 20, 1937; s. Sidney Elliot Weathermon and Evelyn Marie (Landreth) Parker. BA, U. Colo., 1962, MA, 1968, EdD, 1976. Cert. K-12 reading thcr., elem. edn. tchr., K-12 reading specialist. Tchr. Jefferson County (Colo.) Pub. Schs., 1963-66; grades 5-6 tchr. Boulder (Colo.) Valley Pub. Schs., 1962-63, reading tchr., 1968-71, consortium dir. right-to-read project Louisville Mid. Sch., 1974-75, comm. skills program coord. Vocat.-Tech. H.S., 1976, K-12 dist. reading specialist, 1971-85, chpt. 1 tchr. grades 1-6, 1985-89, chpt. 1 kindergarten project coord., 1985-89, grade 1 tchr., 1989—; instr. U. Colo., Boulder, 1971-72, U. No. Colo., Greeley, 1977; adj. faculty Regis U., Denver, 1972—, dept. edn. instr., 1982. Contbr. articles to profl. jours. Recipient Celebrate Literacy award, Boulder Coun. Internat. Reading Assn., 1986, IBM Corp. Tchr. of Yr. award, 1989, Colo./Nat. Educator, Milkin Family Found., 1990; NDEA fellow, 1966-68. Mem. NEA, Internat. Reading Assn., Colo. Edn. Assn., Boulder Valley Edn. Assn. (chair tchr. adv coun., assoc. rep., tchrs. rights and activities commn., negotiations team, profl. leave com.), Phi Delta Kappa (certs. of recognition 1987, 90), Kappa Delta Pi. Democrat. Home: 449 S Shore Dr Osprey FL 34229-9657 Office: Martin Park Elem Sch 3740 Martin Dr Boulder CO 80303-5448

WEATHERS, WARREN RUSSELL, forester, appraiser, consultant; b. La Jolla, Calif., Feb. 17, 1947; s. Warren Obert and Cicely Joanne (Hawken) W.; m. Terri Ruth Pillette, May 5, 1988; children: Nathan, Stuart, Erik. BS in Forestry, Oreg. State U., 1970; MBA, U. Oreg., 1985. Chief forester Pacific Timber Products, Haines, Alaska, 1972-75; exec. v.p. Shee Atika, Inc., Sitka, Alaska, 1975-82; cons. forester, 1982—; commr. Alaska State Bd. Forestry, Juneau, 1979-80. Mem., pres. Lowell (Oreg.) City Coun., 1987-91, chmn. budget com., 1987-88; mayor City of Lowell, 1991—. 1st lt. U.S. Army Res., 1971-80. Mem. Nat. Trappers Assn., Am. Assn. Cert. Appraisers, Nat. Woodland Owners Assn., Soc. Am. Foresters (chpt. chair 1979-80), Assn. Consulting Foresters. Office: PO Box 39 1/2 Lowell OR 97452-0039

WEATHERUP, ROY GARFIELD, lawyer; b. Annapolis, Md., Apr. 20, 1947; s. Robert Alexander and Kathryn Crites (Hesser) W.; m. Wendy Gaines, Sept. 10, 1977; children: Jennifer, Christine. AB in Polit. Sci., Stanford U., 1968, JD, 1972. Bar: Calif. 1972, U.S. Dist. Ct. 1973, U.S. Ct. Appeals (9th cir.) 1975, U.S. Supreme Ct. 1980. Assoc. Haight, Brown & Bonesteel, L.A., Santa Monica and Santa Ana, Calif., 1972-78, ptnr., 1979—; judge Moot Ct. UCLA, Loyola U., Pepperdine U.; arbitrator Am. Arbitration Assn.; mem. com. Book Approved Jury Instructions L.A. Superior Ct. Mem. ABA, Calif. Acad. Appellate Lawyers, Town Hall Calif., L.A. County Bar Assn. Republican. Methodist. Home: 17260 Rayen St Northridge CA 91325-2919 Office: Haight Brown & Bonesteel 1620 26th St Santa Monica CA 90404

WEAVER, BRYAN H., engineer, producer; b. Denver, Aug. 12, 1957; s. Donald H. and Kazumi (Nakamichi) W.; m. Pamela Jean Scholefield, Aug. 31, 1985. AA in Bus., St. Petersburg Jr. Coll., 1976; BA in Mktd., U. South Fla., 1978; BS in Indsl. and Systems Engring., U. Fla., 1985. Engr. Layne Western, Denver and Pensacola, Fla., 1985-87; spl. forces intelligence analyst Denver, 1987-92; product engr. Paramont Equipment, Denver, 1988-89; pres., CEO Scouting Report of Colo., Denver, 1989-91; gen. ptnr. Mentor Prodns., San Diego, 1990—; cons. Mentor Prodns., 1992-94. Bd. dirs. Mentor Found., Denver, 1991. With USNG, 1987-93. Mem. Soc. Motion Picture and TV Engrs., Internat. TV Assn., Internat. Interactive Computer Soc. Home and Office: 24220 Watt Rd Ramona CA 92065-4153

WEAVER, GRACE MARGARET, minister; b. Phila., Sept. 4, 1909; d. James Henry and Beulah Grace (Davis) W. BA, Morningside Coll., 1947; ThM, Iliff Sch. Theology, 1955. Tchr. elem. West Berlin, N.J., 1929-44, Clementon, N.J., 1944-45; missionary worker United Meth. Ch., Utah, 1948-51; min. Emmett, Glenns Ferry, Fruitland and Am. Falls, Idaho, and Ketchikan, Alaska, 1954-76; ret., 1976. Recipient 4 Golden Poet awards, 1989. Home: 1551 Center St NE Salem OR 97301-4201

WEAVER, HOWARD CECIL, newspaper editor; b. Anchorage, Oct. 15, 1950; s. Howard Gilbert and Lurlene Eloise (Gamble) W.; m. Alice Laprele Gauchay, July 16, 1970 (div. 1974); m. Barbara Lynn Hodgin, Sept. 16, 1978. BA, Johns Hopkins U., 1972; MPhil, Cambridge U., 1993. Reporter, staff writer Anchorage Daily News, 1972-76, columnist, 1979-80, mng. editor, 1980-83, editor, 1983—; editor, owner Alaska Advocate, Anchorage, 1976-79; internat. co-chair Northern News Svc., 1989-94; disting. lectr. journalism U. Alaska, Fairbanks, 1991. Pulitzer Prize juror, 1988, 89, 94, 95. Recipient Pulitzer prize, 1976, 89, Pub. Svc. award AP Mng. Editor's Assn., 1976, 89, Headliner award Press Club of Atlantic City, 1976, 89, Gold medal Investigative Reporters and Editors, 1989. Mem. Am. Soc. Newspaper Editors, Investigative Reporters and Editors, Sigma Delta Chi (Nat. award 1989), Alaska Press Club (bd. dirs. 1972-84), Upper Yukon River Press Club (pres. 1972). Avocations: ice hockey, foreign travel, opera.

WEAVER, JOSEPH STEPHEN, state park administrator; b. Dayton, Ohio, Jan. 5, 1950; s. James Joseph and Phyllis Catherine (Bauer) W.; m. Kathleen Rusnak, Oct. 28, 1972. B in Environ. Design, N.C. State U., 1972, M in Forestry, 1976; AAS in Bus., W. Nev. C.C., Carson City, 1985. Cert. landscape architect. From intern to landscape architect N.C. State Parks, Raleigh, 1972-79; supr., landscape arch., asst. adminstr. Nev. State Parks, Carson City, 1979-83, 85-90, chief planning and devel., 1990—; environ. mgmt. specialist Nev. Divsn. Environ. Protection, Carson City, 1983-85. Co-author: North Carolina State Parks - Now or Never, 1973. Bd. trustees, chmn. Indian Hills Gen. Improvement Dist., Carson City, 1989—. Named Eagle Scout Boy Scouts Am., 1967, Outstanding Vol., Voluntary Action, 1994. Mem. Am. Soc. Landscape Archs., Nature Conservancy, Sierra Club (group conservation chair 1976-78), Tahoe Rim Trail Fund (bd. dirs., Highest Distinction award 1989), Xi Sigma Pi. Roman Catholic.

WEAVER, MARK ARTHUR, finance educator, foreign language educator; b. Visalia, Calif., Feb. 14, 1952; s. Arthur Roy and Dorothy Jean (Sawyer) W. Student, U. Wash., 1972-73; BA in Polit. Sci. with hons., San Francisco State U., 1981, MA in Romance Langs., Lit., 1984; MA in Internat. Bus. with distinction, George Washington U., 1986; D in Bus. Adminstrn., U. Geneva, 1993—. Cert. consecutive interpretation. Freelance writer, import/export rep., sales/mktg. rep., agril. cons. Europe, North Africa and Latin America, 1973-79; asst. to chief editor corr., editor, copy editor Bancroft-Whitney Pub., San Francisco, 1981-82; asst. to dep. asst. sec. trade adjustment assistance U.S. Department of Commerce, Washington, 1985, internat. market analyst office product devel., 1985-86, editor, trade specialist Caribbean Basin Ctr., 1986-87, dir. mktg. Caribbean Basin Ctr., 1987-88; internat. trade specialist U.S. Fgn. Comml. Svc. U.S. Department of Commerce, L.A., 1988-89, sr. internat. trade specialist U.S. Fgn. Comml. Svc., 1990-93; dir., eastern Washington br., U.S. Fgn. Comml. Svc. U.S. Department of Commerce, Kennewick, Wash., 1993—; dir. internat. sales Am. Bur. Collections, Santa Ana, Calif., 1989-90; bd. dirs. Greater L.A. World Ctr. Com.; prof. internat. bus. West Coast U., L.A., Long Beach City (Calif.) Coll., 1990-93, Wash. State U., Richland, 1994-95. Editor jurisprudence law books, 1982—, Caribbean Bus. Bull., 1986-88, L.A.-So. Calif. World Trade Week, 1988-89. Capt. Volvo Amateur Tennis Teams, Washington, 1987, L.A., 1989. Wolcott Pub. Svc. fellow Masonic Lodge, 1984. Mem. French-Am. C. of C. L.A. (bd. dirs. 1988-89), Coun. European C. of C., Calif.-Chile C. of C., Calif.-Columbia C. of C., Torrance C. of C. (founder, chmn. internat. bus. com. 1990—), Long Beach C. of C. (bd. dirs. internat. bus. assn. 1990—), Internat. Trade Edn. and Cultural Assn., Inland N.W. World Trade Coun. Republican. Roman Catholic. Office: US Dept Commerce US Fgn Comml Svc 320 N Johnson St Ste 350 Kennewick WA 99336-2771

WEAVER, MAX KIMBALL, social worker, consultant; b. Price, Utah, Apr. 4, 1941; s. Max Dickson and Ruth (Kimball) W.; m. Janet Hofheins, Sept. 13, 1963; children: Kim, Cleve, Chris, Wendy, Michael, Amyanne, Heather. Student, So. Utah State Coll., 1959-60; BS, Brigham Young U., 1965; MSW, U. Utah, 1967. Lic. clin. social worker and marriage counselor, Utah. Cons. Utah State Tng. Sch., American Fork, 1966; dir. Dept. Pub. Welfare, Cedar City, Utah, 1967-70; social worker Latter Day St. Social Services, Cedar City, 1970-75; with Mental Retardation Devel. Disabled Adult Services Dept. Social Services, Cedar City, 1975—; cons. nursing homes, Utah, 1974—; tchr. So. Utah State Coll., Cedar City, 1972, 77. Contbr. articles to mags. Pres. Am. Little League Baseball, 1977-84, 86, Cedar High Booster Club, 1984—; chmn. Rep. Precinct #1, 1984; v.p. Big League Baseball, 1986—. Mem. Nat. Assn. Social Work (nominating com., licensing com.), Am. Pub. Welfare Assn., Utah Pub. Employees Assn. Mormon. Lodge: Rotary. Home: 116 N 200 E Cedar City UT 84720-2617 Office: Dept Social Svcs 106 N 100 E Cedar City UT 84720-2608

WEAVER, MICHAEL JAMES, lawyer; b. Bakersfield, Calif., Feb. 11, 1946; s. Kenneth James and Elsa Hope (Rogers) W.; m. Valerie Scott, Sept. 2, 1966; children: Christopher James, Brett Michael, Karen Ashley. AB, Calif. State U., Long Beach, 1968; JD magna cum laude, U. San Diego, 1973. Bar: Calif., 1973, U.S. Dist. Ct. (so. dist.) Calif. 1973, U.S. Ct. Appeals (9th cir.) 1975, U.S. Supreme Ct. 1977. Law clk. to chief judge U.S. Dist. Ct. (so. dist.) Calif., San Diego, 1973-75; assoc. Luce, Forward, Hamilton & Scripps, San Diego, 1975-80, ptnr., 1980-86; ptnr. Sheppard, Mullin, Richter & Hampton, San Diego, 1986—; judge pro tem San Diego Superior Ct.; master of the Bench of the Inn, Am. Inns of Ct., Louis M. Welch chpt.; lectr. Inn of Ct., San Diego, 1981—, Continuing Edn. of Bar, Calif., 1983—, Workshop for Judges U.S. Ct. Appeals (9th cir.) 1990. Editor-in-chief: San Diego Law Rev., 1973; contbr. articles to profl. jours. Bd. dirs., pres. San Diego Kidney Found., 1985—; bd. dirs. San Diego Aerospace Mus., 1985—; trustee La Jolla (Calif.) Playhouse, 1990—. Served to lt., USNR, 1968-74. Fellow Am. Coll. Trial Lawyers; mem. San Diego Assn. Bus. Trial Lawyers (founding mem., bd. govs.), San Diego Def. Lawyers Assn. (dir.), Am. Arbitration Assn., 9th Cir. Jud. Conf. (del. 1987-90), Safari Club Internat. (San Diego chpt.), San Diego Sportsmen's Club. Republican. Presbyterian. Office: Sheppard Mullin Richter & Hampton 501 W Broadway Fl 19 San Diego CA 92101-3536

WEAVER, VELATHER EDWARDS (VAL WEAVER), small business owner; b. Union Hall, Va., Feb. 20, 1944; d. Willie Henry and Ethel (Smith) Edwards; m. Ellersn Fitzpatrick Weaver; children: Frankie Lawrence Mattox Jr., Terence Leon Mattox, Christopher Lamar Williams, Sharon, Shelley, Stephanie. Student, Sonoma State Coll., 1972, U. Calif., Berkeley, 1972; BA, Calif. State U., Hayward, 1973; MBA, St. Mary's Coll., Moraga, Calif., 1989. Coach, counselor Opportunities Industrialization Ctr., Oakland, Calif., 1967-69; tchr. Berkeley Headstart, 1969-70; instr., cons. external degree program Antioch Coll.-West, San Francisco, 1971-74; market analyst World Airways, Inc., Oakland, 1972-75, affirmative action adminstr., 1975-78; cons. A.C. Transit, Oakland, 1982; owner, mgr. Val's Designs and Profl. Svcs., Lafayette, Calif., 1980—; mgr. adminstrn., tng. supr. North Oakland Pharmacy, Inc., 1970—, also bd. dirs.; adv. bd. The Tribune, Oakland, 1982-88. Author RAPRO Self Mgmt. Program, 1985. Program coord., publicity Lafayette Arts and Sci. Found., 1982-83; mem. admission bd. grad. bus. sch. St. Mary's Coll., 1990; bd. dirs. Acalanes High Sch., Lafayette, 1980-82, Lafayette Elem. Sch., 1975-80; mem. City of Lafayette Econ. Devel. Task Force, 1994—. Mem. Calif. State Pharmacists Assn. Aux. (pres. Contra Costa Aux. 1980, pres. state aux. 1986-88, recognition award 1987), Calif. Pharmacists Polit. Action Com. (appreciation award 1988), Diablo Valley Bus. and Profl. Women (pub. rels. com. 1986-87, best local orgn. award 1987, author yearbook 1987), No. Calif. Med., Dental and Pharm. Assn. Aux. (bd. dirs., com. chair 1975—, pres. elect 1991, pres. 1991-93), Internat. Platform Assn., Links, Inc. Office: North Oakland Pharmacy Inc 5705 Market St Emeryville CA 94608-2811

WEAVER, WILLIAM SCHILDECKER, electric power industry executive; b. Pitts., Jan. 15, 1944; s. Charles Henry and Louise (Schildecker) W.; m. Janet Kae Jones, Mar. 7, 1981. BA, Hamilton Coll., 1965; JD, U. Mich., 1968. Bar: Wash. 1968. Assoc. Perkins Coie, Seattle, 1968-74; ptnr. Perkins COIE, Seattle, 1975-91; exec. v.p., CFO Puget Sound Power & Light Co., Bellevue, Wash., 1991—; bd. dirs. Puget Sound Power & Light Co., Hydro Electric Devel. Co., Bellevue. Bd. dirs. Wash. Rsch. Coun., Seattle, 1991—; trustee Seattle Reperatory Theatre, 1992—. Mem. ABA, Wash. State Bar Assn., Seattle Yacht Club, Rainier Club. Office: Puget Sound Power & Light Co PO Box 97034-obc- Bellevue WA 98009

WEBB, ERIC SETH, physician; b. Lexington, Ky., Mar. 2, 1958; s. Ross Allen and Ruth Evangeline (Keil) W. BA, Coll. of Charleston, 1980; MD, Med. U. S.C., 1986. Diplomate Am. Bd. Family Practice. Emergency dept. physician Good Samaritan Hosp., Lexington, Ky., 1989-90, Ashland (Oreg.) Comty. Hosp., 1991—; physician and med. dir. Comty. Health Ctr., Medford, Oreg., 1991—. Mem. Am. Acad. Family Physicians, U.S. Tennis Assn., Sierra Club, Hash House Harriers (religious adviser Ashland chpt. 1992—). Office: Cmty Health Ctr 19 Myrtle St Medford OR 97504

WEBB, GILBERT A., obstetrician, gynecologist; b. Oakland, Calif., June 21, 1923; s. Frank Gilbert and Allena Valeria (Prather) W.; m. Donna Jean Meyer, Feb. 24, 1946; children: Paul Gilbert, Pamela Eickmann, Janet Brunsting, Bruce, William. BS, U. Calif., Berkeley, 1943; MD, U. Calif., San Francisco, 1946; postgrad., U.S. Naval Med. Sch., 1947-48. Diplomate Am. Bd. Ob-Gyn. Intern San Francisco City and County Hosp., 1946, Mare Island Naval Hosp. Mil Svc., 1947; asst resident in ob-gyn. U.S. Naval Hosp., Bethesda, Md., 1948-49; asst. resident in psychiatry Langley Porter Clinic/U. Calif. Med. Sch., San Francisco, 1950; from asst. resident to chief resident in ob-gyn. U. Calif. Hosp., San Francisco, 1951-54; from instr. to assoc. clin. prof. ob-gyn. U. Calif. Med. Sch., San Francisco, 1955-72, clin. prof. ob-gyn., 1972—; examiner Am. Bd. Ob-Gyn., 1973-94; com. on in-tng. examination for residents ob-gyn. Coun. Resident Edn. Ob/Gyn, 1969-74; com. on core curriculum for ob-gyn. residency Am. Assn. Ob/Gyn-Coun. Resident Edn. Ob/Gyn, 1974-77; chmn. dept. ob-gyn. Children's Hosp., San Francisco, 1963-80, dir., adolescent maternity ctr., 1967-77, chmn. med. edn. com., 1982-93, chmn. adv. sub-com. on breast health, 1983-1985; sr. staff com. U. Calif., San Francisco, 1967-80, house officer com. 1973-80, 87—; cons. broad-based genetic adv. com. Dept. Pub. Health State of Calif., 1977-83; mem. editorial adv. bd. Ob/Gyn Collected Letters Internat. Corr. Soc., 1975-94. Contbr. articles to profl. jours. Lt. (j.g.) USN, 1947-50. Named Outstanding Tchr. of Yr. Childrens Hosp., San Francisco, 1973-74, U. Calif. Med. Ctr. Dept. Ob-Gyn. and Reproductive Scis., 1977-78, Clin. Faculty Teaching award, 1986, Kaiser award for excellence in teaching, 1983; recipient Ortho Ob-Gyn Spotlight award, 1987, Life Time Achievement award Childrens Hosp., 1990, Charlotte C. Baer meml. award W.C. Med., 1992. Fellow ACS (bd. govs., specialty soc. gov. from Am. Coll. Ob-Gyn. 1984-88), Am. Coll. Ob-Gyn. (Nat. Dist. Svc. award 1986, v.p. 1987-88, capitol devel. com. 1986-88, health care commn. 1986-90, task force on voluntary rev. 1985-88, exec. com. mem. 1981-84, 87-88, chmn. coun. dist. 1983-84, chmn. dist. IX 1982-84, Calif. sect. dist. VIII chmn. 1980-81, vice-chmn. 1978-80); mem. AMA (rep. for ob-gyn. residency rev. com. 1975-81), Calif. Med. Soc., Calif. Med. Assn. (del. 1962-63, 81, 82, 83, relative value study com chmn. ob-gyn panel 1962-65, ob-gyn rep. to com. 1965-69, adv. com. to public 1982-86, adv. panel Ob-Gyn 1982-86), Calif. Acad. Medicine, Pacific Coast Ob-Gyn. Soc. (arrangements chmn. 1969, exec. bd. 1969, 70, 71, pres.-elect 1991-92, pres. 1992-93), San. Francisco County Med. Soc. (chmn. maternal and infant care com. 1973-74, cancer com. 1965-70), San. Francisco Gynecol. Soc. (pres. 1976-77), Med. Friend of Wine. Home: 3838 California St San Francisco CA 94118-1522

WEBB, HENRY ROBERT, theatre arts educator; b. L.A., June 11, 1938; s. Henry and Benita (Terrazas) W. BA, Calif. State U., Fresno, 1970; MA, Calif. State U., Fresno, 1975. Instr. West Hills Coll., Coalinga, Calif., 1970-71; grad. asst. Calif. State U., Fresno, 1972-74; prof. Bakersfield (Calif.) Coll., 1975—. Actor in plays for Cmty. Theatre, 1994, dir., 1993. With USN, 1957-60. Recipient Dept. award Calif. State U., 1968, 69; named Regional finalist Am. Coll. Theatre Festival, 1992. Mem. NEA, Calif. C.C. Coun. Roman Catholic. Office: Bakersfield Coll 1801 Panorama Dr Bakersfield CA 93305-1219

WEBB, JONELL, advertising professional; b. Elko, Nev., Dec. 29, 1945; d. Maurice Ernest and Edith Emily (Tremewan) Hageman; m. Larry Dale Parnell, June 28, 1969 (div. Apr. 1985); m. Thomas Dean Webb. AA, Porterville Coll., 1965. Tchr. St. Anne's Sch., Porterville, Calif., 1965-67, 71-72; adminstrv. sec. Teague Sch., Fresno, Calif., 1967-68; tchr. Woodville (Calif.) Elem. Sch., 1968-70; classified advt. mgr. Recorder, Porterville, 1970-71, 72-93, advt. dir., 1993—. Mem. steering com. Leadership Porterville, 1992; chair Pride in Porterville Com., 1990, Porterville Stampede, 1991; organizer Old Fashioned 4th in the Park, Porterville, 1991-94; bd. dirs. Porterville Coll. Found. Named Woman of Distinction by Soroptimist Internat., 1990, Woman of Yr. by Porterville C. of C., 1993. Mem. Calif. Classified Advt. Execs. (treas., pres.), Calif. Newspaper Advt. Execs. Assn., Western Classified Advt. Assn. Republican. Baptist. Home: PO Box 1904 Porterville CA 93258

WEBB, LEWIS M., retail executive; b. 1934. Owner Webb's Texaco Svc., Los Alamitos, Calif., 1960-72; pres. Bargain Rent-A-Car Inc., Cerritos, Calif., 1960—, L.M. Webb & Sons, Inc., Mission Viejo, Calif., 1988—; pres., CFO Webb Automotive Group, Inc., Cerritos, Calif., 1989—; pres. Buick Mart Inc., Cerritos, Cerritos Body Works, Inc., Irvine, Calif., Kit Fit Inc., Buena Park, Calif., Lew Webb's Irvine Toyota, Mr. Wheels Inc., Cerritos. Office: Webb Automotive Group Inc 18700 Studebaker Rd Cerritos CA 90703-5335

WEBB, RICHARD L., air industry service executive; b. 1932. With USAF, 1948-69; dir. Dynair Svc. Inc., McLean, Va., 1969—; pres., CEO Dynair Tech. Ariz., Inc., Phoenix, 1988—. Office: Dynair Tech of Arizona Inc 3737 E Bonanza Way Phoenix AZ 85034-3701*

WEBB, WELLINGTON E., mayor; BA in Edn. Colo. State Coll., 1964, MA in Edn. Univ. No. Colo., 1970; teacher, 1964-76; elected Colo. House of Reps., 1972, 74, 76; regional dir. HEW, 1977-81, governor's cabinet, 1981-87; elected auditor City of Denver, 1987-91, mayor, 1991—. Chmn. U.S. Conf. of Mayor's Task Forces on Violence, 1993—. Office: Office of Mayor City & County Bldg Rm 350 1437 Bannock St Denver CO 80202-5308

WEBBER, MARILYN ASPEN KAY, writer; b. Abilene, Tex., Nov. 22, 1961; d. George Caswell Sleep and Barbara Maxine (Vick) W. BA in Journalism, U. Okla., 1984; MFA in Screen Writing, Am. Film Inst., 1991. Tchrs. asst. Tarleton State U., Stephenville, Tex., 1988-89; writer, assoc. producer AFI, L.A., 1989-91; TV animation writer Gunther-Wahl Prodns.-ABC, L.A., 1992, Ruby/Spears-ABC, L.A., 1993-94; TV writer children's programs ABC-Greengrass Prodns., L.A., 1993-94, CBS-Allegra Films, L.A., 1994; children's programs animation writer ABC, L.A., 1994; Saturday morning animation writer DIC Entertainment-ABC, L.A., 1994; cons., Tex., 1993. Writer: (screenplays) How to Kill Howie?, 1987 (best screenplay), Mouth of the Cat, 1993 (semi-finalist Am.'s best). Mem. World Wildlife Fund, 1991; supporter Union Rescue Mission, L.A., 1991, Feed the Children, Oklahoma City, 1994, Habitat for Humanity Internat., Americus, Ga., 1994. Recipient Acad. award nomination Motion Picture Acad., 1992, Most Notable Children's Video award Am. Libr. Assn., 1993, nomination Humanitas, 1994, award for advancement of learning in broadcasting NEA, 1994. Episcopalian.

WEBBER, MILO MELVIN, radiologist, educator; b. L.A., Sept. 27, 1930; s. George Clifford and Sophia (Binkowski) W.; m. Vivienne Marie Larson, Dec. 18, 1955 (div. Dec. 1987); children: Sonja Elizabeth, Linda Marie. Student, Calif. Inst. Tech., 1948-51; AB, UCLA, 1952, MD, 1955; LLB, La Salle Extension U., Chgo., 1973. Bar: Calif. 1974. From instr. to assoc. prof. radiology UCLA Sch. Medicine, 1960-74, prof., 1974—; bd. dirs. Omnimedical, Inc., Northbrook, Ill.; examiner Am. Bd. Radiology, 1975-78. Contbr. articles to profl. jours., chpts. to books in field. Chmn. L.A. County Dist. Med. Quality Rev. Com. of Med. Bd. Calif., 1978-87. Recipient rsch. grants NIH, Bethesda, Md., 1976-79, 1977-79, 1988—. Mem. Am. Coll. Radiology, Soc. Nuclear Medicine (pres. So. Calif. chpt. 1971), Radiol. Soc. N.Am., Calif. Med. Assn., L.A. County Med. Assn., Calif. Bar Assn.

WEBBER, PATRICK NEIL, diversified financial services company executive; b. Hanna, Alta., Can., Apr. 17, 1936; s. Charles and Katherine (McAuliffe) W.; m. Dorothy Platzer, Aug. 3, 1957; children: Barbara, Carol, Len, Lorne, Dianne. BS, U. Alta., 1957, BEd, 1962, PhD, 1973; MA, U. Mont., 1963. Mem. Alta. Legis. Assembly, 1975-90; former min. of energy Govt. of Alta., former min. of edn., former min. social svcs. and cmty. health, former assoc. min. telephones for Alta.; head Neil Webber Consulting Ltd., 1989—; chmn. Telus Corp., AGT Ltd.; former chmn. Alta. Govt. Telephones Commn.; bd. dirs. SNC-Lavalin Group Inc., Calgary Rsch. and Devel. Authority. Former mem. Mt. Royal Coll.; bd. govs. Can. Math. Congress. Mem. Assn. Inst. Rsch. Progressive Conservative. Roman Catholic. Home: 210 Edgeview Dr NW, Calgary, AB Canada T3A 4X5 Office: 411-1 Street SE 26th fl, Calgary, AB Canada T2G 4Y5

WEBBER, WILLIAM ALEXANDER, university administrator, physician; b. Nfld., Can., Apr. 8, 1934; s. William Grant and Hester Mary (Constable) W.; m. Marilyn Joan Robson, May 17, 1958; children—Susan Joyce, Eric Michael, George David. M.D., U. B.C., Can., Vancouver, 1958. Intern Vancouver Gen. Hosp., 1958-59; postdoctoral fellow Cornell U. Med. Coll., N.Y.C., 1959-61; asst. prof. medicine U. B.C., 1961-66, assoc. prof., 1966-69, prof., 1969—, dean faculty medicine, 1977-90, assoc. v.p. acad., 1990—. Mem. B.C. Med. Assn., Can. Assn. Anatomists, Am. Assn. Anatomists, Can. Nephrological Soc. Home: 2478 Crown St, Vancouver, BC Canada V6R 3V8 Office: U BC Old Adminstrn Bldg, 6328 Memorial Rd Rm 132, Vancouver, BC Canada V6T 1Z2

WEBEL, CHARLES PETER, human science and psychology educator; b. L.A., Dec. 23, 1948; s. James Webel and Jeanne (Herbert) Mackavanagh. BA, U. Calif., Berkeley, 1969, PhD, 1976; postgrad., Harvard U., 1989-91. Chair Ctr. Ednl. Change, Berkeley, 1968-70; filmmaker Nat. Ednl. TV, N.Y.C., 1969-70; lectr. social scis. U. Calif., Berkeley, 1976-78; dir. grad. programs Western Inst. Social Rsch., Berkeley, 1977-78; asst. prof. sociology New Coll., Sarasota, Fla., 1978-79; exec. editor social scis. Columbia U. Press, N.Y.C., 1980-83; asst. prof. philosophy Calif. State U., Chico, 1984-89; teaching fellow gen. edn. Harvard U., Cambridge, Mass., 1990-91; gen. editor scholarly book series Peter Lang Pub., N.Y.C., 1990—; rsch. assoc. dept. anthropology U. Calif., Berkeley, 1990—; prof. human sci. and psychology Saybrook Inst., San Francisco, 1990—. Author, editor: Marcus Critical Theory and The Promise of Utopia, 1988; filmmaker: Lifestyle, 1969. Organizer Congress Racial Equality, N.Y.C., 1965-66; West Coast sec. Internat. Philosophers for Prevention Nuclear Omnicide, 1985-89. Fulbright scholar Fulbright Commn., Germany, 1971-72; regents fellow U. Calif., Berkeley, 1972-73, dissertation fellow Social Sci. Rsch. Coun., N.Y.C., 1974-76, grad. fellow Harvard U., 1989-91, NEH summer fellow Harvard U., 1986. Mem. Am. Philos. Assn., Am. Sociol. Assn., Internat. Soc. Polit. Psychology, Commonwealth Club Calif., World Affairs Coun. Office: Saybrook Inst 450 Pacific Ave San Francisco CA 94133-4640

WEBER, ARNOLD I., lawyer; b. Little Cedar, Iowa, Oct. 4, 1926. PhB, Marquette U., 1949; MA, Harvard U., 1950; JD, George Washington U., 1954, LLM, 1956. Bar: D.C. 1954, Md. 1961, Calif. 1962, U.S. Dist Ct. D.C. 1954, (no. dist.) Calif. 1962, (cen. dist.) Calif. 1992, U.S. Ct. Claims 1960, U.S. Tax Ct. 1965, U.S. Ct. Appeals (D.C. cir.) 1954, (9th cir.) 1962, (fed. cir.) 1991, U.S. Supreme Ct. 1959. Lawyer Housing and Home Fin., Washington, 1954, Tariff Commn., Washington, 1954-55, FCC, Washington, 1955-56, IRS, Washington, 1956-61; assoc. Brobeck, Phleger & Harrison, San Francisco, 1961-64; sr. gen. atty. So. Pacific Transp., San Francisco, 1964-84; western tax counsel Santa Fe Pacific Corp., San Francisco, 1985-88; pvt. practice San Francisco, 1988—. With USNR, 1944-46, PTO. Mem. Olympic Club, San Francisco C. of C., ABA, Bar Assn. San Francisco, State Bar of Calif. Office: 57 Post St Ste 612 San Francisco CA 94104-5023

WEBER, CHARLENE LYDIA, social worker; b. Phila., Mar. 2, 1943; d. Walter Gotlieb and Dorothy (Peart) W.; m. Billy Mack Carroll, Oct. 3, 1959 (div. Sept. 1974); children: Dorothy Patricia, Robert Walter, Lydia Baker, Billy Bob, Elizabeth Louise; m. John Edward Thomaston, Sept. 26, 1974 (div. July 1986); m. Stan Koski, Dec. 31, 1994. BSW with honors, Coll. Santa Fe, 1983; MSW, N.Mex. Highlands U., 1988. Client service agt. I Social Svcs. div. Dept. Human Svcs., Albuquerque, 1975-78, client service agt. IV, 1978-83; social worker II Social Svcs. div. Dept. Human Svcs., Bernalillo, N.Mex., 1983, social worker III, 1983—. Mem. Nat. Assn. Social Workers, N.Mex. Council on Crime and Deliquency, Albuquerque Retarded Assn., Child Welfare League. Democrat. Home: 72 Umber Ct NE Albuquerque NM 87124-2454 Office: Dept Human Svcs Div Social Svcs PO Box 820 Bernalillo NM 87004-0820

WEBER, CHARLES EUGENE, property management company executive; b. Tokoma Park, Md., Mar. 22, 1947; s. John Harrington and Gale (Lough) W.; m. Nina Weber, July 21, 1975; children: David, Lory, Adam. BBA, U. Miami, Coral Gables, Fla., 1969; postgrad., Calif. State U., L.A., 1976-

real estate broker. Sales mgr. Kay Pro Computers, Calif.; real estate broker A-Z Real Estate, La Mesa, Calif.; pres. A-Z Property Mgmt., La Mesa, Child Devel. Ctr., 1986—. Coach Little League. Home: 1443 San Elijo Ave # B Cardiff By The Sea CA 92007-2419

WEBER, CHARLES WALTER, nutrition educator; b. Harold, S.D., Nov. 30, 1931; s. Walter Earl and Vera Jean (Scott) W.; m. Marylou Merkel Adam, Feb. 3, 1961; children: Matthew, Scott. BS, Colo. State U., 1956, MS, 1958; PhD, U. Ariz., 1966. Research asst. U. Ariz., Tucson, 1963-66, asst. prof., 1966-68, assoc. prof., 1969-72, prof. nutrition, 1973—; cons. Hermosillo, Mex., 1970-74, Inst. of Health, Cairo, 1981-82, U. Fortaleza, Rio de Janiero, 1986. Contbr. articles to sci. jours. Served as cpl. U.S. Army, 1952-54. Mem. Am. Assn. Cereal Chemists, Am. Inst. Nutrition, Inst. Food Technologists, N.Y. Acad. Scis., Am. Soc. Clin. Nutrition, Poultry Sci. Assn., Ariz. Referees Assn., Sigma Xi. Club: Randolph Soccer (Tucson) (pres. 1976-79). Home: 4031 E Calle De Jardin Tucson AZ 85711-3410 Office: U Ariz Dept Nutritional Sci 309 Shantz Bldg Tucson AZ 85721

WEBER, CONSTANCE LYNN, dietitian; b. Santa Monica, Calif., Aug. 17, 1955; d. Richard Harry and Loretta Mary Estelle (Kennedy) Bayne; m. Dennis James Weber, Aug. 19, 1989; 1 child, Megan Anne. BA, Whittier Coll., 1977; MS, U. Ariz., 1978. Registered dietitian. Staff dietitian Mayo Clinic, Rochester, Minn., 1980-87; lead dietitian Mayo Clinic, Scottsdale, Ariz., 1987-95, staff dietitian, 1995—. Author book chpts. Recipient Svc. Recognition award Mayo Clinic, Scottsdale, 1993. Mem. Am. Dietetic Assn., Ctrl. Ariz. Dist. Assn., Nat. Kidney Found., PEO (chaplain, treas., v.p.).

WEBER, DAVID C(ARTER), librarian; b. Waterville, Maine, July 25, 1924; s. Carl J. and Clara (Carter) W.; m. Natalie McLeod, Dec. 26, 1952; children: L. Jefferson, Christopher Q., Douglas McLeod, Sarah N. A.B., Colby Coll., 1947; student, Bowdoin Coll., 1946; B.S., Columbia U., 1948; A.M., Harvard U., 1953; postgrad., Rutgers U., 1956. Cataloger, asst. to dir., asst. dir. libraries Harvard U., 1948-61; asst. dir., assoc. dir. Stanford (Calif.) U., 1961-69, dir. libraries, 1969-91, Ida M. Green chair, 1987-91, dir. librs. emeritus, 1991; cons. to acad. libraries, pub. and pvt. instns. and orgns., U.S. and Can. Author: (with others) College and University Accreditation Standards, 1958, (with R.D. Rogers) University Library Administration, 1971; (with P.D. Leighton) Planning Academic and Research Library Buildings, 1986; editor: Studies in Library Administrative Problems, 1960; contbr. articles to profl. jours. Served with AUS, 1943-46. Council on Library Resources fellow, 1970. Mem. ALA, Assn. Coll. and Rsch. Libraries (pres. 1981-82), Assn. Libr. Collections and Tech. Svcs. (pres. 1967-68). Clubs: Roxburghe (San Francisco); Book of Calif. Office: 863 Lathrop Dr Stanford CA 94305-1054

WEBER, DAVID OLLIER, journalist; b. Cin., Feb. 28, 1938; s. George W. Jr. and Eleanor Marchant (Kilby) W.; m. Christine Heath Leigh-Taylor, Nov. 28, 1964; children: Alexandra Leigh-Taylor, Peter Christian, Erec-Michael Ollier. Cert. Norwegian studies, U. Oslo, 1958; BA in Philosophy, U. Cinn., 1959; postgrad., Columbia U., 1959-60, U. Calif., Berkeley, 1964. Gen. assignment reporter The Daily Review, Hayward, Calif., 1964-66; freelance sci. writer and tech. editor, 1966-74; pub. rels. rep. Port of Oakland, Calif., 1975-79; sr. editor Pacific Gas and Electric Co., San Francisco, 1979-80; free-lance writer and editor, 1980—. Author: Health for the Harvesters, 1970, Oakland: Hub of the West, 1981; contbg. editor: The Healthcare Forum Jour., 1994—, Strategies For Healthcare Excellence, 1994—; editor: MRI Industry Report, 1994—. Lt. (j.g.) USNR, 1961-64. Recipient Gold Quill awards Internat. Assn. Bus. Communicators, 1975, 79, Best Bus. Mag. Feature award L.A. Press Club, 1980, Best Feature Story award Assn. Area Bus. Publs., 1984, Golden Hammer award Nat. Assn. Home Builders, 1985; fellow Woodrow Wilson Fellowship Found., Princeton, N.J., 1959. Mem. Phi Beta Kappa. Home: 1186 Euclid Ave Berkeley CA 94708-1640

WEBER, EICKE RICHARD, physicist; b. Muennerstadt, Germany, Oct. 28, 1949; s. Martin and Irene (Kistner) W.; m. Magdalene Graff (div. 1983); m. Zuzanna Liliental, June 10, 1985. BS, U. Koeln, Fed. Republic of Germany, 1970, MS, 1973, PhD, 1976, Dr.Habil., 1983. Sci. asst. U. Koeln, 1976-82; rsch. asst. U. Lund, Sweden, 1982-83; asst. prof. Dept. Material Sci. U. Calif., Berkeley, 1983-87, assoc. prof., 1987-91, prof. materials sci., 1991—; prin. investigator Lawrence Berkeley Lab., 1984—; vis. prof. Tohoku U., Sendai, Japan, 1990; cons. in field; internat. fellow Inst. for Study of Defects in Solids, SUNY, Albany, 1978-79; chmn. numerous confs.; lectr. in field. Editor: Defect Recognition and Image Processing in III-V Compounds, 1987, Imperfections in III-V Compounds, 1993; co-editor: Chemistry and Defects in Semiconductor Structures, 1989, others; series co-editor: Semiconductors and Semimetals, 1991—, Growth and Characterization of Semiconductor Materials, 1992—; contbr. over 200 articles to profl. jours. Recipient IBM Faculty award, 1984, Humboldt U.S. Sr. Scientist award, 1994; rsch. grantee Dept. of Energy, 1984—, Office Naval Rsch., 1985—, Air Force Office Sci. Rsch., 1988—, NASA, 1988-90, Nat. Renewable Energy Lab., 1992—. Mem. IEEE (sr.), Am. Phys. Soc., Materials Rsch. Soc. Office: 587 Evans Hall Dept Materials Sci U Calif Berkeley CA 94720

WEBER, EUGEN, historian, educator, author; b. Bucharest, Romania, Apr. 24, 1925; came to U.S., 1955; s. Emanuel and Sonia (Garrett) W.; m. Jacqueline Brument-Roth, June 12, 1950. Student, Institut d'etudes politiques, Paris, 1948-49, 51-52; M.A., Emmanuel Coll., Cambridge U., 1954, M.Litt., 1956. History supr. Emmanuel Coll., 1953-54; lectr. U. Alta., 1954-55; asst. prof. U. Iowa, 1955-56; asst. prof. history UCLA, 1956, assoc. prof., 1959-63, prof., 1963—, Joan Palevsky prof. modern European history, 1984—, chmn. dept., 1965-68; dir. study center UCLA, France, 1968-70; dean social scis. UCLA, 1976-77, dean Coll. Letters and Scis.,, 1977-82; Ford faculty lectr. Stanford U., 1965; Patten lectr. Ind. U., 1981; vis. prof. Collège de France, Paris, 1983; directeur d'études Ecole des hautes études, Paris, 1984-85; Christian Gauss lectr., Princeton U., 1990. Author: Nationalist Revival in France, 1959, The Western Tradition, 1959, Paths to the Present, 1960, Action Française, 1962, Sata Franc-Maçon, 1964, Varieties of Fascism, 1964 (with H. Rogger) The European Right, 1965, A Modern History of Europe, 1970, Europe Since 1715, 1972, Peasants into Frenchmen, 1976 (Commonwealth prize Calif. 1977), La Fin des terroirs, 1983 (Prix de la Socièté des gens de lettres 1984), France Fin-de-siècle, 1986 (Commonwealth prize Calif. 1987), My France, 1990, Movements, Currents, Trends, 1991, The Hollow Years, 1994, Prix littéraire Etats-Unis, 1995; adv. editor Jour. Contemporary History, 1966—, French History, 1985—, French Cultural Studies, 1990—, Am. Scholar, 1992. Served as capt. inf. Brit. Army, 1943-47. Recipient Luckman Disting. Teaching award UCLA Alumnae Assn., 1992; decorated Ordre Nat. des Palmes Academiques, France; Fulbright fellow, 1952, 82-83; research fellow Am. Philos. Soc., 1959, Social Sci. Research Council, 1959-61, Am. Council Learned Socs., 1962; Guggenheim fellow, 1963-64; NEH sr. fellow, 1973-74, 82-83. Fellow Netherlands Inst. Advanced Studies, Assn. française de science politique, Am. Acad. Arts and Scis.; mem. Am. Hist. Assn., Soc. d'histoire moderne, Soc. French Hist. Studies, Phi Beta Kappa (hon., Ralph Waldo Emerson prize 1977, senator 1988—).

WEBER, FRED J., retired state supreme court justice; b. Deer Lodge, Mont., Oct. 6, 1919; s. Victor N. and Dorothy A. (Roberts) W.; m. Phyllis M. Schell, June 2, 1951; children: Anna Marie, Donald J., Mark W., Paul V. B.A., U. Mont., 1943, J.D., 1947. Bar: Mont. 1947. Atty. Kuhr & Weber, Havre, Mont., 1947-55, Weber, Bosch & Kuhr, and successors, 1956-80; justice Supreme Ct. Mont., Helena, 1981-95. Served to capt. inf. U.S. Army, 1943-46. Fellow Am. Bar Found., Am. Coll. Probate Counsel; mem. ABA, Am. Judicature Soc. Office: Mont Supreme Ct Justice Bldg 215 N Sanders St Helena MT 59601-4522

WEBER, GAIL L., lawyer; b. Tacoma, June 14, 1955; d. Arthur Dean and Vera Martha (Grimm) Lundgren; AB cum laude, Vassar Coll., 1977; JD cum laude, U. Puget Sound., 1980. Bar: Wash. 1981. Legal intern Reed, McClure, Moceri & Thonn, Seattle, 1979, Burgess & Kennedy, Tacoma, 1979-80; legal intern Lee, Smart, Cook, Martin & Patterson, P.S., Inc., Seattle, 1980-81, assoc., 1981-92; prin. Law Offices Gail L. Weber, Bothell, Wash., 1992—. Vestry com. Queen Anne Luth. Ch., 1983-86, v.p. of congregation, 1988, 89, mem. worship and music com., 1982-83, 84-86, parish edn. com., 1983-84. Recipient Am. Jurisprudence Book award in Criminal [illegible] ...tions and Business Planning, 1980. Mem. ABA, Fed. Bar Assn., Am. Trial Lawyers Assn., Wash. State Bar Assn., King County Bar Assn., Wash. State Trial Lawyers Assn., Order of Barristers, Wash. State Vassar Club (chmn. alumni admissions 1983-85, rep. 1986-92). Democrat. Avocations: scuba diving, tennis, classical music, needlepoint and stitchery. Office: Law Offices Gail L Weber 19125 Northcreek Pky Ste 120 Bothell WA 98011

WEBER, GEORGE RICHARD, financial consultant, writer; b. The Dalles, Oreg., Feb. 7, 1929; s. Richard Merle and Maud (Winchell) W.; m. Nadine Hanson, Oct. 12, 1957; children: Elizabeth Ann Weber Katooli, Karen Louise Weber Zaro, Linda Marie. BS, Oreg. State U., 1950; MBA, U. Oreg., 1962. CPA, Oreg. Sr. trainee U.S. Nat. Bank of Portland (Oreg.), 1950-51; jr. acct. Ben Musa, CPA, The Dalles, 1954; tax and audit asst. Price Waterhouse, Portland, 1955-59; sr. acct. Burton M. Smith, CPA, Portland, 1959-62; pvt. practice, Portland, 1962—; lectr. acctg. Portland State Coll.; expert witness fin. and tax matters. Sec.-treas. Mt. Hood Kiwanis Camp, Inc., 1965. Exec. counselor SBA; mem. fin. com., powerlifting team U.S. Powerlifting Fedn., 1984, amb. People to People, China, 1987. With AUS, 1951-53. Decorated Bronze Star. Mem. AICPA, Internat. Platform Assn., Oreg. Hist. Soc.,Oreg. City Traditional Jazz Soc., Order of the Holy Cross Jerusalem, Order St. Stephen the Martyr, Order St. Gregory the Illuminator, Knightly Assn. St. George the Martyr., World Literary Acad., Portland C.S. Lewis Soc., Beta Alpha Psi, Pi Kappa Alpha. Republican. Lutheran. Clubs: Kiwanis, Portland Track, City (Portland); Multnomah Athletic; Sunrise Toastmasters. Author: Small Business Long-term Finance, 1962, A History of the Coroner and Medical Examiner Offices, 1963, CPA Litigation Service References, 1991; contbr. to profl. publs. and poetry jours. Home: 2603 NE 32nd Ave Portland OR 97212-3611

WEBER, JOAN L., library director; b. Renton, Wash., June 21, 1948; d. Karl J. and Mildred C. Weber. Br. clk., head bookmobile, pub. info. officer Spokane (Wash.) County Libr. Dist., 1971-74; part-time tech. lab. asst. U. Denver, 1976-77; dir. Learning Resource Ctr. Northeastern Jr. Coll., Sterling, Colo., 1977-80; dir. Pend Oreille County Libr. Dist., Newport, Wash., 1980-81; br. libr. Manito br. and East Side br. Spokane Pub. Libr., 1981-89, acting mgr. facilities, 1989, mgr. Manito br., 1990-91, mgr. Shadle br., 1991-92; dir. libr. and media svcs. Yakima (Wash.) Valley C.C., 1992—; tchr. mgmt. courses Nat. Mgmt. Assn., Inst. Cert Profl. Mgrs., Spokane; mem. Wash. State Coun. on Continuing Edn.; mem. Wash. State Adv. Coun. on Librs. Apptd. facilitator Wash. State Libr. Gov.'s Conf. on Libr. and Info. Svcs.; charter commr. Greater Spokane Women's Commn.; apptd. chair Older Women's Task Force; mem. Spokane City Women's Issues Adv. Com. Recipient Nat. Mgmt. Chpt. Exec. of Yr., City of Spokane, 1991-92. Mem. ALA, Am. Assn. Women in C.C.s, Assn. Coll. and Rsch. Librs., Nat. Coun. Instnl. Adminstrs., Wash. Libr. Assn. (1st v.p. com., publicity chair 1994 ann. conf.), P.E.O. (state chair scholar award, chpt. pres., pre. internat. conv.), Rotary (exec. bd., chair scholarship com.), Beta Phi Mu. Office: Yakima Valley CC PO Box 1647 Yakima WA 98907-1647

WEBER, MARIAN FRANCES, laboratory administrator, educator; b. L.A., Mar. 25, 1951; d. Charles Robert and Dorothy Elizabeth (Welch) Howseman; m. Daniel Mark Babcock, July 13, 1972 (div. 1977); 1 child, Angela Dawn Babcock; m. Michael Patrick Weber, July 24, 1984; 1 child, Benjamin Michael. ScB in Chemistry, Brown U., 1973. Lab. tech. Med. Coll. Ga., Augusta, 1973; analytical sci. United Mchts. & Mfg., Langley, S.C., 1973-75; analytical chemist Saw River Ecology Lab., Aiken, S.C., 1976-82; chief chemist Enwright Lab., Greenville, S.C., 1983-86; chief chemist Laidlaw Environ. Svcs., Roebuck, S.C., 1986-90, lab. mgr., 1990-92; lab. mgr. U.S. Pollution Control, Inc., Salt Lake City, 1993-95; lab. supervisor FMC Wyo. Corp., Green River, 1995—. Mem. Am. Chem. Soc., S.C. Lab. Mgmt. Soc. (v.p. 1986, pres. 1992), Am. Assn. Lab. Analysts. Baptist. Office: FMC Westvaco Rd Green River WY 82935

WEBER, MOLLY SMITH, sales executive; b. Durham, N.C., Sept. 4, 1957; d. H. Ralph and Sally Ann (Simmons) Smith; m. Walter Charles Weber, July 13, 1985 (dec.). BA in Psychology, Yale U., 1979; MA in Edn., Stanford U., 1980. Dir. aquatics SUNY, Purchase, 1980-81; sales rep. Prentice-Hall, Inc., Englewood Cliffs, N.J., 1981-83; sales rep. West Ednl. Pub., St. Paul, 1983-85, acquisitions editor, 1985-89; sales mgr. western region MacMillan Pub. Co., 1989-92; sales mgr. western region Houghton Mifflin Co., 1992-93, v.p., 1993-95. Active Dem. Polit. Campaigns, 1987—. Mem. NOW. Avocations: swimming, snow and water skiing, running, photography. Home: 1626 S Syracuse St Denver CO 80221

WEBER, ROBERT J., education educator, law educator; b. Detroit, June 6, 1936. BS, Ariz. State Univ., 1959; PhD in Psychology, Princeton U., 1962; NSF Postdoctoral Fellow, Princeton Univ., 1962-63. Asst. prof. C.W. Post Coll. of Long Island Univ., N.Y., 1963-64, Kenyon Coll., Gambier, Ohio, 1964-67; assoc. prof. Okla. State Univ., Stillwater, 1967-73, prof., 1973-93; cons. on tech., creativity, collaboration, 1995—; vis. prof. Univ. Oregon, 1974-75, Harvard Univ., 1985-86, Univ. N.Mex., 1992-95; adv. Assn. Sci. and Tech. Ctrs. Co-author: (with R.J. & Perkins) Inventive Minds: Creativity in Technology, 1992, (with R.J.) Forks, Phonographs and Hot Air Balloons: A Field Guide to Inventive Thinking, 1992. contbg. numerous articles to profl. jours; canadian broadcasting series for t.v.: Suddenly a Light Come On, 1987. Woodrow Wilson fellow Princeton Univ., 1959-60, NIH Predoctoral Rsch. fellow Princeton Univ., 1962-63, NIMH Rsch. grantee. Mem. Psychonomic Soc., Southwestern Psychol. Assn., Am. Assn. Univ. Profs., Okla. Inventors Congress, Invention Devel. Soc., Soc. for the Social Studies of Sci., Am. Psychol. Soc. Office: 9516 Avenida De La Luna NE Albuquerque NM 87111-1602

WEBER, SAMUEL, editor; b. N.Y.C., July 31, 1926; s. Bernard and Gertrude (Ellenberg) W.; m. Eileen Gloria Hornstein, Mar. 5, 1950; children—Bruce Jay, Robert Matthew. B.S. in Elec. Engring, Va. Poly. Inst., 1947. Engr. N.Y. Bd. Transp., 1948-50, U.S. Naval Shipyard, Bklyn., 1950-52, Barlow Engring. Co., N.Y.C., 1952-54; engring. supr. Curtiss Wright Corp., Woodridge, N.J., 1954-56; electronics engr. Loral Electronics Corp., N.Y.C., 1957-58; with Electronics mag., N.Y.C., 1958-67, assoc. mng. editor, 1968-70, exec. editor, 1970-79, editor in chief, 1979-84, exec. tech. editor, 1984-88, editor-at-large, 1988-92; editor in chief Electrotechnology mag., N.Y.C., 1968—; pres. Samuel Weber & Assocs., 1988-91, Samuel Weber & Assocs., Inc., 1991—; contbg. editor Asic & Eda Magazine, 1991—; spl. projects editor Electronic Engring. Times, 1992—. Author: Modern Digital Circuits, 1964, Optoelectronic Devices and Circuits, 1968, Large and Medium Scale Integration, 1974, Circuits for Electronics Engineers, 1977, Electronic Circuits Notebook, 1981. Served with AUS, 1944-46. Mem. IEEE (life). Home and Office: 4242 E Allison Rd Tucson AZ 85712-1039

WEBER, SUSAN LEE, marketing consultant; b. Honolulu, Nov. 30, 1948; d. Kenneth Charles and Valerie (June) W. BBA, San Jose (Calif.) State U., 1970; postgrad., U. Calif., Berkeley, 1972-73, Pepperdine U., 1977-78; Cert. in Mktg., Harvard U. Small bus. organizer VISTA, Roseville, N.C., 1970-72; cosmetics buyer USN Commissary Supply, Oakland, Calif., 1972-74; cosmetics product mgr. Shaklee Corp., San Francisco, 1974-76; mktg. mgr. Max Factor, Inc., Hollywood, Calif., 1976-81; v.p. electronic mktg. Bank of Am., San Francisco, 1981-83, v.p. bank card merchandising, 1983-85, v.p., upscale mktg., sales, 1985-88; pres. Mktg. Fundamentals, San Francisco, 1988—. Mem. Am. Mktg. Assn., Bank Mktg. Assn., Bay Area Women's Network, NAFE, Fin. Insts. Mktg. Assn. Republican. Presbyterian. Office: Mktg Fundamentals 977 E Stanley Blvd Ste 227 San Francisco CA 94102-2873

WEBER, WILHELM K., language professional; b. Cologne, Germany, Dec. 13, 1939; came to U.S., 1978; naturalized, 1985; s. Matthias and Maria (Eck) W.; m. Maria Angela Gradenigo, Nov. 30, 1968; children: Armelle, Philippe. MA, U. Geneva, 1964. Freelance conf. interpreter German, English, Spanish, Italian, Dutch langs. Geneva, 1964-78; adj. prof. U. Geneva, 1964-78; program head Monterey (Calif.) Inst. Internat. Studies, 1978-80, dept. chair, 1980-85, dean grad. div. translation and interpretation, 1985-91; pres. Lang. Svcs. Internat., Inc., Carmel, Calif., 1991—; cons. Govt. of Hong Kong, Govt. of Province of Ont., Govt. of France in Guadalupe, U.S. Dept. State; presenter program Moscow Sch. Translation and Interpretation, Hankuk U. Fgn. Studies, Seoul, Korea; speaker at internat. confs. and seminars. Contbr. articles to profl. publs. Vol., trained shelter mgr. ARC. Mem. No. Calif. Translators Assn., Am. Translators Assn., Internat. Assn. Conf. Interpreters (past. exec. sec.), UN Assn. of USA (past pres. Monterey Bay chpt., past treas. No. Calif. div.), Sons of Italy in Am. Republican. Roman Catholic. Office: Lang Svcs Internat Inc 26555 Carmel Rancho Blvd Carmel CA 93923-8748

WEBER, WILLIAM PALMER, chemistry educator; b. Washington, Nov. 7, 1940; s. Frederick Palmer and Lillian (Dropkin) W.; m. Heather Ross Wilson, Oct. 10, 1963; children: Edward Palmer, Robert Owen, Justin Sprague, Nathaniel Pitman. BS in Chemistry, U. Chgo., 1963; MS in Chemistry, Harvard U., 1965, PhD in Chemistry, 1968. Rsch. chemist Dow Chem. Co., Wayland, Mass., 1967-68; asst. prof. chemistry U. So. Calif., L.A., 1968-72, assoc. prof., 1972-78, prof., 1978—, chmn. dept. chemistry, 1986-89; exec. assoc. dir. Loker Hydrocarbon Rsch. Inst., 1992—; chair univ. admissions com. U. So. Calif., 1980-84, pres. faculty senate, 1985-86. Author: Phase Transfer Catalysis in Organic Synthesis, 1977, Silicon Reagents for Organic Synthesis, 1983. Mem. Phi Beta Kappa (U. Chgo. chpt.), Phi Kappa Phi (recipient award for scholarly work 1983). Home: 3341 Country Club Dr Los Angeles CA 90019-3535 Office: U So Calif Loker Hydrocarbon Rsch Inst Los Angeles CA 90089-1661

WEBSTER, GARY DEAN, geology educator; b. Hutchinson, Kans., Feb. 15, 1934; s. John Raymond and Mable Fae (Randles) W.; m. Beverly Eileen Wilson, Aug. 30, 1964; children—Dean, Karissa. Student Hutchinson Jr. Coll., 1951-53; B.S. in Geol. Engring., U. Okla., 1956; M.S. in Geology, U. Kans., 1959; Ph.D. in Geology, UCLA, 1966. Geologist, Amerada Petroleum Corp., Williston, N.D., 1956-57, Belco Petroleum Corp., Big Piney, Wyo., 1960; lectr. Calif. Luth. Coll., Thousand Oaks, 1963-64; curator UCLA, 1964-65; asst. prof. San Diego State U., 1965-68, prof. geology Wash. State U., Pullman, 1968—, chmn. dept., 1980-85 . Contbr. numerous articles to profl. jours. Fellow Geol. Soc. Am.; mem. Am. Inst. Profl. Geologists, Paleontol. Soc. Am. (Western regional chmn. 1979-80), Soc. Econ. Paleontologists and Mineralogists, Paleontol. Assn. Office: Wash State U Dept Geology Pullman WA 99164

WEBSTER, JOHN M., biologist, educator; b. Wakefield, Yorkshire, England, May 5, 1936; s. Colin Ernest and Marion Webster; m. Carolyn Ann McGillivray, May 15, 1970; children: Gordon John, Sandra Jane. BSc, Imperial Coll. London U., 1958, PhD, 1962, DSc, 1988. Scientific officer Rothamsted Experimental Sta., Harpenden, England, 1961-66; rsch. scientist Agrl. Can. Rsch. Inst., Belleville, Can., 1966-67; assoc. prof. dept. biol. scis. Simon Fraser U., Burnaby, B.C., Can., 1967-71, prof., 1971—, chmn. dept. biol. scis., 1974-76, dean sci., 1976-80, assoc. v.p. acad., 1980-85, dean grad. studies, 1982-85, rsch. prof., 1987; pres. Sci. World, Vancouver, 1980-82, Vancouver Pub. Aquarium, 1990-92; mem. Sci. Coun. Can., 1982-89, Premier's Adv. Coun. on Sci. and Tech., 1991—; v.p. Tynehead Zool. Soc., Vancouver, 1984-88. Editor: Economic Nematology, 1972; co-editor: Plant Parasitic Nematodes in Temperate Agriculture, 1993. Fellow Linnean Soc. London, Soc. Nematologists (pres. 1982-83); mem. Can. Soc. Zoologists, Can. Phytopathol. Soc., European Soc. Nematologists, British Soc. Parasitology, Am. Soc. Parasitology. Office: Simon Fraser U, Dept Biol Scis, Burnaby, BC Canada V5A 1S6

WEBSTER, ROBIN WELANDER, interior designer; b. Bethesda, Md., Sept. 24, 1956; d. Robert Oscar and Patricia (Benson) W.; m. Bryan Douglas Webster, Oct. 9, 1982. BA, Mary Washington Coll., Fredericksburg, Va., 1978. Design asst. Del Mar (Calif.) Designs, 1983-84; ptnr., interior designer Corp. Design, Solana Beach, Calif., 1984-86; owner, mgr. R Designs, San Diego, 1986—. Bd. dirs. Save Our Heritage Orgn., San Diego, 1986-92, pres., 1988-89; vol. San Diego Mus. Art, 1986—; bd. dirs. Contemporaries San Diego Mus. Art, 1989-95; del. Calif. Legis. Conf. on Interior Design. Lt. USN, 1978-83. Mem. Internat. Interior Design Assn. (com. chmn. San Diego 1989—), Nat. Coun. Interior Design (cert.), Calif. Coun. Interior Design (cert.), Color Mktg. Group.

WEBSTER, RONALD LEWIS, structural engineer; b. Salt Lake City, Aug. 23, 1936; s. Wesley Owen and Ruth (Holmes) W.; m. Linda Helen Hall, Apr. 16, 1960; children: Mark, Adeena, David, Ronna, Ann, John, Paul, Scott, Brent, Lori Jo, Brian, Adam, Chelsea. Student, U. Utah, 1955-57; BS in Math., Utah State U., 1965; MS in Mech. Engring., Brigham Young U., 1969; PhD in Civil Engring., Cornell U., 1976. Registered profl. engr., N.Y. Rsch. technician Raytheon Co., Lawrence, Mass., 1960; asst. engr. Thiokol Corp., Brigham City, Utah, 1960-64; engr. Thiokol Chem. Corp., Brigham City, Utah, 1966-67; sr. staff engr. Theokol Chem. Corp., Brigham City, Utah, 1977—; scientific programmer Boeing Airplane Co., Seattle, 1965-66; engr. Lockheed Propulsion Co., Redlands, Calif., 1967-68, GE Co., ESD, Syracuse, N.Y., 1969-77; cons. Brigham City, 1977—. Author: (computer program) SEADYN, 1976; contbr. articles to profl. jours. Mem. AIAA (assoc. fellow), ASME, Phi Kappa Phi. Home: 720 Eliason St Brigham City UT 84302-2268

WECHSLER, MARY HEYRMAN, lawyer; b. Green Bay, Wis., Jan. 8, 1948; d. Donald Hubert and Helen (Polcyn) Heyrman; m. Roger Wechsler, Aug. 1971 (div. 1977); 1 child, Risa Heyrman; m. David Jay Sellinger, Aug. 15, 1981; 1 stepchild, Kirk Benjamin; 1 child, Michael Paul. Student, U. Chgo., 1966-67, 68-69; BA, U. Wash., 1971; JD cum laude, U. Puget Sound, 1979. Bar: Wash. 1979. Assoc. Law Offices Ann Johnson, Seattle, 1979-81; ptnr. Johnson, Wechsler, Thompson, Seattle, 1981-83, Mussehl, Rosenbert et al, Seattle, 1987-88; pvt. practice, Seattle, 1984-87; ptnr. Wechsler, Besk, Erickson, Ross & Rubik, Seattle, 1988—; mem. Walsh Commn. on Jud. Selection; presenter in field. Author: Family Law in Washington, 1987, rev. edit., 1988, Marriage and Separation, Divorce and Your Rights, 1994; contbr. articles to legal pubs. Mem. Wash. State Ethics Adv. Com., 1992—; bd. dirs. Seattle LWV, 1991-92. Fellow Am. Acad. Matrimonial Lawyers (trustee Wash. state chpt. 1994, mem. Walsh commn. on jud. selection 1995); mem. ABA (mem. chmn. Wash. state 1987-88), Wash. State Bar Assn. (exec. com. family law sect. 1985-91, chair 1988-89, legis. com. 1991—, Outstanding Atty. of Yr. family law sect. 1988), Wash. Women Lawyers, King County Bar Assn. (legis. com. 1985—, vice chmn. 1990-91, chair family law sect. 1986-87, chair domestic violence com. 1986-87, trustee 1988-90, policy planning com. 1991-92, 2d v.p. 1992-93, 1st v.p., 1993-94, pres. 1994-95); mem. Walsh com. on jud. selection (1995), Nat. Conf. of Bar Pres. (comms. com. 1994—). Office: Wechsler Besk Erickson Ross & Roubik 701 5th Ave Seattle WA 98104-7016

WEDDLE, JUDITH ANN, social services administrator; b. Burlington, Iowa, Aug. 28, 1944; d. Kenneth Ivan and Betty Ruth (Neiswanger) Shipley; 1 child, Brian Douglas. BA, Midland Coll., 1966. Social worker Dodge County Welfare Dept., Fremont, Nebr., 1967-68; social worker L.A. County Dept. Pub. Social Svcs., 1969-71, appeals hearing specialist, 1971-78; supr., appeals hearing specialist L.A. Welfare Dept., 1978-86; human svcs. adminstr. Los Angeles Welfare Dept., 1986—. Pres. Gardena (Calif.) Hotline, 1971-72, Gardena Swimteam Parents, 1978-79; elder Presbyn. Ch., Gardena, 1987—; active Torrance (Calif.) Civic Chorale, 1989—.

WEDEL, MILLIE REDMOND, secondary school educator; b. Harrisburg, Pa., Aug. 18, 1939; d. Clair L. and Florence (Heiges) Aungst; BA, Alaska Meth. U., 1966; MEd, U. Alaska, Anchorage, 1972; postgrad. in comm. Stanford U., 1975-76; m. T.S. Redmond, 1956 (div. 1967); 1 child, T.S. Redmond II; m. Frederick L. Wedel, Jr., 1974 (div. 1986). Lic. third class broadcasting, FCC. Profl. model Charming Models & Models Guild of Phila., 1954-61; public rels. staff Haverford (Pa.) Sch., 1959-61; asst. dir. devel. in charge public rels. Alaska Meth. U., Anchorage, 1966, part-time lectr., 1966, 73; comm. tchr. Anchorage Sch. Dist., 1967—; owner Wedel Prodns., Anchorage, 1976-86; pub. rels. staff Alaska Purchase Centennial Exhibit, U.S. Dept. Commerce, 1967; writer gubernatorial campaign, 1971; part-time instr. Chapman Coll., 1990-93; adj. instr. U. Alaska, Anchorage, 1972, 77-79, 89—; cons. Cook Inlet Native Assn., 1978, No. Inst., 1979; judge Ark. Press Women's Writing Contest, 1990-91; sec. exec. bd. Alaska Dept. Edn. Profl. Tchg. Practices Commn., 1993—. Bd. dirs. Sta. KAKM, Alaska Pub. TV, membership chmn., 1978-80, nat. lay rep. to Pub. Broadcasting Svc. and Nat. Assn. Pub. TV Stas., 1979; bd. dirs. Ednl. Telecom. Consortium for Alaska, 1979, Mid-Hillside Community Coun., Municipality of Anchorage, 1979-80, 83-88, Hillside East Cmty. Coun., 1984-88, pres. 1984-85; rsch. writer, legal asst. Vinson & Elkins, Houston, 1981; v.p., bd. dirs. inlet view ASD Cmty. Sch., 1994-95, pres. 1995—; mem. Valley Forge Freedoms Found., Murdoch Scholarships, Valley Forge; bd. dirs. Rev.

Richard Gay Trust, Alaska and Pa., 1992—, Inlet View ASD Cmty. Sch., 1995—; comm. dept. edn. profl. teaching practices commn. State Alaska, 1993-95, sec. exec. bd. 1993—; active Anchorage Opera Guild, Anchorage Concert Assn. Recipient awards for newspapers, lit. mags.; award Nat. Scholastic Press Assn., 1968, 74, 77, Am. Scholastic Press Assn., 1981, 82, 83, 84; Alaska Coun. Econs., 1982, Merits award Alaska Dept. Edn., 1982, 93, Legis. commendation State of Alaska, Blue Ribbon award State Alaska, 1982, 93. Mem. NEA (AEA bldg. rep., state del. 70s, 80s, 94-95), Nat. Assn. Secondary Sch. Prins., Nat. Fedn. Interscholastic Speech and Debate Assn., Assn. Pub. Broadcasting (charter mem., nat. lay del. 1980), Indsl. TV Assn. (San Francisco and Houston 1975-81), Alaska Press Club (chmn. high sch. journalism workshops, 1968, 69, 73, awards for sch. newspapers, 1972, 74, 77), Alaska Fedn. Press Women (dir. 1978-86, 94-95, pres. 1995—, h.s. journalism competition youth projects dir., award for brochures, 1978, chair youth writing contest, 1994-95, pres. 1995—), Internat. Platform Assn., World Affairs Coun., Alaska Coun. Tchrs. of English, Chugach Electric (chair 1990, nomination com. for bd. dirs. 1988-90) Stanford Alumni Club (pres. 1982-84, 90-92), Capt. Cook Athletic Club, Alaska (Anchorage), Edgewater Beach Club, Glades Country Club (Naples, Fla.), Delta Kappa Gamma. Presbyterian. Office: PO Box 730 Girdwood AK 99587-0730

WEDGLE, RICHARD JAY, lawyer; b. Denver, Dec. 2, 1951; s. Joseph M. and Lillian E. (Brown) W.; m. Susan R. Mason, Oct. 17, 1987. BA, U. Calif., Berkeley, 1974; JD, U. Denver, 1978. Bar: Colo. 1978, U.S. Dist. Ct. Colo. 1978, U.S. Ct. Appeals (10th cir.) 1980. Ptnr. Cox, Wedgle & Padmore, P.C., Denver, 1978-85, Barnes, Wedgle & Shpall, P.C., Denver, 1986-87, Wedgle and Shpall, P.C., Denver, 1987—. Vol. coord. Dick Lamm for Gov., 1974, citizen adv. office, 1975; bd. dirs. Cherry Creek Improvement Assn., 1985-88. Mem. ABA, Colo. Bar Assn., Denver Bar Assn. Club: Denver Athletic. Home: 365 Marion St Denver CO 80218-3927 Office: Wedgle & Shpall PC 730 17th St Ste 230 Denver CO 80202-3506

WEED, RONALD DE VERN, engineering consulting company executive; b. Indian Valley, Idaho, Sept. 1, 1931; s. David Clinton and Grace Elizabeth (Lavendar) W.; m. Doris Jean Hohener, Nov. 15, 1953; children: Geraldine Gayle, Thomas De Vern, Cheryl Ann. BSChemE, U. So. Calif., 1957; MS in Chem. Engring., U. Wash., 1962; LLB, La Salle U., Chgo., 1975; postgrad., Century U., Beverly Hills, Calif., 1979—. Registered profl. engr., Washington, Calif. Devel. engr. GE Co., Richland, Washington, 1957-65, Battelle N.W. Labs., Richland, 1965-68; oper. plant engr. NIPAK, Inc., Kerens, Tex., 1968-72; aux. systems task engr. Babcock & Wilcox Co., Lynchburg, Va., 1972-74; materials and welding engr. Bechtel Group Cos., San Francisco, 1974-85; cons. engr. Cygna Energy Svcs., Walnut Creek, Calif., 1985-91; with inter city fund Cygna Energy Svcs., Oakland, Calif., 1991-94; with Gen. Physics Corp., Oakland, 1994—. Contbr. rsch. reports, papers and chpts. in books; patentee in field. With U.S. Army, 1951-53. Mem. Am. Inst. Chem. Engrs., Am. Welding Soc., Nat. Assn. Corrosion Engrs. (cert., sect. vice chmn. and chmn. 1962-68). Home and Office: 74 Sharon St Pittsburg CA 94565-1527

WEEDEN, MARY ANN, organizational development executive; b. Troy, N.Y., July 23, 1948; d. John James and Antionette Catherine Foley; m. Paul Joseph Weeden, Aug. 31, 1968; 1 child, Eric Paul. BSBA, Russell Sage Coll., 1978. Corp. rels .rep. Ariz. Pub. Svc., Phoenix, 1983-85, contract adminstr., 1985-88, sr. trainer mgmt. devel., internal cons., 1988-91; organizational devel. adminstr. Data Mgmt. div. Ariz. Dept. Adminstrn., Phoenix, 1991; quality circle leader and facilitator Ariz. Nuclear Power Project, Phoenix, 1988-91; cons., trainer Inroads of Phoenix, 1988-91. Editor The Signature, 1973. Candidates' forum coord. LWV, Albany, 1975-80; coord. Project S.H.A.R.E., Phoenix, 1984-85; exec. advisor Jr. Achievement, Phoenix, 1985-87, Bus. Leader Advisor award, 1986, 87; environ. issues coord. Maricopa County Platform, Phoenix, 1986. Recipient Community Action award Salvation Army, 1985. Mem. Am. Mgmt. Assn., Am. Bus. Women's Assn. (exec. bd. mem., edn. com. chmn. 1984-86), World Affairs Coun.

WEEKS, DOROTHY MAE, publishing executive; b. Shanghai, China, Jan. 18, 1924; d. Herbert Clarence and Anna Louise (Johnson) White; m. Howard Benjamin Weeks, Dec. 12, 1946; children: John Howard, Douglas Alan, Carolyn M., Donna Louise. RN, Glendale Adventist Med. ctr., 1946; BA, Columbia Union Coll., 1961; MA, Loma Linda U., 1964. Assoc. prof. nursing Loma Linda (Calif.) U. Sch. of Nursing, 1964-73; instr., inservice tng. Cottage Hosp., Santa Barbara, Calif., 1973-74; sec., bd. mgr. Woodbridge Press Pub. Co., Santa Barbara, Calif., 1974-84, pres., 1984-91, chmn. bd., 1991—. Mem. Santa Barbara Seventh-day Adventist Ch. Office: Woodbridge Press 815 De La Vina St Santa Barbara CA 93101-3254

WEEKS, ROBERT LEE, electronic engineer, test facility administrator; b. Woonsocket, R.I., Mar. 8, 1957; s. Joseph Bernard and Claire Lorraine (Jolicoeur) W.; m. Christine Ann Bentley; children: Barbara Ann, Christopher Lee. BSEE, U. Ariz., 1985, postgrad., 1987; postgrad., U. Phoenix, 1994—. Laborer ASARCO Mine Inc., Sahuarita, Ariz., 1979-82; test engr. EMI and TEMPEST br. U.S. Army Electronic Proving Ground, Ft. Huachuca, Ariz., 1985-88, chief EMI and TEMPEST br., 1988—; mem. MIL-STD-461 Joint Working Group, 1989-94; mem. DOD and industry E3 standards com. Dept. Def., 1994—. Bd. dirs. Bristol Park Neighborhood Assn., Tucson, 1994—. Served with USMC, 1975-79. Mem. IEEE (named Engr. of Yr. local chpt. 1994), Electromagnetic Compatibility Soc. of IEEE, Nat. Assn. Radio and Telecomms. Engrs. (cert. electromagnetic compatibility engr.). Democrat. Roman Catholic. Office: US Army Electronic Proving Ground STEEP-MT-E Fort Huachuca AZ 85613

WEEKS, WILFORD FRANK, geophysics educator, glaciologist; b. Champaign, Ill., Jan. 8, 1929; married; 2 children. BS, U. Ill., 1951, MS, 1953; PhD in Geology, U. Chgo., 1956. Geologist mineral deposits br. U.S. Geol. Survey, 1952-55; glaciologist USAF Cambridge Research Ctr., 1955-57; asst. prof. Washington U., St. Louis, 1957-62; adj. prof. earth scis. Dartmouth Coll., Hanover, N.H., 1962-85; glaciologist Cold Regions Rsch. and Engring. Lab., Hanover, 1962-89; chief scientist Alaska Synthetic Aperture Radar Facility, Fairbanks, 1986-93; prof. geophysics Geophys. Inst. U. Alaska, Fairbanks, 1986—; vis. prof. Inst. Low Temperature Sci. Hokkaido U., Sapporo, Japan, 1973; chair Arctic marine sci. USN Postgrad. Sch., Monterey, Calif., 1978-79; mem. earth sys. sci. com. NASA, Washington, 1984-87; advisor U.S. Arctic Rsch. Commn., divsn. polar programs NSF, Washington, 1987-88; chmn. NAS Com. on Cooperation with Russia in Ice Mechanics, 1991-92; mem. environ. task force MEDEA Cons. Group, 1992—. Capt. USAF, 1955-57. Fellow Arctic Inst. N.Am., Am. Geophys. Union; mem. NAE, Internat. Glaciological Soc. (v.p. 1969-72, pres. 1973-75, Seligman Crystal award 1989). Office: U Alaska Fairbanks Geophys Inst PO Box 757320 Fairbanks AK 99775-7320

WEESE, BRUCE ERIC, pharmaceutical industry lobbyist; b. Chewelah, Wash., Mar. 22, 1942; s. Harry M. and Roberta B. (Carman) W.; m. Elaine M. Smith, June 18, 1962 (div. July 1972); children: Sandra G., Michael D.; m. Vera B. Reed, Mar. 22, 1975; stepchildren: Kevin E. Bayton, Kelly M. Bayron. BA in Edn., Ea. Wash. State U., Cheney, 1964; MBA, Pepperdine U., 1981. Tchr. Grant Joint Union High Sch. Dist., Sacramento, 1964-70; pharm. sales McNeil Labs., San Jose, Calif., 1970-77, Adria Labs., San Francisco, 1977-83, Serono Labs., San Francisco, 1983-84, Boehringer Ingelheim, Santa Rosa, Calif., 1984-91; mgr. govt. affairs (lobbyist) Boehringer Ingelheim, 9 western states, 1991—. Bd. dirs. Russian River Health Ctr., Guerneville, Calif., 1994—. Mem. United Anglers, Sequoia Paddlers, Santa Rosa Sailing Club. Democrat. Home: 17550 Summit Ave PO Box 135 Guerneville CA 95446-0135 Office: Boehringer Ingelheim PO Box 368 Ridgefield CT 06877-0368

WEESE, WILLIAM CURTIS, physician; b. Chgo., Dec. 13, 1944. BS with distinction, U. Mich., 1965; MD, U. Chgo., 1969. Diplomate Nat. Bd. Med. Examiners, Am. Bd. Internal Medicine, specialty bd. pulmonary diseases. Intern U. Iowa Hosps., 1969-70, resident in internal medicine, 1970-72; fellow in pulmonary diseases Mass. Gen. Hosp., Boston, 1972-74, asst. in medicine, 1974-75; instr. medicine Harvard Med. Sch., Boston, 1974-75; pvt. practice chest diseases Phoenix, 1975—; chmn. dept. internal medicine St. Joseph's Hosp., Phoenix, 1983-87; med. dir. St. Joe's Preferred Choice Health Plan, Phoenix, 1990—; mem. exec. com. St. Joseph's Hosp., Phoenix, 1983-86, 90-92; med. advisor Social Security Adminstrn. Health and Human Svcs. Dept., Phoenix, 1979—. Fellow ACP, Am. Coll. Chest Physicians; mem. AMA, Ariz. Med. Assn., Ariz. Thoracic Soc. (pres. 1984-86), Maricopa County Med. Soc., Osler Club, Am. Lung Assn., Am. Thoracic Soc., Am. Coll. Health Care Execs., Am. Coll. Physicians Execs., Med. History Club Ariz. (pres. 1977-80), Ariz. Lung Assn. (bd. dirs. 1984—, pres. bd. 1990-92). Office: 375 E Virginia Ave Ste C Phoenix AZ 85004-1202

WEESNER, LOWELL MICHAEL, distribution management executive; b. Marion, Ind., May 15, 1949; s. Lowell Max and Ruth Evangeline (Riley) W.; m. Hilary Fiona Goodson, Dec. 9, 1967; children: Catriona Ann, David Michael. AA in Data Processing, Fullerton (Calif.) Coll., 1970; student, Calif. State U., Fullerton, 1970-73. Quality control mgr. Essex Wire and Cable, Anaheim, Calif., 1966-74; mdse. control mgr. Thrifty Corp., L.A., 1974-93; warehouse and inventory control mgr. Steadi Sys., Hollywood, Calif., 1994-95; inventory control mgr. Conco Paint Co., Commerce, Calif., 1995—. Mem. Diamond Bar (Calif.) High Sch. Booster Club, 1991-92. Recipient 1st Pl. amateur gun dog western field classic, Am. Kennel Club, 1985, Sullivan award Am. Weimaraner Club, 1985. Mem. Orange Coast Weimaraner Club (treas. 1984-85, field trial chmn. 1985-86). Mem. Soc. of Friends. Home: 1704 Autumnglow Dr Diamond Bar CA 91765-2710 Office: Steadi Sys 1041 N Highland Ave Los Angeles CA 90038-2406

WEGENER, ALBERT WILLIAM, engineering executive; b. Abington, Pa., June 7, 1959; s. Adolph H. and Elfriede (Wunderlich) W.; m. Joye Claire Cazanjian, Mar. 12, 1983; children: Adam Stephen, Eric Randall. BSEE, Bucknell U., 1981; MS in Computer Sci., Stanford U., 1986. Engr. GTE Govt. Sys. Corp., Mountain View, Calif., 1981-83; mem. tech. staff Atari Corp. Rsch., Sunnyvale, Calif., 1983-85; sect. mgr. GTE Govt. Sys. Corp., Mountain View, 1985-90; sr. digital signal processing engr. Studer Editech Corp., Menlo Park, Calif., 1990-93, dir. engring., 1993—; cons. Multimedia Sys. Corp., San Jose, 1992-94, Macrovision Inc., Mountain View, Calif., 1993—, Local Silence Inc., Palo Alto, Calif., 1994—. Mem. IEEE, Audio Engring. Soc. Democrat. Presbyterian. Home: 867 Jasmine Dr Sunnyvale CA 94086-8145 Office: Studer Editech Corp 1370 Willow Rd Menlo Park CA 94025-1516

WEGENER, GARY RAYMOND, municipal official; b. Detroit, Mar. 4, 1948; s. Eliot Brede and Margy Lou (Scheer) W.; m. Mary Ann Rita Minghi, June 19, 1971; children: Christin Ann, Michelle Marie. BCE, U. Calif., 1971; MS in Mgmt., U.S. Naval Postgrad. Sch., Monterey, Calif., 1983. Registered profl. engr., Pa., Calif. Ensign civil engr. corps. USN, 1971-73; base maint USN, Midway, 1973-76; const. mgmt. USN, Philippines, 1976-78; with Seebees, 1978-81; pgm. mgr. Norfolk, Va., 1983-86; base engr., contract mgr. Oakland, Calif., 1987-90; fac pgm mgr. Hawaii, 1990-92; base engr. Concord, Calif., 1992; ret., 1992. Mem. ASCE, APWA. Office: City of Woodland 300 1st St Woodland CA 95695-3413

WEGENSTEIN, MARTIN WILLI, electric company executive; b. Zurich, Switzerland, May 23, 1950; came to U.S., 1976; s. Willi Otto and Doris (Maya) W.; m. Jill Schneier, June 3, 1979; children: Danielle Maya, Michelle Andrea. Diploma in math., Swiss Fed. Inst. Tech., 1976; MS in Computer Sci., Union Coll., 1977. Rsch. asst. Swiss Fed. Inst. Tech., Zurich, 1976.; ops. analyst Emerson Electric Co., St. Louis, 1977-78, corp. hardware specialist, 1978-80, mgr. corp. data planning, 1980-81; dir. systems planning Skil Corp. subs., Chgo., 1981-82; dir. systems and planning Skil Netherland BV, Breda, 1982-85; dir. corp. mgmt. info. systems parent co. Emerson Electric Co., St. Louis, 1985-92; v.p. info. tech. Raychem Corp., Menlo Park, Calif., 1992—; chmn. European meeting Round Table, Breda, 1984-85. Bd. advisors Pontikes Ctr. for Mgmt. of Info., So. Ill. U., Carbondale, 1989—, Internat. Bus. Edn. Ctr., Memphis State U. and So. Ill. U., Carbondale, 1990-92. Office: Raychem Corp 300 Constitution Dr Menlo Park CA 94025

WEGGE, LEON LOUIS FRANÇOIS, economics educator; b. Breendonk, Antwerp, Belgium, June 9, 1933; came to U.S., 1959; s. Petrus Maria and Alberta (De Maeyer) W.; m. Beate Maria Teipel, Nov. 22, 1962; children: Simone, Robert, Elizabeth. B in Thomistical Philosophy, Cath. U. Louvain, Belgium, 1957, Licentiate in Econ. Sci., 1958; PhD in Indsl. Econs., MIT, 1963. Assoc. lectr. U. New S. Wales, Kensington, Australia, 1963-66; prof. econs. U. Calif., Davis, 1966—; vis. prof. U. Bonn, Fed. Republic Germany, 1980-81. Assoc. editor Jour. Internat. Econs., 1971-84; contbr. articles to profl. jours. Rsch. fellow Ctr. for Ops. Rsch. and Econometrics, 1972-73, fellow The Netherlands Inst. for Advanced Study, 1987-88. Mem. Econometric Soc., Am. Statistical Assn. Roman Catholic. Home: 26320 County Rd # 98 Davis CA 95616 Office: U Calif Davis Dept Econs Davis CA 95616

WEGNER, SAMUEL JOSEPH, historical society executive; b. Twin Falls, Idaho, Aug. 27, 1952; s. Albert Henry and Eleanor Esther (Wright) W.; m. Linda Louise Talley, May 27, 1972; children: Ethan, Elena. BA, U. Ariz., 1973; MA, U. Idaho, 1975. Curator Mansion Mus.-Oglebay Inst., Wheeling, W.Va., 1975-76; curator of edn. State Hist. Soc. Wis., Madison, 1976-78; asst. supt. Region I Mo. Dept. Nat. Resources, Brookfield, 1978-85; dir. ops. So. Oregon Hist. Soc., Jacksonville, Oreg., 1985-87; exec. dir. So. Oregon Hist. Soc., Medford, Oreg., 1987—; mem. Nat. Adv. Com. Common Agenda for History Mus., 1990-92, Nat. Adv. Com. Phila. Documentation Project for Common Agenda, 1989-91; chmn. Region 11 Am. Assn. State and Local History Awards Program, 1989-90, chmn. Oregon State chpt., 1987-88; chmn. Western Region Assn. Living History Farms and Agrl. Mus., 1986-87; mem. Am. Assn. Mus. Ad Hoc Com. for Hist. Sites and Mus. in Pks., 1984-85. Adv. com. Medford (Oreg.) Vis. and Conv. Bur., 1988—. Mem. Am. Assn. Mus., Nat. Trust for Hist. Preservation, Internat. Coun. Mus., Oregon Mus. Assn. Home: 3196 Springbrook Rd Medford OR 97504-4972 Office: So Oreg Hist Soc 106 N Central Ave Medford OR 97501-5926

WEH, ALLEN EDWARD, airline executive; b. Salem, Oreg., Nov. 17, 1942; s. Edward and Harriet Ann (Hicklin) W.; m. Rebecca Ann Roberton, July 5, 1968; children: Deborah Susan, Ashley Elizabeth, Brian Roberton. BS, U. N.Mex., 1966, MA, 1973. Asst. to chief adminstrv. officer Bank N.Mex., Albuquerque, 1973; pres., owner N.Mex. Airways, Inc., Albuquerque, 1974; dep. dir. N.Mex. Indochina Refugee Program, Santa Fe, 1975-76; dir. pub. affairs UNC Mining & Milling Co., Albuquerque, 1977-79; pres., chief exec. officer Charter Svcs., Inc., Albuquerque, 1979—, Mpls., Minn., 1993—. Mem. steering com. Colin McMillan for lt. gov., Albuquerque, 1982; bd. dirs. N.Mex. Symphony Orgh., Albuquerque Conv. and Visitors Bur., 1982; mem. Albuquerque Police Adv. Bd., 1977-78; treas., bd. dirs. Polit. Action Com., Albuquerque, 1982. Capt. USMC, 1966-71, Vietnam; col. USMCR, 1971-90, Col. USMC, 1990-91, Persian Gulf, 1992-93, Somalia. Decorated Bronze Star, Purple Heart with two gold stars, Air medal, Merit Svc. medal. Mem. Marine Corps. Res. Officers Assn. (life, bd. dirs. 1973, 86), Res. Officers Assn. U.S. (life), SCV (life), Mil. Order Stars and Bars (life), N.Mex. Amigos. Republican. Episcopalian. Home: 6722 Rio Grande Blvd NW Albuquerque NM 87107-6330 Office: Charter Svcs Inc 3700 Rio Grande Blvd NW Albuquerque NM 87107-3042

WEHDE, ALBERT EDWARD, lawyer; b. Milw., Feb. 14, 1935; s. Albert Christian and Mary Hubbel (Dewey) W.; m. Joan M. Forney, Nov. 4, 1978; children: John C., Edward T. BS, Marquette U., 1956, JD, 1960. Bar: Wis. 1960, Calif. 1968. Atty. AEC, Albuquerque, 1963-66; counsel Lockheed Aircraft Co., Sunnyvale and Redlands, Calif., 1966-73; assoc. Schultz & Manfield, Palo Alto, Calif., 1973-74; sr. counsel FMC Corp., Santa Clara, Calif., 1974-95; with AEW Internat. Cons., Santa Clara, 1995—; bd. dirs. Tech. Fed. Credit Union, San Jose, Calif., chmn., 1994-96. Pres. Mountain View (Calif.) Babe Ruth League, 1976; trustee Mid-Peninsula Family Services Assn., Palo Alto, 1973-74. Served to capt. U.S. Army, 1960-63. Mem. ABA (chmn. region VII pub. contracts sect. 1977-81), Santa Clara County Bar Assn. (co-chmn. corp. counsel sect. 1983-84, mem. exec. com.), Am. Corp. Counsel Assn. (chpt. sec., pres. 1988, bd. dirs. 1983—). Democrat. Roman Catholic. Home: 1106 Lorne Way Sunnyvale CA 94087-5157 Office: AEW Internat Cons 1400 Coleman Ave Ste F27 Santa Clara CA 95050

WEHMHOEFER, RICHARD ALLEN, lawyer, educator; b. Minot, N.D., Mar. 15, 1951; s. Leo W. and Myrtle C. (Wickman) W.; m. Gail M. Prostrollo, July 9, 1983. BA, U. Colo., 1973, MA, 1974, PhD, 1979, M in Urban Adminstrn., 1977, MPA, 1978; JD, U. Denver, 1982. Bar: Colo. 1983, U.S. Dist. Ct. Colo. 1983, S.D. 1994, U.S. Dist. Ct. S.D. 1994. Rsch. assoc. Denver Urban Obs., 1974-78; exec. asst. to regional adminstr. HUD, Denver, 1978-81; pvt. practice Denver, 1982—; asst. prof. mgmt. U. Denver, 1985-88, disting. prof. ethics, 1988-89; exec. dir., gen. counsel Colo. Commn. on Jud. Discipline, Denver, 1986—; cons. in ethics Pub. Svc. Co. Colo., Denver, 1987—; mem. core curriculum com. U. Denver, 1987-89. Author: Statistics in Litigation, 1985, Agriculture's Legal Rights Under the Bankruptcy Laws, 1987. Com. Colo. Dem. Party, Denver, 1980—; mem. Mayor's Com. on Keeping Denver a Great City, 1974—. Henderson fellow Fed. Exec. Inst., Charlottesville, Va., 1977. Mem. ABA (bd. dirs. jud. performance and conduct com. 1987—), Am. Judicature Soc., Assn. Jud. Disciplinary Counsel, Colo. Bar Assn., Colo. State Mgrs. Assn., Denver Bar Assn., S.D. Bar Assn. Home: 2277 Holly St Denver CO 80207-3842 Office: Colo Commn Jud Discipline 1301 Pennsylvania St Ste 260 Denver CO 80203-5012

WEHR, WESLEY CONRAD, museum curator; b. Everett, Wash., Apr. 17, 1929; s. Conrad John and Ingeborg (Hall) W. BA, U. Washington, 1951, MA, 1953. Affiliate curator paleontology Burke Mus. U. Wash., Seattle, 1976—; cons. Stonerose Interpretive Ctr., Republic, Wash., 1990—; guest curator Cheney Cowles Mus., Spokane, 1987, 88, State Capitol Mus., Olympia, Wash., 1986, Frye Art Mus., Seattle, 1984. Mem. Internat. Soc. Paleontology, Botanical Soc. Am., U. Wash. Pres. Club, U. Wash. Deans Club. Democrat. Home: PO Box 45221 Seattle WA 98145-0221 Office: Burke Mus U Wash Seattle WA 98195

WEHRLI, JOHN ERICH, biotechnology executive; b. Bogota, Colombia, Dec. 1, 1963; came to U.S., 1969; s. Werner Freiderich and Graciela Wehrli; m. Vicki Lee Burnett, Aug. 18, 1991; 1 child, Sophia Cristina. BS summa cum laude in Mgmt. and Econs., Golden Gate U., 1993; Tax cert., Foothill Coll., 1994; student, U. Calif., San Francisco, 1994—, U. Calif., Berkeley, 1995—. Analytical chemist dept. Chem. Analysis Syva Diagnostics Co., 1985-87; part-time fin. cons. assoc. Shearson Lehman Bros., San Francisco, 1989; robotics specialist dept. Automation Tech. Syntex Rsch. Inc., 1987-89; v.p. Precision Instrument Design Inc., Los Altos, Calif., 1989—; rsch. chemist Inst. Pharm. Scis., dept. Pharm. Chemistry Syntex Rsch. Inc., 1987-91, sr. sci. analyst programmer, sys. mgr. Rsch. Info. Sys., 1991-93, sys. analyst, sr. sys. mgr., 1993-94; legal intern patenet and tech. licensing Lawrence Berkeley Nat. Lab., 1995—. Contbr. articles to profl. jours. Enterprise scholar Golden Gate U., 1992, Kanze scholar, 1993, Univ. Honors scholar, 1993, Pres.'s scholar Foothill Coll., 1993. Mem. ABA (sci. and tech. sect.), AAAS, Am. Chem. Soc. (chem. info. and computer scis. sect.), Phi Alpha Delta. Home: 1879 Springer Rd Apt B Mountain View CA 94040-4052 Office: Precision Instrument Design Tahoe City CA 96145

WEHRLY, JOSEPH MALACHI, industrial relations executive b. County Armagh, Ireland, Oct. 2, 1915; s. Albert and Mary Josephine (Gribbon) W.; came to U.S., 1931, naturalized, 1938; student L.A. City Coll., evenings 1947-49; certificate indsl. relations U. Calif. at Berkeley Extension, 1957; m. Margaret Elizabeth Banks, July 3, 1946; children: Joseph Michael, Kathleen Margaret, Stephen Patrick. Mgr. interplant relations Goodyear Tire & Rubber Co., L.A., 1935-42; dir. indsl. rels. Whittaker Corp., L.A., 1946-60, Meletron Corp., L.A., 1960-61; asst. indsl. rels. mgr. Pacific Airmotive Corp., Burbank, Calif., 1961-63; pers. mgr. Menasco Mfg. Co., Burbank, 1963-66; indsl. rels. adminstr. Internat. Electronic Rsch., Burbank, 1966; dir. indsl. rels. Adams Rite Industries, Inc., Glendale, Calif., 1966-75, cons., 1975-76; pers. mgr. TOTCO div. Baker Hughes Corp., Glendale, 1975-80; instr. indsl. rels. and supervision L.A. Pierce Coll., 1949-76. Served with U.S. Army, 1942-46. Mem. Pers. and Indsl. Rels. Assn., Mchts. and Mfrs. Assn. Republican. Roman Catholic. Home: 90 Shorebreaker Dr Laguna Niguel CA 92677-9304

WEI, JEN YU, physiologist, researcher, educator; b. Fukien, China, Jan. 26, 1938; came to U.S., 1979; s. Soen Yu Wei and Soen Sang Hoeng; m. Lian Shen, Jan. 19, 1966; 1 child, Ching Wei. BS, Fu-Dan U., Shanghai, China, 1962; PhD in Neurophysiology, Shanghai Inst. Physiology, Chinese Acad. Scis., 1966; PhD in Sensory Physiology, U. Utah, 1987. Rsch. assoc. Inst. of Physiology, Shanghai, 1966-77, asst. rschr., 1977-78; rsch. assoc. dept. physiology U. Hong Kong, China, 1979; rsch. assoc. U. Utah, Salt Lake City, 1979-81, rsch. instr., 1981-87, rsch. asst. prof., 1987-89, asst. rsch. neurophysiologist, 1989-91; assoc. rsch. neurophysiologist dept. medicine Brain Rsch. Inst. and Ctr. Ulcer Rsch. and Edn./Gastroenteric Biol. Ctr., VA Wadsworth Med. Ctr. UCLA, 1991—. NIH Individual Investigator Rsch. grantee, 1990—. Mem. AAAS, The Chinese Physiology Soc., Soc. for Neurosci., Internat. Brain Rsch. Orgn., Sigma Xi. Office: UCLA Dept Medicine & Brain Rsch Inst 10833 Le Conte Ave Los Angeles CA 90024

WEIDE, JANICE LEE, librarian; b. Baker, Oreg., Aug. 12, 1948; d. Albert L. and Woodie Rue (Jeffords) Crowson; m. Roy Karl Weide, June 13, 1971; children: Megan, Alison. BA, Oreg. State U., 1971; MLA, U. Oreg., 1974. Online coord. Salem (Oreg.) Pub. Libr., 1974—. Contbr. articles to profl. publs. Recipient On the Frontline award OCLC, 1991. Office: Salem Pub Libr 585 Liberty St SE Salem OR 97301-3513

WEIDENHOFER, NEAL, systems programer, computer company executive; b. Chgo., June 18, 1940; s. William Joseph and Pearl Martha (Miller) W.; m. Joan Foster, June 17, 1962 (div. 1974); children: Mark Raymond, Lisa Marie; m. Dennise Marie Harrington, June 18, 1988. BS, U. N.Mex., 1964, MA, 1965; MA, Dartmouth Coll., 1967, PhD, 1968. Grad. asst. Dartmouth Coll., Hanover, N.H., 1965-68; asst. prof. U. Ill., Urbana, 1968-69; systems programmer United Computing Systems, Kans. City, Mo., 1969-80; researcher United Telecommunications, Mission, Kans., 1981-83; asst. to v.p. software lang. Denelcor, Aurora, Colo., 1983-85; systems programmer Amdahl, Sunnyvale, Calif., 1986-94. Mem. Am. Nat. Standards Inst. (X3J11 and X3J16 lang. standards coms.). Libertarian.

WEIDNER, JOE C., jewelry designer, silversmith; b. Mineral Wells, Tex., Nov. 23, 1948; s. Alvin and Frances Marion (Shook) W. BS, Tarleton Jr. Coll., Stephenville, Tex., 1969; BFA, Baylor U., 1973. Art instr. Waco Mental Health/Mental Retardation Ctr., Waco, Tex., 1972-73; owner Turquoise Unique, Tularosa, N.Mex., 1979-80; owner vehicle customizing J.C.'s Custom Shop, Tularosa, 1981-82; owner Turquoise and Such, Tularosa, 1981-82, Weidner's Video City, Tularosa, 1985-92; owner jewelry design and silversmith shop T. & S., Tularosa, 1993&; stone cons., Alamogordo and Tularosa, 1974—. Author: (book of poetry) Fellings of Love and Other Treasures, 1976; songwriter Simple Little Words, 1986, Bad Love, 1993, In Loving Memory, 1993. Sgt. USAF, 1973-77. Mem. Singles Together (mem. notifier program com. 1994), Tularosa C. of C., Alamogordo C. of c. Republican. Christian. Office: T & S PO Box 1245 Tularosa NM 88352-1245

WEIDNER, MARK, environmental research executive; b. 1952. MS in Analytical Chemistry, Purdue U., 1976. With Mich. State U., East Lansing, 1976-78; instr. Finnigan Corp., San Jose, Calif., 1978-80; sr. chemist Metro Lab., Seattle, 1980-85; now pres., treas. Analytical Resources, Inc., Seattle, 1985—. Office: Analytical Resources Inc 333 9th Ave N Seattle WA 98109-5122*

WEIDNER, NOEL, pathologist and surgeon; b. Douglas, Ariz., Oct. 5, 1949. BA summa cum laude in Chemistry/Zoology, U. Wyo., 1971; MD with distinction in rsch., U. Rochester, 1975. Diplomate Nat. Bd. Med. Examiners, Am. Bd. Pathology in anatomic and clin. pathology; lic. physician, Calif. Resident in lab. medicine Washington U./Barnes Hosp., St. Louis, 1975-77; fellow in clin. chemistry Barnes Hosp., St. Louis, 1977-78; resident in anatomic pathology U. N.Mex., Albuquerque, 1978-80; fellow in surg. pathology U. Iowa Hosps. and Clinics, Iowa City, 1983-84; staff pathologist, dir. gen. chemistry lab. Penrose Hosp., Colorado Springs, Colo., 1980-83; asst. prof. pathology Bowman Gray Sch. Medicine, Wake Forest U., Winston-Salem, 1984-87; nephropathologist and surg. pathologist N.C. Bapt. Hosp., Winston-Salem, 1984-87; asst. prof. pathology to assoc. prof. Harvard Med. Sch., Boston, 1987-91; assoc. prof. pathology and dir. surg. pathology U. Calif., San Francisco, 1991-93; prof. pathology and dir. surg. pathology U. Calif., 1993—; surg. pathologist, dir. electron microscopy Brigham and Women's Hosp., Boston, 1991; cons. oral pathology seminar Ellis Fischel State Cancer Hosp., Columbia, Mo., 1980-91; cons. Roswell Park Cancer Inst., Buffalo, 1991—; dir./originator surg. pathology panel Pathology dept. Brigham and Women's Hosp./UCSF, 1986-93; cons. clin. pathology Harvard Cmty. Health Plan, Watertown, Mass., 1987-89, West Roxbury VA Med. Ctr., Boston, 1988-91; [illegible]

Pathology, 1994—; staff organizer conf. Brigham & Women's Hosp., Boston, Moffitt-Long Hosp., San Francisco, 1990—; mem. pathology com. Radiation Therapy Oncology Group, 1994—; lectr./cons. in field. Bd. cons.: Robbins Pathologic Basis of Disease, 1989-91; sect. editor Ultrastructural Pathology, 1992; guest editor Seminars in Diagnostic Pathology, 1993-94; editl. bd. Jour. Cellular Biochemistry, 1994—, Applied Immunohistochemistry, 1994—; sect. editor Ultrastructural Pathology, 1994; contbr. numerous articles, abstracts to profl. jours., chpts. to books.; editor: The Difficult Diagnosis in Surgical Pathology, 1994; manuscript reviewer numerous sci. jours. including Caner, Lancet, Cancer Rsch. Winner 1987 slide competition, Am. Rheumatism Assn., 1988; recipient Clin. Oncology Career Devel. award Am. Cancer Soc., 1988-91; Nat. Rsch. Svc. fellow in blood banking Washington U. Med. Sch./Barnes Hosp., 1976; rsch. p[rofiled in Harvard Med. Sch. Perspectives, 1991, Focus: Harvard Medical Area, 1991, Science, 1993; career profiled by Am. Cancer Soc. in Clin. News, Vol. 3, 1992; NIH grantee, 1989-94. Fellow Am. Soc. Clin. Pathologists, Coll. Am. Pathologists; mem. AMA, Am. Assn. Pathologists, Internat. Acad. Pathology (abstract rev. bd. 1993—), New Eng. Pathology Soc., Arthur Purdy Stout Soc. (program com. 1993—), Assn. of Dirs. of Anatomic and Surg. Pathology, Soc. for Ultrastructural Pathology, Calif. Soc. Pathology, Phi Beta Kappa, Phi Kappa Phi, Alpha Epsilon Delta. Home: 71 Lopez Ave San Francisco CA 94116-1450 Office: U Calif Dept Pathology San Francisco CA 94143

WEIGAND, WILLIAM KEITH, bishop; b. Bend, Oreg., May 23, 1937. Ed., Mt. Angel Sem., St. Benedict, Oreg., St. Edward's Sem. and St. Thomas Sem., Kenmore, Wash. Bishop Diocese Salt Lake City, 1980—; Ordained priest Roman Cath. Ch., 1963. Office: Pastoral Ctr 27 C St Salt Lake City UT 84103-2302*

WEIGEND, GUIDO GUSTAV, geographer, educator; b. Zeltweg, Austria, Jan. 2, 1920; came to U.S., 1939, naturalized, 1943; s. Gustav F. and Paula (Sorgo) W.; m. Areta Kelble, June 26, 1947 (dec. 1993); children: Nina, Cynthia, Kenneth. B.S., U. Chgo., 1942, M.S., 1946, Ph.D., 1949. With OSS, 1943-45; with mil. intelligence U.S. War Dept., 1946; instr. geography U. Ill., Chgo., 1946-47; instr. then asst. prof. geography Beloit Coll., 1947-49; asst. prof. geography Rutgers U., 1949-51, assoc. prof., 1951-57, prof., 1957-76, acting dept. chmn., 1951-52, chmn. dept., 1953-67, assoc. dean, 1972-76; dean Coll. Liberal Arts, Prof. geography Ariz. State U., Tempe, 1976-84, prof. geography, 1976-89; ret., 1989; Fulbright lectr. U. Barcelona, 1960-61; vis. prof. geography Columbia U., 1963-67, NYU, 1967, U. Colo., summer 1968, U. Hawaii, summer 1969; liaison rep. Rutgers U. to UN, 1950-52; invited by Chinese Acad. Scis. to visit minority areas in Chinese Cent. Asia, 1988; mem. U.S. nat. com. Internat. Geog. Union, 1951-58, 61-65; chmn. Conf. on Polit. and Social Geography, 1968-69. Author articles, monographs, bulls. for profl. jours.; contbr.: (4th edit.) A Geography of Europe, 1977; geog. editor-in-chief: Odyssey World Atlas, 1966. Bd. adjustment Franklin Twp., N.J., 1959; mem. Highland Park (N.J.) Bd. Edn., 1973-75, v.p., 1975; mem. Ariz. Coun. on Humanities and Pub. Policy, 1976-80; vice chmn. Phoenix Com. on Fgn. Rels., 1976-79, chmn., 1979-81; mem. exec. com. Fedn. Pub. Programs in Humanities, 1977-82; bd. dirs. Coun. Colls. Arts and Scis., 1980-83, Phoenix Chamber Music Soc., 1983—; commr. N. Cen. Assn. Colls. and Schs., 1976-80, bd. dirs. commn. on instns. of higher edn., 1980-83. Research fellow Office Naval Research, 1952-55, Rutgers Research Council, 1970-71; grantee Social Sci. Research Council, 1956, Ford Found., 1966, Am. Philos. Soc., 1970-71, German Acad. Exchange Service, 1984; Fulbright travel grantee Netherlands, 1970-71. Mem. Assn. Am. Geographers (chmn. N.Y. Met. div. 1955-56, editorial bd. 1955-59, mem. coun. 1965-66, chmn. N.Y.-N.J. div. 1965-66), Am. Geog. Soc., Sigma Xi (pres. Ariz. State U. chpt. 1989-91). Home: 2094 E Golf Ave Tempe AZ 85282-4046 Office: Ariz State U Dept Geography Tempe AZ 85287

WEIGHT, GEORGE DALE, banker, educator; b. Salt Lake City, Mar. 25, 1934; s. Sheldon J. and Florence (Noe) W.; m. Carilee Kesler, June 16, 1959; children: Camille, Kristene, Denise, Marcie, Nancy. BS, U. Utah, 1961; MS, U. Oreg., 1965, PhD, 1968. Instr. U. Oreg., Eugene, 1963-68; economist Fed. Res. Bank, Cleve., 1968-69; asst. v.p. fiscal ops. Fed. Res. Bank, Pitts., 1969-71; v.p. bank ops. Fed. Home Loan Bank Bd., Pitts., 1971-73; exec. v.p. Syracuse Savs. Bank, N.Y., 1972-73, pres., chief exec. officer, 1973-83; chmn., chief exec. officer Ben Franklin Fed. Savs. and Loan Assn., Portland, Oreg., 1983-90; dean Atkinson Grad. Sch. Mgmt. Willamette U., Salem, Oreg., 1990—; adj. prof. Oreg. Grad. Inst. Sci. & Tech., 1994—, Syracuse U., 1974; chmn. bd. Savs. Banks Life Ins. Fund, N.Y.C., bd. dirs. Onondaga County Indsl. Devel. Agy., Fed. Res. Bank San Francisco, Portland Br., State Accident Ins. Fund, Fed. Home Loan Bank Seattle; chmn. Oreg. State Bd. Edn., 1991. Pres. Hiawatha coun. Boy Scouts Am., Syracuse, 1974-77; chmn. bd. Crouse-Irving Meml. Hosp., 1978-83; mem. Gov.'s Commn. Edn. Reforms, 1988, Oreg. State Bd. Edn., 1989-95, chmn., 1991-92; chmn. Associated Oreg. Industries Found., 1993—; pres. Canal Mus.; bd. dirs. Oreg. Bus. Coun. Recipient Silver Beaver award Boy Scouts Am., 1978; recipient Vol. of Yr. award Am. Heart Assn., 1980, Community Service award Rotary, Syracuse, 1982. Mem. Am. Fin. Assn., Arlington Club, Beta Gamma Sigma. Republican. Home: 16057 NW Claremont Dr Portland OR 97229-7841 Office: Willamette U Atkinson Grad Sch Mgmt 900 State St Salem OR 97301-3930

WEIGHT, MICHAEL ANTHONY, lawyer, former judge; b. Hilo, Hawaii, Jan. 5, 1940; s. Leslie A. and Grace B. (Brown) W.; m. Victoria Noel; children: Rachael R., Elizabeth G. BS in History, U. Rochester, 1961; LLB, Vanderbilt U., 1967. Bar: Hawaii 1967, U.S. Ct. Appeals (9th cir.) 1968, U.S. Supreme Ct. 1972. Pvt. practice, Honolulu; former judge Dist. Ct. (1st cir.) Hawaii. Bd. dirs. Bishop Mus. Assn. 1st lt. USMC, 1961-63. Mem. ABA, Hawaii Bar Assn. Office: 735 Bishop St Ste 430 Honolulu HI 96813-4820

WEIGHTMAN, JUDY MAE, lawyer; b. New Eagle, Pa., May 22, 1941; d. Morris and Ruth (Gutstadt) Epstein; children: Wayne, Randall, Darrell. BS in English, California U. of Pa., 1970; MA in Am. Studies, U. Hawaii, 1975; JD, U. Hawaii, 1981. Bar: Hawaii 1981. Tchr. Fairfax County Sch. (Va.), 1968-72, Hawaii Pub. Schs., Honolulu, 1973-75; lectr. Kapiolani Community Coll., Honolulu, 1975-76; instr. Olympic Community Coll., Pearl Harbor, Hawaii, 1975-77; lectr. Hawaii Pacific Coll., Honolulu, 1977-78; law clk. to atty. gen. Hawaii & Case, Kay & Lynch, Davis & Levin, 1979-81, to chief judge Intermediate Ct. Appeals State of Hawaii, 1981-82; dep. pub. defender Office of Pub. Defender, 1982-84; staff atty. Dept. Commerce & Consumer Affairs, State of Hawaii 1984-86; pres., bd. dirs. Am. Beltwrap Corp., 1986—; asst. prof. law, dir. pre-admission program, asst. prof. Richardson Sch. Law, U. Hawaii, 1987—, faculty senator; faculty senate exec. com. U. Hawaii Manua. Author: Days of Remembrance: Hawaii Witnesses to the Holocaust; producer (documentary) The Panel: The First Exchange, Profile of An Aja Soldier, Profile of a Holocaust Survivor; prodr., dir. From Hawaii to The Holocaust: A Shared Moment in History; patentee in field; mem. Richardson Law Rev., 1979-81. Mem. neighborhood bd. No. 25 City and County Honolulu, 1976-77; vol. Legal Aid Soc., Honolulu, 1977-78; bd. dirs. Jewish Fedn., Protection and Advocacy Agy.; parent rep. Wheeler Intermediate Adv. Coun., Honolulu, 1975-77; trustee Carl K. Mirikitani Meml. Scholarship Fund, Arts Coun. Hawaii; membership dir. ACLU, 1977-78, bd. dirs., Hawaii, 1988—, treas. Amicus; founder Hawaii Holocaust Project; trustee Jewish Fedn. Hawaii. Community scholar, Honolulu, 1980; Internat. Rels. grant Chaminade U., 1976; recipient Hawaii Filmmakers award Hawaii Internat. Film Festival, 1993, Golden Eagle award CINE, 1995, Silver Apple Nat. Edn. Film & Video Festival, 1995. Mem. ABA, Afro-Am. Lawyers Assn. (bd. trustee), Hawaii Women Lawyers, Assn. Trial Lawyers Am., Hawaii State Bar Assn., Am. Judicature Soc., Richardson Sch. Law Alumni Assn. (alumni rep. 1981-82), Advocates for Pub. Interest Law, U. Hawaii Senate Faculty (senator), Phi Delta Phi (v.p. 1980-81), Hadassah Club, Women's Guild Club. Democrat. Jewish. Office: U Hawaii William S Richardson Sch Law 2515 Dole St Honolulu HI 96822-2328

WEIGLE, WILLIAM OLIVER, immunologist, educator; b. Monaca, Pa., Apr. 28, 1927; s. Oliver James and Caroline Ellen (Alsing) W.; m. Kathryn May Lotz, Sept. 4, 1948 (div. 1980); children—William James, Cynthia Kay; m. Carole G. Romball, Sept. 24, 1983. B.S., U. Pitts., 1950, M.S., 1951, Ph.D., 1956. Research assoc. pathology U. Pitts., 1955-58, asst. prof. immunochemistry, 1959-61; assoc. div. exptl. pathology Scripps Rsch. Inst., La [illegible] Calif. 1961-62, assoc. mem. div., 1962-63; mem. dept. exptl. pathology Scripps Rsch. Inst., La Jolla, 1963-74, mem. dept. immunopathology, 1974-82, chmn. dept. immunopathology, 1980-82, mem., vice chmn. dept. immunology, 1982-85, mem. dept. immunology, 1982—, chmn. dept. immunology, 1985-87; adj. prof. biology U. Calif., San Diego; McLaughlin vis. prof. U. Tex., 1977; mem. adv. bd. Immunetech Pharms., San Diego, 1988—; cons. in field. Author: Natural and Acquired Immunologic Unresponsiveness, 1967; assoc. editor: Clin. and Exptl. Immunology, 1972-79; Jour. Exptl. Medicine, 1974-84; Immunochemistry 1964-71; Procs. Soc. Exptl. Biology and Medicine, 1967-72; Jour. Immunology, 1967-71; Infection and Immunity, 1969-86, Aging: Immunology and Infectious Disease, 1987—; sect. editor: Jour. Immunology, 1971-75; editorial bd.: Contemporary Topics in Immunobiology, 1971-93; Cellular Immunology, 1984—; contbr. articles to profl. jours. Trustee Lovelace Med. Found., Albuquerque. With USNR, 1945-46. Pub. Health Research fellow, Nat. Inst. Neurol. Diseases and Blindness, 1956-59; NIH sr. research fellow, 1959-61, Research Career award, 1962. Mem. Am. Assn. Immunologists, Am. Soc. Exptl. Pathology (Parke Davis award 1967), Am. Soc. Microbiology, N.Y. Acad. Scis., Am. Assn. Pathologists, Soc. Exptl. Biology and Medicine. Home: 688 Via De La Valle Solana Beach CA 92075-2461 Office: Scripps Rsch Inst Dept Immunology IMM9 10666 N Torrey Pines Rd La Jolla CA 92037-1027

WEIGNER, BRENT JAMES, secondary education educator; b. Pratt, Kans., Aug. 19, 1949; s. Doyle Dean and Elizabeth (Hanger) W.; m. Sue Ellen Weber Hume, Mar. 30, 1985; children: Russell John Hume, Scott William Hume. BA, U. No. Colo., 1972; MEd, U. Wyo., 1977, PhD, 1984. Counselor, coach Olympia Sport Village, Upson, Wyo., summer 1968; dir. youth sports F.E. Warren AFB, Cheyenne, summers 1973, 74; instr. geography Laramie County Community Coll., Cheyenne, 1974-75; tchr. social sci. McCormick Jr. High Sch., Cheyenne, 1975—, Laramie County Sch. Dist. 1, Cheyenne, 1975—; head social studies dept. McCormick Jr. High Sch., 1987—; curriculum adv. coun. chmn. Laramie County Sch. Dist. No. 1, 1988-89; lectr. ednl. methods U. Wyo., 1989, mem. clin. faculty, 1992-94; nat. chmn. Jr. Olympic cross-country com. AAU, Indpls., 1980-81; pres. Wyo. Athletic Congress, 1981-87; tchr. cons. Nat. Geog. Soc. Geography Inst., summer 1991; bd. dirs. Shadow Mountain Lodge, Aspen, Colo., 1992-93, United Med. Ctr. of Wyo. Found., 1995—. Fgn. exch. student U. Munich, 1971-72; head coach Cheyenne Track Club, 1976—, pres., 1980; deacon 1st Christian Ch., Cheyenne, 1987-90, elder, 1991-93; rep. candidate gen. election Wyo. Legis., 1991. Named Wyo. U.S. West Outstanding Tchr., 1989, Wyo. Coun. for the Social Studies K-8 Tchr. of Yr., 1994-95; fellow Taft Found., 1976, Earthwatch-Hearst fellow, Punta Allen, Mex., summer 1987, Christa McAuliffe fellow, 1991-92, Wyo. Christa McAuliffe Selection Com., 1994; Fulbright grantee, Jerusalem, summer 1984; Fulbright scholar Ghana and Senegal, 1990; People-to-People Internat. Ambassador to Vietnam, 1993; recipient Masons of Wyo. Disting. Tchr. award 1994. Mem. ASCD, NEA, Nat. Network for Ednl. Renewal, Nat. Coun. Social Studies, Nat. Coun. Geog. Edn., Dominican Rep. Nat. Coun. for Geog. Edn. (Cram scholarship 1992), Wyo. Geog. Alliance (steering com.), Cheyenne Tchrs. Edn. Assn. (govtl. rels. com., instrn. and profl. devel. com.), U. No. Colo. Alumni Assn., Cheyenne C. of C., Wyo. Heritage Soc., Wyo. Edn. Assn. (World Book Ency. classroom rsch. project cons. 1976—, accountability task force 1989-90), Fulbright Alumni Assn. (life), U. Wyo. Alumni Assn. (life), Lions (bd. dirs. Cheyenne 1987, pres. 1995—, 1st v.p. 1993-94, Melvin Jones Fellowship, 1995), Cheyenne Sunrise Lions Club (pres. 1995—), Phi Delta Kappa (life, bd. dirs. Cheyenne 1989—, v.p., edn. award for rsch. 1990, pres. 1992-93, ednl. found. rep. 1993—, area 4-D coord. 1994-95, Gerald Read Internat. Seminar scholar 1994; mem. outstanding doctoral dissertation coom. 1994). Home: 3204 Reed Ave Cheyenne WY 82001-2578 Office: McCormick Jr High Sch 3204 Reed Ave Cheyenne WY 82001-2578

WEIHAUPT, JOHN GEORGE, geosciences educator, scientist, university administrator; b. La Crosse, Wis., Mar. 5, 1930; s. John George and Gladys Mae (Ash) W.; m. Audrey Mae Reis, Jan. 28, 1961. Student, St. Norbert Coll., De Pere, Wis., 1948-49; B.S., U. Wis., 1952, M.S., 1953; M.S., U. Wis.-Milw., 1971; Ph.D., U. Wis., 1973. Exploration geologist Am. Smelting & Refining Co., Nfld., 1953, Anaconda Co., Chile, S.Am., 1956-57; seismologist United Geophys. Corp., 1958; geophysicist Arctic Inst. N.Am., Antarctica, 1958-60, Geophys. and Polar Research Center, U. Wis., Antarctica, 1960-63; dir. participating Coll. and Univ. program, chmn. dept. phys. and biol. sci. U.S. Armed Forces Inst., Dept. Def., 1963-73; assoc. dean for acad. affairs Sch. Sci., Ind. U.-Purdue U., Indpls., 1973-78; prof. geology Sch. Sci., Ind. U.-Purdue U., 1973-78; asst. dean (Grad. Sch., prof. geoscis. Purdue U.), 1975-78; prof. geology, assoc. acad. v.p., dean grad. studies and research, v.p. Univ. Research Found., San Jose (Calif.) State U., 1978-82; vice chancellor for acad. affairs U. Colo., Denver, 1982-86, prof. geoscis., 1987—; Sci. cons., mem. sci. adv. bd. Holt Reinhart and Winston, Inc., 1967—; sci. editor, cons. McGraw-Hill Co., 1966—; hon. lectr. U. Wis., 1963-73; geol. cons., 1968—; editorial cons. John Wiley & Sons, 1968; editorial adv. bd. Dushkin Pub. Group, 1971—. Author: Exploration of the Oceans: An Introduction to Oceanography; mem. editorial bd. Internat. Jour. Interdisciplinary Cycle Research, Leiden; co-discoverer USARP Mountain Range (Arctic Inst. Mountain Range), in Victoria Land, Antarctica, 1960; discoverer Wilkes Land Meteorite Crater, Antarctic. Mem. Capital Community Citizens Assn.; mem. Madison Transp. Study Com., Found. for Internat. Energy Research and Tng.; U.S. com. for UN Univ.; mem. sci. council Internat. Center for Interdisciplinary Cycle Research; mem. Internat. Awareness and Leadership Council; mem. governing bd. Moss Landing Marine Labs.; bd. dirs. San Jose State U. Found. Served as 1st lt. AUS, 1953-55, Korea. Mt. Weihaupt in Antarctica named for him, 1966; recipient Madisonian medal for outstanding community service, 1973; Outstanding Cote Meml. award, 1974; Antarctic medal, 1968. Fellow Geol. Soc. Am., Explorers Club; mem. Antarctican Soc., Nat. Sci. Tchrs. Assn., Am. Geophys. Union, Internat. Council Corr. Edu., Soc. Am. Mil. Engrs., Wis. Alumni Assn., Soc. Study Biol. Rhythms, Internat. Soc. for Chronobiology, Marine Tech. Soc., AAAS, Univ. Indsl. Adv. Council, Am. Council on Edn., Expdn. Polaire France (hon.), Found. for Study Cycles, Assn. Am. Geographers, Nat. Council Univ. Research Adminstrs., Soc. Research Adminstrs., Man-Environ. Communication Center, Internat. Union Geol. Scis., Internat. Geog. Union, Internat. Soc. Study Time, Community Council Pub. TV, Internat. Platform Assn., Ind., Midwest assns. grad. schs., Western Assn. Grad. Schs., Council Grad. Schs. in U.S., Wis. Alumni Assn. of San Francisco, Kiwanis, Carmel Racquet Club (Rinconada), The Ridge at Hiwan (Evergreen, Colo., pres. 1991-93). Home: 23906 Currant Dr Golden CO 80401-9243 Office: U Colo Campus Box 172 PO Box 173364 Denver CO 80204-5310

WEIL, LOUIS ARTHUR, III, newspaper publishing executive; b. Grand Rapids, Mich., Mar. 14, 1941; s. Louis Arthur, Jr. and Kathryn (Halligan) W.; m. Mary Elizabeth Buckingham, Sept. 7, 1963 (div. June 1977); children: Scott Arthur, Christopher Davison, Timothy Buckingham; m. Daryl Hopkins Goss, Jan. 26, 1980. B.A. in English, Ind. U., 1963; DHL (hon.), Mercy Coll., Grand Valley State U. Various positions Times Herald, Port Huron, Mich., 1966-68; personnel dir., pub. Journal and Courier, Lafayette, Ind., 1968-73; gen. mgr., pub. Gannett Westchester Rockland Newspapers, White Plains, N.Y., 1973-74, pres., gen. mgr., 1974-77, pres., pub., 1977-79; v.p. devel. Gannett Co., Inc., N.Y.C., 1979-83, sr. v.p. planning and devel., 1982-86; chmn., pub. Gannett Westchester Rockland Newspapers, White Plains, 1984-86; pres. The Detroit News, 1986-89, pub., 1987-89; U.S. pub. Time Mag., 1989-91; pub., chief exec. officer, exec. v.p. Ariz. Republic, Phoenix Gazette, Ariz. Bus. Gazette, 1991—; bd. dirs. Ctrl. Newspapers, Inc., Prudential. Chmn. membership Trustee Found. for Am. Comm.; mem. Greater Phoenix Leadership; trustee Cronkite Endowment Sch. Journalism and Telecomm. Ariz. State U., Phoenix Art Mus.; bd. dirs. Found. Am. Comms.; mem. adv. bd. Ariz. Cancer Ctr. U. Ariz.; campaign chmn. Valley of the Sun United Way, 1992. With USN. Office: Phoenix Newspapers Inc 120 E Van Buren St Phoenix AZ 85004-2227*

WEIL, PAMELA MARION, interior designer; b. Sacramento, Nov. 1, 1949; d. George Edward and Marion Claire (Azevedo) Rader; m. Robert L. Weil, Nov. 22, 1969; children: Melisa Marion, Matthew Erich, Mark Richard. AA in Interior Design, Am. River Coll., Sacramento, 1984; profl. cert. in Interior Design, Am. River Coll., 1988; BA, Calif. State U., Sacramento, 1992. Cert. interior designer. Kitchen and bath designer Marion Claire Interior Designer, Sloughhouse, Calif., 1982; interior designer Regency House, Sacramento, 1984; salesperson/lighting cons. Welco Interiors/World of Lighting, Carmichael, Calif., 1984-87; space planner/interior designer Employment Devel. Dept. State of Calif., Sacramento, 1987-94. Mem. Crocker Art Mus. Assn. (vol. touring docent). Mem. Am. Soc. Interior Designers (profl.). Home: 4509 Hazelwood Ave Sacramento CA 95821-6720

WEILAND, I. HYMAN, psychiatrist; b. Cin., Sept. 17, 1921; s. Jonah and Goldie (Ginsburg) W.; m. Ruth Kissa Mirsky, Feb. 2, 1946 (div. 1969); children: Sally Ann, Arthur Ronald, Nancy Cottrell; m. Sue Davis, Sept. 14, 1970; children: Elizabeth Anne Bauer, Jonah David, Sharon Anne. BS, U. Cin., 1943, MD, 1946; postgrad. in Psychoanalysis, Phila. Psychoanalytic Inst., 1959-62; PhD, So. Calif. Psychoanlytic Inst., 1971. Diplomate Am. Bd. Psychiatry and Neurology. Intern So. Pacific Gen. Hosp. (now Harkness Hosp.), San Francisco, 1946-47; from asst. resident to resident dept. pscyhiatry Coll. Medicine, U. Cin., 1947-49; sr. resident dept. psychiatry, fellow child guidance home U. Cin., 1949-51; assoc. clin prof. child and gen. psychiatry Sch. Medicine UCLA, 1967-79; clin. prof. dept. psychiatry Sch. Medicine UCLA., 1979—; assoc. instr. So. Calif. Psychoanalytic Inst., Beverly Hills, Calif., 1976-84; instr. So. Calif. Psychoanalytic Inst., Beverly Hills, 1984—; pvt. practice psychiatry L.A., 1972—; instr. Sch. Social Work, U. Louisville, 1949-51, dept. psychiatry U. Cin., 1951, dept. psychiatry Coll. Medicine U. Wash., Seattle, 1951-55, dept. psychiatry Sch. Medicine U. Pa., Phila., 1957-62; dir. psychiatry Pinel Found. Hosp., Seattle, 1951-55, San Fernando Guild Guidance Clinic, L.A., 1961-71, San Fernando Valley Cmty. Health Ctr., L.A., 1967-71; cons. in child psychiatry Seattle Children's Home, 1951-55; asst. dir. children's unit Ea. Pa. Psychiatric Inst., Phila., 1967-62, others. Contbr. numerous articles to profl. jours.; presenter many confs. and convs. profl. groups. Mem. select com. on psychiatric care and evaluation, sponsered by Dept. Defense, Am. Psychiat. Assn., NIMH, Cmty. Adv. Bd., KOST radio; bd. dirs. Grad. Ctr. for Child Devel. and Psychotherapy, 1981-90, chmn. 1983-86, sec.-treas., 1986-88; adolescent med. dir. dept. psychiatry, Northridge Hosp., 1987—. Lt. cmdr. US Navy, 1955-56. Grantee: NIMH, 1959-61, 63-68, 64-71, 65-67, 67-74, L.A. County Dept. Mental Health, 1964-71. Fellow Am. Psychiat. Assn. (life, commn. on childhood and adolescence), Am. Orhtopsychiat. Assn. (life), Acad. Child and Adolescent Psychiatry (life); mem. So. Calif. Psychiatric Soc. (task force on allied mental health workers, pvt. practice com.), So. Calif. Soc. for Child and Adolescent Psychiatry, So. Calif. Psychoanalytic Soc., So. Calif. Psychoanalytic Inst. Home: 9351 Shoshone Ave Northridge CA 91325 Office: 18530 Roscoe Blvd Ste 211 Northridge CA 91324-4631

WEILER, DOROTHY ESSER, librarian; b. Hartford, Wis., Feb. 21, 1914; d. Henry Hugo and Agatha Christina (Dopp) Esser; A.B. in Fgn. Langs., Wash. State U., 1935; B.A.L., Grad. Library Sch., U. Wash., 1936; postgrad. U. Ariz., 1956-57, Ariz. State U., 1957-58, Grad. Sch. Librarianship, U. Denver, 1971; m. Henry C. Weiler, Aug. 30, 1937; children—Robert William, Kurt Walter. Tchr.-librarian Roosevelt Elem. Schs., Dist. #66, Phoenix, 1956-59; extension librarian Ariz. Dept. Library and Archives, Phoenix, 1959-67; library dir. City of Tempe (Ariz.), 1967-79; assoc. prof., dept. library sci. Ariz. State U., 1968; vis. faculty Mesa Community Coll., 1980-84. Mem. public relations com. United Fund; treas. Desert Samaritan Med. Ctr. Aux., 1981, v.p. community relations Hosp., 1982, vol. asst. chaplain, 1988—, pastoral care vol. Named Ariz. Librarian of Yr., 1971; recipient Silver Book award Library Binding Inst., 1963. Mem. Tempe Hist. Soc., Ariz. Pioneers Hist. Soc., Am. Radio Relay League, Am. Bus. Women's Assn., ALA, Southwestern Library Assn., Ariz. State Libr. Assn. (pres. 1973-74), Ariz. Libr. Pioneer. Roman Catholic. Clubs: Our Lady of Mt. Carmel Ladies' Sodality, Soroptimist Internat. Founder, editor Roadrunner, Tumbling Tumbleweed; contbr. articles to mags. Home: PO Box 26018 Tempe AZ 85285-6018

WEILL, SAMUEL, JR., automobile company executive; b. Rochester, N.Y., Dec. 22, 1916; s. Samuel and Bertha (Stein) W.; student U. Buffalo, 1934-35; m. Mercedes Weil, May 20, 1939 (div. Aug. 1943); children: Rita and Eric (twins); m. Cléanthe Kimball Carr, Aug. 12, 1960 (div. 1982); m. Jacqueline Natalie Bateman, Jan. 5, 1983. Co-owner, Brayton Air Coll., St. Louis, 1937-42; assoc. editor, advt. mgr., bus. mgr. Road and Track Mag., Los Angeles, 1951-53; pres. Volkswagen Pacific, Inc., Culver City, Calif., 1953-73, Porsche Audi Pacific, Culver City, 1953-73; chmn. bd. Minto Internat., Inc., London; v.p. fin. Chieftain Oil Co., Ojai, Calif. Recipient Tom May award Jewish Hosp. and Research Center, 1971. Served with USAAF, 1943-45. Home: 305 Palomar Rd Ojai CA 93023-2432 Office: Chieftain Oil Co 214 W Aliso St Ojai CA 93023-2502

WEIMER, ROBERT JAY, geology educator, energy consultant, civic leader; b. Glendo, Wyo., Sept. 4, 1926; s. John L. and Helen (Mowrey) W.; m. Ruth Carol Adams, Sept. 12, 1948; children: Robert Thomas, Loren Edward (dec.), Paul Christner, Carl Scott. BA, U Wyo., 1948, MA, 1949; PhD, Stanford U., 1953. Registered profl. engr., Colo. Geologist Union Oil Co. Calif., 1949-54; cons. geologist U.S. and fgn. petroleum exploration, 1954—; prof. geology Colo. Sch. Mines, 1957-83, prof. emeritus, 1983—, Getty prof. geology, 1978-83; vis. prof. U. Colo., 1961, U. Calgary, Can., 1970, Inst. Tech., Bandung, Indonesia, 1975; Fulbright lectr. U. Adelaide, South Australia, 1967; disting. lectr. and continuing edn. lectr. Am. Assn. Petroleum Geologists, Soc. Expl. Geophysicists; ednl. cons. to petroleum cos., 1964—; mem. energy rsch. adv. bd. Dept. Energy, 1985-90, Bd. on Mineral and Energy Resources, NAS, 1988. Editor: Guide to Geology of Colorado, 1960, Symposium on Cretaceous Rocks of Colorado and Adjacent Area, 1959, Denver Earthquakes, 1968, Fossil Fuel Exploration, 1974, Studies in Colorado Field Geology, 1976. Trustee Colo. Sch. Mines Research Found., 1967-70; pres. Rockland Found., 1982-83. With USNR, 1944-46. Recipient Disting. Alumnus award U. Wyo., 1982, Mines medal Colo. Sch. Mines, 1984, Brown medal, 1990, Parker medal Am. Inst. Profl. Geologists. Fellow Geol. Soc. Am. (chmn. Rocky Mountain sect. 1966-67), AAAS; mem. Am. Assn. Petroleum Geologists (pres. elect 1990, Sidney Powers medal), Soc. Econ. Paleontologists and Mineralogists (hon., sec.-treas. 1966-67, v.p. 1971, pres. 1972, Twenhofel medal 1995), Colo. Sci. Soc. (hon., pres. 1981), Rocky Mountain Assn. Geologists (pres. 1969, hon. mem., Scientist of Yr. 1982), Wyo. Geol. Assn. (hon.), Colo. Sch. Mines Alumni Assn. (hon., Coolbaugh award), Am. Geol. Inst. Found. (sec., treas. 1984-88), Nat. Acad. Engring., Mt. Vernon Country Club (Golden, bd. dirs. 1956-59, 81-84, pres. 1983-84). Home: RR 3 25853 Mt Vernon Rd Golden CO 80401-9699

WEINBERG, ALVIN HOWARD, engineer; b. Buffalo, N.Y., June 30, 1956; s. Sidney Roger and Evelyn (Miller) W.; m. Lisa Prechter, Nov. 1, 1986; children: Alyson Rae, Nash Devereau. BE, Vanderbilt U., 1978; MS, Drexel U., 1981. Engring. mgr. Cordis Corp., Miami, Fla., 1981-87, Pacesetter, Inc., Sylmar, Calif., 1987—. Patentee in field; contbr. articles to profl. jours. Mem. Internat. Soc. for Hybrid Microelectronics (Tech. Achivement award, 1991), Internat. Electronics Packaging Soc., ASM Internat., IEEE. Home: 11859 Maple Crest St Moorpark CA 93021-3171 Office: Pacesetter Inc 15900 Valley View Ct Sylmar CA 91342-3577

WEINBERG, BERND, management educator; b. Chgo., Jan. 30, 1940; s. Berthold and Freda (Gramms) W.; children: John, Katherine, Mark. BA, SUNY, Fredonia, 1961; MA, Ind. U., 1963, PhD, 1965. Instr. Ind. U. Schs. Medicine and Dentistry, Indpls., 1964-66, 68-74; asst. prof., 1968-71, assoc. prof., 1971-74; rsch. fellow NIH, Bethesda, Md., 1966-68; assoc. prof. Purdue U., West Lafayette, Ind., 1974-76; prof. Purdue Rsch. Found., West Lafayette, 1976-87; assoc. dir. div. sponsored programs Office of Patents and Copyrights, West Lafayette, 1985-87; dir. instnl. rels. Rsch. Corp. Technologies, Inc., Tucson, 1987—. Author: Readings in Speech Following Total LAryngectormy, 1980, (with D. Shedd) Approaches to Surgical Prosthetic Speech Rehabilitation, 1980, (with I. Meitus) Diagnosis in Speech-Language Pathology, 1983; contbr. over 75 articles to profl. jours., 15 chprs. to books; patentee in field. Recipient Disting. Alumni award SUNY-Fredonia, 1981. Fellow Am. Speech/Lang. and Hearing Assn. (cert.); mem. Acoustical Soc. Am., Assn. Univ. Tech. Mgrs. Home: 4950 N Apache Hills Trl Tucson AZ 85715-5909 Office: Rsch Corp Technologies Inc 101 N Wilmont Rd Ste 600 Tucson AZ 85711-3335

WEINBERG, DARIN THOMPSON, sociologist, researcher; b. Stanford, Calif., Feb. 6, 1963; s. Phillip Ivan Weinberg and Karen (Blom) Rogers; m. Diana Leticia Chapa, Sept. 17, 1994. BA, U. Calif., San Diego, 1984; MSc, London Sch. Econs., 1985; MA, UCLA, 1991. Rsch. cons. RAND, L.A., 1990—; rschr., educator UCLA, 1991—. Fellow UCLA, 1989-90, Nat. Inst. Drug Abuse, 1993—. Mem. Am. Sociol. Assn., Soc. Study Social Problems.

Home: 432 S Cochran Ave Apt 3 Los Angeles CA 90036-3313 Office: UCLA Dept Sociology 405 Hilgard Ave Los Angeles CA 90024-1301

WEINBERG, JOHN LEE, federal judge; b. Chgo., Apr. 24, 1941; s. Louis Jr. and Jane Kitz (Goldstein) W.; m. Sarah Kibbee, July 6, 1963; children: Ruth, Leo. BA, Swarthmore Coll., 1962; JD, U. Chgo., 1965. Bar: Ill. 1966, Wash. 1967, U.S. Dist. Ct. (we. dist.) Wash. 1967, U.S. Ct. Appeals (9th cir.) 1967. Law clk. to Hon. Henry L. Burman Ill. Appellate Ct., Chgo., 1965-66; law clk. to Hom. Walter V. Schaefer Ill. Supreme Ct., Chgo., 1966; law clk. to Hon. William T. Beeks U.S. Dist. Ct. Wash., Seattle, 1967-68; atty. Perkins Coie Law Firm, Seattle, 1968-73; judge U.S Magistrate Ct., Seattle, 1973—. Author: Federal Bail and Detention Handbook, 1988. Mem. ABA, Am. Judicature Soc., Wash. State Bar Assn., Seattle-King County Bar Assn., Fed. Magistrate Judges Assn. (nat. pres. 1982-83). Office: US Magistrate Judge 304 US Courthouse 1010 5th Ave Seattle WA 98104-1130

WEINBERG, WILLIAM HENRY, chemical engineer, chemical physicist, educator; b. Columbia, S.C., Dec. 5, 1944; s. Ulrich Vivian and Ruth Ann (Duncan) W. BS, U. S.C., 1966; PhD in Chem. Engring, U. Calif., Berkeley, 1970; NATO postdoctoral fellow in phys. chemistry, Cambridge U., Eng., 1971. Asst. prof. chem. engring. Calif. Inst. Tech., 1972-74, asso. prof., 1974-77, prof. chem. engring. and chem. physics, 1977-89, Chevron disting. prof. chem. engring. and chem. physics, 1981-86; prof. chem. engring. and chemistry U. Calif., Santa Barbara, 1989—, assoc. dean Coll. Engring., 1992—; vis. prof. chemistry Harvard U., 1980, U. Pitts., 1987-88, Oxford U., 1991; Alexander von Humboldt Found. fellow U. Munich, 1982; cons. E.I. DuPont Co. Author: (with Van Hove and Chan) Low-Energy Electron Diffraction, 1986; editor 4 books in field; mem. editorial bd. Jour. Applications Surface Sci., 1977-85, Handbook Surfaces and Interfaces, 1978-80, Surface Sci. Reports, 1980—, gen. editor, 1992—, Applied Surface Sci., 1985—, Langmuir, 1990—, Surface Sci., 1992—; contbr. articles to profl. jours., chpts. to books. Recipient Giuseppe Parravano award Mich. Catalysis Soc., 1989; fellow NSF, 1966-69, Alfred P. Sloan Found., 1976-78, Camille and Henry Dreyfus Found. fellow 1976-81. Fellow Am. Phys. Soc. (Nottingham prize 1972), Am. Vacuum Soc.; mem. AAAS, AIChE (Colburn award 1981), Am. Chem. Soc. (LaMer award 1973, Kendall award 1991, Arthur W. Adamson award 1995), N.Am. Catalysis Soc., Nat. Acad. Engring., Phi Beta Kappa. Home: 877 Summit Rd Santa Barbara CA 93108-2321 Office: U Calif Dept Chem Nuclear Engr Santa Barbara CA 93106

WEINBERGER, FRANK, information systems advisor; b. Chgo., Sept. 18, 1926; s. Rudolph and Elaine (Kellner) W.; m. Beatrice Natalie Fixler, June 27, 1953; children: Alan J., Bruce I. BSEE, Ill. Inst. of Tech., 1951; MBA, Northwestern U., Evanston, 1959. Registered profl. engr., Ill, Calif. Engr. Admiral Corp., Chgo., 1951-53; sr. engr. Cook Rsch., Chgo., 1953-59; mem. tech. staff Rockwell Internat., Downey, Calif., 1959-80, info. systems advisor, 1980-95; info. mgmt. cons. Los Alamitos, Calif., 1995—. Pres. Temple Israel, Long Beach, Calif., 1985-87, bd. dirs. 1973-85. With USN, 1944-46. Mem. Assn. for Computer Machinery. Democrat. Jewish. Home and Office: 3231 Yellowtail Dr Los Alamitos CA 90720-5253

WEINER, DORA B., medical humanities educator; b. Furth, Germany, 1924; d. Ernest and Emma (Metzger) Bierer; m. Herbert Weiner, 1953; children—Timothy, Richard, Antony. Baccalaureat, U. Paris, 1941; B.A. magna cum laude, Smith Coll., 1945; M.A., Columbia U., 1946, Ph.D., 1951. Lectr. gen. studies Columbia U., N.Y.C., 1949-50, instr., 1950-52, vis. lectr. Tchrs. Coll., 1962-63; instr. Barnard Coll., 1952-56; fellow in history of medicine Johns Hopkins U., Balt., 1956-57; mem. faculty dept. social sci. Sarah Lawrence Coll., 1958-62; asst. prof. history Manhattanville Coll., 1964-65, assoc. prof., 1966-78, prof., 1978-82; adj. prof. med. humanities UCLA Sch. Medicine, Los Angeles, 1982—, prof., 1987—; cons. and lectr. in field. Author: Raspail: Scientist and Reformer, 1968; The Clinical Training of Doctors: An Essay of 1793, 1980, The Citizen-Patient in Revolutionary and Imperial Paris, 1993; editor: Jacques Tenon's Memoirs of Paris Hospitals, 1995; co-editor: From Parnassus; Essays in Honor of Jacques Barzun, 1976; contbr. chpts. to books, articles to profl. jours. Grantee numerous profl. and ednl. instns. Mem. Am. Hist. Assn. (nominating com. 1979-82, Leo Gershoy award com. 1985-88), AAUP, Am. Assn. History Medicine (past mem. numerous coms.), Soc. 18th Century Studies, Soc. for French Hist. Studies (exec. com. 1978-81), History of Sci. Soc. Office: UCLA 12-138 Ctr Health Scis Los Angeles CA 90024

WEINER, NORMAN, pharmacology educator; b. Rochester, N.Y., July 13, 1928; m. Diana Elaine Weiner, 1955; children: Steven, David, Jeffrey, Gareth, Eric. BS, U. Mich., 1949; MD, Harvard U., 1953. Diplomate Am. Bd. Med. Examiners. Intern 2d and 4th Harvard Med. Svc., Boston City Hosp., 1953-54; rsch. med. officer USAF, 1954-56; instr. dept. pharmacology-biochemistry Sch. of Aviation Medicine, San Antonio, 1954-56; from instr. to asst. prof. Harvard Med. Sch., Boston, 1956-67; prof. pharmacology U. Colo. Health Sci. Ctr., Denver, 1967—, disting. prof., 1989, chmn. dept. pharmacology, 1967-87; vis. prof. U. Calif., Berkeley, 1973-76; interim dean U. Colo. Sch. Medicine, 1983-84; Allan D. Bass lectr. sch. medicine Vanderbilt U., Nashville, 1983, divsn. v.p. Abbott Labs., Abbott Park, Ill., 1985-87; Pfizer lectr. Tex. Coll. Osteo. Medicine, Ft. Worth, 1985; disting. prof. UCHSC, 1989. Editor: Drugs and the Developing Brain, 1974, Structure and Function of Monoamine Enzymes, 1977, Regulation and Function of Monoamine Enzymes, 1981, Neuronal and Extraneuronal Events in Autonomic Pharmacology, 1984. Recipient Rsch. Career Devel. award USP HS, 1963, Kaiser Permanente award, 1974, 81, Otto Krayer award Am. Soc. Pharmacology and Exptl. Therapeutics, 1985; Spl. fellow USPHS, London, 1961-62; Disting. Volwiler Rsch. fellow Abbott Labs., 1988; Norman Weiner Festschrift, 1993; Julius Axelrod medal for outstadning scholarship in catecholamine rsch., 1993. Mem. AAAS, Am. Soc. for Pharmacology and Exptl. Therapeutics (Otto Krayer award 1985), N.Y. Acad. Scis., Assn. Med. Sch. Pharmacology, Am. Soc. Neurochemistry, Western Pharmacology Soc., Am. Coll. Neuropsychopharmacology, Soc. Neurosci., Biochem. Soc., Internat. Brain Rsch. Orgn., Internat. Soc. Neurochemistry, Rsch. Soc. on Alcoholism, Phi Beta Kappa, Sigma Xi, Alpha Omega Alpha, Phi Eta Sigma, Phi Lambda Upsilon, Phi Kappa Phi. Office: U Colo Health Sci Ctr Pharmacology Dept 4200 E 9th Ave Denver CO 80220-3706

WEINER, RICHARD S., healthcare administrator; b. Yonkers, N.Y., July 14, 1951; s. Joseph and Muriel (Zucker) W.; m. Kathryn, Aug. 25, 1985; children: Jason C., Rebecca E. BA, U. Del., 1976, MC, 1978, PhD, 1981. Nat. cert. counselor, crt. behavioral medicine, mediator; diplomate med. psychotherapy, profl. counseling; diplomate in pain mgmt. Exec. dir. Inst. Pain Mgmt., Ceres, 1983-90; assoc. dir. planning Meml. Hosp., Ceres, Calif., 1987-90; exec. dir. Am. Acad. Pain Mgmt., 1988—. Contbr. articles to profl. jours. Hon. citizen ambassador Med. Exch. Program to People's Republic China, coleader to Russia, Czechoslovakia, Hungary, Vietnam, Singapore, Thailand. Mem. Am. Pain Soc. (profl. edn. com.), Am. Mental Health Counseling (editorial rev. bd.). Home: 19240 Michigan Dr Twain Harte CA 95383-9794

WEINGARTEN, SAUL MYER, lawyer; b. Los Angeles, Dec. 19, 1921; s. Louis and Lillian Dorothy (Alter) W.; m. Miriam Ellen Moore, Jan. 21, 1949; children: David, Steven, Lawrence, Bruce. AA, Antelope Valley Coll., 1940; AB, UCLA, 1942; cert., Cornell U., 1943; JD, U. Southern Calif., 1949. Prin. Saul M. Weingarten, Inc., Seaside, Calif., 1954—; pres, CEO Quaestor Inc., Seaside, Calif., 1995—; atty. City of Gonzales, Calif., 1968-74, City of Seaside, 1955-70; gen. counsel Redevel. Agy., Seaside, 1955-76, Security Nat. Bank, Monterey, Calif., 1968-74; bd. dirs., exec. com. Frontier Bank, Cheyenne, Wyo., 1984—, Mariposa Hall Inc., 1989—. Author: Practice Compendium, 1950; contbr. articles to profl. jours. Del. Internat. Union of Local Authorities, Brussels, Belgium, 1963, 73; candidate state legislature Dem. Com., Monterey County, 1958; counsel Monterey Peninsula Mus. of Art, Inc., 1972-80; gen. counsel Monterey County Symphony Assn., Carmel, Calif., 1974—, Mountain Plains Edn. Project, Glasgow, Mont., 1975-81; chmn. fund raising ARC, Monterey, 1964; chmn., bd. dirs. fund raising United Way, Monterey, 1962-63; pres., bd. dirs. Alliance on Aging, Monterey, 1968-82; bd. dirs. Family Svc. Agy., Monterey, 1958-66, Monterey County Cultural Council, 1986—; dir., mem. exec. com. Monterey Bay Cultural Arts Ctr., 1990. Served to commdr. USN, 1942-46, 50-54, Korea. Grad. fellow Coro Found., 1949-50. Mem. Calif. Bar Assn., Monterey County Bar Assn., Monterey County Trial Lawyers Assn., Rotary (pres. 1970-71, 82-83), Commonwealth Club, Meadowbrook Club. Jewish. Home: 4135 Crest Rd Pebble Beach CA 93953-3008 Office: 1123 Fremont Blvd Seaside CA 93955-5759

WEINHOLD, ALBERT RAYMOND, plant pathologist; b. Evans, Colo., Feb. 14, 1931; s. Albert Raymond and Ruth Evelyn (Stocks) W.; m. Connie Marie Seastrand, Mar. 15, 1952; children: Albert Raymond, Kathryn Beth. BS, Colo. State U., 1953, MS, 1955; PhD, U. Calif., Davis, 1958. Asst. prof. to prof. plant pathology U. Calif., Berkeley, 1960-93; prof. emeritus U. Calif., 1993—, chmn. dept. plant pathology, 1976-84, acting dean Coll. Natural Resources, 1984-86. Contbr. articles to profl. jours., chpts. to books; editor-in-chief Phytopathology, 1973-76. 1st Lt. USAF, 1958-60. Mem. AAAS, Am. Phytopathol. Soc. (pres. 1987-88); mem. Mira Vista Golf and Country Club (dir. 1989-92, pres. 1991-92). Republican. Presbyterian. Home: 213 Arlington Ave Kensington CA 94707-1401 Office: U Calif Dept Plant Pathology Berkeley CA 94720

WEINIG, RICHARD ARTHUR, lawyer; b. Durango, Colo., Mar. 23, 1940; s. Arthur John and Edna (Novella) W.; m. Barbara A. Westerland, June 16, 1964. B.A. in Polit. Sci., Stanford U., 1962, postgrad. in Soviet Studies, 1962-65; J.D., U. Calif.-San Francisco, 1971. Bar: Alaska, 1971, U.S. Dist. Ct. Alaska 1971, U.S. Ct. Appeals (9th cir.) 1978, U.S. Supreme Ct. 1979. Assoc. Burr, Pease & Kurtz, Anchorage, 1971-73; assoc. Greater Anchorage Area Borough, 1973-75, Municipality of Anchorage, 1975-82; ptnr. Pletcher & Slaybaugh, Anchorage, 1982-88, Pletcher, Weinig, Moser & Merriner, 1988—. Active, Stanford U. Young Republicans, 1961-65, Sierra Club, Mountaineering Club, Knik Canoyers and Kayakers of Alaska, Alaska Ctr. for Environ. Mem. ABA, Alaska Bar Assn., Anchorage Bar Assn., Nat. Rifle Assn. Republican. Presbyterian. Mem. editorial bd. Hastings Law Jour. Office: Pletcher Weinig Moser & Merriner 800 E Dimond Blvd Ste 3-620 Anchorage AK 99515-2046

WEINMAN, GLENN ALAN, lawyer; b. N.Y.C., Dec. 9, 1955; s. Seymour and Iris Rhoda (Bergman) W. BA in Polit. Sci., U. Calif., Los Angeles, 1978; JD, U. So. Calif., 1981. Bar: Calif. 1981. Assoc. counsel Mitsui Mfrs. Bank, Los Angeles, 1981-83; assoc. McKenna, Conner & Cuneo, Los Angeles, 1983-85, Stroock, Stroock & Lavan, Los Angeles, 1985-87; sr. counsel Buchalter, Nemer, Fields & Younger, Los Angeles, 1987-91; ptnr. Keck, Mahin & Cate, 1991-93; sr. v.p., gen. counsel Western Internat. Media Corp., L.A., 1993—. Mem. ABA (corp. banking and bus. law sect., com. on savs. instns., com. on banking law), Calif. Bar Assn. (bus. law sect., com. fin. instns. 1989-91, com. consumer svcs. 1991-94), L.A. County Bar Assn. (corp. legal depts. sect., bus. and corps. law sect., subcom. on fin. instns.), Legion Lex., U. So. Calif. Law Alumni Assn., Phi Alpha Delta. Office: Western Internat Media Corp 8544 W Sunset Blvd Los Angeles CA 90069-2310

WEINMAN, ROBERTA SUE, marketing and financial communications consultant; b. Bennington, Vt., Sept. 22, 1945. BA, U. Calif., Berkeley, 1967; MA, Stanford U., 1975, MLA, 1994; MBA, Pepperdine U., 1982. Tech. editor SRI Internat., Menlo Park, Calif.; adminstr. consumer affairs Fed. Home Loan Bank, San Francisco, 1977-79; legal research asst. Townsend and Townsend, San Francisco, 1979-80; ind. cons. mktg. and fin. comm., 1981—. Editor, writer, developer various mktg., pub. relations and fin. documents, primarily for high-tech. industry. Home and Office: 99 Orchard Hills Atherton CA 94027

WEINMANN, ROBERT LEWIS, neurologist; b. Newark, Aug. 21, 1935; s. Isadore and Etta (Silverman) W.; m. Diana Weinmann, Dec. 13, 1980 (dec. Dec. 1989); children: Paul, Chris, Dana, Paige. BA, Yale U., 1957; MD, Stanford U., 1962. Diplomate Am. Bd. of EEG and Neurophysiology, v.p.; diplomate Am. Acad. Pain Mgmt. Intern Pacific Presbyn. Med. Ctr., San Francisco, 1962-63; resident in neurology Stanford U. Hosp., 1963-66, chief resident, 1965-66; pvt. practice San Jose, Calif., 1969—. Chmn. editorial bd. Clin. EEG Jour.; mem. editorial bd. Jour. Am. Acad. Pain Mgmt.; formerly mem. editorial bd. Clin. Evoked Potentials Jour.; contbr. articles to various publs. Capt. M.C., U.S. Army, 1966-68, Japan. Award recipient State of R.I., Santa Clara County Med. Soc., Epilepsy Soc., other orgns.; fellow Univ. Paris, 1957-58. Union of Am. Physicians and Dentists (pres. 1990—, bd. dirs. 1972—, pres. Calif. fedn. 1990—). Office: Union Am Physicians & Dentists 1330 Broadway Ste 730 Oakland CA 94612-2506

WEINREB, BRADLEY ALLEN, deputy attorney general; b. Great Neck, N.Y., Sept. 29, 1966; s. Marshall Alan and Marcia Lee (Saltsburg) W.; m. Lisa Beth Selbst, Aug. 13, 1989. MA in Govt., U. Tex., 1988; JD, U. San Diego, 1991. Bar: Calif. 1991. Dep. atty. gen. Office of Atty. Gen., San Diego, 1992—. Assoc. editor Journal of Contemporary Legal Issues, 1991. Mem. Nat. Trial Team, 1991, Nat. App. Moot Ct. Bd., 1991. Mem. State Bar Calif., Federalist Soc. (exec. com. San Diego chpt. 1992—), Calif. Dist. Attys. Assn. Office: Office of Atty Gen PO Box 85266 San Diego CA 92186-5266

WEINREB, ROBERT NEAL, ophthalmologist, educator; b. N.Y.C., Nov. 23, 1949; s. David and Ruth (Kramer) W. S.B., MIT; M.D., Harvard U., 1975. Diplomate Am. Bd. Ophthalmology. Resident in ophthalmology U. Calif.-San Francisco, 1976-80, fellow in glaucoma, 1981; mem. faculty U. Calif.-San Diego, La Jolla, 1984—, prof. ophthalmology, 1984—, vice chair, 1984—, chief glaucoma div., 1984—. Chief editor Focus on Glaucoma, 1986—; assoc. editor Jour. Glaucoma, 1992—. Recipient Hogan prize U. Calif.-San Francisco, 1981, Alcon prize Alcon Research Inst., 1983, 92. Fellow Am. Acad. Ophthalmology (Honor award 1986); mem. Internat. Soc. Eye Research, Assn. Research in Vision and Ophthalmology (Helmholtz award 1979). Office: U Calif San Diego Glaucoma Ctr and Rsch Labs 9415 Campus Point Dr La Jolla CA 92093

WEINRICH, JAMES DONALD, psychobiologist, educator; b. Cleve., July 2, 1950; s. Albert James and Helen (Lautz) W. AB, Princeton U., 1972; PhD, Harvard U., 1976. Postdoctoral fellow, then instr. Johns Hopkins U., Balt., 1980-82; rsch. assoc., then asst. rsch. prof. psychiatry Boston U., 1983-87; asst. rsch. psychobiologist, project mgr. U. Calif., San Diego, 1987-89, asst. rsch. psychobiologist, ctr. mgr., 1989-91, sr. investigator sexology, 1991-93, prin. investigator sexology project, 1994—; bd. dirs. Found. Sci. Study of Sexuality, Mt. Vernon, Iowa. Author: Sexual Landscapes, 1987; co-editor: Homosexuality: Social, Psychological and Biological Issues, 1982, Homosexuality: Research Implications for Public Policy, 1991. Mem. Internat. Acad. Sex Rsch., Soc. for Sci. Study of Sex (Hugo Beigel award 1987), Am. Coll. Sexologists (cert.), Phi Beta Kappa. Office: Univ Calif San Diego 2760 5th Ave Rm 200 San Diego CA 92103-6325

WEINSHIENK, ZITA LEESON, federal judge; b. St. Paul, Apr. 3, 1933; d. Louis and Ada (Dubov) Leeson; m. Hubert Troy Weinshienk, July 8, 1956 (dec. 1983); children: Edith Blair, Kay Anne, Darcy Jill; m. James N. Schaffner, Nov. 15, 1986. Student, U. Colo., 1952-53; BA magna cum laude, U. Ariz., 1955; JD cum laude, Harvard U., 1958; Fulbright grantee, U. Copenhagen, Denmark, 1959; LHD (hon.), Loretto Heights Coll., 1985; LLD (hon.), U. Denver, 1990. Bar: Colo. 1959. Probation counselor, legal adviser, referee Denver Juvenile Ct., 1959-64; judge Denver Mcpl. Ct., 1964-65, Denver County Ct., 1965-71, Denver Dist. Ct., 1972-79, U.S. Dist. Ct. Colo., Denver, 1979—. Precinct committeewoman Denver Democratic Com., 1963-64; bd. dirs. Crime Stoppers. Named one of 100 Women in Touch with Our Time Harper's Bazaar Mag., 1971, Woman of Yr., Denver Bus. and Profl. Women, 1969; recipient Women Helping Women award Soroptimist Internat. of Denver, 1983, Hanna G. Solomon award Nat. Coun. Jewish Women, Denver, 1986. Fellow Colo. Bar Found., Am. Bar Found.; mem. ABA, Denver Bar Assn., Colo. Bar Assn., Nat. Conf. Fed. Trial Judges (exec. com.), Dist. Judges' Assn. of 10th Cir. (past pres.), Colo. Women's Bar Assn., Fed. Judges Assn., Denver Crime Stoppers Inc. (bd.dirs.), Devner LWV, Women's Forum Colo., Harvard Law Sch. Assn., Phi Beta Kappa, Phi Kappa Phi, Order of Coif (hon. Colo. chpt.). Office: US Dist Ct 1929 Stout St Denver CO 80294-2900*

WEINSTEIN, GERALD D., dermatology educator; b. N.Y.C., Oct. 13, 1936; m. Marcia Z. Weinstein; children: Jeff, Jon, Debbie. BA, U. Pa., 1957, MD, 1961. Diplomate Am. Bd. Dermatology. Intern Los Angeles County Gen. Hosp., 1961-62; clin. assoc. dermatology br. Nat. Cancer Instn. NIH, Bethesda, Md., 1962-64; resident Dept. Dermatology U. Miami, Fla., 1964-65, asst. prof., 1966-71, assoc. prof., 1971-74, prof., 1975-79; prof. U. Calif., Irvine, 1979—, acting dean Coll. Medicine, 1985-87; attending staff VA Med. Ctr., Long Beach, Calif., 1979—, UCI Med. Ctr., Orange, Calif., 1979—, St. Joseph Hosp., Orange, 1980—; cons. Naval Regional Med. Ctr., San Diego, 1980—. Contbr. articles to profl. jours., chpts. to books. Spl. postdoctoral fellow NIH, 1965-67; co-recipient Award for Psoriasis Research Taub Internat. Meml., 1971. Mem. Am. Acad. Dermatology (chmn. task force on psoriasis 1986—, bd. dirs. 1984-88). Office: U Calif Irvine Calif Coll Medicine Office of Dean Irvine CA 92717

WEINSTEIN, NORMAN CHARLES, writer; b. Phila., Jan. 26, 1948; s. Emanuel Weinstein and Gertrude (Zamarin) Shaffer; m. Julie Jane Hall. BA, Bard Coll., 1969; MA in Tchg., SUNY, New Paltz, 1975. Instr. SUNY, New Paltz, 1971-73, Boise (Idaho) Sr. Ctr., 1981-85, Boise State U., 1981-93. Author: Gertrude Stein and the Literature of Modern Consciousness, 1970, (poetry) Nigredo, 1982, A Night in Tunisia, 1992. Recipient Deems Taylor award ASCAP, 1989. Mem. NARAS, African Studies Assn., Ctr. for Black Music Rsch. (assoc.). Home: 730 E Bannock St Boise ID 83712-6409

WEINSTEIN, STEVEN SAMUEL, marketing executive; b. N.Y.C., May 18, 1942; s. Jack Sidney and Fannie (Reiss) W.; m. Judith Ruhlman, Dec. 15, 1968; children: Rachel, Brian. BS, Rensselaer Poly. Inst., 1964; PhD, U. N.H., 1969; MBA, U. Conn., 1975. Product mgr. Becton-Dickinson Co., Cockeysville, Md., 1973-77; mktg. mgr. Tex. Instruments Corp., Lubbock, 1977-83; v.p. mktg. Spectravideo Inc., N.Y.C., 1983-84; pres. Databar Corp., Eden Prairie, Minn., 1984-85; mktg. cons. S.S. Weinstein & Assocs., Wayzata, Minn., 1985-87; v.p. mktg. Micro Display Systems, Inc., Hastings, Minn., 1987-89, Jr. Achievement Inc., Colorado Springs, Colo., 1989—; instr. Coll. St. Thomas, St. Paul, 1985—. Little League coach, Lubbock, 1978-80; bd. mem. Shaareth Israel Temple, Lubbock, 1981-82. Jewish. Home: 2225 Angelbluff Ct Colorado Springs CO 80919-3847

WEINSTOCK, CAROL ANN, manufacturing executive; b. San Francisco, July 19, 1946; d. Vernon A. and Kathleen (Taylor) Davison; D. Michael Romano, Apr. 4, 1971 (div. Mar. 1979); children: Michael G. Romano, Kimbely A. Romano; m. Ronald D. Weinstock, Jan. 12, 1984 (div.). BA in Edn., U. Ariz., 1964-70, grad. work, 1977-82; MS in Photography, Brooks Inst. Photography, 1982-84. Exhibits Shalom-Salaam Liese Communal Svcs. Bldg., Tucson, 1980; photographer Jews of Ethiopia, 1982, Nat. Jewish Community Rels. Adv. Coun., 1983, Jews of Ireland, 1985-87, Bet Hatefutsot Mus. of Diaspora, Tel Aviv, Israel, 1987-88, Westside Jewish Community Ctr., L.A., 1989, Irish Jewish Mus., Dublin, Ireland, 1992—; pres., owner EthnoGraphics Greeting Cards, 1987—. exec. bd., adv. com. Jewish Fedn. So. Ariz., 1979-82 chmn. Run for Soviet Jewry, 1983-84. Recipient Internat. Greeting Card awards, 1988, 91, 92, 93, 94, Cmty. Svc. award Jewish Fedn. So. Ariz., 1981, Simon Rockower award for excellence in Jewish journalism, Excellence in Photography mag. category, 1992. Mem. Am. Soc. Media Photographers, Greeting Card Assn. (bd. dirs. 1994—). Office: 417 Santa Barbara St # B 7 Santa Barbara CA 93101-2348

WEINSTOCK, RONALD JAY, research and development company executive; b. L.A., Mar. 14, 1960; s. Howard Frank and Anne Carol (Schneider) W.; m. Sigrid Lipsett, June 11, 1988; children: Rachel, Brent. Student, U. Calif., San Diego, 1978-80, U. Calif., Santa Barbara, 1980-81. CEO Magnetic Resonance Diagnostics Corp., Thousand Oaks, Calif., 1989—; vice chmn. Magnetic Resonance Rsch. Soc., Tokyo, 1991—; lectr. in field. Co-developer Magnetic Resonance Analyzer; contbr. articles to profl. jours. CPR instr. Am. Heart Assn., Beverly Hills, 1981; EMT, UCLA, 1980.

WEIR, ALEXANDER, JR., utility consultant, inventor; b. Crossett, Ark., Dec. 19, 1922; s. Alexander and Mary Eloise (Field) W.; m. Florence Forschner, Dec. 28, 1946; children: Alexander III, Carol Jean, Bruce Richard. BSChemE, U. Ark., 1943; MChemE, Poly Inst. Bklyn., 1946; PhD, U. Mich., 1954; cert., U. So. Calif. Grad. Sch. Bus. Adminstrn., 1968. Chem. engr. Am. Cyanamid Co., Stamford Rsch. Labs., 1943-47; with U. Mich., 1948-58; rsch. assoc., project supr. Engring. Research Inst., U. Mich., 1948-57; lectr. chem. and metall. engring. dept. U. Mich., 1954-56, asst. prof., 1956-58; cons. Ramo-Wooldridge Corp., Los Angeles, 1956-57, mem. tech. staff, sect. head, asst. mgr., 1957-60, incharge Atlas Missile Captive test program, 1956-60; tech. adv. to pres. Northrop Corp., Beverly Hills, Calif., 1960-70; prin. scientist for air quality So. Calif. Edison Co., Los Angeles, 1970-76, mgr. chem. systems research and devel., 1976-86, chief research scientist, 1986-88; utility cons. Playa Del Rey, Calif., 1988—; rep. Am. Rocket Soc. to Detroit Nuclear Council, 1954-57; chmn. session on chem. reactions Nuclear Sci. and Engring. Congress, Cleve., 1955; U.S. del. AGARD (NATO) Combustion Colloquium, Liege, Belgium, 1955; Western U.S. rep. task force on environ. research and devel. goals Electric Research Council, 1971; electric utility advisor Electric Power Research Inst., 1974-78, 84-87; industry advisor Dept. Chemistry and Biochemistry Calif. State U., Los Angeles, 1981-88. Author: Two and Three Dimensional Flow of Air through Square-Edged Sonic Orifices, 1954; (with R.B. Morrison and T.C. Anderson) Notes on Combustion, 1955, also tech. papers; inventor acid rain prevention device used in 5 states. Sea Scout leader, Greenwich, Conn., 1944-48, Marina del Rey, Calif., 1965-70; bd. govs., past pres. Civic Union Playa del Rey, chmn. sch., police and fire, nominating, civil def., army liaison coms; mem. Senate, Westchester YMCA, chmn. Dads sponsoring com., active fundraising; chmn. nominating com. Paseco del Rey Sch. PTA, 1961; mem. Los Angeles Mayors Community Adv. Com.; asst. chmn. advancement com., merit badge dean Cantinella dist. Los Angeles Area council Boy Scouts Am. Recipient Nat. Rsch. Coun. Flue Gas Desulfurization Industrials Scale Reliability award NAS, 1975, Power Environ. Achievement award EPA, 1980, Excellence in Sulfur Dioxide Control award EPA, 1985. Mem. AICE, Am. Geophys. Union, Navy League U.S. (v.p. Palos Verdes Peninsula coun. 1961-62), N.Y. Acad. Scis., Sci. Rsch. Soc. Am., Am. Chem. Soc., U.S. Power Squadron, St. Andrews Soc. So. Calif., Clan Macnachtan Assn., Clan Buchanan Soc. in Am., Betty Washington Lewis Soc. of Children of Am. Revolution (past pres.), Ark. Soc. of Children of Am. Revolution (past pres.), Santa Monica Yacht Club, Sigma Xi, Phi Kappa Phi, Phi Lambda Upsilon, Alpha Chi Sigma, Lambda Chi Alpha. Office: 8229 Billowvista Dr Playa Del Rey CA 90293-7807

WEIR, JIM DALE, small business owner; b. Phoenix, Feb. 2, 1956; s. Jim Earl and Laverne Alice (Mahan) W.; m. Myra Yvonne Anglin, July 19, 1980; children: Justin, Kevin, Amanda, Jordan. Student, Phoenix Coll., 1978; BS, Grand Canyon Coll., 1980. Owner Quality S Mfg., Phoenix, 1980—. Vol. Tempe (Ariz.) Ch. of the Nazarene, 1987-89, Latin Am. Ch. of the Nazarene, Phoenix, 1988-89. Recipient Key of City award Phoenix, 1987, Fast Growth award Inc. mag., 1988. Republican. Home: PO Box 23910 Phoenix AZ 85063-3910

WEIR, PETER DOUGLAS, accountant; b. Glendale, Calif., Oct. 11, 1959; s. Douglas Brenton and Diane Isabel (Leppert) W.; m. Allison Margaret Bowen, June 7, 1986; children: Heather Elizabeth, Michelle Christine. BA, U. Calif., Santa Barbara, 1981. CPA. Acct. Stonefield Josephson, An Accountancy Corp., L.A., 1981-87; ptnr. Brown & Weir, An Accountancy Corp., Glendale, 1987-94; pvt. practice Glendale, Calif., 1995—. Office: Peter D Weir An Accountacy Corp 505 N Brand Blvd Ste 750 Glendale CA 91203

WEISBROD, MARVIN LESTER, tax company executive; b. Schenectady, Mar. 22, 1928; s. Sidney Saul and Frances Helen (Miller) W.; m. Harriet Rose Grant, Feb. 5, 1950; children: Richard Allen, Sandra Lee. BS in Math. cum laude, Sienna Coll., 1954. Sr. actuarial clk. N.Y. State Employees' Retirement System, Albany, 1952-53; jr. actuary accident and health rates sect. N.Y. State Ins. Dept., Albany, 1953-54; mgr. actuarial dept., group sec. Empire State Mut. Life Ins. Co., Jamestown, N.Y., 1954-60; mgr. tax dept. to v.p., adminstrv. officer bd. dirs. Occidental Life Ins. Co. Calif., L.A., 1960-73; tax planner, v.p., treas. Equity Funding Corp. Am., Century City, Calif., 1973-74; office mgr., v.p. Triple Check Income Tax, Burbank, Calif., 1976—; mem. Pacific Stock Exch.; chmn. tax study com. Assn. Calif. Life Ins. Cos.; bd. dirs. Transam. Ins. Corp., 2nd v.p., tax officer Transam. Occidental Life; v.p., treas., trustee Equity Funding Corp. Am. Author manual. Pres. bd. trustees Congregation Temple Beth Torah; exec. v.p. Temple Ahavat Shalom; coach Little League; dist. mgr. [illegible] ship drive Campfire Girls; pack chmn. Cub Scouts. With U.S. Army, 1946-47, Japan. Mem. Am. Acad. Actuaries (enrolled agt.), Tax Execs. Inst., Nat. Assn. Securities Dealers (prin., fin. prin.), Pacific States Actuarial Club, L.A. Actuarial Club., Nat. Soc. Pub. Accts. Office: 727 S Main St Burbank CA 91506-2528

WEISBURD, HARRY NOAH, artist, educator; b. N.Y.C., Feb. 18, 1938; m. Guang Xin, Mar. 10, 1990; 1 child, Jing-Lin. Cert., Parsons Sch. Design, N.Y.C., 1959; student, San Francisco Art Inst., 1963; BFA, Calif. Coll. Arts & Crafts, 1965, MFA, 1966. Prof. art U. Conn., Storrs, 1966-71, Westfield (Mass.) State Coll., 1971-78; art instr. DeYoung Mus. Art, San Francisco, 1981; head Ctr. for the Visual Arts, Oakland, 1984-87. Work exhibited in numerous group exhbns., one-person shows, art galleries and pvt. collections; contbr articles to mags. With USAR, 1958-64. Recipient Purchase award North Bay Artists Assn., Benecia, Calif., 1963, Ford Found. grant Calif. Coll. Arts and Crafts, Oakland, 1964, Faculty grants for exptl. film making and sculpture U. Conn., Storrs, 1966-71. Mem. Coll. Art Assn. Home: PO Box 10036 Oakland CA 94610-0036

WEISENBURGER, THEODORE MAURICE, judge, poet, educator, writer; b. Tuttle, N.D., May 12, 1930; s. John and Emily (Rosenau) W.; children: Sam, Jennifer, Emily, Todd, Daniel, Dwight, Holly, Michael, Paul, Peter; m. Maylyne Chu, Sept. 19, 1985; 1 child, Irene. BA, U. N.D., 1952, LLB, 1956, JD, 1969; BFT, Am. Grad. Sch. Internat. Mgmt., Phoenix, 1957. Bar: N.D. 1963, U.S. Dist. Ct. N.D. 1963. County judge, tchr. Benson County, Minnewaukan, N.D., 1968-75, Walsh County, Grafton, N.D., 1975-87; tribal judge Devils Lake Sioux, Ft. Totten, N.D., 1968-84, Turtle Mountain Chippewa, Belcourt, N.D., 1974-87; U.S. magistrate U.S. Dist. Ct., Minnewaukan, 1972-75; Justice of the Peace pro tem Maricopa County, Ariz., 1988-92; instr. Rio Salado C.C., 1992—; tchr. in Ethiopia, 1958-59. 1st lt. U.S. Army, 1952-54. Author: Poetry and Other Poems, 1991. Recipient Humanitarian award U.S. Cath. Conf., 1978, 82, Right to Know award Sigma Delta Chi, 1980, Spirit of Am. award U.S. Conf. Bishops, 1982. Home: 2708 E Grovers Ave Phoenix AZ 85032-1647

WEISGERBER, JOHN SYLVESTER, provincial legislator; b. Barrhead, Alta., Can., June 12, 1940; s. Sylvester and Eva (Kilshaw) Harrison; m. Judith Muriel Janke, June 30, 1961; children: Joanne, Pamela. BBA, N. Alta. Inst. Tech., 1962. Owner Carland Ltd., 1975-81; econ. devel. commr. Peace River-Liard Regional Dist., Dawson Creek, 1982-84; sales mgr. Timberline Pontiac Buick GMC Ltd., Dawson Creek, 1984-86; mem. legis. assembly Govt. of B.C. (Can.), Victoria, 1986—, parliamentary sec. to min. of state, 1987-88, min. of state for Nechako and N.E., 1988-89, min. native affairs, 1989—; chmn. Cabinet Com. on Native Affairs, Victoria, 1988-90; mem. Cabinet Com. on Sustainable Devel., Victoria, 1988-90; mem. Select Standing Com. of Forests and Lands, Victoria, 1988-90; mem. Select Standing Com. on Agr. and Fisheries, Victoria, 1988-90; interim leader B.C. Social Credit Party, 1992-93; leader Reform Party of B.C., 1995. Bd. dirs., pres. Dawson Creek and Dist. Fall Fair, 1980-86. Mem. Rotary (past pres.), Mile O Riding Club (bd. dirs., pres. 1976-81). Office: Parliament Bldgs, Rm 101, Victoria, BC Canada V8V 1X4

WEISKOPF, WILLIAM HARVARD, accountant; b. Chgo., Feb. 18, 1938; s. William Herman and Josephine (Marron) W.; m. Carol Ruth Soderstrom, June 14, 1958; children: Cheryl Ruth, William Helge, Richard Harvard. BSBA, Northwestern U., 1960, MBA, 1967. CPA, Colo., Ill. Controller Clare Ceramics, Cary, Ill., 1960-63; chief fin. officer S.C. Lawlor Co., Melrose Park, Ill., 1964-65; staff acct. Ernst & Young, Chgo., 1967-69; staff acct. Ernst & Young, Denver, 1970-71, mgr., 1972-75, sr. mgr., 1976-78, ptnr., 1979-91; exec. dir. Colo. Sch. Mines Found., Inc., Golden, Colo., 1992—. Mem. exec. bd. Denver Coun. Boy Scouts Am., 1981—. Mem. AICPA (coun. mem. 1989-92), Colo. Soc. CPAs (pres. 1988-89), Leadership Denver Assn., Colo. Alliance of Bus. (dir., treas. 1986-91). Republican. Office: Colo Sch Mines Found Inc 923 16th St Golden CO 80401

WEISMAN, JEB, university administrator; b. Las Palmas, Spain, June 7, 1960; came to U.S., 1962; s. Edward B. and Joan (Murray) W.; m. Frances H. Harris, Mar. 24, 1989. BA in Anthropology, Vassar Coll., 1982; MA in Anthropology, N.Y. New Sch. Social Rsch., 1991; postgrad., N.Y. Sch. Social Rsch., 1991—. Fellow East-West Ctr., Honolulu, 1982-83; cons. computing and systems mgmt., 1983—; instr. phys. and cultural anthropology U. Hawaii - Manoa, Honolulu, 1982-83; supervising editor, microcmputer cons. Curriculum Concepts, Inc., N.Y.C., 1985-88, systems trainer/software developer, 1985-88; info. systems and techs. cons. The Children's Health Fund, N.Y.C., 1988-93; info. systems and techs. dir. divsn. community pediatrics Montefiore Med. Ctr. - Albert Einstein Coll. Medicine, N.Y.C., 1988-93; UNIX systems and internet adminstr. Pacific U., Forest Grove, Oreg., 1994—. Mem., activist Computer Profls. for Social Responsibility, 1993—, Electronic Frontier Found., 1993—. Mem. AAAS, IEEE Computer Soc., Assn. Computing Machinery, USENIX Assn., System Adminstrs. Guild, Info. Systems Security Assn., N.Y. Acad. Sci., Am. Anthropol. Assn., The Internet Soc. Office: Pacific U Forest Grove OR 97116

WEISMAN, MARTIN JEROME, manufacturing company executive; b. N.Y.C., Aug. 22, 1930; s. Lewis E. and Estelle (Scherer) W.; m. Sherrie Cohen, Jan. 27, 1952; children: Jane Dory, Andrea Sue, Amy Ellen. B in Chem. Engring., N.Y.U., 1951. Sr. chem. engr. Ideal Toy Corp., Hollis, N.Y., 1951-57; research chemist Chesebrough-Ponds, Stamford, Conn., 1957-62; mgr. nail products lab. Max Factor and Co., Hollywood, Calif., 1962-81; v.p., tech. dir. Sher-Mar Cosmetics div. Weisman Industries, Inc., Canoga Park, Calif., 1981—. Patentee in field. Mem. Soc. Cosmetic Chemists, Los Angeles Soc. Coatings Tech., Am. Chem. Soc. Office: Sher-Mar Cosmetics 8755 Remmet Ave Canoga Park CA 91304-1519

WEISMAN, PAUL HOWARD, lawyer; b. Los Angeles, Oct. 14, 1957; s. Albert L. and Rose J. (Zimman) W.; m. Allison L. Minas, Oct. 19, 1985. BA cum laude, U. Calif., Davis, 1979; JD, Loyola U., Los Angeles, 1982. Bar: Calif. 1982. Tax atty. legis. and regulations div. office of chief counsel Dept. of Treasury IRS, Washington, 1982-83; tax atty. dist. counsel/office of chief counsel Dept. of Treasury IRS, L.A., 1983-87; tax atty. Law Offices of Paul H. Weisman, L.A., 1987—; registered players contract rep. Nat. Football League Players Assn. Co-author BNA Tax Mgmt. Portfolio 404 2d Federal Tax Collection Procedure, publs. in field. Mem. Community and Rsch. Info. Ctr., 1989—; participant vol. Income Tax Assistance, L.A., 1981-83. Mem. San Fernando Valley Bar Assn., L.A. County Bar Assn. (co-chmn. tax ct. prose program). Republican.

WEISMAN, ROBERT EVANS, caterer; b. N.Y.C., Feb. 11, 1950; s. Arnold and Selma (Leinow) W.; m. Margaret Lavin, july 3, 1983; children: Sarah Miriam, Michael Samuel. BA, U. Wis., 1972. Gen. mgr. Medieval Manor, Boston, 1976-80, Ruppert's Restaurant, N.Y.C., 1980-82; owner Bobby Weisman Caterers, Los Angeles, 1983—. Office: Bobby Weisman 1105 S La Brea Ave Los Angeles CA 90019-6908

WEISMEYER, RICHARD WAYNE, academic administrator; b. Loma Linda, Calif., Oct. 15, 1943; s. Norman Glenn and Nedra Aileen (McGinniss) W.; m. Carol Mae Siebenlist, Aug. 16, 1970; children: Michael Brett, Marci Diann. BA in English, Loma Linda U., Riverside, Calif., 1966. Editorial asst. Loma Linda U., Loma Linda, 1966-70, editor new publs., 1970-75, dir. pub. rels., 1975—; mem. panel Heart Transplantation and Pub. Rels. sponsored by USA Today and fellows of ACS; bd. dirs. Sta. KSGN-FM, Riverside, Loma Linda Acad. Press; mem. group on pub. rels. Am. Med. Colls. Bd. dirs. Loma Linda Acad., Adventist Editors Internat. Mem. Pub. Rels. Assn. So. Calif., Coun. for Advancement and Support of Edn. Adventist. Home: 143 Browning St Riverside CA 92507-1245 Office: Loma Linda U Dept Pub Rels 24941 Stewart St Loma Linda CA 92350

WEISS, AMY LEE, interior designer; b. Mpls., Dec. 8, 1950; d. August Carl and Margaret Amelia (Wittman) W. AA in Home Econs., Cerritos Coll.; student, Long Beach State U., Santa Ana Jr. Coll. Asst. to interior designer Pati Pfahler Designs, Canoga Park, Calif., 1974-75; interior designer B.A. Interiors, Fullerton, Calif., 1976-78, Birns Cos., Rancho Mirage, Calif., 1978-79, Carole Eichen Interiors, Fullerton, 1981, Sears, Roebuck and Co., Alhambra, Calif., 1982-84; staff interior designer Assoc. Design Studios, Costa Mesa, Calif., 1979-81; sr. corp. designer, mgr. design studio Barratt Am., Irvine, Calif., 1984-88; owner Amy Weiss Designs, Coronado, Calif., 1988—; designer in residence San Diego Design Ctr., 1990-94. Mem. Am. Soc. Interior Designers (Globe-Guilders steering com. 1989-92, chmn. Christmas party, co-chmn. Christmas on Prado 1989, 89, designer for ASID showcase house 1992, 93), Bldg. Industry Assn. (sales and mktg. coun. awards com. 1993, mem. sales and mktg. coun. 1986-88, mem. home builders coun. 1994, 2d place M.A.M.E. award 1987, 1st place M.A.M.E. award 1986, 2d place S.A.M. award 1987), Building Industry Assn. Remodeler's Coun., Nat. Kitchen and Bath Assn., Coronado C. of C., Coronado Rotary; participant in Pacific Design Ctr. Designer on Call progarm, L.A. Home and Office: Amy Weiss Designs 10 Admiralty Cross Coronado CA 92118

WEISS, DICK JOSEPH, artist; b. Everett, Wash., June 24, 1946; s. Karl and Ann Weiss; m. Linda Soley (div.); m. June Simpson (div.); m. Sonja Blomdahl; 1 child, Melissa. BA, Yale U., 1968. faculty mem. flat glass summer session UCLA, 1980; artist-in-residence Pilchuck Glass Sch., Stanwood, 1982, faculty mem., 1983-84, 93; co-curator show Bellevue Art Mus., 1994. One-man shows include Traver Sutton Gallery, Seattle, 1979, 81, 88, William Traver Gallery, Seattle, 1990; exhibited in group shows at N.Y. Experimental Glass Workshop, N.Y.C., 1978, Jacksonville (Fla.) Art Mus., 1979, The Works Gallery, Phila., 1981, State Capitol Art Mus., Olympia, Wash., 1985, Bellevue (Wash.) Art Mus., 1988, 91, 93, The Glass Gallery, Bethesda, Md., 1991; represented in permanent collections including Pilchuck Glass Sch., Stanwood, Wash., Corning (N.Y.) Mus. Glass, Victoria and Albert Mus., London, etc. Grantee Nat. Endowment for Arts, 1981, 87. Democrat. Home: 811 N 36th St Seattle WA 98103-8806

WEISS, EDWARD ABRAHAM, lawyer; b. Chgo., Jan. 26, 1931; s. Morris Isaac and Gizella (Zeiger) W.; m. Phyllis Seibel, Oct. 1, 1983; children: Jennifer, Nathan, Chris, Darin, Corey. BSBA, U. Calif.-Berkeley, 1953; JD (Frank M. Angellotti scholar, John Norton Pomeroy scholar), Hastings Coll. Law, U. Calif.-San Francisco, 1959. Bar: Calif. 1960, U.S. Supreme Ct. 1971; CPA, Calif. Acct., Aitel & Aitel, CPAs, San Francisco, 1953, 55-57; assoc. Dreher & Frankel, Oakland, Calif., 1959-61; sole practice, Oakland, 1961-71, Walnut Creek, Calif., 1973—; sr. ptnr. Weiss & Paul, Oakland, 1967-69, Weiss & Wald, Oakland, 1969-71, Weiss & Pincus, 1988-89; exec. v.p., gen. counsel Am. Plan Investment Corp., San Francisco, 1971-72; lectr., instr. J.F. Kennedy Law Sch., 1973-75. Mem. aviation adv. com. Bd. Suprs.; bd. dirs. Jewish Welfare Fedn. Alameda and Contra Costa Counties, 1963-69; founder, bd. dirs. Beth Olam Meml. Chapel, 1971-72; bd. dirs. Jewish Community Relations Council Alameda and Contra Costa Counties, 1963-65, 67-68; pres. Congregation B'nai Sholom, 1969-71. Mem. Comml. Law League, ABA, State Bar Calif., Alameda County Bar Assn., Contra Costa County Bar Assn., Lawyer-Pilots Bar Assn., Thurston Honor Soc., Order of Coif. Home: 115 Bando Ct Walnut Creek CA 94595-2701

WEISS, HERBERT KLEMM, aeronautical engineer; b. Lawrence, Mass., June 22, 1917; s. Herbert Julius and Louise (Klemm) W.; m. Ethel Celesta Giltner, May 14, 1945 (dec.); children: Janet Elaine, Jack Klemm (dec.). B.S., MIT, 1937, M.S., 1938. Engr. U.S. Army Arty. Bds., Ft. Monroe, Va, 1938-42, Camp Davis, N.C., 1942-44, Ft. Bliss, Tex., 1944-46; chief WPN Systems Lab., Ballistic Research Labs., Aberdeen Proving Grounds, Md, 1946-53; chief WPN systems analysis dept. Northrop Aircraft Corp., 1953-58; mgr. advanced systems devel. mil. systems planning aeronutronic div. Ford Motor Co., Newport Beach, Calif., 1958-61; group dir., plans devel. and analysis Aerospace Corp., El Segundo, Calif., 1961-65; sr. scientist Litton Industries, Van Nuys, Calif., 1965-82; cons. mil. systems analysis, 1982—; Mem. Sci. Adv. Bd. USAF, 1959-63, sci. adv. panel U.S. Army, 1965-74, sci. adv. commn. Army Ball Research Labs., 1973-77; advisor Pres.'s Commn. Law Enforcement and Adminstrn. Justice, 1966; cons. Office Dir. Def., Research and Engring., 1954-64. Contbr. articles to profl. jours. Patentee in field. Recipient Commendation for meritorious civilian service USAF, 1964, cert. appreciation U.S. Army, 1976. Fellow AAAS, AIAA (assoc.); mem. IEEE, Ops. Research Soc. Am. Republican. Presbyterian. Club: Cosmos. Home: PO Box 2668 Palos Verdes Peninsula CA 90274-8668

WEISS, IRWIN KEVIN, pediatrician, educator; b. Bklyn., Nov. 13, 1961; married; 2 children. BA magna cum laude, Yeshiva U., 1982, MD Albert Einstein Coll. Medicine, 1986. Diplomate Am. Bd. Pediatrics, sub bd. pediatric critical care medicine, Nat. Bd. Med. Examiners. Intern. in Pediatrics North Shore U. Hosp. Cornell U. Mcd. Coll., Manhasset, N.Y., 1986-87; resident in Pediatrics North Shore U. Hosp., clin. assoc. Cornell U. Hosp., Manhasset, 1987-89; fellow Pediatric Critical Care The N.Y. Hosp. Cornell U. Med. Ctr., N.Y.C., 1989-92; asst. prof. Pediatrics divsn. Critical Care UCLA Med. Ctr., L.A., 1992—. Contbr. articles to profl. jours. Mem. AMA, Am. Acad. Pediatrics, Soc. Critical Care Medicine, N.Y. Soc. Pediatric Critical Care Medicine. Office: UCLA Med Ctr 10833 Le Conte Ave Los Angeles CA 90024

WEISS, LOREN ELLIOT, lawyer, educator; b. Cleve., Sept. 28, 1947; s. Harry and Gertrude (Rapport) W.; m. Gina Dalton. BA with honors, UCLA, 1969; JD cum laude, U. San Diego, 1972. Bar: Calif. 1972, U.S. Dist. Ct. (so. dist.) Calif. 1972, Utah 1983, U.S. Dist. Ct. (cen. dist.) Calif. 1983, U.S. Dist. Ct. Utah 1983, U.S. Ct. Appeals (9th cir.) 1972, U.S. Ct. Appeals (10th cir.) 1986. With various law firms, San Diego, 1972-80; owner, gen. mgr. Mid-Mountain Lodge, Park City, Utah, 1980-83; pvt. practice, Salt Lake City, 1983-89, 93—; of counsel Purser, Okazaki & Berrett, Salt Lake City, 1989-93; mem. Utah Com. Bar Examiners, Salt Lake City, 1986-90, mem. annual meeting com. Utah State Bar, 1985-91, chmn., 1994-95. Contbr. articles to legal jours. Trustee Utah Trout Found., Salt Lake City, 1988—. Mem. FBA, Calif. Bar Assn., Utah BAr Assn., Nat. Assn. Criminal Def. Lawyers (co-chmn. continuing legal edn. com. 1992-93, co-chair indigent svcs. com. 1994—), Utah Assn. Criminal Def. Lawyers (pres. 1993). Office: 1000 Boston Bldg Nine Exchange Pl Salt Lake City UT 84111

WEISS, MARTIN HARVEY, neurosurgeon, educator; b. Newark, Feb. 2, 1939; s. Max and Rae W.; m. R. Debora Rosenthal, Aug. 20, 1961; children: Brad, Jessica, Elisabeth. A.B. magna cum laude, Dartmouth Coll., 1960, B.M.S., 1961; M.D., Cornell U., 1963. Diplomate Am. Bd. Neurol. Surgery (bd. dirs. 1983-89, vice chmn. 1987-88, chmn. 1988-89). Intern Univ. Hosps., Cleve., 1963-64; resident in neurosurgery Univ. Hosps., 1966-70; sr. instr. to asst. prof. neurosurgery Case Western Res. U., 1970-73; asso. prof. neurosurgery U. So. Calif., 1973-76, prof., 1976-78, prof., chmn. dept., 1978—; chmn. neurology B study sect. NIH; mem. residency rev. com. for neurosurgery Accreditation Commn. for Grad. Med. Edn., 1989—, vice chmn., 1991-93, chmn., 1993—; Courville lectr. Sch. Medicine, Loma Linda U., 1989; W. James Gardner lectr. Cleve. Clinic, 1993; Edwin Boldrey vis. prof. U. Calif., San Francisco, 1994; hon. guest San Francisco Neurol. Soc., 1994; Edgar Kahn vis. prof. U. Mich., 1987; Arthur Ward vis. prof. U. Wash., 1988; Afrox traveling prof. South African Cong. of Neurol. Surgeons, 1989; Loyal Davis lectr. Northwestern U., 1990; John Raff lectr. U. Oreg., 1995. Author: Pituitary Diseases, 1980; mem. editl. bd. Neurosurgery, 1979-84, Neurol. Rsch., 1980—, Jour. Neurosurgery, 1987—, chmn., 1995—; editor-in-chief Clin. Neurosurgery, 1980-83; assoc. editor Bull. L.A. Neurol. Socs., 1976-81, Jour. Clin. Neurosci., 1981—. Served to capt. USAR, 1964-66. Spl. fellow in neurosurgery NIH, 1969-70. Mem. ACS (adv. coun. neurosurgery 1985-88), Soc. Neurol. Surgeons, Neurosurg. Soc. Am., Am. Acad. Neurol. Surgery (exec. com. 1988-89, v.p. 1992-93), Rsch. Soc. Neurol. Surgeons, Am. Assn. Neurol. Surgeons (bd. dirs. 1988-91, sec. 1994-97), Congress Neurol. Surgeons (v.p. 1982-83), Western Neurosurg. Soc., Neurosurg. Forum, So. Calif. Neurosurg. Soc. (pres. 1983-84), Phi Beta Kappa, Alpha Omega Alpha. Home: 357 Georgian Rd La Canada Flintridge CA 91011-3520 Office: 1200 N State St Los Angeles CA 90033-4525

WEISS, ROBERT STEPHEN, medical manufacturing and services company financial executive; b. Honesdale, Pa., Oct. 25, 1946; s. Stephen John and Anna Blanche (Lescinski) W.; BS in Acctg. cum laude, U. Scranton, 1968; m. Marilyn Annette Chesick, Oct. 29, 1970; children: Christopher Robert, Kim Marie, Douglas Paul. CPA, N.Y. Supr., Peat, Marwick, Mitchell & Co., N.Y.C., 1971-76; asst. corp. contr. Cooper Labs., Inc., Parsippany, N.J., 1977-78, v.p., corp. contr. Palo Alto, Calif., 1981-83; v.p., corp. contr. The Cooper Cos., Inc. (formerly CooperVision, Inc.), Palo Alto, Calif., 1984-89; v.p., treas., CFO The Cooper Cos., Inc., Pleasanton, Calif., 1989—, sr. v.p., 1992—; v.p. fin., contr. CooperVision Pharms., Mountain View, Calif., 1979, v.p. fin., group contr., 1980; bd. dirs. The Cooper Cos., Inc., Ft. Lee, N.J., 1992-94. With U.S. Army, 1969-70. Decorated Bronze Star with oak leaf cluster, Army Commendation medal. Mem. AICPA, N.Y. State Soc. CPAs. Home: 446 Arlington Ct Pleasanton CA 94566-7708 Office: The Cooper Cos Inc 6140 Stoneridge Mall Rd Pleasanton CA 94588-3232

WEISS BIZZOCO, RICHARD LAWRENCE, biology educator; b. N.Y.C., Dec. 28, 1940; s. Louis Lawrence Weiss and Annette Bizzoco; divorced; children: Shaynon Andrew, Wendy Alicia. BA, U. Conn., 1964; MS in Microbiology, Calif. State U., 1970; PhD in Microbiology/Biophysics, Ind. U., 1972. Am. Cancer Soc. rsch. fellow U. Calif., Berkeley, 1973; EM lab. dir. Harvard U., Cambridge, Mass., 1973-74, NIH fellow, 1975; assoc. med. microbiologist U. Calif. Med. Sch., Irvine, 1976-77; prof. San Diego State U., 1977—. NSF Instrumentation award, 1986. Mem. Phycological Soc. Am., Sigma Xi. Roman Catholic. Office: San Diego State U Dept Biology 5300 Campanile Dr San Diego CA 92115-1338

WEISSENBUEHLER, WAYNE, bishop. Bishop of Rocky Mountain Evang. Luth. Ch. in Am., Denver. Office: Rocky Mountain Synod ABS Bldg #101 7000 Broadway Denver CO 80221-2907

WEISSMAN, JERROLD, metal products executive; b. Great Falls, Mont., June 25, 1936; m. Nadyne B. Weissman; children: Aaron, Leila. Student, Denver U., 1953, U. Mont., 1954-55; AB in History and Econs., U. Miami (Fla.), 1958, postgrad. in history, 1958-61. Chmn. bd. dirs., chief operating officer, chief exec.officer N.W. Steel, Inc., 1962-81; chief exec. officer N.W. Steel of Idaho, Inc., 1973-81; sales mgr., asst. v.p., exec. v.p., pres., chief exec. ofcr. Carl Weissman & Sons, Inc., Great Falls, 1987—; pres., bd. dirs. Mont. Compressed Steel, Inc., N.W. Fence Products Co., Nat. Gen. Supply, Inc.; pres., bd. dirs. N. Warehouse Distbrs. Bd. dirs. Great Falls Children's Receiving Home, 1971-75; active United Way, 1961—; mem. City Trade Commn., 1983-85; fundraiser ARC; chmn. univ. com. Forward Great Falls, 1984; asst. scout master Boy Scouts Am., 1985-86; pres. Great Falls Hebrew Assn., 1984-86, 94-95, v.p. 1987, bd. dirs., 1990—; mem. Mont. Assn. Jewish Communities, 1986—; founding mem. N.W. Assn. Against Malicious Harassment; mem. Mont. Hist. Soc., various mus.; campaign worker, del. Rep. Party. Mem. Inst. Scrap Iron and Steel (chpt. officer, bd. dirs. 1963-86), Nat. Assn. Recycling Industries (mem. nat. legis. com. 1967-86), Inst. Scrap Recycling Industries, Nat. Assn. Steel Pipe Distbrs. (bd. dirs.1976-80, mem. standards com. 1976-80, convention dir. 1976-80), Masons (master 1969-70, mem. jr. exec. com. 1964-67, pres. jr. exec. com. 1966-67), Shriners, Meadowlark Country Club. Home: 2777 Greenbrier Dr Great Falls MT 59404-3639 Office: Carl Weissman & Sons Inc PO Box 1609 Great Falls MT 59403-1609

WEISSMAN, ROBERT ALLEN, lawyer, real estate broker; b. Los Angeles, May 26, 1950; s. Joseph Jonas and Shirley Rhoda (Solitare) W.; m. Susan Renee Bashner, Apr. 5, 1975; children: Evan Gregory, Russell Joseph, Dustin Raymond. Student, Chapman Coll., World Campus Afloat, 1970-71; BA, UCLA, 1972; JD, Southwestern U., 1975. Bar: Calif. 1975, U.S. Dist. Ct. Calif. 1976, D.C. 1980, U.S. Supreme Ct. 1982, U.S. Ct. Appeals (9th cir.) 1982. Ptnr., U.S. Dist. Ct. (no. dist.) Calif. 1985. Weissman & Weissman, L.A., 1975-81, prin., 1981—; speaker to profl. and trade groups. on creditor's rights, constrn. and mechanics' lien law. Contbg. author Calif. Real Property Jour., 1987; columnist on creditors rights and mechanics' lien law L.A. Daily Jour. contbr. articles to profl. jours. Pres.'s adv. coun. City of Hope, 1981-86. Named one of Outstanding Young Men of Am., U.S. Jaycees, 1980. Mem. ABA, State Bar Calif., L.A. County Bar Assn. (L.A. county founding mem., pre-judgement remedies sect., trustee 1994-95), San Fernando Valley Bar Assn. (co-chair bus. law sect. 1989-91, trustee 1991-92, treas. 1992-93, sec. 1993—, pres.- elect 1994, pres. 1995—), Calif. Land Title Assn., Bus. Trial Lawyers Assn., Comml. Law League Am., Assn. Real Estate Attys., Calif. Lawyers for Arts, Acad. Magical Arts, Inc. Club, Northridge Tennis Club, Masons. Democrat. Jewish. Office: Weissman & Weissman 16130 Ventura Blvd Ste 600 Encino CA 91436-2503

WEISSMANN, PAUL MARTIN, state legislator; b. Denver, Colo., June 9, 1964; s. Max Ludwig and Arlene Frances (Bloom) W. BA in Polit. Sci., U. Colo., 1986. Bartender Blue Parrot Restaurant, Louisville, Colo., 1989—; mem. Colo. State Senate, Denver, 1992—. Democrat. Jewish. Home: 822 La Farge Ave Louisville CO 80027-1824 Office: Colo State Senate State Capitol Denver CO 80203

WEISS-SWEDE, FRANCES ROBERTA See **ZAMIR, FRANCES ROBERTA**

WEITZ, SHERI LEE, dietitian; b. Canoga Park, Calif., Sept. 7, 1962; d. Walter Franklin Wissman and Debbie Mae (Keltz) Robbins; m. Gary Robin Weitz, Sept. 20, 1992. BS, Calif. State U., Northridge, 1986; intern in Dietetics, VA Med. Ctr., LaJolla, Calif., 1987. Clin. dietitian Martin Luther King Hosp., L.A., 1987-88, Midway Hosp., L.A., 1988-90, Rader Inst., L.A., 1990—; massage therapist Westland Health Ctr., West Los Angeles, Calif., 1990-94; nutritionist pvt. practice Playa del Rey, Calif., 1989—; massage therapist pvt. practice Paya del Rey, 1990—; spkrs. bur. Rader Inst., L.A., 1992—; nutrition cons. Cell Tech. Klamath Falls, Oreg., 1993—. Vol. speaker Heal the Bay, Santa Monica, Calif., 1992—. Recipient acad. scholarships Calif. State U. Northridge, 1984, 85, 86. Mem. Am. Dietetic Assn. (registered dietitian), Assn. Bodywork and Massage Profls., Omicron Nu, Phi Kappa Phi. Democrat. Jewish. Home and Office: 8505 Gulana Ave Spt 6103 Playa Del Rey CA 90293

WEITZ, SUE DEE, academic administrator; b. Coeur D'Alene, Idaho, Oct. 16, 1948; d. Donald and Larraine (Kiefer) W.; m. Greg Intinarelli, Nov. 25, 1984; children: Derek, Lauran, Marcus. BA cum laude, Coll. Idaho, 1971, MEd, 1975; postgrad., Ind. U., 1979-81; PhD, Gonzaga U., 1990. Coord. student activities, then asst. dean students Coll. Idaho, Caldwell, 1971-73, dean student life, 1974-76; assoc. dean students U. Cen. Ark., 1976-78; v.p. student affairs St. Mary-of-the-Woods (Ind.) Coll., 1978-81; dean of students Gonzaga U., Spokane, Wash., 1981-87, v.p. student life, 1987—; cons. Seattle U., 1989; evaluator Commn. on Colls., Seattle, 1990. Contbr. to profl. publs. Mem. Nat. Assn. Student Pers. Adminstrs., N.W. Assn. Coll. and Univ. Housing Officers, Nat. Assn. Coll. Activities, N.W. Coll. Pers. Assn. Office: Gonzaga Univ 502 E Boone Ave Spokane WA 99258-1774

WEITZE, WILLIAM FREDERICK, mechanical engineer; b. Westwood, N.J., May 4, 1960; s. Joseph Harry and May Elizabeth (Donnelly) W.; m. Sylvia Bankston Garcia, June 1, 1985 (div. Nov. 1991). BS in Mech. Engring., Rutgers U., 1982; MS in Mech. Engring., U. Calif., Berkeley, 1985. Lic. profl. engr., Calif. Program engr. nuclear energy GE, San Jose, Calif., 1982-85, engr., 1985-91, sr. engr., 1991—; cons. Engring. Cons. Svcs., San Jose, 1990—. Editor newsletter Silicon Valley Engring. Coun., 1991-92; contbr. articles to popular publs. Mem. ASME (treas., Santa Clara Valley 1990-91, sec. 1991-92, vice chmn. 1992-93, chmn. 1993-94, editor newsletter, 1988-90). Office: GE Nuclear Energy 175 Curtner Ave # C 747 San Jose CA 95125-1014

WEITZEL, JOHN QUINN, bishop; b. Chgo., May 10, 1928; s. Carl Joseph and Patricia (Quinn) W. BA, Maryknoll (N.Y.) Sem., 1951, M of Religious Edn., 1953; PMD, Harvard U. Ordained priest Roman Cath. Ch., 1955. With ednl. devel. Cath. Fgn. Mission Soc. of Am., Maryknoll, 1955-63, nat. dir. vocations for Maryknoll, dir. devel. dept. and info. services, 1963-72, mem. gen. council, 1972-78; asst. parish priest Cath. Ch., Western Samoa, 1979-81, pastor, vicar gen., 1981-86; consecrated bishop, 1986; bishop Cath. Ch., Am. Samoa, 1986—. Office: Diocese Samoa-Pago Pago Fatuoaiga PO Box 596 Pago Pago AS 96799-0596*

WELBORN, VICTORIA LEE, science librarian, educator; b. Thomasville, N.C., Feb. 17, 1953; d. Ivan Edward and Mary Christine (Murphy) W.; m. Craig K. Weatherington, Apr. 20, 1993. BA, Wake Forest U., 1975; MLS, Kent State U., 1979. Ref. libr. Health Scis. Libr. Ohio State U., Columbus, 1980-83, head Biol. Scis. Libr., 1983-88; head sci. libr. U. Calif., Santa Cruz, 1988—; adj. instr. Libr. Sch., Kent (Ohio) State U., 1987-88. Mem. Internat. Assn. Marme Scis. Librs. and Info. Ctrs. Office: U Calif Sci Libr Santa Cruz CA 95063

WELBORNE, JOHN HOWARD, lawyer; b. Los Angeles, July 24, 1947; s. William Elmo and Pauline Cornwell (Schoder) W.; m. Mary Martha Lampkin, Oct. 8, 1994. AB, U. Calif.-Berkeley, 1969; MPA, UCLA, 1974; JD, U. Calif.-Davis, 1977. Bar: Calif. 1977, D.C. 1980. Congl. intern Congressman John V. Tunney, Washington, 1969; assoc. firm Adams, Duque & Hazeltine, L.A., 1979-84, of counsel, 1984—; gen. counsel Magnum Software Corp., Chatsworth, Calif., 1989—; mgmt. cons., 1971—; dir. Pueblo Viejo Devel. Corp., 1979-88, Union Hardware & Metal Co. Contbr. articles to profl. jours. Mem. cen. bus. dist. project adv. com., downtown strategic plan adv. com., chmn. open space task force, mem. South Park task force City of L.A. Community Redevel. Agy.; mem. L.A. Philharm. Men's Com., 1978-89; pres. Los Angeles County Host Com. for Olympic Games, 1984; mem. exec. com. Citizens' Task Force for Cen. Libr. Devel., L.A., 1981-83; bd. dirs. L.A. chpt. ARC, 1986-89, Children's Bur. L.A., 1982-88, El Pueblo Park Assn., 1983-89, Inner City Law Ctr., 1992-95, Los Amigos del Pueblo, L.A. Libr. Assn., 1983-89, 92—, Windsor Sq. Assn., 1980-87, L.A. Beautiful, 1982-85, Pershing Sq. Restoration Campaign, 1986-87; bd. dirs. In the Wings div. Music Ctr. Los Angeles County, 1982-86, pres., 1984-85; bd. dirs., officer L.A. 200 Com., 1978-91; bd. councilors U. So. Calif. Sch. Pub. Adminstrn., 1983-89; mem. adv. bd. The L.A. Conservancy; trustee Windsor Sq.-Hancock Park Hist. Soc., 1983-86; fellow Amundsen Inst. U.S.-Mex. Studies, 1987. Capt. Adj. Gen.'s Corps, U.S. Army, 1970-71, USAR, 1972-79. Decorated Army Commendation medal with oak leaf cluster; Cross of Merit 1st class (Fed. Republic Germany). Mem. ABA, D.C. Bar Assn., State Bar Calif., Los Angeles County Bar Assn., Ordre des Coteaux de Champagne, Confrerie Saint-Etienne d'Alsace, Calif. Vintage Wine Soc. Episcopalian. Office: Magnum Software Corp 21115 Devonshire St Ste 337 Chatsworth CA 91311-2317

WELCH, BOBBY O'NEAL, dean; b. Brunswick, Ga., Sept. 26, 1937; s. Thomas Joseph and Inez (Gibbs) W.; m. Margaret Ann Sias, Oct. 1, 1960; children: Linda Ailieen, Carol Ann. BBA, U. Miami, 1961; MS in Sys. Mgmt., U. So. Calif., L.A., 1968; PhD in Mgmt. and Adminstrn., Walden U., 1994. Commd. 2d lt. USAF, 1961, advanced through grades to lt. col., 1975, ret., 1982; tech. staff Logicon, Ft. Walton Beach, Fla., 1985-88; sr. contract adminstr. Logicon, San Pedro, Calif., 1988-91, Intermetrics, Inc., Huntington Beach, Calif., 1991-92; pres., CEO Harbour Corp., Laguna Hills, Calif., 1992-93; assoc. dean Sch. Bus. and Mgmt., West Coast U., L.A., 1989—; v.p. Nat. Contract Mgmt. Assn., Huntington Beach, 1989-91. V.p. Village Pk. Homeowners Assn., Irvine, 1990-91, pres., 1991-92. Decorated Air medal, Bronze Star. Mem. Air Force Assn. Republican. Methodist. Home: 118 Sequoia Tree Ln Irvine CA 92715-2228

WELCH, CLAUDE (RAYMOND), theology educator; b. Genoa City, Wis., Mar. 10, 1922; s. Virgil Cleon and Deone West (Grenelle) W.; m. Eloise Janette Turner, May 31, 1942 (div. 1970); children—Eric, Thomas, Claudia; m. Theodosia Montigel Blewett, Oct. 5, 1970 (dec. 1978); m. Joy Neuman, Oct. 30, 1982. BA summa cum laude, Upper Iowa U., 1942; postgrad., Garrett Theol. Sem., 1942-43; BD cum laude, Yale U., 1945, PhD, 1950; DD (hon.), Ch. Div. Sch. of Pacific, 1972, Jesuit Sch. Theology, 1982; LHD (hon.), U. Judaism, 1976. Ordained to ministry Meth. Ch., 1947. Instr. religion Princeton (N.J.) U., 1947-50, asst. prof., 1950-51, vis. prof., 1962; asst. prof. theology Yale U. Div. Sch., New Haven, 1951-54, assoc. prof., 1954-60; Berg prof. religious thought, chmn. dept. U. Pa., Phila., 1960-71, assoc. dean Coll. Arts and Scis., 1964-68, acting chmn. dept. philosophy, 1965-66; prof. hist. theology Grad. Theol. Union, Berkeley, Calif., 1971—, dean, 1971-87, pres., 1972-82; vis. prof. Garrett Theol. Sem., 1951, Pacific Sch. Religion, 1958, Hartford Sem. Found., 1958-59, Princeton Theol. Sem., 1962-63, U. Va., 1987; Fulbright sr. lectr. U. Mainz, Germany, 1968; Sprunt lectr. Union Theol. Sem., Richmond, Va., 1958; Willson lectr. Southwestern U., Georgetown, Tex., 1994; dir. study of grad. edn. in religion Am. Coun. Learned Socs., 1969-71; del. World Conf. on Faith and Order, 1963. Author: In This Name: the Doctrine of the Trinity in Contemporary Theology, 1952, (with John Dillenberger) Protestant Christianity, interpreted through its Development, 1954, 2d rev. edit., 1988, The Reality of the Church, 1958, Graduate Education in Religion: A Critical Appraisal, 1971, Religion in the Undergraduate Curriculum, 1972, Protestant Thought in the 19th Century, vol. 1, 1799-1870, 1972, vol. 2, 1870-1914, 1985; Editor, translator: God and Incarnation in Mid-19th Century German Theology (Thomasius, Dorner and Biedermann), 1965; Contbr. to publs. in field. Recipient decennial prize Bross Found., 1970; Guggenheim fellow, 1976; NEH research fellow, 1984, Fulbright research fellow, 1956-57. Mem. Am. Acad. Religion (pres. 1969-70), Coun. of Socs. for Study of Religion (chmn. 1969-74, 85-90), Soc. for Values in Higher Edn. (pres. 1967-71), Am. Soc. Ch. History, Am. Theol. Soc., Phi Beta Kappa. Home: 123 Fairlawn Dr Berkeley CA 94708-2107

WELCH, LLOYD RICHARD, electrical engineering educator, communications consultant; b. Detroit, Sept. 28, 1927; s. Richard C. and Helen (Felt) W.; m. Irene Althea Main, Sept. 12, 1953; children—Pamela Irene Welch Towery, Melinda Ann, Diana Lia Welch Worthington. B.S. in Math., U. Ill., 1951; Ph.D. in Math., Calif. Inst. Tech., 1958. Mathematician NASA-Jet Propulsion Lab., Pasadena, Calif., 1956-59; staff mathematician Inst. Def. Analyses, Princeton, N.J., 1959-65; prof. elec. engring. U. So. Calif., L.A., 1965—; cons. in field. Contbr. articles to profl. jours. Served with USN, 1945-49, 51-52. Fellow IEEE; mem. Nat. Acad. Engring., Am. Math. Soc., Math. Assn. Am., Soc. for Indsl. and Applied Math., Phi Beta Kappa, Sigma Xi, Phi Kappa Phi, Pi Mu Epsilon, Eta Kappa Nu. Office: U So Calif Elec Engring Bldg 500A Los Angeles CA 90089

WELCHERT, STEVEN JOSEPH, public affairs consultant; b. Davenport, Iowa, June 16, 1956; s. Richard Marshall and Norma Jean (Waters) W.; m. Kathleen Ann Agnitsch, June 13, 1981; children: Sarah Elizabeth, Matthew Joseph. BGS, U. Iowa, 1979. Nat. field staff Ted Kennedy for President, 1979-80; polit. dir. Lucero for U.S. Senate, Denver, 1984; legis. dir. for Gov. Richard Lamm, Denver, 1984-87, sr. edn. advisor for, 1985-87; issues dir. for Mayor Federico Peña, Denver, 1987; v.p. Bonham/Shlenker & Assocs., Denver, 1988-90; pres. The Welchert Co., Denver, 1990—; staff chmn. Nat. Govs. Assn., Washington and Denver, 1986; on-air analyst Sta. KMGH-TV, Denver, 1987—; Wis. dir. Gore for Pres., Milw., 1988; floor whip Dem. Nat. Platform Com., 1988. Writer radio series Ind. Thinking, 1987-88. Advisor Cultural Facilities Dist., Denver, 1988; bd. dirs. Citizens for Denver's Future, 1989-90; active Denver Baseball Commn., 1986-89, also chmn. govt. com., Rocky Mt. chpt. Am. Ireland Fund. Named Rising Leader for 90's Colo. Bus. Mag., 1990. Mem. Am. Assn. Polit. Cons. Democrat. Roman Catholic. Office: The Welchert Co 1525 Market St # 200 Denver CO 80202-1607

WELD, ROGER BOWEN, clergyman; b. Greenfield, Mass., Dec. 1, 1953; s. Wayland Mauney and Luvycie (Bowen) W.; m. Patricia Ann Kaminski, June 7, 1978 (div. 1979); m. Cynthia Lou Lang, Apr. 15, 1995. Grad., Sacred Acad. Jamilian U. of the Ordained, Reno, 1976-77, Seminary, 1978-82; student, U. Nev., 1983-85; postgrad., Sacred Coll. Jamilian Theology, 1988-90. Ordained to ministry, Internat. Comty. of Christ Ch. of Second Advent, 1977; appointed Rabban priest Internat. Comty. of Christ, 1993. Adminstrv. staff Internat. Community of Christ Ch. of Second Advent, Reno, 1977—, exec. officer dept. canon law, 1985—, exec. officer advocates for religious rights and freedoms, 1985—, exec. officer speakers bur., 1985—, exec. officer office pub. info., 1986—, mgr. Jamilian Univ. Press, 1987—, dir. advt. prodns., 1988—; founder, pres. Crown Rsch. Found., 1992—. Author: Twelve Generations of the Family of Weld: Edmund to Wayland Mauney, 1986; dir. photography, supervising editor: (video documentary) Gene Savoy's Royal Roads to Discovery. Staff sgt. USAF, 1971-75. Named Life Mem., Sacred Oversee, 1991. Mem. Nev. Clergyman's Assn., Andean Explorers Found. (Explorer's medal 1990), Ocean Sailing Club (exec. sec. 1988—, Participant's Silver Medallion 1989). Office: Internat Community Christ 643 Ralston St Reno NV 89503-4436

WELK, RICHARD ANDREW, plastic surgeon; b. Aug. 9, 1956. BS, U. Mich., 1977, MD, 1981. Diplomate Am. Bd. Surgery, Am. Bd. Plastic Surgery. Resident gen. surgery Grand Rapids, Mich., 1981-86; resident plastic surgery U. Calif., Irvine, 1986-88; plastic surgeon pvt. practice, Kirkland, Wash., 1988-91, Polyclinic, Seattle, 1991—. Mem. AMA, Am. Soc. Plastic & Reconstructive Surgery, Am. Soc. Aesthetic Plastic Surgery, Wash. State Med. Assn., Wash. Soc. Plastic Surgeons (pres. 1995—). Office: Polyclinic 1145 Broadway Seattle WA 98122-4201

WELLBORN, CHARLES IVEY, company executive, lawyer; b. Houston, Dec. 9, 1941; s. Fred W. and Emily R. (Gladu) W.; m. J.D. McCausland, Aug. 14, 1965; children: Westly O., Kerry S. BA in Econs., U. N.Mex., 1963, JD, 1966; LLM, NYU, 1972. Bar: N.Mex. 1966, U.S. Dist. Ct. N.Mex. 1966. Assoc. Neal & Matkins, Carlsbad, N.Mex., 1966-68; Robinson & Stevens, Albuquerque, 1969-71; ptnr. Schlenker, Parker, Payne & Wellborn, Albuquerque, 1971-76, Parker & Wellborn, Albuquerque, 1976-82; ptnr. Modrall, Sperling, Roehl, Harris & Sisk, Albuquerque, 1982-95; pres. Sci. and Tech. Corp. at U. N.Mex., Albuquerque, 1995—. Bd. dirs. N.Mex. Symphony Orch., 1988-91; bd. dirs. U. N.Mex. Anderson Schs. Mgmt. Found., 1989-94; vice chair U. N.Mex. Found., Inc., 1990-94; mem. Gov.'s Bus. Adv. Coun., 1989—; Small Bus. Adminstrn. Fin. Svcs. Adv., N.Mex., 1989; mem. venture capital mgmt. adv. com. N.Mex. State Investment Coun., 1991—; mem. Econ. Forum, vice-chair, 1993—; chmn. Roots & Wings Found., 1989—; v.p. N.Mex. Dem. Bus. Coun., 1992—; bd. dirs. Accion N.Mex., 1994—. Contbr. articles to law revs. Sgt. USAF, 1968-69, Korea. Fellow Am. Bar Found.; mem. ABA (ho. of dels. 1984-91), Albuquerque Bar Assn. (pres. 1977-78), N.Mex. Bar Found. (pres. 1980-82), State Bar N.Mex. (pres. 1982-83). Democrat. Roman Catholic. Office: Sci and Tech Corp at U NMex 851 University Blvd SE Ste 200 Albuquerque NM 87106

WELLER, DONALD MIGHELL, graphic designer, illustrator; b. Colfax, Wash., Aug. 13, 1937; s. Harry Charles and Margaret Genevieve (Mighell) W.; m. Camille Ann Iantosca, 1964 (div.); children: Anna Margaret, Nancy Rosetta, Julie Casamire, Kathy Ruth; m. Chikako Matsubayashi, Dec. 27, 1976. BA, Wash. State U., 1960. Prodn. artist The May Co., L.A., 1960-61; designer UCLA Ext., 1961-63, Robert H. Haddad, L.A., 1962-63, Will Martin Design, L.A., 1965-68; art dir. Ron Grauer, Pasadena, Calif., 1964-65; owner, art dir. Weller & Juett Inc., L.A., 1968-72; founder, owner Weller Inst. for Cure of Design Inc., L.A., 1972-84, Park City, Utah, 1984—; co-founder, dir. The Design Conf. that Just Happens to be in Park City, design conf., Park City, 1978—. Designer, illustrator, pub.: Park City, 1985; photographer, designer, pub.: Seashells and Sunsets, 1988, The Cutting Horse, 1990 (award N.Y. Art Dirs. 1991). Recipient gold medal N.Y. Art Dirs. Club, 1971, The One Show, N.Y.C., 1973, 76, L.A. Art Dirs. Show, 1974, 75. Mem. Salt Lake Art Dirs. Club (bd. dirs. 1991-93), L.A. Soc. Illustrators (pres., bd. dirs., Lifetime Achievement award 1983), L.A. Art Dirs. Club (sec., bd. dirs. 1966-84), Utah Cutting Horse Assn. (bd. dirs. 1993-94). Office: PO Box 518 Oakley UT 84055

WELLER, GUNTER ERNST, geophysics educator; b. Haifa, June 14, 1934; came to U.S., 1968; s. Erich and Nella (Lange) W.; m. Sigrid Beilharz, Apr. 11, 1963; children: Yvette, Kara, Britta. BS, U. Melbourne, Australia, 1962, MS, 1964, PhD, 1968. Meteorologist Bur. Meteorology, Melbourne, 1959-61; glaciologist Australian Antarctic Exps., 1964-67; from asst. prof. to assoc. prof. geophysics Geophys. Inst., U. Alaska, Fairbanks, 1968-72, prof., 1973—, dep. dir., 1984-86, 90—; project dir. NASA-UAF Alaska SAR Facility, Fairbanks, 1983-93; program mgr. NSF, Washington, 1972-74; pres. Internat. Commn. Polar Meteorology, 1980-83; chmn. polar rsch. bd. NAS, 1985-90, Global Change Steering Com. Sci. com. on Antarctic Rsch., 1988-92; chmn. Global Change Working Group Internat. Arctic Sci. Com., 1990—; dir. Ctr. for Global Change and Arctic System Rsch., U. Alaska, 1990; dir. Coop. Inst. Arctic Rsch., 1994—. Contbr. numerous articles to profl. jours. Recipient Polar medal Govt. Australia, 1969; Mt. Weller named in his honor by Govt. Australia, Antarctica; Weller Bank named in his honor by U.S. Govt., Arctic. Fellow AAAS (exec. sec. arctic divsn. 1982—), Arctic Inst. N.Am.; mem. Internat. Glaciological Soc., Am. Meteorol. Soc. (chmn. polar meteorology com. 1980-83), Am. Geophys. Union. Home: PO Box 81024 Fairbanks AK 99708-1024 Office: U Alaska Geophys Institute Fairbanks AK 99775

WELLES, JOHN GALT, museum director; b. Orange, N.J., Aug. 24, 1925; s. Paul and Elizabeth Ash (Galt) W.; m. Barbara Lee Chrisman, Sept. 15, 1951; children: Virginia Chrisman, Deborah Galt, Barton Jeffery, Holly Page. BE, Yale U., 1946; MBA, U. Pa., 1949; LHD (hon.) U. Denver, 1994. Test engr. Gen. Electric Co., Lynn, Mass., 1947; labor relations staff New Departure div. Gen Motors Corp., Bristol, Conn., 1949-51; mem. staff Mountain States Employers Coun., Denver, 1952-55; head indsl. econs. div. U. Denver Research Inst., Denver, 1956-74; v.p. planning and devel. Colo. Sch. Mines, Golden, 1974-83; regional adminstr. EPA, Denver, 1983-87; exec. dir. Denver Mus. Natural History, 1987-94, dir. emeritus, 1994—. Sr. cons. Secretariat, UN Conf. Human Environment, Geneva, 1971-72; cons. Bus. Internat., S.A., Geneva, 1972; trustee Tax Free Fund of Colo., N.Y., 1987—; exec. com. Denver Com. on Fgn. Rels., 1987—; bd. dirs Gulf of Maine Found., 1995—; chmn. Colo. Front Range Project, Denver, 1979-80. Contbr. articles to profl. jours., newspapers. Recipient Disting. Svc. award Denver Regional Coun. Govts., 1980, Barnes award EPA, 1987. Mem. AAAS, Am. Assn. Museums (ethics commn. 1991-94, v.p. 1992-95), Sustainable Futures Soc. (nat. adv. bd. 1994—), Met. Denver Exec. Club (pres. 1967-68), World Future Soc., Univ. Club (Denver) Denver Athletic Club, Tau Beta Pi, Blue Key. Republican. Episcopalian.

WELLES, MELINDA FASSETT, artist, educator; b. Palo Alto, Calif., Jan. 4, 1943; d. George Edward and Barbara Helena (Todd) W. Student, San Francisco Inst. Art, 1959-60, U. Oreg., 1960-62; BA in Fine Arts, UCLA, 1964, MA in Spl. Edn., 1971, PhD in Ednl. Psychology, 1976; student fine arts and illustration Art Ctr. Coll. Design, 1977-80. Cert. ednl. psychologist, Calif. Asst. prof. Calif. State U., Northridge, 1979-82, Pepperdine U., L.A., 1979-82; assoc. prof. curriculum, teaching and spl. edn. U. So. Calif., L.A., 1980-89; mem. acad. faculty Pasadena City Coll., 1973-79, Art Ctr. Coll. Design, 1978—, Otis Coll. Art and Design, L.A., 1986—, UCLA Extension, 1980-84, Coll. Devel. Studies, L.A., 1978-87, El Camino C.C., Redondo Beach, Calif., 1982-86; cons. spl. edn.; pub. adminstrn. analyst UCLA Spl. Edn. Rsch. Program, 1973-76; exec. dir. Atwater Park Ctr. Disabled Children, L.A., 1976-78; coord. Pacific Oaks Coll. in svc. programs for L.A. Unified Schs., Pasadena, 1978-81; mem. Southwest Blue Book, Freedom's Found. at Valley Forge, Friends of French Art, bd. dirs. Costume Coun. L.A. County Mus. of Art., Assistance League of So. Calif. Author: Calif. Dept. Edn. Tech. Reports, 1972-76; editor: Teaching Special Students in the Mainstream, 1981, Educating Special Learners, 1986, 88, Teaching Students with Learning Problems, 1988, Exceptional Children and Youth, 1989; group shows include: San Francisco Inst. Art, 1960, U. Hawaii, 1978, Barnsdall Gallery, L.A., 1979, 80; represented in various pvt. collections. HEW fellow, 1971-72; grantee Calif. Dept. Edn., 1975-76, Calif. Dept. Health, 1978. Mem. Am. Psych. Assn., Calif. Learning Disabilities Assn., Am. Council Learning Disabilities, Calif. Scholarship Fedn. (life), Alpha Chi Omega. Office: 700 Levering Ave Apt 1 Los Angeles CA 90024-2795

WELLINGER, CHARLES H., health services company executive; b. 1945. BBA, Wichita State U., 1972; MPH, U. Mo., 1972. Various positions Kamen Supply Co., Wichita, Kans., 1963-72; adminstrv. resident St. Luke's Hosp., Kansas City, Mo., 1972-73, assoc. dir., 1977-80, assoc. exec. dir., 1980; adminstr., CEO Spelman Meml. Hosp., Smithville, Mo., 1980-82; sr. adminstr., COO Good Samaritan Med. Ctr., Phoenix, 1982-86, CEO, 1989-91; CEO Thunderbird Samaritan Hosp. and Health Ctr., Glendale, Arix., 1986-89; exec. v.p., COO Samaritan Health Svcs., Phoenix, 1991—; also chmn. Ariz. Physicians IPA Inc., Phoenix. Office: Ariz Physicians IPA Inc 4041 N Central Ave Bldg B Phoenix AZ 85012

WELLISCH, WILLIAM JEREMIAH, social psychology educator; b. Vienna, Austria, July 3, 1938; came to U.S., 1940; s. Max and Zelda (Schanser) W.; m. Geraldine Eve Miller (dec. Feb. 1970); children: Garth Kevin, Miriam Rhoda; m. Claudine Abbey Truman, Sept. 5, 1971; children: Rebecca Colleen, Marcus Joshua, Gabriel Jason. MA in Sociology, U. Mo., 1965, PhD in Sociology, 1968. Researcher urbanization Hemispheric Consultants, Columbia, Mo., 1968-69; cons. to local govt. ofcl. on L.Am. Bicultural Consultants, Inc., Denver, 1969-70; prof. Red Rocks Coll., Lakewood, Colo., 1970-76, 77—. Author: Bi-Cultural Development, 1971, Honduras: A Study in Sub-Development, 1978. Mem. citizen's adv. bd. Sta. KCFR Pub. Radio, Denver, 1989—. Republican. Mem. Unification Ch. Home: 2325 Clay St Denver CO 80211-5123 Office: Red Rocks CC 13300 W 6th Ave Lakewood CO 80401

WELLIVER, CHARLES HAROLD, hospital administrator; b. Wichita, Kans., Feb. 14, 1945; married. BA, Wichita State U., 1972; MHA, U. Mo., 1974. Asst. dir. St. Luke's Hosp., Kansas City, 1974-79, assoc. dir., 1979-80; adminstr. Spelman Meml. Hosp., Smithville, Mo., 1980-82; sr. adminstr., COO Good Samaritan Med. Ctr., Phoenix, 1982-86, v.p., CEO, 1989—; v.p., CEO Thunderbird Samaritan Hosp., Glendale, Ariz., 1986-89. Office: Good Samaritan Regional Med Ctr 1111 E McDowell Rd Phoenix AZ 85006-2837

WELLS, CHRISTINE LOUISE, physical education educator; b. Buffalo, N.Y., Mar. 22, 1938; d. Harold Edward and Edythe Adelina (Burton) W. BS in Edn., U. Mich., 1959; MS, Smith Coll., 1964; PhD, Pa. State U., 1969. Phys. edn. tchr. Grosse Pointe (Mich.) Pub. Schs., 1959-62; instr. Smith Coll., Northampton, Mass., 1962-66; NDEA scholar Pa. State U., University Park, 1969-72; asst. prof. Dalhousie U., Halifax, N.S., Can., 1969-72; NIH postdoctoral fellow U. Calif., Santa Barbara, 1971-73; assoc. prof. Temple U., Phila., 1973-76; assoc. prof. Ariz. State U., Tempe, 1976-80, prof., 1980—; Lorraine C. Snell vis. prof. Northeastern U., Boston, 1984; mem. adv. bd. Rodale Press, Emmaus, Pa., The Women's Sports Found., Eisenhower Park, N.Y., 1992—; presenter more than 100 papers in field, 1970—; cons. U.S. Olympic Physiology Com., 1982—, Granville Corp., 1982, Whittle Corp., 1986-91; mem. adv. bd. Internat. Dance-Exercise Assn., 1982-90, Melpomene Inst. Women's Health Rsch., 1983—, Nat. Inst. Fitness and Sport, 1985-91. Author: Women, Sport and Performance: A Physiological Perspective, 1985, 2d edit., 1991, (with E.M. Haymes) Environment and Human Performance, 1986, (with others) Research and Practice in Physical Education, 1977, Female Endurance Athletes, 1986, Physical Activity and Human Well-Being, 1986, Future Directions in Exercise and Sport Science Research, 1989; mem. editorial bd. Cycling Sci., Women in Sport and Phys. Activity Jour., 1990—, biol. rev. editor; mem. adv. bd. Walking Mag., 1987—, Time-Life Fitness Series, 1987, Moxie, 1989-90, Shape Mag., 1993—, Bicycling Mag., 1987—, Runner's World, 1987—; contbr. articles to profl. jours., chpts. to books; jour. reviewer in field. Alumni fellow Pa. State U., 1984; recipient Wonder Woman Found. award 1982, Women's Sport Found. Individual Contbn. to Women's Sports award 1983, Disting. Alumna award U. Mich., 1994. Fellow AAHPERD, Rsch. Consortium, (chmn. position statements 1976-77, pres. 1978-79, exec. v.p. search com. 1986, alliance scholar com. chair 1988-89), Am. Coll. Sports Medicine (trustee 1979-92, v.p. for edn. 1982-84, chmn. meetings evaluation 1976-77; pres. S.W. chpt. 1989-90, chmn. student breakfast 1984, position statements com. 1984, Citation award 1995); mem. Ariz. State Assn. of Health, Phys. Edn. and Recreation, Am. Acad. Kinesiology and Phys. Edn. (membership com. chairperson 1986-87, 93-94, program com. 1988-89), Sigma Xi, Phi Lambda Theta, Phi Sigma. Office: Ariz State U Dept Exercise Sci Phys Edn Tempe AZ 85287-0404

WELLS, DAVID CONRAD, lawyer; b. L.A., June 22, 1938; s. Glenn W. and Maxine B. Wells; m. D. Charlene Moore, Apr. 6, 1963; children: Karen A., Michael V. BA, U. Colo., 1960, LLB, 1963. Bar: Colo. 1963. Assoc., Mack, Johnson & Doty, Boulder, Colo., 1963-66; ptnr. Zook & Wells, Boulder, 1966-68; sole practice, Boulder, 1969-75; ptnr. Wells, Love & Scoby, Boulder, 1975—; lectr. Constable, Boulder County, 1960-63; fire chief Boulder Heights Fire Protection Dist., 1972-78. Mem. ABA, Colo. Bar Assn., Boulder County Bar Assn., Am. Arbitration Assn. Author legal articles. Office: 225 Canyon Blvd Boulder CO 80302-4920

WELLS, GEORGE DOUGLAS, corporate executive; b. Clydebank, Scotland, Aug. 6, 1935; came to U.S., 1960; m. Roberta S. Rennie, 1959; children: Carole, George Leslie, Neil. BSc with honors, U. Glasgow, Scotland, 1957, MS, 1959. With Fairchild Camera & Instrument Corp., Mountain View, Calif., successively gen. mgr. diode div., gen. mgr. transistor div., gen. mgr. discrete group, gen. mgr. analog and discrete group, sr. v.p., from 1977, exec. v.p., until 1983; pres. Intersil Inc. div. GE, Cupertino, Calif., 1983-85; pres., chief oper. officer, mem. Office Chief Exec. L.S.I. Logic Corp., Milpitas, Calif., 1985-92; pres., CEO Exar Corp., 1992—. Home: 14580 Carnelian Cir Saratoga CA 95070-5966 Office: LSI Logic Corp 1551 Mccarthy Blvd Milpitas CA 95035-7424

WELLS, JEFFREY M., state senator, lawyer, judge; b. Springfield, Mass., Sept. 26, 1948; s. William and Paulina Wells; m. Sherri; children: Pamela, Kimberly, Tom. BA, Duke U., 1970; MBA, Fla. State U., 1972, J.D., 1974. Ptnr. firm Wilder & Wells, P.C., Colorado Springs, Colo.; mem. Colo. State Senate, 1982—, majority leader, 1987—. Mem. El Paso Bar Assn., Colo. Bar Assn., Fla. Bar Assn., Colo. Trial Lawyers Assn., Moose Club. Republican. Presbyterian. Office: Wilder & Wells 524 S Cascade Ave Ste 1 Colorado Springs CO 80903-3934 Office: Office State Senate State Capitol Denver CO 80203

WELLS, LU, artist; b. Althouse, Oreg., May 10, 1915; d. Joseph Lee and Emma (Hervey) Sowell; m. Charles Keith Wells, May 4, 1933; children: Tommy Lee, Donald Eugene. Comml. Art Design and Illus., Oreg. Inst. Tech., 1955. instr. pvt. classes and local galleries, Tri-Hue Watercolor, Klamath Falls, 1989-92. Exhibited in group shows at Crater Lake Nat. Park, Oreg. Caves Chateau, first tri-hue show Maui, Hawaii. With USAF, 1945-58. Recipient Spl. Svc. award The Favell Mus., Klamath Falls, 1991. Mem. Watercolor Soc. Oreg. (recipient awards), Daus. Am. Colonists (regent 1962-64), Daus. Am. Revolution (registrar). Home: 256 1/2 N Laguna St Klamath Falls OR 97601-2344

WELLS, MARK ALAN, systems manager; b. Burlington, Vt., Jan. 16, 1960; s. Charles H. and Sally (Temple) Whitson; m. Michelle M. Murphy, Feb. 23, 1985; children: Benjamin Mark, Richard Alan, Kendall Colby. Grad., Boulder Vo-Tech, 1977. Screen dept. mgr. Centerline Cirs., Longmont, Colo., 1978-87; prodn. mgr. GTE Corp., Printed Cir. Bd. Operation, Muncy, Pa., 1987-88; card store mgr. Heinrich Mktg., Denver, 1988—, mgr. prodn., MIS; bus. owner Reflective Images, Longmont, Colo., 1984-87; cons. MW Svcs., Arvada, Colo., 1990-91. With U.S. Army, 1977. Home: 10363 W 68th Way Arvada CO 80004-1512 Office: Heinrich Mktg Inc 1350 Independence St Lakewood CO 80215-4629

WELLS, MERLE WILLIAM, historian, state archivist; b. Lethbridge, Alta., Can., Dec. 1, 1918; s. Norman Danby and Minnie Muir (Huckett) W.; student Boise Jr. Coll., 1937-39; A.B., Coll. Idaho, 1941, L.H.D. (hon.), 1981; M.A., U. Calif., 1947, Ph.D., 1950; L.H.D., U. Idaho, 1990. Instr. history Coll. Idaho, Caldwell, 1942-46; assoc. prof. history Alliance Coll., Cambridge Springs, Pa., 1950-56, 58, dean students, 1955-56; cons. historian Idaho Hist. Soc., Boise, 1956-58, historian and archivist, 1959—; hist. preservation officer, archivist State of Idaho, Boise, 1968-86. Treas., So. Idaho Migrant Ministry, 1960-64, chmn., 1964-67; nat. migrant adv. com. Nat. Council Chs., 1964-67, gen. bd. Idaho council, 1967-75; bd. dirs. Idaho State Employees Credit Union, 1964-67, treas., 1966-67; mem. Idaho Commn. Arts and Humanities, 1966-67; mem. Idaho Lewis and Clark Trail Commn., 1968-70, 84-88; mem. Idaho Bicentennial Commn., 1971-76; bd. dirs. Sawtooth Interpretive Assn., 1972—, dept. history United Presbyn. Ch., 1978-84; v.p. Idaho Zool. Soc., 1982-84, bd. dirs., 1984-94, treas., 1988-90, historian, 1990—. State Hist. Preservation Officers (dir. 1976-81, chmn. Western states council on geog. names 1982-83), Am. Hist. Assn., Western History Assn. (council 1973-76), AAUP, Am. Assn. State and Local History (council 1973-77), Soc. Am. Archivists, Assn. Idaho Historians (pres., 1994), others. Author: Anti-Mormonism in Idaho, 1978, Boise: An Illustrated History, 1982, Gold Camps and Silver Cities, 1984, Idaho: Gem of the Mountains, 1985. Office: Idaho State Hist Soc 210 Main St Boise ID 83702-7264

WELLS, PATRICK HARRINGTON, biology educator; b. Palo Alto, Calif., June 19, 1926; s. Harrington and Doris Virginia (Lacsten) W.; m. Pearl Marie Pernich, July 27, 1951; children: Harrington, Patricia Ann, John Thomas. BA, U. Calif., Santa Barbara, 1948; PhD, Stanford U., 1951. Asst prof. biology U. Mo., Columbia, 1951-57; from asst. prof. to prof. biology Occidental Coll., L.A., 1957—, prof. emeritus, 1991. Co-author (book) Anatomy of a Controversy: the Question of a Language Among Bees, 1990; contbr. articles to profl. jours. Fellow AAAS, So. Calif. Acad. Sci. (dir. 1972-78, mem. adv. bd. 1977—); mem. Am. Zoologists Soc., Zool. Soc. Japan, History of Sci. Soc., Internat. Bee Rsch. Assn., Western Soc. of Naturalists. Office: Occidental Coll Dept Biology 1600 Campus Rd Los Angeles CA 90041-3384

WELLS, RICHARD H., gaming research executive; b. Stillwater, Okla., June 24, 1940; s. James R. and Edna Ruth (McKnight) W.; m. Peggy P.

Puyear, Aug. 7, 1988; children: Shanley Renne, Richard Carlyle, Amy Luru. BS in Gen. Bus., Okla. State U., 1964; student systems dynamics program, MIT, 1985-86. Sr. fin. analyst Conoco, Houston, 1964-69; v.p. planning Union Planters Nat. Bank, Memphis, 1969-75; v.p. fin. planning Inn devel. Holiday Inns, Memphis, 1975-78, v.p. corp. adminstrn., 1979-80; sr. v.p. planning-adminstrn. Harrah's, Reno, 1980-86; v.p. Bally's Casino Hotels, Reno, 1986-90; co-owner Pennington & Assocs., Reno, 1990—; founder, owner Casino Player Count Svc., Reno, 1990—; founder, pres. Wells Gaming Rsch., Reno, Nev., 1995—. Mem. Reno Downtown Redevel. Com., 1983-84, Reno Task Force for Econ. Diversification, 1984, Nev. Gov.'s Econ. Adv. Com., 1983-84, Reno-Sparks Conv. Authority Rsch. Coun., 1990; chmn. Washoe Med. Found. Project Mgmt. Group, 1990; mem. dir. Econ. Devel. Authority Western Nev., 1992—. Served with USAR, 1958-61. Mem. Reno C. of C. (dir. 1983-84), Fin. Execs. Inst. (pres. 1974-75). Home: PO Box 3781 Reno NV 89505-3781

WELLS, ROGER STANLEY, software engineer; b. Seattle, Apr. 13, 1949; s. Stanley A. and Margaret W. BA, Whitman Coll., 1971; postgrad., U. Tex., Austin, 1973-74; BS, Oreg. State U., 1977. Software evaluation engr. Tektronix, Beaverton, Oreg., 1979-83; computer engr. Aramco, Dhahran, Saudi Arabia, 1983-84; software engr. Conrac Corp., Clackamas, Oreg., 1984-85, Duarte, Calif., 1985; software analyst Lundy Fin. Systems, San Dimas, Calif., 1986-89; contract software analyst for various orgns. Seattle, 1989-92; software engr. U.S. Intelco, Olympia, Wash., 1993—. Bd. dirs. The Science Fiction Mus., Salem, Oreg., 1993—. Sgt. USAF, 1971-75. Mem. Am. Philatelic Soc., Am. Inst. Parliamentarians, Portland Sci. Fiction Soc., N.W. Sci. Fiction Assn., Internat. Platform Assn., Assn. Computing Machinery, L.A. Sci. Fantasy Soc., Oreg. Sci. Fictin Convs. (pres., co-founder 1979-81) Melbourne (Australia) Sci. Fiction Club, Toastmasters Internat. (club pres. 1980, v.p. edn. 1994-95, area gov. 1994-95). Home: 4820 Yelm Hwy SE Apt B-102 Lacey WA 98503

WELLS, WILLIAM ADRAIN, non-profit executive; b. San Antonio, Jan. 16, 1951; s. Jarold Adrain and Sarah Ferne (Cain) W. BA, Trinity U., San Antonio, 1972; MA, 1974; cert. in History, Woodbrooke Coll., U.K., 1976. Instr. Trinity U., San Antonio, 1972-76; nat. dir. Programs Rsch. Epilepsy Found. Am., Washington, 1978-81; nat. dir. Planning and Evalulation Fund Raising Am. Heart Assn., Dallas, 1981-83; exec. dir. Am. Heart Assn., Washington, 1983-86; exec. v.p. Am. Heart Assn., L.A., 1986-88, Childrens Hosp. Found., L.A., 1989-92; exec. dir. Ctr. for Living, L.A., 1992-93; v.p. Weingart Ctr. Assn., L.A., 1993—; adv. coun. George Washington U., 1980-81; exec. com. Calif. Biomedical Rsch. Found., Berkeley, Calif., 1986-88; founding assoc. Lymphoma Rsch. Found., L.A., 1991-92; bd. dirs. Am. Heart Assn., Hollywood, Calif., 1991-92. Author, producer: (video series) New Directions in Rehabilitation, 1980; author: Epilepsy Research, 1981, Prentice-Hall Fund Raising Sries, 1984. Ofcl. participant Jeunesse-Carnegie Hall, N.Y.C., 1980; mem. Rotary L.A., 1986-89; com. mem. L.A. Com. Nat. Inst. Health Centennial, 1987; city commn. Ethical Standards, L.A. Social Svcs., 1990. Mem. Nat. Soc. Fund Raising Execs. Republican. Home: 913 Dolores Rd Altadena CA 91001-1740

WELSCH, SUZANNE CAROL, mathematics educator; b. Chgo., Nov. 23, 1941; d. James Dumont Seiler and Lotta May Marjorie (Grayson) Langford; m. Ralph Kelley Ungermann, Mar. 31, 1962 (div. Mar. 1980); children: Annette Carol, Scott Kelley; m. John Henry Welsch, Jan. 2, 1981; children: James Henry, Lee William. AA in Math., Ventura Coll., 1962; BA in Stats., U. Calif., Berkeley, 1964; MA in Math., U. Calif., Irvine, 1972. Computer programmer N.Am. Space & Info. Systems, Downey, Calif., 1964-65; biostatistician U. Calif., Irvine, 1969-73; owner, mgr. Ungermann Assocs., developers Logcap software, Los Altos, 1972-80; prof. math., stats. and computers Sierra Nevada Coll., Incline Village, Nev., 1983—; chmn. sci. dept. Sierra Nevada Coll., Incline Village, 1989—; founder, owner, mgr. Zilog, Los Altos, Calif., 1974; cons. Long Beach Heart Assn., 1972-75. Contbr. articles to profl. jours. Neighborhood chmn., bd. dirs., coun., treas., leader Girl Scouts U.S., 1971—, treas., Reno, 1985-86; pres. Parents Advocation Givted Edn. for Students, 1989-95; bd. dirs. Nev. State Odyssey of the Mind. Recipient appreciation pin Sierra Nevada coun. Girl Scouts U.S.A., 1986; Outstanding Tchr. award Sierra Nevada Coll., 1987, svc. award, 1990. Mem. AAUW, Math. Assn. Am., Am. Statis. Assn., Nat. Coun. Tchrs. Math., Assn. Women in Math., Nat. Assn. Advisors for Health Professions, Consortium of Math. Programs, Nev. Assn. for Gifted, U. Calif. Alumni Assn. Home: 680 Saddlehorn Dr Incline Village NV 89451-8500 Office: Sierra Nevada Coll 800 College Dr Incline Village NV 89451-9114

WELSH, DORIS MCNEIL, early childhood education specialist; b. Kansas City, Mo.; d. Zelbert Melbourne and Anna May (Main) McNeil; children: J. Randall, Valerie M. BA, U. Calif., Berkeley, 1950, MA, 1952; postgrad., U. San Francisco, 1980-82. Cert. tchr., counselor, supr., Calif. Asst. dir. Bing Sch., Stanford, Calif., 1966-76; family devel. specialist Children's Hosp., Stanford, 1976-78; rsch. cons. Stanford U. Med. Ctr., 1970-87; dir. One Fifty Parker Sch., San Francisco, 1978—; citizen ambassador del. edn. & childcare People to People Internat., St. Petersburg, Russia, Vilnius, Lithuania, Budapest, Hungary, 1993; pres. bd. dirs. Support for Parents of Spl. Children, San Francisco, 1986-87; bd. dirs. Family Svc. Assn. Mid-Peninsula, Palo Alto, Calif., 1970-80; leader Summer Camp for Pre-Schoolers, East Palo Alto, 1970-73; leader parenthood discussion groups U. Chgo., 1963-64; lectr. in field. Vol. Irving Mental Hosp., Chgo., 1963. Mem. Nat. Assn. Edn. Young Children, Assn. Childhood Edn. Internat., World Affairs Coun., Audubon Soc., Sierra Club. Office: One Fifty Parker Sch 150 Parker Ave San Francisco CA 94118

WELSH, JOHN BERESFORD, JR., lawyer; b. Seattle, Feb. 16, 1940; s. John B. and Rowena Morgan (Custer) W. Student U. Hawaii, 1960, Georgetown U., 1960; BA, U. Wash., 1962, LLB, 1965. Bar: Wash. 1965. Staff counsel Joint Com. on Govtl. Cooperation, 1965-66; asst. atty. gen. Dept. Labor and Industries, 1966-67; atty. Legis. Coun., acting as counsel to Pub. Health Com., Labor Com., Pub. Employees Collective Bargaining Com., Com. on State Instns. and Youth Devel., State of Wash., 1967-73; sr. counsel Wash. Ho. of Reps., counsel to Ho. Com. on Social and Health Svcs., Olympia, 1973-86; counsel Ho. Com. Human Svcs., 1987-91, 93-95, Ho. Com. on Health Care, 1987—, Ho. Com. on Trade and Econ. Devel., 1995—; legal cons. Gov.'s Planning Commn. Vocat. Rehab., 1968, Gov.'s Commn. on Youth Involvement, 1969; envoy from Gov. Wash. to investiture of Prince of Wales, London, 1969; faculty Nat. Conf. State Legislatures, Denver, 1977, New Orleans, 1977, San Francisco, 1984, Orlando, Fla., 1985, Denver 1986, Kansas City, Mo., 1987, Washington, 1988, Indpls., 1989, Seattle, 1990, Ft. Lauderdale, Fla., 1991, Albuquerque, 1992, Boston, 1994, chmn. legis. issues com., 1986, mem. steering com., 1986-90, legis. issues com., 1986—, Coun. of State Govts. Coun. on Licensure, Enforcement and Regulation, 1984, 86-90, 87-88, Coun. of State Govts. com. on suggested state legis., 1988—, sub com. scope and agenda, 1988—. Hon. prof. health adminstrn. Eastern Wash. U., 1982. Mem. Wash. Bar Assn., Govtl. Lawyers Assn., Nat. Health Lawyers Assn., Soc. des Amis du Musée de l'Armée, Paris, English Speaking Union, La Societé Napoleonienne and Medals Soc. Am., Sons of Union Veterans of the Civil War, Custer Battlefield Hist. & Mus. Assn., 8th Army Air Force Hist. Assn., Napoleonic Assn Am., Phi Delta Phi. Office: Wash Ho Reps Olympia WA 98504

WELSH, JOHN RICHARD, state official; b. Neillsville, Wis., May 27, 1938; s. Francis Richard and Bernice Margaret (Schneider) W.; m. Carol Kay Ableidinger, Sept. 30, 1961; children: Tony, Becky, Cathy, Michael, Chelley. BBA, Loyola U., Chgo., 1977; postgrad., No. Ariz. State U. Benefit mgr. George F. Brown & Sons, Chgo., 1968-69, Marsh & McLennon, Chgo., 1969-71; adminstrv. mgr. Kemper Ins. Group, Long Grove, Ill., 1971-73; benefits mgr. 1st Nat. Bank of Chgo., 1973-79, The Arizona Bank, Phoenix, 1979-81; cons. Phoenix, 1981-84; benefits mgr., arbitrator Frontier Airlines, Inc., Denver, 1984-85; benefits mgr. Dept. Adminstrn., State of Ariz., Phoenix, 1985-91; retirement officer, seminar facilitator Ariz. State Retirement Sys., Phoenix, 1991—; team leader, benefits adv. Total Quality Mgmt. Ariz. State Retirement System, Phoenix, 1995. High sch. football ofcl. Ariz. Interscholastic Assn., Phoenix, 1980-93; football coach Portage Park Sports, Chgo., 1969-79, baseball coach, 1969-79; basketball coach K.C., Durand, Wis., 1966-68. With USN, 1956-59. Mem. Nat. Assn. for Pre-Retirement Edn., Loyola U. Alumni Assn. (Phoenix chpt.). Roman Catholic. Home: 4141 W Hayward Ave Phoenix AZ 85051-5751 Office: Ariz ... Sys 3300 N Central Ave Phoenix AZ 85012-2501

WELSH, MARY MCANAW, educator, family mediator; b. Cameron, Mo., Dec. 7, 1920; d. Francis Louis and Mary Matilda (Moore) McA.; m. Alvin F. Welsh, Feb. 10, 1944 (dec.); children: Mary Celia, Clinton F., M. Ann. AB, U. Kans., 1942; MA, Seton Hall U., 1960; EdD, Columbia U., 1971. Reporter, Hutchinson (Kans.) News Herald, 1942-43; house editor Worthington Pump & Machine Corp., Harrison, N.J., 1943-44; tchr., housemaster, coordinator Summit (N.J.) Pub. Schs., 1960-68; prof. family studies N.Mex. State U., Las Cruces, 1972-85; adj. faculty dept. family practice Tex. Tech. Regional Acad. Health Ctr., El Paso, 1978-82, Family Mediation Practice, Las Cruces, 1986—. Mem. AAUW (pres. N.Mex. 1981-83), N.Mex. Council Women's Orgn. (founder, chmn. 1982-83), Delta Kappa Gamma, Kappa Alpha Theta. Democrat. Roman Catholic. Author: A Good Family is Hard to Found, 1972; Parent, Child and Sex, 1970; contbr. articles to profl. jours.; writer, presenter home econs. and family study series KRWG-TV, 1974; moderator TV series The Changing Family in N.Mex./LWV, 1976. Home and Office: PO Box 3483 University Park Las Cruces NM 88003

WELSOME, EILEEN, journalist; b. N.Y.C., Mar. 12, 1951; d. Richard H. and Jane M. (Garity) W.; m. James R. Martin, Aug. 3, 1983. BJ with honors, U. Tex., 1980. Reporter Beaumont (Tex.) Enterprise, 1980-82, San Antonio Light, 1982-83, San Antonio Express-News, 1983-86, Albuquerque Tribune, 1987-94. Recipient Clarion award, 1989, News Reporting award Nat. Headliners, 1989, John Hancock award, 1991, Mng. Editors Pub. Svc. award AP, 1991, 94, Roy Howard award 1994, James Aronson award, 1994, Gold Medal award Investigative Reporters and Editors, 1994, Sigma Delta Chi award, 1994, Investigative Reporting award Nat. Headliners, 1994, Selden Ring award, 1994, Heywood Broun award, 1994, George Polk award, 1994, Sidney Hillman Found. award, 1994, Pulitzer Prize for nat. reporting, 1994; John S. Knight fellow Stanford U., 1991-92.

WELTER, COLE H., artist, educator; b. Watertown, S.D., July 26, 1952; s. Phillip Henry and Jane (Lambert) W.; m. Lisa Dawn Jones, June 18, 1988. BFA with honors in Studio Art, U. Tex., 1974, MFA in Painting, 1976; PhD in Fine Art, Tex. Tech. U., 1989. Teaching asst. U. Tex., Austin, 1975-76; sr. designer MacMillan Pub., N.Y.C., 1976-81; art dir. Random House Pub., N.Y.C., 1981-82; pres. Welter & Assocs., N.Y.C., 1982-86; grad. fellow Tex. Tech. U., Lubbock, 1986-88; asst. prof. art U. Alaska, Anchorage, 1988-92, assoc. prof. art, 1992—, chair dept. art, 1990—. Editor Alaska Jour. Art, 1989—; contbr. articles to profl. jours.; exhbns. include Butler Inst. Am. Art, 1975, Abilene Mus. Art, 1988 (Juror's Citation 1988). Exec. bd. dirs. Anchorage Mus. Art, 1988-92. Recipient Reston Prize in writing Nat. Assn. Schs. Art, Theatre and Music, 1987, Disting. Alumni award Tex. Tech. U., 1991; named Alaska Art Educator of the Yr., Alaska Art Edn. Assn., 1990, 92; Ford Found. painting fellow, 1975, 76, Tex. Tech. U./DeVitt-Jones fellow, 1986. Mem. Coll. Art Assn., Nat. Art Edn. Assn. Office: University of Alaska 3211 Providence Dr Anchorage AK 99508-4614

WELTER, LINDA ALLAIRE, developer; b. Bayonne, N.J., Aug. 11, 1949; d. Godfrey Adolf and Grace Elizabeth (Buss) W. BA in Philosophy and Polit. Sci., Drew U., 1971, postgrad., 1972-73; postgrad., Harvard U., 1985; MBA, Boston Coll., 1987. Development asst. Harvard U., Cambridge, Mass., 1980-83, development assoc., 1983-85, dir. class and area programs, 1985-86, sr. development officer, 1986-87; from capital campaign dir. to asst. v.p. for resources Wellesley (Mass.) Coll., 1987-93; v.p., gen. mgr. for development ops. ARC, Washington, 1993-94; dir. major gifts U. Calif., Berkeley, 1994—; instr. Stonehill Coll., Easton, Mass.; lectr. Northeastern U., Boston; cons. Vassar Coll.; fundraising cons. Dimock Comty. Health Ctr., Boston, 1992. Vol. co-chair fundraising Ruah; mem. capital campaign com. Fenway Cmty. Health Ctr.; vol. Nat. Network on Women as Philanthropists. Mem. Women in Development (bd. dirs., chair city svc. project), Coun. for Advancement and Support of Edn. (teaching faculty 1985—), Women in Philanthropy. Office: U Calif Univ Rels 2440 Bancroft Way Berkeley CA 94720

WELTON, CHARLES EPHRAIM, lawyer; b. Cloquet, Minn., June 23, 1947; s. Eugene Frances and Evelyn Esther (Koski) W.; m. Nancy Jean Sanda, July 19, 1969; children: Spencer Sanda, Marshall Eugene. BA, Macalester Coll., 1969; postgrad., U. Minn., 1969-70; JD, U. Denver, 1974. Bar: Colo. 1974, U.S. Dist. Ct. Colo. 1974, U.S. Supreme Ct. 1979, U.S. Ct. Appeals (10th cir.) 1980. Assoc. Davidovich & Assocs., and predecessor firm, Denver, 1974-77, Charles Welton and Assocs., Denver, 1978-80, 1984-88; ptnr. Davidovich & Welton, Denver, 1981-84, OSM Properties, Denver, 1982—; prin. Charles Welton, P.C., 1988—; adj. prof. Inst. Advanced Legal Studies U. Denver, 1991—; lectr. in field. Author study; contbr. articles to profl. jours. Sch. pres. PTSA, Denver, 1983-84; coach Colo. Jr. Soccer League, 1980-85; coach Odyssey of the Mind (formerly Olympics of the Mind), 1986-88; bd. dirs. Virginia Vale Swim Club, officer, 1989-91, Pioneer Jr. Hockey Assn., 1990-92. Served alt. mil. duty Denver Gen. Hosp., 1970-72. Mem. Denver Bar Assn. (law week case mediator, legal fee arbitration com.), Colo. Bar Assn. (legal fee arbitration com.), Assn. Trial Lawyers Am., Colo. Trial Lawyers Assn. (bd. dirs. 1985-90, chmn. seminar com. 1986-88, exec. com. 1987-88, legis. com. 1988—), Am. Bldg. a Lasting Earth (founder), Exec. Ventures Group of Am. Leadership Forum (adv. bd. 1987-90). Democrat. Lutheran. Home: 615 E 7th Ave Denver CO 80207 Office: Old Smith Mansion 1751 Gilpin St Denver CO 80218-1205

WELTON, DAVID GERALD, telecommunications educator, writer, researcher; b. Oakland, Calif., Jan. 31, 1957. AA in Media Arts, Lassen Coll., Susanville, Calif., 1984, AA in Liberal Arts, 1986; BA in Comm., Calif. State U., Chico, 1988, MA in Social Sci., 1993. Instr. comm. studies and media prodn. technician Lassen Coll., Susanville, 1984-86; rsch. asst. Survey Rsch. Ctr. Calif. State U., Chico, 1988-90; tech. editor Videomaker Mag., Chico, 1990-93; assoc. faculty telecomm. dept. Butte Coll., Chico, 1993—; rschr. video project No. Calif. Cmty. Rsch. Group, U. Calif., Davis, 1993—; lectr. in field. Contbg. writer MGW Newspaper, Sacramento, 1991—, Videomaker Mag., Chico, 1993—; editor Sociologists Lesbian and Gay Caucus Newsletter, 1989, CenterStone, the newsletter of the Stonewall Alliance, 1990-92; contbr. articles to profl. jours.; prodr. videos including AIDS Ednl. Videos for African Am. Audiences, 1994, Videomaker: The Video Series, 1991, 93, Healthy Chico 2000, 1992, Telephone Interviewer Training, 1990, Virginia Satir, 1989, Becoming Employable, 1984, others. Mem. Chico Dem. Club, 1988—, Dem. Nat. Com., 1988—, River City Dem. Club, 1989—, Nat. Gay and Lesbian Task Force, 1989—; founding mem. Stonewall Alliance of Chico, bd. dirs., 1991-92; mem. ACLU. Mem. Sociologists Lesbian and Gay Caucus, Sociologists AIDS Network, Nat. Lesbian and Gay Journalists Assn. Home: PO Box 3375 Chico CA 95927-3375 Office: No Calif Cmty Rsch Group Psychology Dept Univ Calif-Davis Davis CA 95616

WELTY, JOHN DONALD, university president; b. Amboy, Ill., Aug. 24, 1944; s. John Donald and Doris (Donnelly) W.; children: Anne, Elisabeth. B.S., Western Ill. U., 1965; M.A., Mich. State U., 1967; Ed.D., Ind. U., 1974. Asst. v.p. for student affairs SW State U., Marshall, Minn., 1973-74; dir. residences SUNY-Albany, 1974-77, assoc. dean for student affairs, 1977-80; v.p. for student and univ. affairs Indiana U. of Pa., 1980-84, pres., 1984-91; pres. Calif. State U., Fresno, 1991—; lectr. in field. Contbr. articles to profl. jours. Chmn. Small Bus. Incubator of Indiana, 1985-91; bd. dirs. Open Door Crises and Counseling Ctr., Indiana, Big Bros./Big Sisters, Indiana, 1980-84. Recipient Chancellor's award SUNY, 1977. Mem. Pa. Assn. Student Personnel Adminstrs., Am. Coll. Personnel Assn., Am. Assn. State Colls. and Univs., Nat. Assn. Student Personnel Adminstrs., Indiana C. of C. (bd. dirs.), Assn. Gov. Bds. Roman Catholic. Lodge: Rotary. Office: Calif State U 5241 N Maple Ave Fresno CA 93740-8027

WELTY, ROBERT G., petroleum company executive. Pres., CEO Bow Valley Industries Ltd., Calgary; chmn. Asamera Inc., Calgary. Office: Bow Valley Industries Ltd, PO Box 6610 Station D, Calgary, AB Canada T2P 3R2

WEMISCHNER, ROBERT BARRY, culinary educator; b. Newark, July 11, 1951; s. Harry and Elsie (Steinholtz) W.; m. Leslie Jo Raffel, June 27, 1982; children: Lauren, Chad. BA in Oriental Studies, U. Pa., 1972. Chef, owner Creative Catering, Westfield, N.J., 1972-75, Le Grand Buffet, Beverly Hills, Calif., 1976-85; culinary instr. Balt. Internat. Culinary Arts Inst., 1986; chef, owner What's Cookin'?, Balt., 1987-91; culinary instr. L.A. Trade Tech. Coll., 1991—; cons. start-up bakeries and food prodn. cos., Calif., 1970—. Author: The Vivid Flavors Cookbook, 1994; contbr. articles to Fine Cooking and Cook's Illustrated mags. Recipient 2d pl. Spice of Life award Food Mgmt. Mag., 1993. Mem. Internat. Assn. Cooking Profls., Am. Culinary Fedn. (cert. exec. chef, cert. culinary educator), Retail Bakers Assn. Office: LA Trade Tech Coll 400 W Washington Blvd Los Angeles CA 90015-4108

WEMPLE, JAMES ROBERT, psychotherapist; b. Hardin, Mont., May 31, 1943; s. Charles Clifford and Lillian Louise (Smith) W.; m. Sarah Ann House, May 7, 1983; children: Brian Matthew, Laura Ashley. BA, U. Mont., 1966, MA, 1970, postgrad., 1970-71; PhD, Wash. State U., 1979. Diplomate Am. Acad. Pain Mgmt. Tchr., coach Custer County High Sch., Miles City, Mont., 1966-67; sch. psychologist Missoula, Mont., 1970-71; grad. asst. U. Mont., Missoula, 1970-71; dir. counseling Medicine Hat (Alberta) Coll., Canada, 1971-73; counselor Lethbridge (Alberta) C.C., 1973-76; head resident Wash. State U., Pullman, 1976-79; mental health specialist Missoula Rehab., 1979-82; clin. mental health counselor Missoula, 1982—. With U.S. Army, 1960-69, Korea. Fellow Am. Bd. Med. Psychotherapists; mem. Am. Psychol. Assn., Soc. for Clin. and Exptl. Hypnosis, Am. Soc. for Clin. Hypnosis, Internat. Soc. for Hypnosis, Nat. Acad. Cert. Clin. Mental Health Counselors, Soc. for Personality Assessment, AACD, Phi Kappa Phi. Home: 2410 Clydesdale Ln Missoula MT 59801-9297 Office: 715 Kensington Ave Ste 9 Missoula MT 59801-5700

WEN, CHAUR SHYONG, chemical engineer; b. Kaohsiung, Taiwan, Mar. 15, 1947; came to U.S., 1972; s. I-chun and Pien (Kuo) W.; m. Limei C. Wen, July 4, 1972; children: Kenneth C., Katherine T. BS in Chem. Engring., Cheng Kung U., 1969, MS in Chem. Engring., 1971; MS in Environ. Health, U. Cin., 1974; PhD in Chem. Engring., U. So. Calif., L.A., 1976. Cert. environ. health profl. Rsch. asst. Kettering Labb., Cin., 1972-73; rsch. asst./rsch. assoc. dept. chem. engring. U. So. Calif., 1973-77; rsch. engr. to sr. rsch. engr. Gulf Rsch. and Devel. Co., Pitts., 1977-86; sr. devel. engr. to prin. engr. Solar Turbines, Inc., San Diego, Calif., 1986—. Patentee in field; contbr. articles to profl. jours. and books. Mem. Am. Chem. Soc., Am. Inst. Chem. Engring., Sigma Xi, Phi Tau Phi. Home: 13036 Candela Pl San Diego CA 92130-1800 Office: Solar Turbines Inc PO Box 85376 2200 Pacific Hwy San Diego CA 92101-1745

WENDEL, JEANNE LAURETTA, economics educator; b. Cleve., May 24, 1951; d. Charles William and Patricia (O'Reilly) Seelbach; 1 child, Nathan. BA in Econs. and History summa cum laude, Rice U., 1973; PhD in Econs., So. Meth. U., 1977. Economist Fed. Res. Bank, Dallas, 1977; asst. prof. Miami U., Oxford, Ohio, 1977-80; economist Sverdrup & Parcel, St. Louis, 1980-83; instr. U. Louisville, Bellarmine Coll., 1983-85; assoc. prof. U. Nev., Reno, 1985—; quality improvement advisor Washoe Med. Ctr., Reno, 1993—; cons. Bur. Bus. and Econ. Rsch. Projects. Contbr. articles to profl. jours. Home: 1720 Rockhaven Dr Reno NV 89511-8663 Office: U Nev Coll Bus Dept Econs Reno NV 89557

WENDRUCK, LOUIS, publisher, television personality, consultant; b. Hollywood, Calif., Apr. 8, 1957; s. Albert and Anna (Goldberger) W. BA in Commerce, McGill U., 1977; BA in Biology, Occidental Coll., L.A., 1978; MBA, Pepperdine U., 1985. Sys. analyst/computer programmer cons. L.A., 1978-86; ind. pub., owner Fan Club Pub., West Hollywood, Calif., 1986—; pres., pub. club newsletter for The Dark Shadows Fan Club, The Munsters and the Addams Family Fan Club, The Girl Groups 60's Rock 'n Roll Fan Club, The Gay Airline and Travel Club, The Mil. and Police Uniform Assn. Office: Fan Club Publishing PO Box 69A04 Dept WW West Hollywood CA 90069

WENDT, JOHN ARTHUR FREDERIC, JR., lawyer; b. Cleve.; s. John Arthur Frederic and Martha Ann (Hunter) W.; m. Marjorie Rickard Richardson, Oct. 2, 1962; children: Wendy Wendt Wood, Eric A., John A. F. III, Hilary H.; m. 2d Dorothy Fay Nuttall, Dec. 29, 1976. AB with honors, U. Mich., 1942; JD, U. Colo., Boulder, 1951. Bar: Colo. 1951, U.S. Dist. Ct. Colo. 1951, U.S. Ct. Appeals (10th cir.) 1957, U.S. Sup. Ct. 1971. Assoc., Tippit, Haskell & Welborn, Denver, 1953-58; ptnr. Wendt & Kistler, Denver, 1958-62; ptnr. Clark & Wendt, Aspen, Colo., 1962-71; ptnr. Wendt Law Offices, Aspen, Colo., 1971-81, Delta, Colo., 1985—; dist. atty. 9th Jud. Dist. Colo., 1965-69; judge Pitkin County, Colo., 1971-78; dist. atty. 7th Jud. Dist. Colo., 1981-85; farmer. Chmn. Delta County Planning Commn., 1991-94. Served to maj. U.S. Army, 1942-46, 51-53. Decorated Purple Heart, Silver Star, Bronze Star. Mem. Am. Arbitration Assn. (mem. panel), Acad. Family Mediators, Colo. Bar Assn. (gov. 1965-71, 82-85, 87—), Pitkin County Bar Assn. (pres. 1971-72), Delta County Bar Assn. (pres. 1986-89), Am. Judicature Soc., 7th Jud. Dist. Bench-Bar Com., Colo. Coun. Mediation, Phi Kappa Psi, Phi Delta Phi, Phi Beta Kappa. Republican. Episcopalian. Clubs: U.S. Equestrian Team (chmn. Colo. chpt. 1976-86), Masters of Fox Hounds Assn., M.F.H. Roaring Fork Hounds, Black Canyon Pony Club (dist. commr. 1992—). Home: Lenado Farm 2130 Spruce Lane Cedaredge CO 81413 Office: PO Box 94 540 Main St Delta CO 81416

WENDT, MICHAEL JAMES, production potter, business owner; b. Bemidji, Minn., Jan. 7, 1948; s. George Rudolph and Isabel Mary (Zimmermann) W.; m. Rosemary Ann Pittenger, Nov. 10, 1972; children: Natalie Kathleen, Elizabeth Mary. BA, U. Idaho, 1971. Cert. secondary edn. tchr. Idaho. Tchr. German, English Lewiston (Idaho) High Sch., 1971-73; tchr. art Culdesac (Idaho) Sch. Dist., 1974; research asst. U. Idaho, 1976; instr. Walla Walla Community Coll., Clarkston, Wash., 1979, Lewis Clark State Coll., Lewiston, 1985; instr. math., 1994; owner Wendt Pottery, Lewiston, 1973—. Mem. Phi Beta Kappa, Phi Kappa Phi, Am. Field Service Club (pres. 1978), Computer Literacy Support Soc. Home: 1510 9th Ave Lewiston ID 83501-3108 Office: Wendt Pottery 2729 Clearwater Ave Lewiston ID 83501-3234

WENDT, STEVEN WILLIAM, business educator; b. Rockford, Ill., Sept. 18, 1948; s. Roy W. Wendt and Betty Lou (Phillips) Wendt Oser. AAS, Clark County Community Coll., North Las Vegas, Nev., 1982; BS, U. Nev., 1985, MBA, 1987. Cert. vocat. adult educator, Nev. Electronics tech. engr. Rockford Automation, Inc., 1972-74; owner, operator S.W. Ltd., Rockford, 1972-76, S.W. Enterprises, Henderson, Nev., 1977—; instr. electronics Nev. Gaming Sch., Las Vegas, 1977-83; gen. mgr., corp. sec. treas. Customs by Peter Schell, Las Vegas, 1977-83; field engr. Bell & Howell Mailmobile Ops. div., Zeeland, Mich., 1982-90; instr. bus. U. Nev., Las Vegas, 1985—; dir. Wing Fong & Family Microcomputer Labs. Coll. Bus. and Econs. U. Nev., 1990—; sr. arbitrator Better Bus. Bur., Las Vegas, 1982—; bus. cons. Small Bus. Devel. Ctr., Las Vegas, 1985—; incorporator, v.p. Info. Sys., Warren, Mich., 1990-91; fin. officer, gen. ptnr. Obsidian Pub. Press, Henderson, Nev., 1991—; mem. faculty senate U. Nev., 1993—; bd. dirs. Gem Crafters Inc., Warren. Author: Intro to Microcomputers, For Future PC Experts, 1992. Treas. U. Nev. Grad. Student Assn, 1986-87. Served with USN, 1967-71. Recipient Cert. Appreciation UNICEF, 1984. Mem. IEEE, Computer Soc., Fin. Mgmt. Assn. (Nat. Honor Soc. 1985), Strategic Gaming Soc., U. Nev. Computer User Group (exec. com., chair stds. com.), U. Nev. Alumni Assn., Am. Legion, Phi Lambda Alpha. Home: 1325 Chestnut St Henderson NV 89015-4208 Office: U Nev 4505 S Maryland Pky Las Vegas NV 89154-9900

WENN, DEREK JAY, marketing professional; b. New Orleans, Aug. 8, 1956; s. Julian George Jr. and Jane Marilyn (Canone) W.; m. Karen Kunz, Sept. 4, 1986; children: Jared Ian, Colton Ryan, Jamie Lauren. BA in Arts, Humanities and Architecture, U. Southwestern La., 1981. Architect, developer Tom Isbell Devel., Lafayette, La., 1980-82; vol. missionary LDS Ch., Washington, 1982-85; archtl. designer Walker, Lee, Halander Architects, Provo, Utah, 1985-87; mktg. cons. The McKinley Inst., Orem, Utah, 1987-89; dealer consumer affairs mgr. Rick Warner Nissan, Salt Lake City, 1989-90; tech. and mktg. dir. Hayes Bros. Buick, Jeep, Eagle, Salt Lake City, 1990—; prin., owner D. Wenn & Co. Devel., Salt Lake City, 1986—; ptnr. Target Market Rsch., Sandy, Utah, 1991—; owner Alta West Distbg., Draper, Utah, 1994—, PoBoys LLC Restaurant, Salt Lake City, 1995—. Elder LDS Ch., 1983—. Mem. AIA, Pi Kappa Alpha. Office: Alta West 11675 S Brisbane Dr Sandy UT 84094

WENNIK, ROBERTA SCHWARTZ, dietitian; b. San Francisco, June 12, 1948; d. Ernest and Annette Louise (Lamdan) Schwartz; m. Lawrence Paul Wennik, Oct. 24, 1971; children: Deborah, Shari. BA in Interior Design, U. Calif., Berkeley, 1970; MS in Nutrition, U. Wash., 1991. Registered dietician. Interior designer Interiors and Textiles Corp., Burlingame, Calif.,

1970-72; cons. dietitian, owner HealthPro, Edmonds, Wash., 1991—; tchr. Edmonds C.C., Lynnwood, Wash., 1993—. Author: Drawing the Line of Fat and Cholesterol, 1992; patentee in field; contbr. articles to popular mags. Spkr. om nutrition issues civic and women's groups, 1993—. Scholarship U. Wash., 1988. Mem. Am. Dietetic Assn., Wash. State Dietetic Assn., Greater Seattle Dietetic Assn. Office: HealthPro PO Box 83 Lynnwood WA 98046-0083

WENTS, DORIS ROBERTA, psychologist; b. L.A., Aug. 26, 1944; d. John Henry and Julia (Cole) W. BA, UCLA, 1966; MA, San Francisco State U., 1968; postgrad., Calif. State U., L.A., 1989-90, Claremont (Calif.) Grad. Sch., 1990—. Lic. ednl. psychologist, credentialed sch. psychologist, Calif. Sch. psychologist Diagnostic Sch. for Neurologically Handicapped Children, L.A., 1969-86; pvt. practice Monterey Park, Calif., 1986—; instr. Calif. State U., L.A., 1977. Co-author: Southern California Ordinal Scales of Development, 1977. Mem. Western Psychol. Assn., L.A. World Affairs Coun., L.A. Conservancy, Zeta Tau Alpha (officer Santa Monica alumnae chpt. 1970—, Cert. of Merit 1979), Sigma Xi. Office: Claremont Grad Sch Dept Psychology Claremont CA 91711

WENTWORTH, THEODORE SUMNER, lawyer; b. Bklyn., July 18, 1938; s. Theodore Sumner and Alice Ruth (Wortmann) W.; AA, Am. River Coll., 1958; JD, U. Calif., Hastings, 1962; m. Sharon Linelle Arkush, 1965 (dec. 1987); children: Christina Linn, Kathryn Allison; m. Diana Webb von Welanetz, 1989; 1 stepchild, Lexi von Welanetz. Bar: Calif. 1963, U.S. Dist. Ct. (no., ctrl. dists.) Calif., U.S. Ct. Appeals (9th cir.), U.S. Supreme Ct.; cert. civil trial specialist; diplomate Nat. Bd. Trial Advocacy; assoc. Am. Bd. Trial Advocacy. Assoc. Adams, Hunt & Martin, Santa Ana, Calif., 1963-66; ptnr. Hunt, Liljestrom & Wentworth, Santa Ana, 1967-77; pres. Solabs Corp., 1990—; chmn. bd., exec. v.p. Plant Warehouse, Inc., Hawaii, 1974-82; prin. Law Offices of Theodore S. Wentworth, specializing in personal injury, product liability, profl. malpractice, bus. fraud, fire loss litigation, human rights issues, Newport Beach and Temecula, Calif.; judge pro tem Superior Ct. Attys. Panel, Harbor Mcpl. Ct.; owner Eagles Ridge Ranch, Temecula, 1977—. Pres., bd. dirs. Santa Ana-Tustin Community Chest, 1972; v.p., trustee South Orange County United Way, 1973-75; pres. Orange County Fedn. Funds, 1972-73; bd. dirs. Orange County Mental Health Assn. Mem. ABA, Am. Bd. Trial Advocates (assoc.), State Bar Calif., Orange County Bar Assn. (dir. 1972-76), Am. Trial Lawyers Assn., Calif. Trial Lawyers Assn. (bd. govs. 1968-70), Orange County Trial Lawyers Assn. (pres. 1967-68), Lawyer-Pilots Bar Assn., Aircraft Owners and Pilots Assn., Bahia Corinthian Yacht Club, Balboa Bay Club, Corsair Yacht Club, The Center Club, Pacific Club, Newport, Fourth of July Yacht Club (Catalina Island). Research in vedic prins., natural law, quantum physics and mechanics. Office: 4631 Teller Ave Ste 100 Newport Beach CA 92660-8105 also: Wells Fargo Bank Bldg 41530 Enterprise Cir S Temecula CA 92590-4816

WENTZ, JEFFREY LEE, information systems consultant; b. Philippi, W.Va., Nov. 29, 1956; s. William Henry and Edith Marie (McBee) W. AS in Data Processing, BS in Acctg., Fairmont (W.Va.) State Coll., 1978. Programmer/analyst U.S. Dept. Energy, Morgantown, W.Va., 1978-79; analyst Middle South Svcs., New Orleans, 1979-81; sr. analyst Bank of Am., San Francisco, 1981-83; pres., cons. Wentz Cons. Inc., San Francisco, 1983—. Office: Wentz Cons Inc 1378 34th Ave San Francisco CA 94122-1309

WERBACH, MELVYN ROY, physician, writer; b. N.Y.C., Nov. 11, 1940; s. Samuel and Martha (Robbins) W.; m. Gail Beth Leibsohn, June 20, 1967; children: Kevin, Adam. BA, Columbia Coll., N.Y.C., 1962; MD, Tufts U., Boston, 1966. Diplomate Am. Bd. Psychiatry and Neurology. Intern VA Hosp., Bklyn., 1966-67; resident in psychiatry Cedars-Sinai Med. Ctr., L.A., 1969-71; dir. psychol. svcs., clin. biofeedback UCLA Hosp. and Clinics, 1976-80; pres. Third Line Press, 1986—; asst. clin. prof. Sch. Medicine, UCLA, 1978—; mem. nutritional adv. bd. Cancer Treatment Ctrs. Am., 1989—; mem. adv. com. The Dead Sea Confs., Israel, 1990—. Author: Third Line Medicine, 1986, Nutritional Influences on Illness, 1987, 2d edit., 1993, Nutritional Influences on Mental Illness, 1991, Healing Through Nutrition, 1993; co-author: Botanical Influences on Illness, 1994; mem. editl. bd. Jour. of Nutritional Medicine, 1993—, Health News and Rev., 1991—, Jour. Optimal Nutrition, 1993—, Alt. Medicine Digest, 1994—; mem. med. adv. bd. Let's Live Mag., 1989-93; columnist Jour. Alt. and Complementary Medicine, 1992—, Townsend Letter for Doctors, 1993—, Australian Jour. Nutrition and Environ. Medicine, 1995—; mem. panel What Doctor's Don't Tell You, 1993—; contbr. articles to med. jours. Mem. Am. Coll. Clin. Nutrition, Biofeedback Soc. Calif. (life, pres. 1977, Cert. Honor 1985).

WERLEIN, DONNA DABECK, community health care administrator; b. Ishpeming, Mich., Sept. 29, 1956; d. Walter J. and Ann M. (Paquette) Dabeck; m. Mark S. Werlein, June 19, 1981; 1 child, Stephanie Marie. BS in Nursing, U. Wis., OshKosh, 1978. Area mgr. Quality Care, Rockwell Center, N.Y., 1984-86; western div. tng. mgr. Kimberly Quality Care, Boston, 1986-88; dir. tng. and manpower devel. CarePoint, Walnut Creek, Calif., 1988-89, v.p. orgnl. devel., 1989-90; v.p. ops. Alliance Home Care Mgmt., Walnut Creek, 1990-92; v.p. clin. svcs. Western Med. Svcs., Walnut Creek, 1992—.

WERNER, E. LOUIS, JR., lawyer, retired insurance company executive; m. Sandra M. Johnston; children: E. Louis III, Eric R., Matthew J. BA, Princeton U., 1949; BS, Washington U., St. Louis, 1950, LLB, 1952, JD, 1952. Bar: Mo. 1952, U.S. Ct. Mil. Appeals 1963, U.S. Supreme Ct. 1963; CPCU 1957; lic. pilot single, multi-engine and instrument ratings. Exec. v.p. TOR Mgmt., Shawnee Mission, Kans.; mng. ptnr. Dukes Deux Leasing Co., Scottsdale, Ariz.; dir. ABC Moving and Storage Co., Inc., Phoenix; v.p. devel. Phoenix (Ariz.) Country Day Sch.; chmn. emeritus, dir. Insurers Svc. Corp., Briarcliff Manor, N.Y.; magistrate judge Town of Paradise Valley, Ariz.; v.p., bd. dirs. Butch Baird Enterprises, Inc., Hialeah, Fla., Pacific Tooling Corp.; exec. v.p. Frank B. Hall Svcs., Briarcliff Manor; chmn., chief exec. officer Insurers Svc. Corp., St. Louis; exec. v.p., bd. dirs. Safety Mutual Casualty Corp., St. Louis; v.p., bd. dirs. St. Louis Indoor Soccer Club; bd. dirs., past pres. Nat. Assn. Safety and Claims Orgn.; v.p., bd. dirs. Chester Broadcasting Corp., St. Louis; mem. bd. dirs. Phoenix Symphony; mem. bd. trustees San Francisco Theol. Seminary. Trustee Scottsdale Meml. Health Found., Valley Presbyn. Found., San Francisco Theol. Sem.; mem. Fiesta Bowl Com., Tempe, Ariz.; bd. dirs. Playgoers of St. Louis, Inc., Rossman Sch., St. Louis; former deacon, trustee, ruling elder Ladue Chapel, St. Louis; ruling elder Valley Presbyn. Ch., Paradise Valley, Ariz. Mem. Fed. Bar Assn., Mo. Bar Assn., St. Louis Bar Assn., Mo. Athletic Club, USPGA (assoc.), Assn. Corp. Growth (Ariz. chpt.), Am. Soc. CPCU, Aircraft Owners and Pilots Assn., Econ. Club of Phoenix, Paradise Valley Country Club, Forest Highlands Golf Club, Desert Mtn. Golf Club, Desert Highland Golf Club. Home: 5715 N Cameldale Way Paradise Vly AZ 85253-5207 Office: 6900 E Camelback Rd Ste 700 Scottsdale AZ 85251-2443

WERNER, MARLIN SPIKE, speech pathologist and audiologist; b. Portland, Maine, Aug. 15, 1927; s. Leonard Matthews and Margaret (Steele) W.; m. Caroline Emma Paul, Dec. 23, 1985; children: Leo Hart, Joseph Hart. BA in Sociology and Social Work, U. Mo., 1950; ScM in Audiology and Speech Pathology, Johns Hopkins U., 1957; PhD in Speech and Hearing Sci., Ohio State U., 1966. Lic. in audiology, hearing aid dispensing, speech pathology, Hawaii; lic. in audiology and speech pathology, Calif. Audiologist/speech pathologist, dir. Speech and Hearing Ctr. Asheville (N.C.) Orthopedic Hosp., 1960-64; assoc. prof. speech pathology and audiology We. Carolina U., Cullowhee, N.C., 1965-69; assoc. prof. speech pathology, audiology and speech sci. Fed. City Coll. (now U. D.C.), Washington, 1969-73; pres. Friends of Nepal's Hearing Handicapped, Oakland, Calif., 1979-84; hearing aid dispenser, audiologist, speech pathologist pvt. practice, Oakland and Lafayette, Calif., 1973-85; pvt. practice Lafayette, 1985-87; pvt. practice speech pathology and audiology Hilo, Hawaii, 1987—; speech and hearing cons. VA Hosp., Oteen, N.C., 1960-64; clin. cons. Speech and Hearing Clinic, Asheville Orthopedic Hosp., 1966-67; lectr., presenter in field. Contbr. articles to profl. jours.; contbr. to Ency. Brit., Am. Heritage Book of Natural Wonders, others. Mem. hearing impaired svcs. task force State of Hawaii Dept. Health, 1987-88; mem. Hawaii County Mayor's Com. for Persons with Disabilities, 1988-94; adv. bd. Salvation Army, 1992; bd. dirs. Hawaii chpt. Am. Arthritis Found.; past pres. Big Island Safety Assn.; mem. Hawaii Gov.'s bd. Hearing Aid Dealers and Fitters; mem. adv. com., pres. Older Adult Resource Ctr., Laney Coll., Oakland, Calif.; v.p. Hawaii Speleological Survey; chmn. Hawaii Grotto of Nat. Speleological Soc.; others. MCH fellow Johns Hopkins U., 1954, Pub. Health fellow Ohio State U., 1964. Fellow Nat. Speleological Soc.; mem. AAAS, Am. Speech and Hearing Assn., Acoustical Soc. Am., Calif. Speech and Hearing Assn., Calif. Writers Club (bd. dirs., past pres.), Hawaii Speech/Lang. Hearing Assn. Home: PO Box 11509 Hilo HI 96721-6509

WERNER, MICHAEL WOLOCK, astrophysicist; b. Chgo., Oct. 9, 1942; s. Louis and Zelda (Wolock) W.; m. Edwenna Merryday Rosser, Sept. 23, 1967; children: Erica, Alexander. BA, Haverford Coll., 1963; PhD, Cornell U., 1968. Rsch. fellow Cambridge (Eng.) Univ., 1968-69; vis. lectr. Univ. Calif., Berkeley, 1969-72; asst. prof., physics Caltech, Pasadena, Calif., 1972-79; rsch. scientist NASA-Ames Rsch. Ctr., Moffett Field, Calif., 1979-90; sr. mem. tech. staff, sr. rsch. scientist Jet Propulsion Lab., Pasadena, 1990—; project scientist and sci. working group chmn. NASA-Space Infrared Telescope Facility, 1984—; vis. fellow Johns Hopkins U., Balt., 1987-88; Phillips lectr. Haverford Coll., 1991. Contbr. over 150 articles to profl. jours. Alfred P. Sloan fellow Sloan Found., 1972-74. Mem. AAAS, Am. Astron. Soc., Astron. Soc. of the Pacific. Office: Jet Propulsion Lab 4800 Oak Grove Dr Pasadena CA 91109-8001

WERNER, RICHARD ALLEN, entomologist; b. Reading, Pa., Feb. 20, 1936; s. Roy M. and Hazel (Rightmeyer) W.; m. Patricia Thomas, Aug. 25, 1973; children: Sarah T., Luke O. BS in Forestry, Pa. State U., 1958, BS in Entomology, 1960; MS in Entomology, U. Md., 1966; PhD in Entomology, N.C. State U., 1971. Forester Forest Svc., USDA, Roseberg, Oreg., 1957-60; rsch. entomologist Forest Svc., USDA, Juneau, Alaska, 1960-64; insect toxicologist Forest Svc., USDA, Research Triangle Park, N.C., 1965-74; rsch. entomologist Forest Svc., USDA, Fairbanks, Alaska, 1974-85, project leader, 1985-91, chief rsch. entomologist, 1991—; adj. prof. U. Alaska, Fairbanks, 1980—; prin. rsch. assoc. Inst. Arctic Biology, U. Alaska, 1985—. Author: Insects and Diseases of Alaskan Forests, 1980, 2d edit. 1985. Counselor Boy Scouts Am., Fairbanks, 1989—. Mem. Entomol. Soc. Am., Soc. Am. Foresters, Ga. Entomol. Soc., Entomol. Soc. Can., Chem. Ecology Soc. Am., Western Forest Insect Wk. Conf. (sec.-treas. 1980-82), N. Am. Forest Insect Wk. Conf. (steering com. 1989-91). Office: Inst of No Forestry USDA 308 Tanana Dr Fairbanks AK 99775

WERNER, ROGER HARRY, archaeologist; b. N.Y.C., Nov. 11, 1950; s. Harry Emile and Rena (Roode) W.; m. Kathleen Diane Engdahl, Feb. 20, 1982; children: Meryl Lauren, Sarah Melise, Jeremy Marshall; 1 stepchild, Amber Fawn. BA, Belknap Coll., 1973; MA, Sonoma State U., Rohnert Park, Calif., 1982. Curatorial aide Anthro. Lab. Sonoma State Coll., 1975-76, curatorial asst., 1976-77, staff archaeologist, 1977-80; staff archaeologist Planning Dept., Lake County, Calif., 1977; cir. riding archaeologist western region Nat. Park Service, Tucson, Ariz., 1978; prin. investigator Archaeol. Services, Inc., Stockton, Calif., 1979—; cons. Calif. Indian Legal Services, Ukiah, 1977, Geothermal Research Impact Projection Study, Lakeport, Calif., 1977; instr. Ya-Ka-Ama Indian Ednl. Ctr., Santa Rosa, Calif., 1978-79; lead archaeologist No. Calif., WESTEC Services, Inc., San Diego, 1979-81; adj. prof. U. Puget Sound, Summer 1995. Sec. Colonial Hts. PTA, 1983-84, 2d v.p., 1985-86, historian, 1986-87, v.p., 1987-88; cons., instr. Clovis Adult Sch., 1984-85; instr. U. Pacific Lifelong Learning Ctr., 1987—, San Joaquin Delta Coll., 1990—, Calif. State U., Fresno, 1992—; bd. dirs. Valley Mountain Regional Ctr., 1987-88, treas., 1988-89, v.p., 1989-90, pres.-elect, 1990-91, pres., 1991-92; bd. trustees Stockton Chorale, treas., 1992-93, youth chorale rep., 1993-94; active Spl. Olympics, Stockton, Calif. Anthropology dept. research grantee, Sonoma State U., 1980. Mem. Geol. Soc. Am., Soc. for Am. Archaeologists, Great Basin Anthropol. Conf., Soc. for Calif. Archaeology, Soc. Profl. Archaeologists, Soc. for Hist. Archeology, Assn. for Retarded Citizens, Am. Soc. Photogrammetry and Remote Sensing, Urban Regional Info. Systems Assn., Bay Automated Mapping Assn., Kiwanis. Democrat. Lodge: Kiwanis (Stockton). Home: 1117 Aberdeen Ave Stockton CA 95209-2625 Office: ASI Cartography & GIS 8026 Lorraine Ave Ste 218 Stockton CA 95210-4241

WERNER, ROY ANTHONY, aerospace executive; b. Alexandria, Va., June 30, 1944; s. William Frederick and Mary Audrey (Barksdale) W.; m. Paula Ann Privett, June 8, 1969; children: Kelly Rene, Brent Alastair. BA, U. Cen. Fla., 1970; MPhil, Oxford U., 1973; MBA, Claremont (Calif.) Grad. Sch., 1986. Reporter St. Petersburg (Fla.) Times, 1968-69; assoc. dir. White House Conf. on Youth, 1970-71; exec. sec. Oxford Strategic Studies Group, 1971-73; internat. officer Fed. Energy Adminstrn., 1973-74; mem. legis. staff U.S. Senate, Washington, 1974-79; prin. dept. asst. Sec. of The Army, Washington, 1979-81; dir. policy rsch. Northrop Corp., L.A., 1982-83, spl. asst. to sr. v.p., mktg. to mgr. program planning and analysis electronics system divsn., 1989-94; sr. internat. bus. advisor Internat. Offset and Countertrade Northrop Corp., 1994, bus. devel. mgr. Asia & Pacific, 1995—; chmn. U.S. delegation/polit. com. Atlantic Treaty Assn. Meeting, Brussels, 1989, mem. U.S. delegation, Paris, 1990, Athens, 1993, others; staff dir. East Asian and Pacific Affairs subcom. U.S. Sentate Fgn. Rels. Com., 1977-79; mem. Atlantic Coun. of U.S., 1985—; speaker Pacific Parliamentary Caucus, numerous acad. confs. in U.S. and East Asia. Editorial bd. Global Affairs, 1982-86; contbr. numerous articles to profl. jours./publs. Pres. Irvine (Calif.) Boys and Girls Club, 1990-92, v.p., 1989-90, bd. dirs., 1987—; treas. Irvine Temporary Housing, 1988-91, bd. dirs., 1986-91; chmn. City of Irvine Fin. Commn., 1986-89; mem. fin. com. Irvine Barclay Theater, 1989—; chair Oxford U. L.A. Phonathon, 1995; nat rep. Oriel Coll. Oxford Devel. Trust, 1994—; chmn. fin. com. Outreach Univ. United Meth. Ch., Irvine, 1989-90, others; corp. sec. Irvine Housing Opportunities, 1988-89, pres., 1993—; bd. dirs. Harbor Area Boys and Girls Cl. Recipient Disting. Alumnus award U. Ctrl. Fla. Alumni Assn., Orlando, 1982, Outstanding Civilian Svc. medal Dept. Army, 1981, Fed. Energy Adminstr., 1974; sr. rsch. fellow Atlantic Coun. of the U.S., 1988-89. Mem. Am. Fgn. Svc. Assn., Am. Def. Preparedness Com. Methodist. Home: 28 Fox Hill Irvine CA 92714-5493

WERNER, WILLIAM ARNO, architect; b. San Francisco, Dec. 11, 1937; s. William Arno and Sophie (Menutis) W.; m. Wendy Rolston Wilson, Feb. 3, 1963 (div. Jan. 1983); 1 child, Christa Nichol. BA with honors, Yale U., 1959, BArch, 1962, MArch, 1963. Drafter Serge Chermayeff, Paul Rudolph and Charles Brewer, New Haven, 1961-63; project designer Johnson, Poole & Storm, San Francisco, 1963-64; project designer Leo S. Wou & Assocs., Honolulu, 1965-66, v.p. of design, 1971-72; project architect John Tatom Assocs., Honolulu, 1965-66; sr. designer Skidmore, Owings & Merrill, San Francisco, 1968-71, assoc./project architect, 1972-76; prin. W.A. Werner Assocs., San Francisco, 1976-80; ptnr. Werner & Sullivan, San Francisco, 1980—; chmn. Design Rev. Bd., City of Sausalito, Calif.; bd. govs. Yale U., New Haven; visitorship in architecture U. Auckland Found., New Zealand, 1994. Prin. works include Alameda Mcpl. Credit Union, Lane Pub. Co., Menlo Park, Calif., Pacific Data Images, Mountain View, Calif., Saga Corp., Menlo Park, Tiffany & Co., Union Square, San Francisco, Somerset Collection, Troy, Mich., Touche Ross & Co., Oakland, U.S. Post Office, San Francisco, (renovations) Fed. Express Co., San Francisco, KD's Grog N' Grocery, San Francisco, Jessie Street. Substation, San Francisco, Lakeside Tower Health Ctr./Mt. Zion Hosp., Qantas Bldg, San Francisco, Women's Care, San Francisco, Moon Residence, Dillon Beach, Calif., Shenkar Residence, San Francisco, Tacker Residence, Denver, Lasky Residence, San Francisco, Starring Residence, San Francisco, Whitehead Residence, Monte Rio, Calif., various laboratories, theatres and rsch. facilities, urban design. Recipient Progressive Architecture Design award Jessie St. Substation, 1980, DuPont Co. Design award Touche Ross & Co., 1983, award of Excellence Woodwork Inst. of Calif., 1989, USPS/NEA Nat. Honor award for Design Excellence, 1990, Tucker Design Excellence award Bldg. Stone Inst., Tiffany & Co., 1992. Mem. AIA (San Francisco chpt.), Found. for San Francisco's Architectural Heritage (hon.). Home: 213 Richardson St Sausalito CA 94965-2422

WERNER, WILLIAM EUGENE, protein biochemist; b. San Diego, Nov. 8, 1958; s. Norbert Marcellus and Doris Mae (McFarlane) W.; m. Jo Lynn Williams, Aug. 22, 1987; children: Alicia Jayne, Andrea Lane. BS, U. Puget Sound, Tacoma, Wash., 1980; MA, Wake Forest U., Winston-Salem, 1983; PhD, U. Calif., Berkeley, 1988. Postdoctoral fellow Protos Corp./Chiron Corp., Emeryville, Calif., 1988-89; rsch. chemist GS-11 USDA-Agrl. Resch. Svc., Albany, Calif., 1990-91; scientist/cons. Biocircuits Corp., Burlingame, Calif., 1991; scientist Applied Biosystems divsn. Perkin-Elmer, Foster City, Calif., 1991—. Contbr. articles to profl. jours.; patentee in field. Office: Perkin Elmer Applied Biosystems Divsn 850 Lincoln Centre Dr Foster City CA 94404-1128

WERTH, ROGER ALAN, photojournalist; b. Portland, Oreg., Apr. 17, 1957; s. Dean Erwin and Patricia Ann (Loehner) W.; m. Belinda Marie Campbell, Sept. 6, 1985 (Apr. 1991); 1 child, Shardé Marie. BS, Oreg. State U., 1980. Intern in photography The Daily News, Longview, Wash., 1978, part-time photojournalist, 1978, photojournalist, 1978-79, photo editor, photojournalist, 1979—. Photographer cover Time Mag., 1980. Recipient Pulitzer prize for photos of eruption of Mt. St. Helens, 1981. Mem. Nat. Press Photographers Assn. Office: The Daily News 770 11th St PO Box 189 Longview WA 98632

WERTHEIMER, ROBERT E., paper company executive; b. 1928; married. BSME, U. Wash., 1950; MBA, Harvard U., 1952. With Longview (Wash.) Fibre Co., 1952—, package engr., 1955-59, asst. mgr. container ops., 1959-60, asst. mgr. container sales, 1960-63, v.p. container sales West, 1963-75, v.p. prodn., 1975, group v.p. containers, now exec. v.p., dir. Office: Longview Fibre Co 120 Montgomery St Ste 2200 San Francisco CA 94104-4325 Office: Longview Fiber Co Longview WA 98632

WERTZ, GARY RANDALL, secondary education educator, counselor; b. Lewistown, Pa., Feb. 19, 1958; s. Harold Ira and Beverly Arlene (Miller) W.; m. Iris Christine Holloway, Sept. 26, 1981; children: Christopher, Joss, Morgan, Cord. BS in Wildlife, Fisheries Mgmt., U. Idaho, 1982; MEd in Gen. and Sch. Counseling, Coll. Idaho, 1991. Cert. tchr., Idaho. Tchr., football coach, counselor O'Leary Jr. H.S., Twin Falls, Idaho, 1984-85; football coach, driver edn. instr. Cambridge (Idaho) Schs., 1985—; dir. Natural Helpers, Cambridge, 1988—; mem. bd. dirs. Adams Co. Child Abuse Prevention Team, Council, Idaho, 1994—. singer Cambridge Cmty. Choir, Cambridge, 1986—, Treasure Valley Cmty. Choir, Ontario, Oreg., 1988—; bishop Jesus Christ Latter-Day Saints, Cambridge, 1992—. Mem. Idaho Sch. Counselors Assn.

WERTZ, JAMES RICHARD, space mission engineer; b. Kingman, Ariz., Feb. 20, 1944; s. Emerson Dunkle and Beryl Bernice (Barber) W.; m. Alice Frances Valerie, Sept. 2, 1967; children: Laura Ellen, Cheryl Lynn, Julie Ann. SB, MIT, 1966; PhD, U. Tex., 1970; MS in Adminstrn. of Sci., George Washington U., 1978. Asst. prof. Moorhead (Minn.) State U., 1970-73; sect. mgr. Computer Scis. Corp., Silver Spring, Md., 1973-78; dir. spacecraft engrng. Western Union Space Communications, Upper Saddle River, N.J., 1978-80; sr. staff engr. TRW, Inc., El Segundo, Calif., 1980-84; owner, pres. Microcosm, Inc., Torrance, Calif., 1984—. Co-author, editor: Spacecraft Attitude Determination and Control, 1978, 8th printing, 1994, Space Mission Analysis and Design, 1st edit., 1991, 2d edit., 1992, Reducing Space Mission Cost, 1995; mng. editor book series: Space Technology Library Series, 1985—; contbr. over 30 articles to profl. publs. Fellow AAIA (assoc.), Brit. Interplanetary Soc.; mem. AAAS, Am. Astronautical Soc., Am. Astron. Soc., Am. Phys. Soc. Home: 2362 W 228th St Torrance CA 90501-5327 Office: Microcosm Inc 2601 Airport Dr Ste 230 Torrance CA 90505-6142

WESLEY, VIRGINIA ANNE, real estate property manager; b. Seattle, Apr. 29, 1951; d. Albert William and Mary Louise (Heusser) W. BA in Speech, U. Hawaii, Hilo, 1978. Cert. property mgr. Mgr. office, traffic Sta. KIPA-Radio, Hilo, 1972-74; reporter West Hawaii Today, Kailua-Kona, Hawaii, 1974; mgr. office U. Hawaii, Hilo, 1975-78; dir. property mgmt. First City Equities, Seattle, 1978-88, Winvest Devel. Corp., Seattle, 1988-89; with Quadrant Corp, Bellevue, Wash., 1992—; instr. Bellevue (Wash.) Community Coll., 1982-85. Bd. dirs. Mayor's Small Bus. Task Force, Seattle, 1981-83, 1st Hill Improvement Assn., Seattle, 1982—; active Goodwill Games, Seattle, 1990, Kauri Investments, Ltd., Seattle, 1991-92. Mem. Inst. Real Estate Mgmt., Internat. Coun. Shopping Ctrs., Comml. Real Estate Women, Women's Bus. Exch., Seattle-King County Bd. Realtors, Big Island Press Club, Phi Kappa Phi. Home: 906 Lake Washington Blvd S Seattle WA 98144-3314

WESSLER, MELVIN DEAN, farmer, rancher; b. Dodge City, Kan., Feb. 11, 1932; s. Oscar Lewis and Clara (Reiss) W.; grad. high sch.; m. Laura Ethel Arbuthnot, Aug. 23, 1951; children: Monty Dean, Charla Cay, Virgil Lewis. Farmer-rancher, Springfield, Colo., 1950—; dir., sec. bd. Springfield Co-op. Sales Co., 1964-80, pres. bd., 1980—. Pres., Arkansas Valley Co-op. Council, SE Colo. Area, 1965-87, Colo. Co-op. Council, 1969-72, v.p. 1974, sec. 1980-86; community com. chmn. Baca County, Agr. Stablzn. and Conservation Svc., Springfield, 1961-73, 79—, vice chmn. Baca County Com., 1980-90; mem. spl. com. on grain mktg. Far-Mar-Co.; mem. adv. bd. Denver Bapt. Bible Coll., 1984-89; chmn., bd. dirs. Springfield Cemetery Bd., 1985—; apptd. spl. com. Farmland Industries spl. project Tomorrow, 1987—. Recipient The Colo. Cooperator award The Colo. Coop Coun., 1990. Mem. Colo. Cattlemen's Assn., Colo. Wheat Growers Assn., Southeast Farm Bus. Assn. (bd. dirs. 1991—), Big Rock Grange (yes. 1964-76, master 1976-82). Address: 18363 County Road Pp Springfield CO 81073-9210

WEST, BILLY GENE, public relations executive; b. Richmond, Ind., Nov. 22, 1946; s. Billy D. and Jean C. (Cox) W. AA, Cerritos Coll., 1966; BA, U. So. Calif., 1969; MA, U. Minn., 1971. Salesman, Marina Art Products, L.A., 1967-73; v.p. Am. Telecon Network, Dallas, 1974-77; gen. mgr. Phoenix Publs., Houston, 1977-78; pres. San Dark, Inc., San Francisco, 1978-82; gen. ptnr. Billy West & Assocs., 1982—; pres. V.G. Prodns., 1983—; chief exec. officer Westmarking, San Francisco, 1989— ; exec. dir. Young Ams. for Freedom, Minn. and Wis., 1970-72; pres. S.F.P.A., San Francisco, 1982-83. Mem. Assn. MBA Execs. Mem. Am. Ref. Ch.

WEST, CYNTHYA THOMAS, municipal agency administrator; b. Massillon, Ohio, Sept. 12, 1947; d. Anthony Frank and Beverly Elaine Thomas; m. William Alan West, Oct. 13 1985. BS, Kent (Ohio) State U., 1969. Purchasing agt. Masoneilan/Dresser, Houston, 1981-85; purchasing supr. commodity and svcs. contracts Purchasing and Transp., Orange County Gen. Svcs. Agy., Santa Ana, Calif., 1985-93; purchasing supr. City of Costa Mesa, Calif., 1993—; dir. County of Orange Vendor Products Fair, 1991. Assisted in restoration of the Hist. Orange County Courthouse, Santa Ana, 1985-87; negotiated contract for design and devel. of mus. exhibit gallery, 1988; assisted in preparing Rancho Del Rio, Calif. for Visit from Pres. George Bush, 1989; mem. Friends of Costa Mesa Libr., Friends of San Juan Capistrano Libr. Mem. Nat. Inst. Govtl. Purchasing (chair 1992, bd. dirs. Calif. chpt. 1993), Nat. Assn. Purchasing Mgmt., Purchasing Mgmt. Assn. Houston (co-chmn. pub. rels. com. 1984-85), Purchasing Mgmt. Assn. Orange County (chmn. planning com. 1988—), Calif. Assn. Pub. Purchasing Officers (Organce County group chair 1995, chair conf. registration com. 1986), Friends of South Coast Repertory and Orange County Performing Arts Ctr. Office: City of Costa Mesa Purchasing Divsn 77 Fair Dr Costa Mesa CA 92626

WEST, DELNO CLOYDE, JR., history educator, writer; b. Skyler County, Mo., Apr. 8, 1936; s. Delno C. Sr. and Elsie (Cornett) W.; m. Jean Donald, Aug. 31, 1958; children: Douglas, Delisa, Dawn. BS, N.E. Mo. StateU., 1961; MA, U. Denver, 1962; PhD, UCLA, 1970. Prof. history No. Ariz. U., Flagstaff, 1969—. Author: Joachim in Christian Thought, 1975, Joachim of Fiore, 1983, Christopher Columbus, 1991, The Libro de las Profecías of Christopher Columbus, 1991. Mem. Ariz.-Mex. Commn., Phoenix, 1975-79; chmn. Milligan House Hist. Trust Commn., Flagstaff, 1983-85, Flagstaff Coconino County Libr., 1987—. Recipient Bronze medal, Congresso Internazionale Studi Gioachimiti, Italy, 1984, 1989, Scholar of Year award, Phi Kappa Phi, 1984. Fellow Ariz. Ctr. for Medieval and Renaissance Studies, Ctr. Theol. Inquiry; mem. Am. Hist. Assn., Medieval Acad. Am., Cath. Hist. Assn., Soc. for History of Discoveries, UCLA Ctr. for Medieval and Renaissance Studies (corr.), Rocky Mountain Medieval and Renaissance Assn. (pres. 1975, 1979). Home: 3120 Walkup Dr Flagstaff AZ 86001-8978 Office: No Ariz U PO Box 6023 Flagstaff AZ 86011

WEST, DONNA C., licensing executive; b. Lancaster, Pa., Oct. 10, 1956; d. Donald A. and Catherine M. (Sammet) Ziegler; m. Robert C. West, May 16, 1987; 1 child, Cathy. Student, U. Nev., 1974, Nat. Judicial Coll., 1985. DUI adjudicator DMV & PS, Carson City, Nev.; so. dist. mgr. DMV & PS, Las Vegas, asst. chief fraudulent divsn. Gov. award for team bldg., 1995.

Mem. So. Nev. DUI Task Force, Organ Donor Coalition, Leadership Las Vegas. Office: Dept Motor Vehicles 8250 W Flamingo Rd Las Vegas NV 89117

WEST, EDWARD ALAN, graphics communications executive; b. L.A., Dec. 25, 1928; s. Albert Reginald and Gladys Delia (White) W.; m. Sonya Lea Smith, Jan. 2, 1983; children: Troy A., Tamara L.; stepchildren: Debra, Chris, Donna. A.A., Fullerton Coll., 1966; student, Cerritos Coll., 1957, UCLA, 1966-67. Circulation mgr. Huntington Park (Calif.) Signal Newspaper, 1946-52; newspaper web pressman Long Beach (Calif.) Press Telegram, 1955-62; gravure web pressman Gravure West, Los Angeles, 1966-67; sales engr. Halm Jet Press, Glen Head, N.Y., 1968-70; salesman Polychrome Corp., Glen Head, 1970-74; supr. reprographics Fluor Engring & Construction, Irvine, Calif., 1974-81; dir. reprographics Fluor Arabia, Dhahran, Saudi Arabia, 1981-85, Press Telegram, Long Beach, 1986—; printing advisor Saddleback C.C., Mission Viejo, Calif., 1979, 80. Author: How to Paste up For Graphic Reproduction, 1967. Sgt. USMC, 1952-55. Decorated 3 Battle Stars. Mem. In-Plant Printing Assn. (cert. graphics comm. mgr. 1977, editor newsletter 1977, pres. Orange County chpt. 1979-80, Internat. Man of Yr. award 1980), 1st Marine Divsn. Assn. (life), VFW (life), Am. Legion, Masons, Shriners (pres. South Coast club 1991, editor blue and gold unit Legion of Honor El Bekala Temple 1989—, life mem., comdr. Legion of Honor 1992, Shriner of Yr. award 1994), KT (life), High Twelve # 500 (Capistrano pres. 1995). Presbyterian. Home: 198 Monarch Bay Dr Dana Point CA 92629-3437 Office: 604 Pine Ave Long Beach CA 90844-0003

WEST, HUGH STERLING, aircraft leasing company executive; b. Kansas City, Kans., Apr. 5, 1930; s. Gilbert Eugene and Dorothy (Johnson) W.; BS, U. Va., 1952; BS in Aero., U. Md., 1959; grad. U.S. Naval Test Pilot Sch., 1959; m. Willa Alden Reed, Jan. 16, 1954; children: Karen, Phillip, Susan. Commd. 2d lt. U.S. Marine Corps., 1948, advanced through grades to maj., 1961; exptl. flight test pilot, U.S. Naval Air Test Center, Patuxent River, Md.; resigned, 1961; program mgr. Boeing Aircraft Co., Seattle and Phila., 1961-66, dir. airworthiness, comml. airplane divsn., 1969-71; dir. aircraft sales Am. Airlines, Tulsa, 1971-76; v.p. equipment mgmt. GATX Leasing Corp., San Francisco, 1976-80; v.p. tech., partner Polaris Aircraft Leasing Corp., San Francisco, 1980-85; v.p., co-founder U.S. Airlease, Inc. divsn. Ford Motor Co., 1986—; aircraft cons. Mem. Soc. Exptl. Test Pilots, Army Navy Country Club. Republican. Episcopalian. Home: 387 Darrell Rd Hillsborough CA 94010-6763 Office: US Airlease Inc 733 Front St San Francisco CA 94111-1808

WEST, JACK HENRY, petroleum geologist; b. Washington, Apr. 7, 1934; s. John Henry and Zola Faye (West) Pigg; m. Bonnie Lou Ruger, Apr. 1, 1961; children: Trent John, Todd Kenneth. BS in Geology, U. Oreg., 1957, MS, 1961. Cert. petroleum geologist. Geologist Texaco Inc., L.A and Bakersfield, Calif., 1961-72; asst. dist. devel. geologist Texaco Inc., L.A., 1972-78; geologist Oxy Petroleum Inc., Bakersfield, 1978-80, div. geologist, 1980-83; exploitation mgr. Oxy U.S.A. Inc./Cities Svc. Oil and Gas, Bakersfield, 1983-89; sr. petroleum advisor WZI Inc., Bakersfield, 1990-92, petroleum cons., 1993—. Active Beyond War, Bakersfield, 1983-90. Mem. Am. Assn. Petroleum Geologists (pres. Pacific sect. 1988-89, adv. coun. 1992-94, sec. divsn. profl. affairs 1995—), San Joaquin Geol. Soc. (pres. 1984-85), Alfa Romeo Owners Club. Republican. Methodist.

WEST, JAMES STUART, small business owner; b. Modesto, Calif., Jan. 22, 1935; s. Donald Hayden and Ruby Edith (Garrison) W.; m. Sandra Lee Hedman, June 7, 1958 (div.); m. Jessie Lee Dunn, May 23, 1973; children: Jason sTephan, Janet Lynn. AA, Menlo Jr. Coll., Menlo Park, Calif., 1955; student, Kans. State U., 1957-58. V.p. J.S. West & Co., Modesto, Calif., 1958—. Bd. dirs., sec.-treas. Delta Blood Bank, Stockton, Calif., 1972—; bd. dirs., vice-chmn. Modesto C. of C., 1980-89 (Disting. Svc. award 1989). Recipient Good Egg of Yr. award Annual Good Egg Breakfast Com., 1992. Mem. Calif. Egg Com. (bd. dirs. 1985-92, pres. 1992-95), Pacific Egg and Poultry Assn. (bd. dirs. 1984-92, pres. 1992, 93), Am. Egg Bd. (bd. dirs. 1989—, treas. 95—), Rotary (pres. Modesto club 1979-80, Paul Harris fellow 1977). Republican. Home: 224 Patricia Ln Modesto CA 95354-0262

WEST, JERRY ALAN, professional basketball team executive; b. Chelyan, W.Va., May 28, 1938; s. Howard Stewart and Cecil Sue (Creasey) W.; m. Martha Jane Kane, May, 1960 (div. 1977); children: David, Michael, Mark; m. Karen Christine Bua, May 28, 1978; 1 son, Ryan. BS, W.Va. Coll.; LHD (hon.), W.Va. Wesleyan Coll. Mem. Los Angeles Lakers, Nat. Basketball Assn., 1960-74, coach, 1976-79, spl. cons., 1979-82, gen. mgr., 1982-94; exec. v.p. basketball operations L. A. Lakers, 1994—; mem. first team Nat. Basketball Assn. All-Star Team, 1962-67, 70-73, mem. second team, 1968, 69. Author: (with William Libby) Mr. Clutch: The Jerry West Story, 1969. Capt. U.S. Olympic Basketball Team, 1960; named Most Valuable Player NBA Playoff, 1969, All-Star Game Most Valuable Player, 1972; named to Naismith Meml. Basketball Hall of Fame, 1979, NBA Hall of Fame, 1980; mem. NBA 35th Anniversary All-Time Team, 1980. Office: LA Lakers 3900 W Manchester Blvd PO Box 10 Inglewood CA 90306*

WEST, MADELINE FLORENCE, elementary education educator; b. San Francisco, Mar. 10, 1944; d. John Victor Hughes and Daisy Elizabeth (Darling) Irwin; m. Victor Vance West, Mar. 27, 1965; children: Amanda Elizabeth West Sutter, Aaron Frederick. BA, La Sierra Coll., Riverside, Calif., 1966; MA, Loma Linda U., Riverside, 1982. Tchr. Alvord Unified Sch. Dist., Riverside, 1966-71, 78—, sci. coord., 1992—, learning facilitator, 1993—. Author: The Constitutional Convention of 1787: The Delegates in Profile, 1987 (mentor award 1987), Women Who Made a Difference, 1988 (mentor award 1988). Mem. World Affairs Coun., Riverside, 1983-92. Recipient mentor tchr. award Alvord Unified Sch. Dist., 1987, 88, Tchr. of Yr. award S. Christa McAuliffe Sch., Riverside, 1988, outstanding contbns. award Inland Empire Calif. chpt. Internat. Reading Assn., 1988. Mem. NEA (rep. 1992-94, del. 1994). Office: S Christa McAuliffe Elem Sch 4100 Golden Ave Riverside CA 92505

WEST, MICHELLE LYNNE, television personality; b. Cleve., July 20, 1961; d. Leonard Carlton and Anne (Braxton) W.; m. Michael Donell Scott, Nov. 29, 1986; children: Michael Donell II, Brittany Anne Scott. BA in Journalism, Calif. State U., Northridge, 1983. Anchorwoman, reporter KIEM-TV, Eureka, Calif., 1984-85, KJEO-TV, Fresno, Calif., 1985—. Campaign worker Dukakis for Pres., Fresno, 1988. Mem. Nat. Assn. Black Journalists. Democrat. Office: KJEO-TV 4880 N 1st St Fresno CA 93726-0514

WEST, RICHARD VINCENT, art museum official; b. Prague, Czechoslovakia, Nov. 26, 1934; came to U.S., 1938, naturalized, 1947; s. Jan Josef and Katherine Frieda (Mayer) Vyslouzil; 1 child, Jessica Katherine. Student, UCLA, 1952-55, Music Acad. of the West, 1958-60; BA with highest honors, U. Calif., Santa Barbara, 1961; postgrad., Akademie der Bildenden Kuenste, Vienna, 1961-62, Hochschule fur Musik und darstellende Kuenste, Vienna, 1961-62; MA, U. Calif., Berkeley, 1965. Curatorial intern Cleve. Art Mus., 1965-66, Albright-Knox Art Gallery, Buffalo, 1966-67; curator Mus. Art Bowdoin Coll., Brunswick, Maine, 1967-69, dir., 1969-72; dir. Crocker Art Mus., Sacramento, Calif., 1973-82, Santa Barbara Mus. Art, Calif., 1983-91; pres. Artmuse Assocs., Benicia, Calif., 1991-92; dir. Newport (R.I.) Art Mus., 1992-94, Frye Art Mus., Seattle, 1995—; mem. Joint Yugoslav-Am. Excavations at Sirmium, 1971; bd. dirs. Sacramento Regional Art Coun., 1973-77; bd. overseers Strawbery Banke, 1993—. Author: Painters of the Section d'Or, 1967, Language of the Print, 1968; The Walker Art Building Murals, 1972, Munich and American Realism in the 19th Cen., 1978, An Enkindled Eye: The Paintings of Rockwell Kent, 1985, Standing in the Tempest: Painters of the Hungarian Avant-Garde, 1991, America in Art, 1991, A Significant Story: American Painting and Decorative Arts from the Karolik Collection, 1993; exhbn. catalogues, also various revs. and articles. Active Newport Reading Room; founding mem. New England Community Mus. Consortium. Served with USN, 1956-57. Ford Found. fellow, 1965-67; Smithsonian fellow, 1971. Mem. Am. Assn. Mus., Coll. Art Assn., Internat. Coun. Mus., Western Assn. Art Mus. (pres. 1975-78), Calif. Assn. Mus. (bd. dirs. 1980-82, v.p. 1986-91), Newport Reading Rm., Rotary. Office: Frye Art Mus PO Box 3005 Seattle WA 98114-3005

WEST, ROBERT SUMNER, surgeon; b. Bowman, N.D., Nov. 20, 1935; s. Elmer and Minnie (DeBode) W.; m. Martha W. Hopkins, Mar. 23, 1957; children: Stephen, Christopher, Anna Marie, Catherine, Sarah. BA, U. N.D., 1957, BS in Medicine, 1959; MD, Harvard U., 1961. Diplomate Am. Bd. Surgery. Intern U.S. Naval Hosp., Chelsea, Mass., 1961-62; resident in surgery U. Vt. Med. Ctr. Hosp., 1965-69; pvt. practice Coeur d'Alene, Idaho, 1969—; coroner Kootenai County, Coeur d'Alene, 1984—. Trustee, pres. Coeur d'Alene Sch. Dist. 271 Bd. Edn., 1973-77. Lt. M.C., USN, 1960-65. Fellow ACS (pres. Idaho chpt. 1985, gov. at large); mem. Idaho Med. Assn. (pres. 1989-90, trustee), Kiwanis. Republican. Lutheran. Office: 920 W Ironwood Dr Coeur D Alene ID 83814-2643

WEST, SHELBY JAY, insurance agent; b. Salt Lake City, Feb. 21, 1938; s. Shelby J. and Grace (Hunsaker) W.; m. Judene Casper, Apr. 14, 1961; children: Shauri Lynne, Pamela Joy, Christopher J., Troy Jay. Student, U. Utah, 1956-57, Utah State U., 1961-62. CLU, Utah, chartered fin. cons., Utah. Ins. agt. State Farm Ins. Cos., Salt Lake City, 1961—. Rep. dist. chmn., Midvale, Utah, 1984. Mem. Valley Assn. Life Underwriters (sec. 1983-84, v.p. 1984-85, pres. 1985-86, mem. nat. com. 1986-87), Rotary (Ft. Union, Midvale, sec. 1971-73, v.p. 1973-74, pres. 1974-75, sec. 1977-79, bd. dirs. 1990-92, pres. 1993-94). Mormon. Home: 635 Marquette Dr Midvale UT 84047-3617 Office: Jay West Ins Agy 114 W 7200 S Midvale UT 84047-3721

WEST, STEPHEN MCCALLUM, editor; b. Midland, Tex., May 22, 1948; s. Thomas M. and Elizabeth (Williams) W.; m. Anna Tartaglini. BA in Sociology, Yale U., 1970; MFA in Photography and Design, Calif. Inst. of the Arts, 1972; MBA in Fin. and Mktg., UCLA, 1983. Co-founder, editor Popular Psychology, 1971-73; asst. editor The Village Voice, N.Y.C., 1974-75; publs. editor L.A. County Mus. of Art, 1978-81; bus. reporter, copy editor Herald-Examiner, L.A., 1981-84; asst. bus. editor L.A. Times, 1984-91; exec. editor Daily Variety, L.A., 1991—; editor, writer, 1973-74, 75-78. Office: Daily Variety 5700 Wilshire Blvd Ste 120 Los Angeles CA 90036-3659

WEST, STERLING GAYLORD, physician; b. St. Petersburg, Fla., Aug. 4, 1950; s. Curtis Gaylord and Patricia (Bottome) W.; m. Brenda Sue White, June 20, 1972; children: Dace Nichole, Matthew Sterling. Grad., U.S. Mil. Acad., 1972; MD, Emory U., 1976. Diplomate Nat. Bd. Med. Examiners, Am. Bd. Internal Medicine, subspecialty rheumatology. Commd. 2d lt. U.S. Army, 1972, advanced through grades to col., 1992; intern, resident Fitzsimons Army Med. Ctr., Denver, 1976-79, chief resident in medicine, 1979, chief rheumatology, 1981-95; fellowship rheumatology Walter Reed Army Med. Ctr., Washington, 1979-81; cons. in rheumatology to U.S. Army Surgeon Gen., 1991-94; prof. of medicine and rheumatology fellowship program dir. U. Colo. Health Scis. Ctr., Denver, 1995—. Contbr. articles to profl. jours., rev. in field. Col. U.S. Army, 1972-95. Recipient Legion of Merit; Sr. fellow rsch. Merck, Sharp and Dohme, 1981; recipient AMSUS Phillips Hench award, 1983; rsch. grantee Rocky Mountain chpt. Arthritis Found., Denver, 1994. Fellow Am. Coll. Rheumatology, Am. Coll. Physicians; mem. AMA, Am. Coll. Physicians, Rocky Mountain Rheumatism Assn., Alpha Omega Alpha. Office: U Colo Health Sci Ctr 4200 E 9th Ave # B115 Denver CO 80220-3706

WEST, TONY, state official; b. Phoenix, Ariz., Oct. 29, 1937; m. Margaret O'Malley, 1962; 3 children: William A., III, John Patrick, Stephen Michael. BS, Ariz. State Univ., 1961. Formerly pres., chief exec. officer Shenendoah Ranches; Ariz. state rep., 1973-82, former Ariz. state senator, dist. 18, now Ariz. state treas. Mem. Ariz. Club (formerly pres.), Ariz. Found. for Handicapped (pres.), John C. Lincoln Hosp. Found. Republican. Office: Office of the State Treas 1700 W Washington St Phoenix AZ 85007-2812*

WESTBO, LEONARD ARCHIBALD, JR., electronics engineer; b. Tacoma, Wash., Dec. 4, 1931; s. Leonard Archibald and Agnes (Martinson) W.; B.A. in Gen. Studies, U. Wash., 1958. Electronics engr. FAA, Seattle Air Route Traffic Control Center, Auburn, Wash., 1961-72; asst. br. chief electronics engring. br. 13th Coast Guard Dist., Seattle, 1972-87. Served with USCG, 1951-54, 1958-61. Registered profl. engr., Wash. Mem. Aircraft Owners and Pilots Assn., IEEE, Am. Radio Relay League. Home and Office: 10528 SE 323rd St Auburn WA 98092-4734

WESTBROOK, T. L., bishop. Bishop of Wash. Ch. of God in Christ, Spanaway. Office: Ch of God in Christ 1256 176th St Spanaway WA 98387-7901

WESTCOTT, BRIAN JOHN, manufacturing executive; b. Rexford, N.Y., June 19, 1957; s. John Campbell and Norma (Cornell) W.; m. Andrea Belrose, Apr. 23, 1988; children: Sarah Katharine, Paul Brian. BS, Lehigh U., 1979; MS, Stanford U., 1980, PhD, 1987. Engr. Combustion Engring., Windsor, Conn., 1980-81; rsch. engr. Gen. Electric Corp. Rsch., Niskayuna, N.Y., 1981-83; rsch. fellow Stanford (Calif.) Grad. Sch. Bus., 1987-88; mgr. Gen. Electric Corp. Mgmt., Bridgeport, Conn., 1988-89; prin. A.T. Kearney Tech. Inc., Redwood City, Calif., 1989-91; chief exec. officer Westt, Inc., Menlo Park, Calif., 1990—. Author: (with others) Paradox and Transformation, 1988; contbr. articles to profl. jours.; inventor, patentee in field. Campaign com. James Buckley Senate Campaign, Conn., 1980; mem. Dean's Panel Campus Housing, Stanford, 1987-88; mem. Menlo Park Vitality Task Force, 1993-94. Postdoctoral rsch. fellow Stanford U. Grad. Sch. Bus., 1987, 88; rsch. fellow Electric Power Rsch., Stanford, 1983-87. Mem. ASME, Soc. Mfg. Engrs. Office: Westt Inc 980 O'Brien Dr Menlo Park CA 94025-1407

WESTCOTT, JAY YOUNG, pulmonary and critical care medicine educator; b. Phila., Jan. 5, 1953; m. Jamie L. English, June 14, 1989; children: Claire, Jay. BS in Biology, SUNY, Albany, 1975; PhD in Biology, Purdue U., 1981. Teaching asst. Purdue U., West Lafayette, Ind., 1976-77, grad. asst., 1977-81; postdoctoral fellow pharmacology dept. U. Colo. Health Sci. Ctr., Denver, 1981-85; instr. dept. medicine Cardiovasc. Pulmonary Rsch. Lab. U. Colo. Healath Scis. Ctr., Denver, 1986-88, asst. prof. divsn. Pulmonary Critical Care Medicine, 1988—. Contbr. articles to sci. jours., chpts. to books. Grantee NIH, 1977-80, NIH, 1988-95, Abbott Labs., 1992-93; fellow Nat. Inst. on Alcohol Abuse and Alcoholism, 1982-84, rsch. fellow Am. Lung Assn., 1987-89. Mem. Am. Thoracic Soc. Home: 2211 Vine St Denver CO 80205-5651 Office: U Colo Health Scis Ctr Div. Pulm-Critical Care Med 4200 E 9th Ave Denver CO 80220-3706

WESTER, KEITH ALBERT, film and television recording engineer, television executive; b. Seattle, Feb. 21, 1940; s. Albert John and Evelyn Grayce (Nettell) W., m. Judith Elizabeth Jones, 1968 (div. Mar. 1974); 1 child, Wendy Elizabeth. AA, Am. River Coll., Sacramento, 1959; BA, Calif. State U., L.A., 1962; MA, UCLA, 1965. Lic. multi-engine rated pilot. Prodn. asst. KCRA-TV, Sacramento, 1956; announcer KSFM, Sacramento, 1960; film editor, sound rec. technician Urie & Assocs., Hollywood, Calif., 1963-66; co-owner Steckler-Wester Film Prodns., Hollywood, 1966-70; owner Profl. Sound Recorders, Studio City, Calif., 1970—, Aerocharter, Studio City, 1974—; owner Wester Devel., Sun Valley, Coeur d'Alene, Idaho, 1989—, also Studio City, 1989—; ptnr. Sta. KDQ-TV, Coeur d'Alene/Spokane, Idaho, 1993—. Mem. NATAS (Emmy award An Early Frost 1986, Emmy nominations in 1982, 84, 85, 87), Acad. Motion Picture Arts and Scis. (Acad. award nomination for best sound Black Rain 1990), Cinema Audio Soc. (sec. 1985-91, Sound award 1987), Soc. Motion Picture and TV Engrs., Internat. Sound Technicians, Local 695, Assn. Film Craftsmen (sec. 1967-73, treas. 1973-76), Screen Actors Guild, Aircraft Owners and Pilots Assn. (Confederate Air Force col.), Am. Radio Relay League. Home: 4146 Bellingham Ave Studio City CA 91604-1601 Office: Profl Sound Recorders 22440 Clarendon St Woodland Hills CA 91367-4467

WESTERDAHL, JOHN BRIAN, nutritionist, health educator; b. Tucson, Dec. 3, 1954; s. Jay E. and Margaret (Meyer) W.; m. Doris Mui Lian Tan, Nov. 18, 1989. AA, Orange Coast Coll., 1977; BS, Pacific Union Coll., 1979; MPH, Loma Linda U., 1981. Registered dietitian; chartered herbalist; cert. nutrition specialist. Nutritionist, health educator Castle Med. Ctr., Kailua, Hawaii, 1981-84, health promotion coord., 1984-87, asst. dir. health promotion, 1987-88, dir. health promotion, 1988-89; dir. nutrition and health rsch. Health Sci., Santa Barbara, Calif., 1989-90; sr. nutritionist, project mgr. Shaklee Corp., San Francisco, 1990—; talk show host Nutrition and You, Sta. KGU Radio, Honolulu, 1983-89; nutrition com. mem. Hawaii div. Am. Heart Assn., Honolulu, 1984-87; mem. nutrition study group Govs. Conf. Health Promotion and Disease Prevention for Hawaii, 1985. Mem. AAAS, Am. Coll. Sports Medicine, Am. Dietetic Assn., Am. Nutritionists Assn., Am. Coll. Nutrition, Soc. for Nutrition Edn., Nat. Wellness Assn., Nutrition Today Soc., Am. Soc. Pharmacognosy, Inst. Food Technologists, Hawaii Nutrition Coun. (v.p. 1983-86,m pres.-elect 1988-89, pres. 1989), Hawaii Dietetic Assn., Calif. Dietetic Assn., N.Y. Acad. Scis., Seventh-day Adventist Dietetic Assn., several other profl. assns. Republican. Seventh-Day Adventist. Office: Shaklee Corp 444 Market St San Francisco CA 94111-5325

WESTERMAN, JOHN HAROLD, health administrator; b. Mpls., July 24, 1933; s. Harold V. and Kay S. Westerman; children: James, Laura (dec.), Eric, Peter. B.S., U. Minn., 1954, B.B.A., 1958, M.H.A., 1960. Asst. adminstr., sr. instr. U. Rochester (N.Y.) Med. Center, 1961-64; research assoc. Sci. Planning Office, U. Minn., Mpls., 1964-66; assoc. prof. pub. health, gen. dir. hosps. and clinics, coordinator health systems research and devel. Sci. Planning Office, U. Minn. (Office Vice pres.), 1967-82; pres. Allegheny Health, Edn. and Research Corp., 1982-85, Allegheny Gen. Hosp., Allegheny Diagnostic Services, Inc., Allegheny Singer Research Corp.; chief exec. officer Allegheny Health Services, Inc.; pres., chief exec. officer Hosp. of the Good Samaritan, Los Angeles, 1985-92; interim pres. Assn. of Univ. Programs in Health Adminstrn., Arlington, Va., 1993; CEO Hilo (Hawaii) Med. Ctr., 1993—; mem. bd. Minn. Blue Cross-Blue Shield, 1972-78; mem. bd. commrs. Joint Commn. Accreditation Hosps., Chgo., 1976-82; pres., mem. bd. Minn. Bd. Health, 1972-78; mem. clin. research adv. com. NIH, 1976-80; accrediting mem. Commn. Edn. for Health Services Adminstrn., 1977; mem. adv. panel on multi-instnl. arrangements Am. Hosp. Assn., 1977-83; mem. Nat. End Stage Renal Disease Planning Com., 1980-81; pres. Consortium for Study Univ. Hosps., 1980-81; mem. Vol. Hosp. Am., 1983-85, Premier Health Alliance, 1988-92; chmn. Big Island Health Consortium, 1994. Author articles in field; mem. editl. bd. Jour. Med. Edn, 1972-78, Health Care Mgmt. Rev, 1979-82, Frontiers of Health Svcs. Mgmt., 1992-95. Served with USAF, 1955-58. Recipient Distinguished Service award. Democrat. Episcopalian. Office: Hilo Med Ctr 1190 Waianuenue Ave Hilo HI 96720-2020

WESTERMAN, KATY DOROTHEA, former vocational education administrator; b. Swink, Colo., Feb. 16, 1930; d. Orval Ernest and Beatrice Alzina (Cloud) Krout; m. Hugh Abraham Westerman, Oct. 15, 1955 (div. Apr. 1971); children: Vincent Hugh, Theodore Lynn, Michael Darryl Dean, Christopher Wayne, Mark Alan. BA, U. No. Colo., 1954; MEd, Colo. State U., 1979. Tchr. Eagle (Colo.) County High Sch., 1954-57, Sangre De Cristo High Sch., Mosca, Colo., 1957-61, Sierra Grande High Sch., Ft. Garland, Colo., 1961-70; instr., coord. power sewing program San Luis Valley Area Vocat. Sch., Monte Vista, Colo., 1970-74; instr., coord. spl. coop. program Alamosa (Colo.) High Sch., 1974-81; coord. cmty. edn., supr. adult basic edn. and GED Alamosa Pub. Schs., 1981-84; asst. dir. San Luis Valley Area Vocat. Sch., 1984-87; dir. secondary vocat. edn. San Luis Valley, 1988-92; adminstr. Carl Perkins Consortium San Luis Valley Area Vocat. Sch., 1990-92; ret., 1992; instr. Ford Found. Rocky Mountain Area Small High Schs. Project, Mosca, 1957-61; mem. Gov.'s Coun. on Status of Women, Monte Vista, 1971-74; adminstr. Community Recreation Bd., Alamosa, 1981-84; cons. Chinese Spl. Needs Program, People's Republic of China, 1986; sec. Colo. Vocat. Hall of Fame Found., 1979-84, pres., 1988-92. Member Alamosa C. of C., 1986-90; precinct rep. Alamosa County Cen. Dem. Com., 1984-90. Inducted into Colo. Vocat. Hall of Fame, 1994. Mem. NEA, Am. Vocat. Assn., Colo. Vocat. Assn. (sec. new and related svcs. div. 1980-82, pres. elect new and related svcs. div. 1983, pres. 1984-85), Nat. Assn. Vocat. Spl. Needs Pers. (sec. Colo. chpt. 1980-82, pres. elect 1983, pres. 1984-85), Colo. Edn. Assn., Colo. Assn. Vocat. Adminstrs., Colo. Assn. Sch. Execs., Iota Lambda Sigma, Beta Sigma Phi (Woman of the Yr. 1986). Roman Catholic. Home: 8481A County Road 8 S Alamosa CO 81101-9193

WESTERNOFF, W. GARY, construction company executive; b. Oakland, Calif., Nov. 20, 1941; s. Walter Herbert and Ada Wardlow (Blake) W.; m. Peggy Jean Plummer, Oct. 19, 1942; children: Thomas Gary, John Walter. AA in Architecture, Laney Coll., 1966; BA in Constrn. Tech., San Francisco State U., 1968. Lic. gen contractor, Calif., Hawaii; lic. real estate agent, Calif. Arch., design draftsman Montgomery Ward Co., Oakland, 1968-70; project engr. Lucky Stores, Inc., San Leandro, Calif., 1970-75; dir. design and contrn. A&P Stores, Montvale, N.J., 1975-78; dir. planning and constrn. Liberty House, Honolulu, 1978-81; v.p. design and constrn Joseph Magnin Co., Inc., San Francisco, 1981-83; owner The Westernoff Group, Moraga, Calif., 1983—; prof. constrn. mgmt. Diablo Valley Coll., Pleasant Hill, Calif.; presentor constrn. mgmt. seminar, 1992. Contbr. articles to profl. jours.; patentee jousting game. Pres. Rotary Club, Lafayette, Calif., 1992-93. With U.S. Army, 1959-62, Korea. Mem. Profl. Assn. Constrn. Inspectors, Profl. Coun. Condominium Homeowner Assns., Masons. Home: 4 Doral Dr Moraga CA 94556-1041 Office: The Westernoff Group 370 Park St # 15 PO Box 153 Moraga CA 94556

WESTIN, ROBERT LEE, management consultant; b. Center, Colo., Nov. 5, 1932; s. Henri Charles and Catherine Lucile (Head) W.; m. Leontine Mae Eckhardt, Jan. 11, 1953; children: Patricia, Robert, Theresa, Susan, Richard, Katherine. BSBA, U. Denver, 1956. CPCU. Gen. mgr. Home Ins. Co., L.A., 1956-65; sr. v.p. Penn Gen. Agys. Inc., L.A., 1965-78; pres. Physicians and Surgeons Exch., L.A., 1978-83, Victus, Inc., Pasadena, Calif., 1983—; chmn., founder Brookside Savs. & Loan, Pasadena, 1982-85; pres. Flying V Ranch, Lompoc, Calif., 1985—; bd. dirs. M.H. Ross Co., Inc., Sepulveda, Calif., Medex Internat. Corp., Balt. Author: Management by Objectives for Insurance Agents and Brokers, 1978; contbr. over 70 articles to profl. jours. Bd. dirs. Am. Heart Assn., L.A., 1982-84; chmn. ins. com. AAU, L.A., 1988-90. With USN, 1951-53. Mem. Am. Inst. Property and Casualty Underwriters. Republican. Roman Catholic.

WESTON, EDWARD, art dealer, consultant; b. N.Y.C., Feb. 25, 1925; s. Joseph and Mona Weston; m. Ann Jean Gould, May 4, 1974; children: Jon Marc, Cari Alyn Rene. News editor Sta. WMCA, N.Y.C., 1940-41; announcer news dept. Sta. WSAV, Savannah, Ga., 1941-43; newscaster, disc jockey Sta. WNOX, Knoxville, Tenn., 1943-45; program dir. Sta. WXLH, Okinawa, Japan, 1945-47; newscaster, announcer Sta. WAVZ, New Haven, 1947-48; program dir. Sta. WCCC, Hartford, Conn., 1948-49; asst. gen. mgr. Sta. WCPO AM-FM-TV, Cin., 1949-59; pres., gen. mgr. Sta. WZIP, Cin., 1959-61; pres. Weston Entertainment, Northridge, Calif., 1961—, Edward Weston Fine Art; chmn. bd. Fulton J. Sheen Communications; pres. Inspirational Programs, Inc., 1983—, Weston Editions, 1970—, Marilyn Monroe Editions, 1975—. Producer TV/video cassettes Life Is Worth Living; PBS TV series How to Paint with Elke Sommer, 1984. Founder Cin. Summer Playhouse, 1950. Served with U.S. Army, 1945-46. Recipient Outstanding News Coverage award Variety mag., 1949, Outstanding Sta. Ops. award Variety mag., 1950, Best Programming award Nat. Assn. Radio TV Broadcasters, 1951. Mem. Nat. Franchise Assn. (founder). Home: 10511 Andora Ave Chatsworth CA 91311-2004 Office: Weston Entertainment 19355 Business Center Dr Northridge CA 91324-3503

WESTON, JANE SARA, plastic surgeon, educator; b. Oceanside, N.Y., May 21, 1952; m. Jan K. Horn; 1 child, Jonathan Spencer Horn. MD, Stanford U., 1975-79. Diplomate Am. Bd. Plastic Surgery. Resident gen. surgery Sch. Medicine Stanford (Calif.) U., 1979-82, resident plastic surgery Sch. Medicine, 1982-83; fellow craniofacial surgery Hopital des Enfants Malades, Paris, 1983-84; plastic surgeon Kaiser Permanente Med. Group, San Jose, Calif., 1985-90; pvt. practice Palo Alto, Calif., 1990—; plastic surgeon Stanford U. Med. Sch., 1994—. Active Leadership Palo Alto, 1993. Fellow ACS; mem. Am. Soc. Plastic and Reconstructive Surgeons (chair women plastic surgeons com. 1993—), Interplast (assoc. dir.). Office: 750 Welch Rd Ste 321 Palo Alto CA 94304-1510

WESTON, JOHN FREDERICK, business educator, consultant; b. Ft. Wayne, Ind., Feb. 6, 1916; s. David Thomas and Bertha (Schwartz) W.; children: Kenneth F., Byron L., Ellen J. B.A., U. Chgo., 1937, M.B.A., 1943, Ph.D., 1948. Instr. U. Chgo. Sch. Bus., 1940-42, asst. prof., 1947-48; prof. Anderson Grad. Sch. Mgmt. UCLA, 1949—, Cordner prof. Anderson Grad. Sch. Mgmt., 1981-94; prof. emeritus Anderson Grad. Sch. Mgmt. UCLA, 1986—; econ. cons. to pres. Am. Bankers Assn., 1945-46; disting.

lecture series U. Okla., 1967, U. Utah, 1972, Miss. State U., 1972, Miami State U., 1975; dir. UCLA Anderson Grad. Sch. Mgmt. Rsch. Program in Competition and Bus. Policy, 1969—, Ctr. for Managerial Econs. and Pub. Policy, 1983-86. Author: Scope and Methodology of Finance, 1966, International Managerial Finance, 1972, Impact of Large Firms on U.S. Economy, 1973, Financial Theory and Corporate Policy, 1979, 2d edit., 1983, 3d edit., 1988, Managerial Finance, 9th edit, 1992; assoc. editor: Jour. of Finance, 1948-55; mem. editorial bd., 1957-59; editorial bd. Bus. Econs., Jour. Fin. Rsch., Managerial and Decision Econs.; manuscript referee Am. Econ. Rev., Rev. of Econs. and Statistics, Engring. Economist. Bd. dirs. Bunker Hill Fund. Served with Ordnance Dept. AUS, 1943-45. Recipient Abramson Scroll award Bus. Econs., 1989-93; McKinsey Found. grantee, 1965-68; GE grantee, 1967; Ford Found. Faculty Rsch. fellow, 1961-62. Mem. Am. Finance Assn. (pres. 1966, adv. bd. 1967-71), Am. Econ. Assn., Western Econ. Assn. (pres. 1962), Econometric Soc., Am. Statis. Assn., Royal Econ. Soc., Fin. Analysts Soc., Fin. Mgmt. Assn. (pres. 1979-80). Home: 258 Tavistock Ave Los Angeles CA 90049-3229 Office: UCLA Anderson Grad Sch Mgmt Los Angeles CA 90095-1481

WESTOVER, KRISTINE ELIZABETH, dietitian, nutritionist; b. San Mateo, Calif., Aug. 6, 1958; d. Maurice Parkinson and Olive Elizabeth (McFate) Monson; m. Layne D. Westover, Dec. 27, 1978; children: Brian Jason, Sean Monson, Thomas Layne. BS, Brigham Young U., 1979, MS, 1983. Registered dietitan. Rsch. asst. McKesson Corp., San Francisco, 1979-80; instr. Utah Tech. Coll., Provo/Orem, 1979-81, FSN Dept., Brigham Young U., Provo, 1980-82; health educator March of Dimes, So. Utah Chpt., Provo, 1980-83; rsch. nutritionist U. Utah Sch. Medicine, Salt Lake City, 1982-84; sr. instr. Oreg. Health Sci. U., Portland, 1984-86; pvt. cons., 1986—; clin. dietitian Kaiser Permanente Med. Ctr., Vallejo/Richmond, Calif., 1986-87; med. writer Bristol-Myers USPNG, Evansville, Ind., 1989—; nutrition cons. The Westover Grp., Salem, Oreg., 1986—; fitness instr. various orgns. Contbg. author: Handbook of Clinical Dietetics, 1986; contbr. articles to profl. jours. Brigham Young U. scholar, 1975. Mem. Am. Dietetic Assn., Sigma Xi. Republican. Mem. Ch. of Jesus Christ of Latter Day Saints. Home: 4174 Sunray Ave S Salem OR 97302

WESTPHAL, MARJORIE LORD, lawyer; b. Erie, Pa., July 24, 1940; d. Thomas and Dorothy (Hofft) Lord; m. David Melvin Zurn, Sept. 2, 1960 (div. Sept. 1970); children: Rena Zurn Fulweiler, Amelie Susan, Christopher F.; m. Lester Roy Westphal, May 26, 1971. Student, Brown U., 1958-60; BS, Gannon U., 1974; JD, Case Western Res. U., 1978. Bar: Ohio 1979. Assoc. Kohrman, Jackson, Weiss, Cleve., 1980-81; sole practice Cleve., 1981-92. Trustee Emma Willard Sch., Troy, N.Y., 1978-80; dir. Ohioans for Merit Selection of Judges, Cuyahoga County, 1979; mem. Vol. Lawyers for the Arts, Citizens League of Cleve., Women's City Club Found.; treas. Women's Community Fund, 1991-92; publicity chmn. Desert Foothills Music Fest, 1994—. Mem. ABA, Ohio Bar Assn., Cleve. Bar Assn., Cleve. Women's Bar Assn, Pi Gamma Mu. Club: Cleve. Skating, Desert Mountain.

WESTPHAL, PAUL, professional basketball coach; b. Torrance, Calif., Nov. 30, 1950; m. Cindy Westphal; children: Victoria, Michael Paul. Degree in phys. edn., U. So. Calif., 1972. Player Boston Celtics, 1972-75, Phoenix Suns, 1975-80, 83-84, Seattle Supersonics, 1980-81, N.Y. Knicks, 1981-83; coach S.W. Coll., Phoenix, 1985-86, Grand Canyon Coll., 1986-88; asst. coach. Phoenix Suns, 1988-92, head coach, 1992—. Named All-Star 5 times, Comeback Player of Yr.; uniform number retired by Suns, 1989. Office: Phoenix Suns 201 E Jefferson St Phoenix AZ 85004-2412*

WESTPHAL, RUTH LILLY, educational audiovisual company executive, author, publisher; b. Glendale, Calif., July 27, 1931; d. Glen R. and Margaret E. (John) Lilly; m. H. Frederick Westphal, June 25, 1953. B.A. in Edn., UCLA, 1953; M.A. in Instructional System Tech., Chapman Coll., 1968. Cert. tchr. Calif. Tchr. pub. schs., Los Angeles, Glendale, Whittier, Calif., 1953-65; instuctional systems analyst Litton Industries, Anaheim, Calif., 1965-67; dir. devel. Trainex Corp., Garden Grove, Calif., 1967-69; owner, pres. Concept Media, Inc., Irvine, Calif., 1969—, Westphal Pub., Irvine, 1980—. Co-founder Friends of City Library, LaHabra, Calif., 1960-65; mem. Los Angeles County Mus. Art, 1975—, Laguna Beach Mus. Art, 1979—, Nautical Heritage Soc. Dana Point, Calif. 1982—. Author, editor numerous ednl. filmstrip and video programs. Author: Plein Air Painters of California: The Southland, 1982 (Western Books award 1982), Plein Air Painters of California: The North, 1986 (Western Books award 1986), American Scene Painting: California, 1930s and 1940s, 1991. Recipient numerous awards Info. Film Producers Am., Internat. Film and TV Festival N.Y., Chgo. Film Festival, Am. Jour. Nursing Media Festival, Author Recognition award U. Calif., 1983. Mem. Nat. Audiovisual Assn., Assn. Media Producers. Avocations: Art history. Office: Concept Media Inc 2493 Du Bridge Ave Irvine CA 92714-5022

WETTERHAHN, RALPH FRANCIS, freelance writer; b. N.Y.C., Apr. 20, 1942; s. John William and Marie Bernadette (Hackenberg) W.; m. Mary Ann Bowers, June 26, 1963 (div. June 1985); children: Scott Gerald, Thomas Michael, Michael David; m. Carol L. Leviton, May 28, 1986. BS, USAF Academy, 1963; MBA, Auburn U., 1973. Commd. 2d lt. USAF, 1963, advanced through grades to col.; fighter pilot 1st TAC Fighter Wing Langley AFB, Va., 1976-82; dep. dir. internat. program Washington, 1983-86; dep. dir. plans Pacific Air Command Honolulu, 1986-87, chief of safety Pacific Air Command, 1987-88; chief air force div. Joint U.S. Mil. Adv. Group, Bangkok, Thailand, 1989-92; ret., 1992; chmn. R&R Aviation Svc., Ltd., Bangkok, 1992-93; freelance writer Long Beach, Calif., 1993—. Recipient Silver Star USAF, 1966. Mem. Air Force Assn., Long Beach Writers Group.

WETZEL, JODI (JOY LYNN WETZEL), history and women's studies educator; b. Salt Lake City, Apr. 5, 1943; d. Richard Coulam and Margaret Elaine (Openshaw) Wood; m. David Nevin Wetzel, June 12, 1967; children: Meredith (dec.), Richard Rawlins. BA in English, U. Utah, 1965, MA in English, 1967; PhD in Am. Studies, U. Minn., 1977. Instr. Am. studies and family social sci. U. Minn., 1973-77, asst. prof. Am. studies and women's studies, 1977-79, asst. to dir. Minn. Women's Ctr., 1973-75, asst. dir., 1975-79; dir. Women's Resource Ctrs. U. Denver, 1980-84, mem. adj. faculty history, 1981-84, dir. Am. studies program, dir. Women's Inst., 1983-84; dir. Women in Curriculum U. Maine, 1985-86, mem. coop. faculty sociology, social work and human devel., 1986—; dir. Inst. Women's Studies and Svcs. Met. State Coll. Denver, 1986—, assoc. prof. history, 1986-89, prof. history, 1990—; speaker, presenter, cons. in field; vis. prof. Am. studies U. Colo., 1985. Co-author: Women's Studies: Thinking Women, 1993; co-editor: Readings Toward Composition, 2d edit., 1969; contbr. articles to profl. publs. Del. at-large Nat. Women's Meeting, Houston, 1977; bd. dirs. Rocky Mountain Women's Inst., 1981-84; treas. Colo. Women's Agenda, 1987-91. U. Utah Dept. English fellow, 1967; U. Minn. fellow, 1978-79; grantee NEH, 1973, NSF, 1981-83, Carnegie Corp., 1988; named to Outstanding Young Women of Am., 1979. Mem. Am. Hist. Assn., Nat. Assn. Women in Edn., Am. Assn. for Higher Edn., Am. Studies Assn., Nat. Women's Studies Assn., Golden Key Nat. Honor Soc. (hon.), Alpha Lambda Delta, Phi Kappa Phi. Office: Met State Coll Denver Campus Box 36 PO Box 173362 Denver CO 80217-3362

WETZEL, KARL JOSEPH, physics educator, university official and dean; b. Waynesboro, Va., May 29, 1937; s. Mark Ernest and Margaret K. (Jungbluth) W.; m. Barbara Carol Damutz, Aug. 3, 1968; children: Sebastian P., Christopher M. BS in Physics, Georgetown U., 1959; MS in Physics, Yale U., 1960, PhD in Physics, 1965. Physicist Nat. Bur. Standards, Washington, 1959; postdoctoral fellow Inst. Nuclear Physics, Darmstadt, Germany, 1965-67, Argonne (Ill.) Nat. Lab., 1967-69; asst. prof. physics U. Portland, Oreg., 1969-72, assoc. prof., 1972-80, prof., 1980—, chmn. sci. dept., 1980-86, dean Grad. Sch., 1987—, asst. acad. v.p.; cons. in field; adj. prof. State of Oreg. Dept. Continuing Edn., Portland, 1976—. Contbr. articles to profl. publs. Bd. dirs. Friendly House Ctr., Portland, 1979-82, Choral Arts Ensemble, Portland, 1988—. NSF fellow, 1965, 76-77; recipient Pres.' award Oreg. Mus. Sci. and Industry, 1972, Outstanding Advisor award Am. Coll. Test/Nat. Academic Advising Assn., 1984. Mem. Am. Phys. Soc., AAUP. Office: U Portland 5000 N Willamette Blvd Portland OR 97203-5743

WEVURSKI, PETER JOHN, newspaper editor; b. Jersey City, Sept. 10, 1948. BA in English, St. Peter's Coll., Jersey City, 1970. Editor night sports, columnist The Jersey Jour., Jersey City, 1969-79; editor night sports, sportswriter The Pitts. Press, 1979-85; dep. sports editor L.A. Herald Examiner, 1985-87; sports editor The Morning News Tribune, Tacoma, 1987-90; exec. news editor The Nat. Sports Daily, N.Y.C., 1990-91; asst. sports editor The Newark Star-Ledger, 1991-92; exec. sports editor Alameda Newspaper Group, Hayward, Calif., 1992—. Past juror N.Y. Film Festival. With U.S. Army, 1971-74, capt. Res. Recipient 20 individual writing and editing awards. Mem. Associated Press Sports Editors, Investigative Reporters & Editors. Office: Alameda Newspaper Group 4770 Willow Rd Pleasanton CA 94588-2762

WEWER, WILLIAM PAUL, lawyer; b. San Diego, May 27, 1947; s. William P. and Helen E. (Helm) Wewer; m. Katheleen Marquardt, Dec. 6, 1987. BA with honors, Pomona Coll., 1970; JD with high honors, George Washington U., 1977. Bar: D.C. 1977, U.S. Ct. Appeals (D.C. cir.) 1977, Calif. 1980, U.S. Ct. Appeals (9th cir.) 1980, U.S. Dist. Ct. D.C. 1981, U.S. Dist. Ct. (no. dist.) Calif. 1982, U.S. Supreme Ct. 1982, Colo. 1989, Mont., 1994. Legisl. asst. U.S. Senator Howard W. Cannon, Washington, 1970-74; profl. staff mem. Rules Com. U.S. Senate, Washington, 1974-77; assoc. Sutherland, Asbill & Brennan, Washington, 1977-79; ptnr. Wewer & Mann, P.C., Washington, 1979-83, Wewer Law Firm, Washington, L.A., Denver, Helena, 1983—, Bleak House Publishing Co., Bethesda, Md., 1988-89; cons. various candidates nationwide, 1966-76. Contbr. articles to profl. jours. and nationally syndicated newspaper column. Bd. dirs. Am. Tax Reduction Movement, Washington, 1980-89, pres., 1989-91; bd. dirs. Howard Jarvis Taxpayers Assn., L.A., 1980-89, Am. Tax Reduction Found., Washington, 1983-90, Nat. Com. to Preserve Social Security and Medicare, Washington, 1982-87, Montanans for Better Govt. Found., Helena, 1995—; sec. Beer Drinkers of Am., Sacramento, Calif., 1994—; treas. Dr. Lynch Found., L.A., 1995—, various non-profit groups nationwide; mem. legal adv. bd. and exec. com. Defenders of Property Rights, Washington; sec. Subscription TV Assn., Washington, 1979-83, Calif. Apt. Law Info. Found., L.A., 1989—. Mem. ABA. Republican. Home: 533 5th Ave Helena MT 59601-4359 also: Ste 292-A 4401 Connecticut Ave NW Washington DC 20008 also: 621 S Westmoreland Ave Ste 200 Los Angeles CA 90005-3981

WEXLER, JUDIE GAFFIN, sociology educator, researcher; b. N.Y.C., Apr. 15, 1945; d. Isaac and Sara (Widensky) Pearlman; m. Howard M. Wexler, Mar. 11, 1973; children—Robyn, Matthew. B.A. in Sociology, Russell Sage U., Troy, N.Y., 1965; M.A. in Demography, U. Pa., 1966; Ph.D. in Sociology, U. Calif.-Berkeley, 1975. Researcher N.Y. Mental Health Dept., Albany, 1966-67; demographer City Planning Dept., San Francisco, 1967-68; prof. Holy Names Coll., Oakland, Calif., 1974—, dean of acad. affairs, 1992—, v.p. acad. affairs, 1993; cons. in field. Contbr. articles to profl. jours. Fellow Ford Found., NDEA. Mem. Am. Sociol. Assn., Am. Psychol. Assn. Home: 23 Cresta Vista Dr San Francisco CA 94127-1632 Office: Holy Names Coll 3500 Mountain Blvd Oakland CA 94619-1627

WEYAND, FREDERICK CARLTON, retired military officer; b. Arbuckle, Calif., Sept. 15, 1916; s. Frederick C. W. and Velma Semans (Weyand); m. Lora Arline Langhart, Sept. 20, 1940; children: Carolyn Ann, Robert Carlton, Nancy Diane. A.B., U. Calif.-Berkeley, 1939; LL.D. (hon), U. Akron, 1975. Officer U.S. Army, advanced to gen. chief of staff, 1940-76; sr. v.p. First Hawaiian Bank, Honolulu, 1976-82; trustee Estate of S.M. Damon, Honolulu, 1982—; bd. dirs. First Hawaiian, Inc., Ltd., First Hawaiian Bank, First Hawaiian Credit Corp. Chmn. ARC, Honolulu, 1982, Hawaiian Open golf Tourney, 1981-82. Decorated D.S.C. U.S. Army, 1967, D.S.M. Army (3), Dept. Def. (1), 1966-76, other U.S. and fgn. mil. decorations. Mem. Am. Def. Preparedness Assn., Assn. U.S. Army, U.S. Strategic Inst. (v.p. 1976—), USAF Assn. Lutheran. Clubs: Waialae Country. Lodge: Masons. Home: 2121 Ala Wai Blvd Ph 1 Honolulu HI 96815-2211 Office: SM Damon Estate 1132 Bishop St Ste 1520 Honolulu HI 96813-2830

WEYERHAEUSER, GEORGE HUNT, forest products company executive; b. Seattle, July 8, 1926; s. John Philip and Helen (Walker) W.; m. Wendy Wagner, July 10, 1948; children: Virginia Lee, George Hunt, Susan W., Phyllis A., David M., Merrill W. BS with honors in Indsl. Engring., Yale U., 1949. With Weyerhaeuser Co., Tacoma, 1949—, successively mill foreman, br. mgr., 1949-56, v.p., 1957-66, exec. v.p., 1966-88, pres., chief exec. officer, 1988, chmn. bd., chief exec. officer, 1988-91, chmn. bd., past CEO, also bd. dirs.; bd. dirs. Boeing Co., SAFECO Corp., Chevron Corp.; mem. Bus. Coun., Bus. Roundtable, Wash. State Bus. Roundtable. Office: Weyerhaeuser Fin Svcs 33663 Weyerhaeuser Way S Auburn WA 98001-9646*

WEYGAND, LEROY CHARLES, service executive; b. Webster Park, Ill., May 17, 1926; s. Xaver William and Marie Caroline (Hoffert) W.; BA in Sociology cum laude, U. Md., 1964; m. Helen V. Bishop, Aug. 28, 1977; children: Linda M. Weygand Vance (dec.), Leroy Charles, Cynthia R., Janine P. Enlisted in U.S. Army, 1944, commd. 2d lt., 1950, advanced through grades to lt. col., 1966; service in Korea, 1950; chief phys. security U.S. Army, 1965-70; ret., 1970; pres. Weygand Security Cons. Srvcs., Anaheim, Calif., 1970—, W & W Devel. Corp., 1979—; security dir. Jefferies Banknote Co., 1972-78; pres. Kern County Taxpayers Assn., 1986—; dir. Mind Psi-Biotics, Inc. Bd. dirs. Nat. Assn. Control Narcotics and Dangerous Drugs. Decorated Legion of Merit. Mem. Am. Soc. Indsl. Security. Contbr. articles profl. jours. Patentee office equipment locking device. Home: 12110 Backdrop Ct Bakersfield CA 93306-9707 Office: Kern County Taxpayers Assn 1415 18th St Ste 407 Bakersfield CA 93301-4442

WHALEN, ALBERTA DEAN, community health nurse; b. Oakland, Calif., Apr. 27, 1929; d. Govie and Lula (Rutledge) Smith; m. Joseph T. Whalen, May 29, 1954; children: Michael, Joseph, William. RN, Providence Coll. Nursing, Oakland, 1951; postgrad., Chabot Coll., Las Positas Coll. RN, Calif. Surgical/recovery room nurse Peralta Hosp., Oakland, Calif., 1951-55; surg., recovery rm. nurse Providence Hosp., Oakland, 1956; recovery room nurse Eden Hosp., Castro Valley, Calif., 1957; pvt. duty nurse Valley Meml. Hosp., Livermore, Calif., 1966-68; doctor's office nurse Daphne M. Chisolm, MD, Livermore, 1984-86; home nursing Livermore, 1987—; part-time pvt. duty nurse Hacienda Care Ctr., Livermore, Calif., 1993—. Vol. ARC, 1976—, CPR and std. 1st aid instr., rep. in fair booths and 1st aid stas., disaster teams, coord. Tri Valley Area, 1995; vol. cmty. health nurse for Livermore Libr. sr. blood pressure clinics, 1984—; rec. sec. Cath. Nurses Assn., South Alameda County, 1958-60; found. mem. Newly Merged Summit Med. Group, Oakland, Calif.; active St. Rose Hosp. Found., Hayward, Calif.; mem. welcoming com. St. Michaels Cath. Ch., Livermore, 1962—, Golden Friends, 1988—, Eucharistic min., 1991—. Recipient ARC nursing pin 1981, 20 yr. pin 1995; named instr. of yr. TriValley ARC Ctr., 1995. Mem. ARC, Providence Hosp. Valley Meml. Hosp. Founds.

WHALEN, MARGARET CAVANAGH, retired secondary school educator; b. Des Moines, Iowa, Mar. 9, 1913; d. Thomas J. and Ann Lenore (Paul) Cavanagh; m. George Hubert Whalen, Aug. 3, 1946; children: Michael T., Ann Whalen Carrillo, George Patrick (dec.), Cheryl. BS in Commerce, St. Teresa Coll., Winona, Minn., 1935. Head bus. dept. St. Augustine High Sch., Austin, Minn., 1935-36, Parochial High Sch., Caledonia, Minn., 1936-37; clk., typist U.S. Govt., Dept. Socicl Security, Des Moines, 1937-38; county investigator for old age asst., aid to blind Marion County, Knoxville, Iowa, 1938; hydro dept. U.S. Weather Bur. Regional Office, Iowa City, Kansas City, Mo., 1939-42; head bills/warrants dept. IRS, Des Moines, 1942-46; substitute tchr. Los Gatos High Sch., Calif., 1961-65, Saratoga High Sch., Calif., 1961-65. Vol. Girl Scouts U.S.A., Boy Scouts Am., Saratoga, Calif., 1957-62; poll insp. Santa Clara County Regional Voters, Saratoga; precinct insp. Saratoga for Santa Clara County Registrar of Voters; organizer, vol. Saratoga Area Sr. Coord. Coun., 1979—; Eucharistic minister, lector, commentator Sacred Heart Ch., Saratoga, 1986—; charter pres. Oz chpt. Children's Home Soc., Saratoga; mem. Sacred Heart Women's Club, Our Lady of Los Gatos # 197 Young Ladies Inst. Recipient Papal Bronze medal for Pub. Rels. Nat. Coun. Cath. Women, Saratoga, 1958, Merit award Friends of Saratoga Librs., 1975—, Merit award Saratoga Area Sr. Coord. Coun., 1981. Mem. AAUW (corr. sec. Los Gatos-Saratoga br., chmn. social arts, bridge, hospitality, Friday Matinee sect., book rev. sect.), Saratoga Hist. Found., Alumnae Assn. St. Theresa Coll., Montalvo Assn., Saratoga Foothill Club. Democrat. Roman Catholic. Home: 14140 Victor Pl Saratoga CA 95070-5425

WHALEN, MARTIN J., transportation executive, lawyer; b. Chgo., May 6, 1940; s. Frank Gervais and Beatrice (Granger) W.; m. Mary-Jo McMahon, Aug. 17, 1963; children: Maureen, Michael, Cathryn, Matthew. JD, DePaul U., 1965. Bar: Ill., U.S. Tax Ct., U.S. Supreme Ct. Dir. labor relation-flight Ea. Airlines Inc., Miami, Fla., 1973-76; dir. labor rels. Hughes Airwest div. Hughes Air Corp., San Francisco and Phoenix, 1976-77, gen. atty., 1977-79, sr. dir. pers., 1979-80; assoc. gen. counsel Hughes Helicopters, Inc., Culver City, Calif. and Mesa, Ariz., 1980-84; v.p. adminstrn. McDonnel Douglas Helicopter Co., Mesa, 1984-86; sr. v.p. adminstrn., gen. counsel Am. West Airlines, Inc., Phoenix, 1986—; exec. com. Airline Indsl. Rels. Conf., Washington, 1986—. Chmn. Mesa Econ. Growth Assn., 1989, treas., 1985-87, vice chmn., 1988; bd. dirs. Prehab of Ariz., Mesa, 1988—, East Valley Partnership, 1989. Roman Catholic. Office: Am W Airlines Inc 4000 E Sky Harbor Blvd Phoenix AZ 85034-3802

WHALEN, MICHELLE O., senior workers' compensation underwriter; b. Bloomington, Ill., Jan. 14, 1964; d. Michael Bernard and Dorothy (Juanita) W. BS, No. Ariz. U., 1986; MBA, U. Redlands, 1991. Display artist Levitz Furniture, San Diego, 1987-88; underwriter Indsl. Indemnity, San Diego, 1988-91; sr. underwriter Transamerica Ins. Group, San Diego, 1991-93, Fremont Compensation, San Diego, 1993—. Named one of Outstanding Young Women in Am., 1991. Roman Catholic.

WHALLEY, LAWRENCE ROBERT, computer engineer, consultant; b. L.A., Dec. 13, 1943; s. Robert George Whalley and Victoria (Campiglia) Grier; m. E.M. Keremitsis, Apr. 1, 1985. BS in Physics, U. So. Calif., 1966, MS in Physics, 1970; PhD in Physics, U. Ill., 1974. Postdoctoral fellow, asst. prof. U. Maine, Orono, 1975-79; founder, chief technologist Maine Sci. Assocs., Orono, 1979-84; sr. design engr. Digital Sound Corp., Santa Barbara, Calif., 1984-87; mgr. prodn. cert. Telebit Corp., Mountain View, Calif., 1987-89; founder, prin. Rhinoceros Cons., San Francisco, 1989—. Contbr. articles to profl. jours. Mem. IEEE, Am. Phys. Soc., Assn. for Computing Machinery. Home: 46 Grand View Ter San Francisco CA 94114-2311

WHAM, DOROTHY STONECIPHER, state legislator; b. Centralia, Ill., Jan. 5, 1925; d. Ernest Joseph and Vera Thelma (Shafer) Stonecipher; m. Robert S. Wham, Jan. 26, 1947; children: Nancy S. Wham Mitchell, Jeanne Wham Ryan, Robert S. II. BA, MacMurray Coll., 1946; MA, U. Ill., 1949; D of Pub. Adminstrn. (hon.), MacMurray Coll., 1992. Counsellor Student Counselling Bur. U. Ill., Urbana, 1946-49; state dir. ACTION program, Colo./Wyo. U.S. Govt., Denver, 1972-82; mem. Colo. Ho. of Reps., 1986-87; mem. Colo. Senate, 1987—, chair jud. com., 1988—; with capital devel. com., health, environ, welfare, instns., fin. appropriations, legal svcs. Mem. LWV, Civil Rights Commn. Denver, 1972-80; bd. dirs. Denver Com. on Mental Health, 1985-88, Denver Symphony, 1985-88. Mem. Am. Psychol. Assn., Colo. Mental Health Assn. (bd. dirs. 1986-88), Colo. Hemophilia Soc. Republican. Methodist. Lodge: Civitan. Home: 2790 S High St Denver CO 80210-6352 Office: State Capitol Rm 342 Denver CO 80203

WHARTON, CHARLES ELLIS, legal administrator; b. Shelbyville, Tenn., Apr. 5, 1943; s. Frank Mears and Myra (Green) W.; m. Julie Anne Kitchen, Dec. 23, 1967. BS in Indsl. Engring., U. Tenn., 1965; MBA, U. Chgo., 1970. Systems engr. Chrysler Corp., Huntsville, Ala., 1966-68, Gen. Electric, Houston, 1968-69; sr. assoc. McKinsey & Co., Chgo., 1971-73; asst. to pres. North Am. Royalties, Inc., Chattanooga, 1973-77; v.p., chief fin. officer Glover, Inc., Roswell, N.Mex., 1977-79; exec. v.p. Carbon Co. Internat., Houston, 1980; chief adminstrv. officer Fulbright & Jaworski, Houston, 1980-85; exec. dir. O'Melveny & Myers, L.A., 1985—; bd. govs. U. Tenn., 1987-89. Mem. devel. coun. U. Tenn., 1993—. With USAF, 1965. Mem. L.A. Soc. Prevention of Cruelty to Animals (bd. dirs., exec. com.), L.A. Athletic Club. Office: O'Melveny & Myers 400 S Hope St Los Angeles CA 90071-2801

WHARTON, DAVID C., data processing administrator; b. Caldwell, Ohio, Aug. 2, 1945; s. Clyde W. and Margaret (Fetkovich) W.; m. Maria E. Avelino, June 5, 1965 (div. Sept. 1990); 1 child, Theresa; m. Beryle I. Matsumura, Oct. 12, 1990; children: Nathan, Evan, Megan. BA in Bus. Adminstrn., Otterbein Coll., Westerville, Ohio, 1984; Cert. in Pub. Adminstrn., U. Hawaii, 1990. Systems analyst Miles Labs., Inc., Worthington, Ohio, 1968-72, Drs. Hosp., Columbus, Ohio, 1972-74; sr. systems analyst Hughes Helicopters, L.A., 1978-79, NCR, Inc., Cambridge, Ohio, 1974-78, 79-80; project mgr. Gold Circle Stores, Worthington, 1980-83; quality assurance analyst BancOhio Nat. Bank, Columbus, 1983; project mgr. Online Computer Libr. Ctr., Dublin, Ohio, 1983-85; mgmt. analyst Hawaii Med. Svc. Assocs., Honolulu, 1985-87; mgr. data processing Dept. Land and Natural Resources, Honolulu, 1987—. Served with U.S. Army, 1963-68, Vietnam. Office: DLNR 1151 Punchbowl St Honolulu HI 96813-3007

WHARTON, THOMAS WILLIAM, mining executive; b. St. Louis, Nov. 20, 1943; s. Thomas William and Elaine Margaret (Bassett) W.; divorced; children: Thomas William, Christopher John. BSc in Econs., U. Mo., 1967; M in Health Adminstrn., U. Ottawa, Ont., Can., 1978. Asst. to exec. dir. Ottawa Civic Hosp., 1978-80; exec. dir. Caribou Meml. Hosp., Williams Lake, B.C., Can., 1980-83; dir. clinic and rehab. services Workers' Compensation Bd., Vancouver, B.C., 1983-89; dir. Conquistador Goldmines, Vancouver, 1989—; pres. Diagnostic and Health Cons., Vancouver, 1989—; dir. PHL Pinnacle Holdings, Ltd., Vancouver, B.C., Can., 1994—; ptnr., dir. Lynn Valley Med. Ctr., North Vancouver, B.C., 1993. Recipient Founder award Cariboo Musical Soc., 1983; named Lord of the Manors of Wharton and Kirkby Stephen (Eng.), 1991. Mem. Can. Coll. Health Service Execs., Am. Coll. Health Execs., Am. Acad. Med. Adminstrs., Health Adminstrs. Assn. B.C., U. Ottawa Health Service Alumni Assn. (pres. 1983-84).

WHATCOTT, MARSHA RASMUSSEN, elementary educator; b. Fillmore, Utah, Mar. 29, 1941; d. William Hans and Evangelyn (Robison) Rasmussen; m. Robert LaGrand Whatcott, Sept. 14, 1961; children: Sherry, Cindy, Jay Robert, Justin William. Assoc., So. Utah State U., 1962; BS, Brigham Young U., 1968. Cert. tchr. early childhood, Utah. Tchr. Provost Elem. Sch., Provo, Utah, 1968-84, 91—, kindergarten tchr., 1984-91, music specialist, 93-94, art specialist, 1984-85, math. specialist, 1988-89, sci. specialist, 1994—; music specialist Provost Elem., 1984-87, 91-92, 93-94, art specialist, 1984-85, math. specialist, 1988-89, sci. specialist, 1994—; del. Utah Edn. Assn., 1989-90; bldg. rep. Provo Edn. Assn., 1993-94, 94-95. Mem. polit. action com. Provo Sch. Dist., 1982, 90, mem. profl. devel. com., 1972-79; mem. profl. devel. com. Benniville Uniserve (Provo, Alpine and Nebo Sch. Dist.), 1994-95. Recipient Millard County Utah PTA scholarship, 1959-62, Golden Apple award Provo City PTA, 1984, Recognition Disting. Svc. in Edn. award Utah State Legis., 1992; named Outstanding Educator in Utah Legis. Dist. # 64, 1992. Mem. Utah Edn. Assn. (del. 1989-90), Provo Edn. Assn. (bldg. rep. 1983—), Bonneville Uniserve (profl. devel. com.). Mem. LDS Ch. Office: Provost Elem Sch 629 S 1000 E Provo UT 84606-5204

WHEATLEY, MELVIN ERNEST, JR., retired bishop; b. Lewisville, Pa., May 7, 1915; s. Melvin Ernest and Gertrude Elizabeth (Mitchell) W.; m. Lucile Elizabeth Maris, June 15, 1939; children: Paul Melvin, James Maris, John Sherwood. AB magna cum laude, Am. U., 1936, DD, 1958; BD summa cum laude, Drew U., 1939; DD, U. of Pacific, 1948. Ordained to ministry Meth. Ch., 1939. Pastor area Meth. ch., Lincoln, Del., 1939-41; assoc. pastor First Meth. Ch., Fresno, Calif., 1941-43; pastor Centenary Meth. Ch., Modesto, Calif., 1943-46, Cen. Meth. Ch., Stockton, Calif., 1946-54, Westwood Meth. Ch., L.A., 1954-72; bishop Denver Area, 1972-84, ret., 1984; instr. philosophy Modesto Jr. Coll., 1944; summer session instr. Hebrew-Christian heritage U. of Pacific; instr. Homiletics U. So. Calif., So. Calif. Sch. Theology, Claremont; lectr. St. Luke's Lectures, Houston, 1966; mem. Bd. of Ch. and Soc., Commn. on Status and Role of Women, United Meth. Ch., 1976-84; condr. European Christian Heritage tour, 1961, Alaska and Hawaii Missions, 1952, 54. Author: Going His Way, 1957, Our Man and the Church, 1968, The Power of Worship, 1970, Family Ministries Manual, 1970, Christmas Is for Celebrating, 1977; contbr. articles to profl. jours. Chmn. Community Rels. Conf. So. Calif., 1966-69; pres. So. Calif.-Ariz. Conf. Bd. Edn., 1960-68; hon. trustee Iliff Sch. Theology; hon. dir., active mem. Parents and Friends of Lesbians and Gays, 1980—. Recipient Disting. Alumnus award Am. U., 1979, Ball award Meth. Fedn. Social Action, 1984, Prophetic Leadership award The Consultation on Homosexuality, Tolerance and Roman Cath. Theology, 1985, Human Rights award

Universal Fellowship of Met. Community Congregations, 1985. Home: 859A Ronda Mendoza Laguna Hills CA 92653-5964

WHEATLEY, ROBERT RAY, III, marketing executive; b. Amarillo, Tex., Sept. 24, 1934; s. Robert Ray Jr. and Lila Amanda (Townsend) W.; m. Nora Joan Madden, Aug. 25, 1972; children: James Ray, Robert Todd. BS, West Tex. A&M U., 1956; MBA, Calif. Coast U., 1985, PhD, 1988. Sr. contract adminstr. Martin Marietta, Denver, 1968-76; owner, operator John Deere Dealership, Broomfield, Colo., 1976-80; engring. analyst Rockwell Internat., Houston, 1980-84; mktg. mgr. ICC Space Systems, Houston, 1984-85; v.p. bus. devel. Presearch, Inc., Houston, 1985-07; dir. NASA mktg. QuesTech Rsch. Corp., McLean, Va., 1988; mktg. mgr. Space Systems, Houston, 1988-90; mktg. cons., Colorado Springs, Colo., 1990—. Capt. U.S. Army, 1955-60. Mem. Am. Mktg. Assn., Sons of Confederate Vets., Am. Legion, Elks. Lutheran. Home and Office: 46 White Eagle Cir Woodland Park CO 80863

WHEATON, ALICE ALSHULER, secretary; b. Burbank, Calif., Mar. 20, 1920; d. Elmore and Anzy Jeanette (Richards) Wheaton; m. Robert Edward Alshuler, Sept. 19, 1942 (div. 1972); children: John Robert, Katherine Dennis. BA in Edn., UCLA, 1942. Cert. profl. sec. Owner, dir. The Fitness Studio, Washington, 1974-85; staff asst. Pres. Coun. Phys. Fitness and Sports, Washington, 1980-89; coord. Fed. Inter Agy. Health Fitness Coun., Washington, 1986-89; expert advisor U.S. Office Pers. Mgmt., Washington, 1986-89; sec. Pala Mesa Village Homes Assn., 1994—; cons. Pres. Coun. Phys. Fitness and Sports. Editor: The Federal FitKit-Guidelines for Federal Agencies, 1988. Recipient Gold Key award L.A. Area United Way, 1966. Mem. Profl. Secs. Internat. (pres. Palomar chpt. 1993-95), UCLA Gold Shield Hon. (pres.), UCLA Alumni Assn. (v.p., Disting. Com. Svc. award 1968), San Diego Hist. Soc., North County Kappa Kappa Gamma Alumnae Assn. (pres. 1995—). Republican. Episcopalian.

WHEATON, MARY EDWINA, health facility administrator, educator; b. Clifton, N.Y., Aug. 19, 1950; d. James E. and Beatrice C. (Preston) Potter; m. Gerald B. Wheaton, Sept. 10, 1968; children: Shelley L., Laura Ann. ADN, Chabot Coll., 1986. RN, Calif.; cert. med/surg. nurse. Staff nurse St. Rose Hosp., Hayward, Calif., 1986-88, mem. clin. ladder task force, chairperson rev. bd., 1988-90, charge nurse, 1988-91, mem. nursing standards com., 1990—, chairperson nursing practice com., 1990-92, clin. coord., supr., 1991—; clin. examiner Chabot Coll., Hayward, 1989—. Instr. basic life support Am. Heart Assn., San Ramon, Calif., 1984-86; leader Livermore (Calif.) Girl Scouts U.S., 1976-86, chairperson, 1982-84. Mem. Am. Acad. Med. and Surg. Nursing. Baptist.

WHEELER, DAVID MCMAKIN, software engineer; b. Leominster, Mass., Feb. 23, 1965; s. Alfred Lawrence and Nancy Lee (McMakin) W.; m. Jill Christine Rhodes, June 30, 1984; 1 child, Christine Eileen. BS in Computer Sci., Grand Canyon U., 1990. Software engr. Bull HN, Phoenix, 1989-92; staff engr. Motorola Inc. GSTG, Scottsdale, Ariz., 1992—; security assn. panel mem. Nat. Computer Security Conf., Washington, 1994. Author (protocol) Security Assn. Mgmt. Protocol, 1991. Adult Sunday sch. leader N.W. Community Ch., Phoenix, 1993—, juvenile leader, 1990-92. With U.S. Army, 1984-88. Mem. Assn. Computing Machinery. Office: Motorola GSTG PO Box 1417 8201 E McDowell Scottsdale AZ 85252

WHEELER, DOUGLAS PAUL, conservationist, government official, lawyer; b. Bklyn., Jan. 10, 1942; s. Robert S. and Lottie (Neubauer) W.; m. Heather A. Campbell, Aug. 28, 1965; children—Clay Campbell, Christopher Campbell. AB in Govt. with honors, Hamilton Coll., Clinton, N.Y., 1963; LLB, Duke U., 1966. Bar: N.C. 1966. Assoc. Levine, Goodman & Murchison, Charlotte, N.C., 1966-69; legis. atty. to asst. legis. counsel U.S. Dept. Interior, Washington, 1969-72, dep. asst. sec. Fish and Wildlife and Pks., 1972-77; exec. v.p. Nat. Trust for Hist. Preservation, Washington, 1977-80; pres. Am. Farmland Trust, Washington, 1980-85, now life mem.; exec. dir. Sierra Club, San Francisco, 1985-86; v.p. Land Heritage and Wildlife Conservation Found., Washington, 1986-88, exec. v.p., 1989-91; sec. for resources State of Calif., 1991—; advisor Pres.'s Commn. on Am. Outdoors. Bd. dirs. Calif. Nature Conservancy, Calif. Environ. Forum; mem. nat. coun. World Wildlife Fund, Am. Farmland Trust; candidate N.C. Ho. of Reps., 1968; mem. D.C. Rep. Ctrl. Com., 1984-85. Lt. JAGC, USNR, 1969-75. Recipient commendation U.S. Dept. Interior, 1976, Achievement award, 1980; Conservation award Gulf Oil Corp., 1985. Mem. N.C. Bar Assn., Sierra Club (life). Episcopalian. Home: PO Box 3164 El Macero CA 95618-0764

WHEELER, ELTON SAMUEL, financial executive; b. Salinas, Calif., Oct. 25, 1943; s. Luther Elton and Naomi E. (Beatty) W.; m. Patricia Lynne McCleary, Sept. 2, 1967; children: Pamela Kathleen, Leslie Elizabeth-Anne, Deborah Suzanne, Jonathan Samuel. BS, Calif. State U., 1966. CPA, Calif. Acct. Coopers & Lybrand, Oakland, Calif., 1967-70; contr. Adams Properties, Inc., San Francisco, 1970-71, treas., 1972-75, v.p., chief fin. officer, 1976-77; v.p., chief fin. officer Adams Capital Mgmt. Co., San Francisco, 1977-79, pres., chief exec. officer, 1979-87; pres., chief exec. officer, bd. dir. Calif. Real Estate Investment Trust, 1980-88, Franklin Select Real Estate Income Trust, 1989—, Franklin Advantage Real Estate Income Trust, 1990—. With USMCR, 1966-72. Mem. Nat. Assn. Real Estate Investment Trusts, Inc. (sec., treas., bd. govs. 1984-89), Am. Inst. CPAs, Calif. Soc. CPAs, Olympic Club, Rotary (Sonora, Calif.). Office: PO Box 3718 Sonora CA 95370-3718

WHEELER, GLORIA, database analyst; b. Huron, S.D., Dec. 28, 1955; d. Joseph Julian and Agnota W. (Christensen) Wheeler; m. Douglas J. Wolf, Jan. 23, 1982; children: Alexander, Ilsa. BS in Home Econ., N.D. State U., 1978; MPH in Pub. Health Nutrition, U. Minn., 1983. Registered dietitian; cert. secondary sch. tchr., Calif. Project dir. N.D. State U., Fargo, 1978; nutritionist Quality Child Care, Inc., Mound, Minn., 1978-84; tng. analyst Science Applications Internat. Corp., San Diego, 1992-94; database analyst SAIC, San Diego, 1994—. Author: Advanced User's Guide to Sprint, 1988, Paradox, A Self-Teaching Guide, 1991, 1-2-3 for Windows, A Self-Teaching Guide, 1992, Paradox for Windows, A Self-Teaching Guide, 1993; co-author: (with Douglas J. Wolf) Sprint Simplified, 1988, Using Microsoft Works, 1989; editor: Act 2 for Windows, 1994; contbr. articles to profl. jours. Vol. Rudy Boschwitz for Senate campaign, Minn., 1982; cub scout den leader Boy Scouts Am., Calif., 1993-94; child care com. SAIC, 1992-93; apptd. mem. Mpls. Pub. Health Bd., 1981-83; mem. Maternal and Child Health Adv. Bd., Mpls., 1981-83. Recipient APLE award State of Calif., 1991. Mem. Am. Dietetic Assn., Calif. Dietetic Assn., San Diego Dietetic Assn. (Heartfest com. 1993).

WHEELER, HELEN RIPPIER, writer, educator, consultant. BA, Barnard Coll., 1950; MS, Columbia U., 1951; MA, U. Chgo., 1954; PhD, Columbia U., 1964. Media adminstr. Chgo. City Colls., 1958-62; Latin Am. coord. Columbia U. Librs., N.Y.C., 1962-64; assoc. prof. La. State U., Baton Rouge, 1971-73; cons. Womanhood Media, Berkeley, Calif., 1973—; vis. lectr. U. Calif., Berkeley, 1978-87; cons. U. Hawaii Community Coll. System. Author: Womanhood Media, 1972, The Bibliographic Instruction Course Handbook, 1988, Getting Published in Women's Studies, 1989, others; contbr. chpts. to books, articles to profl. jours, scripting for instructional media. Presdl. appointee Comm. on Status of Women, Internat. Rels. Com.; subcom. mem. Sexist Subject-Heads; caucus mem. Nat. Women's Studies Assn. Mem. ALA, NOW (chpt. founder), Josei to Toshokan No Tameno Network, Women's Inst. for Freedom of Press. Democrat. Address: 1909 Cedar St Apt 107 Berkeley CA 94709-2035

WHEELER, LARRY RICHARD, accountant; b. Greybull, Wyo., Nov. 30, 1940; s. Richard F. and Olive B. (Fredrickson) W.; m. Marjorie A. Frady, Dec. 20, 1961; m. Patricia C. Marturano, Dec. 3, 1977; children: Anthony, Richard, Teresa, Kara. BS, U. Wyo., 1965. CPA, Colo. Staff acct. H. Greger CPA, Ft. Collins, Colo., 1965-66, sr. acct. Lester Draney & Wickham, Colorado Springs, Colo., 1966-67; acct., controller/treas., J.D. Adams Co., Colorado Springs, 1967-74; ptnr. Wheeler Pierce & Hurd, Inc., Colorado Springs, 1974-80; gen. mgr., v.p. Schneebeck's, Inc., Colorado Springs, 1980-81; prin. L.R. Wheeler & Co., P.C., Colorado Springs, 1981-94; pres. Wheeler & Gilmartin Assocs., P.C., Colorado Springs, 1994—, L.R. Wheeler & Co., P.C., 1995; dir. Schneebeck's Industries, Williams Printing, Inc. Mem. U.S. Taekwondo Union; bd. dirs. Domestic Violence Prevention Ctr. Paul Stock Found. grantee, 1962. Mem. Internat. Assn. Fin. Planners, Am. Inst. CPA's, Nat. Contract Mgmt. Assn., Colo. Soc. CPA's (map. com.), Colo. Litigation Support Group. Office: 317 E San Rafael St Colorado Springs CO 80903-2405

WHEELER, MALCOLM EDWARD, lawyer, law educator; b. Berkeley, Calif., Nov. 29, 1944; s. Malcolm Ross and Frances Dolores (Kane) W.; m. Donna Marie Stambaugh, July 21, 1981; children: Jessica Ross, M. Connor. SB, MIT, 1966; JD, Stanford U., 1969. Bar: Calif. 1970, Colo. 1992, U.S. Dist. Ct (cen. dist.) Calif. 1970, U.S. Ct. Appeals (9th cir.) 1970, U.S. Ct. Appeals (10th cir.) 1973, U.S. Dist. Ct. (no., so., ea. and cen. dists.) Calif. 1975, U.S. Ct. Appeals (11th cir.) 1987, U.S. Ct. Appeals (D.C. cir.) 1987, U.S. Supreme Ct. 1976, U.S. Ct. Appeals (3d cir.) 1989, (4th cir.) 1992. Assoc. Howard, Prim, Smith, Rice & Downs, San Francisco, 1969-71; assoc. prof. law U. Kans., Lawrence, 1971-74; assoc. Hughes Hubbard & Reed, Los Angeles, 1974-77, ptnr., 1977-81, 83-85, cons., 1981-83; ptnr. Skadden, Arps, Slate, Meagher & Flom, Los Angeles, 1985-91; dir. Parcel, Mauro, Hultin & Spaanstra P.C., Denver, 1991—; vis. prof. U. Iowa, 1978, prof., 1979; prof. U. Kans., Lawrence, 1981-83; chief counsel U.S. Senate Select Com. to Study Law Enforcement Undercover Activities, Washington, 1982-83. Mem. editorial bd. Jour. Products Liability, 1984—; bd. editors Fed. Litigation Guide Reporter, 1986—; contbr. articles to profl. jours. Mem. ABA, Calif. Bar Assn., Colo. Bar Assn., Am. Law Inst. Office: Parcel Mauro Hultin & Spaanstra PC 1801 California St Denver CO 80202-2658

WHEELER, MICHELE LYNN, financial analyst; b. Santa Maria, Calif., Jan. 5, 1964; d. Thomas Almon and Patricia (O'Bid) W. BSBA, U. Nev., 1986, MBA, 1990. Acct. exec. Citicorp, Las Vegas, 1986; mgmt. analyst I Clark County, Las Vegas, 1986-88, mgmt. analyst, 1988-91, sr. fin. analyst, 1991—. Participant, mem. Clark County Leadership Forum, 1993. Named Outstanding Mgmt. Student U. Nev., 1986. Mem. ASPA, Am. Pub. Works Assn., Govt. Fin. Officers Assn., Jr. League Las Vegas (chmn. 1993-94, 94-95), U. Nev. Alumni Soc., Phi Kappa Phi. Republican. Roman Catholic. Home: 918 Clipper Dr Henderson NV 89015-5646 Office: Clark County 225 Bridger Ave Las Vegas NV 89101-6112

WHEELER, RALPH MERRILL, pharmacist, state senator; b. American Falls, Idaho, Aug. 10, 1932; s. Ralph Merrill and Monne May (Zemo) W.; m. Patricia J. Howard Wheeler (dec.); children: Vickie D., Michael M., Jodi L.; m. Ann F. Reed Wheeler, June 19, 1965; children: Clark R., Ryan M. BS, Idaho State U., 1954. Registered pharmacist. Owner Rockland Pharmacy, 1960-88, part-time staff, 1988—; pres. Assn. Idaho Cities, Boise, 1971-72, Idaho State Pharmaceutical Assn., 1979-80. Pres. Lion's Club, American Falls, 1962; rep. State Legis. Boise, Idaho, 1972-76; county commr. Power County, American Falls, 1982-94; senator State of Idaho, 1994—. Named Pharmacist of Yr., Idaho Pharmaceutical Assn., 1972. Republican. Roman Catholic. Home: 659 Gifford Ave American Falls ID 83211-1315

WHEELER, ROBERT ROSS, medical director; b. Milw., Sept. 12, 1949; s. Ross W. and Mary Lou Wheeler. AB with honors, U. Calif., Berkeley, 1972; MD, U. Calif., San Francisco, 1976. Resident U. Calif., San Francisco, 1979; physician internal medicine pvt. practice, Cottage Grove, Oreg., 1981-92; med. dir. Lane Individual Practice Assn., Eugene, Oreg., 1992—. Author: (software) OHP Linefinder, 1994. Med. advisor Ambulence Svc., Cottage Grove, 1983-92. Mem. AAAS, Am. Coll. Physician Execs., Am. Coll. Physicians, Internat. Soc. Tech. Assessment, Soc. Med. Decisionmaking, Phi Beta Kappa. Office: Lane Individual Practice Assn 1200 Exec Pky Ste 200 Eugene OR 97401

WHEELON, ALBERT DEWELL, physicist; b. Moline, Ill., Jan. 18, 1929; s. Orville Albert and Alice Geltz (Dewell) W.; m. Nancy Helen Hermanson, Feb. 28, 1953 (dec. May 1980); children—Elizabeth Anne, Cynthia Helen; m. Cicely J. Evans, Feb. 4, 1984. B.Sc., Stanford U., 1949; Ph.D., Mass. Inst. Tech., 1952. Teaching fellow, then rsch. assoc. physics MIT, Boston, 1949-52; with Douglas Aircraft Co., 1952-53, Ramo-Wooldridge Corp., 1953-62; dep. dir. sci. and tech. CIA, Washington, 1962-66; with Hughes Aircraft Co., L.A., 1966-88, chmn., chief exec. officer, 1987-88; vis. prof. MIT, 1989; mem. Def. Sci. Bd., 1968-76; mem. Pres.'s Fgn. Intelligence, 1983-88; mem. Presdl. Commn. on Space Shuttle Challenger Accident, 1986; trustee Aerospace Corp., 1990-93, Calif. Inst. Tech., Rand Corp. Author 30 papers on radiowave propagation and guidance systems. Recipient R.V. Jones Intelligence award, 1994. Fellow IEEE, AIAA (Von Karman medal 1986); mem. NAE, Am. Phys. Soc., Sigma Chi. Republican. Episcopalian. Address: 181 Sheffield Dr Montecito CA 93108-2242

WHELCHEL, SANDRA JANE, writer; b. Denver, May 31, 1944; d. Ralph Earl and Janette Isabelle (March) Everitt; m. Andrew Jackson Whelchel, June 27, 1965; children: Andrew Jackson, Anita Earlyn. BA in Elem. Edn., U. No. Colo., 1966; postgrad. Pepperdine Coll., 1971, UCLA, 1971. Elem. tchr. Douglas County Schs., Castle Rock, Colo., 1966-68, El Monte (Calif.) schs., 1968-72; br. librarian Douglas County Libraries, Parker, Colo., 1973-78; zone writer Denver Post, 1979-81; reporter The Express newspapers, Castle Rock, 1979-81; history columnist Parker Trail newspapers, 1985-93; columnist Gothic Jour. 1994; writing tchr. Aurora Parks and Recreation, 1985-91; writing instr. Arapahoe C.C., 1991—; exec. dir. Nat. Writers Assn., 1991—; editor Authorship mag., 1992—; contbr. short stories and articles to various publs. including: Writer's World, Writer's Open Forum, Writer's Jour., Reunions, Ancestry Newsletter, Empire mag., Calif. Horse Rev., Host mag., Jack and Jill, Child Life, Children's Digest, Peak to Peak mag.; author (non-fiction books): Your Air Force Academy, 1982, A Guide to the U.S. Air Force Acad., 1990, Parker, Colorado: A Folk History, 1990; (coloring books): A Day at the Cave, 1985, A Day in Blue, 1984, Pro Rodeo Hall of Champions and Museum of the American Cowboy, 1985, Pikes Peak Country, 1986, Mile High Denver, 1987; co-author: The Register, 1989; lectr. on writing. Mem. Internat. Platform Assn., Nat. Writers Club (treas. Denver Metro chpt. 1985-86, v.p. membership 1987, sec. 1990, bd. dirs. 1990-91, pres. 1990-91, v.p. programs 1992), Parker Area Hist. Soc. (pres. 1987, 88, 89).

WHETTEN, JOHN THEODORE, geologist; b. Willimantic, Conn., Mar. 16, 1935; s. Nathan Laselle and Theora Lucille (Johnson) W.; m. Carol Annette Jacobsen, July 14, 1960; children—Andrea, Krista, Michelle. A.B. with high honors, Princeton U., 1957; Ph.D., 1962; M.S., U. Calif.-, Berkeley, 1959. Mem. faculty U. Wash., Seattle, 1963-81; research instr. oceanography U. Wash., 1963-64, asst. prof., 1964-68, assoc. prof., 1968-72, prof. geol. scis. and oceanography, 1972-81, chmn. dept. geol. scis., 1969-74; assoc. dean Grad. Sch., 1968-69; geologist U.S. Geol. Survey, Seattle, 1975-80; asst. div. leader geoscis. div. Los Alamos Nat. Lab., 1980-81, dep. div. leader earth and space scis. div., 1981-84, div. leader earth and space scis. div., 1984-86, assoc. dir. energy and tech., 1986-92, assoc. dir. quality, policy and performance, 1992-93; lab. affiliate, 1994—; cons. in environ., safety and health and mfg. techs. Motorola Corp., 1994—. Contbr. articles to profl. jours. Fulbright fellow, 1962-63. Home: 154 Piedra Loop Los Alamos NM 87544-3837 Office: Los Alamos Nat Lab MS J-591 Los Alamos NM 87545

WHIDDEN, MARY BESS, English language educator; b. San Angelo, Tex., Aug. 14, 1936; d. James Edgar and Bess (Mullican) W. BA, U. Tex., 1957, PhD, 1965; MA, U. N.C., 1959. Rsch. assoc. U. Tex., Austin, 1956-58, spl. instr., 1962-63; asst. prof. English, U. N.Mex., Albuquerque, 1963-71, assoc. prof., 1971-95, prof., 1995—; bd. dirs. N.Mex. Endowment for Humanities, Albuquerque, 1987-93. Author: Provincial Matters, 1985; co-editor: Staging Howells, 1994; contbr. essays to various publs. Recipient Disting. Svc. award N.Mex. Endowment for Humanities, 1993; Woodrow Wilson fellow, 1958-59, 61, Univ. fellow U. Tex., 1960-61. Mem. MLA, NAACP. Democrat. Home: 421 Richmond Dr SE Albuquerque NM 87106-2241 Office: U NMex Dept English Humanities Bldg Albuquerque NM 87131

WHIDDON, CAROL PRICE, writer, editor, consultant; b. Gadsden, Ala., Nov. 18, 1947; d. Curtis Ray and Vivian (Dooly) Price; m. John Earl Caulking, Jan. 18, 1969 (div. July 1987); m. Ronald Alton Whiddon, Apr. 13, 1988. Student, McNeese State U., 1966-68; BA in English, George Mason U., 1984. Flute instr. Lake Charles, La., 1966-68; flutist Lake Charles Civic Symphony, 1966-69, Beaumont (Tex.) Symphony, 1967-68; freelance editor The Washington Lit. Rev., 1983-84, ARC Hdqrs., Washington, 1984; writer, editor Jaycor, Vienna, Va., 1985-87; writer, editor Jaycor, Albuquerque, 1987-90, publs. mgr., 1990-91; writer, editor Proteus Corp., Albuquerque, 1991-92; owner Whiddon Editorial Svcs., Albuquerque, 1989—; mem. S.W. Writer's Workshop, 1991—. Co-author: The Spirit That Wants Me: A New Mexico Anthology, 1991; contbr. various articles to Albuquerque Woman and mil. dependent pubs. in Fed. Rpublic Germany. Bd. dirs. Channel 27-Pub. Access TV, 1991-93, exec. bd. sec., 1992, v.p., 1993; dep. mgr. Fed. Women's Program, Ansbach, Fed. Republic Germany, 1980-81; pres. Ansbach German-Am. Club, 1980-82; sec. Am. Women's Activities, Fed. Republic Germany, 1980-81, chairwoman, 1981-82. Recipient cert. of appreciation from Am. amb. to Germany Arthur T. Burns, 1982, medal of appreciation from comdr. 1st Armored Div., Ansbach, Germany, 1982. Mem. NAFE, Women in Comm. (newsletter editor 1989-90, 91-92, 94-95, v.p. 1990-91, pres.-elect 1992-93, pres. 1993-94, chair programs com. Nat. Profl. Conf. 1994), Soc. Tech. Comm. (membership dir. 1993-94), Nat. Assn. Desktop Pubs., Am. Mktg. Assn., Greater Albuquerque C. of C., N.Mex. Caucus Soc. (historian 1989-94, sec. 1991, newsletter editor 1992—, various show ribbons 1989-91). Republican. Home: 1129 Turner Dr NE Albuquerque NM 87123-1917

WHIMBEY, ARTHUR EMIL, writer; b. New York, Sept. 18, 1940. BA in Psychology, U. Miami, 1961; PhD, Purdue U., 1964. Asst. prof. psychology U. Ill., Urbana, 1965-67; from asst. to assoc. prof. psychology Calif. State U., Hayward, 1967-71; sr. postdoctoral fellow NIMH Inst. Human Learning, Berkeley, Calif., 1971-72; assoc. prof. psychology Dillard U., 1974-75; dir. rsch. CUE project Bowling Green State U., 1976-77, coord. math. and comm. labs. devel. edn. program, 1977-78; acad. support specialist Bethune-Cookman Coll., 1983; reading specialist Miami-Dade Pub. Schs., 1988; adj. prof. math. CCNY, fall, 1978; vis. prof. math. dept. Xavier U., spring, 1979; cons. Ventures in Edn., Coll. Bd., N.J. State Dept. Edn.; assoc. editor On TRAC Text Reconstrn. Across the Curriculum Newsletter, 1993—; speaker in field. Author: Intelligence Can Be Taught, 1973, Analytical Reading and Reasoning, 2d edit., 1989; (with M.J. Linden) Analytical Writing and Thinking: Facing the Tests, 1990; (with J. Lochhead) Problem Solving & Comprehension, 1991; (with others) Thinking Through Math Word Problems, 1990, Keys to Quick Writing Skills: Sentence Combining and Text Reconstruction, 1992, Blueprint for Educational Change: Improving Reasoning, Literacies, and Science Achievement, 1993; contbr. articles to profl. jours. Resident scholar CCNY, 1978, Clark Coll., 1980-82. Home and Office: 3920 Avalon Rd NW Albuquerque NM 87105-1814

WHIPKEY-LOUDEN, HARRIET BEULAH, fine arts and theatre productions executive; b. Willmar, Minn., Mar. 9, 1932; d. Frank Leroy and Annetta Cecelia (Cafferty) Whipkey; m. James William Louden, Aug. 20, 1956; children: Liza Katherin, Cheryl Anne. BS, St. Cloud State U., 1954; MA, Montclair State Coll., 1978. English-speech tchr. Minn. Dept. Edn., Verndale, Sauk Centre, Sauk Rapids, Minn., 1954-57; English-speech tchr. Bd. of Edn., Marquette, Mich., 1958-62, Slinger, Wis., 1963-67; drama dept. chair Bd. Edn., Pattonville High, St. Louis, 1967-69; speech and theatre dept. chair Bd. of Edn., Westfield, N.J., 1969-85; v.p. Louden Enterprises, Phoenix, 1990—; dir.-producer The Scholarship Show, Marquette, Mich., 1960; drama cons. New Faces of Charleston, Charleston, N.C., 1986-89, Internat. Models Talent Competition, Scottsdale, Ariz., 1986-89; edn. cons. Nat. Assn. Restaurant Mgrs., Scottsdale, 1988. Co-founder, chair 1st All Upper Peninsula Art Show, 1960; founder, pres. Ariz. State U. Theatre Assn., 1985-88; creator, dir. Children's Touring Theatre, St. Louis, 1968, Westfield, N.J., 1971, Summer Theatre Workshop, Pine-Strawberry, Ariz., 1990; founding bd. mem. N.J. Theatre Forum, 1979; TV talk show host Channel 9 Cable, Scottsdale, 1986-88; bd. mem. Phoenix East Valley Social Svcs.; founder Youth Theatre, Pine, Ariz., 1995. Grantee N.J. Dept. Edn., 1978; recipient Gov.'s Citation, State of Mich., 1960. Mem. AAUW (pres. Marquette chpt. 1960), Ariz. Arts Commn., Ariz. for Cultural Devel., Ariz. Theatre Edn. Assn., Ariz. State U. Toastmasters, Friends of Ariz. State U. Art Mus. Home and Office: 5836 E Angela Dr Tempe AZ 85284-3460

WHISENHUNT, DONALD WAYNE, history educator; b. Meadow, Tex., May 16, 1938; s. William Alexander Whisenhunt and Beulah (Johnson) King; m. Betsy Ann Baker, Aug. 27, 1960; children: Donald Wayne Jr., William Benton. BA, McMurry Coll., 1960; MA, Tex. Tech U., 1962, PhD, 1966. Tchr. Elida (N.Mex.) High Sch., 1961-63; from asst. to assoc. prof. history Murray (Ky.) State U., 1966-69; assoc. prof., chmn. dept. Thiel Coll., Greenville, Pa., 1969-73; Dean Sch. Liberal Arts and Scis., Ea. N.Mex. U., Portales, 1973-77; v.p. acad. affairs U. Tex., Tyler, 1977-83; v.p., provost Wayne (Nebr.) State Coll., 1983-91, interim pres., 1985; prof. history, chmn. dept. Western Wash. U., Bellingham, 1991—; Fulbright lectr. Peoples Republic of China, 1995. Author: Environment and American Experience, 1974, Depression in the Southwest, 1979, Chronological History of Texas, Vol. 1, 1982, Vol.2, 1987, Texas: Sesquicentennial Celebration, 1984; editor: Encyclopedia USA, 1988—. Democrat. Methodist. Office: Western Wash U Dept History Bellingham WA 98225

WHISLER, JAMES STEVEN, lawyer, mining and manufacturing executive; b. Centerville, Iowa, Nov. 23, 1954; s. James Thomas and Betty Lou (Clark) W.; m. Ardyce Dawn Christensen, Jan. 20, 1979; children: James Kyle, Kristen Elyse. BS, U. Colo., Boulder, 1975; JD, U. Denver, 1978; MS, Colo. Sch. Mines, Golden, 1984. Bar: Colo. 1978; CPA, Ariz. Assoc. gen. counsel, sec. Western Nuclear, Inc., Denver, 1979-81; exploration counsel Phelps Dodge Corp., N.Y.C., 1981-85; legal and adminstrv. mgr. Phelps Dodge Corp., Phoenix, 1985-87, v.p., gen. counsel, 1987-88, sr. v.p., gen. counsel, 1988-91; pres. Phelps Dodge Mining Co., Phoenix, 1991—; bd. dirs. Unocal Corp., 1st Interstate Bank Ariz., N.A.; chmn. Western Regional Coun.'s Working Group on Environ. Texas, 1990-93; mem. Ariz. Fed. Dist. Ct. Adv. group, 1991-92. Trustee Heard Mus., Phoenix, 1989-94, Rocky Mountain Mineral Law Found., 1989-92; mem. Dean's Coun. of 100, Ariz. State U., 1992—; mem. nat. bd. advisors Coll. Bus. and Pub. Adminstrn., U. Ariz., 1992—; bd. dirs. Met. Phoenix YMCA, 1989-92, Copper Bowl Found., Tucson, 1990-91, Ariz. Town Hall, 1991—, We. Regional Coun., 1991—; mem. Maricopa County Sports Authority, Phoenix, 1990—; mem. Phoenix Com. on Fgn. Rels., 1991-94. Mem. AICPA, AIME, Am. Corp. Counsel Assn., Soc. Mining Engrs., Colo. Bar Assn., Phoenix Thunderbirds, Phoenix Country Club. Home: 11438 N 54th Pl Scottsdale AZ 85254-5712 Office: Phelps Dodge Corp 2600 N Central Ave Phoenix AZ 85004-3050

WHITACRE, JOHN, apparel executive; b. 1953. Student, U. Wash. With Nordstrom Inc., 1976—; co-chmn. Nordstrom Inc., Seattle, 1995—. Office: Nordstrom Inc 1501 5th Ave Seattle WA 98101-1603*

WHITAKER, JUDY ERICKSON, career counselor; b. Salt Lake City, June 13, 1948; d. Delmon and Marilyn (Geertsen) Erickson; m. Bruce A. Whitaker, May 28, 1977; children: Wendy, Cindy, RB, Jeff. BA in English, U. Utah, 1970, BA in German, 1972, MEd, 1974, MEd in Sch. Psychology, 1991. Cert. tchr., counselor. Tchr. Spanish and German langs. Bountiful (Utah) High Sch., 1976-89; guidance counselor Cyprus High Sch., Salt Lake City, 1989-93; dir. career ctr. Taylorsville High Sch., Salt Lake City, 1993—; carrer cons. KUED TV; adv. bd. Gender Equity Ctr., Salt Lake C.C.; comprehensive guidance steering com., Granite Sch. Dist., 1993-95. Mem. Utah Edn. Assn. Polit. Action, women's caucus, 1993-95. Fulbright scholar, 1976. Mem. Am. Counseling Assn., AAUW, Am. Sch. Counseling Assn., Utah Sch. Counseling Assn. (secondary v.p. 1994-95), Am. Vocat. Assn., Utah Vocat. Assn., Nat. Career Devel. Assn. Office: Taylorsville High Sch 5225 S Redwood Rd Salt Lake City UT 84123-4213

WHITAKER, MORRIS DUANE, university administrator; b. Pocatello, Idaho, Apr. 4, 1940; s. Mirl William and Ada Belle (Bruesch) W.; m. Marguerite Fae Benson, Sept. 3, 1963; children: Jacqueline, Cynthia, Angela, Carolyn, Melinda, James, William, Christina. BS in Econs., Utah State U., 1965, MS in Econs., 1966; PhD in Agrl. Econs., Purdue U., 1970. Asst. prof. econs. Utah State U., Logan, 1970-75, assoc. prof. econs., 1976-83, prof. econs., 1983—; co-dir. planning Bolivian Ministry of Agr., La Paz, 1973-76; dep. exec. dir. Bd. for Internat. Food and Agrl. Devel., Washington, 1978-82; sr. advisor, adminstr. U.S. AID, Washington, 1981-82, policy advisor agr. programs, Quito, Ecuador, 1987-90, cons. on Asia, Near East, Latin Am., 1971-90; dir. internat. programs Utah State U., Logan, 1982-87, 90—. Author: Status of Bolivian Agriculture, 1975, Agricultural Development in Bangladesh, 1984, Agriculture and Economic Survival/Ecuador, 1990; contbr. articles to profl. jours. Com. mem. sch. bd. Cotopaxi Acad., Quito, 1987-90; asst. scoutmaster troop 240 Boy Scouts Am., Quito, 1987-90; mem. U.S. Presidential Task Force in Agr. to Ecuador, 1984. Mem. Am.

Agrl. Econs. Assn., Consortium for Internat. Devel. (bd. trustees). Republican. LDS. Office: Utah State U Internat Programs Logan UT 84322-9500

WHITAKER, RUPERT EDWARD DAVID, neuroimmunologist and behavioral scientist, consultant, writer; b. London, May 6, 1963; came to U.S., 1985; BSc in Psychology with honors, London U., 1984; PhD, Boston U., 1990. Instr. in medicine New Eng. Med. Ctr., Boston, 1989-90; rsch. fellow Dept. Psychiatry U. Mich., 1990-91, Immunology Rsch. Lab. Dept. Lab. Medicine U. Calif., San Francisco, 1992—; dir. Prime Directive Cons. Inc., Guerneville, Calif. Author: (with others) AIDS Care, 1991, Hospital Formulary, 1991, (with Edwards R.K.) AIDS and Public Policy Jour., 1991, Am. Jour. Pub. Health, 1990. Co-founder, trustee Terrence Higgins Trust, London, 1984-88; mem. AIDS Action Com., Boston, 1986-88; active Internat. AIDS Soc. Mem. Internat. Soc. Neuroimmunomodulation. Buddhist. Home: PO Box 951 Guerneville CA 95446-0951

WHITBY, WILLIAM MELCHER, Spanish language and literature educator; b. Phila., Apr. 1, 1920; s. Stephen Sturgis and Charlotte Patten (Melcher) W.; m. Lynn S. Whitby, Feb. 1, 1946; children: Barbara C. Jann, Christopher W. BA summa cum laude, Haverford Coll., 1948; PhD, Yale U., 1954. Instr. Yale U., New Haven, 1949-54, U. So. Calif., L.A., 1954-60; asst. prof. Spanish lang. and lit. U. Ariz., Tucson, 1960-61, assoc. prof., 1961-65, prof., 1965-68; prof. Spanish lang. and lit. Purdue U., West Lafayette, Ind., 1968-87, prof. emeritus, 1987—; mem. editorial bd. Purdue U. Monographs in Romance Langs., West Lafayette, 1975-87. Editor: (with Robert R. Anderson) La fianza satisfecha Attributed to Lope de Vega, 1971. 1st lt., field arty. U.S. Army, 1942-45; ETO. Fulbright rsch. grantee, Madrid, 1966-67. Mem. Hispanic Soc. Am. (corr.).

WHITCHURCH, CHARLES AUGUSTUS, art gallery owner, humanities educator; b. Long Beach, Calif., Sept. 29, 1940; s. Charles Augustus and Frances Elizabeth (White) W.; m. Michèle Elizabeth Cartier, Aug. 17, 1968 (div. 1977); 1 child, Gialisa Elizabeth; m. Mary Susan Ornelas, Jan. 28, 1984; 1 child, Marisa Tatiana. BA in History, Santa Clara U., Irvine, 1962; MA in Comparative Lit., U. Calif., Irvine, 1970. Cert. grad. secondary teaching credential. Asst. ops. officer United Calif. Bank, Inglewood, 1965-66; tchr. English Laguna Beach (Calif.) High Sch., 1966-68; teaching assoc., fellow U. Calif., Irvine, 1968-70; prof. lit. and humanities Golden West Coll., Huntington Beach, Calif., 1971—; owner, dir. Charles Whitchurch Fine Arts, Huntington Beach, Calif., 1978—; cons. Pyo Gallery, Seoul, Dem. Peoples Rep. Korea, 1989-90, Nichols-Ward Gallery, Mission Viejo, Calif., 1989-92; judge, spkr. in field. Author mus. catalogues; contbr. articles to profl. jours. Founding mem., mem. adv. coun. Modern Mus. Art, Santa Ana, Calif., 1987-92; bd. dirs. Robert Gumbiner Found. for the Arts. NEA grantee; named One of Outstanding Young Men Am., 1977. Mem. Nat. Coun. Tchrs. English, Art Dealers Assn. of Calif. (bd. dirs. 1988—, sec. 1988-90, pres. 1990-92), Huntington Beach Art Assn. (founding mem. 1990), Robert Gumbiner Found. for the Arts (bd. dirs. 1994—), The Libra Group (pres. 1994—), Santa Clara Alumni Assn., Alpha Sigma Nu, Phi Sigma Tau.

WHITE, ALVIN MURRAY, mathematics educator, consultant; b. N.Y.C., N.Y., June 21, 1925; s. Max and Beatrice White; m. Myra Goldstein, Dec. 4, 1946; children: Louis, Michael. BA, Columbia U., 1949; MA, UCLA, 1951; PhD, Stanford U., 1961. Acting instr. Stanford (Calif.) U., 1950-54; asst. prof. U. Santa Clara, Calif., 1954-61; prof. Harvey Mudd Coll., Claremont, Calif., 1962—; vis. scholar MIT, 1975; initiator-facilitator humanistic math. network of over 1400 mathematicians worldwide; cons. coop. learning tutorial program Claremont Unified Sch. Dist. Author: Interdisciplinary Teaching, 1981; pub., editor: Mathematics Network Jour.; contbr. articles to profl. jours. Served with USN, 1943-46, PTO. Grantee Fund for Improvement of Post-secondary Edn., Exxon Found. Mem. Am. Math. Soc., Math. Assn. Am., Nat. Coun. Tchrs. Math., Profl. Organizational Developers Network, Fedn. Am. Scientists, AAUP, Sigma Xi. Office: Harvey Mudd Coll 1250 N Dartmouth Ave Claremont CA 91711

WHITE, BETTY, actress, comedienne; b. Oak Park, Ill., Jan. 17, 1922; m. Allen Ludden, 1963 (dec.). Student pub. schs., Beverly Hills, Calif. Appearances on radio shows This Is Your FBI, Blondie, The Great Gildersleeve; actress: (TV series) including Hollywood on Television, The Betty White Show, 1954-58, Life With Elizabeth, 1953-55, A Date With The Angels, 1957-58, The Pet Set, 1971, Mary Tyler Moore Show, 1974-77, The Betty White Show, 1977, The Golden Girls, 1985-92 (Emmy award for best actress 1986), The Golden Palace, 1992-93, Maybe This Time, 1995—; (TV miniseries) The Best Place to be, 1979, The Gossip Columnist, 1980, (film) Advise and Consent, 1962; guest appearances on other programs; summer stock appearances Guys and Dolls, Take Me Along, The King and I, Who Was That Lady?, Critic's Choice, Bells are Ringing. Recipient Emmy award NATAS, 1975, 76, 86; L.A. Area Emmy award, 1952. Mem. AFTRA, Am. Humane Assn., Greater L.A. Zoo Assn. (dir.). Office: care William Morris Agy 151 S El Camino Dr Beverly Hills CA 90212-2704*

WHITE, BONNIE YVONNE, management consultant, educator; b. Long Beach, Calif., Sept. 4, 1940; d. William Albert and Helen Iris (Harbaugh) W. BS, Brigham Young U., 1962, MS, 1965, EdD in Ednl. Adminstrn., 1976. Tchr., Wilson High Sch., Long Beach, Calif., 1962-63; grad. asst. Brigham Young U., Provo, Utah, 1963-65; instr., dir. West Valley Coll., Saratoga, Calif., 1965-76; instr., evening adminstr. Mission Coll., Santa Clara, Calif., 1976-80; dean gen. edn. Mendocino Coll., Ukiah, Calif., 1980-85; dean instrn. Porterville (Calif.) Coll., 1985-89, dean adminstrv. svc., 1989-93; rsch. assoc. SAGE Rsch. Internat., Orem, Utah, 1975—. Del. Tulare County Ctrl. Com. Rep. Party, 1993-94; pres. community adv. bd. Calif. Conservation Corps, 1989-93; v.p. Porterville Community Concerts, 1990-94; bd. dirs. United Way North Bay, Santa Rosa, Calif., 1980-85, St. Vincent de Paul, 1993—; mem. Calif. Commn. on Basic Skills, 1987-89, Calif. Commn. on Athletics, 1987-90. Mem. AAUW, Faculty Assn. Calif. Community Colls., Calif., Coun. Fine Arts Deans, Assn. Calif. Community Coll. Adminstrs. Assn. Calif. Community Coll. Adminstrs. Liberal Arts, Zonta (intern), Soroptimists (intern). Republican. Mormon.

WHITE, BRIAN WILLIAM, investment company executive; b. Seattle, Sept. 5, 1934; s. George Carlos and Mary Mae (McCann) W.; m. Christine C. Nelson, Oct. 21, 1955 (div. 1970); children: Catherine, Teresa, Patrick, Melissa, Christopher; m. B. Maureen Scott, June 21, 1972; children: Meghan Mary, Erin Maureen. Acctg. mgr. Pacific Northwest Bell, Seattle, 1960-68; rep. Dominick and Dominick, Inc., Seattle, 1968-74; dir. Western Search Assn., San Diego, 1974-80; acct. exec. Bateman Eichler Hill Richards, San Diego, 1982-90; pres. White Securities, La Mesa, Calif., 1990—. Republican. Roman Catholic. Office: White Securities Inc 8363 Center Dr # 600 La Mesa CA 91942

WHITE, BRITTAN ROMEO, manufacturing company executive; b. N.Y.C., Feb. 13, 1936; s. Brittan R. and Matilda H. (Baumann) W.; m. Esther D. Friederich, Aug. 25, 1958 (dec. May 1981); children: Cynthia E., Brittan R. VII; m. Peggy A. Lee, Aug. 30, 1990. BSChemE, Drexel U., 1958; MBA, Lehigh U., 1967; JD, Loyola U., Los Angeles, 1974; MA, Pepperdine U., 1985. Bar: Calif., U.S. Dist. Ct. Calif.; registered profl. engr., Calif. Process engr. Air Reduction Co., Bound Brook, N.J., 1958-64; area supr. J.T. Baker Chem. Co., Phillipsburg, N.J., 1964-66; asst. plant mgr. Gamma Chem. Co., Great Meadows, N.J., 1966-69; plant mgr. Maquite Corp., Elizabeth, N.J., 1969-70; purchasing mgr. Atlantic Richfield Co., Los Angeles, 1970-79; dir. mfg. Imperial Oil, Los Angeles, 1979-82; mgr. chem. mgmt. program Hughes Aircraft Co., Los Angeles, 1982-94; pres. The Crawford Group, 1994—; bd. dirs. Diversified Resource Devel. Inc., Los Angeles, 1979—; seminar moderator and speaker Energy Conservation Seminars, 1979-83. Editor Rottweiler Rev., 1979-81; chief award judge Chem. Processing mag., 1976, 78, 80; contbr. articles to profl. jours. Vice chmn. Bd. Zoning and Adjustment, Flemington, N.J., 1970-72; pres. bd. dirs. Homeowners' Assn., Palm Springs, Calif., 1983-90. Capt. C.E., U.S. Army, 1958-60, res., 1960-68. Mem. AIChE, Am. Inst. Chem. Engrs., Am. Chem. Soc., Mensa, Psi Chi. Republican. Lodge: Elks. Home: 3664 Vigilance Dr Rancho Palos Verdes CA 90275 Office: The Crawford Group 3664 Vigilance Dr Rancho Palos Verdes CA 90275

WHITE, CECIL RAY, librarian, consultant; b. Hammond, Ind., Oct. 15, 1937; s. Cecil Valentine and Vesta Ivern (Bradley) W.; m. Frances Ann Gee, Dec. 23, 1960 (div. 1987); children—Timothy Wayne, Stephen Patrick. B.S. in Edn., So. Ill. U., 1959; cert. in Czech., Syracuse, U., 1961; M. Div., Southwestern Bapt. Sem., 1969; M.L.S., N. Tex. State U., 1970, Ph.D., 1984. Librarian, Herrin High Sch. (Ill.), 1964-66; acting reference librarian Southwestern Sem., Ft. Worth, 1968-70, asst. librarian, 1970-80; head librarian Golden Gate Bapt. Sem., Mill Valley, Calif., 1980-88; head librarian West Oahu Coll., Pearl City, Hawaii, 1988-89; dir. spl. projects North State Coop. Library System, Yreka, Calif., 1989-90; dir. library St. Patrick's Sem., Menlo Park, Calif., 1990—; library cons. Hist. Commn., So. Bapt. Conv., Nashville, 1983-84, mem. Thesaurus Com., 1974-84. Bd. dirs. Hope and Help Ctr., 1986-88, vice chmn. 1987-88. With USAF, 1960-64. Lilly Found. grantee Am. Theol. Library Assn., 1969. Mem. Am. Theol. Library Assn. (coord. consultation svc. 1973-78, program planning com. 1985-88, chmn., 1986-88), Nat. Assn. Profs. Hebrew (archivist 1985—), ALA, Assn. Coll. and Rsch. Librarians, Cath. Libr. Assn., Phi Kappa Phi, Beta Phi Mu. Democrat. Baptist. Home: 105 Poplar Ave Apt 3 Redwood City CA 94061-3068 Office: St Patricks Sem 320 Middlefield Rd Menlo Park CA 94025

WHITE, CLARA JO, graphoanalyst; b. County Cherokee, Tex., June 26, 1927; d. William and Elmira (Johnson) Walker; m. Jeff Davis White, May 5, 1950; children: Anita, Jackie, Mona Lisa, Jeris, Gina. Cert., Ft. Worth Bus. Coll., 1947; AA, Riverside City Coll., 1986; cert. mgmt. and supervisory devel., U. Calif., Riverside, 1986, cert. counseling skills, 1990. Cert. Graphoanalyst 1977; cert. master graphoanalyst 1979; cert. mus. docent tng., 1977. Owner, pres. White Handwriting Analysis Svc., Riverside, Calif., 1982—; lectr., cons. Graphoanalysis, Riverside, 1977—; instr. Internat. Congress and Resident Inst. sponsored by Internat. Graphoanalysis Soc., 1989, discussion group leader, 1988; presented in field; analyzed handwriting Lady Margaret Beauford, 1992, Mary Queen of Scots, 1993, Hillary Rodham Clinton, 1993. Asst. editor: (commemorative book) Reflections, 1986; contbr. poems to anthologies. Mem. YWCA, Riverside; mem. children's conf. planning com. Riverside Mental Health Assn., 1981—; mem. U.S. Olympic Com., 1984; v.p. Heritage House Mus., Riverside, 1981—, co-pres., 1985-86, pres. 1986-87; historian Riverside Juvenile Hall Aux., 1984—, pres., 1987—; vol. teacher's aide County of Riverside Juvenile Ct. Schs., 1979—; mem. Riverside Mus. Assocs., bd. dirs., 1985-87, vol. 1985-88, aux. historian 1984—, pres., 1987-88; mem. Met. Mus. Assocs., 1960—. Recipient Cert. of Appreciation vol. svcs. program Riverside County Probation Dept., 1986, County Riverside Suprs., 1988; award F.H. Butterfield Sch., 1980, Golden Poet award The Homer Honor Soc., 1987, 90; named Vol. of Yr., recipient community svc. cert. Riverside City Coll., 1982; named to Hall of Fame, Riverside Juvenile Hall Aux., 1984; recipient Cert. of Appreciation, Riverside Mental Health, 1990, First Pl. award writing-poetry Am. Biog. Rsch. Assn., 1991, Trophy award for Outstanding Svc. to Community Sta. KQLH-FM, Trophy Pl. Vol. Ctr. of Riverside, 1991, Trophy award and Individual Svc. award, Riverside County Juvenile Hall of Fame, 1990-91, Cert. Recognition Riverside County Probation Dept., 1991, Cert. Recognition Calif. Legis.-State Assembly, 1991, Cert. Appreciation So. Calif. Chpt. IGAS, 1990-91, Cert. Appreciation Riverside County Bd. Suprs. and Riverside County Probation Dept., 1993, Participation award 21st Internat. Congress Arts and Comm. in Scotland, 1994; her poem Peace included in Scottish Library Archives, 1994. Mem. NAFE, Internat. Graphoanalysis Soc. (life, cert. master graphoanalyst, 2d and 1st v.p., pres. So. Calif. chpt., pres. excellence award 1982, 83, 84, Merit cert. 1981, Pres. Merit citation 1988, Achievement cert. 1995), U.S. Olympic Soc., Smithsonian Inst. (assoc.), Riverside C. of C., The Rsch. Coun. of Scripps Clinic and Rsch. Found., Women's Networking Club (Riverside), Confederation of Chivalry (life, grand coun., dame officer). Club: Women's Networking (Riverside). Home and Office: 7965 Helena Ave Riverside CA 92504-3513

WHITE, DANNY LEVIUS, counselor, consultant, educator; b. Temple, Tex., Oct. 9, 1956; s. Chester Allen and Elizabeth (Jimmerson) W.; m. Phemonia Lyvette Miller, July 23, 1988; 1 child, Amadi Najuma. AA, Mesa (Ariz.) Community Coll., 1976; BA, Ottawa (Kans.) U., 1982; postgrad., Chapman Coll., 1989-90; MEd magna cum laude, No. Ariz. U., 1993. Cert. lifetime jr. coll. instr., Ariz. Clinician V Phoenix South Mental Health, 1982-85; therapist I Ariz. Dept. of Correction, Tucson, 1985-87; cons. Tucson Urban League, 1987-88; counselor, assessment specialist Pima County Atty.'s Office, Tucson, 1988—; adj. faculty Pima C.C.; mem. com. So. Ariz. Task Force Against Domestic Violence, Tucson, 1989—, outreach coord. Dem. precinct committeeman, Tucson, 1988-92; del. 1988 Nat. Dem. Conv.; dep. registrar Pima & Maricopa County Recorders Office, Phoenix and Tucson, 1983-90; mem. citizens adv. coun. Phoenix Elem. Sch. Dist. 1, 1983-85; chair radiothon membership drive com. Tucson chpt. NAACP, 1990-93, chair health fair drive, 1992-93; pres. bd. dirs. P.A.S.A.R., Tucson, 1989-91; booster Spl. Olympics, 1980-90; spl. friend Ariz. Children's Home Foster Care, 1990; implemented Will to Win and Stay In Sch. drive programs, 1987-91; vol., blooddrive coord. United Blood Svcs., Phoenix, 1983-87. Mem. United Parent and Youth League Inc. (pres. bd. dirs. 1984-85), Gov.'s Alliance Against Drugs (bd. dirs. 1989-91), Omega Psi Phi (named Man of Yr. Ariz. chpts. 1983, 85, pres. Tucson grad. chpt. 1991—), Delta Alpha Alpha. Home: PO Box 1135 Tucson AZ 85702-1135

WHITE, DAVID OLDS, education researcher; b. Fenton, Mich., Dec. 18, 1921; s. Harold Bancroft and Doris Caroline (Olds) W.; m. Janice Ethel Russell, Sept. 17, 1923; children: John Russell, David Olds Jr., Benjamin Hill. BA, Amherst Coll., 1943; MS, U. Mass., 1950; PhD, U. Oreg., 1970. Tchr. human physiology Defiance (Ohio) Coll., summer 1950; sci. tchr. Roosevelt Jr. High Sch., Eugene, Oreg., 1951-52; prin. Glide (Oreg.) High Sch., 1952-56; tchr. Munich Am. Elem. Sch., 1957-69; prin. Wurzburg (Fed. Republic Germany) Am. High Sch., 1959-60, Wertheim (Fed. Republic Germany) Am. Elem. Sch., 1960-61; tchr. Dash Point Elem. Sch., Tacoma, 1961-63, Eugene (Oreg.) Pub. Schs., 1963-81; internat. rschr. in field. Contbr. articles to profl. publs.; patentee electronic model airplane. Staff sgt. U.S. Army, 1942-45, PTO. Fulbright grantee, 1956-57, 72-73. Mem. NEA, Fulbright Alumni Assn., Phi Delta Kappa. Home: 4544 Fox Hollow Rd Eugene OR 97405-3904

WHITE, DON WILLIAM, banker; b. Santa Rita, N.Mex., June 27, 1942; s. Thomas Melvin and Barbara (Smith) W.; m. Jacqueline Diane Bufkin, June 12, 1965; children: Don William Jr., David Wayne. BBA, Western N.Mex. U., 1974, MBA, 1977. Field acct. Stearns Roger Corp., Denver, 1967-70; controller, adminstrv. mgr. USNR Mining and Minerals Inc., Silver City, N.Mex., 1970-72; devel. specialist County of Grant, Silver City, 1973-77; divisional controller Molycorp. Inc., Taos, N.Mex., 1977-78; mgr. project adminstrn. Kennecott Minerals Co., Hurley, N.Mex., 1978-83; sr. v.p. Sunwest Bank Grant County, Silver City, N.Mex., 1983-84, exec. v.p., 1984-85, pres., chief exec. officer, 1985—; bd. dirs. Bank of Grant County. Bd. dirs. Sunwest Bank of Grant County, Silver City/Grant County Econ. Devel., 1983—; councilman Town of Silver City, 1977; chmn. Dems. for Senator Pete Domenici, 1986; pres. Gila Regional Med. Found., 1989-92; pres. SWNM Econ. Devel. Corp., 1984—; trustee Indian Hills Bapt. Ch., 1988-89; chmn. State of N.Mex. Small Bus. Adv. Coun.; mem. vocat. edn. adv. com. Western N.Mex. U., 1989; mem. Silver Schs.-Sch./Bus. Partnership Coun. Named Outstanding Vol., Silver City/Grant County Econ. Devel., 1987, 94, FFA, 1985. Mem. Am. Bankers Assn., N.Mex. Bankers Assn., Bank Adminstrn. Inst., Assn. Commerce and Industry (bd. dirs. 1988-91), N.Mex. Mining Assn. (assoc.), Rotary (past pres., dist. gov. rep.). Office: Sunwest Bank of Grant County 1203 N Hudson St Silver City NM 88061-5519

WHITE, DONALD HARVEY, physicist, educator; b. Berkeley, Calif., Apr. 30, 1931; s. Harvey Elliott and Adeline White; m. Beverly Evalina Jones, Aug. 8, 1953; children: Jeri, Brett, Holly, Scott, Erin. AB, U. Calif., Berkeley, 1953; PhD, Cornell U., 1960. Rsch. physicist Lawrence Livermore (Calif.) Nat. Lab., 1960-71, cons., 1971-90; prof. physics Western Oreg. State Coll., Monmouth, 1971—; vis. rsch. scientist Inst. Laue-Langevin, Grenoble, France, 1977-78, 84-85, 91-92. Author: (with others) Physics, an Experimental Science, 1968, Physics and Music, 1980. Pres. Monmouth-Independence Community Arts, 1983; pres. E. Smith Fine Arts Series, Monmouth, 1987. DuPont scholar, 1958; Minna-Heineman Found. fellow, Hannover, Fed. Republic Germany, 1977. Mem. Am. Phys. Soc., Am. Assn. Physics Tchrs. (pres. Oreg. sect. 1974-75), Oreg. Acad. Sci. (pres. 1979-80), Phi Kappa Phi (pres. West Oreg. chpt. 1989-90). Democrat. Presbyterian. Home: 411 S Walnut Dr Monmouth OR 97361-1948 Office: Western Oreg State Coll Dept Phys Earth Scis Monmouth OR 97361

WHITE, DOUGLAS R., anthropology educator; b. Mpls., Mar. 13, 1942; s. Asher Abbott and Margaret McQuestin (Richie) W.; m. Jayne Chamberlain (div. Feb. 1971); m. Lilyan Amdur Brudner, Mar. 21, 1971; 1 child, Scott Douglas. BA, U. Minn., 1964, MA, 1967, PhD, 1969. Asst. prof. U. Pitts., 1967-72, assoc. prof., 1972-76; assoc. prof. U. Calif., Irvine, 1976-79, prof., 1979—; dep. dir. Lang. Attitudes Rsch. Project, Dublin, Ireland, 1971-73; vis. prof. U. Tex., Austin, 1974-75; chmn. Linkages: World Devel. Res. Coun., Md., 1986—, pres. 1986-90. Co-editor: Research Methods in Social Networks, 1989, Anthropology of Urban Environments, 1972; founder, gen. editor World Cultures Jour., 1985-90; author sci. software packages; contbr. articles to profl. jours. Fellow Ctr. for Advanced Studies, Western Behavioral Sci. Inst., La Jolla, Calif., 1981-84; recipient Sr. Scientist award Alexander von Humboldt Stiftung, Bonn, Germany, 1989-91, Bourse de Haute Niveau award Ministry of Rsch. and Tech., Paris, 1992. Mem. Social Sci. Computing Assn. (pres. elect 1991, pres. 1992.). Democrat. Home: 8888 N La Jolla Scenic Dr La Jolla CA 92037-1608 Office: U Calif Irvine School of Social Sci Irvine CA 92717

WHITE, EDWARD MICHAEL, English language educator; b. Bklyn., Aug. 16, 1933; s. Joseph and Ida (Eisen) W.; m. Carol Moore, June 2, 1956 (div. 1976); m. Volney S. Douglas, Dec. 11, 1976; children: Katherine Lorimer, Elizabeth Spencer; stepchildren: Douglas, Dina, Frank. BA, NYU, 1955; MA, Harvard U., 1956, PhD, 1960. Teaching asst. Harvard U., Cambridge, Mass., 1958-60; asst. prof. Wellesley (Mass.) Coll., 1960-65; assoc. prof., prof. English Calif. State U., San Bernardino, 1965—; coord. writing improvement program Calif. State U., 1975-80, dir. English equivalency exam., 1973-81; dir., cons. evaluator program Coun. Writing Program Adminstrn., 1988-94. Author: The Writer's Control of Tone, 1970, The Pop Culture Tradition, 1972, Teaching and Assessing Writing, 1985, 2nd edit. 1994, Developing Successful College Writing Programs, 1989, Assigning, Responding, Evaluating, 1992, 3rd edit., 1995, Inquiry, 1993, Composition in the 21st Century, 1995. Officer Am. Field Svc., San Bernardino, 1980-88. Mem. MLA (publs. com. 1989-92), Nat. Coun. Writing Program Adminstrs. (bd. dirs. 1988-94). Democrat. Home: 933 W Edgehill Rd San Bernardino CA 92405-2018 Office: Dept English Calif State U 5500 University Pky San Bernardino CA 92407-2318

WHITE, EUGENE R., computer manufacturing company executive. With Gen. Electric Co., Fairfield, Conn., 1958-70, Fairchild Camera & Instrument Corp., 1970-74; chmn., chief exec. officer Amdahl Corp., Sunnyvale, Calif., from 1974, now vice chmn., also bd. dirs. Office: Amdahl Corp PO Box 3470 1250 E Arques Ave Sunnyvale CA 94088

WHITE, GARY RICHARD, electrical engineer; b. Detroit, Nov. 15, 1962; s. Thomas Richard and Davene (Reynolds) W. BS in Elec. Engring., Wayne State U., 1986. Electronics engr. U.S. Army Info. Sys. Engring. Command, Ft. Belvoir, Va., 1987-88, Ft. Shafter, Hawaii, 1988-92; elec. worker U.S. Navy Pub. Works Ctr., Pearl Harbor, Hawaii, 1992—. Mem. IEEE, NRA, Nat. Soc. Profl. Engrs., Assn. Computing Machinery, Nat. Republican Senatorial Com., Am. Assn. Individual Investors, Am. Mgmt. Assn. Home: 2430 Kini Pl Honolulu HI 96819

WHITE, GAYLE CLAY, aerospace company executive; b. Wyandotte, Mich., Sept. 28, 1944; s. John Leonard and Irene Francis (Clay) W.; m. Sharon Wong, June 8, 1968; children: Lai Jean, Quinn Yee. BBA, Ea. Mich. U., 1967; MBA, Utah State U., 1971; MPA, Auburn U., 1976; postgrad., Nova U., 1985—. Computer system analyst USAF Logistics Command, Odgen, Utah, 1967-71, U.S.-Can. Mil. Officer Exec., Ottawa, Ont., 1971-73; mgr. software devel. USAF Data System Design Ctr., Montgomery, Ala., 1973-77; data base adminstr. Supreme Hdqrs. Allied Powers Europe, Casteau, Belgium, 1977-81; mgr. software configuration System Integration Office, Colorado Springs, Colo., 1981-83; mgr. computer ops. N.Am. Aerospace Def. Command, Colorado Springs, 1983-84; dir. ops. 6 Missile Warning Squadron, Space Command, Cape Cod, Mass., 1984-86, comdr., 1986-87; mgr. program devel. Rockwell Internat., Colorado Springs, 1987—; mem. faculty computer sci. and bus. Regis U., Colorado Springs, 1981—. Treas. Christian Ctr. Ch., Colorado Springs, 1989—; v.p. European Parents, Tchrs. and Students Assn., 1979-81. Recipient Mil.-Civilian Rels. award Otis Civilian Adv. Coun., 1987, awarded cert. Data Processing Mgmt. Assn., 1973. Mem. Am. Mgmt. Assn., Armed Forces Comm. Electronics Assn., Inst. Navigation, Global Positioning Sys. Internat. Assn., Air Force Assn., SHAPE Officers Assn., Nat. Security Indsl. Assn. (bd. dirs. Rocky Mountain chpt. 1990—), Christian Businessmen's Assn., Air Force Assn., Lynmar Racquet Club, Alpha Kappa Psi. Republican. Home: PO Box 17184 Colorado Springs CO 80935-7184 Office: Rockwell Internat 1250 Academy Park Loop Colorado Springs CO 80910-3708

WHITE, GEOFFREY MILES, cultural studies program director; b. Bridgeport, Conn., Nov. 11, 1949; s. Stephen Theodore and Marjorie Elizabeth (Richardson) W.; m. Nancy Ann Montgomery, June 17, 1978; 1 child, Michael Geoffrey. BA in Sociology and Anthropology, Princeton U., 1971; PhD in Anthropology, U. Calif. San Diego, La Jolla, 1978. Rsch. assoc. East-West Ctr., Honolulu, 1978-92, sr. fellow, dir. cultural studies, 1992—. Author: Identity Through History, 1991; co-author: Island Encounters, 1990; co-editor: The Pacific Theater, 1989 (award 1992), New Directions in Psychological Anthropology, 1992; editl. bd. The Contemporary Pacific, 1987—, Ethos: Jour. of the Soc. for Psychological Anthropology, 1990—. Recipient Masayoshi Ohira Meml. Book prize, Japan, 1992; Intrepretive Rsch. Project grantee NEH, 1987-89, Summer Seminar dir. NEH, 1991, 93, 95, Rsch. grantee Wenner-Gren Found., N.Y. Mem. Am. Anthropol. Assn. (Stirling award 1978), Am. Ethnol. Soc., Soc. for Psychol. Anthropology (bd. dirs. 1988-90). Office: East-West Ctr 1777 E West Rd Honolulu HI 96822-2323

WHITE, JACK RAYMOND, lawyer; b. Lincoln, Nebr., Oct. 12, 1936; s. Raymond John and Twila Helen (Leonard) W.; m. Jane Eliot Brown, Sept. 1, 1990; children: Ann C., Raymond A., Arline C., Kathleen M., Colleen M. A.B., U. So. Calif., 1958, LL.B., 1961, cert. in tax and bus. litigation, 1962—. Bar: Calif. 1962, U.S. Dist. Ct. (cen. dist.) Calif. 1962, U.S. Ct. Appeals (9th cir.) 1964, U.S. Ct. Claims 1967, U.S. Supreme Ct. 1982, U.S. Tax Ct. 1964. Assoc. Hill, Farrer and Burrill, Los Angeles, 1961-71, ptnr., 1971—. Mem. ABA, Calif. Bar Assn., Los Angeles County Bar Assn., Order Coif, Legion Lex. Office: Hill Farrer & Burrill 445 S Figueroa St Fl 35 Los Angeles CA 90071-1602

WHITE, JAMES MACKEY, computer and telecommunications consultant; b. Washington, Jan. 3, 1941; s. Markey W. and Florence (Gerlich) W.; m. Anne Goddin, Apr. 28, 1964; children: Catherine, Eric. BS in Math., Duke U., 1963; postgrad., U. Ill., 1963-64; MBA, U. Del., 1968. Supr. telecommunications E.I. du Pont de Nemours & Co., Inc., Wilmington, Del., 1968-72, mgr. systems devel., 1977-81, mgr. remote systems support, 1982-87, sr. cons. telecom, 1988-92; mgr. European computer systems E.I. du Pont de Nemours & Co., Inc., Geneva, 1972-76; v.p. tech. planning and architecture Charles Schwab & Co., San Francisco, 1992-94; pres. Internat. Info. Tech., Inc., Walnut Creek, Calif., 1994—. Pres. West Chestnut Hill Resident Assn., Newark, Del., 1986-88; mem. Com. to Elect Amick, Newark, 1986-92; chmn. steering com. Mfg. Area Prorocols/Tech. and Office Protocols, Las Lomas H. S. Tech. Com., Walnut Creek Sch. Dist. Tech Com. Republican. Home: 1224 Chesterton Ct Walnut Creek CA 94596-6639

WHITE, JANE SEE, journalist; b. St. Louis, Aug. 26, 1950; d. Robert Mitchell and Barbara Whitney (Spurgeon) W.; 1 child, Laura Mitchell. BA in History and Am. Studies, Hollins Coll., 1972. Reporter Roanoke (Va.) Times, 1972-73, Kansas City (Mo.) City Star, 1973-76, AP, N.Y.C., Hartford, 1976-78; spl. writer AP, N.Y.C., 1978-81; sr. writer, chief news and bur., chief profl. div. Med. Econs. Mag., Oradell, N.J., 1981-87; dep. city editor, city editor Roanoke Times World News, 1987-91; asst. metro. editor Phoenix Gazette, 1991-93; asst. city editor Ariz. Rep., Phoenix, 1993, features editor, 1993—; asst. mng. editor adminstrn. Ariz. Rep., Phoenix, 1995—. Editor: Medical Practice Management, 1985; contbr. articles to profl. jurs. Home: 7143 N 15th Pl Phoenix AZ 85020-5416 Office: Ariz Rep PO Box 2243 Phoenix AZ 85002-2243

WHITE, J(OB) BENTON, retired religion educator; b. Birmingham, Ala., Sept. 3, 1931; s. Edith Branch (Benton) White; m. Mary Lou White, July 19, 1958; children: Thomas Raymond, Matthew Louis. BS, U. Ala., 1953; BD,

Emory U., 1956; MTh, Pacific Luth. Theol. Sem., 1969. Ordained to ministry United Meth. Ch., as deacon, 1954, as elder, 1956. Assoc. dir. Wesley Found., U. Nebr., Lincoln, 1959-61; dir. Wesley Found. San Jose (Calif.) State U., 1961-67, dir. United Campus Christian Ministry, 1968-69, assoc. prof., 1968-69, asst. to pres., 1969-70, prof. religious studies, 1970—, ombudsman, 1967-68; vis. prof. Santa Clara U., 1992—. Author: From Adam to Armageddon: A Survey of the Bible, 1986, 3d edit., 1994, Taking the Bible Seriously: Honest Differences About Biblical Interpretation, 1993; contbr. articles to profl. jours., mags. Capt. USAF, 1956-59. Mem. Am. Acad. Religion (v.p., pres. western region). Democrat. Home: 2503 Briarwood Dr San Jose CA 95125-4902

WHITE, JOHN ABIATHAR, pilot, consultant; b. Chgo., May 29, 1948; s. Abiathar Jr. and Gretchen Elizabeth (Zuber) W.; m. Therese Ann Denz, June 21, 1980; children: Kathryn Ann, Laura Ellen. Student, Art Ctr. Coll. of Design, 1969-70, Calif. Inst. Tech., 1966-67; BArch, U. Ill., 1972. Archtl. apprentice Farner Und Gründer Industriearchitekten, Zürich, Switzerland, 1972; archtl. draftsman Walter Carlson Assocs., Elk Grove, Ill., 1973; architectural job capt. Unteed Assocs., Palatine, Ill., 1974-75; flight instr. Planemasters, Inc., West Chicago, Ill., 1976; pilot Aero Am. Aviation, West Chicago, 1977, Beckett Aviation, Cleve., 1978; pilot Am. Airlines, Chgo. and L.A., 1979—, capt., 1988—; archtl. cons. Nat. Accelerator Lab., Batavia, Ill., 1980, Constrn. Collaborative, Park Ridge, Ill., 1982, L.K. White Assocs., San Diego, 1988-92. Nat. Coun. Tchrs. of English scholar, 1966. Mem. Nat. Assn. Flight Instrs. Unitarian. Home: 25400 N Bridge Rd Hawthorn Woods IL 60047 Office: Am Airlines O'Hare Internat Airport Chicago IL 60666

WHITE, JOY MIEKO, communications executive; b. Yokohama, Japan, May 1, 1951; came to U.S., 1951; d. Frank Deforest and Wanda Mieko (Ishiwata) Mellen; m. George William, June 5, 1948; 1 child, Karen. BA in Communications, Calif. State U., Fullerton, 1974, teaching cert., 1977; cert. bus. mgmt., Orange Coast Coll., 1981; cert. teaching, Community Coll., 1990. Cert. secondary tchr., Calif. Secondary tchr. Anaheim (Calif.) Union High Sch. Dist., 1977-80; tech. writer Pertec Computer Corp., Irvine, Calif., 1980-81; supr. large systems div. Burroughs, Mission Viejo, Calif., 1981-83; mgr. Lockheed div. CalComp, Anaheim, 1983-86; owner, pres. Communicator's Connection, Irvine, Calif., 1986-90; pres. Info Team, Inc., 1989—; adj. faculty, coord. tech. comm. program Golden West Coll., Huntington Beach, Calif., 1987-90; instr. U. Calif., Irvine, 1987—, Calif. State U., Fullerton, 1988-91; condr. numerous workshops, profl. presentations, 1982—; sec. Santa Ana Dist. chpt. U.S. SBA, Assn. for Minority-Owned Bus., 1991-95. Active Performing Arts, Costa Mesa, 1986—. Mem. NAFE, Soc. Tech. Communication (sr.), Soc. Profl. Journalists, Women in Communications (pres. Orange County Profl. chpt. 1989-90), Nat. Assn. Women Bus. Owners, Rembrandts Wine Club (Yorba Linda). Democrat. Home: 21651 Vintage Way Lake Forest CA 92630-5760 Office: 22365 El Toro Rd # 265 Lake Forest CA 92630-5053

WHITE, JOYCE LOUISE, librarian; b. Phila., June 7, 1927; d. George William and Louisa (Adams) W. BA, U. Pa., 1949; MLS, Drexel U., 1963; MA in Religion, Episc. Sem. S.W., 1978. Head libr. Penniman Libr. Edn. U. Pa., Phila., 1960-76; archivist St. Francis Boys' Home, Salina, Kans., 1982-84; libr. Brown Mackie Coll., Salina, 1983-86; libr., dir. St. Thomas Theol. Sem., Denver, 1986—. Author: Biographical and Historial Yarnall Library, 1979; asst. editor: Women Religious History Sources, 1983; contbr. articles to profl. jours. and chpts. to books. Vol. libr. St. John's Cath., Denver, 1993—. Mem. Ch. and Synagogue Libr. Assn. (life, founding, pres. 1969-70, exec. sec. 1970-72, exec. bd. 1967-76). Office: Saint Thomas Sem 1300 S Steele St Denver CO 80210-2526

WHITE, JUDITH LOUISE, social worker; b. Lodi, Ohio, Feb. 27, 1939; d. Henry and Charlotte Virginia (Spahr) Schmelzer; m. Downer Dale White, Sept. 4, 1959; children: Mark, Kelly, Kristy, David. AA, Northland Pioneer Coll., Holbrook, Ariz., 1980; postgrad., No. Ariz. U., 1984—, Ariz. State U., 1985—; BS in Human Svcs. Prescott Coll., 1992. Tchr. White Mountain Apache Head Start Program, Whiteriver, Ariz., 1976-80, child services coord., 1980-87; cons. Nat. Indian Head Starts, 1980—; trainer Indian Child & Family Conf., Phoenix and Albuquerque, 1982-86, Fetal Alcohol Syndrome-Indian Health Services, Whiteriver, 1984—; cons. White Mountain Apache Head Start Resource Access Project, 1984—; assoc. tchr. Northland Pioneer Jr. Coll., Holbrook, Ariz., 1985—; trainer pilot parent program; coord. Whiteriver Pilot Parents. Mem. Coalition for Chronically Ill Children, Phoenix, 1985—. Mem. NASW (presentor conf. 1990), Council Exceptional Children, Nat. Assn. for Edn. Young Children, White Mt. Assn. for Edn. Young Children. Avocations: music, reading, theater, art. Home: PO Box 707 Whiteriver AZ 85941-0707 Office: Whiteriver Elem Sch PO Box 190 Whiteriver AZ 85941-0190

WHITE, KATHLEEN MERRITT, geologist; b. Long Beach, Calif., Nov. 19, 1921; d. Edward Clendenning and Gladys Alice (Merritt) White; m. Alexander Kennedy Baird IV, Oct. 1, 1965 (dec. 1985); children: Pamela Roberts, Peter Madlem, Stephen Madlem, Mari Afify. Attended, Sch. Boston Mus. Fine Arts, 1939-40, Art Students League, 1940-42; BS in Geology, Pomona Coll., 1962; MS in Geochemistry, Claremont Grad. Sch., 1964. Rsch. asst. geology Pomona Coll., Claremont, Calif., 1962-66, rsch. assoc. geology, 1966-75; cons. geology Claremont, Calif., 1975-77; sr. scientist Jet Propulsion Lab./NASA, Pasadena, 1977-79, mem. tech. staff, 1979-86; ind. rschr. Claremont, 1986-95; owner Kittie Tales, Videos and CDs for Children, Claremont, 1992—. Contbr. Geosat Report, 1986; contbr. articles to profl. jours. Grantee NASA, 1984, 85; Pomona Coll. scholar, 1963. Mem. Geol. Soc. Am. (invited paper 1994), Am. Geophys. Union, Pomona Coll. Alumni Assn. Republican. Home: 265 W 11th St Claremont CA 91711-3804

WHITE, KENTON STOWELL, writer, publisher; b. Long Beach, Calif., July 9, 1933; s. Ernest Euliel (Ballenger) W.; m. Elizabeth Mills Laurenson, June 22, 1957; 1 child, Corey Ross. BA, U. Calif., Berkeley, 1955, MLS, 1964. Cert. secondary tchr., Calif. Tchr. English Alameda (Calif.) High Sch., 1958-60, San Lorenzo (Calif.) High Sch., 1960-61; libr. intern Alameda County, Fremont, Calif., 1962-63; ref. libr. San Bernardino (Calif.) Pub. Libr., 1964-65; audio visual coord. Inland Libr. System, San Bernardino, 1966-69; asst. city libr. Huntington Beach (Calif.) Pub. Libr., 1969-74; pub., v.p. Lightning Pubs., Fullerton, Calif., 1992; pub. North Hills Pub. Co., Costa Mesa, Calif., 1994—. Author: Buying America Back, 1988, Winning the Peace, 1992; columnist San Diego Rev. Campaign dir. Ron Pattison for City Coun., huntington Beach, 1975-76; Dem. cand. for Congress, 40th Dist., Claif., 1983-84. Mem. Am. Fiction Soc. (pres. 1993—), Nat. Writers Assn., Neighborhood Watch (pres. Huntington Beach club 1975-76), Exch. Club (pres. Huntington Beach club 1975-76). Democrat. Home: 2824 Shantar Dr Costa Mesa CA 92626-3539 Office: Am Fiction Soc 22824 Shantar Dr Costa Mesa CA 92626

WHITE, LERRILL JAMES, clinical pastoral educator; b. Lafayette, Ind., Mar. 13, 1948; s. Joe Lloyd and Wanita Irene (Robertson) W.; m. Deborah June Brown, Dec. 27, 1969; children: Krister Colin Brant, Kourtney Cassidy Benay. BA, Abilene Christian U., 1970, MS, 1973; MDiv, Princeton Theol. Sem., 1975; postgrad., Pa. State U., 1980-89. Ordained to ministry Ch. of Christ, 1975. Clin. chaplain Ft. Logan Mental Health Ctr., Denver, 1975-76, Meml. Med. Ctr., Corpus Christi, Tex., 1976-78; sr. pastor Centre Community Ch. of Christ, State Coll., Pa., 1978-87; assoc. dir. pastoral care Geisinger Med. Ctr., Danville, Pa., 1983-87; dir. pastoral care Yuma (Ariz.) Regional Med. Ctr., 1987-95; pres. well i b enterprises inc., 1995—; author, presenter tng. courses, 1987—. Contbr. articles to profl. jours.; creator interview instrument P.C. Ranking Instrument, 1981. Bd. dirs. Behavioral Health Svcs., Yuma, 1991—; mem. Yuma High and Pecan Grove PTO, 1987—; mem., coach Yuma Youth Soccer Assn., 1987-93. Fellow Coll. Chaplains (state rep.- Ariz.); m. Assn. Clin. Pastoral Edn. (supr. 1983—, regional cert. com. Pacific region 1990—), Ariz. Chaplain's Assn. (exec. com. 1988-93, pres. 1989-90), Greater Yuma Ministerium.

WHITE, LORAY BETTY, public relations executive, writer, actress, producer; b. Houston, Nov. 27, 1934; d. Harold White and Joyce Mae (Jenkins) Mills; m. Sammy Davis Jr., 1957 (div. 1959); 1 child, Deborah R. DeHart. Student, UCLA, 1948-50, 90-91, Nichiren Shoshu Acad., 1988-92; AA in Bus., Sayer Bus. Sch., 1970; study div. mem. dept. L.A., Soka U., Japan, 1970-86. Editor entertainment writer L.A. Community New, 1970-81; exec. sec. guest rels. KNBC Prodns., Burbank, Calif., 1969-75; security specialist Xerox X10 Think Tank, L.A., 1975-80; exec. asst. Ralph Powell & Assocs., L.A., 1980-82; pres., owner, producer LBW & Assocs. Pub. Rels., L.A., 1980—; owner, producer, writer, host TV prodn. co. Pub. Pub. Rels., L.A., 1987—; dir., producer L.B.W. Prodn. "Yesterday, Today, Tomorrow, L.A., 1981—. Actress (film) Ten Commandments, 1956, (Broadway) Joy Ride; appeared in the following endorsements including Budweiser Beer, Old Gold Cigarettes, Salem Cigarettes, TV commls. including Cheer, Puffs Tissue, Coca Cola, Buffern, others; entertainment editor L.A. Community News, 1970-73; writer (column) Balance News, 1980-82. Mem. Soka Gakkai Internat. Youth divsn. ARC, Urban League, Nat. Audubon Found., Nat. Parks Assn., Smithsonian Instn., Lupus Found. of Am. (so. Calif. chpt.), World Peace Cultural Festival '72, Bicentennial Celebration '76, United High Blood Pressure Telethon, Com. for Sr. Citizens, Beverly Hills-Westwood Sr. Citizen Cmty. Ctr. Recipient award ARC, 1955, Cert. of Honor, Internat. Orgn. Soka Gakkai Internat. of Japan, Cmty. Vols. of Am. award, 1994; named Performer of Yr. Cardella Demillo, 1976-77. Mem. ARC (planning, mktg., prodn. event com. 1995), ULCA Alumni Assn., Lupus Found. Am. (so. Calif. chpt.). Buddhist.

WHITE, LYLA LEE, religious organization administrator; b. Watsonville, Calif., Apr. 20, 1940; d. Lyle Verne Loehr and Marjorie (Rhoades) Smith; m. J. Melville White, Sept. 7, 1962 (Jan. 1987); children: Erinn Kathleen, Michael Christopher. BA in English and History, Warner Pacific Coll.; postgrad., Pepperdine U. Tchr. of English Crescenta Valley High Sch./Glendale (Calif.) C.C., 1964-74; v.p. Mel White Prodns., 1964-84; editor Harper and Row Pubbs., 1983-86; dir. devel. All Saints Ch., Pasadena, Calif., 1986-94; dir. devel. and pub. rels. Grace Cathedral, San Francisco, 1994—; bd. dirs. The Psychol. Ctr. of Fuller Theol. Sem., 1977-88. Coauthor: In the Presence of Mine Enemies, 1973, Tested by Fire, 1976. Mem. Leadership Calif., 1993—; fundraising cons., conf. spkr., San Francisco, 1990—. Mem. LWV, Nat. Assn. Fundraising Execs., San Francisco Planned Giving Round Table, San Francisco City Club. Office: Grace Cathedral All Saints Church 1051 Taylor St San Francisco CA 94108-2209

WHITE, MATTHEW, family practice physician; b. Phila., May 21, 1941; s. Frank and Minerva (Shiffmann) W.; m. Kristina J. Johnson, Aug. 15, 1978. AB in Chemistry, Temple U., 1963; MD, Jefferson Med. Coll., 1967. Diplomate Am. Bd. Family Practice. Commd. lt. USN, 1967, advanced through grades to comdr., 1975; intern U.S. Naval Hosp., Newport, R.I., 1967-68; resident U.S. Naval Hosp., Jacksonville, Fla., 1968-70; family practice medicine USN, Japan, 1970-73, Bremerton, Wash., 1973-77; family practice medicine Sand Pt. Naval Air Sta., Seattle, 1977-78; resigned USN, 1978; family practice medicine Tacoma, 1978—; mem. active staff, bd. dirs., exec. com. St. Claire Hosp.; mem. courtesy staff Humana Hosp., Multicare Hosp., St. Joseph's Hosp.; pres. med. staff Lakewood Hosp., 1989-90. Mem. utilization rev. com. Georgian House Nursing Home, Meadow Park Nursing Home, Lakewood Health Care N.H. Fellow Am. Acad. Family Practice; mem. AMA (nat., state and county chpts.). Republican. Jewish. Office: #304 11311 Bridgeport Way SW Tacoma WA 98467

WHITE, MICHAEL LEE, executive producer, writer; b. Rochester, Minn., Aug. 2, 1967; s. Floyd Leroy and Yvonne Cecile (Jarrett) W. Student, U. Ariz., 1984-85. Glazier Sunset Glass & Mirror, Tucson, 1980-84; assoc. astronomer Flandrau Planetarium, Tucson, 1984-85; owner W.A.V. Enterprises, Hemet, Calif., 1985-88; exec.producer, writer Nine Star-Domestic, Hemet, 1989-95; news/program dir. Buffalo Comms., San Jacinto, Calif., 1992, gen. mgr., 1993; co-owner Mail Depot, Hemet, 1994—, Aero Pig Ltd., Hemet, 1995—; co-owner, producer, writer Mide Prodns., Hemet, 1995—. Editor Hemet Valley Bull. Bd. List, 1990—, Tucson Bull. Bd. List, 1987—; contbr. author: Computer Phone Book, 1986. Founder, spokesperson Pro-Am. Found., Tucson, 1985—, internat. pres., 1986-88, 92; pres. Tucson Jr. Civitan, 1982-83. Republican. Lutheran. Home: 44135 Oak Glen Rd Hemet CA 92544 Office: Mail Depot 3007 W Florida Ave Hemet CA 92545-3617

WHITE, PAUL VERLIN, electronics marketing executive; b. Sioux Falls, S.D., Apr. 12, 1941; s. Verlin J.A. and Dorothy M. (Bates) W.; m. Judi Maureen Greene, July 3, 1965; children—Paul H., Sean M. B.S.E.E., Ariz. State U., 1964. Quality engr. mil. div. Motorola, Scottsdale, Ariz., 1962-65, dist. sales mgr. semicondr. div., Los Angeles, 1965-71, mgr. hi-rel mktg., Mesa, Ariz., 1971-74, mktg. mgr., Phoenix, 1974-75, dir. mktg. power products, 1976-82, v.p., dir. mktg. discrete and spl. technologies group, 1982-95, mem. adv. council to bd. dirs., 1984; v.p. dir. mktg. Analog I/C divsn., 1995—. Bd. dirs. Grace Community Ch., Tempe, 1983—, treas., 1984—. Author articles in field. Mem. Motorola PAC, 1983—. Phoenix Coll. scholar, 1962. Mem. Am. Mktg. Assn. (award 1978). Republican. Home: 2062 E Malibu Dr Tempe AZ 85282-5966 Office: Motorola Inc 2100 E Elliott Scottsdale AZ 85254

WHITE, RAYMOND, health facility administrator. BS in Microbiology, U. Oreg., 1965; PhD in Microbiology, MIT, 1971; postdoctoral study, Stanford U. Assoc. prof. Microbiology Dept. U. Mass. Sch. Medicine, Worcester, 1978-80; assoc. prof. Cellular, Viral & Molecular Biology U. Utah Sch. Medicine, Salt Lake City, 1980-84; investigator Howard Hughes Med. Inst. U. Utah, 1980-94; co-chair Human Genetics Dept. U. Utah Sch. Medicine, 1985—, dir. Huntsman Cancer Inst., 1994—, chmn. Dept. Oncological Scis., 1994—. Recipient Rosenthal Found. award Am. Assn. Cancer Rsch., Charles S. Mott prize for Cancer Rsch. Gen. Motors Found., Nat. Med. Rsch. award Nat. Health Coun., Allen award for Cancer Rsch. Am. Soc. Human Genetics, Friedrich von Recklinghausen award Nat. Neurofibromatosis Found., Lewis S. Rosenstiel award for Disting. Work in Med. Scis. Brandeis U. Mem. NAS. Office: Huntsman Cancer Inst Bldg 533 Ste 7410 U Utah Sch Medicine Salt Lake City UT 84112*

WHITE, RAYMOND EDWIN, JR., astronomer, educator, researcher; b. Freeport, Ill., May 6, 1933; s. Raymond Edwin White and Beatrice Ellen (Rahn) Stone; m. Ruby Elaine Fisk, Oct. 16, 1956; children: Raymond Edwin III, Kathleen M., Kevin D. BS, U. Ill., 1955, PhD in Astronomy, 1967. Instr. astronomy U. Ariz., Tucson, 1964-65, asst. prof. astronomy, 1965-71, lectr. astronomy, 1972-81, assoc. prof. astronomy, 1981-93, prof. astronomy, 1993—, disting. prof., 1995—; program officer astronomy NSF, Washington, 1971-72. Editor: Observational Astrophysics, 1992; editor Astronomy Quar. jour., 1989-91; North Am. editor Vistas in Astronomy jour., 1992—. 1st lt. U.S. Army, 1955-58. Fellow AAAS, Royal Astron. Soc.; mem. Am. Astron. Soc., Am. Assn. Physics Tchrs., Math Assn. Am., Internat. Astron. Union, Sigma Xi. Office: Univ Ariz Steward Observatory Tucson AZ 85721

WHITE, RICHARD CLARENCE, lawyer; b. Sioux City, Iowa, Oct. 31, 1933; m. Beverly Frances Fitzpatrick, Feb. 22, 1955; children—Anne, Richard, William, Christopher. B.A.; LL.B., Stanford U., 1962. Bar: Calif. 1963, U.S. Supreme Ct. 1970, N.Y. 1983. Assoc. O'Melveny & Myers, L.A., 1962-70, ptnr., 1970—. Lectr. in field. Bd. dirs. Equal Employment Adv. Coun., Washington, 1976-80, 83, Performing Arts Ctr. of Orange County 1983-86. Capt. USMC, 1954-59; Mem. ABA (co-chmn. com. on practice and procedure labor and employment law sect. 1977-80, mem. equal opportunity law com. 1980-85, co-chmn. com. on insts. and meetings 1985-87, coun. 1987—), Orange County Bar Assn., Lincoln Club (Orange County). Republican. Contbr. articles to profl. publs.

WHITE, ROBERT C., air transportation executive; b. 1943. Student, Wake Forest U., 1961-65. With Procter & Gamble, Columbus, Ohio, 1971-73; asst. dir. Shreveport (La.) Airport Authority, 1973-75; airport mgr. Gainesville (Fla.) Regional Airport, 1975-78; dep. dir. aviation Jacksonville (Fla.) Port Authority, 1978-80; exec. dir. Peninsula Airport Commn., Newport News, Va., 1980-82; dir./cons. Lockheed Air Terminal, Burbank, Calif., 1982—; with Reno Cannon Internat. Airport, 1988—. With USN, 1966-71. Office: Reno Cannon Internat Airport PO Box 12490 Reno NV 89510-2490*

WHITE, ROBERT GORDON, educator, researcher, research director; b. Lithgow, NSW, Australia, Jan. 17, 1938; s. Richard Robert and Francis Elsie (Schubert) W.; m. Sandra Elizabeth Ferrier, Dec. 9, 1961; children: Robert Ian, Andrew Douglas. B. in Agrl. Sci., Melbourne U., Australia, 1962; M in Rural Sci./Physiology, U. New Eng., Australia, 1968, PhD, 1974. Rsch. asst. Melbourne U., 1962-63; demonstrator U. New Eng., Armidale, Australia, 1963-66, teaching fellow, 1966-69; asst. prof. zoophysiology and nutrition Inst. Arctic Biology, U. Alaska, Fairbanks, 1970-75; assoc. prof. U. Alaska, Fairbanks, 1975-81, prof., 1981—; acting dir. Inst. Arctic Biology, U. Alaska, Fairbanks, 1985, 92, dir., 1993—; dir. Large Animal Rsch. Sta., 1979—. Co-editor: (with Hudson) Bioenergetics of Wild Herbivores, 1985; editor: (proceedings, with Klein, Keller) First International Muskox Symposium, 1984 (proceedings, with Luick, Lent, Klein) First International Reindeer and Caribou Symposium, 1975; editorial bd.: Rangifer/Biol. Papers U. Alaska; contbr. over 100 papers to profl. jours. Pipe major Fairbanks Red Hackle Pipe Band, 1975-90; pres. Fairbanks Nordic Ski Club, 1973-75. NATO Rsch. fellow, Trondheim, Norway, 1975-76. Fellow AAAS (Alaska chmn. 1985, 94), Arctic Inst. N.Am.; mem. Am. Physiol. Soc., Wildlife Soc., Am. Soc. Mammologists, The Wildlife Mgmt. Soc., Australasian Soc. Wildlife Mgmt., Australian Soc. of Animal Prodn., Australian Soc. Biochemistry and Molecular Biology, Sigma Xi. Office: U Alaska Inst Arctic Biology Fairbanks AK 99775

WHITE, ROBERT LEE, electrical engineer, educator; b. Plainfield, N.J., Feb. 14, 1927; s. Claude and Ruby Hemsworth Emerson (Levick) W.; m. Phyllis Lillian Arlt, June 14, 1952; children: Lauren A., Kimberly A., Christopher L., Matthew P. BA in Physics, Columbia U., 1949, MA, 1951, PhD, 1954. Assoc. head atomic physics dept. Hughes Rsch. Labs., Malibu, Calif., 1954-61; head magnetics dept. Gen. Tel. and Electronics Rsch. Lab., Palo Alto, Calif., 1961-63; prof. elec. engring., materials sci. and engring. Stanford U., Palo Alto, 1963, chmn. elec. engring. dept., 1981-86; William E. Ayer prof. elec. engring. Stanford U., 1985-88; exec. dir. The Exploratorium, San Francisco, 1987-89; dir. Inst. for Electronics in Medicine, 1973-87, Stanford Ctr. for Rsch. on Info. Storage Materials, 1991—; initial ltd. ptnr. Mayfield Fund, Mayfield II and Alpha II Fund, Rainbow Co-Investment Ptnrs., Halo Ptnrs.; vis. prof. Tokyo U., 1975; cons. in field. Author: (with K.A. Wickersheim) Magnetism and Magnetic Materials, 1965, Basic Quantum Mechanics, 1967; Contbr. numerous articles to profl. jours. With USN, 1945-46. Fellow Guggenheim Oxford U., 1969-70, Canton Hosp., Swiss Fed. Inst. Tech., Zurich, 1977-78, Christensen fellow Oxford U., 1986; Sony sabbatical chair, 1994. Fellow Am. Phys. Soc., IEEE; mem. Sigma Xi, Phi Beta Kappa. Home: 450 El Escarpado Stanford CA 94305-8431 Office: Stanford U Dept Material Sci Engr Stanford CA 94305

WHITE, ROBERT MICHAEL, small business owner, executive; b. Ravenswood, W.Va., Aug. 30, 1942; s. Thomas Michael and Margaret (Blazier) W.; m. Geraldine Noack (div. 1969); children: Thomas, Gary, Greg; m. Henrietta Delikowski (div. 1988, remarried 1995); 1 child, Robert; m. Diana Lynn, July 1, 1988 (div. 1994); children: Levi, Megan, Alicia, Emily. Diploma, East High Sch., Green Bay, Wis., 1960. Br. mgr. Local Loan Co., Milw., 1962-69; owner, pres. Marketmasters, Milw., 1967-69; sr. cons. Sales Dynamics Inst., N.Y.C., 1969-71; pres. Mind Dynamics, inc., San Rafael, Calif., 1971-73; chmn., CEO Arc Internat., Ltd., Tokyo, Hong Kong, Singapore and Denver, 1974—. Author: One World One People, 1984. Chmn. Republicans Abroad, Tokyo, 1983-86, Internat. Eagles, Washington, 1984-86; bd. dirs. Rocky Mountain World Trade Ctr.; bd. advs. Japan Am. Soc. Colo., Ctr. for the New West; adv., underwriter New Dimensions Radio, San Francisco, 1986—. Baden Powell fellow, 1985. Mem. ASTD, Pacific Basin Econ. Coun. (vice chmn. 1986—), Am. C. of C.-Japan (gov. 1984-86), Am. Mgmt. Assn., Instructional Systems Assn. (v.p. 1989—). Republican. Home: 2114 McClain Flats Rd Aspen CO 81611 Office: ARC Internat Ltd PO Box 12396 Aspen CO 81612-9207

WHITE, ROBERT RANKIN, writer and historian, hydrologist; b. Houston, Feb. 8, 1942; s. Rankin Jones and Eleanor Margaret (White) W. BA in Geology, U. Tex., 1964; MS in Hydrology, U. Ariz., 1971; PhD in Am. studies, U. N.Mex., 1993. Hydrologist Tex. Water Devel. Bd., Austin, 1972-74; hydrologist U.S. Geol. Survey, Las Cruces, N.Mex., 1974-78, Santa Fe, 1978-80, Albuquerque, 1980-89; writer, historian Albuquerque, 1989—; mem. planning bd. N.Mex. Art History Conf., Taos, N.Mex., 1987—. Author: The Lithographs and Etchings of E. Martin Hennings, 1978, The Taos Soc. Artists, 1983, (with others) Pioneer Artists of Taos, 1983, Bert Geer Phillips and The Taos Art Colony, 1994; contbr. articles to profl. jours. Bd. dirs. Friends of U. N.Mex. Librs., Albuquerque, 1984-90. With U.S. Army, 1965-68. Mem. Western History Assn., Hist. Soc. N.Mex. (pres. 1991-93), N.Mex. Book League (pres. 1994), Taos County Hist. Soc., NRA (life). Episcopalian. Home and Office: 1409 Las Lomas Rd NE Albuquerque NM 87106-4529

WHITE, ROBERT STEPHEN, physics educator; b. Ellsworth, Kans., Dec. 28, 1920; s. Byron F. and Sebina (Leighty) W.; m. Freda Marie Bridgewater, Aug. 30, 1942; children: Nancy Lynn, Margaret Diane, John Stephen, David Bruce. AB, Southwestern Coll., 1942, DSc hon., 1971; MS, U. Ill., 1943; PhD, U. Calif., Berkeley, 1951. Physicist Lawrence Radiation Lab., Berkeley, Livermore, Calif., 1948-61; head dept. particles and fields Space Physics Lab. Aerospace Corp., El Segundo, Calif., 1962-67; physics prof. U. Calif., Riverside, 1967-92, dir. Inst. Geophysics and Planetary Physics, 1967-92, chmn. dept. physics, 1970-73, prof. emeritus physics dept., rsch. physicist, 1992—; lectr. U. Calif., Berkeley, 1953-54, 57-59. Author: Space Physics, 1970; contbr. articles to profl. jours. Officer USNR, 1944-46. Sr. Postdoctoral fellow NSF, 1961-62; grantee NASA, NSF, USAF, numerous others. Fellow Am. Phys. Soc. (exec. com. 1972-74); mem. AAAS, AAUP, Am. Geophys. Union, Am. Astron. Soc. Home: 5225 Austin Rd Santa Barbara CA 93111-2905 Office: U Calif Inst Geophysics & Planetary Physics Riverside CA 92521

WHITE, ROBERTA LEE, comptroller; b. Denver, Sept. 18, 1946; d. Harold Tindall and Araminta (Campbell) Bangs; m. Lewis Paul White, Jr., Jan. 23, 1973 (div. Sept. 1974). BA cum laude, Linfield Coll., 1976; postgrad., Lewis & Clark Coll. Office mgr. Multnomah County Auditor, Portland, Oreg., 1977-81; rsch. asst. Dan Goldy and Assocs., Portland, 1981-83; regional asst. Vocat. Rehab., Eugene, Oreg., 1983-85; internal auditor Multnomah County, Portland, Oregon, 1985-89; cons. Portland, 1989-91; fin. analyst City of Portland, 1991-93; comptroller Wordsmith Svcs., Portland, 1993—; mem. Com. for Implementation of the ADA, Portland, 1991-93. Treas. Mary Wendy Roberts for Sec. of State, Portland, 1992, Re-Elect Mary Wendy Roberts, Portland, 1990, Elect Hank Miggins Com., 1994; mem. Oreg. Women's Polit. Caucus, Portland, 1982-85, City Club, Portland, 1978-81. Democrat. Mem. Disciples of Christ. Office: Wordsmith Svcs 1500 NE Irving Ste 350 Portland OR 97232

WHITE, RONALD CEDRIC, JR., religion educator; b. Mpls., May 22, 1939; s. Ronald Cedric and Evelyn Ann (Pearson) W.; m. Sherrie Rosalind Derrick, June 18, 1964 (div. Nov. 1988); children: Melissa Gale White Clawson, Bradley Derrick; m. Cynthia Conger, Nov. 23, 1991. BA, UCLA, 1961; MDiv, Princeton Theol. Sem., 1964; MA, Princeton U., 1970, PhD, 1972. Ordained to ministry Presbyn. Ch., 1964. Min. First Presbyn. Ch., Colorado Springs, Colo., 1964-68; lectr. history Colo. Coll., Colorado Springs, 1965-66; chaplain, asst. prof. Am. studies Rider Coll., Lawrenceville, N.J., 1972-74; chaplain, assoc. prof. religion Whitworth Coll., Spokane, Wash., 1974-80, assoc. prof., chair dept. religion and philosophy, 1980-81; lectr. in ch. history, dir. continuing edn. Princeton (N.J.) Theol. Sem., 1981-88; rsch. scholar The Huntington Libr., San Marino, Calif., 1988—; Presby. Eccles. prof. Fuller Theol. Sem., Pasadena, Calif., 1988-92; lectr. in history UCLA, 1991—; vis. prof. ch. history San Francisco Sem./Grad. Theol. Union, San Anselmo/Berkelry, Calif., 1979;. Author: The Social Gospel: Religion and Reform in Changing America, 1976, Liberty and Justice for All, 1990; editor, author: American Christianity: A Case Approach,1986, An Unsettled Arena: Religion and the Bill of Rights, 1990. Founding dir. Martin Luther King Edn. Fund, Colorado Springs, 1968; trustee Spokane Peace and Justice Ctr., Spokane, 1976-80, Wesley-Westminster Found., Princeton U., 1984-86. World Coun. Chs. scholar Lincoln Theol. Coll., Eng., 1966-67; Ford Found. fellow, 1970-72; Haynes-Huntington fellow; Lilly Endowment scholar, 1992-94. Mem. Am. Hist. Assn., Am. Soc. Ch. History, Orgn. Am. Historians, Assn. of Case Teaching (bd. dirs.). Democrat. Home: 5328 Godbey Dr La Canada CA 91011

WHITE, STANLEY ARCHIBALD, research electrical engineer; b. Providence, Sept. 25, 1931; s. Clarence Archibald White and Lou Ella (Givens) Arford; m. Edda María Castaño-Benítez, June 6, 1956; children: Dianne, Stanley Jr., Paul, John. BSEE, Purdue U., 1957, MSEE, 1959, PhD, 1965.

Registered profl. engr., Ind., Calif. Engr. Rockwell Internat., Anaheim, Calif., 1959-68, mgr., 1968-84, sr. scientist, 1984-90; pres. Signal Processing and Controls Engring. Corp., 1990—; adj. prof. elec. engring. U. Calif., 1984—; cons. and lectr. in field; bd. dirs. Asilomar Signals, Systems and Computers Conf. Corp. Publisher, composer music; contbr. chpts. to books; articles to profl. jours.; patentee in field. Fellow N.Am. Aviation Sci. Engring., 1963-65; recipient Disting. Lectr. award Nat. Electronics Conf., Chgo., 1973, Engr. of Yr. award Orange County (Calif.) Engring. Coun., 1984, Engr. of Yr. award Rockwell Internat., 1985, Leonardo Da Vinci Medallion, 1986, Sci. Achievement award, 1987, Disting. Engring. Alumnus award Purdue U., 1988, Meritorious Inventor's award Rockwell Internat. Corp., 1989, Outstanding Elec. Engr. award Purdue U., 1992. Fellow AAAS, AIAA, IEEE (founding chmn. Orange County chpt.), Acoustics, Speech and Sigmal Processing Soc. (vice chmn. 1983, gen. chmn. Internat. Symposium Cirs. and Sys. 1992, Internat. Conf. Acoustics, Speech and Signal Processing 1984, Centennial medal 1984), IEEE Signal Processing Soc. (disting. lectr. 1991-92), Inst. Advancement Engring., N.Y. Acad. Scis.; mem. Air Force Assn., Sci. Rsch. Soc., Sigma Xi (founding pres. Orange County chpt.), Tau Beta Pi, Eta Kappa Nu (internat. dir. emeritus). Home: 433 E Avenida Cordoba San Clemente CA 92672-2350

WHITE, TERRY WAYNE, hospital administration executive; b. Rocky Mountain House, Alta., Can., Mar. 27, 1952; s. Arnold N. and Mildred J. W.; m. Darlene Y. Rockwell, July 31, 1977; children: Danae, Derek. BSc, Pacific Union Coll., 1973; MPH, Loma Linda U., 1977. Sr. v.p. Shawnee Mission (Kans.) Med. Ctr., 1977-84; pres. Castle Med. Ctr., Kailua, Hawaii, 1984—; mem. nat. adv. bd. The Healthcare Forum, San Francisco, 1986—; chmn. pacific region Inst. Svc. Excellence, 1993, Quality Mgmt. Exchange Forum, 1993. Trustee Le Jardin Academy, Kailua, 1989—. Maffly scholar The Healthcare Forum, 1993. Fellow Am. Coll. Healthcare Execs.; mem. Am. Hosp. Assn. (del. for state 1993—), Am. Soc. Quality and Control, Healthcare Assn. Hawaii (bd. dirs. 1991-93, chmn. 1990, Disting. Svc. award 1992), Rotary. Office: Castle Med Ctr 640 Ulukahiki St Kailua HI 96734-4454

WHITE, THOMAS JEFFREY, healthcare management educator; b. Boston, Oct. 25, 1945; m. Tomoe Niijima White, Nov. 6, 1970; children: Tammy P., Treacy C. BA in Bus., U. Md., 1972; MS in Edn., Troy State U., 1974; MS in Sys. Mgmt., U. So. Calif., L.A., 1977; MBA in Healthcare Mgmt., Western New Eng. Coll., 1985. Bd. cert. hosp. adminstr. Commd. 2d lt. USAF, 1963, advanced through grades to lt. col., devel. officer edn. program USAF Air U., 1972-74, asst. adminstr. pers. adminstrn., 1974-75, asst. adminstr. resources mgmt., 1975-76, asst. adminstr. patient affairs mgmt., 1976-80; adminstr., CEO USAF Hosp., Yokota Air Base, Japan, 1980-81, USAF Comty. Med. Group Facility, L.A. AFB, El Segundo, Calif., 1981-83; adminstr., COO USAF Comty. Med. Group Facility, Hanscom AFB, Boston, 1983-86; mgmt. fellow spl. assignment Arthur D. Little, Inc., 1986-87; healthcare mgmt. cons./auditor Air Force Med. Inspection Ctr., 1987-90; chief plans and programs Air Force Inspection & Safety Ctr., 1990-91; sr. devel. officer Brim Enterprises, 1991-92; mem. adj. faculty grad. program health svcs. adminstrn. Chapman U., 1990—. Recipient So. Calif. Fed. Exec. Bd. Profl. Devel. award, 1983. Fellow Am. Coll. Healthcare Execs., Am. Hosp. Assn. Roman Catholic. Home: 29127 Lake Ridge Ln Highland CA 92346-3907 Office: Chapman U Graeber St Riverside CA 92518

WHITE, THOMAS S., lawyer; b. Sharon, Pa., Aug. 27, 1949; s. Herbert F. and Ruth J. W.; m. Linda K. Clark, May 12, 1973; children: Kimberly, Nicholas. BA, Case Western Reserve U., 1973; JD, Gonzaga U., 1976. Bar: Wash. 1980, U.S. Dist. Ct. (we. dist.) Wash. 1983, U.S. Dist. Ct. (we. dist.) Pa. 1983, U.S. Ct. Appeals (3rd cir.) 1983. Legal advisor Spokane Legal Services, Wash., 1977; revenue officer State of Wash., Everett, 1979-80; dep. pros. atty. Snohomish County, Everett, 1980; postal insp. U.S. Postal Service, Pa., W.V., 1981-84; regional insp. atty. U.S. Postal Service, Phila., 1984-85; insp. atty., nat. money laundering advisor U.S. Postal Svc., Washington, 1985-93; insp. atty. Seattle divsn. U.S. Postal Svc., Seattle, 1993—. Active Spotsylvania County Boy Scouts, Fredericksburg, Va., 1988-89; trustee Peace United Meth. Ch., Fredricksburg, 1988-89. Recipient Meritorious Svc. honor award U.S. Postal Svc., 1988, 90, 91, Spl. Achievement award, 1988, 93. Mem. ABA (criminal justice sect.), Wash. State Bar Assn. Methodist. Office: 3d & Union PO Box 400 Seattle WA 98111

WHITE, VICTOR DEA, airport management executive; b. Ft. Worth, Tex., Mar. 16, 1951; s. Victor George and Louise Emily (Roach) W.; m. Denise Sue Bonzo, Sept. 3, 1977; children: Kathy, Tiffany, Daniel. BS in Bus. and Transportation with honors, St. Louis U., 1974. Airport mgmt. intern St. Louis Internat. Airport, 1974-75; airport mgmt. cons. Landrum & Brown, Cinn., 1975-77; airport duty mgr. Dallas/Ft. Worth Internat. Airport, 1977-81; exec. dir Waukegan (Ill.) Port Authority, 1981-83; dir. airports City of Midland (Tex.)/Odessa, 1983-90; dep. dir. airports Salt Lake City Airport Authority, 1990—; pres. U.S. Airport Svcs. Corp., Salt Lake City, 1983—, Bedford Industries Corp., Ft. Worth, 1977—. Author: Small Hub Airport Management, 1985. Chmn. Midland/Odessa Interant. Task Force, 1986-90, Mayor's Transp. Task Force 1991-95, Mayor's Americans with Disabilities Task Force 1991-94, Internat. Airport Rescue/Firefighting Acad. 1986-89, Internat. Airport Facilities Conf. 1993; mem. The Midland Com., 1986-90. Alpha Sigma Nu scholar, 1974, Alpha Chi scholar, 1974. Mem. Am. Assn. Airport Execs (pres. Northwest chpt. 1993-95, Southcentral chpt. 1988-90), Midland C. of C. (chmn. aviation task force 1986—). Republican. Roman Catholic. Office: Salt Lake City Internat Airport AMF Box 22084 776 N Terminal Dr Salt Lake City UT 84122*

WHITEAKER, RUTH CATHERINE, retired secondary education educator, counselor; b. Monte Vista, Colo., Mar. 3, 1907; d. Samuel sigel and Vina Catherine (Becraft) Heilman; m. George Henry Whiteaker, June 23, 1946. BA, U. Denver, 1930, MA, 1954; student, Columbia U., Ohio State, and others, 1933-66. cert. tchr. Tchr./drama coach Brighton (Colo.) High Sch., 1930-36; tchr. Meeker Jr. High Sch., Greeley, Colo., 1936-42; tchr. South High Sch., Denver, 1942-52, couselor, 1952-61; tchr. Thomas Jefferson High Sch., Denver, 1961-66; organizer first career day Greeley High Sch., 1939, Future Tchrs. Am. in Colo. High Schs. Colo. Edn. Assn., 1949-55; co-organizer Wyo. Future Tchrs. Am. Wyo. Edn. Assn., 1951; com. mem. Nat. Future Tchrs. Am. Adv. Bd., 1954. Author: (English speech units) Colo. English Guide, 1939, Denver K-12 Program, 1951; editor: (guidebook) South High Syllabus, 1952-60. Chmn. 50th reunion U. Denver Class 1930, 1980. Grantee U.S. Dept. Edn. and Ministry of Edn. Mex., Mexico City, 1945; recipient plaque Colo. Future Tchrs. Am., 1955, Student Nat. Edn. Assn., Colo., 1955; Yearbook dedication South Denver High Sch., 1958. Mem. AAUW, Bus. and Profl. Women's Club (pres. 1933, 38), Colo. Bus. and Profl. Women's Club (v.p. 1944), Columbia U. Women's Club Colo. (pres. 1975-77), Rep. Ladies Roundtable, Colo. Symphony Guild, PEO Sisterhood, Meth. Women's Assn., Terr. Daus., Columbia U. Alumni Club, Alpha Gamma Delta (regional sec.-treas. 1934-36, pres. 1936-40), Delta Kappa Gamma (v.p. Colo. chpt. 1959). Republican. Methodist. Home: 6930 E Girard Ave Apt 108 Denver CO 80224-2900

WHITEHEAD, ARDELLE COLEMAN, advertising and public relations executive; b. Carrollton, Ohio, May 13, 1917; d. James David and Gilsie Dale (Hendricks) Coleman. BS, Wittenberg U., 1938. Account exec. Steve Hannagan Assocs., N.Y.C., 1946-52; dir. publicity Fieldcrest Mills, Inc., N.Y.C., 1952-55; account and pub. rels. exec. Calkins & Holden, N.Y.C., 1956-59; creative dir. Leslie Advt. Agy., Greenville, S.C., 1960-62; dir. advt. Lanz Originals, Los Angeles, 1962-64; account exec., copywriter, consumer affairs specialist Jennings & Thompson, Phoenix, 1965-73; mgr. pub. communications Valley Nat. Bank, Phoenix, 1974-75; pres. The Whiteheads, Inc., Phoenix, 1976—. Author: (pamphlets) How to Be a Client, 1979, Advertising Isn't Everything, 1981; contbr. articles to various Phoenix and regional art mags. Recipient Lulu award Los Angeles Advt. Women, 1974; named Adperson of Yr. Ad II of Phoenix, 1978. Mem. Pub. Relations Soc. (Percy award 1985), Women in Communications (Woman of Achievement award for west region 1981), Phoenix Advt. Club (hon. life mem.). Office: The Whiteheads Inc 5242 N 15th Dr Phoenix AZ 85015-3001

WHITEHEAD, JAMES FRED, III, lawyer; b. Atlanta, July 3, 1946; s. James Fred Jr. and Jessie Mae (Turner) W.; m. Joanne Christina Mayo, June 21, 1969 (div. Feb. 1992); children: Matthew Nicholas, Rebecca Catherine; m. Nancy Karean Hatley, May 28, 1992; stepchildren: Brandon, Madison. AB with distinction, Stanford U., 1968; JD, U. Mich., 1975. Bar: Wash. 1975, U.S. Dist. Ct. (we. dist.) Wash. 1975, U.S. Ct. Appeals (9th cir.) 1975, U.S. Supreme Ct. 1976. Assoc. LeGros, Buchanan, Paul & Madden, Seattle, 1975-79; dir., officer LeGros, Buchanan, Paul & Whitehead, Seattle, 1979-92; ptnr. McGee, Reno & Whitehead, Seattle, 1993; of counsel Faulkner, Banfield, Doogan & Holmes, Seattle, 1993—; organizer, lectr. Pacific Northwest Admiralty Law Inst., Seattle, 1981—. Assoc. editor Am. Maritime Cases, 1991—; contbr. articles to profl. jours. Mem. ABA, Maritime Law Assn. of U.S. Office: Faulkner Banfield Doogan Holmes First Interstate Center Ste 2600 Seattle WA 98104

WHITEHEAD, PAUL LEON, physician; b. Salt Lake City, May 23, 1936; s. Rolland N. and Marva B. (Bullock) W.; m. Marilyn Davis, Sept. 5, 1964; children: Anne, Paul D., Kathryn, Emily. BS, U. Utah, 1957, MD, 1960. Diplomate Am. Bd. Psychiatry and Neurology-Psychiatry (examiner child and adolescent psychiatry 1976—, examiner gen. psychiatry 1994—), Am. Bd. Psychiatry and Neurology-Child Psychiatry. Pvt. practice of child, adolescent and adult psychiatry, 1967—; clin. prof. psychiatry U. Utah Coll. Medicine, 1977—; pub. affairs rep. Utah Psychiat. Assn., 1977-89, 91-93; psychiat. cons. Salt Lake Alliance for the Mentally Ill, 1991—; active med. staff Primary Children's Med. Ctr., 1967—, dir. children's psychiat. ctr., 1967-75, chmn. dept. child psychiatry, 1975-81, chmn. human subjects com., 1978-81; cons. child psychiatry Utah State Divsn. Health, 1966-80, Wyo. State Hosp., 1976-77; cons. Children's Ctr. Group Home, Salt Lake City, 1968-69; chmn. adv. coun. children's svcs. Utah State Divsn. Mental Health, 1968-73; mem. Utah State Mental Health Task Force, 1969-71; mem. adv. bd. Salt Lake City Cmty. Mental Health Ctr., 1971-75; courtesy med. staff St. Mark's Hosp., LDS Hosp.; chmn. Norman S. Anderson, M.D. award Fund bd., 1993-95; del. Intermountain Acad. of Child and Adolescent Psychiatry to Assembly of Regional Orgns., Am. Acad. of Child and Adolescent Psychiatry, 1987-91; psychiat. admissions rev. com. to advise Utah State Legis., 1989-90; med. dir. CPC Olympus View Hosp., Salt Lake city, 1986-88; instr. psychiatry coll. medicine U. Utah, 1969-70, asst. prof., 1970-76, dir. divsn. child and adolescent psychiatry, 1977-78; mem. med. evaluation com. St. Mark's Hosp., 1985, chmn. libr. com., 1986; mem. Spl. Rev. Task Force Valley Mental Health, 1988-89; presenter in field. Contbr. numerous articles to profl. jours. Gen. Med. Officer USAF, 1961-63. Ford Early Admissions scholarship, 1953-57; recipient Norman S. Anderson, MD award, 1989. Fellow Am. Psychiat. Assn., Am. Acad. Child and Adolescent Psychiatry (continuing edn. com. 1977-90); mem. AMA, Utah State Med. Assn. (dangerous drugs com. 1971-75, del. ho. dels. 1975-79, legis. com. 1976-77, bd. dirs. acad. continuing med. edn. 1978-84, chmn. psychiat. sect. ann. sci. meeting 1987), Salt Lake County Med. Soc., Utah Psychiat. Assn. (pres. 1977-78), Intermountain Acad. Child and Adolescent Psychiatry (pres. 1969-70), Alpha Omega Alpha (pres. 1959-60), Phi Beta Kappa. Office: Paul L Whitehead MD & Assocs 1580 East 3900 South #200 Salt Lake City UT 84124

WHITEHOUSE, CHARLES BARTON, avionics educator; b. Boston, Sept. 7, 1933; s. John Clifford and Pauline Barbara (Larkin) W.; m. Diana Bernier, June 9, 1962; 1 child, Clifford Bernard. B.S., Central Conn. State Coll., 1957; M.S., U. Northern Colo., 1974, D.Edn., 1977. Cert. profl. tchr., Colo.; cert. flight instr., aircraft & instrument, advanced ground instr., Colo. Electrician, Killywatt Elec. Co., Newington, Conn., 1951-56, Guerrard Elec. Co., New Britain, Conn., 1956-57; technician electric curriculum Opportunity Sch., Denver, 1958-60, elec. instr., 1960-68, avionics, communications instr., 1968-92; ret.; founder, owner, seminar leader, mfr. InterTech Aviation Svcs., Littleton, Colo., 1980—; radio engr. Pacific Nomad, 1989; adj. prof. avionics aerospace dept. Met. State Coll. of Denver, 1990—. Author: FCC Exam Guide, 1991, Avionics for Aviators, 1994; contbr. manuals, study guides on avionics. Mem. AAAS, Colo. Aviation Hist. Soc., Air Power West, Am. Field Svc. Com., Sister Cities Internat., Wings Over the Rockies Aviation & Space Mus., Colo. Pilots Assn., Assn. for Avionics Edn., Denver Radio League, Exptl. Aircraft Assn., Aircraft Owners and Pilot's Assn., Antique Wireless Assn., Silver Wings Aviation Frat., Radio Club Am. Republican. Unitarian. Home: 3 Sunset Ln Greenwood Village Littleton CO 80121 Office: Metro State Coll West Class Bldg Mail Box 30 PO Box 173362 Denver CO 80217-3362

WHITEHOUSE, JACK PENDLETON, public relations executive; b. Los Angeles, Aug. 18, 1924; s. Marvin and Lola Katherine (Gerber) W.; m. Phyllis Jeanne Stockhausen, Mar. 6, 1964 (div. 1983); 1 child, Mark Philip. Student, The Principia Coll., 1942-43, UCLA, 1945-49. Editor L.A. Ind. Pub. Co., 1946-48; writer UCLA Office Pub. Info., 1948-51; mng. editor Yuma (Ariz.) Daily Sun, 1951-53; assoc. editor Desert Mag., 1953-54; owner Whitehouse & Assocs., L.A., 1954-55; dir. West Coast press rels. Shell Oil Co., L.A., 1955-56; pub. rels. dir. Welton Becket & Assocs., L.A., 1956-58; owner, pres. Whitehouse Assocs. Inc., L.A., 1958—, Internat. Pub. Rels. Co. Ltd., L.A., 1959—; exec. dir. Japan Steel Info. Ctr., L.A., 1966—; U.S. Justice Dept. fgn. agt. Consulate-Gen. Japan, L.A., 1971—; frequent guest lectr. to colls., univs. Author: International Public Relations, 1978. Mem. Los Angeles World Affairs Council; advisor Japanese Philharmonic Soc., 1975—. With AC, U.S. Army, 1943-45. Recipient Fgn. Minister's award govt. of Japan, 1994. Mem. Pub. Rels. Soc. Am., Japan-Am. Soc. (exec. coun. 1968-94, hon. dir. 1994—), Fgn. Trade Assn. (bd. dirs. 1978-80), Japan-West Coast Assn., Greater L.A. Press Club, L.A. Athletic Club. Office: Internat Pub Rels Co Ltd 523 W 6th St Los Angeles CA 90014-1217

WHITE-HUNT, KEITH, business executive; b. Rowlands Gill, Eng., Sept. 6, 1950; s. Thomas William and Louisa (Robson) W-H.; m. Brenda Liddle, Jan. 1, 1970; children: Keith Brendan, John Roland, Daniel Thomas, Brooke Arran, Edward James, Ross Andrew. BA in Econ. Studies with honors, U. Exeter, United Kingdom, 1973; MS in Indsl. Mgmt., U. Bradford, Eng., 1975; cert. in edn., U. Leeds, 1976; DSc in Bus. Econs., U. Lodz, Poland, 1982; postgrad., Cornell U., 1986, Stanford U., 1987. Registered cons. in info. tech., registered cons. in export sales. Asst. prof. U. Bradford, 1973-77; assoc. prof. U. Sokoto, Nigeria, 1977-78, U. Stirling, Scotland, 1978-80; v.p. corp. devel. Lithgows Ltd., Scotland, 1980-83; deputy chief exec.. & pres. N. Am. Yorkshire & Humberside Devel. Assn., Eng., 1983-90; dir. Internat. Devel. Regent Pacific Mgmt. Corp., Cupertino, Calif., 1990—; vis. prof. U. R.I., 1980-88, Tech. U. of Lodz, 1985-90, adj. prof. internat. bus. San Francisco State U., 1991; bd. dirs. White-Hunt Industries Ltd., Eng., GKWH Inc. and British Market Inc., Calif., Tex. contbr. numerous articles to profl. jours. Recipient David Forsyth award U. Leeds, 1976, Amicus Poloniae award for Contbn. to Coop. Acad. Research in Poland, 1981. Fellow British Inst. Mgmt., Inst. Sales and Mktg. Mgmt., Inst. Petroleum, Internat. Inst. Social Econs., Chartered Inst. Mktg.; mem. Inst. Info. Scientists, Inst. of Wastes Mgmt. Home: 141 Pepper Ct Los Altos CA 94022-3754 Office: 10600 N De Anza Blvd Cupertino CA 95014-2059

WHITEHURST, HARRY BERNARD, chemistry educator; b. Dallas, Sept. 13, 1922; s. Clement Monroe and Grace Annette (Walton) W.; m. Audry Lucile Hale, June 12, 1948; children: Jonathan Monroe, Katherine Annette Whitehurst Hilburn. BA, Rice U., 1944, MA, 1948, PhD, 1950. Rsch. chemist Manhattan Project, Oak Ridge, Tenn., 1944-46, U.S. Naval Radiol. Def. Lab., San Francisco, 1959; postdoctoral fellow U. Minn., Mpls., 1950-51; rsch. chemist Owens-Corning Fiberglas Corp., Newark, Ohio, 1951-55, rsch. dept. head, 1955-59; assoc. prof. chemistry Ariz. State U., Tempe, 1959-70, prof., 1970-92. Contbr. articles on oxides to profl. jours.; patentee glass fibers field. With C.E., AUS, 1944-46. Fellow Am. Inst. Chemists, AAAS, Ariz. Acad. Sci. (pres. 1960-61); mem. Am. Chem. Soc., Phi Lambda Upsilon. Democrat. Baptist. Home: 630 E Concorda Dr Tempe AZ 85282-2319

WHITENER, PHILIP CHARLES, aeronautical engineer, consultant; b. Keokuk, Iowa, July 9, 1920; s. Henry Carroll and Katherine Ethel (Graham) W.; m. Joy Carrie Page, Oct. 9, 1943; children: David A., Barbara C., Wendy R., Dixie K. BSME, U. N.Mex., 1941. Ordained to elder Presbyn. Ch., 1956. Engr. Boeing Airplane Co., Seattle, 1941-47, supr. wind tunnel model design, 1947-57, project engr. B-52 flight test, 1957-62, engring. mgr. Fresh I hydrofoil, 1962-65, configurator supersonic transport, 1965-70, with preliminary design advanced concepts, 1970-83, ret., 1983; pres., chief engr. Alpha-Dyne Corp., Bainbridge Island, Wash., 1983—. Inventee in field. Organizer Trinity Ch., Burien, Wash., 1962, Highline Reformed Presbyn., Burien, 1970, Liberty Bay Presbyn., Poulsbo, Wash., 1978; pres. Whitener Family Found., Bainbridge Island, 1979; bd. dirs. Mcpl. League of Bainbridge, 1993—, v.p., 1994; pres. Mcpl. League Found., 1994—. Republican. Home: 5955 Battle Point Dr NE Bainbridge Island WA 98110

WHITESIDE, CAROL GORDON, state official, former mayor; b. Chgo., Dec. 15, 1942; d. Paul George and Helen Louise (Barre) G.; m. John Gregory Whiteside, Aug. 15, 1964; children: Brian Paul, Derek James. BA, U. Calif., Davis, 1964. Pers. mgr. Emporium Capwell Co., Santa Rosa, 1964-67; pers. asst. Levi Strauss & Co., San Francisco, 1967-69; project leader Interdatum, San Francisco, 1983-88; with City Coun. Modesto, 1983-87; mayor City of Modesto, 1987-91; asst. sec. for intergovtl. rels. The Resources Agy., State of Calif., Sacramento, 1991-93; dir. intergovtl. affairs Gov.'s Office, Sacramento, 1993—. Trustee Modesto City Schs., 1979-83; nat. pres. Rep. Mayors and Local Ofcls., 1990. Named Outstanding Woman of Yr. Women's Commn., Stanislaus County, Calif., 1988, Woman of Yr., 27th Assembly Dist., 1991. Republican. Lutheran. Office: Governor's Office 1400 10th St Sacramento CA 95814-5502

WHITESIDE, LOWELL STANLEY, seismologist; b. Trinidad, Colo., Jan. 7, 1946; s. Paul Edward and Carrie Belle (Burgess) W. BS, Hamline U., 1968; postgrad., Oswego State U. of N.Y., 1970-72; MS, U. Nebr., 1985; postgrad., Ga. Inst. of Tech., 1986-88, U. Colo., 1990-94. Instr. U.S. Peace Corps, Mhlume, Swaziland, 1968-71; rsch. assoc. CIRES, U. Colo., Boulder, 1988-90; geophysicist in charge of internat. earthquake data base NOAA, Nat. Geophys. Data Ctr., Boulder, 1990—. Scoutmaster Boy Scouts Am., St. Paul, Lincoln, Nebr., 1968-80, camp counselor, 1966-76. Recipient Eagle Scout award Boy Scouts Am., 1968, NGDC/DOAA Customer Svc. award, 1995. Mem. AAAS (chmn. 1986-87, vice chmn. 1985-86, Geology-Geography, Rocky Mountain sect., Outstanding Articles Referee 1992, Best Student Paper award 1984, 85), Seismol. Soc. of Am., Am. Geophys. Union, Sierra Club, Planetary Soc. Presbyterian. Home: PO Box 3141 Eldorado Springs CO 80025-3141 Office: NOAA/NGDC/NESOIS 325 Broadway St Boulder CO 80303-3337

WHITE-VONDRAN, MARY ELLEN, retired stockbroker; b. East Cleveland, Ohio, Aug. 21, 1938; d. Thomas Patrick and Rita Ellen (Langdon) White; m. Gary L. Vondran, Nov. 25, 1961; children: Patrick Michael, Gary Lee Jr. BA, Notre Dame Coll., South Euclid, Ohio, 1960; postgrad., John Carroll U., 1960, U. Mass., 1961, U. S.C., 1969, San Jose State U., 1971-75, U. Santa Clara, Calif., 1972, Stanford U., 1989; MSL, Peninsula U., Mountain View, Calif., 1994. Cert. life secondary tchr., Calif.; lic. NASD series 7, 11 & 18 broker. Tchr. Cleve. Sch. Dist., 1960-61, East Hartford (Conn.) Sch. Dist., 1961-62, San Francisco Bay Area Sch. Dist., 1970-75; life and disability agt. Travelers Ins. Co. and BMA Ins. Co., San Jose, Calif., 1975-77; stockbroker Reynolds, Bache, Shearson, Palo Alto, Calif., 1977-78, Schwab & Co., San Francisco, 1980; adminstr. pension and profit Crocker Nat. Bank, San Francisco, 1980-82; stockbroker Calif. Fed./Invest Co., San Francisco, 1982-83; head trader, br. mgr. Rose & Co., San Francisco, 1983-84; ret., 1984; tchr. citizenship for fgn. born adult community edn. Fremont Union High Sch. Dist., Sunnyvale, Calif., 1988—. Author: Jo Mora-Renaissance Man, 1973, Visit of Imperial Russian Navy to San Francisco, 1974, John Franklin Miller, 1974, 1905 Quail Meadow Road. Sec. Quota Internat., Los Altos, Calif., 1987; constn. chairperson LWV, Los Altos, 1985—, lectr. speakers bur. 1987, moderator, co-producer TV programs; precinct capt. 1988 & 90 Elections, Los Altos; appointee ad hoc com. for transp. of mobility impaired Santa Clara County, 1988; vol. tchr. English in Action; usher lively arts Stanford U.; mem. tele com. Peninsula Dem. Coalition; active Internat. Vis. Com., Palo Alto, People for Accessible Health Care, Women in History Mus., Calif. History Ctr., Cupertino, Palo Alto Neighbors Abroad. Recipient Valley Cable Recognition award, 1988. Mem. AAUW, ACLU, NOW (speakers bur. coord.), World Affairs Forum, Women in History Assn., The Great War Soc., Am. Assn. Retired Persons, Older Women's League, Los Altos Women in Bus., Women's Internat. League for Peace & Freedom, Commonwealth Club (steering com., program com. Palo Alto/Midpeninsula chpt.), Kenna Club. Democrat. Roman Catholic.

WHITING, ARTHUR MILTON, diversified company executive; b. St. Johns, Ariz., 1928. With Kaibab Industries, chmn., chief exec. officer; formerly bd. dir. Western Savs. & Loan, Western Fin. Corp. Office: Kaibab Industries 4602 E Thomas Rd Phoenix AZ 85018-7710*

WHITING, JAMES VINCENT, cartoonist; b. Canton, Pa., May 19, 1926; s. George Edward and Grace Electa (Dann) W.; m. Bernita Mae Blanchard, Nov. 20, 1945; children: James, Donna, John, Andrea, David. Student, Chgo. Acad. of Fine Arts, 1948, Sch. Visual Arts, 1949-51. Radio sales, air work Sta. WFLR-AM & FM, Dundee, N.Y., 1956-84; free-lance cartoonist Solana Beach, Calif., 1984—. Mem. team producing Ad Libs for syndicated newspaper panel; produced panels Wee Women, Li'l Ones, Gen. Features Corp., L.A. Times Syndicate, 1957-72. With USN, 1944-46. Mem. Southern Calif. Cartoonists Soc. (pres. 1986—, co-founder), Upstate Cartoonists League Am. (co-founder). Home and Office: 773 S Nardo Ave Apt 10 Solana Beach CA 92075-2337

WHITLEY, DAVID SCOTT, archaeologist; b. Williams AFB, Ariz., Mar. 5, 1953; s. Edgar Duer and Yvonne Roca (Wightman) W.; m. Tamara Katherine Koteles, Feb. 13, 1987; 1 child, Carmen. AB in Anthrop. & Geog. (magna cum laude), U. Calif., 1976, MA in Geography, 1979, PhD in Anthropology, 1982. Soc. Profl. Archeology. Chief archeologist Inst. Archeology UCLA, L.A., 1983-87; rsch. fellow Archeology Dept. U. Witwatersrand, Johannesburg, S. Africa, 1987-89; pres. W&S Cons., Simi Valley, Calif., 1989—; U.S. rep. internat. com. rock art Internat. Com. Monuments and Sites, 1992—. Author: Rock Art of Ancient America, 1983; editor: archeological monographs; contbr. articles to profl. jours. Prehistoric Archeologist, State of Calif. Hist. Resources Commn., 1986-87. Recipient post doctoral fellowship, Assn. for Field Archeology, 1983, tech. specialist grant, U.S. Aid, 1986. Fellow Am. Anthrop. Assn.; mem. Soc. Am. Archeology, SAR, Sons of the Indian Wars. Home: 447 3rd St Fillmore CA 93015-1413 Office: W&S Consultants 2422 Stinson St Simi Valley CA 93065

WHITLOCK, TIMOTHY SCOTT, commercial pilot; b. Eugene, Oreg., Oct. 3, 1948; s. Kenneth Gerald and Shirley Louise (Multhauf) W.; m. Ann Marie Yoder, June 24, 1972; children: Robert Scott, Scott Thomas. BS in Biology, USAF Acad., 1972. Commd. 2d lt. USAF, 1973, advanced through grades to lt. col., 1980, ret., 1985; capt. Am. Airlines, San Francisco, 1985—. Liaison USAF Acad., Napa, Calif., 1979—. Decorated Disting. Flying Cross, Air medal. Mem. Allied Pilots Assn., Air Force Assn., Piano Tchrs. Assn. Republican. Baptist. Home: 1055 Stonebridge Dr Napa CA 94558-5347

WHITLOW, DONNA MAE, daycare and primary school administrator; b. Buffalo, S.D., May 23, 1933; d. Carl Axel and Esther Johanna (Wickman) Magnuson; married, June 13, 1953; children: Debra Diane Reasy, Cathleen Denise Corallo, Lisa Mae. Diploma, Eugene Bible Coll., 1956; BA in Religious Edn., Internat. Seminary, 1985, MA, 1986. Corp. sec. various orgns., 1953-56; asst. registrar, prof. child edn. Calif. Open Bible Inst., Pasadena, 1956-57; dir. religious edn. and music, sec. to gen. bd. Jamaica Open Bible Inst., 1958-59; dir. religious edn. and music, sec. to gen. bd.. prof. on staff, bus. mgr. Trinidad Open Bible Inst., 1960-65; asst. to full-charge bookkeeper Jennings Strouss Law Firm, 1966-68; dir. religious edn. and music., mem. gen. bd., assoc. pastor Biltmore Bible Ch., Phoenix, Ariz., 1967-93; founder, dir. Biltmore Bible Day Care & Kindergarten, Phoenix, 1977—; founder bible schs. in South Africa, Argentina, Ctrl. Am., Europe, Carribean. Author: How To Start a Daycare in the Local Church, 1986. Republican. Home: 2144 E Lamar Rd Phoenix AZ 85016-1147 Office: Biltmore Bible Ch 3330 E Camelback Rd Phoenix AZ 85018-2310

WHITMAN, KENNETH JAY, advertising executive; b. N.Y.C., May 4, 1947; s. Howard Jay and Suzanne Marcia (Desberg) W.; m. Susan M. Hall, Feb. 8, 1995. Student, Berklee Sch. Mus., 1965-66, Hubbard Acad., 1968-70. Nat. dep. dir. Pub. Relations Bur., Los Angeles, 1970-75; pres. Creative Cons., Los Angeles, 1975-82; pres., creative dir. Whitman & Green Advt., Toluca Lake, Calif., 1982-86, Whitman-Olson, Toluca Lake, 1986-92; v.p. mktg. Maxa Corp., 1992-93; creative dir. Whitman-Hall, L.A., 1993—. Co-author: Strategic Advertising, 1986; editor Freedom news jour., 1971-79; contbr. newspaper column Shape of Things, 1971-79. Pres. Los Angeles

Citizens Commn. Human Rights, 1971-75. Recipient Cert. of Design Excellence Print Regional Design Ann., 1985, 87, Award of Excellence Consolidated Papers, 1985, Award of Excellence Print Mag., 1985, 87, 1st place award Sunny Creative Radio, 2 Telly awards, 1988, Belding award Advt. Club Los Angeles, Excellence award Bus. and Profl. Advt. Assn., 1987, Internat. Gold Medallion award Broadcast Promotion and Mktg. Execs. Mem. Art Dirs. Club of Los Angeles, VSC (pres. 1964-65), CEOs Circle. Office: Whitman-Hall 2820 Griffith Park Blvd Apt 7 Los Angeles CA 90027-3367

WHITMORE, DONALD CLARK, retired engineer; b. Seattle, Sept. 15, 1932; s. Floyd Robinson and Lois Mildred (Clark) W.; m. Alice Elinor Winter, Jan. 8, 1955; children: Catherine Ruth, William Owen, Matthew Clark, Nancy Lynn, Peggy Ann, Stuart John. BS, U. Wash., 1955. Prin. engr. The Boeing Co., Seattle, 1955-87, ret., 1987; developer, owner mobile home pk., Auburn, Wash., 1979—. Author: Towards Security, 1983, (monograph) SDI Software Feasibility, 1990, Characterization of the Nuclear Proliferation Threat, 1993, Rationale for Nuclear Disarmament, 1995. Activist for arms control, Auburn, Wash., 1962—; chmn. Seattle Coun. Orgns. for Internat. Affairs, 1973, Auburn Citizens for Schs., 1975; v.p. Boeing Employees Good Neighbor Fund, Seattle, 1977, Spl. Svc. award, 1977; bd. dirs. 8th Congl. Dist. Sane/Freeze, 1992—; pres., founder Third Millennium Found., 1994—. Home and Office: 16202 SE Lake Moneysmith Rd Auburn WA 98092-5274

WHITNER, JANE MARVIN, analyst programmer; b. Oakland, Calif., Aug. 29, 1935; d. Chauncey Hill and Alice Belle (Cromwell) Whitner. BA in Biol. Sci., San Jose State U., 1958; MA in Biostatistics, U. Calif., Berkeley, 1960. EDP programmer San Mateo County EDP Ctr., Redwood City, Calif., 1962-65; sci. programmer Lockheed Missiles & Space Co., Sunnyvale, Calif., 1967-68, Stanford U. Med. Ctr., 1969-73; sci. sys. programmer Physics Internat. Co., San Leandro, Calif., 1980-84; analyst programmer Syntex Rsch. Corp., Palo Alto, Calif., 1985—. Mem. ACM, AAUW, Astron. Soc. Pacific, Planetary Soc., Smithsonian Instn., U. Calif. Alumni Assn., Commonwealth Club of Calif.

WHITNEY, DAVID CLAY, business educator, consultant, writer; b. Astoria, Oreg., May 30, 1937; s. Rolla Vernon and Barbara (Clay) W.; m. Kathleen Donnelley, 1956 (div. 1963); children: David Jr., Sandra, Sara; m. Zelda Gifford, 1967 (div. 1973); m. Emily Jane Williams, 1992. BS in Chemistry, San Diego State U., 1959; PhD in Chemistry, U. Calif., Berkeley, 1963. Cert. data processor, cert. data educator. Acting asst. prof. U. Calif., Davis, 1962-63; chemist, mathematician Shell Devel. Corp., Emeryville, Calif., 1963-72; dir. computer services Systems Applications, Inc., San Rafael, Calif., 1973-77; prof. Sch. Bus. Coll. Bus. San Francisco State U., 1977—; info. systems cons. numerous cos., 1977—; textbook reviewer numerous pubs., 1979—. Author: Instructors' Guides to Understanding Fortran, 1977, 83, 87, Understanding Fortran, 1984, 88, Basic, 1988, 89, 95. Mem. Assn. Computing Machinery, Data Processing Mgmt. Assn., Soc. Data Educators, Mensa. Home: 1501 S Norfolk St San Mateo CA 94401-3605 Office: San Francisco State U Coll of Bus San Francisco CA 94132

WHITNEY, JANE, foreign service officer; b. Champaign, Ill., July 15, 1941; d. Robert F. and Mussette (Cary) W. BA, Beloit Coll., 1963; CD, U. Aix, Marseille, France, 1962. Joined Fgn. Service, U.S. Dept. State, 1965, vice consul, Saigon, Vietnam, 1966-68, career counselor, 1968-70, spl. asst. Office of Dir. Gen., 1970-72, consul, Stuttgart, Fed. Republic Germany, 1972-74, Ankara, Turkey, 1974-76, spl. asst. Office of Asst. Sec. for Consular Affairs, 1976-77, mem. Bd. Examiners Fgn. Service, 1977-78, 79-81, consul, Munich, Germany, 1978-79, Buenos Aires, 1981-82, Argentina, ethics officer Office of Legal Adviser, 1982-85, advisor Office of Asst. Sec. for Diplomatic Security, 1985-86, dep. prin. officer, consul, Stuttgart, 1986-90, prin. officer, consul gen., Perth, Australia, 1990-91. Recipient awards U.S. Dept. State, 1968, 70, 81, 85, 87, 90. Mem. Presbyterian Ch.

WHITNEY, LISA VANDERSLUIS, software engineer; b. Oak Ridge, Tenn., Mar. 3, 1960; d. Kenneth Leory and Joan (Harvie) VanderSluis; m. David John Whitney, June 3, 1995. BA in Computer Sci./Bus. Adminstrn., U. Tenn., 1982; MS in Computer Sci., Rensselaer Poly. Inst., 1992. Computer scientist, computer programmer/analyst Naval Underwater Sys Ctr., Newport, R.I., 1983-87; project computer programmer analyst Tech. Applications, Inc., New London, Conn., 1987-92; sr. programmer analyst Cray Rsch. Inc., Eagan, Minn., 1992-93; software engr., new tech. specialist Sterling Software, Moffett Field, Calif., 1993—. Contbr. articles to profl. jours. Mem. IEEE, IEEE Computer Soc. Home: 22364 Salem Ave Cupertino CA 95014-0907 Office: Sterling Software NASA Ames Rsch Ctr MS233-10 Moffett Field CA 94035

WHITNEY, STAN, marriage and family therapist; b. Wellsboro, Pa., Jan. 15, 1935; m. Ida G. Shoop, Dec. 29, 1960 (div. Jan. 1984); children: Rebecca Whitney Jones, Mark Daniel; m. Gloria Leon LeFleur, Jan. 30, 1988. BS, Bob Jones U., Greenville, S.C., 1961, MA, 1962; PhD, San Antonio Theol. Sem., St. Paul, 1989. Diplomate Am. Bd. Cert. Managed Care Providers. Pastoral counselor various area chs., Ottawa, Ill., 1964-74; bus. cons. Rental Real Estate Co., Ottawa, 1974-87; pastoral counselor various area chs., Las Vegas, Nev., 1987-92; founder, clin. dir. Hope Counseling Inc., Bullhead City, Ariz., 1992—; exec. bd. and cons. Blasingame Found., Dallas, 1987—. Fellow Am. Acad. Clin. Sexologists; mem. Am. Counseling Assn., Am. Assn. Christian Counselors, Am. Acad. Clin. Family Therapists. Office: Hope Counseling Inc PO Box 1068 Bullhead City AZ 86430-1068

WHITSEL, RICHARD HARRY, biologist, entomologist; b. Denver, Feb. 23, 1931; s. Richard Elstun and Edith Muriel (Harry) W.; children by previous marriages: Russell David, Robert Alan, Michael Dale, Steven Deane. BA, U. Calif., Berkeley, 1954; MA, San Jose State Coll., 1962. Sr. rsch. biologist San Mateo County Mosquito Abatement Dist., Burlingame, Calif., 1959-72; environ. program mgr., chief of watershed mgmt., chief of planning Calif. Regional Water Quality Control Bd., Oakland, 1972—; mem. grad. faculty water resource mgmt. U. San Francisco, 1987-89. Served with Med. Service Corps, U.S. Army, 1954-56. Mem. Entomol. Soc. Am., Entomol. Soc. Wash., Am. Mosquito Control Assn., Calif. Alumni Assn., The Benjamin Ide Wheeler Soc., Nat. Parks and Conservation Assn. (life), Sierra Club. Democrat. Episcopalian. Contbr. articles to profl. jours. Home: 4331 Blenheim Way Concord CA 94521-4258 Office: Calif Regional Water Quality Control Bd 2101 Webster St Oakland CA 94612-3027

WHITTEMORE, LOREN R., rancher, real estate broker, county commissioner; b. Colorado Springs, Colo., Apr. 24, 1935; s. Roy Volney and Ida Lorene (Fellers) W.; m. Judy Mae Cowger, Sept. 30, 1963; children: Charlotte Dee, Cynthia Dawn, Celeste Dana. Rancher Whittemore Ranch, El Paso County, Colo.; real estate broker Hatton Land & Cattle, Colorado Springs, Colo., 1980—; pres. Colo. Counties, Inc., Denver, 1989, treas., 1993-94; chmn. Pikes Peak Coun. Govts., Colorado Springs, 1992-93. Author: Ranching in Pikes Peak Region, 1968; editor, pub.: Rocky Mountain Quarter Horse, 1968-88, Colo. Thoroughbred, 1979-82; contbr. articles to profl. jours. County commr. El Paso County, Colorado Springs, 1985—, chmn. bd., 1985-86. With U.S. Army, 1958-60. Recipient cert. of recognition Farm Bur., El Paso County, 1989, award of excellence Grand Lodge of Colo., 1989. Mem. Pikes Peak Cattlemens (pres. 1984), El Paso County Farm Bur. (pres. 1979), Rocky Mountain Quarter Horse (v.p. 1986). Republican. Baptist. Home: 12335 Whittemore Rd Rush CO 80833-8726 Office: El Paso County 27 E Vermijo Ave Colorado Springs CO 80903-2213

WHITTEMORE, PAUL BAXTER, psychologist; b. Framingham, Mass., Apr. 11, 1948; s. Harry Ballou and Margaret (Brown) W.; m. Jane Manson, Apr. 22, 1995. BA in Religion, Ea. Nazarene Coll., 1970; MDiv., Nazarene Theol. Sem., 1973; MA in Theology, Vanderbilt U., 1975, PhD in Theology, 1978; PhD in Clin. Psychology, U. Tenn., 1987. Lic. psychologist. Asst. prof. philosophy and edn. Trevecca Nazarene Coll., Nashville, Tenn., 1973-76; asst. prof. philosophy and theology Point Loma Coll., San Diego, Calif., 1976-80; asst. prof. philosophy Middle Tenn. State U., Murfreesboro, 1980-83; clin. psychology intern. LAC/U. So. Calif. Med. Ctr., L.A., 1986-87; coord. behavior health ctr. Calif. Med. Ctr., L.A., 1987-88; clin. asst. prof. family medicine sch. medicine U. So. Calif., L.A., 1988—; pvt. practice psychologist Newport Beach, Calif., 1989—; mem. behavioral sci. faculty Glendale Adventist Family Practice Residency Program, Glendale, Calif., 1989-90; inpatient group therapist Ingleside Hosp., Rosemead, Calif., 1990-92; founder, pres. The Date Coach, 1992—. Contbr. articles to profl. jours. Recipient Andrew W. Mellon Postdoctoral Faculty Devel. award Vanderbilt U., 1981. Mem. Am. Acad. Religion, Am. Philosophical Assn., Am. Assn. Univ. Prof. (chpt. v.p. 1982-83), Am. Psychological Assn. Office: 3901 Macarthur Blvd Ste 200 Newport Beach CA 92660-3011

WHITTENBURG, RUSSELL THOMAS, finance executive; b. Ponca City, Okla., Jan. 23, 1957; s. William Robert and Jerry Lee (Mullins) W.; m. Barbara Rose Billard, Sept. 17, 1983; children: Jocelyn Rose, Jamie Lee. BSME, U. Tex., 1978; MBA, Harvard U., 1980. From sr. planning analyst to fin. dir. Atlantic Richfield Co., L.A., 1980-86; engagement leader Boston Consulting Group, L.A., 1986-90; chief fin. officer, agribus. Roll Internat. Corp., L.A., 1990—. Bd. dirs. Westside Food Bank; mem. fin. com. 1st United Meth. Ch., Santa Monica, Calif.; active Rotary, Santa Monica. Home: 409 18th St Santa Monica CA 90402-2429 Office: Roll Internat Corp 12233 W Olympic Blvd # 380 Los Angeles CA 90064-1034

WHITTIER, MONTE RAY, lawyer; b. Pocatello, Idaho, June 28, 1955; s. Raymond Max and Marjorie Lucille (Pea) W.; m. Denise Womack, May 29, 1982; children: Jason Dennis, Sarah Michell, Sadie McKenzie. BS in Accfg., U. Utah, 1976; JD, U. Idaho, 1978. Bar: U.S. Dist. Ct. Idaho, 1979, U.S. Supreme Ct. 1985, U.S. Tax Ct. 1989, U.S. Ct. Appeals (9th cir.) 1991, Idaho, 1979. Ptnr., shareholder Whittier & Souza, Pocatello, 1979-89; shareholder, mng. atty. Whittier, Souza & Clark, Pocatello, 1989—; head pub. defender 6th Jud. Dist., 1989-95; bd. dirs. Spl. Workers Industries for Tng., Pocatello. Vol. Internat. Spl. Olympics, South Bend, Ind., 1987, Mpls., 1991; mem. Magistrate Commn. 6th Jud. Dist., Pocatello, 1989-91. Mem. Assn. Trial Lawyers Am. (bd. dirs., 6th Jud. Dist. Pro Bono award 1994), Idaho Trial Lawyers Assn. (bd. dirs.), Civitan (pres. Bannock chpt. 1983-84, bd. dirs. 1981-87, 92-93, lt. gov. Intermountain chpt. 1986-87, Outstanding Pres. award 1984, Outstanding Svc. award 1982, 83, 86, 87, 88, 91), Rotary. Office: Whittier Souza & Clark PO Box 4048 Pocatello ID 83205-4048

WHITTINGHAM, CHARLES EDWARD, thoroughbred race horse owner and trainer; b. San Diego, Apr. 13, 1913; s. Edward and Ellen (Taylor) W.; m. Peggy Boone, Oct. 12, 1944; children: Michael Charles, Charlene. Trainer thoroughbred horses, Calif., 1930-42; asst. trainer Luro Pub. Stable, N.Y., 1945-49; owner, trainer Whittingham Pub. Stable, Sierra Madre, Calif., 1949—; winner Ky. Derby with Ferdinand, 1986, with Sunday Silence, 1989. Mem. Rep. Senatorial Inner-Circle, Washington, 1983—, nat. advisor bd. Am. Security Council, Washington, 1976—; campaigner mem. Rep. Nat. Com., Washington, 1976—. Served to master sgt. USMC, 1942-45, PTO. Recipient Eclipse awards Thoroughbred Race Track Assn./Daily Racing Form/Nat. Turf Writers Assn., 1971, 82, 89; named to Nat. Racing Hall of Fame, 1974, Brietbard Hall of Fame/Hall of Champions, San Diego, 1993. Mem. Horsemens Benevolent & Protective Assn. (v.p 1976—). Republican. Roman Catholic. Home: 88 Lowell Ave Sierra Madre CA 91024-2510 Office: Charles Whittingham Inc 145 S Baldwin Ave Sierra Madre CA 91024-2556

WHITTLE, PAUL DAY, educational products manufacturing executive; b. Bronxville, N.Y., Nov. 9, 1946; s. Harold Day and Mary Agnes Whittle; children: Leslie Margaret, Matthew Day; m. Linda S. Gutman, Jan., 1993. B.B.A. magna cum laude, Midwestern U., 1971; M.B.A., U. Colo., 1972. Fin. analyst, fin. mgr. Storage Tech. Corp., Louisville, 1972-75; dir. fin., treas., controller NBI, Inc., Boulder, Colo., 1975-76; co-founder, v.p. fin., treas. PurCycle Corp., Boulder, 1976-78; sec. PurCycle Corp., 1976-82, also dir.; pres. Davis-Whittle, Denver, 1978-80; also dir. Davis-Whittle; pres. Synergetics Internat. Inc., Boulder, 1980-82; chmn. bd., chief exec. officer Synergetics Internat. Inc., 1980-84; chmn. bd., chief exec. officer, treas. Colo. Venture Capital Corp., 1981-86; pres., CEO Am. Ednl. Products, Inc., 1986—. Mem. Alpha Chi.

WHITTY, RAYMOND JOHN, hotel company executive; b. N.Y.C., Mar. 22, 1945; s. Raymond John and Agnes (Delaney) W.; m. Jacqueline Rae Howard, June 1, 1968; 1 son, Joseph. B.B.A., U. Portland, 1967. C.P.A., Wash. Acct., Peat Marwick Mitchell, Seattle, 1967-75; controller Arctic Marine Freighters div. Crowley Maritime Corp., Seattle, 1975-76; v.p., controller Westin Hotel Co., Seattle, 1976-84, sr. v.p., treas., 1984—. Trustee Seattle Children's Home, 1981-84. Mem. Am. Inst. C.P.A.s, Wash. Soc. C.P.A.s. Club: Sandpoint Country (Seattle). Office: Westin Hotel Co The Westin Bldg 2001 6th Ave Seattle WA 98121-2522

WHYTE, ROBERT ANDREW, art curator, writer; b. L.A., Jan. 27, 1931; s. James Syme and Mary Josephine (Turner) W. AA, Orange Coast Coll., 1950; BA in History of Art, UCLA, 1958; MA in History of Art, U. Calif., Berkeley, 1965. Dir. edn. San Francisco Mus. Modern Art, 1967-87; exec. dir. Mus. Italo-Americano, San Francisco, 1987-92; curator Mus. Italo Americano, San Francisco, 1992—; lectr. San Francisco State U., 1986-87. Sgt. USAF, 1951-55. Mem. Am. Assn. Mus. (curators com. 1994—, edn. com. 1976-87). Office: Mus Italo Americano Ft Mason Ctr San Francisco CA 94123

WHYTE, RONALD M., federal judge; b. 1942. BA in Math., Wesleyan U., 1964; JD, U. So. Calif., 1967. Bar: Calif. 1967, U.S. Dist. Ct. (no. dist.) Calif. 1967, U.S. Dist. Ct. (cen. dist.) Calif. 1968, U.S. Ct. Appeals (9th cir.) 1986. Assoc. Hoge, Fenton Jones & Appel, Inc., San Jose, Calif., 1971-77, mem., 1977-89; judge Superior Ct. State of Calif., 1989-92, U.S. Dist. Ct. (no. dist.) Calif., San Jose, 1992—; judge pro-tempore Superior Ct. Calif., 1977-89; lectr. Calif. Continuing Edn. of Bar, Rutter Group, Santa Clara Bar Assn., State Bar Calif.; legal counsel Santa CLara County Bar Assn., 1986-89; mem. county select com. Criminal Conflicts Program, 1988. Bd. trustees Santa Clara County Bar Assn., 1978-79, 84-85. Lt. Judge Advocate Gen.'s Corps, USNR, 1968-71. Recipient Judge of Yr. award Santa Clara County Trial Lawyers Assn., 1992, Am. Jurisprudence award. Mem. Calif. Judges Assn., Assn. Bus. Trial Lawyers (bd. govs. 1991-93). Office: US Courthouse 280 S 1st St San Jose CA 95113-3002*

WHYTE-BANKS, HILA JANE, communication technician; b. St. Joseph, Mo., Oct. 21, 1949; d. Everett Louis and Janet Lee (Biggerstaff) Whyte; m. Henry Lee Clark, Feb. 19, 1980 (div. Mar. 1984); children: Haléa Lanay Clark, Heather Lynn Clark; m. Robert Banks Jr., Jan. 2, 1985; 1 child, Robert Banks III. Student, Tarkio Coll., 1967-69; BA, Calif. State U., San Diego, 1972. Mail aide U.S. Post Office, San Diego, 1970-72; order typist Pacific Bell, San Diego, 1972-74, staff clk., 1974-78, frame attendant, 1978-80, communication technician, 1980—; factory worker Whittaker Cable Corp., St. Joseph, summer 1969; illustrator, comedy writer, dramatic writer Reflections of Real Life, San Diego, 1990—. Author musical play, song. Min. music Antioch Ch. of God in Christ, San Diego, 1976-86, Christian Compassion Ctr., San Diego, 1987—; singer Patrick Whyte Singers, San Diego, 1982—, Cox Cable TV, Christian Compassion Ctr., San Diego, 1988—, corp. officer, sec.-treas., 1993—. Scholar Tarkio Coll., 1967. Mem. Word of Faith Ch. Office: Reflections of Real Life PO Box 740422 San Diego CA 92174-0422

WIBORG, JAMES HOOKER, chemicals distribution company executive; b. Seattle, Aug. 26, 1924; s. John R. and Hazel (Hooker) W.; m. Ann Rogers, July 1948; children: Katherine Ann, Mary Ellen, Caroline Joan, John Stewart. B.A., U. Wash., 1946. Owner, Wiborg Mfg. Co., Tacoma, 1946-50; securities analyst Pacific N.W. Co., Seattle, 1950-53; founder Western Plastics Corp., Tacoma, 1953; pres. Western Plastics Corp., 1953-55, chmn. bd., dir., ret.; exec. v.p. Wash. Steel Products Co., Tacoma, 1955-58; mgmt. cons. Tacoma, 1958-60; v.p. United Pacific Corp., Seattle, 1960; pres. Pacific Small Bus. Investment Corp., Seattle, 1961-63; sr. v.p. indsl. div. United Pacific Corp., Seattle, 1963-65; pres., chief exec. officer, dir. United Pacific Corp., 1965; past pres., chief exec. officer, dir. Univar Corp. (formerly VWR United Corp.), Seattle, from 1966; chmn., chief exec. officer Univar Corp. (formerly VWR United Corp.), 1983-86, chief strategist, 1986-91, chmn., 1991—; dir., chmn., chief strategist VWR Corp., 1986—; dir. PACCAR Inc., Gensco Inc., Tacoma, Penwest Ltd., PrimeSource Corp. Clubs: Tacoma Country and Golf, Tacoma, Tacoma Yacht; Rainier (Seattle), Columbia Tower (Seattle). Office: Univar Corp PO Box 34325 Seattle WA 98124-1325

WICK, JAMES EUGENE, physician, pulmonologist; b. Dayton, Ohio, Dec. 15, 1947; s. Glenn Austin and Marjorie Maxine (McAfee) W.; m. Doris Elaine Reed. MS in Elec. Engring., U. Colo., 1971; BME, Gen. Motors Inst., 1972; MD, Med. Coll. of Ohio, 1976. Diplomate Am. Bd. Internal Medicine; bd. cert. internal medicine and pulmonary disease. Intern Presbyn. Med. Ctr., Denver, 1976-77, resident, 1977-80; fellow Ind. U. Med. Ctr., Indpls., 1980-82; pvt. practice specializing in pulmonary disease Aurora, Colo., 1983—. Fellow Am. Coll. Chest Physicians. Office: James E Wick MD PC 750 Potomac St Ste 227 Aurora CO 80011-6744

WICKER, ALLAN WERT, psychology educator; b. Elk Falls, Kans., Aug. 10, 1941; s. Lester Allen and Hazel Katherine (Clum) W.; m. Kathleen O'Brien, Feb. 5, 1973; 1 child, David Allan. BA, U. Kans., 1963, MA, 1965, PhD, 1967. Asst. prof. psychology U. Wis., Milw., 1967-69, U. Ill., Urbana, 1969-71; assoc. then prof. psychology Claremont (Calif.) Grad. Sch., 1971—. Author: Introduction to Ecological Psychology, 1979; contbr. articles to profl.jours., chpts. to books. Rsch. grantee NIMH, 1968-72, NSF, 1972-76, Haynes Found., 1985-87; Fulbright sr. lectr. Coun. for Internat. Exchange of Scholars, Zimbabwe, 1989, Ghana, 1993. Fellow Am. Psychol. Soc.; mem. Acad. Mgmt., Internat. Assn. Applied Psychology. Office: Claremont Grad Sch Ctr Orgnl and Behavioral Sci 130 E 9th St Claremont CA 91711-5907

WICKES, GEORGE, English language educator, writer; b. Antwerp, Belgium, Jan. 6, 1923; came to U.S., 1923; s. Francis Cogswell and Germaine (Attout) W.; m. Louise Westling, Nov. 8, 1975; children by previous marriage: Gregory, Geoffrey, Madeleine (dec.), Thomas, Jonathan. BA, U. Toronto, Ont., Can., 1944; MA, Columbia U., 1949; PhD, U. Calif., Berkeley, 1954. Asst. sec. Belgian Am. Ednl. Found., N.Y.C., 1947-49; exec. dir. U.S. Ednl. Found. in Belgium, 1952-54; instr. Duke U., Durham, N.C., 1954-57; from asst. prof. to prof. Harvey Mudd Coll. and Claremont Grad. Sch., Calif., 1957-70; prof. English and comparative lit. U. Oreg., Eugene, 1970—; dir. comparative lit. U. Oreg., 1974-77, head English dept., 1976-83; lectr. U.S. Info. Service, Europe, 1969, Africa, 1978, 79; vis. prof. U. Rouen, France, 1970, U. Tubingen, W. Ger., 1981. Editor: Lawrence Durrell and Henry Miller Correspondence, 1963, Henry Miller, Letters to Emil, 1989, Henry Miller and James Laughlin: Selected Letters, 1995; author: Henry Miller, 1966, Americans in Paris, 1969, The Amazon of Letters, 1976; adv. editor: N.W. Rev., 1972—; translator: The Memoirs of Frederic Mistral, 1986. Served with U.S. Army, 1943-46. Fulbright lectr. France, 1962-63, 66, 78; sr. fellow Ctr. for Twentieth Century Studies, U. Wis.-Milw., Milwaukee, 1971, Creative Writing fellow Nat. Endowment Arts, 1973, Camargo fellow, 1991. Mem. PEN. Office: U Oreg English Dept Eugene OR 97403

WICKES, MARY, actress; b. St. Louis, June 13; d. Frank A. and Mary Isabella (Shannon) Wickenhauser. A.B., D.Arts (hon.), Washington U., St. Louis; postgrad., UCLA, 1972—. Lectr. seminars on acting in comedy Coll. William and Mary, Williamsburg, Va., Washington U. at St. Louis, Am. Conservatory Theatre, San Francisco. Debut at Berkshire Playhouse, Stockbridge, Mass.; appeared in: Broadway plays Stage Door, 1936, Father Malachy's Miracle, 1937, The Man Who Came to Dinner, 1939, Jackpot (musical), 1944, Hollywood Pinafore (musical), 1945, Town House, 1948, Park Avenue (musical), 1946, Oklahoma (revival), 1979, others; numerous appearances in dramatic and musical stock, including St. Louis Mcpl. Opera, Cape Playhouse, Dennis, Mass., Bucks County Playhouse, Pa., Alliance Theater, Atlanta, The Coconut Grove Playhouse, Miami, Fla., Burt Reynolds Theatre, Jupiter, Fla., Fox Theatre, St. Louis, Mark Taper Forum, Ahmanson Theater and Chandler Pavilion, Los Angeles, Am. Shakespeare Festival, Stratford, Conn., Am. Conservatory Theater, San Francisco, Berkshire Playhouse, Mass., 1937-78; film debut in The Man Who Came to Dinner, 1942; other film appearances include Now Voyager, 1942, Higher and Higher, 1943, June Bride, 1948, Anna Lucasta, 1949, On Moonlight Bay, 1951, By the Light of the Silvery Moon, 1952, The Actress, 1953, White Christmas, 1959, The Music Man, 1962, The Trouble with Angels, 1966, Where Angels Go, Trouble Follows, 1968, Touched by Love, 1979, Postcards from the Edge, 1990, Sister Act, 1992, Sister Act II, 1993, Little Women, 1994; TV debut as Mary Poppins: other TV appearances include Studio One, 1946; regular: TV series Doc, Halls of Ivy, Lucy shows, Dennis the Menace, The Canterville Ghost, Murder, She Wrote, Wonderworks (PBS), Twigs, Highway to Heaven, others; co-star ABC series Father Dowling Mysteries, 1989-91. Mem. aux. Hosp. Good Samaritan, L.A.; chmn. Nat. Crippled Children's Soc., Mo., 1969; bd. dirs Med. Aux. Ctr. for Health Scis., UCLA, 1977—, St. Barnabas Sr. Ctr., L.A., 1994—. Recipient numerous awards including Outstanding Actress award Variety Clubs, 1967; awards for vol. work UCLA; Humanitarian award Masons; elected to St. Louis Mcpl. Opera Hall of Fame, 1987; 1st annual Starbird lectr. Washington U., St. Louis, 1988; nominated best comedy supporting-actress for Sister Act Am. Comedy awards, 1993. Mem. AFTRA, NATAS (Emmy award nomination), SAG, Actors Equity Assn., Acad. Motion Picture Arts and Scis., Phi Mu. Republican. Episcopalian.

WICKIZER, CINDY LOUISE, elementary school educator; b. Pitts., Dec. 12, 1946; d. Charles Sr. and Gloria Geraldine (Cassidy) Zimmerman; m. Leon Leonard Wickizer, Mar. 21, 1971; 1 child, Charlyn Michelle. BS, Oreg. State U., 1968. Tchr. Enumclaw (Wash.) Sch. Dist., 1968—. Mem. NEA, Wash. Edn. Assn., Enumclaw Edn. Assn., Buckley Ednl. Agrl. Coun., Buckley C. of C., Wash. Contract Loggers Assn., Am. Rabbit Breeders Assn. (judge, chmn. scholarship found. 1986-87, pres. 1988-94, dist. dir. 1994—, Disting. Svc. award 1987), Wash. State Rabbit Breeders Assn. (life, Pres.'s award 1983, 94, sec., dir., v.p. 1995—), Vancouver Island Rabbit Breeders Assn. (pres. 1984-88, 94—), Wash. State Rabbit and Cavy Shows Inc. (sec. 1994—), Wash. State Evergreen Rabbit Assn. (sec., v.p., pres.), Alpha Gamma Delta. Home: 26513 112th St E Buckley WA 98321-9258

WICKIZER, MARY ALICE See BURGESS, MARY ALICE

WICKLINE, MARIAN ELIZABETH, former chemical librarian; b. St. Louis, Feb. 18, 1915; d. William Anderson and Grace B. (Gooding) W. BA, Mills Coll., 1935; postgrad., U. Calif., Berkeley, 1935-37. Tech. files asst. Shell Devel. Co., San Francisco, 1938-45; libr. western div. Dow Chem. Co., Pitts. and Walnut Creek, Calif., 1945-75; ret., 1975. Mem. Planning Commn., Danville, Calif., 1982-86, El Dorado County Libr. Commn., Placerville, Calif., 1989-92, policy adv. com. gen. plan, 1989-92; bd. dirs. Greenstone Country Cmty. Svcs. Dist., 1994—. Named Woman of Yr. San Ramon Valley C. of C., Danville, Calif., 1983. Mem. AAUW (Gift Honoree 1982, 84), Am. Hort. Soc., Am. Chem. Soc., Spl. Libr. Assn. (pres. San Francisco Bay region chpt. 1973-74, chair chemistry divsn. 1970-71). Home: 5474 Comstock Rd Placerville CA 95667-8712

WICKLUND, LEE ARTHUR, school superintendent; b. Ft. Atkinson, Wis., Aug. 10, 1938; s. Verner F. and Ellen V. (Anderson) W.; m. Georganne Emilie Trumbull, June 27, 1964; children: Eric Trumbull, Lance Frederick. AA, Wright Jr. Coll., Chgo., 1958; BEd, Chgo. Tchrs. Coll., 1961; MEd, Loyola U., Chgo., 1964; DEd, U. Oreg., 1969. Cert. supt./prin., Oreg., Ill., Wis., Minn. Elem./secondary/adult edn. tchr., asst. prin. Chgo. Bd. Edn., 1961-67; rsch. asst. U. Oreg., Eugene, 1967-69; dir. lab. sch., asst. prof. Idaho State U., Pocatello, 1969-71; R&D specialist N.W. Regional Edn. Lab., Portland, Oreg., 1971-72; assoc. prof., ednl. adminstr. U. Wis., Superior, 1972-75; dir. curriculum and instrn. North Bend (Oreg.) Sch. Dist., 1975-89; assoc. supt. Mercer Island (Wash.) Sch. Dist., 1989-92; supt. Riverdale Sch. Dist., Portland, 1992-94; supt. in residence N.W. Regional Ednl. Lab., Portland, 1994—; chmn. Oreg. State Textbook Commn., Salem, 1981-87; sr. fellow Inst. for Devel. of Edn. Activities, Kettering, Ohio, 1977—; past chair Inter-Luth. Commn. for Continuing Edn., Tacoma, 1982-89. Chair budget com. North Bay Rural Fire Dist., North Bend, 1984-89; mem. adv. com. South Slough Natural Estuarine Res., Coos Bay, Oreg., 1984-90; sec. exec. com. United Way of S.W. Oreg., Coos Bay, 1978-83; mem. exec. com. Music Enrichment Assn., Coos Bay, 1977-81; trustee Lake Oswego (Oreg.) Libr. Bd., 1993—; bd. dirs. Slingerland Inst., vice chmn., 1989-94. Served to sgt. Ill. Air N.G., 1956-65. Mem. Am. Assn. Sch. Adminstrs., Conf. Oreg. Sch. Adminstrs. (prep. and licensure com. 1994—), Lake Oswego Rotary (pres.), Alumni Soc. Coll. Edn. U. Oreg. Lutheran. Home: 16860 Lakeridge Dr Lake Oswego OR 97034-6819 Office: NW Regional Ednl Lab 101 SW Main Ste 500 Portland OR 97204-3297

WICKMAN, PAUL EVERETT, public relations executive; b. Bisbee, Ariz., Aug. 21, 1912; s. Julius and Hilda Wilhelmina (Soderholm) W.; m. Evelyn Gorman, Nov. 22, 1969; children by previous marriage: Robert Bruce, Bette Jane, Marilyn Faye. Student, LaSierra U., Arlington, Calif., 1928-30, Pacific Union Coll., Angwin, Cal., 1931-32; spl. student, Am. U., 1946. Min., 1931-53, Internat. traveler, lectr., writer, 1937-44; assoc. sec Internat. Religious Liberty Assn., 1944-46; travel lectr. Nat. Lecture Bur., 1944-55; exec. sec., dir. internat. radio and TV prodns. Voice of Prophecy Corp., Faith for Today Corp., 1946-53; v.p. Western Advt. Agy., Los Angeles, 1953-55; dir. devel. Nat. Soc. Crippled Children and Adults, Inc., Chgo., 1955-56; exec. dir. Pub. Relations Soc. Am., Inc., N.Y.C., 1956-57; dir. corp. pub. relations Schering Corps., Bloomfield, N.J., 1957-58; pres. Wickman Pharm. Co., Inc., Calif., 1959-83, Paul Wickman Co., 1984—. Mem. Newport Beach CSC, mem. Orange County Children's Hosp. Fund; trustee Walla Walla (Wash.) Coll., 1989-91. Mem. Newcomen Soc., Pub. Rels. Soc. Am. (accredited), Internat. Platform Assn., Swedish Club (L.A., past pres.), Vikings, 552 Hoag Hosp. Club, Elks, Masons, Shriners, Royal Order Jesters, Kiwanis (past pres. Newport Beach club, lt. gov. div. 41 Cal-Neva Hi 1990-91). Home and Office: 28 Point Loma Dr Corona Del Mar CA 92625-1026

WICKWIRE, PATRICIA JOANNE NELLOR, psychologist, educator; b. Sioux City, Iowa; d. William McKinley and Clara Rose (Pautsch) Nellor; m. Robert James Wickwire, Sept. 7, 1957; 1 child, William James. BA cum laude, U. No. Iowa, 1951; MA, U. Iowa, 1959; PhD, U. Tex., Austin, 1971; postgrad. U. So. Calif., UCLA, Calif. State U., Long Beach, 1951-66. Tchr., Ricketts Ind. Schs., Iowa, 1946-48; tchr., counselor Waverly-Shell Rock Ind. Schs., Iowa, 1951-55; reading cons., head dormitory counselor U. Iowa, Iowa City, 1955-57; tchr., sch. psychologist, adminstr. S. Bay Union High Sch. Dist., Redondo Beach, Calif., 1962-82, dir. student svcs. and spl. edn.; cons. mgmt. and edn.; pres. Nellor Wickwire Group, 1981—; mem. exec. bd. Calif. Interagency Mental Health Coun., 1968-72, Beach Cities Symphony Assn., 1970-82; chmn. Friends of Dominguez Hills (Calif.), 1981-85. Lic. ednl. psychologist, marriage, family and child counselor, Calif.; pres. Calif. Women's Caucus, 1993-95. Mem. APA, AAUW (exec. bd., chpt. pres. 1962-72), Nat. Career Devel. Assn. (media chair 1992—), Am. Assn. Career Edn. (pres. 1991—), L.A. County Dirs. Pupil Svcs. (chmn. 1974-79), L.A. County Personnel and Guidance Assn. (pres. 1977-78), Assn. Calif. Sch. Adminstrs. (dir. 1977-81), L.A. County SW Bd. Dist. Adminstrs. for Spl. Edn. (chmn. 1976-81), Calif. Assn. Sch. Psychologists (bd. dirs. 1981-83), Am. Assn. Sch. Adminstrs., Calif. Assn. for Measurement and Evaluation in Guidance (dir. 1981, pres. 1984-85), ACA (chmn. Coun. Newsletter Editors 1989-91, mem. com. on women 1989-92, mem. com. on rsch. and knowledge, 1994—), Assn. Measurement and Eval. in Guidance (Western regional editor 1985-87, conv. chair 1986, editor 1987-90, exec. bd. dirs. 1987-91), Calif. Assn. Counseling and Devel. (exec. bd. 1984—, pres. 1988-89, jour. editor 1990—), Internat. Career Assn. Network (chair 1985—), Pi Lambda Theta, Alpha Phi Gamma, Psi Chi, Kappa Delta Pi, Sigma Alpha Iota. Contbr. articles in field to profl. jours.

WIDAMAN, GREGORY ALAN, financial executive, accountant; b. St. Louis, Oct. 4, 1955; s. Raymond Paul Sr. and Louise Agnes (Urschler) W. BS in Bus. Econs. cum laude, Trinity U., 1978. CPA, Tex. Sr. auditor Arthur Andersen & Co., Houston, 1978-82; sr. cons. Price Waterhouse, Houston, 1983-85; fin. advisor to segment pres. Teledyne, Inc., Century City, Calif., 1985-95; sr. mgr. consumer products ops. planning Walt Disney Co., Burbank, Calif., 1995—; cons. Arthur Andersen & Co., Price Waterhouse, Teledyne, Inc. Mem. AICPAs, Calif. Soc. CPAs, Christian Bus. Mens com. of U.S.A., World Affairs Coun., MIT/Calif. Tech. Enterprise Forum. Republican. Home: 1416 S Barrington Ave # 4 Los Angeles CA 90025-2363 Office: Walt Disney Co Ste 1500 500 S Buena Vista St Burbank CA 91521-6191

WIDDER, PATRICIA A., helicopter company research and engineering technical specialist; b. Lorain, Ohio, Jan. 30, 1953; d. James Russell and Sallie Grace (Fox) W. BS, John Carroll U., Cleve., 1975; postgrad., Ariz. State U., 1978-86, Keller Grad. Sch. Mgmt., 1992—. Programmer Gould/Sel, Williams AFB, Ariz., 1978-81; programmer, analyst USAF, Williams AFB, 1981-84; R & E specialist McDonnell Douglas Helicopter Systems, Mesa, Ariz., 1984—. Contbr. articles to profl. jours. Mem. IEEE Computer Soc., AIAA, Assn. Computing Machinery, Image Soc., Am. Def. Preparedness Assn., Am. Helicopter Soc., Nat. Computer Graphics Assn. Office: McDonnell Douglas Longbow Apache Software B340 5000 E McDowell Rd #531 Mesa AZ 85215-9797

WIDENER, PERI ANN, business development executive; b. Wichita, Kans., May 1, 1956; d. Wayne Robert and LuAnne (Harris) W. BS, Wichita State U., 1978; MBA, Fla. Tech., 1992. Advt. intern Associated Advt., Wichita, 1978; pub. rels. asst. Fourth Nat. Bank, Wichita, 1978-79; mktg. communications rep. Boeing Co., Wichita, 1979-83, pub. rels. rep., Huntsville, Ala., 1983-85, pub. rels. mgr., 1985-92; sr. pub. rels. mgr. Boeing Mil. Airplanes, Seattle, 1992-95; bus. devel. mgr. Boeing Defense & Space Group, Washington, D.C., 1995—. mem. exec. devel. program Boeing Def. & Space Group, 1993—. Preston Huston scholar, Wichita State U., 1978; recipient Best Electronic Ad award Def. Electronics mag., 1982, Best Total Pub. Rels. Program award Huntsville Press Club, 1985, Huntsville Media awards, 1986, 87, 88, 89, 90, 91, Huntsville Advt. Fedn. Addys, 1988. Mem. Pub. Rels. Soc. Am. (Seattle chpt.), Women in Communications, Pub. Rels. Coun. Ala. (bd. dirs. 1985-92, state pres. 1992, officer Huntsville chpt. 1984-91, pres. No. Ala. chpt. 1989, Excellence award 1986-91, Achievement award 1986-91, Pres.'s award Huntsville chpt. 1985, State Practitioner of Yr. 1989, PRCA Medallion award excellence, numerous others), Internat. Assn. Bus. Communicators (D2 Silver Quills award 1985, 91, D6 Silver Quills 1993, 94), Pub. Rels. Soc. Am. (accredited 1989—), So. Pub. Rels. Fedn. (practitioner of yr. 1991, Excellence award 1986-91, Lantern award 1991), Huntsville-Madison County C. of C. (pub. rels. adv. com. 1987-92), Huntsville Press Club (bd. dirs. 1989-92), Sigma Delta Chi (pres.'s award 1991). Methodist. Office: Boeing Mil Airplanes MS 4C-98 PO Box 3707 # 14 Seattle WA 98124-2207

WIDMANN, GLENN ROGER, electrical engineer; b. Newark, Jan. 8, 1957; s. Elmer and Ellen (Eccles) W. BSEE, Rutgers U., 1979; MSEE, Purdue U., 1981, PhDEE, 1988. Engr. N.J. Bell Telephone Co., Hopelawn, 1979; instr. Purdue U., West Lafayette, Ind., 1979-81, 83-88; prof. elec. engring. Colo. State U., Ft. Collins, 1989-91; engr. Hughes Aircraft Co., Canoga Park, Calif., 1980-83, scientist, project mgr., 1991-94; sr. sci. Hughes Rsch. Labs. Hughes Aircraft Co., Malibu, Calif., 1994—; cons. Bur. Reclamation, Denver, 1989, Benjamin Cummings Pub. Co., Ft. Collins, 1989; mem. program com. Internat. Symposium Robotics and Mfg., Santa Fe, N.Mex., 1991—. Contbr. articles to tech. jours.; patentee in robotics field. Recipient presentation award Am. Controls Conf., 1990. Mem. IEEE, Soc. Automotive Engrs., Tau Beta Pi, Eta Kappa Nu. Home: 3434 Delilah St Simi Valley CA 93063-2720 Office: Hughes Aircraft Co Hughes Rsch Labs MS RL 71 3011 Malibu Canyon Rd Malibu CA 90265

WIEBE, J. E. N., province official. Lt. gov. Govt. Saskatchewan, Regina, Can. Office: Government House, 4607 Dewdney Ave, Regina, SK Canada S4P 3V7

WIEBE, JOHN CLEMENT, school director; b. Ootacamund, India, Aug. 17, 1930; s. John Abraham and Viola (Bergthold) Wiebe; m. Carol Hiebert, Dec. 30, 1954; children: Wendell Wiebe-Powell, Roland Philipp, Evelyn Wiebe-Anderson, Rebecca Wiebe-Freed. AB, Tabor Coll., 1953; MA, Kans. State U. Tchr. South Humboldt Unified Dist., Miranda, Calif., 1960-65; tchr., adminstr. Kodaikanal (India) Internat. Sch., 1968-78; tchr., facilitator ARAMCO Schs., Abgaig, Saudi Arabia, 1978-83; dir., developer Lincoln Internat. Sch., Kampala, Uganda, 1984-86; dir. archeology ICRISAT, Pattancheru, India, 1972-73; coach, activity dir., 1960-86; mgmt. com. Kodaikahal Internat. Sch., 1974-78; facilitator environ. edn. ARAMCO, Saudi Arabia, 1978-83; builder, developer Lincoln Internat., Kampala, 1984-86,. Cartoonist, illustrator various publs., 1953-70; contbr. articles to profl. jours., newspapers, sport manuals, 1968—. Founder, sec. Kodaikanal Conservation Coun., 1969-75; charter mem., organizer Westhaven (Calif.) Com. Devel. Coun., 1992—. Mem. Sierra Club (exec. com. North Group Redwood chpt. 1988-89, 94—). Mem. Mennonite Ch. Home: 1026 Westhaven Dr S Trinidad CA 95570-9731

WIEBE, MICHAEL EUGENE, microbiologist, cell biologist; b. Newton, Kans., Oct. 1, 1942; s. Austin Roy and Ruth Fern (Stucky) W.; m. Rebecca Ann Doak, June 12, 1965; children: Brandon Clark, Thomas Huntington. BS, Sterling Coll., 1965; PhD, U. Kansas, 1971. Rsch. assoc. Duke U. Med. Ctr., Durham, N.C., 1971-73; asst. prof. Cornell U. Med. Coll., N.Y.C., 1973-81, assoc. prof., 1981-85; assoc. dir. rsch. and devel. N.Y. Blood Ctr., N.Y.C., 1980-83, dir. Leukocyte products, 1983-84; sr. scientist Genentech Inc., South San Francisco, Calif., 1984-88, assoc. dir. medicinal and analytical chemistry, 1988-90, dir. quality control, 1990—; mem. biol. scis. alumni adv. bd. U. Kans., 1994—. Contbr. articles to profl. jours. Mem. bd. trustees Sterling Coll., 1990—, chmn., 1994—. Postdoctoral fellow NIH, 1971-73. Mem. AAAS, Am. Soc. for Microbiology, Am. Soc. Virology, Soc. Exptl. Biology and Medicine, Parenteral Drug Assn. Presbyterian. Home: 44 Woodhill Dr Redwood City CA 94061-1827 Office: Genentech Inc 460 Point San Bruno Blvd South San Francisco CA 94080-4918

WIEBELHAUS, PAMELA SUE, school administrator, educator; b. Stanley, Wis., May 28, 1952; d. Wilbur Leroy and Marjorie Jean (Bernse) Thorne; m. Mark Robert Wiebelhaus, Apr. 27, 1985; 1 child, Sarah Jean. AS in Nursing, No. Ariz. U., 1973, BS in Gen. Home Econs., 1974. R.N. Ariz., Colo; cert. post secondary vocat. tchr., Colo. Nurse Flagstaff (Ariz.) Community Hosp., 1973-75, Children's Hosp., Denver, 1975, St. Joseph's Hosp., Denver, 1980; office nurse, surg. asst. OB-Gyn Assocs., P.C., Aurora, Colo., 1975-78; nursing coordinator perinatal services Community Hosp. Smaritan Health, Phoenix, 1978-79; nurse, mem. personnel pool Good Samaritan Hosp., Phoenix, 1979-80, J. Bains, MD, Phoenix, 1979-80; file clk. Pharm. Card Systems, Inc., Phoenix, 1979-80; office nurse S. Eisenbaum, MD, Aurora, Colo., 1980; instr., coordinator med. office program T.H. Pickens Tech. Ctr., Aurora (Colo.) Pub. Schs., 1980—; med. supr. healthfair sites, Denver, 1982-85; mem. adf. com. Emily Griffith Opportunity Sch., Denver, 1984-90; mem. survey team North Ctrl. Bd. Edn., 1985, Colo. Bd. Edn., Denver, 1987; book reviewer proposal and new edit. ins. text-reference book W.B. Saunders, 1992—. Acad. scholar No. Ariz. U., 1970, nat. def. grantee, 1970-74; PTA and Elks Club scholar, 1970. Mem. Am. Assn. Med. Assts. (cert.; membership chmn. Capitol chpt. Colo. Soc. 1981). Lutheran.

WIECHEC, DONALD, photographer; b. Phila., Jan. 28, 1943; s. Frank and Kathryn (Reinhart) W.; m. Betty Wiechec, Aug. 27, 1966. BA, U. Pitts., 1966; MFA, NYU, 1970. Asst. to program dir. Corp. for Pub. Broadcasting, N.Y.C., 1968-70; filmmaker, photographer Herman Miller, Inc., Zeeland, Mich., 1970-73; supervising producer Sandy Co., Detroit, 1974; documentary filmmaker Agoura Hills, Calif., 1975-86, photographer, 1987—. Exhibited photographs in numerous shows including purchase of portfolio for permanent exhibit Bibliotheque Nationale, France, 1992, Smithsonian Instn., 1981, High Mus. Art, Atlanta, 1970. Bd. dirs. Santa Monica (Calif.) Mountains Parkland Assn., 1986-87; mem. planning adv. com. City of Agoura Hills, 1982; del. Las Virgenes Homeowners Fedn., 1983-87. Capt. USMC, 1965-68. Grantee Sierra Club, 1970; recipient 2d prize Columbus Film Festival, 1970, Award of Excellence, 1972. Mem. DAV (life). Home and Office: 4039 Liberty Canyon Rd Agoura Hills CA 91301-3550

WIEDEN, DAN G., advertising executive; b. 1945. With Georgia-Pacific Corp., Portland, Oreg., 1967-72; free-lance writer, 1972-78; with McCann-Erickson, Portland, OR, 1978-80, William Cain, Portland, OR, 1980-82; pres. Wieden & Kennedy, Portland, OR, 1982—. Office: Wieden & Kennedy Inc 320 SW Washington St Portland OR 97204-2640*

WIEDERHOLT, WIGBERT C., neurologist, educator; b. Germany, Apr. 22, 1931; came to U.S., 1956, naturalized, 1966; m. Carl and Anna-Maria (Hoffmann) W.; student (Med. Sch. scholar), U. Berlin, 1952-53; M.D., U. Freiburg, 1955; M.S., U. Minn., 1965; children—Sven, Karen, Kristin. Intern in Ob-Gyn, Schleswig (W. Ger.) City Hosp., 1955-56; rotating intern Sacred Heart Hosp., Spokane, Wash., 1956-57; resident in medicine Cleve. Clinic, 1957-58, 60-62, U.S. Army Hosp., Frankfurt, W. Ger., 1958-59; resident in neurology Mayo Clinic, Rochester, Minn., 1962-65; assoc. prof. medicine, dir. clin. neurophysiology Ohio State U. Med. Sch., Columbus, 1966-72; prof. neuroscis. U. Calif. Med. Sch., San Diego, 1972—, neurologist-in-chief, 1973-83, chmn. dept. and group in neuroscis. 1978-83, 90-93; chief neurology VA Hosp., San Diego, 1972-79. Fulbright scholar, 1956-58. Diplomate Am. Bd. Psychiatry and Neurology. Fellow Am. Acad. Neurology (S. Weir Mitchell award 1956); mem. Internat. Brain Research Orgn., Am. Assn. EEG and Electrodiagnosis (sec.-treas. 1971-76, pres. 1977-78), AAAS, Soc. for Neurosci., Am. Neurol. Assn., Am. EGG Soc., Western EEG Soc., Calif. Neurol. Soc., San Diego Neurol. Soc., N.Y. Acad. Scis., AMA, Calif. Med. Assn., San Diego County Med. Soc. Club: La Jolla Tennis. Contbr. numerous articles to med. jours. Office: Univ Calif at San Diego Dept Neuroscis 0624 9500 Gilman Dr La Jolla CA 92093-5003

WIEDLE, GARY EUGENE, real estate management company executive; b. San Antonio, July 28, 1944; s. Eugene Wiley and Melba Frances (Keeney) W.; m. Regena Zokosky, July 7, 1977 (div. June 1983); children: Ana Lauren, Aric Brandt. AA, Coll. of the Desert, Palm Desert, Calif., 1975; BA, Calif. State U., Long Beach, 1967; MA, U. So. Calif., 1973. Lic. real estate broker, Calif.; cert. profl. community assn. mgr. Adminstrv. asst. City of Inglewood, Calif., 1967-68, asst. city mgr., 1970-74; exec. dir. Coachella Valley Assn. of Govts., Palm Desert, 1974-84; mgr. The Springs Country Club, Rancho Mirage, Calif., 1984-87; prof. polit. sci. Coll of the Desert, Palm Desert, 1987-90; owner Fortune West Mgmt., Palm Desert, 1990—; cons. polit. orgns., bus. and community groups, Riverside County, Calif., 1984—. State comdr. DAV, Dept. Calif., 1982. 1st lt. U.S. Army, 1968-70, Vietnam. Decorated Bronze Star for valor, Purple Heart, Commendation of valor. Mem. Am. Inst. Cert. Planners (cert. planner), Cmty. Assns. Inst. (pres. 1986-89), Calif. Assn. Cmty. Mgrs., Real Estate Educators Cert. Inst., Bd. Realtors Palm Desert, Am. Planning Assn., Western Govtl. Rsch. Assn., Gideons Internat. Republican. Lutheran. Home: 82-362 Gable Dr Indio CA 92201-7439 Office: Fortune West Mgmt GE Wiedle Co 73-900 El Paseo Rear Palm Desert CA 92260-4336

WIEGMAN, EUGENE WILLIAM, minister, former college administrator; b. Fort Wayne, Ind., Oct. 27, 1929; s. A. Henry and E. Catherine (McDonald) W.; m. Kathleen Wyatt, Apr. 26, 1952; children: Kathryn, Rose Marie, Mark, Jeanine, Gretchen, Matthew. BS, Concordia Coll., 1953; MS, U. Kans., 1956, EdD, 1962; grad., Pacific Luth. Theol. Sem., 1985. Tchr., coach Trinity Luth. Sch., Atchison, Kans., 1954-58; prin. tchr. St. John's Coll., Winfield, Kans., 1958-61; prof. Concordia Coll., Seward, Nebr., 1961-65; adminstrv. asst. to Rep. Clair Callan, Lincoln, Nebr., 1965-66; asst. to adminstr. fed. extension service Dept. Agr., Washington, 1966-67; dean community edn. Fed. City Coll., Washington, 1967-69; pres. Pacific Luth. U., Tacoma, 1969-75, Independent Colls. Wash., 1975-76; dir. Wash. Office Community Devel., 1977-78; commr. Dept. of Employment Security, 1978-81; exec. dir., pres., chief exec. officer Family Counseling Service of Tacoma and Pierce County, Wash., 1987—; assoc. pastor Luther Meml. Ch., Tacoma, 1987-90; pastor Gethsemane Luth. Ch., Tacoma, 1990—; dean clin. pastoral edn. Grad. Sch. of Korea, 1992—; mem. Wash. State Employment and Tng. Council; mem. cabinet Gov. of Wash., 1977-81; lectr., nat. public speaker, 1981—; pres. The Wiegman Inst., Tacoma, 1981—. Candidate for U.S. Congress from 6th dist. Wash., 1976; mem. Council on Washington's Future; exec. bd. dirs. Pacific Harbors Coun. Boy Scouts Am.; bd. dirs. Tacoma Area Urban Coalition; past chmn. Wash. Friends Higher Edn.; bd. dirs. Tacoma Urban League, Nat. Alliance Businessmen, Bellarmine Prep. Sch., Tacoma, Camp Brotherhood; trustee Tacoma Gen. Hosp., Pacific Sci. Center; mem. Commn. on Children for Tacoma and Pierce County, Coalition on Child Sexual Abuse, 1989—; mem. com. Faith Homes for Young Women; pres. Second City chamber of Tacoma. Recipient Disting. Teaching award City Winfield, Kans., 1960, Freedom Found. Teaching award, 1961, Disting. Eagle Scout award, 1982, Pres. award St. Martins Coll., 1980. Fellow Philosophy of Edn. Soc.; mem. Tacoma C. of C., N.W. Assn. Pvt. Colls., Assn. Higher Edn., Kiwanis, Phi Delta Kappa. Home: 405 N Stadium Way Tacoma WA 98403-3228

WIEMANN, JOHN MORITZ, communications educator, consultant; b. New Orleans, July 11, 1947; s. John M. and Mockie (Oosthuizen) W.; m. Mary Eileen O'Loghlin, June 7, 1969; children: Molly E., John M. BA, Loyola U., New Orleans, 1969; postgrad., NYU, 1970-71; MS, Purdue U., 1973, PhD, 1975. With employee comm. dept. IBM, East Fishkill, N.Y., 1969-71; asst. prof. comm. Rutgers U., New Brunswick, N.J., 1975-77; from asst. prof. to prof. U. Calif., Santa Barbara, 1977—, prof., 1988—, prof. comm. and Asian Am. studies, 1994—, acting vice chancellor instnl. advancement, 1994—. Editor: Nonverbal Interaction, 1983, Advancing Communication Science, 1988, Communication, Health and the Elderly, 1990, Miscommunication and the Problematic Talk, 1991, Strategic Interpersonal Communication, 1994, Interpersonal Communication in Older Adulthood, 1994; author: Competent Communication, 1995; series editor Sage Ann. Rev. Communication Rsch., 1988-94. Bd. dirs. Goleta Youth Basketball Assn., 1987-92; mem. sch. site coun. Foothill Elem. Sch., 1987-88; mem. budget adv. com. Goleta Union Sch. Dist., 1982-84. David Ross fellow Purdue U., 1975, W.K. Kellogg Found. fellow, 1980-83; Fulbright-Hayes sr. rsch. scholar U. Bristol, Eng., 1985. Mem. APA, Internat. Comm. Assn. (bd. dirs. 1988-90), Speech Comm. Assn. (bd. dirs. 1984-86), Western States Comm. Assn., Internat. Network on Personal Rels., Internat. Pragmatics Assn., Sigma Xi, Phi Kappa Phi. Democrat. Roman Catholic. Office: U Calif Dept Comm Santa Barbara CA 93106-4020

WIEMER, ROBERT ERNEST, film and television producer, writer, director; b. Highland Park, Mich., Jan. 30, 1938; s. Carl Ernest and Marion (Israelian) W.; m. Rhea Dale McGeath, June 14, 1958; children: Robert Marshall, Rhea Whitney. BA, Ohio Wesleyan U., 1959. Ind. producer, 1956-60; dir. documentary ops. WCBS-TV, N.Y.C., 1964-67; ind. producer of television, theatrical and bus. films N.Y.C., 1967-72; exec. producer motion pictures and TV, ITT, N.Y.C., 1973-84; pres. subs. Blue Marble Co., Inc., Telemontage, Inc., Alphaventure Music, Inc., Betaventure Music, Inc. ITT, 1973-84; founder, chmn., chief exec. officer Tigerfilm, Inc., 1984—; chmn., bd. dirs. Golden Tiger Pictures, Hollywood, Calif., 1988—; pres, CEO Tuxedo Pictures Corp., Hollywood, Calif., 1993—. Writer, prodr., dir.: (feature films) My Seventeenth Summer, Witch's Sister, Do Me a Favor, Anna to the Infinite Power, Somewhere, Tomorrow, Night Train to Kathmandu; exec. prodr.: (children's TV series) Big Blue Marble (Emmy and Peabody awards); dir. (TV episodes) seaQuest DSV, Star Trek: The Next Generation, Deep Space Nine, The Adventures of Superboy; composer (country-western ballad) Tell Me What To Do. Recipient CINE award, 1974, 76, 77, 79, 81, Emmy award, 1978. Mem. NATAS, ASCAP, Info. Film Producers Assn. (Outstanding Producer award), Nat. Assn. TV Programming Execs., Am. Women in Radio and TV, N.J. Broadcasters Assn., Dirs. Guild Am. Office: Golden Tiger Pictures 3896 Ruskin St Las Vegas NV 89117

WIENER, SYDNEY PAUL, investor; b. N.Y.C., Aug. 18, 1918; s. Nathan and Lillian (Fortunoff) W.; m. Charlotte Rosen, Jan. 28, 1945; children: Laura Jane Mills, Barbara Hanawalt. DMD, U. Louisville, 1943. Gen. practice dentistry Flushing, N.Y., 1947-68; pvt. investor El Cajon, Calif., 1968—; mortgage sales rep. El Cajon, 1972—; dentist Booth Meml. Hosp., Flushing, 1963-68; researcher Anti-Coronary Club N.Y.C. Dept. Health, 1962-67. Contbr. articles on coronary disease, remedial edn., intergovt. rels. to profl. jours. Past bd. dirs. Calif. Community and Jr. Colls.; bd. dirs. Calif. Community Coll. Trustees, Sacramento, 1975-89; chmn. bd. trustees Grossmont-Cuyamaca Community Coll. Dist., El Cajon, 1973-90; dep. sheriff San Diego Sheriff Aero-squadron, 1971-82; pres. El Cajon San Diego County Civic Ctr. Authority, 1973-77; fundraiser East County Performing Arts Ctr, El Cajon, cons. to bd. dirs. Capt. U.S. Army, 1941-47. Recipient Commendation, Sheriff Maricopa County, Phoenix, 1981, Sheriff San Diego County, 1981; award, City El Cajon, 1973-74, Associated Students Grossmont Coll., El Cajon, 1975, 91, Grossmont Coll. Learning Skills, 1983, Calif. Community Coll. Trustees award, 1987, Trustee Emeritus award, 1990, Cuyamaca Coll., 1990, Grossmont/Cuyamaca Community Coll. Dist., 1991. Democrat. Jewish.

WIENER, VALERIE, communications executive; b. Las Vegas, Nev., Oct. 30, 1948; d. Louis Isaac Wiener and Tui Ava Knight. BJ, U. Mo., 1971, MA, 1972; MA, Sangamon State U., 1974; postgrad., McGeorge Sch. Law, 1976-79. Producer TV show "Checkpoint" Sta. KOMU-TV, Columbia, Mo., 1972-73; v.p., owner Broadcast Assocs., Inc., Las Vegas, 1972-86; pub. affairs dir. First Ill. Cable TV, Springfield, 1973-74; editor Ill. State Register, Springfield, 1973-74; producer and talent "Nevada Realities" Sta. KLVX-TV, Las Vegas, 1974-75; account exec. Sta. KBMI (now KFMS), Las Vegas, 1975-79; nat. traffic dir. six radio stas., Las Vegas, Albuquerque and El Paso, Tex., 1979-80; exec. v.p., gen. mgr. Stas. KXKS and KKJY, Albuquerque, 1980-81; exec. adminstr. Stas. KSET AM/FM, KVEG, KFMS and KKJY, 1981-83; press sec. U.S. Congressman Harry Reid, Washington, 1983-87; adminstrv. asst Friends for Harry Reid, Nev., 1986; press sec. U.S. Senator Harry Reid, Washington, 1987-88; owner Wiener Comm. Group, Las Vegas, 1988—. Author: Power Communications: Positioning Yourself for High Visibility (Fortune Book Club main selection 1994), Gang Free: Friendship Choices For Today's Youth, 1995; contbg. writer The Pacesetter. Sponsor Futures for Children, Las Vegas, Albuquerque and El Paso, 1979-83; mem. Exec. Women's Coun., El Paso, 1981-83; mem. VIP bd. Easter Seals, El Paso, 1982; appointee, media chair Gov.'s Coun. Small Bus., 1989-93, Clark Coun. Sch. Dist. and Bus. Cmty. PAYBAC Spkrs. and Partnership Programs, 1989-93; media dir. 1990 Conf. on Women Gov. of Nev.; media chair Congl. Awards Coun., 1989-93; media chair, nat. rep. Nat. Assn. Women Bus. Owners, So. Nev., 1990-91, appointee, vice chair Gov.'s Commn. on Postsecondary Edn.; bd. dirs. Better Bus. Bureau So. Nev. Named Outstanding Vol. United Way, El Paso, 1983, SBA Nev. Small Bus. Media Advocate of Yr., 1992; recipient Woman of Achievment in Media award, 1992, numerous 1st place Nev. Press Women Media awards, 1990—, Outstanding Achievement award Nat. Fedn. Press Women, 1991, Disting. Leader award Nat. Assn. for Community Leadership, 1993, Cir. of Excellence award Las Vegas C. of C., 1993, numerous other awards. Mem. Nev. Press Women, Nat. Speakers Assn., Nat. Assn. Women Bus. Owners (Nev. Advocate of Yr. 1992), Dem. Press Secs. Assn., El Paso Assn. Radio Stas., Am. Soc. Assn. Execs., U.S. Senate Staff Club, Las Vegas C. of C. (Circle of Excellence 1993), Soc. Profl. Journalists. Democrat. Office: 1500 Foremaster Ln Ste 2 Las Vegas NV 89101-1103

WIENS, DUANE DATON, matrix-graphic design firm owner; b. Inman, Jan. 13, 1935; s. Jacob D. and Anna Marie (Dirks) W.; m. Barbara A. Hege, Nov. 5, 1959 (div. Nov. 1984); children: Brian V., David K.; m. Paula M. Streiff, Aug. 18, 1990; stepson, Luke Ouellette. Art sch. diploma, Colo. Inst. of Art, 1964. Graphic designer Hesdorfer Comml. Art, Denver, 1964-65, McCormick-Armstrong Printing, Wichita, Kans., 1965-67; co-founder, ptnr. Unit 1/ Graphic Design, Denver, 1967-78; founder, owner Matrix Internat. Assocs., Denver, 1978—. Works published in profl. jours. Inductee Hall of Fame, Colo. Inst. of Art, 1989, Nat. Hall of Fame, Nat. Assn. Trade and Tech. Schs., 1990. Mem. Art Dirs. Club of Denver. Home: 7269 S Cook Cir Littleton CO 80122-1902 Office: Matrix Internat Assocs 50 S Steele St Ste 875 Denver CO 80209-2813

WIESE, NEVA, critical care nurse; b. Hunter, Kans., July 23, 1940; d. Amil H. and Minnie (Zemke) W. Diploma, Grace Hosp. Sch. Nursing, Hutchinson, Kans., 1962; BA in Social Sci., U. Denver, 1971; BSN, Met. State Coll., 1975; MS in Nursing, U. Colo., Denvr, 1978; postgrad., U. N.Mex., 1986—. RN, N.Mex.; CCRN. Cardiac ICU nurse U. N.Mex. Hosp., Albuquerque; coord. critical care edn. St. Vincent Hosp., Santa Fe, charge nurse CCU, clin. nurse III intensive and cardiac care. Recipient Mary Atherton Meml. award for clin. excellence St. Vincent Hosp., 1986. Mem. ANA (cert. med. surg. nurse), AACN (past pres., sec. N.Mex. chpt., Clin. Excellence award 1991), N.Mex. League Nursing (past v.p., bd. dirs., sec., membership com. 1992—).

WIESER, SIEGFRIED, planetarium executive director; b. Linz, Austria, Oct. 30, 1933; came to Can., 1955; s. Florian Wieser and Michaela Josepha (Kaufmann) Wieser-Burgstaller; m. Joan Xaven Quick, Sept. 8, 1962; children: Leonard Franz, Bernard Sidney. BS in Physics, U. Calgary, Alta., Can., 1966. Lead chorus singer, dancer Landes Theatre, Linz, 1949-53; project engr. EBG, Linz, 1952-54; with Griffith Farms Ltd., Eng., 1954-55; seismic computer operator Shell Can., Calgary, 1956-61; GTA systems analyst U. Calgary, 1961-66; planetarium dir. Centennial Planetarium, Calgary, 1966-84, exec. dir., 1984-91; exec. dir. emeritus Alberta Sci. Ctr., 1991—; cons. Electro Controls, Salt Lake City, 1978-79. Contbr. articles to profl. publs. Recipient Violet Taylor award U. Calgary, 1964; Queen Elizabeth scholar Province Alta., 1961; Paul Harris fellow Rotary Internat. Mem. AAAS, Royal Astron. Soc. Can., Internat. Planetarium Soc., Can.

Planetarium Soc., Can. Mus. Assn., Alberta Coll. of Art Alumni Assn. (pres. 1991-92). Anglican. Club: Magic Circle (Calgary).

WIEST, WILLIAM MARVIN, education educator, psychologist; b. Loveland, Colo., May 8, 1933; s. William Walter and Katherine Elizabeth (Buxman) W.; m. Thelma Lee Bartel, Aug. 18, 1955; children: William Albert, Suzanne Kay, Cynthia May. BA in Psychology summa cum laude, Tabor Coll., 1955; MA, U. Kans., 1957; PhD, U. Calif., 1962. Rsch. asst. psychol. ecology U. Kans., 1955-57; rsch. asst. measurement cooperative behavior in dyads U. Calif., Berkeley, 1958-59; from asst. to assoc. prof. Reed Coll., Portland, Oreg., 1961-74, prof., 1974—; adj. investigator Ctr. Health Rsch., Portland, 1985—; project coord. WHO, Geneva, 1976-84; fgn. travel leader Assiniboine Travel, Winnipeg, Manitoba, Can., 1990-91, Willamette Internat. Travel, Portland, 1993-95; lectr. Fgn. Travel Club, Portland, 1990, 94; vis. scientist Oceanic Inst., Waimanalo, Hawaii, 1967-68; chmn. dept. psychology Reed Coll., Portland, 1973-75, 86; social sci. adv. com. Population Resource Ctr., N.Y.C., 1978—; vis. investigator Health Svcs. Rsch. Ctr., Portland, 1975-76, cons. 1976-80; com. protection human subjects Kaiser Permanente Med. Care Program, Portland, 1978-81; cons. WHO, 1980-81, U.S. Dept. Energy, 1980-83; mem. panel population study sect. HHS. Consulting editor Population and Environment, 1981—; jour. referee Health Psychology, Jour. Social Biology, Jour. Personality and Social Psychology, Memory and Cognition; contbr. articles to profl. jours. Sloan Found. Faculty Rsch. fellow, 1972-73, NSF fellow, 1975-76, USPSH fellow U. Calif., 1957-58, Woodrow Wilson Found. fellow U. Calif., 1960-61. Mem. AAAS, APHA, Am. Hist. Soc. Germans from Russia (conv. speaker 1991), Germans from Russia Heritage Soc., Am. Psychol. Assn., Population Assn. Am., Phi Beta Kappa, Sigma Xi. Home: 5009 SE 46th Ave Portland OR 97206-5048 Office: Reed Coll Psych Dept SE Woodstock Blvd Portland OR 97202

WIGGINS, CHARLES EDWARD, federal judge; b. El Monte, Calif., Dec. 3, 1927; s. Louis J. and Margaret E. (Fanning) W.; m. Yvonne L. Boots, Dec. 30, 1946 (dec. Sept. 1971); children: Steven L., Scott D.; m. Betty J. Koontz, July 12, 1972. B.S., U. So. Calif., 1953, LL.B., 1956; LL.D. (hon.) Ohio Wesleyan, 1975, Han Yang. U., Seoul, Korea, 1976. Bar: Calif. 1957, D.C. 1978. Lawyer, Wood & Wiggins, El Monte, Calif., 1956-66, Musick, Peeler & Garrett, Los Angeles, 1979-81, Pierson, Ball & Dowd, Washington, 1982-84, Pillsbury, Madison & Sutro, San Francisco, 1984; mem. 90-95th congresses from 25th and 39th Calif. Dists.; judge U.S. Ct. Appeals 9th Circuit, 1984—. Mayor City of El Monte, Calif., 1964-66; mem. Planning Commn. City of El Monte, 1956-60; mem. Commn. on Bicentennial of U.S. Constitution, 1985—, mem. standing com. on rules of practice and procedure, 1987—. Served to 1st lt. U.S. Army, 1945-48, 50-52, Korea. Mem. ABA, State Bar Calif., D.C. Bar Assn. Republican. Lodge: Lions. Office: US Ct Appeals 9th Cir 50 W Liberty St Ste 950 Reno NV 89501-1949

WIGGINS, KIM DOUGLAS, artist, art dealer; b. Roswell, N.Mex., Apr. 8, 1959; s. Walton Wray Wiggins and Barbara Jo (Chesser) Ortega; m. Mary Allison Raney, Sept. 4, 1977 (div. May 1984); children: Rebekah, Mona; m. Cynthia Meredith, Sept. 29, 1985 (div. Oct. 1994); m. Maria C. Trujillo, June 17, 1995. Student, Ea. N.Mex. U., Roswell, 77, 83, 84, San Antonio Coll., 1978, 79, Ind. Bapt. Coll., Dallas, 1982, 83, Santa Fe Inst. Fine Art, 1989. Dir. Clarke-Wiggins Fine Art, Palm Springs, Calif., 1986-89; owner, mgr. Wiggins Fine Art, Santa Fe, 1989-93, Wiggins Studio, Roswell, 1991—; cons. Mus. N.Mex., Santa Fe, 1992—, Cline Fine Art, Santa Fe, 1993—. One man shows at Altermann Morris Galleries, Houston, 1992-95; exhibited in group shows Pa. Acad. Fine Art, Phila., 1992-95, M.H. DeYoung Mus., San Francisco, 1993-95; represented in permanent collections Mus. of N.Mex., Anschutz Collection, Denver; editor: K. Douglas Wiggins: Sense of Spirit, 1993. Mem. Soc. Am. Impressionists, Coun. for Art of West, Gladney Ctr., Assurance Home. Republican. Home: 6 El Arco Iris Roswell NM 88201 Studio: Cline Fine Art 526 Canyon Rd Santa Fe NM 87501-2720

WIGGLESWORTH, DAVID CUNNINGHAM, business and management consultant; b. Passaic, N.J., Sept. 23, 1927; s. Walter Frederick and Janet (Cunningham) W.; m. Rita Domínguez, Mar. 15, 1956 (dec.); children: Mitchell Murray, Marc David, Miles Frederick, Janet Rose; m. Gayle Coates, Aug. 1, 1981; 1 child, Danielle. BA, Occidental Coll., 1950, MA, 1953; postgrad. U. de las Ams., 1954-56; PhD, U. East Fla., 1957; LHD (hon.), Arubaanse Handels Academie, 1969. Dir., Spoken English Inst., Mexico City, also lectr. Mexico City Coll., 1954-56; headmaster Harding Acad., Glendale, Calif., also lectr. Citrus Jr. Coll., 1956-58; dir. Burma-Am. Inst., Rangoon, 1958-60; project dir. Washington Ednl. Rsch. Assocs., Washington, Conakry, Guinea, Benghazi, Libya, Carbondale, Ill., 1960-64; mng. editor linguistics div. T. Y. Crowell Pub. Co., N.Y.C., 1964-66; dir. linguistic studies Behavioral Rsch. Labs., Palo Alto, Calif., 1966-67; pres. D.C.W. Rsch. Assocs. Internat., Foster City, Calif., 1967—. Author: PI/LT-Programmed Instruction/Language Teaching, 1967, Career Education, 1976, ASTD in China, 1981, Resources for Workforce Diversity, 1993; contbr. articles to profl. publs.; mem. editorial bd. Vision/Action; mem. editorial rev. bd. Human Resource Devel. Quar. Trustee, City U. L.A.; mem. adv. bd. Martin Luther King Reading Acad., L.A., Internat. Ctr. Cultural Ergonomics, 1990—; mem. tng. systems design and prodn. program adv. bd. U. Calif.-Santa Cruz; U.S. rep. Internat. Com. Human Resources Devel., Kuwait, 1990—; ordained minister Universal Life Ch., 1969. Served with U.S. Army, 1945-46, 52-54. Mem. Am. Mgmt. Assn., Orgn. Devel. Network, Am. Soc. Tng. and Devel. (bd. dirs. internat. div., named Practitioner of Yr. 1988), Internat. Fedn. Tng. and Devel. Organs. (task force), Soc. Internat. Edn. Tng. and Rsch., 1st World Congress Internat. Orgn. Devel., Orgn. Devel. Forum, Peninsula Orgn. Devel. Support, Mideast Am. Bus. Conf., World Future Soc., Peninsula Exec. Club (Los Altos), SEDUMEX (Mexico City), Benghazi Sailing Club, Orient Club (Rangoon). Office: DCW Rsch Assocs Internat PO Box 4400 San Mateo CA 94404-0400

WIGHTMAN, THOMAS VALENTINE, rancher, researcher; b. Sacramento, Oct. 7, 1921; s. Thomas Valentine and Pearl Mae (Cutbirth) W.; m. Lan Do Wightman. Student, U. Calif., Berkeley, 1945-46; B of Animal Husbandry, U. Calif., Davis, 1949; student, Cal. Poly. Inst., 1949-50. Jr. aircraft mechanic SAD (War Dept.), Sacramento, Calif., 1940-42; rancher Wightman Ranch, Elk Grove, Calif., 1950-59; machinest Craig Ship-Bldg. Co., Long Beach, Calif., 1959-70; rancher Wightman Ranch, Austin, Nev., 1970-88; dir. Wightman Found., Sacramento, 1988—. Dir. med. rsch. Staff sgt. U.S. Army, 1942-45. Recipient scholarship U.S. Fed. Govt., 1945-50. Fellow NRA, VFW, U. Calif. Alumni Assn., U. Calif. Davis Alumni Assn., Bowles Hall Assn.; mem. Confederate Air Force. Republican. Home and Office: Wightman Found PO Box 278016 Sacramento CA 95827-8016

WIGNARAJAH, KANAPATHIPILLAI, plant physiologist, researcher, educator; b. Batticaloa, Sri Lanka, Dec. 26, 1944; came to U.S., 1988; s. Sinnathoamby and Nagaratnam (Nallathamby) K.; m. Asha Vasanti Ramcharan, Aug. 2, 1984; children: Avisha Nia, Amira Tari. BS in Botany, U. Ceylon, Colombo, Sri Lanka, 1969; PhD in Plant Physiology, U. Liverpool, Eng., 1974. Asst. lectr. in botany U. Ceylon, Sri Lanka, 1969-71; rsch. assoc. agronomy dept. U. Western Australia, 1974-75; lectr. U. Malawi, Africa, 1975-76, U. West Indies, Trinidad, 1976-84; sr. lectr. U. Guyana, S. Am., 1985-86; rsch assoc. U. Wales, Bangor, United Kingdom, 1986-87; rsch. assoc. Ctr. Nat. de la Recherche Sci., Montpellier, France, 1987-88, U. Okla., Norman, 1988-89, U. Calif., Santa Cruz, 1989-90; plant scientist The Bionetics Corp., Moffett Field, Calif., 1990—; cons. Nat. Inst. for Sci. and Tech., Georgetwon, Guyana, 1985-86; Inter-Am. Inst. for Coop. in Agrl., 1985-86; reviewer for Tropical Agrl., 1980-86, Oecologia Plantarium, 1986-87, Environ. and Exptl. Botany, 1990—, Grant Proposals to NASA, 1991—. Contbr. articles to profl. jours. Sec. Ceylon Nat. Hist. Soc., Sri Lanka, 1969-71. Recipient Wheat Bd. Rsch. grant, Australian Res. Bank, Nedlands, 1974, Swedish Guest scholarship The Swedish Inst., Stockholm, 1980, King Gustav Lectr. medal U. Stockholm, 1980, Yamani Found. U. fellowship U. Wales, 1986, European Econ. Commn., Centre Nat. de la Recherche Scientifique fellowship, Montpellier, France, 1987. Fellow Indian Chem. Soc.; mem. Scandinavian Soc. Plant Physiologists, Phytochem. Soc. Europe. Hindu. Office: The Bionetics Corp Nasa Ames Rsch Ctr Moffett Field CA 94035

WIITA, KATHRYN CARPENTER, public relations company executive; b. Casper, Wyo., Sept. 15, 1961; d. Hugh Lewis and Kathryn Estelle (Pepper) Carpenter; m. Thomas A. Wiita, Sept. 1, 1991. BS in Mass Communications, U. Utah, 1983. Mcht. rep. Tracy Collins Bank & Trust, Salt Lake City, 1983-84; communications specialist Arthur Young & Co., Salt Lake City, 1984-88; officer, dir. pub. rels. 1st Interstate Bank Utah, Salt Lake City, 1988-89; pres. KC Communications, Jackson, Wyo., 1989—; cons. Mountain West Venture Group, Salt Lake City, 1984-87, Catheter Tech. Inc., Salt Lake City, 1986-89, Sta. KTVX, Salt Lake City, 1986, Inter Therapy, Inc., Costa Mesa, Calif., 1990, Stop Gap, Santa Ana, Calif., Jackson Peak Outfitters, 1992—, M W Med., 1990—, Jackson Hole Cowboy Ski Challenge, 1994; mktg. cons.Wines & Spirits, 1992—. Mem. Pub. Rels. Soc. Am. (accredited; officer 1988-89), Pub. Rels. Soc. Am. Counselors Acad., Women in Comms. (officer 1988-89), Jr. League Orange County, Calif. Inc. (pub. rels. coord. 1991-92, dir. pub. rels. c992—), Kappa Kappa Gamma. Home and office: 1630 Woodland Ter Lake Oswego OR 97034-5837

WIKER, STEVEN FORRESTER, industrial engineering educator; b. Alhambra, Calif., Sept. 29, 1952; s. Bruce Forrester and Joan (Centers) W.; m. Jody Louise Wiker, Jan. 24, 1976; children: Douglas Forrester, James McCallum. BS in Physiology, U. Calif., Davis, 1975; MS in Biol. Scis., Washington U., 1981; MS in Indsl. Engring., U. Mich., 1982, PhD in Indsl. Engring., 1986. Rsch. project officer USCG, Washington, 1976-79; rsch. asst. U. Mich., Ann Arbor, 1979-86; rsch. engr. Naval Ocean Systems Ctr. Lab., Kailua, Hawaii, 1986-87, Naval Ocean Systems Ctr., San Diego, 1987-88; asst. prof. indsl. engring. U. Wis., Madison, 1988-93, head indsl. ergonomics rsch. lab., 1989-93; assoc. prof.dept. environ. health U. Wash., Seattle, 1993; assoc. prof. Dept. Environ. Health, U. Wash., Seattle, 1993—; sr. rsch. engr. James Miller Engring., Inc., Ann Arbor, 1981-88; dirs. telerobotics lab. Wis. Ctr. for Space Automation and Robotics, 1991-93. Contbr. articles to profl. jours. Comdr. USCGR, 1976—. Recipient Achievement medal USCG, 1988, 92, Humanitarian Svc. medal, 1993; fellow Ford Motor Co., Detroit, 1983-86; grantee Nat. Inst. Occupational Safety and Health, Washington, 1979-84, NASA, Ctrs. for Disease Control. Mem. Am. Soc. Safety Engrs., Inst. Indsl. Engrs., Internat. Soc. Biomechs., Aerospace Med. Soc., Human Factors Soc., Res. Officers Assn., N.Y. Acad. Scis., Sigma Xi, Alpha Pi Mu. Office: Univ of Wash SC-34 Dept Environ Health Seattle WA 98195

WIKSTROM, KAREN, economic planner; b. Ogden, Utah, Dec. 25, 1958; d. John H. and Dorothy T. (Maher) W.; m. Erik Strindberg, Sept. 24, 1983. BA in Econs., Smith Coll., 1981; MS in Fin., U. Utah, 1988. Sr. assoc. Wallace Assoc. Consulting, Salt Lake City, 1981-86; v.p. Wallace Assocs. Consulting Group, Salt Lake City, 1986-89; pres. Wikstrom Economic & Planning Consultants, Inc., Salt Lake City, 1989—; adj. instr. U. Utah, Salt Lake City, 1989. Pres. bd. trustees ASSIST, Inc., Salt Lake City, 1984-90; mem. adv. bd. Utah Womens Bus. Devel. Coun., Salt Lake City, 1991-92; chair Salt Lake Housing Adv. Appeals Bd., Salt Lake City, 1990-93; v.p. bd. Salt Lake Cmty. Devel. Corp., 1989-90; bd. mem. Childrens Aid Soc. of Utah, Ogden, 1993-94; pres. bd. trustees ArtSpace II, Salt Lake City, 1994. Grantee Garn Inst. of Fin., 1988. Mem. Am. Inst. Cert. Planners, Am. Real Estate and Urban Econs. Assn., Am. Inst. Planners, Urban Land Inst., Alta Club. Office: Wikstrom Economic and Planning Consultants 24 S 600 E Ste 1 Salt Lake City UT 84102-1017

WILBUR, COLBURN SLOAN, foundation administrator, chief executive officer; b. Palo Alto, Calif., Jan. 20, 1935; s. Blake Colburn and Mary (Sloan) W.; m. Maria Grace Verburg, Sept. 1, 1961; children: Marguerite Louise, Anne Noelle. BA in Polit. Sci., Stanford U., 1956, MBA, 1960. Asst. cashier United Calif. Bank, San Francisco, 1960-65; v.p. Standata, San Francisco, 1965-68; adminstrv. mgr. Tab Products, San Francisco, 1968-69; exec. dir. Sierra Club Found., San Francisco, 1969-76, David and Lucile Packard Found., Los Altos, Calif., 1976—; bd. dirs., mem. adv. bd. Coun. Founds., Washington, Found. Ctr., N.Y.C. Former bd. dirs., mem. adv bd. Global Fund Women, Palo Alto, Calif.; past bd. dirs. Big Bros. San Francisco, Calif. Confederation Arts, Peninsula Grantmakers, Women's Fund Santa Clara; former bd. dirs., pres. Big Bros. Peninsula, North Fork Assn., Peninsula Conservation Ctr.; past bd. dirs., chmn. No. Calif. Grantmakers; bd. dirs., mem. adv. bd. Sierra Club Found., Stanford Theater Found., Palo Alto, U. San Francisco/Inst. Nonprofit Orgn. Mgmt. With U.S. Army, 1957-58. Office: David and Lucile Packard Found 300 2nd St Los Altos CA 94022-3621

WILBUR, LESLIE EUGENE, education educator; b. Modesto, Calif., Jan. 11, 1924; s. Horace Gilbert and Grace (King) W.; m. Norma June Lash, June 14, 1946; children: Stuart Alan, Lesley Lynn. AA, Modesto Jr. Coll., 1943; BA, U. Ill., 1948; MA, U. Calif., Berkeley, 1951; PhD, U. So. Calif., 1962. Instr. Bakersfield (Calif.) Coll, 1950-58, assoc. dean, 1958-62; pres. Barstow (Calif.) Coll., 1962-65; prof. edn. U. So. Calif., L.A., 1965-89, chmn. higher edn. dept., 1968-85, pres. faculty senate, 1972-73; cons. L.A. County Office Schs., 1966-79; dir. Pullias Lecture Programs, L.A., 1978—; v.p. So. Calif. TV Consortium, Cypress, 1976-90. Co-author: Improving English Skills, 1965, Teaching in the Community Junior College, 1972, Principles and Values for College and University Administration, 1984. With AUS, 1943-46, ETO. Recipient We Honor Ours award Calif. Tchrs. Assn., 1972; Faculty Rsch. grantee U. S.C. Sch. Edn., 1986, 87, 88. Mem. Am. Assn. for Higher Edn., Assn. for Study Higher Edn., Community Coll. Rsch. Assn. (bd. dirs. 1975—), Calif. Coll. and Univ. Faculty Assn. (pres. U. So. Calif. chpt. 1965-68). Democrat. Mem. United Ch. of Christ. Home: 1434 Punahou St Apt 1031 Honolulu HI 96822-4740

WILBUR, MARGUERITE LOUISE, redevelopment manager; b. Palo Alto, Calif., Nov. 7, 1962; d. Colburn Sloan and Maria Grace (Verberg) W.; m. John Charles Christiansen, June 27, 1987. BS, Calif. Poly. State U., 1984; M Planning, U. Va., 1986; cert. arch., landscape arch., fine arts, Ecole D'Art Americaines, France, 1983. Asst. to project mgr. Monterey (Calif.) Bay Aquarium, 1982-85; assoc. Inst. Environ. Negotiation, U. Va., Charlottesville, Va., 1985-86; devel. officer Redevel. Agy. City San Jose, Calif., 1987-89; project mgr. Redevel. Agy. City of Seaside, Calif., 1989-91; redevel. mgr. Redevel. Agy. City of Santa Cruz, Calif., 1992—; adv. mem. Santa Cruz (Calif.) County Conf. and Visitors Coun., 1993—; mem. adv. bd. Ctrl. Coast Small Bus. Devel. Corp., Santa Cruz County, 1993—. Alumni Leadership Santa Cruz County, 1992-93. Assoc. Urban Land Inst. Office: Redevel Agy City Santa Cruz 323 Church St Santa Cruz CA 95060-3811

WILCK, CARL THOMAS, public relations executive; b. Quantico, Va., May 26, 1933; s. Carl and Glennie Alma (Jones) W.; m. Tommie England, June 16, 1961 (dec. Sept. 1985); m. Nadine Bagley Henry, May 21, 1989; 1 child, Jacqueline Leigh Henry. AA, Santa Monica Coll., 1955; BA in Polit. Sci., UCLA, 1957. Pres. Thomas Wilck Assocs., L.A., 1960-70, chmn., pres.; asst. adminstr. SBA, Washington, 1971; dep. chmn. Rep. Nat. Com., Washington, 1972-73; v.p. pub. affairs Irvine Co., Newport Beach, Calif., 1973-85; pres. Thomas Wilck Assocs., Orange County, 1985—. Bd. chmn. Coro Found., L.A., 1982-83. Sgt. USMC, 1950-52, PTO. Mem. Fellow Pub. Rels. Soc. Am. (Silver Anvil award 1964, 77); mem. CORO Found. (bd. dirs.), Orange County C. of C.. Republican. Presbyterian. Office: 2600 Michelson Dr Ste 1570 Irvine CA 92715-1550 Office: Thomas Wilck Assocs 2600 Michelson Dr Irvine CA 92715-1550

WILCOCK, JOHN, TV producer, writer, editor; b. Sheffield, Eng., Aug. 4, 1927; s. Richard Barker Wilcock and Edith Clara Gambling; divorced. Grad. high sch., Halifax, Eng. Reporter Sheffield Telegraph, 1944-48, The Daily Mail, London, 1948-50, The Daily Mirror, London, 1950-52, Liberty mag., Saturday Night mag., Toronto, Ont., Can., 1952-54; asst. travel editor N.Y. Times, N.Y.C., 1957-60; producer The John and Joanna Show Wait a Minute!, N.Y.C., L.A., 1980—. Author: The Village Square, 1957, Magical and Mystical Sites, 1977, Occult Guide to South America, 1978, Traveling in Venezuela, 1978, travel books about Greece, India, Japan, California, Italy, Vancouver, Mexico and Seattle, 1960-95; West Coast editor Insight Guides. Home: 814 Robinson Rd Topanga CA 90290-3627

WILCOX, CALVIN HAYDEN, mathematics educator; b. Cicero, N.Y., Jan. 29, 1924; s. Calvin and Vara (Place) W.; m. Frances I. Rosekrans, May 29, 1947; children: Annette Faye, Victor Hayden, Christopher Grant. Student, Syracuse U., 1947-48; A.B. magna cum laude, Harvard U., 1951, A.M., 1952, Ph.D., 1955. Mem. faculty Calif. Inst. Tech., Pasadena, 1955-61; asst. prof. math. Calif. Inst. Tech., 1957-60, asso. prof., 1960-61; prof. U. Wis.-Madison, 1961-66; prof., head dept. U. Ariz., Tucson, 1966-69; prof. U. Denver, 1969-70, U. Utah, Salt Lake City, 1971—; vis. prof. U. Geneva, 1970-71, U. Liege, Belgium, 1973, U. Stuttgart, Fed. Republic Germany, 1974, 76-77, Kyoto (Japan) U., 1975, Ecole Polytechnique Fédérale, Lausanne, Switzerland, 1979, U. Bonn (W. Ger.), 1980. Author: Lectures on Scattering Theory for the d'Alembert Equation in Exterior Domains, 1975; monograph Scattering Theory for Diffraction Gratings, 1983, Sound Propagation in Stratified Fluids, 1983; Editor: Asymptotic Solutions of Differential Equations and Their Applications, 1964, Perturbation Theory and its Application in Quantum Mechanics, 1966. Served with AUS, 1945-47. NSF predoctoral fellow, 1952-53; Sr. U.S. Scientist award Alexander von Humboldt Found., W. Ger., 1976-77. Mem. AAAS, Soc. Indsl. and Applied Math., Am. Math. Soc., Math. Assn. Am. Office: Univ Utah Dept Math Salt Lake City UT 84112

WILCOX, CHARLES STEVEN, pharmacology administrator; b. June 21, 1955. BS, U. So. Calif., 1978, MPA, 1979, MBA, 1982, PhD, 1989. Spanish/English tutor Joint Ednl. Project U. So. Calif., 1976; legis. analyst Am. Petroleum Inst., Washington, 1977; asst. policy analyst Office of Planning and Rsch. Gov.'s Office, State of Calif., Sacramento, 1978; rsch. adminstr. psychopharmacology unit U. Calif., Irvine, 1978-79, adminstrv. analyst psychopharmacology unit, 1979-81; exec. dir. Psychopharmacology Rsch. Assocs., Inc., Irvine, Calif., 1981-84, Pharmacology Rsch. Inst., Long Beach, Calif., 1984—; mktg. rsch., pharm. rsch. and personnel mgmt. cons. Contbr. articles to profl. jours. Vol. L.A. Alzheimer's Assn. Speakers Bur., L.A. Mem. ASPA (life), Soc. for Clin. Trials, Regulatory Affairs Profls. Soc., Internat. Personnel Mgmt. Assn., Am. Soc. Clin. Psychopharmacology, Assocs. of Clin. Pharmacology (cert.), Pi Alpha Alpha. Home: 177 Bay Shore Ave Long Beach CA 90803-3452 Office: 3505 N Long Beach Blvd Ste 2F Long Beach CA 90807-3947

WILCOX, DEBRA KAY, lawyer; b. Colorado Springs, Colo., Sept. 7, 1955; children: Justin, Lauren. BA in English, U. No. Colo., 1977; JD, U. Denver, 1986. Bar: Colo. 1987, U.S. Dist. Ct. Colo. 1988. Rsch. analyst Colo. Legis. Coun., Denver, 1978-80, 81-83; govt. affairs staff Alliance of Am. Insurers, Chgo., 1980-81; law clk. and assoc. Rotole, Jaunarajs, Walker & Lumbye, Denver, 1986-88; of counsel Jay M. Finesilver, P.C., Denver, 1988-90, Cogswell & Eggleston, Denver, 1990, Kobayashi & Assocs., P.C., Denver, 1990-94, Pencom, Inc., Denver, 1994—; mem. jud. tchg. faculty Colo. Dept. Jud. Adminstrn., P.C., Denver, 1988, mem. state collection agy. bd., 1992. Co-author: A History of Colorado's Legislative Leaders, 1979. Recipient Arnold M. Chuktow award, U. Denver, 1986; named Outstanding Young Women in Am., 1976, 1986. Mem. ABA (mem. host com. young lawyers divsn. 1988), Colo. Bar Assn. (mem. availability of legal svcs. com.), Denver Bar Assn., Sigma Sigma Sigma (v.p. 1988-90, mem. nat. ednl. found. bd. 1990-92). Office: Pencom Inc 511 16th St Ste 400 Denver CO 80202-4229

WILCOX, MICHAEL JOHN, vision systems researcher, medical educator; b. Detroit, Mar. 20, 1948; s. Fred Edwin and LaVergne Elizabeth (Anderson) W.; m. Claudie Nicole Zamet, June 26, 1980; children: Christopher, Marc. BS, Purdue U., 1971, MS, 1976, PhD, 1980. Teaching asst. Purdue U., West Lafayette, Ind., 1972-74, rsch. assoc., 1974-80; postdoctoral fellow Fogarty Internat. Ctr., Bethesda, Md., 1980-82; chercheur associé Centre Nat. de la Recherche Scientifique, Marseille, France, 1982-83; chercheur boursié Fondation de la Recherche Medicale, Paris, 1983-84, Delduca Found., Marseille, 1984-85; asst. prof. U. P.R., Mayaguez, 1984-86, U. So. Calif., L.A., 1987-89; staff scientist Doheny Eye Inst., L.A., 1986-89; rsch. asst. prof. U. N.Mex., Albuquerque, 1989—; cons. Allergan Pharms., Irvine, Calif., 1986-89, Kirtland AFB, Albuquerque, 1990—; co-founder Interdisciplinary Computational Sys. Group, Albuquerque, 1993-95; pres. Hyperacuity Sys. Author chpts. and articles. Leader Boy Scouts Am., Albuquerque, 1989-92. NIH grantee, 1985-90; Office of Naval Rsch. grantee, 1989—. Mem. AAAS, IEEE, Assn. for Rsch. in Vision and Ophthalmology, N.Y. Acad. Scis., Am. Soc. for Cell Biology, Internat. Neural Network Soc. Office: U NMex Dept Anatomy Albuquerque NM 87131-5211

WILCOX, RHODA DAVIS, elementary education educator; b. Boyero, Colo., Nov. 4, 1918; d. Harold Francis and Louise Wilhelmina (Wilfert) Davis; m. Kenneth Edward Wilcox, Nov. 1945 (div. 1952); 1 child, Michele Ann. BA in Elem. Edn., U. No. Colo., 1941; postgrad., Colo. Coll., 1955-65. Life cert. tchr., Colo. Elem. tchr. Fruita (Colo.) Pub. Sch., 1938-40, Boise, Idaho, 1940-42; sec. civil service USAF, Ogden, Utah, 1942-43, Colorado Springs, Colo., 1943-44; sec. civil service hdqtrs. command USAF, Panama Canal Zone; sec. Tech. Libr., Eglin Field, Fla., 1945-46; elem. tchr. Colorado Springs Sch. Dist. 11, 1952-82, mem. curriculum devel. com., 1968-69; lectr. civic, profl. and edn. groups, Colo.; judge for Excellence in Literacy Coldwell Bankers Sch. Dist. 11, Colo. Coun. Internat. Reading. Assn. Author: Man on the Iron Horse, 1959, Colorado Slim and His Spectackler, 1964, (with Jean Pierpoint) Changing Colorado (Social Studies), 1968-69, Founding Fathers and Their Friends, 1971, The Bells of Manitou, 1973, (with Ben Froisland) In the Footsteps of the Founder, 1993. Mem. hist. adv. bd. State Colo., Denver, 1976; mem. Garden of the Gods master plan rev. com. City of Colorado Springs, 1987—; mem. cemetery adv. bd. City of Colorado Springs, 1988-91; mem. adv. bd. centennial com., 1971; mem. steering com. Spirit of Palmer Festival, 1986; judge Nat. Hist. Day, U. Colo., Colorado Springs, and Colo. Coll., Colorado Springs; hon. trustee Palmer Found., 1986—; mem. Am. the Beautiful Centennial Celebrations, Inc., 1992-93; active Friends of the Garden of the Gods, Friends of Winfield Scott Stratton, Friends of the Libr. Named Tchr. of the Yr., Colorado Springs Sch. Dist. 11, 1968. Mem. AAUW (Woman of Yr. 1987), Colo. Ret. Educators Assn., Colorado Springs Ret. Educators Assn., Helen Hunt Jackson Commorative Coun., Women's Ednl. Soc. Colo. Coll. Home: 1620 E Cache La Poudre St Colorado Springs CO 80909-4612

WILCOXEN, WILLIAM MERRITT, lawyer; b. Des Moines, May 19, 1932; s. Frank Crombie and Helen (Stevenson) W.; m. Lois Christensen, Oct. 22, 1955; children: Jennifer Merritt, Amy Allen, Elizabeth Corwin, Katherine Kristen. BA, Grinnell Coll., 1954; JD, U. Calif., Berkeley, 1959. Bar: Calif. 1960., U.S. Dist. Ct. Calif. (so. dist.) 1960, U.S. Supreme Ct. 1987. Dep. dist. atty. Orange County, Calif., 1960-62; pvt. practice, Laguna Beach, Calif., 1962—; lectr. U. Calif. Irvine, 1974-75. Trustee Laguna Beach Unified Sch. Dist., 1965-71; mem. Laguna Beach City Council, 1981-82; bd. dirs. Planning and Conservation League, Sacramento, 1971—. Served with U.S. Army, 1954-56. Mem. ABA, Orange County Bar Assn. (bd. dirs. 1970-75), Orange County Trial Lawyers Assn. Democrat. Congregationalist. Avocations: backpacking, swimming. Home: 499 Legion St Laguna Beach CA 92651-2555 Office: 801 Glenneyre St Ste A Laguna Beach CA 92651-2751

WILCZEK, JOHN FRANKLIN, history educator; b. San Francisco, Jan. 9, 1929; s. Leonard Matthew and Teresa Edith (Silvey) W.; m. Kuniko Akabane, Nov. 14, 1966; 1 child, Mary Theresa Wilczek. BA in History with honors, U. Calif., Berkeley, 1952; MA, U. Calif., 1953; PhD, Pacific Western U., Encino, Calif., 1978. Cert. secondary tchr., Calif. Instr. history and polit. sci. City Coll. of San Francisco, 1956-94; retired, 1995; instr. Kobe (Japan) Women's Coll., 1979-81; instr. Seido Lang. Inst., Kobe, 1979-81; sec.-treas. Tokyo TV Broadcasting Corp., San Francisco, 1975—. Author: The Teaching of Japanese History on the Community College Level, 1978. Sgt. U.S. Army, 1953-55. Mem. U. Calif. Alumni Assn. Republican. Roman Catholic. Home: 5 Windsor Dr Daly City CA 94015-3257 Office: City Coll of San Francisco 50 Phelan Ave San Francisco CA 94112-1821

WILDE, DAVID, publisher, writer; b. Hereford, Nov. 12, 1944; s. Elizabeth Lillian (Price-Slawson) W. Diploma, Kneller Hall, London, 1965; pvt. mus. studies with Carmello Pace, Malta, 1964-68; student, Cardiff (Wales) Coll. Music, 1970-71; diploma in art, Open U., Leicester, Eng., 1980; student, Lancaster (Eng.) U., 1980-81, U. N.Mex., 1984. With BBC Radio, Eng., 1975-79; resident mem. wind ensemble Loughborough (Eng.) U., 1976-79; oil field worker Western Oceanic Inc., North Sea, Scotland, 1983-84; tutor U. N.Mex., Albuquerque, 1986-88, tchr. dept. continuing edn., 1989-90; musician/composer Civic Orch., Albuquerque, 1988-89; legal rschr. Wilde & Sprague, Albuquerque, 1988-90; pub., author Wilde Pub., Albuquerque, 1989—; clerical officer Severn-Trent Water, Eng., 1972-74, Social Security, Eng., 1983. Author: In the South: The Five Year Diary of a Journey Across America, 1991, Route 66: The Five Year Diary of a Journey Across America, 1991, Wildeland: Prose, 1992, North Sea Saga, 1960s: Opera of Oil, 1993, Desert Meditations: A Fairy Tale of New Mexico, 1993, Black Innocence: The Immigrant, 1993, Poems, People, Places: Travels on My Own, 1994, Basic Horn Technique: Studies for the French Horn, 1994; editor 6 books;

actor Geronimo prodn. Turner Network TV, 1993; extra various prodns., 1969-84. rschr. SRIC, Albuquerque, 1989-94; cons. N.Mex. Bd. Appraisers, Albuquerque, 1989-90. Roman Catholic. Office: 105 Stanford Dr SE Albuquerque NM 87106-3537 also: Wilde Pub PO Box 4524 Albuquerque NM 87196-4524

WILDE, JAMES DALE, archaeologist, educator; b. Las Vegas, N.Mex., May 9, 1950; s. Ralph M. and Joyce (Anderson) W.; m. Deborah Thompson, Oct. 6, 1973 (div. 1979); 1 child, Colin James Post; m. Deborah E. Newman, June 4, 1983; children: Matthew Catlow, Russell James. BA, U. N.Mex., 1972; MA, U. Oreg., 1978, PhD, 1985. Archaeologist Deerlodge Nat. Forest, U.S. Forest Svc., Butte, Mont., 1977, Earth Tech. Corp., Seattle, 1981-82, Geo-Recon Internat., Ltd., Seattle, 1982-84; asst. dir. office pub. archaeology Brigham Young U., Provo, Utah, 1984-88, dir., 1988-95, adj. prof. dept. anthropology, 1985-95; archaeologist Hdqrs. Force Ctr. for Environ. Excellence, San Antonio, 1995—; mem. com. on archaeologist Brigham Young U., 1986-90, mem. mus. adv. com., 1990-95; mem. subcom. on antiquities legis. Utah Legislature, Salt Lake City, 1988-90. Author: Utah Avocational Archaeologist Certification Program: Teaching Guide (vols. I-III), 1988, Utah Avocational Archaeologist Certification Program: Student Handbook (vols. I-III), 1988; contbr. articles to profl. publs., encys. Mem. vestry St. Mary's Episc. Ch., Provo, 1992-95. Mem. Am. Anthropol. Assn., Soc. Am. Archaeology, Soc. Profl. Archaeologists, Utah Profl. Archaeol. Coun. (treas. 1986-88, pres. 1988-90), Am. Quaternary Assn., Sigma Xi. Democrat. Home: 7923 Moon Walk San Antonio TX 78250 Office: HQ AFCEE/ECR 8106 Chennault Rd Brooks AFB TX 78235-5318

WILDER, JAMES D., geology and mining administrator; b. Wheelersburg, Ohio, June 25, 1935; s. Theodore Roosevelt and Gladys (Crabtree) W.; children: Jaymie Deanna, Julie Lynne. Graduated high sch., Wheelersburg. Lic. real estate agt., Ohio. Real estate agt. Portsmouth, Ohio; mgr. comml. pilots, fixed base operator Scioto County Airport, Ohio; mgr. and part owner sporting goods store, Portsmouth; cons. geologist Paradise, Calif., 1973-81; pres. Mining Cons., Inc., Paradise, 1981-84; dir. geology and devel. Para-Butte Mining, Inc., Paradise, 1984-88, pres., 1988-90, pres., chief exec. officer, 1990—. Served with U.S. Army, 1956-57. Home and Office: Para-Butte Mining Inc PO Box 564 Paradise CA 95967-0564

WILDER, JENNIFER ROSE, interior designer; b. Washington, Nov. 23, 1944; d. Winfield Scott and Blanche Irene (Taylor) Wilder; m. Scott Harris Smith, 1973 (div. 1987); children: Jason W., Adam S., Molly L., Whitney W. AA, Colo. Woman's Coll., Denver, 1965, BA, 1967. Interior designer Jamaica St. Interiors, Aurora, Colo., 1969-71; mgr./interior designer Interior Systems, Denver, 1971-73; owner/interior designer Jennifer Smith Designs, Denver, 1973-85, Inside Image Ltd., Castle Rock, Colo., 1985-86; interior designer Greenbaum Home Furnishings, Bellevue, Wash., 1986-94, Westbay Interiors, Gig Harbor, Wash., 1994—; instr. Tacoma C.C., Gig Harbor, Wash., 1995—. Recipient Design for Better Living award Am. Wood Coun., Seattle, 1987, Silver Mame awards Master Bldrs. Assn., 1992, 1st place Internat. Design Competition, Shintaku Daiwa, Hokaido, Japan,1 992. Mem. Am. Soc. Interior Design. Office: Westbay Interiors 5790 Soundview Dr Gig Harbor WA 98335

WILDER, KAY MARIDEL, home economics educator; b. Seattle, July 23, 1945; d. John and Violet (Precious) Wordsworth; m. Dean B. Wilder, Aug 26, 1967 (div. Mar. 1981); 1 child, Anne Elizabeth. BA, N.W. Nazarene Coll., Idaho, 1967; MS, Simmons Coll., Mass., 1972; EdD, No. Ariz. U., 1986. Tchr. home econs. Fruitland (Idaho) High Sch., 1968, North Quincy High Sch., Quincy, Mass., 1968-72, West Windsor-Plainsboro High Sch., Princeton Junction, N.J., 1972-75, Maple Park Mid. Sch., Kansas City, Mo., 1979-81; instr. William Jewell Coll., Liberty, Mo., 1976-77; prof., chmn. dept. human environ. sci. Point Loma Nazarene Coll., San Diego, 1981—; cons. Fresh Produce Coun. Calif., L.A., 1988-89; seminar speaker Elderhostel, San Diego, 1989-92; Calif. Home Econs. Articulation Liaison Com., 1990-95; speaker Nutrition Edn. Substance Abuse and Child Abuse at workshops, 1989—, Women's Day seminar, 1994, 95. Author: Season with Love, 1985. Speaker on child abuse Assn. Christian Schs., L.A., 1991, 92, AAUW, Poway, Calif., 1992. Mem. Am. Assn. Family and Consumer Scis., Internat. Fedn. for Home Econs., Calif. assn. of Family and Consumer Sci. (bd. dirs. San Diego dist. 1988—, pres. 1991-93). Office: Point Loma Nazarene Coll 3900 Lomaland Dr San Diego CA 92106-2810

WILDERMUTH, RONALD E., public relations professional; married; two children. BA in Internat. Rels. and Sociology, St. Ambrose Coll.; MS in Pub. Rels. with honors, Am. U.; MS in Naval Sci., Naval War Coll.; honor. grad., U. Okla. Commd. ensign USN, 1968, advanced through grades to capt., 1992; line officer USS Catamount, Comphibron 5, 1968-71; pub. rels. for Navy recruiting USN, 1971-75, pub. rels. staff Office of Info. dept., 1975-78; pub. rels. officer U.S. European Command, 1978-81; student Naval War Coll., Newport, R.I., 1981-82; dep. dir. pub. rels. U.S. Atlantic Command, Norfolk, Va., 1982-84; pub. rels. advisor Joint Chiefs of Staff, 1984-86; pub. rels. dir. Naval Air Forces, Pacific Fleet, 1986-88; dir. corp. rels. The Parsons Corp., Pasadena, Calif., 1992—; spokesman, pub. rels. counselor, speech writer in field, 1984-91. Active Feline Conservation Ctr., Greater Pasadena Bus. Ptnrs., Pasadena NOW; bd. dirs., mem. exec. com. Pasadena-Foothill br. L.A. Urban League. Decorated two Meritorious Svc. medals Dept. Def., two Meritorious Svc. medals USN, Personal Achievement medal USN, Legion of Merit medal Gen. H. Norman Schwarzkopf; recipient Accolades award for cmty. svc., Easter Seals Appreciation award for cmty. svc., Navy League Appreciation award for cmty. svc., Armed Forces YMCA Appreciation award for cmty. svc., others. Mem. Pub. Rels. Soc. Am., Am. Mktg. Assn., L.A. C. of C., Pasadena C. of C. (bd. dirs., mem. exec. com.), U.S. C. of C. Office: The Parsons Corp 100 W Walnut St Pasadena CA 91124-0001

WILDFOGEL, JEFFREY ALAN, psychologist, educator; b. N.Y.C., July 3, 1950; s. Paul and Sylvia W. BA, CUNY, 1972; PhD, Stanford U., 1978. Asst. prof. psychology Baruch Coll. CUNY, N.Y.C., 1980-83; cons. prof. psychology Stanford (Calif.) U., 1983—; pres. The Mental Edge, Mountain View, Calif., 1985—; cons. Stanford U. Baseball Team, 1985-88, Women's Basketball Team, 1985-89. Mem. Nat. Speakers Assn. No. Calif. (bd. dirs. 1991-92), Assn. for Advancement of Applied Sports Psychology, Peninsula Executives Assn., Mountain View C. of C., Phi Beta Kappa. Office: The Mental Edge 201 San Antonio Cir Ste 212 Mountain View CA 94040-1234

WILENSKY, HAROLD L., political science and industrial relations educator; b. New Rochelle, N.Y., Mar. 3, 1923; s. Joseph and Mary Jane (Wainsten) W.; children: Stephen David, Michael Alan, Daniel Lewis. Student, Goddard Coll., 1940-42; AB, Antioch Coll., 1947; MA, U. Chgo., 1949, PhD, 1955. Asst. prof. sociology U. Chgo., 1951-53, asst. prof. indsl. relations, 1953-54; asst. prof. sociology U. Mich., Ann Arbor, 1954-57, assoc. prof., 1957-61, prof., 1961-62; prof. U. Calif., Berkeley, 1963-82, prof. polit. sci., 1982—, research sociologist Inst. Indsl. Relations, 1963—, project dir. Inst. Internat. Studies, 1970-90; project dir. Ctr. for German and European Studies, Berkeley, 1994—; mem. research career awards com. Nat. Inst. Mental Health, 1964-67; cons. in field. Author: Industrial Relations: A Guide to Reading and Research, 1954, Intellectuals in Labor Unions: Organizational Pressures on Professional Roles, 1956, Organizational Intelligence: Knowledge and Policy in Government and Industry, 1967, The Welfare State and Equality: Structural and Ideological Roots of Public Expenditures, 1975, The New Corporatism, Centralization, and the Welfare State, 1976, (with C.N. Lebeaux) Industrial Society and Social Welfare, 1965, (with others) Comparative Social Policy, 1985, (with L. Turner) Democratic Corporatism and Policy Linkages, 1987; editor: (with C. Arensberg and others) Research in Industrial Human Relations, 1957, (with P.F. Lazarsfeld and W. H. Sewell) The Uses of Sociology, 1967; contbr. articles to profl. jours. Recipient aux. award Social Sci. Rsch. Coun., 1962, Book award McKinsey Found., 1967; fellow Ctr. for Advanced Study in Behavioral Scis., 1956-57, 62-63, German Marshall Fund, 1978-79; Harry A. Millis rsch. awardee U. Chgo., 1950-51. Fellow AAAS; mem. Internat. Sociol. Assn., Internat. Polit. Sci. Assn., Indsl. Relations Research Assn. (exec. com. 1965-68), Soc. for Study Social Problems (chmn. editorial com.), Am. Polit. Sci. Assn., Am. Sociol. Assn. (exec. council 1969-72, chmn. com. on info. tech. and privacy 1970-72), Council European Studies (steering com. 1980-83), AAUP, ACLU. Democrat. Jewish. Office: U Calif Dept Polit Sci 210 Barrows Hall Berkeley CA 94720

WILETS, LAWRENCE, physics educator; b. Oconomowoc, Wis., Jan. 4, 1927; s. Edward and Sophia (Finger) W.; m. Dulcy Elaine Margoles, Dec. 21, 1947; children—Ileen Sue, Edward E., James D.; m. Vivian C. Wolf, Feb. 8, 1976. B.S., U. Wis., 1948; M.A., Princeton, 1950, Ph.D., 1952. Research asso. Project Matterhorn, Princeton, N.J., 1951-53, U. Calif. Radiation Lab., Livermore, 1953; NSF postdoctoral fellow Inst. Theoretical Physics, Copenhagen, Denmark, 1953-55; staff mem. Los Alamos Sci. Lab., 1955-58; mem. Inst. Advanced Study, Princeton, 1957-58; mem. faculty U. Wash., Seattle, 1958—; prof. physics U. Wash., 1962-95, prof. emeritus, 1995—; cons. to pvt. and govt. labs.; vis. prof. Princeton, 1969, Calif. Inst. Tech., 1971. Author: Theories of Nuclear Fission, 1964, Nontopological Solitons, 1989; contbr. over 170 articles to profl. jours. Del. Dem. Nat. Conv., 1968. NSF sr. fellow Weizmann Inst. Sci., Rehovot, Israel, 1961-62; Nordita prof. and Guggenheim fellow Lund (Sweden) U., also Weizmann Inst., 1976—; Sir Thomas Lyle rsch. fellow U. Melbourne, Australia, 1989; recipient Alexander von Humboldt sr. U.S. scientist award, 1983. Fellow Am. Phys. Soc., AAAS; mem. Fedn. Am. Scientists, AAUP (pres. chpt. 1969-70, 73-75, pres. state conf. 1975-76), Phi Beta Kappa, Sigma Xi. Club: Explorers. Office: U Washington Dept Physics FM 15 Seattle WA 98195

WILEY, BONNIE JEAN, journalism educator; b. Portland, Oreg.; d. Myron Eugene and Bonnie Jean (Galliher) W. BA, U. Wash., 1948; MS, Columbia U., 1957; PhD, So. Ill. U., 1965. Mng. editor Yakima (Wash.) Morning Herald; reporter, photographer Portland Oregonian; feature writer Seattle Times; war correspondent PTO AP; western feature editor AP, San Francisco; reporter Yakima Daily Republic; journalism tchr. U. Wash., Seattle, Cen. Wash. U., Ellensburg, U. Hawaii, Honolulu; mem. grad. faculty Bangkok U., Thailand, 1991; mem. faculty journalism program U. Hawaii, Honolulu, 1992—; Adminstr. Am. Samoa Coll., Pago Pago; news features advisor Xinhua News Agy., Beijing, Yunnan Normal U., Kumming, China, 1995. Mem. Women in Communications (Hawaii Headliner award 1985, Nat. Headliner award 1990), Theta Sigma Phi. Home: 1434 Punahou St Apt 722 Honolulu HI 96822-4729

WILFRIED, GRAU, hotel executive officer. Pres., c.e.o. Ramada Internat. Hotels and Resorts (sub. New World Hotels Inc.), Phoenix, Ariz. Office: Ramada Internat Hotels 3838 E Van Buren St Phoenix AZ 85008-6906

WILHELM, ROBERT OSCAR, lawyer, civil engineer, developer; b. Balt., July 7, 1918; s. Clarence Oscar and Agnes Virginia (Grimm) W.; m. Grace Sanborn Luckie, Apr. 4, 1959. B.S. in Civil Engring., Ga. Tech. Inst., 1947, M.S.I.M., 1948; J.D., Stanford U., 1951. Bar: Calif. 1952, U.S. Supreme Ct. Mem. Wilhelm, Thompson, Wentholt and Gibbs, Redwood City, Calif., 1952—; gen. counsel Bay Counties Gen. Contractors; pvt. practice civil engring., Redwood City, 1952—; pres. Bay Counties Builders Escrow, Inc., 1972-88. With C.E., AUS, 1942-46. Mem. Bay Counties Civil Engrs. (pres. 1957), Peninsula Builders Exchange (pres. 1958-71, dir.), Calif. State Builders Exchange (tres. 1971). Clubs: Mason, Odd Fellows, Eagle, Elks. Author: The Manual of Procedures for the Construction Industry, 1971, Manual of Procedures and Form Book for Construction Industry, 9th edit., 1995; columnist Law and You in Daily Pacific Builder, 1955—; author: Construction Law for Contractors, Architects and Engineers. Home: 134 Del Mesa Carmel Carmel CA 93923-7950 Office: 600 Allerton St Redwood City CA 94063-1504

WILHELMS, DON EDWARD, geologist; b. L.A., July 5, 1930; s. William Leslie and Allene Marie (Schmitt) W. BA, Pomona Coll., 1952; MA, UCLA, 1958, PhD, 1963. Geologist U.S. Geol. Survey, Menlo Park, Calif., 1962-86; ret., 1986—. Contbr. chpt.: Geology of the Terrestrial Planets, 1984, Planetary Mapping, 1990; author: The Geologic History of the Moon, 1987, To A Rocky Moon: A Geologist's History of Lunar Exploration, 1993; contbr. articles to profl. jours. With U.S. Army, 1953-55. Fellow AAAS, Am. Geophys. Union, Geol. Soc. Am. (G.K. Gilbert award 1988).

WILHITE, WILSON CECIL, JR., anesthesiology educator; b. Birmingham, Ala., Apr. 19, 1935; s. Wilson Cecil and Lorraine (Gibbs) W.; m. Patricia Sewell, Aug. 13, 1957; children: Jennifer Lee Wilhite Pierce, Tiffany Wilhite Lynch. BA, Samford U., 1956; MD, U. Ala., 1960. Diplomate Am. Bd. Anesthesiology. Intern U. Miami, Fla., 1960-61; resident in anesthesiology Wilford Hall USAF Med. Ctr., San Antonio, 1962-64; chmn. dept. anesthesiology Carraway Meth. Med. Ctr., Birmingham, 1966-82, pres. med. staff, 1975-77; vice chmn. dept. anesthesiology Bapt. Med. Ctr.-Montclair, Birmingham, 1982-83, chmn. dept., 1983-87; attending anesthesiologist Phenix Med. Park Hosp., Phenix City, Ala., 1987-89; prof. U. Tex. Med. Sch., Houston, 1989-91; prof., vice chmn. dept. anesthesiology UCLA Sch. Medicine, 1991—; nat. lectr. in field. Hon. dep. sheriff Jefferson County (Ala.) Sheriff's Dept., 1971—. Capt. M.C., USAF, 1961-66. Named Outstanding Clin. Instr. Dept. Anesthesiology, U. Tex. Med. Sch., 1990, 91. Fellow Am. Coll. Anesthesiologists; mem. Am. Soc. Anesthesiologists (bd. dirs. dist. 9 1971-80 asst. treas. 1980-85, treas. 1985-91, 1st v.p. 1991-92, pres. elect 1993, pres. 1994), Assn. Anesthesiology Clin. Dirs., So. Med. Assn., Internat. Anesthesia Rsch. Soc., Soc. Cardiovascular Anesthesiologists, Calif. Soc. Anesthesiologists (ex officio mem. bd. dirs. and ho. of dels. 1991-92), Am. Soc. Post Anesthesia Nurses (hon. life), Ala. Post Anesthesia Nurses Assn. (hon. life). Republican. Baptist. Home: PO Box 17438 Beverly Hills CA 90209-3438 Office: UCLA Sch Medicine 10833 Le Conte Ave Los Angeles CA 90024

WILK, DIANE LILLIAN, architect, educator; b. L.A., July 14, 1955; d. Stefan Piotr and Wanda Helen (Harasimowicz) W. BS in Architecture, U. So. Calif., 1977; MArch, Yale U., 1981; postgrad., Stanford U., 1981-82. Registered architect, Calif., Colo.; cert. Nat. Coun. Archtl. Registration Bds. Project designer Daniel, Mann, Johnson & Mendenhall, L.A., 1981, Boyd Jenks Architect, Palo Alto, Calif., 1982-84; project arch. HED Architects, Redwood City, Calif., 1984-86; assoc. prof. architecture U. Colo., Denver, 1986—, assoc. dir. architecture program, 1991-92. Author: Historic Denveer Guides, 1995; contbg. author: The Avant Garde and The Landscape, 1991; editor: Avant Garde; contbr. articles to profl. jours. Cellist Redwood Symphony, Redwood City, 1982-85. Recipient faculty rsch. award U. Colo. Sch. Architecture, 1988, 92; grantee Graham Found., 1989. Mem. AIA, Soc. Archtl. Historians, Tau Sigma Delta (award student chpt. 1990), Alpha Rho Chi, Alpha Lambda Delta. Office: U Colo Campus Box 126 PO Box 173364 Denver CO 80217

WILKERSON, KENNETH L., retail department stores executive. Chmn. Famous-Barr Co., St. Louis. Office: Robinson's 600 W 7th St Los Angeles CA 90017-3802

WILKES, JOHN SOLOMON, III, land commissioner; b. Birmingham, Ala., Sept. 13, 1937; s. John Solomon Jr. and Lola Louise (Day) W. BS, U.S. Mil. Acad., 1960; M in Engring., Tex. A & M U., 1966. Commd. officer U.S. Army, 1960, advanced through grades to lt. col.; dep. dist. engr. St. Louis (Mo.) Dist. Corps of Engrs., 1977-80; ret. U.S. Army, 1980; mgr. Arch Mineral Corp., St. Louis, 1980-82; campaign staff Gov. Richard D. Lamm, Colo., 1982-83; facility engr., engring. mgr. FELEC Svcs., Inc., Clear, Alaska, 1983-85; mem. State Bd. Land Commrs., Denver, 1985—; coun. mem. Colo. Natural Areas, Denver, 1985—; pres. Western States Land Commrs. Assn., Colo., 1989-90; com. mem. Colo. Geog. Names, Denver, 1993—. Precinct chair Rep. Party, Denver, 1985-90. Decorated Legion of Merit, Bronze Star medal with two oak leafs, Meritorious Svc. medal, Joint Svcs. Commendatin medal, Army Commendation medal. Mem. West Point Soc. Denver, Army Athletic Assn., Denver Coal Club, Soc. Am. Mil. Engrs., Assn. U.S. Army, West Point Alumni Assn., Engrs. Club St. Louis, U.S. Com. on Large Dams. Republican. Episcopalian. Home: Unit Y-386 9725 E Harvard Ave Denver CO 80231-3961 Office: Bd Land Commrs 1313 Sherman St Rm 620 Denver CO 80203-2236

WILKES, SHAR (JOAN CHARLENE WILKES), elementary education educator; b. Chgo., July 15, 1951; d. Marcus and Hattie (Ehrich) Wexman; 1 child, McKinnon. Student, U. Okla., 1973, U. Wyo., 1975—. Rsch. dirs., exhibit designer Nicolaysen Art Mus.-Children's Ctr., Casper, Wyo., 1984-85; tchr. Natrona County Sch. Dist. 1, Casper, Wyo., 1974—; enrichment coord. Paradise Valley Elem. Sch., 1993-94; co-coord. Children's Health Fair/Body Works Healthfair, Ptnrs. in Edn., Paradise Valley Elem. Sch./Wyo. Med. Ctr. and Blue Envelope, 1994. Author: Fantastic Phonics Food Factory. Democrat candidate Wyo. State Legis., 1986, 88; edn. chair United Way, Casper, 1988; chairperson Very Spl. Arts Festival, 1988, March of Dimes, 1989; grants person Casper Smphony, 1990; NCSD coord. Bear Trap Meadow Blue Grass Festival, 1995. Mem. NEA, LWV, Coun. Exceptional Children, Nat. Coun. Edn. Assn., Wyo. Edn. Assn., Natrona County Sch. Dist. # 1 (spelling bee coord.), Soroptimist (charter), Phi Delta Kappa (exec. bd. 1988-90), Delta Kappa Gamma. Home: 4353 Coffman Ct Casper WY 82604 Office: Natrona County Sch Dist # 1 Paradise Valley Casper WY 82604

WILKIE, DONALD WALTER, biologist, aquarium museum director; b. Vancouver, B.C., Can., June 20, 1931; s. Otway James and Jessie Margaret (McLeod) W.; m. Patricia Ann Archer, May 18, 1980; children: Linda, Douglas, Susanne. B.A., U. B.C., 1960, M.Sc., 1966. Curator Vancouver Pub. Aquarium, 1961-63, Phila. Aquarama, 1963-65; exec. dir. aquarium-mus. Scripps Instn. Oceanography, La Jolla, Calif., 1965-93, ret., 1993; aquarium cons.; sci. writer and editor naturalist-marine edn. programs. Author books on aquaria and marine ednl. materials; contbr. numerous articles to profl. jours. Mem. Am. Soc. Ichthyologists and Herpetologists, San Diego Zool. Soc. (animal health and conservation com.). Home: 4548 Cather Ave San Diego CA 92122-2632 Office: U Calif San Diego Scripps Instn Oceanography Libr 9500 Gilman Dr La Jolla CA 92093-5003

WILKIN, EUGENE WELCH, broadcasting executive; b. North Attleborough, Mass., May 14, 1923; s. Laurence Welch and Ruth Marion (Totten) W.; m. Anita Drake, Sept. 10, 1949; children: Judith Louise, Lawrence Welch 2d, Diana Lewis, William Alexander. A.B., Dartmouth Coll., 1948; postgrad., Grad. Sch. Bus. Adminstrn., Harvard, July 1963. Surety rep. Aetna Casualty Ins. Co., Boston, Providence, 1949-50; asst. to pres., graphic arts salesman J.C. Hall Co., Pawtucket, R.I., 1950-51; copywriter T. Robley Louitt Advt. Agy., Providence, 1951-52; sales rep., local sales mgr. WPRO, Providence, 1952; sales mgr. WPRO-Am-TV, 1953, nat. sales mgr. TV, 1955-61; gen. mgr. WGAN-TV, Portland, Maine, 1961-63; v.p., dir. Guy Gannett Broadcasting Services, Portland, 1963-68; dir. corporate devel. Guy Gannett Broadcasting Services, 1966-68; gen. mgr. King Broadcasting Co., Spokane, 1968-73; pres. Wilkin Broadcast Cons., Inc., 1974-90; with Wilkin Communications, 1990—. Author: Where Does Daddy Go, 1962, Broadcasting Directions, 1965. Chmn. for Maine Radio Free Europe Fund, 1963-65; pres. Northeast HEaring and Speech Ctr., Portland, 1965-68; mem. Gov.'s Com. on Voluntary Programs, 1973-75; chmn. pub. assistance com., citizens adv. bd. Wash. Dept. Social/Health Svcs.; bd. dirs., chmn. 1973 sustaining fund drive Spokane Symphony Soc.; mem. devel. com. Whitworth Coll.; ex-officio mem. devel. com. Mental Health Ctr.; chmn. pub. rels. com. United Fund; vice chmn. pub. rels. com. Retail Trade Bd. ; mem. Am. Com. on E.W. Accord/Communications sub com.; sec. ad hoc coalition Sopkane County Homeowners Assns.; pres. Los Verdes Homeowners Assn., 1993; vol. comm. United Way San Luis Obispo, 1993-94; pres. SLO Affiliate Nat. Coun. Drug & Alcohol Abuse; sr. warden St. Paul's Anglican Ch.; ; chair media com. SLO County Master Plan to Reduce Drug & Alcohol Abuse; mem. Internat. Exec. Svc. Corps. Vol. Exec. (Eastern Europe). Served to capt. C.E. U.S. Army, 1942-46, PTO. Mem. Advt. Fedn. Am. (gov. 1960, bd. dirs. 1966-67), San Juan C. of C., Nat. Assn. Broadcasters, Nat. Assn. TV Program Execs., Spokane and Inland Empire Dartmouth Alumni Assn. (pres. 1970-73), Orange County (Calif.) Dartmouth Alumni Assn. (pres. 1979-82, sec. 1982-85), Delta Upsilon (life). Home: 11 Villa Ct San Luis Obispo CA 93401-7722

WILKINS, CAROLINE HANKE, consumer agency administrator, political worker; b. Corpus Christi, Tex., May 12, 1937; d. Louis Allen and Jean Guckian Hanke; m. B. Hughel Wilkins, 1957; 1 child, Brian Hughel. Student, Tex. Coll. Arts and Industries, 1956-57, Tex. Tech. U., 1957-58; BA, U. Tex., 1961; MA magna cum laude, U. Ams., 1964. Instr. history Oreg. State U., 1967-68; adminstr. Consumer Svcs. divsn. State of Oreg., 1977-80, Wilkins Assoc., 1980—; mem. PFMC Salmon Adv. subpanel, 1982-86. Author: (with B. H. Wilkins) Implications of the U.S.-Mexican Water Treaty for Interregional Water Transfer, 1968. Dem. precinct committeewoman, Benton County, Oreg., 1964-90; publicity chmn. Benton County Gen. Election, 1964; chmn. Get-Out-the Vote Com., Benton County, 1966; vice chmn. Benton County Dem. Ctrl. Com., 1966-70; vice chmn. 1st Congl. Dist., Oreg., 1966-68, chmn., 1969-74; mem. exec. com. Western States Dem. Conf., 1970-72; vice chmn. Dem. Nat. Com., 1972-77, mem. arrangements com., 1972, 76, mem. Dem. charter commn., 1973-74; mem. Dem. Nat. Com., 1972-77, 85-89, mem. size and composition com., 1987-89, rules com., 1988; mem. Oreg. Govt. Ethics Commn., 1974-76; del., mem. rules com. Dem. Nat. Conv., 1988; 1st v.p. Nat. Fedn. Dem. Women, 1983-85, pres., 1985-87, parilamentarian, 1993-95; mem. Kerr Libr. bd. Oreg. State U., 1989-95, pres., 1994-95, Corvallis-Benton County Libr. Found., 1991—, sec., 1993, v.p., 1994—. Named Outstanding Mem., Nat. Fedn. Dem. Women, 1992. Mem. Nat. Assn. Consumer Agy. Adminstrs., Soc. Consumer Affairs Profls., Oreg. State U. Folk Club (pres. faculty wives 1989-90), Zonta (vice area bd. dirs. dist. 8 1992-94, area dir., bd. dist. 8 1994—). Office: 3311 NW Roosevelt Dr Corvallis OR 97330-1169

WILKINS, CHARLES L., chemistry educator; b. Los Angeles, Calif., Aug. 14, 1938; s. Richard and Lenore M. (McKean) W.; m. Susan J., Oct. 17, 1966; 1 child, Mark R. BS, Chapman Coll., 1961; PhD, U. Oreg., 1966. Prof. chemistry U. Nebr., Lincoln, 1967-81; prof. U. Calif., Riverside, 1981—. Office: Univ of Calif-Riverside Dept Of Chemistry Riverside CA 92521

WILKINS, ELIZABETH ANN, staff development and training consultant; b. Honolulu, June 12, 1964; d. William Ralph and Susan May (Bower) W.; 1 child, Ashley Elizabeth Wilkins Hummell. BA in History, Wash. State U., 1988; MS in Instrnl. Leadership/Curr. Devel. with distinction honors, Nat. U., San Diego, 1994. Ops. mgr. Video Unltd., Inc., Spokane, Wash., 1983-86; ops. mgr. Koala Blue, Inc., Van Nuys, Calif., 1989-90, dir. corp. stores, cons. ops. and leadership, 1990-91; sr. sales mgr. TMC/Crazy Shirts, Inc., San Diego, 1991-92; ops. cons. Hummell Chiropractic, San Diego, 1993-94; tng. and devel. mgr. CSR-West, Everett, Wash., 1995—; practicum facilitator Wash. State U., Pullman, 1987-88. Vol. Am. Cancer Soc., San Diego, 1993; student rep. Nat. U., San Diego, 1992-94; vol. donations Women's Resource Ctr., San Diego, 1994; alumni mem. Gonzaga Prep. Sch. Bldg. Found., 1987—. Leadership scholar Nat. U., 1993. Mem. ASCD, Assn. Tng. and Devel., Nat. Assn. Hist. Preservation, Assn. Early Childhood Devel., Kappa Alpha Theta (adv. bd. Zeta Rho chpt. 1994—, chmn/historian 75 yr. reunion 1987-88, sr. of yr. 1988). Republican. Home: 14406 24th Ave SE Mill Creek WA 92012

WILKINS, SHEILA SCANLON, management consultant; b. Oakland, Calif., Sept. 23, 1936; d. Michael Joseph and Joan (Daly) Scanlon; m. Thomas Wayne Wilkins, Aug. 14, 1965; children: Mary, John, Kathleen. BMusic, AB Liberal Arts maxima cum laude, Holy Names Coll., Oakland, 1958, MA in Music, 1972; MA in Ednl. Adminstrn., St. Mary's Coll., Moraga, Calif., 1983. Cert. tchr., Calif.; cert. in human resources mgmt., human resources tng. and devel. Tchr., dir. student activities Vallejo (Calif.) Unified Sch. Dist., 1962-63; tchr. Berkeley (Calif.) Unified Sch. Dist., 1963-66; pub. rels. asst. Alta Bates Hosp., Berkeley, 1973-74; tchr., adminstr. Walnut Creek (Calif.) Sch. Dist., 1974-80; dist. tchg. Moraga Sch. Dist., 1980-83; tech. tng. adminstr. Crocker Nat. Bank, Walnut Creek, Calif., 1984-85; tng. officer Wells Fargo Bank, Concord, Calif., 1985-86; tng. mgr. Fab 3 Intel Corp, Livermore, Calif., 1986-91; orgn. cons. CIS ops. Intel Corp, Folsom, Calif., 1991-92; mgr. profl. devel. corp. edn. Intel Corp, Santa Clara, Calif., 1992-94; prin. The Wilkins Group, Walnut Creek, Calif., 1994—. Contbr. articles to profl. jours. Chair parent com. Boy Scouts Am., Concord, 1977-80; pres. Parents Club of St. Francis Sch., Concord, 1978-79; v.p. Parents Club of Carondelet High Sch., Concord, 1983-84. Mem. ASTD, Nat. Soc. Performance and Instrn. (v.p. fin. 1988-89, pres. 1989-91), No. Calif. Human Resources Coun., Inst. Mgmt. Cons. Home: 2182 Gill Port Ln Walnut Creek CA 94598-1150 Office: 712 Bancroft Rd Ste 250 Walnut Creek CA 94598-1531

WILKINSON, FRANCES CATHERINE, librarian, educator; b. Lake Charles, La., July 20, 1955; d. Derrell Fred and Catherine Frances (O'Toole) W.; div.; 1 child, Katrina Frances. BA in Communication with distinction, U. N.Mex., 1982, MPA, 1987; MLS, U. Ariz., 1990. Mktg. rsch. auditor Mktg. Rsch. N.Mex., Albuquerque, 1973-78; freelance photographer, 1974-75; libr. supr. gen. libr. U. N.Mex., Albuquerque, 1978-89, libr., asst. dept.

head, 1989-90, libr., dept. head, 1990—; cons., trainer ergonomics univs. and govt. agys. across U.S., 1986—; bd. dirs. Friends of U. N.Mex. Librs., Aubuquerque, 1991—; mediator Mediation Alliance, 1991-94. Contbr. articles to profl. jours. Counselor, advocate Albuquerque Rape Crisis Ctr., 1981-84. Mem. ALA (mem. com. 1990—), N.Am. Serials Interest Group (mem. com. 1994—), N.Mex. Libr. Assn., N.Mex. Preservation Alliance, (vice chair 1995—), Phi Kappa Phi (chpt. treas. 1991-92, chpt. pres. 1992-94), Pi Alpha Alpha. Home: PO Box 8102 Albuquerque NM 87198-8102 Office: U NMex Gen Libr Acquisitions and Serials Dept Albuquerque NM 87131

WILKINSON, JOAN KRISTINE, nurse, pediatric clinical specialist; b. Rochester, Minn., June 15, 1953; d. A. Ray and Ruth Audrey (Wegwart) Kubly; m. Robert Morris Wilkinson, June 14, 1975; children: Michael Robert, Kathryn Ann. BS in Nursing, U. Wis., 1975; MS, U. Colo., 1986. RN. Team leader Mendota Mental Health Inst., Madison, Wis., 1975-76; care leader Boulder (Colo.) Psychiat. Inst., 1976-78; pub. health nurse, head nurse Rocky Mountain Poison Ctr., Denver, 1978-83; research teaching asst. U. Colo. Health Scis. Ctr., Denver, 1986-87. Disaster nurse ARC, Boulder, 1976—; participant community service United Way, Denver, 1981-84; vol. nurse Channel 9 Health Fair, Boulder, 1983. Fellow U. Colo. Health Scis. Ctr., 1986; recipient Recognition cert. ARC, Madison, 1978, Gold award United Way, Denver, 1981, Outstanding Citizen award Boulder, 1990, Torch award for outstanding leader Girl Scouts, 1995. Mem. Colo. Nurses Assn. (dist. 12 scholar 1983-86), Am. Nurses Assn., World Health Assn., Sigma Tau Theta. Lutheran. Home: 1195 Hancock Dr Boulder CO 80303-1101 Office: U Colo Health Scis Ctr Sch Nursing 9th and Colorado Denver CO 80206

WILL, GARY DEAN, JR., director of public safety; b. Silverton, Oreg., Jan. 29, 1961; s. Gary Dean and Mary Louise (Bockelman) W.; m. Tamara Lynn Luther, Dec. 19, 1981; children: Kristina S. M., Rebecca E. A., Gary Dean III, Shelby Donald. Student, Southwestern Oreg. C.C., 1985-87; AS, Clackamas Community Coll., 1988; student, Ea. Oreg. State Coll., 1988-94. Police officer, reserve, cadet City of Hubbard, Oreg., 1976-82; police officer City of Molalla, Oreg., 1983-84, City of Toledo, Oreg., 1984-85, City of Coquille, Oreg., 1985-87; chief of police City of Gervais, Oreg., 1987-89, City of Elgin, Oreg., 1989-91; police officer City of Umatilla, Oreg., 1991, City of Sweet Home, Oreg., 1991-92; dir. pub. safety City of Klawock, Alaska, 1992—; chairperson So. S.E. LEPC, Klawock, 1993-95. Mem. Alaska State Emergency Response Commn., 1994—. With Alaska Army N.G., 1994—. Recipient Non-criminal lifesaving award Oreg. Peace Officers Assn., 1988. Mem. Internat. Assn. Chiefs of Police, Nat. Assn. Chiefs of Police, Oreg. Assn. Chiefs of Police, Alaska Assn. Chiefs of Police. Democrat. Roman Catholic. Home: 801 B Spring St PO Box 138 Klawock AK 99925-0138 Office: Klawock Dept Pub Safety 650 Hemlock St PO Box 113 Klawock AK 99925-0113

WILL, JOHN EMMETT, electrical engineer; b. Rome, N.Y., Nov. 2, 1960; s. Robert F. and Verda E. (House) W.; m. Barbara J. Byrne, May 4, 1984; children: David J., Daniel R. BA in Physics, SUNY, Geneseo, 1983; BSEE, Clarkson U., 1983; MSEE, Syracuse U., 1990; postgrad., Colo. U., 1992—. Cert. engr., Colo. Mem. staff to sr. staff to assoc. Rome Rsch. Corp., Verona, N.Y., 1983-88; sr. scientist, office mgr. JAYCOR, Rome, 1988-90; sr. scientist JAYCOR, Colorado Springs, Colo., 1990-93, prin. scientist, 1993—; mem. office of sec. of def. high power microwave exec. steering group, Rome, 1988-90. Co-inventor: Auto-arrester, 1994. N.Y. state regents scholar, 1978-82. Mem. IEEE, IEEE EMC Soc. (chmn. Pike Peak sect. 1994—), N.Y. Acad. Scis., Armed Forces Comm. and Electronics Assn., Sigma Pi Sigma, Tau Beta Pi, Eta Kappa Nu, Eta Kappa Nu. Home: 8415 Avens Cir Colorado Springs CO 80920-5710 Office: JAYCOR 25 N Cascade Ave Ste 300 Colorado Springs CO 80903

WILLARD, H(ARRISON) ROBERT, electrical engineer; b. Seattle, May 31, 1933; s. Harrison Eugene and Florence Linea (Chelquist) W.; BSEE, U. Wash., 1955, MSEE, 1957, PhD, 1971. Staff assoc. Boeing Sci. Research Labs., Seattle, 1959-64; rsch. assoc. U. Wash., 1968-72, sr. engr. and rsch. prof. applied physics lab., 1972-81; sr. engr. Boeing Aerospace Co., Seattle, 1981-84; dir. instrumentation and engring. MetriCor Inc. (previously Tech. Dynamics, Inc.), 1984—. Served with AUS, 1957-59. Lic. profl. engr., Wash. Mem. IEEE, Am. Geophys. Union, Phi Beta Kappa, Sigma Xi, Tau Beta Pi. Contbr. articles to tech. jours. Patentee in field. Office: 17525 NE 67th Ct Redmond WA 98052-4939

WILLARD, JAMES DOUGLAS, health care administrator; b. St. Edward, Nebr., Aug. 13, 1945; s. Merrell and Eloise Vanell (Andreasen) W.; m. Sylvia Lawrence, Jan. 2, 1970; children: James Christopher, Elizabeth. BS, Colo. State U., 1967; MHA, U. Minn., 1972. Asst. adminstr. People to People Health Found (HOPE), Washington, 1968-70; assoc. dir. Comprehensive Health Plan Agy., Worcester, Mass., 1973-74; v.p., adminstr. Luth. Med. Ctr., Wheat Ridge, Colo., 1974-80, exec. v.p., 1980-82, pres., 1982—, chief exec. officer, 1984—, also dir.; bd. dirs. InterHealth, 1985—, Luth. Hosp. Assn. Am., 1986—, Lakeside Nat. Bank. Bd. dirs. MetroNet; trustee Winter Park Recreation Assn. Mem. AHA (del. region 8 policy bd. 1988—, sect. for met. hosps. governing bd.), Colo. Hosp. Assn. (bd. dirs. 1986—). Presbyterian. Lodge: Rotary of Denver. Office: Luth Med Ctr 8300 W 38th Ave Wheat Ridge CO 80033-6005

WILLARD, ROBERT EDGAR, lawyer; b. Bronxville, N.Y., Dec. 13, 1929; s. William Edgar and Ethel Marie (Van Ness) W.; m. Shirley Fay Cooper, May 29, 1954; children: Laura Marie, Linda Ann, John Judson. B.A. in Econs., Wash. State U., 1954; J.D., Harvard U., 1958. Bar: Calif. 1959. Law clk. to U.S. dist. judge, 1958-59; pvt. practice L.A., 1959-82; assoc. firm Flint & Mackay, 1959-61; pvt. practice, 1962-64; mem. firm Willard & Baltaxe, 1964-65, Baird, Holley, Baird & Galen, 1966-69, Baird, Holley, Galen & Willard, 1970-74, Holley, Galen & Willard, 1975-82, Galvin & Willard, Newport Beach, Calif., 1982-86; pvt. practice Newport Beach, 1987-89; mem. firm Davis, Punelli Keathley & Willard, Newport Beach, 1990—; Dir. various corps. Served with AUS, 1946-48, 50-51. Mem. ABA, Los Angeles County Bar Assn., State Bar Calif., Assn. Trial Lawyers Am., Am. Judicature Soc., Acacia Frat. Congregationalist. Club: Calcutta Saddle and Cycle. Home: 1840 Oriole Dr Costa Mesa CA 92626-4758

WILLARDSON, ROBERT KENT, physicist, manufacturing technology executive; b. Gunnison, Utah, July 11, 1923; s. Anthony Robert and Alice Eva (Pierce) W.; m. Beth Marie Bennett, Sept. 12, 1947; children: Amanda Marie Ballou, Elizabeth Ann Engar, Jennie Lynette. B.S. in Physics, Brigham Young U., 1949; M.S. in Solid State Physics, Iowa State U., 1951. Asst. chief phys. chemistry div. Battelle Meml. Inst., Columbus, Ohio, 1951-60; gen. mgr. electronic materials div. Bell & Howell Co., Pasadena, Calif., 1960-72; pres. Electronic Materials Corp., Pasadena, 1973; sales mgr., sr. scientist Cominco Am. Inc., Spokane, Wash., 1973-82; pres. Willardson Cons., Spokane, 1982-84; pres., dir. Cryscon Techs. Inc., Phoenix, 1984-87; tech. dir. EniChem Ams., Inc., Phoenix, 1988-91; pres. Willardson Cons., 1991—. Editor: Compound Semiconductors, 1962; Semiconductors and Semimetals, 52 vols., 1966—. Served as sgt. USAF, 1942-46. Mem. Am. Phys. Soc., IEEE (sr., chmn. San Gabriel chpt. 1967-68), Am. Chem. Soc., Electrochem. Soc. Democrat. Mormon. Home: 12722 East Spokane WA 99216-0327

WILLBANKS, ROGER PAUL, publishing and book distributing company executive; b. Denver, Nov. 25, 1934; s. Edward James and Ada Gladys (Davis) W.; m. Beverly Rae Masters, June 16, 1957; children: Wendy Lee, Roger Craig. B.S., U. Denver, 1957, M.B.A., 1965. Economist, bus. writer, bus. forecaster Mountain States Tel. Co., Denver, 1959-66; dir. pub. relations Denver Bd. Water Commrs., 1967-70; pres. Royal Publs. Inc., Denver, 1971—, Nutri-Books Corp., Denver, 1971—, Inter-Sports Book and Video, 1986—. Editor Denver Water News, 1967-70, Mountain States Bus., 1962-66. Mem. Gov. of Colo.'s Revenue Forecasting Com., 1963-66. Served with U.S. Army, 1957-58. Recipient Pub. Rels. award Am. Water Works Assn., 1970, Leadership award Nat. Inst. of Nutritional Edn., 1989, Medal of Freedom, U.S. Senate, 1994. Mem. Am. Booksellers Assn., Nat. Nutritional Foods Assn., Pub. Rels. Soc. Am. (charter mem. health sect.), Denver C. of C., SAR. Republican. Lutheran. Clubs: Columbine Country, Denver Press, Auburn Cord Duesenberg, Rolls Royce Owners, Classic Car of Am., Denver U. Chancellor's Soc., Ferrari. Address: Royal Publs Inc PO Box 5793 Denver CO 80217-5793

WILLBANKS, SUE SUTTON, investor, writer, artist; b. Luling, Tex., Sept. 24, 1935; d. William Herbert and Melba Ophelia (Ward) Sutton; m. Charles Walter Willbanks, Nov. 21, 1953 (dec. Feb. 1979); children—Jill Ann, Brenda Kay. B.S., Tex. Tech. U., 1955; M.A., U. Tex. Permian Basin, 1980. Cert. secondary, vocat. and elem. tchr., Tex. Tchr., Big Spring Ind. Sch. Dist., Tex., 1964-68, 1972-79, dept. chmn., 1980-82; owner, pres. Sutwill Co., Tucson, Ariz., 1981—; pvt. practice psychotherapy, Tex., Hawaii, Ariz., 1979—. Author short stories and poems. Contbr. articles to profl. jours. Organizer Silver Heels Vol. Fire Dept., Howard County, Tex., 1970-71; bd. dirs. Permian Basin Planned Parenthood Assn., Odessa, Tex., 1980-82; co-leader N.W. support group Multiple Sclerosis Soc., Tuczon, Ariz., 1990—; organist Immaculate Heart of Mary Ch., Big Spring, Tex., 1975-78. Methodist. Avocations: interior decorating, acting. Home: 6644 N Amahl Pl Tucson AZ 85704-1212

WILLER, KENNETH HENRY, library director; b. Buffalo, N.Y., May 24, 1954; s. Harold and Ruth (Kroll) W. BA, SUNY, Buffalo, 1977, MLS, 1984. Audiovisual technician Sunbird Teleproductions, Williamsville, N.Y., 1978; acct. exec. Beam-Cast, Inc., Buffalo, 1979-81; sales and mktg. rep. Wine Merchants, Ltd., Buffalo, 1981-82; asst. to head of circulation SUNYAB Health Scis. Libr., Buffalo, 1983-84; asst. slide libr. Albright-Knox Art Gallery, Buffalo, 1984; reference/media libr. Medaille Coll., Buffalo, 1984-85; med. info. svcs. coord. L.I. Libr. Resources Coun., Inc., Stony Brook, N.Y., 1985-87; libr. United Hosp. Fund N.Y., N.Y.C., 1987-90; libr., cons. Tech. Engring. Libr., Lockheed Missile and Space Co., Sunnyvale, Calif., 1990; dir. Med. Resource Facility Los Gatos, Calif., 1990—. Host, producer: (cable TV show) Here's To Your Health!, 1991—. Pub. speaker local healthcare support groups, Santa Clara Valley, Calif., 1992—. Mem. Am. Libr. Assn., Med. Libr. Assn., Spl. Libr. Assn. Home: 1649 Brookvale Dr # 1 Sunnyvale CA 94087-2134 Office: Med Resource Fclt Los Gatos 815 Pollard Rd Los Gatos CA 95030-1438

WILLEY, CHARLES WAYNE, lawyer; b. Dillon, Mont., Oct. 7, 1932; s. Asa Charles and Elizabeth Ellen Willey; m. Helene D., July 21, 1962 (div.); children: Stephen Charles, Heather Helene, Brent David, Scott D.; m. Alexis W. Grant, Jan. 26, 1986. BS with honors, Mont. State U., 1954; JD with high honors, U. Mont., 1959. Bar: Mont. 1959, Calif. 1960, U.S. Ct. Claims 1975, U.S. Tax Ct. 1975, U.S. Ct. Appeals (9th cir.) 1959, U.S. Ct. Appeals (Fed. cir.) 1983, U.S. Supreme Ct. 1972. Law clk. to presiding judge U.S. Ct. Appeals (9th cir.), 1959-60; ptnr. Price, Postel & Parma, Santa Barbara, Calif., 1960-77; pvt. practice Santa Barbara, 1977-91; ptnr. Willey & Beckerman, Santa Barbara, 1991—; instr. Santa Barbara City Coll., 1961-63, U. Calif., Santa Barbara, 1963-64, prof. law corp. now mem. of Willey & Beckerman; lectr. Mont. Tax Inst., 1990, 92, Am. Agr. Law Assn. Chief editor Mont. Law Rev., 1958-59. Pres. Legal Aid Found. Santa Barbara, 1970; mem. Laguna Blanca Sch. Bd., pres. 1980-81; v.p. Phoenix of Santa Barbara. Served to capt. USAF, 1954-56. Mem. Santa Barbara County Bar Assn. (pres. 1972-73), Phi Kappa Phi, Phi Eta Sigma, Phi Delta Phi. Republican. Episcopalian. Lodge: Kiwanis. Office: 812 Presidio Ave Santa Barbara CA 93101-2210

WILLEY, ELIZABETH LOU, lawyer, advanced practice nurse; b. Salt Lake City, Oct. 7, 1952; d. Walter Wilson and Dorothy Leola (Ryan) W.; m. Dale Stephen Vranes, July 23, 1993. BSN, U. Utah, 1976; M Nursing in Physiol., U. Wash., 1979; JD, U. Utah, 1989. Lic. nurse clinician, Utah; bar: Utah, U.S. Dist. Ct. Utah 1990, U.S. Ct. Appeals (D.C. cir.) 1992. ICU primary nurse Children's Med. Ctr., Salt Lake City, 1976-77; staff nurse ICU Holy Cross Hosp., Salt Lake City, 1979; faculty Coll. of Nursing Brigham Young U., Provo, Utah, 1979-89; assoc. law clk. Strong & Hanni, 1987—; mem. State Bd. Nursing, 1981-87, chmn. edn. com., 1983-84, mem. rules and regulations com., edn. com., 1983-87, chmn. state bd., 1984-87; mem. Nursing Leadership Forum, 1984-87; chmn. Utah State Bd. Nursing Entry into Practice Task Force, Nat. Coun. state Bds. Nursin Entry into Practice Com., 1985-86; mem. SBN/UNA Ad Hoc Com., Nurse Practice Act, 1983-84; lectr. in field. Author: (with others) Risk Management in Health Care: An Updated Service, 1990; contbr. articles to profl. jours. NIH Nursing Edn. grantee, 1978; recipient Outstanding Young Women of Am. award 1983, Outstanding Young Women award Bountiful (Utah) Jaycee Aux., 1983, Tchr. of Yr. award Utah Student Nurses Assn., 1985, 86, Nurse Visible in Politics award Utah Nurse Assn., 1987. Mem. ABA, ANA, Salt Lake County Bar Assn., Washington D.C. Bar, Utah Bar Assn., Utah Nurses' Assn., Mortar Bd., Sigma Theta Tau, Phi Kappa Phi. Democrat. Mem. LDS Church. Office: Strong & Hanni 600 Boston Bldg Salt Lake City UT 84110-3810

WILLHIDE, GARY L., educational administrator; b. Chambersburg, Pa., Oct. 6, 1944; s. Leon Seaton and Annabelle (Nye) W. BS in Edn., Shippensburg U., 1966, MS in Communications, 1974. Staff writer, bur. chief Harrisburg (Pa.) Patriot-News, 1966-70; asst. dir., then dir. pub. rels. Shippensburg U. Pa., 1970-88; dir. pub. affairs Oreg. Inst. Tech., Klamath Falls, 1988—; founding bd. dirs., treas., exec. com. Coll. and Univ. Pub. Rels. Assn. Pa., 1976-88; chair pub. info. adv. com. Pa. Assn. Colls. and Univs., 1983-88; chair pub. rels. coun. Pa. State System Higher Edn., Harrisburg, 1985-87. Mem. Cumberland County Bicentennial Commn., Carlisle, Pa., 1970-76; vice chair Cumberland County Drug/Alcohol Commn., Carlisle, 1983-88; mem., treas. Klamath County HIV-AIDS Coun., 1988-90; mem. adv. bd. Stepping Stones Treatment Ctr., Klamath Falls, 1989-94, v.p., 1991, pres., 1992-94. Recipient Disting. Svc. award Cumberland County Drug/Alcohol Commn., 1987. Mem. Am. Assn. State Colls. and Univs. (pub. info. adv. com. 1990-92, 93—), Coun. Advancement and Support of Edn. Home: 2525 Yonna St Klamath Falls OR 97601-1263 Office: Oreg Inst Tech 3201 Campus Dr Klamath Falls OR 97601-8801

WILLHITE, CALVIN CAMPBELL, toxicologist; b. Salt Lake City, Apr. 27, 1952; s. Jed Butler and Carol (Campbell) W.; m. Tandra Pauline Jorgensen, Aug. 14, 1982. BS, Utah State U., 1974, MS, 1977; PhD, Dartmouth Coll., 1980. Toxicologist USDA, Berkeley, Calif., 1980-85; toxicologist Dept. Health Services, State of Calif., Berkeley, 1985—; adj. assoc. prof. toxicol. Utah State U., 1984-94. Contbr. articles on birth defects to profl. jours. Nat. Inst. Child Health and Human Devel. grantee, 1985, 89, 92, March of Dimes Birth Defects Found. grantee, 1987-91, Hoffman LaRoche grantee, 1992-94. Mem. Soc. Toxicology (mem. program com. 1995—, Frank R. Blood award 1986), Teratology Soc. (chair pub. affairs), Am. Conf. Govt. Indsl. Hygienists (TLV com.). Republican. Mem. United Ch. of Christ. Home: 2863 Sanderling Dr Fremont CA 94555 Office: State Calif 700 Heinz Ave Berkeley CA 94710-2721

WILLIAMS, ANGELITA SOPHIA, acquisitions negotiator; b. San Antonio, Apr. 2, 1964; d. Herbert Jr. and Ligaya Williams. BA in Sociel Sci., U. Calif., Berkeley, 1987; MBA, Calif. Poly. State U., 1991. Asst. store mgr., purchasing asst., advt. coord. Cost Plus Imports, Oakland, Calif., 1987-89; lab. asst. mgr. Calif. Poly. State U., San Luis Obispo, 1990-91; intern KSBY Action News/NBC News, San Luis Obispo, 1990-91; sr. buyer, contractor adminstr. IBM, San Jose, Calif., 1991-94; acquisition negotiator Bank of Am. NT & SA, Concord, Calif., 1994—. Asst. campaign mgr. Dist. 28 Assembly, San Jose, 1993-94; vol. March of Dimes, 1995—. Mem. NAFE, Oakland SPCA, Commonwealth Club (San Francisco).

WILLIAMS, ANTHONY MICHAEL, cell biologist; b. Syracuse, N.Y., Aug. 22, 1947; s. Earl Charles and Olga Josephine (Rebec) W. AA, Onondaga C.C., Syracuse, 1967; BA, Syracuse U., 1969, BS, 1987, PhD, 1992. Dishwasher Century Club, Syracuse, 1970-80; electronics technician Instruments for Cardiac Rsch., Liverpool, N.Y., 1981-84; cell biologist Oreg. Health Sci. U., Portland, 1991—. Author: Treatise on Biomembranes, Vol. 5, 1994. Active Coun. of Pk. Friends, Syracuse. Mem. AAAS, Am. Soc. Cell Biology. Home: 9060 SW Oleson Rd D5 Portland OR 97223 Office: Oreg Health Sci Univ Sam Jackson Pk Portland OR 97201

WILLIAMS, ARTHUR COZAD, broadcasting executive; b. Forty Fort, Pa., Feb. 12, 1926; s. John Bedford and Emily Irene (Poyck) W.; m. Ann Cale Bragan, Oct. 1, 1955; children: Emily Williams Van Hoorickx, Douglas, Craig. Student, Wilkes U., 1943-44; B.A. cum laude, U. So. Calif., 1949. With Kaiser Aluminum, 1949, Sta. KPMC, 1950-51; v.p., mgr. KFBK and KFBK-FM Radio Stas., Sacramento, 1951-80; with public relations dept. Sacramento Bee, McClatchy Newspapers, 1981-86; dir.-treas. Norkal Opportunities, Inc.; pres. Sacramento Bee Credit Union. Served with AUS, 1944-46. Mem. Sigma Delta Chi. Clubs: Rotary, Sutter, Valley Hi Country, Masons, Shriners. Home: 1209 Nevis Ct Sacramento CA 95822-2532 Office: 1125 Brownwyk Dr Sacramento CA 95822-1028

WILLIAMS, BEN FRANKLIN, JR., mayor, lawyer; b. El Paso, Tex., Aug. 12, 1929; s. Ben Franklin and Dorothy (Whitaker) W.; m. Daisy Federighi, June 2, 1951; children: Elizabeth Lee, Diane Marie, Katherine Ann, Benjamin Franklin III. BA, U. Ariz., 1951, JD, 1956. Bar: Ariz. 1956. With Bd. Immigration Appeals, Dept. Justice, 1957, ICC, 1959; pvt. practice Tucson, Ariz., 1956—; city atty. Douglas and Tombstone, 1962; atty. Mexican consul, 1960; mayor of Douglas, 1980-88; bd. dirs. Ariz. Pub. Service Co. Pres. Ariz. League Cities and Towns, pres. Douglas Sch. Bd., 1963, 69, 70; mem. bd. Ariz. Dept. Econ. Planning and Devel.; bd. dirs. Ariz.-Mex. Commn., Ariz. Acad. (Town Hall), Merabank & Ariz. Pub. Service Co.; ward committeeman Douglas Republican Com., 1962. Served to 1st lt. AUS, 1951-53. Mem. ABA, Internat. Bar Assn., Ariz. Bar Assn. (treas. 1963), Cochise County Bar Assn. (pres. 1959), Pima County Bar Assn., Am. Judicature Soc., U. Ariz. Law Coll. Assn. (dir.), Ariz. Hist. Soc. (dir.), Sigma Nu, Phi Delta Phi, Blue Key. Episcopalian. Lodge: Elks. Home: 6555 N St Andrews Dr Tucson AZ 85718-2615 Office: 3773 E Broadway Blvd Tucson AZ 85716-5409

WILLIAMS, BETTY LOURENE, volunteer, manager, consultant; b. Topeka, Oct. 3, 1934; d. Jim and Catherine (Sears) Lewis; m. Herman Williams, Sept. 22, 1950; children: Herm Jr., Danny Clay, Iris Angela, John Joseph, Steve Arnold. AA, Compton Coll., 1988. Lic. real estate agt., Calif. Lumbleau Real Estate Sch. Kindergarten, music tchr. St. Catherine Cath. Mission Sch., Guthrie, Okla., 1956-57; real estate agt. Diamond Realty, Compton, Calif., 1964-65; office mgr. J & H Clin. Lab., Inglewood, Calif., 1967-71; exam clk. typist Fed. Office of Personnel Mgmt., L.A., 1981, consulting adminstrv. coord., designer of office ops. system, 1983; vol. Harbor Chpt. AAKP, Long Beach, Calif., 1979—; office orgn., cons. Inglewood Chpt., 1989—; kidney peer patient counseling. Author: (book of poems) Expressions, 1988. Mem. NAACP, Compton, Calif. Br., 1992; mem. Congl. hearing com. Nat. Urologic and Kidney Diseases Adv. Bd. for West Coast, L.A., 1988; organizer Tng. Seminar for So. Calif. State Rehab. Dept., 1988. Recipient Shirley Berman Nat. Outstanding Vol. of Yr. award, 1992, Award for 20 Yrs. of Outstanding Svc., Am. Assn. for Kidney Patients; grantee McDonald Douglas to purchase van for patients, 1993. Mem. Am. Assn. Kidney Patients, Normal Bridge Club (sec. 1986-87), Am. Bridge Assn. (L.A. unit 1986—). Democrat.

WILLIAMS, CHARLES D., bishop. Bishop of Alaska Ch. of God in Christ, Anchorage. Office: Ch of God in Christ 2212 Vanderbilt Cir Anchorage AK 99508-4563

WILLIAMS, CHARLES JUDSON, lawyer; b. Sam Mateo, Calif., Nov. 23, 1930; s. John Augustus and Edith (Babcock) W.; children: Patrick, Victoria, Apphia. AB, U. Calif.-Berkeley, 1952, LLB, 1955. Bar: Calif. 1955, U.S. Supreme Ct. 1970. Assoc. Kirkbride, Wilson, Harzfeld & Wallace San Mateo County, Calif. 1956-59; sole practice Solano County, Calif., 1959-64, Martinez, Calif., 1964—, Benicia, Calif. 1981-88; city atty. Pleasant Hill, Calif., 1962-80, Yountville, Calif., 1965-68, Benicia, 1968-76, 80-82, Lafayette, Calif. 1968—, Moraga, Calif., 1974-92, Danville, Calif., 1982-88, Pittsburg, Calif., 1984-93, Orinda, Calif., 1985—; lectr. Calif. Continuing Edn. Bar 1964-65, U. Calif. Extension 1974-76, John F. Kennedy U. Sch. Law 1966-69; spl. counsel to various Calif. cities; legal advisor Alaska Legis. Council 1959-61; advisor Alaska sup. ct. 1960-61; advisor on revision Alaska statues 1960-62; atty. Pleasant Hill Redevel. Agy. 1978-82; sec., bd. dirs. Vintage Savs. & Loan Assn., Napa County, Calif., 1974-82; bd. dirs. 23d Agrl. Dist. Assn., Contra Costa County, 1968-70. Author: California Code Comments to West's Annotated California Codes, 3 vols. 1965, West's California Code Forms, Commercial, 2 vols., 1965, West's California Government Code Forms, 3 vols., 1971, supplement to California Zoning Practice, 1978, 80, 82, 84, 85, 87, 89, 91, 92, 94, 95; contbr. articles to legal jours. Mem. ABA, Calif. Bar Assn., Contra Costa County Bar Assn., Mt. Diablo Bar Assn. Office: 1320 Arnold Dr Ste 160 Martinez CA 94553-6537

WILLIAMS, CHARLES LINWOOD (BUCK WILLIAMS), professional basketball player; b. Rocky Mount, N.C., Mar. 8, 1960; s. Moses and Betty Williams. Student, U. Md. Basketball player New Jersey Nets, NBA, 1981-89, Portland Trail Blazers, 1989—. Mem. U.S. Olympic Team, 1980, NBA All-Rookie Team, 1982; player NBA All-Star Games, 1982, 83, 86; named NBA Rookie of Yr., 1982; named to NBA All-Defensive Team, 1990, 91. Office: Portland Trail Blazers Port of Portland Bldg 700 NE Multnomah St Ste 600 Portland OR 97232-4106*

WILLIAMS, CINDY J., actress; b. Van Nuys, Calif., Aug. 22, 1947; d. Bechard J. and Frances (Bellini) W.; m. William Louis Hudson, May 1, 1982; children: Emily, Zachary. Grad. high sch., Van Nuys. Film appearances include Travels With My Aunt, American Graffiti, The Conversation, More American Graffiti, Rude Awakening, 1989, Bingo; regular in TV series Laverne and Shirley, Normal Life; TV movies include Tricks of the Trade, 1990, Murder at the PTA Luncheon, 1990; producer motion picture Father of the Bride, 1991, The Laverne & Shirley Reunion Special, 1995. Active Actors and Others for Animals, Los Angeles, Greenpeace, Nature Conservancy. Nominated Best Supporting Actress Brit. Acad. Awards, London, 1974; named Honorary Citizen Office of Mayor, New Orleans, 1977, Honorary Mem. Teamsters Union, Milw., 1979, Hon. Texan Office of Gov., Austin, 1987, Disting. Alumni Calif. Jr. Colls., 1987; recipient Hon. Commendation medal U.S. Marine Corps, 1977, Award of Appreciation Blinded Vets Adminstrn., 1979. Democrat. Roman Catholic.

WILLIAMS, CLARENCE, protective services official; b. Shreveport, La., Oct. 1, 1945; s. Leonard and Hearlean (Willis) W.; m. Mary K. Mannings, Nov. 30, 1974 (div. 1982); 1 child, Makala Deloris; m. Paulette Maria Guyton, Nov. 9, 1991; children: Kevin Michael, Maleah Requal. Student, So. U., 1963-64, Seattle C.C., 1968. Aerospace mechanic Boeing Aircraft Co., Seattle, 1965-68; fire fighter Seattle Fire Dept., 1968-76, engr., driver, 1976-82, emergency med. tech., 1976—, lt., 1982—; accreditation inspector Nat. Fire Protection Assn., Quincy, Mass., 1990—. Chmn. bd. trustees Mt. Zion Bapt. Ch., Seattle, 1992—; active Leadership Tomorrow, Seattle, 1986—, N.W. Conf. Black Pub. Ofcls., Wash., 1980—. With Wash. NG, 1965-71. Named one of Outstanding Young Men Am., 1978, 81, Most Outstanding Fire Fighter in State of Wash. Wash. State Jaycees, 1979; recognized for furthering cause of human rights UN Assn. U.S.A., 1979. Mem. Internat. Assn. Black Profl. Fire Fighters (pres. 1984-88), NAACP (membership com. 1976), Seattle Urban League (scholarship com. 1978), Seattle Black Fire Fighters Assn. (pres. 1968), So. U. Alumni Assn. Democrat. Office: Internat Assn Black Profl Fire Fighters PO Box 22005 Seattle WA 98122-0005

WILLIAMS, DARLEEN DOROTHY, librarian; b. Bay City, Mich., May 8, 1938; d. Albert Carl and Irene Dorothy (Szafran) Fritz; m. Joe Lee Williams, June 2, 1966; children: Julie Ann, Amy Louise Williams Huggins. Student, Bay City Jr. Coll., 1956-57; BA, Cen. Mich. U., 1959; MALS, U. Mich., 1963; postgrad., Cath. U. Am., Washington, D.C., 1965, U. Ariz., 1989, No. Ariz. U., 1990. Cert. secondary tchr., Ariz., libr., Ariz. Asst. libr. Handy High Sch., Bay City, 1959-63; libr. Gibson Jr. High Sch., Las Vegas, Nev., 1963-66; asst. reference libr. U. Nev., Reno, 1966-70; interlibr. loan libr. Case Western Res. U., Cleve., 1970-71, assoc. libr., 1971-72; libr. Kingman (Ariz.) High Sch., 1972—. Author: American West Magazine Index (1974-1983), 1985. Mem. Ariz. State Libr. Assn., Kingman Secondary Edn. Assn. Home: 2540 Crozier Ave Kingman AZ 86401-4712 Office: Kingman High Sch North 4182 N Bank St Kingman AZ 86401-2715

WILLIAMS, DAVID MICHAEL, manufacturing executive; b. Bklyn., Feb. 25, 1936; s. Robert Irving and Patricia Margaret (Flanagan) W.; m. Carol Bultmann, Nov. 13, 1965; children: Mark, Jennifer. Cert., NYU, Ctr. for Safety Engring., Manhattan, N.Y., 1960. Mgr. various mfrs., 1956-79; pres. D.M. Williams, Inc., Livermore, Calif., 1979—; cons. various mfrs., 1979—. Candidate for Gov., Calif., 1990; candidate for Congress, Calif., 1986, 88, 89, 92, 94; active Rep. Ctrl. Com., Calif., 1987-88. Cole grantee NYU, 1960. Mem. Inst. Packaging Profls. (bd. dirs. no. Calif. chpt., 1982-85, chmn. 1985-86), ASTM, Mensa (founder interest group 1983-86). Roman Catholic. Office: 1560 Kingsport Ave Livermore CA 94550-6149

WILLIAMS, DAVID WELFORD, federal judge; b. Atlanta, Mar. 20, 1910; s. William W. and Maude (Lee) W.; m. Ouida Maie White, June 11, 1939; children: David Welford, Vaughn Charles. A.A., Los Angeles Jr. Coll., 1932; A.B., UCLA, 1934; LL.B., U. So. Calif., 1937. Bar: Calif. 1937. Practiced in Los Angeles, 1937-55; judge Mcpl. Ct., Los Angeles, 1956-62, Superior Ct., Los Angeles, 1962-69, U.S. Dist. Ct. (cen. dist.) Calif., Los Angeles, 1969—; now sr. judge U.S. Dist. Ct. (cen. dist.) Calif.; judge Los Angeles County Grand Jury, 1965. Recipient Russwurm award Nat. Assn. Newspapers, 1958; Profl. Achievement award UCLA Alumni Assn., 1966. Mem. ABA, Los Angeles Bar Assn., Am. Judicature Soc. Office: US Dist Ct 255 E Temple St Rm 7100 Los Angeles CA 90012-3334

WILLIAMS, DAY ROBERT, lawyer; b. Fresno, Calif., June 2, 1954; s. Rene Harold and Maurine Anne (Elliot) W.; m. Robin Alyss McKee, Aug. 11, 1993; 1 stepchild, Alyss Evans; 1 child, Nathanael Day. BA in English Lit., Reed Coll., Portland, Oreg., 1976; JD, U. Ariz., 1991. Bar: Nev. 1991. Law clk. Pima Savs. & Loan, Tucson, 1989-91; law clk. to Justice of Nev. Supreme Ct., Carson City, 1992; legal rschr. Carson City, 1993, pvt. practice law, 1993—; freelance photographer, Conn., N.Y., Nev., 1976-85. Editor and pub. Daylight newsletter, 1991-95; author: (book of poetry) Daybreak, 1986, (novel) Gambling With Death, 1995. Exec. com. Friends of Pyramid Lake, Reno, Nev., 1991-93; mem. Leadership Reno, 1987; donator of photographs Nev. Hist. Soc.; mem. Parable Prodns. Vineyard Christian Community. U. Ariz. Grad. Christian fellow, 1990-91. Mem. Nat. Acad. Elder Law Attys., State Bar Nev. Republican. Office: 1300 S Curry St Carson City NV 89703-5202

WILLIAMS, DENNIS FÜRST VON BLUCHER, homeopathic physician; b. Tulsa, Aug. 21, 1944; s. Paul Dennis and Catherine Susan (Krischan) B. BFA, Kans. U., 1967; postgrad., London Coll. Homeopathy, 1980; diploma, Royal Acad. Dramatic Arts, London, 1971; assoc. deg., Pasadena (Calif.) Playhouse, 1973; PhD in Nutrition, Donsbach Sch., 1981. Actor, contract player 20th Cent. Fox Studios, Century City, Calif., 1973-74; actor Universal Studios, Universal City, Calif., 1974-84, Embassy TV, Universal City, 1984-86; exec. producer D.W. Prodns., Hollywood, 1986—; dir. and instr. Pasadena Playhouse, 1983-85; instr., Hollywood, Calif., 1983—; bd. dirs. USO, Hollywood. Author: Basic Health and Nutrition, 1986; screenwriter Sunset Heaven, 1978, The Illuminati, 1984; appeared in films Silent Movie, 1975, Gypsy Warriors, 1978, Truce in the Forest, 1979; TV appearances include Nancy Walker Show, 1976, Mary Hartman, Mary Hartman, 1976, Maude, 1976, Operation Petticoat, 1977, Bionic Woman, 1978, E/R, 1984 (Emmy award 1985). Founding mem. Hollywood Preservation Orgn., 1985; mem. Hollywood Heritage, Inc., 1985, Orgn. Police & Sheriffs; mem. com. Save Medicare and Social Security, 1986—; hon. consulate Principality of Wahlstatt. Recipient Resolution award City of L.A., 1985, Disting. Svc. award Hollywood Heritage, Inc., 1985, Bronze Halo award So. Calif. Motion Picture Coun., Star Sapphire award So. Calif. Motion Picture Coun., 1986; named Celebrity of Yr. Calif. Spl. Olympics, 1984; nominated Emmy award, 1985. Mem. AFTRA, NATAS, SAG, WHO, Actors Equity Assn., Royal Acad. Dramatic Arts, British Acad. Film & TV.

WILLIAMS, DONALD SPENCER, scientist; b. Pasadena, Calif., May 28, 1939; s. Charles Gardner and Delia Ruth (Spencer) W. BS, Harvey Mudd Coll., 1961; MS, Carnegie Inst. Tech., 1962; PhD, Carnegie-Mellon U., 1969. Asst. project dir. Learning Rsch. & Devel. Ctr., Pitts., 1965-67; cons. system design, Pitts., 1967-69; mem. tech. staff RCA Corp., Palo Alto, Calif., 1969-72; prin. investigator robot vision Jet Propulsion Lab., Calif. Inst. Tech., Pasadena, 1972-80; chief engr. oper. TRW, Inc., Redondo Beach, 1980—; cons. system design, 1984—. Japan Econ. Found. grantee, 1981. Mem. AAAS, Assn. Computing Machinery, Audio Engring. Soc., Nat. Fire Protection Assn., IEEE, Soc. Motion Picture & TV Engrs., Town Hall Calif. Contbr. articles to profl. jours. Home: PO Box 40700 Pasadena CA 91114-7700 Office: TRW Inc 1 Space Park Dr Redondo Beach CA 90278-1001

WILLIAMS, DONALD VICTOR, office manager, coach; b. Decatur, Ill., May 8, 1936; s. Victor H. and Dorothy M. (Runion) W.; m. Helen Williams (div. 1977); m. Barbara A. Porter, July 4, 1980; children: Kevin, Brian, Michael. Corrections officer State of Oreg., Salem, 1959-69, adminstrv. asst. dept. corrections, 1969-76; spl. dep. Marion County, Salem, 1976-78; job svcs. rep. div. of employment State of Oreg., Gold Beach, 1979; adminstrv. asst. airport mgr. Port of Portland, Oreg., 1980; office mgr. North Opinion Rsch., Portland, 1980; probable shooting sports coord. 4th World Masters Games, Portland, 1998. Contbr. numerous articles to profl. jours. Sport tech. officer U.S. Cerebral Palsy Athletic Assn., Mich., 1990—; exec. bd. Multnomah Art Assn., Portland, 1985-89; com. mem. Portland/Sapporo Sister City Assn., 1989-90; dir. Oreg. Jr. Olympic Shooting Program, Portland, 1980-89; coach Region I Daisy Air Gun Program, Portland, 1980-83; head coach U.S.C.P. Shooting Team 1990 World Championships, Assen, Holland; commr. State Games Oreg., 1986-89. With U.S. ARNG, 1954-88. Recipient Double Bronze medalist 3d World Masters Games, Brisbane, Australia. Mem. Internat. Shooting Coaches Assn. (editor 1988—, life), NRA (endowment 1980—), Oreg. State Rifle/Pistol Assn. (life), Oreg. 4-H Shooting Sports Com. (bd. dirs. 1985-91). Home: 17446 SW Granada Dr Beaverton OR 97007-5364

WILLIAMS, DOROTHY RHONDA, gifted education consultant and teacher; b. Grants, N.M., Aug. 20, 1957; d. Howard Lemuel and Betty Virginia (Bragg) Williams; m. John T. McGill, May 31, 1985. BS in Secondry Edn., U. Ark., 1979, MEd in Gifted Edn., 1985; postgrad studies in Anthropology, U. Ill., 1984-86. Cert. tchr., Class 1, Mont. High sch. math. tchr. Heber Springs (Ark.) Pub. Schs., 1979-80; math. theory instr. Ark. Gov. Sch. for Gifted, 1980; rsch. asst. U. Ark., Fayetteville, 1981-84, U. Ill., Champaign-Urbana, 1984-86; tchr. reading and English Browning (Mont.) Pub. Schs., 1986-87, tchr. 8th grade reading, 1987-91, tchr. critical thinking, 1991-92, bilingual gifted and talented specialist, 1992—; instr. Gifted Inst. Carroll Coll., Helena, Mont., 1991—; instr. Satori Camp Ea. Washington U., Cheney, Wash., 1993—; instr. stress mgmt. for tchrs., 1995—; presenter at peer ednl. confs., 1987—; project success enrichment trainer, 1994—, ednl. cons. 1993—; mem. curriculum writing project Mont. Office Pub. Instrn./law-related edn.; peer mediation and conflict mgmt. trainer Nat. Conf. on Peacemaking and Conflict Resolution, 1995—. Edge scholar Office of Pub. Instrn. Mont., 1990-92; Taft fellow, 1993. Mem. Assn. Gifted and Talented Edn. (planning com., presenter), Nat. Conf. on Gifted and Talented Edn. for Native People (presenter 1993, 94, 95), Glacier Reading Coun. (presenter), Mont. Reading Coun. (presenter), Internat. Reading Assn. Home: PO Box 246 East Glacier Park MT 59434-0246 Office: Browning Pub Schs PO Box 610 Browning MT 59417-0610

WILLIAMS, ELIZABETH YAHN, author, lawyer; b. Columbus, Ohio, July 20, 1942; d. Wilbert Henry and Elizabeth Dulson (Brophy) Yahn. BA cum laude, Loyola-Marymount U., 1964; secondary teaching credential, UCLA, 1965; JD, Loyola U., 1971. Cert. tchr. h.s. and jr. coll. law, English and history. Writer West Covina, Calif., 1964—; designer West Covina, 1966-68; tchr. jr./sr. h.s. L.A. City Schs., Santa Monica, Calif., 1964-65, La Puente (Calif.) H.S. Dist., 1965-67; legal intern, lawyer Garvey, Ingram, Baker & Uhler, Covina, Calif., 1969-72; lawyer, corp. counsel Avco Fin. Svcs., Inc., Newport Beach, Calif., 1972-74; sole practice Santa Ana, Calif., 1974-80, Newport Beach, 1980-87; mem. faculty continuing edn. State Bar of Calif., 1979; adj. prof. Western State U. Sch. Law, Fullerton, Calif., 1980; mem. fed. cts. com. Calif. State Bar, San Francisco, 1977-80. Author: (1-act plays) Acting-Out Acts, 1990, Grading Graciela, 1992, Boundaries in the Dirt, 1993; author, lyricist: (1-act children's musical) Peter and the Worry Wrens, 1995; contbr. articles to profl. jours.; panelist TV show Action Now, 1971; interviewee TV show Women, 1987; scriptwriter, dir. TV show Four/Four, 1994, (3 act adaptation) Saved in Sedona, 1995. Mem. alumni bd. Loyola-Marymount U., L.A., 1980-84; mem. adv. bd. Rancho Santiago Coll., Santa Ana, 1983-84; speaker Commn. on Status on Women, Santa Ana, 1979. French scholar Ohio State U., 1959, acad. scholar Loyola-Marymount U., 1960-64. Mem. Calif. Women Lawyers (co-founder, life, bd. dirs. 1975-76), Orange County Bar Assn. (faculty Orange County Coll. Trial Advocacy 1982, chmn. human and individual rights com. 1974-75, comml. law and bankruptcy com. 1978-79, corp. and bus. law sect. 1980-81), Phi Delta Delta, Phi Alpha Delta, Phi Theta Kappa (hon. life mem.). Address: PO Box 146 San Luis Rey CA 92068

WILLIAMS, EMILY JEAN, dietitian, medical researcher; b. Indpls., July 18, 1928; d. Emil Charles and Vera Pearl (White) Rinsch; m. Donald Eugene Williams, Feb. 21, 1953; children: Donald Eugene, Ronald Owen. BS in Dietetics, Ind. U., 1950, MS, 1979, Dr.Med. Scis., 1983. Registered dietitian. Dietetic intern U. Mich., 1951; therapeutic dietitian Ind. U., 1952-53; asst. prof. Ind. U.-South Bend, 1980, 81, grad. teaching asst., 1978-80; clin. assoc. Ind. U. Med. Ctr., Indpls., 1984-92 ; therapeutic dietitian Desert Hosp., Palm Springs, Calif., 1965-66, 70-71, reviewer Diabetes Care and Edn. Practice Group Jour., 1985—; panel moderator Am. Dietetic Assn., New Orleans, 1985; lectr. in field. Author: Diabetes Care and Education Practice Group Newsletter, 1985. Contbr. articles to profl. jours. Pres. Western Art Coun. Palm Springs Desert Mus., 1993-95; chair mus. svc. coun. Desert Mus., 1994-95. Named Outstanding Mem., Alpha Xi Delta. Mem. DAR, Am. Dietetic Assn., Calif. Dietetic Assn., Am. Diabetes Assn. (profl. sect.), Palm Springs Hist. Soc., Coachella Valley Panhellenic Club (pres. 1970-71), Palm Springs Woman's Club (v.p.), P.E.O., Pi Lambda Theta. Republican. Avocation: needlepoint. Home: 38-681 E Bogert Trl Palm Springs CA 92264-9651

WILLIAMS, FORMAN ARTHUR, engineering science educator, combustion theorist; b. New Brunswick, N.J., Jan. 12, 1934; s. Forman J. and Alice (Pooley) W.; m. Elsie Vivian Kara, June 15, 1955 (div. 1978); children: F. Gary, Glen A., Nancy L., Susan D., Michael S., Michelle K.; m. Elizabeth Acevedo, Aug. 19, 1978. BSE, Princeton U., 1955; PhD, Calif. Inst. Tech., 1958. Asst. prof. Harvard U., Cambridge, Mass., 1958-64; prof. U. Calif.-San Diego, 1964-81; Robert H. Goddard prof. Princeton U., N.J., 1981-88; prof. dept. applied mechs. and engring. scis. U. Calif., San Diego, 1988—. Author: Combustion Theory, 1965, 2d edit., 1985; contbr. articles to profl. jours. Fellow NSF, 1962; fellow Guggenheim Found., 1970; recipient U.S. Sr. Scientist award Alexander von Humboldt Found., 1982, Silver medal Combustion Inst., 1978, Bernard Lewis Gold medal Combustion Inst., 1990. Fellow AIAA (Pendray Aerospace Lit. award 1993); mem. Am. Phys. Soc., Combustion Inst., Soc. for Indsl. and Applied Math., Nat. Acad. Engring., Nat. Acad. Engring Mex. (fgn. corr. mem.), Sigma Xi. Home: 8002 La Jolla Shores Dr La Jolla CA 92037-3230 Office: U Calif San Diego Ctr Energy & Combustion Rsch 9500 Gilman Dr La Jolla CA 92093-5003

WILLIAMS, GORDON ROLAND, librarian; b. Ontario, Oreg., July 26, 1914; s. Herbert Harrison and George Lola (Davis) W.; m. Jane Margaret Smith, Apr. 25, 1942; 1 dau., Megan Davis. AB, Stanford U., 1936; AM, U. Chgo., 1952. Vice pres. Brentano's Inc., Calif., 1945-49; chief asst. librarian UCLA, 1952-59; dir. Center for Research Libraries, Chgo., 1959-80; bd. dirs. Napa Valley Wine Libr., 1984-95; Mem. 1st Japan-U.S. Conf. on Libraries in Higher Edn., Tokyo, 1969, 2d Japan-U.S. Conf. on Libraries in Higher Edn., Wingspread, 1972, Internat. Conf. on Library Automation, Brasenose Coll., Oxford U., 1966; mem. archives and library com. Nat. Conservation Advisory Council, 1973—; Trustee, vice chmn. Bioscis. Info. of Biol. Abstracts, 1977-83; chmn. Conf. Cataloging and Info. Sers. for Machine-Readable Data Files, 1978; mem. Study Com. Libraries and Archives Nat. Conservation Advisory Council, 1973—; chmn. adv. com. McCune Rare Book Collection, 1989—. Author: Ravens and Crows, 1966, Bewick to Dovaston, Letters 1824-1828, 1968, Cost of Owning vs. Borrowing Serials, 1969; hon. editorial adv. Interlending Rev., Eng. Served with USNR, 1942-45. Decorated Commendation medal. Mem. ALA (chmn. com. nat. union catalogue 1960-85), Internat. Inst. Conservation Historic and Artistic Works, Assn. Research Libraries (com. on preservation of research library materials 1960-68, dir. 1964-67), Soc. Am. Archivists (chmn. com. on paper preservation 1970-77). Clubs: Caxton (Chgo., hon.); Rounce and Coffin, Zamorano (Los Angeles); Roxburghe (San Francisco).

WILLIAMS, HAROLD MARVIN, foundation official, former government official, former university dean, former corporate executive; b. Phila., Jan. 5, 1928; s. Louis W. and Sophie (Fox) W.; m. Nancy Englander; children: Ralph A., Susan J., Derek M. AB, UCLA, 1946; JD, Harvard U., 1949; postgrad. U. So. Calif. Grad. Sch. Law, 1955-56; DHL (hon.), Johns Hopkins U., 1987. Bar: Calif. 1950; practiced in Los Angeles, 1950, 53-55; with Hunt Foods and Industries, Inc., Los Angeles, 1955-68, v.p. 1958-60, exec. v.p., 1960-68, pres., 1968; gen., mgr. Hunt-Wesson Foods, 1964-66, pres., 1966-68; chmn. finance com. Norton Simon, Inc., 1968-70, chmn. bd., 1969-70, dir., 1959-77; dir. Times-Mirror Corp., SunAmerica; prof. mgmt., dean Grad. Sch. Mgmt., UCLA, 1970-77; pres., dir. Special Investments & Securities Inc., 1961-66; chmn. SEC, Washington, 1977-81; pres., chief exec. officer J. Paul Getty Trust, 1981—; regent U. Calif., 1983-94. Mem. Commn. for Econ. Devel. State of Calif., 1973-77; energy coordinator City of Los Angeles, 1973-74; public mem. Nat. Advt. Review Bd., 1971-75; co-chmn. Public Commn. on Los Angeles County Govt.; mem. Coun. on Fgn. Rels., Com. for Econ. Devel.; commn. to rev. Master Plan for Higher Edn., State of Calif., 1985-87; trustee Nat. Humanities Ctr., 1987-93; dir. Ethics Resource Ctr.; mem. Pres.' Com. on Arts and Humantities; mem. Commn. on the Acad. Presidency. Served as 1st lt. AUS, 1950- 53. Mem. State Bar Calif. Office: J Paul Getty Trust 401 Wilshire Blvd Ste 900 Santa Monica CA 90401

WILLIAMS, HARRY EDWARD, management consultant; b. Oak Park, Ill., July 20, 1925; s. Harry E. and Mary E.; m. Jean Horner; 1 child, Jeanne. Student, West Coast U., Los Angeles, 1958-60; BS in Engring., Calif. Coast Coll., Santa Ana, 1975; MA, Calif. Coast Coll., 1975; PhD, Golden State U., Los Angeles, 1981. Registered profl. engr., Calif. Mgr. Parker Aircraft Co., Los Angeles, 1958-60, Leach Corp., Los Angeles, 1968-69, Litton, Data Systems, Van Nuys, Calif., 1969-72; dir. Electronic Memories, Hawthorne, Calif., 1972-78, Magnavox Co., Torrance, Calif., 1978-80; v.p. Stacoswitch Inc., Costa Mesa, Calif., 1981-87; mgmt. cons., Seal Beach, Calif., 1987—; cons. in field. Contbr. articles to profl. jours. With USAF, 1943-46. Fellow Internat. Acad. Edn., Am. Soc. Quality Control, Soc. for Advancement Mgmt. (Mgr. of Yr. 1984, Phil Carrol award 1985, Profl. Mgr. award 1985). Republican. Methodist.

WILLIAMS, HENRY STRATTON, radiologist, educator; b. N.Y.C., Aug. 26, 1929; m. Frances S. Williams; children: Mark I, Paul S., Bart H. BS, CCNY, 1950; MD, Howard U., 1955. Diplomate Nat. Bd. Med. Examiners. Intern Brooke Army Hosp., San Antonio, 1956; resident in radiology Letterman Army Hosp., San Francisco, 1957-60; pvt. practice radiology L.A., 1963—; assoc. clin. prof. radiology Charles R. Drew Med. Sch., L.A.; chmn. bd. Charles Drew U. Medicine and Sci. Found.; interim pres. Charles R. Drew U. of Medicine and Sci. Mem. ad hoc adv. com. Joint Commn. Accreditation Hosps. Served to maj. U.S. Army, 1960-63. Fellow Am. Coll. Radiology; mem. Calif. Physicians Service (bd. dirs. 1971-77), Calif. Med. Assn. (counselor, mem. appeals bd., del., chmn. urban health com.), Los Angeles County Med. Assn.

WILLIAMS, HIBBARD EARL, medical educator, physician; b. Utica, N.Y., Sept. 28, 1932; s. Hibbard G. and Beatrice M. W.; m. Sharon Towne, Sept. 3, 1982; children: Robin, Hans. AB, Cornell U., 1954, MD, 1958. Diplomate Am. Bd. Internal Medicine. Intern Mass. Gen. Hosp., Boston, 1958-59, resident in medicine, 1959-60, 62-64, asst. physician, 1964-65; clin. assoc. Nat. Inst. Arthritis and Metabolic Diseases, NIH, Bethesda, MD, 1960-62; instr. medicine Harvard U., Boston, 1964-65; asst. prof. medicine U. Calif., San Francisco, 1965-68, assoc. prof., 1968-72, prof., 1972-78, chief divsn. med. genetics, 1968-70, vice chmn. dept. medicine, 1970-78; prof., chmn. dept. medicine Cornell U. Med. Coll., N.Y.C., 1978-80; physician-in-chief N.Y. Hosp.-Cornell Med. Ctr., N.Y.C., 1978-80; dean Sch. Medicine U. Calif., Davis, 1980-92, prof. internal medicine, 1980—; mem. program project com. NIH, Nat. Inst. Arthritis and Metabolic Diseases, 1971-73. Editor med. staff confs. Calif. Medicine, 1966-70; mem. editl. bd. Clin. Rsch., 1968-71, Am. Jour. Medicine, 1978-88; cons. editor Medicine, 1978-86; assoc. editor Metabolism, 1970-80; mem. adv. bd. physiology in medicine New Eng. Jour. Medicine, 1970-75; contbr. articles to med. jours. With USPHS, 1960-62. Recipient Career Devel. award USPHS, 1968; recipient award for excellence in teaching Kaiser Found., 1970, Disting. Faculty award U. Calif. Alumni-Faculty Assn., 1978; John and Mary R. Markle scholar in medicine, 1968. Fellow ACP; mem. AAAS, Am. Fedn. Clin. Rsch., Am. Soc. Clin. Investigation (sec.-treas. 1974-77), Assn. Am. Physicians, Assn. Am. Med. Colls. (adminstrv. bd., coun. deans 1989-92, exec. coun. 1990-92), Calif. Acad. Medicine (pres. 1984), San Francisco Diabetes Assn. (bd. dirs. 1971-72), Western Assn. Physicians (v.p. 1977-78), Western. Soc. Clin. Rsch., Calif. Med. Assn. (chmn. coun. sci. affairs 1990-95, bd. dirs. 1990-95), Am. Clin. and Climatol. Soc., St. Francis Yacht Club, Alpha Omega Alpha. Office: U Calif Sch Medicine Davis CA 95616

WILLIAMS, HOWARD RUSSELL, lawyer, educator; b. Evansville, Ind., Sept. 26, 1915; s. Clyde Alfred and Grace (Preston) W.; m. Virginia Merle Thompson, Nov. 3, 1942; 1 son, Frederick S.T. AB, Washington U., St. Louis, 1937; LLB, Columbia U., 1940. Bar: N.Y. 1941. With firm Root, Clark, Buckner & Ballantine, N.Y.C., 1940-41; prof. law, asst. dean U. Tex. Law Sch., Austin, 1946-51; prof. law Columbia U. Law Sch., N.Y.C., 1951-63; Dwight prof. Columbia Law Sch., 1959-63; prof. law Stanford U., 1963-85, Stella W. and Ira S. Lillick prof., 1968-82, prof. emeritus, 1982, Robert E. Paradise prof. natural resources, 1983-85, prof. emeritus, 1985—; Oil and gas cons. President's Materials Policy Commn., 1951; mem. Calif. Law Revision Commn., 1971-79, vice chmn., 1976-77, chmn., 1978-79. Author or co-author: Cases on Property, 1954, Cases on Oil and Gas, 1956, 5th edit., 1987, Decedents' Estates and Trusts, 1968, Future Interests, 1970, Oil and Gas Law, 8 vols., 1959-64 (with ann. supplements/rev. 1964-95), abridged edit., 1973, Manual of Oil and Gas Terms, 1957, 9th edit., 1994. Bd. regents Berkeley Bapt. Divsn. Sch., 1966-67; trustee Rocky Mountain Mineral Law Found., 1964-66, 68-85. With U.S. Army, 1941-46. Recipient Clyde O. Martz Tchg. award Rocky Mountain Mineral Law Found., 1994. Mem. Phi Beta Kappa. Democrat. Home: 360 Everett Ave Apt 4B Palo Alto CA 94301-1422 Office: Stanford U Sch Law Nathan Abbott Way Stanford CA 94305

WILLIAMS, HOWARD WALTER, retired aerospace engineer; b. Evansville, Ind., Oct. 18, 1937; s. Walter Charles and Marie Louise (Bollinger) W.; m. Phyllis Ann Scofield, May 4, 1956 (div. Sept. 1970); m. Marilee Sharon Mulvane, Oct. 30, 1970; children: Deborah, Steven, Kevin, Glenn, Lori, Michele. AA, Pasadena City Coll., 1956; BSME, Calif. State U., Los Angeles, 1967; BSBA, U. San Francisco, 1978; PhD in Comml. Sci. (hon.), London Inst. Applied Rsch., 1992. Turbojet, rocket engr. Aerojet-Gen. Corp., Azusa, Calif., 1956-59, infrared sensor engr., 1959-60, rocket, torpedo engr., 1960-66; power, propulsion mgr. propulsion divsn. Aerojet-Gen. Corp., Sacramento, 1967-73, high speed ship systems mgr., 1974-78, combustion, power mgr., rocket engine and energy mktg. mgr., 1979-89, dir. strategic planning, 1989-94; ret., 1994. Author: (with others) Heat Exchangers, 1980, Industrial Heat Exchangers, 1985; co-inventor Closed Cycle Power System, 1969. Recipient Energy Innovation award U.S. Dept. Energy, 1985. Mem. AIAA (sr., Best Paper 1966), Am. Soc. Metals (organizing dir. indsl. heat exch. confs. 1985).

WILLIAMS, JAMES E., food products manufacturing company executive; married. With Golden State foods Corp., 1961—; pres., chief exec. officer Golden State foods Corp., Pasadena, Calif., 1978—. Office: Golden State Foods Corp 18301 Von Karman Ave Ste 1100 Irvine CA 92715-1009

WILLIAMS, JEANNE, writer; b. Elkhart, Kans., Apr. 10, 1930; d. Guy Edwin and Louella Isabel (Salmon) Kreie; m. Gene F. Williams, Jan. 18, 1949 (div. 1968); children: Michael Williams, Kristian Williams; m. John Creasey, 1970 (div. 1973); m. Robert Joseph Morse, Feb. 13, 1981. Student, U. Okla. Author: Beasts with Music, 1967, Bride of Thunder, 1978, The Cave Dreamers, 1983, Daughter of the Sword, 1979, Harvest of Fury, 1981, The Heaven Sword, 1985, A Lady Bought with Rifles, 1976, Lady of No Man's Land, 1988, A Mating of Hawks, 1983, No Roof but Heaven, 1990, River Guns, 1962, So Many Kingdoms, 1986, Texas Pride, 1987, The Valiant Women, 1980, A Woman Clothed in Sun, 1977, Home Mountain, 1990, Island Harp, 1991, The Longest Road, 1993, Daughter of the Storm, 1994, The Unplowed Sky, 1994, Home Station, 1995, (novels as Megan Castell) The Queen of a Lonely Country, 1980, (novels as Jeanne Crecy) The Evil Among Us, 1975, Hands of Terror, 1972, The Lightning Tree, 1973, My Face Beneath the Stone, 1975, The Night Hunter, 1982, The Winter Keeper, 1975, (novels as Jeanne Foster) Deborah Leigh, 1981, Eden Richards, 1982, Women of the Three Worlds, 1984, (novels as Kristin Michaels) Enchanted Journey, 1977, Enchanted Twilight, 1976, Magic Side of the Moon, 1979, Make Believe Love, 1977, Song of the Heart, 1977, A Special Kind of Love, 1976, To Begin With Love, 1975, Voyage to Love, 1977, (novels as Deirdre Rowan) Dragon's Mount, 1973, Ravensgate, 1977, Shadow of the Volcano, 1975, Silver Wood, 1973, Time of the Burning Mask, 1976, (books for young adults) The Confederate Fiddle, 1962, rev. edit. 1995, Coyote Winter, 1966, Freedom Trail, 1973, The Horsetalker, 1961, Mission to Mexico, 1958, New Medicine, 1972 (new edit. 1994), Oh! Susanna, 1963, Oil Patch Partners, 1967, Promise of Tomorrow, 1959, Tame the Wild Stallion, 1957, To Buy a Dream, 1958, Trails of Tears, 1972 (new edit. 1993), Winter Wheat, 1975. Bd. dirs. Internat. Soc. for Animal Rights, Clark's Summit, 1982-86, Defenders of Wildlife, Washington, 1988-90; vol. EMT, Portal, Ariz., 1986—. Mem. Western Writers Am. (pres. 1974-75, Levi Strauss Golden Saddleman 1962, Spur award Best Novel of the West 1981, 91, Best Western Juvenile 1962, 74), Tex. Inst. of Letters, Authors Guild. Democrat. Unitarian. Home: Cave Creek Canyon Rd Portal AZ 85632

WILLIAMS, JEFFREY THOMAS, economist; b. Duluth, Minn., Sept. 30, 1952; s. Bruce Foch Pershing and Kathleen (Griffee) W.; m. Theresa Ann Moore, May 29, 1987; children: Spencer Thomas, Sarah Christine. BS in Finance, U. Utah, 1975, BS in Econs., 1975, MS in Econs., 1981. Research fellow Utah Ctr. for Pub. Affairs, U. Utah, Salt Lake City, 1981; economist Utah Energy Office, State of Utah Dept. of Nat. Resources, Salt Lake City, 1981-85; sr. economist com. consumer svcs. Utah Dept. Commerce, Salt Lake City, 1985-90; econ. cons. Evergreen, Colo., 1990—; mem. Salt Lake Community Coll. Computer Tech. Adv. Com., Salt Lake City, 1985-89; expert witness PacificCorp cost allocation case, 1990, merger case, 1988, fuel procurement cases, 1986, Utah Power and Light Co. Co-author: State Review of the Bonneville Unit Central Utah Project, 1984; author, editor: Study of a Conceptual Nuclear Energy Center at Green River, 1982 and others. Vol. Nat. Ski Patrol System, Park City, Utah, 1980-89. Mem. Internat. Assn. Energy Economists. Roman Catholic. Home and Office: 3077 S Hiwan Dr Evergreen CO 80439-8951

WILLIAMS, JESS, editor; b. Las Cruces, N.Mex., Jan. 18, 1959; s. Jess Carlton Jr. and Betty (Harlan) W. B of Print Journalism, N.Mex. State U., 1985; postgrad., La. State U., 1985. Assoc. editor Puerto de Sol, 1983-85; editor N.Mex. State U. Round Up, 1984-85; copy editor Las Cruces (N.Mex.) Sun-News, 1986-87, Albuquerque Tribune, 1987; mng. editor The Raton (N.Mex.) Range, 1987-89; editor Stephenville (Tex.) Empire-Tribune, 1989-91, The Taos (N.Mex.) News, 1991—. Named 1st Pl. Feature Writing, N.Mex. Press Assn., 1986, , Pub. Svc. Writing, 1988, Edit. Writing, 1988, 92, News Writing, 89, Column Writing, 1989, 2d Pl. Edit. Writing, 1986, News Writing, 1988, Column Writing, 1988, 93, Edit. Writing, 1989, Feature Writing, 1992, Column Writing 3d Pl. Nat. Newspaper Assn., 1993, 1st Pl. Column Writing, 1994. Mem. Nat. Lesbian and Gay Journalists Assn. (pres. N.Mex. chpt. 1993-95). Home: PO Box U Taos NM 87571

WILLIAMS, JOHN BRINDLEY, English language educator, writer; b. N.Y.C., Aug. 4, 1919; s. Elmer Reed and Stella (Brindley) W.; m. Jean Elizabeth Humphrey, Aug. 24, 1951; children: Marilyn, Evelyn, Heather, Laura. BA, U. So. Calif., L.A., 1948; MA, UCLA, 1955; PhD, U. Southern Calif., 1965. Suburban editor San Pedro (Calif.) News-Pilot, 1948-53; instr. in English Glendale (Calif.) Coll., 1955-66; prof. English Calif. State U., Long Beach, 1966-92. Author: Style and Grammar, 1973, White Fire: The Influence of Emerson on Melville, 1990. With U.S. Army, 1943-45, ETO. Recipient Disting. Faculty Teaching, 1987. Mem. Modern Lang. Assn., Melville Soc. Republican. Presbyterian. Home: 9791 El Tulipan Cir Fountain Valley CA 92708

WILLIAMS, JOHN CHRISTOPHER RICHARD, bishop; b. Sale, Cheshire, Eng., May 22, 1936; arrived in Can., 1960; s. Frank Harold and Ceridwen Roberts (Hughes) W.; m. Rona Macrae Aitken, Mar. 18, 1964; children: Andrew David, Judith Ann. BA in Commerce, Manchester U., Eng., 1958; diploma in theology, Cranmer Hall, Durham, Eng., 1960. Ordained deacon Anglican Ch. of Can., 1960, priest, 1962. Missionary in charge Anglican Ch. Can., Sugluk, Que., Can., 1961-72, Cape Dorset, N.W.T., Can., 1972-75, Baker Lake, N.W.T., 1975-78; archdeacon of the Keewatim Anglican Ch. Can., 1975-87; rector Holy Trinity Anglican Ch. Can., Yellowknife, N.W.T., 1978-87; bishop suffagan Diocese of the Arctic, Can., 1987-90, diocesan bishop, 1990—; trustee Can. Churchman, Anglican Ch. Can., 1976-82, mem. nat. exec. com., 1976-79, 92—. Coord., trans. into

Eskimo Inukkitut New Testament, 1992. Office: Diocese of the Arctic, Box 89, Iqaluit, NT Canada X0A 0H0

WILLIAMS, JOHN JAMES, JR., architect; b. Denver, July 13, 1949; s. John James and Virginia Lee (Thompson) W.; m. Mary Serene Morck, July 29, 1972. BArch, U. Colo., 1974. Registered architect, Colo., Calif., Idaho, Virginia, Utah. Project architect Gensler Assoc. Architects, Denver, 1976, Heinzman Assoc. Architects, Boulder, Colo., 1977, EZTH Architects, Boulder, 1978-79; prin. Knudson/Williams PC, Boulder, 1980-82, Faber, Williams & Brown, Boulder, 1982-86, John Williams & Assocs., Denver, 1986—; panel chmn. U. Colo. World Affairs Conf.; vis. faculty U. Colo. Sch. Architecture and Planning, Coll. Environ. Design, 1986-91. Author (with others) State of Colorado architect licensing law, 1986. Commr. Downtown Boulder Mall Commn., 1985-88; bd. dirs. U. Colo. Fairway Club, 1986-88; mem. Gov.'s. Natural Hazard Mitigation Coun., State of Colo., 1990. Recipient Teaching Honorarium, U. Colo. Coll. Architecture and Planning, 1977, 78, 79, 80, 88, Excellence in Design and Planning award City of Boulder, 1981, 82, Citation for Excellenc, WOOD Inc., 1982, 93, Disting. Profl. Svc. award Coll. Environ. Design U. Colo., 1988. Mem. AIA (sec. 1988, bd. dirs. Colo. North chpt. 1985-86, Design award, 1993, pres. 1990, v.p. 1989, sec. 1987, sec. Colo. chpt. 1988, ednl. fund Fisher I traveling scholar 1988, state design conf. chair 1991, North chpt. Design award 1993), Intersoc. Color Coun., Architects and Planners of Boulder (v.p. 1982), Nat. Coun. Architect Registration Bd., Nat. Golf Found. (sponsor), Kappa Sigma (chpt. pres. 1970). Home: 1031 Turnberry Cir Louisville CO 80027-9594 Office: John Williams & Assocs 1475 Lawrence St Ste 302 Denver CO 80202-2212

WILLIAMS, JOHN PERSHING, industrial relations consultant, retired manufacturing and mining company executive; b. Bluefield, W.Va., July 25, 1919; s. Deck Christopher and Zeora Monte (Brocklehurst) W.; m. Ruth Elizabeth Jones, Sept. 10, 1947; 1 child, Jeanne Lynn. BS, U. Mich., 1951. Mem. indsl. rels. staff King-Seeley Thermos Co., Ann Arbor, Mich., 1950-63; personnel mgr., then indsl. rels. mgr. Butler Mfg. Co., Kansas City, Mo., 1963-66; dir. indsl. rels. Mueller Brass Co., Port Huron, Mich., 1966-69; v.p. indsl. rels. Mueller Brass Co., Port Huron, 1969-78; dir. indsl. rels. U.S. Smelting, Refining & Mining, N.Y.C., 1966-78; indsl. rels. cons. UV Industries, N.Y.C., 1969-78; dir. indsl. rels. Fed. Pacific Electric Co., Newark, 1970-76; dir. labor rels. Anamax Mining Co., Sahuarita, Ariz., 1978-85; pres. Alert Consulting Corp., Tucson, 1985—. Co-author: Collective Bargaining, 1985, Strike Planning, 1985. Pres., Perry Nursery Sch., Ann Arbor, Mich., 1957; rd. commr., Scio Twp., Ann Arbor, 1961; del. State Rep. Conv., Detroit, 1961; mem. parents coun., Adrian (Mich.) Coll., 1973-74; bd. dirs., Blue Cross-Blue Shield Mich., Detroit, 1971-77. Mem. Masons. Methodist. Home and Office: Alert Consulting Corp 775 W Samalayuca Dr Tucson AZ 85704-3233

WILLIAMS, JOHN PHILLIP, physician, researcher; b. Detroit, Dec. 29, 1954; s. Edward Theodore and Marjorie Ann (Logan) W. BS, Tex. A&M Coll., 1977; MD, Baylor U., 1979. Intern St. Joseph Hosp., Houston, 1979-80; resident in anesthesiology U. Tex. Med. Sch., Houston, 1980-82, instr., 1983-85, asst. prof., 1985-90, assoc. prof., 1990—; fellowship Guy's Hosp., London, 1982-83; instr. U. Tex., Houston, 1983-85; attending anesthesiologist Tex. Heart Inst., Houston, 1987-88, clin. asst. prof., 1987-88; dir. cardiothoracic anesthesiology U. Tex. Med. Sch., 1987—; fellow Guy's Hosp. London, 1982-83; instr. anesthesiology U. Tex. Med. Sch., Houston, 1983-85; asst. prof. anesthesiology U. Tex. Med. Sch., Houston, 1985-90; clin. asst. prof. anesthesiology Tex. Heart Inst., Houston, 1987-88; dir. cardiothoracic anesthesiology U. Tex. Med. Sch., Houston, 1987—, assoc. prof. anesthesiology, 1990—; vis. prof. U. Utah, 1984; lectr. in field. Contbr. numerous articles to profl. jours. Recipient Rink Prize award Guy's Hosp., 1983. Mem. Tex. Soc. Anesthesiologists, Am. Soc. Anesthesiology, Anesthesia Rsch. Soc. (Eng.), Harris County Med. Soc., Internat. Anesthesia Rsch. Soc., Soc. Cardiovascular Anesthesiologists, Tex. Med. Assn., Tex. Gulf Coast Anesthesia Soc. (v.p. 1989). Office: UCLA Dept Anesthesiology 10833 Le Conte Ave Los Angeles CA 90024

WILLIAMS, JOHN RAY, electronics engineering executive; b. Kosciusko, Miss., Nov. 20, 1962, s. Charles V. and Mary Christine (Miller) W.; 1 child, Seth J. Fullilove. BSEE, U. Miss., 1984; cert. in bus. mgmt., U. Calif., Riverside, 1992. Lic. sales assoc. Calif. Dept. Real Estate. Electronics engr. Fleet Analysis Ctr. (name now Naval Warfare Assessment Ctr.), Corona, Calif., 1985-90, acquisition/logistics engr., 1990-92, sr. electronics engring. project leader, 1990—; coll. recruiter Naval Warfare Assessment Divsn., Corona, 1990—. Soc. Minority Engrs. scholar, 1980-84. Democrat. Baptist. Home: 3091 Manchester Cir Corona CA 91719-6528

WILLIAMS, JUDITH ANN, technical and engineering services company executive; b. Lancaster, Calif., Aug. 10, 1954; d. Robert Melvin Williams and Cora Lee (Clemow) Williams Campbell. AA, Ventura Coll., 1979; BA in Communications, U. Wash., 1982. Editor NOAA, Seattle, 1982; liaison asst. Naval Ship Weapon Systems Engring. Sta., Washington, 1983; mgmt. analyst Triton Assocs., Inc., 1983-84; program mgr. Tech. Applications, Inc., Alexandria, Va., 1984-86; logistics analyst Value Systems Engring. Corp., Alexandria, 1986-87; tng. analyst Designers & Planners, Inc., Arlington, Va., 1987; prin. Ind. Profl. Writers & Assoc., Alexandria, 1987-88; sr. logistician Support Mgmt. Svcs., Inc., Oxnard, Calif., 1989-91; sys. engr. GE Govt. Svcs., Oxnard, 1991-93, Martin Marietta Svcs., Inc., Oxnard, 1994—. Author newsletter articles, 1986-88. Mem. Soc. Naval Architects and Marine Engrs. (assoc.; dir. 1987-88), Navy League U.S. (dir. pub. affairs 1986-87, mng. editor newsletter 1986), Soc. Logistics Engrs., Ventura County Writers' Club.

WILLIAMS, JUDITH LORRAINE, pediatric emergency nurse; b. Little Chute, Wis., Mar. 29, 1948; d. Joseph Leo and Mary Theresa (Bowers) Hermes; m. Robert John Van Eyck, Aug. 10, 1968 (div. 1970); m. William Clarence Williams, Sept. 6, 1975; children: Erin Brooke, Justin David. Diploma in Practical Nursing, Neenah-Menasha Vocat. Sch., Wis., 1968; BSN, Calif. State U., Fresno, 1989. Cert. provider BLS, ACLS and pediat. advanced life support, Am. Heart Assn.; cert. emergency nurse, trauma nurse. Nurse's aide St. Elizabeth's Hosp., Appleton, Wis., 1966-68, LVN, 1970-71; LVN Newport (R.I.) Hosp., 1968-70, Country Care Convalescent Hosp., Atascadero, Calif., 1971-72, Appleton Meml. Hosp., 1972-73, Ross-Loss Med. Ctr., L.A., 1973-74, L.A. Children's Hosp., 1974-75, Valley Children's Hosp., Fresno, 1975-77, Milford (Iowa) Nursing Home, 1977-79; staff nurse Valley Children's Hosp., Fresno, 1989—; mem. career advancement program task force Valley Children's Hosp., 1991—, mem. protocol and standards task force, 1990—. Bd. dirs. Sch. Site Coun., Pacific Union Sch., Bowles, Calif., 1982. Mem. Emergency Nurses Assn., Mid-Valley Emergency Nurses Assn. (chairperson edn. com. 1992, sec. 1993-94, pres. 1995—, Calif. state pediat. chairperson 1995), Sigma Theta Tau. Pentecostal Ch. Home: 4345 E Springfield Ave Fresno CA 93725-9691 Office: Valley Children's Hosp 3151 N Millbrook Ave Fresno CA 93703-1425

WILLIAMS, KEITH ROY, museum director; b. Sunnyside, Wash., Sept. 5, 1958; s. Charles N. Williams and Ruth Arlene (Plank) Hicks; m. Nancy Maxson, 1980 (div. 1984); m. Deanna Lynn Murphy, Oct. 26, 1987; children: Steven, Jeremy. AA in Gen. Studies, Columbia Basin C.C., Pasco, Wash., 1979; BA in Anthropology, Wash. State U., 1981, MA in History/Pub. History, 1984, PhD in History, 1991. Interpretive ranger Nez Perce Nat. Hist. Pk. Nat. Pk. Svc., 1984; historian Alaska regional office Nat. Pk. Svc., Anchorage, 1986; dir. North Ctrl. Wash. Mus., Wenatchee, 1987—; cons. Office Archaeology and Hist. Preservation, 1985, Batelle N.W. DOSE Reconstruction Project, Hanford, 1987, 88; instr. Wenatchee Valley C.C., 1988, 93—; speaker in field. Author: (video, booklet) The People and The Plow, 1987; contbr. articles to profl. jours. Active Wash. State Heritage Coun., Olympia, 1988-90, Wash. Centennial Com., Wenatchee, 1989; mem. design com. Wenatchee Downtown Assn., 1993—; bd. dirs. Wash. Friends Humanities, Seattle, 1990—, Wenatchee Centennial Com., 1992. Grantee Assn. Humanities Idaho, Wash. Commn. Humanities, various other founds. Mem. Wash. Mus. Assn. (bd. dirs. 1988-90, 94—), Kiwanis (bd. dirs.). Office: North Central Washington Museum 127 S Mission St Wenatchee WA 98801-3039

WILLIAMS, KENNETH JAMES, retired county official; b. Eureka, Calif., Apr. 28, 1924; s. E. J. and Thelma (Hall) W.; student Humboldt State Coll., 1942-43; B.S., U. Oreg., 1949, M.Ed., 1952; m. Mary Patricia Warring, Sept. 3, 1949; children—James Clayton, Susan May, Christopher Kenneth. Engaged as mountain triangulation observer with U.S. Coast and Geodetic Survey, 1942; instr. bus. and geography Boise (Idaho) Jr. Coll., 1949-51; tchr. Prospect High Sch., 1952-54; prin. Oakland (Oreg.) High Sch., 1954-58; supt. prin. Coburg Public Schs., 1958-64; supt. Yoncalla (Oreg.) Public Schs., 1964-66, Amity (Oreg.) Public Schs., 1966-72; adminstr. Yamhill County, McMinnville, Oreg., 1974-85; cons., 1985—; county liaison officer Land and Water Conservation Fund, 1977-85. Dist. lay leader Oreg.-Idaho ann. conf. United Methodist Ch., 1968-80, bd. dirs. western dist. Ch. Extension Soc., 1976; mem. Mid-Willamette Manpower Council, 1974-85; bd. dirs. Lafayette Noble Homes, 1970-72; mem. adv. com. local budget law sect. State of Oreg. Served with AUS, 1943-46. Decorated Purple Heart. Mem. NEA, Oreg. Edn. Assn., Oreg. Assn. Secondary Prins., Nat. Assn. Secondary Prins., AAUP, Oreg., Am. Assn. Sch. Adminstrs., Assn. Supervision and Curriculum Devel., Nat. Sch. Pub. Relations Assn., Phi Delta Kappa. Mason (Shriner), Lion. Home: 21801 SE Webfoot Rd Dayton OR 97114-8832

WILLIAMS, KNOX, water conditioning company executive; b. Grandfield, Okla., Aug. 9, 1928; s. Knox B. and Clara Mae (Butler) W.; m. Juanita June Wood, Sept. 9, 1951; children—Jodi Ann and Jeri Ruth (twins), Drue Knox. B.A., UCLA, 1951. With Wilson-McMahan Furniture Stores, Santa Barbara, Calif., 1951-61; prin., pres. Rayne of North San Diego County, Vista, Calif., 1961—, Aqua Fresh Drinking Water Systems, Inc., San Diego, 1980—. Mem. bd. counsellors UCLA; chmn. Santh Margarita Br. YMCA, 1991-93. With USNR, 1947-48. Mem. Carlsbad C. of C., Pacific Water Quality Assn. (pres. 1975-76), Water Quality Assn. (bd. dirs. 1980-83). Republican. Presbyterian. Clubs: El Camino Rotary (pres. 1989-90) (Oceanside, Calif.), Masons (Santa Barbara). Office: Rayne of North San Diego County 2011 W Vista Way Vista CA 92083-6013 also: Aqua Fresh Drinking Water Systems 7370 Opportunity Rd Ste 1 San Diego CA 92111

WILLIAMS, LEE DWAIN, lawyer; b. Enid, Okla., Sept. 2, 1950; s. Lawrence and Wilma Jean (Richards) W. BA Polit. Sci., U. Calif., Santa Barbara, 1974; postgrad., U. Calif., 1974; JD, UCLA, 1977. Bar: Calif. 1977, U.S. Dist. Ct. (cen. dist.) Calif. 1977. Assoc. Irell & Manella, L.A., 1977-79, Riordan & McKinzie (formerly Riordan, Caps, Carbone & McKinzie), L.A., 1979-84; prin. Law Offices of Lee D. Williams, L.A., 1984-88; ptnr. Williams & Kilkowski, L.A., 1988—; bd. dirs. RJS Enterprises, Inc., Monrovia, Calif. Vol. atty. Pub. Counsel, La., 1978-80; trustee Children's Inst. Internat., L.A., 1981—, v.p., 1982-83, treas., v.p., 1993—. Mem. Calif. State Bar. Democrat. Office: Fox Plaza 2121 Avenue of the Stars 22d Fl Los Angeles CA 90067

WILLIAMS, LEONA RAE, lingerie retailer; b. Fairfield, Nebr., July 1, 1928; d. Melton M. and Helga D. (Sorensen) Brown; m. Eugene F. Williams, June 6, 1946; 1 child, Dennis D. Grad. high sch., Fairfield. Owner Alice Rae Apparel Shop, Tucson, 1953—, second location 1967—, Green Valley, Ariz., 1976-93, Sun City, Ariz., 1979—. Sponsor Distributive Edn. Program, 1978-82; coord. fashion shows Am. Cancer Soc., Tucson, 1987, 88, 89. Mem. Exec. Women's Internat. Assn. (chpt. pres. 1994), Mchts. Assn. (pres. 1987-89), Soroptomists, C. of C. Better Bus. Bur. Republican. Baptist. Office: Alice Rae Intimate Apparel 2954 N Campbell Ave Tucson AZ 85719-2813

WILLIAMS, MARION LESTER, government official; b. Abilene, Tex., Dec. 1, 1933; s. Martin Lester and Edde Faye (Wilson) W.; m. Johnnie Dell Ellinger, Dec. 14, 1957; children: Tammy Dawn Cole, Pamela DeAnn Ritterbush. BS, Tex. A&M U., 1956; MS, U. N.Mex., 1967; PhD, Okla. State U., 1971. Test engr. Sandia Nat. Labs., Albuquerque, 1959-61; weapons sys. engr. Naval Weapons Evaluation Facility, Albuquerque, 1961-66; ops. rsch. analyst Joint Chiefs of Staff/Joint Task Force II, Albuquerque, 1966-68; chief reliability div. Field Command DNA, Albuquerque, 1969-71; prin. scientist SHAPE Tech. Ctr., The Hague, Netherlands, 1971-74; chief tech. advisor HQ AF Test & Evaluation Ctr., Albuquerque, 1974-81; chief scientist HQ AF Operational Test & Evaluation Ctr., Albuquerque, 1981-89; tech. dir. HQ AF Operational Test & Evaluation Ctr., 1989—; vis. adv. com. Okla. State U., Stillwater, 1988—; adv. com. U. N.Mex., Albuquerque, 1985—. Editor T&E Tech. Jour., 1987—; contbr. articles to profl. jours. Sci. advisor N.Mex. Sci. & Tech. Oversigh Com., Albuquerque, 1988; bd. advisors U. N.Mex. Cancer Ctr., 1987—; bd. dirs. Contact Albuquerque, 1986-87. 1st lt. USAF 1956-59. Recipient Presdl. Rank award, 1987, 92. Fellow Mil. Ops. Rsch. Soc. (pres. 1982-83, bd. dirs. 1976-81, Wanner award 1991), Internat. Test & Evaluation Ctr. (bd. dirs. 1984-86, 88-90, v.p. 1990, pres. 1992-93), Ops. Rsch. Soc. Am., Tau Beta Pi, Phi Eta Sigma, Alpha Pi Mu, Sigma Tau, Kappa Mu Epsilon. Democrat. Baptist. Home: 1416 Stagecoach Ln SE Albuquerque NM 87123-4429 Office: HQ AF Operational Test Ctr Kirtland AFB Albuquerque NM 87117-7001

WILLIAMS, MARK TULLY, foundation executive; b. Bishop, Calif., Jan. 20, 1948; s. Paul Jacob Williams and Gertrude Margaret (Melsheimer) W.; m. Paula Marie Fink, June 20, 1970 (div. 1980); 1 child, Joshua Glen; m. Melinda Kay Bell, Aug. 14, 1982; children: Brian, Mark. BA magna cum laude, Pacific Union Coll., 1970; MDiv cum laude, Andrews U. SDA Theol. Sem., 1973; MA in Health Sys. Mgmt., Webster U., 1987. Pastor, tchr. Seventh-Day Adventist Ch., 1970-80; editor, publisher The Bldg. and Real Estate Jour., Hemet, Calif., 1980-83; asst. adminstr. Anacapa Adventist Hosp., 1983-85; v.p. mktg. and devel. Boulder (Colo.) Meml. Hosp., 1985-89; v.p. devel. San Antonio Cmty. Hosp., Upland, Calif., 1989-90; pres., CEO Riverside (Calif.) Cmty. Hosp. Found., 1990—; ptnr. Philanthropic Mgmt. Group. Bd. dirs. Vol. Ctr. of Riverside. mem. Nat. Assn. for Healthcare Philanthropy (cert. mem.), Riverside Rotary Club (bd. dirs.), La Sierra U. Sch. of Bus. and Mgmt. (adv. coun.), So. Calif. Assn. for Hosp. Devel., Nat. Soc. of Fund Raising Execs. Republican. Office: Riverside Cmty Hosp Found 4445 Magnolia Ave # A Riverside CA 92501-4135

WILLIAMS, MARSHA KAY, data processing executive; b. Norman, Okla., Oct. 26, 1963; d. Charles Michael and Marilyn Louise (Bauman) Williams; m. Dale Lee Carabetta, Dec. 13, 1981. Student, Metro. State Coll., Denver. Data processing supr. Rose Mfg. Co., Englewood, Colo., 1981-84, Mile High Equip. Co., Denver, 1984-88; supr. info. tech. Ohmeda Monitoring Sys., Louisville, Colo., 1988—. Mem. info. tech. adv. bd. Warren Tech. Sch., 1994—. Mem. Bus. and Profl. Women's Assn. (Young Careerist award 1991), Data Processing Mgmt. Assn. Home: 3302 W 127th Ave Broomfield CO 80020-5800 Office: Ohmeda Monitoring Systems 1315 W Century Dr Louisville CO 80027-9560

WILLIAMS, MARY D(ENNEN), psychologist; b. Cin.; d. Frank Eugene and Katharine Powell (Wiley) D.; children from previous marriage: John Wiley Hartung, Katharine D. Hartung, Denny Hartung. AB, Radcliffe Coll., 1943; MS, U. Vt., 1948; MPA in Pub. Health, U. R.I., 1965; PhD, U. Oreg., 1982. Lic. psychologist, Oreg., Idaho. Instr. zoology U. R.I., Kingston, 1950-51, asst. prof. zoology in Pub. Health, 1957-59; grad. teaching fellow U. Oreg., Eugene, 1978-80; resident psychologist Portland, Oreg., 1982-85; pvt. practice psychologist Portland, 1985—. Mem. APA, Oreg. Psychol. Assn., Portland Psychol. Assn., Oreg. Psychoanalytic Found., Sigma Xi, Pi Sigma Alpha, Phi Kappa Phi.

WILLIAMS, MARY IRENE, college administrator; b. Hugo, Okla., June 30, 1944; d. Primer and Hyler B. (Tarkington) Jackson; m. Lee A. Williams (div. June 1981); 1 child, Monica Ariane. BS in Bus. Edn., Langston U., 1967; MS in Bus., Emporia (Kans.) State U., 1973; EdS, U. Nev., Las Vegas, 1977; D of Bus. Adminstrn. in Internat. Bus., U.S. Internat. U., 1992. Instr. Spokane (Wash.) C.C., 1967-70; tchr. bus. Topeka Pub. Schs., 1970-73; instr. Clark County C.C., Las Vegas, Nev., 1973—; assoc. dean of bus. Clark County C.C., Las Vegas, 1978-93; dean acad. support svcs. C.C. So. Nev., 1993—. Named Educator of Yr. Nucleus Plaza Assn., 1985, New Visions, Inc., 1986. Mem. NAFE, AAUW, Internat. Assn. Bus. Communicators, Nat. Bus. Edn. Assn., Nat. Coun. on Black Affairs, Am. Assn. Cmty. and Jr. Colls., Nat. Assn. Instrnl. Adminstrs., Nat. Rainbow Coalition. Office: CC So Nev 3200 E Cheyenne Ave North Las Vegas NV 89030-4228

WILLIAMS, MATT (MATTHEW DERRICK WILLIAMS), professional baseball player; b. Bishop, Calif., Nov. 28, 1965. Student, U. Nev., Las Vegas. With San Francisco Giants, 1986—; player Nat. League All-Star Team, 1990, 94. Recipient Gold Glove award, 1991, 93, 94, Silver Slugger award, 1990, 93-94; named to Sporting News Nat. League All-Star team, 1990, 93-94, Coll. All-Am. team Sporting News, 1986; Nat. League RBI Leader, 1990. Office: San Francisco Giants Candlestick Park San Francisco CA 94124*

WILLIAMS, MICHAEL EDWARD, lawyer; b. Ft. Worth, Aug. 10, 1955; s. Jerrol Evans and Helen Louise (Hoffner) W.; m. Jackie Ann Gordinier, Dec. 30, 1978; children: Margaret Eileen, James Andrew. BA, U. Calif., Riverside, 1977; JD, U. San Diego, 1980. Bar: Calif. 1980, U.S. Dist. Ct. (so. dist.) Calif. 1980, U.S. Tax Ct. 1981, U.S. Dist. Ct. (ea. and cen. dists.) Calif. 1982, U.S. Dist. Ct. (no. dist.) Calif. 1985. Assoc. Jamison & McFadden, Solana Beach, Calif., 1980-86, Dorazio, Barnhorst & Bonar, San Diego, 1986; sole practice Encinitas, Calif., 1987—. Atty. pro bono Community Resource Ctr., Encinitas, Calif., 1984—. Mem. Calif. State Bar Assn. (fee arbitrator 1992—), San Diego County Bar Assn. (client rels. com. 1990—, fee arbitration com. 1991—, ct. arbitrator). Democrat. Presbyterian. Office: 4405 Manchester Ave Ste 206 Encinitas CA 92024-7902

WILLIAMS, MICHAEL JAMES, editor; b. San Antonio, May 12, 1940; s. Daniel Arla and Sibyl Hortense (Kimmey) W.; children: Charles Keller, Kimberly Grace. BA in English, N. Ga. Coll., 1962; MA in Journalism, U. Wis., 1971. Commd. 2d lt. U.S. Army, 1962, advanced through grades to major; platoon leader U.S. Army, Ft. Hood, Tex., 1962-64; staff officer U.S. Army, 1964-67; comdr. U.S. Army, Vietnam, 1967, staff officer, 1971-72; staff officer U.S. Army, various locations, 1973-82; instr., trainer Nat. Ass. Underwater Instrs., Profl Assn. Diving Instrs., YMCA, ARC, Am. Heart Assn., 1973-76. Editor: Sources-The Journal of Underwater Education, 1989—. Patron Oreg. Shakespeare Festival, Ashland, 1990—. Mem. NRA (life), Pub. Rels. Soc. Am., Am. Assn. Desktop Pubs., Nat. Assn. Underwater Instrs. (dir. 1982—, Service award 1979). Episcopalian. Office: Nat Assn Underwater Instrs 4650 Arrow Hwy # 1 Montclair CA 91763-1223

WILLIAMS, MICHAEL KNIGHTON, social worker; b. Charleston, W.Va., Oct. 5, 1953; s. John Alexander and Barbara Ann (Knighton) W. BA, Northeastern U., 1976; MA, Boston U., 1982. Adoption social worker dept. pub. welfare Adoption Placement Unit, Boston, 1976-79; affirmative action/EEO officer Mass. Bay C.C., Wellesley, 1979-80; fin. aid counselor Talent Search Program, Boston, 1980-81; dir. Bromley/Cooper Collaborative, Jamaica Plain, Mass., 1981-83; account exec., radio announcer Sta. WXAZ-AM, St. Albans, W.Va., 1984; child placement counselor Maclaren Children's Ctr., El Monte, Calif., 1984-86; children svcs. worker II Dept. Childrens Svcs., L.A. County, Calif., 1986-93, Black Family Investment Project Rights of Passage Program, L.A., 1993—; adult-youth sports dir. Weingart YMCA, L.A., 1989—; film editor Sta. WVAH, Hurrican, W.Va., 1984; host, producer Inner City Beat Sta. WRKO, Boston, 1976-81. Founder Skip Wright Meml. Fund. Recipient award UPI, 1977. Mem. So. Calif. Mcpl. Athletic Fedn., CAL Basketball Ofcls. Assn., Masons, Elks, Iota Phi Theta (grad. chpt. pres.). Home: 833 S Mansfield Ave Apt 202 Los Angeles CA 90036-4949 Office: Dept Children Svcs Rites of Passage Program 11390 W Olympic Blvd Los Angeles CA 90064-1607

WILLIAMS, NANCY ELLEN-WEBB, social services administrator; b. Quincy, Ill., Aug. 1; d. Charles and Garnet Naomi (Davis) Webb; m. Jesse B. Williams, Apr. 11, 1959; children: Cynthia L. Williams Clay, Troy Andrea Williams Redic, Bernard Peter. BA, Quincy Coll., 1957; postgrad., Tenn. A&I U., 1961; M Pub. Adminstrn., U. Nev., Las Vegas, 1977; LHD (hon.), U. Humanistic Studies, 1986. Cert. peace officer, Nev. (chmn. Standards and Tng. Com., 1978-81); cert. social worker. Tchr. Shelby County Tng. Sch., Memphis, 1957-61; dep. probation officer Clark County Juvenile Ct., Las Vegas, 1961-66, supervising probation officer, 1966-74, dir. probation services, 1974-80, dir. intake admissions, 1980-81, dir. Child Haven, 1989—; mem. Nev. Crime Commn., 1970-81. Author: When We Were Colored, 1986, Dinah's Pain and Other Poems of the Black Life Experience, 1988, Them Gospel Songs, 1989; contbr. poetry to various mags. Mem. exec. com. Clark County Econ. Opportunity Bd., Las Vegas, 1963-71; chmn. So. Nev. Task Force on Corrections, 1974-81; mem. Gov.'s Com. on Justice Standards and Goals, 1979-81; bd. dirs. U. Humanistic Studies, Las Vegas, 1984—. Recipient Friend of Golden Gloves award Golden Gloves Regional Bd., 1981, Tribute to Black Women award U. Nev., Las Vegas, 1984, Commr.'s award HHS, 1991, Folklore mini-grant Nev. Coun. of the Arts, 1992. Fellow Am. Acad. Neurol. and Orthopedic Surgeons (assoc.); mem. AAUW, Nat. Council Juvenile Ct. Judges, Nat. Writers Assn. Democrat. Office: Flamingo Pecos Plaza 3430 E Flamingo Rd Ste 210 Las Vegas NV 89121-5064

WILLIAMS, NATHAN DALE, counselor; b. Vancouver, B.C., Can., Nov. 25, 1968; s. Douglas Niel and Marian Verna (Olson) W.; m. Sandra Ann Cobbs, Dec. 4, 1993. AA and Scis., Clark Coll., Vancouver, Wash., 1991; BA in Psychology magna cum laude, Colo. Christian U., Lakewood, 1993; MA in Counseling, Denver Sem., 1995. Technician Sun Heating & Air Conditioning, Vancouver, 1986-87; security officer Ram's Specialized Security Svcs., Inc., Portland, Oreg., 1991-92; athletic trainer Lakewood Athletic Club, 1992-93; dir. counseling and mental health Health Styles, Inc. at Lakewood Athletic Club, Lakewood, Colo., 1994-95; counselor, intern Christian Counseling Clinic, Denver, 1994-95, Heritage Christian Ctr., 1995; dir. counseling and testing U. Mary Hardin-Baylor, Belton, Tex., 1995—. With USAF, 1987-91. Mem. ACA, Christian Assn. Psychol. Studies.

WILLIAMS, PAMELA AVONNE, nutritionist and technical writer; b. Bklyn., July 18, 1958; d. Rogis and Erma Alison (Bennett) W.; 1 child, Erica Ashley. BS in Home Econs., Oakwood Coll., Huntsville, Ala., 1980; MPH in Nutrition and Health Edn., Loma Linda (Calif.) U., 1983; postgrad., U. Phoenix. Pub. health nutritionist Pub. Health Found.-WIC, Monterey Park, Calif., 1983-85; clin. nutritionist Charles R. Drew Postgrad. Med. Sch., L.A., 1985-88; nutrition program coord. Charles R. Drew U. Medicine and Sci., L.A., 1988-90, nutrition program dir., 1990-93; tech. nutrition writer Nutrilite Products Inc., Buena Park, Calif., 1993—; lctr. English as a Second Lang./Bible instr. Sam Yook Yang-a Hak Won, Seoul, Korea, 1978-79; lectr. in field. Contbr. articles to jours.; author: (poetry) Sleeping Giant, 1990 (1st pl. award 1990). Recipient Outstanding Tchr. of Yr. award C.R. Drew U. Medicine and Sci., 1993. Mem. Am. Dietetic Assn. (registered, asst. chair L.A. Dist. minority recruitment com. 1986-87). Office: Nutrilite Products Inc 5600 Beach Blvd Buena Park CA 90621-2007

WILLIAMS, PAMELA R., secondary school administrator; b. Tacoma, Feb. 9, 1950; d. Richard Bartle and Elaine Staab; m. Raymond L. Williams, 1972. BA in Edn. with distinction, Wash. State U., 1972; MA in Adminstrn., Washington U., St. Louis, 1983. Cert. tchr., Mo., Colo., adminstr., Colo. Tchr. Countryside Elem., DeSoto, Kans., 1972-77, U. Chgo. Lab Sch., 1977-78, Francis Parker Sch., Chgo., 1978-80; mid. sch. tchr., coord. English, Mary Inst., St. Louis, 1980-88; elem. bilingual tchr. Boulder (Colo.) Valley Schs., 1988-91, asst. prin, 1991—. Mem. ASCD, NEA, Am. Assn. Sch. Adminstrs. (women's caucus), Nat. Assn. Secondary Sch. Prins., Boulder Valley Edn. Assn., CORO Women in Leadership Alumnae Assn., Phi Delta Kappa. Office: Base Line MS 700 20th St Boulder CO 80302-7702

WILLIAMS, PAT, congressman; b. Helena, Mont., Oct. 30, 1937; m. Carol Griffith, 1965; children: Griff, Erin, Whitney. Student, U. Mont., 1956-57, William Jewell U.; BA, U. Denver, 1961; postgrad., Western Mont. Coll.; LLD (hon.), Carroll Coll., Montana Coll. of Mineral Sci. and Tech. Mem. Mont. Ho. of Reps., 1967, 69; exec. dir. Hubert Humphrey Presdl. campaign, Mont., 1968; exec. asst. to U.S. Rep. John Melcher, 1969-71; mem. Gov.'s Employment and Tng. Council, 1972-78, Mont. Legis. Reapportionment Commn., 1973; co-chmn. Jimmy Carter Presdl. campaign, Mont., 1976; mem. 96th-102nd Congresses from 1st Mont. dist., 1979—; ranking mem. postsecondary edn. subcom. Coordinator Mont. Family Edn. Program, 1971-78. Served with U.S. Army, 1960-61; Served with Army N.G., 1962-69. Mem. Mont. Fedn. Tchrs. Democrat. Lodge: Elks. Office: House of Representatives 2329 Rayburn Ho Office Bldg Washington DC 20515

WILLIAMS, PHYLLIS CUTFORTH, retired realtor; b. Moreland, Idaho, June 6, 1917; d. William Claude and Kathleen Jessie (Jenkins) Cutforth; m. Joseph Marsden Williams, Jan. 21, 1938 (dec. 1986); children: Joseph Marlis,

Bonnie L. Williams Thompson, Nancy K. Williams Stewart, Marjorie Williams Karren, Douglas Claude, Thomas Marsden, Wendy K. Williams Clark, Shannon I. Williams Ostler. Grad., Ricks Coll., 1935. Lic. realtor, Idaho. Tchr. Grace (Idaho) Elem. Sch., 1935-38; realtor Williams Realty, Idaho Falls, Idaho, 1972-77; mem. Idaho Senate, Boise, 1977; owner, mgr. river property. Compiler: Idaho Legisladies Cookbook, Cookin' Together, 1981. With MicroFilm Ctr., LDS Ch. Mission, Salt Lake City, 1989-90; block chmn. March of Dimes Soc.; active Idaho State Legisladies Club, 1966-84, v.p., 1982-84. Republican. Home: 1950 Carmel Dr Idaho Falls ID 83402-3020

WILLIAMS, QUINN PATRICK, lawyer; b. Evergreen Park, Ill., May 6, 1949; s. William Albert and Jeanne Marie (Quinlan) W.; children: Michael Ryan, Mark Reed, Kelly Elizabeth. BBA, U. Wis., 1972; JD, U. Ariz., 1974. Bar: Ariz. 1975, N.Y. 1984, U.S. Dist. Ct. Ariz. 1976. Vice pres., sec., gen. counsel Combined Comm. Corp., Phoenix, 1975-80; v.p., sec., gen. counsel Swensen's Ice Cream Co., Phoenix, 1980-83; sr. v.p. legal and adminstrn. Swensen's Inc., Phoenix, 1983-86; of counsel Winston & Strawn, Phoenix, 1985-87, ptnr., 1987-89, ptnr. Snell & Wilmer, Phoenix, 1989—. Vice chmn., treas. Combined Comm. Polit. Action Com., Phoenix, 1976-80; chmn. Ariz. Tech. Inventor, Ariz. Tech. Incubator, Ariz. Venture Capital Conf.; co-chair Gov. Small Bus. Advocate Exec. Coun., 1993—. Served with USAR, 1967-73. Mem. ABA, Maricopa County Bar Assn., N.Y. Bar Assn., State Bar Ariz., Internat. Franchise Assn., Paradise Valley Country Club, Phi Alpha Delta. Republican. Roman Catholic. Home: 8131 N 75th St Scottsdale AZ 85258-2781 Office: Snell & Wilmer One Arizona Ctr Phoenix AZ 85004

WILLIAMS, RANDY LEE, special education educator; b. Downey, Calif., Dec. 30, 1947; s. Leland Harold and Valerie Clara (Herman) W.; m. Betty Fry Williams, Mar. 10, 1977; children: Lee Timothy, Maileen. BA in Psychology, Pomona Coll., Claremont, Calif., 1970; MA in Clin. Psychology, Western Mich. U., 1973; PhD in Devel. and Child Psychology, U. Kans., 1976. Home and sch. therapist Multicap Ctr., Kalamazoo, 1971-73; dist. adviser, coord. rsch. devel., assoc. dir. For Project Follow Through, U. Kans., Lawrence, 1973-78; assoc. dir. follow through program U. Kans., Lawrence, 1973-78; dir. comm. disorders Gonzaga U., Spokane, Wash., 1981-85, asst. prof. spl. edn., 1979-83, assoc. prof. spl. edn., 1983-87, prof. spl. edn., 1987—; adj. asst. prof. human devel. U. Kans., Lawrence, 1977-79; cons. in field. Assoc. editor: Education and Treatment of Children, 1983-86; guest editor, reviewer, chair various jours.; contbr. articles to profl. jours. Mem. Mayor's Com. on Handicapped, Spokane, 1982-84; cons., vol. various sch. and cmty. activities. Mem. N.W. Assn. Behavior Analysis (conf. chair 1990-91), Assn. Behavior Analysis, Coun. for Exceptional Children, Assn. Direct Instrn., Assn. Retarded Citizens, Parent Tchr. Student Assn. Office: Gonzaga U Dept Spl Edn Ad Box 25 Spokane WA 99258

WILLIAMS, RICHARD JAMES, food service executive; b. Goliad, Tex., Aug. 19, 1942; s. L. D. and Freida Irene (Watkins) W.; m. Shirley Ann Mihalik, July 11, 1967; children: Kenneth F., Dawn L. AA, Santa Ana Jr. Coll. (Calif.), 1965. Area mgr. Jack in the Box Restaurant, San Diego, 1972-80; v.p. ops. Franchise Dirs., Inc., Bradley, Ill., 1980-81; area supr. Pizza Hut of Am., Inc., Lombard, Ill., 1981-83; regional dir. of food svc. Montgomery Ward Co., Chgo., 1983-84, v.p. ops. Golden Bear Restaurants, Mt. Prospect, Ill., 1983-84; franchise area dir. Wendy's Internat., Oakbrook Terrace, Ill., 1984-85; regional mgr. franchise ops. Godfather's Pizza, Inc., 1985-89; franchise dist. mgr. Tony Roma's "A Place for Ribs", Dallas, 1989—, franchise owner, Phoenix, Ariz. Author: Anthology of American High School Poetry, 1959. Served with USMC, 1960-72. Decorated Silver Star, Bronze Star. Republican. Mem. Chs. of Christ. Home: 3541 E Renee Dr Phoenix AZ 85024-3248 Office: Jest Ent 15025 N 74th St Scottsdale AZ 85260-2406

WILLIAMS, RICHARD STANLEY, chemistry educator; b. Kodiak, Alaska, Oct. 27, 1951; s. Bobby Lebe and Shirley Ann (Tweten) W.; m. Jennifer C.-Y. Kao, June 30, 1990. BA, Rice U., 1974; MS, U. Calif., Berkeley, 1976, PhD, 1978. Mem. tech. staff AT&T Bell Labs., Murray Hill, N.J., 1978-80; asst. prof. chemistry UCLA, 1980-84, assoc. prof., 1984-86, prof., 1986—, vice chmn. dept. chemistry, 1991-94. Mem. editorial bd. Chem. Physics Letters Sci. Jour., 1986-93, Jour. of Materials Rsch., 1988-92, Accounts of Chem. Rsch., 1995—; contbr. articles to profl. jours. Fellow NSF, 1974-77, Alfred P. Sloan Found., 1984-86; Camille and Henry Dreyfus Found. scholar, 1983-88. Mem. AAAS, Am. Chem. Soc., Am. Phys. Soc., Am. Vacuum Soc., Materials Research Soc., Alpha Chi Sigma (Glenn T. Seaborg award 1984, Herbert Newby McCoy award 1989). Office: UCLA Dept Chemistry PO Box 951569 Los Angeles CA 90095-1569

WILLIAMS, RICHARD T., hospital administrator; b. 1931. With Dow Chem. Corp., Midland, Mich., 1958-88, Janis Pacific Inc., San Luis Obispo, Calif., 1988-90, Long Beach Meml. Health Ctr., Calif., 1990-93; with Childrens Hosp. L.A. Inc., 1993—, pres., chief exec. officer. Office: Childrens Hosp Los Angeles Inc 4650 W Sunset Blvd Los Angeles CA 90027-6016

WILLIAMS, ROBERT JASON, psychotherapist, consultant; b. Kansas City, Mo., Nov. 1, 1956; s. Glenn L. and Verna May (Long) W.; m. Patricia Mae Gloodt, Nov. 6, 1973 (div. Dec. 1991); children: Anthony Lee, Robert Jason Jr.; m. Virginia K. Wescott, Dec. 6, 1991. Grad. of Theology, Bapt. Bible Coll., 1983, BA, 1984; ThD, Christian Bible Coll., 1986; ThM (hon.), Fundamental Bapt. Theol. Sem., 1986; MA, Liberty U., 1991. Cert. doctoral diplomat Internat. Assn. Counselors & Therapists. Sr. pastor Pine Grove Bapt. Ch., Marshfield, Mo., 1982-84, Sulphur Springs Bapt. Ch., El Dorado Springs, Mo., 1985-90; dir. Dr. R.J. Williams & Assocs., Englewood, Colo., 1990—; cons. Woodland Park (Colo.) Med., 1990-93, Christian Counselor, Independence, Mo., 1990—, Continental Corp., Englewood, Colo., 1993-94. With USMC, 1974-80. Office: Williams & Assocs 6535 S Dayton Ste 1400 Englewood CO 80111

WILLIAMS, ROBERT STONE, protective services official; b. Mathews, Va., Jan. 22, 1952; s. Charles H. and Anne (Stone) W.; m. Danielle Williams, July 1987. AAS, Rowan Tech. Inst., 1972; BS in Fire Protection and Safety Engring., Okla. State U., 1975, MBA, 1976. Adminstrv. specialist Oklahoma City Fire Dept., 1977-79; dep. fire chief Clovis Fire Dept., N.Mex., 1979-82; fire chief Billings Fire Dept., Mont., 1982-88; fire chief City of Spokane, Wash., 1988—. Mem. Wash. State Bldg. Code Coun., 1989-94; bd. dirs. Salvation Army, Billings, 1984-85, Am. Heart Assn., Clovis, N.Mex., 1980-82; chmn. Internat. Fire Code Inst., 1993-94, 94-95, mem., 1990—. Named Fireperson Yr. Billings Downtown Exchange Club, 1988. Mem. Western Fire Chiefs Assn. (1st v.p. 1984-85, pres. 1985-86), Internat. Assn. Fire Chiefs, Nat. Fire Protection Assn., Curry County Jaycees (v.p. 1981-82, Jaycee of Yr. 1982), Billings Jaycees (bd. dirs. 1983-87, v.p. community devel. 1985, Outstanding Jaycee 1983, Disting. Service award 1985), Mont. Jaycees (treas. 1986-87, speak-up program mgr. 1986-87, Outstanding Young Montanan award 1985-86). Roman Catholic. Office: Spokane Fire Dept 44 W Riverside Ave Spokane WA 99201-0114

WILLIAMS, ROBERT WILMOT, actuary; b. N.Y.C., Sept. 6, 1943; s. Roger and Odessa Roane (Lastrapes) W.; m. Arleen Rolling, Aug. 13, 1965 (div.); children: Laura Roane, Keith Clayon; m. Margaret Carol Slyter, May 13, 1989. BA, La. State U., 1965; postgrad., Am. U., Washington, 1966-67, Ariz. State U., Tempe, 1975-78. Statistician USPHS, Washington, 1965-68; chief statistician V.I. Health Dept., St. Thomas, 1968-71; actuary Ariz. State Compensation Fund, Phoenix, 1972—; cons. Ariz. State Personnel Com., Phoenix, 1975-82; chmn. stats. com. Am. Assn. State Funds, 1983. Contbr. articles to profl. jours. Mem. Villa Montessori Sch. Bd. Dirs., Phoenix, 1978-82. Mem. Ariz. Statis. Assn. (pres. 1979), Mensa, 20-30 Internat. Office: State Compensation Fund 3031 N 2nd St Phoenix AZ 85012-3015

WILLIAMS, RONALD LEE, pharmacologist; b. Koleen, Ind., June 26, 1936; s. Marion Raymond and Doris May (Lynch) W.; m. Sondra Sue Cobb, June 7, 1957; children: Robin Lee, Christopher P., David R., Jonathon V. BS, Butler U., 1959, MS, 1961; PhD, Tulane U., 1964. Registered pharmacist, Colo. From instr. to assoc. prof. pharmacology La. State U., New Orleans, 1964-84, assoc. prof. medicine, 1978-84, ret., 1984; asst. dir. Dept. of Corrections Hosp. Pharmacy, Canon City, Colo., 1986—; expert adv. panel renal drugs U.S. Pharmacopeia Drug Info., 1981-85; cons. in field. Editorial bd. jour. Pharmacology, 1979; reviewer jour. Pharmaceutical Sci., 1976; contbr. articles to profl. jours. La. Heart Assn. grantee, 1964, 66. Mem. Am. Soc. Pharmacology, N.Y. Acad. Sci., Fedn. Am. Soc. Exptl. Biology, So. Colo. Soc. Hosp. Pharm. Assn., Sigma Xi. Republican. Baptist.

WILLIAMS, RONALD OSCAR, systems engineer; b. Denver, May 10, 1940; s. Oscar H. and Evelyn (Johnson) W. BS in Applied Math., U. Colo. Coll. Engring., 1964, postgrad. U. Colo., U. Denver, George Washington U. Computer programmer Apollo Systems dept., missile and space divsn. Gen. Electric Co., Kennedy Space Ctr., Fla., 1965-67, Manned Spacecraft Ctr., Houston, 1967-68; computer programmer U. Colo., Boulder, 1968-73; computer programmer analyst def. systems divsn. System Devel. Corp. for NORAD, Colorado Springs, 1974-75; engr. def. systems and command-and-info. systems Martin Marietta Aerospace, Denver, 1976-80; systems engr. space and comm. group, def. info. systems divsn. Hughes Aircraft Co., Aurora, Colo., 1980-89; rsch. analyst, 1990—. Vol. fireman Clear Lake City (Tex.) Fire Dept., 1968; officer Boulder Emergency Squad, 1969-76, rescue squadman, 1969-76, liaison to cadets, 1971, pers. officer, 1971-76, exec. bd., 1971-76, award of merit, 1971, 72, emergency med. technician 1973—; spl. police officer Boulder Police Dept., 1970-75; spl. dep. sheriff Boulder County Sheriff's Dept., 1970-71; nat. adv. bd. Am. Security Coun., 1979-91, Coalition of Peace through Strength, 1979-91. Served with USMCR, 1958-66. Decorated Organized Res. medal; recipient Cost Improvement Program award Hughes Aircraft Co., 1982, Systems Improvement award, 1982, Top Cost Improvement Program award, 1983. Mem. AAAS, AIAA, Math. Assn. Am., Am. Math. Soc., Soc. Indsl. and Applied Math., Math. Study Unit of the Am. Topical Assn., Armed Forces Comm. and Electronics Assn., Assn. Old Crows, Am. Def. Preparedness Assn., Marine Corps Assn., Air Force Assn., U.S. Naval Inst., Nat. Geog. Soc., Smithsonian Instn., Soc. Amateur Radio Astronomers, Met. Opera Guild, Colo. Hist. Soc., Hist. Denver, Inc., Historic Boulder, Inc., Hawaiian Hist. Soc., Denver Botanic Gardens, Denver Mus. Natural History, Denver Zool. Found., Inc., Mensa. Lutheran.

WILLIAMS, RUTH LEE, clinical social worker; b. Dallas, June 24, 1944; d. Carl Woodley and Nancy Ruth (Gardner) W. BA, So. Meth. U., 1966; M Sci.in Social Work, U. Tex., Austin, 1969. Milieu coordinator Starr Commonwealth, Albion, Mich., 1969-73; clin. social worker Katherine Hamilton Mental Health Care, Terre Haute, Ind., 1973-74; clin. social worker, supr. Pikes Peak Mental Health Ctr., Colorado Springs, Colo., 1974-78; pvt. practice social work Colorado Springs, 1978—; pres. Hearthstone Inn, Inc., Colorado Springs, 1978—; practitioner Jin Shin Jyutsu, Colorado Springs, 1978—; pres., v.p. bd. dirs. Premier Care (formerly Colorado Springs Mental Health Care Providers Inc.), 1986-87, chmn. quality assurance com., 1987-89, v.p. bd. dirs., 1992-93. Author, editor: From the Kitchen of The Hearthstone Inn, 1981, 2d rev. edit., 1986, 3d rev. edit., 1992. Mem. Am. Bd. Examiners in Clin. Social Work (charter mem., cert.), Colo. Soc. Clin. Social Work (editor 1976), Nat. Assn. Soc. Workers (diplomate), Nat. Bd. Social Work Examiners (cert.), Nat. Assn. Ind. Innkeepers, So. Meth. U. Alumni Assn. (life). Home: 11555 Howells Rd Colorado Springs CO 80908-3735 Office: 536 E Uintah St Colorado Springs CO 80903-2515

WILLIAMS, SALLY, landscape designer; b. Kansas City, Mo., June 30, 1955; d. Douglas John and Margaret Ann (Paul) Williams; m. Siegfried Peter Duray-Bito, June 16, 1984; children: Cassie, Alana. BA, Metro State Coll., Denver, 1979. Bus. mgr. Muse, Denver, 1985-87; exec. dir. Colo. Fedn. of the Arts, Denver, 1987-88; owner Perennial Garden Planning, Littleton, Colo., 1992—. Advanced master gardener Arapahoe County Ext. Svc., Littleton, 1985—. Home and Office: Perennial Garden Planning 5475 Manitou Rd Littleton CO 80123-2936

WILLIAMS, SPENCER MORTIMER, federal judge; b. Reading, Mass., Feb. 24, 1922; s. Theodore Ryder and Anabel (Hutchison) W.; m. Kathryn Bramlage, Aug. 20, 1943; children: Carol Marcia (Mrs. James B. Garvey), Peter, Spencer, Clark, Janice, Diane (Mrs. Sean Quinn). AB, UCLA, 1943; postgrad., Hastings Coll. Law, 1946; JD, U. Calif., Berkeley, 1948. Bar: Calif. 1949, U.S. Supreme Ct. 1952. Assoc. Beresford & Adams, San Jose, Calif., 1949, Rankin, O'Neal, Center, Luckhardt, Bonney, Marlais & Lund, San Jose, Evans, Jackson & Kennedy, Sacramento; county counsel Santa Clara County, 1955-67; adminstr. Calif. Health and Welfare Agy., Sacramento, 1967-69; judge U.S. Dist. Ct. (no. dist.) Calif., San Francisco, from 1971, now sr. judge; County exec. pro tem, Santa Clara County; adminstr. Calif. Youth and Adult Corrections Agy., Sacramento; sec. Calif. Human Relations Agy., Sacramento, 1967-70. Chmn. San Jose Christmas Seals Drive, 1953, San Jose Muscular Dystrophy Drive, 1953, 54; team capt. fund raising drive San Jose YMCA, 1960; co-chmn. indsl. sect. fund raising drive Alexian Bros. Hosp., San Jose, 1964; team capt. fund raising drive San Jose Hosp.; mem. com. on youth and govt. YMCA, 1967-68; Candidate for Calif. Assembly, 1954, Calif. Atty. Gen., 1966, 70; Bd. dirs. San Jose Better Bus. Bur., 1955-66, Boys City Boys' Club, San Jose, 1965-67; pres. trustees Santa Clara County Law Library, 1955-66. Served with USNR, 1943-46; to lt. comdr. JAG Corps USNR, 1950-52, PTO. Named San Jose Man of Year, 1954. Mem. ABA, Calif. Bar Assn. (vice chmn. com. on publicly employed attys. 1962-63), Santa Clara County Bar Assn., Sacramento Bar Assn., Internat. Assn. Trial Judges (pres. 1995-96), Calif. Dist. Attys. Assn. (pres. 1963-64), Nat. Assn. County Civil Attys. (pres. 1963-64), 9th Cir. Dist. Judges Assn. (pres. 1981-83), Fed. Judges Assn. (pres. 1982-87), Kiwanis, Theta Delta Chi. Office: US Dist Ct 280 S 1st St San Jose CA 95113-3002

WILLIAMS, STANLEY CLARK, medical entomologist, educator; b. Long Beach, Calif., Aug. 24, 1939; s. Thomas and Sadie Elenore (Anderson) W.; m. Charlene E. Fernald; children: Lisa M., Thomas S.; m. Roxanna Berlin, Aug. 30, 1981; 1 child, Erin B. AB, San Diego State Coll., 1961, MA, 1963; postgrad., U. Kans., 1963-64; PhD, Ariz. State U., 1968. Cert. secondary tchr., Calif. Instr. San Diego Mus. Nat. History, 1957-59, asst. curator herpetology, 1957-61; park naturalist U.S. Nat. Park Svc., San Diego, 1960-62; instr. Grossmont (Calif.) High Sch. Dist., 1962-63, Ariz. State U., Tempe, 1964-66; prof. biology San Francisco State U., 1967—; vis. prof. biology USAF Acad., 1993-94; mem. adv. bd. San Francisco Insect Zoo. Contbr. over 60 articles to profl. jours. Grantee NSF, 1968-72; recipient Travel grant T.P. Hearne Co. Fellow Calif. Acad. Sci.; mem. Am. Arachnological Soc., San Francisco Beekeepers Assn. (pres. 1984-85), Pacific Coast Entomol. Soc. (pres. 1987), Assn. Biologists for Computing (pres. 1986-88), Soc. Vector Ecologists (editorial bd. 1986—), Western Apicultural Soc. (v.p. 1987-88, pres. 1988-89), Soc. Systematic Biologists, Willi Hennig Soc., Brit. Arachnological Soc., Classification Soc. N.Am. Office: San Francisco State U Dept Biology San Francisco CA 94132

WILLIAMS, STEPHEN, anthropologist, educator; b. Mpls., Aug. 28, 1926; s. Clyde Garfield and Lois (Simmons) W.; m. Eunice Ford, Jan. 6, 1962; children: Stephen John, Timothy. BA, Yale U., 1949, PhD, 1954; MA (hon.), U. Mich., 1950; MA, Harvard, 1962. Asst. anthropology dept. Peabody Mus., Yale U., 1950-52; mem. faculty Harvard U., Cambridge, Mass., 1958—, prof. anthropology, 1967-72, Peabody prof., 1972-93, prof. emeritus, chmn. dept., 1967-69; rsch. fellow Peabody Mus., Harvard U., Cambridge, Mass., 1954-57, mem. staff, 1954—, dir. mus., 1967-77; curator N.Am. Archaeology, 1962-93, hon. curator 1993—; dir. rsch. of Peabody Mus.'s Lower Miss. Survey, 1958-93. Author books and articles on N.Am. archaeology and "Fantastic" archaeology. Home: 1017 Foothills Trl Santa Fe NM 87505-4537 Office: PO Box 22354 Santa Fe NM 87502-2354

WILLIAMS, STEPHEN JOSEPH, education educator, researcher; b. Washington, Dec. 14, 1948; s. David and Nettie (Robbins) W.; m. Sandra J. Guerra, Jan. 19, 1980; children: Jeffrey, Daniel. BS, Carnegie Mellon U., 1970; MS, MIT, 1971; SM, Harvard U., 1972, ScD, 1974. Assoc. prof. health adminstrn. program Sch. of Pub. Health U. Wash., Seattle, 1975-80; prof., dept. head div. health svcs. adminstrn. Grad. Sch. Pub. Health San Diego State U., 1980—. Adv. editor Internat. Dictionary of Medicine and Biology, 1981-87; series editor, cons.: Wiley Series in Health Services, 1978-89, Delmar Series in Health Services, 1989—; mem. editorial bd. Jour. of Practice in Mgmt., 1989—; contbr. numerous articles to profl. jours. Office: San Diego State U Coll Health Human Svcs San Diego CA 92182

WILLIAMS, STUART VANCE, real estate executive; b. Bloomington, Ind., Aug. 5, 1960; s. Walter and Jacqueline (Block) W.; m. Lucy Keenan, Sept. 5, 1993. BA, Claremont McKenna Coll., Calif., 1982; MBA, Harvard U., 1986. Nat. accounts officer Lloyds Bank calif., L.A., 1982-84; asst. project mgr. Pacific Realty, Dallas, 1985; prin. The Norman Co., Seattle, 1986-92; prin., co-founder Pacific Real Estate Ptnrs., Bellevue, Wash., 1993—. Bd. dirs. Alki Found., Seattle, 1992-94, North End Jewish Cmty. Ctr., Seattle, 1994—; campaign vol. Rice for Mayor, Congress, Seattle, 1989, 91. Mem. Claremont McKenna Coll. Alumni Assn. (bd. dirs. 1988-90), Rotary. Home: 6820 Phinney Ave N Seattle WA 98103-5238 Office: Pacific Real Estate Ptnrs 1975 112th Ave NE Ste 201 Bellevue WA 98004-2942

WILLIAMS, SUE M., corporate communications specialist, writer; b. Sumter, S.C., Aug. 20, 1942; d. Perry Harrington and Ida (Sumter) Taylor; m. Elwood E. Williams, Mar. 9, 1963 (div. 1969); 2 children. Diploma, cert., Communications Inst. of Am., 1968; BA, U. Colo., 1974; R. Sc. F., Ernest Holmes Coll. Ch. of Religious Sci., 1979. Ordained to ministry. Long distance operator Mountain Bell/Penn Bell, Phila. & Colorado Springs, Colo., 1964-69; comml. teller Exch. Nat. Bank, Colorado Springs, 1969-74; ops. trainee Cen. Bank of Denver, 1974-75; legal specialist USAFR, Lowry AFB, Colo., 1975-77; asst. mgr. Western Airlines, L.A., 1974-87; supr. reservation sales Delta Air Lines, L.A., 1987-88; sr. sec., office mgr. U. Colo., Denver, 1988-89; sales coord. Hewlett Packard Co., Englewood, Colo., 1989-90; supr. U.S. Sprint (United Telecom), Denver, 1990—. Contbr. articles to profl. jours. Mem. Vets. Club, Colorado Springs, 1973-74; various offices L.A. Election Dept., 1983-85; appointed vet. com. Calif. Reps., L.a., 1985; participant Hands Across Am., L.A., 1985, The Bolder Boulder, various walking races for local charity; charter mem. Women in Mil. Meml. Found., Washington, 1990. With USAF, 1961-63. Mem. Am. Legion, Coll. Devine Metaphysics Alumni Assn. (area v.p. 1982—). Office: US Sprint 1099 18th St Ste 1210 Denver CO 80202-1908

WILLIAMS, SUSAN EILEEN, urban planner; b. Chgo., Dec. 13, 1952; d. Joseph Andrew and Alice (Regnier) W.; 1 child, Ryan Joseph. AA in Polit. Sci., Coll. of Desert, Palm Desert, Calif., 1971; BA in Polit. Sci., U. Calif., Riverside, 1973; M of Pub. Adminstrn., Consortium Calif. State Colls. and Univs., 1982. Planning trainee City of Indio, Calif., 1975-79, assoc. planner, 1979-80, prin. planner, 1980-90, prin. planner redevel. agy., 1983-90; supervising planner J.F. Davidson Assocs., Inc., Palm Desert, Calif., 1990-94; dir. cmty. devel. City of Coachella, Calif., 1994—. Mem. Am. Planning Assn., Assn. Environ Profls., Ill. Geneal. Soc., Geneal. Club Am. Roman Catholic. Office: City of Coachella 1515 6th St Coachella CA 92236-1713

WILLIAMS, THEODORE EARLE, industrial distribution company executive; b. Cleve., May 9, 1920; s. Stanley S. and Blanche (Albaum) W.; m. Rita Cohen, Aug. 28, 1952; children: Lezlie, Richard Atlas, Shelley, William Atlas, Wayne, Marsha, Patti Blake, Jeff Blake. Student, Wayne U., 1937-38; BS in Engring, U. Mich., 1942, postgrad. in bus. adminstrn, 1942. Pres. Wayne Products Co., Detroit, 1942-43, L.A., 1947-49; pres. Williams Metal Products Co., Inglewood, Calif., 1950-69; chmn. bd., pres., chief exec. officer Bell Industries, L.A., 1970—; instr. U. Mich., 1942. Patentee in field. Served to 1st lt. AUS, 1943-46. Recipient Humanitarian award City of L.A., 1977. Democrat. Home: 435 N Layton Way Los Angeles CA 90049-2022 Office: Bell Industries Inc 11812 San Vicente Blvd Los Angeles CA 90049-5022

WILLIAMS, T(HOMAS) PATRICK, psychologist; b. Wichita, Kans., Mar. 7, 1950; s. Vernon Lowell and Marjorie Irene (Melton) W.; m. Priscilla Ann Wingent, Oct. 7, 1972 (div. Nov. 1993); children: Megan, Briana. BA in Psychology, BA in Human Rels., Kans. U., 1972; MA Psychology, West Ga. Coll., 1975; EdD in Psychology, U. No. Colo., 1977. Lic. psychologist, Colo. Counselor U. No. Colo., Greeley, 1975-77; instr. Alms Coll., Greeley, 1975-77; dir. clin. svcs. Foothills Gateway Rehab. Ctr., Ft. Collins, Colo., 1977-87; pvt. practice psychology Loveland, Colo., 1977—; cons. Williams and Assocs., Loveland, 1987—; mediator Resolutions Inc., Loveland, 1994—. Author: Transpersonal Psychology: An Introductory Guidebook, 1980. Mem. City Coun. City of Loveland, 1989-93; mem. Task Force on Future of Childrenand Families in Am., 1990-93. Mem. APA, Colo. Psychol. Assn., Rotary (pres. 1993-94). Democrat. Methodist. Office: Front Range Psychotherapy Assocs 101 E 6th St Loveland CO 80537

WILLIAMS, VIVIAN LEWIE, college counselor; b. Columbia, S.C., Jan. 23, 1923; d. Lemuel Arthur Sr. and Ophelia V. (McDaniel) Lewie; m. Charles Warren Williams, Apr. 4, 1947 (div. Dec. 1967); children: Pamela Ann Williams-Coote, Charles Warren Jr. BA, Allen U., 1942; MA, U. Mich., 1946, postgrad., 1946, 48; MS, U. So. Calif., 1971, postgrad., 1971-72. Cert. marriage, family and child counselor, Calif.; cert. Calif. C.C. counselor. Asst. prof. psychology Tenn. State Agrl. and Indsl. U., Nashville, 1946-47; asst. prof. edn. Winston-Salem (N.C.) State U., 1947-50; asst. prof. edn., dir. tchr. edn. Allen U., Columbia, S.C., 1951-53; specialist reading, coord. lang. arts Charlotte (N.C.) Mecklenburg Schs., 1963-67, cons. comprehensive sch. improvement project, 1967-69; asst. prof. edn., psychology Johnson C. Smith U., Charlotte, 1967-69; counselor, team leader Centennial, U. So. Calif. Tchr. Corps, L.A., 1970-73; counselor Compton (Calif.) C.C., 1973—, adv. fgn. student, 1975-85; co-developer Hyde Park Estates and The Moors, Charlotte, N.C., 1960-63. Pres. bd. dirs. Charlotte Day Nursery, 1956-59; bd. dirs. Taylor St. USO, Columbia, S.C., 1951-53; sec. southwest region Nat. Alliance Family Life, 1973-74; sec. bd. dirs. NCCJ, Charlotte, 1959-62. Recipient Faculty Audit Program award Ford/Carnegie Found., Harvard U., Cambridge, Mass., 1968, Pub. Svc. Achievement award WSOC Broadcasting Co.; fellow U. Mich., 1946. Mem. NAACP (life, Golden Heritage mem. 1992), AAUW (life), NEA (life), Am. Fedn. Tchrs., Faculty Assn. Calif. C.C., Nat. Acad. Counselors and Family Therapists (life, clin. mem., pres. S.W. region 1989), C.C. Counselors Assn., The Links, Inc. (Harbor area chpt. historian 1985-87, chaplain 1990-94), Jack and Jill Am. (charter mem., organizer Charlotte chpt., pres. 1954-56), Women on Target, Calif. Tchrs. Assn., Delta Sigma Theta, Alpha Gamma Sigma (Golden Apple award 1981). Democrat. Methodist. Home: 6621 Caro St Paramount CA 90723-4755 Office: Compton Community Coll 1111 E Artesia Blvd Compton CA 90221-5314

WILLIAMS, WALTER BAKER, mortgage banker; b. Seattle, May 12, 1921; s. William Walter and Anna Leland (Baker) W.; m. Marie Davis Wilson, July 6, 1945; children: Kathryn Williams-Mullins, Marcia Frances Williams Swanson, Bruce Wilson, Wendy Susan. BA, U. Wash., 1943; JD, Harvard U., 1948. With Bogle & Gates, Seattle, 1948-63, ptnr., 1960-63; pres. Continental Inc., Seattle, 1963-91, chmn., 1991—; bd. dirs. United Graphics Inc., Seattle, 1973-86, Fed. Nat. Mortgage Assn., 1976-77; chmn. Continental Savings Bank, 1991—. Rep. Wash. State Ho. of Reps., Olympia, 1961-63; sen. Wash. State Senate, Olympia, 1963-71; chmn. Econ. Devel. Council of Puget Sound, Seattle, 1981-82; pres. Japan-Am. Soc. of Seattle, 1971-72; chmn. Woodland Park Zoo Commn., Seattle, 1984-85. Served to capt. USMC, 1942-46, PTO. Recipient Brotherhood Citation, NCCJ, Seattle, 1980. Mem. Mortgage Bankers Assn. Am. (pres. 1973-74), Wash. Mortgage Bankers Assn., Fed. Home Loan Mortgage Corp. (adv. com.), Wash. Savs. League (bd. dirs., chmn. 1991-92), Rotary (pres. local club 1984-85), Rainier Club Seattle (pres. 1987-88). Republican. Congregationalist. Office: Continental Inc 2000 Two Union Sq Seattle WA 98101

WILLIAMS, W(ALTER) D(AVID), aerospace executive, consultant; b. Chgo., July 22, 1931; s. Walter William and Theresa Barbara (Gilman) W.; m. Joan Haven Armstrong, Oct. 22, 1960; children: Latham Lloyd, Clayton Chapell, William Haven. BS, Ohio U., 1951; MBA, Harvard U., 1955; MS, MIT, 1972. Supr. fin. policy and systems Hughes Aircraft Co., Culver City, Calif., 1955-57; staff mem. Rand Corp. and SDC, Santa Monica, Calif., 1957-60; mgr. adminstrn. and fin. Microwave Div. TRW Inc., Canoga Park, Calif., 1960-63; exec. asst. Space Labs. Northrop Corp., Hawthorne, Calif., 1963-66; fin. mgr. comml. group Aircraft Div. Northrop Corp., Hawthorne, Calif., 1966-72; dir. internat. plans Northrop Corp., L.A., 1972-74, dir. internat. mkt. devel., 1974-77, exec. dir. internat., 1977-93; pres. Williams Internat. Assocs., L.A., 1994—; export advisor U.S. Sec. Commerce, Washington, 1986—. Author (study/lect. series) Internat. Def. Mktg., 1982. Dir. KCET Men's Coun., L.A., 1970; pres. Westwood Rep. Club, L.A., 1970; assoc. mem. Rep. State Ctrl. Com., Calif., 1968; div. chmn. Rep. Ctrl. Com., L.A. County, 1968. Served to capt. U.S. Army, 1951-53. Recipient fellowship Alfred P. Sloan Found., 1971-72. Mem. AIAA, Soc. Sloan Fellows, MIT Club, Harvard Bus. Sch. Assn., Newcomen Soc., Chaine des Rotisseurs, L.A. Country Club, Harvard Club, Soc. Bacchus Am., Delta Sigma Pi. Office: Williams Internat Assocs PO Box 491178 Los Angeles CA 90049-9178

WILLIAMS, WAYNE DE ARMOND, lawyer; b. Denver, Sept. 24, 1914; s. Wayne Cullen and Lena Belle (Day) W.; m. Virginia Brinton Deal, Sept. 9, 1937 (dec. Feb. 1992); children: Marcia Lee, Daniel Deal; m. Thelma Ralston, Apr. 8, 1995. A.B., U. Denver, 1936; J.D., Columbia U., 1938. Bar: Colo. 1938. Pvt. practice Denver, 1938-43, 46-58; ptnr. firm Williams & Erickson (and predecessors), Denver, 1958-77; gen. counsel Denver Water Dept., 1977-91; asst. city atty. Denver, 1939-43, spl. asst. city atty., 1946-49; chmn. Denver County Ct. Nominating Commn., 1968-69; mem. Denver Dist. Ct. Nominating Commn., 1969-75; lectr. in field U. Denver, 1947-60. Contbr. articles to legal jours. Chmn. Denver Mcpl. Airport Adv. Commn., 1963-65; chancellor Rocky Mountain Meth. Ann. Conf., 1978-86; former mem. governing bd. Colo. chpt. English Speaking Union, Colo. Tuberculosis Assn., Colo. Soc. for Prevention Blindness; mem. adv. bd. Anchor Ctr. for Blind Children. Capt. JAGD U.S. Army, 1943-46. Mem. ABA (Ross Essay prize 1944), Colo. Bar Assn. (gov. 1974-77), Denver Bar Assn. (pres. 1974-75), Sigma Alpha Epsilon, Phi Delta Phi, Omicron Delta Kappa. Democrat. Methodist. Clubs: Lions, Masons. Home: 625 S Alton Way Apt 3A Denver CO 80231-1752

WILLIAMS, WILLIAM ARNOLD, agronomy educator; b. Johnson City, N.Y., Aug. 2, 1922; s. William Truesdall and Nellie Viola (Tompkins) W.; m. Madeline Patricia Moore, Nov. 27, 1943; children—David, Kathleen, Andrew. B.S., Cornell U., 1947, M.S., 1948, Ph.D., 1951. Prof. emeritus U. Calif., Davis, 1993—. Editor agr. sect. McGraw-Hill Ency. Sci. & Tech.; contbr. articles to profl. jours. Mem. Nat. Alliance for Mentally Ill. Served to lt. U.S. Army, 1943-46. Grantee NSF, 1965-82, Kellogg Found., 1963-67; Fulbright scholar, Australia, 1960, Rockefeller Found. scholar, Costa Rica, 1966. Fellow AAAS, Am. Soc. Agronomy, Crop Sci. Soc. Am.; mem. Soil Sci. Soc. Am., Soc. Range Mgmt., Am. Statis. Assn., Assn. for Tropical Biology, Fedn. Am. Scientists, Am. Math. Soc., Math Assn. Am. Democrat. Home: 718 Oeste Dr Davis CA 95616-3531 Office: Univ California Dept Agronomy And Rang Davis CA 95616

WILLIAMS, WILLIAM COREY, Old Testament educator, consultant; b. Wilkes-Barre, Pa., July 12, 1937; s. Edward Douglas and Elizabeth Irene (Schooley) W.; m. Alma Simmenroth Williams, June 27, 1959; 1 child, Linda. Diploma in Ministerial Studies, NE Bible Inst., 1962; BA in Bibl. Studies, Cen. Bible Coll., 1963, MA in Religion, 1964; MA in Hebrew and Near Ea. Studies, NYU, 1966, PhD in Hebrew Lang. and Lit., 1975; postgrad., Hebrew U., 1977-78, Inst. Holyland Studies, 1986. Ref. libr. Hebraic section Libr. of Congress, Washington, 1967-69; prof. Old Testament So. Calif. Coll., Costa Mesa, 1969—; adj. prof. Old Testament Melodyland Sch. Theology, Anaheim, Calif., 1975-77; vis. prof. Old Testament Fuller Theol. Sem., Pasadena, Calif., 1978-81, 84, Asian Theol. Ctr. for Evangelism and Missions, Singapore and Sabah, E. Malaysia, 1985, Continental Bible Coll., Saint Pieters-Leeuw, Belgium, 1985, Mattersey Bible Coll., Eng., 1985, Inst. Holy Land Studies, Jerusalem, 1986, Regent U., 1994; transl. cons. and reviser New Am. Standard Bible, 1969-94; transl. cons. The New Internat. Version, New Century Version, 1991, A New Translation, 1992—, New Internat. Version, Simplified, 1993-94; transl. cons. and editor Internat. Children's Version, 1985-86; transl. editor: Everyday Bible, 1990. Author: (books, tapes) Hebrew I: A Study Guide, 1986, Hebrew II: A Study Guide, 1986; transl. editor: Everyday Bible, 1990; contbr. articles to International Standard Bible Encyclopedia, New International Dictionary of Old Testment Theology and Evangelical Dictionary of Biblical Theology; contbr. articles to profl. jours.; contbr. notes to Spirit Filled Life Study Bible. Nat. Def. Fgn. Lang. fellow NYU, 1964-67; Alumni scholar N.E. Bible Inst., 1960-61; NEH fellow, summer 1992. Mem. Soc. Bibl. Lit., Evang. Theol. Soc. (exec. office 1974-77), Am. Acad. Religion, Nat. Assn. Profs. of Hebrew, Inst. Bibl. Rsch., The Lockman Found. (hon. mem. bd. dirs. 1992-94, mem. editorial bd. 1974-94). Home: 1817 Peninsula Pl Costa Mesa CA 92627-4591 Office: So Calif Coll 55 Fair Dr Costa Mesa CA 92626-6520

WILLIAMS, WILLIAM HARRISON, retired librarian; b. Seattle, Apr. 18, 1924; s. William E. and Letah M. (Hollenback) W.; m. Mary Helen Sims, Apr. 19, 1945; children: Linda Lee, Dee Ann. B.S., Brigham Young U., 1969, M.L.S., 1970. Dir. Provo Pub. Library, Utah, 1969-70; Wyo. State Librarian, 1970-78; dir. Wyo. state Archives and Hist. dept., 1971-78; exec. sec. Wyo. Hist. Soc., 1971-78; sr. research analyst Wyo. Taxpayers Assn., 1978-84. Served to lt. col. USAAF, 1943-64. Decorated USAF commendation with oak leaf cluster. Mem. Beta Phi Mu, Phi Alpha Theta. Home: 21607 N 123rd Dr Sun City West AZ 85375-1950

WILLIAMS, WILLIE, protective services official; b. 1943; m. Evelina; children: Lisa, Willie Jr., Eric. AS, Phila. Coll. Textiles and Sci., 1982; postgrad., St. Joseph U., 1991. Police officer City of Phila., 1964-72, police detective, 1972-74, police sgt., 1974-76, police lt. juvenile aid div., 1976-84, police capt. 22nd and 23rd dists., 1984-86, police inspector, head tng. bur., civil affairs div., North police div., 1986-88, dep. commr. adminstrn., 1988, police commr., 1988-92; chief of police L.A. Police Dept., 1992—; lecture, instr. Temple U., Univ. Pa., Univ. Del. Former scoutmaster Boy Scouts Am.; mem. Pa. Juvenile Officers' Assn., Southeastern Pa. Chiefs of Police, West Angeles Ch. of God in Christ; past bd. dirs. Rebuild L.A. Mem. Nat. Orgn. Black Law Enforcement Execs. (past nat. pres.), Internat. Assn. Chiefs of Police, Alpha Sigma Lambda. Office: Office of Police Chief 150 S Los Angeles St Los Angeles CA 90012-3750

WILLIAMS, WILLIS RAY, paint manufacturing company executive; b. Iaeger, W. Va., Mar. 8, 1937; s. Hobart Virgil and Thelma Belle (Blankenship) W.; m. Gale Jacqueline Scott, Aug. 27, 1956; children: Ray, Scott, Michael, Mark. B.S. in Chemistry, Marshall U., 1963. Chemist, Columbia Paint Co., Huntington, W.Va., 1957-63, tech. dir., 1963-66, v.p., 1966-71, pres., 1971-79; pres., owner Wiltech Corp., Wash., 1979—. Mem. Nat. Paint and Coatings Assn., Portland Paint and Coatings Assn. (pres. 1984-85). Huntington Kiwanis (pres. 1978). Methodist. Home: 4400 Sunset Way Longview WA 98632-9581 Office: Wiltech Corp PO Box 517 Longview WA 98632-7337

WILLIAMSON, DAVID HENRY, data processing professional; b. Ogden, Utah, Aug. 21, 1952; s. Arthur Williamson; m. Kathleen Price, May 20, 1972 (dec. July 1974); children: Arthur Larry, Tiffany; m. Cindy Ann Singleton, Feb. 21, 1976. BS, Weber State Coll., 1981. Computer operator Envirtech, Salt Lake City, 1974-75, control clk., 1975-76, programmer, 1977-80; programmer State of Utah Office of Edn., Salt Lake City, 1981-83, database analyst, 1984—. With USN, 1971-74. Mem. Software AG Rocky Mountain West User Group (pres. 1989-92). Mem. LDS Ch. Office: Utah State Office of Edn 250 E 500 S Salt Lake City UT 84111-3204

WILLIAMSON, EDWARD HENRY, chaplain, army officer; b. Jackson, Miss., Dec. 9, 1957; s. Oliver Frank and Edith Elise (Berch) W.; m. Jeanne Marie Lazio, May 28, 1988. B History, Miss. Coll., 1983; MDiv, Golden Gate Sem., 1988. Ordained to ministry So. Bapt. Ch., 1988. Commd. capt. U.S. Army, 1991; chaplain Letterman Army Med. Ctr. USAR, San Francisco, 1988-90; post chaplain U.S. Army, Camp Parks, Calif., 1990; chaplain U.S. Army, Ft. Rucker, Ala., 1990-93; chaplain 1-503rd rgt. U.S. Army, Camp Casey, South Korea, 1993-94; chaplain 5-29th Field arty. U.S. Army, Ft. Carson, Colo., 1994—. Mem. Army Aviator Assn. Am., Pi Gamma Mu, Phi Alpha Theta. Republican. Home: PO Box 13907 Fort Carson CO 80913-2202

WILLIAMSON, EDWIN LEE, wardrobe and costume consultant; b. Downey, Calif., Dec. 2, 1947; s. Cecil Earnest and Edwina Louise (Tedie) W. AA, L.A. City Coll., 1967-70; BA in Theater and Music Edn., 1971, MA in Theater and Music Edn., 1973; student, U. So. Calif., 1971-73. Wardrobe master Ice Capades, 1973-76; mem. wardrobe dept. Paramount Studios, 1976-78, Disney Studios, 1978-81; freelance wardrobe and costume cons., L.A., 1981—. Appeared as Michael in original mus. Peter Pan. Mem. adv. bd. Halfway House and AIDS Hospsice, Valley Presbyn. Hosp.; founder West Coast Singers L.A., Inner City Athletic Union L.A.; founding mem. Gay Mens Chorus, Gt. Am. Yankee Freedom Band L.A., L.A. Gay and Lesbian Community Ctr.; hon. mem. bd. dirs. U. So. Calif. Idylwild Sch. Music and Arts.; bd. dirs. One Christopher St. West; founding vol. Gay Community Svc. Ctr.; emperor Imperial Ct. of San Fernando Valley. Scholar U. So. Calif., 1971-73. Mem. SAG, AFTRA, Wardrobe Union, Masons. Lutheran. Home and Office: 4741 Elmwood Ave Apt 4 Los Angeles CA 90004-3135

WILLIAMSON, GEORGE EUGENE, lawyer; b. Danville, Ill., Nov. 2, 1946; s. Eugene Victor and Marie Elaine (Rekau) W.; m. Diana F. Williamson, July 18, 1981; 1 child, Lance Eugene. BS in Material Sci. Engring., Purdue U., 1974; JD, U. West L.A., 1982. Bar: Calif. 1982. Chief metallurgist, asst. tech. dir., lab. supr. Harrison Steel casting Co., Attic, Ind., 1974-79; law clk. Ronald P. Slates, A Profl. Corp., L.A., 1980-82; trial atty. Stapleton & Stapleton, Lawndale, Calif., 1982-85, Rogers & Hartley, A Law Corp., Huntington Beach, Calif., 1985-88; assoc. R.W. Harlan & Assocs., Newport Beach, Calif., 1988-91; sr. trial atty. Law Offices of Alexander Gelman, Fountain Valley, Calif., 1991-92, Koester, Brislin & Gelman, Santa Ana, Calif., 1992—. With U.S. Army, 1966-69. Mem. State Bar of Calif., Orange County Bar Assn., Assn. of So. Calif. Def. Counsel. Republican. Office: Koester Brislin & Gelman 1633 E 4th St Santa Ana CA 92701-5163

WILLIAMSON, JERRY DEAN, radio station executive; b. Appleton City, Mo., Mar. 14, 1934; s. Charles Murry and Eunice Lee (Davis) W.; m. Joan Hawkes, Apr. 22, 1955; children: Kirk Dean, Vicky Lynn, Kimberly Dawn, Gregory Alan, Robert Todd. Student, Idaho State U., 1952-56, Ea. Wash. U., 1956-57. Radio announcer Sta. KOSI, Denver, 1957-61; sales mgr. Sta. KLAK-AM-FM, Denver, 1961-76; account exec. Sta. KIRO, Seattle, 1976-78; gen. mgr. Stas. KIDO, KIDQ, Boise, Idaho, 1978-80, Sta. KART/KFMA, Twin Falls, Idaho, 1980-82; gen. sales mgr. Sta. KUTV-TV, Salt Lake City, 1982-85; nat. sales mgr. Stas. KLTQ, KUTR, Salt Lake City, 1985; sta. mgr. Sta. KGHL/KIDX, Billings, Mont., 1985—; sales cons. Sta. KART/KFMA, Twin Falls, 1982—. Mem. Mont. Broadcasters Assn., Billings Advt. Club., Rotary. Republican. Mormon. Home: 2589 Granite St Idaho Falls ID 83402-1400 Office: Sta KGHL 2070 Overland Ave Ste 103 Billings MT 59102-7429

WILLIAMSON, LAIRD, stage director, actor; b. Chgo., Dec. 13, 1937; s. Walter B. and Florence M. (Hemwell) W. B.S. in Speech, Northwestern U., 1960; M.F.A. in Drama, U. Tex., 1965. Dir. Am. Conservatory Theatre, San Francisco, 1974—; stage dir. A Christmas Carol, 1976-81, The Matchmaker (tour of Soviet Union), 1976, A Month in the Country, 1978, The Visit, 1979, Pantagleize, 1980, Sunday in the Park, 1986, End of the World, 1988, Imaginary Invalid, 1990; dir. Oreg. Shakespearean Festival, Ashland, 1972-74, Western Opera Theatre, San Francisco, 1976-77, Theater Fest, Santa Maria, Calif., 1971-84, Denver Theater Ctr., 1981, Bklyn. Acad. Music, 1981, Denver Ctr. Theatre Co., 1985-94, Seattle Repertory Theatre, 1990, Old Globe Theatre, San Diego, 1977, 92, 94; artistic dir. Theater Fest, Solvang, Calif., 1981-83, Intiman Theatre, 1986, 88, Seattle Repertory Theatre, 1990, Berkeley Shakespeare Festival, 1990, Guthrie Theatre, 1991, 93, The Shakespeare Theatre, Washington, 1995; actor in Othello, 1973, Twelfth Night, 1974, Cyrano, 1974, Enrico IV, 1977, Judas, 1978, Hamlet, 1979, The Bacchae, 1981. Mem. Soc. Stage Dirs. Actors Equity Assn., Screen Actors Guild.

WILLIAMSON, NEIL ROBERT, psychiatrist; b. LaGrande, Oreg., Oct. 14, 1940; s. Robert Elton and Lorene Adeline (Johnson) W. BS, U. Oreg., Eugene, 1962; MD, U. Oreg., Portland, 1967; postgrad. in Advanced Studies Social Welfare, Heller Sch., Brandeis U., 1973-77. Intern Balt. City Hosps., 1967-68; fellow in medicine Johns Hopkins U. Hosps., Balt., 1967-68; staff physician Hall Health U. Wash., Seattle, 1970-72; resident in psychiatry Worcester (Mass.) State Hosp., 1973-77, assoc. outpatient treatment clin., 1977-78; instr. U. Mass. Med. Sch., Worcester, 1978-82; cons. Josephine County Mental Health Program, Grants Pass, Oreg., 1982-88; pvt. practice in psychiatry Grants Pass, Oreg., 1982—; med. dir. Southern Oreg. Adolescent Study and Treatment Ctr., Grants Pass, Oreg., 1986—; med. dir. Josephine County Coun. on Alcohol and Drug Abuse, 1987—; cons.-supr. Basics, Inc. Substance Abuse Treatment Program, 1989-92; cons. Western Med. Cons., 1989—; cons. appeals and hearings Social Security Sys., 1991—; supr. to pvt. practice counselors, 1987—; supr. treatment planning decisions ALC program, 1992—. Bd. dirs. Josephine County Human Rights Alliance, 1992-94, Rural Organizing Project for Oreg., 1995—. Capt. U.S. Army, 1968-70. Mem. Oreg. Med. Assn., Josephine County Med. Soc., Grants Pass C. of C. Democrat. Office: Williamson MD PC 243 NE C St Grants Pass OR 97526-2153

WILLIAMSON, OLIVER EATON, economics and law educator; b. Superior, Wis., Sept. 27, 1932; s. Scott Gilbert and Lucille S. (Dunn) W.; m. Dolores Jean Celeni, Sept. 28, 1957; children: Scott, Tamara, Karen, Oliver, Dean. SB, MIT, 1955; MBA, Stanford U., 1960; PhD, Carnegie-Mellon U., 1963; PhD (hon.), Norwegian Sch. Econs. and Bus. Adminstrn., 1986; PhD in Econ. Sci. (hon.), Hochschule St. Gallen, Switzerland, 1987, Groningen U., 1989; Turku Sch. Econs. & Bus. Admin, 1995. Project. engr. U.S. Govt., 1955-58; asst. prof. econs. U. Calif., Berkeley, 1963-65; assoc. prof. U. Pa., Phila., 1965-68, prof., 1968-83, Charles and William L. Day prof. econs. and social sci., 1977-83; Gordon B. Tweedy prof. econs. law and orgn. Yale U., 1983-88; Transam. prof. of bus., econs. and law U. Calif., Berkeley, 1988-94, Edgar F. Kaiser prof. bus. adminstrn., prof. econs. and law, 1994—; spl. econ. asst. to asst. atty. gen. for antitrust Dept. Justice, 1966-67; dir. Ctr. for Study of Organizational Innovation, U. Pa., 1976-83; transam. prof. of bus., econs. and law U. Calif., Berkeley, 1988—; cons. in field. Author: The Economics of Discretionary Behavior, 1964, Corporate Control and Business Behavior, 1970, Markets and Hierarchies, 1975, The Economic Institutions of Capitalism, 1985, Economic Organization, 1986, Antitrust Economics, 1987; assoc. editor: Bell Jour. Econs., 1973-74, editor, 1975-82; co-editor: Jour. Law, Econs., and Orgn., 1983—. Fellow Ctr. for Advanced Study in Behavioral Scis., 1977-78; Guggenheim fellow, 1977-78; Am. Acad. Arts and Scis. fellow, 1983; recipient Alexander Henderson award Carnegie-Mellon U., 1962, Alexander von Humboldt Rsch. prize, 1987, Irwin award Acad. of Mgmt., 1988. Fellow Econometric Soc.; mem. NAS, Am. Econ. Assn. Office: U Calif Dept Econs Berkeley CA 94720

WILLIG, KARL VICTOR, computer firm executive; b. Idaho Falls, Idaho, June 4, 1944; s. Louis Victor and Ethel (McCarty) W.; m. Julianne Erickson, June 10, 1972; 1 son, Ray. BA magna cum laude, Coll. of Idaho, 1968; MBA (Dean Donald Kirk David fellow), Harvard U., 1970. Pres. Ariz. Beef, Inc., Phoenix, 1971-73; group v.p. Ariz.-Colo. Land & Cattle Co., Phoenix, 1973-76; v.p. Rufenacht, Bromagen & Hertz, Inc., Chgo., 1976-77; pres. Sambo's Restaurants, Inc., Santa Barbara, Calif., 1977-79; ptnr. Santa Barbara Capital, 1979-85; pres. EURUSA Equities Corp., 1985-86; pres., chief exec. officer InfoGenesis, 1986—; trustee Am. Bapt. Sem. of West, 1977-85. Named one of Outstanding Young Men of Am., 1972; recipient Assn. of U.S. Army award, 1964.

WILLIS, CHARLES DUBOIS, neuropsychiatrist, writer; b. N.Y.C., Dec. 30, 1925; s. William Charles and Alma Anna (Lazear) W.; m. Shirley Mae Clarke, Jan. 28, 1951; children: Carol, Nancy, John, Sarah, James. BA in Religion, Atlantic Union Coll., 1949; MD, Loma Linda U., 1955. Diplomate Am. Bd. Psychiatry and Neurology. Intern Orange (Calif.) County Hosp.; resident in psychiatry Met. State Hosp., Norwalk, Calif., 1956, 57-60; resident in neurology U. Calif. Med. Ctr., San Francisco, 1966-68; pres. Ancient World Found., Pinedale, Calif., 1990—; staff psychiatrist Dept. Corrections, Corcoran, Calif., 1983—; leader Mt. Ararat Expdns., 1983, 84, 86, 88. Author: End of Days=1971-2001, 1973. Capt. U.S. Army Med. Corps, 1957-60. Republican. Office: Ancient World Found PO Box 3118 Fresno CA 93650-3118

WILLIS, CLIFFORD LEON, geologist; b. Chanute, Kans., Feb. 20, 1913; s. Arthur Edward and Flossie Duckworth (Fouts) W.; m. Serreta Margaret Thiel, Aug. 21, 1947 (dec.); 1 child, David Gerard. BS in Mining Engring., U. Kans., 1939; PhD, U. Wash., 1950. Geophysicist The Carter Oil Co. (Exxon), Tulsa, 1939-42; instr. U. Wash., Seattle, 1946-50, asst. prof., 1950-54; cons. geologist Harza Engring. Co., Chgo., 1952-54, 80-82, chief geologist, 1954-57, assoc. and chief geologist, 1957-67, v.p., chief geologist, 1967-80; pvt. practice cons. geologist Tucson, Ariz., 1982—; cons. on major dam projects in Iran, Iraq, Pakistan, Greece, Turkey, Ethiopia, Argentina, Venezuela, Colombia, Honduras, El Salvador, Iceland, U.S. Lt. USCG, 1942-46. Recipient Haworth Disting. Alumnus award U. Kans., 1963. Fellow Geol. Soc. Am., Geol. Soc. London; mem. Am. Assn. Petroleum Geologists, Soc. Mining, Metallurgy and Exploration Inc., Assn. Engring. Geologists, Sigma Xi, Tau Beta Pi, Sigma Tau. Republican. Roman Catholic. Home: 4795 E Quail Creek Dr Tucson AZ 85718-2630

WILLIS, DAWN LOUISE, paralegal, small business owner; b. Johnstown, Pa., Sept. 11, 1959; d. Kenneth William and Dawn Louise (Joseph) Hagins; m. Marc Anthony Ross, Nov. 30, 1984 (div.); m. Jerry Wayne Willis, Dec. 16, 1989. Grad. high sch., Sacramento, Calif. Legal sec. Wilcoxen & Callahan, Sacramento, 1979-87, paralegal asst., 1987-88; legal adminstr. Law Office Jack Vetter, Sacramento, 1989—; owner, mgr. Your Girl Friday Secretarial and Legal Support Svcs., Sacramento, 1991—; with Amway Distbr., 1992—. Vol. ARC, 1985. Mem. NAFE, Assn. Legal Adminstrs., Calif. Trial Lawyers Assn., Sacramento Legal Secs. Assn. Republican. Lutheran. Address: Apt 487 4339 Galbrath Dr Sacramento CA 95842-4156

WILLIS, EDWARD CHARLES, legislator; b. Barstow, Calif., Nov. 29, 1923; s. Charlie Brice and Mary Elizabeth (Indihar) W.; m. Joyce Houtz, June 23, 1949; children: Steve (dec.), Rodney, Charles, Linda, Marla. Student, San Bernardino C.C., 1941-42. Lessee, operator svc. sta. Barstow, 1948-49; power plant engr. Dept. of Army, Alaska, 1950-74; maintenance worker State of Alaska, 1979-84. Rep. Alaska Ho. of Reps., 1993—; senator Alaska State Senate, 1975-78; assemblyman Anchorage Borough Assembly, 1966-74, pres., 1973-74, 69-70; mem. Chugiak (Alaska) Adv. Sch. Bd., 1961-63; co-chair Operation Chugiak High Sch., 1961-63. With USCG/Merchant Marines, 1944-47, PTO. Decorated Mcht. Marine emblem Pacific War Zone Bar; recipient Bear Paw award Chugiak-Eagle River C. of C., 1970, Appreciation honor Alaskan VFW, 1993. Mem. NRA, Mothers Against Drunk Driving, Alaska Retarded Citizens Assn., Am. Legion (life; Alaska Legionnaire of Yr. 1994), Alpine Alternatives (bd. dirs. 1990), Am. Assn. Ret. Persons, Ret. Officers Assn. (hon.), Elks. Office: 11940 Business Blvd Eagle River AK 99577-7742

WILLIS, HAROLD WENDT, SR., real estate developer; b. Marion, Ala., Oct. 7, 1927; s. Robert James and Della (Wendt) W.; student Loma Linda U., 1950, various courses San Bernardino Valley Coll.; m. Patsy Gay Bacon, Aug. 2, 1947 (div. Jan. 1975); children: Harold Wendt II, Timothy Gay, April Ann, Brian Tad, Suzanne Gail; m. Vernette Jacobson Osborne, Mar. 30, 1980 (div. 1984); m. Ofelia Alvarez, Sept. 23, 1984; children: Ryan Robert, Samantha Ofelia. Ptnr., Victoria Guernsey, San Bernardino, Calif., 1950-63, co-pres., 1963-74, pres., 1974—; owner Quik-Save, 9th & Waterman shopping ctr., 1966—, Ninth and Waterman Shopping Ctr., San Bernardino, 1969—; pres. Energy Delivery Systems, Food and Fuel, Inc. San Bernardino City water commr., 1965—, pres. bd. water commrs., 1994—. Bd. councillors Loma Linda (Calif.) U., 1968-85, pres., 1971-74; mem. So. Calif. Strider's Relay Team (set indoor Am. record in 4x800 1992, set distance medley relay U.S. and World record for 60 yr. old 1992). Served as officer U.S. Mcht. Marine, 1945-46. Mem. Calif. Dairy Industries Assn. (pres. 1963, 64), Liga Internat. (2d v.p. 1978, pres. 1982, 83). Seventh-day Adventist (deacon 1950-67). Lic. pvt. pilot; rated multi engr. Office: PO Box 5607 San Bernardino CA 92412-5607

WILLIS, NELL ELAINE, small business owner; b. Anderson, S.C., June 19, 1940; d. Howard Sidney and Nell (Foster) Behr; m. Norman E. Willis, Jan. 9, 1989. BA, Western Wash. U., 1962. Stewardess Pan Am. Airways, Seattle, 1962-63; clk. Sea-First Bank, Seattle, 1963-65; customer contact Wash. Natural Gas, Seattle, 1965-66; programmer NCR, Seattle, 1966-72; rsch. analyst Boeing Computer Systems, Seattle, 1972-82; owner Nelco Ent., Seattle, 1982—. Mem. N.W. Bead Soc. Home and Office: 7811 SE 27th St Ste 246 Mercer Island WA 98040-2961

WILLIS, PAUL JONATHAN, English language educator; b. Fullerton, Calif., Nov. 8, 1955; s. David Lee and Earline Louise (Fleischman) W.; m. Sharon Gail Leitzel, Aug. 25, 1979; children: Jonathan David, Johanna Leitzel. BA in Biblical Studies, Wheaton Coll., 1977; MA in English, Washington State U., 1980, PhD in English, 1985. Wilderness guide Sierra Treks, Bridgeport, Calif., 1974—; English instr. Whitworth Coll., Spokane, Wash., 1981-85; asst. prof. English Houghton (N.Y.) Coll., 1985-88; assoc. prof. English Westmont Coll., Santa Barbara, Calif., 1988—. Author: No Clock in the Forest, 1991, The Stolen River, 1992 (award Christianity Today 1993). Mem. MLA, Assn. Study of Lit. and Environment, So. Calif. C.S. Lewis Soc., Conf. on Christianity and Lit., Sierra Club (chair wilderness com. 1983-84), Wilderness Soc. Democrat. Mem. Evangelical Covenant Ch. Office: Westmont Coll 955 La Paz Rd Santa Barbara CA 93108

WILLIS, SELENE LOWE, electrical engineer; b. Birmingham, Ala., Mar. 4, 1958; d. Lewis Russell and Bernice (Wilson) Lowe; m. André Maurice Willis, June 12, 1987. BSEE, Tuskegee (Ala.) U., 1980; postgrad. in Computer Programing, UCLA, 1993-94. Component engr. Hughes Aircraft Corp., El Segundo, Calif., 1980-82; reliability and lead engr. Aero Jet Electro Systems Corp., Azusa, Calif., 1982-84; sr. component engr. Rockwell Internat. Corp., Anaheim, Calif., 1984, Gen. Data Comm. Corp., Danbury, Conn., 1984-85; design engr. Lockheed Missile & Space Co., Sunnyvale, Calif., 1985-86; property mgr. Penmar Mgmt. Co., L.A., 1987-88; aircraft mechanic McDonnell Douglas Corp., Long Beach, 1989-93; Unix system adminstrn. Santa Cruz Ops., 1994; mem. tech. staff Space Applications Corp., El Segunda, Calif., 1995; cons., software designer Nat. Advancement Corp., Santa Ana, Calif., 1995—; cons., software designer Kern & Wooley, attys., Westwood, Calif., 1995. Vol. Mercy Hosp. and Children's Hosp., Birmingham, 1972-74; mrm. L.A. Gospel Messengers, 1982-84, West Angeles Ch. of God and Christ, L.A., 1990; cons., mgr. bus. ops. New Start/Santa Monica (Calif.) Bay Area Drug Abuse Coun., 1995. Scholar Bell Labs., 1976-80. Mem. IEEE, ASME, Aerospace and Aircraft Engrs., So. Calif. Profl. Engring. Assn., Tuskegee U. Alumni Assn., UCLA Alumni Assn., Eta Kappa Nu. Mem. Christian Ch.

WILLISON, BRUCE GRAY, banker; b. Riverside, Calif., Oct. 16, 1948; s. Walter G. and Dorothy (Phillips) W.; m. Gretchen A. Illig; children: Patrick, Bruce G., Kristen, Jeffery, Geoffrey, Lea. B.A. in econs., UCLA, 1970; M.B.A., U. So. Calif., 1973. With Bank of Am., Los Angeles, 1973-79; dir. mktg. First Interstate Bancorp, Los Angeles, 1981; sr. v.p. corp. banking group First Interstate Bank, L.A., 1982, mgr. trust divsn., 1983; exec. v.p. world banking group First Interstate Bank, Los Angeles, 1983-85; pres., chief exec. officer First Interstate Bank Ltd., 1985-86; chmn., chief exec. officer First Interstate Bank Oreg., Portland, 1986-91; chmn., pres., chief exec. officer First Interstate Bank of Calif., L.A., 1991—. Served to lt. USN, 1970-72. Office: First Interstate Bank Calif 707 Wilshire Blvd Los Angeles CA 90017-3501

WILLMAN, ARTHUR CHARLES, healthcare executive; b. N.Y.C., Oct. 25, 1938; s. Arthur Charles Willman and Irene (Lamb) Meyer; m. Mary McHugh, Dec. 30. 1961; children: Jean, Susan, Brian, Kevin. BS in Pharmacy, St. Johns U., 1960; MS, Columbia U., 1968. Staff pharmacist St. Vincent's Hosp., S.I., N.Y., 1960-61, Valentine Pharmacy, S.I., 1961; commd. ensign USPHS, 1962, advanced through grades to capt., 1982; chief pharmacist USPHS Hosp., Kotzebue, Alaska, 1962-63, adminstr., 1963-66; svc. unit dir. USPHS Hosp., Sitka, Alaska, 1971-86; ret. USPHS Hosp., 1991; adminstrv. resident So. Nassau Communities Hosp., Oceanside, N.Y., 1967-68; exec. officer Gallup (N.Mex.) Indian Med. Ctr., 1968-71; dir. Phys. Asst. Tng. Program, Gallup, N.Mex., 1971; v.p. S.E. Alaska Regional Health Corp., Sitka, 1986—; chmn. bd. dirs. S.E. Alaska Health Systems Agy., Ketchikan, 1980-83; instr. mgmt. U. Alaska, Sitka, 1975-85. Active Ad hoc Com. on Diversification, Sitka, 1993. Fellow APHA, Am. Coll. Healthcare Execs.; mem. Sitka Rotary Club (v.p., chmn.). Roman Catholic. Home: 1203 Seward Ave Sitka AK 99835-9418 Office: SE Alaska Regional Health Corp 222 Tongass Dr Sitka AK 99835-9416

WILLMOTT, PETER SHERMAN, retail executive; b. Glens Falls, N.Y., June 1, 1937. B.A., Williams Coll., 1959; M.B.A., Harvard U., 1961. Sr. fin. analyst Am. Airlines, N.Y.C., 1961-63; mgr. cons. Booz, Allen & Hamilton, N.Y.C., 1964-66; treas. Continental Baking Co., Rye, N.Y., 1966-69, v.p., 1969-74; sr. v.p. fin. Fed. Express Corp., Memphis, 1974-77, exec. v.p. fin. and adminstrn., 1977-80, pres., chief operating officer, 1980-83, now bd. dirs.; pres., chief exec. officer Carson Pirie Scott & Co., Chgo., 1983—, chmn., 1984—, also bd. dirs. Office: Pic N Save Corp 2430 E Del Amo Blvd Compton CA 90220-6306

WILLMS, ARTHUR HENRY, gas executive; b. Namaka, Alta., Can., Oct. 28, 1939; m. June Gladstone, 1961; children: Tara Nicole, Jordan Peter. BEd in Math., U. Calgary, Alta., Can., 1965, BA in Math., 1967, MA in Econs., 1970. Pub. sch. teacher Strathmore, Alta., 1961-63, Calgary

Pub. Sch. Bd., 1965-67; lectr. in econs. U. Calgary, 1969-70; exec. v.p., chief operating officer pipeline div. Westcoast Transmission Co. Ltd., Vancouver, B.C., 1971—; also bd. dirs.; bd. dirs. Westcoast Petroleum Ltd., Pacific Northern Gas Ltd., Foothills Pipe Lines Ltd. Mem. Canadian Gas Assn. (bd. dirs. 1983). Clubs: Vancouver, Hollyburn Country. Office: Westcoast Transmission Co Ltd, 1333 W Georgia St, Vancouver, BC Canada V6E 3K9

WILLNER, ALAN ELI, electrical engineer, educator; b. Bklyn., Nov. 16, 1962; s. Gerald and Sondra (Bernstein) W.; m. Michelle Frida Green, June 25, 1991. BA, Yeshiva U., 1982; MS, Columbia U., 1984, PhD, 1988. Summer tech. staff David Sarnoff Rsch. Ctr., Princeton, N.J., 1983, 84; grad. rsch. asst. dept. elec. engring. Columbia U., N.Y.C., 1984-88; postdoctoral mem. tech. staff AT&T Bell Labs., Holmdel, N.J., 1988-90; mem. tech. staff Bell Communications Rsch., Red Bank, N.J., 1990-91; assoc. prof. U. So. Calif., L.A., 1992—, assoc. dir. Ctr. Photonic Tech., 1994—; head del. Harvard Model UN Yeshiva U., 1982; instr. Columbia U., 1987; rev. panel mem. NSF, Washington, 1992, 93, 94; invited optical comm. workshop NSF, Washington, 1994, chair panel on optical info. and comm., 1994. Author 1 book; contbr. articles to IEEE Photonics Tech. Letters, Jour Lightwave Tech., Jour. Optical Engring., Jour. Electrochem. Soc., Electronics Letters, Applied Physics Letters, Applied Optics; assoc. editor Jour. Lighwave Tech., guest editor. Mem. faculty adv. bd. U. So. Calif. Hillel Orgn., 1992. Grantee NSF, Advanced Rsch. Projects Agy., Packard Found., Powell Found.; fellow Semiconductor Rsch. Corp., 1986, NATO/NSF, 1985, Sci. and Engring. fellow David and Lucile Packard Found., 1993, Presdl. faculty fellow NSF, 1994; recipient Armstrong Found. prize Columbia U., 1984, Young Investigator award NSF, 1992. Mem. IEEE (sr. mem.), IEEE Lasers and Electro-Optics Soc. (mem. optical comm. tech. com., bd. govs., chmn. optical comm. tech. com., chmn. optical comm. subcom. ann. meeting 1994, mem. optical networks tech. com.), Optical Soc. Am. (vice-chair optical comm. group, symposium organizer ann. meeting 1992, 95, panel organizer ann. meeting 1993, 95, program com. for conf. on optical fiber commn. 1996), Soc. Photo-Instrumentation Engring. (program chair telecomm. engring. photonics west 1995, chmn. conf. on emerging technologies for all-optical networks, photonics west, 1995, program com. for Conf. on Optical Fiber Comm., 1996, conf. program com. components for WDM), Sigma Xi. Home: 1200 S Shenandoah St Apt 201 Los Angeles CA 90035-2265 Office: U So Calif Dept Elec Engring EEB 538 Los Angeles CA 90089-2565

WILLNER, JAY R., consulting company executive; b. Aurora, Ill., Sept. 22, 1924; s. Charles R. and Ida (Winer) W.; m. Suzanne Wehmann, July 17, 1958; 1 child, Adam. Student U. Calif., Los Angeles, 1946-48; BS, MIT, 1950; MBA, Rutgers U., 1959. Researcher Andrew Brown Co., Los Angeles, 1950-52; tech. salesman Glidden Co., Los Angeles, 1952-54; market researcher Roger Williams Inc., N.Y.C., 1954-59; sr. market analyst Calif. Chem. Co., San Francisco, 1959-63; mgr. planning chem. coatings div. Mobil Chem. Co., N.Y.C., 1963-68; pres. WEH Corp., San Francisco, 1968—; lectr. U. Calif., Berkeley, 1962—; adj. faculty U. San Francisco, 1977—; U.S. corr. German mag. Farbe & Lack. Contbg. editor Jour. Protective Coatings and Linings; editor The WEH Report. Served to 2d lt. A.C., AUS, 1943-46. Mem. Am. Chem. Soc., San Francisco Comml. Club, Chemists Club (N.Y.C.), MIT Club No. Calif. Home: 700 Presidio Ave San Francisco CA 94115-2956 Office: WEH Corp PO Box 470038 San Francisco CA 94147-0038

WILLOUGHBY, JAMES RUSSELL, artist; b. Toronto, Ohio, Apr. 22, 1928; s. Russell Lee and Edna Gertrude (McKeown) W.; m. Dorothy M. Ponder, Sept. 12, 1952 (div. 1958); children: Jim Jr., David; m. Susan N. Boettjer, Nov. 28, 1980. AA, Pasadena City Coll., 1951; postgrad., Art Ctr. Sch. Mem. staff Chrysler Corp., Maywood, Calif., 1951-57; adminstrv. asst., tech. artist Ramo-Wooldridge, El Segundo, Calif., 1957-59; adminstr. asst. Space Tech. Labs., El Segundo, 1959-61; intelligence analyst Aerospace Corp., El Segundo, 1961-65; freelancer Calif., 1965-72, Filmation Studios, Reseda, Calif., 1972-82, various orgns., 1982—; storyboard designer Hanna-Barbera, Disney Studios, 1987-90. Author/Illustrator Cowboy Country Cartoons, 1988; co-author, illustrator Cowboy Cartoon Cookbooks, 1990, Cactus County, 1992. Mem. Nat. Cartoonist Soc., Westerners Internat., Prescott Corral. Home: 1407 Sierra Vista Dr Prescott AZ 86303-4545

WILLOUGHBY, STUART CARROLL, contractor; b. Tucson, Mar. 19, 1951; s. Stuart Carroll and Margeret Ann (Thornton) W.; children: Julie Ann, Aimee Sue, Scott Tyler. Student, U. Ariz., 1970-74, U. Ariz., 1973. Owner Willcox (Ariz.) Realty and Constrn. Co., 1974-75, Willoughby Constrn. and Devel. Corp., Tucson, 1975—; owner, broker Red Baron Realtors, Inc., Tucson, 1978—; owner Willoughby Plumbing Corp., Tucson, 1985—, Sunshine Solar Co., Tucson, 1980—. Leader 4H Club. Mem. So. Ariz. Home Builders Assn. (bd. dirs. 1978—, life dir., Bd. Mem. of Yr. award 1981, honored PAC com. 1985, 86, 87), Tucson Bd. Realtors, Nat. Assn. of Home Builders (Life Spike award 1980). Republican. Home: 7979 S Camino Loma Alta Tucson AZ 85747-9372

WILLOUGHBY, SUSAN NELL, museum director; b. Flint, Mich., Dec. 3, 1941; d. Arthur Francis and Fay R. (Randolph) Boettjer; m. Joe Stuard, June 29, 1961 (div. 1977); children: Sherri B. Carlsberg, Nick Stuard; m. James R. Willoughby Sr., Nov. 28, 1980. Grad. h.s., Glendale, Calif. Pers. dir. Kaufman & Broad Home Sys., L.A., 1971-72; dir. adminstrv. svcs. Carlsberg Corp., Santa Monica, Calif., 1972-85; dir. Phippen Mus. of Western Art, Prescott, Ariz., 1987-88, 91—; chair Prescott Mus. Coalition, 1993-94; program chair Prescott Art Docents, 1988-90. Co-author: Cowboy Country Cookbook, 1990—, Cactus Country, 1993. Sheriff Westerners Corral, Prescott, 1992. Mem. Am. Assn. of Mus., Ariz. Assn. of Mus., Mus. Educators of Ctrl. Ariz., Western Registrars Com., Westerners Internat. (Heads Up award 1993). Republican. Office: Phippen Mus of Western Art 4701 Hwy 89 North Prescott AZ 86301

WILLRICH, MASON, utility company executive, consultant; b. L.A., 1933; m. Patricia Rowe, June 11, 1960; children: Christopher, Stephen, Michael, Katharine. BA magna cum laude, Yale U., 1954; JD, U. Calif., Berkeley, 1960. Atty. Pillsbury Madison and Sutro, San Francisco, 1960-62; asst. gen. coun. U.S. Arms Control and Disarmament Agy., 1962-65; assoc. prof. law U. Va., 1965-68, prof. law, 1968-75, John Stennis prof. law, 1975-79; dir. internat. rels. Rockefeller Found., N.Y.C., 1976-79; v.p. Pacific Gas & Electric, San Francisco, 1979-84, sr. v.p., 1984-88, exec. v.p., 1988-89; CEO, pres. PG&E Enterprises, San Francisco, 1989-94; exec. Pacific Gas and Electric Co., San Francisco, 1979-94; cons., 1994—. Author: Non-Proliferation Treaty, 1969, Global Politics of Nuclear Energy, 1971, (with T.B. Taylor) Nuclear Theft, 1974, Administration of Energy Shortages, 1976 (with R.K. Lester) Radioactive Waste Management and Regulation, 1977. Trustee, past chmn. bd. dirs. World Affairs Coun. No. Calif.; pres. Midland Sch.; mem. Resources for the Future, Atlantic Coun. U.S. Guggenheim Meml. fellow, 1973. Mem. Phi Beta Kappa, Order of Coif. Office: 1452 Hamilton Ave Palo Alto CA 94301-3124

WILLS, DONALD ALLISON, lawyer; b. Phoenix, May 3, 1946; s. William Donald Wills and Mary Polly Alice (Ernst) Burdick; m. Joy Charlene Martin, Sept. 14, 1969; children: Eric Donald, Warren Bradley. BS, Calif. Poly. State U., 1968; JD, U. West L.A., 1978; postgrad., Sch. of Theology of Claremont, 1993—. Bar: Calif. 1978. Assoc. atty. Bralley, Bentley & Dickinson, L.A., Pasadena, 1978-81; ptnr. Bralley, Bentley & Wills, Pasadena, 1981-82; owner Law Offices Donald A. Wills, Arcadia, South Pasadena, 1982-86; owner, ptnr. Wills & Rifkin, South Pasadena, 1986-88; owner Law Offices Donald A. Wills, South Pasadena, 1988-92; owner, ptnr. Wills & Griepp, South Pasadena, 1992-93; owner, ptnr. Wills & Kliger, South Pasadena, 1993-94, Pasadena, 1994—; adj. prof. Pasadena (Calif.) C.C., 1983-87, U. West L.A. Sch. of Law, 1988; instr. Ins. Edn. Assn., 1986-91; dir. Calif. State Bar Workers' Compensation Exec. Com., San Francisco, 1989-91. Transp. com. mem. City of South Pasadena, 1989-91; fin. dir. South Pasadena Tournament of Roses Assn., 1990-93. Capt. U.S. Army, 1969-72, West Berlin. Mem. L.A. County Bar Assn. (dir. Workers' Compensation sect. 1991—), State of Calif. Divsn. Indsl. Rels. (judge pro-tem Workers' Compensation Appeals bd. 1988-94), Workers' Compensation Def. Attys. Assn., Calif. Self Ins. Assn., So. Calif. Coun. of Self-Insurers, Oneonta Club (dir. 1989-92, Lyons/Adams award 1991-92). Republican. Office: Wills & Kliger 547 S Marengo Ave Pasadena CA 91101-3114

WILLSON, GEORGE BIGELOW, civil engineer, consultant; b. Douglas, Wyo., May 12, 1929; s. Eugene P. and Marie V. (Lipe) W.; m. Lois Ann Goodman, Dec. 21, 1959; children: John A., Carol A. Phifer. BS in Civil Engring., U. Wyo., 1951, MS, 1963. Registered profl. engr. and surveyor, Wyo. Project engr. mcpl. engring. projects J.T. Banner and Assocs., Laramie, Wyo., 1956-58; tchr., rschr. gen. and agrl. engring. U. Wyo., Laramie, 1958-65; rschr. on agrl. and mcpl. waste mgmt. ARS, USDA, Md., 1966-87; cons. composting tech. and organic waste recycling, prin. George B. Willson Assocs., Laurel, Md., 1988-93, Loveland, Colo., 1993—; facilitator workshops and seminars; cons. on numerous projects. Contbg. author: On-Farm Composting Handbook, 1992; mem. editorial bd. BioCycle Jour. of Waste Recycling; contbr. numerous articles to profl. jours. Recipient Md. Gov.'s citation, 1982, other awards. Mem. Am. Soc. Agrl. Engrs., Water Environment Fedn. Home: 1535 Park Dr Loveland CO 80538-4285 Office: George B Willson Assocs Ste 103 407 N Lincoln Ave Loveland CO 80537

WILLSON, JOHN MICHAEL, mining company executive; b. Sheffield, England, Feb. 21, 1940; s. Jack Desmond and Cicely Rosamond (Long Price) W.; m. Susan Mary Partridge, Aug. 26, 1942; children: Marcus J., Carolyn A. BSc in Mining Engring. with honors, Imperial Coll., London, 1962, MSc in Mining Engring., 1985. With Cominco Ltd., 1966-74; v.p. No. Group Cominco Ltd., Vancouver, B.C., Can., 1981-84; pres. Garaventa (Canada) Ltd., Vancouver, 1974-81; pres., CEO Western Can. Steel Ltd., Vancouver, 1985-88, Pegasus Gold Inc., Spokane, Wash., 1989-92, Placer Dome Inc., Vancouver, B.C., Can., 1993—; chmn. bd. dirs. Placer Pacific Ltd., Sydney, Australia, Placer Dome U.S., San Francisco, Placer Dome Can. Ltd., Placer Dome Latin Am. Pres. N.W.T. Chamber Mines, Yellowknife, Can., 1982-84; chmn. bd. dirs. Western States Pub. Lands Coalition, Pueblo, Colo., 1990-91; bd. dirs. World Gold Coun. Mem. AIME, Can. Inst. Mining and Metallurgy, Inst. Mining and Metallurgy (London), Assn. Profl. Engrs. B.C., Assn. Profl. Engrs. and Geologists N.W.T., N.W. Mining Assn. (bd. dirs. Corp. Leadership award 1991), Am. Mining Congress (bd. dirs.), World Gold Coun. (bd. dirs.). Home: 4722 Drummond Dr, Vancouver, BC Canada V6T 1B4 Office: Placer Dome Inc, 1055 W Dunsmuir St Ste 1600, Vancouver, BC Canada V7X 1P1

WILLSON, MARY F., ecology researcher, educator; b. Madison, Wis., July 28, 1938; d. Gordon L. and Sarah (Loomans) W.; m. R.A. von Neumann, May 29, 1972 (dec.). B.A. with honors, Grinnell Coll., 1960; Ph.D., U. Wash., 1964. Asst. prof. U. Ill., Urbana, 1965-71, assoc. prof., 1971-76, prof. ecology, 1976-90; rsch. ecologist Forestry Scis. Lab., Juneau, Alaska, 1989—; adj. prof. zoology Wash. State U., Pullman; prin. rsch. scientist, affiliate prof. biology Inst. Arctic Biology U. Alaska, Fairbanks; faculty assoc. divsn. biol. scis. U. Mont., Missoula. Author: Plant Reproductive Ecology, 1983, Vertebrate Natural History, 1984; co-author: Mate Choice in Plants, 1983. Fellow AAAS, Am. Ornithologists Union; mem. Soc. for Study Evolution, Am. Soc. Naturalists (hon. mem.), Ecol. Soc. Am., Brit. Ecol. Soc. Office: Forestry Scis Lab 2770 Sherwood Ln Juneau AK 99801-8545

WILLSTATTER, ALFRED, diplomat; b. Landsberg, Germany, Oct. 17, 1925; came to the U.S., 1938; s. Louis M. and Lucia (Cahn) W.; m. Edith R. Klabunde, Dec. 24, 1955; children: Kurt, Karl, Steve. BA, U. Minn., 1951. Commd. 2d lt. U.S. Army, 1944, advanced through grades to lt. col., 1966, ret., 1979; owner, operator Twin Plunges, Ashland, Oreg., 1966-77; fraud investigator L.A. County Charities, 1957-66. Coun. mem. City of Ashland, 1969-72, chmn., 1971; bd. dirs. Rogue Valley Transit Dist., Medford, Oreg., 1975—, original chmn., vice chmn.; vol. probation officer Project Misdemeanant, Medford, 1969—; vol., arbitrator BBB, Portland, Oreg., 1985—. Recipient Cert. of Svc. Project Misdemeanant, 1992; named Outstanding Bd. Mem. Spl. Dists., 1991. Mem. Nat. Counter Intelligence Corps Assn., Spl. Dist. of Oreg. Assn. (mem. budget com. 1993). Home: 128 Central Ave Ashland OR 97520-1715

WILNER, PAUL ANDREW, journalist; b. N.Y.C., Feb. 12, 1950; s. Norman and Sylvia (Rubenstein) W.; m. Alyson Paula Bromberg, June 3, 1980; children: Anne Charlotte, Daniel Joseph. Student, U. Calif., Berkeley, 1968; BA, CUNY, 1976. Copy clk. N.Y. Times, 1976-80; reporter L.A. Herald Examiner, 1980-85; mng. editor Hollywood Reporter, L.A., 1985-87; asst. mng. editor features San Francisco Examiner, 1987—; sr. instr. U. So. Calif., L.A., 1983-85. Author: (poetry) Serious Business, The Paris Rev., 1977. Office: San Francisco Examiner Mags. 110 5th St San Francisco CA 94103-2918

WILSEY, H. LAWRENCE, management consultant; b. Montaque, Calif., Aug. 17, 1923; s. Lawrence and Viola Louise (DeMuth) W.; m. Luana E. Jones, Feb. 26, 1944; 1 child, Kathryn Louise Wilsey Lerch. BS, U. So. Calif., 1944, MA, 1946; PhD, Cornell U., 1951. Asst. dean sch. bus. U. So. Calif., L.A., 1948-50; fgn. svc. officer U.S. Embassy, Oslo, 1950-52, Manila, 1952-54; chief China div. AID, Washington, 1954-55; sr. v.p. Booz, Allen & Hamilton, Chgo., 1955-76; pres., chief exec. officer Booz, Allen & Hamilton, Tokyo, 1972-74; exec. vice chancellor Tex. Christian U., Ft. Worth, 1976-79; chmn., chief exec. officer Lakewood Bank & Trust Co., Dallas, 1979-83; cons. Dallas and Pebble Beach, Calif., 1983—; chmn. Crown Charter Nat. Bank, Dallas, 1984-93. Trustee Evanston (Ill.) Hosp., 1960-76; bd. dirs. Dallas Opera, 1980-86. Lt. (j.g.) USN, 1944-46. Mem. Beach and Tennis Club. Presbyterian. Home: PO Box 396 Pebble Beach CA 93953-0396

WILSHIRE, HOWARD GORDON, research geologist; b. Shawnee, Okla., Aug. 19, 1926; s. Leslie Maynard and Mae Pearl (Craig) W.; m. Jane Ellen Nielson, June 1, 1984; children: Ruth, Paul, David. BA, U. Okla., 1952; PhD, U. Calif., 1956. Lectr. U. Sydney, 1956-60; rsch. fellow Australian Nat. U., Canberra, Australia, 1960-61; geologist U.S. Geol. Survey, Menlo Park, Calif., 1961—; mem. panel on surface processes Nat. Rsch. Coun.; cons. Pres.'s Coun. on Environ. Quality, Washington, 1979. Author, editor: Environmental Effects of Offroad Vehicles, 1983; contbr. numerous articles to profl. jours. Pres. Com. for Green Foothills, Palo Alto, 1981-82; bd. dirs. Desert Protective Coun., Palm Springs, Calif., 1988-90; exec. bd. mem. Pub. Employees for Environ. Responsibility, Washington, 1994. Recipient Meritorious Svc. award Dept. of Interior, 1988. Fellow AAAS, Geol. Soc. of Am. (com. on environ. and pub. policy); Am. Geophys. Union. Office: US Geological Survey MS/975 345 Middlefield Rd # Ms/975 Menlo Park CA 94025-3561 Home: 1348 Isabelle Ave Mountain View CA 94040-3038

WILSON, ARCHIE FREDRIC, medical educator; b. L.A., May 7, 1931; s. Louis H. and Ruth (Kert) W.; m. Tamar Braverman, Feb. 11, 1937; children: Lee A., Daniel B. BA, UCLA, 1953, PhD, 1967; MD, U. Calif., San Francisco, 1957. Intern L.A. County Gen. Hosp., 1957-58; resident U. Calif., San Francisco, 1958-61; fellow in chest disease dept. medicine UCLA, 1966-67, asst. prof., 1967-70; asst. prof. U. Calif., Irvine, 1970-73, assoc. prof., 1973-79, prof., 1979—. Editor: Pulmonary Function Test: Interpretation, 1986; contbr. articles to profl. jours. Bd. mem. Am. Lung Assn., Orange County, 1970-90, Am. Heart Assn., Calif., 1990—. Capt. USMC, 1961-63. Mem. Am. Fedn. Clin. Rsch., Western Soc. Clin. Investigation. Office: Univ Calif 101 The City Dr S Orange CA 92668-3201

WILSON, A(RNOLD) J(ESSE), city manager, consultant, communications executive; b. St. Louis, Oct. 18, 1941; s. Arnold Jesse and Eleanor (Zinn) W.; m. Patricia Ann Wilson, Mar. 7, 1961 (div. Aug. 1970); children: Mark, Mary Beth; m. Sara Roscoe, Aug. 29, 1970; children: Kristin, Jesse. AA, S.W. Bapt. Coll., 1961; BA in Psychology, William Jewell Coll., 1963; BD, Yale U., 1966, ThM, 1967. Assoc. minister, community cons. United Ch. on the Green, New Haven, 1964-67; salesperson Clark Peeper Co., St. Louis, 1967-68; dir. human resources City of University City, Mo., 1968-69; exec. dir. St. Louis County Mcpl. League, Clayton, Mo., 1969-70; exec. asst. to mayor City of St. Louis, 1971-76; mgr. City of Portland, Maine, 1976-80, City of Santa Ana, Calif., 1980-83, City of Kansas City, Mo., 1983-85; pres. Wilson Communications, Kansas City and Fallbrook, Calif., 1985-88; city adminstr. City of Pomona, Calif., 1988-90; exec. dir. Western Riverside (Calif.) Coun. Govts., 1990—; cons. U.S. Dept. HUD, Washington, 1975-76, U.S. Dept. HHS, Washington, 1978, 1st Nat. Bank of Boston, 1979-80, Nat. League of Cities, Washington, 1988—. Contbr. articles to profl. jours. Mem. human devel. com. Nat. League of Cities, Washington, 1978-84, 88; mem. resolutions com. Mo. Mcpl. League, 1978-79; mem. com. on revenue and fin. Calif. League of Cities, 1980-83; chmn. exec. adv. com. St. Louis Regional Coun., 1975. Recipient Golden City award City of Santa Ana, 1983, Community Svc. award Orange County (Calif.) Bd. of Suprs., 1983, Life Svc. award S.W. Bapt. Coll., 1984. Mem. Internat. City Mgmt. Assn., Am. Soc. Pub. Adminstrn., Govt. Fin. Officers Assn., Internat. Assn. Human Rights Orgn., Nat. Assn. Housing Redevel. Officers, Calif. Community Renewal Assn., Women and Minorities in Mgmt., City Mgrs. Assn. (social action com. 1987-88). Home: 1523 Green Canyon Rd Fallbrook CA 92028-4329 Office: Western Riverside Coun Govt 3880 Lemon St #300 Riverside CA 92501-3335

WILSON, BARY WALLACE, neuroendocrinologist; b. Moscow, Idaho, Dec. 12, 1945; s. Arlin Chadwick and June (Rawlings) W.; m. Martha Ericka Ruf, Aug. 21, 1967; children: Melanie, Mark, Meaghan, Miranda, Brandon, Benjiman. BS, U. Wash., Seattle, 1972; PhD, U. London, 1977; post doctoral assoc., MIT, 1977-78. Engr. Varian Mat, Bremen, Germany, 1973-74; biochemist St. Bartholomew's Med. Sch., London, 1974-76; sr. rsch. scientist, staff scientist Battelle Northwest, Richland, Wash., 1978—; founder, prin. Tecna Corp., San Bernardino, Calif., 1983—; founder Columbia Magnetics Inc., Kennewick, Wash., 1993—; founder, chief scientist Gulf Tech. Ctr., Abu Dhabi, U.A.E., 1994—; cons. SCA Assocs., McLean, Va., 1990-93, Univ. Petroleum & Minerals RI, Dhahran, Saudi Arabia, 1986-87; mem. EPA sci. adv. bd. NIEMF com., Washington, 1990—; bd. dirs. Bioelectromagnetics Soc., Falls Church, Md. Author, editor Extremely LF EMF: The Question of Cancer, 1990; patentee: Microbial Solubilization of Coal, 1990, Methods and Treatment of NIDDM, 1989; contbr. articles to profl. jours. Sgt. USMCR, 1965-72. Recipient Mentor award Internat. Sci. and Engring. Fair, 1991. Home: 4727 Tripple Vista Dr Kennewick WA 99337 Office: Pacific Northwest Lab 617 Battelle Blvd Richland WA 99352

WILSON, BLENDA JACQUELINE, university chancellor; b. Woodbridge, N.J., Jan. 28, 1941; d. Horace and Margaret (Brogsdale) Wilson; m. Louis Fair Jr. AB, Cedar Crest Coll., 1962; AM, Seton Hall U., 1965; PhD, Boston Coll., 1979; DHL (hon.), Cedar Crest Coll., 1987, Loretto Heights Coll., 1988, Colo. Tech. Coll., 1988, U. Detroit, 1989; LLD (hon.), Rutgers U., 1989, Ea. Mich. U., 1990, Cambridge Coll., 1991, Schoolcraft Coll., 1992. Tchr. Woodbridge Twp. Pub. Schs., 1962-66; exec. dir. Middlesex County Econ. Opportunity Corp., New Brunswick, N.J., 1966-69; exec. asst. to pres. Rutgers U., New Brunswick, N.J., 1969-72; sr. assoc. dean Grad. Sch. Edn. Harvard U., Cambridge, Mass., 1972-82; v.p. effective sector mgmt. Ind. Sector, Washington, 1982-84; exec. dir. Colo. Commn. Higher Edn., Denver, 1984-88; chancellor and prof. pub. adminstrn. & edn. U. Mich., Dearborn, 1988-92; pres. Calif. State U., Northridge, 1992—; Am. del. U.S./U.K. Dialogue About Quality Judgments in Higher Edn.; adv. bd. Mich. Consolidated Gas Co., Stanford Inst. Higher Edn. Rsch., U. So. Col. Dist. 60 Nat. Alliance, Nat. Ctr. for Rsch. to Improve Postsecondary Teaching and Learning, 1988-90; bd. dirs. Alpha Capital Mgmt.; mem. higher edn. colloquium Am. Coun. Edn., vis. com. Divsn. Continuing Edn. in Faculty of Arts & Scis., Harvard Coll., Pew Forum on K-12 Edn. Reform in U.S.; trustee Children's TV Workshop. Dir. U. Detroit Jesuit High Sch., Northridge Hosp. Med. Ctr., Arab Cmty. Ctr. for Econ. and Social Svcs., Union Bank, J. Paul Getty Trust, James Irvine Found., Internat. Found. Edn. and Self-Help, Achievement Coun., L.A.; dir., vice chair Met. Affairs Corp.; exec. bd. Detroit area coun. Boy Scouts Am.; bd. dirs. Commonwealth Fund, Henry Ford Hosp.-Fairlane Ctr., Henry Ford Health System, Met. Ctr. for High Tech., United Way Southeastern Mich.; mem. Nat. Coalition 100 Black Women, Detroit, Race Rels. Coun. Met. Detroit, Women & Founds., Greater Detroit Interfaith Round Table NCCJ, Adv. Bd. Valley Cultural Ctr., Woodland Hills; trustee assoc. Boston Coll.; trustee emeritus Cambridge Coll.; trustee emeritus, bd. dirs. Found. Ctr.; trustee Henry Ford Mus. & Greenfield Village, Sammy Davis Jr. Nat. Liver Inst. Mem. AAUW, Assn. Governing Bds. (adv. coun. of pres.'s), Edn. Commn. of the States (student minority task force), Am. Assn. Higher Edn. (chair-elect), Am. Assn. State Colls. & Univs. (com. on policies & purposes, acad. leadership fellows selection com.), Assn. Black Profls. and Adminstrs., Assn. Black Women in Higher Edn., Women Execs. State Govt., Internat. Women's Forum, Mich. Women's Forum, Women's Econ. Club Detroit, Econ. Club, Rotary. Office: Calif State Univ Office of President 18111 Nordhoff St Northridge CA 91330-0001

WILSON, BRANDON LAINE, writer, advertising and public relations consultant, explorer; b. Sewickley, Pa., Oct. 2, 1953; s. Edgar C. and Mary Beth (Tuttle) W.; m. Cheryl Ann Keefe, June 23, 1989. BA, U. N.C., 1973; Cert. Am. Acad. Dramatic Arts, 1974. Asst. acct. exec. Hill & Knowlton Pub. Rels., Pitts., 1973; dir. video Seattle Repertory Theatre, 1975-76; asst. dir., cameraman Pub. Broadcasting Network, Chapel Hill, 1976-77; dir. advt. and TV Prodn. N.Am. Films, Eugene, Oreg., 1977-79; gen. mgr. Boulder Community Coops., 1980-81; pub. info. officer, asst. to mayor City of Barrow, Alaska, 1981-82; dir. advt. and promotion Anchorage Conv. and Visitors Bur., Anchorage, 1983-85; mgr. mktg. communications GTE, Honolulu, 1986-87; v.p., sr. copywriter, producer Peck, Sims, Mueller Advt. (NW Ayer affiliate), Honolulu, 1987-89; pres., creative dir. Wilson & Assoc., Inc., Hawaii, 1987—, pres. Brandon Wilson Lit. Svcs., 1991—. Author: Dead Men Don't Leave Tips, A Couple's Trans-African Odyssey, 1991 Yak Butter Blues, 1994; prin. works (TV) include The General Assembly Today, 1976-77, (films) Sasquatch, Mystery of the Sacred Shroud, Buffalo Rider; contbr. articles to nat. mags. and newspapers. Named Eagle Scout Boy Scouts Am., one of Exceptionally Able Youth, 1970, Literary award U. Pitts., 1970, one of Outstanding Young Men in Am., 1986, Men of Achievement award U.K., 1987, 93, Dict. of Internat. Biography, U.K., 1993; recipient Order of the Arrow, two Ike Pono Gold awards Internat. TV Assn., 6 creative advt. awards, (AAF). Mem. Am. Advt. Fedn., (accreditation), PRSA, Soc. of Friends, Mensa, Internat. Campaign for Tibet, Amnesty Internat. Journeyed length of Africa overland (Ceuta to Cape Town), 1990; half of first western couple to cross Himalayas from Lhasa, Tibet to Kathmandu, Nepal, 1992; climbed Mt. Nyragongo, Mt. Kilimanjaro, Mt. Olympus, Mt. Everest Base Camp, Tibet, Mt Miyajima, Crough Patrick, Te Rua Manga; rafted down the Zambezi River; tracked mountain gorillas in Zaire; journeyed overland across C.Am.; explored Eastern Europe, 1989.

WILSON, BRIAN CHARLES, civil engineer; b. St. Paul, Apr. 25, 1950; s. Robert L. and Helen L. Wilson. BSCE, U. Minn., 1972. Registered profl. engr., N.Mex. Rural devel. advisor U.S. Peace Corps, Latoka, Fiji Islands, 1973-75; asst. engr. New Zealand Ministry of Works, Wellington, 1975-76; water resource engring. specialist N.Mex. State Engr. Office, Santa Fe, 1978—. Author tech. report on water use. Office: NM State Engr Office Bataan Meml Bldg PO Box 25102 Santa Fe NM 87504

WILSON, CARL ARTHUR, real estate broker; b. Manhasset, N.Y., Sept. 29, 1947; s. Archie and Florence (Hefner) W.; divorced; children: Melissa Starr, Clay Alan. Student UCLA, 1966-68, 70-71. Tournament bridge dir. North Hollywood (Calif.) Bridge Club, 1967-68, 70-71; computer operator IBM, L.A., 1967-68, 70-71; bus. devel. mgr. Walker & Lee Real Estate, Anaheim, Calif., 1972-76; v.p. sales and mktg. The Estes Co., Phoenix, 1976-82, Continental Homes Inc., 1982-84; pres. Roadrunner Homes Corp., Phoenix, 1984-86, Lexington Homes, Inc., 1986, Barrington Homes, 1986-90; gen. mgr. Starr Homes, 1991—; pres. Offsite Utilities, Inc., 1992—; adv. dir. Liberty Bank. Mem. Glendale (Ariz.) Citizens Bond Coun., 1986-87, Ariz. Housing Study Commn., 1988-89, Valley Leadership, 1988—; pres.'s coun. Am. Grad. Sch. Internat. Mgmt., 1985-89; vice-chmn. Glendale Planning and Zoning Commn., 1986-87, chmn., 1987-91; mem. bd. trustees Valley of Sun United Way, 1987-92, chmn. com. Community Problem Solving and Fund Distbn., 1988-89; mem. City of Glendale RTC Task Force, 1990, Maricopa County Citizens Jud. Reform Com., 1990-92, Maricopa County Citizens Jud. Adv. Coun., 1990-91; co-founder, bd. dirs. Leaderhsip West, Inc., 1993—; mem. Maricopa County Trial Ct. Appointment Commn., 1993—. Mem. Nat. Assn. Homebuilders (bd. dirs. 1985-93, nat. rep. Ariz. 1990-92), Cen. Ariz. Homebuilders Assn. (adv. com. 1979-82, treas. 1986, sec. 1987, v.p. 1987-89, chmn. 1989-90, bd. dirs. 1985—, life dir. 1994—); mem. bd. adjustments City of Glendale, 1976-81, chmn., 1980-81, mem. bond coun., 1981-82; mem. real estate edn. adv. coun. State Bd. Community Coll., 1981-82; precinct committeeman, dep. registrar, 1980-81. With U.S. Army, 1968-70. Mem. Glendale C. of C. (dir. 1980-83, 89-91), Sales and Mktg. Coun. (chmn. edn. com. 1980, chmn. coun. 1981-82, Mame grand award 1981). Home: PO Box 39985 Phoenix AZ 85069-0985 Office: Starr Homes Inc Offsite Utilities Inc 2432 W Peoria Ave Ste 1190 Phoenix AZ 85029-4736

WILSON, CARTER, writer, educator; b. Washington, Dec. 27, 1947; s. George and Harriet W.; life partner, Reynolds S. Martinez, Oct. 29, 1977. BA, Harvard Coll., 1963; MA, Syracuse U., 1966. Lectr. Stanford U., Calif., 1965-66; Briggs-Copeland lectr. Harvard U., Cambridge, Mass., 1966-69; from lectr. to asst. prof. Tufts U., Medford, Mass., 1969-72; from asst. prof. to prof. U. Calif., Santa Cruz, 1972—. Author: Crazy February, 1966, I Have Fought the Good Fight, 1967 (children's book) On Firm Ice, 1969, A Green Tree and a Dry Tree, 1972, Treasures on Earth, 1981, Hidden in the Blood, 1995, contbr. (films) The Times of Harvy Milk, 1983, Common Threads, 1989, Where Are We? A Trip Across America. Recipient achievement award Assn. Gay & Lesbian Artists, 1984. Office: U Calif College 8 Steno Pool Santa Cruz CA 95064

WILSON, CHARLES B., neurosurgeon, educator; b. Neosho, Mo., Aug. 31, 1929; married; 3 children. BS, Tulane U., 1951, MD, 1954. Resident pathologist Tulane U., 1955-56, instr. neurosurgery, 1960-61; resident Ochsner Clinic, 1956-60; instr. La. State U., 1961-63; from asst. prof. to prof. U. Ky., 1963-68; prof. neurosurgery U. Calif., San Francisco, 1968—. Mem. Am. Assn. Neurol. Surgery, Soc. Neurol. Surgery. Office: U Calif Sch Medicine Box 0350 San Francisco CA 94143

WILSON, CHARLES E., air industry service executive; b. 1941. With White Motor Co. & Fresno (Calif.) Truck Ctr., 1962-77; pres. Exec. Wings, Fresno, 1977-87; now pres. Corp. Aircraft Inc., Fresno, 1987—. Office: Corp Aircraft Inc 4885 E Shields Ave Fresno CA 93726-6420*

WILSON, CHARLES R., research chemist; b. San Francisco, Oct. 11, 1946; s. Charles G. Wilson Jr. and Eleanore R. (Muzzin) Samarzes. BS, St. Mary's Coll. of Calif., 1968; PhD in Inorganic Chemistry, Stanford U., 1973. Research chemist Corning (N.Y.) Glass Works, 1973-74, ARCO Chem. Co., Glenolden, Pa., 1974-77; sr. research chemist Air Products and Chem., Inc., Marcus Hook, Pa., 1977-81; cons. scientist Chevron Rsch. and Tech. Co., Richmond, Calif., 1981—. Patentee in field. Mem. AAAS, Am. Chem. Assn., Phila. Catalysis Soc., Calif. Catalysis Soc. Home: 1101 Diamond St San Francisco CA 94114-3630 Office: Chevron Rsch & Tech Co 100 Chevron Way Richmond CA 94801-2016

WILSON, CHARLES ZACHARY, JR., newspaper publisher; b. Greenwood, Miss., Apr. 21, 1929; s. Charles Zachary and Ora Lee (Means) W.; m. Doris J. Wilson, Aug. 18, 1951 (dec. Nov. 1974); children: Charles III, Joyce Lynne, Joanne Catherine, Gary Thomas, Jonathan Keith; m. Kelly Freeman, Apr. 21, 1986; children: Amanda Fox, Walter Bremond. BS in Econs., U. Ill., 1952, PhD in Econs. and Stats., 1956. Asst. to v.p. Commonwealth Edison Co., Chgo., 1956-59; asst. prof. econs. De Paul U., Chgo., 1959-61; assoc. prof. bus. SUNY, Binghamton, 1961-67, prof. econs. and bus., 1967-68; prof. mgmt. and edn. UCLA, 1968-84, vice chancellor acad. programs, 1985-87; CEO, pub., pres. Cen. News-Wave Publs., L.A., 1987—; pres. Czamd Assoc., Pacific Palisades, Calif., 1994—; mem. adv. council Fed. Res. Bank, San Francisco, 1986-88, 2001 com. Office of Mayor of Los Angeles, 1986-89. Author: Organizational Decision-Making, 1967; contbr. articles on bus. to jours. Bd. dirs. Los Angeles County Mus. Art, 1972-84; com. on Los Angeles City Revenue, 1975-76, United Nations Assn. panel for advancement of U. and Japan Relations, N.Y.C. 1972-74; chmn. Mayor's task force on Africa, 1979-82. Fellow John Hay Whitney, U. Ill., 1955-56, Ford Found., 1960-61, 81-82, 84, Am. Council of Edn., UCLA, 1967-68, Aspen Inst. for Human Studies; named one of Young Men of Yr., Jaycees, 1965. Mem. AAAS, Am. Econ. Assn., Nat. Newspaper Pub. Assn., Am. Mgmt. Assn., Alpha Phi Alpha (pres., pledgemaster 1952-54), Phi Kappa Phi, Order of Artus (pres.). Home: 1053 Tellem Dr Pacific Palisades CA 90272-2243 Office: Cen Newspaper Publs 2621 W 54th St Los Angeles CA 90043-2614

WILSON, DALE OWEN, JR., physiology educator; b. Euclid, Ohio, Jan. 7, 1955; s. Dale Owen and Lois (Cyr) W.; m. Polly Meg Wilson, Aug. 17, 1974; children: Gregg, Susan, Kathrine. BS, U. Wis., 1977; MS, Ohio State U., 1983, PhD, 1986. Assoc. prof. S.W. Idaho Rsch. and Ext. Ctr. U. Idaho, Parma, 1986—. Contbr. articles profl. jours. Mem. AAAS, Am. Soc. Agronomy, Nat. Sweet Corn Breeders Assn., Sigma Xi. Mem. Evang. Christian Ch. Office: Parma Rsch Ext Ctr 29603 U Of I Ln Parma ID 83660-6590

WILSON, DAVID ALLEN, political scientist, science policy consultant; b. Rockford, Ill., May 1, 1926; s. Allen C. and Margaret (McKay) W.; m. Marie Wilson; children: Elizabeth, Stephen; m. Belle Lifson Cole, Jan. 1, 1989. BA, U. Toledo, 1948; PhD, Cornell U., 1960. Prof. UCLA, 1959—; pres. The PMR Group, Westwood, Calif., 1988—; cons. The Rand Corp., Santa Monica, Calif., 1963-68, Aid U.S. Ops. Mission Thailand, Bangkok, 1968-71, Dept. Def./Office Sec. Def., Washington, 1982-86. Author: Politics In Thailand, 1961, United States and Future of Thailand, 1970; editor: Universities And Military, 1988; co-editor: Future of State University, 1986. Ford Found. fellow, 1955-58. Fellow AAAS; mem. Am. Pol. Sci. Assn. Office: UCLA Dept Polit Sci Los Angeles CA 90024

WILSON, DAVID EUGENE, magistrate judge; b. Columbia, S.C., Jan. 12, 1940; s. David W. and Emma (Moseley) W.; m. Nancy Ireland, Sept. 5, 1964; children: Amy R., Cara S. BA, U. S.C., 1963, JD, 1966; MA, Boston U., 1971. Bar: Vt. 1972, D.C. 1973, Wash. 1980, U.S. Dist. Ct. Vt. 1972, U.S. Dist. Ct. (we. dist.) Wash. 1976. Asst. atty. gen. State of Vt., Montpelier, 1972-73; asst. U.S. atty. U.S. Dist. Ct. D.C., Washington, 1973-76; asst. U.S. atty. U.S. Dist. Ct. (we. dist.) Wash., Seattle, 1976-89, U.S. atty., 1989, asst. U.S. atty., chief criminal div., 1989-92; U.S. magistrate judge Seattle, 1992—; mem. faculty Atty. Gen.'s Advocacy Inst., Washington, 1979—, Nat. Inst. Trial Advocacy, Seattle, 1987—. Capt. U.S. Army, 1966-71, col. USAR. Recipient Disting. Community Svc. award B'nai Brith, 1987. Fellow Am. Coll. Trial Lawyers; mem. Fed. Bar Assn., Wash. State Bar, Seattle-King County Bar. Office: 304 US Courthouse Seattle WA 98104

WILSON, DAVID JEAN, ophthalmologist; b. Houston, July 24, 1955; s. Joseph William and Mary Catherine (Fitter) W.; m. Nancy Reva Greene, July 17, 1982; children: Reid, Eric, Claire. BS in Chemistry, Stanford U., 1977; MD, Baylor Coll. of Medicine, 1981. Diplomate Am. Bd. Ophthalmology. Resident in ophthalmology Oreg. Health Scis. U., Portland, 1981-85; fellow ophthalmic pathology Wilmer Eye Inst. Johns Hopkins U., Balt., 1985-87; fellow retina vitreous Ophthalmic Cons. of Boston Harvard U., 1987-88; asst. prof. ophthalmology Oreg. Health Scis. U., Portland, 1988-93, assoc. prof. ophthalmology, 1993—. Office: Casey Eye Inst 3375 SW Terwilliger Blvd Portland OR 97201-4146

WILSON, DOUGLAS BROWNLOW, language educator; b. Denver, Aug. 19, 1930; s. Brownlow Villers and Joyce Means (Gow) W.; m. Carmen Diana Armas, June 23, 1956; children: Antonia Joy, Andrea, Fiona, Miranda. BA, Williams Coll., 1952; MA, Oxford Coll., 1962; PhD, Harvard U., 1964. Instr. U. Houston, 1958-59; asst. prof. Williams Coll., Williamstown, Mass., 1964-68; from asst. prof. to prof. U. Denver, 1968—; lectr. Colo. Endowment for Humanities, 1989-93; mem. seminar for coll. tchrs. NEH, Stanford, Calif., 1982. Author: The Romantic Dream, 1993; contbr. articles, notes to profl. jours. and book. 1st lt. USAF, 1952-55. Grantee ACLS, 1984, Faculty Rsch. Fund, 1993, 94. Mem. MLA (assembly del. 1985-88), Wordsworth Coleridge Assn., Friends of Coleridge, Keats Shelley Soc. Democrat. Home: 2551 E Floyd Ave Englewood CO 80110-7602 Office: U Denver Dept English Denver CO 80208

WILSON, EMILY MARIE, sales executive; b. Aberdeen, Wash., Mar. 24, 1951; d. Charles Robert and Alice Adele (Robinson) W.; m. Michael A. Rich, July 1, 1976. Student, U. Puget Sound, 1969-71, Austro-Am. Inst., Vienna, 1971; BA in Polit. Sci., U. Wash., 1973. U.S. sales mgr. Clairol, Inc., Seattle, 1975-81, sales rep. N.W. Wash., drug-mass mdse. div., 1975-77, sales rep. Met. Seattle, 1977-78, dist. mgr. sales western Wash., 1978-81; trainer territorial sales reps., mgr. dist. dollar sales, and dist. sales mgr. of Wash., Oreg., Idaho and Mont., Clorox, Inc., Seattle, 1981-82, assoc. regional mgr. Western div. spl. markets, 1982-83; regional mgr. Olympic Stain Co., Bellevue, Wash., 1983-86; dir. sales Inscape Products The Weyerhauser Co., Tacoma, 1986-88; dir. ops. Wildland Journeys, Seattle, 1988-89; Traveller World Wide Explorations, 1989—; sales mgr. Adventures Abroad, Seattle, 1990-92; owner Emily Unltd. Organizational Svcs. and Mgmt., 1992—. Mem. Transcendental Meditation Soc., Oreg. Hist. Soc., Sons and Daus. of Oreg. Pioneers, Pioneer Assn. Wash., Seattle Hist. Soc., Sidha of the Age of Enlightenment World Govt. Assn., Grad. Sci. of Creative Intelligence, Women's Profl. Managerial Network. Office: 4417 54th Ave NE Seattle WA 98105-4942

WILSON, ERVIN MCDONALD, music consultant; b. Pacheco, Mex., June 11, 1928; came to U.S., 1944; s. Marion Lyman and Luisa (McDonald) W. Student, Brigham Young U., 1949-52. Draftsman Douglas Aircraft, Santa Monica, Calif., 1953-57; microtonal music cons. L.A. Editorial bd. XenHarmonikon, 1974—; inventor keyboard musical instruments; contbr. articles on speculative music theory to XenHarmonikon. Cpl. USAF, 1946-49. Home: 844 N Avenue 65 Los Angeles CA 90042-1541

WILSON, FRANK DOUGLAS, geneticist; b. Salt Lake City, Dec. 17, 1928; s. Frank LeRoy and Nellie Mae (Roach) W.; m. Beverly Ann Urry, Nov. 27, 1950; children: Kerry, Leslie, Eileen, John, Greg, Cynthia, Angela, David. BS, U. Utah, 1950, MS, 1953; PhD, Wash. State U., 1957. Rsch. geneticist agrl. rsch. svcs. U.S. Dept. Agr., Belle Glade, Fla., 1957-65; geneticist agrl. rsch. svcs. U.S. Dept. Agr., College Station, Tex., 1965-71, USDA, Phoenix, 1971-93; biol. scis. collaborator USDA, College Station, Tex., 1993—. Bd. dirs., tng. chmn. Boy Scouts Am., Phoenix, 1977-88. Recipient Silver Beaver award Boy Scouts Am., 1984, Cotton Genetics Rsch. award Joint Cotton Breeding Policy Com., 1991. Mem. Agronomy Soc. Am. (assoc. editor 1978-80), AAAS, Ariz-Nev. Acad. Sci. Mormon. Office: USDA Western Cotton Rsch 4135 E Broadway Rd Phoenix AZ 85040-8803

WILSON, GARY THOMAS, engineering executive; b. Pitts., Sept. 26, 1961; s. Charles Zachary and Doris Jean (Thomas) W. AB, Dartmouth Coll., 1983, BEEE, 1984; MSEE, Calif. State U., Long Beach, 1992; postgrad., UCLA, 1992—. Elec. engr. AiResearch, Man., Garrett, Torrance, Calif., 1983; sr. mem. tech. staff TRW Space & Electronics Group, Redondo Beach, Calif., 1984-93; v.p. of R&D CZAND Assocs., L.A., 1993—; rsch. asst. UCLA Flight System Rsch. Ctr., Westwood, Calif., 1994—; cons. CZAND Assocs., L.A., 1985-93. Tutor math. and sci. TRW Bootstrap, Redondo Beach, 1991-93. Recipient Meritorious Svc. award United Negro Coll. Fund, 1989; TRW master's fellow, doctoral incentive fellow Calif. State U., 1993. Mem. IEEE, Nat. Soc. Black Engrs. (pres. Dartmouth chpt. 1982-83), Dartmouth Soc. Engrs.

WILSON, GERALD ALAN, retail executive; b. Portland, Oreg., Jan. 30, 1951; s. Stanley Edward and Frances (O'Brien) McBarron; m. Francee Lee Davies, Aug. 21, 1972 (div. Nov. 1980); 1 child, Joel Alan. BS in Biology, U. Oreg., 1973, MS in Curriculum and Instrn., 1975. Cert. tchr., Oreg. Tchr. biology Molalla (Oreg.) Union High Sch., 1974-75; instr. biology Lane Community Coll., Eugene, Oreg., 1975; with sci. curriculum, design and implementation dept. Oaklea Mid. Sch., Junction City, Oreg., 1975-78; ptnr. Wilson Music House, Eugene, 1978-83, prin., 1983—; adviser small bus. mgmt. com. Lane Community Coll., Eugene, 1983-93. Mem. budget com. City of Eugene, 1978-80; chairperson Westside Neighborhood Orgn., 1977-78; mem. bachelor auction Lane County March of Dimes, 1987-91; trustee Wilson Trusts. Mem. U. Oreg. Alumni Assn. (dir. Lane County chpt. 1987-92). Republican. Methodist. Club: Downtown Athletic (Eugene) (charter). Office: Wilson Music House 943 Olive St Eugene OR 97401-3006

WILSON, HERMAN T., JR., agricultural products supplier; b. 1941. Food divsn. mgr. Granada Corp., Houston, 1986-88; chmn., co-founder Western Farm Svc. Inc., Fresno, Calif., 1988—. Office: Western Farm Svc Inc 3705 W Beechwood Ave Fresno CA 93711-0650

WILSON, HERSCHEL MANUEL (PETE WILSON), retired journalism educator; b. Candler, N.C., July 17, 1930; s. Shuford Arnold and Ida Camilla (Landreth) W.; m. Ruby Jean Herring, Aug. 10, 1952. AB in Journalism, San Diego State U., 1956; MS in Journalism, Ohio U., Athens, 1959; postgrad., U. So. Calif., 1966-70. Reporter, copy editor, picture editor The San Diego Union, 1955-58; reporter, wire editor Long Beach (Calif.) Ind., 1959-65; prof. journalism Calif. State U., Northridge, 1965-71; fgn. desk copy editor L.A. Times, 1966-71; prof. and former chmn. journalism Humboldt State U., Arcata, Calif., 1971-91; ret., 1991; cons. KVIQ-TV News Dept., Eureka, Calif., 1985-87. Contbr. articles to profl. jours. Publicity dir. Simi Valley (Calif.) Fair Housing Coun., 1967; bd. dirs., publicity dir. NAACP, Eureka, Calif., 1978-80. With USN, 1948-52, Korea. Named Nat. Outstanding Advisor, Theta Sigma Phi, 1970. Mem. Soc. Profl. Journalists. (named Disting. Campus Advisor 1982), San Fernando Valley Press Club (v.p. 1969-70), Beau Pre Men's Golf Club (McKinleyville, Calif., pub. rels. dir., treas. 1978). Democrat. Methodist. Home: 115 Bent Creek Ranch Rd Asheville NC 28806-9521

WILSON, IAN HOLROYDE, management consultant, futurist; b. Harrow, England, June 16, 1925; came to U.S., 1954; s. William Brash and Dorothy (Holroyde) W.; m. Page Tuttle Hedden, Mar. 17, 1951 (div. Dec. 1983); children: Rebecca, Dorothy, Ellen, Holly, Alexandra; m. Adrianne Marcus, July 12, 1992. MA, Oxford U., 1948. Orgn. cons. Imperial Chem. Industries, London, 1948-54; various staff exec. positions in strategic planning, mgmt. devel. Gen. Electric Co., Fairfield, Conn., 1954-80; sr. cons. to maj. U.S. and internat. cos. SRI Internat., Menlo Park, Calif., 1980-93; prin. Wolf Enterprises, San Rafael, Calif., 1993—; exec. in residence Va. Commonwealth U., Richmond, 1976. Author: Planning for Major Change, 1976, The Power of Strategic Vision, 1991, Rewriting the Corporate Social Charter, 1992, Managing Strategically in the 1990s, 1993; mem. editorial bd. Planning Rev., Oxford, Ohio, 1973-81; Am. editor Long Range Planning Jour., London, 1981-89; sr. editor Planning Review, 1993—. Mem. adv. bd. Technol. Forecasting and Social Change, 1989—; chmn. Citizen's Long Range Ednl. Goals Com., Westport, Conn., 1967-70; mem. strategic process com. United Way of Am., Alexandria, Va., 1985-94. Capt. Brit. Army, 1943-45, ETO. Mem. AAAS, Planning Forum, World Future Soc. Unitarian. Office: 79 Twin Oaks Ave San Rafael CA 94901-1915

WILSON, IAN ROBERT, food company executive; b. Pietermaritzburg, South Africa, Sept. 22, 1929; s. Brian J. and Edna C. W.; m. Susan Diana Lasch, Jan. 14, 1970; children: Timothy Robert, Christopher James, Diana Louise, Jason Luke. B.Commerce, U. Natal, South Africa, 1952; postgrad., Harvard U. Bus. Sch., 1968. With Coca-Cola Export Corp., Johannesburg, South Africa, 1956-74; mgr. Coca-Cola Export Corp., 1969-72, v.p., regional mgr., 1972-73, area mgr., 1973; pres., chief exec. officer Coca-Cola Ltd., Toronto, Ont., Can., 1974-76; chmn. bd., dir. Coca-Cola Ltd., 1976-81; exec. v.p. Coca-Cola Co., Atlanta, 1976-79; vice chmn. Coca-Cola Co., 1979-81, pres. Pacific group; dir. Coca-Cola Export Corp., Atlanta, 1976-81; pres., chief exec. officer, dir. Castle & Cooke, Inc., San Francisco, 1983-84, Wyndham Foods, Inc., 1985-89; chmn. bd., chief exec. officer Windmill Corp., San Francisco, 1989-94; mng. ptnr. Dartford Partnership and Induna Ptnrs., San Francisco, 1993—; also bd. dirs. Dartford Partnership and Induna Ptnrs.; bd. dirs. Novell Inc., Golden State Foods, Inc., Egoli Ptnrs., New Age Beverages Ltd., U.S./Asean Coun., East-West Ctr.; chmn. bd. dirs. Windy Hill Pet Foods and Van de Kamp Inc. Mem. Church of Eng. Clubs: Durban Country and Johannesburg Country, Inanda Hunt and Polo, Atlantic Salmon, San Francisco Golf, Pacific Union, Burlingame Country. Home: 945 Green St San Francisco CA 94133-3639 Office: Dartford Partnership 801 Montgomery St Ste 400 San Francisco CA 94133-5164

WILSON, JAMES BARKER, lawyer, writer; b. Visalia, Calif., Jan. 29, 1926; s. John Fleming and Helen Mae (Barker) W.; m. Joanne Bailey, Apr. 27, 1956. BA, U. Wash., 1948, JD, 1950. Bar: Wash. 1950, U.S. Supreme Ct. 1955. Asst. atty. gen. Wash. State Atty. Gen., Seattle, 1951-52; prin. Harlow, Ringold & Wilson, Seattle, 1953-63; asst. atty. gen. U. Wash., Seattle, 1963-65, sr. asst. atty. gen., 1965-89; gen. counsel U. Wash., 1965-89; pres. Intourex, Inc. 1988-92. Contbr. chpts. to books, articles to profl. jours. Democrat candidate for U.S. Congress, 1st Dist., Wash., 1956; del. Dem. Nat. Conv., 1952, 60; pres. bd. trustees Group Health Credit Union, 1954-61; v.p. Group Health Co-op, Seattle, 1963-64; bd. dirs. Henry Gallery, U. Wash., 1972-80, Allied Arts of Seattle, 1973-75; pres. Pacific Basin Council, 1988-92. Served with USAAF, 1944-45. Mem. ABA, Wash. State Bar Assn., Seattle-King County Bar Assn., Nat. Assn. Coll. and Univ. Attys. (bd. dirs. 1972-73, 75-82, pres. 1979-80, cert. of merit 1980, life mem. 1990), Phi Alpha Delta, Theta Chi.

WILSON, JAMES ERNEST, petroleum consultant, writer; b. McKinney, Tex., Apr. 19, 1915; s. James Ernest and Agnes (Neill) W.; m. Elloie Barkely, Apr. 4, 1940; children: Judith Wilson Grant, Elizabeth Wilson. BS, Tex. A&M U., 1937. Surface geologist Shell Oil Co., Tex., 1938-41, various positions, 1945-59, v.p., Houston, New Orleans and Denver, 1959-73; cons., Denver, 1973—. Trustee and chmn. Am. Assn. Petroleum Geologists Found., 1975-79; trustee Children's Hosp. Denver, 1970-83, Denver Symphony, 1968-82, Inst. Internat. Edn., Denver, 1968-82; mem. bd. University Park Meth. Ch., 1968—. Maj. U.S. Army, 1941-45; ETO. Recipient Geosciences and Earth Resources medal Tex. A&M, 1986, Disting. Alumnus, 1991. Fellow Geol. Soc. Am., Soc. Petroleum Engrs., Am. Assn. Petroleum Geologists (hon., recipient Sidney Powers Meml. medal, 1988). Republican. Methodist. Clubs: Cherry Hill Country (Denver); Confrerie des Chevaliers du Tastevin (pres. 1983-93, grand officier honoraire). Home: 4248 S Hudson Pky Englewood CO 80110-5015

WILSON, JAMES ROBERT, lawyer; b. Meade, Kans., Dec. 3, 1927; s. Robert J. and Bess O. (Osborne) W.; m. Marguerite Jean Reiter, Nov. 27, 1960; 1 son, John Ramsey. B.A., Kans. U., 1950, LL.B., 1953. Bar: Kans. 1953, Nebr. 1961, Colo. 1981. Pvt. practice Meade, Kans., 1953-57, Lakewood, Colo., 1989-93; county atty. Meade County, 1954-57; city atty. Meade, 1954-57; asst. gen. counsel Kans. Corp. Commn., 1957-59, gen. counsel, 1959-61, mem., 1961; atty. KN Energy, Inc., 1961-75, personnel dir., 1964-67, v.p., treas., 1968-75, exec. v.p., 1975-78, pres., chief operating officer, 1978-82, pres., chief exec. officer, 1982-85, chmn., pres., chief exec. officer, 1985-88, chmn., 1988-89; bd. dirs. Alliance Ins. Cos. With USNR, 1945-46. Mem. Phi Kappa Sigma. Home: 1725 Foothills Dr S Golden CO 80401-9167

WILSON, JAY, tapestry weaver; b. Clarksburg, W.Va., May 21, 1947; s. William Hall Wilson and Elizabeth Wamsley. BArch, Auburn U., 1971. Archtl. designer Architects Hawaii, Honolulu, 1972-75; pvt. practice Honolulu, Hawaii, 1976—; juror numerous art exhbns., 1989—. Represented in pvt., corp. and pub. collections in Hawaii, on U.S. mainland and Can.; exhibited in numerous juried & invitational art exhbns., 1972—, including solo exhbn. at Contemporary Arts Ctr., Honolulu, 1980, 3 tapestries with juried exhibit Artists of Hawaii, Honolulu Acad. Arts, 1987, 1 tapestry at 25th Anniversary of Hawaii State Found. on Culture & the Arts Exhbn., Contemporary Mus., Honolulu, 1990, 1 tapestry 30 yrs. of Honolulu Advertiser Gallery, 1991. Named Master Artist Hawaii State Found. on Culture and Arts; featured in art and craft publs. Mem. Hawaii Craftsmen (ann. exhbn. cash award 1972, jurors spl. mention 1980), Am. Tapestry Alliance, Internat. Tapestry Network, Handweaver's Guild Am. (award of merit 1989). Home and Office: 3155 Nahenahe Pl Kihei HI 96753-9314

WILSON, JOHN FRANCIS, religion educator; b. Springfield, Mo., Nov. 4, 1937; s. Frederick Marion and Jesse Ferrel (Latimer) W.; m. L. Claudette Faulk, June 9, 1961; children: Laura, Amy, Emily. BA, Harding U., Searcy, Ark., 1959; MA, Harding U., Memphis, 1961; PhD, U. Iowa, 1967. Dir. Christian Student Ctr., Springfield, 1959-73; prof. religious studies S.W. Mo. State U., Springfield, 1961-83; prof. of religion, dean Seaver Coll. Arts, Letters and Scis. Pepperdine U., Malibu, Calif., 1983—. Author: Religion: A Preface, 1982, 2d edit., 1989; co-author: Discovering the Bible, 1986, Excavations at Capernaum, 1989; contbr. articles, revs. to profl. publs. Mem. Archaeol. Inst. Am., Am. Schs. of Oriental Rsch., Soc. Bib. Lit., Am. Numismatic Soc., Am. Coun. Acad. Deans. Mem. Ch. of Christ. Office: Pepperdine U Seaver Coll 24255 Pacific Coast Hwy Malibu CA 90263-0001

WILSON, JOHN JAMES, federal judge; b. Boston, Dec. 23, 1927; s. John J. and Margaret (Thomas) W.; m. Joan Ellen Bostwick, Sept. 1, 1951 (div. Sept. 1975); children: Jeffrey, John, Julie; m. Elizabeth Brower, Dec. 4, 1975; 1 child, Stephane. AB, Tufts U., 1951; LLB, Stanford U., 1954. Bar: Calif. 1954, Mass. 1954, Oreg. 1982, U.S. Dist. Ct. (no., cen., ea. and so. dists.) Calif., U.S. Dist. Ct. Oreg. Asst. U.S. atty. L.A., 1958-60; ptnr. Hill, Farrer & Burrill, L.A., 1960-85; bankruptcy judge U.S. Dist. Ct. Calif., San Bernardino, 1985-88, Santa Ana, Calif., 1989—. Lt. (j.g.) USN, 1945-50. Seventh Day Adventist. Office: US Bankruptcy Ct 506 Fed Bldg PO Box 12600 34 Civic Center Plz Santa Ana CA 92701-4025

WILSON, JOHN LEWIS, university official; b. Columbus, Ohio, Mar. 18, 1943; s. John Robert and Betty Marie (Barker) W.; m. Linda Patricia Kiernan, Apr. 23, 1966; 1 child, Heidi Annette. BA in Internat. Rels., Am. U., 1963, MA in Econs., 1973, PhD, 1977. Staff asst. Congressman Paul N. McCloskey, Washington, 1968-72; sr. assoc. Govt. Affairs Inst., Washington, 1973-77; pres. Experience Devel., Inc., Tucson, 1978-85; from asst. to assoc. dean faculty sci. U. Ariz., Tucson, 1985-93, acting asst. to sr. v.p. adminstrn. and fin., 1988-89, dir. decision and planning support, 1994—; instr. U. Phoenix, Tucson, 1980-83. Author: (with others) Managing Planned Agricultural Development, 1976. 1st lt. U.S. Army, Vietnam, 1964-68. Decorated Bronze Star with oak leaf cluster and V device. Mem. Am. Econ. Assn., Am. Soc. Quality Control, Assn. for Instnl. Rsch., Tucson Met. C. of C. Democrat. Home: 8030 E Garland Rd Tucson AZ 85715-2830 Office: U Ariz Adminstration 116 Tucson AZ 85721

WILSON, JOHNNY LEE, editor-in-chief; b. Santa Maria, Calif., Oct. 20, 1950; s. John Henry and Bobbie Lou (Henson) W.; m. Susan Lynne Leavelle, Aug. 28, 1970; children: Jennifer Lynne, Jonathan Lee. BA, Calif. Bapt. Coll., Riverside, 1972; MDiv, Golden Gate Bapt. Seminary, Mill Valley, Calif., 1975; ThM, So. Bapt. Theol. Seminary, Louisville, 1978, PhD, 1981. Pastor Rollingwood Bapt. Ch., San Pablo, Calif., 1974-75, Temple Bapt. Ch., Sacramento, Calif., 1975-77, Hermosa-Redondo Beach (Calif.) Ministries, 1981-82, Immanuel. Bapt. Ch., La Puente, Calif., 1982-86; asst. editor Computer Gaming World, Anaheim, Calif., 1986-89, editor, 1989-94; editor-in-chief Computer Gaming World, Anaheim, 1993—; pres. and prof. of Old Testament Calif. Korean Bapt. Seminary, Walnut, 1990-93; adj. prof. Old Testament studies So. Calif. Ctr., Garden Grove, Calif., 1981-86; com. mem. Software Pub. Assn. Ratings Group, Washington, 1994. Author: The Sim City Planning Commission Handbook, 1990, The Sim Earth Bible, 1991; co-author: The Mercer Dictionary of Bible, 1990, Sid Meier's Civilization: Rome on 640K A Day, 1992. Named to Outstanding Young Men of Am., Jaycees, Ala., 1977, Best Software Reviewer, Software Pubs. Assn., Washington, 1990. Mem. Am. Film Inst. Tech. Coun. Home: 41513 Avenida De La Reina Temecula CA 92592-5474 Office: Ziff-Davis Publishing 130 Chaparral Ct #260 Anaheim CA 92808

WILSON, JOSEPH MORRIS, III, lawyer; b. Milw., July 26, 1945; s. Joseph Morris Jr. and Phyllis Elizabeth (Cresson) W.; children: Elizabeth J., Eric M.; m. Dixie Lee Brock, Mar. 23, 1984. BA, Calif. State U., Chico, 1967; MA, U. Washington, 1968; JD summa cum laude, Ohio State U., 1976. Bar: Alaska 1976, U.S. Dist. Ct. Alaska 1976, U.S. Ct. Appeals (9th cir.) 1986. Recruiter and vol. U.S. Peace Corps, People's Republic of Benin, 1969-73; legal intern U.S. Ho. of Reps., Washington, People's Republic of Benin, 1975; ptnr. Guess & Rudd P.C., Anchorage, 1976-88, chmn. comml. dept., 1981-82, ptnr. compensation com., 1982-84; mgr. Alaska taxes, sr. tax atty. BP Exploration Inc., Alaska, 1990—; bus. law instr. U. Alaska, Anchorage, 1977-78. Counsel Tanaina Child Devel. Ctr., Anchorage, 1982-84, Alaska Child Passenger Safety Assn., Anchorage, 1983-86; bd. dirs. Alaska Alcohol Safety Action Program, Anchorage, 1977-79. Mem. ABA, Alaska Bar Assn. (taxation sect.), Anchorage Bar Assn. Democrat. Club: UAA Basketball Boosters, World Affairs Coun. Home: 1779 Morningtide Ct Anchorage AK 99501-5722 Office: MB6-4 PO Box 196193 Anchorage AK 99519-6193

WILSON, KAREN LEROHL, lawyer; b. Albuquerque, Sept. 15, 1950; d. John Kenneth Sr. and Ann Castleman (Lawrence) LeRohl; children: Teddy, Tommy. BA, William & Mary U., 1972; JD, Am. U., 1978; LLM, George Washington U., 1982. Bar: Va. 1979, Calif. 1984, U.S. Claims Ct. 1980, U.S. Ct. Appeals (4th cir.) 1981, U.S. Supreme Ct. 1982. Supr. law dept. Prudential Ins. Co., Washington, 1972-74; law clk. Arnold & Porter, Washington, 1975-78; atty., advisor Def. Logistics Agy., Alexandria, Va., 1978-80, Office Sec. Def., Washington, 1980-84; counsel TRW Corp., Redondo Beach, Calif., 1984-87; asst. group counsel Hughes Aircraft Co., El Segundo, Calif., 1987-92; group contr., dir. govt. rels. and compliance Allied Signal Aerospace, Torrance, Calif., 1992—. Contbr. articles to profl. jours. Recipient Presdl. Sports award Pres. Carter, Washington, 1980; Disting. Youth award U.S. Army, 1976. Mem. ABA (dep. chmn. 1980), Fed. Bar Assn., Va. Bar

Assn., Calif. Bar Assn., Nat. Contract Mgmt. Assn., Fin. Execs. Inst. (com. govt. bus.), Ethics Officers Assn., Inst. Mgmt. Accts., Inst. Internal Auditors, William and Mary Coll. Alumni Assn. (v.p. greater L.A. 1987-88), Am. Corp. Counsel Assocs., Cameron Sta. Tennis Club (pres. 1980), Michelob Light Tennis Club (capt. 1983). Republican. Office: Allied Signal Aerospace Dept 14-22 M/S T-52 2525 W 190th St Torrance CA 90504-6002

WILSON, KATHERINE SCHMITKONS, biologist; b. Lorain, Ohio, Jan. 22, 1913; d. H. William and Katherine (Bauman) Schmitkons; AB, Oberlin Coll., 1933; MS, Northwestern U., 1935; PhD, Yale U., 1944; m. George E. Woodin, Nov. 23, 1961. Instr. biology Muskingum Coll., New Concord, Ohio, 1935-40; bot. researcher Yale U., 1941-44, Sessel fellow in biology, 1948-49, instr. biology, 1953-56; biologist div. research grants NIH, Bethesda, Md., 1956-58, scientist adminstr. genetics, 1958-77; ret., 1977; cons., lectr. genetics, 1978—. Recipient High Quality Service award HEW, NIH, 1966. Fellow AAAS, N.Y. Acad. Sci.; mem. Am. Soc. Human Genetics (spl. citation 1973), Genetics Soc. Am. (Service citation 1979), Environ. Mutagen Soc., Am. Inst. Biol. Scis., Am. Genetic Assn., Sigma Xi. Congregationalist. Club: PEO. Author: Botany—Principles and Problems, 6th ed., 1963; contbr. articles to profl. jours. Home: 77 235 Indiana Ave Palm Desert CA 92211

WILSON, LINDA, librarian; b. Rochester, Minn., Nov. 17, 1945; d. Eunice Gloria Irene Wilson. BA, U. Minn., Morris, 1967; MA, U. Minn., 1968. Libr. rsch. svcs. U. Calif., Riverside, 1968-69, head dept. phys. scis. catalog, 1969-71; city libr. Belle Glade (Fla). Mcpl. Libr., 1972-74; instr. part-time Palm Beach Jr. Coll., Belle Glade, 1973; head adult-young adult ext. Kern County Libr. Sys., Bakersfield, Calif., 1974-80; dir. dist. libr. Lake Agassiz Regional Libr. System, Crookston, Minn., 1980-85; supervising libr. San Diego County Libr., 1985-87; county libr. Merced (Calif.) County Libr., 1987-93; learning network mgr. Merced Coll., 1994-95; libr. Monterey Park (Calif.) Bruggemeyer Meml. Libr., 1995—. Active Leadership Merced, 1987-88; mem. East Site Based Corodinating Coun., Merced, 1990-92, Merced Gen. Plan Citizens Adv. Com., 1992—, Sister City Com., Merced, 1992—. Recipient Libr. award Eagles Aux., 1984, Woman of Achievement award Commn. on the Status of Women, 1990, Libr. award Calif. Libr. Trustees and Commrs., 1990, Woman of Yr. award Merced Bus. and Profl. Women, 1987. Mem. ALA (sec. pub. libr. systems sect. 1988-89), Calif. Libr. Assn. (sec. govt. rels. com. 1991-92, continuing edn. com. 1993-94), Minn. Libr. Assn. (pres. pub. libr. div. 1985), Merced County Mgmt. Coun. (pres. 1989), Bus. and Profl. Women (pres. 1988-89). Democrat. Lutheran. Home: 1000 E Newmark Ave # 22 Monterey Park CA 91754

WILSON, MELVIN EDMOND, civil engineer; b. Bremerton, Wash., Aug. 3, 1935; s. Edmond Curt and Madeline Rose (Deal) W.; m. Deanna May Stevens, Nov. 22, 1957 (div. Mar. 1971); children: Kathleen, Debra Wilson Frank. BSCE, U. Wash., 1957, MSCE, 1958. Registered profl. engr., Wash. Asst. civil engr. City of Seattle, 1958-60, assoc. civil engr., 1960-64, sr. civil engr., 1964-66, supervising civil engr., 1966-75, sr. civil engr., 1975-77, mgr. X, 1977-88; owner Wilson Cons. Svcs., Seattle, 1988-89; transp. systems dir. City of Renton, Wash., 1989—; owner Mel Wilson Photographer, Seattle, 1975-84. Contbr. reports to profl. jours. Rep. Renton transp. work group King County (Wash.) Growth Mgmt. Policy Com.; rep. Renton tech. adv. com. South County Area Transp. Bd., King County, 1992—. Mem. ASCE, Am. Pub. Works Assn., Inst. Transp. Engrs., Tau Beta Pi, Sigma Xi. Office: City of Renton 200 Mill Ave S Renton WA 98055-2132

WILSON, MICHAEL GREGG, film producer, writer; b. N.Y.C., Jan. 21, 1942; s. Lewis Gilbert Wilson and Dorothy (Natol) Broccoli; m. Coila Jane Hurley; children: David, Gregg. BS, Harvey Mudd Coll., 1963; JD, Stanford U., 1966. Bar: D.C., Calif., N.Y. Legal advisor FAA-DOT, Washington, 1966-67; assoc. Surrey, Karasik, Gould, Green, Washington, 1967-71; ptnr. Surrey and Morse, Washington and N.Y.C., 1971-74; legal advisor Eon Prodns., London, 1974-78, producer, mng. dir., 1978—. Writer/prodr.: For Your Eyes Only, 1981, Octopussy, 1983, View to a Kill, 1985, The Living Daylights, 1987, Licence to Kill, 1989; prodr.: Goldeneye, 1995; author: Pictorialism in California, Getty Museum, 1994.

WILSON, MIRIAM GEISENDORFER, physician, educator; b. Yakima, Wash., Dec. 3, 1922; d. Emil and Frances Geisendorfer; m. Howard G. Wilson, June 21, 1947; children—Claire, Paula, Geoffrey, Nicola, Marla. B.S., U. Wash., Seattle, 1944, M.S., 1945; M.D., U. Calif., San Francisco, 1950. Mem. faculty U. So. Calif. Sch. Medicine, L.A., 1965—, prof. pediatrics, 1969—. Office: U So Calif Med Ctr 1129 N State St Los Angeles CA 90033-1069*

WILSON, MYRON ROBERT, JR., former psychiatrist; b. Helena, Mont., Sept. 21, 1932; s. Myron Robert Sr. and Constance Ernestine (Bultman) W. BA, Stanford U., 1954, MD, 1957. Diplomate Am. Bd. Psychiatry and Neurology. Dir. adolescent psychiatry Mayo Clinc, Rochester, Minn., 1965-71; pres. and psychiatrist in chief Wilson Ctr., Faribault, Minn., 1971-86; ret., 1986; chmn. Wilson Ctr., 1986-90; ret., 1990; assoc. clin. prof. psychiatry UCLA, 1985—. Contbr. articles to profl. jours. Chmn., chief exec. officer C.B. Wilson Found., L.A., 1986—; mem. bd. dirs. Pasadena Symphony Orchestra Assn., Calif., 1987. Served to lt. comdr., 1958-60. Fellow Mayo Grad. Sch. Medicine, Rochester, 1960-65. Fellow Am. Psychiat. Assn., Am. Soc. for Adolescent Psychiatry, Internat. Soc. for Adolescent Psychiatry (founder, treas. 1985-88, sec. 1985-88, treas. 1988-92); mem. Soc. Sigma Xi (Mayo Found. chpt.). Episcopalian. Office: Wilson Found 8033 W Sunset Blvd # 4019 West Hollywood CA 90069-1925

WILSON, NONA B. KAHOKUKAUAHIAHI, critical care nurse; b. Honolulu, Nov. 10, 1941; d. John B. and Helen H. (Enos) Kramer; m. Les Schneider (div.; 1 child, Guy Keoni; m. Herbert R. Wilson, Sept. 30, 1983. LPN, Clark County C.C., Las Vegas, 1978; AA, U. Nev., 1980, BSN, 1982; MSA, Cen. Mich. U., 1991. Stewardess Hawaiian Airlines and United Airlines; profl. entertainer various; staff nurse Humana Hosp., Las Vegas, 1978-82; staff nurse Kaiser Med. Care Program, Honolulu, 1982-85, charge nurse, emergency dept., 1985-86, supr., emergency dept., 1986-90, dir. emergency svcs., 1990—; mem. diabetic adv. coun., Honolulu, 1989—; cons. in field. Mem. State Health Planning Devel. Agy., Honolulu, 1989—, Prince Kuhio Hawaiian Civic Club Choral Group. Mem. Emergency Nurses Assn. (CEN), Disaster Coms. Hosp. Assn. of Hawaii, Ka'ahumanu Soc., others. Home: 51-262 Kamehameha Hwy Kaaawa HI 96730-9807 Office: Kaiser Med Care Program 3288 Moanalua Rd Honolulu HI 96819-1469

WILSON, PATRICIA POPLAR, electrical manufacturing company executive; b. Chgo., Sept. 20, 1931; d. George and Leona (O'Brien) Poplar; BS U. Wash., 1966, MA 1967, PhD 1980; m. Chester Goodwin Wilson, Jan. 30, 1960; children: Susan Spadafora, Chester Wilson. Instr., U. Wash., Seattle, 1967-74; women's editor Nor'westing Mag., Seattle, 1969—; pres. Wilson & Assos. N.W. Inc., Seattle, 1974—; v.p. N.W. Mfg. & Supply, Inc., 1977-87, pres., 1987—; pres. Trydor Sales Alberta Ltd., Can. Mem. Electric League, N.W. Mfg. & Supply. Episcopalian. Club: Seattle Yacht. Author: Household Equipment, Guide to Surplus Equipment. Contbr. articles to profl. jours. Office: 4045 7th Ave S Seattle WA 98108-5240

WILSON, PETE, governor of California; b. Lake Forest, Ill., Aug. 23, 1933; s. James Boone and Margaret (Callaghan) W.; m. Betty Robertson (div.); m. Gayle Edlund, May 29, 1983. B.A. in English Lit., Yale U., 1955; J.D., U. Calif., Berkeley, 1962; LL.D., Grove City Coll., 1983, U. Calif., San Diego, 1983, U. San Diego, 1984. Bar: Calif. 1962. Mem. Calif. Legislature, Sacramento, 1966-71; mayor City of San Diego, 1971-83; U.S. Senator from Calif., 1983-91; gov. State of Calif., 1991—. Trustee Conservation Found.; mem. exec. bd. San Diego County council Boy Scouts Am.; hon. trustee So. Calif. Council Soviet Jews; adv. mem. Urban Land Inst., 1985-86; founding dir. Retinitis Pigmentosa Internat.; hon. dir. Alzheimer's Family Ctr., Inc., 1985; hon. bd. dirs. Shakespeare-San Francisco, 1985. Recipient Golden Bulldog award, 1984, 85, 86, Guardian of Small Bus. award, 1984, Cuauhtemoc plaque for disting. svc. to farm workers in Calif., 1991, Julius award for outstanding pub. leadership U. So. Calif., 1992, award of appreciation Nat. Head Start, 1992; named Legislator of Yr., League Calif. Cities, 1985, Man of Yr. N.G. Assn. Calif., 1986, Man of Yr. citation U. Calif. Boalt Hall, 1986; ROTC scholar Yale U., 1951-55. Mem. Nat. Mil. Family Assn. (adv. bd.), Phi Delta Phi, Zeta Psi. Republican. Episcopalian. Office: State Capitol Office Of Governor Sacramento CA 95814*

WILSON, PETER TRIMBLE, fisheries development consultant. Cons. Global Ocean Cons., Inc., 1982—; cons. Societe Nouvelle Conserveries du Senegal, 1990, Kosrae State, 1991—, Dept. Agriculture, 1989, Mankoadze and Pioneer, 1988, Asian devel. Bank, 1988, Seychelles Tuna Cannery, 1988, Cannery Devel. Plan, Indonesia, 1992, Papua New Guinea Tuna Cannery Devel. Plan, 1993. Contbr. numerous articles to profl. jours. Office: Global Ocean Consultants Inc 1130 Mano Dr # A Kula HI 96790-9500

WILSON, RHEA, newspaper editor; b. Asbury Park, N.J., July 3, 1946; d. Abraham H. and Gertrude (Kassack) W.; m. Frederic L. Levy, Feb. 29, 1972; 1 child, Jemma Alix. B.A., Harvard U., 1967; postgrad., MIT, 1968-71. Faculty Goddard Coll., Plainfield, Vt., 1971-73; lectr. San Jose State U., Calif., 1975-76, Mills Coll., Oakland, Calif., 1976; lectr. U. Calif., Santa Cruz, 1977-78, Berkeley, 1978; assoc. editor McClatchy Newspapers, Sacramento, 1978—; juror for Pulitzer prizes, 1990-91. John S. Knight fellow Stanford U., 1986-87. Office: McClatchy Newspapers 1626 E St Fresno Fresno CA 93786

WILSON, RICHARD ALLAN, landscape architect; b. Chgo., Feb. 5, 1927; s. Edgar Allan and Lois Helena (Hearn) W.; m. Lisabet Julie Horchler, May 31, 1958; children: Gary Allan, Carl Bruce. BS, U. Calif., Berkeley, 1952. Engring. draftsman Freeland Evanson & Christenson, San Diego, 1952-53; designer, estimator Blue Pacific Nursery & Landscape Co., San Diego, 1955-59; prin. Richard A. Wilson, FASLA and Assocs., San Diego, 1959—; sec. Calif. Coun. Landscape Architects, 1982-85; expert witness for law firms, 1983—. Designer Phil Swing Meml. Fountain, 1967. Mem. landscape com. Clairemont Town Coun., San Diego, 1955. With U.S. Army, 1944-46, Korea. Recipient First Pl. award for landscape So. Calif. Expdn., Del Mar, 1963. Fellow Am. Soc. Landscape Architects (del. coun. 1982-85), Am. Inst. Landscape Architects (treas. 1970, 2d v.p. 1971). Republican. Home and Office: 2570 Tokalon Ct San Diego CA 92110-2232

WILSON, RICHARD RANDOLPH, lawyer; b. Pasadena, Calif., Apr. 14, 1950; s. Robert James and Phyllis Jean (Blackman) W.; m. Catherine Goodhugh Stevens, Oct. 11, 1980; children: Thomas Randolph, Charles Stevens. BA cum laude, Yale U., 1971; JD, U. Wash., 1976. Bar: Wash. 1976, U.S. Dist. Ct. (we. dist.) Wash. 1976, U.S. Ct. Appeals (9th cir.) 1977. Assoc. Hillis, Phillips, Cairncross, Clark & Martin, Seattle, 1976-81, ptnr., 1981-84; ptnr. Hillis, Cairncross, Clark & Martin, Seattle, 1984-87; ptnr. Hillis Clark Martin & Peterson, Seattle, 1987—, chmn. land use and environ. group; bd. dirs. Quality Child Care Svcs., Inc., Seattle, Plymouth Housing Group, Seattle; mem. legal com. Bldg. Industry Assn. Wash.; lectr. various bar assns., 1980—. Contbr. articles to profl. jours. Mem. Seattle Mayor's Kidsplace Adv. Task Force, Seattle, 1985; chmn. class agts. Yale U. Alumni Fund, New Haven, 1985-87, class agt., 1971—, mem. class foun., 1991—, mem. western Wash. exec. com. Yale capital campaign, vice chmn. leadership gifts com. Yale 25th reunion, 1995-96; mem., vice cihmn. Medina (Wash.) Planning Commn., 1990-02; chmn. capital campaign Plymouth Congl. Ch., Settle, 1995. Mem. ABA, Wash. State Bar Assn. (dir. environ. and land use law sect. 1985-88), Seattle-King County Bar Assn., Kingsley Trust Assn., Yale Assn. of Western Wash. Congregationalist. Home: 2305 86th Ave NE Bellevue WA 98004-2416 Office: Hillis Clark Martin & Peterson 1221 2nd Ave Ste 500 Seattle WA 98101-2942

WILSON, ROBERT LEE, geological consultant; b. Peoria, Ill., Dec. 16, 1918; s. Harry James and Alta May (Matthews) W.; m. Annabell June Tullis, May 25, 1941; children: Cheryl D., Sandra J., David L. Geol. Engr., Colo. Sch. Mines, 1941; PhD, U. Ariz., 1956. Registered geologist, Calif.; cert. engring. geologist, Calif. Asst. regional geologist Bur. Reclamation, Colo., Nev., Ariz., 1946-51; dist. geologist Corps of Engrs., Ga., Fla., S.C., 1951-53; pvt. practice geol. cons. Ariz., 1953-55, Calif., 1984—; raw materials geologist Kaiser Steel Corp., Calif., Utah, N.Mex., 1956-66; chief geologist Kaiser Steel Corp., Calif., Utah, N.Mex., also Can., 1967-70; exploration mgr. Kaiser Steel Corp., U.S. and 25 other countries, 1970-84. Contbg. author and editor articles to profl. jours. Maj. Corps of Engrs., U.S. Army, 1941-46. Fellow Navajo Indian Svc., 1953-55. Mem. AIME, Am. Inst. Profl. Geologists, Geol. Soc. Am., Soc. Econ. Geologists, Sigma Xi, Community Club (Walnut Creek chpt.). Home and Office: 2646 Saklan Indian Dr # 3 Walnut Creek CA 94595-3014

WILSON, ROBERT MCCLAIN, plastic surgeon, educator; b. Cornwall, N.Y., Dec. 6, 1942; s. James Van Gorder and Isabel Mae (Steele) W.; m. Dorothea Louise Figge; children: Michael McClain, Sara Malia. MD, U. Colo., Denver, 1968. Diplomate Am. Bd. Surgery, Am. Bd. Plastic Surgery. Commd. U.S. Army, 1967, advanced through ranks to Col., 1993; intern Tripler Army Med. Ctr., Honolulu, 1968-69, resident gen. surgery, 1970-74; resident orthopaedic surgery Martin Army Hosp., Ft. Benning, Ga., 1969-70; resident plastic surgery Walter Reed Army Med. Ctr., Washington, 1974-76, asst. chief plastic surgery svcs., 1976-78; chief plastic surgery svcs. Landstuhl Army Regional Med. Ctr., Germany, 1978-81, 90-93, Fitzsimons Army Med. Ctr., Aurora, Colo., 1993—; plastic surgeon Wenatchee (Wash.) Valley Clinic, 1981-90. Fellow ACS; mem. AMA, Am. Soc. Plastic Surgeons, Assn. Mil. Surgeons of U.S., Northwest Soc. Plastic Surgeons, Colo. Soc. Plastic Surgeons. Luth. Home: 790 Madison St Denver CO 80206 Office: Fitzsimons Army MC Attn MCHG-SGP Plastic Surg Serv Aurora CO 80045-5001

WILSON, ROBIN SCOTT, university president, writer; b. Columbus, Ohio, Sept. 19, 1928; s. John Harold and Helen Louise (Walker) W.; m. Patricia Ann Van Kirk, Jan. 20, 1951; children: Kelpie, Leslie, Kari, Andrew. B.A., Ohio State U., 1950; M.A., U. Ill., 1951, Ph.D., 1959. Fgn. intelligence officer CIA, Washington, 1959-67; prof. English Clarion State Coll., (Pa.), 1967-70; assoc. dir. Com. Instnl. Cooperation, Evanston, Ill., 1970-77; assoc. provost instrn. Ohio State U., Columbus, 1977-80; univ. pres. emeritus Calif. State U., Chico, 1980—. Author: Those Who Can, 1973; short stories, criticism, articles on edn. Lt. USN, 1953-57. Mem. AAAS, Phi Kappa Phi.

WILSON, RODERICK T., food products executive; b. 1944. BS, JD, U. Kans., 1970. Officer Arvida Corp., Boca Raton, Fla., 1971-84, Wilson Miller Capital Corp., Boca Raton, Fla., 1984-88; now pres., CEO Amfac/JMB Hawaii Inc., Honolulu, 1988—. Office: Amfac/JMB Hawaii Inc PO Box 3230 Honolulu HI 96801-3230*

WILSON, SHARON ROSE, educator, researcher; b. Denver, May 13, 1941; d. John William Wilson and Rose Schlagel; m. Roger Lloyd Brown, May 5, 1973; 1 child, Stephen Roger Wilson-Brown. BA, Colo. State Coll., 1963; MA, Purdue U., 1967; PhD in Eng., U. Wis., 1976. Cert. secondary edn., Colo. Teaching asst. Purdue U., West Lafayette, Ind., 1963-65, U. Wis., Madison, 1965-70; instr. U. Northern Colo., Greeley, 1970-73, asst. prof., 1974-78, assoc. prof., 1978-84, prof. eng., women's studies, 1985—; cons. Marly Rusoff, 1993; vis. humanist Boulder County Women's Resources Ctr., 1980; speaker and lectr. in field. Author: Margaret Atwood's Fairy-Tale Sexual Politics, 1993, The Self-Conscious Narrator and His Twentieth-Century Faces, 1976; contbr. articles to profl. jours. Founding mem. local Nat. Orgn. for Women, 1982; women's issues chairperson League of Women Voters, Longmont, 1978-85; founding co-pres. Margaret Atwood Soc., 1983-88. Recipient numerous rsch. grants. Mem. MLA (organizer of spl. sessions 1980, 85, 88), Colo. Seminars (adv. bd. 1980—, coord. of program), Colo. Women's Studies Assn. (conf. coord. 1977), Margaret Laurence Soc., Samuel Beckett Soc. (charter), Doris Lessing Soc., Internat. Assn. Fantastic in the Arts, Assn. for Canadian Studies in the U.S., Popular Culture Assn., Pacific Ctrl. Canadian Studies Network, Western Canadian Studies Assn., Rocky Mountain MLA. Office: U Northern Colo Eng Dept Greeley CO 80639

WILSON, SHERYL J., state agency administrator; b. Shelton, Wash., May 23, 1936; d. Kenneth F. and Bernice (Angell) Sturdevant; m. Daniel I. Stuckey, Sept. 8, 1956 (div. June 1967); children: Mark, Ann, David, Noni; m. Donald R. Wilson, Aug. 9, 1968. Student, Wash. State U., 1954-57; BA, Evergreen State Coll., 1985. Rsch. analyst Wash. Pub. Pension Commn., Olympia, 1967-75; budget analyst Wash. State Senate, Olympia, 1975-80; retirement and ins. officer U. Wash., Seattle, 1980-83; asst. dir. Wash. Dept. Retirement Sys., Olympia, 1983-89, dir., 1993—; exec. dir. Oreg. Pub. Employees Retirement Sys., Portland, 1989-93; mem. exec. com. Nat. Coun. Tchr. Retirement, Austin, 1992—; pres., mem. exec. com. Nat. Preretirement Edn. Assn., 1985-91; vice chair Wash. State Investment Bd., Olympia, 1993—; mem. steering com. cert. employee benefit specialist program U. Wash., 1983—. Chair Interagy. Com. Status of Women, Olympia, 1987-88. Mem. Nat. Assn. State Retirement Adminstrs. (legis. com. 1989—), Women in Pub. Adminstrn. (founder Oreg. chpt. 1990), Govt. Fin. Officers (retirement and benefits adminstrn. com. 1992—), Zonta Internat.

WILSON, SONJA MARY, secondary education educator, consultant, poet; b. Lake Charles, La., Mar. 28, 1938; d. Albert Ronald and Annelia (DeVille) Molless; m. Willie McKinley Williams, Apr. 28, 1956 (div. May 1969); children: William P., Dwayne L., Rachelle A., Devon A., Lisa M., Ricardo Soto; m. Howard Brooks Wilson, Nov. 12, 1982; stepchildren: Howard N. Wilson, Yvonne Wilson. AA in Social and Behavioral Scis., Mt. St. Jacinto Jr. Coll., 1992; Designated Subjects Credential, U. Calif., San Bernardino, 1983; student, Calif. State Poly. U., 1986, Laverne U., 1984-85; BS in Edn., So. Ill. U., 1995; student, Riverside (Calif.) City Coll., 1988-89, 94. Prin.'s sec. Elsinore (Calif.) H.S., Elsinore Jr. H.S., 1974-83, tchr. bus. and adult vocat. edn., 1979-84, notary pub., 1981-85, coord. vocat. edn., 1983-84, class adviser, 1983-88; long-term substitute tchr. Perris H.S. Dist., 1991-94. Clk., v.p., pres. Lake Elsinore Unified Sch. Dist. Bd., 1988—; pres., clk., mem. Lake Elsinore Elem. Sch. Bd., 1979-88, v.p., 1988-89; pres., sec., treas., v.p. Riverside County Sch. Bds. Assn., 1979—; assoc. sponsor, advisor Black Student Union/Future Leaders of Am., 1984-90; svc. unit rep., leader Girl Scouts U.S.; den mother Boy Scouts Am.; mem. Ctrl. Dem. Com., 1989-91; del. PTSA, 1991-93. Tribute in her honor Black Student Union/Future Leaders Am., 1989; recipient Excellence in Edn. award Hilltop Community Ctr. Club, 1989, Leadership award Black Art and Social Club, 1989, Svc. award Sojourner Truth Media Network, 1989, Proclamation award City of Elsinore, 1989, County of Riverside, 1984; named Outstanding Poet, Nat. Libr. of Congress, 1994, 95. Mem. NAACP (Lake Elsinore affiliate, plaque), Calif. Sch. Bds. Assn. (regional dir. 1988-92, conf. planning com. 1989, legis. com. 1981—, nominations com. 1988, media com., dir. at large black 1993-95, audit com. 1993, dir./del. trainer 1993, alt. del., sgt. at arms 1994, 95, Fed. Rels. Network del. 1992, 95), Calif. Elected Women Ofcls. Assn., Calif. Sch. Employees Assn. (pres., treas., regional rep. asst., state negotiation com., del. to conf.), Internat. Soc. Poets, Lake Elsinore C. of C., Calif. Coalition Black Sch. Bd. Mems. (v.p. 1989, pres. 1990, program liaison 1989), Nat. Sch. Bds. Assn. (alt. del. 1994, 95), Nat. Coalition Black Sch. Bd. Mems. (dir. 1989-94, v.p. 1995—), Nat. Coun. Negro Women (charter, Willa Mae Taylor sect.), Black Art and Social Club, Hilltop Cmty. Club (plaque), Sojourner Truth Media Network (plaque), Eta Phi Beta (treas., sec. Gamma Alpha chpt., plaque, pres. 1992—). Home: 21330 Waite St Lake Elsinore CA 92530-9503

WILSON, STAN LE ROY, mass communications educator; b. Orange, Calif., May 24, 1935. AA, Modesto Jr. Coll., 1955; BA, Calif. State U., Fresno, 1958; MA, Calif. State U., Stanislaus, 1966; EdD, U. So. Calif., 1973. Newspaper reporter, editor Turlock Daily Jour., 1957-60; news reporter KYNO-Fresno, 1960-61; asst. to exec. dean Calif. State U., Stanislaus, 1961-66, part-time prof. journalism and radio-TV, 1961-65; lectr. in mass comm. Calif. State U., Fullerton, 1975-76; prof. mass comm. Coll. of the Desert, Palm Desert, Calif., 1975-94, chmn. dept. comm., 1967-94; mem. acad. adv. bd. telecomm. course WGBH-TV, Boston, 1989-90; pub. rels. cons. Medic-Alert Found., 1963-64; speaker in field. Author: Mass Media/Mass Culture: An Introduction, 3rd edit., 1995; contbr. articles to profl. publs. Mem. Palm Desert City Coun., 1977-95; mayor City of Palm Desert, 1980-82, 88-89, 93-94; mem. Palm. Desert Planning Commn., 1974-77, chmn., 1975-77; mem. Riverside County Transp. Commn., 1980-95, chmn., 1982-83, 86-87; Riverside Cities rep. bd. dirs., South Coast Air Quality Mgmt. Dist., 1988-95; chmn. adminstrv. com., 1988-91, chmn. trip reduction program adv. com., 1993-95; vice chmn. Riverside County Mayors' and Councilmens' Conf., 1986-87; adv. bd. Chapman Coll. Residence Ctr., 1982-88; bd. dirs. Coachella Valley Counseling, 1982-93, pres. 1989-90; bd. dirs. Valley Partnership, 1992-95. Named Outstanding Journalism Educator, Calif. Newspaper Pubs. Assn., 1978, Outstanding Cmty. Leader, Coll. of the Desert Alumni Assn., 1987, Outstanding Community Svc. award Palm Desert C. of C., 1995. Mem. Coachella Valley Assn. Govts. (exec. bd. 1979-84, 88-89, 93-94, chmn. energy and environ. com. 1983-84), Am. Legion, Coachella Valley Mex. Am. C. of C., Assn. for Edn. in Journalism and Mass Comm. (nat. adv. bd. 1987-88), Soc. Profl. Journalists (charter sec. Desert chpt. 1976-77), Nat. C.C. Journalism Assn. (pres. 1987-88), Calif./Ariz. Journalism Assn. C.C. (pres. 1979-80). Office: County of Riverside 46209 Oasis St Ste 414 Indio CA 92201-5964

WILSON, STEPHEN EDWIN, geologist, consultant; b. Middletown, Ohio, Apr. 13, 1951; s. Edwin Gustin and Mildred Francis (Forbes) W.; m. Catherine Anne Young, June 12, 1971; children: Matthew S., John M. BS in Geology, Ea. Ky. U., Richmond; MS in Mgmt., U. W.Va., 1987. Lic. geologist, N.C., Ky. Sr. geologist ARMCO, Inc., Middletown, 1979-84; mgr. geology Peabody Devel. Co., St. Louis, 1984-91; mgr. mktg. Christensen Boyles Corp., Salt Lake City, 1991-94; v.p. Geol. Data Svc., Sandy, Utah, 1994—. Author: (tech. manual) Drilling, Sampling and Analysis of Coal, 1992. Served to sgt. USAF, 1971-73, Eng. Mem. Soc. Mining, Metallurgy and Exploration (treas. Salt Lake City 1994-95).

WILSON, STEPHEN JAY, psychiatrist, consultant; b. Syracuse, N.Y., Aug. 23, 1940; s. Louis L. and Esther A. (Alderman) W.; children from previous marriage: Leigh, Eric; m. Anne Nadel, Aug. 26, 1986. BA, Cornell U., 1961; MD, SUNY, Syracuse, 1965. Diplomate Am. Bd. Psychiat. and Neurology. Intern Med. Coll. of Va. Hosps., Richmond, 1965-66; resident in psychiat. Neuropsychiat. Inst. U. Mich., Ann Arbor, 1969-72; UCLA legal psychiat. fellow, 1972-73; pvt. practice psychiat. Tarzana, Calif., 1973—; cons. Vista Del Mar Child Care Svc., L.A., 1974-75, Tarzana Psychiat. Hosp., 1974-75, L.A. Unified Sch. Dist., 1983-85, L.A. Superior Ct. Adult Criminal Psychiat. Evaluations, 1985—, Children of Our Future Group Home, 1990—, Passageway Group Home, 1990—, Pioneer Boys Ranch, Newhall, Calif., 1982—, Walden Environ., Mission Hills, Calif., 1988—, Stirling Acad., Reseda, Calif., 1989—, Pain Care Ctr. Van Nuys, Calif. Valley Presbyn. Hosp., 1988—, Dr.'s Co. Malpractice Revs., 1992—; cons., psychiat. evaluator L.A. Juvenile Ct., 1983—, L.A. Superior Ct. Family Law Sect., 1974—, Ventura Family Law Sect., 1988—; cons. pvt. industry issues mgmt. and devel., 1982—; instr. dept. cmty. medicine SUNY Upstate Med. Ctr., Syracuse, 1968-69; clin. asst. prof. dept. psychiat. Neuropsychiat. Inst. UCLA, 1973-86, Calif. Sch. Profl. Psychology, L.A., 1975-78; med. dir. Western Ctr. for Emotionally Handicapped, Tarzana, 1972-73, staff psychiatrist Calif. Dept. Corrections Parole Outpatient Clinic, L.A., 1972-73; pres. med. staff Van Nuys Hosp., 1976-78, v.p. med. staff, 1990-91, mem. exec. com., 1976-80, mem. utilization rev. com., 1985-92, chmn. com. impaired physicians, 1978-80, med. dir. adolescent program, 1985-89, dir. cmty. rels., 1989-91; mem. med. exec. com. Woodview Calabasas Hosp., Calif., 1976-78, 80-82; agreed med. examiner, ind. med. examiner Calif. Workers' Compensation Appeals Bd., 1979—; expert witness L.A. and Ventura County Superior Cts., 1982—; expert, lectr. in field; dir. behavioral scis. ALTA Health Strategies, 1990-91, psychiat. reviewer, 1990—; mem. quality assurance com. Los Robles Regional Med. Ctr., Thousand Oaks, Calif., 1989-94, mem. emergency room com., 1987-88; hosp. affiliations include Pine Grove Hosp., West Hills, Calif., 1989-92, Los Robles Regional Med. Ctr., 1987—, Simi Valley (Calif.) Adventist Hosp., 1988-89, Westlake Cmty. Hosp., Westlake Village, Calif., 1985-91, Valley Hosp. Med. Ctr., Van Nuys, 1983-86, Tarzana Med. Ctr., 1981—, Northridge (Calif.) Hosp., 1979-90, Valley Presbyn. Hosp., 1973-74, 88—, Woodview-Calabasas Hosp., 1973-84, Van Nuys Psychiat. Hosp., 1973-90. Contbr. articles to profl. jours. Physician Free People's Clin., Ann Arbor, 1969-72, Goose Lake Rock Festival, Ann Arbor, 1969; bd. dirs. San Fernando Valley Cmty. Mental Health Ctr., Northridge, 1974-76, mem. profl. adv. coun. 1976-77; mem. drug, alcohol and tobacco adv. com. Las Virgenes Sch. Dist., 1990-92. Peace Corps. physician USPHS, 1966-68. Recipient Achievement award for meritorious svc. Guyana Lions Club, 1968. Mem. Am. Psychiat. Assn., So. Calif. Psychiat. Soc. (drug abuse and alcoholism com. 1973-75, peer rev. com. 1982-91), So. Calif. Soc. Adolescent Psychiat., Am. Acad. Psychiat. and the Law (So. Calif. chpt.). Office: 18370 Burbank Blvd Ste 503 Tarzana CA 91356-2804

WILSON, STEPHEN VICTOR, federal judge; b. N.Y.C., Mar. 26, 1942; s. Harry and Rae (Ross) W. B.A. in Econs., Lehigh U., 1963; J.D., Bklyn. Law Sch., 1967; LL.M., George Washington U., 1973. Bars: N.Y. 1967, D.C. 1971, Calif. 1972, U.S. Ct. Appeals (9th cir.) U.S. Dist. Ct. (so., cen. and no. dists.) Calif. Trial atty. Tax div. U.S. Dept. Justice, 1968-71; asst. U.S. atty., L.A., 1971-77, chief spl. prosecutions, 1973-77; ptnr. Hochman, Salkin &

Deroy, Beverly Hills, Calif., from 1977; judge U.S. Dist. Ct. (cen. dist.) Calif., L.A., 1985—; adj. prof. law Loyola U. Law Sch., 1976-79; U.S. Dept. State rep. to govt. W.Ger. on 20th anniversary of Marshall Plan, 1967; del. jud. conf. U.S. Ct. Appeals (9th cir.), 1982-86. Recipient Spl. Commendation award U.S. Dept. Justice, 1977. Mem. ABA, L.A. County Bar Assn., Beverly Hills Bar Assn. (chmn. criminal law com.), Fed. Bar Assn. Jewish. Contbr. articles to profl. jours. Home: 9100 Wilshire Blvd Beverly Hills CA 90212-3415 Office: US Dist Ct 312 N Spring St Los Angeles CA 90012-4701*

WILSON, THEODORE HENRY, retired electronics company executive, aerospace engineer; b. Eufaula, Okla., Apr. 23, 1940; s. Theodore V. and Maggie E. (Buie) W.; m. Barbara Ann Tassara, May 16, 1958 (div. 1982); children: Debbie Marie, Nita Leigh, Wilson Axten, Pamela Ann, Brenda Louise, Theodore Henry II, Thomas John; m. Colleen Fagan, Jan. 1, 1983 (div. 1987); m. Karen L. Lerohl, Sept. 26, 1987. BSME, U. Calif., Berkeley, 1962; MSME, U. So. Calif., 1964, MBA, 1970, MSBA, 1971. Sr. rsch. engr. N.Am. Aviation Co. div. Rockwell Internat., Downey, Calif., 1962-65; propulsion analyst, supr. div. applied tech. TRW, Redondo Beach, Calif., 1965-67, mem. devel. staff systems group, 1967-71; sr. fin. analyst worldwide automotive dept. TRW, Cleve., 1971-72; contr. systems and energy group TRW, Redondo Beach, 1972-79; dir. fin. control equipment group TRW, Cleve., 1979-82, v.p. fin. control indsl. and energy group, 1982-85; mem. space and def. group TRW, Redondo Beach, 1985-93, ret., 1993; lectr., mem. com. acctg. curriculum UCLA Extension, 1974-79. Mem. Fin. Execs. Inst. (com. govt. bus.), Machinery and Allied Products Inst. (govt. contracts coun.), Nat. Contract Mgmt. Assn. (bd. advisors), Aerospace Industries Assn. (procurement and fin. coun.), UCLA Chancellors Assocs., Tau Beta Pi, Beta Gamma Sigma, Pi Tau Sigma. Republican. Home: 3617 Via La Selva Palos Verdes Peninsula CA 90274-1115

WILSON, VINCENT LEE, geneticist, toxicologist, educator; b. Kentfield, Calif., Dec. 4, 1950; s. Thomas H. Wilson and Elizabeth I. Vincent; married; 2 children. BS in Chemistry, Sonoma State Coll., 1973; MS in Phys. Chemistry, U. Calif., Davis, 1976; PhD in Pharmacology and Toxicology, Oreg. State U., 1980. Cert. clin. lab. dir. in genetic testing svcs., N.Y. Postdoctoral fellow U. So. Calif. Comprehensive Cancer Ctr. and Childrens Hosp., L.A., 1980-82; sr. staff fellow Nat. Cancer Inst./NIH, Bethesda, Md., 1982-88; dir. molecular genetics/oncology The Children's Hosp., Denver, 1988-94; affiliate faculty Colo. State U., Ft. Collins, 1994—; assoc. prof. U. Colo. Sch. Medicine, Denver, 1989—; vis. assoc. prof. La. State U., Baton Rouge, 1994—; cons. BioServe Biotechs. Ltd., Laurel, Md., 1994—; chmn. molecular genetics com. Mountain States Regional Genetic Svcs. Network, Denver, 1991-93; mem. ad hoc subcom. on genetics and ins. Gov.'s Commn. on Life and the Law, Denver, 1993. Contbr. numerous articles to profl. jours. Recipient numerous grants in field. Mem. AAAS, Am. Chem. Soc., Am. Assn. for Cancer Rsch., Am. Soc. for Cell Biology, Am. Soc. for Human Genetics, Environment Mutagenesis Soc., Sigma Xi, Phi Kappa Phi, Rho Chi. Home: 3435 W 101st Pl Westminster CO 80030-6753

WILSON, VIRGIL JAMES, III, lawyer; b. San Jose, Calif., July 25, 1953; s. Virgil James Wilson Jr. and Phyllis Emily (Mothorn) Brasser; m. Sara Fahey; children: Gabriel, Alexander, Hayley Noelani. BA with honors, U. Calif., Santa Cruz, 1975; JD cum laude, U. Santa Clara, 1981. Bar: Calif. 1981, U.S. Dist. Ct. (no. dist.) Calif. 1981, Hawaii 1982, U.S. Dist. Ct. Hawaii 1982, U.S. Supreme Ct. 1987, U.S. Ct. Appeals (9th cir.) 1987, Oreg. 1990; lic. pvt. investigator, Hawaii. Atty. James Krueger P.C., Wailuku, Maui, 1981-83; resident counsel Sterns & Ingram, Honolulu, 1983-89; pvt. practice Kailua, Hawaii, 1989-94; atty. Law Offices of Ian L. Mattoch, 1994—; owner Wilson Investigations, Santa Cruz, 1978-81, Honolulu, 1981—; panel of arbitrators Am. Arbitration Assn. Mem. ATLA, ABA, Hawaii Bar Assn., Calif. State Bar Assn. Office: 737 Bishop St Ste 1835 Honolulu HI 96813-3209

WILSON, WARREN BINGHAM, artist, art educator; b. Farmington, Utah, Nov. 4, 1920; s. Alma L. and Pearl E. (Bingham) W.; B.S. in Edn., Utah State U., 1943; M.F.A., U Iowa, 1949; m. Donna Myrle VanWagenen, Dec. 22, 1948; children—Vaughn Warren, Michael Alma, Annette, Pauline, Douglas George, Craig Aaron, Robert Kevin. Asst. prof. art Utah State U., Logan, 1949-54; vis. instr. Salt Lake Art Center, Utah, 1952-53; prof. art and edn. Brigham Young U., Provo, Utah, 1954-83; ret., 1983 vis. lectr. ceramics U. Calif., Davis, 1968; fellow in residence Huntington Hartford Found., Pacific Palisades, Calif., 1960-61; vis. instr. Pioneer Crafthouse, Salt Lake City, 1969-70; one-man shows of paintings and/or sculpture include: Salt Lake Art Center, 1951, Yakima Valley Coll., 1962, UCLA, 1962, Mont. State U., Bozeman, 1963, Stanford U., 1963, Wash. State U., Pullman, 1964, Central Wash. State Coll., Ellensburg, 1964, Nev. So. U., Las Vegas, 1967, Ricks Coll., Rexburg, Idaho, 1976, 80, Brigham Young U., Provo, Utah, 1970, 75, 79, 82, retrospective retirement exhbn. of sculpture, ceramics and paintings, 1983; group shows include: Denver Art Mus., 1951, Colorado Springs (Colo.) Fine Arts Center, 1951, Santa Fe Art Mus., 1953, Madison Sq. Gardens, N.Y.C., 1958, Wichita Art Center, 1960, Ceramic Conjunction Invitational, Glendale, Calif., 1973; represented in permanent collections: Utah State Inst. Fine Arts Salt Lake City, Utah State U., Logan, Utah State Fair Assn., Utah Dixie Coll., St. George, Coll. So. Utah, Cedar City, Brigham Young U., also numerous pvt. collections. Asst. dist. commr. Boy Scouts Am., 1975-80; counselor in Ward Bishopric, Ch. of Jesus Christ of Latter-day Saints, 1981-83; scoutmaster, 1954-75; served L.D.S. Mission, Nauvoo, Ill., 1984-85. Served with USAAF, 1943-46. Recipient Am. Craftsman Council merit award, 1964; Silver Beaver award Boy Scouts Am. Republican. Home: 1000 Briar Ave Provo UT 84604-2868

WILSON, WILLIAM J., construction executive. Northwestern U., Evanston, Ill., 1972, Northwestern U., Evanston, Ill., 1974. Pres. Dillingham Constrn. Co., Honolulu, Hawaii, 1974—. Office: Dillingham Constr Corp 614 Kapahulu Ave Honolulu HI 96815-3846*

WILSON-HART, JESSICA HELEN, mental health counselor, writer; b. London, July 3, 1965; came to U.S., 1988; d. Alan Brian and Audrey Irma (Sherrard) Wilson; m. Patrick Alan Hart, Nov. 19, 1988. BS in Psychology with honours, U. Warwick, Coventry, Eng., 1987; MA in Counseling Psychology, Lewis and Clark Coll., 1994. Registered counselor, Wash. Residential counselor Columbia River Mental Health, Vancouver, Wash., 1989-90, 93—, children's case mgr., 1990-92; mental health counselor Nelson Counseling & Cons., Vancouver, 1994—; mental health therapist YWCA, Vancouver, 1994—. Democrat. Office: Nelson Counseling & Cons 1211 Manzanita Way Vancouver WA 98661-6356

WIMBERLY, GEORGE JAMES, architect; b. Ellensburg, Wash., Jan. 16, 1915; s. George Welch and Eurma (Bezdechek) W.; m. Janet Harrietta Brebner, July 7, 1939 (div. Sept. 1969); 1 child, Heather Mary; m. Walton Jeffords, Dec. 12, 1969. B.Arch., U. Wash., 1937; student in, Mex., 1938. Draftsman, designer Seattle, Los Angeles, Phoenix, 1938-40; architect U.S. Civil Service, Pearl Harbor, 1940-45; practice architecture Honolulu, 1945—; partner Wimberly & Cook, 1945-59; pres., dir. Wimberly, Whisenand, Allison, Tong & Goo, Architects, Ltd., 1959-87; con.s Wimberly, Allison, Tong & Goo, Inc., 1987—; cons. for tourist facilities, Western Samoa, 1967-69, Ceylon, 1968, New Zealand, 1968, Australia, 1969, Singapore, 1970, 85, Taiwan, 1971, Malaysia, 1971, Fiji, 1972, India, 1972, Nepal, 1975; mem. Hawaii Bd. Registration Profl. Architects and Engrs., 1959-67; pres. Waikiki Assn., 1951-53. Prin. works include Keelikolani State Bldg., Honolulu, 1950, Canlis Restaurant, Seattle, 1951, Coco Palms Hotel, Kauai, Hawaii, 1952, First Nat. Bank, Waikiki, 1953, Canlis Restaurant, Honolulu, 1954, Honolulu Gas Co. Bldg., 1955, Hawaiian Trust Co. Bldg., Honolulu, 1956, Windward City Shopping Ctr., Kaneohe, Hawaii, 1957, First Nat. Bank, Kapiolani br., Honolulu, 1958, Fin. Factors home office bldg., Honolulu, 1958, Home Ins. Bldg., Honolulu, 1959, Prince Kaiulani Hotel Waikiki, 1960, Hotel Tahiti, 1960, 3019 Kalakaua Ave. Apt., 1961, Sheraton Maui Hotel, 1962, Civic Auditorium, American Samoa, 1963, Pago Pago Intercontinental Hotel, American Samoa, 1965, Bank of Hawaii Bldg., Waikiki, 1967, Visitor Ctr., Mt. Rainier Nat. Park, 1967, Kona-Hilton Hotel, 1968, Taharaa's Intercontinental Hotel, Tahiti, 1968, Fijian Hotel, Nadi, Fiji, 1968, Sheraton Kauai Hotel, Kauai, 1968, Mauna Kea Beach Hotel South Wing, Kamuela, Hawaii, 1968, New Surfrider Hotel, Waikiki, 1969, Royal Hawaiian Diamond Head Wing, Waikiki, 1969, Tokyu Djakarta Hotel, Indonesia, 1971, Sheraton Waikiki Hotel, Honolulu, 1971, Hawaiian Telephone Office Bldg., Honolulu, 1972, Ibusuki Kanko Hotel, Tokyo, 1972, Maui Land and Pineapple Co. Bldg., 1972, Mauna Kea Beach Hotel Addition, Kamuela, 1972, First Hawaiian Bank, Waianae, Oahu, 1972, Hayashida Onsen Hotel, Japan, 1973, Iwasaki Hotel, Japan, 1973, Wailea Golf Clubhouse, Maui, 1973, Hanalei Beach and Racquet Club, 1975, Hyatt Regency at Hemmeter Ctr., Waikiki, 1976, Aloha Towers Condominium, Waikiki, 1977, Sheraton Molokai Hotel, 1977, Tangjong Jara Beach Hotel, Malaysia, 1978, Shangri-La Hotel Addition, Singapore, 1978, Hyatt Maui Hotel, 1980, Hilton Tapa Tower, 1982, Bangkok Peninsula Hotel, 1983, Arcadia Condominiums, Singapore, 1984, Ritz-Carlton Hotel, Laguna Nigel, Calif., 1985, Four Seasons Hotel, Newport Beach, Calif., 1986. Bd. dirs. Honolulu Community Theatre, 1961-64, 80-84, Honolulu Theatre for Youth, 1960-63; mem. Hawaii Visitors Bur., 1952—, bd. dirs., 1973-77; mem. U.S. Dept. Commerce Hawaii/Pacific Dist. Export Council, 1979-83. Recipient Institutions Mag. Design awards; Holiday Mag. Design award; White Cement award of excellence Portland Cement Assn., 1972; Aga Kahn award for architecture Tanjong Jara Beach Hotel and Rantau Abang Visitor Ctr., 1983; Platinum Circle award Restaurant and Hotel Design mag., 1989. Fellow AIA (pres. Hawaii 1953, hon. awards Hawaii chpt. 1955, 60 (3), 1962, 64, 66, 68 (2), 1972, 73-75, 79, 82, 84); mem. Pacific Area Travel Assn. (life mem., contbg. mem., alt. dir. 1972-77, chmn. Devel. Authority 1979-81, award of merit 1979), Honolulu C. of C., Waikiki Improvement Assn., Tau Sigma Delta (pres. 1936). Clubs: Sports Car Club Am., Les Chevaliers du Deuxième Hemisiècle, Le Grand Chevalier Intérimaire (sr. steward); Pacific (Waikiki), Outrigger Canoe (Waikiki). Office: Wimberly Allison Tong & Goo 1000 Quail St Ste 190 Newport Beach CA 92660-2721 also: 2260 University Dr Newport Beach CA 92660-3319

WIMER, BRUCE MEADE, hematologist/oncologist, researcher; b. Tuckerton, N.J., Aug. 31, 1922; s. John Wade and Margaret Ellen (Brugh) W.; m. Polly Reynolds Wheaton, Nov. 18, 1950; children: Susan Hewett Chapman, Bruce Woodruff, Katherine Wade Wimer-Tawney. BS, Franklin and Marshall Coll., 1943; MD, Jefferson Med. Coll., 1946. Diplomate Am. Bd. Internal Medicine and Hematology. Intern Jefferson Med. Coll. Hosp., Phila., 1946-47, resident in internal medicine and hematology, 1948-51; gen. resident Williamsport (Pa.) Hosp., 1947-48; internist, hematologist Guthrie Clinic, Sayre, Pa., 1953-59, Overlook Hosp., Summit, N.J., 1959-60; asst. med. dir. Squibb Inst. Med. Rsch., New Brunswick, N.J., 1960-62; chief sect. hematology-oncology Lovelace Med. Ctr., Albuquerque, 1962-81; assoc. prof. hematology Tex. Tech. U., Lubbock, 1982-89; biotherapy rschr. JBMW Immunotherapeutics, Albuquerque, 1990—. Mem. editl. bd.: Molecular Biotherapy, 1991-92, Cancer Biotherapy, 1993—; contbr. articles to profl. publs. Capt. U.S. Army, 1951-53. Fellow ACP; mem. AMA., Am. Soc. Hematology, Internat. Soc. Hematology. Republican. Episcopalian. Home and Office: 1609 Catron Ave SE Albuquerque NM 87123-4255

WIMMER, GEORGE ALBERT, chiropractor, consultant; b. Ogden, Utah, Sept. 3, 1918; s. Charles Warren and Neta Hortense (Benson) W.; m. Fern Bernice Holley, Oct. 19, 1942; children: Holly Kay, Michael Warren, Connie Louise, Douglas Max, Debra. BS, Weber State Coll., 1980; D Chiropractic, Tex. Chiropractic Coll., 1948, Philosopher of Chiropractic cum laude, 1948. Cook Bob's Bar-b-que, Ogden, 1935-36; night watchman Hill AFB, Ogden, 1941; assoc. Turley Chiropractic Clinic, San Antonio, 1948-50, Wheeler Chiropractic Ctr., Ogden, 1952-59; chiropractor Ogden, 1959-86; sr. cons., assoc. mem. Wimmer Chiropractic Ctr., Ogden, 1986—. Contbr. articles to profl. jours. Pres. Five Pts. Lions Club, Ogden, 1956; v.p. Lake Bonneville Coun., Boy Scouts Am., Ogden, 1957; pres. Ogden (Utah) City Sch. Bd. With USAF, 1941-45. Named Father of Yr., Ogden (Utah) City Coun., 1964. Mem. Lewis Peak Lions Club (bd. dirs., pres. 1990, Pres.'s award 1990). Republican. LDS Ch. Home: 1246 S 775 E Ogden UT 84404-5826

WIN, KHIN SWE, anesthesiologist; b. Rangoon, Burma, Sept. 27, 1934; came to U.S., 1962; d. U Mg and Daw Aye (Kyin) Maung; m. M. Shein Win, May 28, 1959; children: Tha Shein, Thwe Shein, Maw Shein, Thet Shein, Htoo Shein. Intermediate of Sci. Degree, U. Rangoon, 1954, MB, BS, 1962. Intern Waltham (Mass.) Hosp., 1962-63; resident anesthesiology Boston City Hosp., 1963-65; fellow pediatric anesthesiology New Eng. Med. Ctr. Hosps., Boston, 1965-66; fellow anesthesiology Martin Luther King Jr. Gen. Hosp., L.A., 1978-79; pvt. practice anesthesiology Apple Valley, Calif., 1984—; asst. prof. anesthesiology Martin Luther King Jr./Charles R. Drew Med. Ctr., L.A., 1979-84. Republican. Buddhist. Home: 13850 Pamlico Rd Apple Valley CA 92307-5400 Office: St Mary Desert Valley Hosp Dept Anesthesiology 18300 Us Highway 18 Apple Valley CA 92307-2206

WINARSKI, DANIEL JAMES, mechanical engineer; b. Toledo, Dec. 16, 1948; s. Daniel Edward and Marguerite (Pietersien) W.; BS in Engring., U. Mich., 1970, PhD (NSF fellow), 1976; MS, U. Colo., 1973; m. Donna Ilene Robinson, Oct. 10, 1970; 1 son, Tyson York. Mech. engr. Libbey Owens Ford Co., Toledo, summers 1968, 69, 72; petroleum engr. Exxon Production Research, Houston, 1976-77; staff engr. mech. engring. sect. IBM storage systems divsn., Tucson, 1977-84, adv. engr., 1984-86, systems engr., performance evaluator, 1986-94, sr. engr., 1994—; assoc. prof. dept. civil/mech. engring. U.S. Mil. Acad., 1980—; instr. minority computer edn. No. Ariz. U., 1983-85. Served to 1st lt. U.S. Army, 1970-72; lt. col., Res., 1991. Recipient 13 IBM Invention Achievement award, 1981-94, IBM Mfg. award, 1986; registered profl. engr., Ariz., Colo. Mem. ASME (pub. chmn. U. Mich. 1974), Phi Eta Sigma, Pi Tau Sigma, Tau Beta Pi. Republican. Methodist. Designer adjustable artificial leg; patentee tape reel hub, tape loose-wrap check, tape reel sizing, tape reel-cartridge, calibrating optical disk drives, automated storage library. Office: IBM Storage Systems Divsn P83/031-2 Tucson AZ 85744

WINCHELL, RICHARD G., urban planning educator, consultant; b. Waverly, Iowa, Aug. 16, 1949; s. Clark D. and Minnie F. (Eckhoff) W.; m. Susan M. Mitchell, Mar. 21, 1990; children: Matthew James, Anne Elizabeth. BA in Sociology and Philosophy, Wartburg Coll., 1971; M of Urban and Regional Planning, U. Colo., Denver, 1972; PhD, Ariz. State U., Tempe, 1982. Cert. planner. Asst. planner City of Huntington Beach, Calif., 1972-73; assoc. planner City of Scottsdale (Ariz.) Long Range Planning, 1973-74; planner Schoneberger, Straub, Florence Assoc. Architects, Phoenix, 1974-75; planning dir. Ft. McDowell (Ariz.) Yavapai Indian Community, 1975-80; dir. Native Am. pub. adminstrn. prog. Ctr. for Pub. Affairs, Ariz. State U., Tempe, 1978-80; asst. prof. geography West Ga. Coll., Carrollton, 1982-86; assoc. prof. urban and regional planning Ea. Wash. U., Cheney, Wash., 1986-93, prof. urban and regional planning, 1993—; mem., vice chair Spokane Housing Authority, 1993—; chair Inland Empire Planner's Assn., 1990-91. Author: (with others) Geography in America, 1992, Human Geography in North America, 1995; co-editor: Planning American Indian Lands, 1995; contbr. articles to profl. jours. Co-founder, bd. dirs. Habitat for Humanity Spokane, 1987-90. Office: Dept Urban and Regional Planning Ea Wash U Cheney WA 99004

WINCHELL, ROBERT ALLEN, government agency administrator, accountant; b. Ft. Monmouth, N.J., Oct. 28, 1945; s. Robert Winslow Winchell; B.A., U. Calif., Santa Barbara, 1967; M.B.A., U. Pa., 1969. CPA, Calif. Air Force Audit Agy., El Segundo, Calif., 1972-73; accountant Scholefield, Bellanca & Co., W. Los Angeles, 1974-75, So. Calif. Gas Co., Los Angeles, 1975-76; auditor Def. Contract Audit Agy., Dept. Def., Los Angeles, 1976-86, supervisory auditor, 1986—. Served with AUS, 1969-71; Vietnam. Decorated Bronze Star. Mem. Assn. Govt. Accountants, Am. Inst. C.P.A.'s, Alpha Kappa Psi. Republican. Presbyterian. Club: Los Angeles Country. Home: 2008 California Ave Santa Monica CA 90403-4506

WINCOR, MICHAEL Z., psychopharmacology educator, clinician, researcher; b. Chgo., Feb. 9, 1946; s. Emanuel and Rose (Kershner) W.; m. Emily E.M. Smythe; children: Meghan Heather, Katherine Rose. SB in Zoology, U. Chgo., 1966; PharmD, U. So. Calif., 1978. Rsch. project specialist U. Chgo. Sleep Lab., 1968-75; psychiat. pharmacist Brotman Med. Ctr., Culver City, Calif., 1979-83; asst. prof. U. So. Calif., L.A., 1983—; cons. Fed. Bur. Prisons Drug Abuse Program, Terminal Island, Calif., 1978-81, Nat. Inst. Drug Abuse, Bethesda, Md., 1981, The Upjohn Co., Kalamazoo, 1982-87, 91-92, Area XXIV Profl. Stds. Rev. Orgn., L.A., 1983, Brotman Med. Ctr., Culver City, Calif., 1983-88, SmithKline Beecham Pharms., Phila., 1990-93, Tokyo Coll. of Pharmacy, 1991, G. D. Searle & Co., Chgo., 1992—. Contbr. over 30 articles to profl. jours., chpts. to books, papers presented at nat. and internat. meetings and reviewer. Mem. adv. coun. Franklin Ave. Sch., 1986-89; bd. dirs. K.I. Children's Ctr., 1988-89; trustee The Sequoyah Sch., 1992-93; mem. tech. com. Ivanhoe Sch., 1993—. Recipient Cert. Appreciation, Mayor of L.A., 1981, Bristol Labs Award, 1978; Faculty scholar U. So. Calif. Sch. Pharmacy, 1978. Mem. Am. Coll. Clin. Pharmacy (chmn. constn. and bylaws com. 1983-84, mem. credentials com. 1991-93, 95, mem. ednl. affairs com. 1994), Am. Assn. Colls. Pharmacy (focus group on liberalization of profl. curriculum), Am. Soc. Hosp. Pharmacists (chmn. edn. and tng. adv. working group 1985-88), Am. Pharm. Assn. (del. ann. meeting ho. dels. 1989), Sleep Rsch. Soc., Am. Sleep Disorders Assn., U. So. Calif. Sch. Pharmacy Alumni Assn. (bd. dirs. 1979—), Rho Chi. Office: U So Calif 1985 Zonal Ave Los Angeles CA 90033-1058

WINDER, CHARLES L., real estate executive; b. Ontario, Oreg., Nov. 21, 1945; s. Henry J. and Dorothy (Bridwell) W.; m. Dianne P. Winder, June 7, 1968; children: Elizabeth Nelson, David C. BA in Polit. Sci., Coll. of Idaho, 1968. Asst. to pres. Makad, Inc., Nampa & Boise, Idaho, 1972-73; v.p. devel. Emkay Devel. Inc., Boise, 1973-79; pres. Winder Devel. Svc. Inc., and The Winder Co., Boise, 1979—. Commr. Boise City Planning & Zoning Commn., 1976-81, Ada County Hwy. Dist., Boise, 1981-93; Rep. candidate for Gov. of Idaho, 1994; pres. Jr. Achievement Idaho, Boise, 1989-91. Lt. USN, 1968-79. Mem. Nat. Assn. Realtors, Arid Club. Presbyterian. Office: The Winder Co 877 Main St Boise ID 83702-5858

WINDER, DAVID KENT, federal judge; b. Salt Lake City, June 8, 1932; s. Edwin Kent and Alma Eliza (Cannon) W.; m. Pamela Martin, June 24, 1955; children: Ann, Kay, James. BA, U. Utah, 1955; LLB, Stanford U., 1958. Bar: Utah 1958, Calif. 1958. Assoc. firm Clyde, Mecham & Pratt Salt Lake City, 1958-66; law clk. to chief justice Utah Supreme Ct., 1958-59; dep. county atty. Salt Lake County, 1959-63; chief dep. dist. atty., 1965-66; asst. U.S. atty. Salt Lake City, 1963-65; partner firm Strong & Hanni, Salt Lake City, 1966-77; from judge to chief judge U.S. Dist. Ct., Dist. Utah, Salt Lake City, 1979—; examiner Utah Bar Examiners, 1975-79, chmn., 1977-79. Served with USAF, 1951-52. Mem. Am. Bd. Trial Advocates, Utah State Bar (Judge of Yr. award 1978), Salt Lake County Bar Assn., Calif. State Bar. Democrat. Office: US Dist Ct 350 S Main St Salt Lake City UT 84101-2106*

WINDHAM, EDWARD JAMES, bank executive, leasing company executive; b. Salt Lake City, Dec. 13, 1950; s. James Rudolph and Margaret Ann (Griffith) W.; m. Marilyn Ann Kenyon, Mar. 27, 1973; children: Ian James (dec.), Kendra Ann. Student, U. Calif., San Diego, 1969-70, 72-74. Cert. mortgage credit examiner HUD; accredited residential originator. Salesman Bonanza Properties, Tustin, Calif., 1976; loan officer Medallion Mortgage, Santa Cruz, Calif., 1976-80; sr. loan officer Cen. Pacific Mortgage, Santa Cruz, 1980-83, v.p., 1983-86; ptnr. Winn Leasing Co., Santa Cruz, 1983-90; v.p. Community West Mortgage, 1986-89, Central Pacific Mortgage, Citrus Heights, Calif., 1989-95; trainer GMAC Mortgage Western Region, 1995—; cons. Contour Inc., San Jose, Calif., 1983-85. Pres. Evergreen Estates Homeowners Assn., Soquel, Calif., 1983-85; treas. Sacramento/Placer chpt. MADD. No. Calif. State champion #3 Nat. Age Group award Am. Bicycle Assn., 1991. Mem. Nat. Assn. Rev. Appraisers and Rev. Underwriters (sr., cert.), Mortgage Bankers Assn. (Willis Bryant scholar 1994), Mensa, Intertel. Republican. Lodge: Masons (master Santa Cruz 1987). Home: 1451 Rocky Ridge Dr Apt 1713 Roseville CA 95661-3013 Office: GMAC Mortgage 1406 Highland Ave Melbourne FL 32935

WINDROTH, WILLIAM E., architect, building and safety executive; b. Balt., Nov. 23, 1931; s. William E. and Elizabeth C. (Schnepf) W.; m. Alvina A. Bonilla, Nov. 30, 1952 (div.); children: Michelle, Lillian (dec.), Alicia, Stefan, Barbara; m. Norma Jean Hobbs, Windroth, Dec. 27, 1970; children: Cherylan, Deanna K., Joellyn F. AA in Architecture, Md. Inst., 1951; student, U. Cincinnati, 1995—. registered architect, Calif. Pvt. practice Santa Barbara, Calif., 1964-75; architect, code cons. Saudi Arabia, Yanbu, 1975-80; asst. dir. bldg. and safety City of Santa Barbara (Calif.), 1980-84; dir. bldg. and safety County of Ventura, Calif., 1984-94; ret., 1994. With USN, 1951-55, Japan. Mem. Internat. Conf. of Bldg. Officials (chpt. pres. Whittier, Calif. 1987-93, com. mem. 1988-93). Republican. Roman Catholic. Home: 5937 Viewcrest Ct Ventura CA 93003

WINDSOR, WILLIAM E., consulting engineer, sales representative; b. Evansville, Ind., Jan. 24, 1927; s. Charles H. and Lora E. (Archey) W.; divorced; children: Kim, William, Robert. Student, Purdue U., 1946-50. Field engr. Philco Corp., Phila., 1950-53; studio ops. engr. Sta. WFBM, Indpls., 1953-55; field engr. RCA Svc. Co., Cherry Hill, N.J., 1955-56; audio facilities engr. ABC, N.Y.C., 1956-62; rsch. engr. Fine Recording, Inc., N.Y.C., 1962-66; chief engr. A & R Recording, Inc., N.Y.C., 1966-68; chief engr., corp. sec. DB Audio Corp., N.Y.C., 1968-70; pres. Studio Cons., Inc., N.Y.C., 1970-72; sr. v.p., v.p., gen. mgr. Quad Eight Electronics-Quad Eight/Westrex, San Fernando, Calif., 1972-85; sr. mktg. exec. Mitsubishi Pro Audio Group, San Fernando, Calif., 1985-89; pres., CEO Quad Eight Electronics, Inc., Valencia, Calif., 1989-90; ind. cons., Valencia, 1991—. Inventor monitor mixer for multitrack audio consoles, 1967, update function for audio console automation, 1973; designer of new architecture for film scoring and film re-recording sound mixing consoles (Academy award), 1974. Served with USNR, 1945-50. Fellow Audio Engring. Soc.; mem. Soc. Motion Picture & TV Engrs. Home and Office: 23112 Yvette Ln Valencia CA 91355-3060

WINEBERG, HOWARD, research director; b. N.Y.C., Aug. 30, 1955; s. Moe and Ruth (Blinder) W. BA, Bowling Green (Ohio) State U., 1977, MA, 1980; PhD, Johns Hopkins U., 1985. Demographer Indian Nations Coun. of Govts., Tulsa, 1985; asst. dir. Population Rsch. Ctr., assoc. prof. urban studies and planning Portland (Oreg.) State U., 1986—; co-founder Oreg. Demographic Group, Portland, 1990; Oreg. rep. to Fed.-State Coop. Program for Population Estimates, 1986—. Author: Do All Trails Lead to Oregon?, Population Estimates for Oregon 1980-90, 91, 92, 93, 94; contbr. articles to profl. jours. Johns Hopkins U. fellow, 1980-82; Children's Svcs. Commn., grantee, 1989. Mem. Internat. Soc. for Philos. Enquiry, Population Assn. Am., Population Reference Bur., Soc. for Study of Social Biology, So. Demographic Assn., Oreg. Acad. Sci., Internat. Platform Assn. Office: Portland State U Population Rsch Ctr 632 SW Hall St Portland OR 97201-5215

WINFIELD, ARMAND GORDON, international plastics consultant, educator; b. Chgo., Dec. 28, 1919; grad. Newark Acad. 1937; BS, Franklin and Marshall Coll., 1941; postgrad. U. N.Mex., 1941, State U. Iowa, 1944, Washington U., St. Louis, 1948-50; m. Lillian Tsukea Kubota, June 8, 1951 (dec. Dec. 1965); m. Barbara Jane La Barge, July 23, 1966 (dec. May 1992). Undergrad. tchg. fellow Franklin and Marshall Coll., 1939-41; owner Winfield Fine Art in Jewelry, N.Y.C., 1945-48; rsch. dir. Hanley Plastics Co. divsn. Wallace Pencil Co., St. Louis, 1955-57; plastic cons. engr. DeBell & Richardson, Inc., Hazardville, Conn., 1957-64; exec. v.p. Crystopal Ltd., Hazardville, Conn., 1963-64; pres., CEO Armand G. Winfield Inc., Santa Fe, 1963-93; rsch. prof. mech. engring., dir. Tng. and Rsch. Inst. for Plastics, U. N.Mex., Albuquerque, 1993—; mem. faculty Harris Tchrs. Coll., 1950, dept. English Washington U., St. Louis, 1956, Yale U., 1960-61; adviser USIA on plastics show to tour USSR, 1960-61; chmn. SPR Traveling Exhibition: Plastics-A New Dimension in Bldg., 1960-62; vis. critic in plastics Sch. Architecture, CCNY, 1968-69; plastics cons. indsl. design dept., faculty Pratt Inst., Bklyn., 1964-70, instr. prodn. methods, 1968-70; lectr. U. Hartford, U. Kans., 1970, U. Ariz., 1978, Calif. Poly. State U., 1980, numerous others; adj. prof. plastics engring. U. Lowell (Mass.), 1978-81; spkr. Acoplásticos conf., Cartagena, Colombia, 1986; conceived and directed the building of 13 installations at the N.Y. Worlds Fair, 1962-63. Mem. Vol. in Tech. Assistance, 1983—; bd. dir. Santa Fe Crime Stoppers, 1980-94, chmn., 1986, 87, carnival chmn., 1983, 84. U.S. State Dept. Am. Specialist grantee to USSR, 1961, UNIDO grantee, 1968-69, 1971; recipient Sci. award, 1980-94, 94. UNIDO expert in newer fibers and composites, India, 1977, cons. glass fibers and composites, Colombia, 1979. Fellow Plastics and Rubber Inst. (Eng., 1970); mem. Soc. Advancement Materials and Process Engring. (chpt. chmn. 1986, 87, 94, 95, editor newsletter 1987, 94, 95, special status hon. sr. mem. life, 1994), Soc. Plastics Engrs. (pres. Western New Eng. sect. 1963-64, v.p. N.Y. sect. 1968-69, chmn. regional tech. conf. 1967, historian am. tech. conf. 1968), Soc. Plastic Industry, Plastics Pioneers Assn. Author: The Alexian Brothers, 1951; The Merchants Exchange of St. Louis, 1953, Plastics For Architects, Artists and Interior Designers, 1961, 100 Years Young, 1968, Inventors Handbook, 1990; also chpts. in books, monthly column in Display

World Mag., 1965-68, Designer Mag., 1971-72, Museum Scope, 1976-77; spl. exhibitions at The Smithsonian Inst., Washington, 1988—, Cooper Hewitt, N.Y.C., 1993, Mus. Sci. and Industry, 1994; numerous articles on plastics; patentee of mass-producible process for embedding specimens in acrylics; patentee in the field. Office: U NM Sch Engring TRIP 109 Pine St NE Albuquerque NM 87106

WINFREY, DIANA LEE, lawyer; b. Kansas City, Mo., July 17, 1955; d. James William and Louise Augusta (Harrison) W. BA in Spanish, U. Mo., 1978, JD, 1984. Bar: Mo. 1984, Calif. 1985. Tchr. Pan-Am. Workshop, Mexico City, 1979; law clk. Mo. Ct. of Appeals, Kansas City, 1984-85; assoc. Early, Maslach, Leavy & Nutt, L.A., 1985-87, Wilson, Elser, et al, L.A., 1987-88, Wood, Lucksinger & Epstein, L.A., 1988-90, Coony & Bihr, Beverly Hills, Calif., 1990-95; sole practitioner Woodland Hills, Calif., 1995—. Asst. editor The Urban Lawyer Jour., 1983-84. Member Heal the Bay, Santa Monica, Calif., 1991—. Recipient Outstanding Achievement and Svc. award U. Mo., 1978. Mem. ABA, Calif. Bar Assn., Mo. Bar Assn., L.A. County Bar Assn., Beverly Hills Bar Assn., Am. Bd. Trial Attys., Inns of Ct. Democrat. Office: 21112 Ventura Blvd Woodland Hills CA 91364-2103

WING, JANET ELEANOR SWEEDYK BENDT, nuclear scientist; b. Detroit, Oct. 12, 1925; d. Jack and Florence C. (Springman) Sweedyk; m. Philip J. Bendt, Sept. 4, 1948 (div. Jan. 1972); children: Karen Ann Bendt Sox, Paul Philip, Barbara Jean Bendt Medlin, Linda Sue; m. G. Milton Wing, Aug. 26, 1972 (div. Jan. 1987). BSEE with distinction, Wayne State U., 1947; MA in Physics, Columbia U., 1950; postgrad., U. Oreg., 1966-67, U. N.Mex., 1968-71. Research engr. Gen. Motors Corp., Detroit, 1944-48; physicist, mathematician Manhattan Project Columbia U., N.Y.C., 1950-51; mem. research staff Los Alamos (N.Mex.) Nat. Lab, 1951-57, 68—, project leader, 1976-81, asst. group leader, 1980-84, assoc. group leader, 1985—. Bd. dirs., treas. Esperanza Shelter, Santa Fe, N. Mex., 1984—. Mem. Am. Nuclear Soc., AAAS, Women in Sci. and Engring., Los Alamos Women in Sci., Sigma Xi, Tau Beta Pi. Office: Los Alamos Nat Lab Los Alamos NM 87545

WING, MICHAEL JAMES, marketing research company executive; b. Tucson, Ariz., July 1, 1959; s. James and Bess (Acton) W.; m. Pamela Constantz Wing, May 18, 1980; children: Lindsay Leann, Jacqueline McKenna, Broderick James. BA in Internat. Affairs/Internat. Bus., U. Colo., 1981; MBA in Mktg./Fin., Denver U., 1986; M Pub. Policy, Georgetown U., 1988. Head baseball coach U. Colo., Boulder, 1980-81; area rep. Kansas City Fellowship Christian Athletes, Denver, 1982; divsn. mgr., ops. mgr. Boyd Distbn. Co., Inc., Denver, 1982-84; pres. U.S. ops. Soft Am., Inc., Denver, 1984-88; pres. Lundby of Sweden U.S.A., Inc., N.Y.C. and Tucson, Ariz., 1985-90, InfoPlan, Inc./Info Plan Internat. Inc., Houston, 1987—; spl. asst. to sec. Dept. Interior, 1993; spl. asst. to chmn. FCC, 1992-93; pub. speaker to profl. sports teams, collegiate teams, luncheons, banquets, others. Author: Talking With Your Customers, 1993. Bd. dirs. Young Life and Fellowship Christian Athletes; mem. Leadership Fairfax, Va., Leadership Tucson. White House fellow, Washington, 1992-93. Mem. C.of C. (legis. affairs com.). Republican. Baptist. Home: 5741 N Placita Del Trueno Tucson AZ 85718-3930 Office: InfoPlan Internat Inc 14505 Torrey Chase Blvd Ste 420 Houston TX 77014-1025

WING, ROGER, management consultant; b. N.Y.C., May 26, 1945; s. John A. and Norma M. (LeBlanc) W.; m. Judith A. King, June 7, 1963 (div. 1980); m. Peggy J. McFall, Aug. 27, 1983; children: Roger, Karin, Nicole, Sean, Nathan, Alexandra. BBA, Cleve. State U., 1972, MBA, 1975. Supr. Am. Greetings Co., Brooklyn, Ohio, 1969-74; dir. Revco D.S. Inc., Twinsburg, Ohio, 1974-78; mgr. Hughes Aircraft Co., Los Angeles, 1978-79; sr. dir. Continental Airlines, Los Angeles, 1979-81; dir. Coopers & LyBrand, Los Angeles, 1981-83; pres. Huntington Cons. Group, Huntington Beach, Calif., 1983—; prof. Cleve. State U., 1977-78. Named Systems Man of Yr., Assn. Systems Mgmt., 1978. Office: The Huntington Cons Group 8531 Topside Cir Huntington Beach CA 92646-2117

WING, THOMAS, micrometrologist, engineer, consultant; b. Shanghai, China, Mar. 12, 1929; came to U.S., 1930, naturalized, 1950; s. Lim and Fong Shee W.; B.S. in Engring. cum laude, Purdue U., 1953, postgrad., 1957-60; postgrad. CCNY, 1953-55; m. Catherine Amajelia Scambia, Nov. 27, 1954; children—Karen Elyse, Thomas Scambia, Robert Frank Joseph, David Anthony. Sr. project mgr. Gulton Industries, Metuchen, N.J., 1960-63; adv. engr. IBM, Lexington, Ky., 1963-65; with guidance and control systems div. Litton Industries, Woodland Hills, Calif., 1966-69, mem. tech. staff, 1976-92; cons. in field, 1992—; staff cons. Devel. Consultants, Cin., 1965-66; image tech. mgr. Fairchild Semiconductor, Mountain View, Calif., 1969-71; gen. mgr. research and devel., v.p., Jade Corp., HLC Mfg. Co., Willow Grove, Pa., 1971-75; pres. Photronic Engring. Labs., Inc., Danbury, Conn., 1975-76; lectr. in micro-photo lithography, Inst. Graphic Communication, Boston; cons. engr. in micro image tech. and metrology; founding mem. Thermo Phys. Properties Research Center, Purdue U.; pres., staff cons. Zantec Inc., North Hollywood, Calif., 1981-86; cons. Kasper Instruments, Sunnyvale, Calif., 1977-79, Quintel Corp., San Jose, Calif., 1979—. Coach, v.p. Roadrunners Hockey Club, 1972-75, founder, 1972, Bristol, Pa.; founder, pres. Eastridge Jr. Hockey Club, San Jose, Calif., 1970-71; coach Belmont (Calif.) Jr. Hockey Club, 1969; v.p. Greater Los Angeles Minor Hockey Assn., 1968-69; v.p., coach West Valley Minor Hockey Club, Tarzana, Calif., 1968-69; coach Topanga Plaza Jr. Hockey Club, 1967. Mem. ASME, ASTM (mem. F-1 com. on microelectronics 1972-75), Soc. Photog. Instrumentation Engrs., Soc. Photog. Scientists and Engrs., Tau Beta Pi, Pi Tau Sigma, Phi Eta Sigma. Organizer first internat. lecture series on micro photo lithography, Boston, 1974; contbr. articles to profl. publs.; patentee currency counter, trimming inductor, damped high frequency accelerometer, three phase dithered pivot, auto focus for step and repeat camera, temperature compensated dither drive for laser gyro, proximity printing mechanism, equilbrator for howitizer. Home and Office: 6261 Jumilla Ave Woodland Hills CA 91367-3822

WINGATE, MARCEL EDWARD, speech educator; b. New Castle, Pa., Feb. 27, 1923; s. Morton Harvey and Elizabeth (Martin) Wingett; m. Elaine C. Kayser, June 8, 1948 (div. July 1968); children: Nancy, Amy, Jennifer; m. Cicely Anne Johnston, June 7, 1969; children: Marcel Richard, Cicely Anna Marie. BA, Grinnell (Iowa) Coll., 1948; MA, U. Wash., 1952, PhD, 1956. Lic. psychologist, Wash., N.Y. Psychologist Childrens Hosp., Seattle, 1953-57, Wash. State C.P. Ctr., Seattle, 1954-57; asst. prof. U. Wash., Seattle, 1957-65, assoc. prof., 1965-68; prof. SUNY, Buffalo, 1968-73, U. Ariz., Tucson, 1973-75; prof. speech, hearing sci. Wash. State U., Pullman, 1975—; cons. psychologist St. Mary's Hosp., Lewiston, N.Y., 1969-73. Author: Stuttering: Theory and Treatment, 1976, Structure of Stuttering, 1988; assoc. editor Jour. Speech/Hearing Disorders, 1966-73; editorial cons. Jour. Speech/Hearing Rsch., 1974-80; editorial bd. Jour. Fluency Disorders, 1974—; contbr. articles to profl. jours., chpts. to books. With U.S. Army, 1942-45, ETO. Fellow Am. Speech and Hearing Assn. Home: RR 2 Box 102 Pullman WA 99163-9605 Office: Wash State U Speech and Hearing Sci Pullman WA 99164

WINGO, MICHAEL, artist, educator; b. L.A.; s. W.R. and Katie Lois (Hall) Mahan. BA, Claremont McKenna Coll., 1964; BFA, MFA, Otis Art Inst., L.A., 1967. Instr. Pasadena (Calif.) Art Mus., 1968-72, Otis Art Inst./Parsons Sch. Design, L.A., 1984-95; instr. Calif. State Summer Sch. Arts Calarts, Loyola Marymount U., L.A., 1987, 88; vis. artist San Francisco Art Inst., 1987, guest lectr., 1984. Prin. works exhibited in numerous one-man shows including Terry DeLapp Gallery, L.A., 1985, Janet Steinberg Gallery, San Francisco, 1984, Turnbull Lutjeans Kogan Gallery, Costa Mesa, Calif., 1983, Newport Harbor Art Mus., Newport Beach, Calif., 1976, Santa Barbara Mus. Art, 1970, others; works represented in numerous pub. and pvt. collections; contbr. works to profl. publs. NEA Visual Artists fellow in painting, 1989-90; Adolph and Esther Gottlieb Found. grantee in painting, 1992. Office: 7051 N Figueroa St Los Angeles CA 90042-1276

WINKLER, AGNIESZKA M., advertising agency executive; b. Rome, Italy, Feb. 22, 1946; came to U.S., 1953, naturalized, 1959; d. Wojciech A. and Halina Z. (Owsiany) W.; children from previous marriage: children: Renata G. Ritcheson, Dana C Sworakowski.; m. Arthur K. Lund. BA, Coll. Holy Name, 1967; MA, San Jose State U., 1971; MBA, U. Santa Clara, 1981. Teaching asst., San Jose State U., 1968-70; cons. to ea. European bus., Palo Alto, Calif., 1970-72; pres./founder Commart Communications, Palo Alto, 1973-84; pres./founder, chmn. bd. Winkler McManus, Santa Clara, Calif., 1984—; bd. dirs. Supercuts, Inc., Reno Air. Trustee Santa Clara U., 1991—; trustee O'Connor Found., 1987-93, mem. exec. com., 1988—, mem. Capital Campaign steering com., 1989; mem. nat. adv. bd. Comprehensive Health Enhancement Support System, 1991—; mem. mgmt. west com. A.A.A.A. Agy., 1991—; project dir. Poland Free Enterprise Plan, 1989-92; mem. adv. bd. Normandy France Bus. Devel., 1989-92; mem. bd. regents Holy Names Coll., 1987—; bd. dirs. San Jose Mus. Art, 1987; mem. San Jose Symphony, Gold Baton, 1986; mem. nat. adv. com. CHESS, 1991—; dir. Bay Area Coun., 1994—. Recipient CLIO award in Advt., Addy award and numerous others; named to 100 Best Women in Advt., Ad Age, 1988, Best Woman in Advt., AdWeek and McCall's Mag., 1993. Mem. Family Svc. Assn. (trustee 1980-82), Am. Assn. Advt. Agys. (agy. mgmt. west com. 1991), Bus. Profl. Advt. Assn., Polish Am. Congress, San Jose Advt. Club, San Francisco Ad Club, Beta Gamma Sigma (hon.), Pi Gamma Mu, Pi Delta Phi (Lester-Tinneman award 1966, Bill Raskob Found. grantee 1965). Office: Winkler McManus 150 Spear St Fl 16 San Francisco CA 94105-1535

WINN, ROBERT CHARLES, retired military officer, aeronautical engineer, consultant; b. Chgo., Sept. 4, 1945; s. Bart James and Dorothy Eleanor (Smith) W.; m. Kathleen Nowak, Aug. 3, 1968; children: Eric Michael, Kara Michelle. BSME, U. Ill., 1968, MSME, 1969; PhD in Mech. Engring., Colo. State U., 1982. Registered profl. engr., Colo. Enlisted USAF, 1969, advanced through grades to lt. col., 1991; instr. pilot 14 student squad USAF, Columbus AFB, Mo., 1970-74; instr. pilot 61 Tactical Airlift Squad USAF, Little Rock AFB, 1974-76; asst. prof. dept. aeronautics USAF Acad., Colorado Springs, Colo., 1976-79, assoc. prof., 1982-90; chief scientist USAF European Office of Aerospace R&D, London, 1986-88; prof. USAF Acad., 1988-91; adj. prof. Colo. Tech. Coll., 1991—; cons. Colorado Springs, 1991-94; sr. cons. Engring. Sys., Inc., Colorado Springs, 1994—. Contbr. articles to profl. jours. Mem. AIAA (assoc. fellow, vice chmn. Rocky Mountain sect. 1985, sec. 1984, mem. terrestrial energy systems nat. tech. com. 1984-91, dep. dir. energy conversion 1989). Roman Catholic. Office: 4775 Centennial Blvd Ste 106 Colorado Springs CO 80919-3309

WINN, SUZANNE BARBARA, marketing professional; b. Passaic, N.J., Feb. 11, 1957; d. Roger Emmett and Claire Louise (Nicholson) Behre; m. Mitchell D. Winn, May 13, 1978; children: Casey Anne, Amanda Christine. BS in Communications, U. Idaho, 1992; postgrad. in sports mgmt., 1995—. Asst. mgr. Jay Jacobs Clothing, Moscow, Idaho, 1980, Small World Toys and Pets, Moscow, 1980-81; mgr. Fitness Unlimited, Moscow, 1983-87; office mgr., exec. asst. Moscow C. of C., 1987-89; sales mgr. Creative Workshops, Moscow, 1992-93; telecomms. specialist athletic dept. U. Idaho, Moscow, 1993-94, compliance/programs asst. athletic dept., 1994-95; athletic ticket mgr., 1995. Bd. dirs. Moscow Mardi Gras, 1989, Deary Latchkey Program, 1994. Mem. Moscow C. of C. (tourism com. 1988-89, retail com. 1988-89, chair awards banquet 1989, bd. dirs. Latah County Vandal Boosters 1995—). Office: U Idaho Athletics KAC 235E Moscow ID 83844-2302

WINNER, KARIN, newspaper editor. Editor San Diego Union-Tribune. Office: Copley Press Inc 350 Camino De La Reina San Diego CA 92108-3003

WINSKILL, ROBERT WALLACE, manufacturing executive; b. Tacoma, Oct. 30, 1925; s. Edward Francis William and Margaret Eyre (Myers) W. BA, Coll. Puget Sound, Tacoma, 1947. Field rep. Ray Burner Co., San Francisco, 1954-57, nat. sales mgr., 1960-69; v.p. sales Western Boiler Co., L.A., 1957-60; gen. sales mgr. Ray Burner Co., San Francisco, 1973-82; v.p., chief exec. officer Orr & Sembower, Inc., Middletown, Pa., 1969-73; pres. Combustion Systems Assocs., Inc., Mill Valley, Calif., 1982—; bd. dirs. Sino-Am. Boiler Engring. Co., Shanghai, China, S. T. Johnson Co., Oakland, Calif. Contbr. articles to profl. jours.; columnist Marin Scope, Mill Valley Harold, 1991—. With U.S. Army, 1943-44. Mem. ASME, Olympic Club (San Francisco), Rotary. Office: Combustion Systems Assocs Inc PO Box 749 Mill Valley CA 94942-0749

WINSLOW, DAVID ALLEN, chaplain, naval officer; b. Dexter, Iowa, July 12, 1944; s. Franklin E. and Inez Maude (McPherson) W.; m. Frances Lavinia Edwards, June 6, 1970; children: Frances, David. BA, Bethany Nazarene Coll., 1968; MDiv, Drew U., 1971, STM, 1973. Ordained to ministry United Meth. Ch., 1969. Clergyman, 1969—; assoc. minister All Sts. Episcopal. Ch., Millington, N.J., 1969-70; asst. minister Marble Collegiate Ch., N.Y.C., 1970-71; min. No. N.J. Conf., 1971-75; joined chaplain corps USN, 1974, advanced through grades to lt. comdr., 1980, ret., 1995; exec. dir. Marina Ministries, 1995—. Author: Road to Bethlehem: Advent, 1993, The Utmost for the Highest, 1993, Epiphany: God Still Speaks, 1994, Be Thou My Vision, 1994, Evening Prayers at Sea, 1995, Wise Men Still Adore Him, 1995, (with Walsh) A Year of Promise: Meditations, 1995; editor: Preparation for Resurrection, 1994, God's Promise: Advent, 1994, The Way of the Cross: Lent, 1995; contbr. articles to profl. jours. Bd. dirs. disaster svcs. and family svcs. ARC, Santa Ana, Calif., 1988-91, Child Abuse Prevention Ctr., Orange, Calif., 1990-91; bd. dirs. Santa Clara County Coun. Chs., 1993-94, del., 1995—. Mem. ACA, Internat. Soc. Traumatic Stress Studies, Mil. Chaplain Assn. USA, Commonwealth Club Calif., USN League (hon.), Sunrise Exch. Club (chaplain 1989-91), Dick Richards Breakfast Club (chaplain 1988-91), Masons (charter) Shriners, Scottish Rite. Home: 20405 Via Volante Cupertino CA 95014-6318

WINSLOW, FRANCES EDWARDS, city official; b. Phila., Sept. 12, 1948; d. Harry Donaldson and Anna Louise (McColgan) E.; m. David Allen Winslow, June 6, 1970; children: Frances Lavinia, David Allen Jr. BA, Drew U., 1969, MA, 1971; M Urban Planning, NYU, 1974, PhD, 1978; cert. hazardous material mgmt., U. Calif., Irvine. Adminstrv. asst. Borough of Florham Park, N.J., 1970-73; instr. Kean Coll., Union, N.J., 1973-75; adminstrv. analyst Irvine (Calif.) Police Dept., 1984-86; coord. emergency svcs. City of Irvine, 1986-91; dir. emergency svcs. City of San Jose, Calif., 1991—; instr. U. Calif., Irvine Extension; commr. Calif. Seismic Safety Commn., 1991-95, Calif. Hosp. Bldg. Safety Bd., 1994-95. Editor NCEER Workshop Procs., 1990, 92; contbr. chpts. in books and articles to profl. jours. Vice pres. San Diego Chaplain's Wives, 1976-79; treas. Girl Scouts U.S.A., Yokohama, Japan, 1980-81; treas. Camp Pendleton Officer's Wives Club, 1982-83, pres., 1983-84; vice chmn. curriculum ARC Disaster Acad., 1989-90, chmn., 1991; mem. community disaster preparedness com. ARC, 1992—; del. Nat. Coordinating Com. on Emergency Mgmt., 1990—. Recipient Vol. Svc. award Navy Relief Soc., 1984; Lasker Found. fellow, 1972; named one of Women of Distinction, Soroptimists Internat., 1991. Mem. ASPA (program chmn. Orange County 1984-85, chmn. criminal justice sect. award com. 1988-92, Santa Clara County bd. dirs., co-chmn. mini-conf. 1993, sec. 1994-95, pres. 1995—, bd. mem. Sect. Emergency Mgmt., Nat. Policy Com.), Am. Planning Assn. (regional conf. planning com. 1989-90), Internat. City Mgrs. Assn., Assn. Environ. Profls., Assn. Police Planning and Res. Officers (past sec., v.p. Orange County 1984-90), Creekers Club (pres. 1985-88), San Jose Mgmt. Assn. (bd. dirs.), Calif. Emergency Svcs. Assn. (conf. program com. 1992, 95). Republican. Methodist. Home: 20405 Via Volante Cupertino CA 95014-6318 Office: City of San Jose 855 N San Pedro St # 404 San Jose CA 95110-1718

WINSLOW, KENELM CRAWFORD, mining engineer; b. Albany, N.Y., Jan. 24, 1921; s. Leon Loyal and Lois Esther (Crawford) W.; m. Bette Jean Killingsworth, Sept. 5, 1947; children: Katherine, Jeanette, Kenelm, Elizabeth, Priscilla. BS in Liberal Arts, Bowling Green State U., 1941; diploma in Mil. Meteorology, N.Y.U., 1943; BS in Mining Engring., Mich. Tech. U., 1948, BS in Geol. Engring., 1948. Registered profl. engr. and land surveyor, N.Mex. Mining engr. Hanna Coal and Ore Corp., DeGrasse, N.Y., 1948-50, Warren Foundry & Pipe Corp., Dover, N.J., 1950-53, Cleve.-Cliffs Iron Co., Ishpeming, Mich., 1953-64, Molybdenum Corp. Am., Questa, N.Mex., 1964-66; pvt. practice cons. engr. El Prado, N.Mex., 1966—. Cpt. Air Corps U.S. Army, 1943-46; lt. col. USAFR, ret. 1981. Mem. Soc. Mining Engrs. of AIME, Soc. Am. Mil. Engrs., Tau Beta Pi. Republican. Presbyterian. Home and Office: PO Box 927 El Prado NM 87529-0927

WINSLOW, NORMAN ELDON, business executive; b. Oakland, Calif., Apr. 4, 1938; s. Merton Conrad and Roberta Eilene (Drennen) W.; m. Betty June Cady, Jan. 14, 1962 (div. Aug. 1971); 1 child, Todd Kenelm; m. Ilene Ruth Jackson, Feb. 3, 1979. BS, Fresno (Calif.) State U., 1959. Asst. mgr. Proctors Jewelers, Fresno, 1959-62; from agt. to dist. mgr. Allstate Ins. Co., Fresno, 1962-69; ins. agt. Fidelity Union Life Ins., Dallas, 1969-71; dist. and zone mgr. The Southland Corp., Dallas, 1971-78; owner Ser-Vis-Etc., Goleta, Calif., 1978—. Pub./editor FranchiserviceNews; author: Hands in Your Pockets, 1992; contbr. numerous articles to profl. jours. With USAFNG, 1961-67. Mem. Nat. Coalition of Assn. of 7-11 Franchises (affiliate, mem. adv. bd. Glendale, Calif. chpt. 1984-90), Am. Arbitration Assn. (expert witness/cons. Calif. superior cts.). Republican. Methodist. Home: 1179 N Patterson Ave Santa Barbara CA 93117-1813 Office: Ser-Vis-Etc PO Box 2276 Goleta CA 93118-2276

WINSLOW, PAUL DAVID, architect; b. Phoenix, June 12, 1941; s. Fred D. and Thelma E. (Ward) W.; m. Carole Lynn Walker, June 13, 1964; 1 child, Kirk David. B.Arch., Ariz. State U., 1964. Lic. architect, Ariz., Calif. Ptnr. The Orcutt/Winslow Partnership, Phoenix, 1972—; speaker solar energy workshops, Phoenix, 1986-89; adjunt prof. Ariz. State Univ., 1991. Mem. profl. adv. council Ariz. State U. Coll. Architecture, Tempe, 1970—, bd. dirs. Architecture Found., 1972-76; mem. adv. com. City of Phoenix Bldg. Safety Bd., 1981. Bd. dirs. Central Ariz. Project Assn., Phoenix, 1971-74, Ariz. Ctr. for Law in the Pub. Interest, Phoenix, 1979-86; chmn. Encanto Village Planning Com., Phoenix, 1981-86; mem. council City of Phoenix, chmn. adv. com. Indian Sch. Citizens adv. com. Ind. Sch. Land Use Planning Team; lectr. on planning Ariz. State Univ. planning dept., 1989, city of Presott, Phoenix and Tempe, 1988-89. Mem. AIA (bd. dirs. Central Ariz. chpt. also sec., treas. and pres.), Ariz. Soc. Architects (bd. dirs. 1970-71, 78-82), Bldg. Owners and Mgrs. Assn. Greater Phoenix (pres. 1985-91), Boar Valley Forward Assn.. (exec. com. 1994—). Methodist. Club: Plaza (Phoenix). Home: 816 E Circle Rd Phoenix AZ 85020-4144 Office: The Orcutt.Winslow Partnership 1130 N 2nd St Phoenix AZ 85004-1806

WINSLOW, PHILIP CHARLES, agriculturist, marketing consultant; b. Carthage, Ind., Jan. 13, 1924; s. William Howard and Ione (Morris) W.; m. Arlis Brown, Oct. 6, 1951; children: Mark, Jay, Julie. BS, Purdue U., 1948. Successively dist. mgr., regional product mgr., asst. div. sales mgr., div. sales mgr., nat. product mgr., nat. mktg. mgr. Ralston Purina Co., 1950-1970; v.p. mktg. Namolco, Inc., Willow Grove, Pa., 1971-84; dir. mktg. molasses div. Cargill, Inc., Willow Grove, 1984-85; nat. mktg. cons. Cargill, Inc., Mpls., 1986-88; v.p. The Montgomery Group, Indpls., 1989—; pres., dir. Winslow Farms, Inc., Carthage, 1982—. Sgt. U.S. Army, 1948-50. Mem. Am. Feed Industry Assn. (com. chmn. 1975-76, com. sec. 1982-83), Big 10 Club Phila. (pres. 1981), Shadowridge Golf Club (sec.-treas. 1992, pres. 1993, bd. govs. 1993—), Purdue Club Phila. (v.p. 1982-83, pres. 1983-86), Masons. Republican. Lutheran. Home and Office: 1305 La Salle Ct Vista CA 92083-8945

WINSLOW, RICHARD PAUL, computer science educator, consultant; b. Washington, Oct. 28, 1939; m. Nancy J. Kelley, Aug. 17, 1991; 1 child, Krista. BS, Ohio State U., 1965, U. Wyo., 1979; MEd, Lesley Coll., 1987. Cert. tchr., Wyo. Programmer The Trinity Cos., Dallas, 1970-73, systems analyst, 1973-74; programmer analyst State Wyo., Cheyenne, 1974-78; tchr. Platte County Sch. Dist. #1, Wheatland, Wyo., 1979-87; instr. Cen. Wyo. Coll., Riverton, 1987-90, asst. prof., 1990-93, assoc. prof., 1993—; cons. Custom Computer Svcs., Riverton, 1992—,. Capt. USAF, 1962-70. Mem. IEEE Computer Soc., Phi Beta Kappa. Republican. Pentecostal. Office: Ctrl Wyo Coll 2660 Peck St Riverton WY 82501-2215

WINSOR, DAVID JOHN, cost consultant; b. Duluth, Minn., May 27, 1947; s. Alphonse Joseph and Sylvia Mae (Petrich) W.; m. Linda Kay Sanders, Dec. 22, 1968 (div. Mar. 1974). BA in Bus., U. Puget Sound, 1978; M of Mech. Engring., Pacific Western U., 1979. Jr. engr. J.P. Head Mech., Inc., Richland, Wash., 1965-67; estimator, project engr. Subs. of Howard S. Wright Co., Seattle, 1972-75; sr. estimator Massart Co., Seattle, 1975-76; project mgr. Univ. Mechanical, Portland, Oreg., 1976; cons. Kent, Wash., 1976-79; owner Leasair, Federal Way, Wash., 1978-83; pres., owner Expertise Engring. & Cons., Inc., Bellevue, Wash., 1979-82, 90—; cons. Winsor & Co., Walnut Creek, Calif., 1983—; cons. NASA, Mountain View, Calif., 1986, Lockheed Missile & Space, Sunnyvale, Calif., 1984-87, The Boeing Co., Seattle, 1979-82. Author: (with others) Current Construction Costs, 1987, 88, 89, Construction Materials Inventory Systems, 1973, 74, Construction Inflation Trends, 1975, 76, 77, 78, 79, 80, 81, Construction Claims and Prevention, 1981, 82. Served to sgt. USAF, 1967-71. Mem. Jaycees (state dir. 1972-73, state chmn. 1973-74). Republican. Roman Catholic. Office: Expertise Engring 1611 116th NE Bellevue WA 98004

WINTER, DONALD CHRISTOPHER, computer systems architect; b. Hull, Eng., Feb. 23, 1944; came to U.S., 1966; s. Henry and Ethel (Bradley) W.; m. Christine Alice Kopp, June 6, 1969; 1 child, Henry Christopher. BSc with honors, U. Southampton, Eng., 1965; MS, U. Cin., 1970. Engr. Avco Electronics, Cin., 1966-70, Xerox Electro-optical sys., Pasadena, Calif., 1970-83; sys. engr. Xerox Spl. Info. Sys., Pasadena, 1983-93; solutions architect Xerox Integrated Sys., Pasadena, 1993; sys. architect Xerox Printing Sys., El Segundo, Calif., 1994—. Mem. IEEE, Assn. for Computing Machinery, Instn. of Elec. Engrs. (assoc.), Mensa.

WINTER, RICHARD SAMUEL, JR., computer training company owner, writer; b. Denver, Mar. 17, 1958; s. Richard Samuel and Jerryl Dene (Gano) W.; m. Karen Annette Hansen, May 27, 1989. Student, Griffith U., Brisbane, Australia, 1979; BA in Internat. Environment, Colo. Coll., 1981; MA in Pub. Adminstrn., U. Colo., Denver, 1989. Range aide U.S. Forest Svc., Desert Exptl. Station, Utah, 1976-77; pub. health investigator, lab. technician Denver Health Dept., 1982-84; projects mgr. Colo. Statesman, Denver, 1984-85; editor Mile Hi Prep, Denver, 1985; fin. analyst Pan Am. World Airways, N.Y.C., 1985-88; sr. ptnr., owner PRW, Denver, 1988—; pres. info. systems Trainers, Denver, 1994. Co-author, revisor: MicroRef Quick Reference Gd. Lotus 1-2-3 Rel. 3.0, 1990, MicroRef Quick Reference Gd. Lotus 1-2-3 Rel. 2.2, 1990, Que Q&A QueCards, 1991, Que 123 Release 2.3 QuickStart, 1991, Que 123 Release 3.1 QuickStart, 1991, Que 123 Release 2.4 QuickStart, 1992, Que Look Your Best with Excel, 1992, Que 123 Release 3.4 QuickStart, 1992, Que Excel for Windows Sure Steps, 1993, Que Using Lotus 123 Release 4, 1994, Que Using Excel 5, 1994, Que Using Microsoft Office, 1994, Que Using Microsoft Office, 1995. Chmn. N.Y. Victims for Victims, N.Y.C., 1986-87; bd. dirs. Colo. Common Cause, Denver, 1984-85; steering com. Voter Registration "Motor Voter" Amendment, Denver, 1983-84; pres. Broadway Commons Homeowners Assn., Denver, 1982-84. Recipient Vigil Honor, Order of the Arrow, 1976. Mem. Phi Beta Kappa, Alpha Lambda Delta.

WINTERBAUER, RICHARD HILL, physician, medical researcher; b. Springfield, Ill., June 11, 1936; s. Henry Thomas and Helen Louise (Hill) W.; m. Dianna Marie Heuer, Dec. 27, 1958; children: Michael James, Steven Hill, Andrew Mark. BA, Yale U., 1958; MD, Johns Hopkins U., 1962. Diplomate Am. Bd. Internal Medicine, Am. Bd. Pulmonary Disease. Resident in internal medicine Johns Hopkins Hosp., Balt., 1962-64, 66-69; mem. staff Va. Mason Clin., Seattle, 1969—, chief sect. pulmonary and critical care medicine, 1976—; clin. prof. medicine U. Wash., Seattle, 1984—; bd. dirs., treas. Va. Mason Clinic, 1986-92. Contbr. more than 110 articles to profl. jours. With USPHS, 1964-66. Fellow ACP, Am. Coll. Chest Physicians (editorial bd.), Sigma Xi; mem. Am. Thoracic Soc. (sec.-treas. 1980-81), Alpha Omega Alpha. Republican. Roman Catholic. Office: Va Mason Clinic 1100 9th Ave Seattle WA 98101-2756

WINTERLIN, WRAY LAVERN, environmental chemist emeritus, educator; b. Sioux City, Iowa, July 20, 1930; s. William and Nettie (Larson) W.; m. Arlene Fay Harper, Nov. 15, 1929; children: Jerry and Larry (twins), Dwight. Student, Morningside Coll., 1948-50, Iowa State U., 1950-51; BS, U. Nebr., 1955, MS, 1956. Jr. chemist Calif. Dept. Water Resources, Sacramento, 1958-59; staff rsch. assoc., exptl. sta. specialist U. Calif., Davis, 1959-79, lectr., environ. chemist, 1979—, dir. pesticide residue and trace analysis lab., 1965-84, acting chmn. dept. environ. toxicology, 1972; instr. workshops Nat. Inst. Environ. Health Scis., Cairo, Egypt, 1982. Contbr. to numerous profl. publs. With U.S. Army, 1951-53, Korea. Grantee numerous fed. and state agys., indsl. orgns. Mem. AAAS, Am. Chem. Soc., Sigma Xi, Gamma Sigma Delta. Republican.

WINTERMUTE, MARJORIE MCLEAN, architect, educator; b. Great Falls, Mont., Sept. 15, 1919; d. Allan Edward and Gladys Pearl (Pelton)

McLean; m. Charles Richard Wintermute, June 14, 1947 (div.); children: Lynne Wintermute, Lane. BA, U. Oreg., 1941; postgrad. Portland State U., 1969-72. Registered architect, Oreg. Archtl. draftsman Def. Projects, Portland and San Francisco, 1941-43; architect Pietro Belluschi, Portland, 1943-47; free-lance architect, Portland, 1948—; architect-in-residence Edn. Service Dist., Portland, 1978-91, ret.; instr. Portland State U., 1973—; architect-in-residence Dept. Def. Dependents Sch., Asian Region Hdqrs. Japan, 1981-83; with Upshur Group Collaborative, 1976-87; architect-in-residence program coord. Oreg. Arts Commn., 1987—, AIA; leader archtl. tours to Europe, 1969, 71, 73, Greece and Turkey, 1989, 91. Author: Students, Structures, Spaces, 1983, Blueprints: A Built Environment Education Program, 1984, Architecture As A Basic Curriculum Builder, 1987-90; editor: Pitter Patter (Gold medal 1965), 1960-69. Prin. archtl. works include comml. and residential bldgs. and restoration and mus. installation Timberline Lodge, Oreg., 1983, 2d Timberline Restoration project, 1993. Bd. dirs. Oreg. Heart Assn., Portland, 1960-70, pres. 1968-69; bd. dirs. Friends of Timberline, Creative Arts Community, pres. 1993—; program devel. cons. Am. Heritage Assn., Lake Oswego, Oreg., 1969-83, Mt. Angel Abbey, St. Benedict, Oreg., 1970-73; bd. dirs., com. chmn. Environ. Edn. Assn., Portland, 1978-85. Recipient Disting. Citizen award Environ. Edn. Assn., 1983; role model award area coun. Girl Scouts, 1994; Woman of Achievement award Inst. Profl. and Managerial Women, 1984; Woman of Distinction award Women in Arch., 1993, named Disting. Citizen Portland Hist. Landmarks Commn., 1988, fellowship in The Am. Inst. of Architects, 1978. Fellow AIA (pub. edn. com. 1970-80, chair 1972-73); mem. Women's Archtl. League (bd. dirs., com. chmn. 1980—), Fashion Group Internat. (facilitator 1983-84), Ednl. Futures Inc. (Western rep. 1978-83), Oreg. State Dept. Edn. (adv. bd. 1980-83). Republican. Presbyterian. Home: 6740 SW Canyon Ln # 1 Portland OR 97225-3606

WINTERS, BARBARA JO, musician; b. Salt Lake City; d. Louis McClain and Gwendolyn (Bradley) W. AB cum laude, UCLA, 1960, postgrad., 1961; postgrad., Yale, 1960. Mem. oboe sect. L.A. Philharm., 1961-94, prin. oboist, 1972-94; ret.; clinician oboe, English horn, Oboe d'amore. Recs. movie, TV sound tracks. Home: 3529 Coldwater Canyon Ave Studio City CA 91604-4060 Office: 135 N Grand Ave Los Angeles CA 90012-3013

WINTERS, RICHARD ALLEN, mineral economist; b. Butte, Mont., Feb. 19, 1963; s. Allen S. and Doris Ellen (Taylor) W.; m. Malinna J. Winters, June 30, 1994. BS in Fin., Econs., U. Mont., 1986; MS in Mineral Econs., Colo. Sch. Mines, 1990, postgrad. mineral econs. dept., 1991—. Office engr. Morrison Knudsen Engrs., Richland, Wash., 1986-88; project acct. Morrison Knudsen Engrs., Richland, 1987-88; ops. analyst Echo Bay Mines, Denver, 1989; instr. Colo. Sch. Mines, Golden, Colo., 1991-92; cons. Coors Brewing Co., Golden, 1991-92; sr. rsch. engr. Phelps Dodge Mining Co., Morenci, Ariz., 1992-94; gold analyst Robertson, Stephens and Co., San Francisco, 1994—. Pres. Mineral Econ. Grad. Student Assn., 1989-90. Mem. Soc. Mining, Metallurgy and Exploration, Assn. Environ. Resource Economists, Mineral, Econs. and Mgmt. Soc. Home: 184 12th Ave San Francisco CA 94118-1111 Office: Robertson Stephens & Co San Francisco CA 94104

WINTERS, RICHARD KEITH, social services administrator; b. Salt Lake City, Sept. 11, 1931; s. Elwood Grant and Elizabeth Louise (Bennett) W.; m. Mary Janet Nebeker, Dec. 22, 1953; children: Richard Jr., Steven, Katherine, Elizabeth, David, Sidney. Ann. BS in Polit. Sci., U. Utah, 1954. Credit mgr. Western Steel Co., Salt Lake City, 1956-61; exec. v.p. Bennetts, Salt Lake City, 1961-81; land developer Edge of Eden, Laketown, Utah, 1981-88; owner, mgr. Cedars & Shade Campground, St. Charles, Idaho, 1981—; exec. dir. Cmty. Svcs. Coun., Salt Lake City, 1988—. Mem. citizens adv. bd. Salt Lake Detention Ctr., 1987-93; bd. dirs. Bd. Juvenile Justice & Delinquency Prevention, Salt Lake City, 1990-92; bd. dirs., chmn. Utah Bd. Youth Correction, Salt Lake City, 1992—; With U.S. Army, 1954-56. Mem. Sons of Utah Pioneers (life). Republican. Mem. LDS Ch.

WINTER-SWITZ, CHERYL DONNA, travel company executive; b. Jacksonville, Fla., Dec. 6, 1947; d. Jacqueline Marie (Carroll) Winter; m. Frank C. Snedaker, June 24, 1974 (div. May 1976); m. Robert William Switz, July 1, 1981. AA, City Coll. of San Francisco, 1986; BS, Golden Gate U., 1990, MBA, 1992. Bookkeeper, agt. McQuade Tours, Ft. Lauderdale, Fla., 1967-69; mgr. Boca Raton (Fla.) Travel, 1969-76; owner, mgr. Ocean Travel, Boca Raton, 1976-79; ind. contractor Far Horizons Travel, Boca Raton, 1979-80; mgr. Tara/BPF Travel, San Francisco, 1981-84; mgr. travel. dept. Ernst & Whinney/Lifeco Travel, San Francisco, 1984-86; travel cons. Siemer & Hand Travel, San Francisco, 1989—; instr. Golden Gate U., 1986—, U. San Francisco. Mem. Amateur Trapshooting Assn., Hotel and Restaurant Mgmt. Club. Republican. Episcopalian. Home: 642 Brussels St San Francisco CA 94134-1902 Office: Siemer & Hand Travel 101 California St Ste 1750 San Francisco CA 94111-5862

WINTHROP, JOHN, real estate executive, lawyer; b. Salt Lake City, Apr. 20, 1947; m. Marilyn MacDonald, May 17, 1975; children: Grant Gordon, Clayton Hanford. AB cum laude, Yale U., 1969; JD magna cum laude, U. Tex., 1972. Bar: Calif. 1972. Law clk. 9th cir. U.S. Ct. Appeals, L.A., 1972-73; conseil juridique Coudert Freres, Paris, 1973-75; v.p. gen. counsel MacDonald Group, Ltd., L.A., 1976-82; pres., CEO MacDonald Mgmt. Corp. and MacDonald Group Ltd., L.A., 1982-86; pres., chief exec. officer MacDonald Corp. (gen. contractors), L.A., 1982-86; chmn., CEO Comstock Mgmt. Co., L.A., 1986—; pres., CEO Winthrop Investment Properties, Los Angeles, 1986—; bd. dirs. Plus Prods., Tiger's Milk Prods., Irvine, Calif., 1977-80. Bd. dirs., sec. L.A. Sheriff's Dept. Found.; bd. dirs. L.A. Opera. Mem. Calif. Bus. Properties Assn. (mem. bd. advisors 1981-87), Internat. Coun. Shopping Ctrs., Nat. Eagle Scout Assn. (life), French-Am. C. of C. (bd. dirs. 1982-87), Urban Land Inst., Nat. Realty Bd., Regency Club, Yale Club N.Y., Calif. Club, The Beach Club, Elizabethan Club. Republican. Office: Comstock Mgmt Co Penthouse 9460 Wilshire Blvd Beverly Hills CA 90212

WINTHROP, KENNETH RAY, insurance executive; b. N.Y.C., Dec. 29, 1950; s. Ralph and Lore (Bruck) W.; m. Sharon Swinnich, 1976 (div. 1978); m. Diane Louise Denney, June 27, 1981; children: Alyssa Louise, Matthew Lawrence, Andrew Lee. BA in English, SUNY, Buffalo, 1972. Agt. Northwestern Mut. Life Ins., Woodland Hills, Calif., 1975-78, Nat. Life of Vermont, L.A., 1978-93; mgr. Mass Mut., L.A., 1993—. Mem. Million Dollar Round Table. Democrat. Home: 7609 W 83rd St Playa Del Rey CA 90293-7979 Office: 3d Fl 4601 Wilshire Blvd Fl 3 Los Angeles CA 90010-3880

WINTHROP, LAWRENCE FREDRICK, lawyer; b. L.A., Apr. 18, 1952; s. Murray and Vauneta (Cardwell) W.; BA with honors, Whittier Coll., 1974; JD magna cum laude, Calif. Western Sch., 1977. Bar: Ariz. 1977, Calif. 1977, U.S. Dist. Ct. Ariz. 1977, U.S. Dist. Ct. (so. dist.) Calif. 1981, U.S. Ct. Appeals (9th cir.) 1981, U.S. Dist. Ct. (cen. dist.) Calif. 1983, U.S. Supreme Ct. 1983. Assoc. Snell and Wilmer, Phoenix, 1977-83, ptnr., 1984-93, Doyle, Winthrop, Oberbillig & West, P.C., Phoenix, 1993—. judge pro tem Maricopa County Superior Ct., 1987—, Ariz. Ct. Appeals, 1992—; lectr. Ariz. personal injury law and practice and state and local tax law Tax Exec. Inst., Nat. Bus. Inst., Profl. Edn. Systems, Inc., Ariz. Trial Lawyers Assn., Maricopa County Bar Assn.; chmn. bd. dirs. Valley of the Sun Sch., 1989—; mem. Vol. Lawyers Program, Phoenix, 1980—. Fellow Ariz. Bar Found., Maricopa Bar Found.; mem. ABA, Calif. Bar Assn., Ariz. Bar Assn., Ariz. Tax Rsch. Assn. (bd. dirs. 1989-93), Maricopa County Bar Assn., Ariz. Assn. Def. Counsel (bd. dirs., pres. 1988-89, chmn. med.-malpractice com. 1993—). Republican. Methodist. Clubs: Fairfield Flagstaff, LaMancha Racquet. Avocations: music, golf, tennis. Editor-in-chief Calif. Western Law Rev., 1976-77. Home: 6031 N 2nd St Phoenix AZ 85012-1210 Office: Doyle Winthrop Oberbillig & West PC PO Box 10417 2800 N Central Ave Ste 1550 Phoenix AZ 85016-4666

WINZELER, JUDITH KAY, foundation administrator; b. Canton, Ohio, Dec. 17, 1942; d. Charles and Pauline Doris (Werstler) Wenzlawski; m. Robert Lee Winzeler, Nov. 4, 1961; children: Elizabeth Ann, Alice Louise Winzeler Smith. BA, U. Nev., 1971, MA, 1981. Instr. anthropology Western Nev. C.C., Reno, 1976-77; program developer Nev. Humanities Com., Reno, 1977-78, asst. dir., 1978-80, assoc. dir., 1980-84, exec. dir., 1984—; panelist NEH, 1991; mem. Hilliard Found. Com., Reno, 1984—; mem. program com. Fedn. of State Humanities Couns., Washington, 1989; mem. selections com. Grace A. Griffen Chair in History, Reno, 1992. Mem. Nev. Commn. on Bicentennial of U.S. Constn., 1985-91; pres. Luth. Ch. of Good Shepherd, Reno, 1987-89; mem. nominating com. Evang. Luth. Ch. of Am., Sierra Synod, Oakland, Calif., 1991—; bd. dirs., officer Reno/Sparks Metro Min., Reno, 1987—; active Nev. Hist. Soc., Nev. State Mus., Nev. Mus. Art, Western Folklife Ctr., Friends of Washoe County Libr. Mem. Asian Pacific Assn. of No. Nev., Sierra Art Found., Reno Rotary Club, Nev. Corral, Westerners Internat. Home: 1579 Belford Rd Reno NV 89509-3907 Office: Nev Humanities Com 1034 N Sierra St Reno NV 89503-3721

WINZENRIED, JESSE DAVID, retired petroleum executive; b. Byron, Wyo., June 13, 1922; s. Fritz and Margaret Smith W.; m. Marion Suzan Jacobson, Mar. 15, 1945 (dec. 1984); children: Suzan Winzenried Carlston, Jay Albert, Keith Frederic; m. Lela Madsen, Mar. 12, 1988. B.S., U. Wyo., 1945; M.S., U. Denver, 1946; Ph.D., NYU, 1955. Dir. research Tax Found., N.Y.C., 1947-56; sr. v.p. Husky Oil Ltd., Cody, Wyo., 1956-65, Calgary, Alta., Can., 1965-67; v.p. firm Booz, Allen & Hamilton, Cleve., 1968-69; v.p. Coastal States Gas Corp., Houston, 1969-74; group v.p., dir. Crown Central Petroleum Corp., Balt., 1974-81; vice chmn., dir. Securities Investor Protection Corp., Washington, 1988—; lectr. mgmt. NYU, 1955-56. Contbr. articles to profl. jours. Served with US Air Corps, 1942-43. Republican. Mem. Ch. Jesus Christ of Latter-day Saints. Office: Securities Investor Protection Corp 805 15th St NW Ste 800 Washington DC 20005-2207

WIRAM, WAYNE CURTIS, interior designer; b. Washington, Apr. 29, 1942; s. Kenneth Charles and Margaret (Lois) W. Cert., Corcoran Art Sch., 1961; BFA, Richmond (Va.) Profl. Inst., 1965. Display mgr. W&J Sloane & Co., Washington, 1965-66; interior design dir. The Hecht Co., Washington, 1966-68; interior designer Ursells, Inc., Washington, 1968-70, C.S. Wo & Sons, Honolulu, 1970-73, Interior Systems, Honolulu, 1973-78; practice interior design Aiea, Hawaii, 1978—. Contbr. articles to newspapers and mags. Served with U.S. Army, 1966. Mem. Am. Soc. Interior Designers (cert., local offices including pres. 1986—). Republican. Home and Office: 99-524 Kahilinai Pl Aiea HI 96701-3535

WIRKKALA, JOHN LESTER, software company executive; b. Wadena, Minn., Sept. 25, 1947; s. Rueben Richard and Virginia Grace (Plank) W.; m. Connie Lee Cardarelle (div.); children: Scott, Todd; m. Lynn Diane Braund, Feb. 14, 1984; children: Scott, Seth, Shawn. AS in Electronic Tech., Brown Inst., 1982. Acct. La Maur Inc., Mpls., 1969-72, regional sales mgr., 1976-78; controller Nat. Beauty Supply, Mpls., 1972-76; store mgr. Schaak Electronics, Mpls., 1980-82; divsn. mgr. Mktg. Link, Denver, 1982-85; owner, operator Computer Systems Cons., Aurora, Colo., 1985-87; v.p. sales and mktg. Mgmt. Info. Support, Lakewood, Colo., 1987-89; sales mgr. Foothills Software Inc., Littleton, Colo., 1989-93; ops. mgr. Data Packaging Corp., Denver, 1993—. With U.S. Army, 1966-69, Vietnam. Mem. VFW (quartermaster post # 6331 1993-94). Home: 19682 E Purdue Cir Aurora CO 80013-4520 Office: Data Packaging Corp 2635 S Santa Fe Dr Denver CO 80223-4429

WIRSING, DALE ROBERT, journalist, educator; b. Tacoma, Nov. 7, 1936; s. Werner Ludwig and Hazel Edna (Robinson) W.; m. Karla Marchant, Sept. 8, 1958 (div. Sept. 1965); children: Karl Steven, Paul Mikel; m. Marlene Helen Nelson, Aug. 12, 1967; children: Eric Robert, Andrea Wirsing Lyon. BA with honors, U. Puget Sound, 1958; MA, Stanford U., 1959; PhD, Wash. State U., 1972. Reporter, bus. editor The News Tribune, Tacoma, 1959-65; reporter, drama critic Madison (Wis.) Capital Times, 1965-66; asst. city editor The New Tribune, Tacoma, 1966-67; pub. info. officer, instr. in journalism Tacoma C.C., 1967-72; dir. edn. and info. Metro. Devel. Coun., Tacoma, 1972-73; copy desk chief The News Tribune, Tacoma, 1974-82, news editor, 1983-84, sr. copy editor, 1984—; instr. English, journalism, sociology at area colls. Author: Builders, Brewers and Burghers: Germans of Washington State, 1977. Bd. dirs. Friends of Tacoma C.C. Libr., Tacoma German Lang. Sch., 1983-88; pres. U. Puget Sound Alumni Assn., Tacoma, 1975-76; scouter Boy Scouts Am., Tacoma, 1983-85. Recipient Russell Sage fellowship U. Wis., 1965-66, Friendship award Fed. Republic of Germany, 1981. Mem. Soc. Profl. Journalists, Phi Delta Kappa (Rainier chpt. pres. 1975-76). Lutheran. Home: 429 Harvard Ave Fircrest WA 98466-7306 Office: The News Tribune 1950 S State St Tacoma WA 98405-2817

WIRTHLIN, DAVID BITNER, hospital administrator; b. Salt Lake City, Sept. 19, 1935; s. Joseph L. and Madeline (Bitner) W.; m. Anne Goalen, Apr. 25, 1961; children: Kimberly, Jennifer, David, Deborah, John, Marianne. B.S. in Bus. Adminstrn. cum laude, U. Utah, 1960; M.H.A., U. Minn., 1963. Asst. adminstr. Idaho Falls (Idaho) Latter Day Saints Hosp., 1963-66; asst. to adminstr. Latter Day Saints Hosp., Salt Lake City, 1966-67; 1st asst. adminstr. Latter Day Saints Hosp., 1967-70, assoc. adminstr., 1970-73, adminstr., 1973-85; regional v.p. IHC Hosps., Inc., 1985—, Primary Children's Med. Ctr., 1973-75; v.p. cen. region Intermountain Health Care, Salt Lake City, 1984—; trustee Utah State Hosps.; mem. rev. com. Great Salt Lake Health Planning Agy., 1974; mem. Comprehensive Health Planning Rev. Com., 1975; chmn. Met. Hosp. Coun., 1975; mem. bd. Utah Profl. Rev., 1985-89; adv. com. Robert Wood Johnson Found.'s Hosp.-based Rural Health Care Program. Active with Mission for the LDS Ch., 1989-92, exec. dir. Inc Fund Devel., 1992—, exec. dir. LDS desert Hosp. found., 1992. Fellow Am. Coll. Hosp. Adminstrs. (regent, editoral bd. 1989, Gold Com. Mem. award 1989); mem. Am. Hosp. Assn., Utah Hosp. Assn. (past pres.), Western Assn. Hosps. (del. from Utah Hosp. Assn.), Coun. Teaching Hosps., Rotary, Timpanogos Club, Bonneville Knife and Fork Club. Republican. Mormon. Home: 2757 St Marys Way Salt Lake City UT 84108-2071 Office: Intermountain Health Care 36 S State St Ste 2200 Salt Lake City UT 84111

WIRTZ, DAVID REINER, enologist; b. Hillsboro, Oreg., May 22, 1952; s. Reiner Shogren and Mary Ellen (Greip) W.; m. Mary Lois Wirtz, Oct. 28, 1978; 1 child, Thatcher. BS, Portland State U., 1976. Cellar master Coury Vineyards, Forest Grove, Oreg., 1971-77; wine maker Rueter Hill Vineyards, Forest Grove, 1977-80; instr. Clackamas Coll., Oregon City, 1980-84; wine grower Writz Vineyards, Forest Grove, 1966—; cons. Oreg. Wine Industry, 1980—; mem. adv. bd. Viticulture and Winemaking, Clackamas Coll., Oregon City, 1980-84. Author: Wheels of Time, 1992. Mem. Am. Soc. Enologists, Sons and Daus. of Oreg. Pioneers, Am. Truck Hist. Soc. (historian 1988-93), Pacific N.W. Truck Mus., Antique Truck Club of Am., N.W. Car Collectors, Oreg. Winegrowers Assn. Home: 49690 NW Hillside Rd Forest Grove OR 97116-7631

WISE, HELENA SUNNY, lawyer; b. Ridgecrest, Calif., Dec. 3, 1954; d. Strother Eldon and Mary Helen (Harinek) W.; children: Marie Evelyn, Shawnie Helene. BA with honors, UCLA, 1976; JD with highest honors, Loyola Marymount U., 1979. Bar: Calif. 1979, U.S. Dist. Ct. (ctrl. dist.) Calif. 1980, U.S. Ct. Appeals (9th cir.) 1980, Nev. 1992, Ariz. 1992. Ptnr. Geffner & Satzman, Los Angeles, 1980-87; pvt. practice Burbank, Calif., 1987—. Columnist Los Angeles Lawyer mag., 1985-86. Chmn., founder Barristers Child Abuse Com., L.A., 1982-86; mem. exec. bd. Vols. in Parole, L.A., 1983-90; mem. Dem. Chair's Circle, L.A., 1985; mem. adv. bd. Over Easy Found., 1987—; vol. Love is Feeding Everyone. Fellow ABA (exec. coun. labor and employment law 1986-89, liaison young lawyers sect., bd. dirs. young lawyers divsn. 1986-88, mem. MSN team Nat. Com. on Child Abuse, del., teller Ho. of Dels. 1978-79), L.A. County Bar Assn. (v.p. sr. bar 1984-86, pres. young lawyers sect.), State Bar Calif. (bd. dirs. Calif. Young Lawyers Assn., labor law ad hoc com. on wrongful discharge, mem. juv. law com., UCLA alumni rep., USAC 1992-94, student rels. com. 1992-94), Am. Legion Women's Auz. Office: 1100 N Hollywood Way Ste A Burbank CA 91505-2527

WISE, JANET ANN, college official; b. Detroit, Aug. 8, 1953; d. Donald Price and Phyllis (Licht) W.; m. Peter Anthony Eisenklam, Oct. 16, 1976 (div. Aug. 1982); m. Edward Henry Moreno, Mar. 31, 1984; 1 child, Talia. Student, U. N.Mex., 1971-73; BA in English, Coll. of Santa Fe, 1989. Editorial asst., writer The New Mexican, Santa Fe, 1975-77; press asst., press sec. Office of Gov. N.Mex., Santa Fe, 1979-82; dir. pub. relations City of Santa Fe, 1983-84, Coll. of Santa Fe, 1984—. Bd. dirs. Santa Fe Bus. Bur., 1984-87, Santa Fe Girl's Club, 1986-89. Recipient Exemplary Performance award Office Gov. of N.Mex., Santa Fe., 1981, Outstanding Service award United Way of Santa Fe, 1982. Mem. PRSA, N.Mex. Press Women, Santa Fe Media Assn. (pres. 1989-91), Infolink (bd. dirs.). Democrat. Unitarian. Home: 7 Conchas Ct Santa Fe NM 87505-8803 Office: Coll of Santa Fe 1600 Saint Michaels Dr Santa Fe NM 87505-7615

WISE, RALPH EDMUND, electronic engineer; b. San Diego, June 27, 1951; s. Alfred Edmund and Gladys Marie (Smith) W. AS, San Diego City Coll., 1971. Electronic technician CIR, El Cajon, Calif., 1976-78; electronic engr. Cubic Comms., Oceanside, Calif., 1978-90, San Diego, 1990—. With USAF, 1971-76. Office: Cubic Communications 4285 Ponderosa Ave San Diego CA 92123-1525

WISE, WOODROW WILSON, JR., small business owner; b. Alexandria, Va., Mar. 9, 1938; s. Woodrow Wilson Sr. and Helen (Peverill) W.; m. Barbara Jean Hatton, Oct. 6, 1956 (div. 1975); m. Sandra Kay Habitz, Dec. 17, 1983; children: Anthony P., Laura J. Gen. mgr. Alexandria (Va.) Amusement Corp., 1956-73; curator Harold Lloyd Estate, Beverly Hills, Calif., 1973-75; pres. Discount Video Tapes, Inc., Burbank, Calif., 1975—. Office: Discount Video Tapes Inc PO Box 7122 833 "A" N Hollywood Way Burbank CA 91510

WISEHEART, TESS, social services administrator; b. Grand Rapids, Mich., Mar. 5, 1944; d. Lou Nelson and Evelyn Ruby (Fuson) Zeek; children: John Brown, Anthony Brown, Carole Peterson, Andrew Peterson. AA, Grand Rapids Jr. Coll., 1964; BA, Olivet Coll., 1966; MA, Ea. Mich. U., 1973. H.S. English tchr. Huron Valley Schs., Milford, Mich., 1967-71; adult H.S. tchr. Grand Rapids Pub. Schs., 1973-79, curriculum developer, 1977-80; English tchr. Ctrl. H.S., Grand Rapids, 1984-86, Ottawa Hills H.S., Grand Rapids, 1985-86; exec. dir. Portland (Oreg.) Women's Crisis Line, 1988—; cons. women's studies Portland State U., 1987-89; cons. Internat. Women's Day, Portland, 1987-90. Author: Government Access Packet, 1988, English for Adults Only, 1988, Women's History/Women's Choice, 1989. Coord. Mich. Women's Music Festival, Walhalla, 1975-95; mem. adv. bd. Waverly Children's Home, Portland, 1993—; spkr. in field, 1988—. Office: Portland Women's Crisis Line PO Box 97242 Portland OR 97242

WISELEY, RICHARD EUGENE, securities corporation executive; b. Tulsa, Oct. 20, 1945; s. Jess Porter and Gussie (Wright) W.; m. March McCoy, May 29, 1965; children: Jessica, March Elizabeth, Katherine. B.S. in Econs., U. Tulsa, 1970. Stock broker Bache & Co., Tulsa, 1972-75; resident mgr. Bache, Halsey, Stuart, Shields, Inc., Ft. Worth, 1975-78; regional dir., sr. v.p. Prudential-Bache Securities Inc., Ft. Lauderdale, Fla., 1978-84; with Oppenheimer & Co. Inc., N.Y.C., 1984—; gen. ptnr. Oppenheimer & Co. Inc., 1985—. Author book on recruiting, 1975. Mem. Securities Industry Assn., Nat. Assn. Security Dealers. Republican. Presbyterian. Club: Safari Club Internat. (pres. Carolinas). Office: Oppenheimer & Co Inc 10880 Wilshire Blvd Los Angeles CA 90024-4101

WISEMAN, JAY DONALD, photographer, mechanical designer and contractor; b. Salt Lake City, Dec. 23, 1952; s. Donald Thomas and Reva (Stewart) W.; m. Barbara Helen Taylor, June 25, 1977; children: Jill Reva, Steve Jay. Ed. Utah State U., Logan, U. Utah. Cert. profl. photographer. Pvt. practice photography; owner, pres. JB&W Corp. Recipient Grand prize Utah State Fair, 1986, Kodak Crystal for Photographic Excellence, 1986, 87, Master of Photography degree, 1989, Best of Show award, 1991-92; Profl. Photographer Mag. cover photo, 1988; numerous photos inducted for permanent collection Internat. Photographic Hall of Fame, 1989; photo named one of World's Greatest, Kodak, 1987-88; 2 photos named among World's Best, Walt Disney World and Profl. Phototgraphers Assn., 1988, 2 prints tied for Best of Show award RMPPA Regional contest, 1991; recipient Gold Medallion award Best in Show (world wide). Mem. Profl. Photographers Assn. Am. (one of top 10 scores internat. photo contest), Rocky Mountain Profl. Photographers (Best of Show, highest score ever 1987, Master Photographer of Yr. 1991, Ct. of Honour 1981-91), Intermountain Profl. Photographers Assn. (Master's Trophy Best of Show 1982, 86, 88, Photographer of Yr. award 1986, Ct. of Honour 1981-91), Photographers Soc. Am (Best of Show award Utah chpt. 1986). Latter Day Saints. Represented in Salt Lake City Internat. Airport permanent photo exhibit, various traveling loan collections, U.S. and Europe, 1988, loan collection Epcot Ctr., 1988-91; photographs published numerous profl. jours.

WISENER, MAUREEN MAYDEN, public relations, marketing executive; b. Hialeah, Fla., Apr. 17, 1961; d. Harry and Joyce Adele (Christensen) Mayden; m. Charles (Chuck) Richard Wisener, June 3, 1984; 1 child, Jeffrey Stewart. BA, So. Coll. Seventh Day Adventists, 1984. Pub. rels. asst. Park Ridge Hosp., Fletcher, N.C., 1984-86; pers. receptionist Fla. Hosp., Orlando, 1986-87; mktg. asst. San Joaquin Cmty. Hosp., Bakersfield, Calif., 1987-89; assoc. dir. mktg., comms. Paradise Valley Hosp., San Diego, 1989—. Contbr. articles to Adventist Review. Mem. Internat. Assn. Bus. Communicators (newsletter editor, 1990-91, v.p. San Diego chpt. 1991-92), Am. Mktg. Assn., Am. Soc. Health Care Mktg. and Pub. Rels., Acad. for Health Svcs. Mktg. Republican. Office: Paradise Valley Hosp 2400 E 4th St National City CA 91950-2026

WISHEK, MICHAEL BRADLEY, lawyer; b. Pasadena, Calif., June 25, 1959; s. Homer Cedric and Donna Jean (Arnold) W.; m. Shari Patrice Rubin, June 7, 1981 (div. Feb. 1986); m. Dorothea Jean Palo, Feb. 12, 1988; children: Kirstin Alyce, Lauren Ashley. BS in Polit. Sci and Philosophy, Claremont Men's Coll., 1981; JD, U. Calif., Davis, 1985. Bar: Calif. 1986, U.S. Dist. Ct. (ea. dist.) Calif. 1986. Assoc. Michael S. Sands, Inc., Sacramento, 1986-91; ptnr. Rothschild & Wishek, Sacramento, 1991—; mem. Anthony M. Kennedy Am. Inn of Ct., 1989-91, Milton L. Schwartz Am. Inn of Ct., 1992—. Mem. ABA, Calif. Bar Assn., Sacramento County Bar Assn. (co-chmn. criminal law sect. 1988-90), Calif. Attys. for Criminal Justice, Criminal Def. Lawyers of Sacramento (bd. dirs. 1993—, treas. 1994—). Democrat. Office: 901 F St Ste 200 Sacramento CA 95814-0715

WISHNER, STANLEY HERMAN, cardiologist; b. Czernovitz, Romania, June 25, 1939; came to U.S., 1948; BA cum laude, Franklin & Marshall Coll., 1961; MD cum laude, Harvard U., 1965. Diplomate Am. Bd. Internal Medicine, Am. Bd. Cardiovascular. Instr. medicine Harvard Med. Sch., Boston, 1967-70; dir. coronary care U. So. Calif./Good Samaritan Hosp., L.A., 1972-80; co-dir. cardiology dept. Good Samaritan Hosp., L.A., 1980-84; clin. prof. medicine U. So. Calif. Found., L.A., 1982—; pvt. practice L.A., 1984—. Contbr. articles to profl. jours. Maj. USAF, 1970-72. Fellow Am. Coll. Cardiology, Coun. of Am. Heart Assn. Office: 1245 Wilshire Blvd Ste 707 Los Angeles CA 90017-4807

WISKOWSKI, EUGENE, health facility administrator. CFO Eisenhower Med. Ctr., Rancho Mirage, Calif. Office: Eisenhower Med Ctr 39000 Bob Hope Dr Rancho Mirage CA 92270-3221

WISMER, PATRICIA ANN, secondary education educator; b. York, Pa., Mar. 23, 1936; d. John Bernhardt and Frances Elizabeth Loreen Marie (Fry) Feiser; m. Lawrence Howard Wismer, Aug. 4, 1961. BA in English, Mt. Holyoke Coll., 1958; MA in Speech/Drama, U. Wis., 1960; postgrad., U. Oreg., 1962, Calif. State U., Chico, 1963-64, U. So. Calif., 1973-74. Tchr., co-dir. drama program William Penn Sr. High Sch., York, 1960-61; instr. English, dir. drama York Jr. Coll., 1961-62; assoc. church editor San Francisco Examiner, 1962-63; reporter, publicist News Bur. Calif. State U., Chico, 1963-64; chmn. English Dept. Chico Sr. H.S., 1964—; mentor tchr. Chico Sr. High Sch., Chico Unified Sch. Dist., 1983-93; judge writing awards Nat. Coun. Tchr. English, 1970—; cons. No. Calif. Writing Project, 1977—. Mem. Educators for Social Responsibility, Calif. Assn. for Gifted, Upper Calif. Coun. Tchrs. English (bd. dirs. 1966-85, pres. 1970-71), Calif. Assn. Tchrs. English, Nat. Coun. Tchrs. English, NEA, Calif. Tchrs. Assn., Chico Unified Tchrs. Assn. Democrat. Lutheran. Home: 623 Arcadian Ave Chico CA 95926-4504 Office: Chico Sr High Sch 901 Esplanade Chico CA 95926-3908

WISNER, LINDA ANN, advertising agency executive, publishing company executive, interior designer; b. Sidney, N.Y., Apr. 28, 1951; d. Herbert and Ruth W. B.A. in Theatre and Art, Macalester Coll., 1973, postgrad. in journalism, 1974; postgrad. in graphic design Mpls. Coll. Art and Design, 1973-74; postgrad. in advtg. and mktg. U. Minn., 1974. Designer, publs.

asst. Macalester Coll., St. Paul, 1973-76; designer Stretch & Sew Inc., Eugene, Oreg., 1976-78; free-lance designer, Eugene, 1978-79; owner, creative dir. Wisner Assocs., Eugene, 1979-87, Portland, 1987—, Interludes, Eugene, 1981—; ptnr. Instant Interiors, Eugene, 1979-88; design dir. Palmer/Pletsch Assocs., 1988—, v.p., 1992—; chmn. Bus. Images Exhibit, Eugene, 1983. Author: Creative Serging for the Home, 1991 (Best Sewing Book award 1991); designer/author, editor booklet series: Instant Interiors, 1979-83 (Woodie award 1980-83); designer, illustrator: Palmer/Pletsch Sewing Books, 1981—. Ambassador, City of Eugene, 1985-87; bd. dirs. Maude Kerns Art Ctr., Eugene, 1984-85, Oreg. Repertory Theatre, 1986-87, Oreg. Sales and Mktg. Exec., 1986, Lloyd Dist. Transportation Mgmt. Assn.; bd. dirs Portland Culinary Alliance, 1989—, pres., 1992-93. Nat. Merit scholar Macalester Coll., 1969. Mem. Designers' Forum (pres. 1983-84, Designer of Yr. 1983), Sales and Mktg. Execs., Graphic Artists Guild, Exec. Bus. Women (pres. 1983-84), Mid Oreg. Ad Club (numerous certs. and trophy 1980-85), Eugene C. of C. (M.V.P. Leadership Program award 1986), Sullivan's Gulch Neighborhood Assn. (chairperson land use planning com., 1993—, bd. dirs 1990—). Avocations: design, illustration, soft sculpture, event planning, catering.

WISNIEWSKI, STEPHEN ADAM, professional football player; b. Rutland, Vt., Apr. 7, 1967. Student, Pa. State U. Offensive guard L.A. Raiders, 1989—. Named All-Pro Team Guard by Sporting News, 1990-93, Coll. All-Am. Team, 1987, 88. Office: L A Raiders 332 Center St El Segundo CA 90245-4047*

WISNOSKY, JOHN G., artist, educator; b. Springfield, Ill., Mar. 21, 1940; s. August Peter and Ann Alice (Tisckos) W.; m. Merium Norma Corl, June 22, 1966; 1 child, Merium Evelyn. BFA, U. Ill., 1962, MFA, 1964. Instr. Va. Poly. Inst., Blacksburg, Va., 1964-66; chmn. art dept. U. Hawaii, Honolulu, 1976-85; acting chmn. George Mason U., Fairfax, Va., 1987-88; prof. U. Hawaii, Honolulu, 1966—, chmn. grad. field in art, 1990-93. Co-designer: (permanent exhbn.) Onizuka Ctr. for Internat. Astronomy, 1985; numerous one man shows; represented in permanent collections The Honolulu Acad. of Art, The Contemporary Arts Ctr. Hawaii, Bank of Hawaii and numerous private collections. Recipient Purchase award State Found. on Culture and the Arts, 1990, Dept. of Edn. Hawaii, 1990, Commns. award Toyota Corp., Beta West, Inc., 1992. Office: U Hawaii Dept Art 2535 The Mall Honolulu HI 96822-2233

WITEMEYER, HUGH HAZEN, English language educator; b. Flint, Mich., June 10, 1939; s. Benton Diehl and Dorothy June (Hazen) W.; m. Sharon Kay Bristol Dec. 28, 1967 (div. Sept. 1980); 1 child, Hazen Allison; m. Barbara Ellen Watkins, Aug. 21, 1987. BA, U. Mich., 1961, Oxford U., 1963; PhD, Princeton U., 1966. Asst. prof. English U. Calif., Berkeley, 1966-73; assoc. prof. English U. N.Mex., Albuquerque, 1973-79, prof. English, 1979—; bd. govs. N.Mex. D.H. Lawrence Festival, Santa Fe, 1979-80; selection com. Marshall Scholarships, San Francisco, 1977-80. Author: Poetry of Ezra Pound 1908-1920, 1969, George Eliot and the Visual Arts, 1979; editor: William Carlos Williams and James Laughlin: Selected Letters, 1989; co-editor: W.B. Yeats, Letters to the New Island, 1989; mem. editorial bd. George Eliot/George Henry Lewes Rev., 1992—. Fulbright fellow, 1984, 89, NEH fellow, 1977, ACLS fellow, 1971-72. Mem. AAUP (pres. campus chpt. 1995—), MLA, PEN N.Mex., George Eliot Fellowship, Ezra Pound Soc. (pres. 1972—), Soc. for Textual Scholarship. Office: Dept English U NMex Albuquerque NM 87131

WITHERELL, ELIZABETH HALL, scholarly editor; b. Columbus, Ohio, Aug. 15, 1948; d. Donivan Lester and Elizabeth Jane (Mason) Hall; m. Michael Stewart Witherell, Dec. 27, 1969. BA, U. Mich., 1969; MA, U. Wis., 1972, PhD, 1979. Editor writings of Henry David Thoreau Princeton (N.J.) U., 1975-80, editor-in-chief writings of Henry David Thoreau, 1980-83; editor-in-chief writings of Henry David Thoreau U. Calif., Santa Barbara, 1983—; bd. dirs. Mark Twain Project, Berkeley; mem. adv. bd. Am.: History and Life, Santa Barbara, 1991-93, 93-95. Editor: Henry David Thoreau, A Week on the Concord and Merrimack Rivers, 1980, Henry David Thoreau, Journal 1:1837-44, 1981. NEH grantee, 1980-87, 89-95, summer stipend, 1988. Mem. MLA (mem. com. on scholarly edits. 1981-85, 93—), ALA, Thoreau Soc. (bd. dirs. 1993—), Assn. Documentary Editing (pres. 1992-93), Soc. Am. Archivists. Office: Univ Calif Davidson Libr Santa Barbara CA 93106-9010

WITHERS, HUBERT RODNEY, radiotherapist, radiobiologist, educator; b. Queensland, Australia, Sept. 21, 1932; came to the U.S., 1966; s. Hubert and Gertrude Ethel (Tremayne) W.; m. Janet Macfie, Oct. 9, 1959; 1 child, Genevieve. MBBS, U. Queensland, Brisbane, Australia, 1956; PhD, U. London, 1965, DSc, 1982. Bd. cert. Ednl. Coun. for Fgn. Med. Grads. Intern Royal Brisbane (Australia) and Associated Hosps., 1957; resident in radiotherapy and pathology Queensland Radium Inst. and Royal Brisbane (Australia) Hosp., 1958-63; Univ. Queensland Gaggin fellow Gray Lab., Mt. Vernon Hosp., Northwood, Middlesex, Eng., 1963-65, Royal Brisbane (Australia) Hosp., 1966; radiotherapist Prince of Wales Hosp., Randwick, Sydney, Australia, 1966; vis. rsch. scientist Lab. Physiology, Nat. Cancer Inst., Bethesda, Md., 1966-68; assoc. prof. radiotherapy sect. exptl. radiotherapy U. Tex. Sys. Cancer Ctr. M.D. Anderson Hsop. & Tumor Inst., Houston, 1968-71, prof. radiotherapy, chief sect. sect. exptl. radiotherapy, 1971-80; prof. dir. exptl. radiation oncology dept. radiation oncology UCLA, 1980-89, prof., vice-chair dir. exptl. radiation oncology dept. radiation oncology, 1991—, Am. Cancer Soc. Clin. Rsch. prof. dept. radiation oncology, 1992—, interim dir. Jonsson Comprehensive Cancer Ctr., chmn. radiation oncology, 1994—; assoc. grad. faculty U. Tex., Grad. Sch. Biomed. Scis., Houston, 1969-73, mem. grad. faculty, 1973-80; prof. dept. radiotherapy Med. Sch., U. Tex. Health Sci. Ctr., Houston, U. Tex. Med. Sch., Houston, 1975-80; prof., dir. Inst. Oncology, The Prince of Wales Hosp., U. NSW, Sydney, Australia, 1989-91; mem. com. mortality mil. pers. present at atmosphere tests of nuclear weapons Inst. Medicine, 1993-94; mem. radiation effects rsch. bd. NRC, 1993—; mem. com. neutron dose reporting Internat. Commn. Radiation Units and Measurements, 1982—, mem. report com. clin. dosimetry for neutrons, 1993—; mem. task force non-stochastic effects radiation Internat. Com. Radiation Protection, 1980-84, mem. com. 1, 1993—; mem. radiobiology com. Radiation Therapy Oncology Group, 1979—, mem. dose-time com., 1980—, mem. gastroenterology com., 1982—; mem. edn. bd. Royal Australian Coll. Radiology, 1989-91; mem. cancer rsch. coord. com. U. Calif., 1991—, mem. standing curriculum com. UCLA biomed. physics grad. program, 1983-84; cons. exptl. radiotherapy U. Tex. System Cancer Ctr., 1980—. Mem. Am. editorial bd.: Internat. Jour. Radiat. Oncol. Biol. Phys., 1982-89, 91—, internat. editorial bd., 1989-91; cons. editor: The European Jour. Cancer, 1990—; editorial bd. dirs.: Endocurietherapy/Hyperthermia Oncology, 1991—, Radiation Oncology Investigations, 1992—; assoc. editor: Cancer Rsch., 1993-94. Mem. Kettering selection com. Gen. Motors Cancer Rsch. Found., 1988-89, chmn., 1989, awards assembly, 1990-94. Recipient Medicine prize Polish Acad. Sci., 1989, Second H.S. Kaplan Disting. Scientist award Internat. Assn. for Radiation Rsch., 1991, Gray medal Internat. Commn. Radiation Units, 1995; named Gilbert H. Fletcher lectr. U. Tex. Sys. Cancer Ctr., 1989, Clifford Ash lectr. Ont. Cancer Inst., Princess Margaret Hosp., 1987, Erskine lectr. Radiol. Soc. N.Am., 1988, Ruvelson lectr. U. Minn., 1988, Milford Schultz lectr. Mass. Gen. Hosp., 1989, Del Regato Found. lectr. Hahnemann U., 1990, Bruce Cain Meml. lectr. New Zealand Soc. Oncology, 1990, others. Fellow Royal Australasian Coll. Radiologists (bd. cert.), Am. Coll. Radiology (bd. cert. therapeutic radiology, adv. com. patterns of care study 1988—, radiation oncology advisory group 1993—, others), Am. Radium Soc. (membership and credentials com. 1986-89, 93-94, treas. 1993—, others), Am. Soc. Therapeutic Radiology and Oncology (awards com. 1993, publs. com. 1993, keynote address 1990, Gold medal 1991, others); mem. Nat. Cancer Inst. (various ad-hoc rev. coms. 1970—, radiation study sect. 1971-75, cons. U.S.-Japan Coop. Study High LET Radiotherapy 1975-77, cancer rsch. emphasis grant rev. com. 1976, clin. cancer-79, toxicology working group 1977-78, reviewer outstanding investigator grants 1984—, bd. sci. counselors 1986-88), Nat. Cancer Inst. Can. (adv. com. rsch. 1992—), Pacific N.W. Radiol. Soc. (hon.), Tex. Radiol. Soc. (hon.), So. Calif. Radiation Oncology Soc. (sec., treas. 1992-94), European Soc. Therapeutic Radiology and Oncology (hon.), Polish Oncology Soc. (hon.), Austrian Radiation Oncology Soc. (hon.), Phila. Roentgen Ray Soc. (hon.), Radiation Rsch. Soc. (pres. 1982-83, honors and awards com. 1984-88, ad hoc com. funds utilization 1987-89, adv. com. Radiation Rsch. Jour., 1988—, Failla award 1988). Office: UCLA Med Ctr 10833 LeConte Ave Los Angeles CA 90095-1714

WITHERS, JAMES CLYDE, executive high technology company; b. Buna, Tex., Nov. 5, 1934; s. James W. and Vera I. (Owens) W.; m. Marilyn Johnson, Feb. 14, 1956 (div. 1968); children: Marc, Chris, Laura; m. Tiffany Heppich, Apr. 17, 1969. BS in Chemistry, Am. U., Washington, 1958; PhD in Chemistry, Clayton U., St. Louis, 1980. Chemist Melpar, Inc., Falls Church, Va., 1954-58; mgr. chem. sect. Am. Machine & Foundry, Inc., Alexandria, Va., 1958-62; v.p. Gen. Technologies Corp., Alexandria, 1962-67; pres. Gen. Technologies Corp., Reston, Va., 1967-72; chmn. bd. Deposites & Composites, Corp., Reston, 1972-76; pres. Pora, Inc., Berea, Ohio, 1976-81; mgr. materials Atlantic Richfield, Co., Tucson, 1981-85; chief exec. officer Keramont Research Corp., Tucson, 1986-88; CEO MER Corp., Tucson, 1988—; chmn. bd. Potomac Savs. & Loan, Reston, Va., 1970-76. Contbr. articles to profl. jours.; patentee in field. Republican. Episcopalian. Home: 7261 E Ventana Canyon Dr Tucson AZ 85715-0826 Office: MER Corp 7960 S Kolb Rd Tucson AZ 85706-9237

WITHERSPOON, GREGORY JAY, financial services company executive; b. Quantico, Va., Sept. 30, 1946; s. Thomas Sydenham and Dorothy M. (Jordan) W.; m. Judith A. Klein, Feb. 11, 1966 (dec. Oct. 1984); children: Lisa Marie, Michelle, Rene. BS, Calif. State U., Long Beach, 1970. CPA, Calif. Sr. acct. Peat, Marwick & Main, L.A., 1969-72; sr. mgr. Deloitte & Touche & Co., L.A., 1972-79; v.p. fin. Nanco Enterprises, Santa Barbara, Calif., 1979-84; pres. Pea Soup Andersen's, Buellton, Calif., 1984-86, VWB & P Cons., Santa Barbara, 1986-87; sr. v.p. fin. and adminstrn. Aames Fin. Svcs., L.A., 1987—; owner, founder Witherspoon Properties Ltd., L.A., 1976—; owner, mgr. Witherspoon Leasing, L.A., 1976—. Mem. Calif. Rep. Com., 1978—, Nat. Rep. Com., 1978—. Mem. AICPA, Calif. Inst. CPA's, Tennis Club, Ski Clubs. Office: Aames Fin Svcs 3731 Wilshire Blvd Fl 10 Los Angeles CA 90010-2830

WITKIN, JOEL-PETER, photographer; b. Bklyn., Sept. 13, 1939; s. Max and Mary (Pellegrino) W.; m. Cynthia Jean Bency, June 30, 1978; one child, Kersen Ahanu. B.F.A., Cooper Union, 1974; M.F.A., U. N.Mex., 1986; student (fellow), Columbia U., 1973-74. Exhibited in Projects Studio One, N.Y.C., 1980, Galerie Texbraun, Paris, 1982, Kansas Ctiy Art Inst., 1983, Stedelijk Mus., Amsterdam, 1983, Fraenkel Gallery, 1983-84, 87, 91, 93, 95, Pace/MacGill Gallery, N.Y.C., 1983, 84, 87, 89, 91, 93, 95, San Francisco Mus. Modern Art, 1985, Bklyn. Mus., 1986, Galerie Baudoin Lebon, Paris, 1987, 89, 91, 95, Centro de Arte Reina Sofia Mus., Madrid, 1988, Palais de Tokyo, Paris, 1989, Fahey/Klein Gallery, L.A., 1989, 92, 93, Mus. Modern Art, Haifa, Israel, 1991, Photo Picture Space Gallery, Osaka, Japan, 1993, Guggenheim Mus., N.Y.C., 1995, Interkamera, Prague, 1995; group shows: Mus. Moder Art, N.Y.C., 1959, San Francisco Mus. Moder Art, 1981, Whitney Biennial, 1985, Palais de Tokyo, Paris, 1986; represented in permanent collections, Mus. Modern Art, N.Y.C., San Francisco Mus. Modern Art, 1980, Nat. Gallery Art, Washington, Victoria and Albert Mus., London, George Eastman House, N.Y., The Getty Collection, Moder Museet, Stockholm, Sweden, Whitney Mus., N.Y.C., The Guggenheim Mus., N.Y.C.; represented by Pace/MacGill, N.Y.C., Fraenkel Gallery, San Francisco, Baudoin Lebon Gallery, Paris; sugject of monographs: Joel-Peter Witkin, 1985, 88, 89, 91, 93, 95; editor: Masterpeices of Medical Photography, 1987, Harms Way, 1994. Served with U.S. Army, 1961-64. Decorated Chevalier Des Arts et de Letters (France), 1990; recipient Disting. Alumni award The Cooper Union, 1986, Internat. Ctr. Photography award, 1988; Ford Found. grantee, 1977, 78, Nat. Endowment in Photography grantee, 1980, 81, 86, 92. Address: 1707 Five Points Rd SW Albuquerque NM 87105-3017

WITKIN, SUSAN BETH, broadcast journalist, reporter; b. Denver, June 10, 1959; d. Bernard Theodore and Sharon Elaine (Ginsberg) W. BA in Communications Arts, Fort Lewis Coll., 1982. Anchor, gen. assignment reporter Sta. KBCO-FM/KADE-AM, Boulder, Colo., 1982-83; asst. news dir. Sta. KSPN-FM/TV, Aspen, Colo., 1983-84, Sta. KIUP/KRSJ-FM, Durango, Colo., 1984-85; anchor, gen. assignment reporter Sta. KOA, Denver, 1985-90; anchor, reporter Sta. KGO ABC/Capital Cities, San Francisco, 1990-94. Producer, reporter series on st. gangs Nothing To Do, No Place To Go, 1986 (1st place gen. reporting category Soc. Profl. Jours., 2nd place feature category AP). Bd. dirs. Allied Jewish Fedn. Women's Div., Denver, 1987-89, March of Dimes, San Francisco, 1991—. Named one of Outstanding Young Women of Am., 1987; recipient 2d Pl. award Spl. Report Saudi Arabia AP, 1990, 1st Place award L.A. Riot Coverage, 1992, 1st Place award RTNDA, 1992. Mem. AFTRA, AP, Bus. Profl. Women's Orgn., Soc. Profl. Jours. Democrat. Office: Sta KGO 900 Front St San Francisco CA 94111-1427

WITT, DAVID L., curator, writer; b. Kansas City, Mo., Nov. 3, 1951; s. Lloyd Vernon and Dean W. B.S. in Polit. Sci., Kans. State U., 1974. Naturalist Naish Nature Ctr., Edwardsville, Kans., summers 1967-70; asst. curator Seton Mus., Cimarron, N.Mex., summers 1972-74; curatorial asst. Riley County Hist. Mus., Manhattan, Kans., 1973-74; mus. asst. Millicent Rogers Mus., Taos, N.Mex., 1976-77; curator The Gaspard House Mus., Taos, N.Mex., 1978-79, The Harwood Found., Taos; 1979—; Author: The Taos Artists, 1984, Taos Moderns: Art of the New, 1992 (Southwest Book award Border Regional Libr. Assn. 1993); contbr. articles to profl. jours. Organizer first N.Mex. Art History Conf., 1986; founder Southwest Art History Coun., 1990. Mem. PEN, Mountain-Plains Mus. Assn. (council mem. 1983-85), N.Mex. Assn. Mus. (pres. 1986-88). Democrat. Home: PO Box 317 Taos NM 87571-0317 Office: PO Box 4081 Taos NM 87571

WITT, ROBERT LOUIS, materials manufacturing and sales company executive, lawyer; b. Vallejo, Calif., Feb. 22, 1940; s. Charles Louis and Encie Lyndell (Bates) W.; m. Myrna Doreen Harvey; 1 child, Mark Louis. A.A., Solano Coll., 1959; student, Oreg. State U., 1959-61; J.D., San Francisco Law Sch., 1968. Sec., corp. counsel Hexcel Corp., San Francisco, 1969-76, v.p., sec., 1976-80, v.p. adminstrn., 1980-82, sr. v.p. internat., 1982-84, exec. v.p., 1984-85, pres., 1985—, CEO, 1986—, chmn. bd. dirs., 1986. Office: Hexcel Corp 11555 Dublin Blvd Dublin CA 94568-2854

WITTEN, MARK LEE, lung injury research scientist, educator; b. Amarillo, Tex., June 23, 1953; s. Gerald Lee and Polly Ann (Warren) W.; m. Christine Ann McKee, June 10, 1988; 1 child, Brandon Lee. BS in Phys. Sci., Emporia State U., 1975; PhD, Ind. U., 1983. Postdoctoral fellow U. Ariz., Tucson, 1983-88; instr. in medicine Harvard Med. Sch., Boston, Mass., 1988-90; rsch. assoc. prof. U. Ariz., Tucson, 1990—; grant cons. USAF, Washington, 1991—. Contbr. articles to profl. jours. Grantee USAF, 1991—, Tng. grant Dept. of Def., 1992—, NIH, 1991—, Upjohn Pharm., 1992, Dept. of Army, 1993. Mem. Am. Physiol. Soc., Soc. Critical Care Medicine, Am. Thoracic Soc., N.Y. Acad. Scis., Soc. Toxicology. Methodist. Office: U Ariz Dept Pediatrics AHSC 1501 N Campbell Ave Tucson AZ 85724

WITTENSTEIN, GEORGE JUERGEN, surgeon, educator; b. Tubingen, Germany, Apr. 26, 1919; s. Oskar Juergen and Elisabeth (Vollmoeller) W.; m. Elisabeth Hartert, Apr. 26, 1947 (dec. Jan. 1966); m. Christel J. Bejenke, July 1, 1966; children: E. Deirdre, Nemone E., W. Andreas, Catharina J. MD, U. Munich, 1944; MSc in Surgery, U. Colo., 1956, MD, 1956. Diplomate Am. Bd. Surgery and Thoracic Surgery. Instr. U. Colo. Sch. Medicine, Denver, 1953-60; instr., clin. asst., then prof. UCLA Sch. Medicine, 1964-73, prof. surgery, 1974-90, prof. surgery emeritus, 1990—; chmn. dept. surgery Olive View Med. Ctr., Sylmar, Calif., 1947-90; pvt. practice surgery Santa Barbara, Calif., 1989—; vis. prof. at various European med. sch., 1958—. Contbr. sci. articles to profl. publs. Bd. dirs. Friends of U. Calif.-Santa Barbara Libr., 1965-75; trustee Santa Barbara Mus. Art, 1968-75. Boettcher Found. scholar, 1955. Home: 4004 Cuervo Ave Santa Barbara CA 93110-2412 Office: 2410 Fletcher Ave Ste 204 Santa Barbara CA 93105-4828

WITTER, WENDELL WINSHIP, financial executive, retired; b. Berkeley, Calif., Oct. 16, 1910; s. George Franklin Jr. and Mary Ann (Carter) W.; m. Florence Corder, Oct. 18, 1935 (div. Oct. 1973); 1 child, Wendelyn; m. Janet Hutchinson Alexander, Dec. 12, 1973 (dec. 1977); m. Evelyn Grinter Harkins Gooding, Mar. 26, 1978. BA, U. Calif., Berkeley, 1932; Diploma, Investment Bankers Inst., Wharton Bus. Sch., 1955. Salesman Dean Witter & Co., San Francisco, 1933-50, ptnr., 1950-68, exec. v.p., 1968-76; cons. Dean Witter, Reynolds, Inc., San Francisco, 1976-82, retired cons., 1982—. Past Regent U. Calif., 1969-70; mem. Coordinating Coun. Higher Edn., Calif., 1970-71; trustee State Univs., Long Beach, Calif., 1971-79. Lt. col. Army Air Force, 1941-46. Mem. San Francisco Bond Club (pres. 1955), Assn. of Stock Exch. Firms (pres. 1962), Investment Bankers Assn. Am. (pres. 1965), U. Calif. Alumni Assn. (pres. 1969-70), Berkeley Fellows, Pacific Union Club, San Francisco Golf Club, Bohemian Club, Zeta Psi. Republican. Episcopalian. Home: 1400 Geary Blvd Apt 2109 San Francisco CA 94109-6572 Office: PO Box 7597 101 California St San Francisco CA 94120

WITTERS, ROBERT DALE, chemist educator; b. Cheyenne, Wyo., May 2, 1929; s. Alva Oscar and Vera Leona Witters; m. Brenda M. Marlow, Dec. 13, 1987. BA in Chemistry, U. Colo., 1951; PhD of Phys. Chemistry, Mont. State U., 1964. Chemist duPont, Parlin, N.J., 1951-53; asst. prof. SUNY, Plattsburgh, 1959-60, 61-62, Mont. State U., Bozeman, 1962-63; postdoctoral fellow Harvey Mudd Calif., Claremont, 1964-65; from asst. prof. to prof. Colo. Sch. Mines, Golden, 1965—. With U.S. Army, 1953-55. Recipient Outstanding Tchg. award Amoco Found., 1972-73, 76-77. Mem. Am. Chem. Soc., Am. Crystallographic Assn., Sigma Xi, Alpha Chi Sigma. Office: Colo Sch Mines Golden CO 80401

WITTICH, WILLIAM VINCENT, academic administrator, educator; b. N.Y.C., Jan. 17, 1941; s. Fred W. and Gertrude L. (Pildegard) W.; 1 child, Tami Lynn; m. Ann Argo, May 18, 1991. BA, Calif. State U., L.A., 1965; MA, Calif. State U., Long Beach, 1969; EdD, U. So. Calif., L.A., 1975. Tchr. Bellflower Unified Sch. Dist., Lakewood, Calif., 1963-66; prof. Calif. State U., Long Beach, 1967—, dept. chair, 1988—; cons. Del Mar Pubs., Albany, N.Y., 1987—, Glencoe McGraw Hill, Mission Hills, Calif., 1988—; reviewer Nat. Ctr. for Rsch., Berkeley, 1988—, U.S. Dept. Edn., Washington, 1989—. Recipient Orange award Advt. Fedn., 1986. Mem. Nat. Assn. Vocat. Leadership Devel. (pres. 1988-90), Internat. Tech. Edn. Assn., Nat. Photo Instrs. Assn. (pres. 1972-74), U. So. Calif. Alumni Assn. (pres. 1988-90). Home: 3932 N Cielo Pl Fullerton CA 92635-1102 Office: Calif State U 1250 N Bellflower Blvd Long Beach CA 90840-0006

WITTIG, ERLAND PAUL, research chemist; b. Fairbury, Ill., July 2, 1955; s. William M. and Isabelle F. (Nelson) W.; m. Pamela S. Schaefer, June 23, 1984 (div. Dec. 1994); children: Anne E., Katherine N. AB, Wartburg Coll., 1976; PhD in Analytical Chemistry, Ind. U., 1981. Rsch. chemist Chevron Rsch. Co., Richmond, Calif., 1981-88; sr. rsch. chemist Chevron Rsch. and Tech. Co. (formerly Chevron Rsch. Co.), Richmond, 1988-91; sr. chemist Chevron USA Products Co., El Segundo, Calif., 1991—; adj. prof. So. Oreg. State Coll., Ashland, 1988-91. V.p. Richmond Unified Edn. Fund, 1988-89, pres., 1989-90, bd. dirs., 1986-91, Young Human Resources Devel. Corp., Richmond, 1986-91. Mem. Soc. Applied Spectroscopy, Am. Chem. Soc. Office: Chevron USA Products Co Lab Divsn 324 W El Segundo Blvd El Segundo CA 90245-3641

WITTKOWER, ROBERT STEVEN, electronics executive; b. Atlanta, Feb. 26, 1951; s. Louis David Jr. and Pauline Catherine (King) W. BS in Chemistry, U. Tex., Arlington, 1976; MBA, No. Tex. State U., 1986; post-grad., Northwestern U., 1991. Cert. safety profl. Chemist Morton Salt Co., Grand Saline, Tex., 1976-78; safety sect. mgr. United Techs. Mostek, Carrollton, Tex., 1978-85; corp. dir. safety, health E-Systems, Inc., Dallas, 1985-88; mgr. environmental health and safety, western region Xerox Corp., El Segundo, Calif., 1988—; also pres. Bob Wittkower Cons.; Hazardous materials adv. to fire dept. City of Carrollton, Tex., 1979-85; spokesman Industry Task Force on Hazardous Materials, St. Petersburg, Fla., 1986; mem. oversight com. drug abuse prevention education for sch. children, State of Tex. Region X, 1987-88. Mem. Mayor's Task Force on Drug Abuse City of Garland, Tex., 1987, Calif. OSHA Standards Bd. subcom., 1990. Recipient Extraordinary Management Effectiveness award United Techs. Corp., 1983. Mem. Semicondr. Safety Assn. (life, bd. dirs. 1979-87, treas. 1983-86), Semicondr. Industry Assn. (occupational safety, health and environ. com.), Internat. Conf. Bldg. Officials, Nat. Fire Protection Assn., Beta Gamma Sigma.

WITTLER, SHIRLEY JOYCE, former state official, state commissioner; b. Ravenna, Nebr., Oct. 10, 1927; d. Earl William and Minnie Ethel (Frink) Wade; m. LeRoy F. Wittler, Dec. 31, 1946; children: Julie Diane, Barbara Liane. Student, U. Nebr., 1944-47. Real estate saleswoman Harrington Assocs., Lincoln, Nebr., 1965-69; real estate broker Tom Searl Realty, Inc., Cheyenne, Wyo., 1970-76; dep. state treas. Wyo., 1976-78; state treas., 1979-83; chmn. state tax commn. and bd. equalization State of Wyo., 1985-90; ret., 1990. Pres. LWV, Lincoln, 1965-69; bd. dirs. LWV Wyo., 1970-72; fin. chmn. Republican Central Com. Laramie County, Wyo., 1974-76; chmn. Laramie County Pres. Ford Com., 1976; Rep. precinct committeewoman, 1972-77; mem. Laramie County Library Bd., 1976, Community Devel. Adv. Bd., 1974-77. Mem. Cheyenne Bd. Realtors (pres. 1976, Cheyenne Realtor of Yr. 1974), Women's Civic League (treas. 1974, legis. chmn. 1975-76). Lutheran. Home: 5022 Hoy Rd Cheyenne WY 82009-4850

WITTY, JAMES H., journalist, consultant; b. Pasadena, Calif., Mar. 11, 1958; s. Henry Vincent and Edna Ruth (Doty) W.; m. Donell Jean Allen, Aug. 29, 1981; 1 child, Keven Vincent. BS in Journalism, Calif. Polytech. State U., San Luis Obispo, 1982. Reporter Corning (Calif.) Daily Observer, 1984-86; govt. reporter Vacaville (Calif.) Reporter, 1986-88; city editor The Hemet (Calif.) News, 1988-90; lifestyle editor Hawaii Tribune-Herald, Hilo, 1990-94; freelance writer, cons. Hilo, 1994—. Contbg. editor Bldg. Industry Mag., 1991; contbr. articles to profl. jours. Election observer LWV, Hilo, 1990, 92; mem. adv. bd. Wailoa Ctr., Hilo, 1993. Recipient Outstanding Feature Writing award Calif. Newspaper Pubs. Assn., Outstanding Column award Riverside County Press Club, Outstanding Column award Inland Empire Press Club, 1989, Outstanding Mag. Feature award Orange County Fair Best Reporters Contest, 1990. Mem. Big Island Press Club (pres. 1994). Home and Office: PO Box 5509 Hilo HI 96720-8509

WITTY, ROBERT MILTON, editor; b. Grove, Okla., May 15, 1930; s. Curt Edward and May Ellen (Thomas) W.; m. Judith Eshenfelder, Jan. 28, 1961; children: Elizabeth Ellen Scheibner, Stephen Curt. BA in journalism, U. Okla., 1952. Editor Holdenville (Okla.) Daily News, 1954-57; state editor Dallas (Tex.) Times Herald, 1957-61; reporter, columnist Evening Tribune, San Diego, 1961-73; editor, exec. v.p. San Diego Daily Transcript, 1973-81; deputy editor San Diego Tribune, 1981-92; assoc. editor San Diego Union-Tribune, 1992-93; editor, exec. v.p. Copley News Svc., San Diego, 1993—. Author: Marines of the Margarita, 1970. Capt. U.S. Army Res., 1952-54. Mem. Soc. Profl. Journalists (pres. 1975), San Diego Press Club (pres. 1976). Office: Copley New Svc PO Box 190 San Diego CA 92112-0190

WITWER, JEFFREY GARTH, marketing executive; b. Elkhart, Ind., July 18, 1944. BSME, Northwestern U., 1966; MSME, U. Calif., Berkeley, 1967, PhD in Mech. Engring., 1971; MBA, Golden Gate U., 1982. Registered profl. engr., Calif. Asst. prof. Sch. Aerospace, Mech. and Nuclear Engring. U. Okla., Norman, 1972-74; with SRI Internat., Menlo Park, Calif., 1974-78, 79-81; ASME Congl. fellow Com. on Interstate and Fgn. Commerce, U.S. Ho. of Reps., Washington, 1978-79; mktg. and mgmt. cons. Strategies Unltd., Mountain View, Calif., 1981-84; from mgr. bus. and mktg. devel. to dir. draftstation programs GE Calma, Milpitas, Calif., 1984-87; from mgr. MCAE major accounts/bus. devel. to dir. internat. mktg. Silicon Graphics, Mountain View, 1987-91; v.p. mktg. and bus. devel. Centric Engring. Systems, Palo Alto, Calif., 1991-93; v.p. internat. ops. Knowledge Revolution, San Mateo, Calif., 1994—. Bd. dirs. Jr. Achievement Santa Clara County. Recipient Ralph Teetor award Soc. Automotive Engrs., 1992; named Sports Car Club Am. Class Champion, 1991. Mem. ASME. Home: 27030 Elena Rd Los Altos CA 94022-3346 Office: Knowledge Revolution 66 Bovet Rd Ste 200 San Mateo CA 94402

WIZARD, BRIAN, publisher, author; b. Newburyport, Mass., June 24, 1949; s. Russell and Ruth (Hidden) Willard. BA, Sonoma (Calif.) State U., 1976. Pvt. practice as jeweler, sculptor and craftsman Calif., 1974-79; Wallowa, Oreg., 1991—; prin. The Starquill Pub., Port Douglas, Queensland, Australia, 1981-86; owner Starquill Internat., Wallowa, Oreg. Author: (novels) Permission to Kill, 1985, Shindara, 1987, Heaven on Earth, 1990, Coming of Age, 1990, Permission to Dive, 1992, Pollution IV, 1993, (short stories) Tropical Pair, 1986, Metempsychosis, 1988, (In Search Of) The Silver Lining, 1994, The Moon Whistling by on a Cloud, 1994, (The Princess of the) Wildflowers, 1995; contbt. to SpaceArc; prodr.: (video documentaries)

Thunderhawks, 1987, Swift Action Newsteam, Tope Creek Lookout, 1995; songwriter, prodr.: (cassette) Brian Wizard Sings for His Supper, 1989 (Cert. of Achievement Billboard 1993); songwriter, prodr., singer: (music videos) (I don't want) Permission to Kill, 1989, Busker Themes Song, Living in North Queensland, Circus Act, Hitch Hiking Man, Self-Portrait; songwriter: The Love We Share Will Never End, 1994. Renovator hist. landmark The Tope Creek Lookout (Skyship); sponsor Adopt A Hwy., 1995. With U.S. Army, 1967-70. Decorated Air medals (26), Aviator Flight Wings; recipient Cert. of Appreciation, Pres. Richard M. Nixon. Mem. Vietnam Helicopter Crewmember Assn., 145th Combat Aviation Bn. Assn., Vietnam Combat Vets. Assn., Vietnam Vets. Am., Vietnam Vets. Australia Assn. Office: PO Box 42 Wallowa OR 97885-0042

WLODARSKI, ROBERT JAMES, archaeologist; b. L.A., July 17, 1948; s. Matthew Bill and Henrietta Barbara (Rokita) W.; m. Linda Marie Porfilio, Oct. 19, 1974 (div. Aug. 14, 1985); m. Anne Walker Powell, Nov. 22, 1990. AA, Fullerton (Calif.) Jr. Coll., 1968; BA, Calif. State U., Northridge, 1971, 72, MA, 1975. Clk. Fullerton Jr. Coll. Bookstore, 1967-68; archaeol. asst. UCLA Archaeol. Survey, Westwood, Calif., 1973-74; staff archaeologist Calif. State U., Northridge, 1974-78; archaeol. asst. Greenwood & Assocs., Pacific Palisades, Calif., 1973-83; archaeol. project leader Calif. Dept. Transp., L.A., 1983-85; pres. H.E.A.R.T., Calabasas, Calif., 1978—, Mayan Moon Prodns., Calabasas, 1988—; tech. cons. Ironwood Prodns., L.A., 1985. Author: Out of Mind, 1989; author 6 screenplays: The Crawling Eye, Illusion, No Innocents, Shattered Secrets, Cool Change, Cities of Stone; contbr. articles to profl. jours. Author: Out of Mind, 1989; co-author 6 screenplays: The Crawling Eye, Illusion, No Innocents, Shattered Secrets, Cool Change, Cities of Stone; co-author: A Guide to the Haunted Queen Mary and Haunted Catalina; contbr. articles to profl. jours. Recipient Spl. Archaeol. Recognition, Candelaria Am. Indian Coun., Oxnard, 1988. Mem. Soc. Profl. Archaeologists, Calif. Com. for Promotion of History. Democrat. Roman Catholic. Home and Office: 5516 Las Virgenes Rd Calabasas CA 91302-1080

WNUCK, KENNETH L., software engineer; b. Yonkers, N.Y., July 6, 1957; s. Adolph Lloyd and Grace (Evjen) W. BS, SUNY, Stony Brook, 1979; MS, Poly. U. N.Y., 1985. Rsch. scientist Revlon Health Care Group, Tuckahoe, N.Y., 1979-81, CIBA-Geigy Corp., Ardsley, N.Y., 1981-85; tech. staff AT&T Bell Lab., Denver, 1985—; pres. KJ Custom Software; cons. in field. Contbr. articles to profl. jours. Mem. IEEE. Home: 11632 W 75th Cir Arvada CO 80005-5336 Office: AT&T Bell Labs 11900 Pecos St Denver CO 80234-2703

WODELL, GEOFFREY ROBERT, management consultant; b. Madison, Wis., June 15, 1949; s. Robert Holland and Juanita Jacqueline (Francisco) W.; m. Lynn Johnson, Aug. 2, 1975; 1 child, Haaland Johnson. BA, U. Wis., 1971; postgrad., Met. State U., 1987, U. Oslo, Norway, 1987, Loretto Heights U., 1987-88; MA, Webster U., 1990. Mgr. Contact Electronics, Madison, 1972-74; buyer, mgr. Cecil's Boot Ranch, Madison, 1974-76; salesman Miller Stockman div. Miller Internat., Denver, 1976-77, asst. mgr., 1977-78; mgr. Miller Internat., Inc., Denver, 1978-79; buyer Miller Internat., Inc., 1979-80, real estate exec., 1980-89; human resource devel. cons. Nyveg Cons., Lakewood, Colo., 1989—; dir. of training Colo. De Molay. Mem. Econ. Devel. and Revitalization Commn. of Wheat Ridge. Mem. Internat. Transactional Analysis Assn., Nat. Assn. Neuro-Linguistic Programmers, Sons of Norway (mgmt. trainer 1980—, pres. 6th dist. 1988, internat. dir. 1988—), Nordmanns Forbundet, Nat. Wildlife Fedn., World Wildlife Fedn., Better World Soc., Nature Conservancy, Eagles Soccer Club, Kicker Sports, Masons. Lutheran. Home: 3935 Garland St Wheat Ridge CO 80033-4210 Office: 6610 W 14th Ave Denver CO 80214-1999

WOELLMER, RALPH, hotel executive; b. White Plains, N.Y., Nov. 13, 1958; s. Helmut Erich and Christa (Hurrle) W.; m. Shelley Lynn Godown, July 1, 1989. BS, No. Ariz. U., 1984. Cert. hotel adminstr. Owner, operator Matterhorn Motor Lodge, Sedona, Ariz., 1980-85, 93—; v.p., gen. mgr. Best Western Inn of Sedona, 1994—; gen. mgr. Archbishops Mansion Inn, San Francisco, 1987-88, Kensington Park Hotel, San Francisco, 1988-90; v.p., gen. mgr. Bodega Bay (Calif.) Lodge, 1990-93.; v.p. Matterhorn Shoppes Inc., Sedona, 1984—. Bd. dirs. Sonoma County Conv. and Visitors Bur., Santa Rosa, 1992-94. Mem. Sedona Oak Creek Canyon C. of C. (bd. dirs. 1993—). Republican. Roman Catholic. Home: 230 Apple Ave Sedona AZ 86336-4806 Office: Matterhorn Motor Lodge 230 Apple Ave Sedona AZ 86336-4806

WOERNER, ROBERT LESTER, landscape architect; b. Rochester, N.Y., Jan. 31, 1925; s. William John and Loretta Bertha (Hettel) W.; m. Mary Jane Warn, May 12, 1952; children: Jane Marie, Anne Louise. B.S., SUNY Coll. Forestry, Syracuse, 1949. Cert. landscape architect, Wash., Idaho. Draftsman N.A., Rotunno Landscape Architects, Syracuse, 1947-49; landscape architect Park Dist., Plan Commn., Yakima, Wash., 1949-50; asst. supt. parks Spokane Park Dept., Spokane, Wash., 1950-56; dir. Denver Bot. Gardens, 1956-58; pvt. practice landscape architect Spokane, 1959—; chmn. bd. registration Landscape Architects State of Wash., 1976-78; pres. Council Landscape Archtl. Registration Bds., 1978-79. Mem. Zoning Bd. Adjustment, Spokane, 1983; mem. Urban Design Com., 1983; mem. Capitol Campus Design Adv. Com., 1982-94. Cpl. U.S. Army, 1943-45, ETO. Recipient Indsl. Landscaping Award Am. Assn. Nurserymen, Lincoln Bldg., Spokane, 1966; recipient Cert. of Merit Wash. Water Power, 1967, State Indsl. Landscaping award Wash State Nurserymen's Assn., Wash. Water Power, 1968. Fellow Am. Soc. Landscape Architects (pres. 1979-80, Disting. Svc. award 1976). Republican. Roman Catholic. Lodge: Kiwanis.

WOESSNER, FREDERICK T., composer, pianist; b. Teaneck, N.J., July 23, 1935; s. Fred and Bertha W.; m. Lise, Feb. 14, 1960 (div. 1973); children: Betty, Allison. Student, Peabody Conservatory of Music, Balt., 1960-61; MBA, NYU, 1968; MA, Calif. State U., Los Angeles, 1975; pvt. study with, David Diamond, Charles Haubiel, Albert Harris. Owner Al-Fre-Bett Music, Los Angeles, 1980—. Composer (for orch.) Nursery Song, Variations on an Irish Air, Reflections for Strings, Fanfare for Winds, String Quartet, Concerto for piano improvisations and orch., Secret Gospels (Cantata), Sonic studies for Piano I, (music for films) Sky Bandits, Gunbus, Pale Horse, Pale Rider, The Curb Your Appetite Diet, Centerfold, (title music for TV) Actors Forum, (for stage) From Berlin to Broadway, Oh Atlantis, Kurt, Lil Nell, Another Town, Victorian Atmospheres; composer and pianist, album-film/video, Vincent Moreaux, His Finest Hour In My Forest Cathedral, Songs from the Sea; rec. artist Sonic Arts and Repertoire Records. Pres. bd. dirs. Inst. for Recording and Multimedia Arts; mem. bd. govs.Music and the Arts Found. of Am., Inc. Mem. ASCAP, Nat. Acad. Recording Arts and Scis., Dramatists Guild, Soc. Composers and Lyricists, Am. Fedn. Musicians, Am. Soc. Music Arrangers and Composers (treas. 1978—), Composers and Arrangers Found. Am. (sec.). Democrat. Office: Al-Fre-Bett Music PO Box 45 Los Angeles CA 90078-0045

WOGSLAND, JAMES WILLARD, retired heavy machinery manufacturing executive; b. Devils Lake, N.D., Apr. 17, 1931; s. Melvin LeRoy and Mable Bertina (Paulson) W.; m. Marlene Claudia Clark, June 1957; children: Karen Lynn, Steven James. BA in Econs., U. Minn., 1957. Various positions fin. dept. Caterpillar Tractor Co., Peoria, Ill., 1957-64, treas., 1976-81; mgr. fin. Caterpillar Overseas S.A., Geneva, 1965-70, sec.-treas., 1970-76; dir.-pres. Caterpillar Brasil S.A., São Paulo, 1981-87; exec. v.p. Caterpillar, Inc., Peoria, 198-90, also bd. dirs., vice-chmn., 1990-95; bd. dirs. First of Am. Bank Corp., Kalamazoo, Protection Mut. Ins. Co., Park Ridge, Ill., Cipsco, Inc., Springfield, Ill. Mem. adv. bd. St. Francis Hosp., Peoria, 1987-95; bd. dirs. Peoria Area Cmty. Found., 1986-92; trustee Eureka Coll., 1987-95. Sgt. USAF, 1951-55. Mem. Hayden Lake Golf & Country Club, Peoria. Republican. Presbyterian. Home: 9675 Easy St Hayden ID 83835-9526

WOHL, ARMAND JEFFREY, cardiologist; b. Phila., Dec. 11, 1946; s. Herman Lewis and Selma (Paul) W.; m. Marylouise Katherine Giangrossi, Sept. 4, 1977; children: Michael Adam, Todd David. Student, Temple U., 1967; MD, Hahnemann U., 1971. Intern Bexar County Hosp., San Antonio, 1971-72; resident in internal medicine Parkland Hosp., Dallas, 1972-74; fellow in cardiology U. Tex. Southwestern Med. Ctr., Dallas, 1974-76; chief of cardiology USAF Hosp. Elmendorf, Anchorage, 1976-78; chief cardiologist Riverside (Calif.) Med. Clin., 1978-79; cardiologist Grossmont Cardiology Med. Group, La Mesa, Calif., 1980-84; pvt. practice, La Mesa, 1985—; chief of cardiology Grossmont Hosp., La Mesa, 1988-90; asst. clin. prof. Sch. Medicine. U. Calif., San Diego, 1990—. Contbr. articles to profl. jours. Bd. dirs. San Diego County chpt. Am. Heart Assn., 1981-87, Grossmont Hosp. Dist., 1995—. Maj. USAF, 1976-78. Fellow Am. Coll. Cardiology (councilor Calif. chpt. 1991—), Am. Coll. Physicians, Coun. on Clin. Cardiology. Office: 5565 Grossmont Center Dr La Mesa CA 91942-3020

WOHL, CHARLES MARTIN, business development executive; b. Cambridge, Mass., June 12, 1959; s. Martin and Ann Hedges (Findley) W.; m. Martha Ellen Fleming, Apr. 30, 1988; children: Amelia Ann, Diana Catherine. BA, Calif. State U., Long Beach, 1981; BS, U. So. Calif., L.A., 1985, MS, 1985. Project engr. Hughes Aircraft Co., El Segundo, Calif., 1979-85; project mgr. Northrop Corp., Hawthorne, Calif., 1985-89; sr. product mgr. Magnavox Electronics, Torrance, Calif., 1989-94; cons. Group L, Newport Beach, Calif., 1994—; gen. mgr., ptnr. Significant Improvements, Long Beach, 1991—. Dist. commrs. Boy Scouts Am., Long Beach, 1987-88, asst. scoutmaster, 1979-86. Mem. Alamitos Bay Yacht Club, Snipe Class Internat. Racing Assn. (dist. gov. 1986-89). Methodist. Home: 3907 Marron Ave Long Beach CA 90807-3613 Office: 2599 28th St Ste 206 Signal Hill CA 90805

WOHLETZ, KENNETH HAROLD, volcanologist; b. Chico, Calif., Jan. 19, 1952; s. Norbert Harlod and Martha Deborah (Focht) W.; m. Ann Grayson Barker. BA, U. Calif., Santa Barbara, 1974; MS, Ariz. State U., 1976, PhD, 1980. Grad. rsch. asst. Ariz. State U., Tempe, 1974-79, postdoctoral rsch. asst., 1980-81; vis. scientist Consiglio Nationale della Ricerche, Pisa, Italy, 1980; postdoctoral rsch. asst. Ariz. State U., Tempe, 1980-81; geology instr. U. N.Mex., Los Alamos, 1982-83; vis. staff mem. Los Alamos (N.Mex.) Nat. Lab., 1975-80, postdoctoral fellow, 1981-83, staff mem., 1983—; volcanology prof. U. N.Mex., Albuquerque, 1991—; Ariz. coord. Internat. Kimberlite Conf., Tempe, 1977-78; vis. prof. U. Naples Federico II, Italy, 1992—. Author: Explosive Volcanism, 1984, Volcanic Ash, 1985 (award of excellence 1986), Volcanology and Geothermal Energy, 1992; contbr. articles to profl. jours. Mem. Internat. Assn. Volcanology and Chemistry of the Earth's Interior (organizer gen. assembly 1989), Am. Geophys. Union, Geol. Soc. Am., Sigma Xi. Roman Catholic. Home: 4 Karen Cir Los Alamos NM 87544-3797 Office: Los Alamos Nat Lab EES -1 Ms D462 Los Alamos NM 87545

WOHLETZ, LEONARD RALPH, soil scientist, consultant; b. Nekoma, N.D., Oct. 22, 1909; s. Frank and Anna (Keifer) W.; m. Jane Geisendorfer, Sept. 1, 1935; children: Mary Jane, Leonard Ralph Jr., Elizabeth Ann, Catherine Ellen, Margaret Lee. BS, U. Calif., Berkeley, 1931, MS, 1933. Jr. soil expert USDA Soil Erosion Svc., Santa Paula, Calif., 1934; asst. regional chief soil surveys USDA Soil Conservation Svc., Santa Paula, 1935; asst. regional chief soil surveys USDA Soil Conservation Svc., Berkeley, 1939-42, soil survey supr., 1942-45, state soil scientist, 1945-68, asst. to state conservationist, 1969-71; cons. soil scientist Berkeley, 1973—. Author: Survey Guide, 1948; contbr. articles to profl. publs. including Know Calif. Land, Soils and Land Use Planning, Planning by Foresight and Hindsight. Mem. Waste Mgmt. Commn., Berkeley, 1981; chmn. com. Rep. for Congress, 8th Dist. Calif., 1980; pres. State and Berkeley Rep. Assembly, 1985—. Recipient Soil Conservationist of Yr., Calif. Wildlife Fedn., 1967. Mem. Soil and Water Conservation Soc. (chmn. organic waste mgmt. com. 1973—, sect. pres., Dist. Svc. award, charter and life mem., Disting. Svc. award 1971, Outstanding Svc. award 1983), Soil Sci. Soc. Am. (emeritus), Internat. Soc. Soil Sci., Profl. Soil Sci. Assn. Calif., Commonwealth Club Calif., San Francisco Farmers Club. Roman Catholic. Home: 510 Vincente Ave Berkeley CA 94707-1522

WOHLFORTH, ERIC EVANS, lawyer; b. N.Y.C., Apr. 17, 1932; s. Robert Martin and Mildred Campbell (Evans) W.; m. Caroline Penniman, Aug. 3, 1957; children: Eric Evans, Charles Penniman. AB, Princeton U., 1954; LLB, U. Va., 1957. Bar: N.Y. 1958, Alaska 1967. Assoc. Hawkins, Delafield & Wood, N.Y.C., 1957-66; ptnr. McGrath & Wohlforth, Anchorage, 1966-70; commr. revenue State of Alaska, Anchorage, 1970-72; ptnr. McGrath, Wohlforth & Flint, Anchorage, 1972-74, Wohlforth & Flint, Anchorage, 1974-87, Wohlforth, Flint & Gruening, 1987-88, Wohlforth, Argetsinger, Johnson & Brecht, 1988—; mem. Alaska Investment Adv. Com., 1973-80. Chancellor Episcopal Diocese of Alaska, 1972—; mem., trustee, vice-chair Alaska Permanent Fund Corp., 1995—. Mem. Alaska Bar Assn., Assn. of Bar of City of N.Y. Home: 7831 Ingram St Anchorage AK 99502-3965 Office: 900 W 5th Ave Ste 600 Anchorage AK 99501-2029

WOHLMUT, THOMAS ARTHUR, communications executive; b. Perth, Australia, Feb. 19, 1953; came to U.S., 1956, naturalized, 1963; s. Arthur John and Georgine Elfreida (Pipek) W.; B.A. cum laude, UCLA, 1975; m. Debra Lynn Hansen, Aug. 1, 1979 (div. 1990); 1 child, Katherine Emily; m. Michele Ann Mc Carthy, May 9, 1992. TV prodn. asst. (All in the Family, Mary Tyler Moore Show, Carol Burnett Show, Emmy Awards Show), CBS, Hollywood, Calif., 1971-74; video disc producer I/0 Metrics Corp., Calif., 1975-77; dir., writer Innovative Media Inc., Menlo Park, Calif., 1977-78; pres. Wohlmut Media Services, Union City, 1978—; cons. Bechtel Power Corp., Sunset Mag., Xerox-Diablo Systems, Pacific Gas & Electric Co., Elec. Power Research Inst., Advanced Micro Devices, Amdahl Corp., IBM-Rolm, Intel Corp., Mervyn's, Shaklee Corp., Kelly-Moore Paint Co.; lectr. in field. Contbr. articles to profl. jours. Recipient Bronze Anvil award Pub. Rels. Soc. Am., 1988, Cindy award Assn. Visual Communicators, 1988, Joey award, 1991, award ITVA Golden Vision, 1991. Mem. Internat. TV Assn. (past. pres. San Francisco chpt., v.p. for Alaska, Wash., Idaho, Oreg., Utah, Nev., No. Calif., Joyce Nelson award 1987), Soc. Visual Communicators, Internat. Interactive Communications Soc. (founder, 1st pres.), Am. Soc. Tng. and Devel., Am. Film Inst., San Francisco C. of C. Office: 2600 Central Ave Ste L Union City CA 94587-3187

WOHLSTETTER, ALBERT JAMES, defense research executive; b. N.Y.C., Dec. 19, 1913; s. Philip and Nellie (Friedman) W.; m. Roberta Morgan, June 7, 1939. BA in Mathematical Logic, Columbia U., MA, 1938. Vis. prof. UCLA and U. Calif. Berkeley, 1962-64; asst. to pres. Rand Corp., 1950-64; prof. U. Chgo., 1964-80; pres., dir. rsch. PAN Heuristics Svcs. Inc., L.A., 1979—; v.p. Security Conf. on Asia and Pacific, 1980—; mem. Pres.' Fgn. Intelligence Adv. Bd., 1985-88, Def. Policy Bd.; advisor to under sec. def. for policy and chief naval ops.; former advisor to asst. to Pres. for nat. security, dir. ACDA, Dept. State; advisor Geneva Conf. on Surprise Attack, 1958. Author and co-author of several books; contbr. numerous articles to profl. publs. Recipient Disting. Pub. Svc. medal Dept. Def., 1965, 76, Presdl. Medal of Freedom, 1985, Freedom Flame award Ctr. for Security Policy, 1993; fellow All Souls Coll., Oxford U., Rand Grad. Sch.; sr. fellow Hoover Instn., Stanford U. Fellow AAAS; mem. European Am. Inst. for Security Rsch. (pres. 1975—).

WOJAHN, R. LORRAINE, state legislator; b. Tacoma, Wash.; m. Gilbert M. Wojahn (dec.); children: Mark C, Gilbert M. Jr. (dec.). Mem. Wash. State Ho. of Reps., 1969-76, Wash. State Senate, 1977—, pres. pro tempore; vice chmn. rules, health and human svcs. com.; mem. labor and commerce, ways and means coms. Bd. dirs. Allenmore Hosp.; trustee Comsumer Credit Counseling Svcs., Inc., Tacoma-Pierce County; active, past pres. mem. Eastside Boys' and Girls' Club, Tacoma-Pierce County; active Wash. State Hist. Soc. Democrat. Office: State Senate State Capital Olympia WA 98504 Other: 2515 S Cedar St Tacoma WA 98405-2323

WOJAK, DEBORAH J., nursing consultant and educator; b. Chgo., June 8, 1950; d. Ben F. and Josephine (Hertelendi) W.; 1 child, Megan Yvette. Diploma, Freeport Meml. Hosp., 1976; BS, No. Ill. U., 1979; MS, Ariz. State U., 1981; AS, Highland Community Coll., Freeport, Ill., 1972. RN, Ariz. Educator tng. and devel. Scottsdale (Ariz.) Meml. Health Systems, 1980-82; instr. Maricopa Community Colls., Phoenix, 1982-85, 87-90; nursing educator, dir. Waddell Inst. for Longer Life Phoenix Meml. Hosp., 1990; educator health and staff devel. coord. Meml. Family Health Ctr., Phoenix, 1991; psychiatric nurse Desert Vista Hosp., Meza, Ariz., 1989-90; dir. tng. and devel. Pla. Healthcare, Thatcher, Ariz., 1992-93; dir. nursing and allied health care Ea. Ariz. Coll., Thatcher, 1993—; cons. Med. Legal Litigation, Scottsdale, 1986—; qualified expert witness; profl. svcs. coord. Health Internat., 1993—; dir. tng. and devel. Plaza Healthcare, Scottsdale, 1994; dir. nursing and allied health Ea. Ariz. Coll., Thatcher, 1994—. Dir. producer (slide tape) Nursing Negligence, 1982, (video) Ostomy Appliance Application, 1990. NIMH trainee, 1980-81. Mem. Nat. League Nursing, Nat. Student Nurse Assn. (dist. pres. 1974-75), Ariz. League Nursing (bd. dirs. 1992). Home: PO Box 639 Thatcher AZ 85552-0639

WOJCIK, RICHARD FRANK, pharmaceutical company executive; b. Chgo., Apr. 1, 1936; s. Francis Joseph and Marie Cora (Szalecki) W.;m. Kathleen Mary Janousek, Nov. 18, 1961; children: Richard, Margaret, Christopher. BS, S.D. State U., 1958; cert., Columbia U., Harrison, N.Y., 1976. Registered pharmacist, Ill. Various sales positions Eli Lilly & Co., Chgo., 1960-67; market rsch. analyst Eli Lilly & Co., Indpls., 1967-68; dist. mgr. Eli Lilly & Co., Buffalo, 1968-71; mktg. plans mgr. Eli Lilly & Co., Indpls., 1971-72; regional mgr. southern region Dista Products, Atlanta, 1972-75; dir. sales eastern region Eli Lilly & Co., Boston, 1975-76; U.K. dir. mktg. Eli Lilly Internat., Basingstoke, Eng., 1976-79; European dir. mktg. Eli Lilly Internat., London, 1979; v.p. sales pharm. div. Eli Lilly & Co., Indpls., 1979-92; sr. v.p. sales and customer svc. McKesson Drug Co., San Francisco, 1992—. Fund raiser Indpls. Ballet Co., 1989, Indpls. Art Mus., 1990; adv. bd. U. Tex. Pharmacy Sch., Austin, 1986-92. Capt. U.S. Army, 1958-59; capt. USAR, 1959-67. Mem. Meridian Hills Country Club, Hawthorne Golf and Country Club (bd. dirs.), Noble Ctrs. (adv. bd. govs.). Office: McKesson Drug Co One Post St San Francisco CA 94104-5296

WOJTYLA, WALTER HAASE, artist; b. Chgo., Feb. 10, 1933; s. Louis Walter and Helen Julia (Haase) W.; m. Susan Virginia Leonard, Sept. 2, 1967 (div.); 1 child, Anthony Lewis. BFA, U. Ill., 1956; MFA, U. Cin., 1967. Solo exhbns. include San Diego Art Inst., 1992, 93; group exhbns. include Spanish Village Art Ctr., San Diego, 1991, La Jolla (Calif.) Art Exhbn. 1991, San Diego-Tijuana Yokohama Art Exch., 1992, The Paladion, San Diego, 1994, others; works collected at Mus. of Contemporary Art, San Diego, 1993; contbr. to profl. publs.; (TV documentary) Artists-in-Residence, San Diego, 1983. Mem. San Diego Art Guild. Home: 2102 C St San Diego CA 92102-1835

WOLANER, ROBIN PEGGY, magazine publisher; b. Queens, N.Y., May 6, 1954; d. David H. and Harriet (Radlow) W.; m. Steven J. Castleman, 1992; 1 child, Terry David. BS in Indsl. and Labor Rels., Cornell U., 1975. Sr. editor Viva Mag., N.Y.C., 1975-76; editor Impact Mag., N.Y.C., 1976-77; circulation mgr. Runner's World Mag., Mountain View, Calif., 1977-79; cons. Ladd Assocs., San Francisco, 1979-80; gen. mgr. Mother Jones Mag., San Francisco, 1980-81, pub., 1981-85; founder, pub. Parenting Mag., San Francisco, 1985-91, pres., 1991-92; v.p. Time Pub. Ventures, 1990—; pres., CEO Sunset Pub. Corp., 1992—; trustee Muir Investment Fund, 1991-94. Mem. bd. advisors Grad. Sch. Journalism, U. Calif., Berkeley, 1991—; bd. dirs. Bay Area Coun., 1992—. Jewish. Office: Sunset Pub Corp 80 Willow Rd Menlo Park CA 94025-3661

WOLBERS, HARRY LAWRENCE, engineering psychologist; b. L.A., Jan. 29, 1926; s. Harry Lawrence and Edith Christine (Nordeen) W.; m. Mary Lou Jordan Call, Feb. 18, 1972; children: Harry L., Richard C., Leslie A., Suzanne M. BS, Calif. Inst. Tech., 1946; MA, U. So. Calif., L.A., 1949, PhD, 1955. Lic. psychologist Calif. V.p. Psychol. Svcs., Inc., L.A., 1948-54; chief systems rsch. Douglas Aircraft Co., El Segundo, Calif., 1954-63; chief program engr. space systems Douglas Aircraft Co., Santa Monica., Huntington Beach, 1963-74; chief systems engr. advanced space systems McDonnell Douglas Astronautics Co., Huntington Beach, Calif., 1974-85; adj. prof. dept. indsl. and systems engrng. U. So. Calif., L.A., 1954-85; dep. dir. flight crew systems McDonnell Douglas Space Systems Co., Huntington Beach, 1985-91; ret.; mem. USAF Sci. Adv. Bd., Washington, 1991—; cons. NASA, Washington, 1988—. Contbr. articles to profl. jours. Lt. (j.g.) USN, 1943-47; ATO; PTO. Recipient Engrng. Merit award San Fernando Valley Engrs. Coun., Calif., 1988. Fellow Human Factors and Ergonomics Soc. (Orange County chpt. pres. 1989); mem. APA, Soc. Indsl. and Orgnl. Psychologists, Sigma Xi, Psi Chi.

WOLBRINK, DONALD HENRY, landscape architect, city planner; b. Ganges, Mich., May 13, 1911; s. Isaac M. and Ruby (Payne) W.; m. Florence Theresa Stack, Dec. 24, 1938; 1 child, Gretchen. B.A., U. Mich., 1932, M. Landscape Design, 1933. Landscape architect Nat. Park Service, Washington, 1934-41; landscape architect C.E., Omaha, 1941-44; assoc. Bartholomew Assocs., Honolulu, 1946-58, ptnr., 1958-64; pres. Donald Wolbrink, Honolulu, 1964-87, ret., 1989; dir. emeritus First Fed. Savs. and Loan, Honolulu; chmn. bd. Hawaii Architects and Engrs., Honolulu, 1979-84 (project dir. Melbourne strategy plan 1972-73); dir. Interplan, Melbourne, Australia, 1972-80. Co-author Hawaii State Law (land use law), 1961, sociophysical planning process, 1980; dir. (book) Tourism Standards, 1972. Bd. dirs. Oahu Devel. Conf., Honolulu, 1975-86 (project dir. 9 prin. Micronesian Islands 1961-75), C. of C., Honolulu, 1971-73, Downtown Improvement Assn., Honolulu, 1973-79; pres. Foresight, Inc., Honolulu, 1972-85. Served to lt. USN, 1944-46. Recipient Victorian Archtl. award Royal Australian Inst., 1977, Disting. Service award Engrng. Assn. Hawaii, 1983, Spl. Achievement award Am. Plan Assn., 1990. Fellow ASCE, Am. Soc. Landscape Architects (trustee 1960-66, 77-78, merit award Hawaii chpt. 1983); mem. Am. Inst. Cert. Planners, Nat. Hist. Planning Pioneer Am., Inst. Consulting Planners. Club: Pacific (Honolulu). Home: 900 W Alpine Way Shelton WA 98584

WOLCOTT, OLIVER, psychiatrist, educator; b. Barneveld, N.Y., Feb. 25, 1930; s. George N. and Magdalen (Ames) W.; m. Helen Louise Mag, Aug. 29, 1950; children: Steven, Betsy, Peter, Andrew, Jennifer. BA, Western Res. U., 1951; MD, U. Rochester, 1955. Diplomate Am. Bd. Psychiatry and Neurology. Intern USPHS Hosp., San Francisco, 1955-56; resident in psychiatry U. Colo. Sch. Medicine, Denver, 1958-61, instr., then asst. prof., 1961-65, clin. asst. prof., 1965—; pvt. practice, Denver, 1965—; staff psychiatrist Mental Health Corp. Denver, 1982—; mem. staff State Hosp., Mental Health Ctr. Med. dir. USPHS, 1955-58, mem. Res. Fellow (life) Am. Psychiat. Assn.; mem. Colo. Psychiat. Soc., Am. Soc. Hispanic Psychiatrists. Democrat. Unitarian. Office: 1514 Fairfax St Denver CO 80220-1322

WOLD, DAVID C., bishop. Bishop of Southwestern Wash. Evang. Luth. Ch. in Am., Tacoma. Office: Synod of Southwestern Washington 420 121st St S Tacoma WA 98444-5218

WOLD, JOHN SCHILLER, geologist, former congressman; b. East Orange, N.J., Aug. 31, 1916; s. Peter Irving and Mary (Helff) W.; m. Jane Adele Pearson, Sept. 28, 1946; children: Peter Irving, Priscilla Adele, John Pearson. AB, St. Andrews U., Scotland and Union Coll., Schenectady, 1938; MS, Cornell U., 1939; LLD (hon.), U. Wyo., 1991. Dir. Fedn. Rocky Mountain States, 1966-68; v.p. Rocky Mountain Oil and Gas Assn., 1967, 68; mem. Wyo. Ho. of Reps., 1957-59; Wyo. Republican candidate for U.S. Senate, 1964, 70; mem. 91st Congress at large from, Wyo.; chmn., CEO Wold Trona Co., Inc.; pres., chmn. Wold Oil & Gas Co.; ret. Wold Nuclear Co., Wold Mineral Exploration Co., Casper, Wyo.; founding pres. Wyo. Heritage Soc.; founder Central Wyo. Ski Corp.; chmn. Wyo. Natural Gas Pipeline Authority, 1987-91; chmn. bd. Nuclear Exploration and Devel. Corp., Mineral Engrng. Co. Contbr. articles to profl. jours. Chmn. Wyo. Rep. Com., 1960-64, Western State Rep. Chmns. Assn., 1963-64; mem. exec. com. Rep. Nat. Com., 1962-64; chmn. Wyo. Rep. State Fin. Com.; Active Little League Baseball, Boy Scouts Am., United Fund, YMCA, Boys Clubs Am.; former pres. bd. trustees Casper Coll.; trustee Union Coll. Served to lt. USNR, World War II. Named Wyo. Man of Yr. AP-UPI, 1968; Wyo. Mineral Man of Yr., 1979, Wyo. Heritage award, 1992; named Benefactor of Yr., Nat. Coun. for Resource Devel., 1993. Mem. Wyo. Geol. Assn. (hon. life, pres. 1956), Am. Assn. Petroleum Geologists, Ind. Petroleum Assn. Am., AAAS, Wyo. Mining Assn., Sigma Xi, Alpha Delta Phi. Episcopalian (past vestryman, warden). Home: 1231 W 30th St Casper WY 82604-4738 Office: Mineral Resource Ctr 139 W 2d St Casper WY 82601

WOLD, NANA BEHA, social services administrator; b. N.Y.C., Nov. 4, 1943; d. William John and Margaret (Robinson) Beha. BA, Tex. Women's U., 1965; M in Social Welfare, U. Calif., Berkeley, 1967. Lic. clin. social worker, Calif. Psychiat. social worker Mendocino State Hosp., Talmage, Calif., 1967-70, Calif. State Dept. Mental Health, San Diego, 1972-74; supervising psychiat. social worker Calif. State Dept. Health, San Diego, 1974-81; assoc. chief, case mgmt. services San Diego Regional Ctr. Devel. Disabled, 1981—; instr. social work Chapman Coll., San Diego, 1972; mem.

adv. com. Community Living Project, San Diego, 1973-76, Sr. Citizens Day Care Ctr., San Diego, 1976-77; mem. Assembly Woman Bentley adv. com. on devel. disabilities, San Diego, 1984-92; co-chair Com. Community Care for Devel. Disabled, San Diego, 1978—. Co-author: Sex Education for the Mentally Retarded, 1975, (pamphlet) Happiness is a Good Home, 1977. Vol. Army Community Services, Ft. Wolters, Tex., 1968-69. Mem. NASW (diplomate in clin. social work), Assn. for Severely Handicapped. Republican. Roman Catholic. Office: San Diego Regional Ctr Devel Disabled 4355 Ruffin Rd Ste 306 San Diego CA 92123-4309

WOLDA, HINDRIK, research biologist; b. Wageningen, Netherlands, May 24, 1931; s. Willem Derk and Gepke (Paap) W.; m. Trientje Smit, Mar. 27, 1958; children: Hetty, Willem D., Jacob, Marianne. BS, U. Groningen, Netherlands, 1955, MS, 1958, PhD, 1963. Sci. officer U. Groningen, 1958-64, chief sci. officer, 1964-68, prof., 1968-71; rsch. biologist Smithsonian Tropical Rsch. Inst., Panama, 1971-91; vis. prof. U. Wash., Seattle, 1987-88. Contbr. numerous articles to profl. jours. 1st lt. Dutch Army, 1950-52. Recipient Dir.'s award Smithsonian Tropical Rsch. Inst., 1977, award Smithsonian Instn., 1984. Fellow Linnean Soc. London, Royal Entomology Soc. London; mem. Royal Dutch Acad. Scis., Ultar Pradesh Zool. Soc., Wash. State Entomol. Soc., Japanese Soc. for Population Ecology, Ecol. Soc. Am. Office: 1626 106th Ave SE Bellevue WA 98004-7102

WOLF, ALFRED, rabbi; b. Eberbach, Germany, Oct. 7, 1915; came to U.S., 1935, naturalized, 1941; s. Hermann and Regina (Levy) W.; m. Miriam Jean Office, June 16, 1940; children: David B., Judith C. (dec.), Dan L. BA, U. Cin., 1937; MHL, Hebrew Union Coll., 1941; DD, 1966; PhD, U. So. Calif., 1961; DHL, U. Judaism, 1987, Loyola Marymount U., 1990. Ordained rabbi, 1941. Rabbi Temple Emanuel, Dothan, Ala., 1941-46; S.E. regional dir. Union Am. Hebrew Congregations, 1944-46; Western regional dir. Union Am. Hebrew Congregations, Los Angeles, 1946-49; rabbi Wilshire Blvd. Temple Los Angeles, 1949-85, rabbi emeritus, 1985—; dir. Skirball Inst. on Am. Values of Am. Jewish Com., 1985—; lectr. U. So. Calif., 1955-69, Hebrew Union Coll., Jewish Inst. Religion, Calif., 1963-65, 74; lectr. religion Seven Seas div. Chapman Coll., 1967; adj. prof. theology Loyola U. Los Angeles, 1967-74; lectr. sociology Calif. State U., Los Angeles, 1977; co-chair First Nationwide Conf. for Cath. Jewish and Protestant seminiaries, Chgo., 1993. Author: (with Joseph Gaer) Our Jewish Heritage, 1957, (with Monsignor Royale M. Vadakin) Journey 0f Discovery - A Resource Manual for Catholic-Jewish Dialogue, 1989; editor Teaching About World Religions: A Teacher's Supplement, 1991. Mem. camp commn. adminstrv. com. Camp Hess Kramer, 1951—; mem. L.A. Com. on Human Rels., 1956-72, mem. exec. bd., 1960—, chmn., 1964-66, hon. mem., 1972—; pres. Anytown U.S.A., 1964-66; mem. United Way Planning Coun. Bd., chmn., 1974-78; mem. youth adv. com. NCCJ, 1968-72, exec. bd., 1972-93; founding pres. Interreligious Coun. So. Calif., 1970-72; chmn. clergy adv. com. L.A. Sch. Dist., 1971-81; chmn. Nat. Workshop on Christian-Jewish Rels., 1978; bd. govs. Hebrew Union Coll., bd. alumni overseers, 1972—; mem. L.A. 2000 Com., 1986-89, The 2000 Partnership, 1989-95, Berlin Sister City Com., L.A., 1987-89; bd. dirs. Jewish Fedn. Coun., 1978-85, bd. govs., 1985—; bd. dirs. Jewish Family Svc. L.A., sec., 1978-80. Recipient Samuel Kaminker award as Jewish educator of year Western Assn. Temple Educators, 1965, John Anson Ford Human Relations award County Commn. on Human Relations, 1972, 90, Harry Hollzer Meml. award Los Angeles Jewish Fedn. Council, 1978, Volpert Community Service award, 1986, Community Service award United Way of Los Angeles, 1980, Leadership award Los Angeles Bd. Edn., 1981, Service to Edn. award Associated Adminstrs. Los Angeles, 1983, Pub. Service award Jewish Chautauqua Soc., 1986, N.Am. Interfaith Leadership award Nat. Workshop for Christian-Jewish Rels., 1990. Mem. Bd. Rabbis So. Calif. (pres.), Am. Jewish Com. (exec. com. Los Angeles chpt., Max Bay Meml. award 1986), Central Conf. Am. Rabbis (exec. bd., mem. commn. on Jewish edn. 1970-72, treas. 1975-79, chmn. interreligious activities com. 1975-79, hon. mem. 1991—), Pacific Assn. Reform Rabbis (pres.), So. Calif. Assn. Liberal Rabbis (pres.), Synagogue Council Am. (mem. com. interreligious affairs), Alumni Assn. Hebrew Union Coll.-Jewish Inst. Religion, Town Hall, Los Angeles World Affairs Council, U. So. Calif. Alumni Assn. Home: 3389 Ley Dr Los Angeles CA 90027-1315 Office: Skirball Inst on Am Values 635 S Harvard Blvd Los Angeles CA 90005-2586

WOLF, CHARLES, JR., economist, educator; b. N.Y.C., Aug. 1, 1924; s. Charles and Rosalie W.; m. Theresa van de Wint, Mar. 1, 1947; children: Charles Theodore, Timothy van de Wint. B.S., Harvard U., 1943, M.P.A., 1948, Ph.D. in Econs., 1949. Economist, fgn. service officer U.S. Dept. State, 1945-47, 49-53; mem. faculty Cornell U., 1953-54, U. Calif., Berkeley, 1954-55; sr. economist The Rand Corp., Santa Monica, Calif., 1955-67; head econs. dept. The Rand Corp., 1967-81; dean The Rand Grad. Sch., 1970—; sr. economist, 1981—; sr. fellow Hoover Inst., 1988—; bd. dirs. Fundamental Investors Fund, Capital Income Builder Fund, Am. Capital Fund, Capital World Growth Fund; mem. exec. com. Rand-UCLA Health Policy Ctr.; mem. adv. com. UCLA Clin. Scholars Program; mem. exec. com. Rand Ctr. for Russian and Eurasian Studies; lectr. econs. UCLA, 1960-72; mem. adv. bd. grad. sch. pub. policy Carnegie-Mellon U., 1992—. Author: The Costs and Benefits of the Soviet Empire, 1986, Markets or Governments: Choosing Between Imperfect Alternatives, 1988, 93, (with others) The Improverished Superpower: Perestroika and the Soviet Military Burden, 1990, Linking Economic Policy and Foreign Policy, 1991, Promoting Democracy and Free Markets in Eastern Europe, 1992, Defense Conversion and Economic Reform in Russia and Ukraine, 1994; contbr. articles to profl. jours. Mem. Assn. for Public Policy Analysis and Mgmt. (pres. 1980-81), Am. Econs. Assn., Econometric Soc., Coun. on Fgn. Rels., Internat. Inst. Strategic Studies London. Clubs: Cosmos (Washington); Riviera Tennis (Los Angeles); Harvard (N.Y.). Office: RAND Grad Sch Policy Studies 1700 Main St Santa Monica CA 90401-3208

WOLF, CYNTHIA TRIBELHORN, librarian, library educator; b. Denver, Dec. 12, 1945; d. John Baltazar and Margaret (Kern) Tribelhorn; m. H.Y. Rassam, Mar. 21, 1969 (div. Jan. 1988); children: Najma C., Yousuf J.; adopted children: Leonard Joseph Lucero, Lakota E. Rassam-Lucero. BA, Colo. State U., 1970; MLS, U. Denver, 1985. Cert. permanent profl. librarian, N.Mex. Elem. tchr. Sacred Heart Sch., Farmington, N.Mex., 1973-78; asst. prof. library sci. edn. U. N.Mex., Albuquerque, 1985-90, dir. libr. sci. edn. divsn., 1989-90; pres. Info. Acquisitions, Albuquerque, 1990—; libr. dir. Southwestern Coll., Santa Fe, 1992-94; mem. youth resources Rio Grande Valley Libr. Sys., Albuquerque, 1994—; fine arts resource person for gifted edn. Farmington Pub. Schs., 1979-83; speaker Unofficial Mentorships & Market Research, 1992—. Mem. Farmington Planning and Zoning Commn., 1980-81; bd. dirs. Farmington Mus. Assn., 1983-84; pres. Farmington Symphony League, 1978. Mem. ALA, N.Mex. Library Assn., LWV (bd. dirs. Farmington, 1972-74, 75, pres.). Office: Rio Grande Valley Libr Sys Albuquerque NM 87000

WOLF, DAN C., real estate associate broker; b. Palmer, Alaska, Mar. 23, 1957; s. Daniel Frederick and Sylvia Ann Wolf; children: Corene Danielle, Ryan Daniel. Grad., Palmer High Sch., 1974. GRI, CRS. Real estate assoc. broker Vista Real Estate, Anchorage, 1981-85, RE/MAX Properties, Inc., Anchorage, 1985—. Recipient real estate awards. Office: RE/MAX Properties Inc 2600 Cordova St Ste 100 Anchorage AK 99503-2745

WOLF, G. VAN VELSOR, JR., lawyer; b. Balt., Feb. 19, 1944; s. G. Van Velsor and Alice Roberts (Kimberly) W.; m. Ann Holmes Kavanagh, May 19, 1984; children: George Van Velsor III, Timothy Kavanagh (dec.), Christopher Kavanagh, Elisabeth Huxley. BA, Yale U., 1966; JD, Vanderbilt U., 1973. Bar: N.Y. 1974, Ariz. 1982, U.S. Dist. Ct. (so. dist.) N.Y. 1974, U.S. Dist. Ct. Ariz. 1982, U.S. Ct. Appeals (2d cir.) 1974, U.S. Ct. Appeals (9th cir.) 1982. Agrl. advisor U.S. Peace Corps, Tanzania and Kenya, 1966-70; assoc. Milbank, Tweed, Hadley & McCloy, N.Y.C., 1973-75; vis. lectr. law Airlangga U., Surabaya, Indonesia, 1975-76, U. Ariz. 1990, Vanderbilt U., 1991, U. Md., 1994, Ariz. State U., 1995; editor in chief Environ. Law Reporter, Washington, 1976-81; cons. Nat. Trust for Historic Preservation, Washington, 1981; assoc. Lewis & Roca, Phoenix, 1981-84, ptnr., 1984-91; ptnr. Snell & Wilmer, Phoenix, 1991—. Bd. dirs. Ariz. div. Am. Cancer Soc., 1985—, sec. 1990-92, vice chmn. 1992-94, chmn., 1994—. Editor: Toxic Substances Control, 1980; contbr. articles to profl. jours. Bd. dirs. Phoenix Little Theater, 1983-90, chmn., 1986-88. Mem. ABA (vice chmn. SONREEL commn. state and regional environ. coop.), Assn. Bar City N.Y., Ariz. State Bar Assn. (coun. environ. & nat. res. law sect. 1988-93, chmn. 1991-92), Maricopa County Bar Assn., Ariz. Acad., Union Club (N.Y.C.), Univ. Club (Phoenix). Office: Snell & Wilmer 1 Arizona Ctr Phoenix AZ 85004-0001

WOLF, GAIL POKELA, psychometrist, counselor; b. Mpls., Nov. 30, 1940; d. Earle M. and M. Millicent (Moody) Pokela; m. David Lawrence Wolf, June 3, 1961; children: Brady Lawrence, Justin David. BA, U. Puget Sound, Tacoma, Wash., 1962, MA, 1975; cert. chem. dependency, Seattle U., 1990; postgrad., U. Oreg., Boise State U. Tchr. English Curtis High Sch., Tacoma, 1962-64; psychologist Elk's Rehab., Boise, Idaho, 1975-77; grad. asst. U. Oreg., Eugene, 1978-80; bookkeeper Cascadian, Eugene, 1980-83; substitute tchr. Eugene Sch. Dist., 1984-85; cons. RDA, Tacoma, 1985-88; intern Cabrini Recovery Ctr., Seattle, 1990-91; chem. dependency counselor Swedish Hosp., Seattle, 1992-94; pres. 1st Hill Video Corp., Seattle, 1994—; cons. Eugene Jr. League, 1980-85; pvt. cons. in organizational devel. Parent leader Churchill H.S., Eugene, 1982-84; mem. Oreg. Shakespeare Festival, 1987—, Ctr. for Marine Conservation, Washington, 1990-91; bd. dirs. Muscular Distrophy, Eugene, 1982-85, Cerebral Palsy, Boise, 1977-78; bd. dirs. Millionair Club, 1993—. Mem. Internat. Platform Assn., Assn. for Psychol. Type, Mortar Bd., Psi Chi, Alpha Phi. Home and Office: 1301 Spring # 10D Seattle WA 98104-3504

WOLF, HANS ABRAHAM, retired pharmaceutical company executive; b. Frankfurt, Fed. Republic Germany, June 27, 1928; came to U.S., 1936, naturalized, 1944; s. Franz Benjamin and Ilse (Nathan) W.; m. Elizabeth J. Bassett, Aug. 2, 1958; children: Heidi Elizabeth, Rebecca Anne, Deborah Wolf Streeter, Andrew Robert. AB magna cum laude, Harvard U., 1949, MBA, 1955; PhB, Oxford U., 1951. Math instr. Tutoring Sch., 1946-47; statis. research Nat. Bur. Econ. Research, N.Y.C., 1948-49; researcher Georgetown U., 1951-52; confidential aide Office Dir. Mut. Security, Washington, 1952; analyst Ford Motor div. Ford Motor Co., Dearborn, Mich., summer 1954; foreman prodn. M&C Nuclear Inc., Attleboro, Mass., 1955-57; asst. supt. prodn. Metals & Controls Corp., Attleboro, 1957-59, mgr. product dept., 1959-62, controller, 1962-67; asst. v.p., controller materials and services group Tex. Instruments Inc., Dallas, 1967-69, treas., v.p., 1969-75; v.p. fin., chief fin. officer Syntex Corp., Palo Alto, Calif., 1975-78, exec. v.p., 1978-86, vice chmn., chief adminstrv. officer, 1986-92, vice chmn., 1992-93, also bd. dirs., 1986-93; bd. dirs. Clean Sites, Inc., Alexandria, Va., Tab Products Co., Palo Alto, Calif., chmn. 1995—; bd. dirs. Network Equipment Techs., Redwood City, Calif., Satellite Dialysis Ctrs., Inc., Redwood City, Hyal Pharms., Toronto, Ont. Author: Motivation Research—A New Aid to Understanding Your Markets, 1955. Mem. Norton (Mass.) Sch. Bd., 1959-62, chmn., 1961-62; pres., bd. dirs. Urban League Greater Dallas, 1971-74; bd. dirs. Dallas Health Planning Coun., mem. community adv. com., 1973-75; bd. dirs., pres. Children's Health Coun. of the Mid Peninsula; cubmaster Boy Scouts Am., 1976-78; elder United Ch. Christ, 1970-73, vice chmn. gen. bd., 1970-71, moderator, 1978-80; trustee Pacific Sch. Religion, 1986-94, chmn., 1990-94; trustee World Affairs Coun. San Francisco, 1986-92, 94—; dir. Tech Mus. San Jose. With USAF, 1952-53. Mem. Am. Mgmt. Assn. (planning council fin. div. 1970-76), Phi Beta Kappa.

WOLF, JOSEPH ALBERT, mathematician, educator; b. Chgo., Oct. 18, 1936; s. Albert M. and Goldie (Wykoff) W. BS, U. Chgo., 1956, MS, 1957, PhD, 1959. Mem. Inst. for Advanced Study, Princeton, 1960-62, 65-66; asst. prof. U. Calif., Berkeley, 1962-64, assoc. prof., 1964-66, prof., 1966—, Miller research prof., 1972-73, 83-84; prof. honorario Universidad Nacional de Cordoba, Argentina, 1989; vis. prof. Rutgers U., 1969-70, Hebrew U., Jerusalem, 1974-76, Tel Aviv U., 1974-76, Harvard U., 1979-80, 86. Author: Spaces of Constant Curvature, 1967, 72, 74, 77, 84, Unitary Representations on Partially Holomorphic Cohomology Spaces, 1974, Unitary Representations of Maximal Parabolic Subgroups of the Classical Groups, 1976, Classification and Fourier Inversion for Parabolic Subgroups with Square Integrable Nilradical, 1979; co-editor, author: Harmonic Analysis and Representations of Semisimple Lie Groups, 1980, The Penrose Transform and Analytic Cohomology in Representation Theory, 1993; editor Geometriae Dedicata, Math Reports, Jour. of Math. Systems, Estimation and Control, Letters in Math. Physics, Jour. of Group Theory in Physics; contbr. articles to profl. jours. Alfred P. Sloan rsch. fellow, 1965-67, NSF fellow, 1959-62; recipient Médaille de l'Université de Liège, 1977, Humboldt prize, 1995. Mem. Am., Swiss math. socs. Office: U Calif Dept Math Berkeley CA 94720

WOLF, JOSEPH GORDON (PEPE LOBO), marketing communicator, television producer; b. Ft. Sill, Okla., Apr. 23, 1944; s. Gordon Joseph Wolf and Amanda Roth Block; 1 child, Harrison; m. Celeste Miles, Dec. 25, 1992. BA, Yale U., 1966; MBA, Columbia U., 1968. Photographer Bldg. News Inc., L.A., 1973-74; free-lance photojournalist L.A., 1975; mag. editor Fluor Corp., L.A., 1976-77; mag. editor TRW, L.A., 1978-79, with mktg. comms., 1980—; TV producer and dir. Lobo Prodns., L.A., 1980—. Producer, dir. film Three Miles High, 1981, tapes Gt. American, 1983, CRWTH, 1983, TV shows Space Sta., 1985, Lost or Last Frontier, 1986, TV series Space Capsules, 1987, tapes Craig Internat., 1989, O'Hare Com. and Cont., 1992, Hits!, 1993; photojournalist. Vol. Peace Corps., Columbia, S.Am., 1968-70. Recipient CINE Golden Eagle, U.S. Internat. Film and Video Festival Silver Screen awrd, others. Mem. Bus. Mktg. Assn. (bd. dirs. 1992—), Am. Def. Preparedness Assn., Navy League of U.S. (life), Assn. U.S. Army, Armed Forces Comms. and Electronics Assn., Air Force Assn. Republican. Jewish. Home: 2304 Gardner Pl Glendale CA 91206-3013 Office: TRW R2/1028 One Space Park Redondo Beach CA 90278

WOLF, LAWRENCE JOSEPH, mechanical engineering educator; b. St. Louis, Aug. 10, 1938; s. Vincent F. and Clara A. (Holtkamp) W.; m. Barbara Ann Bieber, Aug. 12, 1961; children: Theresa, Carl, Lawrence V. AA, Harris Tchrs. Coll., 1959; BSME, Washington U., St. Louis, 1961, MS, 1962, DSc, 1971. Registered profl. engr., Tex., Mo., Ind., Ill. Engr. Monsanto Corp., St. Louis, 1962-63; design engr. McDonnell Douglas, St. Louis, 1963-64; from instr. to assoc. prof. to dept. head St. Louis C.C.-Florissnat Valley, 1964-72, assoc. dean, 1975-78; assoc. prof. U. Petroleum and Minerals, Dhahran, Saudi Arabia, 1972-74; dean instrn. Wentworth Inst., Boston, 1974-75; dept. head Purdue U.-Calumet, Hammond, Ind., 1978-80; dean tech. U. Houston, from 1980; pres., prof. Oreg. Inst. of Tech., Klamath Falls, 1991—; cons. engr. Nooter Corp., St. Louis, 1965-72; guest scientist Brookhaven Nat. Lab. and Superconducting Supercollider Lab., 1989—; founder Tex. Assn. Schs. Engring. Tech.; bd. dirs. United Way of Klamath Falls, Cascades East Area Health Edn. Ctr. Author: Understanding Structures...A Parallel Approach to Statics and Strength of Materials; editor Jour. Engring. Tech., 1983-87; contbr. 40 articles to profl. jours. Leader Webelos Boy Scouts Am., Houston; chmn. Sesquicentennial Cannon Com., Houston, 1986; bd. dirs. Klamath County United Way; founder, chmn. Cascades-East Health Edn. Ctr. Served with U.S. Army, 1956-57. Recipient Fellow Members awd., Am. Soc. for Engineering Education, 1992. Fellow Accrediting Bd. Engring. and Tech. (TAC chmn.); mem. ASME, Am. Soc. Engring. Edn. (div. chmn., James H. McGraw award 1987), Soc. Mfg. Engrs. Office: Oreg Inst Tech Office of Pres 3201 Campus Dr Klamath Falls OR 97601-8801

WOLF, MONICA THERESIA, procedures analyst; b. Germany, Apr. 26, 1943; came to U.S., 1953, naturalized, 1959; d. Otto and Hildegard Maria (Heim) Bellemann; children: Clinton, Danielle. BBA, U. Albuquerque, 1986. Developer Word Processing Ctr., Pub. Service of N.Mex., Albuquerque, 1971-74, word processing supr., 1974-78, budget coordinator, 1978-80, lead procedures analyst, 1980-88; owner Monica's Woodworks, 1988-91; founder Monidan Blue, 1992—; mem. adv. bd., student trainer APS Career Enrichment Ctr. Instr. firearm safety and pistol competition. Mem. Internat. Word Processing Assn. (founder N.Mex. chpt.), Nat. Assn. Female Execs., Nat. Rifle Assn., N.Mex. Shooting Sports Assn. Democrat. Club: Sandia Gun (adv. bd., coach). Home and Office: 305 Alamosa Rd NW Albuquerque NM 87107-5312

WOLF, RICHARD JAY, software designer; b. Boston, May 11, 1952; s. Fred A. and Ruth (Alpert) W.; m. Sarah McKim Chalfant, Sept. 21, 1985; 1 child, Lucy Chalfant. BA, U. Pa., 1978; MS, U. Mass., 1982. Mem. tech. staff Xerox Corp., Palo Alto, Calif., 1982-85; sys. arch. Lotus Devel. Corp., Cambridge, Mass., 1985-93; sr. program mgr. Microsoft Corp., Redmond, Wash., 1993—. Office: Microsoft Corp 1 Microsoft Way Redmond WA 98052-8300

WOLF, ROSE BARRY, tax consultant, educator; b. Colchester, Conn., Apr. 27, 1921; d. Samuel David and Lena Sylvia (Hoffman) Barry; grad. in acctg. Pace Inst., 1946; m. Lester Wolf, Sept. 28, 1947 (dec.); children—Beverly Sheila, Perry Stewart. Office mgr. HY & D. Agar Realty, Inc., Bklyn., 1946-47, Joseph Love, Inc., N.Y.C., 1947-48; real estate accountant, tax accountant Benjamin Pasilla, N.Y.C., 1948-67; acct. Val Stream Volkswagen, Valley Stream, N.Y., 1967-67; sr. tax acct. Columbia Pictures Industries, Inc., N.Y.C., 1968-73; comptroller Matthews, Inc., Beverly Hills, Calif., 1973-74, Alexander & Friends., Inc., El Segundo, Calif., 1974-76; tax cons., pres. Group Services Internat., Tarzana, Calif., 1976—; treas. Travel Group Inc., Anaheim, Calif.; employment sec.-treas. Midway Energy Inc., Tarzana, 1978; citizens adv. com. Valley Coll. Accredited in accountancy; enrolled to practice before IRS. Mem. Nat. Soc. Pub. Accts., Am. Soc. Profl. Accts. (pres. 1985-86), Am. Soc. Women Accts. (corr. sec., pres. 1986—), Nat. Assn. Enrolled Agts. (chmn. Yellow Pages advt. Los Angeles chpt.), Am. Bus. Women's Assn. (treas.). Democrat. Clubs: B'nai B'rith, Seaford Dramatic. Columnist, Weekend mag., San Fernando Valley. Office: Ste 105 6442 Coldwater Canyon Ave North Hollywood CA 91606-1137

WOLFE, BARBARA AHMAJAN, stock brokerage company executive, administrator; b. Providence, Aug. 1, 1943; d. Michael Ashod and Liberty (Hagopian) A.; m. Thomas Francis Wolfe, Apr. 7, 1984. B.A., Mills Coll., 1965. Mktg. analyst Calif. Blue Shield, San Francisco, 1967-70; research analyst Pacific Maritime Assn., San Francisco, 1970-73; corp. adminstr. Lawrence Systems, Inc., San Francisco, 1973-75; analyst Stanford Research Inst., Calif., 1975; exec. v.p., adminstr. Charles Schwab & Co., San Francisco, 1976—, dir.; corp. sec. Charles Schwab & Co., 1976—. Bd. govs. Mills Coll., Oakland, Calif., 1977-80. Home: 1221 Jones St # 3hc San Francisco CA 94109-4228 Office: Charles Schwab & Co Inc 101 Montgomery St San Francisco CA 94104-4122

WOLFE, BRIAN AUGUSTUS, sales executive; b. Mexico City, Nov. 23, 1946; came to U.S., 1947; s. Steward Augustus and Vivia Idalene (Fouts) W.; m. Holly Joyce Gilhart, Dec. 29, 1981; 1 child, Derek Augustus. BSME, Tex. A&M U., 1968. Project engr. Tex. Power & Light Co., Dallas, 1968-72; service engr. Babcock & Wilcox, Chgo., 1972-74; sales engr., New Eng. dist. Babcock & Wilcox, Boston, 1974-79; area mgr., Far East, internat. bus. Babcock & Wilcox, Barberton, Ohio, 1979-81; dist. sales mgr. Babcock & Wilcox, Lakewood, Colo., 1981—. Mem. Rocky Mountain Elec. League (bd. dirs. 1988—, v.p. 1990-91, pres.-elect 1991-92, pres. 1992-93). Home: 7285 W Vassar Ave Denver CO 80227-3303 Office: Babcock & Wilcox 7401 W Mansfield Ave Ste 410 Denver CO 80235-2224

WOLFE, CHRISTOPHER LANE, cardiologist, educator; b. Saginaw, Mich., Sept. 23, 1951; s. Richard Allen and Ellen Marie (Lane) W.; m. Cynthia Marie Soghikian, Sept. 26, 1981; children: Lena Marie, Laura Anne. BA, Am. U. Beirut, 1974; MD, Wayne State U., 1978. Diplomate Am. Bd. Internal Medicine, subspecialty cardiovasc. disease. Med. intern and resident Emory U. Affiliated Hosps., Atlanta, 1978-81; cardiology fellow U. Tex. Health Sci. Ctr., Dallas, 1982-85; rsch. fellow U. Oxford, Eng., 1985-86; asst. prof. medicine U. Calif., San Francisco, 1986-94, assoc. prof. medicine, 1994—; assoc. dir. cardiac care unit Moffitt-Long Hosp.-U. Calif., San Francisco, 1986-95; med. dir. intensive cardiac care Moffitt-Long Hosp.-U. Calif. San Francisco, San Francisco, 1995—. Author 9 book chpts., numerous sci. and rev. articles, peer-reviewed sci. publs. Deacon Westminster Presbyn. Ch., Tiburon, Calif., 1992-94; fellow coun. clin. rsch. Am. Heart Assn., 1987—. Recipient Clinician Scientist award Am. Heart Assn., 1985, Clin. Investigator award Nat. Heart, Lung and Blood Inst., 1986, Nat. Grant-in-Aid Am. Heart Assn., 1992; Brit.-Am. rsch. fellow Am. Heart Assn., 1985. Fellow Am. Coll. Cardiology; mem. Am. Fedn. Clin. Rsch. (2 Henry Christian Meml. awards 1991), Soc. Nuclear Medicine, Soc. Magnetic Resonance, Western Soc. Clin. Investigation. Office: U Calif 505 Parnassus Ave San Francisco CA 94122-2722

WOLFE, CLIFFORD EUGENE, architect, writer; b. Harrington, Wash., Mar. 26, 1906; s. Delwin Lindsley and Luella Grace (Cox) W.; m. Frances Lillian Parkes, Sept. 12, 1936 (dec.); children: Gretchen Yvonne Wolfe Mason, Eric Von; m. Mary Theye Worthen. A.B. in Architecture, U. Calif.-Berkeley, 1933. Registered architect, Calif. Assoc. architect John Knox Ballantine, Architect, San Francisco, 1933-42; supervising architect, prodn. engr. G.W. Williams Co. Contractors, Burlingame, Calif., 1942-44; state-wide coord. med. schs. and health ctrs. office archs. and engrs. U. Calif.-Berkeley, San Francisco and Los Angeles, 1944-52; sec. council on hosp. planning Am. Hosp. Assn., Chgo., 1952-59; dir. planning dept. Office of York & Sawyer, Architects, N.Y.C., 1959-74; prin. Clifford E. Wolfe, AIA-E, Oakland, Calif., 1974-88; ret.; assoc. designer State of Calif. Commn. for Golden Gate Internat. Exposition, San Francisco, 1938-39; cons. Fed. Hosp. Council, Washington, 1954-60; mem. Pres.'s Conf. on Occupational Safety, Washington, 1955; rsch. architect Hosp Rsch. and Ednl. Trust, Chgo., 1957-59; instr. hosp. planning Columbia U., N.Y.C., 1961-73. Author, editor manuals on hosp. planning, engring. and safety, 1954-58. Author: Ballad of Humphrey The Humpback Whale, 1985; contbr. poetry to Tecolote Anthology, 1983, The Ina Coolbrith Circle, 1985, 87, 89, 91, 93, 95 (Grand prize Ina Coolbrith award 1986, Cleone Montgomery award 1990), Islandia, 1986, Tidings, 1989, Calif. Fedn. Chaparral Poets (pres. Tecolote chpt. 1982-86, 91-95). Hosp. planning research grantee USPHS, 1956. Mem. AIA (chmn. honor awards com. Chgo. chpt. 1958-59, chmn. activities com. N.Y. chpt. 1972-74, mem. emeritus East Bay chpt. 1974—). Address: 3900 Harrison St Apt 306 Oakland CA 94611-4525

WOLFE, EDWARD WILLIAM, II, music educator, composer; b. Albuquerque, Sept. 24, 1946; s. Edward William and Mary Ellen (Gabriele) W.; m. Nancy Jean Brown, Aug. 16, 1980. B in Music Edn., U. N.Mex., 1968, MA, 1973. Cert. tchr., N.Mex., Calif. Tchr. Grant Jr. High Sch., Albuquerque, 1970-75, Manzano High Sch., Albuquerque, 1974-75, Hoover Mid. Sch., Albuquerque, 1975-77, San Dimas (Calif.) High Sch., 1977-85; instr. music Calif. Poly. State U., Pomona, Calif., 1984; tchr. Bonita High Sch., LaVerne, Calif., 1985-89, Lone Hill Mid. Sch. and Feeders, San Dimas, Calif., 1989—; tchr. Hummingbird Music Camp, Jemez, N.Mex., 1970-76; cons. BUSD, San Dimas, 1980—. Author: The Language of Music, 1974, rev. 1993; composer Quartet for Horns, 1967, Oboe Sonata, 1967, Trio for Flute, Violin and Horn, 1968, Caverna, 1972, Quintet for Brass, 1993, numerous compositions and jazz arrangements, 1972—. Mem. Task Force on Mid. Sch. Reform, 1990. Recipient award Juvenile Justice Commn. City of San Dimas, 1984, 93; named to BUSD Hall of Fame, 1991. Mem. Music Educators Nat. Conf. (adjudicator 1969-77, 80—, v.p. dist. 7 1972, pres. 1975-76), Calif. Music Educators Assn. (task force on mid. sch. reform 1990, Outstanding Music Edn. cert. 1991), Nat. Assn. Jazz Educators (adjudicator 1980—, treas. N.Mex. chpt. 1972), Calif. Tchrs. Assn., So. Calif. Sch. Band and Orch. Assn., Bonita United Teaching Assn., Phi Mu Alpha. Home: 817 S Dumaine Ave San Dimas CA 91773-3808

WOLFE, GERRY, office administrator; b. Safford, Ariz., Nov. 2, 1929; d. Moroni and Ruth (Elliott) Jensen; m. Don Pickens, Nov. 29, 1947 (div. 1959); m. Billy E. Wolfe, Oct. 13, 1959 (div. 1972); 1 child, James Elliott. Lic. ins. agt., N.Mex. Credit mgr. Sears, Roebuck & Co., Safford, 1950-55; adminstrv. clk., sec. U.S. Forest Svc., Safford, 1955-61; sec., bookkeeper Groos, Clift & Ball, Architects, Odessa, Tex., 1961-65; sec. Mike Mason, Esq., Odessa, 1967-72; legal asst. Gene Ater, Esq., Odessa, 1967-72, Rodey Law Firm, Albuquerque, 1972-77; office adminstr. Keleher & McLeod, P.A., Albuquerque, 1983-94; office mgr. Intercontinental Devel. Co., Scottsdale, Ariz., 1979-80; sec. Sandia Labs., Albuquerque, 1981-82. Mem. Nat. Legal Adminstrs. Assn. Republican. Mem. LDS Ch. Home: 11308 Mahlon Ave NE Albuquerque NM 87112-4359 Office: Keleher & McLeod PA 414 Silver NW Albuquerque NM 87102

WOLFE, JONATHAN SCOTT, mortgage company executive, lawyer; b. San Francisco, Feb. 28, 1950; s. Lawrence Irving and Charlotte Ione (Avrick) W.; m. Constance Jarvis, Sept. 15, 1974; children: Alexandra Wickersham, Graham William Avrick. AB, Stanford U., 1972; JD, Harvard U., 1976; LLB, U. Cambridge, Eng., 1976. Bar: Calif. 1977, U.S. Dist. Ct. (no. dist.) Calif. 1977, U.S. Ct. Appeals (9th cir.) 1977. Assoc. Davis, Stafford, Kellman & Fenwick, Palo Alto, Calif., 1976-78, Dinkelspiel, Pelavin, Steefel & Levitt, San Francisco, 1979-80; prin. Steefel, Levitt & Weiss, San Francisco, 1981-84; assoc. counsel, v.p. Bank of Calif., N.A., San Francisco, 1984-85; gen. counsel, v.p., sec. N. Am. Mortgage Co. (successor to IMCO

Realty Svcs., Inc.), Santa Rosa, Calif., 1986-92; sr. v.p., gen. coun., sec. Fleet Mortgage Group, Inc., Columbia, S.C., 1992-93; sr. v.p., gen. counsel Headlands Mortgage Co., Larkspur, Calif., 1993-95; judge pro tem, arbitrator Sonoma Mcpl. Ct., 1979-80; lectr. World Trade Inst., N.Y.C., 1979, Am. Mgmt. Assn., San Francisco, 1979-80; v.p., gen. counsel, sec. Sonoma Conveyancing Corp., Santa Rosa, 1986-92, Sonoma Ins. Agy., Santa Rosa, 1986-92; sec. IMCO Capital Co., Inc., 1989-92; sec. IC Capital Co., Inc., 1989-92; Sec. North Am. Mortgage Co.; sen. v.p., gen. coun. and sec., Fleet Mortgage, Inc., Columbia, S.C., 1992-94; v.p. Marin Co.; co-chmn. Berger Kahn's Multimedia Group; ptnr., mng. ptnr. Berger, Kahn, Shafton, Moss, Figler, Simon and Gladstone, San Rafael, L.A. and Irvine, Calif.; sr. v.p., gen. counsel, sec. Fleet Realty; dir. Marin Ins. Agy., 1992-95. Author: (with others) The Dream Sellers, 1972, Surveillance and Espionage in a Free Society, 1972; cons. editor: Controlling Drugs: International Handbook, 1973. Mem. planning group subcom. on intelligence and security Dem. Nat. Com., Washington, 1971-72; spl. counsel Campfire Girls, Santa Clara County, Calif., 1977, Am. Lives Endowment, Portola Valley, Calif., 1980-82. Mem. ABA (consumer fin. ins. products com. 1987), Calif. Bar Assn., Sonoma County Bar Assn., Calif. Mortgage Bankers Assn. (legis. com. 1988—), Mortgage Bankers Assn. Am. (legal affairs com. 1987—, compliance com. 1988—), Phi Beta Kappa. Office: Berger Kahn et al 101 Lucas Valley Rd Ste 300 San Rafael CA 94903

WOLFE, STEVEN ALBERT, secondary education educator; b. Des Moines, Iowa, Feb. 24, 1949; s. Edward Jr. and Necia Lee (Hill) W.; m. Nina Joyce Wagner, Apr. 25, 1973; children: Ivan Angus, Rebekah, Nina Ellen, Rainbow, Tamara, Ross, Rosemary. BS, Brigham Young U., 1974; Masters Arts Teaching, Alaska Pacific U., 1988. Cert. tchr., Idaho, Alaska. Tchr. North Gem High Sch., Bancroft, Idaho, 1974-76, Homer (Alaska) Mid. Sch., 1976-77, Homer Jr. High Sch., 1977-85, Homer High Sch., 1985—; coach wrestling Homer High Sch., 1976-91, coach football, 1983-90. Author: Comprehensive Index to Wrestling Rules, 1991. Scoutmaster troop 365 Boy Scouts Am., Homer, 1988—; coach state championship wrestling teams Alaska Sch. Activities Assn., 1982, 85, 86. Named Nat. Coach of Yr., Franklin Inst., 1988. Mem. Alaska Wrestling Coaches Assn. (pres. 1989-91, inductee Hall of Fame 1990), Kenai Penninsula Wrestling Ofcls. Assn. (pres. 1992—). LDS. Home: 5007 Clover Ln Homer AK 99603-8116 Office: Homer High Sch 600 E Fairview Ave Homer AK 99603-7661

WOLFE, WILLIAM JEROME, librarian, English language educator; b. Chgo., Feb. 24, 1927; s. Fred Wiley and Helen Dorothea (Lovaas) W.; m. ViviAnn Lundin O'Connell, June 25, 1960 (div. 1962); 1 child, Lund. AB, U. Chgo., 1948; BA, Roosevelt U., Chgo., 1953; MEd, Chgo. State U., 1963; AA with high honors, Pima C.C., 1992; BAA magna cum laude, U. Ariz., 1994. Tchr. English John Marshall High Sch., Chgo., 1956-60; libr. Safford Jr. High Sch., Tucson, Ariz., 1961-71, Santa Rita High Sch., Tucson, 1971-75, Tucson High Sch., 1975-87; tutor Eastside Ctr., Tucson Adult Lit. Vols., 1988—, supr., 1993—. Co-founder Tucson Classic Guitar Soc., 1969-72; docent U. Ariz. Mus. Art, Tucson, 1989—; singer U. Ariz. Collegium Musicum, Sons of Orpheus Male Chorus. With U.S. Army, 1945-46, ETO. Mem. Sons of Norway, U. Chgo. Century Club, Roosevelt U. Sparling Soc., U. Ariz. Pres. Clun, U. Ariz. Hon. Fellows Soc., Tucson Post Card Exch. Club, Nat. Assn. Scholars, Assn. Lit. Scholars and Critics, Norsemen's Fedn., Phi Kappa Phi. Mem. Sons of Norway, U. Chgo. Century Club, Roosevelt U. Sparling Soc., U. Ariz. Pres. Club, U. Ariz. Hon. Fellows Soc., Tucson Post Card Exch. Club, Nat. Assn. Scholars, Assn. Literary Scholars & Critics, Norsemen's Fedn., Phi Kappa Phi. Republican. Mem. Ch. of Christ Scientist. Home: 8460 E Rosewood Tucson AZ 85710

WOLFF, BRIAN RICHARD, metal manufacturing company executive; b. L.A., Dec. 11, 1955; s. Arthur Richard and Dorothy Virginia (Johnson) W.; divorced; children: Ashley Rachael, Taryn Nicole. BSBA, Calif. State U., Chico, 1980; postgrad., U. Phoenix, 1990—. Sales rep. Federated Metals Corp./ASARCO, Long Beach, Calif., 1980-82, dist. sales mgr., 1983-84; sales mgr. Copper Alloys Corp., Beverly Hills, Calif., 1982-83; dir. mktg. Federated-Fry Metals/Cookson, Long Beach, Industry and Paramount, Calif., 1984-87; regional sales mgr. Colonial Metals Co., L.A., 1987-91; nat. sales mgr. Calif. Metal X/Metal Briquetting Co., L.A., 1991-93; sales engr. Ervin Industries, Inc., Ann Arbor, Mich., 1993 ; tech. sales mgr. GSP Metals & Chems. Co., 1987-91; cons. sales Calif. Metal Exch., L.A., 1987-91, Atlas Pacific Inc., Rialto, Calif., 1993—. Mem. citizens adv. com. on bus. Calif. Legis., 1983. Mem. Non Ferrous Founders Soc., Am. Foundrymen Soc., Calif. Cast Metals Assn., Steel Structures Painting Coun. Republican. Presbyterian.

WOLFF, DAVID JONATHAN, foreign affairs consultant; b. Cardiff, Wales, U.K., Sept. 12, 1962; came to U.S., 1962; s. Gayle William and Jeannene Collette W. BA in Polit. Sci., U. Hawaii, 1986; MA in Internat. Affairs magna cum laude, George Washington U., 1989. Fgn. affairs asst. to Senator David Durenberger U.S. Senate, Washington, 1986-87, sr. office systems analyst, 1987-89; rschr. in internat. rels. East-West Ctr., Honolulu, 1990—; chief aide to Senator Mary George Hawaii State Senate, Honolulu, 1990-94; cons. Pacific Forum/Ctr. for Strategic and Internat. Studies, Honolulu, 1990. Editor, contbg. author Asia-Pacific Current Affairs, 1991-93; contbr. articles to profl. jours. Pres. Quayside Cons. Fgn. Affairs Analysis. Roman Catholic. Office: East West Ctr 1777 E West Rd Honolulu HI 96822-2323

WOLFF, EDITH ANN, biochemist; b. Midland, Mich., Nov. 8, 1960; d. Manuel Daniel and Roselyn Elaine (Walth) W.; m. Martyn Nicholas Walker, Aug. 20, 1988. BS in Cell Biology, U. Kans., 1982; MS in Applied Genetics, Birmingham U., Eng., 1983. Rsch. biochemist Genetic Systems Corp., Seattle, Wash., 1984-87; rsch. scientist Bristol-Myers Squibb, Seattle, 1987—; cons. Banso Hosp., Cameroon, Africa, 1981, Resort for Eco-Tourism, Costa Rica, 1993. Contbr. articles to profl. jours. Recipient Student Rsch. award Sci. and Engring. Rsch. Coun., Birmingham, Eng., 1982-83. Mem. AAAS.

WOLFF, HOWARD KEITH, computer science educator, consultant; b. L.A., Mar. 28, 1948; s. Fred and Yvonne (Primock) W.; m. Anna Bornino, Dec. 6, 1966 (div. June 1971); children: Francesea, Jeffrey; m. Cindy Brattan, June 4, 1981; children: Jeffrey, Mariya. BA, Calif. State U., Dominguez Hill, 1969; MPA, U. So. Calif., 1971, PhD, 1973; MS, Calif. State U., Chico, 1992. Prin. investigator U. Simon Fraser, Vancouver, B.C., Can., 1970-71; prof. U. So. Calif., L.A., 1971-73, Tribhuuan (Nepal) U., 1974-75, Calif. State U., Chico, 1976-85, 87—, Colo. State U., Ft. Collins, 1985-87; evaluation cons. Nat. Planning Commn., Kathmandu, Nepal,. 1973-75; statis. cons. Nat. Population Commn., Kathmandu, 1983-87; cons. Butte Canyon Rsch. Assocs., Chico, 1979—; evaluator migrant edn. program Calif. State Dept. Edn., 1992—. Author: Social Science and Thesis Handbook, 1974; contbr. articles to profl. jours. Research grantee Can. Govt., Vancouver, 1970. Mem. IEEE, Am. Assn. Computing Machinery, Am. Soc. Pub. Adminstrn., Soc. Computer Simulations. Democrat. Club: Gears (Chico). Home: 1966 Honey Run Rd Chico CA 95928-8835 Office: Calif State U Dept Computer Sci Dept Polit Sci Chico CA 95929

WOLFF, JOEL HENRY, human resources engineer; b. New Rochelle, N.Y., Oct. 29, 1966; s. s. Richard Eugene and Elise Leonora (Wolff) A. BA, U. Nev. at Las Vegas, 1991; JD, Gonzaga U., 1995. Computer operator Sun Teleguide, Henderson, Nev., 1987-90; engring. aide Wojcik Engring., Las Vegas, 1989-90; computer cons. Ax Med. Interfaces, Las Vegas, 1990-91; programmer Biosoft, Las Vegas, 1991-92; rule 9 legal intern, 1994-95, univ. legal assistance, 1994. Named Eagle Scout Boy Scouts Am., 1984. Mem. ASCE (sec. student chpt. 1986-87), ABA (Law Student Divsn., 1992—), Internat. Law Soc. of Gonazaga Univ., Nat. Eagle Scout Assn., Phi Alpha Delta, Sigma Nu. Home: PO Box 858 Spokane WA 99210-0858

WOLFF, MARK ROBERT, elementary and secondary education educator; b. North Hollywood, Calif., Jan. 5, 1961; s. Hanns and Elke (Lohmayr) W. AA, L.A. Pierce Coll., Woodland Hills, Calif., 1983; BA in History, Calif. State U., Northridge, 1987. Elem., jr. and sr. high sch. tchr. L.A. Unified Sch. Dist. Author and editor: The Illustrated Math Book on Animal Cules, 1992. Home: 8703 Ranchito Ave Panorama City CA 91402-3315

WOLFF, SIDNEY CARNE, astronomer, observatory administrator; b. Sioux City, Iowa, June 6, 1941; d. George Albert and Ethel (Smith) Carne; m. Richard J. Wolff, Aug. 29, 1962. BA, Carleton Coll., 1962, DSc (hon.), 1985; PhD, U. Calif., Berkeley, 1966. Postgrad. research fellow Lick Obs. Santa Cruz, Calif., 1969; asst. astronomer U. Hawaii, Honolulu, 1967-71, assoc. astronomer, 1971-76; astronomer, assoc. dir. Inst. Astronomy, Honolulu, 1976-83, acting dir., 1983-84; dir. Kitt Peak Nat. Obs., Tucson, 1984-87, Nat. Optical Astronomy Observatories, 1987—; dir. Gemini Project Gemini 8-Meter Telescopes Project, 1992-94. Author: The A-Type Stars--Problems and Perspectives, 1983, (with others) Exploration of the Universe, 1987, Realm of the Universe, 1988, Frontiers of Astronomy, 1990; contbr. articles to profl. jours. Trustee Carleton Coll., 1989—. Rsch. fellow Lick Obs. Santa Cruz, Calif., 1967; recipient Nat. Meritorious Svc. award NSF, 1994. Mem. Astron. Soc. Pacific (pres. 1984-86, bd. dirs. 1979-85), Am. Astron. Soc. (coun. 1983-86, pres.-elect 1991, pres. 1992-94). Office: Nat Optical Astronomy Obs PO Box 26732 950 N Cherry Ave Tucson AZ 85719-4933

WOLFGANG, BONNIE ARLENE, musician, bassoonist; b. Caribou, Maine, Sept. 29, 1944; d. Ralph Edison and Arlene Alta (Obetz) W.; m. Eugene Alexander Pridonoff, July 3, 1965 (div. Sept. 1977); children: George Randall, Anton Alexander, Stephan Eugene. MusB, Curtis Inst. Music, Phila., 1967. Soloist Phila. Orch., 1966; soloist with various orchs. U.S., Cen. Am., 1966-75; prin. bassoonist Phoenix Symphony, 1976—, with Woodwind Quintet, 1986—. Home: 9448 N 106th St Scottsdale AZ 85258-6056

WOLFLE, DAEL LEE, public affairs educator; b. Puyallup, Wash., Mar. 5, 1906; s. David H. and Elizabeth (Pauly) W.; m. Helen Morrill, Dec. 28, 1929 (dec. July 1988); children: Janet Helen (Mrs. Wilhelm G. Christophersen), Lee Morrill, John Morrill. B.S., U. Wash., 1927, M.S., 1928; postgrad., U. Chgo., summers 1929, 30; Ph.D., Ohio State U., 1931, D.Sc., 1957; D.Sc., Drexel U., 1956, Western Mich. U., 1960. Instr. psychology Ohio State U., 1929-32; prof. psychology U. Miss., 1932-36; examiner in biol. scis. U. Chgo., 1936-39, asst. prof. psychology, 1938-43, assoc. prof., 1943-45; on leave for war work with Signal Corps, 1941-43; with OSRD, 1944-45; exec. sec. Am. Psychol. Assn., 1946-50; dir. commn. on human resources and advanced tng. Assoc. Research Councils, 1950-54; exec. officer AAAS, 1954-70; editor Sci., 1955, pub., 1955-70; prof. pub. affairs U. Wash., Seattle, 1970-76; prof. emeritus U. Wash., 1976—; mem. sci. adv. bd. USAF, 1953-57; mem. def. sci. bd. Dept. Def., 1957-61; mem. adv. council on mental health NIMH, 1960-64; mem. nat. adv. health council USPHS, 1965-66; mem. commn. on human resources NRC, 1974-78; mem. adv. bd. Geophys. Inst., Fairbanks, Alaska., 1970-93, chmn. adv. bd., 1972-81. Author: Factor Analysis to 1940, 1941, Science and Public Policy 1959, The Uses of Talent, 1971, The Home of Science, 1972, Renewing a Scientific Society, 1989; editor: America's Resources of Specialized Talent, 1954. Trustee Russell Sage Found., 1961-78, Pacific Sci. Cent. Found., 1962-80, Biol. Scis. Curriculum Study, 1980-85; chmn. bd. J. McK. Cattell Fund, 1962-82. Named Alumnus Summa Laude Dignatus, U. Wash., 1979. Mem. AAAS (pres. Pacific div. 1991-92), AAUP, Am. Psychol. Assn., Am. Acad. Arts and Scis. (exec. com. western sect. 1985-92), Sigma Xi. Home: 4545 Sand Point Way NE Apt 805 Seattle WA 98105-3932 Office: U Wash Grad Sch Pub Affairs Seattle WA 98195

WOLFLEY, VERN ALVIN, dentist; b. Etna, Wyo., Aug. 4, 1912; s. Rudolf E. and Eliza (Neuenschwander) W.; m. Bernice Michaelson, June 12, 1936; children: Norda Beth Wolfley Brimley, Vern A. Jr., Paul R., Carol Jo Wolfley Bennett. BS, U. Wyo., 1934; BS in Dentistry and DDS, U. Nebr., 1947. Farm mgmt. specialist USDA, 1934-43; placement officer War Relocation Authority, 1943; pvt. practice, Idaho Falls, Idaho, 1947-57, Phoenix, 1957—. Pres. Ariz. Children's Soc., Phoenix, 1960-61. With AUS, 1943; 1st lt. USAF, 1954. Mem. ADA (life), Ariz. Dental Assn. (life), Idaho Falls Dental Soc. (pres. 1949-50), Upper Snake River Dental Soc. (pres. 1955-56), Am. Soc. Dentistry for Children (life), Acad. Gen. Dentistry, Internat. Assn. Orthodontics (life), Am. Assn. Functional Orthodontists (charter), Fedn. Dentaire Internat., Cen. Ariz. Dist. Dental Soc. (life), Am. Legion, Lions (v.p. 1956), Omicron Kappa Upsilon, Alpha Zeta. Republican. Mem. LDS Ch. Office: 2837 W Northern Ave Phoenix AZ 85051-6646

WOLFRED, MORRIS M., pharmacologist and toxicologist; b. L.A., Apr. 30, 1920; s. Harry and Sylvia (Stern) W.; m. Rita R. Baer, Apr. 18, 1948; children: Robin Jan, Karen Lynn, Joan Daryl. BS in Pharmacy, U. So. Calif., L.A., 1941, MS in Pharm. Chemistry, 1942; PhD in Pharmacology, U. Wash., 1945. Diplomate Am. Bd. Diplomates in Pharmacy, Am. Bd. Diplomates in Pharmacy Internat; registered pharmacist Calif., Ariz. Teaching asst. U. So. Calif., L.A., instr.; assoc. toxicology State of Wash. Toxicology Lab.; S.B. Penick Rsch. fellow State U. Wash.; assoc. prof. pharmacology and toxicology U. So. Calif., dept. dir. grad. rsch.; cons. in field; drug evaluator rsch. and devel. of pharms.; lectr. in field; bd. advisors Intrasci. Rsch. Inst.; v.p. pharm. rsch. and devel. Med. Testing Sys., Inc.; pres. Prescription Ctrs. of Beverly Hills and L.A.; drug cons. Calif. Medicare Program; pharm. cons. ednl. planning com. U. Calif. Western Ctr. for Continuing Edn. in Hosps. and Related Health Instns.; bd. dirs., med. adv. bd. Cancer Detection Svcs., Inc.; mem. sci. coun. Intrasci. Rsch. Found., others. Pharm. editor Calif. Pharmacy Jour.; assoc. editor Bull. Lab. Medicine; editl. bd. Guidelines to Profl. Pharmacy. Founding mem. bd. dirs. The Comprehensive Health Planning Assn. L.A. County; chair Calif. Pharm. Assn. liaison com. on drugs to State of Calif. Pub. Assistance Med. Care Program; bd. drug cons. Smith Kline & French Labs.; apptd. to Calif. State Task Force on Profl. Svcs. ad hoc Com. to the Drug Adv. Com.; bd. advisors Paid Prescriptions; advisor, cons. Minister of Health of Republic of China, many others. Recipient Wisdom Award of Honor, Advancement of Knowledge, Learning and Rsch. in Edn., Man of the Yr. award Calif. Pharm. Assn., Merck Scholastic award. Fellow AAAS, Am. Inst. Chemists, Royal Soc. Health, Acad. Psychomatic Medicine, Internat. Acad. Law and Sci., Am. Coll. Pharmacists, Am. Coll. Apothecaries, Louis Pasteur Lib. and Sci. Found.; mem. N.Y. Acad. Sci., Internat. Soc. Comprehensive Medicine, Am. Soc. Hosp. Pharmacists, Am. Chem. Soc., So. Calif. Chem. Soc., So. Calif. Soc. Clin. Hypnosis, Western Soc. Pharmacology, Am. Pharm. Assn., Calif. Pharm. Assn., Acad. Pharm. Scis., Nat. Assn. Retail Pharmacy, Sigma Xi, Rho Chi, Phi Delta Chi.

WOLFSBERG, MAX, chemist, educator; b. Hamburg, Germany, May 28, 1928; came to U.S., 1939, naturalized, 1945; s. Gustav and Ida (Engelmann) W.; m. Marilyn Lorraine Fleischer, June 23, 1957; 1 dau., Tyra Gwendolen. A.B., Washington U., St. Louis, 1948, Ph.D., 1951. Assoc. chemist Brookhaven Nat. Lab., Upton, N.Y., 1951-54; chemist Brookhaven Nat. Lab., 1954-63, sr. chemist, 1963-69; prof. chemistry SUNY, Stony Brook, 1966-69; vis. prof. chemistry Ind. U., Bloomington, 1965, Cornell U., Ithaca, N.Y., 1963; prof. chemistry U. Calif., Irvine, 1969—, chmn. dept., 1974-80; Deutsche Forschungs Gemeinschaft guest prof. U. Ulm, Fed. Republic Germany, 1986; Forchheimer vis. prof. Hebrew U., 1993. Assoc. editor: Jour. Chem. Physics, 1968-70; editor: Comments on Chemical Physics, 1986-89; mem. editorial bd. Isotopenpraxis, 1987—; contbr. articles to profl. jours. AEC fellow, 1950-51; NSF sr. postdoctoral fellow, 1958-59; Alexander von Humboldt awardee, 1977, reinvitations 1982, 93. Mem. Am. Chem. Soc., Phi Beta Kappa, Sigma Xi. Jewish. Home: 4533 Gorham Dr Corona Del Mar CA 92625-3111 Office: U Calif Dept Chemistry Irvine CA 92717

WOLFSON, MARSHA, internist, nephrologist; b. Bklyn., Feb. 14, 1944; d. Murray and Rose (Cohen) W. Student, Boston U., 1961-63; BS, Fairleigh Dickinson U., 1965; MD, Med. Coll. Pa., 1970. Diplomate Am. Bd. Internal Medicine, Am. Bd. Nephrology. Staff physician NIH, Bethesda, Md., 1975-77; clinic instr. Georgetown U. Sch. Medicine, Washington, 1975-77; asst. prof. medicine Oreg. Health Scis. U., Portland, 1977-82; attending physician VA Hosp., Portland, 1983-87, chief nephrology, 1977-95; assoc. prof. medicine Oreg. Health Scis. U., Portland, 1982-95, prof., 1995—; med. dir. nutrition support svc. VA Hosp., Portland, 1987-95; Baxter Healthcare Corp., McGaw Park, Ill., 1995—; cons. in field. Co-author: The Science and Practice of Clinical Medicine, 1980, Clinical Dialysis, 1984, 90, Current Nephrology, 1984, Progress in Clinical Kidney Disease and Hypertension, 1985, Dialysis Therapy Handbook, 1986, Clinical and Physiological Applications of Vitamin B6, 1988, Acute Renal Failure: Diagnosis, Treatment, and Prevention, 1989; contbr. numerous articles to profl. jours. Bd. dirs. Kidney Assn. Oreg., Portland. Lt. comdr. USPHS, 1975-77. Mem. ACP, Women in Nephrology (pres. 1988), Multnomah County Med. Soc., Oreg. Med. Assn., Am. Soc. Parenteral and Enteral Nutrition, Am. Soc. Artificial Internal Organs, Am. Soc. Clin. Nutrition, Am. Inst. Nutrition, Am. Fedn. for Clin. Rsch., Internat. Soc. Nephrology, Am. Soc. Nephrology, Alpha Omega Alpha. Office: Baxter Healthcare Corp Renal Divsn 1620 Waukegan Rd Mc Gaw Park IL 60085

WOLFSON, MURRAY, economics educator; b. N.Y.C., Sept. 14, 1927; s. William and Bertha (Finkelstein) W.; m. Betty Ann Goessel, July 21, 1950; children: Paul G., Susan D., Deborah R. BS, CCNY, 1948; MS, U. Wis., 1951, PhD, 1964; postgrad., Marquette U., 1958-59. Cert. secondary tchr., Wis., Mich. Tchr. math. Montrose (Mich.) High Sch., 1959-61; instr. econs. Thornton Jr. Coll., Harvey, Ill., 1961-63; prof. Oreg. State U., Corvallis, 1963-86, Calif. State U., Fullerton, 1986—; vis. prof. numerous univs., including Ahamdu Bello U., Zaria, Nigeria, U. Canterbury, Christchurch, New Zealand, U. Wis., Milw., Marquette U., Milw., U. Durham, Eng., U. Oreg., U. So. Calif., Haifa (Israel) U., U. Adelaide, Australia; Fulbright specialist lectr., Japan, 1976-77, Tokyo U., Hitotsubashi U., Waseda U., Keio U.; docent Groningen U., The Netherlands; vis. fellow history of ideas unit Australian Nat. U., Sofia U., 1993-94; adj. prof. U. Calif., Irvine, 1986—; others. Author: A Reappraisal of Marxian Economics, 1968, (transl. into Japanese and Portuguese), Karl Marx, 1971, Spanish transl., 1977, A Textbook of Economics: Structure, Activities, Issues, 1978, Marx: Economist, Philosopher, Jew, 1982, Japanese transl., 1987, Economic Activities: Microeconomics, 1989, rev. edit., 1991, Essays on the Cold War, 1992, (with Vincent Buranelli) In the Long Run We Are All Dead, A Macroeconomic Murder Mystery, 1983, 2d edit., 1989; also numerous articles. Adv. bd. Yale U. Civic Edn. Project. With USN, 1945-46. Scholar N.Y. Bd. Regents, 1943; staff devel. fellow Oreg. State U., 1976; travel grantee Am. Coun. Learned Socs., 1979; recipient 1st nat. prize for excellence in teachng coll. econs. Joint Coun. on Econ. Edn., 1970. Mem. AAUP (chpt. pres. 1983-84), Am. Econ. Assn., Hist. of Econs. Soc., Peace Sci. Soc., Def. Econs. Assn., Western Econs. Assn., Peace Sci. Soc. (pres.). Home: 2022 Via Mariposa E # D Laguna Hills CA 92653-2247

WOLIN, MERLE LINDA, journalist, consultant; b. Cheyenne, Wyo., Jan. 1, 1948; d. Morris Aaron and Helen (Sobol) W. AA, Pine Manor Coll., 1968; BA, U. Calif., Berkeley, 1970. Co-founder, philanthropic cons. Pacific Change, San Francisco, 1971-73; mem editorial staff City Mag., San Francisco, 1974-75; co-founder, assoc. pub. Mother Jones mag., San Francisco, 1973-74; freelance writer N.Y Times, L.A. Times, People, 1976-79; Latin affairs writer L.A. Herald Examiner, 1979-82; nat. Latin affairs writer Wall Street Journal, L.A., 1982-83; correspondent Latin Am. L.A. Herald Examiner, Mexico City, 1983-86; freelance journalist Life, Premier Mag., The New Republic, 1986—; tv. news feature producer BBC, Fox TV., 1991—, ABC News, CBS News, 1991—. Recipient Mark Twain prize, regional prize AP, 1981, Journalism Atrium award U. Ga. 1981, econ. understanding award Dartmouth Coll., 1981, disting. writing award Hearst Newspapers, 1981, Paul Tobenkin Meml. award Columbia U., 1982, Robert F. Kennedy award, 1982, best investigative reporting award, L.A. Press Club, 1982, best fgn. press writing award, 1985, Clarence Darrow award ACLU, 1982, Unity award Lincoln U. Mo., 1982. Mem. Writers Guild Am., PEN Internat. (Gold Pen award for meritorious achievement, 1982).

WOLINSKY, LEO C., newspaper editor. BA in Journalism, U. So. Calif., 1972. Journalist, 1972—; staff writer L.A. Times, 1977-86, chief Sacramento bur., 1987-89, city editor, 1990, Calif. polit. editor, 1991, metro editor, 1994—. Office: Los Angeles Times Times Mirror Sq Los Angeles CA 90053

WOLINSKY, RICHARD BARRY, writer; b. N.Y.C., July 10, 1950; s. Melvin Wolinsky and Judith Sally (Weisberg) Green. BA, SUNY, Binghampton, 1971; MA, The New Sch. for Social Rsch., 1975. Asst. publicity dir. KPFA-FM, Berkeley, Calif., 1977; pub. dir. KPFA-FM, 1978, editor folio program guide, 1978-92; editor Perspectives Alonzo Printing, Hayward, Calif., 1993—; freelance editor, writer, 1977—; host Probabilities KPFA, 1977—, Broadway Madness, 1991—. Office: PO Box 1173 El Cerrito CA 94530-1173

WOLK, MARTIN, electronic engineer, physicist; b. Long Branch, N.J., Jan. 13, 1930; s. Michael and Tillie (Barron) W.; 1 child, Brett Martin. BS, George Washington U., 1957, MS, 1968; PhD, U. N.Mex., 1973. Physicist Naval Ordnance Lab., White Oak, Md., 1957-59, Nat. Oceanic and Atmospheric Adminstrn., Suitland, Md., 1959-66; solid state physicist Night Vision Lab., Fort Belvoir, Va., 1967-69, rsch. asst. U. N.Mex., Albuquerque, 1969-73; electronics engr. Washington Navy Yard, 1976-83, TRW, Inc., Redondo Beach, Calif., 1983-84; physicist Metrology Engring. Ctr., Pomona, Calif., 1984-85; electronics engr. Naval Aviation Depot North Island, San Diego, 1985—; cons. Marine Corps Logistics Base, Barstow, Calif., 1985—, Naval Weapons Station, Fallbrook, Calif., 1987-89, Naval Weapons Support Ctr., Crane, Ind., 1989—. Contbr. articles to Jour. Quantitative Spectroscopy and Radiative Transfer, Monthly Weather Rev., Proceedings of SPIE. Cpl. U.S. Army, 1946-49, Japan. Mem. IEEE, Soc. Photo-Optical Instrumentation Engring., Sigma Pi Sigma, Sigma Tau. Home: 740-91 Eastshore Ter Chula Vista CA 91913

WOLKOWITZ, OWEN MARK, physician, psychiatrist, researcher; b. Washington, Oct. 3, 1952; s. Gabriel Wolkowitz and Mandzia (Wroclawska) Wolkowitz-Murik; m. Janet Anne Negley, Sept. 9, 1984. BA, NYU, 1974; MD, U. Md., 1979. Diplomate Am. Bd. Psychiatry and Neurology. Intern in psychiatry Stanford (Calif.) U. Med. Ctr., 1979-80, resident in psychiatry, 1980-82, chief resident in psychiatry, 1983; med. staff fellow NIMH, Bethesda, Md., 1983-86; attending psychiatrist, assoc. prof., rschr. U. Calif., San Francisco, 1986—, staff psychiatrist, team leader Adult Inpatient Svcs., 1991-95; dir. Psychopharmacology and Exptl. Therapeutics Clinic, San Francisco, 1995—; mem. dean's award com. U. Calif., San Francisco, 1986-93, mem. student rsch. fellowship com., 1986-87, mem. residency tng. objective com., 1986-87; jour. reviewer Archives of Gen. Psychiatry, Biol. Psychiatry, Gen. Hosp. Psychiatry, Hosp. & Cmty. Psychiatry, Jour. Clin. Psychopharmacology, Jour. Nervous & Mental Disease, Jour. Neurosci., Jour. Psychiat. Rsch., Psychiatry Rsch., Psychosomatics, Schizophrenia Bull., Schizophrenia Rsch., Western Jour. Medicine; mem. behavioral scis. rev. bd. VA, 1988, 90, rsch. adv. group, 1993; mem. adv. bd. for clin. investigation Western Jour. Medicine, 1993; mem. steering com. Napa State Hosp., 1988—. Contbr. more than 100 articles to profl. jours. Recipient Young Rschr. Neurosci. award Calif. Assn. for the Mentally Ill, 1989, Stanley award Nat. Assn. for the Mentally Ill, 1993, Young Investigator award Nat. Alliance for Rsch. in Schizo and Affective Disorder, 1989; grantee S. Henderson Fund, 1988-90, Biomed. Rsch. Support, 1989-91, 93, AIDS Clin. Rsch. Ctr., 1990-91, NIMH, 1987-93, Scottish Rite Found., 1993-95, Stanley Found., 1993-95. Mem. AAAS, Am. Psychiat. Assn. (session chmn. ann. meeting 1993), Psychiat. Rsch. Soc., Soc. for Biol. Psychiatry, Am. Soc. Clin. Psychopharmacology, Internat. Soc. for Psycho-Neuro-Endocrinology (Carl P. Richter prize 1992), Collegium Internationale Neuropsychopharmacoligicum, World Fedn. Socs. Biol. Psychiatry, West Coast Coll. Biol. Psychiatry (consensus conf. on benzodiazepine regulation 1993—), No. Calif. Psychiat. Soc., Internat. Soc. for Neuroimaging in Psychiatry, Psi Chi. Office: U Calif/Dept Psychiatry Langley Porter Psychiat 401 Parnassus Ave Box F0984 San Francisco CA 94143

WOLLENBERG, DAVID ARTHUR, real estate developer; b. Longview, Wash., Aug. 6, 1947; s. Richard Peter and Leone (Bonney) W.; m. Katrina Moulton, Aug. 30, 1975; children: Andrew Richard, Blake Endicott. BA, Brown U., 1969; MBA, Stanford U., 1973. Front office mgr. Caneel Bay Plantation, St. John, V.I., 1969-71; adminstrn. asst. AMFAC Communities-Hawaii, Honolulu, 1973-77; exec. v.p. The Cortana Corp., Palo Alto, Calif., 1977-83, pres., 1983—; dir. Longview Fibre Co., Wash. 1979—. Bd. dirs. Peninsula Ctr. for Blind, Palo Alto, 1984-90; bd. dirs. Christmas in April, Mid-Peninsula, 1992, pres., 1994-95, treas., 1995-96. Mem. Outrigger Canoe Club (Honolulu), Menlo Circus Club, Palo Alto Club. Republican. Office: The Cortana Corp 800 El Camino Real Ste 175 Menlo Park CA 94025-4808

WOLLENBERG, RICHARD PETER, paper manufacturing company executive; b. Juneau, Alaska, Aug. 1, 1915; s. Harry L. and Gertrude (Arnstein) W.; m. Leone Bonney, Dec. 22, 1940; children: Kenneth Roger, David Arthur, Keith Kermit, Richard Harry, Carol Lynne. BSME, U. Calif., Berkeley, 1936; MBA, Harvard U., 1938; grad., Army Indsl. Coll., 1941; D in Pub. Affairs (hon.), U. Puget Sound, 1977. Prodn. control Bethlehem Ship, Quincy, Mass., 1938-39; with Longview (Wash.) Fibre Co., 1939—, safety engr., asst. chief engr., chief engr., mgr. container operations, 1951-57, v.p., 1953-57, v.p. ops., 1957-60, exec. v.p., 1960-69, pres., 1969-78, pres., chief exec. officer, 1978-85, pres., chief exec. officer, chmn. bd., 1985—, also bd. dirs.; mem. Wash. State Council for Postsecondary Edn., 1969-79, chmn., 1970-73; mem. western adv. bd. Allendale Ins. Bassoonist SW Washington Symphony. Trustee Reed Coll., Portland, 1962—, chmn. bd. 1982-90. Served to lt. col. USAAF, 1941-45. Recipient Alumni Achievement award Harvard U., 1994. Mem. NAM (bd. dirs. 1981-86), Pacific Coast Assn. Pulp and Paper Mfrs. (pres. 1981-92), Inst. Paper Sci. and Tech. (trustee), Wash. State Roundtable, Crabbe Huson (bd. dirs.). Home: 1632 Kessler Blvd Longview WA 98632-3633 Office: Longview Fibre Co PO Box 606 Longview WA 98632-7391

WOLLINS, DAVID H., lawyer; b. N.Y.C., Nov. 1, 1952; s. Donald J. Wollins and Constance Joy Graham; m. Leslie Bjerg Lilly, Apr. 1, 1989;1 child, Alexander Bjerg Lilly. BS in Fin. and Mktg., U. Pa., 1974; JD, New Eng. Sch. Law, 1978. Bar: N.Y. 1979, U.S. Dist. Ct. (ea. and so. dists.) N.Y. 1989, U.S. Dist. Ct. Colo., U.S. Ct. Appeals (10th cir.) 1986, U.S. Ct. Appeals (fed. and 2d cirs.) 1990, U.S. Ct. Claims 1983, U.S. Supreme Ct. 1994. Pres. Nature's Way Recycling Co., Boston, 1974-75; summer assoc. Phillips, Nizer, Benjamin, Krim & Ballon, N.Y.C., 1976-77, assoc., 1978-86; of counsel Cortez and Friedman, P.C., Englewood, Colo., 1986-87; mem. firm, co-head litigation dept. Brenman, Raskin, Friedlob & Tenenbaum, P.C., Denver, 1987-91; shareholder, head litigation dept. McGeady Sisneros & Wollins, P.C., Denver, 1991-95; spl. counsel Jonathan T. Hellman & Assocs., P.C., Englewood, Colo., 1995—; pro bono atty., City N.Y., 1978-86. Author short stories and numerous poems. Mem. ABA, N.Y. Bar Assn., Colo. Bar Assn., Denver Bar Assn. Home: 311 Bannock St # C Denver CO 80223-1103 Office: Jonathan T. Hellman & Assocs PC Tower 2, 5th Fl 12835 E Arapahoe Rd Englewood CO 80112

WOLLMAN, ARTHUR LEE, urologist; b. Bklyn., Apr. 30, 1943; s. Leo and Eleanor (Rakow) W.; m. Maxine Marsha Mandel, Aug. 23, 1964; 1 child, D. Bruce. AB, Middleburg Coll., 1963; PhD, Downstate Med. Ctr., Bklyn., 1967, MD, 1969. Diplomate Nat. Bd. Med. Examiners, Am. Bd. Urology. Intern U.S. Pub. Health Svc. Hosp., Staten Island, N.Y., 1969-70; resident in gen. surgery U.S. Pub. Health Svc. Hosp., Staten Island, 1970-71, resident in urology, 1971-74; fellowship in nephrology Meml. Sloan Kettering Inst., N.Y.C., Jan.-Mar. 1972; fellowship in pediatric urology Presbyn. Hosp., Columbia U., N.Y.C., July-Dec., 1972; ptnr., urologist So. Calif. Permanente Med. Group, San Diego, 1974—; mem. active surg. staff Kaiser Permanente Med. Ctr., San Diego, 1974—. Cmmdr. PHS, 1969-74. Mem. Phi Beta Kappa, Sigma Xi, Alpha Omega Alpha. Republican. Jewish. Office: So Calif Permanente Med Group 4647 Zion Ave San Diego CA 92120-2507

WOLLMER, RICHARD DIETRICH, statistics and operations research educator; b. L.A., July 27, 1938; s. Herman Dietrich and Alice Myrtle (Roberts) W. BA in Math., Pomona Coll., 1960; MA in Applied Math., Columbia U., 1962; MS in Engring. Sci., U. Calif., Berkeley, 1963, PhD Engring. Sci., 1965. Scientist Rand Corp., Santa Monica, Calif., 1965-70; prof. info. systems Calif. State U., Long Beach, 1970—; vis. prof. Calif. State U., Northridge, 1981-82; cons. McDonnell Douglas, Long Beach, Calif., 1978-80, 82, 85-91, Logicon, San Pedro, Calif., 1979-81; vis. assoc. prof. Stanford U., 1976; rsch. scientist Electric Power Rsch. Inst., Palo Alto, Calif., 1977; rsch. engr. Jet Propulsion Lab., Pasadena, Calif., 1971. Contbr. articles to profl. jours. Deacon Bel Air Presbyn. Ch., L.A., 1982-84, treas. 1983. Mem. So. Calif. Inst. Mgmt. Sci.-Ops. Rsch. Soc. (chmn. 1981, 89, vice chmn., 1980, 88, treas. 1979), Ops. Rsch. Soc. Am., Inst. Mgmt. Sci. Republican. Home: 6132 Fernwood Dr Huntington Beach CA 92648-5574 Office: Calif State U 1250 N Bellflower Blvd Long Beach CA 90840-0006

WOLLUM, OWEN LEE, entrepreneur; b. Yakima, Wash., July 27, 1959; s. Leo and Dolores Lucille (Ringer) W.; m. Sandra Ellen Larsen, Nov. 26, 1988. AAS, Yakima Valley Coll., 1981; BA in Psychology, Pacific Luth. U., Tacoma, 1983. Software designer Pacific Luth. U., 1983-84; prin. Johnson & Wollum, Tacoma, 1984-87; pres., dir. Pinnacle Pub., Inc., Federal Way, Wash., 1987-91; pres., chmn. Palisade Press, Inc., Auburn, Wash., 1991—. Democrat. Lutheran.

WOLSEY, THOMAS DEVERE, middle school educator; b. Salt Lake City, Mar. 6, 1962; d. T. Mark and Lynn Wolsey. BS, So. Utah State Coll., 1986; MA in Ednl. Adminstrn., Calif. State U., San Bernardino, 1990. Cert. tchr., Utah; mid. sch. endorsement, reading, English tchr., adminstrv. svcs., Calif. Tchr. adult edn., tchr. English San Bernardino City Unified Sch. Dist., 1986-89; ESL tutor Alpine Sch. Dist., American Fork, Utah, 1981-84; Chpt. One resource and English tchr., dir. activities Lake Elsinore (Calif.) Unified Sch. Dist., 1989—. Mem. Nat. Coun. Tchrs. English, Internat. Reading Assn., Calif. Network of Mid. Grades Partnership Schs. (rep.). Home: 31996 Corte Ruiz Temecula CA 92592 Office: Elsinore Mid Sch 1203 W Graham Ave Lake Elsinore CA 92530

WOLTERBEEK, MARC WILLIAM, English language educator; b. San Francisco, July 7, 1951; s. Robert Daniel Wolterbeek and Mary Bella (Chiapetta) Muse; m. Kim Silveira, Dec. 11, 1951; 1 child, Marc William Jr. BA, U. Calif., Berkeley, 1972, MA, 1974, PhD, 1984. Cert. C.C. instr., Calif. English instr. Contra Costa Coll., San Pablo, Calif., 1974-85, Napa (Calif.) Coll., 1975-82, Chabot Coll., Hayward, Calif., 1984-85; tchg. asst. French dept. U. Calif., Berkeley, 1980-81, tchg. asst. comparative lit. dept., 1982-83, acting instr. comparative lit., 1983-84; lectr. English Calif. State U., Hayward, 1984-85, U. of the Pacific, Stockton, Calif., 1985-87; assoc. prof., head English dept. Coll. of Notre Dame, Belmont, Calif., 1987—. Author: Comic Tales of the Middle Ages, 1991; contbr. articles to profl. publs. Chair, judge poetry contest San Mateo (Calif.) County Fair, 1990-94; chair 4th Ann. Jack London Writers' Conf., Belmont, 1992. Mem. Philol. Assn. of Pacific Coast (sec. session on medieval lit. 1994—), Pacific Coast Writing Ctrs. Assn. (pres. 1991-92). Office: Coll of Notre Dame 1500 Ralston Ave Belmont CA 94002-1908

WOLTERS, CHRISTOPHER FREDERICK, performing company executive; b. Oceanside, Calif., Dec. 27, 1959; s. Gerald Frederick and Charlene Ann (Peters) W.; m. Jill Annette Posey, July 24, 1982 (div. Dec. 12, 1989). BA in Psychology, U. Calif., Santa Cruz, postgrad. in edn.; postgrad. in edn., Ariz. State U. Dir. Evening of One Acts The Moore Theater, 1977-78; learning asst. kindergarten De La Veaga Elem. Sch., Santa Cruz, 1983; coach and instr. Santa Cruz Gymnastics Ctr., 1982-84; performing arts specialist City of Sacramento, 1984-86; expressive arts coord. Sacramento Children's Home, 1986-87; achievement specialist Cruddas Family Home, 1987-89; performing arts cons. Santa Cruz City Sch. Dist., 1992-94; program asst. U. Calif., Santa Cruz, 1989—; artistic dir., owner Life in Motion Musical Theatre Co., Santa Cruz, 1982—; creative arts cons. Santa Cruz City Sch. Dist., 1983-94, Sacramento City Schs., 1984-87, Davis City Schs., 1984-87, Yolo County, 1984-87, San Diego Sch. Dist., 1991-92, Pajaro Valley Sch. Dist., 1994-95; instr. U. Calif.-Davis Exptl. Coll., 1986. Editor The Children's Musical Theatre News, 1991—; rec. artist: I Heard the Children Say, 1991, Soup of Stone, 1992, Jack and the Beanstalk, 1992, Sarah and Her Brother, 1992; live radio performer KUSP Radio, Santa Cruz; choreographer GATE Dance Concerts, Santa Cruz; profl. dancer Pamela Trokansky Dance Theatre, 1986-87; contbr. articles to jours.; author children's plays and musicals including: Soup of Stone, 1984, Aladdin, 1985, Jack and the Beanstalk, 1986, Substitute Blues, 1994, others. Vol. Santa Cruz AIDS Project, 1992; dir./children's musical fund-raiser Santa Cruz Natural History Assn., 1994. Schs. Plus Found. grantee, 1988, 92, 93, Title VII Fund grantee, 1994. Mem. No. Calif. Songwriters Assn. (Award for Best Song/Performance 1989), Broadcast Music Inc., Santa Cruz Performing Arts Alliance. Office: Life in Motion Children Mus PO Box 267 Santa Cruz CA 95061-0267

WOLTERS, GALE LEON, range science professional; b. Portis, Kans., Apr. 25, 1939; s. Lester Orin and Dalice Marie (Smith) W.; m. Justine Louise Beatty, May 29, 1960; children: Ty, Amy. BS, Ft. Hays State U., 1961, MS, 1962; PhD, N.D. State U.. 1968. Instr. N.D. State U., Fargo, 1965-66; range scientist Southern Forest Experiment Sta. USDA, Alexandria, La., 1966-75; project leader Pacific Southwest Forest and Range Experiment Sta. USDA, Fresno, Calif., 1975-80; range rsch. br. chief U.S. Forest Svc., Washington, 1980-87; range scientist Rocky Mountain Forest and Range Experiment Sta., Albuquerque, 1987—; del. 2d Internat. Rangeland Congress, Adelaide, Australia, 1984, 4th Internat. Rangeland Congress, Montpellier, France, 1991, Agr. Goodwill Tour, People-to-People program, People's Republic of China, 1986. Contbr. to Jour. Range Mgmt. Mem. Soc. Range Mgmt. (pres. regional sects., 1972, 82), Wildlife Soc., Soc. Am. Foresters, Sigma Xi, Beta Beta Beta. Home: 801 Navarra Way SE Albuquerque NM 87123-4517 Office: Rocky Mountain Exptl Sta 2205 Columbia Dr SE Albuquerque NM 87106-3222

WOLVINGTON, WINSTON WARREN, retired judge; b. Denver, July 10, 1923; s. William Thomas and Bessie Maude (Roberts) W.; m. Shirley Anne Vail, Sept. 9, 1944; children: Gloria, Judith, Donald, Glenn. JD, U. Mich., 1948; BA, Oberlin (Ohio) Coll., 1949. Bar: Colo. 1949. Assoc. Wolvington & Wormwood, Denver, 1949-54, ptnr., 1954-73; dist. judge State of Colo., Golden, 1973-89, sr. judge, 1989-94; retired, 1994. Mem. ABA, Am. Judicature Soc., Colo. Bar Assn., Colo. Judicature Soc., 1st Judicial Bar Assn. (pres., v.p.). Democrat. Home: 1391 S Winston Dr Golden CO 80401-8040

WOMACK, THOMAS HOUSTON, manufacturing company executive; b. Gallatin, Tenn., June 22, 1940; s. Thomas Houston and Jessie (Eckel) W.; Linda Walker Womack, July 20, 1963 (div. Dec. 1989); children: Britton Ryan, Kelley Elizabeth; m. Pamela Ann Reed, Apr. 20, 1991. BSME, Tenn. Tech. U., Cookeville, 1963. Project engr. U.S. Gypsum Co., Jacksonville, Fla., 1963-65; project mgr. Maxwell House Div. Gen. Foods Corp., Jacksonville, 1965-68; mfg. mgr. Maxwell House Div. Gen. Foods Corp., Hoboken, N.J., 1968-71, div. ops. planning mgr., 1971-73; industry sales mgr. J.R. Schneider Co., Tiburon, Calif., 1973-79; pres. Womack Internat., Inc., Novato, Calif., 1979—. Holder 4 U.S. patents. Mem. Soc. Tribologists and Lubrication Engrs., Am. Filtration Soc., Soc. Mfg. Engrs., Am. Soc. Chem. Engrs. Office: Womack Internat Inc One Digital Dr Novato CA 94949

WONDER, JOHN PAUL, educator; b. Long Beach, Calif., July 29, 1921; s. John Paul and Etta (Jones) W.; m. Jane Josephine Walder, Dec. 22, 1946; children: John Walder, Peter Charles. A.B., Stanford U., 1943, A.M., 1948, Ph.D., 1952; Exchange scholar, Universidad Central, Madrid, 1950-51. Grad. fellow Stanford, 1946-50; instr., asst. prof. Spanish U. Ariz., 1951-56; dir. Binational Center, Belo Horizonte, Brazil; with USIA, also Rio de Janeiro and Port-au-Prince, Haiti, 1956-62; asst. prof. Los Angeles State Coll., 1962-63; prof. Spanish U. Pacific, Stockton, Calif., 1963-91; chmn. dept. modern langs. U. Pacific, 1964-75; dir. Center for Internat. Programs, 1979-82. Author: (with Aurelio M. Espinosa, Jr.) Gramática Analítica, 1976; assoc. editor: (theoretical linguistics) Hispania, 1979-89. Served as 1st lt., arty. M.I. AUS, 1943-46, ETO. Mem. Alpha Tau Omega. Home: 660 W Euclid Ave Stockton CA 95204-1819

WONDERS, WILLIAM CLARE, geography educator; b. Toronto, Apr. 22, 1924; s. George Clarence and Ann Mary (Bell) W.; m. Lillian Paradise Johnson, June 2, 1951; children—Karen Elizabeth, Jennifer Anne, Glen William. B.A. with honors, Victoria Coll., U. Toronto, 1946; M.A., Syracuse U., 1948; Ph.D., U. Toronto, 1951; Fil. Dr. h.c., Uppsala U., 1981. Teaching asst. dept. geography Syracuse U., 1946-48; lectr. dept. geography U. Toronto, 1948-53; asst. prof. geography dept. polit. economy U. Alta., 1953-55, assoc. prof. geography, 1955-57, prof., head dept. geography, 1957-67, prof. dept. geography, 1967-87, Univ. prof., 1983—, prof. emeritus, 1987—; vis. prof. geography U. B.C., 1954, U. Okla., 1965-66, St. Mary's U., 1977, U. Victoria, 1989, J.F. Kennedy Inst., Free U. Berlin, 1990; guest prof. Inst. Geography, Uppsala (Sweden) U., 1962-63; rsch. fellow in Geography U. Aberdeen, Scotland, 1970-71, 78; vis. fellow in Can. Studies, U. Edinburgh, Scotland, 1987. Author: Looking at Maps, 1960, The Sawdust Fusiliers, 1991, Norden and Canada-A Geographer's Perspective, 1992, Alaska Highway Explorer, 1994; (with T. Drinkwater et al) Atlas of Alberta, 1969, (with J.C. Muller et al) Junior Atlas of Alberta, 1979; contbr., editor: Canada's Changing North, 1971, The North, 1972, The Arctic Circle, 1976, Knowing the North, 1988; contbr. articles to jours. and encys., chpts. to books. Mem. Nat. Adv. Com. on Geog. Rsch., 1965-69; mem. Can. Permanent Com. on Geog. Names, 1981-94, Alta. Historic Sites Bd., 1978-93; mem. policy bd. Can. Plains Rsch. Centre, U. Regina (Sask.), 1975-86; mem. adv. bd. Tyrrell Mus. Paleontology, 1984-89; bd. dirs. The Muttart Found., 1986-93, 95—, v.p., 1991-93, mem., 1991—. NSF sr. fgn. scientist fellow, 1965-66; Canada Council leave fellow, 1969-70, 77-78; Nuffield Found. fellow, 1970-71. Fellow Arctic Inst. N.Am., Royal Soc. Can.; mem. Canadian Assn. Geographers (past. pres.), Royal Scottish Geog. Soc., Canadian Assn. Scottish Studies (councillor 1974-77), Scottish Soc. Northern Studies, Champlain Soc. (councillor 1981-86), Sigma Xi, Gamma Theta Upsilon.

WONG, ALEXANDER SHIH-WEI, electrical engineer; b. Lawrence, Kans., Apr. 26, 1966; s. Sheh and Eugenia J.K. Wong. BS in Computer Engring., U. Ill., 1987; MSEE, U. Calif., Berkeley, 1989, PhD in Elec. Engring., 1992. Customer engr. GE, Research Triangle Park, N.C., 1985; sr. tech. assoc. AT&T Bell Labs., Murray Hill, N.J., 1986; engr. Lawrence Livermore (Calif.) Lab., 1987-88; cons. Motorola Corp., Mesa, Ariz., 1989; sr. CAD engr. Intel Corp., Santa Clara, Calif., 1992-93, staff CAD engr., 1994—; chmn. tech. CAD wafer subcom. CAD Framework Initiative, Austin Tex., 1989—. Editor CAD Framework Initiative wafer TCAD, 1992. Mem. IEEE, Phi Kappa Phi, Tau Beta Pi, Eta Kappa Nu. Republican. Office: Intel Corp 2200 Mission College Blvd Santa Clara CA 95052

WONG, ASTRIA WOR, cosmetic business consultant; b. Hong Kong, Oct. 23, 1949; came to U.S., 1970; B in Vocat. Edn., Calif. State U., Long Beach, 1976. Cert. coll. tchr. (life), Calif. West coast sales trainer Revlon Inc., N.Y.C, 1975-82; nat. tng. dir. diReniel Internat., Palm Springs, Calif., 1982; dir. Beauty Cons. Service Agy., Long Beach, Calif., 1983—; pres. Boutique Astria, Scottsdale, Ariz., 1994—. Author: The Art of Femininity, 1971; editor (newsletter) So. Calif. Cosmetic, 1983-86. Chair Cmty. Involvement Paradise Rep. Woman's Club. Named Salesperson of Yr., Revlon, Inc., N.Y.C., 1978. Mem. So. Calif. Cosmetic Assn. (correspondence sec. 1982—), Women's Coun., Cosmetologist Tchr. Assn., Bus. and Profl. (ind. devel. chair.), Fashion Group Internat. Republican. Office: Beauty Cons Service Agy 7121 E 1st Ave Scottsdale AZ 85251-4305

WONG, BERNARD P., anthropologist; b. China, Feb. 12, 1941; came to U.S., 1969; s. Maurice S. and Theresa S. (Chau) W.; m. Rosemarie Deist, Apr. 14, 1973; children: Veronica, Alexandra. BA, Berchmans Coll., Quezon City, Philippines, 1966; post grad., Ateneo de Manila, Philippines, 1968; MA, U. Wis., 1971, PhD, 1974. Asst. prof. U. Wis., Anthropology Dept., Janesville, 1974-81, assoc. prof., 1981-86; assoc prof. San Francisco State U., Anthropology Dept., 1986-88, prof., 1988—; dir. San Francisco State U., Ctr. Urban Anthropology, 1988—, chair anthropology dept., 1990. Author: A Chinese American Community, 1979, Chinatown, 1982, Patronage Brokerage, 1988; editor: Bridge: An Asian American Perspective, 1978-80; contbr. articles to profl. jours. Coun. mem. Gov's. Asian Adv. Coun. Wis., 1983-86. Fellow; Am. Anthrop. Assn., Soc. Applied Anthropology; mem. Am. Ethnological Soc., Soc. Urban Anthopology, Soc. Anthropology Work, Chinese Hist. Soc. Am. (bd. dirs.). Office: San Francisco State Univ Dept of Anthropology 1600 Holloway Ave San Francisco CA 94132-1722

WONG, BONNIE LEE, systems analyst; b. L.A., Nov. 30, 1957; d. Robert Lee and Betty Rose (Woo) W. Student, Cambridge (Eng.) U., 1979; BS, U. So. Calif., L.A., 1979, MPA, 1981. Resident, adminstrv. asst. Olive View Med. Ctr., Sylmar, Calif., 1980-81; quality assurance coord. Lincoln Hosp. Med. Ctr., L.A., 1982; cons. Ernst & Whinney, L.A., 1983-85; systems coord., analyst, then cons. Am. Med. Internat., L.A., 1985-87; client svcs. rep. McDonnell Douglas Health Systems, L.A., 1987-89; mktg. support rep. Sci. Dynamics Corp., Torrance, Calif., 1989; bus. analyst The Hosp. of the Good Samaritan, L.A., 1990-93; sys. analyst UniHealth, Burbank, Calif., 1994—. Mem. Healthcare Fin. Mgmt. Assn. (mem. roster com. 1985, info. systems com. 1988), U. So. Calif. Healthcare Alumni. Office: UniHealth Info Svcs 3400 Riverside Dr Burbank CA 91505

WONG, CHOY-LING, interior designer; b. Hong Kong, Nov. 25, 1949; d. Teh-Chung Wang; m. Francis Michael Wong, Feb. 7, 1975; children: Shelby, Kenton. BFA in Environ. Design, BA in Art, U. Hawaii, 1973. Graphics/mapping artist Hawaii, 1972-73; asst. Lanai Urban Planning Project, Hawaii, 1973; interior designer C.S. Wo & Sons, Inc., Honolulu, 1973-83; pres. Choy-Ling Wong, Inc., Honolulu, 1984—, Furniture Catalog Libr., Honolulu, 1986—. Contbr. articles to profl. jours. Active Hist. Hawaii Preservation Parade, Honolulu, 1985-88. Recipient Design awards Bldg. Industry Assn., 1990, Cert. of Appreciation, U. Hawaii, 1990, Outstanding Vol. award First Lady of Hawaii, 1990. Mem. Am. Soc. Interior Designers (profl., participant showhouse 1978, 80, 82, 85, 87, Sunday snoop, 1988, 91-94, Presdl. citations 1993, 94), Assn. Chinese Univ. Women, U. Hawaii Internat. Students Alumni Assn. (charter), U. Hawaii Sch. Architecture Alumni Assn. (bd. dirs. 1993-95). Office: Choy-Ling Wong Inc 931 Hausten St Honolulu HI 96816

WONG, HARRY CHOW, anesthesiologist, educator; b. Beloit, Wis., June 26, 1933; s. Charles T. and Yee S. W.; m. Jean A. Nagahiro, June 21, 1958; children: Jeffrey, Stacey, Daphne, Steven. BS, U. Wis., 1955, MD, 1958. Diplomate, Am. Bd. Anesthesiology. Intern Providence Hosp., Portland, Oreg., 1958-59; resident in anesthesiology U. Wis., Madison, 1959-61; pvt. practice Salt Lake City, 1961-88; chmn. dept. anesthesiology, Latter-day Saints Hosp., 1966-67, 74-76, chmn. ICU com., 1971-75; pres. med. staff, Salt Lake Surg. Ctr., 1976-88; mem. Joint Commn. Accreditation Health Orgns., 1983—, cons. surveyor, 1985—; prof. anesthesiology, U. Utah, Salt Lake City, 1988—. Mem. AMA, Am. Soc. Anesthesiologists (chmn. com. ambulatory surgical care 1983-85, patient safety 1986-88, com peer review 1986—, chmn. 1993—), Internat. Anesthesia Rsch. Soc., Am. Heart Assn., Federated Ambulatory Surg. Assn. (bd. dirs. 1976—), Soc. Ambulatory Anesthesia (bd. dirs. 1985—, pres. 1990), Utah Med. Ins. Assn. (bd. govs. 1980-90), Utah State Soc. Anesthesiologists (pres. 1966). Home: 1060 Oak Hills Way Salt Lake City UT 84108-2073 Office: Dept Anesthesiology 50 N Medical Dr Salt Lake City UT 84132-0001

WONG, ING LIONG, nephrologist; b. Sibu, Malaysia, Feb. 16, 1945; came to the U.S., 1971; s. Tiong Keng and Kieu Hung (Su) W.; m. Chu Fong, Nov. 8, 1969; children: Yu-Tian, Yu-Tung, Adrienne. BS, U. Manitoba, 1969, MD, 1971. Diplomate Am. Bd. Internal Medicine. Intern U. So. Calif. Med. Ctr., L.A., 1971-72; resident in internal medicine VA Hosp., 1972-74; nephrology fellowship UCI and affiliated hosps., 1974-76; asst. clin. prof. U. Calif., Irvine, 1979—; pres. Alamitos Renal-Med. Group Inc., Los Alamitos, Calif., 1978—, Hemotech, Inc., Los Alamitos, 1979—; med. dir. Norwalk (Calif.) Dialysis Ctr., 1991—, Lakewood Dialysis Ctr., Calif., 1995—; chmn. credential com. Bellwood Gen. Hosp., Bellflower, Calif., 1990—. Founding mem. Chinese Ams. United for Self-Empowerment, L.A., 1994. Mem. ACP, Am. Soc. Nephrology, Internat. Soc. Nephrology. Democrat. Office: Alamitos Renal Med Group 3801 Katella Ave Los Alamitos CA 90720-3338

WONG, JAMES BOK, economist, engineer, technologist; b. Canton, China, Dec. 9, 1922; came to U.S., 1938, naturalized, 1962; s. Gen Ham and Chen (Yee) W.; m. Wai Ping Lim, Aug. 3, 1946; children: John, Jane Doris, Julia Ann. BS in Agr., U. Md., 1949, BS in Chem. Engring., 1950; MS, U. Ill., 1951, PhD, 1954. Rsch. asst. U. Ill., Champaign-Urbana, 1950-53; chem. engr. Standard Oil of Ind., Whiting, 1953-55; process design engr., rsch. engr. Shell Devel. Co., Emeryville, Calif., 1955-61; sr. planning engr., prin. planning engr. Chem. Plastics Group, Dart Industries, Inc. (formerly Rexall Drug & Chem. Co.), L.A., 1961-66, supr. planning and econs., 1966-67, mgr. long range planning and econs., 1967, chief economist, 1967-72, dir. econs. and ops. analysis, 1972-78, dir. internat. techs., 1978-81; pres. James B. Wong Assocs., L.A., 1981—; chmn. bd. dirs. United Pacific Bank, 1988—; tech. cons. various corps. Contbr. articles to profl. jours. Bd. dirs., pres. Chinese Am. Citizens Alliance Found.; mem. Asian Am. Edn. Commn., 1971-81. Served with USAAF, 1943-46. Recipient Los Angeles Outstanding Vol. Service award, 1977. Mem. Am. Inst. Chem. Engrs., Am. Chem. Soc., VFW (vice comdr. 1959), Commodores (named to exec. order 1982), Sigma Xi, Tau Beta Pi, Phi Kappa Phi, Pi Mu Epsilon, Phi Lambda Upsilon, Phi Eta Sigma. Home: 2460 Venus Dr Los Angeles CA 90046-1646

WONG, JEFFREY YUN CHUNG, radiation oncologist, medical researcher; b. Honolulu, Nov. 5, 1955; s. Tom Kam Yee and Rose Ah Moy (Chun) W.; m. Julia Kyoko Yoshikawa, Oct. 17, 1987; 1 child, Marisa Midori. BS in Biology, Stanford U., 1977; MD, Johns Hopkins U., 1981. Diplomate in radiation oncology Am. Bd. Radiology. Intern Harbor-UCLA Med. Ctr., Torrance, 1981-82; resident U. Calif., San Francisco, 1982-85; staff physician City of Hope Med. Ctr., Duarte, Calif., 1985—. Contbr. articles to profl. jours. Am. Cancer Soc. clin. fellow, 1984. Mem. Am. Soc. Therapeutic Radiology and Oncology, Am. Soc. Clin. Oncology, Soc. Nuclear Medicine, Radiation Rsch. Soc., Phi Beta Kappa.

WONG, KAR-YIU, economist educator; b. Canton, China, Sept. 19, 1950; came to U.S., 1983; s. Kong Ming and Wai Yu Wong; m. Yunkin Leung, May 17, 1973; 1 child, Licyau. BSc in Engring., U. Hong Kong, 1972; MPhil in Econs., Chinese U., Hong Kong, 1979; PhD in Econs., Columbia U., 1983. Asst. prof. U. Wash., Seattle, 1983-90, assoc. prof., 1990—. Mem. Chinese Econ. Assn. N.Am. (v.p. 1994, 95), Am. Econ. Assn., Can. Econ. Assn. Office: Univ Wash Dept Econs Seattle WA 98195

WONG, KENNETH LEE, import executive, software engineer, consultant; b. L.A., Aug. 15, 1947; s. George Yut and Yue Sam (Lee) W.; m. Betty (Louie) Wong, June 29, 1975; children: Bradford Keith, Karen Beth. BS in Engring., UCLA, 1969, MS in Engring., 1972, postgrad., 1972-73, 76-78. Cert. community coll. instr., Calif. Engring. aide Singer Librascope, Glendale, Calif., 1972-73; computer system design engr. Air Force Avionics Lab., Wright-Patterson AFB, Ohio, 1973-75; mem. tech. staff Hughes Aircraft Co., various cities, Calif., 1976-78, 79-81, TRW Def. and Space Systems Group, Redondo Beach, Calif., 1975-76, 78-79; engring. specialist Northrop Corp., Hawthorne, Calif., 1981-84; mem. tech. staff Jet Propulsion Lab., Pasadena, Calif., 1984-87; software cons. EG&G Spl. Projects, Las Vegas, Nev., 1987, AT&T Bell Labs., Warren, N.J., 1987-88, Westinghouse Electric Corp., Linthicom, Md., 1988, E Systems, Inc., Greenville, Tex., 1984-89; prin. Wong Soft Works, L.A., 1989—; pres. Oriental Silk Co., L.A., 1989—. Author tech. reports. Coach, Tigers Youth Club, L.A. 1st lt. USAF, 1973-75. Mem. AIAA, IEEE, Assn. Computing Machinery, Upsilon Pi Epsilon. Republican. Home: 3385 McLaughlin Ave Los Angeles CA 90066 Office: Oriental Silk Co 8377 Beverly Blvd Los Angeles CA 90048

WONG, KIN-PING, university dean, biotechnology researcher, company executive, educator, science administrator; b. Guangzhou, China, Aug. 14, 1941; s. Kwok-Keung and Yuan-Kwan (Loo) W.; m. Anna S.K. Koo, Sept. 16, 1968; children: Voon-Chung Wong, Ming-Chung Wong. BS, U. Calif., Berkeley, 1964; PhD, Purdue U., 1968. Postdoctoral fellow Duke U., Durham, N.C., 1968-70; asst. and assoc. prof. chemistry U. South Fla., Tampa, 1970-75; vis. scientist Max Planck Inst. Molecular Genetics, Berlin, 1972; vis. prof. U. Uppsala, Sweden, 1975; assoc. and prof. biochemistry U. Kans., Kansas City, 1975-83, dean grad. studies, 1980-83; vis. prof. biochemistry U. Tokyo, 1979; program dir. of biophysics NSF, Washington, 1982-83; sci. dean, prof. Calif. State U., Fresno, 1983—; mng. dir., CEO Hong Kong Inst. Biotechnology, 1992-93; founder, chmn., pres., CEO RiboGene Inc., Menlo Pk., Calif., 1989-91; vis. prof. biochemistry Stanford U. Med. Ctr., summer 1985; adj. prof. medicine U. Calif. San Francisco Med. Sch., 1986—; adj. prof. biochemistry and biophysics, U. Calif., San Francisco, 1987—; mem. U.S. Govt. Interagency Com. on Radiation, Washington, 1982-83; gov. Moss Landing (Calif.) Marine Labs., 1983—; cons. HHS, Washington, 1985—; trustee U. Calif., San Francisco, Fresno 1986—; mem. rev. panel NSF; mem. sci. expert panel Calif. Commn. Tchr. Credentialing. Contbr. over 50 research articles to prof. jours.; 32 pub. research abstracts; author various keynote speeches, convocation lectures. Chmn. sci. com. Fresno Met. Mus., 1983-85; co-chmn. planning com. Cen. Calif. Biomed. Rsch. Inst., Fresno, 1987—; co-chmn. multicultural coun. Clovis Unified Sch. Dist., 1988-90. Recipient cancer research grants and awards, Damon Runyan Fund, Milheim Found., Am. Cancer Soc., Eli Lilly Corp., Research Corps., Am. Heart Assn., 1980-81; grantee HHS, 1986-89, Nat. Inst. Heart Lung and Blood, 1972-87, Nat. Inst. Gen. Med. Scis., 1972-80; research career devel. awardee NIH, 1972-75; sr. research fellow European Molecular Biology Orgn., 1975; NSF summer rsch. professorship Stanford U., 1985; Laval Research award in innovative scis. and tech. Calif. State U., Fresno, 1985; scholarship Pepperdine U. presdl. and key exec. program, 1986-88; Calif. Sea grant Dept. Commerce, 1987-90. Fellow Royal Soc. Chemistry, Am. Inst. Chemists; mem. Am. Soc. Biol. Chemistry (membership com. 1983-86), AAAS, Biophys. Soc., Am. Chem. Soc., Sigma Xi. Office: Calif State U Sch Natural Sci Fresno CA 93740-0090

WONG, NANCY L., dermatologist; b. Chung King, China, Aug. 23, 1943; came to U.S., 1947; d. Alice (Lee) Wong; m. Robert Lipshutz; children: Seth, Alison, David. BS magna cum laude, Pa. State U., 1963; MS in Physics, Columbia U., 1965; MD, Jefferson Med. Coll., Phila., 1971. Diplomate Am. Bd. Dermatology. Intern Wilmington Med. Ctr., 1972; resident Jackson Meml. Hosp., Miami, Mount Sinai Med. Ctr., Miami, 1977; physician Kaiser Med. Ctr., Redwood City, Calif., 1987—. NSF fellow, AEC fellow, Woodrow Wilson fellow. Fellow Am. Acad. Dermatology, Woodrow Wilson , Atomic Enery Commn. Office: 910 Maple St Redwood City CA 94063-2034

WONG, OTTO, epidemiologist; b. Canton, China, Nov. 14, 1947; came to U.S., 1967, naturalized, 1976; s. Kui and Foon (Chow) W.; m. Betty Yeung, Feb. 14, 1970; children: Elaine, Jonathan. BS, U. Ariz., 1970; MS, Carnegie Mellon U., 1972; MS, U. Pitts., 1973, ScD, 1975. Cert. epidemiologist, Am. Coll. Epidemiology, 1982. USPHS fellow U. Pitts., 1972-75; asst. prof. epidemiology Georgetown U. Med. Sch., 1975-78; mgr. epidemiology Equitable Environ. Health Inc., Rockville, Md., 1977-78; dir. epidemiology Tabershaw Occupational Med. Assocs., Rockville, 1978-80; dir. occupational rsch. Biometric Rsch. Inst., Washington, 1980-81; exec. v.p., chief epidemiologist, ENSR Health Scis., Alameda, Calif., 1981-90; chief epidemiologist, pres. Applied Health Scis., San Mateo, Calif., 1991—; cons. Nat. Cancer Inst., Nat. Inst. Occupational Safety and Health, Occupational Safety and Health Adminstrn., Nat. Heart, Lung and Blood Inst., Ford Motors Co., Gen. Electric, Mobil, Chevron, Union Carbide, Fairfax Hosp., Va. U. Ariz. scholar, 1967-68. Fellow Am. Coll. Epidemiology, Human Biology Council; mem. Am. Pub. Health Assn., Biometric Soc., Soc. Epidemiologic Rsch., Phi Beta Kappa, Pi Mu Epsilon. Republican. Contbr. articles to profl. jours. Office: Applied Health Scis PO Box 2078 181 Second Ave Ste 628 San Mateo CA 94401

WONG, SUN YET, engineering consultant; b. Honolulu, Dec. 6, 1932; s. Chip Tong and Shiu Inn (Chang) W.; m. Janet Siu Hung Law; children: Cathleen, Bryan, Jonathan. BS in Civil Engring. with honors, U. Hawaii, 1954; MS in Civil Engring., Yale U., 1955. Exec. v.p., treas., tech. dir. Mechanics Rsch. Inc., 1964-77; treas. System Devel. Corp., 1977-79; chmn. bd., pres., treas. Applied Rsch. Inc., 1979-81; ind. tech. cons. Rolling Hills Estates, Calif., 1981—; engring. cons. Acurex, Mountain View, Calif., 1983, Ampex, Redwood City, Calif., 1991, Applied Tech., Mountain View, 1983-85, Astron, Mountain View, 1983-85, E Systems, Garland, Tex., 1986-93, Electromech. Systems Inc., Anaheim, 1984, Hughes, El Segundo, Calif., 1992, 94—, Intercon, Cerritos, Calif., 1982-84, J.H. Wiggins Co., Redondo Beach, Calif., 1982-84, Kodak Datatape, Pasadena, Calif., 1989, Measurement Analysis Corp., Torrance, Calif., 1984—, MRJ, Fairfax, Va., 1984, Odectics, Anaheim, 1990, Swales & Assocs., Beltsville, Md., 1992-93, Statistical Scis. Inc., Beverly Hills, Calif., 1986, Tompkins and Assocs., Torrance, 1984—, TRW, Redondo Beach, 1984. Home and Office: 7 Club View Ln Rolling Hills Estates CA 90274

WONG, WALLACE, medical supplies company executive, real estate investor; b. Honolulu, July 13, 1941; s. Jack Yung Hung and Theresa (Goo) W.; m. Amy Ju, June 17, 1963; children: Chris, Bradley, Jeffery. Student, UCLA, 1960-63. Chmn., pres. South Bay Coll., Hawthorne, Calif., 1965-86; chmn. Santa Barbara (Calif.) Bus. Coll., 1975—; gen. ptnr. W B Co., Redondo Beach, Calif., 1982—; CEO Cal Am. Med. Supplies, Rancho Santa Margarita, Calif., 1986—, Cal Am. Exports, Inc., Rancho Santa Margarita, 1986—, Pacific Am. Group, Rancho Santa Margarita, 1991—; chmn., CEO Alpine, Inc., Rancho Santa Margarita, Calif., 1993—; pres. Bayside Properties, Rancho Santa Margarita, 1993—; bd. dirs. Metrobank, L.A. FFF Enterprises; chmn. bd. 1st Ind. Fin. Group., Rancho Santa Margarita. Acting sec. of state State of Calif., Sacramento, 1982; founding mem. Opera Pacific, Orange County, Calif., 1985; mem. Hist. and Cultural Found., Orange County, 1986; v.p. Orange County Chinese Cultural Club, Orange County, 1985. Named for Spirit of Enterprise Resolution, Hist. & Cultural Found., Orange Country, 1987; recipient resolution City of Hawthorne, 1973. Mem. Westren Accred Schs. & Colls. (v.p. 1978-79), Magic Castle (life), Singapore Club. Office: Alpine Inc 23042 Arroyo Vis Rancho Santa Margarita CA 92688

WONG, WALTER FOO, county official; b. San Francisco, Apr. 11, 1930; s. Harry Yee and Grace (Won) W. AA, Hartnell Coll., 1952; BS, U. Calif., Berkeley, 1955; MPH, U. Hawaii, 1968. Registered sanitarian, Calif. Sanitarian Stanislaus County Health Dept., Modesto, Calif., 1955-56; sanitarian Monterey County Health Dept., Salinas, Calif., 1956-67, sr. sanitarian, 1968-69, supervising sanitarian, 1969-70, dir. environ. health, 1971—; sec. Monterey County Solid Waste Mgmt. Com., 1976—, Monterey County Hazardous Wast Mgmt. Com., 1987—; coord. Monterey County Genetic Engring. Rev. Com., 1987—; mem. Monterey County Hazardous Materials Response Task Force, 1988—; mem. tech. adv. com. Monterey Peninsula Water Mgmt. Dist., 1985—, Monterey Regional Water Pollution Control Agy., 1985—; chmn. task force Monterey Regional Wastewater Reclamation Study for Agr., EPA and State of Calif. Chmn. Salinas Bicentennial Internat. Day Celebration, 1974, Pollution Clean-up Com. of Fort Ord Task Force, 1992; mem. Calif. Bare Closure Environ. adv. com., 1993. Mem. Calif. Conf. Dirs. Environ. Health (pres. 1982-83), Assn. Environ. Health Adminstrs. (pres. 1982-83), Salinas C. of C. (Mem. of Yr. award 1971), U. Calif. Berkeley Alumni Assn., U. Hawaii Alumni Assn. (Disting. Alumni award 1992), Monterey County Hist. Soc. (1st v.p. 1995), Ethnic Cultural Coun. (chmn. 1995). Republican. Presbyterian. Home: 234 Cherry Dr Salinas CA 93901-2807 Office: Monterey County Health Dept 1270 Natividad Rd Rm 301 Salinas CA 93906

WONG, WAYNE D., nutritionist; b. San Francisco, May 13, 1950; s. Chaney Noon and La Dean Maryan (Mah) W. m. Betty Lee, Oct. 16, 1977; children: Michael Gabriel, Elizabeth Catherine, Whitney Forbes, Ellesse Florence. BS in Dietetic Adminstrn., U. Calif., Berkeley, 1972; MS in Sch. Bus. Mgmt., Pepperdine U., 1976; student, Nikon Sch. Photography, San Francisco, 1969. Cert. Food Svc. Dir., Calif. Community Coll. tchr.; Registered Dietitian, Sch. Bus. Official, Benefit specialist. Food svc. worker, lab. asst. U. Calif., Berkeley, 1968-69, 70-71; mgmt. intern Mich. State U., East Lansing, 1970; dietetic intern Milw. Pub. Schs., 1972-73; food svc. cons. Trader Vic's, San Francisco, 1973; dir. food svcs. Bakersfield (Calif.) City Sch. Dist., 1973—; instr. Bakersfield Coll., 1978—; cons. Wong, R.D., Bakersfield, 1978—; registered Benefit Specialist Investors Retirement Mgmt., Carpenteria, Calif., 1988—; Nat. Child Nutrition Adv. Coun. USDA, Washington, 1977-79; first v.p. Partners in Nutrition Coop., Lancaster, Calif., 1988-90; food svc. edn. task force Calif. Dept. Edn., Sacramento, 1979—; project coord. nutrition edn. and tng. exemplary program adoption grant Bakersfield City Sch. Dist., 1982; project dir. basic skills, basic foods course, curriculum and recipe devel. grant Calif. Dept. Edn., 1985, cons. teaching course, 1985-88; mem. adv. coun. Calif. State U. Long Beach Child Nutrition Program Mgmt. Tng. Ctr., 1991; mem. Sch. Nutrition Adv. Coun., Bakersfield, 1990—. Author: Food Service Equipment-How Long Should It Last?, 1985; co-author (videotape) Bettermade Plastics, 1991, Recycle: Save Earth's Resources Now; programmer Food Svc. Pers. Database, 1988, Dishmachine Labor and Energy Matrix, 1991; contbr. articles to profl. jours. BBQ fund-raiser co-chmn. Citizens for Yes on Measure B, Bakersfield, 1989; legis. com. Child Nutrition Facilities Act 1975, Sacramento, 1973-76; expert witness State Senate Select Subcom. on Nutrition and Human Needs, Sacramento, 1973; asst. troop leader Boy Scouts Am., Troop 219, San Francisco, 1965-67; participant Chinese Family Life Study U. Calif., Berkeley; dir. polystyrene recycling project Bakersfield City Sch. Dist., 1990; team leader Healthy Kids, Healthy Calif. program Calif. Dept. Edn., 1985-87; sponsor Christian Broadcasting Network Satellite Communications Ctr., 1978; world vision sponsor India Community Devel. Program, 1974-92. Recipient Leadership award Calif. State Dept. Edn., 1987, Outstanding Sch. Lunch Program award USDA, 1989; 1st pl. Calif. Sch. Food Svc. Assn. Country Cook-off, 1983, 84; Toto Wizard nominee Sabatasso Foods, 1985, Best Practice award USDA, 1992. Mem. Am. Dietetic Assn. (Young Dietitian of Yr. 1976), Am. Sch. Food Svc. Assn. (child nutrition mktg. bike ride 1991, Cycle Across Am. for Child Nutrition and Fitness 1993), Am. Running and Fitness Assn., Calif. Assn. Sch. Bus. Ofcls. (photographer 1985, food svc. R&D chmn. 1985-87, recognition 1987, food and nutrition R&D com. 1984), Calif. Sch. Food Svc. Assn. (edn. tng. chmn. 1975-76, wellness awareness bike ride 1990-91, child nutrition bike ride 1991, 1st pl. photo contest 1993, cover photographer assn. jour. Poppyseeds 1992), Sports and Cardiovascular Nutritionists, Kern County Sch. Food Svc. Assn. (pres. 1987-90, recipient Golden Poppy award 1990), Kern Wheelmen (v.p. 1992), Pi Alpha Phi, Omicron Nu. Republican. Baptist. Home: 4901 University Ave Bakersfield CA 93306-1773

WONG, WILLIAM, newspaper editor, columnist; b. Oakland, Calif., July 7, 1941; m. Joyce Ann Mende, Nov. 23, 1968; 1 child, Sam Mende-Wong. AB, U. Calif., Berkeley, 1962; MS, Columbia U., 1970. Reporter San Francisco Chronicle, 1962, San Leandro (Calif.) Morning News, 1962-63, San Francisco News-Call-Bull., 1963-64; editl. assoc. Nat. Com. for Support of Pub. Schs., Washington, 1968-69; reporter Wall St. Jour., Cleve. and San Francisco, 1970-79; bus. editor Oakland Tribune, 1979-81, asst. mng. editor, 1981-84, 86-88, ombudsman, 1984-86; assoc. editor, columnist, 1988-92, columnist, 1992—; lectr. Sch. Journalism U. Calif., 1990-91; lectr. Asian Am. studies San Francisco State U., 1988-92, lectr. journalism, 1991-92. Vol. U.S. Peace Corps, The Philippines, 1964-68. Jefferson fellow East-West Ctr., Honolulu, 1983; recipient Thomas Storke Internat. Jour. award No. Calif. sect. World Affairs Coun., 1989, Print Journalism award Media Alliance, San Francisco, 1990, Cert. of Merit, NCCJ, N.Y.C., 1991. Mem. Asian Am. Journalists Assn. (nat. v.p. 1989-91, Spl. Recognition award 1990). Office: Oakland Tribune 66 Jack London Sq Oakland CA 94607-3700

WONG, WILLIE, mayor, automotive executive; b. Mesa, Ariz., Oct. 12, 1948; m. Cobina Wong; children: Kevin, Jeremy. Grad., Ariz. State U. Vice mayor City of Mesa (Ariz.), 1988-90; councilmem., 1990-91; mayor City of Mesa (Ariz.), 1992—; pres. Wilky's Performance Ctr., Mesa, Ariz.; prev. employment with AT&T. Treas. Regional Pub. Transp. Authority; chmn. Williams Redevel. Ptnrship., Maricopa Assn. Govts. Regional Devel. Policy Com.; vice-chmn. Williams Gateway Airport Authority, Mesa Sister Cities; exec. com. League of Ariz. Cities and Towns; bd. dirs. YMCA (past pres.), Child Crisis Ctr., Southwest Pub. Recycling Assn. Named Outstanding Young Man Mesa Leadership, Tng., & Devel. Assn., 1989. Mem. MAG Regional Coun., Econ. Devel. Adv. Bd., Rotary Club-Mesa West. Home: 1343 E McLellan Mesa AZ 85203 Office: Office of the Mayor 55 N Center St PO Box 1466 Mesa AZ 85211-1466 also: Wilky's Performance Ctr 402 E Main Mesa AZ 85203

WONG, Y(ING) WOOD, real estate investment company executive, venture capital investment company executive; b. Hong Kong, Apr. 28, 1950; came to U.S., 1969; s. Loyee K.H. and Margaret M.C.L. Wong; m. Leslie K. P. Chan, Dec. 18, 1977; children: Joshua H., Jonathan H. AA in Biology, Menlo Coll., 1971, BSBA, 1974; BA in Zoology, U. Calif., Berkeley, 1972; M in Mgmt., Northwestern U., 1976. Auditor, Touche Ross & Co., CPA's, San Francisco, 1976-78; founder, mng. dir. Wong Properties, Palo Alto, Calif., 1976—; founder, gen. ptnr. Wongfratris Co., Palo Alto, 1986—; instr. Golden Gate U., 1977. Trustee Crystal Springs Uplands Sch., Hillsborough, Calif. Mem. Internat. Platform Assn., Commonwealth Club Calif., Beta Alpha Psi. Office: 51 Jordan Pl Palo Alto CA 94303-2903

WONG-DIAZ, FRANCISCO RAIMUNDO, lawyer, educator; b. Havana, Cuba, Oct. 29, 1944; came to U.S., Nov. 1961; s. Juan and Teresa (Diaz de Villegas) Wong; 1 child, Richard Alan. BA with honors, No. Mich. U., 1963; MA with highest honors, U. Detroit, 1967; PhD, MA, U. Mich., 1974; JD, U. Calif.-Berkeley, 1976. Bar: Calif. 1980, U.S. Dist. Ct. (no. dist.) Calif. 1990, Fla. 1987. Asst. prof. San Francisco State U., 1977; vis. scholar U. Calif. Berkeley Sch. Bus., Berkeley, 1983-84; prof. City Coll. San Francisco, 1975—, dept. chmn., 1978-85; rsch. atty. Marin Superior Ct., 1980-81; ct. arbitrator Marin Mcpl. Ct., 1985; solo practice, Kentfield, Calif., 1980—; assoc. dean Miami-Dade Coll., 1986; dir. Cutcliffe Consulting, Inc., Hawthorne, LaFamila Ctr., Inc., San Rafael, Calif., 1980-85, Small Bus. Inst., Kentfield, 1982-86; cons. ICC Internat., San Francisco, 1980-82. Bd. editors Indsl. Relations Law Jour., 1975-76; mem. editl. bd. California Lawyer, 1991-93; lector St. Sebastian's Ch., 1984—, Parish Coun., 1995. Diplomat-scholar U.S. Dept. State, Washington, 1976; Horace C. Rackham fellow U. Mich., 1970, fellow U.C. Berkeley, 1995. Summer fellow U. Calif., Berkeley, 1995. Mem. Am. Polit. Sci. Assn., Latino Ednl. Assn. (treas. 1985), Cuban Am. Nat. Coun., World Affairs Coun. (seminar leader San Francisco 1980). Roman Catholic. Club: Commonwealth.

WOO, RAYMOND, aerospace engineer; b. Tokyo, Japan, Nov. 22, 1949; came to U.S., Sept. 7, 1966; s. Eric Dee and Alice Chi-Hua (Chang) W. BS in Engring., UCLA, 1972, MS in Engring., 1975; engr. degree, U. So. Calif., 1988. Tech. staff Rockwell Internat., Downey and El Segundo, Calif., 1975-78, TRW (Aerospace), Redondo Beach, Calif., 1978-82, Logicon (Aerospace), San Pedro, Calif., 1982-84; tech. staff, engr. Jet Propulsion Lab., Pasadena, Calif., 1984-87; dept. staff, engr. TRW (Aerospace), Redondo Beach, Calif., 1988-89; electronics engr. naval air warfare ctr. USN, China Lake, Calif., 1989—. Contbr. article to profl. jour. Dept. scholar UCLA Sch. Engring., 1971. Mem. AIAA, IEEE (exec. com. 1971—). Republican. Baptist. Home: 1301 S Atlantic Blvd No 118 Monterey Park CA 91754 Office: Naval Air Warfare Ctr Code Sec 471260D Ridgecrest CA 93555

WOO, TIMOTHY DAVID, JR., state senate clerk, lawyer; b. Hilo, Hawaii, Oct. 30, 1944; s. Timothy David and Evelyn Momi (Goo) W.; m. Donna May Lee, Aug. 2, 1948; 1 child, Tiffany Wing Yan. BA, Northwestern U., 1967; MBA, Golden Gate U., 1968; JD, U. Calif., 1971. Bar: U.S. Supreme Ct. Hawaii, Calif. Assoc. atty. Evans, Jackson & Kennedy, Sacramento, 1973-74; asst. U.S. atty. U.S. Dept. Justice, Honolulu, 1974-78; ptnr. Chang & Woo, Attys., Honolulu, 1978-80; law clerk to Judge Philip C. Wilkins U. S. Dist. Cts., Sacramento, 1971-73; asst. clerk of the senate Hawaii State Senate, Honolulu, 1979-82, clerk of the senate, 1982—. Mem. Waialae County Club. Democrat. Office: State Capital Honolulu HI 96813

WOO, VERNON YING-TSAI, lawyer, real estate developer; b. Honolulu, Aug. 7, 1942; s. William Shu-Bin and Hilda Woo; m. Arlene Gay Ischar, Feb. 14, 1971; children: Christopher Shu-Bin, Lia Gay. BA, U. Hawaii, 1964, MA, 1966; JD, Harvard U., 1969. Pres. Woo Kessner Duca & Maki, Honolulu, 1972-87; pvt. practice law Honolulu, 1987—; judge per diem Honolulu Dist. Ct., 1978-84, 95—. Bd. dirs. Boys and Girls Club of Honolulu,. 1985—, pres., 1990-92. Mem. ABA, Hawaii Bar Assn., Honolulu Bd. Realtors, Waikiki Yacht Club, Pacific Club. Home: 2070 Kalawahine Pl Honolulu HI 96822-2518 Office: 1019 Waimanu St Ste 205 Honolulu HI 96814-3409

WOOD, BEVERLY PHYLLIS, pediatric radiologist, educator; b. Fayetteville, Ark., Mar. 17, 1939; d. Emil Felix and Julia Louise (Finger) Helbling; m. Lawrence Warren Wood, Aug. 10, 1963; children: Sarah, Rebecca, Steven, Thomas. AB, Harvard U., 1961; MD, U. Rochester, 1965. Diplomate Am. Bd. Radiology; added qualification in pediatric radiology. Intern St. Elizabeth's Hosp., Boston, 1965-66; resident in diagnostic radiology U. Rochester Med. Ctr., 1967-71, fellow in pediatric radiology, 1971-72, from asst. prof. to prof. radiology and pediatrics, 1972-89; prof. radiology and pediatrics U. So. Calif., L.A., 1989—; radiologist in chief Children's Hosp. of L.A., 1987—. Author: Caffey's X-Ray Diagnosis, 1991, Pediatric Orthopaedics in Primary Care, 1993; editor Pediatric Learning File, Am. Coll. Radiology; exec. editor Am. Jour. Roentgenology. Served to capt. U.S. Army, 1966-68, Korea. Mem. AMA, Am. Coll. Radiology (commn. on edn.), Am. Roentgen Ray Soc. (treas.), Radiol. Soc. N.Am., Soc. Pediatric Radiology, Assn. Univ. Radiologists, Am. Acad. Pediatrics, Am. Assn. Computing in Edn., Am. Assn. Women Radiologists, Am. Inst. Ultrasound Medicine, Soc. Thoracic Radiology, Soc. Radiologists Ultrasound, Harvard-Radcliffe Club of So. Calif. (sec. 1994), Phi Beta Kappa.

WOOD, DANIEL B., educational consultant; b. Roseburg, Oreg., Mar. 5, 1960; s. Jack Livingston and E. June (Gamble) W. BS, U. Oreg., 1982, MS, 1985, PhD, 1989. Cert. folklore and ethnic studies. Fare policy analyst Lane Transit Dist., Eugene, Oreg., 1984-85; asst. to dean for internships Univ. Oreg., Eugene, 1987-88; rsch. analyst Oreg. System Higher Edn., Eugene, 1988; pvt. practice, ednl. rsch. Eugene, 1988—; co-designer, coauthor statewide exam. and analysis of transfer student performance in Oreg. higher edn.; manuscript reviewer for refereed jours.; vis. asst. prof., rsch. assoc. U. Miss., 1992-93; active Statewide Task Force on Transfer Followup, 1987-88. Reviewer Internat. Jour. Intercultural Rels., 1995—; contbr. articles to profl. jours. Mem. Am. Soc. Pub. Adminstrn., Oreg. Sect. Pub. Adminstrn. Edn., Pi Lambda Theta (pres.), Phi Delta Kappa. Home: 122 E Howard Ave Eugene OR 97404-2617 Office: EdCon 3 Ednl Cons 122 E Howard Ave Eugene OR 97404-2617

WOOD, DAVID BRUCE, naturopathic physician; b. Fayetteville, N.C., Jan. 21, 1954; s. Marvin James and Rachel Elenor (Thom) W.; m. Wendy Ann McKiernan, Aug. 1974 (div. Aug. 1976); m. Cheryl Lynn Garbarino, Aug. 17, 1980. BS in Microbiology, U. Wash., 1977; D in Naturopathic Medicine, Bastyr U., Seattle, 1983. Pres., co-founder Trinity Family Health Clinic, Inc., P.S., Edmonds, Wash., 1984—. Singer Sound of Praise Choir, Overlake Christian Ch., Kirkland, Wash., 1987-92; narrator Easter Pagent, 1989. Mem. Am. Assn. Nutritional Cons., Nat. Health Fedn., Am. Assn. Naturopathic Physicians, Wash. Assn. Naturopathic Physicians (trustee, exec. bd. 1989-92). Home: 13721 Cascadian Way Everett WA 98208-7345 Office: Trinity Family Health Clinic Inc PS 7614 195th St SW Edmonds WA 98026-6260

WOOD, DAVID DUANE, clinical psychologist, marriage and family counselor; b. Pasadena, Calif., Feb. 22, 1950; s. Robert Andrew and Carolyn Irene (Cartier) W.; m. Laurel Beth Roska, Sept. 23, 1973; 1 child, Daniel Cody. Student, U. Bergen, Norway, 1971-72; BA in Psychology with high honors, U. Calif., Santa Barbara, 1973; MA in Clin. Psychology, U. Utah, 1980, PhD in Clin. Psychology, 1985. Lic. psychologist, Calif.; lic. marriage, family and child counselor, Calif. Rsch. tech. Psychophysiology Rsch. Lab. Camarillo (Calif.) Neuropsychiatric Inst. Rsch. Ctr. Camarillo State Hosp., 1970-71, rsch. asst. behavior analysis and modification project, 1972-73, rsch. asst. hosp. improvement project, 1973-74; psychology trainee II pilot alcohol drug abuse treatment unit Salt Lake VA Med. Ctr., 1974-75, psychology trainee III behavior modification unit and day hosp., 1975-76, intern medicine and neurology, 1977-78; instr. dept. psychology divsn. continuing edn. U. Utah, 1979-81; postdoctoral fellow behavioral pediatrics Sch. Medicine U. Md., Balt., 1983-85; psychologist mental health program Turning Point, Visalia, 1985-86; clin. dir. Visalia Children's Svcs. Clinic Tulare County Children's Mental Health Svcs. Consortium, 1986-89, consulting chief psychologist, 1989-90, consulting psychologist, 1990—; consulting psychologist Tulare County Dept. Mental Health, 1993—; mem. med. staff Charter Behavioral Health Care Systems Hosp., Visalia, 1994—; therapist Behavioral Pediatric Clinic U. Md. Sch. Medicine, 1983-85; clinician, cons. Balt. youth health project City of Balt. Health Dept., 1983-85; cons. Lyndhurst Elem. Sch., Balt. City Sch. Dist., 1983-85; cons. James L. Kernan Hosp., Balt., 1984-85; mem. adj. faculty Calif. State U., Fresno, 1987-88, U. San Francisco, 1987, Calif. Sch. Profl. Psychology, Fresno, 1989; rep. med. staff, community governing bd. Mill Creek Hosp., Visalia, 1993-94; mem. med. staff Cedar Vista Hosp., Fresno, 1989—, Mill Creek Hosp., 1990-94; textbook reviewer Holt, Rinehart & Winston; presenter in field. Contbr. chpts. to Evaluation of Behavioral Programs in Cmommunity, Residential and School Settings, 1974, International Handbook of Behavior Modification and Therapy, 1982, 2d edit., 1990; ad hoc editorial cons. Behavior Therapy, Behavioral Assessment, Jour. Adolescent Health Care, Jour. Consulting and Clin. Psychology, Jour. Devel. and Behavioral Pediatrics, Pediatrics, Psychotherapy Bulletin; contbr. articles to profl. jours. Cons. behavior counseling Ventura County Dept. Social Welfare, Calif., 1974, behavioral contracting workshop dist. 2 Juvenile Ct., State of Utah, 1976; program dir. Sports Camp Salt Lake Jewish Community Ctr., Salt Lake City, 1975; program cons. behavioral intervention outpatient chronic schizophrenic program Salt Lake Community Mental Health Ctr., Salt Lake City, 1977; sub. house parent, clin. cons. Child Abuse Intervention/Family Support Ctr., Salt Lake City, 1978-81; lectr. sch. health Balt. City Schs., 1985; cons. venereal disease control program Dept. Health and Mental Hygiene, State of Md., 1985, Tulare County Dept. Mental Health, 1986-87, Visalia Unified Sch. Dist., 1987. Recipient Outstanding Mental Health Advocate award Calif. Mental Health Advocates for Children & Youth, 1989; grantee Calif. Dept. Mental Health/Tulare County Mental Health Calif., 1988—. Mem. APA, Calif. State Psychol. Assn., Soc. for Behavioral Pediatrics, Assn. Advancement Psychology, Assn. Advancement Behavior Therapy, Sigma Xi. Office: 208 N Jacob St Visalia CA 93291-4733

WOOD, DONALD FRANK, transportation educator, consultant; b. Waukesha, Wis., Feb. 22, 1935; s. Frank Blaine and Uilah (Mathson) W.; m. Doreen Johnson, July 5, 1968; children: Frank, Tamara. BA, U. Wis., 1957, MA, 1958; PhD, Harvard U., 1970. Transp. planner State of Wis., Madison, 1960-70; prof. San Francisco State U., 1970—. Author: El Camino, 1982; (with others) Motorized Fire Apparatus of the West, 1991, Contemporary Transportation, 1993, Contemporary Logistics, 1993, American Volunteer Fire Trucks, 1993, Commercial Trucks, 1993, International Logistics, 1994, Wreckers and Two Trucks, 1995; contbr. Ency. Britannica. 2d lt. U.S. Army, 1958. Mem. Coun. of Logistics Mgmt. (chpt. pres. 1975-76), Transp. Rsch. Forum (chpt. pres. 1974), Am. Truck Hist. Soc. Presbyterian. Home: 321 Riviera Cir Larkspur CA 94939-1508 Office: San Francisco State U. Coll Bus San Francisco CA 94132

WOOD, EDWARD NEWTON, civil and mechanical engineer; b. Smethwick, Eng., Aug. 3, 1928; came to U.S., 1930; s. Harold Arthur and Maud (Newton) W.; m. Eileen Magginis, May 5, 1952 (div. 1962); children: Mary, Wendy; m. Mary Rose Daniels, Feb. 25, 1965; children: Dennis, Gary, Pamela. Student, Columbia U., 1948-50; BS, UCLA, 1957. Lic. profl. engr., Calif., Oreg. Engr. Nat. Presto Industries, Eau Claire, Wis., 1958-59; engr. Aerojet Gen., Downey, Calif., 1958-60, Rohr Corp., Riverside, Calif., 1960-62, Atlantic Rsch. Corp., Costa Mesa, Calif., 1962-69; city engr. City of Seal Beach, Calif., 1970-73, City of Roseburg, Oreg., 1973-75; pres. Wood Engring. Inc., Umpqua, Oreg., 1975—; asst. bldg. official Douglas County Oreg., 1984-86; mem. Nat. Defense Exec. Res., 1982—. Mem. and chmn. Douglas County Planning Commn., 1978-87, mem. and chmn. Douglas County Traffic Safety Commn., 1976—. Mem. ASCE, ASME, Profl. Engrs. Oreg. (pres. Umpqua chpt. 1983-84, 88-94), Masons, Elks. Home and Office: 311 Smethwick Dr Umpqua OR 97486-9731

WOOD, FAY S., marketing executive; b. Phila., Aug. 22; d. Paul and Dorothy (Berkowitz) Wiener; children: Deborah, Esther. BA in English, Pa. State U.; grad. RCA Corp. Real estate sales rep., 1968-70; cons. Hearing Ctrs., Inc., 1970-72; dist. sales mgr. Beltone Hearing Aid Ctrs., Inc., 1972-76; v.p. PHD Hearing Ctrs., Inc.; with RCA Svcs. Co., 1976-79, sales mgr., 1977-79, regional sales mgr., N.Y. dist., 1979; v.p. sales and mktg. Full Line Repair Ctrs., Inc., 1979-81; v.p. sales and mktg. Quantech Electronics Corp., Freeport, N.Y., 1981-85; v.p., gen. mgr. Elite Group, Inc., Torrance, Calif., 1985-87, exec. v.p., 1987-88; pres. Prestige Resources, Inc., Palos Verdes, Calif., 1987-88; pres., chief exec. officer KeyPrestige, Inc., Cypress, Calif., 1988—. Mem. adv. bd. Dept. Consumer Affairs, mem. N.Y.C. Commn. on Status of Women. Recipient audiology cert. Dahlberg Electronics, Master Cons. award Beltone Electronics; 1st degree Black Belt in Tae Kwon Do Karate. Named Sales Mgr. of Yr., RCA. Mem. AAUW, LWV, NAFE, Nat. Fedn. Bus. and Profl. Women, B'nai Brith, Fedn. Bus. and Profl. Women Club. Home and Office: 4012 Montego Dr Huntington Beach CA 92649

WOOD, FERGUS JAMES, geophysicist, consultant; b. London, Ont., Can., May 13, 1917; came to U.S., 1924, naturalized, 1932; s. Louis Aubrey and Dora Isabel (Elson) W.; student U. Oreg., 1934-36; AB, U. Calif., Berkeley, 1938, postgrad., 1938-39; postgrad. U. Chgo., 1939-40, U. Mich., 1940-42, Calif. Inst. Tech., 1946; m. Doris M. Hack, Sept. 14, 1946; children: Kathryn Celeste Wood Madden, Bonnie Patricia Wood Ward. Teaching asst. U. Mich., 1940-42; instr. in physics and astronomy Pasadena City Coll., 1946-48, John Muir Coll., 1948-49; asst. prof. physics U. Md., 1949-50; assoc. physicist Johns Hopkins U. Applied Physics Lab., 1950-55; sci. editor Ency. Americana, N.Y.C., 1955-60; aero. and space rsch. scientist, sci. asst. to dir. Office Space Flight Programs, Hdqrs., NASA, Washington, 1960-61; program dir. fgn. sci. info. NSF, Washington, 1961-62; phys. scientist, chief sci. and tech. info. staff U.S. Coast and Geodetic Survey, Rockville, Md., 1962-66, phys. scientist Office of Dir., 1967-73, rsch. assoc. Office of Dir., 1973-77, Nat. Ocean Svc.; cons. tidal dynamics, Bonita, Calif., 1978—; mem. Am. Geophys. Union, ICSU-UNESCO Internat. Geol. Correlation Project 274, Working Group #1-Crescendo Events in Coastal Environments, Past and Future (The Millennium Project), 1988—. Capt. USAAF, 1942-46. Recipient Spl. Achievement award Dept. Commerce, NOAA, 1970, 74, 76, 77. Mem. Sigma Pi Sigma, Pi Mu Epsilon, Delta Phi Alpha. Democrat. Presbyterian. Author: The Strategic Role of Perigean Spring Tides in Nautical History and North American Coastal Flooding, 1635-1976, 1978; Tidal Dynamics: Coastal Flooding, and Cycles of Gravitational Force, 1986, Synergetic Gravitational Forces in Tides and the Solar System, 2 vols., 1995; contbr. numerous articles to encys., reference sources, profl. jours.; writer, tech. dir. documentary film: Pathfinders from the Stars, 1967; editor-in-chief: The Prince William Sound, Alaska, Earthquake of 1964 and Aftershocks, vols. 1-2A and sci. coordinator vols. 2B, 2C and 3, 1966-69. Home: 3103 Casa Bonita Dr Bonita CA 91902-1735

WOOD, GLADYS BLANCHE, retired secondary education educator, journalist; b. Sanborn, N.D., Aug. 12, 1921; d. Charles Kershaw and Mina Blanche (Kee) Crowther; m. Newell Edwin Wood, June 13, 1943 (dec. 1990); children: Terry N., Lani, Brian R., Kevin C.; m. F.L. Stutzman, Nov. 30, 1991. BA in Journalism, U. Minn., 1943; MA in Mass Comm., San Jose State U., 1972. Cert. secondary tchr., Calif. Reporter St. Paul Pioneer-Dispatch, 1943-45; editor J.C. Penney Co., N.Y.C., 1945-46; tchr. English and journalism Willow Glen H.S., San Jose, Calif., 1968-87; freelance writer, photographer, 1947—; cons. in field. Named Secondary Journalism Tchr. of Yr. Calif. Newspaper Pubs. Assn., 1977. Mem. AAUW, Soc. Profl. Journalists, Journalism Edn. Assn., Calif. Tchrs. English, Calif. Ret. Tchrs. Assn., Women in Comm., Santa Clara County Med. Assn. Aux., Montalvo Assn., LWV, Friends of Libr., Delta Kappa Gamma, Alpha Omicron Pi. Republican. Methodist. Home: 14161 Douglass Ln Saratoga CA 95070-5535

WOOD, HAROLD SAMUEL, retired educator; b. Long Beach, Calif., Mar. 8, 1913; s. Samuel Bury and Helen Imogene (Hawkins) W. BA, U. Redlands, 1942; MBA, U. So. Calif., 1947; AM, Columbia U., 1954; LLD (hon.), St. Louis U., 1985. With cargo ops. Trans World Airlines, L.A., 1946-49; prof. St. Louis U., 1949-80, prof. emeritus, 1980; cons. Air Afrique, 1970-75, Air Nippon Airways, 1975-85, S.A.S. Airline, Copenhagen, 1975-77, TWA, 1972-79. Author: Organization and Management of College Flying Clubs, 1965. With U.S. Army, 1941-46. Recipient Brewer Trophy Nat. Aeronautic Assn., 1971, Disting. Svc. award Dept. of Transp., 1982. Fellow U. Aviation Assn. (pres. 1961-63, sr. advisor 1964-80, emeritus 1980—), Nat. Inter-Collegiate Flying Assn. (exec. dir. 1978-83, emeritus 1983—), Aviation-Space Edn. Assn., Flying Assn. Exec. (dir. 1967-83, emeritus 1983—), Phi Delta Kappa, Delta Nu Alpha. Republican. Baptist. Home: 1325 Las Villas Way Apt 302 Escondido CA 92026-1949 Office: Alpha Eta Rho Palamar Coll San Marcos CA 92069

WOOD, HUGH BERNARD, retired education educator; b. Angola, Ind., Feb. 18, 1909; s. Weir and Merle (Saylor) W.; m. Helen Launa Croyle, Oct. 19, 1928 (dec. June 1984); children: Wayne Bernard, Pamela Lynn. BA, U. Toledo, 1931; MA, U. Colo., 1935; EdD, Columbia U., 1937. Cert. elem. and secondary tchr., curriculum design specialist. Prof. of edn. U. Oreg., Eugene, 1939-74, prof. emeritus, 1974—; co-founder, exec. dir., pres. Am. Nepal Edn. Found., 1955—; Fulbright lectr., India, 1953-54; ednl. advisor, Govt. of Nepal, chief Edn. Div. of US Ops. Mission in Nepal, 1953-59; dir. for curriculum devel. Tongue Point Job Corps Ctr., Astoria, Oreg., 1965-66; convocation speaker Tribhuvan U., Nepal, 1983, others. Author 300 publs. including Curriculum Planning and Development, 1940, revised edit. 1960, Evaluation of Pupil Growth and Development, 1940, Manual for Educational Research, 1950, Nepal Diary, others; contbr. articles to profl. jours. and books. Lt. comdr. USN, 1942-45. Recipient Svc. awards, Nepal, 1959-62, 81, Outstanding Adminstrv. Svc. medal Souh Vietnam, 1968, Birendra Prajnalankar award Nepal, 1988, others. Home: 2790 Cape Meares Loop Tillamook OR 97141-9328

WOOD, JAMES LESLIE, sociology educator; b. Aug. 30, 1941. BA in Sociology, U. Calif., Berkeley, 1963, postgrad., MA in Sociology, 1966, PhD in Sociology, 1973. Asst. prof. San Francisco State U., summer 1972; instr. in sociology Holy Names Coll., 1971-73; lectr. in sociology U. Calif., Riverside, 1973-75; lectr. in sociology San Diego State U., 1975-76, asst. prof. sociology, 1976-78, assoc. prof. sociology, 1978-81, prof. sociology, 1981—, chmn. sociology, 1991—; SDSU mem. Promotions com., Executive com., Curriculum Com., Methodology com., Syposium com., Post-Tenure review com. (chair), San Diego Poll com., Personnel com., Rsch. Human Subjects com., Applied Social Rsch. Group com., Reappointment Tenure com. (chair), Master's essay com., Graduate com., Master's Degree theory and Methodology Exam com., Colloquium com., Teaching Eval. com.; lectr. in field; resident scholar U. London, Goldsmiths' Coll., 1984. Author: The Sources of American Student Activism, 1974, (co-author) Sociology: Traditional and Radical Perspectives, Adapted for the United Kingdom, 1982, Social Movements: Development, Participation and Dynamics, 1982, 3d printing, 1985, Sociology: Traditional and Radical Perspectives, 2d edit., 1990; author: (monographs) Political Consciousness and Student Activism, New Left Ideology: Its Dimensions and Development, 1975, Aging in America; works presented at profl. organizations; contbr. articles to profl. jours. U. Calif. grantee, 1969, 73-74, 75, San Diego State U. grantee, 1976, 79, 81, 82, 88, 83, 85, 90. Mem. Am. Sociol. Assn. (collective behavior and social movements sect., polit. sociology sect.), Internat. Soc. Polit. Psychology, Pacific Sociol. Assn., Soc. for the Study of Social Problems, Calif. Sociol. Assn., Phi Beta Delta, Alpha Kappa Delta. Office: San Diego State U Dept of Sociology 5300 Campanile Dr San Diego CA 92115-1338

WOOD, JEANNINE KAY, state official; b. Dalton, Nebr., Apr. 22, 1944; d. Grover L. and Elsie M. (Winkelman) Sanders; m. Charles S. Wood, Dec. 7, 1968; children: Craig C., Wendi L. Wood Armstrong. Exec. sec. Idaho Hosp. Assn., Boise, 1966-71; com. sec. Idaho State Senate, Boise, 1976-81, jour. clk., 1981-85, asst. to sec. of senate, 1985-91, sec. of senate, 1991—; pvt. practice typing svc. Boise, 1979-86. Precinct committeeman Rep. Party. Mem. Am. Soc. Legis. Clks. and Secs. (vice chmn. legis. adminstr. com.), Nat. Assn. Parliamentarians, Idaho Assn. Parliamentarians. Methodist. Home: 3505 S Linder Meridian ID 83642 Office: Idaho State Capitol PO Box 83720 Boise ID 83720-0081

WOOD, JOHN MORTIMER, aerospace executive, aeronautical engineer; b. New Orleans, July 7, 1934; s. John Mortimer Sr. and Annie Jeff (Gates) W.; m. Bonnie Ann Blanchette, June 6, 1958 (div. Oct. 1977); m. Barbara Lee Butler, Aug. 12, 1978; 1 child, Mark Douglas. BA in Aero. Engring., U. Tex., 1957. Project engr. Gen. Dynamics/Convair, San Diego, 1957-58, Rocket Power, Inc., Mesa, Ariz., 1961-64; sales mgr. S.E. region Rocket Power, Inc., Huntsville, Ala., 1964-67; dir. mktg. Quantic Industries, San Carlos, Calif., 1967-70; sr. mktg. mgr. Talley Industries of Ariz., Mesa, 1970-77; dir. mktg. Universal Propulsion Co., Inc., Phoenix, 1977-85, v.p. mktg., 1985-91, v.p. contract mgmt., 1992-94, v.p. mktg., 1994—. 1st lt. USAF, 1958-61. Mem. Am. Def. Preparedness Assn., Assn. for Unmanned Vehicle Sytsems, Tech. Mktg. Soc. of Am., Survival and Flight Equipment Assn. Republican. Home: 111 W Canterbury Ln Phoenix AZ 85023-6252 Office: Universal Propulsion Co Inc 25401 N Central Ave Phoenix AZ 85027-7837

WOOD, KAREN SUE, theatre manager, stage producer, consultant; b. Artesia, Calif., May 14, 1950; d. Frank Leon and Edith Jeanette (DeLong) Wray; m. Lawrence Anthony Wood (div. 1972); 1 child, Kimberly. BA in Theatre Arts, Calif. State U., Fullerton, 1975; MFA in Theatre Mgmt., UCLA, 1977. Assoc. mgr. Huntington Hartford Theatre, L.A., 1978-81; gen. mgr. Sch. Drama, U. So. Calif., L.A., 1986-88, Mark Taper Forum, Ctr. Theatre Group, L.A., 1988—; lectr. dept. theatre Irvine Coll. and UCLA, 1989-93; mgr. theatre co. USIA, Czechoslovakia and Poland, 1988; chair mgmt. com. Music Ctr. Oper. Co., L.A., 1989—, burning tissues com. Theatre L.A., 1992-94; participant Gov.'s Conf. on Arts, Sacramento, 1992-95; founding mem. L.A. Theatre Ctr. Coop., 1992. Producer: (play) Buddies, 1978-79, Uncommon Women and Others, 1982; line producer: 1984 Olympic Arts Festival Theatre du Soleil, 1984, Piccolo Teatro di Milano, 1984, Robert Wilson/King Lear, 1985; assoc. producer 50/60 Vision, 1989-90 (Spl. Prodn. award L.A. Drama Critics Cir. 1989); author: Ambassador Auditorium Box Office Procedures, 1985; also theatre overviews. Trustee, bd. dirs. Odyssey Theatre, L.A., 1980; bd. dirs. Open Fist Theatre, 1995; spkr. Nat. Assn. Schs. of Theatre, 1987. Recipient L.A. Weekly Theatre award, 1979, Dramalogue Theatre award, 1979. Mem. NOW, NAFE, Women in Theatre, Assn. Theatrical Press Agts. and Mgrs., League of Resident Theatres (legue of resident theatres exec. com.), Theatre Commn. Group (charter mem.). Democrat. Office: Ctr Theatre Group Mark Taper Forum 135 N Grand Ave Los Angeles CA 90012-3013

WOOD, KENNETH ARTHUR, retired newspaper editor, writer; b. Hastings, Sussex, Eng., Feb. 25, 1926; came to U.S., 1965; s. Arthur Charles and Ellen Mary (Cox) W.; m. Hilda Muriel Harloe, Sept. 13, 1952. Educated in Eng. Editor Stamp Collector newspaper Van Dahl Publs., Albany, Oreg., 1968-80, editor emeritus, 1980—. Author (ency.) This Is Philately, 1982, (atlas) Where in the World, 1983, Basic Philately, 1984, Post Dates, 1985, Modern World, 1987; author several hundred articles and columns published in the U.K. and U.S.A., 1960—. Served with Brit. Army WW II. Recipient Disting. Philatelist award Northwest Fedn. Stamp Clubs, 1974, Phoenix award Ariz. State Philatelic Hall of Fame, 1979, Disting. Philatelist award Am. Topical Assn., 1979. Fellow Royal Philatelic Soc. (London); mem. Am. Philatelic Soc. (Luff award 1987, Hall of Fame Writers Unit, 1984). Office: Van Dahl Pub PO Box 10 520 E First Albany OR 97321-0006

WOOD, KEVIN MICHAEL, sales consultant; b. Troy, N.Y., Jan. 19, 1948; s. August Elwood and Marion Frances (O'Connell) W. Student, Onondaga C.C., Syracuse, N.Y., 1967-69. Master practitioner neuro-linguistic programming. Owner Coast Chimney Sweep & Stoves, Newport, Oreg., 1978-85; pres., owner Wood/West & Assocs., Nederland, Colo., 1985—; pres. Unltd. Futures, Inc., Nederland, Colo., 1993—; asst. trainer NLP-Comprehensive, Boulder, 1993-94; bd. dirs. Wood Energy Inst.-West, Seattle, 1985-91, pres., 1991-92. Co-author: The Owner's Manual for Your Brain, 1994; editor The Hearthtender newsletter, 1993-94. Mem. wood smoke reduction group Regional Air Quality Coun., denver, 1992-94; mem. Clean Air Consortium, Boulder, 1992-94. Recipient Improving Air Quality award Clean Air Colo., Denver, 1993, Appreciation award Wood Energy Inst.-West, 1992; named to Wood Energy Inst.-West Hall of Fame, 1988. Mem. Inst. of Noetic Scis., World Future Soc., Hearth Products Assn. (govt. rels. com. 1993-94), Wood Heating Alliance of Colo. (pres., exec. dir. 1989-90), Rocky Mountain Hearth Products Assn. (negotiator/polit. liaison 1990-94), Colo. Solar Energy Industries Assn., Inst. for Internat. Connections (spkr./trainer 1993-94), Inst. for Specialized Studies (founder, pres. 1994), Colo. Assn. Psychotherapists (co-founder, exec. dir.). Office: Wood West & Assocs PO Box 1449 125 S 8th St Nederland CO 80466

WOOD, LARRY (MARY LAIRD), journalist, author, university educator, public relations executive, environmental consultant; b. Sandpoint, Idaho; d. Edward Hayes and Alice (McNeel) Small; children: Mary, Marcia, Barry. BA summa cum laude, U. Wash., 1939, MA summa cum laude, with highest honors, 1940; postgrad., Stanford U., 1941-42, U. Calif., Berkeley, 1946-47; cert. in photography, U. Calif., Berkeley, 1971; postgrad. journalism, U. Wis., 1971-72, U. Minn., 1971-72, U. Ga., 1972-73; postgrad. in art, architecture and marine biology, U. Calif., Santa Cruz, 1974-76, Stanford Hopkins Marine Sta., Santa Cruz, 1977-80. Lifetime secondary and jr. coll. teaching cert., Wash., Calif. Feature writer and columnist Oakland Tribune and San Francisco Chronicle, Calif., 1939—; archtl. and environ. feature and travel writer and columnist San Jose (Calif.) Mercury News (Knight Ridder), 1972-90; teaching fellow Stanford U., 1940-43; dir. pub. rels. 2-counties, 53-parks East Bay Regional Park Dist., No. Calif., 1948-68; pres. Larry Wood Pub. Rels., 1946—; prof. (tenure) pub. rels., mag. writing, journalism and investigative reporting, San Diego State U., 1974, 75; disting. vis. prof. journalism San Jose State U., 1976; assoc. prof. journalism Calif. State U., Hayward, 1978; prof. sci. and environ. journalism U. Calif. Berkeley Extension grad. div., 1979—; press del. nat. convs. Am. Geophys. Union Internat. Conf., 1986—, AAAS, 1989—, Nat. Park Svc. VIP Press Tour, Yellowstone after the fire Nat. Pk. Svc. VIP Press Tour, 1989, Nat. Assn. Sci. Writers, 1989, George Washington U./Am. Assn. Neurol. Surgeons Sci. Writers Conf., 1990, Am. Inst. Biol. Scis. Conf., 1990, Nat. Conf. Sci. Writers Am. Heart Assn., 1995, Internat. Cardiologists Symposium for Med./Sci. Writers, 1995; EPA del. to USSR and Ea. Europe; mem. Am. Bd. Forensic Examiners, 1994; expert witness on edn., affirmative action, pub. rels., journalism and copyright; cons. sci. writers interne project, Stanford U., 1989—; spl. media guest Sigma Xi, 1990—; mem. numerous spl. press corps; selected White House Special Media, 1993—; internat. press guest Swiss Nat. Tourist Offices, Lake Geneva Region Celebration, 1994, Can. Consulate Gen. Dateline Can., 1995, Ministerio delle Risorse Agricole Alimentari e Forestali and Assocs. Conf., 1995; mem. Am. Bd. Forensic Examiners, 1994; appeared in TV documentary Larry Wood Covers Visit of Queen Elizabeth II. Contbr. over 5,000 articles on various topics for newspapers, nat. mags., nat. and internat. newspaper syndicates including L.A. Times-Mirror Syndicate, Washington Post, Phila. Inquirer, Chgo. Tribune, Miami Herald, Oakland Tribune, Seattle Times, San Francisco Chronicle, Parade, San Jose Mercury News (Nat. Headliner award), Christian Sci. Monitor, L.A. Times/Christian Monitor News Syndicate, Hawaiian Airlines In Paradise and other in-flight mags., MonitoRadio, Sports Illus., Mechanix Illus., Popular Mechanics, Parents, House Beautiful, Am. Home (awards 1988, 89), National Geographic World, Travel & Leisure, Chevron USA/Odyssey (Calif. Pub.'s award 1984), Xerox Edn. Publs., Europe's Linguapress, PSA Mag., Hawaiian Airlines In Paradise Mag., Off Duty, Oceans, Sea Frontiers, AAA Westways, AAA Motorland, Travelin', others. Significant works include home and garden columnist and editor, 5-part series Pacific Coast Ports, 5-part series Railroads of the West, series Immigration, Youth Gangs, Endangered Species, Calif. Lighthouse Chain, Elkhorn Slough Nat. Estuarine Res., Ebey's Landing Nat. Hist. Res., Calif. Water Wars, BLM's Adopt a Horse Program, Mt. St. Helen's Eruption, Loma Prieta Earthquake, Oakland Firestorm, Missing Children, Calif. Prison Reform, Columbia Alaska's Receding Glacier, Calif. Underwater Parks, and many others; author: Wonderful U.S.A.: A State-by-State Guide to Its Natural Resources, 1989; co-author over 21 books including: McGraw-Hill English for Social Living, 1944, Fawcett Boating Books, 1956-66, Fodor's San Francisco, Fodor's California, 1982-les Merrill Focus on Life Science, Focus on Physical Science, Focus on Earth Science, 1983, 87, Earth Science, 1987; contbr. Earth Science 1987; 8 works selected for use by Europe's Woltors-Nordoff-Longman English Language Texts, U.K., Netherlands, 1988; author: (with others) anthology West Winds, 1989; reviewer Charles Merrill texts, 1983-84; book reviewer Profl. Communicator, 1987—; selected writings in permanent collections Oakland Pub. Libr., U. Wash. Main Libr.; environ. works included in Dept. Edn. State of Md. textbook; contbr., author Journalism Quar.; author script PBS/AAA America series, 1992. Nat. chmn. travel writing contest for U.S. univ. journalism students Assn. for Edn. in Journalism/Soc. Am. Travel Writers, 1979-83; judge writing contest for Nat. Assn. Real Estate Editors, 1982—; Italy; press del. 1st Internat. Symposium Volcanism and Aviation Safety, 1991, Coun. for the Advancement of Science Writing 1977—, Rockefeller Media Seminar Feeding the World-Protecting the Earth, 1992, Global Conf. on Mercury as Pollutant, 1992, Earth Summit Global Forum, Rio de Janeiro, 1992; invited Nat. Park Svc. Nat. Conf. Sci. Writers, 1985, Postmaster Gen.'s 1992 Stamps, 1991, Internat. Geophysical Union Cong., 1982-95, The Conf. Bd., 1995, Corp. Comm. Conf., Calif. Inst. Tech.'s Media and Sci. Sem., 1995, EPA and Dept. Energy Tech. Conf., 1992, Am. Soc. Photogammetry and Remote Sensing Internat. Conv. Mapping Global Change, 1992, N.Y. Mus. Mod. Art Matisse Retrospective Press Rev., 1992, celebration 150th anniversary Oreg. Trail 1993, coun. advancement sci. writing 1993, 94, Sigma Xi Nat. Conf. 1988—, PRSA Travel and Tourism Conf. 1993, Internat. Conf. Environment, 1994, 95, Quality Life Europe, Prague, 1994, and many others; press guest State of Conn., 1993; mem. Gov.'s Conf. Tourism N.C., 1993, 94, 95, Calif., 1976—, Fla., 1987—; mem. planning com. U. Wash. Purple and Gold Soc., 1995. Recipient numerous awards, honors, citations, speaking engagements, including induction into Broadway Hall of Fame, U. Wash., 1984, Broadway Disting. Alumnus award, 1995; citations for environ. writing Nat. Park Svc., U.S. Forest Svc., Bur. Land Mgmt., Oakland Mus. Assn., Oakland C. of C., Chevron USA, USN plaque and citation, best mag. articles citation Calif. Pubs. Assn., 1984; co-recipient award for best Sunday newspaper mag. Nat. Headliners, citation for archtl. features Oakland Mus., 1983; honoree for achievements in journalism Nat. Mortar Bd., 1988, 89; selected as one of 10 V.I.P. press for Yellowstone Nat. Park field trip on "Let Burn" rsch., 1989; named one of Calif.'s top 40 contemporary authors for writings on Calif. underwater parks, 1989, nat. honoree Social Issues Resources Series, 1987; invited V.I.P. press, spl. press guest numerous events worldwide. Mem. Am. Bd. Forensic Examiners, Calif. Acad. Scis., San Francisco Press Club, Nat. Press Club, Pub. Rels. Soc. Am. (charter mem. travel, tourism, environment and edn. divs.), Nat. Sch. Pub. Rels. Assn., Environ. Cons. N.Am., Am. Assn. Edn. in Journalism and Comm. (exec. bd. nat. mag. div. 1978, panel chmn. 1979, 80, author Journalism Quar. jour.), Women in Comm. (nat. bd. officer 1975-77, book reviewer Prof. Communicator), Soc. Profl. Journalists (nat. bd. for hist. sites 1980—), Nat. Press Photographers Assn. (hon. life, cons. Bay Area interne project 1989—, honoree 1995), Investigative Reporters and Editors (charter), Bay Area Advt. and Mktg. Assn., Nat. Assn. Sci. Writers, Calif. Writers Club (state bd., Berkeley bd. 1989—, honoree ann. conv. Asilomar, Calif. 1990), Am. Assn. Med. Writers, Internat. Assn. Bus. Communicators, Am. Film Inst., Am. Heritage Found. (citation 1986, 87, 88), Soc. Am. Travel Writers, Internat. Oceanographic Found., Oceanic Soc., Calif. Acad. Environ. News Writers, Seattle Advt. and Sales Club (former officer), Nature Conservancy, Smithsonian Audubon Soc., Nat. Wildlife Fedn., Nat. Parks and Conservation Assn., Calif. State Parks Found., Fine., San Francisco, Seattle Jr. Advt. Club (charter), U. Wash. Comm. Alumni (Sch. Comm. alumni, life, charter mem. ocean scis. alumni, Disting. Alumni 1987), U. Calif., Berkeley Alumni (life, v.p., scholarship chmn. 1975-81), Stanford Alumni (life), Mortar Board Alumnae Assn. (life, honoree 1988, 89), Am. Mgmt. Assn., Nat. Soc. Environ. Journalists (charter), Phi Beta Kappa (v.p., bd. dirs. Calif. Alumni Assn., statewide chmn. scholarship awards 1975-81), Annenberg Washington D.C. Program Electronic Media Symposium, U. Wash. Purple and Gold Soc. (planning com., charter, 1995—), Pi Lambda Theta, Theta Sigma Phi. Home: Piedmont Pines 6161 Castle Dr Oakland CA 94611-2737

WOOD, LINCOLN JACKSON, aerospace engineer; b. Lyons, N.Y., Sept. 30, 1947; s. William Hulbert and Sarah Brock (Strumsky) W. BS with distinction, Cornell U., 1968; MS in Aeronautics and Astronautics, Stanford U., 1969, PhD, 1972. Staff engr. Hughes Aircraft Co., El Segundo, Calif., 1974-77; mem. tech. staff Jet Propulsion Lab. Calif. Inst. Tech., Pasadena, 1977-81, tech. group supr. Jet Propulsion Lab., 1981-89, tech. mgr., 1989-91, dep. tech. section mgr., 1991—; Bechtel instr. engring. Calif. Inst. Tech., Pasadena, 1972-74, lectr. in systems engring., 1975-76, vis. asst. prof., 1976-78, vis. assoc. prof., 1978-84; cons. in field. Contbr. articles on space navigation and optimal control theory to profl. jours. Bd. dirs. Boys Republic, Chino, Calif., 1991. Assoc. fellow AIAA (Tech. com. on astrodynamics 1985-86, chmn. 1986-88, assoc. editor Jour. Guidance, Control and Dynamics 1983-89); sr. mem. Am. Astro. Soc. (space flight mechanics com. 1980—, chmn. 1993—, assoc. editor Jour. of Astro. Scis. 1980-83, gen. chmn. AAS/AIAA Space Flight Mechanics Meeting 1993), IEEE (sr. mem.), AAAS, Los Solteros (pres. 1991), Sigma Xi. Office: Jet Propulsion Lab 4800 Oak Grove Drive Mail Stop 301-125L Pasadena CA 91109

WOOD, LINDA GAYE, real estate development company executive; b. South Haven, Mich., May 12, 1959; d. Gene A. and Beatrice (McKamey) W.; m. Terry M. Shaw, July 20, 1980 (div. 1982). Sr. loan processor Shearson Am Express Mktg., San Diego, 1977-80; office mgr. Lomas & Nettleton Mfg. Co., San Diego, 1980-81; escrow coord. Barratt Developers, San Diego, 1981-83, Tara Escrow Inc., 1983-84; sales mgr. real estate devel. Watt Industries Inc., Rancho Sante Fe, Calif, 1984-85; asst. v.p., dir. sales and mktg. The Buie Corp., Laguna Niguel, Calif., 1985-90; dir. mktg. Bramalea Calif., Inc., Irvine, 1990-91; v.p. sales, mktg. Kaufman and Broad S. Calif., Anaheim, 1991-92; dir. sales and mktg. Kaufman and Broad Sacramento, 1992—; dirs., mem. exec. com. Sales and Mktg. Coun., So. Calif., 1990-92. Named Mktg. Dir. of Yr., 1989, Laurel Mktg. Dir. of Yr., 1989 . Mem. NAFE, So. Calif. Sales and Mktg. Coun. (bd. dirs. 1985-88, 90-91, mem. exec. bd. 1988, 90—, Pres.'s Achievement award 1988, 89), Assn. Profl. Mktg. Women (rec. sec. 1984-85), Niguel Beach Terr. Homeowners Assn. Republican. Avocations: Swimming, walking, hiking, travel, cycling. Avocations: swimming, walking, hiking, travel, cycling.

WOOD, LINDA MAY, librarian; b. Fort Dodge, Iowa, Nov. 6, 1942; d. John Albert and Beth Ida (Riggs) Wiley; m. C. James Wood, Sept. 15, 1964 (div. Oct. 1984). BA, Portland State U., 1964; M in Librarianship, U. Wash., 1965. Reference libr. Multnomah County Libr., Portland, Oreg., 1965-67, br. libr., 1967-72, adminstrv. asst. to libr., 1972-73, asst. libr., asst. dir., 1973-77; asst. city libr. L.A. Pub. Libr., 1977-80; libr. dir. Riverside (Calif.) City and County Pub. Libr., 1980-91; county libr. Alameda County Libr., Fremont, Calif., 1991—; adminstrv. coun. mem. Bay Area Libr. and Info. Svcs., Oakland, Calif., 1991—. Chair combined charities campaign County of Alameda, Oakland, 1992; bd. dirs. Inland AIDS Project, Riverside, Calif., 1990-91; vol. United Way of Inland Valleys, Riverside, 1986-87, Bicentennial Competition on the Constitution, 36th Congl. Dist., Colton, Calif., 1988-90. Mem. ALA (CLA chpt. councilor 1992-95), Calif. Libr. Assn. (pres. 1985, exec. com., ALA chpt. councilor 1992-95), Calif. County Librs. Assn. (pres. 1984), League of Calif. Cities (cmty. svcs. policy com. 1985-90), OCLC Users Coun. (Pacific Network del. 1986-89). Democrat. Avocations: folk dancing, opera, reading. Office: Alameda County Libr 2450 Stevenson Blvd Fremont CA 94538-2326

WOOD, NAOMI ALICE, language services firm executive; b. San Francisco, Feb. 28, 1964; d. William Hunt and Winifred Ruth (Jaeger) W. BA in Internat. Affairs, U. Colo., 1986; MA in Internat. Rels. with distinction, U. So. Calif., London, 1991; postgrad., Goethe Inst., London, 1989-91, Monterey Inst. Internat. Stud., 1991. Legal asst. Sea Containers Ltd., London, 1986-87; conf. technician Design Specialists Multilingual Conf. Svcs., Mountain View, Calif., 1980-86, ops. mgr., 1987-89, exec. v.p., 1991—. Recipient Rotary Club Cmty. Svc. award, 1982; U. Colo. Merit scholar, 1982, 83, 84, 85, 86. Mem. Internat. Studies Assn., Am. Fgn. Svc. Assn., Internat. Soc. Meeting Planners, Acad. Polit. Sci., World Affairs Coun. No. Calif., CATO Inst., Commonwealth Club, Phi Beta Kappa. Home: 1575 Kensington Cir Los Altos CA 94024-6030 Office: Design Specialists PO Box 4221 Mountain View CA 94040-0221

WOOD, NATHANIEL FAY, editor, writer, public relations consultant; b. Worcester, Mass., June 23, 1919; s. Henry Fletcher and Edith (Fay) W.; m. Eleanor Norton, Dec. 19, 1945; children: Gary Nathaniel, Janet Ann. BS in Journalism, Bus. Adminstrn., Syracuse U., 1946. Editor, writer various publs., various cities, 1946-51; mng. editor Butane-Propane News, L.A., 1951-52; editor Western Metalworking Mag., L.A., 1952-62; western editorial mgr. Penton Pub. Co. Cleve., L.A., 1962-71; editor Orange County Illustrated, Orange County Bus., Newport Beach, Calif., 1971-72; western editor Hitchcock Pub., L.A., 1972-75; co-owner, mgr. Norton-Wood Pub. Rels. Svcs., Pasadena, Calif., 1975—; editorial dir. Security World, SDM and SCA Mags., Culver City, Calif., 1975-80; mgr. trade show Cahners Pub. and Expo Group, L.A., 1979-82; sr. editor Alarm Installer Dealer Mag., L.A., 1982-89; editor CNC West Mag., Long Beach, Pasadena, Calif., 1982—. Freelance indsl. writer miscellaneous bus. pubs. Organizer Willkie Presdl. Campaign, Syracuse, N.Y., 1940; advisor various GOP campaigns, L.A., Washington, 1940-92; charter mem. Rep. Nat. Com., 1995; nat. adv. bd. Am. Security Coun.; donor L.A. Civic Light Opera; mem., donor L.A. Mus. Art, 1989—; founding mem. Western Heritage Mus., L.A., 1989—; active Met. Opera Guild, Colonial Williamsburg Found., Mus. Natural History L.A. 2nd lt. U.S. Army, 1943-45, PTO. Decorated Purple Heart; recipient Silver, Bronze and Gold medals for Editorial Excellence Gov. of Calif., 1959, 60, 62. Mem. Am. Legion. Scabbard and Blade, L.A. World Affairs Coun., Smithsonian Instn., Alpha Epsilon Rho, Sigma Delta Chi. Home: 1430 Tropical Ave Pasadena CA 91107-1623 Office: Norton-Wood Pub Rels Svcs 1430 Tropical Ave Pasadena CA 91107-1623

WOOD, NICOLA, artist; b. Gt. Crosby, Lancashire, Eng., Oct. 18, 1936; d. John Wood and Eva Wood Heyes; m. Theodore Cartan, Mar. 25, 1965 (dec. 1972); m. Emmet Baxter June 11, 1981 (dec. 1994). Diploma with 1st class honors, Manchester (Eng.) Coll. Art, 1959, Royal Coll. Art, London, 1960; postgrad. degree, Parsons Sch. Design, N.Y.C., 1963. Freelance textile designer, 1959-84; graphic designer N.Y.C., 1960-63; wallpaper designer Rasch Tapeten Fabric, Osnabruck, Germany, 1965-84; lectr. Farnham (Eng.) Coll. Art, 1975, Ctrl. Coll. Art, London, 1976-78, Claremont (Calif.) Coll., 1992-93, 95. Represented in permanent collections Sherry Frumkin Gallery, Santa Monica, Calif., Bruce Lewin Gallery, N.Y.C., O.K. Harris/David Klein Art Gallery, Detroit; group shows include Jerry Silverman Gallery, L.A., 1987, Pebble Beach Concours d'Elegance, Carmel, Calif., 1987-95, Lancaster (Calif.) Mus., 1988, Butler Inst., Ohio, 1988, Harrahs Mus., Las Vegas, 1989, Kresle Art Ctr., Mich., 1991, The Automobile in Art Gallery, Long Beach, Calif., 1992, Bakersfield (Calif.) Mus. Art, 1994, PEterson Automotive Mus., L.A., 1994, others. Work auctioned for charity Pebble Beach Concourse d'Elegance. Proctor Meml. Travel scholar, 1959, Fulbright scholar, 1960, Am. Travel scholar Royal Coll. Art, 1960; recipient Excellence award Pebble Beach Concours d'Elegance, 1992, Peter Helk award, 1993, Raymond E. Holland award, 1993. Mem. Automotive Fine Art Soc. Studio: 1728 S Bedford St Los Angeles CA 90035-4321

WOOD, RAYMUND FRANCIS, retired librarian; b. London, Nov. 9, 1911; came to U.S., 1924; s. George S. and Ida A. (Lawes) W.; m. Margaret Ann Peed, Feb. 26, 1943; children: Paul George, Gregory Leo, David Joseph. AB, St. Mary's U., Balt., 1931; MA, Gonzaga U., 1939; PhD, UCLA, 1949; MS in Libr. Sci., U. So. Calif., L.A., 1950. Instr. English U. Santa Clara (Calif.), 1939-41; rehab. officer VA, L.A., 1946-48; reference libr. Fresno (Calif.) State Coll., 1950-66; prof. libr. sci. UCLA, L.A., 1966-77, prof. emeritus, 1977—, from asst. dean to assoc. dean Grad. Sch. Libr. &

Info. Sci., 1970-77. Author: California's Agua Fria, 1952, Life and Death of Peter Lebec, 1954, The Saints of the California Landscape, 1987; co-author: Librarian and Laureate: Ina Coolbrith of California, 1973, many others. Vol. driver ARC, Van Nuys, Calif., 1977—; pres. Friends of the Encino/Tarzana Br. Libr., Tarzana, Calif., 1977-80, Jedediah Smith Soc., Stockton, Calif., 1987-90, knight comdr. Order of St. Gregory, 1994. With U.S. Army, 1942-46, ETO. Travel grantee Am. Book Found., 1964, Del. Amo Found., 1974. Mem. ALA (book reviewer 1974—), Calif. Libr. Assn. (many offices), Mariposa County Hist. Assn. (life), Oral History Assn. (life), Fresno County Hist. Soc. (editor 1959-66), Westerners L.A. Corral (editor of Brand Book 1982). Democrat. Byzantine Catholic. Home: 18052 Rosita St Encino CA 91316-4217

WOOD, ROBERT CHARLES, financial consultant; b. Chgo., Apr. 8, 1956; s. Roy Edward and Mildred Lucille (Jones) W.; m. Jennifer Jo Briggs, Oct. 1984; children: Jacqueline Jones, Reagan Keith. BA in History, BBA in Real Estate, So. Meth. U., 1979, JD, 1982. Bar: Tex. 1983. Appraiser McClellan-Massey, Dallas, 1977-79; researcher, acquisitions officer Amstar Fin. Corp., Dallas, 1979-80; prin. Robert Wood Cons., Dallas, 1981—; cons. Plan Mktg. Cos., 1983-84; pvt. practice law, Dallas, 1983-84; gen. counsel Diversified Benefits, Inc., Dallas, 1984-86; nat. accountants mgr. L.omas & Nettleton Real Estate Group, Dallas, 1987-88; sr. pension cons., prin. Eppler, Guerin & Turner, 1988-93; chmn. adv. coun. on devel. Medisend, 1991; nat. consulting coord. fin. advisors coun., v.p. Callan Assocs., San Francisco, 1995—. Author: Electionomics: How the Money Managers View the Election, 1992, After the Congress Vote: How the Managers See Things Now, 1993; mem. So. Meth. U. Law Rev., 1981-82; contbr. articles to profl. publs. Bd. dirs. Am. Cancer Soc., Dallas unit, 1982-87, mem. spl. events com., 1986-87, crusade com., 1987-88, corp. devel. bd. chmn. 1989—. Mem. Tex. Bar Assn., Phila. Bar Assn., Phi Gamma Delta. Avocations: tennis, bicycling.

WOOD, ROBERT EARLE, artist, educator; b. Gardena, Calif., Feb. 4, 1926; s. Earle Charlton and Ruth Marie (Stewart) W.; m. Jane E. Clark, Dec. 14, 1975. BA, Pomona Coll., 1950; MFA, Claremont Grad. Sch., 1952. Dir. Robert E. Wood Ann. Summer Sch. of Painting, 1961-94; instr. U. Minn., Otis Art Inst., L.A., Scripps Coll., Claremont, Calif., Claremont Grad. Sch., Riverside (Calif.) Art Ctr., Rex Brandt Summer Sch., Corona del Mar, Calif.; presenter many workshops. One-man shows include Reinike Gallery, Atlanta, Stary/Sheets Gallery, Irvine, Calif., Huntsman Galleries, Aspen, Colo., Challis Galleries, Laguna Beach, Calif., The Gallery, Burlingame, Calif., A Gallery, Palm Desert, Calif., Beretich Gallery, Claremont, Calif., Galeria Blu Di Prussia, Naples, Italy; Gallery Eight, Claremont, Zachary Waller Gallery, La Cienega, Calif., The Jones Gallery, La Jolla, Calif, others; contbr. articles to profl. jours. Recipient Exhbn. award Nat. Acad. Design, 1993, Nat. Watercolor Soc., 1958, 63, 64, 68, 70, 73, 76, Am. Watercolo Soc., 1969, 71, 78, 81, 82, 83, 85, 87, Silver medal 1982, High Winds medal 1985, exhbn. award Watercolor U.S.A., 1963, 66, 72, Rocky Mountain Nat. Watermedia Exhbn., 1974, 78, 86, Watercolor West, 1970, 71, 72, 73, 74, 75, 76, 77, Nat. Orange Show, Calif., 1961, 64, 67, 70, 73, 76, 79, many others. Home and Office: PO Box 8216 Green Valley Lake CA 92341-8216

WOOD, ROBERT WARREN, lawyer; b. Des Moines, July 5, 1955; s. Merle Warren and Cecily Ann (Sherk) W.; m. Beatrice Wood, Aug. 4, 1979; 1 child, Bryce Mercedes. Student, U. Sheffield, Eng., 1975-76; AB, Humboldt State U., 1976; JD, U. Chgo., 1979. Bar: Ariz. 1979, Calif. 1980, U.S. Tax Ct. 1980, N.Y. 1989, D.C. 1993. Assoc. Jennings, Strouss, Phoenix, 1979-80, McCutchen, Doyle, San Francisco, 1980-82, Broad, Khourie, San Francisco, 1982-85; assoc. Steefel, Levitt & Weiss, San Francisco, 1985-87, ptnr., 1987-91; ptnr. Bancroft & McAlister, San Francisco, 1991-93; prin. Robert W. Wood, P.C., San Francisco, 1993—; instr. in law U. Calif. San Francisco, 1981-82. Author: Taxation of Corporate Liquidations: A Complete Planning Guide, 1987, The Executive's Complete Guide to Business Taxes, 1989, Corporate Taxation: Complete Planning and Practice Guide, 1989, S Corporations, 1990, The Ultimate Tax Planning Guide for Growing Companies, 1991, Taxation of Damage Awards and Settlement Payments, 1991, Tax Strategies in Hiring, Retaining and Terminating Employees, 1991, The Home Office Tax Guide, 1991; (with others) California Closely Held Corporations: Tax Planning and Practice Guide, 1987, Legal Guide to Independent Contractor Status, 1992, Home Office Money & Tax Guide, 1992, Tax Aspects of Settlements and Judgements, 1993; editor-in-chief The M & A Tax Report; mem. editorial bd. Real Estate Tax Digest, The Practical Accountant. Mem. Calif. Bd. Legal Specialization (cert. specialist taxation), Internat. Platform Assn., Bohemian Club, Internat. Order of St. Hubert. Republican. Office: 235 Montgomery St Ste 972 San Francisco CA 94104-2902

WOOD, ROGER HOLMES, financial planner, educator; b. Corning, N.Y., Apr. 26, 1920; s. James Orville and Helen Lucille (Winemiller) W.; m. Phyllis Elizabeth Anderson, Dec. 26, 1947; children: Stephen, David, Elizabeth. AB, U. Pitts., 1944; MS, Columbia U., 1945; MA, San Francisco State U., 1951; PhD, Internat. Coll., 1978. CLU, Calif.; CFP, Calif., ChFC, Calif. Tchr. Oakdale (Calif.) High Sch., 1947-49, Galileo High Sch., San Francisco, 1949-54; instr. Coll. San Mateo, Calif., 1960-70; mem. nat. faculty Am. Coll., Bryn Mawr, Pa., 1960-70; lectr. Golden Gate U., San Francisco, 1983-84; agt. N.Y. Life Ins. Co., San Francisco, 1954—; tchr. Jefferson High Sch. Dist., Daly City, Calif., 1965—; pres. Leading Life Ins. Producers, San Francisco, 1960-62. Contbg. editor Western Underwriter, 1959-63. Mem. bd. dirs. San Francisco Coun. Chs., 1954-60. With U.S. Army, 1940-42. Mem. Internat. Assn. Fin. Planning, Internat. Soc. Descendants of Cherlemogne, Internat. Transactional Analysis Assn., Am. Risk and Ins. Assn., Am. Soc. CLU and Chartered Fin. Cons., Nat. Soc. Descendants of Early Quakers, San Francisco Estate Planning Coun., San Francisco Life Underwriters Assn. (v.p. 1960-62), Peninsula Estate Planning Coun., Soc. Genealogists (London), Soc. of The War of 1812, Soc. Col. Wars, Hon. Order Ky. Cols., SAR, Phi Delta Kappa, Phi Gamma Delta. Republican. Presbyterian. Home: 65 Capay Cir South San Francisco CA 94080-4117

WOOD, STEPHEN, minister. Dir. Native Am. Ministry Dist. of the Christian and Missionary Alliance. Office: 10454 S Hyacinth Pl Highlands Ranch CO 80126

WOOD, STUART KEE, retired engineering manager; b. Dallas, Mar. 8, 1925; s. William Henry and Harriet (Kee) Wood; m. Loris V. Poock, May 17, 1951 (dec. June 1990); children: Linda S. Kuehl, Thomas N., Richard D.; m. Lois H. Morton, Nov. 25, 1994. BS in Aero. Engring., Tex. A&M U., 1949. Aircraft sheet metal worker USAF SAC, Kelly Field, San Antonio, Tex., 1942-45; structural design engr. B-52, 367-80, KC-135, 707 Airplanes Boeing, Seattle and Renton, Wash., 1949-55; thrust reverser design engr. 707 and 747 Airplanes Boeing, Renton, 1955-66; supr. thrust reverser group 747 Airplane Boeing, Everett, Wash., 1966-69; supr. rsch. basic engine noise 727 airplane FAA, NASA, 1969-74; supr. jetfoil propulsion Jetfoil Hydrofoil Boeing, Renton, 1974-75; supr. rsch. basic engine performance loss JT9D Pratt & Whitney, 1975-79; supr. propulsion systems 757 Airplane Boeing, Renton, 1979-90; supr., propulsion systems thrust reverser 737, 747, 757, 767 Boeing, Kent, Wash., 1990-94, ret., 1994. Patentee in field. Recipient Ed Wells award AIAA, N.W. chpt., Bellevue, Wash., 1992. Republican. Presbyterian. Home: 3831 46th Ave SW Seattle WA 98116-3723

WOOD, THOMAS COWAN, physician; b. Denver, Oct. 4, 1938; s. Gerald Cowan and Virginia Elizabeth (Sevier) W.; m. Kathryn Louise Francis, June 12, 1964 (div. Mar. 1993); children: Karen, Robert, Paul. BA, Dartmouth Coll., 1960; postgrad., Denver U., 1961; MD, U. Colo., 1965. Intern Letterman Gen. Hosp., San Francisco, 1965-66; resident U. Wash., Seattle, 1968-70, fellowship in nephrology, 1970-71; pvt. practice Anchorage, 1971—; med. dir. Alaska Kidney Ctr., Anchorage, 1973-94; chief of medicine Providence Hosp., 1978-80; gov. Am. Coll. Physicians, Phila., 1985-89; adv. bd. Providence Hosp., Anchorage, 1992—, N.W. Organ Procurement Agy., Seattle, 1985—. Initiator, tchr. Paramedic Sys., Anchorage, 1972-76; initiator Alaska Kidney Found., Anchorage, 1973. With U.S. Army, 1965-68. Fellow ACP (gov. 1985-89); mem. Renal Physicians Assn. (state leader 1985—), N.W. Renal Soc., Alaska State Med. Assn., Anchorage Med. Soc. Office: Providence Med Office Bldg #55 3340 Providence Dr Ste 551 Anchorage AK 99508-4643

WOOD, WILLIS BOWNE, JR., utility holding company executive; b. Kansas City, Mo., Sept. 15, 1934; s. Willis Bowne Sr. and Mina (Henderson) W.; m. Dixie Gravel, Aug. 31, 1955; children: Bradley, William, Josh. BS in Petroleum Engring., U. Tulsa, 1957; grad. advanced mgmt. program, Harvard U., 1983. Various positions So. Calif. Gas Co., L.A., 1960-74, v.p. then sr. v.p., 1975-80, exec. v.p., 1983-84; pres., CEO Pacific Lighting Gas Supply Co., L.A., 1981-83; sr. v.p. Pacific Enterprises, L.A., 1984-85, exec. v.p., 1985-89, pres., 1989-91, pres., CEO, 1991-92, chmn., pres., CEO, 1992-93, chmn., CEO, 1993—; bd. dirs. Gt. Western Fin. Corp., Gt. Western Bank, L.A.; dir. Automobile Club So. Calif.; trustee U. So. Calif.; bd. visitors Rand Grad. Sch. Trustee, vice chmn. Harvey Mudd Coll., Claremont, Calif., 1984; vice chmn. Calif. Med. Ctr. Found., L.A., 1983—; trustee, past pres. S.W. Mus., L.A., 1988—; bd. dirs. L.A. World Affairs Coun., 1994—; dir., past chmn. bus. coun. Sustainable Energy Future, 1994—. Mem. Soc. Petroleum Energy Engrs., Am. Gas Assn., Pacific Coast Gas Assn. (past bd. dirs.), Pacific Energy Assn., Calif. Bus. Roundtable, Calif. State C. of C. (bd. dirs.), Nat. Assn. of Mfrs. (bd. dirs.), Hacienda Golf CLub, Ctr. Club, Calif. Club. Republican. Office: Pacific Enterprises 633 E 5th St Ste 5400 Los Angeles CA 90013-2109

WOODARD, ALVA ABE, business consultant; b. Roy, N.Mex., June 28, 1928; s. Joseph Benjamin and Emma Lurania (Watkins) W.; m. Esther Josepha Kaufmann, Apr. 5, 1947 (div. Sept. 1991); children: Nannette, Gregory, Loreen, Arne, Mark, Kevin, Steven, Curtis, Marlee, Julie, Michelle; m. Margaret Adele Evenson, Oct. 1, 1994. Student, Kinman Bus. U., 1948-49, Whitworth Coll., 1956, Wash. State U., 1953-54. Sec.-treas., dir. Green Top Dairy Farms, Inc., Clarkston, Wash., 1948-52; v.p., treas., sec., dir. ASC Industries, Inc. (subs. Gifford-Hill and Co.), Spokane, Wash., 1953-75; dir. Guenther Irrigation, Inc., Pasco, Wash., 1966-71; mng. dir. Irrigation Rental, Inc., Pasco, 1968-75, Rain Chief Irrigation Co., Grand Island, Nebr., 1968-75; sec., dir. Keeling Supply Co., Little Rock, 1969-72; pres., dir. Renters, Inc., Salt Lake City, 1971-75, Woodard Western Corp., Spokane, 1976-86, Woodard Industries, Inc., Auburn, Wash., 1987-90; cons. Woodard Assocs., Spokane, Wash., 1985—; pres., dir. TFI Industries, inc., Post Falls, Idaho, 1989-90; v.p., sec., treas., dir. Trans-Force, Inc., Post Falls, 1989-90, TFI Computer Scis., Inc., Post Falls, 1989-90. Newman Lake (Wash.) Rep. precinct committeeman, 1964-80; Spokane County del. Wash. Rep. Conv., 1968-80. Mem. Adminstrv. Mgmt. Soc. (bd. dirs. 1966-68), Optimists. Home and Office: 921 E 39th Ave Spokane WA 99203

WOODARD, DOROTHY MARIE, insurance broker; b. Houston, Feb. 7, 1932; d. Gerald Edgar and Bessie Katherine (Crain) Floeck; student N.Mex. State U., 1950; m. Jack W. Woodard; June 19, 1950 (dec.); m. Norman W. Libby, July 19, 1982 (dec. Dec. 1991). Ptnr. Western Oil Co., Tucumcari, N.Mex., 1950—; owner, mgr. Woodard & Co., Las Cruces, N.Mex., 1959-67; agt., dist. mgr. United Nations Ins. Co., Denver, 1968-74; agt. Western Nat. Life Ins. Co., Amarillo, Tex., 1976—. Exec. dir. Tucumcari Indsl. Commn., 1979—; dir. Bravo Dome Study Com., 1979—; owner Libby Cattle Co., Libby Ranch Co.; regional bd. dirs. N.Mex., Eastern Plains Council Govts., 1979—. Mem. NAFE, Tucumcari C. of C., Mesa Country Club. Home: PO Box 823 Tucumcari NM 88401-0823

WOODARD, JOHN HENRY, quality control professional; b. Alameda, Calif., Mar. 25, 1948; s. Charles A. and Louise E. (Fick) W.; m. Nancy L. Smith, Apr. 8, 1972; 1 child, Victoria A. BA in Psychology, Calif. State Coll., Hayward, 1970. Quality control supr. Hunt Wesson Foods, Hayward, Calif., 1969-75; quality control mgr. Hunt Wesson Foods, Davis, Calif., 1975-92; quality control and bulk paste mgr. Hunt Wesson Foods, Davis, 1992—. Mem. Woodland (Calif.) Davis Rail Study, 1993-94. Mem. Alpha Phi Omega (historian, treas., pres.). Republican. Episcopalian. Home: 614 Ashley Ave Woodland CA 95695-3671 Office: Hunt Wesson Foods 1111 E Covell Blvd Davis CA 95616-1209

WOODARD, LARRY L., college official; b. Lebanon, Oreg., Apr. 16, 1936; s. Hugh Frank and Ima Ellen (Bilyeu) W.; m. Bette Jeanette Brown, Aug. 10, 1956; children: Perry, Craig, Stacy. BS in Forestry, Oreg. State U., 1957. Forester Bur. of Land Mgmt., Oreg., 1957-69, Washington, 1969-72; dist. mgr. Bur. of Land Mgmt., Coeur d'Alene, Idaho, 1972-76; assoc. state dir. Bur. of Land Mgmt., Boise, Idaho, 1976-78, Santa Fe, 1978-82, Boise, 1982-86; state dir. Bur. of Land Mgmt., Santa Fe, 1987-93; dir. devel. Boise Bible Coll., 1993—. Author: A to Z, The Biography of Arthur Zimmerman, 1988, Before the First Wave, 1994. Bd. dirs. Boise Bible Coll., 1977-87; trustee N.Mex. Nature Conservancy, 1987-90. Recipient Disting. Svc. award U.S. Dept. Interior, 1986, Sec.'s Stewardship award U.S. Dept. Interior, 1989, Pres.'s Meritorious Exec. award, 1991. Republican. Home: PO Box 365 Meridian ID 83680-0365 Office: Boise Bible Coll 8695 Marigold St Boise ID 83714-1220

WOODBRIDGE-KIRADJIAN, FRANCES WOLSEY, marketing professional; b. Cleve., Jan. 20, 1953; d. Allon W. and Stefanie (Herman) Wolsey; m. Robert S. Woodbridge, Oct. 1979 (div. Dec. 1992); 1 child, Angela Michele Setters; m. Varouj Kiradjian, Dec. 27, 1993. Cert. in bus. mgmt., Calif. State U., Northridge, 1985; cert. in mgmt. effectiveness, U. So. Calif., 1993. Cert. corp. travel exec. Adminstr. to dir. mfg. ITT Gilgillan, Van Nuys, Calif., 1972-78; adminstrv. asst., then corp. rels. adminstr./travel mgr. Datametrics Corp., Northridge, 1978-87; nat. account mgr. Carlson Travel Network, L.A., 1987-93; dir. mktg. Computerized Corp. Rate Assn., Woodland Hills, Calif., 1993-94; speaker Corp. Travel East & West, N.Y.C. and San Francisco, 1987, 87; presenter/lectr. numerous corp. travel confs. and internat. travel meetings; past exec. dir. recreation club, past sr. human resources adminstr., mng. editor newsletter Datametrics Corp., 1985-87. Vol. Haven Hills Home for Battered Women/Children, Pediatric AIDS Found. Mem. NAFE, Profl. Women in Travel (founder L.A. chpt., past pres., past internat. dir., editor newsletter 1989-92), L.A. Bus. Travel Assn. (mem. exec. bd. 1987-88). Home: 22370 Macfarlane Dr Woodland Hills CA 91364-2914

WOODBURY, JAMES ROBERTS, electronics consultant; b. Hollywood, Calif., May 24, 1931; s. Walter Edgar Woodbury and Gladys Rose Rockwell (Roberts) Woodbury Abberley; m. Joyce Elaine Albaugh, June 27, 1953; children: Jennifer Lynne, Neal Walter, Elaine Dorothy. BSc in Electronics and Aero. Engring., Brown U., 1953; MSEE, Stanford U., 1962, MS in Math., 1964. Mem. tech. staff Bell Telephone Labs., Whippany, N.J., 1953-56, TRW (formerly Ramo Wooldridge), L.A., 1956-59; rsch. engr. SRI Internat., Menlo Park, Calif., 1959-76; mem. tech. staff Phillips (formerly Signetics), Mountain View, Calif., 1976-81, Fairchild Semi Conductor, Mountain View, 1981-84; sr. mem. tech. staff MTel (formerly M/A Com Linkabit), San Diego, 1984-87; sr. design engr. Hughes Network Systems, San Diego, 1987-93; cons. Woodbury Electronics Cons., San Diego, 1993—. Mem. IEEE, Tau Beta Pi. Baptist. Home and Office: Woodbury Electronics Cons 11745 Avenida Sivrita San Diego CA 92128-4525

WOODBURY, LAEL JAY, theatre educator; b. Fairview, Idaho, July 3, 1927; s. Raymond A. and Wanda (Dawson) W.; m. Margaret Lillian Swenson, Dec. 19, 1949; children: Carolyn Inez (Mrs. Donald Hancock), Shannon Margaret (Mrs. Michael J. Busenbark), Jordan Ray, Lexon Dan. BS, Utah State U., 1952; MA, Brigham Young U., 1953; PhD (Univ. fellow), U. Ill., 1954. Teaching asst. U. Ill., 1953; assoc. prof. Brigham Young U., 1954-61; guest prof. Colo. State Coll., 1962; asst. prof. Bowling Green State U., 1961-62; asso. prof. U. Iowa, 1962-65; producer Ledges Playhouse, Lansing, Mich., 1963-65; prof. speech and dramatics, chmn. dept. Brigham Young U., 1966-70, assoc. dean Coll. Fine Arts and Communications, 1969-73, dean Coll. Fine Arts and Communications, 1973-82; vis. lectr. abroad; bd. dirs. Eagle Systems Internat.; bd. dir. workshop Fedn. for Asian Cultural Promotion, Republic of China; dir. European study tour. Author: Play Production Handbook, 1959, Mormon Arts, vol. I, 1972, Mosaic Theatre, 1976, also articles, original dramas; profl. actor PBS and feature films. Chmn. gen. bd. drama com. Young Men's Mut. Improvement Assn., 1958-61; bd. dirs. Repertory Dance Theatre, Utah ARC; chmn. Utah Alliance for Arts Edn.; mem. adv. coun. Utah Arts Festival; missionary LDS Ch., N.Y.C., 1994. With USN, 1942-46. Recipient Creative Arts award Brigham Young U., 1971, Disting. Alumni award, 1975, Tchr. of Yr. award, 1988, Excellence in Rsch. award, 1992, Disting. Svc. award, 1992. Mem. Rocky Mountain Theatre Conf. (past pres.), Am. Theatre Assn. (chmn. nat. com. royalties 1972—, mem. fin. com. 1982—), NW Assn. Univs. and Colls. (accrediting officer), Am. Theatre Assn. (v.p. Univ. and Coll. Theatre Assn.), Theta Alpha Phi, Phi Kappa Phi. Home: 1303 Locust Ln Provo UT 84604-3651

WOODBURY, MARDA LIGGETT, librarian, writer; b. N.Y.C., Sept. 20, 1925; d. Walter W. and Edith E. (Fleischer) Liggett; m. Philip J. Evans, Sept. 1948 (div. 1950); 1 child, Mark W. Evans; m. Mark Lee Woodbury, 1956 (div. 1969); children: Brian, Heather. Student, Bklyn. Coll., 1942-44; BA in Chemistry and Polit. Sci., Bard Coll., 1946; BS in Libr. Sci., Columbia U., 1948; postgrad., U. Calif., Berkeley, 1955-56, 60-61. Cert. tchr. Libr. various spl., med. and pub. librs., San Francisco, 1946-60, Coll. Pk. High Sch., Mt. Diablo, Calif., 1962-67; elem. sch. libr. Oakland and Berkeley, Calif., 1967-69; libr. dir. Far West Lab. Ednl. Rsch. & Devel., San Francisco, 1969-73; libr., editor Gifted Resource Ctr., San Mateo, Calif., 1973-75; libr. cons. Rsch. Ventures, Berkeley, Calif., 1975—; libr. dir. Life Chiropractic Coll., San Lorenzo, Calif., 1980—. Author: A Guide to Sources of Educational Information, 1976, 2d edit., 1982, Selecting Instructional Materials, 1978, Selecting Materials for Instruction, Vol. I: Issues and Policies, 1979, Vol. II: Media and the Curriculum, 1980, Vol. III: Subject Areas and Implementation, 1980, Childhood Information Resources, 1985 (Outstanding Ref. Work, Assn. Ref. Librs. 1985), Youth Information Resources, 1987; mem. editorial bd. Ref. Libr., 1980—. Mem. Med. Libr. Assn. (editor Chiropractic Librs. 1990-92). Home: 2411 Russell St Berkeley CA 94705-2019 Office: Life Chriopractic Coll 2005 Via Barrett San Lorenzo CA 94580-1315

WOODEN, JOHN ROBERT, former basketball coach; b. Martinsville, Ind., Oct. 14, 1910; s. Joshua Hugh and Roxie (Rothrock) W.; m. Nellie C. Riley, Aug. 8, 1932; children: Nancy Anne, James Hugh. B.S., Purdue U., 1932; M.S., Ind. State U., 1947. Athletic dir., basketball and baseball coach Ind. State Tchrs. Coll., 1946-48; head basketball coach UCLA, 1948-75; lectr. to colls., coaches, business. Author: Practical Modern Basketball, 1966, They Call Me Coach, 1972; Contbr. articles to profl. jours. Served to lt. USNR, 1943-46. Named All-Am. basketball player Purdue U., 1930-32, Coll. Basketball Player of Yr., 1932, to All-Time All-Am. Team Helms Athletic Found., 1943, Nat. Basketball Hall of Fame, Springfield (Mass.) Coll., as player 1960, as coach, 1970, Ind. State Basketball Hall of Fame, 1962, Calif. Father of Yr., 1964, 75, Coach of Yr. U.S. Basketball Writers Assn., 1964, 67, 69, 70, 72, 73, Sportsman of Yr. Sports Illustrated, 1973, GTE Acad. All-Am., 1994; recipient Whitney Young award Urban League, 1973, 1st ann. Velvet Covered Brick award Layman's Leadership Inst., 1974, 1st ann. Dr. James Naismith Peachbasket award, 1974, medal of excellence Bellarmine Coll., 1987.

WOODFORD, CHARLES WALTER, bank executive, economist; b. Sharon, Wis., Dec. 23, 1931; s. John Chauncey and Pauline Sweet (Goelzer) W.; B.A. in Econs. with honors, Beloit Coll., 1956; postgrad. Northwestern U. Grad. Sch. Bus., 1956-58, U. Chgo. Grad. Sch. Bus., 1958-60, Stanford U., summer 1969; m. Barbara J. Johnsen, Aug. 25, 1956; children: Mark Mallory, Stuart Allen, Geoffrey James. Investment advisor Brown Bros. Harriman, Chgo., 1956-66; asst. state treas. State of Ill., Springfield, 1967-71, state treas., 1971; treas., chief investment officer Horace Mann Ins. Corp., Springfield, 1972-75; adminstrv. v.p. Am. Nat. Bank, Chgo., 1975-78; sr. v.p., head trust and personal banking dept. First Nat. Bank of Chgo., 1978-83; pres. Ft. Dearborn Income Securities, 1978-82; chmn., chief exec. officer Trust Services Am., 1982-91; exec. v.p. Sanwa Bank Calif., 1992—; bd. dirs. Japan Am. Soc. of So. Calif.; vice-chmn. Town Hall of So. Calif., L.A., 1987-89. Author econ. newsletter Economic Horizons. Mem. Ill. Bd. Investments, 1971-74, chmn., 1973-74; chmn. Budget Task Force State of Ill., 1971-72; mem. platform com. Ill. Dem. Party, 1976-80; dir. Japanese Philarmonic Soc. L.A. Recipient Commendation City of L.A., 1986. Mem. Nat. Assn. Bus. Economists, Fin. Analysts Fedn., Am. Econ. Assn., Hong Kong Assn. of So. Calif., L.A. World Affairs Coun. (internat. circle), exec. v.p., divsn. head Sanwa Trust & Investment, 1991—. Democrat. Methodist. Home: 2222 Canalda Dr La Canada CA 91011-1203 Office: Sanwa Trust 601 LS Figueroa St W10-2 Los Angeles CA 90017

WOODHULL, JOHN RICHARD, electronics company executive; b. LaJolla, Calif., Nov. 5, 1933; s. John Richard Woodhull and Mary Louise (Fahey) Hostetler; m. Barbara Adams; children: Elizabeth A., John A. BS in Engring. Physics, U. Colo., 1957, MS in Applied Math., 1960. Engr. Space Tech. Labs. (now TRW Systems), Redondo Beach, Calif., 1960-63; mgr., engr. Northrop Corp., Hawthorne, Calif., 1964; mem. tech. staff Logicon, Inc., San Pedro, Calif., 1964-69, pres., chief exec. officer, Torrance, Calif., 1969—, also bd. dirs.; instr. physics U. Colo., 1959-60; bd. dirs. 1st Fed. Fin. Corp. Bd. mgrs. San Pedro (Calif.) and Peninsula YMCA; bd. dirs. Los Angeles YMCA, 1985—, Sunrise Med., Torrance, 1986—. With USN, 1956-59. Mem. Chief Execs.' Orgn., World Bus. Coun., Nat. Indsl. Security Assn. (bd. dirs. 1986—). Avocations: sailboat racing, tennis, skiing. Office: Logicon Inc 3701 Skypark Dr Ste 200 Torrance CA 90505-4712*

WOODRESS, JAMES LESLIE, JR., English language educator; b. Webster Groves, Mo., July 7, 1916; s. James Leslie and Jessie (Smith) W.; m. Roberta Wilson, Sept. 28, 1940. A.B., Amherst Coll., 1938; A.M., NYU, 1943; Ph.D., Duke U., 1950; DLitt, U. Nebr., 1995. News editor Sta. KWK, St. Louis, 1939-40; rewriteman, editor UPI, N.Y.C., 1940-43; instr. English, Grinnell (Iowa) Coll., 1949-50; asst. prof. English, Butler U., Indpls., 1950-53; asso. prof. Butler U., 1953-58; asso. prof. English, San Fernando Valley (Calif.) State Coll., 1958-61, prof., 1961-66, chmn. dept., 1959-63, dean letters and scis., 1963-65; prof. English, U. Calif.-Davis, 1966-87, chmn. dept., 1970-74; vis. prof. Sorbonne, Paris, 1974-75, 83. Author: Howells and Italy, 1952, Booth Tarkington: Gentleman from Indiana, 1955, A Yankee's Odyssey: The Life of Joel Barlow, 1958, Dissertations in American Literature, 1957, 62, 68, Willa Cather: Her Life and Art, 1970, 75, 81, American Fiction 1900-50, 1974, Willa Cather: A Literary Life, 1987; editor: Eight American Authors, 1971, American Literary Scholarship: An Annual, 1965-69, 75-77, 79, 81, 87, Critical Essays on Walt Whitman, 1983, Cather's The Troll Garden, 1983, (with Richard Morris) Voices from America's Past, anthology, 1961-62, 75. Served to lt. AUS, 1943-46. Ford Fund for Advancement Edn. fellow, 1952-53; Guggenheim fellow, 1957-58; Fulbright lectr. France, 1962-63; Fulbright lectr. Italy, 1965-66; recipient Hubbell medal, 1985. Mem. MLA (sec. Am. Lit. group 1962-63), AAUP, Phi Beta Kappa. Address: 824 Sycamore Ln Davis CA 95616-3225 Office: U Calif Dept English Davis CA 95616

WOODROW, KENNETH M., psychiatrist; b. Yonkers, N.Y., Mar. 20, 1942; s. Jack H. and Grace (Lewis) W.; m. Mary Mack, June 9, 1968 (div. 1985); 1 child, Laura; m. Patricia Robin Stokes, July 1, 1989. BA, Wesleyan U., 1964; postgrad., U. Calif., Davis, 1964; MD, U. Md., 1968. Diplomate Am. Bd. Psychiatry and Neurology. Intern Kaiser Found. Hosp., Oakland, Calif., 1968-69; resident psychiatry Stanford (Calif.) U. Med. Ctr., 1969-72; clin. assoc. NIMH Lab. Clin. Pschopharmacology, USPHS, 1972-74; pvt. practice psychiatry Menlo Park, Calif., 1977—; clin. assoc. prof. dept. psychiatry Stanford U. Sch. Medicine, 1975—; staff psychiatrist, chmn. pharmacy and therapeutics com. Stanford U. Hosp.; staff psychiatrist Sequoia Hosp., Redwood City, Calif.; examiner Am. Bd. Psychiatry and Neurology; rsch. assoc. NIH, Lab. Socioenviron. Studies, 1963-65; rsch. fellow U. Md. Psychiat. Inst., Balt., 1966; cons. Kaiser Permanente Med. Group, 1969; grant rev. cons. nSF, 1970; psychiat. emergency svc. and med. cons. Highland Alameda Hosp., 1970-72; clin. assoc. NIMH, 1972-74; exec. com. Com. for Concerned Psychiatrists, 1972-74; staff psychiatrist Palo Alto VA Hosp., 1974-76; psychiat. cons. Job Corps, San Jose, 1975-82; lectr. San Jose Hosp., 1976-83. Fellow Am. Psychiat. Assn. Mem. Am. Psychiat. Assn. Office: 1225 Crane St Ste 106 Menlo Park CA 94025-4253

WOODRUFF, FAY, paleoceanographer, geological researcher; b. Boston, Jan. 23, 1944; d. Lorande Mitchell and Anne (Fay) W.; m. Alexander Whitehill Clowes, May 20, 1972 (div. Oct. 1974); m. Robert G. Douglas, Jan. 27, 1980; children: Ellen, Katerina. RN, Mass. Gen. Hosp. Sch. Nursing, Boston, 1965; BA, Boston U., 1971; MS, U. So. Calif., 1979. Rsch. assoc. U. So. Calif., L.A., 1978-81, rsch. faculty, 1981—; keynote spkr. 4th Internat. Symposium on Benthia Foraminiferi, Sendai, Japan, 1990. Contbg. author: Geological Society of America Memoir, 1985; contbr. articles to profl. jours. Life mem. The Nature Conservancy, Washington, 1992. NSF grantee, 1986-88, 88-91, 91-94. Mem. Am. Geophys Union, Geol. Soc. Am., Internat. Union Geol. Scis. (internat. commn. on stratigraphy, subcommn. on neogene stratigaphy 1991-92), Soc. Women Geographers (sec. So. calif.

chpt. 1990-96), Soc. Econ. Paleontologists and Minerologists (sec., editor North Am. Micropaleontology sect. 1988-90), Oceanography Soc. (chpt. mem.), Sigma Xi. Episcopalian. Office: U So Calif Dept Geol Scis Los Angeles CA 90089-0740

WOODRUFF, JAMES ROBERT, engineer; b. Akron, Ohio, Oct. 13, 1929; s. James Henry and Grace Eunice (Titus) W.; m. Mary Arlene Pancharian, Dec. 20, 1959; children: Katherine Arlene Waite, Mary Lucinda Ruefenacht, James Thomas. BA in Phys. Sci., Chapman U., 1951. Aerospace technologist NASA Ames Rsch. Ctr., Sunnyvale, Calif., 1959-75; engr. Systron Donner, Concord, Calif., 1975-88; rsch. specialist Allied Signal, Redmond, Wash., 1988—. With USN, 1951-55. Mem. AAAS, IEEE. Home: 7910 146th Ave NE Redmond WA 98052-4169 Office: Allied Signal 15001 NE 36th St Redmond WA 98052-5317

WOODRUFF, SHIRLEY, middle school educator; b. Richmond, Calif., May 30, 1951; d. Vern LeRoy and Betty Jo (Salyer) Cole; m. Carl Woodruff, June 22, 1974; children: Dan, David, Ben, Mark, Joseph. AA, Solano C.C., Rockland, Calif., 1971; BA in Social Sci., Calif. State U., Sacramento, 1973; postgrad., Idaho State U., 1972-73; student, Contra Costa Jr. Coll., San Pablo, Calif., 1969-70; postgrad., Brigham Young U. Cert. reading specialist, secondary and elementary credentials, kindergarten endorsement, reading endorsement K-12, social studies K-12, Idaho, Calif. Tchr. grades 5 and 6, tchr. art and music Sch. Dist. 91, Idaho Falls, Idaho, 1973-74; chpt. I tchr., 1979-82; tchr. kindergarten Bonneville Joint Dist. 93, Idaho Falls; 3rd grade tchr., 1982-85; elem. tchr. Bonneville Joint Dist. 93, Idaho Falls; 9th grade reading tchr., Book Fair chmn. Sandcreek Mid. Sch., Idaho Falls, Idaho, 1992-95; tchr. reading Bonneville Joint Dist. 93, Idaho Falls; 7th grade reading, geography, and lit. tchr., 1985—. Editor Hi-Hopes newsletter; past editor Edn. Coalition Newsletter, Idaho Falls, 1992-93. Libr. Sunday sch. tchr.; chmn. Multiple Sclerosis Read-a-thon Iona Elem. Sch., 1980; team leader Team of Tchrs., Sandcreek Mid. Sch., 1992-93, book fair chmn., 1992-95; bldg. rep. East Idaho Reading Coun., 1992-95, BEA, 1994-95; mem. steering com. Edn Coalition, Idaho Falls, 1991-93. Mem. NEA, Nat. Coun. Tchrs. English, Internat. Reading Assn. (Pres.'s award Idaho coun.), East Idaho Reading Coun. (v.p. 1994-95, membership chair, bldg. rep. 1994-95), Idaho Edn. Assn., Idaho Coun. Internat. Reading Assn., Bonneville Edn. Assn. (bldg. rep. 1994-95). Home: 5511 Concord Circle Idaho Falls ID 83401-5244

WOODRUFF, VIRGINIA, television and radio host, producer; b. Morrisville, Pa.; d. Edwin Nichols and Louise (Meredith) W.; m. Raymond F. Beagle Jr. (div.); m. Albert Plaut II (div.); 1 child, Elise Meredith. Student, Rutgers U. News corr. Sta. WNEW-TV Metromedia, N.Y.C., 1967; nat., internat. critic-at-large Mut. Broadcasting System, 1968-75; lectr. Leigh Bur., 1969-71; byline columnist N.Y. Daily Mirror, N.Y.C., 1970-71; first Arts critic Teleprompter and Group W Cable TV, 1977-84; host/producer The First Nighter N.Y. Times Primetime Cable Highlight program, 1977-84; pres., chief exec. officer Starpower, Inc., 1984-91; affiliate news corr. ABC Radio Network, N.Y.C., 1984-86; pres. Promarket People Inc., 1991-93; S.W. freelance corr. Voice of Am., USIA, 1992—; S.W. contbg. corr. Am. in the Morning, First Light, Mut. Broadcasting System, 1992; perennial critic Off-Off Broadway Short Play Festival, N.Y.C., 1984—; was 1st Woman on 10 O'Clock News, WNEW-TV, 1967. Contbg. feature writer Vis a Vis mag., 1988-91. Mem. celebrity panel Arthritis Telethon, N.Y.C., 1976. Selected episodes of First Nighter program in archives N.Y. Pub. Libr., Billy Rose Theatre Collection, Rodgers and Hammerstein Collection, Performing Arts Rsch.Ctr. Mem. Drama Desk. Presbyterian; National Arts Club.

WOODS, ALMA JEAN, elementary educator; b. Pueblo, Colo., Aug. 26, 1937; d. Melvin Leroy and Lillian Roberta (Ullrich) W. Assoc., Pueblo (Colo.) Jr. Coll., 1958; BA, Western State Coll., Gunnison, Colo., 1960; MA, U. No. Colo., Greeley, 1964. Lic. elem. educator. Elem. tchr. Sch. Dist. 60, Pueblo, 1960-93; travel-cultural spkr., educator So. Colo. Sch., Colorado Springs. Bd. mem. Pueblo United Way Allotment Com., 1993—; vol. to patients Sangre de Cristo Hospice, Pueblo, 1994—; historic docent Rosemount Mus. Mem. Colo. Ret. Educators, Ark. Valley Audubon, Pueblo YWCA Internat. Club, Alpha Delta Kappa (chpt. pres. 1982-84). Democrat. Methodist. Home: 98 Bonnymede Rd Pueblo CO 81001-1337

WOODS, BOBBY JOE, transportation executive; b. Frederick, Okla., June 20, 1935; s. Vivin Richard and Mattie Marie (Malone); divorced; children: Donald B., Kathryn M., David R., Lynda J. Student, U. Calif., Berkeley, 1955-56; AA, Phoenix Coll., 1955; student, Glendale (Ariz.) Coll., 1968, 75. Pres. Southwest Prorate Inc., Phoenix, 1967—, TCAB Registration Cons., Inc., 1993—; office mgr. Menke Transp., Phoenix, 1967-68; dist. exec. Boy Scouts Am., Phoenix, 1968-76; pres. Facing E's Enterprises, Inc., Yarnell, Ariz., 1991—. Commr. Boy Scouts Am., Ariz., N.Mex. Mem. Profl. Trucking Svcs. Assn. (pres. 1989-90), Lions Club (dist. gov. 1992-93, zone chmn. 1983-84, dep. dist. gov. 1984-85, lt. gov. 1991-92, dist. sight and hearing chmn. 1985-91, Sight and Hearing Found. state hearing chmn. 1985-89). Republican. Home: 918 W Cochise Dr Phoenix AZ 85021-2343 Office: TCAB Registrtion Cons Inc 2045 W Glendale Ave Phoenix AZ 85021-7841

WOODS, DONALD PETER, real estate executive, marketing professional; b. Seneca Falls, N.Y., Oct. 14, 1911; s. James Henry and Isabell Teresa (McDonald) W.; m. June 17, 1935; children: Donald Peter Jr., Richard, Terrence, Lynn, Thomas. PhB, Niagara U., Niagara Falls, N.Y., 1933; postgrad., Bklyn. Law Sch., 1933-36. Law clk. N.Y. State Ins. Dept., N.Y.C., 1933-36; title examiner Abstract Title and Mortgage, Rochester, N.Y., 1936-38; title officer Monroe Abstract & Title, Rochester, 1938-43; pres., chief exec. officer D.P. Woods, Inc., Rochester, 1945-54, Don Woods Realty, Phoenix, 1954-82; assoc. v.p. Colliers Internat., Phoenix, 1982—. Lt. USNR, 1943-45, PTO. Mem. Cert. Real Estate Appraisal, Internat. Coun. of Shopping Ctrs., Ariz. Club, Camelback Racquet Club (pres. Phoenix chpt. 1959—), Phi Delta Phi. Republican. Roman Catholic. Home: 5301 E Palomino Rd Phoenix AZ 85018-1911 Office: Colliers Internat 3636 N Central Ave Ste 600 Phoenix AZ 85012-1935

WOODS, GURDON GRANT, sculptor; b. Savannah, Ga., Apr. 15, 1915; s. Frederick L. and Marion (Skinner) W. Student, Art Student's League N.Y.C., 1936-39, Bklyn. Mus. Sch., 1945-46; Ph.D. (hon.), Coll. San Francisco Art Inst., 1966. exec. dir. San Francisco Art Inst., 1955-64; dir. Calif. Sch. Fine Arts, 1955-65; prof. Adlai E. Stevenson Coll., U. Calif. at Santa Cruz, 1966-74; dir. Otis Art Inst., Los Angeles, 1974-77; asst. dir. Los Angeles County Mus. Natural History, 1977-80; Sculptor mem. San Francisco Art Commn., 1954-56; mem. Santa Cruz County Art Commn., Regional Arts Council of Bay Area. Exhibited: N.A.D., 1948, 49, San Francisco Art Assn. anns., 1952-54, Denver Mus. Anns., 1952, 53, Whitney Mus. Ann., 1953, Sao Paulo Biennial, 1955, Bolles Gallery San Francisco, 1969, 70, 72, Los Angeles Mcpl. Gallery, 1977, San Jose Inst. Contemporary Art (Calif.), Washington Project for the Arts retrospective, 1968-1985, Washington, 1985, Retrospective Art Mus. Santa Cruz County, Calif., 1987, d.p. Fong Gallery, 1993, 94; commns. include: cast concrete reliefs and steel fountain, IBM Center, San Jose, Calif., fountain, Paul Masson Winery, Saratoga, Calif., McGraw Hill Pubs. (now Birkenstock), Novato, Calif.; work in permanent collection Oakland (Calif.) Mus.; papers in Archives of Am. Art, Smithsonian Instn., Washington. Recipient citation N.Y.C., 1948; prize N.A.D., 1949; Chapelbrook Found. research grantee, 1965-66; Sequoia Fund grantee, 1967; Research grantee Creative Arts Inst., U. Calif., 1968; grantee Carnegie Corp., 1968-69. Mem. Artists Equity Assn (pres. No. Calif. chpt. 1950-52, nat. dir. 1952-55). Address: 133 Seascape Ridge Dr Aptos CA 95003-5890

WOODS, JAMES PATRICK, JR., writer; b. N.Y.C., Nov. 27, 1954; s. James Patrick and Kathleen Theresa (Granville) W.; m. Kathryn Ann Depman, Oct. 17, 1992. BA, Georgetown U., 1976. Mgr. Saville Book Shop, Washington, 1976-77, Kramer Books & Afterwords, Washington, 1977; exec. prodr. Jack Morton Prodns., Washington, 1978-80; editor, primary author ABC Sports/Cap Cities/Nylac/ABC Wide World of Sports, N.Y.C., 1986-88; editor-in-chief Visa U.S.A. Inside the Rings, Foster City, Calif., 1993—; founder, pres. Creative Writing Svcs., San Francisco, 1980—; cons. Integral Systems, Walnut Creek, Calif., 1993-94, Pansophic, Chgo., 1992, Panoramic Techs., San Jose, Calif., 1991. Author: (video) Information Please, 1992 (Cindy award 1993); author, editor: (book) ABC's Wide World of Sports: 25 Years, 1988, (film) Commitment to Excellence, 1985 (N.Y. Film Festival Silver medal). Chairperson pub. rels. St. Paul's Roman Cath. Ch., San Francisco, 1993—, sec., 1991—, bd. dirs. parish coun., 1993—; pub. rels. rep. Noe Valley Merchants Assn., San Francisco, 1992—; active City Dem. Club, San Francisco, 1990—. Mem. San Francisco Press Club, Georgetown U. No. Calif. Alumni Assn., Christian Bros. Acad. Alumni Assn. Home and Office: 550 30th St San Francisco CA 94131

WOODS, LAWRENCE MILTON, airline company executive; b. Manderson, Wyo., Apr. 14, 1932; s. Ben Ray and Katherine (Youngman) W.; m. Joan Frances Van Patten, June 10, 1952; 1 dau., Laurie. B.Sc. with honors, U. Wyo., 1953; M.A., N.Y. U., 1973, Ph.D., 1975; LL.D., Wagner Coll., 1973. Bar: Mont. 1957; C.P.A., Colo., Mont. Accountant firm Peat, Marwick, Mitchell & Co. (C.P.A.'s), Billings, Mont., 1953; supervisory auditor Army Audit Agy., Denver, 1954-56; accountant Mobil Producing Co., Billings, Mont., 1956-59; planning analyst Socony Mobil Oil Co., N.Y.C., 1959-63; planning mgr. Socony Mobil Oil Co., 1963-65; v.p. North Am. div. Mobil Oil Corp., N.Y.C., 1966-67; gen. mgr. planning and econs. North Am. div. Mobil Oil Corp., 1967-69, v.p., 1969-77, exec. v.p., 1977-85, also dir.; pres., chief exec. officer, dir. Centennial Airlines, Inc., 1985-87; pres., dir. Woshakie Travel Corp., 1988—, High Plains Pub. Co. Inc., 1988—; bd. dirs. The Aid Assn. for Lutherans Mutual Funds. Author: Accounting for Capital, Construction and Maintenance Expenditures, 1967, The Wyoming Country Before Statehood, 1971, Sometimes the Books Froze, 1985, Moreton Frewen's Western Adventures, 1986, British Gentlemen in the Wild West, 1989; editor: Wyoming Biographies, 1991; co-author: Takeover, 1980; editor: Wyoming Biographies, 1991; contbr.: Accountants' Encyclopedia, 1962. Bd. dirs. U. Wyo. Research Corp. Served with AUS, 1953-55. Mem. ABA, Mont. Bar Assn., Am. Inst. CPA's, Chgo. Club. Republican. Lutheran. Office: High Plains Pub Co PO Box 1860 Worland WY 82401-1860

WOODS, MELANIE ANN, sales professional; b. Oakley, Kans., Oct. 24, 1957; d. Richard L. and Myrle E. (Arie) Stanfield; m. George K. Woods Jr., Oct. 16, 1982. BSBA, Kans. State U., 1979. Sales rep. George A. Hormel & Co., Kansas City, Mo., 1980-82; sales rep. Hershey Chocolate USA, Phoenix, 1985-86, key account rep., 1987-88, dist. account supr., 1988—. Mem. Kans. State U. Alumni Assn., Kappa Kappa Gamma Alumni Assn. Republican. Home: 3838 E Mountain Sky Ave Phoenix AZ 85044-6618

WOODS, ROBERT OCTAVIUS, aerospace engineer; b. Evanston, Ill., Feb. 17, 1933; s. Robert and Anna Margaret (Welch) W.; m. Judith Charlene Neese, Dec. 27, 1965; children: Lisa Ann, Robert David. BS in Engring., Princeton U., 1962, MS in Engring., 1964, MA, 1965, PhD, 1967. Registered profl. engr., Pa., N.Mex. From draftsman to profl. engr. Allstates Engring. Co., Trenton, N.J., 1950-60; sr. mem. Sandia Nat. Labs., Albuquerque, 1967—. Contbr. articles to profl. jours.; patentee in field. Fellow Ford Found., 1963, NSF, 1965. Fellow Brit. Interplanetary Soc., ASME (congl. sci. fellow 1991-92); mem. AAAS, Am. Phys. Soc., Albuquerque Soaring Club (v.p. 1972-74), Princeton Club (pres. 1976-91), Sigma Xi, Tau Beta Pi (Eminent Engr. award 1978). Republican. Presbyterian. Home: 7513 Harwood Ave NE Albuquerque NM 87110-1479 Office: Sandia Nat Labs Sandia Nat Labs 2171 Albuquerque NM 87185

WOODS, TRUDY ANN OLSON, gallery director; b. Mason City, Iowa, Mar. 14, 1946; d. Arnold E. and Audrey A. (Makeever) Olson; m. Michael G. Woods, June 15, 1969. BA, Grinnell (Iowa) Coll., 1968; MA in Tchg., Northwestern U., Evanston, Ill., 1969. Tchr. Highland Park (Ill.) Sch. Dist., 1968-69, Moreno Valley High Sch., Sunnymead, Calif., 1970-72, McNary High Sch., Salem, Oreg., 1974-76, Hoquiam (Wash.) High Sch., 1976-78; tchr. Lower Columbia Coll., Longview, Wash., 1988-89, art gallery dir., 1991—; founder, treas. Broadway Gallery, Longview, 1982—. Bd. dirs., pres. LWV of Grays Harbor, Aberdeen, Wash., 1978-81, LWV of Cowlitz County, Longview, Wash., 1981-93. Mem. Oreg. Potters Assn. Office: Art Gallery Lower Columbia Coll 1600 Maple St Longview WA 98632-3907

WOODSIDE, GEORGE ROBERT, computer software developer; b. Meadville, Pa., Oct. 29, 1949; s. William Clinton and Bernadette Lorena (Greene) W.; m. Diane Claire Hickenlooper, June 14, 1980. Grad. h.s., Fairview, Pa. Program GE Co., Erie, Pa., 1967-69; programmer-analyst Lovell Mfg. Co., Erie, 1969-70; mgr. data processing Eriez Mfg. Co., Erie, 1970-74; owner Woodside-Benson Assocs., Fairview, Pa., 1974-78; prin. mem. tech. staff Transaction Tech. Inc. (now Citicorp/TTI), Santa Monica, Calif., 1978-92; owner GRW Sys. and Programming, Gardnerville, Nev., 1993—. Contbr. articles to mags.; developer software to detect and eliminate computer viruses. Mem. IEEE. Office: 1590 Lombardy Rd Gardnerville NV 89410

WOOD-TROST, LUCILLE MARIE, educator, writer, psychotherapist; b. Candor, N.Y., Nov. 4, 1938; d. Stiles and Alice E. (Keim) Wood; m. Charles Trost, June 18, 1960 (div. 1981); 1 child, Scott. BS in Zoology, Pa. State U., 1960; MS in Biology, U. Fla., 1964; PhD in Human Behavior, Union Grad. Sch., Cin., 1975. Dir. Tamarack Learning Coop., Pocatello, Idaho, 1969-74; freelance writer, 1960-75, 82—; asst. prof. Westminster Coll., Salt Lake City, 1975-80; therapist, planner, writer Garden of Peace Healing Ctr., Stanwell Tops, NSW, Australia, 1980-81; pvt. practice psychotherapy Bellingham, Wash., 1982-84; assoc. prof. Northwest Indian Coll. (formerly Lummi Community Coll.), Bellingham, 1984—; dir. student svcs. N.W. Indian Coll., Bellingham, 1989-92, dir. individualized studies, 1992—. Author: Lives and Deaths in a Meadow, 1973 (award, Am. Assn. Sci. Tchrs.-Children's Book Coun. 1976), others. Mem. Sigma Xi, Phi Sigma. Mem. Science of Mind Church. Home: 2611 Mckenzie Rd Bellingham WA 98226-9203 Office: Northwest Indian Coll 2522 Kwina Rd Bellingham WA 98226-9278

WOODWARD, JAMES FRANCIS, humanities educator; b. Chgo., Sept. 17, 1946; s. Harry Herbert and Mary Winifred (O'Brien) W.; m. Julia Ann Gerber Woodward, June 3, 1978; 1 child, Katherine Julia. BA, Carleton Coll., Northfield, Minn., 1968; PhD, U. Tex., 1977. Asst. prof. U. Wis., LaCrosse, 1976-79, Coll. Charleston, S.C., 1980-81, Memphis State U., 1981-83; Mellon postdoctoral fellow in philosophy Calif. Inst. Technol., Pasadena, 1983-85; asst. prof. Caltech, Pasadena, 1986-88, assoc. prof., 1988-92, prof., 1992—, exec. officer Humanities, 1992—. Contbr. articles to profl. jours. Fellow Mellon Postdoctoral Caltech, 1983-85; grantee Nat. Sci. Found., 1994-95. Mem. Philosophy of Sci. Assn. Home: 694 S Oakland Ave Pasadena CA 91106-3797 Office: Calif Inst Tech Mail Code 228-77 Pasadena CA 91125

WOODWARD, JOHN RUSSELL, motion picture production executive; b. San Diego, July 10, 1951; s. Melvin C. and Dora M. (Rorabaugh) W. BA in Visual Arts, U. Calif., San Diego, 1973; MA in Cinema Prodn., U. So. Calif., 1978. V.p. prodn. World Wide Motion Pictures Corp., 1982—. Prodn. asst. various commls., 1977; asst. producer The Manitou, 1977; 1st asst. dir. Mortuary, 1981, They're Playing with Fire, 1983, Prime Risk, 1984, Winners Take All, 1986, Kidnapped, 1986, Slam Dance, 1986, Honor Betrayed, 1986, The Hidden, 1987, New Monkees, 1987, Bad Dreams, 1987, Night Angel, 1988, Disorganized Crime, 1988, UHF, 1988, The Horror Show, 1988, Fear, 1989, Tremors, 1989, Young Guns II, 1990, Shattered, 1990, Tales from the Crypt, 1990, Two-Fisted Tales, 1990, Buried Alive, 1990, Dream On, 1991, Strays, 1991, Universal Soldier, 1991, An Army of One, 1992, The Vanishing, 1992, Ghost in the Machine, 1992, The Shawshank Redemption, 1993, City Slickers II, 1993, Tour of Duty, 1994; location mgr. Star Chamber, 1982, To Be or Not to Be, 1983, Flashdance, 1983, Two of a Kind, 1983, Touch and Go, 1984, Explorers, 1984, Sweet Dreams, 1985, The Long Shot, 1985, The Running Man, 1985, A Different Affair, 1985, Walk Like a Man, 1986.

WOODWARD, KESLER EDWARD, artist, educator; b. Aiken, S.C., Oct. 7, 1951; s. Norman Edward and Bebe Helen (Kneece) W.; m. Marianna Boaz, May 15, 1971. BA, Davidson Coll., 1973; MFA, Idaho State U., 1977. Curator temporary exhibits Alaska State Mus., Juneau, 1977-78; artistic dir. Visual Arts Ctr. Alaska, Anchorage, 1978-79; curator visual arts Alaska State Mus., 1979-81; asst. prof. art U. Alaska, Fairbanks, 1981-88, assoc. prof., 1989—; gallery dir. U. Alaska Fine Arts Gallery, 1982—; dir. fine arts and humanities project Inst. on Can., Dartmouth Coll., Hanover, N.H., 1988-91, vis. rsch. fellow, 1988-91; acad. affiliate U. Alaska Mus., 1991—; workshop instr. U. Alaska Mus., others.; bd. dirs. Western States Arts Found, 1987-88; council mem. Alaska State Council on Arts, 1983-88; mem. adv. panel Visual Arts Ctr., Anchorage, 1979-92, Alaska Pub. Art Adv. Panel, 1979—. One-man exhbns. include Alaska State Mus., 1985, U. Alaska Mus., 1985, 91, Davidson Coll. Art Gallery, 1986, Anchorage Fine Arts Mus., 1983, 91, U. Ala., Huntsville, 1990, Anderson (S.C.) Art Ctr., 1994; exhbn. juror; author: Sydney Laurence, Painter of the North, 1990, Painting in the North, 1993, A Sense of Wonder: Art in Alaska, 1995. Alaska State Council Arts fellow, 1981. Mem. Mus. Alaska, Anchorage Fine Arts Mus. Assn., Coll. Art Assn., Friends of U. Alaska Mus. Lutheran. Home: PO Box 82211 Fairbanks AK 99708-2211 Office: Art Dept Alaska Fairbanks AK 99701

WOODWARD, STEPHEN RICHARD, newspaper reporter; b. Fukuoka City, Japan, July 27, 1953; came to U.S., 1954; s. Leonard Edwin and Etsuko (Okumura) W.; m. Sandra Elizabeth Richardson, Dec. 31, 1979; children: Daniel Joseph, Elizabeth Etsuko. BA in English, Wright State U., 1975; MA in Journalism, U. Mo., 1979. Advt. coordinator Wright State U., Dayton, Ohio, 1976-77; reporter Kansas City (Mo.) Star, 1979-82; assoc. editor then editor Kansas City Bus. Jour., 1982-83; editor then gen. mgr. Portland (Oreg.) Bus. Jour., 1984-86; exec. bus. editor The Hartford (Conn.) Courant, 1986-87; editor San Francisco Bus. Times, 1987-88; bus. editor The Oregonian, Portland, 1989-93, reporter, 1993—. Recipient 1st Place Investigative Reporting award Assn. Area Bus. Publs., 1983, 1st Place Column Writing award Assn. Area Bus. Publs., 1985. Mem. Investigative Reporters and Editors Inc. Home: 3309 NE Irving St Portland OR 97232-2538 Office: The Oregonian 1320 SW Broadway Portland OR 97201-3469

WOODWARD, WILLIAM WALTER, news anchor, journalism educator; b. Marlin, Tex., Dec. 15, 1943; s. Clarence Walter and Marie Margaret (Frick) W.; m. Gloria Jean Fredericks, Dec. 31, 1965 (div. Dec. 1969); m. Marilyn June Davis, June 26, 1971; children: Arlene Marie, Frederick Walter, Jonathan Walter. AD in Gen. Studies, Arapahoe Community Coll., Littleton, Colo., 1988, AA, 1989; MA, U. No. Colo., Greeley, 1991. News dir. KTVS-TV, Sterling, Colo., 1973-78; news editor, anchor KLZ/KAZY Radio, Denver, 1979-85; news dir. KCOL AM/FM, Ft. Collins, Colo., 1985-89; news stringer KUNC FM, Greeley, 1989-90; news anchor KYGO AM, Denver, 1989—; instr. Resource Tng. Inst., Ft. Collins, 1989; teaching asst. U. No. Colo., 1990-91, instr., 1991—; broadcast coord. Colo. State U., Ft. Collins, 1991-92; cons. Colo. State Alumni Assn., 1991-92, Sterling Kiwanis Club, 1977-78, Sterling Jaycees, 1967-70. Contbr. articles to profl. jours. Bd. dirs. Four Season Homeowners Assn., Ft. Collins, 1989-91, pres., 1991-92; bd. dirs. RE-1 Sch. Bd., Sterling, 1977-78. With U.S. Army, 1962-64. Recipient Best Investigative Report award AP, 1988; recipient scholarships. Mem. Radio-TV News Dirs. Assn., Pub. Rels. Soc. Am., Soc. Profl. Journalists, Colo. Press Assn. (mem. journalism edn. com.), No. Colo. Media Profls., Elks. Democrat. Lutheran. Home: 713 Arbor Ave Fort Collins CO 80526-3101 Office: U No Colo Candelaria # 123 Greeley CO 80639

WOODWORTH, STEPHEN DAVIS, business and financial consultant, investment banker; b. Stillwater, Okla., Nov. 4, 1945; s. Stanley Davis and Elizabeth (Webb) W.; m. Robin Woodworth; children: Lisa Alexander, Ashley Ives. BA, Claremont McKenna Coll., 1967; MBA, Calif. Lutheran U., 1975; grad. Mgmt. Policy Inst., U. So. Calif., 1981. Div. mgr. Security Pacific Bank, L.A., 1970-86; pres. Channel Island Equities, Oxnard, Calif., 1988—; prin. Woodworth Assocs., Westlake Village, Calif., 1987-88; advisor to bd. Hanson Lab Furniture Ind., Inc., Newbury Park, Calif., 1992-93; trustee Calif. Luth. Edn. Found., Thousand Oaks, Calif., 1983-93; chmn. Cen. Coast MIT Enterprise Forum, Santa Barbara, Calif., 1992-93; instr. fin. and banking Calif. Luth. U., 1978-79. Contbr. articles to profl. jours. Chmn. Alliance for the Arts, Thousand Oaks, Calif., 1982-94; vice chmn. Conejo Symphony Orch., Thousand Oaks, 1986-90. 1st lt. U.S. Army, 1968-70, Korea. Recipient Outstanding Alumnus Calif. Lutheran U., 1986. Mem. Res. Officers Assn. of the U.S., Ventura County Economic Devel. Assn., Am. Mgmt. Assn., Conejo Future Found., Marine Meml. Club, Tower Club. Republican. Roman Catholic. Home: 163 Stanislaus Ave Ventura CA 93004-1172 Office: Channel Island Equities 300 E Esplanade Dr Ste 900 Oxnard CA 93030-1251

WOOLARD, HENRY WALDO, aerospace engineer; b. Clarksburg, W.Va., June 2, 1917; s. Herbert William and Elsie Marie (Byers) W.; m. Helen Stone Waldron, Aug. 16, 1941; children: Shirley Ann, Robert Waldron. BS in Aero. Engring., U. Mich., 1941; MSME, U. Buffalo, 1954. Aero. engr. NACA, 1941-46; assoc. prof., acting dept. head, aero. engr. W. Va. U., Morgantown, W.Va., 1946-48; rsch. aerodynamicist Cornell Aero. Lab., Buffalo, 1948-57; sr. staff engr. applied physics lab. Johns Hopkins U., Silver Spring, Md., 1957-63; sr. rsch. specialist Lockheed Calif. Co., Burbank, Calif., 1963-67; mem. tech. staff TRW Systems Group, Redondo Beach, Calif., 1967-70; pres. Beta Tech. Co., Palos Verdes, Calif., 1970-71; aero. engr. Air Force Flight Dynamics Lab., Wright-Patterson AFB, Ohio, 1971-85; aero. cons. Dayton, Ohio, 1985-87, Fresno, Calif., 1987—. Contbr. articles to profl. jours. Recipient Scientific Achievement award Air Force Systems Command, 1982. Assoc. fellow AIAA; mem. ASME, Sigma Xi, Sigma Pi Sigma. Office: Consultant Aerospace 1249 W Magill Ave Fresno CA 93711-1428

WOOLF, NANCY JEAN, neuroscientist, educator; b. Ft. Sill, Okla., July 27, 1954; d. Lee Allen and Rachel Christine (Sedjo) W.; m. Larry Lee Butcher, Dec. 24, 1983; children: Lawson Frederick, Ashley Ellen. BS, UCLA, 1978, PhD, 1983. Grad. researcher UCLA, 1979-83, asst. rsch. neuroscientist, 1984-92, adj. assoc. prof., 1992—, assoc. rsch. neuroscientist, 1992—. Author: (review article) Progress in Neurobiology, 1991; contbr. 40 articles to various sci. pubs. Recipient Colby prize Sigma Kappa Found., Indpls, 1990; named Woman of Yr. Coll. of the Desert, Palm Desert, Calif., 1976. Mem. AAAS, Assn. Acad. Women (Grad. Woman of Yr. UCLA 1983), Internat. Neural Network Soc., Soc. for Neurosci. Office: U Calif Dept Psychology 405 Hilgard Ave Los Angeles CA 90095-1563

WOOLF, ROBERT HANSEN, periodontist; b. Salt Lake City, Jan. 29, 1945; s. Robert McCarthy and Dorthy (Hansen) W.; m. Linda Gail Maddux, Aug. 18, 1967; children: Robert David, Laura Elizabeth. BS in Molecular and Genetic Biology, U. Utah, 1967; DDS, U. of the Pacific, 1971; cert. in periodontics, U. Oreg., 1976. Lic. dentist, Calif., periodontist, Oreg. Commd. 2d lt USAR, 1963, advanced through grades to capt., 1978; dental intern U.S. Army Hosp., Ft. Jackson, S.C., 1972; clin. instr. depts. geriodontology, periodontology Sch. Dentistry U. Oreg., Portland, 1974-76; asst. prof. dept. periodontology Sch. Dentistry Oreg. Health Scis. U., Portland, 1976—; mem. dental staff Meridian Pk. Hosp., Tualatin, Oreg., 1976—; pvt. practice Lake Oswego, Oreg., 1976—. Mem. YMCA. Fellow Am. Coll. Dentists, Internat. Coll. Dentists; mem. ADA, Am. Acad. Periodontology, Am. Acad. Gen. Dentistry, Am. Acad. Dental Anesthesiology, Am. Acad. Dentistry for Children, Oreg. Dental Assn., Oreg. Soc. Periodontists, Oreg. Acad. Gen. Dentistry, Oreg. Acad. Dental Anesthesiology, Oreg. Acad. Dentistry for Children, Oreg. Soc. Craniomandibular Disfunction, Clackamus County Dental Assn., Western Soc. Periodontology, Rotary Internat. (Paul Harris fellow), Xi Xi Phi (pres. local chpt. 1971), Pi Kappa (chpt. v.p. 1966), Omicron Kappa Upsilon. Republican. Home: 17346 Canal Cir Lake Oswego OR 97035-5620 Office: 320 A Ave Lake Oswego OR 97034-3056

WOOLF-SCOTT, HELENE LYDA, real estate developer; b. N.Y.C., Apr. 2, 1938; d. Harry and Eleanor (Wolfson) Burke; m. William Woolf, Aug. 17, 1958 (div. 1982); 1 child, Gina Karen; m. Walter Scott Jr., May 1, 1987. BA, NYU, 1959. Lic. real estate agt. Calif. Realtor Wright & Co., Los Altos, Calif., 1974-80; v.p. Munsey Devel. Corp., Los Altos, Calif., 1978—; v.p. McKeon, Scott, Woolf & Assocs., 1982-84; pres. GKW Enterprises, Inc. 1978—, Scott, Woolf & Assocs., 1984—; bd. dirs. Mulford, Moreland, Scott & Assocs., San Jose. Mem. Los Altos Bd. Realtors, Am. Mgmt. Assn., Nat. Trust for Historic Preservation, Nat. Assn. Realtors, Calif. Assn. Realtors. Democrat. Home: 564 Santa Rita Ave Palo Alto CA 94301-4035 Office: Scott Woolf & Assocs 701 Welch Rd Ste 323 Palo Alto CA 94304-1709

WOOLLEY, DONNA PEARL, timber land management executive; b. Drain, Oreg., Jan. 3, 1926; d. Chester A. and Mona B. (Cheever) Rydell; m. Harold Woolley, Dec. 27, 1952 (dec. Sept. 1970); children: Daniel, Debra, Donald. Diploma, Drain High Sch. Sec. No. Life Ins. Co., Eugene, Oreg., 1943-44; sec., bookkeeper D & W Lumber Co., Sutherlin, Oreg., 1944, Woolley Logging Co. & Earl Harris Lumber Co., Drain, 1944-70; pres.

Woolley Logging Co., 1970—, Smith River Lumber Co., 1970—, Mt. Baldy Mill, 1970-81, Drain Plywood Co., 1970-81, Woolley Enterprises, Inc., Drain, 1973—, Eagle's View Mgmt. Co., Inc., Eugene, 1981—; bd. dirs. Douglas Nat. Bank, Roseburg, Oreg. Bd. dirs. Oreg. Cmty. Found., Portland, Oreg., 1990—, Wildlife Safari, Winston, Oreg., 1986; trustee emeritus U. Oreg. Found., Eugene, 1979—; trustee Linfield Coll. Found., McMinnville, Oreg., 1990—; v.p. Oreg. Trail coun. Boy Scouts Am., Eugene, 1981—; mem. Yoncalla Rodeo. Recipient Pioneer award U. Oreg., 1982, Econ. and Social Devel. award Soroptimist Club, 1991. Mem. Oreg. Women's Forum, Pacific Internat. Trapshooting Assn., Amateur Trapshooting Assn., Eugene C. of C. (bd. dirs. 1989-92), Arlington Club, Town Club (bd. dirs., pres.), Shadow Hills County Club, Sunnydale Grange, Cottage Grove/Eugene Rod & Gun Club. Republican. Office: Eagle's View Mgmt Co Inc 1399 Franklin Blvd Eugene OR 97403-1979

WOOLLEY, J(ONATHAN) MICHAEL, health economist, economic consultant; b. Norfolk, Va., Mar. 2, 1958; s. Herbert Thomas Woolley and Jane Kennedy (Dodson) Genet; m. Diana Elaine Gorrie, Aug. 1, 1987; children: Christian David, Thomas Michael, Jonathan James. BA in Econs., U. Calif., San Diego, 1981; MA in Econs., U. Calif., Santa Barbara, 1983, PhD in Econs., 1987. Economist Fed. Res. Bd., Washington, 1987-89; asst. prof. Sch. Pub. Adminstrn. U. So. Calif., L.A., 1989-93; health economist Amgen Inc., Thousand Oaks, Calif., 1993—; econ. cons. Econ. Analysis Corp., L.A., 1990—. Co-author: (book) Handbook for Microeconomic Principles, 1983; bd. editors Internat. Jour. of Econs. of Bus., 1993—; contbr. articles to profl. jours. Regents fellow U. Calif., Santa Barbara, 1981-82, Earhart Found. fellow, 1985-86, Haynes Found. fellow, 1990-91. Mem. Internat. Health Econs. Assn., Am. Econ. Assn., Am. Fin. Assn., Western Econ. Assn., Health Econ. Rsch. Orgn. Home: 301 Regal Oak Ct Thousand Oaks CA 91320 Office: Amgen Inc MS 17-1-C-311 1840 De Havilland Dr Thousand Oaks CA 91320-1701

WOOLLIAMS, KEITH RICHARD, arboretum and botanical garden director; b. Chester, Eng., July 17, 1940; s. Gordon Frank and Margaret Caroline W.; m. Akiko Narita, Apr. 11, 1969; children: Frank Hiromi, Angela Misako. Grad., Celyn Agrl. and Hort. Inst., North Wales, 1955; student, U. Liverpool, various horticultural insts., 1956-59; Kew Cert., Royal Bot. Gardens, Kew, U.K., 1963. Cert. Horticulture Union Cheshire and Lancs. Insts., 1955, Royal Hort. Soc., 1956, 57, 58, Nat. Cert. Horticulture, 1958, Cert. Arboriculture, 1962. Supt. field sta. U. London Queen Mary Coll., Brentwood, Essex, Eng., 1963-65; horticulturist Horizons Ltd., Bermuda, 1965-67; dept. forests, supt. botanic gardens Papua, New Guinea, 1967-68; instr. Eng. staff indsl. cos., Japan, 1968-71; supt., horticulturist Nat. Tropical Bot. Garden, Kauai, Hawaii, 1971-74; horticulturist Waimea Arboretum and Botanical Garden, Haleiwa, Hawaii, 1974-80, dir., 1980—; Contbr. articles to profl. jours., New Royal Horticultural Society's Dictionary of Gardening, 1992. Field assoc. botany Bishop Mus., Honolulu, 1981—; bd. dirs. Friends of Honolulu Bot. Gardens, 1980—; v.p., founder Waimea Arboretum Found., 1977—; bd. dirs. Condominium Estate, Wahiawa, Hawaii, 1990—. Mem. Am. Assn. Botanical Gardens and Arboreta, Am. Hort. Soc., Hawaii Audubon Soc., Hawaiian Botanical Soc. (pres. 1979), Internat. Assn. Plant Taxonomists, Royal Hort. Soc., Kew Guild. Office: Waimea Arboretum & Bot Garden 59-864 Kamehameha Hwy Haleiwa HI 96712-9406

WOOLMAN, BRUCE ALAN, family practice physician; b. Watonga, Okla., June 16, 1955; s. William Werner and Gwendolyn (DuPree) W.; m. Debra May Smith, Aug. 24, 1985; children: Brittany, David, Christopher, Stephanie. BS in Biology, Southwestern Okla. State U., 1977; DO, Okla. Coll. Osteopathic Med., Tulsa, 1980. Diplomate Am. Bd. Family Physicians. Intern William Beaumont Army Med. Ctr., El Paso, Tex., 1980-81; family practice resident Madigan Army Med. Ctr., Tacoma, 1983-85; commd. U.S. Army, 1980—, advnced through grades to lt. col., 1992; family physician Reynolds Army Community Hosp., Ft. Sill, Okla., 1985-89, Evans Army Community Hosp., Ft. Carson, Colo., 1990-95; residency tchg. staff Madigan Army Med. Ctr., 1995—. Fellow Am. Acad. Family Physicians; mem. Am. Osteopathic Assn., Uniformed Svcs. Acad. Family Practice, Aerospace Med. Assn., Soc. of U.S. Army Flight Surgeons, Assn. Mil. Osteopathic Physicians and Surgeons. Methodist. Home: 1809 28th St SE Puyallup WA 98372 Office: Madigan Army Med Ctr Dept Family Practice Tacoma WA 98431

WOOLSCHLAGER, LAURA TOTTEN, sculptor, artist, printmaker; b. Dallas, Sept. 1, 1932; d. Johns McCleave and Katherina (Smith) Totten; m. Hawley Lee Woolschlager, Jan. 22, 1955; children—Christy Catherine Nielsen, Layne Gay Sawyer, Wilson Johns. Student Redlands U., 1950-51; B.A. magna cum laude, Syracuse U., 1954. Mus. display advisor Okanogan County Hist. Soc., Okanogan, Wash., 1974-84. One-woman shows: Mus. Native Am. Cultures, Spokane, Wash., 1979, Wickiup, Coeur d'Alene, Idaho, Wolfwalker Gallery, Sedona, Ariz., 1984, Am. Indian Art Gallery, Ashland, Oreg., 1994; group shows include: Am. Artists Rockies Ann., 1983, Mus. Rockies, Bozeman, Mont., 1983, Choice Ann. Art Show Mus. History and Industry, Seattle, 1984, Ceres (Calif) Western Art Show, 1993, 94, 95; represented in permanent collections: Favell Mus., Klamath Falls, Oreg., Carnegie Library, Lewiston, Idaho, Mus. Native Am. Cultures, Spokane; series of triptych paintings include: Singing Down the Buffalo Moon (Western Art Assn. Best of Show award 1979); artist adv. Ellensburg (Wash.) Nat. Western Art Show and Auction, 1995—; featured artist at Quest Gallery, Bozeman, Mont., 1994, Gallery I, Ellensburg, Wash., 1995. Mem. Am. Artists of the Rockies Assn. (v.p. 1982-83, pres. 1983—). Home and Studio: 28 Dixon Rd Omak WA 98841

WOOLSEY, LYNN, congresswoman; b. Seattle, Nov. 3, 1937. BA, U. San Francisco, 1980. Mem. 103rd-104th Congresses from 6th Calif. dist., 1993—; mem. Ho. Reps. coms. on budget, & econ. & ednl. opportunity. Office: US House of Reps 439 Cannon Bldg Washington DC 20515-0003*

WOOLSEY, ROY BLAKENEY, electronics company executive; b. Norfolk, Va., June 12, 1945; s. Roy B. and Louise Stookey (Jones) W.; m. Patricia Bernadine Elkins, Apr. 17, 1988. Student, Calif. Inst. Tech., 1962-64; BS with distinction, Stanford U., 1966, MS, 1967, PhD, 1970. Sr. physicist Tech. for Communications Internat., Mountain View, Calif., 1970-75; mgr. radio direction finding systems Tech. for Communications Internat., Mountain View, 1975-80, program mgr., 1980-83, dir. strategic systems, 1983-88, dir. research and devel., 1988-91, v.p. engring., 1991-92; v.p. programs Tech. for Communications Internat., Sunnyvale, Calif., 1992—; bd. dirs. Merit Software Corp., Menlo Park, 1990—. Author: (with others) Applications of Artificial Intelligence to Command and Control Systems, 1988, Antenna Engineering Handbook, 1993; contbr. articles to profl. jours. Active YMCA, Palo Alto, Calif. Fellow NSF, 1966-70. Mem. AFCEA, Stanford Club, Sequoia Yacht Club, Sigma Xi, Phi Beta Kappa. Republican. Presbyterian. Home: 26649 Snell Ln Los Altos Hills CA 94022-2039 Office: Tech for Communications Internat 222 Caspian Dr Sunnyvale CA 94089-1014

WOOTEN, FREDERICK (OLIVER), applied science educator; b. Linwood, Pa., May 16, 1928; s. Frederick Alexander and Martha Emma (Guild) W.; m. Jane Watson MacPherson, Aug. 30, 1952; children: Donald, Bartley. BS in Chemistry, MIT, 1950; PhD in Chemistry, U. Del., 1955. Sr. scientist Lawrence Livermore (Calif.) Lab., 1957-72; prof. applied sci. U. Calif., Davis, 1972—, chmn. dept. applied sci., 1973-93; vis. prof. physics Drexel U., Phila, 1964, Chalmers Tekniska Hogskola, Goteborg, Sweden, 1967-68, Heriot-Watt U., Edinburgh, Scotland, 1979, Trinity Coll., Dublin, Ireland, 1986, Mich. State U., East Lansing, 1993; vis. scholar math. U. Mass., Amherst, 1991; staff physicist All-Am. Engring. Co., Wilmington, Del., 1955-57; cons. in field. Author: Optical Properties of Solids, 1972. Mem. AAAS, AM. Phys. Soc., N.Y. Acad. Sci., Materials Rsch. Soc., Sigma Xi. Home: 2328 Alameda Diablo Diablo CA 94528 Office: Univ Calif Dept Applied Sci Davis CA 95616

WOOTEN, MICHAEL ERIC, military officer; b. San Diego, June 12, 1959; s. James Willis and Elease (Lewis) W.; m. D'Andrea Michele Wilson, Feb. 1, 1988; children: John Michael Christopher, Sarah Mary Elizabeth. AA, DeKalb C.C., 1981; BA in Psychology, Chapman U., 1987; postgrad., Norwich U., 1994—. Cert. tower operator. Air traffic controller Hdqs. & Hdqs. Squadron, Tustin, Calif., 1983-86; commd. 1st lt. USMC, 1989, advanced through grades to capt., 1991; officer student, 1987-88; asst. supply officer Second Maintenance Battalion, Camp LeJeune, N.C., 1988-89; supply officer Second Landing Support Battalion, Camp LeJeune, N.C., 1989-90; protocol officer Marine Corps Logistics Base, Albany, Ga., 1990; asst. br. head Mgmt. Br. Integrated Logistics Support, Albany, Ga., 1990-91; aide-de-camp Marine Corps Logistics Base, Albany, Ga., 1991-92; logistics officer Hdqs. Battalion, Albany, Ga., 1992-93; supply officer Second Light Anti Aircraft Missile Battalion, Yuma, Ariz., 1993—; nonresident dir. Navy Mut. Aid Assn., Arlington, Va., 1994. Recipient Navy Commendation medal. Mem. Nat. Naval Officer Assn., Masons, Phi Beta Sigma. Episcopalian. Home: 2282 Green Forrest Dr Decatur GA 30032-7175 Office: Capt M E Wooten 2d LAAM Battalion Box 99280 Yuma AZ 85368-9280

WOOTEN, PATRICIA CAROL, critical care nurse, humor educator, consultant; b. Springfield, Ill., Dec. 22, 1946; d. Richard Leland and Yvonne (Nebel) Savercool; m. Deakin Caleb, Sept. 1, 1968 (div. Sept. 1973); 1 child, Kenneth Alan. BSN, U. Calif., San Francisco, 1969. CCRN; cert. life-death transition counselor. Staff nurse cardiac surgery ICU Los Angeles County Hosp., 1969-70; dist. pub. health nurse, clinic nurse Los Angeles County Dept. Pub. health, Watts, Calif., 1970-71; charge nurse ICU-CCU Alameda (Calif.) Hosp., 1971-73, 76-79; charge nurse respiratory-neurosurgery ICU U. Calif. San Diego Med. Ctr., 1974-76; nursing supr. Prather Convalescent Home, Alameda, 1979-80; hospice nurse, home IV and chemotherapy nurse Vis. Nurses Assn., Oakland, Calif., 1980-81; staff nurse ICU-CCU post cardiac surgery unit French Hosp., San Luis Obispo, Calif., 1981-94; dir., humor educator, speaker Jest For The Health Of It Seminars, Davis, Calif., 1985—; rsch. presenter 8th Internat. Conf. on Humor, Sheffield, Eng., July 1990. Author: (workshop) Jest for the Health of It, 1985, (book) Heart Humor and Healing, 1994, (video) Healing Power of Humor; moderator, co-presenter with Norman Cousins and Allen Funt: (video) The Healing Power of Humor, 1989; contbg. editor Jour. Nursing Jocularity, 1991—. Mem. AACN (cert.), ANA, Calif. Nurses Assn., Internat. Soc. Humor Studies, Clowns of Am. Internat., Am. Assn. Therapeutic Humor (v.p.), Sigma Theta Tau. Office: Jest For The Health Of It PO Box 4040 Davis CA 95617-4040

WORDELL, DOUGLAS RAY, nutrition services director, consultant; b. Spokane, Wash., May 15, 1965; m. Lori Anne Haughen, Aug. 6, 1988; children: Chelsea, Spencer, Andrew. BS in food science human nutrition, Wash. State U., 1989. Registered dietitian. Food svc. mgr. Marriott Corp., Salem, Oreg., 1989-91; nutrition svc. dir. Bend-LaPine Sch. Dist., Bend, Oreg., 1991—; wellness coord. Bend-LaPine Pub. Schs., Bend, 1993—; cons. Beaverton Sch. Food Svc., Beaverton, Oreg., 1994. Spl. Friends Bend Schs., 1992-94; young youth group tchr., West Side Ch., Bend., 1992—; treas., mem. Bend-LaPine Adminstrn. & Supr. Team, 1992—. Republican. Home: 520 NE 6th St Bend OR 97701-4905 Office: Bend-LaPine Pub Schs 520 NW Wall St Bend OR 97701-2608

WORKS, MADDEN TRAVIS, JR. (PAT WORKS), operations executive, author, skydiving instructor, skydiving publications executive; b. Harris County, Tex., Mar. 17, 1943; s. Madden Travis and Vivian Alle (Browning) W.; m. Janet Elaine Allen, Dec. 19, 1970. Student Tex. A&M U., 1962-64; B.A., U. Houston, 1967, MS C.I.S. Claremont Grad. Sch., 1992. Engr. in tng. Cameron Iron Works, Houston, 1963-65; promotion planner, supr. field advt. Procter & Gamble, Cin., 1967-70; mgr. sta. promotions Union Oil Co. Calif., Chgo., 1970-73; mgr. sales promotion Hunt Wesson Foods, Fullerton, Calif., 1973-76; mgr. promotions Knott's Berry Farm Holdings, 1976-77; owner RWU Parachuting Publs., Fullerton, 1975—; mgr. opers. automation Aerojet-GenCorp, Azusa, 1983—; supr. mfg. engring., chmn. change bd. HITCO, ARMCO, Gardena, Calif., 1981-83; cons. engr. D.A.R. Enterprises; instr. advanced freefall in 9 countries; pub. speaker. Nat. bd. dirs. U.S. Parachute Assn., 1980-86. Served with Army NG, 1962. Recipient medal for merit Australian Parachute Fedn., 1972, Medal for Services French Nat. Team, 1972, certs. appreciation YMCA, 1980, 82, numerous awards and medals related to parachuting. Mem. AIAA (sr.), Computer and Automated Systems Assn. (sr., cert. systems engr., mem. tech. council), Soc. Mfg. Engrs. (sr., cert. mfg. engr., artificial intelligence in mfg. com.), BMW Owners Assn., Am. Motorcycle Assn., U.S. Parachute Assn. (dir. 1980-86), Club: Toastmasters (v.p. 1977). Author: Parachuting, English, German, French and Spanish edits.; Parachuting: United We Fall, 1978; The Art of Freefall, 1979, 2d edit., 1988, CIM Planning Guide, 1986, 2d edit., 1988, Configuration and CIM, 1987; contbr. articles to parachuting publs. Inventor flight suit, parachute line knife; nat. champion Nat. Collegiate Parachuting League, 1967; nat. winner Point of Purchase Profl. Inst., 1974. Home: 1656 E Beechwood Ave Fullerton CA 92635-2149 Office: Aerojet GenCorp 1100 W Hollyvale St Azusa CA 91702-3305

WORLEY, LLOYD DOUGLAS, English language educator; b. Lafayette, La., Sept. 11, 1946; s. Albert Stiles and Doris (Christy) W.; m. Maydean Ann Mouton, Apr. 4, 1966; children: Erin Shawn, Albert Stiles II. BA, U. SW La., 1968, MA, 1972; PhD, So. Ill. U., 1979. Ordained priest, Liberal Cath. Ch. Tchr. Lafayette H.S., 1969-74; vis. asst. prof. dept. English So. Ill. U., Carbondale, 1979-80; asst. prof. dept. English Pa. State U., DuBois, 1980-87; assoc. prof., assoc. dir. composition dept. English U. No. Colo., Greeley, 1987-88, prof. dept. English, 1988—; acting dir. Writing Component Ctr. Basic Skills, So. Ill. U., 1980. Editor: Ruthven Literary Bull., 1988-92; contbr. book chpts., articles. Rector Parish of St. Albertus Magnus, sec-treas. Am. Province; mem. Am. Clerical Synod Chpt. Decorated Knight Comdr. Star of Order of Merit St. Angilbert, 1993, Prelate Comdr. Order of Noble Companions of Swan, 1993; created hereditary Baron of Royal and Serene House of Alabona-Ostrogojsk by HRSH Prince William I Fedn. of Princes of Holy Roman Empire-in-Exile, 1993. Fellow Philalethes Soc.; mem. ASCD, Internat. Assn. for Fantastic in Arts (divsn. head Am. Lit. 1987-93), Lord Ruthven Assembly (pres. 1988-94), Conf. Coll. Composition and Commn., Nat. Coun. Tchrs. English, Am. Conf. Irish Studies, Sigma Tau Delta (bd. dirs. 1990—, high plains regent various states 1992—), Masons (century lodge #190), Order of DeMolay (chevalier, corss of honor, legion of honor), Knights Holy Sepulchre (Sov. Grand Master), Rose & Crox Martinist Order (pres. premier nat. coun.). Democrat. Office: 2644 11th Ave # D-109 Greeley CO 80631-8441

WOROBEC, BRUCE WILLIAM, computer systems analyst; b. Montreal, Que., Can., Jan. 9, 1963; came to U.S., 1971; s. William and Marie (Gancer) W. BS magna cum laude, Gonzaga U., 1985; MS, Wash. State U., 1986. Teaching asst. Wash. State U., Pullman, 1985-87; sr. mem. tech. staff, computer systems analyst U S West, Bellevue, 1987-93; pres. Worobec Cons., Renton, Wash., 1993—; v.p. Ritax Corp., 1994—; bd. dirs. Vis. Nurse Svcs. of Northwest, 1992—. Mem. Assn. for Computing Machinery, Data Resource Mgmt. Assn. Office: PO Box 2751 Renton WA 98056-0751

WORRALL, ROGER CHARLES, investor, management consultant; b. Colorado Springs, Colo., Nov. 15, 1938; s. Charles Ross and Blanche Freeman (McCann) W.; m. Judith Ann Tyer, May 30, 1964; children: Beth Ann Worrall Catt, Joanna Marie. BS, Marylhurst, 1984, MS in Mgmt., 1991. V.p. ops. Aviation Assistance, Inc., Des Moines, 1969-75; owner, capt. Bee Jay Salmon Trawler, Ilwaco, Wash., 1975-78; change mgr. Intel Corp., Hillsboro, Oreg., 1978—; dir. R. Worrall Investments, Newberg, 1992—; COO Julia's Child Inc., Newberg, 1993—; v.p. mfg. mgr. Profab, Newberg, Oreg., 1973-78. Bd. dirs. Rainbow Lodge, MacMinnville, Oreg., 1984-85; commr. Newberg (Oreg.) Planning Commn., 1993—. Lt. col. USAF, 1959-67. Recipient Flight Navigator cert. FAA, 1973. Home: 215 N Center St Newberg OR 97132-2707

WORRELL, JANE CARSON, insurance adjustor; b. L.A., July 13, 1934; d. Felix Adelbert and Minnie Alice (Heuser) Barney; m. Norman Carson, Aug. 31, 1951 (div. 1964); children: Richard, Norma, Daniel; m. Charles L. Worrell, June 2, 1969 (div.). Grad. high sch., Bell Gardens, Calif. With order desk Burke Rubber Co., L.A., 1964-66; with line desk Airlane Aviation, Roswell, N.Mex., 1966-69; mgr. Avis Rent A Car, Roswell, 1969-71; owner, mgr. Worrell Enterprise dba Nat. Car Rental, Roswell, 1971-73, Airport Security, Roswell, 1973-77; office mgr. P.B. Moorhead, MD, Roswell, 1977-82; adjuster GAB Bus. Svcs. Inc., Roswell, 1982-87, Am. States Ins. Co., Albuquerque, 1987—. Author poetry. Mem. N.Mex. Claims Assn. (sec. 1987, 89, treas. 1988), Ins. Women Albuquerque (bd. dirs. 1994—). Republican. Office: Am States Ins Co PO Box 35969 Albuquerque NM 87176-5969

WORRELL, RICHARD VERNON, orthopedic surgeon, college dean; b. Bklyn., June 4, 1931; s. John Elmer and Elaine (Callender) W.; BA, NYU, 1952; MD, Meharry Med. Coll., 1958; m. Audrey Frances Martiny, June 14, 1958; children: Philip Vernon, Amy Elizabeth. Intern Meharry Med. Coll., Nashville, 1958-59; resident gen. surgery Mercy-Douglass Hosp., Phila., 1960-61; resident orthopedic surgery State U. N.Y. Buffalo Sch. Medicine Affiliated Hosps., 1961-64; resident in orthopedic pathology Temple U. Med. Ctr., Phila., 1966-67; pvt. practice orthopedic surgery, Phila., 1964-68; asst. prof. acting head div. orthopedic surgery U. Conn. Sch. Medicine 1968-70; attending orthopedic surgeon E.J. Meyer Meml. Hosp., Buffalo, Millard Fillmore Hosp., Buffalo, VA Hosp., Buffalo, Buffalo State Hosp.; clin. instr. orthopedic surgery SUNY, Buffalo, 1970-74; chief orthopedic surgery VA Hosp., Newington, Conn., 1974-80; asst. prof. surgery (orthopedics) U. Conn. Sch. Medicine, 1974-77, assoc. prof., 1977-83, asst. dean student affairs, 1980-83; prof. clin. surgery SUNY Downstate Med. Ctr., Bklyn., 1983-86; dir. orthopedic surgery Brookdale Hosp. Med. Ctr., Bklyn., 1983-86; prof. of orthopedics U. N.Mex. Sch. of Medicine, 1986—; dir. orthopedic oncology U. N.Mex. Med. Ctr., 1987—; mem. med. staff U. N.Mex. Cancer Ctr., 1987—; chief orthopedic surgery VA Med. Ctr., Albuquerque, 1987—; cons. in orthopedic surgery Newington (Conn.) Children's Hosp., 1968-70; mem. sickle cell disease adv. com. NIH, 1982-86. Bd. dirs. Big Bros. Greater Hartford. Served to capt. M.C., U.S. Army Res., 1962-69. Diplomate Am. Bd. Orthopedic Surgery, Nat. Bd. Med. Examiners. Fellow ACS, Am. Acad. Orthopedic Surgeons, Royal Soc. Medicine, London; mem. AMA, Am. Orthopaedic Assn., Orthopedic Rsch. Soc., Internat. Soc. Orthopedic Surgery and Traumatology, Internat. Fedn. Surg. Colls. (assoc.), Alpha Omega Alpha. Office: U NMex Med Ctr Albuquerque NM 87131-5296

WORRILOW, RICHARD CHARLES, small business owner; b. L.A., Feb. 28, 1944; s. Richard Morris and Helen Elizabeth (Charleston) W.; m. Janice Joanne Ludwick, Mar. 9, 1944 (div. Dec. 1977); 1 child, Lisa Anne. BA in Polit. Sci., Calif. State U., Northridge, 1971; MS in Recreation Mgmt., Calif. State U., L.A., 1978. Profl. model Robert Black Agy., Tempe, Ariz., 1958—; sr. account rep. Travelers Ins. Co., L.A., Hartford, Conn., 1971-85; owner Villa Maria Pasta Products, Mesa, Ariz., 1987-88; ptnr. Rickman Assocs., Scottsdale, 1987-88; owner Gourmet Imports Wild Game, Phoenix, 1982—, Gourmet Delicacies, Phoenix, 1988—, Scottsdale Cookie Co., 1985-89, Vis a'Vis, Phoenix, 1984—. Pres. Men's League of Scottsdale, 1986-87. With U.S. Army, 1966-69, Vietnam. Mem. Scottsdale C. of C., Phoenix C. of C. Republican. Office: Gourmet Imports 128 E Wood Dr Phoenix AZ 85022-5236

WORSTELL, KAREN FREEMAN, data processing executive; b. Tacoma, Wash., Apr. 30, 1954; d. Robert Mark and Ethel Viola (Cox) Freeman; m. Garner Jay Smith, Aug. 14, 1976 (div. 1988); children: Jessica Erin Freeman, Jared Scott; m. Craig David Worstell, Sept. 15, 1990. BS in Molecular Biology, U. Wash., 1976, BS in Chemistry, 1980; MS, Pacific Luth. U., 1987. Tech. project mgr. computing security Boeing Computer Svcs. Rsch. and Tech., Seattle, 1990-93, program mgr., 1993—; mem. adv. com. Stanford Rsch. Inst. Internat. Info. Integrity Inst., Menlo Park, Calif., 1993—. Lay leader United Meth. Ch., Covington, Wash., 1994. Mem. Assn. for Computing Machinery, IEEE, Aerospace Industries Assn. (vice chair tech. security subcom. 1993-94). Office: Boeing Computer Svcs PO Box 24346 MS 7L-15 Seattle WA 98124

WORTH, VONNE NOELL, newspaper publisher, editor, writer, disability rights activist; b. Dayton, Ohio, Jan. 5, 1950; d. William Dewey Worth and Donna Jean (Clay) Klammer; m. Harry Louderback Young Jr., Mar. 25, 1984 (dec. Dec. 1987). BA in English, Transylvania U., 1972; BA in Journalism, Seattle U., 1986. Proofreader The Kernel, U. Ky. newspaper, 1973, staff writer, 1974-75; fiction editor Amanuensis, U. Ky. lit. mag., 1975-76; freelance writer Lexington (Ky.) Herald-Leader, 1975-76; reporter The Univ. News, Kansas City, Mo., 1978; editorial page editor, reporter, copy editor The Spectator, Seattle, 1985-86; reporter Flaherty Newspapers, Seattle, 1986-87; freelance writer Diversity, Seattle, 1993; founder, editor, pub. Different TIMES, Seattle, 1987—; speaker in field. Bd. dirs. Girl Scouts Totem Coun., 1993—, co-chair diversity team; mem. choir St. Mark's Episcopal Cathedral, 1993—; chair spl. ministries commn. St. George's Episcopal Ch., 1992-93; pres. Seattle Disabled Businesswomen's Network, 1990-92. Episcopalian. Home and Office: 201 NW 39th St Apt 206 Seattle WA 98107-4953

WORTHEY, CAROL, composer; b. Worcester, Mass., Mar. 1, 1943; d. Bernard Krieger and Edith Lilian (Cramer) Symonds; m. Eugene Worthey III, June 1969 (div. 1980); 1 child, Megan; m. Raymond Edward Korns, Sept. 21, 1980. BA in Music Composition, Columbia U., 1965; grad., Dick Grove Sch. Music., L.A., 1979; grad. filmscoring prog., UCLA, 1978; music studies with Darius Milhaud, Walter Piston, Elliot Carter, Vincent Persichetti, Grant Beglarian, Karl Korte, Otto Luening, Eddy Lawrence Manson, Dick Grove; studied, RISD, 1948-54, Columbia U., 1965. Sr. composer, arranger Celebrity Ctr. Internat. Choir, Hollywood, Calif., 1985—. Composer, arranger The Hollywood Chorale; composer ballets Athena, 1963, The Barren, 1965; composer, lyricist, librettist full-length musical The Envelope Please, 1988; composer piano works performed in France, Italy, Germany, Can., U.S. and Eng. by Mario Feninger, 1982; composer Pastorale performed in Mex., 1994, Neighborhood of the Heart, 1994, (choir) Unquenchable Light, 1993; composer film score The Special Visitor, 1992; compositions performed at Aspen Music Festival, 1963, Carnegie Hall, 1954, Dorothy Chandler Pavilion, 1986-89; appeared as singer-songwriter on L.A. Songwriter's Showcase, 1977; arranger Merv Griffin Show, 1981, The Night Before Christmas, L.A. Children's Theatre, 1988-91, Capistrano Valley Symphony, 1994, Very Old Merry Old Christmas, Dorothy Chandler Pavillion, 1994; author: Treasury of Holiday Magic, 1992, (poems) The Lonely Wanderer Comes Home, 1994; art work exhibited RISD, 1952, Folk and Craft Mus., L.A., 1975, 1st Internat. Art Exhibit Celebrity Ctr. Pavillion, 1992. Vol. performer various childcare ctrs., old folks homes, etc. Recipient Silver Poet award World of Poetry, 1987, 2nd place winner, 1st BarComposers and Songwriters Competition for "Fanfare for Joy & Wedding March", 1990, Golden Poet award World of Poetry, 1992. Mem. Nat. Assn. Composers, USA, Broadcast Music Inc., Nat. Acad. Songwriters, Songwriters and Composers Assn., Toastmasters Internat. Jewish.

WORTHY, JAMES AGER, former professional basketball player; b. Gastonia, N.C., Feb. 27, 1961; m. Angela Worthy. Grad., U. N.C., 1985. Basketball player L.A. Lakers, 1982-94. Named to Sporting News All-Am. First Team, 1982; named MVP, NCAA Divsn. I Tournament, 1982, MVP, NBA playoffs, 1988, mem. All-Star team, 1986-92; mem. NCAA Divsn. I Championship Team, 1982, NBA All-Rookie Team, 1983. Office: LA Lakers Great Western Forum 3900 W Manchester Blvd Inglewood CA 90305-2200*

WOSKOW, ROBERT MARSHALL, management consultant; b. N.Y.C., Aug. 1, 1951; s. Martin and Marion (Kloder) W.; m. Gail Berrin, Apr. 1, 1979; children: Belle Ilysa, Benjamin Hale. BSEE, UCLA, 1973; MSEE, Calif. State U., Northridge, 1976; MBA, Pepperdine U., 1982. Elec. engr. various orgns., L.A., 1973-84; engring. dir. Arts and Sci. Tech., L.A., 1984-85; programs mgr. Pacesetter Systems, Sylmar, Calif., 1985-87; chief exec. officer Robert Marshall and Assocs., Encino, Calif., 1982—. Patentee in field. Home and Office: Robert Marshall and Assocs 16801 Severo Pl Encino CA 91436-4033

WOTRUBA, DAVID LAWRENCE, marriage and family therapist; b. Bremerton, Wash., July 1, 1942; s. Joe Lawrence Cook and Louise (Powell) Smith; m. Diane Gayle Mason, Mar. 21, 1986; 1 child, Elizabeth Louise Cook. BS, U. Wash., 1967; MS, Seattle Pacific U., 1995. Registered counselor, Wash.; lic. pharmacist, Wash., Calif., Hawaii. Pharmacist, 1967—; family therapist Cath. Cmty. Svc., Bremerton, Wash., 1994—; cert. mediator Dispute Resolution Ctr., Bremerton, 1988-92; faculty mem. Inst. Reality Therapy, 1992—. Registered lobbyist, Hawaii, 1975-76. Mem. ACA, Am. Assn. Marriage and Family Therapists, Am. Pharm. Assn., Hawaii Pharmacists Assn. (pres. 1975-76). Home: 13133 Central Valley Rd NW Poulsbo WA 98370-8105

WOTTON, ROBERT H., JR., small business owner; b. Renton, Wash., Nov. 14, 1963; s. Robert H. and Ruth E. (Hart) W. BA, U. Puget Sound,

1986. Adminstrv. intern Sec. of State, Olympia, Wash., 1986; mgr. Red Wing Shoe Store, Silverdale, Wash., 1987-88, The Shoe Hutch, Corvallis, Oreg., 1988-89; owner Wotton's of Shelton, Wash., 1990—; pres. Western Ind. Shoe Enterprises, 1993-94; instr. Olympic Coll. Shelton, 1995—; vice chair Wash. delegation White House Conf. Small Bus., 1995. Chmn. Mason County Rep. Party, Shelton, 1991-94, state committeeman, 1994—; chmn. Mason Dist. Boy Scouts, Shelton, 1987; chmn., co-founder Shelton-Talsi Latvia Sister City Project, Shelton, 1991—; mem. adv. bd. Shelton Vocat. Edn., mktg. chair, 1991-93, chmn. bd. dirs., 1995—; founder Edn. First, 1993—. Named Eagle Scout Boy Scouts Am., 1981, Dist. award of Merit, 1987. Mem. Shelton Lions Club (pres. 1995—), Shelton-Mason County C. of C., Evergreen Apparel Guild. Republican. Methodist. Office: Wotton's of Shelton 331 W Railroad Ave Shelton WA 98584-3542

WOU, LEO S., architect, planner; b. Tianjin, Republic of China, Sept. 4, 1927; s. Henri and Irene (Chu) W.; m. Mary Fong, Apr. 15, 1955; children—Loring, Jacqui, Tia. B.Arch., U. Pa., 1950; postgrad., Yale U., 1952-54; M.Arch., UCLA, 1984. Pres. Leo S. Wou & Assoc., Inc., Honolulu, 1960, San Francisco, 1968-78; pres. Wou Internat. Inc., Houston, 1978-82; ptnr. Ross/Wou Internat., Los Angeles, 1982—; cons. Golemon & Rolfe, Houston, 1978-79, Pierce, Goodwin, Alexander, Houston, 1978-79. Prin. works include: Master Plan for downtown Honolulu, 1963, Fin. Plaza of Pacific, Hdqrs. of Castle & Cooke and Bank of Hawaii, Honolulu, 1968, Houston Internat. Airport, Terminal D., 1978, Tex. A&M Stadium, 1978, The Crystal Palace Hotel, Tianjin, People's Republic China, 1984, Long Beach (Calif.) World Trade Ctr., 1984, USN 700 sta. Weapons System Lab., Calif., 1985, UCLA Ambulatory Care Complex, Calif., 1986, 400 bed Presbyn./St. Luke's Med. Ctr., Denver, 1987, USN 550 Sta. Automatic Data Processing Ctr., Calif., 1990, Proposed 56-story Office Tower, Singapore, 1992, Proposed Master Plan for Nanyang Polytechnic U., Singapore, 1993, 36-story Tianjin News Bldg., Tianjin, China, 1994. Served with U.S. Army, 1954-56. Fellow AIA. Home: 3600 Montrose Blvd Houston TX 77006-4658 Office: RossWou Inc 2450 Broadway Ste 650 Santa Monica CA 90404-3064

WOYSKI, MARGARET SKILLMAN, retired geology educator; b. West Chester, Pa., July 26, 1921; d. Willis Rowland and Clara Louise (Howson) Skillman; m. Mark M. Woyski, June 19, 1948; children: Nancy Elizabeth, William Bruno, Ronald David, Wendelin Jane. BA in Chemistry, Wellesley (Mass.) Coll., 1943; MS in Geology, U. Minn., 1945, PhD in Geology, 1946. Geologist Mo. Geol. Survey and Water Resources, Rolla, 1946-48; instr. U. Wis., Madison, 1948-52; lectr. Calif. State U., Long Beach, 1963-67; lectr. to prof. Calif. State U., Fullerton, 1966-91, assoc. dean Sch. Natural Sci. and Math., 1981-91, emeritus prof., 1991—. Contbr. articles to profl. jours.; author lab. manuals; editor 4 guidebooks. Fellow Geol. Soc. Am. (program chmn. 1982); mem. South Coast Geol. Soc. (hon. pres. 1974), Mineral Soc. Am. Home: 1843 Kashlan Rd La Habra CA 90631-8423

WOZNIAK, JOYCE MARIE, sales executive; b. Detroit, Aug. 3, 1955; d. Edmund Frank and Bernice (Liske) W. BA, Mich. State U., 1976; MA, Nat. U., San Diego, 1988; postgrad., U.S. Internat. U., 1989-90. Probation officer San Diego County Probation, 1979-81; prodn. engr. Tuesday Prodns., Inc., San Diego, 1981-85; nat. sales mgr. Advance Rec. Products, San Diego, 1986-88; account exec. Joyce Enterprises, San Diego, 1986-95; sales exec. Audio-Video Supply Inc., San Diego, 1988—. Producer (video) Loving Yourself, 1987, southwest cable access program, 1986-95; registered marriage, family and child counselor-intern, Calif., 1989. Active Zool. Soc. San Diego. Mem. Art Glass Assn. So. Calif., Calif. Assn. Marriage and Family Therapists, Internat. TV Assn. (treas. San Diego chpt. 1990-91), Nat. Acad. TV Arts and scis.

WRAY, TOM C., state senator, electrical engineering consultant; b. Converse, La., Feb. 4, 1949; s. Joe O. Wray and Joyce (Tyler) Griffin; 1 child, Tyler Mark Manning-Wray. BSEE, La. State U., 1971; MBA, U. N.Mex., 1984; MSEE, Colo. U., 1988. Cert. profl. engr., N.Mex. Div. engr. Pub. Svc. Commn. of N.Mex., Santa Fe, 1972-75; sr. distbn. standards engr. Pub. Svc. Commn. of N.Mex., Albuquerque, 1975-77; supervising engr. Albuquerque div. Pub. Svc. Commn. of N.Mex., 1977-78, mgr. div. svcs., 1978-84, mgr. strategic planning, 1988; exec. v.p., sec., treas. Dineh Power Project, Albuquerque, 1984-88; cons. Mgmt. Analysis Co., San Diego, 1988-90; ptnr. Groves, Wray & Assoc., Albuquerque, 1991—; mem. N.Mex. State Senate, Albuquerque, 1993—. Exec. v.p. N.Mex. Cystic Fibrosis Found., Albuquerque, 1987—; bd. dirs. U.S. Selective Svc. System Region IV, 1988—; legis. asst. Sen. Les Houston, Albuquerque, 1989. Mem. IEEE, Am. Mgmt. Assn., Nat. Soc. Profl. Engrs. Republican. Home: 1835 Tramway Terrace Loop NE Albuquerque NM 87122-1325

WRIGHT, BARTON ALLEN, ethnologist, author; b. Bisbee, Ariz., Dec. 21, 1920; s. Roy Joline and Anna Sophronia (Harris) W.; m. Margaret Anna Nickelson, Apr. 16, 1949; children: Frances Elena, Matthew Allen. BA, U. Ariz., 1952, MA, 1954. Tech. illustrator Ariz. State Mus., 1946-53; archaeologist N.C. State U., 1949-41; archaeologist, artist Amerind Found., Dragoon, Ariz., 1953-55; mus. curator Mus. of No. Ariz., Flagstaff, 1955-76; sci. dir. San Diego Mus. of Man, 1978-82; rsch. anthropologist Heard Mus., Phoenix, 1983-85; contractor Nat. Park Svc., 1955-82; cons. Nat. Geographic Soc., Washington, 1965-85; bd. dirs. Indian Arts & Crafts Assn., Albuquerque; rep. Western Mus. League, 1975-77. Author: Kachinas, Hopi Artist, 1973 (Wolfe award 1984), Hopi Kachinas, 1977, Zuni Kachinas, 1986 (S.W. Librs. award), Mythic World of the Zuni, 1988, Hallmarks of the Southwest, 1989, Clowns of the Hopi, 1994; author, artist; Unchanging Hopi, 1975 (Rounce award 1975). Committeeman Bicentennial/Centennial, Flagstaff, 1976, Hopi Cultural Values, Hopi Reservation, Ariz., 1976—; judge Intertribal Ceremonial Gallup, N.Mex., 1964-93, chief judge, 1993-94. With U.S. Army, 1943-46, PTO. Harvey Found. fellow, 1965-77; NEA grantee, 1974, NEH grantee, 1975, NSF grantee, 1978; Inst. Mus. Svcs. scholar, 1979. Mem. Am. Assn. Mus. (accreditor 1970-80), Ariz. Nev. Acad. Sci. (charter), Western Regional History Assn. Home and Office: 4143 W Gelding Dr Phoenix AZ 85023-5327

WRIGHT, BERNARD, artist; b. Pitts., Feb. 23, 1938; s. Garfield and Emma (Jefferson) W.; m. Corrine Westley, Mar. 7, 1964; 1 son, Jeffrey. Student Otis Art Inst., Los Angeles, 1969-70, Los Angeles Trade Tech. Coll., 1971-73. Exhibited traveling art show Moscow, Baku, Leningrad, Alma Alta, USSR, European capitals, 1966, Los Angeles City Hall Rotunda Gallery, 1967, Calif. Lutheran Coll., Thousand Oaks, 1967, Alley Gallery, Beverly Hills, 1968, Florenz Art Gallery, Los Angeles, 1969, San Diego Mus., 1969, Phillip E. Freed Gallery of Fine Arts, Chgo., 1969, Art West Gallery, Los Angeles, 1973, N.J. State Mus., Trenton, Detroit Inst. Arts, Mich., 1974, U. So. Calif., Calif. Mus. Sci. and Industry, 1974, City Art Mus., St. Louis, 1976, N.Y.C. Pub. Library, 1977, Pitts. City Hall Rotunda, 1982, The Mus. of African Am. Art, Los Angeles, 1982, Main Bridge Art Gallery, Los Angeles City Hall, 1983; represented in pvt. and pub. collections including Howard U., Library of Congress. collections past pres. co-founder Wright's & Westley Prodns., furniture and garment designers. Cited by U.S. Rep. Cardiss Collins, Ill., 1978, state senator Bill Greene, Calif, 1981, Mayor Richard S. Callguiri, Pitts., 1981, Mayor Coleman A. Young, Detroit, 1981, Mayor Tom Bradley, Los Angeles. bd. supr. Kenneth Hahn, Los Angeles, 1981; active community involvement Sta. KHJ-TV, 1982. Mem. Art West Assn. (bd. dirs.). Contbr. articles to profl. jours. Home: PO Box 76169 Los Angeles CA 90076-0169

WRIGHT, CAROLE DEAN, reading specialist; b. Mt. Clemens, Mich., Aug. 18, 1943; d. Edward Lawrence and Alice Agnes (Roshinski) Hundt; m. David John Wright, Dec. 20, 1964 (div. Sept. 1984); 1 child, Amy Elizabeth. BA, Mich. State U., 1964, MA, 1967. Reading specialist Holt (Mich.) Pub. Schs., 1965-70, Ypsilanti (Mich.) Pub. Schs., 1970-71, Aurora (Colo.) Pub. Schs., 1972—; pres. Aurora Edn. Assn., 1978-80, Colo. Edn. Assn., Denver, 1982; mem. adv. com. Nat. Assessment of Ednl. Progress, Denver, 1975; chair unit accreditation bd. Nat. Coun. Accreditation of Tchr. Edn., Washington, 1990—; trustee Pub. Employees Retirement Assn. Colo., 1993—. Contbg. author to Idea's for Children's Literature, 1976. Mem. Colo. Commn. on Tchr. Edn. and Accreditation, Denver, 1976-82; vice chair Gov.'s Chpt. 2 Adv. Com., Denver, 1987-93. Named Outstanding Educator, Fed. Programs Adminstr. Coun. U.S. Dept. Edn., 1991. Mem. NEA (bd. dirs. 1984-87), Internat. Reading Assn., Colo. Edn. Assn. (v.p. 1980-84), Phi Delta Kappa. Home: 2268 Clermont St Denver CO 80207-3740

WRIGHT, CAROLE YVONNE, chiropractor; b. Long Beach, Calif., July 12, 1932; d. Paul Burt and Mary Leoan (Staley) Fickes; 1 child, Morgan Michelle. D. Chiropractic, Palmer Coll., Davenport, Iowa, 1976. Instr. Palmer Coll., 1975-76; dir., owner Wright Chiropractic Clinic, Rocklin, Calif., 1978-88, Woodland, Calif., 1980-81; co-owner Ft. Sutter Chiropractic Clinic, Sacramento, 1985-89; owner Wright Chiropractic Health Ctr., Sacramento, 1989—, Capitol Chiropractic, Sacramento, 1993—; cons. in field; lectr., speaker on radio and TV programs, at seminars. Contbr. articles to profl. jours. Co-chmn. Harold Michaels for Congress campaign, Alameda, Calif., 1972; dist. dir. 14th Congl. Dist., 1983—. Mem. Internat. Chiropractic Assn. Calif. (bd. dirs. 1978-81, pres. 1983-85), Palmer Coll. Alumni Assn. (Calif. state pres. 1981-83), Rocklin C. of C. (bd. dirs. 1979-81). Republican. Avocations: reading, travel. Home: 1404 Stonebridge Way Roseville CA 95661-5456 Office: Capitol Chiropractic 1972 Stockton Blvd Sacramento CA 95816-6638

WRIGHT, CHARLES LEE, information systems consultant; b. Dalton, Ga., Dec. 18, 1949; s. Charlie William and Catherine Christine (Quarles) W.; children: Charles Lee, Christina. AA in Bus., Dalton Jr. Coll., 1971; BS in Bus., U. Tenn., Chattanooga, 1977; also numerous IBM classes on various machines and systems;. Trainee Ludlow Carpets, Dalton, 1971, EDP supr., 1971-73, EDP mgr., 1973-77; ops. mgr. Walter Carpet Mills, Industry, Calif., 1977-80; ptnr., cons. TCT Systems, San Dimas, Calif., 1978-92; ptnr., CEO Williams, Wright and Assocs., Upland, Calif., 1978-92; dir. ops. Roland Corp., U.S., 1993—. Served as sgt. U.S. Army, 1969-71; Vietnam, Cambodia. Decorated Bronze Star, Army Commendation medal with oak leaf and oak leaf cluster, Air medal. Mem. Data Processing Mgmt. Assn., Am. Mgmt. Assn., Small Systems User Group, COMMON. Home and Office: 3708 Palamino Place Ontario CA 91761-5107

WRIGHT, DAVID LEE, special events producer, design consultant; b. Peoria, Ill., Nov. 8, 1946; s. Lowell Grandon Wright and Helen Joann (Snyder) Hohstadt; m. Barbara Jane Wick, 1971 (div. 1974); 1 child, Rachael Elizabeth. BA in English, Ill. State U., 1975; MA in English, U. Ill., 1977. Mgr. Studio Instrument Rentals, Chgo., 1980-81; prodn. mgr. Chip Monck Industries, Redondo Beach, Calif., 1981-83; ops. mgr. Greek Theatre, L.A., 1983-84; exec. producer Simas & Assocs., Ventura, 1984-94; prodn. mgr. Del Mar (Calif.) Fair, 1983-94; pres. Stage Wright Prodns., Inc., Rancho La Costa Oceanside, Calif., 1980—; prodn. mgr. 22d Dist. Agrl. Assn., Del Mar, 1984-94, chief exposition events, 1994—; prodn. mgr. SouthLand Concerts, San Deigo, 1985-87; dept. supr. Del Mar Satellite Wagering, 1987-94; tech. dir. Western Fairs Assn., Sacramento, 1988—; prodn. cons. Hard Rock Cafe, San Deigo, 1988-94. Campaign worker Hunter S. Thompson, Aspen, Colo., 1980; event coord. Missing Children's Found., San Diego, 1988. With U.S. Army, 1966-68. Mem. Am. Mus. Natural History, Nat. Geog. Soc., San Deigo Mus. Fine Art, Audubon Soc., Smithsonian Instn., U.S. Golf Assn., Am. Legion. Home: 1832 Bailey Dr Oceanside CA 92054-6126 Office: Del Mar Fair 2260 Jimmy Durante Blvd Del Mar CA 92014-2216

WRIGHT, EDWARD N., political science educator; b. Chillicothe, Ohio, Mar. 20, 1945; s. Herbert Wright and Martha A. (Boden) Grant; m. June Claire Goodwin, Apr. 26, 1969; children: Edward II, Robert E., Benjamin J. BS in Polit. Sci. and Econs. with highest honors, U. So. Miss., Hattiesburg, 1971, MA in Polit. Sci., 1973; PhD in Govt., Georgetown U., 1985. Commd. 2d lt. USAF, 1965, advanced through the grades to lt. col, 1990; politico military affairs officer Project Peace Hawk, U.S. Air Force, Alkhabar, Saudi Arabia, 1977-78; staff analyst Office of Sec. of Defense, Washington, 1978-79; instr. polit. sci. USAF Acad., Colorado Springs, Colo., 1979-80; rsch. assoc. Carnegie Endowment for Internat. Peace, Washington, 1980-81; assoc. prof. polit. sci. USAF Acad., Colorado Springs, Colo., 1983-87; spl. asst. to the Atty. Gen., U.S. Dept. Justice, Washington, 1987-88; assoc. prof. polit. sci. USAF Acad., Colorado Springs, Colo., 1988-90; prof. pub. adminstrn. Grad Sch. of Pub. Affairs, U. Colo., Colorado Springs, Colo., 1990-91; assoc. prof. polit. sci. U. So. Colo., Pueblo, Colo., 1991—; assoc. provost U. Soc. Colo., 1995—; mem. nat. advisory coun. Ctr. for Study of the Presidency, N.Y.C., 1990—. Editor: (book) American Defense Policy, 1990. V.p. Rocky Mt. Coun. Boy's Scouts of Am., Pueblo, Colo., 1992—; mem. 2010 commn. Comm. of Pueblo Strategic Plan, Pueblo, 1994—; mem. state bd. agrl. Colo. State Govt., 1994—. Mem. Am. Polit. Sci. Assn., Western Polit. Sci. Assn., Phi Kappa Phi, Phi Sigma Alpha, Omicron Delta Kappa. Republican. Roman Catholic. Home: 457 W Hahns Peak Ave Pueblo West CO 81007-2860 Office: U So Colo Office of the Provost 2200 Bonforte Blvd Pueblo CO 81001-4901

WRIGHT, ELLEN FLORENCE, consultant; b. Seattle, Aug. 29, 1939; d. Edwin Sherman and Mildred (Redfield) W.; children: Michael Stanley Tetelman, Margaret Elaine. BA in English and Speech, U. Calif., L.A., 1962; MA in Edn., Stanford U., 1965, postgrad., 1970-74. Gen. adminstrv. credential, Calif.; C.C. credential; tchg. credential grades 7-12. Prin. Piedmont (Calif.) H.S., 1978-79; dir. devel. Packard Children's Hosp., Palo Alto, Calif., 1983-85; exec. dir. Peninsula Ctr. for Blind and Visually Impaired, Palo Alto, 1987-90; dir. devel. The Nueva Sch., Hillsborough, Calif., 1990-92; owner Ellen Wright Consulting Co., Menlo Park, Calif., 1992—; mem. Calif. Post Secondary Edn. Commn., Sacramento, 1994—; mem. Western Interstate Commn. for Higher Edn., 1995—; bd. dirs. Alumni Cons. Team Stanford U. Sch. Bus.; bd. dirs. Children's Health Coun., Palo Alto; bd. dirs. Garfield Charter Sch., Spl. Olympics. Mem. Nat. Soc. Fund Raising Execs., Phi Delta Kappa, Lincoln Club No. Calif. Republican. Office: Bldg 3 Ste 140 3000 Sandhill Rd Menlo Park CA 94025

WRIGHT, ERIC R., physician assistant; b. Fremont, Mich., Apr. 8, 1952; s. Owen Aaron and Ethlyn Emily (Crandall) W.; m. Teresa Christine Harrison, May 3, 1979; 1 child, Natalie Ann. Grad., Hackley Hosp. Sch. Radiol.Tech, Muskegon, Mich., 1975; AS in Physician Assisting with honors, Kettering (Ohio) Coll. Med.Art, 1984. Diplomate Colo. Bd. Med. Examiners. Physician asst. Peak Nine Med. Ctr./Family & Emergency Med. Assocs., Breckenridge, Colo., 1984-85, Richard Wageman, M.D., Monument, Colo., 1985-86, Dennis Caldwell, M.D., Colorado Springs, Colo., 1986-88, Sheldon Ravin, D.O., Skyway Family Practice, Colorado Springs, 1988-90, The People's Clinic, Boulder, Colo., 1990-95, Columbine Family Practice Ctr., Loveland, Colo., 1991-93, Poudre Valley Otolaryngology, Ft. Collins, Colo., 1993—. Author: PA Protocols: A Guidebook, 1992. Mem. Am. Registry of Radiologic Technologists, Beaven-Black Student Soc. Physician Assts. (v.p. 1982-83), Am. Acad. Physician Assts., Colo. Assn. Physician Assts. (membership chmn. 1990-92), Soc. Physician Assts. in Otolaryngology. SDA. Home: 3411 N Douglas Loveland CO 80538-2574

WRIGHT, ERNEST MARSHALL, physiologist, consultant; b. Belfast, Ireland, June 8, 1940; came to U.S., 1965; BSc, U. London, 1961, DSc, 1978; PhD, U. Sheffield, Eng., 1964. Research fellow Harvard U., Boston, 1965-66; from asst. prof. to full prof. physiology UCLA Med. Sch., 1967—, chmn. dept. physiology, 1987—; cons. NIH, Bethesda, Md., 1982—, Senator Jacob K. Javits neurosci. investigator, 1985. Office: UCLA Sch Med Dept Physiology 10833 Le Conte Ave Los Angeles CA 90024

WRIGHT, EUGENE ALLEN, federal judge; b. Seattle, Feb. 23, 1913; s. Elias Allen and Mary (Bailey) W.; m. Esther Ruth Ladley, Mar. 19, 1938; children: Gerald Allen, Meredith Ann Wright Morton. AB, U. Wash., 1935, JD, 1937; LLD, U. Puget Sound, 1984. Bar: Wash. 1937. Assoc. Wright & Wright, Seattle, 1937-54; judge Superior Ct. King County, Wash., 1954-66; v.p., sr. trust officer Pacific Nat. Bank Seattle, 1966-69; judge U.S. Ct. Appeals (9th cir.), Seattle, 1969—; acting municipal judge, Seattle, 1948-52; mem. faculty Nat. Jud. Coll., 1964-72; lectr. Sch. Communications, U. Wash., 1965-66, U. Wash. Law Sch., 1952-74; lectr. appellate judges' seminars, 1973-76, Nat. Law Clks. Inst., La. State U., 1973; chmn. Wash. State Com. on Law and Justice, 1968-69; mem. com. on appellate rules Jud. Conf., 1978-85, mem. com. on courtroom photography, 1983-85, com. jud. ethics, 1984-92, com. Bicentennial of Constn., 1985-87. Author: (with others) The State Trial Judges Book, 1966; also articles; editor: Trial Judges Jour., 1963-66; contbr. articles to profl. jours. Chmn. bd. visitors U. Puget Sound Sch. Law, 1979-84; mem. bd. visitors U. Wash. Sch. Law, 1989—; bd. dirs. Met. YMCA, Seattle, 1955-72; lay reader Episc Ch. Served to lt. col. USAR, 1941-46, col. Res., ret. Decorated Bronze Star, Combat Inf. badge; recipient Army Commendation medal, Disting. Service award U.S. Jr. C. of C., 1948, Disting. Service medal Am. Legion. Fellow Am. Bar Found.; mem. ABA (coun. div. jud. adminstrn. 1971-76), Fed. Bar Assn. (Disting. Jud. Svc. award 1984), Wash. Bar Assn. (award of merit 1983), Seattle-King County Bar Assn. (Spl. Disting. Svc. award 1984), Appellate Judges Conf., Order of Coif, Wash. Athletic Club, Rainier Club, Masons (33 deg.), Shriners, Delta Upsilon (Disting. Alumni Achievement award 1989), Phi Delta Phi.

WRIGHT, FRANCES JANE, educational psychologist; b. Los Angeles, Dec. 22, 1943; d. step-father John David and Evelyn Jane (Dale) Brinegar. BA, Long Beach State U., 1965, secondary tchr. cert., 1966; MA, Brigham Young U., 1968, EdD, 1980; postgrad. U. Nev., 1970, U. Utah, 1972-73; postdoctoral Utah State U., 1985-86. Cert. tchr., adminstr. Utah. Asst. dir. Teenpost Project, San Pedro, Calif., 1966; caseworker Los Angeles County, 1966-67; self-care inservice dir. Utah State Tng. Sch., American Fork, Utah, 1968, vocat. project designer, 1968; tchr. mentally handicapped Santa Ana Unified Schs., Calif., 1968-69; state specialist intellectually handicapped State Office Edn., Salt Lake City, 1969-70; vocat. counselor Manpower, Salt Lake City, 1970-71; tchr. severely handicapped Davis County Schs., Farmington, Utah, 1971-73, diagnostician, 1973-74, resource elem. tchr., 1974-78; instr. Brigham Young U., Salt Lake City, 1976-83; resource tchr. jr. high Davis County Schs., Farmington, 1978-90; ednl. cons., Murray, Utah, 1973-90; chief ednl. diagnostician Ctr. for Evaluation of Learning and Devel., Layton, Utah, 1989-90; clin. dir. assessment and observation program Idaho Youth Ranch, 1990—, clin. dir. intake program, 1992-94, supr. family preservation svc./aftercare teams, 1993—, co-ranch treatment dir. and placement officer, 1995—; cons. and lectr. in field. Author curriculums in spl. edn.; contbr. articles to profl. jours. Named Profl. of Yr., Utah Assn. for Children with Learning Disabilities, 1985. Mem. Assn. Children/Adults with Learning Disabilities (del. 1979-85, 87, nat. nominating com. 1985-86, nat. bd. dirs. 1988-91), Utah Assn. Children/Adults with Learning Disabilities (exec. bd. 1978-84, profl. adv. bd. 1985-90, coord. LDA orgn. Idaho 1991—), Coun. Exceptional Children (div. learning disabilities, ednl. diagnostics, behavioral disorders), Council Learning Disabilities, Assn. Supervisors and Curriculum Devel. (regional adv.), Windstar Found., Smithsonian Found., Cousteau Soc., Am. Biographical Inst. (life, hon. advisor rsch. bd. advisors nat. div.), Nat. Assn. Sch. Adminstrs. Democrat. Mormon. Lodge: Job's Daughters. Avocations: geneology research, horseback riding, sketching, crafts, reading. Home and Office: Idaho Youth Ranch Rupert ID 83350

WRIGHT, FREDERICK HERMAN GREENE, II, computer systems engineer; b. Quincy, Mass., Feb. 23, 1952; s. Frederick Herman Greene and Dorothy Louise (Harrold) W. Student, MIT, 1968-69. Test and measurement technician The Foxboro (Mass.) Co., 1968; hardware and software designer MIT Project MAC, Cambridge, Mass., 1969, Info. Internat., Brookline, Mass., 1969, Stanford Artificial Intelligence Lab, Palo Alto, Calif., 1971-73, Systems Concepts, San Francisco, 1970, 73-74, 1976-90; hardware and software designer, then pres. Resource One, San Francisco, 1974-76; pvt. cons. San Rafael, Calif., 1991—; computer cons. Langley-Porter Neuropsychiatric Inst., San Francisco, 1976. Membership chmn. Pacific Soaring Coun., San Francisco, 1983-85, bd. dirs., 1984-85; active Mayflower Cmty. Chorus, 1994—. Recipient Gold Soaring Badge Fed. Aeronautique Internat., 1983. Mem. Digital Equipment Corp. Users Soc., Bay Area Soaring Assn. Home and Office: 251 C St San Rafael CA 94901-4916

WRIGHT, GEORGE THADDEUS, humanities educator; b. S.I., N.Y., Dec. 17, 1925; s. George Thaddeus and Tekla Alida (Anderson) W.; m. Jerry Honeywell, Apr. 28, 1955. A.B., Columbia, 1946, M.A., 1947; student, U. Geneva, Switzerland, 1947-48; Ph.D. (Dr. Benjamin P. Wall meml. fellow 1955-56), U. Calif. at Berkeley, 1957. Lectr. English U. Calif. at Berkeley, 1956-57; instr., then asst. prof. U. Ky., 1957-60; asst. prof. San Francisco State Coll., 1960-61; assoc. prof. U. Tenn., 1961-68; prof. English U. Minn., Mpls., 1968-89, Regents' prof., 1989-93, prof. emeritus, 1993—, chmn. dept. English, 1974-77; Fulbright lectr. Am. lit. U. d'Aix Marseille, France, 1964-66, U. Thessaloniki, Greece, 1977-78. Author: The Poet in the Poem: The Personae of Eliot, Yeats and Pound, 1960, W.H. Auden, 1969, rev. edit., 1981, Shakespeare's Metrical Art, 1988, paperback edit., 1991; also articles, poems.; Editor: Seven American Literary Stylists from Poe to Mailer, 1973. Served with U.S. Army, 1944-46. NEH stipend, 1981; Guggenheim fellow, 1981-82; NEH fellow, 1984-85. Mem. Shakespeare Assn. Am., MLA (William Riley Parker prize 1974, 81), Phi Kappa Phi. Home: 2617 W Crown King Dr Tucson AZ 85741-2569

WRIGHT, GEORGIA SOMMERS, scholar, video producer; b. St. Paul, Minn., Jan. 23, 1937; d. Ben and Mary (Crosby) Sommers; m. David Herndon Wright, July 14, 1967; 1 child, Elizabeth. BA, Swarthmore Coll., 1959; MA, Columbia U., 1961, PhD, 1966; MBA, U. Calif., Berkeley, 1981. Vis. lectr U. Minn., Mpls., 1962, 64; vis. lectr U. Calif., Berkeley, 1966-67, Davis, 1967-68; asst. prof. Mills Coll., Oakland, Calif., 1968-76; vis. assoc. prof. Stanford (Calif.) U. Dir., prod. 2 edn. videos; contbr. articles to profl. jours. Grantee NEH, 1993-94; named Chevalier in the Order of Academic Palms, Govt. of France, 1989. Mem. Nat. Coalition of Ind. Scholars (editor 1986-93), Inst. for Hist. Study (pres. 1985-87, 1995—). Home: 105 Vicente Rd Berkeley CA 94705-1605

WRIGHT, GORDON BROOKS, musician, conductor, educator; b. Bklyn., Dec. 31, 1934; s. Harry Wesley and Helen Philomena (Brooks) W.; m. Inga-Lisa Myrin Wright, June 13, 1958 (div. 1979); children: Karin-Ellen Blindenbacher, Charles-Eric, Daniel Brooks. MusB, Coll. Wooster, 1957; MA, U. Wis., 1961; postgrad., Salzburg Mozarteum, 1972, Loma Linda U., 1979; studied with, René Leibowitz, Carl Melles, Wilfred Pelletier, Herbert Blomstedt, Hans Swarowsky. Founder, music dir. Wis. Chamber Orch., 1960-69; music dir. Fairbanks (Alaska) Symphony Orch., 1969-89; prof. music Univ. Alaska, Fairbanks, 1969-89, prof. emeritus, 1989—; founder, music dir. Arctic Chamber Orch., Fairbanks, 1970-89; exec. dir. The Reznicek Soc., Indian, Alaska, 1982—. Guest condr. Philharmonia Hungarica, Philomusica London, Norwegian Radio Orch., Orch. St. Luke's, Anchorage Symphony Orch.; composer: Suite of Netherlands Dances, 1965, Six Alaskan Tone Poems, 1974, Symphony in Ursa Major, 1979 (Legis. award 1979), 1984 Overture, Scott Joplin Suite, 1987, Toccata Festiva, 1992; columnist Alaska Advocate. Founder, bd. dirs. No. Alaska Environ. Ctr., Fairbanks, 1971-78. Served as pvt. AUS, 1957-59. Mem. Am. Musicol. Soc., Royal Musical Assn., Am. Symphony Orch. League, Condr.'s Guild, Arturo Toscanini Soc., Am. Fedn. Musicians, Royal Mus. Assn., Sierra Club (chmn. Fairbanks Group 1969-71), Friends of Earth-Alaska (bd. dirs. 1978—), Wilderness Soc., Audubon Soc., Alaska Conservation Soc. (editor Rev. 1971-78), Ctr. for Alaskan Coastal Studies (bd. dirs. 1982—). Home: HC 52 Box 8899 Indian AK 99540-9604

WRIGHT, H. S., III, pilot; b. Seattle, May 2, 1953; s. Howard S. Wright and Theiline Ada (Pigott) Scheumann; m. Katherine Ann Janeway, Apr. 9, 1983. BA, Wash. State U., 1976. Credit analyst Seattle First Nat. Bank, 1978-80; pres. Renton (Wash.) Aviation, 1981-84; pilot Horizon Air, Seattle, 1984-86; pilot Delta Airlines, Seattle, 1986-88, Cin., 1988-93, L.A., 1993—; prin. Sprague Capital, 1994—; co-owner Grousement Assocs., Seattle, 1985—, Space Needle, Coast Hotels; bd. dirs., officer Wright Roberts & Co., Seattle, 1985—. Grad. Leadership Tomorrow, Seattle, 1988; bd. dirs. Intiman Theatre, Seattle, 1980-85, Market Found., Seattle, 1987—; chair com. Renton C. of C., 1983; trustee Wash. State U. Found., 1991—, Vt. Acad. Mem. Seattle Tennis Club, Seattle Yacht Club, Wash. Athletic Club.

WRIGHT, HELENE SEGAL, editor; b. L.A., Jan. 31, 1955; d. Alan and Lila E. (Hambro) Segal; m. David Scott Wright, May 6, 1979. Student, Calif. State U., Fullerton, 1973-75; BA in English, U. Calif., Santa Barbara, 1978. Library asst. ABC-CLIO, Santa Barbara, 1979-80, editorial asst., 1980-81, asst. editor, 1981-83; mng. editor ABC POL SCI, ABC-CLIO, Santa Barbara, 1983—. Mem. Am. Polit. Sci. Assn., Current World Leaders (adv. bd. 1989—). Home: 142 La Vista Grande Santa Barbara CA 93103-2817 Office: ABC-CLIO 130 Cremona Dr Santa Barbara CA 93117-3075

WRIGHT, JAMES BARON, electrical engineer; b. San Francisco, Sept. 17, 1933; s. George Baron and Louise Henerette (Vallee) Boyd; m. Judith Clarice Gehring, May 25, 1962; children: Peter Baron, Erich Paul, John Conrad. BSEE, U. Calif., Berkeley, 1958. Engr. elec. design divsn. Sandia Labs., Livermore, Calif., 1958-60, engr. W55 project engrng. divsn., 1960-61, engr. electronic support divsn., AF&F designer, 1961-63, engr. preliminary analysis divsn., 1963-64, lead elec. engr. Pebbles/W68 devel. team, 1964-69, supr. nuclear safety divsn., 1969-71, supr. preliminary design div.,

1971-74, supr. B77/B83 elec. sys. div., 1974-82, mgr. solar ctrl. receiver dept., 1982-85, mgr. W89 program sys. devel. dept., 1985-92, dir. Calif. Weapon Devel. Ctr., 1992—. With USN, 1950-54. Mem. IEEE. Home: 2141 Hampton Rd Livermore CA 94550-6509 Office: Sandia National Labs Ctr 5300 MS9005 Box 969 Livermore CA 94551

WRIGHT, JAMES CORWIN, international management consultant; b. Watertown, S.D., 1959; s. Patrick and Delores Wright; m. Susan Kathleen Mohr, Nov. 7, 1981 (div. Oct. 1983); m. Lynda Renelle Prettyman, Jan. 4, 1986. HHD (hon.), 1993, D in Internat. Mgmt. (hon.), 1993. With delivery dept. San Juan (P.R.) Star Newspaper, 1972-74; asst. diving instr. Caribbean Sch. of Aquatics, San Juan, 1973-74; freelance musician various locations, 1975-81; detail draftsman AiResearch Mfg. Co. of Ariz., Phoenix, 1977-79; project designer McMartin Industries, Inc., Omaha, 1980-82; chief exec. officer Aztron Corp., Council Bluffs, Iowa, 1982-86; pres. Aztron Prodns., Fountain Hills, Ariz., 1986-88; chief exec. officer Jalyn Entertainment Group, Scottsdale, Ariz., 1988—; pub. Roadrunner Mag., Phoenix, 1988-89; v.p. Zent & Assocs., 1989-93; cons. Tripp and Assocs., Inc., Blair, Nebr., 1982-85, Control Data Corp., Omaha, 1984, Fast Lane Mag., Omaha, 1984-87, Salt River Project, Ariz., 1986-87, MEMCON, Nebr., 1984, Tricon, Ltd., Iowa, 1982-84, Doane Western Co. Inc., Nebr., 1984; gen. mgr. Tight Fit Enterprises, Council Bluffs, 1983-85; trustee Jalyn Internat. Trust, 1991-94, Bus. Intercontinental Trust, 1991-94, West African Devel. Trust, 1991-93; writer syndicated column, 1984-89. Author: Newsletters: A Report, 1985, Developing Presentation Skills; editor: (jour.) The Wintight Letter, 1985; contbr. articles to profl. jours. Active Nat. Congl. Com., 1985-86, Rep. Nat. Com., 1985; chmn. G.P.V. Community Assistance Team, Inc., 1990-92. Recipient Cert. of Merit Pres. Ronald Reagan, 1984, Cert. of Merit Presdl. Task Force, 1986, Cert. of Appreciation Nat. Congl. Com., 1985-86, World Decoration Excellence award, 1990, Disting. Leadership award, 1991, Medal of Honor, 1993; named Cert. Internat. Financier Internat. Soc. of Financiers, 1987, 89; Decorated titled knight Paupers Commilitones Christi Templique Solomonis, cpt. Légion de L'Aigle de Mer Baron. Mem. Internat. Traders, Internat. Parliment for Safety and Peace, Internat. Platform Assn., Inst. des Affaires Internat. (assoc.), Maison Internat. des Intellectuels-Academie Midi (sec., pres.), Am. Mgmt. Assn., Nat. Assn. of Underwater Instrs., Liberia-Am. C. of C. (trustee 1991-93). Office: Jalyn Internat Trust PO Box 5065 Scottsdale AZ 85261-5065

WRIGHT, J(AMES) LAWRENCE, lawyer; b. Portland, Oreg., Apr. 12, 1943; s. William A. and Esther M. (Nelson) W.; m. Mary Aileene Roche, June 29, 1968; children: Rachel, Jonathan, Christopher. BBA, Gonzaga U., 1966, JD, 1972; LLM, NYU, 1977. Bar: Wash. 1972, U.S. Ct. Mil. Appeals 1974, U.S. Tax Ct. 1976, U.S. Supreme Ct. 1976. Prin. Halverson & Applegate, P.S., Yakima, Wash., 1972-74, 77—. Mem. St. Elizabeth Hosp. Found., Yakima, 1986-89, Yakima Meml. Hosp. Found., 1990—; pres. fin. bd. St. Paul's Cathedral, Yakima, 1979—; mem. fin. coun. Diocese of Yakima, 1994—; v.p. Apple Tree Racing Assn., 1986-87; bd. dirs Capital Theatre, Yakima, 1985—. Capt. U.S. Army, 1966-68, 74-76. Mem. ABA, Wash. Bar Assn., Yakima County Bar Assn., Rotary. Roman Catholic. Office: Halverson & Applegate PS PO Box 22730 311 N 4th St Yakima WA 98907-2715

WRIGHT, JANET SCRITSMIER, investment consultant; b. Pomona, Calif., May 21, 1960; d. Jerome Lorenzo and Mildred Joan (Lloyd) Scritsmier; children—Justin Michael, Corey Gray, Cody James. Student Calif. State Poly. U., 1978-79. Vice pres. sales E.L.A. Co., Industry, Calif., 1979-84; investment cons. Cameron Properties Inc., Covina, Calif., 1980—. Asst. instr. Dale Carnegie Sales Course, 1981-82, Human Relations, 1983. Republican. Mormon. Home: 436 N Washington Ave Glendora CA 91741-2560

WRIGHT, JEFF, minister, non-profit religious administrator; b. Jan. 15, 1960; s. James Lee and Mary E. (Shelton) W.; m. Debra Yvonne Thesman, June 6, 1981; children: Bethany Nicole, Jordan Nicholas. BA, Tabor Coll., Hillsboro, Kans., 1981; postgrad., Kans. State U., 1981-83; Ctrl. Bapt. Theol. Sem., 1983; MDiv, Mennonite Brethren Bibl. Sem., Fresno, Calif., 1986; MBA, Grad. Theol. Found., Donaldson, Ind., 1995. Ordained to ministry, Gen. Conf. Mennonite Ch., 1989. Pastoral intern Fairlawn Mennonite Brethren Ch., Topeka, Kans., 1981-83; youth pastor Zion Mennonite Brethren Ch., Dinuba, Calif., 1983-85; assoc. minister Meml. United Meth. Ch., Clovis, Calif., 1985-86; pastor First Mennonite Ch., Upland, Calif., 1986-89; founding pastor Peace Mennonite Fellowship, Rancho Cucamonga, Calif., 1989-92; coord. Pacific S.W. Mennonite Conf., Downey, Calif., 1992—; dir. ministry devel. Shalom Ministries, Inc., Downey, 1992—. Author column Youth Guide, 1990—. Bd. dirs. Urban Health Care Ctr., Inglewood, Calif., 1993—, Shalom Homes, Inc., Glendora, Calif., 1987-95, Peace and Justice Ctr. of Pomona Valley, La Verne, Calif., 1993—; mem. Commn. on Edn., Gen. Conf. Mennonite Ch., Newton, Kans., 1992—. Mem. Christian Mgmt. Assn., Nat. Network of Youth Ministries, Mennonite Econ. Devel. Assocs., Christian Community Devel. Assocs., Religious Conf. Mgmt. Assn. Democrat. Office: Shalom Ministries Inc 11821 Old River School Rd Downey CA 90241-4625

WRIGHT, JOHN MACNAIR, JR., retired army officer; b. L.A., Apr. 14, 1916; s. John MacNair and Ella (Stradley) W.; m. Helene Tribit, June 28, 1940; children: John MacNair III, Richard Kenneth. B.S., U.S. Mil. Acad., 1940; grad., Airborne Sch., 1947, Strategic Intelligence Sch., 1948; advanced course, Inf. Sch., 1951, Command and Gen. Staff Coll., 1953; M.B.A., U. So. Calif., 1956; grad., Army Logistics Mgmt. Sch., 1957, Advanced Mgmt. Program, U. Pitts., 1959, Nat. War Coll., 1961, Army Aviation Sch., 1965; M.S. in Internat. Affairs, George Washington U., 1973. Enlisted U.S. Army, 1935, comd. 2d. lt., 1940, advanced through grades to lt. gen., 1970; comdr. Battery Wright Corregidor, P.I., 1942; with intelligence div. War Dept. Gen. Staff, 1946-48; mil. attache Am. embassy, Paraguay, 1948-50; bn. comdr. 508th Airborne Regtl. Combat Team, 1951-52; asst. chief of staff for pers. 7th Inf. Div., Korea, 1953, asst. chief staff logistics, 1954; assigned office U.S. Army Chief of Staff, 1956-60; chief staff 8th Inf. Div., 1961-62, asst. chief staff plans and ops. 7th Corps, 1962-63, asst. chief staff plans and ops. 7th Army, 1963-64, asst. div. comdr. 11th Air Assault Div., 1964-65; asst. div. comdr. 1st Cav. Div. (Airmobile) Vietnam, 1965-66; assigned office asst. Chief Staff Force Devel., 1966-67; comdg. gen. U.S. Army Inf. Ctr., 1967-69; comdt. U.S. Army Inf. Sch., 1967-69; comdg. gen. 101st Airborne Div. (Airmobile), Vietnam, 1969-70; controller of the Army Washington, 1970-72; ret., 1973. Dir. R&D Boy Scouts Am., 1973, nat. dir. program, 1974-77, nat. dir. program support, 1977-78; nat. dir. exploring, 1978-81, mem. nat. exploring com., 1981—; pres. Chattahoochee (Ga.) coun. Boy Scouts Am., 1968-69, mem. exec. bd. region 5, 1967-69; mem. nat. coun., 1964-73; tech. adviser Vietnamese Boy Scout Assn., 1965-66; Regent for Life Nat. Eagle Scout Assn., 1988—; exploring chmn. five nations dist. Calif. Inland Empire Coun., 1992—. Decorated D.S.M. with 2 oak leaf clusters, Silver Star with oak leaf cluster, Legion of Merit with oak leaf cluster, D.F.C., Bronze Star with oak leaf cluster, Air medal with 59 oak leaf clusters, Army Commendation medal, Prisoner of War medal, Purple Heart with oak leaf cluster, Combat Inf. badge, Master Parachutist, Sr. Army Aviator, numerous area and campaign ribbons, fgn. decorations; recipient Silver Beaver award Boy Scouts Am., 1961, Silver Antelope award, 1969, Distinguished Eagle Scout award, 1971, Disting. Svc. award Founders and Patriots Am., 1988, Freedoms Found. at Valley Forge Hon. medal, 1992; elected Army Aviation Hall of Fame, 1986. Mem. Assn. U.S. Army, Army Aviation Assn. Am. (pres. 1974-76), 101st Airborne Divsn. Assn., 1st Cavalry Divsn. Assn., SAR (pres. Tex. Soc. 1987-88, pres. Inland Empire chpt. 1992-93, Silver Good Citizenship medal 1984, 87, Meritorious Svc. medal 1986, Patriot, Liberty and Gold Good Citizenship medals 1988), Ret. Officers Assn., West Point Soc., Mil. Order World Wars (Patrick Henry award 1986, 90, comdr. Dalls chpt. 1985-86, vice comdr. dept. ctrl. Calif. 1991-92, comdr. Inland Empire chpt. 1992-93), Nat. Order Founders and Patriots of Am. (sec.-gen. 1986-88, gov. gen. 1988-90, councillor gen. Calif. Soc. 1990-95), Soc. Descendants of Colonial Clergy, Flagon and Tchr. Soc., Soc. Colonial Wars (lt. gov. Calif. soc. 1992—), Sons of the Revolution in State of Calif. (pres. 1993-94), Soc. War of 1812 (dist. dep. pres. gen. 1991—, v.p. Calif. soc. 1993-94, pres. 1994-95), Nat. Huguenot Soc., Soc. Sons and Daus. of Pilgrims, Order Ams. Armorial Ancestry, Soc. Descendants Founders of Hartford, Old Plymouth Colony Descendants, Mil. Order of the Loyal Legion of the U.S., Mil. Order Fgn. Wars of the U.S., Hereditary Order of First Families of Mass., Masons, Shriners, Sojourner, Phi Kappa Phi, Beta Gamma Sigma, Alpha Kappa Psi. Home: 21227 George Brown Ave Riverside CA 92518-2881

WRIGHT, KATHRYN MICHELE, grocery retail chain coordinator; b. Boise, Idaho, Apr. 10, 1959; d. Richard William and Helga Marie (Stipa) Madland; m. Robert C. Wright, June 14, 1981; children: Robert William, Alexander Ian. BBA, Boise State U., 1981. Checker Albertsons Inc., Boise, 1978-84, mgr. ge. mdse., 1984-86, scan coord., 1986-88, pricing clk., 1988-92, dir. store delivery coord., 1992—. Mem. Alpha Kappa Psi. Republican. Office: Albertsons Inc 1404 S Phillippi St Boise ID 83705-2627

WRIGHT, MICHAEL EUGENE, chemistry educator, researcher; b. San Diego, Oct. 10, 1956; s. Howard Eugene and Jean Carolyn (Soderquist) W.; m. Janet DeJonghe, July 4, 1981; children: Christopher E., Matthew D., Cori A. BS, San Diego State U., 1979; MS, U. Ariz., 1981, PhD, 1983. Postdoctoral assoc. Colo. State U., Ft. Collins, 1983-84; asst. prof. chemistry Utah State U., Logan, 1985-91, assoc. prof., 1991—. Contbr. numerous articles to Jour. Am. Chem. Soc., Jour. Organic Chemistry, others. Alexander Von Humboldt fellow, Germany, 1993-94. Mem. Am. Chem. Soc. (chair local sect. 1993). Home: 1392 Maple Dr Logan UT 84321-3628 Office: Utah State U Dept Chemistry/Biochemistry Logan UT 84322

WRIGHT, MICHAEL RAGSDALE, artist, educator; b. La Grande, Oreg., Jan. 26, 1944; s. Thomas Wright and Chris (Rieden) Wu; m. Jo-Ann Morgan, Aug. 14, 1993; 1 child, Marcy Jean. BFA in Painting and Drawing, U. Wash., 1970, BA in European History, 1970. Instr. Shoreline Coll., Seattle, 1969-70, Cabrillo Coll. Cmty. Edn., Santa Cruz, Calif., 1974-80, U. Calif. Extension, Santa Cruz, 1978-81, U. Calif. Kresge Coll., Santa Cruz, 1979, Foothill Coll., Los Altos Hills, Calif., 1980-81, DeAnza Coll., Cupertino, Calif., 1980-82, Santa Cruz County Cultural Coun., Santa Cruz, 1980-90, West Valley Coll., Saratoga, Calif., 1978-84, Rancho Santago Coll., Santa Ana, Calif., 1985-89, Otis Coll. Art and Design, L.A., 1986-95, Performing Tree, L.A., 1986-95, Calif. State U., L.A., 1988-94, L.A. H.S. For the Arts, 1989-95, Crossroads Sch. For the Arts and Scis., Santa Monica, 1989-95, Mt. San Antonio Coll., Walnut, Calif., 1994-95, L.A. CountyMus. Art, L.A.; mem. resource com. Cultural Action Plan for Santa Cruz County, 1979; dir., curator The Gallery Santa Cruz Public Library, 1978-79; arts commr. first dist. Santa Cruz County, 1978-82; spokesperson Artists Coalition Convention Ctr. Expension Project, 1987-88; arts specialist Santa Cruz County Cultural Coun., 1980-90; mem. bd. dirs. Artists Equity of L.A., 1989-90; mem. adv. coun. L.A. H.S. for the Arts, 1991-95; arts educator L.A. County Mus. of Art, 1988-95; gallery dir. Sam Francis Gallery Crossroads Sch. for Arts and Scis., Santa Monica, 1989-95; guest artist, vis. artist numerous orgns. One person exhbns. include First Interstate Bank, Brentwood, Calif., 1994-95, Cerro Coso Coll. Fine Arts Gallery, Ridgecrest, Calif., 1993, The Wilshire Hobart Bldg., L.A., 1992, Buena Park City Coun. Chambers Gallery, Buena Park, Calif., 1991, numerous others; group exhbns. include Curator Mus. of Contemporary Art, L.A., Downey (Calif.) Mus. Art, 1995, Mt. San Antonio Coll. Art Gallery, Walnut, Calif., 1995, Cheekwood Mus. Art, Nashville, 1994, The Conejo Valley Art Mus., Thousand Oaks, Calif., 1994, L.A. Mcpl. Art Gallery, 1994, San Francis Gallery, Crossroads Sch. for Arts & Scis., Santa Monica, 1994, Pres's. Gallery No. Aberdeen State U., S.D., 1994, Univ. Art Gallery Calif. State U., Chico, 1994, Mt. San Antonio Coll. Art Gallery, Walnut, 1994, Downtown Artists Devel. Assn., L.A., 1993, La Grand Gallery Loyola Marymount U., Joslyn Fine Arts Ctr., Torrance, Calif., 1995, Cafe, N.Y.C., 1995, L.A. Conv. Ctr., 1995, numerous others; also numerous public works, Calif.; contbr. articles to jours. in field. Recipient Cultural Affairs grant The City of L.A., 1990, Otis Parsons award Otis Art Inst. Parsons Sch. Design, 1990. Mem. Coll. Art Assn. Am., Calif. Art Edn. Assn., L.A. Mural Conservancy, L.A. County Mus. Art, Santa Monica Mus. Art, L.A. Contemporary Exhbns., L.A. Arts Coun., Artists Equity Assn., Inc., Found. For the Cmty. of Artists, Mus. Contemporary Art. Office: M Ragsdale Wright Studios 2021 S Alameda # 10 Los Angeles CA 90058

WRIGHT, PATRICIA, state legislator; b. South Bend, Ind., Feb. 28, 1931; m. Paul J. Wright, 1951; children: Timothy, Patrick M. Mem. Ariz. State Senate. Republican. Home: 9374 E Hunter Ct Scottsdale AZ 85262-2300 Office: Ariz Senate State House Phoenix AZ 85007

WRIGHT, RICHARD OSCAR, III, pathologist, educator; b. La Junta, Colo., Aug. 9, 1944; s. Richard O. Sr. and Frances R. (Curtiss) W.; m. Bernale Trout, May 31, 1969; children: Lauren Diane, Richard O. IV. BS in Biology, Midwestern State U., 1966; MS in Biology, U. Houston, 1968; DO, U. Health Sci., 1972. Cert. anatomic pathology and lab. medicine Am. Osteo. Bd. Pathology. Sr. attending pathologist Normandy Met. Hosps., St. Louis, 1977-81; sr. attending pathologist Phoenix (Ariz.) Gen. Hosps., 1981—, dir. med. edn., 1989-92; clin. asst. prof. pathology Coll. Osteo. Medicine, Pomona, Calif., 1985—; clin. instr. pathology Ohio U. Coll. Osteo. Medicine, Athens, 1976-77; clin. asst. prof. pathology Kirksville (Mo.) Coll. Osteo. Medicine, 1985-87; vis. lectr. pathology New Eng. Coll. Osteo. Medicine, Biddeford, Maine, 1989-92; cons. pathologist Phoenix (Ariz.) Indian Med. Ctr., 1992-94; adv. bd. Inter Soc. Coun. Pathology, Chgo., 1992—. Active Ariz. Rep. Party, Phoenix, Rep. Nat. Com., Washington; chmn. bd. trustees Phoenix (Ariz.) Gen. Hosp., 1994—. Recipient Mead-Johnson award Nat. Osteo. Assn., 1975. Fellow Am. Osteo. Coll. Pathologists (pres. 1989-90, bd. govs. 1984-91), Coll. Am. Pathologists; mem. Ariz. Osteo. Med. Assn. Ariz. Soc. Pathologists, Century Club Alumni Assn., AAAS, Alpha Phi Omega, Rho Sigma Chi, Psi Sigma Alpha. Presbyterian. Office: Anatomic Pathology Assoc 19829 N 27th Ave Phoenix AZ 85027-4001

WRIGHT, ROSALIE MULLER, newspaper and magazine editor; b. Newark, June 20, 1942; d. Charles and Angela (Fortunata) Muller; m. Lynn Wright, Jan. 13, 1962; children: James Anthony Meador, Geoffrey Shepard. BA in English, Temple U., 1965. Mng. editor Suburban Life mag., Orange, N.J., 1960-62; assoc. editor Phila. mag., 1962-64, mng. editor, 1969-73; founding editor Womensports mag., San Mateo, Calif., 1973-75; editor scene sect. San Francisco Examiner, 1975-77; exec. editor New West mag., San Francisco and Beverly Hills, Calif., 1977-81; features and Sunday editor San Francisco Chronicle, 1981-87, asst. mng. editor features, 1987—; tchr. mag. writing U. Calif., Berkeley, 1975-76; participant pub. procedures course Stanford U., 1977-79; chmn. mag. judges at conf. Coun. Advancement and Support of Edn., 1980, judge, 1984. Contbr. numerous mag. articles, critiques, revs., Compton's Ency. Mem. Am. Assn. Sun and Feature Editors (treas. 1984, sec. 1985, 1st v.p. 1986, pres. 1987), Am. Newspaper Pub. Assn. (pub. task force on minorities in newspaper bus. 1988-89, Chronicle minority recruiter 1987—), Calif. Soc. Newspaper Editors, Internat. Women's Forum, Women's Forum West (bd. dirs. 1993—, sec. 1994). Office: Chronicle Pub Co 901 Mission St San Francisco CA 94103-2905

WRIGHT, SUSIE, stage manager; b. Huntington Station, N.Y., Mar. 8, 1964; d. Robert L. and Carol A. (Wellersdick) Wright; m. John E. Peel, May 15, 1993. BA in European and Asian History, Dowling Coll., Oakdale, N.Y., 1988. Notary pub., 1994. Asst. to dir. ops. Islip (N.Y.) Arts Coun., 1982-88; asst. tech. dir. Theatre Three, Port Jefferson, N.Y., 1986; house mgr. L.I. Philharm., Islip, 1987; stage mgr. Arena Players, Farmingdale, N.Y., 1988; sound technician San Jose (Calif.) State Co., 1991; stage mgr. Bayside Entertainment/Phoenix Prodns., Sunnyvale, Calif., 1991-93; asst. stage mgr. Star Shakespeare Festival, Saratoga, Calif., 1993; stage mgr. Mac's Murder Mystery, Los Altos, Calif., 1993—; mem. Theatre Bay Area, San Francisco, 1992—. Co-playwright: America? Sounds Good to Me, 1980, Who's On First, 1982. Mem. Am. Mgmt. Assn., Nat. Notary Assn., Amnesty Internat., Human Rights Watch. Democrat. Zen Existentialist.

WRIGHT, THEODORE OTIS, forensic engineer; b. Gillette, Wyo., Jan. 17, 1921; s. James Otis and Gladys Mary (Marquiss) W.; m. Phyllis Mae Reeves, June 21, 1942 (div. 1968); children: Mary Suzanne, Theodore Otis Jr., Barbara Joan; m. Edith Marjorie Jewett, May 22, 1968; children: Marjorie Jane, Elizabeth Carter. BSEE, U. Ill., 1951, MS in Engring., 1952; postgrad., Air Command and Staff Coll., 1956-57, UCLA, 1958. Registered profl. engr. Wash. 2d lt. U.S. Air Force, 1942-65, advanced through grades to lt. col., 1957, ret., 1965; dep. for engring. Titan SPO, USAF Sys. Command, L.A., 1957-65; rsch. engr. The Boeing Co., Seattle, 1965-81; pres. The Pretzelwich, Inc., Seattle, 1981—; cons., forensic engr. in pvt. practice Bellevue, Wash., 1988—; adj. prof. U. Wash., Greenriver Jr. Coll., both 1967-68. Contbr. articles to nat. and internat. profl. jours. Decorated Purple Heart, Air medal. Mem. NSPE (v.p. western region 1985-87), ASTM (com. E-43 metric practice 1988—), Nat. Coun. Weights and Measures, Wash. Soc. Profl. Engrs. (state pres. 1981-82, Disting. Svc. award 1980), U.S. Metric Assn. (life, cert. advanced metrication specialist), Am. Nat. Metric Coun. (bd. dirs. 1978-94), Air Force Assn. (life, state pres. 1974-76, 90-91, Jimmy Doolittle fellow 1975), Order of Daedalians (life), Sigma Tau, Eta Kappa Nu, Pi Mu Epsilon, Tau Beta Pi. Democrat. Presbyterian. Home: 141 140th Pl NE Bellevue WA 98007-6939

WRIGHT, TIM EUGENE, packaging development executive; b. Weed, N.Mex., Oct. 13, 1943; s. Clyde Everett and Juanita Delores (Barrett) W.; m. Nancy Ann Ausenbaugh, Oct. 2, 1965 (div. 1975); 1 child, Ramsey Jordan. Diploma, Dayton Art Inst., 1967, M.F.A., U. Idaho, 1969. Designer, Lawson Mfg. Co., Troy, Idaho, 1968-70, Boise Cascade, Burley, Idaho, 1970-72; project coord. Boise Cascade, Golden, Colo., 1972-76, product devel. mgr., Wallula, Wash., 1976-84; mng. ptnr. Matrix Applications Co., Pasco, Wash., 1984—. Patentee folding carton, spacer for rolls, collapsible pallet. Recipient Silver award for packaging, 1978. Mem. Inst. Packaging Profls., Western Packaging Assn. (bd. dirs., past pres. Columbia chpt.), Soc. Plastics Engrs., TAPPI. Office: Matrix Applications Co PO Box 3668 Pasco WA 99302-3668

WRIGHT-QUASTLER, REBA, urban planner; b. Glendale, Calif., Dec. 11, 1946; d. Glenn Holiday and Nellie Fern (Brandon) Wright; m. Cornelis Daniel Touw, May 17, 1968 (div. Aug. 1987); 1 child, Thomas; m. Imre Ernest Quastler, Aug. 24, 1988. BA, Chapman Coll., 1967; Doctor, U. Utrecht, Utrecht, The Netherlands, 1983. Project mgr. The Nowland Orgn., Greenwich, Conn., 1969-70; translator Dun & Bradstreet, Rotterdam, The Netherlands, 1971-73; asst. mgr. P-E Consulting Group, Staines, Middlesex, Eng., 1973; assoc. planner City of Costa Mesa, Calif., 1978-86; dir. planning City of Poway, Calif., 1986—; adj. prof. San Diego State U., 1992—. Contbr. articles to profl. jours. Mem. Am. Inst. Cert. Planners (cert.), Am. Planning Assn. (San Diego sect. chair various coms., San Diego sect. Contbn. to Women in Planning award 1991, Calif. chpt. pres., v.p. adminstrn.). Office: City of Poway 13325 Civic Center Dr Poway CA 92064-5755

WRIGLEY, ELIZABETH SPRINGER (MRS. OLIVER K. WRIGLEY), foundation executive; b. Pitts., Oct. 4, 1915; d. Charles Woodward and Sarah Maria (Roberts) Springer; BA U. Pitts., 1935; BS, Carnegie Inst. Tech., 1936; m. Oliver Kenneth Wrigley, June 16, 1936 (dec. July 1978). Procedure analyst U.S. Steel Corp., Pitts., 1941-43; rsch. asst. The Francis Bacon Found., Inc., Los Angeles, 1944, exec., 1945-50, trustee, 1950—, dir. rsch., 1951-53, pres., 1954—, dir. Francis Bacon Libr.; mem. adv. coun. Shakespeare Authorship Roundtable, Santa Monica, Calif.; mem. regional Fine Arts adv. coun. Calif. State Poly. U., Pomona. Mem. ALA, Calif. Libr. Assn., Renaissance Soc. Am., Modern Humanities Rsch. Assn., Cryptogram Assn., Alpha Delta Pi. Presbyn. Mem. Order Eastern Star, Damascus Shrine. Editor: The Skeleton Text of the Shakespeare Folio L.A. (by W.C. Arensberg), 1952. Compiler: Short Title Catalogue Numbers in the Library of the Francis Bacon Foundation, 1958; Wing Numbers in the Library of the Francis Bacon Foundation, 1959; Supplement To Francis Bacon Library Holdings in the STC of English Books, 1967; (with David W. Davies) A Concordance to the Essays of Francis Bacon, 1973. Home: 4805 N Pal Mal Ave Temple City CA 91780-4129 Office: Francis Bacon Libr 655 N Dartmouth Ave Claremont CA 91711-3960

WRIGLEY, WILLIAM, corporation executive; b. Chgo., Jan. 21, 1933; s. Philip Knight and Helen Blanche (Atwater) W.; m. Alison Hunter, June 1, 1957 (div. 1969); children: Alison Elizabeth, Philip Knight, William Jr.; m. Julie Burns, Nov. 28, 1981. Grad., Deerfield Acad., 1950; B.A., Yale, 1954. With Wm. Wrigley Jr. Co., Chgo., 1956—, v.p., 1960-61, pres., CEO, 1961—, also bd. dirs.; dir. Wrigley Philippines, Inc., Wrigley Co. Ltd. (U.K.), The Wrigley Co. (N.Z.) Ltd., Wrigley Co. Pty. Ltd., Australia, The Wrigley Co. (H.K.) Ltd., The Wrigley Co. (P.N.G.) Pty. Ltd., New Guinea, Wrigley & Co. Ltd., Japan, Wrigley Poland S.P.Z.O.O., Wrigley Chewing Gum Co. Ltd., China, Wrigley d.o.o., Slovenia, Blvd. Bancorp, Inc., Chgo., mem. compensation com.; chmn., trustee William Wrigley Jr. Co. Found.; chmn., mem. pension com., mem. fin. com. Texaco Inc.; bd. dirs., mem. com. non-mgmt. dirs., mem. nominating com. Texaco Inc.; bd. dirs., exec. com., chmn., CEO Santa Catalina Island Co.; mem. corp. issues com., nominating com. Am. Home Products Corp. Bd. dirs. Wrigley Meml. Garden Found.; life trustee Northwestern Meml. Hosp.; benefactor, mem. Santa Catalina Island Conservancy; mem. Geneva. Nat. Bd. Govs.; trustee U. So. Calif., CEO bd. advisor, mem. devel. com.; life mem. Cataline Island Mus., Art Inst. Chgo.; founding mem. Cowboy Artists Am. Mus. Lt. (j.g.) USNR, 1954-56; lt. comdr. Res., 1956-77. Mem. Navy League U.S., Chgo. Hist. Soc. (hon. life) Field Mus. Nat. Hist. (life), Wolf's Head Soc., U. So. Calif. Oceanographic Assocs. (hon. life), Catalina Island Mus. Soc. (life), The Calif. Club, Saddle and Cycle Club, Racquet Club, Chgo. Yacht Club, Tavern Club, Comml. Club, 410 Club (chmn.), Catalina Island Yacht Club (hon. life), Tuna Club of Santa Catalina Island, L.A. Yacht Club, Lake Geneva Country Club (Wis.), Lake Geneva Yacht Club, Brook Club (N.Y.C.), Delta Kappa Epsilon. Office: Wm Wrigley Jr Co 701 N Loara St Anaheim CA 92803-9000

WRITER, SHARON LISLE, secondary education educator; b. L.A., Aug. 29, 1939; d. Harlan Lawerance and Emma Mae (Cordery) Lisle; m. Robert Vincent Writer, Dec. 30, 1961; children: Martin Carl, Cynthia Louise, Brian Robert, Scott Andrew. BS, Mt. St. Marys Coll., 1961; MS in Sci. Edn., Calif. State U., Fullerton, 1989; postgrad., U. Calif., Irvine, 1987, Colo. Sch. Mines, 1994. Cert. secondary tchr., Calif. Tchr. St. Mary's Acad., L.A., 1961-62, Escambia High Sch., Pensacola, Fla., 1962-63; rsch. asst. U. So. Calif., L.A., 1964-65, U. Calif., Irvine, 1965-66; tchr. aide Cerro Villa Jr. High Sch., Villa Park, Calif., 1975-76, tchr., 1976-88; tchr. Villa Park High Sch., 1988—, mentor tchr., 1990—; tchr. of yr. com. Orange (Calif.) Unified Sch. Dist., 1992, supt. adv. coun., 1990—, curriculum sci. com., 1991—. Active Villa Park Womens League, 1975—, Assistance League of Orange, 1991—; project leader, county coord. Orange County 4-H Assn., Anaheim, Calif., 1975-84; bd. sec. Orange County Sci. Fair, 1986-91, awards chmn., 1991-94, pres., 1994—. Recipient Outstanding Sci. Tchr. award Orange County Sci. Tchrs. Assn., 1993; named Tchr. of Yr. Villa Park High Sch., 1990, 94, Outstanding Coach Orange County Sci. Olympiad, 1990, 92, 94, Calif. State Sci. Olympiad, 1987. Mem. NSTA (conv. hospitality com. 1989, 90, hospitality co-chair 1994 nat. conv.), Am. Chem. Soc., Calif. Sci. Tchr. Assn., Orange County Sci. Educators Assn. (Disting. Sci. Tchr. award 1993). Roman Catholic. Home: 18082 Rosanne Cir Villa Park CA 92667-6431 Office: Villa Park High School 18042 Taft Ave Villa Park CA 92667-4148

WROLSTAD, HELEN LOUISE, interior designer, business owner; b. Portland, Oreg., Aug. 2, 1931; d. J. Sanford and Annette (Robins) Wrolstad; m. Glen Edward Dillon, Dec. 27, 1953 (div. Apr. 1976); children: Eric Edward, Karl Douglas, Nancy Sue. BS, Oreg. State U., 1953. Tchr. Millbrae (Calif.) H.S., 1953-54, Martinez (Calif.) H.S., 1954-57, Skagit Valley Coll., Mt. Vernon, Wash., 1970; shop-at-home design cons. Meier & Frank, Portland, 1976-86; owner interior design bus. Portland, 1987—; interior designer St. Luke Luth. Ch. Bldg. Projects, 1978, 88; interior designer Home in St. of Dreams Show, Portland, 1981. Photograph printed in Marine Biology Textbook, 1971; exhibited in Creative Stitchery Profl. Art Show, 1968. Pres. AAUW, Anacortes, Wash., 1970, PTA, Anacortes, 1971; co-chmn. Sch. Bond Drive, Anacortes, 1974; Sunday Sch. Supt. Anacortes Luth. Recipient 1981 Best Kitchen award Portland St. of Dreams Homebuilders; named Woman of Distinction in Design and Architecture, Columbia River Girl Scouts Coun., 1994. Mem. Am. Soc. Interior Designers (profl. mem.), Oreg. Remodelers Assn., Portland Art Mus., Oreg. Hist. Soc. (designer Kitchen of the 90's, 1992), Sons of Norway Lodge, Bergfreunde Ski Club, Kappa Alpha Theta Alumni, Kappa Alpha Theta, Phi Kappa Phi, Omicron Nu. Lutheran.

WRONA, PETER ALEXANDER, structural engineer; b. Cracow, Poland, Feb. 19, 1955; came to U.S., 1970; s. Wlodzimierz Stefan and Anna Maria (Czech) W.; m. Bernadette Maria Waskowska, Oct. 9, 1984; 1 child, Marie. BS in Civil Engring., U. Calif., Berkeley, 1976, MS in Structural Engring., 1980. Registered profl. engr., Calif.; lic. pvt. pilot. Staff engr. Bechtel Power Corp., San Francisco, 1977-79; project engr. S. Medwadowski Cons. Engrs., San Francisco, 1980-82, 85-87; cons. Bechtel Power Corp., San Francisco, 1982-83; sr. engr. Forell and Elsesser Engrs., San Francisco, 1983-85; project engr. C.H. Wells & Assocs., San Mateo, Calif., 1987-88; assoc. Dasse Design Inc., San Francisco, 1988—; pres., bd. dirs. Polam Fed. Credit

Union, Redwood City, Calif., 1986—; cert. vol. engr. Office of Emergency Svcs., State of Calif., 1986—. Bd. dirs., treas. Skyview Homeowners Assn., Hayward, Calif., 1986-89. Mem. ASCE, Structural Engrs. Assn. No. Calif. (mem. continuing edn. com. 1984-86), Internat. Assn. for Shell and Spatial Structures, Chi Epsilon. Home: 28091 Ziele Creek Dr Hayward CA 94542-2425 Office: Dasse Design Inc 33 New Montgomery St San Francisco CA 94105-4506

WU, ELLEN YUNG-HUA, pharmacology research scientist; b. Georgetown, Penang, Malaysia, Apr. 15, 1961; came to U.S., 1966; d. Sinmin and Betty (Chang) W. BA, St. Olaf Coll., 1983; PhD, U. Calif., San Francisco, 1988. Rsch. scientist Calif. Inst. for Med. Rsch.-Calif. Parkinson's Found., San Jose, 1989-91; sr. toxicologist Parametrix, Inc., Kirkland, Wash., 1991-93; rsch. scientist Agouron Pharms., Inc., San Diego, 1993—. Co-author book chpts.: MPTP: A Neurotoxin Producing a Parkinsonian Syndrome, 1986, Progress in Catecholamine Research, Part B: Central Aspects, 1988, Zenobiotics Metabolism and Disposition: Proceedings of the 2nd International ISSX Symposium, Kobe, Japan, 1989, Molecular Basis of Neurological Disorders and their Treatment, 1991, Neurotoxins and Neurodegenerative Diseases, 1992; contbr. articles to profl. jours. NSF grad. fellow, 1984-87. Mem. Internat. Soc. for Study of Xenobiotics, Am. Assn. Pharm. Scientists, Soc. Toxicology. Democrat. Lutheran. Office: Agouron Pharms Inc 3565 General Atomics Ct San Diego CA 92121-1122

WU, HUNG-HSI, mathematician, educator; b. Hong Kong, May 25, 1940; came to U.S., 1956; s. Tsao-Chih and Mary Tsun (Ouyang) W.; m. Charlotte Lee, July 1967; m. Kuniko Weltin, Aug. 9, 1976; 1 child, Colin Weltin-Wu. AB, Columbia Coll., 1961; PhD, MIT, 1963. Rsch. assoc. MIT, Cambridge, 1963-64; mem. Inst. for Advanced Study, Princeton, N.J., 1964-65; from asst. prof. to assoc. prof. U. Calif., Berkeley, 1965-73, prof., 1973—. Author: The Bochner Technique in Differential Geometry, 1988; co-author: (with R.K. Sachs) General Relativity for Mathematicians, 1977.

WU, JONATHAN CHARNGHAU, accountant, consultant; b. Chungli, Republic of China, Feb. 12, 1953; came to U.S., 1980; s. Fupei and Lianmei (Liu) W.; m. Liming Han, Mar. 25, 1979. BS, Fujen U., Taipei, Republic of China, 1975; M in Mgmt., Northwestern U., 1982; MA, U. Ill., Chgo., 1985. CPA, Tex. Asst. to v.p. Shus Found., Taipei, 1977-78; ptnr. Bianko Co., Taipei, 1978-80; adj. lectr. Roosevelt U., Chgo., 1983-84; sr. fin. systems analyst Tex. Dept. Community Affairs, Austin, 1984-86, asst. dir. acctg. system, 1986-87, dir. data services, 1987; chief fin. officer Full Employment Council, Kansas City, Mo., 1987-89; v.p. MC2 Internat., Pullman, Wash., 1989-92, pres., 1992—; mng. dir. The Changhao Group (China), Nanjing, 1993—; acctg. and tax systems cons., Austin, 1984-89. Author, editor: Job Tng. Ptnrship. Act Fin. Mgmt. Manual, 1986, Food Science, 1978; also articles. Served to 2d lt. Chinese Air Force, 1975-77. Mem. Am. Inst. CPA's, Tex. Soc. CPA's, Inst. Mgmt. Accts. (cert.), Inst. Internal Auditors (cert.), Northwestern Mgmt. Assn. Home: SW 360 State Pullman WA 99163 Office: MC2 Internat PO Box 246 Pullman WA 99163-0246

WU, QINGYUN, Chinese language and literature educator; b. Zhengding, China, Aug. 28, 1950; came to U.S., 1985; d. Ming and Xuejin (Zhao) W.; m. Yulong Jin, Jan. 23, 1979; 1 child, Lin Jin. BA in English, Kaifeng (China) Normal U., 1975; Diploma in English, Ctrl. London Poly., 1978; MA in English, So. Ill. U., 1987; PhD in Comparative Lit., Pa. State U., 1991. Lectr. English Zhengzhou (China) U., 1978-85; grad. lectr. Chinese Pa. State U., State College, 1987-91, coord. for Chinese Summer Intensive Lang. Inst., 1990-91; asst. prof. Chinese Calif. State U., L.A., 1991—, dir. Chinese Studies Ctr., 1991—. Author: (novel) Clouds and Rain: A China-to-America Memoir, 1994, (criticism) Female Rule in Chinese and English Literary Utopias, 1995, others; translator: (novel) Remote Country of Women, 1994. Recipient Bayard award Pa. State U., 1991, Acad. Merit prize for translation, 1986; Brit. Coun. fellow, 1976-77; Calif. State U. grantee, 1991-92, 94-95. Fellow Asian Rsch. Ctr. (Hong Kong); mem. MLA, Assn. Asian Studies. Home: 1233 Hartview Ave La Puente CA 91744-2328 Office: Calif State U 5151 State University Dr Los Angeles CA 90032

WU, SENG-CHAI, financial planner, life insurance agency official; b. Amoy, Fuchian, China, Oct. 19, 1930; came to U.S., 1954; s. Eng-Hwa and Lian-Hoe (Iu) W.; m. Evelyn M. Mangaser, Sept. 9, 1975; children: Patrick O., Michael L., Andrew J. BA, Union Coll., Lincoln, Nebr. CLU; ChFC. Sales rep., also regional sales mgr. Home Health Edn. Svc., Richardson, Tex., 1959-68; sales rep., mgr. Met. Life Ins. Co., N.Y.C., 1968-85; sales mgr. Met. Life Ins. Co., Arcadia, Claremont, Calif., 1982-85; fin. cons. Fin. Design, Rancho Cucamonga, Calif., 1985—; gen. agy. mgr. Franklin Fin. Svcs. Corp., Springfield, Calif., 1988—, Am. Mut. Life Ins. Co., Des Moines, 1991—. Active Philippines and Chinese Assn., Dallas, 1969-75; nominated to participate LIMRA Internat. Rsch. Mem. Pomona Valley Life Underwriter Assn., Arrowhead CLU Assn. Republican. Adventist. Home: 10988 Wilson Ave Alta Loma CA 91737-2438

WU, SHAUN-INN, computer science educator; b. Taipei, Aug. 11, 1953; s. Ger-tin and Yi (Dru) Wu; m. Li-Huey Wu, Jan. 17, 1981; children: John, Jimmy. BS in Math., Soochow U., 1975; MS in Math., U. Tex., 1979; MS in Computer Sci., N.Mex. State U., 1982, PhD in Computer Sci., 1988. Sr. sys. and software analyst Holguin Corp., El Paso, Tex., 1982-85; rsch. and tchg. asst. Dept. Computer Sci., N.Mex. State U., Las Cruces, 1985-88; asst. prof. computer sci. U. Minn., Morris, 1988-91; asst. prof. computer sci. Calif. State U., San Marcos, 1991-94, assoc. prof. computer sci., 1994—, computer sci. program dir., 1994—; steering com. mem. Small Coll. Computing Symposium, 1989—, conf. co-chair, 1991; program com. mem. Internat. Conf. on Artificial Neural Networks, Taiwan, 1994; sys. mgr. Choral Corp., San Diego, 1993-94. Contbr. articles to profl. jours. Bd. dirs. San Diego Chinese Cultural Assn., 1993-94; judge for speech contests Chinese Sch., San Diego, 1992; exhibit judge Minn. State Fair, 1989-90. 2d lt. Army of Republic of China, 1975-77. Grantee Sun Microsystems, 1994. Mem. Assn. for Computing Machinery, IEEE Computer Soc., Phi Kappa Phi. Office: Calif State U 333 S Twin Oaks Valley Rd San Marcos CA 92096-0001

WU, WILLIAM LUNG-SHEN (YOU-MING WU), aerospace medical engineering design specialist, foreign intelligence analyst; b. Hangchow, Chekiang Province, China, Sept. 1, 1921; came to U.S., 1941, naturalized, 1955; s. Sing-Chih and Mary (Ju-Mei) Wu. AB in Biochemistry, Stanford U., 1943, MD, 1946; MS in Chemistry and Internal Medicine, Tulane U., 1955; diploma, U.S. Naval Sch. Aviation Medicine, Pensacola, Fla., 1956, USAF Sch. Aviation Medicine, USAF Aerospace Med. Ctr., 1961; cert. of tng. in aviation medicine, U. Calif., Berkeley, 1962, 1964. Diplomate Am. Bd. Preventive Medicine, Am. Bd. Internal Medicine, Am. Bd. Psychiatry, Am. Bd. Pathology. Gen. rotating intern U. Iowa Hosps., Iowa City, 1945-46; resident Lincoln (Nebr.) Gen. Hosp., 1946-47, resident in pathology, 1947-48; resident in pathology Bryan Meml. Hosp., Lincoln, 1947-48; fellow, instr. in internal medicine Tulane U., New Orleans, 1948-54; asst. vis. physician Charity Hosp. and Hutchinson Meml. Teaching and Diagnostic and Cancer Detection Clinics, New Orleans, 1948-51; vis. physician Charity Hosp. and Hutchinson Meml. Teaching and Diagnostic Clinics, New Orleans, 1951-54; staff physician Holderman (Army) Hosp., Napa, Calif., 1958; staff physician Aviation Space and Radiation Med. Group Gen. Dynamics/Convair, San Diego, 1958-61; aerospace med. specialist, med. monitor for Life Sciences Sect. Gen. Dynamics/Astronautics, San Diego, 1961-65; aerospace med. and bioastronautic specialist Lovelace Found. for Med. Edn. and Rsch., Albuquerque, 1965-68; staff physician Laguna Honda Hosp., San Francisco, 1968-74; ret.; staff physician Kaiser-Permanente Hosp. all-night med. clinic, San Francisco, 1971-73; safety rep. and med. examiner U.S. Civil Aeronaut. Adminstrn., 1959; med. examiner Fed. Aviation Adminstrn., 1961; expert witness in forensic medicine and/or medicolegal jurisprudence for cts. Author 8 books and 100 tech. papers in field. Active mem. Planning, Rsch. and Devel. Commn. Redwood City; bd. dirs. Legal Aid Soc. Santa Clara County, U.S. Congl. Adv. Bd., Am. Security Coun. Found., Little House Sr. Multipurpose Ednl. Ctr.; Life Fellow Royal Soc. of Lichtenstein, Zurich, Switzerland, Oxford Club (N.Y. and Fla.), Royal Coll. of Heraldry. Comdr., flight surgeon M.C., USN, 1954-57. Recipient Gold medal Internat. Inst. Community Svc., 1976, J. Edgar Hoover Gold Disting. Pub. Svc. award Am. Police Hall of Fame, 1991, Albert Einstein Bronze medal, 1986, Cambridge Gold medal, Dedication Insignia. Fellow San Diego Biomed. Rsch. Inst. (bd. dirs. 1961-65, sec. of fellows 1961-62, chmn. of fellows 1963), Inst. Environ. Scis. (chmn. specifications and standards com.), AIAA (mem. nominating com. San Diego sect., plant rep. life sci. sect. 1963-65); mem. IEEE (vice chmn. San Diego chpt. profl. tech. group on biomed. electronics 1962-65), N.Y. Acad. Scis., Internat. Univ. Found. (hon. pres.), Internat. Acad. Found. (hon. registrar-sec.), Computer Club, Sigma Xi, U.S. Naval Inst. (life), Naval League of U.S. West-pac (life). Home: 250 Budd Ave Campbell CA 95008

WU-CHU, STELLA CHWENYEA, nutritionist, consultant; b. Kaohsiung, Taiwan, Sept. 22, 1952; came to U.S., 1976; d. Jin-Shoui and Sue-Tuan (Ling) Wu; m. T.K. Chu, Dec. 25, 1975; children: Christine, Whitney. BS, Fu-Jen Cath. U., Taiwan, 1974; MA, San Francisco State U., 1979. Registered dietitian. Intership U C berkeley, 1978; food svc. supr. Calif. Surgery Hosp., Oakland, 1979-80; nutritionist, cons. Solano Napa Agy. on Aging, Vallejo, Calif., 1980—; nutrition cons. Marin County Div. of Aging, San Rafael, Calif., 1981—; nutritionist San Francisco Commn. on Aging, San Francisco, 1990—; nutritional advisor Veggie Life Mag., Walnut Creek, Calif., 1993—. Chief editor quar. publ. Taiwanese Assn. publ., 1991-94. Cmty. liaison East Bay Taiwanese Assn., Walnut Creek, 1992-93; v.p. No. Calif. Formosan Fedn., 1993. Mem. Am. Dietetic Assn., Am. Pub. Health Assn., Jacob Inst. of Women's Health, Nat. Assn. Nutrition and Aging Svcs., Formosan Assn. for Pub. Affairs. Home: 7 Haven Ct Moraga CA 94556-2366 Office: San Francisco Commn Aging 25 Van Ness Ave Ste 650 San Francisco CA 94102-6033

WUDL, FRED, chemistry educator, consultant; b. Cochabamba, Bolivia, Jan. 8, 1941; came to U.S., 1958; s. Robert and Bertha (Schorr) W.; m. Linda Raimondo, Sept. 2, 1967. BS, UCLA, 1964, PhD, 1967. Postdoctoral rsch. fellow Harvard U., 1967-68; asst. prof. dept. chemistry SUNY, Buffalo, 1968-72; mem. tech. staff AT&T Bell Labs., Murray Hill, N.J., 1972-82; prof. chemistry and materials U. Calif., Santa Barbara, 1982—. Recipient Arthur C. Cope scholar award Am. Chem. Soc., 1993, Natta medal Italian Chem. Soc., 1994, Wheland medal U. Chgo., 1994. Fellow AAAS. Office: U Calif Dept Chemistry Santa Barbara CA 93106

WULBERT, DANIEL ELIOT, mathematician, educator; b. Chgo., Dec. 17, 1941; s. Morris and Anna (Greenberg) W.; children: Kera, Noah. BA, Knox U., 1963; MA, U. Tex., Austin, 1964, PhD, 1966. Research assoc. U. Lund (Sweden), 1966-67; asst. prof. U. Wash., Seattle, 1967-73; prof. U. Calif.-San Diego, La Jolla, 1973—; vis. prof. Northwestern U., Evanston, Ill., 1977. Contbr. articles in field. World champion cyclist Masters World Cup Track Points Race, 1990. Office: U Calif San Diego Dept Math # 0112 La Jolla CA 92093

WUNDER, HAROLDENE FOWLER, accounting educator; b. Greenville, S.C., Nov. 16, 1944; d. Harold Eugene Fowler and Sarah Ann (Chaffin) Crooks. BS, U. Md., 1971; M Acctg., U. S.C., 1975, PhD, 1978. CPA, Ohio. Vis. asst. prof. U. S.C., Columbia, 1977-78; asst. prof. U. Pa., Phila., 1978-81; vis. asst. prof. U. N.C., Chapel Hill, 1981-82; asst. prof. U. Mass., Boston, 1982-86; vis. assoc. prof. Suffolk U., Boston, 1986-87; assoc. prof. U. Toledo, 1987-93; prof. acctg. Calif. State U., Sacramento, 1993—. Contbr. articles to acad. and profl. publs. George Olson fellow, 1975. Mem. NAFE, AICPA, Calif. Soc. CPAs, Am. Acctg. Assn., Am. Taxation Assn., Nat. Tax Assn.-Tax Inst. Am., Beta Gamma Sigma. Office: Calif State U Sch Bus Adminstrn Sacramento CA 95819-6088

WUNDERLY, STEPHEN WALKER, chemist, researcher; b. Cleve., May 24, 1945; s. Ernest Edward and Lucille (Walker) W.; m. Bonnie Lynn Barrows, Oct. 4, 1969; children: Jennifer, Chris. BA, Coll. Wooster, 1967; MS, U. Cin., 1971, PhD, 1974. Postdoctoral fellow dept. chemistry U. B.C., Vancouver, B.C., Can., 1974-76; postdoctoral fellow dept. pharmacy and chemistry U. Calif., San Francisco, 1976; postdoctoral fellow dept. chemistry U. So. Calif., L.A., 1977; tchr. Ashland (Ohio) City Schs., 1968-70, St. Bernard (Ohio) City Schs., 1970-71; scientist Beckman Instruments, Fullerton, Calif., 1978—. Contbr. 17 articles to profl. jours. Fellow Am. Inst. Chemists, mem. Am. Chem. Soc. Evangelical Christian. Office: Beckman Instruments 2500 N Harbor Blvd Fullerton CA 92635-2607

WURDINGER, STEPHANIE ROSE, software engineer; b. Appleton, Wis., Feb. 8, 1951; d. John Lyle and Jacquelyn Mary (Bartlein) W. BA in Russian, U. Wis., 1978; MS in Geology, U. Minn., Duluth, 1980; BS in Computer Sci., No. Ariz. U., 1990. Geologist St. Joe Am., Tucson, 1981-85, Asarco, Reno, Nev., 1987, Echo Bay Mines, Reno, 1988; data processing supr. U. Ariz., Tucson, 1985-87; software engr. Honeywell Inc., Phoenix, 1988-91, 93, Metro Software Inc., Tucson, 1991-93, Artisoft Inc., Tucson, 1993—. Contbr. articles to profl. publs. Mem. IEEE, Ariz. Geol. Soc. Democrat. Home: 3640 E Lee St Apt D Tucson AZ 85716-3761 Office: Artisoft Inc 691 E River Rd Tucson AZ 85704-5824

WUSTRACK, KARL OTTO, plastic surgeon; b. Rochester, N.Y., Mar. 6, 1944; s. Otto Henry and Dorothy (Haversack) W.; m. Diane Harris Maurel, July 9, 1966; children: Gretchen, Sonja, Rosanna. BS, Stanford U., 1966; MD, Yale U., 1970. Diplomate Am. Bd. Plastic Surgery. Resident in gen. surgery Oreg. Hosp. State U., Portland, 1970-76; resident in plastic surgery UCLA, 1976-78; pvt. practice Oregon City, Oreg., 1976—. Bd. dirs. Willamette Falls Hosp., Oregon City, 1988—, chmn., 1994, 95. Named Most Valuable Player Masters Basketball 45 Over Tournament, Ft. Lauderdale, Fla., 1989; Oreg. State 3 on 3 over 40 champion, 1991. Fellow ACS; mem. Am. Soc. Plastic and Reconstructive Surgeons, Am. Soc. for Aesthetic Plastic Surgery. Republican. Office: 605 High St Oregon City OR 97045-2202

WUTZ, MICHAEL, English language educator; b. Leutershausen, Bavaria, Fed. Republic of Germany, Jan. 10, 1960; came to U.S., 1985; s. Josef and Else (Hannweg) W.; m. Marilee Rohan, June 3, 1990. Student, Julius-Maximilians-Universitat, Würzburg, Fed. Republic of Germany, 1983; MA in English, U. Mont., 1986; PhD in English, Emory U., 1991. Teaching asst. U. Mont., 1985-86, Emory U., Atlanta, 1987-89, 90-91; Asst. prof., asst. prof., 1991-92; asst. prof. Weber State U., Ogden, Utah, 1992—. Asst. editor Weber Studies; contbr. articles to profl. jours. German Acad. Exch. Svc. fellow, 1983, Inst. Internat. Edn./UN fellow, 1988, Emory U. fellow, 1989; Dartmouth Coll. grantee, 1991—. Office: Weber State U Dept English Ogden UT 84408

WYATT, EDITH ELIZABETH, elementary education educator; b. San Diego, Aug. 13, 1914; d. Jesse Wellington and Elizabeth (Fultz) Carne; m. Lee Ora Wyatt, Mar. 30, 1947 (dec. Jan. 1966); children: Glenn Stanley (dec.), David Allen. BA, San Diego State Coll., 1936. Elem. tchr. Nat. Sch. Dist., National City, Calif., 1938-76. Sec. San Diego County Parks Soc., 1986—; librarian Congl. Ch. Women's Fellowship, Chula Vista, Calif., 1980—; active Boy Scouts Am, 1959—. Recipient Who award San Diego County Tchrs. Assn., 1968, Silver Fawn award Boy Scouts Am. Mem. AAUW (sec. 1978-80, pub. rels. 1985—), Calif. Ret. Tchrs. Assn. (scholarship com. 1985-90, 92-95), Starlite Hiking Club (sec.-treas. 1979—). Home: 165 E Millan St Chula Vista CA 91910-6255

WYATT, LENORE, civic worker; b. N.Y.C., June 12, 1929; d. Benedict S. Rosenfeld and Ora (Copel) Kanner; m. Bernard D. Copeland, May 17, 1953 (dec. March 1968); children: Harry (dec.), Robert (dec.); m. C. Wyatt Unger, Mar. 26, 1969 (dec. Feb. 1992); 1 child, Amy Unger; m. F. Lowry Wyatt, Sept. 12, 1992. Student, Mills Coll., 1946-48; BA, Stanford U., 1950, MA, 1952; postgrad., NYU, 1952-53. Instr. Stanford U., Palo Alto, Calif., 1952, Hunter Coll., N.Y.C., 1052-53, Calif. State U., Sacramento, 1056-60, U. Calif., Davis, 1965-69; property mgr. Unger, Demas & Markakis, Sacramento, 1974-83; former actress and model. Pres. Sacramento Opera Assn., 1972-73; treas. Sacramento Children's Home, 1990-92, v.p., 1992—; former mem. bd. dirs. Sutter Hosp. Aux., Sutter Hosp. Med. Rsch. Found., Sacramento Symphony League, Temple B'nai Israel Sisterhood, Sacramento chpt. Hadassah, Sacramento Children's Home Guild; active Sacramento Opera Assn., Crocker Soc. of Crocker Art Gallery, Sacramento Symphony Assn., Sacramento Reportory Theater Assn.; founding mem. Tacoma Communities Art Sch.; mem. Temple Beth El of Tacoma. Mem. Joint Adventure Investment Club, Am. Contract Bridge League, Sacramento Pioneer Assn., Stanford U. Alumni Assn. (past bd. dirs. Sacramento) Sutter Club, Kandahar Ski Club, Sutter Lawn Tennis Club, DelPaso Country CLub (capt. women's golf 1983), Tacoma Country and Golf Club, Maui Country Club, Wash. Athletic Club, Tacoma Club. Republican. Jewish.

WYCKOFF, MARGO GAIL, pyschologist; b. Omaha, Jan. 30, 1941; d. Winfield Jennings and Gail Claudia (Leach) Hartland; m. Tom Lawrence Wyckoff, Mar. 17, 1971; children: Ted, Elizabeth. BA, U. Wash., 1973, MSW, 1975; PhD, Union Grad. Sch., Seattle, 1978; cer. Licensed psychologist. Clin. lectr. U. Wash. Med. Sch., Seattle, 1976-78, asst. prof. univ. Pain Ctr., 1980-87; assoc. dir. pain ctr. Swedish Med. Ctr., Seattle, 1979-83, dir. behavioral svcs., 1979-83; pvt. practice Seattle, 1983—; psychology cons. Providence Med. Ctr., Seattle, 1979-87. Contbr. articles to jours., chpts. to books. Mem. Wash. Psychol. Assn. (bd. dirs. 1986-87), Nat. Orgn. Soc. Workers, Internat. Assn. for the Study of Pain, Psychoanalytic Assn. (bd. dirs. 1982-84), Wash. Environ. Council. Democrat.

WYCOFF, CHARLES COLEMAN, retired anesthesiologist; b. Glazier, Tex., Sept. 2, 1918; s. James Garfield and Ada Sharpe (Braden) W.; m. Gene Marie Henry, May 16, 1942; children: Michelle, Geoffrey, Brian, Roger, Daniel, Norman, Irene, Teresa. AB, U. Calif., Berkeley, 1941; MD, U. Calif., San Francisco, 1943. Diplomate Am. Bd. Anesthesiology. Founder The Wycoff Group of Anesthesiology, San Francisco, 1947-53; chief of anesthesia St. Joseph's Hosp., San Francisco, 1947-52, creator residency tng. program in anesthesiology, 1950; creator residency tng. program in anesthesiology San Francisco County Hosp., 1954, chief anesthesia, 1953-54; practice anesthesiology, tchr. Presbyn. Med. Ctr., N.Y.C., 1955-63; asst. prof. anesthesiology Columbia U., N.Y.C., 1955-63; clin. practice anesthesiology St. Francis Meml. Hosp., San Francisco, 1963-84. Producer, dir. films on regional anesthesia; contbr. articles to sci. jours. Scoutmaster Boy Scouts Am., San Francisco, 1953-55. Capt. M.C., U.S. Army, 1945-47. Mem. Alumni Faculty Assn. Sch. Medicine U. Calif.-San Francisco (councilor-at-large 1979-80). Democrat. Home: 394 Cross St Napa CA 94559-3840

WYCOFF, ROBERT E., petroleum company executive; b. Tulsa, 1930; married. B.S.M.E., Stanford U., 1952, M.S.M.E., 1953. With Atlantic Richfield Co., L.A., 1953—, various engring. and mgmt. positions, 1957-70, mgr. western region Internat. div., 1971-73, v.p., resident mgr. Alaska region N.Am. Producing div., 1973-74, corp. planning v.p., 1974-77, sr. v.p. planning and fin., 1977-80, exec. v.p., 1980-84, chief corp. officer, 1984, vice chmn., 1985, pres., chief operating officer, 1986-93, also dir.; chmn. Lyondell Petrochem. Co., Houston. Mem. ASME, Am. Petroleum Inst. Office: Atlantic Richfield Co PO Box 2579 515 S Flower St Los Angeles CA 90071*

WYDEN, RONALD LEE, congressman; b. Wichita, Kans., May 3, 1949; s. Peter and Edith W.; m. Laurie Oseran, Sept. 5, 1978; 1 child, Adam David. Student, U. Santa Barbara, 1967-69; A.B. with distinction, Stanford U., 1971; J.D., U. Oreg., 1974. Campaign aide Senator Wayne Morse, 1972, 74; co-founder, co-dir. Oreg. Gray Panthers, 1974-80; dir. Oreg. Legal Services for Elderly, 1977-79; instr. gerontology U. Oreg., 1976, U. Portland, 1980, Portland State U., 1979; mem. 97th-104th Congresses from 3d Oreg. dist., Washington, D.C., 1981—; mem. Commerce com., subcom. telecom. and fin., health and environment, small bus. com. Recipient Service to Oreg. Consumers award Oreg. Consumers League, 1978, Citizen of Yr. award Oreg. Assn. Social Workers, 1979, Significant Service award Multnomah County Area Agy. on Aging, 1980; named Young Man of Yr. Oreg. Jr. C. of C., 1980. Mem. Am. Bar Assn., Iowa Bar Assn. Democrat. Jewish. Office: 1111 Longworth House of Representatives Washington DC 20515-3703*

WYLE, EWART HERBERT, clergyman; b. London, Sept. 12, 1904; s. Edwin and Alice Louise (Durman) W.; B.A., U. Louisville, 1930; B.D., Lexington Theol. Sem., 1933; postgrad. Louisville Presbyn. Theol. Sem., Temple U., 1933-35; D.D., Tex. Christian U., 1953; m. Prudence Harper, June 12, 1959; 1 son, Ewart Herbert. Ordained to ministry Christian Ch., 1935; pastor First Ch., Palestine, Tex., 1935-37, First Ch., Birmingham, Ala., 1937-41, First Ch., Tyler, Tex., 1944-54, Country Club Ch., Kansas City, Mo., 1954-59; minister Torrey Pines Ch., La Jolla, Calif., 1959-79, minister emeritus, 1979—. Bd. dirs. Scripps Meml. Hosp., pres., 1980-81. Served as chaplain, maj., AUS, 1941-44. Mem. Mil. Order World Wars, Am. Legion, Tau Kappa Epsilon, Pi Kappa Delta. Clubs: Masons (32 deg.), Shriners, Rotary, LaJolla Beach and Tennis. Home: 8850 N La Jolla Scenic Dr La Jolla CA 92037-1608

WYLE, FREDERICK S., lawyer; b. Berlin, Germany, May 9, 1928; came to U.S., 1939, naturalized, 1944; s. Norbert and Malwina (Mauer) W.; m. Katinka Franz, June 29, 1969; children: Susan Kim, Christopher Anthony, Katherine Anne. B.A. magna cum laude, Harvard U., 1951, LL.B., 1954. Bar: Mass. 1954, Calif. 1955, N.Y. 1958. Teaching fellow Harvard Law Sch., 1954-55; law clk. U.S. Dist. Ct., No. Dist. Calif., 1955-57; assoc. firm Paul, Weiss, Rifkind, Wharton & Garrison, N.Y.C., 1957-58; pvt. practice San Francisco, 1958-62; spl. asst. def. rep. U.S. del. to NATO, Paris, 1962-63; mem. Policy Planning Council, Dept. State, Washington, 1963-65; dep. asst. sec. def. for European and NATO affairs Dept. Def., Washington, 1966-69; v.p. devel., gen. counsel Schroders, Inc., N.Y.C., 1969-71; atty., cons. Schroders, Inc., 1971-72; chief exec. officer Saturday Rev. Industries, Inc., San Francisco, 1972-76; individual practice law San Francisco, 1976—; internat. counsel to Fed. States Micronesia, 1974-82; cons. Rand Corp., Dept. of Def., Nuclear Regulatory Commn.; trustee in bankruptcy, receiver various corps since 1974. Contbr. to: Ency. Brit, 1972, also articles in profl. publs., newspapers. Served with AUS, 1946-47. Mem. World Affairs Coun., Internat. Inst. Strategic Studies, Phi Beta Kappa. Office: 2500 Russ Bldg 235 Montgomery St San Francisco CA 94104-2902

WYLIE, KAREN ELIZABETH, local government official; b. Midway Island, Hawaii, Dec. 20, 1965; d. Gary Owen and Judith Ann (Stevens) Sauer; m. Steven Ware Wylie, June 26, 1993. BA in Sports Sci., U. Denver, 1986; MPA, San Diego State U., 1987. Mgmt. asst., adminstrv. svcs. City of Coronado, Calif., 1988-89; mgmt. analyst City Mgr.'s Office City of Carlsbad, Calif., 1989-91; mgmt. analyst Housing & Redevel. Dept. City of Carlsbad, Calif., 1991-93; adminstrv. analyst comml. devel. City of Burbank, Calif., 1993, adminstrv. officer comml. devel., 1993—. Bd. dirs. The Villas Homeowners Assn., Carlsbad, 1990-91, pres., 1991-92. Mem. Mcpl. Mgmt. Assts. So. Calif. (bd. dirs., regional chair 1991-92, regional liaison 1992-93, v.p. 1993-94), Internat. City Mgrs. Assn. Office: City of Burbank 275 E Olive Ave Burbank CA 91502

WYLIE, LAURIE JEAN, nursing administrator; b. Seattle, Mar. 13, 1951; d. Alexander James and Edna O. (Pulis) Wylie II; m. John W. Iverson, Sept. 21, 1974 (div.); children: Sara Jean, John Berger. BS in Nursing, U. Wash., Seattle, 1975, postgrad., 1977; MA in Nursing, Columbia U., 1990. Cert. sch. nurse practitioner, community health nurse, nursing adminstr. Nurse practioner Child Devel. & Mental Retardation Ctr., Seattle, 1975-76; EPSDT nurse coord. State of Wash., Seattle, 1976; sch. nurse Snohomish (Wash.) Sch. Dist., 1976-80; interim sch. nurse Lake Stevens (Wash.) Sch. Dist., 1980-81; cons. nurse Group Health Coop., Redmond, Wash., 1980-91; maternal infant nurse cons. Vis. Nurse Assn. Snohomish, 1986-88; nursing practice and govt. rels. coord. King County Nurses Assn., Seattle, 1987-90; exec. dir. Western Wash. Area Health Edn. Ctr., Seattle, 1990—. Mem. ANA (senatorial coord., congl. dist. coord., com. of examiners for sch. nurse practitioner cert.), Wash. State Nurses Assn. (PAC trustee, dist. pres.). Home: 923 N 195th St Seattle WA 98133-3503

WYLIE, PAUL RICHTER, JR., lawyer; b. Livingston, Mont., Dec. 25, 1936; s. Paul Richter and Alice (Dredge) W.; m. Arlene Marie Klem, Mar. 6, 1982; children—Lynne Catherine, John Michael, Thomas Robert. BS in Chem. Engring., Mont. State U., 1959; JD, Am. U., 1965. Bar: Calif. 1970, Utah 1967, U.S. Supreme Ct. 1971, Mont. 1990. Patent examiner U.S. Patent and Trademark Office, Washington, 1962-64; asst. gen. patent counsel Dart Industries Inc., L.A., 1967-81; pvt. practice law, L.A., 1981-86, Pacific Palisades, Calif., 1986-90, Bozeman, Mont., 1990—. Mem. ABA, L.A. County Bar Assn., Am. Intellectual Property Law Assn., L.A. Patent Law Assn., Am. Inst. Chem. Engrs., Am. Chem. Soc., Licensing Execs. Soc., Tech. Transfer Soc. Home: 106 Silverwood Dr Bozeman MT 59715-9255 Office: 1805 W Dickerson St Ste 3 Bozeman MT 59715-4131

WYLLIE, PETER JOHN, geologist, educator; b. London, Feb. 8, 1930; came to U.S., 1961; s. George William and Beatrice Gladys (Weaver) W.; m.

Frances Rosemary Blair, June 9, 1956; children: Andrew, Elizabeth (dec.), Lisa, John. B.Sc. in Geology and Physics, U. St. Andrews, Scotland, 1952, B.Sc. with 1st class honours in Geology, 1955, Ph.D. in Geology, 1958, D.Sc. (hon.), 1974. Glaciologist Brit. W. Greenland Expdn., 1950; geologist Brit. N. Greenland Expdn., 1952-54; asst. lectr. geology U. St. Andrews, 1955-56; research asst. geochemistry Pa. State U., State College, 1956-58, asst. prof. geochemistry, 1958-59, asso. prof. petrology, 1961-65, acting head, dept. geochemistry mineralogy, 1962-63; research fellow chemistry Leeds (Eng.) U., 1959-60, lectr. exptl. petrology, 1960-61; prof. petrology geochemistry U. Chgo., 1965-77, Homer J. Livingston prof., 1978-83, chmn. dept. geophys. scis., 1979-82, master phys. scis. collegiate div., asso. dean coll., asso. dean phys. scis. div., 1972-73; chmn. div. geol. and planetary scis. Calif. Inst. Tech., Pasadena, 1983-87, prof. geology, 1987—; chmn. commn. exptl. petrology high pressures temperatures Internat. Union Geol. Scis.; mem. adv. panel earth scis. NSF, 1975-78, chmn. adv. com. earth scis. div., 1979-82; mem. U.S. Nat. Com. on Geology, 1978-82; mem. U.S. Nat. Com. Internat. Union Geodesy and Geophysics, 1980-84, U.S. Nat. Com. Geochemistry, 1981-84; chmn. com. on objectives in solid-earth scis. NRC, 1988-93. Author: The Dynamic Earth, 1971, The Way the Earth Works, 1976; editor: Ultramafic and Related Rocks, 1967; chmn. editorial & writing com. Solid-Earth Sciences and Society, 1993; editor Jour. Geology, 1967-83; editor-in-chief Minerals Rocks (monograph series), 1967—. Served with RAF, 1948-49. Recipient Polar medal H.M. Queen Elizabeth, Eng.; Quantrell award, 1979; Wollaston medal Geol. Soc. London, 1982, Abraham-Gottlob-Werner-Medaille German Mineral. Soc., 1987. Fellow Am. Acad. Arts and Sci., Royal Soc. London, Edinburgh Geol. Soc. (corr.), Mineral. Soc. Am. (pres. 1977-78, award 1965), Am. Acad. Scis. (fgn. assoc.), Am. Geophys. Union, Indian Geophys. Union (fgn.), Nat. Acad. Sci. India (fgn.), Russian Acad. Scis. (fgn.), Russian Mineral. Soc. (fgn., hon.), Indian Nat. Sci. Acad. (fgn.), Geol. Soc. Am.; mem. Mineral. Soc. Gt. Britain and Ireland (hon.), Internat. Mineral. Assn. (2d v.p. 1978-82, lst v.p. 1982-86, pres. 1986-90), Internat. Union of Geodesy and Geophysics (v.p. 1991—). Office: Calif Inst Tech Geol Planetary Scis 17 # 25 Pasadena CA 91125

WYMER, NANCY ELAINE, plant taxonomist, consultant, habitat restorationist, educator; b. Kittanning, Pa., Oct. 5, 1948; d. Ernest and Helen Irene (Rattigan) Ruhland; children: Jason, Shawn. BS in Horticulture, U. Ariz., 1971, MS in Plant Ecology & Physiology, 1979; cert. in hazardous waste mgmt., U. Calif., Davis, 1989. Lab. technician USPA Bee Rsch. Lab., Tucson, 1969; landscape supr. Estes Constrn. Co., Tucson, 1974-76; pub. sch. tchr. Ariz., 1980-82; instr. Calif. State U., Sacramento, 1982-83; environ. intern Aerojet Corp., Sacramento, 1983, mem. sci. real world community rels. program, 1983-90; owner, prin. investigator Wymer and Assocs., Citrus Heights, Calif., 1984—; sr. ecologist Kleinfelder, Sacramento, 1991—; continuing edn. instr. Calif. State U., Sacramento, 1982-83. Author: Planetary Geology, 1988. Mem. Am. Geophys. Union, Calif. Native Plant Soc., Women Geoscience, Soc. Wetland Scientists. Office: 8100 Oak Ave Citrus Heights CA 95610-3219

WYNN, ROBERT E., retired career officer, electronics executive; b. Dallas, Jan. 31, 1942; s. Wendell W. and Thelma (Smart) W.; m. Lavenia K. Davis, Mar. 25, 1972; children: Leslie, Lauren. Bachelors degree, West Point, 1964; MEE, U. Tenn., 1971. Commd. 2d lt. U.S. Army, 1964, advanced through grades to commdg. gen., 1990; chief comm. Ops. Divsn. 5th Signal Command, Heidelberg, Germany, 1979-81; chief of staff 5th Signal Command, Worms, Germany, 1984-85; chief plans and programs, dep. chief staff Ops. and Plans DCS for OPS and PLANS, Washington, 1981-84; comdr. 2d Signal Brigade, Mannheim, Germany, 1986-88, U.S. Army Info. Systems Command/Tng. Doctrine Command, Ft. Monroe, Va., 1988-90; commdg. gen. 7th Signal Command, Ft. Ritchie, Md., 1990-92, U.S. Army Info. Systems Engring. Command, Ft. Huachuca, Ariz., 1992—; ret., 1995; dir. tech. staff Electrospace sys., Inc., Richardson, Tex., 1995—. Decorated Bronze Star, Legion of Merit, Silver Order of Mercury. Mem. Assn. U.S. Army Assn. Grads. (life), Armed Forces Comm. and Electronics Assn. (life, bd. dirs.), Sky Soldier (life, 173d airborne brigade), Signal Corps Regiment (life). Home: 703 Laredo Cir Allen TX 75002-5444

WYNN, ROBERT RAYMOND, engineer; b. Omaha, Mar. 4, 1929; s. Horace Oscar and Yvonne Cecil (Witters) W.; m. Joann Elizabeth Swicegood, June 28, 1974; children: Kay, William, Frederick, Andrew, Emma, Lawrence, Robert. Diploma in Nuclear Engring., Capitol Radio Engring. Inst., 1964; BSEE, Pacific Internat. Coll. Arts and Scis., 1964; AA in Bus. Adminstrn., Allen Hancock Coll., 1969; MSEE, Pacific Internat. Coll. Arts and Scis., 1971; MSMS, West Coast U., 1975, ASCS, 1985; BSCS, U. State of N.Y., 1985. Registered profl. engr., Calif. Meteorologist United Air Lines, Calif., 1949-53; engring. planner Aircraft Tools Inc., Inglewood, Calif., 1953-55; field service engr. N. Am. Aviation, Inglewood, Calif., 1955-59; R&D engr. Carstedt Research Inc., N. Long Beach, Calif., 1959-60; test engr. Martin Marrietta Corp., Vandenburg AFB, Calif., 1960-64; project engr. Fed. Electric Corp., Vandenburg AFB, Calif., 1965-69; systems engr. Aeronutronic Ford Corp., Pasadena, Calif., 1970-75; MTS Jet Propulsion Lab., Pasadena, Calif., 1975-83; engring. mgr. Space Com., Redondo Beach, Calif., 1983-84; engring. specialist Boeing Service Inc., Pasadena, 1984-86; cons., mem. tech. staff Jet Propulsion Lab., Pasadena, 1986—; instr. computer sci. and CAD, Jet Propulsion Lab., 1980-82. With USAAF, 1946. Mem. Calif. Soc. Profl. Engrs., Exptl. Aircraft Assn. (pres. Lompoc chpt. 1968), W. Coast U. Alumni Assn. Democrat. Home: PO Box 4138 Sunland CA 91041-4138 Office: Jet Propulsion Lab 4800 Oak Grove Dr Pasadena CA 91109-8001

WYRICK, DANIEL JOHN, science/health textbook editor, science specialist; b. Oakland, Calif., May 22, 1952; s. Charles Truman and Thelma Lillian (White) W.; m. Christine Evelyn Ingels, Nov. 10, 1972; children: Aimee, Emilie. BA, Pacific Union Coll., 1977, MA, 1984. Cert. tchr., Calif. Tchr. Pine Hills Jr. Acad., Auburn, Calif., 1977-81; prin., tchr. Fort Bragg (Calif.) Seventh Day Adventist Elem. Sch., 1981-85; sci. tchr. Lodi (Calif.) Adventist Elem. Sch., 1985-89; sci./health textbook editor N.Am. Div. of Seventh Day Adventist, Silver Spring, Md., 1989-95; sci. specialist Lodi Adventist Elem. Sch., 1995—. Author science curriculum; co-author: Every Friday, 1987, Life Science Health Series, 1993—. Youth leader Fairmont Seventh Day Adventist Ch., Lodi, 1986-91, ch. elder, 1988; youth leader English Oaks Seventh Day Adventist Ch., Lodi, 1991-93, ch. elder, 1991—; mem. Lodi Acad. Sch. Bd., 1992-95. Mem. Nat. Sci. Tchrs. Assn., Calif. Sci. Tchrs. Assn., Calif. Assn. Pvt. Schs. Republican. Office: Lodi Acad 1230 S Central Ave Lodi CA 95240-5907

WYRICK, WES(LEY), air force officer; b. Abilene, Tex., July 21, 1953; s. Edward Thomas and Floreene (Burgess) W.; m. Joy Ann Frank, Dec. 27, 1974; 1 child, Thomas Joseph. B in Maths., North Tex. State U., 1974; MS in Computer Info. Systems, Boston U., 1981. Cert. airline transport pilot. Commd. 2d lt. USAF, 1974, advanced through grades to lt. col., 1991; ops. officer, pilot USAF, Nev. and Saudi Arabia, 1989-91; chief F-117A tactics and test USAF, Nellis AFB, Nev., 1991-95; pilot Northwest Airlines, Mpls., 1995—. Writer songs; appeared in Discovery channel TV spl. Desert Storm, 1991. Decorated DFC, Air medals, Aerial Achievement medals. Republican. Office: Northwest Airlines Minneapolis MN

WYSOCKI, JO ANN, elementary education educator, librarian; b. Loup City, Nebr., Sept. 28, 1935; d. Mathew Robert and Evelyn Lucille (Dilla) W. BA, U. So. Calif., 1957, MLS, 1957; MA in History, Calif. State U., Long Beach, 1978. Cert. gen. elem., jr. high sch., gen. secondary, jr. coll., reading tchr., ESL credentials, Calif. Libr., jr. high sch. tchr. Compton (Calif.) Unified Sch. Dist., 1957-62; K-9 tchr. Erlangen (Fed. Republic Germany) Elem.-Jr. High Sch., 1962-63; elem. and jr. coll. libr., elem. tchr. gifted edn. Long Beach (Calif.) Unified Sch. Dist., 1963-73; libr. South Australian Sch. System, 1973-75; elem. tchr. L.A. Unified Sch. Dist., 1978—; libr. L.A. Pub. Librs., 1980—, Long Beach Pub. Librs., 1980-90. Pres. Harbor Coalition Against Toxic Waste, Wilmington, Calif., 1982—; v.p. Wilmington (Calif.) Home Owners, 1985-90, pres., 1991—; v.p. Friends Wilmington Br. Libr., 1985—, Family Fed. Credit Union, Wilmington, 1987—; vice chmn. 54th, 57th, 58th Assembly Dists., 1990-91, chmn., 1991—; mem. L.A. Citizens Adv. Com., 1985—; v.p., treas. Drumm Barracks Soc., 1988-91; mem. Rep. Nat. Com., 1990—. Named hon. mayor City of Wilmington, 1987; recipient Amicus Collegii award L.A. Harbor Community Coll., 1989. Mem. Wilmington Bus. and Profl. Women (pres. 1982-83, publicity chmn. 1990-91), Greenpeace, Sierra Club, Isaac Walton League, Am. Soc. Prevention Cruelty to Animals, Claremont Inst., Audubon Soc. Roman Catholic. Home: 1006 King Ave Wilmington CA 90744-3204 Office: Miles Avenue Elem Sch 6720 Miles Ave Huntington Park CA 90255-5012

WYSOCKI, MICHAEL, architect, artist; b. Gary, Ind., Aug. 24, 1953; s. Michael and Julia (Resanov) W.; m.Rachel Tolmachoff, June 12, 1986 (div. Sept. 1992); 1 child, Paris Michael. BS, Carnegie-Mellon U., 1973; MArch, U. Tex., 1979. Registerd architect, Calif., Sweden. Rsch. assoc. Sch. Architecture, U. Tex., Austin, 1979-80; archtl. designer Harrison Fraker Architects, Princeton, N.J., 1980-81; asst. prof. Sch. Architecture, U. Lund, Sweden, 1981-84; architect Salö Arkiteckter, Malmö, Sweden, 1984-86, Whisler-Patri Assocs., San Francisco, 1986-88; prin. architect Oneiros Architects, Santa Rosa, Calif., 1988—; mem. adv. bd. Sonoma Arts Coun., Santa Rosa, 1990-94, Alliance for Responsible Bldg., Sebastopol, Calif., 1993-94. Editor Foment, 1985-87; contbr. articles to profl. jours. Mem. adv. bd. North Bay League, 1989-91; bd. dirs. Sonoma Select, Sonoma County, 1991—, Lewlli Found., San Rafael, Calif., 1989—; mem. Design Rev. Bd., Sonoma County, 1988-90; participant Leadership Santa Rosa, 1990-91. Recipient Isanoff prize Rice Found., 1993, Design award Napa Valley Vintners Assn., 1991; Swedish Edn. coun. travel grantee, 1983; U. Tex. fellow, 1977-79. Mem. AIA, Svensk Architects Riksförbund, Commonwealth Club, Olympic Club, Bohemian Club, Sonoma County Exec. Assn. Office: Oneiros Architects PO Box 7808 Santa Rosa CA 95407-0808

WYSS, JUDITH ANN, artist; b. Spokane, Wash., Jan. 19, 1938; d. Maurice Landon and Catherine Evangeline (Deemy) Thomson; m. Loren L. Wyss, June 9, 1962; children: Emily Alison, Jennifer Ann, Isabel Jean, Edmund John. BA in English, San Francisco State U., 1961; BFA in Drawing, Mus. Art Sch., Portland, Oreg., 1981. Mem. Inkling Printmaking Studio, Portland, 1982-86, Blackfish Co-operative Gallery, Portland, 1992—, Graystone Gallery, Portland, 1984-92, Troy Co-operative Studios, Portland, 1981—. Exhibited in Oreg., Wash., and Eng. Past pres. and sec. Cmty. Music Ctr., Portland, 1975—, Alumni and Friends of PNCA, Portland, 1982-94; mem. bd. govs. Pacific Northwest Coll. of Art, Portland, 1993—; mem. awards/fellowships Adv. Coun. Literary Arts, 1991—; bd. dirs. Burdock/Burn Art Resource; sec., v.p. Wyss Found. Award for Best Unbuilt Chair, Table, Lamp & Chair, Portland, 1988; participant-juried show Oreg. Biennial/Portland Art Mus., 1985. Mem. Artists' Equity, Met. Art's Com. Per-Cent for Art Coms., Tri-Met Art (adv. com. 1993—), Oreg. Cello Soc. Democrat. Presbyterian. Home: 3028 SE Crystal Springs Blvd Portland OR 97202-8561 Office: Troy Studios 221 SE 11th Ave Portland OR 97214-1316

YABLUN, RONN, secondary education educator, small business owner; b. Chgo., July 11, 1950; s. Sidney and Phyllis (Bender) Y.; m. Anna Yablun, Dec. 17, 1977 (div. Jan. 1987); children: Melissa, Alex, Mark. BS in Edn., No. Ill. U., 1972. Cert. tchr., Ill., Calif. Tchr. art Page Sch., Beverly Hills, Calif., 1977-78; tchr. math. Calif. Prep. Sch., Encino, 1978-80; dir. of instruction The Reading Game, Encino, 1980-83; tchr. math. and computers Northridge (Calif.) Jr. High Sch., 1983—, math. dept. chairperson, 1991—; owner, dir. Mathamazement, Tarzana, Calif., 1983—; leadership sponsor Northridge Jr. High Sch., 1985-88, pentathlon coach, 1985-89, theatrical dir., 1989—. contbr. articles to jours.; freelance editor and writer ednl. manuscripts, 1991—. GTE fellow, 1989; grantee L.A. Unified Schs.; recipient Outstanding Classroom Tchr. award L.A. Unified Schs.. 1989. Mem. NEA, United Tchrs. L.A., Calif. Tchrs. Assn., Phi Kappa Sigma (sec., social chmn.). Office: Mathamazement 6047 Tampa Ave Ste 303 Tarzana CA 91356-1157

YACK, PATRICK ASHLEY, editor; b. Little Rock, Oct. 25, 1951; s. Leo Patrick and Sarah Ann (Dew) Y.; m. Susan Marie Courtney, June 7, 1980; children: Alexander Ryan, Kendall Elizabeth. BFA, So. Meth. U., 1974. Staff asst. U.S. Rep. Alan Steelman, Washington, 1975-76; press aide U.S. Senator Charles Percy, Chgo., 1977-78; reporter Fla. Times-Union, Jacksonville, 1979-80; regional reporter Fla. Times-Union, Atlanta, 1981-82; reporter The Denver Post, 1983-85, Washington bur. chief, 1985-87; nat. editor Atlanta Constitution, 1987-89; mng. editor The Register-Guard, Eugene, Oreg., 1989-94; editor News & Record, Greensboro, N.C., 1994—. Mem. Am. Soc. Newspaper Editors, AP Mng. Editors Assn., Nat. Assn. Black Journalists.

YACOB, YOSEF, lawyer, economist; b. Dire Dawa, Harar, Ethiopia, Nov. 12, 1947; s. Yacob and Egziaraya (Osman) Zanios; m. Betsy Ann Boynton; children: Sarah Ann, Matthew Yosef, Ezra Yosef, Jarred Yosef, Rachel Helen. BA, Linfield Coll., 1971; JD, Lewis and ClarkU., 1974. Bar: Oreg. 1975, U.S. Dist. Ct. Oreg. 1979, U.S. Ct. Appeals (9th cir.) 1980. Rschr. criminal justice State of Oreg., Salem, 1974, sr. administrv. analyst, 1974-76; adjudications specialist, legal counsel, law enforcement coun. Office of the Gov. State of Oregon, Salem, 1976-78; chief administrv. law judge State of Oregon, Milwaukie, 1978-83, dir. hearings, appeals, 1982-84; mng. atty. Hyatt Legal Services, Clakamas, Oreg., 1984-86; pres., sr. ptnr. Yacob & Assocs. P.C., Clackamas, 1986-93; dir. gen. for legal affairs, gen. counsel Ministry of Fgn. Affairs, Govt. of Ethiopia, 1993—. Co-author: Evaluation of Multwomah County District Attorney's High Impact Project, 1978. Home: 6885 SW Montgomery Way Wilsonville OR 97070-9702 Office: Yacob & Assocs PC Northwest Legal Svcs 6885 SW Montgomery Way Wilsonville OR 97070-9702

YAFFE, BARBARA MARLENE, journalist; b. Montreal, Que., Can., Mar. 4, 1953; d. Allan and Ann (Freedman) Y.; m. Wilson E. Russell, Aug. 30, 1985. Student, McGill U., 1970-73; BA, U. Toronto, 1974; B in Journalism, Carleton U., 1974. Reporter Montreal Gazette, 1975-76, Toronto Globe and Mail, 1976-79; reporter, columnist Toronto Globe and Mail, Halifax, N.S., 1979-81; TV bur. chief CBC-TV, St. Johns, Nfld., 1981-84, Edmonton, Alta., 1983; reporter Toronto Globe and Mail, St. John's, 1984-86; editor Sunday Express, St. John's, 1987-88; editor Vancouver Sun, 1988-93, columnist, 1993—. Recipient Gov. Gen.'s award Roland Michener Found., 1977. Jewish. Office: c/o Vancouver Sun, 2250 Granville St, Vancouver, BC Canada V6H 362

YAFFE, JAMES, author; b. Chgo., Mar. 31, 1927; s. Samuel and Florence (Scheinman) Y.; m. Elaine Gordon, Mar. 1, 1964; children: Deborah Ann, Rebecca Elizabeth, Gideon Daniel. Grad., Fieldston Sch., 1944; B.A. summa cum laude, Yale U., 1948. Prof. Colo. Coll., Colo. Springs, 1968—; dir. gen. studies Colo. Coll., 1981—. Author: Poor Cousin Evelyn, 1951, The Good-for-Nothing, 1953, What's the Big Hurry?, 1954, Nothing But the Night, 1959, Mister Margolies, 1962, Nobody Does You Any Favors, 1966, The American Jews, 1968, The Voyage of the Franz Joseph, 1970, So Sue Me!, 1972, Saul and Morris, Worlds Apart, 1982, A Nice Murder for Mom, 1988, Mom Meets Her Maker, 1990, Mom Doth Murder Sleep, 1991, Mom Among the Liars, 1992; play The Deadly Game, 1960, (with Jerome Weidman) Ivory Tower, 1967, Cliffhanger, 1985; also TV plays, stories, essays, revs. Served with USNR, 1945-46. Recipient Nat. Arts Found award, 1968. Mem. P.E.N., Authors League, Writers Guild of Am., Dramatists Guild, A.A.U.P., Mystery Writers of Am., Phi Beta Kappa. Jewish. Club: Elizabethan (Yale). Address: 1215 N Cascade Ave Colorado Springs CO 80903-2303 Office: Colo Coll Colorado Springs CO 80903

YAGER, JOEL, psychiatry educator; b. Bronx, N.Y., June 27, 1941; s. Edward and Natalie (Schwartzman) Y.; m. Eileen Danies, Oct. 8, 1964; children: Jonathan Eric, Alison Rachel. BS, CCNY, 1961; MD, Albert Einstein Coll. Medicine, 1965. Diplomate Am. Bd. Psychiatry and Neurology. Asst. prof. psychiatry U. Calif., San Diego, 1971-73; asst. prof. psychiatry U. Calif., L.A., 1973-82, assoc. prof. psychiatry, 1982-88, prof., 1988—; assoc. chair for edn., dir. residency edn. U. Calif. Neuropsychiat. Inst., L.A., 1991—, dept. psychiatry and biobehavioral scis. West L.A. VA, 1991—. Editor: Teaching Psychiatry and Behavioral Science, 1982, The Future of Psychiatry as a Medical Specialty, 1989, Special Problems in Managing Eating Disorders, 1991. Maj. U.S. Army, 1969-71. Recipient Joseph B. Goldberger award in clin. nutrition AMA, 1989, ANAD award Nat. Assn. for Anorexia Nervosa and Related Disorders, 1991. Fellow Am. Psychiat. Assn. (chair coun. on med. edn. and career devel. 1988-89), Am. Assn. Dirs. Psychiat. Residency Tng. (pres. 1979-80). Office: UCLA Neuropsychiat Inst 760 Westwood Plz Los Angeles CA 90024-8300

YAGER, PAUL, molecular bioengineering educator; b. N.Y.C., Feb. 7, 1954; s. George and Rose (Gsintermann) Y.; m. Teresa D. Sparkman, June 10, 1982; children: Sofie L. Sparkman-Yager, David W. Sparkman-Yager. AB, Princeton U., 1975; PhD, U. Oreg., 1980. Resident rsch. assoc. Naval Rsch. Lab., Washington, 1980-82, rsch. chemist, 1982-87; assoc. prof. Ctr. for Bioengring., U. Wash., Seattle, 1987-95, prof., 1995—. Contbr. articles to profl. jours. Mem. AAAS, Am. Chem. Soc., Biophys. Soc. Office: U Wash Box 352255 Seattle WA 98195

YAGJIAN, ANITA PALEOLOGOS, lawyer; b. Fresno, Calif., Apr. 5, 1954. BA in Philosophy, Stanford U., 1976, MA in Philosophy, 1977; JD, U. Santa Clara, 1980. Bar: Calif. 1980, U.S. Dist. Ct. (cen. dist.) Calif. 1983, U.S. Tax Ct. 1983. Atty. Sanford, Harmssen & Wilson, San Jose, Calif., 1980-82; assoc. Deering, Walther & Sands, Santa Monica, Calif., 1982-86; assoc. counsel Autoclub of So. Calif., Los Angeles, 1986—. Commr. Santa Monica Fair Election Practice Commn., 1985; appointed by Gov. Deukmejian to Santa Monica Mountains Conservancy Adv. Com., 1986-90; mem. L.A. Opera League; bd. dirs. Santa Monica Rep. Club, 1984-85. Assoc. editor Santa Clara Law Review, 1979-80. Mem. ABA, Calif. Bar Assn., Santa Monica Bar Assn., Westside Women Lawyers, Los Angeles Profl. Rep. Women (v.p., treas. 1984-85), Stanford Profl. Women.

YAGJIAN, MICHAEL ARTHUR, food company executive; b. Lynn, Mass., May 10, 1949; s. John Peter and Cora (Mekalian) Y.; m. Anita Paleologos, May 25, 1987. BA, U. So. Calif., 1970, JD, 1973. Bar: Calif. 1973. Founder, pres. Sub Station Ltd., L.A., 1971—, Gourmet's Fresh Pasta, L.A., 1971—; also bd. dirs. Sub Station Ltd., L.A., 1971—, Gourmet Fresh Pasta, L.A., 1971—; bd. dirs. DMD Food Products, L.A., 1987-89. Bd. dirs. Community Counseling Svcs., L.A., 1986—. Mem. Calif. Bar Assn., Nat. Pasta Assn., Assn. Inst. Food Technologists, Calif. Restaurant Assn., L.A. County Bar Assn., MENSA. Republican. Office: Gourmets Fresh Pasta 2200 S Figueroa St Los Angeles CA 90007-2049

YAKAN, MOHAMAD ZUHDI, political science educator; b. Tripoli, Lebanon, Aug. 28, 1938; came to U.S., 1988; s. Zuhdi Rasheed and Habibah (Shaaban) Y.; m. Sibylle Nickle, Apr. 8, 1988. HS, Internat. Coll., Beirut, Lebanon, 1956; BA, Am. U. Beirut, 1959; MA, A.U.B., Beirut, 1961; PhD, U. Mich., 1965. Asst./acting mgr. Prodeco/Pub. Rels.-Mktg., Beirut, 1965-71; asst. prof. Beirut U. Coll., 1965-71; lectr. law faculty Lebanese U., Beirut, 1966-71; asst. prof., dir. devel. and rel. Beirut U. Coll., 1971-88; lectr. Wayne State U., Detroit, 1988-89, Henry Ford Coll., Dearborn, Mich., 1988-89; v.p., gen. mgr. internat. I.A.S. Group, San Diego, 1989-90; lectr. U. San Diego, 1990-91; adj. prof. U.S. Internat. U., San Diego, 1991-93, assoc. prof., 1994—. Author: Lebanon and Challenges of Future, 1978, Political Authority in Lebanon, 1979, Hijrah Calendar, 1981; editor: Lebanese Constitutional Issues, 1975, Roman Law and Muslin Shari'a, 1975, Diwan Al-Mu'atamid Bin Abbad, 1975, Diwan Al-Shafi'e, 1981, Diwan Al-Baghdadi, 1983, Constitutional Law and Political Systems, 1982; co-editor: documents on Lebanon's Political System, 1975; author more than 100 articles and papers. Founding mem. Salwa Nassar Found., Beirut, 1970, Lebanese Polit. Sci. Assn., Beirut, 1959, Lebanese Assn. for Human Rights, Beirut, 1985, Internat. Coun. for Muslim-Christian Dialogue, Beirut, 1985. Recipient H.B. Earhart Found. award, 1965. Mem. Am. Polit. Sci. Assn., Middle East Inst. (assoc. Middle East rsch. and info. project), Acad. Polit. Sci., Western Polit. Sci. Assn., Acad. Polit. and Social Sci., Middle East Studies Assn., Fgn. Policy Assn., UN Assn., Internat. Studies Assn., World Affairs Coun. San Diego. Home: 9051 Westmore Rd San Diego CA 92126 Office: USIU Dept Liberal & Interdisciplinary Studies 10455 Pomerado Rd San Diego CA 92131-1717

YAKICH, DAVID ELI, international sales executive; b. Denver, May 31, 1957; s. Eli and Josephine (Goodnough) Y. Jr.; m. Carrie Elizabeth. BS, Colo. State U., 1979; postgrad., U. Minn., 1980-82; BA, U. Colo., 1984. Geophys. tech. Amoco Prodn. Corp., Denver, 1980-81; cons. geophycist Lear Petroleum, Denver, 1982-84; computer svc. mgr. Daniel Geophys., Denver, 1984-87; nat. sales mgr. Graphics Info. Inc., Denver, 1987-89; area mgr. Far East Auto-trol Tech., Denver, 1989-91; v.p. sales and support GeoGraphix Inc., Denver, 1991; dir. internat. sales Visual Numerics Inc., 1992-93; telesales mgr. NeoCAD, Inc., 1994—; computer cons. Daniel Geophysical, Denver, 1983. Mem. Soc. Exploration Geophysics, Denver C. of C. Republican. Roman Catholic.

YALAM, ARNOLD ROBERT, allergist, immunologist, consultant; b. N.Y.C., Apr. 1, 1940; s. Herman and Sylvia (Taber) Y.; m. Carol Ann Strocker, June 16, 1964; children: John, Matthew. AB, Johns Hopkins U., 1960; MD, U. Md., Balt., 1964. Diplomate Am. Bd. Internal Medicine, Am. Bd. Allergy and Immunology. Intern Jackson Meml. Hosp., Miami, Fla., 1964-65; resident in internal medicine SUNY Downstate Med. Ctr., Bklyn., 1965-67; fellow Scripps Clinic and Rsch. Found., La Jolla, Calif., 1967-68; cons. allergist and immunologist San Diego, 1970—. Maj. US Army, 1968-70. Fellow Am. Acad. Allergy and Immunoloy; mem. Am. Soc. Addiction Medicine (cert.), San Diego Allergy Soc. Office: 8929 University Center Ln San Diego CA 92122-1006

YALMAN, ANN, judge; b. Boston, June 9, 1948; d. Richard George and Joan (Osterman) Y. BA, Antioch Coll., 1970; JD, NYU, 1973. Trial atty. Fla. Rural Legal Svcs., Immokalee, Fla., 1973-74; staff atty. EEO, Atlanta, 1974-76; pvt. practice Santa Fe, N.Mex., 1976—; part time U.S. Magistrate, N.Mex., 1988—. Commr. Met. Water Bd., Santa Fe, 1986-88. Mem. N.Mex. Bar Assn. (commr. Santa Fe chpt. 1983-86). Home: 441 Calle La Paz Santa Fe NM 87501-2821 Office: 304 Catron St Santa Fe NM 87501-1806

YAMADA, STEPHEN KINICHI, lawyer; b. Honolulu, July 19, 1946; s. Harold Kiyoshi and Frances Sadako (Uchida) Y.; m. Amy M. Chiemi, Apr. 23, 1965 (div.); 1 child, Tammy Lynn; m. Kwi Nam Kim, Nov. 18, 1984. BA, U. Hawaii, 1968; JD, U. Calif., San Francisco, 1971. Bar: Hawaii 1972, U.S. Dist. Ct. Hawaii 1972; lic. real estate broker. Dep. atty. gen. State of Hawaii, Honolulu, 1971-74; pvt. practice law Honolulu, 1974—, pvt. practice real estate, 1975—; instr. Chaminade U., Honolulu, 1975, owner Sky Sch. Real Estate, Honolulu, 1976. Mem. exploring com. Boy Scouts Am., Honolulu, 1974; second vice chmn. 7th Dem. Dist., Honolulu, 1978. Fellow Hawaii Trial Lawyers Assn.; mem. ABA, Assn. Trial Lawyers Am., Hawaii Jaycees (state legal counsel 1976). Democrat. Lodge: Rotary. Office: 820 Mililani St Ste 712 Honolulu HI 96813-2937

YAMADA, TOMOKIYO TOM, advertising executive; b. Seattle, May 8, 1924; s. Toyojiro and Toku (Fukumoto) Y.; m. Miye Yamagishi, June 5, 1948; children: Mark, Ann Ellen, Grant. B in Design, U. Mich., 1950. Cert. tchr., Mich. Art dir. J. Walter Thompson, Detroit, 1950-53, San Francisco, 1954-60; art group supr. J. Walter Thompson, N.Y.C., 1960-65; v.p., creative dir. J. Walter Thompson, Tokyo, 1965-74; v.p., sr. art dir. J. Walter Thompson, N.Y.C., 1974-77; sr. v.p., design dir. J. Walter Thompson, San Francisco, 1978-91; exec. dir. world identity program J. Walter Thompson, San Francisco, N.Y.C., 1990-91; creative cons. Compass Group, Oakland, Calif., 1991—; instr. Golden Gate Coll., San Francisco, 1957. Contbr.: Designing Education in Values, 1958, Japan's Market and Foreign Business, 1971. Cons. Med. Edn. for South African Blacks, Washington, 1989-93, Japanese Am. Soc. East Bay, 1987-92. Recipient Silver award Clio, 1977, Andy award Advt. Club N.Y., 1982; named Best of Show San Francisco Ad Club, 1981. Mem. Oakland Asian Cultural Ctr., Oakland Art Mus., Berkeley Hist. Soc. Office: Compass Group 801 Franklin St Apt 603 Oakland CA 94607-4233

YAMAGATA, LESLIE CRAIG, contract specialist; b. Sacramento, Calif., Aug. 15, 1961; s. Mitsuru and Dorothy Tsuyumi (Toyota) Y. BA in History magna cum laude, San Diego State U., 1984; postgrad., Calif. State U., Sacramento, 1983-86. Exec. intern State of Calif., Sacramento, 1979; asst. forensic coach, 1980; life ins. analyst CalFarm Life Ins. Co., Sacramento, 1988-90, life/annuity specialist, 1989-90; contract specialist intern Gen. Svcs. Adminstrn., San Francisco, 1990-92, contract specialist, 1993—, contracting officer, 1994—. Mem. Japanese-Am. Citizens League, San Francisco, 1990, Very Spl. Arts Calif., 1991, Commonwealth Club San Francisco, 1992. Mem. Am. Mgmt. Assn., Nat. Contract Mgmt. Assn. (cert. assoc. contracts mgr., cert. profl. contracts mgr.), Nat. Forensic League, Profl. Mgrs. Assn., San Diego State U. Alumni Assn., Phi Alpha Theta, Phi Beta Kappa.

YAMAGUCHI, KIRK CHARLES, psychotherapist, educator; b. Denver, Oct. 4, 1956; s. Charles Shigero and Chiseko (Morishige) Y.; m. Jane Louise Stelzer, June 9, 1985; children: Wade Charles, Joseph Sean. BS in Comml. Recreation, U. Colo., 1980; MA in Counseling, Denver Sem., 1988. Wilderness ranch dir. Young Life, Creede, Colo., 1980-82; area dir. North Jeffco Young Life, Denver, 1982-84; Mountview sch. chaplain Youth for Christ, Lakewood, Colo., 1985-89; Lookout Mountain sch. chaplain Youth for Christ, Golden, Colo., 1989-91; program supr. Jacob Ctr. West, Grand Junction, Colo., 1991-94, program dir., 1994—; pvt. practice Arvada, Colo., 1988-91, Grand Junction, Colo., 1991—; prof. Colo. Christian U., Grand Junction, Colo., 1993—; pub. spkrs., trainer for various orgns., chs., and retreats, 1988—. Chairperson Mesa County Domestic Violence Treatment Providers Cert. Bd., Grand Junction, 1993-94; agy. rep. Mesa County Cmty. Evaluation Team, Grand Junction, 1993-94, Cmty. Evaluation Team, Grand Junction, 1993—; deacon Trinity Bapt. Ch., Wheat Ridge, Colo., 1989-91; mem. Senate Bill 94 Mgmt. Team, Grand Junction, 1994—. Republican. Office: Jacob Center West 1415 Main Canon City CO 81212

YAMAKAWA, DAVID KIYOSHI, JR., lawyer; b. San Francisco, Jan. 25, 1936; s. David Kiyoshi and Shizu (Negishi) Y. BS, U. Calif., Berkeley, 1958, JD, 1963. Bar: Calif. 1964, U.S. Supreme Ct. 1970. Prin. Law Offices of David K. Yamakawa Jr., San Francisco, 1964—; dep. dir. Cmty. Action Agy., San Francisco, 1968-69; dir. City Demonstration Agy., San Francisco, 1969-70; mem. adv. coun. Calif. Senate Subcom. on the Disabled, 1982-83, Ctr. Mental Health Svcs. and Substance Abuse Mental Health Svcs. Administrn. U.S. Dept. Health and Human Svcs., 1995—; chmn. cmty. residential treatment system adv. com. Calif. Dept. Mental Health, 1980-85, San Francisco Human Rights Commn., 1977-80; pres. Legal Assistance to the Elderly, 1981-83; 2d v.p. Nat. Conf. Social Welfare, 1983—; v.p. Region IX, Nat. Mental Health Assn., 1981-83; vice-chmn. Mt. Zion Hosp. and Med. Ctr., 1986-88; bd. dirs. United Neighborhood Ctrs. of Am., 1977-83, ARC Bay Area, 1988-91, Mt. Zion Inst. on Aging, 1993—, v.p., 1994—; bd. trustees Mt. Zion Med. Ctr., U. Calif., San Francisco, 1993—; chmn. bd. trustees United Way Bay Area, 1983-85; chief fin. officer Action for Nature, Inc., 1987—; v.p. Friends of Legal Assistance to the Elderly, 1984—; bd. dirs. Ind. Sector, 1986-92, Friends of the San Francisco Human Rights Commn., 1980—, CFO, 1980-85, vice chmn., 1985-94, CFO, 1994—, La Madre de los Pobres, 1982—, v.p., 1994—, Nat. Concilio Am., 1987—, Hispanic Community Found. of the Bay Area, 1989—, legal coun., 1989—; bd. dirs., pres. Non-Profit Svcs., Inc., 1987—, sec., 1987-90, chmn., 1990—; pres. Coun. Internat. Programs, San Francisco, 1987-89; mem. citizens adv. com. San Francisco Hotel Tax Fund Grants for the Arts Program, 1991—. Recipient John B. Williams Outstanding Planning and Agy. Rels. vol. award United Way of the Bay Area, 1980, Mortimer Fleishhacker Jr. Outstanding Vol. award United Way, 1985, Spl. Recognition award Legal Assistance to the Elderly, 1983, Commendation award Bd. Suprs. City and County of San Francisco, 1983, cert. Honor, 1985, San Francisco Found. award, 1985, 1st Mental Health Awareness award Mental Health Assn. San Francisco, 1990; David Yamakawa Day proclaimed in San Francisco, 1985. Mem. ABA (Liberty Bell award 1986), Internat. Inst. San Francisco (bd. dirs., 1989-95, pres. 1990-93). Office: 582 Market St Ste 410 San Francisco CA 94104-5305

YAMAMOTO, FUMIICHIRO, molecular biologist, educator; b. Osaka, Japan, Feb. 8, 1955; came to U.S., 1983; s. Takichi and Fumiko (Kurimoto) Y.; m. Miyako Azuma, Feb. 25, 1979; children: Fumiya, Ami. BS in Biology, Osaka City U., 1978, PhD in Developmental & Cellular Biology, 1983. Postdoctoral fellow SUNY, Stony Brook, 1983-86, rsch. assoc. dept. biochemistry, 1986; staff scientist, head of molecular biology The Biomembrane Inst., Seattle, 1987—, biosafety officer, 1987-89, radiation safety officer, 1991—; rsch. asst. prof. dept. pathobiology Sch. Pub. Health and Community Medicine U. Wash., Seattle, 1988-93, mem. grad. faculty, 1992—, faculty in Interdisciplinary Molecular and Cellular Biology Program, 1992—, rsch. assoc. prof. dept. pathobiology Sch. Pub. Health & Community Medicine, 1993—. Nihon Ikueikai fellow, 1974-78, 78-83; Osaka Prefectural Ikueikai fellow, 1974-78; Daido Seimei Ikueikai fellow, 1974-78. Mem. Am. Assn. Blood Banks, Am. Soc. Biochemistry and Molecular Biology, Am. Soc. Microbiology, Internat. Soc. Blood Transfusion (Jean Juilliard prize 1992). Office: The Biomembrane Institute 201 Elliott Ave W Seattle WA 98119-4230

YAMAMOTO, MICHAEL TORU, journalist; b. San Francisco, July 9, 1960; s. Harry Naoto and Noriko (Yoshitomi) Y.; m. Marianne Chin, Oct. 9, 1993. BA Psychology, San Francisco State U., 1981, BA Journalism, 1981. Editor San Francisco State U. Phoenix, 1980; news editor Hayward (Calif.) Daily Rev., 1979-80, Long Beach (Calif.) Press-Telegram, 1981; nat. desk editor L.A. Times, 1981-85; night news editor L.A. Times, Washington, 1986-87, investigative projects editor, 1988; dep. city editor San Francisco Chronicle, 1989-92, exec. projects editor, 1993, city editor, 1993—; adj. prof. Am. U., Washington, 1987, Calif. State U. at Northridge, Calif., 1984-85; vis. faculty mem. Am. Press Inst., Reston, Va., 1994, Poynter Inst. for Media Studies, St. Petersburg, Fla., 1995, San Francisco Unified Sch. Dist., 1994; fellow Coro Found., San Francisco, 1990-91. Recipient Dow Jones Newspaper Fund scholarship, Princeton, N.J., 1980. Mem. Asian Am. Journalism Assn., White House Corr. Assn., Soc. Profl. Journalists., World Affairs Coun. Office: San Francisco Chronicle 901 Mission St San Francisco CA 94103

YAMAN, F. M., JR., airport terminal executive; b. 1942. BA, U. So. Calif., 1964, MBA, 1969. Chief acct. Lockheed Corp., Burbank, Calif., 1965—; v.p. fin. treas. Lockheed Air Terminal Inc., Burbank, Calif., 1972—. Office: Lockheed Air Terminal Inc 2550 N Hollywood Way Burbank CA 91505-1055*

YAMANI, ELAINE REIKO, computer-peripheral company executive; b. Ogden, Utah, Apr. 2, 1945; d. Joe and Chieko (Kato) Yamani; m. Victor G. Sugihara, Aug. 10, 1970 (div. June 1973); 1 dau., Jo Ann Renae. B.S. in English and Psychology, Weber State U., 1965, A.A., 1967; M in Human Resource Mgmt., U. Utah, 1975-79. Personnel generalist Weber State U., Odgen, Utah, 1973-78; personnel specialist Cutter Lab., Ogden, 1978-81; human resource mgr. Iomega, Ogden, 1981-83, compensation and benefits mgr., 1983-85; dir. human resources Cericor Inc., 1983; personnel mgr., Hewlett-Packard, 1983—. Mem. Utah Personnel Assn. (pres. 1988), No. Utah Personnel Assn. (pres. 1980-81).

YAMAOKA, SEIGEN HARUO, bishop; b. Fresno, Calif., Aug. 21, 1934; s. Haruichi and Rika (Ogawa) Y.; m. Shigeko Masuyama, Apr. 3, 1966; children—Jennifer Sae, Stacy Emi. B.A., Calif. State U.-Fresno, 1956; M.A., Ryukoku U., Kyoto, Japan, 1961; M.R.E., Pacific Sch. Religion, Berkeley, Calif., 1969, D.Min., 1979. Ordained to ministry Buddhist Chs. Am., 1961. Minister Oakland Buddhist Ch., Calif., 1964-71; registrar Inst. Buddhist Studies, Berkeley, 1969-71, lectr., mem. Curriculum com., 1969-81, pres., 1981—; minister Stockton Buddhist Temple, Calif., 1971-81; treas. No. Calif. Radio Ministry, 1975-76; cons. ethnic studies Stockton Unififed Sch. Dist., 1974-76; chmn. Buddhist Chs. Am. Ministers Assn., 1979-81; bishop Buddhist Chs. Am., San Francisco, 1981—, research com., 1970-79; English sec. Ministerial Assn., 1972-75; assoc. in doctrinal studies Hokyo, Kyoto, 1974; mem. Bd. Buddhist Edn., 1975; vice chmn. No. Calif. Ministers Assn., 1976; trustee Numata Ctr. for Buddhist Translation and Research, Buddhist Dharma Kyokai Soc. of Am. Author: Compassion in Encounter, 1970, Teaching and Practice Jodo Shinshu, 1974, Jodo Shinshu: Religion of Human Experience, 1976, Meditation-Gut-Enlightenment... Way of Hara, 1976, Awakening of Gratitude in Dying, 1978; editor, advisor, writer: Dharma School Teachers Guide, 1979. Mem. Japan Karate Fedn., Shinshu Acad. Soc., San Francisco-Japanese Am. Citizens League, Calif. State U.-Fresno Alumni Assn., Pacific Sch. Religion Alumni Assn., Internat. Assn. Shin Buddhist Studies, Internat. Translation Ctr. Kyoto, Hongwanji Bishops Council Kyoto. Home: 37 Waterloo Ct Belmont CA 94002-2936 Office: Buddhist Chs of Am 1710 Octavia St San Francisco CA 94109-4341*

YAMASAKI, MITCH, history educator; b. Tokyo, Apr. 7, 1951; came to the U.S., 1959; s. Hisao and Fusako (Hirose) Y. BA in History, U. Hawaii, 1974, MA in History, 1978, PhD in History, 1989. Rsch. statistician State Dept. Social Svcs., Honolulu, 1980-84; sr. rsch. analyst Hawaii State Judiciary, Honolulu, 1984-88; assoc. prof. history Chaminade U. Honolulu, 1988—; state coord. Nat. History Day, College Park, Md., 1991—. Editor: Chaminade Hist. Rev. Named Outstanding Tchr. and Leader, Sears, Roebuck & Co., 1991. Mem. Am. Hist. Assn., Orgn. Am. Historians (com. on tchg. 1994—), Nat. Coun. for History Edn. Office: Chaminade U 3140 Waialae Ave Honolulu HI 96816-1510

YAMASHITA, JOHN HIROSHI, engineer; b. Tachikawa, Japan, Dec. 9, 1958; s. Saburo and Ruth Nobuko (Tokuhisa) Y. B of Mech. Engrng., U. Wash., 1980. Engr., stress analysis Boeing Comml. Airplane Co., Seattle, 1981-88. Republican. Presbyterian.

YAMAYEE, ZIA AHMAD, engineering educator, dean; b. Herat, Afghanistan, Feb. 2, 1948; came to U.S., 1974; s. Sayed and Merjan Ahmad. BSEE, Kabul (Afghanistan) U., 1972; MSEE, Purdue U., 1976, PhD, 1978. Registered profl. engr., Calif., Wash. Mem. faculty of engrng. Kabul U., 1978; engr. Systems Control, Inc., Palo Alto, Calif., 1979-81; sr. engr. Pacific N.W. Utilities, Portland, Oreg., 1981-83; assoc. prof. elec. engrng. Clarkson U., Potsdam, N.Y., 1983-85; assoc. prof. Gonzaga U., Spokane, 1985-87, dean Sch. Engrng., 1988—; prof., chair elec. engrng. dept. U. New Orleans, 1987-88; part-time rsch. engr. La. Power and Light Co., New Orleans, 1987-88; sr. cons. Engrng. and Cons. Svcs., Spokane, 1989—. Contbr. articles, reports to profl. jours. Bd. dirs. Wash. State Math., Engrng. Sci. Achievement, Seattle, 1989—; mem. Spokane Intercollegiate Rsch. and Tech. Inst. Adv. Coun., 1990—. NSF grantee. Mem. Am. Soc. Engrng. Edn., IEEE (sr.). Office: Gonzaga U Sch Engrng 502 E Boone Ave Spokane WA 99258-1774

YAMREUDEEWONG, WEERANUJ, clinical pharmacist, educator; b. Bangkok, Thailand, Aug. 1, 1952; came to U.S., 1984; d. Su and Wha (Woo) Chow. BS in Pharmacy, Mahidol U., 1976; BS in Pharmacy cum laude, Mass. Coll. Pharmacy, 1987, D Pharmacy, 1987. Clin. pharmacy resident Jewish Hosp. St. Louis, 1987-88; asst. prof. sch. pharmacy U. Wyo., Laramie, 1992—; cons. clin. pharmacy coord. VA Med. Ctr., Cheyenne, 1992. Roman Catholic. Home: 2120 E 17th St Cheyenne WY 82001-5016 Office: VA Med Ctr 2360 E Pershing Blvd Cheyenne WY 82001-5356

YAN, QIAO, neurobiologist; b. Shanghai, People's Republic of China, Dec. 20, 1955; came to U.S., 1983; s. Weinian and Ji Chang (Xia) Y.; m. Lilian Huacong Jiang, July 14, 1985; children: Heather H., Iris H., Johathan H. BSc, Fudan U., Shanghai, China, 1982; PhD, Washington U., St. Louis, 1989. Postdoctoral fellow in devel. biology Genentech, Inc., San Francisco, 1989-90; rsch. scientist I dept. neurobiology Amgen, Inc., Thousand Oaks, Calif., 1990-93, rsch. scientist II dept. neurobiology, 1993—; vis. scientist dept. of CNS rsch. FIDIA Rsch. Labs., Pardova, Italy, 1989. Contbr. chpts. to books and articles to profl. jours. Olin Med. fellow Washington U., 1987. Mem. Soc. for Neurosci., Internat. Brain Rsch. Orgn. Home: 1840 Marview Dr Thousand Oaks CA 91362-1846 Office: Amgen Inc 1840 De Havilland Dr Thousand Oaks CA 91320-1701

YANDELL, GEORGE WILSON, physician, psychiatrist; b. Greenwood, Miss., Mar. 30, 1924; s. George Wilson Sr. and Beatrice (Parsons) Y.; m. Margaret Ann King, Sept. 24, 1950; children: Brian Stuart, Lynn, Paul Reid, George W. III, Bruce Parsons. BA, U. Calif., Berkeley, 1943; MD, U. Rochester, 1947. Diplomate Am. Bd. Psychiatry and Neurology, Am. Bd. Child Psychiatry. Intern Evanston (Ill.) Hosp. Assn., 1947-48; rotating resident Seaside Meml. Hosp., Long Beach, Calif., 1948-49; resident in psychiatry Fairfield State Hosp., Newtown, Conn., 1953-54, Phila. Gen. Hosp., 1954-55; NIMH fellow in child psychiatry Langley Porter Psychiat. Inst., U. Calif. Med. Ctr., San Francisco, 1955-57; asst. clin. prof., supervising psychiatrist children's svc. U. Calif., San Francisco, 1957-68; lectr., asst. rsch. educator U. Calif., Berkeley, 1968-82; sr. psychiatrist Calif. Med. Facility Dept. of Corrections, Vacaville, Calif., 1981-83; pvt. practice psychiatry Orinda, Calif., 1957-93; ret. Contbr. articles to profl. jours. Pres., Orinda, Lafayette, Moraga Coun. Civic Unity, Contra Costa County, Calif., 1964-65. With USPHS, 1951-53. Fellow Am. Psychiat. Assn. (life), Am. Orthopsychiat. Assn. (life), Am. Acad. Child and Adolescent Psychiatry (life); mem. Calif. Med. Assn., Alameda-Contra Costa Med. Assn., No. Calif. Psychiat. Soc. (chmn. awards com. 1983-88), East Bay Psychiat. Assn. (pres. 1982-83), No. Calif. Regional Orgn. Child and Adolescent Psychiatry.

YANG, ANAND ALAN, history educator; b. Shantineketan, India, Jan. 12, 1949; came to U.S., 1966; s. Yun Yuan and Heng (Lo) Y. BA, Swarthmore Coll., 1970; PhD, U. Va., 1976. Instr. Sweet Briar (Va.) Coll., 1975; asst. prof. U. Utah, Salt Lake City, 1975-81, assoc. prof., 1981-92, prof., 1992—, chair dept. history, 1989-94. Author: The Limited Raj, 1989; editor: Crime and Criminality in British India, 1986; editor Jour. Asian Studies, 1995—. Mem. nat. bd. Reportory Dance Theater, Salt Lake City, 1985—; bd. dirs. Chinese Cmty Action, Salt Lake City, 1977—, Asian Assn. Utah, Salt Lake City, 1980-82, Wimmer & Wimmer Dance Co., Salt Lake City, 1979-80. Fulbright Hays scholar, 1994—; Travel to Collections grantee NEH, 1990, Bernadotte E. Schmitt grantee, Am. Hist. Assn., 1988-89; ACLS/SSRC grantee, 1985. Mem. Am. Hist. Assn. (profl. divsn. 1991-93, program com. 1986-87, 94-95), Assn. Asian Studies (asst. editor 1993-94, bd. dirs. 1991-92, 95—, coun. confs. 1989-92), World History Assn., Phi Alpha Theta. Office: U Utah Dept History 211 Carlson Hall Salt Lake City UT 84112

YANG, HENRY CHANG-LIEN, oncology educator, physician; b. Shanghai, China, Oct. 7, 1947; came to U.S., 1955; s. Li-Ching and Ling-Ta (Ling) Y. BA, Johns Hopkins U., 1968; MD, U. Pa., 1972; MTS, Boston U., 1983. Diplomate Am. Bd. Internal Medicine, Hematology, Med. Oncology. Asst. prof. Medicine U. Mass., Worcester, 1975-78, Tufts U., Boston, 1978-83; vis. lectr. in Pharmacology Harvard Med. Sch., Dana-Farber Cancer Inst., Boston, 1984-86; asst. prof. Medicine UCLA, 1986-92, assoc. prof. Medicine, 1992—; dir. outpatient oncology svcs. Harbor Med. Ctr. UCLA, Torrance, Calif., 1992—; dir. hemophilia rsch. lab. Meml. Hosp., Worcester, 1975-78; med. dir. South Cove Cmty. Health Ctr., Boston, 1978-82; mem. adv. com. Boston Area Health Edn. Ctr., Boston, 1979-80, adv. com. on health promotion Med. Found., Boston, 1980-82; cons. in med. oncology Magan Med. Clinic, Covina, Calif., 1991—. Contbr. articles to profl. jours. Vol. physician Sage Meml. Hosp., Ganado, Ariz., 1976; participant Mini-White House Conf. on the Asian-Am. Elderly, 1981; mem. Citizens Rev. com. United Way, Boston, 1984-86; bd. dirs. Pacific-Ackworth Sch. Found., Temple City, Calif., 1989-91. Johns Hopkins U. scholar, 1964-68. Fellow ACP; mem. Am. Assn. Cancer Rsch., Phi Beta Kappa. Home: 1618 Harper Ave Redondo Beach CA 90278-2725 Office: Divsn Med Oncology Harbor UCLA Med Ctr 1000 W Carson St Torrance CA 90502-2004

YANG, HENRY T., university chancellor, educator; b. Chungking, China, Nov. 29, 1940; s. Chen Pei and Wei Gen Yang; m. Dilling Tsui, Sept. 2, 1966; children: Maria, Martha. BSCE, Nat. Taiwan U., 1962; MSCE, W.Va. U., 1965; PhD, Cornell U., 1968. Rsch. engr. Gilbert Assocs., Reading, Pa., 1968-69; asst. prof. Sch. Aeros. and Astronautics, Purdue U., West Lafayette, Ind., 1969-72, assoc. prof., 1972-76, prof., 1976-94, Neil A. Armstrong Disting. prof., 1988-94, sch. head, 1979-84; dean engrng. Purdue U., 1984-94; chancellor U. Calif., Santa Barbara, 1994—; mem. sci. adv. bd. USAF, 1985-89; mem. aero. adv. com. NASA, 1985-89; mem. engrng. adv. com. NSF, 1988-91; mem. mechanics bd. visitors ONR, 1990-93; mem. def. mfg. bd. DOD, 1988-89, def. sci. bd., 1989-91; mem. acad. adv. bd. Nat. Acad. Engring., 1991-94; mem. tech. adv. com. Pratt & Whitney, 1993-95; bd. dirs. Space Industries Internat., 1993—. Recipient 12 Best Tchg. awards Purdue U., 1971-94, Centennial medal Am. Soc. Engrng. Edn., 1993. Fellow AIAA, ASEE; mem. NAE, Academia Sinica. Home: University House University Calif Santa Barbara CA 93106 Office: Chancellor's Office U California Santa Barbara CA 93106

YANG, HSIN-MING, immunologist; b. Taipei, Taiwan, Dec. 2, 1952; came to U.S., 1980; s. Sze Piao and Yun-Huan (Chang) Y.; m. Yeasing Yeh, June 28, 1980; children: Elaine, Albert. BS, Nat. Taiwan U., 1976, MS, 1983; PhD, U. Wash., 1985. Rsch. assoc. Tri-Svc. Gen. Hosp., Taipei, 1979-80; fellow Scripps Clinic and Rsch. Found., La Jolla, Calif., 1986-88, sr. rsch. assoc., 1988-90; asst. prof. U. Nebr. Med. Ctr., Omaha, 1990-91; sr. rsch. scientist Pacific Biotech, Inc., San Diego, 1991-95; mgr. Scantibodies Lab., Inc., Santee, Calif., 1995—; lectr. Yun-Pei Coll. Med. Tech., Shinchiu, Taiwan, 1979-80. Contbr. articles to profl. jours., chpt. to book; inventor in field; patentee on analyte detection device including a hydrophobic barrier for improved fluid flow. Joseph Drown Found. fellow, 1986, Nat. Cancer Ctr. fellow, 1987-88. Mem. Am. Assn. for Cancer Rsch., Am. Assn. Clin. Chemistry, N.Y. Acad. Scis. Office: Scantibodies Lab Inc 9336 Abraham Way Santee CA 92071

YANG, JEN TSI, biochemistry educator; b. Shanghai, China, Mar. 18, 1922; came to U.S., 1947; s. Dao Kai and Ho Ching (Yu) Y.; m. Yee-Mui Lee, Aug. 8, 1949; children—Janet Nancy, Frances Ann. B.S., Nat. Central U., China, 1944; Ph.D., Iowa State U., 1952, postdoctoral fellow, 1952-54; postdoctoral fellow Harvard U., 1954-56. Research chemist Am. Viscose Corp., Marcus Hook, Pa., 1956-59; assoc. prof. Med. Sch. Dartmouth Coll., Hanover, N.H., 1959-60; assoc. prof. U. Calif., San Francisco, 1960-64, prof. biochemistry, 1964—; vis. prof. Nat. Sci. Coun., Taiwan, 1967; Shanghai Inst. Biochemistry, Acad. Simica, 1978. Guggenheim fellow, 1959-60; Commonwealth fellow, 1967; vis. fellow Japan Soc. for Promotion of Scis., 1975. Mem. Am. Chem. Soc., Am. Soc. Biochemistry and Molecular Biology, Biophys. Soc., Protein Soc., Sigma Xi. Achievements include research interests in chiroptical phenomena of biopolymere and protein conformation in solution. Home: 1375 20th Ave San Francisco CA 94122-1707 Office: U Calif CVRI Box 0130 San Francisco CA 94143-0130

YANG, JERRY ZEREN, obstetrician/gynecologist, researcher; b. Xi Chong, Sichuan, People's Republic of China, July 2, 1958; came to U.S., 1989; s. Di De and Suhua (Zeng) Y.; m. Li-Ling Liao, Mar. 30, 1964. MD, West China U. of Med. Scis., Chengdu, Sichuan, 1983, MS, 1986. Intern West China U. of Med. Scis., Chengdu, 1982-83, resident, 1983-88, asst. prof., 1986-88, lectr., 1988-94, assoc. prof., 1994—; postdoctoral fellow U. Calif., San Francisco, 1989-92; fellow Stanford U., 1992—. Assoc. editor-in-chief An English-Chinese Dictionary of Ob/Gyn, 1989; contbr. articles to profl. jours. Cheng's scholar U. Calif., 1989; Nat. Com. of Scis. of Beijing, 1987. Mem. Chinese Assn. of Ob./Gyn., Anti-Cancer Assn. of China. Office: Stanford U Sch Medicine Falk Cardiovascular Rsch Ctr CV 194 Stanford CA 94305

YANG, LINDA TSAO, financial executive; b. Shanghai, China, Sept. 5, 1926; came to U.S., 1946; d. Ying Yung and Yu-shun (Ng) Tsao; m. An Tzu Yang, June 20, 1953; children—Yuelin T., Eton Y. B.A., St. John's U., Shanghai, 1945; M.S., Grad. Sch. Bus., Columbia U., 1948, M.Phil. in Econs., 1975. Econ. analyst Am. Overseas Fin. Corp., N.Y.C., 1955-58; founder, dir. Mother Lode Savs., Sacramento, 1977-80; savs. and loan commr. State of Calif., San Francisco and Los Angeles, 1980-82; prin. Linda Tsao Yang & Assocs., Davis, Calif., 1983—; dir. The Hong Kong Assn. of No. Calif.; bd. dirs., mem. budget and fin. com. Blue Cross Of Calif.; vice chmn. investment com., v.p. bd. adminstrn. Pub. Employees Retirement System, State of Calif., 1977-80; invited expert on restructuring fin. instrn. Senate Banking Com., Senate Fin. Com., Washington, 1981-82. Mem. policy adv. com. Coll. Agrl. and Environ. Scis., U. Calif.-Davis, 1979-85; mem. policy adv. com. Ctr. for Real Estate and Urban Econs., Grad. Sch. Bus., U. Calif.-Berkeley, 1980-82; mem. fairness commn. Dem. Nat. Com., 1984-85, compliance assistance commn., 1986-88; commr. Calif. Commn. on Teaching Profession, 1984-86. Recipient award Am. Savs. and Loan League, 1982, Achievement award Los Angeles YWCA, 1982, Outstanding Service award United Chinese-Am. League, 1982. Mem. Am. Econ. Assn., Acad. Polit. Sci., Orgn. Chinese-Ams., Trusteeship for Betterment of Women, Los Angeles, Asian-Pacific Women's Network Calif., Nat. Assn. State Savs. and Loan Suprs. (bd. dirs., nat. legis. com. 1980-82), Nat. Economists Club (Washington), Downtown Economists Luncheon Group (N.Y.C.). Office: 1619 Holly Ln Davis CA 95616-1010

YANG, SAMUEL CHI-AN, software engineer; b. Taipei, Taiwan, June 21, 1956; s. Chia Shan and Yuen Chen (Tsui) Y.; m. Connie Wong, June 21, 1992. BA in Biology and Computer Sci., U. Pa., 1979; MS in Computer Sci., Rensselaer Polytech. Inst., 1984. Data base analyst AT&T, Piscataway, N.J., 1979-82; programmer IBM, Poughkeepsie, N.Y., 1982, 83; software engr. Xerox Corp., El Segundo, Calif., 1984—; researcher in genetic algorithms and artificial life, UCLA, 1977—. Mem. Mensa, IEEE, Pi Mu Epsilon. Democrat. Office: Xerox Corp 701 S Aviation Blvd # 366 El Segundo CA 90245-4806

YANG, SHIGUANG, parasitologist, educator; b. Ma'anshan, Anhui, China, Nov. 21, 1954; came to U.S., 1986; s. Guilin and Xiufang Zhu; m. Chunwei Du, Jan. 30, 1984; children: Hongfei, Annie. DVM, Anhui Agrl. U., 1981; MS, Nanjing Agrl. U., Jiangsu, China, 1984; PhD, Purdue U., 1989. Grad. rsch. asst. Nanjing Agrl. U., 1982-84, instr., 1985; grad. rsch. asst. Purdue U., West Lafayette, Ind., 1986-89; postdoctoral rsch. assoc. U. Wyo., Laramie, 1989-91; rsch. asst. prof. Utah State U., Logan, 1991—. Contbr. articles to sci. jours. Grantee Utah State U., 1992-94. Mem. AAAS, Am. Soc. Parasitologists. Home: 1747 E 1550 North St Logan UT 84341 Office: Utah State U ADVS Dept UMC 5600 Logan UT 84322

YANG, XUEMING, research chemist; b. Huzhou, Zhejiang, China, Oct. 11, 1962; came to U.S., 1985; s. Fatang and Xingzi Yang; m. Mona Pan, May 25, 1988. BS in Physics, Zhejiang Normal U., Jinhua, China, 1982; MS in Chemistry, Dalian Inst. Chem. Physics, China, 1985; PhD in Chemistry, U. Calif., Santa Barbara, 1991. Rsch. assoc. Princeton (N.J.) U., 1991-93; rsch. chemist Lawrence Berkeley (Calif.) Lab., 1993—. Contbr. numerous articles to profl. jours. U. Calif.-Santa Barbara Regents fellow, 1989-90. Home: 2924 Santa Clara Ave Apt 4 El Cerrito CA 94530 Office: Lawrence Berkeley Lab 1 Cyclotron Rd Berkeley CA 94720

YANICK, MILES, architect; b. Clinton, Iowa, Sept. 25, 1935; s. Nickolas Miles and Marie Cathrine (Thede) Y.; m. Barbara Taze, Dec. 13, 1963 (div. Mar. 1975); children: Aaron, Taze; m. Molly Louise Gordon, Mar. 25, 1978. BArch, U. Wash., 1962. Assoc. landscape architect Richard Haag/Landscape Architects, Seattle, 1963-68; prin. architect Miles Yanick & Co./Architects, Landscape Design, Planners, Seattle/Bainbridge Island, Wash., 1968—. Vice chair Seattle Landmarks Preservation Bd., 1970-73; mem. Bainbridge Island Planning Adv. Bd., 1978-81. Recipient Dirs. Honor award West Coast Art Dirs., 1972; Kent Beautiful award City of Kent, 1970, U.S. Dept. Housing and Urban Devel. Cultural Design Energy Conservation award, 1994. Mem. AIA (Honor award 1971, Cert. of Achievement 1993). Office: Miles Yanick & Co Architects/Landscape Design 600 Winslow Way E Bainbridge Island WA 98110

YANOFSKY, CHARLES, biology educator; b. N.Y.C., Apr. 17, 1925; s. Frank and Jennie (Kopatz) Y.; m. Carol Cohen, June 19, 1949, (dec. Dec. 1990); children: Stephen David, Robert Howard, Martin Fred; m. Edna Crawford, Jan. 4, 1992. BS, CCNY, 1948; MS, Yale U., 1950, PhD, 1951, DSc (hon.), 1981; DSc (hon.), U. Chgo., 1980. Rsch. asst. Yale U., 1951-54; asst. prof. microbiology Western Res. U. Med. Sch., 1954-57; mem. faculty Stanford U., 1958—, prof. biology, 1961—, Herzstein prof. biology, 1966—; career investigator Am. Heart Assn., 1969-95. With AUS, 1944-46. Recipient Lederle Med. Faculty award, 1957; Eli Lilly award bacteriology, 1959; U.S. Steel Co. award molecular biology, 1964; Howard Taylor Ricketts award U. Chgo., 1966; Albert and Mary Lasker award, 1971; Townsend Harris medal Coll. City N.Y., 1973; Louisa Gross Horwitz prize in biology and biochemistry Columbia U., 1976; V.D. Mattia award Roche Inst., 1982; medal Genetics Soc. Am., 1983; Internat. award Gairdner Found., 1985; named Passano Laureate Passano Found., 1992. Mem. NAS (Selman A. Waksman award in microbiology 1972), Am. Acad. Arts and Scis., Genetics Soc. Am. (pres. 1969, Thomas Hunt Morgan medal 1990), Am. Soc. Biol. Chemists (pres. 1984), Royal Soc. (fgn. mem.), Japanese Biochem. Soc. (hon.). Home: 725 Mayfield Ave Stanford CA 94305-1016 Office: Stanford U Dept Of Biological Sci Stanford CA 94305

YAO, LAWRENCE, radiologist; b. Chgo., June 23, 1959; s. John and Eleanor Yao. BA, Brown U., 1981, MD, 1985. Diplomate Am. Bd. Radiology, Nat. Bd. Med. Examiners. Med. intern Miriam Hosp., Brown U., Providence, 1985-86; radiology resident Albany (N.Y.) Med. Ctr. Hosp., 1986-90; fellow musculoskeletal imaging dept. radiol. scis. UCLA Ctr. for the Health Scis., 1990-91, asst. prof. dept. radiol. scis., 1991—. Reviewer Radiology, 1993—; contbr. numerous articles to profl. jours. Home: 11044 Ophir Dr Apt 601 Los Angeles CA 90024-2003 Office: Dept Radiol Scis UCLA Med Ctr 10833 Le Conte Ave Los Angeles CA 90024

YAO, MENG-CHAO, molecular geneticist; b. Taipei, Taiwan, Mar. 21, 1949; s. Da-Liang and Shing (Huang) Y.; m. Ching-Ho Chang, Nov. 8, 1974;

1 child, Kairu. BS, Nat. Taiwan U., 1971; PhD, U. Rochester, 1975. Postdoctoral assoc. Yale U., New Haven, Conn., 1975-78; asst. prof. Washington U., St. Louis, 1978-84, assoc. prof., 1984-86; mem. Fred Hutchinson Cancer Rsch. Ctr., Seattle, Wash., 1986—; affil. prof. U. Wash., 1988—; rev. bd. Jour. Eukanyotic Microbiology, 1991-95. Editl. bd.: Jour. Protozoology, 1989-91, various NIH publs.; contbr. articles to profl. jours. Recipient career devel. award NIH, Bethesda, Md., 1983, rsch. grantee NIH, NSF. Mem. AAAS, Am. Assn. Cell Biology, Soc. Chinese Bioscientist in Am. Home: 3724 Cascadia Ave S Seattle WA 98144-7220 Office: Fred Hutchinson Cancer Rsch 1124 Columbia St Seattle WA 98104-2015

YAO, STEPHEN APUY, health services administrator; b. Quezon City, The Philippines, May 20, 1968; came to U.S., 1981; s. Jimmy and Sol (Apuy) Y. BS in Biol. Scis., U. Calif., Irvine, 1990; M of Health Adminstrn., U. La Verne, 1994. Acct. asst. Hershey Comms. & Characters Restaurant & Ent., Inc., Irvine, 1986-91; researcher developmental cell biology dept. U. Calif., Irvine, 1987-89; blood gas technician internal medicine dept. L.A. County-U. So. Calif. Med. Ctr., 1991—, adminstrv. resident, 1993—; adminstrv. resident El Monte (Calif.) Comprehensive Health Ctr., 1993—; mem. L.A. County Dept. Health Svcs. Mgmt. Forum; mem. quality assurance com. and automation com. Pulmonary Physiology Lab., L.A. County-U. So. Calif. Med. Ctr. Sponsor World Vision, Pasadena, Calif., 1986—; vol. Interfaith, Tijuana, Mex., 1987-89, Palamores Home for Aged, Pomona, Calif., 1992; tutor Calif. Literacy Program, Pomona, 1992; vol. Fred Jordan Mission, Pomona Valley Hosp., 1985-86, Orange Shelter for Homeless. Coll. scholar Pomona Valley Hosp. Med. Ctr., 1985-86. Mem. Am. Coll. Healthcare Execs. (pres., founder local student chpt. 1993-94), Nat. Mgmt. Assn. (asst. to mktg. dir. local chpt. 1993-94), Chicanos for Creative Medicine, Internat. Student Club, World Vision. Office: LAC & U So Calif Med Ctr Internal Medicine Dept 1200 N State St Los Angeles CA 90033-4525

YAPLE, HENRY MACK, library director; b. Vicksburg, Mich., May 30, 1940; s. Henry J. and Pauline B. (Spencer) Y.; m. Marilyn Lou Bales, Dec. 31, 1971; children: Sean H., Kendra S. BA in English with hons., Kalamazoo Coll., 1963; MA, U. Idaho, 1966; postgrad., U. d'Aix-Marseille, France, 1965-66, U. Toronto, 1966-69; MLS, W. Mich. U., 1972. Order libr. Mich. State U., E. Lansing, 1972-74, humanities bibliographer, 1974-78; acquisitions libr. U. Wyo., Laramie, 1978-87; libr. dir. Whitman Coll., Walla Walla, Wash., 1987—; Mem. Wyo. Coun. for the Humanities, 1982-86. U. Toronto scholar, 1966-69; Rotary fellow, 1965, 66; U. Wyo. rsch. grantee, 1982, 86. Mem. ALA, Wyo. Libr. Assn. (pres. 1984-85), Nat. Ski Patrol System (sr. patroller 1978—, nat. #6946 1988), Wash. Libr. Assn., Northwest Assn. of Pvt. Colls. and U. Librs. (pres. 1987-88, 94-95), Rotary (Walla Walla), Beta Phi Mu. Home: 1889 Fern St Walla Walla WA 99362-9393 Office: Whitman Coll Office Libr 345 Boyer Ave Walla Walla WA 99362-2067

YARAR, BAKI, metallurgical engineering educator; b. Adana, Turkey, Feb. 28, 1941; came to U.S., 1980; s. Salih and Sidika Yarar; m. Ruth G. Yarar; children: Deniz, Defne. BSc in Chemistry, Mid. East Tech. U., Ankara, Turkey, 1965, MSc in Chemistry, 1966; PhD in Surface Chemistry, U. London, 1969; DIC in Mineral Tech., Imperial Coll. London, 1969. Instr. Mid. East Tech. U., 1970-71, asst. prof., 1971-76, assoc. prof., 1976-79; vis. prof. U. B.C., Vancouver, Can., 1979-80; assoc. prof. Colo. Sch. of Mines, Golden, 1980-86, prof., 1986—; pvt. practice cons. in mineral processing, worldwide, 1980—. Author chpts. to books, over 120 papers; editor books; mem. editl. bd. 4 jours. Lt. Turkish Army, 1970-71. Holder numerous awards and certificates of recognition. Mem. Soc. Mining Engrs. (chmn. fundamental com. 1989), Am. Chem. Soc., Materials Rsch. Soc., Sigma Xi (life, pres. CSM chpt.). Home: 13260 Braun Rd Golden CO 80401-1643 Office: Colo Sch Mines Dept Metal Engring Golden CO 80401

YARBOROUGH, MARK ASHLEY, philosophy educator, bioethicist; b. Brimingham, Ala., Nov. 14, 1955; s. Joseph Franklin and Jocelyn (Allen) Y.; m. Pirjo Paula Jauhiainen, Nov. 13, 1981. BA cum laude, Berry Coll., Rome, Ga., 1977; MA, U. Tenn., 1980, PhD, 1984. Instr. Auburn (Ala.) U., 1982-84; asst. prof. U. Colo., Denver, 1984-91, assoc. prof., 1991—; presenter in field. Author: Medicine and Money, 1990; contbr. articles to profl. jours. Grantee GTE, 1991, faculty U. Colo., 1991-93. Mem. Am. Philos. Assn., Soc. Health and Human Values, Alpha Chi. Office: U Colo Health Sci Ctr 4200 E 9th Ave Denver CO 80220-3706

YARIV, AMNON, electrical engineering educator, scientist; b. Tel Aviv, Israel, Apr. 13, 1930; came to U.S., 1951, naturalized, 1964; s. Shraga and Henya (Davidson) Y.; m. Frances Pokras, Apr. 10, 1972; children: Elizabeth, Dana, Gabriela. B.S., U. Calif., Berkeley, 1954, M.S., 1956, Ph.D., 1958. Mem. tech. staff Bell Telephone Labs., 1959-63; dir. laser research Watkins-Johnson Co., 1963-64; mem. faculty Calif. Inst. Tech., 1964—, Thomas G. Myers prof. elec. engring. and applied physics, 1966—; chmn. bd. ORTEL Inc., Accuwave Corp.; cons. in field. Author: Quantum Electronics, 1967, 75, 85, Introduction to Optical Electronics, 1971, 77, 89, Theory and Applications of Quantum Mechanics, Propagation of Light in Crystals. Served with Israeli Army, 1948-50. Recipient Pender award U. Pa., Harvey prize Technion, Israel, 1992. Fellow IEEE (Quantum Electronics award 1980), Am. Optical Soc. (Ives medal 1986), Am. Acad. Arts and Scis.; mem. NAS, NAE, Am. Phys. Soc. Office: 1201 E California Blvd Pasadena CA 91125-0001

YARRIGLE, CHARLENE SANDRA SHUEY, realtor, investment counselor; b. Redlands, Calif., July 25, 1940; d. Troy Frank and Anna (Miskew) Shuey; m. Robert Charles Yarrigle, Oct. 16, 1965 (div. July 1985); children: Stephanie Ann, Steven Charles. AA, San Bernardino (Calif.) Coll., 1965; student, Ariz. State U., 1965-66; BS, Northern Mich. U., 1976, postgrad., 1976-77. Clk. Bungalow Grocery, Redlands, 1957-59; operator Pacific Telephone Co., San Bernardino, 1958-61; service rep. So. Calif. Gas, San Bernardino, 1961-66; tchr. bus. Gwinn (Mich.) High Sch., 1976-78; realtor, investment counselor Remax Fair Oaks, Fair Oaks, Calif., 1978—; broker, 1990—; tchr. Project 100,000, Sheppard AFB, Wichita Falls, Tex., 1966-70. Mem. steering com., adv. bd. Sacramento (Calif.) Bd. Realtors, 1981—; vol. Easter Seal Soc., ARC San Bernardino, 1968-72. Mem. NAFE, Nat. Assn. Realtors (lic.), Calif. Assn. Realtors, Sierra Club, Eagles. Republican. Office: Lyons Real Estate 5207 Sunrise Blvd Ste 200 Fair Oaks CA 95628

YARYMOVYCH, MICHAEL IHOR, manufacturing company executive; b. Bialystok, Poland, Oct. 13, 1933; came to U.S., 1951, naturalized, 1956; s. Nicholas Joseph and Olga (Kruczowy) Y.; m. Roxolana Abramiuk, Nov. 21, 1951; children—Tatiana, Nicholas. B.Aero. Engring., NYU, 1955; M.S. in Engring. Mechanics, Columbia U., 1956, D. Engring. Sci., 1969. Dep. asst. sec. research and devel. U.S. Air Force, Washington, 1967-70; dir. AGARD, NATO, Paris, 1970-73; chief scientist U.S. Air Force, 1973-75; asst. adminstr. field ops. ERDA, 1975-77; v.p. engring. N.Am. aerospace ops. Rockwell Internat. Corp., Seal beach, Calif., 1977-81; v.p. advanced systems devel. Rockwell Internat. Corp., El Segundo, Calif., 1981-86, v.p., assoc. dir. Sys. Devel. Ctr., 1986—; mem. Air Force Sci. Adv. Bd., 1990—; chmn. NATO Adv. Group for Aerospace R&D, 1994—; cons. in field. Author papers in field. Translator Russian books and periodicals. Recipient Exceptional Civilian Svc. award Dept. Air Force, 1968, 73, 75, 94, Disting. Svc. award ERDA, 1977; Guggenheim fellow, 1956-58. Fellow AIAA (dir., pres., gen. chmn. ann. meeting 1978); mem. Air Force Assn., Nat. Mgmt. Assn., Nat. Security Industries Assn., AAAS, Am. Astronautical Soc., Aerospace Industry Assn., Internat. Acad. Astronautics (v.p. sci. programs). Office: Rockwell Internat Sys Devel Ctr 2800 Westminster Ave Seal Beach CA 90740-5606

YASNYI, ALLAN DAVID, communications company executive; b. New Orleans, June 22, 1942; s. Ben Z. and Bertha R. (Michalove) Y.; BBA, Tulane U., 1964; m. Susan K. Manders; children: Benjamin Charles, Evelyn Judith, Brian Mallut. Free-lance exec. producer, producer, writer, actor and designer for TV, motion picture and theatre, 1961-73; producer, performer The Second City; dir. fin. and adminstrn. Quinn Martin Prodns., Hollywood, Calif., 1973-76, v.p. fin., 1976-77, exec. v.p. fin. and corp. planning, 1977; vice chmn., CEO QM Prodns., Beverly Hills, Calif., 1977-78, chmn. bd., CEO, 1978-80; pres., CEO The Synapse Communications Group, Inc., 1981—; exec. dir., adj. prof. U. So. Calif. Entertainment Tech. Ctr., 1994—; participant IC IS Forum, 1990—; exec. prodr. first live broadcast combining Intelsat, Intersputnik, The Voice of Am., and The Moscow World Radio Svc., 1990; resource guest Aspen Inst. Exec. Seminars, 1990; chmn. bd. dirs. Found. of Global Broadcasting, Washington, 1987-93. Trustee Hollywood Arts Coun., 1980-83; exec. v.p., trustee Hollywood Hist. Trust, 1981-91; bd. dirs. Internat. Ctr. for Intergative Studies, N.Y.C., 1988-92; bd. dirs. Asthma and Allergy Foun. Am., 1981-85. Logistical combat officer U.S. Army, 1964-66, Viet Nam. Named to Tulane U. Hall of Fame. Mem. Acad. TV Arts and Scis., Inst. Noetic Scis., Hollywood Radio and TV Soc., Hollywood C. of C. (dir., vice-chmn. 1978-93), Screen Actors Guild, Assn. Transpersonal Pyschology (keynote speaker 1988).

YASSIN, ROBERT ALAN, museum administrator, curator; b. Malden, Mass., May 22, 1941; s. Harold Benjamin and Florence Gertrude (Hoffman) Y.; m. Marilyn Kramer, June 9, 1963; children: Fredric Giles, Aaron David. BA (Rufus Choate scholar), Dartmouth Coll., 1962; postgrad., Boston U., 1962-63; M.A., U. Mich., 1965, postgrad. (Samuel H. Kress Found. fellow), 1968-70, Ph.D. candidate, 1970; postgrad (Ford Found. fellow), Yale U., 1966-68. Asst. to dir. Mus. Art U. Mich., 1965-66, asst. dir., 1970-72, asso. dir., 1972-73, acting dir., 1973, instr. dept. history of art, 1970-73; co-dir. Joint Program in Mus. Tng., 1970-73; chief curator Indpls. Mus. Art, 1973-75, 87-89, acting dir., 1975, dir., 1975-89; exec. dir. Tucson Mus. Art, 1990—; adj. prof. Herron Sch. Art Ind. U./Purdue U., 1975-89. Contbr. to mus. publications. Mem. Ariz. Hist. Soc., Ariz. Mus. Assn., Tucson Mus. Assn., Tucson Arts Coalition., Tucson Downtown Adv. Coun. Mem. Am. Assn. Mus. (bd. dirs. Internat. Coun. Mus. 1986-89), Assn. Art Mus. Dirs., Coll. Art Assn. Am., Intermus. Conservation Assn. (chmn. exec. com. 1977-78), Tucson C. of C. (cultural affairs com., econ. devel. com.), Nat. Trust Historic Preservation, Rotary. Jewish. Office: Tucson Mus Art 140 N Main Ave Tucson AZ 85701-8218

YASUI, BYRON KIYOSHI, musician, music educator; b. Honolulu, Dec. 13, 1940; s. Shigeo and Helen Shizue (Kimura) Y. BE in Music, U. Hawaii, 1965; MusM in Composition, Northwestern U., 1967, D of Mus. Arts in Composition, 1972. Prof. music U. Hawaii, Honolulu, 1972—; double bassist Honolulu Symphony, 1963—. Composer Music for Timpani and Brass, 1974, Four Pieces (double bass quartet), 1984; co-author: Basic Sight Singing, 1988. Served with USAFNG, 1959-65. Named MacDowell Colony fellow, 1979, Nat. Orch. Assn. fellow, 1988. Mem. Am. Soc. Univ. Composers, ASCAP(Std. award ann. 1985—), Internat. Soc. Bassists. Office: U Hawaii Music Dept 2411 Dole St Honolulu HI 96822-2329

YATCHAK, MICHAEL GERARD, electrical engineer; b. Wakefield, Mich., July 3, 1951; s. Roman C. and Mary A. (Zorich) Y.; m. Sachiko Kim, Jan. 29, 1987; 1 child, Rika M. BSEE, Mich. State U., 1974. Assoc. engr. Eagle Signal, Davenport, Iowa, 1974-76; engr. computer lab. Mich. State U., East Lansing, 1977-84; sr. engr. Martin Marietta Corp., Denver, 1984-86; sr. engr. McDonnell Douglas Corp., Huntington Beach, Calif., 1986-92, mgr., 1992-93, prin. engr., 1993—. Mem. IEEE.

YATES, ALBERT CARL, university administrator, chemistry educator; b. Memphis, Sept. 29, 1941; s. John Frank and Sadie L. (Shell) Y.; m. Ann Young; children: Steven, Stephanie, Aerin Alessandra. B.S., Memphis State U., 1965; Ph.D., Ind. U., 1968. Research assoc. U. So. Calif., Los Angeles, 1968-69; prof. chemistry Ind. U., Bloomington, 1969-74; v.p. research, grad. dean U. Cin., 1974-81; exec. v.p., provost, prof. chemistry Washington State U., Pullman, 1981-90; pres. Colo. State U., Fort Collins, 1990—; chancellor Colo. State U. System, Fort Collins, 1990—; mem. grad. record exam. bd. Princeton (N.J.) U., 1977-80, undergrad. assessment program council, 1977-81; cons. NRC, 1975-82, Office End., HEW, 1978-80; mem. exec. council acad. affairs NASULGC, 1983-87, ACE, 1983-87,. nat adv. council gen. med. scis. NIH, 1987—. Contbr.: research articles to Jour. Chem. Physics; research articls to Phys. Rev.; research articles to Jour. Physics, Phys. Rev. Letters, Chem. Physics Letters. Served with USN, 1959-62. Recipient univ. and State honors and awards. Mem. Am. Phys. Soc., Am. Chem. Soc., AAAS, Nat. Assn. State Univs. and Land Grant Colls. (mem. exec. council academic affairs), Am. Council Edn. (mem. exec. com. academic affairs), Sigma Xi, Phi Lambda Upsilon. Home: 1744 Hillside Dr Fort Collins CO 80524-1965 Office: Colo State U 102 Administration Bldg Fort Collins CO 80523

YATES, DAVID JOHN C., chemist, researcher; b. Stoke-on-Trent, Staffordshire, Eng., Feb. 13, 1927; came to U.S., 1958; s. Eric John and Beatrice Victoria (Street) Y.; m. Natalie Chmelnitsky, June 22, 1983. B.S. with honors, U. Birmingham, U.K., 1949; Ph.D., U. Cambridge, Eng., 1955, Sc.D., 1968. Rsch. physicist Kodak Labs., Wealdstone, London, 1949-50; rsch. chemist Brit. Ceramic Rsch. Assn., Stoke-on-Trent, 1950-51; rsch. assoc. dept. colloid sci. U. Cambridge, 1951-58; lectr. Sch. Mines and dept. chemistry Columbia U., N.Y.C., 1958-60; sr. rsch. fellow Nat. Phys. Lab., Teddington, U.K., 1960-61; rsch. assoc. corp. labs. Exxon Rsch. and Engring., Annandale, N.J., 1961-86; rsch. prof. dept. of chem. engring. Lafayette Coll., Easton, Pa., 1986-87; rsch. prof. dept. materials sci. Rutgers U., Piscataway, N.J., 1987-88; cons. San Diego, 1988—. Contbr. over 70 articles to profl. jours., chpts. to books; 13 U.S. patents, numerous fgn. patents. Fellow Inst. of Physics (U.K.), Royal Soc. Chemistry (U.K.), N.Y. Catalysis Club (chmn. 1966-67). Club: N.Y. Catalysis (chmn. 1965-66).

YATES, HELEN LOUISE, labor and delivery, critical care nurse; b. Neosho, Mo., Mar. 2, 1941; d. John Merlin and Ella Mae Pratt; children: Roger Dean, Rogenia Louise. Grad., Sch. Cosmetology, Neosho, 1974; lic. in practical nursing, Crowder Coll., 1977; ADN, Northeastern Okla. A&M Coll., 1981. RN, Calif., Tex., Ariz.; cert. in phlebotomy, intravenous therapy, chemotherapy, thermoregulation and critical care of infant, fetal heart monitoring I, II and advanced, neonatology outreach edn., critical care/emergency nursing; cert. provider ACLS, Am. Heart Assn. Team leader proarrhythmic effects of antiarrhythmic drugs Sale Hosp., Neosho, 1978-83; cons. nurse King Fahad Hosp., Riyadh, Saudi Arabia, 1983; team leader nurse N.W. Hosp., Tucson, 1984-85; labor/delivery nurse Sierra Vista (Ariz.) Hosp., 1985-88; travel nurse Judy's Nurses, Tucson, 1988—, SEAMC Hosp., Douglas, Ariz., 1988—; cons. HCA, Saudi Arabia, 1983. Author: Financial Care Plan, 1992. Cert. provider ACLS, Am. Heart Assn., 1990—. Home: 1440 S Via Viento Sierra Vista AZ 85635-4523

YATES, KEITH LAMAR, retired insurance company executive; b. Bozeman, Mont., Oct. 29, 1927; s. Thomas Bryan and Altha (Norris) Y.; m. Dolores Hensel, Aug. 30, 1948; children: Thomas A., Molly Yates McIntosh, Richard A., Nancy Yates Sands, Penny Dannielle Yates, Pamela Yates Beeler. BA, Eastern Wash. State U., 1953. Salesman Ancient Order United Workmen, Spokane, Wash., 1952-53, sales mgr., 1953-56, corp. sec., 1956-73; corp. sec. Neighbors of Woodcraft, Portland, Oreg., 1973-89, pres., 1989-92; ret., 1992. Author: Life of Willie Willey, 1966, The Fogarty Years, 1972, History of The Woodcraft Home, 1975, An Enduring Heritage, 1992. Pres. Wash. State Christian Mens Fellowship, Seattle, 1965-67; pres. Met. Area Assn. Christian Chs., 1981-83; mem. regional bd. Christian Chs. Oreg., 1990-94. Command sgt.-maj., ret., 1987; served with USN, USAF, USANG, 1946-87. Mem. Wash. State Frat. Cong., (cert. Commendation 1969, sec. 1957-68, pres., mem. exec. bd., chmn. conv. program advt. com. 1960-73), Oreg. State Frat. Cong. (Outstanding Frat. 1975-76, Spl. Appreciation award 1984, Frat. Family of Yr. 1986, sec. 1975-87, pres., mem. exec. bd. 1974—), Nat. Fraternal Congress Am. (conv. arrangement com. 1964, 90, publicity com. 1964, 65, 68, 90, credentials com. 1970, 77, 78, pres. press & pub. rels. sec. 1971-72, pub. rels. com. 1971-73, chmn. 1972, co-chmn. press and pub. rels. frat. seminar 1972, frat. monitor com. 1974-75, mem. com. 1975-76, family life com. 1978-80, constitution com. 1980, pres. state frat. congs. sec. 1981-82, historian 1987—, Washington County's Disting. Patriot, 1988), Portland Ins. Acctg. and Statis. Soc. Assn. Records Mgrs. and Adminstrs. (Oreg. chpt.), Portland C. of C., Wash. Ins. Coun., Wash. Claims Assn., Seattle Underwriting Assn. Home: 29860 SW Buckhaven Rd Hillsboro OR 97123-8706

YATES, MARGERY GORDON, educator; b. Walton, N.Y., July 3, 1910; d. McClellan Gordon and Marcia Beulah (Ramsdell) Gordon-Strahl; m. James McKendree Yates, Aug. 11, 1933; 1 child, Sally. Cortland Normal Sch.; BS, U. Houston, 1943, MS, 1948; MA, Stanford U., 1952. Tchr. Baldwin (N.Y.) Sch. Dist., 1928-34, Houston Sch. Dist., 1943-48; supr. primary edn. Watsonville (Calif.) Sch. Dist., 1948-53; edn. cons. San Mateo County Office Edn., Redwood City, Calif., 1953-58; supr. primary edn. Jefferson Elem. Sch. Dist., Daly City, Calif., 1958-65; tchr. Hillsborough (Calif.) Sch. Dist., 1965-75; instr. U. Houston, 1956, San Jose State Coll., 1957. Mem. AAUW (edn. area rep. 1987-88, 89-90, 91-92, 92-93, 93-94, Fellowship award honoree 1991), burlingame Music Club (pres. 1992-93, 93-94), Alpha Delta Kappa (corr. sec. Calif. state bd. 1981-82, Gamma Beta chpt. pres. 1971-74, treas. 1985-89, 94—). Republican. Mem. Ch. Christian Sci. Home: 2731 Summit Dr Burlingame CA 94010-6039

YAU, STEPHEN SIK-SANG, computer science and engineering educator, computer scientist, researcher; b. Wusei, Kiangsu, China, Aug. 6, 1935; came to U.S., 1958, naturalized, 1968; s. Pen-Chi and Wen-Chum (Shum) Y.; m. Vickie Liu, June 14, 1964; children: Andrew, Philip. BS in Elec. Engring, Nat. Taiwan U., China, 1958; MS in Elec. Engring, U. Ill., Urbana, 1959, PhD, 1961. Rsch. asst. elec. engring. rsch. lab. U. Ill., Urbana, 1959-61; asst. prof. elec. engring. Northwestern U., Evanston, Ill., 1961-64, assoc. prof., 1964-68, prof., 1968-88, prof. computer scis., 1970-88, Walter P. Murphy prof. Elec. Engring. and Computer Sci., 1986-88, also chmn. dept. computer scis., 1972-77; chmn. dept. elec. engring. and computer sci. Northwestern U., 1977-88; prof. computer and info. sci., chmn. dept. U. Fla., Gainesville, 1988—; conf. chmn. IEEE Computer Conf., Chgo., 1967; symposium chmn. Symposium on feature extraction and selection in pattern recognition Argonne Nat. Lab., 1970; gen. chmn. Nat. Computer Conf., Chgo., 1974, First Internat. Computer Software and Applications Conf., Chgo., 1977; Trustee Nat. Electronics Conf., Inc., 1965-68; chmn. organizing com 11th World Computer Congress, Internat. Fedn. Info. Processing, San Francisco, 1989; gen. co-chmn. Internat. Symposium on Autonomous Decentralized Systems, Japan, 1993. Editor-in-chief Computer mag., 1981-84; assoc. editor Jour. Info. Scis., 1983—; editor IEEE Trans. on Software Engring., 1988-91; contbr. numerous articles on software engring., distributed and parallel processing systems, computer sci., elec. engring. and related fields to profl. publs.; patentee in field. Recipient Louis E. Levy medal Franklin Inst., 1963, Golden Plate award Am. Acad. of Achievement, 1964, The Silver Core award Internat. Fedn. Info. Processing, 1989, Spl. award, 1989. Fellow IEEE (mem. governing bd. Computer Soc. 1967-76, pres. 1974-75, dir. Inst. 1976-77; Richard E. Merwin award Computer Soc. 1981, Centennial medal 1984, Extraordinary Achievement 1985, Outstanding Contbn. award Computer Sci. Soc. 1985), AAAS, Franklin Inst.; mem. Assn. for Computing Machinery, Am. Fedn. Info.-Processing Socs. (mem. exec. com. 1974-76, 79-82, dir. 1972-82, chmn. awards com. 1979-82, v.p. 1982-84, pres. 1984-86; chmn. Nat. Computer Conf. Bd. 1982-83), Am. Soc. Engring. Edn., Sigma Xi, Tau Beta Pi, Eta Kappa Nu, Pi Mu Epsilon. Office: AZ State U Computer Sci & Eng GWC 206 Tempe AZ 85287

YAU, TE-LIN, corrosion engineer; b. Ton-Chen, Anhuei, China, Apr. 9, 1945; s. Chiu-Ho and Chih (Yang) Y.; m. Jue-Hua Tsai, Mar. 19, 1979; children: Kai-Huei, Ian-Huei, Jean-Huei. BS in Engring. Sci., Cheng Kung U., Taiwan, 1969; MS in Engring. Sci., Tenn. Technol. U., 1972; PhD in Metall. Engring., Ohio State U., 1979. Mech. engr. Taiwan Shipbuilding Corp., Keelung, Taiwan, 1970-71; corrosion group head Teledyne Wah Chang, Albany, Ore., 1979—; cons. Fontana Corrosion Ctr., Ohio State U., Columbus, 1979. Author: ASTM STP, 1984, 85, 86, 90, 92, 95, ASM Metals Handbook, 1987, ASM Stress Corrosion Cracking, 1992; contbr. over 60 articles to profl. jours. Mem. Nat. Assn. Corrosion Engrs. Internat. (chmn. T-5A-38 task group on reactive metals 1993—), Electrochem. Soc., TAPPI, Sigma Xi. Home: 1445 Belmont Ave SW Albany OR 97321-3765 Office: Teledyne Wah Chang Albany 1600 Old Salem Rd NE Albany OR 97321-4548

YAZDANI, MEHRI, artist; b. Tehran, Iran, Oct. 4, 1944; came to U.S., 1971; m. James Joseph Reid, Nov. 24, 1972. BA, U. Tehran; MA, UCLA, 1977. One-woman shows include Mangel Gallery, Phila., 1989, 91, 93, Town Hall, Rethymno, Crete, Greece, 1991, Town Hall, Senden-Aufheim, Germany, 1993, Calif. State U., Sacramento, 1994. Recipient Cresson Meml. Traveling scholarship Pa. Acad. Fine Arts, Phila., 1986, Liqui-Tex Fine Arts award Pa. Acad. Fine Arts, Phila., 1987, Pa. Gov.'s award Pa. Acad. Fine Arts, Phila., 1987, Binney & Smith Fine Arts award Allentown (Pa.) Art Mus., 1989. Office: Vryonis Ctr 3140 Gold Camp Dr Ste 50 Rancho Cordova CA 95670-6023

YEAGER, DAVID CLARK, product designer, education specialist; b. Hinsdale, Ill., July 1, 1951; s. William Frances and Helen Gerrity (Clark) Y.; m. Tina Alden, Jan. 4, 1974; 1 child, Christopher Alden. BA, U. Colo., 1975. Cert. tchr., Colo. Tchr. Boulder (Colo.) Valley Schs., 1976-86, ednl. cons., 1986-90; aide to Gov. Romer State of Colo., Denver, 1990-91; devel. dir. Boulder Valley Schs. and Colo. Partnership Ednl. for Renewal, 1991-94; ednl. product designer InGenius, Englewood, Colo., 1994—; cons. Va. Commonwealth U., Richmond, 1990, 91; coord. Am. Coun. Learned Socs. Elem. and Secondary Curriculum Devel. Project, 1992—. Author several math. books; film reviewer McArthur Found., 1989; contbr. articles to profl. jours. Active Safehouse for Children, Boulder County, 1994. Recipient numerous grants. Home: 3745 Birchwood Dr Boulder CO 80304-1423 Office: InGenius Ste 210 5970 Greenwood Plaza Blvd Englewood CO 80111-4703

YEAGER, MYRON DEAN, English language educator, business writing consultant; b. Evansville, Ind., Oct. 27, 1950; s. Robert Paul and Sarah Mazol (Hunt) Y. BA, Grace Coll., 1972; MA, Purdue U., 1974, PhD, 1980. Cert. tchr., Calif. Assoc. prof. Grace Coll., Winona Lake, Ind., 1976-84, Chapman U., Orange, Calif., 1984—; cons. numerous firms, 1980—; faculty chmn. Chapman U., Orange, 1991-92, dept. chmn., 1990-93; dept. chmn. Grace Coll., Winona Lake, 1981-84. Author: (chpt.) Business Writing, 1989; contbr. articles to profl. jours. and mags. Recipient UCLA Clark postdoctoral fellowship, 1982, David Ross fellowship Purdue U., 1980. Mem. ACLU, AAUP, Am. Soc. Eighteenth-Century Studies, Johnson Soc. Western Region, Assn. Bus. Communication, Phi Beta Delta. Office: Chapman Univ 333 N Glassell St Orange CA 92666-1011

YEAMAN, MICHAEL ROBERT, microbiologist, infectious diseases consultant; b. Roswell, N.Mex., Mar. 10, 1963; s. Donald Lee and Barbara Jane (Banck) Y. BS cum laude, U. N.Mex., 1985; MS, U. N.Mex. Sch. Medicine, 1987, PhD in Microbiology cum laude, 1990. Instr. Med. Microbiology U. N.Mex., Albuquerque, 1985-90; NIH fellow Infectious Diseases UCLA Sch. Medicine, 1990-92, fellow Am. Heart Assn., 1992-93, asst. prof. medicine, 1994—; cons. Nat. Weather Svc., Washington, 1985-87, Nat. Oceanic and Atmosphere Adminstrn., 1987-89, Aquascapes, 1987-92; contbg. editor Freshwater and Marine Aquarium Mag., L.A., 1987-92. Author: Aquarium Technique, 1987; writer Acoustica, 1980-83; patents pending in field. Cons. Anti-Infective Program, Heart-to-Heart Internat. Childrens Med. Alliance, 1992—; invited judge N.Mex. Sci. Fair, 1987, Regional Sci. Fair, U. N.Mex., 1987-90; speaker Discover U N.Mex. Program for H.S. Seniors, 1986-88; spl. cons. N.Mex. Acad. Decathlon, 1989. Recipient Kodak award for Excellence in Sci., 1980, USAF Acad. Excellence award, 1980, Sizemore Found. Elite Acad. scholarship, 1981-85, U. N.Mex. Excellence in Teaching awards, 1985-90, Nat. Oceanic and Atmospheric Adminstrn. Spl. award, 1989; named Biol. Soc. of N.Mex. Outstanding Tchr., 1987, U. N.Mex. Outstanding Teaching Assoc., 1987, Dean's Honor List Coll. Arts and Scis., U N.Mex., 1981-85. Mem. AAAS, Am. Soc. for Microbiology, Infectious Diseases Soc. Am., Am. Soc. for Rickettsiology and Rickettsial Diseases, N.Y. Acad. Scis., Phi Kappa Phi. Office: UCLA Sch Medicine Harbor-UCLA MC 1000 W Carson St Torrance CA 90502-2004

YEARLEY, DOUGLAS CAIN, mining and manufacturing company executive; b. Oak Park, Ill., Jan. 7, 1936; s. Bernard Cain and Mary Kenny (Howard) Y.; m. Elizabeth Anne Dunbar, Feb. 8, 1958; children: Sandra, Douglas Jr., Peter, Andrew. BMetE, Cornell U., 1958; postgrad., Harvard U., 1968. Engr. welding Gen. Dynamics, Groton, Conn., 1958-60; dir. rsch., project engr. Phelps Dodge Copper Products, Elizabeth, N.J., 1960-68; mgr. ops. Phelps Dodge Internat. Co., N.Y.C., 1968-71; v.p. ops. Phelps Dodge Tube Co., L.A., 1971-73; exec. v.p. Phelps Dodge Cable and Wire Co., Yonkers, N.Y., 1973-75; pres. Phelps Dodge Brass Co., Lyndhurst, N.J., 1975-79; pres. Phelps Dodge Sales Co., N.Y.C., 1979-82, v.p. mktg., 1979-82; sr. v.p. Phelps Dodge Corp., N.Y.C., 1982-87, exec. v.p., 1987-89; chmn., chief exec. officer Phelps Dodge Sales Co., N.Y.C., 1989-91; chmn., pres., CEO Phelps Dodge Sales Co., Phoenix, 1991—; also bd. dirs. Phelps Dodge Corp., N.Y.C.; bd. dirs. USX Corp., Pitts., J.P. Morgan and Co., Inc. and Morgan Guaranty Trust Co., N.Y.C., Lockheed Corp., Calabasas, Calif., So. Peru Copper Co. Mem. Ariz. Econs. Coun., 1989—, Conf. Bd., 1989—; bd.

dirs. Am. Grad. Sch. Internat. Mgmt., 1990-92, Phoenix Symphony, 1988-94; chmn. Arts Coalition, 1989-90; trustee Phoenix Art Mus., 1994—. Mem. Nat. Elec. Mfrs. Assn. (bd. dirs. 1983-92), Internat. Cooper Assn. (bd. dirs. 1987—, chmn. 1990—), Am. Mining Congress (vice chmn.), Copper Devel. Assn. (chmn. 1989-93, dir. 1993—), Nat. Assn. Mfrs. (bd. dirs. 1988-94), Bus. Roundtable, Bus. Coun., Skyu Club, Echo Lake Country Club, Paradise Valley Country Club, Ariz Club, Blinf Brook Country Club. Republican. Congregationalist. Home: 8201 N Via De Lago Scottsdale AZ 85258-4215 Office: Phelps Dodge Corp 2600 N Central Ave Phoenix AZ 85004-3050*

YEDLICKA, WILLIAM GEORGE, retired sales professional; b. Apollo, Pa., Dec. 25, 1922; s. Joseph Frank and Katie (Cadena) Y.; m. Theresa Rosamond Unger, July 17, 1970; 1 child, Monte. BS, U. Pitts., 1949, M Letters, 1957. Asst. sales mgr. Bowers Battery & Spark Plug Co. div. Gen. Battery Co., Reading, Pa., 1965-66; regional sales mgr. Gen. Battery Co., Atlanta, 1966-67; spl. products mgr. East Pa. Mfg. Co., Inc., Lyon Station, 1967-74, sales mgr. R.R. and mining, 1974-79, v.p. sales, indsl., R.R. and mining, 1979-88; bd. dirs., Molds Corp., Kansas City, Mo. Author tech. papers, procedural manuals. Lt. col. USAF, 1942-46. Decorated, DFC, Air medal with 4 clusters. Mem. Material Handling Inst., Material Handling Equipment Dealers Assn., Nat. Elec. Mfrs. Assn., Ind. Battery Mfrs. Assn., Battery Coun. Internat. (chmn. indsl. battery com.), Indsl. Truck Assn., Indsl. Battery Soc., Pinehurst Country Club, Shriners, Elks. Republican. Presbyterian. Home: 15305 W Blue Verde Dr Sun City West AZ 85375-6506

YEE, BEN, import-export business executive; b. Seattle, June 16, 1946; s. Sam and Gertrude (Jue) Y. BA in Mktg. and Bus., Seattle Coll., 1980; BA in Hotel and Restaurant Mgmt., Wash. State U., Pullman, 1982. Importer/exporter, distbr. Internat. Distbr. and Svcs., San Francisco, 1980-86; import/export cons., direct factory contact in China By Enterprises, Inc., Seattle, 1986—, pres., 1986-92, CEO, 1992—; bd. dirs. World Trade Inst., Seattle. Patentee Create-A-Lite; speaker in field. Bd. dirs. Chinese Am. U., Seattle, 1993—. Mem. World Trade Ctr., China Trade Rels. Orgn. Home: 23110 30th Ave S Des Moines WA 98198-7287 Office: By Enterprise Inc PO Box 68305 Seattle WA 98168

YEE, BRUCE JAMES, anesthesiologist; b. San Francisco, Nov. 27, 1950; s. William James and Mildred Ann Y.; m. Pauline J. Tom, July 3, 1977; children: Catherine, Stephanie, Christopher. BS, Rensellaer Poly. Inst., 1974; MD, Albany Med. Coll., 1974. Diplomate Am. Bd. Anesthesiology, Am. Acad. Pain Mgmt. Intern U. So. Calif. Med. Ctr., 1974-75; resident anesthesiology New England Med. Ctr., 1976-78; anesthesiologist Luth. Care Home, Mesa, Ariz., 1981—; chmn. dept. anesthesiology Mesa Luth. Hosp., 1985-87. Mem. exec. bd. Phoenix House-Chinese Am. Citizen Alliance. Fellow Am. Acad. Anesthesiology; mem. Rotary. Home and Office: Luth Hosp 525 W Brown Rd Mesa AZ 85201-3202

YEE, DARLENE, gerontological health educator; b. N.Y.C., Sept. 19, 1958; d. Jimmy Tow and Yuen Hing (Chin) Y. BA in Biology, Barnard Coll., 1980; MS in Gerontology, Coll. New Rochelle, 1981; MS in Health Edn., Columbia U., 1984, EdD in Health Edn., 1985. Cert. Nat. Commn. Health Edn. Asst. dir. biology lab. Barnard Coll., N.Y.C., 1980-83; rsch. assoc. safety rsch. and edn. project Columbia U. Tchrs. Coll., N.Y.C., 1983-85; asst. prof. health and phys. edn. York Coll., N.Y.C., 1985-88; cons. Transp. Rsch. Bd., NAS, Washington, 1987, N.Y. State Dept. Edn., Albany, 1987, U.S. Dept. Edn., Washington, 1991; assoc. prof. clin. gerontology, health edn. and promotion U. Tex. Med. Br., Galveston, 1988-90; assoc. prof. health edn. San Francisco State U., 1990-93; prof. health edn., 1994-95; prof. gerontology San Francisco State U., 1995—. Contbr. articles to profl. jours. Mem. Am. Coll. Health Care Adminstrs., Gerontol. Soc. Am., Am. Soc. on Aging, Assn. for Advancement Health Edn., Nat. Coun. on Aging, Sigma Xi. Home: 40 Meadow Park Cir Belmont CA 94002-2947 Office: San Francisco State U Gerontology Programs 20 Tapia Dr San Francisco CA 94132-1717

YEE, KANE SHEE-GONG, mathematician, electrical engineer; b. Canton, Kwangtung, China, Mar. 26, 1934; came to U.S., 1951; s. Wing Dye Yee and Check Wah Fong; m. Maxine Big-Shung Fong, Aug. 19, 1962; children: Audrey, Albert. BS, U. Calif., Berkeley, 1957, MS in Elec. Engring., 1958, PhD in Applied Math., 1963. Scientist, mathematician Lawrence Livermore Nat. Lab., Livermore, Calif., 1964-87; assoc. prof. math. U. Fla., Gainesville, 1966-68; prof. math. and elec. engring. Kans. State U., Manhattan, 1968-84; cons. sr. scientist Lockheed Missiles and Space Co., Sunnyvale, Calif., 1987—; advisor NSF, Washington, 1989-92. Originator finite difference time domain method in numerical solution of Maxwell's equations; frequent reviewer for IEEE Jours., 1968—; author more than 30 tech. papers. Recipient scholarships and fellowships. Mem. IEEE. Democrat. Home: 23350 Toyonita Rd Los Altos CA 94022

YEE, KEITH PHILIP, accountant; b. Luton, Eng., Apr. 26, 1958; came to the U.S., 1985; m. Ginny Sung, Feb. 9, 1985; children: Ashley, Brittany. BA in Acctg. with honors, Exeter (Eng.) U., 1979. CPA, Calif. Audit sr. Ernst & Whinney, London, 1979-83; investigation supr. Ernst & Whinney, Hong Kong, 1983-85; audit mgr. Ernst & Whinney, Memphis, 1985-86; audit sr. mgr. Ernst & Young, San Francisco, 1986-91; internat. resident Ernst & Young, 1991-93; audit sr. mgr. Ernst & Young, San Francisco, 1993-95, Price Waterhouse, San Jose, Calif., 1995—. Vice chmn. adv. coun. for svcs. to srs. Salvation Army, San Francisco, 1989. Grad. leadership San Francisco program San Francisco C. of C., 1990. Fellow Inst. Chartered Accts. in Eng. and Wales; mem. AICPA, Asian Am. CPAs (mem. adv. bd. 1994—), Calif. Soc. CPAs, Inst. for Internat. Edn. (student programs com. 1990—), Asian Bus. League, Hong Kong Assn., Commonwealth Club, San Francisco C. of C. (internat. bus. devel. com. 1993—). Office: Price Waterhouse 150 Almaden Blvd Ste 1200 San Jose CA 95113

YEE, MARCUS CHARLES, software developer; b. Sacramento, Calif., Sept. 4, 1963; s. Fan and Viola (Fong) Y.; m. Kelly Matsudaira, June 25, 1994. BS, U. Calif., Davis, 1986. Software engr. TelWatch, El Dorado Hills, Calif., 1987-88; programmer analyst Dilts Kappeler Durham & Co., Rocklin, Calif., 1988-90, Affordable Healthcare Concepts, Sacramento, 1990-93; sys. analyst Healthcare Compare, West Sacramento, 1993—. Recipient Eagle Scout award Boy Scouts Am., 1981. Mem. IEEE Computer Soc., Assn. for Computing Machinery.

YEE, STEPHEN, airport executive. Adminstrv. asst. health dept. City of L.A., 1958-63, sr. adminstrv. asst. dept. airports, 1963-72, fed. aid coord., 1972-75, project mgr., 2d level roadway and terminal improvements, airport facilities planner, 1975-83, staff asst. to bd. airport commrs., 1983-85, airport mgr. L.A. Internat. Airport, 1985—. Office: Los Angeles Intl Airport Los Angeles Dept of Airports 1 World Way Los Angeles CA 90045-5803*

YEGGE, ROBERT BERNARD, lawyer, college dean emeritus, educator; b. Denver, June 17, 1934; s. Ronald Van Kirk and Fairy (Hill) Y. A.B. magna cum laude, Princeton U., 1956; M.A. in Sociology, U. Denver, 1958, J.D., 1959. Bar: Colo. 1959, D.C. 1978. Ptnr. Yegge, Hall and Evans, Denver, 1959-78; with Harding & Ogborn successor to Nelson and Harding, 1979—; prof. U. Denver Coll. Law, 1965—, dean, 1965-77, dean emeritus, 1977—; asst. to pres. Denver Post, 1971-75; v.p., exec. dir. Nat. Ctr. Preventive Law, 1986-91. Author: Colorado Negotiable Instruments Law, 1960, Some Goals; Some Tasks, 1965, The American Lawyer: 1976, 1966, New Careers in Law, 1969, The Law Graduate, 1972, Tomorrow's Lawyer: A Shortage and Challenge, 1974, Declaration of Independence for Legal Education, 1976. Mng. trustee Denver Ctr. for Performing Arts, 1972-75; chmn. Colo. Coun. Arts and Humanities, 1968-80, chmn. emeritus, 1980—; mem. scholar selection com. Henry Luce Found., 1975—; Active nat. and local A.R.C., chmn. Denver region, 1985-88; trustee Denver Symphony Soc., Inst. of Ct. Mgmt., Denver Dumb Friends League, 1992—, Met. Denver Legal Aid Soc., 1994—, Colo. Acad.; trustee, vice chmn. Nat. Assembly State Arts Agys.; vice chmn. Mexican-Am. Legal Edn. and Def. Fund, 1970-76. Recipient Disting. Svc. award Denver Jr. C. of C., 1965; Harrison Tweed award Am. Assn. Continuing Edn. Adminstrs., 1985, Alumni Faculty award U. Denver, 1993. Mem. ABA (chmn. lawyers conf. 1987-88, chmn. accreditation commn. for legal asst. programs 1980-90, standing com. legal assts. 1987-92, standing com. delivery legal svcs. 1992-95, del. to jud. adminstrn. coun. 1989-95, standing com. on gavel awards 1995—), Law and Soc. Assn. (life, pres. 1965-70), Colo. Bar Assn. (bd. govs. 1965-77), Denver Bar Assn., D.C. Bar Assn., Am. Law Inst., Am. Judicature Soc. (bd. dirs. 1968-72, 75-85, Herbert Harley award 1985), Am. Acad. Polit. and Social Sci., Am. Sociol. Soc., Assn. Am. Law Schs., Order St. Ives, Phi Beta Kappa, Beta Theta Pi, Phi Delta Phi, Alpha Kappa Delta, Omicron Delta Kappa. Home: 3472 S Race St Englewood CO 80110-3138 Office: Harding & Ogborn 1200 17th St Ste 1950 Denver CO 80202-5810

YEGIAN, RICHARD, real estate executive. BSME, Harvey Mudd Coll., 1985; MCE, MBA, Northwestern U., 1986. Co-founder Admiral Devel. Co., Burbank, Calif., 1986—; pres., CEO Admiral Realty, Glendale, Calif., 1989—. Mem. Mensa. Office: Admiral Realty 100 N Brand Blvd 2d Fl Glendale CA 91203-2614

YEH, PAUL PAO, electrical and electronics engineer, educator; b. Sung Yang, Chekiang, China, Mar. 25, 1927; came to U.S., 1956, naturalized, 1963; s. Tsung Shan and Shu Huan (Mao) Y.; m. Beverley Pamela Eng, May 15, 1952; children: Judith Elaine, Paul Edmond, Richard Alvin, Ronald Timothy. Student, Nat. Cen. U., Nanking, China, 1946-49; BA Sc in Elec. Engring., U. Toronto (Ont., Can.), 1951; MSEE, U. Pa., 1960, PhD, 1966. Registered profl. engr., Ont. Design engr. Can. Gen. Electric Co., Toronto, 1951-56; asst. prof. SUNY, Binghamton, 1956-57; sr. engr. H.K. Porter, ITE & Kuhlman, Phila. and Detroit, 1957-61; assoc. prof. N.J. Inst. Tech., Newark, 1961-66; supr. rsch. and devel. N.Am. Rockwell, Anaheim, Calif., 1966-70; sr. R&D engr. Lockheed Advanced Devel. Co., Burbank, Calif., 1970-72, 78-89; mem. tech. staff The Aerospace Corp., El Segundo, Calif., 1972-78; chief scientist Advanced Systems Rsch., Pasadena, Calif., 1989—; cons. Consol. Edison Co., N.Y.C., 1963-64; sr. lectr. State U. Calif., Long Beach, 1967-73; vis. prof. Chung Shan Inst., 1989-92, Tsinghua U., 1993—, S.E. U., 1994—, Zhejiang U., 1994—; cons. prof. Northwestern Poly. U., 1993—, Shanghai U., 1994—; hon. prof. Beijing U. Aeros. and Astronautics, 1993—, Zhejiang U. Sci. and Tech., 1994—; rschr. power sys. design and control, 1951-66; investigator R&D Stealth tech. electronic warfare, avionics, nuclear hardening, anti-submarine warfare,. Recipient Achievement award for anti-submarine warfare/magnetic anomaly detection sys. Lockheed Corp. Mem. IEEE (sr., life), Nat. Mgmt. Assn., Am. Def. Preparedness Assn., Assn. Old Crows, Chines Am. Engring./Sci. Assn. So. Calif. (pres. 1969-71), Nat. Ctrl. U. Alumni Assn. (pres. 1977), Nat. Security Indsl. Assn., Beijing Assn. for Sci. and Tech. Exchs. with Fgn. Countries (hon. dir.), Assn. Profl. Engrs. of Ont. Can., N.Y. Acad. Scis., Air Force Assn. Republican. Presbyterian. Home: 5555 Via De Campo Yorba Linda CA 92687-4916 Office: Advanced Systems Rsch Inc 33 S Catalina Ave Ste 202 Pasadena CA 91106-2426

YELLEN, PAMELA GAY, sales and marketing consultant; b. Buffalo, Nov. 16, 1952; d. Arthur Irwin and Carole (Swartz) Y.; m. James Joseph Donahoe, Dec. 28, 1975 (div. Apr. 1984). BA, Lone Mountain Coll., San Francisco, 1974; postgrad., Calif. Inst. Integral Studies, San Francisco, 1974-76. V.p. sales and mktg. Bench Press, Oakland, Calif., 1974-84; nat. sales mgr. Camp-orama, Sarasota, Fla., 1984-87; speaker, cons. Prospecting and Mktg. Inst., Phoenix, 1987—; cons. Chevron, Phoenix, 1989—, Apple One, Phoenix, 1990—; prodr. (tng. program) Magnetic Recruiting, 1995. Author: (video cassett tng. programs) Supercharge Your Commissions, 1993; editor: Dream Reality, 1974, Enigma, 1979, Professional Prospecting: How to Succeed at the Ultimate Contact Sport, 1994; author audio cassette album: Simple Selling, 1990, Stay Out of the Cold, 1991, rev. edit., 1993, Growing Your Business, 1992, Women in Business, 1992. Pres. Nat. Fedn. Jewish Youth, Buffalo, 1969-70; mem. networking com. Ariz. Coun. Excellence, Phoenix, 1989—; facilitator MMS Self-Esteem Workshops, Phoenix, 1988-90. Mem. Nat. Speakers Assn., Nat. Assn. Life Underwriters (presenter, speaker 1991—). Democrat. Office: PO Box 51657 Phoenix AZ 85076

YEN, DUEN HSI, corporate executive, physicist; b. Nyack, N.Y., Apr. 24, 1949; s. Ernest Chu and Louise (Loo) Y.; m. Linda Leiko Takai, June 22, 1989. BS in Physics, Rensselaer Polytech. Inst., 1971; MA in Biophysics, Johns Hopkins U., 1974; MSEE, U. Vt., 1978. Mem. tech. staff Bell Telephone Labs., Holmdel, N.J., 1978-83; pres. Multipath Systems, Inc., Honolulu, 1984—; Violinist Oahu Civic Orch. Inventor noise detector, electronic travel aids for blind; contbr. articles to profl. jours. Violinist Oahu Civic Orch. Small Bus. Innovation Rsch. grantee, NSF grantee 1984, Nat. Eye Inst. grantee 1988, 89, 91. Mem. Acoustical Soc. Am., Audio Engring. Soc., Sigma Pi Sigma.

YEN, I-KUEN, chemical engineer, environmental engineer, industrial hygiene consultant; b. Singapore, May 29, 1930; came to U.S., 1955; s. Shang and Juei-hung (Wang) Y.; m. Chen-wan Liu, Feb. 4, 1958; children: Alfred, Albert. BS, Nat. Taiwan U., Taipei, 1954; SM, MIT, 1956, ScD, 1960. Cert. indsl. hygienist; registered environ. assessor. Rsch. asst. Crucible Steel Co., Pitts., 1959-61; rsch. engr. Am. Std. Corp., New Brunswick, N.J., 1961-64; group leader C.F. Braun & Co., Alhambra, Calif., 1964-68; dir. Occidental Rsch. Corp., Irvine, Calif., 1968-83; prin. Ike Yen Assocs., Claremont, Calif., 1983—. Mem. Am. Inst. Chem. Engrs., Am. Chem. Soc., Am. Acad. Indsl. Hygiene, N.Y. Acad. Scis. Office: Ike Yen Assocs 867 Marymount Ln Claremont CA 91711-1513

YEN, TEH FU, civil and environmental engineering educator; b. Kun-Ming, China, Jan. 9, 1927; came to U.S., 1949; s. Kwang Pu and Ren (Liu) Y.; m. Shiao-Ping Siao, May 30, 1959. B.S., Cen. China U., 1947; M.S., W.Va. U., 1953; Ph.D., Va. Poly. Inst. and State U., 1956; hon. doctoral degree, Pepperdine U., 1982. Sr. research chemist Good Yr. Tire & Rubber Co., Akron, 1955-59; fellow Mellon Inst., Pitts., 1959-65; sr. fellow Carnegie-Mellon U., Pitts., 1965-68; assoc. prof. Calif. State U., Los Angeles, 1968-69; assoc. prof. U. So. Calif., 1969-80, prof. civil engring. and environ. engring., 1980—; hon. prof. Shanghai U. Sci. and Tech., 1986, U. Petroleum, Beijing, 1987, Daqing Petroleum Inst., 1992; cons. Universal Oil Products, 1968-76, Chevron Oil Field Rsch. Co., 1968-75, Finnigan Corp., 1976-77, GE, 1977-80, United Techs., 1978-79, TRW Inc., 1982-83, Exxon, 1981-82, DuPont, 1985-88, Min. Petroleum, Beijing, 1982—, Biogas Rsch. Inst.-UN, Chengdu, 1991. Author numerous tech. books; contbr. articles to profl. jours. Recipient Disting. Svc. award Tau Beta Pi, 1974, Imperial Crown Gold medal, Iran, 1976, Achievement award Chinese Engring. and Sci. Assocs. So. Calif., 1977, award Phi Kappa Phi, 1982, Outstanding Contbn. honor Pi Epsilon Tau, 1984, Svc. award Republic of Honduras, 1989, Award in Petroleum Chemistry ACS, 1994. Fellow Royal Chem. Soc., Inst. Petroleum, Am. Inst. Chemists; mem. Am. Chem. Soc. (bd. dirs. 1993, councillor, founder and chmn. geochemistry divsn. 1979-81, Chinese Acad. Scis. (standing com.), Acad. Scis. Russian Fedn. (academician, fgn. mem.). Home: 2378 Morslay Rd Altadena CA 91001-2716 Office: U So Calif University Park KAP 224A Los Angeles CA 90089

YENER, MUZZ, civil engineer, educator; b. Iskenderun, Turkey, June 30, 1947; s. Celal and Rahmiye (Koraltan) Y.; m. Barbara Ann Valovage, Dec. 14, 1980; children: Devren Adem, Alden Efrem, Erin Esra, Suzan Nora. BCE, NYU, 1969, MS, 1971; PhD, Cornell U., 1979. Design engr. Herbert Fleisher Assocs., N.Y.C., 1970; teaching asst., rsch. assoc. Cornell U., Ithaca, N.Y., 1974-80; design engr. Turkish Army Engring. Corps., 1976; supervising engr. Dalsar Corp., Turkey, 1977; asst. prof. Purdue U., West Lafayette Ind., 1980-86; prof. civil engring. Utah State U., 1986—; cons. Served with Turkish Army, 1976. Recipient govt. grants for coll. edn., 1966-72. Mem. ASCE, Am. Concrete Inst., Sigma Xi, Chi Epsilon. Author: Dynamics of Bridge Structures, 1984; contbr. articles to profl. jours. Office: Utah State U Dept Civil Engring Logan UT 84322

YENSON, EVELYN P., lottery official; b. Johannesburg, Republic of South Africa, Dec. 20, 1944; came to U.S., 1963; d. T. and P.F. Yenson; children: Megan Y. Sun, Elliot H. Sun. BA, Coll. New Rochelle, 1967; MA, U. Wis., Milw., 1968. Planner/evaluator Seattle Pub. Schs., 1971-73; dir. planning divsn., various other positions Dept. Cmty. Devel., Seattle, 1973-83; planning dir. Seattle Ctr., 1983-84; pvt. practice as cons. Seattle, 1984-85; dir., dep. commr. Expo '86, Vancouver, B.C., Can., 1985-86; dir. Wash. State Lottery, Olympia, 1987—; presenter in field. Mem. Mcpl. League Bd., Seattle, 1991-92; bd. dirs. Seattle Arts Commn., 1989-93; bd. dirs. Camp Brotherhood, Seattle, 1994—, treas., 1995; sec. bd. dirs. Sunhill, Inc., Seattle. Mem. N.Am. Assn. State and Provincial Lotteries (pres. 1991-93, past pres.), Intertoto (bd. dirs.). Roman Catholic. Home: 2350 34th Ave S Seattle WA 98144-5554 Office: Wash State Lottery PO Box 43001 Olympia WA 98504-3001

YEP, LAURENCE MICHAEL, author; b. San Francisco, June 14, 1948; s. Thomas Kim and Franche (Lee) Y. B.A., U. Calif., Santa Cruz, 1970; Ph.D., SUNY, Buffalo, 1975. Tchr. San Jose (Calif.) City Coll., part-time 1975-76, Foothill Coll., Mountain View, Calif., 1975, U. Calif., Berkeley, 1987-89; writer in residence U. Calif., Santa Barbara, 1990; Book-of-the-Month writing fellow, 1970; teaching fellow SUNY, Buffalo, 1970-73, research fellow, 1973-74. Author sci. fiction stories, children's stories, 1968—: Sweetwater, 1973, Dragonwings (Newbery Honor Book award ALA 1976, Children's Book award Internat. Reading Assn. 1976), (Carter G. Woodson award Nat. Council Social Studies 1976), 1975, Child of the Owl, 1977, Seademons, 1977, Sea Glass, (Commonwealth Club lit. award 1979), 1979, Kind Hearts and Gentle Monsters, 1982, The Mark Twain Murders, 1982, Dragon of the Lost Sea, 1982, Liar, Liar, 1983, Tom Sawyer Fires, 1984, Dragon Steel, 1985, Mountain Light, 1985, Shadow Lord, 1985, Monster Makers, Inc., 1986, Curse of the Squirrel, 1987, The Rainbow People, 1989; author one-act plays Pay the Chinaman, 1987, FairyBones, 1987, Dragon Cauldron, 1991, The Lost Garden, 1991, The Star Fisher, (Christopher award 1992), 1991, Tongues of Jade, 1991, theatrical adaption of Dragonwings, 1991, Dragon War, 1992, American Dragons, 1992, also editor, Butterfly Boy, 1993, Dragon's Gate, (Newbery Honor Book award ALA 1994), 1993, The Ghost Fox, 1993, The Man Who Tricked a Ghost, 1993, The Shell Woman and the King, 1993, The Boy Who Swallowed Snakes, 1994, The Junior Thunder Lord, 1994, The Tiger Woman, 1994. Literature fellow Nat. Endowment for Arts, 1990. Address: 921 Populus Pl Sunnyvale CA 94086-9050

YESKE, DAVID BRENT, investment advisor; b. Albany, Calif., May 21, 1957; s. Ronald and JoAnn (Huntsman) Y.; m. Virginia Folwell, Jan. 10, 1987. BS in Applied Econs., U. San Francisco, 1988, MA in Econs., 1994. CFP. Mng. gen. ptnr. PCM Ltd., Napa, Calif., 1977-83; wire trader Goldberg Securities, San Francisco, 1984-85; brokerage cons. The Paul Revere Cos., San Francisco, 1985-89; pres. Yeske & Co., Inc., San Francisco, 1990—. Mem. Inst. Cert. Fin. Planners (pres. San Francisco chpt. 1993—), Commonwealth Club of Calif., Security Analysts of San Francisco. Office: Yeske & Co Inc 220 Bush St Ste 1109 San Francisco CA 94104-3513

YESNER, DAVID R., anthropology educator; b. Hartford, Conn., Jan. 15, 1948; s. Raymond and Bernice (Lieberman) Y.; m. Kristine June Sanger Crossen, Jun. 9, 1989; 1 child, Daniel Robert Yesner. AB, Cornell U., 1971; MA, U. Conn., 1974, PhD, 1977. Teaching asst. U. Conn., Storrs, Conn., 1973-75; instr. Anchorage C.C., Anchorage, 1975-77; asst. prof. U. So. Maine, Portland, Maine, 1977-81; vis. prof. Mc Gill U., Montreal, Quebec, Can., 1981-82; assoc. prof. U. So. Maine, Portland, Maine, 1982-87; assoc. prof. U. Alaska, Anchorage, 1987-94, prof. anthropology, 1994—; bd. dirs. So. Alaska Mus. Nat. History, Anchorage, 1991—. Editor: (book) As The World Warmed, 1995, Alaska's People, 1995; book rev. editor: Man in the Northeast, 1982-85; contbr. to profl. jours. Mem. Alaska Anthropol. Assn. (editor 1988-91, book review editor 1995), Soc. for Am. Archaeology, Am. Quaternary Assn., Cornell Club of Alaska (alumni mem. 1990-95). Democrat. Jewish. Office: U Alaska Dept Anthropology 3211 Providence Dr Anchorage AK 99508-4614

YGUADO, ALEX ROCCO, economics educator; b. Lackawanna, N.Y., Jan. 17, 1939; s. Manuel and Rose (Barrillio) Y.; m. Patricia Ann Rieker; children: Gary Alexander, Melissa Rose, Charissa Ann. BA, San Fernando State Coll., Northridge, 1968; MA, Calif. State U., Northridge, 1970; MS, U. So. Calif., 1972. Contractor Los Angeles, 1962-69; instr. Calif. Poly. State U., San Luis Obispo, 1969-70, U. So. Calif., Los Angeles, 1970-74; prof. econs. L.A. Mission Coll., San Fernando, Calif., 1975—, acad. senate pres., 1992-93, cluster chair profl. studies, 1993—; cons. Community Service Orgn., Los Angeles, 1969-71. Author: Principles of Economics, 1978; contbr. chpts. to books. Served with U.S. Army, 1957-60. Recipient: Blue Ribbon landscape design City of Albuquerque, 1962, Cert. Appreciation Los Angeles Mission Coll., 1978; Fulbright scholar, 1986-87. Mem. Calif. Small Bus. Assn. Democrat. Roman Catholic. Clubs: Newman (Los Angeles), Sierra Retreat (Malibu, sponsor). Home: 30960 N Romero Cyn Castaic CA 91384 Office: LA Mission Coll 13356 Eldridge Ave Sylmar CA 91342-3244

YIH, MAE DUNN, state legislator; b. Shanghai, China, May 24, 1928; d. Chung Woo and Fung Wen (Feng) Dunn; m. Stephen W.H. Yih, 1953; children: Donald, Daniel. B.A., Barnard Coll., 1951; postgrad. Columbia U., 1951-52. Asst. to bursar Barnard Coll., N.Y.C., 1952-54; mem. Oreg. Ho. of Reps. from 36th dist., 1977-83, Oreg. Senate from 19th dist., 1983—. Mem. Clover Ridge Elem. Sch. Bd., Albany, Oreg., from 1969-78, Albany Union High Sch. Bd., from 1975-79, Joint Legis. Ways and Means Com., Joint Legis. Audit Com., Senate Transp. Com., Western States Forestry Task Force, 1993, senate pres. pro-tempore, 1993. Episcopalian. Home: 34465 Yih Ln NE Albany OR 97321-9557 Office: Oreg State Senate 206 State St Salem OR 97301-3444

YIN, GERALD ZHEYAO, technology and engineering executive; b. Beijing, Jan. 29, 1944; came to U.S., 1980; s. Huaixing and Halumi Yin; m. Junling June Yen, Feb. 28, 1971; 1 child, John Chengjiang. BS in Chem. Physics, U. Sci. & Tech. China, Beijing, 1967; postgrad., Beijing U., 1978-80; PhD in Chemistry, UCLA, 1984. Process engr. Lanzhou Oil Refinery, Lanzhou, People's Republic of China, 1968-73; mgr. research staff Chinese Acad. Sciences, Lanzhou, 1973-78; sr. process engr. Intel Corp. Santa Clara TD, Santa Clara, Calif., 1984-86; mgr., staff engr. Lam Rsch. Corp., Rsch. & Devel., Fremont, Calif., 1986-91; dir. etch tech. and engring. new product devel. Applied Materials, Inc., Santa Clara, Calif., 1991. Author: Introducing Orthogonal Design to Semiconductor Industry, 1985; inventor multistep power reduction plasma etching, Rainbow oxide etcher, 200mm enhanced Electron Cyclotron Resonance reactor, High Density Plasma oxide and Decoupled Plasma Source metal etch plasma source and reactors. Recipient Nat. Acad. award People's Republic of China, 1979, Nat. Acad. Invention award, People's Republic of China, 1980. Mem. Electrochem. Soc., Am. Chem. Soc., Am. Vacuum Soc., Silicon Valley Chinese Engring. Assn. (founder, first pres.). Office: Applied Materials Inc 3320 Scott Blvd M/S 1111 Santa Clara CA 95054

YINGLING, ROBERT GRANVILLE, JR., accountant; b. Lakewood, Ohio, Nov. 8, 1940; s. Robert Granville and Natalie (Phillips) Y.; m. Linda Kay Patterson, Mar. 30, 1968; 1 child, Michael Philip. AB in Polit. Sci., U. Mo., 1963; postgrad., U. Ariz., 1966-67, Portland State U., 1971-73. CPA, Oreg. Mgmt. trainee Mich. Nat. Bank, Flint, 1963-65; comml. note teller First Nat. Bank Ariz., Tucson, 1965-67; spl. asst. Travelers Ins. Cos., Phoenix, then Portland, Oreg., 1967-70; chief acct. Am. Guaranty Life Ins. Co., Portland, 1970-73; supr. Peat, Marwick, Mitchell & Co., Portland, 1973-79; ptnr. Dietrich, Bye, Griffin & Youel, Portland, 1979-84; prin. Isler, Collins & McAdams, Portland, 1984-85; owner, acct. R.G. Yingling Jr., CPA, Portland, 1985—; adj. asst. prof., U. Portland, 1988. Treas. Portland Amateur Hockey Assn., 1977-78; mem. exec. bd. Columbia Pacific coun. Boy Scouts Am., 1980—, asst. treas., 1986-87, treas. 1988-91, dist. chmn. Mt. View, 1991; bd. dirs. Artist Repertory Theatre, Inc., 1992—,St. Andrew Legal Clinic, Inc., 1992—, treas. Recipient Silver Beaver award, Boy Scouts Am., 1986. Mem. AICPA, Oreg. Soc. CPAs, Nat. Assn. Accts. (nat. dir. 1985-87), Assn. Govt. Accts. (nat. v.p. 1983), Nat. Conf. CPA Practitioners, Rotary.

YNDA, MARY LOU, artist, educator; b. Los Angeles, Apr. 4, 1936; d. Ernest Pastor Ynda and Mary Estella (Ruiz) Zapotocky, m. Gary Lynn Coleman, Sept. 1, 1956 (div. Feb. 1983); children: Debra Lynn, Lisa Annette, David Gary; m. Miles Ciletti, May 25, 1991. Student, Immaculate Heart Coll., Los Angeles, 1973-79; AA in Fine Arts, Los Angeles City Coll., 1976; BA, Calif. State U., L.A., 1993. Instr. Fashion Inst. Design, L.A., 1980-81; tchr. art to disabled First St. Gallery, Claremont, Calif., 1991-94; tchr. art Tierra Del Sol Found., Sunland, Calif., 1994—. Group shows include Double Rocking G Gallery, L.A., 1983, Improv Theater West, West Hollywood, Calif., 1983, Exposition Gallery Calif. State U., L.A., 1983, L.A. Art Core Gallery, 1985, Poly. Tech. Sch., Pasadena, Calif., 1986, Bad Eye Gallery, L.A., 1987, Art in the Hall VI West Hollywood City Hall, 1989, Echo Park Gallery, L.A., 1991, Art N Barbee Gallery, 1992, A Celebration of City Life, 1993, DADA Show-Downtown Lives, L.A., 1994; designer Spoken Word CD Long Days and Monster Nights, 1994; contbg. author poetry Spoken Word Voices of the Angels, 1982; book rev. Yesterday and Tomorrow: California Women Artists, 1989. Mem. Women's Caucus for Art. Democrat. Office: 2118 E 7th Pl Los Angeles CA 90021-1762

YOCAM, DELBERT WAYNE, communication company executive; b. Long Beach, Calif., Dec. 24, 1943; s. Royal Delbert and Mary Rose (Gross) Y.; m. Janet McVeigh, June 13, 1965; children—Eric Wayne, Christian Jeremy, Elizabeth Janelle. B.A. in Bus. Adminstrn., Calif. State U.-Fullerton, 1966; M.B.A., Calif. State U., Long Beach, 1971. Mktg.-supply changeover coordinator Automotive Assembly div. Ford Motor Co., Dearborn, Mich., 1966-72; prodn. control mgr. Control Data Corp., Hawthorne, Calif., 1972-74; prodn. and material control mgr. Bourns Inc., Riverside, Calif., 1974-76; corp. material mgr. Computer Automation Inc., Irvine, Calif., 1976-78; prodn. planning mgr. central staff Cannon Electric div. ITT, World hdqrs., Santa Ana, Calif., 1978-79; exec. v.p., chief ops. officer Apple Computer, Cupertino, Calif., 1979-91; pres., COO Textronix Inc., Wilsonville, Oreg., 1992-95; mem. faculty Cypress Coll., Calif., 1972-79; bd. dirs. Adobe Sys. Inc., Mountain View, Calif., 1991—, Oracle Corp., Redwood Shores, Calif., 1992—, AST Rsch. Inc., Irvine, Calif., 1992—, Tech. Ctr. of San Jose, Calif., 1987-93, vice chmn., 1989, 90. Mem. Am. Electronics Assn. (bd. dirs. 1988-89), Control Data Corp. Mgmt. Assn. (co-founder 1974), L.A. County Heart Assn. (active 1966). *

YOCHEM, BARBARA JUNE, sales executive, lecturer; b. Knox, Ind., Aug. 22, 1945; d. Harley Albert and Rosie (King) Runyan; m. Donald A. Yochem (div. 1979); 1 child, Morgan Lee; m. Don Heard, Dec. 12, 1987. Grad. high school, Knox, Ind., 1963. Sales rep. Hunter Woodworks, Carson, Calif., 1979-84, sales mgr., 1984-87; sales rep. Comml. Lumber and Pallet, Industry, Calif., 1987-92; owner By By Prodns., Glendora, Calif., 1976—. Author: Barbara Yochem's Inner Shooting; contbr. articles to profl. jours. Head coach NRA Jr. Olympic Shooting Camp, 1989-94; foster parent, 1992-94. Recipient U.S. Bronze medal U.S. Olympic Com., 1976, World Bronze medal U.S Olympic Com., 1980; nominated Calif. Trapshooting Hall of Fame, 1994. Address: By By Prodns PO Box 1676 Glendora CA 91740-1676

YOCUM, HARRISON GERALD, horticulturist, botanist, educator, researcher; b. Bethlehem, Pa., Apr. 2, 1923; s. Harrison and Bertha May (Meckes) Y. BS, Pa. State U., 1955; MS, Rutgers U., 1961. Horticulture instr. U. Tenn., Martin, 1957-59; biology tchr., libr. asst. high schs., El Paso, Tex., 1959-60; rsch. asst. geochronology lab. U. Ariz., Tucson, 1960-67, rsch. asst. environ. rsch. lab., 1969-76; landscaping supt. Tucson Airport Authority, 1976-82; instr. Pima C.C., Tucson, 1976—. Contbr. articles to profl. jours. Founder Tucson Bot. Gardens, 1964. Mem. Am. Hort. Soc., Men's Garden Club Tucson (pres. 1991), Tucson Cactus & Succulent Soc. (pres. 1991, 92), Internat. Palm Soc. (charter), El Paso Cactus and Rock Club, Tucson Gem & Mineral Soc., Old Pueblo Lapidary Club, Deming Mineral Soc., Nat. Geog. Soc., Ariz.-Sonora Desert Mus., Huachuca Vigilantes, Penn State Alumni Assn., Pa. Club Tucson, Fraternal Order Police Assocs., N.Am. Hunting Club (life), Shriners, Masons, Scottish Rite. Lutheran. Home: 1628 N Jefferson Ave Tucson AZ 85712-4204

YOHE, JOHN SPENCER, financial analyst; b. Lawrence, Kans., Jan. 5, 1954; s. Delton Spencer and Betty Claire (Foster) Y.; m. Sherri Sue Kendall, Sept. 1, 1979; 1 child, Darrell. BS in Acctg., U. Kans., 1977, BSBA, 1977. CPA; cert. quality analyst. Cost acct. Greyhound Exposition Svcs., Kansas City, Mo., 1977-78; systems analyst Gates Learjet, Tucson, Ariz., 1978-82; supr., cost acctg. Hughes Aircraft Co., Tucson, 1982-84; supr. bus. practices Sperry Corp., Phoenix, 1984-86; supr. fin. systems Motorola, Inc., Scottsdale, Ariz., 1986—. Home: PO Box 54252 Phoenix AZ 85078-4252

YOKLEY, RICHARD CLARENCE, fire department administrator; b. San Diego, Dec. 29, 1942; s. Clarence Ralph and Dorothy Junese (Sackman) Y.; m. Jean Elizabeth Liddle, July 25, 1964; children: Richard Clarence II, Karin Denise. Student, San Diego City Coll., 1967; AS, Miramar Coll., 1975. Cert. fire officer, fire instr., Calif. Disc jockey Sta. KSDS-FM, San Diego, 1966-67; bldg. engr. Consolidated Systems, Inc., San Diego, 1968-72; with Bonita-Sunnyside Fire Dept., Calif., 1972—; ops. chief Bonita-Sunnyside Fire Dept., 1991-93, maintenance officer, 1993—; med. technician Hartson Ambulance, San Deigo, 1978-80, Bay Gen. Hosp. (now Scripps Hosp.), Chula Vista, Calif., 1980-83; chmn. South Bay Emergency Med. Svc., 1988. Contbr. articles to jours., newspapers and mags. Asst. curator Firehouse Mus., San Diego, 1972-89, docent, 1990-93; scoutmaster troop 874 Boy Scouts Am., Bonita, Calif., 1978-79. With USAF, 1962-66. Recipient Heroism and Community Svc. award Firehouse Mag., N.Y.C., 1987, Star News Salutes award Chula Vista Star News, 1987, Golden Svc. award San Diego County Credit Union, 1988. Mem. Internat. Assn. Firefighters (pres. local chpt. 1981-82), Calif. State Firefighters Assn. (dep. dir. so. divsn. 1994—), San Diego County Fire Prevention Officers (v.p. 1984, pres. 1985), Bonita Bus. and Profl. Assn. (bd. dirs. 1991-93, Historian award 1987), South Bay Commn., Bonita Hist. Mus. (co-founder 1986), Sport Chalet Dive Club (v.p. 1991). Republican. Methodist. Office: Bonita-Sunnyside Fire Dept 4900 Bonita Rd Bonita CA 91902-1725

YON, JOSEPH LANGHAM, gynecologist, oncologist; b. Charlotesville, Va., Feb. 9, 1936; s. Joseph Langham and Sallie Pugh (Haden) Y.; m. Dagmar Camilla Halmagyi, June 27, 1959 (div. 1979); children: Joseph III, Steven A., Lura C.; m. Edith Jane Maffeo, Nov. 26, 1979. BA in Biology, Va. Mil. Inst., 1957; MD, U. Va., 1961. Diplomate Am. Bd. Ob-Gyn. With med. corps USN, Jacksonville, Fla., 1961-62; med. officer U.S.S. Yellowstone, USN, Jacksonville, 1962-63; resident Ob-Gyn USN, Portmouth, Va., 1962-66; staff Ob-Gyn USN, Quantico, Va., 1967-69, Oakland, Calif., 1970-72; fellow Gyn-Oncology Jackson Meml. Hosp., Miami, 1972-74; staff Gyn-Oncology USN, San Diego, 1974-80; head gyn-oncology Va. Mason Clinic, Seattle, 1983—; clin. prof. U. Wash. Sch. Medicine, Seattle, 1983—. Contbr. articles to profl. jours. Fellow Am. Coll. Ob-Gyn (vice chmn. sect. 1971-80), Am. Coll. Surgery, Soc. Gynecology Oncologists (bd. cert. Gyn-Oncology), Am. Soc. Clin. Oncologists, Western Assn. Gynecology Oncologists. Republican. Office: Virginia Mason Clinic 1100 9th Ave Seattle WA 98101-2756

YOON, IN-JIN, social sciences educator; b. Hong Seong, South Korea, June 30, 1963; came to U.S., 1985; s. Hee-Ro and Ok-Hee (Song) Y.; m. Hyang-Ju Lee, June 8, 1991; 1 child, Joan Yoon. BA, Korea U., Seoul, 1985; MA, U. Chgo., 1988, PhD, 1991. Rsch. cons., interviewer Social Svc. Adminstrn. U. Chgo., 1987-88, rsch. cons., 1990-91, post-doctoral fellow Irving B. Harris Grad. Sch. Pub. Policy, 1991-92; asst. prof. Asian-Am. Studies U. Calif., Santa Barbara, 1991—; columnist Korea Times, L.A., 1992—; manuscript referee Am. Jour. Sociology, Chgo., 1992—, Temple U. Press, Phila., 1993—, Princeton U. Press, N.Y.C., 1994—. Author: Papers of the East-West Center Population Institute, 1993; contbr. articles to profl. jours. Deacon Pyong Kang Ch., Isla Vista, Calif., 1992—; adviser Korean Christian Fellowship, U. Calif. Santa Barbara, 1992—. Recipient Marc Galler prize U. Chgo., 1992, Urban Poverty post-doctoral fellowship, U. Chgo., 1991-92, Hewlett Demographic Tng. scholarship, U. Chgo., 1986-91. Mem. Am. Sociol. Assn., Assn. for Asian-Am. Studies, Pacific Sociol. Assn. Presbyterian. Office: U Calif Asian Am Studies Program Santa Barbara CA 93106

YOON, JI-WON, virology, immunology and diabetes educator, research administrator; b. Kang-Jin, Chonnam, Korea, Mar. 28, 1939; came to U.S., 1965; s. Baek-In and Duck-Soon (Lee) Y.; m. Chungja Rhim, Aug. 17, 1968; children: John W., James W. MS, U. Conn., 1971, PhD, 1973. Sr. investigator NIH, Bethesda, Md., 1978-84; prof., chief div. virology U. Calgary, Alta., Can., 1984—, prof., assoc. dir. diabetes rsch. ctr., 1985-90, prof., dir. diabetes rsch. ctr., 1990—; mem. edit. bd. Annual Review Advances Present Rsch. Animal Diabetes, 1990—, Diabetes Rsch. Clin. Practice, 1989—; scientific coord. 10th Internat. Workshop on Immunology Diabetes, Jerusalem, 1989-90; sr. investigator NIH, 1976-84. Contbg. author: Current Topics in Microbiology and Immunology, 1990, Autoimmunity and Pathogenesis of Diabetes, 1990; contbr. articles to New England Jour. Medicine, Jour. Virology, Sci., Nature, The Lancet, Jour. Diabetes. Rsch. fellow Sloan Kettering Cancer Inst., 1973-74, Staff fellow, Sr. Staff fellow NIH, 1974-76, 76-78; recipient NIH Dir. award, 1984, Heritage Med. Scientist award, Alberta Heritage Found. Med. Rsch., 1984, Lectrship. award, 3d Asian Symposium Childhood Diabetes, 1989, 8th Annual Meeting Childhood Diabetes, Osaka, Japan, 1990, 9th Korean/Can. Heritage award, 1989. Mem. Am. Soc. Immunologists, Am. Diabetes Assn., Am. Soc. Microbiology, N.Y. Acad. Sci., Soc. Virology, Internat. Diabetes Fedn. Baptist. Home: 206 Edgeview Dr NW, Calgary, AB Canada T3A 4W9 Office: Julia McFarlane Diabetes Rsch Ctr, 3330 Hospital Dr NW, Calgary, AB Canada T2N 4N1

YORK, DOUGLAS ARTHUR, manufacturing and construction company executive; b. Centralia, Ill., June 5, 1940; s. Harry Bernice and Violet Alvera (Johnstone) Y.; student San Diego State Jr. Coll., 1957; m. Linda Kay McIntosh, Sept. 13, 1958; children—Deborah Ann, Darren Anthony. With Meredith & Simpson Constrn. Co./DBA Pressure Cool Co., Indio, Calif., 1958—, v.p., 1968—, sec., gen. mgr., 1976-82, pres., 1982—. Mem. Bldg. and Housing Appeals Bd. City of Indio, City of Coachella, Calif.; bd. dirs. Coachella Valley wild Bird Ctr.; trustee Eisenhower Med. Ctr., Rancho Mirage, Calif. Mem. ASHRAE, Internat. Conf. Bldg. Officials. Republican. Office: 83-801 Ave 45 Indio CA 92201

YORK, EARL DANA, oil company executive, engineering consultant; b. Gary, Ind., July 28, 1928; s. Emil and Irene (Fink) Y.; m. Feb. 12, 1961 (div. June 1988); 1 child, Earl D. II. BS in Chem. Engrng., Purdue U., 1950; postgrad., Poly. Inst. Bklyn., 1950-51, U. Tenn., 1951-52, Purdue U.-Calumet, Hammond, Ind., 1959-62. Engr. Otto H. York Co., Inc., East Orange, N.J., 1950-52; devel. engr. Oak Ridge (Tenn.) Nat. Lab., 1952-53; various positions Amoco Oil Co., Whiting, Ind., 1953-64; dir. rsch. assocs. R & D dept. Amoco Oil Co., Naperville, Ill., 1975-79; various positions Amoco Internat., N.Y.C. and Chgo., 1964-69; mgr. tech. svcs. Amoco U.K. Ltd., London and Milford Haven, Wales, 1969-74; spl. engrng. assignment Kharg Chem. Co., Tehran, Iran, 1974-75; rsch. assoc., dir. Amoco Oil R&D, Naperville, Ill., 1976-79; v.p. Rio Blanco Oil Shale Co. div. Amoco Corp., Denver, 1979-86, pres., 1986-92; retired Amoco Corp., 1992. Patentee in field. With U.S. Army, 1954-56. Mem. Am. Chem. Soc., Am. Inst. Chem. Engrs., AAAS. Lutheran. Home: 23 Talana Cir # 723 Hot Springs National Park AR 71909-7412

YORK, JESSE LOUIS, chemical engineering and environmental consultant; b. Plains, Tex., May 1, 1918; s. Jesse Lewis and Alma Terrell (Sealy) Y.; m. Eva Jean Woods, Dec. 15, 1945 (div. Sept. 1975); children: Terrell Mae, Kathleen Lenore; m. Ruth Roberta Robinson, Sept. 17, 1975. BS in Engrng., U. N.Mex., 1938; MS, U. Mich., 1940, PhD in Chem. Engrng., 1950. Registered profl. engr., Mich., Colo., N. Mex. From instr. to prof. dept. chem. and metall. engrng. U. Mich., Ann Arbor, 1941-70; chief environ. scientist Stearns-Roger Engrng. Corp., Denver, 1970-83; v.p. Sr. Mgmt. Cons., Denver, 1984—; engrng. cons., Denver, 1983—. Author: Unit Operations, 1950; contbr. articles to tech. mags.; patentee in field. Chmn. planning bd. Scio Twp., Washtenaw County, Dexter, Mich., 1963-70; bd. dirs. Colo. Sch. Mines Found., Golden, 1973-94, exec. dir., 1989-92; bd. dirs. Denver Symphony Orch., 1982-89; mem. nat. adv. bd. Santa Fe Opera, 1985-92. Mem. ASME, Am. Inst. Chem. Engrs., Am. Chem. Soc., Am. Acad. Environ. Engrs. (diplomate), Air and Waste Mgmt. Assn. Republican. Home and Office: 3557 S Ivanhoe St Denver CO 80237-1122

YORK, ROBERT DEVEREUX, anthropologist, archaeologist; b. Phoenix, Apr. 5, 1944; s. John Devereux and Mary Elizabeth (Potter) Y.; m. Patricia Louise Rochon, Aug. 20, 1966 (div. July 1988); m. Gigi G. Grover, Dec. 28, 1991; children: Adrian D., Sara. BS, No. Ariz. U., 1969; MA, U. Ariz., 1971. State archeologist U.S. Dept. Interior, Bur. of Land Mgmt., Reno, 1974-78; archeologist, cultural resource mgr., history officer San Juan Nat. Forest, Durango, Colo., 1978-89; archeologist, cultural resources mgr. Wyo. zone USDA Forest Svc., Laramie, Wyo., 1989-90; cultural resources mgr. Office of Navajo-Hopi Indian Relocation, Flagstaff, Ariz., 1990-94; archaeologist Medicine Wheel Project Bighorn Nat. Forest, Sheridan, Wyo., 1994—; pres. Nev. Archaeol. Soc., Reno, 1975. Editor Nev. Bur. of Land Mgmt. Cultural Resource Mgmt. Pubs., 1976-78; contbr. articles to profl. jours. Bd. mem. Assn. for Retarded Citizens, Durango, 1984; v.p. El Rancho Florida Homeowners, Durango, 1984-88; mem. San Juan Nat. Forest Handicap Access Com., Durango, 1986-89. With USCG, 1962-66. Recipient Excellence in Govt. award Denver (Colo.) Fed. Exec. Bd., 1989. Mem. Soc. Profl. Archaeologists, Colo. Archaeol. Soc. (advisor 1990—), Fed. Preservation Forum (nominating com.). Office: Bighorn Nat Forest 1969 S Sheridan Ave Sheridan WY 82801-6108

YORK, THEODORE ROBERT, consulting company executive; b. Mitchel Field, N.Y., May 4, 1926; s. Theodore and Helen (Zierak) Y.; m. Clara Kiefer, Jan. 3, 1952; children: Theodore R. II, Sharon L., Scott K., Krista A. Jarman. BS, U.S. Mil. Acad., 1950; MBA, George Washington U., 1964; MPA, Nat. U., 1984. Commd. 2d lt. USAF, 1950, advanced through grades to col., 1970, ret., 1974; pres. T. R. York Cons., Fairfax, Va., 1974-79, T. R. Cons., San Diego, 1979-85, ULTRAPLECS Intelligent Bldgs., Sandy, Utah, 1991—; dir. Software Productivity Consortium, Herndon, Va., 1985-90. Mem. Loudoun County Rep. Com., Leesburg, Va., 1990-91. Decorated DFC, Air medal (5), Meritorius Svc. medal, Joint Svcs. Commendation medal, Air Force Commendation medal (5). Mem. Internat. Facilities Mgmt. Assn., Intelligent Bldgs. Inst. (advisor), Instituto Mexicana Del Edificios Intelegente (hon.), Office Planners and Users Group, Shriners, Masons. Office: ULTRAPLECS Intelligent Bldg 1289 S Bluff View Dr Sandy UT 84092-5922

YOSHIDA, AKIRA, biochemist; b. Okayama, Japan, May 10, 1924; came to U.S., 1961; s. Isao and Etsu (Kagawa) Y.; m. Michiko Suzuki, Nov. 10, 1954; 1 child, Emmy. MSc, U. Tokyo, 1947, DSc, 1954. Assoc. prof. U. Tokyo, 1952-60; sr. rsch. fellow U. Pa., Phila., 1960-63; rsch. scientist NIH, Bethesda, Md., 1963-65; rsch. prof. U. Wash., Seattle, 1965-72; dir. dept. biochem. genetics City of Hope Med. Ctr., Duarte, Calif., 1972—. Contbr. over 250 articles to profl. jours. Rockefeller Found. scholar, 1955-56; recipient Merit award Japanese Soc. Human Genetics, 1980, Achievement award City of Hope, 1981, Merit Grant award NIH, 1988. Mem. AAAS, Am. Soc. Biol. Chemists, Am. Soc. Human Genetics (assoc. editor), Am. Soc. Hematology, N.Y. Acad. Scis. Home: 2140 Pinecrest Dr Altadena CA 91001-2121 Office: City of Hope Beckman Inst 1450 Duarte Rd Duarte CA 91010-3011

YOSHIDA, KANETAKA, banking executive; b. 1938. With Bank of Tokyo, Ltd., 1962-90, Union Bank, San Francisco, 1990—. Office: Union Bank 350 California St San Francisco CA 94104-1402*

YOSHIDA, KAREN KAMIJO CATEEL, public relations professional; b. Honolulu, Sept. 18, 1964; d. William Francis and Masako (Kamijo) Cateel; m. Ken Yutaka Yoshida, Aug. 4, 1990. BSBA in Mktg., Hawaii Pacific Coll., 1989. Jour. editorial asst. Univ. Press, U. Hawaii, Honolulu, 1983; customer svc. rep. GTE Hawaiian Tel, Honolulu, 1988; account coord. Ogilvy & Mather Hawaii, Honolulu, 1989; pub. rels. asst. McCormick Communications, Honolulu, 1989-90; account dir. Joyce Timpson & Assocs., Honolulu, 1989-90; mgr. communications and pub. rels. Hawaii State Bar Assn., Honolulu, 1990—; tchr. spl. edn. Kahi Mohala Sch., 1994—; mng. mag. editor, dir. membership benefits Hawaii State Bar Assn., 1990—; mem. Pub. Radio Community Adv. Bd., 1993; instr. Honolulu C.C., 1993. Vol. Easter Seal Soc., Hawaiian Humane Soc., Lanakila Elem. Sch. State contest winner Exec. Women's Internat., 1982. Mem. Sons. and Daus. 442nd RCT (newsletter and membership coms. 1993), Hawaii Pacific U. Alumni Assn. (comm. com. 1993). Home: 2807 Pacific Heights Rd Honolulu HI 96813-1019 Office: Kahi Mohala School 91-2301 Ft Weaver Rd Ewa Beach HI 96706

YOSHIDA, KOSAKU, quantitative methods educator; b. Tokyo, July 23, 1938; s. Sakujiro and Shizu (Arita) Y.; m. Chizu Matsuda, Oct. 30, 1977; 1 child, Kayo. BA in Commerce, Waseda U., Tokyo, 1962; MS in Bus. Adminstrn., U. Mont., 1968; PhD in Bus. Adminstrn., NYU, 1975. Asst. prof. Calif. State U., Dominquez Hills, 1975-79, assoc. prof., 1979-84, prof., 1984—; cons. in quality mgmt., 1987—. Author: Elementary Statistics, 1989; contbr. articles to profl. jours. Productivity commr. City of L.A., 1988-92. Mem. Decision Scis. Inst., Am. Statis. Assn., Inst. of Mgmt. Scis., Am. Soc. for Quality Control. Office: Calif State U Sch Mgmt Dominguez Hls Carson CA 90747

YOSHIMOTO, CEDRIC MITSUO, physician; b. Kansas City, Mo., Aug. 22, 1951; s. Mitsuru and Annie Nakami (Koga) Y.; 1 child, Walden Emil Bjorn. AB, U. Calif., Berkeley, 1972; MD, U. Hawaii, 1977; DTM&H, London Sch., 1990; MPH, U. Hawaii, 1993. Integrated Flexible resident U. Hawaii, Honolulu, 1977-78; staff physician Tumutumu Hosp., Karatina, Kenya, 1979-80; locum tenans physician Kalihi-Palama Clinic, Honolulu, 1982; cons. Hawaii State Dept. of Health, Honolulu, 1983-91; staff physician Waianae Coast Comprehensive Health Ctr., 1983—; cons. U.S. Fish and Wildlife Svc., Honolulu, 1990—; preceptor Hawaii Dept. of Health, Waianae, 1991-92; cons. Ebeye Hosp., Marshall Islands, 1992; cons. Health Care Orgn. for Africa, The Gambia, 1994; asst. clin. prof. Dept. Family Practice and Cmty. Health, John A. Burns Sch. Medicine, U. Hawaii, Honolulu, 1992—, asst. clin. prof. dept. pub. health sci. Sch. Pub. Health, 1994—. Mem. Amnesty Internat., Honolulu, 1983. Fellow Am. Acad. of Family Physicians, Royal Soc. of Tropical Medicine and Hygiene; mem. Am. Soc. of Tropical Medicine and Hygiene, Physicians for Social Responsibility, Wilderness Med. Soc., Sierra Club (instr., cons. 1990—, outing leader, 1990—). Office: Waianae Coast Comprehensive Health Ctr 86-260 Farrington Hwy Waianae HI 96792-3128

YOSHIMOTO, HIROKO, art educator, artist; b. Kobe, Japan, Apr. 23, 1943; came to U.S., 1958; d. Akira and Teiko (Takahashi) Y. BA with highest honors, UCLA, 1965, MA with highest honors, 1967. Cert. tchr., Calif. Freelance designer Los Angeles, 1967-68; graphic designer Zamparelli Graphics, Los Angeles, 1968; with IBM Japan, Tokyo, 1968-70; instr. studio art Ventura (Calif.) Coll., 1970—; instr. Santa Ana (Calif.) Coll., 1970; pres. Studio 83, Ventura, 1983-85, 92-93. One-woman shows include Ventura Hist. Mus., 1978, Gallery 932, Ventura, 1982, Ventura County Govt. Ctr. Atrium Gallery, 1983, 91, New Media Gallery at Ventura Coll., 1989, Tokyo Mcpl. Art Space, 1994, Osaka Contemporary Art Ctr., 1994, Amitage Cleo, Tokyo, 1994; exhibited in group shows at Grandview Gallery, L.A., L.A. Artcore Gallery, 1984, 86, L.A. County Mus. Art Rental Gallery, 1987, 92; art dir. (video tapes) Art and Anatomy, 1989, Sumi-e and Western Watercolor, 1989. Recipient Outstanding Faculty Recognition award Ventura Coll. Acad. Senate, 1990. Mem. Am. Fedn. Tchrs., Ventura Art Assn., Asian Am. Women Artists Assn. Democrat. Home: 352 Lupine Way Ventura CA 93001-2221 Office: Ventura Coll 4667 Telegraph Rd Ventura CA 93003-3872

YOSHINO, GEORGE, food products executive; b. Kennewick, Wash., June 25, 1928; s. Frank H. and Kazuye (Hada) Y.; m. Frances T. Kaku, Dec. 29, 1951 (div. 1979); children: Jean Frances, Frankie Jo, Michael Stanton, Harry Walter; m. Marguerite Shirley Mosley, Dec. 8, 1990. Grad. high sch., Weiser, Idaho. Owner Yoshino Farms, Quincy, Wash., 1948—; pres. Columbia Growers Inc, Quincy, 1956-62, Yoshino Western, Inc., Quincy, 1962-68, Wyco, Inc., Seattle, 1968-74; asst. sr. v.p. U & I Inc., Pasco, Wash., 1974-79; dir., gen. mgr. Spad Distributing, Inc., Pasco, 1979-86; pres. Century 21 Products, Inc., Pasco, 1987—; bd. dirs. Am. Nat. Bank, Kennewick; exec. bd. Benton-Franklin Govtl. Conf., 1993—; dir. Assoc. Wash. Bus. Mem. City Coun. Quincy, 1964-66; bd. dirs. Columbia Basin Commn., Olympia, Wash., 1964-68; dir. Associated Wash. Bus., 1994—; dir. exec. com. Benton Franklin Regional Coun., 1993—. Mem. Produce Mktg. Assn., Associated Wash. Bus. Republican. Office: Century 21 Products Inc 1917 N 2nd Ave Pasco WA 99301-3722

YOSHIZUMI, DONALD TETSURO, dentist; b. Honolulu, Feb. 18, 1930; s. Richard Kiyoshi and Hatsue (Tanouye) Y.; BS, U. Hawaii, 1952; DDS, U. Mo., 1960, MS, 1963; m. Barbara Fujiko Iwashita, June 25, 1955; children: Beth Ann E., Cara Leigh S., Erin Yuri. Clin. instr. U. Mo. Sch. Dentistry, Kansas City, 1960-63; pvt. practice, Santa Clara, Calif., 1963-70, San Jose, Calif., 1970—. With USAF, 1952-56. Mem. Am. Dental Assn., Calif. Dental Assn., Santa Clara County Dental Soc., Omicron Kappa Upsilon, Delta Sigma Delta. Contbr. articles to profl. jours. Home: 5054 Parkfield Ave San Jose CA 95129-3225 Office: 2011 Forest Ave San Jose CA 95128

YOST, DARLENE R., geriatrics and psychiatric/mental health nurse; b. Leonard, N.D., Sept. 15, 1933; d. Richard Frank and Rose Myrtle (Nesemeier) Greuel; m. Donald R. Walker (dec.); children: Darrell R. Walker, Douglas R. Walker, Deborah R. Walker Barry, Donna R. Walker Gregory; m. James J. Yost, Nov. 4, 1961; children; Yvonne M. Yost Michael, Mary R. Yost Camarillo, Katherine A. Yost Jones. ADN, Community Coll. Denver, 1973. RN, Colo.; cert. EMT. Nurse night supr. Sunny Acres Villa, Northglenn, Colo.; pvt. duty nurse CPQ Nurses, Denver; charge and supervisory nurse Lifelines Inc., Denver; nursing supr. Poplar Grove Care Ctr., 1993—; night supr. St. Paul Care Ctr., Denver; camp nurse Salvation Army, Denver, 9 summers. Mem. Colo. Nurses Against Abortion, Part Time and Non-Practicing Nurses Assn. Home: 501 W 70th Pl Denver CO 80221-3001

YOST, DOUGLAS LEIGHTON, data processing executive; b. Chgo., Mar. 3, 1948; s. George William and Ruthe Edith (Felberg) Y.; m. Barbara Jeanne Beavin, July 20, 1968. BA, North Ctrl. Coll., Naperville, Ill., 1970; MPA, U. Denver, 1975. Cert. data processor. Project mgr. Rocky Mountain Bank Note, Lakewood, Colo., 1970-86; dir. info. svcs. U. Colo. Found., Boulder, 1986—. Mem. Data Processing Mgmt. Assn., Focus Users Group. Home: 3531 Bryant St Denver CO 80211-2852 Office: Univ of Colo Found PO Box 1140 Boulder CO 80309

YOST, KELLY LOU, pianist; b. Boise, Idaho, Aug. 10, 1940; d. Roy Daniel and Helen Roberta (Kingsbury) Frizzelle; m. Nicholas Peter Bond, Dec. 27, 1961 (div. 1973); 1 child, Brook Bernard; m. Samuel Joseph Yost, June 16, 1984. BA in Music, U. Idaho, 1962; postgrad., U. So. Calif., 1965-69. Pvt. tchr. classical piano Twin Falls, Idaho, 1962-88; rec. artist, co-owner ind. record label Channel Prodns., Twin Falls, 1986—; soloist U. Idaho Symphony Orch., Moscow, 1962; pianist, keyboardist Magic Valley Symphony Orch., Twin Falls, 1985, 86; touring guest piano soloist Vandaleer Concert Choir, Moscow, 1961. Recorded record albums: Piano Reflections, 1987, Quiet Colors, 1991. Mem. NARAS, Nat. Assn. Ind. Record Distbrs., Music Tchrs. Nat. Assn., Idaho Music Tchrs. Assn. (sec. 1981-82), Magic Valley Community Concert Assn. (bd. dirs. 1964-87), Phi Beta Kappa. Office: Channel Prodns PO Box 454 Twin Falls ID 83303-0454

YOUNG, C. CLIFTON, judge; b. Nov. 7, 1922, Lovelock, Nev.; m. Jane Young. BA, U. Nev., 1943; LLB, Harvard U., 1949. Bar: Nev. 1949, U.S. Dist. Ct. Nev. 1950, U.S. Supreme Ct. 1955. Justice Nev. Supreme Ct., Carson City, 1985—, former chief justice, from 1989. Office: Nev Supreme Ct 201 S Carson St Carson City NV 89701

YOUNG, CAPRICE YVONNE, municipal official; b. Palo Alto, Calif., Oct. 11, 1965; d. Michael G. and Nancy (Schwartz) Y. BA in History with Stats., Yale U., 1988; MPA in Pub. Fin., U. So. Calif., 1991. Coro Pub. Policy fellow Coro Found., 1988-89; dir. tng. Liaison Citizen Program, L.A., 1989-90; chief mgmt. analyst, fin. and adminstrn. L.A. County Transp. Commn., 1990-93; special asst. to CEO Met. Transp. Authority, 1993-94; asst. deputy mayor City of L.A., 1994—. Author: Local Youth Group Programs, 1985, Giving Sanctuary, 1986. Gant rev. panel mem. fund for a Just Soc., 1992—; bd. sec. Liaison Citizen Program, 1990-94; 2d v.p. SFV Mental Health Ctr., 1993—; bd. dirs. Friends of Hollygrove, 1993—. Mem. Govt. Fin. Officers' Assn., Am. Soc. Pub. Adminstrn., Yale Club So. Calif. Home: 3750 Lankershire Blvd Los Angeles CA 90068 Office: City of L A 200 N Spring St Ste M-1 Los Angeles CA 90012-4801

YOUNG, CEDRIC JAN-YEE, laboratory director, microbiologist; b. Macau, Feb. 23, 1942; came to U.S., 1953; s. Tim-Oy and Sui-On Young; m. Selina Chui-Wah, Sept. 1, 1973; children: Derek Park-Shing, Edmund Park-Wei. BA, Calif. State U., San Francisco, 1970; MS, Calif. State U., Fresno, 1979; postgrad., Loma Linda (Calif.) U., 1981. Pub. health microbiologist Fresno County Pub. Health Dept., 1970-73; dir. pub. health lab. Madera (Calif.) County Pub. Health Dept., 1973-87, Stanislaus County Pub. Health Lab., Modesto, Calif., 1987—; mem. Stanislaus County Tobacco Control Coalition, Modesto, 1990-91. Mem. Am. Cancer Soc., Madera County, 1977-87, Stanislaus and Tuolumne Counties, 1990—, Stanislaus Chinese Assn., Modesto, 1990—. Recipient Cert. San Joaquin (Calif.) Valley Health Consortium, 1985; named to the Order of the Golden Sword Am. Cancer Soc., 1979. Mem. Am. Soc. for Microbiology, Calif. Assn. Pub. Health Lab. Dirs., Calif. Assn. for Med. Lab. Tech. (pres. Stanislaus chpt. 1989-90), Conf. of Pub. Health Laboratorians. Republican. Office: Stanislaus Co Pub Hlth Lab 820 Scenic Dr Modesto CA 95350-6194

YOUNG, CHARLES EDWARD, university chancellor; b. San Bernardino, Calif., Dec. 30, 1931; s. Clayton Charles and Eula May (Walters) Y. AA, San Bernardino Coll., 1954; AB, U. Calif., Riverside, 1955; MA, UCLA, 1957, PhD, 1960; DHL (hon.), U. Judaism, L.A., 1969. Congl. fellow Washington, 1958-59; adminstrv. analyst Office of the Pres., U. Calif., Berkeley, 1959-60; asst. prof. polit. sci. U. Calif., Davis, 1960; asst. prof. polit. sci. UCLA, 1960-66, assoc. prof., 1966-69, prof., 1969—, asst. to chancellor, 1960-62, asst. chancellor, 1962-63, vice chancellor, adminstrn., 1963-68, chancellor, 1968—; bd. dirs. Intel Corp.; cons. Peace Corps., 1961-62, Ford Found. on Latin Am. Activities, 1964-66; mem. bd. govs. L.A. Met. Project. Mem. Knight Found. Commn. on Intercollegiate Athletics, Calif. Coun. on Sci. and Tech., NCAA Pres.'s Commn., Coun. for Govt.-Univ.-Industry Rsch. Roundtable and the Nat. Rsch. Coun. Adv. Bd.-Issues in Sci. and Tech., Nat. Com. on U.S.-China Rels., chancellor's assocs. UCLA, coun. trustees L.A. Ednl. Alliance for Restructuring Now; past chair. Assn. Am. Univs., Nat. Assn. State Univs. and Land-Grant Colls.; mem. adminstrv. bd. Internat. Assn. Univs.; bd. govs. Found. Internat. Exchange Sci. and Cultural Info. by Telecommunications, The Theatre Group Inc.; v.p. Young Musicians Found.; bd. dirs. Los Angeles Internat. Visitors Council, Greater Los Angeles Energy Coalition, Los Angeles World Affairs Coun.; trustee UCLA Found. With USAF, 1951-52. Named Young Man of Year Westwood Jr. C. of C., 1962. Fellow AAAS. Office: UCLA Office of Chancellor Office of Chancellor 405 Hilgard Ave Los Angeles CA 90095

YOUNG, CHARLITA LUCILLE, community and educational administrator; b. Chgo., Oct. 5, 1958; d. Bernarr Elbert and Janean Elizabeth (Romig) Y. AA, Palomar Community coll., 1974; M of Ednl. Adminstrn., Nat. U., Chico, 1994; MA, Calif. State U., Long Beach, 1981. Mgmt. trainee J.W. Robinson's Dept. Store, Los Angeles, 1977-78; screening coordinator Riverview Hearing, Speech and Lang. Ctr., Long Beach, 1978-81, speech pathologist, 1981-84; speech pathologist, dir. Speech Pathology Svcs., Carlsbad, Calif., 1984—; dir. comty. outreach and student/alumni rels. Kelsey-Jenney Coll., San Diego; mem. adv. com. for Developmentally Disabled, San Diego, 1985-91; coord. pub. svc. announcements for Disabilities Awareness Week, ABC-TV, 1986, Inside San Diego program, 1988. Producer (cable TV series), Communicative Disorders, 1983. Active Carlsbad Hist. Soc., 1993—. Mem. Am. Speech, Lang. and Hearing Assn. (cert. charter mem. adminstrn. and supervision divsn. 1990, augmentative and alternative comm. divsn. 1993, 94), Calif. Speech, Lang. and Hearing Assn. (divsn. rep. 1985-88, Outstanding Achievement award 1987), Calif. Speech Pathologists and Audiologists in Pvt. Practice, Nat. Assn. Hearing and Speech Action (chmn. Disney benefit 1983-84), Assn. for Retarded Citizens, Calif. Scholastic Fedn., Sierra Club, Zeta Tau Alpha, Phi Delta Gamma (sec. 1982-88, v.p. 1983-84). Republican. Home: 1263 Robinson Ave Unit 9 San Diego CA 92103 Office: Kelsey-Jenney Coll 201 A St San Diego CA 92101-4003

YOUNG, CHRISTOPHER MICHAEL, skier; b. San Diego, Dec. 26, 1961; s. Darryl Thomas and Shirley Young; divorced; 1 child, Brandon. Mem. A team U.S. Disabled Ski Team, Park City, Utah, 1988—. Guard Denver Wheelchair Nuggets, 1987—; counselor Rocky Mountain Jr. Wheelchair Sports Camp, Denver, 1987—. Recipient 1st place giant slalom, 2nd place slalom, 3rd place super G, 3rd place combined World Disabled Ski Champs, Winter Park, Colo., 1990, 1st place super G, 2nd place giant slalom, 7th place slalom, U.S. Disabled Alpine Ski Champs, 1991, 1st place downhill, 1st place salom, Subaru U.S. Disabled Apline Ski Championship, 1993, Disabled Am. Vets. Comdrs. trophy, 1990. Mem. Paralyzed Vets. Am., U.S. Ski Assn., Nat. Wheelchair Basketball Assn. Democrat. Home: 224 29th St Boulder CO 80303-3314

YOUNG, CONNIE SUE, public affairs specialist; b. Oxnard, Calif.. BS in Psychology with honors, Colo. State U., 1977; MA in Journalism, U. Colo., 1987. Adminstrv. officer Divsn. Mental Health, Denver, 1980-86; asst. dir. mktg. Bethesda Hosp., Denver, 1986; writer U. Colo., Boulder, 1987; pub. rels. cons. Boulder, 1987-88; pub. info. specialist Colo. Divsn. Wildlife, Denver, 1988-93; pub. affairs specialist U.S. Fish and Wildlife Svc., Lakewood, Colo., 1993—. Contbr. articles to profl. jours. Recipient 2nd Pl. award print media advt. Nat. Fedn. Press Women, 1990. Mem. Pub. Rels. Soc. Am. (Silver Pick award Colo. chpt. 1994), Phi Beta Kappa. Office: US Fish & Wildlife Svc 134 Union Blvd Ste 440 Lakewood CO 80228

YOUNG, DON WILLIAM, hydrologist, educator; b. Erie, Pa., Dec. 17, 1941; s. Kenneth William and Helen Amelia (Waldinger) Y.; m. Mary Jane Driscoll (div.); 1 child, Natalie A. BS, U. Miami, Coral Gables, Fla., 1964; MS, Edinboro U. of Pa., 1971; PhD, U. Ariz., 1994. Chief chemist Bur. of Water City of Erie, Pa., 1964-66; gen. mgr. Wanakah Water Co., Hamburg, N.Y., 1966-71; tchg. and rsch. asst. dept. hydrology and water resources U. Ariz., Tuscon, 1972-76, lectr., rsch. assoc., 1976-77; from hydrologist to water resource supv.-sr. hydrologist Divsn. Natural Resources, Ariz. State Land Dept., Phoenix, 1977-87; dir. water rights litigation divsn., water resources mgr., chief hydrologist Criminal divsn., Office Atty. Gen., Phoenix, 1987—; mem. mineral extraction task force tech. adv. com. Ctrl. Ariz. Assn. Govts., 1981-83; mem. instream flow task force Ariz. Dept. Water Resources, 1987—; mem. rsch. adv. com. Water Resources Rsch. Ctr. U. Ariz., Tuscon, 1987—; mem. steering com. Gov. Riparian Habitat Task Force, 1990-91; mem. natural areas adv. com. Ariz. State Parks Bd., 1991—, vice chmn., 1991—; mem. Riparian areas coordinating coun. Ariz. Commn. on Environ., 1991—; chmn. ad hoc com. on hydrology field camp U. Ariz. Dept. Hydrology and Water Resouces, 1993—; expert witness in field. Contbr. articles to profl. jours. Vol. Lake View (N.Y.) Vol. Fire Assn., 1967-71; committeeman Lake View (N.Y.) Boy Scouts, 1970-71; treas. Quatros I Homeowners Condominium Assn., Phoenix, 1982-84, ins. com. chmn., 1983-84, 92, v.p., 1984-85, pres., 1986-87, archtl. com. chmn., 1987-88, mem. nominating com., 1987-90, chmn. paradise corridor com., 1988-89, mem. exec. com., 1989-90. Mem. NRA, Am. Water Resources Assn. (chmn. exhibits com. for ann. conf. 1977, pres. Ariz. sect. 1979-80, mem. law com. 1986, mem. conf. planning com. 1986-92, S.W. dist. dir. 1991-94, mem. student activities com. 1992—; mem. exec. planning com. for ann. conf. 1993, chmn. promotions com. for ann. conf. 1994), Am. Water Works Assn., Ariz. Hydrology Soc. (charter mem., co-chmn. spl. projects com.), Ariz. Riparian Coun., Ariz./Nev. Acad. Scis. (chmn. hydrology sect. 1980-81), Assn. Arid Land Studies, Renewable Natural Resources Found., Ariz. State Rifle and Pistol Assn., Ariz. Wildlife Fedn., Cousteau Soc., Ducks Unltd., Exempt Firefighters Assn. (life), The Nature Conservancy, U. Miami Alumni Assn., U. Ariz. Alumni Assn. Republican. Home: 5311-A N 35th Ave Phoenix AZ 85017-2812 Office: Office Atty Gen Crim Divsn EES WRAT 1275 W Washington St Phoenix AZ 85007-2926

YOUNG, DONALD ALLEN, writer, consultant; b. Columbus, Ohio, June 11, 1931; s. Clyde Allen and Helen Edith (Johnston) Y.; m. Rosemary Buchholz, Feb. 26, 1955 (div. Nov. 1976); children: Kent Allen, Kelly Ann; m. Marjorie Claire Shapiro, Aug. 20, 1977; stepchildren: Jo Alene, Andrea Lynn, Beth Ellen. Student, Ohio State U., 1949-51, Columbia Coll., 1952, North Cen. Coll., Naperville, Ill., 1956, Coll. DuPage, 1978. Editor various newspapers, mags., Detroit, Chgo., Columbus, 1946-63, 1973-74, 1978-79; v.p. Frydenlund Assocs., Chgo., 1963; pub. relations mgr. info. systems div. Gen. Electric Co., Phoenix, 1963-70; publs. dir. Data Processing Mgmt. Assn., Park Ridge, Ill., 1970-72; pub. relations mgr. Addressograph-Multigraph Corp., Arlington Heights, Ill., 1975-76; acct. exec. John Ripley & Assocs., Glenview, Ill., 1977-78; editorial dir. Radiology/Nuclear Medicine mag., Des Plaines, Ill., 1979-81; pres. Young Byrum Inc., Hinsdale, Ill., 1982-83; writer, consultant Tucson, 1983—; cons. various companies, 1973—; sports reporter, Copley newspapers, 1975-83; mem. adv. council Oakton Community Coll., 1970-75. Author: Principles of Automatic Data Processing, 1965, Data Processing, 1967, Rate Yourself as a Manager, 1985, Nobody Gets Rich Working for Somebody Else, 1987, 2d edit., 1993, Rate Your Executive Potential, 1988, If They Can...You Can, 1989, The Entrepreneurial Family, 1990, How to Export, 1990, Women in Balance, 1991, Sleep Disorders: America's Hidden Nightmare, 1992, Small Business Troubleshooter, 1994. Arbitrator Better Bus. Bur., Tucson, 1987-92; docent Ariz. Sonora Desert Mus., 1988-92. With USAF, 1952-56. Recipient Jesse Neal awards Assn. of Bus. Pub., 1959, 61, Silver Anvil award Pub. Rels. Soc. of Am., 1976. Mem. Publicity Club of Chgo. (pres. 1978-79). Soc. Southwestern Authors (pres. 1992), Glen Ellyn (Ill.) Jaycees (bd. dirs., SPOKE award 1959, Outstanding Jaycee 1960), Young Reps. Club (v.p. 1960). Home: 4866 N Territory Loop Tucson AZ 85715-5948

YOUNG, DONALD CHARLES, research chemist; b. Fremont, Ohio, June 29, 1944; s. Charles William and Mildred Murlyleen (Miller) Y.; m. Janet Weaver, June 29, 1968 (div. May 1979); children: Steven Donald, Michael Justin; m. Mary Katherine Garland, Nov. 1, 1980 (div. 1989); 1 child, Justin Thomas; m. Shari A. O'Neal Finn, Sept. 20, 1991. AB, Harvard U., 1966; PhD, U. N.C., 1971. Postdoctoral research assoc. Purdue U., West Lafayette, Ind., 1971-72; asst. prof. chemistry Oakland U., Rochester, Mich., 1972-78; project chemist Gulf Oil Corp., Harmarville, Pa., 1978-84; sr. research chemist Chevron Oil Corp., Richmond, Calif., 1984—, staff scientist, 1989-91, analytical coord., 1992—. Contbr. articles to profl. jours. Mem. Am. Chem. Soc., Soc. Applied Spectroscopy, Sigma Xi. Office: Chevron Research Corp PO Box 1627 Richmond CA 94802-1796

YOUNG, DONALD E., congressman; b. Meridian, Calif., June 9, 1933; m. Lula Fredson; children—Joni, Dawn. AA, Yuba Jr. Coll., 1952; BA ., Chico (Calif.) State Coll., 1958. Former educator, river boat capt.; mem. Fort Yukon City Council, 6 years, mayor, 4 years; mem. Alaska Ho. of Reps., 1966-70, Alaska Senate, 1970-73, 93rd-104th Congresses from Alaska, 1973—; mem. transp. & infrastructure com., chmn. resources com. With U.S. Army, 1955-57. Republican. Episcopalian. Office: US House of Representatives 2331 Rayburn Bldg Ofc B Washington DC 20515-0005*

YOUNG, EDNA ELIZABETH, art consultant and broker; b. Chgo., July 12, 1936; d. Henry and Josephine (Dunkel) Zimmerman; m. C. Farley Young, Dec. 1, 1972; children: Camella Rainwater, Robin Rainwater. Dir. Young Gallery, Saratoga, Calif., 1972-93. Bd. dirs. San Jose Mus. of Art, 1984-86.

YOUNG, EDWARD MEDHARD, JR., dermatologist; b. Long Beach, Calif., Apr. 27, 1954. BA in Biology summa cum laude, UCLA, 1976; MD, U. Calif., San Diego, 1980. Diplomate Am. Bd. Dermatology. Intern in gen. surgery U. Calif., San Diego, 1980-81, resident in dermatology, 1981-84; fellow in dermatopathology U. Calif., Irvine; dermatologist, dermatopathologist Sidell, Erickson, McCleary and Young Dermatology Surg. Group, L.A., 1985—. Co-author: Geriatric Dermatology: Color Atlas and Practitioner's Guide, 1991; co-editor: Geriatric Dermatology: Clinical Diagnosis and Practical Therapy, 1989; contbg. author: Problems in Aesthetic Surgery: Biological Causes and Clinical Solutions, 1986, Geriatric Dermatology, 1989; contbr. articles to profl. jours. Mem. UCLA Alumni Band, 1976—. Fellow Am. Acad. Dermatology; mem. Internat. Soc. Dermatopathology, L.A. Met. Dermatol. Soc., Dermatology Radiotherapy Soc., Am. Soc. Dermatologic Surgery, Los Angeles County Med. Assn. (ethics com. 1989), Phi Beta Kappa, Phi Eta Sigma, Kappa Kappa Psi. Office: Sidell Erickson McCleary Young Dermatology Surg Med 4955 Van Nuys Blvd Ste 200 Sherman Oaks CA 91403-1814

YOUNG, EDWIN S. W., federal agency official; b. Honolulu, Nov. 13, 1943; s. Hoon Kwan and Clara (Lee) Y.; m. Joan Tay, May 19, 1978. BA, U. Hawaii, 1966; MBA, U. Utah, 1975; MS, U. So. Calif., 1983. Asst. gen. mgr. Royal Men's Shops, Inc., Honolulu, 1973-75; mgmt. analyst U.S. Gen. Acctg. Office, Denver and Honolulu, 1976-83; audit mgr. USAF Audit Agy., L.A., 1983-84, 87-90; fgn. svc. officer Dept. State, 1984-87; with Office of Insp. Gen., Office Policy & Program Rev., Washington, 1984-87; divsn. dir., asst. dir., dir. prodn. Naval Audit Svc. Western Region, Vallejo, Calif., 1990-95; desk officer, planning and policy dir. Naval Audit Svc., Washington, 1995—; U.S. govt. rep. Pacific and Asian Affairs Coun., Honolulu, 1978-83; USN audit svc. rep. World Affairs Coun. No. Calif., 1990—; exec. dir. The Asian-Am. Found., Phoenix, 1990—. Community coord. Kailua Neighborhood Bd., Honolulu, 1978-83; area rep. Urban Mass Transit Authority, Honolulu, 1978-83; active John F. Kennedy Ctr. for Arts, Corcoran Gallery Art, L.A. County Mus. Art, San Francisco DeYoung Mus. Art. Capt. USAF, 1966-72. Recipient Commendation awards U.S. Gen. Acctg. Office, 1980, USAF Audit Agy., 1983, 88, 90, USAF Acctg. and Fin. Ctr., 1984, U.S. Naval Audit Svc. award, 1992, 94. Mem. Assn. Govt. Accts., Soc. Mil. Compts., Inst. Internal Auditors, Nat. Geog. Soc., Chinese C. of C., World Affairs Council, Smithsonian Inst. Roman Catholic.

YOUNG, FELIX KUN CHINN, organization financial executive, consultant; b. Honolulu, Sept. 11, 1960; s. Randolph K.C. and Rose S.J. (Ng) Y. BBA, U. Hawaii, 1982; MBA, U. Wash., 1985. CPA, Hawaii. Auditor Coopers & Lybrand, CPA's, Honolulu, 1985-88, cons., 1988-90; dir. fin. and adminstrn. Hawaiian Humane Soc., Honolulu, 1990—. Mem. AICPA, Hawaii Soc. CPAs, John Howard Assn. Hawaii (treas. 1991-93, bd. dirs. 1991—), Honolulu Japanese Jr. C. of C., U. Wash. Alumni Assn.

YOUNG, HOWARD THOMAS, foreign language educator; b. Cumberland, Md., Mar. 24, 1926; s. Samuel Phillip and Sarah Emmaline (Frederick) Y.; m. Carol Osborne, Oct. 5, 1949 (div. 1966); children—Laurie Margaret, Jennifer Anne; m. Jennifer Bunker, July 15, 1966 (div. 1980); m. Edra Lee Airheart, May 23, 1981; 1 child, Timothy Howard. B.S. summa cum laude, Columbia U., 1950, M.A., 1952, Ph.D., 1954. Lectr. Columbia U., N.Y.C., 1950-54; asst. prof. Romance langs. Pomona Coll., Claremont, Calif., 1954-60; assoc. prof. Pomona Coll., Claremont, 1960-66, Smith prof. Romance langs., 1966—; vis. prof. Middlebury Program in Spain, Madrid, 1986-87, U. Zaragoza, 1967-68; chief reader Spanish AP Ednl. Testing Service, Princeton, 1975-78, chmn. Spanish lang. devel. commn., 1976-79; mem. fgn. lang. adv. commn. Coll. Bd., N.Y.C., 1980-83; mem. West Coast selection commn. Mellon Fellowships for Humanities, Princeton, 1984-86, European selection com., 1987, 90. Author: The Victorious Expression, 1964, Juan Ramón Jiménez, 1967, The Line in the Margin, 1980; contbr. numerous articles and book revs. to profl. jours. Dir. NEH summer seminar for Sch. tchrs., 1993. Served with USNR, 1944-46, ETO. Fellow Del Amo Found., 1960-61, NEH, 1975, 89-90; Fulbright fellow; 1967-68; Rockefeller Study Ctr. scholar, 1976. Mem. MLA, Assn. Tchrs. Spanish and Portuguese, Am. Comparative Lit. Assn., Acad. Am. Poets. Home: 447 W Redlands Ave Claremont CA 91711-1638 Office: Pomona Coll Modern Lang Dept 550 Harvard Ave Claremont CA 91711

YOUNG, J. LOWELL, soil chemist, biologist; b. Perry, Utah, Dec. 13, 1925; s. I.A. and Elzada (Nelson) Y.; m. Ruth Ann Jones, Sept. 15, 1950; children: Gordon, LoAnn, Colene, Kathryn. BS, Brigham Young U., 1953; PhD, Ohio State U., 1956. Rsch. asst. Ohio Agrl. Expt. Sta., Columbus, 1953-56, postdoctoral fellow, 1956-57; chemist Agrl. Research Service USDA, Corvallis, Oreg., 1957-64, rsch. chemist, 1964-78; asst. prof. Oreg. State U., Corvallis, 1957-63, assoc. prof., 1963-78, prof. soil sci., 1978-90, Courtesy prof. soil sci., 1990—; rsch. chemist Horticultural Crops Rsch. Unit USDA, Corvallis, 1978-88; collaborator Horticultural Crops Rsch. Unit U.S. Dept. Agrl., Corvallis, 1988-91. Contbr. articles to profl jours. Served with USAAF, 1944-46. Mem. AAAS, Internat. Soil Sci. Soc., Internat. Humic Substances Soc., Soil Sci. Soc. of Am. (officer 1972-75, assoc. editor jour. 1975-80), Am. Soc. Agronomy (officer western 1966-72), Western Soc. Soil Sci. (officer 1966-71), Inst. for Alternative Agrl. Office: Oreg State U Crops & Soil Sci Dept Corvallis OR 97331

YOUNG, JACK DONALD, middle school educator; b. Pontiac, Mich., May 12, 1960; s. Harold Richard and Charlott Lucille (Eckler) Y.; m. Robyn Carol Stewart, July 28, 1990; 1 child, Heather Stewart. B Music Edn., U. Mich., Flint, 1982; MusM, Baylor U., 1986. Cert. tchr., Calif., Mich., Tex. Music educator San Felipe Del Rio (Tex.) Sch. Dist., 1982-84, orch. dir., 1986-89; rec. engr., tchg. asst. Baylor U., Waco, Tex., 1984-86; music educator Ontario (Calif.) Montclair Sch. Dist., 1989—, mentor tchr., 1992—. Vol. fireman Del Rio Fire Dept., 1987-89; county rep. Rep. Party, Flint, 1978; condr. Civic Orch. of Del Rio, 1987-89. Mem. Am. Musicol. Soc., Ontario Montclair Tchrs. Assn., So. Calif. Sch. Band and Orch. Assn., Musicians Local 47, Ontario Radio Amateur Civil Emergency Svc. (ham radio operator). Office: Imperial Mid Sch 1450 E G St Ontario CA 91764-4410

YOUNG, JACQUELINE EURN HAI, state legislator; b. Honolulu, May 20, 1934; d. Paul Bai and Martha (Cho) Y.; m. Harry Valentine Daniels, Dec. 25, 1954 (div. 1978); children: Paula, Harry, Nani, Laura; m. Everett Kleinjans, June 4, 1988. BS in Speech Pathology, Audiology, U. Hawaii, 1969; MS in Edn., Spl. Edn., Old Dominion U., 1972; advanced cert., Loyola Coll., 1977; PhD in Communication, Women's Studies, Union Inst., 1989. Dir. dept. speech and hearing Md. Sch. for the Blind, Balt., 1975-77; dir. deaf-blind project Easter Seal Soc. Oahu, Hawaii, 1977-78; project dir. equal ednl. opportunity programs Hawaii State Dept. Edn., Honolulu, 1978-85, state ednl. specialist, 1978-90; state rep. dist. 20 Hawaii State Legislature, Honolulu, 1990-92, state rep. dist. 51, 1992—; vice-speaker Hawaii Ho. of Reps., Honolulu; apptd. to U.S. Dept. Def. Adv. Commn. on Women in the Svc.; cons. spl. edn. U.S. Dept. Edn., dept. edn. Guam, Am. Samoa, Ponape, Palau, Marshall Islands, 1977-85; cons. to orgns. on issues relating to workplace diversity; adj. prof. commn., anthopology, mgmt. Hawaii Pacific U. Guest moderator Sta. KGMB-TV. 1st v.p. Nat. Women's Polit. Caucus, 1988-90; chair Hawaii Women's Polit. Caucus, 1987-89; bd. dirs. YWCA Oahu, Kalihi Palama Immigrant Svc. Ctr., Hawaii Dem. Movement, Family Peace Ctr.; appointee Honolulu County Com. on the Status of Women, 1986-87; mem. Adv. Coun. on Family Violence. Recipient OUtstanding Woman Leader award YWCA of Oahu, 1994, Pres.'s award Union Inst., 1993, Fellow of the Pacific award Hawaii-Pacific U., 1993, Headliner award Honolulu chpt. Women in Commn., 1993. Mem. Soroptimist Internat. (Kailua chpt.), Orgn. Women Leaders, Kailua C. of C., Korean C. of C., Kook Min Hur, Sierra Club, Korean Univ. Club. Home: 212 Luika Pl Kailua HI 96734-3237

YOUNG, JEFFREY ROBERT LUNN, data processing executive; b. Kailua, Hawaii, Sept. 22, 1965; s. Forrest James Lunn and Jodee Morrison Hunt. BS in Computer Sci., Hawaii Pacific U., 1987. Sr. software engr. Comml. Data Systems, Honolulu, 1986-89; asst. mgr. MIS Frito-Lay of Hawaii, 1989-91; MIS mgr. FMALI Herb Co., Inc., Santa Cruz, Calif., 1992—; cons. Island Paradise Sch., Honolulu, 1990-92, Muffet Mktg., Kailua, Hawaii, 1988—.

YOUNG, JOAN CRAWFORD, advertising executive; b. Hobbs, N.Mex., July 30, 1931; d. William Bill and Ora Maydelle (Boone) Crawford; m. Herchelle B. Young, Nov. 23, 1971 (div.). BA, Hardin Simmons U., 1952; postgrad. Tex. Tech. U., 1953-54. Reporter, Lubbock (Tex.) Avalanche-Jour., 1952-54; promotion dir. Sta. KCBD-TV, Lubbock, 1954-62; account exec. Ward Hicks Advt., Albuquerque, 1962-70; v.p. Mellekas & Assocs., Advt., Albuquerque, 1970-78; pres. J. Young Advt., Albuquerque, 1978—. Bd. dirs. N.Mex. Symphony Orch., 1970-73, United Way of Greater Albuquerque, 1985-89; bd. trustees N.Mex. Children's Found., 1994—. Recipient Silver medal N.Mex. Advt. Fedn., 1977. Mem. N.Mex. Advt. Fedn. (bd. dirs. 1975-76), Am. Advt. Fedn., Greater Albuquerque C. of C. (bd. dirs. 1984), Albuquerque Petroleum Club (membership chmn. 1992-93, bd. dirs. 1993—, sec. 1994—, v.p. 1995—). Republican. Author: (with Louise Allen and Audre Lipscomb) Radio and TV Continuity Writing, 1962. Home: 1638 Tierra Del Rio NW Albuquerque NM 87107 also: 500 Marquette NW Albuquerque NM 87102

YOUNG, JOHN ALAN, electronics company executive; b. Nampa, Idaho, Apr. 24, 1932; s. Lloyd Arthur and Karen Eliza (Miller) Y.; m. Rosemary Murray, Aug. 1, 1954; children: Gregory, Peter, Diana. B.S. in Elec. Engring, Oreg. State U., 1953; M.B.A., Stanford U., 1958. Various mktg. and finance positions Hewlett Packard Co. Inc., Palo Alto, Calif., 1958-63, gen. mgr. microwave div., 1963-68, v.p. electronic products group, 1968-74, exec. v.p., 1974-77, chief oper. officer, 1977-78, pres., 1977-92, chief exec. officer, 1978-92; ret., 1992; bd. dirs. Wells Fargo Bank, Wells Fargo and Co., Chevron Corp., SmithKline Beecham Plc, Affymetrix, Inc., Shaman Pharms., Inc., Ciphergew, Novell, Inc. and Gen. Magic; chmn. Smart Valley, Inc. Chmn. ann. fund Stanford U., 1966-73, nat. chmn. corp. gifts, 1973-77, mem. adv. coun. Grad. Sch. Bus., 1967-73, 75-80, Univ. trustee, 1977-87; bd. dirs. Mid-Peninsula Urban Coalition, 1971-80, co-chmn., 1983-85; chmn. Pres.'s Commn. on Indsl. Competitiveness, 1983-85, Nat. Jr. Achievement, 1983-84; pres. Found. for Malcolm Baldrige Nat. Quality Award; mem. Adv. Com. on Trade Policy and Negotiations, 1988-92. With USAF, 1954-56. Mem. Nat. Acad. Engring., Coun. on Competitiveness (founder, founding chair computer systems policy project 1986), Bus. Coun.

YOUNG, JON NATHAN, archeologist; b. Hibbing, Minn., May 30, 1938; s. Robert Nathan Young and Mary Elizabeth (Barrows) Roy; m. Karen Sue Johnson, June 5, 1961 (div. May 1980); children: Shawn Nathan, Kevin Leigh; m. Tucker Heitman, June 18, 1988. BA magna cum laude, U. Ariz., 1960, PhD, 1967; MA, U. Ky., 1962. Archeologist Nat. Park Svc. Southwest Archeol. Ctr., Globe and Tucson, Ariz., 1967-75; exec., camp dir. YMCA of Metro. Tucson, 1976-77; asst. dir. Kit Carson Meml. Found., Taos, N.Mex., 1978; co-dir. Las Palomas de Taos, 1979; archeologist Nat. Forest Svc., Carson Nat. Forest, Taos, 1980—; exec. order cons. U.S. Sec. Interior, 1973-75. Author: The Salado Culture in Southwestern Prehistory, 1967; co-author: Excavation of Mound 7, 1981, First-Day Road Log in Techtonic Development of the Sangre de Cristo Mountains, 1990. Advisor Boy Scouts Am.; active YMCA White Rag Soc. Grantee NEH, 1978; Ariz. Wilson Found., NSF, Ky. Rsch. Found. fellow, 1960-62; Baird Found., Bausch and Lomb, Elks; recipient cert. merit USDA, 1987, 89. Fellow AAAS, Am. Anthrop. Assn., Explorers Club, Royal Anthrop. Inst.; mem. Current Anthropology (assoc.), Ariz. Archaeol. and Hist. Soc., Ariz. Hist. Soc., Coun. on Am.'s Mil. Past, Soc. Hist. Archaeology, Soc. Am. Archaeology, Harwood Found., Millicent Rogers Mus., Taos Archaeol. Soc., Taos County Hist. Soc., Sigma Xi, Phi Beta Kappa, Alpha Kappa Delta, Phi Kappa Phi, Delta Chi. Home: PO Box 2207 Taos NM 87571-2207 Office: Nat Forest Svc Suprs Office PO Box 558 Taos NM 87571-0558

YOUNG, JOYCE HENRY, adult education educator, consultant; b. Oak Park, Ill., July 3, 1930; d. Jesse Martin and Adelina Patti (Gillander) H.; m. James Edward Young, Apr. 26, 1958; children: Richard Allen, Patti Ann. BA, Calif. State U., Fresno, 1951; MA, Northwestern U., 1952; EdD, U. So. Calif., 1986. Tchr. Glencoe (Ill.) Pub. Schs., 1952-53, Hayward (Calif.) Schs., 1953-59, Honolulu Dept. Edn., 1969-83, Kamehameha Schs., Honolulu, 1987; instr. Hawaii Pacific Coll., Honolulu, 1987, Honolulu Community Coll., 1988, Chaminade U., Honolulu, 1990, Kansai Gaidai Hawaii Coll., 1991-93, U. Hawaii, Manoa, 1994—; cons. Computer Lab., Honolulu, 1988. Mem. AAUW, Am. Ednl. Rsch. Assn., Educom, Delta Epsilon, Kappa Delta Pi, Pi Lamda Theta. Democrat. Presbyterian.

YOUNG, KATHERINE ANN, education educator; b. Castleford, Idaho, Apr. 9, 1941; d. Ross and Norna (Scully) Stoner; m. Virgil Monroe Young, Dec. 20, 1964; 1 child, Susan Annette. BS in Elem. Edn., U. Idaho, 1965; MEd, Ea. Washington U., 1969; EdD, Utah State U., 1980. Cert. advanced elem. tchr., Idaho. Tchr. spl. edn. Coeur d'Alene (Idaho) Sch. Dist., 1965-66; tchr. elem. grades Coeur d' Aleue (Idaho) Sch. Dist., 1966-67, Boise (Idaho) Sch. Dist., 1967-88; assoc. prof. edn. Boise State U., 1988-93, prof., 1993—. Co-author: (resource book) The Story of Idaho Author's, 1977, The Story of Idaho Guide and Resource Book, 1993; author: The Utah Activity Book, 1980, Constructing Buildings, Bridges, and Minds, 1993; cons., contbr. (nat. edn. jour.) Learning, 1991—. Named Idaho Tchr. of Yr., State Dept. of Edn., Boise, 1983; invited to luncheon at White House, Pres. Ronald Reagan, Washington, 1983; Recipient Outstanding Young Educator award Boise Jaycees, 1983; profiled in Idaho Centennial pub., 1990; travel to Japan grantee Rocky Mountain Region Japan Project, 1990. Mem. ASCD, Nat. Coun. for Social Studies, Idaho Law Found., Alliance Idaho Geographers (state coord.). Office: Boise State U Dept Tchr Edn 1910 University Dr Boise ID 83725-0001

YOUNG, LESTER REX, engineering company administrator; b. Marion, Ind., Aug. 26, 1946; s. Harold Leroy and Willow Marie (May) Y.; m. Bonnie Darline Denison, Sept. 5, 1965; children: Tamara Lynn, Kelby Gene, Kadee Lynn. BSEE, Kans. State U., 1969; MBA, Wichita State U., 1979. Reg. engr. Colo., Kans., Ohio, Mont., Utah, La. Plant engr. Beech Aircraft Corp., Wichita, Kans., 1973-75; asst. to v.p. mfg. Beech Aircraft Corp., Wichita, 1975-77; sr. project mgr. Smith & Boucher, Inc., Overland Park, Kans., 1977-80; dir. engring. R.M. Henning, Inc., New Philadelphia, Ohio, 1980-82; mgr. indsl. engring. Williams Internat., Ogden, Utah, 1982-84; mgr. plant engring. Sundstrand Corp., Denver, 1984-86; pres. ECS Engrs. Inc., Arvada, Colo., 1986-90; dir. bus. devel. Morrison Knudsen Corp., Denver, 1990—; cons. Compliance Recycling Industires, Denver, 1984-87. Author: (reference manuals) Selection of Reverse Osmosis for Boiler Applications, 1987, Applications for Enzyme Activated Carbon, 1989, Integrated Refinery Waste Management, 1992. Capt. U.S. Army, 1969-73, Europe. Republican. Nazarene. Office: Morrison Knudsen 7100 E Belleview Ave Ste 300 Englewood CO 80111-1636

YOUNG, LIH-JIUAN SHIAU, energy research and development company manager; b. Taiwan, Republic of China, Mar. 3, 1951; d. Jia-Jen and Yeh-Horn (Shieh) Shiau; m. Masefield J. Young, Apr. 9, 1976; 1 child, Jason S. BS in Nutrition, U. Chinese Culture, Taipei, 1973, MS in Nutrition, 1975; MS in Biochemistry, Duquesne U., 1978, PhD in Phy. Chemistry, 1982. Assoc. rsch. chemist Food Industry R&D Inst., Taiwan, 1975-76; postdoctoral rsch. assoc. Scripps Clinic and Rsch. Found., San Diego, 1984-85, U. Calif., San Diego, 1985-86; R & D lab. mgr. Ahlstrom Pyropower, Inc., San Diego, 1986—. Contbr. articles to profl. jours. Active San Diego Chinese Hist. Soc. Mem. Am. Chem. Soc. Office: Ahlstrom Pyropower Inc 8970 Crestmar Pt San Diego CA 92121-3222

YOUNG, LOWELL SUNG-YI, medical administrator, educator; b. Honolulu, Dec. 5, 1938. AB, Princeton U., 1960; MD, Harvard U., 1964. Di;omate Am. Bd. Internal Medicine with subspecialty in infectious diseases. Intern, jr. asst. resident, sr. asst. resident med. divsn. Bellevue Hosp. and Meml. Hosp., N.Y.C., 1964-67; fellow in medicine Cornell U. Med. Coll., 1965-67; epidemic intelligence officer bacterial diseases br. Nat. Communicable Disease Ctr., Atlanta, 1967-69, chief spl. pathogens sect., 1968-69; spl. postdoctoral rsch. fellow Nat. Inst. Allergy and Infectious Diseases, 1969-70; rsch. fellow in medicine Meml. Hosp./Cornell U. Med. Coll., 1969-70; clin. asst. physician infectious disease svc. dept. medicine Meml. Hosp., 1970-72, assoc. dir. microbiology lab., 1971-72; instr. in medicine Cornell U. Med. Coll., 1970-72; asst. clinician Sloan-Ketterin Inst. for Cancer Rsch., 1971-72; adj. prof. pharmacy U. of Pacific, San Francisco, 1989—; mem. microbiology and invectious diseases adv. com. Nat. Inst. Allergy and Infectious Diseases, 1981-85, mem. allergy and immunology rsch. com., 1975-79; mem. staff Calif. Pacific Med. Ctr., Mt. Zion Hosp. and Med. Ctr., U. Calif., San Francisco; mem. sci. adv. bd. Am. Found. for AIDS Rsch. Mem. editl. bd. Infection, Infectious Diseases in Clin. Practice, Antimicrobic Newsletter, Diagnostic Microbiology and Infectious Diseases, Antimicrobial Agts. and Chemotherapy; contbr. numerous articles to profl. jours., chpts. to books. Recipient Alexander D. Langmuir prize Epidemic Intelligence Svc., 1970, Garrod medal Brit. Soc., 1992. Fellow ACP (mem. med. self-assessment com.), Infectious Diseases Soc. Am. (councillor 1983-85); mem. Am. Soc. for Clin. Investigation, Am. Fedn. for Clin. Rsch., Am. Soc. for Microbiology, Western Soc. for Clin. Rsch., Internat. Immunocompromised Host Soc., Brit. Soc. Antimicrobial Chemotherapy. Office: Calif Pacific Med Ctr Kuzell Inst 2200 Webster St Ste 305 San Francisco CA 94115-1821

YOUNG, MARGARET BUCKNER, civic worker, author; b. Campbellsville, Ky.; d. Frank W. and Eva (Carter) Buckner; m. Whitney M. Young, Jr., Jan. 2, 1944 (dec. Mar. 1971); children: Marcia Elaine, Lauren Lee. BA, Ky. State Coll., 1942, MA, U. Minn., 1946. Instr. Ky. State Coll., 1942-44; instr. edn. and psychology Spelman Coll., Atlanta, 1957-60; dir. emeritus N.Y. Life Ins. Co.; alt. del. UN Gen. Assembly, 1973. Mem. pub. policy com. Advt. Coun. Trustee emerita Lincoln Ctr. for Performing Arts; chmn. Whitney M. Young, Jr. Meml. Found., 1971-92; trustee Met. Mus. Art, 1976-90; bd. govs. UN Assn., 1975-82; bd. visitors U.S. Mil. Acad., 1978-80; dir. Philip Morris Cos., 1972-91. Author: The First Book of American Negroes, 1966, The Picture Life of Martin Luther King, Jr., 1968, The Picture Life of Ralph J. Bunche, 1968, Black American Leaders-Watts, 1969, The Picture Life of Thurgood Marshall, 1970, pub. affairs pamphlet.

YOUNG, MARGARET CHONG, elementary education educator; b. Honolulu, May 8, 1924; d. Henry Hon Chin and Daisy Kyau (Tong) Chong; m. Alfred Y.K. Young, Feb. 21, 1948; children: Robert S.W., Richard S.K., Linda S.K. EdB, 5th yr. cert., U. Hawaii, 1945. Cert. tchr., Hawaii. Tchr. Waipahu (Hawaii) Elem. Sch., Manoa Housing Sch., Hawaii Dept. Edn., Honolulu, Pauoa Elem. Sch., Honolulu. Author: And They Also Came, History of Chinese Christian Association, Hawaii's People From China; contbr. numerous articles to profl. jours. Ch. sch. tchr., supt. United Ch. Christ-Judd St. Grantee San Francisco State Coll. Mem. NEA, Hawaii State Tchrs. Assn., Hawaii Congress of Parents and Tchrs. (hon. life mem.), Kappa Kappa Iota (Disting. Educator award 1986-87), Delta Kappa Gamma (internat.).

YOUNG, MARY JANE, American studies and folklore educator; b. Apollo, Pa., Oct. 25, 1950; d. Floyd Clark and Lillian Grace (Deemer) Y.; m. Robert Henry Leibman, June 12, 1982. BA, St. John's Coll., 1973; MA, U. Pa., 1978, PHD, 1982. Math. tchr. Severn Sch., Severna Park, Md., 1973-75; asst. dir. admissions St. John's Coll., Annapolis, Md., 1975-76; rsch. asst. U. Pa., Phila., 1976-79, teaching fellow dept. folklore, 1979-80, lectr. dept. folklore, 1979-82; asst. prof. folklore ctr. U. Tex., Austin, 1982-87; assoc. prof. Am. studies U. N.Mex., Albuquerque, 1987—; cons. Tribal Mus. Com., Zuni, N.Mex., 1980—. Author: Signs from the Ancestors, 1988; editorial bd. Jour. of the Am. Studies Assn. Tex., 1988—, Archaeoastronomy, bull. for Ctr. for Archaeoastronomy, 1979—; contbr. articles to profl. jours. Fellow Roothbert Found., 1976-79, dissertation fellow AAUW, 1981-82; recipient rsch. assistantship Smithsonian Inst., 1978. Office: U NMex Dept Am Studies 305 Ortega Hall Albuquerque NM 87131-1176

YOUNG, MICHAEL EDWARD, music educator; b. San Francisco, June 25, 1939; s. John Davis and Mary Katherine (Polese) Y. BA in Music, U. Wash., 1964, MA in Music, 1966. Organist First Presbyn. Ch., Seattle, 1961-65, St. Paul's Episcopal Ch., Seattle, 1966-70; instr. music Cornish Sch. Allied Arts, Seattle, 1966-70; organist Sts. Peter and Paul Ch., Vancouver, B.C., 1970-74, Cathedral of Our Lady of Lourdes, Spokane, Wash., 1979-83, Messiah Luth. Ch., Spokane, 1988-92; asst. to assoc. prof. music Whitworth Coll., Spokane, 1976—. Composer: Season's Song for Baritone and Piano, 1992, Give Glory, All Creation for Trumpet, Choir and Organ, 1991, A Mountain Symphony for Orchestra, 1987-88, Mountain Sketches, Set 5, 1988, String Quartet No. 2, 1986, Northwest Images Horn, Cello, Piano, 1981. With U.S. Army, 1957-60. Mem. Am. Guild Organists (assoc.; 25th Creative Ann award 1983), Christian Fellowship of Art Music Composers, Glacier Mountaineering Soc. (charter mem.). Orthodox. Office: Whitworth Collge Station 1701 Spokane WA 99251

YOUNG, ROBERT ANTHONY, association director; b. Syracuse, N.Y., May 21, 1943; s. Frank A. and Grace (Farnett) Y. BS, Le Moyne Coll., 1965; MS, Long Beach State Coll., 1966. Exec. dir. Cystic Fibrosis Found., Syracuse, 1974-75; dir. pub. rels. & programs Am. Heart Assn., New Orleans, 1975-76; dir. programs La. State Bar Assn., New Orleans, 1976-84; exec. dir. Am. Coll. Trial Lawyers, Irvine, Calif., 1984—. With USAF, 1966-67. Mem. Am. Soc. Assn. Execs., Nat. Assn. Bar Execs. (leadership award 1986, chmn's. award pub. rels. sect. 1984). Office: Am Coll of Trial Lawyers 8001 Irvine Center Dr Ste 960 Irvine CA 92718-2921

YOUNG, ROBERT ARTHUR, electrical engineer; b. Columbus, Ohio, Feb. 16, 1950; s. Arthur Peck and Norma Jean (Rownd) Y.; m. Roberta Jeanne Husted, Oct. 14, 1989. BSEE, Ohio State U., 1972; postgrad., Air Force Inst. Tech., Dayton, Ohio, 1977-78, U. So. Calif., 1991—. Commd. 2d lt. USAF, 1972, advanced through grades to capt., 1976; elec. engr. USAF, Omaha, 1972-77, Dayton, 1977-78, L.A., 1978-82; ret., 1982; with USAFR, 1982—; systems analyst OAO Corp., L.A., 1982-84, project mgr., 1984-88; project mgr. Hughes Aircraft Co., El Segundo, Calif., 1988—. Mem. IEEE, Armed Forces Communications and Electronics Assn., Maserati Owners Club N.Am. (tech. editor 1987-89). Republican. Office: Hughes Space and Comm Co PO Box 92919 Los Angeles CA 90009-2919

YOUNG, ROBERT EDWARD, finance company executive; b. L.A., Nov. 28, 1943; s. David and Sue (Wise) Y. Student, E. Los Angeles Coll., 1973, Santa Monica Coll., 1975; BA, UCLA, 1978. Cert. securities analyst N.Y. Inst. Fin., 1972. Computer operator Rocketdyne Corp., Canoga Park, Calif., 1963-65; computer ops. supr. Hughes Aircraft Corp., El Segundo, Calif., 1965-67; with investment securities dept. Smith, Tilton & Co., Inc., Santa Ana, Calif., 1967-70, Morton Seidel & Co., Inc., L.A., 1970-78; sales mgr. of comml. interior constrn. NICO Constrn. Co., Inc., L.A., 1978-80; sales mgr. Strauss Constrn. Co., Inc., L.A., 1981-82; v.p., instl. investment officer FCA Asset Mgmt./Am. Savs., Los Angeles, 1982-87; pres., chief exec. officer Avalon Fin. Group, Inc., Los Angeles, 1988-90; prin. Robert Young & Co., 1991—; bd. dirs. RESA Prodns. 1973-80, Edu Care, L.A., 1981-90, ASC Edn. Svcs. Inc., L.A., chmn. fin. com.; mktg. cons. Shehata Enterprises, L.A., 1978-79; sales tng. cons. Versailles Gallery, L.A., Schwartz Constrn., L.A., 1982; cons. PC Etcetera, L.A., 1990-91. Photographer: prin. works include Man at Work or Play UN, Geneva, 1976, Cat of Yr. photo, 1977, Photomontage U. So. Calif. Early Childhood Edn. Ctr., 1977; producer weekly pub. affairs prog. for family fin. planning sta. KPOL Radio, 1974, Stocks and Bonds Show KWHY-TV, 1975-78, MacRadio show, Am. Radio Network, 1989, WinRadio Show, 1990, MacWin Radio, 1991—. Fin. cons. Hofheinz Fund, Houston, 1988. Served with USCGR, 1964-70. Mem. AIA, Cosmopolitan Internat. (pres. 1967-68), Soc. Archtl. Historians, L.A. Conservancy, West L.A. Constitution Observance Day (chmn. 1970), Archtl. Hist. Soc. (life mem. So. Calif. chpt.), Valley MacIntosh User Group, Downtown High Teslve Club (past pres.), Reel Sports Club, Masons, Toastmasters (Outstanding Troasmaster 1973-74, 76), Wind n' Sea Sailing GLub. Home: 4531 Don Arturo Pl Los Angeles CA 90008-2803 Office: Robert Young & Co 8306 Wilshire Blvd Ste 499 Beverly Hills CA 90211-2382

YOUNG, ROGER CARL, computer company executive; b. Clayton, Mo., Mar. 21, 1932; s. Gerald Lee Young and Bertha Augusta (Schlottach) McCulloh; m. Nadine Fay Basch, Apr. 27, 1952; children: Julia Allyn, David Ford. Student, Washington U., St. Louis, 1956-57, U. Calif., Berkeley, 1957-60, Contra Costa Coll., 1970. V.p. and div. mgr. Crocker Nat. Bank, San Francisco, 1967-75; nat. accts. mgr. Wang Labs., San Francisco, 1975-78; industry cons. Fortune 500, 1978-81; pres. ComTrak, Richmond, Calif., 1981-83; dir. mktg. Delphi Systems, Inc., Westlake Village, Calif., 1983-89; regional sales mgr. Applied Systems, Inc., Chgo., 1991-92. Served with USAF, 1951-55. Mem. Data Processing Mgmt. Assn. (cert., bd. dirs., sec. San Francisco chpt. 1965-67), Am. Contract Bridge League (life master 1959), Green Tree Golf Club. Republican. Home and Office: 779 Arbor Oaks Dr Vacaville CA 95687-5252

YOUNG, ROSABEL RIBARES, neurologist; b. Laredo, Tex., June 1, 1960; d. Arthur and Rosario Ribares; m. Anthony O. Young, Nov. 25, 1984. AB, U. Chgo., 1982, MS in Pharmacology and Physiology, 1984; MD, U. Ill., 1987. Diplomate Am. Bd. Psychiatry and Neurology; cert. Am. Bd. Electrodiagnostic Medicine. Intern in neurology The Nat. Hosp., London, 1987; intern in internal medicine UCLA-Wadsworth VA Med. Ctr., 1987-88; resident in neurology Ctr. for Health Scis., UCLA, 1988-91; neurologist CIGNA Health Care, L.A., 1991-94; fellow neurophysiology EEG, EMG Harbor-UCLA Med. Ctr., 1994—; attending neurologist UCLA Neurology Clinic; chair edn. com. CIGNA Health Care, L.A., 1993—, cons. pharmacy and therapeutics, 1991—, mem. instnl. rev. bd., 1991—; dir. Doctors-to-Schs. Sci. Advisors Program, Chgo. and L.A., 1989—. Contbr. articles to profl. jours. judge advisor L.A. County Schs., 1990—; judge and awards contbr. Calif. State Sci. Fair, L.A., 1992—. Rsch. fellow Pharm. Mfrs. Assn., UCLA, 1984-85, NIH, 1983, Epilepsy Found. Am., 1984; recipient scholarships Bertram Richardson Internat. Studies, 1987, Joseph K. Narat Found., 1985, U. Chgo. MacArthur Found., 1982-86, U. Chgo. Becker Warburg, 1982-87, U. Chgo. Joseph Blazek, 1980-81, Ill. Gen. Assembly, 1984-85, 85-86, Nat. Med. Fellowship, 1983, 85, Chgo. Edmondson Rsch. award, 1981. Mem. AMA (Leadership in Cmty. Svc. award 1989, 90, RPS resource com. rep. to AMA ho. dels. 1989-90), Am. Electroencephalographers Soc., Am. Assn. Electrodiagnostic Medicine, Am. Acad. Neurology (legis. affairs com., subcom. on edn. of non-neurologists, chair Neurosci. Prize subcom., chair comms. and liaison com.), Calif. Med. Assn., L.A. County Med. Assn., L.A. Soc. for Neurol. Scis. Office: UCLA Harbor Med Ctr 1000 W Carson St Ste 432 Torrance CA 90502-2004

YOUNG, SCOTT THOMAS, business management educator; b. Oak Park, Ill., Dec. 28, 1949; s. Thomas Menzies and Grace (Butler) Y.; m. Teresa M. Foskey, Jan. 2, 1981; children: Reginald, Galen. BA, U. Ga., 1974; MBA, Ga. Coll., 1982; PhD, Ga. State U., 1987. Asst. prof. U. Utah, Salt Lake City, 1987-92, assoc. prof., 1992—, chmn. mgmt. dept., 1994—; mgmt. cons. to numerous orgns., 1987—; lectr., speaker, cons. on ops., quality and project mgmt. Author: Managing Global Operations; contbr. numerous articles to profl. jours. With U.S. Army, 1971-73. Decorated Commendation medal; grantee Nat. Assn. Purchasing Mgmt., 1986. Mem. Decision Sci. Inst., Acad. Mgmt., Prodn. and Ops. Mgmt. Soc. Democrat. Office: U Utah David Eccles Sch Bus Salt Lake City UT 84112

YOUNG, STEPHEN JEROME, investment banker; b. Berkeley, Calif., Oct. 20, 1956; s. William Jordan and Marina Solveig (Amdahl) Y.; m. Amy Marie Seminario, Feb. 21, 1987; 1 child, Alden Edward. BA, U. Pa., 1978; MBA, U. Calif., Berkeley, 1983, JD, 1983. Bar: Calif. 1983, Mass. 1986. V.p. real estate investment banking group E.F. Hutton & Co., Inc., San Francisco, 1982-85; assoc. Csaplar & Bok (name changed to Gaston & Snow), Boston and San Francisco, 1986-91; ptnr. Cooper, White & Cooper, San Francisco, 1991-92; v.p. Krambo Corp., San Francisco, 1993—. Mem. Commonwealth Club Calif., Phi Beta Kappa. Office: Krambo Corp 100 Spear St Ste 1510 San Francisco CA 94105-1527

YOUNG, STEVEN, professional football player; b. Salt Lake City, Oct. 11, 1961. JD, Brigham Young, 1993. With L.A. Express, USFL, 1984-85, Tampa Bay Buccaneers, 1985-87; quarterback San Francisco 49ers, 1987—. Davey O'Brien Award, 1983, All-America team quarterback, The Sporting News, 1983; Named NFL's Top-rated quarterback, 1991, named NFL Most Valuable Player, The Sporting News, 1992, NFL All-Pro team quarterback, The Sporting News, 1992, Superbowl Most Valuable Player, 1995. Office: San Francisco 49ers 4949 Centennial Blvd Santa Clara CA 95054-1229*

YOUNG, SUZANNE MARYE, management consultant; b. Kansas City, Mo., Nov. 1, 1946; d. Charles S. and Anne M. (Ceccone) Y. BA, U. Mich., 1968; MS in Organizational Devel., Pepperdine U., 1990. Comml. coord. Sta. WXYZ-TV, Southfield, Mich., 1968; prodn. mgr. Daystar Multi-Media, Ann Arbor, Mich., 1969-74; dir. major events U. Mich., Ann Arbor, 1974-78; exec. dir. The Mich. Union, Ann Arbor, 1978-80; adminstr. Tourism Promotion Bur., Jackson Hole, Wyo., 1983-85; exec. dir. Jackson Hole C. of C., 1985-91; interim town administr. Jackson, Wyo., 1995. Chmn. tourism task force Wyo. Futures Project, 1986-87; bd. dirs. Old West Trail Found., 1988-90, Jackson Hole Land Trust, Nat. Mus. Wildlife Art, 1988—, Community Found. of Jackson Hole; Dem. candidate Wyo. legislature, 1992. Named Promoter of Yr., Billboard mag., 1975, 77, Local Woman of Yr. award, Bus. and Profl. Women, 1988. Home and Office: PO Box 3351 Jackson WY 83001-3351

YOUNG, TAMRA ANN, pediatrics nurse; b. Bremerton, Wash., Jan. 9, 1959; d. Alexander Blanger and Dana D. (Magden) Park; m. Earl Thomas Young, Oct. 17, 1981; children: Christopher Michael, Jacob Adam. ADN, San Juan Coll., 1985; BSN, U. N.Mex., 1991; diploma, Inst. Children's Lit., 1989. Cert. pediatric advanced life support Am. Heart Assn.; cert. newborn resuscitation, N.J.; cert. BLS Am. Heart Assn. Newborn nursery nurse San Juan Regional Med. Ctr., Farmington, N.Mex., 1985-90, pediatrics nurse, 1990—; spkr. for outreach programs in child abuse and parenting, 1994—; spkr. for outreach asthma programs, 1995—; instr. in field. Author: (book of study) NCLEX, 1992; developer Asthma Program for Kids, Parenting Classes; creator child abuse prevention mascot the "Hug Bug". Spkr. San Juan Coll., 1989; cmty. spkr. in parent edn. and child abuse, Pub. Schs.-Parent Edn., San Juan Coll.; mem. San Juan County for Prevention of Child Abuse Coun., Farmington, 1992—. Recipient Award of Merit, San Juan Coll., 1991, Award of Svc., San Juan Regional med. Ctr., 1986. Mem. Young Am. Bowling Aliance (bd. dirs. 1987), Women's Internat. Bowling Aliance (pres. 1991-92), U. N.Mex. Alumni Assn. Republican. Episcopalian. Home: 7 Road 5759 Farmington NM 87401-9536

YOUNG, VIRGIL M., education educator; b. Santa Rosa, Calif., Sept. 24, 1936; s. Virgil M. and Vesta May (Huyett) Williams; stepson Louis H. Young; m. Katherine Ann Young, Dec. 20, 1964; 1 child, Susan Annette. BS, U. Idaho, 1958, EdD, 1967. Cert. advanced secondary sch., sch. supt., Idaho. Tchr. Moscow (Idaho) Sch. Dist.; adminstrv. asst. to supt. Coeur d'Alene (Idaho) Sch. Dist.; prof. edn., dept. head Boise (Idaho) State U. Author: (elem., jr. high textbook) The Story of Idaho, 3 editions; co-author: The Story of the Idaho Guide and Resource Book, 1993. Capt. USAR. Mem. N.W. Assn. Tchr. Educators (past pres.), Idaho Assn. Colls. Tchr. Edn. (past pres.), Phi Delta Kappa (past pres.).

YOUNG, WILLIAM CLARENCE, career officer, training specialist; b. Catasauqua, Pa., Jan. 6; s. William Henry and Catherine (Romanko) Y.; m. Jeanne Elinore Lienhard, Sept. 30, 1942; children: Barbara E. McLellan, Suzanne M. Young, Janet D. Goodling. Commd./Staff, Naval War Coll., Newport, R.I., 1954; BA, Fla. State U., 1965; MS, George Wash. U., 1970, U. Ark., 1975. Enlisted seaman to comdr. USN, various, 1940-65; ASW program mgr. Bur. Naval Personnel, Washington, 1967-72; ASW tng. program coord. Chief of Naval Tech. Tng., Millington, Tenn., 1972-84; ASW tng. program mgr. Comdr./Tng. Command U.S. Pacific Fleet, San Diego, Calif., 1984—; cons. Naval Sea Systems Command/Contractors, Washington, 1967—. Author: Naval Gunnery: 20 MM, 40MM, Small Arms, 1943; editor: Anti-Submarine Warfare and Underwater Fire Control Systems, Sonars, 1967-94. Comdr. USN, 1940-65, WWII, Korea, Vietnam. Decorated Legion of Merit Venezuelan Commandant/Navy, others. Mem. U.S. Naval Inst., Am. Def. Preparedness Assn., BMW Club of Am., Mature Outlook Assn. Home: 12594 Cresta Pl San Diego CA 92128-2312 Office: Comtrapac 33055 Nixie Way San Diego CA 92147-5105

YOUNG, ZORA ORAL, psychiatrist; b. Baytown, Tex., Nov. 30, 1922; s. Zora Oral Sr. and Kathryn (Litzler) Y.; m. Mary Ella Young (div.); children: Richard, Jame, John; m. Rosemary Ruth Young, Oct. 18, 1980. BS, U. Ariz., 1947; MD, U. So. Calif., 1952. Diplomate Am. Bd. Psychiatry and Neurology. Intern Santa Fe Coast Lines Hosp., L.A., 1950-51; resident Langley Porter Neuropsychiat. Inst., San Francisco, 1951-54; med. dir. No. Nev. Child and Adolescent Svcs., Reno, 1980—. Office: Childrens Behavioral Svc 2655 Enterprise Rd Reno NV 89512-1666

YOUNGBLOOD, DEBORAH S., lawyer; b. Fairview, Okla., July 29, 1954; d. G. Dean and Beatrice J. (Hiebert) White. BS with honors, Okla. State U., 1976, MA with honors, 1979; JD cum laude, Boston Coll. Law Sch., 1991; MPH in Health Care Mgmt., Harvard U., 1992. Speech-lang. pathologist Mesa Sch. Dist. 51, Grand Junction, Colo., 1979-82 summer, Fed. Migrant Presch., Grand Junction, 1980-81; dir. clin. services, acting exec. dir. Idaho Easter Seal Soc., Boise, 1982-84; chief audiology and speech pathology Boise VA Med. Ctr., 1984-86; pvt. practice speech-lang. pathology Colorado Springs, 1987-88; judicial law clk. Colo. Supreme Ct., 1992-94; assoc. atty. Patton Boggs, L.L.P., 1994—; grad. asst. Okla. State U., Stillwater, 1976-78; speech-lang. cons. Boise Cleft Lip-Palate Team, 1982-84, Idaho Migrant Health Adv. Council, Boise, 1982-86; speech pathology cons. St. Alphonsus Med. Ctr., Boise, 1984-85. Recipient Superior Performance award VA, 1985. Mem. Am. Speech-Lang.-Hearing Assn. (cert.), Nat. Health Lawyers Assn., Phi Kappa Phi.

YOUNGBLOOD, RONALD FRED, religious educator; b. Chgo., Aug. 10, 1931; s. William C. and Ethel V. (Arenz) Y.; m. Carolyn J. Johnson, Aug. 16, 1952; children: Glenn, Wendy. BA, Valparaiso U., 1952; BD, Fuller Seminary, Pasadena, Calif., 1955; PhD, Dropsie Coll., Phila., 1961; post-grad., NYU, 1966. Prof. Old Testament Bethel Theol. Seminary, St. Paul, 1961-78; dean, prof. Old Testament Wheaton (Ill.) Coll., 1978-81; prof. Old Testament Trinity Evang. Divinity Sch., Deerfield, Ill., 1981-82, Bethel Seminary West, San Diego, 1982—. Author: Heart of the Old Testament, 1971, Themes From Isaiah, 1983, Exodus, 1983, Book of Genesis: An Introductory Commentary, 1991; editor: The Genesis Debate, 1986, NIV Study Bible, 1985. Owen D. Young fellow Gen. Electric Found., 1959-61, Hebrew Union Coll. fellow, 1967-68. Mem. Evang. Theol. Soc. (editor 1976—), Near East Archaeol. Soc. (sec. 1978—), Inst. for Bibl. Rsch., Internat. Bible Soc. (bd. dirs. 1989—). Office: Bethel Seminary West 6116 Arosa St San Diego CA 92115-3902

YOUNGER, BOB, aerospace executive; b. Sacramento, Sept. 24, 1936; s. Harold Payne and Nina Jo (Greenway) Y.; 1 child, Christian L. BSME, Calif. Poly. Inst., San Luis Obispo, 1964; MBA, U. Santa Clara, 1971. Engring. aide Aerojet, Sacramento, 1955-56, test engr., 1959-64; engr. Lockheed Missiles & Space, Sunnyvale, Calif., 1964-84, supr. post boost control sys., 1984-85; mgr. project engring. Lockheed Space Ops., Vandenberg, Calif., 1985-88; staff engr. new bus. Lockheed Missiles & Space, Sunnyvale, 1988-89; dir. ASRM support equipment Lockheed Missiles & Space, Iuka, Miss., 1989-93; mgr. propulsion status controls Lockheed Missiles & Space, Sunnyvale, 1994—. With USAF, 1955-59. Mem. AIAA. Home: 279 Camphor Ave Fremont CA 94539-7502 Office: LMSC PO Box 504 Sunnyvale CA 94086

YOUNGQUIST, ANDREW LANCE, construction executive; b. Newport Beach, Calif., Nov. 30, 1940; s. Vincent R. and Elizabeth (Tebbs) Y.; children: Bill, Jennifer; m. Linda Kay, May 17, 1980. Student, Orange Coast Coll. Pres. Decco Constrn., Orange, Calif., 1970-78; v.p. Capitol Systems, Newport Beach, 1976-77; with Saffell & McAdam, Irvine, Calif., 1977-79; pres. Birtcher Constrn. Ltd., Laguna Niguel, Calif., 1979—. Dir. Girl Scout Coun., Orange Empire, Girl Scouts U.S., 1991; bd. mem. Orange County Together. Mem. Nat. Assn. Indsl. Office Pks., Internat. Coun. Shopping Ctrs., Associated Gen. Contractors (bd. mem. Orange County dist.), Bldg. Industry Assn., Balboa Bay Club, Pacific Anglers. Republican. Home: 1851 Braemer Way Newport Beach CA 92660-3724 Office: Birtcher Constrn Ltd 24051 Shelley Rd Laguna Beach CA 92656-3912

YOUNGQUIST, WALTER LEWELLYN, consulting geologist; b. Mpls., May 5, 1921; s. Walter Raymond and Selma Regina (Knock) Y.; m. Elizabeth Salome Pearson, Dec. 11, 1943; children: John, Karen, Louise, Robert. BA, Gustavus Adolphus Coll., St. Peter, Minn., 1942; MSc, U. Iowa, 1943, PhD, 1948. Registered profl. geologist, Oreg. Jr. geologist U.S. Geol. Survey, 1943-44; rsch. assoc. U. Iowa, Iowa City, 1945-48; asst. prof. geology U. Idaho, Moscow, 1948-51; sr. geologist Internat. Petroleum Co., Talara, Peru, 1951-54; prof. geology U. Kans., Lawrence, 1954-57, U. Oreg., Eugene, 1957-66; cons. geologist Minerals dept. Exxon Corp., Houston, 1968-73; geothermal cons. Eugene Water & Electric Bd., 1973-92; ind. cons. Eugene, 1992—. Author: Mineral Resources and the Destinies of Nations, 1990, Investing in Natural Resources, 1980; co-author: Ordovician Cephalopod Fauna of Baffin Island, 1954. Ensign, USNR, 1944-45. Recipient Lowden Prize in Geology, U. Iowa, 1943. Fellow AAAS, Geol. Soc. Am.; mem. Am. Assn. Petroleum Geologists, Geotherman Resources Coun., N.W. Energy Assn. Lutheran. Office: PO Box 5501 Eugene OR 97405-0501

YOUNGS, JACK MARVIN, cost engineer; b. Bklyn., May 2, 1941; s. Jack William and Virginia May (Clark) Y.; BEngring., CCNY, 1964; MBA, San Diego State U., 1973; m. Alexandra Marie Robertson, Oct. 31, 1964; 1 child, Christine Marie. Mass properties engr. Gen. Dynamics Corp., San Diego, 1964-68, rsch. engr., 1968-69, sr. rsch. engr., 1969-80, sr. cost devel. engr., 1980-81, cost devel. engring. specialist, 1981—; prin. estimator Martin Marietta Astronautics, 1994—. Dist. dir. Scripps Ranch Civic Assn., 1976-79; pres. Scripps Ranch Swim Team, 1980-82; dir., 1986-87; judge Greater San Diego Sci. and Engring. Fair, 1981-92. Mem. Princeton U. Parents Assn. Recipient 5th place award World Body Surfing Championships, 1987, 6th place award, 1988. Mem. AIAA, N.Y. Acad. Scis., Alumni Assn. CUNY, Bklyn. Tech. High Sch. Alumni Assn., Inst. Cost Analysis (cert., charter mem., treas. Greater San Diego chpt. 1986-90), Soc. Cost Estimating and Analysis (cert. cost estimator/analyst, pres. San Diego chpt. 1990-91), Internat. Soc. Parametric Analysts (bd. dirs. San Diego chpt. 1987-90), Nat. Mgmt. Assn. (space systems div. charter mem. 1985, award of honor Convair chpt. 1975), Assn. MBA Execs., San Diego State U. Bus. Alumni Assn. (charter mem. 1986), Scripps Ranch Swim and Racquet Club (dir. 1977-80, treas. 1978-79, pres. 1979-80), Beta Gamma Sigma, Chi Epsilon, Sigma Iota Epsilon. Lutheran. Research in life cycle costing and econ. analysis. Home: 11461 Tribuna Ave San Diego CA 92131-1907 Office: PO Box 85990 San Diego CA 92186-5990

YOUNGS, JAMES MURRAY, freelance writer, photographer; b. Abilene, Tex., Apr. 15, 1947; s. William Murray and Mary Nell (Brown) Y.; m. Carolyn Sue Allen, Aug. 14, 1971; children: James Murray Jr., Monica Sue. BA in Journalism, Pepperdine U., 1972. Adminstrv. asst. Los Angeles County Bd. Suprs., 1966-67; photography coord. Pepperdine U., Malibu, Calif., 1971-72; photographer, draftsman Brehler Legal Photos, Los Angeles, 1973; pub. relations, advt. mgr. Griswolds Restuarants, Inc., Claremont, Calif., 1973-74; gen. mgr. Cinemodule, Hollywood, Calif., 1974-77; editor-in-chief Trailer Boats Mag., Carson, Calif., 1977-88; freelance writer Englewood, Colo., 1988—. Contbr. Trailer Boats Mag., Boating Mag., Lakeland Boating, Water Ski, Sports Illustrated, Popular Mechanics, Specialty Car. With USN, 1966-70. Mem. Boating Writers Internat. (dir. 1987-90), Nat. Marine Mfg. Assn., Sigma Delta Chi. Republican. Church of Christ. Home and Office: 8 Mountainview Rd Greenwood Village CO 80111-1736

YOUNT, CHARLES ROBERT, electrical and computer engineer; b. Hickory, N.C., Jan. 9, 1965; s. Charles Ivo and Thelma Gay (Lane) Y.; m. Sharron Lynn Stevens, Oct. 19, 1991; children: Danielle Christine, Sydney Ann. BS in Computer Engring., N.C. State U., 1987; MS in Elec. and Computer Engring., Carnegie Mellon U., 1990, PhD in Elec. and Computer Engring., 1993. Free-lance computer programmer Hickory, N.C., 1982-85; with personal comm. products dept. IBM, Research Triangle Park, N.C., 1984; with transmission tech. dept. IBM, Research Triangle Park, 1985, with material and logistics support dept., 1986, with Very Large-Scale Integration application design dept., 1986-87, 87-88; with Advanced Tech. Ctr. Boeing Computer Svcs., Bellevue, Wash., 1989-90; head software engr. Omniview, Inc., Pitts., 1992; sr. software engr. Inter-Nat. Rsch. Inst., San Diego, 1993—; tchg. asst. Carnegie Mellon U., Pitts., 1988, 89, guest lectr. Carnegie BOSCH Inst., 1991, seminar instr. Pa. Jr. Acad. Sci., 1991. Contbr. articles to profl. jours. Bd. dirs. United Campus Ministry of Pitts., corp. treas., 1992-93; adult edn. coord. Pine Run United Meth. Ch., 1993. Mem. IEEE, IEEE Computer Soc., IEEE Reliability Soc., Assn. Computing Machinery (spl. interest group in design automation), Phi Kappa Phi, Eta Kappa Nu, Tau Beta Pi (rec. sec. 1986-87). Home: 17916 Pueblo Vista Ln San Diego CA 92127-1276

YOUNT, DAVID EUGENE, physicist, educator; b. Prescott, Ariz., June 5, 1935; s. Robert Ephram and Jeannette Francis (Judson) Y.; m. Christel Marlene Notz, Feb. 22, 1975; children—Laura Christine, Gregory Gordon, Steffen Jurgen Robert, Sonja Kate Jeannette. B.S. in Physics, Calif. Inst. Tech., 1957; M.S. in Physics, Stanford U., 1959, Ph.D. in Physics, 1963. Instr. Princeton U., 1962-63, asst. prof. physics, 1963-64, Minn. Mining and Mfg. fellow, 1963; NSF postdoctoral fellow U. Paris, Orsay, France, 1964-65; rsch. assoc. Stanford Linear Accelerator Ctr. Stanford U., 1965-69; assoc. prof. U. Hawaii, 1969-73, prof., 1973—, chmn. dept. physics and astronomy, 1979-85, acting asst. v.p. for acad. affairs, 1985-86, v.p. rsch. and grad. edn., 1986-95. Mem. Am. Phys. Soc., Undersea and Hyperbaric Med. Soc., Am. Chem. Soc., U.S. Tennis Assn., Sigma Xi. Republican. Lutheran. Home: 5468 Opihi St Honolulu HI 96821-1924 Office: U Hawaii 2505 Correa Rd Honolulu HI 96822-2219

YOUNT, GEORGE STUART, paper company executive; b. Los Angeles, Mar. 4, 1949; s. Stanley George and Agnes (Pratt) Y.; m. Geraldine Marie Silvio, July 18, 1970; children: Trisha Marie, Christopher George. Postgrad., Harvard U., 1983-86. Mgmt. trainee Fortifiber Corp., L.A., 1969-71, asst. to v.p. ops., 1971-75, adminstrv. v.p., treas., sec., 1975-85, exec. v.p., sec., chief fin. officer, 1985-90, chmn., chief exec. officer, 1991—; pres., dir. Fonzia Corp., 1993—; pres., bd. dirs. Fonzia Corp.; treas., bd. dirs. Stanwall Corp., L.A., Pres., 1989, past pres. Hollister Ranch Cattle Coop., Gaviota, Calif., 1986-88; bd. dirs. Consol. Media Corp., Pasadena, Calif., Electrocel Tech. Systems, Santa Fe Springs, Calif. Team leader L.A. United Way, 1981-86; bd. dirs. Big Bros. Greater L.A., 1984-87, L.A. coun. Boy Scouts Am., 1992—; mem. Young Pres. Orgn., 1991, forum moderator, 1993-95. Mem. Am. Paper Inst. (dir. 1993—, splty. coaters and extrusion sect. 1990—), Nat. Assn. Corp. Dirs., Harvard Bus. Club So. Calif., Harvard Owner/Pres. Mgmt. Program Club, Jonathan Club (L.A.), San Marino City Club (Calif.), Rotary (bd. dirs. L.A. club 1992-94). Home: PO Box 3592 Incline Village NV 89450 Office: Fortifiber Corp 4489 Bandini Blvd Los Angeles CA 90023-4709

YOUNT, PHILIP RICHARD, insurance company executive; b. Hartwick, Iowa, Feb. 7, 1937; s. Fred Austin and Katherine Elizabeth (Gross) Y.; m. Mary Maxine White, June 3, 1956 (div. Jan. 1989); children: Jo Ann Yount Pearson, Mary Beth Yount King, Douglas Alan; m. Donna Mae Eki, Sept. 4, 1989; stepchildren: Maile Hitomi Solis, Gabriella Chiharu Solis, Ayala Masayo Solis. BA magna cum laude, Parsons Coll., 1959. CPCU; cert. in data processing, assoc. in mgmt. Staff acct., instr. Grinnell (Iowa) Coll., 1959-60; from acct. to pres. and chief exec. officer Grinnell Mut. Reins. Co., 1960-91; v.p., sec., treas. Grange Mut. Ins. Co., Tigard, Oreg., 1992—; pres., bd. dirs. Big M Agy., Inc., Grinnell, 1983-91, Grinnell Realty, Inc., 1985-91; bd. dirs. Grinnell Life Ins. Co., 1985-91, pres., 1985-89. Pres. pk. bd. City of Grinnell, 1972-78; pres., founder Grinnell Cmty. Taxpayers Assn., 1974-78; pres., bd. dirs. Greater Poweshiek Cmty. Found., Grinnell, 1988-92, GMG Found., Grinnell, 1989-91; bd. dirs. Grinnell Gen. Hosp., 1989-92. Recipient Meritorious Svc. award Nat. Assn. Mut. Insurers, 1989. Mem. CPCU Soc., Ins. Inst. Am., Data Processing Mgmt. Assn., Toastmasters, Chi Beta Chi, Phi Kappa Phi. Office: Grange Mut Ins Co PO Box 230969 7105 SW Varns St Tigard OR 97281-0969

YOUSEF, MARJAN, gerontologist, psychology educator; b. Amsterdam, The Netherlands, Apr. 10, 1945; came to the U.S., 1966; d. Theodorus Antonius Johannus and Johanna Maria (ter Beek) Lowies; m. Fathi S. Yousef, June 24, 1994; children: Monique El-Faizy, Robert El-Faizy. RN, Wilhelmina Gasthuis, 1966; BA, U. Calif., Irvine, 1987, MA, 1993. Grad. rsch. asst. dept. phys. medicine and rehab. U. Calif., 1988-93; adj. prof. Concordia U., Irvine, Calif., 1991—. Author articles in psychology and gerontology. Ombudsman Orange County Coun. on Aging, Irvine, 1987-88; vol. Hospice Orange County, Santa Ana, 1979-80. Mem. Gerontol. Soc. Am., Am. Psychol. Assn., Phi Eta Sigma. Office: Concordia U 1530 Concordia Irvine CA 92715-3203

YU, CHONG HO, educational researcher; b. Hong Kong, Aug. 9, 1963. BS in Mass Comm., BA in Art, Bemidji State U., 1989; cert. in profl. photography, N.Y. Inst. Profl. Photography, 1991; advanced cert. in liberal studies in philosophy, Hamline U., 1993; M Human Rels., U. Okla., 1992, MEd in Ednl. Psychology, 1993; PhD in Measurement of Stats., Ariz. State U., 1995. Cert. in computer programming. Sales mgr. Youth Lit. Book Co., Hong Kong, 1985-86; rsch. asst. human rels. U. Okla., Norman, 1990-92, rsch. asst. rsch. bur., 1992-94; faculty assoc. Ariz. State U., Tempe, 1994—; presenter in field. Columnist Macau Daily News, 1986—, Tin Tin Daily News, 1987, Ming Pao Daily News, Olive, others. Mem. APA, Am. Ednl. Rsch. Assn., Am. Statis. Assn., Assn. Computing Machinery, Assn. Ednl. Commn. and Tech., Psychometric Soc., Internat. Freelance Photographers Assn., Sooner Macintosh Users Group, Judgment and Decision Making Soc. Office: Ariz State U Divsn Measurement Statistic Dept Psychology Coll Edn Tempe AZ 85287-0611

YU, KITSON SZEWAI, computer science educator; b. Toishan, Kwangtung, China, Apr. 4, 1950; came to U.S., 1969; s. Ho Yee and Yin Sang (Chan) Y.; m. Mabel Griseldis Wong, July 15, 1972; 1 child, Robin Roberta Emily. BS, Troy State U., 1974, MS, 1977, BS, 1980. Cert. systems profl.; cert. data processing educator. V.p. Troy (Ala.) Computer Ctr., 1976-81; computer instr. Tory State U., 1980-81, Linn Benton Community Coll., Albany, Oreg., 1981—; dir. real estate program Linn Benton Community Coll., 1985—; mng. broker Kitson Realty, Corvallis, Oreg., 1975—. Vice pres. econ. devel. Daleville C. of C., Ala., 1976; dir. Corvalis Youth Symphony, 1990-93. Mem. Data Processing Mgmt. Assn. (bd. dirs. at large 1982-93, v.p. 1984-85, pres. 1985-86), Greater Albany Rotary (treas. 1985—), Corvallis Multiple Listing Exch. (bd. dirs. 1990-94), Gamma Beta Phi. Home: 2768 NW Wintergreen Pl Corvallis OR 97330-3550 Office: Linn Benton Community Coll 6500 Pacific Blvd SW Albany OR 97321-3755

YU, ZENG-QI, engineer, researcher; b. Jiansu, China, Nov. 26, 1941; came to U.S., 1980; s. Zu-An Yu and Pin-Yue Yin; m. Hao Jiang, Feb. 4, 1975; 1 child, Hong. BS, Fudan U., Shanghai, Peoples Republic of China, 1965; MS, Colo. State U., 1982, PhD, 1990. Asst. prof., researcher vacuum physics Fudan U., Shanghai, 1965-67, instr. laser physics, 1967-84; vis. scientist Colo. State U., Ft. Collins, 1980-82, rsch. asst., 1985-88, rsch. assoc., 1988-90, rsch. scientist, 1991-94; sr. engr. Storage Tech. Corp., Louisville, Colo., 1995—; tech. advisor Industry Bur. So. Dist. Shanghai, 1973-77; cons. Applied Electron Corp., Albuquerque, 1986-87, Hewlett Packard Co., Ft. Collins; technique cons. Electronics R&D Nippon Seiko K.K., Kanagawa, Japan, 1990, Quantum Rsch. Corp., 1990-93. Co-author: The Lasers, 1971, Laser Applications on Industry, 1972, Handbook of Thin Film Deposition Processes and Technologies, 1988; contbr. numerous articles to profl. jours.; patentee in field. Recipient Ann. Rschrs. Recognition award Rsch. Found. Bd., Colo. State U., 1987-95. Mem. IEEE (sr.), Optical Soc. Am., Am. Vacuum Soc. Home: 2830 Michener Dr Fort Collins CO 80526-6290 Office: Storage Tech Corp 2270 S 88th St Louisville CO 80028-0224

YUAN, ROBIN TSU-WANG, plastic surgeon; b. Boston, July 2, 1954; s. Robert Hsun-Piao and Grace I. (Chen) Y. AB, Harvard U., 1974, MD, 1978. Diplomate Am. Bd. Plastic Surgery. Resident in gen. surgery UCLA Med. Ctr., 1978-80, Cedars-Sinai Med. Ctr., L.A., 1980-81, 83-84; resident in plastic surgery U. Miami (Fla.)-Jackson Meml. Hosp., 1985-87; pvt. practice L.A., 1987—; clin. instr. div. plastic surgery UCLA, 1987—; vice-chief div. plastic surgery Cedars-Sinai Med. Ctr., L.A., 1991—; pres., chief exec. officer, founder Family of Independent Reconstructive Surgery Teams (F.I.R.S.T.), 1990—. Contbr. numerous articles to med. jours. Mem. Am. Soc. Plastic and Reconstructive Surgery, Am. Cleft Palate Assn., Calif. Med. Assn. (del.), L.A. County Med. Assn. (bd. govs. dist. 1), Phi Lambda (co-mgr. 1991—). Office: 150 N Robertson Blvd Ste 315 Beverly Hills CA 90211-2145

YUAN, SHAO WEN, aerospace engineer, educator; b. Shanghai, China, Apr. 16, 1914; came to U.S., 1934, naturalized, 1954; s. Ti An and Chieh-huang (Chien) Y.; m. Hui Chih Hu, Nov. 5, 1950. B.S., U. Mich., 1936; M.E., Stanford U., 1939; M.S., Calif. Inst. Tech., 1937, Ph.D., 1941. Rsch. engr. Glenn Martin Co., 1942-43; chief of rsch. Helicopter div. McDonnell Aircraft Corp., 1943-45; instr. Washington U., St. Louis, 1944-45; adj. prof. Poly. Inst. Bklyn., 1946-49, assoc. prof., 1949-54, prof., 1954-57; ptnr. von Kármán, Yuan & Arnold Assocs., 1955-63; prof. aerospace engring. U. Tex., 1958-68; prof., chmn. mech. engring. div. George Washington U., 1968-78, chmn. civil, mech. and environ. dept., 1973-78, 80-81, prof. emeritus, 1984; pres. RISE, Inc., 1977-85; Canadair Chair prof. U. Laval, Can., 1957-58; chmn. adv. com. Joint Inst. for Advancement of Flight Sci., 1970-84; hon. prof. Zhejiang U., 1987—; cons. Edo Aircraft Corp., Aerojet Corp., Cornell Aero. Lab., Dept. of Interior, Oak Ridge Nat. Lab., N.Am., Aviation, Inc., Fairchild-Hiller Corp., McDonnell-Douglas Corp., The World Bank; hon. adviser Nat. Center Research of China, Taiwan, 1958-68; chmn., founder 1st U.S.-China Conf. on Energy, Resources, and Environment, 1982; founder Consortium of Univs. for Promoting Grad. Aerospace Studies, 1984; founder Disting. Lecture Series on Founds. of Aerospace Research and Devel., 1986. Author: Foundations of Fluid Mechanics, 1967; Contbr. to: High Speed Aerodynamics and Jet Propulsion series, 1959, Energy, Resources, and Environment: Procs. at 1st U.S.-China Conf., 1982. Recipient Outstanding Achievements award George Washington U., 1981; named Outstanding Educator of Am., 1970, Outstanding Chinese American, 1983. Fellow AAAS, AIAA; mem. ASME (life), Am. Soc. Engring. Edn., Soc. Engring. Sci. (bd. dirs. 1973-78, pres. 1977), Torchbearers Caltech, Founding Grant Soc. of Stanford U. (charter), John Montieth Soc. of U. Mich. (charter), Sigma Xi, Phi Kappa Phi, Phi Tau Phi, Sigma Gamma Tau, Pi Tau Sigma, Tau Beta Pi, Tau Xi Sigma. Home: 1400 Geary Blvd Apt 1505 San Francisco CA 94109-6570

YUAN, SHAO-YUEN, management consultant; b. Shanghai, China, July 30, 1929; came to U.S., 1947; m. Cecilia X. Zhou, Nov. 30, 1989; children: Chris, Mark. BSChemE, Ill. Inst. Tech., 1950; MSChemE, U. Louisville, 1951. Rsch. engr. E.I. DuPont De Nemours Co., Phila., 1951-56; sr. rsch. engr. Chevron Rsch. Co., Richmond, Calif., 1956-69; regional exec. Chevron Rsch. Co., San Francisco, 1977-84; plant mgr. Chevron Chem. Co., Anaheim, Calif., 1966-69; sr. engring. assoc. Chevron Chem. Co., San Francisco, 1969-77; country mgr. Chevron Overseas Petroleum, Ltd., Beijing, 1984-89; licensing exec. Chevron Rsch. & Tech. Co., Richmond, Calif., 1989-92; prin. Yuan & Assocs., San Rafael, Calif., 1992—. Contbr. articles to profl. jours.; patentee in field. V.p. Am. C. of C. in China, Bejing, 1987, pres., 1988. AIChe, Am. Chem. Soc., Commonweatlh Club Calif. Office: Yuan & Assocs 70 Heritage Dr San Rafael CA 94901-8308

YUE, AGNES KAU-WAH, otolaryngologist; b. Shanghai, Peoples Republic China, Dec. 1, 1947; came to U.S., 1967; d. Chen Kia and Nee Yuan (Ying0 ; m. Gerald Kumata, Sept. 25, 1982; children: Julie, Allison Benjamin. BA, Wellesley Coll., 1970; MD, Med. Coll. Pa., 1974; postgrad., Yale U., 1974-78. Intern Yale-New Haven Hosp., 1974-75, resident, 1975-78; fellow U. Tex. M.D. Anderson Cancer Ctr., Houston, 1978-79; asst. prof. U. Wash., Seattle, 1979-82; physician Pacific Med. Ctr., Seattle, 1979-90; pvt. practice Seattle, 1991—. Fellow Am. Acad. Otolaryngology, Am. Coll. Surgeons; mem. Northwest Acad. Otolaryngology. Office: 1801 NW Market St Ste 410 Seattle WA 98107-3909

YUE, ALFRED SHUI-CHOH, metallurgical engineer, educator; b. China, Nov. 12, 1920; s. Choy Noon-woo and Sze Man-hun (Tom) Y.; m. Virginia Chin-wen Tang, May 21, 1944; children: Mary, Raymond Yuan, John, Ling Tsao, David, Nancy Chang. B.S., Chao-tung U., 1942; M.S., Ill. Inst. Tech., 1950; Ph.D., Purdue U., 1956. Assoc. engr. Taiwan Aluminum Co., 1942-47; instr. Purdue U., 1952-56; research engr. Dow Chem. Co., Midland, Mich., 1956-62; sr. mem. Lockheed, Palo Alto Research Lab., 1962-69; now cons.; prof. engring. and applied sci. U. Calif., Los Angeles, 1969—; hon. prof. Xian Jiao-tong U., China, 1980; cons. LTV Aerospace Co., Lockheed Missile & Space Co., Atlantic Richfield Co.; Sec.-gen. Chinese Culture Assn. in, U.S.A., 1967, also; bd. dirs. Chinese scholar to U.S.A. Fellow AIAA (assoc.); mem. AAAS, AIME, Am. Soc. Metals, Materials Rsch. Soc., Sigma Xi, Sigma Pi Sigma, Tau Beta Pi, Phi Tau Phi (pres. 1978-82). Office: U of Calif Los Angeles CA 90095-1595

YUEN, ANDY TAK SING, electronics executive; b. Wanchai, Hong Kong, Aug. 26, 1952; came to U.S., 1984; s. Yan Chong and Chi Oi (Tse) Y.; m. Kathy Man Kwan Chan, Jan. 29, 1983; children Lambert Hann Shi, Robin Hann Lang. Higher Cert. in Elec. Engring., Hong Kong Poly., 1975; Diploma in Bus. Mgmt., Hong Kong Bapt. Coll., 1976; Diploma in Exec. Devel., Chinese U., Hong Kong, 1981; MBA, Chui Hai Coll., Hong Kong, 1981; PhD in Bus. Mgmt., Calif. Coast U., 1987. Supervising engr. Teledyne Semiconductor Ltd., Kowloon, Hong Kong, 1976-79; ops. mgr. Microsemi (Hong Kong) Ltd., Kowloon, 1979-81, gen. mgr., 1981-84; corp. mgr. Microsemi Corp., Santa Ana, Calif., 1984-89, corp. v.p., 1989—; corp. dir. Semcon Electronics Pvt. Ltd., Bombay, 1984—. Author (books): Can Quality Circles Bring the Breakthrough to Hong Kong Industrial Management, 1982, Harnessing Japanese Quality Circles in Hong Kong, 1987. Fellow Inst. Sales and Mktg. Mgmt., Brit. Inst. Mgmt., Inst. Elec. and Electronics Inc. Engrs. Office: Microsemi Corp PO Box 26890 Santa Ana CA 92799-6890

YUEN, KARSTEN BRANDON, programmer analyst, consultant; b. Saigon, Vietnam, June 19, 1966; came to the U.S., 1975; s. Van Loi and Long Thi (Le) Nguyen. BS, Hawaii Pacific U., 1990. UNIX/CATIA cons. Boeing Aeroplane Co., Seattle, 1991-93; programmer analyst Island Mortgage Corp., Honolulu, 1993—; software cons. Quasidmodo Software Cons., Honolulu, 1984—. Vol. March of Dimes, Honolulu, 1984-94. Mem. U.S. Jr. C.of C. Home: 99-703 Halawa Dr Aiea HI 96701-3142 Office: P O Box 3707 MS7XRL Seattle WA 98124-2207

YUEN, RICHARD JOSEPH, university dean; b. San Francisco, Mar. 1, 1956; s. Joseph Edward Yuen and Nancy Jair Louie; m. Mabel Sikmei Teng, Dec. 10, 1983; children: Tania, Leticia. BA in Sociology/BA in Asian Am. Studies, U. Calif., Berkeley, 1978; MA in Social Work Edn., San Francisco State U., 1983. Rare book handler John Howell Books, San Francisco, 1973-82; supr. youth svcs. Oakland (Calif.) Chinese Cmty. Coun., 1982-84, supr. adult vocat., 1984-86; acad. counselor City Coll. of San Francisco, 1986-89; asst. dean of students Stanford (Calif.) U., 1989—, dir. Asian Am. Activities Ctr., 1989—. Founding mem. Asian Pacific Student Union, U. Calif., Berkeley, 1978, Nat. Coalition for Redress and Reparations, San Francisco, 1980, Asian Pacific Dem. Club, Oakland, 1985; bd. dirs. Chinese Am. Dem. Club, 1989—. Recipient Dir.'s award Black Cmty. Svcs. Ctr., Stanford, 1992, Dedicated Svc. award Stanford U. Nikkei, 1993; Children, Youth and Family fellow Frederick Burke Found., San Francisco, 1980. Mem. Asian Pacific Ams. in Higher Edn., Nat. Assn. of Student Pers. Adminstrs., Orgn. Chinese Ams., Chinese for Affirmative Action, Asian Staff Forum-Stanford (chair 1989-95), Kappa Delta Phi (Outstanding Svc. award 1994). Democrat. Roman Catholic. Office: Stanford University Old Union Clubhouse Stanford CA 94305-3064

YURIST, SVETLAN JOSEPH, mechanical engineer; b. Kharkov, USSR, Nov. 20, 1931; came to U.S., 1979, naturalized, 1985; s. Joseph A. and Rosalia S. (Zoilman) Y.; m. Imma Lea Erlikh, Oct. 11, 1960; 1 child, Eugene. M.S. in Mech. Engring. with honors, Poly. Inst., Odessa, USSR, 1954. Engr. designer Welding Equipment Plant, Novaya Utka, USSR, 1954-56; sr. tech. engr. Heavy Duty Automotive Crane Plant, Odessa, 1956-60, asst. chief matallugist, 1971-78; supr. research lab. Inst. Spl. Methods in Foundry Industry, Odessa, 1960-66, project engr. sci. research, 1966-71; engr. designer Teledyne Cast Product, Pomona, Calif., 1979-81; sr. mech. engr. Walt Elliot Disney Enterprises, Glendale, Calif., 1981-83; foundry liaison engr. Pacific Pumps div. Dresser Industries, Inc., Huntington Park, Calif., 1984-86; casting engr. Superior Industries Internat., Inc., Van Nuys, Calif., 1986-89; mech. engr. TAMCO Steel, Rancho Cucamonga, Calif., 1989—. Recipient award for design of automatic lines for casting electric motor parts USSR Ministry Machine Bldg. and Handtools Mfr., 1966, for equipment for permanent mold casting All Union Exhbn. of Nat. Econ. Achievements, 1966-70. Mem. Am. Foundrymen's Soc. Contbr. reports, articles to collections All Union Confs. Spl. Methods in Foundry, USSR; USSR patentee permanent mold casting. Home: 184 W Armstrong Dr Claremont CA 91711-1701 Office: TAMCO Steel 12459 Arrow Hwy Rancho Cucamonga CA 91739-9601

YUSE-MILLER, MARY ADONNA, dietitian, holistic nutrition therapist; b. Walla Walla, Wash., Mar. 3, 1960; d. Francis Theodore and Adonna Helen (Nuxoll) Yuse; m. Keith Michael Miller, Oct. 13, 1990; stepchildren: Sarah, Seth, Dustin. BS in Food and Nutrition, Eastern Wash. U., 1982; postgrad., Portland State U., 1987-90. Lic. dietitian, Oreg. Clin. dietitian Ctrl. Wash. Hosp., Wenatche, 1983; asst. food svc. mgr. Rogue Valley Manor, Medford, Oreg., 1984-86; nutrition specialist Area Agy. on Aging, Yreka, Calif., 1986-87; field mgr. Nutrition Svcs. Portland (Oreg.) Pub. Schs., 1987-90; cons. dietitian Beverly Enterprises, Portland, 1990-94; pres., founder Mary's Holistic Nutrition Therapy, Carlton, Oreg., 1994—; nutrition advisor McMinnville Wellness Found., 1994—; yoga instr. Chemetaka C.C., McMinnville, 1994—; cookbook reviewer Vegetarian Jour., 1993. Author: Yoga-Fit, 1994; editor newspaper G St. Sentinel, 1972. Founder, chair St. John Peace Group, Yamhill, Oreg., 1992—. Recipient scholarship Tony's Pizza and Food Svcs., Wo-He-Lo medallion Camp Fire, 1978, Quadrathon Woman's Winner Graham's Rowing Shells, 1987. Mem. Am. Dietetic Assn. (registered, vegetarian nutrition practice group 1991—), Oreg. Dietetic Assn., Toastmasters Internat. (pres., v.p., pub. rels., sec., area gov. Newberg chpt. 1986—). Roman Catholic. Office: Mary's Holistic Nutrition Therapy 10800 Modaffari Carlton OR 97111

YUWILER, ARTHUR, neurochemist; b. Mansfield, Ohio, Apr. 4, 1927; s. Max and Esther (Swartz) Y.; m. Alice Lubin, Dec. 16, 1950; children: Janice Anne, Michael Jeffrey, Kenneth Craig. BS, UCLA, 1950, PhD, 1956. Rsch. biochemist U.S. VA, L.A., 1957-58, chief neurobiochemistry rsch., 1962—; mental health trainee dept. anatomy UCLA, 1958-59, asst. rsch. biochemist dept. psychiatry and biochemistry, 1962-64, asst. prof. dept. psychiatry, 1965-70, assoc. prof. dept. psychiatry, 1972-77, prof., 1977—; dir. biochemistry schizophrenia joint rsch. project U. Mich., Ann Arbor, 1959-60, dir. biochemistry, dir. lab., 1960-62, rsch. biochemist Mental Health Rsch. Inst., 1960-62; adj. assoc. prof. dept. psychiatry UCLA, 1970-71; vis. sr. scientist Weizmann Inst. Sci., Israel, 1972-73; vis. prof. Karolinska Inst., Stockholm, 1990; mem. VA basic sci. com., Washington, 1966-69; mem. NIMH career devel. award com., Washington, 1971-76, chmn., 1976. Co-author: Biochemistry Behaviour, 1964; editorial bd. Jour. of Autism, Neurochem. Rsch.; contbr. articles to profl. jours., publs. Scientific adv. bd. Dystonia Found., 1976-83, 85-88, chmn. 1982-83. Mem. AAAS, Am. Coll. Neuropsychopharmacology, Am. Soc. Biol. Chemistry and Molecular Biology, Am. Soc. Neurochemistry, Internat. Soc. Neurochemistry, Soc. Bio. Psychiatry, Soc. for Neurosci. Jewish. Office: Neurobiochemistry Lab T-85 VAMC Brentwood Wilshire And Sawtelle Blvd Los Angeles CA 90073

YUZEITIS, JAMES RICHARD, information specialist; b. Chgo., Nov. 11, 1942; s. Stanley J. and Amy B. (English) Y.; m. Susan C. London, Oct. 7, 1967; children: Timothy, David, Amy. BA in Econs., Loyola U., Chgo., 1965, MS in Personnel Mgmt., 1968. Personnel adminstr. Chgo. Police Dept., 1965-67; personnel asst. McDonald's Corp., Chgo., 1967-69; ops. trainee McDonald's Corp., Washington, 1969-70; personnel mgr. McDonald's Corp., Detroit, 1970-72; licensing mgr. McDonald's Corp., Columbus, Ohio, 1972-73; internat. personnel cons. McDonald's Corp., Oakbrook, Ill., 1973-80, dir. of human resources, 1980-86, dir. human resources devel., 1986-91; pres. Quality Surveys, Inc., Big Timber, Mont., 1991—; cons. Ronald McDonald Children's Charities, Chgo., 1986-88. Cons. and vol. Ronald McDonald Houses, Chgo., 1987; vol. Crazy Mont. Mus. Soc., Big Timber, 1991-92; bd. dirs. Pioneer Med. Ctr., Big Timber, 1993—. Recipient medal of Merit Cath. Youth Orgn., Chgo., 1960. Mem. Soc. for Human Resource Mgmt., Human Resource Planning Soc., Indsl. Rels. Rsch. Soc. Home: PO Box 1244 Big Timber MT 59011-1244 Office: Quality Surveys Inc PO Box 1089 Big Timber MT 59011-1089

ZABANAL, EDUARDO OLEGARIO, lawyer; b. Legazpi City, Albay, The Philippines, Aug. 8, 1952; came to U.S., 1986; s. Jose Agas and Maria Soledad (Olegario) Z.; m. Leorosie Rebodos Nabor, June 18, 1983; children: Shalimar Rosary, Angelica Almira, Regina Tatiana. BA, Aquinas U., The Philippines, 1972; BL, U. The Philippines, 1978. Bar: Hawaii 1990, The Philippines 1979, U.S. Dist. Ct. Hawaii 1990. Assoc. Pacis & Reyes, Manila, 1979-86; pvt. practice Honolulu, 1990—. Contbr. articles to profl. jours. Bd. dirs. Kahaluu Neighborhood Bd., Honolulu, 1991-93; active Filipino Coalition for Solidarity, Honolulu, 1991—. Mem. ABA, Assn. Trial Lawyers Am., Hawaii State Bar Assn., Hawaii Filipino Lawyers Assn., Integrated Bar The Philippines, Philippine Bar Assn., Nat. Assn. Life Underwriters (Nat. Sales Achievement award 1992), West Honolulu Assn. Life Underwriters, Filipino C. of C. Hawaii. Roman Catholic. Home: 1031 Nuuanu Ave Apt 404 Honolulu HI 96817-5602

ZABINSKY, ZELDA BARBARA, operations researcher, industrial engineering educator; b. Tonawanda, N.Y., Oct. 31, 1955; d. Joseph Marvin and Helen Phyllis (Kava) Z.; m. John Clinton Palmer, July 15, 1979; children: Rebecca Ann Zabinsky, Aaron Zeff Palmer. BS, U. Puget Sound, Tacoma, 1977; MS, U. Mich., 1984, PhD, 1985. Tutor math. U. Puget Sound, 1975-77; programmer, analyst Nat. Marine Fisheries, Seattle, 1977, Boeing Computer Svcs., Seattle, 1977-78; sr. systems analyst Vector Rsch. Inc., Ann Arbor, Mich., 1980-84; asst. prof. indsl. engring. U. Wash., Seattle, 1985-93, assoc. prof. indsl. engring., 1993—; cons. Boeing Corp., Seattle, 1987, Numerical Methods, Inc., Seattle, 1989-90, METRO, Seattle, 1992. Contbr. articles to tech. jours. Mem. faculty adv. bd. Women in Engring., U. Wash., 1990—. Recipient E. Goman Math. award, 1977, Rsch. Initiation award NSF, 1992-95; Howarth-Thompson scholar, 1973-77; Benton fellow, 1983-84; rsch. grantee NSF, NASA-Langley, Nat. Forest Svc., NATO, Boeing, 1985—. Mem. Ops. Rsch. Soc. Am., Inst. Indsl. Engrs. (sr.), Math. Programming Soc., Mortar Board, Phi Kappa Phi. Jewish. Office: U Wash Dept Indsl Engring FU-20 Seattle WA 98195

ZABRISKIE, ROBERT, performing arts association administrator, data processing manager; b. Monroe, Utah, July 22, 1929; s. John Peter and Violet (Harding) Z.; m. Betty Ross, Feb. 2, 1952 (div.); m. Beverly Young, Oct. 16, 1970; children: Michael, Christie, Lara. BA in Music, Brigham Young U., 1953. Missionary Ch. of Jesus Christ of Latter Day Saints, Germany, 1957-60; owner Utah Conv. Svc., Salt Lake City, 1961-63; stockbroker G.L. Jones and Assocs., Salt Lake City, 1963-74; data processing mgr. Utah Dept. Transp., Salt Lake City, 1974—; founder, dir. Salt Lake Opera Theatre, 1978—; adj. prof. Westminster Coll., Salt Lake City, 1989—. condr. Murray Intermtn. Symphony, 1987—, operas and musicals including Pagliacci, Faust, Madame Butterfly, Rigoletto, The Mikado and My Fair Lady, The King & I; dir. La Boheme, The Mikado, Suor Angelica, Il Tabarro, Gianni Schicchi, Lucia di Lammermoor, Tales of Hoffman, Verdi Requiem, Brahms Requiem. Mem. Mormon Tabernacle Choir. Tech. sgt. USAF, 1951-55. Home and Office: Salt Lake Opera Theatre Am Towers 807-S 44 W 300 S Salt Lake City UT 84101-3201

ZABSKY, JOHN MITCHELL, engineering executive; b. Joplin, Mo., Apr. 18, 1933; s. Joseph Anthony and Joan (Lucas) Z. AS, Joplin Jr. Coll., 1953; BSME, U. Mo., 1956; MSME, U. Kans., 1965. Profl. engr., Mo. System engr. Bendix KCD, Kansas City, Mo., 1958-62; rsch. engr. Rocketdyne, Neosho, Mo., 1962-65, Boeing Co., Huntsville, Ala., 1965-66; prin. rsch. engr., scientist Honeywell Inc., St. Paul, 1966-71; chief engr. Pressure Tank & Pipe Fabrication Co., Nashville, 1971-72, Engring. for Industry, Danville, Va., 1972-73; area mgr. fluid machinery Dresser Adv. Tech. Ctr., Irvine, Calif., 1973-85; v.p. ops. ATI, Laguna Niguel, Calif., 1985-93; pres.

Cytoprobe, San Diego, 1993-94, v.p. ops., 1994-95; cons. Oral Care Products, L.A., 1990-92. Patentee in field. Pres. Mpls.-St. Paul Singletons, 1969-72. Mem. AIAA, ASME, Mo. Soc. Profl. Engrs., Soc. Mfg. Engrs. Home: 3640C S Main St Santa Ana CA 92707-5720

ZACCHINO, NARDA, newspaper editor. Assoc. editor L.A. Times, Calif. Office: Los Angeles Times Times Mirror Sq Los Angeles CA 90053

ZACHARIAS, RICHARD ALLEN, electrical engineer; b. Fresno, Calif., Dec. 3, 1953; s. John Henry and Georgia Margaret (Botts) Z.; m. Janice Anne Carter, Aug. 24, 1974; children: Eric, Nicole, Laura, Nathan, Karen. BSEE, U. of the Pacific, 1977; MSEE, U. So. Calif., 1979. Radio person, sta. engr. KSTN/AM, KUOP/FM, Stockton, Calif., 1972-74; engr. Concord (Calif.) Naval Weapons Sta., 1974-79; tech. staff mem. Hughes Aircraft Co., El Segundo, Calif., 1977-79; project engr., group leader, dep. program leader L.L.N.L., Livermore, Calif., 1979—. Author IEEE Systems, 1992. Soccer referee Manteca (Calif.) Area Soccer League, 1987-92. Named Disting. alumni U. of the Pacific Engring., 1980. Republican. LDS. Office: Lawrence Livermore Nat Lab Mail Code L-153 700 East Ave Livermore CA 94550

ZACHER, VALERIE IRENE, interior designer; b. Woodland, Calif., Dec. 12, 1942; d. Albert Richard and Laura Ruth (Mast) Z.; m. William Robert Wallace, June 14, 1964 (div. Oct. 1968); 1 child, Jason Zachery Wallace. BA in Polit. Sci., Stanford U., 1964; AS in Interior Design, West Valley Coll., 1982; cert. TESL, U. Calif. Santa Cruz, Santa Clara, 1994. Owner, operator Artefactorage, Fresno, Calif., 1968-77; owner, designer Viz a Viz, Los Gatos, Calif., 1978-82; facilities project mgr. Nat. Semiconductor, Santa Clara, Calif., 1982-85; project supr. Mervyns, Hayward, Calif., 1985-86; interior designer, project mgr. Charles Schwab & Co., San Francisco, 1986-87; small bus. advisor US Peace Corps, Gaborone, Botswana, 1987-89, Swedish Coop. Ctr., Gaborone, 1989-90; English tchr. YCC Am. Club, Yokohama, Japan, 1992-93; interior design cons. Los Gatos, 1993—; design/facilities cons. Octel Comm. Corp., Milpitas, Calif., 1994; interior designer Am. Cancer Soc. Designers Showcase, 1994-95. Home and Office: 16721 Madrone Ave Los Gatos CA 95030-4120

ZACK, JAMES G(ORDON), JR., construction claims executive, consultant; b. Springfield, Mass., Sept. 6, 1946; s. James Gordon and Marione Mildred (Langevin) Z.; m. Yvonne Eileen Beezley, Oct. 26, 1970; children: Jennifer Yvonne, Stacy Rebecca, James William, Trevor David. AB in Polit. Sci., Assumption Coll., 1968; MPA, U. S.C., 1975. Dir. budgets and grants adminstrn. S.C. Dept. Health and Environ. Control, Columbia, 1972-78; mgr. constrn. contracts group CH2M Hill, Inc., Milw., 1978-85; mgr. scheduling and claims dept. CH2M Hill, Inc., L.A., 1986-95; asst. gen. mgr. High-Pont Rendel, L.A., 1995—; cons. EPA, 1977-88; reviewer Engring. Mgmt. Jour., 1987—; expert witness on constrn. litigation; lectr. profl. devel. seminars. Contbr. articles to profl. jours. Commr. Pacifica dist. Boy Scouts Am., 1987-94, scoutmaster, 1994—; mem. Calif. Compact Com., Huntington Beach, 1988-92. Mem. ASCE, Am. Assn. Cost Engrs., Project Mgmt. Inst., Constrn. Mgmt. Assn. Am., Am. Arbitration Assn.,. Methodist. Home: 9531 Netherway Dr Huntington Beach CA 92646-6051 Office: High Point 515 S Flower St Ste # 3510 Los Angeles CA 90071

ZACKS, ARTHUR, retired radiologist; b. Winnipeg, Manitoba, Can., Mar. 12, 1926; came to U.S., 1946; s. Peter and Elizabeth (Ducan) Z.; m. Betty Lynn Sadis, June 15, 1952; 1 child, Dorothy. Student, U. B.C., Vancouver, Can., 1944-46; BS, U. Wash., 1948, MD, 1952. Diplomate Am. Bd. Radiology. Resident radiology Jewish Hosp., Children's Hosp., Gen. Hosp., Cin., 1953-56; radiologist Kaiser-Permanente Med. Ctr., San Francisco, 1956-58; chief radiology Kaiser-Permanente Med. Ctr., Honolulu, 1958-62; radiologist St. Mary's Hosp., San Francisco, 1962-65; pvt. practice radiology San Francisco, 1962-65; radiologist Kaiser-Permanente Med. Ctr., San Francisco, 1965-71; chief radiology Kaiser-Permanente Med. Ctr., San Rafael, Calif., 1971-80, sr. cons., 1980-86; sr. cons., exec. sec., founding mem. Hawaii Permanente Med. Group, Honolulu, 1958-62; exec. com, Kaiser-Permanente Ctr., San Rafael, 1971-80; mem. radiology chief's com. Kaiser-Permanente Med. Ctrs., no. Calif., 1971-80. Contbr. articles to profl. jours. Mem. World Affairs Coun. No. Calif., San Francisco, 1989-92; docent San Francisco Mus. Modern Art, 1987—; vol. Friends of Photography, Ansel Adams Ctr., San Francisco, Calif. Acad. Sci., San Francisco, 1989—, docent, 1993—. Fellow Royal Soc. Health (U.K.); mem. AAAS, Soc. Nuclear Medicine, N.Y. Acad. Scis., Commonwealth Club Calif. (San Francisco).

ZAFFARONI, ALEJANDRO C., biochemist, medical research company executive; b. Montevideo, Uruguay, Feb. 27, 1923; came to U.S., 1944; s. Carlos and Luisa (Alfaro) Z.; m. Lyda Russomanno, July 5, 1946; children—Alejandro A., Elisa. B., U. Montevideo, 1943; Ph.D. in Biochemistry, U. Rochester, 1949; Doctorate (hon.), U. Republic, Montevideo, 1983; M.Divinity, Cen. Bapt. Seminary, 1987. Dir. biochem. research Syntex S.A., Mexico City, 1951-54, v.p., dir. research, 1954-56; exec. v.p., dir. Syntex Corp., Palo Alto, Calif., 1956-68; pres. Syntex Labs. Inc., Palo Alto, Calif., 1962-68, Syntex Research, Palo Alto, Calif., 1962-68; founder, co-chmn. ALZA Corp., Palo Alto, Calif., 1968—, also CEO; founder, mem. policy bd. and exec. com. DNAX Research Inst. of Molecular and Cellular Biology, Inc., Palo Alto, Calif., 1980—, chmn., 1980-82; founder, chmn., chief exec. officer Affymax, N.V., Palo Alto, 1989—; chmn. Internat. Psoriasis Research Found., Palo Alto; incorporator Neuroscis. Research Found. MIT, Brookline, Mass.; bd. govs. Weizmann Inst. Sci., Rehovot, Israel; mem. pharm. panel of com. on tech. and internat. econs. and trade issues Nat. Acad. Engring. Office of Fgn. Sec. and Assembly of Engring., Washington; hon. prof. biochemistry Nat. U. Mex., 1957, U. Montevideo, 1959. Contbr. numerous articles to profl. jours.; patentee in field. Recipient Barren medal Barren Found., Chgo., 1974; Pres.'s award Weizmann Inst. Sci., 1978; Chem. Pioneer award Am. Inst. Chemists, Inc., 1979. Fellow Am. Acad. Arts and Scis., Am. Pharm. Assn.; mem. AAAS, Am. Chem. Soc., Am. Found. Pharm. Edn., Am. Inst. Chemists, Inc., Am. Soc. Biol. Chemists, Inc., Am. Soc. Microbiology, Am. Soc. Pharmacology and Exptl. Therapeutics, Biomed. Engring. Soc., Calif. Pharmacists Assn., Internat. Pharm. Fedn., Internat. Soc. Chronobiology, Internat. Soc. Study of Biol. Rhythms, Soc. Exptl. Biology and Medicine, Sociedad Mexicana de Nutricion y Endocrinologia, Biochem. Soc. Eng., Endocrine Soc., Internat. Soc. Research in Biology of Reproduction, N.Y. Acad. Scis., Christian Legal Soc. (Mo. bd. dirs. 1973—), Tau Kappa Epsilon (internat. pres. 1953-57). *

ZAFREN, KEN, physician; b. Cin., Oct. 12, 1953; s. Herbert Cecil and Miriam (Koenigsberg) Z.; m. Christina Tower, June 29, 1984. BA in Math., New Coll., Sarasota, Fla., 1975; MD, U. Wash., 1984. Diplomate Nat. Bd. Med. Examiners, Am. Bd. Emergency Medicine. Transitional intern Presbyn.-St. Luke's Med. Ctr., Denver, 1985-86; pvt. practice Anchorage, 1986-91, Kern Med Ctr, Bakersfield, Calif., 1991-94; emergency physician Alaska Regional Hosp., Anchorage, 1994—, Providence Hosp., Anchorage, 1994—; asst. med. dir. North Care, 1990-91; mem. Alaska Mountain Rescue Group, 1988—, chmn., 1991. Mem. Rocky Mountain Rescue Group, Boulder, 1976-80, Mountain Rescue Council, Seattle, 1979-83. NIH tng. grantee, 1979-83; grand prize winner 1988 MD Magazine photo contest. Mem. Am. Alpine Club, Mountaineering Club Alaska (bd. dirs. 1990-91), Himalayan Rescue Assn. (life, assoc. dir. USA 1993—), Wilderness Med. Soc. (bd. dirs. 1991—, program co-chair 2d World Congress on Wilderness Medicine, 1995).

ZAHARIA, ERIC STAFFORD, developmental disabilities program administrator; b. Pomona, Calif., Aug. 24, 1948; s. Edgar A. and Dorothy (Stafford) Z.; m. Caryle Koentz, Dec. 23, 1967; children: Tye W., Tieg A. BA, Pomona Coll., 1970; MEd, U. Ariz.-Tucson, 1973; PhD, George Peabody Coll., 1978; postgrad., Govt. Execs. Inst. U. N.C., Chapel Hill, 1981. Mental retardation worker Ariz. Tng. Program, Tucson, 1970-71, unit dir., 1971-73; dir. residential svcs. Willmar State Hosp., (Minn.), 1973-76; rsch. asst. Inst. on Mental Retardation and Intellectual Devel., Nashville, 1976-78; dir. mental retardation program svcs. Dept. Mental Health/Mental Retardation, State of Tenn., Nashville, 1978-79; dir. Caswell Ctr., Kinston, N.C., 1979-86; program adminstr. Colo. Div. of Devel. Disabilities, Denver, 1986-90; dir. Utah div. Svcs. for People with Disabilities, Salt Lake City, 1990—; mem. adj. faculty East Carolina U., Greenville, 1979-86; bd. dirs. Neuse Enterprises Inc., Kinston. Chmn. Big Bros./Sisters Kinston Inc., 1980-83; mem. N.C. Coalition for Community Svc., 1982-85. Mem. Am. Assn. Mental Retardation, Nat. Assn. Supts., Pub. Residential Facilities, Assn. Retarded Citizens, Kinston C. of C. (bd. dirs. 1983-86). Home: 8010 Juniper Dr Park City UT 84060-5370 Office: 120 N 200 W Salt Lake City UT 84103-1550

ZAIDI, IQBAL MEHDI, biochemist, scientist; b. Bijnor, India, June 30, 1957; s. Iqbal Haider and Habib (Zehra) Z.; m. Nuzhat Shikoh, Jan. 2, 1993; 1 child, Shan Zehra. BS in Chemistry with honors, Aligarh M. U., 1976, MS in Biochemistry, 1978, PhD in Biochemistry, 1984. Cert. in radiation. Rsch. fellow Indsl. Toxicology Rsch. Ctr., Lucknow, India, 1979-83; rsch. affiliate N.Y. State Health Dept., Albany, 1984-91; scientist Applied Biosystems div. Perkin Elmer Corp., Foster City, Calif., 1991—. Contbr. articles to profl. jours. Mem. AAAS, Am. Chem. Soc. (biochem. tech. div. 1992—), Shia Assn. Bay Area, N.Y. Acad. Scis. Office: Perkin Elmer Corp Applied Biosystems Divsn 850 Lincoln Center Dr Foster City CA 94404

ZAJAC, JOHN, semiconductor equipment company executive; b. N.Y.C., July 21, 1946; s. John Andrew and Catherine (Canepa) Z.; m. Vera Barbagallo, Jan. 13, 1973; children: Jennifer, Michelle. AAS, NYU, 1966; BEE, U. Ky., 1968. Project engr. B.C.D. Computing, N.Y.C., 1968-70; v.p. Beacon Systems, Commack, N.Y., 1970-73, E.T. Systems, Santa Clara, Calif., 1973-77; v.p. research and devel. Eaton Corp., Sunnyvale, Calif., 1977-81; pres. Semitech/Gen. Signal, Los Gatos, Calif., 1981-83; mgr. advanced product div. Tegal/Motorola Inc., Novato, Calif., 1983-86; v.p. research and devel. U.S.A. Inc., San Jose, Calif., 1986—. Author: Delicate Balance, 1988; holder of 19 patents in field; guest TV and radio. Office: PO Box 21237 San Jose CA 95151-1237

ZAKARIN, KEITH, lawyer; b. Bklyn., Dec. 24, 1958; s. Leonard Zakarin and Rozlyn Dolling. Student, Mesa Coll., 1979-81; BA in Polit. Sci., U. Calif., San Diego, 1983; JD, U. Calif., Berkeley, 1986. Bar: Calif. 1986, U.S. Dist. Ct. (so., cen., ea. and no. dists.) Calif. 1986, U.S. Tax Ct. 1986, U.S. Ct. Appeals (9th cir.) 1986, U.S. Supreme Ct. 1991. Assoc. Pillsbury, Madison & Sutro, San Diego, 1985-94; ptnr. Rice, Fowler, Booth & Banning, San Diego, 1994—; mem. fed. ct. com. So. Dist. With USN, 1976-81. U. Calif. scholar, San Diego, 1983. Mem. ABA, Calif. Bar Assn., San Diego County Bar Assn., U. Calif. Alumni Assn. Office: Rice Fowler Booth & Banning Emerald-Shapery Ctr San Diego CA 92101

ZAKY, AMR MOHAMED, computer scientist, educator; b. Cairo, Apr. 20, 1957. BSc, Alexandria (Egypt) U., 1979, MSc, 1982; PhD, Ohio State U., 1989. Software engr. Computer Ctr. Alexandria U., 1979, instr. computer sci. dept., 1979-82; grad. teaching asst. Ohio State U., Columbus, 1983-89; asst. prof. dept. computer sci. Naval Postgrad.Sch., Monterey, Calif., 1989—. Office: Naval Postgrad Sch Dept Computer Sci Monterey CA 93943-5000

ZALE, COOPER JONATHAN CAMPBELL, computer systems analyst, information systems consultant; b. Ann Arbor, Mich., Apr. 2, 1955; s. Eric Michael and Jane (Roberts) Z.; m. Sally Rosloff, Dec. 18, 1983; children: Eric Rosloff, Emma Rosloff. BA magna cum laude, U. Mich., 1978; BS summa cum laude, Calif. State U., L.A., 1986. Film location scout L.A., 1980-81; field organizer NOW, L.A., 1981-86; computer software designer L.A., 1986-90; computer systems analyst Syncor Internat. Corp., Chatsworth, Calif., 1990-94; ind. info. sys. cons., 1994—. Pres. Sepulveda Unitarian Universalist Soc., North Hills, Calif., 1994—. Mem. NOW (v.p. L.A. chpt. 1980-86, sec. 1989—, Women's Rights Advocacy award 1982). Home: 17806 Lorne St Reseda CA 91335-1530 Office: Syncor Internat Corp 20001 Prairie St Chatsworth CA 91311-6508

ZALESKI, BRIAN WILLIAM, chiropractor; b. Trenton, N.J., Oct. 27, 1962; s. Joseph Rudolph and Roseline (Moore) Z.; m. Petra Gertrude Tucker, Apr. 10, 1983; children: Natasha Reneé, Tatyana Amber. Student, Def. Lang. Inst., Monterey, Calif., 1980-81; BS, Palmer Coll., 1992, D of Chiropractic, 1992. Grad. researcher Palmer Coll. of Chiropractice, Davenport, Iowa, 1991-92; chiropractor Peninsula Spinal Care, Daly City, Calif., 1992, Creekside Family Chiropractic, Vacaville, Calif., 1992—; prin. investigator, presenter Internat. Conf. on Spinal Manipulation, 1992. Baseball umpire Iowa High Schs., Davenport, 1989-92, Men's Sr. League, Davenport, 1989-91, No. Calif. Umpires Assn., San Mateo, Calif., 1992. Sgt. U.S. Army, 1980-85. Recipient scholarship Internat. Chiropractors Assn., 1989, 90, Cecil M. Grogan scholarship Palmer Internat. Alumni Assn., 1991, Alma Nielsen scholarship Internat. Chiropractors Assn. Aux., 1991, Student Rsch. grant Palmer Coll. Chiropractic, 1992; named to Dean's List, 1991-92. Mem. Internat. Chiropractors Assn. (coun. on chiropractic pediatrics), Calif. Chiropractic Assn., Assn. for History of Chiropractic, Internat. Chiropractors Assn. Calif., Napa/Solano Chiropractic Soc. (sec.), Palmer Internat. Alumni Assn., Masons, Delta Sigma Chi, Chi Rho Theta. Republican. Office: Creekside Family Chiropractic 3000 Alamo Dr Ste 104 Vacaville CA 95687-6345

ZALKIND, JOSEPH GARY, fundraiser, writer, speaker; b. Fall River, Mass., Apr. 16, 1946; s. David and Anne M. (Dondis) Z.; m. Sheila A. Zalkind, Aug. 11, 1979; stepchildren: Lee Rosenbaum, Alison Rosenbaum. BA, U. Mass., 1968. Devel. dir. Loretto Heights, Denver, 1985-87, Denver Art Mus., 1987-89; chief fundraiser Provenant Health Ptnrs., Denver, 1990-94. Author: Guide to Corporations, 1974; contbr. articles to profl. jours. Colo. liaison Friends of Peace Now, 1983-93; midwest coord. New Jewish Agenda, Denver, 1985-93; advisor Assn. of Sr. Citizens, Denver, 1988; adv. com. Am. Friends of Svc. Com., Denver, 1982-94. Mem. Nat. Soc. of Fund Raising Execs. Democrat. Jewish. Home: 200 W 60th St Apt 20H New York NY 10023-8508 Office: 200 W 60th St #20H New York NY 10023

ZALLE, PAUL MARTIN, financial services company executive; b. L.A., Aug. 13, 1945; s. Morris D. and Esther M. (Kahn) Z.; m. Judith Ann Willen, Mar. 31, 1968; children: Melissa Elise, Michael Brandon. BSBA, Calif. State. U., Northridge, 1968; postgrad. in acctg., Calif. State U., L.A., 1969-71. Cert. internal auditor, cert. info. sys. auditor, cert. fraud examiner. Sr. acct. Cohen & Cohen, CPA's, L.A., 1968-72; mgr. auditing Carte Blanche Corp., L.A., 1973-77; regional audit mgr. Avco. Corp., Newport Beach, Calif., 1978-82; regional dir. auditing Textron Corp., Irvine, Calif., 1983-86; v.p. auditing Avco Fin. Svcs., Inc., Irvine, 1987—; cons. to pres. Bus. Spltys., Inc., Newport Beach, Calif., 1986—; cons. to chmn. Imperial Thrift & Loan Assn., Burbank, Calif., 1987-93. Contbr. articles to profl. publs. Family advisor prosthetic program for handicapped UCLA, 1975—. Mem. Am. Fin. Svcs. Assn. (nat. audit com. 1985—, chmn. 1990-92, chmn. 1995-96), Inst. Internal Auditors (editor, advisor 1980—, hon. svc. award 1983, bd. govs. Orange County chpt. 1990—), EDP Auditors Assn., Orange County Pvt. Investment Club. Democrat. Jewish. Home: 30 Ocean Vista Newport Beach CA 92660 Office: Avco Fin Svcs Inc 17770 Cartwright Rd Irvine CA 92714

ZALTA, EDWARD, otorhinolaryngologist, utilization review physician; b. Houston, Mar. 2, 1930; s. Nouri Louis and Marie Zahde (Lizmi) Z.; m. Carolyn Mary Gordon, Oct. 8, 1971; 1 child, Ryan David; children by previous marriage: Nouri Allan, Lori Ann, Barry Thomas, Marci Louise. BS, Tulane U., 1952, MD, 1956. Diplomate Am. Bd. Quality Assurance and Utilization Rev. Physicians. Intern Brooke Army Hosp., San Antonio, 1956-57; resident in otolaryngology U.S. Army Hosp., Ft. Campbell, Ky., 1957-60; practice medicine specializing in otolaryngology Glendora, West Covina and San Dimas, Calif., 1960-82; ENT cons. City of Hope Med. Ctr., 1961-76; mem. staff Foothill Presbyn.; past pres. L.A. Found. Community Svc., L.A. Poison Info. Ctr., So. Calif. Physicians Coun., Inc.; founder, chief exec. officer, chmn. bd. dirs. CAPP CARE, INC.; chmn. bd. MDM; founder Inter-Hosp. Coun. Continuing Med. Edn. Author: (with others) Medicine and Your Money; mem. editorial staff Managed Care Outlook, AAPPO Jour., Med. Interface; contbr. articles to profl. jours. Pres. bd. govs. Glendora Unified Sch. Dist., 1965-71; mem. Calif. Cancer Adv. Coun., 1967-71, Commn. of Californias, L.A. County Commn. on Economy and Efficiency, U. Calif. Irvine Chief Exec. Roundtable. Served to capt. M.C. AUS, 1957-60. Recipient Award of Merit Order St. Lazarus, 1981. Mem. AMA, Calif. Med. Assn., Am. Acad. Otolaryngology, Am. Coun. Otolaryngology, Am. Assn. Preferred Provider Orgns. (past pres.), Am. Coll. Med. Quality, L.A. County Med. Assn. (pres. 1980-81), Kappa Nu, Phi Delta Epsilon, Glendora CountryClub, Centurion Club, Sea Bluff Beach and Racquet Club; Center Club (Costa Mesa, Calif.), Pacific Golf Club (San Juan, Capistrano). Republican. Jewish. Home: 3 Morning Dove Laguna Niguel CA 92677-5331 Office: West Tower 4000 Macarthur Blvd Ste 10000 Newport Beach CA 92660-2526

ZALUCKY, ALEXANDER DAVID, automation company executive; b. Warsaw, Poland, Mar. 24, 1960; came to U.S., 1967; s. Henry K. and Maria Zalucky. BSME, Purdue U., 1980; MSME, MIT, 1982. Mem. tech. staff IBM, Boca Raton, Fla., 1982-83; mgr. application engring. Adept Tech., Inc., San Jose, Calif., 1983-86; pres., founder Robotic Development, Sunnyvale, Calif., 1986—. Patentee in field of active beam bending compensation. Office: Robotic Development 1156-A Aster Ave Sunnyvale CA 94086

ZALUTSKY, MORTON HERMAN, lawyer; b. Schenectady, Mar. 8, 1935; s. Albert and Gertrude (Daffner) Z.; m. Audrey Englebardt, June 16, 1957; children: Jane, Diane, Samuel. BA, Yale U., 1957; JD, U. Chgo., 1960. Bar: Oreg. 1961. Law clk. to presiding judge Oreg. Supreme Ct., 1960-61; assoc. Hart, Davidson, Veazie & Hanlon, 1961-63, Veatch & Lovett, 1963-64, Morrison, Bailey, Dunn, Cohen & Miller, 1964-69; prin. Morton H. Zalutsky, P.C., 1970-76; ptnr. Dahl, Zalutsky, Nichols & Hinson, 1977-79, Zalutsky & Klarquist, P.C., Portland, Oreg., 1980-85, Zalutsky, Klarquist & Johnson, Inc., Portland, 1985-94; Zalutsky & Klarquist, P.C., Portland, 1994—; instr. Portland State U., 1961-64, Northwestern Sch. of Law, 1969-70; assoc. prof. U. Miami Law Sch.; lectr. Practicing Law Inst., 1971—, Oreg. State Bar Continuing Legal Edn. Program, 1970, Am. Law Inst.-ABA Continuing Legal Edn. Program, 1973—, 34th, 37th NYU ann. insts. fed. taxation, So. Fed. Tax Inst., U. Miami Inst. Estate Planning, Southwestern Legal Found., Internat. Foun. Employee Benefit Plans, numerous other profl. orgns. Author: (with others) The Professional Corporation in Oregon, 1970, 82; contbg. author: The Dentist and the Law, 3d edit.; editor-in-chief (retirement plans) Matthew Bender's Federal Tax Service, 1987—; contbr. to numerous publs. in field. Mem. vis. com. U. Chgo. Law Sch. Mem. ABA (vice chair profl. svcs. 1987-89, mem. coun. tax sect. 1987-89, spl. coord. 1980-85), Am. Law Inst., Am. Bar Retirement Assn. (trustee, bd. dirs., vice chair 1990-91, 91-92, A-E-F-C pension plan 1994—), Multnomah County Bar Assn., Am. Coun. Tax Lawyers (charter mem.), Oreg. Estate Planning Coun. Jewish. Home: 3118 SW Fairmount Blvd Portland OR 97201-1466 Office: 215 SW Washington St Fl 3D Portland OR 97204-2636

ZAMBETTI, DENIS EGAN, product specialist; b. Riverdale, N.Y., Oct. 18, 1953; s. Emil John and Teresa Veronica (McSherry) Z. BS, U.S. Mil. Acad., 1977; MBA, Golden Gate U., 1985; grad., Command and Gen. Staff Coll., 1993. Commd. 2d lt. U.S. Army, 1977, advanced through ranks to capt., 1977-81, resigned, 1985; platoon leader B Co. 2d/22d Inf., Wiesbaden, Fed. Republic Germany, 1977-78, mortar platoon leader, 1978-79, exec. officer, 1979-80; communications and electronics officer HHC Co. 2d/22d Inf., Wiesbaden, 1980-81; morale support fund custodian U.S. Mil. Command Activity Group, Bad Kreuznach, Fed. Republic Germany, 1981-82; equal opportunity staff officer HQ Presidio of San Francisco, 1982-83, chief reserve pay, 1983-85; peninsula area mgr. Beringer Wines/Wineworld, San Francisco, 1985-87; nat. accts. mgr. SW region Beringer Wines/Wineworld, Mission Viejo, Calif., 1987—; v.p. product devel. IQUEST Bus. Devel., Santa Clara, Calif., 1988—; nat. accts. mgr. Sutter Home Winery, 1988-92; mgr. sales Union Camp Corp., Stockton, Calif., 1992—. Maj. USAR, 1991—. Named One of Outstanding Young Men of Am. Jaycees, 1983. Mem. Knights of the Vine, West Point Soc. of Bay Area (bd. govs. 1982-85), West Point Soc. Orange County (admissions rep. 1987—, mil. liaison officer 1991—). Democrat. Roman Catholic. Home: 4843 Kimberly Common Livermore CA 94550-7707

ZAMBOUKOS, CYNTHIA SOTERIA, office manager, travel consultant; b. San Francisco, June 17, 1957; d. James Neal and Nafsika Vasiliki (Katsoulos) Z. BA in French and Italian, San Francisco State U., 1980. Asst. sec.-treas. Pacific Am. Group, Inc., San Francisco, 1980-84; freelance travel cons. and legal asst., San Francisco, 1984-86, adminstrv. asst. Wells Fargo Bank, 1987-89, office mgr., 1989-93, compliance rep., 1993—. Mem. Hellenic Am. Profl. Soc. Democrat. Greek Orthodox.

ZAME, WILLIAM R., economist, educator, mathematician; b. Long Beach, N.Y., Nov. 4, 1945; s. Herbert and Miriam Zame; m. Elaine Bennett, Sept. 13, 1989. BS, Calif. Inst. Tech., Pasadena, 1965; PhD, Tulane U., 1970. Instr. Rice U., Houston, 1970-72; from asst. prof. to prof. SUNY, Buffalo, 1972-91; assoc. prof. Tulane U., New Orleans, 1975-78; prof. Johns Hopkins U., Balt., 1990-93, UCLA, 1991—. Contbr. over 55 articles to profl. jours. NSF grantee, 1970-93. Office: UCLA Dept Econs 405 Hilgard Ave Los Angeles CA 90024

ZAMENHOF, STEPHEN, researcher, biochemistry educator; b. Warsaw, Poland, June 12, 1911; came to U.S., 1939; s. Henry Gregory and Sabina (Szpinak) Z.; m. Patrice J. Driskell, May 2, 1961. D in Tech. Scis., Warsaw Poly., 1936; PhD in Biochemistry, Columbia U., 1949. Asst. prof. Columbia U., N.Y.C., 1951-56, assoc. prof., 1956-64; prof. biochemistry UCLA, 1964—. Author: The Chemistry of Heredity, 1959. Contbr. over 247 articles to profl. jours. Guggenheim fellow, 1958-59. Home: 333 S Medio Dr Los Angeles CA 90049-3913 Office: Dept Microbiology and Immunology UCLA Sch Medicine Los Angeles CA 90024

ZAMIR, FRANCES ROBERTA (FRANCES ROBERTA WEISS-SWEDE), assistant principal; b. Bklyn., Nov. 6, 1944; d. Martin and Jean (Roskosky) Swede. BA in English, Calif. State U., Northridge, 1967, MA in Spl. Edn., 1975; MA in Ednl. Adminstrn., Calif. State U., L.A., 1987. Credential adminstrv. svcs., std. elem, spl. edn.-learning handicapped, Calif; cert. resource specialist. Childrens' ctr. tchr. L.A. Unified Sch. Dist., 1966-68, elem. tchr., 1968-76, spl. edn. tchr., 1976-80, resource specialist tchr., 1980-86, mentor tchr., 1984-86, program specialist/region advisor, 1986-90, asst. prin., 1990—; owner, ptnr. Best Bet Ednl. Therapy/Tutoring Referral Svc., 1979-81; cons. Academics Plus Tutoring Referral Svc., 1984-86; asst. prof. resource specialist cert. program Calif. State U., Dominguez Hills, 1987-90; instr. early and regular edn. credential program UCLA, 1990—; mem. asst. prin. steering com. L.A. Unified Sch. Dist., Region C, 1992—; adminstr. portfolio documentation subcom. Adminstrv. Tng. Acad., 1991; sch. site rev. coms. Calif. State Dept. Edn., 1985-87, ad hoc com. on quality indicators, 1985. Mem. Speakers Bur. Commn. on Jews With Disabilities, 1985-86. Mem. NEA, Assn. Adminstrs. L.A. Rep. Coun. (elem. asst. prin. rep. 1992-94), Friends of Cal State, Calif. Assn. Program Specialists (So. Calif. regional rep. 1988-90), Calif. Assn. Sch. Adminstrs. (spl. edn. com. L.A. chpt. 1985-86, 87-88), Calif. Assn. Resource Specialists (state pres. 1984-85, bd. dirs. 1983-86), Calif. Tchrs. Assn., Women in Ednl. Leadership, Kappa Delta Pi, Phi Beta Kappa. Office: L A Unified Sch Dist 450 N Grand Ave Los Angeles CA 90012-2100

ZAMPINI, MARY LEE, Spanish and Portuguese educator; b. Syracuse, N.Y., Apr. 18, 1964; d. Joseph John and Elizabeth Anne (Coughlin) Z. Student, Instituto Internat., Madrid, 1984-85; BA in Spanish, St. Bonaventure U., 1986; postgrad., U. Lisbon, Portugal, 1986; MS in Spanish Linguistics, Georgetown U., 1989, PhD in Hispanic Linguistics, 1993. Lectr. in Spanish Georgetown U., Washington, 1989-92; instr. summer program East Tenn. State U., Madrid, 1990; instr. Lang. Immersion Inst. SUNY-New Paltz, Washington, 1991; asst. prof. Spanish and Portuguese U. Ariz., Tucson, 1992—; grad. fellow Georgetown U., Washington, 1986-89. Contbg. editor Hispania, 1991; contbr. articles to profl. jours. Vol. interpreter Univ. Med. Ctr., Tucson, 1994—. Presdl. scholar St. Bonaventure U., 1982-86, Bolsa de Estudo scholar, 1987; internat. travel grantee U. Ariz., 1993. Mem. MLA, Am. Assn. Tchrs. of Spanish and Portuguese. Roman Catholic. Office: U Ariz Dept Spanish & Portuguese Modern Langs 532 Tucson AZ 85721

ZANETTA, JOSEPH MICHAEL, university administrator, lawyer; b. Jamestown, N.Y., Apr. 26, 1953; s. Joseph A. and Freda (Felanzo) Z.; m. Ellen L. Leggett, June 2, 1979. BS, Cornell U., 1975, JD, 1978. Bar: N.Y. 1980. Mem. Hartley & Fessenden, Attys., Jamestown, 1978-79; devel. officer Cornell U., Ithaca, N.Y., 1979-82; assoc. dir. maj. gifts Tufts U., Medford, Mass., 1982-83; dir. devel. Belmont Hill Sch., Belmont, Mass., 1983-86; exec. dir. external affairs Sch. Bus. Adminstrn. U. So. Calif., L.A., 1986-93; v.p. advancement Whittier (Calif.) Coll., 1993—; chmn. Pasadena Enterprise Ctr. Sec.-treas. Lord Found. of Calif., L.A., 1988-93. Mem. Coun. for Advancement and Support of Edn. (chair nat. confs. 1990, 92), Univ. Club of L.A. (bd. dirs. 1991—), Phi Kappa Phi (bd. dirs. 1991—). Roman Catholic.

Home: 391 S Parkwood Ave Pasadena CA 91107-5037 Office: Whittier College 13406 Philadelphia St Whittier CA 90601-4446

ZANINOVICH, MARKO B., food products executive; b. 1942; s. Marko Zaninovich. With Marko Zaninovich Inc., Delano, Calif., 1962—, pres., 1966—. Office: Marko Zaninovich Inc 31560 Peterson Rd Delano CA 93215*

ZANT, JOHN DONALD, journalist; b. L.A., Sept. 19, 1946; s. John Lewis and Mary Constance (Richter) Z.; m. Nancy Lou Alberty, Dec. 21, 1974 (div. Dec. 1991); children: Joseph A., Francie J., Joanna K., Christopher M. BA in Anthropology, U. Calif., Santa Barbara, 1968. Reporter, columnist, sports editor Santa Barbara (Calif.) News-Press, 1968—. Mem. Associated Press Sports Editors, Track and Field Writers Assn. Roman Catholic. Office: Santa Barbara News Press PO Box 1359 Santa Barbara CA 93102-1359

ZAREM, HARVEY ALAN, plastic surgeon; b. Savannah, Ga., Feb. 13, 1932; s. Harry A. and Rose (Gold) Z.; m. Beth McCanghey, July 11, 1981; children: Harold, Allison, Melissa, Kathryn, Michael, Robert. BA, Yale U., 1953; MD, Columbia U., 1957. Diplomate Am. Bd. Surgery, Am. Bd. Plastic Surgery; lic. physician, Md., Ill., Calif. Intern Johns Hopkins Hosp., Balt., 1957-58, resident in plastic surgery, 1964-66; rsch. fellow Peter Bent Brigham Hosp., Boston, 1958-59, asst. resident in surgery, 1959-61; resident in surgery then chief resident Boston City Hosp., 1961-63; postdoctoral fellow NYU, N.Y.C., 1963-64; from asst. prof. to assoc. prof. surgery U. Chgo., 1966-73; prof. surgery U. Calif., L.A., 1973-87, prof. emeritus, 1987—; mem. med. staff Pacific Surgicenter, Santa Monica, Calif., 1987—; physician Sepulveda (Calif.) VA Hosp., 1974—; mem. med. staff St. Johns Hosp., Santa Monica, Calif., 1987—, Santa Monica Hosp., 1988—; vis. prof. So. Ill. U., 1983, Lackaland AFB, 1986, Creighton U., 1987, Comesa, Milan, 1989, Baylor Coll. Medicine, 1990; Kazanjian vis. prof. Mass. Gen. Hosp., 1986, 88; cons. and presenter in field. Contbr. numerous articles to profl. jours. Grantee NIH, 1964-75, NIH, 1967-72, Sheldon and Carol Appel Family Found., 1982—, Chantal Pharms., 1983-84, Mentor Corp./Heyer-Schulte Products, 1985—, Michael Jackson Burn Found., 1986-87. Fellow ACS; mem. AMA, Am. Soc. Plastic Reconstructive Sugeons, Inc., Am. Burn Assn., Am. Cleft Palat Assn., Am. Assn. Plastic Surgeons, Am. Soc. Aesthetic Plastic Surgery, Am. Assn. Hand Surgery, Am. Assn. Surgery of Trauma, Calif. Med. Asssn., Calif. Soc. Plastic Surgeons, New Eng. Soc. Plastic Surgeons (hon.), L.A. Cunty Med. Assn., Johns Hopkins Med. and Surg. Soc., Plastic Surgery Rsch. Coun., Soc. Head and Neck Surgeons (sr.), Soc. U. Surgeons, N.W. Soc. Plastic Surgeons (hon.), others. Office: Pacific Surgicenter 1301 20th St Ste 470 Santa Monica CA 90404-2050

ZARIAN, LARRY, mayor; children: Vincent, Lawrence, Gregory. Student, Glendale Coll.; B in Polit. Sci., UCLA. Ptnr. Glenmont Property Mgmt. Co., Glendale, Calif.; vice-chmn. Lama Devel.; mayor City of Glendale, 1986—; mem. Glendale City Council, Glendale Devel. Council, 1983—, State Regional Water Quality Control Bd., 1986; commr. Glendale Planning, 1984, Glendale Pub. Service, 1981; pres. Pub. Service Commn., 1979-81; past v.p. Glendale Coordinating Council; vice chmn. Nat. Hwy. Safety Com., 1986; chmn. Glendale Housing Authority, 1983-85; vice chmn. Glendale Redevel. Agy., 1984, chmn., 1985. Co-chmn. protocol and linguistics U.S. Olympics, 1984; del. 1980 Nat. Conv.; past mem., organizer Com. To Help Delinquent Youth; fundraiser United Way, St. Mary's Ch.; mem. Glendale Traffic Safety, Los Angeles County Econ. Devel. Authority, Glendale Beautiful, Glendale BPW, Glendale Coordinationg Council, Rep. Cen. Com., 1965, Rep. Associates, Glendale Law and Order Orgn., exec. bd. Boy Scouts Am., adv. bd. Verdugo Hills Hosp.; past mem. Glendale PTA; past mem., v.p. Calif. Jaycees; past pres. Glendale Young Reps., mem. Glendale-Verdugo Rep. Assembly; chmn. Young Businessmen for Ronald Reagan for Gov.; active numerous polit. campaigns; trustee Calif. Bicentennial Found for U.S. Constn., 1987—; bd. dirs. Self-Aid Workshop; chmn. bd. dirs. Los Angeles County Indsl. Devel. Authority, 1981—. Mem. Glendale C. of C., Bell Gardens C. of C. (bd. dirs.). Clubs: Buck and Ballot, VIPS. Lodges: Elks, Toastmasters. Home: 1770 Golf Club Dr Glendale CA 91206-1350 Office: Office of Mayor 613 E Broadway Ste 200 Glendale CA 91206-4308

ZARO, BRAD A., research company executive, biologist; b. San Jose, Calif., Dec. 4, 1949; s. Raymond J. and Irene R. (Cunha) Z.; m. Angela M. Greenan, Nov. 20, 1971; children: Amy C., Kristen E. BA in Zoology, San Jose State U., 1974, MA in Biology, 1981. Chemist, Dept. Drug Metabolism Syntex Rsch., Inc., Palo Alto, Calif., 1976-78, chemist II, Dept. Drug Metabolism, 1978-81, chemist III, Dept. Drug Metabolism, 1981-84, clin. rsch. assoc. I, Inst. of Clin. Medicine, 1984-85, clin. rsch. assoc. II, Inst. of Clin. Medicine, 1985-87, sen. clin. rsch. assoc., Inst. of Clin. Medicine, 1985-87; sen. clin. rsch. assoc. Triton Biosciences, Inc., Alameda, Calif., 1988, mgr. clin. trials, 1988; pres. Clinimetrics Rsch. Assoc., Inc., San Jose, 1988—. Contbr. articles to scholarly jours. Mem. Am. Coll. Clin. Pharmacology, Am. Assoc's. for the Advancement of Sci., Assoc's. of Clin. Pharmacology, Prof. Tech. Cons's. Democrat. Roman Catholic. Office: Clinimetrics Rsch Assocs 2025 Gateway Pl Ste 403 San Jose CA 95110-1006

ZATLOUKAL, CHARLENE ANN, distribution company executive; b. Tecumseh, Nebr., Aug. 28, 1950; d. Billy Ardean and Patricia Jean (Gates) Murray; m. Patrick Eugene Zatloukal, Dec. 15, 1976; children: Dean LaRue, Wendy Jo, Patrick Arthur, Richard Joseph, Jaime Lyn, Ryan John. Student, Kearney State Coll., 1968-69, Lincoln State Coll., 1971. Owner Designs in Time, Omaha, 1981-84, Ron's Restaurant, Goldfield, Iowa, 1984-85; v.p. A.R.S., Nashville, 1989-90; owner Zatco Enterprises, Lander, Wyo., 1990—. Author: An American Tradition, 1990, A Very Merry Christmas, 1993; editor: The Wyo. Traveler, 1994. Vol. Coalition for Homeless, Nashville, 1987; chairperson St. Patrick Family Life, Nashville, 1989; organizer Seeds of Hope, Lander, 1994—; bd. dirs. Respond, Nashville, 1986-87. Democrat. Roman Catholic. Office: Zatco Enterprises Box 863 444 Amoretti Lander WY 82520

ZAVALA, ALBERT, research psychologist; b. Chgo., Mar. 10, 1930; s. Edward and Maria Soledad (Herrejon) Z.; div.; children—Camille, Sally, Elena, Jenifer, Alexis. B.A., Willamette U., Salem, Oreg., 1959; M.A. Mich. State U., 1961; Ph.D., Kans. State U., 1966. Prof., head life scis. Calspan, Buffalo, 1967-73; prof. SUNY Coll. at Buffalo, 1968-78; exec. dir. Corp. IV, Cheektowaga, N.Y., 1973-77; dir. projects Inpsych, Cupertino, Calif., 1978-80; sr. research psychologist SRI Internat., Menlo Park, Calif., 1980-85; sr. staff engr., Lockheed Missiles and Space Co., Sunnyvale, Calif., 1985-94. Mem. Erie County (N.Y.) sheriff's sci. staff, 1972-78. Served with U.S. Army, 1955-57. Dunlap fellow, 1964; Greater Kans. City Mental Health Found. fellow, 1962-63. Mem. Am. Psychol. Assn., Human Factors Soc., Sigma Xi, Psi Chi, Phi Kappa Phi. Author: (with J.J. Paley) Personal Appearance Identification, 1972. Contbr. numerous articles to profl. jours.

ZEAMER, RICHARD JERE, engineer, executive; b. Orange, N.J., May 13, 1921; s. Jay and Margery Lilly (Herman) Z.; m. Jean Catherine Hellens, July 8, 1944 (div. 1966); children: Audrie Dagna, Richard Warwick, Geoffrey Hellens; m. Theresa Elizabeth Taborsky, Mar. 27, 1969; children: Emily Elizabeth, Charlotte Anne. BSME, MIT, 1943, MSCE, 1948; PhD in Mech. Engring., U. Utah, 1975. Registered profl. engr., Utah. Civil engr. Morton C. Tuttle, Boston, 1949-53; process design engr. Nekoosa Edwards Paper Co., Port Edwards, Wis., 1953-55; process engr. W.Va. Pulp and Paper Co., Luke, Md., 1955-60; rocket engr., supr. Allegany Ballistics Lab., Rocket Ctr., W.Va., 1960-65; engring. supr. Hercules Powder Co., Magna, Utah, 1965-69; engr. structures, heat, flow, combustion & failure analysis Hercules Rocket Plant, Magna, 1969-83; project engring. mgr. Hercules Aerospace Div., Magna, 1983-89; pres., mgr. Applied Sci. Assocs., Salt Lake City, 1989—; chmn. policy studies UN Assn. Utah, 1990—; project leader world problem analyses, 1990—. Contbr. papers, articles, reports to profl. publs. Judge sci. fair, Salt Lake County, Utah, 1985—; chmn. citizens policy panel Utah chpt. UN Assn., U.S.A., N.Y.C., 1990—; mem. Utah State Hist. Soc., Salt Lake City, 1968-91, Mil. History Soc. Utah, Salt Lake City, 1990—. 1st lt. U.S. Army, 1943-46. Recipient commendation for presentation on world population problem Utah's Forum on Global Environ., 1992. Fellow AIAA (astronautics assoc.); mem. Cons. Engrs. Coun. Utah (article award 1992), League Utah Writers, Wasatch Mountain Club (hike leader 1987—). Home and Office: Applied Sci Assocs 843 13th Ave Salt Lake City UT 84103-3327

ZEEB, JAMES LAWRENCE, software company executive; b. Ann Arbor, Mich., Sept. 18, 1945; s. Lawrence Edward and Dorothy Ann (Waters) Z.; m. Marcia Morgan Witty, Sept. 30, 1967; children: Eric, Benjamin. BS, Allegheny Coll., 1967. Cert. in data processing ICCP. Systems engr. Electronic Data Systems, Dallas, 1972-79; cons., founder Just Tech. Assoc., Inc., Dallas, 1979-87; pres., chmn. Pyramid Computing Inc., Evergreen, Colo., 1987—. Capt. USAF, 1968-72. Mem. Data Processing Mgmt. Assn. Home: 333 Red Lily Pl Evergreen CO 80439-4216 Office: Pyramid Computing Inc PO Box 1119 Evergreen CO 80439-1119

ZEGANS, LEONARD SAUL, psychiatry educator; b. N.Y.C., Apr. 12, 1934; m. Susan S. Zegans; children: Marc, Michael. AB cum laude, Princeton U., 1955; MD, NYU, 1959; postgrad., Wash. Sch. Psychiatry, 1963-65. Diplomate Am. Bd. Psychiatry and Neurology. Intern Greenwich (Conn.) Hosp., 1959-60; psychiatric resident U. Mich., Ann Arbor, 1960-63; NIMH spl. postdoctorate rsch. fellow Tavistock Clinic, London, 1965-66; jr. clin. instr. U. Mich., Ann Arbor, 1962-63; instr. psychiatry Howard U., Washington, 1963-65; assoc. prof. dept. psychiatry Yale U., 1966-71, assoc. prof. clin. psychiatry dept. psychiatry, 1971-78, fellow Jonathan Edwards Coll., 1969-78; prof. psychiatry dept. psychiatry U. Calif., Sch. Medicine, San Francisco, 1978—; staff psychiatrist USPHS, St. Elizabeth Hosp., Washington, 1963-65; staff physician Conn. Mental Health Ctr., New Haven, 1966-78; attending physician Yale New Haven (Conn.) Hosp., 1966-78, Langley Porter Psychiat. Inst., San Francisco, 1979—; dir. grad. and postgrad. edn. dept. psychiatry Yale U., 1971-78; dir. edn. and profl. stds., dept. psychiatry, U. Calif., Sch. Medicine, San Francisco, 1978—, dir. residency tng. program, 1980-89, acting dir. Ctr. Deafness dept. psychiatry, 1982-84, others. Editl. bd. U. Calif. San Francisco Mag., 1978—; editl. cons. Free Press, MacMillan Pub. Co., 1978, Grune & Stratton, Inc., 1980, Gastroentereology, 1986, Western Medicine, 1986; editl. reviewer Jour. AMA, 1989, Internat. Jour. Psychiatry in Medicine, 1989; series editor Mind & Medicine Series Grune & Stratton, Inc., 1983-88, Mind & Medicine Series Rutgers U. Press, 1989, others; contbr. articles to profl. jours. Cons. Com. on Re-Orgn., Butler Hosp., Providence, 1969-70, VA Med. Ctr., West Haven, Conn., 1972-78, Dept. Corrections, San Quentin Prison, 1978-82, Behavioral Medicine Clinic, Divsn. Gen. Internal Medicine, U. Calif. San Francisco, Langley Porter Psychiat. Inst., 1981—, NIMH AIDS Edn. Program, 1988-89, Napa State Hosp. Ednl. Planning, 1989, NIH Sect. on Alt. Medicine Grant Revs., 1993, others. Recipient Pawlowski Peace prize Pawlowski Peace Found., 1972; Tng. grantee NIMH, 1978-82, 81-82, 83-86, 86-89, 89-92; grantee Nat. Inst. Handicapped Rsch., 1983-87; Behavioral Sci. Rsch. grantee U. Calif. San Francisco, 1988-89; others. Fellow Am. Psychiat. Assn. (grad. edn. com. No. Calif. Psychiat. Soc. 1979), Royal Soc. Health; mem. AMA, AAAS, Am. Acad. Polit. and Social Scis., Am. Assn. Dirs. Psychiatric Residency Tng., Assn. for Acad. Psychiatry, Physicians for Social Responsibility. Office: Univ Calif San Francisco 401 Parnassus Ave San Francisco CA 94122-2720

ZEHM, STANLEY JAMES, education educator; b. Seattle, Dec. 3, 1936; s. Howard Ernest and Rene (Martin) Z.; m. Andrea Sue Johnson, Oct. 25, 1969; children: Kristofor Michael, Erin Jennifer Zehm Burton. BA, St. Edward's Sem., 1959; MDiv, St. Thomas Sem., 1963; MA in English, Gonzaga U., 1966; PhD in English Edn. with distinction, Stanford U., 1973. Tchr. English Carroll High Sch., Yakima, Wash., 1963-67, McFadden Intermediate Sch., Santa Ana, Calif., 1967-71; supr. student interns, then rsch. asst. Stanford (Calif.) U., 1971-73; prof. edn. Wash. State U., Pullman, 1973-81; dir. curriculum Richland (Wash.) Sch. Dist., 1981-82; asst. supt. Selah (Wash.) Sch. Dist., 1982-86; dean div. edn. and psychology Heritage Coll., Toppenish, Wash., 1987-90; prof. and chair dept. instructional and curricular studies U. Nev., Las Vegas, 1990—; marriage, family and child counselor Graden Grove (Calif.) Counseling Ctr., 1967-71; adv. com. Wash. State Lang. Arts Curriculum Com., Olympia, 1985; adv. bd. Wash. State Arts Commn., Olympia, 1989-90. Co-author: On Being A Teacher, 1993, Classrooms Under the Influence, 1993; contbr. to profl. publs. Bd. Trustees St. Jude's Ranch for Children, Boulder City, Nev., 1993—. Named one of 100 Outstanding English Tchrs., State of Calif., 1968; grantee U.S. Dept. Edn., Dept. Labor, NSF, Nat. Endowment for Humanities. Mem. ASCD, Internat. Reading Assn. (media awards chair 1974-76), Nat. Coun. Tchrs. English, Orange County Tchrs. English (v.p. 1969-70), Phi Delta Kappa. Roman Catholic. Home: 8116 Lake Hills Dr Las Vegas NV 89128-7090 Office: U Nev Las Vegas Instrnl/Curricular Studies 4505 S Maryland Pky Las Vegas NV 89154-9900

ZEHNER, WILLIAM BRADLEY, II, marketing educator, consultant; b. Albuquerque, May 7, 1944; s. William B. and Mathilda Ida (Metz) Z.; m. Linda C. Trickett, Oct. 12, 1968 (div. 1974); 1 child, Clinton Bradley; m. Tamra Anne Weber, Mar. 26, 1988; children: Christopher Bradley, Jacquelyn Anne. BA in Polit. Sci., U. Calif., Riverside, 1966; MBA in Fin., U. So. Calif., 1968, MS in Mktg., 1970; MA in Psychology, Pepperdine U., 1983. Mng. dir. LEFAR, Hong Kong, 1974-75; v.p. sales Latin Am. and Asia Leesona Corp., Warwick, R.I., 1976-79; v.p. western ops. Leesona Corp., L.A., 1979-82; v.p. strategic planning John Brown PLC, London, 1982-84; pres. worldwide sales John Brown Plastics Machinery, Warwick, R.I., 1984-86; pres., founder Zetec, Westlake Village, Calif., 1987—; mem. MBA faculty, Pepperdine U., 1989—. Mem. Am. Mktg. Assoc., Am. Psychol. Assn. Republican. Roman Catholic. Home: 1665 Berwick Pl Westlake Village CA 91361-1502 Office: Pepperdine U 400 Corporate Pointe Culver City CA 90230-7615

ZEHR, NORMAN ROBERT, association administrator; b. Niagara Falls, N.Y., May 19, 1930; s. George Andrew and Ina Kate (Morrell) Z.; Engr. of Mines, Colo. Sch. Mines, 1952, M.S., 1956; m. Janet Hutchinson, Apr. 24, 1976; children—Jeannette Ann, Leslie. Sales trainee Ingersoll-Rand Co., N.Y.C., 1955-56, sales engr., Lima, Peru, 1956-64, regional mgr. mining and constrn. sales, Lima, Peru and N.Y.C., 1964-68, gen. sales mgr. Latin Am., N.Y.C., 1968-69, gen. mgr. Latin Am. ops., N.Y.C., 1969-71, v.p. Ingersoll Rand Internat., Woodcliff Lake, N.J., 1971-72, pres., 1972-83, , v.p. Ingersoll-Rand Co., 1975-83; exec. dir. Colo. Sch. Mines Alumni Assn., 1984—. Served with AUS, 1952-54. Recipient Colo. Sch. Mines Disting. Achievement medal, 1977. Mem. AIME, Scabbard and Blade, Nat. Soc. Pershing Rifles, Mining Club , Sigma Nu. Office: Colo Sch Mines Twin Towers Golden CO 80401

ZEIG, JEFFREY KENNETH, psychologist; b. N.Y.C., Nov. 6, 1947; s. Martin Joel and Ruth (Epstein) Z.; divorced; 1 child, Nicole Rachel. BS in Zoology, Mich. State U., 1969; MS in Clin. Psychology, San Francisco State U., 1973; PhD, Ga. State U., 1977. Lic. psychologist, Ariz.; lic. and cert. marriage, family and child counselor, Calif., Ariz. Psychologist Ariz. State Hosp., Phoenix, 1978-79; dir. Milton H. Erickson Found., Phoenix, 1979--; lectr. in field. Author: Experiencing Erickson, 1985; editor: The Evolution of Psychotherapy, 1988; editor and/or co-editor numerous books and monographs. Recipient Milton H. Erickson award Netherlands Soc. Clin. Hypnosis, 1980. Fellow Am. Soc. Clin. Hypnosis (Milton H. Erickson award 1981), Am. Psychol. Assn. Office: Milton H Erickson Found 3606 N 24th St Phoenix AZ 85016-6509

ZEIGEL, HENRY ALAN, architect; b. Vernal, Utah, Aug. 17, 1933; s. Emmett Ray and Willa Meddie (Hahn) Z.; m. Laura Belle Miller, Dec. 21, 1953; children: Shonda G. Zeigel Cortez, Désha K. Zeigel Davis, Brad A. BArch, U. Colo., 1957, postgrad., 1981-83. Lic. architect. Assoc. J.H. Johnson, FAIA, Denver, 1961-64; prin. Everett-Zeigel, Boulder, Colo., 1965—. Prin. works include Chautauqua Auditorium. Chmn. City Landmarks Bd., Boulder, 1975-79, Com. on Ch. Architecture and Arts, 1970-80; active Nat. Trust for HIst. Preservation, Washington, 1970—. Served to 1st lt. U.S. Army, 1957-60. Mem. AIA, Boulder C. of C. Episcopalian. Home: 1510 Wazee St # 2 Denver CO 80202-1312 Office: OZ Architecture 1580 Lincoln St Ste 200 Denver CO 80203-1504

ZEIGER, ROBERT S., allergist; b. Bklyn., July 31, 1942; s. Murray and Mildred (Oransky) Z.; m. Karen P. Zeiger, June 25, 1967; children: Joanna, Laurie. BA with honors, Tulane U., 1963; MD, PhD, SUNY, Bklyn., 1969. Diplomate Am. Bd. Pediatrics, Am. Bd. Allergy-Immunology. Intern pediatrics Harriet Lane Johns Hopkins Hosp., Balt., 1969-70; staff assoc. NIH, Bethesda, Md., 1970-72; resident pediatrics Boston Children's Hosp., 1972-73, allergy fellow, 1973-75; instr. Harvard Med. Sch., Boston, 1975-76; chief of allergy Kaiser Permanente, San Diego, 1976—; clin. assoc. prof. U. Calif., San Diego, 1980-87, clin. prof., 1987—. Editorial bd. Family Practice Survey, 1983-85, Jour. Allergy Clin. Immunology, 1985-91, Pediatric Allergy Immunology Jour., 1990; author: Nasal Manifestations of Systemic Diseases, 1990; contbr. articles to profl. jours. Lt. comdr. USPHS, 1970-72. Phizer Honor scholar Phizer Corp., 1967-69, Charles A. Janeway scholar Harvard U., 1975; Hood Found. grantee, 1975-77. Fellow Am. Acad. Pediatrics, Am. Acad. Allergy Clin. Immunology (Travel award 1975), Phi Beta Kappa, Alpha Omega Alpha. Democrat. Office: So Calif Permanente Med Group 7060 Clairemont Mesa Blvd San Diego CA 92111-1003

ZEIHEN, LESTER GREGORY, geology educator; b. Stevensville, Mont., Feb. 8, 1913; s. Gregory Sylvester and Francis M. (Haigh) Z.; m. Jeannette A. McMahon, July 10, 1941; children: Marilyn, Nancy, Donna, Gregory. BS in Geol. Engring., Mont. Sch. Mines, 1935, MS, 1937, profl. degree, 1961. Jr. engr. Anaconda Copper Mining Co., Butte, 1937-38; mine geologist Chile Exploration Co., Chuquicamata, 1938-52; rsch. geologist The Anaconda Co., Butte, 1952-73, cons. mineralogist, 1973-79; adj. assoc. prof. geology, adj. curator mineral mus. Mont. Coll. Mining Sci. and Tech., Butte, 1979—. Author in field. Pres. Silver Bow Humane Soc., Butte, 1971—; bd. dirs. Butte Sheltered Workshop, 1968—, Butte Silver Bow Arts Found., 1979-86, World Mus. Mining, Butte, 1984. Mem. AAAS, AIME (chmn. sect. 1964, Legion of Honor award), Am. Assn. for Advancement Sci., 1990—, Am. Mineral. Assn. (life), Soc. Econ. Geologists, Geochem. Soc., Mineral. Assn. Can., Mont. Tech. Alumni Assn. (sec.-treas. 1977—), Rotary (pres. Butte club 1980-81, Svc. Above Self award 1976, Paul Harris award 1990), Sigma Xi. Republican. Roman Catholic. Home: 834 W Silver St Butte MT 59701-1548 Office: Mont Coll Mineral Sci and Tech W Park St Butte MT 59701

ZEILINGER, ELNA RAE, tutor, educator; b. Tempe, Ariz., Mar. 24, 1937; d. Clayborn Eddie and Ruby Elna (Laird) Simpson; m. Philip Thomas Zeilinger, June 13, 1970; children: Shari, Chris. BA in Edn., Ariz. State U., 1958, MA in Edn., 1966, EdS, 1980. Bookkeeper First Nat. Bank of Tempe, 1955-56; with registrar's office Ariz. State U., 1956-58; piano tchr., recreation dir. City of Tempe; tchr. Thew Sch., Tempe, 1958-61; elem. tchr. Mitchell Sch., Tempe, 1962-74, intern prin., 1976, personnel intern, 1977; specialist gifted edn. Tempe Elem. Schs., Tempe, 1977-86; elem. tchr. Holdeman Sch., Tempe, 1986-89; tchr. Zeilinger Tutoring Svc., 1991—; grad. asst. ednl. adminstrn., Iota Workshop coordinator Ariz. State U., 1978; presenter Ariz. Gifted Conf., 1978-81; condr. survey of gifted programs, 1980; reporter public relations Tempe Sch. Dist., 1978-80, Access com. for gifted programs, 1981-83. Author: Leadership Role of the Principal in Gifted Programs: A Handbook, 1980; Classified Personnel Handbook, 1977, also reports, monographs and paintings. Mem. Tempe Hist. Asns., liaison, 1975; mem. Tempe Art League; mem. freedom train com. Ariz. Bicentennial Commn., 1975-76; bd. dirs. Maple Property Owners Assn., 1994—. Named Outstanding Leader in Elem. and Secondary Schs., 1976' Ariz. Cattle Growers scholar, 1954-55; Elks scholar, 1954-55; recipient Judges award Tempe Art League, 1970, Best of Show, Scottsdale Art League, 1976. Mem. Tempe Hist. Assn., liaison, 1975, Tempe Art League; Freedom Train com. Ariz. Bicentennial Commn., 1975-76; bd. mem. Maple Property Owners Assn., 1994—. Democrat. Congregationalist.

ZEILINGER, PHILIP THOMAS, aeronautical engineer; b. David City, Nebr., Feb. 13, 1940; s. Thomas Leroy and Sylvia Dorothy Zeilinger; m. Elna Rae Simpson, June 13, 1970; children: Shari, Chris. AS, Wentworth Mil. Acad., Lexington, Mo., 1959; BSME, Kans. U., 1962. Estimator, engr. Reynolds Electronics and Engring. Co., El Paso, Tex., 1966-68; accessories coord. ITI Garrrett, Phoenix, 1974-79, cntrl. access engr., 1968—, controls coord. ITEC, 1983-84, integrated support specialist ITEC, 1984-86, mgr. systems software light helo turbine engring. co. div., 1986-91, FAA designated engr. rep. engine div., 1991—; chmn. Light Helicopter Turbine Engine Company Computer Aided Acquistion and Logistics Working Group. V.p. Indsl. Devel. Authority, Tempe, Ariz., 1979-84; pres. Univ. Royal Garden Homes Assn., Tempe, 1984-90. 1st lt. U.S. Army, 1962-66. Recipient Vol. Svc. award City of Tempe, 1984, Grand Cross of Color, Internat. Order of Rainbow Girls, 1978. Mem. AIAA, Aircraft Owners and Pilots Assn., Explt. Aircraft Assn. (v.p. chpt. 228 1974-79), Masons (master 1990-92, chmn. statewide picnic 1992, Mason of the Yr. 1992). Democrat. Unitarian. Home: 760 N Sycamore Pl Chandler AZ 85224-6925 Office: 111 S 34th St Phoenix AZ 85010

ZEITLER, BILL LORENZ, aviation engineer; b. Columbus, Ohio, July 14, 1920; s. Walter Andrew and Naomi Lee (Limes) Z.; BSCE, Calif. State U., Long Beach, 1965; m. Betty Eileen Thomas, Nov. 8, 1942; children: Eddie, Naomi Parker. Cert. vocat. tchr., Calif. Loftsman, Curtiss Wright Corp., Columbus, 1941-45; linesman Lockheed Corp., Burbank, Calif., 1946-49; linesman N.Am. Rockwell (and predecessor firms), Inglewood, Calif., 1950-58, airframe designer, 1958-62, supr. engring. coll. unit, 1962-65, project engr. life scis., health care delivery systems, 1965-68, project dir. health care delivery systems, Princeton, W.Va., 1968-69, mem. tech. staff, Downey, Calif., 1946-85; project engr. space shuttle design, 1971-75, shuttle alignment and mating, 1975-77, space shuttle design support extra vehicular stowage and testing, 1978-85; ret., 1985; mem. Space Shuttle Speakers Bur. Instr. 55 Alive-mature driving classes; former pres. Big Bear Valley Sr. Citizens; mem. Annual Mayor's Prayer Breakfast Com.; chairperson Living Forest Task Force; v.p. Friends of Moonridge Zoo; bd. dir. Sr. Center; citizen adv. coun. mem. BBL Dept Water & Power. Mem. AIAA, Nat. Space Inst., Nat. Geog. Soc., Smith Instn. Assocs., Rockwell Mgmt. Club, Toastmasters, Kiwanis, Big Bear Mcpl. Water Dist. Citizens Adv. Com., Annual Mayors Prayer Breakfast Erwin Lake Home Owners Assoc., Friends Moonridge Zoo, Living Forest Task Force.

ZEITLIN, EUGENIA PAWLIK, librarian, educator; b. N.Y.C., Jan. 29; d. Charles and Pauline Pawlik; m. Herbert Zakary Zeitlin, July 3, 1949; children: Mark Clyde, Joyce Therese Zeitlin Harris, Ann Victoria, Clare Katherine. BA in English, Bklyn. Coll., 1945; MA in English, NYU, N.Y.C., 1951; MALS, Rosary Coll., 1968. Teaching credential N.Y., Ariz., Calif., Ill. English tchr. Sea Cliff, L.I., N.Y., 1945-47; English, math. tchr. Merrick (N.Y.) Sch. Dist., 1948-49; English tchr. Wilson Sch. Dist., Phoenix, 1949-50; counselor West Phoenix (Ariz.) High Sch., 1953-56; asst. prof. English Wright Coll., Chgo., 1965-66; asst. prof. English, asst. to v.p. curriculum and instrn. Oakton C.C., Des Plaines, Ill., 1970-76; libr. Pasadena City Coll., L.A. C.C. Dist., L.A., 1979-91. Contbr. articles to profl. jours. Named Northridge City Employee of Yr., 1986. Mem. AAUW (br. pres. Lancaster, Calif. 1958-60), Thoreau Soc. (life), Beta Phi Mu. Home: 20124 Phaeton Dr Woodland Hills CA 91364-5633

ZEITLIN, GERALD MARK, electrical engineer; b. Phila., May 7, 1937; s. David Edward and Charlotte (Freedman) Z.; m. Frances Loretta Scherr, May 17, 1983 (div. 1988). BEE, Cornell U., 1960; MSEE, U. Colo., 1969. Electronic engr. Nat. Security Agy., Ft. Meade, Md., 1962-64, Westinghouse Georesearch Lab., Boulder, Colo., 1966-69; owner Sunrise Books, Estes Park, Colo., 1969-71; asst. research computer sci. U. Calif., San Francisco, 1972-78; assoc. devel. engr. U. Calif., Berkeley, 1978-82; sr. systems engr. EEG Systems Lab., San Francisco, 1982-86; computer cons., expert systems design Pacific Bell, San Francisco, 1986-87; mgr. microcomputer security Pacific Bell, San Ramon, Calif., 1987-89; dir. Alliance for Innovation tech. devel. ctr., Scottsdale, Ariz., 1990-91; pres. Centauri Secure Computing, Scottsdale, 1990; computer security cons. Bedford Cons., San Francisco, 1991; owner, operator Mono Communications, Oakland, Calif., 1991—; also bd. dirs. Mono Communications, Lee Vining and Oakland, Calif. Contbr. articles to profl. jours. Served to 1st lt. U.S. Army, 1960-62. Summer Faculty fellow NASA-Am. Soc. Engring. Edn., Ames Research Ctr., 1981. Mem. IEEE, Civil Air Patrol. Jewish.

ZEITLIN, HARRY LEON, artist; b. Denver, Apr. 29, 1952; s. Cecil and Sandra (Rothenberg) Z.; m. Beth Leslie Ackerman, Aug. 20, 1984; children: Naomi, Avital, Yael, Aaron. BA, Yale U., 1974. Novelist N.Y.C., Denver, Bloomingt, 1974-76; journalist, photographer Newfoundland, Can., 1976; artist L.A., Jerusalem, Seattle, 1976—. One-man exhibitions include Colo. Photographic Art Cen., Denver, 1979, Am. Cultural Ctr., Jerusalem, 1986, Bezalel Acad. Art, Jerusalem, 1986, Bertha Urdang Gallery, N.Y.C., 1988, The Jewish Quarter, L.A., 1988, Henry Art Gallery, Seattle, 1991, Bertha Urdang Gallery, 1991, Silver Image Gallery, Seattle, 1991, 93, C.G. Jung Inst. Chgo., 1994; group shows include Susan Spiritus Gallery, Newport

Beach, Ca., 1980, West Colo. Gallery, Pasadena, 1981, White Bird Gallery, Portland, 1993 and others. Founder Young Israel of Santa Monica, 1981, Congregation Zechut Avotainu, Seattle, 1993. Mem. Seattle Art Mus., Friends of Photography. Jewish.

ZEITLIN, MARILYN AUDREY, museum director; b. Newark, July 14, 1941; d. Sidney M. and Theresa Feigenblatt) Litchfield; widowed; children: Charles C. Sweedler, Milo Sweedler. Student, Vanderbilt U., 1963-65; AB in Humanities, Harvard U., 1966, MA in Teaching of English, 1967; postgrad., Cornell U., 1971-74. Dir. Ctr. Gallery, Bucknell U., Lewisburg, Pa., 1975-78; Freedman Gallery, Albright Coll., Reading, Pa., 1978-81, Anderson Gallery, Va. Commonwealth U., Richmond, 1981-87; curator, acting co-dir. Contemporary Arts Mus., Houston, 1987-90; exec. dir. Washington Projects for the Arts, 1990-92; dir. Univ. Art Mus., Ariz. State U., Tempe, 1992—; juror Dallas Mus. of Arts, McKnight Awards, Mpls.; grant evaluator IMS; grant evaluator, panelist NEH; lectr., cons. in field. Editor, contbr. essays to art publs. Bd. dirs. Cultural Alliance Washington; curator, commr. for U.S. for 1995 Venice Biennale. Samuel H. Kress fellow, 1972-73. Mem. Assn. Coll. and Univ. Mus. and Galleries (v.p. 1986-88), Am. Assn. Mus., Coll. Art Assn. (U.S. commr. Venice Bieniale 1995). Office: Ariz State U Art Mus PO Box 872911 Tempe AZ 85287-2911

ZEITLIN, MAURICE, sociology educator, author; b. Detroit, Feb. 24, 1935; s. Albert J. and Rose (Goldberg) Z.; m. Marilyn Geller, Mar. 1, 1959; children: Michelle, Carla, Erica. BA cum laude, Wayne State U., 1957; MA, U. Calif., Berkeley, 1960, PhD, 1964. Instr. anthropology and sociology Princeton (N.J.) U., 1961-64, research assoc. Ctr. Internat. Studies, 1962-64; asst. prof. sociology U. Wis.-Madison, 1964-67, assoc. prof., 1967-70, prof., 1970-77, dir. Ctr. Social Orgn., 1974-76; prof. sociology UCLA, 1977—, also research assoc. Inst. Indsl. Relations; vis. prof. polit. sci. and sociology Hebrew U., Jerusalem, 1971-72. Author: (with R. Scheer) Cuba: An American Tragedy, 1963, 1964, Revolutionary Politics and the Cuban Working Class, 1967, 1970, The Civil Wars in Chile, 1984, Landlords and Capitalists, 1988, The Large Corporation and Contemporary Classes, 1989; Latin Am. editor Ramparts mag., 1967-73; editor-in-chief: Political Power and Social Theory, 1980-90; mem. editorial adv. bd. The Progressive mag., 1985—; editor: (with J. Petras) Latin America: Reform or Revolution?, 1968, American Society, Inc., 1970, 1977, Father Camilo Torres: Revolutionary Writings, 1972, Classes, Class Conflict, and the State, 1980, How Mighty a Force?, 1983, Insurgent Workers: The Origins of Industrial Unionism, 1987. Chmn. Madison Citizens for a Vote on Vietnam, 1967-68; chmn. Am. Com. for Chile, 1973-75; mem. exec. bd. U.S. Com. for Justice to Latin Am. Polit. Prisoners, 1977-84; mem. exec. com. Calif. Campaign for Econ. Democracy, 1983-86. Ford Found. fellow, 1965-67, 70-71; Guggenheim fellow, 1981-82; NSF grantee, 1981, 82; recipient Project Censored award Top Censored Story, 1981; named to Ten Best Censored list, 1978. Mem. Am. Sociol. Assn. (governing council 1977-80, Disting. Contbn. Scholarship award in Pol. Sociology 1992), Internat. Sociol. Assn. (editorial bd. 1977-81), Latin Am. Studies Assn., Orgn. Am. Historians. Democrat. Jewish.

ZEKMAN, TERRI MARGARET, graphic designer; b. Chgo., Sept. 13, 1950; d. Theodore Nathan and Lois (Bernstein) Z.; m. Alan Daniels, Apr. 12, 1980; children: Jesse Logan, Dakota Caitlin. BFA, Washington U., St. Louis, 1971; postgrad, Art Inst. Chgo., 1974-75. Graphic designer (on retainer) greeting cards and related products Recycled Paper Products Co., Chgo., 1970—, Jillson Roberts, Inc., Calif.; apprenticed graphic designer Helmuth, Obata & Kassabaum, St. Louis, 1970-71; graphic designer Container Corp., Chgo., 1971; graphic designer, art dir., photographer Cuerden Advt. Design, Denver, 1971-74; art dir. D'Arcy, McManus & Masius Advt., Chgo., 1975-76; freelance graphic designer Chgo., 1976-77; art dir. Garfield Linn Advt., Chgo., 1977-78; graphic designer Keiser Design Group, Van Noy & Co., Los Angeles, 1978-79; owner and operator graphic design studio Los Angeles, 1979—. Recipient cert. of merit St. Louis Outdoor Poster Contest, 1970, Denver Art Dirs. Club, 1973.

ZELDITCH, BERNICE OSMOLA, English language educator; b. Detroit, May 19, 1929; d. Steven M. and Mary (Skrompulska) Osmola; m. Morris Zelditch, Jr., June 1, 1950; children: Miriam Lea, Steven Morris. BA, Oberlin Coll., 1951; MA, Stanford U., 1965. Cert. tchr., Calif. Indexer, picture editor 11 pub. firms including Random House, Knopf, McGraw Hill, N.Y.C., 1955-61; instr., asst. prof., assoc. prof. English, Foothill Coll., Los Altos Hills, Calif., 1966-69, prof., 1969—; vis. prof. Stanford (Calif.) U. Sch. Edn., 1974-76, mem. adv. bd. Friends of Mary Schofield Collection, 1985-90. Contbr. poems to lit. publs. Info. officer Internat. Yr. of Child, UNICEF, Palo Alto, Calif., 1978-80. Conf. grantee Calif. Coun. for Humanities, NEH, 1975. Mem. MLA, NOW, AAUW, Children's Lit. Assn., also local art and music guilds. Democrat. Office: Foothill Coll 12345 El Monte Los Altos CA 94022

ZELENCIK, STEPHEN J., electronics company executive; b. East Chicago, Ind., Mar. 8, 1935; s. Stephen John and Catherine Edith (Churilla) Z.; m. Harriet Sarnecki, Oct. 18, 1958; 1 child, Mary Kathryn. B.S. in Elec. Engring., Purdue U. Sales mgr. Amphenol Corp., Broadview, Ill., 1961-65; nat. sales mgr. Fairchild Semi condr., Mount View, Calif., 1965-70; area sales mgr. Advance Micro Devices, Sunnyvale, Calif., 1970-76, dir. distbn. ops., 1976-80, sr. v.p. sales mktg., 1980—. Served with U.S. Army, 1956-58. Office: Advanced Micro Devices 901 Thompson Pl Sunnyvale CA 94086-4518

ZELENY, WILLIAM BARDWELL, physics educator; b. Mpls., Mar. 14, 1934; s. Lawrence and Olive Z.; m. Pimporn Chavasant, 1960 (div. 1983); children: Thomas, Indira; m. Ylda Portillo, 1988. BS, U. Md.-College Park, 1956; MS, Syracuse U., 1958, PhD, 1960. Lectr. physics U. Sydney, Australia, 1960-62; from asst. prof. to assoc. prof. Naval Postgraduate Sch., Monterey, Calif., 1962—, assoc. chmn. dept. physics, 1980—. Author: (textbook) Introduction to Relativistic Quantum Mechanics, 1975. Contbr. articles to profl. jours. Mem. Sigma Xi. Home: PO Box 8656 Monterey CA 93943-0656 Office: Dept Physics Naval Postgraduate Sch Monterey CA 93943

ZELEZNY, WILLIAM FRANCIS, retired physical chemist; b. Rollins, Mont., Sept. 5, 1918; s. Joseph Matthew and Birdie Estelle (Loder) Z.; m. Virginia Lee Scarcliff, Sept. 14, 1949. BS in Chemistry, Mont. State Coll., 1940; MS in Metallurgy, Mont. Sch. Mines, 1941; PhD in Phys. Chemistry, State U. Iowa, 1951. Scientist NACA, Cleve., 1951-54; metallurgist div. indsl. research Wash. State Coll., Pullman, 1954-57; scientist atomic energy div. Phillips Petroleum Co., Idaho Falls, Id., 1957-66, Idaho Nuclear Corp., Idaho Falls, 1966-70; mem. staff Los Alamos (N.Mex.) Nat. Lab., 1970-80; instr. metallurgy State U. Iowa, Iowa City, 1948-49; asst. prof. metallurgy Wash. State Coll., 1956-57; instr. U. Idaho, Idaho Falls, 1960-68. Contbr. articles to profl. jours.; patentee in field. Served with AUS, 1944-46. Mem. Am. Chem. Soc. (sec. N.Mex. sect. 1978-79), Microbeam Analysis Soc., Am. Soc. Metals, The Minerals, Metals & Materials Soc., Sigma Xi, Alpha Chi Sigma. Democrat. Methodist. Home: PO Box 37 Rollins MT 59931-0037

ZELLER, KATHARINE MARGRET, physician; b. Portland, Oreg., May 21, 1957; d. Herbert Arnold and Margret Katharine (Zwald) Z.; m. David Walker Hill, May 2, 1987. BA, Linfield Coll., 1979; MD, Oreg. Health Scis. U., 1985. Intern Case We. Reserve U., Cleve.; resident Oreg. Health Scis. U., Portland; gen. internist Northwest Internal Medicine, Portland, 1988—. Vol. Neighborhood Health Clinic, Portland, 1987—. Mem. AMA, Soc. Gen. Internal Medicine, Am. Med. Women's Assn., Oreg. Med. Assn., Multnomah County Med. Soc., Alpha Omega Alpha. Home: 4720 SW Dosch Park Ln Portland OR 97201-1284 Office: Northwest Internal Medicine 2222 NW Lovejoy Ste 315 Portland OR 97210

ZELLMER, ARLENE, special education educator; b. Audubon, Iowa, Aug. 21, 1920; d. Clyde Lewis and Susan (Law) Hogueisson; m. Neale Albert Zellmer, June 21, 1953; children: Alan Neale, Scott Lewis. BA in Psychology, San Diego State U., 1948, teaching credential, 1951; postgrad., Coll. Notre Dame, Belmont, Calif.; learning handicapped specialist cert., U. Santa Clara, 1978. Cert. learning handicapped specialist, Calif. Tchr. of mentally gifted San Diego Sch. Dist., La Jolla, Calif., 1949-51; tchr. San Diego Sch. Dist., Valencia Park, Calif., 1951-53; tchr. San Carlos (Calif.) Sch. Dist., 1953-57, home tchr. spl. edn. dept., 1967-86; home tchr. spl. edn. dept. Belmont (Calif.) Sch. Dist., 1967-86; ret., 1986; pvt. tutor of learning handicapped, Belmont, 1979—. Contbr. poetry to World of Poetry, 1991. Active Peninsula Symphony Aux., Belmont, 1963-68; cub leader Boy Scouts Am., Belmont, 1966-68; vol. 4-H Clubs Am., Belmont, 1967-73, Am. Heart Assn., Belmont, 1968-78; deacon 1st Presbyn. Ch., San Mateo, 1966, 77; hon. life mem. 1st Presbyn. Ch. Women; mem. bd. Presbyn Women, U.S.A., 1990-91. Mem. AAUW, Calif. Tchrs. Assn., Calif. Ret. Tchrs. Assn., Ind. Order for Foresters, Daughters of Norway, Commonwealth Club (San Francisco), PEO Sisterhood. Republican. Home: 1588 Harbor Blvd Belmont CA 94002-3709

ZEMEL, NORMAN PAUL, orthopaedic surgeon; b. Bklyn., Oct. 15, 1939; s. Nathan M. and Mary (Sklarevsky) Z.; m. Mary P. Kane. BSN, Rutgers U., 1961; MD, Thomas Jefferson Med. Sch., 1965. Bd. cert. orthopaedic surgery with added qualification in hand surgery Am. Bd. Orthopaedic Surgery. Orthopaedic surgery resident Northwestern U., Chgo., 1969-73; hand surgery fellow Boyes Hand Fellowship, L.A., 1973-74; hand surgery physician Boyes, Stark, Ashworth, L.A., 1974-88, Kerlan-Jobe Orthopaedic Clinic, Inglewood, Calif., 1989—; clin. assoc. prof. dept. orthopaedics U. So. Calif. Sch. Medicine, L.A., 1977—. Contbr. chpts. to books and articles to profl. jours. Lt. USNR, 1966-68, Vietnam. Mem. ACS, Am. Acad. Orthopaedic Surgery (bd. councilors), Am. Soc. for Surgery of the Hand, Western Orthopaedic Assn. (pres. L.A. chpt. 1993-94), Soc. Internat. de Orthopedique et de Traumatologie. Office: Kerlan-Jobe Orthopaedic Clinic 501 E Hardy St Ste 300 Inglewood CA 90301

ZEMKE, (E.) JOSEPH, computer company executive. CEO Auto-Trol Tech., Denver, 1981-84; chief operating officer Amdahl Corp., Sunnyvale, Calif., 1985—, pres., 1987—; CEO, 1992—. Office: Amdahl Corp PO Box 3470 1250 E Arques Ave Sunnyvale CA 94086-4730*

ZENEV, IRENE LOUISE, museum curator; b. Albuquerque, Nov. 18, 1948; d. Stanley D. and Louise Marie (Risler) Z.; 1 child, Carson M. Bell. BA, U. N.Mex., 1971. Dir. Umpqua Valley Arts Assn., Roseburg, Oreg., 1978-82; edn. coord. Douglas County Mus., Roseburg, 1985-86, curator history, 1986—; publs. rschr. Oreg. Mus. Assn., Portland, 1989-92. Reviewer The Roseburg News-Review, 1989-93. Chairperson Douglas County Oreg. Trail Sesquicentennial Celebration Com., 1991-93. Mem. Nat. Assn. for Mus. Exhbn. (Oreg. State rep. 1994).

ZEPEDA, SUSAN GHOZEIL, county official; b. N.Y.C., Aug. 8, 1946; d. Harry S. and Anne (Golden) Kantor; m. Isaac Ghozeil, Jan. 29, 1967 (div. Oct. 1979); children: Daniel Jacob, Adam Leo; m. Fernando Zepeda, Jan. 2, 1983; children: Paloma Andrea, Sofia Elisa. BA, Brown U., 1967; MA, U. Ariz., 1971, postgrad., 1971-75; PhD, Internat. Coll., 1985. Rsch. assoc. div. bus. and econ. rsch. U. Ariz., Tucson, 1971-73, rsch. assoc. Coll. Medicine, 1975-76; assoc. dir. Pima Alcoholism Consortium, Tucson, 1976-79, exec. dir., 1979-80; dep. dir. pub. health Orange County Health Care Agy., Santa Ana, Calif., 1980-89; dir. policy, planning Orange County Health Care Agy., Santa Ana, 1989-90; dir. pub. fin. Orange County, 1990-92; dir. San Luis Obispo County Health Agy., 1993—; cons. Tucson Sch. Dist. No. 1, 1973-75, U.S. Dept. Labor, Washington, 1976-79, Indian Health Svc., Rockville, Md., 1984-85; ptnr. Zepeda Assocs., Fullerton, Calif., 1987-93; presenter confs. Mem. Fullerton Planning Commn., 1984-91, chmn., 1990-91; mem. Calif. Task Force on Comparable Worth, 1984-85, Calif. Dist. Appeal Bd. No. 510, L.A., 1986—. Recipient Woman of Achievement award Orange County Bd. Suprs., 1988, Disting. Achievement awards Nat. Assn. Counties, 1985, 86, 87, 89. Mem. APHA, County Health Execs. Assn. Calif. (exec. com.), U.S.-Mex. Border Health Assn., County Alcohol Program Adminstrs. Assn. Calif. (v.p. 1983, pres. 1984-85), Rotary (San Luis Obispo de Tolosa). Home: 109 Cerro Romauldo San Luis Obispo CA 93405 Office: San Luis Obispo County Health Agy 2191 Johnson Ave San Luis Obispo CA 93401-4534

ZEPP, THOMAS MILLARD, economic consultant; b. Bklyn., Feb. 17, 1943. AB magna cum laude, Wofford Coll., 1965; MA in Econs., U. Fla., 1968, PhD in Econs., 1971. Asst. prof. Ctrl. Mich. U., Mt. Pleasant, 1970-71; sr. economist Oreg. Pub. Utility Commn., Salem, 1976-81, Zinder Cos., Salem, 1981-85; v.p., economist Utility Resources, Inc., Salem, 1985—. Office: Utility Resources Inc 1500 Liberty St SE Salem OR 97302-4365

ZERBE, RICHARD OLIS, public affairs educator; b. Nitro, W.Va., Oct. 2, 1938; s. Richard Olis and Fanny Hammond (Carter) Z.; m. Evelyn A. Ashe Benoit, June 1966 (div. 1970); 1 child, Robert Riley; m. E. Diane Husband, June 24, 1971; 1 child, Richard Alexander. AB in Polit. Sci., U. Okla.; PhD in Econs., Duke U., 1969. Lectr. Marshall U., 1964-66; asst. prof. York U., 1966-69; rsch. fellow law and econs. U. Chgo., 1969-71; assoc. prof. econs. Roosevelt U., 1971-76; rsch. assoc. dept. econs. U. Chgo., 1972-76; prof. Grad. Sch. Pub. Affairs U. Wash., Seattle, 1981—, acting dir. program in mgmt. of tech., 1976-77, adj. prof. dept. econs., 1990, adj. prof. civil engring., 1980-92, adj. prof. Sch. Law, 1990—; Gether Inst. invitee; scholar in residence Am. Bar Found.; fellow law and econs. U. Chgo., 1969-71; bd. econ. advisors to econs. com. ABA, antitrust sect.; cons. FTC; scholar in residence Am. Bar Found., 1971-72, affiliated scholar, 1972-74; vis. assoc. prof. econs. Northwestern U., 1972-76; vis. rsch. scholar FTC, Washington, 1989; cons. Novell Corp., Jones, Day, McDonald Hogue andBayless, Mann and Simon, Abloni and Foster, City of Seattle Legal Dept., Perkins Coie, others. Sr. editor Jour. Rsch. in Law and Econs.; author: (with K. Croke) Urban Transportation and the Environment: The Cost-Effectiveness Approach, 1975; (with D. Dively) Benefit Cost Analysis in Theory and Practive, 1994; contbr. articles to profl. jours., chpt. to books; referee Jour. Polit Economy, Am. Econ. Rev., Jour. Law and Econs., Econ. Inquiry. Commr. Regional Taxicab Commn.; cubmaster pack 9 Boy Scouts Am. Olinfellow Yale Law Sch., 1990; sea grantee, 1977-78, Ford Found. grantee, 1969, Ont. Dept. Pub. Health rsch. grantee, 1968, Rand Rsch. grantee, 1994; recipient Rsch. award Nat. Bureau of Econ. Rsch., 1978. Mem. ABA (assoc.), Am. Law and Econs. Assn. (bd. dirs. 1990-94), Am. Econ. Assn., Law and Soc. Assn., Western Econs. Assn. (exec. com. 1994-99). Home: 939 21st Ave E Seattle WA 98112-3510 Office: U Wash Grad Sch Pub Affairs DC-13 Seattle WA 98195

ZERETZKE, FREDERICK FRANK H., artist, educator; b. Milw., July 4, 1919; s. Herman and Hertha Hildegarde (Riebow) Z.; m. Marian Louise Elfers, Dec. 7, 1942; children: Frederick J., David L., Mary J., John E. Student, Milw. Art Inst., 1938-39, Layton Sch. of Art, Milw., 1940-41, Rockford (Ill.) Coll., 1947. Art tchr. Burpee Art Gallery, Rockford, Ill., 1946-48; mural artist People's Real Estate Agy., Rockford, 1958, Grace Luth. Ch., Loves Park, Ill., 1960, Sweden House, Rockford, 1972; artist oil meml. young girl First United Presbyn. Ch., Greeley, Colo., 1963; mural artist Linos, Rockford, 1974; art tchr. pvt. studio, Rockford, Ill., 1968-78; art. tchr. pvt. studio, Burlington, Wash., 1978—; artist and tchr. art in nat. def. Camp Callan, San Diego, 1942-43, Rock Valley Coll., Rockford, Ill., 1970-77, Skagit Valley Coll., Mt. Vernon, Wash., 1978-80. Prin. works include mural in Hadamar, Germany, exhibits in galleries in Wis., Calif., Wash., Ill., Elements Gallery, Bellingham, Wash., 1988-90, Fox Glove Art Gallery, Mt. Vernon, Wash., 1989-92, Twisted Willow Gallery, Mt. Vernon, 1993-94, Arts & Frame Gallerie, Canyon Lake, Calif., 1993, juried show Arts Coun. Snohomish County, Everett, Wash., 1993, Concrete Wash. Art Show (1st prize watercolor 1992), Bald Eagle Art Show, Concrete, 1993 (4 awards), Sculpture in Mt. Vernon, 1983, portraits, 1941—; water color demonstrations at Daniel Smith Art, Seattle, 1994-95. Sec. Loves Park (Ill.) Zoning Bd., 1949-56. With U.S. Army, 1941-45, ETO. Scholar Milw. Art Inst., 1939, Layton Sch. Art, 1940; awarded commission for design for Swedish Tour of Sveas Soner Chorus of Rockford, 1965; named Artist of Yr. Winnebago County, 1974. Mem. Tamaroa Water Color Soc. Rockford (hon. lifetime, founder, pres. 1964), Skagit Art Assn. (pres. 1987-88). Mem. Unitarian Ch. Home: 722 Peterson Rd Burlington WA 98233-2656

ZERNOW, LOUIS, physicist; b. N.Y.C., Dec. 27, 1916; s. Meyer and Lena (Fradkin) Z.; m. Edith Hazel Weinstein, Nov. 2, 1940; children: Lenore R., Elaine, Melvin R., Richard H. BChemE, Cooper Union Inst. Tech., 1938; PhD in Physics, Johns Hopkins U., 1953. Chief detonation physics br. Ballistic Rsch. Lab., Aberdeen Proving Ground, Md., 1940-55; mgr. ordnance rsch. div. Aerojet Gen. Corp., Downey, Calif., 1955-63; pres. Shock Hydrodynamics Inc., Sherman Oaks, Calif., 1963-67, Shock Hydrodynamics div. Whittaker Corp., N. Hollywood, Calif., 1967-81, Zernow Tech. Svcs. Inc., San Dimas, Calif., 1981—. Contbr. over 200 tech. reports to Dept. Def. agys.; 6 patents in field. Recipient Meritorious Civilian Svc. award U.S. Army Ballistic Rsch. Lab., 1945. Mem. AIME, Am. Phys. Soc., Accoustical Soc. Am., Am. Soc. for Metals, Am. Def. Preparedness Assn. (exec. bd. ballistics div. 1973—, Outstanding Leadership award 1987), Internat. Ballistics Com. Home: 1103 E Mountain View Ave Glendora CA 91741-3165 Office: Zernow Tech Svcs Inc 425 W Bonita Ave San Dimas CA 91773-2541

ZERZAN, CHARLES JOSEPH, JR., gastroenterologist; b. Portland, Oreg., Dec. 1, 1921; s. Charles Joseph and Margaret Cecelia (Mahony) Z.; BA, Wilamette U., 1948; MD, Marquette U., 1951; m. Joan Margaret Kathan, Feb. 7, 1948; children: Charles Joseph, Michael, Kathryn, Paul, Joan, Margaret, Terrance, Phillip, Thomas, Rose, Kevin, Gregory. Commd. 2d. lt., U.S. Army, 1940, advanced through grades to capt., 1945, ret., 1946, re-enlisted, 1951, advanced through grades to lt. col., M.C., 1965; intern Madigan Gen. Hosp., Ft. Lewis, Wash., 1951-52; resident in internal medicine Letterman Gen. Hosp., San Francisco, 1953-56, Walter Reed Gen. Hosp., Washington, 1960-61; chief of medicine Rodriquez Army Hosp., 1957-60, U.S. Army Hosp., Fort Gordon, Calif., 1962-65; chief gastroenterology Fitzsimmons Gen. Hosp., Denver, 1965-66; chief profl. services U.S. Army Hosp., Ft. Carson, Colo., 1967-68; dir. continuing med. edn. U. Oreg., Portland, 1968-73; ptnr. Permanente Clinic, Portland, 1973—; assoc. clin. prof. medicine U. Oreg., 1973—; individual practice medicine, specializing in gastroenterology, Portland, 1968-92; staff Northwest Permanente, P.C.; dir., 1980-83. Mem. Portland Com. Fgn. Rels., 1986—. Decorated Legion of Merit, Army Commendation medal with oak leaf cluster; Meritorious Alumnus award Oreg. Health Scis. U., 1990. Diplomate Am. Bd. Internal Medicine. Fellow A.C.P.; mem. Am. Gastroenterol. Assn., Oreg. Med. Assn. (del. Clackamas County), Ret. Officers Assn. Republican. Roman Catholic. Home and Office: 6364 SE Mcnary Rd Portland OR 97267-5119

ZEWE, JUDITH LYNN, human resources professional; b. Monongahela, Pa., May 2, 1947; d. Norman Edward and Martha Ellen (Harkins) Kenny; m. Dennis Dale Zewe, Aug. 17, 1964; children: Dennis Dale Jr., Donna Lynn. BA in Mgmt., Mercyhurst Coll., 1979; cert. of mgmt., U. Colo., Denver, 1982, postgrad.; postgrad., Regis U. Dir. pers. Mercyhurst Coll., Erie, Pa., 1975-79; compensation mgr. Community Coll. of Denver System, 1979-83, dir. employee rels., 1983-85; founder, pres., career cons. Lynn Dale & Co., Southfield, Mich., 1985-88; dir. pers., affirmative action Colo. Sch. Mines, Golden, 1988-93; dir. human resources Arapahoe C.C., Littleton, Colo., 1993—; compensation cons. Colo. Bd. Community Colls., 1981. Author: Successful Job Search Strategies. Vol. Make-a-Wish Found. Colo., 1990—, Children's Hosp. Denver, 1990—. Named Outstanding Vol. Make-a-Wish Found. Colo., 1991. Mem. Coll. and Univ. Pers. Assn. (nat. benefits coun. 1983-84), Colo. Higher Edn. Affirmative Action Adminstrs., Coll. and Univ. Pers. Assn. Colo. (pres. 1992-93). Home: 10244 Owens St Broomfield CO 80021-6656 Office: Arapahoe C C 2500 W College Dr Littleton CO 80120-1956

ZHANG, GUORUI, software engineer; b. Jiexi, Guangdong, China, Nov. 11, 1946; came to U.S., 1986; s. Longwen Zhang and Lanmei Peng; m. Yuegui Li, Feb. 5, 1975; 1 child, Hua. BSc in Computer Software Engr., Tsinghua U., Beijing, 1970; PhD in Elec. Engring., UMIST, Manchest, Eng., 1984. Rsch. fellow Nanjing (China) Automation Rsch. Inst., 1985-86; vis. faculty assoc. Ariz. State U., Tempe, 1986-88; prin. software engr. ABB Network Control, Baden, Switzerland, 1988-93, ABB Systems Control, Santa Clara, Calif., 1993—; vis. researcher R&D Delft (The Netherlands) U. Tech., 1979-82. Contbr. articles to profl. jours. Mem. IEEE Power Engring. Soc. (sr.). Home: 1501 Chaumont Dr San Jose CA 95118

ZHANG, JIM ZENHUA, artist, consultant; b. Xuzhou, Jiangsu, China, July 21, 1957; came to the U.S., 1987; s. Shaojun and Peiyin (Gao) Z.; m. Xiaoxing Yu, July 20, 1983; 1 child, Jon Z. BA, Nanjing (China) Art Inst., 1982, MA, 1985; MFA, La. Tech. U., 1990. Artist-in-residence Chisholm Inst. Tech., Melbourne, Australia, 1986-87; tchg. asst. art dept. La. Tech. U., Ruston, 1987-90; pres., owner Zhang & Yu Art, Irvine, Calif., 1990—; sr. staff artist Images Internat. Hawaii, Honolulu, 1991—. Artist: Beyond the Open Door, 1987; artist for various jours. Chmn. arch. com. Northwood Homeowners Assn., Irvine, 1993-94. Scholar La. Tech. U., Ruston, 1989; grantee The Pollock-Krasner Found., N.Y.C., 1990. Mem. Orange County Chinese Artists' Assn. Home: 15 New Hvn Irvine CA 92720-3286

ZHANG, LONGXI, educator, literary critic; b. Chengdu, Sichuan, China, June 10, 1947; came to U.S., 1983; s. Xidu and Yufang (Guan) Z.; m. Weilin Tang, Jan. 26, 1979; children: Celia Youhuan, Caroline Ruihuan. MA, Peking U., 1981; PhD, Harvard U., 1989. Asst. prof. comparative lit. U. Calif., Riverside, 1989-93, assoc. prof., 1993—; mem. adv. bd. Oxford Univ. Press, Hong Kong; mem. editorial bd. Modern China, Newbury Park, Calif. Author: The Tao and the Logos, 1992 (Joseph Levenson award 1994). Pres.'s rsch. fellow in humanities U. Calif., 1991-92. Mem. MLA, Assn. for Asian Studies (Levenson prize 1994). Office: U Calif Riverside University Ave Riverside CA 92521

ZHANG, ZHEN, electrical engineer; b. Beijing, Dec. 6, 1945; came to U.S., 1982; s. Liyan and Jingxin (Zhu) Z.; m. Xiaolu Zhang, Oct. 1, 1977; 1 child Ruonan (Nancy). B in Math., Nankai U., Tianjin, China, 1969, M in Math., 1980; PhD in Applied Math., Cornell U., 1984; Habilitation in Math., Bielefeld (Germany) U., 1988. Lectr. Nankai U., Tainjin, 1981-82; rsch. assoc. Cornell U., Ithaca, N.Y., 1984-85, Stanford U., Palo Alto, Calif., 1985, Bielefeld U., 1986-88; asst. prof. U. So. Calif., L.A., 1988-92, assoc. prof., 1992—. Contbr. articles to profl. jours. Rsch. grantee NSF, 1989—. Mem. IEEE (sr. mem.). Home: 19329 Red Hawk Rd Walnut CA 91789-4229 Office: Univ So Calif EEB 508 Los Angeles CA 90089-2565

ZHAO, LI, fine arts company executive, teacher, consultant; b. Tianjin, China, Mar. 16, 1958; came to U.S., 1984; d. Robert Yunnian Chao and Qizhen Cao; m. Shiyi Zhang, Aug., 1984 (div. 1987); m. Kenneth Lloyd Schoolland, Aug. 8, 1988 (div. 1994); 1 child, Kenli Dulcinea. BA, Foreign Lang. Inst., Tianjin, China, 1983; MA, U. Minn., 1987; Mgmt. Sci. (Japanese), Japan-Am. Inst. Mgmt. Sci., Honolulu, 1988; MS in Japanes Bus. Study, Chaminade U., Honolulu, 1988. Steel mill worker Guang Xi, China, 1969-78; tchr. Liu-Zhou Steel Mill High Sch., Guang Xi, 1978; translator, researcher China Dept. Transp., Beijing, 1983-84; teaching asst. U. Minn., Mpls., 1985-87; intern trainee Tobu Dept. Store, Tokyo, Japan, 1988; pres. Schoolland Internat., 1988—; sales mgr. trainee Duty Free Shops, Honolulu, 1989-92; gen. mgr. Double-Eye Hawaii, Honolulu, 1989-92, 1989—; gen. mgr. Tianjin Victor Entertainment Co. Ltd., Tianjin, China, 1994—. Editor: (newsletters) Double-Eye News, 1989-92, Libertarian Party Hawaii News, 1991-93. Chmn. membership com. U.S.-China People's Friendship Assn., 1988-89; mem. legis. com. Small Bus. Hawaii; bd. dirs. Libertarian Party Hawaii, 1992. Recipient Model Citizen award Mpls. Police Dept., 1992; named Outstanding Grad. Student, U. Minn., 1992. Mem. Am. Mktg. Assn. (bd. dirs.), Am. Soc. Interior Designers, Sales and Mktg. Execs. of Honolulu, Honolulu Japanese C. of C. (chair com.), Honolulu Acad. Art, Japan-Am. Assn. Hawaii, Assn. Hawaii Artists (corr. sec.), Chinese C. of C. Honolulu.

ZHAO, TIEMIN, electrical engineer; b. Beijing, June 1, 1963; came to U.S., 1988; s. Yunfei Zhao and Jinqing Liu; m. Shuye Lily Huan, Jan. 19, 1988; 1 child, Michael H. BS in Microelectronics, Peking U., Beijing, 1985, MS in Microelectronics, 1988; PhD in Elec. Engring., Stanford U., 1994. Instr. Stone Group Corp., Beijing, 1987-88; device engr. Cypress Semicondr., San Jose, Calif., 1991-92; vis. rschr. Matsu Shita Electric, Osaka, Japan, 1992; sr. engr. Xilinx, San Jose, 1994—. Inventor in field. Outstanding student scholar Peking U., 1981-84; rsch. fellow Cypress Semicondr., 1990-94. Mem. IEEE, AAAS.

ZHENG, YOULU, computer scientist, educator; b. Hangzhou, Zhejiang, People's Republic of China, Nov. 3, 1942; came to U.S., 1984; s. Fat-Lai and Yi (Tong) Cheng;m. Li Sun, June 20, 1970; 1 child, Nan. BS, Sichuan (People's Republic of China) U., 1967; MS, Zhejiang U., 1981; PhD, Wash. State U., 1987. Engr. Chongqing (People's Republic of China) Automobile Co., 1967-75, Yunnan (People's Republic of China) Electronic Equipment Co., 1975-79, ISC Systems Co., Spokane, Wash., 1986; lectr. Chengdu (People's Republic of China) U. Sci. and Tech., 1981-84; computer scientist, sr. engr. EXP Group, Inc., Fremont, Calif., 1990—; prof. U. Montana, Missoula, 1987—; cons. Meswell Tech., San Leandro, Calif., 1990—; advisor SunLabs, Missoula, Mont., 1991—; dir. computer graphics and visualization lab. U. Mont., 1992—; invited lectr. info. tech. summer sch. Chinese Acad. Scis., Beijing, 1993; bd. dirs. Progressive Tech., Inc., Missoula. Contbr. articles on computer sci. to acad. jours., 1981-94. NSF grantee and prin. investigator. Mem. Math. Assn. Am., Assn. Computer Machinery. Home: 110 Ben Hogan Dr Missoula MT 59803-2423 Office: U Mont Missoula MT 59812

ZHOU, CHIPING, mathematician, educator; b. Shanghai, People's Republic of China, Jan. 21, 1957; s. Xingui Zhou and Qi Zhu; m. Xiaoyu He, June 22, 1986; children: Kevin K., Brandon K. BS, Fudan U., Shanghai, 1983, MS, 1986; PhD, U. Hawaii, 1990. Asst. prof. Fudan U., Shanghai, 1986-; lectr. Chaminade U., Honolulu, 1990; instr. U. Hawaii, Honolulu, 1990-. Author: Some Problems for Elliptic and Hyperbolic Equations, 1986, Maximum Principles and Liouville Theorems for Elliptic Partial Differential Equations, 1991; contbr. articles to profl. jours. Recipient rsch. fellowship Rsch. Corp. of U. Hawaii, 1989. Mem. Am. Math. Soc., Math. Assn. Am. Office: U Hawaii - HCC Math Dept 874 Dillingham Honolulu HI 96817

ZHOU, MING DE, aeronautical scientist, educator; b. Zhejiang, China, June 26, 1937; s. Pin Xiang and Ang Din (Xia) Z.; m. Zhuang Yuhua, Aug. 12, 1936; children: Zhengyu, Yan Zhuang. BS, Beijing U. Aeros.-Astronautics, 1962; MS, Northwestern U. Tech., 1967; PhD, Internat. Edn. Rsch. Found., 1992. Tchr. Harbin (China) U. Tech., 1962-64, 67-73; from lectr. to prof. Nanjing (China) U. Aeronautics and Astronautics, 1973-86, 86—; dean bd. postgrad. studies Nanjing (China) U. Aeros. and Astronautics, 1985-89; nationally qualified PhD advisor China, 1989—; rsch. scientist U. Ariz., Tucson, 1991-93, rsch. prof., 1993—; vis. scholar Cambridge (England) U., 1980-82; guest scientist Inst. Exptl. Fluid Mechanics, Göttingen, Germany, 1983-84, 85, 87; sr. vis. scientist Tech. U. Berlin, 1988, 90; rsch. assoc. U. So. Calif., L.A., 1989-90. Mem. editorial com. Chinese Jour. Exptl. Mechanics, 1986-89; author: (with others) Viscous Flows and Their Measurements, 1988, (with others) Introduction to Vorticity and Vortex Dynamics, 1992; contbr. articles to Aero. Jour. U.K., Experiments in Fluids, AIAA Jour., Chinese Jour. Aeronautics. Co-recipient Nat. award Progress in Sci. and Tech. first class, Peoples Republic of China, 1985. Mem. AIAA (sr.), Am. Phys. Soc., Chinese Soc. Aeronautics, Chinese Soc. Mechanics (mem. acad. group exptl. fluid mechanics 1986-89), Chinese Soc. Aerodynamic Rsch. (acad. group unsteady flow and vortex control 1985-89).

ZHU, JUN, mathematics educator; b. Suzhou, Jiangsu, People's Republic of China, June 13, 1957; arrived in Can, 1989; s. Chengyan and Ronghua (Jiang) Z.; m. Yunfang Xu, Jan. 1, 1985; 1 child, Chenchong. Student, Suzhou U., 1982. Tchr. Suzhou (Peoples Republic of China) U., 1982-89; researcher U. B.C., Vancouver, 1989—. Contbr. articles to profl. jours. Office: U BC Dept Math, 1984 Math Rd, Vancouver, BC Canada V6T 1Z2

ZHU, YU, neurologist, neurophysiologist, researcher; b. Shanghai, China, Aug. 10, 1946; came to U.S., 1988; s. Jia Nai Zhu and Yue Rou Sun; m. Ming Tao, May 20, 1975; 1 child, Jay. MD, Zhejiang Med. U., China, 1970; MS, Shanghai Second Med. Coll., 1981. Neurologist Lishui Hosp., Zhejiang, 1971-78, Shanghai Second Med. Coll., Renji Hosp., 1978-82; clin. neurophysiologist U. Montpellier (France) Med. Coll., 1983-88; vis. scientist U. Brussels Brain Rsch. Unit, 1984-85; asst. rschr. U. Calif., Irvine, 1988—. Contbr. articles to profl. jours. Mem. Am. Assn. Electrodiagnostic Medicine, N.Y. Acad. Scis., Soc. d'Eletroencephalographie et de Neurophysiologie Clinique de Lanque Française. Home: 3 Newton Ct Irvine CA 92715-4038 Office: U Calif Irvine Campus Dr Irvine CA 92717

ZICK, LESTER GEORGE, actor, systems consultant; b. Sumter, S.C., Jan. 6, 1944; s. William Henry and Frances (Fauntleroy) Z. BS, U.S. Naval Acad., 1966. Commd. ensign USN, 1966, assigned to Vietnam,, 1966-68; resigned, 1968; systems programmer Internat. Harvester, Broadview, Ill., 1968-73; systems cons. Atlantic Richfield, L.A., 1973-80; self-employed theoretical physicist, L.A., 1980-90, actor,, 1990—; systems cons. Data Products, Woodland Hills, Calif., 1985. Author: Theory of Predication, 1982, Metaphysics of Matter, 1987; appeared in movies Line of Fire: The Moris Dees Story, 1992, Never Forget, 1992. Mem. AFTRA.

ZIDEK, JAMES VICTOR, statistician, educator; b. Acme, Alta., Can., Sept. 26, 1939; s. John and Anne (Marik) Z.; m. Patricia Lynne Donald, Aug. 5, 1961. B.Sc. with honors, U. Alta., 1961, M.Sc., 1963; Ph.D., Stanford U., 1967. Mem. faculty U. B.C., Vancouver, 1967—, prof. stats., 1976—, head dept., 1984-89; prof. dept. stats. U. Wash., Seattle, 1983-84; hon. research fellow Univ. Coll., London, 1971-72; vis. sr. research scientist Commonwealth Sci. and Indsl. Research Orgn., 1976-77; chmn. statis. scis. com. Natural Sci. and Engring. Research Council Can., 1980-81, chmn. math. sci. group, 1988-91. Editor Statis. Sci., 1988-91, Chapman and Hall Math Stat Series; sr. assoc. editor Can. Jour. Stats., 1980; contbr. articles to profl. jours. Fellow Inst. Math. Stats., Am. Statis. Assn.; mem. Internat. Statis. Inst., Internat. Assn. Survey Statisticians, Royal Statis. Soc., Can. Statis. Soc., Elec. Stats. Soc. Can. (pres. 1987-88). Office: U B C, Vancouver, BC Canada V6T 1Z2

ZIEGAUS, ALAN JAMES, public relations executive; b. Bremerton, Wash., May 8, 1948; s. Alan Moon and Dorothy (Lamont) Z.; m. Constance Jean Carver, 1972; children: Jennifer, Ashley. BJ, San Diego State U., 1970. Staff writer San Diego Tribune, 1972-77; exec. asst. San Diego City Council, 1977-78; v.p. Gable Agy., San Diego, 1978-80; pres. Stoorza, Ziegaus & Metzger, San Diego, 1980—. Mem. planning com. County San Diego, 1980-82; mem. sewage task force City of San Diego, 1986-88, civil svc. com., 1992—; trustee armed forces YMCA, San Diego, 1984—. Recipient Best Investigative Series award AP, 1975. Mem. San Diego Press Club (Best News Story award 1973). Home: 12351 Brassica St San Diego CA 92129-4127 Office: Stoorza Ziegaus & Metzger 225 Broadway Ste 1600 San Diego CA 92101-5018*

ZIEGLER, GLENN I., manufacturing company executive; b. Queens, N.Y., June 26, 1962; s. Howard I. and Barbara (Cohen) Z. BS in Computer Sci., SUNY, Albany, 1984; MBA in Mgmt., Pepperdine U., Malibu, Calif., 1991. Systems analyst NBC, N.Y.C., 1984-86; sr. systems analyst NBC, Burbank, Calif., 1986-88; project leader Candle Corp., L.A., 1988-91; mgr. comml. parts BW/IP Internat., Inc., Vernon, Calif., 1991—. Mem. Am. Prodn. and Inventory Control Soc., U.S. Triathlon Fedn., Delta Mu Delta. Home: 5700 Etiwanda Ave Apt 217 Tarzana CA 91356-2573 Office: BW/IP Internat Inc 2300 E Vernon Ave Vernon CA 90058-1623

ZIEGLER, R.W., JR., lawyer, consultant; b. Pitts.; children: Caroline, Gretchen, Jeremy, Benjamin, Phoebe, Polly. Student, Carnegie Tech., U. Pitts.; JD, Duquesne U., 1972. Bar: Pa. 1972, Calif. 1981, U.S. Ct. Appeals (3d cir.) 1977, (9th cir.) 1982, U.S. Dist. Ct. (we. dist.) Pa. 1972, Calif., 1982, U.S. Tax Ct. 1978, U.S. Supreme Ct. 1977. Ptnr. Ziegler & Ombres, Pitts., 1973-79; pres. Ziegler Ross Inc., San Francisco, 1979—; lectr. for Bar Assns. Author: Law Practice Management; editor: Law Office Guide in Computing. Mem. ABA, Am. Mgmt. Assn., Pa. State Bar Assn., Calif. State Bar Assn. Office: 1350 Bayshore Hwy Ste 440 Burlingame CA 94010-1813

ZIELKE, PATRICK MICHAEL, aerospace company executive; b. San Antonio, Dec. 4, 1945; s. Albert J. and Ruth Grace (Crissey) Z.; m. Patriaia Ann Krikorian, Dec. 30, 1966; 1 child, Christopher Patrick. BS in Physics, Wayne State U., 1967; MBA, U. Phoenix, 1991. Engr. Boeing Aircraft, Seattle, 1967-69; lead engr. Beech Aircraft, Wichita, 1969-73; project engr. Grumman Corp., Cleve., 1973-74; engring. mgr. Crescent Metal Products, Cleve., 1974-75; pres. Almont Insulation, Gunnison, Colo., 1975-82; program mgr. GE, Moffett Field, Calif., 1982-86; dir. tech. svcs. Thiokol Corp., Ogden, Utah, 1986—; cons. in pvt. practice, Willard, Utah, 1986-93. Fundraiser Make-A-Wish Found., Ogden, 1993; mem. allocation com. United Way, Ogden, 1993, Corinth, Miss., 1994; mem. Almont Vol. Fire Dept., 1975-82. Roman Catholic. Home: 906 E 3400 N Ogden UT 84414 Office: Thiokol Corp PO Box 707 Brigham City UT 84302

ZIEMANN, G. PATRICK, bishop; b. Pasadena, Calif., Sept. 13, 1941. Attended, St. John's Coll. and St. John's Sem., Camarillo, Calif., Mt. St. Mary's Coll., L.A. Ordained priest Roman Cath., 1967. Titular bishop, aux. bishop Diocese Santa Rosa, Obba, 1986-92; bishop Diocese Santa Rosa, Santa Rosa, Calif., 1992—. Office: Chancery Office PO Box 1297 547 B St Santa Rosa CA 95401-5249*

ZIERATH, MARILYN JEAN, medical/surgical and pediatrics nurse; b. Centralia, Wash., Jan. 24, 1942; d. Lloyd and Lolita Jeneva (Francis) Reese; m. David William Zierath, Dec. 1963; children: Carolyn, Robert, Michael. Diploma in nursing, Tacoma Gen. Hosp., 1964; BSN, U. Puget Sound, 1965; MS in Nursing, Calif. State U., Fresno, 1975. RN, Wash.; cert. in enterostomal therapy; advanced nurse practitioner. Instr. nursing Calif. State U., Fresno, 1973-75; nursing supr. med.-surg. Good Samaritan Hosp., Puyallup, Wash., 1977; clin. instr. Pacific Luth. U., Tacoma, 1977-79; med.-surg. clin. specialist, enterostomal therapy nurse Tacoma Gen. Hosp., 1979-92, nurse oper. rm., 1992-95; enterostomal therapy nurse Quad-C, Tacoma Terrace, Wash., 1995—. Contbr. articles to nursing jours. Mem. ANA (cert. med.-surg. clin. nurse specialist), Wound, Ostomy and Continence Nurses, Assn. Enterostomal Therapy Nurses, Puget Sound Enterostomal Nurses, Clin. Nurse Specialists Puget Sound, Phi Kappa Phi, Alpha Phi. Office: Tacoma Terrace Health Care Ctr 3625 East B St Tacoma WA 98405

ZIERNICKI, RICHARD MIECZYSLAW, engineering firm executive; b. Krakow, Poland, Feb. 3, 1950; came to U.S., 1981; m. Mila Kristine Czarnecka, Apr. 1, 1952; children: Maciek, Daniel. BS in Mech. Design, U. Mining and Metallurgy, Krakow, 1973, MS in Mech. Engring., 1975, PhD in Tech. Sci. cum laude, 1979. Registered profl. engr., Colo., Calif., Tex. and Wyo. Asst. prof. engring. Inst. Vibrations and Acoustics, Krakow, 1975-80; mgr. rsch. and devel. Inst. Tech., Krakow, 1980-81; mgr. mech. engring. Over-Lowe Co., Denver, 1981-84; sr. cons., pres. Knott Lab., Denver, 1984—; invited speaker Denver U. Dept. Engring. Contbr. articles to profl. jours.; patentee in field. Mem. ASME, NSPE, Soc. Automotive Engrs., Soc. for Exptl. Stress Analysis, Robotic Internat. Soc. Mfg. Engrs., Profl. Engrs. Colo., Nat. Assn. Profl. Accident Reconstruction Specialists, Nat. Forensic Ctr., Nat. Acad. Forensic Engrs. Home: 8809 S Blue Mountain Pl Highlands Ranch CO 80126-2802 Office: Knott Lab Inc 2727 W 2d Ave Denver CO 80219

ZIGMAN, PAUL EDMOND, environmental consultant, executive; b. L.A., Mar. 10, 1924; s. Fernand and Rose (Orlijan) Z.; m. children: Andrea, Eric. BS in Chemistry, UCLA, 1948. Supr., applied research U.S. Naval Radiol. Def. Lab., San Francisco, 1949-59, head tech. mgmt. office, 1961-69; supr., analytical chemistry Atomics Internat., Canoga Park, Calif., 1960-61; pres. Environ. Sci. Assocs., San Francisco, 1969-94, chmn., bd. dirs, 1969—. Contbr. articles to profl. jours. Served as pvt. U.S. Army, 1943. Recipient USN Meritorious Civilian Service award, 1968. Mem. Am. Chem. Soc., Nat. Assn. Environ. Profls. (v.p. 1977), Assn. Environ. Profls. (pres. 1974-76) (Outstanding Service award 1977, Cert. Appreciation 1984). Home: 2311 Crystal Downs Ct Oxnard CA 93030-7755

ZIKA, FRANK JOSEPH, sculptor, designer; b. L.A., Aug. 13, 1955; s. Frank Joseph and Lorraine Ada (Burdick) Z.; m. Josephine Nora Laing, May 12, 1984. BS in Ornamental Horticulture, Calif. Poly. State U., 1978. Lic. landscape contractor, Calif. Owner, designer Zika Archtl. Glass, San Luis Obispo, Calif., 1984—; sculptor San Luis Obispo, 1980—. Fused glass sculptor, 1980—. Recipient Calif. Design '94 award Contemporary Craft Coun., 1994. Mem. Am. Craft Coun. Home: 141 Cuesta Dr San Luis Obispo CA 93405-1132 Office: Zika Archtl Glass 141 Cuesta Dr San Luis Obispo CA 93405-1132

ZIL, JOHN STEPHEN, psychiatrist, physiologist; b. Chgo., Oct. 8, 1947; s. Stephen Vincent and Marilyn Charlotte (Jackson) Zilius; 1 child, Charlene-Elena. BS magna cum laude, U. Redlands, 1969; MD, U. Calif., San Diego, 1973; MPH, Yale U., 1977; JD with honors, Jefferson Coll., 1985. Intern, resident in psychiatry and neurology U. Ariz., 1973-75; fellow in psychiatry, advanced fellow in social and community psychiatry, Yale community cons. to Conn. State Dept. Corrections, Yale U., 1975-77, instr. psychiatry and physiology, 1976-77; instr. physiology U. Mass., 1976-77; acting unit chief Inpatient and Day Hosp. Conn. Mental Health Ctr., Yale-New Haven Hosp. Inc., 1975-76, unit chief, 1976-77; asst. prof. psychiatry U. Calif., San Francisco, 1977-82, assoc. prof. psychiatry and medicine, 1982-86, vice-chmn. dept. psychiatry, 1983-86; adj. prof. Calif. State U., 1985-87; assoc. prof. bioengring. U. Calif., Berkely and San Francisco, 1982-92, clin. faculty, Davis, 1991—; chief psychiatry and neurology VA Med. Ctr., Fresno, Calif., 1977-86, prin. investigator Sleep Rsch. & Physiology Lab., 1980-86; dir. dept. psychiatry and neurology U. Calif.-San Francisco, Fresno-Cen. San Joaquin Valley Med. Edn. Program and Affiliated Hosps. and Clinics, 1983-86; chief psychiatrist State of Calif. Dept. Corrections cen. office, 1986—; chmn. State of Calif. Inter-Agy. Tech. Adv. com. on Mentally Ill Inmates & Parolees, 1986-92; mem. med. adv. com. Calif. State Personnel Bd., 1986—; appointed councillor Calif. State Mental Health Plan, 1988-93; cons. Nat. Inst. Corrections, 1992—; invited faculty contbr. and editor Am. Coll. Psychiatrist's Resident in Tng. Exam., 1981—. Author: The Case of the Sleepwalking Rapist, 1992, Mentally Disordered Criminal Offenders, 5 vols., 1989, reprinted, 1991; contbg. author: The Measurement Mandate: On the Road to Performance Improvement in Health Care, 1993; assoc. editor Corrective and Social Psychiatry Jour., 1978—, referee, 1980—, reviewer, 1981—; contbr. articles in field to profl. jours. Nat. Merit scholar, 1965; recipient Nat. Recognition award Bank of Am., 1965, Julian Lee Roberts award U. Redlands, 1969, Kendall award Internat. Symposium in Biochemistry Research, 1970, Campus-Wide Profl. Achievement award U. Calif., 1992, Career Achievement award U. Redlands, 1994. Fellow Royal Soc. Health, Am. Assn. Social Psychiatry; mem. Am. Assn. Mental Health Profls. in Corrections (nat. pres. 1978—), Calif. Scholarship Fedn. (past pres.), AAUP, Am. Psychiat. Assn., Nat. Council on Crime and Delinquency, Am. Pub. Health Assn., Delta Alpha, Alpha Epislon Delta. Office: PO Box 163359 Sacramento CA 95816-9359

ZILLY, THOMAS SAMUEL, federal judge; b. Detroit, Jan. 1, 1935; s. George Samuel and Bernice M. (McWhinney) Z.; divorced; children: John, Peter, Paul, Luke; m. Jane Greller Noland, Oct. 8, 1988; stepchildren: Allison Noland, Jennifer Noland. BA, U. Mich., 1956; LLD, Cornell U., 1962. Bar: Wash. 1962, U.S. Ct. Appeals (9th cir.) 1962, U.S. Supreme Ct. 1976. Ptnr. Lane, Powell, Moss & Miller, Seattle, 1962-88; judge U.S. Dist. Ct. (we. dist.) Wash., Seattle, 1988—; judge pro tem Seattle Mcpl. Ct., 1972-80. Contbr. articles to profl. jours. Mem. Cen. Area Sch. Council, Seattle, 1969-70; scoutmaster Thunderbird Dist. council Boy Scouts Am. Seattle, 1976-84; bd. dirs. East Madison YMCA. Served to lt. (j.g.) USN, 1956-59. Recipient Tuahku Dist. Service to Youth award Boy Scouts Am., 1983. Mem. ABA, Wash. State Bar Assn., Seattle-King County Bar Assn. (treas. 1979-80, trustee 1980-83, sec. 1983-84, 2d v.p. 1984-85, 1st v.p. 1985-86, pres. 1986-87). Office: US Dist Ct 410 US Courthouse 1010 5th Ave Seattle WA 98104-1130

ZIMAN, RONALD BERT, physician, researcher, consultant; b. Chgo., Oct. 20, 1948. MD, Washington U., St. Louis, 1973. Diplomate Am. Bd. Psychiatry & Neurology, Am. Bd. Internal Medicine. Rotating medicine intern, 1973-74; medicine intern UCLA, Wadsworth, Va., 1974-75, neurology resident, 1975-78; pres. Northridge (Calif.) Neurol. Ctr., 1979—; med. dir. electrophysiology Northridge Hosp. Med. Ctr., 1983—; med. dir. care program Granada Hills. (Calif.) Community Hosp., 1986—, bd. dirs., 1989—, vice chair bd. dirs., 1994—; assoc. clin. prof. neurology & dentistry UCLA, 1993—, clin. faculty exec. com., 1993—. Recipient Lange Med. Book award Lange Publs., 1973. Fellow ACP, Am. Acad. Neurology, Am. EEG Soc., Royal Soc. Medicine. Office: Northridge Neurol Ctr 18433 Roscoe Blvd # 210 Northridge CA 91325-4108

ZIMERMANN, ALFRED EARLE, software engineering educator; b. Bethesda, Md., June 23, 1951; s. Richard Galt and Dorothy Mae (Dungan) Z.; m. Adrienne Whitely Radulovic, Dec. 22, 1979. AB, Duke U., 1973; M Bus. Info. Systems, Ga. State U., 1985. Fin. analyst E.F. Hutton, Atlanta, 1984-86; software cons. Unisys, Atlanta, 1986-89; asst. prof. software engring., dept. head computer sci. and info. sys. Hawaii Pacific U., Honolulu, 1990—; bd. dirs. Avant Techs., Inc., Atlanta; owner Avant Technology West, Honolulu; software cons. Computer Systems, Internat., Honolulu, 1991. Mem. Inman Park Restoration, Atlanta, 1981—; mem. city councilman election campaign, Atlanta, 1982. Lt. comdr. USN, 1973-81. Mem. Assn. Computer Machinists, IEEE Computer Soc., Japan-Am. Soc. Ga. Democrat. Episcopalian. Home: 1100 Austin Ave NE Atlanta GA 30307-1918 Office: Hawaii Pacific U 1188 Fort Street Mall Honolulu HI 96813-2713

ZIMKAS, CHARLES PATRICK, JR., space foundation director; b. Scranton, Pa., Sept. 8, 1940; s. Charles Zimkas Sr. and Margaret (Bakunas) Sullick; m. Ursula Frediel Marten; children: Robert L., Uwe F., Michael P., Brian David. Enlisted USAF, advanced through grades to chief master sgt., 1958; dep. chief of staff, personnel adminstrv. div. Aerospace Def. Command, Colorado Springs, Colo., 1971-74; exec. to dep. chief of staff personnel Aerospace Def. Command, Colorado Springs, 1975-80; chief of adminstrn. Air Forces Iceland, Keflavik, 1974-75; first sr. enlisted advisor USAF Space Command, Colorado Springs, 1980-84; ret., 1984; dir. regional devel. Noncommissioned Officers Assn., San Antonio, 1984-86; dir. ops. U.S. Space Found., Colorado Springs, 1986—. Named Air Force Outstanding Airman of Yr., 1978; recipient Air Force Legion Merit. Mem. Noncommissioned Officers Assn. (bd. dirs. 1978-84, chmn. bd. dirs. 1982-84, excalibur award 1979, Order of Sword 1978); Lance P. Sijan (exec. v.p. Air Force Assn. chpt.). Home: 729 Drew Dr Colorado Springs CO 80911-2606 Office: US Space Found 2860 S Circle Dr Ste 2301 Colorado Springs CO 80906-4107

ZIMMER, DONALD WILLIAM, former professional baseball manager; b. Cin., Jan. 17, 1931; s. Harold Lesley and Lorraine Bertha (Ernst) Z.; m. Jean Carol Bauerle, Aug. 16, 1951; children: Thomas Jeffrey, Donna Jean. Student pub. schs., Cin. Baseball player Dodger Farm Clubs, 1949-54, Bklyn. Dodgers, 1954-57, Los Angeles Dodgers, 1958-59, Chgo. Cubs, 1960-61, N.Y. Mets, 1962, Cin. Reds, 1962, Los Angeles Dodgers, 1963, Washington Senators, 1963-65, Toei Flyers, Tokyo, 1966; mgr. Cin. Reds Farm Clubs, Knoxville and Buffalo, 1967, Indpls., 1968; mgr. San Diego Padre Farm Clubs, Key West, Fla., 1969, Padre Farm Club, Salt Lake City, 1970; coach Montreal Expos, Que., Can., 1971; mgr. San Diego Padres, 1972-73; coach Boston Red Sox, 1974-76, mgr., 1976-80; mgr. Tex. Rangers, 1981, 82; coach N.Y. Yankees, 1983, fall 1986, Chgo. Cubs, 1984, 85, 86, San Francisco Giants, 1987; mgr. Chgo. Cubs, 1988-91; coach Boston Red Sox, 1992, Colo. Rockies, Denver, 1993-95; mem. minor league All-Star Teams, Hornell, N.Y., 1950, Elmira, N.Y., 1951, Mobile, Ala., 1952, St. Paul, 1953; player World Series teams, 1955, 56, 59, coach, 1975. Recipient Bill Stern award NBC, 1949; named St. Paul Rookie of Yr., 1953; mem. All Star Team, 1961, 78, 81, 90; named Nat. League Mgr. of Yr. 1989. Mem. Profl. Baseball Players Am. (life), Old Time Ball Players Wis.

ZIMMERER, KATHY LOUISE, university art gallery director; b. Whittier, Calif., Dec. 9, 1951. BA cum laude, U. Calif., Berkeley, 1974; MA, Williams Coll., 1976. From tour guide to curatorial asst. Sterling and Francine Clark Inst., Williamstown, Mass., 1975-76; spl. asst. dept. modern art L.A. County Mus. Art, 1976-77; mus. edn. fellow Fine Arts Mus. San Francisco, 1977-78; dir. coll. art gallery SUNY, New Paltz, 1978-80; cons. in field, 1980-81; dir. univ. art gallery Calif. State U., Dominguez Hills, 1982—. Mem. Internat. Assn. Art Critics, ArtTable. Office: Univ Art Gallery Calif State U 1000 E Victoria St Carson CA 90747-0001

ZIMMERMAN, HAROLD SAMUEL, newspaper executive, state senator, state administrator; b. Valley City, N.D., June 1, 1923; s. Samuel Alwin and Lulu (Wylie) Z.; m. Julianne Williams, Sept. 12, 1946; children—Karen, Steven, Judi Jean (dec.). B.A., U. Wash., 1947. News editor Sedro-Woolley (Wash.) Courier-Times, 1947-50; editor, pub. Advocate, Castle Rock, Wash., 1950-57; pub. Post-Record, Camas, Wash., 1957-80; assoc. pub., columnist, 1980; assoc. pub., columnist, dir. Eagle Publs., Camas, 1980-88. Mem. Wash. Ho. of Reps., 1967-80; mem. Wash. Senate, 1981-88, Wash. State Environ. Hearings Bd., Lacey, 1988-93. Served with USAAF, 1943-46. Mem. Grange, Sigma Delta Chi, Sigma Chi. Republican. United Methodist. Clubs: Lions, Kiwanis.

ZIMMERMAN, MICHAEL DAVID, state supreme court chief justice; b. Chgo., Oct. 21, 1943; s. Elizabeth Porter; m. Lynne Mariani (dec. 1994); children: Evangeline Albright, Alessandra Mariani, Morgan Elisabeth. BS, U. Utah, 1966, JD, 1969. Bar: Calif. 1971, Utah 1978. Law clk. to Chief Justice Warren Earl Burger U.S. Supreme Ct., Washington, 1969-70; assoc. O'Melveny & Myers, L.A., 1970-76; assoc. prof. law U. Utah, 1976-78, adj. prof. law, 1978-84, 89—; of counsel Kruse, Landa, Zimmerman & Maycock, Salt Lake City, 1978-80; spl. counsel Gov. of Utah, Salt Lake City, 1978-80; ptnr. Watkiss & Campbell, Salt Lake City, 1980-84; assoc. justice Supreme Ct. Utah, Salt Lake City, 1984-93, chief justice, 1994—; co-moderator Justice Soc. Program of Snowbird Inst. for Arts and Humanities, 1991, 92; moderator, Tanner lecture panel dept. philosophy U. Utah, 1994—; faculty, Judging Sci. Program Duke U., 1992. Editor: Utah Law Rev., 1968-69; contbr. numerous articles to legal publs. Mem. Project 2000, Coalition for Utah's Future. Named Utah State Bar Appellate Ct. Judge of Yr., 1988; recipient Excellence in Ethics award, Ctr. for Study of Ethics, 1994, fellowship Justice and Soc. Program of Aspen Inst. for Humanistic Studies, 1988, co-moderator, 1989. Mem. ABA (faculty mem. judges' seminar 1993), Am. Law Inst., Utah Bar Assn., Salt Lake County Bar Assn., Jud. Conf. U.S. (adv. com. civil rules 1985-91), Utah Jud. Coun. (supreme ct. rep. 1986-91, chair 1994—, chair com. on alternative dispute resolution 1993-94), Utah Constnl. Revisions Commn., Snowbird Inst. for Arts and Humanities (bd. dirs), Am. Inns of Ct. VIII, Am. Judicature Soc. (bd. dirs.), U. Utah Coll. of Law Alumni Assn. (pres. 1991-92), Order of Coif, Phi Kappa Phi. Office: Utah Supreme Ct 332 State Capitol Salt Lake City UT 84114-1181

ZIMMERMAN, NIEL THOMAS, academic administrator; b. Blackduck, Minn., Aug. 27, 1943; s. Roy Arthur and Nielen Carlisle (Lien) Z.; m. Judith Ann Wortman, Mar. 21, 1964; children—Kurt Raymond, Joelle Marie. B.A., U. Calif.-Riverside, 1965, M.A., 1966, Ph.D., 1970. Instr. polit. sci. Mankato State Coll., Minn., 1966-67; from asst. prof. govt. to assoc. prof. govt. Eastern Wash. U., Cheney, 1970-89, prof., 1986—; dir. DSHS Contract, 1973-82, dean Sch. Pub. Affairs, 1978-90, accreditation liaison officer, 1990-92, dean Coll. of Letters and Scis., 1990-92, spl. asst. to pres., 1992-93; v.p., legis. rep. Cheney Sch. Bd., 1986—, pres. 1987-92; chmn. com. Boy Scouts Am., Cheney, 1984. Mem. Am. Judicature Soc., Wash. State Sch. Dir.'s Assn. (mem. interscholastic activities com., 1988-90, nomination com.). Democrat. Lutheran. Lodge: Kiwanis (Spokane). Home: 519 S Presley Dr Cheney WA 99004-1338 Office: Ea Wash U Mailstop # 30 Cheney WA 99004

ZIMMERMAN, ROBERT LEONARD, internist, cardiologist; b. Bklyn., Apr. 2, 1918; s. Louis A. and Jennie (Marx) Z.; m. Phyllis Maude Wright, May 20, 1946; children: Susan D'Andrea, Barbara Lynn Estomin, Robert L. Zimmerman, Jeanne M. Walz, Phyllis M. Rosenthal, Mary L. Rodriguez. AB, Harvard Coll., 1938; MD, SUNY, Bklyn., 1942. Diplomate Am. Bd. Internal Medicine. Intern Mt. Sinai Hosp., N.Y.C., 1942-43, resident, 1948-49; resident S.W. Med. Sch., McKinney, Tex., 1946-48; pvt. practice N.Y.C., 1949-54, Colorado Springs, Colo., 1954—; chief of staff Meml. Hosp., Colorado Springs, 1980. Capt. AUS, 1943-46, ETO. Mem. AMA, Colorado State Med. Assn., El Paso County Med. Assn., Am. Heart Assn. (coun. on clin. cardiology 1963—), Am. Coll. Cardiology, Assn. Harvard Chemists, Christian Med. Dental Soc. Methodist. Home: 1603 Wood Ave Colorado Springs CO 80907-7352 Office: 22 E Monument St Colorado Springs CO 80903-1018

ZIMMERMANN, JOHN PAUL, plastic surgeon; b. Milw., Mar. 9, 1945; s. Paul August and Edith Josephine (Tutsch) Z.; m. Bianca Maria Schadach Zimmermann, June 13, 1970; children: Veronica, Jean-Paul. BS in Biology, Chemistry, Marquette U., 1966; MD, Med. Coll. Wis., 1970. Diplomate Am Bd. Plastic Surgery. Internship surgery Stanford U. Sch. of Medicine, Calif., 1970-71; flight surgeon USAF, 1971-73; residency in gen. surgery, plastic & reconstructive surgery, 1974-79; fellowship head & neck surgery Roswell Park Meml. Cancer Inst., Buffalo, N.Y., 1977; pvt. practice Napa, Calif., 1979—; dir. Aesthetic Surgery Ctr. of Napa Valley, Calif., 1993—; clinical asst. prof. of plastic surgery Stanford U. Sch. of Medicine, Calif., 1993—; bd. dirs. Interplast, Palo Alto, Calif. (pres., bd. dirs. 1991-94, chmn. bd. dirs 1994-95). Mem. Am. Soc. Plastic & Reconstructive Surgeons, Am. Soc. Aesthetic Plastic Surgeons, Lipoplasty Soc., Calif. Soc. Plastic Surgeons (bd. dirs.), Calif. Med. Assn., Napa County Med. Assn. Republican. Roman Catholic. Office: 3344 Villa Ln Ste 10 Napa CA 94558

ZIMMERMANN, LAURA KRISTINE, psychology educator; b. Charlotte, N.C., Dec. 12, 1968; d. G. Floyd and Janet (Snow) Z. BA cum laude in

Psychology, Emory U., 1990, BA in Religion, 1990; MS in Developmental Psychology, U. N.Mex., 1993. Teaching assoc., asst. U. N.Mex., Albuquerque, 1991—; rsch. coord., clin. asst. Wesley Woods Geriatric Hosp., Atlanta, 1990-91; rsch. asst. Emory U., Atlanta, 1990-91, student computing instr., 1991, computer lab. cons., 1991. Mem. Soc. for Rsch. in Child Devel. Republican. Methodist. Office: U NMex Psychology Dept Logan Hall Albuquerque NM 87131

ZIMRING, STUART DAVID, lawyer; b. L.A., Dec. 12, 1946; s. Martin and Sylvia (Robinson) Z.; m. Eve Axelrad, Aug. 24, 1969 (div. 1981); m. Carol Grenert, May 24, 1981; children: Wendy Lynn Grenert, Joseph Noah, Matthew Kevin Grenert, Dov Shimon. BA in U.S. History, UCLA, 1968, JD, 1971. Bar: Calif. 1972, U.S. Dist. Ct. (cen. dist.) Calif. 1972, U.S. Dist. Ct. (no. dist.) Calif. 1984; U.S. Supreme Ct., 1994; cert. specialist in estate planning, probate and trust law. Assoc. Law Offices Leonard Smith, Beverly Hills, Calif., 1971-73; ptnr. Law Offices Smith & Zimring, Beverly Hills, Calif., 1973-76; assoc. Levin & Ballin, North Hollywood, Calif., 1976-77; prin. Levin, Ballin, Plotkin, Zimring & Goffin, A.P.C., North Hollywood, 1978-91, Law Offices Stuart D. Zimring, North Hollywood, 1991—; lectr. Los Angeles Valley Coll., Van Nuys, Calif., 1974-82. Author: Inter Vivos Trust Trustees Operating Manual, 1994, Lending to Inter Vivos Trusts--A Guide for Bankers and their Counsel, 1995, Durable Powers of Attorney for Health Care--A Practical Approach to an Intimate Document, 1995. Bd. dirs. Bet Tzedek, Jewish Legal Svcs., L.A., 1975-88, chmn. legal svcs. com., 1978-82; bd. dirs. Brandeis-Bardin Inst., Simi Valley, Calif., 1976-80; bd. dirs. Bur. Jewish Edn., L.A., 1973-88, chmn. com. on parent and family edn., 1985-87; trustee Adat Ari El Synagogue, L.A., 1982—; bd. dirs. Orgn. for the Needs of the Elderly, 1994—. Recipient Circle award Juvenile Justice Connection Project, L.A., 1989, Wiley W. Manuel award for pro bono legal svcs., 1994, 95. Mem. State Bar Calif., San Fernando Valley Bar Assn. (trustee 1979-86), Nat. Acad. Elder Law Attys. Democrat. Office: 12650 Riverside Dr North Hollywood CA 91607

ZINK, MELISSA ELLIS, artist; b. Kansas City, Mo., June 9, 1932; d. Everett Elgin and Margaret Iola (Logan) Ellis; m. William Morgan Howell, Dec. 20, 1952 (div. 1973); 1 child, Mallery Logan Howell Downs; m. Nelson John Zink, June 23, 1975. Student, Swarthmore Coll., 1950-53, U. Chgo., 1953, Kansas City (Mo.) Art Inst., 1959-60. One-person shows include Bellas Artes, N.Y.C., 1992, U. Colo., Boulder, 1993, The Parks Gallery, Taos, N.Mex., 1994; works appeared in groups shows including Munson Gallery, Santa Fe, 1993, J. Cacciola Galleries, N.Y.C., 1993, Santa Fe Mus., 1993; represented in permanent collections Santa Fe (N.Mex.) Mus., Albuquerque (N.Mex.) Mus., The Harwood Found., Taos, The Old Jail Found., Albany, Tex. Mem. Nat. Sculpture Soc.

ZINK, STEVEN DOUGLAS, librarian; b. Salem, Ind., Aug. 30, 1954; s. Victor I. and Anita P. (Clark) Z.; m. Lois C. Bowers, May 17, 1975; children: Joel, Ryan. BS, Ind. State U., 1974; MA, U. Wis., Madison, 1975; MLS, La. State U., 1979; PhD, Nova Southeastern U., 1991. Documents libr. The Coll. of Wooster (Ohio), 1979-80; head govt. publs. U. Nev., Reno, 1980-85, dir. pub. svcs., 1985-93, dean, 1993—; mem. Depository Libr. Coun. U.S. Pub. Printer, Washington, 1982-85; editor in chief Jour. Government Information, N.Y.C., 1984—. Author (book) United States Government Publications Catalogs, 1981, 1988, Guide to the Presidential Advisory Commissions 1973-84, 1987; co-editor (book) Government Documents and Microforms, 1984; contbr. articles to profl. jours. Mem. ALA (dir.-at-large div. Reference & Adult Svcs. 1989-92), Assn. for Bibliography of History, Soc. for History in Fed. Govt. Home: 160 Gooseberry Dr Reno NV 89523-9610 Office: U Nev MS 322 Reno NV 89557

ZINK, STEVEN MARTIN, software engineer; b. Bronx, N.Y., May 30, 1946; s. Robert and Florence Blanche (Katz) Z. BS in Math. and Humanities, MIT, 1968. Instr. math. and physics Maine Maritime Acad., Castine, 1968-69; math. tchr. Sharon (Mass.) Jr. High Sch., 1969-70; systems analyst John Hancock Ins., Boston, 1970-73; software devel. engr. Control Data, Sunnyvale, Calif., 1973-75, Hewlett Packard, Cupertino, Calif., 1975-90; sr. software devel. engr. Tandem Computers, Cupertino, 1990-92, mgr. quality initiatives, 1992-93; software engring. cons. Silicon Graphics, Mountain View, Calif., 1994—; software cons. Systems Ptnrs., Orinda, Calif, 1994; librettist (with composer Randol Bass) In Praise of Music, 1994; coun. mem. comm. South Bay Eckankar, Cupertino, 1990-93. Author: (poetry) At Days End, 1994. Facilitator, vol. ARIS Project, Campbell, Calif., 1987-92; team capt. Walk for AIDS, Cupertino, 1992; pres., treas. Eastridge Townhouse Homeowners Assn., San Jose, Calif., 1979-80. Mem. Coun. for Continuous Improvement, Barbary Coast Boating Club, Alumni Assn. MIT, Alumni Assn. Bronx High Sch., Calif. Satsang Soc. Inc. (communications dir. 1992-93). Mem. Green Party. Mem. Eckist Ch. Home: 24 Trillium Ln San Carlos CA 94070-1525

ZINKE, SALLY GRIFFITHS, geophysicist, consultant; b. St. Louis, Aug. 30, 1951; d. John William II and Ada Dorothy (Agnew) Griffiths; m. Val Philip Zinke, June 23, 1984; 1 child, Allyson Marie. BS in Geology and Geophysics, U. Wis., 1973; MS in Geophysics, Pa. State U., 1979; MBA, U. Denver, 1987. Registered profl. geologist, Wyo. Sr. exploration geologist Mobil Oil Corp., Denver, 1973-80, sr. prodn. geologist, 1980-81; regional geophysicist Pan Can. Petroleum Co., Denver, 1981-89; rsch. assoc. Bureau Econ. Geology U. Tex., Austin, 1989-90; sr. dist. geophysicist Pacific Enterprises Oil Co., Denver, 1990-91; ind. geophys. cons. Denver, 1991—. Bd. dirs. Parent's Day Out, Denver, 1994—. Mem. Am. Assn. Petroleum Geologists (del. 1980—), Denver Geophys. Soc. (treas. 1987, v.p. 1988, pres. 1989), Denver Internat. Petroleum Assn., Rocky Mountain Assn. Geologists, Soc. Exploration Geophysicists (sec., treas. 1992-93, fin. com. 1992-94, chmn. policy and procedures com. 1994, chmn. profl. affairs com. 1990-92, coun. 1988-91, constitution and bylaws com. 1989-92). Home and Office: 3060 Oak St Denver CO 80215-7176

ZINSER, ELISABETH ANN, university president; b. Meadville, Pa., Feb. 20, 1940; d. Merle and Fae Zinser. BS, Stanford U., 1964; MS, U. Calif., San Francisco, 1966, MIT, 1982; PhD, U. Calif., Berkeley, 1972. Nurse VA Hosp., Palo Alto, Calif., 1964-65, San Francisco, 1969-70; instr. Sch. Nursing U. Calif., San Francisco, 1966-69; pre-doctoral fellow Nat. Inst. Health, Edn. and Welfare, 1971-72; adminstr. Sch. Medicine U. Wash., Seattle, 1972-75, Coun. Higher Edn., State of Ky., 1975-77; prof., dean. Coll. Nursing U. N.D., Grand Forks, 1977-83; vice chancellor acad. affairs U. N.C., Greensboro, 1983-89; pres. Gallaudet U., Washington, 1988, U. Idaho, Moscow, 1989—; cons. Ctr. Leadership Devel. Am. Coun. Edn., Washington, Boeing Aircraft Co., Seattle, Nat. Workshop Acad. Deans, Higher Edn. Exec. Assocs., Denver, Bush Found., St. Paul; chmn. commn. on outreach and tech. transfer Nat. Assn. State Univs. and Land Grant Colls., 1993—, mem. bd. dirs., 1994—. Author: (with others) Contemporary Issues in Higher Education, 1985, Higher Education Research, 1988; co-author: Nurse: A Changing Word in a Changing World, 1982. Bd. dirs. Humana Hosp., Greensboro, 1986-88; v.p., bd. dirs. Ea. Music Festival, Greensboro, 1987-89; trustee N.C. Coun. Econ. Edn., 1985-89, Greensboro Day Sch., 1987-89. Leadership fellow Bush Found., 1981-82. Mem. Am. Assn. Higher Edn., Assn. Am. Colls. (Coun. Liberal Learning), Am. Assn. Univ. Adminstrs., AAUP, AAUW, Rotary, Pi Lambda Theta, Sigma Theta Tau. Home: 1026 Nez Perce Dr Moscow ID 83843-4138 Office: U Idaho Office of the President Moscow ID 83843*

ZIOMEK, STEPHEN PHILLIP, business owner; b. East Chicago, Ind., Nov. 8, 1950; s. John Joseph and Marian Louise Ziomek; m. Jeannine Marie Mayone, Feb. 13, 1993; 1 child, Alexander Stephen. BS, U.S. Coast Guard Acad., 1972; postgrad., U. So. Calif., 1976. Lic. real estate broker, Ariz.; cert. flight instr., Calif. Aviation safety officer, rescue pilot U.S. Coast Guard, Chgo. and San Francisco, 1973-82; pres., owner Personal Dynamics, Scottsdale, Ariz., 1982-83; v.p. investments Prudential Securities, Inc., Scottsdale, 1983-94; co-founder, chief oper. officer FAS-HOTLINE, Inc., Scottsdale, 1989—; founder, pres. Scottsdale Bus. Assn., 1986-87; founder, exec. dir. Scottsdale Exec. Alliance, 1987-88; pres. Maricopa Bus. Alliance, Phoenix, 1985-86. Alpine skiing sponsor and fund raiser Ariz. Spl. Olympics Winter Games, Scottsdale, 1992-94. Lt. USCG, 1972-82. Decorated Air medal, USCG commendation medal; recipient numerous awards. Mem. Scottsdale C. of C., Far West Ski Assn. (trustee 1994-95, Man of Yr. 1992-93), Ariz. Ski Coun. (founder, pres. 1991-93), Scottsdale Area Sea and Ski Club (founder, pres. 1986-89), U.S. Coast Guard Acad. Alumni Assn., Harley Owners Group, Ancient Order of the Pterodactyl. Republican. Roman Catholic.

ZISLIS, PAUL MARTIN, software engineering executive; b. Chgo., Feb. 8, 1948; s. Harold Solomon and Beatrice (Bossen) Z.; m. Sharon Margo Kaufmann, June 8, 1969; children: Daniel, Benjamin, Rachel. BS in Computer Sci., U. Ill., 1969; SM in Info. Sci., U. Chgo., 1971; PhD in Computer Sci., Purdue U., 1974. Mem. tech. staff AT&T Bell Labs., Naperville, Ill., 1969-72, 74-77; supr. data network devel. AT&T Bell Labs., Holmdel, N.J., 1977-81, dept. head data network architecture, 1981-82; dept. head advanced software tech. AT&T Bell Labs., Naperville, 1982-90; dir. software engring. Ericsson Raynet Corp., Menlo Park, Calif., 1990-92, dir. product validation, 1993—. Contbr. articles to profl. jours. Grad. fellow IBM, 1973-74. Mem. IEEE Computer Soc., Assn. for Computing Machinery, Phi Beta Kappa. Office: Ericsson Raynet 155 Constitution Dr Menlo Park CA 94025-1106

ZITO, MICHAEL ANTHONY, advertising and graphics design typesetting company owner; b. San Diego, Feb. 25, 1957; s. Richard and Margaret Jane (Greggs) Z. Student, El Paso Community Coll., 1976-77, Grossmont Coll., 1977-78. Emergency med. technician E&E Ambulance Svc., Colorado Springs, Colo., 1972-73; psychiat. technician Alvarado Hosp., San Diego, 1975-78; surg. technician, orderly Eisenhower Osteopathic Hosp., Colorado Springs, 1973-75; mktg. mgr. Calif. Dept. Forestry Fire Fighters, San Diego, 1978-79; mktg. rep. Mort Fin. Svcs., San Diego, 1980-81, Mil.-Civil Svc. Yellow Pages, San Diego, 1983-84; nuclear technician San Onofre (Calif.) Nuclear Power Plant, 1982-83; mktg. rep. Stas. XPRS, XHRM, KMLO, 1982-84; pres. Discount Yellow Pages, San Diego, 1984-87, 3-D Advt. Graphics and Typesetting Co., San Diego, 1987—, Anthony Industries and Am. Fin. Svcs., San Diego, 1990—; nat. coord. Robbins Rsch. Internat., La Jolla, Calif., 1993-94. Actor TV documentary and movies, San Diego, 1987 (award Nat. Movie Arts Festival and Movies 1988). Instr. YMCA/USO, 1971-72. Recipient award Nat. Movie Arts Festival, 1988. Roman Catholic.

ZIVELONGHI, KURT DANIEL, artist; b. Barstow, Calif., Oct. 3, 1960; s. Vincent Otto and Beverly Dean (Schwind) Z. Student, Pasadena (Calif.) City Coll., 1984-85; BFA, Art Ctr. Coll. of Design, 1993. Mgr. Foothill Airplane Washing Svc., Claremont, Calif., 1980-82; sales rep. Valley Group Fin. Svc., Claremont, 1986-88; loan rep. Pacific Group Funding, Claremont, 1989-90; self employed fine artist Alhambra, Calif., 1990—. One man show at Coll. of Design Art Ctr., Pasadena, 1993, two man show at Flux Gallery, Eagle Rock, Calif., 1993, group show at Art Students League, N.Y.C., 1989; represented by Gallery 57, Fullerton, Calif. Mem. Ctr. for the study of Popluar Culture, Studio City, Calif., 1994. Mem. Am. Soc. of Portrait Artists.

ZLAKET, THOMAS, state judge. State justice Ariz. Supreme Ct. Mem. ABA, State Bar Ariz. (pres.). Office: Office of Supreme Ct 1501 W Washington St Phoenix AZ 85007-3231*

ZOBEL, JAN ARLEEN, tax consultant; b. San Francisco, Feb. 8, 1947; d. Jerome Fremont and Louise Maxine (Purwin) Z. BA, Whittier Coll., 1968; MA, U. Chgo., 1970. Tchr. Chgo. Pub. Schs., 1969-70, San Francisco Pub. Schs., 1971-78; editor, pub. People's Yellow Pages, San Francisco, 1971-81; pvt. practice tax cons. San Francisco, 1978—; tchr. community coll. dist., San Francisco, 1986-91; tax lectr. U. Hawaii, 1989—, U. Calif., San Francisco State U., Marin C.C. Editor: People's Yellow Pages, 1971-81 (cert. of honor San Francisco Bd. Suprs. 1974), Where The Child Things Are, 1977-80. Com. mem. Bay Area Career Women's Fund. Named Acct. Advocate of Yr. SBA, 1987; presented with Key to Buffalo, 1970. Mem. Nat. Assn. Enrolled Agts., Calif. Assn. Enrolled Agts., Nat. Assn. Tax Preparers, Bay Area Career Women. Home: 3045 Holyrood Dr Oakland CA 94611-2541 Office: 1197 Valencia St San Francisco CA 94110-3026

ZOBEL, LOUISE PURWIN, author, educator, lecturer, writing consultant; b. Laredo, Tex., Jan. 10, 1922; d. Leo Max and Ethel Catherine (Levy) Purwin; m. Jerome Fremont Zobel, Nov. 14, 1943; children: Lenore Zobel Harris, Janice A., Robert E., Audrey Zobel Dollinger. BA cum laude, Stanford U., 1943, MA, 1976. Cert. adult edn. and community coll. tchr., Calif. Freelance mag. writer and author Palo Alto, Calif., 1942—; writer, editor, broadcastor UP Bur., San Francisco, 1943; lectr. on writing, history, travel No. Calif., 1964—; lectr., educator U. Calif. campuses, other colls. and univs., 1969—; writing cons. to pvt. clients, 1969—; editorial asst. Assn. Coll. Unions Internat., Palo Alto, 1972-73; acting asst. prof. journalism San Jose State U., 1976; keynote speaker, seminar leader, prin. speaker at nat. confs. Author: (books) The Travel Writer's Handbook, 1980, (paperback), 1982, 83, 84, 85, rev. edit., 1992; author, narrator (90 minute cassette) Let's Have Fun in Japan, 1982; contbr. articles to anthologies, nat. mags. and newspapers; writer advertorials. Bd. dirs., publicity chair Friends of Palo Alto Libr., 1985—; officer Santa Clara County Med. Aux., Esther Clark Aux., others; past pres. PTA. Recipient award for excellence in journalism Sigma Delta Chi, 1943, awards Writers Digest, 1967-75, 94, Armed Forces Writers League, 1972, Nat. Writers Club, 1976. Mem. Am. Soc. Journalists and Authors, Travel Journalists Guild, Internat. Food, Wine and Travel Writers Assn., Pacific Asia Travel Assn., Calif. Writers Club (v.p. 1988-89), AAUW (v.p. 1955-57, Nat. writing award 1969), Stanford Alumni Assn., Phi Beta Kappa. Home and Office: 23350 Sereno Ct Unit 30 Cupertino CA 95014-6543

ZOBELL, GREGORY GRANT, hospital administrator; b. Billings, Mont., Jan. 29, 1950; s. Rex Scholes and Bernice (Gunnell) Z.; m. Suzanne Taylor, Apr. 19, 1975; children: Gregory Grant Jr., Jeff, Natalie, Stephanie, Joshua. BS, Brigham Young U., 1975; MS, Trinity U., San Antonio, 1979. CEO, Kino Cmty. Hosp., Tucson, 1990-92; assoc. adminstr. Good Samaritan Hosp., Phoenix, 1980-89, 93—. Fellow Am. Coll. Healthcare Execs. Mem. LDS Ch. Home: 1704 E Enrose St Mesa AZ 85203 Office: Good Samaritan Reg Med Ctr 1111 E Mcdowell Rd Phoenix AZ 85006-2612

ZOBELL, KARL, lawyer; b. La Jolla, Calif., Jan. 9, 1932; s. Claude E. and Margaret (Harding) ZoB.; m. Barbara Arth, Nov. 22, 1968; children: Bonnie, Elizabeth, Karen, Claude, Mary. Student, Utah State U., 1949-51, Columbia U., 1951-52; AB, Columbia U., 1953, student of law, 1952-54; JD, Stanford U., 1958. Bar: Calif., 1959. Assoc., lawyer Gray, Cary, Ames and Frye, San Diego, 1959-64, ptnr., lawyer, 1964—, chmn., 1989-90; dir., officer San Diego Digital Multimedia Assn., San Diego, 1994; bd. dirs., founder La Jolla (Calif.) Bank and Trust Co.; v.p. bd. dirs. Geisel-Seuss Enterprises, Inc. Trustee La Jolla Town Coun., 1962-87, chmn. bd. trustees, 1967-68, pres. 1976-77, 80-81, v.p., 1986-87; trustee La Jollans Inc., 1964-80, founder, 1964, pres. 1965-68, 73-76, 78-79, Dr. Seuss Found., 1992—, James C. Copley Charitable Found., 1992—; mem. charter rev. com. City San Diego, 1968, 73; chmn. City of San Diego Planning Commn., 1988-93; trustee La Jolla Mus. Art, 1964-72, San Diego Mus. Contemporary Art, 1990-92; pres. 1967-70, bd. dirs Scripps Meml. Hosp. Found., 1980-84, bd. overseers, Stanford Law Sch., 1977-80, U. Calif., San Diego, 1974-76. Served to lt. USCG, 1954-57. Fellow Am. Coll. Trust and Estate Counsel; mem. ABA, Calif. Bar, La Jolla Beach and Volleyball Club (pres. 1982—), La Jolla Beach and Tennis Club, Lambda Alpha. Republican. Home: Po Box 1 555 Coast Walk La Jolla CA 92037-3731 Office: Gray Cary Ames & Frye 1200 Prospect St Ste 575 La Jolla CA 92037-3608

ZODL, JOSEPH ARTHUR, international trade executive, consultant; b. Hackensack, N.J., Aug. 13, 1948; s. Joseph Frank and Edna Josephine (Hokanson) Z. BA in Polit. Sci., Fordham Coll., 1970; MA in Polit. Sci., New Sch. for Social Rsch., N.Y.C., 1991. Lic. customs broker U.S. Treasury Dept. Export mgr. Savage Universal Corp., Tempe, Ariz., 1984-93; corp. transp. mgr. Nat. Media Corp., Phoenix, 1993—; adj. instr. internat. bus. Rio Salado C.C., 1989—. Author: Export-Import: Everything You and Your Company Need To Know To Compete in World Markets, 1992, rev., 1995; contbr. articles to profl. jours. Vice chmn. Legis. Dist. 20 Dems., 1978-80, chmn., 1980-82; mem. Ariz. State Dem. Com., 1978-89; cand. Ariz. Ho. Reps., 1986. Named Eagle Scout, Boy Scouts Am., 1966. Mem. Am. Polit. Sci. Assn., Ariz. World Trade Ctr., Internat. Transp. Mgmt. Assn. (dir. 1990-91), Phoenix Traffic Club, Phoenix Customs Brokers Assn., Delta Nu Alpha (pres. 1980-81, Ariz. Transp. Man of Yr. 1980), Alpha Phi Omega. Roman Catholic.

ZOECKLER, LINDA KAY, librarian art historian; b. Chgo., Ill., Dec. 11, 1946; d. Harold David and Catherine (Welch) Davies; m. John Carr Zoeckler, Mar. 17, 1967. BA in Art History cum laude, U. Calif., Riverside, 1970, M in Art History, 1976; M in Lib. and Info. Sci., UCLA, 1985. Art cataloguer, bibliographer U. Calif., Riverside, 1969-81; head of lib. Otis Art Inst., L.A., 1981-83; curator of collections Edward Dean Mus., Cherry Valley, Calif., 1984-85; head tech. info. ctr. Singer Librascope Corp., Glendale, Calif., 1985-88; head art reference lib. Huntington Lib. Art Collections and Bot. Gardens, San Marino, Calif., 1988—; adj. prof. art Golden West Coll., Huntington Beach., Calif., 1989—; vice chair Art Librs. Soc. N.Am., So. Calif. chpt., 1993-94; mem. rsch. com. Art Librs. Soc.-N.Am., 1993-94. Contrb. article to profl. jour. Honorable mention Gerd Muehsam award ARLIS/NA, 1985. Mem. Coll. Art Assn. Episcopalian. Home: 23227 Forest Canyon Dr Diamond Bar CA 91765 Office: Huntington Lib Art Collections Bot Gardens 1151 Oxford Rd San Marino CA 91108

ZOELLNER, ROBERT WILLIAM, chemistry educator; b. Marshfield, Wis., May 30, 1956; s. Willard Rudolph and Marie Martha (Prihoda) Z.; m. Barbara Moore, Feb. 5, 1983; children: Joan Moore, Thaddeus Barak. BS, St. Norbert Coll., De Pere, Wis., 1978; PhD, Kans. State U., 1983. Postdoctoral assoc. Cornell U., Ithaca, N.Y., 1983-84; vis. scientist U. Aix-Marseille (France) III, 1984-85; asst. prof. No. Ariz. U., Flagstaff, 1986-92, assoc. prof., 1992—; sabbatical assoc. Istituto per lo Studio della Stereochimica Consiglio Nazionale delle Ricerche, 1994-95. Mem. AAAS, AAUP, Am. Chem. Soc., Internat. Coun. on Main Group Chemistry, N.Y. Acad. Sci., N.D. Acad. Sci., Wis. Acad. Sci., Arts and Letters, Sigma Xi, Alpha Chi Sigma, Phi Lambda Upsilon. Office: No Ariz U PO Box 5698 Flagstaff AZ 86011

ZOHNER, STEVEN K., environmental scientist; b. Driggs, Idaho, June 8, 1953; s. LaVar Orin and Shirley Elizabeth (Kempton) Z.; m. Marivene Amelia List, Apr. 26, 1977; children: Suzanne, Nathan, Julie, Audrey. AS with high honors, Ricks Coll., 1976; BSmagna cum laude, Brigham Young U., 1978, student, 1978-79, MS magna cum laude, 1982; grad., Dept. Energy/Westinghouse Sch. Environ. Excellence, Idaho, 1992. Rsch. chemist Brigham Young U., Provo, Utah, 1978-81; plant chemist Martin Marietta, Lemington, Utah, 1981-82; engr. prodn. dept. Exxon Nuclear Idaho, Idaho Falls, 1982-85; sr. engr. tech. dept. Westinghouse Idaho Nuclear, Idaho Falls, 1985-91, sr. scientist environ. dept., 1991-94; sr. scientist environ. safety & health dept. Lockheed Idaho Tech. Co., Idaho Falls, 1994—; staff scientist environ. characterization Lockheed Martin Idaho Technologies, 1994—; cons. EG&G Idaho, Idaho Falls, 1986, Fernald Nuclear Facility, Cin., 1991. Inventor decontamination solution (Recognition award 1990). Lay minister Ch. Jesus Christ Latter Day Sts., Stockholm, 1972-74, ward clerk, 1985—; active Boy Scouts Am., Idaho Falls, 1982—, PTO, Idaho Falls, 1986—. Mem. Am. Chem. Soc., Phi Kappa Phi. Republican. Home: 1042 Grizzly Ave Idaho Falls ID 83402-3822 Office: Lockheed Idaho Tech Co MS-3202, MS-5117 1955 Fremont Ave Idaho Falls ID 83404

ZOLLINGER, THOMAS TENNANT, lawyer; b. Louisville, Feb. 13, 1945; s. Robert William and Betty Beatrice (Benkert) Z.; m. Anne Marie Green, April 9, 1993. B.S., Murray State U., 1969; J.D., U. Wyo., 1972. Bar: Wyo. 1972, U.S. Dist. Ct. Wyo. 1972, U.S. Ct. Appeals (10th cir.) 1979. Sole practice, Lander, Wyo., 1972-74, Rock Springs, Wyo., 1975—; prosecuting atty. Sweetwater County, 1987-91; surpervising atty. territorial pub. defender St. Croix, U.S. Virgin Island, 1993; sr. asst. pub. defender Wyo., Gillette, Wyo., 1994—. commr. Wyo. State Bar, Cheyenne, 1983-85. Chmn., Sweetwater County central com. Republican Party, 1975-76, state committeeman, 1977-80, 88-91; bd. dirs. S.W. Wyo. Alcohol Rehab. Assn., 1981-87. Mem. Assn. Trial Lawyers Am., ABA, Am. Judicature Soc. Methodist. Lodges: Elks, Eagles. Home: 18 W Sage St Pine Haven WY 82721-9764 Office: 500 S Gillette Ave Gillette WY 82716

ZOLOTH-DORFMAN, LAURIE SUSAN, bioethicist; b. L.A., June 15, 1950; d. Arthur and Helen (Cohen) Zoloth; m. Henry Levy (div. June 1980); m. Daniel Zoloth Dorfman, Aug. 17, 1986; children: Matthew, Noah, Benjamin, Joshua, Sarah. BA cum laude, U. Calif., Berkeley, 1974; BSN, U. State of N.Y., 1982; MA in English, San Francisco State U., 1991; MA in Theology and Jewish Studies, PhD, Grad. Theol. Union, 1993. Instr. adult edn. in Jewish studies Lehrahaus Judaica, 1988-93; cons. ethicist Nat. Kaiser Permanente HMO, Berkeley, Calif., 1987—; asst. prof. Calif. State U., Sonoma, summer, 1994; instr. bioethics program Grad. Theol. Union/Stanford U., spring, 1994, lectr. clin. bioethics program, 1991-92; instr. ethics Chapman Coll., spring, 1989; teaching asst. Grad. Theol. Union, spring. 1988, 91. Co-author: The Ethics Proctic & Consultation Firm. Jewish. Home and Office: 1104 Euclid Ave Berkeley CA 94708-1603

ZONGOLOWICZ, HELEN MICHAELINE, education and psychology educator; b. Kenosha, Wis., July 22, 1936; d. Edmund S. and Helen (Ostrowski) Z.; EdB, Dominican Coll., 1966; MA, Cardinal Stritch Coll., 1973; EdD, U. No. Colo., 1977. Tchr. elem. schs. Kenosha, 1956-58, Center Line, Mich., 1958-59, Taft, Calif., 1960-61, Lake Wales, Fla., 1962-63, Albuquerque, 1963-65; tchr., asst. prin. St. Mary's Sch., Taft, 1965-69; asst. sch. supt. Diocese of Fresno, Calif., 1969-70; tchr. primary grades Greasewood Boarding Sch., Ganado, Ariz., 1970-72, coord. spl. projects, 1972-75, liaison to parent adv. coun., 1972-75, tchr. supr., 1972-76; ednl. specialist Ft. Defiance Agy., Navajo Area, Ariz., 1974-75, ednl. diagnostician, 1979-80; asst. prof. Auburn (Ala.) U., 1977-79; asst. prof. U. N.Mex.-Gallup, 1981-94, prof. edn. and psychology, 1994—, dir. child care ctr.; prin. Chuska Sch., 1980-93; chair dept. psychology/edn. CDA dir.; vis. prof. U. Colo., 1976; mem. N.Mex. State Articulation Task Force. Recipient Spl. Achievement award U.S. Dept. Interior, 1971, 73, Points of Light award, 1990, Superior Performance award, 1982, Achievement award Navajo Nation, 1993; named Prin. of Yr. Bur. of Indian Affairs, 1990; named Prin. of Yr. Navajo Area Sch. Bd. Assn., 1991. Mem. AAUW, AAUP, Nat. Assn. Edn. of Young Children, Nat. Staff Devel. Coun., Am. Assn. Mental Deficiency, Assn. for Supervision and Curriculum Devel., Coun. for Exceptional Children, Coun. for Basic Edn., Am. Ednl. Rsch. Assn., NAFE, Internat. Reading Assn., Assn. for Children with Learning Disabilities Nat. Coun. Tchrs. of English., Assn. Childhood Edn. Internat., Navajo Nation North Cen. Assn. (mem. exec. bd.), Kappa Delta Pi, Phi Delta Kappa. Address: 604 Mckee Dr Gallup NM 87301-4830

ZOOK, KAY MARIE, nursing administrator; b. O'Neill, Nebr.; d. Roy W. and Elsie B. Carroll; m. Larry A. Zook, Aug. 17, 1957; children: David, Debra Zook Wickizer. Diploma, Mary Lanning Sch. Nursing, Hastings, Nebr., 1955; BS, Hastings Coll., 1957; MS, St. Francis Coll., Joliet, Ill., 1984. RN, Nebr., Minn., Colo. Instr. nursing Mary Lanning Meml. Hosp., Hastings; instr. med.-surg. nursing Bryan Meml. Hosp., Lincoln, Nebr.; asst. DON Lincoln Gen. Hosp.; charge nurse St. Luke's Hosp., Duluth, Minn.; edn. coord. Rose Med. Ctr., Denver; v.p. patient svcs. St. Joseph Hosp., Denver, 1973—. Author: (bulletin) A New Threat to Health Care Delivery: The Nursing Shortage, 1988. Active Denver Leadership Forum, 1987. Fellow The Wharton Sch. U. Pa., Phila., 1985. Mem. Am. Orgn. Nurse Execs., Colo. Soc. Nurse Execs., Colo. League Nursing. Office: St Joseph Hosp 1835 Franklin St Denver CO 80218-1126

ZOOK, WAYNE BOWMAN, physician; b. Cresco, Iowa, Oct. 2, 1927; s. Ray Edward and Mildred Bernice (Bowman) Z.; m. Evelyn Viola Johnson, June 11, 1950; children: Teresa Kay, Kim Wayne, Dale Johnson. BA, Manchester Coll., 1949; MD, Ind. U., 1953. Physician Wenatchee (Wash.) Family Practice, 1956—. Capt. USAF, 1953-56. Fellow Am. Acad. Family Physicians (del.); mem. AMA, Rotary (pres.), Wenatchee Area C. of C. (pres. 1988). Mem. Ch. of the Brethren. Home: 201 Elliott Ave S Apt 16 Wenatchee WA 98801-6325 Office: Wenatchee Family Practice 707 N Emerson Ave Wenatchee WA 98801-2032

ZORICH, ROBERT SAM, semiconductor engineer; b. Montgomery, Ala., Oct. 14, 1957; s. Sam and Mary Jeanne (Hestand) Z.; m. Cathleen Mary Coles, Oct. 19, 1985; children: Michelle, Scott. BS in Physics, U. Idaho, 1979. Process engr. Nat. Semiconductor, Salt Lake City, 1980-83; product engr., engring. data processing mgr. Intel Corp., Santa Clara, Calif., 1983-85; sr. process engr. LSI Logic Corp., Santa Clara, 1985-87; sr. process engr. supr. Photolytics, Inc., Santa Clara, 1987-88; staff applications engr. Nanometrics, Corp., Sunnyvale, 1988-90; product mgr. Schumacher, 1991—; chief exec. officer, programmer ACRO Tech., Sunnyvale, Calif., 1983—.

Author: (software) Scicalc Math Utilities, 1985, (book) Handbook of Quality Integrated Circuit Manufacturing, 1991; contbr. articles to profl. jours. Mem. AAAS, Am. Phys. Soc., Nat. Space Soc., The Planetary Soc., Nature Conservancy, Union Concerned Scientists. Democrat. Home: 7051 Snapdragon Carlsbad CA 92009-8353

ZORNES, MILFORD, artist; b. Camargo, Okla., Jan. 25, 1908; s. James Francis and Clara Delphine (Lindsay) Z.; m. Gloria Codd, 1935; 1 son, Franz Milford; m. Patricia Mary Palmer, Nov. 8, 1942; 1 dau., Maria Patricia. Student, Otis Art Inst., Los Angeles, 1929, Pomona Coll., 1930-34. Instr. art Pomona Coll., 1946-50; art dir. Vortox and Padua Hills Theatre, Claremont, 1954-66. Exhibited, Calif. Watercolor Soc., Met. Mus., Am. Watercolor Soc., Corcoran Gallery, Bklyn. Mus., Denver Mus., Cleve. Mus., L.A. Mus., Brooks Gallery, London, Bombay Art Assn., Chgo. Art Inst., Butler Mus., Gallery Modern Masters, Washington, Santa Barbara (Calif.) Mus., Cin. Mus., Laguna (Calif.) Art Gallery, Oklahoma City Mus., Springville (Utah) Mus.; represented in permanent collections at L.A. Mus., White House Collection, Met. Mus., Pentagon Bldg., Butler Mus., UCLA, Nat. Acad., San Diego Mus., L.A. County Fair, Home Savs. and Loan Assn., L.A., Corcoran Gallery, Washington; mem. art com., Nat. Orange Show, San Bernardino, Calif., 1963-65; author: A Journey to Nicaragua, 1977, The California Style: California Watercolor Artists, 1925-1955, 1985; subject of book by Gordon McClelland: Milford Zornes, Hillcrest Press, 1991. Served with U.S. Army, 1943-45, CBI. RecipientPaul Prescott Barrow award Pomona Coll., 1987, David Prescott Burrows award, 1991, A Most Disting. Citizen award So. Utah State Coll., 1988, Am. Artist Achievement award Am. Artist Mag., 1994. Mem. NAD, Am. Watercolor Soc., Southwestern Watercolor Soc., Watercolor West, Nat. Watercolor Soc., Utah Watercolor Soc. Address: PO Box 176 Orderville UT 84758-0176

ZOTTNICK, LISA ISOBEL, educational therapist; b. Sacramento, Calif., May 9, 1958; d. James T. and Rhoda (VanAllen) McElree. BS, Calvary Bible Coll., 1980; MS, Clayton U., 1991. Cert. ednl. therapist, Calif. Learning disabilities program tchr. New Vistas Christian Sch., Pleasant Hill, Calif., 1981-83; jr. high sch. tchr. Bethel Christian Acad., El Sobrante, Calif., 1983-85; jr. high learning disabilities tchr. Anchor Acad., Pleasant Hill, 1985-91; adminstr. sch.-based day treatment Clipper Acad. for Pvt. Study, Concord, Calif., 1991; pvt. practice ednl. therapist Lifeline Testing and Counseling Svcs., Pleasant Hill, 1986—; speaker at seminars, workshops and convs. in field. Author: Understanding A.D.D., 1992. Mem. Calif. Adv. Bd. on Attention Deficit Disorders, Sacramento, 1992—, chair advocacy and info. com. Mem. Assn. Ednl. Therapists, Learning Disabilities Assn., Children and Adults with Attention Deficit Disorders (coord. Contra Costa County chpt. 1991-94), Orton Dyslexia Soc. Office: Lifeline Testing and Counseling Svcs 140 Gregory Ln Ste 250 Pleasant Hill CA 94523-3357

ZUBER, NORMA KEEN, career counselor, educator; b. Iuka, Miss., Sept. 27, 1934; d. William Harrington and Mary (Hebert) Keen; m. William Frederick Zuber, Sept. 14, 1958; children: William Frederick Jr., Michael, Kimberly, Karen. BS in Nursing, U. Southwestern La., 1956; MS in Counselling, Calif. Luth. U., 1984. Nat. cert. counselor, nat. cert. career counselor. Intensive care nurse Ochsner Found. Hosp., New Orleans, 1956-59; career devel. counselor BFC Counseling Ctr., Ventura, Calif., 1984-87; founder, prin., counselor Career & Life Planning-Norma Zuber & Assocs., Ventura, 1987—; instr. adult continuing edn. Ventura C.C., 1987—; instr. Calif. State U., Northridge, 1988-89; instr. U. Calif. Santa Barbara, Antioch U.; mem. adv. coun. on tchr. edn. Calif. Luth. U., Thousand Oaks, 1984-87; mem. adv. bd. for development of profl. career counseling cert. program U. Calif., San Diego, 1991—. Co-author: The Nuts and Bolts of Career Counseling: Setting Up and Succeeding in Private Practice, 1992. Chmn. bd. dirs. women's ministries Missionary Ch., Ventura, 1987-90. Recipient profl. contbn. award H.B. McDaniel Found.-Stanford U. Sch. Edn., 1988, Govt. Rels. Com. Cert. of Appreciation, Am. Assn. for Counseling and Devel. Mem. NAFE, ACA, Nat. Career Devel. Assn., Calif. Assn. Couseling and Devel. (chmn. legis. task force 1987-89, So. Calif. coord. area cons. for Calif. Career Devel. Assn. 1990, Jim Saum govt. rels. award 1989), Internat. Platform Assn., Nat. Career Devel. Assn. (western regional trustee 19095—), Calif. Career Devel. Assn. (bd. dirs. 1985-91, membership dir. 1991-92, pres. 1992-93, Leadership and Professionaliam award 1988, 89), Calif. Career Conf. (program chair 1993), Ventura County Profl. Women's Network (dir. membership 1990-91), Calif. Registry Profl. Counselors and Paraprofls. (vice chmn. bd. dirs. 1990—). Republican. Home: 927 Sentinel Ct Ventura CA 93003-1202 Office: Career and Life Planning Norma Zuber and Assocs 3585 Maple St Ste 237 Ventura CA 93003-3508

ZUBERI, SHAKIR H., management consultant; b. Aligarh, India, July 1, 1940; came to U.S., 1970; s. Sabir Husain and Niaz Bano Zuberi; m. Shaila K., Mar. 14, 1972; children: Sana, Sahar. BS in Geology with honors, U. Sind, Hyderabad, Pakistan, 1962; MS in Internat. Bus., MBA, St. Mary's Coll., Moraga, Calif., 1978. Registered geologist, Calif.; cert. project mgmt. profl. Jr. geologist Water and Power Devel. Authority, Lahore, Pakistan, 1962-65; geologist Khanpur (Pakistan) Dam Project, 1966-69; sr. project geologist Woodward-Clyde Cons., San Francisco, 1970-77, program mgr., 1978-89; project mgr. Davy Internat., 1990-92; mgr. environ. restoration projects ICF Kaiser Hanford Co., Richland, Wash., 1993—. State advisor U.S. Congl. Adv. Bd., Washington, 1985; constrn. panel mem. Am. Arbitration Assn., N.Y.C., 1986. Mem. Project Mgmt. Inst. (chmn. contract and procurement com. 1985-87, mem. mktg., edn. coms., 1986—), Am. Security Council, Internat. Strategic Studies Assn., Am. Def. Preparedness Assn., Nat. Contracts Mgmt. Assn. Moslem. Home: 178 Llandwood Ct Richland WA 99352-9403 Office: ICF Kaiser Hanford PO Box 888 Richland WA 99352-0888

ZUBRIN, ROBERT MAYNARD, astronautical engineer, educator; b. Bklyn., Apr. 9, 1952; s. Charles and Roslyn (Fallenberg) Z.; m. Maggie Gagnon, 1991; 1 child, Rachel; stepchildren: Eliot, Sarah. BA in Math., U. Rochester, 1974; MS in Nuclear Engring., U. Washington, 1984, MS in Aero. and Astronautics, 1986, PhD in Nuclear Engring., 1992. Cert. math. and sci. tchr., N.Y., N.J., Wash. Tchr. various pub. schs., N.Y., 1974-83; grad. research assoc. Los Alamos (N.Mex.) Nat. Lab., 1985; recording sec. magnetic fusion adv. com. U.S. Dept. of Energy, Washington, 1986-88; health physicist Wash. State Office of Radiation Protection, Seattle, 1987-88; sr. engr. Martin Marietta Astronautics, Denver, 1988—. Inventor Mars Direct Mission Plan, NIMF, magnetic sail, integral power and propulsion stage, nuclear salt water rocket, Mars aerial photography mission, Three Player Chess Game, 1972; author (play) Benedict Arnold, 1983; contbr. articles to profl. jours. Mem. AIAA, AAAS, Am. Nuclear Soc. (v.p. U. Wash. chpt., pub. speaker 1986-88) Am. Phys. Soc., Planetary Soc., Moutaineers Club, Wash. Yacht Club, Tau Beta Pi, Alpha Nu Sigma. Home: PO Box 273 Indian Hills CO 80454-0273

ZUCCARELLI, ANTHONY JOSEPH, molecular biology and biochemistry educator; b. N.Y.C., Aug. 11, 1944; m. Sharron Adele Ames; children: Cara N., A. Alexandar. BS in Bacteriology, Cornell U., 1966; MS in Microbiology with honors, Loma Linda U., 1968; PhD in Biophysics, Calif. Inst. Tech., 1974; postdoctoral studies in molecular biology, U. Konstanz, Fed. Republic Germany, 1974-76. Asst. prof. grad. sch. biology Loma Linda (Calif.) U., 1976-80, assoc. prof. microbiology sch. medicine, 1980-91; prof. microbiology Sch. Medicine, 1991—; assoc. mem. grad. faculty biology program Loma Linda (Calif.) U., 1982—, mem. grad. faculty microbiology program, 1982—, mem. grad. faculty biochemistry program, 1986—, asst. dir. med. scientist program, grad. coord., 1989-91, dir. med. scientist program, grad. coord., 1991—; mem. Ctr. for Molecular Biology and Gene Therapy, 1994—; grad. student rsch. mentor, chmn., mem. numerous coms. including mem. sch. medicine basic sci. course coords. com., 1987—, sch. medicine basic sci. faculty coun., 1987—, acad. rev. com., 1987—, med. scientist curriculum com., 1989—, microbiology dept. faculty search com., 1988—, grad. sch. coun. Loma Linda U.; instr. microbial genetics, molecular biology Nat. Med. Sch. Rev., 1987—; outside reviewer grant applications NSF, 1977-78, 81-82,. Contbr. articles to profl. jours. Fellow NSF, 1968-71, Am. Cancer Soc., 1974-76; trainee NIH, 1971-74; recipient First Prize for Sci. Exhibit award Macpherson Soc., 1989, Basic Sci. Student-Faculty Rsch. award, 1990, grantee Loma Linda U., 1977, 78, 79, 81, 82, 83, 85, 86, 87, 90. Mem. Am. Soc. Microbiology, Am. Soc. Advancement Sci., Am. Soc. Biotechnology, Am. Chem. Soc., N.Y. Acad. Scis., Sigma Xi. Mem. Seventh Day Adventist Ch. Office: Loma Linda U AH115 Dept Microbiol/Molec Genet Loma Linda CA 92350

ZUCKER, ALFRED JOHN, English educator, academic adminstrator; b. Hartford, Sept. 25, 1940; s. Samuel and Rose (Zucker) Z.; AA, L.A. Valley Coll., 1960; AB in English, UCLA, 1962, AB in Speech, MA in English, 1962, MA in Speech, 1963, PhD, 1966, postgrad., UCLA, U. So. Calif., Harvard U.; m. Sallie Lea Friedheim, Dec. 25, 1966; children—Mary Anne, John James, Jr., James Patrick, Patrick Jonathan, Anne-Marie Kathleen, Kathleen Mary. Lectr. English, Los Angeles City Coll., 1963-68; prof. English, philosophy, chmn. div. humanities Los Angeles Southwest Coll., 1968-72, chmn. English dept., 1972-74, asst. dean instruction, 1974—; prof. English El Camino Coll., 1985—; prof. English L.A. Valley Coll., 1989—. Mem. Los Angeles Coll. Dist. Senate, 1969—. Mem. Los Angeles Coll. Tchrs. Assn. (dir.), Calif. Jr. Coll. Assn., Calif. Tchrs. Assn., AAUP, World Affairs Coun., Mensa, Phi Beta Kappa, Phi Delta Kappa (pres. U. Calif. at Los Angeles chpt. 1966-67, v.p. 1967-68), Tau Alpha Epsilon. Lodge: KC. Contbr. articles to profl. jours. Office: 5800 Fulton Ave Van Nuys CA 91401-4062

ZUMBRUN, RONALD ARTHUR, lawyer; b. Oak Park, Ill., Dec. 12, 1934; s. Arthur Raymond and Jean (Crandall) Z.; m. Ann Hartley, July 14, 1957; children: Kevin Ronald, Richard Douglas, Heidi Ann. BA in Econs., Pomona Coll., 1957; LLB, U. Calif., Berkeley, 1961. Bar: Calif. 1962, U.S. Dist. Ct. (no. dist.) Calif. 1962, U.S. Ct. Appeals (9th cir.) 1962, U.S. Dist. Ct. (cen. dist.) Calif. 1963, U.S. Supreme Ct. 1974, U.S. Dist. Ct. (ea. dist.) Calif. 1974, U.S. Ct. Appeals (D.C. cir.) 1975, U.S. Dist. Ct. (so. dist.) Calif. 1978, U.S. Ct. Appeals (3d, 5th, 7th, 8th, 9th and 11th cirs.) 1981, D.C. 1985, U.S. Ct. Appeals (fed. cir.) 1994. Sr. trial atty. Calif. State Dept. Pub. Works, Sacramento, 1961-71; dep. dir. legal affairs Calif. State Dept. Social Welfare, Sacramento, 1971-73; spl. counsel HEW, Washington, 1973; legal dir., pres. Pacific Legal Found., Sacramento, 1973-94, pres. emeritus, 1994—; pres., mng. atty. Zumbrun, Best & Findley, Sacramento, 1991—. Mem. Gov. Reagan's Task Force on Pub. Assistance, Sacramento, 1970, exec. office of Pres. Welfare Reform Study Team, 1972, Gov. Reagan's Task Force Project: Safer Calif., 1974, Carmichael (Calif.) adv. commn. on Parks and Recreation, 1969—. Served to capt. U.S. Army, 1957-70.9. Mem. Calif. Bar Assn., Sacramento Bar Assn., Phi Alpha Delta. Republican. Episcopalian. Lodge: Rotary. Office: Zumbrun Best & Findley 2150 River Plaza Dr Ste 255 Sacramento CA 95833-3880

ZUMPF, YORDIS ETHANA, nursing supervisor; b. Oakes, N.D., Aug. 24, 1941; d. Wesley Ralph and Yordis Frederika (Olsen) Spear; m. John Paul Zumpf, Sept. 1, 1963; children: Paul, Steven, Doreen. Diploma in Nursing, St. Lukes Sch. Nursing, Fargo, N.D., 1962. Asst. clin. instr. St. Luke's Sch. Nursing, Fargo, 1962-64; staff nurse St. Mary's Hosp., Rochester, Minn., 1964; office nurse, pvt. operating rm. tech. Garberson Clinic, Miles City, Mont., 1981-94, nursing supr., 1989—; task force Robert Johnson Wood/Pew Grant Holy Rosary Hosp., Miles City, 1992-93. Mem. Cmty. Concert Series, Miles City, 1989, 90, 92, 94; chair 1st Luth. Ch. Women, Miles City, 1987-90; lay communion com. 1st Luth. Ch., 1985—. Named Outstanding Young Woman of Am., 1977. Republican. Home: RR 2 Box 3042 Miles City MT 59301-9103 Office: Garberson Clinic 2200 Box Elder St Miles City MT 59301-2843

ZUMWALT, ROGER CARL, hospital administrator; b. Eugene, Oreg., Oct. 26, 1943; s. Robert Walter and Jean Elaine (Adams) Z.; m. Sharon Marlene Ryan, Aug. 22, 1970; children: Kathryn Nicole, Timothy Robert. Student, Boise State U., 1963-65; BA, Western Oreg. State Coll., 1969; postgrad., U. Iowa, 1969-71; MA cum laude, Oreg. State U., 1973. Adminstr. Coulee Community Hosp., Grand Coulee, Wash., 1973-75, Eastmoreland Hosp., Portland, Oreg., 1975-81; hosp. surveyor Am. Osteopathic Assn., Chgo., 1977—; exec. dir. Community Hosp., Grand Junction, Colo., 1981—; speaker numerous local and nat. presentations on healthcare, hosp. mktg./success/costs, etc., 1981—; bd. dirs. Healthcare Fin. Mgmt. Assn., Portland, 1978-80; chief exec. officer Community Med. Pla., 1984—, Community Health Care Providers Orgn., 1986—, Community Hosp. Found., 1988—. Newspaper columnist, 1973-75; contbr. articles, presentations to profl. publs. Commr. Multnomah County Health Care Commn., Portland, 1978-81; health cons. Grant County Housing Authority, Grand Coulee, 1974-75; mem. park bd. City of Tigard, Oreg., 1976-78; caucus rep. Mesa County Rep. Party, Grand Junction, 1988; mem. adv. com., pres.'s office Mesa State Coll., Grand Junction, 1989; bd. dirs. Hospice of Grand Valley, Grand Junction, Colo., 1992—, mem. devel. com., 1993—. With USAF, 1961-65. Fellow Coll. Osteopathic Healthcare Execs. (bd. dirs. 1985-88, pres. 1987, examiner 1989—, Disting. Svc. award 1989); mem. Am. Osteopathic Hosp. Assn. (bd. dirs. 1987—, treas. 1992-93, 1st v.p. 1994—, 2d v.p. 1993-94, bd. mem. ex officio 1995—), Am. Osteopathic Assn., Bur. Healthcare Facilities Accreditation (v.p., 1994), Joint Commn. on Am. Healthcare Organ. (Task Force on Small and Rural Accreditation, 1994), Colo. Hosp. Assn. (bd. dirs. 1987-92), Grand Valley Hospice (bd. dirs. 1992—), Mountain States Voluntary Hosp. Assn. (bd. dirs. 1984—, exec. com. 1991—, v.p. 1993, vice chmn. bd. 1992—), Western Col. Ind. Practice Assn. (medicine mauls measles com., fin. com. 1991-92), Western Colo. Health Care Alliance (bd. dirs. 1989-94, v.p. 1992, chmn. bd. 1993, past chmn. 1994), Mesa County Mental Health Assn. (bd. dirs. 1988-89, 1991-92), Grand Junction C. of C. (bd. dirs. 1991-93), Rotary, Masons, Shriners (pres. Grand Junction club 1989, bd. dirs. El Jebel 1986-90, 1st v.p. Western Colo. club 1989). Republican. Methodist. Home: 2515 Snowmass Ct Grnd Junction CO 81503-1752 Office: Community Hosp 2021 N 12th St Grand Junction CO 81501-2980

ZUND, JOSEPH DAVID, mathematical sciences educator; b. Ft. Worth, Apr. 27, 1939; s. Emil A. and Lillian A. (Braxton) Z. BS in Math., Tex. A&M U., 1961, MS in Math., 1961; PhD in Math., U. Tex., 1964. From asst. prof. to assoc. prof. N.C. State U., Raleigh, 1965-69; assoc. prof. Va. Poly. Inst. and State U., Blacksburg, 1969-70; assoc. prof. N.Mex. State U., Las Cruces, 1970-72, prof., 1972—. Contbr. rsch. papers to profl. jours. Grantee NSF, 1967-68, USAF Phillips Lab., 1986-88, 89-94. Fellow Royal Astron. Soc., Internat. Assn. Geodesy; mem. London Math. Soc., Am. Geophys. Union, Am. Metereol. Soc., The Tensor Soc. Office: NMex State U Dept Math Scis Las Cruces NM 88003

ZUNKER, RICHARD E., insurance company executive; b. 1938. BS, U. Wis., 1964. With Employers Ins. Wausau, Wis., 1964-69, Northwestern Nat. Investors Life, 1969-75; with Safeco Life Ins. Co., Seattle, 1975—, pres., also bd. dirs. With U.S. Army, 1956-58. Office: Safeco Life Ins Co PO Box 34690 Seattle WA 98124-1690*

ZUSSY, NANCY LOUISE, librarian; b. Tampa, Fla., Mar. 4, 1947; d. John David and Patsy Ruth (Stone) Roche; m. R. Mark Allen, Dec. 20, 1986. BA in Edn., U. Fla., 1969; MLS, U. So. Fla., 1977, MS in Pub. Mgmt., 1980. Cert. librarian, Wash. Ednl. evaluator State of Ga., Atlanta, 1969-70; media specialist DeKalb County Schs., Decatur, Ga., 1970-71; researcher Ga. State Libr., Atlanta, 1971; asst. to dir. reference Clearwater (Fla.) Pub. Libr., 1972-78, dir. librs., 1978-81; dep. state libr. Wash. State Libr., Olympia, 1981-86, state libr., 1986—; chmn. Consortium Automated Librs., Olympia, 1982—; cons. various pub. librs., Wash., 1981—; exec. officer Wash. Libr. Network, 1986-90; v.p. WLN (non-profit orgn.), 1990-93. Contbr. articles to profl. jours. Treas. Thurston-Mason Community Mental Health Bd., Olympia, 1983-85, bd. dir., 1982-85; mem. race com. Seafair Hydroplane Race, Seattle, 1986—, mem. milk carton derby team, 1994—. Mem. ALA, Assn. Specialized and Coop. Libr. Agys. (legis. com. 1983-86, chmn. legis. com. 1985-87, vice chmn. state libr. agys. sect. 1985-86, chmn. state libr. agys. sect. 1986-87, chmn. govt. affairs com. Libr. Adminstrn. and Mgmt. Assn. 1986-87), Freedom to Read Found. (bd. dirs. 1987-91), Chief Officers of State Libr. Agys. (dir.-at-large 1987-90, v.p./pres. elect 1990-92, pres. 1992-94), Wash. Libr. Assn. (co-founder legis. planning com. 1982—, fed. rels. coord. 1984—), Fla. Libr. Assn. (legis. and planning com. 1978-81), Pacific N.W. Libr. Assn., Rotary, Phi Kappa Phi, Phi Beta Mu. Home: 904 E Bay Dr NE # 404B Olympia WA 98506-3970 Office: Wash State Libr PO Box 42464 Olympia WA 98504-2464

ZWACK, RAYMOND THEODORE, engineer; b. East Orange, N.J., Nov. 14, 1907; s. Anthony Theodore and Minnie Helena (Weidner) Z.; m. Louise Stark, May 25, 1937 (dec. 1985); children: Robert, David, Donna, Jeffrey. ME, Stevens Inst. Tech., 1930. Registered profl. engr., N.J. Project engr., then sr. project engr. Bendix Corp., Teterboro, N.J.; chief design engr. Walter Kidde and Co., Belleville, N.J.; staff engr. Curtiss-Wright Corp., Caldwell, N.J.; mgr. devel. engring. div. Solar Aircraft Co., Des Moines, Iowa; asst. mgr. devel. engring. div. Thiokol Chem. Corp., Brigham City, Utah; asst. mgr. vehicle systems br. N.Am. Rockwell Corp., Downey, Calif.; staff engr., mgr. polaris propulsion div. Lockheed Missiles & Space Co., Sunnyvale, Calif.; ind. cons. in aerospace field San Jose, Calif., 1968—. Patentee (17) in field. Fellow AIAA (assoc.); mem. ASME, Soc. Automotive Engrs. Home and Office: 3925 Teale Ave San Jose CA 95117-3431

ZWAHLEN, FRED CASPER, JR., journalism educator; b. Portland, Oreg., Nov. 11, 1924; s. Fred and Katherine (Meyer) Z.; m. Grace Eleanor DeMoss, June 24, 1959; children: Molly, Skip. BA, Oreg. State U., 1949; MA, Stanford U., 1952. Reporter San Francisco News, 1949-50; acting editor Stanford Alumni Rev., Palo Alto, Calif., 1950; successively instr. journalism, news bur. asst., prof. journalism, chmn. journalism dept. Oreg. State U., Corvallis, 1950-91, prof. emeritus, 1991—; Swiss tour guide, 1991—; corres. Portland Oregonian, 1950-67. Author: (with others) Handbook of Photography, 1984. Coord. E.E. Wilson Scholarship Fund, 1964—; active budget com. Corvallis Sch. Dist., 1979. Recipient Achievement award Sch. Journalism U. Oregon, 1988. Mem. Assn. for Edn. in Journalism and Mass Communications (conv. chmn. 1983, pres.' award 1988), Oreg. Newspaper Pubs. Assn. (bd. dirs. 1980-85, student loan fund named in his honor 1988), Soc. Profl. Journalists (nat. svc. citation 1988), Corvallis Country Club, Shriners, Masons, Elks, Moose, Eagles, Delta Tau Delta. Republican. Presbyterian. Home: 240 SW 7th St Corvallis OR 97333-4551 Office: Oreg State U Dept Student Activities Corvallis OR 97331

ZWEIFEL, RICHARD GEORGE, curator; b. L.A., Nov. 5, 1926; s. Harold Charles and Kathleen Marguerite (Garland) Z.; m. Frances Ann Wimsatt, July 30, 1956; children: Matthew Karl, Kenneth Paul, Ellen Katrina. B.A., UCLA, 1950; Ph.D., U. Calif. at Berkeley, 1954. Mem. staff Am. Mus. Natural History, N.Y.C., 1954-89, chmn. curator dept. herpetology, 1968-80, curator emeritus, 1989—; sci. attaché Gondwana, 1974-75. Served with AUS, 1945-46. Mem. Soc. Study Evolution, Am. Soc. Icthyologists and Herpetologists. Home: PO Box 354 Portal AZ 85632-0354

ZWEIG, BELLA, humanities educator; b. Bad Reichenhal, Germany, Oct. 6, 1946; came to U.S., 1951; d. Osias and Deborah (Taubenfeld) Z. Student, UCLA, 1964-66; BA, Columbia U., 1973; PhD, Stanford U., 1982. Instr. Stanford (Calif.) U., 1977-81; asst. prof. Emory U., Atlanta, 1982-87; sr. lectr. U. Ariz., Tucson, 1987—. Contbr. articles to prfl. jours. Coord. No on 6 & 7 Campaign, Davis, Calif., 1978, Big Mountain Support Group, Atlanta, 1982-87, Tucson, 1987-92. NEH study grantee, 1994; Whiting Dissertation fellow Whiting Found., 1977-78. Mem. Am. Philological Assn. (women's classical caucus 1982—, steering com. 1988-89, chair status of women and minority groups com. 1993—), Nat. Women's Studies Assn., Classical Assn. of Midwest and South. Jewish. Office: U Ariz Humanities Program Harvill 347 Tucson AZ 85721

ZWERVER, PETER JOHN, linguistics educator; b. Grouw, Friesland, The Netherlands, Sept. 3, 1942; came to U.S., 1959; m. Margot Anne Otters, July 16, 1978. AA in Fgn. Langs., Cerritos Coll., 1963; BA in German and English, Calif. State U., Long Beach, 1963; MA in Edn., Azusa Pacific U., 1971; PhD in Edn., Pacific Western U., 1980; PhD in Linguistics, Clayton U., 1988; BS in Liberal Studies, SUNY, Albany, 1989; BA in Archtl. Arts, Clayton U., 1995. Cert. standard elem., jr. high sch. and gen. secondary tchr., Calif.; cert. in standard supervision and adminstrv. svcs. grades kindergarten through 12, Calif. Tchr. math. and woodworking Monrovia (Calif.) Unified Sch. Dist., 1966—; assoc. prof. applied linguistics Pacific Western U., L.A., 1984-92, prof., 1992—; v.p. adminstrv. svcs. Am. M & N U., Metairie, La., 1993—; fellow in community arts and architecture Am. Coastline U., New Orleans, 1989; mem. acad. adv. coun. Pacific Western U., 1984—; chmn. acad. coun. Am. Coastline U., 1988—. Editor jour. Internat. Inst. for Ind. Scholarship, Pacific Western U., 1983-87; contbg. author: Poetic Voices of America, 1993; columnist Foothill Inter-City Newspapers, 1983-86. Pres. Monroe Sch. PTA, 1975, Santa Anita Family Svc., Monrovia, 1982, Arcadian Christian Sch., Arcadia, Calif., 1974. Recipient Hon. Svc. award Nat. Congress of Parents and Tchrs., 1976. Mem. NEA, Nat. Assn. Scholars, Calif. Tchrs. Assn., Monrovia Tchrs. Assn., Doctorate Assn. N.Y. Educators, Phi Beta Kappa, Phi Delta Kappa (rsch. rep. U. So. Calif. chpt. 1990-91, Rsch. award 1987, Intrnat. Svc. Key, 1993).

ZWICK, BARRY STANLEY, newspaper editor, speechwriter; b. Cleve., July 21, 1942; s. Alvin Albert and Selma Davidovna (Makofsky) Z.; m. Roberta Joan Yaffe, Mar. 11, 1972; children: Natasha Yvette, Alexander Anatol. BA in Journalism, Ohio State U., 1963; MS in Journalism, Columbia U., 1965. Copy editor Phila. Inquirer, 1964; night news editor Detroit Free Press, 1965-67; West Coast editor L.A. Times/Washington Post News Svc, 1967-77; makeup editor L.A. Times, 1978—; adj. prof. U. So. Calif., L.A., 1975-77. Author: Hollywood Tanning Secrets, 1980. NEH profl. journalism fellow Stanford U., 1977-78. Jewish. Office: LA Times Times Mirror Sq Los Angeles CA 90012

ZWICK, SHELLY CRITTENDON, university official; b. Cin., Dec. 27, 1941; d. Kenneth Shelby and Rosa Henrietta (Ruda) Crittendon; m. Peter Ronald Zwick, July 6, 1963. BA, Stetson U., Deland, Fla., 1963; JD, La. State U., 1976. Bar: La. 1977, U.S. Dist. Ct. (mid. dist.) La. 1977, U.S. Ct. Appeals (5th cir.) 1979, (11th cir.) 1981, U.S. Dist. (ea. dist.) La. 1988, (we. dist.) La. 1988, U.S. Supreme Ct. 1990. Asst. U.S. atty. mid. dist. Dept. Justice, Baton Rouge, 1978-84, chief civil div., 1981-84; magistrate U.S. Cts., Baton Rouge, 1984-86; ptnr. Roy, Kiesel, Aaron, Tucker & Zwick, Baton Rouge, 1986-90; dir. affirmative action Calif. State U., San Marcos, 1992-94; adj. prof. La. State U., Baton Rouge, 1987-90, lectr., 1979-90, La. State Police, Baton Rouge, 1980-84. Contbr. articles to profl. jour. Recipient Disting. Alumni award Stetson U., 1985. Mem. Fed. Bar Assn., La. State Bar Assn., Nat. Assn. Coll. and Univ. Attys., Am. Assn. for Affirmative Action, Dean Henry George McMahon Inn of Ct. Episcopalian. Home: 849 N Rios Ave Solana Beach CA 92075

ZWOYER, EUGENE MILTON, consulting engineering executive; b. Plainfield, N.J., Sept. 8, 1926; s. Paul Ellsworth and Marie Susan (Britt) Z.; m. Dorothy Lucille Seward, Feb. 23, 1946; children: Gregory, Jeffrey, Douglas. Student, U. Notre Dame, 1944, Mo. Valley Coll., 1944-45; BS, U. N.Mex., 1947; MS, Ill. Inst. Tech., 1949; PhD, U. Ill., 1953. Mem. faculty U. N.Mex., Albuquerque, 1948-71, prof. civil engring., dir. Eric Wang Civil Engring. Rsch. Facility, 1961-70; rsch. assoc. U. Ill., Urbana, 1951-53; owner, cons. engr. Eugene Zwoyer & Assocs., Albuquerque, 1954-72; exec. dir., sec. ASCE, N.Y.C., 1972-82; pres. Am. Assn. Engring. Socs., N.Y.C., 1982-84; exec. v.p. T.Y. Lin Internat., San Francisco, 1984-86, pres., 1986-89; owner Eugene Zwoyer Cons. Engr., 1989—; chief oper. officer, treas. Polar Molecular Corp., Saginaw, Mich., 1990, exec. v.p., 1991-92. Trustee Small Bus. Research Corp., 1976-80; trustee Engring. Info., Inc., 1981-84; internat. trustee People-to-People Internat. 1974-86; v.p. World Fedn. Engring. Orgns., 1982-85. Served to lt. (j.g.) USN, 1944-46. Named Outstanding Engr. of Yr. Albuquerque chpt. N.Mex Soc. Profl. Engrs., 1969, One Who Served the Best Interests of the Constrn. Industry, Engring. News Record, 1980; recipient Disting. Alumnus award the Civil Engring. Alumni Assn. at U. Ill., 1979, Disting. Alumnus award Engring. Coll. Alumni Assn., U. N.Mex., 1982, Can.-Am. Civil Engring. Amity award Am. Soc. Civil Engrs., 1988, Award for Outstanding Profl. Contbns. and Leadership Coll. Engring. U. N.Mex., 1989. Mem. AAAS, ASCE (dist. bd. dirs. 1968-71), NSPE, Am. Soc. Engring. Edn., Am. Concrete Inst., Nat. Acad. Code Adminstrn. (trustee, mem. exec. com. 1973-79), Engrs. Joint Coun. (bd. dirs. 1978-79), Engring. Soc. Commn. on Energy (bd. dirs. 1977-82), Sigma Xi, Sigma Tau, Chi Epsilon. Home: 6363 Christie Ave Apt 1326 Emeryville CA 94608-1940 Office: 1172 San Pablo Ave Ste 200C Berkeley CA 94706-2245

ZYGAS, KESTUTIS PAUL, architectural historian, educator; b. Kaunas, Lithuania, June 29, 1942; came to U.S., 1949; s. Kestutis Anthony and Ona (Matulevicius) Z.; m. Nijole Garla,June 6, 1964 (dec. June 1985); children: Jonas, Laura; m. Daiva Ciapaite, Mar. 6, 1992. AB, Harvard U., 1964, MArch, 1968; PhD, Cornell U., 1978. Asst. prof. U. So. Calif., L.A., 1977-84; assoc. prof. Ariz. State U., Tempe, 1984—. Editor: F.L. Wright - The Phoenix Papers: Broadacre City; author: Form Follows Form, 1981; contbr.

articles on archtl. history to profl. jours. Mem. Soc. Archtl. Historians, Coll. Art Assn. Office: Ariz State U Sch Architecture Tempe AZ 85287

ZYGELMAN, BERNARD, physicist; b. Tirol, Austria, Jan. 6, 1952; came to U.S., 1959; s. Mordecai and Agnes Hinterholzer Z.; m. Judith Ann Villani, Sept. 24, 1983. BS, CCNY, 1975; PhD in Physics, CUNY, 1983. Postdoctoral fellow Harvard Coll. Observatory, Cambridge, Mass., 1983-86; rsch. assoc. Harvard Coll. Observatory, Cambridge, 1986-90; vis. rsch. physicist Inst. for Theoretical Physics, Santa Barbara, Calif., 1988; sci. cons. Spectral Scis., Inc., Burlington, Mass., 1990-95; asst. prof. physics U. Nev., Las Vegas, 1990-94, assoc. prof., 1994—. Contbr. articles to Physical Review Letters, Am. Inst. Physics Proceedings. Mem. Am. Physical Soc. Office: U Nev Dept Physics Las Vegas NV 89154

ZYROFF, ELLEN SLOTOROFF, information scientist, classicist, educator; b. Atlantic City, N.J., Aug. 1, 1946; d. Joseph George and Sylvia Beverly (Roth) Slotoroff; m. Jack Zyroff, June 21, 1970; children: Dena Rachel, David Aaron. AB, Barnard Coll., 1968; MA, The Johns Hopkins U., 1969, PhD, 1971; MS, Columbia U., 1973. Instr. The Johns Hopkins U., Balt., 1970-71, Yeshiva U., N.Y.C., 1971-72, Bklyn Coll., 1971-72; libr., instr. U. Calif., 1979, 81, 91, San Diego State U., 1981-85, 94; prof. San Diego Mesa Coll., 1981—; dir. The Reference Desk Rsch. Svcs., La Jolla, Calif., 1983—; prin. libr. San Diego County Libr., 1985—; v.p. Archaeol. Soc. Am., Balt., 1970-71. Author: The Author's Apostrophe in Epic from Homer Through Lucan, 1971, Cooperative Library Instruction for Maximum Benefit, 1989. Pres. Women's Am. ORT, San Diego, 1979-81. Mem. ALA (chair divsn. coms. 1982—), Am. Philol. Assn., Calif. Libr. Assn. (elected to assembly 1993—), Am. Soc. Info. Sci., Am. Classical League, Toastmasters, Beta Phi Mu. Office: PO Box 12122 La Jolla CA 92039-2122

Professional Index

AGRICULTURE

UNITED STATES

ARIZONA

Green Valley
McGibbon, William Alexander *rancher, photographer*

Paradise Valley
Twist, Robert Lanphier *farmer, rancher, cattleman*

Phoenix
Ramos, Christina Sierra *natural resource specialist*

Tucson
Thacker, Gary William *agricultural extension agent*

CALIFORNIA

Berkeley
Perloff, Jeffrey Mark *agricultural and resource economics educator*

Caliente
Rankin, Helen Cross *cattle rancher, guest ranch executive*

Calistoga
Davies, Jack Lloyd *vintner, consultant*

Davis
Carter, Harold O. *agricultural economics educator*

Fresno
Petrucci, Vincent Emilio *retired viticulture educator, consultant*
Wilson, Herman T., Jr. *agricultural products supplier*

Hanford
Hall, Richard Dennis *agribusiness and international trade writer*

La Jolla
Foxley, William Coleman *cattleman*

Lebec
Hunt, Jack *animal breeder*

Los Angeles
Dickason, James Frank *land and farming company executive*

Napa
Chiarella, Peter Ralph *corporate executive*

Orange
Barry, James Paul *consulting arborist, educator*

Oxnard
Hansen, J. Woodford *agricultural products supplier*

Pacific Palisades
Jennings, Marcella Grady *rancher, investor*

Porterville
Wall, Fred Willard *agricultural products supplier*

Rutherford
Eisele, Milton Douglas *viticulturist*

Sacramento
Wightman, Thomas Valentine *rancher, researcher*

Salinas
Merrill, Thomas M. *produce executive*

San Diego
Caughlin, Stephenie Jane *organic farmer*

San Jose
D'Arrigo, Stephen, Jr. *agricultural company executive*

San Luis Obispo
McCorkle, Robert Ellsworth *agribusiness educator*

Sanger
Hackett, Ralph *agricultural products supplier*

Shingletown
Denny, James Clifton *tree farm administrator, forestry consultant*

Sierra Madre
Whittingham, Charles Edward *thoroughbred race horse owner and trainer*

Visalia
Hein, Martin Henry *farm manager*

West Hollywood
Harting, Trip *equine trainer*

COLORADO

Brighton
Mitchell, Ken *retired government executive, insurance agent*

Colorado Springs
Whittemore, Loren R. *rancher, real estate broker, county commissioner*

Greeley
McKee, Byron Duncan *livestock broker*
Oppelt, Norman Theodore *park ranger, retired psychology educator*

Kersey
Guttersen, Michael *cattle rancher*

Ridgway
Decker, Peter Randolph *rancher, former state official*

Springfield
Wessler, Melvin Dean *farmer, rancher*

IDAHO

Boise
Hennessey, Alice Elizabeth *forest products company executive*
Johnson, Ronald Douglas *business executive*

Buhl
Ray, Leo Eldon *fish breeding and marketing company executive*

Mountain Home
Salvo, Ginger Calhoun *horse trainer, sculptor*

Nezperce
Branson, Robert Dale *farm owner*

Twin Falls
Garnand, Gary L. *produce broker*
Jones, Douglas Raymond *farming executive, state legislator*

MONTANA

Butte
Anderson, Richard Ernest *energy and chemical research and development company executive, rancher*

Choteau
De Bruycker, Lloyd Henry *rancher, feedlot operator*

Polson
Marchi, Jon *cattle rancher, former investment brokerage executive*

Utica
Hollatz, Sarah Schoales *rancher, business owner*

NEVADA

Yerington
Scatena, Lorraine Borba *rancher, women's rights advocate*

NEW MEXICO

Cebolla
Berryman, Donald Carroll *cattle rancher*

Clovis
Atchley, Robbie Rene *farmer*

OREGON

Corvallis
Ripple, William John *forestry researcher, educator*

Eugene
Stogsdill, Robin Lynn *horse trainer, barn manager and owner*
Woolley, Donna Pearl *timber land management executive*

Forest Grove
Wirtz, David Reiner *enologist*

Grants Pass
Miller, Richard Alan *agricultural consultant*

Lake Oswego
Green, Daniel Fred *forester*

Lowell
Weathers, Warren Russell *forester, appraiser, consultant*

Riley
Cowan, Richard John *cattle rancher*

WASHINGTON

Pullman
Clement, Stephen Le Roy *agricultural researcher*

Toppenish
Hefflinger, LeRoy Arthur *agricultural manager*

Yakima
Grandy, Jay Franklin *fruit processing executive*

WYOMING

Douglas
Sanford, Leroy Leonard *rancher*

Dubois
Betts, Robert Budd, Jr. *dude ranch owner*

Fort Laramie
Hageman, James C. *rancher*

Lander
Raynolds, David Robert *buffalo breeder, author*

Wheatland
Bunker, John Birkbeck *cattle rancher, retired sugar company executive*

ADDRESS UNPUBLISHED

Erwin, Elmer Louis *vintager, cement consultant*
Gordon, Emmajean Elizabeth *farmer, investor, consultant*
Green, Allan Wright *winery owner*
Hanley, Joan Corette *vineyard owner*

ARCHITECTURE AND DESIGN

UNITED STATES

ALASKA

Anchorage
Maynard, Kenneth Douglas *architect*

ARIZONA

Bisbee
Bogatay, Todd Cunningham *architect*

Carefree
Robbins, Conrad W. *naval architect*

Green Valley
Schirmer, Henry William *architect*

Mesa
Shill, Victor Lamar *architect*

New River
Bruder, William Paul *architect*

Paradise Valley
Blumer, Harry Maynard *architect*

Phoenix
DeBartolo, Jack, Jr. *architect*
Elmore, James Walter *architect, retired university dean*
Klien, Wolfgang Josef *architect*
Lendrum, James Thoburn *architect*
Salazar, Luis Adolfo *architect*
Saletta, Charles Anthony, Jr. *architect*
Schiffner, Charles Robert *architect*
Winslow, Paul David *architect*

Scottsdale
Ball, Donald Edmon *architect*
Clapp, James Ford, Jr. *architect*
Hersker, Susan Catherine Utke *interior designer*
Hooker, Jo *interior designer*
Kelsey, Floyd Lamar, Jr. *architect*
LeForce, Jacquetta K. *interior designer*
Munninger, Michael Joseph *architect*
Panks, Gary Allen *golf course architect*
Rutes, Walter Alan *architect*
Schick, Janelle Keysar *interior designer*
Walker, Lisa Lee *interior designer, artist*

Sedona
Iverson, Wayne Dahl *landscape architect, consultant*

Sun City West
Madson, John Andrew *architect*
Mc Cune, John Francis, III *retired architect*

Tempe
Cutler, Lorraine Masters *interior designer, facilities manager*
Goodwin, Kemper *retired architect*
Kenyon, David Lloyd *architect, architectural firm executive*
Menefee, Merritt Marie *interior designer*
Thums, Charles William *designer, consultant*
Walker, Theodore Delbert *landscape architect*

Tucson
Breckenridge, Klindt Duncan *architect*
Chafee, Judith Davidson *architect*
Dinsmore, Philip Wade *architect*
Mc Connell, Robert Eastwood *architect, educator*
Nelson, Edward Humphrey *architect*
Riggs, John B. *architect*
Wallach, Leslie Rothaus *architect*

CALIFORNIA

Albany
Sullivan, Robert Scott *architect, graphic designer*

Bakersfield
McAlister, Michael Hillis *architect*
Renfro, Donald William *architect*

Belvedere
Gale, Daniel Bailey *architect*

Berkeley
Arbegast, David Elwood *landscape architect*
Blake, Laura *architect*
Burger, Edmund Ganes *architect*
Cardwell, Kenneth Harvey *architect, educator*
Eckbo, Garrett *landscape architect, urban designer*
Hester, Randolph Thompson, Jr. *landscape architect, educator*
Hunt, Frank Bouldin *architect, water color artist*
Lyndon, Donlyn *architect, educator*
Shaw, Morgan Albert *architect, consultant*
Stoller, Claude *architect*

Beverly Hills
Blakeley, James Edward, III *interior designer*

Bodega Bay
King, Leland W. *architect*

Bolinas
Carpenter, Arthur Espenet *furniture designer*

Burbank
Watson, Raymond Leslie *architect*

Burlingame
Castleberry, Arline Alrick *architect*
Tanzi, Carol Anne *interior designer*

Calabasas
Colton, Stanley *landscape architecture company executive*

Cardiff By The Sea
Farrell, Kevin *architect*

Carmel
Merrill, William Dickey *architect*

Carmichael
Hummel, Fred Ernest *architect*

Chula Vista
Quisenberry, Robert Max *architect, industrial designer*

Coronado
Wagener, Hobart D. *retired architect*
Weiss, Amy Lee *interior designer*

Culver City
Korney, Ellen Lemer *interior designer*
Moss, Eric Owen *architect*
Ray, Mary-Ann *architect, educator*
Sussman, Deborah Evelyn *designer, company executive*

Dana Point
Robinson, Theodore Gould *golf course architect*

El Cerrito
Hand, Harland Julius *garden designer, consultant, retired educator*

Encino
Beshlian, Lisa *interior designer*
Rance, Quentin E. *interior designer*

Fair Oaks
Muller, David Webster *architectural designer*

Fallbrook
Burge, Henry Charles *architect*

Fresno
Darden, Edwin Speight, Sr. *architect*
Patnaude, William E. *architect*
Pings, Anthony Claude *architect*
Putman, Robert Dean *golf course architect*
Saito, Paul Makoto *landscape architect*

Glendale
Colby, Barbara Diane *interior designer, consultant*
O'Connor, Pauline R. *interior design consultant*

Healdsburg
Disrud, Carol Ann *interior designer*

Huntington Beach
Lans, Carl Gustav *architect, economist*

Irvine
Danielian, Arthur Calvin *architect*
Dorius, Kermit Parrish *architect*
Jacobs, Donald Paul *architect*
Kraemer, Kenneth Leo *architect, urban planner, educator*

La Jolla
Baesel, Stuart Oliver *architect*
Brandt, Maryclare *interior designer, educator*

Lafayette
Harlock, Michael J. *architect*

Laguna Hills
Burrows, Gates Wilson *retired architect*

Laguna Niguel
Hassouna, Fred *architect, educator*

Los Angeles
Adams, William Wesley, III *architect*
Axon, Donald Carlton *architect*
Fickett, Edward Hale *architect, planner, arbitrator*
Hanciulesco, Barbu *architectural design professional*
Harding, Teresa J. *interior designer*
Holzbog, Thomas Jerald *architect, planner*
Johnson, Scott *architect*
Kline, Lee B. *architect*
Krag, Olga *interior designer*
Li, Gerald *architect, film producer*
Martin, Albert Carey *architect*
Moe, Stanley Allen *architect, consultant*
Murdoch, Paul Allan *architect*
Myers, Christopher Charles *interior designer, sales associate*
Neutra, Dion *architect*
Phelps, Barton Chase *architect, educator*
Thoman, John Everett *architect, mediator*
Verger, Morris David *architect, planner*

Los Gatos
Chapson, Lois Jester *interior designer*
Zacher, Valerie Irene *interior designer*

Manhattan Beach
Blanton, John Arthur *architect*

Marina Del Rey
Crockett, Robert York *architect*
Hadavi, Fouad Fred *interior designer*
Tanaka, Ted Tokio *architect, educator*

Marshall
Evans, Robert James *architect*

Menlo Park
Sidells, Arthur F. *architect*

Mill Valley
D'Amico, Michael *architect, urban planner*
Pflueger, John Milton *architect*

Monterey
Shaw, William Vaughan *architect*

Montrose
Greenlaw, Roger Lee *interior designer*

Morgan Hill
Halopoff, William Evon *industrial designer, consultant*

Mount Shasta
Anderson, Lee Roger *landscape architect, solar, environmental, recreation and site planner*
Guill, John Russell *architect*

Mountain View
Kobza, Dennis Jerome *architect*

Napa
Chernoff-Pate, Diana *interior designer, small business owner*

Newport Beach
Bauer, Jay S. *architect*
Deal, Lynn Eaton Hoffmann *interior designer*
Dougherty, Betsey Olenick *architect*
Hench, Robert Irving *architect*
Morgridge, Howard Henry *architect*
Morrelli, Gino J. *yacht designer*
Paul, Courtland Price *landscape architect, planner*
Richardson, Walter John *architect*
Strock, Arthur Van Zandt *architect*
Wimberly, George James *architect*

Oakland
Brocchini, Ronald Gene *architect*
Nicol, Robert Duncan *architect*
Wolfe, Clifford Eugene *architect, writer*

Orange
Bogart, Wanda Lee *interior designer*
Mason, Naomi Ann *interior designer*

Oxnard
O'Connell, Hugh Mellen, Jr. *architect, retired*
Okuma, Albert Akira, Jr. *architect*

Palm Springs
Broderick, Harold Christian *interior designer*
Frey, Albert *architect*

Palo Alto
Jones, Robert Trent, Jr. *golf course architect*
Knott, Donald Joseph *golf course architect*
Linn, Gary Dean *golf course architect*

Pasadena
Goei, Bernard Thwan-Poo (Bert Goei) *architectural and engineering firm executive*
Heaton, Culver *architect*
Thomas, Joseph Fleshman *architect*

Pleasanton
Dunbar, Frank Rollin *landscape architect*
Fehlberg, Robert Erick *architect*

Pomona
Lyle, John Tillman *landscape architecture educator*

Rancho Mirage
Chambers, Milton Warren *architect*

Rancho Palos Verdes
Lunden, Samuel Eugene *architect*

Redondo Beach
Shellhorn, Ruth Patricia *landscape architect*

Redwood City
Morrison, Murdo Donald *architect*

Sacramento
Cox, Whitson William *architect*
Craigo, Steade Richard *architect, preservationist*
Dahlin, Dennis John *landscape architect*
Hallenbeck, Harry C. *architect*
Lionakis, George *architect*
Nacht, Daniel Joseph *architect*
Ross, Terence William *architect*
Wasserman, Barry L(ee) *architect*
Weil, Pamela Marion *interior designer*

San Diego
Delawie, Homer Torrence *architect*
Donaldson, Milford Wayne *architect, educator*
Eichman, Patricia Frances *interior designer*
Holl, Walter John *architect, interior designer*
Hope, Frank Lewis, Jr. *retired architect*
Livingston, Stanley C. *architect*
Paderewski, Clarence Joseph *architect*
Rosen, Manuel Morrison *architect, educator*
Stepner, Michael Jay *architect*
Watts, James Harrison *architect*
Wilson, Richard Allan *landscape architect*

San Francisco
Armsby, Robert *architect*
Brown, Joseph E. *landscape architecture executive*
Bruneau, Bill *architect*
Brutting, Thomas Charles *architect*
Budzinski, James Edward *interior designer*
Bull, Henrik Helkand *architect*
Burk, Gary Maurice *health care facility planner*
Costa, Walter Henry *architect*
Del Campo, Martin Bernardelli *architect*
Dodge, Peter Hampton *architect*
Emmons, Donn *architect*
Field, John Louis *architect*
Hardison, Donald Leigh *architect*
Hooper, Roger Fellowes *architect*
Judd, Bruce Diven *architect*
Keenan, Robert *architect*
Kennedy, Raymond McCormick, Jr. *interior designer, educator*
Kriken, John Lund *architect*
MacDonald, Donald William *architect*
Mc Laughlin, Herbert E. *architect*
McMahan, Celeste Tina *architect, construction and real estate project manager, organizational psychologist*
Painter, Michael Robert *landscape architect, urban designer*
Perez, Oscar Alfredo *architect*
Raeber, John Arthur *architect, construction specifier consultant*
Ream, James Terrill *architect, sculptor*
Rockrise, George Thomas *architect*
Rockwell, Burton Lowe *architect*
Simon, Cathy Jensen *architect*
Sowder, Robert Robertson *architect*
Taggart, Paulett Long *architect, educator*
Thistlethwaite, David Richard *architect*
Turnbull, William, Jr. *architect*
Valentine, William Edson *architect*
Volkmann, Daniel George, Jr. *architect*

San Jose
Dyer, Kecia Carole *interior project designer*
Olson, Bernadette Lucienne *holographer*
Tanaka, Richard Koichi, Jr. *architect, planner*

San Luis Obispo
Deasy, Cornelius Michael *architect*
Fraser, Bruce Douglas, Jr. *architect, artist*
Tickell, William Earl *architect, educator*

San Marino
Man, Lawrence Kong *architect*
Rendon, Leonard *interior designer*

San Mateo
Sadilek, Vladimir *architect*

San Rafael
Badgley, John Roy *architect*
Ciampi, Mario Joseph *architect, planner*
Clark, Charles Sutter *interior designer*
Elliott, Edward Procter *architect*
Thompson, Peter L. H. *golf course architect*

San Simeon
Izenour, Christine *lighting designer*

Santa Barbara
Frizzell, William Kenneth *architect*
Kruger, Kenneth Charles *retired architect*
Powell, Herbert J. *architect*

Santa Clara
Kwock, Royal *architect*

Santa Cruz
Oberdorfer, Jeff *architect, firm executive*

Santa Monica
Eizenberg, Julie *architect*
Koning, Hendrik *architect*
Miller, Leroy Benjamin *architect*
Naidorf, Louis Murray *architect*
Wou, Leo S. *architect, planner*

Santa Rosa
Gilger, Paul Douglass *architect*
Roland, Craig Williamson *architect*
Sohm, Irene Maxine *interior designer*
Wysocki, Michael *architect, artist*

Sausalito
Leefe, James Morrison *architect*
Werner, William Arno *architect*

Seal Beach
Rossi, Mario Alexander *architect*

Sherman Oaks
Cochrane, Peggy *architect, writer*

Somerset
Setzekorn, William David *architect, consultant*

Sonoma
Allen, Rex Whitaker *architect*
Lackey, Lawrence Bailis, Jr. *retired architect, urban designer*

South Pasadena
Girvigian, Raymond *architect*

Sunnyvale
Holt, Steven Hamilton Skov *strategic design company executive, educator*

Tarzana
Neiswander, Laurel Ann *interior designer*
Smith, Mark Lee *architect*

Thousand Oaks
Nahmias, Victor Jay *architect*

Torrance
Ryniker, Bruce Walter Durland *industrial designer, manufacturing executive*

Venice
Baldon, Cleo *interior designer*
Ehrlich, Steven David *architect*

Ventura
Ruebe, Bambi Lynn *interior, environmental designer*
Windroth, William E. *architect, building and safety executive*

Villa Park
Buffington, Linda Brice *interior designer*

Visalia
Heidbreder, Gail *architect, educator*

Walnut
Muszynski, L. Jane *interior designer*

Walnut Creek
Caddy, Edmund Harrington Homer, Jr. *architect*
Kuechle, Roland Koerner *architect*

West Hollywood
Luckman, Charles *architect*

Woodland Hills
O'Rourke, William Patrick *architect*

COLORADO

Aspen
Alstrom, Sven Erik *architect*
Caudill, Samuel Jefferson *architect*
Ensign, Donald H. *landscape architect*

Aurora
Hynek, Frederick James *architect*

Boulder
Carlson, Devon McElvin *architect, educator*
Forssander, Paul Richard *inventor, artist, entrepreneur*
Hoffman, Charles Fenno, III *architect*
Vander Vorste, James LeRoy *architect*

Colorado Springs
Phibbs, Harry Albert *interior designer, professional speaker, lecturer*

Denver
Abo, Ronald Kent *architect*
Anderson, John David *architect*
Brownson, Jacques Calmon *architect*
Decker, David B. *architect, educator*
Dominick, Peter Hoyt, Jr. *architect*
Falkenberg, William Stevens *architect, contractor*
Fuller, Kenneth Roller *architect*
Fuller, Robert Kenneth *architect, urban designer*
Hatami, Marvin *architect, educator, urban designer*
Havekost, Daniel John *architect*
Hoover, George Schweke *architect*
Hornbein, Victor *architect*
Larson, Dayl Andrew *architect*
Mason, Ronald Leonard *architect*
Nagel, Jerome Kaub *architect*
Steenhagen, Robert Lewis *landscape architect, consultant*
Voigt, Donald Bernard *tool designer*
Wilk, Diane Lillian *architect, educator*
Williams, John James, Jr. *architect*
Zeigel, Henry Alan *architect*

Englewood
Eccles, Matthew Alan *golf course and landscape architect*
Sharkey, Richard David *product designer, architect, musician*
Stead, Timothy *architect*

Evergreen
Gerou, Phillip Howard *architect*

Lakewood
Franta, Gregory Esser *architect, energy consultant*

Littleton
Williams, Sally *landscape designer*

Steamboat Springs
Gamble, Lee St. Clair *architectural and interior designer*

Vail
Nelson, Nevin Mary *interior designer*
Vosbeck, Robert Randall *architect*

FLORIDA

West Palm Beach
Mc Neal, Martha von Oesen *landscape architect*

HAWAII

Aiea
Wiram, Wayne Curtis *interior designer*

Honolulu
Ayer, David Clay *architect*
Botsai, Elmer Eugene *architect, educator, former university dean*
Cain, Raymond Frederick *landscape architect, planning company executive*
Chun, Lowell Koon Wa *architect, land planner, consultant*
Cruthers, Evan Douglas *architect*
Ferraro, Joseph James *architect*
Hale, Nathan Robert *architect*
Hamada, Duane Takumi *architect*
Hara, Ernest Hideo *architect*
Ho, Owen Matthew *store planning consultant, caterer/event planner*
Hong, Norman G. Y. *architect*
Lau, Charles Kwok-Chiu *architect, architectural firm executive*
Lee, Marvin Jun Hung *architectural firm executive*
Sutton, Charles Richard *architect, designer*
Vidal, Alejandro Legaspi *architect*
Wong, Choy-Ling *interior designer*

Kahului
Riecke, Hans Heinrich *architect*

Kailua
Thompson, Arthur Kimbal *architect*

Kamuela
Moss, Susan Jean *interior designer*

Kaneohe
Fisette, Scott Michael *golf course designer*
Jackson, Jane W. *interior designer*

IDAHO

Boise
Cline, Glen Edwin *retired architect and planner*
Shneider, Jeffrey A. *architect*
Turney, Steven Craig *architect*

Sun Valley
Bryant, Woodrow Wesley *architect*
McLaughlin, James Daniel *architect*
McMillen, Darryl Charles *architect*

MONTANA

Bozeman
DeHaas, John Neff, Jr. *retired architecture educator*
Mattson, George Arthur *architect*
Sisson, Carole McDonald *interior designer*

Great Falls
Davidson, David Scott *architect*
Hoiland, Andrew Calvin *architect*

Livingston
Russell, Carina Boehm *interior designer*

Missoula
Snavely, Sharon Martin *interior designer*

NEVADA

Gardnerville
Harlander, Leslie Albert *naval architectural consultant*

Las Vegas
Dillon, Charles G. *architect*
Koppa-Whitney, Diane Lynn *interior designer*
Kruger-Hamilton, Erica *interior designer, small business owner*
Serfas, Richard Thomas *architecture educator, urban planner, county official*
Thomas, Roger Parry *interior designer, art consultant*

Reno
Casazza, Ralph Anthony *architect*
Schweigert, Lynette Aileen *interior designer, consultant*

NEW MEXICO

Albuquerque
Armijo, Jacqulyn Doris *interior designer*
Campbell, C(harles) Robert *architect*
Crawford, Dale Lee *architect*
Davis, Bruce Warren *architect*
Hakim, Besim Selim *architecture and urban design educator*
McCabe, Robert R. *architect, city planner*
Pearl, George Clayton *architect*
Sabatini, William Quinn *architect*
Smith, Jean *interior design firm executive*

Farmington
Freimuth, William Richard *architect*

Santa Fe
Conron, John Phelan *architect*
Leon, Bruno *architect, educator*

OREGON

Clackamas
Merrill, William Dean *architect, medical facility planning consultant*

Medford
Skelton, Douglas H. *architect*

Newport
Gordon, Walter *architect*

Portland
Frasca, Robert John *architect*
Gunsul, Brooks R. W. *architect*
Hacker, Thomas Owen *architect*
Kilbourn, Lee Ferris *architect, specifications writer*
Loeb, Joyce Lichtgarn *interior designer, civic worker*
Michael, Gary Linn *architect*
Ritz, Richard Ellison *architect, architectural historian, writer*
Scott, George Larkham, IV *architect*
Stastny, Donald Joseph *architect*
Wintermute, Marjorie McLean *architect, educator*

Scappoose
Emmert, Russell LeRoy *interior designer*

Springfield
Lutes, Donald Henry *architect*

Sunriver
Sawyer, Gerald *interior designer*

Tualatin
Broome, John William *retired architect*
Harrington-Lloyd, Jeanne Leigh *interior designer*

UTAH

Provo
Gifford, Lisa Bonnie *interior designer*

Salt Lake City
Beall, Burtch W., Jr. *architect*
Blackner, Boyd Atkins *architect*
Brems, David Paul *architect*
Daniels, George Nelson *architect*
Miller, William Charles *architect, educator*
Stowe, Neal P. *architect*

WASHINGTON

Auburn
Keimig, Alan Charles *architect*

Bainbridge Island
Yanick, Miles *architect*

Bellevue
Flom, Robert Michael *interior designer*
Roselle, Richard Donaldson *industrial, marine and interior designer*

Bellingham
Christensen, David Earl *architect*
Kienast, Charlotte D. *interior designer*

Bothell
Sakkal, Mamoun *architect, interior designer*

Deer Harbor
Hoag, Paul Sterling *architect*

Edmonds
Petersen, Aimee Bernice *interior designer, artist, landscape designer*

Everett
Arbogast, Genevieve L. *interior designer*
King, Indle Gifford *industrial designer, educator*

Gig Harbor
Bowman, Michael O. *interior designer*
Wilder, Jennifer Rose *interior designer*

Hansville
Griffin, DeWitt James *architect, real estate developer*

Issaquah
Browne, Gretchen Lynn *interior designer*

Kirkland
Mitchell, Joseph Patrick *architect*
Steinmann, John Colburn *architect*

Mount Vernon
Hall, David Ramsay *architect*
Klein, Henry *architect*

Ocean Shores
Morgan, Audrey *architect*

Olympia
John, Yvonne Maree *artist, interior designer*
Moffett, Frank Cardwell *architect, civil engineer, real estate developer*

Seattle
Bain, William James, Jr. *architect*
Bassetti, Fred Forde *architect*
Bosworth, Thomas Lawrence *architect, educator*
Buursma, William F. *architect*
Bystrom, Arne *architect*
Castanes, James Christopher *architect*
Cichanski, Gerald *golf course architect*
Dermanis, Paul Raymond *architect*
Durham, Robert Lewis *architect*
Freed, Aaron David *architect*
Grossman, Robert James *architect*
Hastings, L(ois) Jane *architect, educator*
Hinshaw, Mark Larson *architect, urban planner*
Jacobson, Phillip Lee *architect, educator*
Jonassen, James O. *architect*
Jones, Grant Richard *landscape architect, planner*
Jones, Johnpaul *architect*
Kelbaugh, Douglas Stewart *architect, urban designer, architecture educator*
Klontz, James Mathias *architect*
Kolb, Keith Robert *architect, educator*
Malcolm, Garold Dean *architect*
Meyer, C. Richard *architect*
Miles, Don Clifford *architect*
Morse, John Moore *architect, planner*
Olson, James William Park *architect*
Perthou, Alison Chandler *interior designer*
Polk, William Merrill *architect*
Sanders, James Joseph *architect*
Shinbo, Robert *landscape architect*
Small, Robert E. *architect, architecture educator*
Springer, Floyd Ladean *architect*
Swain, Robert Edson *architect*

Shelton
Wolbrink, Donald Henry *landscape architect, city planner*

Spokane
Haines, Jim Allen *architect*
Stone, Michael David *landscape architect*

Tacoma
Harris, James Martin *architect*
Liddle, Alan Curtis *architect*
McGovern, Ricky James *architect, educator*

Vancouver
Graffis, Julie Anne *interior designer, entrepreneur*

MILITARY ADDRESSES OF THE UNITED STATES

ATLANTIC

APO
González, Arthur Eliseo *architectural designer*

CANADA

ALBERTA

Edmonton
Manasc, Vivian *architect, consultant*

BRITISH COLUMBIA

Vancouver
Erickson, Arthur Charles *architect*
Hirshen, Sanford *architect, educator*
Oberlander, Cornelia Hahn *landscape architect*
Patkau, John *architect*
Patkau, Patricia *architect, architecture educator*

SASKATCHEWAN

Saskatoon
Henry, Keith Douglas *architect*

ADDRESS UNPUBLISHED

Attoe, Wayne Osborne *architecture educator, author, designer*
Awbrey, Mary Stuart *interior designer*
Bilezikjian, Edward Andrew *architect*
Blair, Frederick David *interior designer*
Chao, James Min-Tzu *architect*
Cowee, John Widmer, Jr. *architecture company executive*
Crowther, Richard Layton *architect, consultant, researcher, author, lecturer*
Dobbel, Rodger Francis *interior designer*
Ely, Marica McCann *interior designer*
Funte-Radford, Deidrea Lea *interior designer, consultant*
Gensler, M. Arthur, Jr. *architect*
Goodwin, Marcy *architectural coordinator, consultant*
Guthrie, James Bryan *architect*
Hargreaves, George Julian *landscape architect*
Hecht, Sasanna Bettina *architect/design educator*
Helmich, Pamela Pence *architect*
Henderson, John Drews *architect*
Hopkins, Pamela Withers *architect*
Jones, Jeffrey Dean *interior designer*
Kirk, Paul *architect*
Leaman, Jack Ervin *landscape architect, community/regional planner*
Macdonald, Virginia Brooks *architect*
Maltzan, Michael Thomas *architect*
Matas, Myra Dorothea *interior designer, kitchen and bath designer*
McGraw, Susan Catherine *interior designer*
Moore, Richard Alan *landscape architect*
Parke, Janet Diane *interior designer*
Peters, Robert Woolsey *architect*
Renne, Janice Lynn *interior designer*
Rubenstein, Michael Alan *architect*
Rupp, Sigrid Lorenzen *architect*
Sande, Barbara *interior decorating consultant*
Siefer, Stuart B. *architect*
Stein, Janice Marie *interior designer*
Stockwell, Sherwood Beach *architect*
Sutton, Marcella French *interior designer*
Thornton, Ival Crandall *interior architect*
Tomasi, Donald Charles *architect*
Webster, Robin Welander *interior designer*
Woerner, Robert Lester *landscape architect*

Wrolstad, Helen Louise *interior designer, business owner*

ARTS: LITERARY. *See also* COMMUNICATIONS MEDIA.

UNITED STATES

ALASKA

Anchorage
Starratt, Patricia Elizabeth *writer, actress, composer*
Strohmeyer, John *writer, former editor*
Thomas, Lowell, Jr. *author, lecturer, former lieutenant governor, former state senator*

Fairbanks
Anderson, Jean Blanche *fiction writer*

Juneau
Albanese, Mary Dalene *writer, educator, geologist*
Rogers, Jean Clark *writer*

Tok
Blasor-Bernhardt, Donna Jo *screenwriter, poet, author, photographer*

ARIZONA

Carefree
Ripley, Robert Elliott *author, psychologist*

Cave Creek
Gose, Celeste Marlene *writer*

Cottonwood
Nauman, Ruth Eileen *author*

Flagstaff
Cline, Platt Herrick *author*

Mesa
Tillman, Henry Barrett *author*

Phoenix
Chorlton, David *writer*

Portal
Williams, Jeanne *writer*

Scottsdale
Lanier-Graham, Susan D. *writer*
Perkins, Wendy Frances *author, speaker*

Sedona
Rubin, Charles Alexis *writer*
Thorne, Kate Ruland *writer, publisher*

Sun City West
Ault, Phillip Halliday *author, editor*

Tempe
Nolle, Richard *writer, astrological consultant*
Raby, William Louis *author*
Sylvester, Edward Joseph *science writer, journalism educator*

Tucson
Hallett, Jane Martin *writer, educator*
Ingalls, Jeremy *poet, educator*
King, Harry Alden *author*
Leydet, François Guillaume *writer*
Mason, Judith Ann *freelance writer*
Vicker, Ray *writer*

ARKANSAS

Fayetteville
Jones, Douglas Clyde *author*

Little Rock
Brown, Dee Alexander *author*

CALIFORNIA

Albany
Luhn, Robert Kent *writer, magazine editor*
Meyers, Carole Terwilliger *writer*

Alpine
Butler, Evelyn Anne *writer, educator, editor*

Altadena
Burden, Jean (Prussing) *poet, writer, editor*

Apple Valley
McCormick, Alma Heflin *writer, retired educator, psychologist*

Arcadia
Sloane, Beverly LeBov *writer, consultant*

Berkeley
Bardhan, Kalpana *translator, writer*
Harrison, Helen Herre *writer, volunteer, advocate*
Milosz, Czeslaw *poet, author, educator*
Ogg, Wilson Reid *poet, lyricist, curator, publisher, lawyer, retired judge, educator*
Rosenwasser, Rena Sue *poet*
Scott, Peter Dale *writer, retired English language educator*
Temko, Allan Bernard *writer*
Wheeler, Helen Rippier *writer, educator, consultant*

Beverly Hills
Basichis, Gordon Allen *author, screenwriter*
Blakeley, Linda *writer, producer, psychologist*
Hacker, Richard Carleton *author*
Hearle, Kevin James *poet, educator*
Livingston, Myra Cohn *poet, writer, educator*
McGee, Rex Alan *motion picture screenwriter*

Camarillo
Alexander, John Charles *editor, writer*

Canoga Park
Katz, Ilana Paulette *writer*

Carmel
Aurner, Robert Ray *author, corporate executive*

Claremont
Mezey, Robert *poet, educator*

Concord
Headding, Lillian Susan (Sally Headding) *writer, forensic clairvoyant*

Coronado
Boggess, Tyree M *technical writer*

Corte Madera
Nicosia, Gerald Martin *author, freelance writer*

Costa Mesa
White, Kenton Stowell *writer, publisher*

Cottonwood
Hocking, Phoenix Jeanne (Sandra J. Hocking) *writer*

Covina
Phillips, Jill Meta *novelist, critic, astrologer*

Cromberg
Kolb, Ken Lloyd *writer*

Culver City
de Seigne, Pascal (Lawrence) *author, art appraiser*

Cupertino
Zobel, Louise Purwin *author, educator, lecturer, writing consultant*

Cypress
Edmonds, Ivy Gordon *writer*

Davenport
Ann, Karen *author, lecturer, concept design artist*

Davis
Major, Clarence Lee *novelist, poet, educator*

Del Mar
Smith, Robert Hamil *author, fund raiser*

Duncans Mills
Schuett, Stacey Lynn *writer, illustrator*

El Cerrito
Wolinsky, Richard Barry *writer*

El Segundo
Halloran, James Vincent, III *technical writer*

Escondido
Aplon, Roger Laurence *writer, poet*

Fieldbrook
Schaaf, Miv *writer, graphic designer, composer*

Fremont
Jenkins, Creed Harold *writer*

Fresno
Garrison-Finderup, Ivadelle Dalton *writer*
Levine, Philip *poet, educator*

Fullerton
Conway, James F. *writer, counselor, minister*

Gardena
Baker, Lillian L. *author, historian, artist, lecturer*

Georgetown
Lengyel, Cornel Adam (Cornel Adam) *author*

Granada Hills
Spolter, Pari Dokht *scientific books writer*

Gualala
Alinder, Mary Street *writer*

Hillsborough
Atwood, Mary Sanford *writer*

Kensington
Nathan, Leonard Edward *writer, educator*

La Jolla
Freilicher, Melvyn Stanley *writer, educator*
Havis, Allan Stuart *playwright, theatre educator*
Movius, Alice Whitney Burton *writer, educator, speaker*

Laguna Niguel
Stern, Matthew Arnold *technical writer*

Landers
Landers, Vernette Trosper *writer, educator, association executive*

Long Beach
Datsko, Tina Michelle *writer, producer*

Los Angeles
Branch, Taylor *writer*
Chetwynd, Lionel *screenwriter, producer, director*
Cray, Ed *writer, educator*
Engelbach, David Charles *scriptwriter, television producer*
Hinerfeld, Susan Hope Slocum *writer, editor*
Hughes, Marvis Jocelyn *poet, photographer*

Kenner, Ronald W. *writer, editor*
Kraft, Scott Wallace *writer, actor*
Larbalestrier, Deborah Elizabeth *writer*
Maker, Janet Anne *author, lecturer*
Malcor, Linda A. *writer, researcher*
Meeks, Christopher Nelson *writer*
Messerli, Douglas *author, publisher*
Monroe, Keith *writer, consultant*
Myers, Katherine Donna *writer, publisher*
Noguchi, Thomas Tsunetomi *author, forensic pathologist*
Racina, Thom (Thomas Frank Raucina) *television writer, editor*
Rhoads, Rick *writer, editor*
Shuman, James Burrow *writer, consultant*
Swartz, Charles S. *screenwriter, producer, educator*
Thomas, Shirley *author, educator, business executive*

Magalia
Stadley, Pat Anna May Gough (Mrs. James M. Stadley) *writer*

Malibu
Klevit, Alan Barre *business executive, motivational speaker*

Marina Del Rey
Eckermann, Gerald Carlton *writer, corporate executive*

Mendocino
Shep, Robert Lee *editor, publisher, textile book researcher*

Menlo Park
Phillips, Jeffrey Richard *magazine writer*

Mill Valley
Haspiel, George Sidney *writer, illustrator*
Swan, James Albert *environmental psychologist, writer, actor*

Monterey
Wayne, Kyra Petrovskaya *writer*

Moorpark
Stewart, Sharon Diane *writer*

Mountain View
Allen, Bruce John *writer, activist*

Murrieta
Brandenburgh, Donald Carter *literary agent*

North Hollywood
Kuter, Kay E. *writer, actor*
Leavengood, William Samuel *playwright*

Northridge
Boberg, Dorothy Kurth *author*

Norwalk
Reagan, James Dale *writer, editor*

Oakland
Berlak, Harold *writer, educator, consultant*
Grzanka, Leonard Gerald *writer, consultant*

Oceanside
Bengelsdorf, Irving Swem *science writer, consultant*
Humphrey, Phyllis A. *writer*

Orange
DeCarlo, Angela Rocco *writer, journalist*

Pacific Grove
O'Shaughnessy, Ellen Cassels *writer*

Palm Springs
Curran, Jan Barer *writer, editor, public relations consultant*
Shaeffer, Claire Brightwell *writer, educator*

Palo Alto
Drexler, Kim Eric *researcher, author*
Morris, Bruce Dorian *technical writer, scholar, educator*
Sanna, Lucy Jean *writer*

Palomar Mountain
Day, Richard Somers *author, editorial consultant, video producer*

Pasadena
Alwan, Ameen *writing educator*
Rasmussen, R. Kent *writer*

Petaluma
Pronzini, Bill John (William Pronzini) *author*

Piedmont
Phillips, Betty Lou (Elizabeth Louise Phillips) *author, interior designer*

Rancho Palos Verdes
Stockwell, Shelley Lessin *writer, hypnotherapist*

Rancho Santa Fe
Simon, William Leonard *film and television writer and producer, author*

Riverside
Simon, Maurya *poet, educator*

Rohnert Park
Haslam, Gerald William *writer, educator*

Sacramento
Blackwell, Charles Curtis *writer, visual artist*
de Vontine, Julie Elisabeth (The Marchioness de Roe Devon) *writer, lawyer*
Hauck, Dennis William *author, technical writer*

Salinas
Canada, Stephen Andrew *writer*

San Diego
Ashley, Rosalind Minor *writer*
Hart, Anne *author*
Prescott, Lawrence Malcolm *medical and health science writer*
Seifert, Miki *scriptwriter, producer*
Self, Susan Carolyn *technical writer*
Stutz, Frederick Paul *writer, educator*

San Francisco
Anderson, Walter Truett *author*
Boutilier, Nancy W. *writer, secondary English educator*
Ferris, Russell James, II *freelance writer*
Field, Carol Hart *writer, journalist, foreign correspondent*
Graham, Toni *writer*
Hopkins, Lee Wallace *writer*
Jundis, Orvy Lagasca *writer, consultant, educator*
Lai, Him Mark *writer*
Lippitt, Elizabeth Charlotte *writer*
Preuss, Paul Frederick *writer*
Quick, William Thomas *author, consultant*
Reinhardt, Richard Warren *writer*
Rogers, Michael Alan *writer*
Wayburn, Peggy (Cornelia E. Wayburn) *author, editor*
Woods, James Patrick, Jr. *writer*

San Jose
Fitzgerald, Timothy Kevin *writer*
Loventhal, Milton *writer, playwright, lyricist*

San Luis Rey
Williams, Elizabeth Yahn *author, lawyer*

San Marcos
Sauer, David Andrew *writer, computer consultant*

San Mateo
Cerepak, Julia Lee *poet, writer*
Korn, Walter *writer*

San Rafael
Turner, William Weyand *author*

Santa Ana
Fluor, Marjorie Letha Wade *author*
Neeper, Frederic Allen *advertising copywriter*

Santa Barbara
Bock, Russell Samuel *author*
Easton, Robert (Olney) *author, environmentalist*
Gibbs, Wolcott, Jr. *writer, editor*
Jackson, Beverley Joy Jacobson *columnist, lecturer*

Santa Cruz
Sward, Robert Stuart *author*
Wilson, Carter *writer, educator*

Santa Monica
Casty, Alan Howard *author, retired humanities educator*
Spataro, Janie Dempsey Watts *writer*

Santa Ynez
Walker, Burton Leith *engineering writer, psychotherapist*

Sausalito
Follett, Carolyn Brown *poet, artist*

Scotts Valley
O'Mahony, Kieran T. *writer*

Sherman Oaks
MacMullen, Douglas Burgoyne *writer, editor, retired army officer, publisher*
Schilling, Vivian *novelist, screenwriter and actress*

Simi Valley
Bolton, Martha O. *writer*
Jones, Jordan Douglas *writer, publisher*

Sonoma
Jayme, William North *writer*

Sunland
Porter, Albert Wright *author, artist, educator*

Sunnyvale
Yep, Laurence Michael *author*

Taft
Miller, Katherine Toy *writer*

Thousand Oaks
Finney, Richard S. *screenwriter*
Hagey, Robin Greene *writer*

Van Nuys
Coen, Dana *playwright, TV and film scriptwriter*
Fanning, Don Brian *poet, computer services consultant*

Venice
Moran, Thomas Francis *writer*

Ventura
King, Elizabeth Ann *writer*

West Hollywood
Fuchs, Thomas *writer*

Westminster
Amato, Carol Joy *writer, anthropologist*

Yorba Linda
Magnuson, Donald Richard (Blaine Nellington) *motion picture and television screenwriter, producer, director*

COLORADO

Aurora
Bower, Donald Edward *author*
McClendon, Irvin Lee, Sr. *technical writer, editor*

Boulder
Dorn, Edward Merton *poet, educator*
Jason, Debra Ann *copywriter*
Kaye, Ivan Nathaniel *writer*

Colorado Springs
Hicks, David Earl *author, inventor*
Leasure, Robert Ellis *writer, photographer*
Van Ness, Lottye Gray *author, genealogist*
Yaffe, James *author*

Denver
Goss, Georgia Bulman *translator*
Mead, Beverly Mirium Anderson *author, educator*

Fort Collins
Mark, Maxine Catherine Schlieker *writer*

Golden
Greenberg, Joanne *author, anthropologist*

Greenwood Village
Youngs, James Murray *freelance writer, photographer*

Ouray
Hall, Hal *writer, economic, political, social and religious critic*

Pueblo
Moffeit, Tony Archie *poet, librarian*

Salida
Quillen, Edward Kenneth, III *freelance writer, columnist*

Vail
Knight, Constance Bracken *writer, realtor, interior decorator, corporate executive*

Westminster
Finton, Kenneth Harper *writer, publishing executive*

CONNECTICUT

Old Saybrook
Hamilton, Donald Bengtsson *author*

DISTRICT OF COLUMBIA

Washington
Cavnar, Samuel Melmon *author, publisher, activist*

HAWAII

Hanalei
Ludwig, Myles Eric *writer, editor, publishing executive, art director*

Honolulu
Edel, (Joseph) Leon *biographer, educator*

IDAHO

Boise
Weinstein, Norman Charles *writer*

Emmett
Silva, Yvonne Joan *writer*

Idaho Falls
Collins, Matthew *poet*

MONTANA

Anaconda
Adams, Duncan Macleod *writer, psychotherapist*

Livingston
Clarke, Urana *writer, musician, educator*

Mc Leod
Hjortsberg, William Reinhold *author*

NEVADA

Las Vegas
Caro, Mike *writer, editor, publisher*
Charles, Frederick C. *publisher, editor, writer*
Eikenberry, Arthur Raymond *writer, service executive, researcher*

NEW HAMPSHIRE

Hanover
Bryan, Sharon Allen *writer, humanities educator*

NEW MEXICO

Albuquerque
Davidson, Juli *writer, entrepreneur*
Evans, Max Allen *writer, artist*
Miller, Louise Dean *writer, retired journalist*
Spencer, Gwynne Carol *writer*
Whiddon, Carol Price *writer, editor, consultant*
Whimbey, Arthur Emil *writer*

Corrales
Englade, Kenneth Francis *writer*
Page, Jake (James K. Page, Jr.) *writer, editor*

Las Cruces
Medoff, Mark Howard *playwright, screenwriter, novelist*

Los Alamos
Parker, Kathleene *writer, publishing executive*

Santa Fe
Bergé, Carol *author*
Harter, Penny *poet, English educator*
Knight, Carol Bell *author, lecturer, clergyperson*
Tarn, Nathaniel *poet, translator, educator*

Taos
Dickey, Robert Preston *author, educator, poet*

NEW YORK

New York
Burland, Brian Berkeley *novelist, poet, artist, scenarist, playwright*
Hawke, Simon Nicholas *writer, educator*
Heifner, Jack L. *writer*
Kass, Jerome Allan *writer*
Kluger, Steve *writer, scriptwriter*
Salter, James *writer*

Sunnyside
Wallmann, Jeffrey Miner *author*

OREGON

Boring
Gentry, Jeanne Louise *lecturer, writer*

Coos Bay
Reynolds, David Kent *writer, educator*

Eugene
Ailor, Karen Tana *magazine writer, proposal consultant*
Kannenberg, Ida Marguerite *writer*

Grants Pass
Stafford, Patrick Purcell *poet, writer, management consultant*

Hillsboro
Cornish, Linda Sowa Young *children's books author and illustrator, educator*

Lake Oswego
Carman, LauraLee *writer, personal development coach, speaker*

Newport
Kennedy, Richard Jerome *writer*

Otis
King, Frank William *writer*

Pleasant Hill
Kesey, Ken *writer*

Portland
DePrez, Daniel Robert *writer*
Lum, Paul *writer*
Milholland, David Marion *writer, editor*

Salem
Hays, Daniel William *writer, counselor, lecturer*

Terrebonne
Siebert, Diane Dolores *author, poet*

SOUTH CAROLINA

Sullivans Island
Ralston, Gilbert Alexander *writer, educator*

UTAH

Ivins
Riggs, June Rosemary *author, interior designer*

Provo
Hart, Edward LeRoy *poet, educator*
Hickman, Craig Ronald *author*

Salt Lake City
Becher, Stuart Lorenz *writer, planetarium show producer*
Bowes, Florence (Mrs. William David Bowes) *writer*
Ghiselin, Brewster *author, English language educator emeritus*
Salmon, William Irwin *writer*

WASHINGTON

Auburn
Johnson, Douglas Scott *writing educator*

Bellevue
Auestad, Amy Eileen *freelance writer, poet*
Habbestad, Kathryn Louise *writer*

Bellingham
Skinner, Knute Rumsey *poet, English educator*

Bremerton
Hanf, James Alphonso *poet, government official*

Edmonds
Swindler, Kathryn Elizabeth *writer*

Federal Way
Scott, Otto *writer*

Friday Harbor
Hill, Ruth Beebe *author, editor*

Issaquah
Trask, Robert Chauncey Riley *author, lecturer, foundation executive*

Kent
Raymond, Eugene Thomas *technical writer, retired aircraft engineer*

Lynnwood
Bear, Gregory Dale *writer, illustrator*

Olympia
Perkins, Gary Michael *writer, political consultant*

Port Townsend
Osborne, Jerry Paul *writer*

Roslyn
Lamb-Brassington, Kathryn Evelyn *writer, genealogist*

Seattle
Hawthorne, Nan Louise *writer, editor, trainer*
Kunkel, Georgie Myrtia *writer, retired school counselor*
Loeb, Paul Rogat *writer, lecturer*
Pearce, Jeannie *writer, real estate agent*
Sonenberg, Maya *writer, educator*
Wason, Betty (Elizabeth Wason) *author*

Vancouver
Larson, Charles Lester *television writer, producer, author*

WYOMING

Laramie
Boresi, Arthur Peter *author, educator*

CANADA

ALBERTA

Edmonton
Fenton, Terry Lynn *author, artist, consultant*

BRITISH COLUMBIA

Victoria
Harris, Christie Lucy *author*
Hodgins, Jack Stanley *author*

ADDRESS UNPUBLISHED

Bach, Muriel Dunkleman *author, actress*
Baird, Alan C. *screenwriter*
Barnes, Joanna *author, actress*
Barrows, Robert Guy *scriptwriter*
Bassett, Carol Ann *magazine, video, and radio documentary writer, producer, journalism educator*
Baum, Thomas Henle *writer, director, producer*
Bostwick, Angelina Celeste *technical writer*
Boswell, Winthrop Palmer *writer*
Briles, Judith *writer, speaker, consultant*
Bussewitz, M. Walter *writer*
Cairns, Diane Patricia *motion picture literary agent*
Campbell, Addison James, Jr. *writer*
Char, Carlene *writer, publisher, editor*
Claes, Gayla Christine *writer, editorial consultant*
Codye, Corinn *writer, editor*
Dahl, Bren Bennington *screenwriter*
D'Alessandro, Mary Patricia *essayist, poet, photographer, retired*
Dawdy, Doris Ostrander *writer*
Dawson, Frances Emily *poet, nurse*
Dean, Charles Albert *writer, educator, clergy member*
Delffs, Dudley J. *writer, educator*
Doig, Ivan *writer*
Drohojowska-Philp, Hunter *author, critic*
Ebersole, Martha C. *writer and producer*
Eckley, Alicia Kathryn *editor, writer, public relations specialist*
Elliott, Corinne Adelaide *retired copywriter*
Fraser, Kathleen Joy *poet, creative writing educator*
Fritz, Ethel Mae Hendrickson *writer*
Gallagher, Sarah Woodside *writer, producer*
Gottlieb, Sherry Gershon *author, editor*
Grant, John Barnard *writer*
Green, Joey *writer*
Green, Marilyn Virginia *writer*
Hall, Charles McAllister *writer*
Heffern, Richard Arnold *author*
Herbert, Mary Katherine Atwell *freelance writer*
Herman, George Adam *writer*
Humphries, Stephen Edward *writer*
Hyland, Penelope *writer, artist*
Isbell, Harold M(ax) *writer, investor*
Jacobs, Wilbur Ripley *writer, history educator*
Jones, Janet Dulin *writer, film producer*
Katchen, Carole Lee *writer, artist*
Kearse, David Grier *stage and screen writer, journalist*
Keenan, Gerald Kean *writer, retired publishing company executive*
Kellerman, Faye Marder *novelist, dentist*
Kelly, Florence Ann *writer, poet*
Kimbrell, Grady Ned *author, educator*
King, Gary Curtis *author, lecturer*
Kyd, Marilyn Gratton *writer, editor*
Lane, Linda Patricia *scriptwriter*
Lawrence, Jerome *playwright, director, educator*
Leininger, Robert Farnes *author, screenwriter*
Lightwood, Carol Wilson *writer*
London, Adele *poet*
Longstreet, Stephen (Chauncey Longstreet) *author, painter*
Madril, Lee Ann *writer*
Marx, Wesley *writer, environmental educator*
McPeak, William John *science and technical author, consultant*
Morang, Diane Judy *writer, television producer, business entrepreneur*
Muro, Vincent *author*
O'Neill, Elizabeth Stone *writer*
Orenstein, Peggy Jo *writer, editor*
Overby, Paul *writer, political analyst*
Paul, Paula Griffith *writer*
Peters, Barbara Humbird *writer, editor*
Poppoff, Ilia George *science writer, consultant*
Preminger, Erik Lee *writer, television producer*
Rising, Catharine Clarke *author*
Roberts, Wess *author*
Rosenberg, Jane *author, illustrator*
Ross, Jonathan *film writer, producer, director*
Schenkkan, Robert Frederic *writer, actor*
Scott, Latayne Colvett *writer*
Sears, Steven Lee *screenwriter, consultant*
Sharpe, Wenonah Finch *writer, educator, editor*
Simmons, Ted Conrad *writer*
Soler, Dona Katherine *poet*
Sorrell, Paul A. *writer*
Spada, James *author, publisher*
Spiegel, Marcia Cohn *writer*
Spies, Karen Bornemann *writer, education consultant*
Stone, Arlene *writer*
Storey, Isabel Nagy *writer, television producer*
Tobias, Sheila *writer, educator*
Topham, Douglas William *writer, consultant*
Ulam, Françoise *freelance writer, editor*
Wetterhahn, Ralph Francis *freelance writer*
Whelchel, Sandra Jane *writer*
Wilson, Brandon Laine *writer, advertising and public relations consultant, explorer*

ARTS: PERFORMING

UNITED STATES

ALASKA

Anchorage
Hood, Michael James *theatre educator*

Fairbanks
Riccio, Thomas Patrick *theater director*

Indian
Wright, Gordon Brooks *musician, conductor, educator*

ARIZONA

Flagstaff
Aurand, Charles Henry, Jr. *music educator*

Glendale
Neff, John *recording engineer, producer*
Reed, Lynda Bernal *video producer, writer*

Mesa
Black, Eric *conductor*
Feldaverd, Nicholas Edward, III *music educator, musician*
Harrop, Donald Bruce *film company executive*
Missal, Joshua Morton *composer, conductor*

Paradise Valley
Alcantara, Theo *conductor*

Phoenix
Aschaffenburg, Walter Eugene *composer, music educator*
Lambert, Dennis Alvin *radio news director*
Shaw, Lillie Marie King *vocalist*

Prescott
Moses, Elbert Raymond, Jr. *speech and dramatic arts educator*

Scottsdale
Fosgate Heggli, Julie Denise *producer*
Wolfgang, Bonnie Arlene *musician, bassoonist*

Sedona
Gregory, James *actor*
Griffin, (Alva) Jean *entertainer*

Sun City
Albright, Lois *operetta company executive director*

Tempe
Lombardi, Eugene Patsy *orchestra conductor, violinist, educator, recording artist*
Moore, Dianne Lea *recording studio owner*
Reber, William Francis *music educator, conductor*
Saldaña, Johnny *theatre educator, researcher*
Whipkey-Louden, Harriet Beulah *fine arts and theatre productions executive*

Tucson
Armstrong, R(obert) Dean *entertainer*
Brault, Marguerite Bryan *theatre organization administrator*
Malmgren, René Louise *educational theater administrator*
Roe, Charles Richard *baritone*
Ross, Glynn *opera administrator*
Seaman, Arlene Anna *musician, educator*

CALIFORNIA

Alameda
Austen, Shelli *actress*

Altadena
Chambers, Jonathan Goetz *film producer*

Antioch
Adams, Liliana Osses *music performer, harpist*

Apple Valley
Beller, Gerald Stephen *magician, former insurance company executive*

Aptos
Swenson, Kathleen Susan *music and art educator*

Bakersfield
Mason, Jeffrey Daniel *theatre educator*
Webb, Henry Robert *theatre arts educator*

Benicia
Cummings, Barton *musician*

Berkeley
Kleiman, Vivian Abbe *filmmaker*
Matsumura, Vera Yoshi *pianist*
Quick, John Antony *film and video producer*
Reid, Frances Evelyn Kroll *cinematographer, director, film company executive*
Ridgway, David Wenzel *educational film producer, director*

Beverly Hills
Becks, Ronald Arthur *film producer*
Bellisario, Donald P. *television director*
Brokaw, Norman Robert *talent agency executive*
Chritton, George A. *film producer*
Farley, Bill Thomas *entertainment industry executive*
Foch, Nina *actress, creative consultant, educator*
Greenberg, Barry Michael *talent executive*
Griffin, Merv Edward *former entertainer, television producer, entrepreneur*
Hunt, Peter Huls *director, theatrical lighting designer*
Jordan, Glenn *theater director*
Kantor, Igo *film and television producer*
Linkletter, Arthur Gordon *radio and television broadcaster*
Lynn, Jonathan Adam *director, writer, actor*
Martinson, Constance Frye *television program hostess, producer*
Matovich, Mitchel Joseph, Jr. *motion picture producer, executive*
Mischer, Donald Leo *television director and producer*
Nichols, Mike *stage and film director*
Robinson, Phil Alden *director*
Uffner, Beth Marilyn *television and film agent*
White, Betty *actress, comedienne*

Burbank
Berg, Dave *television producer, writer*
Cowings, Everett Alvin *entertainment manager, film/television producer*
Ett, Alan Paul *composer*
Girolami, Lisa S. *film producer*
Gobetti, Maria Cecilia *acting coach, director, producer*
Kaplan, Martin Harold *writer, producer*
Sutter, Diane *radio and television group executive*
Tatum, Thomas Deskins *film and television producer, director*

Calabasas
Albrecht, Joie *television and film producer, director, writer*

Canoga Park
Peirson, George Ewell *art director, educator*

Castaic
Goren, Bruce Neal *television engineer, computer graphics company executive*

Chico
King, Claudia Louan *film producer, lecturer*
Pate, Susan Lee Hargrave *theatre arts educator, choreographer*

Claremont
Doty, Horace Jay, Jr. *theater administrator, arts consultant*
Eisel, Gunnar Georg *music educator*
Pronko, Leonard Cabell *theater educator*

Clovis
Speace, Oscar Kimbrough *television producer and director, writer*

Costa Mesa
Taussig, H. Arthur *film analyst, film and photography educator*

Crockett
Moors, Leonard Jerald, Jr. (Jerry Moors) *musician*

Culver City
Stark, Ray *motion picture producer*
Trebek, Alex *television game show host*

Cypress
Tischler, David William *music educator*

Del Mar
Curl, James Michael *special event producer, manager*

Encino
Eves, Jeffrey P. *entertainment industry executive*

Fresno
Seaberg, Eric Dayle *audio engineer*
West, Michelle Lynne *television personality*

Fullerton
Linahon, James Joseph *music educator, musician*
Stedman, William Preston *music educator*

Glendale
Allen, Norm *entertainer, marketing entrepreneur*
Ernst, Donald William *producer*
Grillo, Leo *actor, photographer, animal rescuer*

Glendora
Del Vecchio, Dawn Marie *theatre manager*

Hemet
Bible, Frances Lillian *mezzo-soprano, educator*
White, Michael Lee *executive producer, writer*

Hidden Hills
Andrews, Ralph Herrick *television producer*

Irvine
Ruyter, Nancy Lee Chalfa *dance educator*

Joshua Tree
Styles, Beverly *entertainer*

La Crescenta
James, Mark William *cameraman*
Kessler-Hodgson, Lee Gwendolyn *actress, corporate executive*

La Honda
Beckman, Kenneth Oren *film and video specialist, researcher*

La Jolla
Corrigan, Mary Kathryn *theatre educator*
Gall, Sally Moore *librettist, poet, scholar*
Mullin, Constance Hammond *performing arts organization administrator*
Reynolds, Roger Lee *composer*

Laguna Hills
Herold, Ralph Elliott *motion picture arts educator*

Lake Hughes
La Mont, Tawana Faye *video director, public relations executive*
LaMont-Wells, Tawana F. *video director*

Littlerock
Caston, Jonathon Craig *radio producer*

Los Angeles
Amey, Rae *television and video developer, producer*
Archuletta, Patti Stolkin *performing arts association administrator*
Balestrero, Dan Charles *voice teacher, TV producer*
Banner, Bob *television producer, director*
Barker, Robert William *television personality*
Bartley, Opelene *actress, consultant*
Bell, Lee Phillip *television personality, television producer*
Benson, Francis M. *production coordinator, radio producer*
Bialosky, Marshall Howard *composer*
Brosnan, Peter Lawrence *documentary filmmaker*
Burrows, James *television and motion picture director, producer*
Burton, Al *producer, director, writer*
Calman, Craig David *writer, actor*
Carnicke, Sharon Marie *drama educator, theatre specialist and director*
Carroll, Pat *actress*
Chomsky, Marvin J. *director*
Conner, Lindsay Andrew *screenwriter, producer*
Cury, Ivan N. *producer, director, educator*
Davidson, Gordon *theatrical producer, director*
Dillingham, Charles, III *performing arts executive*
Dumas, William Joseph *filmmaker*
Fleischmann, Ernest Martin *music administrator*
Gazdag, Gyula *film director, educator*
Glick, Samuel David *entertainment/communications executive, shop owner*
Hancock, Herbert Jeffrey (Herbie Hancock) *composer, pianist, publisher*
Healy, Kieran John Patrick *lighting designer, consultant*
Hemion, Dwight Arlington *television producer, director*
Hemmings, Peter William *orchestra and opera administrator*
Hicklin, Ronald Lee *music production company executive*
Hunt, Peter Roger *film director, writer, editor*
Jackson, Isaiah *conductor*
Kahan, Sheldon Jeremiah *musician, singer*
Kuyper, Peter Walk *motion picture company executive*
Lewitzky, Bella *choreographer*
Magner, Martin *theatrical producer and director*
Mann, Rachel Kronstadt *writer, producer*
Mansoor, Christine Marie-Dominique *television producer*
Mason, Marshall W. *theater director*
Mc Coy, Frank Milton *concert pianist, educator, lecturer*
McDonald, Jeanne Gray (Mrs. John B. McDonald) *television producer*
Michaels, Stacey Qualls *recording engineer*
Michelson, Sonia *music educator, author*
Mueller, Carl Richard *theater arts educator, author*
Newton, Richard Edward *filmmaker*
Nichols, Mark Allan *theatre administrator*
Rafkin, Alan *television and film director*
Richmond, Rocsan *television/video producer, publicist, inventor, interior designer*
Salloum, Glenn Richard *film company assistant*
Salzman, David Elliot *entertainment industry executive*
Schurmann, Gerard *composer, conductor*
Schwartzman, Arnold Martin *film director, graphic designer*
Schwortz, Barrie Marshall *video/film producer*
Sherman, Eric *director, writer, educator*
Slonimsky, Nicolas *conductor, composer*
Stanfill, Shelton G. *performing arts administrator*
Steen Olson, Christopher J. *film producer/director, computer consultant*
Stevenson, Robert Murrell *music educator*
Termini, Olga Ascher *music educator*
Tesh, John *television talk show host*
Vannatter, Michael Steven *art director*
Vintas, Gustavo Horacio *actor, psychiatrist*
Warner, Paul Wellman *film and theater director, educator*
Williamson, Edwin Lee *wardrobe and costume consultant*
Wilson, Ervin McDonald *music consultant*
Winters, Barbara Jo *musician*
Woessner, Frederick T. *composer, pianist*
Wood, Karen Sue *theatre manager, stage producer, consultant*

Malibu
Georgopoulos, Dean Elias *film producer, real estate developer*
Page, Richard Edward *entertainment company executive, business owner*

Menlo Park
Gioia, Ted *musician, writer*

Mill Valley
Singleton, Harold Craig *music educator*
Walters, Bruce Allen *special effects designer*

Montrose
Twitchell, Theodore Grant *music educator and composer*

Morongo Valley
Groves, William Ralph *actor*

Mountain Center
De Forest, Edgar Lester *actor, poet, educator*

Nevada City
Simpson, Dave *radio producer*

Newbury Park
Issari, M(ohammad) Ali *film producer, educator, consultant*

Newport Beach
Bryant, Janet Hough *actress, voice teacher, performing artist*

North Hollywood
Epcar, Richard Michael *actor, writer, director*
Frost, Mark *director, producer, writer*
Harper, Joseph Stafford *theater educator, performer*
Levin, Alvin Irving *composer*
Martell, William Claise *screenwriter, film producer, writer*

Novato
Valentino, Stephen Eric *production and entertainment company executive, actor, singer*

Oakland
DeFazio, Lynette Stevens *dancer, choreographer, educator, chiropractor, author, actress*
Randle, Ellen Eugenia Foster *opera and classical singer, educator*

Pacific Palisades
Nachmanovitch, Stephen *violinist, composer, author and educator*

Palm Springs
Garris, Sidney Reginald *artist management company executive*

Palmdale
Nuse, Deland Lynn *film director, writer, producer*

Palo Alto
Mitchell, William E. *video game producer*
Nadel, James Oliver *musician, music educator*

Pasadena
Mantle, Larry Edward *radio director*

Pomona
Stone, Jeffrey Thomas *musician*

Rancho Cucamonga
Robertson, Carey Jane *musician, educator*

Redwood City
Curotto, Michael Lloyd *professional musician, educator*

Sacramento
Nice, Carter *conductor, music director*

San Anselmo
Farr, David Donald *musician, educator, administrator*

San Bruno
Hansen, Julia *music educator*

San Diego
Burge, David Russell *concert pianist, composer, piano educator*
Campbell, Ian David *opera company director*
Elaine, Karen *musician, educator*
Flettner, Marianne *opera administrator*
Gandelman, Joel Leslie *ventriloquist*
Lakoff, Evelyn *music association executive*
Price, Betty Jeanne *choirchime soloist, writer*

San Dimas
Wolfe, Edward William, II *music educator, composer*

San Francisco
Adessa, Anthony Thomas *violinist, music educator, conductor*
Bergen, Christopher Brooke *opera company administrator, translator, editor*
Blasdale, Allan Walter *organist, choirmaster, pianist*
Caspe, Naomi *children's entertainer, educator*
Davis, John Jeffrey *musician*
De Coteau, Denis *music director, conductor*
Dupont, Colyer Lee *television and film producer, video and film distributing company executive*
Eilenberg, Lawrence Ira *theater educator, artistic director*
Getty, Gordon Peter *composer, philanthropist*
Kennedy, Matthew Lawry *dance educator, writer*
Marks, William J. *cable television executive*
Mendonça, Maria Luisa *video producer, educator*
Pastreich, Peter *orchestra executive director*
Peterson, Wayne Turner *composer, pianist*
Ram, Tracy Schaefer *ballet company manager*
Runnicles, Donald *conductor*
Sullivan, John *theater administrator*
Tiano, Anthony Steven *television producer, book publishing executive*

San Jose
Dalis, Irene *mezzo-soprano, opera company administrator, music educator*
Grin, Leonid *conductor*

San Pedro
Sprung, John Leon *film company engineer, cinematographer, auctioneer*

Santa Ana
Isaacson, Gene Lester *fine arts educator*
Ogle, Joseph Womack *composer, retired piano teacher*

Santa Barbara
Behrenbruch, William David *filmmaker, educator*
Potter, Robert Alonzo *dramatic art educator*
Wayland, Newton Hart *conductor*

Santa Clarita
Powell, Mel *composer*

Santa Cruz
Wolters, Christopher Frederick *performing company executive*

Santa Margarita
Baker, Janita Lou *musician, luthier*

Santa Monica
Alenikov, Vladimir *motion picture director and writer*
Black, Noel Anthony *television and film director*
Edwards, Sarah Anne *radio, cable television personality, clinical social worker*
Gossage, James Dearl *quality control administrator*
Kalb, Benjamin Stuart *television producer, director*
Kaplan, Mike *film and video producer, director, and distributor, marketing executive*
London, Andrew Barry *film editor*
Owens, Gary *broadcast personality, entrepreneur, author*
Schroeder, William Robert *actor, graphic designer, linguist*
Simons, Annette *performing company executive*

Santa Rosa
Nelson, Jon R. *music educator*

Sherman Oaks
Graham, Steven Piddington *entertainment production company executive*
Hansch, Joachim Horst *music director*
Marshall, Meryl Corinblit *television producer, lawyer*
Peterson, Lowell *cinematographer*

Simi Valley
Durst, Eric *television and commercial director*

Springville
Montana, Montie, Jr. *performing arts producer*

Stanford
Rehm, Maurice Pate *drama and classics educator, actor, director*

Stockton
Coburn, Robert James *music educator, composer*
Hull, Grant Warren *music educator, composer*
Jennings, Charles Raymond *music educator, bands director*
Roche, Catherine Mary *music educator*

Studio City
Autry, Gene (Orvon Gene Autry) *actor, entertainer, broadcasting executive, baseball team executive*
Bergen, Polly *actress*
Cockrell, Frank Boyd, II *film production company executive*
McClellan, Bennett Earl *producer*
Sertner, Robert Mark *producer*

Sunset Beach
Bettis, John Gregory *songwriter*

Sylmar
Foster, Dudley Edwards, Jr. *musician, educator*

Thousand Oaks
Hagopian, Jacob Michael *documentary film producer, political scientist, educator*
Mathias, Harry Michael *cinematographer, consultant, author*

Toluca Lake
Friedman, Alan Ira *make-up artist*
Rustam, Mardi Ahmed *film and television producer, publisher*

Topanga
Wilcock, John *TV producer, writer, editor*

Turlock
Klein, James Mikel *music educator*

University Park
Cheng, Meiling *theatre arts educator*

Valencia
Millar, Michael William *trombonist*

Vallejo
Allen, Rick (Frederick Allen Klycinski) *magician, advertising and publicity consultant*

Van Nuys
Allen, Stephen Valentine Patrick William *television comedian, author, pianist, songwriter*
Kazle, Elynmarie *producer*
King-Ettema, Elizabeth Dorothy *video and film editor, writer, photographer*
Morgan, Lanny *musician*

Venice
Furman, Will *film producer, director, cinematographer, writer*
Nathan, Adele Marcia *research director*

West Hollywood
Sherman, Robert B(ernard) *composer, lyricist, screenwriter*

Woodland Hills
Taylor, Rowan Shaw *music educator, composer, conductor*
Wester, Keith Albert *film and television recording engineer, television executive*

Yountville
Damé-Shepp, Diane *art management administrator*

COLORADO

Arvada
Pettit, Margaret Esta *broadcasting executive*

Aspen
Eirman, Thomas Fredrick *music festival manager*
Harth, Robert James *music festival executive*

Basalt
Puente, Tito Anthony *orchestra leader, composer, arranger*
Severinsen, Doc (Carl H. Severinsen) *conductor, musician*

Boulder
Blake, Bambi Reva *international fine artist*
Boydston, James Christopher *composer*
Brakhage, James Stanley *filmmaker, educator*
Duckworth, Guy *musician, educator*
Fink, Robert Russell *music theorist, former university dean*
Hayes, Deborah *musicology educator, college administrator*
Sarson, John Christopher *television producer, director, writer*
Spanier, Nancy Louise *artistic director, educator, choreographer*
Symons, James Martin *theater and dance educator*
Tolliver-Palma, Calvin Eugene *violist, instructor, performer*

Cherry Hills Village
Stapleton, Katharine Hall (Katie Stapleton) *food broadcaster, author*

Denver
Ceci, Jesse Arthur *violinist*
Folger, William Montraville *actor, journalist*
Fredmann, Martin *ballet artistic director, educator, choreographer*
Rule, Daniel Rhodes *opera company executive*
Schwartz, Cherie Anne Karo *storyteller*

Littleton
Fortna, Valerié Annette *dance and performing company owner, instructor*

Pueblo
Park, Dale Lee *standup comedian, author*

Steamboat Springs
Norris, Mary Beth *flutist, educator*

Sterling
Kuebler, Richard Arthur *theatre educator, consultant*

FLORIDA

North Palm Beach
Hayman, Richard Warren Joseph *conductor*

HAWAII

Honolulu
Baker, Kent Alfred *television news director*
Cohen, Warren *musician, writer*
Engle, Robert Irwin *music educator, musician, composer, writer*
Greenberg, Marvin *retired music educator*
Johanos, Donald *orchestra conductor*
Kelin, Daniel Allen, II *theatre director*
Landovsky, John *artistic director*
McGinn, Susan Frances *musician*
Smith, Barbara Barnard *music educator*
Yasui, Byron Kiyoshi *musician, music educator*

Waimanalo
Dougherty, Michael *writer, filmmaker*

IDAHO

Moscow
Bray, R(obert) Bruce *music educator*
Klimko, Ronald James *music educator*
Samaniego, Pamela Susan *executive producer*

Twin Falls
Yost, Kelly Lou *pianist*

INDIANA

Fort Wayne
Compton, Tamara Lynn *theatre director, educator*

MASSACHUSETTS

Boston
Moriarty, John *opera administrator, artistic director*
Sellars, Peter *theater director*

MICHIGAN

Interlochen
Smith, Henry Charles, III *symphony orchestra conductor*

MONTANA

Billings
Barnea, Uri N. *music director, conductor, composer, violinist*
Pihlaja, Maxine Muriel Mead *orchestra executive*

Missoula
Crump, Juliette Taft *dance educator*
Knowles, William Leroy (Bill Knowles) *television news producer, journalism educator*
Marquand, Ian MacDonald *television producer*

NEBRASKA

Omaha
Johnson, James David *concert pianist, educator*

NEVADA

Las Vegas
Capelle, Madelene Carole *opera singer, educator, music therapist*
Castro, Joseph Armand *music director, pianist, composer, orchestrator*
Wiemer, Robert Ernest *film and television producer, writer, director*

NEW JERSEY

Manalapan
Armstrong, Andrew Robert *film director, producer*

NEW MEXICO

Albuquerque
Ellingboe, Bradley Ross *musician, educator*
Grealish, Jeanne Blair *voice educator*
Smyer, Myrna Ruth *drama educator*

Edgewood
Hamilton, Jerald *musician*

Santa Fe
Baustian, Robert Frederick *conductor*
Crosby, John O'Hea *conductor, opera manager*
Gaddes, Richard *performing arts administrator*
Jackson, Sally *location casting director*
Kanegis, Arthur L.D. *film producer, screenwriter*

NEW YORK

New York
Bernardi, Mario *conductor*
Fryer, Robert Sherwood *theatrical producer*
Harrell, Lynn Morris *cellist*
Hawkanson, David Robert *theatre company executive*
Penn, Arthur Hiller *film and theatre producer*
Schwarz, Gerard *conductor, musician*
Talmi, Yoav *conductor, composer*
Tilson Thomas, Michael *symphony conductor*

OREGON

Ashland
Hirschfeld, Gerald Joseph *cinematographer*

Eugene
Bailey, Exine Margaret Anderson *soprano, educator*
Hsu, Apo *conductor*
Valdez, Stephen Kenneth *music educator, researcher, consultant*

Lake Oswego
Edwards, Andrew *arts administrator*

Medford
Shinn, Duane K. *music publisher*
Tevis, Barry Lee *television producer, marketing executive*

Portland
Bailey, Robert C. *opera company executive*
Brown, Deborah Elizabeth *television producer, marketing professional*
Cole-McCullough, Daniel *music educator*
DePreist, James Anderson *conductor*
Hill, Andrew William *jazz musician, composer*
Leyden, Norman *conductor*

Talent
O'Rourke, Michael *artistic director*

UTAH

American Fork
Johnson, Lois Jean *music educator*

Cedar City
Cook, Douglas Neilson *theatre educator, producer, artistic director*

Ogden
Howard, Sherwin Ward *theatre educator*

Orem
Karr, Cheryl Lofgreen *film producer, consultant*

Provo
Pratt, Rosalie Rebollo *harpist, educator*
Woodbury, Lael Jay *theatre educator*

Saint George
Belnap, Norma Lee Madsen *musician*
Brock, James Wilson *drama educator, playwright, researcher*

Salt Lake City
Ewers, Anne *opera company director*
Hahn, Joan Christensen *drama educator, travel agent*
Morey, Charles Leonard, III *theatrical director*
Thompson, Edgar Joseph *musician, educator*
Zabriskie, Robert *performing arts association administrator, data processing manager*

Sandy
George, Mary Gae *music educator*

VIRGINIA

Norfolk
Allen, Russell Plowman *opera company executive*

WASHINGTON

Auburn
Overholt, Miles Harvard *cable television consultant*

Bellevue
Hilbert, Stephanie Mayer *actress, director, producer*

College Place
Spring, Glenn Ernest *composer*

Gig Harbor
Ramsey, Jerry Virgil *radio broadcaster, educator, financial planner*

Issaquah
Hunt, Robert William *theatrical producer, data processing consultant*

Lynnwood
Krause, Thomas Evans *record promotion consultant*

Marysville
Philpott, Larry La Fayette *horn player*

Mercer Island
Francis, Carolyn Rae *music educator, musician, author, publisher*

Renton
Pettigrew Welch, Dana Mary *musician, insurance agent*

Seattle
Bensinger, Lenore Cooper *theater director*
Coleman, Dennis G. *conductor*
Dempster, Stuart Ross *trombonist, composer, music educator*
Forbes, David Craig *musician*
Jenkins, Speight *opera company executive, writer*
Jensen, Helen *musical artists management company executive*
Kopta, Jean Marilyn *voice educator, vocal performer*
Nishitani, Martha *dancer*
Nolte, Scott Lloyd *artistic director, actor*
Russell, Francia *ballet director, educator*
Rutter, Deborah Frances *orchestra administrator*
Ryder, Hal *theatre educator, director*
Sateren, Terry *theater technical production*
Stowell, Kent *ballet director*

Spokane
Fowler, Betty Janmae *dance company director, editor*
Pugh, Kyle Mitchell, Jr. *musician, music educator*
Young, Michael Edward *music educator*

Sumner
Poppe, Donna *music educator*

Tacoma
Haas, Catherine May *performing arts executive*

Woodinville
McGowan, Mitchell Joseph *director, stage manager*

WYOMING

Cheyenne
Rohla, Dru Allen *civic center director*

CANADA

ALBERTA

Banff
Fruchtman, Milton Allen *film and television producer, director*

Calgary
Graf, Hans *conductor*
LaHay, David George Michael *ballet company director*
Lauchlan, Douglas Martyn *performing arts administrator*

Edmonton
McPhee, W. R. (Bob McPhee) *orchestra managing director*

BRITISH COLUMBIA

Saanichton
Little, Carl Maurice *performing arts administrator*

Vancouver
Hallam, Robert J. *performing company executive, consultant*

COSTA RICA

Santa Ana
Latham, Debra Lynne *radio station administrator*

ENGLAND

London
Foster, Lawrence *concert and opera conductor*
Salonen, Esa-Pekka *conductor*

ISRAEL

Tel Aviv
Mehta, Zubin *conductor, musician*

ADDRESS UNPUBLISHED

Adelson, Mervyn Lee *entertainment and communication industry executive*
Aguiar, William, Jr. *music and dance critic*
Akiyama, Carol Lynn *motion picture industry executive*
Alberts, David *artistic director, mime*
Aldag, Richard Jeffrey *composer*
Allen, Denise Newbold *music educator*
Askin, Leon *artistic director, actor, producer, writer*
Baerwald, Susan Grad *television broadcasting executive producer*
Behlmer, Rudy H., Jr. *director, writer, film educator*
Berman, Sanford Solomon *motion picture sound designer, composer, arranger, artist*
Birrell, G. William (Bill Birrell) *special effects executive*
Brady, Mary Rolfes *music educator*
Campobasso, Craig *casting director*
Collard, Lorraine Fullmer *violin educator*
Craft, Brian Thomas *stand up comedian, embetterment consultant*
Curry, Jane Kathleen *theater educator*
Dean, Dearest (Lorene Glosup) *songwriter*
Debus, Eleanor Viola *retired business management company executive*
Dechario, Tony Houston *symphony orchestra executive*
D'Elia, William Vincent *film director*
Elikann, Lawrence S. (Larry Elikann) *television and film director*
Favre, June Marie *actress, singer*
Flood, James Tyrrell *broadcasting executive*
Foley, Mary Kathleen *theatre arts educator*
Frank, Laurie *screenwriter*
Frankish, Brian Edward *film producer, director*
Goldstein, William M. *composer, producer*
Gordon, Claude Eugene *musician*
Great, Don Charles *composer, music company executive*
Greenlick, Vicki Ruth *film producer*
Greenspan, Evan Martin *music industry executive*
Guttentag, William Sidney *television producer*
Guttman, Irving Allen *opera stage director*
Hanket, Arthur Anthony *actor, marketing and sales analyst, consultant*
Hansen, Christine Merri *music educator*
Harper, Richard Henry *film producer, director*
Harris, Edward A. *producer, writer, director*
Hartman, Terry A. *filmmaker*
Heard, Ronald Roy *motion picture producer*
Hislop, Kare Elizabeth *music director, educator*
Hite, Catharine Leavey *orchestra manager*
Howard, Mel *film producer, educator*
Huning, Deborah Gray *actress, dancer, audiologist, photographer/video producer-editor*
Iacangelo, Peter August *actor*
Kaylan, Howard Lawrence *musical entertainer, composer*
Kennedy, Orin *film company executive*
Kinberg, Jud *producer*
Knobeloch, James Joseph *actor*
Little, Loren Everton *musician, ophthalmologist*
Lobanov-Rostovsky, Oleg *arts association executive*
Lucas, Beth Anne *television producer*
Main, Robert Gail *communications educator, training consultant, television and film producer, former army officer*
Malouf-Cundy, Pamela Bonnie *visual arts editor*
Mandel, Jeff *writer, director, composer*
Mansouri, Lotfollah *opera stage director*
Marinacci, Teresa Denise *theater director*
Mason, Elizabeth Frye *violinist, educator*
Matthau, Charles Marcus *film director*
McClain, Richard Stan *cinematographer*
Megalos, Bill *film director*
Miller, Steve *television director, producer*
Murjee, Tara Bonita *choreographer, dance educator*
Myerson, Alan *director, film and television writer*
Neary, Patricia Elinor *ballet director*
Newhart, Bob *entertainer*
O'Brien, Jack George *artistic director*
Porter, Richard Kane *audio engineer, consultant*
Price, Thomas Frederick *theatre educator*
Pryor, Carolyn Ann *church musician, educator*
Reda, Mark Anthony *television producer*
Robinett, Ann *music educator*
Rosenthal, Emily Sarah *television producer*
Salvatore, Richard John *cinematographer, company executive*
Sandrich, Jay H. *television director*
Schaefer, George Louis *theatrical producer and director, educator*
Sikes, Cynthia Lee *actress, singer*
Sisemore, Claudia *educational films and videos producer, director*
Smith, Carter Blakemore *broadcaster*
Smith, Irby Jay *film producer*
Smoot, Hazel Lampkin *retired piano teacher, poet*
Solow, Herbert Franklin *film producer, writer*
Spier, Luise Emma *film editor, director*
Steinberg, Russell *composer*
Summers, Cathleen Ann *film producer*
Sutherland, Bruce *composer, pianist*
Symmes, Daniel Leslie *three-dimensional technology executive, producer, director*
Tanner, Lynn *actress*
Tarbuck, Barbara Joan *actor*
Taylor, Guy Watson *symphonic conductor*
Timmons, William Milton *producer, freelance writer, retired cinema arts educator, publisher, film maker*
Tokofsky, Jerry Herbert *film producer*
Topilow, Carl S. *conductor*
Truffaut, Michelle *film director*
Veselack, Marilyn Sue *musician, silversmith, massage therapist*
Wickes, Mary *actress*
Williams, Cindy J. *actress*
Williamson, Laird *stage director, actor*
Wilson, Michael Gregg *film producer, writer*
Woodruff, Virginia *television and radio host, producer*
Worthey, Carol *composer*
Wright, Susie *stage manager*
Yasnyi, Allan David *media communications executive*
Zhao, Li *fine arts company executive, teacher, consultant*
Zick, Lester George *actor, systems consultant*

ARTS: VISUAL

UNITED STATES

ALASKA

Anchorage
Shadrach, (Martha) Jean Hawkins *artist*
Welter, Cole H. *artist, educator*

Cooper Landing
Downer, Spelman Evans *artist, consultant*

Cordova
Bugbee-Jackson, Joan *sculptor*

Fairbanks
Brody, Arthur William *artist, educator*
Chin, Wanda Won *graphics designer*
Mollett, David L. *artist*
Woodward, Kesler Edward *artist, educator*

Ketchikan
McDermott, David (John) *artist, writer, photographer*

ARIZONA

Carefree
Harris, Robert George *illustrator*

Cornville
Waddell, John Henry *sculptor*

Flagstaff
Arentz, Dick *photographer*
Salsig, Doyen *photographer, photography studio owner*

Green Valley
Easton, Roger David *art history educator*
Nasvik-Dennison, Anna *artist*

Lake Montezuma
Burkee, Irvin *artist*

Mesa
Dawson, John Alan *artist*
Kaida, Tamarra *art and photography educator*

Oracle
Rush, Andrew Wilson *artist*

Paradise Valley
Heller, Jules *artist, writer*
Maxey, Diane Meadows *artist*

Phoenix
Braverman, Donna Caryn *fiber artist*
Nisula, Larry William *artist*
Reade, James Garretson *artist, illustrator*

Prescott
Farrar, Elaine Willardson *artist*
McClure, Thomas Fulton *artist, retired educator*
Willoughby, James Russell *artist*

Scottsdale
Lang, Margo Terzian *artist*
Lehrman, Lewis Barrett *artist, writer*

Sedona
DeMille, Leslie Benjamin *artist*
Jennerjahn, Warren P. *artist, educator*

Tempe
Fahlman, Betsy Lee *American art history educator*
Kinney, Raleigh Earl *artist*
McFarland, Timothy Andrew *artist, artisan-craftsman*
Pile, James William *artist educator*
Turk, Rudy Henry *artist, retired museum director*

Tucson
Bloomfield, Suzanne *artist*
Bredlow, Thomas Gayle *metals designer, craftsman*
Denniston, Douglas *artist, educator*
Flint, Willis Wolfschmidt (Willi Wolfschmidt) *artist*
Geoffrion, Moira Marti *artist, educator*
Goodman, Mary A. *photographer*
Hamilton, Ruth Hellmann *design company owner*
Quiróz, Alfred James *art educator, artist, lecturer*
Root, Nile *photographer, educator*
Teiwes, Helga *photographer*

Whiteriver
Cosay, Bennett Wayne *photographer*

CALIFORNIA

Agoura Hills
Wiechec, Donald *photographer*

Altadena
Green, David Oliver, Jr. *sculptor, designer*

Anaheim
Nelipovich, Sandra Grassi *artist*

Angwin
Seyle, Robert Harley *artist, educator*

Aptos
Woods, Gurdon Grant *sculptor*

Arcata
Hess, Ivan Edward *set designer, educator*
Land-Weber, Ellen *photography educator*

Aromas
Nutzle, Futzie (Bruce John Kleinsmith) *artist, author, cartoonist*

Auburn
Blaney, Suzanne Avery *artist*
Schulzke, Margot Seymour *artist, educator*

Avalon
Burns, Denise Ruth *artist*

Azusa
Tarkington, Dickey Edward *artist, educator*

Bakersfield
Kerzie, Ted L., Jr. *painter, fine arts educator*

Baldwin Park
Phillips, Donna Rose *production artist, writer*

Belmont
Harris, David Jack *artist, painter, educator*
Pava, Esther Shub *artist, educator*

Berkeley
Edwards, John David *artist*
Felter, June Marie *artist*
Genn, Nancy *artist*
Hartman, Robert Leroy *artist, educator*
Healy, Anne *sculptor*
Hoare, Tyler James *sculptor*
Mitchell, Margaretta Kuhlthau *photographer*
Miyasaki, George Joji *artist*
Sussman, Wendy Rodriguez *artist, educator*

Beverly Hills
Potter, Stephen Arnold *production designer*
Ting, Shao Kuang *artist, educator*

Brentwood
Peters, William Frank *art educator*

Burbank
Merrill, Thomas St. John *medical photographer*

Calistoga
Nechis, Barbara *artist*
Thollander, Earl Gustave *artist, author*

Camarillo
Jones, Jeanne Rae *art director*

Canoga Park
Duzy, Merrilyn Jeanne *artist, educator*

Carmel
Bergfors, Judith Lyn *photographer*
Kennedy, John Edward *art dealer, appraiser, curator*
Skalagard, Hans Martin *artist*

Carmel Valley
Corser, Kira Dorothy *photographic artist*
Sands, Sharon Louise *graphic design executive, art publisher, artist*

Carmichael
Sahs, Majorie Jane *art educator*
Wang, Jian Chuan-Qiu *artist*

Castro Valley
Soldahl-Hertzog, Nan *architectural illustrator, artist*

Chatsworth
Luebtow, John Gilbert *artist*

Claremont
Benjamin, Karl Stanley *artist, educator*
Furman, David Stephen *art educator, artist*
Leabhart, Thomas Glenn *art educator*
Macko, Nancy *artist, educator*

Concord
Tackitt, James William *graphic arts/photography educator, genealogical researcher*

Coronado
Hubbard, Donald *marine artist, writer*

Costa Mesa
Muller, Jerome Kenneth *photographer, art gallery director, editor*

Culver City
Apple, Jacqueline B. (Jacki Apple) *artist, writer, educator*

Cypress
Mathiesen, Timothy Rollin *photographer*

Daggett
Bailey, Katherine Christine *artist, writer*

Daly City
Leong, Lam-Po (Lanbo Liang) *artist, educator*

Davis
Rivers, Victoria Z. *textile design educator, artist*
Storey, Phoebe Reed *artist*

Dillon Beach
Petersen, Roland *artist, printmaker*

El Cajon
Harvey, Elaine Louise *artist, educator*

Emeryville
Grafton, Frederick Wellington *artist*
Jones, David *artist*

Encinitas
Budek, Allin Alla *artist*
Conrad, John Wilfred *fine arts educator, ceramist*

Encino
Baciu, Michael *photographer*
LaCom, Wayne Carl *artist, writer*

Fillmore
Timmons, Terry Lee *photographer, educator*

Fresno
Stuart, Dorothy Mae *artist*

Fullerton
Corsi, Sandro *artist, educator*

Gilroy
Decker, Bo *artist*

Glendale
Lebejoara, Ovidiu *artist*
Sweet, Harvey *theatric, scenic and lighting designer*
Turner, Nancy Elizabeth *artist, designer*

Green Valley Lake
Wood, Robert Earle *artist, educator*

Hawthorne
Palmer, Charles Ray *graphics specialist and production controller*

Hayward
Jordahl, Geir Arild *photographer, educator*

Hollywood
Shersher, Zinovy Israil *artist*

Huntington Beach
McNally, Brian Craig *creative director, philosopher, publisher*

Indio
Lloyd, Douglas George *watercolor artist, educator*

Irvine
Kingman, Dong *artist, educator*
Koo, Grace *artist*
Varo, Marton-Geza *sculptor*
Zhang, Jim Zenhua *artist, consultant*

Kelseyville
Fletcher, Leland Vernon *artist*

La Jolla
Fredman, Faiya Rubenstein *artist*
Imana, Jorge Garron *artist*
Silva, Ernest R. *visual arts educator, artist*

La Mirada
Feldman, Roger Lawrence *artist, educator*

La Puente
Collins, Dick (rkc) *artist*

Lafayette
Beaumont, Mona *artist*
Kapp, Eleanor Jeanne *impressionistic artist, writer, researcher*
Shurtleff, Akiko Aoyagi *artist, consultant*

Laguna Beach
Darrow, Paul Gardner *painter, printmaker, cartoonist, illustrator*
DiGenova, Silvano Antonio *rare coin and fine art dealer*
Jacques, Michael Louis *artist, educator*

Laguna Niguel
Pierce, Hilda (Hilda Herta Harmel) *painter*

Lake Arrowhead
Barnes, Clifford V. *artist*

Lake Elsinore
Bouchard, Paul Eugene *artist*

Lakeport
Twitchell, Kent *mural artist*

Lancaster
Coleman-Levy, Jack Robin *photographic laboratory design consultant*

Larkspur
Frances, Harriette (Sherana) *painter, printmaker, consultant*

Lodi
Eger, Marilyn Rae *artist*

Long Beach
Braunstein, Terry Malikin *artist*
Ferreira, Armando Thomas *sculptor, educator*
Sanchez-H., Jose *fine arts educator, producer, director, media consultant*

Los Alamitos
Lucas, Elizabeth Helene *artist, calligrapher, educator*

Los Altos
Linn, David Edward *artist*

Los Angeles
Adams, Lisa Kay *artist*
Anderegg, Ronald Henry *artist*
Ankrum, Joan Wheeler *art dealer*
Asano, Hisako *fine arts educator*
Bachenheimer, Beth Adair *artist, educator*
Bangs, Cate (Cathryn Margaret Bangs) *film production designer, interior designer*
Bayless, Raymond *artist*
Bernier, Michael Scott *graphic/sportswear designer, artist*
Bothwell, Dorr, Jr. *artist*
Burke, Kristin Marie *costume designer*
Cassell, Beverly Anne *artist, art association executive*
Cossutta, Renée Claire *graphic designer*
Danziger, Louis *graphic designer, educator*
Decter, Betty Eva *artist*
Doolin, James Lawrence *artist, educator*
Douke, Daniel Wayne *art educator, artist*
Elias, Sheila *artist*
Ewing, Edgar Louis *artist, educator*
Goins, Ronald L. *art director*
Heinecken, Robert Friedli *art educator, artist*
Hockney, David *artist*
Hopkins, Glenn Ernest *artist, educator*
Hueter, James Warren *painter, sculptor*
Karabay, Adnan Sami *artist*
Kienholz, Lyn Shearer *international arts projects coordinator*
Korelov, Nikolai *artist*
Lang, Wendy Frances *artist, photographer*
Lark, Raymond *artist, art scholar*
Leeson, Thomas Aubert *painter*
Lem, Richard Douglas *painter*
Lukather, Christian Eric *graphic designer and author*
Manolakas, Stanton Peter *watercolor artist*
Marrow, Marva Jan *photographer, writer, video and multimedia producer*
McAuley, Skeet *artist*
Miller, Harriet Sanders *art center director*
Schnitzler, Beverly Jeanne *designer, art educator, writer*
Sherburn, Earl Franklin *community arts director, tour consultant*
Simon, Steven Adam *sculptor, educator*
Smith, Alexis *artist*
Sorensen, Vibeke *artist, educator*
Tanaka, Janice *artist, educator*
Welles, Melinda Fassett *artist, educator*
Wingo, Michael *artist, educator*
Wood, Nicola *artist*
Wright, Bernard *artist*
Wright, Michael Ragsdale *artist, educator*
Ynda, Mary Lou *artist, educator*

Los Banos
Peterson, Stanley Lee *artist*

Los Osos
Musselman, Darwin B *artist, educator*

Malibu
Almond, Joan Harwood Elkins *photographer*
Altfeld, Merwin Richard *artist, educator*
Bowman, Bruce *art educator, writer, artist*

Manhattan Beach
Millar, Robert *artist*
Stulz, Dale Warren *photographic consultant, appraiser*

Mariposa
Rogers, Earl Leslie *artist, educator*

Menlo Park
Domingo, Estrella Tina *fashion designer, consultant, paralegal*
Mayes, Sharon Suzette *sculptor, educator*

Mill Valley
Baruch, Ruth-Marion Evelyn *photographer, writer*
Blatt, Morton Bernard *medical illustrator*

Millbrae
Dawdy, Faye Marie Catania *photographer, lecturer*

Montrose
Handford, Jack *fashion education consultant*

Moraga
Schmaltz, Roy Edgar, Jr. *artist, art educator*

Napa
Kravjansky, Mikulas *artist*

North Hollywood
Brommer, Gerald Frederick *artist, writer*
Powell, Stephanie *visual effects director*

Northridge
Harden, Marvin *artist, educator*
Weston, Edward *art dealer, consultant*

Oakland
Beasley, Bruce Miller *sculptor*
Bowen-Forbes, Jorge Courtney *artist, author, poet*
Donahue, Philip Richard *artist, educator*
Hardy, David Whittaker, III *artist, educator*
Kagemoto, Patricia Jow (Pat Jow) *artist, printmaker*
Margosian, Lucille Manougian (Mrs. Ervin M. Margosian) *artist, educator*
Mendenhall, Jack L. *artist, educator*
Rath, Alan T. *sculptor*
Weisburd, Harry Noah *artist, educator*

Occidental
Chester, Elfi *artist*

Oceanside
Sarkisian, Pamela Outlaw *artist*

Ojai
McIntosh, Gregory Stephen *artist*
Sylvester, Stephen Thomas *artist*

Orange
Felisky, Barbara Rosbe *artist*
Metcalf, Eugene Max *artist, educator*

Orange Cove
Paris, Vreda *artist, educator*

Oroville
Rugenstein, Robert Wayne *clothing designer*

Oxnard
Carlson, Doris Catherine *art educator, retired publications specialist*

Pacific Palisades
Sherman, Zelda Charlotte *artist*

Pacifica
Torlakson, James Daniel *artist*

Palm Desert
Bell, Helen Lavin *artist*

Palm Springs
Maree, Wendy *painter, sculptor*

Palmdale
Handley, Sue Ann *professonal quiltmaker, educator*

Palo Alto
Chu, Christopher Kar Fai *graphic designer*
McCluskey, Lois Thornhill *photographer*
Miller, Judith Juntura *artist*

Panorama City
Jones, John Harding *photographer*

Pasadena
Goldstein, Debbe *art history educator*
Mesquita, Rosalyn Anaya *artist, educator*

Paso Robles
Chase, Jacoline B. *designer, career consultant, educator*

Pebble Beach
Mortensen, Gordon Louis *artist, printmaker*

Petaluma
Reichek, Jesse *artist*

Pinole
Gerbracht, Robert Thomas (Bob Gerbracht) *painter, educator*

Placentia
Galvez, William *artist*

Port Costa
Bailey, Clayton George *artist, educator*

Poway
Runkle, Ethel Mona *artist*

Rancho Cordova
Yazdani, Mehri *artist*

Richmond
Huckeby, Karen Marie *graphic arts executive*

Riverside
Divola, John *artist*
Jones, Amelia Gwen *art history educator, curator*
Medel, Rebecca Rosalie *artist*

Rosemead
Ensign, Donald Dale *art director*

Running Springs
Gordon, Steven Eric *animator, designer*

Sacramento
Drachnik, Catherine Meldyn *art therapist, artist*
LaPena, Frank Raymond *art educator*
McCullough, Gayle Jean *graphic artist, publisher*
Merta, Paul James *cartoonist, photographer, engineer, restaurateur, real estate developer*
Moment, Joan *artist, educator*
Thomas, Laura Marlene *artist, private antique dealer*

Salinas
Kirby, Thomas Paul *artist*
Smith, Gary Thomas *fine arts educator, curator*

San Anselmo
Torbet, Laura *graphic designer, author*

San Clemente
Lopina, Louise Carol *artist*

San Diego
Braley, Jean (J. McNeil Sargent) *artist, educator*
Carter, Michael Ray *freelance artist, singer, composer*
Chandler, Floyd Copeland *fine arts educator*
Farmer, Janene Elizabeth *artist, educator*
Jung, Kwan Yee *artist*
Jung, Yee Wah *artist*
Lauer, Stefanie Dorothea *painter, writer*
Markarian, Alexia Mitrus *artist*
Nyiri, Joseph Anton *sculptor, art educator*
Penney, Roger Lee *artist*
Sowinski, Stanislaus Joseph *artist, retired naval officer*
Wojtyla, Walter Haase *artist*

San Francisco
Adams, Mark *artist*
Arnitz, Rick *artist*
Babcock, Jo Warren *artist, educator*
Beall, Dennis Ray *artist, educator*
Bechtle, Robert Alan *artist, educator*
Chin, Sue Soone Marian (Suchin Chin) *conceptual artist, portraitist, photographer, community affairs activist*
DeSoto, Lewis Damien *art educator*
Helder, David Ernest *artist, educator*
Hendricks, Mark Kenneth *animator, artist*
Hershman, Lynn Lester *artist*
Huntting, Cynthia Cox *artist*
Katano, Marc *artist*
Kehlmann, Robert *artist, critic*
Komenich, Kim *photographer*
Krempel, Ralf Hugo Bernhard *artist, art gallery owner*
Lemkhin, Mikhail *photographer*
Lew, Weyman *artist*
Lobdell, Frank *artist*
Lupper, Edward *artist*
Marioni, Tom *artist*
McNamara, John Stephen *artist, educator*
Murch, Anna Valentina *artist, lecturer*
Oropallo, Deborah *artist, educator*
Phill, Daniel Stouffer *artist*
Preble, Patricia Joan *visual artist, writer*
Raciti, Cherie *artist*
St. Louis, Nena *artist, performance artist*
Saunders, Raymond Jennings *artist, educator*
Schmalz, Charles Joseph *artist, photographer, creative consultant*
Shepp, Alan *artist, educator*
Stermer, Dugald Robert *designer, illustrator, writer, consultant*
Sultan, Larry *photographer*
Tavenner, Patricia May *artist, printmaker*
Taylor, Sandra Ortiz *artist, educator*
Vignes, Michelle Marie *photographer, educator*

San Jose
Helprin, Benson Raimon *fine arts educator*
Johnson, Gwenavere Anelisa *artist*
Milnes, Robert Winston *artist, educator*
Olson, Ronald Burr *holographer*
Suggs, Patricia Ann *artist*
Thurston, Jacqueline Beverly *art educator*

San Leandro
Chilcoat, Dale Allen *artist, visual and performing arts educator*
Waldron, Vanis Roy *artist, educator*

San Luis Obispo
Dickerson, Colleen Bernice Patton *artist, educator*
Zika, Frank Joseph *sculptor, designer*

San Marino
Roberts, Ann Bayard Price *oil painting artist*

San Mateo
Chester, Sharon Rose *photographer, natural history educator*

Santa Barbara
Braiden, Rose Margaret *art educator, illustrator, calligrapher*
Brown, Gary Hugh *artist, art educator*
Eguchi, Yasu *artist*
Kavish, Kimberly Layne *art director, photographer*
Nideffer, Robert Foster *artist, educator*
Torbert, Meg Birch *artist, design and color consultant*

Santa Clara
Hernandez, Sam *sculptor, educator*
Hofstetter, Jane Robinson *artist, educator*

Santa Cruz
Lanting, Frans Marten *photographer, writer*
Rydell, Amnell Roy *artist, landscape architect*
Stolpe, Daniel Owen *artist, printmaking educator*

Santa Monica
Cheng, Carl Fu Kang (John Doe Co.) *artist*
Chu, Julia Nee *artist*
Fellows, Alice Combs *artist*
Fukuhara, Henry *artist, educator*
Getman, Sheryl Marie *artist*
Gilbert-Rolfe, Jeremy Denton *artist, art critic, educator*
Mitchell, Kathleen Ann *illustrator, graphic designer*
Mitchell, Robin *artist, educator*
Scott, James Michael *artist, filmmaker*

Santa Rosa
Monk, Diana Charla *artist, stable owner*
Rider, Jane Louise *artist, educator*

Santa Ynez
Bornell, Cecil Jean *computer graphics designer, small business owner*

Sausalito
Kuhlman, Walter Egel *artist, educator*

Sebastopol
Greene, Richard Martin *artist*
Stanford, Ginny Crouch *painter*

Sepulveda
Field, Jeffrey Frederic *designer*

Sherman Oaks
Carl, Joan Strauss *sculptor, painter*
Studley, Helen Ormson *artist, poet, writer, designer*

Simi Valley
Gilligan-Ivanjack, Claudia Marlene *motion picture set artist, writer*

Solana Beach
Beck-von-Peccoz, Stephen George Wolfgang *artist*

Somis
Kehoe, Vincent Jeffré-Roux *photographer, author, cosmetic company executive*

Sonora
Hay, Sherman Colin *artist, art educator*
Price, Joe (Allen) *artist, former educator*

South Lake Tahoe
Darvas, Endre Peter *artist*

Stanford
Maxmin, Jody Lewis *art educator*

Stinson Beach
Chapline, Claudia Beechum *artist, art dealer*

Stockton
Miller, Carl Vosburgh *artist*
Oak, Claire Morisset *artist, educator*

Sunnyvale
Lopez, Angelo Cayas *freelance illustrator*

Tahoe City
Cutten, Betty Bancroft *lighting designer, interior designer*

Thousand Oaks
Heyer, Carol Ann *illustrator*
Villegas, Richard Junipero *artist*

Trinidad
Simmons, Ned Lee *landscape artist, art dealer, consultant*

Turlock
Piskoti, James *artist, educator*

Vacaville
Ford, John T., Jr. *art, film and video educator*

Valencia
Fiskin, Judith Anne *artist, educator*
Lawson, Thomas *artist*

Vallejo
Bullock, James Benbow *sculptor*

Venice
Barth, Uta *artist, educator*
Chipman, Jack Ernest *artist*
Eversley, Frederick John *sculptor, engineer*
Shimogori, Kotaro *designing company executive*

Ventura
Radley, Gregory Norman *custom furniture maker, educator*
Yoshimoto, Hiroko *art educator, artist*

Vista
Simmons, Cleda Marie *artist*

Walnut
Boerem, Ronald Merle *educator*
Owen, Carol Thompson *artist, educator*

Westlake Village
Newman, Ruth Tantlinger *artist*

Westminster
Nguyen, Tam Van *artist, photographer*

Woodacre
Uzilevsky, Marcus *artist*

Woodland
Nye, Gene Warren *art educator*

Woodland Hills
Blaisdell, Donald Charles *artist, educator*
Reed, Harold Ervin *artist, educator*

Yorba Linda
Stirm, Eugene Robert *sculptor*

Yreka
Fiock, Shari Lee *design entrepreneur, researcher*
McFadden, Leon Lambert *artist, inventor*

COLORADO

Aurora
Hickman, Grace Marguerite *artist*

Boulder
Cline, Clinton Clifford *art educator, printmaker*
Donovan-Johnson, D.J. *artist, educator*
Friedman, Pamela Ruth Lessing *art consultant, financial consultant*
Hakeem, Muhammad Abdul *artist, educator*
Matthews, Eugene Edward *artist*
Sampson, J. Frank *artist, educator*
Vielehr, William Ralph *sculptor, business executive*

Colorado Springs
Cook, Judith Ann Polus *art educator*
Dwight, Donald Stearns *artist, retired military officer*
Kosta, Ivan *sculptor*

Denver
Bumiller, Trine Roberts *artist*
Carter, Melvin Whitsett (Mel Carter) *artist, educator*
Enright, Cynthia Lee *illustrator*
McKee, Melissa Marie *animator, artist*
Navratil, Greg Allan *artist, screenprinter*
Norman, John Barstow, Jr. *designer, educator*
Shwayder, Elizabeth Yanish *sculptor*
Smith-Warren, Katharine *art advisor, educator*
Speer, Andrew Kevin *art educator*
Thompson, Richard Craig *artist*

Dolores
Wagner, Richard *artist*

Elizabeth
Kaplinski, Buffalo *artist*

Englewood
Lamb, Darlis Carol *sculptor*
Walter, Patricia Ann *graphic designer*
Yeager, David Clark *product designer, education specialist*

Evergreen
Desrochers, Jeri Kilzer *artist*

Fort Collins
Jacobs, Peter Alan *artist, educator*
Refvem, Robert Loren *sculptor*
Scott, Sandra Lynn (Sandy Scott) *artist, sculptor, printmaker*

Glen Haven
Sorby, J(oseph) Richard *artist, educator*

Golden
Acevedo, Angelique Marie *art educator*

Lakewood
Binkley, Joan Vivian (Jody Binkley) *artist, educator, gallery owner*
Denton, Patry Redding *artist, educator*

Larkspur
Bierbaum, Janith Marie *artist*

Littleton
Barnes, Cloyd Ray *sculptor, retired engineer*

Longmont
King, Jane Louise *artist*

Louisville
Qualley, Charles Albert *fine arts educator*

Loveland
Cole, Julie Kramer *artist*

Pueblo
Wands, Robert James *art educator*

Salida
Ragan, Susan Swartz *art educator*

Sedalia
Nickerson, John Henry *artist, sculptor, designer*

Telluride
Smith, Samuel David *artist, educator*

Trinidad
Louden, Willard Charles *artist, environmental consultant*

HAWAII

Haiku
Cost, James Peter *artist*

Honolulu
Amor, Simeon, Jr. *photographer, historian*
Betts, Barbara Stoke *artist, educator*
Bushnell, Kenneth Wayne *artist, educator*
Chang, Rodney Eiu Joon *artist, dentist*
Hansen, Peter Ulrich *art educator*
Head, Dwight Terry *art educator*
Lo, Waituck *artist*
Morita, John Takami *artist*
Scott, Kenneth Craig *artist*
Uhl, Philip Edward *marine artist*
Wisnosky, John G. *artist, educator*

Kahului
Miller, Barbara Darlene *art educator*

Kaneohe
Kubota, Miyoko *artist*

Kapaau
Jankowski, Theodore Andrew *artist*

Kihei
Wilson, Jay *tapestry weaver*

Kurtistown
Campbell, Christopher Mark *artist, singer, songwriter*

Lahaina
Killingsworth, Kathleen Nola *artist, photographer, company executive*
Sato, Tadashi *artist*

Lihue
Lai, Waihang *art educator*

Makawao
Kratka, Ilene *artist, sculptor*

Waianae
Kadota, Mark Fumio *artist*

IDAHO

Boise
Watia, Tarmo *artist*

Coeur D Alene
Hosack, Kathleen Elizabeth *art consultant, artist*

Lewiston
Wendt, Michael James *production potter, business owner*

Weiser
Hough, Michael James *sculptor, educator*

Yellow Pine
Auth, Robert Ralph *art educator*

ILLINOIS

Chicago
Mantor-Clarysse, Justine Claire *fine arts educator*

MARYLAND

Saint Mary's City
Jackson, Suzanne Fitzallen *painter, poet, scenographer*

MINNESOTA

Golden Valley
Jiang, Tiefeng *artist*

MISSOURI

Kansas City
Bransby, Eric James *muralist, educator*

MONTANA

Big Sky
Doll, Linda A. *artist, educator*

Browning
Scriver, Robert Macfie *sculptor*

Helena
Cleary, Shirley Jean *artist, illustrator*

Kalispell
Abbrescia, Joseph Leonard *artist, educator*
von Krenner, Walther G. *artist, writer, art consultant and appraiser*

Livingston
Bauer, Erwin Adam *photographer*

Victor
Merrell, Cyrus Walbridge, Jr. *artist, rancher*

West Yellowstone
Carter, Gary Lee *artist*

NEVADA

Elko
Sweetwater, Sarah *art educator*

Fallon
Stevenson, Patricia Kennard *artist, journalist*

Henderson
Hara-Isa, Nancy Jeanne *graphic designer*
Turner, Florence Frances *ceramist*

Incline Village
Flagg, Keoki Scott *photographer*

Las Vegas
Gideon-Hawke, Pamela Lawrence *fine arts small business owner*
Goldblatt, Hal Michael *photographer, accountant*
Holder, Thomas Jay *art educator*
Ijams, Jan Allison *lighting technician*
Lesnick, Stephen William *artist*
Newquist, Donald Stewart *designer, technical director, consultant*

North Las Vegas
Purcell, Roy Everett *artist*

Reno
Fowles, Janice *graphic designer*
Goin, Peter Jackson *art educator*
Harder, Kelsie T. *artist, educator*
Newberg, Dorothy Beck (Mrs. William C. Newberg) *portrait artist*
Olmsted, Suzanne M. *photographer*

Zephyr Cove
Green, Ferderick Bardon *photographer*

NEW MEXICO

Albuquerque
Abrams, Jane Eldora *artist*
Adams, Clinton *artist, historian*
Antreasian, Garo Zareh *artist, lithographer, art educator*
Armstrong, Glenn Garnett *artist, retired postal executive*
Barrow, Thomas Francis *artist, educator*
Barry, Steve *sculptor, educator*
Cia, Manuel Lopez *artist*
Clark, Patricia Sue *antiques dealer*
Easley, Loyce Anna *painter*
Gonzalez, Enrico Raul *art educator, artist*
Good, Deborah Anne *art therapist, counselor, consultant*
Hahn, Betty *artist, photographer, educator*
Hammersley, Frederick Harold *artist*
Kellar, Martha Robbins *artist*
Kenarov, Miroslav Ivanov (Miro Kenarov) *artist, printmaker*
McReynolds, Barbara *artist*
Moyers, William Taylor *artist*
Multhaup, Merrell Keyes *artist*
Nelson, Mary Carroll *artist, author*
Phillips, Ronald Edward *artist, sales executive*
Ramirez, Joel Tito *artist*
Robb, Peggy Hight *artist, educator*
Witkin, Joel-Peter *photographer*

Angel Fire
Shanhouse, Bill *sculptor, educator*

Anthony
Porter, L(awrence) B(enjamin) *artist*

Arroyo Hondo
Ferguson-Huntington, Kathleen Elizabeth *artist, educator*

Corrales
Eaton, Pauline *artist*
Leis, Marietta Patricia *artist*
Nieto, John Wesley *artist*
Townsend, Storm Diana *sculptor*

Galisteo
Merrick, Nicholas Gregory *photographer*

Gallup
Cattaneo, Jacquelyn Annette Kammerer *artist, educator*

Grants
Lowney, Bruce Stark *artist*

Las Cruces
Jacobs, Sallie Ritter *painter, sculptor*

Ranchos De Taos
Koehler, Jeremy *tapestry artist*

Rociada
Reed, Carol Louise *designer*

Roswell
Avery, Keith Willette *artist, educator*
Hallenbeck, Pomona Juanita *artist*
Wiggins, Kim Douglas *artist, art dealer*

Ruidoso Downs
Knapp, Thomas Edwin *sculptor, painter*

Santa Fe
Ancona, George Ephrain *photographer, film producer, author*
Bass, David Loren *artist*
Burgess, Joseph James, Jr. *artist, educator*
Clift, William Brooks, III *photographer*
Dean, Nat *artist, educator*
Dechert, Peter *photographer, writer, foundation adminstrator*
Fangor, Voy *painter*
Fincher, John Henry *artist*
Handell, Albert George *artist*
Harroun, Dorothy Summer *painter, educator*
Hartford, Jane Davis *textile artist*
Hatch, John Davis *design consultant, art historian*
Hensley, Jackson Morey *artist*
Johnson, James Ralph *artist, writer*
Lindsay, Richard Paul *artist, jewelry designer*
Lippincott, Janet *artist, art educator*
Orduno, Robert Daniel *artist, painter, sculptor*
Price, Patricia Anne *artist*
Scheinbaum, David *photography educator*
Shubart, Dorothy Louise Tepfer *artist, educator*
Steinke, Bettina *artist*
Tidwell, Enid Eugenie *sculptor, advocate*
Vala, Robert (Donald Robert Mann) *artist*

Taos
Bell, Larry Stuart *artist*
Crespin, Leslie Ann *artist*
Harmon, Cliff F. *artist*
Lee, Caroline Dured *art appaiser, consultant, curator*
Lerner, Alexandria Sandra *artist*
Macpherson, Kevin Dan *artist*
Manzo, Anthony Joseph *painter*
Ray, Robert Donald *artist*
Stewart, William R. *artist, painter, educator*

Tijeras
Sweet, Mary French *artist*

Tularosa
Weidner, Joe C. *jewelry designer, silversmith*

OREGON

Applegate
Boyle, (Charles) Keith *artist, educator*

Ashland
Anderson, Arthur Lee *gem cutter, writer*
Hay, Richard Laurence *theater scenic designer*

Bandon
Lindquist, Louis William *artist, writer*

Brookings
Lang, Norma Ellen *art educator*

Cannon Beach
Greaver, Harry *artist*

Eugene
Buckner, Matthew Eric *sculptor*
Joyce, John David *art educator, artist*
O'Connell, Gwyneth Pieta *art educator, graphic artist*
O'Connell, Kenneth Robert *artist, animator, educator*

Jacksonville
Bennett, Eugene Peart *artist*

Klamath Falls
Wells, Lu *artist*

Lake Oswego
Van Leunen, Alice Louise *artist, educator*

Medford
Puckett, Richard Edward *artist, consultant, retired recreation executive*
Schubert, Ruth Carol Hickok *artist, educator*

Newberg
Keith, Pauline Mary *artist, illustrator, writer*

Pendleton
Harper, Gloria Janet *artist, educator*

Portland
Borgeson, Bet *artist*
Bruneaux, Debra Louise *costume designer*
Dente, Michael Florin *sculptor, art educator*
Giannotti, Stephen Paul *graphic designer*
Gimbolo, Aleksei Frank Charles *artist, philosopher, author*
Montone, Kenneth Alan *art director, creative director, consultant*
Pander, Hendrik Pieter *artist*

Shannon, Brian Lee *artist, education educator*
Stephens, Alice Elizabeth (Alice Wanke Stephens) *artist*
Waddingham, John Alfred *artist, journalist*
Wyss, Judith Ann *artist*

Salem
Hall, Carl Albin *artist*
Pierre, Joseph Horace, Jr. *commercial artist*

PENNSYLVANIA

Harrisburg
Sturgen, Winston *photographer, printmaker, artist*

UTAH

Ivins
Riggs, Francis Porter *sculptor*

Monroe
Kirby, Orville Edward *potter*

Oakley
Weller, Donald Mighell *graphic designer, illustrator*

Orderville
Zornes, Milford *artist*

Orem
Laney, Stephen Fayne *art educator*

Provo
Barsch, Wulf Erich *artist, educator*
Myer, Peter Livingston *artist, educator*
Wilson, Warren Bingham *artist, art educator*

Saint George
Collett, Farrell Reuben *art educator*

Salt Lake City
Meyers, Randal Curtis *sculptor*
Powell, Ted Ferrell *micrographics specialist*
Reinhold, Allen Kurt *graphic design educator*

Smithfield
Rasmuson, Brent (Jacobsen) *photographer, graphic artist*

West Valley City
Johnson, D. Arlo *artist*

WASHINGTON

Anacortes
Mc Cracken, Philip Trafton *sculptor*

Bainbridge Island
Carlson, Robert Michael *artist*

Battle Ground
Hansen, James Lee *sculptor*

Bellevue
Sogabe, Akiko *artist*

Bellingham
Johnston, Thomas Alix *artist, educator*

Bothell
Scannell, Faye Naomi *art educator*

Burlington
Zeretzke, Frederick Frank H. *artist, educator*

Carnation
Santucci, Selene Marie *artist, educator*

Eastsound
Phillips, Gertrude Marilynn *fine artist, educator, transformational psychologist*

Edmonds
Johnson, d'Elaine Ann Herard *artist*

Ellensburg
Stillman, George *artist*

Everett
Huffman, Linda Rae *artist, educator, cartoonist*

Gig Harbor
Schutzky, Marilyn Horsley *artist*

Kent
Broer, Roger L. *artist*

Lilliwaup
McGrady, Corinne Young *design company executive*

Longview
Werth, Roger Alan *photojournalist*

Marysville
Colvin, Dorisjean Mittmann *artist, educator*

Mercer Island
Langhout-Nix, Nelleke *artist*
Steinhardt, Henry *photographer*

Ocean Park
Lee, Martha *artist, writer*

Olalla
Kimura, Joan Alexandra *artist, educator*

Olympia
Davis, Steven Arthur *photographer, educator*

Omak
Woolschlager, Laura Totten *sculptor, artist, printmaker*

Pullman
Coates, Ross Alexander *art educator*
Lee, Paul Pak-hing *artist, educator*
Siler, Patrick Walter *drawing and ceramics educator*
Watts, Christopher John *artist, educator*

Puyallup
Chalk, Earl Milton *retired art director*

Redmond
Scharf, Barry W. *artist*
Skiles, Violet Denice *artist*
Swerda, Patricia Fine *artist, author, educator*

Seattle
Allen, Judith Syma *art educator, artist*
Berger, Paul Eric *artist, photographer*
Campos, Mark Henry *cartoonist*
Christenson, Charles Elroy *art educator*
Cohen, Jonathan Jacob *furniture artist*
Du Pen, Everett George *sculptor, educator*
Katz, Richard Emanuel *photographer, educator*
Kucera, Gregory Michael *art dealer*
MacKenzie, Peter Sean *publications designer, writer*
Maki, Robert Richard *sculptor, draftsman, educator*
Myers, Joseph John *graphic designer*
Pawula, Kenneth John *artist, educator*
Ross, Sueellen *artist*
Skoor, John Brian *art educator, art consultant*
Spafford, Michael Charles *artist*
Tanzi, Ronald Thomas *artist, educator*
Theobald, Gillian Lee *artist*
Vaness, Margaret Helen *artist, consultant*
Washington, James Winston, Jr. *artist, sculptor*
Weiss, Dick Joseph *artist*

Spokane
Flahavin, Marian Joan *artist*
Fyfe, Jo Suzanne *artist*
Kalapacs, Ildiko *visual artist, dancer*

Tacoma
Colby, Bill *artist*

Vashon
Dyer, Carolyn Price *artist, writer*

Walla Walla
Meitzler, Neil *artist*

WYOMING

Casper
Seeger, Sondra Joan *artist*

Centennial
Russin, Robert Isaiah *sculptor, educator*

Cheyenne
Craft, Robbie Wright *artist*
Lawes, Patricia Jean *art educator*
Moore, Mary French (Muffy Moore) *potter, community activist*

Cody
Jackson, Harry Andrew *artist*
Patrick, Lucille Nichols *artist, rancher*

Laramie
Flach, Victor Hugo *designer, educator*
Reif, (Frank) David *artist, educator*

CANADA

ALBERTA

Calgary
Esler, John Kenneth *artist*

Edmonton
Jungkind, Walter *design educator, writer, consultant*

BRITISH COLUMBIA

Duncan
Hughes, Edward John *artist*

Vancouver
Smolarek, Waldemar *artist, printmaker*

Victoria
Harvey, Donald *artist, educator*

SASKATCHEWAN

Saskatoon
Bornstein, Eli *artist, sculptor*

SPAIN

Seville
Sanchez, Leonedes Monarrize Worthington (Duke de Leonedes) *fashion designer*

ADDRESS UNPUBLISHED

Beckmann, Robert Owen *artist*
Benton, Fletcher *sculptor*
Blanchette, Jeanne Ellene Maxant *artist, educator, performer*
Blinder, Janet *art dealer*
Bowers, Jack (John Burton Bowers, Jr.) *artist, graphics and digital color executive*
Bowman, Brice *artist, educator*
Broadbent, Amalia Sayo Castillo *graphic arts designer*
Brodie, Howard *artist*
Brown, Theophilus *artist*
Brun, Kim Eric *photographer*
Buckner, Kay Lamoreux *artist*
Cabot, Hugh, III *painter, sculptor*
Calzolari, Elaine *sculptor*
Campbell, Demarest Lindsay *artist, designer, writer*
Cannon, Kevin Francis *sculptor*
Chaykin, Howard Victor *cartoonist, screenwriter*
Chinn, Thomas Wayne *typographic company executive*
Chowdhury, Debra Cofer *photographer, administrative assistant*
Conway, Robert P. *art dealer*
Cooper, Susan *artist*
Cowell, Ernest Saul *lighting designer, consultant*
Crabs, Donald Benjamin *scenic and lighting designer, theater consultant*
Crispo, Richard Charles *artist, ethnologist, minister*
Dickau, Keith Michael *artist, secondary science educator*
Dill, Laddie John *artist*
Dixon, Michael Wayne *designer, writer*
Donath, Therese *artist, author*
Drage, Starla Rae *fashion designer*
Eder, James Alvin *artist, educator*
Engle, Stephen Eugene *artist*
Enyart, Gregory Leonard *art dealer*
Erden, Sybil Isolde *artist*
Ettenberg, Frank Joseph *artist*
Farnham, Mary Glade Siemer *artist*
Flower, Renée Beville *artist*
Frutkoff, Gary *production designer*
Garrison, Gene Kirby *artist, writer, photographer*
Gifford, Leslie Jane *artist, writer, educator*
Golubic, Theodore Roy *sculptor, designer, inventor*
Goodwill, Margaret Jane *artist*
Gregory, Eleanor Anne *artist, educator*
Groat, Jenny Hunter (LaVida June Groat) *painter, artist, choreographer, writer*
Gurwitz-Hall, Barbara Ann *artist*
Guthrie, Edgar King *artist*
Haley, Sally Fulton *artist*
Hasegawa, Noriko *artist*
Heilman, Marlin Grant *photographer*
Hertel, Howard Jay *photographer*
Hess, Frederick Scott *artist*
Hogle, Ann Meilstrup *painter, art educator*
Holbrook, Peter Greene *artist*
Hurley, Bruce Palmer *artist*
Jay, Norma Joyce *artist*
Johnson, Douglas Walter *artist*
Johnson, Lloyd Warren *artist, real estate investor*
Jones, Thomas William *artist*
Katona, Robert Roy *artist, sculptor*
Kirkpatrick, Joey J. *artist*
Klein, M(ary) A(lice) *fiber artist*
Klotz, Suzanne Ruth *artist*
Kramer, James Joseph *artist, painter*
Langager, Craig T. *artist*
Lefranc, Margaret (Margaret Schoonover) *artist, illustrator, editor, writer*
Lipman, Carol Koch *designer*
Liu, Katherine Chang *artist, art educator*
Lord, Carolyn Marie *artist*
McCracken, John Harvey *painter, sculptor*
Merchey, Ruth Ann *artist, designer*
Milant, Jean Robert *art dealer*
Minami, Robert Yoshio *artist, graphic designer*
Moyer, Linda Lee *artist, educator*
Nadel, Ann Honig *sculptor, educator*
Nemiroff, Maxine Celia *art educator, gallery owner, consultant*
Neykov, George Strahilov *photographer*
Nilles, Darrell F. *artist, inventor, architectural consultant*
Noble, Helen Bonner *artist*
Orland, Ted Norcross *artist*
Parker, Wilma Joan *artist*
Phillips, Billy Saxton *artist, designer, painter*
Pincus, Laurie Jane *artist*
Pomeroy, Mary Barnas *artist, illustrator, writer*
Preston, Astrid Deborah *artist*
Quigley, Richard Lawrence *artist, educator*
Raymond, Susan Grant *sculptor*
Reed, Helen Bernice *artist*
Roberts, Holly Lynn *artist*
Rogers, Keith Johnathan *artist*
Root, Doris Smiley *portrait artist*
Ross, Molly Owings *gold and silversmith, jewelry designer, small business owner*
Rossbach, Caroletta *art consultant*
Rubin, Sandra Mendelsohn *artist*
Ryan, Jodell *fine artist*
Saturen, Ben B. *oceanic wildlife artist*
Simmons, Christopher Laird *graphic designer, art director*
Skirvin, William David *artist, art director*
Smith, Serafina Gangemi *artist, drug counselor*
Soto, Thomas De *photographer*
Steel, Claudia Williamson *artist*
Stevens, Ann L. Hense *art educator, artist*
Stevens, Michael Keith *artist*
Stewart, Cherie Anita *painter*
Strawn, Evelyn Rae *artist*
Swensen, Mary Jean Hamilton *graphic artist*
Swig, Roselyne Chroman *art advisor*
Turner, Bonese Collins *artist, educator*
Vaccarino, Robin *artist*
Valesco, Frances Kay *artist, educator*
Villa, Theodore B. *artist, educator*
Walker, Edward Donald (Rusty Walker) *artist, educator*
Wiseman, Jay Donald *photographer, mechanical contractor, designer*
Zeitlin, Harry Leon *artist*
Zekman, Terri Margaret *graphic designer*
Zink, Melissa Ellis *artist*
Zivelonghi, Kurt Daniel *artist*

ASSOCIATIONS AND ORGANIZATIONS. *See also* specific fields.

UNITED STATES

ALASKA

Anchorage
Jones, Mark Logan *educational association executive, educator*
Ronan, James Douglas, Jr. *counselor, writer, photographer*

Soldotna
Parker, Linda Susan Dennis *nonprofit organization executive*

Unalakleet
Katchatag, Stanton Oswald *civic and political worker*

ARIZONA

Dewey
Burch, Mary Lou *organization consultant, housing advocate*

Lake Havasu City
Chambers, Virginia Ellen *community volunteer, retired photographer*

Mesa
Boyce, James Ward, Jr. *association director, retired military officer*

Phoenix
Carpenter, Peter Rockefeller *social services agency administrator*
Coomer, John Harner *association administrator*
Haynes, James Earl, Jr. *association executive*
Hoyt, Diana Vaughn *fundraising executive*
Lloyd, Llyn Allan *association executive*
Orton, Mary C. *nonprofit administrator*
Rodriguez, Leonard *foundation administrator*
Sallman, Jeanne Larraine *volunteer, administrator*
Smith, Stuart Robert *foundation executive*
Stewart, Donald Edwin *association director*

Scottsdale
Carney, Richard Edgar *foundation executive*
Smith, Susan Bitter *trade association executive, consultant*

Sedona
Stoufer, Ruth Hendrix *community volunteer*

Tempe
Sullivan-Boyle, Kathleen Marie *association administrator*

Tucson
Belk, John Blanton *educational and cultural organization executive*
Langum, W. Sue *civic worker*
McConkey, Max *association executive*
Mullen, Rod Gorden *nonprofit organization executive*
Pack, Phoebe Katherine Finley *civic worker*
Putterman, William Zev *foundation executive, television producer*
Riggs, Frank Lewis *foundation executive*
Shenk, Howard Fred *association executive*
Sickel, Joan Sottilare *foundation administrator*
Vandiver, Robert Sanford *civic association executive*

CALIFORNIA

Alamo
Chew, Linda Lee *fundraising management consultant*

Alhambra
Arellanes, Audrey Spencer *society administrator*

Altadena
Griswold, Martha Kerfoot *social worker*
Staehle, Robert L. *foundation executive*
Wells, William Adrain *non-profit executive*

Anaheim
Richards, Morris Dick *social work administrator, environmental analyst, educator*

Angwin
St. Clair, Shane Scott *communications and international health specialist*

Arcadia
Day-Gowder, Patricia Joan *association executive, consultant*

Arcata
Clary, Patricia May *nonprofit administrator*

Atherton
Heyns, Roger William *retired foundation executive and educator*
King, Jane Cudlip Coblentz *volunteer, educator*

Avalon
Olson, Edward Charles *conservation foundation executive, writer, television producer*

Bakersfield
Clark, Michal Charles *social services director*
Stanley, Forrest Edwin *fundraiser, university program director*

Belvedere Tiburon
Cook, Lyle Edwards *retired fund raising executive, consultant*

Berkeley
Bettelheim, Ann Elise *nonprofit organization executive*
Cohen, Andrew Neal *activist, writer, scientist*
Jefferds, Mary Lee *environmental education executive*
Malmstrom, Patricia Elizabeth *social service agency administrator, consultant*
Welter, Linda Allaire *developer*

Beverly Hills
Prusan, Lilian *fundraising executive*

Boonville
Wayburn, Laurie Andrea *environmental and wildlife foundation administrator, conservationist*

Boulder Creek
Martin, James Lowrey, Jr. *foundation administrator*

Brea
Tamura, Cary Kaoru *fundraiser*

Burbank
Angele, Alfred Robert *police labor union executive*

Campbell
Throndson, Edward Warner *residential association administrator*

Canoga Park
Lederer, Marion Irvine *cultural administrator*

Carlsbad
Vincent, John Graham *administrator*

Carmel
Allan, Robert Moffat, Jr. *corporate executive, educator*
Chester, Lynne *foundation executive, artist*
Criley, Richard Lawrence *retired advocate*
Faridany, Nancy Lofton *cultural organization executive*

Citrus Heights
Clawson, Mary *social services administrator*

Claremont
Arnn, Larry Paul *foundation executive, editor*
Pendleton, Othniel Alsop *fundraiser, clergyman*
Wrigley, Elizabeth Springer (Mrs. Oliver K. Wrigley) *foundation executive*

Colton
Arnquist, Jeanette Green *charitable foundation administrator*

Culver City
Netzel, Paul Arthur *fundraising management executive, consultant*

Davis
Boulton, Lyndie McHenry *professional society administrator*
Redenbach, Sandra Irene *educational consultant*

El Cerrito
Kerr, Catherine Spaulding *environmental advocate*

El Monte
Last, Marian Helen *social services administrator*

Encino
Mc Carthy, Patricia Margaret *retreat house administrator, social worker*

Fontana
Cory, Rolland Wayne *business administrator*
Tomiska, Cora Lorena *civic worker*

Glendora
Schiele, Paul Ellsworth, Jr. *educational business owner, writer*

Hawthorne
Gruenwald, James Howard *association executive, consultant*

Hayward
Evanoff, Mark Evan *advocate*
Feldman, Annette Young *civic worker*

Hercules
Guynn, Stefanie Carol *social work administrator, trainer, consultant*

Hollister
Schiffner, Joan Lessing *consultant*

Irvine
Moore, David Lewis *trade association executive*
Young, Robert Anthony *association director*

Kentfield
Blum, Joan Kurley *fundraising executive*

La Crescenta
Stubbs, Daniel Gaie *labor relations consultant*

La Jolla
Fishman, Lillian *research foundation executive*

Laguna Hills
Prusa, James Graham *association executive*

Lodi
Nusz, Phyllis Jane *fundraising consultant, meeting planner*

Lompoc
Politte, Richard Andrew *social services administrator*

Los Alamitos
Breunig, Robert Henry *foundation executive*

Los Altos
Wilbur, Colburn Sloan *foundation administrator, chief executive officer*

Los Angeles
Ball, Bert *foundation executive, arts consultant*
Brandlin, Thomas E. *nonprofit association consultant*
Caldwell-Portenier, Patty Jean Grosskopf *advocate, educator*
Ennis, Thomas Michael *health foundation executive*
Fields, Willie, Jr. *social welfare administrator*
Fox, Joel David *political association executive*
Gottlieb, Leonard *association administrator*
Harris, Barbara Hull (Mrs. F. Chandler Harris) *social agency administrator*
Headlee, Rolland Dockeray *association executive*
Henricksen, Lisa Alaine *development director*
Hubbs, Donald Harvey *foundation executive*
Kim-Han, Jeannie Hyun *educational administrator*
Lindley, F(rancis) Haynes, Jr. *foundation president, lawyer*
Lovato, Roberto *association executive*
Mack, J. Curtis, II *civic organization administrator*
Millman, Paul Richard *fundraiser*
Orsatti, Alfred Kendall *organization executive*
Schaffer, Jeffrey Lee *nonprofit organization executive*
Schine, Wendy Wachtell *foundation administrator*
Schwartz, Jeffrey Alan *fundraising executive*
Shmavonian, Gerald S. *association executive*
Smith, Peggy Anne *fundraising executive*

Manhattan Beach
Devitt-Grasso, Pauline Virginia *civic volunteer, nurse*

Menlo Park
Altman, Drew E. *foundation executive*
Gardner, David Pierpont *foundation executive*
Morrison, James Ian *research institute executive*
Nichols, William Ford, Jr. *foundation executive, business executive*
Pallotti, Marianne Marguerite *foundation administrator*

Modesto
Richardson, Ernest Ray (Rocky Richardson) *housing program supervisor*

Moffett Field
Scott, Donald Michael *educational association administrator, educator*

Monterey Park
Besen, Jane Phyllis Triptow *retired civic worker*

Mountain View
Michalko, James Paul *library association administrator*

Nevada City
Hudson, Lee (Arlene Hudson) *environmental activist*

Newbury Park
McCune, Sara Miller *foundation executive, publisher*

Newport Beach
Ford, Michael Q. *not-for-profit association administrator*
Machoskie, Katie Herbert *fundraising executive*

North Highlands
Bauer, Cecile Ruth *grant coordinator*

North Hollywood
Grasso, Mary Ann *theatre association administrator*

Norwalk
Gould, D. Joy *social services administrator*

Oakland
Borchardt, Marilyn *development administrator*
Dozier, Flora Grace *civil and human rights activist, entrepreneur*
Hackbarth, Dorothy Alice *association executive*
Misner, Charlotte Blanche Ruckman *community organization administrator*
Oberti, Sylvia Marie Antoinette *rehabilitation counselor and administrator, career advisor, textile consultant*
Smith, Jeffrey Alan *international educational aid administrator*
Wagner, Steve *social service program director*

Oceanside
Roberts, James McGregor *retired professional association executive*

Ojai
Mankoff, Albert William *cultural organization administrator, consultant*

Orange
Reed, David Andrew *foundation executive*

Oxnard
Daughenbaugh, Mary Jane *foundation administrator*

Pacific Palisades
Snowhook, Ann Laferty *social services administrator*

Pacoima
Syms, Helen Maksym *educational administrator*

Palm Desert
Berkman, Susan C. Josephs *association executive*

Palm Springs
Hearst, Rosalie *philanthropist, foundation executive*

Palo Alto
Clark, Dwight DeLong *voluntary organization administrator*

Pasadena
King, Rheta Baron *rehabilitation consultant*

Pauma Valley
Magee, Dennis *cultural organization administrator*

Pebble Beach
Gianelli, William Reynolds *foundation administrator, civil engineering consultant, former federal agency commissioner*

Pleasanton
Brooks, Stephen Volume *foundation executive*

Pomona
Lyon, Carolyn Bartel *civic worker*

Rancho Cordova
Smith, Milton Jay *fundraising executive*

Rancho Palos Verdes
Vanderlip, Elin Brekke *professional society executive*

Redlands
Ledbetter, Carl Scotius *counselor, educator*
Sandlin, Marlon Joe *planned giving director, financial planner*

Redwood City
Patterson, Francine G. P. *foundation administrator*

Riverside
Mellon, William Knox *foundation executive, consultant*
Williams, Mark Tully *foundation executive*

Rolling Hills Estates
King, Lea Ann *community volunteer and leader*
Lamkins, Robert Gerald *fundraising executive*

Sacramento
Hayward, Fredric Mark *social reformer*
Leighton, Larry J. *nonprofit organization administrator*
Naglestad, Frederic Allen *legislative advocate*
Oberlink, James Richard *environmental association executive, lawyer*

San Anselmo
Tomsky, Judy *fundraiser and event planner, importer*

San Bruno
Eckert, Steven Paul *social services administrator*

San Clemente
Buck, Lawrence Richard *fundraising executive*

San Diego
Ballinger, Charles Edwin *educational association administrator*
Boersma, Lawrence Allan *animal welfare administrator*
Brown, James Cooke *nonprofit organization administrator, game inventor, educational administrator, writer*
Carleson, Robert Bazil *public policy consultant, corporation director*
Dolan, James Michael, Jr. *zoological society executive*
Douglas, Lee Wayland *association executive*
Gallison, H(arold) Bailey, Sr. *youth agency administrator, public relations and marketing consultant*
Hinsvark, Don George *social services agency professional*
Lane, Gloria Julian *foundation administrator*
Robinson, Paulette Jean *educational association administrator*
Schlotter, Wally *chamber of commerce executive, television director*
Turnipseed, Victoria Lee *foundation administrator, public relations executive*
Wold, Nana Beha *social services administrator*
Young, Charlita Lucille *community and educational administrator*

San Francisco
Ahn, Tina Marie *association executive*
Aldrich, Michael Ray *organization executive*
Collins, David Michael *foundation administrator*
Collins, Dennis Arthur *foundation executive*
Eastham, Thomas *foundation administrator*
Evankovich, George Joseph *labor union administrator*
Fisher, Robert M. *foundation administrator, university administrator*
Fitch, Jack *association executive*
Giovinco, Joseph *nonprofit administrator, writer*
Gordon, Gloria Kathleen *business association executive, magazine editor*
Grose, Andrew Peter *association executive*
Hasenkamp, Bruce Henry *foundation executive*
Hickman, Maxine Viola *social services administrator*
Horn, Robert Eldon *university researcher, think-tank executive, entrepreneur*
Jacobs, John Howard *association executive*
Krasney, Martin *organization executive, educator*
Lord, Mia W. *peace activist*
Mack, Charles Daniel, III *labor union executive*
McIntyre, Robert Wheeler *conservation organization executive*
Morris, Richard Ward *nonprofit organization administrator, author*
Onek, David Alexander *social services organization researcher*
Reichbach, Naomi Estelle *social service administrator*
Salazar, Wayne Hardy *arts and social services administrator*
Schuchat, Samuel Price *professional society administrator*
Thelen, Max, Jr. *foundation executive, lawyer*

San Jose
Bennett, Charles Turner *social welfare administrator*
Callan, Patrick M. *educational executive, educator*
Dargis, Jean Anthony *retired voluntary health agency executive*
Lind, Terrie Lee *social services administrator*

San Luis Obispo
Jamieson, James Bradshaw *foundation administrator*

San Marino
Hull, Suzanne White *retired cultural institution administrator, writer*
Spear, Margaret C. *development officer*

San Mateo
Hongo, Florence Makita *educational association administrator*

San Rafael
Lee, Robert *association executive, former theological educator, consultant, author*
Raphael, Tamar Amita *development director*

Santa Barbara
Bailey, Marsha Ann *association executive*
Conklin, Hal (Harold Conklin) *arts association executive*
Doll, Nancy Marie *arts administrator and curator*
Golden, Nancy McAleer *fundraising consultant*
Mc Coy, Lois Clark *emergency services executive, retired county official, magazine editor*
Walker, Sally C. *fundraising executive*

Santa Monica
Fredricks, Shirley Jean *foundation director, consultant*
Greene, Michael C. *art association administrator*
Liddicoat, Richard Thomas, Jr. *association executive*
Williams, Harold Marvin *foundation official*

Santa Rosa
Harris, David Joel *foundation executive*

Scotts Valley
Bourret, Marjorie Ann *educational advocate, consultant*

Sherman Oaks
Green, Marjorie Biller *educational administrator*
Marckwardt, Harold Thomas *association executive*

Simi Valley
Bumgardner, Larry G. *foundation administrator, communications educator*

Sloughhouse
Uhde, Larry Jackson *joint apprentice administrator*

Sonoma
Stadtman, Verne August *former foundation executive, editor*

Sonora
Coffill, Marjorie Louise *civic leader*

Spring Valley
Drake, Stanley Joseph *association executive*

Stanford
Dickinson, Ann *fundraiser*
Lyman, Richard Wall *foundation and university executive, historian*
Matisoff, Susan *cultural research organization administrator*

Stockton
Blodgett, Elsie Grace *association executive*

Studio City
Barrett, Dorothy *performing arts administrator*

Sylmar
Froelich, Beverly Lorraine *foundation director*

Thousand Oaks
Brittan, John Scott *cultural exchange society executive*

Trinidad
Harper, Sharyne Rae *social services administrator*

Truckee
Johnston, Bernard Fox *foundation executive*

Tustin
Parker, Kimberly Jane *nonprofit association executive, paralegal*
Silverstein, Richard Mark *fundraiser*

Van Nuys
Miller, Robert Steven *educational association administrator*

Ventura
Downs, Florella McIntyre *civic worker, pilot*

Watsonville
Cane, William Earl *nonprofit organization executive*

West Hollywood
Hoffenblum, Allan Ernest *political consultant*

West Sacramento
Hill, Nathan Scott *art organization executive, cultural consultant, lecturer*

Woodland
Sandrin, Colleen Louise *healthcare philanthropist*

Woodland Hills
Harris, Helen Josephine *foundation administrator*
O'Meara, Sara *foundation administrator*
Sigholtz, Sara O'Meara *nonprofit organization executive*

COLORADO

Arvada
Kent, Sheila Kelly *community volunteer*
Meiklejohn, (Lorraine) Mindy June *political organizer, realtor*
Parro, Douglas Arthur *nonprofit child care center administrator*

Aurora
Fish, Ruby Mae Bertram (Mrs. Frederick Goodrich Fish) *civic worker*

Boulder
Brandauer, Nancy Ellsworth *resource center executive*
Cross, Christopher S. *fundraising executive*
Eberl, Patricia Jo *professional society administrator, editor*
Forstrom, June Rochelle *professional society administrator*
Hill, Norbert S., Jr. *professional society executive*
Jensen, C. Neil *association executive, lobbyist*
Neinas, Charles Merrill *athletic association executive*

Broomfield
Bryan, A(lonzo) J(ay) *service club official*

Castle Rock
Graf, Joseph Charles *retired foundation executive*

Colorado Springs
Deiotte, Margaret Williams Tukey *nonprofit consultant, grants writer*
Eskew, Cathleen Cheek *social services administrator*
Killian, George Ernest *association executive*
Libby, Lauren Dean *foundation executive*
Loo, Katherine Haughey *nonprofit organization consultant*
Loux, Gordon Dale *organization executive*
MacLeod, Richard Patrick *foundation administrator*
Miller, Zoya Dickins (Mrs. Hilliard Eve Miller, Jr.) *civic worker*
Prensner, Steven R. *nonprofit organization executive*
Rochette, Edward Charles *retired association executive*
Sanner, Monty Ray *nonprofit organization administrator*

Deer Trail
Mergl, Betty Mae *senior center executive director*

Denver
Andrews, John Kneeland *youth worker*
Blish, Eugene Sylvester *trade association administrator*
Coté, Robert Dean *social activist*
Daley, Richard Halbert *foundation executive*
Darkey, Kermit Louis *association executive, lawyer*
Dinner, Marie Bernice *social services program administrator*
Fielden, C. Franklin, III *educational administrator*
Gloss, Lawrence Robert *fundraising executive*
Hirschfeld, Arlene F. *civic worker, homemaker*
Hogan, Curtis Jule *union executive, industrial relations consultant*
Knorr, Tom Johnson *cultural organization administrator*
Koch, Gerald Douglas *social services administrator*
Konrad, Peter Allen *foundation administrator*
Low, Merry Cook *civic worker*
Parr, John David *not-for-profit executive*
Pederson, Clay Leonard *nonprofit organization administrator*
Phillips, Kay Randelle *association executive*
Proctor, Bettina Rea *fish and wildlife organization administrator*
Raughton, Jimmie Leonard *educational foundation administrator, urban planner*
Schlottman, James L. *not-for-profit organization executive, consultant*
Walker, Mary Christine *community services facilitator, educator*
Ward, Lester Lowe, Jr. *arts association executive, lawyer*

Durango
Conrad, Barbara Ann *association executive*

Englewood
Massey, Leon R. *association executive*
Reese, Monte Nelson *agricultural association executive*

Fort Collins
Adams, Frank Stewart *family service agency director, pastor/chaplain*
Fetters, Joan Frances *child care center administrator, educator*

Golden
Zehr, Norman Robert *association administrator*

Grand Junction
Morris, Rusty Lee *administrative executive*

Lakewood
Froehlich, Robert Elmer *association director, management consultant*
Gansauer, Diane H. *wildlife association executive*
Isely, Henry Philip *association executive, integrative engineer, writer, educator*

Littleton
Walker, Eljana M. du Vall *civic worker*

Snowmass
Lovins, L. Hunter *public policy institute executive*

U S A F Academy
Coppock, Richard Miles *nonprofit association administrator*

CONNECTICUT

Ridgefield
Weese, Bruce Eric *pharmaceutical industry lobbyist*

DISTRICT OF COLUMBIA

Washington
Peck, Robert David *educational foundation administrator*
Siciliano, Rocco Carmine *institute executive*

HAWAII

Hilo
Fopiano, Lois Mae *institute administrator, psychotherapist,*

Honolulu
Blackfield, Cecilia Malik *civic volunteer, educator*
Botti, Richard Charles *association executive*
Lee, Beverly Ing *educational administrator*
McCall, Stephen Shawn *philanthropist*
Mirikitani, John Masa *foundation administrator*
Olmsted, Ronald David *foundation executive, consultant*
Staub, Scott Christopher *fundraiser*

Kapaa
Atkins, William Theodore *community volunteer, retired insurance executive*

Lihue
Pironti, Lavonne De Laere *association executive*

Pearl City
Trahan, Ellen Vauneil *nonprofit association executive, public administrator*

IDAHO

Boise
Guerber, Stephen Craig *community foundation executive*

Idaho Falls
Hoopes, Sidney Lou *educational association administrator*

MISSOURI

Kansas City
Bugher, Robert Dean *association executive*

MONTANA

Big Timber
Sanddal, Nels Dodge *foundation executive, consultant*

Billings
Sample, Joseph Scanlon *foundation executive*

Bozeman
Chambers-Sweeney, Linda J. *association administrator, small business owner*
Cummins, John Thomas, Jr. *lobbyist, writer, speaker*

Great Falls
Ebbinga, Crystalle Yvonne *social services administrator*

Harrison
Jackson, Peter Vorious, III *retired association executive*

Helena
Marquardt, Kathleen Patricia *association executive*
Munck, Michael George *fundraising executive*

Libby
Symmons, Clare Payne *foundation administrator*

Missoula
Amundson, Eva Donalda *civic worker*
Chapman, Judi *Indian tribes and organizations consultant, lobbyist*
Gunstream, Robby Dean *music society executive*

NEVADA

Carson City
Ayres, Janice Ruth *social service executive*

Ely
Rajala, Karen Rae *economic and community development administrator*

Henderson
Freyd, William Pattinson *fund raising executive, consultant*

Las Vegas
Chinn-Hechter, Mamie May *nonprofit organization executive*
Deacon, Maxine Shirley *grant writer, fundraiser*
Horner, Lee *foundation executive, speaker, consultant, computer specialist*
Lowman, Mary Bethena Hemphill (Mrs. Zelvin D. Lowman) *civic worker, realtor*
Williams, Nancy Ellen-Webb *social services administrator*

Pahrump
Hersman, Marion Frank *professional administrator, lawyer*

Reno
LePome, Penelope Marie *rehabilitation counselor, educator*
Winzeler, Judith Kay *foundation administrator*

NEW JERSEY

Lyndhurst
McCuaig, Ian Carruthers *fundraising consultant*

NEW MEXICO

Albuquerque
Cole, Terri Lynn *organization administrator*
Roberts, Dennis William *association executive*

Angel Fire
Dillon, Robert Morton *retired association executive, architectural consultant*

Church Rock
Linford, Laurance Dee *cultural organization administrator*

Farmington
Mathers, Margaret *charitable agency consultant, political activist*

Las Cruces
Coombs, Michael John *research center administrator*
Eriksson, Anne-Marie *social services executive, educator*

Playas
Clifton, Judy Raelene *association administrator*

Santa Fe
Cardinale, Robert Lee *foundation executive, art administrator*
Chatfield, Cheryl Ann *nonprofit organization executive, educator*
Johnson, William Stewart *cultural arts administrator*
Kolman, Marc Rand *public health administrator*
Melnick, Alice Jean (aj Melnick) *counselor*

NEW YORK

New York
Zalkind, Joseph Gary *fundraiser, writer, speaker*

OREGON

Bandon
Millard, Esther Lound *foundation administrator, educator*

Beaverton
Henderson, George Miller *foundation executive, former banker*
Hoffman, Marianne Macina *nonprofit organization administrator*

Bend
Denney, Teresa Marie *nonprofit association executive*

Corvallis
Krug, Al John *social services administrator*
Wilkins, Caroline Hanke *consumer agency administrator, political worker*

Eugene
Hale, Dean Edward *social services administrator*

Grants Pass
Boling, Judy Atwood *civic worker*

Junction City
Humphry, Derek *association executive*

Klamath Falls
Ehlers, Eleanor May Collier (Mrs. Frederick Burton Ehlers) *civic worker*

Lake Oswego
Miller, Barbara Stallcup *development consultant*

Medford
Wegner, Samuel Joseph *historical society executive*

Oregon City
Alldredge, Rendel Burdette *volunteer, retired government official*

Pendleton
Marko, Chris Emery *social services administrator*

Portland
Barnett, Erna Justine *nonprofit organization administrator*
Beaird, Steven Edward *fundraising professional*
Bloch, Ernest, II *foundation administrator*
Bruce, John Allen *foundation executive, educator*
Culver, Wesley Ellsworth *relief and development organization executive*
Dailey, Joseph Charles *development executive*
May, John Stuart *fundraising executive*
O'Hollaren, Paul Joseph *former international fraternity administrator*
Rianda, David Noel *medical foundation administrator*
Rooks, Charles S. *foundation administrator*
Schultz, James Michael *nonprofit marketing administrator*
Underwood, Jerry Lawrence *nonprofit corporation executive, writer*
Wiseheart, Tess *social services administrator*

Redmond
Johnson, Elizabeth Hill *foundation administrator*

Salem
Gann, Jo Rita *social services administrator, association executive*
Johnston, Marilyn Elaine (Greene) *nonprofit organization executive director*

UTAH

Bountiful
Pedersen, Gaylen *organization executive, marketing consultant*

Cedar City
Weaver, Max Kimball *social worker, consultant*

Ogden
Littleton, Gaye Darlene *nonprofit executive director*
Pappas, Leah Aglaia *civic worker, political consultant, educator*

Provo
Lee, Blaine Nelson *educational executive, consultant, educator*

Salt Lake City
Barry, Bonnie B. *trade association executive*
Cofield, Philip Thomas *educational association administrator*
Dolcourt, Joyce Linda *social service administrator*
Evans, Max Jay *historical society administrator*
Julander, Paula Foil *association administrator*
Lowry, Candace Elizabeth *human resource administrator, consultant*
Melich, Doris S. *public service worker*
Oswald, Delmont Richard *humanities organization executive, writer*

WASHINGTON

Auburn
Piraino, Ann Mae *seminar trainer, leader, vocational counselor*

Bainbridge Island
Rosner, Robert Allan *advocate*

Bellevue
Arnold, Ronald Henri *nonprofit organization executive, consultant*
Brown, Eric *developer*
Kiest, Alan Scott *social services administrator*

Bellingham
Green, Michael *foundation administrator*

Blaine
James, Herb Mark (Jay James) *foundation and insurance executive, free trade consultant*

Centralia
Olson, Steven Stanley *social service executive*

Edmonds
Thyden, James Eskel *professional society administrator, former diplomat, educator*

Everett
Corkran, John Rogerson *fundraising executive*

Ferndale
Lane-Oreiro, Laverne Teresa *former tribal official*

Olympia
Gray, Donovan Michael *cultural development specialist*
St. John, Eugene Logan *labor union director*

Redmond
Andrew, Jane Hayes *nonprofit organization executive*

Seattle
Baker, Bruce Frederick *health services association administrator*
Cole, Kenneth James *advocate*
Conlin, Richard Byrd *association administrator*
Hirstel, Robert *labor relations consultant*
Jones, Louisa Elsa *medical association executive*
Moberly, David Lindsey *foundation executive*
Ray, Marianne Yurasko *social services administrator*
Rooney, Alice Gregor *art society executive*
Rotenberg, Susan *association administrator*
Sayward, Jenny *cultural organization executive*
Swain, Nola V. *foundation administrator, marketing professional*
Thompson, Dwight Alan *vocational rehabilitation expert*

Selah
Ballard, James Kenneth *association executive, horticulture executive*

Spokane
Bowker, Gary Ades *development executive*
Falkner, James George *foundation executive*
Murphy, Mary Ann *human services administrator*
Rowe, Marjorie Douglas *retired social services administrator*

Tacoma
Graybill, David Wesley *chamber of commerce executive*
Robison, William Thomas *trade association executive*

Vancouver
Anderson, Ford A., II (Drew Anderson) *foundation executive*
Campbell, Cindy Irene *social service administrator*
Smith, Sam Corry *retired foundation executive, consultant*

Yakima
Nelson, Bryan H(erbert) *educational association administrator*

WYOMING

Cheyenne
Smith, Shane Dale *cultural organization administrator, consultant*

Cody
Coe, Margaret Louise Shaw *community service volunteer*

Laramie
Freeman, John Francis *foundation executive*
Powers, Judith Kay *educational administrator, English educator*

Sundance
Rowe, Randy Roland *nonprofit organization executive, consultant*

CANADA

ALBERTA

Calgary
Raeburn, Andrew Harvey *performing arts association executive, record producer*

Medicine Hat
Sorensen, Elizabeth Julia *cultural administrator*

BRITISH COLUMBIA

Vancouver
Saywell, William George Gabriel *foundation administrator*

ENGLAND

London
Abrams, Ossie Ekman *fundraiser*

ADDRESS UNPUBLISHED

Ackles, Janice Vogel *fundraising executive, writer*
Allison, Andrew M. *foundation administrator*
Anderson, Ned, Sr. *Apache tribal executive*
Anguiano, Lupe *advocate*
Black, Karen L. *not-for-profit administrator, social worker, advocate*
Blair, Kathie Lynn *social services worker*
Blum, Joanne Lee *development executive, educator*
Boal, Dean *retired arts center administrator, educator*
Burns, Mary Ferris *society administrator*
Cazares, Roger *community improvement executive*
Chirumbolo, Paul *arts organization executive*
Cilek, Jeffrey Robert *nonprofit executive*
Clark, Alicia Garcia *political party official*
Eliot, Theodore Lyman, Jr. *international consultant*
Fiedler, Bobbi *community agency director, former congresswoman*
Furman, James Merle *foundation executive*
Hansen, Michael Joseph *association executive, writing educator*
Harris, Cynthia Viola *educational administrator*
Hobbs, Kenneth Burkett *foundation administrator, consultant*
Hybl, William Joseph *foundation executive, lawyer*
Ikeda, Tsuguo (Ike Ikeda) *social services center administrator, consultant*
Joyner, Darla Jean *trade association executive*
Klopfleisch, Stephanie Squance *social services agency administrator*
MacMillan, Kip Van Metre *foundation executive*
McCall, Franceen Kay *social services administrator*
McCarthy, Mary Frances *hospital foundation administrator*
Migden, Chester L. *association executive*
Morgan, Kat C. *political activist*
Parker, Alan Dale *financial development executive*
Peri, Winnie Lee Branch *educational director*
Powell, Julia Gertrude *volunteer*
Ramo, Virginia M. Smith *civic worker*
Reagan, Nancy Davis (Anne Francis Robbins) *volunteer, wife of former President of United States*
Robbins, John *foundation executive, writer*
Rosen, Rosalie *association executive*
Schiff Bernard, Ellie *political and nonprofit fundraiser*
Scott, Jacqueline Delmar Parker *educational association administrator, business administrator, consultant, fundraiser*
Scribner, Dorothy Nesbitt *community relations executive, consultant*
Shuman, Thomas Alan *correctional operations executive, consultant*
Simmons, Glori Louise *nonprofit development officer*
Sinnex, Ceil *nonprofit foundation founder, newsletter publisher*
Siri, Jean Brandenburg *citizen advocate*
Smith, Alice Murray *civic worker, mathematician*
Smith, Marcia Taylor *special event planning and fundraising consultant*
Spoehel, Jerri Hoskins *volunteer agency executive*
Steiner, Roberta Pearl *not-for-profit foundation administrator*
Stewart, Paul Anthony, II *building association executive, author*
Stout, Elizabeth West *administrator*
Terrill, W(allace) Andrew *international security analyst*
Van Ness, John Ralph *university foundation administrator*
Viking, Nancy Lee *special events management and marketing consultant*
Weddle, Judith Ann *social services administrator*
Williams, Betty Lourene *volunteer, manager, consultant*
Winters, Richard Keith *social services administrator*
Wyatt, Lenore *civic worker*
Young, Margaret Buckner *civic worker, author*

ATHLETICS

UNITED STATES

ARIZONA

Phoenix
Barkley, Charles Wade *professional basketball player*
Bidwill, William V. *professional football executive*
Colangelo, Jerry John *professional basketball team executive*
Fitzsimmons, (Lowell) Cotton *professional basketball executive, broadcaster, former coach*
Johnson, Kevin Maurice *professional basketball player*
Joyner, Seth *professional football player*
Majerle, Daniel Lewis *professional basketball player, Olympic athlete*
Manning, Daniel Ricardo *professional basketball player*
Ryan, Buddy (James Ryan) *professional football coach*
Simmons, Clyde *professional football player*
Starks, Rosalyn June *physical education and health educator*
Van Arsdale, Dick *professional basketball team executive*
Westphal, Paul *professional basketball coach*

Tempe
Hoke, Judy Ann *physical education educator*
Wells, Christine Louise *physical education educator*

Tucson
Olson, Lute *university athletic coach*

CALIFORNIA

Agoura Hills
Patano, Patricia Ann *health and fitness professional, marketing and public relations specialist*

Alta Loma
Tolan, Vicki Irvena *physical education educator*

Anaheim
Brown, Richard M. *professional baseball team executive*
Frontiere, Georgia *professional football team executive*
Jackson, Bo (Vincent Edward Jackson) *professional baseball, former football player*
Lachemann, Marcel *professional baseball manager*
Langston, Mark Edward *professional baseball player*
Smith, Lee Arthur *professional baseball player*
Stark, Milton Dale *sports association executive*

Bakersfield
Friedman, Gloria A. *tennis coach*

Beverly Hills
Shoemaker, Bill (William Lee Shoemaker) *retired jockey, horse trainer*

Coronado
Axelson, Joseph Allen *professional athletics executive, publisher*

Danville
Behring, Kenneth E. *professional sports team owner*

El Cajon
Addis, Thomas Homer, III *professional golfer*

El Dorado Hills
Mansoor, John Jirius *sports management executive*

El Segundo
Brown, Timothy Donell *professional football player*
Davis, Allen *professional football team executive*
Gossett, Jeffrey Alan *professional football player*
Herrera, John *professional football team executive*
Hostetler, Jeff W. *professional football player*
Jaeger, Jeff Todd *professional football player*
Mosebar, Donald Howard *professional football player*
Townsend, Greg *professional football player*
Wisniewski, Stephen Adam *professional football player*

Escondido
Mueller, Elizabeth Suzanne *physical education educator*

Fullerton
Garrido, Augie *university athletic coach*

Inglewood
Harris, Tim Ray *sports promoter, agent*
Johnson, Earvin (Magic Johnson) *professional sports team executive, former professional basketball coach*
Kurri, Jari *professional hockey player*
McNall, Bruce *professional sports executive, numismatist*
Sharman, William *professional basketball team executive*
Vachon, Rogatien Rosaire (Rogie Vachon) *professional hockey team executive*
West, Jerry Alan *professional basketball team executive*
Worthy, James Ager *former professional basketball player*

Irvine
Farrell, Dennis *sports association executive*

Los Angeles
Barretta-Keyser, Jolie *professional athletics club coach, author*
Baylor, Elgin Gay *professional basketball team executive*
Carrica, Xavier *health and fitness professional*
Chamberlain, Wilton Norman *retired professional basketball player*
Claire, Fred *professional baseball team executive*
Dismukes, Valena Grace Broussard *physical education educator*
Fitch, William C. *professional basketball coach*
Harrick, Jim *university athletic coach*
Karros, Eric Peter *professional baseball player*
Kelly, Roberto Conrado (Bobby Kelly) *professional baseball player*
Lasorda, Thomas Charles (Tommy Lasorda) *professional baseball team manager*
Levy, Louis *chess master*
O'Malley, Peter *professional baseball club executive*
Piazza, Michael Joseph *professional baseball player*
Raveling, George *former university athletic coach*
Sterling, Donald T. *professional basketball team executive*

Malibu
Louganis, Greg E. *former Olympic athlete, actor*

Manhattan Beach
Kamin, Aviva *sports association administrator*

Mentone
Stockton, David Knapp *professional golfer*

Napa
Miller, John Laurence *professional golfer*

Oak Park
Caldwell, Stratton Franklin *kinesiologist*

Oakland
Dolich, Andrew Bruce *professional basketball team executive*
Eckersley, Dennis Lee *professional baseball player*
Finnane, Daniel F. *professional basketball team executive*
Haas, Walter J. *professional baseball team executive*
Hardaway, Timothy Duane *basketball player*
Henderson, Rickey Henley *professional baseball player*
McGwire, Mark David *professional baseball player*
Mullin, Chris(topher) Paul *professional basketball player*
Sierra, Ruben Angel Garcia *professional baseball player*

Oceanside
Lomelí, Refugio (Jesse Lomelí) *athletics educator*

Palm Springs
Jumonville, Felix Joseph, Jr. *physical education educator, realtor*

Rancho Santa Margarita
Griffith Joyner, Florence DeLorez *track and field athlete*

Riverside
Hamerslough, Walter Scott *health and physical education educator*

Sacramento
Russell, Bill *former professional basketball team executive, former professional basketball player*
St. Jean, Garry *professional basketball coach*
Thomas, Jim *professional basketball team executive*

San Bernardino
Rizzo, Terry Lee *physical education educator*

San Diego
Beathard, Bobby *professional football team executive*
Benes, Andrew Charles *professional baseball player*
Freeman, Dick *professional baseball team executive*
Gwynn, Anthony Keith (Tony Gwynn) *professional baseball player*
Seau, Junior (Tiana Seau, Jr.) *professional football player*
Spanos, Alexander Gus *professional football team executive*

San Francisco
Baker, Dusty (Johnnie B. Baker, Jr.) *professional baseball team manager*
Beck, Rodney Roy *professional baseball player*
Bonds, Barry Lamar *professional baseball player*
Magowan, Peter Alden *professional baseball team executive, grocery chain executive*
Mays, Willie Howard, Jr. (Say Hey Kid) *former professional baseball player*
McGee, William Dean (Willie McGee) *professional baseball player*
Thompson, Robert Randall (Robby Thompson) *professional baseball player*
Williams, Matt (Matthew Derrick Williams) *professional baseball player*

San Gabriel
Sandvig, Kipp Ray *physical education educator*

San Luis Obispo
Buccola, Victor Allan *physical education educator, sports association executive*

Santa Ana
Muzila, Thomas Walter *marital arts and karate educator, consultant*

Santa Clara
Carroll, Pete *professional football coach*
Dent, Richard Lamar *professional football player*
Hanks, Merton Edward *professional football player*
Jackson, Rickey *professional football player*
McDonald, Tim *professional football player*
McVay, John Edward *professional football club executive*
Rice, Jerry Lee *professional football player*
Seifert, George *professional football coach*
Young, Steven *professional football player*

Sausalito
Casals, Rosemary *professional tennis player*

Sherman Oaks
Hamilton, Scott Scovell *professional figure skater, former Olympic athlete*

Simi Valley
De Angelis, Deborah Ann Ayars *university athletics official*

Stanford
Van Derveer, Tara *university athletic coach*
Walsh, William *former football coach*

Sunnyvale
Cognata, Joseph Anthony *football commissioner*

Torrance
Reeves, Daniel Morton *shotgun shooting coach, writer*

Walnut
Ashford, Evelyn *track and field athlete*

Walnut Creek
Hallock, C. Wiles, Jr. *athletic official*
Hansen, Thomas Carter *college athletics conference commissioner*

Yorba Linda
Sargent, Harry Tompkins *professional golfer*

COLORADO

Alamosa
Straub, Richard Neal *coach*

Boulder
Young, Christopher Michael *skier*

Colorado Springs
Badger, Sandra Rae *health and physical education educator*
Essick, Raymond Brooke, III *amateur sports administrator*
Groebli, Werner Fritz (Mr. Frick) *professional ice skater, realtor*
Haag, Carrie H. *sports association executive*

Denver
Baylor, Don Edward *professional baseball manager*
Bickerstaff, Bernard Tyrone, Sr. *professional basketball team executive*
Galarraga, Andres Jose *professional baseball player*
Gebhard, Bob *professional baseball team executive*
Johnson, Mary Bettina Black *physical education educator, athletic trainer*
Mutombo, DiKembe (Dikembe Mutombo Mpolondo Mukamba Jean Jacque Wamutombo) *professional basketball player*
Swift, William Charles *professional baseball player, Olympic athlete*

Englewood
Atwater, Stephen Dennis *professional football player*
Beake, John *professional football team executive*
Craw, Nicholas Wesson *motor sports association executive*
Elway, John Albert *professional football player*
Mecklenburg, Karl Bernard *professional football player*
Perry, Michael Dean *professional football player*
Phillips, Wade *former professional football team coach*
Sharpe, Shannon *professional football player*
Smith, Dennis *professional football player*

Fort Collins
Cebrick, Joan Alice *fitness educator*

Littleton
Kearney, Joseph Laurence *athletic conference administrator*

Louisville
Tobin, Robert Manford, Jr. *karate instructor*

FLORIDA

Gainesville
Lopez, Andy *university athletic coach*

Opa Locka
Clark, Gary C. *football player*

HAWAII

Kihei
Fowler, Charles Edward, Jr. *tennis management company executive*

MICHIGAN

Detroit
Davis, Eric Keith *former professional baseball player*

MONTANA

Billings
Hahn, Woody *sports association executive*

NEVADA

Las Vegas
Allen, Vicki Lynette *physical education educator*

NEW MEXICO

Albuquerque
Unser, Al *professional auto racer*

OHIO

Youngstown
DeBartolo, Edward John, Jr. *professional football team owner, real estate developer*

OREGON

Eugene
Decker Slaney, Mary Teresa *Olympic athlete*

Portland
Carlesimo, P. J. (Peter J. Carlesimo) *former college basketball coach, professional basketball coach*
Kolde, Bert *professional basketball team executive*
Thorpe, Otis Henry *professional basketball player*
Williams, Charles Linwood (Buck Williams) *professional basketball player*

TEXAS

Arlington
Burkett, John David *professional baseball player*
Clark, Will (William Nuschler Clark, Jr.) *professional baseball player*

Houston
Camarillo, Richard Jon *professional football player*
Drexler, Clyde *professional basketball player*

Leander
Erickson, Ralph D. *retired physical education educator, small business owner, consultant*

UTAH

Ephraim
Trythall, Robert C. *athletic director*

Park City
Kelly, Thomas J. *sports association executive*

Salt Lake City
Hornacek, Jeffrey John *professional basketball player*
Layden, Francis Patrick (Frank Layden) *professional basketball team executive, former coach*
Malone, Karl (The Mailman) *professional basketball player*
Miller, Larry H. *professional sports team executive, automobile dealer*
Sloan, Jerry (Gerald Eugene Sloan) *professional basketball coach*

Sandy
Schneiter, George Malan *golf professional, development company executive*

Tropic
Heywood, Thomas Kay *physical education educator, coach*

WASHINGTON

Kirkland
Allen, Chuck *football team executive*
Erickson, Dennis *professional football coach, former university football coach*
Flores, Thomas R. *professional football team executive*
Kennedy, Cortez *professional football player*

Seattle
Ackerley, Barry *professional basketball team executive, communications company executive*
Carey, Stan *sports administrator, football coach*
Ellis, John W. *professional baseball team executive, utility company executive*
Griffey, Ken, Jr. (George Kenneth Griffey, Jr.) *professional baseball player*
James, Don *university athletic coach*
Johnson, Randall David (Randy Johnson) *professional baseball player*
Karl, George *professional basketball coach*
Kemp, Shawn T. *professional basketball player*
Martinez, Edgar *professional baseball player*
Piniella, Louis Victor *professional baseball team manager*

Spokane
Moe, Orville Leroy *racetrack executive*

Tacoma
Sundquist, Leah Renata *physical education specialist*

CANADA

ALBERTA

Calgary
Cheveldae, Tim *professional hockey player*
Hay, William Charles *professional hockey team executive*
Housley, Phil F *professional hockey player*
King, W. David *professional hockey coach*

Edmonton
Burnett, George *professional hockey coach*
Sather, Glen Cameron *professional hockey team executive, coach*

BRITISH COLUMBIA

Vancouver
Bure, Pavel *professional hockey player*
Griffiths, Arthur R. *professional hockey team executive*
Quinn, Pat (John Brian Patrick Quinn) *professional sports team manager*

QUEBEC

Montreal
Damphousse, Vincent *professional hockey player*

ADDRESS UNPUBLISHED

Herzog, Whitey (Dorrel Norman Elvert Herzog) *former professional baseball team executive*
Lindsey, D. Ruth *physical education educator*
Massimino, Roland V. *former university basketball coach*
McIntyre, Guy Maurice *professional football player*
Oates, Bart Steven *professional football player*
Risebrough, Doug *professional hockey team executive*
Ross, Robert Joseph *head professional football coach*
Schrempf, Detlef *professional basketball player*
Stadler, Craig Robert *professional golfer*
Wooden, John Robert *former basketball coach*
Zimmer, Donald William *former professional baseball manager*

BUSINESS. *See* FINANCE; INDUSTRY.

COMMUNICATIONS. *See* COMMUNICATIONS MEDIA; INDUSTRY: SERVICE.

COMMUNICATIONS MEDIA. *See also* ARTS: LITERARY.

UNITED STATES

ALASKA

Anchorage
Atwood, Robert Bruce *publisher*
Levi, Steven C(hanning) *freelance writer, historian*
Lindauer, John Howard, II *newspaper publisher*
Pearson, Larry Lester *journalism educator, communication consultant*
Tobin, William Joseph *newspaper editor*
Unruh, Leon Dale *newspaper editor*

Fairbanks
Cole, Dermot Matthew *newspaper columnist, historian*
Crawford, Sarah Carter (Sally Crawford) *broadcast executive*

Juneau
Silvas-Ottumwa, Sally *publishing executive*

Seward
Blatchford, Edgar Pleasant *editor, publisher*
Leary, Lory Diane Mary B. *publishing executive*

ARIZONA

Apache Junction
Files, James Lincoln *editor*

Bisbee
Eppele, David Louis *columnist, author*

Casa Grande
Kramer, Donovan Mershon, Sr. *newspaper publisher*

Flagstaff
Aitchison, Stewart Wayne *photojournalist*
Hammond, Howard David *retired botanist and editor*
Helford, Paul Quinn *communications educator, academic administrator*
Morrow, Brian R. *publishing executive*

Glendale
Joseph, Gregory Nelson *media critic*

Green Valley
Lasch, Robert *former journalist*

Phoenix
Benson, Stephen R. *editorial cartoonist*
Cheshire, William Polk *newspaper columnist*
Chesterfield, Mary *editor*
DeBruhl, Richard R. *television reporter*
Dulude, Gary Joseph *copywriter*
Early, Robert Joseph *magazine editor*
Edens, Gary Denton *broadcasting executive*
Ellison, Cyril Lee *publisher*
Fessler, Diane Marcia *publisher*
Floyd, Barbara Irene *newspaper editor-in-chief*
Floyd, Marguerite Marie (Maita Floyd) *publisher*
Forder, Reg Arthur *publishing executive*
Genrich, Mark L. *newspaper editor*
Grafe, Warren Blair *cable television executive*
Gruver, William Rand, II *journalist, educator*
Gunty, Christopher James *newspaper editor*
Kolbe, John William *newspaper columnist*
Leach, John F. *newspaper editor, journalism educator*
Moyer, Alan Dean *retired newspaper editor*
Murian, Richard Miller *book company executive*
Oppedahl, John Fredrick *newspaper editor*
Perlman, Janet *indexer, editor, writer*
Schatt, Paul *newspaper editor*
Stahl, Richard G. C. *journalist, editor*
Weil, Louis Arthur, III *newspaper publishing executive*
White, Jane See *journalist*

Prescott
Kimball, Richard Wilson *reporter*

Scottsdale
Bowie, Herbert Hughes, Jr. *magazine editor*
Everingham, Harry Towner *editor, publisher*
Fox, Kenneth L. *retired newspaper editor, writer*
Friedman, Diana Patricia *editor*
Frischknecht, Lee Conrad *retired broadcasting executive*
Gates, Sheldon Wilbur *publishing executive*
Godwin, Mary Jo *editor, librarian consultant*
Reidy, Richard Robert *publishing company executive*
Ross, Roger *publishing executive*
Schweiker, Maxine Aynes *magagine editor*
Searight, Patricia Adelaide *retired radio and television executive*
Smyth, Bernard John *retired newspaper editor*
Walsh, Mason *retired newspaperman*

Sedona
Chicorel, Marietta Eva *publisher*
Sasmor, James Cecil *publisher representative, educator*
Stinnett, Leia Ann *publisher*

Sun City West
Edwards, F(loyd) Kenneth *journalist, educator, management consultant, marketing executive*

Tempe
Aynesmith, Lawrence *publishing executive*
Craft, John Edward *communications educator, media consultant*
Gorder, Cheryl Marie *book publisher*
Koppes, Steven Nelson *public information officer, science writer*
Milner, Joe W. *journalism educator*
Rankin, William Parkman *communications educator, former publishing company executive*

Tucson
Annerino, John Joseph *photojournalist, author*
Collins, Conchita Ryan *writer*
Copenhaver, Larry James *journalist*
Evers, Mark *media research firm executive*
Gasparrini, Claudia *publishing company executive, scientist, writer*
Hatfield, Charles Donald *newspaper executive*
Hutchinson, Charles Smith, Jr. *book publisher*
Johnson, James William, III *journalism educator*
Martin, June Johnson Caldwell *journalist*
Meehan, Eileen R. *communications educator*
Neal, James Madison, Jr. *editor*
Reel, James *music critic, writer*
Roos, Nestor Robert *consultant*
Silva, John Philip Costa *newspaper editor*
Stickler, John Cobb *publisher, journalist, author*
Villa, Jacqueline I. *newspaper editor*
Weber, Samuel *editor*
Young, Donald Allen *writer, consultant*

CALIFORNIA

Agoura Hills
Chagall, David *journalist, author*
Teresi, Joseph *publishing executive*

Alhambra
Duke, Donald Norman *publisher*

Alpine
Greenberg, Byron Stanley *newspaper and business executive, consultant*

Alta Loma
Rollins, Lanier *recording company executive*

Anaheim
Wilson, Johnny Lee *editor-in-chief*

Antioch
Chu, Valentin Yuan-ling *author*

Arcata
Dominitz, Sidney *editor, journalist*

Atherton
Alexander, Marie Bailey *consulting editor, family economist*

Auburn
Renner, Jeannette Irene (Jay Renner) *publishing executive*

Avila Beach
Kamm, Herbert *journalist*

Belmont
Lake, David S. *publisher, lawyer*

Belvedere Tiburon
Kramer, Lawrence Stephen *journalist*
Moffitt, Phillip William *magazine editor*

Berkeley
Bagdikian, Ben Haig *journalist, emeritus university educator*
Brodsky, Bart Lou *publisher*
Brooke, Tal (Robert Taliaferro) *company executive, author*
Craib, Ralph Grant *reporter*
Drechsel, Edwin Jared *retired magazine editor*
Elkus, Jonathan Britton *music publisher, music educator*
Lesser, Wendy *literary magazine editor, writer, consultant*
McQuillin, Cynthia Ann *music publishing company executive*
O'Brien, Mark David *poet, journalist*
Salski, Andrzej M. *journalist, editor*
Warwick, Mal *publisher, consultant, author*
Weber, David Ollier *journalist*

Beverly Hills
Bland, Janeese Myra *editor*
Corwin, Stanley Joel *book publisher*
Farhat, Carol S. *motion picture company executive*
Hinton, Leslie Frank *media executive*
Jenner, Bruce *sportscaster, former Olympic athlete*
Levy, David *broadcasting executive*
Madden, John *television sports commentator, former professional football coach*
Summerall, Pat (George Allan Summerall) *sportscaster*
Thompson, Tina Lewis Chryar *publisher*

Bishop
Ferrey-Laughon, Barbara Eloyce *journalist, newspaper editor*

Burbank
Brogliatti, Barbara Spencer *television and motion picture executive*
Chiolis, Mark Joseph *television executive*
Eisner, Michael Dammann *entertainment company executive*
Griffith, Robert Douglas *broadcasting company executive*
Wallach, Paul *publishing executive, author*

Calabasas
Mann, Brian Roland *editor*

Camino
Miller, Carole Ann Lyons *editor, publisher, retail advertising specialist*

Campbell
Duncan, James Richard *broadcast engineer*

Canoga Park
Bloomfield, Masse *publishing executive, writer*

Carlsbad
Brown, Jack *magazine editor*
Coleman, Kenneth William *publishing company executive*
Lynn, Fredric Michael *sportscaster, former professional baseball player*

Carmel
Bohannon-Kaplan, Margaret Anne *publisher, lawyer*
Koeppel, Gary Merle *publisher, art gallery owner*

Carson
Davidson, Mark *writer, educator*

Chula Vista
Blankfort, Lowell Arnold *newspaper publisher*
Pasqua, Thomas Mario, Jr. *journalism educator*

Claremont
Ringen, Randy Mark *editor, writer*

Columbia
Martin, Donald Walter *author, publisher*

Concord
Anderberg, Roy Anthony *journalist*

Cool
Toren, Robert *photojournalist*

Costa Mesa
Billiter, William Overton, Jr. *journalist*
Jensen, Gerald Randolph *editor, graphics designer*

Cotati
Carroll, Bonnie *publisher, editor*

Culver City
Fetter, Trevor *film executive*
Lyou, Keith Weeks (Kay Lyou) *editor*

Cupertino
Lim, Kenneth Ting *interactive multimedia analyst*

Dana Point
Hawk, Steve J. *magazine editor*

Davis
Anderson, Lorraine Pearl *editor, writer*
Manea-Manoliu, Ion S. *journalist, editor*

Del Mar
Faludi, Susan C. *journalist, scholarly writer*
Kaye, Peter Frederic *newspaper editor*

El Cajon
Saulpaugh, Christopher Francis *publishing executive*

El Centro
Lokey, Frank Marion, Jr. *broadcast executive, consultant*

El Cerrito
Macauley, Charles Cameron *media appraiser, consultant*

El Dorado
Traylor, William Robert *publisher*

Emeryville
Rybarski, Michael Anton *publishing company executive*
Schwartz, David Marcus *magazine editor-in-chief*

Encinitas
Newman, Katharine Dealy *author, consultant*

Eureka
Shepard, William Wayne *editor*

Fair Oaks
Davidson, Marie Diane *publisher*

Fall River Mills
Caldwell, Walter Edward *editor, small business owner*

Forestville
Benyo, Richard Stephen *magazine editor, writer*

Fountain Valley
Kumagai, Stacey *broadcast executive*

Frazier Park
Nelson, Harry *journalist, medical writer*

Fremont
Rockstroh, Dennis John *journalist*

Fresno
Bochin, Hal William *speech communication educator*
Hart, Russ Allen *telecommunications educator*
Setencich, Eli John *columnist*
VeZolles, Janet Lee *newspaper publisher*
Wilson, Rhea *newspaper editor*

Fullerton
Burrowes, Carl Patrick *communications educator*
Long, Emmett Thaddeus *communication educator*

Glendale
McKellar, James Louis *publisher*

Svetlik, John Anthony *entertainment company executive*

Half Moon Bay
Bonham, George Wolfgang *magazine editor, writer, foundation executive*

Happy Camp
Brown, Barbara Black *publishing company executive*

Hayfork
Oviatt, Katy Valentine *editor, publisher*

Hayward
Hammerback, John Clark *communications educator*
Roberts, Timothy Wynell *journalist*

Hollywood
Israel, David *journalist, screenwriter, producer*
Purcell, Patrick B. *motion picture company executive*
Sarley, John G. *broadcast executive, writer*

Huntington Beach
Frye, Judith Eleen Minor *editor*
McReynolds, Rochelle Sharon *broadcast executive*

Indio
Ellis, Lee *publisher, editor*
Wilson, Stan Le Roy *mass communications educator*

Irvine
Lesonsky, Rieva *editor-in-chief*
Madera, Marie Louise *magazine publishing executive*
Segal, D. Robert *publishing and broadcast company executive*

La Canada
Paniccia, Patricia Lynn *television news reporter, lawyer*

La Crescenta
Blackburn, Daniel M. *correspondent*

La Habra
Oliver, Joyce Anne *journalist, editorial consultant, columnist*

La Jolla
Copley, Helen Kinney *newspaper publisher*
Hornaday, Aline Grandier *publisher, independent scholar*
Jones, Charlie *television sports announcer*
McGilvery, Laurence *book publisher, dealer*

La Mesa
Raftery, Miriam Genser *writer, columnist*

Laguna Beach
Fisher, Marla Jo *newspaper reporter*

Lakewood
Fenwick, James H(enry) *editor*

Linden
Smith, Donald Richard *editor, publisher*

Lodi
Wyrick, Daniel John *science/health textbook editor, science specialist*

Loma Linda
Bell, Denise Louise *newspaper reporter, photographer, librarian*

Long Beach
Christensen, Christina Marie *newspaper columnist*
Frohnen, Richard Gene *journalism educator*
Ridder, Daniel Hickey *newspaper publisher*
Ruszkiewicz, Carolyn Mae *newspaper editor*

Los Altos
Miller, Ronald Grant *journalist*

Los Angeles
Askin, Richard Henry, Jr. *entertainment company executive*
Barrie, Lita *editor, publisher, art critic, cultural theorist*
Bart, Peter Benton *newspaper editor, film producer, novelist*
Bell, Alan *publishing company executive*
Beniger, James Ralph *communications educator, writer*
Berger, Dan Lee *newspaper wine columnist*
Berman, Arthur Malcolm *newspaper editor*
Boyarsky, Benjamin William *journalist*
Brogan, Maurice Kenneth *visual media consultant, photographer*
Brown, J'Amy Maroney *journalist, media relations consultant*
Brown, LaRita Early Dawn Ma-Ka-Lani *publisher*
Camron, Roxanne *editor*
Cannon, Louis Simeon *journalist, author*
Cash, William *correspondent, columnist*
Cate, Benjamin Wilson Upton *journalist*
Coffey, C. Shelby, III *newspaper editor*
Comeau, Jack Francis *lighting and photography director*
Crippens, David Lee *broadcast executive*
Day, Anthony *newspaper correspondent*
Del Olmo, Frank *newspaper editor*
Delugach, Albert Lawrence *journalist*
de Passe, Suzanne *record company executive*
Diamond, Aviva *communications consultant*
Dolan, Mary Anne *journalist, columnist*
Dorrell, Torrie Ann *recording industry executive*
Dreyfuss, John Alan *journalist*
Dwyre, William Patrick *journalist, public speaker*
Erburu, Robert F. *media and information company executive*
Farmer, James David *journalist*
Flanigan, James J(oseph) *journalist*
Foster, Mary Christine *motion picture and television executive*
Friedman, Arthur Meeker *magazine editor, professional motorcycle racer*
Fromson, Murray *communications educator, journalist*
Garry, William James *magazine editor*
Garza, Oscar *newspaper editor*
Grad, Laurie Burrows *food editor*
Green, Marc Edward *editor*
Groves, Martha *newspaper writer*
Hessler, Curtis Alan *newspaper publishing company executive*
Hines, William Everett *publisher, producer, cinematographer, writer*
Hogarth, Burne *cartoonist, illustrator*
Jacobson, Steve Evan *production company executive*
James, Garry *executive editor*
Jampol, Jeffrey *music industry executive*
Jarmon, Lawrence *developmental communications educator*
Kaye, Jeffrey Kenneth *television reporter*
Kelly, Gabrielle Mary *film production executive*
Kephart, Floyd W. *entertainment company executive*
Knittle, William Joseph, Jr. *media executive, psychologist, religious leader, management and marketing consultant*
Ladd, Alan Walbridge, Jr. *motion picture company executive*
Laird, Jere Don *news reporter*
Laventhol, David Abram *newspaper editor*
Lipstone, Howard Harold *television executive*
Loehwing, Rudi Charles, Jr. *publicist, radio broadcasting executive*
Lond, Harley Weldon *editor, publisher*
Macdonald, Katharine March *journalist, public relations executive*
Mack, Donald *publisher*
Margulies, Lee *newspaper editor*
Marsh, Dave Rodney *writer, publisher, editor*
Martinez, Al *journalist, screenwriter*
Maslin, Harry *recording industry executive, producer*
Maxwell, Donald Stanley *publishing executive*
Michaud, Michael Gregg *publishing executive, writer*
Miller, Norman Charles, Jr. *newspaper editor*
Murphy, Philip Edward *broadcast executive*
Murray, James Patrick *newspaper columnist*
Parks, Michael Christopher *journalist*
Pearlman, Nancy Sue *environmental broadcaster*
Perenchio, Andrew Jerrold *film and television executive*
Phillips, Geneva Ficker *editor*
Podber, Jake *broadcasting educator*
Rense, Paige *editor, publishing company executive*
Romo, Cheryl Annette *writer, editor*
Saltzman, Joseph *journalist, producer, educator*
Sanello, Frank Anthony *journalist, columnist*
Sansweet, Stephen Jay *journalist, author*
Schneider, Wolf *magazine editor, writer*
Scott, Kelly *newspaper editor*
Scully, Vincent Edward *sports broadcaster*
Shaw, David Lyle *journalist, author*
Shuster, Alvin *journalist, newspaper editor*
Smith, Jack Clifford *journalist, author*
Sommers, Bill *radio broadcast executive*
Stanton, Lewis Harris *publishing company executive*
Sturken, Marita Louise *communications educator, writer, critic*
Trembly, Cristy *television executive*
Trousdale, Stephen Richard *newspaper editor*
Vanzi, Max Bruno *editor*
Ward, Leslie Allyson *journalist, editor*
West, Stephen McCallum *editor*
Wilson, Charles Zachary, Jr. *newspaper publisher*
Wolinsky, Leo C. *newspaper editor*
Zacchino, Narda *newspaper editor*
Zwick, Barry Stanley *newspaper editor, speechwriter*

Los Gatos
Lee, Edmund *photojournalist*

Malibu
Blakemore, Paul Henry, Jr. *retired publishing executive*
Hudson, Christopher John *publisher*
MacLeod, Robert Fredric *editor, publisher*

Marina
Grenfell, Gloria Ross *freelance journalist*

Marina Del Rey
Seligson, Marcia Sue *journalist*

Menlo Park
Browne, Millard Child *former newspaper editor*
Marken, William Riley *magazine editor*
Wolaner, Robin Peggy *magazine publisher*

Merced
Boese, Sandra Jean *publishing executive*

Mill Valley
Brady, Lee Burnett *columnist, playwright*
Cushing, Richard Gollé *journalist*
Daigon, Ruth *editor, poet*
Leslie, Jacques Robert, Jr. *journalist*
Mandelstein, Paul Stanley *book publishing executive*
McNamara, Kay Copeland *publishing executive*
McNamara, Stephen *newspaper executive*

Modesto
LaMont, Sanders Hickey *journalist*

Montara
Tyler-Parker, Sydney Billig *publishing executive, author, consultant*

Montclair
Williams, Michael James *editor*

Monterey
Dedini, Eldon Lawrence *cartoonist*

Monterey Park
Hendricks, Glenn Richard *publishing executive*
Stapleton, Jean *journalism educator*

Mountain View
Richards, Evelyn Jean *journalist*

Newport Beach
Barber, Steven Alden *telecommunications analyst*
Bryant, Thos Lee *magazine editor*
Dean, Paul John *magazine editor*
Douglas, Stephen *publishing company executive*
Homan, Rich *magazine editor*
Michaels, Patrick Francis *broadcasting company executive*
Snow, Alan Albert *publisher*

Nicasio
Hopkin, John Barton *publisher, editor*

North Hollywood
Boyle, Barbara Dorman *motion picture company executive*
Cramer, Douglas Schoolfield *broadcasting executive*
Hulse, Jerry *journalist*
Koran, Dennis Howard *publisher*
Loper, James Leaders *broadcasting executive*

Oakland
Dailey, Garrett Clark *publisher, lawyer*
Kees, Beverly *newspaper editor*
Knight, Jeffrey William *publishing and marketing executive*
Lavoie, Steven Paul *columnist, library director*
Poole, Monte LaRue *sports columnist, consultant*
Powell, Lane Alan *editor*
Torrez, Naomi Elizabeth *copyright review editor, librarian*
Wong, William *newspaper editor, columnist*
Wood, Larry (Mary Laird) *journalist, author, university educator, public relations executive, environmental consultant*

Oceanside
Howard, Robert Staples *newspaper publisher*

Orange
Alonzo, R. Gregory *professional speaker*
Fletcher, James Allen *video company executive*
Galambos, Suzanne Julia *editor, writer, institute administrator*

Oxnard
Morgan, Gary B. *journalism educator*

Pacific Grove
Verduin, Claire Leone *publishing company executive*

Pacific Palisades
Hadges, Thomas Richard *media consultant*

Palm Springs
Behrmann, Joan Gail *newspaper editor*
Behrmann, Joan Metzner *newspaper editor*
Browning, Norma Lee (Mrs. Russell Joyner Ogg) *journalist*
Pricer, Jamie Lee *magazine editor*

Palmdale
Grooms, Larry Willis *newspaper editor*

Palo Alto
Andreopoulos, Spyros George *writer*
Hamilton, David Mike *publishing company executive*
McNeil, John Stuart *publisher*
Much, Kathleen *editor*
Rusk, Lauren *editor*

Panorama City
Hugen, Michael Frank *journalist, publisher*

Pasadena
Bergholz, Richard Cady *political writer*
Diehl, Digby Robert *journalist*
Drutchas, Gerrick Gilbert *publishing executive*
Faulkner, Dexter Harold *magazine publishing executive, editor*
Hopkins, Philip Joseph *journalist, editor*
Ozminkowski, Mariusz *journalist, educator*
Post, Jonathan Vos *publishing company executive, aerospace computer consultant*
Wood, Nathaniel Fay *editor, writer, public relations consultant*

Paso Robles
Brown, Benjamin Andrew *journalist*

Pebble Beach
Neswitz, Margye Fulgham *newspaper columnist*

Pilot Hill
Freitas, Robert Archibald, Jr. *periodical editor and publisher*

Pleasant Hill
Gonzalez, Martin Michael *television industry executive*

Pleasanton
Wevurski, Peter John *newspaper editor*

Point Reyes Station
Austen, Hallie Iglehart *author*

Redlands
Kulbin, Vello *publisher, writer*

Redondo Beach
Sakurai, Jennifer M. *editor, writer*

Redwood City
Kassabian, Anahid *media theorist*

Reedley
Kehler, Ruth *newspaper editor*

Reseda
Kinkade, Kate *publishing executive, magazine editor, insurance executive*

Richmond
Doyle, William Thomas *retired newspaper editor*

Riverside
Garrett, John Cecil *newspaper editor*
Hays, Howard H. (Tim Hays) *editor, publisher*
Hays, Jonathan Fincher *newspaper executive*
Holley, Jack K. *journalist*
Locke, Francis Philbrick *retired editorial writer*
Maas, Sally Ann *newspaper editor, journalist*
McQuern, Marcia Alice *newspaper publishing executive*
Parsley, Martie *communications educator*
Scott, Loretta Bernadette *newspaper editor*

Sacramento
Baltake, Joe *film critic*
Biagi, Shirley Anne *journalism educator*
Blum, Deborah *reporter*
Bottel, Helen Alfea *columnist, writer*
Dahlberg, Thomas Robert *columnist, screenwriter, author, attorney*
Dexter, Peter Whittemore *columnist, writer*
Endicott, William F. *journalist*
Giacomo, Gary Christopher *magazine editor, journalist*
Jones, Mark Alan *broadcast technician*
Knudson, Thomas Jeffery *journalist*
Lawler, Rick M. *publishing executive*
Lundstrom, Marjie *newspaper editor*
McClatchy, James B. *editor, newspaper publisher*
McGrath, Daniel Bernard *newspaper editor*
Schrag, Peter *editor, writer*
Shaw, Eleanor Jane *newspaper editor*
Slater, Manning *broadcasting consultant*
Walsh, Denny Jay *reporter*
Walters, Daniel Raymond *political columnist*
Williams, Arthur Cozad *broadcasting executive*

San Anselmo
Alpine, Andrew Elliot *publisher*

San Bernardino
Burgess, Mary Alice (Mary Alice Wickizer) *publisher*
Fairley Raney, Rebecca *journalist*
Garson, Arnold Hugh *newspaper editor*
Hamm, Catharine Margaret *journalist*
Phillips, Anna *publisher, editor-in-chief newspaper*

San Carlos
Barnard, William Calvert *retired news service executive*

San Clemente
Singer, Kurt Deutsch *news commentator, author, publisher*
Stallknecht-Roberts, Clois Freda *publisher, publicist*

San Diego
Abrams, Morris Alec *book company executive*
Bennett, Ronald Thomas *photojournalist*
Brooks, Jeanne Freeman *journalist*
Cushman, Thomas Henry *sports editor, columnist*
Derrough, Neil E. *television executive*
Fine, Nikki Paige *acquisitions editor*
Freedman, Jonathan Borwick *journalist, author, lecturer*
Hall, TennieBee M. *editor*
Hope, Douglas Olerich *newspaper editor*
Kaufman, Julian Mortimer *broadcasting company executive, consultant*
Kopp, Harriet Green *communication specialist*
Krulak, Victor Harold *newspaper executive*
Leach, Deanna Darlene *publisher*
Lee, Marianna *editor*
Mc Kinnon, Clinton D. *editor, former congressman*
Mickelson, Sig *broadcasting executive, educator*
Owen, Charles Theodore *journalist, publisher*
Pfeiffer, John William *publisher, management consultant*
Phillips, Frank Sigmund *business executive*
Ristine, Jeffrey Alan *reporter*
Salamone, Gary P. (Pike Salamone) *newspaper editor-in-chief, cartoonist*
Schneider, Joseph Francis *journalism educator, editor*
Simms, Maria Kay *publishing and computer services executive*
Slater, Leonard *writer, editor*
Steen, Paul Joseph *retired broadcasting executive*
Vandiver, Linton Mitchell, II *publisher*
Warren, Gerald Lee *newspaper editor*
Winner, Karin *newspaper editor*
Witty, Robert Milton *editor*

San Francisco
Allen, Sally Rothfus *editor*
Batlin, Robert Alfred *editor*
Bauer, Michael *newspaper editor*
Benet, Thomas Carr *journalist*
Blakey, Scott Chaloner *journalist, writer*
Caen, Herb *newspaper columnist, author*
Carman, John Elwin *journalist*
Carroll, Jon *newspaper columnist*
Cavagnaro, Edmund Walter *radio station executive*
Chapin, Dwight Allan *columnist, writer*
Close, Sandy *journalist*
Curley, John Peter *sports editor*
Donnally, Patricia Broderick *newspaper fashion editor*
Duscha, Julius Carl *journalist*
Garchik, Leah Lieberman *journalist*
George, Donald Warner *newspaper editor, writer, lecturer*
German, William *newspaper editor*
Graham, Robert Arlington *newspaper entertainment editor*
Hill, Greg *newspaper bureau chief*
Hoppe, Arthur Watterson *columnist*
Hudson, Heather Elizabeth *telecommunications educator, consultant, lawyer*
Jenkins, Bruce *sportswriter*
Johns, Roy (Bud Johns) *publisher, author*
Kayfetz, Victor Joel *writer, editor, translator*
Kinney, Jay MacNeal *editor, author, illustrator*
Klein, Jeremy Stephen *editor*
Klein, Marc S. *newspaper editor and publisher*
Knee, Richard Alan *journalist*
Lara, Adair *columnist, writer*
Lefevre, Greg *bureau chief*
Lufkin, Liz *newspaper editor*
MacDonald, Kenneth Richard *writer*
Morgan, Michael Brewster *publishing company executive*
Nachman, Gerald Weil *columnist, critic, author*
Nichols, Robert E(dmund) *editor, writer, journalist*
O'Flaherty, Terrence *journalist*
Ostler, Scott *newspaper sports columnist*
Perlman, David *science editor, journalist*
Rice, Jonathan C. *educational television executive*
Rivers, Christopher Beaumont, III *newspaper publisher, sales executive*
Roberts, Gerald Jeffrey *newspaper editor, journalist*
Roberts, Jerry *newspaper editor*
Rubenstein, Steven Paul *newspaper columnist*
Rusher, William Allen *writer, commentator*
Ryan, Joan *sportswriter*
Saunders, Debra J. *columnist*
Schwarz, Glenn Vernon *editor*
Sinton, Peter *newspaper editor, journalist*
Spander, Art *sportswriter*

Susskind, Teresa Gabriel *publisher*
Tulsky, Fredric Neal *journalist*
Vistica, Jerrold Francis *publishing executive*
Wilner, Paul Andrew *journalist*
Witkin, Susan Beth *broadcast journalist, reporter*
Wright, Rosalie Muller *newspaper and magazine editor*
Yamamoto, Michael Toru *journalist*

San Jose
Carey, Peter Kevin *reporter*
Ceppos, Jerome Merle *newspaper editor*
Chan, Loren Briggs *technical writing specialist*
Cohen, David Edward *publisher*
Edmonds, Charles Henry *publisher*
Elder, Robert Laurie *newspaper editor*
Frymer, Murry *columnist, theater critic, critic-at-large*
Ingle, Robert D. *newspaper editor, newspaper executive*
Langberg, Mike *newspaper reporter, columnist*
Pulcrano, Dan Michael *newspaper executive*
Ritzheimer, Robert Alan *educational publishing executive*
Sumrall, Harry *journalist*
Trounstine, Philip J. *editor, journalist*

San Luis Obispo
Carr, Peter Emile *publisher*
Shea, B(arbara) Christine *communications educator, consultant*
Wilkin, Eugene Welch *broadcasting executive*

San Mateo
Carter, Michelle Adair *editor*
Golding, George Earl *journalist*
Morgan, Miriam Rae *journalist*
Waring, Rebecca Lynn *magazine editor, freelance writer*

San Pedro
Bowling, Lance Christopher *record producer, publisher*

Santa Ana
Cheverton, Richard E. *newspaper editor*
Katz, Tonnie *newspaper editor*
Rosenberg, Donald Lee *magazine publisher*
Stern, Sherry Ann *journalist*

Santa Barbara
Bull, Nancy Ann *publishing executive*
Delmerico, George Anthony *publications executive*
Gibney, Frank Bray *publisher, editor, writer, foundation executive*
Poynter, Daniel Frank *publisher*
Stacey, Pamela *editor, writer*
Tapper, Joan Judith *magazine editor*
Weeks, Dorothy Mae *publishing executive*
Wiemann, John Moritz *communications educator, consultant*
Witherell, Elizabeth Hall *scholarly editor*
Wright, Helene Segal *editor*
Zant, John Donald *journalist*

Santa Clara
Charles, Mary Louise *newspaper columnist, photographer, editor*
Fedore, Ronald J. *telecommunications company executive*

Santa Clarita
Adams, Jack *film company executive, screenwriter, producer, educator*
Osborn, Susan Titus *editor*

Santa Fe Springs
Madsen, William Marshall *media specialist*

Santa Monica
Jacobson, Sidney *editor*
Palmatier, Malcolm Arthur *editor, consultant*
Renetzky, Alvin *publisher*
Roggero, Miguel Leonardo (Mike Roggero) *motion picture company executive, consultant*
van Allen, Philip Andrew *multimedia production company executive, educator*

Santa Rosa
Pipal, George Henry *journalist*
Swofford, Robert Lee *newspaper editor, journalist*

Santee
Hosler, Laddie *editor*

Sebastopol
Hutchison, John Nelson *correspondent*

Sherman Oaks
Davidson, Bill (William John Davidson) *entertainment journalist, author*

Sierra Madre
Dewey, Donald William *magazine publisher, editor, writer*
Steele, Susan *art editor*

Simi Valley
Killion, Jack Charles *newspaper columnist*

Solana Beach
Doyle, Richard James *photojournalist, photo software developer*
Parker, John Brian *broadcast executive*
Whiting, James Vincent *cartoonist*

Somis
Gius, Julius *retired newspaper editor*

Sonoma
Beckmann, Jon Michael *publisher*
Lynch, Robert Montgomery *newspaper publisher*

Soquel
Thacker, Netha Lynn *editor*

South San Francisco
Alvarez, Robert Smyth *editor, publisher*

Stanford
Chaffee, Steven Henry *communications educator*
Maharidge, Dale Dimitro *journalist, educator*
Salisbury, David Francis *newspaper, television science writer*

Stockton
Kraus, Joe *editor and publisher, writer*

Studio City
Gordon, Robert William *editor*

Sunnyvale
Noon, John Patrick *editor, publisher*

Tarzana
Shaw, Carole *editor, publisher*
Shaw-Cohen, Lori Eve *magazine editor*

Tehachapi
Mitchell, Betty Jo *publisher, writer*

Thousand Oaks
Van Mols, Brian *publishing executive*

Torrance
Adelsman, (Harriette) Jean *newspaper editor*
Barnett, Jeanie Maureen *writer, editor*
Kass, Jeffrey Robert *journalist*
Roberts, Jerry Keith (Gerald Keith Roberts) *film critic, author*

Union City
Funston, Gary Stephen *publishing and advertising executive*

Universal City
Horowitz, Zachary I. *entertainment company executive*

Ventura
Greig, William Taber, Jr. *publishing company executive*
Shedenhelm, William Rex Charles *writer*

Victorville
Barsky, Martin *editor, publisher*

Walnut Creek
Haswell, T. Clayton *newspaper editor*
Lesher, Margaret Lisco *newspaper publisher, songwriter*
Parkhurst, Gary Stephen *publishing company executive*

West Hollywood
Watanabe, Hiroshi *film production company executive*
Wendruck, Louis *publisher, television personality, consultant*

Westminster
Rillera, Marri J. *publisher, writer*

Winnetka
Robbins, Karen Diane *editor*

Woodland Hills
DeWitt, Barbara Jane *journalist*
Fisher, Gerald Saul *publisher, financial consultant, lawyer*
Gray, Thomas Stephen *newspaper editor*
Neill, William Alexander *magazine editor*
Rapoport, Ronald Jon *journalist*
Timmermann, Thomas Joseph *journalist*

Yreka
Smith, Vin *sports editor, business owner, novelist*

COLORADO

Arvada
Ashby, Edward Howard *publisher*

Aspen
Hayes, Mary Eshbaugh *newspaper editor*
Jenkins, Loren B. *publisher, writer*
Klusmire, Jon Dalton *editor, writer*

Aurora
Vaughan, Suzanne Lowe *professional speaker, consultant*

Boulder
Birkenkamp, Dean Frederick *editor, publishing executive*
Brink, Glen Arthur *publisher, wholesaler*
Davis, Donald Alan *author, news correspondent, lecturer*
Everett, Stephen Edward *advertising and communications educator, researcher*
Hauser, Gerard Alan *communication educator*
Quint, Bert *journalist*

Broomfield
Marrs, Roy Alonzo *magazine editor, educator*

Colorado Springs
Mansfield, Roger Leo *astronomy and space publisher*

Denver
Ballentine, Lee Kenney *publishing company executive*
Bates, James Robert *newspaper editor*
Boczkiewicz, Robert Eugene *freelance journalist*
Brom, Libor *journalist, educator*
Carlson, Robert Ernest *freelance writer, architect, lecturer*
Clark, Nancy Jo *publisher*
Cubbison, Christopher Allen *editor*
Dallas, Sandra *correspondent, writer*
Dance, Francis Esburn Xavier *communication educator*
Dobbs, Gregory Allan *journalist*
Doyle, Alfreda Carrol *publisher, writer*
Dubroff, Henry Allen *journalist*
Engdahl, Todd Philip *newspaper editor*
Giffin, Glenn Orlando, II *music critic, writer, newspaper editor*
Green, Charles Walter *newspaper editor*
Hirschfeld, A. Barry *publishing executive*
Kerver, Thomas Joseph *editor, consultant*
May, Clifford Daniel *newspaper editor, journalist*
McGowan, Joseph Anthony, Jr. *news executive*
Otto, Jean Hammond *journalist*
Person, Tom (Stanley Thomas Person) *publisher, editor*
Price, Kathleen McCormick *book editor, writer*
Spencer, Frederick Gilman *newspaper editor in chief*
Stanton, Grace Patricia *communications educator, consultant*
Willbanks, Roger Paul *publishing and book distributing company executive*

Durango
Ballantine, Morley Cowles (Mrs. Arthur Atwood Ballantine) *newspaper editor*
Hansen, Leonard Joseph *author, journalist, marketing consultant*

Estes Park
Asbury, Timothy Edward *editor*

Fort Collins
Holzberlein, Kurt W. *cablevision news director*
MacLauchlin, Robert Kerwin *communications artist, educator*
Sons, Raymond William *journalist*

Golden
Baron, Charlotte Foehner *publishing executive*
Baron, Robert Charles *publishing executive*
Jamieson Nichols, Jill *journalist*

Grand Junction
Hammer, Jan Harold *television station manager*
Reed, Kristen King *broadcast sales manager*

Greeley
Woodward, William Walter *news anchor, journalism educator*

Littleton
Keogh, Heidi Helen Dake *publishing executive*
Ostendorf, Virginia Angelita *publishing executive, communications executive*
Rothman, Paul Alan *publisher*
Syring, James John *telecommunications company editor*

Longmont
Lehman, Ruth Gillespie *newspaper executive*

Manitou Springs
James, Georg LeRoy *broadcasting executive*

Masonville
Hammond, Alan David *public speaker*

Mc Coy
Hastings, Merrill George, Jr. *publisher, marketing consultant*

Montrose
Day, Richard Elledge *newspaper executive*
Gillette, Ethel Morrow *columnist*

Paonia
Marston, Edwin H. *newspaper publisher*

Pueblo
Noblit, Betty Jean *publishing technician*
Rawlings, Robert Hoag *newspaper publisher*
Vigil, Karen LaVerne *reporter*

Salida
Shovald, Arlene Elizabeth *newspaper reporter*

Silverton
Denious, Jon Parks *publishing executive*
Denious, Sharon Marie *publisher*

Steamboat Springs
Olsen, Deborah Jean *journalist, writer*

Sterling
Muldoon, William Henry, III *newspaper publisher*

Winter Park
Johnson, William Potter *newspaper publisher*

CONNECTICUT

Middletown
Mac Lam, Helen *editor, periodical*

DISTRICT OF COLUMBIA

Washington
Herman, Andrea Maxine *newspaper editor*

HAWAII

Hilo
Witty, James H. *journalist, consultant*

Honolulu
Chaplin, George *newspaper editor*
Flanagan, John Michael *editor, publisher*
Jellinek, Roger *editor*
Kamemoto, Garett Hiroshi *reporter*
Keir, Gerald Janes *newspaper editor*
Kim, Joung-Im *communication educator, consultant*
Novick, Stuart Allan *publishing executive*
Parma, Florence Virginia *magazine editor*
Roth, Michael James *magazine publisher*
Simonds, John Edward *newspaper editor*
Smith, Christopher Case *newspaper editor*
Smyser, Adam Albert *newspaper editor*
Sparks, Robert William *publishing executive*
Twigg-Smith, Thurston *newspaper publisher*
Wiley, Bonnie Jean *journalism educator*

Kailua
Bone, Robert William *writer, photojournalist*

Kaneohe
Berry, Ken *publishing company executive*

Kihei
Isbell, Alan Gregory *editor, writer, publisher*

Lahaina
Arnold, Joan Dean *publisher*

Wailuku
Martin, Doris Ellen *publisher, management consultant*

IDAHO

Boise
Lemmon, Philip Douglas *publishing company executive*

Caldwell
Gipson, Gordon *publishing company executive*

Idaho Falls
Harris, Darryl Wayne *publishing executive*

Moscow
Anderson, Clifton Einar *editor, writer*
Haarsager, Sandra Lynn *author, communications educator*

Pocatello
Morrison, Joy South *journalist*

ILLINOIS

Champaign
Meyer, August Christopher, Jr. *broadcasting company executive, lawyer*

Deerfield
Thorne, Oakleigh Blakeman *publishing company executive*

Normal
Mc Knight, William Warren, Jr. *publisher*

INDIANA

Indianapolis
Pulliam, Eugene Smith *newspaper publisher*

MISSOURI

Saint Louis
Godsey, C. Wayne *broadcasting executive*

MONTANA

Bigfork
Blumberg, Nathan(iel) Bernard *journalist, educator, writer and publisher*

Billings
Abendroth, Kent Allen *broadcast engineer, electronic engineer*
Cox, Meridith Brittan *publishing executive, risk manager, consultant*
Rye, David Blake *television news anchor*
Svee, Gary Duane *newspaper editor, author, journalist*

Bozeman
Burns, Paul Andrew *sports editor*
O'Donnell, Victoria J. *communication educator*

Dillon
Ross, Deborah Lynn (Debbie Ross) *reporter, photographer*

Great Falls
Newhouse, Eric *newspaper editor*

Havre
Gallus, Charles Joseph *journalist*

Helena
Korson, Gerald Michael *newspaper editor*
Malcolm, Andrew Hogarth *journalist, writer*

Joliet
Jarecke, Kenneth John *photojournalist*

Kalispell
James, Marion Ray *magazine founder, editor*
Ruder, Melvin Harvey *retired newspaper editor*

Livingston
Sullivan, John Charles *journalist, editor, publisher*

Polson
Randle, Kathe McGehee *publisher, writer*

NEVADA

Carson City
Christensen, Jon Allan *journalist*

Henderson
Furimsky, Stephen, Jr. *freelance writer*

Incline Village
McCartney, Patrick Kevin *newspaper reporter*
Scheller, Erin Linn *publishing company executive*

Las Vegas
Baker, Chuck *journalist, author*
Carleton, Mary Ruth *journalist, educator, consultant*
Castaldi Toddre, Gwen *journalist*
Dennis, Sonya Reneé *television station official*
Engstrom, Erika Julie *communications educator*
Hill, Michael John *newspaper editor*
Mische, Kurt Andrew *broadcast executive*
Rossin, Herbert Yale *television broadcaster*

Reno
Lerude, Warren Leslie *journalism educator*
Sheeran, Angela Maureen *information specialist*

NEW MEXICO

Alamogordo
McQuiddy, Marian Elizabeth *publisher, editor*

Albuquerque
Burton, Johanna King *journalist*
Danziger, Jerry *broadcasting executive*
Davis, Anthony J. *journalist*
Goldston, Barbara M. Harral *editor*
Guthrie, Patricia Sue *newspaper reporter, free-lance writer*
Hadas, Elizabeth Chamberlayne *publisher*
Johnson, Robert Hersel *journalist*
Kinlen, James Gilbert *publishing executive*
Looney, Ralph Edwin *newspaper editor, author, photographer*
Mc Million, John Macon *retired newspaper publisher*
Wilde, David *publisher, writer*

Artesia
Hunter, Lynn (Koenig) *reporter, historian*

Glenwood
Tackman, Arthur Lester *newspaper publisher, management consultant*

Las Cruces
Dickinson, James Gordon *editor*
Matson, Eva Jane *publisher*

Los Alamos
Mendius, Patricia Dodd Winter *editor, educator, writer*

Mesilla
Rossi, Guy Anthony *publishing executive*

Santa Fe
Atkinson, John Christopher *magazine editor, critic, writer*
Bowman, Jon Robert *editor, film critic*
Calloway, Larry *columnist*
Forsdale, (Chalmers) Louis *education and communication educator*
Mc Kinney, Robert Moody *newspaper editor and publisher*
Moyes, Terence E. *publishing executive*
Ott, Robert William *publishing executive*
Slaughter, Paul Damien *photojournalist*
Stieber, Tamar *writer*

Taos
Bacon, Wallace Alger *speech communications educator, author*
Williams, Jess *editor*

NEW YORK

Buffalo
Peradotto, Nicole Anne *journalist*

Farmingdale
Steckler, Larry *publisher, editor*

New York
Perera, Victor Haim *journalism educator, writer*

NORTH CAROLINA

Asheville
Wilson, Herschel Manuel (Pete Wilson) *retired journalism educator*

OHIO

Athens
Friedenberg, Walter Drew *journalist*

OREGON

Albany
Wood, Kenneth Arthur *retired newspaper editor, writer*

Ashland
Major, Marguerite Louise *retired magazine editor*

Astoria
Harlan, David *reporter*

Baker City
Brinton, Byron Charles *publishing executive, editor*

Beaverton
Challem, Jack Joseph *editor, health, advertising and public relations writer*

Bend
Bagwell, Steven Kent *newspaper editor*
Hill, Geoffrey William *publisher*

Coquille
Taylor, George Frederick *newspaper publisher, editor*

Corvallis
Donnelly, Margarita Patricia *editor*
Smullin, Donald Evan *communications company executive*
Zwahlen, Fred Casper, Jr. *journalism educator*

Eugene
Baker, Alton Fletcher, III *newspaper editor, publishing executive*
Baker, Bridget Downey *newspaper executive*
Baker, Edwin Moody *retired newspaper publisher*
Franklin, Jon Daniel *journalist, writer, educator*
Hager, Thomas Arthur *editor, writer*
Ismach, Arnold Harvey *journalism educator*
Lee, Michael Eric *magazine editor*
Lemert, James Bolton *journalist, educator*
McGlone, David Anthony Joseph *publishing executive*
Robinson, Donald Wallace *journalist*
Sherriffs, Ronald Everett *communications and film educator*
Sommer, Tripp *radio journalist*
Toké, Arun Narayan *editor, educator, electrical engineer*
Tykeson, Donald Erwin *broadcasting executive*

Gleneden Beach
Marks, Arnold *journalist*

Gold Beach
Van Leer, Robert Roy *editor, publisher*

Lake Oswego
Luther, Luana Mae *editor*

Madras
Matheny, Susan Kay *news editor*

Medford
Taylor, Gregory Hobbs *publisher*
Twitchell, Cleveland Edwards *journalist, writer*

Newport
O'Donnell, Leslie Ann *newspaper editor*

North Bend
Kocher, Charles Rodney *journalist*

Ontario
Croner, John Alton *journalist*

Pacific City
Anderson, Carl E. *newspaper reporter, editor, writer*

Pendleton
Rupp, Virgil William *journalist, editor*

Portland
Abel, Richard Eugene *book publishing consultant*
Arnst, Albert *editor, forester*
Bhatia, Peter K. *editor, journalist*
Bradley, Jean Eleanor *newspaper executive, public relations consultant*
Carlson, Paula Jean *publishing executive*
Cornyn-Selby, Alyce Patricia *publishing company executive*
Crabbs, Roger Alan *publisher, consultant, small business owner, educator*
Franks, Thomas Allen *editorial cartoonist*
Freiser, Helen *editor*
Graves, Earl William, Jr. *journalist*
Johnston, Virginia Evelyn *editor*
Lewis, Gerald Anthony *film company executive*
Lieberman, Brandon Stuart *broadcast executive*
Loewenthal, Nessa Parker *communications educator*
Mainwaring, William Lewis *publishing company executive, author*
Mapes, Jeffrey Robert *journalist*
Murphy, Francis Seward *journalist*
Rowe, David Alan *magazine publisher*
Rowe, Sandra Mims *newspaper editor*
Smith, Donald Kendall *communication educator*
Sterling, Donald Justus, Jr. *retired newspaper editor*
Woodward, Stephen Richard *newspaper reporter*

Saint Helens
Parsons-Petersen, Pamela Anne *publishing executive*

Salem
Bergel, Peter Robin *editor*
Johnson, Gloria Lee *publisher, writer*

South Beach
Gilbert, David Heggie *retired educational publisher, consultant*

Tigard
Clark, Earl Ernest *publisher*
Nokes, John Richard *retired newspaper editor, author*

Tualatin
Evans, Victoria Lynn *publishing executive*

Wallowa
Wizard, Brian *publisher, author*

Woodburn
Stollery, Rodger Gordon *publisher*

Yamhill
Kristof, Nicholas Donabet *journalist*

UTAH

Ogden
Larson, Brent T. *broadcasting executive*

Orem
Bearnson, Lisa Downs *editor-in-chief*

Provo
Hatch, Steven Graham *publishing company executive*
Hughes, (Robert) John *journalist, educator*
Tata, Giovanni *publishing executive*

Saint George
Skinner, E. Morgan, Jr. *broadcast executive*

Salt Lake City
Anderson, Arthur Salzner *publishing company executive, marketing executive*
Bauman, Joseph Matthew *journalist, author*
Berkes, Howard *radio news reporter*
Brady, Rodney Howard *broadcast company executive, former college president, former government official*
Brown, Carolyn Smith *communications educator, consultant*
Cutrubus, Christina Nina *publisher*
Fehr, J. Will *newspaper editor*
Fogo, Fred Richard *communications educator*
Hatch, George Clinton *television executive*
Kimball, K. Randall *broadcasting executive*
Lustica, Katherine Grace *publisher, artist, marketing consultant*
Lythgoe, Dennis Leo *newspaper columnist*
Mortimer, William James *newspaper publisher*
Paulsen, Vivian *magazine editor*
Robison, Barbara Ann *retired newspaper editor*
Shelledy, James Edwin, III *editor*
Smith, Donald E. *broadcast engineer, manager*
Trahant, Mark Neil *newspaper editor*
Trapp, Gerald Bernard *journalist*

WASHINGTON

Bellevue
Berkley, James Donald *clergyman*
Smith, Lester Martin *broadcasting executive*
Van Mechelen, Roderick Daniel *publisher*

Bellingham
Clark, Silvana Marie *professional speaker, author*
Doerper, John Erwin *publisher, editor*
McKay, Floyd John *journalist, educator*

Bothell
Brown, Gregory Donald *sportswriter, author*

Centralia
MacCracken, Gordon Stuart *columnist, wire editor*

Edmonds
Owen, John *retired newspaper editor*

Everett
Haines, David Wayne *commercial printing executive*

Friday Harbor
Leeming, Frank, Jr. *newspaper editor, publisher*
Schonberger, Howard *news reporter*

Kirkland
Ferraiuolo, Perucci DiAndrea *journalist*

Mercer Island
Bowne, Martha Hoke *magazine editor, consultant*
Hicks, James Kenneth *entertainment industry executive*

Monroe
Snyders, Rebecca Elaine *communications specialist*

Oak Harbor
Adams, Ann Louise *publisher*
Batdorf, Kurt Richard *editor*

Olympia
McClelland, Kamilla Kuroda *news reporter, proofreader, book agent*

Oroville
DeVon, Gary Albert *newspaper editor*

Pasco
Turnbow, Jeffery Theodore *radio news director*

Port Townsend
Buhler, Jill Lorie *editor, writer*
Rollins, Louis Arthur *editor*

Pullman
Bird, Robert Kenton *journalist, educator*
Limburg, Val Evert *media educator*

Redmond
Lamb, Ronald Alfred *computer book editor*
Mollman, John Peter *book publisher, consultant electronic publishing*

Renton
Gifford, Arthur Roy *publishing executive, aircraft executive*

Roy
Pledger, Leland James (Lee Pledger) *publisher, travel writer*

Seattle
Anderson, Ross *columnist*
Arends, Jack *journalist*
Boardman, David *newspaper editor*
Brennan, Michael Joseph *news service executive*
Buckner, Philip Franklin *newspaper publisher*
Cameron, Mindy *newspaper editor*
Cochran, Wendell *science editor*
Dietrich, William Alan *reporter*
Ellegood, Donald Russell *publishing executive*
Enlow, Clair Lou *newspaper editor, journalist*
Even, Jan *newspaper editor*
Fancher, Michael Reilly *newspaper editor, newspaper publishing executive*
Fluke, Lyla Schram (Mrs. John M. Fluke) *publisher*
Gold, Jerome *publisher, novelist*
Gormèzano, Keith Stephen *editor, arbitrator*
Gouldthorpe, Kenneth Alfred Percival *publisher, state official*
Gwinn, Mary Ann *newspaper reporter*
Henkel, Cathy *newspaper sports editor*
Hills, Regina J. *journalist*
Hobart, Willis Lee *editor*
Jacobson, Lynn *newspaper editor*
Johnson, P. Anna *publishing executive*
Johnson, Wayne Eaton *writer, editor, former drama critic*
Kelly, Carolyn Sue *newspaper executive*
Krepky, Cynthia D. *technical publishing administrator*
Lacitis, Erik *journalist*
Nalder, Eric Christopher *investigative reporter*
Nash, Cynthia Jeanne *journalist*
Nelson, Daniel Alan *editor, columnist*
Ng, Assunta *newspaper publisher*
Nickson, Christopher Howard *music journalist*
Ostrom, Carol Marie *reporter*
Parks, Michael James *publisher, editor*
Rathe, Karen Marie *editor*
Stanton, Michael John *newspaper editor*
Szeto, Hung *publisher*
Thiel, Arthur Warren *journalist*
Turner, Wallace L. *reporter*
Voorhees, John Lloyd *columnist*
Worth, Vonne Noell *newspaper publisher, editor, writer, disability rights activist*

Spokane
Feigenbaum, Clifford Scott *newsletter editor, financial consultant*
Gilbert, Reta Alice *communications educator*
Gray, Alfred Orren *journalism educator, research and communications consultant*
Herdrich, Norman Wesley *magazine editor*
Kafentzis, John Charles *journalist, educator*
Kaufman, Stephan *news director*
Meisfjord, Eric Palmer *newspaper editor*
Roberts, Larry Paul *broadcasting executive*

Tacoma
Jasinek, Gary Donald *newspaper executive*
Johnson, Charles Robert *television news anchor, reporter*
Marcotte, Michael Vincent *journalist, public radio executive*
Mottram, Robert Hugh *journalist*
Shipman, Keith Bryan *sportscaster*
Wirsing, Dale Robert *journalist, educator*

Vancouver
Wagner, Diane Masters *newspaper editor*

Vashon
Mann, Claud Prentiss, Jr. *retired television journalist, real estate agent*

Woodinville
Margeson, Douglas William *reporter*

WYOMING

Casper
MacKinnon, Anne *editor*
Rosenthal, Jack *broadcasting executive*

Cheyenne
Occhipinti, Carl Joseph *broadcasting executive*

Glendo
Curtis, Nancy Nell *publisher, rancher*

Jackson
Ninneman, Thomas George *broadcast executive*

Laramie
Bieber-Roberts, Peggy Eilene *communications educator, journalist*

Yellowstone National Park
Schullery, Paul David *editor, writer, consultant*

TERRITORIES OF THE UNITED STATES

GUAM

Agana
Crisostomo, Manny *photographer*

CANADA

ALBERTA

Calgary
Peterson, Kevin Bruce *newspaper editor, publishing executive*
Poole, Robert Anthony *journalist*
Russell, Gary *broadcast executive*
Speers, J. Alvin *editor, publisher, accountant*

Edmonton
Hughes, Linda J. *newspaper publisher*
MacLean, Victoria Graham *journalist, editor*
Poignant, Gary Donald *newspaper editor*
Stanway, Paul William *newspaper editor*

BRITISH COLUMBIA

Vancouver
Dykk, LLoyd Henry *journalist*
Hume, Stephen *writer, editor*
Yaffe, Barbara Marlene *journalist*

ONTARIO

Toronto
Newman, Peter Charles *journalist*

SASKATCHEWAN

Regina
Hughes, Robert Lachlan *newspaper executive*

Saskatoon
Knycha, Josef *journalist*

ENGLAND

London
Montalbano, William Daniel *foreign correspondent, novelist*

INDIA

New Delhi
Dahlburg, John-Thor Theodore *newspaper correspondent*

ADDRESS UNPUBLISHED

Agner, Wayne Richard *journalist*
Ainsworth, Harriet Crawford *journalist, public relations consultant*
Allen, Mitchell Jack *publisher, archaeologist*
Ashby, Norma Rae Beatty *journalist, beauty consultant*
Barham, Patte (Mrs. Harris Peter Boyne) *publisher, author, columnist*
Barnhurst, Christine Louise *broadcast executive*
Barry, Rick (Richard Francis Dennis Barry, III) *sportscaster, retired professional basketball player, marketing professional*
Bassett, Barbara Wies *editor, publisher*
Bender, Gary Nedrow *television sportscaster*
Bennett, Paul Lester *producer, manager*
Berke, Judie *publisher, editor*
Blackstock, Joseph Robinson *newspaper editor*
Broussard, Carol Madeline *writer, literary consulting agent, photographer*
Capell, Cydney Lynn *editor*
Carey, Margaret Theresa Logan *newspaper education consultant*
Carlson, Natalie Traylor *publisher*
Cherwin, Sunah Caroline *publisher, editor*
Collins, Amy Denise *reporter*
Cooper, Jon Hugh *public television executive*
Cullen, Robert John *publishing executive, financial consultant*
Curtin, David Stephen *newswriter*
Dahl, Donald Douglas *newswriter*
Dinkel, John George *magazine editor*
Dore, Bonny Ellen *film and television production company executive*
Draznin, Jules Nathan *journalism and public relations educator, consultant*
Farah, Joseph Francis *newspaper editor, writer*
Ferro, James Michael *publishing executive*
Fraser, Laura Jane *journalist*
Gatchell, Howell Lamborn, Jr. *radio and television news executive*
Golum, Robert Bruce *journalist*
Hahn, Helene B. *motion picture company executive*
Harden, Patrick Alan *journalist, news executive*
Heath, Scott Richard *instructional designer, hypermedia developer*
Herdeck, Donald Elmer *publishing executive, retired humanities educator*
Hibler, Jude Ann *photojournalist*
Hogarth, Christopher Grant *documentation specialist*
Humes, Edward *journalist, writer*
Jacobs, Joanne Lee *journalist*
Jenkins, Billie Beasley *film company executive*
Jennings, Max *newspaper editor*
Johnson, Ciri Diane *graphic design firm owner*
Johnson, Frank Edward *newspaper editor*
Koppett, Leonard *columnist, journalist, author*
Kounalakis, Markos *foreign correspondent*
Kummer, Edward Wolfgang *film company executive*
Laird, Andrew Kenneth *radio broadcast engineer*
Leason, Jody Jacobs *newspaper columnist*
Lee, Robert W(illiam) *journalist, researcher*
Lister, Keith Fenimore *publishing executive*
Loges, William Earl *communications educator*
Love, Laurie Miller *science editor*
Lush, Pamela Grace Meine *international publishing company executive*
MacAller, Natasha Jeannette *dancer*
Manley, Joan A(dele) Daniels *retired publisher*
Manning, Richard Dale *writer*
Martin, Hugo Casillas *staff writer*
Medavoy, Mike *motion picture company executive*
Melendez, James Patrick *editor*
Moskowitz, Robert Arthur *publishing executive*
Murray, J(ames) Edward *retired newspaper editor, publisher*
Nish, Albert Raymond, Jr. *retired newspaper editor*
Noeth, Louise Ann *journalist*
Oster, Patrick Ralph *journalist*
Paige, Woodrow Wilson *columnist*
Payne, Ancil Horace *retired broadcasting executive*
Pedersen, Kim Aasberg *newsletter publisher, video producer*
Petron, Donald Robert *magazine editor*
Prigge, Liz Maynard *publishing executive*
Prine, Stephen Brent *publisher*
Pudney, Gary Laurence *television executive*
Radke, Linda Foster *publishing consultant*
Rayner, William Alexander *retired newspaper editor*
Rhodes, Gerald Lee *writer*
Robinson, Frank Robert *radio station executive*
Roche, Lisa Riley *reporter*
Rosenkrantz, Linda *writer*
Rosenthal, Donna *broadcast producer*
Ryan, Cathrine Smith *publisher*
Sapsowitz, Sidney H. *entertainment and media company executive*
Schacht, Linda Joan *broadcast journalist*
Sevey, Robert Warren *retired broadcasting executive, journalist*
Silveira, Ronald Louis *video company executive*
Skaar, Sarah Henson *editor*
Smith, Chester *broadcasting executive*
Smith, Martin Bernhard *journalist*
Spitaleri, Vernon Rosario *newspaper publisher*
Steiner, Shari Yvonne *publisher, editor*
Stennett, William Clinton (Clint Stennett) *radio and television station executive, state legislator*
Thompson, Anne Marie *newspaper publisher*
Vandenberg, Peter Ray *magazine publisher*
Voight, Joan *publisher*
Vree, Dale *editor*
Weaver, Howard Cecil *newspaper editor*
Webber, Marilyn Aspen Kay *writer*
Welsome, Eileen *journalist*
Wolin, Merle Linda *journalist, consultant*
Wollum, Owen Lee *entrepreneur*
Woodward, John Russell *motion picture production executive*
Yack, Patrick Ashley *editor*

EDUCATION. For postsecondary education, *See also* specific fields.

UNITED STATES

ALASKA

Anchorage
Behrend, Donald Fraser *university administrator*
Collins, Michael Paul *secondary school educator, earth science educator, consultant*
Davis, Bettye Jean *academic administrator, state official*
Mitchell, Michael Kiehl *elementary and secondary education educator, minister*
Skladal, Elizabeth Lee *elementary school educator*

Fairbanks
Barsdate, Mary Kathryn *educator*
Gaylord, Thomas Alan *academic administrator*
Komisar, Jerome Bertram *university administrator*
Wadlow, Joan Krueger *university chancellor*

Girdwood
Wedel, Millie Redmond *secondary school educator*

Haines
Haas, June F. *special education educator, consultant*

Homer
Wolfe, Steven Albert *secondary education educator*

Napaskiak
Bajczyk, William Richard *secondary education educator*

North Pole
Kilbourn, Aldean Gae *secondary school educator*

Tuntutuliak
Daniel, Barbara Ann *secondary education educator, English educator*

Wasilla
Hogue, Bonnie Marie Kifer Gosciminski *child care educator, consultant*
Rydolph, Simmie Tommy *middle school educator*

ARIZONA

Arizona City
Donovan, Willard Patrick *retired elementary education educator*

Bisbee
Skinner, David Cooper *school administrator, educator*

Chandler
Barnard, Annette Williamson *elementary school educator*
Fordemwalt, James Newton *microelectronics educator, consultant, engineer*
Malcolm, Richard Ward *college administrator, consultant*
Meibert, Catherine Welch *secondary school educator, administrator*
Toth, Elizabeth Levay *retired educational organization executive, lawyer*

Chinle
Greenfield, Sarah C. *school counselor*

Flagstaff
Bloom, John W. *counselor, educator*
Chambers, Stephen L.E. *university official*
Ratzlaff, Vernon Paul *elementary education educator, consultant*

Fountain Hills
Humes, Charles Warren *counselor educator*

Glendale
Horner, Jennie Linn *retired educational administrator, nurse*
Voris, William *educational administrator*

Green Valley
Carpenter, John Everett *retired principal, educational consultant*

Kingman
Miller, Clara Burr *education educator*

Lake Havasu City
Rheinish, Robert Kent *university administrator*

Mesa
Adams, Heidi-Christa *counselor*
Bydalek, David Allen *education educator*
Colledge, Deborah Gail *gifted and talented elementary educator*
Markey, Thomas Adam *school business manager*
Philbrick, Douglas Robert *principal, librarian, mental health professional*
Ramirez, Janice L. *assistant school superintendent*
Smets, Tobias Charles *elementary education educator*

Morristown
Rosehnal, Mary Ann *educational administrator*

Page
Hart, Marian Griffith *retired reading educator*
Tsinigine, Allen *educator*

Paradise Valley
Dickerson, Barbara Ann Ransom *dean, education educator, consultant*
Hendrickson, Robert J. *educational administrator*

Peoria
Jones, Lillie Agnes *retired elementary education educator*

Phoenix
Barela, Bertha Cicci *retired elementary education educator, artist*
Boston, Marcia Ann *elementary school educator*
Buehler, Marilyn Kay Hasz *secondary education educator*
Cain, Robert Joseph *elementary school educator*
Comprone, Joseph John *dean*
Field, Earl Lyle *dean, education educator*
Forsyth, Ben Ralph *academic administrator, medical educator*
Gibbs, William Harold *university administrator*
Gibson, Treva Kay *university official*
Hunt, Holly *elementary education educator*
Kumler, Rose Marie *career counselor, educator*
Straka, Donald Joseph *technical educator*
Thor, Linda Maria *college president*
Whitlow, Donna Mae *daycare and primary school administrator*

Prescott
Baca, Sherry Ann *secondary school educator*
Daly, Paul Sylvester *retired academic administrator*
Sasmor, Jeannette Louise *educational consulting company executive*

Safford
Riddlesworth, Judith Himes *elementary education educator*

San Manuel
Hawk, Dawn Davah *secondary education educator*
Hawk, Floyd Russell *secondary school educator*

Scottsdale
Churchill, William DeLee *retired education educator, psychologist*
Cisar, Catherine Ann *special education educator*
Esquer, Deborah Anne *elementary education educator*
Phillips, Wanda Charity *secondary education educator, writer*
Tubbs, Janet Carolyn *educational consultant*

Sierra Vista
Casteel, Cheryl Theodora *security officer*

Sun City West
Conner, Jeanne Williams *retired educator*

Sun Lakes
Johnson, Marian Ilene *education educator*

Tempe
Brandt, Beverly Kay *university administrator, educator*
Coor, Lattie Finch *university president*
Ordini, John, Jr. *accountant*
Richardson, Richard Colby, Jr. *higher education educator, researcher*
Sackton, Frank Joseph *university official, lecturer, retired army officer*
Saunders, Karen Estelle *secondary education educator*
Scott, Judith Myers *elementary education educator*
Thompson, Anna Blanche *retired educator*
Valentine, Carol Ann *educational program director, consultant*
Yu, Chong Ho *educational researcher*

Tucson
Bjorhovde, Patricia Ordonez *university development director*
Dyer-Raffler, Joy Ann *special education diagnostician, educator*
Gallagher, Rosanna Bostick *elementary educator, administrator*
Garcia, Juan Ramon *historian, educator*
Garner, Girolama Thomasina *educational administrator, educator*
Golden, Bonnie Jane *counselor*
Heins, Marilyn *college dean, pediatrics educator, author*
Humphrey, John Julius *university program director, historian, writer*
Johnson, Maryanne Elizabeth *private school educator*
Pacheco, Manuel Trinidad *university president*
Porreca, Betty Lou *education educator*
Powers, Stephen *educational researcher, consultant*
Reid, Charles Phillip Patrick *academic administrator, researcher, professor*
Shafer, Susan Wright *elementary education educator*
Starr, Melvin Lee *counselor*
Tomoeda, Cheryl Kuniko *academic researcher*
Treat, James Michael *secondary education educator*
Ungar, Lisa Elaine *school counselor, education educator*
White, Danny Levius *counselor, consultant, educator*
Wilson, John Lewis *university official*

Yuma
Badgley, Judeth Birdwell *motivational learning consultant*
Drysdale, Valerie Micole *elementary education educator*
Farland, Eugene Hector *retired educational consultant*
Rhodes, James Lamar, Jr. (Grizzly Bear Rhodes) *educator, research historian*

CALIFORNIA

Alameda
Carter, Roberta Eccleston *counselor, therapist*
Sakamoto, Katsuyuki *college chancellor, psychology educator*

Alamo
Hardy, Lois Lynn *educational seminar training company executive*

Alhambra
Anton, William R. *retired school system administrator, consutant*

Alta Loma
Doyle, Michael James *educational administrator, organist*
Lucas, Elizabeth Coughlin *educator*
Rhoades, Jacqueline Jo *education educator, consultant, writer*

Anaheim
Grennan, Cynthia *school superintendent*
Grose, Elinor Ruth *retired elementary education educator*

Angwin
Bell, Charles Vester *college administrator*

Aptos
Hirsch, Bette G(ross) *college administrator, foreign language educator*

Arcata
Mc Crone, Alistair William *university president*
Peters, Barbara M. Stratton *career counselor, administrator*
Slinker, John Michael *academic director*

Atherton
Lane, Joan Fletcher *educational administrator*

Azusa
Gray, Paul Wesley *university dean*

Bakersfield
Arciniega, Tomas Abel *university president*
Guyton, Robert Armour, Jr. *secondary school educator, business administrator*
Hess, Helen Elizabeth *retired secondary school educator, musician*
Neumann, Herman Ernest *elementary and special education educator*
Olsen, Carl Franklin *school superintendent*
Skillin, Therese Jeno *elementary school educator*

Beaumont
Ullman, Patricia *secondary education educator*

Belmont
Zellmer, Arlene *special education educator*

Ben Lomond
Sikora, James Robert *educational business administrator*
Sparks, Jack Norman *college dean*

Benicia
Dunaway, Phillip Lee, Jr. *secondary school education educator*
Garrop, Barbara Ann *elementary education educator*

Berkeley
Bucher, Glenn Richard *academic administrator*
Cross, Kathryn Patricia *education educator*
Damaschino, Ann Toothman *school development administrator*
Geist, Karin Ruth Tammeus Mcphail *secondary education educator, realtor, musician*
Lilly, Luella Jean *university administrator*
McConnell, Patricia Lynn *vocational consultant*
Ralston, Lenore Dale *academic policy and program analyst*
Rice, Robert Arnot *school administrator*
Tien, Chang-Lin *chancellor*
Ullman, Dana Gregory *educational administrator, publisher, author*

Beverly Hills
Grant, Michael Ernest *educational administrator, institutional management educator*
Harris, Ellen Stern *foundation administrator, public policy educator, writer*

Buena Park
Conrady, James Louis *audio visual technician*
Papin, Nancy Sue *educational computer coordinator*

Burlingame
Yates, Margery Gordon *educator*

California City
Friedl, Rick *former academic administrator, lawyer*

Campo
Charles, Blanche *retired elementary education educator*
Jermini, Ellen *educational administrator, philosopher*

Canyon Lake
Knight, Vick, Jr. (Ralph Knight) *dean, education educator, counselor*

Carlsbad
Gardner, David Chambers *education educator, psychologist, business executive, author*

Carmichael
Marmaduke, Arthur Sandford *educational administrator*

Carson
Detweiler, Robert Chester *university president, historian*

Castro Valley
Parris, Anne Witmer *secondary education educator, writer*

Chico
DuFour, Kim *university official*
Esteban, Manuel Antonio *university administrator, educator*
Wismer, Patricia Ann *secondary education educator*

Chino
Rodríguez, Paul Anthony *elementary school educator*

Chula Vista
Clement, Betty Waidlich *literacy educator, consultant*
Hanson, Eileen *principal*
Livziey, James Gerald *secondary school educator*
Wyatt, Edith Elizabeth *elementary education educator*

Claremont
Alexander, John David, Jr. *college administrator*
Bekavac, Nancy Yavor *academic administrator, lawyer*
Douglass, Enid Hart *educational program director*
Faranda, John Paul *college administrator*
Gamer, Nancy Crews Schaefer *alumni relations director, fundraiser*
Hess, Dorothy Haldeman *college official*
Maguire, John David *university administrator, educator, writer*
Platt, Joseph Beaven *former college president*
Riggs, Henry Earle *college president, engineering management educator*
Stark, Jack Lee *college president*
Taulbee, Amy Louise *college administrator*

Clarksburg
Palacio, Thomas *secondary education educator, coach, sports official*

Clovis
Bitters, Conrad Lee *biological sciences educator*

Colton
Dybowski, Douglas Eugene *education educator, economist*
Slider, Margaret Elizabeth *elementary education educator*

Compton
Williams, Vivian Lewie *college counselor*

Concord
Langley, Michael Douglas *secondary education educator*
Snyder, Lynn Nelson *special education educator*
Thall, Richard Vincent *education program director*

Coronado
Trent-Ota, Jane Suzanne *elementary school educator*

Covelo
Dixon, Michel LaVon *educational administrator*

Covina
Aguilar-Posada, Gladys Maria *counselor*

Crockett
De Maranville, Nancy Joan *secondary education educator*

Culver City
Maxwell-Brogdon, Florence Morency *school administrator, educational adviser*

Cupertino
Campbell, William Joseph *academic director*
Mirk, Judy Ann *elementary educator*
Reza, Jacquelyn Valerie *counselor, consultant*

Daly City
Patnaik, Obadiah *principal*

Danville
Brown, Merlinde Maria *elementary school educator*

Davis
Bittlingmayer, George *educator*
Denison, Michael Steven *education educator*
Green, Bonnie Jean *early childhood administrator*
Ramey, Felicenne Houston *dean academic affairs, educator*
Springer, Sally Pearl *university administrator*
Vanderhoef, Larry Neil *university administrator*

Desert Center
Reinhart, Maria Rinna *secondary education educator*

Downey
Gogolin, Marilyn Tompkins *educational administrator, language pathologist*

El Cajon
Thomas, Esther Merlene *elementary education educator*

El Cerrito
Herzberg, Dorothy Crews *middle school educator*

Encino
O'Connor, Patricia Ranville *secondary and special education educator*

Escondido
Hodges, Rose Marie *secondary education educator*

Fairfield
Lederer, Thomas Felix *secondary education educator, consultant*

Fontana
Marks, Sharon Lea *primary school educator, nurse*
Smith, Jerilynn Suzanne *educational coordinator*

Forestville
Kielsmeier, Catherine Jane *school system administrator*

Fortuna
Fisher, Bruce David *elementary educator*
Fullerton, Gail Jackson *university president emeritus*

Fountain Valley
Carrozzo, Guy A. *former school principal, mayor*
Otto, (Bertha) Marie *educational administrator, educational consulting company executive*

Fremont
Brown, David Richard *school system administrator, minister*
de Roque, Barbara Penberthy *special education educator, consultant*
Riley, Dawn C. *educational philosopher, special education educator, researcher*

Fresno
Howard, Katsuyo Kunugi *counselor, educator, consultant*
Nickel, Rosalie Jean *reading specialist*
Tanner, David Earl *education educator*
Tudman, Cathi Graves *elementary education educator, music director*
Welty, John Donald *university president*
Wong, Kin-Ping *university dean, biotechnology researcher, company executive, educator, science administrator*

Fullerton
Baker, Kathleen Ann *student services counselor*
Gordon, Milton Andrew *academic administrator*
Voorhees, Lorraine Isobel *college dean*

Garden Valley
Silver, Monte S. *elementary education educator, consultant*

Glendale
Case, Lee Owen, Jr. *retired academic administrator*
Leeds-Horwitz, Susan Beth *school system administrator, speech-language pathology educator*
Levine, Benjamin Jacob *secondary education educator*

Glendora
Lindly, Douglas Dean *elementary school educator, administrator*

Grass Valley
Dolan, Grace Frances *elementary education educator*

Grover Beach
Betita, Kenneth Simon *academic counselor*

Hacienda Heights
Thiessen, Betty Jean *special education educator*

Hanford
Bartel, Arthur Gabriel *educational administrator, city official*
Canady, Gloria Diane *secondary education educator, business owner*

Hayward
McCune, Ellis E. *retired university system chief administrator, higher education consultant*
Rees, Norma S. *university president, educator*

Huntington Beach
De Massa, Jessie G. *media specialist*
Olson, Gerald Theodore *educational consultant*
Olson, Wayne Roger *community college dean*

Huntington Park
Wysocki, Jo Ann *elementary education educator, librarian*

Imperial
Patterson, Melissa *elementary education educator*

Indian Wells
Trotter, F(rederick) Thomas *retired university president*

Indio
Houghton, Robert Charles *secondary education educator*

Inglewood
Guzy, Marguerita Linnes *secondary education educator*
McDuffie, Annie Laura *special needs educator*

Irvine
Garretson, Steven Michael *elementary education educator*
Kleeman, Nancy Gray Ervin *special education educator*
Payne, Lisa Mossman *middle school educator*
Welch, Bobby O'Neal *dean*

Kentfield
McCarthy, Marie Geraldine *program director, coordinator*

Kerman
Fischle, Daniel Karl *school system administrator*

La Canada Flintridge
Lamson, Robert Woodrow *retired school system administrator*

La Jolla
Atkinson, Richard Chatham *academic administrator, cognitive psychologist, educator*
Caserio, Marjorie Constance *academic administrator*
Fitch, Noel Riley *writer, educator*
Rachmeler, Martin *university administrator*

La Mesa
Black, Eileen Mary *elementary school educator*
Tarson, Herbert Harvey *university administrator emeritus*

La Palma
Akubuilo, Francis Ekenechukwu *secondary school educator*

La Verne
Coray, Jeffrey Warren *assistant principal, instructor*
Morgan, Stephen Charles *academic administrator*

Lafayette
Dietz, Donald Arthur *vocational education educator*

Laguna Beach
Ryder, Virginia Pinkus *retired school system administrator*
Strong, Winifred Hekker *educational counselor, consultant*

Laguna Hills
Penkava, Richard Anton *secondary school administrator*

Lake Elsinore
Wilson, Sonja Mary *secondary education educator, consultant, poet*
Wolsey, Thomas DeVere *middle school educator*

Lakeport
Jones, Brenda Gail *school district administrator*

Lakewood
Bogdan, James Thomas *secondary education educator, electronics researcher and developer*

Lancaster
Dumas, Louise Isabelle *elementary school educator*

Lemon Grove
Mott, June Marjorie *school system administrator*

Lemoore
Krend, William John *secondary education educator*

Littlerock
Eggleston, Rose Mary Lewis Quarrels *elementary education educator, clergywoman*

Livermore
Daniel, Helen Anderson *secondary education educator, psychotherapist, intern*
Lucas, Linda Lucille *dean*
Roshong, Dee Ann Daniels *dean, educator*

Loma Linda
Johnston, Patricia Kathleen *college dean*
Weismeyer, Richard Wayne *academic administrator*

Lomita
Malm, Royce Elliott *secondary education educator*

Lompoc
Duke, Pamela Ruth *reading specialist*

Long Beach
Armstrong, Joanna *education educator*
Beljan, John Richard *university administrator, medical educator*
Bozanich, Lawrence Anthony *school system administrator*
Hobgood, E(arl) Wade *college dean*
Lunderville, Gerald Paul *bilingual education educator*
Martinez, Patricia Ann *middle school educator, administrator*
McCutchen, Edna Elizabeth *counselor*
Munitz, Barry *university administrator, English literature educator, business consultant*
Reichard, Gary Warren *university administrator, history educator*
Stewart, Gail Benita *alumni development director, editor*
Wittich, William Vincent *academic administrator, educator*

Los Altos
Gonzales, Richard Robert *academic administrator*
Lee, Hamilton H. *education educator*

Los Angeles
Aguilar, Raul Abraham *adult school administrator*
Alexander, Henry Alan *academic administrator*
Anderson, Henry Lee Norman *academic administrator*
Ansley, Julia Ette *elementary education educator, consultant, poet, writer*
Armstrong, Lloyd, Jr. *university official, physics educator*
Cahill, Eileen Mary *secondary education educator*
Cavanaugh, Michael Arthur *secondary education educator, retired sociologist*
Chang, Wung *business advisor*
Darmstaetter, Jay Eugene *secondary education educator*
Dewey, Donald Odell *university dean*
Gilbert, Richard Keith *education educator, researcher*
Gothold, Stuart E. *school system administrator, educator*
Harris, F. Chandler *retired university administrator*
Harvey, James Gerald *educational consultant, counselor, researcher*
Haynes, Michael Scott, Sr. *resource specialist*
Herscher, Uri David *academic administrator, history educator, rabbi*
Hirson, Estelle *retired school educator*
Kennelly, Sister Karen Margaret *college administrator*
La Mothe, Suzanne Marie *career counselor*
Lee, Dorothy Wong *secondary art educator*
Lim, Larry Kay *university official*
Lucente, Rosemary Dolores *educational administrator*
McDonough, Patricia M. *education educator*
Moore, Donald Walter *academic administrator, school librarian*
Moran, Thomas Harry *academic administrator*
Mori, Allen Anthony *university dean, consultant, researcher*
Patterson, Dawn Marie *dean, consultant, author, educator*
Peterson, Vance Tullin *academic administrator, educator*
Polon, Linda Beth *elementary school educator, writer, illustrator*
Prager, Susan Westerberg *dean, law educator*
Rappaport, Michael David *college dean, labor arbitrator*
Rideout, Phyllis McCain *university official, educator*
Rosser, James Milton *university president*
Rothman, Judith Ellen *associate dean*
Sample, Steven Browning *university president*
Slaughter, John Brooks *university president*
Steinberg, Warren Linnington *principal*
Wagner, William Gerard *university dean, physicist, consultant, information scientist, investment manager*
Young, Charles Edward *university chancellor*
Zamir, Frances Roberta (Frances Roberta Weiss-Swede) *assistant principal*

Los Gatos
Gangwere, Heather Hendry *secondary education educator*
Hartinger, Patricia Bernardine Curran *elementary school educator*

Lynwood
Herschler, Leslie Norman *elementary education educator*

Malibu
Luft, Herbert *former dean*
Mollner, Frederick Richard *director publications, graphic designer*

Manhattan Beach
Brooks, Edward Howard *college administrator*

Marina Del Rey
Nixon, Nora *educational director*

Marysville
DeVore, Marilyn Ruth *education educator, consultant*

Menlo Park
Wright, Ellen Florence *consultant*

Merced
Roberts, Lillian *retired principal*

Midway City
Leong, Yvonne C. *literacy consultant*

Millbrae
Carlson, Sydney Anne *secondary school educator and counselor*

Milpitas
Lobig, Janie Howell *special education educator*

Mission Viejo
Hough, J. Marie *vocational education educator*
O'Banion, Terry Underwood *academic administrator, consultant*

Modesto
Peyton, Mary Johanna *secondary educator*
Price, Robert William *school superintendent, consultant*
Sibitz, Michael William *school superintendent*

Mojave
Morrin, Virginia White *retired educator*

Montebello
Dible, Rose Harpe McFee *special education educator*

Monterey
Oder, Broeck Newton *school emergency management consultant*

Monterey Park
Choyke, George Raymond *safety educator, consultant*

Moreno Valley
McMurty, Judy Jean *school counselor*

Mountain View
Cicora, Mary Angela *researcher, author*

Murrieta
Hofman, Edmond John *secondary school educator, police official*

Napa
Ervin, Margaret Howie *elementary educator, special education educator*
Nemko, Barbara Gail *academic director*
Rada, Alexander *university official*

Newport Beach
Rodasta, Joanne Cook *elementary education educator*

Northridge
Brotman, Carol Eileen *adult education educator, advocate*
Cohea, Melinda Ruth *school business executive*
Wilson, Blenda Jacqueline *university chancellor*

Norwalk
McCamly, Jerry Allen *secondary education educator*

Oakland
Caulfield, Carlota *education educator*
Charbonneau, Robert Bruce *university official, natural resourcess consultant*
Dibble, David Van Vlack *visually impaired educator, lawyer*
Fries, Lita Linda *school system administrator*
Gantt, Barry *secondary school educator*
Lawrence, Gary Sheldon *academic administrator*
Peltason, Jack Walter *university president*

Ontario
Kennedy, Mark Alan *middle school educator*
Morton, Laurel Anne *elementary education educator*
Young, Jack Donald *middle school educator*

Orange
Gerhard, Nancy Lucile Dege *counselor, educator*
Hamilton, Harry Lemuel, Jr. *academic administrator*
Shukla, Pradip Kantilal *academic administrator, educator, consultant*

Orinda
Glasser, Charles Edward *university president*
Odermatt, Diana B. *educational administrator, educational consultant*

Orosi
McKittrick, Joseph Terrence *principal, educator*

Oroville
Rasmussen, Mike Joseph *college financial aid administrator*
Tamori, David Isamu *secondary education educator*

Oxnard
Hamm, George Ardeil *retired secondary education educator, hypnotherapist, consultant*
Herrera, Sandra Johnson *school system administrator*
Steele, Julius Raynard *special education educator*

Palm Springs
Hartman, Rosemary Jane *special education educator*
Schreiman, Howard Leslie *special education educator*

Palmdale
Bowen, Jimmie Carl *vocational education educator*

Palo Alto
Attig, John Clare *secondary education educator, consultant*
Bolitho, Louise Greer *educational administrator, consultant*
Gong, Mamie Poggio *secondary education educator*
Haertel, Geneva DiLuzio *educational researcher*
Liddell, Barbara Anne *school administrator*
Robinson, John Thomas *arts education administrator, designer*
Rogaway, Betty Jane *retired school system administrator, social worker*

Palos Verdes Estates
Bacher, Rosalie Wride *educational administrator*

Palos Verdes Peninsula
Copeland, Phillips Jerome *former university administrator, former air force officer*

Panorama City
Wolff, Mark Robert *elementary and secondary education educator*

Pasadena
Almore-Randle, Allie Louise *special education educator*
Brown, David R. *academic administrator*
Everhart, Thomas Eugene *academic administrator, engineering educator*
Freise, Earl Jerome *univeristy administrator, materials engineering educator*
Lawler, Alice Bonzi (Mrs. Oscar T. Lawler) *retired college administrator, civic worker*
Levy, David Steven *college administrator*
Moore, Kathleen Green *educational administrator*
Siemon-Burgeson, Marilyn M. *education administrator*
Stork, William Willis *secondary education educator*

Pebble Beach
Roth, Frederic Hull, Jr. *secondary education educator*

Petaluma
O'Hare, Sandra Fernandez *secondary education educator*

Piedmont
Marinelly, Ralph *secondary educator*

Pinole
Grogan, Stanley Joseph *educational educator, consultant*

Pleasant Hill
Lundgren, Susan Elaine *counselor, educator*
Zottnick, Lisa Isobel *educational therapist*

Pomona
Bullock, Molly *educator*
Gugelchuk, Gary Michael *academic administrator*
Lawrence, William, Jr. *elementary education educator*
Markham, Reed B. *education educator, consultant*
Schmitt, Catherine Laura *academic career counselor*

Portola Valley
Oscarson, Kathleen Dale *writing assessment coordinator, educator*

Poway
Shippey, Lyn *reading center director*

Rancho Cordova
Hendrickson, Elizabeth Ann *secondary education educator*

Rancho Cucamonga
Callaway, Linda Marie *special education educator*
Jones, Joanna Patricia *education educator, college official, consultant*

Redlands
Proffitt, Lawrence Alan *secondary school educator*
Ritchie, C(laude) Alen *middle school educator, tax preparer*

Redondo Beach
Fix, Tobie Lynn *special education educator*
Takahashi, Tomoko *education educator, writer*

Reseda
Moss, Debra Lee *school counselor*

Rialto
Jackson, Betty Eileen *music and elementary school educator*
Johnson, Ruth Floyd *secondary education educator, consultant*
Straight, James Wesley *secondary education educator*

Richmond
Colfack, Andrea Heckelman *elementary education educator*

Ridgecrest
Smith, Howard Norman, Jr. *educational coordinator, anthropology educator*

Riverside
Allen, William Merle *university administrator, educator*
Chou, Yue Hong *education educator, researcher*
Danger, Suzan Elizabeth *elementary education educator*
Diamond, Richard *secondary education educator*
Finan, Ellen Cranston *secondary education educator, consultant*
Lacy, Carolyn Jean *elementary education educator, secondary education educator*
Leo, Louis J. *university administrator*
Peterson, Leroy *retired secondary education educator*
Schlax, Sharon Lynn Newell *physical education educator*
Thomas, Sylvia Ann *community college dean*
Tweddle, Jennifer Lynne *academic mental health counselor*
West, Madeline Florence *elementary education educator*

Rohnert Park
Arminana, Ruben *university president, educator*
Babula, William *university dean*

Rosemead
Hansen, Robert Dennis *educational administrator*

Rowland Heights
Perfetti, Robert Nickolas *career education coordinator, educator*

Sacramento
Branch, Barbara Lee *elementary education educator*
Chaim, Robert Alex *academic administrator, educator*
Denardo, Gerald Louis *academic director*
Evans, James Handel *university administrator, architect, educator*
Gerth, Donald Rogers *university president*
Johnson, Chris Alan *education educator*
Kerschner, Lee R(onald) *former university president, political science educator*
Lawrence, Paul Frederic *educational consultant*
Martell, Charles Rennie, Jr. *dean, librarian*
McKim, Harriet Megchelsen *education educator*
Reed-Graham, Lois L. *administrator, secondary education educator*
Riles, Wilson Camanza *educational consultant*
Shoemaker, Cameron David James *dean, educator*
Stalling, Charlesetta *educational consultant, trainer*
Stark, Mary Barbara *retired educator*

San Andreas
Millsaps, Rita Rae *elementary school educator*

San Bernardino
Evans, Anthony Howard *university president*
Norton, Ruth Ann *education educator*

San Diego
Arenson, Barbara Levine *special education educator*
Ashton-Coombs, Tamarah M. *learning disabilities specialist, consultant*
Berrian, James Edwin *biology teacher*
Campbell, Robert Madison *university program director*
Clifton, Mark Stephen *administrator*
Day, Thomas Brennock *university president*
Eisemann, Kurt *director computer center, mathematics educator*
Fellows, Donald Matthew *university official*
Hoye, Walter Brisco *retired college administrator*
Hoyt, Jack Wallace *engineering educator*
Lomeli, Marta *elementary education educator*
Mir, Marilyn *retired educator*
Oviatt, Larry Andrew *educator*
Rose, Faye Schuman *university department director communications*
Schade, Charlene Joanne *adult and early childhood education educator*
Trybus, Raymond J. *higher education executive, psychologist*
Uribe, Jennie Ann *elementary school educator*
Williams, Stephen Joseph *education educator, researcher*

San Dimas
Cameron, Judith Lynne *secondary education educator, hypnotherapist*
Lawson, Scott Lawrence *dean, consultant*

San Francisco
Ada, Alma Flor *education educator, writer*
Adcock, Muriel W. *special education educator*
Balzer, Anthony James *academy director*
Barrett, William Owen *academic administrator*
Buidang, George (Hada Buidang) *education educator, administrator, consultant, writer*
Corrigan, Robert Anthony *academic administrator*
Counelis, James Steve *education educator*
Essa, Lisa Beth *elementary education educator*
Fong, Elaine Chun *principal*
Fromm, Hanna *educational administrator*
Hasan, Mahmood Ul *secondary school educator*
Kane, Kathleen Lillian *university administrator, lawyer*
Kelley, James Charles, III *dean*
Krevans, Julius Richard *university administrator, physician*
Manson, Malcolm Hood *educational administrator*
Marshall, Lucille Taylor *educator, receptionist*
Pierce, Deborah Mary *educational administrator*
Pinsky, Charlotte Lee (Cherie Pinsky) *academic administrator*
Runyon, Steven Crowell *university administrator, communications educator*
Schlegel, John Peter *university president*
Stephens, Elisa *academic administrator*
Tahmassian, Ara Zarneh *university director*
Threadgill, Mae Ellen *educational administrator*
Welsh, Doris McNeil *early childhood education specialist*

San Gabriel
Provenzano, Maureen Lynn *secondary educator*

San Jacinto
Tausig, Michael Robert *college administrator, higher education planning consultant*

San Jose
Cryer, Rodger Earl *educational administrator*
Elsorady, Alexa Marie *secondary education educator*
French, Stephen Warren *university administrator, educator, artist*
Holyer, Erna Maria *adult education educator, writer, artist*
Liehr, Robert Joseph *private school educator*
Sanders, Adrian Lionel *education consultant*

San Leandro
Cipriano, Patricia Ann *secondary education educator, consultant*
Nehls, Robert Louis, Jr. *school system administrator*

San Luis Obispo
Bailey, Philip Sigmon, Jr. *university official, chemistry educator*
Baker, Warren J(oseph) *university president*
Cota, Harold Maurice *educator*
Maas, Donald Kenneth *education educator, consultant*
Rathbun, Larry Peter *education consultant*

San Marcos
Wood, Harold Samuel *retired educator*

San Marino
Footman, Gordon Elliott *educational administrator*

San Mateo
Copello, Angelo Gene *health services administrator*

San Pedro
Allison, Lynn Dee *university program administrator, consultant*

San Rafael
Blum, Arthur Marvin *academic administrator*
Cloud, James Merle *university and hospital administrator*
Geoffey, Ruth *director activities, artist*

Santa Ana
Boroskin, Alan *counselor, psychotherapist*
Castruita, Rudy *school system administrator*
Howard, Darcie Sheila *special education educator*
Vail, Michael George *academic director*

Santa Barbara
Allaway, William Harris *retired university official*
O'Dowd, Donald Davy *retired university administrator*
Robeck, Mildred Coen *early childhood education educator*
Tettegah, Sharon Yvonne *education educator*
Yang, Henry T. *university chancellor, educator*

Santa Clara
Abdaljabbar, Abdalhameed A. *educational administrator*
Achabal, Dale Domingo *business educator*
Grafft, William Davis *retired school system administrator*
Jiménez, Francisco *academic administrator*
Locatelli, Paul Leo *university administrator*
Nordmeyer, Mary Betsy *vocational educator*
Shoup, Terry Emerson *university dean, engineering educator*

Santa Clarita
Boyer, Carl, III *secondary education educator, city official*
Lavine, Steven David *college president*
Schwartz, Betty Barsha *secondary education educator, writer, artist*

Santa Cruz
Coate, Lester Edwin *university administrator*

Santa Maria
Dunn, Judith Louise *secondary school educator*
Torbert, George Kenneth *elementary educator*

Saratoga
Whalen, Margaret Cavanagh *retired secondary school educator*
Wood, Gladys Blanche *retired secondary education educator, journalist*

Seal Beach
Melton, Cheryl Ann *special education educator, small business owner*

Seaside
Livermore, Donald Raymond *elementary education educator, library media specialist, educational consultant*
Wall, Janet E. *assessment and testing professional*

Sepulveda
Davison, Helen Irene *secondary education educator, counselor*

Sherman Oaks
Barron, Tiana Luisa *educator*
O'Neill, Sallie Boyd *education educator, business owner, sculptor*

Simi Valley
Bullock, Donald Wayne *elementary education educator, educational computing consultant*

Solana Beach
Aker, Dianne Lee *academic administrator, consultant*
Zwick, Shelly Crittendon *university official*

Sonoma
Hobart, Billie *education educator, consultant*
Venturini, Donald Joseph *special education educator*

South Lake Tahoe
Grutter, Judith Appley *career counselor*

South Pasadena
Sato, Irving Shigeo *education consultant*

Stanford
Bridges, Edwin Maxwell *education educator*
McClanahan, Clarence Edward *academic administrator*
Raisian, John *public policy institute executive, economist*
Steele, Charles Richard *applied mechanics educator*
Strena, Robert Victor *research laboratory manager*
Strober, Myra Hoffenberg *education educator, consultant*
Yuen, Richard Joseph *university dean*

Stinson Beach
Metz, Mary Seawell *university dean, retired college president*

Stockton
Addie, Harvey Woodward *retired secondary education educator, music director*
Jantzen, J(ohn) Marc *retired education educator*
Minden, R. Doyle *university administrator*
Needler, Martin Cyril *university dean, political science educator*
Peters, Rita *university administrator*

Suisun City
Bishop, Carol Ward *dean*
Kirkorian, Donald George *college official, management consultant*

Sylmar
Lisalda, Sylvia Ann *primary educator*

Tarzana
Brook, Winston Rollins *audio-video design consultant*
Yablun, Ronn *secondary education educator, small business owner*

Tehachapi
Stewart, Susan Kay *school administrator*

Thousand Oaks
Cammalleri, Joseph Anthony *academic administrator, security firm executive, retired air force officer*
Dunkel, Peter Carl *university administrator*
LaGuardia, Ronald Paul *career counselor, educator*
Tennant, Mary Jo *secondary education educator*

Torrance
McNamara, Brenda Norma *secondary education educator*

Tracy
Moore, Joseph Mark *secondary education educator*
Penner-Sekera, Cynthia Dawn *elementary education educator*

Trinidad
Lundeen, Samuel Edward *elementary education educator*
Wiebe, John Clement *school director*

Tustin
Greene, Wendy Segal *special education educator*

Twentynine Palms
Clemente, Patrocinio Ablola *psychology educator*

Upland
Hung, Jenny *development specialist*

Valencia
Hugo, Joan Lyall *academic administrator, art critic, curator*
Looney, Claudia Arlene *academic administrator*

Vallejo
Bonham, Charlie Leonard *college official*
Goldstone, Stephen A. *superintendent*
Pelkey, Teena Ferris *elementary education educator, consultant*

Van Nuys
Altshiller, Arthur Leonard *secondary education educator*
Burri, Glenn Alan *middle school educator*
Gilbert, Terence Neil *education educator, musician*
Meier, Robert John *secondary education educator*

Ventura
Zuber, Norma Keen *career counselor, educator*

Villa Park
Writer, Sharon Lisle *secondary education educator*

Vista
Castle, Alfred *administrator*
Miller-Tiedeman, Anna Louise *counselor, writer*
Palmer, William Earl *private school educator*

Walnut Creek
Carver, Dorothy Lee Eskew (Mrs. John James Carver) *retired secondary education educator*

Weed
Edwards, Edith Louise *principal*

West Covina
Adler, Laurel Ann *educational administrator, consultant*
Carter-Goldston, Catherine Angotti *principal*

West Hills
Oborn, Kathleen Marie *college administrator, educator*

West Hollywood
Lewis, Ian David *special education educator*

Westlake Village
Steadman, Lydia Duff *elementary school educator, symphony violinist*

Westminster
Hill, Debra Lee *school counselor, educator*

Whittier
Ashworth, Wayne Oliver *school system administrator*
De Lorca, Luis E. *educational administrator, educator, speaker*
Drake, E Maylon *academic administrator*
Tunison, Elizabeth Lamb *education educator*
Zanetta, Joseph Michael *university administrator, lawyer*

Woodland Hills
Swaim, Ruth Carolyn *secondary education educator*
Tapper, Lance Howard *secondary education educator*

Yorba Linda
Lunde, Dolores Benitez *retired secondary education educator*

Yuba City
Dalpino, Ida Jane *secondary education educator*
Hendrix, Louise Butts *retired educator, author*
Higdon, Bernice Cowan *retired elementary education educator*

Yucaipa
Gomez, Louis Salazar *college president*
Reed, Patricia Colleen *adult education educator*

COLORADO

Alamosa
Rickey, June Evelyn Million *retired educator*
Westerman, Katy Dorothea *former vocational education administrator*

Arvada
Bert, Carol Lois *educational assistant*

Aurora
Fair, Mary Louise *retired elementary school educator*
Hartenbach, David Lawrence *school system administrator*
Jones, Sandra Lou *college program director*
Killian, C(harles) Rodney *school administrator, researcher*
Shearer, Carolyn Juanita *secondary education educator*
Verniero, Joan Evans *special education educator*
Walker, Joyce Marie *secondary school educator*

Boulder
Albino, Judith E. N. *university president*
Bernucci, Leopoldo Marcos *educator*
Carroll, Stephen Graham *university publications administrator, writer*
Healy, James Bruce *cooking school administrator, writer*
Kneebone, Alice Jeannette *child care coordinator*
Malmgren, Dick *school principal, teacher*
Maresh, Nancy Mae *educational entrepreneur*
Park, Roderic Bruce *university chancellor*
Saltzman, Joanne Ellen *cooking school administrator*
Tonso, Cheryl Jackson *retired secondary education educator*
Vigil, Daniel Agustin *academic administrator*
Weathermon, Sidney Earl *elementary school educator*
Williams, Pamela R. *secondary school administrator*

Broomfield
Rodriguez, Linda Takahashi *secondary education educator*

Colorado Springs
Adams, Bernard Schroder *retired college president*
Grady, Dolores Anne *academic administrator, educator, consultant*
Graf, Bob Lee *secondary education educator*
Guy, Mildred Dorothy *retired secondary school educator*
Hodgson, Steven Scott *educational administrator*
Paris, Edward Marvin *education administrator*
Peterson, Glenn Viggo *industrial arts educator*
Shade, Linda Bunnell *academic administrator*
Wilcox, Rhoda Davis *elementary education educator*

Deer Trail
Malson, Verna Lee *special education educator*

Denver
Antonoff, Steven Ross *educational consultant, author*
Bautista, Michael Phillip *school system administrator*
Clark, Drew *secondary education educator, state legislator*
Craig, Lexie Ferrell *career development specialist, career guidance counselor, educator*
Dennis, Evie *retired school system administrator*
DePew, Marie Kathryn *retired secondary educator*
Fevurly, Keith Robert *educational administrator*
Fulkerson, William Measey, Jr. *college president*
Goodchild, Lester Francis *higher education educator*
Hill-Jones, Kathleen Lois *performing art school executive*
Judson, Cheryl Jean *college administrator, management consultant*
Kao, Fa-Ten *education researcher*
Loeup, Kong *counselor*
Lofthouse, Russ Wilbert *school administrator*
Mayer, Adolph *university official*
McCall, Laura *education educator, writer*
Mirich, David Gage *secondary education language educator*
Ritchie, Daniel Lee *university administrator*
Sager, Nancy Wynne *special education consultant*
Scheuneman, Dana Lynn *school counselor*
Tucker, James Raymond *elementary educator*
Whiteaker, Ruth Catherine *retired secondary education educator, counselor*
Wright, Carole Dean *reading specialist*

Durango
Jones, Joel Mackey *college president*

Edgewater
Haynes, Emily Louise *secondary school educator*

Englewood
Leo, Mary Gaye *school administrator*
Ross, Kerry Lynn *secondary education educator*
Shields, Marlene Sue *elementary school educator*

Fort Collins
Cook, Dierdre Ruth Goorman *school administrator, secondary education educator*
Fotsch, Dan Robert *elementary education educator*
Green, Ronnie David *education educator*
Jaros, Dean *university official*
Revier, Charles Franklin *academic administrator, economics educator*
Rewerts, Milan Alvin *university administrator*
Treaster, Melba Mauck *educational consultant*
Yates, Albert Carl *university administrator, chemistry educator*

Fort Morgan
Bond, Richard Randolph *college administrator, legislator*

Frisco
Gibson, Elisabeth Jane *principal*

Golden
Arden, Wayne Richard *automotive technology educator, consultant, systems analyst*
Klug, John Joseph *secondary education educator, director of dramatics*
Lyons, Cherie Ann *educational administrator, author*
Tomczyk, Theodore Clayton *secondary education educator*

Grand Junction
Bergen, Virginia Louise *principal, language arts educator*
Gray, Ronald Frederick *college administrator, engineer*
Moberly, Linden Emery *educational adminstrator*

Greeley
Drake, Lucius Charles, Jr. *school administrator, university consultant*
Eldridge, Roger Gilbert, Jr. *education educator*
Lujan, Herman D. *university president*
Meis, Jeanette Kay *elementary educator*
Murry, Francie Roberta *special education educator*
Townsend, Susan Louise *elementary school administrator*

Highlands Ranch
Hager, Shirley Ann *school counselor*

Johnstown
Norby-Loud, Marie Barbara *secondary education educator*

Keystone
Craig, Robert Wallace *educational and policy center administrator*

Lakewood
Addison, John Robert *counselor*
Forrest, Kenton Harvey *middle school educator, historian*
Frank, Margot Gilbert *middle school educator, investor, philanthropist*

Littleton
Anderson, Judith Anne *academic administrator*
Bush, Stanley Giltner *secondary education educator*
Lening, Janice Allen *physical education educator*
Rothenberg, Harvey David *educational administrator*

Montrose
McDonald, Harry Alonzo, Jr. *school counselor*

Northglenn
Shaeffer, Thelma Jean *primary school educator*

Parker
Nelson, Paula Morrison Bronson *educator*

Pueblo
Jacobsen, Pamela *special education director, consultant, counselor*
Shirley, Robert Clark *university president, strategic planning consultant, educator*
Tenorio, Victor *community college official, researcher*
Vest, Rosemarie Lynn Torres *secondary educator*
Woods, Alma Jean *elementary educator*

Sheridan
Bosworth, Bruce Leighton *school administrator, educator, consultant*

Sterling
Milander, Henry Martin *community college president*

Trinidad
Amari, Kathryn Jane *elementary education educator*
Rocha, Pedro, Jr. *academic administrator*

Westminster
Eaves, Stephen Douglas *vocational administrator, educator*
La Plante, Patricia Ann *counselor, radio broadcaster*
Reed, John Howard *school administrator*

DISTRICT OF COLUMBIA

Washington
Maxwell, David E. *academic administrator, educator*

GEORGIA

Morrow
Becker, Robert Dean *academic administrator, educator, author, consultant*

HAWAII

Ewa Beach
Pedesky, Geraldine Golick *school administrator*

Hilo
Best, Mary Lani *program coordinator*
Perrin, Kenneth Lynn *university chancellor*

Honolulu
Bess, Henry David *dean*
Blumhardt, Jon Howard *college administrator*
Hatzenbeler, Michael Joseph *academic director*
Hee, Vivian Sanae Mitsuda *principal*
Inaba, Lawrence Akio *educational director*
Jackson, Miles Merrill *university dean*
Karelitz, Raymond *secondary school educator and writer*
Keith, Kent Marsteller *academic administrator, corporate executive, government official, lawyer*
Liu, Robert Shing-Hei *chemistry educator, researcher*
Masagatani, Ernesta *school superintendent*
McMath, Carroll Barton, Jr. *past college administrator, retired Army officer*
Meyer, Robert Allen *human resource management educator*
Miyahira, Sarah Diane *college dean, psychologist, educator*
Pacific, Joseph Nicholas, Jr. *educator*
Pickens, Alexander Legrand *education educator*
Ramler, Siegfried *school administrator*
Rogers, Barbara A. *secondary education educator*
Scronce, Ronald Guy *academic counselor*
Smith, David Alan *counseling administrator, writer*
Tune, Suelyn Ching *secondary education educator*
White, Geoffrey Miles *cultural studies program director*
Wilbur, Leslie Eugene *education educator*

Kaneohe
Ko, Seung Kyun *educator, consultant*
Masters, Elaine *educator, writer*

Pahoa
Rodgers, Marilyn Carol *special education educator*

Pearl City
Uyeno, Lani Akemi *education educator*

Waipahu
Stevens, Muriel Kauimaeole Lee *elementary educator*

IDAHO

Blackfoot
Patton, Anne Jewell *elementary school counselor*

Boise
Andrus, Cecil Dale *academic administrator*
Cook, Sharon Evonne *university official*
Ellis-Vant, Karen McGee *special education educator, consultant*
Greear, Michael Allyn *employment counselor and consultant*
Griffin, Gloria Jean *elementary school educator*
Griffin, Sylvia Gail *reading specialist*
Jones, Daryl Emrys *university administrator, English educator*
Kaupins, Gundars Egons *education educator*
Maloof, Giles Wilson *academic administrator, educator, author*
Pletcher, Peggy Jo *program director*
Ruch, Charles P. *university official*
Slone, Ronald Rich *academic consultant*
Steinfort, James Richard *university program director*
Thomas, Janet Verline *counselor*
Woodard, Larry L. *college official*
Young, Katherine Ann *education educator*

Caldwell
Hendren, Robert Lee, Jr. *academic administrator*

Coeur D Alene
Dunnigan, Mary Ann *former educational administrator*
Kotnour, Mary Margaret *elementary physical education educator*

Idaho Falls
Woodruff, Shirley *middle school educator*

Lewiston
Duley, Charlotte Dudley *vocational counselor*

Mackay
Hauck, Joann Rae *secondary education educator*

Mc Call
Evans, Darrell J. *secondary education educator*

Meridian
Angell, Karla Michelle *school counselor*
Babcock, Dale Arlan *school psychologist, counselor*

Middleton
Brown, Ilene De Lois *special education educator*

Moscow
Zinser, Elisabeth Ann *university president*

Nampa
Riley, John Eckel *retired academic administrator*

Pocatello
Bowen, Richard Lee *academic administrator, political science educator*

Post Falls
Ketchum, Robert George *college administrator*

Rexburg
Hart, Eldon Charles *educator*

Twin Falls
Anderson, Marilyn Nelle *elementary educator, librarian, counselor*

Wallace
Paroni, Genevieve Marie Swick *retired secondary education educator*

Wendell
Hall, Brenda Denise *preschool special education educator*

ILLINOIS

Chicago
Watkins, William Henry *education educator*

Decatur
McCray, Curtis Lee *university president*

IOWA

Le Mars
Balch, Glenn McClain, Jr. *academic administrator, minister, author*

KANSAS

Shawnee Mission
Kaplan, Marjorie Ann Pashkow *school district administrator*

KENTUCKY

Louisville
Carden, Joy Cabbage *educational consultant*

MARYLAND

Baltimore
Moszkowski, Lena Iggers *secondary school educator*

MINNESOTA

Northfield
Kohl, Herbert Ralph *education educator*

MONTANA

Antelope
Olson, Betty-Jean *elementary education educator*

Bigfork
Keller, Barbara Lynn *special education educator*

Billings
Abbott, Patti Marie *middle school educator*
Bryngelson, Jim *educational administrator*
Heiny, Robert Wayne *special education educator*
May, Michael Wayne *technical school executive*
Nordlund, Patricia Jean *school system administrator*
Surwill, Benedict Joseph, Jr. *college dean, educator*

Bozeman
Carparelli, Peter Louis *school system administrator*
Dawson, Robert Charles *educational and health care consultant*
Malone, Michael Peter *academic administrator, historian*
Pagenkopf, Andrea LeSuer *university official*

Browning
Williams, Dorothy Rhonda *gifted education consultant and teacher*

Chester
Rasmussen, Renee M. *secondary education educator*

Gallatin Gateway
Monaco, Paul *academic administrator, educator, artist, writer*

Great Falls
Johnson, Pamela Kay *counselor, educator, farmer*

Havre
Daehling, William A. *academic administrator*
Lanier, William Joseph *college program director*

Helena
Argenbright, Ed Frank *school administrator*
Noonan, Edward James *student activity director*

Kalispell
Ormiston, Patricia Jane *elementary education educator*

Missoula
Fisher, William Henry *education educator*
Kindrick, Robert LeRoy *academic administrator, dean, English educator*
Patton, Charlie C. *biologist*

Victor
Stewart, JoAnne *secondary school educator*

NEVADA

Hawthorne
Graham, Lois Charlotte *retired educator*

Incline Village
Hollis, Susan Tower *college dean*

Las Vegas
Flemming, Naomi Verneta *elementary school educator*
Freeman, Herbert James *educational administrator*

Garn, Susan Lynn *secondary computer graphics educator*
Gaspar, Anna Louise *retired elementary school teacher, consultant*
Grubaugh, Steven Jack *education educator*
Hair, Kittie Ellen *secondary educator*
Holmes, Barbara Ann Krajkoski *secondary education educator*
Iorio, John Emil *retired education educator*
Jerrytone, Samuel Joseph *trade school executive*
McDonald, Malcolm Gideon *education educator*
Mirkovich, Thomas Reid *business information educator*
Obenhaus, Kathy Ann *special education educator*
Sestini, Virgil Andrew *secondary education educator*
Simon, Matthew James *dean, educator, educational facilities planner*
Zehm, Stanley James *education educator*

North Las Vegas
Williams, Mary Irene *college administrator*

Reno
Clarke, Janice Cessna *principal*
Crowley, Joseph Neil *academic administrator*
Davies, Robert Oakley *university program director*
Graham, Margaret Katherine *secondary school educator*
Lord, Jacklynn Jean *student services representative*
McKay, Alice Vitalich *school system administrator*
Richardson, James Troy *sociology educator, consultant*

Sun Valley
Olbrantz, Patricia *school counselor*

Zephyr Cove
Bisbee, Diane Parks *guidance counselor*

NEW MEXICO

Albuquerque
Abrams, Helayne Joan *preschool educator*
Bass, Martha Postlethwaite *high school principal*
Benson, Sharon Stovall *primary school educator*
Caplan, Edwin Harvey *university dean, accounting educator*
Drummond, Harold Dean *education educator*
Gutierrez, Mary Cecilia *vocational school counselor*
Howard, Jane Osburn *educator*
Kozojet, Christine Hoffman *university official*
Lattman, Laurence Harold *retired academic administrator*
May, Gerald William *university administrator, educator, civil engineering consultant*
McCutcheon, Randall James *educator*
Mc Reynolds, Mary Barbara *retired secondary school educator, community volunteer*
Peniston, Lorraine Carol *special education educator, therapeutic recreation specialist*
Reed, Alan Barry *university executive, consultant, investor*
Sanders, Roberta Mae *secondary educator*
Van Why, Rebecca Rivera *guidance counselor*
Weber, Robert J. *education educator, law educator*

Artesia
Sarwar, Barbara Duce *school system administrator*

Clovis
Ingram, Peggy Joyce *secondary education educator*

Farmington
Matthews, Marilyn Ann *college development director*

Gallup
Lindenmeyer, Mary Kathryn *secondary education educator*
Zongolowicz, Helen Michaeline *education and psychology educator*

Grants
Marquez, Martina Zenaida *elementary education educator*

Hobbs
Stanley, Sheryl Lynn *college administrator*

Las Cruces
Elliott, Richard L. *school administrator*
Giordano, Gerard Raymond *special education educator, author*
Morehart, Thomas Berton *academic administrator*
Tombes, Averett Snead *academic administrator*
Wang, Joseph *education educator, scientist*

Los Alamos
Engel, Emily Flachmeier *school administrator*

Los Lunas
Rain, Rhonda L. *counselor, educator*

Portales
Gee, Donna Beth *elementary education educator*

Roswell
Dyess, Edwin Earl *academic administrator*
Roark, Denis Darel *college dean*

Ruidoso
Coe, Elizabeth Ann *elementary education educator*
LaCounte, Cheryl DeWerff *academic director, educator*

Santa Fe
Bowdich, Cary Ann *college administrator*
Harcourt, Robert Neff *educational administrator, journalist*
Sandifer, Sandra Ann *moving image educator*
Wise, Janet Ann *college official*

Santa Teresa
Clement, Shirley George *educational services executive*

Socorro
Lopez, Daniel Heraldo *academic administrator*

Univ Of New Mexico
Hull, McAllister Hobart, Jr. *retired university administrator*

Zuni
Smith, Cindy Jean *secondary education educator, coordinator*

NORTH CAROLINA

Durham
Trask, Tallman Harlow, III *university administrator*

OREGON

Ashland
Brown, James Chandler *college administrator*
Strauman, Bruce Edwin *secondary school educator*

Beaverton
Chaney, Victor Harvey *secondary education educator, historical dramatist*
Duncan, Richard Fredrick, Jr. *secondary education educator, travel consultant*
Gretzinger, Wilda Virginia *educator*
Houseman, Kimberly Lynn *special education educator, counselor*

Cave Junction
Maxcy, Lawrence Stahl *education administrator*

Coos Bay
Teyler, Sharon Marie *secondary educator*

Coquille
de Sá e Silva, Elizabeth Anne *secondary education educator*

Corvallis
Bruce, Robert Kirk *college administrator*
Byrne, John Vincent *academic administrator*
Harding, Anna Kristine *education educator*
Thielges, Bart Arthur *university adminstrator*
Verts, Lita Jeanne *university administrator*

Cottage Grove
Miller, Joanne Louise *middle school educator*

Eugene
Cox, Joseph William *academic administrator*
Hosticka, Carl Joseph *academic administrator, educator, legislator*
Katz, Steven Joseph *school counselor*
Lindholm, Richard Theodore *educator*
Matthews, Esther Elizabeth *education educator, consultant*
McDonald, Penny S(ue) *educational administrator*
Reinmuth, James E. *college dean*
Waggoner, David Carl *college administrator*
Weatherhead, Andrew Kingsley *educator*
White, David Olds *education researcher*
Wood, Daniel B. *educational consultant*

Forest Grove
Hosley, Edward Howard *career development organization executive*
Singleton, Francis Seth *dean*
Weisman, Jeb *university administrator*

Gaston
Kohn, Art *education educator*

Hood River
Mitchell, Lynn Lee *secondary education educator*

Independence
Layton, William Frederick, Jr. *school counselor*

Klamath Falls
Porter, Roberta Ann *counselor, educator, school system administrator*
Willhide, Gary L. *educational administrator*

Lake Oswego
Shaff, Beverly Gerard *educational administrator*

Mcminnville
Edwards, Wayne A. *school administrator, religious studies educator*
Howland, Peter McKinnon *academic administrator*
McGillivray, Karen *elementary school educator*

Newberg
Rickey, Jeffrey Barton *academic administrator, consultant*

Portland
Bartlett, Thomas Alva *educational administrator*
Bennett, Charles Leon *vocational and graphic arts educator*
Braun, Stephen Baker *academic administrator*
Edwards, Peter John *secondary education educator, historic preservation consultant, coach*
Frolick, Patricia Mary *retired elementary education educator*
Groff, David Huston *academic administrator, director, educator*
Harris, Michael Hatherly *educational administrator*
Hazel, Joanie Beverly *elementary educator*
Hunter, Richard William *educational director*
Jones, Joe W. *educational research laboratory executive*
Kreinberg, Penelope Pettit *counselor*
McCready, Eric Scott *academic administrator, educator*
Ramaley, Judith Aitken *university president, endocrinologist*
Ricks, Mary Frances *university administrator, anthropologist*
Rosenfeld, Sandra Kaye *elementary school educator*
Tufts, Robert B. *academic administrator*
Ward, James Hubert *dean, social work educator, researcher, consultant*
Wicklund, Lee Arthur *school superintendent*
Wiest, William Marvin *education educator, psychologist*
Wineberg, Howard *research director*

Roseburg
Johnson, Doris Ann *educational administrator*
Plummer, Charles McDonald *retired community college administrator*

Salem
Erekson, Laurie Ida *school administrator*
Hudson, Jerry E. *university president*
Kearns, Homer H. *school system administrator*
Miller, David Foster *academic administrator, educator*

Tillamook
Wood, Hugh Bernard *retired education educator*

Toledo
MacKenroth, Joyce Ellen *secondary school educator*

Waldport
Hockett, Lorna Dee *elementary education educator*

Warrenton
Thompson, Linda Lee *educational consultant*

TEXAS

Austin
Brewer, Thomas Bowman *retired university president*

McAllen
Cowart, Bill F(rank) *academic administrator*

UTAH

American Fork
Rocque, Rebecca Homedew *mathematics educator*
Swenson, Shirley Ruth *elementary education educator*

Cedar City
Sherratt, Gerald Robert *college president*
Thompson, Georgia Beth *university department administrator*

Kaysville
Stevens, Linda Tollestrup *school counselor*

Kearns
De Wreede, Clarice Evans *retired special education educator*

Layton
Daniels, Blake H. *education counselor*

Logan
Allen, Thomas Lavern *university development administrator*
Brown, Rodney Jay *dean, consultant*
Gay, Charles W., Jr. *academic administrator*
Harris, April Lee (April Lee Hill) *higher education public relations professional*
Lyons, Janet Peplow *career advisor*
Price, Susan Kay Lind *employment training organization administrator*
Whitaker, Morris Duane *university administrator*

Ogden
Alexander, Robb Smith, Jr. *academic program director*
Grant, Sandra Kay *adult education educator*
McCulloch, Terri *secondary school educator*
Thompson, Paul Harold *university president*

Paradise
Dobson, L. Kristine *career counselor, counselor educator*

Provo
Allred, Ruel Acord *education educator*
Lee, Rex E. *university president, lawyer*
Randall, Earl Vance *educational leadership educator, consultant*
Taylor, Janice LaRue *elementary education educator*
Whatcott, Marsha Rasmussen *elementary educator*

Salt Lake City
Bennion, John Warren *urban education educator*
Burton, Loren G. *school system administrator*
Elmquist, Donna Lois *educator, consultant, writer, researcher*
Fink, Kristin Danielson *secondary education educator*
Makowski, Heidi Michelle *academic program director*
Morris, Sylvia Marie *university official*
Newell, L. Jackson *education educator*
Peterson, Chase N. *university president*
Pickering, AvaJane *specialized education facility executive*
Simmons, Lynda Merrill Mills *educational administrator*
Smith, Arthur Kittredge, Jr. *university official, political science educator*
Whitaker, Judy Erickson *career counselor*

Sandy
Sabey, J(ohn) Wayne *academic administrator, consultant*
Volpe, Ellen Marie *middle school educator*

VIRGINIA

Arlington
Hill, Donald Wain *education accreditation commission executive*

WASHINGTON

Auburn
Burton, Michael Webster *secondary education educator*

Bellevue
Pastore, Michael Anthony *college administrator*

Bellingham
Masland, Lynne S. *university official*
May, Scott C. *special education educator*
Pierce, George Adams *university administrator, educator*

Bothell
Banks, Cherry Ann McGee *education educator*

Buckley
Wickizer, Cindy Louise *elementary school educator*

Centralia
Kirk, Henry Port *academic administrator*

Cheney
Zimmerman, Niel Thomas *university administrator*

Chimacum
Hollenbeck, Dorothy Rose *special education educator*

Clarkston
Johnson, Maryann Elaine *educational administrator*

Clinton
Hubbard, Kendall Bruce *educational administrator*

East Wenatchee
Nanto, Roxanna Lynn *career planning administrator, consultant*

Edmonds
Carlstrom, R. William *retired special education educator*

Ellensburg
Jones, Gail Kathleen *educational administrator*
Nelson, Ivory Vance *university president*

Everett
Thunder, Spencer K *retired elementary school principal*

Federal Way
Usitalo, Irene Joann *vocational school educator, small business owner*

Hansville
Blalock, Ann Bonar *special policy analyst, evaluation researcher*

Kennewick
Knight, Janet Ann *elementary education educator*
Sauer, Henry Jack *elementary school educator, small business owner*

Kent
Dunayeva, Dina Gavriilovna *cross-cultural training program administrator*

Kirkland
Davis, Dennis Albert *college president*

Lacey
Auer, Benedict LeRoy *education educator, college official, priest*
Kuniyasu, Keith Kazumi *secondary education educator*

Longview
Hutchins, Earl Leroy *retired school system administrator*

Mill Creek
Larson, Mary Bea *elementary education educator*

Mount Vernon
Cline, Pauline M. *educational administrator*

Nine Mile Falls
Payne, Arlie Jean *parent education administrator*

Olympia
Coontz, Stephanie Jean *history and family studies educator, author*
Jervis, Jane Lise *academic administrator, science historian*
Walkup, Hugh Robert *education adminstrator*

Port Angeles
Kilmer, Joseph Charles *secondary school educator*
Ross, Robert King *retired educator*

Prosser
Deffenbaugh, Kay Anne *secondary education art educator*

Pullman
Lewis, Norman G. *academic administrator, researcher, consultant*
Smith, Robert Victor *university administrator*
Smith, Samuel Howard *university president, plant pathologist*

Renton
Tajon, Encarnacion Fontecha (Connie Tajon) *retired educator, association executive*

Richland
Haler, Lawrence Eugene *technology educator, councilman*

Seattle
Banks, James Albert *educational research director, educator*
Bassett, Edward Powers *university official*
Benally, Courage Clah *elementary education educator*
Brown, Lillie McFall *elementary school principal*
Cottingham, Mary Patricia *vocational rehabilitation counselor*
Counsell, Ann Berner *academic administrator*
Debro, Julius *university dean, sociology educator*

Dobel, J. Patrick *graduate studies director, educator*
Eliason, Leslie Carol *comparative public policy educator*
Fialkow, Philip Jack *academic administrator, medical educator*
Hampton, Shelley Lynn *hearing impaired educator*
Nellams, Jane Harris *communications director, journalist*
Olguin, Victor Hugo *school counselor, educator*
Omenn, Gilbert Stanley *university dean, physician*
Pizzorno, Joseph Egidio, Jr. *college president*
Ransmeier, Denis Sirera *university administrator*
Reevis, Maureen Patricia *academic adminstrator*
Schulte, Henry Gustave *college administrator*
Stringer, William Jeremy *university official*
Terrell, W(illiam) Glenn *university president emeritus*
Trzyna, Thomas Nicholas *college dean*
Tschernisch, Sergei P. *academic administrator*

Spokane
Baker, Danial Edwin *director, consultant, pharmacy educator*
Becker, Eleen Marie *secondary education educator*
Gray, William Hiram *university dean*
Sladich, Harry Hamill *university administrator*
Sweeney, William James *special education educator*
Waters, J. Kevin *university administrator, educator*
Weitz, Sue Dee *academic administrator*
Williams, Randy Lee *special education educator*

Springdale
Morrell, June Elizabeth *elementary educator*

Sunnyside
Aiken, Dorothy Louise *secondary education educator*
Charvet, Kathy Delaine *counselor, psychologist*

Tacoma
Jones, Stanley Belmont *counselor*
King, Gundar Julian *retired university dean*
Maloney, Patsy Loretta *university official, nursing educator*
Minnerly, Robert Ward *headmaster*
Noble-Perry, Deborah Ashley *school counselor, horse trainer*
Olson, David Mark *college dean, physical education educator*
Reisberg, Leon Elton *education educator*

Toppenish
Ross, Kathleen Anne *college president*

Vancouver
Ferguson, Larry Emmett *educational administrator*
Fulton, Richard Delbert *dean*
Mangino, Kristin Mikalson *secondary education educator*
McGee, Linda Jeanne Danner *school counselor*

Walla Walla
Cronin, Thomas Edward *academic administrator*
Macduff, Nancy *adult education educator*

Yakima
Corpron, Karen Kae *childhood education specialist*
Eyer, Bruce Jarrett *school district administrator*

WISCONSIN

Platteville
Hundley, Patrick David *college program administrator*

WYOMING

Casper
Fedje, Laurie Anne *special education educator*
Wilkes, Shar (Joan Charlene Wilkes) *elementary education educator*

Centennial
Houston, Jane Hunt *retired educator*

Cheyenne
Jeffrey, Ronald James *youth director, educator*
Reynolds, Glenda Carol *elementary school educator*
Rice, Wallace William *secondary education educator*
Weigner, Brent James *secondary education educator*

Cody
Fees, Nancy Fardelius *special education educator*

Cowley
Thorne, Linda Marie *elementary education educator*

Ethete
McCann, Barbara Ann *school director*

Gillette
Brown, Toni Cyd *secondary education educator*
Buus, Linda Lee Pannetier *secondary education educator*
Thoms, Bonnie Anne *elementary school educator*

Lander
van Barselaar, Leslie Frances *private school director*

Laramie
Darnall, Roberta Morrow *academic administrator*
Forster, Bruce Alexander *dean*
Marston, Richard Alan *geography educator, consultant*
Simpson, Peter Kooi *university official*

Powell
Kitchen, Mark Scott *college administrator, college dean*

Rock Springs
Bonham, J. Lee *special education educator, consultant*
deLeur, Robbie Lynn *university program director*
Kathka, David Arlin *director educational services*

Sheridan
Schatz, Wayne Ardale *middle school educator*

Wheatland
Smith, Freda L. *retired elementary education educator*

CANADA

ALBERTA

Calgary
Samuels, Barbara Ann *university administrator, planner, educator, information architect*

Camrose
Schwabe, Marcus Christopher *college administrator*

Edmonton
Horowitz, Myer *retired university president, education educator*
Strembitsky, Michael Alexander *school administrator*

Grande Prairie
Harper, Donald Calvin *dean*

Lethbridge
Tennant, Howard Edward *academic administrator*

BRITISH COLUMBIA

Vancouver
Griffith, William Samuel *adult education educator*
Webber, William Alexander *university administrator, physician*

SASKATCHEWAN

Saskatoon
Stewart, John Wray Black *college dean*

ADDRESS UNPUBLISHED

Anderson, Carol Ruth *secondary school educator*
Anderson, Iris Anita *retired secondary education educator*
Asperin, Milagros R. *career counselor, educator, journalist*
Bachtel, Ann Elizabeth *educational consultant*
Baker, C. B. *retired day care director, organizer, communicator*
Baldwin, C. Andrew, Jr. *retired science educator*
Barville, Rebecca Penelope *elementary school educator*
Bassist, Donald Herbert *academic administrator*
Bennett, Brenda G. *secondary school counselor, mathematics educator*
Beyersdorf, Marguerite Mulloy *elementary education educator*
Birman, Linda Lee *elementary education educator*
Bishop, Margaret *retired educator, writer*
Black, Barbara Crowder *educational consultant*
Blummer, Kathleen Ann *counselor*
Brunson, Kathleen Kay *elementary educator*
Carrell, Heather Demaris *educational consultant*
Cederberg, Dolores Katherine *elementary education educator, school administrator*
Chook, Edward Kongyen *academic administrator, disaster medicine educator*
Christensen, Caroline *vocational educator*
Conover, Mona Lee *retired adult education educator*
Crump, Rene *school counselor*
Darke, Charles Bruce *academic administrator, dentist*
De Long, Katharine *retired secondary education educator*
Dey, Carol Ruth *secondary education educator*
DiSalle, Michael Danny *secondary education educator*
Eckardt, Charles Lincoln *university official, accountant*
Edwards, Ardis Lavonne Quam *retired elementary education educator*
Evans, Neil *retired secondary school science educator*
Frost, Everett Lloyd *academic administrator*
Gamble, Carol Irene Davis *secondary education educator*
Garza, Deborah Jane *educational administrator*
Gaston, Harrison L. *guidance counselor, consultant, therapist*
Giblett, Phylis Lee Walz *middle school educator*
Goffe, Esther *elementary school educator*
Graham, Denis David *retired curriculum coordinator*
Gray, Richard Moss *retired college president*
Gronli, John Victor *college administrator, minister*
Guilbert, Irene West *educational consultant*
Hale, Violet Elaine *director food service, master graphoanalyst*
Hansen, Anne Moloney *parent educator*
Hansen, Nancy C. Urdahl *special education educator*
Heaton, Jean *early childhood educator*
Hensley, Dorothy Sue *elementary educator*
Hoffman, Judy Greenblatt *preschool director*
Huff, Janet House *special education educator*
Hughes, Eugene Morgan *university president*
Jimmink, Glenda Lee *retired elementary school educator*
Johnson, Sylvia Sue *university administrator, educator*
Johnson, Warren Lyle *educator*
Keiper, Marilyn Morrison *elementary education educator*
Kirk, Rea Helene (Rea Helene Glazer) *school administrator, educator*
Kolb, Dorothy Gong *elementary education educator*
Kormondy, Edward John *university official, biology educator*
Lacey, Ronald Edward *minority outreach advisor*
Ledbury, Diana Gretchen *adult education educator*
Legington, Gloria R. *middle school educator*
Lindegren, Jack Kenneth *elementary and secondary education educator*
Lockart, Barbetta *counselor, jeweler, artwear designer, artist*
Lundgren, Leonard, III *retired secondary education educator*
Lynch, Linda Lou *reading and language arts specialist/educator*
Maclise, James Raymond *secondary education educator*
Mahaffey, Marcia Jeanne Hixson *secondary school administrator*
Maltin, Freda *retired university administrator*
Matera, Frances Lorine *elementary educator*
McAdams, Charles Michael *academic administrator*
McLaughlin, Constance Nethken *science educator*
Meskin, Estelle Rose *college/vocational counselor, educational consultant*
Meyer, Robert Lee *secondary education educator*
Milanovich, Norma JoAnne *occupational educator, training company executive*
Miller, Richard Franklin *educational consultant, researcher*
Miller, Susan Wise *career counselor, consultant*
Moore, Bonnie Lee *secondary school educator*
Morita, Toshiyasu *technical institute administrator*
Mounds, Leona Mae Reed *educational administrator*
Munroe, Mary Hills *preschool/daycare operator*
Newman, Pamela Ann *secondary education educator*
Nichols, Judith Ellen *academic administrator*
O'Driscoll, Marilyn Lutz *kindergarten educator*
Oldham, Elaine Dorothea *retired secondary education educator*
Palsma, Mary J(acobson) *secondary education educator*
Perry, Joyce Fitzwilliam *secondary school educator*
Potts, Sandra D. *elementary education educator*
Richardson, Elsie Helen *retired elementary educator*
Richardson, Judy McEwen *educational consultant, cartoonist*
Rife, Mary Lou *school counselor*
Riggs, Jacki Pieracci *administrator, special education educator*
Ritchie, Anne *educational administrator*
Rohrer, Jane Carolyn *gifted education specialist, administrator, consultant*
Roletta, Richard Peter *education administrator*
Ross, Mary Beth *academic administrator*
Rosvall, Gene Howard *elementary education educator*
Roux, Ann Taylor *gifted/talented education educator*
Rutland, Henry Lee *educational administrator, consultant*
Sampedro, Yvette Yrma *secondary education educator*
Sanchez, Gilbert *retired university president, microbiologist, researcher*
Scholl, Allan Henry *retired school system administrator, education consultant*
Sciaroni, Linda Gillingham *middle school educator*
Shagam, Marvin Hückel-Berri *private school educator*
Shin, Edward Sung-Shik *bilingual education educator*
Silvius, Donald Joe *educational consultant*
Snow, W. Sterling *secondary education educator, sports coach*
Spingola, Jeannie Saundra *college, special education and adult educator*
Stacy, Bill Wayne *college president*
Steinberg, Joan Emily *retired middle school educator*
Steinhauser, Janice Maureen *university administrator, artist*
Tarbi, William Rheinlander *secondary education educator, curriculum consultant, educational technology researcher*
Thomas, Ethel Colvin Nichols (Mrs. Lewis Victor Thomas) *counselor, educator*
Tonjes, Marian Jeannette Benton *education educator*
Trujillo, Lucy Ann *elementary education counselor*
Von Flotow, Andreas Hubertus *university educator, consultant*
Walker, Rubylee France *counselor*
Walsh, Dolores Ann Gonczo *special education educator*
Wertz, Gary Randall *secondary education educator, counselor*
Wiebelhaus, Pamela Sue *school administrator, educator*
Wilson, Robin Scott *university president, writer*
Young, Joyce Henry *adult education educator, consultant*
Young, Margaret Chong *elementary education educator*
Young, Virgil M. *education educator*
Zeilinger, Elna Rae *tutor, educator*

ENGINEERING

UNITED STATES

ALASKA

Anchorage
Jumao-as, Alex Baronda *engineer*
Leman, Loren Dwight *civil engineer*
Pressley, James Ray *electrical engineer*
Riendl, Paul Alex *electrical engineer*
Thomas, Howard Paul *civil engineer, consultant*
Watts, Michael Arthur *materials engineer*

Fairbanks
Bennett, Fred Lawrence *engineering educator*
Ogunsola, Olayinka I. *mineral, fuel and energy engineering educator*
Sengupta, Mritunjoy *mining engineer, educator*

Juneau
Hansen, Ronald Gregory *civil engineer*

Ketchikan
Harney, William John, Jr. *electronics engineer*

ARIZONA

Chandler
Gadberry, Michael Dale *electrical engineer*
Heckman, James Kent *metallurgical engineer*
Higgs, Timothy Gerald *environmental engineer*
Kreutel, Randall William, Jr. *electrical engineer*
Meieran, Eugene Stuart *material scientist*

Flagstaff
Damon, James Christian *communications engineer*

Fort Huachuca
Weeks, Robert Lee *electronic engineer, test facility administrator*

Fredonia
Vredenburgh, Mark De *chemical engineer*

Gilbert
Pemberton, Randall Grant *industrial engineer*

Glendale
Landrum, Larry James *computer engineer*
Lehman, Robert George *electrical engineer*

Litchfield Park
Heermans, John Michael *electrical, chemical engineer*
Miller, Kenneth Edward *mechanical engineer, consultant*

Mesa
Eldridge, Terrance Foy *avionics engineer*
Sampson, William Paul *process engineer, researcher*
Scaven, Gregory Joseph *chemical engineer*
Scofield, Larry Allan *civil engineer*
Stemple, Alan Douglas *aerospace engineer*
Tidwell, Joseph Paul, Jr. *systems safety engineer*

Nogales
Suozzi, Mary-Ann *engineering executive*

Paradise Valley
Russell, Paul Edgar *electrical engineering educator*
Swan, Peter Alfred *systems engineer*

Phoenix
Adams, Richard *electro-mechanical engineer*
Ayraud, Paul Frank *engineer*
Bachus, Benson Floyd *mechanical engineer, consultant*
Blevins, Willard Ahart *electrical engineer*
Brown, John Lafayette, III *civil engineer*
Carver, Darrel R. *computer engineer*
Cazier, Barry James *electrical engineer, software developer*
Chisholm, Tom Shepherd *environmental engineer*
Courtright, Morris *electrical engineer and educator*
Hamilton, Darden Cole *flight test engineer*
Harris, Warren Lynn *development engineer*
Hejhall, Roy Charles *electrical engineer*
Jordan, Raymond Alan *forensic engineer, consultant*
Jorgensen, Gordon David *engineering company executive*
Konkol, Peter Adam *engineer*
Leary, Tim *software microbiologist, electrical engineer*
Lolmaugh, Scott Devere *engineering executive*
McGhay, Jon Davies *engineer*
Myers, Gregory Edwin *aerospace engineer*
Nishioka, Teruo (Ted Nishioka) *electrical engineer*
Puente, Jose Garza *safety engineer*
Sarsam, Mumtaz Bashir *bridge engineer*
Sochacki, Andrzej *mechanical engineer, researcher*
Thomas, Harold William *avionics systems engineer, flight instructor*
Watson, Harold George *engineering executive, mechanical engineer*
Zeilinger, Philip Thomas *aeronautical engineer*

Prescott
Bass, David Jason *manufacturing engineer*
Murray, William Wallace *electrical engineer*

Scottsdale
Bodensieck, Ernest Justus *mechanical engineer*
Clark, Ezekail Louis *chemical engineering consultant*
Cunningham, Larrie John *retired engineering executive, arbitrator*
Diaz, Michael Anthony *electrical engineer, software engineer*
Gilson, Arnold Leslie *engineering executive*
Gookin, Thomas Allen Jaudon *civil engineer*
Kline, Arthur Jonathan *electronics engineer*
Leeland, Steven Brian *electronics engineer*
Miller, Kevin Lane *software engineer/architect, consultant*
Millett, Merlin Lyle *aerospace consultant, educator*
Newman, Marc Alan *electrical engineer*
Ragland, Samuel Connelly *industrial engineer*

Sedona
Silvern, Leonard Charles *retired engineering executive*

Sierra Vista
Plum, Richard Eugene *retired flight engineer*
Ricco, Raymond Joseph, Jr. *computer systems engineer*

Tempe
Culy, Douglas Gale *mechanical engineer*
Kaufman, Irving *retired engineering educator*
Moor, William Chattle *industrial engineering educator*
Ostler, David Val *engineering executive*
Roberts, Peter Christopher Tudor *engineering executive*
Vondrak, Robert Richard *environmental engineer*

Tonopah
Brittingham, James Calvin *nuclear engineer*

Tucson
Armaleh, Sonia Hanna *civil engineer, educator*
Arnell, Walter James William *mechanical engineering educator, consultant*
Battistelli, Joseph John *electronics executive*
Bryan, Gordon Redman, Jr. *nuclear power engineering consultant*
Coates, Wayne Evan *agricultural engineer*
Desai, Chandrakant S. *civil engineering and engineering mechanics educator*
Gilbert, Stephen L. *electrical engineer, chemist*
Gill, Rebecca LaLosh *aerospace engineer*
Gross, Joseph Francis *retired bio-engineering educator*
Heynssens, Julie B. *electrical engineer*
Hunnicutt, Robert William *engineer*
Jones, Roger Clyde *retired electrical engineering educator*

Kececioglu, Dimitri Basil *reliability engineering educator*
Kerwin, William James *electrical engineering educator, consultant*
Kulatilake, Pinnaduwa H.S.W. *mining and geological engineering educator*
Levinson, David W. *engineering educator, consultant*
Lyons, Paul M. *mechanical engineer*
Marefat, Michael M. *electrical and computer engineering educator*
Petersen, Margaret Sara *civil engineering consultant, retired civil engineering educator*
Slack, Donald Carl *agricultural engineer, educator*
Speas, Robert Dixon *aeronautical engineer, aviation company executive*
Szilagyi, Miklos (Nicholas) *electrical and computer engineering educator*
Tellington, Wentworth Jordan *engineer*
Winarski, Daniel James *mechanical engineer, educator*
Wurdinger, Stephanie Rose *software engineer*

CALIFORNIA

Agoura Hills
Hokana, Gregory Howard *engineering executive*

Alameda
Klehs, Henry John Wilhelm *civil engineer*

Alhambra
Moeller, Ronald Scott *mechanical engineer*

Alpine
Roberts, Dwight Loren *management engineering consultant, novelist*

Alta Loma
Bordner, Gregory Wilson *environmental engineer*

Altadena
Edgar, Herman Burton *aerospace engineer, managment and tax consultant*
McConnell, Ross Ferguson *engineering executive*

Anaheim
Acosta, Nelson John *civil engineer*
Bashardoost, Fred *structural engineer*
Hubbard, Charles Ronald *engineering executive*
Jacobs, Henry Stephen *computer engineer*
Kimme, Ernest Godfrey *communications engineer*
Uyehara, Otto Arthur *mechanical engineering educator emeritus, consultant*
Watson, Oliver Lee, III *aerospace engineering manager*

Antioch
Davis, Stanford Evol *civil engineer*
Nelson, Barry Vernon *engineering executive*

Aptos
Herman, James Jerome *electrical engineer, lawyer*

Arcadia
Broderick, Donald Leland *electronics engineer*

Arcata
Chaney, Ronald Claire *environmental engineering educator, consultant*

Atherton
Morel-Seytoux, Hubert Jean *civil engineer, educator*

Auburn
Perilloux, Bruce Edgar *optical engineer*

Avila Beach
Riches, Kenneth William *nuclear regulatory engineer*

Bakersfield
van Dorp, Johan Jacobus *oil company engineer*

Berkeley
Bray, Jonathan Donald *engineering educator, consultant*
Cairns, Elton James *chemical engineering educator*
Chua, Leon O. *electrical engineering and computer science educator*
Desoer, Charles Auguste *electrical engineer*
DiBartolomeo, Dennis *data acquisition and process control engineer*
Fuerstenau, Douglas Winston *mineral engineering educator*
Harris, Guy Hendrickson *chemical research engineer*
Hsu, Chieh Su *applied mechanics engineering educator, researcher*
Kuh, Ernest Shiu-Jen *electrical engineering educator*
Lewis, Edwin Reynolds *biomedical engineering educator*
May, Adolf Darlington *civil engineering educator*
Mote, Clayton Daniel, Jr. *mechanical engineer, educator, administrator*
Ott, David Michael *engineering company executive*
Pestana-Nascimento, Juan M. *civil, geotechnical and geoenvironmental engineer, consultant*
Prausnitz, John Michael *chemical engineer, educator*
Ray, David Christian *aerospace engineer*
Shen, Hsieh Wen *civil engineer, consultant, educator*
Smith, Otto J. M. *electrical engineering educator*
Susskind, Charles *engineering educator, author, publishing executive*
Swaminathan, Venkates Vadakanchery *electrical engineer, software company executive*
Zwoyer, Eugene Milton *consulting engineering executive*

Bermuda Dunes
Smith, Walter J. *engineering consultant*

Bodega Bay
Stone, Richard Lehman *chemical engineer, consultant*

Boron
Potrovitza, Nicholas Pompei *mechanical engineer, solar energy researcher*

Boulder Creek
Ruch, Wayne Eugene *microlithography engineer*

Burbank
Halpert, Leslie Dean *engineering executive*
Strain, John Thomas *electronics engineer*

Burlingame
Chen, Basilio *engineering executive*

Calabasas
Chiang, Albert Chin-Liang *electrical engineer*

California City
Rutledge, Albert Henry *architectural engineer, architect*

Camarillo
MacDonald, Norval (Woodrow) *safety engineer*
Parker, Theodore Clifford *electronics engineer*

Campbell
Landman, Howard Andrew *electronics engineer*
Ross, Hugh Courtney *electrical engineer*

Canoga Park
Gay, Richard Leslie *chemical engineer*
Lin, Ching-Fang *engineering executive*
Ng, Chooon Meng *design engineer, consultant*
Norman, Arnold McCallum, Jr. *engineering executive*
Vinson, Connie Sue *aerospace engineer*
Vinson, John William *aerospace engineer*

Capitola
Barna, Arpad Alex *electrical engineering consultant*

Carlsbad
Pantos, William Pantazes *mechanical engineer, consultant*
Zorich, Robert Sam *semiconductor engineer*

Carmel
Brahtz, John Frederick Peel *civil engineering educator*

Castro Valley
Heckman, Richard Ainsworth *chemical engineer*
Hill, Anthony Whiting *electronic sales engineer*

Cayucos
Theurer, Byron W. *business owner, aerospace engineer*

Cerritos
Jones, Cleon Boyd *research engineer*

Chatsworth
Levine, Arnold Milton *retired electrical engineer, documentary filmmaker*

Chico
Pennock, Cecil Alan *electronic engineer*

China Lake
Gardner, Peter Alston *electronic warfare systems engineer*
Meyer, Steven John *electrical engineer*

Chino
Ellington, James Willard *mechanical design engineer*

Chula Vista
Goldkamp, Kenneth James *civil engineer*
Rusconi, Louis Joseph *marine engineer*
Wolk, Martin *electronic engineer, physicist*

Claremont
Dym, Clive Lionel *engineering educator*
Monson, James Edward *electrical engineer, educator*
Phillips, John Richard *engineering educator*
Shore, John James, III *materials and environmental engineering consultant*
Sparling, Rebecca Hall *materials engineer, energy consultant*
Tanenbaum, Basil Samuel *engineering educator*
Yen, I-Kuen *chemical engineer, environmental engineer, industrial hygiene consultant*

Concord
Middleton, Michael John *civil engineer*

Corona
Sudbeck, Richard James *medical imaging engineer*
Tillman, Joseph Nathaniel *engineering executive*
Williams, John Ray *electronics engineering executive*

Corona Del Mar
Richmond, Ronald LeRoy *aerospace engineer*

Corona Hills
Blanche, Joe Advincula *aerospace engineer, consultant, educator*

Coronado
Crilly, Eugene Richard *engineering consultant*

Costa Mesa
Buchtel, Michael Eugene *optical mechanical engineer*
Carpenter, Frank Charles, Jr. *retired electronics engineer*
Churchyard, James Nohl *engineer, consultant*
Slocum, Michael Scott *satellite systems design engineer*

Crockett
Leporiere, Ralph Dennis *quality engineer*

Culver City
Siri, Kasemsan *power electronics researcher*

Cupertino
Ahlstrom, John *computer infosystem engineer, educator*
Andresen, Mark Nils *electrical engineer*
Bird, Lesley Ann *computer engineer*
Dhuey, Michael Joseph *computer engineer*
Franson, C(arl) Irvin *aerospace material and process engineer, educator*
Ganesh, Shivaji L. *computer engineer*
Kull, William Franklin *civil engineer, land surveyor*

Savage, Thomas Warren *engineering manager*
Schmitt, Richard George *industrial engineer*

Danville
Hill, Ernest Elwood *nuclear engineer*
Karpenko, Victor Nicholas *mechanical engineer*

Davis
Copley, John Duane *civil engineer*
Diemer, William David *retired engineer, research analyst*
Dorf, Richard Carl *electrical engineering and management educator*
Gardner, William Allen *electrical engineering educator*
Gates, Bruce Clark *chemical engineer, educator*
Hull, Maury Lane *mechanical engineering educator*
Larock, Bruce Edward *civil engineering educator*
Margolis, Donald L. *mechanical engineering educator, consultant*

Diamond Bar
Mirisola, Lisa Heinemann *air quality engineer*

Downey
Baumann, Theodore Robert *aerospace engineer, consultant, army officer*
Demarchi, Ernest Nicholas *aerospace company executive*
Flagg, Robert Finch *research aerospace engineer*
Nash, Richard Eugene *aerospace engineer*
Nguyen, Han Van *mechanical engineer*
Nichols, Mark Edward *engineer*

Duarte
Chou, Chung-Kwang *bio-engineer*

Dublin
Parruck, Bidyut *electrical engineer*

East Rancho Dominguez
Chodera, Jerry *mechanical engineer*

Edwards
Bauer, Jeffrey Ervin *aerospace engineer*
Bertapelle, Allen Louis *flight test engineer*
Hamlin, Edmund Martin, Jr. *engineering manager*
Henry, Gary Norman *flight test and astronautical engineer, educator*
Plews, Larry Dale *aerospace engineer*
Ryan, George Wesley, III *aerospace engineer*
Tilley, Dennis Lane *research engineer*

El Cerrito
Chao, Chih Hsu *mechanical research engineer*

El Dorado Hills
Huppert, Merle Cecil *mechanical engineer*

El Monte
Onik, Frank Joseph, Jr. *electronics engineer*

El Segundo
Bauer, Jerome Leo, Jr. *chemical engineer*
Chang, I-Shih *aerospace engineer*
Cummings, Darold Bernard *aircraft engineer*
Daughaday, Douglas Robert *computer engineer*
Gross, Allen *engineer*
Hantos, Peter *computer engineer*
Kerr, James Arthur *logistics engineer*
Kramer, Gordon *mechanical engineer*
Lantz, Norman Foster *electrical engineer*
Mackey, Wayne Allison *electrical engineer*
Mitchell, John Noyes, Jr. *electrical engineer*
Moriarty, Donald Peter, II *engineering executive, military officer*
Myles, Winnfort Joseph *project engineer, real estate broker*

El Sobrante
Bloom, Rose Ellen Giehl *engineer*

Elk Grove
Arakaki, Duke Tsuyoshi *computer engineer, consultant*

Encinitas
Frank, Michael Victor *risk assessment engineer*

Encino
Knuth, Eldon Luverne *engineering educator*
Meckler, Milton *engineering consultant*

Escondido
Thomas, Patrick A. *civil engineer*

Fair Oaks
Agerbek, Sven *mechanical engineer*
Smiley, Robert William *industrial engineer*

Fillmore
Walker, Ernest K. *engineer, educator*

Forest Ranch
Morrison, Martha Kaye *photolithography engineer*

Fountain Valley
Kingsbury, Carolyn Ann *systems engineer*

Fremont
Bush, Mary Elizabeth *mechanical engineer*
Chou, Tai-Yu *electrical engineer*
Gupta, Praveen *engineering executive, software engineer*
Hill, John Earl *mechanical engineer*
Ritter, Terry Lee *electrical engineer, educator*

Fresno
Beekman, William Arthur *technical executive*
Brahma, Chandra Sekhar *civil engineering educator*
Huffman, David George *electrical engineer*
Sit, Chung Sheung *quality engineer*
Woolard, Henry Waldo *aerospace engineer*

Fullerton
Pringle, Weston Stewart, Jr. *traffic engineer*
Tehrani, Fleur Taher *electrical engineer, educator, researcher*

Tuazon, Jesus Ocampo *electrical engineer, educator, consultant*

Gardena
Kucij, Timothy Michael *engineer, composer, organist, pianist, conductor, minister, theologian*

Gilroy
Hackett, Randall Scott *engineer*

Glendale
Knoop, Vern Thomas *civil engineer, consultant*
Nay, Samuel Wesley *retired mechanical engineer*
Patel, Navin J. *electronics engineer, consultant*
Stemmer, Jay John *safety engineer, consultant*
Vilnrotter, Victor Alpár *research engineer*

Glendora
Haile, Benjamin Carroll, Jr. *retired chemical engineer, mechanical engineer*

Hawthorne
Burns, Brent Emil *electrical engineer*
Pi, Wen-Yi Shih *aircraft company engineer, researcher*
Silverstein, Robert Louis *aerospace executive*
Turner, David Winburn *aerospace engineer*

Hayward
Hunnicutt, Richard Pearce *metallurgical engineer*
Kimbell, Marion Joel *retired engineer*
King, Douglas James Christopher *mechanical engineering manager*

Healdsburg
Stucki, Kim Nolan *mechanical engineer*

Hercules
Emmanuel, Jorge Agustin *chemical engineer, environmental consultant*

Huntington Beach
Anderson, David Elliott *aeronautical engineer*
Badzey, Peter Gyula Gusztav *aerospace engineer*
Bartlett, Steven Thade *aerospace engineer*
Forkert, Clifford Arthur *civil engineer*
Hildebrant, Andy McClellan *retired electrical engineer*
Leveton, Ian Sinclair *civil engineer*
Nowlan, Daniel Ralph *engineering executive*
Radtke, Clayton Walter *structural engineer, engineering administrator*

Hydesville
Holton, William Chester *engineer, consultant*

Idyllwild
Peters, Cal Anthony *engineer*

Inglewood
Moghadam, Amir *engineering educator, consultant*

Irvine
Bromm, Robert Dale *nuclear engineer*
Jackson, Albert Smith *electronics engineer*
Kinsman, Robert Preston *biomedical plastics engineer*
Korb, Robert William *former materials and processes engineer*
McCraw, Leslie G. *engineering and construction company executive*
Minot, Mark Morton *engineering executive*
Sheldon, Mark Scott *research engineer*
Sirignano, William Alfonso *aerospace and mechanical engineer, educator*
Sklansky, Jack *electrical and computer engineering educator, researcher*
Sweeney, James Stevens, Jr. *design engineer*
Walen, James Robert *engineering specialist*
Werner, Roy Anthony *aerospace executive*

Kensington
Oppenheim, Antoni Kazimierz *mechanical engineer*

Kentfield
Jordan, Lawrence William *engineering educator*

La Canada Flintridge
Price, Humphrey Wallace *aerospace engineer*

La Habra
Eden, Ralph Moseley *aeronautical engineer*

La Jolla
Elkan, Charles Peter *engineer educator*
Johnson, Jeffrey Paul *systems engineer*
Liu, Shu Qian *biomedical engineer, researcher*
Rudolph, Walter Paul *engineering research company executive*
Schmid-Schoenbein, Geert Wilfried *biomedical engineer, educator*
Skalak, Richard *engineering mechanics educator, researcher*
Williams, Forman Arthur *engineering science educator, combustion theorist*

La Mesa
Kropotoff, George Alex *civil engineer*
Threlkeld, Steven Wayne *transportation/civil engineer*

La Puente
Caudron, John Armand *forensic engineer, technical forensic investigator*
Molinaro, David *design engineer*

Lafayette
Marco, David Duane *biomedical engineer*
Peirano, Lawrence Edward *civil engineer*

Laguna Beach
Bushman, Edwin Francis Arthur *engineer, plastics consultant, rancher*
Kramarsic, Roman Joseph *engineering consultant*

Laguna Niguel
Born, Robert Heywood *consulting civil engineer*
Rediess, Herman Arthur *engineering executive*

Lancaster
Hodges, Vernon Wray *mechanical engineer*

Lincoln
Tovar, Nicholas Mario *mechanical engineer*

Livermore
Cassens, Nicholas, Jr. *ceramics engineer*
Dalder, Edward Neil Cliff *materials engineer*
Hauber, Janet Elaine *mechanical engineer*
King, Ray John *electrical engineer*
Sengupta, Sailes Kumar *engineering researcher, statistical consultant*
Sheem, Sang Keun *fiber optics engineering professional*
Twogood, Richard Edward *electrical engineer*
Wright, James Baron *electrical engineer*
Zacharias, Richard Allen *electrical engineer*

Lomita
Balcom, Orville *engineer*
Mitchell, David Glen *research aerospace engineer*

Long Beach
Appleberry, Walter Thomas *aerospace engineering project executive*
Calkins, Robert Bruce *aerospace engineer*
Dillon, Michael Earl *engineering executive, mechanical engineer, educator*
Elliott, John Gregory *aerospace design engineer*
Kumar, Rajendra *electrical engineering educator*
Long, William Robert *automotive engineer*
Raiklen, Harold *aerospace engineering consultant*
Schwartz, Eric Robert *aerospace engineer*
Sparrevohn, Frederic Reidtz *engineering executive*
Tallman, Cory Roger *aerospace engineer*
Valla, Robert *aeronautical engineer, aerodynamicist*

Los Alamitos
Karkia, Mohammad Reza *energy engineer, educator*

Los Altos
Bergrun, Norman Riley *aerospace executive*
Gough, William Cabot *engineer*
Peterson, Victor Lowell *aerospace engineer, management consultant*
Sharpe, Roland Leonard *retired engineering company executive, earthquake and structural engineering consultant*

Los Angeles
Amer, Kenneth Benjamin *helicopter engineer*
Arbet-Engels, Vincent Paul *electrical engineer, researcher*
Bittenbender, Brad James *environmental safety and industrial hygiene manager*
Breuer, Melvin Allen *electrical engineering educator*
Bucy, Richard Snowden *aerospace engineering and mathematics educator, consultant*
Chobotov, Vladimir Alexander *aerospace engineer, educator*
Cole, Harold Spencer *engineer*
Cross, Glenn Laban *engineering executive, development planner*
Dest, Leonard Ralph *aerospace engineer, telecommunications specialist*
Ferro, Robert Joseph *electronics engineer, researcher*
Fitzsimmons, Jeffrey Lynn *astronautical engineer, military officer*
Frederking, Traugott Heinrich Karl *chemical engineering educator*
Friedlander, Sheldon Kay *chemical engineering educator*
Friedmann, Peretz Peter *aerospace engineer, educator*
Gordon, Kenneth Jay *aerospace engineer*
Incaudo, Joseph August *engineering company executive*
James, William Langford *aerospace engineer*
Kelly, Robert Edward *engineer, educator*
Klehn, Henry, Jr. *engineering company executive*
Kumar, Anil *nuclear engineer*
Leal, George D. *engineering company executive*
Li, Victor On-Kwok *electrical engineering educator*
Liu, Jia-ming *electrical engineering educator, physicist, researcher*
Lynn, Katherine Lyn *engineer, chemist*
Marmarelis, Vasilis Zissis *engineering educator, author*
Marsh, Frank Raymond *engineering technical writer*
Maxworthy, Tony *mechanical and aerospace engineering educator*
McSpedon, Edward *engineering company executive*
Meecham, William Coryell *engineering educator*
Meyer, Rudolf X. *engineering educator, retired space technology executive*
Mortensen, Richard Edgar *engineering educator*
Newman, Richard *engineering executive*
Perkins, Gladys Patricia *retired aerospace engineer*
Pugay, Jeffrey Ibanez *mechanical engineer*
Ramo, Simon *engineering executive*
Rosenstein, Allen Bertram *electrical engineering educator*
Schubert, Gerald *planetary and geophysics educator*
Shen, Jianping *acoustical engineer*
Speyer, Jason Lee *engineer, educator*
Tolliver, James David, Jr. *aerospace engineer*
Udwadia, Firdaus Erach *engineering educator, consultant*
Urena-Alexiades, Jose Luis *electrical engineer*
Wagner, Christian Nikolaus Johann *materials engineering educator*
Welch, Lloyd Richard *electrical engineering educator, communications consultant*
Willner, Alan Eli *electrical engineer, educator*
Yen, Teh Fu *civil and environmental engineering educator*
Young, Robert Arthur *electrical engineer*
Yue, Alfred Shui-choh *metallurgical engineer, educator*
Zhang, Zhen *electrical engineer*

Los Gatos
Fischer, Jay Edward *consulting service company executive*
Kuta, Charles Stanley *computer engineer*

Malibu
Hooper, Catherine Evelyn *developmental engineering senior*
Widmann, Glenn Roger *electrical engineer*

Marina
Lambert, Mark Allen *aero-mechanical engineer*

Marysville
Klein, Stephen Paul *engineering and mathematics educator*

Mcclellan AFB
Walser, Milton Wesley (Buddy Walser) *systems engineer*

Menlo Park
Abdou, Ikram Escandar *engineering consultant*
Edson, William Alden *electrical engineer*
Fishman, Norman *engineering consultant*
Kohne, Richard Edward *retired engineering executive*
Means, James Andrew *engineer*
Milanfar, Peyman *research engineer*
Olson, Henry Dexter *electrical engineer*
Schnebly, F(rancis) David *aerospace and electronics company executive*
Shelton, Robert Charles *electrical engineer*
Wegener, Albert William *engineering executive*

Milpitas
Costa, Vincenzo Francesco *engineer*
Dennison, Ronald Walton *engineer*
Mian, Guo *electrical engineer*
Nagasamy, Vijay *mechanical and aerospace engineer*
Wang, Huai-Liang William *mechanical engineer*

Mission Viejo
Duringer, Jacob Clyde *project engineer, researcher*
Gray, Gavin Campbell, II *computer information engineer, computer consultant*
Ljubicic Drozdowski, Miladin Peter *consulting engineer*
Neely, Alfred William *electrical engineer, marketing professional*
Pohl, John Henning *chemical engineer, consultant*
Subramanian, Sundaram *electronics engineer*

Moffett Field
Bogdanoff, David Wells *aerospace research engineer*
Goldstein, Howard Edward *chemical engineer*
Jardin, Matthew Robert *aerospace engineer*
Rogers, Stuart Eames *aerospace engineer*
Ross, James Carl *aerospace engineer*

Mojave
Cooney, Daniel Ellard *aeronautical engineer*

Monrovia
Leka, Fantu Wolde *quality assurance engineer*
Pray, Ralph Emerson *metallurgical engineer*

Monterey
Ball, Robert Edwin *engineering educator*
Bank, Milton Harold, II *aviation safety and aeronautical engineering educator*
Newberry, Conrad Floyde *aerospace engineering educator*

Morgan Hill
Sailor, J. Douglas *engineering consultant*

Mountain View
Earl, William John *software engineer*
Emerson, Thomas James *mathematician, software engineer*
Erickson, Calvin Howard *computer systems engineer*
Farmwald, Paul Michael *inventor, engineer*
Fujitani, Martin Tomio *software quality engineer*
Huang, Sungrung *engineer*
Jung, Henry Hung *mechanical engineer*
Perrella, Anthony Joseph *electronics engineer, consultant*

Newport Beach
Kraus, John Walter *former aerospace engineering company executive*
Magnuson, Jon Allan *research engineer*

Norco
Lu, Guiyang *electrical engineer*

Northridge
Bekir, Nagwa Esmat *electrical engineer, educator, consultant*
Costea, Ileana *civil engineer, educator, consultant, researcher*
Epstein, Melvin *engineering educator*
Lampson, Francis Keith *metallurgical engineer*
Rengarajan, Sembiam Rajagopal *electrical engineering educator, researcher, consultant*
Stout, Thomas Melville *control system engineer*

Oak View
Hanchett, William A. Barton *mechanical engineer, designer*

Oakland
Avery, Roger Michael *engineering executive*
Elliott, Jon Frederick *environmental consultant, educator, lawyer*
Hintz, Charles Ray *television engineer*
Musihin, Konstantin K. *electrical engineer*
Schell, Farrel Loy *transportation engineer*
Tsztoo, David Fong *civil engineer*
Veltfort, Theodore Ernst *electrical engineer, physicist*

Oceanside
Morin, Robert Warner *civil engineer*

Orange
Fisk, Edward Ray *retired civil engineer, author, educator*
Toeppe, William Joseph, Jr. *retired aerospace engineer*
Vasudevan, Ramaswami *engineering consultant*

Orinda
Calderwood, Neil Moody *retired telephone traffic engineer, consultant*

Oxnard
Lust, Peter, Jr. *microwave engineer, consultant*
Rosenbluth, Murray Joseph *chemical engineer*

Palmdale
Baker, Richard W. *structural and architectural engineer*
Figueiredo, Hubert Fernandes *aerospace engineer*
Moule, William Nelson *electrical engineer*
Olmstead, Richard Gale, Jr. *engineering manager*

Palo Alto
Adapa, Rambabu *electrical engineer*
Aitken, Robert Campbell *engineer*
Geng, Hwai-yu *manufacturing engineer, plant manager*
Johnson, Conor Deane *mechanical engineer*
Kapoor, Ashok Kumar *engineer*
Szczerba, Victor Bogdan *electrical engineer, sales engineer*
Thompson, David Alfred *industrial engineer*
Wada, David Russell *biomedical engineer, researcher*

Palos Verdes Estates
Aro, Glenn Scott *environmental and safety executive*

Palos Verdes Peninsula
Abbott, Anton Dwight *aerospace engineer*
Denke, Paul Herman *aircraft engineer*
Lowi, Alvin, Jr. *mechanical engineer, consultant*
Serafini, Victor Renato *aerospace engineer*
Weiss, Herbert Klemm *aeronautical engineer*

Pasadena
Barney, Kline Porter, Jr. *engineering company executive, consultant*
Basilio, Eleanor Vasco *electronics and aerospace engineer*
Boulos, Paul Fares *civil and environmental engineer*
Craymer, Loring Goddard *engineer*
Dawson, Gilbert Edward, II *systems engineer*
Gawronski, Wodek K. *aerospace engineer*
Hall, William E. *engineering and construction company executive*
Harstad, Kenneth Gunder *mechanical engineer, researcher*
Hatheway, Alson Earle *mechanical engineer*
Hess, Ann Marie *systems specialist, electronic data processing specialist*
Holbeck, Herbert John *mechanical engineer*
Holmgren, Richard S., Jr. *environmental engineering executive*
Jennings, Paul Christian *civil engineering educator, academic administrator*
Joffe, Benjamin *mechanical engineer*
Karnik, Avinash Ramkrishna *electronics engineer*
Kayalar, Selahattin *electrical engineer*
Knowles, James Kenyon *applied mechanics educator*
Losh, Samuel Johnston *engineering administrator*
Mathur, Ashok *telecommunications engineer, educator, researcher*
Nguyen, Tien Manh *communications systems engineer*
Otoshi, Tom Yasuo *electrical engineer*
Perez, Reinaldo Joseph *electrical engineer*
Presecan, Nicholas Lee *civil, environmental engineer, consultant*
Sartor, Luigi *chemical engineering researcher, consultant*
Sayano, Reizo Ray *electrochemical engineer*
Schober, Robert Charles *electrical engineer*
Sims, Robert Reynold *civil engineer*
Smith, Louis *maintenance engineer*
Stelzried, Charles Thomas *engineer*
Swass, Matthew J. *electrical engineer*
Tolaney, Murli *environmental engineering executive*
Wood, Lincoln Jackson *aerospace engineer*
Wynn, Robert Raymond *engineer*
Yariv, Amnon *electrical engineering educator, scientist*
Yeh, Paul Pao *electrical and electronics engineer, educator*

Penryn
Bryson, Vern Elrick *nuclear engineer*

Pico Rivera
Jager, Merle LeRoy *aerospace engineer*
Peavey, Charles Carman *engineering executive*

Pismo Beach
Parker, Roy Alfred *transportation engineer, planner*

Pittsburg
Weed, Ronald De Vern *engineering consulting company executive*

Placentia
Jackson, Frank Thomas *engineering manager*

Placerville
Burnett, Eric Stephen *environmental consultant*

Playa Del Rey
Copperman, William H *value engineer, consultant*
Tai, Frank *aerospace engineering consultant*

Pleasant Hill
Hopkins, Robert Arthur *retired industrial engineer*

Pleasanton
Meany, David William *civil engineer*

Point Mugu
South, Matthew Todd *aerospace engineer*

Pomona
Georgiades, Gabriel George *aerospace engineering educator*
Teague, Lavette Cox, Jr. *systems educator, consultant*

Ramona
Weaver, Bryan H. *engineer, producer*

Rancho Cucamonga
Yurist, Svetlan Joseph *mechanical engineer*

Rancho Palos Verdes
Frassinelli, Guido Joseph *retired aerospace engineer*

Redding
Robles, Arturo Perret *electrical engineer, musician*

Redondo Beach
Briggs, Robert Nathan *electrical engineer*
Buchta, Edmund *engineering executive*
Chazen, Melvin Leonard *chemical engineer*
Cohen, Clarence Budd *aerospace engineer*
Fesq, Lorraine Mae *aerospace and computer engineer*
Heller, Anthony Ferdinand *electronics engineer*
Hughes, James Arthur *electrical engineer*
Sackheim, Robert Lewis *aerospace engineer, educator*
Subramanya, Shiva *aerospace systems engineer*
Williams, Donald Spencer *scientist*

Redwood City
Bertrand, Keith Jay *electrical engineer*
Chu, K. David *engineer*
Nicolet, William Edward *mechanical engineer*

Reseda
Cornog, Robert Aiden *engineering consultant*

Richmond
Pyle, Walter Robert *mechanical engineer, consultant*

Ridgecrest
Pearson, John *mechanical engineer*
Woo, Raymond *aerospace engineer*

Riverside
Beni, Gerardo *electrical and computer engineering educator, robotics scientist*
Carrillo, Gilberto *engineer*

Rohnert Park
Lord, Harold Wilbur *electrical engineer, electronics consultant*

Rolling Hills Estates
Diaz-Zubieta, Agustin *nuclear engineer, executive*
Wong, Sun Yet *engineering consultant*

Sacramento
Ackerly, Wendy Saunders *aeronautic engineer, systems analyst*
Carleone, Joseph *aerospace and defense company executive*
Cavigli, Henry James *petroleum engineer*
Collins, William Leroy *telecommunications engineer*
Diaz-Flores, Hebert De Jesus *scientist, engineer, consultant*
Ferguson, Billy Coker *civil engineer*
Forsyth, Raymond Arthur *civil engineer*
Ishmael, William Earl *land use planner, civil engineer*
Karkoski, Joseph *environmental engineer*
Khandekar, Shekhar Dinkar *electrical engineer*
Lathi, Bhagawandas Pannalal *electrical engineering educator*
Peck, Raymond Charles, Sr. *driver and traffic safety research specialist*
Simeroth, Dean Conrad *chemical engineer*

Salinas
Layton, Donald Merrill *aeronautics educator*
Safdar, Syed Mohammed *quality assurance engineer*

San Bernardino
Bauer, Steven Michael *cost containment engineer*
French, Kirby Allan *transportation engineer, computer programmer*
Holtz, Tobenette *aerospace engineer*

San Carlos
Symons, Robert Spencer *electronics engineer*
Zink, Steven Martin *software engineer*

San Clemente
McCreless, Thomas Griswold *nuclear engineer*
White, Stanley Archibald *research electrical engineer*

San Diego
Anderson, Karl Richard *aerospace engineer, consultant*
Beasley, Gregory Dean *electrical engineer*
Burke, Arthur Thomas *engineering consultant*
Buss, Teresa Thacker *software engineer*
Butler, Geoffrey Scott *systems engineer, educator, consultant*
Chapelle, Gregory Philippe *electronics engineer, researcher*
Chiles, Wilton Richardson *electrical engineer*
Crook, Sean Paul *aerospace systems engineering manager*
Dang, Ngon Trung *engineering executive*
Doliber, Darrel Lee *design engineer, consultant, laboratory manager*
Eckelman, Richard Joel *engineering specialist*
Fernandez, Fernando Lawrence *research company executive, aeronautical engineer*
Fraitag, Leonard Alan *mechanical and manufacturing engineer*
Hall, Harold Robert *retired computer engineer*
Hanna, Nabil *biomedical engineer*
Hills, Linda Launey *advisory systems engineer*
Huang, Chien Chang *electrical engineer*
Kiefer, Robert John *mechanical engineer*
Klumph, Mark Jon *electrical engineer*
Lee, Long Chi *electrical engineering and chemistry educator*
Martin, Gordon Eugene *electrical engineer*
Maynard, John Herbert *electronics engineer*
McLeod, John Hugh, Jr. *mechanical and electrical engineer*
Mohanty, Bibhu Prasad *electrical engineer*
Moroz, Andrew *chemical engineer*
Paget, John Arthur *mechanical engineer*
Riparbelli, Carlo *aerospace engineer*
Schiff, Leonard Norman *electrical engineer*
Schryver, Bruce John *safety engineer*
Sell, Robert Emerson *electrical engineer*
Simpson, Patrick Kenneth *research and development engineer, engineering company executive*
Sweeney, James Augustus *retired marine engineer*
Taylor, John O'Mara *engineer*
Tom, Lawrence *engineering executive*
Tran, Jean-Marie *electrical engineer*
Tricoles, Gus Peter *electromagnetics engineer, physicist, consultant*
Wen, Chaur Shyong *chemical engineer*
Wise, Ralph Edmund *electronic engineer*
Woodbury, James Roberts *electronics consultant*
Youngs, Jack Marvin *cost engineer*

San Dimas
Philpott, Lindsey *civil engineer, researcher, educator*

San Fernando
Bridges, Robert McSteen *mechanical engineer*

San Francisco
Bechtel, Stephen Davison, Jr. *engineering company executive*
Beers, Robert Charles *metallurgical engineer, separations consultant*
Coté, Ralph Warren, Jr. *retired mining engineer, nuclear engineer*
Keller, Edward Lowell *electrical engineer, educator*
Laubscher, Roderick *engineering company executive*
Lipps, Douglas Jay *mechanical engineer*
Luft, Rene Wilfred *civil engineer*
McConn, Donavon J. *engineer*
Morrin, Thomas Harvey *engineering research company executive*
Smith, Bernard Joseph Connolly *civil engineer*
Taussig, Robert Trimble *engineering executive*
Vreeland, Robert Wilder *electronics engineer*
Whalley, Lawrence Robert *computer engineer, consultant*
Wrona, Peter Alexander *structural engineer*
Yuan, Shao Wen *aerospace engineer, educator*

San Jose
Barton, David M. *electronics engineer, consultant*
Bordelon, Scott Lee *computer systems engineer*
Bouldin, Danny Lee *electrical engineer*
Chandramouli, Ramamurti *electrical engineer*
Cingo, Ralph Paul *aerospace executive*
Contos, Paul Anthony *engineer, investment consultant*
Cruz, Antonio Jose, Jr. *engineer*
Dao, Tom Trinh *electrical engineer*
Ferrante, John Anthony *engineering consultant*
Gallar, John Joseph *mechanical engineer, educator*
Hodgson, Gregory Bernard *software systems engineer*
Huang, Francis Fu-Tse *mechanical engineering educator*
Lala, Tapan Kanti *computer and communications engineering manager, consultant, researcher*
Lashley, Robert H. *engineering manager*
Lehane, Andrew Desmond *civil engineer*
McCarthy, Mary Ann Bartley *electrical engineer*
Mitchell, Robert Campbell *nuclear consultant*
Morimoto, Carl Noboru *computer system engineer, crystallographer*
Nouban, Behzad *design engineer, researcher*
Papamarcos, Mark Stanley *electronic design automation consultant*
Pugliese, John David *mechanical engineer, consultant, programmer*
Schenk, William Henry *mechanical engineer*
Shaw, Charles Alden *engineering executive*
Susich, Robert Stephenson *electrical engineer*
Tran, Jack Nhuan Ngoc *gas and oil reservoir engineer*
Weitze, William Frederick *mechanical engineer*
Zwack, Raymond Theodore *engineer*

San Leandro
Reed, Dale Devon *engineering executive*

San Lorenzo
Thompson, Lyle Eugene *electrical engineer*

San Luis Obispo
Cummings, Russell Mark *aerospace engineer, educator*
Hoffmann, Jon Arnold *aeronautical engineer, educator*
Oliver, Stephen Ronald *communications engineer, educator*

San Marcos
Jeffredo, John Victor *aerospace engineer, manufacturing company executive, inventor*

San Mateo
Arnold, Rocky Richard *business and marketing consultant*

San Pedro
Birkenbach, Adam Stephen *engineer*
Ellis, George Edwin, Jr. *chemical engineer*

San Rafael
Godfrey, Douglas *tribologist, consultant*
Taylor, Irving *mechanical engineer, consultant*
Wright, Frederick Herman Greene, II *computer systems engineer*

San Ramon
Christensen, Thomas Craig *engineering executive*
Leonte, Dinu Ioan *software engineer*
Mizer, Richard Anthony *technology consultant*

Santa Ana
Bentley, William Arthur *engineer, electro-optical consultant*
Do, Tai Huu *mechanical engineer*
Loarie, John Adams *engineer*
Zabsky, John Mitchell *engineering executive*

Santa Barbara
Bernstein, Robert David *design engineer*
Bruch, John Clarence, Jr. *engineer, educator*
Crispin, James Hewes *engineering and construction company executive*
Fordyce, Samuel Wesley *electrical engineer, communications company executive, consultant*
Frederic, Brad *engineering company executive*
Kluge, Arthur I. *engineering company executive*
Lucas, Glenn Eugene *materials engineering educator, consultant*
Mitra, Sanjit Kumar *electrical and computer engineering educator*
Vanyo, James Patrick *engineering educator*
Weinberg, William Henry *chemical engineer, chemical physicist, educator*

Santa Clara
Anderson, Richard Alan *mechanical engineer*
Barker, Nancie Lynne *engineer*
Falgiano, Victor Joseph *electrical engineer, consultant*
Gates, John Allen *engineer, consultant*
Henry, William Rader *mechanical engineering consultant*
Kagan, Yishai *electronics engineer*
Lacy, Steven Douglas *bio-electrical engineer*
Luo, Horng J. *electrical engineer*
Nee, Christopher Chi-Huang *computer software engineer*
Pease, Robert Allen *electrical engineer*
Raghavan, Vijaya Nadipuram *engineering manager*
Ran, Xiaonong *research and development engineer*
Roylance, Lynn Michelle *electrical engineer*
Wong, Alexander Shih-Wei *electrical engineer*
Yin, Gerald Zheyao *technology and engineering executive*

Santa Clarita
Abbott, John Rodger *electrical engineer*
Granlund, Thomas Arthur *engineering executive, consultant*

Santa Cruz
Alchalabi, Neal Kamal *manufacturing engineer*
Luzovich, Steven Albert *computer engineer*
Pister, Karl Stark *engineering educator*

Santa Fe Springs
Koons, William Albright *quality engineer*

Santa Maria
Spellman, John David *retired electrical engineer*

Santa Monica
Digby, James Foster *research engineer*
Horn, Kenneth Porter *aeronautical/astronautical engineering administrator*
Ishler, Michael William *structural engineer*
Kayton, Myron *engineering company executive*
Mc Guire, Michael John *environmental engineer*
Thomas, Frank Joseph *nuclear engineer*

Santa Rosa
Cortelyou, Robert J(ohn) *civil engineer*
Hinch, Stephen Walter *manufacturing engineer*
Kelley, Terry Wayne *mechanical engineer*
Makker, Virender Kumar *engineer, scientist*

Saratoga
Boyd, John Willard *engineer, educator*
Brown, Paul Fremont *aerospace engineer, educator*

Scotts Valley
Reinisch, Ronald Fabian *materials engineer*

Seal Beach
Harsha, Philip Thomas *aerospace engineer*

Sierra Madre
O'Neil, William J. *aerospace engineer*

Simi Valley
Deisenroth, Clinton Wilbur *electrical engineer*

Sonora
Walasek, Otto Frank *chemical engineer, biochemist, photographer*

South Pasadena
Coston, Malcolm McGregor *chemical engineer*
Glad, Dain Sturgis *retired aerospace engineer, consultant*

Stanford
Barkan, Philip *mechanical engineer*
Bracewell, Ronald Newbold *electrical engineering educator*
Carlson, Robert Codner *industrial engineering educator*
Ferziger, Joel Henry *mechanical engineering educator, mathematician*
Goltz, Mark Neil *environmental engineer*
Goodman, Joseph Wilfred *electrical engineering educator*
Herrmann, George *mechanical engineering educator*
Kane, Thomas Reif *engineering educator*
Kruger, Charles Herman, Jr. *mechanical engineering educator*
Kruger, Paul *nuclear civil engineering educator*
Madix, Robert James *chemical engineer, educator*
Nelson, Drew Vernon *mechanical engineering educator*
Orr, Franklin Mattes, Jr. *petroleum engineering educator*
Ott, Wayne Robert *environmental engineer*
Sweeney, James Lee *engineering and economic systems educator*
White, Robert Lee *electrical engineer, educator*

Stockton
Turpin, Richard Harold *electrical engineering educator*

Sunnyvale
Forester, John *cycling transportation engineer*
Ghosh, Abhijit *electrical engineer*
Golden, Constance Jean *aerospace engineer*
Haggerty, Francis James *manufacturing engineer*
Israel, Paul Neal *computer design engineer, author*
Ma, Fengchow Clarence *agricultural engineering consultant*
Miller, Joseph Arthur *manufacturing engineer, educator, consultant*
Pearce, Hugh Morris *engineering executive*
Robbins, James Edward *electrical engineer*
Sankar, Subramanian Vaidya *aerospace engineer*
Schubert, Ronald Hayward *retired aerospace engineer*
Swanson, Richard Marker *electrical engineering educator*
Thorne, Richard Page *software engineer, consultant*
Watson, David Colquitt *electrical engineer, educator*

Sylmar
Farr, Donald Eugene *engineering scientist*
Madni, Asad Mohamed *engineering executive*
Weinberg, Alvin Howard *engineer*

Tarzana
Macmillan, Robert Smith *electronics engineer*

Temecula
Petersen, Vernon Leroy *communications and engineering corporations executive*

Thousand Oaks
Motamedi, Manouchehr Edward *electrical engineer, scientist*

Tiburon
Heacox, Russel Louis *mechanical engineer*

Torrance
Das, Subhendu *electrical engineer*
Deibel, Farrell Lee *aerospace engineer*
Gran, Robert *engineering company executive*
Opfell, John Burton *chemical engineer, educator*
Sheh, Robert Bardhyl *environmental management company executive*
Sorstokke, Susan Eileen *systems engineer*
Wertz, James Richard *space mission engineer*

Tracy
Nelson, Kenneth Arthur *electrical engineer*

Tustin
Dorneman, Robert Wayne *manufacturing engineer*

Ukiah
Eschenbach, Richard Corey *mechanical engineer*

Valencia
Windsor, William E. *consulting engineer, sales representative*

Van Nuys
Lagasse, Bruce Kenneth *structural engineer*
Milan, John Maurice *engineering executive*
Schultz, Kenneth W. *engineering executive*

Vandenberg AFB
Stevens, Thomas Edward *aerospace engineer*

Ventura
Bonge, Nicholas Jay, Jr. *biological engineering company executive*
Gaynor, Joseph *technical and management consultant*
Matley, Benvenuto Gilbert (Ben Matley) *computer engineer, educator, consultant*
Roberts, Darryl Jay *software engineer*

Victorville
Pagani, Albert Louis *aerospace system engineer*

Walnut
Lee, Peter Y. *electrical engineer, consultant*

Walnut Creek
Burgarino, Anthony Emanuel *environmental engineer, consultant*
Sanborn, Charles Evan *retired chemical engineer*
Van Maerssen, Otto L. *aerospace engineer, consulting firm executive*

Watsonville
Sicular, George Myer *civil engineer, educator, consultant*

Westlake Village
Frederick, Norman L., Jr. *electrical engineer*
Scully, John Kenneth *engineering executive, consultant*

Westminster
Armstrong, Gene Lee *systems engineering consultant, retired aerospace company executive*

Whittier
Braithwaite, Charles Henry *chemist, chemical engineering consultant*

Woodland Hills
Higginbotham, Lloyd William *mechanical engineer*
Myer, Jon Harold *engineering physicist*
Portney, Joseph Nathaniel *aerospace executive*

COLORADO

Arvada
Fuhrman, Kendall Nelson *software engineer*
Stewart, Larry Ray *engineer, financial director, quality consultant*

Aurora
Bauer, Richard Patrick *electrical engineer*

Boulder
Breddan, Joe *systems engineering consultant*
Burr, John Charles *software engineer*
Chow, Chuen-Yen *engineering educator*
Donges, Samuel Arnold *process control engineer*
Gardner, Homer Jay *electrical engineer*
Hanna, William Johnson *electrical engineering educator*
Hill, David Allan *electrical engineer*
Imad, Azmi Philip *environmental health and safety engineer*
Kompala, Dhinakar Sathyanathan *chemical engineering educator, biochemical engineering researcher*
Krantz, William Bernard *chemical engineering educator*
Mickelson, Alan Rolf *electrical engineering educator, optoelectronics researcher*
Siewert, Sam Burk *aerospace engineer*
Sture, Stein *civil engineering educator*
Uberoi, Mahinder Singh *aerospace engineering educator*
Wald, Robert Gray *electro-optical engineer*
Waters, M. Bruce *engineering technician*

Castle Rock
Franch, Nora *re-engineering specialist*

Colorado Springs
Anderson, Lawrence Keith *electrical engineer*
Borrego, Jesus Garcia *engineer*
Carroll, David Todd *computer engineer*
Chambon, Charles William *electrical engineer*
Harris, Debra Sue *development engineer*
Heilman, John Edward *engineering consultant*
Hutchens, John Gregory *engineering/management consultant*
Jacobsmeyer, Jay Michael *electrical engineer*
James, Wayne Edward *electrical engineer*
McKenzie, Richard Elvin *aerospace engineer*
Rima, Richard Herbert *satellite communications engineer*
Sherman, Donald H. *civil engineer*
Tirman, Valentin Woldemar, Jr. *engineering executive and educator*
Wainionpaa, John William *systems engineer*
Watts, Oliver Edward *engineering consultancy company executive*
White, Gayle Clay *aerospace company executive*
Will, John Emmett *electrical engineer*

Conifer
Powers, Edwin Malvin *consulting engineer*

Denver
Bivins, Susan Steinbach *systems engineer*
Bogart, Frank Jeffrey *system/product planning engineer*
Colvis, John Paris *aerospace engineer, mathematician, scientist*
Ervin, Patrick Franklin *nuclear engineer*
Fay, Richard James *mechanical engineer*
Ferguson, Lloyd Elbert *manufacturing engineer*
Flanders, George James *mechanical engineer, engineering development manager*
Hill, Eugene DuBose, Jr. *consulting engineer*
Hinch, William Harry *retired consulting engineer*
Keating, Larry Grant *electrical engineer, educator*
Mehring, Clinton Warren *engineering executive*
Peters, Douglas Cameron *mining engineer, geologist*
Riese, Arthur Carl *environmental engineering company executive, consultant*
Ross, Douglas Arthur *electrical engineering educator, consultant*
Shapiro, Alison Esther *software engineer*
Slosky, Leonard C. *environmental consultant*
Stephens, Larry Dean *engineer*
Wagner, Bruce Dieter *environmental engineer*
Whitehouse, Charles Barton *avionics educator*
York, Jesse Louis *chemical engineering and environmental consultant*
Ziernicki, Richard Mieczyslaw *engineering firm executive*

Durango
Langoni, Richard Allen *civil engineer*

Englewood
Bailly, Julie Ann *manufacturing engineer*
Bingham, Paris Edward, Jr. *electrical engineer, computer consultant*
Kelly, William States *data network engineer*
Kent, Darrel Arthur *systems engineer*
McLellon, Richard Steven *aerospace engineer, consultant*
Slater, Shelley *document and training manager*
Wallace, William Arthur, Jr. *environmental engineering executive*
Young, Lester Rex *engineering company administrator*

Fort Collins
Balza, John Joseph *research and development manager*
Cochran, Leighton Scott *wind engineering consultant, research scientist*
Emslie, William Arthur *electrical engineer*
Frasier, Gary W. *hydraulic engineer*
Mesloh, Warren Henry *civil and environmental engineer*
Ramirez, Jorge Alberto *civil engineering educator*

Glenwood Springs
Violette, Glenn Phillip *construction engineer*

Golden
Ansell, George Stephen *metallurgical engineering educator, academic administrator*
Chance, Kenneth Donald *engineer*
Clausen, Bret Mark *industrial hygienist, safety professional*
Davenport, Roger Lee *research engineer*
Gupta, Bimleshwar Prasad *mechanical engineer, manager*
Jones, Leonard Dale *facilities engineer*
Loomis, Christopher Knapp *metallurgical engineer*
Nozik, Arthur Jack *research physical chemist*
Salamon, Miklos Dezso Gyorgy *mining educator*
Sloan, Earle Dendy, Jr. *chemical engineering educator*
Yarar, Baki *metallurgical engineering educator*

Indian Hills
Zubrin, Robert Maynard *astronautical engineer, educator*

Lafayette
Hutchison, James Donald *retired engineer, historian*

Lakewood
Burton, Charles Edward *electrical engineer, systems engineer*
Lu, Paul Haihsing *mining engineer, geotechnical consultant*

Littleton
Ballard, Jack Stokes *strategic systems educator*
Brychel, Rudolph Myron *engineer*
Cox, Joe Howard, Jr. *petroleum engineer*
Miller, Gordon Holman *chemical, nuclear and environmental engineering consultant*
Montgomery, Robert Louis *chemical engineer*
Paredes, Bert (Norbert Paredes) *computer systems engineer*
Paynter, Howard Lager *mechanical engineer, educator, consultant*
Tom, Creighton Harvey *aerospace engineer, consultant*
Ulrich, John Ross Gerald *aerospace engineer*

Longmont
Hongsermeier, Martin Karl *software and systems architect, consultant*
Peever, Robert Leroy *electronic engineer*

Louisville
Cope, J. Robert *engineer*
Donze, Jerry Lynn *electrical engineer*
Harney, Francis Paul *mechanical engineer, consultant*
Prodan, Richard Stephen *electrical engineer*
Yu, Zeng-Qi *engineer, researcher*

Loveland
Sleeper, Andrew Duke *electrical engineer, statistician*
Willson, George Bigelow *civil engineer, consultant*

Lyons
Schmidt, Alan Frederick *consulting cryogenic engineer*

Niwot
Tabler, Ronald Dwight *snow and wind engineering consultant*

Parker
Shrestha, Pranaya *electrical engineer, consultant*

Pueblo West
Giffin, Walter Charles *retired industrial engineer, educator, consultant*

Sedalia
Burke, Pamela Ann *systems engineer*

Westminster
Dalesio, Wesley Charles *former aerospace educator*
Talbott, Jonathan Lee *electrical engineer*

Wheat Ridge
Gulman, Paul James *engineer*
Scherich, Erwin Thomas *civil engineer, consultant*

FLORIDA

Delray Beach
Jain, Arvind *engineer*

Melbourne
Hill, Robert Gilbert *aeronautical engineer*

Ocala
MacKay, John *mechanical engineer*

GEORGIA

Atlanta
Briggs, James Henry, II *engineering administrator*

HAWAII

Honolulu
Brock, James Melmuth *engineer, futurist*
Cheng, Ping *engineering educator*
Cotlar, Morton *organizational scientist, educator*
Hirota, Dennis Isao *engineering executive, civil engineer*
Holmes-Smith, David Michael *computer engineer, consultant, priest, dean*
Nakatani, Henry Masatoshi *structural engineer*
Saxena, Narendra K. *marine research educator*
Syrmos, Vassilis Lambros *electrical engineering educator*
Terawaki, Derek Kunio *engineer*
Wataru, Weston Yasuo *civil engineer*
White, Gary Richard *electrical engineer*

Kailua
Tetreault, Mark David *nuclear engineer and financial planner*

Kapolei
Sakamoto, Norman Lloyd *civil engineer*

Makawao
Lester, John James Nathaniel, II (Sean Lester) *engineer, environmental analyst, human rights activist*

Mililani
Savara, Arun Madan *engineering executive, management educator*

IDAHO

Boise
Allen, Jeffrey Douglas *engineering manager*
Baily, Everett Minnich *electrical engineer*
Nuttall, Michael Lee *engineer, educator*
Sandhu, Gurtej Singh *engineer, reseacher*
True, Leland Beyer *civil engineer, consultant*

Idaho Falls
Brown-Van Hoozer, Stefania Alenka *electrical engineer, human factor specialist*
Dahl, Christian Adam *engineer*
Daniher, John M. *retired engineer*
Greenwade, Lance Eric *scientific visualization specialist, mathematician*
Mortensen, Glen Albert *chemical engineer*
Stevens, John Gerald *nuclear engineer*
Towersap, Marc Errol *nuclear engineer*

Moscow
Jacobsen, Richard T. *mechanical engineering educator*

Pocatello
Bennion, John Stradling *engineering educator, consultant*

Rigby
Peterson, Erle Vidaillet *retired metallurgical engineer*

ILLINOIS

Rockford
Vincenti-Brown, Crispin Rufus William *engineering executive*

MONTANA

Bozeman
Gibson, David Frederic *engineering dean and educator*
McLeod, Bruce Royal *electrical engineering educator, consultant*

Butte
Studebaker, Irving Glen *engineering educator, researcher*

Helena
Johnson, David Sellie *civil engineer*
Johnson, Qulan Adrian *software engineer*

Missoula
Rice, Steven Dale *electronics educator*

NEVADA

Beowawe
Vokt, Eric Stephen *hydrogeological engineer*

Carson City
Chabot-Fence, Dene *industrial engineer*
Hughes, Robert Merrill *control system engineer*
James, Daryl Norman *environmental engineer*
Kvam, Robert Lars *geological engineer, educator*
O'Kuinghttons, Camilo Octavio *mechanical engineer*

Elko
Hodkiewicz, Melinda Jane *maintenance engineer*

Fallon
Kelley, Harold Edward *metallurgical engineer*

Las Vegas
Boehm, Robert Foty *mechanical engineer, educator, researcher*
Broca, Laurent Antoine *aerospace scientist*
Broselow, Stanley David *electrical engineer*
Bullock, Richard Lee *mining engineer*
Davis, Richard Ernest *engineer*
Grace, John William *retired electrical company executive*
Graebel, William Paul *engineering educator*
Haas, Robert John *aerospace engineer*
Mavady, Kaykham *electrical engineer, drafting*
Messenger, George Clement *engineering executive, consultant*
Peng, Zhong *electrical engineer*
Ramos, Albert A. *electrical engineer*

Mercury
Schwichtenberg, Daryl Robert *drilling engineer*

Minden
Bently, Donald Emery *electrical engineer*

Reno
Brugger, Paul Raymond *gaming professional*
Daemen, Jaak Joseph K. *mining and geotechnical engineering educator*
Gates, William Chester Bruce *geological engineering executive*
Snyder, Martin Bradford *mechanical engineering educator*

Silver City
Bloyd, Stephen Roy *environmental manager, educator*

Sparks
Byrd, Ronald Dallas *civil engineer*

Verdi
Kmetovicz, Ronald Eugene *new product development educator, writer*

Winnemucca
Bhaduri, Rahul Sankar *metallurgical engineer*

NEW MEXICO

Albuquerque
Allard, Thurman J. *electrical engineer*
Arvizu, Dan Eliab *mechanical engineer*
Benthem, Jack J. *electrical engineer*
Blouin, Scott E. *engineering company executive*
Chua, Koon Meng *civil engineering educator*
Clark, Arthur Joseph, Jr. *retired mechanical and electrical engineer*
Cooper, Susan Carol *environmental, safety and health professional*
Davis, Joel Stephen *systems engineer, scientist*
Doerr, Stephen Eugene *research engineer*
Dorato, Peter *electrical and computer engineering educator*
Doughty, John Robert *mechanical engineer, college president*
Eaton, George Wesley, Jr. *petroleum engineer, oil company executive*
Fuchs, Beth Ann *research technician*
Geyer, David Warren *aerospace scientist, software engineer*
Gruchalla, Michael Emeric *electronics engineer*
Haddad, Edward Raouf *civil engineer, consultant*
Higgins, Cornelius J. *engineering executive*
Kelly, Brian Matthew *industrial hygienist*
Loehman, Ronald Ernest *materials scientist*
McGovern, Douglas Edward *mechanical engineer*
McGowan, John Joseph *energy manager*
Nath, Robert Henry *high technology company executive*
Nelson, Burke Edward *engineering executive*
Orman, John Leo *software engineer, writer*
Palmer, Miles R. *engineering scientist, consultant*
Passman, Stephen Lee *theoretical mechanics scientist*
Plamondon, Maynard Alfred *civil engineer*
Plough, Charles Tobias, Jr. *electronic research and development executive*
Prindle, Robert William *civil and geotechnical engineer*
Rand, Ruth A. *science and computer educator*
Reed, Ray Paul *engineering mechanics measurement consultant*
Robinett, Rush Daleth, III *research engineer*
Sharp, Robert Lee *aerospace engineering consultant, test pilot*
Travis, John Richard *nuclear and mechanical engineer*
Woods, Robert Octavius *aerospace engineer*

Belen
Toliver, Lee *mechanical engineer*

Carlsbad
Wayman, Cooper Harry *environmental legal counsel*

El Prado
Winslow, Kenelm Crawford *mining engineer*

Farmington
Finch, Thomas Wesley *corrosion engineer*
Garretson, Owen Loren *engineer*
Rollstin, Gary Raymond *electrical engineer*

Holman
Bagley, Fenton Lloyd *mechanical engineer*

Kirtland AFB
Baum, Carl Edward *electromagnetic theorist*
Horrocks, John Charles *chemical engineer*

Las Cruces
Blevins, Bruce Allyn *electrical engineer*
Boykin, James Lester *aerospace engineer, consultant*
Colbaugh, Richard Donald *mechanical engineer, educator, researcher*
Vick, Austin Lafayette *civil engineer*

Los Alamos
Doss, James Daniel *electrical engineer, writer*
Gac, Frank David *materials engineer*
Hinrichs, Mark Christian *electrical engineer*
McDonald, Thomas Edwin, Jr. *electrical engineer*
Nunz, Gregory Joseph *program manager, aerospace engineer, educator*
Sicilian, James Michael *research engineer*
Wing, Janet Eleanor Sweedyk Bendt *nuclear scientist*

Mayhill
Carter, Joy Eaton *electrical engineer, consultant*

Santa Fe
Wilson, Brian Charles *civil engineer*

Silver City
La Fleur, Walter J. *engineering executive*

Tijeras
Sholtis, Joseph Arnold, Jr. *nuclear/aerospace engineer, consultant*
Vizcaino, Henry P. *mining engineer, consultant*

White Sands Missile Range
Arthur, Paul Keith *electronic engineer*

OHIO

Cincinnati
Gardner, Leonard Burton, II *former industrial automation engineer*

OREGON

Albany
Yau, Te-Lin *corrosion engineer*

Aloha
Esralian, Michael Jim *process engineer*
Rojhantalab, Hossein Mohammad *chemical engineer, researcher*

Beaverton
Davis, Stanford Melvin *engineering executive, publishing consultant*
Edsall, Ronald Scott *electrical engineer*
Getreu, Ian E(dwin) *electronics engineer*
Melott, Ronald K. *fire protection engineer, consultant*
Pierce, Paul Robert *software engineer*

Corvallis
Calder, Clarence Andrew *mechanical engineer, educator, researcher*
Forbes, Leonard *engineering educator*
Hall, Philip G. *engineering executive*
Hassebroek, Lyle G. *engineering company executive*
Huber, Wayne Charles *engineering educator*
Miner, John Ronald *bioresource engineer*
Peterson, Ralph R. *engineering executive*
Rapier, Pascal Moran *chemical engineer, physicist*
Temes, Gabor Charles *electrical engineering educator*

Eugene
Goodson, John Earl *civil engineering executive*
Kovtynovich, Dan *civil engineer*
Richards, James William *electromechanical engineer*

Grants Pass
Strain, John Willard *consulting aerospace engineer, landscape artist*

Hillsboro
Abel, Mark Jeffrey *electrical engineer, communications researcher*
Chen, James Jen-Chuan *electrical engineer*
Kahn, Kevin Comerford *software engineering executive*
Li, Zhi *process engineer*
Miller, Gregory Stewart *civil engineer*

Klamath Falls
Wolf, Lawrence Joseph *mechanical engineering educator*

Medford
Horton, Lawrence Stanley *electrical engineer, apartment developer*

Portland
Antoch, Zdenek Vincent *electrical engineering educator*
Becker, Bruce Douglas *mechanical engineer*
Cassidy, Richard Arthur *environmental engineer*
Dragoon, Kenneth Myer *electric utility engineer*
Forsberg, Charles Alton *computer, infosystems engineer*
Lewitt, Miles Martin *computer engineering company executive*
Li, Fu *electrical engineering educator, editor*
McCoy, Eugene Lynn *civil engineer*
Nice, James William *electronics educator*
Perkowski, Marek Andrzej *electrical engineering educator*
Pham, Kinh Dinh *electrical engineer, educator, administrator*
Pierzchala, Edmund *electronics engineer*
Prasad, Jayasimha Swamy *electrical engineer*
Rubio, Ivan Patricio *engineering executive*
Sutter, Harvey Mack *engineer, consultant*
Waymire, Evan Sage *automotive engineer*

Salem
Butts, Edward Perry *civil engineer, environmental consultant*
Mooney, Mark Alvin *systems manager*

Umpqua
Wood, Edward Newton *civil and mechanical engineer*

Wilsonville
Isberg, Reuben Albert *radio communications engineer*
Knierim, Robert Valentine *electrical engineer, consultant*

PENNSYLVANIA

Plymouth Meeting
Bulick, Willard James *project management and safety engineer*

UTAH

Alpine
Bateman, Robert Earl, II *technology management consultant*

Brigham City
Krejci, Robert Henry *aerospace engineer*
Webster, Ronald Lewis *structural engineer*

Fort Duchesne
Cameron, Charles Henry *petroleum engineer*

Hill Air Force Base
Oestreich, Paul Christopher *electronics engineer*

Kaysville
Calder, Robert Mac *aerospace engineer*

Logan
Folkman, Steven Lee *engineering educator*
Peralta, Richard Carl *groundwater engineer*
Stevens, David King *civil engineer, educator*
Yener, Muzz *civil engineer, educator*

Ogden
Babcock, John Walter *engineering executive*
Davidson, Thomas Ferguson *chemical engineer*
Hagen, Kirk Dee *mechanical engineer, educator*

Orem
Nordgren, William Bennett *engineering executive*
Shipp, James P. *systems engineer*

Provo
Jensen, David Warren *structural, aerospace and civil engineering educator*

Salt Lake City
Anderson, Charles Ross *civil engineer*
Anderson, Robert Ernest *safety engineer, consultant*
Bhayani, Kiran Lilachand *environmental engineer, programs manager*
De Vries, Kenneth Lawrence *mechanical engineer, educator*
Epperson, Vaughn Elmo *civil engineer*
Gandhi, Om Parkash *electrical engineer*
Gregersen, Max A. *structural, earthquake and civil engineer*
Hogan, Mervin Booth *mechanical engineer, educator*
Judd, Thomas Eli *electrical engineer*
Koller, Thomas John *engineering executive*
Lee, Hosin *civil engineer, educator*
Lee, James Norman *bioengineering researcher, educator*
Ligrani, Phillip Meredith *mechanical engineering educator, consultant*
Loggins, William Conley *industrial engineer*
Priebe, Norman Frank *electronics engineer*
Seale, James Richard *structural engineer*
Zeamer, Richard Jere *engineer, executive*

Sandy
Bennett, Carl McGhie *engineering company executive, consultant, army reserve and national guard officer*
Jorgensen, Leland Howard *aerospace research engineer*

VIRGINIA

Afton
Anderson, Donald Norton, Jr. *retired electrical engineer*

WASHINGTON

Auburn
Duhnke, Robert Emmet, Jr. *aerospace engineer*
Westbo, Leonard Archibald, Jr. *electronics engineer, educator*
Whitmore, Donald Clark *retired engineer*

Bainbridge Island
Whitener, Philip Charles *aeronautical engineer, consultant*

Bellevue
Erickson, Virginia Bemmels *chemical engineer*
Faris, Charles Oren *civil engineer*
Hibbard, Richard Paul *industrial ventilation consultant, lecturer*
Liang, Jeffrey Der-Shing *retired electrical engineer, civil worker, diplomat*
Parks, Donald Lee *mechanical engineer, human factors engineer*
Tien, Jonathon *engineer*
Walsh, John Breffni *aerospace consultant*
Wright, Theodore Otis *forensic engineer*

Bellingham
Albrecht, Albert Pearson *electronics engineer, consultant*
Johnstone, Kenneth Ernest *electronics and business consultant*

Bothell
Blackburn, John Lewis *consulting engineering executive*
Cao, Thai-Hai *industrial engineer*
Piroozmandi, Farid *mechanical engineer*

Bremerton
Joseph, James Edward *engineering technician*

Camas
Prouty, Alan Leslie *environmental engineer*

Edmonds
Landau, Henry Groh *geoenvironmental consulting engineer*
Peckol, James Kenneth *consulting engineer*

Edwall
Sobek, Irvin Gene *consulting engineer, sales engineer, farmer*

Ephrata
Neumann, Charles August *regional drainage engineer*
Reynolds, Donald Dean *retired civil engineering technician*

Kelso
Vincent, Steve *environmental engineer*

Kennewick
Cobb, William Thompson *environmental consultant*

Kent
Bangsund, Edward Lee *aerospace company executive*

Kingston
Pichal, Henri Thomas *electronics engineer, physicist, consultant*

Kirkland
Evans, Robert Vincent *engineering executive*

Mercer Island
Bridgforth, Robert Moore, Jr. *aerospace engineer*
Gravitz, Sidney Isaac *aerospace engineer*

Moses Lake
Silver, Barnard Joseph Stewart *mechanical engineer, consultant*

Mukilteo
Bohn, Dennis Allen *electrical engineer, consultant, writer*

Olympia
Saari, Albin Toivo *electronics engineer*

Pullman
Petersen, James Niels *chemical engineering educator*

Quincy
Gonzales, Anthony Ralph *industrial engineer*

Redmond
Anderson, Patrick Lee *electrical/electronics engineer*
Lane, James F. *software engineer*
Oh, Seho *research engineer*
Willard, H(arrison) Robert *electrical engineer*
Woodruff, James Robert *engineer*

Renton
Wilson, Melvin Edmond *civil engineer*

Richland
Andre, James P. *nuclear engineer*
Chapman, Elaine Grace *engineer*
Davis, Robert Bruce *metallurgical engineer, consultant*
Fouad, Hussein Yehya *electrical engineer*
Henager, Charles Henry *civil engineer*
Pillay, Gautam *chemical engineer, electrochemist*
Schmidt, John Wesley *advanced engineer, environmental scientist*
Schwinkendorf, Kevin Neil *nuclear engineer*
Umek, Anthony Matthew *engineering development company administrator, school system administrator*

Seattle
Allen, Gary King *aerospace advance development engineer*
Arthur, William Lynn *environmental advocate*
Bates, Dwight Lee *mechanical engineer*
Choi, Jai Joon *scientist, researcher, educator*
Drinkard, Terrell DeWayne *aeronautical engineer*
Fadden, Delmar McLean *electrical engineer*
Fox, Warren Leonard John *electrical engineer*
Haralick, Robert Martin *electrical engineering educator*
Hom, Richard Yee *research engineer*
Ii, Jack Morito *aerospace engineer*
Kim, Yongmin *electrical engineering educator*
Kinnison, Harry Austin *transportation engineer*
Levinson, Mark *retired engineering educator*
Mao, Kent Keqiang *engineering executive*
Martin, Thomas Henry, Jr. *water resource engineer, software writer*
Meditch, James Stephen *electrical engineering educator*
Morris, David John *mining engineer, consultant, mining executive*
Nathanson, Theodore Herzl *aeronautical engineer, architect*
Olson, Ronald Charles *aerospace executive*
Pabisz, Michael Joseph *electrical engineer*
Pihl, James Melvin *electrical engineer*
Robinson, Ronald Howard *aeronautical engineer*
Roeder, Charles William *structural engineering educator*
Rudolph, Thomas Keith *aerospace engineer*
Savrun, Ender *engineering executive, researcher, engineer*
Schuldt, Everett Arthur *engineer, consultant*
Somani, Arun Kumar *electrical engineer, educator*
Tencer, Allan Fred *mechanical engineer, medical educator*
Tweney, George Harrison *aeronautical engineer*
Wang, Robert Ching-Huei *engineer*
Weidner, Mark *environmental research executive*
Wiker, Steven Forrester *industrial engineering educator*
Wood, Stuart Kee *retired engineering manager*

South Bend
Heinz, Roney Allen *civil engineering consultant*

Spokane
Maus, John Andrew *computer systems engineer*
Mote, Karl William *mining engineer*
Nandagopal, Mallur R. *engineer*
Pfeuffer, Joseph John *electrical engineer, director*
Wolff, Joel Henry *human resources engineer*
Yamayee, Zia Ahmad *engineering educator, dean*

Steilacoom
Morgenthaler, John Herbert *chemical engineer*

Tacoma
Avril, Jack Joseph *ceramic engineer, forensic scientist*
MacGinitie, Laura Anne *electrical engineer*
Pontsler, Donald N. *electrical engineer*

Vancouver
Chartier, Vernon Lee *electrical engineer*

Vashon
Moser, Sarah Gunning *manufacturing engineer, small business owner*

Woodinville
Lanter, Sean Keith *software engineer*
McGavin, Jock Campbell *airframe design engineer*

Woodland
Mairose, Paul Timothy *mechanical engineer, consultant*

Yakima
Brown, Randy Lee *systems engineer*

WYOMING

Casper
Hinchey, Bruce Alan *environmental engineering company executive*

Dubois
Cummins, Nancyellen Heckeroth *electronics engineer*

Fe Warren AFB
Gardner, Autrey Thaddeus, Jr. *industrial technology educator*

Gillette
Sharp, Pamela Ann *quality assurance engineer*

Green River
Schwartz, John Charles *chemical engineer*

Lander
Hoyt, Anthony Ross *mechanical engineer*

Laramie
Bellamy, John Cary *civil engineer, meteorologist*

Powell
Hecht, Scott James *mechanical engineering executive*

Riverton
Pursel, Harold Max, Sr. *mining, civil and architectural engineer*

CANADA

ALBERTA

Edmonton
Morgenstern, Norbert Rubin *civil engineering educator*

ENGLAND

Feltham
Doerfling, Hank *aerospace engineer*

ADDRESS UNPUBLISHED

Alfriend, Kyle Terry *aerospace engineer*
Avakian, James Lawrence *engineering executive*
Ayler, Maynard Franklin *mining engineer*
Barnes-Roberts, Philip Irwin *engineer*
Barnett, David Hughes *software engineer, network engineer*
Beck, John Roland *environmental consultant*
Bertin, John Joseph *aeronautical engineer, educator, researcher*
Blankenship, Dale Clifford *electrical engineer*
Bowen, Douglas Glenn *electrical engineer, educator, consultant*
Brimacombe, James Keith *metallurgical engineering educator, researcher, consultant*
Broderick, Glen Reid *engineer, consultant*
Brown, Ronald Malcolm *engineering corporation executive*
Burlingham, Aragon *aerospace engineer*
Carter, Peter Lenn *electrical engineer*
Chandra, Abhijit *engineering educator*
Cline, Bryan M. *industrial engineer*
Constant, Clinton *chemical engineer, consultant*
Cooper, Austin Morris *chemist, chemical engineer, consultant, researcher*
Cramer, Eugene Norman *nuclear power engineer, computer educator*
Cramer, Frank Brown *engineering executive, combustion engineer, systems consultant*
Dahlstrom, Norman Herbert *retired engineering executive*
Davis, Clyde Wayne *engineering technician*
Dietz, Patricia Ann *engineering administrator*
Divine, Theodore Emry *electrical engineer*
Dodd, Joe David *safety engineer, consultant*
Field, Charles William *metallurgical engineer, small business owner, consultant*
Fok, Samuel Shiu-Ming *engineer, consultant*
Fritcher, Earl Edwin *civil engineer, consultant*
Gannatal, Joseph Paul *electronics engineer*
Gee, Ken *aerospace research executive*
Glassman, Arthur Joseph *software engineer*
Godo, Einar *computer engineer*
Goetzel, Claus Guenter *metallurgical engineer*
Hang, Soei-Shin *design engineer*
Harris, Martin Stephen *aerospace engineering executive*
Hollmann, Martin *aircraft design engineer*
Hood, Paul *reservoir engineer*
Hunsberger, Robert Earl *mechanical engineer, manufacturing executive*
Johnson, Stewart Willard *civil engineer*
Kahn, Irwin William *industrial engineer*
Kaplan, Laurence Scott *computer engineer*
Kersey, Terry L(ee) *astronautical engineer*
Ketchum, Milo Smith *civil engineer*
Kincheloe, William Robertson, Jr. *electrical engineering educator*
King, Donald Latham, Jr. *computer software engineer*
Kocaoglu, Dundar F. *engineering management educator, industrial and civil engineer*
Koltai, Stephen Miklos *mechanical engineer, consultant, economist, writer, educator*
Kontny, Vincent L. *engineering and construction company executive*
Lancaster, John Howard *civil engineer*
Lara, Tony Richard *industrial engineer, consultant*
Laurance, Mark Rodney *optics instrumentationist*
Laure, Phillip John *industrial engineer*
Lee, Ho John *electrical engineer*
Linhardt, Anthony Lakatos *electrical engineer*
Liu, Alan Fong-Ching *mechanical engineer*
Lowery, Douglas Lane *retired environmental engineer*
Lutze, Robert Stephen *engineering manager*
MacDonough, Robert Howard *consulting engineer*
Maples, James Alfred *software consultant*
Mayenkar, Krishna Vaman *environmental engineer, consultant*
McQuiston, Stevan Loy *electronics engineer*
Meinel, Marjorie Pettit *optical engineer*
Morgan, Lynn James *computer engineer*
Morrison, Robert Thomas *engineering consultant*
Mouch, Thomas Norman *aerospace engineering educator*
Muri, John Imre *mechanical engineer*
Nahman, Norris Stanley *electrical engineer*
Nour, Mohammad *computer engineer*
Nyman, David Harold *nuclear engineer*
Nyquist, Michael S. *civil engineer*
Olson, Donald Harold, Jr. *marine engineer*
Parker, William Elbridge *consulting civil engineer*
Pezeshki, Kambiz A. *metallurgical engineer*
Plambeck, Tom *mechanical engineer*
Pomraning, Gerald Carlton *engineering educator*
Poon, Peter Tin-Yau *engineer*
Remen, John Fredrick *aerospace engineer*
Remer, Donald Sherwood *chemical engineer, engineering economist, educator, administrator*
Richardson, Jean McGlenn *retired civil engineer*
Rodriguez, Dennis *electrical engineer*
Rubin, Sheldon *aerospace engineer*
Ruther, Christine L. *biomedical engineer*
Schimmel, Walter P. *aerospace engineer, educator*
Seldner, Betty Jane *environmental engineer, consultant, aerospace company executive*
Shank, Maurice Edwin *aerospace engineering executive, consultant*
Sheaffer, Richard Allen *electrical engineer*
Silverman, Steven Lee *aerospace engineer*
Singh, Rakesh *computer engineer*
Siyan, Karanjit Saint Germain Singh *software engineer*
Snover, Richard Lester *software engineer*
Spencer, Tamar Lish *aerospace engineer*
Stiglich, Jacob John, Jr. *engineering consultant*
Stout, Roger Paul *mechanical engineer*
Sweeney, James D. *computer engineer*
Ting, Albert Chia *bioengineering researcher*
Toupin, Edward Bernard *engineer, mathematician and computer scientist*
Trussell, R(obert) Rhodes *environmental engineer*
Tyler, Steven Anthony *aerospace engineer*
Valdes, Alfonso J. *research engineer*
Vobejda, William Frank *aerospace engineer*
Wang, Tony Kar-Hung *automotive and aerospace company executive*
Williams, Howard Walter *retired aerospace engineer*
Williams, Judith Ann *technical and engineering services company executive*
Williams, Ronald Oscar *systems engineer*
Willis, Selene Lowe *electrical engineer*
Wilson, Gary Thomas *engineering executive*
Yamashita, John Hiroshi *engineer*
Yatchak, Michael Gerard *electrical engineer*
Zeitler, Bill Lorenz *aviation engineer*
Zeitlin, Gerald Mark *electrical engineer*
Zhao, Tiemin *electrical engineer*

FINANCE: BANKING SERVICES. *See also* FINANCE: INVESTMENT SERVICES.

UNITED STATES

ALASKA

Anchorage
Harris, Roger J. *mortgage company executive, entrepreneur*
Rasmuson, Elmer Edwin *banker, former mayor*
Reed, Frank Metcalf *bank executive*
Sieberts, Jan Kristian *bank executive*

Juneau
Beedle, Joseph Michael, Sr. *bank executive, financial consultant*

ARIZONA

Gilbert
Duran, Michael Carl *bank executive*

Peoria
Kiser, Teri Denise *bank analyst*

Phoenix
Hilton, Eva Mae (Eve Hilton) *banker*
Moore, Elizabeth Jane *banker*
Stewart, Patricia Ann *bank executive*
Thompson, Caryn Elizabeth *banker*
Wallace, Kenneth Alan *investor*

Tempe
Fullmer, Steven Mark *banker*

Tucson
Sniezek, Patrick William *real estate loan officer*

CALIFORNIA

Albion
Harris, Richard Anthony Sidney *trust company executive*

Beverly Hills
Spivak, Jacque R. *bank executive*

Burbank
Miller, Clifford Albert *merchant banker, business consultant*

Campbell
Duke, Ellen Kay *mortgage company professional, community activist*

Chatsworth
Montgomery, James Fischer *savings and loan association executive*

Costa Mesa
Riordan, George Nickerson *investment banker*

Crestline
Holloway, Cindy *mortgage company executive*

Danville
Puffer, Sharon Kaye *residential loan officer*

Davis
Morgan, Charles Edward Phillip *bank executive*

Encino
Callos, John Douglas *banker*
Reser, Daniel M. *trust banker*

Glendale
Bean, James Woolson, Jr. *bank executive*
Masline, Richard Charles *financial executive*
Trafton, Stephen J. *banking executive*

Glendora
Mestad, Orville Laverne *bank executive*

Grass Valley
Apple, Daniel Bryce *finance company executive, financial planner*

Irvine
Butler, Merrill *bank executive*
De Roes, Nanda Yvonne *banker*
Jamshidipour, Yousef *bank executive, economist, financial planner*
Kuhn, Robert Lawrence *investment banker, corporate financier, strategist, author, educator*
Rady, Ernest S. *thrift and loan association executive*

Irwindale
Rinehart, Charles R. *savings and loan association executive*

La Jolla
Robbins, John Michael, Jr. *mortgage company executive*

La Mesa
Ford, Richard Christian *mortgage banker*

Laguna Beach
Flynn, Thomas Charles *banker*

Laguna Hills
Pelton, Harold Marcel *mortgage broker*

Long Beach
Keller, J(ames) Wesley *credit union executive*
Netherton, Jane *bank executive*

Los Angeles
Carson, Edward Mansfield *banker*
Crawford, Philip Stanley *bank executive*
Dockson, Robert Ray *savings and loan executive*
Floyd, Brett Alden *mortgage banker, consultant*
Lenard, Michael Barry *merchant banker, lawyer*
McLarnan, Donald Edward *banker, corporation executive*
Medina, Daniel Andrew *banker*
Miller, Gary Alan *commerical banker*
Reynolds, Jo-Anne Elaine *banker*
Siart, William Eric Baxter *banker*
Van Asperen, Morris Earl *banker*
Willison, Bruce Gray *banker*
Woodford, Charles Walter *bank executive, economist*

Monterey
Spitler, Lee William *banker*

Monterey Park
Hsieh, Rudy Ru-Pin *banker*

Newport Beach
Harley, Halvor Larson *banker, lawyer*
McAlister, Maurice L. *savings and loan association executive*
Prough, Stephen W. *savings and loan executive*

Oakland
Sandler, Herbert M. *savings and loan association executive*
Sandler, Marion Osher *savings and loan association executive*

Orange
Sneed, Gail *mortgage company executive*

Palo Alto
Fletcher, Rose Marie *mortgage banker, consultant*

Pebble Beach
Burkett, William Andrew *banker*

Piedmont
Hoover, Robert Cleary *retired bank executive*

Playa Del Rey
Blomquist, Carl Arthur *medical trust company executive, insurance executive*

Pleasant Hill
Tyran, Garry Keith *banker*

Pomona
Wagemann, Douglas Gerald *banker*

Sacramento
Waller, Larry Gene *mortgage banking executive*

San Bernardino
MacCauley, Hugh Bournonville *banker*

San Francisco
Bloch, Julia Chang *bank executive, former government official*
Case, Daniel Hibbard, III *investment banker*
Coombe, George William, Jr. *banker, lawyer*
Curran, Mark Albert *investment banker*
Dinkelspiel, Paul Gaines *investment banking and public financial consultant*
Dusanic, Linda Nelson *bank executive*
Eckersley, Norman Chadwick *banker*
Gillette, Frankie Jacobs *retired savings and loan executive, social worker, government administrator*
Gordon, Roger L. *savings and loan association executive*
Hamm, William Giles *banking executive*
Hazen, Paul Mandeville *banker*
Miller, John Nelson *banker*
Musick, William C. *bank systems manager*
Oliver, John Edward *bank training consultant*
Readmond, Ronald Warren *investment banking firm executive*
Rosenberg, Richard Morris *banker*
Saavedra, Charles James *banker*
Trowbridge, Thomas, Jr. *mortgage banking company executive*
Vogt, Evon Zartman, III *merchant banker*
Yoshida, Kanetaka *banking executive*
Young, Stephen Jerome *investment banker*

San Marino
Ng, Dominick *bank executive*

San Mateo
Brubaker, John E. *bank executive*
Douglass, Donald Robert *banker*

San Rafael
Wolfe, Jonathan Scott *mortgage company executive, lawyer*

Santa Ana
Cacioppo, Peter Thomas *government bank liquidator*

Santa Monica
Barber, John William McKenzie *private investor*
Heimbuch, Babette E. *bank executive*
Mortensen, William S. *banking executive*
Uberstine, Mitchell Neil *bank executive*

Sherman Oaks
Magner, Rachel Harris *banker*

Thousand Oaks
Tschacher, Darell Ray *mortgage banking executive*

Turlock
Wallström, Wesley Donald *bank executive*

Vista
Cosh, John Morton *bank executive*

Walnut Creek
Sweeney, Kathy A. *bank executive*

COLORADO

Denver
Davidson, John Robert Jay *banking executive*
Malone, Robert Joseph *bank executive*

Englewood
Corboy, James McNally *investment banker*

Fowler
Fox, Maxine Randall *banker*

Georgetown
Hildebrandt-Willard, Claudia Joan *banker*

Lakewood
Orullian, B. LaRae *bank executive*

FLORIDA

Melbourne
Windham, Edward James *bank executive, leasing company executive*

HAWAII

Honolulu
Dods, Walter Arthur, Jr. *bank executive*
Hoag, John Arthur *retired bank executive*
Johnson, Lawrence M. *banker*
MacDonald, Thomas Joseph, Jr. *trust company executive*
Stephenson, Herman Howard *banker*

IDAHO

Boise
Ellis, Ted Ellsworth *banker*
Jones, D. Michael *banker*
Keane, Edmund J., Jr. *banker*
Nelson, Daniel R. *bank executive*

Nampa
Luttrell, Dan Curtis *savings and loan company executive*

IOWA

West Des Moines
Ripper, Rita Jo (Jody Ripper) *strategic planner, researcher*

NEVADA

Henderson
Campbell, David Martin *bank executive*
Magnuson, Alan Douglas *retired banking executive, real estate broker*

Las Vegas
Hoefer, Gregory Allen *banker*
Thomas, Keith Vern *bank executive*

NEW MEXICO

Albuquerque
Constantineau, Constance Juliette *banker*

Carlsbad
Kidd, Melvin Don *banker*

Farmington
Hoyt, Rosemary Ellen *trust officer*

Las Cruces
Papen, Frank O'Brien *banker, former state senator*

Silver City
White, Don William *banker*

OREGON

Eugene
Drennan, Michael Eldon *banker*

Florence
Mehlum, Johan Arnt *banker*

Portland
Breezley, Roger Lee *banker*
Jensen, Edmund Paul *bank holding company executive*
Marek, Tammy Ann *banking consultant*
McAlmond, Russell Wayne *bank executive*
Pierson, Wayne George *trust company executive*
Shankland, Scott Edwin *mortgage company executive*

Salem
Weight, George Dale *banker, educator*

UTAH

Salt Lake City
Eccles, Spencer Fox *banker*
Hemingway, W(illiam) David *banker*
Hurst, C. Grant *bank executive, state agency administrator*
Studdert, Stephen Mark *investment banker*

WASHINGTON

Bellevue
Davidson, Robert William *merchant banker*

Mill Creek
Holmstrom, David Edwin Arthur *mortgage banking executive, consultant*

Oak Harbor
Piercy, Gordon Clayton *bank executive*

Seattle
Andrew, Lucius Archibald David, III *bank executive*
Campbell, Robert Hedgcock *investment banker*
Pinkerton, Guy Calvin *savings and loan executive*
Williams, Walter Baker *mortgage banker*

Sequim
Laube, Roger Gustav *retired trust officer, financial consultant*

Spokane
Sandifur, Cantwell Paul, Sr. *mortgage company executive*

Tacoma
Harlow, Steven Michael *banker*
Wallerich, Peter Kenneth *banker*

Vancouver
Inman, Claudia Jean *banker*

Walla Walla
Oliver, Dan David *banker*

WYOMING

Casper
Hotle, Jackie Lee *credit union executive*

Cheyenne
Knight, Robert Edward *banker*

Rock Springs
Hay, John Woods, Jr. *retired banker*

ADDRESS UNPUBLISHED

Barbera, Sharon Gail *banker*
Barker, Peter Keefe *investment banker*
Birnbaum, Stevan Allen *investment company executive*
Buckels, Marvin Wayne *savings and loan executive*
Burkart, Jordan V. *financial consultant*
Clark, James A. *banker*
Clark, Raymond Oakes *banker*
Coleman, Lewis Waldo *bank executive*
Dickson, Eva Mae *credit bureau executive*
Fielding, Harold Preston *bank executive*
Hausdorfer, Gary Lee *mortgage banker*
Horton, Michael L. *mortgage company executive, publishing executive*
Lacombe, Rita Jeanne *bank consultant*
Lankford, Duane Gail *investment banker, mountaineer*
MacGregor, Donald Lane, Jr. *retired banker*
Roberts, Julia B. *banker*
Tammany, Albert Squire, III *trust and bank executive*

FINANCE: FINANCIAL SERVICES

UNITED STATES

ALASKA

Anchorage
Branson, Lisa Jane *controller*
Mehner, William Michel *financial company executive*
Price, Margaret Ruth *financial services company executive*
Rylander, Robert Allan *financial service executive*

Dillingham
Parkin, Sharon Kaye *bookkeeper*

Fairbanks
Rice, Michael Lewis *business educator*

ARIZONA

Avondale
Rosztoczy, Ferenc Erno *business executive*

Douglas
Stickney, Philip Michael *accountant, educator*

Eagar
Saunders, James Harwood *accountant*

Glendale
Ricks, David Artel *business educator, editor*
Troan, Gordon Trygve *accountant, financial planner, entrepreneur*

Mc Neal
Smith, Clifford Neal *business educator, writer*

Peoria
Molinsky, Bert *tax consultant*

Phoenix
Barnes, Stephen Paul *financial planner*
Bauman, William Winter *financial company executive*
Burg, Jerome Stuart *financial planning consultant*
Cousins, Richard Francis *diversified financial services company executive*
Jungbluth, Connie Carlson *senior tax compliance specialist*
Khan, Ahmed Mohiuddin *finance, insurance executive*
Kolanoski, Thomas Edwin *financial company executive*
Krueger, John Charles *financial planner, investment advisor*
Leonard, George Edmund *finance company executive, consultant*
Linxwiler, Louis Major, Jr. *retired finance company executive*
Loucks, Gordon Craig *business educator, consultant*
Marshall, Anne Carolyn *financial services company official*
Schabow, John William *accountant*
Stern, Richard David *investment company executive*
Veit, William Arthur *financial planner*
Williams, Robert Wilmot *actuary*
Yohe, John Spencer *financial analyst*

Prescott
Larson, Dorothy Ann *business educator*

Scottsdale
Brooke, Edna Mae *retired business educator*
Cannon, James Dean *accountant, division controller, financial analyst, military officer*
Palaniappan, Nat *financial executive*
Rogers, William Cordell *financial executive*
Washburn, Jerry Martin *accountant, corporate executive*

Sun City
Cortright, Inga Ann *accountant*

Sun City West
Abels, Robert Frederick *tax consultant*

Sun Lakes
Relyea, Robert Gordon *management consultant*

Tempe
Files, L(awrence) Burke *financial consultant*
Ger, Shaw-Shyong *accountant*
Kaufman, Herbert Mark *finance educator*
Lastovicka, John Laddie *marketing and advertising educator*
Roy, Asim *business educator*

Tucson
Allardice, Linda Marie *controller, financial executive*
Couture, Richard Edmund *tax auditor*
Dubow, Susan Diane *financial consultant*
Harvey, Jane R. *investment company executive*
Henderson, Arthur James *business educator*
Krasner, Oscar Jay *business educator*
Nixon, Robert Obey, Sr. *business educator*
Norris, D. Wayne *insurance and financial services company executive*
Norvelle, Joan Wilson *forensic accountant, educator, consultant*
Pennington, Joseph Russell *financial services professional*
Schulman, Elizabeth Weiner *financial consultant*
Weinberg, Bernd *management educator*

ARKANSAS

Little Rock
Morgan, Jim Lee *retired business educator*

CALIFORNIA

Alameda
Taveggia, Thomas Charles *management educator*

Alhambra
Lin, Lawrence Shuh Liang *accountant*

Aliso Viejo
Duong, Nghiem Duc *estate planner*

Alta Loma
Wu, Seng-Chai *financial planner, life insurance agency official*

Anaheim
Smith, William Hugh, Sr. *audit manager, consultant*

Artesia
Lee, Jai Jung *accountant*

Bakersfield
Bacon, Leonard Anthony *accounting educator*
Schoenstein, Joseph Roy *accountant*

Berkeley
Blume, James Beryl *financial advisor*
Bucklin, Louis Pierre *business educator, consultant*

Beverly Hills
Matzdorff, James Arthur *investment banker*
McGagh, William Gilbert *financial consultant*
Taggart, Sondra *financial planner*
Young, Robert Edward *finance company executive*

Brea
Coniglio, John Vincent *financial company executive*
Engleman, David S. *diversified financial services executive*

Burbank
Petersen, Gladys *accounting clerk, writer*
Thornton, Cameron Mitchell *financial planner*
Weisbrod, Marvin Lester *tax company executive*
Widaman, Gregory Alan *financial executive, accountant*

Carlsbad
Billingsley, William Scott *accountant, controller*
Gnehm, Max Willi *diversified corporate executive*
Peasland, Bruce Randall *financial executive*
Schechter, Clifford *financial executive, lawyer*

Carmel Valley
Thompson, Billy Dean *accountant*

Castro Valley
Fink, Stuart Howard *accountant*

Chatsworth
Maher, John Francis *financial executive*

Chico
Olsen, Robert Arthur *finance educator*
O'Neill, Michael Foy *business educator*

Chula Vista
Sullivan, Patrick Allen *strategic management educator*

Claremont
Farquhar, Peter Henry *management educator, research director*

Commerce
Cain, Patricia Jean *accountant*

Compton
Bogdan, Carolyn Louetta *financial specialist*

Coronado
Allen, Charles Richard *retired financial executive*

Costa Mesa
Patterson, Joseph Cromwell *financial company executive*

Covina
Cammans, Stephen Charles *finance executive, former controller*
Cottrell, Janet Ann *controller*

Culver City
Abarbanell, Gayola Havens *financial planner*
Eckel, James Robert, Jr. *financial planner*
Hagan, Alfred John *marketing and economics educator*
Haussmann, Norman Joseph *printing account executive*
Richardson, John Edmon *marketing educator*
Zehner, William Bradley, II *marketing educator, consultant*

Cupertino
Davis, Barbara Joyce Wiener *accountant, investment manager, consultant*
Hill, Claudia Adams *tax consultant*
White-Hunt, Keith *business executive*

Cypress
Lowell, Wayne Brian *financial officer*

Daly City
Koga, Elaine *controller*

Dana Point
Kesselhaut, Arthur Melvyn *financial consultant*

Davis
Yang, Linda Tsao *financial consultant*

Diamond Bar
deLlamas, Lloyd Richard *government financial consultant*

Duarte
Fayad, Mike Samih *financial analyst*

El Segundo
Curran, Michael Harvey *finance executive*
Neal, Jerry Eugene *controller*

Encino
Fuld, Steven Alan *financial advisor, insurance tax planning specialist*

Foster City
MacNaughton, Angus Athole *finance company executive*

Fountain Valley
Penderghast, Thomas Frederick *business educator*

Fullerton
Oh, Tai Keun *management educator*
Taylor, James Walter *marketing educator*

Garden Grove
Norsby, Kimberly Lyn *tax specialist, consultant*

Glendale
Greenwood, Richard M. *finance company executive, bank executive*
Katzbeck, Karen Lynn *accounting executive*
Tookey, Robert Clarence *consulting actuary*
Tripoli, Masumi Hiroyasu *financial consultant and diplomat*
Weir, Peter Douglas *accountant*

Harbor City
Lee, Grace Tze *controller*

Hayward
Caywood, Thomas Elias *business educator, consultant*
Kameenui, James Andrew *accountant*

Hemet
Croneberger, Harry Leonard, Jr. *controller*

Inglewood
Lewis, Janie Carol *tax preparer, accounting consultant*

Irvine
Feldstein, Paul Joseph *management educator*
Kaskel, Neal T. *financial services executive*
Lepore, Ken *financial services executive*
Stolz, Neil N. *financial services company executive*
Zalle, Paul Martin *financial services company executive*

La Habra
Schoppa, Elroy *accountant, financial planner*

La Jolla
Simon, Ronald I. *financial consultant*

La Mesa
Bailey, Brenda Marie *accountant*

La Mirada
Barbas, Jeffrey Lawrence *finance company executive*

La Puente
Mc Kee, Raymond Walter *accountant*

La Verne
Rowe, Mary Sue *accounting executive*

Long Beach
Budkevics, Girts Janis *financial planner*
Harlow, Charles Vendale, Jr. *finance educator, consultant*
Lewis, Ralph Jay, III *management and human resources educator*

Los Altos
Sanchez, Marla Rena *finance director*

Los Angeles
Allison, Laird Burl *business educator*
Anderson, Kenneth Jeffery *family financial planner, accountant, lawyer*
Anderson, Roy A. *finance company executive*
Bennis, Warren Gameliel *business administration educator, author, consultant*
Bookman, Mark Andrew *business educator, consultant*
Boysen, Lars *financial consultant*
Brixey, Loretta Sanchez *strategic management consultant*
Broad, Eli *financial services executive*
Cappello, Eve *business educator, writer, international business consultant*
Chapgier, Pierre Andre *financing company executive*
Chase, Richard Barth *operations management educator*
Chavez, Albert Blas *financial executive*
Chesterfield, Rhydonia Ruth Epperson *financial company executive*
Cooper, Glen Alan *financial planner*
Corwin, Jack B. *holding company executive*
Curtis, Gary Lynn *accountant*
Doyle, Peter Thomas *accountant, realtor*
Fisher, Robert John *business educator*
Fitzgerald, Vincent James *controller*
Galloway, Clinton Edmund *accountant, communications executive*
Gillis, Nelson Scott *financial executive*
Goedde, Alan George *financial company executive*
Goldberg, Harvey *financial executive*
Goldfarb, I. Jay *accountant*
Goldwyn, Ralph Norman *financial company executive*
Hayes, Thomas A. *credit manager*
Knapp, Cleon Talboys *business executive*
Kramer, Alexander Gottlieb *financial director*
Leach, Anthony Raymond *financial executive*
Lee, Shi-Chieh (Suchi Lee) *international tax specialist*
Lin, Thomas Wen-shyoung *accounting educator, researcher, consultant*
Linden, Christopher *financial analyst*
Meloan, Taylor Wells *marketing educator*
Miech, Allen C. *financial services company executive*
Moffatt, Robert Henry *accountant, publisher, writer, consultant*
Morrow, Winston Vaughan *financial executive*
Obiora, Emmanuel Chuma *accountant*
Ross, Stan *accounting firm executive*
Ruiz, Luis Rafael *investment and financial planning consultant*
Samuels, Simon J. *finance, insurance company executive*
Scott, William Arthur, III *treasurer, swami*
Sharpstone, Lewis Edward *accountant*
Sidhu, Victor S. *investment executive*
Slouber, James Kirk *accountant*
Stewart, David Wayne *marketing educator, psychologist, consultant*
Talebzadeh, Houman *financial services executive*
Tanaka, Togo W(illiam) *retired real estate and financial executive*
Walendowski, George Jerry *business analyst, accounting educator*
Weston, John Frederick *business educator, consultant*
Whittenburg, Russell Thomas *finance executive*
Witherspoon, Gregory Jay *financial services company executive*

Los Osos
Gonzalez, Elizabeth Farr *accountant, management consultant*

Manhattan Beach
Anderson, Charles Michael *accountant*

Marina Del Rey
Caskie, William Wirt *accountant, securities broker*

Martinez
Mayer, Patricia Jayne *financial officer, management accountant*

Menlo Park
Santry, Barbara Lea *venture capitalist*
Schleh, Edward Carl *business analyst*
Taylor, Henry Stuart *financial consultant*
Timmins, James Donald *venture capitalist*

Mission Viejo
Rodrigues, Mark *financial executive, manpower consultant*

Modesto
Sargent, Diana Rhea *corporate executive*

Monterey Park
Tseng, Felix Hing-Fai *accountant*

Moraga
Horler, Brian Leslie *controller*

Mountain View
Benham, James Mason *mutual fund executive*

Napa
Hennings, Dorothy Ann *financial planner*

Newark
Langdon, Paul Russell *retired accountant*

Newport Beach
Grager, Steven Paul *financial planner*
Gross, William H. *financial analyst, insurance company executive*
Indiek, Victor Henry *finance corporation executive*
Long, Randall Craig *financial advisor*
Masotti, Louis Henry *management educator, consultant*
Plat, Richard Vertin *corporate finance executive*

North Hollywood
Overell, William Lawrence *finance executive*
Wolf, Rose Barry *tax consultant, educator*

Northridge
Lehtihalme, Larry (Lauri) K. *financial planner*
Ruley, Stanley Eugene *cost analyst*
Van Der Westhuizen, Brian Ivan *business educator*

Novato
Moser, Dean Joseph *accountant*

Oakland
Barlow, William Pusey, Jr. *accountant*
Lee, Jong Hyuk *accountant*
Mariscal Zuniga, Jose Luis *funding company executive*
Randisi, Elaine Marie *accountant, educator*
Schwyn, Charles Edward *accountant*

Oceanside
Horsley, Paula Rosalie *accountant*
Taverna, Rodney Elward *financial services company executive*

Ontario
Coney, Carole Anne *accountant*

Orange
Caporaso, Karen Denise *financial planner*
Fipps, Michael W. *corporate executive*
Fullmer, Terry Lloyd *tax consultant, business consultant*
Vines, Henry Ellsworth, III *financial executive, wood product executive, computer and tax consultant*

Oxnard
Woodworth, Stephen Davis *business and financial consultant, investment banker*

Palo Alto
Herrick, Tracy Grant *fiduciary*
Ivy, Benjamin Franklin, III *financial and real estate investment advisor*
Kohler, Fred Christopher *tax specialist*
Rutherford, Reid *finance company executive*
Searby, Daniel MacLeod *venture capitalist*
Supan, Richard Matthew *controller*

Palos Verdes Peninsula
Barab, Marvin *financial consultant*

Pasadena
Caldwell, William Mackay, III *business executive*
Gillis, Christine Diest-Lorgion *financial planner, stockbroker*

Petaluma
Sedlander, John Wingate *controller*

Pleasanton
Vandenberghe, Ronald Gustave *accountant, real estate developer*

Rancho Cordova
Johnson, Cathy *accountant*

Rancho Mirage
Fulton, Norman Robert *home entertainment company executive*

Rancho Palos Verdes
Manning, Christopher Ashley *finance educator*

Rancho Santa Fe
LaPlante, Peggy Lynn *financial executive*

Redlands
Boyce, Mary Elizabeth *management educator, consultant*

Richmond
Feil, Linda Mae *tax preparer*

Riverside
Chatham, Joseph Christopher *financial executive*
Harrison, Ethel Mae *financial executive*
Hodgen, Maurice Denzil *financial development administrator, educator*
Stenger, Martin Lane *financial planner*
Teaman, Richard Alan *accountant*

Rocklin
Dwyer, Darrell James *financial executive*

Sacramento
Kiehn, Ruben Lewis *construction cost estimator*
Putney, Mary Engler *federal auditor*
Wunder, Haroldene Fowler *accounting educator*

Salinas
Lopez, Carlos Celerino *accountant*
Stevens, Wilbur Hunt *accountant*

San Clemente
Petruzzi, Christopher Robert *business educator, consultant*

San Diego
Anderson, Jonpatrick Schuyler *financial consultant, therapist, archivist*
Bradley, Wade Harlow *acquisitions specialist*
Disney, Michael George *financial services executive*
Fox, Jack *financial service executive*
Schneider, Gary Paul *accountant educator*
Sledge, Reginald Leon *industry and compliance analyst*
Stambaugh, Larry G. *finance executive*
Strong, James Thompson *financial/management/security consultant, executive search*
Tennent, Valentine Leslie *accountant*
Turner, Richard Arlen *financial executive*

San Francisco
Ahuruonye, Hyacinth Chidi *accountant, consultant*
Atchison, Oliver Cromwell *retired accountant*
Boone, Norman McKieghan *financial planner*
Brandin, Mark Semple *financial services executive*
Diamond, Stephen Earle *investor, consultant, inventor*
Duff, James George *financial services executive*
Entriken, Robert Kersey *management educator*
Fracchia, Charles Anthony *investment advisor, educator*
Fuller, James William *financial director*
Hallstrom, Robert Chris *government actuary*
Harvey, James Ross *finance company executive*
Herringer, Frank Casper *diversified financial services company executive*
Hollingsworth, Margaret Camille *financial services administrator, consultant*
Jimenez, Josephine Santos *portfolio manager*
Kahn, Paul Markham *actuary*
Kuhns, Craig Shaffer *business educator*
Lee, Pamela Anne *accountant, financial analyst*
Linder, Ronald Jay *accountant, lawyer*
Mack, Cristina Iannone *accountant*
Mansinghka, Surendra Kumar *finance educator*
Mumford, Christopher Greene *corporate financial executive*
Olshen, Abraham Charles *actuarial consultant*
Palmer, William Joseph *accountant*
Scholz, Garret Arthur *financial executive*
Simini, Joseph Peter *accountant, financial consultant, author, former educator*
Skewes-Cox, Bennet *accountant, educator*
Tarlson, Nick Glenn *financial advisor*
Uri, George Wolfsohn *accountant*
Vickers, Thomas Eugene *finance company executive*
Whitney, David Clay *business educator, consultant, writer*
Witter, Wendell Winship *financial executive, retired*
Yeske, David Brent *investment advisor*
Zobel, Jan Arleen *tax consultant*

San Gabriel
Bilecki, Ronald Allan *financial planner*

San Jose
Ball, James William *check cashing company executive*
Belluomini, Frank Stephen *accountant*
Kertz, Marsha Helene *accountant, educator*
Morrison, William Fosdick *business educator, retired electrical company executive*
Wahler, Dennis Daniel *business studies educator, administrator*
Yee, Keith Philip *accountant*

San Luis Obispo
Swartz, Teresa Anne *marketing educator, researcher, consultant*
Weatherford, Alan Mann *business educator*

San Marcos
Waters, George Gary *financial service executive*

San Mateo
Hopkins, Cecilia Ann *business educator*
Lorenz, Brian *finance company executive*
Ravey, Donald Lee *business educator*

San Rafael
Purcell, Stuart McLeod, III *financial planner*

Santa Ana
Hickson, Ernest Charles *financial executive*
Terence, Frank *financial executive*

Santa Barbara
Myerson, Raymond King *investment counseling company executive*
Pybrum, Steven Mark *tax specialist, accountant*

Santa Clara
Delucchi, George Paul *accountant*

Santa Clarita
Bower, William David *credit bureau firm executive*

Santa Monica
Green, Hilarie Cattell *financial consultant*
Lee, Vin Jang Thomas *financial company executive, physicist*
Mazza, John Gamble *financial company executive*
Mc Intyre, James A. *diversified financial services executive*
Taylor, Nigel Brian *financial planner*
Tenney, Robert Nelson *finance company executive*

Santa Rosa
Adolph, Mary Rosenquist *financial company executive*
Dado, Arnold Emmett *financial and insurance consultant*
Root, Charles Joseph, Jr. *finance executive, consultant*

Sausalito
Boothe, Dyas Power, Jr. *emeritus finance company executive*

Sherman Oaks
Rich, Gareth Edward *financial planner*
Tsiros, John Andreas *accountant*

Simi Valley
McBride, Joyce Browning *accountant*

Sonora
Wheeler, Elton Samuel *accountant*

South San Francisco
Wood, Roger Holmes *financial planner, educator*

Stanford
McDonald, John Gregory *financial investment educator*
Serbein, Oscar Nicholas *business educator, consultant*
Spence, Michael *finance educator, dean*

Stockton
Ballot, Michael Harvey *business administration educator, consultant*
Goldstrand, Dennis Joseph *financial planning executive*
Hoverstad, Ronald Alan *marketing educator*
Marchini, Jo Anne *secretary-treasurer*
Mundt, JoNel *marketing educator, consultant*
Van Houten, Adrian James *auditor, controller*

Tarzana
Rouleau, Mark Louis *financial executive*

Temecula
Locklin, William Ray *financial planner*

The Sea Ranch
Coleman, Alan Brouse *financial management educator*

Thousand Oaks
Allen, David Harlow *business educator, consultant*
Detterman, Robert Linwood *financial planner*
Kocen, Lorraine Ayral *accountant*

Toluca Lake
Prystupa, Ester Ana *accountant*

Torrance
Hughs, Mary Geraldine *accountant, social service specialist*
LeBeau, Charles Ray *futures trading advisor*
O'Connor, William Charles *automobile agency finance executive*
Pettersen, Thomas Morgan *accountant, computer company executive*

Upland
Christian, Suzanne Hall *financial planner*
Jones, Nancy Langdon *financial planner, investment advisor*

Vista
Helmuth, Philip Alan *tax consultant*

Walnut Creek
Barton, Ann Elizabeth *financial executive*
Coit, R. Ken *financial planner*
Fridley, Saundra Lynn *internal audit executive*
Hamilton, Allen Philip *financial advisor*
Midanek, Deborah Hicks *portfolio manager, director*

West Hollywood
Felchlin, Mary Kathleen Conroy *financial executive*
Kathol, Anthony Louis *finance executive*
Santillan, Antonio *financial company executive*

Westlake Village
Cucina, Vincent Robert *management and financial consultant, educator*
Pollak, Norman L. *retired accountant*

Westminster
Knapp, Eber Guy *accountant*
Strutzel, J(od) C(hristopher) *escrow company executive*

Whittier
Maxwell, Raymond Roger *accountant*

Willits
Akins, George Charles *accountant*

Woodbridge
Thames, Carroll Thomas *financial consultant*

Woodland Hills
Babayans, Emil *financial planner*
Geuther, Carl Frederick *financial services company executive*
Malick, Peter Benson *accountant*

Woodside
Isaacson, Robert Louis *investment company executive*

COLORADO

Arvada
Hancock, N(ewell) Les(lie) *accountant*
Laidig, Eldon Lindley *financial planner*
Wambolt, Thomas Eugene *financial consultant*

Aurora
Bauman, Earl William *accountant, government official*
Hill, Keith Roland *financial planner, insurance broker*
McColl, Carol Ann *financial executive, educator*

Boulder
Baughn, William Hubert *former business educator and academic administrator*
Lawless, Michael William *strategic management educator*
Mehalchin, John Joseph *entrepreneur, finance company executive*
Richardson, Donn Charles *marketing educator*
Stanton, William John, Jr. *marketing educator, author*

Broomfield
Affleck, Julie Karleen *accountant*
Hartwig, Robert Allen, Jr. *international trade accountant*

Colorado Springs
Bressan, Robert R. *accountant*
Homan, Ralph William *finance company executive*
Scheimer, Janice Schaefer *financial consultant, planner*
Wheeler, Larry Richard *accountant*

Denver
Anderson, Peggy Rees *accountant*
Bennett, Barbara Esther *controller*
Cook, Albert Thomas Thornton, Jr. *financial advisor*
Delk, Richard Allen *accountant, consultant*
Edwards, Phyllis Mae *accountant, graphologist*
Gillis, Paul Leonard *accountant*
Harding, Wayne Edward, III *accountant*
Karras, Donald George *tax administrator*
Lincoln, Alexander, III *financier, lawyer, private investor*
Maatsch, Deborah Joan *trust administrator, compliance officer, paralegal tax specialist*
Ray, David L. *financial planning executive, consultant*
Shannon, Patrick Kavanaugh *finance manager*
Steele, William Arthur *financial analyst, public utilities executive*
Sullivan, Claire Ferguson *marketing educator*
Theis, Joan C. *accountant*

Englewood
Bergmann, Michael Dean *financial services company executive*
Biever, Angela Mary *finance company executive, information transaction processing executive*
Bogard-Reynolds, Christine Elizabeth *financial services executive*
Bondi, Bert Roger *accountant, financial planner*
Frishman, Eileen Steinberg *accountant*
Helfinstine, Kelly Ann *financial planner, securities company executive*
Lager, Douglas Roy *property tax consultant*
Mitchell, Brian John *financial planner*
Shannon, Richard Stoll, III *financial executive*
Sprincz, Keith Steven *financial services company professional*

Fort Collins
Ewing, Jack Robert *accountant*
Garretson, Robert Mark *financial executive*
Johnson, Mildred Irene *retired business educator*
Kinnison, Robert Wheelock *accountant*
Thomas, Jeanette Mae *accountant*
Tucker, Mary Linda *management educator, consultant*

Golden
Weiskopf, William Harvard *accountant*

Greeley
Roessig, John Robert *financial consultant*
Thiesen, Gregory Alan *accountant*

Lakewood
Buxton, Richard Millard *financial planning executive*

Littleton
Barnard, Rollin Dwight *retired financial executive*
Bass, Charles Morris *financial and systems consultant*
McNeil, Robert Duell *family businesses consultant*
Newell, Michael Stephen *finance company executive, international finance, security-protection consultant*
Ryan, Evonne Ianacone *financial planner*
Snyder, William Harry *financial advisor*

Longmont
Simmons, Richard Bryan *finance executive*
Sliker, Todd Richard *accountant, lawyer*

Pueblo
Shah, Abhay *business educator, marketing consultant*

Steamboat Springs
Van Baak, Anthony Edward *resort executive, accountant*

Trinidad
Rausch, Paul Matthew *financial executive*

Wheat Ridge
Leino, Deanna Rose *business educator*
Nichols, Vicki Anne *financial consultant, librarian*

HAWAII

Honolulu
Berni, Betty Catherine *actuary*
Betts, James William, Jr. *financial analyst*
Fukushima, Barbara Naomi *financial consultant*
Haig, David M. *property and investment management specialist*
Hook, Ralph Clifford, Jr. *business educator*
Jacobs, Laurence Wile *marketing educator*
Kam, Thomas Kwock Yung *accountant educator*
McLeod, Malcolm Stewart *financial executive*
Ng, Wing Chiu *accountant, computer software consultant, educator, activist*
Palia, Aspy Phiroze *marketing educator, researcher, consultant*
Sterrett, James Melville *accountant, business consultant*
Tanouye, Marian Natsuko *accountant*

Kihei
Bonfield, Andrew Joseph *tax practitioner*

IDAHO

Boise
Hedrick, Wallace Edward *lottery executive*
Ingram, Cecil D. *accountant, state legislator*
Mock, Stanley Clyde *financial planner, investment advisor*

Caldwell
Allen, Edward Raymond *retired business educator, accountant*

Idaho Falls
Call, Joseph Rudd *accountant*
Papin, Jerry A. *financial adviser, business owner*

Pocatello
Green, David Leroy *accountant*

LOUISIANA

Lafayette
Castellini, Patricia Bennett *business management educator*

Mandeville
Aaron, Shirley Mae *tax consultant*

MASSACHUSETTS

Boston
Rands, Jeffrey Raymond *government consultant*

MONTANA

Billings
Allen, Donald Wayne *accountant, educator*
Elser, Danny Ray *financial planner*

Cut Bank
McCormick, Betty Leonora *accountant*

Great Falls
Christiaens, Chris (Bernard Francis Christiaens) *financial analyst, state senator*
Dickson, Frederic Howard *financial executive*

Livingston
Squillace, Alexander Paul *investment advisor*

NEVADA

Carson City
Larson, Gerald Lee *auditor*
Reid, Belmont Mervyn *brokerage house executive*

Ely
Martin, Sunny *accountant*

Incline Village
Diederich, J(ohn) William *financial consultant*

Las Vegas
Carroll, Jeremiah Patrick, II *auditor*
Helm, George Neville, III *finance and mortgage banking company executive*
Henley, Preston vanFleet *former banker, financial consultant*
Hobbs, Guy Stephen *financial executive*
Wendt, Steven William *business educator*
Wheeler, Michele Lynn *financial analyst*

Reno
Neidert, Kalo Edward *accountant, educator*

NEW MEXICO

Albuquerque
D'Anza, Lawrence Martin *marketing educator*
Lowrance, Muriel Edwards *program specialist*
Mitchell, Lindell Marvin *financial planner*
Strati, Tony J. *accountant*

Las Cruces
Kriegel, Arlyn Alvin *accounting company executive*
Miller, M. Joy *financial planner, real estate broker*

Portales
Hudson, Steven Rex *accountant*

Santa Fe
Martin, Robert Grover *business and computers educator, artist*

OREGON

Ashland
Farrimond, George Francis, Jr. *management educator*

Beaverton
Herron, Carol Christine *financial planner, home economist*

Clackamas
Love, Susan Denise *accountant, consultant, small business owner*
Luchterhand, Ralph Edward *financial advisor*

Corvallis
Brown, Carol Elizabeth *management educator*

Eugene
Hamren, Nancy Van Brasch *bookkeeper*

Lake Oswego
Mylnechuk, Larry Herbert *financial executive*
Stojanik, Kathryn Ann *car accounting manager*

Portland
Adrangi, Bahram *business educator*
Dow, Mary Alexis *auditor*
Epperson, Eric Robert *financial executive, film producer*
Finley, Lewis Merren *financial consultant*
Gren, Conrad Roger *auditor*
Himmelberg, Barbara Taylor *controller*
Hsia, Chi-Cheng *finance educator*
Kimball, Curtis Rollin *investment advisor, appraiser*
Kondrasuk, Jack N. (John Kondrasuk) *business educator*
Krahmer, Donald L., Jr. *financial services company executive*
Lanz, Robert Francis *corporate financial officer*
McCoy, Wally Warren *tax consultant*
Morrow, James Thomas *financial executive*
Robinson, Danielle E. *finance educator*
Stewart, Marlene Metzger *financial planner, insurance agent*
Stewart, Thomas Clifford *securities company executive*
Weber, George Richard *financial consultant, writer*
White, Roberta Lee *comptroller*

Salem
Lew, Donald Evan *accountant*

Springfield
Farris, Larry Dean *financial planner*

TEXAS

Dallas
Lerner, Alan Burton *financial service executive, lawyer*

Houston
Robinson, Charles David *financial services executive*

UTAH

Kaysville
Cottle, Craig Hansen *financial executive*

Ogden
Mano, Ronald Makoto *accounting educator*

Roy
Karras, Nolan Eldon *investment advisor*

Salt Lake City
Bonny, Blaine Milan *retired accountant*
Burdette, Robert Soelberg *accountant*
Creer, James Read *financial officer*
Dibb, Roger Alan *accountant*
Snell, Ned Colwell *financial planner*

Sandy
Mitchell, David Campbell *corporate executive*

VIRGINIA

Alexandria
Pastin, Mark Joseph *executive consultant, society administrator*

WASHINGTON

Bellevue
Laing-Malcolmson, Sally Anne *enrolled tax agent, tax consultant*
Stevenson, Robert W. *technologies company executive, financial officer*

Bellingham
Ross, Steven Charles *business administration educator, consultant*

Bothell
Gierlasinski, Kathy Lynn *accountant*

Chelan
Lundberg, Larry Thomas *general manager*

Cheney
Drummond, Marshall Edward *business educator, university administrator*

Everett
Malott, Dwight Ralph *accountant*
Rapp, Nina Beatrice *financial company executive*
Swanson, David Paul *accountant*
Toyer, Richard Henry *accountant*

Issaquah
Gabrielsen, Paul Thomas *financial planner consultant, educational administrator, clergyman*

Kennewick
Weaver, Mark Arthur *finance educator, foreign language educator*

Longview
Petersen, Michael Jon *utility company executive*

Mount Vernon
Gaston, Margaret Anne *business educator*

Olympia
Christensen, Robert Wayne, Jr. *financial and leasing company executive*
Hogenhout, Frank Paul *accounting manager*

Orting
Riddoch, Hilda Johnson *accountant*

Pullman
Stem, Donald Edward, Jr. *marketing educator, researcher*
Wu, Jonathan Charnghau *accountant, consultant*

Puyallup
Curkendall, Brenda Irene *financial planner, business owner*

Seattle
Baxter, Pat Ann *accountant, educator*
Collett, Robert Lee *financial company executive*
DeJarnatt, George Lee *financial executive, business owner*
Dively, Dwight Douglas *finance director*
Erickson, Gary Michael *business and management educator*
Evans, Richard Lloyd *financial services company executive*
Feiss, George James, III *financial services company executive*
Gallik, Janice Susan *finance executive*
Gaskill, Herbert Leo *accountant, engineer*
Gorans, Gerald Elmer *accountant*
Kaminski, Charles Anthony *portfolio manager*
Kasama, Hideto Peter *accountant, real estate consultant*
Larson, Neil Edwin *accountant*
Mueller, Gerhard G(ottlob) *accounting educator*
Pellett, Howard Arthur *tax investigator*
Pitts, Barbara Towle *accountant*
Sandstrom, Alice Wilhelmina *accountant*
Taafe, Peter James *financial consultant*
Tollett, Glenna Belle *accountant, mobile home park operator*
van der Werff, Terry Jay *management consultant, professional speaker*

Sequim
Walker, Raymond Francis *business and financial consulting company executive*

Spokane
Hoyt, Bradley James *account executive*

Tacoma
Adkins, Ronald Vern *financial planner*
LaVelle-Nichols, Robin Ann *accountant*
Patterson, Beverley Pamela Grace *accountant*
Terranova, Patricia Helen *treasurer*

Woodinville
Olsby, Gregory Scott *financial executive*

WYOMING

Afton
Hunsaker, Floyd B. *accountant*

Cheyenne
Case, Rocky Ceciel *finance company executive*
Drummer, Donald Raymond *financial services executive*
Ferrari, David Guy *auditor*
Price, Keith Glenn *accountant*

Gillette
Enzi, Michael Bradley *accountant, state legislator*

Laramie
Spiegelberg, Emma Jo *business education educator*

Sheridan
Ryan, Michael Louis *controller*

CANADA

ALBERTA

Calgary
Schulz, Robert Adolph *management educator, management consultant*
Webber, Patrick Neil *diversified financial services company executive*

BRITISH COLUMBIA

Burnaby
Tung, Rosalie Lam *business educator, consultant*

Powell River
Carsten, Arlene Desmet *financial executive*

Salt Spring Island
Kandler, Joseph Rudolph *financial executive*

Victoria
Dagg, Steven Gregory *accountant*

SASKATCHEWAN

Saskatoon
Irvine, Vernon Bruce *accounting educator, administrator*

AUSTRALIA

Queensland
Tsukiji, Richard Isao *international marketing and financial services consultant*

OMAN

Muscat
Foote, Paul Sheldon *business educator, consultant*

ADDRESS UNPUBLISHED

Allen, Bonnie Lynn *pension actuary*
Ashcraft, Charles Olin *business educator*
Atcheson, Sue Hart *business educator*
Bagnull, Gary Lynn *accountant*
Bishop, Betty Josephine *financial consultant*
Boxer, Alan Lee *accountant*
Brennan, Ciaran Brendan *accountant, independent oil producer, real estate developer*
Brigham, John Allen, Jr. *financial executive, environmentalist*
Bryan, Kevan Fred *treasurer*
Bucher, Anita Marie *investigations specialist*
Chen, Nai-Fu *finance educator*
Chin, Marjorie Scarlett Yee *controller, business executive*
Darany, Michael Anthony *financial executive*
Davis, Robert H. *controller, financial executive*
Dunlap, James Riley, Sr. *former financial executive, credit manager*
Fagerberg, Dixon, Jr. *retired accountant, weather observer*
Gabriel, Rennie *financial planner*
Gaiber, Lawrence Jay *financial company executive*
Galbreath, James Howard *portfolio manager*
Hilliard, Karyn Jean *accountant*
Hutner, Herbert L. *financial consultant, lawyer*
Kaplan, Milton Emanuel *retired accountant, tax consultant*
Kaufman, Charles David *controller*
Larizadeh, M(ohammed) R(eza) *business educator*
Lewis, Gordon Carter *auditor*
Matteson, Sandra Anne *audit manager*
Miller, Robert Stevens, Jr. *finance professional*
Norton, Karen Ann *accountant*
Oldshue, Paul Frederick *financial executive*
Ong, Ernest Grant *auditor, researcher, accountant*
Paullin, JoAnn Marie *accountant, educator*
Pick, James Block *management and sociology educator*
Proud, Eileen Mariel *financial planner*
Ray, Richard Stanley *accountant*
Roller, David Isaac *financial services company executive*
Sax, Herbert *financial planner*
Saxton, Mary Jane *management educator*
Segel, Karen Lynn Joseph *tax professional, lawyer*
Shemer, Martha Evvard *investment company executive*
Smith, Vangy Edith *accountant, consultant, writer, artist*
Smith, Virgil *business education educator*
Smollan, David Leslie *retired tax practitioner*
Spencer, Richard Prail *property management educator, job placement counselor*
Srinivasan, Venkataraman *marketing and management educator*
Taliaferro, Yvon Rochelle *accountant, consultant*
Taunton, Kathryn Jayne *accountant*
VanAtta, Merry Janice *accountant*
van Seventer, A. *accountant*
Wachbrit, Jill Barrett *accountant, tax specialist*
Wales, Hugh Gregory *marketing educator, business executive*
Wood, Robert Charles *financial consultant*
Yingling, Robert Granville, Jr. *accountant*
Young, Felix Kun Chinn *organization financial executive, consultant*

FINANCE: INSURANCE

UNITED STATES

ALASKA

Anchorage
Trevithick, Ronald James *underwriter*

ARIZONA

Fountain Hills
Kramer, JoAnn Mary *insurance agency executive*

Phoenix
Meldman, Burton Alan *insurance salesman*
Sager, Donald Allen *insurance company executive*
Shcolnik, Robert Milton *insurance company executive*

Scottsdale
Prisbrey, Rex Prince *insurance agent, underwriter, financial consultant*

Tempe
Healy, Barbara Anne *insurance company executive, financial planner*

Tucson
Gerhart, Dorothy Evelyn *insurance executive, real estate professional*
Hartley, Albert Edward *insurance agent*

CALIFORNIA

Beverly Hills
Mehdizadeh, Parviz *insurance company executive*

Brea
Spiegel, Ronald Stuart *insurance company executive*

Camarillo
Rojas, Kristine Briggs *insurance sales and marketing professional*

Carlsbad
Haney, Robert Locke *retired insurance company executive*

Chico
Lynch, Patrick Michael *insurance agent, risk management consultant*

Concord
Padget, John E. *insurance executive*

Costa Mesa
Barden, Timothy John *insurance executive*
Gore, Thomas Gavin *insurance and securities broker*

Danville
Frederickson, John Marcus *insurance executive*

El Segundo
Gantzer, John Carroll *insurance company executive*

Encino
Surrell, Kevin Joel *insurance company official*

Fresno
Eaton, Thomas Clark *insurance and financial consultant*

Glendale
Erickson, Richard Beau *life insurance company executive*

Gustine
Carlsen, Janet Haws *insurance company owner, mayor*

Hemet
Treece, Joseph Charles *insurance broker*

Irvine
Bañuelos, Robert Alexander *insurance company executive*
Boynton, Donald Arthur *title insurance company executive*
Evans, Thomas Edgar, Jr. *title insurance agency executive*

La Mesa
Schlador, Paul Raymond, Jr. *insurance agent*

Laguna Hills
Mayfield-Koch, Lori Jayne *insurance processor*

Livermore
Dyer, Richard Hutchins *risk management executive*

Los Angeles
Aasen, Eugene Nels *workers' compensation underwriting manager*
Budlong, Theodore Warren *insurance company executive*
Denlea, Leo Edward, Jr. *insurance company executive*
Grembowski, Eugene *insurance company executive*
Gurash, John Thomas *insurance company executive*
Johnson, E. Eric *insurance executive*
Milgrim, Darrow A. *insurance broker, recreation consultant*
Murphy, Brian Arthur *insurance executive*
Rinsch, Charles Emil *insurance company executive*
Simmons, Victor J. *real estate and insurance broker*
Stewart, James M. *insurance and securities broker*
Thomas, Sean *insurance company president*
Wahl, Michael Frederick *insurance underwriter*
Winthrop, Kenneth Ray *insurance executive*

Merced
Washington, Napoleon, Jr. *insurance agent, clergyman*

Monterey Park
Lim, Sally-Jane *insurance consultant*

Napa
Craig, Dale Allan *insurance company researcher*

Nevada City
Halby, Anthony Wayne *insurance agent*

Newport Beach
Cosgrove, Cameron *insurance executive*
Randolph, Steven *insurance and estate planning agent*

Northridge
Fries, Arthur Lawrence *insurance broker*

Novato
Grove, Douglas David *insurance company executive*

Oakland
Ching, Eric San Hing *health care and insurance administrator*

Orange
Clayton, Bernard Miles, Jr. *insurance company executive*
Van Noy, Terry Willard *insurance company executive*

Pasadena
Christensen, Donn Wayne *insurance executive*

Pismo Beach
Brisbin, Robert Edward *insurance agency executive*

Pleasanton
Mills, Alan Benjamin *insurance company executive*

Rancho Cordova
Basconcillo, Lindy *insurance and financial services company executive*

Riverside
Cunningham, Vernon Carl *insurance company official*

Roseville
Cross, Dennis Ward *insurance company executive*
Dickerson, Tim Edward *insurance executive*
Singer, Frank J. *insurance company executive, lawyer*

San Clemente
Lang, George Frank *insurance executive, consultant, lawyer*

San Diego
Fuhlrodt, Norman Theodore *retired insurance executive*
Keller, Susan Agnes *insurance officer*
Rotter, Paul Talbott *retired insurance executive*

San Francisco
Clark, Edgar Sanderford *insurance broker, consultant*
Enfield, D(onald) Michael *insurance executive*
Levine, Norman Gene *insurance company executive*
Pemberton, Matthew Anthony *insurance agent*

San Jose
Jackson, Patrick Joseph *insurance executive*
Stotz, Natalie Hamer *underwriter*
Triplett, Raymond Francis *insurance underwriter*

San Mateo
MacCorkle, Emmett Wallace, III *insurance agent*

San Pedro
Roberts, James Lewis, Jr. *insurance executive*

San Rafael
Keegan, Jane Ann *insurance executive, consultant*

Santa Ana
Johnson, Joan Bray *insurance company consultant*

Santa Monica
Matheson, Suzanne Adrie *insurance broker*

Santa Rosa
Farrell, Thomas Joseph *insurance company executive, consultant*

Scotts Valley
Baldwin, Larell Hardison *insurance company executive*

Seal Beach
Schaefer, James Bruce *insurance company executive*

Spring Valley
Peterson, Donald Curtis *life care executive, consultant*

Tarzana
Braun, Stanley *insurance company executive*

Thousand Oaks
Gregory, Calvin *insurance service executive*

Torrance
Mehlig, Donald Homer *insurance broker*

Universal City
Holden, William Willard *insurance executive*

Whittier
Davidson, Alan Charles *insurance executive*

Woodland Hills
Berry, Carol A. *insurance executive*
Pellegrini, Cristian Andres *insurance company executive, consultant*

Woodside
Freitas, Antoinette Juni *insurance company executive*

COLORADO

Aurora
Saeger, Daniel Paul *insurance company sales executive*

Colorado Springs
Stephens, Taylor Lane *insurance company executive*
Volpe, Richard Gerard *insurance accounts executive, consultant*

Denver
Gundzik, Michael John *health insurance executive*
Hardy, Wayne Russell *insurance broker*
Kelly, Jerome Bernard *insurance company executive*

Englewood
Manley, Richard Walter *insurance executive*
Moore, Dan Sterling *insurance executive, sales trainer*
Ware, Roger B. *insurance company executive*

Golden
Schendel, Winfried George *insurance company executive*

Longmont
Simpson, Velma Southall *insurance agent*

Pueblo
Kelly, William Bret *insurance executive*

Westminster
Kruger, Paul Robert *insurance broker*

FLORIDA

Osprey
Deering, Fred Arthur *insurance company executive*

HAWAII

Hilo
Thole, Mary Elizabeth *insurance company executive*

Honolulu
Kanehiro, Kenneth Kenji *insurance educator, risk analyst, consultant*
Matthews, Norman Sherwood, Jr. *insurance company executive*
Ronsman, Wayne John *insurance company executive*
Turnipseed, Pamela Jean *insurance company executive*

IDAHO

Idaho Falls
Parkinson, Howard Evans *insurance company executive*

Nampa
Heidt, Raymond Joseph *insurance company executive*

Soda Springs
Hendricks, Brian James *insurance company executive, consultant*

Twin Falls
Lewis, Frederick Thomas *insurance company executive*

MONTANA

Kalispell
Lopp, Susan Jane *insurance underwriter*

Missoula
Pink, Ernest Edwin *insurance agency executive*

NEVADA

Carson City
Marangi, Vito Anthony, Sr. *claim adminstrator*

Las Vegas
Gresham, Robert Lambert, Jr. *insurance company executive*

NEW MEXICO

Albuquerque
Liss, Norman Richard *insurance executive*
Parsley, Steven Dwayne *title company executive*
Rotherham, Larry Charles *insurance executive*
Wainio, Mark Ernest *insurance company consultant*
Worrell, Jane Carson *insurance adjustor*

Deming
Levine, Michael Joseph *insurance company executive*

Tucumcari
Woodard, Dorothy Marie *insurance broker*

NEW YORK

Brooklyn
Rose, Howard D. *insurance company executive*

New York
Nagler, Stewart Gordon *insurance company executive*
Simpson, William Arthur *insurance company executive*

OHIO

Cleveland
Hybil, James J. *insurance agency executive*

OREGON

Hillsboro
Yates, Keith Lamar *retired insurance company executive*

Lake Oswego
Atwood, Kelly Palmer *insurance agency executive*

Medford
Dvorak, Ray P. *insurance company official*

Portland
Galbraith, John Robert *insurance company executive*
Hill, James Edward *insurance company executive*

Salem
Rasmussen, Neil Woodland *insurance agent*

Tigard
Yount, Philip Richard *insurance company executive*

Tualatin
Chambers, Lois Irene *insurance automation consultant*

West Linn
Dunstan, Larry Kenneth *insurance company executive*

UTAH

Midvale
West, Shelby Jay *insurance agent*

Pleasant Grove
Gross, Bruce L. *insurance executive*

Salt Lake City
Allen, Roy Verl *life insurance company executive*
Elliott, Ross Cox *insurance company executive*
Engar, Richard Charles *insurance executive, dentist, educator*
Harnicher, David John *insurance company executive*
Macumber, John Paul *insurance company executive*

WASHINGTON

Auburn
Colburn, Gene Lewis *insurance and industrial consultant*

Bellevue
Eigsti, Roger Harry *insurance company executive*

Bellingham
Fullmer, Donald Kitchen *insurance executive*

Federal Way
English, Donald Marvin *loss control representative*

Kennewick
Stevens, Henry August *insurance agent, educator*

Kirkland
McDonald, Joseph Lee *insurance broker*

Olympia
Schoengarth, R(obert) Scott *life insurance company executive*

Seattle
Dubes, Michael J. *insurance company executive*
Duckworth, Tara Ann *insurance company executive*
Harrington, Glenn Lewis *insurance company executive*
Kibble, Edward Bruce *insurance-investment advisory company executive*
Varga, Steven Carl *reinsurance company official*
Zunker, Richard E. *insurance company executive*

WYOMING

Glenrock
Bennington, Leslie Orville, Jr. *insurance agent*

Green River
Levitt, Lawrence David *insurance agent*

ADDRESS UNPUBLISHED

Armstrong, F(redric) Michael *retired insurance company executive*
Avery, Elaine Elvira *life insurance representative, retired*
Bovey, Terry Robinson *insurance executive*
Clemens, Charles Joseph *insurance agent*
Cochrun, John Wesley *insurance agent*
Dackow, Orest Taras *insurance company executive*
Ipsen, Grant Ruel *insurance and investments professional*
Kolde, Richard Arthur *insurance company executive, consultant*
Lacy, Carol Angela *insurance executive*
Malphurs, Roger Edward *insurance company executive, chiropractor, biomedical technologist, private commodity trader*
Markos, Laura L. *risk management professional*
Morris, Edward J(ames), Jr. *insurance agent, small business owner*
Porter, Dixie Lee *insurance executive, consultant*
Whalen, Michelle O. *senior workers' compensation underwriter*

FINANCE: INVESTMENT SERVICES

UNITED STATES

ALASKA

Anchorage
Hickel, Walter Joseph *investment firm executive, forum administrator*

ARIZONA

Gilbert
Gaustad, Richard Dale *financier*

Mesa
Tennison, William Ray, Jr. *financial planner, stockbroker, recreational facility executive*

Phoenix
Bansak, Stephen A., Jr. *investment banker, financial consultant*
Fischler, Bryant *venture capital executive*
Scarbrough, Ernest Earl *stockbroker, financial planner*
Silverman, Anthony *securities trader, dealer*
Tribble, Richard Walter *brokerage executive*

Scottsdale
Kahn, Jeffrey Hay *retired investment banker*
Luke, David Kevin *investment company executive*
Seckinger, Gerald Edwin *investor*

Tucson
Grubb, L(ewis) Craig *investment company executive, consultant*
Valenzuela, Ricardo *investment banker, rancher*
Willbanks, Sue Sutton *investor, writer, artist*

Vail
Maierhauser, Joseph George *entrepreneur*

Yuma
Stuart, Gerard William, Jr. *investment company executive, city official*

CALIFORNIA

Arcadia
Berkus, David William *venture capitalist*

Beverly Hills
Gambrell, Thomas Ross *investor*
Israel, Richard Stanley *investment banker*
Skromeda, Steve *investment company executive*
Stern, Milford L. *investment company executive*

Brea
Djalatta, Loretta Jean *securities company executive, real estate broker*

Camarillo
Sullivan, Michael Evan *investment and management company executive*

Capitola
Hamrah, Kallen Michael *securities trader*

Carmel
Sweeney, Joseph W., III *investment executive*

Cedarpines Park
Carter, Larry Alexander *brokerage firm executive*

Chula Vista
Hardy, Erwin *entrepreneur, inventor*
Samaras, Mary Stenning *entrepreneur, educator, video producer*

Coronado
Smith, Albert Cromwell, Jr. *investments consultant*

Cupertino
Horn, Christian Friedrich *venture capital company executive*
Markkula, A. C., Jr. *entrepreneur, computer company executive*
Perkins, Thomas James *venture capital company executive*

Dixon
Molina, Rafael Antonio *investment company executive*

Escondido
Allen, Donald Vail *investment executive, author, concert pianist*

Gardena
Ishimatsu, Eiji *investment company executive*

Glendora
Wright, Janet Scritsmier *investment consultant*

Hayward
Morgan, Joe Leonard *investment company executive, former professional baseball player*

Inglewood
Schwary, Richard Joseph *investment company executive*

Irvine
Burns, Donald Snow *registered investment advisor, financial and business consultant*
Cowart, Jim Cash *business executive*
Holmes, Robert C. *securities trader*
Le Bon, Douglas Kent *investment manager*

La Jolla
Dunn, David Joseph *financial executive*
Stone, Donald D. *investment and sales executive*

La Mesa
White, Brian William *investment company executive*

Larkspur
Kirk, Gary Vincent *investment advisor*

Long Beach
Augerbright, Pamela Jean *entrepreneur*

Los Angeles
Davis, Jack *securities dealer*
DeBard, Roger *investment executive*
Emmeluth, Bruce Palmer *investment banker, venture capitalist*
Horning, Robert Alan *securities broker*
Hurwitz, Lawrence Neal *investment banking company executive*
Khan, Sarbuland Bill *inventor, entrepreneur, consultant*
Koffler, Stephen Alexander *investment banker*
Lewis, Edward A. *investment manager*
Mann, Nancy Louise (Nancy Louise Robbins) *entrepreneur*
Michaelis, George H. *securities executive*
Nilles, John Mathias (Jack Nilles) *entrepreneur*
Ogle, Edward Proctor, Jr. *investment counseling executive*
Perry, Donald Lester, II *venture capitalist*
Reed, George Ford, Jr. *investment executive*
Seidel, Joan Broude *stockbroker, investment advisor*
Setlin, Alan John *entrepreneur*
Shanahan, R. Michael *securities dealer*
Wiseley, Richard Eugene *securities corporation executive*

Menlo Park
Bissell, Betty Dickson *retired stockbroker*
Hellman, Robert Barry, Jr. *venture capitalist*
Hsu, Charles *venture capitalist*
Lucas, Donald Leo *private investor*
Marxman, Gerald Albert *venture capital executive*
Roberts, George R. *venture capital company executive*
Walsh, William Desmond *investor*

Monarch Beach
Hartness, Sandra Jean *venture capitalist*

Napa
Strock, David Randolph *brokerage house executive*

Newport Beach
Davidson, David Neal *securities sales executive*

North Hollywood
Marshall, Conrad Joseph *entrepreneur*

Oakland
Bach, Martin Wayne *stockbroker, owner antique clock stores*
Swaney, Thomas Robbins *venture capitalist*

Orinda
Rosenberg, Barr Marvin *investment advisor, economist*

Palos Verdes Estates
Mennis, Edmund Addi *investment management consultant*

Pasadena
Arnott, Robert Douglas *investment company executive*
Gold, Michael Nathan *investment banker, management consultant*
Lauter, James Donald *stockbroker*
Liebau, Frederic Jack, Jr. *investment manager*

Piedmont
Alford, Joan Franz *entrepreneur*
Ames, Lawrence Coffin, Jr. *investment counsellor*

Rancho Santa Fe
Polster, Leonard H. *investment company executive*

Riverside
Walter-Robinson, Carol Sue *investment executive*

Ross
Rosenbaum, Michael Francis *securities dealer*

San Clemente
Tober, Mark Robert *investment representative, stockbroker*

San Diego
Foster, Ken D. *securities trader*
Gengor, Virginia Anderson *financial planning executive, educator*
Holderman, John Loran *financial broker*
Martinez, John Stanley *entrepreneur*
Reiff, Theodore Curtis *investment banker*
Smith, Benjamin Eric *venture capitalist, executive*

San Francisco
Apatoff, Michael John *finance executive*
Bass, Audrey *commodities trader*
Comann, Tyler Kent *investment banker*
Dellas, Robert Dennis *investment banker*
deWilde, David Michael *executive search consultant, financial services executive, lawyer*
Dunn, Richard Joseph *investment counselor*
Gardner, James Harkins *venture capitalist*
George, Michael P. *investment banker, lawyer*
Greber, Robert Martin *financial investments executive*
Guilfoyle, Bill *securities executive*
Gund, George, III *financier, professional sports team executive*
Hagenbuch, John Jacob *investment banker*
Halliday, John Meech *investment company executive*
Hambrecht, William R. *venture capitalist*
Harris, Bob *investment company executive*
Howell, Donna Murray *brokerage executive*
Hsieh, Michael Thomas *venture capitalist*
Korins, Leopold *stock exchange executive*
McGettigan, Charles Carroll, Jr. *investment banker*
Mc Kee, Allen Page *investment company executive*
Minella, David A. *investment company executive*
Nodelman, Jared Robert *investment advisor*
Pottruck, David Steven *brokerage house executive*
Quigley, Ruth Helen *entrepreneur*
Redo, David Lucien *investment company executive*
Ricker, Jeffrey Paul *investment strategist, researcher, consultant*
Rowen, Harvey Allen *investment company executive*
Schwab, Charles R. *brokerage house executive*
Shansby, John Gary *investment banker*
Smelick, Robert Malcolm *investment bank executive*
Stein, Alan L. *investment banker*
Stupski, Lawrence J. *investment company executive*
Vallee, Jacques Fabrice *venture capitalist*
Wolfe, Barbara Ahmajan *stock brokerage executive, administrator*

San Jose
Estruth, Jerry Thomas *financial professional*
Flagler, William Lawrence *financial broker*
Hall, Robert Emmett, Jr. *investment banker, realtor*

San Leandro
Pansky, Emil John *entrepreneur*

Santa Ana
Kiang, Assumpta (Amy Kiang) *brokerage house executive*

Santa Barbara
Vos, Hubert Daniel *private investor*

Santa Rosa
Cooper, Annette Carlesta *entrepreneur*

Sherman Oaks
Hagenbuch, Rodney Dale *stock brokerage house executive*

Stanford
Marotta, George Raymond *money manager*

Tarzana
Smuckler, Harvey Glasgow *financial consultant*

Templeton
Guenther, Robert Stanley, II *investment and property executive*

Thousand Palms
Martin, Kevin Jay *investment and development executive*

Walnut Creek
Cervantez, Gil Lawrence *venture capital company executive*

West Covina
Tuck, Edward Fenton *business consultant, venture capitalist*

Westlake Village
Fredericks, Ward Arthur *venture capitalist, food industry consultant*
Reavill, David William *financial investment company executive*
Valentine, Gene C. *securities dealer*

Woodland
Rogers, Michele Denise *investment consultant*

COLORADO

Aurora
Ericson, Mark Frederick *investment analyst*

Boulder
Kimmel, Mark *venture capital company executive*

Colorado Springs
Bennett, Brian Richard *investment broker*
Ramsay, Robert Henry *investment manager*
Tutt, Russell Thayer *investment company executive*

Denver
Heitler, Bruce F. *entrepreneur*
Leraaen, Allen Keith *financial executive*
Sutton, Robert Edward *investment company executive*
Wagner, Judith Buck *investment firm executive*

Englewood
Van Loucks, Mark Louis *venture capitalist, business advisor*

Grand Junction
Skogen, Haven Sherman *investment company executive*

Placerville
Monferrato, Angela Maria *entrepreneur, investor, writer*

HAWAII

Honolulu
Ho, Stuart Tse Kong *investment company executive*
McDermott, Rose Marie Joan *investment company executive*

Kaneohe
Kemp, Eddy Nelson *investment advisory firm executive*

IDAHO

Boise
Ballantyne, James Henry, IV *investor, developer*
Hendren, Merlyn Churchill *investment company executive*

Ketchum
Martinson, John Robert *merchant banker*

Mountain Home
Bergh, David Morgan *entrepreneur*

MISSISSIPPI

Natchez
Laurant, Van, III *entrepreneur*

MONTANA

Billings
Mulvaney, Janelle Williams *securities trader*

Bozeman
Gorman, Brian Dean *investment professional*

Missoula
Liston, Albert Morris *investor, political science educator*

Troy
Sherman, Signe Lidfeldt *securities analyst, former research chemist*

NEVADA

Boulder City
DeVylder, Emil Raymond *investment executive*

Carson City
Hoskins, Thomas Richard, Jr. *corporate securities agent*

Glenbrook
Jabara, Michael Dean *investment banker*

Incline Village
Dale, Martin Albert *investment banking executive*

Las Vegas
Di Palma, Joseph Alphonse *brokerage house executive, lawyer*
Fernandez, Linda Flawn *entrepreneur, social worker*
Supchak, Paul Henry *business owner, entrepreneur*

Reno
Morgenroth, Earl Eugene *entrepreneur*
Newberg, William Charles *stock and real estate broker, automotive engineer*

NEW MEXICO

Alamogordo
Green, Francis William *investment consultant*

Albuquerque
Huffman, Nona Gay *financial consultant, retirement planning specialist*

Santa Fe
Dreisbach, John Gustave *investment banker*
Goldberg, Fredric I. *investment management company executive*
Proyect, Martin H. *investment banker*

OREGON

Chiloquin
Reed, David George *entrepreneur*

Eugene
Pierce, Gretchen Natalie *investment company executive*

Medford
Hennion, Carolyn Laird (Lyn Hennion) *investment executive*

Newberg
Worrall, Roger Charles *investor, management consultant*

Portland
Emery, Susan Woodruff *investment trust official*
Hay, Andrew Mackenzie *merchant banking and commodities company executive*
Housman, Richard J. *custom house broker*
Rangila, Nancy Arnevna Kusala *investment consultant*
Rutherford, William Drake *investment executive, lawyer*

UTAH

Provo
Anderson, Mark T. *business developer, entrepreneur, financier*

Salt Lake City
Coltharp, Hugh Nelson *investor*
Wallace, Matthew Walker *entrepreneur*

WASHINGTON

Bainbridge Island
Smallman, Gail Elizabeth *entrepreneur*

Bellevue
Dunlap, Ron *investment securities executive*
Jones, John Wesley *entrepreneur*
Ryles, Gerald Fay *private investor, business executive*

Bothell
Browning, Jesse Harrison *entrepreneur*

Everett
Nerod, Steve (Schezepan Alexander Nerod) *entrepreneur, designer*

Seattle
Bayley, Christopher T. *international investment banking executive*
Block, Robert Jackson *investment banker*
Nelson, Allen F. *investor relations and proxy solicitation company executive*
Paup, Martin Arnold *real estate and securities investor*
Ragen, Brooks Geer *investment banker*

Tacoma
Foley, Thomas Michael *financial executive*
Habedank, Gary L. *brokerage house executive*

WYOMING

Cheyenne
Myers, Rolland Graham *investment counselor*

Jackson
Hirschfield, Alan J. *entrepreneur*

Wilson
Chrystie, Thomas Ludlow *investor*

CANADA

ALBERTA

Calgary
King, Frank *investment company executive*

Edmonton
Cormie, Donald Mercer *investment company executive*
Pocklington, Peter H. *business executive*

BRITISH COLUMBIA

Vancouver
Harwood, Brian Dennis *securities industry executive*
Lyons, Terrence Allan *merchant banking, investment company executive*

HONG KONG

Hong Kong
Chun, Wendy Sau Wan *investment company executive*

ADDRESS UNPUBLISHED

Ang, Paul Thienchai *entrepreneur, international business consultant*
Arnold, Robert Lloyd *investment broker*
Bernstein, Arthur Harold *venture capital executive*
Carter, Robert Spencer *private investor*
Christopher, Lee Neil *investment company executive, author*
Cockrum, William Monroe, III *investment banker, consultant, educator*
Ellis, Carlton Case *managed futures trading specialist*
Fehribach, Ronald Steven *investment executive*
Fitzgerald, John Charles, Jr. *investment banker*
Friedlander, Charles Douglas *investment company executive, space consultant*
Friedman, Kenneth Todd *investment banker*
Gelpi, Michael Anthony *entrepreneur*
Greene, Frank Sullivan, Jr. *investment management executive*
Hellman, F(rederick) Warren *investment advisor*
Holman, John Foster *investment banker*
Howard, James Webb *investment banker, lawyer, engineer*
Kockerbeck, Conrad Campbell *investment company executive*
Marler, Larry John *private investor*
Muhammad, Khaleedah *entrepreneur, sales and marketing consultant*
Roberts, Kenneth Melvin *investment advisor*
Robinson, Annettmarie *entrepreneur*
Rock, Arthur *venture capitalist*
Rondeau, Doris Jean *entrepreneur, consultant*
Rosier, David Lewis *investment banker*
Szabo, Peter John *investment company executive, financial planner, mining engineer, lawyer*
Thorp, Edward Oakley *investment management company executive*
White-Vondran, Mary Ellen *retired stockbroker*
Wiener, Sydney Paul *investor*

FINANCE: REAL ESTATE

UNITED STATES

ALASKA

Anchorage
Faulkner, Sewell Ford *real estate executive*
Fournier, Walter Frank *real estate executive*
Kelly, Maxine Ann *property developer*
Wolf, Dan C. *real estate associate broker*

Juneau
Goff, Robert Allen *environmental regulator, geologist*

ARIZONA

Bullhead City
Jones, Vernon Quentin *surveyor*

Cottonwood
Izzo, Mary Alice *real estate broker*

Lake Havasu City
Mac-Noye, Shirley *public trust executive*

Mesa
Bell, Daniel Carroll *realtor, ranch and land manager*
McCollum, Alvin August *real estate company executive*

Phoenix
Clements, John Robert *real estate professional*
Donaldson, Wilburn Lester *property management corporation executive*
Mee, Joy Anne *city planning executive*
Mobley, Lucille Johanna *real estate broker*
Schrader, William P. *organization executive, farmer*
Wilson, Carl Arthur *real estate broker, contractor*
Woods, Donald Peter *real estate executive, marketing professional*

Scottsdale
Funke, Julie Ann *real estate broker*
Kohn, Robert Samuel, Jr. *real estate investment consultant*
Lennox, Gloria (Gloria Demeree) *real estate executive*
Lutin, David Louis *real estate development and finance consultant*
Stapleton, Shirley Ann *retired real estate executive*

Tucson
Acton, William John *real estate appraiser and consultant*
Bodinson, Holt *conservationist*
Broce, Dorothy Diane *real estate broker, interior designer*
Swihart, H. Gregg *real estate company executive*

CALIFORNIA

Agoura Hills
Kaplan, Donald Sheldon *real estate developer and rehabilitator, property management company executive*

Alhambra
Schwartz, Modest Euphemia *real estate company executive*

Anaheim
Vaughan, Sandra Jean *real estate asset manager*

Apple Valley
Ledford, Gary Alan *real estate developer*

Bakersfield
Hutchings, Dale *realtor*

Berkeley
Arazi, Lorri Rosenberg *realtor*
Catlin, James C. *conservationist, land use planner, electrical engineer*
Grimes, Ruth Elaine *city planner*
Koomey, Jonathan Garo *energy and environmental analyst*
Tinker, Irene *city and regional planning educator, women's studies educator*

Beverly Hills
Breedlove, James Felman *real estate broker*
Fitzgerald, Valerie Ann *real estate company executive*
Winthrop, John *real estate executive, lawyer*

Big Sur
Cross, Robert Louis *realtor, land use planner, writer*
Owings, Margaret Wentworth *conservationist, artist*

Bonita
Dresser, Jesse Dale *real estate investor*

Burbank
Sigal, Sanford David *real estate developer*

Burlingame
Berwick, Andrew Struthers, Jr. *real estate executive*

Cardiff By The Sea
Koehler, Agnes Theresa *real estate sales executive, business executive*
Weber, Charles Eugene *property management company executive*

Carlsbad
Rosin, Morris *real estate, land development company executive*

Coachella
Williams, Susan Eileen *urban planner*

Compton
Snare, Carl Lawrence, Jr. *real estate company executive*

Coronado
Stames, William Alexander *realtor, cost management executive*

Dana Point
Gong, Carolyn Lei Chu *real estate agent*

Desert Hot Springs
Hohenstein, Henry John *land use planner, educator*

Diamond Bar
Dayala, Haji Farooq *real estate broker*

El Cerrito
Odland, Robert Oliver *land use consultant*

El Macero
Wheeler, Douglas Paul *conservationist, government official, lawyer*

Encinitas
Smith, Kent Essam *real estate developer, flower grower*

Etna
Pace, Felice *environmentalist*

Fair Oaks
Yarrigle, Charlene Sandra Shuey *realtor, investment counselor*

Fontana
Atkinson, Donald D., Sr. *real estate broker*
Poulsen, Dennis Robert *environmentalist*

Fremont
Nevin, David Wright *real estate broker, mortgage broker*

Fresno
Fey, Russell Conwell *urban and regional planning educator*

Gilroy
Amin, Jamillah Maarij (Joyce Marie Joseph) *real estate agent, food technologist*

Glendale
Bitterman, Melvin Lee *real estate developer*
Lee, Ralph Kelly *real estate developer*
Llewellyn, Frederick Eaton *real estate executive*
Yegian, Richard *real estate executive*

Granite Bay
Tanner, John D. *real estate developer, contractor*

Grass Valley
Ozanich, Charles George *real estate broker*

Greenbrae
Ingerman, Michael Leigh *realtor*

Hayward
Klein, Russ Vincent *real estate developer*

Huntington Beach
Barry, James Michael *property management company executive*

Inglewood
Buss, Jerry Hatten *real estate executive, sports team owner*

Irvine
Stack, Geoffrey Lawrence *real estate developer*

Jackson
Steele, John Roy *real estate broker*

La Jolla
Anthony, Harry Antoniades *city planner, architect, educator*
Ripley, Stuart McKinnon *real estate consultant*

La Mesa
Ligon, Patti-Lou E. *real estate investor, educator*

Laguna Beach
Hanauer, Joe Franklin *real estate executive*
Lorenz, Timothy Carl *real estate agent*

Loma Linda
Huff, Dale Eugene *environmental services executive*

Lompoc
Lehman, Gary Douglas *real estate broker*

Long Beach
McClune, Michael Marlyn *real estate asset management company executive*
Miller, Edmund Severn, Jr. *professional land surveyor*

Los Altos
Getreu, Sanford *city planner*

Los Angeles
Abernethy, Robert John *real estate developer*
Beavers, Lynne *real estate broker, importer company executive*
Best, Roger Norman *real estate investment manager*
Diepholz, Daniel Ray *real estate consultant, accountant*
Eckhert, Curtis Dale *environmental health sciences educator*
Furlotti, Alexander Amato *real estate development company executive*
Grazioli, Albert John, Jr. *real estate management executive*
Krieger, Martin H. *planning and design educator*
Kuraishi, Akari Luke *real estate company executive*
Lazaruk, Kirk Maurice *real estate developer, land use planner, consultant*
Levy, Alan David *real estate executive*
Nelson, James Augustus, II *real estate executive, architect, banker*
Nguyen, Edward Duy *real estate developer*
Osgood, Frank William *urban and economic planner*
Peiser, Richard Bondy *real estate developer, educator*
Swartz, Roslyn Holt *real estate investment executive*
Truman, Edward Crane *real estate manager, consultant, composer*
Wachs, Martin *urban planning educator*

Lynwood
Dove, Donald Augustine *city planner, educator*

Manhattan Beach
Krienke, Carol Belle Manikowske (Mrs. Oliver Kenneth Krienke) *realtor*

Manteca
Raymus, Toni Marie *real estate executive, newspaper publisher*

Mendocino
Carpenter, Donald Blodgett *real estate appraiser*

Menlo Park
Goodman, Beatrice May *real estate professional*
Wollenberg, David Arthur *real estate developer*

Modesto
Griffin, Linda Sue *appraiser*

Napa
Neuman, James Burton *land company executive*

National City
Potter, J(effrey) Stewart *property manager*

Newbury Park
Fredericks, Patricia Ann *real estate executive*
Guggenheim-Boucard, Alan Andre Albert Paul Edouard *business executive, international consultant*

Newport Beach
Bertea, Hyla Holmes *real estate investor*
Caldwell, Courtney Lynn *lawyer, real estate consultant*
Griffith, John Gordon *real estate company officer*
Matteucci, Dominick Vincent *real estate developer*
Mc Cardle, Randall Raymond *real estate developer*
Mickelson, Greg R. *commerical real estate broker*
Mink, Maxine Mock *real estate executive*
Shank, Thom Lewis *real estate executive, entertainment consultant*
Torrianni, Diane Louise *acquisitions specialist*

Northridge
Struhl, Stanley Frederick *real estate developer*

Oakland
Anthony, Elaine Margaret *real estate executive, interior designer*
Fischer, Michael Ludwig *environmental executive*
Kahn, Vivian *urban planner*
Loebig, Larry E. *realtor, consultant*

Ontario
Ariss, David William, Sr. *real estate developer*

Oxnard
Bond, Audrey Mae *real estate broker*
Narula, Mohan Lal *realtor*

Palm Desert
Wiedle, Gary Eugene *real estate management company executive*

Palo Alto
Warne, William Elmo *irrigationist*
Wong, Y(ing) Wood *real estate investment company executive*
Woolf-Scott, Helene Lyda *real estate developer*

Pasadena
Crowley, John Crane *real estate developer*
Freedman, Gregg *real estate appraisal company executive*
Holabird, Timothy Marshall *real estate appraiser*

Patterson
Simpson, Rod Rex *city planner*

Placentia
Bush, June Lee *real estate executive*

Placerville
Craib, Kenneth Bryden *resource development executive, physicist, economist*

Portola Valley
Litton, Martin *conservationist*

Poway
Wright-Quastler, Reba *urban planner*

Rolling Hills
Allbee, Sandra Moll *real estate broker*

Rough and Ready
Nix, Barbara Lois *real estate broker*

Sacramento
Donelson, Irene W. *property manager*
Oliva, Stephen Edward *resource conservationist, lawyer*

San Bernardino
Willis, Harold Wendt, Sr. *real estate developer*

San Diego
Bezer, David Leon *real estate appraiser*
Davis, James McCoy *real estate executive*
DeMarco, Ralph John *real estate developer*
Mabie, Ruth Marie *realtor*
Munson, Lucille Marguerite (Mrs. Arthur E. Munson) *real estate broker*
Oldham, Maxine Jernigan *real estate broker*

San Francisco
Barnes, William Anderson *real estate investment manager*
Brower, David Ross *conservationist*
Freund, Fredric S. *real estate broker, property manager*
Friedman, Bruce David *real estate and finance executive*
Frush, James Carroll, Jr. *real estate development company executive*
Pendleton, Alan R. *conservation agency executive*
Sause, Helen *redevelopment executive*
Schoch, David Henry *real estate executive*

San Jose
Rothblatt, Donald Noah *urban and regional planner, educator*

San Luis Obispo
Havens, Candace Jean *planning consultant*

San Marino
Van Karnes, Kathleen Walker *realtor*

Santa Barbara
Arnold, Michael Neal *real property appraiser, consultant*
Capelli, Mark Henri *coastal planner, university lecturer*

Santa Cruz
Dilbeck, Charles Stevens, Jr. *real estate company executive*

Santa Monica
McGann, John Milton *real estate executive*

Santa Rosa
Brunner, Howard William *professional land surveyor*
Cohen, Mark Jeffrey *real estate owner, broker*

Sausalito
Klingensmith, Arthur Paul *relocation and redevelopment consultant*

Shaver Lake
Robertson, Karen Jean *real estate broker, appraiser*

South Gate
Funk, Milton Albert *real estate broker*

South Pasadena
Bernal, Harriet Jean Daniels *real estate salesperson*

Stockton
Smith, Dana Kruse *real estate developer*

Temecula
Egger, Ernest Alois *urban planner*

Torrance
Alter, Gerald L. *real estate executive*
Krueger, Kurt Edward *environmental management company official*

Tracy
Dittman, Deborah Ruth *real estate broker*

Tustin
Pauley, Richard Heim *real estate counselor*
Prizio, Betty J. *property manager, civic worker*

Venice
Rosenthal, Richard Jay *real estate consultant, mediator, educator*

Yorba Linda
Vilardi, Agnes Francine *real estate broker*

COLORADO

Aurora
Bobrick, Steven Aaron *property manager*

Boulder
Hammell, Grandin Gaunt *real estate consultant*
Morris, John Theodore *planning official*
Stepanek, Joseph Edward *industrial development consultant*

Colorado Springs
Bowers, Zella Zane *real estate broker*
Christensen, C(harles) Lewis *real estate developer*
Everson, Steven Lee *lawyer, real estate executive*
Scott, Robert Keith *economic development executive*

Denver
Greene, James Fiedler *real estate executive*
Halverson, Steven Thomas *lawyer, real estate executive*
Howlett, John David *urban planner, consultant*
Larson, Kenneth Gerard *real estate professional*
Mugler, Larry George *regional planner*
Norman, John Edward *petroleum landman*
Schroff, William K. *real estate professional, business consultant*

Englewood
Smyth, David Shannon *real estate investor, commercial and retail builder and developer*

Fort Collins
Frank, Joe Eugene *city planner*
Sprague, Amaris Jeanne *real estate broker*

Fort Morgan
Ostermiller, John Victor *retired real estate company executive*

Golden
Keatinge, Cornelia Wyma *architectural preservationist consultant, lawyer*
Sacks, Arthur Bruce *environmental and liberal arts educator*

Grand Junction
Nelson, Paul William *real estate broker*

Lakewood
Penwell, Jones Clark *real estate appraiser, consultant*

Littleton
Bettin, Janene Edna *real estate broker*

Longmont
Dell, Kenneth Charles *city planner and urban designer*
Galnick, Mitchell Neil *real estate developer, lawyer*

Monument
Farrar, Lucy Ellen *real estate broker*

Vail
Bowen, Peter Geoffrey *real estate investment advisor*
Jamar, Peter Norton *urban planner*
Kelton, Arthur Marvin, Jr. *real estate developer*

Wheat Ridge
Stuart, Barbara Kathryn *real estate broker, consultant, genealogist*

FLORIDA

Fort Lauderdale
Mooney, Catherine Lee *real estate broker*

Miami
Esslinger, Anna Mae Linthicum *realtor*

HAWAII

Honolulu
Albano, Andres, Jr. *real estate developer, real estate broker*
Ching, Stefanie W. *realtor*
Gillmar, Jack Notley Scudder *real estate company executive*
Henely, Joann Housh *real estate company owner*
Kim, Karl Eujung *urban planning educator*
Kinard, R. Chris *real estate and agricultural company executive*
Latini, Henry Peter *real estate management executive*
Luke, Lance Lawton *real estate and construction consultant*
Lum, Jody Mae Kam Quon *real property appraiser*
Olsen, Harris Leland *real estate and international business executive, educator*
Sofos, Stephany Louise *real estate executive*
Vinton, Alice Helen *real estate company executive*
Walker, Margaret Smith *real estate company executive*

Kailua
Reed, Robert William *city planner, educator*

Koloa
Cobb, Rowena Noelani Blake *real estate broker*

Lahaina
Mitchell, Thomas George *real estate company executive*

Waianae
Armitage, Carinthia Urbanette *realtor*

IDAHO

Boise
Burnham, William A. *wildlife protection society administrator*
Winder, Charles L. *real estate executive*

Idaho Falls
Merritt, Alan Edwin *environmental professional*
Williams, Phyllis Cutforth *retired realtor*

Moscow
Newsome, Edward Baldwin *real estate broker, retired insurance agent*

Payette
Jones, Donna Marilyn *real estate broker, legislator*

Stanley
Kimpton, David Raymond *natural resource consultant, writer*

Troy
Hepler, Merlin Judson, Jr. *real estate broker*

MISSOURI

Chesterfield
Thomas, Violeta de los Angeles *real estate broker*

MONTANA

Great Falls
Stevens, George Alexander *realtor*

Sidney
Beagle, John Gordon *real estate broker*

NEVADA

Carson City
Empey, Gene F. *real estate executive*

Las Vegas
Griffin, James Edward *real estate consultant*
Han, James Sebastian *commercial real estate broker, consultant*
Jeske, Keith William *real estate and mortgage executive*
Maravich, Mary Louise *real estate professional*
Pulliam, Francine Sarno *real estate broker and developer*
Rosenstein, Leonard *real estate company executive*
Thomas, Peter M. *real estate developer*

Reno
Davenport, Janet Lee *real estate saleswomen, small business owner*
Jennison, Brian L. *environmental specialist*

Winnemucca
Clemons, Lynn Allan *land use planner*

NEW MEXICO

Alamogordo
Black, Maureen *realty company executive*

Albuquerque
Davis, Betty Jean Bourbonia *real estate investment executive*
Edenfield, T(homas) Keen, Jr. *real estate developer*
Godfrey, Richard George *real estate appraiser*
Shaw, A. Park, III *commercial real estate broker*
Stahl, Jack Leland *real estate company executive*
Tinnin, Thomas Peck *real estate professional*
Vihstadt, Robert Francis *real estate broker*

Los Alamos
Farmer, George Thomas, Jr. *environmental scientist, consultant*

Mora
Hanks, Eugene Ralph *land developer, cattle rancher, retired naval officer*

Santa Fe
Ingoldsby, William Power *realtor*
Leinberger, Christopher Brown *urban development consultant, writer*
Ohlsen, Gerald G. *real estate developer, lawyer*

OREGON

Beaverton
Standring, James Douglas *real estate developer*

Bend
Hilderbrand, John Ormand *real estate agent, retired rancher*

Eugene
Farkas, Abraham Krakauer *urban developer, educator*
Nelson, Robert William *real estate executive*

Grants Pass
Comeaux, Katharine Jeanne *realtor*

Gresham
Myers, Al *realtor, property manager, mayor*

Lake Oswego
Morse, Lowell Wesley *real estate executive, banking executive*

Mcminnville
Linscheid, Dan Edwin *land surveyor*

Medford
Andersen, Doris Evelyn *real estate broker*
Johnson, Curtis Lee *real estate executive and broker*

Ontario
Rupe, Dallas Gordon, III *real estate property manager, securities arbitrator*

Portland
Dickinson, Janet Mae Webster *relocation consulting executive*
Packard, Robert Goodale, III *urban planner*

Wilsonville
Schurter, Bette Jo *realtor*

UTAH

Blanding
Royer, Theodore Henry *real estate sales, property management*

Midvale
Teerlink, J(oseph) Leland *real estate developer*

Salt Lake City
Stephenson, Ned Eldon *real estate development company executive*

WASHINGTON

Bellevue
Williams, Stuart Vance *real estate executive*

Bellingham
Friedman, Mitch Alan *conservation biologist*
Harmon, John Emery *public housing agency executive*

Cheney
Winchell, Richard G. *urban planning educator, consultant*

Colville
Ames, Norma Harriet *wildlife consultant, writer*

Everett
Edwards, Kirk Lewis *real estate company executive*

Friday Harbor
Padve, Martha Bertonneau *urban planning and arts consultant, fundraiser*

Issaquah
Price, Darold Wayne *real estate investor*

Olympia
Stewart, Jeffree Robert *environmental planner, artist*

Puyallup
DeBock, Ronald Gene *real estate company executive, clergy member*

Redmond
Doman, Margaret Horn *land use planner consultant, civic official*

Rollingbay
Morris, Donald Charles *real estate developer*

Seattle
Baldwin, Richard Eugene *real estate executive*
Boyd, Marc Adam *real estate company executive*
Chandler, Bridgett Ann *urban planner*
Dillard, Marilyn Dianne *property manager*
Gerrodette, Charles Everett *real estate company executive, consultant*
Hoffman, David Wayne, III *real esate appraiser*
McKinnon, James Buckner *real estate sales executive, writer, researcher*
Moudon, Anne Vernez *urban design educator*
Sander, Susan Berry *environmental planning engineering corporation executive*
Saulness, Fiona *real estate executive*
Stevens, Clyde Benjamin, Jr. *property manager, retired naval officer*
Tovar, Carole L. *real estate management administrator*
Wesley, Virginia Anne *real estate property manager*

WYOMING

Green River
Baker, Bonnie Ann *real estate broker*

Rawlins
Pedersen, Martin Albert *consulting engineer, surveyor*

CANADA

BRITISH COLUMBIA

Vancouver
Belzberg, Samuel *real estate investment professional*
Goldberg, Michael Arthur *land policy and planning educator*
Hassan, Tom Andrew *land developer*

ADDRESS UNPUBLISHED

Ahlgren, Gibson-Taylor *real estate broker*
Angevin, Robert Perkins Brown *real estate development executive*
Craig, Michael Scott *real estate executive, pharmacologist*
Dickey, Robert Marvin (Rick Dickey) *property manager*
Doyle, Theresa Lipari *real estate and marketing executive*
Foley, Daniel Edmund *real estate development executive*
Frazier, Gary Lawson *real estate investment executive*
Haberlin, William Earl *real estate company executive*
Hamilton, Calvin Sargent *planning consultant, retired city official*
Hodson, Nancy Perry *real estate agent*
Hufschmidt, Maynard Michael *resources planning educator*
Jemmott, Elizabeth Joy *real estate broker*
Josephson, Harold Allan *real estate developer*
Jungbluth, Kirk E. *real estate appraiser, mortgage banking executive*
Karakey, Sherry JoAnne *financial and real estate investment company executive, interior designer*
Mallen, Bruce *real estate developer, educator, producer, economist, consultant*
Mann, Clarence Charles *real estate company official*
Matthews, Valerie Jo *development company executive*
Meyer, Daniel Kramer *real estate executive*
Montague, Sidney James *real estate developer*
Moore, Matthew Emerson *environmental program planning management specialist*
Moore, Shirley Beaham *real estate professional, civic worker*
Morehouse, Carl Edward *land use planner*
Nakahata, Tadaka *retired consulting engineer, land surveyor*
Ownbey, Lenore F. Daly *real estate investment specialist*
Porosky, Michael Hanny *real estate and investment company executive*
Richman, Marvin Jordan *real estate developer, investor, educator*
Rosenfield, James Steven *real estate developer*
Snidow, Ronald Wayne *real estate agent*
Steblay, Craig Douglas *real estate executive, entrepreneur*
Stern, John Louis *real estate development and management executive*
Tamkin, Curtis Sloane *real estate development company executive*
Taylor, Nathaniel Hutchins *real estate executive*
Wauters, Shirley Stapleton *retired real estate executive*
Wood, Linda Gaye *real estate development company executive*
Ziomek, Stephen Phillip *business owner*

GOVERNMENT: AGENCY ADMINISTRATION

UNITED STATES

ALASKA

Anchorage
Baxter, Duby Yvonne *government official*
Lawrence, Kelly Joy *federal agency administrator*
Lindbeck, Stephen Emanuel *state agency administrator*
Nolan, James Michael *fire chief*
Porter, Brian Stanley *police chief*
Storm, Joette Getse *government agency public relations specialist*

Fairbanks
Davis, Charles Lee *fire marshal*

Juneau
Burke, Marianne King *state agency administrator, financial executive*
Nordlund, James Robert *state agency administrator*

Klawock
Will, Gary Dean, Jr. *director of public safety*

ARIZONA

Flagstaff
Schoner, Steven Ronald *park ranger*

Glendale
Goforth, Nathan Dan *police officer*

Phoenix
Bates, Stanley Francis *public administrator*
Bishop, C. Diane *state agency administrator, educator*
Brunacini, Alan Vincent *fire chief*
Garrett, Dennis Andrew *police official*
Nielson, Theo Gilbert *law enforcement official, university official*

Scottsdale
Hill, Robert Martin *police detective, consultant, lecturer*

Tempe
Pies, Ronald E. *city official*

Tucson
Done, Robert Stacy *criminal investigation specialist, consultant*
Lehner, Gregory Michael *federal agency administrator*
Seastone, Brian Arthur *protective services official, consultant*

CALIFORNIA

Aliso Viejo
Cook, Thomas Edward *federal agency administrator*

Anaheim
Bowman, Jeffrey R. *protective services official*
Colson, Bret Sterling *public information officer*
Gaston, Randall Wallace *chief of police*

Benicia
von Studnitz, Gilbert Alfred *state official*

Bishop
Dodge, Douglas Stuart *federal agency administrator*

Bonita
Yokley, Richard Clarence *fire department administrator*

Burbank
Chaffee, James Albert *protective services official*

Castro Valley
Palmer, James Daniel *inspector*

Claremont
Ffolkes, Marco Rodgers *security specialist, researcher, consultant*

Compton
Fonza, Milford R. *fire protection official*

Concord
Hughes, John Willars *police officer*

Coronado
Hutchins, Jeffrey Carlton *protective services official*

El Centro
Davis, Nathan Chilton *federal agency administrator*
Steensgaard, Anthony Harvey *federal agent*

El Monte
Clayton, Wayne Charles *protective services official, educator*
George, Leslie Earl *protective services official*

Fremont
Jackson, Keith Douglas *police captain*
Steckler, Craig Theodore *law enforcement official*

Galt
Keller, Michael Crosley *correctional facilities official*

Garden Grove
Sherrard, Raymond Henry *retired government official*

Indio
Hare, Paul DeHaven *public safety official*

Inglewood
Thompson, Oliver Maurice *protective services official*

La Jolla
Brueckner, Bonnie Lichtenstein *security administrator*

La Verne
Mautz, Edward John *professor, public information officer*

Lagunitas
Mann, Karen *consultant, educator*

Long Beach
Jeffery, James Nels *protective services official*
Omel, Harold *protective services official*

Los Angeles
Anderson, Marshall L. *law enforcement administrator*
Bangs, John Wesley, III *law enforcement administrator*
Davis, Gray *state controller*
Hernandez, Sergio Joseph *investigator*
Montoya Thompson, Velma *federal agency administrator*
Williams, Willie *protective services official*

Malibu
Edmiston, Joseph Tasker *state official*

Moraga
Laye, John E(dward) *contingency planning and disaster recovery consulting executive*

Napa
Perry, Joseph Martin *fire chief*

Newark
Chan, Allen Fong *protective services official*

Oakland
Ewell, P. Lamont *fire department chief*
Rodgers, Audrey Penn *public information officer*
Samuels, Joseph, Jr. *police chief*

Ontario
Bernard, Alexander *airport police official*

Orange
Rudat, David L. *fire chief*

Palos Verdes Estates
Basnight, Arvin Odell *public administrator, aviation consultant*

Pasadena
Lowenthal, Tina Marie *contract negotiator*
Schander, Mary Lea *police official*
Tribbett, James Vernon *federal agency administrator*

Placerville
Palmieri, Rodney August *state agency administrator, pharmacist*

Redlands
Enslow, Mel Dennis *fire chief*

Richmond
Lansdowne, William M. *police chief*

Riverside
Poole, Harry Wendell *county group probation counselor*

Rocklin
Ha, Chong Wan *state government executive*

Roseville
Simms, Thomas Haskell *chief of police*

Sacramento
Archer, Mary Jane *state agency administrator*
Costamanga, Gary *fire chief*
Drown, Eugene Ardent *federal agency administrator*
Dunaway, Margaret Ann (Maggie Dunaway) *state agency administrator, consultant*
Gentry, James William *retired state official*
Livingston, Alvin Jacob *state official*
McDowell, Marion *state agency director*
Muehleisen, Gene Sylvester *retired law enforcement officer, state official*
Neville, Monica Mary *state assembly program executive*
Peters, Kenneth Darryl, Sr. *contracts administrator*
Pettite, William Clinton *public affairs consultant*
Renfro, Leonard Earl, II *protective services professional*
Strock, James Martin *state agency administrator, lawyer, conservationist*

San Bernardino
Boyles, Gary Edward *protective services official*

San Bruno
Kell-Smith, Carla Sue *federal agency administrator*

San Diego
Sanders, Jerry *protective services official*

San Francisco
Green, Katherine Elizabeth *federal agency administrator*
Honig, Bill *state educational administrator*
Ribera, Anthony D. *protective services official*
Tognetti, Gene *protective services official, consultant*

San Jose
Brooks, Raymond *protective services official*

Santa Ana
Walters, Paul *protective services official*

Santa Barbara
Goddard, Marshall Lewis, Jr. *fire battalion chief*
Los, Stanley Cornelius, Jr. *security consultant, private investigator*
Shelton, Philip Anderson *criminal investigator, writer*

Santa Cruz
Lewis, B(enjamin) Earl *criminal justice system consultant*

Santa Monica
Brucker, Connie *police officer, consultant*
Winchell, Robert Allen *government agency administrator, accountant*

Simi Valley
Schubert, Anne Maureen *industrial waste administrator*

Sonora
Efford, Michael Robert *police administrator, educator*

Stockton
Chavez, Edward *police chief*
Jackson, Jewel *state youth authority executive*

Sunnyvale
Bailey, Frank Ronald *government executive, technology educator*

West Sacramento
Guay, Gordon Hay *postal service executive, marketing educator, consultant*

Westlake Village
Rogge, Richard Daniel *former government executive, security consultant, investigator*

Whittier
Stone, George Alvin *protective services official*

Yuba City
Doscher, Richard John *police captain, division commander*

COLORADO

Aurora
Barnes, Raymond Edward *fire department official*

Boulder
Larson, Kurt Paul *fire chief*

Colorado Springs
Kramer, Lorne C. *protective services official*
Navarro, Manuel *protective services official*

Denver
Andersen, Michael Paul *government agency payroll manager*
Gonzales, Richard L. *fire department chief*

Holmes-Calvert, Jacquelin Ann *workers compensation administrator*
Logan, James Scott, Sr. *emergency management program specialist*
Murphy, Dennis Robert *state motor vehicle technical coordinator*
Nash, Stella B. *government nutrition administrator*
Nyquist, Maurice Otto *government agency administrator and scientist*
Simons, Lynn Osborn *state education official*
Smith, Waldo Gregorius *former government official*
Smith, Walter Rogers *protective services administrator*

Englewood
McBeth, Ruben Jose, Jr. *retired criminal justice administrator*
Trenary, Ralph Hiram, III *federal agency administrator, human resources manager*

Golden
Kirschner, Bruce Herbert *federal official, political science educator*
Olson, Marian Katherine *emergency management executive, consultant, publisher*

Grand Junction
Olson, Sylvester Irwin *government official*

Lakewood
Berger, John Milton *state agency administrator*
Hayes, Roger Matthew *deputy sheriff*
Johnston, Charles *protective services official*
Miller, Neil Allen *police agent*
Young, Connie Sue *public affairs specialist*

Limon
Waide, Lloyd A(rnold) *protective services official*

Littleton
Manos, Christopher Alexander *crime prevention specialist*

Longmont
Kaminsky, Glenn Francis *deputy chief of police retired, business owner, teacher*

Vail
McGee, Michael Jay *fire marshal, educator*

DISTRICT OF COLUMBIA

Washington
Hansen, Frederic J. *state environmental agency director*

HAWAII

Honolulu
Chang, Donald S. M. *fire department chief*
Devaney, Donald Everett *law enforcement official*
Gibb, Douglas Glenn *police chief*
Kudo, Emiko Iwashita *former state official*
Miyamoto, Owen *state agency administrator*
Nakashima, Mitsugi *state agency administrator*
Roseberry, Edwin Southall *state agency administrator*

Kaneohe
Ikeda, Moss Marcus Masanobu *retired state education official, lecturer, consultant*

Lihue
Hunt, John Joseph *state agency administrator*

IDAHO

Boise
Ferrell, Yvonne Signe *state recreation commission administrator*
Heitman, Gregory Erwin *state official*
Humpherys, A. Rich *state police administrator*
Mulvihill, Peter James *fire protection engineer*
Ryals, Connie *state government department administrator*
Turner, Hal Wesley *state agency administrator*
Wood, Jeannine Kay *state official*

Idaho Falls
Macdonald, Donald William *federal agency administrator*

MARYLAND

Bethesda
Varmus, Harold Eliot *government health institutes administrator, educator*

MONTANA

Billings
Ballard, Lorren Lee *fire protection official*
Ward, David Charles *police chief*

Helena
Howe, Adrian Clarence *state agency administrator*

NEVADA

Henderson
Klein, Freda *state agency administrator*

Las Vegas
Chevers, Wilda Anita Yarde *probation officer, educator*
Lally, Norma Ross *federal agency administrator, retired*
Marsh, James Robert *federal law enforcement official*

North Las Vegas
Marchand, Russell David, II *fire chief*

Reno
Richard, Marty *fire chief*

NEW MEXICO

Albuquerque
Dorn, James Martin *police sergeant*
Lucchetti, Lynn L. *government executive*
Polisar, Joseph Michael *protective services official*
Williams, Marion Lester *government official*

Hobbs
Fons, August Marion, III *protective services official, educator*

Las Cruces
True, Virgil *retired government official, consultant*

Santa Fe
Curran, Neil Willis *state police chief*
Humphries, William R. *state land commissioner*
McHenry, Patricia Rose *state agency administrator*
Mitio, John, III *state agency administrator*
Vigil, Robert E. *state government official*

Tucumcari
Brockmeier, Alan Lee *protective services official*

OREGON

Medford
Cole, Richard George *public administrator*

Portland
Belille, Ronald *safety and security coordinator*

Salem
Dunn, Kimberly Ann *state agency administrator, archaeologist*

UTAH

Ogden
Empey, Michael D. *protective services official*

Salt Lake City
Flint, Lou Jean *state education official*
Gold, Rick L. *federal government executive*
Morrison, Ralph Evans *state agency administrator*

VIRGINIA

Alexandria
Chamberlain, Adrian Ramond *state agency executive*

WASHINGTON

Aberdeen
Caster, Ronald Lynn *fire chief*

Bellevue
Lucarelli, Peter Raymond *fire chief*

Federal Way
Staab, Joseph Raymond *retired federal agency administrator*

Olympia
Gose, Karen Kamara *state arts administrator*
Harding, Jim *state agency executive, energy policy specialist*
Merchant, Judith Miriam *state agency administrator*
O'Keefe, Kathleen Mary *state government official*
Yenson, Evelyn P. *lottery official*

Port Townsend
Farmer, James Douglas *park manager*

Renton
Berkley, Robert John *federal agency professional*

Richland
Dunigan, Paul Francis Xavier, Jr. *federal agency administrator*
Ravely, Victoria Alline *postal clerk*

Seattle
Fehr, Larry Michael *state agency administrator, educator*
Harris, Claude *fire department chief*
Hergert, Richard Gary *government official, property tax assessment executive*
Peddy, Julie Ann *federal agent*
Shanahan, Michael George *police officer*
Stamper, Norman H. *police chief*
Williams, Clarence *protective services official*

Spokane
Mangan, Terence Joseph *police chief*
Williams, Robert Stone *protective services official*

Sumas
Hemry, Larry Harold *immigration inspector*

Tacoma
Hansen, Sharon M. *state agency administrator, policy analyst*

Taholah
Knutzen, Raymond Edward *federal official*

Vancouver
Howsley, Richard Thornton *lawyer, regional government administrator*

Walla Walla
Andring, Ronald Paul *protective services official*

WYOMING

Casper
Reed, James Earl *fire department commander*

Cheyenne
Ayers, Everette Lee *highway patrol director*
Karpan, Kathleen Marie *former state official, lawyer, journalist*

Gillette
Oedekoven, Byron Frank *protective services official*

Rock Springs
Simpson, Richard John *police detective, municipal official*

CANADA

SASKATCHEWAN

Regina
Gordon, Hugh Sangster, Jr. *fire services administrator*
Nuttall, Richard Norris *state agency administrator*
Teichrob, Carol *Canadian provincial official*

ADDRESS UNPUBLISHED

Barham, Steven Walter *state official*
Barker, Mitchell Frederick *former government public relations official*
Brubaker, Crawford Francis, Jr. *government official, aerospace consultant*
Choate, Wayne D. *protective services official*
Clark, Thomas Ryan *retired federal agency executive, business and technical consultant*
Duppong, Margie Ann Claus *retired law enforcement official*
Goodrich, Gloria Jean *federal agency administrator*
Gordon, Peter Lowell *immigration administrator*
Hayes, Gladys Lucille Allen *state community care official, poet, writer*
Hedrick, Basil Calvin *state agency administrator, ethnohistorian, educator, museum and cultural institutions consultant*
Johnson, Rodney Dale *law enforcement officer, photographer*
Keala, Francis Ahloy *security executive*
Kelley, Kevin Patrick *security, safety, risk management administrator*
Kornelly, Irene Louise *state government affairs consultant*
Marquardt, Rod Lewis *probation officer*
Pagani, Beverly Darlene *retired government administrator*
Patino, Isidro Frank *law enforcement educator*
Poimiroo, John Robert *state agency administrator*
Ritchie, Catherine D. *correctional officer, deputy constable*
Roberts, Mary Wendy *state agency administrator*
Sandor, John Abraham *state agency administrator*
Scott, William Herbert *state agency administrator*
Shishido, Calvin M. *special services administrator*
Silva, Robert Owen *retired protective service official*
Taylor, Hourie Lee *law enforcement official*
Waggener, Theryn Lee *law enforcement professional*
Weaver, Joseph Stephen *state park administrator*
Wilson, Sheryl J. *state agency administrator*

GOVERNMENT: EXECUTIVE ADMINISTRATION

UNITED STATES

ALASKA

Anchorage
Gumppert, Karella Ann *federal government official*

Elim
Keith, Robert Allen *Native American Indian tribal executive*

Fairbanks
Smith, Robert London *commissioner, retired air force officer, political scientist, educator*

Juneau
Botelho, Bruce Manuel *state official, mayor*
Brown, Kay (Mary Kathryn Brown) *state official*
Coghill, John Bruce *state official*
Cole, Charles Edward *state attorney general*
Knowles, Tony *governor*
Meacham, Charles P. *president, capital consulting*
Twomley, Bruce Clarke *commissioner, lawyer*
Ulmer, Fran *state official*

Ketchikan
Stanton, Alaire Evelyn *mayor, broadcasting company executive*

Kodiak
Selby, Jerome M. *mayor*

Kokhanok
Nelson, John D., Jr. *village administrator*

Nelson Lagoon
Gundersen, Paul Martin, Sr. *Aleut tribe leader, fisherman*

Ninilchik
Oskolkoff, Grassim *Native American Indian tribal chief*

Seward
Kincheloe, Lawrence Ray *state official*
Murphy, Linda Sue *city official*

Tatitlek
Kompkoff, Gary Phillip *chief of native village, fisherman*

Tok
Miller, William J. *village official*

ARIZONA

Bullhead City
Caisse, Jeanne Mae *city official*

Florence
Griffis, Stanley Douglas *county manager*

Gilbert
Carrico, Donald Jefferson *public transit system manager*

Mesa
Wong, Willie *mayor, automotive executive*

Page
Jentzsch, Richard Allen *city manager*

Paradise Valley
Moya, Sara Dreier *municipal government official*

Phoenix
Arauz, Carlos Gaspar *city official*
Besnette, Francis Henry (Frank Besnette) *state official, educator*
Curcio, Christopher Frank *city official*
Eaton, David E. *city administrator*
Griffiths, Marian E. (Mimi Griffiths) *government administrator*
Hull, Jane Dee *state official, former state legislator*
McClennen, Miriam J. *former state official*
McWhorter, Patrick Sean *lobbyist, consultant*
Miel, Vicky Ann *municipal government executive*
Miner, John Edward *city manager*
Rimsza, Skip *mayor*
Skinner, Nancy Jo *municipal recreation executive*
Spurlock, Cynthia Marie *government official*
Symington, J. Fife, III *governor*
Vanderheiden, Richard Thomas *government official, lawyer*
Welsh, John Richard *state official*
West, Tony *state official*

Scottsdale
Drinkwater, Herbert R. *mayor*
Warnas, Joseph John *municipal official*

Tucson
Dicochea, Alfred Quijada *municipal executive*
Miller, George *mayor*
Williams, Ben Franklin, Jr. *mayor, lawyer*

CALIFORNIA

Anaheim
Daly, Tom *mayor*
Hill, Harry David *city official, human resources professional*

Anderson
Murphy, William Arthur *city manager*

Azusa
Guarrera, Joseph Anthony *city administrator, company director*

Bakersfield
Franey, Philip David *county treasurer, tax collector*
Plane, Fredrick Alan *county official*

Banning
Schweitzer, Raymond D. *city manager, author*

Beverly Hills
Covitz, Carl D. *state official, real estate and investment executive*

Brea
Georgino, Susan Martha *city redevelopment services administrator*

Burbank
Wylie, Karen Elizabeth *local government official*

Chula Vista
Vignapiano, Louis John *municipal official*

Citrus Heights
Nichols, John Roger *county official*

Colton
Lewis, Mark Earldon *city manager*

Coronado
Hostler, Charles Warren *international affairs consultant*

Costa Mesa
Hugo, Nancy *county official, alcohol and drug addiction professional*
West, Cynthya Thomas *municipal agency administrator*

Cypress
Kelly, Christine Elise *city planner*

Downey
Schoettger, Theodore Leo *city official*

El Cajon
Shoemaker, Joan *mayor*

El Centro
Pollock, Richard Edwin *former county administrator*

Fall River Mills
Reed, Eva Silver Star *chieftain*

Felicity
Istel, Jacques Andre *mayor*

Fresno
Patterson, James *mayor*

Fullerton
Campbell, Timothy L. *municipal official*
Sa, Julie *mayor, restaurant chain owner*

Glendale
Day, John Francis *city official, former savings and loan executive, former mayor*
Zarian, Larry *mayor*

Hanford
Gilson, Vicki Cheryl *county official*

Hermosa Beach
Meyer, Gregory Tobin *city official, public administration executive*

Inglewood
Vincent, Edward *mayor*

Irvine
Vander Dussen, Sheri Tulley *city official*

Long Beach
Hennessy, Barbara Rose *city controller*
Levi, Herbert A. *deputy city manager, consultant*
O'Neill, Beverly Lewis *mayor, former college president*

Los Altos
Gray, Robert Donald *mayor*

Los Angeles
Kawasaki, Lillian Yuriko *city general manager environmental affairs*
Lynch, Timothy Bruce *city administrator*
Mancini, William F. *diplomat*
Morales, Margo Melinda *government analyst*
Reagan, Ronald Wilson *former President of United States*
Rice, Donald Blessing *former government executive, corporate executive*
Riordan, Richard J. *mayor*
Young, Caprice Yvonne *municipal official*

Modesto
Lang, Richard Arthur *mayor, educator*
Mensinger, Peggy Boothe *retired mayor*

Monterey Park
Smith, Betty Denny *county official, administrator, fashion executive*

Mountain View
Mason, Carter Gregg *government employee*

Napa
Battisti, Paul Oreste *county supervisor*

Oakland
Harris, Elihu Mason *mayor*
Jennings, Judith Madrone *city official*

Oceanside
Lyon, Richard *mayor, retired naval officer*

Orinda
Conran, James Michael *state government official*

Palo Alto
Fleming, June Helena *city manager*

Pasadena
Hawkey, Philip A. *city manager*

Pomona
Smith, Donna *mayor, small business owner*

Rancho Mirage
Ford, Gerald Rudolph, Jr. *former President of United States*

Redlands
Hanson, Gerald Warner *retired county official*

Redwood City
Franklin, Robert Charles *probation officer*

Richmond
Corbin, Rosemary Mac Gowan *mayor*

Riverside
Downs, Keith David *county official*
Romero, Paul David *municipal official*
Shultz, Kim Todd *municipal official*
Steckel, Barbara Jean *city financial officer*
Wilson, A(rnold) J(esse) *city manager, consultant, communications executive*

Sacramento
Betts, Bert A. *former state treasurer, accountant*
Bolden, Rosamond *state official*
Cozad, Lyman Howard *city manager*
Dunnett, Dennis George *state official*
Grissom, Lee Alan *state official*
Lungren, Daniel Edward *state attorney general*
Mitze, Clark Harold *retired arts administrator*
Nelson, Alan Curtis *government official, lawyer*
Peck, Ellie Enriquez *retired state administrator*
Serna, Joe, Jr. *mayor*
Takasugi, Nao *state official, business developer*
Walston, Roderick Eugene *state government official*
Whiteside, Carol Gordon *state official, former mayor*
Wilson, Pete *governor of California*

Salinas
Mora, David Richard *city manager*
Wong, Walter Foo *county official*

San Bernardino
Lenz, Philip Joseph *municipal administrator*
Stark, S. Daniel, Jr. *convention and visitors bureau executive*
Turoci, Marsha May *county official*

San Diego
Bernstein, Sandra Marie *county official*
Bliesner, James Douglas *municipal/county official, consultant*
Cazares, Hector Robert *county executive, director of animal control*
Edblom, Dale Clarence *city official*
Golding, Susan *mayor*
Lipke, James Scott *municipal official*
Partida, Gilbert A. *chamber of commerce executive*
Ramirez, Steven Adrian, Sr. *city official*

San Francisco
Fischer, David Joseph *ambassador*
Grant, Surlene Georgette *public information officer*
Jordan, Frank M. *mayor*
Lee, Richard Carl *government official*
Mayer, Neil Stephen *municipal official*
Migden, Carole *county official*
Quinn, Harry John *government administrator, real estate consultant*
Taylor, John Lockhart *city official*

San Gabriel
Paules, Paul Michael *city administrator*

San Jose
Gonzales, Ron *county supervisor*
Hammer, Susan W. *mayor*
Winslow, Frances Edwards *city official*

San Luis Obispo
Blakely, David Albert *county supervisor*
Zepeda, Susan Ghozeil *county official*

San Rafael
Jindrich, Ervin James *coroner, medical and legal consultant*

Sanger
Haddix, Charles E. *legislative and regulatory consultant*

Santa Cruz
Wilbur, Marguerite Louise *redevelopment manager*

Santa Monica
de La Vega, Dianne Winifred DeMarinis (Mrs. Jorge de La Vega) *government official*

Santa Rosa
Duffy, Barbara Jean *county official, librarian, education consultant, publisher*
Flores, George Raymond *county health officer*

Saratoga
Houston, Elizabeth Reece Manasco *county education official, consultant*
Peacock, Harry Richard *city manager*

Solana Beach
Apple, Steven Anthony *city official*

South Gate
Mosby, Dorothea Susan *municipal official*

Stanford
Shultz, George Pratt *former government executive, economics educator*

Stockton
Darrah, Joan *mayor*

Torrance
Geissert, Katy *mayor*
Ng, Albert Young *city manager*

West Covina
Manners, Nancy *mayor*

West Hollywood
English, Joan Patricia *municipal official*

Westminster
Smith, Charles Vinton *mayor, retired electrical engineer*

Woodland
Wegener, Gary Raymond *municipal official*

Yuba City
Kemmerly, Jack Dale *retired state official, aviation consultant*

COLORADO

Aurora
Tauer, Paul E. *mayor, educator*

Boulder
Callen, Lon Edward *county official*

Colorado Springs
Isaac, Robert Michael *mayor, lawyer*

Denver
Buckley, Vikki *state official*
Farley, Robert Day *metropolitan planning official*
Hackworth, Theodore James, Jr. *city official*
Minger, Terrell John *public administration institute executive*
Norton, Gale A. *state attorney general*
Romer, Roy R. *governor*
Webb, Wellington E. *mayor*
Wilkes, John Solomon, III *land commissioner*

Eads
Rabe, Steven Glen *town manager, consultant*

Eaton
Carsten, Gary A. *city manager*

Grand Junction
Achen, Mark Kennedy *city manager*
Teck, Ronald Jay *county assessor*

Greeley
Jordan, Loyd Edward *county sheriff*

Lakewood
Morton, Linda *mayor*

Loveland
Chen, Eve Y.V. *city official*

Pueblo
Occhiato, Michael Anthony *city official*

Sterling
Gustafson, Randall Lee *city manager*

DISTRICT OF COLUMBIA

Washington
Lau, Cheryl A. *former state official*
Newman, Frank Neil *federal official*
Peña, Federico Fabian *federal official*
Reilly, William Kane *former government official, educator, lawyer, conservationist*
Rohrback, Michael David *policy analyst*

HAWAII

Honolulu
Cayetano, Benjamin Jerome *governor, former state senator and representative*
Harris, Jeremy *mayor*
Marks, Robert Arthur *lawyer, attorney general*
Tom, Clarence Yung Chen *retired city and county official*

IDAHO

Boise
Batt, Philip E. *governor*
Bauer, Barbara Lois *county official*
Cenarrusa, Pete T. *secretary of state*
Hawkins, James Victor *state official*
Peterson, Martin Lynn *public administrator*

Coeur D Alene
Taggart, Tom *county clerk*

Idaho Falls
Hansen, Lisa Young *municipal agency administrator*

Salmon
Sloan, Lanny Gene *municipal official*

Twin Falls
McAlindin, David Peter *municipal employee*

MONTANA

Billings
Haag, Ken Lee *public works director*
Larsen, Richard Lee *former city manager, business, municipal and labor relations consultant, arbitrator*

Bozeman
Petersen, Gerald Michael *city official*

Fairfield
Graf, Ervin Donald *municipal administrator*

Helena
Cooney, Mike *state official*
Marks, Robert L. (Bob Marks) *treasurer ex-officio, rancher*
Racicot, Marc F. *governor*
Ritter, Russell Joseph *mayor, college official*
Schwinden, Ted *former governor of Montana*
Taylor, Dennis Merrill *state official*

Missoula
DeVore, John Paul *county official*
Kemmis, Daniel Orra *mayor, author*

NEVADA

Carson City
Berkich, John *city manager*
Del Papa, Frankie Sue *state attorney general*
Hammargren, Lonnie *lieutenant governor*
Heller, Dean *state official*
Miller, Robert Joseph *governor, lawyer*
Santor, Ken *state treasurer*
Seale, Robert L. *state treasurer*
Wagner, Sue Ellen *former state official*

Henderson
Bradford, Craig Snow *city official*
Head, Samuel *community development executive*
King, Robert Eugene *economic development consultant*

Las Vegas
Jones, Jan Laverty *mayor*
Lurie, Ron *mayor*
Rowe, Carl Osborn *municipal offical*
Thomson, John Rankin *city manager*

Reno
Balentine, John L. *county official*
Sferrazza, Peter Joseph *mayor, lawyer*

NEW MEXICO

Albuquerque
Grossetete, Ginger Lee *gerontology administrator, consultant*
Haulenbeek, Robert Bogle, Jr. *government official*
Hughes, Herbert Howard *public administrator*
Romo, Gene David *municipal official*

Belen
Luna, Casey *retired state official*

Santa Fe
Gonzales, Stephanie *state official*
Johnson, Gary Earl *governor*
King, David W. *state treasurer*
Valdez, Joseph Vincent, II *state government information management executive*

OREGON

Ashland
Willstatter, Alfred *diplomat*

Dayton
Williams, Kenneth James *retired county official*

Hillsboro
Hays, Bonnie Linn *county official*
Kneese, George Vernon *city manager*

Lake Oswego
Campbell, Colin Herald *former mayor*

Oregon City
Newman, Mary Alice *county official*

Portland
Church, Lorene Kemmerer *retired government official*
Katz, Vera *mayor, former college administrator, state legislator*
McMurdo, C(harles) Gregory *state official*

Salem
Hill, Jim *state official*
Keisling, Phillip Andrew *state official*
Kitzhaber, John Albert *governor, physician, former state senator*
Kulongoski, Theodore R. *state attorney general*
Roberts, Barbara *former governor of Oregon*

UTAH

American Fork
Colborn, Richard Melvin *city official*

Layton
Lawrence, Glenn Scott *state official*

Ogden
Haun, David Harding *government official*
Schow, Terry D. *state official*

Saint George
Sizemore, Kenneth Lee *county official*

Salt Lake City
Alter, Edward T. *state treasurer*
Brockert, John Earl *state official*
Corradini, Deedee *mayor*
Dixon, Katie Loosle *county official*
Foxley, Cecelia Harrison *commissioner*
Graham, Jan *state attorney general*
Hilbert, Robert Backus *county water utility administrator*
Johnson, Frank *state official, educator*
Leavitt, Michael Okerlund *governor, insurance executive*
Sorensen, Craig Burg *county official*

Tooele
Ewing, Dennis D. *county clerk, realtor*

WASHINGTON

Dayton
McFarland, Jon Weldon *county commissioner*

Kirkland
Campbell, Barbara Ann *state official, director*

Oak Harbor
Nevins, Keith Patrick *city supervisor*

Olympia
Gardner, Booth *governor*
Hagens, William Joseph *state official, public health educator*
Lowry, Mike *governor, former congressman*
Murphy, Michael Joseph *county official*
O'Brien, Robert S. *state official*
Pritchard, Joel *state lieutenant governor*

Pullman
Halvorson, Alfred Rubin *mayor, consultant, education educator*

Seattle
O'Neill, Maureen Anne *city administrator, arts administrator*
Rice, Norman B. *mayor*
Skidmore, Donald Earl, Jr. *government official*
Smith, Le Roi Matthew-Pierre, III *municipal administrator*

Sequim
Huston, Harriette Irene Otwell (Ree Huston) *retired county official*

Spokane
Giller, Edward Bonfoy *retired government official, retired air force officer*

Hasson, Steven J. *chairman board of county commissioners*
Lenzi, Jerry C. *state official*

Steilacoom
Moseley, David Herron *public administrator*

Tacoma
Vlasak, Walter Raymond *state official, management development consultant*

Vancouver
Ogden, Daniel Miller, Jr. *government official, educator*
Patella, Lawrence M. *city official*

WYOMING

Cheyenne
Geringer, James E. *governor*
Meyer, Joseph B. *state attorney general*
Rubald, Terry Ellen *state official*
Smith, Stanford Sidney *state treasurer*
Thomson, Thyra Godfrey *former state official*
Wittler, Shirley Joyce *former state official, state commissioner*

Evanston
Hansen, Rodney Allan *city official*

Gillette
Darrington, John Charles *city administrator*

TERRITORIES OF THE UNITED STATES

AMERICAN SAMOA

Pago Pago
Lutali, A. P. *governor of American Samoa*

FEDERATED STATES OF MICRONESIA

Kolonia, Pohnpei
Eu, March Fong *United States ambassador, former state official*

CANADA

ALBERTA

Calgary
Duerr, Alfred *mayor*

Edmonton
Reimer, Jan *mayor*
Rostad, Kenneth Leif *provincial government official*
Towers, Gordon Thomas *province official*

BRITISH COLUMBIA

Richmond
Halsey-Brandt, Greg *mayor*

Surrey
Johnston, Rita Margaret *Canadian provincial government official*

Vancouver
Campbell, Gordon Muir *mayor*
Owen, Philip Walter *mayor, business owner*

Victoria
Harcourt, Michael Franklin *premier of Province of British Columbia*
Lam, David C. *lieutenant governor*

NORTHWEST TERRITORIES

Yellowknife
Cournoyea, Nellie J. *Canadian government official*
Kakfwi, Stephen *Canadian government official*

SASKATCHEWAN

Regina
Archer, Douglas Robert *mayor, insurance services executive*
Mitchell, Robert *province official*
Rolfes, Herman Harold *Canadian government official*
Wiebe, J. E. N. *province official*

Saskatoon
Blakeney, Allan Emrys *Canadian government official, lawyer*
Dayday, Henry *mayor*
Hewitt, William James *municipal official*

YUKON TERRITORY

Whitehorse
Phelps, Willard *Canadian government official*

JAPAN

Chita-gun
Hirohata, Laurie Ann *state agency official*

ADDRESS UNPUBLISHED

Allen, Edgar Burns *records management professional*
Anderson, Dee *government relations consultant*
Cain, Stephen Michael *city official*
Donahue, Dennis Donald *foreign service officer*
Donovan, Walter Edgar *retired mayor*
Eckles, Paul David *city manager*
Hecht, Chic *ambassador, former senator*
Hett, Joan Margaret *civic administrator*
Lampert, Eleanor Verna *retired state official*
McGinnis, Deborah Cheryl *county official*
Miller, Jeffrey Robert *mayor, insurance planner*
Neff, Francine Irving (Mrs. Edward John Neff) *former federal government official*
Nielsen, Glade Benjamin *mayor, former state senator*
Phillips, Rondall Van *city manager*
Rich, David Barry *city official, auditor, accountant, entertainer*
Rudin, Anne Noto *former mayor, nurse*
Singer, Richard Louis *chamber of commerce executive*
Tarkowski, Larry Michael *municipal official*
Thomas, Brian Gordon *municipal finance executive*
Whitney, Jane *foreign service officer*
Wilson, James Barker *lawyer*
Young, Edwin S. W. *federal agency official*

GOVERNMENT: LEGISLATIVE ADMINISTRATION

UNITED STATES

ALASKA

Anchorage
Barnes, Ramona *state legislator*
Toohey, Cynthia D. *state legislator*

Eagle River
Willis, Edward Charles *legislator*

Homer
Phillips, Gail *state legislator*

Juneau
Kelly, Timothy Donahue *state senator*
Mackie, Jerry *state legislator, business owner*
Mulder, Eldon Paul *state legislator, real estate agent*
Pearce, Drue *state legislator*

ARIZONA

Phoenix
Aguirre, Linda G. *state legislator*
Alston, Lela *state senator*
Brewer, Janice Kay *state legislator*
Burns, Brenda *state legislator*
Cajero, Carmen *state legislator*
Keegan, John Charles *state legislator, engineer, consultant*
Kyle, Richard Daniel *state legislator, fundraising consultant*
Preble, Lou-Ann M. *state legislator*
Solomon, Ruth *state legislator, teacher*
Turner, Warren Austin *state legislator*
Wright, Patricia *state legislator*

Scottsdale
Pritzlaff, John Charles, Jr. *former state senator*

Tucson
Bartlett, David Carson *state legislator*

CALIFORNIA

Fresno
Maddy, Kenneth Leon *state senator, lawyer*

Glendale
Russell, Newton Requa *state senator*

Hayward
Sweeney, Michael *state representative*

Huntington Beach
Allen, Doris *state legislator*

Lemon Grove
Owens, Howard Benjamin, III *district director, writer*

Los Angeles
Watson, Diane Edith *state legislator*

Modesto
Snyder, Margaret Elizabeth *assemblywoman, paralegal*

Newport Beach
Cox, Christopher *congressman*

Sacramento
Boatwright, Daniel E. *state legislator*
Bowler, Larry Dean *state legislator*
Brown, Valerie *state legislator*
Brown, Willie Lewis, Jr. *state legislator, lawyer*
Connolly, Tom M. *state legislator, lawyer*
Cortese, Dominic L. *state legislator, farmer*
Detwiler, Peter Murray *legislative consultant, educator*
Holmes, Robert Eugene *state legislative consultant, journalist*
Hughes, Teresa P. *state legislator*
Isenberg, Phillip L. *state legislator*
Killea, Lucy Lytle *state legislator*
Knight, William J. (Pete Knight) *state legislator, retired military officer*
Lokey, R. Eugene *legislative consultant*
Napolitano, Grace F. *state legislator*

San Diego
Alpert, Deirdre Whittleton *state legislator*
Herrera, Francisco Rafael *political advisor*

COLORADO

Colorado Springs
Wells, Jeffrey M. *state senator, lawyer, judge*

Denver
Adkins, Jeanne M. *state legislator*
Allen, Deborah Colleen *state legislator*
Berry, Charles Eugene (Chuck Berry) *state legislator*
Bishop, Tilman Malcolm *state senator, retired college administrator*
Faatz, Jeanne Ryan *state legislator*
Gallagher, Dennis Joseph *state senator, educator*
Kerns, Peggy Shoup *state legislator*
Kopel, Gerald Henry *retired state legislator*
Lyle, Glenda Swanson *state legislator*
Meiklejohn, Alvin J., Jr. *state senator, lawyer, accountant*
Morrison, Marcy *state legislator*
Norton, Thomas Edmond *state senator, engineer*
Schaffer, Robert Warren *state senator*
Sullivan, Patrick James *physician, state representative*
Tanner, Gloria Geraldine *state legislator*
Weissmann, Paul Martin *state legislator*
Wham, Dorothy Stonecipher *state legislator*

Golden
Hopper, Sally *state legislator*

DISTRICT OF COLUMBIA

Washington
Abercrombie, Neil *congressman*
Akaka, Daniel Kahikina *senator*
Allard, Wayne A. *congressman, veterinarian*
Baker, William P. (Bill Baker) *congressman*
Baucus, Max S. *senator*
Becerra, Xavier *congressman, lawyer*
Beilenson, Anthony Charles *congressman*
Bennett, Robert F. *senator*
Berman, Howard Lawrence *congressman*
Bilbray, Brain P. *congressman*
Bingaman, Jeff *senator*
Boxer, Barbara *senator*
Brown, George Edward, Jr. *congressman*
Brown, Hank *senator*
Bryan, Richard H. *senator*
Burns, Conrad Ray *senator*
Calvert, Ken *congressman*
Campbell, Ben Nighthorse *senator*
Cantwell, Maria E. *congresswoman*
Condit, Gary A. *congressman*
Cooley, Wes *Congressman*
Craig, Larry Edwin *senator*
Crapo, Michael Dean *congressman, lawyer*
Cubin, Barbara Lynn *congresswoman, former state legislator, public relations consultant*
Cunningham, Randy *congressman*
DeFazio, Peter A. *congressman*
Dellums, Ronald V. *congressman*
Dicks, Norman De Valois *congressman*
Dixon, Julian Carey *congressman*
Domenici, Pete (Vichi Domenici) *senator*
Dooley, Calvin Millard *congressman*
Doolittle, John Taylor *congressman*
Dornan, Robert Kenneth *congressman*
Dougherty, Charlene *legislative staff member*
Dreier, David Timothy *congressman*
Dunn, Jennifer Blackburn *congresswoman*
Edwards, Don *congressman*
Eshoo, Anna Georges *congresswoman*
Farr, Sam Sharon *congressman*
Fazio, Vic *congressman*
Feinstein, Dianne *senator*
Filner, Bob *congressman*
Furse, Elizabeth *congresswoman, small business owner*
Gorton, Slade *senator*
Hamburg, Daniel (Dan Hamburg) *congressman*
Harman, Jane Frank *congresswoman, lawyer*
Hatfield, Mark O. *senator*
Hayworth, John David, Jr. *congressman, sportscaster, commentator, broadcaster*
Hefley, Joel M. *congressman*
Herger, Wally W. *congressman*
Horn, (John) Stephen *congressman, political science educator*
Inouye, Daniel Ken *senator*
Inslee, Jay R. *congressman, lawyer*
Kempthorne, Dirk Arthur *senator*
Kim, Jay *congressman*
Kolbe, James Thomas *congressman*
Kopetski, Mike *former congressman*
Kyl, Jon *senator*
Lantos, Thomas Peter *congressman*
Lewis, Jerry *congressman*
Lofgren, Zoe *congresswoman, former county government official*
Martinez, Matthew Gilbert *congressman*
Matsui, Robert Takeo *congressman*
McCain, John Sidney, III *senator*
Mc Candless, Alfred A. (Al Mc Candless) *congressman*
McDermott, James A. *congressman, psychiatrist*
McInnis, Scott Steve *congressman, lawyer*
McKeon, Howard P. (Buck McKeon) *congressman, former mayor*
Miller, George *congressman*
Mineta, Norman Yoshio *congressman*
Mink, Patsy Takemoto *congresswoman*
Moorhead, Carlos J. *congressman*
Murkowski, Frank Hughes *senator*
Murray, Patty *senator*
Orton, William H. (Bill Orton) *congressman, lawyer*
Packard, Ronald *congressman*
Packwood, Bob *senator*
Pastor, Ed *congressman*
Pelosi, Nancy *congresswoman*
Pombo, Richard *congressman, rancher, farmer*
Radanovich, George P. *congressman*
Richardson, William Blaine *congressman*
Riggs, Frank *congressman*
Rohrabacher, Dana *congressman*
Roybal-Allard, Lucille *congresswoman*
Royce, Edward R. (Ed Royce) *congressman*
Salmon, Matt *congressman*
Schaefer, Dan L. *congressman*
Schiff, Steven Harvey *congressman, lawyer*
Schroeder, Patricia Scott (Mrs. James White Schroeder) *congresswoman*
Shadegg, John B. *congressman*
Shepherd, Karen *former congresswoman, legislative staff member*
Simpson, Alan Kooi *senator*
Skaggs, David E. *congressman*
Skeen, Joseph Richard *congressman*
Stark, Fortney Hillman (Pete Stark) *congressman*
Stevens, Theodore Fulton *senator*
Stump, Bob *congressman*
Thomas, Craig *senator*
Thomas, William Marshall *congressman*
Torres, Esteban Edward *congressman, business executive*
Tucker, Walter Rayford, III *congressman, lawyer, former mayor*
Vucanovich, Barbara Farrell *congresswoman*
Waters, Maxine *congresswoman*
Waxman, Henry Arnold *congressman*
Williams, Pat *congressman*
Woolsey, Lynn *congresswoman*
Wyden, Ronald Lee *congressman*
Young, Donald E. *congressman*

HAWAII

Hilo
Ushijima, John Takeji *state senator, lawyer*

Honolulu
Baker, Rosalyn *state legislator*
Beirne, Danielle Ululani *state legislator*
Cachola, Romy Munoz *state representative*
Chun Oakland, Suzanne Nyuk Jun *state legislator*
Fasi, Frank Francis *state senator*
Fernandes Salling, Lehua *state senator, lawyer*
Fong, Hiram L. *former senator*
Ikeda, Donna Rika *state senator*
Kobayashi, Ann H. *state legislator*
Takumi, Roy Mitsuo *state representative*

Kailua
George, Mary Shannon *state senator*
Young, Jacqueline Eurn Hai *state legislator*

IDAHO

Boise
Aherns, Pamela Bengson *state legislator*
Barrett, Lenore Hardy *state legislator, mining and investment consultant*
Black, Pete *state legislator, educator*
Darrington, Denton *state senator*
Gurnsey, Kathleen Wallace *state legislator*
Nafziger, Pattie Lois *state legislator*
Ricks, Mark G. *state senator, farmer*
Smyser, Charles Arvil (Skip Smyser) *senator, lawyer*
Stone, Ruby R. *state legislator*
Taylor, W. O. (Bill Taylor) *state legislator, business consultant*

Caldwell
Kerrick, David Ellsworth *state senator, lawyer*

Coeur D Alene
Reed, Mary Lou *state legislator*

Eagle
Carlson, Herb *state legislator*

Idaho Falls
Richardson, Melvin Mark *state legislator, broadcast executive*

Jerome
Bell, Maxine Toolson *state legislator, librarian*

Pocatello
Hofman, Elaine D. *state legislator*

Rupert
Antone, Steve *state legislator, farmer*

MONTANA

Anaconda
McCarthy, Bea *state legislator*

Dutton
DeBruycker, Jane Crystal *state legislator*

Galata
Aklestad, Gary C. *state legislater*

Helena
Bartlett, Sue *state legislator*
Brooke, Vivian M. *state legislator*
Cocchiarella, Vicki Marshall *state legislator*
Ewer, David *state legislator, bond program officer*
Kasten, Betty Lou *state legislator*
Swanson, Emily *state legislator*

Laurel
Blaylock, Chet *state legislator*

Miles City
Bergman, Ellen Marie *state legislator*

NEVADA

Carson City
Lowden, Suzanne *state legislator*
O'Connell, Mary Ann *state senator, business owner*
Tiffany, Sandra L. *state legislator*
Titus, Alice Cestandina (Dina Titus) *state legislator*

Las Vegas
Bilbray, James Hubert *former congressman, lawyer, consultant*

Yerington
Dini, Joseph Edward, Jr. *state legislator*

NEW MEXICO

Albuquerque
Hall, Lois Riggs *former state senator, former symphony orchestra administrator*
Riley, Ann J. *state legislator, technology specialist*
Rutherford, Thomas Truxtun, II *state senator, lawyer*
Wray, Tom C. *state senator, electrical engineering consultant*

Hobbs
Reagan, Gary Don *state legislator, lawyer*

Las Cruces
Porter, William Emme *state legislator, small business owner*

Los Alamos
Wallace, Jeannette Owens *state legislator*

Roswell
Casey, Barbara A. Perea *state representative, educator*
Knowles, Richard Thomas *state legislator, retired army officer*

Santa Fe
Morgan, Lynda M. *state legislator*
Nava, Cynthia D. *state legislator*
Sanchez, Raymond G. *state legislator*
Stefanics, Elizabeth T. (Liz Stefanics) *state legislator*

OREGON

Bend
Luke, Dennis Robert *state legislator, home building company executive*

Portland
Lim, John K. *state senator, business executive*

Saint Helens
Federici, Tony *state legislator, small business owner*

Salem
Bradbury, William Chapman, III *state senator*
Brown, Kate *state legislator*
Bunn, James Lee *congressman*
Cohen, Joyce E. *state senator, investment executive*
Gold, Shirley Jeanne *state legislator, labor relations specialist*
Naito, Lisa Heather *state legislator*
Oakley, Carolyn Le *state legislator, small business owner*
Shibley, Gail Rose *state legislator*
Taylor, Jacqueline Self *state legislator*
VanLeeuwen, Liz Susan (Elizabeth VanLeeuwen) *state legislator, farmer*
Yih, Mae Dunn *state legislator*

Scio
Hayden, Cedric L. *state legislator, dentist*

Troutdale
Minnis, John Martin *state legislator, protective services official*

UTAH

Bountiful
Burningham, Kim Richard *former state legislator*

Cedar City
Hunter, R. Haze *state legislator*

Corinne
Ferry, Miles Yeoman *state official*

Kaysville
Simons, Marlene J. *state legislator, rancher*

Layton
Barlow, Haven J. *state legislator, realtor*

Ogden
Montgomery, Robert F. *state legislator, retired surgeon, cattle rancher*

Provo
Valentine, John Lester *state legislator, lawyer*

Roy
Peterson, Douglas Shurtleff *state legislator, packaging company official*

Salt Lake City
Black, Wilford Rex, Jr. *state senator*
Carnahan, Orville Darrell *state legislator, retired college president*
Howe, Bryant Richard *legislative staff member*
Myrin, N. Alarik *senator, rancher, investor*
Peterson, Millie M. *state legislator*

Sandy
Christensen, Arnold *state senator, electrical contractor*

WASHINGTON

Edwall
Barr, Scott *state legislator*

Everett
Nelson, Gary *county councilman, engineer*

Olympia
Belcher, Jennifer Marion *state legislator, management consultant*
Cooke, Suzette Allen *state representative*
Haugen, Mary Margaret *state legislator*
Kessler, Lynn Elizabeth *state legislator*
Kohl, Jeanne Elizabeth *state senator, sociologist, educator*
Long, Jeanine Hundley *state legislator*
McDonald, Daniel Robert *state senator*
Neeld, Michael Earl *legislative staff administrator*
Newhouse, Irving Ralph *state legislator*
Smith, Linda A. *congresswoman, former state legislator*
Thomas, Brian Chester *state legislator, engineer*
Wojahn, R. Lorraine *state legislator*

Ritzville
Schoesler, Mark Gerald *state legislator, farmer*

Seattle
Pullen, Kent Edward *state legislator*

Spanaway
Campbell, Thomas J. *legislator, chiropractor*

Spokane
Dellwo, Dennis A. *state legislator*

Tacoma
Walker, Sally Warden *state legislator*

Walla Walla
Hayner, Jeannette Clare *state legislator*

WYOMING

Casper
Nagel, Patricia Jo *state legislator, consultant, lawyer*

Cheyenne
Mockler, Esther Jayne *state legislator*

Cody
Shreve, Peg *state legislator, retired elementary educator*

Jackson
LaLonde, Robert Frederick *state senator, retired*

Lander
Tipton, Harry Basil, Jr. *state legislator, physician*

Laramie
Maxfield, Peter C. *state legislator, law educator, lawyer*

Rock Springs
Blackwell, Samuel Eugene *state legislator*

TERRITORIES OF THE UNITED STATES

GUAM

Agana
San Agustin, Joe Taitano *Guam government official, financial institution executive, management researcher*

CANADA

ALBERTA

Edmonton
Klein, Ralph *provincial legislator, former city mayor*

BRITISH COLUMBIA

Victoria
Boone, Lois Ruth *legislator*
Weisgerber, John Sylvester *provincial legislator*

NORTHWEST TERRITORIES

Yellowknife
Ballantyne, Michael Alan *legislator*

ADDRESS UNPUBLISHED

Aragon, Manny M. *state legislator*
Arnold, Sheila *former state legislator*
Bluechel, Alan *state senator, wood structural components manufacturing company executive*
Buffmire, Judy Ann *state representative, psychologist, consultant*
De Concini, Dennis *former senator, lawyer*
Gallegly, Elton William *congressman*
Gilbertz, Larry E. *state legislator, entrepreneur*
Gillham, Grant David *political consultant*
Gordly, Avel Louise *state legislator, community activist*
Hansen, James Vear *congressman*
Hatch, Orrin Grant *senator*
Hauser, Daniel Eugene *state assemblyman*
Hayne, Harriet Ann *state legislator, rancher*
Hickey, Winifred E(spy) *former state senator, social worker*
Humphrey, Shirley Joy *state representative, education consultant*
Hunter, Duncan Lee *congressman*
Konnyu, Ernest Leslie *former congressman*
Lazechko, D. M. (Molly Lazechko) *former state legislator*
Mader, Kelly Forbes *public policy executive, senator*
Mesaros, Kenneth Lee *rancher, state senator*
Parry, Atwell J., Jr. *state senator, retailer*
Pascoe, Patricia Hill *state senator, writer*
Pettis-Roberson, Shirley McCumber *former congresswoman*
Reid, Harry *senator*
Rowe, Russell Marc *executive staff member*
Scott, Charles Kennard *state senator, cattle rancher*
Sorensen, Sheila *state senator*
Stickney, Jessica *former state legislator*
Talmadge, Philip Albert *state senator, lawyer*
Zimmerman, Harold Samuel *state senator, state administrator, newspaper executive*

HEALTHCARE: DENTISTRY

UNITED STATES

ARIZONA

Flagstaff
Ririe, Craig Martin *periodontist*

Phoenix
Fournier, Donald Frederick *dentist*
Wolfley, Vern Alvin *dentist*

Prescott
Lange, Gary David *periodontist*

Tucson
Davis, Richard Calhoun *dentist*
Eshelman, Enos Grant, Jr. *prosthodontist*
Hicks, Morris Alvin *dentist*

CALIFORNIA

Arcadia
Gamboa, George Charles *oral surgeon, educator*

Arcata
Hise, Mark Allen *dentist*

Burbank
Pallasch, Thomas John *periodontist, pharmacologist, educator*

Burlingame
Donlon, William Christopher *maxillofacial surgeon, educator, author, editor*
Truta, Marianne Patricia *oral and maxillofacial surgeon, educator, author*

Calipatria
Dedeaux, Paul J. *orthodontist*

Camarillo
Spellman, William John *dentist*

Campbell
Ichikawa, Wayne *oral and maxillofacial surgeon*

Claremont
Valdez, Arnold *dentist*

Downey
Duncker, Michael Charles *dentist*

La Verne
Huigens, Daniel Dean *dentist*

Larkspur
Danielson, Gordon Douglas *dentist*

Long Beach
Domondon, Oscar *dentist*
Gehring, George Joseph, Jr. *dentist*

Los Angeles
Stevenson, Richard Gray, III *dentist*

Manteca
Tonn, Elverne Meryl *pediatric dentist, dental insurance consultant*

Northridge
Logan, Lee Robert *orthodontist*

Sacramento
Jochum, Lester H. *dentist*

San Diego
Barsan, Richard Emil *oral and maxillofacial surgeon*

San Francisco
Khosla, Ved Mitter *oral and maxillofacial surgeon, educator*

San Jose
Higgins, James Bradley *dentist*
Tanno, Ronald Louis *dentist*
Yoshizumi, Donald Tetsuro *dentist*

San Mateo
Wasserman, Bruce Arlen *dentist, mail order company executive*

Sunnyvale
Eng, Roger S.C. *dentist, educator*

Whittier
Lowe, Oariona *dentist*

COLORADO

Alamosa
Cooper, Jack Kyle *dentist*

Boulder
Schaffer, Joel Lance *dentist*

Denver
Doida, Stanley Y. *dentist*
Patterson, Daniel William *dentist*

Englewood
Simpson, Robert Houser *orthodontist*

HAWAII

Honolulu
George, Peter T. *orthodontist*
Tamura, Neal Noboru *dentist, consultant*

Pearl City
Sue, Alan Kwai Keong *dentist*

MONTANA

Hardin
MacClean, Walter Lee *dentist*

NEVADA

Reno
Waltz, Marcus Ernest *retired prosthodontist*

OREGON

Beaverton
Vorhies, Carl Brad *dentist*

Grants Pass
Anderson, Gordon Sutherland *periodontist*

Lake Oswego
Woolf, Robert Hansen *periodontist*

Medford
Barnum, William Laird *periodontist*

Portland
Rosenthal, John David *dentist*
Van Hassel, Henry John *dentist, educator, university dean*

Salem
Gertenrich, Roger L. *dentist, mayor*

UTAH

South Ogden
Thompson, Elbert Orson *retired dentist, consultant*

WASHINGTON

Ashford
Ingle, John Ide *dental educator*

Bellevue
Carlson, Curtis Eugene *orthodontist, periodontist*
Randish, Joan Marie *dentist*

Kent
Dawson, Leland Bradley *dentist*

Seattle
Chapman, Vaughn Vickers *dentist*

Spokane
Bourekis, James George *dentist*
Foster, Ruth Mary *dental association administrator*
Kolsrud, Henry Gerald *dentist*
Steadman, Robert Kempton *oral and maxillofacial surgeon*

Vancouver
Brewer, Michael Alan *dentist*

WYOMING

Casper
Keim, Michael Ray *dentist*

ADDRESS UNPUBLISHED

Herman, David Jay *orthodontist*
Simmons, Ronny Michael *dentist*

HEALTHCARE: HEALTH SERVICES

UNITED STATES

ALASKA

Anchorage
Ackley, Marjorie Rose *health educator*
Burke, John Charles *social worker*
Gier, Karan Hancock *counseling psychologist*
Henderson-Dixon, Karen Sue *psychologist*
Hong, Patricia Anne *nursing educator*
Madsen, Linda Ann *pediatrics nurse*
Mattison, Elisa Sheri *organizational psychologist*
Meddleton, Daniel Joseph *health facility administrator*
Risley, Todd Robert *psychologist, educator*
Shkurkin, Ekaterina Vladimirovna (Katia Shkurkin) *social worker*

Bethel
Mead, Terry Eileen *clinic administrator, consultant*
Selby, Naomi Ardean *women's health nurse, medical/surgical nurse*

Fairbanks
Stinson, Aviva Jochebed *psychosocial nurse*

Sitka
Willman, Arthur Charles *healthcare executive*

Soldotna
Johnson, Janet Kay *nurse*

ARIZONA

Bisbee
Behney, Charles Augustus, Jr. *veterinarian*

Bullhead City
Whitney, Stan *marriage and family therapist*

Casa Grande
McGillicuddy, Joan Marie *psychotherapist, consultant*

Chandler
Hofmann, Timothy Alan *mental health, marital and family counselor*
Reece, David Bryson *health facility administrator, research administrator, nurse consultant, nurse educator*

Chinle
Kipp, June Carol *health science laboratory administrator*

Cottonwood
Culbertson, Cheryl Ann *home health nurse, medical-surgical nurse*
Peck, Donald Harvey *chiropractor*

Fort Huachuca
Neft, Michael William *critical care nurse*

Glendale
Frye, Karolyn Faye *dietitian, educator*
Napoliello, Daniel Andrew *nursing administrator*

Green Valley
Manning, Arlene M. *home care administrator*

Lake Havasu City
Mitchell, Maureen *clinical dietitian, consultant*

Mesa
Beck, Jerome Joseph *health care administrator, biomedical technologist*
Bohanske, Robert Thomas *psychologist*
Boyd, Leona Potter *retired social worker*
Davis, Rick Jeffrey *psychotherapist, educator*
Nagle, Robert David *therapist, educator, author*
Oakland, Nancy Nell *geriatrics nurse*
Schroeter, Vernon Walter *chiropractor*

Paradise Valley
McKinley, Joseph Warner *health science facility executive*
Timmons, Evelyn Deering *pharmacist*

Parker
Helminiak, Clarc *public health service officer*

Phoenix
Ballantyne, Reginald Malcolm, III *healthcare executive*
Benach, Sharon Ann *physician assistant*
Beno, Carolyn Elizabeth *pharmacist, marketing professional*
Binnie, Nancy Catherine *nurse, educator*
Boone, Birthe Schnohr *nurse practitioner*
Braun, Stephen Hughes *psychologist*
Brawley, Edward Allan *social work educator*
Case, Patricia Sullivan *mental health counselor, educator*
Castle, Tris Speaker *physician assistant*
Chan, Michael Chiu-Hon *chiropractor*
Cheifetz, Lorna Gale *psychologist*
Crews, James Cecil *hospital administrator*
DePinto, Joseph Anthony *social worker*
DeSilva, Joseph J. *hospital administrator*
Gibson, Brooks *family services professional*
Harrington, John Leonard, Jr. *hospital administrator*
Hartnell, Agnes E. *dietitian, educator*
Landsborough, Ron James *health care executive*
Lovering, Loreli *nurse practitioner, secretary*
Mitchell, Wayne Lee *health care administrator*
Neman, Edward Louis, III *hospital administrator*
Oberg, Mary Kathleen *paramedic/nurse coordinator*
Packman, Vicki Sue *assessment analyst*
Patty, Ling Cruz *dietitian, health program administrator*
Richardson, Kenneth T., Jr. *psychotherapist, consultant, educator, author*
Rodgers, Anthony D. *hospital administrator*
Sagraves, Michelle Kaye *nursing administrator*
Schmude, Judy Gail *health care administrator*
Schwartz, Arthur Solomon *research psychologist*
Seiler, Steven Lawrence *health facility administrator*
Shah, Bhailal Morarji *pharmacist*
Todd, William Michael *counselor, educator*
Van Halderen, Laurel Lynn *dietitian*
Van Kilsdonk, Cecelia Ann *retired nursing administrator, volunteer*
Watanabe, Takeo *psychology educator*
Wellinger, Charles H. *health services company executive*
Welliver, Charles Harold *hospital administrator*
Zeig, Jeffrey Kenneth *psychologist*
Zobell, Gregory Grant *hospital administrator*

Pima
Shafer, James Albert *health care administrator*

Prescott
Goodman, Gwendolyn Ann *nursing educator*
Grimm, Larry Leon *psychologist*
Markham, Richard Glover *research executive*
Mc Cormack, Fred Allen *state social services administrator*

Safford
Carpenter, Jeannine Nuttall *nurse*

Saint Michaels
Sekayumptewa, Loren *social worker*

Scottsdale
Clancy, Judith Meyer *health facility administrator*
Cohn, Michael Jay *psychologist, consultant, educator*
Gerry, Debra Prue *psychotherapist*
Jenkins, William Walter *psychologist, consultant*
Kizziar, Janet Wright *psychologist, author, lecturer*
Nachbar, Joyce Irwin *critical care nurse*
Pitcher, Helen Ione *healthcare services administrator*
Poll, Max Henry *hospital administrator*
Shannon, Bernard Joseph *optometrist, vision care company executive*
Troxell-Gurka, Mary Theresa (Terry Troxell-Gurka) *geriatrics services professional*

Sedona
Catterton, Marianne Rose *occupational therapist*
Rothschild, Helene *marriage/family therapist and author*

Sierra Vista
Yates, Helen Louise *labor and delivery, critical care nurse*

Sonoita
Scott, William Coryell *medical executive*

Sun City West
Mc Donald, Barbara Ann *psychotherapist*

Tempe
Anchie, Toby Levine *health facility administrator*
Cheal, MaryLou *experimental psychologist*
Gazley, Jef *psychotherapist*
Guinouard, Donald Edgar *psychologist*
Gustavson, Joan Ellen Carlson *psychologist*
Kulhavy, Raymond William *psychology educator*
Landers, Daniel MacArthur *psychology educator*
Leggat, Janet Cochrane *nutritionist*
Linton, Marigold L. *psychology educator*
Mason, Terence K. *critical care nurse*
Palombi, Barbara Jean *psychologist*
Stone, Gregory Orville *cognitive psychology educator*
Uttal, William R(eichenstein) *psychology and engineering educator, research scientist*

Thatcher
Wojak, Deborah J. *nursing consultant and educator*

Tucson
Allen, John Jeffrey Beck *psychology educator*
Avolio, Wendy Freedman *speech and language pathologist*
Beach, Lee Roy *psychologist, educator*
Beards, Julie Ann *medical/surgical nurse, consultant*
Brady, Timothy Scott *health care adminstration educator, management consultant*
Brimm, Larry Eugene *counseling psychologist*
Campbell, Drace Allan *psychiatric technician, student*
Chiasson, Robert Breton *veterinary science educator emeritus*
Crawford, Joyce Catherine Holmes *retired psychologist*
Guerra, Anna O'Bannon *nurse educator, maternal/women's health nurse*
Harris, Emma Earl *nursing home executive*
Horan, Mary Ann Theresa *nurse*
Horton, Jodi *healthcare executive*
Kirk, Samuel Alexander *psychologist, educator*
Klein, Perry Andrew *counselor*
Marks-Katz, Marjorie Louise *medical nutrition therapist, writer*
Morford, James Warren *international health care executive*
Qin, Yulin *cognitive neuropsychologist*
Ruggill, Solomon P. *psychologist*
Sampliner, Linda Hodes *psychologist, consultant*
Schussel, Alan Lewis *rehabilitation counselor*
Shropshire, Donald Gray *hospital executive*
Smith, David Wayne *psychologist*
Vidal, Delia *medical/surgical and oncological nurse*
Weber, Charles Walter *nutrition educator*

Whiteriver
White, Judith Louise *social worker, counselor*

Yuma
Monks, Karen Elizabeth *nursing educator*

CALIFORNIA

Agoura Hills
Copeland, Mary Ellen *nurse*
Ho, Katy *dietitian, real estate broker*
Merchant, Roland Samuel, Sr. *hospital administrator, educator*

Alameda
Boyer, Ford Sylvester *relationship consultant*
Herrick, Sylvia A. *health service administrator*

Albany
Mohrdick, Eunice Marie *nurse, health educator*

Alhambra
Bortell, Linda Lee *psychotherapist, educator*

Alta Loma
Guyan, Cheryl Ann *nurse*

Anaheim
Benson, James Bernard, Jr. *clinical hypnotherapist*
Ermshar, Linda Charline *health services school director*
Lee, Donna Jean *retired hospice and respite nurse*
Occhipinti, Joseph R. *optometrist*

Apple Valley
Poole, Arnetta Marie *neonatal intensive care nurse*

Arcadia
Anderson, Holly Geis *women's clinic executive, radio personality*
Horner, Althea Jane *psychologist*

Atascadero
Lamore, Bette *rehabilitation counselor, motivational speaker*

Bakersfield
Ashley, Mark James *speech pathologist, health facility administrator*
Bridgewater, Nora Jane *medical/surgical nurse*
Buxton, Susan Elaine *critical care nurse*
Hill, Robert Bryant *chiropractor*
Murillo, Velda Jean *social worker, counselor*
Sanchez, Albert *public health nutritionist*
Watkins, Judith Ann *nurse*
Wong, Wayne D. *nutritionist*

Barstow
Osburn, Melvin L. *psychotherapist*

Belmont
Schreiber, Andrew *psychotherapist*

Berkeley
Baumrind, Diana *research psychologist*
Breedlove, S. Marc *psychology educator*
Canfield, Judy Ohlbaum *psychologist*
Day, Lucille Elizabeth *health facility administrator, educator, author*
Enoch, Jay Martin *vision scientist, educator*
Gibbs, Jewelle Taylor *clinical psychologist*
Gough, Harrison Gould *psychologist, educator*
Greene, Albert Lawrence *hospital administrator*
Hancock, Emily Stone *psychologist*
Jensen, Arthur Robert *psychology educator*
Lazarus, Richard Stanley *psychology educator*
Maurer, Adah Electra *psychologist*
Morgan, Meredith Walter *optometrist, retired educator*
Poe, Lenora Madison *psychotherapist and author*
Rosenzweig, Mark Richard *psychology educator*
Segal, Steven Paul *social work educator*
Silva, Joanna Kontaxis *dietitian*
Terrell, Paul L. *social work educator, university administrator*
Tutashinda, Abd Karim Kweli (Brian P. Altheimer) *chiropractic physician, educator*

Beverly Hills
Aguilera, Donna Conant *psychologist, researcher*
Dreifuss-Kattan, Esther *psychoanalyst, art therapy educator*
Evans, Louise *psychologist, investor, philanthropist*
King, Sheldon Selig *medical center administrator, educator*
Marcus, Donald Morton *psychoanalyst*
Mindell, Earl Lawrence *nutritionist, author*
Mojas, Kathleen Marie *psychologist*

Bieber
Jones, James David *health care executive*

Bonita
Sanderson, Richard Alexander *health facility administrator*

Borrego Springs
Simmel, Edward Clemens *psychology educator, consultant*

Brea
Dyer, Alice Mildred *psychotherapist*
Fyler, Patricia Ann *nurse, small business owner*

Buena Park
Silva, Ladon Gay *dietitian*
Williams, Pamela Avonne *nutritionist and technical writer*

Burbank
Altman, Sheldon *veterinarian*
Hartshorn, Terry O. *health facility administrator*

Burlingame
Suyetsugu, Grace Tamiko *nurse*

Carlsbad
Graham-Rogers, Charles Theodore (Ted Rogers) *metapsychologist, lecturer*

Carmel
Elmstrom, George P. *optometrist, writer*

Carmichael
Utley, Donna Lavelle *healthcare human resources administrator*

Carson
Palmer, Beverly Blazey *psychologist, educator*

Cathedral City
Flood, Sheila Theresa *physical therapist*

Cedar Ridge
Bruno, Judyth Ann *chiropractor*

Chatsworth
Shore, Diana Kay *nutritionist*

Chico
Hartman, Andrew Paul, Jr. *hospital association administrator*
Silliman, Kathryn *nutrition educator*

Chula Vista
Cassel, Russell Napoleon *retired clinical research psychologist*
Kemery, William Elsworth *psychotherapist, hypnotherapist*
Schorr, Martin Mark *forensic psychologist, educator, writer*

Claremont
Berger, Dale Edmund *psychologist, educator*
Hartford, Margaret Elizabeth (Betty Hartford) *social work educator, gerontologist*
Johnson, James Lawrence *clinical psychologist, writer*
Leeb, Charles Samuel *clinical psychologist*
Wents, Doris Roberta *psychologist*
Wicker, Allan Wert *psychology educator*

Coloma
Wall, Sonja Eloise *nurse, administrator*

Concord
Clark, Beverly Wyone *nutritionist*

Corona Del Mar
Davis, Arthur David *psychology educator, musician*

Costa Mesa
Crinella, Francis Michael *neuropsychologist, science foundation director*
Gardin, John George, II *psychologist*
Klein, (Mary) Eleanor *retired clinical social worker*

Culver City
Barrios, Alfred Angel *psychologist*
Connellan, D. Michael *health care finance executive*
Edwards, Marie Babare *psychologist*

Cupertino
Norman, Donald Arthur *cognitive scientist*

Cypress
Neiman, Jeri Anne *therapist*

Dana Point
Bullick, Karen Faye *dietitian*

Danville
Davis, James Ivey *company president, laboratory associate*

Davis
Griffey, Stephen Michael *veterinarian*
Hawkes, Glenn Rogers *psychology educator*
Ilkiw, Janet Elizabeth *veterinary science educator*
Maas, John Paul *veterinarian, researcher*
McBride, Linda Carroll *psychologist*
Owings, Donald Henry *psychology educator*
Rhode, Edward Albert *veterinary medicine educator, veterinary cardiologist*
Shaver, Phillip Robert *psychologist, educator*
Wooten, Patricia Carol *critical care nurse, humor educator, consultant*

Downey
Fields, Michelle Reneé *emergency nurse*
Langdon, Stephanie Davis *orthotist, prosthetist, educational coordinator*

El Cajon
Colling, Kenneth Frank *hospital administrator*
Haley, Rhoberta Jones *family nurse practitioner, educator*
Schenk, Susan Kirkpatrick *geriatric psychiatry nurse*

El Cerrito
Conti, Isabella *psychologist, consultant*
Cooper, William Clark *physician*
Schilling, Janet Naomi *nutritionist, consultant*

Encinitas
Colgan, Michael *nutrition scientist, consultant, researcher*

Encino
Bekey, Shirley White *psychotherapist*
House, Karen Sue *nursing consultant*
Krastman, Hank *psychology educator*
Shapiro, Sumner Leroy *psychoanalyst*
Uhlaner, Julius Earl *psychologist, educator*

Escondido
Brown, Sheila Denise *medical/surgical nurse*
Coleman, Robert Trent *social worker, rehabilitation consultant*
Damsbo, Ann Marie *psychologist*
Rich, Elizabeth Marie *nursing educator*
Schmidt-Dowler, Valerie Wood *retired mental health nurse*

Eureka
Jensen, Jon Norman *clinical child psychologist*
Kriger, Peter Wilson *healthcare administrator*

Fairfax
Neuharth, Daniel J., II *psychotherapist*

Fairfield
Hawn, William Eugene *health care company executive*

Fallbrook
Derelian, Doris Virginia *nutrition educator, consultant*

Fontana
Beckner, Ardis Stern *nutrition specialist, educator*

Fort Ord
Evans, Richard Marlowe *educational psychologist*

Fountain Valley
Barras, Bobbi Ann *psychologist, educator, consultant*

Fremont
Allen, Jacquelyn May *school psychologist, consultant*
Alvari, Kimberlee Ann *dietitian*
Davis, Margaret Anne *dietitian and educator*
Feinberg, Richard Alan *psychologist*
Loarie, Thomas Merritt *healthcare executive*
Sahatjian, Manik *nurse, psychologist*
Thompson, Claire Louisa *medical-surgical nurse*

Fresno
Burnett, Lynn Barkley *health science educator*
Coe, William Charles *psychology educator*
Ezaki-Yamaguchi, Joyce Yayoi *renal dietitian*
Jannette, Marcy *rehabilitation nurse, consultant*
Jury, Debra E. (Debbie Jury) *emergency nurse, consultant, author, educator*
Nichols, Tom A. *nurse*
Pankratz, Robert Lee *psychologist*
Punnett, Audrey Frances *clinical psychologist, educator*

Riley, Charles Logan (Rex Riley) *hospital administrator*
Rusch, Patricia Hull *dietitian*
Schroeder, Rita Molthen *retired chiropractor*
Schuster-Artis, Nancy Marie *medical/surgical nurse*
Simonian, Debra Lyn *dietitian, educator*
Williams, Judith Lorraine *pediatric emergency nurse*

Fullerton
Griffin, Kirsten Bertelsen *nursing educator*
Grimley, Cynthia Patrizi *rehabilitation consultant, special education educator*
Kaisch, Kenneth Burton *psychologist, priest*

Gilroy
Gelwicks, Judith Cathay *rehabilitation and career counselor*

Glendale
Quintero, Bernhild Else *health care executive*

Goleta
Smith, Thomas Harry *counselor*

Granada Hills
McCraven, Carl Clarke *health service administrator*

Grass Valley
Cartwright, Mary Lou *laboratory scientist*

Hayward
Burns, Francis Raymond *biofeedback administrator*
Farley, George Francis *veterinarian*

Healdsburg
McGinnis, Michael Patrick *psychotherapist*

Hemet
Hernandez, Lillian A. *health facility administrator*
Lawrence, Paula Denise *physical therapist*
Minnie, Mary Virginia *social worker, educator*

Hollister
Peterlin, Carol Marie *mental health nurse*

Hollywood
Elliott, Bruce David *rehabilitation counselor*

Huntington Beach
Martin, Wilfred Wesley Finny *psychologist, property owner and manager*
Mosing, Lisa *nutritionist, dietitian*

Inglewood
Haskins, Marian McKeen *nursing administrator*
Long, Ophelia *hospital administrator*

Irvine
Bullock, Gayle Nelson *healthcare executive*
Conti, Daniel Joseph *health science association administrator*
Keddy, Diane *nutrition consultant*
Luce, R(obert) Duncan *psychology educator*
Olson, Betty Haak *public health educator*
Turner, Dee Stone *adult nurse practitioner, diabetes researcher*
Yousef, Marjan *gerontologist, psychology educator*

Kentfield
Black, Suzanne Alexandra *clinical psychologist, researcher*

Kenwood
Podboy, John Watts *clinical, forensic psychologist*

La Honda
Waldhauer, Fred Donald *health care executive*

La Jolla
Anderson, Norman Henry *psychology educator, researcher*
Coburn, Marjorie Foster *psychologist, educator*
Cornette, William Magnus *scientist, research director, company executive*
Covington, Stephanie Stewart *psychotherapist, writer, educator*
Lakier, Nancy S. *health facility administrator*
Maher, James R. *laboratory administrator*
Meltzoff, Julian *psychologist*
Pratt, George Janes, Jr. *psychologist, author*
Ruggeri, Zaverio Marcello *medical researcher*
Spinweber, Cheryl Lynn *research psychologist*

Laguna Beach
Banuelos, Betty Lou *rehabilitation nurse*
Clecak, Dvera Vivian Bozman *psychotherapist*
Smith, Leslie Roper *hospital administrator*

Laguna Hills
O'Grady, Barbara Vinson *community health nurse, nursing administrator*

Laguna Niguel
Bridges, Kathleen Erickson *communication disorders specialist*
Freeland, Darryl Creighton *psychologist, educator*

Lake Forest
Boccia, Judy Elaine *home health agency executive, consultant*

Larkspur
Saxton, Lloyd *psychologist and author*

Lemoore
Kmet, Rebecca Eugenia Patterson *pharmacist*

Livermore
Gledhill, Barton LeVan *veterinarian*

Lodi
Bernhoft, Franklin Otto *psychotherapist, psychologist*

Loma Linda
Betancourt, Hector Mainhard *psychology scientist, educator*
Blix, Glen Garry *preventive care educator*
Hinshaw, David B., Sr. *hospital administrator*
Snyder, John Joseph *optometrist*
Swarner, Julia Boyd *nutrition educator*

Lompoc
Redding-Stewart, Deborah Lynn *psychologist*

Long Beach
Blackman, David Ira *health science administrator*
Brault, G(ayle) Lorain *healthcare executive*
Carlton-Adams, Georgia M. *psychotherapist*
Jacob, Mary *nutritional biochemistry educator, researcher*
Keenan, Retha Ellen Vornholt *nursing educator*
Kohn, Gerhard *psychologist, educator*
Lee, Charlton Robert *psychology educator*
Miller, Maureen Denice *pediatrics nurse*
Mullins, Ruth Gladys *pediatrics nurse*
Newman, J. Robert *psychologist, educator*
Ratliff, Leigh Ann *pharmacist*
Schmidt, Edwin Steven *nursing educator*
Utain, Marsha *marriage family child counselor, author, lecturer*
Wallerstein, Bruce Lee *psychologist*
Wilcox, Charles Steven *pharmacology administrator*

Los Alamitos
Anderson, Mitchell *chiropractor*

Los Altos
Carr, Jacquelyn B. *psychologist, educator*
Menke, James Michael *chiropractor*

Los Angeles
Amador, Tamera Diane *nursing director*
Ash, Lawrence Robert *public health educator, administrator*
Baron, Melvin Farrell *pharmacy educator*
Bourque, Linda Anne Brookover *public health educator*
Bowman, Gary Martin *social worker*
Brotzman, Amy Jean *health facility administrator*
Brown, Gay West *school psychologist*
Bunten, Judith Ann *perinatal nurse, educator*
Butterworth, Robert Roman *psychologist, researcher, media therapist*
Carterette, Edward Calvin Hayes *psychologist*
Chen, Peter Wei-Teh *mental health services administrator*
Cohn, Daniel Howard *laboratory director*
Crammer, Terry Lynn *nursing educator*
Curtis, Francine Marco *nurse*
Donaldson, Mary Kendrick *nurse*
Donatoni, Paul J. *pharmacist*
Eamer, Richard Keith *health care company executive, lawyer*
Everette, Mable Louise *nutrition educator*
Gates, Robert C. *health system administrator*
Gelman, Marcella Taylor *dietitian*
Gilman, John Joseph *research scientist*
Girman, Tanya Lynn *dietitian*
Goldberg, Herb *psychologist, educator*
Gross, Sharon Ruth *forensic psychologist, researcher*
Holmes, Doris Lee *nursing administrator*
Horowitz, Ben *medical center executive*
Horton, Gwendolyn *nursing educator emeritus*
Hummel, Joseph William *hospital administrator*
Izadi, Parvin *medical technologist*
Jerison, Harry Jacob *psychology educator*
Johnson, Leonidas Alexander *optometrist*
Kasper, Christine Eleana *nursing educator, researcher*
Kopp, Claire Joan Bernstein *psychologist, educator*
Kronenberg, Jacalyn (Jacki Kronenberg) *nurse administrator*
Landen, Sandra Joyce *psychologist, educator*
Leckart, Bruce *psychologist*
Lien, Eric Jung-chi *pharmacist, educator*
Lopez-Navarro, Eduardo Luis *family therapist*
Mayo, Benjamin Franklin *therapist*
McCarthy, William James *research psychologist, consultant, psychology educator*
Meduski, Jerzy Wincenty *nutritionist, biochemist*
Mensh, Ivan Norman *medical psychology educator*
Miller, Eric Nathan *neuropsychologist*
Mintz-Binder, Ronda Debra *nursing educator, counselor*
Monterrosa, José Napoleón *bilingual school psychologist*
Morales, Cynthia Torres *clinical psychologist, consultant*
Noce, Walter William, Jr. *hospital administrator*
Ratican, Peter Jay *health maintenance organization executive*
Raven, Bertram H(erbert) *psychology educator*
Renford, Edward J. *hospital administrator*
Scanlon, Deralee Rose *registered dietitian, educator, author*
Serafine, Mary Louise *psychologist, educator, lawyer*
Shneidman, Edwin S. *psychologist, educator, thanatologist, suicidologist*
Silberman, Irwin Alan *public health physician*
Sloane, Robert Malcolm *hospital administrator*
Sokolov, Jacque Jenning *health care executive, nuclear cardiologist*
Solomon, Rhonda Hope *school and educational psychologist*
Stoffel, Karen Marie *nursing coordinator*
Strack, Stephen Naylor *psychologist*
Targow, Jeanette Goldfield *clinical social worker*
Taylor, Darla Jean *nurse*
Thompson, Judith Kastrup *nursing researcher*
Tulloch-Reid, Elma Deen *nurse, educator, consultant*
Ver Steeg, Donna Lorraine Frank *nurse, sociologist, educator*
Watson, Sharon Gitin *psychologist, executive*
Williams, Michael Knighton *social worker*
Williams, Richard T. *hospital administrator*
Yao, Stephen Apuy *health services administrator*

Los Gatos
Asher, James John *psychology educator*
Green, Adeline Mandel *psychiatric social worker*
Ramos, Linda Marie *endoscopy technician*

Malibu
Dimitriadis, Andre C. *health care executive*

March AFB
Edwards, Annette Winfrey *nurse*

Marina
Cornell, Annie Aiko *nurse, administrator, retired army officer*

Marina Del Rey
Thro, Broydrick (Elaine Thro) *educator*

Mariposa
Bryant, Carol Lee *public health educator, psychotherapist, consultant*

Martinez
Atkin, Ruth *social worker*
Boltz, Marlys Peterson *nurse administrator*
Miller, Nicole Gabrielle *clinical psychologist*
Smith, Gaynl Beverly *hospice director, nurse*
Strisower, Suzanne *clinical hypnotherapist, counselor*

Marysville
Myers, Elmer *psychiatric social worker*

Mckinleyville
Janssen, Eunice Charlene *healthcare facility administrator*

Menlo Park
Brown, Stephanie Diane *psychologist, consultant, researcher*
Clair, Theodore Nat *educational psychologist*
Powell-Enzmann, Diana Teresa *speech pathologist, administrator*
Ralston, Rachel Walters *developmental psychologist*

Mission Hills
Stevens, Serita Deborah Mendelson *psychiatric nurse, writer*

Mission Viejo
Baker, Mark W. *psychologist*
Sikand, Geeta *dietitian*

Modesto
Berry, John Charles *psychologist*
Lipomi, Michael Joseph *health facility administrator*
Moe, Andrew Irving *veterinarian*
Ramos, Nelson Herbert *healthcare executive*
Young, Cedric Jan-Yee *laboratory director, microbiologist*

Monrovia
Salaman, Maureen Kennedy *nutritionist*

Monterey
Caldwell, Joni *psychology educator, small business owner*
Tonkin, Thomas Elden *health foundation executive*

Moreno Valley
Gull, Paula Mae *nephrology nurse, medical/surgical nurse*

Morro Bay
O'Neill, Margaret E. *psychological counselor*

Moss Landing
Johnston, Gail Liragis *laboratory director*

Mount Shasta
Mariner, William Martin *chiropractor*

Mountain View
Alameda, Russell Raymond, Jr. *radiologic technologist*
Kanchier, Carole *psychologist*
Wildfogel, Jeffrey Alan *psychologist, educator*

Napa
Lee, Margaret Anne *social worker, psychotherapist*
Sedlock, Joy *psychiatric social worker*

Newark
Sherman, Robert Dewayne *radiologic technologist, entrepreneur*

Newhall
Stone, Norman Michael *psychologist*

Newport Beach
Buenviaje, Rosalinda Tagle *dietitian, consultant*
Green, Melanie Jane *speech-language pathologist*
Johnson, Leayn Hutchinson *nursing educator, mental health nurse*
McBurnett, Robert Keith *child and adolescent psychology educator, researcher*
Rikelman, Herman *psychologist*
Stephens, Michael Dean *hospital administrator*
Teslow, Paul Andre *retired health executive*
Whittemore, Paul Baxter *psychologist*

North Hollywood
Hart, Bonita Ellen *registered dietitian analyst*

Northridge
Chan, Peter Wing Kwong *pharmacist*
Mitchell, Rie Rogers *psychologist, counseling educator*
Reagan, Janet Thompson *psychologist, educator*

Novato
Lowe, Claudia Marie *childbirth assistant*

Oakdale
Smith, Heather Lynn *psychotherapist, recreational therapist,*

Oakland
Bangham, Robert Arthur *orthotist*
Beeson, Montel Eileen *human services administrator, gerontologist*
Caulfield, W. Harry *health care industry executive, physician*
Cumming, Janice Dorothy *clinical psychologist*
Donker, Richard Bruce *health care administrator*
Duprat, Jo Ann *pediatric rehabilitation nurse, consultant*
Elgin, Gita *psychologist*
Eslinger, Michael Ronald *nurse anesthetist*
Gaál, Violetta *retired social worker, massage therapist*
Gardner, Robert Alexander *career counselor, career management consultant*
George, Carol Catherine *psychology educator*
Hancock, Nannette Beatrice Finley *mental health educator, consultant*
Hodson, Christine Ann *psychologist*
Kayman, Susan Goldberg *nutritionist, consultant*
Ko, Kathleen Lim *health administrator*
Lawrence, David M. *health facility administrator*
Loughman, William Doster *cytogenetics/pre-natal diagnosis lab director*
Moon, Wayne *health facility administrator*
Nebelkopf, Ethan *psychologist*
Sovatsky, Stuart Charles *psychotherapist*
Stout, Adelia Diane *therapist*
Taigman, Michael Allen *healthcare management development company official*

Oceanside
Anshel, Jeffrey Robert *optometrist*
Harbord, Anne Marie *consulting dietetics company executive*
Hertweck, E. Romayne *psychology educator*
Jones, Barbara Dean *substance abuse counselor*
Mitchell, Laura Ellen *adult critical care and high-risk/critical care obstetrics nurse*

Ontario
Hull, Jane Laurel Leek *retired nurse, administrator*
Tinker, Judy Marie *nutritionist, musician*

Orange
Alexander-King, Pearl Coqueece *nurse*
Becker, Juliette *psychologist, marriage and family therapist*
Briscoe, Barbara June *nurse*
Brown, Lillian Eriksen *retired nursing administrator, consultant*
Courtney, Angela *veterinarian, researcher*
Gonzalez, Imelda *medical nurse*
Levine, Howard Harris *health facility executive*
Pursell, Paul Dennis *rehabilitation director*
Schlose, William Timothy *health care executive*

Oroville
Shelton, Joel Edward *clinical psychologist*

Oxnard
Herlinger, Daniel Robert *hospital administrator*
Kelch, Vincent Charles *clinical pharmacist*

Pacific Palisades
Kosecoff, Jacqueline Barbara *health services researcher*

Pacifica
Kempis, Janet T. *hospital executive*

Palm Springs
Boyajian, Timothy Edward *public health officer, educator, consultant*
Doi, Lois *psychiatric social worker*
Williams, Emily Jean *dietician, medical researcher*

Palmdale
Bragg, Darrell Brent *nutritionist, consultant*
Ellsworth, Richard German *psychologist*

Palo Alto
Bloem, Kenneth D. *healthcare facility executive*
Bodin, Arthur M. *clinical psychologist*
Card, Stuart Kent *psychologist*
Crawford, Charlotte Joanne *psychologist, psychoanalyst, psychological anthropologist*
Goff, James Albert *medical center administrator*
Gordon, Marc Stewart *pharmacist, scientist*
Hammett, Benjamin Cowles *psychologist*
Kelsey, Edith Jeanine *psychotherapist, consultant*
Lindzey, Gardner *psychologist, educator*
McCorkindale, Carolyn Christine *dietitian*
Moses, James Anthony, Jr. *neuropsychologist*
Pelletier, Kenneth R. *behavioral physician, educator, author*
Romanos, Nabil Elias *business development manager*
Saldich, Anne Rawley *counseling psychologist*
Silverthorn, Lee James *clinical psychology*
Skeff, Kelley Michael *health facility administrator*
Turgel, Stuart Charles *hospital administrator*
Unger, Arlene Klein *medical company executive, counselor, consultant*
Ward-Shaw, Sheila Theresa *nurse*

Panorama City
Sendra-Anagnost, Teresa Amor *nurse practitioner, writer*

Pasadena
Blitz-Weisz, Sally *speech pathologist*
Buckingham, Jerry L. *hospital administrator*
Coles, Bettie Johnson *emergency services nurse*
Croswell, Beverly Ann *women's health nurse*
Messenger, Ron J. *health facility administrator*
Sauer, James Edward, Jr. *hospital administrator*

Paso Robles
Rocha, Marilyn Eva *clinical psychologist*

Pebble Beach
Ference, Helen Marie *nursing consultant*
Keene, Clifford Henry *medical administrator*

Petaluma
Hallowell, M. Brooke *speech pathologist, educator*
Nussinow, Jill Anne *nutritionist*

Pico Rivera
Brotman, Richard Dennis *counselor*

Piedmont
Daniels, Lydia M. *health care administrator*

Pittsburg
Gustafson, Sally A. *counselor, cosmetologist, educator*

Playa Del Rey
Weitz, Sheri Lee *dietitian*

Pleasant Hill
Gomez, Edward Casimiro *physician, educator*
Richard, Robert Carter *psychologist*
Toms, Kathleen Moore *nurse*

Pleasanton
Shen, Mason Ming-Sun *medical center administrator*

Portola Valley
Bell, Donald William *experimental psychologist*

Ramona
Ingber, Beth *intuitive practitioner/counselor*

Rancho Cordova
Schmitz, Vincent Herman *healthcare facility executive, finance executive*

Rancho Mirage
Deiter, Newton Elliott *clinical psychologist*
Ford, Betty Bloomer (Elizabeth Ford) *health facility executive, wife of former President of United States*
Kiser, Roberta Katherine *medical administrator, education educator*
Wiskowski, Eugene *health facility administrator*

Rancho Santa Margarita
Hughes, Bessie *nursing administrator*

Redding
Drake, Patricia Evelyn *psychologist*
Mongold, Michael Ray *psychologist*
Skrocki, Edmund Stanley, II *health fair promoter, executive*

Redlands
Grames, George Miller *human services administrator, physician*

Redwood City
Kennedy, Sheila Grace *medical social worker*

Reseda
Hoover, Pearl Rollings *nurse*
Leonard, Angeline Jane *psychotherapist*

Richmond
Terrill, Karen Stapleton *retired medical planning consultant*

Riverside
Chang, Sylvia Tan *health facility administrator, educator*
Coomes, Lisa Ann *critical care nurse*
Ham, Gary Martin *psychologist*
Riesen, Austin Herbert *psychologist, researcher*
Rothhammer, Craig Robert *social worker, consultant*
Seide, Marilyn Bernstein *mental health administrator*
White, Thomas Jeffrey *healthcare management educator*

Rohnert Park
Robinson, Louise Evette *marriage family child counselor*

Rolling Hills Estates
Brody-Watts, Stella *nurse*

Roseville
Bertacchi, Gloria *health company executive*
Dupper, Frank Floyd *health care facility executive*
Jarrett, Ronald Douglas *nurse, lawyer*

Running Springs
Fangerow, Kay Elizabeth *nurse*

Sacramento
Beckwith, Charles Allan *healthcare administrator, consultant*
Bennett, Lawrence Allen *psychologist, criminal justice researcher*
Boylan, Richard John *psychologist, researcher, educator*
Campos, Leonard Peter *psychologist*
Chapman, Loring *psychologist, educator, neuroscientist*
Emburg, Kathryn Maria *social worker, writer*
Engelhardt, Barbara Ann *nutritionist and registered dietitian*
Farrell, Francine Annette *psychotherapist, educator*
Kelley, Lisa Stone *public guardian, conservator*
Krebs, Nina Boyd *psychologist*
Merwin, Edwin Preston *health care consultant, educator*
Papathakis, Peggy Callaghan *registered dietitian*
Rapoza, Glenn Roberts *vocational rehabilitation counselor, teacher*
Roberts, Paul Dale *health services administrator*
Rogers, Janet Sue *nursing administrator*
Wright, Carole Yvonne *chiropractor*

Salinas
Eifler, Carl Frederick *retired psychologist*
Finnberg, Elaine Agnes *psychologist, editor*

San Anselmo
Milos, Marilyn Fayre *health organization administrator*

San Bernardino
Brown-Stigger, Alberta Mae *nurse*
Godager, Jane Ann *social worker*
Maul, Terry Lee *psychologist, educator*
Tacal, Jose Vega, Jr. *public health official, veterinarian*
Timmreck, Thomas C. *health sciences and health administration educator*
Turpin, Joseph Ovila *psychologist, educator*

San Clemente
Fox, Lorraine Esther *psychologist, human services consultant*

San Diego
Bakko, Orville Edwin *retired health care executive, consultant*
Connelly, Diane Maureen *urology service coordinator*
Day, Pietrina Ann *therapist*
Downie, Pamela *psychologist*
Downs, Kathleen Anne *healthcare operations director*
Duester, Karen Christensen *nutritionist, food industry executive*
Ferm, Brita Ellen *public health administrator-educator, researcher*
Hayden, Ann Marie *family nurse practitioner*
Heuschele, Werner Paul *veterinary researcher*
Kent, Theodore Charles *psychologist*
Lewis, Shirley Jeane *psychology educator*
Litrownik, Alan Jay *psychologist, educator*
Maguire, Edward Francis *hospital administrator*
Mayer, Barbara Jean *critical care nurse*
Mc Guigan, Frank Joseph *psychologist, educator*
Riegel, Barbara J. *educator, clinical researcher, editor*
Rosen, Peter *health facility administrator, emergency physician, educator*
Roy, Catherine Elizabeth *physical therapist*
Rymer, Thérèse Elizabeth *family practice nurse practitioner*
Sabatella, Elizabeth Maria *clinical therapist, educator, mental health facility administrator*
Schmidt, Patricia Fain *nurse educator*
Schmidt, Terry Lane *health care executive*
Smith, Raymond Edward *health care administrator*
Thomas, Verneda Estella *perfusionist*
Thompson, Mari Hildenbrand *medical staff services operations coordinator*
Walker, Carolyn Louise *nursing researcher, educator*

San Francisco
Acree, Michael Coy *psychology educator*
Ansak, Marie-Louise *health care executive*
Auerback, Sandra Jean *social worker*
Backlund, Michael Anders *clinical psychologist, priest*
Batki, Steven L. *health facility administrator, educator, physician*
Belt, Audrey E(von) *social worker, consultant*
Cahalan, Marianne Troy *nurse*
Calvin, Allen David *psychologist, educator*
Clarke, Juno-Ann Krohn *nutrition educator*
Cook, Quentin LaMar *healthcare executive*
Cordes, Fauno Lancaster *retired nuclear medicine technologist*
Cummerton, Joan Marie *social work educator*
Dean, Carolynn Leslie *health science technological administrator*
De Cecco, John Paul *psychology and human sexuality educator, author*
Eng, Catherine *health care facility administrator, physician, medical educator*
Engler, Mary B. *physiologist, educator, nurse, researcher*
Harary, Keith *psychologist*
Hatcher, John Christopher *psychologist*
Henkin, William Asher *psychotherapist*
Howatt, Sister Helen Clare *human services director*
Johnson, Herman Leonall *research nutritionist*
Krippner, Stanley Curtis *psychologist*
Kuck, Marie Elizabeth Bukovsky *retired pharmacist*
Kuhn, Jane Elizabeth *nursing administrator*
Malin, Harold Martin, Jr. *sexologist, educator*
Mannino, J. Davis *psychotherapist*
Matteoli, Ralph, Jr. *nursing educator*
McDonald, Marian Richie *nurse epidemiologist*
Moldanado, Swarnalatha Adusumilli *nursing educator, researcher*
Muñoz, Ricardo Felipe *psychology educator*
Nguyen, Tan Dinh *pharmacist*
Phillips, Kathryn Ann *health services researcher*
Rogers, Camille Madeliene *medical technologist*
Rosales, Suzanne Marie *hospital coordinator*
Schmitt, George Herbert *hospital executive*
Sim, Janet Mao *dietitian, food management and dietetics educator*
Stahlke, Richard David *human services administrator*
Staples, Robert Eugene *nursing educator*
Webel, Charles Peter *human science and psychology educator*
Westerdahl, John Brian *nutritionist, health educator*
Wu-Chu, Stella Chwenyea *nutritionist, consultant*
Yee, Darlene *gerontological health educator*
Young, Lowell Sung-yi *medical administrator, educator*

San Jose
Andrews, Mary Ann *nursing services director*
Cedoline, Anthony John *psychologist*
Connolly, Phyllis Marie *nursing educator, clinical specialist*
Cunnane, Patricia S. *medical facility administrator*
Gabriel, Dierdre Chandra *dietitian*
Hicks, Robert Alvin *psychology educator*
Jordan, James Douglas, Jr. *chemical dependency consultant*
Kuhlman, Gloria Jean *mental health and geriatric nurse, educator*
McEntee, James Patrick, Sr. *human relations executive*
Oak, Ronald Stuart *health and safety administrator*
Storz, Donna Marie *clinical dietitian*

San Luis Obispo
Smith, Joey Spauls *mental health nurse, biofeedback therapist, bodyworker, hypnotist*

San Marcos
Knight, Edward Howden *retired hospital administrator*

San Mateo
Ferrang, Antoinette M. *dietitian educator*
Low, Marissa E. *health care administrator*
Richens, Muriel Whittaker *therapist, counselor, educator*

San Pedro
Hoagland, Albert Joseph, Jr. *psychotherapist, hypnotherapist, minister*

San Rafael
Tosti, Donald Thomas *psychologist, consultant*

San Ramon
Luehrs, Paul Richard *hospital administrator*

Santa Ana
DiLuigi, Ronald Richard *health care agency executive*
Jack, Minta Sue *hospital department head*
Lewis, Robert Turner *psychologist*
Oberstein, Marydale *geriatric specialist*
Saravo, Anne Cobble *clinical psychologist, mental health administrator*

Santa Barbara
Campbell, Charles Curtis *healthcare consultant*
Giannetti, Ronald Armand *psychologist*
Kendler, Howard H(arvard) *psychologist, educator*
Narayanamurti, Venkatesh *research administrator*
Patterson, Anne Margaret *nutritionist*
Sherman, Alan Robert *psychologist, educator*
Singer, Janice Gail *psychotherapist, consultant*
Valdez, Jesse Najera *psychologist*

Santa Clarita
Holden, Heidi Joyce Rummel *dietitian*
Stone, Susan Foster *mental health services professional, psychologist*

Santa Cruz
Domhoff, George William *psychology and sociology educator*
Hilyard, David Franklin *optician*
Poulos, Clara Jean *nutritionist*
Rogoff, Barbara *psychology researcher, educator*

Santa Monica
Barbakow, Jeffrey *health facility administrator*
Bradkowski, Keith A. *patient services administrator*
Focht, Michael Harrison *health care industry executive*
Grabowski, Diane Marietta *registered dietitian, nutrition educator*
Kenney, James Joseph *nutrition research specialist*
Meador, Billie Cooeetta *nurse*
Nizze, Judith Anne *physician assistant*
Pettit, John W. *hospital administrator*
Russell, Marlou *psychologist*
Sandford, Paul Allan *biomedical laboratory director, biochemist*
Shirley, Courtney Dymally *nurse*

Santa Rosa
Black, Alice Ann *neonatal and pediatrics nurse educator*
Daniels, Madeline Marie *psychotherapist, author*
Eilerman, Betty Jean *marriage and family counselor*
Lewis, Marion Elizabeth *social worker*
Searight, Mary Dell (Mrs. Paul James Searight) *nursing educator*

Sausalito
Groah, Linda Kay *nursing administrator, educator*

Scotts Valley
Holleran, Donna Marie *nurse*

Seal Beach
Caesar, Carol Ann *psychologist, consultant*
Stillwell, Kathleen Ann Swanger *healthcare consultant*

Sepulveda
Burton, Paul Floyd *social worker*

Sherman Oaks
Casady, Timothy Philip *medical-surgical nurse*
Franklin, Abby *psychotherapist*
Tucker, Annabelle Doris *medical company executive*

Simi Valley
Clipsham, Robert Charles *veterinarian*

Solvang
Hegarty, William Kevin *medical center executive*

Sonora
Reese, Donna Louise *speech language pathologist*

South San Francisco
Becker, Anne Margaret *neonatal nurse*

Stanford
Bardas, Sandra Leigh *pharmacist*
Ganz, Leo *psychologist and educator*
Heeger, David J. *psychology educator*
Marine, Robert James *nursing administrator, consultant, naval officer, researcher*
Mc Namara, Joseph Donald *researcher, retired police chief, novelist*
Monson, Beverly Parry *dietitian*

Stanton
Bodily, Gerald P. *career counselor, consultant*

Stockton
Britto, Charlotte Mary *dietitian, educator*
Datta, Purna Chandra *clinical psychologist, educator*
Gregory, William Edgar *psychologist*
Hutchison, Loyal Dwayne *pharmacist*
Maslow, Richard Emanuel *psychology consultant*
Ross, Sandra K. *critical care nurse*

Studio City
Herrman, Marcia Kutz *child development specialist*

Suisun City
Maher, Christine Rita *emergency room nurse, sexual assault specialist*

Sunnyvale
Cohen, D. Ashley *clinical psychologist, assessment specialist*
Rizzuto, Carmela Rita *nursing administrator*

Sylmar
Manoogian, Terri Lawrence *dietitian, food service administrator*

Taft
Brewer, Lia Harper *marriage and family therapist*

Tarzana
Rinsch, Maryann Elizabeth *occupational therapist*

Temecula
Walker, Kent Pitt *veterinarian*

Thousand Oaks
Emerson, Alton Calvin *physical therapist*
Mulkey, Sharon Renee *gerontology nurse*

Torrance
Culton, Paul Melvin *counselor, educator, interpreter*
Foley, Edward Joseph *hospital administrator*
Prell, Joel James *medical group administrator*
Todd, Frances Eileen *pediatrics nurse*

Turlock
Harris, Lori Renee *dietitian, educator*

Tustin
Sinnette, John Townsend, Jr. *research scientist, consultant*
Stark, Amy Louise *clinical psychologist*

Twain Harte
Weiner, Richard S. *healthcare administrator*

Union City
Glueck, Mary A. *psychiatric and mental health nurse, administrator*

Upland
Rice, Sharon Margaret *clinical psychologist*

Vacaville
Zaleski, Brian William *chiropractor*

Valley Center
Binegar, Gwendolyn Ann *social worker*

Valley Village
Kessler, Lillian Berman *health facility administrator, retired*

Van Nuys
Blue, James Guthrie *veterinarian*
Marei, Ibrahim *medical technologist*
Mathis, Kathleen Marie *drug abuse counselor*
Owens, Warner Barry *physical therapist*
Rosen, Alexander Carl *psychologist, consultant*

Ventura
Boyle, Marylou Olsen *nursing administrator*
Naurath, David Allison *engineering psychologist, researcher*

Visalia
Fortier, Dana Suzanne *psychotherapist*
Wood, David Duane *clinical psychologist, marriage and family counselor*

Walnut
Martin, George *psychologist, educator*

Weldon
Laymon, Stephen Adair *research scientist*

West Covina
Adams, Sarah Virginia *family counselor*
Franden, Blanche M. *nursing educator*
Makowski, Peter Edgar *hospital executive*

Westminster
Murotake, Thomas Hisashi *emergency medicine technologist*

Whittier
Fisher, David Clarence *optometrist*
Johnson, Ruth Eileen *dietician, researcher, home economics educator*

Woodland Hills
Baldwin, Cathy L. *occupational health nurse, consultant*
Blanchard, William Henry *psychologist*
Holley, Elizabeth Shelby *educational therapist*
Neugroschl, Gail E. (Penny Neugroschl) *geriatrics nurse, educator*

Yountville
Jones, Thomas Robert *social worker*

Yucca Valley
Brower, Lester Mayer *physical therapist*
Cornell, Sherry Elizabeth *occupational health nurse*

COLORADO

Alamosa
Blevins, Sandra Kaye *director senior citizens facility*

Arvada
Careswell, Lori Sue *dietitian*
Coen, Michael Dwain *pastoral counselor*
Kent, Karri Ann *dietitian*

Aurora
Clark, Laura Carroll *dietitian, educator, consultant*
Daugherty, Sharon *mental health counselor*
Dunn, Karen K. *mental health center executive, psychotherapist*
Fedak, Barbara Kingry *technical center administrator*
Gardner, Sandra Lee *nurse, outreach consultant*
Oster, Cynthia Ann *critical care nurse*

Boulder
Anderson, Robert K. *health care company executive*
Arnold, Janet Nina *health care consultant*
Healy, Alice Fenvessy *psychology educator, researcher*
Holdsworth, Janet Nott *women's health nurse*
Jacobson, Jacob G. *psychoanalyst*
Kelley, Bruce Dutton *pharmacist*
Luckow, Elizabeth Ellen *retired nurse*
Mueller, Henrietta Waters *psychologist, artist, painter, printmaker*
Pederson, Holly Lynn *critical care administrator*
Rogers, Richard Gregory *sociology educator*

Broomfield
Lybarger, Marjorie Kathryn *nurse*
Vlosky, Mark Alan *psychologist*

Buena Vista
Herb, Edmund Michael *optometrist, educator*

Burlington
Cure, DeAnn Kay *medical facility executive*

Canon City
Tracy, Emily Anne Miller *social services administrator*
Yamaguchi, Kirk Charles *psychotherapist, educator*

Colorado Springs
Cameron, Paul Drummond *research facility administrator*
Farr, Leonard Alfred *hospital administrator*
Knight, Jane Miller *nurse-midwife, air force officer*
Moltzan, Nicoline G. *nurse, administrator*
Moore, Sheryl Stansil *nursing educator*
Moorhouse, Mary Frances *rehabilitation nurse*
Olson, Kenneth Paul *rehabilitation counselor*
Plunkett, Michael C. *psychotherapist*
Potterat, John James *public health officer, researcher*
Shafer, Dallas Eugene *psychology gerontology educator, minister*
Williams, Ruth Lee *clinical social worker*

Cortez
Selzer, Stephen Rashaw *healthcare administrator*

Denver
Barbour, Alton Bradford *human communication studies educator*
Bauder, Sister Marianna *hospital administrator*
Berland, Karen Ina *psychologist*
Brimhall, Dennis C. *hospital executive*
Burns, Alexandra Darrow (Sandra Burns) *health program administrator*
Candlin, Frances Ann *psychotherapist, social worker, educator*
Daniell, Valerie Jean *clinical therapist, counselor*
Dawrant, Stacey Beth *dietitian*
Delay, Eugene Raymond *psychologist, educator, researcher*
Dirks, Jerald Frederick *psychotherapist*
Gollob, Harry Frank *psychology educator*
Gonzalez, Jesus Manuel *social work associate*
Haas, Bradley Dean *clinical pharmacist, consultant*
Hami, Lisa Suzanne *laboratory supervisor, medical technologist*
Hand, Dale L. *pharmacist*
Hitchens, David William *health facility administrator*
Jennett, Shirley Shimmick *hospice executive, nurse*
Jones, Ann Akridge *hospital administration executive*
Jose, Shirley Ann *nurse, critical care educator*
Kalat, Stephen Salman *psychologist*
Kruger, Dennis George *nurse*
Levine, Joel Seth *medical school and hospital administrator*
Martinez, Amos Delfin *health facility administrator, social worker*
Mastrini, Jane Reed *social worker, consultant*
McBurney, Linda Lee *health facility administrator*
Nett, Louise Mary *nursing educator, consultant*
Nicol, Noreen Heer *dermatology nurse practitioner, educator*
Paap, Christopher Mark *pharmacy educator and researcher*
Park, Suegie JA *clinical pharmacist*
Parker, Catherine Susanne *psychotherapist*
Rael, Henry Sylvester *health administrator*
Rizzi, Teresa Marie *bilingual speech and language pathologist*
Stevenson, Marilyn Joyce *dietitian*
Sweet, Andrew Arnold *psychologist*
Watson, Mary Ann *psychologist, educator*
Wilkinson, Joan Kristine *nurse, pediatric clinical specialist*
Yost, Darlene R. *geriatrics and psychiatric/mental health nurse*
Zook, Kay Marie *nursing administrator*

Englewood
Adelstein, Robert Milton *social worker*
Edelman, Joel *medical center executive*
Grego-Heintz, Donna Marie *pediatric physical therapist*
Vollmer, Timothy Lee *medical center executive, educator*
Williams, Robert Jason *psychotherapist, consultant*

Evergreen
Waldmann, Christopher Hawthorne *psychotherapist*

Fort Carson
Johnson, Jacqueline Dolores *community health nurse*

Fort Collins
Allington, Karby Kay *dietitian*
Bennett, Jacqueline Beekman *school psychologist*
Bishop, George Cameron *therapist*
Ervin, Ardith Ann *psychiatric social worker*
Lauri, John Peter *hospital administrator*
Schatz, Mona Claire Struhsaker *social worker, educator*
Smith, Mary Olivia *veterinary medicine educator*
Smith, Nina Maria *mental health nurse, administrator, consultant*

Glenwood Springs
Reinisch, Nancy Rae *therapist, consultant*

Grand Junction
Graves, Thomas Dayle *psychology educator*
Zumwalt, Roger Carl *hospital administrator*

Greeley
Bostwick Baldo, Tracy Dee *counselor, educator*
Engle, Cindy *medical transcriptionist*
Hart, Milford E. *psychotherapist*
Linde, Lucille Mae (Jacobson) *motor-perceptual specialist*
Rhodes, Jess Lynn *counselor*
Rosenberger, Patricia Hirt *psychology educator, researcher*

La Junta
Strong, Mayda Nel *psychologist, educator*

Lakewood
Wellisch, William Jeremiah *social psychology educator*

Lamar
Gamble, Barbara Jean *dietitian and consultant*
Schmeir, Fred Titus *social worker*

LaSalle
Stevenson, James Ralph *school psychologist, author*

Littleton
Panasci, Nancy Ervin *speech pathologist, cookbook writer, communications consultant*
Thornton, Laurie Anne *veterinarian*

Longmont
Dalke, John David *family therapist*
Jones, Beverly Ann Miller *nursing administrator, patient services administrator*

Louisville
Schmidt, Carol Suzanne *hospital administrator*

Loveland
Cattell, Marguerita Briana *veterinarian, researcher*
Williams, T(homas) Patrick *psychologist*

Monument
Adams, Michael Christopher *counselor*

Pueblo
Avery, Julia May *speech pathologist, organizational volunteer*
Hawkins, Robert Lee *health facility administrator*
Kulkosky, Paul Joseph *psychology educator*
Martines, Karen Louise *hospital administrator, nurse*
Parker, Marsha L. *nutrition services administrator*
Pugh, Michael Duane *healthcare executive*
Rose, David William *psychologist, consultant*
Vega, Jose Guadalupe *psychologist, clinical director*
Vislosky, Frank Michael *nursing educator*

Swink
Rockwell, Virginia Considine *school counselor*

Thornton
Hendren, Debra Mae *critical care nurse*

Trinidad
Swett, Dale Everett *physical therapist*

Wheat Ridge
LaMendola, Walter Franklin *human services, information technology consultant*
Willard, James Douglas *health care administrator*

Yuma
Hertneky, Randy Lee *optometrist*

GEORGIA

Clayton
Knepp, Gerald Everett *hospital director*

Richmond Hill
McCormack, Dennis K. *clinical psychologist*

HAWAII

Aiea
Miguel deSousa, Linda J. *critical care nurse, nursing educator*

Hanalei
Snyder, Francine *psychotherapist, registered nurse, writer*

Hilo
Dixon, Paul William *psychology educator*
Swartwout, Glen Martin *optometrist*
Werner, Marlin Spike *speech pathologist and audiologist*
Westerman, John Harold *health administrator*

Honolulu
Behrens, Barbara Blauth *healthcare administrator*
Bitterman, Morton Edward *psychologist, educator*
Corsini, Raymond Joseph *psychologist*
Fischer, Joel *social work educator*
Flannelly, Kevin J. *psychologist, research analyst*
Flannelly, Laura T. *mental health nurse, nursing educator, researcher*
Fullmer, Daniel Warren *psychologist, educator*
Gormley, Francis Xavier, Jr. *social worker*
Hanson, Dennis Michael *medical imaging executive*
Ishikawa-Fullmer, Janet Satomi *psychologist, educator*
Jones, Sally Lewis *healthcare administrator*
Katz, Alan Roy *public health educator*
Kop, Tim M. *psychologist*
Liang, Louise Linda *health facility administrator*
Loh, Edith Kwok-Yuen *oncology nurse*
Lum, Jean Loui Jin *nurse educator*
Roitblat, Herbert Lawrence *psychology educator*
Thompson, Henry Nainoa *hospital administrator*
Toma, Kyle Takeyoshi *recreational therapist*
Waterhouse, Blake E. *health facility administrator*
Watson, David Locke *psychology educator*
Wilson, Nona B. Kahokukauahiahi *critical care nurse*

Kailua
Ditzler, Ann Marie *nutritionist*
White, Terry Wayne *hospital administration executive*

Kaneohe
Spezzano, Charles Lee *psychologist, writer*

Kihei
Ray, Susan Strom *chiropractor*

Koloa
Gustafson, Charles Ivan *hospital administrator*

Lahaina
Miller-Houck, Nancy Joan *nurse, psychotherapist, consultant, educator*
Vonderheid, Arda Elizabeth *nursing administrator*

Mililani
Fukuda, Naomi Nobuko *medical/surgical nurse*
Kiley, Thomas *rehabilitation counselor*

Pearl City
Lajoie, Denise Helena *psychology educator*

Wahiawa
Rabanal, Lisa Louise *youth counselor*

Wailuku
Powley, Linda Galt *dietitian*

Waipahu
Kuwabara, Dennis Matsuichi *optometrist*

IDAHO

American Falls
Wheeler, Ralph Merrill *pharmacist, state senator*

Boise
Brown, Christopher Patrick *health care administrator, educator*
Burleigh-Sparks, Diana Lee *infection control nurse, healthcare consultant*
Callaghan, Kathleen Marie *family nurse practitioner, nursing educator*
Harper, Anthony *counselor, singer*
Jackson, Dawna Darlene *mental health counselor, educator*
Johnson, Bonnie Jean *dietitian, diabetes educator*
Nelson, Willard Gregory *veterinarian, mayor*
Simpson, C. Dene *clinical neuropsychologist, psychophysiologist*
Thomas, Laura Faler *nutrition educator*
Townsend, Sandra Lynnette *nurse*

Coeur D Alene
Chesnut, Tanya Lynn *dietitian*

Idaho Falls
Croft, Richard T. *psychotherapist*

Lewiston
Jenkins, Geni Louise Evans *home health nurse*
Kudronowicz, Juanita Helen *occupational health nurse*
Lorenz, Connie Elizabeth *nutritionist*
Phillips, James Robert *counselor, educator*

Nampa
Denney, Doris Elaine *pharmacist*
Doner, John Roland *hospital administrator*

Payette
Rommel, Yolanda Elizabeth *mental health counselor*

Post Falls
Hamman, Steven Roger *vocational rehabilitation specialist*

Rupert
Wright, Frances Jane *educational psychologist*

Twin Falls
Billings, Patricia Ann Collins *nurse practitioner*

KANSAS

Topeka
Lemire, David Stephen *school psychologist, educator*

MICHIGAN

Grand Rapids
Jackson, Beth Ann *nursing administrator*

MONTANA

Belgrade
Muhs, Elizabeth Mae *marriage and family therapist*

Billings
Furukawa, Dean Kelii *psychotherapist*
Letz, Eileen Korber *community health nurse*
Ostby, Alan Collier *psychotherapist*

Bozeman
Gray, Philip Howard *psychologist, educator*

Circle
Good-Brown, Sue Ann *nurse, small business owner*

Forsyth
Smith, Jeffry Alan *health administrator, physician, consultant*

Glendive
Bruno, Peter Jackson *counselor, consultant, pastor*

Great Falls
Cooper, Susan J. *dietitian, consultant*

Hardin
Martinez, Virginia Marcelina *dietitian*

Havre
DonTigny, Richard Louis *physical therapist*

Helena
Venzke, Ray Frank *psychotherapist*

Livingston
Eaton, Julia H. *counselor*

Miles City
Zumpf, Yordis Ethana *nursing supervisor*

Missoula
Watkins, John Goodrich *psychologist, educator*
Wemple, James Robert *psychotherapist*

Poplar
Gabrielson, Shirley Gail *nurse*

NEVADA

Carson City
Roelke, Ada (Knock-Leveen) *psychotherapist*

East Ely
Alderman, Minnis Amelia *psychologist, educator, small business owner*

Fallon
Bolen, Terry Lee *optometrist*

Hawthorne
Sortland, Trudith Ann *speech and language therapist, educator*

Incline Village
Cordingley, Mary Jeanette Bowles (Mrs. William Andrew Cordingley) *social worker, psychologist, artist, writer*

Las Vegas
Arager, Frances *rehabilitation nurse*
Benbow, Richard Addison *psychologist*
Brandsness, David R. *hospital administrator*
Breckenridge, Rebecca K. *nurse consultant*
Cunningham, Eleanor Elizabeth *nurse*
Dukes, LaJenne Marie *chiropractic physician*
Een, Miriam Blackham *dietitian*
Emerson, Shirley *counseling educator*
Francis, Timothy Duane *chiropractor*
Goldstein, Steven Edward *psychologist*
Gowdy, Miriam Betts *nutritionist*
Huffer, Karin Dianne *marriage and family therapist, writer*
Israel, Joan *social worker*
Kelly, Nancy Anne *nurse*
Law, Flora Elizabeth (Libby Law) *retired community health and pediatrics nurse*
McAllister, Peter Michael *healthcare executive*
McWhirter, Joan Brighton *psychologist*
Minty, Keith Larry *medical services corporation executive*
Ogren, Carroll Woodrow *retired hospital administrator*
Paul, Charla Jo *home health director, chemical abuse counselor*
Pearson, Robert Allen *optometrist*
Pickett, Nancy Elizabeth *vocational rehabilitation consultant, government council executive*
Ronagh-Langroodi, Tahmineh *dietitian, educator, consultant*
Rose, Carol Denise *orthopedic unit nurse administrator, educator*
Roy, Raymond Albert, Jr. *pharmacist*
Stanger, Lynn Beth Carter *orthopedic nurse*
Toadvine, JoAnne Elizabeth *physical therapy foundation executive*

North Las Vegas
Fry, Judy Arline *hypnotherapist*

Pahrump
Taylor, Mary Elizabeth *dietitian, educator*

Reno
Braun, Gerald Curtis *rehabilitation administrator*
Burkholder, Joyce Lynn *clinical social worker*
Cummings, Nicholas Andrew *psychologist*
James, Sondra Mae Margaret *nurse*
Larsen, Patricia Jane *nursing administrator*
Leslie, Sheila Louise *human services consultant*
Lyon, Jean Cozad *family nurse practitioner, educator*
Magruder, Thomas Malone *marriage and family therapist*
Martinson, Julia Ellenor *health science administrator*
Middlebrooks, Deloris Jeanette *nurse, retired*

Sparks
Allen, Judith Martha *nursing administrator, career officer*
Posten, Thomas Allen *emergency nurse*

NEW MEXICO

Alameda
Sherman, Letitia Reid *dietitian*

Albuquerque
Adams, Mary Elizabeth *counselor, psychotherapist, writer*
Chamberlin, Susan Burt *health facility administrator*
Clark, Teresa Watkins *psychotherapist, clinical counselor*
Hadley, Jane Francis *mental health nurse*
Harris, Mary Bierman *psychology educator*
Harris, Richard Jerome *psychology educator*
Johnson, William Hugh, Jr. *hospital administrator*
Kabat, Hugh *pharmacy educator*
Kodituwakku, Piyadasa Wimalaguna *clinical neuropsychologist, educator*
Langereis-Baca, Maria *speech-language pathologist*
Magnussen, Max Gene *psychologist*
Mason, Rose F. *nurse administrator*
Olson, Lenora Mary *health facility administrator, epidemiologist*
Przekurat, Carolyn Bjorkman *dietitian*
Roller, Carolyn Sue *dietitian*
Sanderlin, Terry Keith *counselor*
Solomon, Arthur Charles *pharmacist*
Zimmermann, Laura Kristine *psychology educator*

Bernalillo
Weber, Charlene Lydia *social worker*

Cedar Crest
Despres, Denise Ann *veterinarian*

Clovis
Rehorn, Lois Marie Smith *nursing administrator*

Corrales
Adams, James Frederick *psychologist, educational administrator*

Edgewood
Starr, Ruby *counselor*

Farmington
MacCallum, (Edythe) Lorene *pharmacist*
Young, Tamra Ann *pediatrics nurse*

Las Cruces
Ketchum, Rhonda J. *hospital administrator*
Kutinac, John George, Jr. *psychologist*
McElyea, Ulysses, Jr. *veterinarian*
Pase, Marilyn Nelsen *nurse, educator*
Welsh, Mary McAnaw *family mediator, educator*

Las Vegas
Lewis, Laura Hester Shepherd *clinical psychologist, consultant*

Los Alamos
Thompson, Lois Jean Heidke Ore *industrial psychologist*

Moriarty
Schwebach, Martha Keene *nurse practitioner*

Placitas
Simpson, Gary Lavern *public health medical director*

Portales
Anderson, Charles Ray *health science facility administrator*

Rio Rancho
DeFeo, Sister Theresa F. Marie *health facility administrator, educator*
Hollingsworth, Meredith Beaton *enterostomal therapy clinical nurse specialist*

Roswell
Allen, Janice Faye Clement *nursing administrator*

Ruidoso
Ernest, Dorothetta P. *health facility administrator, critical care nurse*

Santa Fe
Candelaria, Judith (Watt) *nursing administrator*
Clark, Anne deLain Warden *health department executive*
Kuczaj, Stan Abraham, II *comparative psychologist*
Nuckolls, Leonard Arnold *retired hospital administrator*
Phipps, Claude Raymond *research scientist*
Ruybalid, Louis Arthur *social worker, community development consultant*

Truth Or Consequences
Rush, Domenica Marie *health facilities administrator*

Wagon Mound
Abeyta, Jose Reynato *retired pharmacist, state legislator, cattle rancher*

OHIO

Dayton
Pederson, Sanford Lloyd *psychologist*

The Plains
Butler, Granger Hal *hospital administrator*

OREGON

Albany
Chowning, Orr-Lyda Brown *dietitian*
Cluskey, Mary Marshall *dietitian, educator*
Morgan, Carol Louise *home care manager, nurse*

Ashland
Feinstein, (Allan) David *psychologist, author*

Azalea
Massy, Patricia Graham Bibbs (Mrs. Richard Outram Massy) *social worker, author*

Beaverton
Hall, Julia Frances *psychologist*
Hughes, Laurel Ellen *psychologist, educator, writer*
Tieman, Nancy Lee *mental health counselor*

Bend
Calvert, Patricia Viola *dietitian*
Wordell, Douglas Ray *nutrition services director, consultant*

Brookings
Rosenthal, Paul *physical therapist*

Carlton
Yuse-Miller, Mary Adonna *dietitian, holistic nutrition therapist*

Central Point
Berg, Susan Elaine *nursing educator*

Clackamas
Miillé, Carol Ann *counselor*

Corvallis
Gillis, John Simon *psychologist, educator*
Hall, Jean Ann *veterinarian, educator*
Storvick, Clara Amanda *nutrition educator emerita*
Strandberg, Lee R. *pharmacist*

Cove
Kerper, Meike *family violence, sex abuse and addictions abuse rehabilitation educator, consultant*

Eugene
Dresser, Jack William *research psychologist*
DuShane, Phyllis Miller *nurse*
Kahle, Lynn Richard *psychology and marketing educator*
Littman, Richard Anton *psychologist, educator*
Phelps, Kathryn Annette *mental health counseling executive*
Ross, Frances Margaret *medical technologist, artist*
Slovic, Stewart Paul *psychologist*
Smith, Lee R. (Colleen Smith) *family therapist, political activist*
Sundberg, Norman Dale *psychology educator*
Vickers, Laurice Samuel *laboratory administrator, medical examiner*

Florence
Corless, Dorothy Alice *nurse educator*

Hermiston
Brunk, Patrick Charles Roy *mental health professional, counselor*

Klamath Falls
Noonan, Deborah Rae *dietitian*

La Grande
Monahan, Rita Short *nursing educator*

Lake Oswego
Silbert, Amy Foxman *clinical art therapist*

Lebanon
Summers, Wyman Durand *pharmacist*

Marylhurst
Hickcox, Leslie Kay *health educator, counselor*

Medford
Christie, Bradley Scott *mental health services professional*
Linn, Carole Anne *dietitian*
Phelps, Gail Lanita *medical/surgical and oncology nurse*
Smith, Douglas G. *optometrist*

Myrtle Creek
Gillette-Baumann, Muriel Delphine *nurse*

Ontario
Bean, Donna Rae *healthcare facility executive*

Pendleton
Jensen, Judy Dianne *psychotherapist*

Phoenix
Dodd, Darlene Mae *nurse, air force officer*

Portland
Bowyer, Joan Elizabeth *medical technologist, realtor*
Brim, Armand Eugene *health care executive*
Busch, Ann Marie Herbage *medical/surgical clinical nurse specialist*
Cereghino, James Joseph *health facility administrator, neurologist*
Cichoke, Anthony Joseph, Jr. *chiropractor, writer, health consultant*
DuCette, Sheryl Jane *counselor, educator, therapist*
Fedje, Lorreen Ann *dietitian*
Goldfarb, Timothy Moore *hospital administrator*
Hanks, Susan Budlong *physical therapist*
Hemmy, Mary Louise *social work administrator*
Holtorf, Susan Caroline *dietitian*
Houseworth, Steven Michael *court counselor*
Kafoury, Ann Graham *psychotherapist*
Kepner, Jane Ellen *psychotherapist, educator, minister*
Lee, John Patrick *hospital administrator*
Logan, Steve Dean *pharmacy administrator*
Mason, Sara Smith *managed healthcare consultant*
Matarazzo, Joseph Dominic *psychologist*
Maynard, Glenn C. *healthcare administrator, counselor*
McDaniel, Rickey David *senior living executive*
McGuinness, Margaret Elizabeth *pharmacist*
Meighan, Stuart Spence *hospital consultant, internist, writer*
Olson, Roger Norman *health service administrator*
Seyl, Edith J. *occupational therapist*
Shefi, Ellen Leslie *acupuncturist, nutritionist*
Shireman, Joan Foster *social work educator*
Smith, Cathleen Lynne *psychology educator*
Steen, Emma Edith *dietitian, educator*
Tiekotter, Kenneth Louis *electron microscopist*
Waddell, Emilie Jean McCartney *mental health counselor*

Saint Helens
Van Horn, O. Frank *counselor, consultant*

Salem
Callahan, Marilyn Joy *social worker*
Crockett, Ronald Michael *chiropractor*
Fore, Ann *counselor, educator*
Warnath, Maxine Ammer *organizational psychologist, mediator*
Westover, Kristine Elizabeth *dietitian, nutritionist*

Springfield
Orr, Roy Joseph *hospital administrator*

The Dalles
Ponichtera, Brenda Joyce *dietitian, cookbook author*

Tillamook
Rodrique, Sandra Gail *mental health therapist*

Tualatin
Rondorf-Klym, LouAnn M. *clinical investigator, nurse*
Tyler, Darlene Jasmer *dietitian*

West Linn
Clark, Laraine Marie *maternal-child health nurse*

White City
Moore, Charles August, Jr. *psychologist*

Williams
Morrison, Michelle Williams *nursing educator, administrator, author*

TENNESSEE

Memphis
Rieger, Elaine June *nursing consultant*

TEXAS

Fort Worth
Ferdon, Richard Paul *nutritionist, consultant*

Sheppard AFB
Bullard, Donald Lee *health facility administrator*

UTAH

Bountiful
Rowland, Ruth Gailey *hospital official*

Holloday
Reinkoester, Robert William, Jr. *critical care nurse*

Kaysville
Ashmead, Allez Morrill *speech-hearing-language pathologist, orofacial myologist, consultant*

Logan
Athorp, Ann Leslie *mental health services professional*
Curtis, Thom *marriage and family therapist, educator*
Hendricks, Deloy G. *nutrition educator*
Openshaw, Dale Kim *psychology educator, therapist*

Midvale
Katsonis, Michael George *pharmacist*
Smith, Willard Grant *psychologist*

Morgan
Bohman, Verle Rudolph *animal nutritionist*

Ogden
Doxey, Gordon Earl *physical therapist*
Kishimoto, Yoshie Kondo *dietitian*
Wimmer, George Albert *chiropractor, consultant*

Provo
Aldous, Duane Leo *pharmacist*
Bergin, Allen Eric *clinical psychologist, educator*
Daniels, Philip Bliss *psychology educator*
Hancock, Eugene Merrill *dietitian*
Jones, Ronald Charles *hospital administrator*
Kelly, Emma Jane *veterinarian*
McGuire, Diana Harman *dietitian, educator*
Parent, Edward Alphonse *psychologist, consultant, publishing company executive*

Richfield
Bagley, John Neff *social worker, consultant*

Salt Lake City
Benjamin, Lorna Smith *psychologist*
Benson, Joan Ellen *dietetics educator, researcher*
Giles, Gerald Lynn *psychology,learning enhancement,computer educator*
Good, Rebecca Mae Wertman *learning and behavior disorder counselor, hospice nurse*
Goodey, Ila Marie *psychologist*
Grabarz, Donald Francis *pharmacist*
Gunnell, Dale Ray *hospital administrator*
Jorgensen, Lou Ann Birkbeck *social worker*
Kelen, Joyce Arlene *social worker*
Kiernan, Judith Ann *health facility administrator and educator*
Lee, Glenn Richard *medical administrator, educator*
Lindsay, Elena Margaret *nurse*
Mason, James Ostermann *public health administrator*
Morris, Elizabeth Treat *physical therapist*
Morris, Stephen Blaine *clinical psychologist*
Park, Marilyn McKay *mental health nurse*
Parker, Scott Smith *hospital administrator*
Reeves, Bruce *social worker*
Roach, Beverly Hyatt *public health clinic manager*
Samuelson, Cecil O. *health care facility executive*
Sinclair, Sara Voris *health facility administrator, nurse*
Swaner, Paula Margetts *clinical psychologist*
Wall, David Elliott *substance abuse specialist*
Ward, R(obert) Scott *physical therapist*
White, Raymond *health facility administrator*
Wirthlin, David Bitner *hospital administrator*
Zaharia, Eric Stafford *developmental disabilities program administrator*

Sandy
Boyce, Andrea Zygmunt *nurse*

VIRGINIA

Charlottesville
Novak, Julie Cowan *nursing educator, researcher, clinician*

WASHINGTON

Aberdeen
Cartier, Carol Jean McMaster *social worker*

Bellevue
Akutagawa, Donald *psychologist, educator*
Knoepfler, Gayle Stewart *sex therapist*
Lipkin, Mary Castleman Davis (Mrs. Arthur Bennett Lipkin) *retired psychiatric social worker*
Walsh, Marie Leclerc *nurse*

Bellingham
Wood-Trost, Lucille Marie *educator, writer, psychotherapist*

Bremerton
Sanford, Kathleen Diane *nursing administrator*

Burton
Jackson, Deborah Tonge *dietitian, consulting nutritionist*

Chehalis
Overmoen, Mary Ellen *dietitian*

Des Moines
Harper, Vera Jean *convalescent home activity director, music therapist*

Edmonds
Carle, Harry Lloyd *social worker, career development specialist*

Evanston
Thompson, Leigh Lassiter *psychologist, educator*

Everett
Lombard, Lawrence John *chemical dependency counselor*
O'Connell, Michael Alexander *social worker*

Everson
McGulpin, Elizabeth Jane *nurse*

Federal Way
Ruddell, Alysa Ann *clinical psychologist*

Friday Harbor
MacGinitie, Walter Harold *psychologist*

Gig Harbor
Nash, Clarice Aldine Hayes *family nurse practitioner, critical care nurse*

Issaquah
Cernak, Keith Patrick *health care and financial consultant*

Kennewick
Fann, Margaret Ann *counselor*

Leavenworth
Smith, Carin A. *veterinarian, writer*

Lk Forest Park
Calas, Napoleon Evans *medical laboratory administrator*

Longview
Moosburner, Nancy *nutritionist*

Lynnwood
Thompson-Jurich, Susan Kaye *therapist, addictions consultant*
Wennik, Roberta Schwartz *dietitian*

Moses Lake
Andress, Cathy *psychologist, educator*

Napavine
Morgan-Fadness, Corrina May *staff charge nurse*

Oak Harbor
Miller, Robert Scott *mental health professional, social worker*

Olympia
Boruchowitz, Stephen Alan *health policy analyst*
Collins, Fuji *mental health professional*
González, Natalie Louise *dietitian*
Inverso, Marlene Joy *optometrist*
Langer, Stephen Marc *clinical psychologist*
Reilly, Robert Joseph *counselor*

Poulsbo
Wotruba, David Lawrence *marriage and family therapist*

Pullman
Chermak, Gail Donna *audiologist, speech and hearing sciences educator*
Silflow, Ronald Mark *animal scientist, microbiologist*

Puyallup
Edwards, Rapha Olga Jones *social worker*
Walize, Reuben Thompson, III *health research administrator*

Redmond
Adachi, Derek Kasumi *pharmacist, computer programmer*
Jorgensen, Donald Allan *health facility administrator, immunologist*
Sadri, Fereydoon *medical company executive*
Sasenick, Joseph Anthony *health care company executive*

Richland
Rittmann, Paul Douglas *health physicist*

Seattle
Benson, Karen A. *nursing educator*
Boaz, Doniella Chaves *psychotherapist, consultant*
Childs, Marian Tolbert *nutritionist, educator*
Day, Robert Winsor *cancer research administrator*
Dear, Ronald Bruce *social work educator*
DesRoches, Brian *psychotherapist, organizational systems consultant*
Duncan, Elizabeth Charlotte *marriage and family therapist, educator*
Erickson, Elizabeth Ann (Lisa Erickson) *mental health counselor, educator, consultant*
Fisher, Nancy Louise *pediatrician, medical geneticist, former nurse*
Freedman, Edward *health services administrator, management consultant*
Golston, Joan Carol *psychotherapist*
Hansen, Coral June *nurse practitioner, respiratory therapist*
Henry, Holly Jean *nutritionist, researcher*
Hillmer, Robin Lynn *critical care, medical/surgical nurse*
Horton, John Michael *psychoanalyst*
Huey, Constance Anne Berner *mental health counselor*
Hunt, Mary Lou *counselor, small business owner*

Landberg, Ann Laurel *nurse, psychotherapist*
Larson, Eric Hugh *public health scientist*
MacDonald, Don *psychotherapist, educator*
McComb, Ronald Graeme *rolfer*
Meltzoff, Andrew N. *psychologist, educator*
Muilenburg, Robert Henry *hospital administrator*
Neff, John Michael *health facility administrator, educator, dean*
Niemeier, Cynthia Lee *critical care nurse*
Norkool, Diane Marie *nursing administrator, medical/surgical nurse*
Pianetti, Catherine Natalie *occupational therapist*
Prins, David *speech pathologist, educator*
Schaller, Joanne Frances *nursing consultant*
Thompson, Arlene Rita *nursing educator*
Wolf, Gail Pokela *psychometrist, counselor*
Wylie, Laurie Jean *nursing administrator*

Sequim
Kuest, Marilyn Sibyl *school nurse*
Mc Hugh, Margaret Ann Gloe *psychologist*

Shelton
Larsen, Paula Anne *operating room nurse*

Spokane
Armacost, Cathy Loa *nutritionist, consultant*
Burkhead, Virginia Ruth *rehabilitation nurse*
Callen, Elnora Stoller *nurse, mental retardation professional*
Crogan, Neva Lynne *nursing consultant*
Holm, Audrey Christine *health care organization administrator*
Leahy, Gerald Philip *hospital administrator*
Mealey, Anne Roe *mental health nurse, educator, consultant*
Robinson, Herbert Henry, III *counselor, therapist*
Vaux, Dora Louise *sperm bank official, consultant*

Sultan
Canto, Diana Catherine *nurse*

Tacoma
Bobb, Peter Michael *health infection control technician*
Cammermeyer, Margarethe *nurse*
Hendley, Ashley Preston, Jr. *clinical social worker*
Ingram, Artonyon S. *mental health professional, therapist*
Larson, Maureen Inez *rehabilitation consultant*
Reim, Ruthann *career and personal counselor, corporate trainer*
Robinett, Debora Ann *dietitian*
Sims, Linda Geraldine *therapist, educator*
Smith, Leo Gilbert *hospital administrator*
Sweeney, Stacie Mund *critical care nurse*
Zierath, Marilyn Jean *medical/surgical and pediatrics nurse*

Trout Lake
Turner, Tamara Michele *child and family therapist*

Vancouver
Castles, John William *healthcare company executive*
Gantz, Nancy Rollins *nursing administrator, consultant*
Lewis, Karen Maxine *nurse, pharmaceutical sales executive*
Loggans, Susan Von Brockhoeft *nurse*
Nelson, Robert Earl *mental health counselor*
Wilson-Hart, Jessica Helen *mental health counselor, writer*

Wenatchee
Sims, Darcie Dittberner *grief management specialist, psychotherapist, clinical hypnotherapist*

Yakima
McCown, Linda Jean *medical technology educator*
Simonson, Susan Kay *hospital administrator*

WYOMING

Basin
Kennette, Jennie Laura Fakes *medical/surgical nurse*

Burns
Ricciardelli-Dailey, Mary Lynde *health services company executive and author*

Casper
Margo, Kenneth Craig *counselor*

Cheyenne
Hirst, Wilma Elizabeth *psychologist*
Laycock, Anita Simon *psychotherapist*
Yamreudeewong, Weeranuj *clinical pharmacist, educator*

Hanna
Turner, Lillian Erna *nurse*

Laramie
Alleman, Georgia Carmin *medical technologist*
Berger, Bonnie G. *sport psychologist, educator*
Crocker, Sylvia Fleming *psychotherapist, writer*
Lowe, Sue Esther *optometrist*
Meuli, Mindy Denise *clinical dietitian*
Nord, Thomas Allison *hospital administrator*
Pine, Lois Ann Hasenkamp *nurse*
Schroeder, Cheryl Ann *health and educational consultant*

Powell
Brophy, Dennis Richard *psychology and philosophy educator*

Rock Springs
O'Jack, Helen Margaret *clinical social worker*
Thompson, Josie *nursing administrator*

Saratoga
Collamer, Sonja Mae Soreide *veterinary facility administrator*

Sheridan
Roth, Steven D. *mental health counselor*

Sundance
Peters, Roxanne Leigh *nurse practitioner, consultant*

Torrington
Martindale, Jeanie Arlene *nursing administrator and educator*

Wilson
Breitenbach, Mary Louise McGraw *psychologist, drug rehabilitation counselor*

Worland
Munsterteiger, Kay Diane *speech-language pathologist*

CANADA

ALBERTA

Bentley
Manes, John Dalton *retired hospital administrator, anaesthesiologist*

Calgary
Meyers, Marlene O. *hospital administrator*

Edmonton
Fields, Anthony Lindsay Austin *health facility administrator, oncologist, educator*
Hislop, Mervyn Warren *health advocate administrator, psychologist*

BRITISH COLUMBIA

Cobble Hill
Ling, Daniel *audiology consultant, educator emeritus, former university dean*

New Westminster
Fair, James Stanley *hospital administrator*

Vancouver
Hawkes, Elizabeth Lawrence (Bonnie Hawkes) *health facility administrator*
Mulchey, Ronald Douglas *hospital administrator*
Splane, Richard Beverley *social work educator*

Victoria
Fyke, Kenneth John *hospital administrator*

SASKATCHEWAN

Saskatoon
Belovanoff, Olga *retired health care facility administrator*
Randhawa, Bikkar Singh *psychologist, educator*

ZAMBIA

Mumbwa
Hansen, Florence Marie Congiolosi (Mrs. James S. Hansen) *social worker*

ADDRESS UNPUBLISHED

Abernathy, Vicki Marie *nurse*
Altman, Irwin *psychology educator*
Ancoli-Israel, Sonia *psychologist, researcher*
Anderson, Dorothy Fisher *social worker, psychotherapist*
Annon, Jack Stafford *forensic and criminal psychologist, detective*
Badgett, Ann Wilson *mental health nurse, rehabilitation nurse*
Baldridge, Thad Clifton Walker *psychotherapist, consultant*
Barnes, Elizabeth J. *operating room nurse*
Belles, Donald Arnold *pastoral therapist, mental health counselor*
Belmont, Larry Miller *health association executive*
Bjorklund, Janet Vinsen *speech pathologist*
Blacher, Joan Helen *psychotherapist, educator*
Boehm, Paul Eugene *pharmacist*
Brame, Marillyn A. *hypnotherapist*
Bridge, Sherry *clinical dietitian*
Buckley, Linda Anne *critical care, psychiatric-mental health, chemical dependency nurse*
Bullough, Vern LeRoy *nursing educator, historian, sexologist, researcher*
Burgar, Ruby Rich *college health service nurse*
Busch, Morgan David *health care executive*
Callison, Nancy Fowler *nurse*
Carden, Thom(as) Ray *psychologist*
Carlsen, Mary Baird *clinical psychologist*
Cash, Deanna Gail *nursing educator*
Caspers, Corlyn Marie *adult nurse practitioner*
Caspy, Barbara Jane *social worker*
Cave, Alan Wayne *psychologist*
Chase, Gail Anne *geriatrics nurse, nursing executive*
Child, Carroll Cadell *research nursing administrator*
Chipman, Harold Hastings *psychology educator*
Clanon, Thomas Lawrence *retired hospital administrator*
Colby, Robert Lester *psychologist*
Coleman, Arlene Florence *nurse practitioner*
Coleman, William Robert *optometrist*
Condry, Robert Stewart *retired hospital administrator*
Conner, Natalie Ann *community health nurse specialist*
Cook, Todd McClure *health care executive*
Corah, Deborah Jean *respiratory therapist*
Craig, Carol Mills *marriage, family and child counselor*
Cryer, Linda Brooks *women's health nurse*
Dean, Donna Margaret *psychotherapist, writer*
Deems, Andrew William *health facility administrator*
DeMillion, Julianne *health and fitness specialist, personal trainer, rehabilitation therapist, consultant*
Dempsey, Barbara Matthea *medical/surgical and critical care nurse*
Díaz, Elena R. *community health nurse*
Dickey, Patricia Ann *dietitian*
Diedrick, Geraldine Rose *retired nurse*
Docktor, William Jay *pharmacist, educator*
Duke, Melissa Ann *nurse*
Dungan, Gloria Kronbeck *critical care nurse*
Dungworth, Donald L. *veterinary educator, consultant*
Dunmeyer, Sarah Louise Fisher *health care consultant*
Dusserre, Michelle *dietitian, gymnastics coach*
Easter, Gayl Alma *nutritionist*
Fehr, Lola Mae *nursing association director*
Fifer, Linda Sue *speech pathologist, interior designer*
Fletcher, J. Sue *health educator*
French, Glendon Everett, Jr. *health care executive*
Fryer, Gladys Constance *nursing home medical director, educator*
Gabriel, Michael *hypnotherapist, educator*
Garvey, Evelyn Jewel *mental health nurse*
Gaspar, Rogelio G. *laboratory technologist*
Gengler, Sue Wong *health educator*
Gerstman, Buddy Burt *health science educator*
Gilbert, Jo *psychologist*
Giles, Walter Edmund *alcohol and drug treatment executive*
Glick, Stanley Barton *optometrist, photographer*
Goetzke, Gloria Louise *social worker, income tax specialist*
Golden, Gina Louise *psychotherapist*
Gordon, Ruby Daniels *retired nursing educator, counselor*
Govan, Gladys Vernita Mosley *retired critical care and medical surgical nurse*
Grant, Richard Earl *nursing administrator*
Grasso, Monica Marie *home health nurse*
Gray, Deborah Mary *medical corporation executive*
Green, Flora Hungerford *lactation consultant, nurse*
Grushkin, Donald Adam *psychologist*
Hagen, Edna Mae *retired nurse*
Hall, Julie Jane *community health nurse, administrator*
Hardway, James Edward *vocational specialist*
Harris, Michael Gene *optometrist, educator, lawyer*
Harris, Roxanna Marie *emergency room nurse*
Harrison, Bhanu Joy *social worker*
Hart, Jean MacAulay *clinical social worker*
Hart-Kepler, Virginia Lynn *nurse, educator*
Hartzell, Irene Janofsky *psychologist*
Healy, Sonya Ainslie *health facility administrator*
Held, Nancy B. *perinatal nurse, lactation consultant*
Herrmann, Walter *retired laboratory administrator*
Higgins, Ruth Ann *social worker, family therapist*
Hofmann, Paul Bernard *health care consultant*
Holtzapfel Pesante, Patricia Kelly *health facility executive*
Homestead, Susan E. (Susan Freedlender) *psychotherapist*
Hughes, W. James *optometrist*
Hunter, Annarae *mental health counselor*
Hyatt, Laura *healthcare company executive*
Jacobs, Arthur Dietrich *educator, researcher, health services executive*
Jankovitz, Joseph Edward *psychologist, educator, nurse*
Jennings, Reba Maxine *critical care nurse*
Jones, Wanda Carol *nurse*
Juarez, Maretta Liya Calimpong *social worker*
Keiser, Megan Marie *neuroscience nurse specialist*
Kellam, Norma Dawn *medical, surgical nurse*
Kimbrell, Leslie Caitlin *health science consultant*
Klein, Fay Magid *health administrator*
Lagerberg, Randall Erland *mental health specialist*
Lane, Kathleen Madden *emergency/trauma nurse, family nurse practitioner*
Lane, Thomas Alfred *laboratory manager*
Leake, Philip Gregory *exercise physiologist, consultant*
Lee, Aldora G. *social psychologist*
Lewis, Nancy Patricia *speech and language pathologist*
Lilly-Hersley, Jane Anne Feeley *nursing researcher*
Lindsey, Henry Jackson, III *psychologist, educator*
Logan, Glenn Raymond *mental health professional, counselor*
Lousberg, Sister Mary Clarice *hospital executive*
Mansergh, Gordon Dwight *health promotion and health behavior researcher, consultant*
Marshall, L. B. *medical technologist*
Matheson, Lou Thelma *mental health counselor, multicultural specialist*
McClane, Angela Dawn *marriage, family and child counselor*
McDougall, Jacquelyn Marie Horan *therapist*
McLaughlin, Frank E. *nursing educator*
McNair, Norma Diane *nurse*
McPherson, James Willis, III *health care public affairs director*
Mercurio-Muico, Luisa *critical care nurse*
Meyer, Harry Martin, Jr. *retired health science facility administrator*
Mikel, Thomas Kelly, Jr. *laboratory administrator*
Miller, Sonja Glaaser *social worker*
Mills, Celeste Louise *hypnotherapist, professional magician*
Mitchell, Geneva Brooke *retired hypnotherapist*
Moffatt, Hugh McCulloch, Jr. *hospital administrator, physical therapist*
Mosqueira, Charlotte Marianne *dietitian*
Nakagawa, Allen Donald *radiologic technologist*
Nakano-Matsumoto, Naomi Namiko *social worker*
Napier, Maureen Jill *critical care nurse*
Nordel, Patricia A. Olmstead *medical/surgical, critical care, and obstetrical nurse*
Oswald, Regina M. *community health nurse*
Parker, Jo Ann *nurse*
Parker, Joyce Steinfeld *social worker*
Parks, Richard Keith *clinical social worker*
Parrish, Pamela Jo *counselor*
Paule, Lawrence David *chiropractor*
Pawlak, Michelle Evanthe *dietitian, nutrition educator, consultant*
Pelzl, Beverly Ruth *perioperative nurse*
Peters, Shirley Ann *pediatrics nurse*
Petow, Joan Claudia *orthopedic nurse*
Pettit, Ghery DeWitt *retired veterinary medicine educator*
Price, Jeannine Alleenica *clinical psychologist*
Principe, Helen Mary *medical case manager*
Rasmussen, Gail Maureen *critical care nurse*
Ravicchio, Grace Veneta *home health nurse*
Reeves, Carol Swope *marriage and family counselor*
Reider, Carroll Ann *nutritionist, consultant*
Reisch, Michael Stewart *social work educator*
Reynosa, Brenda Iverson *dietitian*
Richardson, Carolyn Jane *social worker*
Ries, Barbara Ellen *alcohol and drug abuse services professional*
Riley, Stanley Robert *psychologist*
Risley-Curtiss, Christina *social worker, educator*
Rodriguez, Margaret Louise *crisis intervention counselor, community debriefer and trainer*
Roodman, Richard David *hospital administrator*
Ropchan, Rebecca G. *nursing administrator*
Rose, Mason H., IV *psychoanalyst*
Salzman, Anne Meyersburg *psychologist*
Sanders, Augusta Swann *retired nurse*
Sanders, Charmaine Yevette *pharmacist*
Sauvage, Lester Rosaire *health facility administrator, cardiovascular surgeon*
Scala, James *health care industry consultant, author*
Shapiro, Alice Kubernick *dietitian, consultant*
Shapiro, Yanina *psychology educator*
Siekman, Grace Anne *nursing administrator*
Simms, Maria Ester *health services administrator*
Simpson, Jocelyn Yvette *pediatric medical/surgical and hematology/oncology nurse*
Skarda, Richard Joseph *clinical social worker*
Skoglund, Elizabeth Ruth *marriage, child and family counselor*
Sloan, Rosalind *nurse, military officer*
Soeth, Sarah Laverne Reedy McMillan *psychiatric nurse*
Solomon, Julius Oscar Lee *pharmacist, hypnotherapist*
Staley, Martha McCalpin *dietitian*
Stein, Ellyn Beth *mental health services professional*
Stezoski-Rodriguez, Lorise Ann *critical care nurse, educator*
Stickles, Bonnie Jean *nurse*
Suber, Robin Hall *former medical/surgical nurse*
Swan, Anna *school nurse*
Tallmadge, Guy Kasten *research psychologist*
Thistel, Cynthia Grelle *nursing educator, nurse epidemiologist*
Thomson, Grace Marie *nurse, minister*
Tice, Elizabeth *counseling educator, corporate trainer, educational adminstrator, consultant*
Tyler, Gail Madeleine *nurse*
Tyler, JoAnn *ultrasonographer*
Uhrich, Richard Beckley *hospital executive, physician*
Ulmer, Harriet Glass *health services administrator*
Usher, Ronald Lee *government health care consultant, retired county official*
Usinger, Martha Putnam *counselor, educator*
Violet, Woodrow Wilson, Jr. *retired chiropractor*
Voelker, Margaret Irene (Meg Voelker) *gerontology, medical/surgical nurse*
Vos, Robert A. *nurse, health care facility executive*
Wagner, Geraldine Marie *nursing educator*
Wagner, Hazel Edith *medical/surgical and neurological nurse*
Walker, Gail Juanice *electrologist*
Watt, Diana Lynn *social worker*
Weber, Constance Lynn *dietetian*
Werlein, Donna Dabeck *community health care administrator*
Whalen, Alberta Dean *community health nurse*
Wheaton, Mary Edwina *health facility administrator, educator*
Wickwire, Patricia Joanne Nellor *psychologist, educator*
Wiese, Neva *critical care nurse*
Williams, Mary D(ennen) *psychologist*
Williams, Nathan Dale *counselor*
Wolbers, Harry Lawrence *engineering psychologist*
Wyckoff, Margo Gail *pyschologist*
Zavala, Albert *research psychologist*

HEALTHCARE: MEDICINE

UNITED STATES

ALASKA

Anchorage
Mala, Theodore Anthony *physician, consultant*
Wald, Robert David *psychiatrist*
Wood, Thomas Cowan *physician*

Fairbanks
Hutchison, Richard Louis *plastic surgeon*
Parry, Richard Gittings *plastic and reconstructive surgeon, writer*

Haines
Feldman, Leonard *family practitioner*

Wasilla
Troxel, John Milton *physician*

ARIZONA

Apache Junction
Stumpf, Michael Howard *psychiatrist*

Chandler
Robrock, James Lawrence *plastic surgeon*

Flagstaff
Giesecke, Mark Ernst *psychiatrist*

Glendale
Kastrul, Jerome Joe *geriatrician*

Mesa
Boren, Kenneth Ray *endocrinologist*
Bunchman, Herbert Harry, II *plastic surgeon*
Coons, David Joel *physician, psychiatrist*
Fiorino, John Wayne *podiatrist*
Hiatt, Karl Brinton *plastic surgeon*
Labovitz, Earl A. *allergist*
Thompson, Ronald MacKinnon *family physician, artist, writer*
Yee, Bruce James *anesthesiologist*

Paradise Valley
Bankoff, Peter Rosner *anesthesiologist*
Butler, Byron Clinton *physician, cosmologist, gemologist, scientist*
Polson, Donald Allan *surgeon*

Peoria
Grumbling, Hudson Virgil, Jr. *internist*
McKee, Margaret Crile *pulmonary medicine and critical care physician*

Phoenix
Ansel, Lee *surgeon*
Baratz, David Michael *physician*
Benchimol, Alberto *cardiologist, author*
Borel, James David *anesthesiologist*
Bull, John Carraway, Jr. *plastic surgeon*
Burgoyne, David Sidney *psychiatrist*
Bybee, Paul Ralph *psychiatrist*
Calkins, Jerry Milan *anesthesiologist, educator, administrator, biomedical engineer*
Callison, James R. *plastic surgeon*
Casano, Salvatore Frank *physician*
Charlton, John Kipp *pediatrician*
Clifford, Nathan Joseph *cardiologist*
Donahue, Edward Joseph *surgeon*
Edwards, Thomas Alun *physician*
Friedland, Jack Arthur *plastic surgeon*
Goldberg, Morris *internist*
Gordon, Alan Leslie *internist*
Haddad, Farid Sami *educator*
Harris, Benjamin Keith *rheumatologist*
Heffner, John Edward *medical educator*
Hernried, Lucy S. *physician*
Holman, Paul David *plastic surgeon*
Jacobson, Albert Dale *pediatrician, accountant*
Karpman, Robert Ronald *orthopedic surgeon*
Koep, Lawrence James *surgeon*
Kuhl, Wayne Elliott *physician*
Kuivinen, Ned Allan *pathologist*
Lee, Gilbert Brooks *retired ophthalmology engineer*
Long, David R. *cardiologist, internist, medical consultant*
Lorenzen, Robert Frederick *ophthalmologist*
Mattioni, Thomas A. *physician, electrophysiologist*
Miller, Robert Jennings *medical board administrator*
Roth, Sanford Harold *rheumatologist, health care administrator, educator*
Singer, Jeffrey Alan *surgeon*
Sonntag, Volker Karl Heinz *neurosurgeon, educator*
Speiser, Burton Lyle *radiation oncologist*
Stern, Stanley *psychiatrist*
Tafur, Mario Humberto *psychiatrist*
Tour, Robert Louis *ophthalmologist*
Weese, William Curtis *physician*
Wright, Richard Oscar, III *pathologist, educator*

Scottsdale
Adler, Charles Howard *neurologist*
Callies, Quinton Carl *allergist*
DeHaven, Kenneth Le Moyne *retired physician*
Friederich, Mary Anna *gynecology and obstetrics consultant*
Friedman, Shelly Arnold *cosmetic surgeon*
Harrison, Harold Henry *physician, scientist, educator*
Irons, George Benton *plastic surgeon*
Lewis, John Christopher *allergist*
Nitz, Gary Lee *psychiatrist*
Offenkrantz, William Charles *psychiatrist*
Pomeroy, Kent Lytle *physical medicine and rehabilitation physician*
Sanderson, David R. *physician*

Sedona
D'Javid, Ismail Faridoon *surgeon*
Hawkins, David Ramon *psychiatrist, writer, researcher*

Sun City
De La Pava, Daniel *plastic surgeon*

Sun City West
Calderwood, William Arthur *physician*

Tempe
Anand, Suresh Chandra *physician*
Levin, Hal Alan *psychiatrist*
Noce, Robert Henry *neuropsychiatrist, educator*

Tucson
Ahern, Geoffrey Lawrence *behavioral neurologist*
Alberts, David Samuel *physician, pharmacologist, educator*
Alfaro, Armando Joffroy *plastic surgeon*
Arabia, Francisco Alberto *cardiovascular and thoracic surgeon*
Auerbach, Bryan Neil *pediatrician*
Bellamy, William Tracey *pathology educator*
Ben-Asher, M. David *physician*
Berg, Robert Allen *pediatrician, educator*
Binkiewicz, Anna I.S. *pediatrician*
Brooks, William James *osteopathic physician, educator*
Burr, John Clarence *physician*
Dommisse, John Vlok *nutritional-metabolic physician, psychiatrist*
Epstein, Norman Richard *internist*
Evans, Bradley Dennis *psychiatrist, industrial consultant*
Harris, David Thomas *immunologist*
Hess, Richard Neal *plastic surgeon*
Houle, Joseph Adrien *orthopaedic surgeon*
Hunter, Tim Bradshaw *radiologist, educator*
Justice, James Walcott *physician, research scientist*
Kaszniak, Alfred Wayne *neuropsychologist*
Kay, Marguerite M. *immunologist, geriatrician, medical educator*
Ketchel, Steven J. *internist*
Kischer, Clayton Ward *embryologist, educator*
Kittredge, John Russell *physician*
Koldovsky, Otakar *pediatrics and physiology educator*
Kurtin, Sandra Elaine *nurse*
Lam, Kit Sang *medical educator*
Lopez, Ana Maria *physician*
Marcus, Frank Isadore *physician, educator*
Martin, Loren Winston *physician*
McCuskey, Robert Scott *anatomy educator, researcher*
Mills, Joseph Loren *vascular surgeon, educator*
Misiaszek, John J. *psychiatrist*
Nathan, Ronald G. *psychiatrist*
Otto, Charles Wilson *anesthesiologist, educator*
Palmer, Craig M. *anesthesiologist, educator*
Pike, Steven *occupational health physician*
Ramsay, Eric Guy *surgeon*
Reinmuth, Oscar MacNaughton *physician, educator*
Ricke, P. Scott *obstetrician/gynecologist*
Russell, Findlay Ewing *physician*
Salmon, Sydney Elias *medical educator, director*
Sampliner, Richard Evan *physician*
Schilling, Jolyon David *vascular and general surgeon*
Sutherland, John Campbell *pathologist, educator*
Thompson, Floyd Henry *cytogenetic oncologist*
Toff, Howard David *psychiatrist*
Witten, Mark Lee *lung injury research scientist, educator*

CALIFORNIA

Agoura Hills
deCiutiis, Alfred Charles Maria *medical oncologist, television producer*

Anaheim
Lim, Timothy Alton *plastic surgeon*
Sweet, Thomas Ira *physician*

Apple Valley
Win, Khin Swe *anesthesiologist*

Atascadero
Gritter, Gordon William *psychiatrist*
Kiersch, Theodore Alexander *psychiatrist*

Auburn
Hanowell, Ernest Goddin *physician*

Bakersfield
Ansfield, Joseph Gilbert *psychiatrist, educator*
Prunes-Carrillo, Fernando *plastic surgeon, educator*
Tavoularis, Marjorie Osterwise *psychiatrist*

Baldwin Park
Blitz, Ira Allen *obstetrician-gynecologist*

Barstow
Sutterby, Larry Quentin *internist*

Bellflower
Gillman, Greta Joanne *physician*
Ho, Wan Chuen *plastic surgeon*
Nguyen Trung, B. *plastic surgeon*

Belvedere
Van Pelt, Meredith Alden *general and vascular surgeon*

Berkeley
Ames, Richard Galyon *epidemiologist*
Caetano, Raul *epidemiologist, educator*
Clarke, Greta Fields *dermatologist*
Fong, David *psychiatrist*
Handwerker, Lisa *medical anthropologist, public health consultant*
Kaye, Brian Randall *rheumatologist, educator*
Manougian, Edward *physician*
Oken, Richard Leslie *pediatrician*
Patterson, Lloyd Clifford *psychiatrist*
Rutherford, George Williams, III *preventive physician*
Seitz, Walter Stanley *cardiovascular research consultant*
Sheen, Portia Yunn-ling *retired physician*
Simburg, Earl Joseph *psychiatrist, psychoanalyst*
Van Brunt, Edmund Ewing *physician*
Waller, Kirsten Orlette *epidemiologist*

Beverly Hills
Allen, Howard Norman *cardiologist, educator*
Cambre, Athleo Louis, Jr. *plastic surgeon*
Catz, Boris *endocrinologist, educator*
Dennis, Karen Marie *plastic surgeon*
Fein, William *ophthalmologist*
Klein, Arnold William *dermatologist*
Kravitz, Hilard L(eonard) *physician*
Leaf, Norman *plastic surgeon, educator*
Marshak, Harry *physician, plastic surgeon*
Mason, Albert Abraham *psychoanalyst, psychiatrist, educator*
Osman, Marvin Phillip *psychiatrist and psychoanalyst*
Reed, Enid *neuropsychologist*
Semel, George Herbert *plastic surgeon*
Sones, Leon Isaac *psychiatrist*
Yuan, Robin Tsu-Wang *plastic surgeon*

Boulder Creek
Piazza, Duane Eugene *biomedical researcher*

Brawley
Jaquith, George Oakes *ophthalmologist*

Brea
Ewing, Russell Charles, II *physician*

Buena Park
Gaspar, Max Raymond *surgeon*

Burlingame
Beattie, George Chapin *orthopaedic surgeon*
Caplin, Abigail Beth *allergist*
Chu, Sally Chen *medical librarian*
Marcus, Hubert C. *ophthalmologist*
Nadell, Andrew Thomas *psychiatrist*

Camarillo
Green, Michael Foster *neuropsychologist, educator*
Hussain, Shakeela Fatima *internist*
Improta, Robert Stephen *plastic surgeon*

Camp Pendleton
Edwards, Bruce George *ophthalmologist, naval officer*

Campbell
Rubenstein, Martin Donald *hematologist*
Schwartz, Steven Michael *cardiothoracic surgeon*
Wu, William Lung-Shen (You-Ming Wu) *aerospace medical engineering design specialist, foreign intelligence analyst*

Capistrano Beach
Roemer, Edward Pier *neurologist*

Carlsbad
Buccigrossi, David Eric *internist*

Carmel Valley
Chapman, Robert Galbraith *retired hematologist, administrator*

Castro Valley
Fernandes, Dionisio A. *physician*

Cerritos
Gulasekaram, Balasubramaniam *psychiatrist, educator*

Chatsworth
Hage, Stephen John *radiology administrator, consultant*

Chico
Incaudo, Gary Arnold *allergist*

Chino
Lamb, Robert Charles *plastic surgeon*

Chula Vista
Allen, Henry Wesley *biomedical researcher*
Cardona-Loya, Octavio *plastic surgeon*

Claremont
Johnson, Jerome Linné *cardiologist*

Clovis
Terrell, Howard Bruce *psychiatrist*

Concord
Latner, Barry P. *pathologist*

Corte Madera
Epstein, William Louis *dermatologist, educator*

Costa Mesa
Coulter, Christopher Harvey *physician, healthcare executive*
Firestone, Frederick Norton *surgeon, educator*
Sharp, Laurence Newton *diagnostic company executive*

Covina
Schneider, Calvin *physician*
Takei, Toshihisa *otolaryngologist*

Cupertino
Andrews, Russell Joseph *neurosurgeon, educator*

Daly City
Shaw, Richard Eugene *cardiovascular researcher*

Dana Point
Bruggeman, Lewis LeRoy *radiologist*
Kaufman, Edward Redding *psychiatrist, educator*
Noyes, Tom Enderby *psychiatrist*

Danville
Bunkis, Juris *plastic surgeon*
Lavey, Elliott Bruce *plastic surgeon*

Davis
Bauer, Herbert *physician*
Hance, Anthony James *retired pharmacologist, educator*
Hoch, William Henry *surgeon, urologist*
Kass, Philip Howard *epidemiology educator*
Ochoa, Enrique Luis-Maria *pediatrician*
Palmer, Philip Edward Stephen *radiologist*
Plopper, Charles George *anatomist, cell biologist*
Schaefer, Saul *cardiologist*
Williams, Hibbard Earl *medical educator, physician*

Deer Park
Anderson, Bruce Nils *psychiatrist*

Del Mar
Lesko, Ronald Michael *osteopathic physician*

Downey
Burger, Emil Ferdinand *allergist, medical group executive*
Gong, Henry, Jr. *physician, researcher*
Kurnick, John Edmund *hematologist, educator*
Magnes, Harry Alan *physician*
Rubayi, Salah *surgeon, educator*
Shapiro, Richard Stanley *physician*

Duarte
Brynes, Russell Kermit *pathologist, educator*
Comings, David Edward *physician, medical genetics scientist*
Vasilev, Steven Anatol *gynecologic oncologist, educator*

El Cajon
Fauskin, Gary Neale *pediatrician*

Emeryville
Dixon, Richard Erwin *physician, medical director*
Wanerman, Leon Ralph *psychiatrist*

Encinitas
Humber, Philip Richard *plastic surgeon*
Jaffe, Charles J. *allergist*
Rummerfield, Philip Sheridan *medical physicist*

Encino
Bergman, Arieh *gynecologist*
Imber, Wayne Evan *allergist*
Venkatesh, Alagiriswami *cardiologist*

Escondido
Everton, Marta Ve *ophthalmologist*
Khoury, Kenneth Alan *psychiatrist*
Spencer, Mary Josephine *pediatrician*

Fair Oaks
Hendry, John Easton, III *physician, surgeon*

Fairfield
Martin, Clyde Verne *psychiatrist*
Munn, William Charles, II *psychiatrist*

Fontana
Mirante, Kathleen Marie *cardiologist*
Resch, Charlotte Susanna *plastic surgeon*

Fortuna
Montgomery, John Alan *surgeon*

Foster City
Park, Tong M. *medical, physics and cybernetics researcher*

Freedom
Ley, Robert Duncan *plastic surgeon*

Fremont
Chen, John Calvin *child and adolescent psychiatrist*
Karipineni, Shakira Baig *obstetrician, gynecologist*

Fresno
Chandler, Bruce Frederick *internist*
Connor, Paul Lyle *medical librarian*
Glassheim, Jeffrey Wayne *allergist, immunologist, pediatrician*
Knapp, Donald Eugene *gastroenterologist*
Murthy, Veeraraghavan Krishna *medical educator*
Shipp, Joseph Calvin *physician, educator*
Tschang, Tai-Po *pathologist*
Willis, Charles Dubois *neuropsychiatrist, writer*

Garden Grove
Anderson, Geoffrey Robert *research manager*

Gardena
Okada, Tsuyoshi *internist*
Rubin, Lawrence Ira *podiatrist*

Gilroy
Grisez, James Louis *physician, plastic surgeon*

Glendale
Dent, Ernest DuBose, Jr. *pathologist*
Hall, Josephine Weissman *obstetrician/gynecologist*
Sachs, Loren Allen *magnetic resonance imaging technology specialist*

Gold River
Forbes, Kenneth Albert Faucher *urological surgeon*

Greenbrae
Denkler, Keith Alan *surgeon*

Guerneville
Whitaker, Rupert Edward David *neuroimmunologist and behavioral scientist, consultant, writer*

Harbor City
Gottschalk, Adele M. *surgeon*

Hawthorne
Nosratian, Farshad Joseph *internist, cardiologist*

Hayward
Hung, Sammy T. *physician*

Hemet
Galletta, Joseph Leo *physician*

Hillsborough
Graff, Norman Irwin *psychiatrist*
Parker, Thomas Gooch *retired surgeon*

Huntington Beach
Appelbaum, Bruce David *physician*
Lee, Sammy *retired physician, surgeon*
Solmer, Richard *surgeon*

Indio
Dickinson, Dan Calvin *medical librarian*

Inglewood
Sukov, Richard Joel *radiologist*
Zemel, Norman Paul *orthopaedic surgeon*

Irvine
Connolly, John Earle *surgeon, educator*
Gwon, Arlene *ophthalmologist*
Kahn, Joel Sheldon *physician*
Lippa, Erik Alexander *ophthalmologist*
Myers, Rhonda Jan *allergist*
Weinstein, Gerald D. *dermatology educator*

La Canada Flintridge
Byrne, George Melvin *physician*

La Crescenta
Riccardi, Vincent Michael *pediatrician, researcher, educator*

La Jolla
Backus, Varda Peller *psychiatrist*
Barrett-Connor, Elizabeth Louise *epidemiologist, educator*
Brems, John Joseph *surgeon*
Caine, Simon Barak *neuroscientist, researcher*
Demeter, Steven *neurologist, publishing company executive*
Franklin, Marshall *cardiologist*
Freeman, William Roseman *ophthalmologist*
Garland, Cedric Frank *epidemiologist, educator*
Goldman, Mitchel Paul *dermatologist*
Goto, Shinya *cardiologist, researcher*
Gruber, Andras *physician, researcher*
Hamburger, Robert N. *pediatrics educator, consultant*
Havran, Wendy Lynn *immunologist*
Hench, Philip Kahler *physician*
Herwig, Karl Robert *physician*
Hofmann, Alan Frederick *biomedical educator, researcher*
Horner, Anthony Adam *pediatrician, educator*
Jaffer, Adrian Michael *physician*
Jorgensen, Judith Ann *psychiatrist*
Keeney, Edmund Ludlow *physician*
Lewis, Carson McLaughl *plastic surgeon*
Liu, Fu-Tong *biomedical researcher, dermatologist*
Masouredis, Serafeim Panagiotis *pathologist, educator*
Mathews, Kenneth Pine *physician, educator*
Miller, Stephen Herschel *surgery educator*

Parry, Barbara Lockhart *psychiatry educator, researcher*
Peebles, Carol Lynn *immunology researcher*
Perkins, Roy Frank *internist, former university official*
Pollard, Kenneth Michael *molecular immunologist, researcher*
Rao, Tadimeti Seetapati *pharmacologist*
Rearden, Carole Ann *clinical pathologist, educator*
Reid, Robert Tilden *medical association administrator, internist*
Roberts, Anne Christine *interventional radiologist, educator*
Rosenblatt, Allan D. *psychiatrist*
Rudolph, Ross *surgeon, researcher, educator*
Saltz, Lori Hodgson *plastic surgeon*
Saven, Alan *oncologist, hematologist*
Schneider, Gerald L. *plastic surgeon*
Schneider, Jerry Allan *pediatrics educator*
Sherman, Linda Arlene *immunologist*
Singer, Robert *plastic surgeon*
Tan, Eng Meng *immunologist, rheumatologist, biomedical scientist*
Teirstein, Paul Shepherd *physician, health facility administrator*
Terry, Robert Davis *neuropathologist, educator*
Utne, John Richard *retired radiation oncologist*
Walker, Richard Hugh *orthopaedic surgeon*
Weigle, William Oliver *immunologist, educator*
Weinreb, Robert Neal *opthalmologist, educator*
Wiederholt, Wigbert C. *neurologist, educator*

La Mesa
Johnson, Keith Ronald *obstetrician/gynecologist*
Wohl, Armand Jeffrey *cardiologist*

La Puente
Betancourt, Nellie *physician*
Goldberg, David Bryan *biomedical researcher*
Good, William Zev *physician*

Laguna Beach
Gordon, Marvin Jay *physician*
Sartini, Richard Lee *retired internist*

Laguna Hills
Askin, Jerald Mark *podiatrist*
Kirshbaum, Jack D. *pathologist*

Laguna Niguel
Strenger, George *surgeon*

Lakewood
Tong, Richard Dare *anesthesiologist*

Loma Linda
Behrens, Berel Lyn *physician, academic administrator*
Bull, Brian Stanley *pathology educator, medical consultant, business executive*
Coggin, Charlotte Joan *cardiologist, educator*
Condon, Stanley Charles *gastroenterologist*
Cress, Charles R. *pharmacology educator*
Houchin, Kenneth Wayne *ophthalmologist, neuro-opthalmologist, educator*
Kohne, Raymond Ernest *physician, educator*
Llaurado, Josep G. *nuclear medicine physician, scientist*
Marais, Henri John *cardiologist*
Slater, James Munro *radiation oncologist*
Stilson, Walter Leslie *radiologist, educator*

Long Beach
Bloomer, William Ernest *thoracic and cardiovascular surgeon, educator*
Bolton, Leon Leslie *plastic surgeon*
Cohen, Manley *gastroenterologist*
Dana, Hugh Richard *internist, educator*
Gonda, Harry Henrik *psychiatrist*
Hickman, Donn Michael *plastic surgeon*
Honning, Bengt Eugene *chiropractic physician, consultant, biochemist*
Jadus, Martin Robert *cellular immunologist*
Leidl, Peter Janos *internist*
Macer, George Armen, Jr. *orthopedic hand surgeon*
MacLeod, Kathleen Bromley *internist*
Mahutte, Cornelis Kees *internist, educator*
Mills, Don Harper *pathology and psychiatry educator*
Parker, Lawrence Neil *medical educator*
Schoendorf, Judson Raymond *allergist*
Sidhu, Mohan *anesthesiologist*
Tabrisky, Phyllis Page *physiatrist, educator*

Los Alamitos
Wong, Ing Liong *nephrologist*

Los Angeles
Ahn, Samuel Seunghae *vascular surgeon, researcher, consultant*
Alkana, Ronald Lee *neuropsychopharmacologist, psychobiologist*
Allada, Vivekanand *pediatric cardiologist, researcher*
Amstutz, Harlan Cabot *orthopaedic surgeon*
Archie, Carol Louise *obstetrician and gynecologist, educator*
Aronowitz, Joel Alan *plastic and reconstructive surgeon*
Ashley, Sharon Anita *pediatric anesthesiologist*
Bao, Joseph Yue-Se *orthopaedist, microsurgeon, educator*
Barbers, Richard George *physician, educator*
Barker, Wiley Franklin *surgeon, educator*
Barnert, Cyril, III *psychiatrist*
Barnes, Peter Francis *physician, researcher, medical educator*
Batzdorf, Ulrich *neurosurgeon, educator*
Belzberg, Howard *critical care physician, educator*
Berke, Gerald Spencer *surgeon*
Bernstein, Sol *cardiologist, educator*
Bodey, Bela *immuno-morphologist*
Braunstein, Glenn David *physician, educator*
Brickman, Harry Russell *psychiatrist, psychoanalytic institute dean*
Brooks, Scott David *medical research analyst*
Brown, Saul Leon *psychiatrist, educator*
Brown, Spencer L. *surgeon*
Bryson, Yvonne J. *pediatrician, virologist*
Campese, Vito Michele *nephrologist*
Carmel, Ralph *hematologist, educator*
Chandor, Stebbins Bryant *pathologist*
Cherkas, Marshall S. *psychiatrist, psychoanalyst*
Cherry, James Donald *physician*
Chopra, Inder Jit *physician, endocrinologist*
Cicciarelli, James Carl *immunology educator*
Cohen, William B. *vascular surgeon*
Comar, Kanwar Dave *surgeon*
Cote, Richard James *pathologist, researcher*
Coyle, Mara Genevieve *physician, pediatrician*
Crues, John Vernon, III *radiologist, educator*
Danoff, Dudley Seth *surgeon, urologist*
Dee, Anthony James *psychiatrist*
De Shazo, Billy W. *physician, plastic surgeon*
Deutsch, Nicholas Andrew *medical educator*
Dixit, Vivek *medical educator*
Edgerton, Bradford Wheatly *plastic surgeon*
Eilber, Frederick Richard *surgeon*
Eth, Spencer *medical educator, psychiatrist*
Fagelson, Harvey J. *emergency physician, dermatologist, educator*
Feig, Stephen Arthur *pediatrics educator, hematologist, oncologist*
Figlin, Robert Alan *physician, hematologist, oncologist*
Fishbein, Michael Claude *physician, pathologist*
Fisher, Mark Jay *neurologist*
Fonkalsrud, Eric Walter *pediatric surgeon, educator*
Forrester, James Stuart *cardiologist, medical educator*
Gambino, Jerome James *nuclear medicine educator*
Garg, Meena *physician, neonatologist*
Geffner, David Lewis *endocrinologist*
Giannotta, Steven Louis *neurosurgery educator*
Go, Vay Liang Wong *physician, medical educator, editor*
Goin, John Morehead *plastic surgeon*
Goldsmith, Jonathan Charles *pediatrician*
Golomb, Beatrice Alexandra *physician, medical researcher*
Gorney, Roderic *psychiatry educator*
Grody, Wayne William *physician*
Gunn, Michela Faith *psychiatrist*
Heckenlively, John Robert *ophthalmology educator*
Hershman, Jerome Marshall *endocrinologist*
Hines, Melissa *neuroscientist*
Hirsch, Anthony T. *physician*
Hoang, Duc Van *theoretical pathologist, educator*
Holland, Gary Norman *ophthalmologist, educator*
Hsiao, Chie-Fang *neuroscientist*
Jacobson, Edwin James *medical educator*
Johnson, Richard Greene *physician, psychiatrist, psychoanalyst*
Jones, Neil Ford *surgeon*
Kalmansohn, Robert Bruce *physician, consultant, lecturer*
Kaplan, Samuel *pediatric cardiologist*
Kato, Norman Scott *cardiac surgeon, educator*
Katz, Roger *pediatrician, educator*
Kerman, Barry Martin *ophthalmologist, educator*
Kilburn, Kaye Hatch *medical educator*
Kim, Kwang Sik *pediatrician, researcher*
King, Hwa-kou *anesthesiologist*
Kinney, Brian Maltbie *plastic surgeon*
Koch, Richard *pediatrician, educator*
Kramer, Barry Alan *psychiatrist*
Krivokapich, Janine *physician, educator*
Labowe, Mark Lawrence *plastic surgeon*
Lamb, H. Richard *psychiatry educator*
Landing, Benjamin Harrison *pathologist, educator*
Lawrence, Sanford Hull *physician, immunochemist*
Leach, Gary Edward *urologist, educator*
Leavitt, Maimon *psychiatrist*
Lesavoy, Malcolm A. *plastic surgeon, educator*
Lesser, Gershon Melvin *physician, lawyer, medical and legal commentator*
Lin, Henry C. *gastroenterologist, researcher*
Looney, Gerald Lee *medical educator, administrator*
Love, Susan Margaret *surgeon, educator, medical administrator*
Machleder, Herbert Ivan *surgeon, educator*
Macy, Jonathan Isaac *ophthalmologist, educator*
Maguen, Ezra *ophthalmologist, researcher*
Mahour, Gholam Hossein *pediatric surgeon, educator*
Mark, Rufus James *physician, educator*
Maronde, Robert Francis *internist, clinical pharmacologist, educator*
Martin, Neil Alfred *neurosurgeon*
Martin, Paul *hepatologist, medical educator*
Metzner, Richard Joel *psychiatrist, psychopharmacologist, educator*
Mihan, Richard *dermatologist*
Miles, Samuel Israel *psychiatrist*
Miller, Timothy Alden *plastic and reconstructive surgeon*
Moss, Charles Norman *physician*
Mower, William Rex *medical educator, researcher*
Moy, Ronald Leonard *dermatologist, surgeon*
Munro, Malcolm Gordon *obstetrician/gynecologist, educator*
Nathwani, Bharat Narottam *pathologist, consultant*
Nuwer, Marc Roman *neuroscientist, physician*
O'Connell, Theodore Xavier *surgical oncologist, educator*
Oizumi, Jun *pediatrician, geneticist*
Parekh, Dilip *surgeon, oncologist, educator*
Parker, John William *pathology educator, investigator*
Paulson, Richard John *obstetrician/gynecologist, educator*
Penny, Robert *pediatrician, educator, researcher*
Pi, Edmond Hsin-Tung *psychiatry educator*
Rachelefsky, Gary S. *medical educator*
Rasheed, Suraiya *pathology educator, cancer and AIDS researcher*
Reynolds, Charles Patrick *pediatric oncologist, researcher*
Rice, Dale Howard *physician, educator*
Rimoin, David Lawrence *physician, geneticist*
Ritvo, Edward Ross *psychiatrist*
Roven, Alfred Nathan *surgeon*
Ryan, Stephen Joseph, Jr. *ophthalmology educator, university dean*
Saad, Mohammed Fathy *medical educator*
Sadun, Alfredo Arrigo *neuro-ophthalmologist educator*
Schechtman, Vicki Lynn *neurophysiologist*
Schmid, Ingrid *medical researcher*
Schneider, Edward Lewis *medicine educator, research administrator*
Schwartz, Lawrence Jay *ophthalmologist*
Shapiro, Matthew Scott *orthopaedic surgery educator, athletic team physician*
Shau, Hungyi *immunologist*
Shekhar, Stephen S. *obstetrician, gynecologist*
Sherman, Randolph *plastic and reconstructive surgeon, educator*
Shields, William Donald *neurologist, educator*
Siegel, Sheldon C. *physician*
Siegel, Stuart Elliott *physician, pediatrics educator, cancer researcher*
Sigman, Melvin Monroe *psychiatrist*
Simmons, Donna Marie *neuroscientist, neurobiology researcher, histotechnologist*
Singer, Elyse Joy *physician*
So, George J.K. *radiologist, researcher*
Solomon, George Freeman *academic psychiatrist*
Sullivan, Stuart Francis *anesthesiologist, educator*
Tannen, Richard Laurence *medical educator, nephrologist*
Terz, Jose Juan *physician, surgical educator*
Titus, Edward Depue *psychiatrist, administrator*
Tuch, Richard Howard *psychoanalyst, psychiatrist*
van Dam, Heiman *psychoanalyst*
Van Der Meulen, Joseph Pierre *neurologist*
van Leeuwen, Kato *psychiatrist*
Vierling, John Moore *physician*
Villablanca, Jaime Rolando *medical scientist, educator*
Wagner, Willis Harcourt *vascular surgeon*
Wang, Sheng-Yong *cardiologist and research physiologist*
Watanabe, Richard Megumi *medical research assistant*
Watring, Watson Glenn *gynecologic oncologist, educator*
Weiner, Dora B. *medical humanities educator*
Weiss, Irwin Kevin *pediatrician, educator*
Weiss, Martin Harvey *neurosurgeon, educator*
Wilhite, Wilson Cecil, Jr. *anesthesiology educator*
Williams, John Phillip *physician, researcher*
Wilson, Miriam Geisendorfer *physician, educator*
Wincor, Michael Z. *psychopharmacology educator, clinician, researcher*
Wishner, Stanley Herman *cardiologist*
Withers, Hubert Rodney *radiotherapist, radiobiologist, educator*
Woolf, Nancy Jean *neuroscientist, educator*
Yager, Joel *psychiatry educator*
Yao, Lawrence *radiologist*

Los Gatos
Coe, Jeffrey Dean *orthopaedic surgeon*
Naughten, Robert Norman *pediatrician*
Segall, Mark M. *physician, colon and rectal surgeon*

Malibu
Morgenstern, Leon *surgeon*

Martinez
Love, Gordon Lee *pathologist, researcher*
McKnight, Lenore Ravin *child psychiatrist*
Swislocki, Arthur L. M. *physician, internist*

Menlo Park
Adams, Robert Monroe *dermatologist, educator*
Chin, Albert Kae *research physician*
Dewey, Richard Ryder *retired internist, educator*
Kaplan, Jonathan *psychiatrist, educator*
Kelly, Richard John *anesthesiologist, physician, lawyer*
Kovachy, Edward Miklos, Jr. *psychiatrist*
Woodrow, Kenneth M. *psychiatrist*

Merced
Irby, Pamela Jo *family practice physician*
Maytum, Harry Rodell *retired physician*

Mill Valley
Deikman, Arthur J. *psychiatrist*
Newman, Nancy Marilyn *ophthalmologist, educator, consultant, inventor, entrepreneur*
Wallerstein, Robert Solomon *psychiatrist*

Milpitas
Chiu, Peter Yee-Chew *physician*

Mission Hills
Tram, Kenneth Khai Kt *internist*

Mission Viejo
Caliendo, Theodore Joseph *pediatrician, neonatalogist*
Waldman, Jerald Paul *orthopedic surgeon*

Modesto
Carroll, Wallace B. *allergist, immunologist*
Jacisin, John James *psychiatrist*

Monrovia
Lasko, Allen Howard *pharmacist*

Monterey
Lehr, Jeffrey Marvin *immunologist, allergist*

Monterey Park
Chiu, Chu-Tsen *surgeon*
Moel, Steven Allen *ophthalmologist*

Morgan Hill
Scates, Steven Michael *hematologist, oncologist*

Mountain View
Goldring, Stanley Donald *medical instrument designer*
Lowen, Robert Marshall *plastic surgeon*
Warren, Richard Wayne *obstetrician/gynecologist*

Murrieta
Ing, Robert Yun Kwin *allergist*

Napa
Wycoff, Charles Coleman *retired anesthesiologist*
Zimmermann, John Paul *plastic surgeon*

Newport Beach
Brown, John Vincent *gynecologic oncologist*
Chiu, John Tang *physician*
Horowitz, Jed H. *plastic surgeon, reconstructive surgeon*
Zalta, Edward *otorhinolaryngologist, utilization review physician*

Nipomo
Brantingham, Charles Ross *podiatrist, ergonomics consultant*

North Hollywood
Adelson, Leonard Joseph *physician*

Northridge
Weiland, I. Hyman *psychiatrist*
Ziman, Ronald Bert *physician, researcher, consultant*

Norwalk
Vo, Huu Dinh *pediatrician, educator*

Novato
Franklin, Robert Blair *cardiologist*
Pappas, Nicholas *psychiatrist*

Oakland
Cody, Patricia Herbert *health educator*
Eisenberg, Ronald Lee *radiologist*
Friedman, Gary David *epidemiologist, research facility administrator*
Grossman, Seymour *gastroenterologist*
Hobson, Donnis Stacy *plastic surgeon*
Kao, Lily Ching-Chiung *neonatologist*
Killebrew, Ellen Jane (Mrs. Edward S. Graves) *cardiologist*
Klatsky, Arthur Louis *cardiologist, epidemiologist*
Lau, Glen K. *plastic surgeon*
Lee, Michael Anthony *cardiologist*
Le Noir, Michael A. *allergist*
Ng, Lawrence Ming-Loy *pediatric cardiologist*
Poor, Clarence Alexander *physician*
Reichel, John Kento *medical care organization official, writer*
Schoen, Edgar Jacob *pediatrician, pediatric endocrinologist*
Weinmann, Robert Lewis *neurologist*

Oceanside
Curtin, Thomas Lee *ophthalmologist*
Folkerth, Theodore Leon *cardiovascular surgeon, educator*

Olympic Valley
Hsu, Shu-Dean *hematologist, oncologist*

Orange
Ammirati, Mario *neurosurgeon*
Armentrout, Steven Alexander *oncologist*
Brandon, Jeffrey Campbell *physician, interventional radiologist, educator*
Chishti, Nadeem Ahmad *physician*
Furnas, David William *plastic surgeon*
Gislason, Irving Lee *psychiatry educator*
Lott, Ira Totz *pediatric neurologist*
MacArthur, Carol Jeanne *pediatric otolaryngology educator*
Manetta, Alberto *gynecologic oncologist*
Newman, Richard Stephen *pathology educator*
Patrizio, Pasquale *reproductive endocrinologist, andrologist*
Rowen, Marshall *radiologist*
Thompson, William Benbow, Jr. *obstetrician/gynecologist, educator*
Trivedi, Narendra Shantilal *physician, educator, researcher*
Waters, Jonathon Hale *anesthesiologist*
Wilson, Archie Fredric *medical educator*

Orinda
King, Alexander Louis *pediatrician*

Oxnard
Niesluchowski, Witold S. *cardiovascular and thoracic surgeon*

Pacific Palisades
Barritt, Clay Franklin *psychiatrist, educator*
Claes, Daniel John *physician*

Palm Desert
Le Winn, Laurence Rynes *plastic & reconstructive surgeon*
Shah, Suresh Chandra *anesthesiologist*

Palm Springs
Grayman, Glen *emergency medicine physician*

Palmdale
Combs, Donald Steven *physician assistant*

Palo Alto
Adamson, Geoffrey David *reproductive endocrinologist, surgeon*
Agras, William Stewart *psychiatry educator*
Amylon, Michael David *physician, educator*
Babcock, Rosemary Ann Douglas *animal behavior researcher, biomedical librarian, naturalist*
Blessing-Moore, Joann Catherine *physician*
Buck, Louise Bryden *psychiatrist*
Charlton, Randolph Seville *psychiatrist, educator*
Dennery, Phyllis Armelle *pediatrician, educator*
Ebi, Kristie Lee *epidemiologist, consultant*
Fann, James Ilin *cardiothoracic surgeon*
Gendzel, Ivan Bennett *psychiatrist, educator*
Gray, Gary Michael *physician, researcher, educator*
Gupta, Suneel Kumar *pharmacologist*
Harris, Robert Francis *psychoanalyst, psychiatrist*
Hentz, Vincent R. *surgeon*
Lane, William Kenneth *physician*
Laub, Donald R. *plastic surgeon*
Lepore, Vincent Donald, Jr. *plastic surgeon*
Link, Michael Paul *pediatrics educator*
Lobel, Charles Irving *physician*
Lunde, Donald Theodore *physician*
Pirofsky, Harvey *psychiatrist*
Relman, David Arnold *physician, educator*
Robinson, Thomas Nathaniel *pediatrician, educator, researcher*
Segre, Eugene Joseph *drug development consultant, physician*
Shortliffe, Edward Hance *internist, medical information science educator*
Stertzer, Simon Henry *cardiologist, educator*
Strober, Samuel *immunologist, educator*
Tinklenberg, Jared Ray *psychiatrist, researcher*
Vistnes, Lars M. *plastic surgeon*
Weston, Jane Sara *plastic surgeon, educator*

Palos Verdes Peninsula
Thomas, Claudewell Sidney *psychiatry educator*

Panorama City
Bass, Harold Neal *pediatrician, medical geneticist*
Pollack, Alan Myron *physician*
Sue, Michael Alvin *physician*

Paramount
Cohn, Lawrence Steven *physician, educator*
Sernaque, Jose David *cardiothoracic and vascular surgeon*

Pasadena
Glovsky, Myron Michael *medical educator*
Harvey, Joseph Paul, Jr. *orthopedist, educator*
Helsper, James T. *surgical oncologist, researcher, educator*
Hillman, Milton Henry *ophthalmologist, lawyer*
Lake, Kevin Bruce *medical association administrator*
Mathies, Allen Wray, Jr. *physician, hospital administrator*
Morgan, Stanley Charles *plastic and reconstructive surgeon*
Niebur, Ernst Dietrich *computational neuroscientist*
Phelan, Jeffrey Patrick *obstetrician/gynecologist*
Procci, Warren R. *psychiatrist*
Riffenburgh, Ralph Sidney *ophthalmologist*
Shalack, Joan Helen *psychiatrist*
Simard, Marie Françoise *endocrinologist*
Singh, Rajesh Kumar *psychiatrist*

Piedmont
Sharpton, Thomas *physician*

Placerville
Bonser, Quentin *retired surgeon*

Pleasanton
Hisaka, Eric Toru *plastic surgeon*
Iverson, Ronald E. *plastic surgeon*

Portola Valley
Rosenthal, Alan Jay *psychiatry educator*

Poway
Venn-Watson, Patricia *psychiatrist*

Rancho Cordova
Desai, Asha *allergist*

Rancho Mirage
Cone, Lawrence Arthur *research medicine educator*
George, Sebastian *hematologist, oncologist*
Macon, James Barbour, III *neurological surgeon*

Rancho Palos Verdes
Chandraratna, Premindra Anthony N. *physician*

Rancho Santa Fe
Rockoff, S. David *radiologist, physician, educator*

Redding
Campbell, Patrick Milton *internist, educator*
Renard, Ronald Lee *allergist*

Redlands
Flores, John A. *internist*
Haddad, Wisam Boulos *surgeon*
Hunter, Kenneth A. *plastic surgeon*
Jones, Galen Ray *physician assistant*
Richardson, A(rthur) Leslie *former medical group consultant*
Skoog, William Arthur *retired oncologist*
Smith, Dunbar Wallace *retired physician, clergyman*

Redwood City
Wong, Nancy L. *dermatologist*

Reedley
Davis, Charles Arthur *psychiatrist*

Represa
Shepard, Kenneth Sihler *physician, surgeon*

Richmond
Erickson, Russell John *pediatrician*
Hoehne, John H. *allergist*
Hurwitz, George K. *allergist*
Lichtenstein, Robert Moohr *allergist*

Riverside
Cook, Robert P. *psychiatrist*
Hatton, Glenn Irwin *medical educator*
Hiler, Emerson Gard *psychiatrist*
Jukkola, George Duane *obstetrician, gynecologist*
Jung, Timothy Tae Kun *otolaryngologist*
Lau, Kam Yung *physician, educator*
Linaweaver, Walter Ellsworth, Jr. *physician*
Schwartz, Louis *radiologist*
Seyfert, Howard Bentley, Jr. *podiatrist*
Shaffer, Audrey Jeanne *medical records administrator, educator*
Sparks, Dale Boyd *allergist, health facility administrator*

Rolling Hills Estates
Bellis, Carroll Joseph *surgeon*

Roseville
Herman, Frederick Flint *allergist*

Rowland Heights
Tsai, Michael Ming-Ping *psychiatrist*

Sacramento
Achtel, Robert Andrew *pediatric cardiologist*
Coe, Tracy L. *internist*
Evrigenis, John Basil *obstetrician-gynecologist*
Flamm, Melvin Daniel, Jr. *cardiologist*
Follette, David Michael *cardiothoracic surgeon*
Fong, Julita Angela *pathologist*
Garcia, Gordon Stanley *physician*
Greenspan, Adam *radiologist, educator*
Ichelson, David Leon *physician*
Laslett, Lawrence J. *physician, educator*
Lavi, Efraim *allergist*
Leong, Albin B. *allergist, educator*
Lilla, James A. *plastic surgeon*
Lim, Alan Young *plastic surgeon*
Lippold, Roland Will *surgeon*
Makker, Sudesh Paul *physician*
Nagy, Stephen Mears, Jr. *physician, allergist*
Rathlesberger, James Howard *medical board executive*
Reiber, Gregory Duane *forensic pathologist*
Rosenthal, Seth A. *radiologist, oncologist*
Sharma, Arjun Dutta *cardiologist*
Tung, Prabhas *plastic surgeon*
Tupin, Joe Paul *psychiatry educator*
Zil, John Stephen *psychiatrist, physiologist*

Salinas
Ginsburg, Jerry Hugh *physician, health facility administrator*
Kellogg, Donald Ray *surgeon, plastic surgeon*
Kellogg, George William *psychiatrist*
Leighton, Henry Alexander *physician, consultant*
Rever, Barbara L. *medical educator, consultant, researcher*

San Bernardino
Gorenberg, Alan Eugene *physician*
Hodes, Abram *pediatrician*
Kuehn, Klaus Karl Albert *ophthalmologist*
Levister, Ernest Clayton, Jr. *physician*
Prendergast, Thomas John, Jr. *physician, epidemiologist*
Russo, Alvin Leon *obstetrician/gynecologist*
Smith, Roger Alexander *surgeon*

San Bruno
Bradley, Charles William *podiatrist, educator*

San Carlos
Ellis, Eldon Eugene *surgeon*

San Clemente
Kim, Edward William *ophthalmic surgeon*
Sperber, James Irving *physician, medical educator*

San Diego
Abrams, Reid Allen *surgeon, educator*
Bejar, Ezra *pharmacologist, biology educator*
Benirschke, Kurt *pathologist, educator*
Blum, John Alan *urologist, educator*
Boynton, Bruce Ryland *pediatrician, neonatologist, educator*
Brookler, Harry Aaron *physician*
Burns, David M. *medical educator*
Chambers, Henry George *orthopaedic surgeon*
Cowen, Donald Eugene *retired physician*
Cramer, Mark Steven *family physician*
Davidson, Terence Mark *surgery educator, otolaryngologist*
Deftos, Leonard John *medical scientist and educator*
Dimsdale, Joel Edward *psychiatry educator*
Dziewanowska, Zofia Elizabeth *neuropsychiatrist, pharmaceutical executive, physician*
Easter, David Wayne *surgery educator*
Gallen, Christopher Charles *neuroscientist, neurologist, psychiatrist*
Gillin, John Christian *psychiatrist*
Goldzband, Melvin George *psychiatrist*
Greener, Yigal *biomedical researcher*
Haroun, Ansar M. *forensic psychiatrist, educator*
Hollan, Carol Angela *plastic surgeon*
Holmes, Ralph Edward *plastic surgeon*
Hourani, Laurel Lockwood *epidemiologist*
Hubbard, David Richardson *neurologist*
Hugh, Michael Young *allergist*
Intriere, Anthony Donald *physician*
Iragui-Madoz, Vicente J. *neurologist, neurosciences educator*
Jablecki, Charles K. *clinical neurologist*
Jackson, Joseph Brian *physician, health facility administrator*
Jeste, Dilip Vishwanath *psychiatrist, researcher*
Kaplan, George Willard *urologist*
Kaweski, Susan *plastic surgeon*
King, Bernard David *cardiologist, pharmaceutical company executive*
Kruggel, John Louis *physician*
Lamberti, John Joseph *cardiovascular surgeon*
Lee, Myung-Shik *medical researcher*
Lerner, Sheldon *plastic surgeon*
Levy, Jerome *dermatologist, retired naval officer*
Lewis, Gregory Williams *scientist*
Moore, Robert Horton *physician*
O'Leary, Michael Joseph *surgeon, neurotologist*
Oliphant, Charles Romig *physician*
Parsons, C. Lowell *surgery educator*
Pitt, William Alexander *cardiologist*
Sartoris, David John *radiologist*
Schmidt, Joseph David *urologist*
Schuckit, Marc Alan *psychiatry educator, researcher*
Selzer, Kenneth A. *neurologist, editor*
Shin, Sung Sik *pathologist, educator, researcher*
Stevens, John Joseph *physician*
Traynor-Kaplan, Alexis Elaine *biomedical researcher*
Turrell, Eugene Snow *psychiatrist*
Wallace, Helen Margaret *physician, educator*
Wallace, Mark Raymond *physician*
Wasserman, Stephen Ira *physician, educator*
Wollman, Arthur Lee *urologist*
Yalam, Arnold Robert *allergist, immunologist, consultant*
Zeiger, Robert S. *allergist*

San Francisco
Aird, Robert Burns *neurologist, educator*
Amend, William John Conrad, Jr. *physician, educator*
Aminoff, Michael Jeffrey *medical educator*
Anthony, James Peter *plastic surgeon, educator*
Arieff, Allen Ives *physician*
Arsham, Gary *medical educator*
Augustyn, Damian Henry *gastroenterologist*
Bainton, Dorothy Ford *pathology educator, researcher*
Bikle, Daniel David *research physician*
Bishop, John Michael *biomedical research scientist, educator*
Brown, Donald Malcolm *plastic surgeon*
Brown, Robert Stephen, Jr. *gastroenterologist*
Cahan, Robert Barmach *psychiatrist, educator*
Capozzi, Angelo *surgeon*
Caputo, Gary Richard *radiology educator*
Chapman, Alger Baldwin, III *pediatrician, researcher*
Cheitlin, Melvin Donald *physician, educator*
Chung, Crawford *physician*
Cline, Carolyn Joan *plastic and reconstructive surgeon*
Connor, Charles Peter *psychiatrist, educator*
Darney, Philip Dempsey *gynecologist, educator*
Donegan, Elizabeth Ann *anesthesiologist*
Duh, Quan-Yang *surgeon*
Erskine, John Morse *surgeon*
Fishman, Robert Allen *educator, neurologist*
Frick, Oscar Lionel *physician, educator*
Fukuyama, Kimie *medical educator*
German, Donald Frederick *physician*
Gooding, Gretchen Ann Wagner *physician, educator*
Gottfried, Eugene Leslie *physician, educator*
Greenberg, Roger L. *plastic and reconstructive surgeon*
Grullón, Kenneth Emanuel *obstetrician-gynecologist*
Halvorsen, Robert Alfred, Jr. *radiologist, educator*
Handagama, Prem Josef *hematopathologist, researcher*
Herbert, Chesley C. *psychiatrist*
Hering, William Marshall *medical organization executive*
Hinman, Frank, Jr. *urologist, educator*
Hoffman, William Yanes *plastic surgeon*
Horton, Jonathan Charles *neuroscientist, neuro-ophthalmologist*
Hwang, David Genpai *ophthalmologist, educator*
Ikeda, Clyde Junichi *plastic and reconstructive surgeon*
Irwin, Charles Edwin, Jr. *pediatrics educator*
Israel, Mark A. *pediatrics and neurological surgery educator*
Jaume, Juan Carlos *physician, educator*
Katz, Barrett *neuro-ophthalmologist*
Katzung, Bertram George *pharmacologist*
Kimmich, Robert André *psychiatrist*
Kline, Howard Jay *cardiologist*
Koblin, Donald Daryl *anesthesiologist, researcher*
Kuzell, William Charles *physician, instrument company executive*
Levin, Barry Sherwin *physician*
Lewis, Rose *plastic surgeon*
Lidofsky, Steven David *medical educator*
Lowe, Rolland Choy *surgeon*
Maibach, Howard I. *dermatologist*
Martin, Joseph Boyd *neurologist, educator*
Mason, Dean Towle *cardiologist*
Massie, Barry Michael *cardiologist*
Mills, Thomas Cooke *psychiatrist*
Mithun, Robert James *physician*
Mohr, Selby *retired ophthalmologist*
Murray, John Frederic *physician, educator*
Mustacchi, Piero *physician, educator*
Ochitill, Herbert Nolan *psychiatrist, educator*
Paiement, Guy Darius *orthopedic surgeon, educator*
Parer, Julian Thomas *obstetrics and gynecology educator*
Peterlin, Boris Matija *physician*
Reus, Victor I. *psychiatry educator, hospital administrator*
Ristow, Brunno. *plastic surgeon*
Roach, Mack, III *radiation oncology educator*
Roe, Benson Bertheau *surgeon, educator*
Rosenthal, Philip *gastroenterologist*
Sandhu, Fatejeet Singh *radiologist, educator*
Schatz, Howard *ophthalmologist*
Schiller, Nelson Benjamin *physician, cardiologist*
Schmid, Rudi (Rudolf Schmid) *internist, educator, university official*
Scholten, Paul *obstetrician/gynecologist, educator*
Schwartz, Janice Blumenthal *cardiologist*
Scotton, Bruce Warren *psychiatrist, educator*
Seebach, Lydia Marie *physician*
Shapiro, Larry Jay *pediatrician, scientist, educator*
Shumate, Charles Albert *retired dermatologist*
Silverman, Norman Henry *cardiologist, educator*
Smith, David Elvin *physician*
Snyder, John David *pediatric gastroenterologist, epidemiologist*
Sokolow, Maurice *physician, educator*
Stamper, Robert Lewis *ophthalmologist, educator*
Steinman, John Francis *psychiatrist*
Szabo, Zoltan *medical science educator, medical institute director*
Taeusch, H. William *pediatrician*
Tessier-Lavigne, Marc Trevor *neurobiologist, researcher*
Trigiano, Lucien Lewis *physician*
Wallerstein, Ralph Oliver *physician*
Waskell, Lucy Ann *anesthesiologist, researcher*
Wayburn, Edgar *internist, environmentalist*
Webb, Gilbert A. *obstetrician, gynecologist*
Weidner, Noel *pathologist and surgeon*
Wilson, Charles B. *neurosurgeon, educator*
Wolfe, Christopher Lane *cardiologist, educator*
Wolkowitz, Owen Mark *physician, psychiatrist, researcher*
Zegans, Leonard Saul *psychiatry educator*

San Jose
Avakoff, Joseph Carnegie *medical and legal consultant*
Boldrey, Edwin Eastland *retinal surgeon, educator*
Cobb, Luther Fuson *surgeon, educator*
Hovey, Leslie Morris *plastic surgeon, educator*
Isaacson, Joseph Morris *allergist*
Leathers, Margaret Weil *foundation administrator*
Lippe, Philipp Maria *neurosurgeon, educator*
Malish, David Marc *physician*
Mallison, Robert Andrew *neurologist*
Mayo, Cesar M. *neurologist*
Multz, Carter Victor *rheumatologist*
Nelson, Randall Erland *surgeon*
Nguyen, Thinh Van *physician*
Quevedo, Sylvestre Grado *nephrologist*
Shatney, Clayton Henry *surgeon*
Stein, Arthur Oscar *pediatrician*
Stevens, David Alec *medical educator*
Waller, Edmund Kemp *oncologist, researcher, educator*

San Juan Capistrano
Fisher, Delbert Arthur *physician, educator*

San Marino
Benzer, Seymour *neurosciences educator*
Liu, Don *ophthalmologist, medical researcher*

San Mateo
Bell, Leo S. *retired physician*
Cotchett, John Craig *obstetrician and gynecologist*
Goble, Elise Joan H. *pediatric ophthalmologist*
Meyerowitz, Basil Ralph *surgeon*
Tatomer, William Reeves *psychiatrist*
Van Kirk, John Ellsworth *cardiologist*
von Doepp, Christian Ernest *psychiatrist*
Wong, Otto *epidemiologist*

San Pablo
Afsari, Khosrow *physician, consultant, internist*
Sandler, Maurice *urologist*

San Pedro
Askren, Misha *physician*

San Rafael
Hicks, Philip Stanley *psychiatrist*
Hinshaw, Horton Corwin *physician*
Meecham, William James *ophthalmologist*

San Ramon
Litman, Robert Barry *physician, author, television and radio commentator*
Schwartz, John Theodore *orthopedic surgeon*

Sanger
Donaldson, Nikki A. *physician, executive*

Santa Ana
Abbruzzese, Carlo Enrico *physician, writer, educator*
Lambros, Vasilios S., II *plastic surgeon*
Rappaport, Irving *immunologist, researcher*
Strong, John Oliver *plastic surgeon, educator*

Santa Barbara
Clark, Ramona Richli *radiologist*
Dennis, Michael T. B. *plastic surgeon*
Ellis, Eugene Joseph *cardiologist*
Formby, Bent Clark *immunologist*
Hanretta, Allan Gene *psychiatrist, pharmacist*
Klakeg, Clayton Harold *cardiologist*
Kohn, Roger Alan *surgeon*
Liebhaber, Myron I. *allergist*
Love, Jack Wayne *surgeon*
MacArthur, John Reed *physician*
Mathews, Barbara Edith *gynecologist*
Patterson, Donald Scott *psychiatrist*
Rockwell, Don Arthur *psychiatrist*
Wittenstein, George Juergen *surgeon, educator*

Santa Clarita
Haq, Abid *physician*

Santa Cruz
Magid, Gail Avrum *neurosurgery educator*
Nelson, Raymond Milford *surgeon*
Pletsch, Marie Eleanor *plastic surgeon*

Santa Maria
Tank, Himat G. *pediatrician*

Santa Monica
Bohn, Paul Bradley *psychiatrist*
Carr, Ruth Margaret *plastic surgeon*
Dollinger, Malin Roy *physician, author*
Feinstein, Beverly *psychiatrist, psychoanalyst*
Frey, Harvey Stuart *radiologist, law student*
Galton, Elizabeth *psychiatrist, psychoanalyst*
Giuliano, Armando Elario *surgical oncologist, educator, author*
Hoefflin, Steven M. *plastic surgeon*
Hurvitz, James S. *plastic surgeon*
Katz, Robert Irwin *retired physician*
Kawamoto, Henry K. *plastic surgeon*
Landau, Joseph White *dermatologist*
McGuire, Michael Francis *plastic and reconstructive surgeon*
Nemazee, Mahmoud *emergency medicine physician, internist, surgeon*
Pearson, Warren Thomas *surgeon*
Resnick, Jeffrey I. *plastic surgeon*
Thompson, Dennis Peters *plastic surgeon*
Warick, Lawrence Herbert *psychiatrist*
Wasserman, Martin Stephen *psychiatrist, psychoanalyst, child psychiatrist*
Zarem, Harvey Alan *plastic surgeon*

Santa Rosa
Bauman, Martin Harold *psychiatrist, therapist*
Harwood, James William *surgeon*
Lassa, Ralph E. *plastic surgeon*
Leissring, John Cother *pathologist*
Leuty, Gerald Johnston *osteopathic physician and surgeon*
Lobue, Ange Joseph *psychiatrist, writer*
Treanor, Walter John *physician*
Trucker, Albert *plastic surgeon*

Santa Ysabel
Tan, Joo Sim *physician consultant*

Santee
Yang, Hsin-Ming *immunologist*

Sausalito
Jewett, Don Lee *medical researcher*

Seal Beach
Carlin, Jean Effal *psychiatrist*

Sepulveda
Nishimura, Robert Neal *physician, medical educator, researcher*
Sattin, Albert *psychiatry and neuropharmacology educator*
Wasterlain, Claude Guy *neurologist*

Sherman Oaks
Stein, Karl N. *plastic and reconstructive surgeon*
Young, Edward Medhard, Jr. *dermatologist*

Somis
Cho, Sung-Nei Charles *physician*

South Laguna
Hermosillo, Carlos J. *plastic surgeon*

South San Francisco
Curd, John Gary *physician, scientist*
Hefti, Franz F. *neuroscientist, educator*
Kern, Donald Michael *internist*
Rodriguez, Roman *child psychiatrist, physician, educator*
Schenk, Dale Bernard *neuroscientist*

Stanford
Bensch, Klaus George *pathology educator*
Blumenkranz, Mark Scott *surgeon, researcher, educator*
Brocke, Stefan *physician, researcher*
Brodsky, Jay Barry *medical educator*
Cohen, Harvey Joel *pediatric hematology and oncology educator*
Conley, Susan Bernice *medical school faculty pediatrician*
Dafoe, Donald Cameron *surgeon, educator*
Fee, Willard Edward, Jr. *otolaryngologist*
Hubert, Helen Betty *epidemiologist*
Hui, Kenneth Chi-Wan *surgeon*
Klima, Roger R. *physiatrist*
Korn, David *educator, pathologist*

Makino, Clint Lawrence *neurobiologist*
Mansour, Tag Eldin *pharmacologist*
Marmor, Michael Franklin *ophthalmologist, educator*
McDougall, Iain Ross *nuclear medicine educator*
McGuire, Joseph Smith *physician*
Merigan, Thomas Charles, Jr. *physician, medical researcher, educator*
Miller, David Craig *cardiovascular surgeon*
Moss, Richard B. *pediatrician*
Reitz, Bruce Arnold *cardiac surgeon, educator*
Swenson, Robert Sanfred *physician*
Terris, David James *head and neck surgeon, research scientist*
Yang, Jerry Zeren *obstetrician/gynecologist, researcher*

Stockton
Holzer, Eric Roland *plastic surgeon*
Lawrence, Robert Don *pathologist, consultant*
Primack, Marvin Herbert *anesthesiologist*

Sunnyvale
Langston, J. William *neurologist*
Ross, Leabelle I. (Mrs. Charles R. Ross) *retired psychiatrist*
Saxena, Amol *podiatrist, consultant*

Sylmar
Dufour, Frank Dennis *plastic surgeon*
Howe, Joseph William *radiologist*
Morrow, Mark Jay *neurologist, educator*
Tully, Susan Balsley *pediatrician, educator*

Tarzana
Wilson, Stephen Jay *psychiatrist, consultant*

Tehachapi
Melsheimer, Harold *obstetrician/gynecologist*

Temecula
Gill, Becky Lorette *addictionist, psychiatrist*

Templeton
Abernathy, Shields B. *allergist, immunologist, internist*
Carey, James C., Jr. *plastic surgeon*
Peterson, Richard Allan *pediatrician*

Thousand Oaks
Merrin, James Steven *internist*
Pardue, A. Michael *plastic and reconstructive surgeon*
Schaffner, Irving *physician, researcher*

Topanga
Citron, Ronald Seth *physician consultant*

Torrance
Anderson, Thomas Leif *physician, researcher*
Canalis, Rinaldo Fernando *surgeon, educator, researcher*
Casaburi, Richard *respiratory and critical care physician*
Elpers, John Richard *psychiatrist, educator*
Emmanouilides, George Christos *physician, educator*
Greenberg, David Paul *pediatrician, researcher*
Hunter, Judy Arlene *pediatrician*
Isenberg, Harold *physician*
Kitano, Masami *neurologist*
Krout, Boyd Merrill *psychiatrist*
Leake, Rosemary Dobson *physician*
McIntyre, Hugh Baxter *neurology educator*
Niihara, Yutaka *physician, educator*
Tabrisky, Joseph *radiologist, educator*
Wan, Yu-Jui Yvonne *educator, scientist*
Yang, Henry Chang-Lien *oncology educator, physician*
Young, Rosabel Ribares *neurologist*

Travis AFB
Krogh, Peter Sundehl, III *family physician*
Morrison, Robert Townsend *nephrologist*
Wardinsky, Terrance David *physician*

Turlock
Maurer, John Irving *psychiatrist*

Ukiah
Aagaard, Earla Gardner *psychiatrist*

Van Nuys
Ferkel, Richard Dennis *orthopedic surgeon, educator*
Handel, Neal *plastic surgeon, researcher*
Kirschner, Melvin Henry *physician*
Lawlor, Glenn Joseph *allergist*

Ventura
Abul-Haj, Suleiman Kahil *pathologist*
Armstrong, Dale P. *plastic surgeon*
Lindsay, Donald Gene *retired dermatologist, educator, writer*

Victorville
Suval, William David *vascular surgeon*

Visalia
Pérez, Raul Antonio *family practitioner*
Riegel, Byron William *ophthalmologist*
Sament, Sidney *neurologist*
Tiss, George John *pediatrician, educator*

Volcano
Prout, Ralph Eugene *physician*

Walnut Creek
Cohen, Alan Jay *psychiatrist*
Farr, Lee Edward *physician*
Wassermann, Franz Walther *physician*

Watsonville
Alfaro, Felix Benjamin *physician*
Stubblefield, James Irvin *emergency medicine physician, health facility administrator*

West Hollywood
Wilson, Myron Robert, Jr. *former psychiatrist*

Westlake Village
Kottler, Dennis Bruce *physician*
Waller, Robert Carl *chiropractor, pharmacist*

Whittier
Arcadi, John Albert *urologist*
Arenowitz, Albert Harold *psychiatrist*
Hilde, Reuben Lynn *plastic surgeon*
Prickett, David Clinton *physician*

Wilton
Shapero, Harris Joel *pediatrician*

Windsor
Dahmer, Joan Marie *physician*

Woodland Hills
Herdeg, Howard Brian *physician*
Kanter, Michael Howard *pathologist*
Shakman, Robert Allan *public health physician*

Yreka
Allred, Eugene Lyle *physician, educator, small business owner*
Hayes, Ernest M. *podiatrist*

Yucaipa
Ludwig, Rolf Martin *internist*

COLORADO

Allenspark
Carter, Dorothy Linnea *child psychiatrist, cultural anthropologist*

Aspen
Oden, Robert Rudolph *surgeon*

Aurora
Abrams, Fredrick Ralph *physician, clinical ethicist*
Burgess, David Bruce *pediatrician*
Wick, James Eugene *physician, pulmonologist*
Wilson, Robert McClain *plastic surgeon, educator*

Boulder
Bock, S. Allan *physician, educator*
Curtis, Sean Patrick *physician*
Curtis, William Shepley *radiologist*
Plazak, Dean James *physician, psychiatrist*
Satter, Susan Edel *medical consultant*

Colorado Springs
Anderson, Judson Truett *psychiatrist*
Anderson, Paul Nathaniel *oncologist, educator*
Barber, Michael J. *cardiologist, educator*
Barley, Leonard Vaughn *physician*
Du Bois, David D. *plastic surgeon*
Gorab, Lawrence Ned *urologist*
Hovenga, Trent LaVern *surgeon*
Hurley, Thomas Jeremiah *psychiatrist*
McCulloch, Alexander Thomas, Jr. *plastic surgeon*
Nathan, Robert A. *allergist, educator*
Rose, Cynthia *psychiatrist*
Sciotto, Cosimo Gino *pathologist, hematopathologist*
Singleton, Albert Olin, III *physician*
Stein, Gerald S. *psychiatrist*
Zimmerman, Robert Leonard *internist, cardiologist*

Denver
Adair, Olivia Vynn *cardiologist*
Adler, Charles Spencer *psychiatrist*
Aikawa, Jerry Kazuo *physician, educator*
Axelrod, Stephen Lee *physician*
Barber, Patricia Louise *clinical specialist*
Bateman, Jane Bronwyn *ophthalmology educator*
Baum, Kenneth Francis *medical educator, physician*
Bearman, Scott Irvin *internist, educator*
Beers, Alvin LaFrance, Jr. *physician*
Beresford, Thomas Patrick *psychiatry educator, alcoholism researcher*
Broughton, Joseph Otis *physician*
Brown, William Carroll *plastic surgeon, microsurgeon*
Bunn, Paul A., Jr. *oncologist, educator*
Cherington, Michael *neurologist, educator*
Chessick, Cheryl Ann *psychiatrist*
Cochran, John Howard *plastic and reconstructive surgeon*
Collier, David Harris *rheumatologist*
Deitrich, Richard Adam *pharmacology educator*
Diamond, David Mark *neurobiologist, educator*
Doherty, Dennis Edwin *immunologist, educator*
Espey, William Malloneé *psychiatrist*
Firminger, Harlan Irwin *pathologist, educator*
Flaxer, Carl *physician*
Freed, Curt Richard *pharmacology educator*
Freed, John Howard *immunologist, educator*
Gabow, Patricia Anne *internist*
Gelfand, Erwin William *immunologist*
Gerber, John G. *medical educator*
Golitz, Loren Eugene *dermatologist, pathologist, clinical administrator, educator*
Hansen, Lowell Howard *physician*
Hathaway, William Ellison *pediatrics educator*
Hoehn, Robert J. *plastic surgeon, educator*
Huang, Linda Chen *plastic surgeon*
Iseman, Michael Dee *medical educator*
Kamada, Alan Katsuki *pharmacology educator*
Kappy, Michael Steven *pediatrics educator*
Khoo, Robert E.H. *colon and rectal surgeon*
Kluck, Clarence Joseph *physician*
Lacy, George M. *plastic surgeon*
La Rosa, Francisco Guillermo *pathologist, researcher, educator*
Law, Christopher K. *plastic surgeon*
Litvak, John *neurosurgeon*
Lubeck, Marvin Jay *ophthalmologist*
Marx, Johann Rudolf *psychiatrist*
McGregor, James Allen *obstetrician/gynecologist*
McIlvaine, William Brown, Jr. *pediatric anesthesiologist*
Mersenstein, Gerald Burton *pediatrician, educator*
Miller, Robert David *forensic psychiatrist*
Nelson, Nancy Eleanor *pediatrician, educator*
Niermeyer, Susan *medical educator*
Parsons, Polly Elsbeth *internist*
Payea, Norman Philip, II *plastic surgeon*
Reiter, Michael Jay *cardiologist educator*
Rewers, Marian Jerzy *pediatrician, epidemiologist*
Rhine, Mark Woodforde *psychiatrist, psychoanalyst*
Rodgers, Christine M. *plastic surgeon, educator*
Roos, David Bernard *surgeon*
Rumack, Carol Masters *radiologist*
Rymer Davis, Carol Ann *radiologist*
Schneck, Stuart Austin *neurologist, educator*
Schooley, Robert T. *educator*
Schwarz, I. Gene *psychiatry educator*
Stienmier, Richard Harold *pathologist*
Tabakoff, Boris *pharmacologist educator*
Washington, Reginald Louis *pediatric cardiologist*
Weiner, Norman *pharmacology educator*
West, Sterling Gaylord *physician*
Westcott, Jay Young *pulmonary and critical care medicine educator*
Wolcott, Oliver *psychiatrist, educator*

Durango
Crue, Benjamin Lane, Jr. *neurosurgeon*
Grossman, Richard *obstetrician/gynecologist*

Englewood
Boone, Jeffrey Lynn *internist*
English, Gerald Marion *otolaryngologist*
Evans, William Thomas *physician*
Georgitis, William Johnson *endocrinologist, medical educator*
Gipstein, Milton Fivenson *psychiatrist, lawyer*
Greenhut, Saul Ephriam *biomedical researcher, engineer*
Kapelovitz, Leonard Herman *psychiatrist*
Klingensmith, William Claude, III *radiologist*
Milligan, Gatewood Carlisle *physician, retired*
Rosenberg, Neil Lloyd *neurologist*
Shimonkevitz, Richard Phillip *immunologist*

Fort Collins
Dennis, David Tappen *epidemiologist*
Dudek, F. Edward *educator*
Lee, Robert Edward *medical educator, researcher*

Fort Garland
Leighninger, David Scott *cardiovascular surgeon*

Golden
Brent, Jeffrey Alan *physician*

Grand Junction
Janson, Richard Anthony *plastic surgeon*

Greeley
Cook, Donald E. *pediatrician*
Jaouen, Richard Matthie *plastic surgeon*

Littleton
Garfein, Arthur Douglas *psychiatrist, psychoanalyst*
Glasco, Donald Glee *psychiatrist*

Loveland
Wright, Eric R. *physician assistant*

Pueblo
Lawrence, Richard A. *plastic surgeon*

Vail
Chow, Franklin Szu-Chien *obstetrician-gynecologist*

Westminster
Silverberg, Stuart Owen *obstetrician/gynecologist*

Wheat Ridge
Brown, Steven Brien *radiologist*
Jones, Arthur Francis *surgeon*

Woodland Park
Burke, Arlene L. *osteopath, surgeon*

FLORIDA

Tampa
Bowen, Thomas Edwin *cardiothoracic surgeon, retired army officer*

HAWAII

Hilo
Taniguchi, Tokuso *surgeon*

Honolulu
Allin, Robert Cameron *obstetrician and gynecologist*
Camara, Jorge de Guzman *ophthalmologist, educator*
Chee, Percival Hon Yin *ophthalmologist*
Chock, Clifford Yet-Chong *family practice physician*
Cordts, Paul Roger *surgeon*
Diamond, Milton *anatomy and reproductive biology educator*
Edwards, John Wesley, Jr. *urologist*
Flowers, Robert Swaim *medical educator, surgeon*
Goldstein, Sir Norman *dermatologist*
Hay-Roe, Victor *plastic surgeon*
Hollison, Robert Victor, Jr. *physician, medical executive*
Hundahl, Scott Alfred *oncologic surgeon*
Ing, Malcolm Ross *eye surgeon, educator*
Ishii, Clyde Hideo *plastic surgeon*
Jackson, Mary Tallmadge *obstetrician/gynecologist*
Kane, Thomas Jay, III *orthopaedic surgeon, educator*
Kaye, Michael Duncan *physician, gastroenterologist, consultant*
Lau, Bennett Mun Kwai *plastic surgeon, educator*
Lewis, Philip Christie *psychiatrist*
Massey, Douglas Gordon *physician, educator*
McCarthy, Laurence James *physician, pathologist*
Meagher, Michael *radiologist*
Oda, Yoshio *physician, internist*
Pang, Herbert George *ophthalmologist*
Paperny, David Mark N. *pediatrician*
Parsa, Fereydoun Don *plastic surgeon*
Person, Donald Ames, Sr. *pediatrician, rheumatologist*
Premaratne, Shyamal *physician, clinical surgery educator*
Smith, Thomas Kent *radiologist*
Stevens, Stephen Edward *psychiatrist*
Sugiki, Shigemi *ophthalmologist, educator*
Sumfest, Joel Michael *pediatric urologist*
Taniguchi, Raymond Masayuki *neurosurgeon*

Kailua
Hellreich, Philip David *dermatologist*

Kamuela
Bracher, George *radiologist*

Kaneohe
Ahmed, Iqbal *psychiatrist, consultant*

Koloa
Donohugh, Donald Lee *physician*

Tripler Army Medical Center
Myers, Jerome Bartholomew *physician, pathologist*

Waialua
DeLuze, James Robert *physician*

Waianae
Yoshimoto, Cedric Mitsuo *physician*

Waikoloa
Copman, Louis *radiologist*

Wailuku
Savona, Michael Richard *physician*

Waipahu
Caldwell, Peter Derek *pediatrician, pediatric cardiologist*

IDAHO

Boise
Khatain, Kenneth George *psychiatrist, air force officer*
Moss, Stanley W. *orthopedic surgeon*
Nyborg, Lester Phil *physician*

Caldwell
Cornwell, Ronald William *surgeon*

Coeur D Alene
West, Robert Sumner *surgeon*

Home AFB
Daniels, Jonathan Pearson *obstetrician-gynecologist*

Lewiston
Chinchinian, Harry *pathologist, educator*
Majure, Joyce Arlene *surgeon*

Moscow
De Santis, Mark Edward *anatomist, neuroscientist and educator*

Nampa
Botimer, Allen Ray *retired surgeon, retirement center owner*

Pocatello
Maloff, Stephen Martin *plastic surgeon*

Priest River
Freibott, George August *physician, chemist, priest*

ILLINOIS

Mc Gaw Park
Wolfson, Marsha *internist, nephrologist*

Rockford
Montes, Ramon G. *pediatric gastroenterologist, career officer*

INDIANA

Evansville
Sidman, Sally *emergency physician*

Indianapolis
Brandt, Ira Kive *pediatrician, medical geneticist*

LOUISIANA

Baton Rouge
Greenway, Frank Lyons, III *medical educator*

MARYLAND

Rockville
Nora, James Jackson *physician, author, educator*

Wheaton
Matthews, Robert Dean *urologist*

MISSOURI

Kansas City
Cronkleton, Thomas Eugene *physician*

MONTANA

Billings
Glenn, Guy Charles *pathologist*

Bozeman
Tietz, William John, Jr. *research institute executive, university president emeritus*

Great Falls
O'Connor, John Edward *physician*

Havre
Reynolds, Stuart Arnold *surgeon*

Helena
Reynolds, James Francis, Jr. *physician*

Miles City
Rauh, J. Randall *physician*
Smisson, David Clayton *physician*

Missoula
Diettert, Gerald Allen *cardiologist*
Evert, John Andrew, Jr. *surgeon*
Hoell, Noel Loraine *psychiatrist*
Murray, Donald Eugene *plasic surgeon*

Wolf Point
Listerud, Mark Boyd *retired surgeon*

NEVADA

Carson City
Meyer, Roger Paul *physician*
Walls, Joseph Patrick *orthopaedic surgeon*

Henderson
Perel, Michael Joseph *dermatologist*
Reyna, Troy Michael *surgeon*
Silver, James Allen *former military physician*

Las Vegas
Abu-Samrah, Sameer Abdallah *internist*
Bandt, Paul Douglas *physician*
Barger, James Daniel *physician*
Canada, William H. *plastic surgeon*
Capanna, Albert Howard *neuroscientist, neurosurgeon*
Garry, Stacey Lynne *pathologist*
Herte, Mary Charlotte *plastic surgeon*
Hetter, Gregory Paulson *plastic surgeon*
Hyson, Morton Isaac *neurologist, vocalist*
Little, Alex Graham *thoracic surgeon, educator*
Mackey, Maureen Elise *rehabilitation medicine physician*
Mauban, Rene Avanzado *physician*
Moritz, Timothy Bovie *psychiatrist*
Perer, Marvin A. *gastroenterologist*
Petty, Leonora Kathleen *psychiatrist*
Sabanas-Wells, Alvina Olga *orthopedic surgeon*
Shearing, Steven Paul *ophthalmic surgeon*
Stone, William Gene *psychiatrist*

Reno
Ascensão, João Luis Afonso *physician, researcher*
Gerow, Lynn Burdette, Jr. *psychiatrist*
Jackson, Michael Vincent *physician, medical educator*
Krumpe, Peter E. *medical educator*
Lloyd, William Judd, Jr. *obstetrician/gynecologist*
MacKintosh, Frederick Roy *oncologist*
Petersen, Christopher Allen *child and adolescent psychiatrist*
Rahe, Richard Henry *psychiatrist, educator*
Sage, Roderick Duncan *dermatologist, educator*
Sandars, Leibert Jovanovich *radiologist*
Walker, Joseph Robert *neurosurgeon*
Young, Zora Oral *psychiatrist*

NEW MEXICO

Alamogordo
Ashdown, Franklin Donald *physician, composer*
Lindley, Norman Dale *physician*

Albuquerque
Aase, Jon Morton *dysmorphologist, pediatrics educator*
Abrums, John Denise *internist*
Arora, Sanjeev *gastroenterology educator*
Baack, Bret Rolyn *plastic surgeon*
Barton, Larry Lumir *mircobiology educator, consultant*
Brya, William John *anesthesiologist*
Buss, William Charles *research pharmacology educator*
Cooperman, Oliver B(urton) *psychiatrist*
Corcoran, George Bartlett *pharmacologist/ toxicologist*
Frank, Alan *retired psychiatry educator*
Fripp, Raymond Ralph *pediatric cardiologist*
Gleeson, Jeremy Michael *physician*
Goss, Jerome Eldon *cardiologist*
Graham, Susan Brandt *gynecologist, anthropologist*
Harvie, Keith William *orthopaedic surgeon*
Herhahn, Frank T. *plastic surgeon*
Hudson, Patrick A. *plastic surgeon*
Irani, Mehraboon S. *pathologist*
Johnson, John David *pediatrician*
Lindeman, Robert Dean *medical educator, researcher, consultant*
Nachbar, James Milton *plastic surgeon, computer programmer*
Omer, George Elbert, Jr. *orthopaedic surgeon, hand surgeon, educator*
Ottensmeyer, David Joseph *neurosurgeon, health care executive*
Papile, Lucille Ann *pediatrician, educator*
Saland, Linda Carol *anatomy educator*
Simpson, Steven Quinton *physician, researcher*
Smith, Kenneth James *hematologist*
Stellman, Roberta Elise *psychiatrist*
Stevenson, James Richard *radiologist, lawyer*
Summers, William K. *neuropsychiatrist, researcher*
Tatum, Ronald Winston *physician, endocrinologist*
Wascher, Daniel Charles *orthopaedic surgeon*
Wimer, Bruce Meade *hematologist/oncologist, researcher*
Worrell, Richard Vernon *orthopedic surgeon, educator*

Las Cruces
Jacobs, Kent Frederick *dermatologist*
Reeves, Billy Dean *obstetrics/gynecology educator emeritus*

Las Vegas
Land, David Benjamin *obstetrician/gynecologist*

Los Alamos
Gilman, Christopher John *radiologist*

Portales
Goodwin, Martin Brune *radiologist*

Roswell
Jennings, Emmit M. *surgeon*

Santa Fe
Cawley, Leo Patrick *pathologist, immunologist*
Mendez, C. Beatriz *obstetrician/gynecologist*
Stennis, William *psychiatrist, educator*
Suhre, E. Dow *internist*
Tashjian, Levon Donald *psychiatrist*

NEW YORK

New York
Gebbie, Kristine Moore *health science educator, health official*

OREGON

Albany
Crow, Kenneth Arthur *pathologist*

Ashland
Kirschner, Richard Michael *naturopathic physician, speaker, author*

Bend
Peters, Lois Ann *healthcare manager, nutritionist*

Cottage Grove
Bolz, Christopher William *family physician*

Eugene
Dreyer, Thomas Morgan *plastic surgeon*
Flanagan, Latham, Jr. *surgeon*
James, Stan Lawrence *surgeon*
Jarrett, John R. *plastic surgeon*
Nissel, Martin *radiologist, consultant*
Starr, Grier Forsythe *retired pathologist*
Strimling, Bruce Sanford *pediatrician, educator*
Teal, Donald F. *physician, surgeon*
Wheeler, Robert Ross *medical director*

Grants Pass
Williamson, Neil Robert *psychiatrist*

Hillsboro
Pinkert, Ted Charles *pathologist, nuclear medicine physician*

Lake Oswego
Stark, Allen Lytton *psychiatrist, educator*

Lebanon
Girod, Frank Paul *surgeon*

Medford
Dibb, Charles Robert *physician, educator*
Luther, Robert Chester *former psychiatrist, consultant*
Schwartz, John Andrew *surgeon*
Webb, Eric Seth *physician*

Oregon City
Wustrack, Karl Otto *plastic surgeon*

Portland
Baer, William Bruce *ophthalmologist*
Barker, Alan Freund *internist*
Berthelsdorf, Siegfried *psychiatrist*
Black, Franklin Owen *physician, researcher*
Bonafede, R. Peter *rheumatologist*
Breda, Michael Alexander *surgeon*
Brummett, Robert Eddie *pharmacology educator*
Buist, Neil Robertson MacKenzie *medical educator, medical administrator*
Burry, Kenneth Arnold *physician, educator*
Campbell, Robert Allen *pediatrician*
Casey, Daniel E. *psychiatrist, educator*
Collins, Michael Sean *obstetrician-gynecologist*
Crawshaw, Ralph *psychiatrist*
Duell, Paul Barton *internist, endocrinologist*
Duncan, Elmore Edward *psychiatrist*
Fraunfelder, Frederick Theodore *ophthalmologist, educator*
Furnary, Anthony Paul *surgeon, educator*
Geist, Howard J. *orthopedic surgeon*
Gold, Bruce Gordon *medical educator*
Hayes, Margaret Mary *physician*
Jacob, Stanley Wallace *surgeon, educator*
Kendall, John Walker, Jr. *medical educator, researcher, university dean*
Kohler, Peter Ogden *physician, educator, university president*
Labby, Daniel Harvey *medical educator, psychiatry educator*
LaFranchi, Stephen Henry *pediatric endocrinologist, educator, researcher*
Lewy, Alfred Jones *psychiatrist, educator*
Loriaux, D. Lynn *internist, endocrinologist*
Martin, Michael Anthony *medical educator*
McClung, Michael Roy *physician, medical educator, researcher*
Morganroth, Melvin Lee *internist, educator*
Morrison, John Carl *ophthalmologist, educator*
Mozena, John Daniel *podiatrist*
Ochoa, Jose Luis *neurologist*
Pillers, De-Ann Margaret *neonatologist*
Prendergast, William John *ophthalmologist*
Riddle, Matthew C(asey) *physician, educator*
Robertson, Joseph E., Jr. *ophthalmologist, educator*
Rosenbaum, James Todd *rheumatologist, educator*
Rosenbaum, Richard Barry *neurologist*
Rosenfeld, Ron Gershon *pediatrics educator*
Sanders, Wyman *psychiatrist, pediatrician, educator*
Schmidt, Waldemar Adrian *pathologist, educator*
Schwartz, Martin Lerner *physician*
Seres, Joel Leonard *neurosurgeon*
Seyfer, Alan Eric *surgeon*
Shapiro, Philip *psychiatrist, consultant*
Sklovsky, Robert Joel *pharmacology educator*
Stalnaker, John Hulbert *physician*
Stevens, Jeffrey S. *chief of nuclear medicine*
Stone, Patrick Scaife *health science educator, consultant*
Swan, Kenneth Carl *physician, surgeon*
Szeto, Erik K. *family practice physician*
Takahashi, Gary Wayne *internist, hematologist, oncologist*
Thurmond, Amy Suzanne *physician, radiologist, educator*
Toffler, William Louis *medical educator*
Turco, Ronald Nicholas *psychiatrist, educator*
Van Buskirk, Edmund Michael *ophthalmologist*
Vea, Henry Walter *radiologist, nuclear medicine specialist*
Wilson, David Jean *ophthalmologist*
Zeller, Katharine Margret *physician*
Zerzan, Charles Joseph, Jr. *gastroenterologist*

Roseburg
Donahoo, Stanley Ellsworth *orthopaedic surgeon*

Silverton
Centerwall, Willard Raymond *physician*
Watson, Milton Russell *surgeon*

Tualatin
Veverka, Michael J. *diagnostic radiologist*

TEXAS

Dallas
Chowdhary, Sultan Aleem *hematologist, oncologist*

Houston
Evans, Christopher Paul *urologist*

UTAH

Murray
Goates, Delbert Tolton *child psychiatrist*

Ogden
Maughan, Willard Zinn *dermatologist*
Seager, Floyd Williams *medical educator*

Park City
Wardell, Joe Russell, Jr. *pharmacologist*

Provo
Blackwell, Elizabeth Kuhlmann *physician*
Heiner, Douglas Cragun *pediatrician, educator*
Hirsche, Blayne Lynn *plastic surgeon*
Thygerson, Alton Luie *health sciences educator*

Salt Lake City
Anderson, Richard Lee *ophthalmologist, educator*
Bauer, A(ugust) Robert, Jr. *surgeon, educator*
Bjorkman, David Jess *gastroenterologist, educator*
Bragg, David Gordon *physician, radiology educator*
Brandon, Kathryn Elizabeth Beck *pediatrician*
Buchi, Kenneth Norman *medical director, educator*
Cataldo, Renzo Mario *cardiologist*
Dayton, Merril Taylor *gastrointestinal surgeon*
Digre, Kathleen B. *neurology and ophthalmology educator*
Dolowitz, David Augustus *otolaryngologist, educator*
Egan, Talmage D. *physician, educator*
Gilbert, Edward Michael *cardiology educator*
Hammond, M(ary) Elizabeth Hale *pathologist*
Harvey, Stewart Clyde *pharmacologist, retired educator*
Heath, Hunter, III *endocrinology researcher, educator*
Hines, Wirt A. *plastic surgeon*
Jacobson, Jay Andrew *physician*
Kanner, Richard Elliot *physician*
Knight, Joseph Adams *pathologist*
Kolff, Willem Johan *internist, educator*
Lewis, Edward C. *plastic surgeon*
Mamalis, Nick *ophthalmologist, researcher*
Matsen, John Martin *pathology educator, microbiologist*
Middleton, Anthony Wayne, Jr. *urologist, educator*
Middleton, Richard George *urologist, educator*
Milley, John Ross *neonatologist, educator*
Nelson, Russell Marion *surgeon, educator*
Odell, William Douglas *physician, scientist, educator*
Petersen, Finn Bo *oncologist, educator*
Petersen, Marta Jean *dermatologist, educator*
Petersen, Phil Brent *psychiatrist, educator*
Rallison, Marvin L. *pediatrician, educator*
Siegler, Richard Louis *pediatric nephrologist, educator*
Siemionow, Maria *hand surgeon, microsurgeon*
Smith, Eileen Pazderka *dermatologist*
Spangrude, Gerald John *hematologist, researcher*
Stanford, Joseph Barney *medical educator, physician*
Stromquist, Don Leonard *rheumatologist*
Swensen, Laird S. *orthopedic surgeon*
Thomas, David Snow *plastic surgeon*
Ueda, Issaku *medical educator, researcher*
Whitehead, Paul Leon *physician*
Wong, Harry Chow *anesthesiologist, educator*

WASHINGTON

Bellevue
Hackett, Carol Ann Hedden *physician*
Knoepfler, Peter Tamas *psychiatrist, organizational consultant*
Maguire, Yu Ping *oncologist, department director, consultant*
Vath, Raymond Eugene *psychiatrist, educator*

Bellingham
Howe, Warren Billings *physician*
James, Helen Ann *plastic surgeon*

Bremerton
Ringler, Robert Lloyd, Jr. *family practice physician, naval officer*

Chelan
Carlton, Thomas Grant *psychiatrist*

Edmonds
Crone, Richard Allan *cardiologist, educator*
Rees, William James *dermatologist, consultant*
Wood, David Bruce *naturopathic physician*

Everett
Beegle, Earl Dennis *family physician*
Smith, Dorsett David *pulmonologist*

Kennewick
Meader, Willard Lingel *health maintenance organization executive*

Kirkland
Dundas, Dennis Franklin *plastic surgeon*
Pheifer, Terrence Albert *obstetrician/gynecologist*

Longview
Kenagy, John Warner *surgeon*
Kirkpatrick, Richard Alan *internist*
Sandstrom, Robert Edward *physician, pathologist*

Maple Valley
Grosskopf, Barry *psychiatrist, consultant*

Mount Vernon
Peterson, Laurence Robert *pathologist*

Mountlake Terrace
Imamura, Eugene Hachiro *osteopathic physician, surgeon*

Olympia
Flemming, Stanley Lalit Kumar *family practice physician, mayor*
Lane, Henry Wallace *physician, consultant*
Smith, Sherwood Paul *plastic surgeon*

Pasco
Rose, Ray Vincent *surgeon*

Port Townsend
Collin, Jonathan *physician*

Poulsbo
Meyer, Roger Jess Christian *pediatrics educator*

Pullman
Craft, Rebecca Miriam *pharmacologist, educator*
Sclar, David Alexander *medical policy educator*

Puyallup
Jackson, Stanley Martin *plastic surgeon*
Stevenson, Patrice Noel *rehabilitative medicine physician*

Redmond
Ransdell, Tod Elliot *pharmaceutical, parenteral and in vitro diagnostics validation specialist*

Richland
Kathren, Ronald Laurence *health physicist*
Wilson, Bary Wallace *neuroendocrinologist*

Seattle
Altman, Leonard Charles *physician*
Artru, Alan Arthur *anesthesiologist, educator*
Baker, William Blake *dermatologist, dermatopathologist*
Benedetti, Thomas Joseph *obstetrician-gynecologist, educator*
Bierman, Charles Warren *physician, educator*
Bird, Thomas D. *neurologist*
Bredfeldt, James Edward *gastroenterologist*
Broudy, Virginia Constance *hematologist, educator*
Brown, Thomas Joseph *immunologist*
Cardenas, Diana Delia *physician, educator*
Carley, Patrick Clare *physician*
Chatard, Peter Ralph Noel Jr. *aesthetic surgeon*
Christianson, Lisa *biomedical researcher*
Clarren, Sterling Keith *pediatrician*
Clowes, Alexander Whitehill *surgeon, educator*
Dailey, David Kevin *psychiatrist*
Dewhurst, Timothy Andrew *clinical cardiologist, researcher*
Domino, Karen Barbara *anesthesiology educator*
Downey, Daniel Lee *plastic surgeon*
Dunner, David Louis *medicine educator*
Engrav, Loren Henry *plastic surgeon*
Furst, Daniel Eric *medical educator*
Garnett, Daniel Joseph *general surgeon*
Geiduschek, Jeremy Mark *pediatric anesthesiologist*
Giedt, Walvin Roland *epidemiologist, educator*
Graham, Clyde Benjamin, Jr. *physician*
Hackett, John Peter *dermatologist*
Hampson, Neil Bradley *physician*
Han, Mao-Tang *surgeon, researcher*
Hargiss, James Leonard *ophthalmologist*
Heidrich, Fred Edmund, III *medical educator*
Hudgins, Louanne *pediatrician, educator*
Huffine, Charles Walter *psychiatrist, child psychiatrist*
Johnston, Robin Reynolds *cardiologist*
Kaplan, Henry George *oncologist, educator*
Karpilow, Craig *physician*
Keith, Donald Malcolm *physician*
Klaus, Stephen John *immunologist*
Klebanoff, Seymour Joseph *medical educator*
Kowdley, Kris V. *gastroenterologist/hepatologist, educator*
Kozarek, Richard Anthony *gastroenterologist, educator*
Kraft, George Howard *physician, educator*
Krieger, John Newton *urology educator*
Krohn, Kenneth Albert *radiology educator*
Langman, Alan Wayne *physician*
Leininger, Chris J. *physician*
Linker, David T. *cardiologist*
Louis, Nikki Nojima *playwright, actress*
Mangham, Charles Adley, Sr. *psychiatrist*
Mannik, Mart *medical educator*
Marks, William H. *organ transplant program director, pharmacologist*
Martin, George M. *pathologist, gerontologist*
Mehlum, David L. *otolaryngologist*
Miller, Donald Wesley, Jr. *cardiac surgeon*
Mitchell, Michael *pediatric urologist, educator*
Nelson, James Alonzo *radiologist, educator*
Neppe, Vernon Michael *neuropsychiatrist, author, educator*
Nguyen, Toan Dinh *gastroenterologist*
Ochs, Hans Dieter *pediatrics educator*
Pauw, Douglas Stephen *medical educator, primary care physician*
Pagon, Roberta Anderson *pediatrics educator*
Pellegrini, Carlos Alberto *surgeon, educator*
Pritchett, James W. *orthopaedic surgeon, educator*

Rettie, Allan Edward *medical educator*
Ries, Richard Kirkland *psychiatrist*
Roy-Byrne, Peter Paul *psychiatrist, educator*
Rutledge, Joe *pathologist, scientist*
Sale, George Edgar *physician*
Sarnat, Harvey Barry *pediatric neurology educator*
Schwartz, Michael Warren *physician investigator*
Scott, John Carlyle *gynecologist, oncologist*
Sever, Lowell Enyeart *epidemiologist*
Spoerl, Otto Heinrich *psychiatrist, educator*
Staheli, Lynn Taylor *pediatric orthopedist, educator*
Stevenson, James Geoffrey *pediatrician and cardiologist*
Stolov, Walter Charles *physician, rehabilitation educator*
Su, Judy Ya Hwa Lin *pharmacologist*
Surawicz, Christina Mathilda *physician*
Tapper, David *pediatric surgeon*
Tenney, William Frank *pediatrician*
Thomas, Edward Donnall *physician, researcher*
Tsu, Vivien Davis *epidemiologist, educator*
Ulrich, Delmont Marion *physician*
Veith, Richard Charles *geriatric psychiatrist, educator*
Vincenzi, Frank Foster *pharmacology educator*
Voigt, Lynda Fay *cancer researcher*
Wasser, Samuel K. *medical educator, conservation center executive*
Welk, Richard Andrew *plastic surgeon*
Winterbauer, Richard Hill *physician, medical researcher*
Yon, Joseph Langham *gynecologist, oncologist*
Yue, Agnes Kau-Wah *otolaryngologist*

Spokane
DeWood, Marcus Albert *nuclear cardiologist, researcher*
Dittman, William Albert *hematologist*
Genung, Sharon Rose *pediatrician*
Gibson, Melvin Roy *pharmacognosy educator*
James, Norman John *plastic and reconstructive hand surgeon*
Manz, Michael Paul *child psychiatrist*

Sunnyside
Chand, Krishna *surgeon*

Tacoma
Cheah, Keong-Chye *psychiatrist*
Chen, Stephen Shau-tsi *psychiatrist, physiologist*
Clabots, Joseph Paul *cardiothoracic surgeon*
Clark, Richard Douglas *radiologist, research scientist*
Fitzsimmons, John Michael *physician, educator*
Hawkins, Richard Scott *physician*
Ho, Vincent Bok *diagnostic radiologist*
Irish, Thomas Judson *plastic surgeon*
May, Eugene Frank *neuro-ophthalmologist*
Nazaire, Michel Harry *physician*
Rawlings, James Scott *neonatologist*
Verhey, Joseph William *psychiatrist, educator*
White, Matthew *family practice physician*
Woolman, Bruce Alan *family practice physician*

Vancouver
Dygert, Harold Paul, Jr. *cardiologist*

Wellpinit
Riley, Richard Leon *psychiatrist, consultant*

Wenatchee
Knecht, Ben Harrold *surgeon*
Sorom, Terry Allen *ophthalmic surgeon*
Zook, Wayne Bowman *physician*

Yakima
Newstead, Robert Richard *urologist*

WYOMING

Buffalo
Watkins, Eugene Leonard *surgeon, educator*

Casper
Cole, Malvin *neurologist, educator*

Cheyenne
Flick, William Fredrick *surgeon*
Merrell, Arthur N. *psychiatrist*

Douglas
Morgan, James Forrest *physician*

Gillette
Naramore, James Joseph *family practice physician, educator*

Newcastle
Lane, Patricia Baumgartner *medical office manager*

Sheridan
Batty, Hugh Kenworthy *physician*

CANADA

ALBERTA

Calgary
Kimberley, Barry Paul *ear surgeon*

Edmonton
Dewhurst, William George *physician, psychiatrist, educator, researcher*

BRITISH COLUMBIA

New Westminster
Bishop, Rodney Philip *physician*

West Vancouver
Knauff, Hans Georg *physician, educator*

SASKATCHEWAN

Saskatoon
Houston, C(larence) Stuart *radiologist, educator*
McDonald, Ian MacLaren *psychiatrist, educator*

ADDRESS UNPUBLISHED

Altman, Adele Rosenhain *radiologist*
Amer, M(ohamed) Samir *pharmacologist, researcher*
Anderson, Bruce Carl *orthopedic medicine physician*
Angel, Armando Carlos *rheumatologist, internist*
Angelov, George Angel *pediatrician, anatomist, teratologist*
Atkinson, Roland Moore *psychiatrist*
Bailey, Joselyn Elizabeth *physician*
Barnard, William Marion *psychiatrist*
Beach, William Brown *psychiatrist, educator*
Bell, Douglas Scott *internist*
Bierman, Howard Richard *physician*
Bleiberg, Leon William *surgical podiatrist*
Boddie, Lewis Franklin *obstetrics-gynecology educator*
Brehove, Theresa M. *physician*
Bryant, Nancy Dru *physician*
Bussey, George Davis *psychiatrist*
Canales, Francisco Luis *hand surgeon*
Cannon, Grant Wilson *physician*
Charlton, Valerie E. *pediatrics professor, neonatologist, researcher*
Chen, Yu-Cheng Jeffrey *cardiologist*
Cozen, Lewis *orthopaedic surgeon*
Crowl, Charles V(erne) *physician, surgeon*
Douglass, John Michael *internist*
Drye, Robert Caldwell *psychiatrist*
Ellis, Harlan Fred *obstetrician and gynecologist*
Fineman, Jo Ann Booze *psychiatrist, psychoanalyst*
Foster, Lawrence Hunt, Jr. *physician, plastic surgeon*
Freilich, William Stuart *emergency physician*
Friedman, Emanuel *physician, educator*
Garcia-Bunuel, Luis *neurologist*
Garvey, Justine Spring *immunochemistry educator, biology educator*
Geis, John Richard *plastic surgeon*
Giem, Ross Nye, Jr. *surgeon*
Gillon, Jean Warren *surgeon*
Graham, James Herbert *dermatologist*
Green, Joseph Martin *psychiatrist, educator*
Greene, Laurence Whitridge, Jr. *surgical educator*
Greenhouse, Lynn *physician*
Groves, Sheridon Hale *orthopedic surgeon*
Hafner-Eaton, Chris *health services researcher, educator*
Halliday, William Ross *retired physician, speleologist, writer*
Harrison, William Orville *physician*
Herson, Michael K. *physician, educator*
Hondl, Edeltraud A. *retired psychiatrist*
Houston, Harry Rollins *retired obstetrician, gynecologist*
Isse, Nicanor G. *plastic surgeon*
Jackman, Jay M. *psychiatrist*
James, Freburn Leroy *pathologist, retired*
Jarcho, Leonard W. *retired neurology educator*
Jervis, William Horace *plastic and reconstructive surgeon*
Jung, Donald T. *pharmacokineticist*
Kalenscher, Alan Jay *surgeon*
Kanner, Steven Brian *immunologist*
Kaunitz, Jonathan Davidson *physician*
Kendall, Harry Ovid *internist*
Kornfeld, Peter *internist*
Kost, Gerald Joseph *physician, scientist*
Kovarik, Joseph Lewis *surgeon*
Layman, Charles Donald *plastic surgeon*
Levin, Alan Scott *pathologist, allergist, immunologist*
Levin, Jack *physician, educator, biomedical investigator*
Lewis, David Howard *nuclear medicine physician*
Lex, Stephen Francis *plastic surgeon*
Lieberman, Carole Ilene *media psychiatrist, consultant*
Mader, Thomas H. *ophthalmologist*
Major, Carol Ann *perinatologist, obstetrician/gynecologist*
Mathews, William Edward *neurological surgeon, educator*
McCleery, Richard Grimes *retired pathologist*
McLeskey, Charles Hamilton *anesthesiology educator*
Mead, Sedgwick *physician*
Metz, Richard Alan *medical administrator*
Metzner, Jeffrey Lee *psychiatrist, educator*
Meyer, Greg Charles *psychiatrist*
Minard, Eugene Watkins *retired psychiatrist*
Nelson, Scott Haviland *psychiatrist, administrator*
Nelson, William Rankin *surgeon*
Okezie, Ngozi Babette *psychiatrist*
Peña, Heather Maria *internist*
Polites, Demetri John *psychiatrist*
Prenner, Bruce Michael *physician*
Pritz, Michael Burton *neurological surgeon*
Prusiner, Stanley Ben *neurology and biochemistry educator, researcher*
Ranahan, Michael Patrick *obstetrician/gynecologist*
Rasgon, Barry Mitchell *otolaryngologist*
Reichman, Ronald Peter *medical educator*
Renson, Jean Felix *psychiatry educator*
Ringel, Steven Peter *neurology educator*
Roberts, Alan Silverman *orthopedic surgeon*
Rowley, William Robert *surgeon*
Sarfeh, James Iraj *surgery educator*
Scanlon, Michael Patrick *medical legal researcher*
Schechter, Robert Jay *ophthalmic surgeon*
Scrimshaw, George Currie *retired plastic surgeon*
Sheldon, Larry F. *physician assistant*
Skolnikoff, Alan Zachary *psychiatrist*
Stillings, Dennis Otto *research director*
Stone, James Robert *surgeon*
Stoney, Ronald J. *vascular surgeon, educator*
Storek, Jan *hematologist, oncologist, researcher*
Tam, Roland Fook Seng *physician*
Theodosakis, Jason J. *physician*
Uman, Stephen Jonas *physician*
Vetto, John Tyson *surgeon, educator*
Vogelsang, Philip John *pathologist*
Walha, Santokh Singh *physician*
Webber, Milo Melvin *radiologist, educator*
Werbach, Melvyn Roy *physician, writer*
Williams, Dennis Fürst von Blucher *homeopathic physician*
Williams, Henry Stratton *radiologist, educator*
Williams, Ronald Lee *pharmacologist*
Wolfred, Morris M. *pharmacologist and toxicologist*
Wong, Jeffrey Yun Chung *radiation oncologist, medical researcher*
Wood, Beverly Phyllis *pediatric radiologist, educator*
Yandell, George Wilson *physician, psychiatrist*
Zacks, Arthur *retired radiologist*
Zafren, Ken *physician*

HUMANITIES: LIBERAL STUDIES

UNITED STATES

ALASKA

Anchorage
Dennison, Elizabeth Jane *history educator, researcher*
Kuhner, Arlene Elizabeth *English language educator, reviewer, academic administrator*

Fairbanks
Krauss, Michael Edward *linguist*

Juneau
Ruotsala, James Alfred *historian, writer*

ARIZONA

Bisbee
Hagstrum, Jean Howard *language professional, educator*

Flagstaff
Marcus, Karen Melissa *foreign language educator*
West, Delno Cloyde, Jr. *history educator, writer*

Green Valley
Beeson, Diane Kay *language educator*
Dmytryshyn, Basil *historian, educator*

Lake Havasu City
Brydon, Ruth Vickery *history educator*

Mesa
Cervantes, James Valentine *English language educator*

Peoria
Bergmann, Fredrick Louis *English language educator, theater historian*

Phoenix
Cristiano, Marilyn Jean *speech communication educator*
Socwell, Margaret Gertrude Osborn Harris *reading and language arts educator, consultant*
Tompkins, Cynthia Margarita *women's studies educator*
Wright, Barton Allen *ethnologist, author*

Prescott
Tapia, John Reyna *foreign language educator*

Scottsdale
Gwinn, Mary Dolores *philosopher*

Surprise
Clark, Lloyd *historian, educator*

Tempe
Burg, Barry Richard *history educator, writer*
Carlson, Ronald Frank *educator, fiction writer*
Fisher, Marvin Mark *English educator, author*
Gordon, Beatrice Schneider *English literature educator*
Hendrickson, William Lee *French language educator*
Iverson, Peter James *historian, educator*
MacKinnon, Stephen R. *Asian studies administrator, educator*
Trennert, Robert Anthony, Jr. *historian, educator*
Vanden Heuvel, Michael John *literature educator*
Zygas, Kestutis Paul *architectural historian, educator*

Tucson
Adamson, H. Douglas *English language educator*
Arrieta, Olivia *humanities educator*
Austin, John Norman *classics educator*
Beck, Jonathan P. *French language educator*
Birkinbine, John, II *philatelist*
Canfield, J(ohn) Douglas *English language educator*
Chisholm, David Hollister *German studies educator*
Eaton, Richard Maxwell *history educator*
Enos, Theresa *English educator, editor*
Evers, Lawrence Joseph *English language educator*
Ferdon, Edwin Nelson, Jr. *ethnologist*
Foley, Peter Wilhelm Christian *humanities educator, researcher, translator*
Furlow, Mary Beverley *English language educator*
Goldman, Alvin Ira *philosopher and educator*
Karimi, Simin *linguist, educator*
Kellogg, Frederick *historian, educator*
Kleese, William Carl *genealogy research consultant*
Kovach, Thomas Allen *educator*
Leibacher, Lise Helene *French language and literature educator*
Martinez, Oscar Jaquez *educator, author*
Medine, Peter Ernest *literature educator*
Monk, Janice Jones *women's studies researcher, university program administrator*
Parry, Ellwood Comly, III *art history educator*
Schulz, Renate Adele *German studies and second language acquisition educator*
Tao, Chia-lin Pao *humanities educator*
Wearing, J.P. *English language educator*
Wright, George Thaddeus *humanities educator*
Zampini, Mary Lee *Spanish and Portuguese educator*
Zweig, Bella *humanities educator*

Winslow
Kaliher, Michael Dennis *historian, book seller*

CALIFORNIA

Alhambra
Nielsen, David Edward *history and physical education educator*

Anaheim
Borges, Stephany Patricia *English language educator*

Angwin
Gill, Linda Lee *English literature educator*

Aptos
Kiehl, Kathleen Suzanne *English language educator*

Arcata
Doty, Kathleen Leilani *English and linguistics educator*

Bakersfield
Boyd, William Harland *historian*
Gordon, Helen Heightsman *English language educator, writer*
Kegley, Jacquelyn Ann *philosophy educator*

Belmont
Rowland, Susan Blake *English language educator*
Wolterbeek, Marc William *English language educator*

Berkeley
Adelman, Janet Ann *English literature educator*
Anderson, William Scovil *classics educator*
Arteaga, Alfred *English educator*
Baas, Jacquelynn *art historian, museum administrator*
Barish, Jonas Alexander *English language educator*
Booth, Stephen Walter *English language educator*
Brinner, William Michael *near eastern studies educator*
Bronstein, Arthur J. *linguistics educator*
Falk, Candace Serena *historian, biographer, documentary editor*
Feldman, Gerald Donald *history educator*
Friedman, Donald M. *English language educator*
Greenblatt, Stephen J. *English language educator*
Guy, Basil *French literature educator*
Heinze, Ruth-Inge *Asian studies educator, researcher, writer*
Jay, Martin Evan *historian, educator*
Johnson, David George *Chinese history educator*
Jordan, John Emory *language professional, educator*
Larson, James Lee *Scandinavian languages educator*
Lloyd, Elisabeth Anne *philosophy educator*
Lovell, Margaretta M. *art history educator, museum curator*
Mazurek, Stephen Jerome *foreign language educator*
Nagler, Michael Nicholas *classics and comparative literature educator*
Partridge, Loren Wayne *art historian, educator*
Richards, Kyungnyun Kim *Korean language educator*
Richmond, Hugh Macrae *English language educator*
Saldivar, José David *humanities educator*
Seeba, Hinrich Claassen *foreign language educator*
Shannon, Thomas Frederic *German language educator*
Stern, David Gerald *philosophy educator*
Ting, Pang-Hsin *linguistics educator*
Tracy, Robert (Edward) *English language educator, poetry translator*
Upton, Dell *historian, educator*
Wright, Georgia Sommers *scholar, video producer*

Beverly Hills
Kravitz, Ellen King *musicologist, educator*
Valente, Michael F. *philosopher, consultant*

Calexico
Shumaker, Jeanette Roberts *English language educator*

Carmel
Feisthamel, Judy *language educator, interpreter, translator*
McGlynn, Betty Hoag *art historian*
Weber, Wilhelm K. *language professional*

Carmichael
Tokmakoff, George *history educator*

Carson
Grenier, Judson A., Jr. *history educator*
Sando, Ephriam *English language educator*

Cayucos
Garrigus, Charles Byford *retired literature educator*

Chico
Burr, Carol Elizabeth *English language educator*
González, María R. *Spanish language educator*

Claremont
Ackerman, Gerald Martin *art historian, consultant*
Atlas, Jay David *philosopher, consultant, linguist*
Beeks, Graydon Fisher, Jr. *musicology educator*
Chávez-Silverman, Suzanne *Chicano/Latino and Latin American literature educator*
Davis, Nathaniel *humanities educator*
Elsbree, Langdon *English language educator*
Lofgren, Charles Augustin *legal and constitutional historian*
Niven, William John *historian, educator*
Rolle, Myra Moss (Myra E. Moss) *philosophy educator, author, translator*
Roth, John King *philosopher, educator*
Sellery, J'nan Morse *English and American literature educator*
Sontag, Frederick Earl *philosophy educator*
Young, Howard Thomas *foreign language educator*

Costa Mesa
Prout, Carl Wesley *history educator*

Culver City
Forman, Joel Jon *numismatic appraiser*

Cupertino
Dunbar, Maurice Victor *English language educator*

Cypress
Chi, Hong *English as Second Language and Chinese educator*

Daly City
Velasquez, Thomas Aquinas *English language educator*

Davis
Alarcón, Francisco Xavier *poet, educator*
Gilbert, Sandra M. *English language educator*
Manoliu-Manea, Maria *linguist*
Osborn, Marijane *language professional/educator, English*
Torrance, Robert Mitchell *comparative literature educator*
Waddington, Raymond Bruce, Jr. *English language educator*
Woodress, James Leslie, Jr. *English language educator*

El Cerrito
Kuo, Ping-chia *historian, educator*

Fallbrook
Burns, Louis Francis *retired history educator*

Fountain Valley
Greenfield, Roseanne *English and history educator*
Williams, John Brindley *English language educator, writer*

Fresno
Chang, Hsu Hsin (Sidney H. Chang) *history educator*
Clifton, Michael Edward *English language educator*
Flores, William Vincent *Latin American studies educator*
Genini, Ronald Walter *history educator, historian*
Kouymjian, Dickran *art historian, Orientalist, educator*

Fullerton
Acosta-Hess, Josefina Elizabeth *Spanish language educator*
Hansen, Arthur August *history educator*
Hardy, Blaine Carmon *history educator*
Hobson, Wayne K. *humanities educator*
Orr, John Christopher *English language educator*

Glendale
DeGrassi, Leonard Rene *art historian, educator*

Granada Hills
Harris, Sheldon Howard *history educator*

Guerneville
Johnston, Andrea Ruth *writer, educator*

Hayward
Reichman, Henry Frederick *history educator*
Sapontzis, Steve F. *philosophy educator, writer*

Huntington Beach
Boyer, Nancy Gail *language educator*

Inverness
Scriven, Michael *philosopher, evaluator*

Irvine
Baker, Harold Dean *foreign language educator and researcher*
Clark, Michael Phillip *English educator*
Key, Mary Ritchie (Mrs. Audley E. Patton) *linguist, author, educator*
Krieger, Murray *English language educator, author*
Lee, Meredith *German language educator*
Maddy, Penelope Jo *philosopher*
Manzor, Lillian *humanities educator*
Navajas, Gonzalo *foreign language educator*
Nester, Robbi Lynne Kellman *writing and literature educator*
Norris, Margot Christa *English language educator*
O'Brien, Patricia Ann *history educator*
Rieckmann, Jens *German educator*
Toliver, Harold Earl *language professional, English*

La Canada
Hart, Monroe Monte *English language and literature educator*

La Jolla
Hughes, Judith Markham *history educator*
McDonald, Marianne *classicist*
Sanchez, Marta E. *literature educator*

La Mesa
Neumeyer, Peter Florian *English language educator*

La Mirada
Buchanan, Paul William *English language educator*
Rambo, Elizabeth Louise *English literature educator*

La Verne
Chu, Esther Briney *retired history educator*

Long Beach
Alkana, Linda Kelly *history educator*
Beebe, Sandra E. *retired English language educator, artist, writer*
Jura, Jean-Jacques *English language and literature educator*
Lau, Beth *English language educator*
Poertner, Lee Anne *English language educator*
Polakoff, Keith Ian *historian, university administrator*
Porter, Richard Ernest *speech educator, author*
Sater, William Frederick *history educator, writer*
Stetler, Charles Edward *English language educator*
Tang, Paul Chi Lung *philosophy educator*

Loomis
Noy, Gary David *history educator, association executive*

Los Altos
Zelditch, Bernice Osmola *English language educator*

Los Angeles
Bahr, Diana Meyers *humanities educator*
Barber, Elizabeth Jane Wayland *archeology and linguistics educator, researcher*
Bowlt, John Ellis *Slavic language educator*
Braudy, Leo Beal *English language educator, author*
Burns, Robert Ignatius *historian, educator, clergyman*
Cherkin, Adina *interpreter, translator*
Cheung, King-Kok *English language educator*
Comrie, Bernard Sterling *linguistics educator*
Cortinez, Veronica *language and literature educator*
Darby, Joanne Tyndale (Jaye Darby) *arts and humanities educator*
Davidson, Herbert Alan *Near Eastern languages and cultures educator*
Dumitrescu, Domnita *Spanish language educator, researcher*
Dyck, Andrew Roy *philologist*
Eckert, Geraldine Gonzales *language professional, educator, entrepreneur*
Ehret, Christopher Paul *history and linguistics educator*
Ellis, Robert Richmond *Spanish language educator*
Frank, Peter Solomon *art critic, curator*
Gómez, Ricardo Juan *philosophy educator*
Jacoby, Russell *history educator*
Jorgensen, Paul Alfred *English language educator emeritus*
Kaplan, Robert B. *linguistics educator, consultant, researcher*
Klein, Snira L(ubovsky) *Hebrew language and literature educator*
Komar, Kathleen Lenore *literature educator*
Masuoka, Susan Naomi *art historian*
Miles, Richard Robert *art historian, writer*
Peditto, Christopher Natale *humanities, English and communications educator*
Plann, Susan Joan *linguist, foreign language educator*
Saint-Aubin, Arthur Flannigan *French language educator, writer*
Sarafian, Arpi *English language educator*
Schaefer, William David *English language educator*
Schutz, John Adolph *historian, educator, former university dean*
Shaw, Stanford J. *history educator*
Shideler, Ross Patrick *foreign language and comparative literature educator, author, translator, poet*
Sonnenfeld, Albert *French language and comparative literature educator, food historian*
Sotiriou, Peter Elias *English language educator, textbook writer*
Steele, Timothy Reid *English language educator, poet*
Stern, Anita Enkel *English language educator*
Villanueva, Donna-Mae *English educator*
Wands, John Millar *English language educator, researcher*
Wu, Qingyun *Chinese language and literature educator*

Los Gatos
Tinsley, Barbara Sher *historian, educator, writer*

Los Olivos
Norris, James Leo *historian, editor, publisher*

Malibu
Randolph, Paul G. *history educator, minister*
Thomason, Phillip Brian *Spanish language educator*

Marina
Boldyrev, Peter Matveevich *Russian language and culture educator, writer*

Marina Del Rey
Hovy, Eduard H. *computational linguist*

Marysville
Moorman, Lawrence Alan *humanities educator*

Menlo Park
Cohn, Robert Greer *literary arts educator*

Merced
Elliott, Gordon Jefferson *English language educator*

Millbrae
Palmer, Patricia Ann Texter *English language educator*

Modesto
Jensen, Barbara Rebecca *English language educator*

Montclair
Haage, Robert Mitchell *retired history educator, organization leader*

Montecito
Atkins, Stuart (Pratt) *German language and literature educator*

Monterey
Gómez, Rafael *Hispanic studies educator*
Kennedy-Minott, Rodney *international relations educator, former ambassador*
Shropshire, Helen Mae *historian*

Monterey Park
Sanchez, Dennis Robert *English language educator*

Moreno Valley
Kari, Daven Michael *humanities educator*

Napa
Rogers, Brian Edward *English language educator, stand-up comedian/monologuist*

Newport Beach
Abramson, Albert *television historian, consultant*

Northridge
Broesamle, John Joseph *history educator*
Larson, Gale Kjelshus *English language educator, consultant*
Lothrop, Gloria Ricci *historian, educator*
Peters, John U. *English language educator*
Prescott, Gerald LeRoy *history educator*
Schaeffer, Colleen Diane *English language educator*

Oakland
Cai, Xing Yi *art historian, educator*
Walkup, Kathleen Ann *English language educator*

Orange
Krug, Donna Rebecca Dondes *history educator, small business owner*
Ozbirn, Katherine Michealle *English language educator and poet*
Yeager, Myron Dean *English language educator, business writing consultant*

Oxnard
Hill, Alice Lorraine *history, geneology, and social researcher, educator*

Pacific Grove
Elinson, Henry David *artist, language educator*

Palo Alto
Guerard, Albert Joseph *retired modern literature educator, author*
MacLean, Edna Ahgeak *language educator, researcher*
Mommsen, Katharina *retired German language and literature educator*

Pasadena
Kevles, Daniel Jerome *history educator, writer*
Kousser, J(oseph) Morgan *history educator*
Woodward, James Francis *humanities educator*

Placentia
Nettleship, Lois E. *history educator*

Pleasant Hill
Rawls, James Jabus *history educator*

Pomona
Cook, Stanley Joseph *English language educator, academic programs administrator, poet*
Jacobsen, Michael Anthony *art historian, educator*
Morsberger, Robert Eustis *English language educator*
Rocklin, Edward Lawrence *English literature educator, writer*

Poway
Terry, Patricia A. *literature educator*

Riverside
Bensick, Carol Marie *English literature educator*
Brinkerhoff, Dericksen Morgan *art history educator*
Cavers-Huff, Dasiea Yvonne *philosopher*
Daviau, Donald George *foreign language educator*
Dunn, Robert Paul *English language educator*
Gericke, Philip Otto *Spanish language educator*
Grimm, Reinhold *humanities educator*
Kollitz, Janice Arlene *English literature educator, freelance writer*
Loveless, Edna Maye *English language educator*
Snyder, Henry Leonard *history educator, bibliographer*
Zhang, Longxi *educator, literary critic*

Rocklin
Dickson, David Douglas *humanities educator*

Rohnert Park
Martinez, Elizabeth Coonrod *Spanish language educator*
Porras, Jorge Enrique *educator*

Sacramento
Castellano, Olivia Guerrero *English language educator*
Meindl, Robert James *English language educator*
Nesbitt, Paul Edward *historian, author, educator*
Schmitz, Dennis Mathew *English language educator*

San Anselmo
Ocker, Christopher Michael *historian, educator*

San Bernardino
Simard, Rodney *literature and communications educator, media consultant*
White, Edward Michael *English language educator*

San Diego
Argenteri, Letizia *history educator*
Butler, Gerald Joseph *English and comparative literature educator*
Chamberlin, Eugene Keith *historian, educator*
Clements, David Eugene *linguist*
Clowers, Myles Leonard *history educator*
Donnelly, John *philosophy educator*
González-Trujillo, César Augusto *Chicano studies educator, writer*
Gross, George Clayburn *English language educator*
Jonsson-Devillers, Edith *foreign language educator*
Kehler, Dorothea Faith *English educator*
Peterson, Richard Hermann *history educator*
Quintana, Leroy V. *English language educator*
Vanderbilt, Kermit *English language educator*
Vanderwood, Paul Joseph *history educator*
Wagner, Ray David *historian, educator, consultant*

San Francisco
Alayeto, Ofelia Luisa *writer, researcher, educator*
Batchelor, Karen Lee *English language educator*
Beck, Kenneth Eugene *English as a second language educator*
Brown, H. Douglas *English language educator*
Compton, James Vincent *history educator*
Costa-Zalessow, Natalia *foreign language educator*
Hansen, Carol Louise *English language educator*
Landar, Herbert Jay *linguistics educator, author*
Nakayama, Randall Shige *English language educator*
Turks, Victor Leonard *English language educator*
Wilczek, John Franklin *history educator*

San Jose
Borovski, Conrad *German and French literature and language educator*
Maio, Samuel Joseph *English language and literature educator*
Nichols, Patricia Causey *linguist*
Pickering, Mary Barbara *history educator, writer*
Reynolds, Edward Bruce *history educator*
Sabalius, Romey *foreign language and literature educator*
Walker, Carolyn Peyton *English language educator*

San Luis Obispo
Battenburg, John Douglas *English educator, consultant*
Cushing, James Byers *English language educator*
Duffy, Bernard Karl *educator*
Estes, Angela M. *English language educator*
Gish, Robert Franklin *English language educator, writer*
Riedlsperger, Max Ernst *history educator*

San Marcos
Christman, Albert Bernard *historian*
Gundersen, Joan Rezner *historian, educator*
Tanner, John Douglas, Jr. *history educator, writer*
Watts, Jill Marie *history educator*

San Marino
Karlstrom, Paul Johnson *art historian*
Ridge, Martin *historian, educator*
Thorpe, James *humanities scholar*

San Rafael
Dougherty, (Mary) Patricia *history educator*

Santa Ana
Jaurequi, Leticia López *English language educator*

Santa Barbara
Avalle-Arce, Juan Bautista *language educator*
Behrens, Laurence *educator, writer*
Brownlee, Wilson Elliot, Jr. *history educator*
Chafe, Wallace LeSeur *linguist, educator*
Hansen, Robert Gunnard *philatelist*
Hoffmeister, Gerhart *German language educator*
Lim, Shirley Geok Lin *English language educator*
Martinez-López, Enrique *Spanish educator*
Moyer, Ann Elizabeth *historian*
Rickels, Laurence Arthur *foreign language educator*
Willis, Paul Jonathan *English language educator*

Santa Clara
Pierson, Peter O'Malley *history educator*

Santa Cruz
Aptheker, Bettina Fay *women's studies educator*
Cioc, Mark *history educator*
Kashap, Surajnayan Paul *philosophy educator*
Lieberman, Fredric *ethnomusicologist, educator*
Suckiel, Ellen Kappy *philosophy educator*

Santa Monica
Heimann-Hast, Sybil Dorothea *retired language arts and literature educator*
Kotansky, Roy D. *ancient languages, religion and culture educator*
Schipper, Merle *art historian and critic, exhibition curator*

Santa Rosa
Aman, Reinhold Albert *philologist, publisher*

Simi Valley
Lee, Nancy Jane McCleary *American studies educator*
Todd, Steven Davis *fine art consultant, agent, company owner*

Spring Valley
Clark, John DeWitt *retired fine arts educator, sculptor*

Stanford
Duus, Peter *history educator*
Haro, Maria-Paz *Spanish language and culture educator*
Kennedy, David Michael *historian, educator*
Moravcsik, Julius Matthew *philosophy educator*
Ruotolo, Lucio Peter *English language educator*
Stansky, Peter David Lyman *historian*

Stockton
Dominik, Jane Kathryn *English language educator, writer*
Rogers, William Darrow *history educator*
Ward, Barry John *historian*
Wonder, John Paul *educator*

Suisun City
Dambrosio, Annette *English language educator*

Sylmar
Hoggatt, Clela Allphin *English language educator*

Torrance
Gutierrez-Medina, Hector *Spanish interpreter*

Turlock
Dean, Britten *history educator*

Vacaville
Warren, Thomas Henry *philosophy educator*

Van Nuys
Front, Theodore *music company executive*
Zucker, Alfred John *English educator, academic administrator*

Walnut
Henrotte, Gayle Allen *linguistics educator and musicologist*

Whittier
Hewitt, Jerene Cline *English language educator*

Woodland Hills
Pickard, Dean *philosophy and humanities educator*

COLORADO

Arvada
Allbee, Charles Eugene *English language educator*
Elrick, Billy Lee *English language educator*

Aurora
Curtis, Linda Jenarie *genealogist*

Johnson, Geraldine Esch *language specialist*

Boulder
Baena, Julio *Spanish language and literature educator*
Colwell, James Lee *humanities educator*
Gonzalez-del-Valle, Luis Tomas *Spanish language educator*
Jamieson, Dale Walter *philosophy and biology educator*
Jordan, Isolde Jahncke *Spanish and Portuguese language educator*
Juhasz, Suzanne *English language educator*
Moulakis, Athanasios *philosopher, educator*
Nickel, James Wesley *philosophy educator*
Ross, Janet *retired English language educator*
Schütrumpf, Eckart Ernst *classical languages and philosophy educator*

Colorado Springs
Anderson, Katheryn Lucille *language arts educator and author*
Bryson, Dorothy Printup *retired educator*
Cramer, Owen Carver *classics educator*

Delta
Burke, Gary Palmer *historian, educator, coach*

Denver
Fain, Karen Kellogg *history and geography educator*
Fleck, Richard Francis *English language educator, writer*
Geddes, Charles Lynn *retired history educator*
Hamp-Lyons, Liz *language educator, consultant*
Lin, Jian-Zhong *English language educator*
Porter, Donna J. *genealogist*
Scott, Gwendolyn Harrison *educator, consultant*
Storey, Brit Allan *historian*
Templin, John Alton *historical theology educator, minister*
Wetzel, Jodi (Joy Lynn Wetzel) *history and women's studies educator*
Wilson, Douglas Brownlow *language educator*
Yarborough, Mark Ashley *philosophy educator, bioethicist*

Evergreen
Engstrom, Sallee Fox *retired English and elementary music educator*

Fort Collins
Keane, Kevin Patrick *philosopher, consultant*
Knight, Thomas Joseph *history educator*
Tremblay, William Andrew *English language educator*

Golden
Joy, Carla Marie *history educator*

Greeley
Arneson, Patricia Ann *speech communication educator*
Hinds, Elizabeth Jane *humanities educator*
Sandstedt, Lynn Alfred *foreign language and humanities educator*
Wilson, Sharon Rose *educator, researcher*
Worley, Lloyd Douglas *English language educator*

Lakewood
Spude, Robert Lester *historian*

Paonia
Fay, Abbott Eastman *history educator*

Pueblo
Farwell, Hermon Waldo, Jr. *parliamentarian, educator, former speech communication educator*
Sheidley, William Edwards *English language educator*
Taylor, Cynthia Hinkel *English literature educator*
Vorpagel, Wilbur Charles *historical consultant*

Sterling
Christian, Roland Carl (Bud Christian) *retired English and speech communications educator*

Tabernash
Black, Robert Clifford, III *history educator*

Westminster
Kroeger, Karl *retired musicologist, librarian, composer, and editor*

HAWAII

Hilo
Doudna, Martin Kirk *English language educator*
Kahaney, Phyllis Sherman *humanities educator*

Honolulu
Ardolino, Frank Richard *English language educator*
Ball, Robert Jerome *classics educator*
Chandler, Paul Michael *Spanish and Portuguese educator, homeless advocate*
Copi, Irving Marmer *philosophy educator*
Fujita, James Hiroshi *history educator*
Gladney, Dru Curtis *Asian studies educator*
Hoffmann, Kathryn Ann *humanities educator*
Hohing, Frederick William *humanities educator*
La Luzerne-Oi, Sally Ann *humanities educator*
McCutcheon, James Miller *history and American studies educator*
Menikoff, Barry *English language educator*
Moore, Willis Henry Allphin *history and geography educator*
Newby, Idus Atwell *historian, educator*
Onopa, Robert Lawrence *English language educator*
Rapson, Richard L. *history educator*
Rehg, Kenneth Lee *linguistics educator*
Tiles, James Edward *philosophy educator*
Uhalley, Stephen, Jr. *history educator*
Wayne, Valerie *English language educator*
Yamasaki, Mitch *history educator*

Kamuela
Piltz, Josephine Amanti *English language educator, writing consultant*

Keaau
Bailey, Charles-James Nice *linguistics educator*

Laie
Spickard, Paul R. *historian, educator, academic administrator*

Pearl City
Roberts, Norman Frank *English composition and linguistics educator*

IDAHO

Boise
Lovin, Hugh Taylor *history educator*
Maguire, James Henry *English language educator*
Nguyen, King Xuan *language educator*
O'Grady, John Patrick *American literature educator, writer*
Wells, Merle William *historian, state archivist*

Moscow
Greever, Janet Groff *history educator*
Schwantes, Carlos Arnaldo *history educator, consultant*

MINNESOTA

Minneapolis
Noble, John Partridge *English language educator*

MISSOURI

Saint Louis
Birdnow, Brian Everett *history educator, essayist, critic, reporter*

MONTANA

Big Timber
Drake, Jessica *dialect and speech coach*

Bozeman
Allard, James Willard, Jr. *philosophy educator*

Columbia Falls
McKay, Kathryn L. *historian*

Missoula
Bier, Jesse *literature educator*
Charbonneau, Joanne Adrienne *literature and humanities educator*
Flores, Dan Louie *history educator*
Kittredge, William Alfred *humanities educator*
Lauren, Paul Gordon *history educator*
Limberis, Lucy Jane *English studies educator*

NEVADA

Las Vegas
Agonia, Barbara Ann *emeritus English language educator, communications consultant*
Goodwin, Joanne Lorraine *historian, educator*
Hilgar, Marie-France *educator, foreign language*
Hudgins, Christopher Chapman *English educator*
Irsfeld, John Henry *English language educator, novelist*
Koester, Rudolf *educator*
Lang-Peralta, Linda Ann *English language educator*
Walton, (Delvy) Craig *philosopher, educator*

North Las Vegas
Schmitt, Paul John *history educator*

Reno
Brown, Richard Elwood *educator*
Casper, Scott E *historian*
Ronald, Ann *English literature educator*

NEW MEXICO

Albuquerque
Bybee, Joan Lea *linguistics educator*
Cárdenas, Anthony J. *foreign language educator*
Feller, Daniel M. *history educator*
Fleming, Robert Edward *English language educator*
Frumkin, Gene *writer, educator*
Himmerich y Valencia, Robert Theron *historian, farmer*
Hutton, Paul Andrew *history educator, writer*
Joost-Gaugier, Christiane L. *art history educator*
Kutvirt, Duda Chytilova (Ruzena) *scientific translator*
Pena, Juan Jose *interpreter*
Rabinowitz, Howard Neil *history educator*
Skelton, Elizabeth Anne *foreign language educator*
Whidden, Mary Bess *English language educator*
White, Robert Rankin *writer and historian, hydrologist*
Witemeyer, Hugh Hazen *English language educator*
Young, Mary Jane *American studies and folklore educator*

Gallup
Glowienka, Emerine Frances *philosophy educator*

Las Cruces
Matray, James Irving *history educator*
Newman, Edgar Leon *historian, educator*

Placitas
Forrest, Suzanne Sims *research historian*

Portales
Matheny, Robert Lavesco *history educator, former university president*

Roswell
Tuso, Joseph Frederick *English language educator, academic dean emeritus*

Santa Fe
Pesic, Peter Dragan *liberal arts educator*

NEW YORK

Buffalo
Riepe, Dale Maurice *philosopher, writer, illustrator, educator, Asian art dealer*

OHIO

Cincinnati
Harris, Diane *history educator*

Wooster
Glasgow, Janis Marilyn *foreign language educator*

OREGON

Ashland
Ettlich, Ernest Earl *communications educator*

Corvallis
King, David Burnett *history educator*
Rudinsky, Norma Leigh *English language educator, translator*

Eugene
Armstrong, Paul Bradford *English educator, dean*
Bingham, Edwin Ralph *history educator*
Birn, Raymond Francis *historian, educator*
Bishop, Louise Marie *English language educator*
Greene, Roland Arthur *literature educator*
Pascal, C(ecil) Bennett *classics educator*
Rendall, Steven Finlay *language educator, editor, translator, critic*
Wickes, George *English language educator, writer*

Forest Grove
Steele, Michael Rhoads *humanities and peace studies educator, writer*

La Pine
Lansdowne, Karen Myrtle *retired English language and literature educator*

Marylhurst
Henderson, Sarah Allan *English language educator*

Mcminnville
Ericksen, Kenneth Jerrold *English literature educator*
Mc Kaughan, Howard Paul *linguistics educator*

Medford
La Lande, Jeffrey Max *historian*

Monmouth
Harding, Carol Elaine *English language educator*
Meyer, Richard Erwin *English language educator*
Strand, Cheryl Marie *Spanish language, literature educator*

North Bend
Shepard, Robert Carlton *English language educator*

Pendleton
Rice, Douglas Alan *foreign language professor*

Portland
Greco, Gina Lyn *French language and literature educator*
Harris, Frederick Philip *retired philosophy educator*
Henning, Martha Louise *English language educator*
Lenzen, Connie Lou *genealogist*
Menke, Timm Reiner *German language educator*
Nguyen, Joseph Kim Quy *foreign language educator*
Rottschaefer, William Andrew *philosophy educator*
Schmidt, Stanley Eugene *retired speech educator*

Salem
Trammell, Martin Gil *humanities educator*
Trueblood, Paul Graham *retired English educator, author, editor*

Tolovana Park
Muñoz-Sandoval, Ana F. *linguist*

Veneta
Vincent, Claudia Gottschall *English and German educator*

RHODE ISLAND

Little Compton
Terras, Rita *German language educator*

UTAH

Logan
Bakker, Jan *English language educator*
Butler, Anne M. *history educator*
Lye, William Frank *history educator*

Ogden
Burton, Thomas Roghaar *English language educator*
Peterson, Levi Savage *English language educator*
Wutz, Michael *English language educator*

Provo
Hatch, Gary Layne *English educator, writer*
Lyon, James Karl *German language educator*
Paxman, David Brockbank *English literature educator*
Skousen, Royal Jon *linguist*
Tanner, John Sears *English language educator, academic administrator*

Saint George
Compton, Merlin David *Spanish language educator*

Salt Lake City
Arrington, Harriet Ann *historian, biographer, writer*
Battin, Margaret Pabst *philosophy educator*
Donavin, Georgiana *English language educator*
Eakle, Arlene Haslam *genealogist*
Engar, Ann Willardson *humanities educator*
Hibbard, Charles Gustin *historian*
Olpin, Robert Spencer *art history educator*
Rashkin, Esther J. *language and literature educator*
Voigt, Milton *English language educator*
Yang, Anand Alan *history educator*

WASHINGTON

Bellevue
Opperman, Hal N. *art historian*

Bellingham
Dietrich, Dawn Yvette *English language educator*
Gallay, Alan *history educator*
Johnson, Ellwood Gerd *English language educator*
Whisenhunt, Donald Wayne *history educator*

Bothell
Heuving, Jeanne Diane *literature educator*

Cheney
Kaufman, Judith Diane *English language educator, consultant*
Kieswetter, James Kay *history educator*
Smith, Grant William *English language educator, civic fundraiser*
Urcia, Ingeborg *English language educator*

College Place
Aamodt, Terrie Dopp *history and English educator*

Edmonds
Leblon, Jean Marcel *retired French language educator, consultant*

Ellensburg
Cummings, D(onald) W(ayne) *English language educator, dean*
Dunning, William Vance *fine arts educator*
Olson, Steven Douglas *English language educator*
Powell, Joseph Edward *English language educator*

Olympia
Beck, Gordon Eugene *art history educator, consultant*
Chang, Sheng-Tai *English language educator*
Daugherty, Leo *literature and language educator*

Pasco
Hartman-Irwin, Mary Frances *retired language professional*

Pullman
Ashby, Darrel LeRoy *history educator*
Frykman, George Axel *history educator, researcher*
Kuhlman, Erika Ann *historian, educator*
McLeod, Susan Margaret *English language educator*
Wingate, Marcel Edward *speech educator*

Seattle
Abrams, Robert Edward *English educator*
Berman, Morris *historian, author*
Bultmann, William Arnold *historian*
Canaday, Nicholas *retired English educator*
Clauss, James Joseph *classics educator*
Gallagher, Susan VanZanten *English literature educator*
Hertling, G. H. *Germanics educator*
Jones, Edward Louis *historian, educator*
Keyt, David *philosophy and classics educator*
Layton, Marilyn Smith *English language educator*
Maxwell, Raymond Samuel, III *history educator*
Rorabaugh, William Joseph *historian*
Sokoloff, Naomi Beryl *Hebrew language and literature educator*
VanArsdel, Rosemary Thorstenson *English studies educator*
Waluconis, Carl Joseph *English language educator, humanities educator*

Spokane
Carlson, Nancy Lee *English language educator*
Carriker, Robert Charles *history educator*
Stackelberg, John Roderick *history educator*

Tacoma
Collier, Richard Bangs *philosopher, foundation executive*
Krieger, William Carl *English language educator*

Walla Walla
Crockett, Dennis *art historian*

WYOMING

Laramie
Calloway, Colin Gordon *historian educator*
Kohler, Eric Dave *history educator*
Moore, William Howard *history educator, writer*
Nye, Eric William *English language educator*
Reverend, Cedric Dwight, II *English language educator*
Roberts, Philip John *history educator*

Powell
Wasden, Winifred Sawaya *English language educator, writer*

Rock Springs
Taylor, Lee Roger, Jr. *English language educator*

Sheridan
Aguirre-Batty, Mercedes *Spanish/English language and literature educator*

CANADA

ALBERTA

Calgary
Mc Kenna, Marian Cecilia *historian*

Edmonton
Lynn, Richard John *Chinese language and literature educator*

BRITISH COLUMBIA

Burnaby
Kitchen, John Martin *historian, educator*

Vancouver
Batts, Michael Stanley *German language educator*
Gomes, Daniel *historian educator*

SASKATCHEWAN

Saskatoon
Brewster, Elizabeth Winifred *English language educator, poet, novelist*
Kent, Christopher Andrew *history educator*

JAPAN

Kyoto
Fowles, Charlotte Marie *English language educator*

ADDRESS UNPUBLISHED

Broadley, Hugh T. *art history educator*
Brody, Jacob Jerome *art history educator*
Bush, Sarah Lillian *historian*
Caldwell, Howard Bryant *English language educator*
Cassel, Susie Lan *humanities educator*
Daly, Kelly Sue *English language educator, medical technician*
Donelson, Kenneth LaVern *English language educator*
Ducker, James Howard *historian, writer*
Fleck, Jade Carlson *literature educator, registered nurse*
Goldstein, Marcia *historian, educator, law office administrator*
Grayson, Sandra Marie *educator*
Hall, Jill *composition and literature educator*
Hanna, Sara L. *English language educator*
Hanson-Smith, Elizabeth *English language educator, computer consultant*
Hutchinson, Joseph Candler *retired foreign language educator*
Jones, Therese Ann *humanities educator*
Le Bard, Jeffrey Mitchell *English language educator*
Lewis, Norman *English language educator, writer*
Lobach, Melissa Renee *English language educator*
Maehl, William Harvey *historian, educator*
McLeod, Jennifer Gail *English language educator*
Merton, Egon Stephen *English literature educator*
Miller, Robert Ryal *history educator*
Niedzielski, Henri Zygmunt *French and English language educator*
Nix, Nancy Jean *librarian, designer*
Nye, Mary Jo *historian, humanities educator*
Osborne, Thomas Joe *history educator*
özkaragöz, Inci Zühra *linguist*
Pace, R(alph) Wayne *organizational behavior educator*
Pearson, Velvet D. *English and composition educator*
Peters, Ann M. *linguistics educator*
Peterson, Barbara Ann Bennett *history educator, television personality*
Porter, James B. *hieroglyphics specialist*
Radford-McGrady, Stephanie Jill *speech communications educator*
Raymond, C. Elizabeth *history educator*
Rothman, Julius Lawrence *retired English language educator*
Samuels, Wilfred D. *English language and humanities educator, department director*
Seidensticker, Edward George *Japanese language and literature educator*
Stewart, Sandra Itzel *language educator*
Thiroux, Emily Lofton *English educator, theater director*
Tilton, Kathleen Joan *English language educator*
Topik, Steven Curtis *history educator*
Udall, Sharyn R. *art historian, writer, curator*
Weber, Eugen *historian, educator, author*
Whitby, William Melcher *Spanish language and literature educator*
Zwerver, Peter John *linguistics educator*

HUMANITIES: LIBRARIES

UNITED STATES

ALASKA

Anchorage
Parham, Robert Bruce *archivist*
Rollins, Alden Milton *documents librarian*

Fairbanks
Hill, Ronald Gregory *library director*

Juneau
Schorr, Alan Edward *librarian, publisher*
Smith, George Vinal *librarian*

Palmer
Madsen, Elizabeth Karlene *librarian*

ARIZONA

Bullhead City
Huelsbeck, Julie Marie *librarian*

Camp Verde
Hazekamp, Phyllis Wanda *library director*

Casa Grande
Gaulke, Mary Florence *library administrator*

Chino Valley
Rothlisberg, Allen Peter *librarian, educator, deacon*

Dewey
Beck, Doris Olson *library media director*

Goodyear
Gillen, Katherine Elizabeth *librarian*

Kingman
Williams, Darleen Dorothy *librarian*

Mesa
Anderson, Herschel Vincent *librarian*

Phoenix
Edwards, Ralph M. *librarian*
Fox, Frances Juanice *retired librarian, educator, retired*
Landers, Teresa Price *librarian*
Norman, Nita Vegamora *librarian, storyteller*

Scottsdale
Dalton, Phyllis Irene *library consultant*
Meyer, Madeline Anna *librarian*

Sun City West
Williams, William Harrison *retired librarian*

Tempe
Borovansky, Vladimir Theodore *librarian*
Metros, Mary Teresa *librarian*
Weiler, Dorothy Esser *librarian*

Tucson
Anderson, Rachael Keller *library administrator*
Grams, Theodore Carl William *librarian, educator*
Hurt, Charlie Deuel, III *library school director, educator*
Irwin, Mildred Lorine Warrick *library consultant, civic worker*
Laird, Wilbur David, Jr. *librarian*
Miller, Liz Rodriguez *public library system director, librarian*
Pintozzi, Chestalene *librarian*
Skorupski, Diane Christine *school library media specialist*
Wolfe, William Jerome *librarian, English language educator*

CALIFORNIA

Albany
Schonbrun, Rena *librarian*

Alhambra
Harnsberger, Therese Coscarelli *librarian*

Altadena
Tema, William John *librarian*

Aptos
Heron, David Winston *librarian*
Smalley, Topsy Neher *librarian*

Arcata
Chadwick, Sharon Stevens *librarian*

Auburn
Sanborn, Dorothy Chappell *retired librarian*

Avalon
Eisenhut, Donna Parson *community library manager*

Bakersfield
Duquette, Diane Rhea *library director*

Berkeley
Danton, Joseph Periam *librarian, educator*
Hanff, Peter Edward *librarian, bibliographer*
Hoehn, Raymond Philip, Jr. *map librarian*
Minudri, Regina Ursula *library director, consultant*
Osegueda, Laura Margaret *librarian*
Purat, Jacek *library director*
Spohrer, James Henry *librarian, consultant*

Camarillo
Dickinson, Charles Tweed *information science administrator, programmer*
Kiser, Nagiko Sato *retired librarian*

Carlsbad
Kennedy, Charlene Farrington *head reference librarian*
Lange, Clifford E. *librarian*

Coalinga
Anthony, Kay Carroll *librarian*

Commerce
Conover, Robert Warren *librarian*

Culver City
Chow, Judy *library studies educator*

Cupertino
Fletcher, Homer Lee *librarian*

Davis
Borg, Axel Edwin *librarian, educator*
Grossman, George Stefan *library director, law eductor*
Sharrow, Marilyn Jane *library administrator*

El Cajon
Freeland, Robert Frederick *librarian*

El Centro
Gotti, Margaret Lynn *library administrator*

El Cerrito
Diliberto, Helen Bratney *librarian, retired educator*
Kao, Yasuko Watanabe *library administrator*

Encino
Wood, Raymund Francis *retired librarian*

Fremont
Wood, Linda May *librarian*

Fresno
Gorman, Michael Joseph *library director, educator*
Kallenberg, John Kenneth *librarian*
Spencer, Dorothy Ann *library director, consultant*

Fullerton
Ayala, John *librarian, dean*
Hansen, Debra Gold *library science educator, historian*

Glendora
Thompson, John Reed *librarian*

Granada Hills
Stump, D. Michael *librarian*

Huntington Beach
Gylseth, Doris (Lillian) Hanson *librarian*
Halvorsen, Jan La Rayne *library services manager*
Hayden, Ron L. *library director*

Inglewood
Alaniz, Miguel José Castañeda *library director*

Irvine
Euster, Joanne Reed *librarian*

Jamestown
Ward, Dennis Francis *librarian*

La Jolla
Goff, William James *librarian*
Lowell, Gerald Ray *librarian, academic information technology administrator*
Mirsky, Phyllis Simon *librarian*

Livermore
Love, Sandra Rae *information specialist*

Long Beach
Lathrop, Ann *librarian, educator*
Scepanski, Jordan Michael *librarian, administrator*

Los Angeles
Bergman, Emily Anne *librarian*
Brecht, Albert Odell *library and information technology administrator*
Bulmer, Connie J. *film librarian*
Chang, Henry Chung-Lien *library administrator*
Ciccone, Amy Navratil *art librarian*
Coolbaugh, Carrie Weaver *librarian*
Coppin, Ann Stacy *information specialist*
Fry, Stephen Michael *music librarian*
Gabbard, Dana Chester *library assistant*
Gilman, Nelson Jay *library director*
Goldberg Kent, Susan *library director*
Helgeson, Duane Marcellus *retired librarian*
Kent, Susan Goldberg *library director, consultant*
Lee, Robert Andrew *librarian*
O'Brian, Bonnie Jean *library services supervisor*
Patron, Susan Hall *librarian, writer*
Peters, Kevin Casey *university library worker*
Polan, Morris *librarian*
Steele, Victoria Lee *librarian*
Sutherland, Michael Cruise *librarian*

Los Gatos
Willer, Kenneth Henry *library director*

Manteca
Hunt, Charles Amoes *librarian*

Menlo Park
White, Cecil Ray *librarian, consultant*

Modesto
Kreissman, Starrett *librarian*

Monterey
Reneker, Maxine Hohman *librarian*

Monterey Park
Wilson, Linda *librarian*

Mountain View
Di Muccio, Mary Jo *retired librarian*

Napa
Telegdy, Maryll Ilona *librarian, archaeologist*

North Hollywood
Pace, Elizabeth Kristin *free lance researcher*
Stover, Mark Edwin *librarian*

Oakland
Bibel, Barbara Mita *librarian*
Engel, Genevieve *library system analyst*
Gomez, Martin *library director*
Lo, Suzanne Jay *librarian*

Ontario
Luce, Susan Marie *library director*

Orange
Miller, Jean Ruth *librarian*

Palmdale
Storsteen, Linda Lee *librarian*

Palo Alto
Van Velzer, Verna Jean *retired research librarian*

Pasadena
Buck, Anne Marie *library director, consultant*
Dowell, David Ray *library administrator*
Gordon, Helen Wilcox *church librarian*

Placerville
Wickline, Marian Elizabeth *former chemical librarian*

Pleasant Hill
Gold, Anne Marie *library director*

Redding
Compton, Miles Stuart *librarian*

Redlands
Canterbury, Leslie John *librarian*

Riverside
Baldwin, Charlene Marie *librarian*

Sacramento
Halteman, Ellen Louise *librarian*
Hogan, Eddy *librarian*
Killian, Richard M. *library director*
Maginnity, Gerald Francis *librarian*
Snow, Marina Sexton *reference librarian, playwright*

Salinas
Shaffer, Dallas Young *library administrator*
Spinks, Paul *retired library director*

San Bernardino
Anderson, Barbara Louise *retired library director*

San Diego
Cain, Seymour *historian , philosopher and writer*
Collins, Dorothy Smith *librarian*
Sannwald, William Walter *librarian*

San Francisco
Anderson, Harold Paul *historian, archivist, bank executive*
Cline, Fred Albert, Jr. *librarian, conservationist*
Dowlin, Kenneth Everett *librarian*
Frantz, John Corydon *librarian*
Geiger, Richard George *librarian*
Schmalz, Rochelle Perrine *library director*

San Jose
Bratman, David Stephen *librarian*
Crowe, Edith Louise *librarian*
Fish, James Henry *library director*
Schmidt, Cyril James *librarian*

San Lorenzo
Woodbury, Marda Liggett *librarian, writer*

San Luis Obispo
Graham, Priscilla Mann *librarian*
Perkins, Dale Warren *library director*
Reynolds, Brian Arthur *library director*
Rockman, Ilene Frances *librarian, educator, editor*
Walch, David Bean *librarian, university official*

San Marcos
Allison, Terry Lane *librarian*
Cater, Judy Jerstad *librarian*
Ciurczak, Alexis *librarian*

San Marino
Zoeckler, Linda Kay *librarian art historian*

Santa Ana
Adams, John M. *library director*
Richard, Robert John *library director*

Santa Barbara
Boisse, Joseph Adonias *library administrator*
Brun, Christian Magnus From *university librarian*
Keator, Carol Lynne *library director*
Korenic, Lynette Marie *librarian*
Lockett, Barbara Ann *librarian*

Santa Clara
Hopkinson, Shirley Lois *library and information science educator*

Santa Cruz
Dyson, Allan Judge *librarian*
Welborn, Victoria Lee *science librarian, educator*

Santa Monica
Ackerman, Helen Page *librarian, educator*
Levin, Barry Raymond *rare book dealer*

Sebastopol
Sabsay, David *library consultant*

Simi Valley
Osburn, Lisa Marie *archives technician*
Soubers, Richard Rodney *archivist*

Stanford
Derksen, Charlotte Ruth Meynink *librarian*
Fortson, Judith Lee *library administrator*
Keller, Michael Alan *librarian, educator, musicologist*
Linder, Gloria Ann *medical librarian, educator*
Ross, Alexander Duncan *art librarian*
Weber, David C(arter) *librarian*

Stockton
Harrison, Isom *librarian*

Thousand Oaks
Brogden, Stephen Richard *library administrator*

Torrance
Buckley, James W. *librarian*

Turlock
Griffin, Jim Allan *librarian*

Ventura
Adeniran, Dixie Darlene *library administrator*

West Hollywood
Baer, D(avid) Richard *film archive administrator*

Whittier
O'Brien, Philip Michael *library administrator*
Topjon, Ann Johnson *librarian*

Willows
Kirks, James Harvey, Jr. *librarian, administrator*

Woodland Hills
Zeitlin, Eugenia Pawlik *librarian, educator*

Yucaipa
Erickson, Cheryl Ann *librarian*

COLORADO

Aurora
Brown, Darmae Judd *librarian*

Boulder
Carter, Laura Lee *academic librarian, psychologist*
Gralapp, Marcelee Gayl *librarian*

Colorado Springs
Budington, William Stone *retired librarian*
Chen, Lynn Chia-Ling *librarian*
Dew, Thomas Roderick *museum librarian*
Jones-Eddy, Julie Margaret *librarian*
Margolis, Bernard Allen *library administrator, antique book merchant and appraiser*
Sheridan, John Brian *librarian*

Denver
Ahern, Arleen Fleming *retired librarian*
Ashton, Rick James *librarian*
Gehres, Eleanor Agnew Mount *librarian*
Kroll, James Xavier *librarian*
Schafer, Gerald Lewis *librarian*
Schertz, Morris *library director*
Stewart, Karen Elaine *librarian*
White, Joyce Louise *librarian*

Englewood
Long, Henry (Hank Long) *librarian*

Fort Collins
Chambers, Joan Louise *dean of libraries*
Saferite, Linda Lee *library director*

Golden
Lerud, Joanne Van Ornum *library administrator*
Mathews, Anne Jones *international consultant, library director*

Grand Junction
Bragdon, Lynn Lyon *library administrator*

Lakewood
Knott, William Alan *library director, library management and building consultant*

Leadville
McCain, Nancy Schloerke *library director*

Pueblo
Bates, Charles Emerson *library administrator*
Cress, Cecile Colleen *retired librarian*
Moore, Beverly Ann *librarian*
Penny, Laura Jean *librarian*

Trinidad
Murphy, Sara Jo *library director*

U S A F Academy
Barrett, Donald John *library administrator*

HAWAII

Fort Shafter
Hanusey, Richard Dmytro *library director*

Honolulu
Kane, Bartholomew Aloysius *state librarian*
King, Charles Lynn *librarian*
Lee, Pali Jae (Polly Jae Stead Lee) *retired librarian, writer*
Spencer, Caroline *library director*
Stevens, Robert David *librarian, educator*
Wageman, Lynette Mena *librarian*

Pearl City
Eldredge, Jeffrey Robert Carleton *librarian*

IDAHO

Boise
Bolles, Charles Avery *librarian*

Moscow
Force, Ronald Wayne *librarian*

Sandpoint
Murray, James Michael *librarian, law librarian, legal educator, lawyer*

INDIANA

Jeffersonville
Boyer, Laura Mercedes *librarian*

MINNESOTA

North Oaks
Brudvig, Glenn Lowell *retired library director*

Rochester
Key, Jack Dayton *librarian*

MISSOURI

Saint Peters
Michel, Victor James, Jr. *retired librarian*

MONTANA

Billings
Cochran, William Michael *librarian*

Helena
Fitzpatrick, Lois Ann *library administrator*

NEVADA

Carson City
Rocha, Guy Louis *archivist, historian*

Las Vegas
Batson, Darrell Lynn *librarian, consultant*
Hunsberger, Charles Wesley *library consultant*
Lorance, Jane *librarian*
Ortiz, Diane *librarian, management analyst*
Smith, Thomas James *reference librarian*

North Las Vegas
Au, Bertha Lin Tai Chang *school librarian, educator*

Reno
Zink, Steven Douglas *librarian*

NEW MEXICO

Albuquerque
Freeman, Patricia Elizabeth *library and education specialist*
Ross, Marie Heise *retired librarian*
Sabatini, Joseph David *librarian*
Snell, Patricia Poldervaart *librarian, consultant*
Wilkinson, Frances Catherine *librarian, educator*
Wolf, Cynthia Tribelhorn *librarian, library educator*

Bernalillo
Liebert, Martha Ann *public librarian*

Deming
Becker-Klicker, Margaret Chan *library director*

Eunice
Suter, Peggy Jean *library director*

Gallup
Fellin, Octavia Antoinette *retired librarian*

Las Cruces
Dresp, Donald Francis *library director*
Myers, R. David *library director, dean*
Townley, Charles Thomas *librarian, educator*

Los Alamos
Bjorklund, Katharine Browne *librarian*
Orndoff, Elizabeth Carlson *retired reference librarian, educator*
Sayre, Edward Charles *librarian*

Portales
Dowlin, Charles Edwin *librarian*

Roswell
Long, Betty Jean *library director*
McLaren, M(alcom) Bruce *library director*

Santa Fe
Brewster, John Weldon, Sr. *librarian, consultant*
Watkins, Karen J. *librarian*

Truth Or Consequences
Sampson, Ellanie Sue *library director*

NEW YORK

Jamaica
Strong, Gary Eugene *librarian*

OREGON

Albany
House, Edward Briley, Jr. *librarian*

Astoria
Foster, Michael William *librarian*

Boardman
Buck, G. Wendell *library director*

Coquille
DePlois, Molly *library director*

Corvallis
Hunt, Donald R. *retired librarian*

Eugene
Hildebrand, Carol Ilene *librarian*
Morrison, Perry David *librarian, educator*
Stirling, Isabel Ann *science librarian*

Gresham
Pierik, Marilyn Anne *librarian*

Helix
Mitchell, Martha L. *library director*

Ontario
Edwards, Dale Leon *library director*

Portland
Browne, Joseph Peter *retired librarian*
Cooper, Ginnie *library director*
Eshelman, William Robert *librarian, editor*
Freiser, Leonard Harold *engineering library director*
Morgan, James Earl *librarian, administrator*

Roseburg
Reenstjerna, Frederick Roberts *librarian, writer*

Salem
Kenyon, Carleton Weller *librarian*
Oberg, Larry Reynold *librarian*
Weide, Janice Lee *librarian*

Wilsonville
Turner, Stephen Wayne *library director*

UTAH

Brigham City
Hill, Susan Holmes *library director*

Logan
Anderson, Janet Alm *librarian*
Heister, Carla Gayle *library director*

Ogden
Ayer, Carol Anne *librarian*

Provo
Albrecht, Sterling Jean *university library director*
Gillum, Gary Paul *librarian*
Hall, Blaine Hill *librarian*
Jensen, Richard Dennis *librarian*
Smith, Nathan McKay *library and information sciences educator*

Salt Lake City
Anderson, Grant Allen *librarian*
Day, Joseph Dennis *librarian*
Karpisek, Marian Ellen *librarian*
Longsworth, Eileen Catherine *library director*
Morrison, David Lee *librarian, educator*
Partridge, Cathleen Flanagan *library director*

WASHINGTON

Bellevue
Mutschler, Herbert Frederick *retired librarian*

Centralia
Miller, Lester Livingston, Jr. *librarian, researcher*

College Place
Gaskell, Carolyn Suzanne *librarian*
Jonish, Arley Duane *retired bibliographer*

Edmonds
Betz-Zall, Jonathan Richard *librarian*

Ferndale
Harris, Kevin Michael *library manager, investigative specialist*

Kennewick
Vickery, Byrdean Eyvonne Hughes (Mrs. Charles Everett Vickery, Jr.) *retired library services administrator*

Kirkland
Rosett, Ann Doyle *librarian*

Lacey
Smith, Donald Evans *library consultant*

Olympia
Zussy, Nancy Louise *librarian*

Pullman
Croft, Vicki Faye *librarian*
Roberts, Elizabeth Porcher *library director*

Renton
Greggs, Elizabeth May Bushnell (Mrs. Raymond John Greggs) *retired librarian*

Roslyn
Johnson, Leona Mindell *librarian, educator*

Seattle
Abendroth, Kathi Judkins *archivist*
Bengtson, Betty Grimes *library administrator*
Bishop, Virginia Wakeman *retired librarian and humanities educator*
Blase, Nancy Gross *librarian*
Boylan, Merle Nelson *librarian*
Gallagher, Marian Gould *librarian, educator*
Haines, Irene Lois *librarian*
Hiatt, Peter *library educator*
Jennerich, Elaine *librarian*
Lidgate, Doreen Wanda *retired librarian*
Lipson, Philip Bruce *librarian*
Privat, Jeannette Mary *bank librarian*
Ptacek, William H. *library director*
Stroup, Elizabeth Faye *librarian*
Turner, Tamara Adele *medical librarian*

Spokane
Bender, Betty Wion *librarian*
Burr, Robert Lyndon *library director*

Tacoma
Chase, Judith Helfer *librarian, educator, musician*
Crisman, Mary Frances Borden *librarian*

Toppenish
Veomett, Colleen Michelle *librarian*

Vancouver
Hall, Madelyn Gael Priebe *medical librarian*
Hammer, Sharon Arlene *library director*

Walla Walla
Haley, Anne Elizabeth *library director*
Yaple, Henry Mack *library director*

Yakima
Weber, Joan L. *library director*

WYOMING

Casper
Boughton, Lesley D. *library director*

Cheyenne
Johnson, Wayne Harold *librarian, county official*
Osborn, Lucie P. *library director*
Rounds, Linnea Paula *library administrator*

Sundance
Collier, Gaydell Maier *library director, writer, rancher*

CANADA

ALBERTA

Calgary
MacDonald, Alan Hugh *librarian, university administrator*
Meek, Gerry *library director*

Edmonton
McDougall, Donald Blake *retired government official, librarian*
McKee, Penelope Melna *library director*

Lethbridge
Rand, Duncan D. *librarian*

BRITISH COLUMBIA

Nanaimo
Meadows, Donald Frederick *librarian*

Vancouver
Aalto, Madeleine *library director*
Piternick, Anne Brearley *librarian, educator*

Victoria
Hamilton, Donald Emery *librarian*

SASKATCHEWAN

Saskatoon
Kennedy, Marjorie Ellen *librarian*

ADDRESS UNPUBLISHED

Agee, Victoria Valentine *librarian, freelance indexer*
Bullard, Sharon Welch *librarian*
Curley, Elmer Frank *librarian*
Dutton, Pauline Mae *fine arts librarian*
Flanary, Kathy Venita Moore *librarian*
Gould, Martha Bernice *retired librarian*
Gregor, Dorothy Deborah *librarian*
Harrison, Carol Anne *librarian*
Hearth, Fred E. *librarian, educator*
Lowell, Waverly B. *archivist*
Miele, Anthony William *retired librarian*
Nelson, Helen Martha *retired library director*
Rafael, Ruth Kelson *archivist, librarian, consultant*
Richards, Vincent Philip Haslewood *librarian*
Sadler, Graham Hydrick *library administrator*
Silvia, Raymond Alan *librarian*
Smith, Howard McQueen *librarian*
Smith, Sallye Wrye *librarian*
Waugh, Kathleen Mary *archivist*
Williams, Gordon Roland *librarian*

HUMANITIES: MUSEUMS

UNITED STATES

ALASKA

Fairbanks
Jonaitis, Aldona Claire *museum administrator, art historian*

Gustavus
Jensen, Marvin O. *national park superintendent*

Juneau
Lonner, Thomas Dunstan *museum director*

ARIZONA

Mesa
Hulick, Diana Emery *museum director, art historian, photographic consultant, educator*
Mead, Tray C. *museum administrator*

Phoenix
Grinell, Sheila *museum director*
Lidman, Roger Wayne *museum director*
Sullivan, Martin Edward *museum director*

Portal
Zweifel, Richard George *curator*

Prescott
Willoughby, Susan Nell *museum director*

Tempe
Zeitlin, Marilyn Audrey *museum director*

Tucson
Davis, Daniel Edward *museum director*
Hancocks, David Morgan *museum director, architect*
Yassin, Robert Alan *museum administrator, curator*

CALIFORNIA

Bakersfield
Czaplewski, Russell Anthony *museum curator*
Enriquez, Carola Rupert *museum director*

Berkeley
Benedict, Burton *retired museum director, anthropology educator*

Beverly Hills
Halpern, Nora R. *museum director, art curator*

Caliente
de Fonville, Paul Bliss *historic organization administrator*

Carmel Valley
Heimann, Janet Barbara *volunteer trail consultant*

Carson
Zimmerer, Kathy Louise *university art gallery director*

Costa Mesa
Botello, Troy James *arts administrator, counselor*
Labbe, Armand Joseph *museum curator, anthropologist*
Linton, Margaret Ann *curator*

Del Mar
Wright, David Lee *special events producer, design consultant*

Fresno
Sobey, Edwin J. C. *museum director, oceanographer, consultant*

Fullerton
McGee, Mike James *gallery director, writer*

Hollywood
Byrnes, James Bernard *museum director emeritus*

La Jolla
Beebe, Mary Livingstone *curator*
Davies, Hugh Marlais *museum director*

Long Beach
Glenn, Constance White *art museum director, educator, consultant*
Nelson, Harold Bernhard *museum director*

Los Angeles
Cohen, Daniel Morris *museum administrator, marine biology researcher*
Ela, Patrick Hobson *museum director*
Gluckman, Dale Carolyn *art museum curator*
Hendler, Gordon Lee *curator*
Hirano, Irene Ann Yasutake *museum director*
Holo, Selma Reuben *museum director, educator*
Hopkins, Henry Tyler *art educator, university gallery director*
Kaye, Carole *museum director and curator*
Koshalek, Richard *museum director, consultant*
Kuwayama, George *curator*
Pal, Pratapaditya *museum curator*
Powell, James Lawrence *museum president*
Stern, Louis *gallery owner*
Stooker, Hendrik Cornelis *curator, gallery director*

Los Osos
Dorland, Frank Norton *art conservator*

Malibu
Hess, Catherine Mary *museum curator*
Naef, Weston John *museum curator*

Monterey
Penwell, Donna Carol *museum director*

Newport Beach
Botwinick, Michael *museum director*
Gaiber, Maxine Diane *museum education director*

Oakland
Burns, Catherine Elizabeth *art dealer*
Heyman, Therese Thau *curator, art historian*
Power, Dennis Michael *museum director*

Pacific Grove
Adams, Margaret Bernice *retired museum official*
Bailey, Stephen Fairchild *museum director and curator, ornithologist*

Palm Springs
Golden, Morton Jay *museum director*

Palo Alto
Gubins, Samuel *museum administrator*

Redding
Becker, Stephen Arnold *museum director*

Ridgecrest
Lundstrom, Mary Meyer *museum curator, museum store manager, educator*

Riverside
Green, Jonathan William *museum administrator and educator, artist, author*

Sacramento
Gray, Walter P., III *museum director, consultant*

San Diego
DiMattio, Terry *historic site administrator*
Harris, James Michael *museum director*
Ollman, Arthur Lee *museum director, photographer*
Petersen, Martin Eugene *museum curator*
Scott, Mary Louise *educator, writer*

San Francisco
Austerer-Williams, Eleonore *art gallery owner, director*
Berggruen, John Henry *art gallery executive*
Lane, John Rodger *art museum director*
Leviton, Alan Edward *museum curator*
Lindsay, George Edmund *museum director*
Robertson, Merle Greene *museum administrator*
Schlesinger, Ruth Hirschland *art curator, consultant*
Shangraw, Clarence Frank *museum official*
Smith, James Weldon *museum director*
Thomas, William Geraint *museum administrator*
Whyte, Robert Andrew *art curator, writer*

San Jose
Callan, Josi Irene *museum director*

San Marino
Skotheim, Robert Allen *museum administrator*
Wark, Robert Rodger *art curator*

San Simeon
Barghini, Sandra Jean *curator*

Santa Ana
Keller, Peter Charles *museum director, mineralogist*

Santa Barbara
Karpeles, David *museum director*
Mills, Paul Chadbourne *museum director*

Santa Clara
Schapp, Rebecca Maria *museum director*

Santa Monica
Walsh, John, Jr. *museum director*

Sausalito
Elliott, James Heyer *retired university art museum curator, fine arts consultant*

Stanford
Ratliff, William Elmore *curator, researcher*
Seligman, Thomas Knowles *museum administrator*

Ukiah
Lee, Lila June *historical society officer, library director*

Watsonville
Hernandez, Jo Farb *museum and curatorial consultant*

West Hills
Preusser, Frank Dietrich *cultural heritage preservation consultant*

Yosemite National Park
Forgang, David M. *museum curator*

Yucca Valley
DeMersman, James Richard *museum director*

COLORADO

Boulder
Danilov, Victor Joseph *museum management program director, consultant, writer, educator*
Hay, William Winn *former museum director, natural history and geology educator*
Lanham, Urless Norton *curator*

Colorado Springs
Conway, Wallace Xavier, Sr. *retired curator*
Hoge, Robert Wilson *museum curator*
LeMieux, Linda Dailey *museum director*
Riggs, William G(erry) *art gallery director, museum studies educator*
Warner, Michael D. *museum director*

Denver
Conn, Richard George *retired art museum curator*
Foxley, Matthew C. *art gallery administrator*
Graham, Linda Marie *museum director, photographer*
Harrison, Carole Alberta *museum curator, restaurateur, civic worker*
Hughes, Paul Lucien *art gallery owner*

Grand Junction
Menard, Michael Joseph *museum director*

HAWAII

Aiea
Vail, Mary Barbara *museum consultant*

Honaunau
Shimoda, Jerry Yasutaka *national historic park administrator*

Honolulu
Ellis, George Richard *museum administrator*
Klobe, Tom *art gallery director*
Magee, Donald Edward *national park service administrator*
Matelic, Candace Tangorra *museum studies educator, consultant, museum director*
Sendzikas, Aldona Marija *museum curator*

Kaneohe
Lagoria, Georgianna Marie *curator, writer, editor, visual art consultant*

IDAHO

Pocatello
Jackson, Allen Keith *museum administrator*

MONTANA

Missoula
Brown, Robert Munro *museum director*
Miles, Sheila Lee *artist, consultant*

West Glacier
Lusk, Harlan Gilbert *national park superintendent*
Mihalic, David Anthony *national park administrator*

NEVADA

Elko
Hall, Shawn Richard *museum director*

Las Vegas
Schefcik, Jerry Allen *art gallery administrator, university official*

Reno
Feinhandler, Edward Sanford *writer, photographer, art dealer, sports mentor, consultant, educator*
Spencer, Howard DaLee *art museum curator*

NEW MEXICO

Alamogordo
House, George Michael *museum curator*

Albuquerque
Kosse, Krisztina Maria *museum curator, archaeologist*

Las Cruces
Way, Jacob Edson, III *museum director*

Placitas
Smith, Richard Bowen *retired national park superintendent*

Roswell
Ebie, William D. *museum director*

Santa Fe
Bell, Michael Steven *art curator*
Cerny, Charlene Ann *museum director*
Conley, Zeb Bristol, Jr. *art gallery director*
Dailey, Charles Andrew *museum director, educator*
Hood, Gary Allen *curator, arts consultant*
Livesay, Thomas Andrew *museum administrator, lecturer*
Rudisill, Richard *museum curator, educator*

Silver City
Bettison, Cynthia Ann *museum director, archaeologist*

Taos
Witt, David L. *curator, writer*

OREGON

Ashland
Kramer, George H. *historic preservation consultant*

Eugene
McTigue, Bernard Francis *curator, consultant*

Klamath Falls
Favell, Gene Hunter *museum director*

Portland
Eichinger, Marilynne H. *museum administrator*
McKinley, Loren Dhue *museum director*
Russo, Laura *gallery director*
Schnitzer, Arlene Director *art dealer*
Theisen, Lee Scott *foundation director*
Tramposch, William Joseph *museum director, consultant*

UTAH

Provo
Mason, James Albert *museum director, university dean*

Salt Lake City
Hague, Donald Victor *museum director*
Kohler, Dolores Marie *gallery owner*
Leonard, Glen M. *museum administrator*
Oman, Richard George *museum curator*

WASHINGTON

Bellevue
Douglas, Diane Miriam *museum director*
Trubner, Henry *museum curator*
Warren, James Ronald *retired museum director, author, columnist*

Bellingham
Clark-Langager, Sarah Ann *director, curator, university official*

Longview
Woods, Trudy Ann Olson *gallery director*

Olympia
Lind, Carl Bradley *retired museum director*

Pullman
Watkinson, Patricia Grieve *museum director*

Seattle
Andrews, Richard Otis *museum director*
O'Donnell, Wilson Edward *museum director*
Rullkoetter, Jill E. *museum education administrator*
Wehr, Wesley Conrad *museum curator*
West, Richard Vincent *art museum official*

Tacoma
Paulson, Dennis Roy *museum director, biology educator, curator*

Toppenish
Neaman, Brycene Allen *museum curator*

Wenatchee
Williams, Keith Roy *museum director*

Yakima
Baule, John Alvin *museum director, consultant*

WYOMING

Casper
Mobley, Karen Ruth *art gallery director*

Cody
Hassrick, Peter Heyl *museum director*

Moose
Neckels, Jack *park superintendent*

Rock Springs
Chadey, Henry F. *museum director*

CANADA

ALBERTA

Calgary
Janes, Robert Roy *museum director, archaeologist,*

Drumheller
Naylor, Bruce Gordon *museum director*

Edmonton
Bogusky, Alf *museum director*

Sherwood Park
Finlay, James Campbell *retired museum director*

BRITISH COLUMBIA

North Vancouver
Joyner, John Brooks *museum director*

Vancouver
Ames, Michael McClean *university museum director, anthropology educator*
Holmes, Willard *art gallery director*

Victoria
Barkley, William Donald *museum executive director*
Segger, Martin Joseph *museum director, art history educator*

NEW BRUNSWICK

Fredericton
Lumsden, Ian Gordon *art gallery director*

SASKATCHEWAN

Regina
Oko, Andrew Jan *art gallery director, curator*

ADDRESS UNPUBLISHED

Bacigalupa, Andrea *art gallery owner, writer, artist*
Black, Craig Call *retired museum administrator*
Braunstein, Ruth *art dealer, gallery owner*
Chenhall, Robert Gene *former museum director, consultant, author*
Douglass, Amy Anita *museum director*
Glad, Suzanne Lockley *retired museum director*
Hodson, Sara Suzanne *manuscripts curator*
Mayfield, Signe *curator of exhibitions*
Perrot, Paul Norman *museum director*
Pitts, Terence Randolph *curator and museum director*
Prakapas, Eugene Joseph *art gallery director*
Summerfield, John Robert *textile curator*
Welles, John Galt *retired museum director*
Whitchurch, Charles Augustus *art gallery owner, humanities educator*
Wieser, Siegfried *planetarium executive director*
Young, Edna Elizabeth *art consultant and broker*
Zenev, Irene Louise *museum curator*

INDUSTRY: MANUFACTURING. *See also* FINANCE: FINANCIAL SERVICES.

UNITED STATES

ALASKA

Anchorage
Bennett, Connie Sue *food products executive, real estate investor*
Cattanach, Richard L. *contractor*
DeLoach, Robert Edgar *corporate executive*
Doran, Vincent James *steel fabricating company consultant*
Easley, George Washington *construction executive*

Haines
Kaufman, David Graham *construction company executive*

Juneau
Lauber, Mignon Diane *food processing company executive*
Smith, Charles Anthony *businessman*

Kotzebue
Huss, Charles Maurice *municipal building official*

ARIZONA

Gilbert
Stroble-Thompson, Colette Mary Houle *plastering and stucco company executive*

Glendale
Lopez, Steven Richard *small business owner, consultant*
Martori, Arthur J., Jr. *food products executive*

Lake Havasu City
Coons, Eldo Jess, Jr. *manufacturing company executive*

Litchfield Park
Reid, Ralph Ralston, Jr. *electronics executive, engineer*

Mesa
Bond, Gregory Buck *construction company executive*
DeRosa, Francis Dominic *chemical company executive*
Mast, Jim *food executive*

Phoenix
Atutis, Bernard P. *manufacturing company executive*
Bolen, Michael D. *construction executive*
Chalmers, James A. *consulting company executive*
Davidson, Arlene Marie *product manager*
Francisco, Wayne M(arkland) *automotive executive*
Frisk, Jack Eugene *recreational vehicle manufacturing company executive*
Kopp, David Eugene *manufacturing company executive*
Locher, Walter *agricultural products company*
Mardian, Daniel *construction company director*
Murphy, Gerald W. *construction executive*
Norling, James A. *electronics company executive*
Pettigrew, Steven Lee *healthcare management company executive, consultant*
Platt, James Robert *business executive*
Pope, Robert S. *agricultural products executive*
Schmieder, Carl *jeweler*
Thompson, Charles Edward *electronics company executive*
Thompson, Herbert Ernest *tool and die company executive*
Turner, Dennis M. J. *pharmaceutical executive*
Van Horssen, Charles Arden *manufacturing executive*
Whiting, Arthur Milton *diversified company executive*

Prescott
Parkhurst, Charles Lloyd *electronics company executive*

Sahuarita
Walden, Richard Keith *agri-business executive*

Scottsdale
Johnson, Lee Carroll *electronics company executive*
Linthicum, Gary Rex *construction company executive*
Malohn, Donald A. *manufacturing executive, retired*
Ruhlman, Terrell Louis *business executive*
Walsh, Edward Joseph *toiletries and food company executive*
Wong, Astria Wor *cosmetic business consultant*

Sedona
Bolton, Robert Floyd *construction executive*

Sierra Vista
Meyer, William Trenholm *defense company official, real estate executive*

Sun City
Van Horssen, Arden Darrell *retired manufacturing executive*

Tempe
Begay, Jefferson Lee *general contracting company executive*
Mousseux, Marc Christian *tree-salvage company executive*
Snyder, William Regis, Jr. *construction company executive*

Tolleson
Etchart, Ferdinand J. *food products executive*
Etchart, Mike *agricultural products company executive*
Rousseau, David *agricultural products executive*
Rousseau, Will *agricultural products executive*

Tucson
Acker, Loren Calvin *medical instrument company executive*
Allison, Loyette E. *construction company executive*
Anderson, Raymond Eugene *land revegetation company executive*
Fedrick, C. Richard *food products executive*
McGuire, Sondra Lee *automotive executive*
Sundt, Harry Wilson *construction company executive*
Willoughby, Stuart Carroll *contractor*
Withers, James Clyde *executive high technology company*

Yuma
Curtis, Michael *food products executive*
Pasquinelli, Gary *agricultural products executive*
Riebe, Norman John *contractor*

CALIFORNIA

Alhambra
Fried, Elaine June *business executive*
Hovsepian, Abraham *metal products executive*

Aliso Viejo
Baker, Susan Leigh *manufacturing company executive*
Basler, Richard Alan *biomedical instruments manufacturer*

Altaville
Overton, John Farrell *electronic manufacturing executive, educator*

Anaheim
Baumgartner, Anton Edward *automotive sales professional*
Price, Richard Taft, Jr. *manufacturing company executive*
Rosenberg, Howard Alan *manufacturing executive*
Valdez, James Gerald *automotive aftermarket executive*
Wrigley, William *corporation executive*

Arcadia
Belcher, Donald David *manufacturing company executive*
Eck, Dennis K. *supermarket chain executive*
Plessner, Gerald Maurice *business executive*

Atherton
Goodman, Sam Richard *electronics company executive*
Hogan, Clarence Lester *retired electronics executive*

Bakersfield
Barker, Douglas P. *food products executive*
Evans, Berne *food products company executive*
Grimm, Bob *food products executive*
Grimm, Rod *food products executive*
Marguleas, Howard P. *agricultural products executive*
Reniers, Robert *food products executive*

Benicia
Lipsky, Ian David *contracting executive*

Berkeley
Dolberg, David Spencer *business executive, lawyer, scientist*

Beverly Hills
Casey, Joseph T. *corporate executive*
dePaolis, Potito Umberto *food company executive*
Hoch, Orion Lindel *corporate executive*
Leonis, John Michael *aerospace executive*
Schoenfeld, Lawrence Jon *jewelry manufacturing company executive, travel industry consultant*
Singleton, Henry Earl *industrialist*

Blythe
Fisher, Bart *agricultural products company executive*
Fisher, Dana B. *food product executive*

Borrego Springs
Bowers, Bobby Eugene *metal products executive, small business owner*

Brawley
Brazeel, Dale Michael *food products executive*
Colace, Joseph J. *agricultural products company executive*
Colace, William M. *food products executive*

Buena Park
DeRossett, Deborah Stanton *food company executive*
Knott, Russell H. *food products executive*
Oliphant, Elizabeth Knott *food products executive*

Burbank
Altschul, David Edwin *record company executive, lawyer*
Beymer, Dale Allen *machine shop manager*
Gold, Stanley P. *chemical company executive, manufacturing company executive*
Joseff, Joan Castle *manufacturing executive*

Calabasas
Cohen, William *construction executive*
Lipchik, Harold *company executive*
Marafino, Vincent Norman *aerospace company executive*
Sperber, Burton S. *construction executive*

Campbell
Baluni, Alice *electronics company executive*

Canoga Park
Weisman, Martin Jerome *manufacturing company executive*

Carlsbad
Crooke, Stanley Thomas *pharmaceutical company executive*
Graham, Robert Klark *lens manufacturer*

Castroville
Boutonnet, Edward *food products executive*
Tottino, Leslie *food products executive*

Cerritos
Reid, Wallace Leo *manufacturing executive*

Chico
Mooney, Steve *food products executive*

Chino
Goodman, Lindsey Alan *furniture manufacturing executive, architect*
Porrero, Henry, Jr. *construction company executive*

Chula Vista
Jahn, E. Mark *research specialist*
Manary, Richard Deane *manufacturing executive*

Clovis
Ricchiuti, Frances *food executive*
Rowe, Dee *vintner*
Tatham, William R. *vintner*

Coachella
Nickerson, Mark *food products executive*

Colusa
Carter, Jane Foster *agriculture industry executive*

Compton
McNamara, E. Michael *cosmetics executive*

Concord
Thompson, Jeremiah Beiseker *international medical business executive*

Corona
Reeder, Samuel Kenneth *analytical laboratory executive*

Corona Del Mar
Hochschild, Richard *medical instruments executive, researcher*

Costa Mesa
Brady, John Patrick, Jr. *electronics educator, consultant*
Cubrilovic, Vel *pharmaceutical company executive*
Foell, Ronald R. *builder*
Hazewinkel, Van *manufacturing executive*
Sognefest, Peter William *manufacturing company executive*

Cupertino
Fallin, William L. *computer manufacturing company official*
Hallin, Karl-Eliv Johann *industrial process control company executive*
Mathias, Leslie Michael *electronic manufacturing company executive*

Cypress
Barman, Robert John *home electronics company executive*
Dorn, Marian Margaret *educator, sports management administrator*

Del Mar
Alcorn, Michael Scott *food products executive*

Del Rey
Enoch, Charles Johnson *raisin packing company executive*
Jones, Walt *food executive*

Delano
Caratan, Anton G. *food products executive*
Caratan, George *food products executive*
Pandol, Jack J. *food products executive*
Pandol, Matt *food products executive*
Zaninovich, Marko B. *food products executive*

Diamond Bar
Szostak, Edward Walter, Jr. *pharmaceutical company executive*
Vorlick, Robert Jerry *construction consultant*

Duarte
Bres, Philip Wayne *automotive executive*

Dublin
Witt, Robert Louis *materials manufacturing and sales company executive, lawyer*

Edison
Giumarra, George, Jr. *vintner*

El Cajon
Anderson, Margaret Allyn *carpet showroom manager*

El Segundo
Amerman, John W. *toy company executive*
Brown, Lorraine Ann *administrative services coordinator*
Clough, Charles Marvin *electronics company executive*
Eskridge, James Arthur *toy company executive*
McDonald, Rosa Nell *federal research and budgets manager*
Tennant, Samuel McKibben *aerospace systems company executive*

Emeryville
Nady, John *electronics company executive*

Encinitas
Friedman, Paul *food products executive*

Encino
Davenport, Alfred Larue, Jr. *manufacturing company executive*
Snir, Sol Bezalel *floor covering company executive*

Escondido
Sampson, Richard Arnim *security professional*

Exeter
Evans, Berne, III *food products executive*

Fairfield
Castro, David Alexander *construction executive*

Felton
Vurich, John David *electronics company executive, engineer*

Firebaugh
Perez, Mark *food products executive*
Perez, Thomas *food products executive*

Foster City
Sletten, Kenneth G. *construction executive*

Fountain Valley
Price, Westcott Wilkin, III *health care company executive*

Fowler
Bedrosian, James Kenneth *food products executive*

Fremont
Cuneo, Dennis Clifford *automotive company executive*
Kiang, Min *manufacturing executive*
Lahri, Rajeeva *electronics executive*
Pugliese, Vincent Joseph Alfred *manufacturing executive*

Fresno
Baloian, Edward *food products executive*
Baloian, Timothy *food products executive*
Burford, Richard S. *agricultural products executive*
Donaldson, George Burney *chemical company executive*
Emigh, Mike *agricultural products company executive*
Mathis, Jennifer *food products executive*

Fullerton
Nesty, Glenn Albert *manufacturing executive*
Rosso, Louis T. *scientific instrument manufacturing company executive*
Stollsteimer, John F. *food company executive*

Gardena
Kanner, Edwin Benjamin *electrical manufacturing company executive*
Salesky, William Jeffrey *manufacturing company executive*

Glendale
Anderson, Bradford William *food company sales executive*

Gold River
Harper, Robert Levell *pharmaceutical company executive*

Gonzales
Silva, Ed *food products executive*
Silva, Evelyn *food products executive*

Greenfield
Munoz, John Joseph *transportation company executive*

Gridley
Tanimoto, George *agricultural executive, farmer*

Guadalupe
Murphy, Tim *food products executive*
Tompkins, Nick *agricultural products executive*

Hawthorne
Reiner, Thomas Karl *manufacturing company executive*
Roberts, George Christopher *manufacturing executive*
Slusser, Robert Wyman *aerospace company executive*

Hayward
Banister, James Henry, Jr. *manufacturing company executive, consultant*
Hwang, Kou Mau *pharmaceutical executive*
Masterson, Linda Histen *medical company executive*
Minzner, Dean Frederick *aviation company executive*

Healdsburg
Long, Zelma Reed *winery administrator*

Hesperia
Butcher, Jack Robert *manufacturing executive*

Huntington Beach
Crane, Steven *financial company executive*
Joseph, Ezekiel (Ed Joseph) *manufacturing company executive*
Kovach, Ronald *footwear manufacturing executive*
McKasson, Cheri Ann *winery executive*
Thomas-Cote, Nancy Denece *office products manufacturing company executive*

Indio
York, Douglas Arthur *manufacturing and construction company executive*

Irvine
Combs, John Francis *manufacturing company executive*
Copeland, Lawrence R. *construction company executive*
Haggerty, Charles A. *electronics executive*
Herbert, Gavin Shearer *health care products company executive*
Moyer, Albert J. *company executive, financial analyst*
Qureshey, Safi U. *electronics manufacturing company executive*
Reeder, Russell Robert *automotive company executive, engineer*
Shepherd, William C. *pharmaceutical company executive*
Wakefield, Howard *medical representative*
Williams, James E. *food products manufacturing company executive*

Ivanhoe
Meling, Eric M. *food executive*
Story, Paul *food products executive*

Kensington
Somogyi, Laszlo Peter *food technologist*

Kenwood
Richardson, Mary Weld *company executive*

King City
Giudici, Francis *food products executive*

Kingsburg
Bliss, Edwin Crosby *business executive, consultant*

Knights Landing
Spahr, Peter *agricultural products executive*

La Canada Flintridge
Spencer, Herbert Ward, III *air pollution control manufacturing company executive*

La Habra
Golleher, George *food company executive*

La Jolla
Johnson, Peter *pharmaceutical executive*
Koplin, Donald Leroy *health products executive, consumer advocate*

Monday, John Christian *manufacturing company executive*

La Mesa
Bourke, Lyle James *electronics company executive, small business owner*

La Puente
Scritsmier, Jerome Lorenzo *manufacturing company executive*

Lafayette
Shurtleff, William Roy *food products executive*

Laguna Beach
Feldman, Fredric Joel *health products executive*
Youngquist, Andrew Lance *construction executive*

Lebec
Haskell, Donald *agricultural products executive*

Livingston
Fox, Robert August *food company executive*
Shamgochian, Theron *food products executive*

Lodi
Elkins, Carl *food products executive*
Mettler, Leeman *food executive*

Long Beach
Bos, John Arthur *aircraft manufacturing executive*
Hood, Robert H., Jr. *aircraft manufacturing company executive*
Kuhn, John Alan *gas products plant executive*
McGihon, Michael Edwin *sheet metal manufacturing executive*
McGuire, James Charles *aircraft company executive*
Sun, Chieh *electronics company executive*

Los Altos
Albin, Randy Clark *record company executive*
Kao, Cheng Chi *electronics executive*

Los Angeles
Andrade, Joe Russell *lumber company executive, artist*
Berger, Robert Sydney *paper company executive*
Borneman, John Paul *pharmaceutical executive*
Brooks, Tempe Boyce-Smith *manufacturing company executive*
Burns, Dan W. *manufacturing company executive*
Castle, Timothy James *food products executive*
Crites, Richard Ray *international franchising company executive*
Dawes, Wallace Ernest *paper specialist, small business owner*
Dodds, Dale Irvin *chemicals executive*
Drake, Hudson Billings *aerospace and electronics company executive*
Dundon, Brian R. *motor company executive*
El Shami, Ahmed Saïd *company executive*
Forester, Bernard I. *recreational equipment company executive*
Gerstell, A. Frederick *aggregates/asphalt/concrete manufacturing exec*
Giacoletto, Joseph Richard *electronics company executive*
Gill, Steven *food products executive*
Handschumacher, Albert Gustave *retired corporate executive*
Huntley, Alice Mae *manufacturing executive*
Irani, Ray R. *oil, gas and chemical company executive*
Jones, Jerve Maldwyn *construction company executive*
Karatz, Bruce E. *business executive*
Kasmer, Irene *fashion and textile executive*
Korn, Lester Bernard *business executive, diplomat*
Kurtzman, Alan *cosmetics company executive*
Murphy, Gerald D. *agricultural products, grain company executive*
Nakra, Naresh Kumar *food products executive*
O'Gara, Barbara Ann *soap company executive*
Perkins, William Clinton *company executive*
Perry, William Joseph *food processing company executive*
Ruth, Craig *business executive*
Rutledge, William P. *manufacturing company executive*
Smith, Richard *construction executive*
Thomas, Christopher Robert *food products company executive*
Yagjian, Michael Arthur *food company executive*
Yount, George Stuart *paper company executive*
Zack, James G(ordon), Jr. *construction claims executive, consultant*

Los Banos
Prudhomme, Ronald Edward *food processing executive*

Los Gatos
Marks, Peter Amasa *technical consulting firm administrator*
Nitz, Frederic William *electronics company executive*

Los Osos
Maddy, Donald Lee *computer company executive, software developer*

Lynwood
Stamps, Peter David *manufacturing administrator*

Madera
Pierre, Phil *food products executive*

Marina Del Rey
Brown, Anthony B. *aerospace executive*
Tan Wong, Lily *textile executive*

Menlo Park
Bremser, George, Jr. *electronics company executive*
Cook, Paul M. *technology company executive*
Saldich, Robert Joseph *electronics company executive*
Sovish, Richard Charles *retired manufacturing executive, consultant*
Wegenstein, Martin Willi *electric company executive*
Westcott, Brian John *manufacturing executive*

Merced
Bianchi, Richard *food products executive*

Mill Valley
Winskill, Robert Wallace *manufacturing executive*

Milpitas
Brown, David A. *computer hardware company executive*
Huyghe, Jacques M. *manufacturing executive*
Roddick, David Bruce *construction company executive*

Mission Viejo
Burns, Daniel Michael *manufacturing company financial executive*
Gilbert, Heather Campbell *manufacturing company executive*
McDonnel, William George *chemical instrumentation executive*
Sheridan, George Edward *manufacturing company executive*

Monterey
Tumelson, Betsy Martin *consulting and training company executive*

Moraga
Westernoff, W. Gary *construction company executive*

Mountain View
Babu, Uma Mahesh *health/medical products executive*
Cusumano, James Anthony *chemical company executive, former recording artist*
Gray, Donald Allan *computer software international sales executive*
Levy, Ricardo Benjamin *chemical company executive*
McCracken, Edward R. *electronics executive*
Morris, Michael H. *computer company executive*

Napa
Graves, David William *winery executive*
Oren, Joseph *pharmaceutical research company executive, physician*

Newport Beach
Jones, Roger Wayne *electronics executive*
Lawson, Thomas Cheney *fraud examiner*
Pritchard, Joan Trehy *retired aerospace company executive*
Rogers, Robert Reed *manufacturing company executive*

Northridge
Toole, Floyd Edward *manufacturing company executive*

Novato
Womack, Thomas Houston *manufacturing company executive*

Oakland
Ausfahl, William Friend *household products company executive*
Hansen, Donald Curtis *manufacturing executive*
Maier, Cornell C. *aluminum and chemical company executive*
Sullivan, G. Craig *chemical executive*

Oakville
Mondavi, Robert Gerald *winery executive*
Mondavi, Robert Michael *vintner*

Oceano
Donovan, Dennis *agricultural products executive*

Oceanside
Garruto, John Anthony *cosmetics executive*
Garruto, Michelle Bartok *cosmetic company executive*
Kolden, Kenneth Dale *semiconductor company executive*

Ojai
Weill, Samuel, Jr. *automobile company executive*

Ontario
Carlson, Ralph William, Jr. *food products company executive*

Orange
Skilling, David van Diest *manufacturing executive*

Oxnard
Boskovich, George, Jr. *food products executive*
Duda, Luther *food products executive*
Gill, David *food products executive*
Hansen, Margaret *food executive*
Jackson, Gene *food products executive*
Poole, Henry Joe, Jr. *business executive*

Pacific Palisades
Bowen, Christine Lyn *billing company executive*

Palmdale
Toney, W. Alan *battery manufacturing company executive*

Palo Alto
Chow, Winston *engineering research executive*
De Passe, Derrel Blauvelt *electronics industry executive*
Early, James Michael *electronics research consultant*
Freiman, Paul E. *pharmaceutical company executive*
Gerstel, Martin Stephen *pharmaceutical company executive*
Hewlett, William (Redington) *manufacturing company executive, electrical engineer*
Kline, Pamela Iris *consulting company executive*
Mario, Ernest *pharmaceutical company executive*
O'Rourke, J. Tracy *manufacturing company executive*
Packard, David *manufacturing company executive, electrical engineer*
Platt, Lewis Emmett *electronics company executive*
Reagan, Joseph Bernard *aerospace executive*
Schreiner, George Frederic *pharmaceutical executive, medical researcher*
Shulman, Michael Geoffrey *pharmaceutical researcher*

Palos Verdes Peninsula
Dalton, James Edward *aerospace executive, retired air force officer*
Leone, William Charles *retired manufacturing executive*
Pfund, Edward Theodore, Jr. *electronics company executive*
Thomas, Hayward *manufacturing company executive*
Wilson, Theodore Henry *retired electronics company executive, aerospace engineer*

Pasadena
Falick, Abraham Johnson *printing company executive*
Glanville, John Hart *construction executive*
Jenkins, Royal Gregory *manufacturing executive*
Langford, Thomas L. *construction executive*
Miller, Charles Daly *lumber company executive*
Neal, Philip Mark *diversified manufacturing executive*
Pieroni, Leonard J. *engineering and construction company executive*
Porter, Peter *food products executive*
Smith, Howard Russell *manufacturing company executive*
Staniszewski, John *food products executive*
Sudarsky, Jerry M. *industrialist*
Watson, Noel G. *construction executive*

Piedmont
Smith, Charles Conard *refractory company executive*

Placentia
Strom, Mark Alan *manufacturing executive*

Pleasanton
Busboom, Larry D. *food products company executive*
Giacolini, Earl L. *agricultural products company executive*
Milton, Henry Benford Hollis *automotive executive*
Perry, James R. *construction company executive*
Resare, Craig *food executive*
Stager, Donald K. *construction company executive*
Weiss, Robert Stephen *medical manufacturing and services company financial executive*

Pomona
Puckett, Paul David *electronics company executive*

Poway
Aschenbrenner, Frank Aloysious *former diversified manufacturing company executive*

Rancho Cordova
Gebhart, John E., III *health products company executive*
Plumlee, Kenneth B. *health products executive*

Rancho Cucamonga
DeTemple, William Charles *technology executive*

Rancho Mirage
Foster, David Ramsey *soap company executive*

Rancho Palos Verdes
White, Brittan Romeo *manufacturing company executive*

Rancho Santa Fe
Jordan, Charles Morrell *retired automotive designer*

Rancho Santa Margarita
Wong, Wallace *medical supplies company executive, real estate investor*

Redding
Schreiber, Otto William *retired manufacturing company executive*

Redondo Beach
Dockstader, Jack Lee *electronics executive*
Hartwick, Thomas Stanley *aerospace company executive*
Kagiwada, Reynold Shigeru *advanced technology manager*
Sabin, Jack Charles *engineering and construction firm executive*

Redwood City
Ellison, Lawrence J. *computer software company executive*
Ford, Freeman Arms *manufacturing company executive*
Hegedus, John S. *medical products executive*
Howe, Lee Martin *electronics marketing executive, army officer*
Kung, Frank F. C. *medical products executive*
Nosler, Peter Cole *construction company executive*
Wang, Chen Chi *electronics company executive, real estate executive, finance company executive, investment services executive, international trade executive*

Reedley
Surabian, Ann *food products executive*
Surabian, Dennis G. *food products executive*

Riverside
Crean, John C. *housing and recreational vehicles manufacturing company executive*
Falbo, Nadine Lois *contractor*
Kummer, Glenn F. *construction and automotive executive*
Smith, Elden Leroy *recreational vehicle company executive*

Rosemead
Doyle, Harley Joseph *senior prep operator*

Sacramento
Brown, William Edwin *construction executive, educator*
Geiken, Alan Richard *contractor*

Salinas
Anderson, David *agricultural products executive*
Armstrong, John A. *food products executive*
Carr, Noel *food products executive*
Church, Tom *food products executive*
Drever, Mark *food products executive*
Escamilla, Richard *farm labor contracting executive*
Esquivel, Joe G. *food products executive*
Esquivel, Mary *agricultural products company executive*
Frudden, Ronald *agricultural products executive*
Gheen, Betty M. *food products executive*
Griffin, Stephen *food products executive*
Long, Howard *agricultural products executive*
Lugg, James R. *agricultural products executive*
Mann, Harold W. *agricultural products executive*
Mills, Basil E. *food products executive*
Mills, Roger E. *food products executive*
Nunes, Frank R., Jr. *food products executive*
Secondo, Mitchell R. *food products executive*
Taylor, Bruce *agricultural products executive*
Taylor, Steven Bruce *agriculture company executive*

San Bruno
Agresti, Jack Joseph *construction company executive*

San Carlos
Gutow, Bernard Sidney *packaging manufacturing company executive*
Ratcliff, Bruce Ephlin *hoist company executive*

San Clemente
Cate, Floyd Mills *electronic components executive*
Lopina, Robert Ferguson *aerospace company executive*

San Diego
Abbott, Robert T. *pharmaceutical company executive*
Anjard, Ronald Paul, Sr. *business and industry executive, consultant, educator, technologist, importer*
Blumberg, Robert Lee *manufacturing executive*
Brent, Richard Samuel *manufacturing company executive*
Carver, Juanita Ash *plastic company executive*
Childs, John David *computer hardware and services company executive*
Chung, Hsin-Hsien *electronics company executive, electrical engineer*
Cobianchi, Thomas Theodore *engineering and marketing executive, educator*
Dendo, Albert Ulysses *electronics executive*
Duddles, Charles Weller *food company executive*
Gordon, Bradley B. *pharmaceutical research executive*
Greene, Howard E., Jr. *pharmaceutical executive*
Harriett, Judy Anne *medical equipment company executive*
Harris, Marcus William *construction executive*
Hausmann, Werner Karl *pharmaceutical executive*
James, Virginia Lynn *contracts executive*
Jones, Ronald H. *computer information systems executive*
Keith, Norman Thomas *aerospace company administrator*
Kranzler, Jay D. *pharmaceutical executive*
Kull, Lorenz A. *scientific research company executive*
Leuthe, Andrew Peter *manufacturing company executive*
Luby, Charles Strong *company executive*
Nussbaum, Jon Kimbal *defense contractor executive*
Oldham, Christopher Russell *wine company executive*
Reff, Mitchell Elliot *pharmaceutical company administrator*
Robinson, David E. *pharmaceuticals executive*
Schonebaum, Alfred *food company executive*
Segal, Carl Michael *electronics company executive*
Shirley, John Jeffery *manufacturing executive*
Thueson, David Orel *pharmaceutical executive, researcher, educator, writer*
Watari, Shinichiro *holding company executive*
Young, Lih-Jiuan Shiau *energy research and development company manager*

San Dimas
Belcher, William Walter, Jr. *electronics company executive*

San Francisco
Brindley, Robert E. *food products executive*
Chiaverini, John Edward *construction company executive*
Clark, Richard Ward *food industry executive, consultant*
Couse, R. D. *construction company executive*
Dreusike, Donald *construction executive*
Gates, Milo Sedgwick *construction company executive*
Grubb, David H. *construction company president*
Gumucio, Fernando Raul *foods and beverage company executive*
Haas, Peter E., Sr. *retired manufacturing company executive*
Haas, Robert Douglas *apparel manufacturing company executive*
Haas, Walter A., Jr. *retired apparel company executive, professional baseball executive*
Hepler, Kenneth Russel *manufacturing executive*
Jacobs, Robert Neil *meat industry executive*
James, George Barker, II *apparel industry executive*
Kaune, James Edward *ship repair company executive, former naval officer*
Kreitzberg, Fred Charles *construction management company executive*
Lee, Lou S. *printing company executive, developer*
McDowell, David E. *pharmaceutical executive*
Mullenix, Travis H. *food products company executive*
Muratore, Marilyn Ann *contractor*
Oppel, Andrew John *apparel company executive*
Richards, John M. *wood and paper products company executive*
Smith, Lee Clark *apparel company executive*
Smith, Theodore W. *construction executive*
Tusher, Thomas William *apparel company executive*
Wertheimer, Robert E. *paper company executive*
Wilson, Ian Robert *food company executive*
Wojcik, Richard Frank *pharmaceutical company executive*

San Jacinto
Minor, Larry J. *food products executive*

San Jose
Benzing, David Warren *semiconductor equipment company executive*
Conner, Finis F. *electronics company executive*
Goodman, Sam *food products executive*

Gudorf, Greg David *marketing and sales executive*
Hill, Anna Marie *manufacturing executive*
Jacobson, Raymond Earl *electronics company executive*
Mariani, Mark A. *food products executive*
Melehan, Joseph P. *food products executive*
Merrill, Robert Edward *special machinery manufacturing company executive*
Scalise, George Martin *electronics company executive*
Schroeder, William John *electronics executive*
Zajac, John *semiconductor equipment company executive*

San Leandro
Kern, Eugene Francis *corporation executive*

San Lorenzo
Downey, James Edgar *manufacturing executive*

San Luis Obispo
Babcock, Rodney Lee *manufacturing manager*
Johanson, Jerry Ray *company executive*

San Luis Rey
Hoar, Warren Thomas *automotive executive, consultant*

San Marcos
Blackburn, Charles Edward *company executive*
Page, Leslie Andrew *disinfectant manufacturing company executive*

San Mateo
Aadahl, Jorg *corporate executive*
Besse, Robert Gale *food technologist*
Boyd, Robert Jamison *construction equipment company executive*
Grammater, Rudolf Dimitri *retired construction executive*
Leong, Carol Jean *electrologist*

San Rafael
Benzler, Bruce C. *healthcare executive*

Sanger
Albertson, David *food products executive*
Chooljian, Leo *food products executive*
Chooljian, Mehran *food products executive*
Reese, Dudley *food products executive*

Santa Ana
Baik, Hyo Whi *automotive import company executive*
Buster, Edmond Bate *metal products company executive*
Ramsay, Mackay *food executive*
Washburn, Lawrence Robert *manufacturing executive*
Yuen, Andy Tak Sing *electronics executive*

Santa Barbara
Weinstock, Carol Ann *manufacturing executive*

Santa Clara
Amberiadis, Kostas G. *electronics company executive*
Amelio, Gilbert Frank *electronics company executive*
Baird, Mellon Campbell, Jr. *electronics industry executive*
Craigie, Earle James *manufacturing consultant*
Dunlap, F. Thomas, Jr. *electronics company executive, engineer, lawyer*
Grove, Andrew S. *electronics company executive*
House, David L. *electronics components company executive*
Moore, Gordon E. *electronics company executive*
Parikh, Anjan *electronics company executive*

Santa Clarita
Fix-Romlow, Jeanne Kay *hair care products company executive*
Mahler, David *chemical company executive*

Santa Cruz
Broadway, Nancy Ruth *landscape design and construction company executive, consultant, model and actress*

Santa Fe Springs
Locke, John Gardner *chemical company executive*
Lovatt, Arthur Kingsbury, Jr. *manufacturing company executive*

Santa Maria
Ardantz, Henri *agricultural products executive*
Ferini, Robert Pat *agricultural products company executive*

Santa Monica
Deckert, Harlan Kennedy, Jr. *manufacturing company official*
Marsden, Eugene Dennis, Sr. *bleacher seating manufacturing executive*
Seymour, Jeffrey Alan *governmental relations consultant*
Warner, Lee Michael *food products executive*

Santa Paula
Dillard, Michael L. *food products company executive*

Santa Rosa
Jackson, Jess S. *vintner*
Scott, Peter, Jr. *vintner*
Stolte, Charles Albert *company executive*

Santa Ynez
Ellion, M. Edmund *engineering executive*

Santee
Canter, Barry Mitchell *electronics specialist, musician*

Saratoga
Eissmann, Walter James *consulting company executive*

Sausalito
Koons, Todd L. *agricultural products executive*
Swanson, Lee Richard *computer security executive*

Seal Beach
Bacon, Paul Caldwell *training system company executive, aviation consultant, engineering test pilot*
Beall, Donald Ray *multi-industry high-technology company executive*
Iacobellis, Sam Frank *aerospace company executive*
Laidlaw, Victor D. *construction executive*
Yarymovych, Michael Ihor *manufacturing company executive*

Sebastopol
Sugrue, Donal *food products executive*

Sherman Oaks
Best, Barbara *personal manager*
Hanlin, Russell L. *citrus products company executive*

Solana Beach
Brody, Arthur *industrial executive*
Daniels, James Arthur *electronics sales company executive*

Soledad
Valdez, Horacio *food products executive*

Sonoma
Sasaki, Y. Tito *business services company executive*

Soquel
Goodman, Charles Schaffner, Jr. *food product executive, consultant*

South San Francisco
Crowley, Jerome Joseph, Jr. *manufacturing company executive*
Gallo, Joseph E. *vintner*
Gorman, Bruce Charles *health care executive*
Henderson, Thomas James *construction company executive*

Stockton
Bahma, Jerry *agricultural products company executive*
Corkern, Robert J. *agricultural products company executive*
Cuff, William, IV *food company executive*
Guardino, Sal *food executive*
Haase, Robert William *executive bottle water company*
Speckman, Herbert *agricultural products executive*
Speckman, Joyce *agricultural products executive*

Sunnyvale
Chang, Kuang-Yeh *microelectronics technologist*
Fairweather, Edwin Arthur *electronics company executive*
Green, Marjorie *automotive distribution, import and manufacturing company executive*
Hind, Harry William *pharmaceutical company executive*
Holbrook, Anthony *manufacturing company executive*
Kempf, Martine *voice control device manufacturing company executive*
Koriat, Raphael *manufacturing company executive*
Lewis, John Clark, Jr. *manufacturing company executive*
Lewis, John Thomson Condell *aerospace company executive*
Sanders, Walter Jeremiah, III *electronics company executive*
Schapira, Morey Rael *electronics sales executive*
Spilker, James J., Jr. *electronics executive*
Stein, Stephen *electronics executive*
Tramiel, Jack *computer game company executive*
Tramiel, Sam *microcomputer and video game company executive*
Woolsey, Roy Blakeney *electronics company executive*
Zalucky, Alexander David *automation company executive*
Zelencik, Stephen J. *electronics company executive*

Tarzana
Broadhurst, Norman Neil *manufacturing executive*

Temecula
Roemmele, Brian Karl *electronics, publishing, financial and real estate executive*
Traner, Norman *food products executive*

Thermal
Kitagawa, Joe *food products executive*
Kitagawa, Kiyoko *food products executive*

Thousand Oaks
Binder, Gordon M. *health and medical products executive*
DeLorenzo, David A. *food products executive*
Huang, Jen-Tzaw *pharmaceutical executive*
Lee, Lily Kiang *scientific research company executive*
Pope, Edward John Andrew *corporate executive, consultant*

Torrance
Berger, Howard Martin *industrial and service company executive*
Chandler, Richard Hill *medical products company executive*
Greaser, Constance Udean *automotive industry executive*
Kasari, Leonard Samuel *quality control professional, concrete consultant*
Lee, James King *technology corporation executive*
Mann, Michael Martin *electronics company executive*
Rohrberg, Roderick George *welding consultant*
Togo, Yukiyasu *automotive executive*
Woodhull, John Richard *electronics company executive*

Tracy
Esformes, Joseph *agricultural products company executive*
Esformes, Nathan *food products executive*

Turlock
Arias, Joe *agricultural products company executive*

Tustin
Breuer, Werner Alfred *plastics company executive*

Valley Ford
Clowes, Garth Anthony *electronics executive, consultant*

Vernon
Ziegler, Glenn I. *manufacturing company executive*

Walnut Creek
Cadieux, Robert D. *chemical company executive*
Myers, Homer Samuel *technology company executive*
Palmer, Vincent Allan *construction company consultant*
Roach, John D. C. *manufacturing company executive*
Roath, Stephen D. *pharmaceutical company executive*
Sullivan, Edward Joseph *electrotype company executive*

Watsonville
Bennett, Paul Grover *agribusiness executive*
Capurro, Frank L. *food products executive*
Costanzo, Patrick M. *constuction executive*
Jordan, William W. *food executive*
Manfre, Michael *food products executive*
Roberts, Richard Heilbron *construction company executive*
Solari, R. C. *heavy construction company executive*
Watts, David H. *construction company executive*

West Hills
Krive, Irwin *new products development company executive*

Westlake Village
Blum, Fred Andrew *electronics company executive*
Day, Janice Eldredge *cosmetic company executive*
Troxell, Lucy Davis *consulting firm executive*

Wilmington
Hamai, James Yutaka *business executive*

Woodside
Skieller, Christian *manufacturing executive*

Yorba Linda
Forth, Kevin Bernard *beverage distributing industry consultant*

Yountville
Farver, Ed *vintner*

Yucaipa
Allen, Kurt Leonard *poultry industry executive*

COLORADO

Arvada
Holden, George Fredric *brewing company executive, policy specialist, consultant*

Aurora
Kile, Raymond Lawrence *aerospace project manager, consultant*

Bayfield
Burton, Clifton Allen *manufacturing company executive*

Boulder
Abbott, Gregory B. *pharmaceutical executive*
Soll, Larry *pharmaceutical executive*
Tetlow, William Lloyd *computer consultant*

Colorado Springs
Deiotte, Charles Edward *computer software company executive*
Devens, Michael William *construction, contract disputes consultant*
Ehrhorn, Richard William *electronics company executive*
Hill, Roger Wendell *sugar company executive*

Denver
Bennett, James P. *construction executive*
Bowlen, Patrick Dennis *holding company executive, lawyer, professional sports team executive*
Clark, Walter W. *construction executive*
Crawford, Richard A., Jr. *corporate executive*
Ferguson, Bruce A. *construction executive, contractor*
Gates, Charles Cassius *rubber company executive*
Gronning, Lloyd Joseph *engineering company executive, civil engineer*
Johnson, James Gibson, Jr. *community recycling specialist*
Lameiro, Paul Ambrose *manufacturing executive*
Lohre, John Owen *retired leasing company executive*
Onofrio, Joe Frederick, III *piano company executive*
Putnam, J. O. *construction executive*
Rosa, Fredric David *residential construction executive*
Shreve, Theodore Norris *construction company executive*
Stephens, William Thomas *forest products manufacturing company executive*
Stevenson, John Francis *beverage company administrator*

Englewood
Bauer, Randy Mark *management training firm executive*
Bui, Tuan Sy *biomedical company executive, researcher*
Routson, Clell Dennis *manufacturing company executive*
Runice, Robert E. *retired corporate executive*

Erie
Hohner, Kenneth Dwayne *retired fodder company executive*

Fort Collins
Watz, Martin Charles *brewery executive*

Golden
Babb, Alvin Charles *beverage company executive*
Coors, Peter Hanson *beverage company executive*
Coors, William K. *brewery executive*
Malone, Michael William *electronics executive, software engineer*
Rechholtz, Robert August *brewing company executive*
Salazar, Olga *brewery official*

Greeley
Carrico, Stephen J. *construction company executive*
Morgensen, Jerry Lynn *construction company executive*
Mueller, Donald Dean *food company executive*

Lakewood
Hackbarth, Dean Robert *manufacturing executive*
Heath, Gary Brian *manufacturing firm executive, engineer*

Littleton
Gammill, Darryl Curtis *business executive*
Gertz, David Lee *homebuilding company executive*
Heath, Edward V. *rubber company executive*
Price, Gayl Baader *residential construction company administrator*

Longmont
Hahn, Yubong *electro-optics company executive*

Louisville
Poppa, Ryal Robert *manufacturing company executive*

Monument
Karasa, Norman Lukas *home builder, geologist*

Pueblo
Emery, Earl Eugene *steel company executive*

Rocky Ford
Holder, Frank *agricultural products executive*
Holder, J. Hal *food products executive*

Wellington
Grant, Lewis O. *agricultural products executive, meteorology educator*

CONNECTICUT

Greenwich
Wearly, William Levi *business executive*

FLORIDA

Fernandina Beach
Eaton, Henry Taft *forest products executive, consultant*

GEORGIA

Marietta
Richards, Joe McCall *chemical company executive*

HAWAII

Captain Cook
Vidgen, Rick *food products executive*

Honolulu
Andrasick, James Stephen *agribusiness company executive*
Barbieri, David Arthur *company executive*
Bawden, Murray G. *construction executive*
Buyers, John William Amerman *agribusiness and specialty foods company executive*
Couch, John Charles *diversified company executive*
Gary, James Frederick *business and energy advising company executive*
Osada, Stan *construction executive*
Schnack, Gayle Hemingway Jepson (Mrs. Harold Clifford Schnack) *corporate executive*
Usui, Leslie Raymond *clothing executive*
Wilson, Roderick T. *food products executive*
Wilson, William J. *construction executive*

Kahului
Ackerman, Linda Diane *manufacturing executive*
Meyer, Paul J. *food products executive*

Kaumakani
Kennett, E. Alan *agricultural products executive*

Keaau
Cole, Guy *food products executive*
Cole, Lecil *agricultural products company executive*

Wailuku
Viglione, Eugene Lawrence *automotive executive*

IDAHO

Boise
Clausner, Marlin David, Jr. *forest products company executive*
Dorman, Rex Lee *forest products executive*
Ferguson, E. Robert *construction and engineering company executive*
Fery, John Bruce *forest products company executive*
Grant, Stephen R. *construction executive, lawyer*
Harad, George Jay *manufacturing company executive*
Parrish, Richard B. *manufacturing executive*
Sullivan, James Kirk *forest products company executive*

Caldwell
Symms, Richard A. *vintner*

Hayden
Wogsland, James Willard *retired heavy machinery manufacturing executive*

Ketchum
Kreitler, Richard Rogers *company executive*

Nampa
Atkinson, Rick Milton *manufacturing executive*

Post Falls
Jacklin, Doyle *food products executive*
Jacklin, Duane *agricultural products executive*

Salmon
Snook, Quinton *construction company executive*

ILLINOIS

Hoffman Estates
Gast, Nancy Lou *chemical company executive*

Itasca
Fowler, Jack W. *printing company executive*

Schaumburg
Brenner, Arnold S. *electronics company executive*

MISSISSIPPI

Pascagoula
St. Pe, Gerald J. *manufacturing company executive*

MISSOURI

Kansas City
Dillon, George Chaffee *manufacturing company executive*

MONTANA

Anaconda
Rustad, Billie Jo *check recovery business owner*

Billings
Coulter, Clark *company executive*

Butte
Tuck, Michael Ray *technical services executive*

Great Falls
Sletten, John Robert *construction company executive*
Weissman, Jerrold *metal products executive*

Helena
Warren, Christopher Charles *electronics executive*

NEVADA

Fallon
Tedford, Jack Nowlan, III *construction executive, small business owner*

Henderson
Walker, Daniel David, Jr. *lime company executive*

Las Vegas
Bernard, Thelma Rene *property management professional*
Joseph, Conrad *home health care executive*
Nicoletti, William Walter *pharmaceutical company executive*
Opfer, Neil David *educator, consultant*
Strahan, Julia Celestine *electronics company executive*
Tabascio, Stefano Antonino *chemical lubricant company executive*
Warthen, John Edward *construction, leasing and finance executive*

Minden
Harker, Roger George *manufacturing company executive*

Reno
Lindemann, George *agricultural products executive*
Mahin, Glenda Gordon *product development specialist, hydrologist*

Sparks
Kramer, Gordon Edward *manufacturing executive*
Root, William Dixon *construction company executive*

NEW JERSEY

East Hanover
Knight, Frank James *medical sciences liaison*

NEW MEXICO

Alamogordo
Linde, Gary J. *goldsmith*

Albuquerque
Foflygen, Ronald Wayne *manufacturing executive*
Friberg, George Joseph *electronics company executive*
Greer, Darrell Stephen *production operator, finance executive*
Karler, Henry *agricultural products executive*
Karler, Jess *agricultural products executive*
Reynolds, Angus Stuart, Jr. *instructional technologist*
Robinson, Arnold *manufacturing executive*
Rust, John Laurence *manufacturing company executive*
Winfield, Armand Gordon *international plastics consultant, educator*

Deming
Rivett, Robert Wyman *retired pharmaceutical company executive*

Kirtland AFB
Ehrhorn, Thomas Frederick *electronics engineer*

Las Cruces
Cowden, Louis Fredrick *electronics executive, engineer*

Rio Rancho
Dougherty, Rae Ann *semiconductor manufacturing company executive*

Roswell
Armstrong, Billie Bert *retired highway contractor*

Santa Fe
Bearwald, Jean Haynes *company executive*
Odell, John H. *construction company executive*
Robinson, Charles Wesley *energy company executive*

NEW YORK

New York
Johnson, Vilia Jocelyn *perfume company executive*
Munera, Gerard Emmanuel *manufacturing company executive*
Sprague, Peter Julian *semiconductor company executive, lecturer*

OHIO

Miamisburg
Northrop, Stuart Johnston *manufacturing company executive*

OREGON

Beaverton
Donahue, Richard King *athletic apparel executive, lawyer*
Hayes, Delbert J. *athletic company executive*
Knight, Philip H(ampson) *shoe manufacturing company executive*
Long, Tom *manufacturing company executive*
Strong, Carolyn Ray *electronics company official*

Bend
Babcock, Walter Christian, Jr. *membrane company executive*
Dory, Gerry R. "Rudy" *food products executive*

Burns
Bishop, James Allen *wood products consultant*

Eugene
Leeds, Elizabeth Louise *miniature collectibles executive*

Grants Pass
Stevens-Allen, David Joseph (Marquess of Aln, Viscount of St. Etienne, Baron of St. John and of Zellan) *construction executive*

Hermiston
Betz, Richard *agricultural products executive*

Hood River
Garcia, David *agricultural products executive*
Girardelli, Ronald K. *food products executive*

Medford
Hannum, Gerald Luther (Lou Hannum) *retired tire manufacturing company official*

Milwaukie
Jones, Alan C. *grocery company executive*

Oregon City
Abbott, Robert Carl *management company executive*

Portland
Bishop, B. H. *textile manufacturing executive*
Bishop, C. M., Jr. *textile company executive*
Cooley, Edward H. *castings manufacturing company executive*
Eberwein, Barton Douglas *construction company executive, consultant*
Faris-Stockem, Debbie Anne *architectural sheet metal executive*
Hassell, H(ugh) Robert *manufacturing company executive*
Kinnune, William P. *forest products executive*
Merlo, Harry Angelo *forest products executive*
Moffitt, Kevin David *food products executive*
Nagel, Stanley Blair *construction and investment executive*
Pamplin, Robert Boisseau, Sr. *textile manufacturing executive*
Parsons, J. A. *paper and wood products company executive*
Ritchie, Eric Robert David *manufacturing executive*
Russell, Marjorie Rose *manufacturing company executive*
Steinfeld, Ray, Jr. *food products executive*
Stott, James Charles *chemical company executive*
Stott, Peter Walter *forest products company executive*
Swindells, William, Jr. *lumber and paper company executive*
Watkins, Charles Reynolds *medical equipment company executive*
Watkinson, W. Grant *distribution company executive*

Springfield
Detlefsen, William David, Jr. *chemist*

Stayton
Badstuebner, Hans Alexander *electric company executive*

Wilsonville
Jones, Donald Forsyth *food equipment company executive*
Kimberley, A. G., Jr. *industrial products, factory representative, management executive*
Meyer, Jerome J. *diversified technology company executive*

PENNSYLVANIA

Barnesboro
Moore, David Austin *pharmaceutical company executive, consultant*

Wyomissing
Garr, Carl Robert *manufacturing company executive*

SOUTH CAROLINA

Greenville
Mickel, Buck *construction company executive*

TEXAS

Midland
Reed, Joel Leston *diversified manufacturing company executive*

UTAH

Logan
Ehman, Michael Frederick *electronics executive*

New Harmony
Roberts, Liona Russell, Jr. *electronics engineer, executive*

Ogden
Corry, Lawrence Lee *sugar company executive*
Garrison, U. Edwin *military, space and defense products manufacturing company executive*
Klepinger, John William *trailer manufacturing company executive*

Park City
El-Bayoumy, Lotfi E. *engineering executive*

Provo
Rosen, David Allen *manufacturing executive*

Salt Lake City
Ablad, Bjorn Eric Bertil *manufacturing executive*
Baker, Charles DeWitt *research and development company executive*
Blake, Gilbert Easton *air conditioning company executive*
Campbell, David Randall *equipment manufacturing company executive*
Christensen, Don M. *general contractor, realtor*
Clark, Jeffrey Raphiel *research and development company executive*
Frank, Thomas *construction design and management executive*
Frary, Richard Spencer *international consulting company executive*
Nelson, Jim *chemicals executive*
Schenk, Ray M(erlin) *electronic company executive*
Sorenson, James Lee *chemical executive*
Steiner, Richard Russell *conglomerate executive*
Ward, Roger Wilson *corporate executive, physicist*

Sandy
Robbins, Charles Dudley, III *manufacturing executive*

Springville
Haymond, J. Brent *chemical company executive, state legislator*

West Jordan
Bland, Dorothy Ann *construction executive, real estate agent*

WASHINGTON

Auburn
Bingham, Charles W. *wood products company executive*
Creighton, John W., Jr. *forest products company executive*
Weyerhaeuser, George Hunt *forest products company executive*

Bainbridge Island
Blumenthal, Richard Cary *construction executive, consultant*

Bellevue
Hamachek, Tod Russell *manufacturing executive*
Hovind, David J. *manufacturing company executive*
Morie, G. Glen *manufacturing company executive, corporate lawyer*
Nelson, Kim Alexander *construction company executive, consultant*
Nowik, Dorothy Adam *medical equipment company executive*
Pigott, Charles McGee *transportation equipment manufacturing executive*

Bellingham
Helsell, Robert M. *construction executive*

Bonney Lake
Muldary, Patrick Farrell *manufacturing company executive*

Brewster
Chapman, George J. *agricultural products executive*
Thomas, Dalton *food products executive*

Camas
Hanby, John Estes, Jr. *technology management executive*

Eastsound
Anders, William Alison *aerospace and defense manufacturing executive*

Edmonds
Bobry, Howard Hale *electronics industry executive*

Federal Way
Simmons, Robert Wayne *synthetics and coating manufacturing company executive*

Fox Island
Tillman, Peggy Louise (Peggy Louise Larson) *human factors company executive*

Kirkland
Bernard, James William *chemical distribution company executive*
Biggs, Thomas Wylie *chemical executive*
Ross, Alvin *manufacturing executive*

Longview
Williams, Willis Ray *paint manufacturing company executive*
Wollenberg, Richard Peter *paper manufacturing company executive*

Orondo
Navone, Bert *agricultural products executive*

Outlook
Monson, Arvid *food products executive*

Pasco
Geisert, Otto *food products executive*
Wright, Tim Eugene *packaging development executive*
Yoshino, George *food products executive*

Prosser
Brulotte, Bennett *agricultural products executive*

Pullman
Frigon, Judith Ann *electronics executive, office systems consultant*

Puyallup
Stover, Miles Ronald *manufacturing executive*

Redmond
Cordray, Richard Lynn *electronics engineering executive*
Darnell, Larry *plant manager*
Huck, Larry Ralph *manufacturers representative, sales consultant*
Martin, Richard Otto *medical device company executive*

Seattle
Balint, Joseph Philip *medical products executive*
Baugh, Robert H. *construction executive*
Bjornsson, Kevin Scott *manufacturing executive, writer*
Bookkey, Gerald C. *agricultural products executive*
Braithwaite, Walt Waldiman *aircraft manufacturing company executive*
Connor, Bruce J. *construction company executive*
Dern, Christopher M. *construction executive*
Ernst, Chadwick Ellsworth *fastener company executive*
Johnson, Franklin McBee *wholesale distribution executive*
Johnson, Raymond A. *apparel executive*
Joyce, Marilyn Schmidt *consulting company executive*
Mennella, Vincent Alfred *automotive manufacturing and airplane company executive*
Rash, David Allen *construction executive*
Shrontz, Frank Anderson *airplane manufacturing executive*
Singh, Mahendra Pratap *manufacturing executive*
Stear, Edwin Byron *corporate executive*
Stumbles, James Rubidge Washington *multinational company executive*
Tanaka, T. *health, medical products executive*
Whitacre, John *apparel executive*
Wiborg, James Hooker *chemicals distribution company executive*
Wilson, Patricia Poplar *electrical manufacturing company executive*

Spokane
Armfield, W. W. *retired agricultural products company executive*
Johnstone, Patrick C. *food products executive*
Lentes, David Eugene *corporate executive*

Tacoma
Hill, Steven Richard *business executive*
Slater, Don Austin *shipyard executive, consultant*
Stockdale, Ronald Allen *grocery company executive*

Vancouver
Vogel, Ronald Bruce *food products executive*

Wapato
Buntain, Jeannine *agricultural products executive*
Doty, Everett *food products executive*

Wenatchee
Birdsall, Brian *food products executive*
Chandler, Allen *food products executive*
Mathison, Thomas K. *food products executive*
Ward, Ron *food products executive*

Woodinville
Egerter, John T. *computer services consultant*

Woodland
Brown, Alan Johnson *chemicals executive*

Yakima
Little, Bill *food products executive*
Sims, Bernard *food products executive*

WYOMING

Casper
Stroock, Thomas Frank *manufacturing company executive*

Cheyenne
Seekins, Anna Marie *manufacturing executive*

Evanston
Horne, Ralph Sheldon, Jr. *manufacturing executive, management consultant, newspaper columnist*

CANADA

ALBERTA

Calgary
Chrisman, James Joseph *management educator*
Newall, James Edward Malcolm *manufacturing company executive*

Edmonton
O'Briain, Niall P. *wood products company executive*

BRITISH COLUMBIA

Burnaby
Forgacs, Otto Lionel *forest products company executive*
Skidmore, Thomas Ernest *automotive and communications company executive*

Vancouver
Bender, Graham I. *forest products executive*
Buell, Thomas Allan *lumber company executive*
Findlay, Robert B. *paper manufacturing company executive*
Smith, Raymond Victor *paper products manufacturing executive*

SASKATCHEWAN

Regina
Phillips, Roger *steel company executive*

Saskatoon
Carr, Roy Arthur *agricultural products applied research, development & communication processing organization executive*

ADDRESS UNPUBLISHED

Adams, James Russell *semiconductor electronics company executive*
Adams, Quentin John *construction engineering analyst*
Arthur, Alan Robert *ink manufacturing company executive*
Barca, George Gino *winery executive, finanial investor*
Breaker, Richard Carroll *construction company executive*
Buck, Linda Dee *recruiting company executive*
Burch, Hamlin Doughty, III *retired sheet metal professional*
Campbell, Richard Alden *electronics company executive*
Carlson, Frederick Paul *electronics executive*
Carrott, John Arden *manufacturing executive*
Castberg, Eileen Sue *construction company owner*
Chaykin, Robert Leroy *manufacturing and marketing executive*
Cupery, Robert Rink *manufacturing executive*
Davis, Darrell L. *automotive executive*
Derbes, Daniel William *manufacturing executive*
Diener, Royce *corporate director, retired health care services company executive*
Dobelis, George *manufacturing company executive*
Fagnani, Michele Ann *production supervisor*
Farrell, John Stanislaus *manufacturing company executive*
Frappia, Linda Ann *management executive*
French, Clarence Levi, Jr. *retired shipbuilding company executive*
Fritz, Rene Eugene, Jr. *manufacturing executive*
Gassman, Victor Alan *cosmetics executive*
Goldaper, Gabriele Gay *clothing executive, consultant*
Goldberg, Lee Winicki *furniture company executive*
Gorman, Michael Stephen *construction executive*
Grass, George Mitchell, IV *pharmaceutical executive*
Harvey, Joseph Emmett *construction executive*
Hemann, Raymond Glenn *aerospace research company executive*
Holcombe, William Jones *manufacturing company executive*
Jacobson, Stuart Neil *biotechnology company executive, consultant*
Jedenoff, George Alexander *steel consultant*
Johnson, Katherine Holthaus *health care marketing professional*
Kern, Lawrence A. *food products executive*
Kostrikin, Marybeth Elaine *excavating company executive*
Lockwood, Robert Wilson *paper and pulp executive*
Lux, John H. *corporate executive*
Madden, Richard Blaine *forest products executive*
Marrington, Bernard Harvey *retired automotive company executive*
Maskell, Donald Andrew *contracts administrator*
Mason, Frank Henry, III *automobile company executive, leasing company executive*
Maxwell, Jerome Eugene *electronics company executive*
Mayeux, Jerry Vincent *biotechnology executive, microbiologist*
Mayhew, Lawrence Lee *electronics company executive*
McCann, Jack Arland *former construction and mining equipment company executive, consultant*
McCooey, Everett David, Jr. *construction company executive*
McMullin, Joyce Anne *general contractor*
Meyers, Theda Maria *textile company executive*
Miller, David Wayne *construction inspector, coordinator*
Miller, Robert Lewis *consulting firm executive*
Mims, Edward Trow *electronics industry executive*
Nelson-Haney, Juliann Dorothea *wire products company executive*
Norman, David A. *business equipment company executive*
Nunes, Thomas P. *food products executive*
Ochomogo, María García *manufacturing company executive*
Peterson, Roland Oscar *retired electronics company executive*
Rymar, Julian W. *manufacturing company executive*
Satre, Rodrick Iverson *environmental consultant, business developer*
Saute, Robert Emile *drug and cosmetic consultant*
Scheid-Raymond, Linda Anne *property management professional*
Schilling, Dean William *manufacturing executive*
Schow, Duane (Jack) Rivers *manufacturing company executive*
Schumacher, Barbara Finton *apparel executive*
Shaw, Richard Melvin *gemologist, gold company executive*
Siegel, Mo J. *beverage company executive*
Simmons, Bradley Williams *pharmaceutical company executive*
Simpson, Barclay *manufacturing company executive*
Smith, James Alexander *metal processing executive*
Stamper, Malcolm Theodore *aerospace company executive*
Stern, Arthur Paul *electronics company executive, electrical engineer*
Stivers, William Charles *forest products company executive*
Svikhart, Edwin Gladdin *equipment manufacturing executive*
Warner, Walter Duke *corporate executive*
Wasson, James Walter *aircraft manufacturing company executive*
Whittle, Paul Day *educational products manufacturing executive*
Wittkower, Robert Steven *electronics executive*
Wolf, Hans Abraham *retired pharmaceutical company executive*
Wolff, Brian Richard *metal manufacturing company executive*
Yen, Duen Hsi *corporate executive, physicist*
Young, John Alan *electronics company executive*

INDUSTRY: SERVICE

UNITED STATES

ALABAMA

Florence
Fischer, Alvin Eugene, Jr. *marketing executive*

ALASKA

Anchorage
Bohne, Coral L. *public relations specialist*
Gottstein, Barnard Jacob *retail and wholesale food company executive, real estate executive*
Holman, Karen Marie *purchasing agent*
King, Sidsel Elizabeth Taylor (Beth King) *hotel catering-hospitality professional*
Klatt, Janet Marie *sales and marketing executive*
Porcaro, Michael Francis *advertising agency executive*
Schmitt, Nancy Cain *public and corporate relations executive, writer*
Schneibel, Vicki Darlene *human resources administrator*
Thoeni, Mary Irene *business consultant*

Fairbanks
Thompson, Daniel Emerson *vending machine service company*

Juneau
Stone, David Guy *public relations executive*

Ketchikan
Kraft, Richard Joe *sales executive*

Petersburg
Hixon, Robin Ray *food service executive, writer*

ARIZONA

Apache Junction
Steckbauer, James J. *quality assurance professional*

Benson
Collmer, Russell Cravener *data processing executive, educator*

Chandler
Brunello-McCay, Rosanne *sales executive*
Johnson, Kim *customer account representative*
Steinbuchel, Maximilian Frederick *contract manager*

Cortaro
Fossland, Joeann Jones *marketing professional, consultant*

Flagstaff
Bolin, Richard Luddington *industrial development consultant*

Glendale
Baum, Phyllis Gardner *travel management consultant*

Green Valley
Crystall, Joseph N. *communications company executive*
Green, Paul Cecil *management consultant*

Hereford
Hanne, William Geron *training development professional, educator*

Kingman
Baker, Richard Earl *business management educator*

Mayer
Davis, Scott Milton *information systems professional*

Mesa
Alto, Ronald Louis *marketing professional*
DeWalt, Brook *theater executive, public relations executive*
Lohn, Roger Lowell *management consultant*
Simpson, Bob Gene *quality assurance professional*

Paradise Valley
Hawranek, Joseph Paul *computer company executive, consultant*
Kahn, Earl Lester *market research executive*

Peoria
Saunders, James *management and training consultant*

Phoenix
Adams, Ann Elizabeth *corporate communications executive, lawyer*
Alsaker, Robert John *information systems specialist*
Andrews, Garth E. *public relations executive*
Babinec, Gehl P. *convenience store company executive*
Boggess-Gallegos, Frances *management consultant*
Booth, John Louis *service executive*
Checinski, Jadwiga, Joanna *computer company executive, electrical engineer*
Collins, Dane H. *marketing executive*
Dellis, Deborah Ruth *assistant corporate secretary*
DeMichele, Barbara Joan *public relations executive*
DeWall-Owens, Karen Marie *marketing consultant*
DuMoulin, Diana Cristaudo *marketing professional*
English, Philip Stephen *account manager, consultant*
Evans, Handel E. *marketing professional*
Evans, Ronald Allen *lodging chain executive*
Gibson, John Allan *marketing professional*
Grier, James Edward *hotel company executive, lawyer*
Haines, Sally Stewart *public relations practitioner*
Herbert, Christopher Jay *marketing professional, management consultant*
Hofford, Harry *marketing professional*
Landis, Richard Preston *corporate executive*
Last, Dianna Linn Schneider *marketing company executive*
Lemon, Leslie Gene *consumer products and services company executive, lawyer*
Manion, Jerry Robert *hotel chain executive*
Mathews, Wilma Kendrick *public relations executive*
Newman, Lois Mae *marketing executive*
Parker, Brad *public relations and advertising executive*
Phillips-Garcia, Gary Lee *equal employment specialist*
Prellberg, Joanne Marie *office manager*
Riley, Marilyn Gledhill *communications executive*
Siegel, Charlotte Douglas *marketing research professional*
Simpson, Charles Robert *marketing professional*
Simunich, Mary Elizabeth Hedrick (Mrs. William A. Simunich) *public relations executive*
Snell, Richard *holding company executive*
Stephens, Lee Amiel *business development executive*
Subach, James Alan *infosystems company executive, consultant*
Teets, John William *diversifed company executive*
Turner, William Cochrane *international management consultant*
Wade, Michael Stephen *management consultant*
Whitehead, Ardelle Coleman *advertising and public relations executive*
Wilfried, Grau *hotel executive officer*
Woods, Melanie Ann *sales professional*
Yellen, Pamela Gay *sales and marketing consultant*

Prescott
Mayol, Richard Thomas *advertising executive, political consultant*
Palmer, Robert Arthur *private investigator*

Red Rock
Mosher, Kirk A. *marketing director*

Rimrock
Elston, Lester Charles *management consultant*

Scottsdale
Adams, Robert Granville *marketing professional*
Bellino, Peter Vincent, Jr. *marketing manager*
Bellus, Ronald Joseph *marketing and communications executive*
Blake, William Benjamin *management and financial consultant*
Blinder, Martin S. *business consultant, art dealer*
Boone, Earle Marion *business executive*
Doglione, Arthur George *data processing executive*
Eller, Debra *management consultant*
Gacioch, Joseph James *public relations executive*
Gall, Donald Alan *data processing executive*
Hess, Robert, Jr. *ambulance service executive*
Irvine, Donald William *telecommunications company executive*
Joaquim, Richard Ralph *hotel executive*
Loomis, Richard Frank *entertainment company executive*
Nunes, Thomas *marketing director*
O'Donnell, William Thomas *management consultant*
Pavlik, Nancy *convention services executive*
Perry, David Niles *public relations executive*
Powers, James Earl *public relations executive*
Randau, Karen Lynette *public relations executive*
Russell, Jay D. *marketing executive*
Stricklan, Charles Leslie, Jr. *advertising executive*
Turoff, Marshall Arnold *consulting company executive*
White, Paul Verlin *electronics marketing executive*
Williams, Richard James *food service executive*
Wright, James Corwin *international management consultant*

Sedona
Braman, Donald William *public relations consultant*
Woellmer, Ralph *hotel executive*

Sierra Vista
Bowen, Harry Ernest *management consultant*
Reynolds, John Curby *sales representative*

Sun City West
Colvin, Donald Andrew *marketing consultant*
Forti, Lenore Steimle *business consultant*
Suttles, Virginia Grant *advertising executive*
Yedlicka, William George *retired sales professional*

Sun Lakes
Donahue, James J., Jr. *retired corporate executive, consultant*

Tempe
Arters, Linda Bromley *public relations consultant, writer*
Dunbar, Richard Paul *sales manager*
Edmunds, Holly Brook *market research consultant*
Goldstein, Mark Alan *information science and research company executive, consultant*
Guinouard, Philip Andre *restaurant executive*
Huntsman, Edward Loyd *business consultant, marketing executive*
LePage, Kerry Leigh *marketing executive*
McKeever, Jeffrey D. *computer company executive*
Saar, Frederick Arthur *data processing executive*

Tucson
Brown, Judith Ellen *community relations executive*
Elsberry, Susan Davise *computer-aided manufacturing engineer*
Emerine, Stephen Edward *communications executive*
Falbaum, Bertram Seymour *investigator*
Farias, James Arthur *resource development planner, writer*
Kohn, David Zalman *human resources director*
Rose, Hugh *management consultant*
Sarlat, Gladys *public relations consultant*
Sohnen-Moe, Cherie Marilyn *business consultant*
Williams, John Pershing *industrial relations consultant, retired manufacturing and mining company executive*

Yuma
Bennewitt, Loi Dene *personnel director*

CALIFORNIA

Agoura
Poy, Glenn Derrick *corporate executive*

Agoura Hills
Naylor-Jackson, Jerry *public relations consultant, entertainer, producer*
Pickman, Phillip *management consultant*
Schmidt, Frank Broaker *executive recruiter*

Alameda
Billings, Thomas Neal *computer and publishing executive, management consultant*

Alamo
Crocker, Kenneth Franklin *data processing consultant*

Alta Loma
Anderson, Jack Joe *communications and training consultant*

Altadena
Fairbanks, Mary Kathleen *data analyst, researcher*
Solomon, Eugene, Jr. *executive consultant*

Anaheim
Bye, Roseanne Marie *marketing professional*
Conlin, William Patrick *computer company executive*
Hayase, Linda Michi *direct mail company executive*
Herzing, Alfred Roy *computer executive*
Kallay, Michael Frank, II *medical devices company official*
Kidde, Andrew Judson *sales executive, consultant*
Noorda, Raymond J. *computer software company executive*
Obnamia, Reynaldo Zaide *quality assurance professional*
Sorenson, Sandra Louise *merchandising manager*

Antelope
Hope, Gerri Danette *telecommunications management executive*

Atherton
Lowry, Larry Lorn *management consulting company executive*
Weinman, Roberta Sue *marketing and financial communications consultant*

Atwater
DeVoe, Kenneth Nickolas *food service executive, mayor*

Auburn
Norsell, Paul Ernest *service executive*

Avalon
Baker Holliday, Karen *hotel executive*

Avila Beach
McLaren, Archie Campbell, Jr. *marketing executive*

Azusa
Broussard, Frederick *sales executive*

Bakersfield
Weygand, Leroy Charles *service executive*

Bell
Loven, Charles John *human resource executive*

Belmont
Andriella, Steven L. *information systems manager*
Simmons, Noel Alexander *human resources executive, consultant*

Vanides, Alexia *marketing consulting executive*

Berkeley
Colwell, Stephen D. *travel industry executive, lawyer*
Harris, Nancy Howard *paper conservator, writer*
Karabela, Leda *public relations and fund raising executive*
Riley, Ann L. *management professional*

Beverly Hills
Barbakow, Jeffery C. *motion picture and television company executive*
Cantor, Alan Bruce *management consultant, computer software developer*
Carlson, Gary Lee *public relations executive, director, producer*
Damon, Michael *systems design and marketing executive*
Galbraith, James Ronald *hotel executive*
Gleason, Douglas Renwick *marketing professional*
Hathaway-Bates, John Hugh *company executive*
Hilton, Barron *hotel executive*
Hilton, Eric Michael *hotel industry executive*
Philon, James Leon *retired hotel executive*
Ratliff, James Conway *hotel executive*
Ribero, Michael Antonio *marketing executive*
Royer, Victor Henry *marketing consultant, author*
Sassoon, Vidal *hair stylist*

Big Sur
Bussinger, Robert Eugene *service executive*

Bishop
Reget, Ione Hozendorf *business services company executive*

Brea
Burgess, Stephen Andrew *company executive*

Buena Park
Thomas, David Stanley *sales executive*
Underwood, Thomas Woodbrook *communications company executive*

Burbank
Gage, Frederick Albert *business development executive*,
Guidera, Ellen Marie *entertainment industry executive*
Korkunis, Tony William *consumer products executive*
McElwee, Jeanette Gaye *management and program consultant*
Tyler, Richard R. *marketing executive*
Wong, Bonnie Lee *systems analyst*

Burlingame
Howard, Victor *management consultant*
Riach, Douglas Alexander *marketing and sales executive, retired military officer*

Calabasas
Chee, Jason S.I. *product marketing management*
Thagard, Shirley Stafford *sales and marketing executive*

Camarillo
Frayssinet, Daniel Fernand *software company executive*
Knight, Jeffrey Richard *systems requirements analyst*
Lonegan, Thomas Lee *restaurant corporation executive*

Cambria
DuFresne, Armand Frederick *management and engineering consultant*
Morse, Richard Jay *human resources and organizational development consultant, manufacturers' representative company executive*

Campbell
Metcalf, Scott *computer company executive*
Panec, Donald John *marketing executive*

Canoga Park
Beckmann, Jane Miluna *acoustical company executive, consultant*
Morris, Henry Madison, III *software manufacturing executive, minister*

Carlsbad
Chereskin, Valerie Lee *marketing professional*
De La Cruz, Jennifer Lyn *marketing executive*
Handel, William Keating *advertising and sales executive*
McDonald, John Peter *management consultant*
Voigt, John Louis *advertising and marketing executive*

Carmel
Krugman, Stanley Lee *international management consultant*
Louvau, Gordon Ernest *management consultant, educator*
Smith, Gordon Paul *management consulting company executive*

Caspar
Tarbell, Jim *printer, publishing executive, writer*

Cerritos
Ayloush, Cynthia Marie *personnel director*
Kong, Xiangli (Charlie Kong) *technical service company executive, educator*
Madden, James Cooper, V *management consultant*
Morlock, Walter O'Malley *marketing professional*
Rice, Barbara Pollak *advertising and marketing executive*

Chatsworth
Sklar, Louise Margaret *service executive*
Urmer, Diane Hedda *management firm executive, financial officer*

Chico
Heinze, David C. *business administration educator*

Chula Vista
Diaz-Barrios, Ana Paulina *manufacturing and marketing consultant*

Claremont
Farnum, Nancy Alyson *communications executive*

Commerce
Girard, Donald Alan *public relations executive*

Compton
Allumbaugh, Byron *grocery company executive*

Concord
Travers, Judith Lynnette *human resources executive*

Corona Del Mar
Wickman, Paul Everett *public relations executive*

Coronado
Walker, Richard Allen *multimedia computing executive, consultant*

Corte Madera
McCarthy, Brian Nelson *marketing and distribution company executive*

Costa Mesa
Bereznay, Frank M. *information systems specialist*
Damsky, Robert Philip *communications executive*
Doherty, Fred Vincent *advertising executive*
Steed, Emmett D. *hotel executive*
Udink, Johnny Ray *printing company executive*

Crescent City
Hight, Harold Philip *retired security company executive*

Crestline
Merrill, Steven William *research and development executive*

Culver City
Byrd, Marc Robert *florist*
Dutt, Birendra *research specialist*
Green, Richard Kevin *special effect company executive*
Jacobs, Alicia Melvina *account executive*

Cupertino
Belshaw, Janine *research and development executive*
Flynn, Ralph Melvin, Jr. *sales executive, marketing consultant*
Graziano, Joseph A. *computer company executive*
Lee, Kai-Fu *computer company executive*
Mattathil, George Paul *communications specialist, consultant*
Ponzetto, Ennio *research and development executive*
Robles, Emilio *public relations professional, journalist*
Spindler, Michael H. *computer company executive*
Treybig, James G. *computer company executive*

Dana Point
Kinney, Marjorie Sharon *marketing executive, artist*
Krogius, Tristan Ernst Gunnar *international marketing consultant, lawyer*
Mardian, Robert Charles, Jr. *restaurateur*

Danville
da Roza, Victoria Cecilia *human resources administrator*
Gorman, Russell William *marketing executive, consultant*
Randolph, Kevin H. *marketing executive*

Davis
Woodard, John Henry *quality control professional*

Del Mar
Wadia, Maneck Sorabji *management consultant, writer*

Discovery Bay
Pfeiffer, Gerald G. *human resources consultant*

El Centro
Feuerstein, Marcy Berry *employee benefits administrator*

El Cerrito
Pape, Thomas Emil *marketing professional, consultant*

El Segundo
Armstrong, Wallace Dowan, Jr. *data processor*
Autolitano, Astrid *consumer products executive*
Barad, Jill Elikann *toy company executive*
Frahmann, Dennis George *computer company executive*
Ginder, Joseph Ronald *computer company executive, software architect*
Honeycutt, Van B. *computer services company executive*
Leff, Robert S. *computer company executive*
Mehlman, Lon Douglas *information systems specialist*
Wagman, David S. *computer company executive*

El Toro
Schuetz, John Michael *sales executive*

Elk Grove
Bundesen, Faye Stimers *investment and management company consultant, educator*
Mark, Arthur *information systems specialist*
Shipley, Veta Fern Wilson *personnel recruiting company executive*

Emeryville
Palanca, Terilyn *information management consultant*
Suppes, Courtney Mervin *hazardous waste executive*

Encino
Kazenelson Deane, Deborah *public relations executive*
Woskow, Robert Marshall *management consultant*

Escondido
Daniels, Richard Martin *marketing communications company executive*

Eureka
Lindsey, John Hall, Jr. *software company executive*

Fair Oaks
Douglas, Marion Joan *labor negotiator*
Joiner, Dennis Ashley *personnel management consultant*
Marigold, Lawrence Lee *international energy consultant*
McCafferty, Robert Maurice *communications and media skills executive, speaker*
Nolan, Mark Gregory *advertising executive*

Fairfax
Delaney, Marion Patricia *advertising agency executive*

Fallbrook
Cralley, Lester Vincent *retired industrial hygienist, editor*

Folsom
Aprea, Sharon Martin *merchandiser*

Fontana
Hood, Edward *data processing executive*

Fort Bragg
Galli, Darrell Joseph *management consultant*

Foster City
Krieger, Michael Raymond *computer manufacturing executive, writer*
Pflug, Eduard *contractor*

Fremont
Brooks, Samuel Everett *purchasing agent*
Pye, David Thomas *computer technology company executive*

French Camp
Hoberg, Michael Dean *management analyst, educator*

Fresno
Bausano, Donna Ann *marketing professional*
Hardison, Roy Lewis *marketing professional*
Vargas, Al Garcia *building contractor*

Fullerton
Gallup, Janet Louise *business official*
Jensen, Carolyn Jean *marketing and public relations researcher*
Nowel, David John *marketing professional*
Smith, Helen Dibell *executive assistant*

Garden Grove
Banks, Ernest (Ernie Banks) *moving company executive, retired professional baseball player*

Gardena
Archer, James Ernest *sales professional*
Tabet, Paul Mark *information services executive*

Gilroy
Aguilar, Gale Ramon *computer industry executive*

Glendale
Collier, Norma Jean *public relations and advertising executive*
Dedes, George Panayotis *direct marketing executive*
Herzer, Richard Kimball *franchising company executive*
Misa, Kenneth Franklin *management consultant*
Sanders, David Clyde *management and marketing consultant*

Glendora
Milhous, Robert E. *advertising executive*
Yochem, Barbara June *sales executive, lecturer*

Gold River
Brown, Daniel Warren *public relations executive*
Terrill, David Philip *fair industry executive*

Goleta
Kirby, George William *quality assurance professional, consultant*

Granada Hills
O'Connor, Betty Lou *service executive*
Shoemaker, Harold Lloyd *infosystem specialist*

Grand Terrace
Allen, John David *sales executive*

Grass Valley
Hutcherson, Christopher Alfred *marketing, recruiting, and educational consultant*

Greenbrae
Catalano, John George *management consultant*

Grover Beach
Barca, Kathleen *marketing executive*

Half Moon Bay
Fennell, Diane Marie *marketing executive, process engineer*
Kinsman, Robert Warren *emergency management consultant*

Hanford
Neos, Peri Fitch *painting contractor, small business owner*

Hawthorne
Goldstein, Simon *credit management executive*
Perry, James Gregory *sales and marketing executive*

Hayward
Connors, Dennis Michael *infosystems executive*
Mackin, Terrence Christian *infosystems consultant*
Tribus, Myron *management consultant, engineer, educator*

Healdsburg
Canfield, Grant Wellington, Jr. *management consultant*

Hermosa Beach
Dietz, Russell Scott *communications company executive*
Le Veque, Matthew Kurt *public affairs and marketing consultant*

Huntington Beach
Wing, Roger *management consultant*
Wood, Fay S. *marketing executive*

Idyllwild
Robinson, Samuel Willis, Jr. *information sciences specialist*

Inglewood
Schepp, George Phillip, Jr. *research consultant*
Turner, Norris *marketing professional*

Irvine
Coad, Dennis L. *marketing executive, management consultant*
Colino, Richard Ralph *communications consultant*
Demetrescu, Mihai Constantin *computer company executive, scientist*
Freeman, Richard Dean *new business start-up service company executive*
Gort, Pamela J. *sales executive*
Habermann, Norman *restaurant group executive*
Krantz, Barry E. *restaurant executive*
Lee, Robert Erich *information technology consultant*
Leets, Peter John *outplacement consulting firm executive*
Looney, J. Anna *corporate affairs executive*
Manara, James Anthony *software executive, consultant*
Maybay, Duane Charles *recycling systems executive*
Miller, Thomas Roy *computer company executive*
Nelson, Robert E. *public relations executive, political consultant*
Panhuyzen, Ralph Philip *trade relations promoter*
Pape, Barbara Karen *administrative assistant*
Pechmann, Cornelia Ann Rachel *marketing professional*
Quershey, Safi U. *computer company executive*
Ruttencutter, Brian Boyle *holding company/ manufacturing company executive*
Seller, Gregory Erol *marketing executive, writer*
Sims, Jack *marketing professional*
Swan, Richard Alan *executive recruiter*
Thayer, Shelley I. *marketing professional*
von Tilsit, Heidemarie *information management specialist*
Westphal, Ruth Lilly *educational audio-visual company executive, author, publisher*
Wilck, Carl Thomas *public relations executive*

Kentfield
Charles, Anne H. *communications executive*

La Canada Flintridge
Stratton, John Maclean *company executive*

La Habra
Burkle, Ronald W. *food service executive*
Hatai, Thomas Henry *international marketing professional*

La Jolla
Barrett, Larry Leon *housing and dining services administrator*
Finn, Sara Shiels *public relations executive*
Levenstein, Roslyn M. *advertising consultant, writer*
MacAuslan, Ian James *business development specialist*
Nelles, Merice Tilman *business development consultant*
Reed, James Anthony *hotel industry executive, consultant*
Short, Jay Milton *biotechnology company executive*
Smith, Patricia Jacquline *marketing executive*

La Mirada
Carino, Linda Susan *financial software company executive*

La Puente
Ogden, Jean Lucille *sales executive*

La Verne
Bearley, William Leon *consulting company executive*

Lafayette
Hemphill, Norma Jo *special event planning and tour company executive*

Laguna Beach
Gamal, Irwin Bert *management consultant*
Hafey, Edward Earl Joseph *precision tool company executive*

Laguna Hills
Pearson, Thomas Carleton *management consultant*
Schulz, Raymond Alexander *medical marketing professional, consultant*

Laguna Niguel
Kursewicz, Lee Z. *marketing consultant*
Wehrly, Joseph Malachi *industrial relations specialist*

Lake Arrowhead
Bauer, Ralph Leroy *business executive*

Lake Elsinore
Kelly, Kathleen Flo *personal and professional development company executive, cleaning service executive, cosmetologist*

Lake Forest
White, Joy Mieko *communications executive*

Larkspur
Finkelstein, James Arthur *management consultant*

Laytonville
Newell, Castle Skip, III *marketing executive, foundation administrator*

Livermore
Brieger, Stephen Gustave *management consultant*
Portway, Patrick Stephen *telecommunications consulting company executive, telecommunications educator*
Williams, David Michael *manufacturing executive*
Zambetti, Denis Egan *product specialist*

Llano
Martin, Nancy L. *communications executive*

Loma Linda
Maurice, Don *personal care industry executive*

Long Beach
Aldrich, David Lawrence *public relations executive*
Arakawa, Mary K. *systems analyst*
Englund, Lori Jean *financial products company executive*
Giles, Jean Hall *retired corporate executive*
Johnson, William Harry *international management consultant*
Scholnick, Joseph B. *public relations executive, journalist*
Simon, Renee Blatt *communications executive*
Smith, Keith Larue *research company executive*
West, Edward Alan *graphics communications executive*

Los Alamitos
Kidde, John Edgar *food company executive*
Weinberger, Frank *information systems advisor*

Los Altos
Bell, Chester Gordon *computer engineering company executive*
Brill, Yvonne Theresa *marketing research company executive, consultant*
Cook, Robert P., II *business development executive*
Doby, Karen Elaine *data processing company executive*
Poonja, Mohamed *business reorganization, financial and management consultant*

Los Angeles
Armstrong, C. Michael *computer business executive*
Barnes, Michael Keith *transit marketing executive*
Beam, William Washington, III *data coordinator*
Beltramo, Michael Norman *management consultant*
Berkhemer-Credaire, Betsy *public relations executive*
Berman, Saul Jay *strategic consultant*
Bermingham, Richard P. *restaurant and food products company executive*
Busse, Michael Clifford *newspaper advertising executive*
Calvo, Debra Lee Goff *public relations executive*
Campbell, Carolyn Margret *communications consultant*
Chesser, Steven Bruce *public relations executive*
Cho, Dean Deuk *computer company executive*
Cochran, Anne Westfall *public relations executive*
Conto, Aristides *advertising agency executive*
Conway, Casey Anthony *health and safety manager*
Curtis, Marie Therese Dodge *executive assistant*
Domantay, Norlito Valdez (Lito Domantay) *communications executive*
Dorfman, Steven David *electronics company executive*
Dostourian, Dick *computer systems executive*
Duke, William Edward *public affairs executive*
Edwards, William H., Sr. *retired hotel corporation executive*
Ehrlich, Alan M. *marketing company executive*
Engoron, Edward David *food service consultant, television and radio broadcaster*
Fairbrother, Kathryn Louise *customer relations executive*
Ferry, Richard Michael *executive search firm executive*
Fisher, Lawrence W. *public relations company executive*
Flynn, Elizabeth Anne *advertising and public relations company executive*
Funk, Susan E. *management consultant*
Garland, G(arfield) Garrett *sales executive, golf professional*
Giffin, Margaret Ethel (Peggy Giffin) *management consultant*
Goldstein, Norton Maurice (Goldy Norton) *public relations consultant*
Gossett, Richard Gerald *management consultant*
Greene, Alvin *service company executive, management consultant*
Gregory, Thomas Lang *restaurant chain executive*
Grody, Mark Stephen *public relations executive*
Hankins, Hesterly G., III *computer systems analyst, inventor, educator*
Harbison, John Robert *management consultant*
Heinisch, Robert Craig *sales and marketing executive, consultant*
Hofert, Jack *consulting company executive, lawyer*
Hotchkiss, Vivian Evelyn *employment agency executive*
Hudson, Michael Elliott, Sr. *human resource specialist*
Hutchings, LeAnne von Neumeyer *communications executive, research consultant, writer*
Jeffers, Gene *association executive*
Johnson, Patricia Gayle *public relations executive, writer*
Johnson, W. Cedric *computer company executive*
Katz, Jerry Paul *corporate executive*
Kelly, Kathleen Suzanne *marketing professional*
Kessler, Robert Allen *data processing executive*
Kitchen, Yvonne Rae *public relations practitioner*
Knox, Robert Leslie *personnel professional*
Kornman, Henry *marketing executive*
Krinsky, Ira Walter *executive search consultant*
Laba, Marvin *management consultant*
Lamonica, John *food executive*
Larsen, Donna Kay *public relations executive, writer, consultant*
Leibert, Richard William *special events producer*
Livingston, Alan Wendell *communications executive*
LoBaugh, Leslie E., Jr. *holding company executive, corporate lawyer*
Marks, Stanley J. *international legal and business consultant*
McFarland-Esposito, Carla Rae *nursing executive*
Montgomery, Richard Alan *sales executive*
Muraszko, Michael Roman *public relations executive*
Nicholaw, George *communications executive*
Noto, Blaise John *film marketing executive*
O'Hara, Kirk Brandt *management consultant*
Oharenko, Maria T. *public relations official*
Oppedahl, Phillip Edward *computer company executive*
Otto, Joseph Clair *information systems educator*
Parrott, Dennis Beecher *sales executive*
Patel, Chandra Kumar Naranbhai *communications company executive, educator, researcher*
Paura, Catherine *marketing professional*
Pearce, Joan DeLap *research company executive*
Peden, Lynn Ellen *marketing executive*
Pekar, Peter, Jr. *business professional*
Ranftl, Robert Matthew *management consulting company executive*
Richman, Anthony E. *textile rental company executive*
Rickley, David Arthur *communications systems manager*
Roeschlaub, Jean Marian Clinton *restaurant chain executive*
Rucker, Thomas Douglas *purchasing executive*
Segal, Morton *public relations executive*
Sherman, Kathleen A. *public relations executive*
Sherwin, Gary Craig *media relations director, convention executive*
Shiffman, Leslie Brown *management executive*
Shlimak, Yan *office assistant, home healthcare provider*
Shonk, Albert Davenport, Jr. *advertising executive*
Skhisov, Eduard *office project assistant*
Snyder, David Markel *marketing executive*
Spindler, Paul *public relations executive*
Spitzer, Peter George *information systems executive, consultant*
Spofford, Robert Houston *advertising agency executive*
Stevens, Eleanor Sandra *professional services executive*
Stoltz, Eric Michael *public relations executive*
Strong, George Gordon, Jr. *litigation and management consultant*
Sylvester, Richard Russell *management consultant*
Tardio, Thomas A. *public relations executive*
Taylor, Richard W. *public relations executive*
Tellem, Susan Mary *public relations executive*
Tulk, Steven Anthony *director information systems*
Van Remmen, Roger *management consultant*
Van Stekelenburg, Mark *food service executive*
Wade, Michael Robert Alexander *marketing specialist*
Weisman, Robert Evans *caterer*
Wemischner, Robert Barry *culinary educator*
Whitehouse, Jack Pendleton *public relations executive*
Whitman, Kenneth Jay *advertising executive*

Los Gatos
Bederka, Stephen Edward *management consultant*
Henley, Jeffrey O. *restaurant executive*
Stone, David Ulric *management executive, author*

Malibu
Spellman, Douglas Toby *advertising executive*

Mammoth Lakes
Buchanan, Lee Ann *public relations executive*

Manhattan Beach
Anderson, Michael Robert *marketing representative*
Horwitz, Kamala Marie *sales professional*
Poster, Vanessa Irene *development administrator*
Sapoch, John Crim, Jr. *management consultant*
Trager, Russell Harlan *advertising consultant*

March AFB
Bond, Vincent Earl *public relations executive*

Marina Del Rey
Holland, Robin Jean *personnel company executive*
Lott, Davis Newton *advertising agency executive, publisher*
McShirley, Susan Ruth *gift industry executive, consultant*

Martell
Grillo, Terry Wilson *public relations executive*

Menlo Park
Castor, Jon Stuart *management consultant*
Chapin, Ned *information systems consultant*
Creswell, Donald Creston *management consultant*
Dolgow, Allan Bentley *consulting company executive*
Fried, Louis Lester *information technology and management consultant*
Hudson, Vinson Jene *market research executive*
Kornfeld, Judith R. *product marketing consultant*
Kuroda, Yutaka *management consultant*
Straubel, John Frederick *public relations and advertising executive*

Merced
Clark, Ronald Ralph *marketing executive*

Mill Valley
Gianturco, Paola *management consulting executive*
Jackson, Sharon Juanita *management consultant*
Nassikas, James Achilles *hotel executive*
Romm, Jessica Beth *management consultant*
Samuels, Michele *public relations and business consultant*
Walrad, Charlene Chuck *software and total quality management consultant*

Millbrae
Mank, Edward Warren *marketing professional*

Milpitas
Berkley, Stephen Mark *computer peripherals manufacturing company executive*
Corrigan, Wilfred J. *data processing and computer company executive*
McVicar, Sherry Fisher *human resources executive*
Miller, William J. *computer company executive*
Robinett, Reneé Mello *marketing executive*
Rostoker, Michael David *micro-electronics company executive, lawyer*
Wells, George Douglas *corporate executive*

Mission Hills
Griset, Robert Paul *publisher*

Mission Viejo
Corey, Jo Ann *management analyst*
Dillon, Francis Patrick *human resources executive, management and sales consultant*
Harder, Wendy Wetzel *marketing and communications executive*
Parady, John Edward *information systems executive, consultant*
Ross, Renae Lynn *marketing professional*

Modesto
Cofer, Berdette Henry *public management consulting company executive*
Ploutz, Lloyd Gene *management executive, marketing professional, historian*

Moffett Field
Baldwin, Betty Jo *computer specialist*
Bousquet, John Frederick *security firm executive, desktop publishing executive, locksmith*
Waller, Peter William *public affairs executive*

Montebello
Norkin, Mark Mitchell *sales executive*

Monterey
Cutino, Bert Paul *chef, restaurant owner*
Gargiulo, Franca *marketing and communications consultant*
Giddings, Debra Lynn *marketing executive, computer consultant*
Kohler, Gary Joseph *hotel and resort sales and marketing executive*
Reierson, Lawrence Edward *organizational development consultant, executive*

Monterey Park
Kwong, Daniel Wai-Kin *management and financial consultant, educator, writer*
Montag, David Moses *computer company executive*

Moraga
Deju, Raul Antonio *environmental company executive*
Grassi, James Edward *recreational facility executive director*
Haag, Carol Ann Gunderson *marketing professional, consultant*

Mountain View
Akeley, Kurt Barton *computer graphics company executive, engineer*
Benrey, Jeff Michael *marketing professional*
Black, Carlin J. *industrial marketing consultant*
Breitmeyer, Jo Anne *sales and marketing executive*
Cargill, Carl Frederick *standards strategist*
de Urioste, George Adolfo, IV *software company executive*
Kirchner, Ernst Karl *company executive*
Korner, Hilda *personnel executive*
Lekashman, John Raymond *company executive*
Mc Nealy, Scott *computer company executive*
Porter, James Neil *marketing executive*
Rondell, Thomas *public relations consultant, marketing communications consultant*
Rulifson, Johns Frederick *computer company executive, computer scientist*
Shah, Girish Popatlal *data processing services company executive*
Thapa, Mukund Narain-Dhami *software company executive*
Wood, Naomi Alice *language services firm executive*

Napa
LaRocque, Marilyn Ross Onderdonk *public relations executive*
Leavitt, Dana Gibson *management consultant*

National City
Simms, Julia Ann *public relations executive*
Wisener, Maureen Mayden *public relations, marketing executive*

Newark
Cohn, Lawrence Sherman *marketing and sales executive*
Joyce, Stephen Francis *human resource executive*

Newbury Park
Lichtenstein, Chase Walter *management consultant*

Newport Beach
Bird-Porto, Patricia Anne *personnel director*
Bullis, Michael A. *hotel executive*
de Garcia, Lucia *marketing professional*
Eastman, Richard Phillip *marketing executive*
Evans, Deborah Lynn *private investigator, writer*
Gellman, Gloria Gae Seeburger Schick *marketing professional*
Gentry, Grant Claybourne *food retail company executive*
Melrose, Albert Joseph *investor relations professional*
Mitchell, Herbert Eugene *management consultant, marketing specialist*
Potocki, Joseph Edmund *marketing company executive*
Skidmore, David Theodore *service executive*
Terrell, A. John *business organization, management and telecommunications consultant*

North Hollywood
Caughey, Cynthia Louise *agency executive director*
Kaye, Lori *travel academy executive, consultant*

Novato
Hiner, Allegra Broughton *business manager*
Howitt, David Andrew *human resources executive*

Oakland
Burd, Steve *food service executive*
Chamberlin, John Howard *economic and management consultant*
Dunn, David Cameron *entrepreneur, business executive*
Herman, Judith Axelrood *marketing research consultant*
Hoffman, George Alan *consulting company executive*
Howard, Bradford Reuel *travel company executive*
Landrum, Brett John David *automobile sales executive*
Misner, Gervase Arthur *personnel administrator*
Morris, Tami Cantua *public relations and communications consultant*
Potash, Stephen Jon *international public relations practitioner*
Yamada, Tomokiyo Tom *advertising executive*

Oakville
Posert, Harvey Peres *public relations professional*

Oceanside
Hoff, Bernadine Ryan *management consultant*

Ontario
Hawley, Nanci Elizabeth *public relations and communications professional*
Kahn, Mario Santamaria *international marketing executive*
Wright, Charles Lee *information systems consultant*

Orinda
Hermann, James Ray *management executive*

Oxnard
Faulconer, Kay Anne *communications executive, dean*
Snasdell, Susan Kathleen *computer company executive*
Zigman, Paul Edmond *environmental consultant, executive*

Pacific Palisades
Adams, Lynn Donelle *pet sitting company executive*
Perse, Aria Leon *international business marketing professional*

Pacifica
Turnbull, Doreen Joyce *electronic data processing consultant*

Palm Desert
Kern, Paul Alfred *advertising company executive, research consultant, realtor*

Palm Springs
Capps, Anthony Thomas (Capozzolo Capps) *international public relations executive*
Patten, Carolyn S. *public relations professional*
Seale, Robert McMillan *office services company executive*
Vivian, Linda Bradt *sales and public relations executive*

Palo Alto
Allen, Vicky *business development technical specialist*
Antelman, Bruce *information delivery company executive*
Curry, William Sims *procurement manager*
Denning, Michael Marion *computer company executive*
Eleccion, Marcelino *marketing executive, computer engineer, programmer, editor, writer, lecturer, artist*
Geddes, Barbara Sheryl *communications executive, consultant*
Kirk, Carmen Zetler *data processing executive*
Kishimoto, Yoriko *business consultant*
Krich, Kenneth L. *computer dealer executive*
Menjo, Hiroshi *management consultant*
Reed, David Patrick *infosystems specialist*
Seethaler, William Charles *international business executive, consultant*

Palos Verdes Peninsula
Rubenstein, Leonard Samuel *communications executive, ceramist, painter, sculptor, photographer*
Savage, Terry Richard *information systems executive*
Tucker, Charles Cyril *information systems consultant*

Paramount
Gorham-Smith, R(osella) Dorita *direct mail and marketing company executive*

Pasadena
Asbury, Judith Smith *public relations professional*
Berger, Jay Vari *executive recruiter, import company executive*
Caine, Stephen Howard *data processing executive*
Dixon, Diane Brooks *communications executive*
Echeveste, John Anthony *public relations consultant*
Griesche, Robert Price *hospital purchasing executive*
Hanson, Noel Rodger *management consultant*
Kaplan, Gary *executive recruiter*
Koenig, Marie Harriet King *public relations director, fund raising executive*
Mangum, William *management consulting company executive*
Mann, Inez Kimiko *public relations professional, consultant*
Pattie, Steven Norris *advertising executive, artist, author*
Wildermuth, Ronald E. *public relations professional*

Paso Robles
Boxer, Jerome Harvey *computer and management consultant, vintner, accountant*

Pebble Beach
Domnie, Scott Harold *real estate investor, country club operator*
Harvie, J. Jason *administrative aide, secretary*
Stracuzzi, Diane Elizabeth *marketing director*
Wilsey, H. Lawrence *management consultant*

Petaluma
Crawford, George Truett *management systems company executive, consultant*
Daniel, Gary Wayne *communications and music industry executive*
Samuel, George *healthcare information company executive*

Pico Rivera
Luevano, Fred, Jr. *computer systems executive*
Rapier, Stephen Michael *marketing executive*

Piedmont
Morrison, John Gill *communications executive*

Pismo Beach
Edwards, Patrick Michael *sales consultant*

Placerville
Hemsley, David Lee *computer company executive*

Playa Del Rey
Rich, Susan Abby *efficiency consultant*

Pleasant Hill
Munch, William David *information systems consultant*
Newkirk, Raymond Leslie *management consultant*

Pleasanton
Lawson, J(enice) Evelyn *quality assurance professional, pharmacist*
Lykins, Jay Arnold *economic development director*
Roberts, Fred Louis *technology marketing company executive*

Point Reyes Station
Harvey, Gregory Alan *microcomputer technology educator, consultant*

Pomona
Kapoor, Sandra A. *restaurant management educator*

Port Hueneme
Bell, Judy Kay *disaster survival planning company executive*
Cobb, Roy Lampkin, Jr. *computer sciences corporation executive*
Haddad, Edmonde Alex *public affairs executive*

Porter Ranch
Rothenberg, Marcy Miroff *public relations consultant*

Porterville
Webb, Jonell *advertising professional*

Poway
Berger, Newell James, Jr. *security professional*

Rancho Cucamonga
Lakatos, Joseph Sandor *software company executive, engineer*
Olson, Carol Lee *public information officer*
Saito, William Hiroyuki *software company executive*

Rancho Mirage
Rotman, Morris Bernard *public relations consultant*

Rancho Murieta
Ragsdale, Christina Ann *public relations executive, consultant*

Rancho Palos Verdes
Marlett, De Otis Loring *retired management consultant*

Rancho Santa Fe
Gruenwald, George Henry *new products development management consultant*
Hurney, Jeanne Muraco *public relations executive*
Schirra, Walter Marty, Jr. *business consultant, former astronaut*

Redondo Beach
Sloan, Michael Dana *information systems specialist*
Wolf, Joseph Gordon (Pepe Lobo) *marketing communicator, television producer*

Redwood City
Bertman, Roger Bruce *marketing executive*
Bertram, Jack Renard *information systems specialist*
Bruno, Kathleen McGinn *management consultant*
Edwards, Dawn Ann *marketing professional*
FitzGerald, Jerry *security specialist*
Fox, Lorraine Susan *marketing professional*
Gagarin, Dennis Paul *advertising agency executive*
Kirkpatrick, Dennis Oerting *management consultant, benefits and health care*
Lee, Elizabeth Anne *marketing executive*
Miller, Anne Kathleen *training company executive, technical marketing consultant*
Rohde, James Vincent *software systems company executive*

Rialto
Schwartz, Robert John *landscape contractor, landscape designer*

Riverside
Burg, Gary G. *vocational expert*
Chute, Phillip Bruce *management consultant*
Walker, Moira Kaye *sales executive*

Roseville
Furen, Shirley Ann *marketing professional*

Ross
Goulet, William Dawson *marketing professional*

Sacramento
Adelman, William James (William Mylar) *information systems analyst, musician, songwriter*
Anderson, Michael Kenneth *marketing professional*
Briscoe, Agatha Donatto *data processing executive, instructor*
Cannon, Samantha Karrie *management consultant, entrepreneur*
Collings, Charles LeRoy *supermarket executive*
Davies, William Ralph *service executive*
Fedorchak, Timothy Hill *facility planning and program consulting executive*
Fertig, Ted Brian O'Day *producer, public relations and association director*
Hackett, Louise *personnel services company executive, consultant*
Heath, Stephen Richard *communications executive*
Hunt, Dennis *public relations executive*
Kline, Fred Walter *communications company executive*
Lowey-Ball, Albert Edward *health plan management consultant, educator*
McElroy, Leo Francis *communications consultant, journalist*
Ray-Sims, Deborah *marketing analyst*
Solone, Raymond Joseph *advertising executive*

Saint Helena
Spann, Katharine Doyle *marketing and communications executive*

Salinas
Jeffries, Russell Morden *communications company official*

San Anselmo
Beene, M. Melanie *arts management consultant*

San Bernardino
Goodwin, Sandra Joan *management trainer, consultant*

San Carlos
Eby, Michael John *marketing research and technology consultant*
Fleishman, Alan Michael *marketing consultant*
von Herrmann, Bruce Anthony *marketing professional*

San Clemente
Dunlap, Jack Stuart *financial investigator*

San Diego
Adams, Russell Francis *computer company executive, consultant*
Adamson, Robert Michael Knaggs *wellness and conflict resolution specialist*
Bader, Stephen Leigh *communications executive*
Bobkoski, Carl F. *research and development executive*
Broom, Glen Martin *communication educator*
Bryan, John Rodney *management consultant*
Bryant, Steven Bradley *management consultant*
Cady, Joseph Howard *management consultant*
Deuble, John L., Jr. *environmental science and engineering services consultant*
DiRuscio, Lawrence William *advertising executive*
Doll, William *computer company executive*
Downs, Kathleen Joan *purchasing supervisor*
Evans, John Joseph *management consultant*
Faulconer, Thomas Pleasant *aircraft and small ships consultant, retired engineering executive*
Galbraith, Nanette Elaine Gerks *forensic and management sciences company executive*
Gilbertson, Oswald Irving *marketing executive*
Gill, Gail Stoorza *public relations executive*
Gloor, Christopher Barta *corporate professional*
Goodall, Jackson Wallace, Jr. *restaurant company executive*
Gordon, Will *information system specialist*
Grunloh, Howard James *research and development company executive*
Gunter, Emily Diane *communications executive, marketing professional*
Hale, David Fredrick *health care company executive*
Harris, Elliott Sholes *office products executive*
Hawkins, Charles Eugene *private investigator, security consultant*
Hayes, Edward Cary *management consultant*
Hays, Diana Joyce Watkins *consumer products company executive*
Hill, Gordon R. *purchasing executive*
Holden, James Todd *publishing executive*
Infante, Christine Marie *communications consultant*
Izzo, John B(aptist) *management consultant*
Jordan, Jeffrey Guy *foodservice marketing executive*
Kilmer, Maurice Douglas *marketing executive*
Kunkel, Scott William *strategic management and entrepreneurship educator*
Lamden, Evelyn Olson *advertising executive*
Long, Marie Katherine *public relations consultant, researcher*
MacCracken, Peter James *marketing executive, communications executive*
Marchetti, Karen J. *advertising executive*
Miles, Gordon Hugh *restaurant company executive, lawyer*
Miller, Bill *management and marketing consultant*
Mitchell, Thomas Edward, Jr. *communications cabling executive*
Moore, Terry Wayne *management consultant*
Mosteller, James Wilbur, III *data processing executive*
Mueller, Michelle Marie *management executive*
Murray, Robert Michael *telecommunications executive*
Nelson, Craig Alan *management consultant*
Neumann, Renée Anne *marketing professional*
North, Anne Via *public relations administrator*
Nugent, Robert J., Jr. *fast food company executive*
Oolie, Darlene *advertising executive*
Ortiz, Antonio Ignacio *public relations executive*
Perrill, Frederick Eugene *information systems executive*
Province, Sharon G. *research and development executive*
Ronci, Curtis Lee *marketing professional*
Samaras, Thomas Theodore *management system specialist, author, researcher*
Schlesinger, Robert Jackson *business administration educator*
Silverberg, Lewis Henry *management consultant*
Spikes, Rozelia Katherine *management and leadership consultant*
Stoorza Gill, Gail *corporate professional*
Techner, Marc *information systems manager*
Trippe, Anthony Philip *business consultant, technology manager, electronics company executive*
Vallbona-Rayner, Marisa *public relations counselor*
Wallace, Ted *wholesale goods distribution executive*
Ziegaus, Alan James *public relations executive*

San Dimas
Harvey-Melleby, Mary Ann *public relations executive*
Smith, Michael Steven *data processing executive*

San Francisco
Acheson, Alice Brewen *publicist*
Adler, Richard Paul *computer company executive, writer*
Amico, Charles William *management consultant*
Bancel, Marilyn *fund raising management consultant*
Bellows, William *public relations executive*
Bennett, Lewis Tilton, Jr. *advertising and communications company executive, actor*
Bernstein, Gerald William *management consultant, researcher*
Butenhoff, Susan *public relations executive*
Calvin, Dorothy Ver Strate *computer company executive*
Carr-Ruffino, Norma *management educator*
Cheung, Jeffrey *sales and marketing professional*
Colton, Roy Charles *management consultant*
Corporon, Nancy Ann *marketing executive*
Cost, Bruce *cooking educator, writer*
Deasy, John Berchmans *environmental health specialist*
Dykstra, Edie M. *human resource director*
Edgar, James Macmillan, Jr. *management consultant*
Gehb, Michael *public relations executive*
Gesner, Bruce David *consulting company executive*
Gibbons, Jerry Lee *advertising executive*
Goldberg, Fred Sellmann *advertising executive*
Goodby, Jeffrey *advertising agency executive*
Gordon, Judith *communications consultant, writer*
Grayson, Ellison Capers, Jr. *human resources executive*
Gross, Richard Philip *retired business executive*
Harrington, Matthew Jerome *public relations company executive*
Henderson, Nancy Grace *marketing and systems executive*
Holding, Carol Pierson *market positioning consultant*
Holland, Henry Norman *marketing consultant*
Humphreys, Joseph Roy *consultant*
Hurlbert, Roger William *information service industry executive*
Husic, Frank *management consultant*
Jay, Deborah *marketing professional*
Jermann, Jerry *administrator*
Jones, J. Gilbert *research consultant*
Kemp, Jeanne Frances *office manager*
Kielarowski, Henry Edward *marketing executive*
Klammer, Joseph Francis *management consultant*
Landis, Richard Gordon *retired food company executive*
Laspino, Andrew Joseph *business executive, consultant*
Lee, Ivy, Jr. *public relations consultant*
Leighton, Peter Elliott *advertising executive*
Leopold, Michelle Raeanna Saevke *public relations executive*
Levy, Aaron *marketing executive*
Marx, Michael Joseph *market researcher*
Mattia, Thomas Gerard *public relations executive*
McEvoy, Nan Tucker *publishing company executive*
Miller, Burton Leibsle *sales executive*
Miller, Daniel Nathan *communications executive*
Moreno, Paul Michael *media relations manager*
Noonan, William Moss *information systems executive, consultant*
Ollander-Krane, Jason Eric *management consultant*
Otus, Simone *public relations executive*
Pivnicka, Barbara Milliken *marketing executive*
Pollack, Jeffrey Lee *restaurateur*
Pratt, Ronald Franklin *public relations executive*
Rochwarger-Vered, Michelle *management consultant*
Rosenberg, Sydney J. *security company executive*
Russell, Carol Ann *personnel service company executive*
Saunders, Sharon *media director*
Schneeweis, Harold Nathan *security specialist*
Schorb, Jodi Rene *market researcher*
Shackley, Douglas John *fire alarm company executive*
Smith, Christopher Allen *technology company executive, marketing professional*
Smith, Jillaine Sue *computer services specialist*
Staub, Anita (Anita Kilpatrick) *management analyst, educator*
Steele, Evelyn Jane *public relations and advertising executive*
Tarter, Blodwen *marketing and information technology executive*
Taylor, Peter van Voorhees *advertising and public relations consultant*
Thompson, Gary W. *public relations executive*
Todd, James Hiram, II *management consultant*
Tonini, Leon Richard *sales professional*
Torme, Margaret Anne *public relations executive, communications consultant*
Weber, Susan Lee *marketing consultant*
Wentz, Jeffrey Lee *information systems consultant*
West, Hugh Sterling *aircraft leasing company executive*
Willner, Jay R. *consulting company executive*
Winkler, Agnieszka M. *advertising executive*

San Gabriel
Di Massa, Ernani Vincenzo, Jr. *broadcast executive, television producer, writer*
Ramirez, Ralph Roy *management consultant*

San Jose
Almon, William Joseph *data processing company executive*
Anderson, Susan Lynne *sales executive*
Beverett, Andrew Jackson *marketing executive*
Bunn, Charles Nixon *strategic business planning consultant*
Castagnetto, Perry Michael *retail sales executive*
Chung, Heon Hwa *research and development executive*
Connor, Gary Edward *manufacturing company marketing executive*
Dornblaser, David W. *marketing professional*
Franson, Paul Oscar, III *public relations executive*
Hale, Carl Dennis *electronics company executive*
Harkins, Craig *management consultant*
Harrus, Alain Simon *marketing professional*
Highlander, Richard William *communications executive*
Honda, Yoshio *computer company executive*
Hutcheson, Jerry Dee *market research company executive*
Lee, Murlin E. *program manager*
Lutvak, Mark Allen *computer company executive*
McCoy, James M. *data processing, computer company executive*
McGuire, Thomas Roger *distribution company executive*
Murase, Teruo *computer executive*
Nguyen, Lam Duc *business executive, consultant*
Nguyen, Thomas *computer executive*
Ostrom, Philip Gardner *computer company executive*
Rokos, John Paul *marketing professional*
Sisco, Dennis G. *marketing professional*
Smith, Charles Richard *marketing executive*
Stegman, Charles Alexander (Chuck Alexander Stegman) *marketing professional*

San Leandro
Ahrens, Erick Karl Frederick *computer software executive*

San Luis Obispo
Bunge, Russell Kenneth *writer*
Vanderspek, Peter George *management consultant, writer*

San Marino
Christy, Thomas Patrick *human resources executive, educator*

San Mateo
Helfert, Erich Anton *management consultant, author, educator*
Larkin, Nelle Jean *computer programmer, analyst*
Nazzaro, David Alfred *sales executive*
Stuart, Brian Michael *employee benefits and insurance sales consultant*
Van Dyke, Elizabeth Artemis *management executive and consultant*
Wigglesworth, David Cunningham *business and management consultant*
Witwer, Jeffrey Garth *marketing executive*

San Pedro
Gammell, Gloria Ruffner *sales executive*

San Rafael
Davis, Linda Jacobs *public affairs development professional*
Friesecke, Raymond Francis *management consultant*
Thompson, John William *international management consultant*
Wilson, Ian Holroyde *management consultant, futurist*
Yuan, Shao-Yuen *management consultant*

San Ramon
Brown, Joan Mazzaferro *telephone company executive*
Donnally, Patrick Andrew *quality management consultant*
Gardner, Nord Arling *management consultant*
Kuhl, Ronald Webster *marketing executive*
Lee, Robert *telecommunications executive*
Leftwich, James Stephen *management consultant*
Moore, Justin Edward *data processing executive*
Saunders, Brian Keith *consulting company executive*
Warren, Sandra Lyn *quality assurance professional*

Santa Ana
Boynton, William Lewis *electronic manufacturing company official*
Caines, Kenneth L.D. *management consulting executive*
de Lespinay, Philippe *auto racing safety industry consultant, small business owner*
Holtz, Joseph Norman *marketing executive*
Keller, Kent Eugene *advertising and public relations executive*
LaGreen, Alan Lennart *public relations executive, radio personality*
Lesly, Craig Edwards *marketing professional*
Mercier, Michael Anthony *advertising executive*
Sieck, Greg R. *advertising executive*
Thompson, David Charles, Sr. *management executive*

Santa Barbara
Amory, Thomas Carhart *management consultant*
Emmons, Robert John *corporate executive*
Green, Russell Peter *management consultant*
Hanley, Kevin Lance *maintenance manager*
Hasler, Geoff Julian *marketing consultant*
Herb, Frederick William *hotel executive*
Maas, Joan Louise *training and development consultant*
Rasher, George Joseph *sales executive*
Trigg, Douglas A. *marketing and business development executive*

Santa Clara
Barrett, Craig R. *computer company executive*
Candia, Tanya Marie *marketing executive*
Cayne, Douglas Andrew *computer company executive*
Gauff, Susan Tyrrell *marketing executive*
Kaner, Cem *lawyer, computer software consultant*
Kenny, Alan Dennis *international sales executive, computer educator*
Li Dessau, Kathryn Dairoh *product manager*
Menkin, Christopher (Kit Menkin) *leasing company executive*
Rudisin, Gerard John *marketing executive*
Rudolph, Ronald Alvin *human resources executive*
Szteinbaum, Samuel *marketing executive, small business owner*
Venuti, Stephen *advertising executive*
Vincent, David Ridgely *management consulting executive*

Santa Cruz
Brough, Bruce Alvin *public relations and communications executive*
Phanes, Margaret Astrid *trainer, visual designer*
Swartz, Ray *data processing executive*

Santa Fe Springs
Hammond, Judy McLain *business services executive*

Santa Monica
Battle, Thomas Howard *human resources executive*
Bershon, Lawrence Chollett *advertising executive*
Cohn, Frederic *business executive*
Corrigan, Gerald F. *executive search consultant*
Donati, Daniel Edward *marketing professional*
Field, Edward C. *research executive*
Frank, Ann-Marie *sales administration executive*
Fraser, Renee *advertising executive*
Jones, Penn Holter *advertising executive*
Krakower, Bernard Hyman *management consultant*
Lucas, James Bruno *public relations consultant*
Nathanson, Joseph S. *public relations professional, writer*
Price, David *recreational facilities executive*

Santa Rosa
Cavanagh, John Charles *advertising agency executive*
Walton, Deborah Gail *advertising agency executive*

Saratoga
Ippoliti, Ralphine Ann *program manager*

Scotts Valley
Delear, Richard Henry *personnel consultant*
Filler, Gary B. *computer company executive*
Shugart, Alan F. *electronic computing equipment company executive*

Seal Beach
Burge, Willard, Jr. *software company executive*

Deutsch, Barry Joseph *management development company executive*
Thompson, Craig Snover *corporate communications executive*

Sherman Oaks
Ghent, Peer *management consultant*
Holst, Sanford *strategic consulting executive, author*
Peters, Claire Leila *public relations, advertising executive*
Rieder, Ronald Frederick *public relations executive*

Sierra Madre
MacGillivray, MaryAnn Leverone *marketing professional*

Signal Hill
Bagarry, Alexander Anthony, III *quality assurance professional*
Jarman, Donald Ray *public relations professional, minister, retired*
Wohl, Charles Martin *business development executive*

Solana Beach
Friedmann, Lynne Timpani *public relations consultant, writer*
Jebens, Arthur Bertram *management consultant, lawyer*

Sonora
Mathias, Betty Jane *communications and community affairs consultant, writer, editor, lecturer*

South Lake Tahoe
Armstrong, Anna Dawn *marketing professional, writer*

South Pasadena
Lowe, Richard Gerald, Jr. *computer programming manager*

South San Francisco
Lewis, Jason Alvert, Jr. *communications executive*
Sorstokke, Ellen Kathleen *marketing executive, educator*

Stanford
Hellyer, Constance Anne *communications executive, writer*
Miller, William Frederick *research company executive, educator, business consultant*

Stockton
Hall-Hackley, Carol Ann *public relations educator, consultant*
Prevo, Randall Murray *personnel administrator*
Viscovich, Andrew John *educational management consultant*

Studio City
Chambers, Clytia Montllor *public relations consultant*
Hahn, Mark Stephen *computer security specialist, educator*
Land, Carol Jeanne *marketing professional, writer*

Suisun City
Schlenker, Edgar Albert *business director, educator, entrepreneur*

Sunnyvale
Anastole, Dorothy Jean *electronics company executive*
Byers, Charles Frederick *public relations executive, marketing executive*
Clinton, John Philip Martin *communications executive*
Griffin, Joseph Edward *multimedia and telecommunications executive*
Hansen, David Lee *sales and marketing executive*
Michals, Lee Marie *travel agency executive*
Palmer, Daniel Lee *data communication manufacturing company executive*
Previte, Richard *computer company executive*
White, Eugene R. *computer manufacturing company executive*
Zemke, (E.) Joseph *computer company executive*

Surfside
Sonne, Maggie Lee *sales executive*

Sylmar
Heekin, Valerie Anne *telecommunications technician*
Pocrass, Richard Dale *management consultant*

Taft
Smith, Lee L. *hotel executive*

Temecula
Coram, David James *marketing professional*

Thousand Oaks
Cobb, Shirley Ann *public relations specialist*
Dunaway, Robert Lee *sales and marketing executive*
Forti, Corinne Ann *corporate communications executive*
Guggenheim, Suzanne *company executive*
Lark, M. Ann *management consultant, strategic planner*

Toluca Lake
Mracky, Ronald Sydney *marketing management and promotion executive, tourism consultant*

Torrance
Carey, Kathryn Ann *advertising and public relations agency executive, consultant*
Cowart, R. Greg *sales executive*
Djujich, David B. *computer software company executive*
Douglass, Craig Bruce *computer technology executive*
Herendeen, David Louis *software company executive*
Hoyt, Leeza Lee *public relations and advertising firm executive*
Ko, Denny R. S. *research & development executive*
McQuillin, Richard Ross *management consultant*
Oda, Todd I. *quality assurance professional*
Signorovitch, Dennis James *communications executive*
Walti, Randal Fred *management consultant*

Tracy
Green, Brian Gerald *marketing executive*
Snedker, Clive John *advertising executive*

Tustin
Ding, Mae Lon *employee compensation consultant*
Jay, David Jakubowicz *management consultant*
Kelley, Robert Paul, Jr. *management consultation executive*
LeBow, Bennett S. *communications executive*
Suski, Sherrie Leigh *human resources specialist*

Twentynine Palms
Fultz, Philip Nathaniel *management analyst*

Union City
Berg, Kevin Allan *management consultant, retail executive*
Wohlmut, Thomas Arthur *communications executive*

Upland
Duffy, Patrick Sean *marketing research executive*
Garrison, Lloyd Robert *marketing and sales professional*
Hext, Kathleen Florence *regulatory compliance consultant*
Lewis, Edward Norman *marketing executive*

Vacaville
Young, Roger Carl *computer company executive*

Vallejo
Sumner, Leo F., II *management consultant*

Van Nuys
Bick, Israel *collectables and memorabilia company executive*
Goldie, Eric Todd *marketing professional*
Kagan, Stephen Bruce (Sandy Kagan) *travel agency executive*

Venice
Chiat, Jay *advertising agency executive*
Giaquinta, Gerald J. *public relations executive*
King, Frederic *health services management executive, educator*
Thomas, Bob *public relations executive*

Villa Park
Britton, Thomas Warren, Jr. *management consultant*

Vista
Beversdorf, Anne Elizabeth *educational marketing consultant, small business owner*
Williams, Knox *water conditioning company executive*

Walnut Creek
Baumann, Frederick *management consultant*
Garlough, William Glenn *marketing executive*
Moore, John D. *consultant*
Raumer, Ronald Jay *management consultant*
Scott, Gloria *publishing marketing consultant*
White, James Mackey *computer and telecommunications consultant*
Wilkins, Sheila Scanlon *management consultant*

Watsonville
Kodis, Mary Caroline *marketing consultant*
Osmer, Frank Edmond *private investigator, consultant*

West Hollywood
Holt, Dennis F. *media buying company executive*
Rajabi-Asl, Ali *information systems specialist, consultant*

Westlake Village
Catrambone, Eugene Dominic *public relations consultant*
Doherty, Patrick Francis *communications executive, educator*
Murdock, David H. *diversified company executive*
Powers, Jeffrey *business executive, speaker*
Tran, Hai Phuoc *purchasing executive, manufacturing engineer*

Whittier
Ittner, Perry Martin *sales and marketing consultant*

Woodland Hills
Maeda, J. A. *data processing executive*
Randall, Craig *financial management consultant, accountant, computer specialist*
Woodbridge-Kiradjian, Frances Wolsey *marketing professional*

Woodside
Giovenco, John V. *hotel corporation executive*

Yorba Linda
Tuttle, Frank Douglas *marketing executive*

Yountville
Buchanan, Teri Bailey *communications executive*

Yucca Valley
Clay, Sean Cochrane *software development company executive*

COLORADO

Arvada
Hulse, Ralph Robert *management consultant*

Aurora
Brunell, David H. *information systems specialist*
Gorman, Barbara Rose *secretarial service administrator*
Hadsall, Debra June *business service and consulting executive*
Harlan, Raymond Carter *communication executive*
Pohlman, David Lawrence *training systems consultant*
Reitan, Harold Theodore *management consultant*
Smith, James Micheal *marketing executive*
Tarin, William Michael *publications engineer*

Avon
Marshall, James Kenneth *consulting services executive*

Boulder
Anderson, Michael George *marketing and advertising executive*
Bryson, Gary Spath *cable television and telephone company executive*
Burns, Michael Edward *technology company executive*
Ciciora, John A. *research and development executive*
Fisher, Joseph Stewart *management consultant*
Fleener, Terry Noel *marketing professional*
Hart, Michael John *environmental management*
Havdala, Ellen *business executive*
Heffron, Michael Edward *computer scientist*
Hibbs, John David *software executive, engineer, business owner*
Jerritts, Stephen G. *computer company executive*
Keim, Elizabeth M. *computer company executive*
Lavallee, Deirdre Justine *marketing professional*
Matten, Jeffrey S. *quality assurance engineer, computer consultant*
Philipsborn, Randall H. *disaster preparedness consultant*
Smith, William B. *research and development executive*
Watson, William Randy *marketing executive*
Yost, Douglas Leighton *data processing executive*

Broomfield
Cole, Lee Arthur *new product development executive*
Thurber, Howard L. *management consultant, writer*

Castle Rock
Danner, Paul Kruger, III *telecommunications executive*

Colorado Springs
Albers, Ardell (Bud Albers) *software development executive*
Bayne, Kim Miklofsky *marketing communications and public relations professional, consultant, author*
Bondurant, David William *marketing professional*
Comes, Robert George *research scientist*
Doray, Andrea Wesley *advertising administrator, writer*
Eitel, Karl Emil *hotel executive*
Ford, James Carlton *human resources executive*
Fortune, James Michael *marketing executive*
Guthrie, David Neal *marketing executive*
Hurley, Rebecca Johnson *marketing professional*
Hyman, Kevin Michael *communications executive*
Ledbetter, Logan Scott *management consultant*
Lewis, Sheila Muriel *retired communications management specialist*
McDevitt, John Alfred *program manager, military officer, retired*
Midkiff, Donald Wayne *program manager*
Mills, Sherry Rae *training and conference planning*
Schoonmaker, Robert Cadbury *management consultant*
Shaddock, Paul Franklin, Sr. *human resources director*
Tanous, Michael Allan *consulting company executive*
Underwood, Ralph Edward *computer systems engineer*
Weinstein, Steven Samuel *marketing executive*

Denver
Avrin, David Lawrence *public relations executive, legislative liason, vocalist*
Ayers, Rendall Paul *public relations consultant*
Callender, Jonathan Ferris *environmental consultant*
Catherwood, Hugh Robert *public administration consultant*
Caudle, Jones Richard, III *marketing and management consultant*
Clinch, Nicholas Bayard, III *business executive*
Cooper, Larry S. *cleaning network executive, textile consultant*
Dolsen, David Horton *mortician*
Duffy, Michael Lee *marketing professional, engineer*
Duke, Harold Benjamin, Jr. *retired holding company executive*
Fisher, Denise Danches *public relations executive, marketing consultant*
Gross, Beatrice Marie *public relations manager*
Hamrick, Joseph Eugene, Jr. *information services specialist*
Harris, Howard Jeffrey *marketing and printing company executive*
Heck, Gary L. *security management company executive*
Henry, David Allen *advertising executive*
Horwich, Franklin M. *software company executive*
Johnston, Gwinavere Adams *public relations consultant*
Kostka, William James, Jr. *public relations executive*
Kurtz, Maxine *personnel executive, lawyer*
Lehmann, Werner Hans *mail order company executive*
Leiweke, Timothy *sales executive, marketing professional*
Mackinnon, Peggy Louise *public relations executive*
Magee, Douglas Scott *public relations executive*
Marcus, Jeffrey Howard *electronic security system company executive*
Martin, Robert Burton *management consultant*
McLean, Robin Jennifer *marketing, advertising professional*
Miller, Mary Anne *marketing professional*
Miller, Thomas Cecil *private investigator, forensic examiner, lawyer*
Muftic, Felicia Anne Boillot *consumer relations professional*
Murdock, Pamela Ervilla *advertising executive*
Murray, James Alan *urban and environmental consultant, investor*
Neu, Carl Herbert, Jr. *management consultant*
Owen, William Frederick *engineering and management consultant*
Patterson, Nadine Warner *communications manager*
Peck, George Holmes *public relations executive*
Perez, Timothy Allen *software company administrator*
Reece Myron, Monique Elizabeth *marketing, advertising and sales consultant*
Robinson, Lisa Hertz *public relations consultant*
Schiell, Charles Randall *leasing company executive*
Schlueter, Jeffrey J. *marketing executive*
Schotters, Bernard William *communications company executive*
Scott, Mark Richard *information services executive*
Self, Vicki Joye *advertising executive*
Servoss, Marcus Edward *public relations executive*
Shuler, Sally Ann Smith *telecommunications, computer services and software company executive*
Stark, Philip Herald *information company executive*
Sundel, Harvey H. *marketing research analyst and consultant*
Weber, Molly Smith *sales executive*
Welchert, Steven Joseph *public affairs consultant*
Williams, Sue M. *corporate communications specialist, writer*
Wirkkala, John Lester *software company executive*
Wodell, Geoffrey Robert *management consultant*
Wolfe, Brian Augustus *sales executive*

Durango
Solt, Gail Ann *marketing professional, consultant*

Englewood
Bowlin, Gregory Lee *marketing professional*
Burgess, Robert John *marketing consultant, writer, educator*
Butler, John Michael, II *international business consultant*
Cooper, Steven Jon *healthcare management consultant, educator*
Hobbs, Stephen Craig *management consultant*
Hughes, Bradley Richard *marketing executive*
Jones, Glenn Robert *cable systems executive*
Kail, Joseph Gerard *computer sales executive, marketing executive*
Kuhn, Donald Marshall *marketing professional*
Lake, Stanley James *security consulting company executive, motel chain executive, locksmith*
Mahadev, Rajesh *strategic marketing professional*
Milford, Peggy R. *communications executive*
Reisinger, George Lambert *management consultant*
Rounds, Donald Michael *public relations executive*
Sutton-Jones, Sue *quality systems executive*
Walsh, Thomas George *information services industry executive*

Estes Park
Thomas, David Timothy *marketing professional*

Evergreen
Fischer, Peter Heinz *public relations specialist*
Kennerly, Linda Anne *marketing executive*
Rodolff, Dale Ward *sales executive, consultant*

Fort Collins
Butcher, Richard Kent *local market manager*
Gilmore, Timothy Jonathan *physician recruiter*
Meyer, Susan Theresa *business and training industry consultant*
Newlin, Douglas Randal *learning products engineer*

Golden
Allen, Sam Raymond *organization development specialist*
Guettich, Bruce Michael *sporting goods company executive*
Nelson, Frances Patricia *food service executive*
Springer, Gerald William *sales executive*

Grand Junction
Stanton, Campbell Edgar *energy consultant*

Greeley
Miller, Diane Wilmarth *human resources director*

Lafayette
Johnson, Holly Rouillard *public relations executive*

Lakewood
Boyd, John Garth *manufacturing production and operations consultant*
Kuehn, JoDee Stahlecker *information technology consultant*
Leaming, Marj P(atricia) *management and marketing consultant, researcher*
Rhamy, Jennifer Frances *marketing professional*
Richards, Robert Charles *management consultant*
Shoe, Stephen Charles *marketing professional*
Walton, Roger Alan *public relations executive, mediator, writer*
Wells, Mark Alan *systems manager*

Littleton
Hopping, William Russell *hospitality industry consultant and appraiser*
VanderLinden, Carl Rene *consulting company executive*
Zewe, Judith Lynn *human resources professional*

Longmont
Cornay, Stacy Shelton *public relations specialist*
Greene, Sharon Louise *computer executive director*
Kleppinger, Moselle Lee *public relations professional*
Nevling, Harry Reed *health care human resources executive*

Louisville
Green, Richard R. *communications executive*
Williams, Marsha Kay *data processing executive*

Nederland
Wood, Kevin Michael *sales consultant*

Parker
Jankura, Donald Eugene *hotel executive, educator*
Pastore, Thomas Michael *telecommunications sales executive*

Pitkin
Cox, Roger Gordon *educational software company executive*

Pueblo
Arveschoug, Steven Neil *communications executive, state representative*
Carter, Jack Ralph *broadcasting administrator, television personality*

Silverthorne
Schaffer, Thomas Ray *waste management executive*

Griggs, Gail *marketing executive*
Hougan, Tom McKay *advertising executive*
Linstone, Harold Adrian *management and systems science educator*
Locke, Timothy Atwater *marketing communications executive*
Martin, Lucy Z. *public relations executive*
Middlewood, Martin Eugene *technical communications specialist, writer, consultant*
Mitchell, James Herbert *public relations consultant*
Rupp, Jean Louise *communications executive, author*
Sackett, Timothy David *information systems specialist*
Schoppe, James Henry *printing company executive*
Scott, Patricia Jean *educational telecommunications administrator*
Smith, Preston Gibson *management consultant, engineering executive*
Sweeney, Christee A. *public relations executive*
Tahan, Mary Rizkallah *advertising executive*
Tobias, Christopher Ord *software company executive*
Urbanowski, John Richard *lighting systems company official*
Waggener, Melissa *public relations executive*
Wieden, Dan G. *advertising executive*

Roseburg
Parkinson, Thomas Brian *marketing executive*
Plunkett, Marvin Wayne *data processing company executive*
Radcliffe, Nancy Jean Dymond *communications analyst*

Salem
Alves, Carol Ann *administrative assistant*
Baker, Edwin Stuart *retired computer consultant*
Franks, David Allan *communications administrator*
Hands, Elizabeth S. (Elizabeth S. Geltz) *nutrition analysis software company executive*
Lytle, Roy Douglas *manufacturing executive*
Nelson, David Samuel *public relations executive*
Sheldon, Susan Frances *data administration manager*

Scappoose
Trudel, John Davis *management consultant*

Tualatin
Peters, Robert Wayne *direct mail and catalog sales specialist*

West Linn
Garcia, Pamela Marcott *supermarket and real estate investments executive*
Ureel, Patricia Lois *retired manufacturing company executive*

Wilsonville
Kehoe, James William, Jr. *marketing manager*

TEXAS

Bedford
Desilva, Ranjit Nihal *leadership training consultant*

Fort Worth
Boyce, Allan R. *human resources executive*

Houston
Wing, Michael James *marketing research company executive*

UTAH

American Fork
Kitto, Franklin Curtis *computer systems specialist*

Bountiful
Carter, Mildred Brown *executive assistant*

Brigham City
Curtis, Glen Russell *program manager*

Dugway
Christensen, Steven Brent *data processing executive*

Farmington
Smith, Marilyn Jean *administrative analyst*

Heber City
McLean, Hugh Angus *management consultant*

Kaysville
Preece, Norma *executive secretary*
Spiel, Robert Freeman *distribution services executive*

Logan
Garner, Jerryle Gail *food service executive, management consultant*
Thomas, Kent Swenson *sales executive*

Murray
Alba, Felix *industrial computer systems company executive*

Ogden
Johnson, Kenneth Louis *education marketing specialist*

Orem
Morey, Robert Hardy *communications executive*
Sawyer, Thomas Edgar *management consultant*
Theurer, Alan Clark *information management specialist*

Park City
Ebbs, George Heberling, Jr. *management consulting company executive*
Kanten, Steven Craig *communications company executive*

Provo
Clark, Loyal Frances *public affairs specialist*
Feller, Wilford Carter *jewelry retailer, manufacturing company executive*
Herrera, Shirley Mae *personnel and security executive*

Hutchison, Merrill Dean *recreation facility professional*
Newell, Gregory John *international business advisor*
Soter, Nicholas Gregory *advertising agency executive*
Valenti, JoAnn Myer *environmental and mass communications researcher, educator*

Roy
Coy, David Dale *marketing professional*

Saint George
Petersen, Mark L. *public relations executive*

Salt Lake City
Adamson, Jack *communications executive*
Brackett, Louis Vincent *recreation and park administration educator*
Davis, Gene *public relations professional, state legislator*
Gardner, Kathleen Harmon *development administrator*
Jones, Clark David *restaurant executive, accountant*
Kinard, J. Spencer *television news executive*
Lund, Victor L. *retail food company executive*
Mills, Carol Margaret *business consultant, public relations consultant*
Olsen, Rodney Wayne *business development manager, technical consultant*
Phillips, Ted Ray *advertising agency executive*
Scott, Howard Winfield, Jr. *temporary help services company executive*
Thomas, Linda Marri Gandy *administrative assistant*
Young, Scott Thomas *business management educator*

Sandy
Wenn, Derek Jay *marketing professional*
York, Theodore Robert *consulting company executive*

Tremonton
Thompson, (Gerry) Maxine Leak *supply manager, inventory director*

VIRGINIA

Alexandria
Feist-Fite, Bernadette *international and business education consultant*

WASHINGTON

Anacortes
Spaulding, John Pierson *public relations executive, marine consultant*

Auburn
Howard, George Harmon *management consultant*

Bellevue
Allen, Paul *computer executive, professional sports team owner*
Dayton, Douglas Emory *computer marketing consultant*
Dykstra, David Charles *management executive, consultant, accountant, author, educator*
Johnson, Gary Kent *management education company executive*
Kraft, Elaine Joy *community relations and communications official*
Magallanes, Deborah Jean *business consulting company executive*
Mittelstaedt, Rick H. *technical communicator*
Ruiz, Anthony *organizational development consultant, educator*
Winsor, David John *cost consultant*

Bellingham
Haverstraw, Dean L. *information systems executive*

Bothell
Burklund, Patricia Helen *marketing professional*
Culver, Larry G. *medical research executive*
Finney, Linnea Ruth *tailor, educator, accountant*
Herron, Sidney Earl *sales executive*

Burlington
Herbaugh, Roger Duane *computer and software company executive*

Centralia
Brown, Stephan Mark *international fundraising and resource development executive, consultant*

Edmonds
Monks, Caron Lorraine *marketing specialist*
Sankovich, Joseph Bernard *cemetery management consultant*

Ellensburg
Lynde, Gary Gray *human resource manager*

Everett
Gerwick-Brodeur, Madeline Carol *marketing and sales professional*

Federal Way
Cole, David Winslow *personal care industry executive*
Muzyka-McGuire, Amy *marketing professional, nutrition consultant*

Gig Harbor
Stoner, Sue *travel consultant*

Issaquah
Giles, David Edward *management consultant*
Handron, Deanne Westfall *management consulting executive*

Kelso
Koethke, Charles Richard *advertising specialist, consultant*

Kennewick
Adams, Warren Dale *resource development and communications director*

Bland-Schricker, Laurel Le Mieux *human resources executive, consultant*

Kent
Bohn, Edward M. *research and development executive*
Brinton, Richard Kirk *marketing executive*
Cheung, John B. *research and development executive*
Krieps, Mara J. *marketing professional*

Kirkland
Alberg, Tom Austin *communications executive, lawyer*
Detlor, John Sydney *security executive*
Holbrook, Michael Edward *communications company executive*

Lacey
La Brue, Terry J. *advertising executive*

Littlerock
Gunderson, Cleon Henry *management consultant corporation executive*

Loon Lake
Ranck, John Stevens *human resources executive, consultant*

Lynnwood
Hoerner, Michael Duane *beauty salon executive*

Maple Valley
Jordan, Michael Aytch *accounts manager*

Mill Creek
Wilkins, Elizabeth Ann *staff development and training consultant*

Oak Harbor
Gailey, Charles Franklin, Jr. *maritime consultant*
Meaux, Alan Douglas *facilities technician, sculptor*

Olympia
Adkins, Ben Frank *management and engineering consultant*
Marcelynas, Richard Chadwick *management consultant*
Mount, Marsha Louise *management consultant*
Ogden, Valeria Juan *management consultant, state representative*
Petersen, Donald Felix *consultant*

Poulsbo
Seteroff, Sviatoslav Steve *management and logistics information systems consultant*

Redmond
Gates, William Henry, III *software company executive*
Gilmore, A. Douglas *retail sales executive*
Mak, Stanley Ming *distributor, importer, trading consultant, radio broadcasting management consultant*
Mauk, Pamela Anne *marketing and development consultant*

Richland
Eckard, Roy Conrad (Connie Eckard) *communications consultant, writer, editor*
Sandlin, Steven Monroe *power company contracts executive*
Towner, Larry Edwin *consulting company executive*
Zuberi, Shakir H. *management consultant*

Seattle
Ager, Stephanie *public relations executive*
Ashworth, Alan A. *human resources professional*
Aufderhaar, Susan *data processing executive*
Bates, Charles Walter *human resources executive, lawyer, educator*
Beer, Joseph Ernest *telecommunications manager*
Beetham, Stanley Williams *international management consultant*
Bianco, James A. *research and development executive*
Carter, Janice Joene *telecommunications executive*
Dangla, Kristine Lindsay *marketing director, consultant*
DeBon, George A. *security services company executive*
Dederer, Michael Eugene *public relations company executive*
DuBois, Patricia LaVonne *retail mobile electronics company executive*
Duryee, David Anthony *management consultant*
Elgin, Ron Alan *advertising executive*
Feinberg, David Allen *computer software executive*
Grover, Stuart Ralph *management consultant*
Hamilton, Charles Edward, Jr. *communication consultant*
Harrison, William Craig *computer company executive*
Hurlow, Randal Thomas *communications executive*
Imre, John VanArsdale *quality improvement consultant*
Kane, Karen Marie *public affairs consultant*
Kaperick, John Anthony *information specialist*
Kelly, Dennis Ray *sales executive*
Kevane, Raymond A. *career consultant, management consultant*
Kimball, Russell Drew *management consultant*
Kolbeson, Marilyn Hopf *retired advertising executive, organization and management consultant, educator*
Kunkel, Gerald Robert *marketing professional, interior designer*
Leale, Olivia Mason *import marketing company executive*
McCallister, Wren Vance *building services company executive*
Miyata, Keijiro *culinary arts educator*
Murray, Connel Lyle *advertising and public relations executive, consultant*
Nordstrom, James F. *department store executive*
Notkin, David *computer science educator*
O'Leary, Thomas Howard *resources executive*
Patten, Richard E. *personnel company owner*
Philips, Peter Maury *magazine advertising executive*
Porad, Laurie Jo *jewelry company official*
Rockey, Jay *public relations company executive*
Scafe, Lincoln Robert, Jr. *retired sales executive*
Simpson, Ann Marcoux *sports marketing executive*
Southwell, Phyllis Arlene *medical transcriptionist*

Steele, Frank Channel *sales executive*
Whitty, Raymond John *hotel company executive*
Widener, Peri Ann *business development executive*
Wilson, Emily Marie *sales executive*
Worstell, Karen Freeman *data processing executive*

Sequim
Lindamood, George Edward *computer consultant*

Spokane
Ballinger, Charles Kenneth *information specialist*
Desautel, James Michael *public relations executive, writer*
Glatzer, Robert Anthony *advertising executive*
Higgins, Shaun O'Leary *media executive*
Nicolai, Eugene Ralph *public relations consultant, editor, writer*
Olson, William Thomas *business executive, educator, consultant*
Storey, Francis Harold *business consultant, retired bank executive*
Tsutakawa, Edward Masao *management consultant*
Woodard, Alva Abe *business consultant*

Tacoma
Bailey, Brian Dennis *management consultant, author, publisher*
Chang, Taiping *marketing executive, magazine publisher*
Crayne, Zonna Marie *information systems executive*
Hudson, Edward Voyle *linen supply company executive*
Keister, Marie Silver *public relations professional*
Knudson, Melvin Robert *management consultant, business executive*
Licens, Lila Louise *administrative assistant*
Lindsey, John Cunningham *sales executive*
Lonergan, Michael Henry *development administrator, journalist*
Metsker, Thomas Charles *map company executive*
Neeb, Martin John *media executive*
Proudfit, Donna Mae *executive search consultant*
Robinson, Richard Allen, Jr. *human resources development trainer, consultant*

Tonasket
Vawter, Donald *retired personnel management consultant*

Vancouver
Barenis, Pat Peaster *wholesale distribution company executive*
Munroe, Donna Scott *marketing executive, healthcare and management consultant, educator*
Soltisiak, Christina Ann *management consultant*

Walla Walla
Drumheller, George Jesse *motel and hotel chain owner*
Potts, Charles Aaron *management executive, writer*

Wenatchee
Montague, Gary Leslie *newspaper advertising executive*

Woodinville
Addams, Robert Jean *business and financial consultant*
Newlands, Sheila Ann *consumer products company executive, controller*

Yakima
Myers, Elizabeth Rouse *management consultant*

WISCONSIN

Monroe
Bishop, Carolyn Benkert *public relations counselor*

WYOMING

Casper
Kennerknecht, Richard Eugene *marketing executive*
Perkins, Dorothy A. *marketing professional*

Cheyenne
Meister, Verle Martin *management recruiter*

Gillette
Missett, Kathryn McAndrew *public relations expert*

Jackson
Eddy, David Maxon *health policy and management educator*
Young, Suzanne Marye *management consultant*

Laramie
Armintrout, Edward Gilbert *human resources executive*
Hanly, Jeri Ryan *computer science educator*
Hashimoto, Lloyd Ken *communications executive*
Rucinski, Robert D. *environmental company executive*

Riverton
Hudson, Gary Michael *corporate executive*

Sheridan
Schellinger, James Raymond *advertising sales executive*
Taylor, Judith Ann *sales executive*

CANADA

ALBERTA

Calgary
Sturgess, P. Kim *management executive consultant*

Edmonton
Cross, Allan Joseph *security software company co-owner, executive*

BRITISH COLUMBIA

Burnaby
Canfield, Brian A. *communications company executive*

Richmond
Smith, Michael C. B. *restaurant executive*

Vancouver
Anglesio, Franco J. *hotel executive*
Chu, Allen Yum-Ching *automation company executive, systems consultant*

ITALY

Stezzano
Lucas, James Gregory *marketing executive*

REPUBLIC OF KOREA

Taegu
Bowman, Larry Wayne *investigator, English and criminal justice educator*

ADDRESS UNPUBLISHED

Akbarian, Shah-Rokh *management consultant*
Alden, Susan Jane *technical writing agency executive*
Allen, Timothy Burbank *recreational company executive*
Allison, William Robert *management consultant*
Ambrose, Thomas Cleary *communications executive*
Anderson, Mark Robert *data processing executive, biochemist*
Anderson, Roscoe Odell (Dale) *retired personnel officer*
Ariss, Rushdi Alberto *marketing professional, systems engineer*
Bailey, John Arthur *management consultant*
Bakeman, Carol Ann *administrative services manager, singer*
Baker, Marjorie Neuman *information broker*
Bartling, Judd Quenton *research corporation executive*
Bauer, Charles Edward *microelectronics consultant*
Beasley, James Mercer *travel environmentalist, consultant*
Beck, Timothy Daniel *human resources specialist, consultant*
Becker, Patricia Winifred *hotel and casino company executive*
Bernstein, Steve Miller *market research specialist*
Blevins, Bryan O'Donnell *management consultant, dentist*
Borson, Robert Oliver *communication executive, consultant*
Bowers, John Charles *computer company executive*
Bradbury, John Wymond *sales executive*
Braden, George Walter, II (Lord of Carrigaline) *company executive*
Brennen, Stephen Alfred *international business consultant*
Brown, Bart A., Jr. *consumer products company executive*
Brown, Thomas Raymond *marketing company executive*
Brun, Margaret Ann Charlene *buyer, planner*
Buel, James Wes *food service executive*
Burney, Victoria Kalgaard *business consultant, civic worker*
Cabanya, Mary Louise *software development executive, rancher*
Calhoun, John Joseph *advertising executive*
Camper, John Saxton *public relations and marketing executive*
Cantor, Mara Judith *human resources executive, management consultant*
Caplan, John Alan *executive search company executive*
Carter, David MacCormick *management consultant*
Cassidy, Adrian Clyde *telephone company executive*
Cerbone, Robert *sales executive*
Chamberlain, William Edwin, Jr. *management consultant*
Chao, Ronald J. *communications executive*
Charles, Lyn Ellen *marketing executive, commercial artist, photographer*
Chesney, Susan Talmadge *human resources specialist*
Chin, Janet Sau-Ying *data processing executive, consultant*
Christensen, John Stanley *management executive*
Clark, Sheri Lynn *public relations and marketing executive*
Clarke, Paul A. *public relations professional*
Clayton, Cathy J. *healthcare marketing executive*
Collett, Merrill Judson *management consultant*
Collings, Celeste Louise (Shorty Vassalli) *marketing executive, professional artist*
Colucci, Chuck Roger *management consultant*
Cook, Galen Bruce *computer company executive*
Cotter, John Catlin *marketing consultant*
Cotter, Lawrence Raffety *management consultant*
Cree, Dean Edward *computer software consultant*
Criswell, Kimberly Ann *public relations executive*
Crombach, Danita Lynn *communications professional*
Crosson, John Albert *advertising executive*
Crum, Robert M. *business management executive*
Cruse, Denton W. *marketing and advertising executive, consultant*
Davis, Randall Scott *public relations executive*
de Bode, Oleg *information systems administrator*
Dickerson, Cynthia Rowe *marketing firm executive, consultant*
Dietz, Janis Camille *sales executive*
Doane, Samuel Wallace *sales executive*
D'Onofrio, Mary Ann *medical transcription company executive*
Dossett, Lawrence Sherman *professional services company official*
Druffel, Ann Bernice *psychic researcher, writer*
Dunbar, Patricia Lynn *product development consultant*
Ehler, Richard Lee *advertising executive, publisher, consultant*
Ellis, Robert Harry *retired television executive, university administrator*
Eltringham, Thomas James Gyger *telecommunications professional*
Erb, Richard Louis Lundin *resort and hotel executive*
Erickson, Joyce Lillian *telephone services company executive*
Farrell, William Edgar *sales executive, infosystems specialist, management consultant*
Finnigan, Dennis Michael *management consultant*
Fischer, Zoe Ann *real estate and property marketing company executive, consultant*
Flagg, Norman Lee *retired advertising executive*
Friedman, Mitchell Scott *public relations consultant*
Frost, Sterling Newell *arbitrator, mediator, management consultant*
Garcia, Curt Jonathan *company executive*
Gates, Glodean Kent Kerkmann *marketing consultant*
Gerber, Barry Eldon *data processing executive, consultant, writer*
Gill, James H. *public relations and marketing executive*
Gillett, George Nield, Jr. *communications executive*
Goldberg, Leslie Roberta *management development, employee relations and training executive*
Gottlieb, Alan Merril *advertising, fundraising and broadcasting executive, writer*
Grace, Kay Sprinkel *management consultant*
Grant, John Carrington *advertising executive*
Green, James Craig *data systems company executive*
Greene, Richard Boyd, Jr. *marketing and sales executive*
Greer, Martin Brad *computer executive*
Grindal, Mary Ann *sales professional*
Gunderson, Ted Lee *security consultant*
Gunst, Robert Allen *consumer products executive*
Hagel, John, III *management executive*
Hallstrom, Carol Rogoff *human relations professional*
Hansen, Leland Joe *communications executive*
Harbour, Kevin George *sales executive*
Harlan, Kathleen T. (Kay Harlan) *business consultant, professional speaker and seminar leader*
Harper, Richard Hilton *marketing executive*
Harris, Kristina Lee *management/computer consultant*
Heeger, Jack Jay *public relations consultant*
Hemphill, Alan Polk *management consultant*
Hirsh, Norman Barry *management consultant*
Hochschild, Carroll Shepherd *medical equipment and computer company executive, educator*
Hockfeld, Marla Gail Gerecht *advertising and public relations executive*
Hofford, Nancy *marketing professional*
Hoover, William R(ay) *computer service company executive*
Hynds, Frances Jane *communications management consultant*
Jacobson, Donald Thomas *management consultant*
James, Dot (Dorothy Ann James) *researcher, writer, fund-raiser, editor*
Jared, Daniel Wade *telecommunications company executive*
Jeffers, Ida Pearle *management consultant, volunteer*
Johnston, Thomas John *management consultant*
Jones, Gayle Clausse *secretary*
Jones, Gerre Lyle *marketing and public relations consultant*
Kalis, Murray *advertising executive, writer*
Karalis, John Peter *computer company executive, lawyer*
Keenan, Edward Joseph *management consultant*
Kelleher, Richard Cornelius *marketing and communications executive*
Kennedy, Charles John *marketing company executive*
Kennedy, Debra Joyce *marketing professional*
Klodzinski, Beatrice Davis *management consultant*
Koelmel, Lorna Lee *data processing executive*
Korody, Anthony Vincent *corporate event producer, photographer*
Kowalczewski, Doreen Mary Thurlow *communications company executive*
Kozar, Martha Cecile *corporate executive*
Larson, Mel *retired hotel facility executive, corporate executive, helicopter pilot*
Leger, Richard Roubine *public relations executive, writer*
LeMaster, Susan M. *marketing consultant, writer*
Levitt, Irene Hansen *secretarial staff, writer*
Lochanko, Elizabeth Alexandra *communications executive*
Locher, Marianne *marketing professional*
Lyles, Dara Lynn *sales executive*
Mackenzie, Linda Alice *computer company executive*
Macon, Carol Ann Gloeckler *micro-computer data base management company executive*
Manoukian, Rita Chake *sales executive*
Martin, Julia L. *public relations account executive*
Mateer, David Arthur *public relations executive*
Matthew, Lyn *sales and marketing executive*
Maule, Randy William *information systems specialist, educator, producer*
McInnis, Susan Musé *corporate communications specialist*
McQuarrie, Terry Scott *technical director*
McVeigh-Pettigrew, Sharon Christine *communications consultant*
Merrill, Frank Harrison *data processing executive, consultant*
Mikhail, Mary Attalla *computer systems development executive*
Miller, Diane Doris *executive search consultant*
Mitrany, Devora *marketing consultant, writer*
Monda, Marilyn *quality improvement consultant*
Moody, Charles Russell *medical sales and marketing professional*
Morgan, Ronald William *sales executive*
Moya, Rita Becker *public affairs executive*
Muttart, Susan Chambless *corporate communications manager*
Myhren, Trygve Edward *communications company executive*
Nason, Dolores Irene *computer company executive, counselor, eucharistic minister*
Nelson, Margaret Rose *public relations consultant*
Nething, Melissa Ann *human resources representative*
Newman, Jan Harlan *marketing consulting firm executive*
Norman, E. Gladys *business computer educator, consultant*
Olson, Kenneth Harvey *computer company executive*
Oppedisano, Suzanne Marie *marketing professional, dentist*
Ortiz, James George *data information services company executive*
Otremba, Bernard Otto *marketing executive*
Parenti, Kathy Ann *sales professional*
Peavy, Frank *management consultant*
Philippi, Ervin William *mortician*
Pierson-Stein, Marjorie Maxine Gordon *property management and investment administrator*
Pottier, Gerald J., Jr. *management consultant*
Probasco, Dale Richard *management consultant*
Puetz, Pamela Ann *human resources executive*
Ralston, Joanne Smoot *public relations counseling firm executive*
Rayner, Steven Robert *management consultant*
Regensburger, Linda Susan *public relations consultant, writer*
Reiner, James Anthony *marketing executive*
Richards, Lynn *company training executive, consultant*
Richardson, Rand Michael *public relations executive*
Robinson, Herbert William *corporate executive, economist*
Rodrigues, Alfred Benjamin Kameeiamoku *marketing consultant*
Roiz, Myriam *foreign trade marketing executive*
Roller, Susan Lorrayne *industrial communications specialist, consultant*
Rose, Barbara *executive recruiter*
Rubin, Jonathan *government relations consultant*
Sanquist, Nancy Johnson *international facility management professional*
Scaglione, Cecil Frank *marketing executive, publisher*
Schultze, Ernst Eugene *marketing communications executive*
Scott, J. Brian *sales executive*
Shank, Bryan Leigh *marketing executive*
Shirley, Michael James *ski area executive*
Skidmore, Eric Dorr *information systems manager*
Smith, Joban Jonathan *security consultant*
Smith, Thomas Winston *cotton marketing executive*
Smith-Thompson, Patricia Ann *public relations consultant, educator*
Souveroff, Vernon William, Jr. *corporate executive, investor, author*
Spann, Alan *business consultant*
Spoor, James Edward *human resources company executive, entrepreneur*
Stentz, Steven Thomas *researcher, systems analyst*
Stern, Dana Lee *computer company executive, writer, consultant*
Stewart, Renice Ann *financial analyst, writer*
Storozum, Steven Lee *marketing professional*
Stuart, William Roy *information services executive*
Sutton, Barbara Powderly *marketing executive, consultant, author*
Terry, Richard Frank *data transcriber*
Thornsley, Randall G. *management consultant*
Thurlow, Scott A. *computer company executive*
Tipton, Gary Lee *retired services company executive*
Trask, Linda Ann *sales executive*
Tytler, Linda Jean *communications and public affairs executive, retired state legislator*
Uitermark, Helen Joan *computing services executive*
Vallerand, Philippe Georges *sales executive*
VanderZanden, Dana Kathleen *public relations professional*
von Berg, Horst Rüdiger *computer company executive*
von Linsowe, Marina Dorothy *information systems consultant*
Wadley, M. Richard *consumer products executive*
Wagner, Richard *business executive, former baseball team executive*
Watson, Dennis Michael *career development and strategy firm executive*
Weeden, Mary Ann *organizational development executive*
West, Billy Gene *public relations executive*
Westin, Robert Lee *management consultant*
Wheaton, Alice Alshuler *secretary*
White, Bonnie Yvonne *management consultant, educator*
White, Loray Betty *public relations executive, writer, actress, producer*
Williams, Angelita Sophia *acquisitions negotiator*
Williams, Harry Edward *management consultant*
Willig, Karl Victor *computer firm executive*
Wisner, Linda Ann *advertising agency executive*
Wozniak, Joyce Marie *sales executive*
Yakich, David Eli *international sales executive*
Yamagata, Leslie Craig *contract specialist*
Yamani, Elaine Reiko *computer peripheral company executive*
Yocam, Delbert Wayne *communication company executive*
Young, Jeffrey Robert Lunn *data processing executive*
Zamboukos, Cynthia Soteria *office manager, travel consultant*
Zito, Michael Anthony *advertising and graphics design typesetting company owner*
Zodl, Joseph Arthur *international trade executive, consultant*

INDUSTRY: TRADE

UNITED STATES

ALASKA

Anchorage
Vandergriff, Jerry Dodson *computer store executive*

Denali National Park
Swenson, Richard Allen *business owner, animal trainer*

ARIZONA

Carefree
Brierley, Richard Greer *business consultant*

Flagstaff
Russell, Dana *small business operator*

Fountain Hills
Blatt, Melanie Judith *small business owner, broker*

Gilbert
Stark, Joseph P. *business owner*

Phoenix
Antioco, John F. *convenience store chain executive*
Niswander, Adam *bookstore owner, real estate broker, writer*
Turner, Robert Eugene *retail executive*
Weir, Jim Dale *small business owner*
Worrilow, Richard Charles *small business owner*

Scottsdale
Barbey, Peter Diener *bookseller*
Boat, Ronald Allen *business executive*
Cunningham, Gilbert Earl *owner florist and gift shop*

Sierra Vista
O'Neal, Dorothy Decker *fabric sales company executive*

Sun City
Meade, Kenneth John *realty company owner, broker*
Thompson, Betty Jane *small business owner*

Tempe
Lack, Larry Henry *small business owner*

Tucson
Ricci, Carolyne Youngblood *print shop owner*
Sakin, Larry Albert *shop owner*
Schultz, Karen Lee *fire and water restoration company executive*
Williams, Leona Rae *lingerie retailer*

CALIFORNIA

Anaheim
Brownhill, H. Bud *small business owner, canine behavior therapist*

Arcadia
Stangeland, Roger Earl *retail chain store executive*

Beverly Hills
Meyers, Roger Joseph *telegram company executive*
Orenstein, (Ian) Michael *philatelic dealer, columnist*

Burbank
Brankovich, Mark J. *restaurateur*
Wise, Woodrow Wilson, Jr. *small business owner*

Camarillo
Foxhoven, Michael John *retail and wholesale company executive, retail merchant*

Cerritos
Webb, Lewis M. *retail executive*

Chatsworth
Stephenson, Irene Hamlen *biorhythm analyst, consultant, editor, educator*

Compton
Willmott, Peter Sherman *retail executive*

Concord
Mackie, Richard Allen *small business owner, publishing company executive*

Covina
O'Hagan, William Gordon *automotive repair shop owner*

El Segundo
Pickett, Michael D. *computer hardware and software distributor*

Emeryville
Weaver, Velather Edwards (Val Weaver) *small business owner*

Gardena
Shoji, June Midori *import and export trading executive*

Goleta
Winslow, Norman Eldon *business executive*

Hemet
Howard, Jo Ann *business owner*

Huntington Beach
Howell, Mary Elizabeth *small business owner*

Irvine
Hoshi, Katsuo Kai *international business executive*

Laguna Beach
Pelton, Virginia Lue *small business owner*

Lake Hughes
Pattison, John Curtis *business owner, researcher*

Lindsay
Gahan, Kathleen Mason *small business owner, retired educational counselor, artist*

Loomis
Keyston, Stephani Ann *small business owner*

Los Altos
Tallmadge, Diane Joyce *bookstore manager*

Los Angeles
Carter, Edward William *retail executive*
Florence, Verena Magdalena *small business owner*
Haas, Edward Lee *business executive, consultant*
Hawley, Philip Metschan *retired retail executive, consultant*
Hecht, Harold Michael *retail executive*
Quitales, Ramon Jun Bonto *import/export company executive, consultant*
Rosenzweig, Carol Barbara *writer, art publisher*
Seigel, Daniel A. *retail executive*
Straus, Leonard Hirsch *retail company executive*
Uhm, Ken Kwang-Heum *trading company executive*
Underwood, Vernon O., Jr. *grocery stores executive*
Weesner, Lowell Michael *distribution management executive*

Wilkerson, Kenneth L. *retail department stores executive*
Williams, Theodore Earle *industrial distribution company executive*
Wong, Kenneth Lee *import executive, software engineer, consultant*

Milpitas
Buswell, Debra Sue *small business owner, programmer, analyst*

Modesto
Cahill, Lawrence Glenn, Jr. *investigation firm owner*
West, James Stuart *small business owner*

Morongo Valley
Beck, Thomas Edwin *business owner, furniture maker*

Moss Beach
Hoffman, Gary Allan *retail executive*

Newark
Ferber, Norman Alan *retail executive*
Moldaw, Stuart G. *venture capitalist, retail clothing stores executive*

Newport Beach
Koon, Robin Charles *retail pharmacy executive*
Rosten, David Bruce *international investment advisor*

Novato
Podd, Marsha Dianne *small business owner, nurse*

Oakland
Albers, William Marion *retail food distribution executive*
Davis, Roderick William *retail executive*
Paige, Alfred Lee *small business owner*
Spitzer, Matthew L. *retail store executive*
Totman, Patrick Steven *lawyer, retail executive*

Paso Robles
Carpenter, Diane Ellen *small business owner*

Pleasant Hill
Dolan, Maryanne McLorn *small business owner, writer, educator, lecturer*
Ryan, Kevin Durwood *retail executive*

Porterville
Swindler, Stephen Francis *distribution company executive*

Rancho Santa Fe
Bilotta, James Louis *small business owner*

Riverside
Anderson, Jolene Slover *small business owner, publishing executive, consultant*
Hill, Ralph Harold *wholesale grocery company executive*
Najjar, Tamara Litchfield *mail order business owner*
Savage, Karleen Sue *small business owner*
White, Clara Jo *graphoanalyst*

Sacramento
Kidd, Reuben Proctor *management engineer*
MacMillan, Catherine Cope *restaurant owner*
McFarlane, William F. *wholesale nut company executive*

San Bernardino
Sagmeister, Edward Frank *business owner, hospitality industry executive, civic official, retired fund raiser consultant, career officer*

San Bruno
DiCero, Suzanne Joan *retail chain executive*

San Diego
Ling, David Chang *international book dealer*
Monaco, Dick Steven *mail order vendor*
Mooney, Patricia Kathryn *business owner*
Saito, Frank Kiyoji *import-export firm executive*

San Francisco
Alband, Linda Ann *small business owner*
Dean, Norman Emerson (Ned Dean) *coffee company executive*
Drexler, Millard S. *retail executive*
Ferrari, Donna Mae *autobody and mechanical shop owner*
Fisher, Donald G. *casual apparel chain stores executive*
Handler, Mark S. *retail executive*
Jensen, Jakki Renee *retail company executive*
Nicolaï, Judithe *international business trade executive*
Seelenfreund, Alan *distribution company executive*
Seifel, Elizabeth Margaret *business owner*
Uwakah, Onyebuchi Timothy *export company executive*

San Jose
Castro, Teresa Harper *small business owner*
Pan, William Jiawei *import/export company executive, consultant*

San Martin
Payne, Darrell Lee *small business owner*

San Rafael
Koetser, David *export company executive*

Santa Ana
Fitzgerald, Robert Lynn *small business owner*
Shahin, Thomas John *dry cleaning wholesale supply company executive*

Santa Barbara
Lynch, Martin Andrew *retail company executive*

Santa Maria
Baker-Lievanos, Nina Gillson *jewelry store executive*
Purdy, Joseph Donald *small business owner*

Santa Monica
Sigoloff, Sanford Charles *retail executive*

Santa Paula
Anderson, William *retail company executive, business education educator*

Saratoga
Rosenblum, Carla Nadine *travel agent, retirement community executive*

Saugus
Hauenstein, Donald Herbert, Jr. *computer consultant*

Sausalito
Rogoff, Arnold M. *book dealer, publisher, management consultant*

Stockton
Simon, Karen Jordan *retail executive*

Upland
Schwarz, Joseph Richard *engineering manager*

Vallejo
Tiger, Paul *import-export company executive, consultant*

Walnut Creek
Jones, Ebon Richard *retail executive*
Long, Robert Merrill *retail drug company executive*
Plomgren, Ronald Arthur *retail executive*

West Hollywood
Gates, Lisa *small business owner, chef, caterer*

Westminster
Edwards, Charles Richard *retired printing equipment and supplies company executive*

Woodland Hills
Vigdor, James Scott *distribution executive*

COLORADO

Aspen
White, Robert Michael *small business owner, executive*

Aurora
Magalnick, Elliott Ben *retail medical supply company executive*
Reynolds, Robert Harrison *retired export company executive*

Boulder
Johnson, Maryanna *Morse business owner*
Pracko, Bernard Francis, II *artist, business owner*

Castle Rock
Sjostrom, Joan Sevier *travel consultant*

Colorado Springs
Carson, Elizabeth Lorraine Neal *small business owner, civilian military employee*

Denver
Cashman, Michael Richard *small business owner*
Green, Steven J. *retail executive*
Nelson, LeAnn Lindbeck *small business owner*
Oakes, Terry Louis *retail clothing store executive*
Schoeni, Douglas Eugene *wholesale distribution executive*
Stocking, Sherl Dee *retail executive*
Tutt, Margaret Honnen *retail store owner*
Wiens, Duane Daton *matrix-graphic design firm owner*

Englewood
Blair, Stewart D. *small business owner*
Foltz, Donald Joseph *franchise development consultant*

Fort Collins
Thompson, Virginia Lou *agricultural products supplier and importer*

Idaho Springs
Mees, Buddie Petruske *retail executive*

Littleton
Baker, Deborah Ann *business owner*
Bowe, Roger Lee *small business owner*

Loveland
Brandt, William Carl *sports memorabilia store owner, chaplain*
Rodman, Alpine Clarence *arts and crafts company executive*
Rodman, Sue Arlene *wholesale Indian crafts company executive, artist, consultant*

Morrison
Graham, Pamela Smith *distributing company executive, artist*

Pueblo
Pisciotta, Samuel James *small business owner*

FLORIDA

Daytona Beach
James, Barry Alan *import-export consultant*

HAWAII

Hanalei
Ching, Lawrence Lin Tai *retail executive*
Vogel, Richard Wiedemann *business owner, ichthyodynamicist*

Honolulu
Jackson, Ronald Edward, Sr. *small business owner*
Lee, Candie Ching Wah *retail executive*
Nakabayashi, Nicholas Takateru *retired retail executive*

Kailua Kona
Luizzi, Ronald *wholesale distribution executive*

Waipahu
Matsui, Jiro *importer, wholesaler, small business owner*

IDAHO

Boise
Ancell, Judith Anne *gemologist, custom/specialty business owner*
Connolly, David I. *retail executive*
Michael, Gary G. *retail supermarket and drug chain executive*
Rudd, Gerald Ray *retail food and drug company executive*
Shaver, Carl Hutchens *retail executive*
Simmons, Randall Craig *librarian, bookseller*
Timm, Jerry Roger *fiberglass manufacturing company executive*
Wright, Kathryn Michele *grocery retail chain coordinator*

Idaho Falls
Gregory, Nelson Bruce *motel owner, retired naval officer*

Post Falls
Chamberlain, Barbara Kaye *small business owner*

MONTANA

Billings
Marcovitz, Leonard Edward *retail executive*

Great Falls
Campbell, David Alan *retail store manager*
Evenson, S. Jeanne *small business owner*

Helena
O'Connell, Kathryn A. *small business owner*

NEVADA

Las Vegas
Ackerman, H. Don *automotive dealership executive*
Faley, Robert Lawrence *instruments company executive*
Miller, Virginia Lee *business owner*
Myers, Helen Dee *small business owner*

Reno
Nelson, Darryl James *small business owner*

Sparks
Rand, Kathleen Suzette *buyer*

NEW HAMPSHIRE

Rye Beach
Nord, Harold Emil, Jr. *small business owner, consultant*

NEW MEXICO

Albuquerque
McCall, Susan Elizabeth *small business owner*

Las Vegas
Cozens, Richard *small business owner*

Santa Fe
Hackett, Dwight Vernon *business owner*

Taos
Lipscomb, Anna Rose Feeny *small business owner, arts organizer, fundraiser*

OREGON

Applegate
Pursglove, Betty Merle *small business owner, technical writer*

Bend
Nosler, Robert Amos *sports company executive*
Rotz, Marta Lynne *small business owner*

Burns
Timms, Eugene Dale *wholesale business owner, state senator*

Eugene
Wilson, Gerald Alan *retail executive*

Hillsboro
Grant, James Rusk *business owner*

Jefferson
Robertson, Marian Ella (Marian Ella Hall) *small business owner, handwriting analyst*

Klamath Falls
Pastega, Richard Louis *retail specialist*

Lake Oswego
Allender, Nancy G. *corporate turnaround specialist, commercial print broker*

Medford
Stong, John Elliott *retail electronic company executive*

Myrtle Creek
Shirtcliff, John Delzell *business owner, oil jobber*

Pacific City
Hampton, Carolyn Seeba *small business owner, minister*

Portland
Bauer, Louis Edward *retail bookstore executive, educator*
Danielson, Craig *wholesale grocery corporation executive*
Green, Cyril Kenneth *retail company executive*
Greenstein, Merle Edward *import and export company executive*
Miller, Robert G. *retail company executive*
Ramsby, Mark Delivan *lighting designer and consultant*

Salem
Sigurdson, Edwin D. *small business owner*

South Beach
Aldrich, Daniel Eugene *small business owner*

Springfield
Smith, Terry Lee *business owner*

Tigard
Baker, Allison Paige *former wholesale distribution executive, photographer, musician, educator*

Tualatin
Holmes, Thomas Leroy *small business owner*
Loffer, Linda V. *small business owner*

UTAH

Saint George
Day, John Denton *retired company executive, cattle and horse rancher, trainer, wrangler, actor*

Salt Lake City
Bergeson, Scott *retail executive*
Cragun, Calvin *business owner*
Day, Gerald W. *wholesale grocery company executive*
Miller, Kuby Susie *dance and modeling school owner*
Plumley, S. Patric *retail executive*
Postma, Steven J. *owner distribution business*
Skaggs, L. Sam *retail company executive*
Smith, Jeffrey P. *supermarket chain executive*
Smith, Richard D. *supermarkets and drug stores executive*
Tanner, William Coats, Jr. *business owner*

Vernal
Kier, Raymond Edward *motel and restaurant owner*

WASHINGTON

Bellevue
Leofsky, Joan Carole *business owner*
O'Byrne, Michael *equipment dealer executive*

Bellingham
Olsen, Mark Norman *small business owner*

Camano Island
Petrakis, Julia Ward *small business owner*

Centralia
Taylor, Timothy Kevin *business owner*

Kirkland
Brotman, Jeffrey H. *variety stores executive*

Mercer Island
Willis, Nell Elaine *small business owner*

Monroe
Kirwan, Katharyn Grace (Mrs. Gerald Bourke Kirwan, Jr.) *retail executive*

Redmond
Moss, Jack *print shop executive, textile chemist, consultant*
Nagel, Daryl David *retail executive*

Seattle
Denniston, Martha Kent *business owner, author*
Hume, Darrell J. *retail executive*
McMillan, John A. *retail executive*
Mizrahi, Yves *retail executive*
Nordstrom, Bruce A. *department store executive*
Nordstrom, John N. *department store executive*
Read, Charles Raymond, Sr. *business executive*
Yee, Ben *import-export business executive*

Shelton
Wotton, Robert H., Jr. *small business owner*

Spokane
Sines, Randy Dwain *business executive*

Yakima
Newland, Ruth Laura *small business owner*

WYOMING

Cheyenne
Caine, Carol Whitacre *business owner*

Green River
Thoman, Mary E. *rancher, vocational and secondary educator*

Lander
Zatloukal, Charlene Ann *distribution company executive*

CANADA

ALBERTA

Calgary
Isenor, Linda Darlene *grocery retailer, marketing professional*

BRITISH COLUMBIA

Vancouver
Addington, Raymond Joseph *wholesale groceries company executive*

ADDRESS UNPUBLISHED

Adler, Shelley *business owner, poet, English educator*
Busch, Joyce Ida *small business owner*
Cavnar, Margaret Mary (Peggy Cavnar) *business executive, former state legislator, nurse, consultant*
Claus, Carol Jean *small business owner*
Debenham, Ray Gene *electric supply company executive*
Decker, Richard Kelsey *equipment distribution company executive*
Dyer, Arlene Thelma *retail company owner*
Edwards, Patricia Burr *small business owner, counselor, consultant*
Eldridge, Maxine Jew *flower grower, shipper, wholesaler*
Galvao, Louis Alberto *import and export corporation executive, consultant*
Gartner, William Joseph *company executive, business owner*
Halfant, Gary D. *small business owner*
Kittlitz, Linda Gale *small business owner*
Martini, Robert Edward *wholesale pharmaceutical and medical supplies company executive*
Metz, Steven William *small business owner*
Nicolas, J. Bernard *home video distribution executive*
Parks, Richard Cameron *outdoor sports professional, small business owner*
Phillips, Darrell *retail executive*
Sadow, Tim N. *distribution center executive*
Sataloff, Ronald Arthur *small business owner*
Smith, Dianne Harris *import/export company executive*
Sutich, Timothy Jay *small business owner*
Thenell, Arthur Lee *retail supermarket executive*
Ullman, Myron Edward, III *retail executive*
Vandertuin, Victoria Elva *book seller*
Winter, Richard Samuel, Jr. *computer training company owner, writer*

INDUSTRY: TRANSPORTATION

UNITED STATES

ALASKA

Anchorage
Harris, Orville D. *transportation executive*
Rueter, Tom William *water transportation executive*

ARIZONA

Bullhead City
Hicks, Norm *airport operations executive*

Hayden
Jacobson, Lowell Steven (Jake Jacobson) *railroad executive*

Litchfield Park
Cox, Gary Evans *aerospace company official, consultant*

Mesa
Widder, Patricia A. *helicopter company research and engineering technical specialist*

Phoenix
Amoako, James Kwaku *transportation services executive, financial analyst*
Beauvais, Edward R. *airline executive*
Bertholf, Neilson Allan, Jr. *aviation executive*
Bonine, Larry Stanley *transportation executive, engineer*
Elien, Mona Marie *air transportation professional*
Emerson, Frederick George *transportation company executive*
Shoen, Edward Joseph *transportation and insurance companies executive*
Webb, Richard L. *air industry service executive*
Whalen, Martin J. *transportation executive, lawyer*
Wood, John Mortimer *aerospace executive, aeronautical engineer*
Woods, Bobby Joe *transportation executive*

Prescott
Morrison, Gladys Mae *pilot training firm executive*

Scottsdale
Aybar, Charles Anton *aviation executive*
Levy, Marian Muller *transportation executive*

Sierra Vista
Montagne, Ernest *operations analyst*

Tempe
Miller, Marc Douglas *airline pilot*
Robertson, Samuel Harry, III *transportation safety research engineer, educator*

Tucson
Burg, Walter A. *airport terminal executive*
Gissing, Bruce *retired aerospace company executive*
Peete, Russell Fitch, Jr. *aircraft appraiser*

ARKANSAS

Harrison
Garrison, F. Sheridan *transportation executive*

CALIFORNIA

Bayside
Pierce, Lester Laurin *aviation consultant*

Borrego Springs
Scannell, William Edward *aerospace company executive, consultant, psychologist*

Brea
Henderson, Jane Whalen *travel company executive*
Kinsler, Bruce Whitney *air traffic controller, consultant, air traffic control engineer, air defense engineer*

Burbank
Bowman, Brian *airport services terminal*
Butler, Viggo M. *airport terminal executive*
Volk, Robert Harkins *aviations company executive*
Yaman, F. M., Jr. *airport terminal executive*

Calabasas
Caren, Robert Poston *aerospace company executive*

Camarillo
McConnel, Richard Appleton *aerospace company official*

Corona Del Mar
Tether, Anthony John *aerospace executive*

Costa Mesa
Florey, Jerry Jay *aerospace company executive, consultant*
Mittermeier, Janice *commercial airport executive*

Edwards
Johnson, Gregory Harold *experimental test pilot, fighter pilot*
Smolka, James William *aerospace research pilot*

Fremont
Smith, Bernald Stephen *retired airline pilot, aviation consultant*

Fresno
Husein, Firoz *airport terminal executive*

Gilroy
Borton, George Robert *airline captain*

Hawthorne
Arieli, Adi *aerospace company executive*

Hermosa Beach
Kokalj, James Edward *retired aerospace administrator*

Huntington Beach
Drubka, Robert Edward *aerospace executive*
Kasulka, Larry Herman *aerospace company executive*
Richman, David William *aerospace executive*

Lancaster
Crew, Aubrey Torquil *aerospace inspector*

Long Beach
Anderson, Gerald Verne *retired aerospace company executive*
Brown, Thomas Adams *aviation executive*
Dorrenbacher, Carl James *aerospace transportation executive*
Mandeville, Craig H. *aircraft company executive, retired military officer*
Moss, Elizabeth Lucille (Betty Moss) *transportation company executive*
Schaufele, Roger Donald *aircraft company executive*

Los Angeles
Benson, Edgar Charles, Jr. *retired pilot*
Coln, William Alexander, III *pilot*
Fiumerodo, Anthony *airline pilot*
Gregg, Lucius Perry, Jr. *aerospace executive*
Kresa, Kent *aerospace executive*
Mishkin, Marjorie Wong *aviation and marketing consultant*
Moore, Walter Dengel *rapid transit system professional*
Williams, W(alter) D(avid) *aerospace executive, consultant*
Yee, Stephen *airport executive*

Manhattan Beach
Smith, Gordon Eugene *pilot*

Menlo Park
O'Brien, Raymond Francis *transportation executive*

Mill Valley
Edgett, Steven Dennis *transportation consultant*

Millbrae
Brown, William Oscar *retired railroad executive*

Mission Viejo
LaRosa, Gianni *aerospace industry executive*

Moffett Field
Dean, William Evans *aerospace agency executive*

Monterey
Horn, Denis Richard *airport executive*

Napa
Whitlock, Timothy Scott *commercial pilot*

Newport Beach
Penso, Pierpaolo *ship repair company executive*
Reisman, Richard S. *publisher*

Oakland
Lillie, John Mitchell *transportation company executive*
Reynolds, Kathleen Diane Foy (K.D.F. Reynolds) *transportation executive*
Rhein, Timothy J. *transportation company executive*

Ontario
Nevius, Lloyd L. *air industry services executive*

Palo Alto
Moffitt, Donald Eugene *transportation company executive*

Palos Verdes Estates
Smith, Stephen Randolph *aerospace executive*

Ramona
Hoffman, Wayne Melvin *retired airline official*

Redlands
McClain, Roger Allen *aerospace industry executive*

Redondo Beach
Wagemaker, David Isaac *human resources development executive*

Redwood Shores
Abrahamson, James Alan *transportation executive, retired military officer*

Sacramento
Engel, Thomas P. *airport executive*

San Diego
Harden, William L. *airport executive*
Henderson, Hollis Allen *transportation consultant, railway executive*
Hidalgo, Miguel *transportation company executive*
Tuccio, Sam Anthony *aerospace executive, physicist*

San Francisco
Collar, Leo Linford *marine transportation company executive*
Hickerson, Glenn Lindsey *leasing company executive*
Holtman, William J. *railroad company executive*
Kahn, Linda McClure *maritime industry executive*
Mohan, D. Mike *transportation company executive*
Ryan, Randel Edward, Jr. *airline pilot*
Turpen, Louis A. *airport terminal executive*
Winter-Switz, Cheryl Donna *travel company executive*
Wood, Donald Frank *transportation educator, consultant*

San Jose
Verlot, Frank Oscar *aerospace executive*

San Mateo
Trabitz, Eugene Leonard *aerospace company executive*

Santa Ana
Glendinning, Iain *airport terminal executive*
Laidlaw, Robert *aircraft maintenance executive*

Shingle Springs
Crotti, Joseph Robert *aviation executive*

South San Francisco
Bonino, Anthony *air transportation executive*
Scherer, Phil *airport terminal executive*

Stockton
Biddle, Donald Ray *aerospace company executive*
DeAngelis, Dan *transportation executive*
Hall, David Stanley *aerospace transportation executive*
Prickett, Robert *transit executive*

Sunnyvale
Finnie, C(larence) Herbert (Herb Finnie) *aerospace company executive*
Younger, Bob *aerospace executive*

Torrance
Pickett, David Franklin, Jr. *aerospace company executive*
Vampola, Alfred Ludvik *aerospace consultant*

Tustin
Thomas, Mitchell, Jr. *aerospace company executive*

Van Nuys
Stender, Charles Frederick *pilot*

Visalia
Miller, Carl Duane *transportation company executive*

Woodland Hills
Bremer, Robert James *aerospace industry executive*

COLORADO

Aspen
Edwards, H. Boyd *air transportation executive*

Aurora
Minnich, Joseph Edward *tourist railway consultant*

Colorado Springs
Ajer, Randolf E. *airport terminal executive*
Brown, Alison K. *aeronautics company executive*
Kahn, Seymour *air transportation executive*
Stienmier, Saundra Kay Young *aviation educator*

Denver
Boulware, Richard Stark *airport administrator*
Burgess, Larry Lee *aerospace executive*
DeLong, James Clifford *air transportation executive*
Harvey, Cannon Y. *railway company executive, lawyer*

Englewood
Claussen, Bonnie Addison, II *aerospace company executive*

Grand Junction
Buescher, Bernard *air transportation executive*
Buescher, Louis *airport service executive*

Littleton
Bragg, Albert Forsey *retired airline captain*
Kalkbrenner, Edward Joseph, Jr. *pilot, consultant*
Strang, Sandra Lee *airline official*

HAWAII

Honolulu
Olsen, Phillip Buck *corporate pilot, retired educator*
Pfeiffer, Robert John *transportation executive*
Stoddard, Arthur Grant *pilot*

Makawao
Fairechild, Diana *aviation health analyst, author, speaker*

IDAHO

Boise
Agee, William J. *transportation, engineering and construction company executive*
DeVilbiss, Jonathan Frederick *aircraft sales engineer*

Idaho Falls
Thorsen, James Hugh *aviation director*

ILLINOIS

Chicago
White, John Abiathar *pilot, consultant*

NEVADA

Las Vegas
West, Donna C. *licensing executive*

Reno
White, Robert C. *air transportation executive*

NEW MEXICO

Albuquerque
Weh, Allen Edward *airline executive*

Farmington
Anderson, Mark Eugene *specialized truck driver, safety inspector*
Risley, Larry L. *air transportation executive*

OREGON

Mcminnville
Driever, Louis Milton, Jr. *airline executive*
Fowler, David *air and aerospace transportation executive*
Lane, Larry K. *air industry service executive*
Spencer, Michael *airport terminal executive*

Medford
Rogers, Gardner Spencer *railroad company executive*

Portland
Cheston, Michael Galloway *airport executive*
Hebe, James L. *trucking executive*
Lewis, Kenneth *shipping executive*

TENNESSEE

Memphis
O'Neill, Norah Ellen *airline pilot*

UTAH

Bountiful
Clement, Walter Hough *retired railroad executive*

Brigham City
Zielke, Patrick Michael *aerospace company executive*

Ogden
Dilley, William Gregory *aviation company executive*

Salt Lake City
White, Victor Dea *airport management executive*

WASHINGTON

Federal Way
Stober, Mason Frederick, Jr. *retired air traffic control educator*

Seattle
Brazier, Robert G. *transportation executive*
Brown, Janiece Alfreida *pilot*
Cella, John J. *freight company executive*
Charbonneau, Ralph Gray *air cargo leasing company executive*
Chittick, Arden Boone *steamship agency executive*

Clarkson, Lawrence William *airplane company executive*
Cline, Robert Stanley *air freight company executive*
Condit, Philip Murray *aerospace executive, engineer*
Elliott, Jeanne Marie Koreltz *transportation executive*
Fowler, John Robert *airline executive*
Gwin, Billy Joe *transportation executive*
Jaeger, David Arnold *aerospace company executive*
McGinnis, Scott George *cruise line executive*
Raisbeck, James David *aircraft design executive*
Robinson, Gary Dale *aerospace company executive*
Strombom, Cathy Jean *transportation planner, consultant*
Vecci, Raymond Joseph *airline executive*

Spokane
Salerno, Joseph Michael *air cargo company executive*

Sumner
Goodman, William Lee *commercial pilot*

Tacoma
Loete, Steven Donald *pilot*

WYOMING

Casper
Bishop, Jeff *airport terminal executive*

Worland
Woods, Lawrence Milton *airline company executive*

CANADA

ALBERTA

Calgary
McCaig, Jeffrey James *transportation company executive*
McCaig, John Robert *transportation executive*
Paquette, Richard *airport executive*

Edmonton
Eng, Howard *airport administrator*

BRITISH COLUMBIA

Vancouver
Joplin, Albert Frederick *company director, consultant*

CHINA

Beijing
Pinoli, Burt Arthur *airline executive*

JAPAN

Tokyo
Shishido, Fumitake *transportation company executive*

ADDRESS UNPUBLISHED

Brauch, Gary James *pilot*
Cassidy, Donald Lawrence *former aerospace company executive*
Cook, Stephen Champlin *retired shipping company executive*
Elwood, James Peter *air transportation executive*
Freitag, Peter Roy *transportation specialist*
Goldstein, Bernard *transportation company executive*
Gray, Richard Arden *transportation executive*
Knott, Wiley Eugene *retired electronic engineer*
Langs, Ted Charles *aerospace company executive*
Quesnel, Gregory L. *transportation company executive*
Reihel, Ronald Ernest *pilot*
Stepp, William Edward *retired military operations analyst*
Tucker, Joel Lawrence *aviation company executive*
Wright, H. S., III *pilot*

INDUSTRY: UTILITIES, ENERGY, RESOURCES

UNITED STATES

ALASKA

Anchorage
Hopkins, Stephen Davis *mining company executive*
Luttrell, Eric Martin *oil company executive*
Posey, James Madison *oil company executive*
Silverstein, Steven B. *oil company executive*
Wade, William Edward, Jr. *oil company executive*

Juneau
Albanese, Thomas *minerals company executive*

Nikiski
Bumbaugh, Robert Warren, Sr. *oil industry executive*

ARIZONA

Benson
Kimball, Donald W. *electric utility corporate executive*

Buckeye
Burton, Edward Lewis *educator, industrial procedures and training consultant*

Cave Creek
LeNeau, Thomas Ervin *gas company executive*

Phoenix
Brown, James Carrington, III (Bing Brown) *public relations and communications executive*
Ekstrom, Walter F. *utility company executive*
Norberg, Jaron B. *public service company executive*
Yearley, Douglas Cain *mining and manufacturing company executive*

Prescott
Bennett, Kenneth R. *oil company executive, school board executive*

Tempe
Clevenger, Jeffrey Griswold *mining company executive*
Hickson, Robin Julian *mining company executive*

Tucson
Davis, James Luther *retired utilities executive, lawyer*
Peeler, Stuart Thorne *petroleum industry executive and independent oil operator*

Wellton
Gould, Clio LaVerne *electric utility and irrigation district executive*

ARKANSAS

Hot Springs National Park
York, Earl Dana *oil company executive, engineering consultant*

CALIFORNIA

Alhambra
Garber, C(harles) Stedman, Jr. *oil and mining industry executive*
Shannon, Edfred L., Jr. *gas and oil drilling company executive*

Aliso Viejo
Cann, William Hopson *former mining company executive*

Anaheim
Fenton, Donald Mason *retired oil company executive*

Beverly Hills
Brann, Alton Joseph *oil field services executive*
Krems, Susan Alexander *telecommunications specialist*
Levingston, John Colville Bowring *telecommunications executive*

Camarillo
MacAlister, Robert Stuart *oil company executive*

Campbell
Paul, David Jacob *nuclear energy industry executive*

Davis
Welton, David Gerald *telecommunications educator, writer, researcher*

Fountain Valley
DeLong, R. Scott *telecommunications executive*

Fresno
Wilson, Charles E. *air industry service executive*

Fullerton
Sadruddin, Moe *oil company executive, consultant*

La Jolla
Ahlfeld, Charles Edward *nuclear industry executive*

Los Angeles
Arnault, Ronald J. *petroleum company executive*
Asquith, Ronald H. *petroleum corporate executive*
Babikian, George H. *petroleum products company executive*
Beach, Roger C. *oil company executive*
Bowlin, Michael Ray *oil company executive*
Cook, Lodwrick Monroe *petroleum company executive*
Dougherty, Michael Joseph *oil company executive*
Jonker, Peter Emile *gas company executive*
Laurance, Dale R. *oil company executive*
Martin, David R. *oil company executive*
McIntyre, Robert Malcolm *utility company executive*
Pickel, Frederick Hugh *energy company executive*
Snyder, Sam A. *oil company executive, lawyer*
Stegemeier, Richard Joseph *oil company executive*
Wood, Willis Bowne, Jr. *utility holding company executive*
Wycoff, Robert E. *petroleum company executive*

Martinez
Meyer, Jarold Alan *oil company research executive*

Newhall
Nelson, Warren James, III *oil company executive, accountant*

Newport Beach
Clark, Earnest Hubert, Jr. *tool company executive*

Oxnard
Lima, Donald Allan *oil company executive*

Palo Alto
Mattice, Jack Shafer *electric power research manager*
Willrich, Mason *utility company executive, consultant*

Palos Verdes Estates
Christie, Hans Frederick *retired utility company subsidiaries executive, consultant*

Pasadena
Clark, Donald B. *utilities executive*
Van Amringe, John Howard *retired oil industry executive, geologist*

Petaluma
Frederickson, Arman Frederick *minerals company executive*

Placentia
Douglas, Donald Wills, Jr. *energy executive*

Playa Del Rey
Weir, Alexander, Jr. *utility consultant, inventor*

Rosemead
Barry, David N., III *utility executive*
Bennett, Brian O'Leary *utilities executive*
Bryson, John E. *utilities company executive*
Noel, Michael Lee *utility executive*
Ray, Harold Byrd *utilities executive*
Rosenblum, Richard Mark *utility executive*

San Diego
Haney, Raymond Lee *gas and electric company executive*
Sifferman, Thomas Raymond *speciality chemical researcher*
Thomas, Jack E. *utility company executive*
Whyte-Banks, Hila Jane *communication technician*

San Dimas
Brown, Marian Van de Water *utilities executive*

San Francisco
Ansar, Jasmin *utilities executive*
Bonney, John Dennis *oil company executive*
Brandin, Alf Elvin *retired mining and shipping company executive*
Carter, George Kent *oil company executive*
Clarke, Richard Alan *electric and gas utility company executive, lawyer*
Conger, Harry Milton *mining company executive*
Crain, William Edwin *oil company executive*
Derr, Kenneth T. *oil company executive*
Grier, William E. *petroleum company executive*
High, Thomas W. *utilities company executive*
Huckabee, Phyllis *gas industry professional*
Hulse, John Edward *former telephone company executive*
Johnstone, Clint *electric power industry executive*
McCrea, Peter *oil company executive*
Millard, Derek *organizational development consultant*
Neerhout, John, Jr. *petroleum company executive*
Price, Willis Joseph *retired oil company executive*
Quigley, Philip J. *telecommunications industry executive*
Reinsch, Harry Orville *power company executive*
Ross, John J. *petroleum products company executive*
Shiffer, James David *utility executive*
Skinner, Stanley Thayer *utility company executive, lawyer*
Sproul, John Allan *retired public utility executive*
Sullivan, James N. *fuel company executive*

San Jose
Dulin, Jacques M. (James Dulin) *lawyer, consultant, pollution control company executive*
Farach Farach, Jose Eduardo *energy executive*

Santa Ana
Mickelson, H(erald) Fred *electric utility executive*

Santa Clara
Shiota, Takao *telecommunication research company executive*

Sausalito
Linton, William Henry *power industry consultant, engineer*

Stockton
Talmage, Kenneth Kellogg *business executive*

Sunnyvale
Hrut, Christopher Boleslaw *sales and marketing executive*
Money, Arthur L. *electronics executive*

Templeton
Gandsey, Louis John *petroleum and environmental consultant*

Thousand Oaks
Sparrow, Larry J. *telecommunications executive*

Van Nuys
Fisher, Earl Monty *utilities executive*

Villa Grande
Shirilau, Mark Steven *utilities executive*

Walnut Creek
Ginn, Sam L. *telephone company executive*
Humphrey, William Albert *mining company executive*

Winchester
Liesman, William Russell *oil company executive*

COLORADO

Alamosa
Mortensen, Carl Evan *oil company owner*

Aurora
Bond, Michael Wayne *industrial gas company executive*

Boulder
Adams, Linda Alcorn *telecommunications policy professional*
Fox, Joseph Leland *utilities executive*
Schwartz, John Benjamin *telecommunications and real estate executive*
Thomas, Daniel Foley *telecommunications company executive*

Colorado Springs
Bauman, Walter Joseph *telecommunication company executive*
Robinson, Ronald Alan *oil company executive*
Sparger, William Harry *gas transmission company executive*
Stoen, J. Thomas *energy company executive, land developer, investor*

Denver
Anderson, Donald H. *gas industry executive*
Dana, Richard E. *oil industry executive*
Gwinnett, James Randall *telecommunications industry executive*
Hock, Delwin D. *utilities company executive*
Isaacs, Jonathan William *oil company executive*
Magness, Bob John *telecommunications executive*
McCoy, James Henry *oil company executive*
Moriarty, Bruce Joseph *oil industry executive*
Pepper, John Roy *oil and gas executive*
Philip, Thomas Peter *mining executive*
Stewart, Gary Crawford *oil company executive*
Taylor, Leslie George *mining and financial company executive*
Valot, Daniel L. *oil industry executive*
Vostiar, John *telecommunications industry executive*

Durango
Thurston, William Richardson *oil and gas industry executive, geologist*

Englewood
Anderson, James Thomas *telecommunications executive*
Chico, Raymundo José *mining and oil executive*
Fisher, Donne Francis *telecommunications executive*
Le, Khanh Tuong *utility executive*
Leahy, John Henry, Jr. *telecommunications executive*
Malone, John C. *telecommunications executive*
McCormick, Richard David *telecommunications company executive*
Osterhoff, James Marvin *telecommunications company executive*
Parker, Gordon Rae *natural resource company executive*
Tedesco, Steven Anthony *oil company executive*

Fort Collins
Kleinschnitz, Barbara Joy *oil company executive, consultant*

Glenwood Springs
Collins, Bruce Alan *consultant, mining company executive*

Golden
O'Connor, Patricia Eryl *telecommunications consultant*

Grand Junction
Gigliotti, Richard Joseph *nuclear security executive*
Pforzheimer, Harry, Jr. *oil consultant*

Highlands Ranch
Morrison, Bradford Cary *oil and gas industry executive*

Lakewood
Gestring, Clark Kent *oil field well evaluation service executive*
Hall, Larry D. *energy company executive, lawyer*

Littleton
Haley, John David *petroleum consulting company executive*
McFadden, Jo Beth *oil company executive*
Nelsen, Craig Joseph *mining company executive, geologist*
VanderLinden, Camilla Denice Dunn *telecommunications industry manager*

Louisville
Futa, Baryn S. *telecommunications industry executive*

DISTRICT OF COLUMBIA

Washington
Winzenried, Jesse David *retired petroleum executive*

HAWAII

Honolulu
Amioka, Wallace Shuzo *retired petroleum company executive*
Bates, George E. *oil industry executive*
Clarke, Robert F. *utilities company executive*
Toole, Lee K. *telecommunications company executive*

IDAHO

Idaho Falls
Newman, Stanley Ray *oil refining company executive*

Mountain Home
Hiddleston, Ronal Eugene *drilling and pump company executive*

MINNESOTA

Minneapolis
Blair, Craig John *utilities executive*

MONTANA

Billings
Joyce, Casey John *grant development specialist, consultant*
Nance, Robert Lewis *oil company executive*

Butte
Bishop, Robert Charles *architect, metals and minerals company executive*
Gannon, Robert P. *utility company executive*

Helena
Thomas, Jack G. *water quality manager*

Missoula
Watson, Julia *women's studies and liberal studies educator*

NEVADA

Fallon
Sanwick, James Arthur *mining executive*

Las Vegas
Buehrer, Roger Dean *communications executive utility company*
Garcia-Borras, Thomas *oil company executive*
Guinn, Kenny C. *utility company executive*
Land, Kenneth Dean *test and balance agency executive, energy and environmental consultant*
Lenzie, Charles Albert *utility company executive*

Reno
Busig, Rick Harold *mining executive*
Dietz, Vida Lee *utility company executive*
Reed, Michael Raybren *utilities executive, journalist*

NEW MEXICO

Albuquerque
Giron, Rick *adminstrative services manager*
Jackson, Steven Alan *telecommunications professional*
Reinders, James W. *petroleum consultant*

Farmington
Swetnam, Monte Newton *petroleum exploration executive*

Glenwood
Rothman, Steven Isaiah *oil explorationist, consultant*

Hobbs
Garey, Donald Lee *pipeline and oil company executive*

Roswell
Anderson, Donald Bernard *oil company executive*
Anderson, Robert Orville *oil and gas company executive*
Manatt, James C., Jr. *oil and gas exploration executive*
Robinson, Mark Leighton *oil company executive, petroleum geologist, horse farm owner*

Santa Fe
Buck, Christian Brevoort Zabriskie *independent oil operator*
Pickrell, Thomas Richard *retired oil company executive*

OKLAHOMA

Bartlesville
Bowerman, Charles Leo *oil company executive*

OREGON

Aloha
Jones, Charles J. *consultant*

Bend
Miller, William Elwood *mining company executive*

Neskowin
Sifford, Benton Alexander, III *energy consultant*

Portland
Bacon, Vicky Lee *lighting services executive*
Frisbee, Don Calvin *retired utilities executive*
Gleason, Alfred M. *telecommunications executive*
Harrison, Ken L. *holding company and electric utility executive*
Heiner, Lawrence Elden *mineral company executive*
Hobbs, C. D. *utilities executive*
McCall, Robert H. *oil and chemical company executive*
McCall, William Calder *oil and chemical company executive*
Storie, Evelyn *public utilities specialist, crisis consultant*

UTAH

Brigham City
Anderson, Robert Wayne *oil company financial officer*

Salt Lake City
Cash, R. D. *natural gas and oil executive*
Cash, R(oy) Don *gas and petroleum company executive*
Groussman, Raymond G. *diversified utility and energy company executive, lawyer*
Joklik, Günther Franz *mining company executive*
Keener, Robert W. *retired gas company executive*

Vernal
Covington, Robert Edward *mining executive, geologist*

WASHINGTON

Bellevue
Thorpe, James Alfred *retired utilities executive*
Weaver, William Schildecker *electric power industry executive*

Richland
Counsil, William Glenn *electric utility executive*
Newman, Darrell Francis *research and development manager, nuclear engineer*

Spokane
Dukich, Thomas Daniel *utility executive*
Harvey, J. R. *utilities company executive*
Redmond, Paul Anthony *utility executive*

Tacoma
Bearson, John Michael *utility company executive*

Vancouver
Robinson, Charles E. *telecommunications industry executive*

WYOMING

Casper
Huff, Kenneth O. *oilfield executive, geologist*
Smith, Dick Martin *oil field service company executive-owner*

Gillette
Shepherd, Thomas Irvin *mining specialist, electrical engineer*

Laramie
Laman, Jerry Thomas *mining company executive*

Riverton
Bebout, Eli Daniel *oil executive*

CANADA

ALBERTA

Calgary
Cochrane, Barrymore Donald *oil industry executive*
Furnival, George Mitchell *petroleum and mining consultant*
Hopper, Wilbert Hill *retired oil industry executive*
Hugh, George M. *pipeline company executive*
Isautier, Bernard François *oil and gas executive*
Maier, Gerald James *natural gas transmission and marketing company executive*
McIntyre, Norman F. *petroleum industry executive*
Mc Kee, John Angus *oil company executive*
Picard, Robert Real *oil company executive*
Pierce, Robert Lorne *petrochemical, oil and gas company executive*
Schaefer, Harry George *utilities company executive*
Watson, George William *oil company executive*
Welty, Robert G. *petroleum company executive*

Edmonton
Lock, Robert Graham *utilities executive*
MacNeill, Brian F. *oil company executive*
Mitchell, David E. *petroleum company executive*
Neldner, Helmut M. *telecommunications industry executive*
Twa, Craighton Oliver *power company executive*

BRITISH COLUMBIA

Vancouver
Bellringer, Stephen Terrence *gas company executive*
Eckersley, John Alan *mining company executive*
Fell, Fraser M. *mining executive*
Phelps, Michael Everett Joseph *energy company executive*
Willms, Arthur Henry *gas executive*
Willson, John Michael *mining company executive*

SASKATCHEWAN

Saskatoon
Childers, Charles Eugene *potash mining company executive*

TAJIKISTAN

Penjikent
Arne, Kenneth George *mining executive, mineral consultant*

ADDRESS UNPUBLISHED

Abram, John Charles *energy consultant*
Ataie, Ata Jennati *oil products marketing executive*
Bankston, Mary Gay *retired gas industry executive*
Bending, David Alexander Glen *mining executive, geoscientist*
Binder, James Kauffman *computer consultant*
Cashatt, Charles Alvin *retired hydro-electric power generation company executive*
Cliff, Ronald Laird *energy company executive*
Eglinton, William Matthew *utility company executive*
Engel, Linda Jeanne *mining executive*
Farley, Frank Frederic *retired oil industry executive*
Gogarty, William Barney *oil company executive, consultant*
Gottenberg, David Andrew *natural gas executive*
Greenberg, Arnold Elihu *water quality specialist*
Hearne, John Q. *telecommunications executive*
Hesse, Christian August *mining and tunneling industries consultant*
Holmes, Michael *oil and gas consultant*
Johnson, Laymon, Jr. *utility analyst*
Krempel, Roger Ernest *public works management consultant*
Ormasa, John *utility executive, lawyer*
Pillar, Charles Littlefield *retired mining consultant*
Ralston, Roy B. *petroleum consultant*
Sundstrom, Virgil Glenn *petroleum company executive*
Wharton, Thomas William *mining executive*

LAW: JUDICIAL ADMINISTRATION

UNITED STATES

ALASKA

Anchorage
Branson, Albert Harold (Harry Branson) *magistrate judge, educator*
Compton, Allen T. *state supreme court justice*
Holland, H. Russel *federal judge*
Moore, Daniel Alton, Jr. *state supreme court justice*
Rabinowitz, Jay Andrew *state supreme court justice*
Singleton, James Keith *federal judge*

Fairbanks
Kleinfeld, Andrew Jay *federal judge*

Valdez
Anderson, Glen Clark *judge*

ARIZONA

Phoenix
Canby, William Cameron, Jr. *federal judge*
Carroll, Earl Hamblin *federal judge*
Carter, James Edward *judge*
Feldman, Stanley George *state supreme court chief justice*
McNamee, Stephen M. *federal judge*
Moeller, James *state supreme court justice*
Muecke, Charles Andrew (Carl Muecke) *federal judge*
Rosenblatt, Paul Gerhardt *federal judge*
Schroeder, Mary Murphy *federal judge*
Strand, Roger Gordon *federal judge*
Weisenburger, Theodore Maurice *judge, poet, educator, writer*
Zlaket, Thomas *state judge*

Tucson
Bilby, Richard Mansfield *federal judge*
Browning, William Docker *federal judge*
Marquez, Alfredo C. *federal judge*
Roll, John McCarthy *federal judge*

CALIFORNIA

Fort Bragg
Lehan, Jonathan Michael *judge*

Fresno
Coyle, Robert Everett *federal judge*
Crocker, Myron Donovan *federal judge*
Price, Edward Dean *federal judge*
Wanger, Oliver Winston *federal judge, educator*

Inglewood
Dorn, Roosevelt F. *judge*

La Mirada
Henderson, Thelton Eugene *federal judge*
Legge, Charles Alexander *federal judge*
Walker, Vaughn R. *federal judge*

Los Angeles
Alarcon, Arthur Lawrence *federal judge*
Armstrong, Orville *judge*
Ashland, Calvin Kolle *federal judge*
Baird, Lourdes G. *federal judge*
Bufford, Samuel Lawrence *federal judge*
Byrne, William Matthew, Jr. *federal judge*
Davies, John G. *federal judge*
Fenning, Lisa Hill *federal judge*
Gadbois, Richard A., Jr. *federal judge*
Groh, Rupert James, Jr. *judge*
Hatter, Terry Julius, Jr. *federal judge*
Hauk, A. Andrew *federal judge*
Hupp, Harry L. *federal judge*
Ideman, James M. *federal judge*
Jaffe, F. Filmore *judge*
Johnson, Earl, Jr. *judge, author*
Kelleher, Robert Joseph *federal judge*
Keller, William D. *federal judge*
Kenyon, David V. *federal judge*
Kronenberg, John Robert *retired magistrate judge*
Lax, Kathleen Thompson *federal judge*
Letts, J. Spencer *federal judge*
Lew, Ronald S. W. *federal judge*
Marshall, Consuelo Bland *federal judge*
Masterson, William A. *state judge*
Mohr, Anthony James *judge*
Mund, Geraldine *bankruptcy judge*
Norris, William Albert *federal judge*
Pfaelzer, Mariana R. *federal judge*
Rafeedie, Edward *federal judge*
Rea, William J. *federal judge*
Real, Manuel Lawrence *federal judge*
Takasugi, Robert Mitsuhiro *federal judge*
Tashima, Atsushi Wallace *federal judge*
Tevrizian, Dickran M., Jr. *federal judge*
Waters, Laughlin Edward *federal judge*
Williams, David Welford *federal judge*
Wilson, Stephen Victor *federal judge*

Modesto
Hedrick, Joseph Watson, Jr. *retired judge*

Monterey Park
Tucker, Marcus Othello *judge*

Moraga
Harrington, Charles Lee *judge, retired*

Newport Beach
Curtis, Jesse William, Jr. *retired federal judge*

Oakland
Jensen, D. Lowell *federal judge, lawyer, government official*
McKinstry, William A. *judge*
Newsome, Randall Jackson *federal judge*

Pasadena
Boochever, Robert *federal judge*
Fernandez, Ferdinand Francis *federal judge*
Files, Gordon Louis *judge, lawyer*
Goodwin, Alfred Theodore *federal judge*
Hall, Cynthia Holcomb *federal judge*
Hogoboom, William Perry *judge, arbitrator, mediator*
Kozinski, Alex *federal judge*
Nelson, Dorothy Wright (Mrs. James F. Nelson) *federal judge*
Rymer, Pamela Ann *federal judge*

Pomona
Moore, S. Clark *judge*

Redwood City
Harrington, Walter Howard, Jr. *judge*

Richmond
Herron, Ellen Patricia *retired judge*

Sacramento
Burrell, Garland E., Jr. *federal judge*
Dahl, Loren Silvester *retired federal judge*
Karlton, Lawrence K. *federal judge*
Levi, David F. *federal judge*
MacBride, Thomas Jamison *federal judge*
Russell, David E. *federal judge*
Schwabe, Peter Alexander, Jr. *judge*
Schwartz, Milton Lewis *federal judge*
Shubb, William Barnet *federal judge*

San Diego
Adler, Louise DeCarl *bankruptcy judge*
Brewster, Rudi Milton *federal judge*
Gilliam, Earl Ben *federal judge*
Gonzalez, Irma Elsa *federal judge*
Hargrove, John James *federal judge*
Huff, Marilyn L. *federal judge*
Keep, Judith N. *federal judge*
Lewis, Gerald Jorgensen *judge*
McKee, Roger Curtis *federal magistrate judge*
Thompson, David Renwick *federal judge*
Thompson, Gordon, Jr. *federal judge*
Turrentine, Howard Boyd *federal judge*
Wallace, J. Clifford *federal judge*

San Francisco
Arabian, Armand *state supreme court justice*
Armstrong, Saundra Brown *federal judge*
Baxter, Marvin Ray *state supreme court judge*
Browning, James Robert *federal judge*
George, Ronald M. *judge*
Jarvis, Donald Bertram *judge*
Kennard, Joyce L. *judge*
Lucas, Malcolm Millar *state supreme court chief justice*
Lynch, Eugene F. *federal judge*
Mosk, Stanley *state supreme court justice*
Noonan, John T., Jr. *federal judge, legal educator*
Patel, Marilyn Hall *federal judge*
Poole, Cecil F. *federal judge*

San Jose
Aguilar, Robert P. *federal judge*
Ingram, William Austin *federal judge*
Morgan, Marilyn *federal judge*
Ware, James W. *federal judge*
Whyte, Ronald M. *federal judge*
Williams, Spencer Mortimer *federal judge*

Santa Ana
Ferguson, Warren John *federal judge*
Lydick, Lawrence Tupper *federal judge*
Ryan, John Edward *federal judge*
Stotler, Alicemarie Huber *federal judge*
Wilson, John James *federal judge*

Santa Monica
Vega, Benjamin Urbizo *retired judge*

South Lake Tahoe
Reece, Monte Meredith *lawyer, judge*

Studio City
Lasarow, William Julius *retired federal judge*

Susanville
Bradbury, Stephen Douglas *judge, rancher*

Van Nuys
Schwab, Howard Joel *judge*

Whittier
Knupp, Larry Sheldon *judge*

Woodland Hills
Pregerson, Harry *federal judge*

COLORADO

Brighton
Bruner, Cindy Hull *judge*

Denver
Abram, Donald Eugene *federal magistrate judge*
Babcock, Lewis Thornton *federal judge*
Carrigan, Jim Richard *federal judge*
Ebel, David M. *federal judge*
Erickson, William Hurt *state supreme court justice*
Finesilver, Sherman Glenn *retired federal judge*
Kirshbaum, Howard M. *judge*
Lohr, George E. *state supreme court justice*
Matsch, Richard P. *federal judge*
McWilliams, Robert Hugh *federal judge*
Moore, John Porfilio *federal judge*
Mullarkey, Mary J. *state supreme court justice*
Nottingham, Edward Willis, Jr. *federal judge*
Pringle, Bruce D. *federal magistrate*
Rovira, Luis Dario *state supreme court justice*
Satter, Raymond Nathan *judge*
Sparr, Daniel Beattie *federal judge*

Vollack, Anthony F. *state supreme court justice*
Weinshienk, Zita Leeson *federal judge*

Golden
Wolvington, Winston Warren *retired judge*

HAWAII

Honolulu
Acoba, Simeon Rivera, Jr. *judge*
Choy, Herbert Young Cho *federal judge*
Ezra, David A. *federal judge*
Kay, Alan Cooke *federal judge*
Klein, Robert Gordon *judge*
Lum, Herman Tsui Fai *retired state supreme court chief justice*
Moon, Ronald T. Y. *state supreme court chief justice*
Soong, Melvin Kaipoleimanu *circuit court judge*

IDAHO

Boise
Callister, Marion Jones *federal judge*
Hagan, Alfred Chris *federal judge*
Johnson, Byron Jerald *state supreme court judge*
Lodge, Edward James *federal judge*
McDevitt, Charles Francis *state supreme court justice*
Nelson, Thomas G. *federal judge*
Trott, Stephen Spangler *federal judge, musician*
Walters, Jesse Raymond, Jr. *state judge*

Nampa
Hoff, Renae *magistrate*

Pocatello
Bacon, William Francis *tribal judge*

KANSAS

Lawrence
Tacha, Deanell Reece *federal judge*

MONTANA

Billings
Battin, James Franklin *judge, former congressman*
Fagg, Russell *judge, lawyer*
Shanstrom, Jack D. *federal judge*

Great Falls
Hatfield, Paul Gerhart *federal judge, lawyer*

Helena
Gray, Karla Marie *state supreme court justice*
Harrison, John Conway *state supreme court justice*
Hunt, William E., Sr. *state supreme court justice*
Lovell, Charles C. *federal judge*
Trieweiler, Terry Nicholas *state supreme court justice*
Turnage, Jean A. *state supreme court chief justice*
Weber, Fred J. *retired state supreme court justice*

NEVADA

Carson City
Gunderson, Elmer Millard *state supreme court justice, law educator*
Rose, Robert E(dgar) *state supreme court justice*
Springer, Charles Edward *state supreme court justice*
Steffen, Thomas Lee *state supreme court justice*
Young, C. Clifton *judge*

Las Vegas
George, Lloyd D. *federal judge*
Parraguirre, Ronald David *judge*
Pro, Philip Martin *federal judge*

Reno
Brunetti, Melvin T. *federal judge*
Hug, Procter Ralph, Jr. *federal judge*
McKibben, Howard D. *federal judge*
Reed, Edward Cornelius, Jr. *federal judge*
Wiggins, Charles Edward *federal judge*

NEW MEXICO

Albuquerque
Conway, John E. *federal judge*
Dal Santo, Diane *judge*
Hansen, Curtis LeRoy *federal judge*
Parker, James Aubrey *federal judge*

Cloudcroft
Duncan, Reginald Wallace *clergyman, former municipal judge and educator*
Walters, Frederick K., Jr. *judge*

Las Cruces
Apodaca, Rudy Samuel *judge*
Bratton, Howard Calvin *federal judge*

Roswell
Baldock, Bobby Ray *federal judge*

Santa Fe
Alarid, Albert Joseph *judge*
Baca, Joseph Francis *state supreme court chief justice*
Campos, Santiago E. *federal judge*
Franchini, Gene Edward *state supreme court justice*
Kelly, Paul Joseph, Jr. *federal judge*
Ransom, Richard Edward *state supreme court justice*
Yalman, Ann *judge*

OREGON

Eugene
Coffin, Thomas M. *federal magistrate judge*
Hogan, Michael R(obert) *federal judge*

Portland
Belloni, Robert Clinton *federal judge*
Burns, James M. *federal judge*
Frye, Helen Jackson *federal judge*
Haas, Harl Henry *judge*
Jones, Robert Edward *federal judge*
Joseph, George Manley *retired judge*
Leavy, Edward *federal judge*
Marsh, Malcolm F. *federal judge*
O'Scannlain, Diarmuid Fionntain *federal judge*
Panner, Owen M. *federal judge*
Redden, James Anthony *federal judge*
Skopil, Otto Richard, Jr. *federal judge*

Salem
Carson, Wallace Preston, Jr. *state supreme court chief justice*
Fadeley, Edward Norman *state supreme court justice*
Graber, Susan P. *judge*
Peterson, Edwin J. *retired supreme court justice, law educator*
Unis, Richard L. *state supreme court justice*
Van Hoomissen, George Albert *state supreme court justice*

UTAH

Salt Lake City
Anderson, Stephen Hale *federal judge*
Benson, Dee Vance *federal judge*
Clark, Glen Edward *federal judge*
Greene, John Thomas, Jr. *federal judge*
Hall, Gordon R. *retired state supreme court chief justice*
Howe, Richard Cuddy *state supreme court justice*
Jenkins, Bruce Sterling *federal judge*
McKay, Monroe Gunn *federal judge*
Sam, David *federal judge*
Winder, David Kent *federal judge*
Zimmerman, Michael David *state supreme court chief justice*

WASHINGTON

Bellevue
Andersen, James A. *retired state supreme court justice*

Federal Way
Hayek, Carolyn Jean *retired judge*

Mount Vernon
Meyer, John Michael *judge*

Olympia
Dolliver, James Morgan *state supreme court justice*
Durham, Barbara *state supreme court justice*
Guy, Richard P. *state supreme court justice*
Johnson, Charles William *state supreme court justice*
Smith, Charles Z. *state supreme court justice*
Utter, Robert French *state supreme court justice*

Seattle
Beezer, Robert Renaut *federal judge*
Coughenour, John Clare *federal judge*
Dimmick, Carolyn Reaber *federal judge*
Dwyer, William L. *federal judge*
Farris, Jerome *federal judge*
Fletcher, Betty B. *federal judge*
Mc Govern, Walter T. *federal judge*
Rothstein, Barbara Jacobs *federal judge*
Weinberg, John Lee *federal judge*
Wilson, David Eugene *magistrate judge*
Zilly, Thomas Samuel *federal judge*

Spokane
Klobucher, John Marcellus *federal judge*
Munson, Ray Eugene *judge*
Nielsen, William Fremming *federal judge*
Quackenbush, Justin Lowe *chief federal judge*
Van Sickle, Frederick L. *federal judge*

Tacoma
Bryan, Robert J. *federal judge*

Yakima
Hovis, James Brunton *federal judge*
McDonald, Alan Angus *federal judge*
Suko, Lonny Ray *judge*

WYOMING

Cheyenne
Barrett, James Emmett *federal judge*
Brimmer, Clarence Addison *federal judge*
Brorby, Wade *federal judge*
Cardine, Godfrey Joseph *state supreme court justice*
Golden, Michael *state supreme court justice*
Johnson, Alan Bond *federal judge*
Macy, Richard J. *state judge*
Taylor, William Al *judge*

Gillette
Michaels, Jeremy Daniel *judge*

Green River
Marty, Lawrence A. *lawyer, magistrate judge*

TERRITORIES OF THE UNITED STATES

GUAM

Barrigada
Diaz, Ramon Valero *retired judge*

NORTHERN MARIANA ISLANDS

Saipan
Dela Cruz, Jose Santos *retired state supreme court chief justice*

CANADA

ALBERTA

Edmonton
Fraser, Catherine Anne *Canadian chief justice*

NORTHWEST TERRITORIES

Yellowknife
de Weerdt, Mark Murray *judge*

SASKATCHEWAN

Regina
Bayda, Edward Dmytro *judge*

ADDRESS UNPUBLISHED

Bistline, Stephen *retired state supreme court justice*
Burke, Edmond Wayne *retired judge*
Callow, Keith McLean *judge*
Christensen, Albert Sherman *federal judge*
Cruze, Deborah Kaye *judge*
Garcia, Edward J. *federal judge*
Ghareeb, Donald L. *judge*
Mai, Harold Leverne *retired federal judge*
Matthews, Warren Wayne *state supreme court justice*
McLaughlin, Linda Lee Hodge *federal judge*
Montgomery, Seth David *retired state supreme court chief justice*
Reinhardt, Stephen Roy *federal judge*
Rodgers, Frederic Barker *judge*
Scott, Gregory Kellam *state supreme court justice*
Shearing, Miriam *justice*
Smith, Fern M. *federal judge*
Stewart, Isaac Daniel, Jr. *state supreme court justice*
Taylor, Gary L. *federal judge*
Wright, Eugene Allen *federal judge*

LAW: LAW PRACTICE AND ADMINISTRATION

UNITED STATES

ALASKA

Anchorage
Anderson, Kathleen Gay *mediator, hearing officer, arbitrator, educator*
Gruenberg, Max F., Jr. *lawyer*
Hayes, George Nicholas *lawyer*
Hughes, Mary Katherine *lawyer*
Linxwiler, James David *lawyer*
Mason, Robert (Burt Mason) *lawyer*
Owens, Robert Patrick *lawyer*
Perkins, Joseph John, Jr. *lawyer*
Roberts, John Derham *lawyer*
Ross, Wayne Anthony *lawyer*
Wagstaff, Robert Hall *lawyer*
Weinig, Richard Arthur *lawyer*
Wilson, Joseph Morris, III *lawyer*
Wohlforth, Eric Evans *lawyer*

Fairbanks
Rice, Julian Casavant *lawyer*

Juneau
Nave, Thomas George *lawyer*

Kodiak
Jamin, Matthew Daniel *lawyer, magistrate judge*
Teal, Gilbert Earle, II *lawyer, coast guard officer*

ARIZONA

Flagstaff
Bertoldo, Joseph Ramon *lawyer*
Cowser, Danny Lee *lawyer, mental health specialist*
Stoops, Daniel J. *lawyer*

Mesa
Le Clair, Douglas Marvin *lawyer*
Volin, John Joseph *lawyer*

Paradise Valley
Houseworth, Laura Jennings *lawyer*

Phoenix
Allen, Robert Eugene Barton *lawyer*
Barclay, Steven Calder *lawyer*
Barry, Edward Louis *lawyer*
Begam, Robert George *lawyer*
Beggs, Harry Mark *lawyer*
Blanchard, Charles Alan *lawyer, former state senator*
Brecher, Sheila Rae *lawyer*
Case, David Leon *lawyer*
Chanen, Steven Robert *lawyer*
Coppersmith, Sam *lawyer*
Corson, Kimball Jay *lawyer*
Craig, Stephen Wright *lawyer*
Derdenger, Patrick *lawyer*
Dunipace, Ian Douglas *lawyer*
Ehmann, Anthony Valentine *lawyer*
Froeb, Donald Forrest *lawyer, former state judge*
Galbut, Martin Richard *lawyer*
Gladner, Marc Stefan *lawyer*
Goldstein, Stuart Wolf *lawyer*
Hay, John Leonard *lawyer*
Howard, William Matthew *lawyer, business executive, arbitrator, author*
Klausner, Jack Daniel *lawyer*
Knoller, Guy David *lawyer*
Koester, Berthold Karl *lawyer, retired honorary consul*
Madden, Paul Robert *lawyer, director*
Martori, Joseph Peter *lawyer*
McDaniel, Joseph Chandler *lawyer*
McRae, Hamilton Eugene, III *lawyer*
Meschkow, Jordan Mark *lawyer*
Meyers, Howard Craig *lawyer*
Moberly, Michael Dean *lawyer*
Mousel, Craig Lawrence *lawyer*
Moya, Patrick Robert *lawyer*
Olson, Robert Howard *lawyer*
Plattner, Richard Serber *lawyer*
Price, Charles Steven *lawyer*
Rosen, Sidney Marvin *lawyer*
Sears, Alan Edward *lawyer*
Silverman, Alan H. *lawyer*
Smith, Susan Kimsey *lawyer*
Spitzer, Marc Lee *lawyer*
Sterbach, Charles Robert *lawyer*
Sterns, Patricia Margaret *lawyer, consultant*
Susman, Alan Howard *lawyer*
Sutton, Samuel J. *lawyer, educator*
Tancer, Shoshana B. *lawyer, business educator*
Thompson, Terence William *lawyer*
Tubman, William Charles *lawyer*
Ulrich, Paul Graham *lawyer, author, publisher, editor*
Whisler, James Steven *lawyer, mining and manufacturing executive*
Williams, Quinn Patrick *lawyer*
Winthrop, Lawrence Fredrick *lawyer*
Wolf, G. Van Velsor, Jr. *lawyer*

Prescott
Dunn, Paul James *lawyer*
Eaton, William Lee *lawyer*
Gose, Richard Vernie *lawyer*

Scottsdale
Barbee, Joe Ed *lawyer*
Basinger, Richard Lee *lawyer*
Berry, Charles Richard *lawyer*
King, Jack A. *lawyer*
Lisa, Isabelle O'Neill *law firm administrator, mergers and acquisitions executive*
Mybeck, Richard Raymond *lawyer*
Roberts, Jean Reed *lawyer, business executive*
Smith, David Burnell *lawyer*
Starr, Isidore *law educator*
Swartz, Melvin Jay *lawyer*
Werner, E. Louis, Jr. *lawyer, retired insurance company executive*

Sedona
Gliege, John Gerhardt *lawyer*

Sun City
Davidson, Robert Lee, III *retired lawyer, author, consultant*
Treece, James Lyle *lawyer*

Tempe
Evans, Lawrence Jack, Jr. *lawyer*

Tucson
Bell, Alan *lawyer, environmental health activist*
Butler, A(rthur) Bates, III *lawyer*
D'Antonio, James Joseph *lawyer*
Doolan, Mariah *lawyer*
Farrell, Patrick Joseph *lawyer*
Franklin, John Orland *lawyer*
Gantz, David Alfred *lawyer, university official*
Glaser, Steven Jay *lawyer*
Gonzales, Richard Joseph *lawyer*
Hyams, Harold *lawyer*
Levitan, Roger Stanley *lawyer*
Liechty, Clinton *lawyer*
Polan, David Jay *lawyer*
Robinson, Bernard Leo *retired lawyer*
Schwanbeck, Victor Raymond *lawyer, civilian military employee*
Tindall, Robert Emmett *lawyer, educator*

Yuma
Hossler, David Joseph *lawyer, educator*

ARKANSAS

Cotter
Naylor, George LeRoy *lawyer, rail transportation executive*

CALIFORNIA

Alameda
Stonehouse, James Adam *lawyer*

Anaheim
Miller, Jeremy *law educator*
Ross, Roger Scott *lawyer*

Antioch
Jawad, Said Tayeb (Said Tayeb Djawad) *paralegal, political commentator, writer*

Bakersfield
Barmann, Bernard Charles, Sr. *lawyer*
Clark, Thomas Sullivan *lawyer*
Farr, G(ardner) Neil *lawyer*
Feer, Charles Lewis *lawyer, consultant*
Kind, Kenneth Wayne *lawyer*
Tornstrom, Robert Ernest *lawyer, oil company executive*

Berkeley
Bond, Thomas Moore, Jr. *labor mediation and arbitration executive*
Concepciōn, David Alden *arbitrator, educator*
Daniel, Christine Stewart *lawyer*
De Goff, Victoria Joan *lawyer*
Goldsmith, Donald William *lawyer, astronomer, writer*
Hetland, John Robert *lawyer, educator*
Kay, Herma Hill *law educator*
Moran, Rachel *lawyer, educator*

Reilley, Kathleen Patricia *lawyer*
Van Winkle, Wesley Andrew *lawyer, educator*

Bethel Island
Mandel, Maurice, II *lawyer*

Beverly Hills
Amado, Honey Kessler *lawyer*
Brown, Hermione Kopp *lawyer*
Dickerson, William Roy *lawyer*
Donaldson, Michael Cleaves *lawyer*
Florence, Kenneth James *lawyer*
Franzen, Don Erik *lawyer*
Horwin, Leonard *lawyer*
Ishiguro, Toyosuke *international business consultant, educator*
Jeffrey, John Orval *lawyer*
Jessup, W. Edgar, Jr. *lawyer*
Ramer, Bruce M. *lawyer*
Rosky, Burton Seymour *lawyer*
Schiff, Gunther Hans *lawyer*
Shacter, David Mervyn *lawyer*
Shire, Harold Raymond *law educator, author, social scientist*
Spears, Melvin Stanley *lawyer*
Thompson, Richard Dickson *lawyer*

Bonita
Calderon, Rebeca Franco *judiciary interpreter*

Buena Park
Waller, John James *lawyer*

Burbank
Keister, Jean Clare *lawyer*
Wise, Helena Sunny *lawyer*

Burlingame
Cotchett, Joseph Winters *lawyer, author*
Ziegler, R.W., Jr. *lawyer, consultant*

Canoga Park
Wainess, Marcia Watson *legal management consultant*

Carlsbad
McCracken, Steven Carl *lawyer*

Carmichael
Halpenny, Diana Doris *lawyer*

Castro Valley
Newacheck, David John *lawyer*

Chatsworth
Watts, Cynthia Gay *lawyer*
Welborne, John Howard *lawyer*

Chico
Ruge, Neil Marshall *retired law educator*

Chino
Van Wagner, Ellen *lawyer, educator*

Chino Hills
Roberts, John Alden *lawyer*

Chula Vista
Santee, Dale William *lawyer, air force officer*

Citrus Heights
Parquette, Jack Robert *lawyer*

Coalinga
Frame, Ted Ronald *lawyer*

Concord
Orlebeke, William Ronald *lawyer*

Corte Madera
Gordon, Robert Eugene *lawyer*

Costa Mesa
Willard, Robert Edgar *lawyer*

Culver City
Pavitt, William Hesser, Jr. *lawyer*
von Kalinowski, Julian Onesime *lawyer*

Cupertino
Simon, Nancy Ruth *lawyer*

Cypress
Olschwang, Alan Paul *lawyer*

Davis
Jordan, Ellen Rausen *law educator, consultant*
Schreiber, Darren Matthew *law clerk*

Downey
Emerson, Virgil Leon *lawyer, retired judge*

El Cajon
Jallins, Richard David *lawyer*
Parker, Marilyn Adele *paralegal*

El Cerrito
Garbarino, Joseph William *labor arbitrator, economics and business educator*

El Monte
Montgomery, Michael Bruce *lawyer, consultant*

El Segundo
Birren, Jeffrey Emmett *lawyer*
Gambaro, Ernest Umberto *lawyer, consultant*

Elverta
Betts, Barbara Lang (Mrs. Bert A. Betts) *lawyer, rancher, realtor*

Encinitas
Williams, Michael Edward *lawyer*

Encino
Hoefflin, Richard Michael *lawyer, judicial administrator, contractor*
Joyce, Stephen Michael *lawyer*
Kaufman, Albert I. *lawyer*
Scharf, Robert Lee *lawyer*
Smith, Selma Moidel *lawyer, composer*
Weissman, Robert Allen *lawyer, real estate broker*

Escondido
Sullivan, Michelle Cornejo *lawyer*

Fairfield
Honeychurch, Denis Arthur *lawyer*
Moore, Marianna Gay *law librarian, consultant*

Fresno
Ewell, A. Ben, Jr. *lawyer, businessman*
Fletcher, Norman L.S. *lawyer, educator*
Grenfell, George Albert, Jr. *assistant district attorney*
Jensen, Douglas Blaine *lawyer*
Sherr, Morris Max *lawyer*

Fullerton
Bakken, Gordon Morris *law educator*
Everett, Pamela Irene *legal management company executive, educator*
Moerbeek, Stanley Leonard *lawyer*
Parsons, Rodney Hunter *lawyer*
Ruby, Charles Leroy *law educator, lawyer, civic leader*

Gilroy
Jacobs, Bruce Marrin *lawyer*

Glendale
Ball, James Herington *lawyer*
Boukidis, Constantine Michael *lawyer*
Cayse, Phyllis *federal mediator*
Farrell, Thomas Dinan *lawyer*
Martinetti, Ronald Anthony *lawyer*
Ofner, William Bernard *lawyer*

Grass Valley
Hawkins, Richard Michael *lawyer*
Lawrence, Dean Grayson *retired lawyer*

Hayward
Smith, John Kerwin *lawyer*

Huntington Beach
Slates, Roger Duane, II *lawyer, sole practitioner*

Irvine
Bastiaanse, Gerard C. *lawyer*
Danser, Bonita Kay *legal administrator, consultant*
Dill, Jeffrey *lawyer, environmental geologist*
Hilker, Walter Robert, Jr. *lawyer*
Levin, William Edward *lawyer*
Petrasich, John Moris *lawyer*
Specter, Richard Bruce *lawyer*

King City
Bolles, Donald Scott *lawyer*

La Jolla
Eischen, James J., Jr. *lawyer*
Karlen, Peter Hurd *lawyer, writer*
Logan, April Charise *lawyer*
Shannahan, William Paul *lawyer*
ZoBell, Karl *lawyer*

Laguna Beach
Wilcoxen, William Merritt *lawyer*

Larkspur
Greenberg, Myron Silver *lawyer*
Marker, Marc Linthacum *lawyer, investment company executive*

Loma Linda
Seheult, Malcolm McDonald Richardson *solicitor*

Long Beach
Blumberg, John Philip *lawyer*
Stolpman, Thomas Gerard *lawyer*

Los Alamitos
Peters, Samuel Anthony *lawyer*

Los Angeles
Abrams, Norman *law educator, university administrator*
Adler, Erwin Ellery *lawyer*
Alschuler, Fred H. *lawyer*
Angelo, Christopher Edmond *lawyer, consultant*
Arbit, Beryl Ellen *legal assistant*
Argue, John Clifford *lawyer*
Arlen, Jennifer Hall *law educator*
Balesh, James R. *lawyer*
Bardach, Sheldon Gilbert *lawyer*
Barnes, Willie R. *lawyer*
Barrett, Eleanor Edie *lawyer, mediator*
Basile, Paul Louis, Jr. *lawyer*
Bell, Wayne Steven *lawyer*
Belleville, Philip Frederick *lawyer*
Berman, Myles Lee *lawyer*
Bice, Scott Haas *lawyer, educator*
Biederman, Donald Ellis *lawyer*
Biele, Hugh Irving *lawyer*
Bierstedt, Peter Richard *lawyer, entertainment industry consultant*
Bodkin, Henry Grattan, Jr. *lawyer*
Bower, Allan Maxwell *lawyer*
Bower, Paul George *lawyer*
Boxer, Lester *lawyer*
Boyd, Harry Dalton *lawyer, former insurance company executive*
Bradford, David Paul *judicial assistant*
Bradshaw, Carl John *investor, lawyer, consultant*
Brassell, Roselyn Strauss *lawyer*
Bressan, Paul Louis *lawyer*
Bricker, Seymour (Murray) *lawyer*
Burch, Robert Dale *lawyer*
Burke, Robert Bertram *lawyer*
Burns, Marvin Gerald *lawyer*
Butler, James Robertson, Jr. *lawyer*
Calhoun, Gordon James *lawyer*
Carr, James Patrick *lawyer*
Carrey, Neil *lawyer, educator*
Castro, Leonard Edward *lawyer*
Clark, R. Bradbury *lawyer*
Cleary, William Joseph, Jr. *lawyer*
Craig, Amelia Audrey *lawyer*
Davis, J. Alan *lawyer, producer, writer*
Deason, Edward Joseph *lawyer*
Decker, Richard Jeffrey *lawyer*
Demoff, Marvin Alan *lawyer*
Diamond, Stanley Jay *lawyer*
Dinel, Richard Henry *lawyer*
Dunlavey, Dean Carl *lawyer*
Fein, Ronald Lawrence *lawyer*
Field, Morton Richard *lawyer*
Field, Richard Clark *lawyer*
Fischer, Dale Susan *lawyer*
Follick, Edwin Duane *law educator, chiropractic physician*
Franceschi, Ernest Joseph, Jr. *lawyer*
Fredman, Howard S *lawyer*
Froilan, Vicente Singzon *educator*
Gartner, Harold Henry, III *lawyer*
Gilbert, Robert Wolfe *lawyer*
Goldie, Ron Robert *lawyer*
Gooch, Robert Francis *lawyer*
Goodman, Max A. *lawyer, educator*
Goul, Richard Masson *lawyer*
Graubart, Jeffrey Lowell *entertainment lawyer*
Gray, Jan Charles *lawyer*
Green, William Porter *lawyer*
Greenberg, Maxwell Elfred *lawyer*
Hahn, Elliott Julius *lawyer*
Haile, Lawrence Barclay *lawyer*
Handzlik, Jan Lawrence *lawyer*
Hanson, John J. *lawyer*
Hayes, Byron Jackson, Jr. *lawyer*
Hayes, Steven Lee *lawyer*
Heller, Philip *lawyer*
Hennigan, James Michael *lawyer*
Heyck, Theodore Daly *lawyer*
Hicks, James B(radley) *lawyer*
Highberger, William Foster *lawyer*
Hutchins, Robert Bruce *lawyer*
Hutter, James Risque *retired lawyer*
Iamele, Richard Thomas *law librarian*
Izuel, Leeanna *lawyer*
Jacobs, Randall Brian *lawyer*
Johnson, Charles Henry, Jr. *lawyer*
Jordan, Robert Leon *lawyer, educator*
Kamine, Bernard Samuel *lawyer*
Kananack, Michael Jesse *lawyer*
Kaplowitz, Karen (Jill) *lawyer*
Kelly, Daniel Grady, Jr. *lawyer*
Kenoff, Jay Stewart *lawyer*
King, Robert Lucien *lawyer*
Klein, Raymond Maurice *lawyer*
Kupperman, Henry John *lawyer*
Lauchengco, Jose Yujuico, Jr. *lawyer*
Lavin, Laurence Michael *lawyer*
Lesser, Joan L. *lawyer*
Levine, Thomas Jeffrey Pello *lawyer*
Lindholm, Dwight Henry *lawyer*
Link, George Hamilton *lawyer*
Lurvey, Ira Harold *lawyer*
Marshall, Arthur K. *lawyer, judge, arbitrator, educator, writer*
Matsunaga, Geoffrey Dean *lawyer*
May, Lawrence Edward *lawyer*
McBurney, George William *lawyer*
McLurkin, Thomas Cornelius, Jr. *lawyer*
Memel, Sherwin Leonard *lawyer*
Merritt, Bruce Gordon *lawyer*
Mersel, Marjorie Kathryn Pedersen *lawyer*
Meyer, Michael Edwin *lawyer*
Millard, Neal Steven *lawyer*
Miller, Milton Allen *lawyer*
Miller, O'Malley Murray *lawyer*
Morgenthaler, Alisa Marie *lawyer*
Mosk, Richard Mitchell *lawyer*
Moyer, Craig Alan *lawyer*
Muhlbach, Robert Arthur *lawyer*
Newman, Michael Rodney *lawyer*
Nibley, Robert Ricks *retired lawyer*
Noble, Richard Lloyd *lawyer*
O'Connell, Kevin *lawyer*
Pascotto, Alvaro *lawyer*
Pieper, Darold D. *lawyer*
Pircher, Leo Joseph *lawyer*
Polley, Terry Lee *lawyer*
Pollock, John Phleger *lawyer*
Porter, Verna Louise *lawyer*
Power, John Bruce *lawyer*
Pugsley, Robert Adrian *legal educator*
Rae, Matthew Sanderson, Jr. *lawyer*
Renwick, Edward S. *lawyer*
Richardson, Arthur Wilhelm *lawyer*
Richardson, Douglas Fielding *lawyer*
Riffer, Jeffrey Kent *lawyer, educator*
Robertson, Hugh Duff *lawyer*
Robison, William Robert *lawyer*
Rolin, Christopher E(rnest) *lawyer*
Roney, John Harvey *lawyer, consultant*
Rosenthal, Sol *lawyer*
Rosett, Arthur Irwin *lawyer, educator*
Rothman, Frank *lawyer, motion picture company executive*
Rutter, Marshall Anthony *lawyer*
Sacks, Robert Neil *lawyer*
Salvaty, Benjamin Benedict *lawyer*
Schroeder, Glenn Carl *lawyer, educator*
Selvin, Peter Sam *lawyer*
Sheehan, Lawrence James *lawyer*
Sherwood, Allen Joseph *lawyer*
Shultz, John David *lawyer*
Silbergeld, Arthur F. *lawyer*
Smolker, Gary Steven *lawyer, educator*
Snyder, Arthur Kress *lawyer*
Spivak, Joel A. *lawyer*
Stashower, Arthur L. *lawyer*
Stromberg, G. Thomas, Jr. *lawyer*
Swain, Philip C., Jr. *lawyer, mechanical engineer*
Tan, William Lew *lawyer*
Taylor, Minna *lawyer*
Thoren-Peden, Deborah Suzanne *lawyer*
Tinsley, Walton Eugene *lawyer*
Valenzuela, Manuel Anthony, Jr. *lawyer*
Valner, Rudy *lawyer*
Van de Kamp, John Kalar *lawyer*
Verrone, Patric Miller *lawyer, writer*
Walton, Brian *lawyer, union negotiator*
Ward, Richard Alan *lawyer*
Weinman, Glenn Alan *lawyer*
Wharton, Charles Ellis *legal administrator*
White, Jack Raymond *lawyer*
Williams, Lee Dwain *lawyer*

Los Gatos
Dumas, Jeffrey Mack *lawyer*

Malibu
Phillips, Ronald Frank *legal educator, university vice chancellor*

Manhattan Beach
Ho, Anna Shao-Fu *lawyer*
Parcells, Dayton Balcom, III *lawyer*

Martinez
Bray, Absalom Francis, Jr. *lawyer*
Williams, Charles Judson *lawyer*

Menlo Park
Crandall, Nelson David, III *lawyer*
Kirk, Cassius Lamb, Jr. *lawyer, investor*
Russell, John Drinker *legal educator and administrator*

Middletown
Downing, James Christie *lawyer*

Milpitas
Small, Jonathan Andrew *lawyer*

Monterey
Schott, David Preston *lawyer*

Monterey Park
Groce, Ewin Petty *lawyer*

Moreno Valley
Cherniss, David Alan *lawyer*

Napa
Kuntz, Charles Powers *lawyer*

Newport Beach
Barclay, John Allen *lawyer*
Damon, James G. *lawyer*
Hancock, S. Lee *lawyer*
Lopez, Ramon Rossi *lawyer*
McEvers, Duff Steven *lawyer*
Mortensen, Arvid LeGrande *lawyer, insurance company executive*
Olsen, Robert Kenneth *lawyer*
Saltarelli, Thomas Richard *lawyer*
Schnapp, Roger Herbert *lawyer*
Spears, Alan Errol *judicial officer*
Thomas, Joseph Edward *lawyer*
Vaccaro, Christopher Mark *lawyer*
Wentworth, Theodore Sumner *lawyer*

North Hollywood
Kreger, Melvin Joseph *lawyer*
Zimring, Stuart David *lawyer*

Novato
Lewin, Werner Siegfried, Jr. *lawyer*
Obninsky, Victor Peter *lawyer*

Oakland
Allen, Jeffrey Michael *lawyer*
Bjork, Robert David, Jr. *lawyer*
Braverman, Robert Allen *lawyer*
Burnison, Boyd Edward *lawyer*
Cline, Wilson Ettason *retired administrative law judge*
Farley, Barbara Suzanne *lawyer*
Fong, Marc Alan *lawyer*
Innes, Kenneth Frederick, III *lawyer*
Leslie, Robert Lorne *lawyer*
Mc Elwain, Lester Stafford *lawyer*
Mendelson, Steven Earle *lawyer*
Sun, Cossette Tsung-hung Wu *law library director*
Tracy, James Jared, Jr. *law firm administrator*
Wallace, Elaine Wendy *lawyer*

Oceanside
Richards, Gerald Thomas *lawyer, consultant*

Orange
Batchelor, James Kent *lawyer*
Parker, Charles Edward *lawyer*

Orinda
Brookes, Valentine *retired lawyer*
Perez, Richard Lee *lawyer*

Oxnard
O'Hearn, Michael John *lawyer*

Pacific Palisades
Dean, Ronald Glenn *lawyer*
Flattery, Thomas Long *lawyer, legal administrator*
Lagle, John Franklin *lawyer*
Nothmann, Rudolf S. *legal researcher*

Palm Desert
Spirtos, Nicholas George *lawyer, financial company executive*

Palm Springs
FitzGerald, John Edward, III *lawyer*

Palo Alto
Bell, Richard G. *lawyer*
Brigham, Samuel Townsend Jack, III *lawyer*
Coats, William Sloan, III *lawyer*
Miller, Michael Patiky *lawyer*
Petty, Keith *lawyer*

Palos Verdes Estates
Toftness, Cecil Gillman *lawyer, consultant*

Pasadena
Armour, George Porter *lawyer*
Cahill, Richard Frederick *lawyer*
Chan, Daniel Chung-Yin *lawyer*
Hale, Charles Russell *lawyer*
Lisoni, Gail Marie Landtbom *lawyer*
Mosher, Sally Ekenberg *lawyer*
Ritchie, David Brian *lawyer*
Tanner, Dee Boshard *lawyer*
Wills, Donald Allison *lawyer*

Pleasanton
Scott, G. Judson, Jr. *lawyer*
Staley, John Fredric *lawyer*

Rancho Cordova
King, Franklin Weaver *lawyer*
Lynch, Robert Berger *lawyer*

Rancho Mirage
Goldie, Ray Robert *lawyer*

Rancho Palos Verdes
Russell, Thomas Arthur *lawyer*

Redding
Montgomery, Carroll Ann. *law educator*

Redlands
Ely, Northcutt *lawyer*

Redondo Beach
Berman-Barrett, Sara Jane *lawyer, educator*
Coffey, Daniel Wayne *lawyer*
Hachmeister, John H. *lawyer, educator, mediator*
Martin, Robert Michael *lawyer*

Redwood City
Heuman, Donna Rena *lawyer*
Silvestri, Philip Salvatore *lawyer*
Wilhelm, Robert Oscar *lawyer, civil engineer, developer*

Rio Linda
Lebrato, Mary Theresa *lawyer, psychologist*

Riverside
Darling, Scott Edward *lawyer*
Marlatt, Michael James *lawyer*
Spriggs, Everett Lee *lawyer*

Rohnert Park
Hoppenstaedt, Jon Kirk *law librarian*

Rolling Hills
Rumbaugh, Charles Earl *lawyer, corporate executive*

Roseville
Robbins, Stephen J. M. *lawyer*

Sacramento
Bobrow, Susan Lukin *lawyer*
Brazier, John Richard *lawyer, physician*
Bremen, Ronald David *lawyer*
Brookman, Anthony Raymond *lawyer*
Burton, Randall James *lawyer*
Callahan, Ronald *federal investigator, historian*
Callison, Russell James *lawyer*
Collentine, John Thomas *arbitrator, public art consultant*
Dressler, Joshua *lawyer, educator*
Fall, Timothy Lee *lawyer*
Henry, Karen Hawley *lawyer*
Kolkey, Daniel Miles *lawyer*
Marquez, Anthony Philip *lawyer*
Perschbacher, Debra Bassett *lawyer*
Phillips, Dana Wayne *lawyer*
Root, Gerald Edward *courts administrator, resource developer*
Roseme, Sharon Day *lawyer*
Schaber, Gordon Duane *law educator, former judge*
Sims, John Cary *law educator*
Spivey, Roberta Lee *paralegal, community counselor*
Taylor, Walter Wallace *lawyer*
Van Camp, Brian Ralph *lawyer*
Waks, Dennis Stanford *lawyer*
Willis, Dawn Louise *paralegal, small business owner*
Wishek, Michael Bradley *lawyer*
Zumbrun, Ronald Arthur *lawyer*

San Bernardino
Eskin, Barry Sanford *court investigator*

San Carlos
Inama, Christopher Roy *lawyer*

San Clemente
Fisher, Myron R. *lawyer*

San Diego
Bowie, Peter Wentworth *lawyer, educator*
Branson, Harley Kenneth *lawyer, finance executive*
Buzunis, Constantine Dino *lawyer*
Campbell, Arthur Waldron *lawyer, educator*
Carter, Nancy Carol *legal educator, law librarian*
Chatroo, Arthur Jay *lawyer*
Endeman, Ronald Lee *lawyer*
Frasch, Brian Bernard *lawyer*
Hinman, George Burke *lawyer*
Hofflund, Paul *lawyer*
Kennerson, Paul *lawyer, author, educator*
Lathrop, Mitchell Lee *lawyer*
LeBeau, Charles Paul *lawyer*
Manoogian, William *lawyer*
McClellan, Craig Rene *lawyer*
Nelson, Craig Stuart *lawyer*
Orfield, Adrienne Adams *lawyer*
Parker, Larry Benson *lawyer*
Patterson, Jamee Jordan *lawyer*
Paupp, Terrence Edward *legal research associate, educator*
Peters, Richard *lawyer*
Pettis, Ronald Eugene *lawyer*
Pletcher, Robert Anthony *lawyer*
Rushing, Don G. *lawyer*
Sampson, Bryan Dirk *lawyer*
Sceper, Duane Harold *lawyer*
Shepersky, Mimi *probate examiner*
Shippey, Sandra Lee *lawyer*
Skelton, David Lee *lawyer*
Slomanson, William Reed *law educator, legal writer*
Snaid, Leon Jeffrey *lawyer*
Stryker, Dennis J(ames) *lawyer*
Von Passenheim, John B. *lawyer*
Ward, Diane Korosy *lawyer*
Weaver, Michael James *lawyer*
Weinreb, Bradley Allen *deputy attorney general*
Zakarin, Keith *lawyer*

San Dimas
Abner, Eddie Lee *lawyer*

San Francisco
Adams, Philip *lawyer*
Alexander, Mary Elsie *lawyer*
Arnold, Kenneth James *lawyer, publishing company executive*
Bauch, Thomas Jay *lawyer, apparel company executive*
Berns, Philip Allan *lawyer*
Bertain, G(eorge) Joseph, Jr. *lawyer*
Bertram, Phyllis Ann *lawyer, communications executive*
Borny, Walter Michael *lawyer, financial planner, general securities representative, real estate investment consultant*
Briscoe, John *lawyer*
Burden, James Ewers *lawyer*
Bushnell, Roderick Paul *lawyer*
Cadwalader, George Lyell *lawyer*
Campbell, Scott Robert *lawyer, former food company executive*
Cannon, Christopher John *lawyer*
Collas, Juan Garduño, Jr. *lawyer*
Connell, William D. *lawyer*
Daggett, Robert Sherman *lawyer*
Davies, Paul Lewis, Jr. *retired lawyer*
Davis, Roland Chenoweth *lawyer*
Drozd, Leon Frank, Jr. *lawyer*
Dryden, Robert Eugene *lawyer*
Dulaney, Andrew G. *lawyer*
Enersen, Burnham *lawyer*
Fergus, Gary Scott *lawyer*
Finberg, James Michael *lawyer*
Fowler, Peter Niles *lawyer*
Frankel, James Burton *lawyer*
Friedman, Robert Eric *lawyer*
Friese, Robert Charles *lawyer*
Gardner, Francesca Marroquin *lawyer, consultant*
Gary, Richard N. *lawyer*
Gelhaus, Robert Joseph *lawyer, publisher*
Gibson, Virginia Lee *lawyer*
Gillmar, Stanley Frank *lawyer*
Glazer, Jack Henry *lawyer*
Goetzl, Thomas Maxwell *law educator, arbitrator*
Guarino, Peter Roserio *corporate lawyer*
Guggenhime, Richard Johnson *lawyer*
Hansell, Walter White *lawyer*
Haynes, William Ernest *lawyer, financial consultant, educator*
Herlihy, Thomas Mortimer *lawyer*
Hing, Lawrence Stewart *lawyer, stock exchange official*
Hurabiell, John Philip, Sr. *lawyer*
Johns, Richard Seth Ellis *lawyer*
Kahn, Merle Deborah *lawyer*
Kimport, David Lloyd *lawyer*
Klott, David Lee *lawyer*
Knebel, Jack Gillen *lawyer*
Ladar, Jerrold Morton *lawyer*
Lawton, Larry David *lawyer*
Lee, John Jin *lawyer*
Levit, Victor Bert *lawyer, foreign representative, civic worker*
Lynch, Timothy Jeremiah-Mahoney *lawyer, theologian, realtor, educator*
Maddux, Parker Ahrens *lawyer*
Maloney, Douglas James *lawyer*
Mandel, Martin Louis *lawyer*
Martin, Joseph, Jr. *lawyer, former ambassador*
McAniff, Edward John *lawyer*
Meadows, John Frederick *lawyer*
Mesina, Dennis G. *lawyer*
Mihan, Ralph George *lawyer*
Morrissey, John Carroll *lawyer*
Mussman, William Edward *lawyer, oil company executive*
Mussman, William Edward, III *lawyer*
Neiman, Tanya Marie *lawyer*
Nemir, Donald Philip *lawyer*
Nichols, Alan Hammond *lawyer*
O'Bryan, Michael Gavin *lawyer*
Peritore, Laura *law librarian*
Philipsborn, John Timothy *lawyer, author*
Preovolos, Penelope Athene *lawyer*
Prince, Patricia *lawyer*
Reese, John Robert *lawyer*
Rosen, Sanford Jay *lawyer*
Rossmann, Antonio *lawyer, educator*
Schlesinger, Rudolf Berthold *lawyer, educator*
Shors, Susan Debra *lawyer*
Simmons, Robert Michael *lawyer*
Smith, Thorn McClellan *lawyer*
Staring, Graydon Shaw *lawyer*
Stern, Claude Michael *lawyer*
Strickland, N(ancy) Kathleen *lawyer, educator*
Sutcliffe, Eric *lawyer*
Suter, Ben *lawyer*
Thissell, Charles William *lawyer*
Thompson, Robert Charles *lawyer*
Tobin, James Michael *lawyer*
Traynor, J. Michael *lawyer*
Truett, Harold Joseph, III (Tim Truett) *lawyer*
Walker, Walter Herbert, III *lawyer, writer*
Weber, Arnold I. *lawyer*
Wood, Robert Warren *lawyer*
Wyle, Frederick S. *lawyer*
Yamakawa, David Kiyoshi, Jr. *lawyer*

San Jose
Alexander, Katharine Violet *lawyer*
Anderson, Edward V. *lawyer*
Blasgen, Sharon Walther *lawyer*
Cummins, Charles Fitch, Jr. *lawyer*
Doan, Xuyen Van *lawyer*
Jensen, Lawrence Robert *lawyer*
Kraw, George Martin *lawyer, essayist*
Laskin, Barbara Virginia *legal association administrator*
Manayan, Henry C. *corporate executive*
Morgan, Robert Hall *lawyer*
Nopar, Alan Scott *lawyer*

San Marcos
Dixon, William Cornelius *lawyer*

San Marino
Arkenberg, Jerome Stephen *law and history researcher*
Cranston, Howard Stephen *lawyer, management consultant*
Mortimer, Wendell Reed, Jr. *lawyer*
Tomich, Lillian *lawyer*

San Mateo
Drysdale, George Marsman *lawyer, venture capitalist*
Kenney, William Fitzgerald *lawyer*
Slabach, Stephen Hall *lawyer*

San Rafael
Drexler, Kenneth *lawyer*
Squarcy, Charlotte Van Horne *lawyer*
Townsend, Russell Henry *lawyer*

San Ramon
Davis, John Albert *lawyer*

Santa Ana
Capizzi, Michael Robert *lawyer*
Chambers, Gary Lee *lawyer*
Dillard, John Martin *lawyer, pilot*
Fay-Schmidt, Patricia Ann *paralegal*
Hamilton, Phillip Douglas *lawyer*
Heckler, Gerard Vincent *lawyer*
Kaye, Stuart Martin *lawyer*
Oliver, Marvin Maurice *lawyer*
Schiff, Laurie *lawyer*
Williamson, George Eugene *lawyer*

Santa Barbara
Cappello, A. Barry *lawyer*
Gaines, Howard Clarke *lawyer*
McEwan, Willard Winfield, Jr. *lawyer, judge*
McGinnes, James Marc *lawyer, lecturer*
Metzinger, Timothy Edward *lawyer*
Moncharsh, Philip Isaac *lawyer*
Nolte, John Michael *lawyer, consultant*
Reed, Frank Fremont, II *retired lawyer*
Willey, Charles Wayne *lawyer*

Santa Clara
Alexander, George Jonathon *legal educator, former dean*
Blawie, James Louis *law educator*
Gough, Aidan Richard *legal educator, consultant*
Wehde, Albert Edward *lawyer*

Santa Clarita
Kotler, Richard Lee *lawyer*

Santa Maria
Montandon, Arther Ronald *city attorney*

Santa Monica
Cohen, Robert F. *lawyer, journalist*
Dickson, Robert Lee *lawyer*
Harwick, Maurice *lawyer*
Landay, Andrew Herbert *lawyer*
Le Berthon, Adam *lawyer*
Prewoznik, Jerome Frank *lawyer*
Weatherup, Roy Garfield *lawyer*

Seal Beach
Bennett, William Perry *lawyer*

Seaside
Weingarten, Saul Myer *lawyer*

Sebastopol
Harriman, Thomas Jarvis, Jr. *lawyer*

Sherman Oaks
Gotcher, James Ronald *lawyer*

Sloughhouse
Ullrich, Donald William, Jr. *lawyer, real estate broker*

Solana Beach
Upp, Robert Dean *lawyer*

Stanford
Bagley, Constance Elizabeth *lawyer, educator*
Baxter, William Francis *lawyer, educator*
Brest, Paul A. *law educator*
Friedman, Lawrence M. *law educator*
Scott, Kenneth Eugene *lawyer, educator*
Williams, Howard Russell *lawyer, educator*

Suisun City
Tucker, Connie *legal assistant, insurance consultant*

Sunnyvale
McReynolds, Stephen Paul *lawyer*
Scheller, James Charles *patent lawyer*

Temecula
Rosenstein, Robert Bryce *lawyer, financial advisor*

Thousand Oaks
Trover, Ellen Lloyd *lawyer*

Toluca Lake
Tice, Robert Galen *paralegal, computer training consultant*

Torrance
Cohen, Seymour I. *lawyer*
Finer, William A. *lawyer*
Johnson, Einar William *lawyer*
Petillon, Lee Ritchey *lawyer*
Ward, Anthony John *lawyer*
Wilson, Karen LeRohl *lawyer*

Turlock
Hillberg, Ronald William *lawyer*

Tustin
Fortner, Hueston Gilmore *lawyer, writer, composer*
Madory, Richard Eugene *lawyer*

Universal City
Peter, Arnold Philimon *lawyer*

Upland
Graves, Patrick Lee *lawyer*

Valley Village
Amack, Lewis Owen *lawyer*

Van Nuys
Kuklin, Jeffrey Peter *lawyer*
Mikesell, Richard Lyon *lawyer, financial counselor*

Ventura
Clabaugh, Elmer Eugene, Jr. *lawyer*

Victorville
Kraft, Henry R. *lawyer*

Visalia
Crowe, John T. *lawyer*
Hart, Timothy Ray *lawyer, dean*
Smukler, Kim Bennett *lawyer*

Walnut Creek
Blackburn, Michael Philip *lawyer*
Newmark, Milton Maxwell *lawyer*
Pinkerton, Albert Duane, II *lawyer*
Weiss, Edward Abraham *lawyer*

West Hollywood
Finstad, Suzanne Elaine *author, lawyer, producer*
Golden, Renée Wayne *lawyer*

Windsor
Greiner, Robert Philip *lawyer, real estate broker*

Woodland Hills
Winfrey, Diana Lee *lawyer*

COLORADO

Arvada
Rakowsky, Ronald John *lawyer*
Trujillo, Lorenzo A. *lawyer*

Aspen
Shipp, Dan Shackelford *lawyer*

Aurora
Halford, Sharon Lee *crime victim services administrator, victimologist, educator*
Kurz, Edward Philip *lawyer*
Schilling, Edwin Carlyle, III *lawyer*
Seybert, Janet Rose *lawyer, military officer*

Boulder
Anuta, Karl Frederick *lawyer*
Danielson, Luke Jeffries *lawyer*
DuVivier, Katharine Keyes *lawyer*
Gamm, Gordon Julius *lawyer*
Hale, Daniel Cudmore *lawyer*
Hofgard, Kurt Christopher *lawyer, insurance executive*
LaVelle, Betty Sullivan Dougherty *legal professional*
Miller, Jonathan Lewis *lawyer, computer consultant*
O'Conner, Loretta Rae *former court reporter*
Purvis, John Anderson *lawyer*
Rich, Ben Arthur *lawyer, university official*
Wells, David Conrad *lawyer*

Breckenridge
Katz, Jeri Beth *lawyer*

Castle Rock
Bell, Brian Mayes *lawyer*

Cedaredge
Andersen, Ernest Christopher *lawyer*

Colorado Springs
Campbell, Frederick Hollister *lawyer, historian*
Gross, Michael David *lawyer*
Kendall, Phillip Alan *lawyer*
MacDougall, Malcolm Edward *lawyer*
Palermo, Norman Anthony *lawyer*
Purvis, Randall W. B. *lawyer*
Rowan, Ronald Thomas *lawyer*
Schumacher, Frederick Richmond *lawyer*
Thomas, Darrell Denman *lawyer*

Commerce City
Stark, Dennis William *paralegal, consultant*

Delta
Wendt, John Arthur Frederic, Jr. *lawyer*

Denver
Abramovitz, Michael John *lawyer*
Allen, Stephanie West *mediator*
Ash, Walter Brinker *lawyer*
Bain, James William *lawyer*
Benkert, Joseph Philip, Jr. *lawyer*
Bolocofsky, David N. *psychology educator, lawyer*
Bragg, Douglas E. *lawyer*
Breggin, Janis Ann *lawyer*
Bryans, Richard W. *lawyer*
Cassidy, Samuel H. *lawyer, lieutenant governor, state legislator*
Cockrell, Richard Carter *lawyer*
Cohen, Jeremy Patrick *lawyer*
Cordova, Donald E. *lawyer*
Cortes, William Patrick *lawyer, telecommunications executive*
Cox, William Vaughn *lawyer*
Deikman, Eugene Lawrence *lawyer*
DeMuth, Alan Cornelius *lawyer*
Dong, Alvin Lim *law librarian, lawyer*
Dowdle, Patrick Dennis *lawyer*
Dunn, Randy Edwin *lawyer*
Edwards, Daniel Walden *lawyer*
Ehrlich, Stephen Richard *lawyer*
Elrod, Richard Bryan *lawyer*
Fautsko, Timothy F. *national court management consultant*
Faxon, Thomas Baker *lawyer*
Felter, Edwin Lester, Jr. *lawyer, agency administrator*
Finesilver, Jay Mark *lawyer*
Fortune, Lowell *lawyer*
Friedberg, Alan Charles *lawyer*
Gallegos, Larry Duayne *lawyer*
Gehres, James *lawyer*
Green, Jersey Michael-Lee *lawyer*
Guinn, Linda Ann *environmental lawyer*
Gutterman, Sheila Maydet *lawyer*
Hagen, Glenn W(illiam) *lawyer*
Harris, Dale Ray *lawyer*
Hawley, Robert Cross *lawyer*
Hodges, Joseph Gilluly, Jr. *lawyer*
Hutchins, John Milton *lawyer*
Jersin, Edward Anthony *lawyer*
Johnson, Robert Leland *lawyer*
Katz, Michael Jeffery *lawyer*
Keely, George Clayton *lawyer*
Kerwin, Mary Ann Collins *lawyer*
Law, John Manning *retired lawyer*
Lerman, Eileen R. *lawyer*
Lidstone, Herrick Kenley, Jr. *lawyer*
Lutz, John Shafroth *lawyer*

Mains, Steve Alan *lawyer, arbitrator, mediator*
Mark, Denis Hugh *lawyer*
Marquess, Lawrence Wade *lawyer*
Mauro, Richard Frank *lawyer, investment manager*
McDowell, Karen Ann *lawyer*
McMichael, Donald Earl *lawyer*
Molling, Charles Francis *lawyer*
Otten, Arthur Edward, Jr. *lawyer, corporate executive*
Phillips, David Parker *legal foundation executive, lawyer*
Pringle, Edward E. *legal educator, former state supreme court chief justice*
Rich, Robert Stephen *lawyer*
Ruppert, John Lawrence *lawyer*
Sayre, John Marshall *lawyer, former government official*
Schauer, Tone Terjesen *lawyer*
Schmidt, Diana Gail *paralegal*
Schmidt, L(ail) William, Jr. *lawyer*
Scott, Peter Bryan *lawyer*
Seawell, Donald Ray *lawyer, publisher, arts center executive, producer*
Seifert, Stephen Wayne *lawyer*
Skok, Paul Joseph *lawyer*
Snead, Kathleen Marie *lawyer*
Spillane, John Michael *lawyer*
Springer, Jeffrey Alan *lawyer*
Starrs, Elizabeth Anne *lawyer*
Syke, Cameron John *lawyer*
Taylor, T. Raber *lawyer*
Tempelman, Steven Carlos *lawyer*
Terry, Ward Edgar, Jr. *lawyer*
Timmins, Edward Patrick *lawyer*
Tisdale, Douglas Michael *lawyer*
Vigil, Charles S. *lawyer*
Wedgle, Richard Jay *lawyer*
Wehmhoefer, Richard Allen *lawyer, educator*
Welton, Charles Ephraim *lawyer*
Wheeler, Malcolm Edward *lawyer, law educator*
Wilcox, Debra Kay *lawyer*
Williams, Wayne De Armond *lawyer*
Yegge, Robert Bernard *lawyer, college dean emeritus, educator*

Englewood
Cross, Christopher Charles *lawyer*
Figa, Phillip Sam *lawyer*
Gardner, Ray Dean, Jr. *lawyer*
Irwin, R. Robert *lawyer*
Karr, David Dean *lawyer*
Kippur, Merrie Margolin *lawyer*
Meyer, Lee Gordon *lawyer, energy company executive*
Smead, Burton Armstrong, Jr. *lawyer*
Steele, Elizabeth Meyer *lawyer*
Steinhauser, John William *lawyer*
Wagner, David James *lawyer*
Wollins, David H. *lawyer*

Evergreen
Harz, G. Michael *lawyer*

Fort Collins
DiFalco, John Patrick *arbitrator, lawyer*
Gamlin, John Paschall *lawyer*
Gandy, H. Conway *lawyer, state official*
Rogers, Garth Winfield *lawyer*

Frisco
Helmer, David Alan *lawyer*

Golden
Wilson, James Robert *lawyer*

Grand Junction
Mayberry, Herbert Sylvester *lawyer*

Greeley
Abbott, Keith Eugene *lawyer, consultant*
Conway, Rebecca Ann Koppes *lawyer*

Lakewood
Guyton, Samuel Percy *retired lawyer*
McElwee, Dennis John *lawyer, former pharmaceutical company executive*
Thome, Dennis Wesley *lawyer*

Leadville
Horstman, Carol Bellhouse *lawyer*

Littleton
Reddien, Charles Henry, II *lawyer, corporate executive, consultant*
Spelts, Richard John *lawyer*
Truhlar, Doris Broaddus *lawyer*

Manassa
Garcia, Castelar Medardo *lawyer*

Parker
Greenberg, Morton Paul *lawyer*

Pueblo
Farley, Thomas T. *lawyer*
Geisel, Henry Jules *lawyer*

Pueblo West
McHardy, John Alexander *lawyer*

Rifle
George, Russell Lloyd *lawyer, legislator*

DISTRICT OF COLUMBIA

Washington
Katz, John W. *lawyer, state official*
McClure, James A. *lawyer, retired senator*
Ryan, Frederick Joseph, Jr. *lawyer, public official*

HAWAII

Honolulu
Bloede, Victor Carl *lawyer, academic executive*
Boggs, Steven Eugene *lawyer*
Chuck, Walter G(oonsun) *lawyer*
Chur, Daniel Eric *lawyer*
Cowan, Stuart Marshall *lawyer*
Dang, Marvin S.C. *lawyer*
Deaver, Phillip Lester *lawyer*
Edmunds, John Sanford *lawyer*
Fong, Peter C. K. *lawyer, judge*
Fukumoto, Leslie Satsuki *lawyer*
Garcia, Ignacio Razon *lawyer*
Gay, E(mil) Laurence *lawyer*
Gebbia Pinetti, Karen Marie *lawyer, educator*
Gelber, Don Jeffrey *lawyer*
Geshell, Richard Steven *lawyer*
Gillin, Malvin James, Jr. *lawyer*
Gunderson, Clarence Joseph, Jr. *lawyer, judge advocate*
Ingersoll, Richard King *lawyer*
Iwai, Wilfred Kiyoshi *lawyer*
Jackson, Bruce George *lawyer*
Kawachika, James Akio *lawyer*
Lau, Eugene Wing Iu *lawyer*
Lilly, Michael Alexander *lawyer*
Lindow, Louisa Rose *lawyer*
Louie, David Mark *lawyer*
Miller, Clifford Joel *lawyer*
Miller, Richard Sherwin *legal educator*
Moore, Willson Carr, Jr. *lawyer*
Moroney, Michael John *lawyer*
Morse, Jack Craig *lawyer*
Omori, Morio *lawyer*
Powers, Philip Hemsley *lawyer, consultant*
Pyun, Matthew Sung Kwan *lawyer*
Reinke, Stefan Michael *lawyer*
Rohrer, Reed Beaver *lawyer*
Takata, Kevin Kenji *lawyer*
Tanaka, Leila Chiyako *lawyer*
Taylor, Carroll Stribling *lawyer*
Weight, Michael Anthony *lawyer, former judge*
Weightman, Judy Mae *lawyer*
Wilson, Virgil James, III *lawyer*
Woo, Timothy David, Jr. *state senate clerk, lawyer*
Woo, Vernon Ying-Tsai *lawyer, real estate developer*
Yamada, Stephen Kinichi *lawyer*
Zabanal, Eduardo Olegario *lawyer*

Kailua Kona
Martin, William Charles *lawyer*

Kula
Rohlfing, Frederick William *lawyer, judge*

Lihue
Budd, Nancy J. *lawyer*

Maunaloa
Rice, V(irgil) Thomas *lawyer, consultant*

Wailuku
Kinaka, William Tatsuo *lawyer*
Krueger, James *lawyer*
Ranken, Anthony L. *lawyer*

IDAHO

Boise
Doolittle, Michael Jim *lawyer*
Fawcett, Charles Winton *lawyer*
Hamlin, Susan Elizabeth *lawyer, educator*
Hoagland, Samuel Albert *lawyer, pharmacist*
Klein, Edith Miller *lawyer, former state senator*
Marcus, Craig Brian *lawyer*
Meyer, Christopher Hawkins *lawyer*

Coeur D Alene
Ayers, Stephen M. *lawyer*

Ketchum
Hogue, Terry Glynn *lawyer*

Lewiston
Tait, John Reid *lawyer*

Moscow
Vincenti, Sheldon Arnold *law educator, lawyer*

Nampa
Duffy, Wayne Edward *lawyer*

Pocatello
Nye, W. Marcus W. *lawyer*
Whittier, Monte Ray *lawyer*

Salmon
Furey, Sherman Francis, Jr. *lawyer*

Sandpoint
Robinson, Philip H. *lawyer*

Twin Falls
Glenn, James D., Jr. *lawyer*
Stubbs, Mark Darwin *lawyer*

ILLINOIS

Chicago
Ettinger, Joseph Alan *lawyer*

Vernon Hills
Michalik, John James *legal association executive*

INDIANA

Carmel
Read, Frank Thompson *law educator*

MONTANA

Billings
Cromley, Brent Reed *lawyer*
Hanson, Norman *lawyer*
Malee, Thomas Michael *lawyer*
Overfelt, Lee *lawyer*
Thompson, James William *lawyer*
Towe, Thomas Edward *lawyer*

Bozeman
Frantz, Paul Lewis *lawyer*
Nelson, Steven Dwayne *lawyer*
Wylie, Paul Richter, Jr. *lawyer*

Butte
Krueger, Kurt Donn *lawyer*
Poore, James Albert, III *lawyer*

Great Falls
Overfelt, Clarence Lahugh *lawyer*

Havre
Moog, Mary Ann Pimley *lawyer*

Helena
MacMaster, John Arthur *state legislative lawyer*
Sweeney, Nancy Louise *district court clerk*
Wewer, William Paul *lawyer*

Kalispell
Dudis, John Betz *lawyer*
Robinson, Calvin Stanford *lawyer*

Missoula
Bowman, Jean Louise *lawyer, civic worker*
George, Alexander Andrew *lawyer*
Morales, Julio K. *lawyer*
Renz, Jeffrey Thomas *lawyer*

NEVADA

Carson City
Rodefer, Jeffrey Robert *lawyer, prosecutor*
Waters, Noel Scott *county district attorney, lawyer*
Williams, Day Robert *lawyer*

Elko
Vaughan, Robert Oren *lawyer*

Henderson
Smallwood, Betty *lawyer*

Las Vegas
Blouke, Milton Baker *lawyer*
Burnett, Gary Boyd *lawyer, real estate consultant*
Chin, Kelvin Henry *legal association executive, mediator, consultant*
Galane, Morton Robert *lawyer*
Gamble, LaDeana *family mediation center official*
Geihs, Frederick Siegfried *lawyer*
Goodwin, John Robert *law educator*
Gray, Patricia Joyce *court administrator*
Greene, Addison Kent *lawyer, accountant*
Han, Ittah *lawyer, political economist, high technology and financial strategist, computer engineer*
Hilbrecht, Norman Ty *lawyer*
Hill, Judith Deegan *lawyer*
Jost, Richard Frederic, III *lawyer*
Mahan, James Cameron *lawyer*
Sawyer, Grant *lawyer*
Singer, Michael Howard *lawyer*
Smith, Stephanie Marie *lawyer*
Thorndal, John LaFleur *lawyer*

Reno
Barkley, Thierry Vincent *lawyer*
Hill, Earl McColl *lawyer*
Kladney, David *lawyer*
Marshall, Robert William *lawyer, rancher*
Martz, John Roger *lawyer*
Richards, Paul A. *lawyer*
Shaffer, Wayne Alan *lawyer*
Springmeyer, Don *lawyer*

NEW MEXICO

Albuquerque
Addis, Richard Barton *lawyer*
Beach, Arthur O'Neal *lawyer*
Branch, Turner Williamson *lawyer*
Caruso, Mark John *lawyer*
Hanna, Robert Cecil *lawyer, lecturer, hotelier*
Lawit, John Walter *lawyer*
Lock, William Joseph *lawyer*
Messinger, J. Henry *lawyer*
Purcell, Charles Kipps *lawyer*
Reinhart, Steven Anthony *lawyer*
Rezler, Julius *labor arbitrator*
Roehl, Jerrald J(oseph) *lawyer*
Schoen, Stevan Jay *lawyer*
Schuler, Alison Kay *lawyer*
Skipp, Tracy John *legal support service company owner*
Stephenson, Barbera Wertz *lawyer*
Thornton, J. Duke *lawyer*
Throckmorton, Rex Denton *lawyer*
Vigil, Douglas Elliott *lawyer*
Walker, Roger Alfred *lawyer*

Carlsbad
Diamond, Jeffrey Brian *lawyer*

Deming
Sherman, Frederick Hood *lawyer*

Farmington
Morgan, Jack M. *lawyer*

Las Cruces
Palacios, Pedro Pablo *lawyer*

Placitas
Hopkins, Richard Lee *educator, writer*

Roswell
Bassett, John Walden, Jr. *lawyer*
Haines, Thomas David, Jr. *lawyer*
Olson, Richard Earl *lawyer, state legislator*

Santa Fe
Bluestone, Stuart Michael *lawyer*
Burton, John Paul (Jack Burton) *lawyer*
Carpenter, Richard Norris *lawyer*
Casey, Patrick Anthony *lawyer*
Hickey, John Miller *lawyer*
McClaugherty, Joe L. *lawyer, educator*
Mellow, Judith Elizabeth *lawyer*
Noland, Charles Donald *lawyer, educator*
Schwarz, Michael *lawyer*
Shaw, Mark Howard *lawyer, business owner, entrepreneur*
Stevens, Ron A. *lawyer, public interest organization administrator*
Walther, David Louis *lawyer*

Taos
Manzanares, Dennis *lawyer*

NEW YORK

Fayetteville
Senungetuk, Vivian Ruth *lawyer*

New York
Ryan, Reade Haines, Jr. *lawyer*

White Plains
Sloan, F(rank) Blaine *law educator*

OREGON

Albany
Boatner, James William *trial court administrator*

Ashland
Berk, Gail Andrea *lawyer, property manager*
Turner, Garrison F. *lawyer*

Astoria
Haskell, Donald McMillan *lawyer*

Cannon Beach
Hillestad, Charles Andrew *lawyer*

Central Point
Richardson, Dennis Michael *lawyer, educator*

Eugene
Dugan, Marianne Guenevere *lawyer*
DuPriest, Douglas Millhollen *lawyer*
Horn, John Harold *lawyer*
Owens, A(rnold) Dean *lawyer*
Scoles, Eugene Francis *legal educator, lawyer*

Gresham
Faus, Richard Duane *lawyer*

Lincoln City
Elliott, Scott Oller *lawyer*

Mcminnville
Hansen, Bernt Allan *lawyer*

Medford
Deatherage, William Vernon *lawyer*

Milwaukie
Anderson, Mark Alexander *lawyer*

Pendleton
Bloom, Stephen Michael *lawyer, judge*
Kottkamp, John Harlan *lawyer*

Portland
Abravanel, Allan Ray *lawyer*
Bauer, Henry Leland *lawyer*
Berger, Leland Roger *lawyer*
Blumm, Michael Charles *law educator*
Drummond, Gerard Kasper *lawyer, retired minerals company executive*
DuBoff, Leonard David *lawyer, educator*
Eakin, Margaretta Morgan *lawyer*
Foraker, David Alan *lawyer*
Frank, Stephen Richard *lawyer*
Fukumoto, Bert Ken *lawyer*
Glasgow, William Jacob *lawyer*
Hanna, Harry Mitchell *lawyer*
Harrell, Gary Paul *lawyer*
Hurd, Paul Gemmill *lawyer*
Jernstedt, Kenneth Elliott *lawyer*
Kamin, Scott Allan *lawyer*
Kennedy, Jack Leland *lawyer*
King, Garr Michael *lawyer*
Matarazzo, Harris Starr *lawyer*
Schuster, Philip Frederick, II *lawyer*
Simpson, Patrick J. *lawyer*
Sokol, Larry Nides *lawyer, educator*
Sullivan, Edward Joseph *lawyer, educator*
Troutwine, Gayle Leone *lawyer*
Zalutsky, Morton Herman *lawyer*

Salem
Brand, Malcolm Leigh *lawyer*
Ferris, Evelyn Scott *lawyer*
Gatti, Daniel Jon *lawyer*
Mannix, Kevin Leese *lawyer*
Nafziger, James Albert Richmond *law educator*
Robertson, Joseph David *lawyer*
Swank, Bradd A *lawyer*

Wilsonville
Yacob, Yosef *lawyer, economist*

UTAH

Logan
Hillyard, Lyle William *lawyer*

Ogden
Mecham, Glenn Jefferson *lawyer, mayor*
Sullivan, Kevin Patrick *lawyer*
Warner, Frank Shrake *lawyer*

Park City
Kennicott, James W. *lawyer*

Pleasant Grove
Harding, Ray Murray, Jr. *lawyer*

Provo
Abbott, Charles Favour, Jr. *lawyer*
Bramhall, Eugene Hulbert *lawyer*

Sutterfield, Kevin James *lawyer, consultant*

Saint George
Gallian, Russell Joseph *lawyer*

Salt Lake City
Barusch, Lawrence Roos *lawyer*
Callister, Louis Henry, Jr. *lawyer*
Cornaby, Kay Sterling *lawyer, former state senator*
Dorius, Earl Fredric *lawyer*
Gaufin, Samuel Oliver *lawyer*
Gustavson, Mark Steven *lawyer*
Holbrook, James Russell *lawyer*
Hunt, George Andrew *lawyer*
Kimball, Spencer Levan *lawyer, educator*
Lochhead, Robert Bruce *lawyer*
Loos, William Christensen *lawyer, academic administrator*
McConkie, Oscar Walter *lawyer*
McIntosh, James Albert *lawyer*
Melich, Mitchell *lawyer*
Mills, Lawrence *lawyer, business and transportation consultant*
Mooney, Jerome Henri *lawyer*
Murray, Kevin Reid *lawyer*
Nash, William Kelly *lawyer*
Nebeker, Stephen Bennion *lawyer*
Oaks, Dallin Harris *lawyer, church official*
Ockey, Ronald J. *lawyer*
Rasmussen, Thomas Val, Jr. *lawyer, small business owner*
Vincent, Mark Kent *lawyer*
Weiss, Loren Elliot *lawyer, educator*
Willey, Elizabeth Lou *lawyer, advanced practice nurse*

Sandy
Bush, Rex Curtis *lawyer*
Gardiner, Lester Raymond, Jr. *lawyer*
Thorpe, Calvin E. *lawyer, legal educator, legal journalist*

Vernal
Judd, Dennis L. *lawyer*

WASHINGTON

Bellevue
Gulick, Peter VanDyke *lawyer*
Landau, Felix *lawyer*
Sullivan, James Jerome *lawyer, consultant*

Bellingham
Anderson, David Bowen *lawyer*
Packer, Mark Barry *lawyer, financial consultant, foundation official*
Raas, Daniel Alan *lawyer*

Bothell
Weber, Gail L. *lawyer*

Centralia
Maynard, Lynn Marie *lawyer*

Everett
Davies, Gregory Lane *lawyer*

Federal Way
Clement, G. Bruce *lawyer*

Kennewick
Hames, William Lester *lawyer*

Mount Vernon
Moser, C. Thomas *lawyer*

Olympia
Edmondson, Frank Kelley, Jr. *lawyer, legal administrator*
Hoglund, John Andrew *lawyer*
Miller, Allen Terry, Jr. *lawyer*
Tytler, Morton Maynard *lawyer, retired state assistant attorney general*
Walker, Francis Joseph *lawyer*
Wang, Arthur C. *law educator, lawyer*
Welsh, John Beresford, Jr. *lawyer*

Port Angeles
Gay, Carl Lloyd *lawyer*

Port Orchard
Shiers, Frank Abram *lawyer*

Poulsbo
Walters, Dennis H. *lawyer*

Renton
Swanson, Arthur Dean *lawyer*

Richland
Barr, Carlos Harvey *lawyer*

Seattle
Bagshaw, Bradley Holmes *lawyer*
Birmingham, Richard Joseph *lawyer*
Blizinsky, Marlin Joel *lawyer*
Boeder, Thomas L. *lawyer*
Bradley, Mark Charles *defender*
Cornell, Kenneth Lee *lawyer*
Dalton, Thomas George *paralegal, social worker, legal consultant*
Diamond, Josef *lawyer*
Dolan, Andrew Kevin *lawyer*
Ellis, James Reed *lawyer*
Freedman, Bart Joseph *lawyer*
Gaunt, Janet Lois *arbitrator, mediator*
George, Nicholas *criminal defense lawyer, entrepreneur*
Gosanko, Gary Nicolas *lawyer*
Gottlieb, Daniel Seth *lawyer*
Graybeal, Lynne Elizabeth *lawyer*
Groff, David Clark, Jr. *lawyer*
Grutz, James Arthur *lawyer*
Haggard, Joel Edward *lawyer*
Hendricks, Katherine *lawyer*
Keating, Robert Clark *lawyer*
Ketter, David E. *lawyer*
Leed, Roger Melvin *lawyer*
Linn, Brian James *lawyer*
Loftus, Thomas Daniel *lawyer*
Martens, Richard Lawrence *lawyer*
McAteer, James Francis *lawyer*
McKay, Michael Dennis *lawyer*
Merkle, Alan Ray *lawyer*
Mines, Michael *lawyer*
Mussehl, Robert Clarence *lawyer*
Narodick, Kit Gordon *lawyer, consultant*
Niemi, Janice *lawyer, former state legislator*
Oles, Stuart Gregory *lawyer*
Oyer, Sarah Elizabeth *lawyer*
Parks, Gerald Thomas, Jr. *lawyer, business executive*
Paul, Thomas Frank *lawyer*
Peterson, Ronald Arthur *business law educator*
Reardon, Mark William *lawyer*
Robblee, Richard Howard *lawyer*
Steinberg, Jack *lawyer*
Stoebuck, William Brees *law educator*
Strichartz, James Leonard *lawyer*
Sussman, Neil A. *lawyer*
Wagoner, David Everett *lawyer*
Wall, William E. *lawyer, former utility executive*
Walter, Michael Charles *lawyer*
Wechsler, Mary Heyrman *lawyer*
White, Thomas S. *lawyer*
Whitehead, James Fred, III *lawyer*
Wilson, Richard Randolph *lawyer*

Spokane
Foley, Thomas Stephen *lawyer, former speaker House of Representatives*
Fredricks, Anthony Theo *retired lawyer*
Harbaugh, Daniel Paul *lawyer*
Riherd, John Arthur *lawyer*
Weatherhead, Leslie R. *lawyer*

Tacoma
Frohmader, Frederick Oliver *lawyer*
Hostnik, Charles Rivoire *lawyer*
Krueger, James A. *lawyer*
Pearson, Claude Meredith *legal consultant*
Sterbick, Peter Lawrence *lawyer*
Thompson, Ronald Edward *lawyer*

Vancouver
Kleweno, Gilbert H. *lawyer*

Walla Walla
Hayner, Herman Henry *lawyer*
Hedine, Kristian Einar *lawyer*

Wenatchee
Aylward, J. Patrick *lawyer*

Yakima
Larson, Paul Martin *lawyer*
Wright, J(ames) Lawrence *lawyer*

WYOMING

Casper
Combs, W(illiam) Henry, III *lawyer*
Durham, Harry Blaine, III *lawyer*
Hjelmstad, William David *lawyer*
Lowe, Robert Stanley *lawyer*

Cheyenne
Argeris, George John *lawyer*
Carlson, Kathleen Bussart *law librarian*
Hanes, John Grier *lawyer, state legislator*
Hathaway, Stanley Knapp *lawyer*
Lummis, Cynthia Marie *lawyer, rancher*

Cody
Stradley, Richard Lee *lawyer*

Gillette
Zollinger, Thomas Tennant *lawyer*

Glenrock
Bunn, Dorothy Irons *court reporter*

Jackson
Schuster, Robert Parks *lawyer*

Laramie
Honaker, Jimmie Joe *lawyer*
Kinney, Lisa Frances *lawyer*
Smith, Thomas Shore *lawyer*

Riverton
Girard, Nettabell *lawyer*

Rock Springs
Honaker, Richard Henderson *lawyer*
Scorsine, John Magnus *lawyer*

Wheatland
Hunkins, Raymond Breedlove *lawyer, rancher*

CANADA

ALBERTA

Athabasca
Rodnunsky, Sidney *lawyer, educator, Prince of Kiev, Prince of Trabzon, Prince and Duke of Rodari, Duke of Chernigov, Count of Riga, Count of Saint John of Alexandria*

Edmonton
Amonson, Johanne Leslie *barrister, solicitor*
Shoctor, Joseph Harvey *barrister, producer, civic worker*

AUSTRIA

Salzburg
Janigian, Bruce Jasper *lawyer, educator*

ENGLAND

London
Fielding, Brian J(ackson) *lawyer*

SAUDI ARABIA

Riyadh
Taylor, Frederick William, Jr. *lawyer*

ADDRESS UNPUBLISHED

Aaron, Roy Henry *lawyer, business consultant*
Alexander, Richard *lawyer, writer*
Atkinson, Sheridan Earle *lawyer*
Bateman, David Alfred *lawyer*
Baughn, Alfred Fairhurst *lawyer*
Berardini, Jacqueline Hernandez *lawyer*
Berry, Robert Worth *lawyer, educator, retired army officer*
Bertram, Manya M. *lawyer*
Blaine, Dorothea Constance Ragetté *lawyer*
Bouvier, Marshall Andre *lawyer*
Brechbill, Susan Reynolds *lawyer, educator*
Brundin, Brian Jon *lawyer*
Bui, Eugene Lee *justice consultant*
Burgess, Hayden Fern (Pōkā Laenui) *lawyer*
Canoff, Karen Huston *lawyer*
Casillas, Mark *lawyer*
Christian, Ann Seger *lawyer*
Clark, David Curtis *lawyer*
Coulter, George Prothro *retired lawyer, real estate executive*
Crawford, Muriel Laura *lawyer, author, educator*
Criscuolo, Wendy Laura *lawyer, interior design consultant*
Davis, Wanda Rose *lawyer*
Eastin, Keith E. *lawyer*
Erickson, David Belnap *lawyer*
Factor, Max, III *lawyer, investment adviser*
Ferguson, Jack Lee *lawyer*
Fine, Richard Isaac *lawyer*
Fowler, Donald Raymond *retired lawyer, educator*
Gillam, Max Lee *lawyer*
Gomez, David Frederick *lawyer*
Gould, Julian Saul *lawyer*
Grajewski, Julian *law librarian, educator*
Hanzlik, Rayburn DeMara *lawyer*
Harriman, John Howland *lawyer*
Hart, Howard Franklin *lawyer*
Heidig, Elizabeth Anne *lawyer*
Helmbold, William Ross *lawyer, educator*
Hicks, Bethany Gribben *lawyer, commissioner*
Hirsch, Joel Gideon *lawyer*
Hitchcock, Vernon Thomas *farmer, lawyer*
Holmes, Michael Gene *lawyer*
Howe, Drayton Ford, Jr. *lawyer*
Jorgensen, Erik Holger *lawyer*
June, Roy Ethiel *lawyer*
Katz, Maurice Harry *lawyer*
Kjos, Victoria Ann *lawyer*
Kleinberg, Judith G. *lawyer, children's advocate*
Knox, Yolanda Yvette Breckenridge *legal/enforcement processor*
Kolodny, Stephen Arthur *lawyer*
Levinson, Kenneth Lee *lawyer*
Levy, David *lawyer, insurance company executive*
Lightstone, Ronald *lawyer*
MacConnell, Robert Monte *lawyer*
MacDougall, William Roderick *lawyer, county official*
Mc Donnell, Loretta Wade *lawyer*
McGinty, Brian Donald *lawyer, author*
McSorley, Cisco *lawyer*
Millard, Malcolm Stuart *retired lawyer*
Miller, Mona Joy Deutsch *lawyer*
Moore, Betty Jo *legal assistant*
Neumann, Rita *lawyer*
Newman, Carol L. *lawyer*
Orloff, Neil *lawyer*
Ousley, Pamela Darlene *legal assistant*
Paulus, Norma Jean Petersen *lawyer, state school system administrator*
Perey, Ron *lawyer*
Pereyra-Suarez, Charles Albert *lawyer*
Peterson, Howard Cooper *lawyer, accountant*
Porter, Michael Pell *lawyer*
Potts, Dennis Walker *lawyer*
Reber, Joseph E. *lawyer*
Robinson, David Howard *lawyer*
Rohrer, George John *retired lawyer*
Rosen, Martin Jack *lawyer*
Roth, Robert Charles *lawyer*
Schuele, Donna Clare *lawyer, educator*
Shambaugh, Stephen Ward *lawyer*
Shink, Shari Francine *legal administrator*
Skratek, Sylvia Paulette *mediator, arbitrator, dispute systems designer*
Smith, Robert Michael *lawyer*
Snyder, William Arthur, Jr. *lawyer*
Squires, Katherine Landey *lawyer*
Stone, Edward Herman *lawyer*
Tanaka, Jeannie E. *lawyer*
Taylor, Ruth Anne *lawyer*
Thompson, James Avery, Jr. *legal intern*
Tolentino, Casimiro Urbano *lawyer*
Torkildson, Raymond Maynard *lawyer*
Treloar, Harriette Ellen *lawyer*
Trimble, Paul Joseph *lawyer*
Underwood, B. Joann *paralegal*
Waldo, Burton Corlett *lawyer*
Walker, John Sumpter, Jr. *lawyer*
Wallace, John Barry *lawyer*
Warren, David Leslie *lawyer*
Weisman, Paul Howard *lawyer*
Westphal, Marjorie Lord *lawyer*
White, Richard Clarence *lawyer*
Wong-Diaz, Francisco Raimundo *lawyer, educator*
Yagjian, Anita Paleologos *lawyer*
Youngblood, Deborah S. *lawyer*

MEDICINE. *See* HEALTHCARE: MEDICINE.

MILITARY

UNITED STATES

ALASKA

Anchorage
Overly, Frederick Dean *civilian military employee, entrepreneur*

Fort Richardson
Schnell, Roger Thomas *retired military officer, state official*

ARIZONA

Davis Monthan AFB
Hutchinson, Edward Paul *air force officer*

Marana
Ogle, Jack Timothy *army officer*

Mesa
Boyd, Edward Hascal *retired military officer*

Phoenix
Beltrán, Anthony Natalicio *military non-commissioned officer, deacon*

Scottsdale
Coffinger, Maralin Katharyne *retired air force officer, consultant*

Tucson
Guice, John Thompson *retired air force officer*
Nikides, Bill *military officer*

Yuma
Hudson, John Irvin *retired marine officer*
Wooten, Michael Eric *military officer*

CALIFORNIA

Alameda
Allman, Clesson Dale *air force officer*

Camp Pendleton
Frank, Kurt Howard *non-commissioned marine officer*

Carmichael
McHugh, James Joseph *retired naval officer, retired associate dean*

Corona
Schwier, Edward George *naval officer*

Edwards
Engel, Richard L. *career officer*
Major, Karl Burce *air force officer*
Ryan, Robert W. *retired air force officer, aeronautical engineer*

Folsom
Aldridge, Donald O'Neal *military officer*

Laguna Hills
Faw, Duane Leslie *retired military officer, law educator, lay worker, author*

Lompoc
Walker, Duncan Edward *military officer*

Long Beach
Moss, Douglas Mabbett *military officer, aerospace executive*

Los Alamitos
Lasser, Thomas Edward *career officer*

Los Angeles
Moss, Steven Walter *air force officer*
Rollins, James Gregory *air force officer*

Martinez
Nelson, Arjay John *naval aviator*

Monterey
Hoivik, Thomas Harry *military educator, international consultant*
Matthews, David Fort *military weapon system acquisition specialist*
Pradier, Jerome Martin *air force officer, educator, administrator, pilot, businessman*

Napa
Smith, Robert Bruce *former security consultant, retired army officer*

Newport Beach
Keeley, Joseph *military officer, marketing professional*

Palm Desert
Stephens, Ronald Carlyle *retired military officer, academic director*

Pebble Beach
Fergusson, Robert George *retired army officer*

Pleasanton
Petersen, Norman William *naval officer, engineering facility administrator*

Point Mugu NAWC
Hull, Roger Kermit *military officer*

Redwood City
Schumacher, Henry Jerold *former career officer, business executive*

Riverside
Mc Cormac, Weston Arthur *retired educator and army officer*
Wright, John MacNair, Jr. *retired army officer*

San Diego
Collins, Harold John, III *military career officer*
Everett, Hobart Ray, Jr. *engineer, naval officer, consultant, researcher, inventor*
King, Charolette Elaine *administrative officer*
Robinson, David Brooks *naval officer*
Vaughan, Mark Bass *naval officer*
Young, William Clarence *career officer, training specialist*

Santa Barbara
Conley, Philip James, Jr. *retired air force officer*

Santa Clarita
Tilton, Ronald William *naval officer*

Santa Maria
Everhart, Leon Eugene *retired air force officer*

Santa Monica
Huber, Arthur Francis, II *military officer*

Santa Rosa
Andriano-Moore, Richard Norvel Graf *naval officer*

Saratoga
Henderson, William Darryl *army officer, writer*

Seaside
Gales, Samuel Joel *retired civilian military employee, counselor*

South Dos Palos
Hirohata, Derek Kazuyoshi *air force reserve officer*

Travis AFB
Meigel, David Walter *musician, military officer*
Shelwood, Howard Raymon *military officer*

Vacaville
Eberle, Michael Lee *air force officer*

Ventura
Ryan, Mary Gene *military officer, occupational health nurse*

COLORADO

Aurora
Dawes, Douglas Charles *retired military officer*

Boulder
Stone, John Helms, Jr. *admiralty advisor*

Colorado Springs
Allery, Kenneth Edward *air force officer*
Bowen, Clotilde Dent *retired army officer, psychiatrist*
Forgan, David Waller *retired air force officer*
Mitchell, John Henderson *retired army officer, management consultant*
Sawyer, Thomas William *air force officer*
Schaeffer, Reiner Horst *air force officer, retired librarian, foreign language professional*
Skora, Wayne Philip *retired air force officer*
Tarulli, Michael Gene *military officer*
Terry, David Lee *enlisted air force officer*
Todd, Harold Wade *retired air force officer, consultant*
Ulrich, Marybeth Peterson *air force officer, political science educator*
Winn, Robert Charles *retired military officer, aeronautical engineer, consultant*

Englewood
Nuce, Madonna Marie *military officer*

Falcon AFB
Riordan, John Stephen *air force officer*

Fort Carson
Catanese, Peter Anthony *military officer*

Fort Collins
Roberts, Archibald Edward *retired army officer, author*

Monument
Erving, Claude Moore, Jr. *military career officer, pilot*

Peterson AFB
Groeninger, Edward John *air force officer*

U S A F Academy
DiMarchi, David Oscar *air force officer*
Hopkins, James William *career officer, educator*
Hosmer, Bradley Clark *retired military officer, educational consultant*

DISTRICT OF COLUMBIA

Washington
Beason, James Douglas *military officer, physicist, writer, educator*
Earner, William Anthony, Jr. *naval officer*
Menoher, Paul Edwin, Jr. *army officer*

GEORGIA

Columbus
Cavezza, Carmen James *career officer*

HAWAII

Hickam AFB
Ray, Jefferey Wayne *military officer*

Honolulu
Greer, Howard Earl *former naval officer*
Hays, Ronald Jackson *naval officer*
Rienzi, Thomas Matthew Michael *retired army officer*
Roberson, Kelley Cleve *army officer*
Weyand, Frederick Carlton *retired military officer*

Kaneohe
McGlaughlin, Thomas Howard *publisher, retired naval officer*

Schofield Barracks
Vissotzky, David Anthony *army officer, aviator*

Tripler Army Medical Center
Gelish, Anthony *air force officer*

MARYLAND

Glen Burnie
Rice, Kimberely Anne Furgason *career officer*

MINNESOTA

Minneapolis
Wyrick, Wes(ley) *air force officer*

MONTANA

Great Falls
DeFreese, Vernon Lee, Jr. *air force officer*
Kracht, Theodore Andrew *career officer*
Loftin, Orrin Keith *career officer*

NEBRASKA

Bellevue
Luckett, Byron Edward, Jr. *air force chaplain*

Lincoln
Heng, Stanley Mark *military officer*

NEVADA

Boulder City
Heinlein, Oscar Allen *former air force officer*

Carson City
Dykstra, Ronald Joseph *military officer*

Fallon
Costarino, F. Thomas *naval officer*

Henderson
Creech, Wilbur Lyman *air force officer*

NEW MEXICO

Albuquerque
Ellis, Norman Derl *air force chaplain*
Kather, Gerhard *retired air force base administrator*

Cedar Crest
Sheppard, Jack W. *retired air force officer*

Cerrillos
Goodwin, Samuel McClure *officer*

Kirtland AFB
Heckathorn, William Gary *military officer*
Murdock, Robert McClellan *military officer*

Las Cruces
Shepard, Earl Alden *retired government official*

Santa Fe
Fox, Jack Rex *military professional*
Sumner, Gordon, Jr. *retired military officer*

Santa Teresa
Leffler, Stacy Brent *government employee*

OHIO

Dayton
Bridges, Roy Dubard, Jr. *career officer*

OREGON

Corvallis
Koller, Duncan G. *military officer*

Salem
Blackwell, Garland Wayne *retired military officer*
Rees, Raymond F. *military officer*

TEXAS

Allen
Wynn, Robert E. *retired career officer, electronics executive*

UTAH

American Fork
Baum, Kerry Robert *retired military officer*

Brigham City
Fife, Dennis Jensen *military officer, chemistry educator*

Salt Lake City
Asmonas, Vladas *career officer, retired*

VIRGINIA

Alexandria
Horton, Edward Carl *military officer*

Portsmouth
McDaniel, William J. *career military officer*

Virginia Beach
Halpin, Timothy Patrick *former air force officer*

WASHINGTON

Fort Lawton
Fragola, Albert Thomas *army officer*

Index
Ward III-Olson, James Day (Edäh Höe) *retired career officer*

Lacey
Giordano, Angela Maria *military officer*

Lynnwood
Jenes, Theodore George, Jr. *retired military officer*

Olympia
March, George Patrick *retired naval officer*

Prosser
Hill, Dale Richard *military officer*

Seattle
Belec, Marguerite Elizabeth *naval officer*

Tacoma
Perry, John C. *retired officer, non-profit development executive*
Russell, James Sargent *retired naval officer*

Whidbey Island
All, William Hamilton, IV *military officer*

WYOMING

Fe Warren AFB
James, Jeffrey Alan *military chaplain*

MILITARY ADDRESSES OF THE UNITED STATES

ATLANTIC

FPO
Girardin, David Walter *chaplain, military officer*

EUROPE

APO
Oatney, Cecilia Kay *army officer*

PACIFIC

APO
Keen, Ronald Lee *career officer*

FPO
Graf, Gary Lynn *career officer*

ADDRESS UNPUBLISHED

Arnold, Michael James *naval officer, aerospace engineer*
Bechtelheimer, Robert Russell *retired career naval officer*
Brooks, James Sprague *retired national guard officer*
Carter, William George, III *army officer*
DiCocco, Marc *flight test engineer*
Eisenberg, George Henry Gilbert, Jr. *retired army officer*
Gerner, Andre Anthony *air force officer*
Giordano, Andrew Anthony *retired naval officer*
Harrigan, Nicholas Paul *military officer*
Henson, Pamela Jane Carlin *air force official*
Huffman, Kevin Wayne *non-commissioned army officer*
Jewell, Edward William *career officer, radiologist, health facility administrator*
Lee, James Gordon *air force officer*
Lowell, Richard William *naval officer*
Mathews, Timothy Leroy *military officer*
Matthews, John Louis *retired military officer, educator*
McMeekin, Karen Ann *air force officer*
Ninos, Nicholas Peter *retired miliatry officer, physician*
Ochotorena, Domingo Rafael *military officer*
Purdie, Robin Stanford *retired air force officer*
Ramsey, Robert John *merchant marine*
Rideout, Bruce William *military officer, process and maintenance engineer*
Rockwell, Richard Thornton *naval engineer*
Sausser, Robert Gary *retired army officer*
Schrader, Harry Christian, Jr. *retired naval officer*
Smith, Charles Lewis *retired naval officer and association executive*
Todaro, Michael Joseph, Jr. *military officer*
Washington-Knight, Barbara J. *military officer, nurse*
Watanabe, Nathan K. *military officer, helicopter pilot*
Watts, Van *retired career navy officer*

RELIGION

UNITED STATES

ALASKA

Anchorage
Dobler, David Lee *pastor*
Hurley, Francis T. *archbishop*
Miller, Ralph Menno *minister, religious organization administrator*
Parsons, Donald D. *bishop*
Williams, Charles D. *bishop*

Fairbanks
Charleston, Steve *bishop*
Kaniecki, Michael Joseph *bishop*

Juneau
Kenny, Michael H. *bishop*

ARIZONA

Flagstaff
Nash, Reford Brooks *minister*

Munds Park
Owens, Robert Raymond *minister*

Oro Valley
Tinker, Robert Eugene *minister, educational consultant*

Paradise Valley
Sapp, Donald Gene *minister*

Phoenix
Darby, Wesley Andrew *minister, educator*
Enniss, Leonard Franklin *religious educator*
Galvan, Elias Gabriel *bishop*
Galvin, Elias *bishop*
Hamilton, Ronald Ray *minister*
O'Brien, Thomas Joseph *bishop*
Taylor-Grigsby, Queenie Delores *minister, consultant*

Safford
MacDonald, Robbin Rieck *clergyman*

Scottsdale
Demetreon, Daiboune Elayne *minister*

Sierra Vista
Puckle, Donne Erving *priest*

Sun City
Lapsley, James Norvell, Jr. *minister, pastoral theology educator*

Sun City West
Schmitz, Charles Edison *evangelist*

Tucson
Elrod, Jerry David *clergyman*
Moreno, Manuel D. *bishop*

CALIFORNIA

Anaheim
Nguyen, Tai Anh *minister*
Oaks, M(argaret) Marlene *minister*

Barstow
Jones, Nathaniel *bishop*

Berkeley
Ernst, Eldon Gilbert *religion educator, seminary dean*
Gall, Donald Arthur *minister*
Schmalenberger, Jerry Lew *pastor, seminary administrator*
Welch, Claude (Raymond) *theology educator*

Canoga Park
Dickey, Gary Alan *minister*

Carmichael
Probasco, Calvin Henry Charles *clergyman, college administrator*

Claremont
Kim, Chan-Hie *educator, clergyman*
Kucheman, Clark Arthur *religion educator*
Mata, Michael Anthony *religion educator*

Concord
Baker, Larry Curtis *minister*

Costa Mesa
Stout, James Tilman *minister*
Williams, William Corey *Old Testament educator, consultant*

Cupertino
Winslow, David Allen *chaplain, naval officer*

Danville
Davis, Ron Lee *clergyman, author*

Davis
Brown, Arthur Carl, Jr. *retired minister*
Hardy, Charles Exter, III *minister*

Downey
Wright, Jeff *minister, non-profit religious administrator*

El Cerrito
Schomer, Howard *retired clergyman, educator, social policy consultant*

Elk Grove
Talbert, Melvin George *bishop*

Escondido
Frame, John McElphatrick *theology educator, pastor*
Shanor, Clarence Richard *clergyman*

Fountain Valley
Einstein, Stephen Jan *rabbi*

Fresno
Armey, Douglas Richard *minister*
Steinbock, John T. *bishop*

Fullerton
Conway, Sally *writer, lecturer, counselor*

Glendora
Richey, Everett Eldon *religion educator*

Irwindale
Arzube, Juan Alfredo *bishop*

Jamul
Dobyns, Zipporah Pottenger *minister, educator, writer*

La Canada
White, Ronald Cedric, Jr. *religion educator*

La Jolla
Clary, Thomas Charles *bishop, psychologist*
Freedman, David Noel *religion educator*
Wyle, Ewart Herbert *clergyman*

La Mirada
McIntosh, Gary Lynn *theology educator, consultant, writer*

Laguna Hills
Wheatley, Melvin Ernest, Jr. *retired bishop*

Lake Forest
Lindsell, Harold *clergyman*

Long Beach
Lowentrout, Peter Murray *religious studies educator*

Los Alamitos
Booth, John Nicholls *minister, magician, writer, photographer*

Los Angeles
Blaire, Stephen E. *bishop*
Borsch, Frederick Houk *bishop*
Breuer, Stephen Ernest *temple executive*
Brown, E. Lynn *minister*
Brown, Kenneth Ray *minister*
Burg, Gerald William *religious organization administrator*
Chedid, John G. *bishop*
Deck, Allan Figueroa *priest*
Eger, Denise Leese *rabbi*
Fitzgerald, Tikhon (Lee R. H. Fitzgerald) *bishop*
Fogel, Norman Irwin *religious organization administrator*
Mahony, Roger M. Cardinal *archbishop*
Mc Pherson, Rolf Kennedy *clergyman, church official*
Phillips, Keith Wendall *minister*
Talton, Chester Lovelle *bishop*
Ward, John J. *bishop*
Wolf, Alfred *rabbi*

Malibu
Pack, Walter Frank *minister, religion educator emeritus*
Wilson, John Francis *religion educator*

Mill Valley
DuBose, Francis Marquis *clergyman*

Mission Hills
Ochoa, Armando *bishop*

Monrovia
Huffey, Vinton Earl *clergyman*

Monterey
Ryan, Sylvester D. *bishop*

Monterey Park
Szeto, Paul (Cheuk-Ching) *religious mission executive*

Newbury Park
Sanchez, Ruben Dario *minister, parochial school educator, writer*

Northridge
Kuzma, George Martin *bishop*

Oakland
Crompton, Arnold *minister, educator*
Cummins, John Stephen *bishop*
Ice, Richard Eugene *retired minister, retirement housing company executive*
Langguth, Earl Leonard *clergyman, writer, poet*
Patten, Bebe Harrison *minister*
Rosenbaum, Lawrence Alan *evangelist*

Orange
Driscoll, Michael P. *bishop*
Goble, Thomas Lee *clergyman*
Mc Farland, Norman Francis *bishop*

Orinda
Oliver, Mary Anne McPherson *religion educator*

Palm Desert
Hunt, Barnabas John *priest, religious order administrator*

Pasadena
Clark, Gary Kenneth *religious ministries executive*
Dyrness, William Arthur *religion educator, dean*
Robeck, Cecil Melvin, Jr. *religious studies educator*
Sand, Faith Annette *writer, publisher religious material*
Sano, Roy I. *bishop*

Placentia
Kintner, William Leroy, II *clergyman, psychotherapist*

Pomona
Lewis, Tony Lloyd *pastor*

Rancho Cucamonga
Spradlin, Byron Lee *minister*

Rancho Palos Verdes
Dunlop, Laurence James *religious studies educator*

Redlands
Benney, Ghislaine Françoise *religious organization executive*

Redwood City
Logie, Dennis Wayne *minister*

Reedley
Dick, Henry Henry *minister*

Sacramento
Cole, Glen David *minister*
Penney, Bryan Le Roy Humphrey *lay pastor, nursing assistant*
Quinn, Francis A. *bishop*
Smith, Freda M. *minister*
Venema, Jon Roger *pastor, educator*

Salinas
Eckerman, Roy Emmanuel *clergyman*
Kadden, Bruce Jay *rabbi*

San Anselmo
Waetjen, Herman Charles *theologian, educator*

San Bernardino
Barnes, Gerald R. *bishop*

San Diego
Boller, John Hall, Jr. *minister*
Brom, Robert H. *bishop*
Carver, Frank Gould *theology educator*
Chavez, Gilbert Espinoza *bishop*
Downing, David Charles *minister*
Eagen, Isaac Brent *priest, academic administrator*
Hughes, Gethin B. *bishop*
Kraft, William Armstrong *retired priest*
Montali, Lawrence Richard, Jr. *religious newspaper editor*
Peck, Paul Lachlan *minister*
Reed, Gerard Alexander *theology educator, history educator*
Savitripriya, Swami *religious leader, author*
Sparks, Irving Alan *biblical scholar, educator*
Youngblood, Ronald Fred *religious educator*

San Fernando
Gosselin, Kenneth Stuart *minister*

San Francisco
Asturias, Joseph Louis *priest, foundation administrator*
Housewright, Alfred Neil *religious organization executive*
Hurley, Mark Joseph *bishop*
McGrath, Patrick Joseph *bishop*
Perlman, Susan Gail *organization executive*
Quinn, John R. *archbishop*
Rosen, Moishe *religious organization administrator*
Sevilla, Carlos A. *bishop*
Swing, William Edwin *bishop*
Turley-Moore, Susan Gwen *minister*
White, Lyla Lee *religious organization administrator*
Yamaoka, Seigen Haruo *bishop*

San Jose
Samy, Edward Antoni *priest and psychologist*
Shariat, Hormoz *pastor*
White, J(ob) Benton *retired religion educator*

San Rafael
Scanlan, John Joseph *retired bishop*

Santa Barbara
Campbell, Robert Charles *clergyman, religious organization administrator*
Hubbard, David Allan *minister, educator, religious association administrator*

Santa Clara
DuMaine, R. Pierre *bishop*

Santa Cruz
Clinch, Harry Anselm *former bishop*
Johnson, M. Earl *clergyman, administrator*

Santa Monica
Boyd, Malcolm *minister, religious author*
Hearn, Charles Virgil *minister*

Santa Rosa
Ziemann, G. Patrick *bishop*

Sherman Oaks
Bower, Richard James *minister*

South Lake Tahoe
Null, Paul Bryan *minister*

Stockton
Frazier, Ronald Lee *minister*
Montrose, Donald W. *bishop*
Nyberg, Walter Lawrence *psychology and religion educator emeritus*

Tustin
Crouch, Paul Franklin *minister, church official*

Vallejo
McGowan, Thomas Randolph *religious organization executive*

Vista
Rader, Paul Alexander *minister, administrator*

Wilmington
Moreno, Guillermo Fernandez *minister*

Yorba Linda
Miller, Robert Lindsey *bishop*

Yuba City
Koury, Aleah George *retired church executive, minister*

COLORADO

Aurora
Stifel, Frederick Benton *pastor, biochemist, nutritionist*

Canon City
Hein, Kenneth Charles Lawrence *priest, educator*

Colorado Springs
Bishop, Leo Kenneth *clergyman, educator*
Coriell, Bruce Richard *clergy*
Hanifen, Richard Charles *bishop*
Perkins, Floyd Jerry *theology educator*
Pickle, Joseph Wesley, Jr. *religion educator*
Sinclair, William Donald *church official, fundraising consultant, political activist*

Denver
Burrell, Calvin Archie *minister*
Fischer, James Adrian *clergyman*
MacDonald, Dennis Ronald *theology educator*
Morgan, David Forbes *minister*
O'Connor, Kevin Thomas *archdiocese development official*
Richards, Kent Harold *religion educator*
Sheeran, Michael John Leo *priest, educational administrator*
Stafford, J. Francis *archbishop*
Sun, Charles Changkyun *minister, college president*
Swenson, Mary Ann *bishop*
Weissenbuehler, Wayne *bishop*

Fort Carson
Williamson, Edward Henry *chaplain, army officer*

Fort Collins
Pape, Arnis Weston *minister*
Rolston, Holmes, III *theologian, educator, philosopher*

Highlands Ranch
Wood, Stephen *minister*

Lafayette
Short, Ray Everett *minister, sociology educator emeritus, author, lecturer*

Lakewood
O'Connell, Robert Houston *religious educator*

Littleton
Hepler, Ovid Mansfield *minister*

Loveland
Harms, Glenn Edward *minister, pastor*

Pueblo
Tafoya, Arthur N. *bishop*

Superior
Randall, Roger Paul *religious organization consultant*

HAWAII

Honolulu
DiLorenzo, Francis X. *bishop*
Gau, Wayne Watson *church abbot, educational consultant*
Russi, John Joseph *priest, educational administrator*
Sammis, Glenn Conover *minister*
Scott, David Irvin *minister*
Strickland, John Arthur Van *minister*
Tanouye, Royce Tsuzuki *religious foundation administrator*

Kailua
Bezanson, Ronald Scott, Jr. *clergyman, army chaplain*
Grimmer, Beverley Sue *church administrator, maritime agency agent*

Kaneohe
Chappell, David Wellington *religion educator*

Ocean View
Gilliam, Jackson Earle *bishop*

Wahiawa
Crisp, George Robert *pastor*

Waipahu
Eng, Christopher Kamuela *minister, educator*

IDAHO

Boise
Brown, Tod David *bishop*
Caufield, Marie Celine *religious organization administrator*
Thornton, John S., IV *bishop*

Moscow
Tate, Stan Davis *priest, clinical bioethicist*

Nampa
Bowes, A. Wendell *minister, religion educator*

Post Falls
Capener, Regner Alvin *minister, electronics engineer*

INDIANA

Indianapolis
Page, Curtis Matthewson *minister*

MASSACHUSETTS

Cambridge
Hart, Donald Purple *bishop*

MONTANA

Froid
Clark, Ruth Ann *lay worker, educator*

Great Falls
Milone, Anthony M. *bishop*

Helena
Brunett, Alexander J. *bishop*
Jones, Charles Irving *bishop*

Laurel
Allen, Arthur William *pastor, educator*

NEBRASKA

Omaha
Curtiss, Elden F. *bishop*

NEVADA

Las Vegas
Flammang, Susann *author, publisher*
Walsh, Daniel Francis *bishop*

Reno
Chrystal, William George *minister*
Frank, Donald Herbert *minister*
Straling, Phillip Francis *bishop*
Walrath, Harry Rienzi *minister*
Weld, Roger Bowen *clergyman*

NEW MEXICO

Albuquerque
Griffin, W. C. *bishop*
Kelshaw, Terence *bishop*
Oden, William Arthur *minister, artist*
Sanchez, Robert Fortune *archbishop*
Sheehan, Michael Jarboe *archbishop*
Sorensen, Kenneth Christ *church administrator, real estate broker*

Clovis
Dotson, Kevin D. *minister*

Farmington
Plummer, Steven Tsosie *bishop*

Gallup
Hastrich, Jerome Joseph *bishop*
McNeill, Douglas Arthur *priest*

Hobbs
Shook, Dale Alford, Jr. *minister*

Las Cruces
Martin, Julius Oren *minister, social services administrator*
Ramirez, Ricardo *bishop*

Portales
Overton, Edwin Dean *campus minister, educator*

Roswell
Skariah, Matthew *religious organization administrator*

OREGON

Albany
Soot, Stephen Ervin *priest, health facility administrator*

Beaverton
Bristow, John Temple *minister, writer*
Mitchell, Bettie Phaenon *religious organization administrator*

Bend
Connolly, Thomas Joseph *bishop*

Corvallis
Goman, Jon Gifford *university chaplain, educator*

Grants Pass
Oestmann, Irma Emma *minister, artist, educator*

Klamath Falls
Ruhl, Roger Donald, Jr. *minister*

Lake Oswego
Ladehoff, Robert Louis *bishop*

Portland
Carver, Loyce Cleo *clergyman*
Held, Jay Allen *pastor*
Levada, William Joseph *archbishop*
Powlison, Howard Whitfield *religious organization administrator*
Richards, Herbert East *minister emeritus, commentator*
Schwanz, Judith Ann *seminary educator*
Sevetson, Donald James *minister, church administrator*
Steiner, Kenneth Donald *bishop*

Salem
Weaver, Grace Margaret *minister*

The Dalles
Kimsey, Rustin Ray *bishop*

West Linn
Bohrer, Richard William *religious writer, editor, educator*

Wilsonville
Gross, Hal Raymond *bishop*

UTAH

Bountiful
Carter, Richard Bert *retired church official, retired government official*

Ogden
Harrington, Mary Evelina Paulson (Polly Harrington) *religious journalist, writer, educator*

Salt Lake City
Bates, George Edmonds *bishop*
Christensen, Joe David *religious organization executive, architect*
Eyring, Henry Bennion *bishop*
Hinckley, Gordon B. *church official*
Maxwell, Neal A. *church official*
Monson, Thomas Spencer *church official, publishing company executive*
Niederauer, George H. *bishop*
Smith, Eldred Gee *church leader*
Weigand, William Keith *bishop*

WASHINGTON

Belfair
Walker, E. Jerry *retired clergyman*

Everett
Flora, Mary Ellen *bishop*

Federal Way
Feir, Scott Eugene *minister*

Greenbank
Tuell, Jack Marvin *retired bishop*

Kirkland
Murren, Douglas Edward *pastor*

Longview
Walston, Rick Lyle Josh *clergyman, seminary executive, educator*

Mossyrock
Shih, Marie *metaphysical healer*

Oak Harbor
Larsen, Samuel Harry *minister, educator*

Prosser
Cooper, Lynn Dale *minister, retired navy chaplain*

Quilcene
Ross, Lanson Clifford, Jr. *religion educator, pastor, author*

Renton
Warren, Larry Michael *clergyman*

Richland
Johnson, Arnold Gordon *clergyman*

Seattle
Anderson, Janette Beryl *clergy member*
Bergeson, John Henning *denominational executive, theological educator*
Leed, Jean Ann *religious organization administrator*
McConnell, Calvin Dale *clergyman*
McKenzie, Michael Carter *seminary educator*
Murphy, Thomas Joseph *archbishop*
Raible, Peter Spilman *minister*
Ruble, Ann *minister*
Warner, Vincent W. *bishop*

Spanaway
Westbrook, T. L. *bishop*

Spokane
Clary, Donald Ray *minister*
Connolly, Michael Joseph *priest, educator*
Keller, Robert M. *bishop*
Lee, Richard Francis James *evangelical clergyman, apologist, researcher*
Polley, Harvey Lee *retired missionary and educator*
Radha, Sivananda (Ursula Sylvia Hellman) *religious association executive*
Skylstad, William S. *bishop*
Swan, Allan Hollister *minister*
Terry, Frank Jeffrey *bishop*

Tacoma
Alger, David Townley *religious organization director*
Schiller, Johannes August *clergyman, educator*
Wiegman, Eugene William *minister, former college administrator*
Wold, David C. *bishop*

Vancouver
Congdon, Roger Douglass *theology educator, minister*

Wenatchee
Edwards, Charles Garland *minister, counselor, health educator*

Yakima
George, Francis *bishop*

WYOMING

Cheyenne
Hart, Joseph H. *bishop*

Cody
Murphy, Warren Charles *rector*

Laramie
Jones, Bob Gordon *bishop*

TERRITORIES OF THE UNITED STATES

AMERICAN SAMOA

Pago Pago
Weitzel, John Quinn *bishop*

GUAM

Agana
Apuron, Anthony Sablan *archbishop*

CANADA

ALBERTA

Calgary
Curtis, John Barry *bishop*
O'Byrne, Paul J. *bishop*

Camrose
Campbell, John D. *religious organization administrator, religious publication editor*

Edmonton
Daciuk, Myron Michael *bishop*
Doyle, Wilfred Emmett *retired bishop*
Genge, Kenneth Lyle *bishop*
Mac Neil, Joseph Neil *archbishop*

McLennan
Légaré, Henri Francis *archbishop*

Saint Paul
Roy, Raymond *bishop*

BRITISH COLUMBIA

Abbotsford
Holdcroft, Leslie Thomas *clergyman, educator*

Kamloops
Cruickshank, James David *bishop*
Sabatini, Lawrence *bishop*

Nelson
Mallon, Peter *bishop*

Prince George
Kerr, Nancy Karolyn *pastoral counselor, mental health consultant*

Prince Rupert
Hannen, John Edward *bishop*

Richmond
Plomp, Teunis (Tony Plomp) *minister*

Surrey
Farley, Lawrence *clergyman*

Vancouver
Exner, Adam *archbishop*

Victoria
De Roo, Remi Joseph *bishop*
Frame, John Timothy *bishop*

NORTHWEST TERRITORIES

Iqaluit
Williams, John Christopher Richard *bishop*

ONTARIO

Sault Sainte Marie
Ferris, Ronald Curry *bishop*

SASKATCHEWAN

Gravelbourg
Delaquis, Noel *bishop*

Prince Albert
Morand, Blaise E. *bishop*

Regina
Bays, Eric *bishop*

Saltcoats
Farquharson, Walter Henry *minister, church official*

Saskatoon
Filevich, Basil *bishop*
Jacobson, Sverre Theodore *retired minister*
Mahoney, James P. *bishop*
Morgan, Thomas Oliver *bishop*

YUKON TERRITORY

Whitehorse
Lobsinger, Thomas *bishop*

HONG KONG

Kowloon
Chiang, Samuel Edward *theological educator, humanities educator*

ADDRESS UNPUBLISHED

Bauer, Judy Marie *minister*
Blemker, Margaret Ruth *educator, world mission executive*
Bowman, Robert William *minister*
Candelaria, Michael Richard *religious studies educator*
Chagoya, Janine Elaine *religious organization administrator, consultant*
Cobb, John Boswell, Jr. *clergyman, educator*
Crabtree, Davida Foy *minister*
Dornette, Ralph Meredith *church organization executive, educator, minister*
Emerson, R. Clark *priest, business administrator*
Finley, Mitchel Brent *writer*
Greiner Makenna, Carrie Ann *religious science practitioner*
Halpern, Linda Caray *minister, author, poet*
Hambidge, Douglas Walter *archbishop*
Hoops, William James *clergyman*
Johnson, Alice Elaine *retired academic administrator*
Lotz, Trey *scientology auditor*
Mangini, Richard Alan *religious organization executive*
McDermott, Lucinda Mary *minister, teacher, philosopher, poet, author*
Millard, George Richard *bishop*
Mumford, Patricia Rae *religious organization administrator*
Olken, Deborah Jeanne *non-profit organization executive*
Parsons, Elmer Earl *retired clergyman*
Pelotte, Donald Edmond *bishop*
Rice, Richard Lee, Jr. *minister, office manager*
Russell, Patrick James *priest*
Setchko, Edward Stephen *minister, theology educator, psychologist*
Shimpfky, Richard Lester *bishop*
Sinishta, Gjon *pastoral associate*
Swanson, Paul Rubert *minister*
White, Lerrill James *clinical pastoral educator*

SCIENCE: LIFE SCIENCE

UNITED STATES

ALASKA

Anchorage
Hatch, Scott Alexander *wildlife research biologist*
Kudenov, Jerry David *zoology educator*

Fairbanks
Kessel, Brina *ornithologist, educator*
Renecker, Lyle Alfred *animal science educator*
Werner, Richard Allen *entomologist*
White, Robert Gordon *educator, researcher, research director*

Homer
Johnson, Steve Michael *flower essence researcher, educator*

Juneau
Helle, John Harold (Jack Helle) *fishery research biologist*
Willson, Mary F. *ecology researcher, educator*

ARIZONA

Bisbee
Johnson, Heidi Smith *science educator*

Dewey
McMahon, James Patrick *ecologist, science association administrator*

Flagstaff
Grim, J(ohn) Norman *biology educator, electron microscopy consultant*
Keim, Paul Stephen *molecular geneticist educator*

Glendale
Devlin, David Stuart *biology educator*

Peoria
Baker, Gladys Elizabeth *retired microbiologist, educator*

Phoenix
Adler, Eugene Victor *forensic toxicologist, consultant*
Bolin, Vernon Spencer *microbiologist, consultant*
Eriacho, Belinda Pearl *environmental scientist*
Idouraine, Ahmed *researcher*
Wilson, Frank Douglas *geneticist*

Tempe
Chandler, Douglas Edwin *zoology educator*
Goldstein, Elliott Stuart *science educator*
Pinkava, Donald John *botany educator, researcher*

Tucson
Budhu, Muniram *soil scientist*
Cortner, Hanna Joan *science administrator, research scientist, educator*
D'Silva, Aecio Moura *aquaculture scientist*
Gerba, Charles Peter *microbiologist, educator*
Glenn, Edward Perry *research scientist, botanist*
Green, Robert Scott *biotechnology company executive*
Kline, Natasha Cale *biologist*
Lai, LiWen *molecular geneticist, educator*
Laird, Hugh Edward, II *pharmacologist, toxicologist*
McCormick, Floyd Guy, Jr. *agricultural educator, college administrator*
McLaughlin, Steven Paul *botany educator*
Mebrahtu, Yemane Berhan *medical microbiologist, entomologist, researcher*
Payne, Claire Margaret *molecular and cellular biologist*
Racowsky, Catherine *reproductive physiologist, researcher*
Shannon, Robert Rennie *optical sciences center administrator, educator*
Spizizen, John *microbiologist*
Terry, Stephen *gynecologist/obstetrician*
Van Voorhies, Wayne Alan *biologist*
Yocum, Harrison Gerald *horticulturist, botanist, educator, researcher*

Willcox
Decker, Donald Daryl *range conservationist*

Window Rock
Hathaway, Loline *zoo and botanic park curator*

CALIFORNIA

Alameda
Paustenbach, Dennis James *environmental toxicologist*

Arcadia
Morse, Judy *science foundation administrator*

Arcata
Bicknell, Susan Marcia Herr *ecology educator*
Botzler, Richard George *wildlife educator*
Slaughter, Anne Marie *biologist*

Atherton
Goodman, Christopher Bettencourt *cytogeneticist*

Belmont
Center, Elizabeth Mercy *biology educator*

Berkeley
Anderson, Olin Darrell *molecular biologist*
Baker, Herbert George *botany educator*
Barrett, Reginald Haughton *biology educator, wildlife management educator*
Blackman, David Lee *research scientist*
Burnside, Mary Beth *biology educator, researcher*
Chemsak, John Andrew *entomologist*
Dahlsten, Donald Lee *enviromental biology and forest entomology educator*
Gold, Lois Swirsky *research scientist*
Howd, Robert Allen *toxicologist*
Janda, John Michael *microbiologist, researcher*
Lidicker, William Zander, Jr. *zoologist, educator*
Liu, Edwin Chiap Henn *biochemical ecologist*
Markell, Edward Kingsmill *medical parasitologist, educator*
Ow, David Wing *research geneticist*
Purcell, Alexander Holmes *entomologist, educator*
Rabovsky, Jean *toxicologist*
Reginato, Robert Joseph *soil scientist*
Robertson, Jacqueline Lee *entomologist*
Sensabaugh, George Frank, Jr. *forensic sciences educator*
Smith, Martyn Thomas *toxicology educator*
Weinhold, Albert Raymond *plant pathologist*
Willhite, Calvin Campbell *toxicologist*
Wohletz, Leonard Ralph *soil scientist, consultant*

Beverly Hills
Spence, Mary Anne *geneticist, medical association executive*

Bishop
Groeneveld, David Paul *plant ecologist*
MacMillen, Richard Edward *biological sciences educator, researcher*

Bonsall
Alling, Abigail Kingsley *scientist, biosphere system executive*

Burlingame
Li, Shengqiang *virologist*

Chico
Kistner, David Harold *biology educator*
Stern, Kingsley Rowland *botanist, educator*

Chino
Pfuntner, Allan Robert *entomologist*

Chula Vista
Neudecker, Stephen K. *marine ecologist, museum professional*
Thomas, Teresa Ann *microbiologist, educator*

Citrus Heights
Wymer, Nancy Elaine *plant taxonomist, consultant, habitat restorationist, educator*

Claremont
Sadava, David Eric *biology educator*

Creston
Scott, Norman Jackson, Jr. *biologist, zoologist, educator, researcher*

Cupertino
Cheeseman, Douglas Taylor, Jr. *wildlife tour executive, photographer, educator*
Nast, Carol Ann *laboratory executive*

Cypress
Bender, Ralph Jay *educator*
Buck, Alan Charles *forensic investigator*

Daly City
Dowlin, Janice Marie *science administrator*

Davis
Allard, Robert Wayne *geneticist, educator*
Amirkhanian, John David *geneticist, researcher, educator*
Armstrong, Peter Brownell *biologist*
Bernoco, Domenico *immunogeneticist, educator*
Borges, Carlos Rego *topology educator*
Britt, Anne Bagg *geneticist*
Butler, Edward Eugene *plant pathology educator*
Carney, Heath Joseph *aquatic ecologist, educator*
Denning, Robert Mark *agricultural aviation sciences research officer*
Ehler, Lester Ervin *entomology educator*
Gasser, Charles Scott *biologist, educator*
Gifford, Ernest Milton *biologist, educator*
Grossman, Yaffa Linda *plant physiological ecologist*
Hess, Charles Edward *environmental horticulture educator*
Hirsh, Dwight Charles, III *microbiologist*
Horwitz, Barbara Ann *physiologist, educator, consultant*
Jones, James Henry *physiology educator, researcher*
Khasimuddin, Syed *entomologist*
Klasing, Susan Allen *environmental toxicologist, consultant*
Kofranek, Anton Miles *floriculturist, educator*
Kunkee, Ralph Edward *viticulture and enology educator*
Laidlaw, Harry Hyde, Jr. *entomology educator*
Nielsen, Donald Rodney *soil and water science educator*
Pappagianis, Demosthenes *microbiology educator, physician*
Quiros, Carlos Francisco *plant genetics educator*
Stewart, James Ian *agricultural water scientist, cropping system developer, consultant*
Torten, Michael *microbiologist, educator*
Williams, William Arnold *agronomy educator*

Del Mar
Farquhar, Marilyn Gist *cell biology and pathology educator*

Duarte
Davagnino, Juan V. *scientist*
Lundblad, Roger Lauren *research director*
McEwen, Joan E. *researcher, microbiology educator*
Natarajan, Rama *research scientist*
Smith, Steven Sidney *molecular biologist*
Vaughn, James English, Jr. *neurobiologist*

El Centro
Flock, Robert Ashby *retired entomologist*

El Cerrito
Parker, Kenneth Dean *toxicologist, criminalist*

Eureka
Roberts, Robert Chadwick *ecologist, environmental scientist, consultant*

Fresno
Immken, La Donna L. *medical geneticist*
Sidhu, Gurmel Singh *geneticist, researcher*

Gilroy
Barham, Warren Sandusky *horticulturist*
McGrogan, Michael Patrick *molecular and cell biologist*

Granada Hills
Lorbeer, George Coe *retired science educator*

Healdsburg
Armstrong, Joe Edwin *energy management educator, consultant*

Irvine
Ayala, Francisco José *geneticist, educator*
Bhalla, Deepak Kumar *cell biologist, toxicologist, educator*
Campbell, Diane Rita *biologist, educator*
Ericson, Jonathon Edward *environmental health science educator, researcher*
Fitch, Walter M(onroe) *molecular biologist, educator*
Gutman, George Andre *molecular biologist, educator*
James, Anthony Amadé *molecular biologist, educator*
Larson, Kirk David *pomologist and extension specialist*
Lawton, Michael James *entomologist, pest management specialist*
Suarez-Villa, Luis *regional science and economic geography, international development educator*
Zhu, Yu *neurologist, neurophysiologist, researcher*

Kensington
Harris, Morgan *zoologist educator*

Kernville
Christenson, Daniel Paul *biologist, conservationist*

La Honda
Dill, Kilian *research scientist*

La Jolla
Bakhiet, Nouna *microbiologist, researcher*
Ballance, Lisa Taylor *marine ecologist*
Burns, Jane Cary *molecular biologist, educator, physician*
Dulbecco, Renato *biologist, educator*
Fishman, William Harold *cancer research foundation executive, biochemist*
Guillemin, Roger C. L. *physiologist*
Huang, Shi *molecular biologist*
Hunter, Tony (Anthony Rex Hunter) *molecular biologist, educator*
Kolinski, Andrzej *molecular biology researcher, educator*
Lewin, Ralph Arnold *biologist*
Maruyama, Ichiro *biologist, educator*
McRee, Duncan Everett *molecular biologist, researcher*
Pineda, Jaime Armando *science educator*
Saltman, Paul David *educational administrator, biologist*
Shalinsky, David Ray. *pharmacologist*
Subramani, Suresh *biology educator*
Wilkie, Donald Walter *biologist, aquarium museum director*

Laguna Hills
Lukos, Glenn Charles *environmental biologist*

Laguna Niguel
Coleman, Roger Dixon *bacteriologist*

Lake Arrowhead
Asher, James Edward *forestry consultant, engineer, arborist, forensic expert*

Livermore
Lucas, Joe Nathan *research scientist*

Loma Linda
Brand, Leonard Roy *biology educator*
Kettering, James David *microbiologist*
Taylor, Barry Llewellyn *microbiologist, educator*
Zuccarelli, Anthony Joseph *molecular biology and biochemistry educator*

Long Beach
Toma, Ramses Barsoum *food science and nutrition educator*

Los Angeles
Abe, Gregory *microbiologist*
Amur-Umarjee, Shashi Gururaj *neurobiologist, researcher*
Bakus, Gerald Joseph *biology educator*
Buth, Donald George *biology educator*
Ebling, Fanny Marmol *microbiologist, medical educator*
Fain, Gordon Lee *physiology educator*
Fraser-Smith, Elizabeth Birdsey *biologist*
Gallup, Marc Richmond *biology educator, paleontologist*
Gibson, Arthur Charles *biologist, educator*
Kadner, Carl George *biology educator emeritus*
Langer, Glenn Arthur *cellular physiologist, educator*
McClure, William Owen *biologist*
Mockary, Peter Ernest *clinical laboratory scientist, researcher*
Mohr, John Luther *biologist, environmental consultant*
Rotter, Jerome Israel *medical geneticist*
Seto, Joseph Tobey *virologist, educator*
Shi, Wenyuan *microbiologist*
Simmons, Dwayne Deangelo *biology educator*
Smulders, Anthony Peter *biology educator*
Sussman, Mark Alan *cell biologist, educator*
Szego, Clara Marian *cell biologist, educator*
Taylor, Charles E. *biologist*
Towner, Howard Frost *biologist, educator*
Valentine, Jane Lee *environmental health sciences educator*
Warren, Dwight William, III *physiology educator*
Wei, Jen Yu *physiologist, researcher, educator*
Wells, Patrick Harrington *biology educator*
Wright, Ernest Marshall *physiologist, consultant*

Malibu
Chen, Mary Yun-Chun *research engineer*
Krozel, Jimmy Alan *research scientist, artist*
Tallman, John Gary *biology educator*

Manteca
Rainey, Barbara Ann *sensory evaluation consultant*

Martinez
Gerlach, William Edward *agriculturist*

Menlo Park
Cardon, Lon Ray *geneticist researcher*
MacGregor, James Thomas *toxicologist*
Robert, Charles Sidney *research neuroscientist, educator*

Merced
Olsen, David Magnor *science educator*

Moffett Field
Fletcher, Douglas Gerald *research scientist*
Green, Steven Morris *research scientist*
Wignarajah, Kanapathipillai *plant physiologist, researcher, educator*

Monterey
Miller, Robert Jonathan *science/technology educator*
Parsons, Christina Marie *science education consultant*

Moreno Valley
Hamill, Carol *biologist, writing educator*

Moss Landing
Nybakken, James Willard *marine biology educator*

Mountain View
Lu, Wuan-Tsun *microbiologist, immunologist*

Oakland
Whitsel, Richard Harry *biologist, entomologist*

Oceanside
Hofmann, Frieder Karl *biotechnologist, consultant*

Orange
Dumars, Kenneth W. *medical geneticist educator, pediatrician*

Orinda
Bowyer, Jane Baker *science educator*

Pacific Palisades
Mays, John Molteno *science educator, consultant*

Palm Desert
Sausman, Karen *zoological park administrator*
Wilson, Katherine Schmitkons *biologist*

Palo Alto
De Smedt, Philippe *research scientist, technologist*
Eggers, Alfred John, Jr. *research corporation executive*
Lichtenwalter, Kay Gilles *molecular biologist*
Lipsick, Joseph Steven *research scientist, medical educator*
Spickler, Joseph William *researcher, physician*
Suermondt, Henri Jacques *research scientist*

Parlier
Stapleton, James Jay *agricultural scientist, consultant*

Pasadena
Allman, John Morgan *neurobiology educator*
Davidson, Eric Harris *molecular and developmental biologist, educator*
Lewis, Edward B. *biology educator*
Medina-Puerta, Antonio *scientist*
Meyerowitz, Elliot Martin *biologist, educator*
Randolph, Linda Marie *geneticist*
Rouzbahani, Lotfollah *cytogeneticist*
Tappan, Janice Ruth Vogel *animal behavior researcher*

Penn Valley
Fletcher, Donald Warren *microbiologist, educator*

Pleasanton
Choy, Clement Kin-Man *research scientist*
Latham, James Richard *research scientist*

Pomona
Stiffler, Daniel Francis *biology educator*

Richmond
Rudin, Norah *forensic DNA consultant, science writer*

Riverside
Eastmond, David Albert *environmental toxicology educator*
Embleton, Tom William *horticultural science educator*
Erwin, Donald Carroll *plant pathology educator*
Hall, Anthony Elmitt *plant physiologist*
Hanks, Lawrence Michael *ecologist, entomologist*
Judelson, Howard Seth *plant pathology educator*
Madireddi, Mallareddy *physiologist*
Martins-Green, Manuela *cell biologist*
Miller, Thomas Albert *entomology educator*
Quinton, Paul Marquis *physiology educator*
Scora, Rainer Walter *botanist*

Roseville
Sydor, Richard Paul *social science educator*

Sacramento
Booze, Thomas Franklin *toxicologist*
Hackney, Robert Ward *plant pathologist, nematologist, parasitologist, molecular genetecist*
Rosenberg, Dan Yale *retired plant pathologist*

San Diego
Boyce, Ker *electrophysiologist, cardiologist*
Burkhart, Brad John *horticulturist, landscape architect*
Cox, George Wyatt *biology educator*
Crick, Francis Harry Compton *science educator, researcher*
Datta, Arun Kumar *molecular biologist*
Mills, Jonathan A. *microbiologist, educator*
Myers, Douglas George *zoological society administrator*
Oechel, Walter Clarence *ecologist*
Panetta, Joseph Daniel *biotechnology executive*
Richardson, Kathleen *microbiologist, educator*
Risser, Arthur Crane, Jr. *zoo administrator*
Walker, Keith Allen *plant genetics company executive*
Weinrich, James Donald *psychobiologist, educator*
Weiss Bizzoco, Richard Lawrence *biology educator*
Wu, Ellen Yung-hua *pharmacology research scientist*

San Fernando
McCraven, Eva Stewart Mapes *health service administrator*

San Francisco
Borson, Daniel Benjamin *physiology educator, inventor, researcher*
Brown, Walter Creighton *biologist*
Bussiere, Jeanine Louise *toxicologist*
Dewitt, John Belton *retired conservation executive*
Ebner, Reinhard *cell biologist*
Furst, Arthur *toxicologist, educator*
Ganong, William F(rancis) *physiologist, physician*
Jameson, David Lee *evolutionary biologist*
McKnight, Steven Lanier *molecular biologist*
Mitchison, Timothy John *cell biologist, pharmacology educator*
Vyas, Girish Narmadashankar *virologist, immunohematologist*
Williams, Stanley Clark *medical entomologist, educator*

San Jose
Barker, John A. *research scientist*
Ellis, Deborah Lynn *horticulturist, arborist, consultant*
Taylor, Kendrick Jay *microbiologist*
Zaro, Brad A. *research company executive, biologist*

San Luis Obispo
Piirto, Douglas Donald *forester, educator*

San Marcos
Liggins, George Lawson *microbiologist, diagnostic company executive*

San Marino
Hanson, George Peter *retired research botanist, real estate investor*

Santa Barbara
Endler, John Arthur *biology educator, researcher*
Kornell, Jim *artificial intelligence researcher*
Lennox Buchthal, Margaret Agnes *neurophysiologist*
Manclark, Charles Robert *microbiologist, researcher*
Samuel, Charles E. *virologist, educator*
Schneider, Edward Lee *botanic garden administrator*
Smith, Dale Metz *biological science educator, researcher*

Santa Clara
Li, Cindy *scientist*
Tauck, David Lawrence *neurobiologist*

Santa Cruz
Beevers, Harry *biologist*
Bernardi, Giacomo *biology educator*
Flegal, A(rthur) Russell, Jr. *toxicologist, geochemist, educator*
Langenheim, Jean Harmon *biology educator*
Soulé, Michael Ellman *biologist*

Santa Monica
Davis, Paul Kensil *research manager, strategic analyst*
Li, Shuguang *research scientist*
Lin, Hun-Chi *molecular biologist*
Mangir, Tulin Erdim *science educator, consultant*

Santa Paula
Thren, Robert *science executive*

Santee
Hardy, Ben(son) (B.) *orchid nursery executive*

Sausalito
Barrett, Peigin Catherine *marine mammal center executive*

Sebastopol
Walton, James Stephen *research scientist*

Sonoma
Shultz, Fred Townsend *geneticist, biologist*

South San Francisco
Biroc, Sandra Lyn *biology educator, biologist*
Levinson, Arthur David *molecular biologist*
Masover, Gerald Kenneth *microbiologist*
Ruppert, Siegfried *scientist*
Wiebe, Michael Eugene *microbiologist, cell biologist*

Stanford
Bjorkman, Olle Erik *plant biologist, educator*
Cavalli-Sforza, Luigi Luca *genetics educator*
Falkow, Stanley *microbiologist, educator*
Francke, Uta *medical geneticist, genetics researcher, educator*
Hoffman, Neil Eugene *cell biologist*
Lammer, Edward James *geneticist*
Matin, Abdul *microbiology educator, consultant*
Sanders, William John *research scientist*
Yanofsky, Charles *biology educator*

Stockton
Anderson, Steven Clement *biology educator*
Magness, Rhonda Ann *microbiologist*

Sunnyvale
Lal, Preeti Gupta *microbiologist, researcher*
Mansfield, Elaine Schultz *molecular geneticist, automation specialist*

Tahoe City
Wehrli, John Erich *biotechnology executive*

Thousand Oaks
Hatherill, John Robert *toxicologist, educator*
Mayron, Lewis Walter *clinical ecology consultant*
Shieh, Jae-Hung *research scientist*
Yan, Qiao *neurobiologist*

Torrance
Yeaman, Michael Robert *microbiologist, infectious diseases consultant*

Valencia
Solano, Nancy Vogt *chemist*

Vandenberg AFB
Ehrsam, Eldon Edward *operations research analyst, real estate broker*

Ventura
Arita, George Shiro *biology educator*
Huszczuk vel Huszcza, Andrew Richard *physiologist*
Parigian, Michael John *forensic scientist*

Visalia
Day, Kevin Ross *pomologist, researcher, consultant, farmer*

Vista
Winslow, Philip Charles *agriculturist, marketing consultant*

Walnut
Smith, Harry Mendell, Jr. *science educator*

Westminster
Allen, Merrill James *marine biologist*

Westwood
Brydon, Harold Wesley *entomologist, writer*

Woodland Hills
Fox, Stuart Ira *physiologist*

Proebsting, Edward Louis, Jr. *retired research horticulturist*

Pullman
Barbosa-Cánovas, Gustavo Víctor *food engineering educator*
Calza, Roger Ernest *animal science genetics and cell biology educator*
Edwards, Gerald Elmo *botany educator*
Hosick, Howard Lawrence *cell biology educator, academic administrator*
Korge, Paavo *cell physiologist*
Pall, Martin Lawrence *geneticist educator*
Sarkar, Dipak Kumar *physiologist, educator*

Richland
Chikalla, Thomas David *science facility administrator*
Molton, Peter Michael *waste conversion researcher, consultant*
Stevens, Todd Owen *research microbiologist*

Seattle
Benson, Keith Rodney *science educator*
Binder, Marc David *physiology educator*
Boersma, P. Dee *ecology educator*
Byers, Breck Edward *geneticist educator*
Cadd, Gary Genoris *molecular biologist*
Calleman, Carl Johan *toxicologist*
Campbell, Lee Ann *microbiology educator*
Conley, Kevin Edward *biologist*
Disteche, Christine M. *geneticist*
Edmonds, Robert Leslie *forestry educator*
Edwards, John Stuart *zoology educator, researcher*
Gentry, Roger Lee *research wildlife biologist*
Ho, Rodney Jin Yong *educator, medical researcher*
Iwasaki, Kouichi *molecular geneticist*
Karayiorgou, Maria *geneticist*
Lee, Qwihee Park *plant physiologist*
Leung, David Wai-Hung *molecular biologist*
Livingston, Patricia Ann *marine biologist, researcher*
Miller, Robert Victor *scientific research administrator*
Mitchell, David *environmental research executive*
Motulsky, Arno Gunther *geneticist, physician, educator*
Ning, Xue-Han (Hsueh-Han Ning) *physiologist, researcher*
Olstad, Roger Gale *science educator*
Rasco, Barbara A. *food chemistry educator*
Sherwood, Anne Lesley *molecular biologist*
Trumble, Robert Jasper *fishery biologist*
Tukey, Harold Bradford, Jr. *horticulture educator*
Yager, Paul *molecular bioengineering educator*
Yamamoto, Fumiichiro *molecular biologist, educator*
Yao, Meng-Chao *molecular geneticist*

Sequim
Pearson, Walter Howard *marine biologist, researcher*

Spokane
Jacobson, Dean Martin *marine biology educator, researcher*
Mork, Daniel Neil *biologist, councilman*
Rowe, Vikki Denae *mental health therapist*

Walla Walla
Paulson-Ehrhardt, Patricia Helen *laboratory administrator*
Trick, Roger Lee *national park ranger*

Wenatchee
Elfving, Don C. *horticulturist, administrator*
Raese, John Thomas *physiologist*
Schrader, Lawrence Edwin *plant physiologist, educator*

WISCONSIN

Madison
Goodman, Robert Merwin *agriculturalist, plant biologist, university educator*

WYOMING

Green River
Weber, Marian Frances *laboratory administrator, educator*

Jackson
Davis, Randy L. *soil scientist*

Lander
Kesselheim, A. Donn *environmental education educator*

Laramie
Cameron, Bruce Andrew *textile science educator*
Field, Ray Arvid *animal science educator*
Legg, David E. *entomologist, educator*
Reiners, William Arnold *botany educator*

CANADA

ALBERTA

Calgary
Yoon, Ji-Won *virology, immunology and diabetes educator, research administrator*

Sherwood Park
Finlay, Audrey Joy *environmental educator, consultant, naturalist*

BRITISH COLUMBIA

Burnaby
Webster, John M. *biologist, educator*

Vancouver
Binkley, Clark Shepard *forester*
Newman, Murray Arthur *aquarium administrator*

Victoria
Loring, Thomas Joseph *forest ecologist*

SASKATCHEWAN

Saskatoon
Shokeir, Mohamed Hassan Kamel *medical geneticist, educator*

ADDRESS UNPUBLISHED

Baker, Joseph Roderick, III *aviculturist*
Barter Bowlus, Nadine Christena *biology educator*
Bautista, Anthony Hernandez *biomedical company executive*
Bennett, Leslie Robert *radiological sciences educator, researcher*
Bricken, William Marion *scientist*
Burns, Gilbert Alexander *science educator*
Cape, Ronald Elliot *biotechnology company executive*
Cheverton, William Kearns *science corporation executive, consultant*
Cusick, Joseph David *science administrator, retired*
DeLoney, Cindy Rae *biologist*
Diamond, Rochelle Anne *biologist*
Dubesa, Elaine J. *biotechnology company executive*
Fraker, Mark Arnott *environmental scientist*
Gennaro, Antonio L. *biology educator*
Glass, Michael John *microbiologist and researcher*
Goin, Olive Bown *biologist*
Hildebrand, Milton *zoology educator, retired*
Janigro, Damir *physiologist, educator*
Jarvik, Gail Pairitz *medical geneticist*
Kidwell, Margaret Gale *ecology and biology educator*
Meador, James Parnell *toxicologist*
Nitta, Eugene Tadashi *endangered species biologist*
Otto, Catherine Nan *clinical laboratory scientist*
Palade, George Emil *biologist, educator*
Proudfoot, James Michael *research and development executive*
Rajagopalan, Malini *molecular and cellular biologist*
Riley, Erin Lee *biology educator, forensic scientist*
Robeson, David John *patent agent, biotechnology consultant*
Rogers, Jack David *plant pathologist, educator*
Salter, Robert Bryan *wildlife biologist*
Southwick, Charles Henry *zoologist, educator*
Starr, Robert Irving *plant physiologist, chemist*
Todsen, Thomas Kamp *botanist*
Weinstock, Ronald Jay *research and development company executive*

SCIENCE: MATHEMATICS AND COMPUTER SCIENCE

UNITED STATES

ALASKA

Anchorage
Mann, Lester Perry *mathematics educator*
Murray, Robert Henry *technical manager*

Fairbanks
Morris, Deanna Ruth *mathematics tutor*

Juneau
Pella, Jerome Jacob *statistician*

ARIZONA

Chandler
Sridharan, Natesa Sastri *software scientist*
Sue, Lawrence Gene *statistician*

Fort Huachuca
Clark, Brian Thomas *mathematical statistician, operations research analyst*
Vernon, David Paul *computer scientist*

Glendale
Lacy, Lee Marva Lou *mathematics educator*

Green Valley
Meserve, Bruce Elwyn *mathematics educator*

Mesa
Stott, Brian *software company executive*

Phoenix
Doto, Irene Louise *statistician*
Tsakiris, Theodora Lydia *mathematics educator*

Prescott
Anderson, Arthur George *laboratory director, former computer company executive, consultant*

Saint Johns
Moore, Martin Dale *software specialist, environmental policy analyst*

Scottsdale
Loch, Patricia Ann *software company executive, consultant*
Wheeler, David McMakin *software engineer*

Tempe
Kessler, Melody Sheryl *information systems professional*
Yau, Stephen Sik-sang *computer science and engineering educator, computer scientist, researcher*

Tucson
Clay, James Ray *mathematics educator*
DeVito, Carl Louis *mathematics educator*
Gregg, Kenneth Stephen *computer scientist*
Karson, Catherine June *computer programmer, consultant*
Neuts, Marcel Fernand *statistician, educator*
Smarandache, Florentin *mathematics researcher, writer*

CALIFORNIA

Arcata
Chinn, Phyllis Zweig *mathematics educator*

Azusa
Works, Madden Travis, Jr. (Pat Works) *operations executive, author, skydiving instructor, skydiving publications executive*

Berkeley
Anderson, Thomas E. *computer scientist, educator*
Basch, Reva *information services company executive*
Bertram, Christopher D. *artificial intelligence researcher*
Bickel, Peter John *statistician, educator*
Blum, Manuel *computer science educator*
Brillinger, David Ross *statistician, educator*
Chern, Shiing-Shen *mathematics educator*
Fateman, Richard J. *computer science educator, researcher*
Ferrari, Domenico *computer science educator*
Graham, Susan Lois *computer science educator, consultant*
Jewell, Nicholas Patrick *statistics educator*
Kwan, Eddy Man Kin *research mechanician, consultant*
Lehmann, Erich Leo *statistics educator*
McKusick, Marshall Kirk *computer scientist*
Osserman, Robert *mathematician, educator*
Pinney, Edmund *educator, mathematician*
Polster, Arnim Henry *computer scientist consultant*
Sequin, Carlo H. *computer science educator*
Speed, Terence Paul *statistician, educator*
Taub, Abraham Haskel *mathematician*
Vojta, Paul Alan *mathematics educator*
Wolf, Joseph Albert *mathematician, educator*

Brea
Thorn, Norman Robert *software development company executive*

Burbank
Paul, Dwayne Glenn *information systems company executive*

Camarillo
Ross, David Edward *software engineer*
Vannix, C(ecil) Robert *programmer, systems analyst*

Carlsbad
Fairhurst, Jeffrey Thomas *software consultant*
Halberg, Charles John August, Jr. *mathematics educator*
Kao, Philip Min-Shien *software consultant*

Carmichael
Givant, Philip Joachim *mathematics educator, real estate investment executive*

Carson
Kowalski, Kazimierz *computer science educator, researcher*
Suchenek, Marek Andrzej *computer science educator*
Yoshida, Kosaku *quantitative methods educator*

Chatsworth
Koerber, John Robert *computer programmer*
Zale, Cooper Jonathan Campbell *computer systems analyst, information systems consultant*

Chico
Wolff, Howard Keith *computer science educator, consultant*

China Lake
Rugg, David Lewis *software engineer*

Claremont
Henriksen, Melvin *mathematician, educator*
Spanier, Jerome *mathematics educator*
White, Alvin Murray *mathematics educator, consultant*

Compton
Juarez, Mark Andrew *computer analyst*

Concord
Fuld, Fred, III *computer consultant, financial consultant*
Moeller, Walter Eugene *management consultant*

Costa Mesa
Arismendi-Pardi, Eduardo J. *mathematics educator*
Babich, Alan Francis *computer scientist*
Fong, Carl S. *systems and operations analyst*
Salinger, Joan Adah *computer graphics, photography and art educator*
Savage, Sandra Hope Skeen *mathematics educator, curriculum writer*

Culver City
Ulin, Samuel Alexander *computer systems developer*

Cupertino
Bateman, George W. *computer systems consultant*
Benghiat, Jacques *computer science engineer, consultant*
Bickford, Peter Richard *computer programmer*
Holmes, Richard Albert *software engineer, consultant*
Lee, Ruby Bei-Loh *computer systems and multimedia architect*
Schwehr, Robert Frederick *software/hardware development professional*
Slutz, Donald Ray *computer scientist*

Cypress
Askelid, Bertil Rune *computer scientist*
Cao, Dac-Buu *software engineer*

Danville
Appel, Jacob J. *information services technology executive*
Lowery, Lawrence Frank *mathematic science and computer educator*

Davis
Mulase, Motohico *mathematics educator*
Olsson, Ronald Arthur *computer science educator*
Reed, Nancy Ellen *educator*

Downey
Sasso, Giuseppe *systems analyst*

Edwards
Boyles, Larry Wayne *computer scientist, consultant*

El Cajon
Donnelly, Donald Frank *mathematics educator, computer consultant*

El Segundo
Hoffmann, Timothy Jay *computer networking executive*
Lucas, Suzanne *statistician, entrepreneur*
Martin, Ronald Gene *logistics program manager*
Sheldon, Marti Reisman *software engineer*
Sizemore, Nicky Lee *computer scientist*
Yang, Samuel Chi-An *software engineer*

Elk Grove
McDavid, Douglas Warren *systems consultant*

Elkhorn
Guglielmo, Eugene Joseph *computer scientist*

Encinitas
Walker, Larry Gilbert *computer scientist*

Escondido
Collins, George Timothy *computer software consultant*

Felton
Parkison, Roger Clyde *computer scientist*

Fremont
Anderson, David Matthew *computer programmer*
Lautzenheiser, Marvin Wendell *computer software engineer*

Fresno
Bohlin, Carol Fry *mathematics educator*
Diestelkamp, Dawn Lea *systems analyst*
Michael, James Daniel *computer scientist*

Garden Grove
Chacon, Michael Ernest *computer networking specialist*

Glendale
Kolpas, Sidney J. *mathematician, educator*

Goleta
McInturff, Kim *design engineer, mathematician*

Hawthorne
Lyashenko, Nikolai Nikolaevich *mathematician, educator*

Hayward
Duncan, Doris Gottschalk *information systems educator*
Fearn, Dean Henry *statistics educator*
Mafnas, Isabel Iglesias *computer lab specialist, computer consultant*
Prada, Gloria Ines *mathematics and Spanish language educator*
Sabharwal, Ranjit Singh *mathematician*

Huntington Beach
Abu-Mostafa, Ayman Said *computer consultant*
Lupash, Lawrence Ovidiu *computer analyst, researcher*

Irvine
Frankfurth, Mark Stephen *computer engineer*
Hoffman, Donald David *cognitive and computer science educator*
Johnson, Richard Lumus *systems analyst*
Juberg, Richard Kent *mathematician, educator*
Lee, Kenneth *computer aided design educator*
Li, Peter Wai-Kwong *mathematics educator*
Nicolau, Alexandru *educator*
Suda, Tatsuya *computer science educator*

La Honda
Melvin, Jay Wayne *computer programmer*

La Jolla
Freedman, Michael Hartley *mathematician, educator*
Lin, James Peicheng *mathematics educator*
Pasquale, Joseph *computer scientist, educator*
Terras, Audrey Anne *mathematics educator*
Wulbert, Daniel Eliot *mathematician, educator*
Zyroff, Ellen Slotoroff *information scientist, classicist, educator*

La Mesa
Allen, David Charles *computer science educator*

La Mirada
Johnson, Stephen Alden *computer programmer*
Norman, Daniel Wiley *computer technician/programmer*

Livermore
Blattner, Meera McCuaig *computer science educator*
Grant, Charles Wayne *computer scientist*
Haga, Enoch John *computer educator, author*
Lindsay, Norman Roy *systems consultant*
Motteler, Zane Clinton *computer science educator*

Long Beach
Gittleman, Arthur Paul *computer science and engineering educator*
Le, Nguyen Minh *computer company executive*
Schroeder, Arnold Leon *mathematics educator*

Turner, Maureen Barbara *mathematics educator, researcher*
Wollmer, Richard Dietrich *statistics and operations research educator*

Los Altos
Yee, Kane Shee-Gong *mathematician, electrical engineer*

Los Angeles
Allswang, John Myers *computer science educator, historian*
Arbib, Michael Anthony *computer scientist, educator, neuroscientist, cybernetician*
Bekey, George Albert *computer scientist, educator, engineer*
Brown, Robert Freeman *mathematics educator*
Campbell, Michael Lee *computer science researcher*
Chacko, George Kuttickal *systems science educator, consultant*
Delaney, Matthew Sylvester *mathematics educator*
DiStefano, Joseph John, III *bioengineering and biocybernetics educator, consultant*
Eggan, Peter Cornelius *mathematician*
Estrin, Gerald *computer scientist, engineering educator, academic administrator*
Ghandeharizadeh, Shahram *computer scientist and educator*
Greenberger, Martin *computer and information scientist, educator*
Han, Junghyun *computer scientist*
Hoffman, Rodney Joseph *computer scientist*
Jacobsen, Laren *programmer, analyst*
King, Todd Allen *programmer, analyst*
Liggett, Thomas Milton *mathematics educator*
Mesrobian, Edmond *computer scientist, researcher*
Redheffer, Raymond Moos *mathematician, educator*
Reich, Simeon *mathematics researcher, educator*
Senevitratne, Sonal Jerard *systems analyst*
Silvers, E. Randall *computer system manager*
Stoner, Michael C. *network specialist*
Stormes, John Max *instructional systems developer*
Swanson, E. Burton *business and information systems educator*
Symonds, Norman Leslie *computer programming specialist*
Taylor, Jeremy Michael George *statistician, educator*
Terwilliger, Cynthia Lou *software designer*

Malibu
Crawford, Natalie Wilson *applied mathematician*
Schindler, Keith William *software engineer*

Marina Del Rey
Johnson, William Lewis *information science eduator*
Neuman, B. Clifford *computer scientist*
Touch, Joseph Dean *computer scientist, educator*

Martinez
Tong, Siu Wing *computer programmer*

Menlo Park
Martin, David Lee *computer scientist*
Neumann, Peter Gabriel *computer scientist*
Perrault, Charles Raymond *computer scientist*
Zislis, Paul Martin *software engineering executive*

Mill Valley
Komissarchik, Edward A. *computer scientist*

Milpitas
Crain, Chester Ray *statistician, consultant*

Mission Viejo
Doig, Beverly Irene *systems specialist*

Moffett Field
Mehra, Pankaj *computer scientist, researcher*
Paluzzi, Peter Ronald *data processing professional*
Saini, Subhash *computer scientist*
Whitney, Lisa VanderSluis *software engineer*

Monte Sereno
Rustagi, Jagdish Sharan *statistics educator*

Monterey
Borges, Carlos Freitas *computational mathematician*
Lundy, Gilbert Moulton, Jr. *computer science educator*
Zaky, Amr Mohamed *computer scientist, educator*

Moorpark
Beron, Alberto *mathematics educator, consultant, lecturer*

Morgan Hill
Mancini, Robert Karl *computer analyst, consultant*

Mountain View
Beaver, William Lawrence *retired scientist, educator, consultant*
Cattell, Roderic geoffrey Galton *computer scientist*
Chapman, Donald Brent *computer network security consultant*
Chow, Billy Ying-Jung *software development executive*
Kessler, Peter Bernard *computer scientist, researcher*
Keutzer, Kurt William *computer scientist, researcher*
Miller, Terrence Clark *software engineer*
Patel, Sukesh Janubhai *software engineer*
Pendleton, Joan Marie *microprocessor designer*
Raugh, Michael Randolph *mathematician*
Scheer, Janet Kathy *mathematics educator*
Shah, Devang Kundanlal *software engineer*
Tugender, Ronald *software executive*

Oakland
Finnegan, Daniel *statistician*
Long, William Joseph *software engineer*
Onyeador, Emmanuel Osita *mathematics and computer educator*
Ramsay, Janice Susan *computer programmer, analyst*

Oceanside
Mallory, Steven Reece *software engineering executive*

Orange
Krichmar, Lee *information systems executive*
Stickney, Douglas Henry *biostatistician, consultant*

Palo Alto
Barford, Lee Alton *computer scientist*
Beretta, Giordano Bruno *computer scientist, researcher*
Brown, Allen Leon, Jr. *computer scientist, educator*
Chaudhuri, Surajit *computer scientist, researcher*
Goldberg, Jacob *computer scientist, researcher*
Kelley, Robert Suma *systems analyst*
Kolarov, Krasimir Dobromirov *computer scientist, researcher*
Mahmood, Aamer *computer system architect*
Mayo, Robert N. *software engineer*
McJones, Paul Robert *computer scientist, software engineer*
Rejman, Diane Louise *systems analyst, aerospace*
Silvers, Abraham *biostatistician, researcher*

Palos Verdes Estates
Morizumi, Shigenori James *applied mathematician*

Pasadena
Brown, James William *information systems development executive*
Chandy, Kanianthra Mani *computer sciences educator, consultant*
Greenhall, Charles August *mathematician*
Lenzo, Thomas John *training and development consultant*
Urista, Juan *computer scientist*

Pleasanton
Meyers, Gene Howard *computer scientist*
Novak-Lyssand, Randi Ruth *computer scientist*
Petersen, Ann Nevin *computer systems administrator, consultant*

Pomona
Riley, Henry Norton *computer scientist educator*
Sang, Fuh-Ching *computer science educator*
Tuul, Johannes *mathematician, educator*

Port Hueneme
Schilbrack, Karen Gail *systems analyst*

Portola Valley
Kuo, Franklin F. *computer scientist, electrical engineer*

Ramona
Bennett, James Chester *computer consultant, real estate developer*

Rancho Cucamonga
Greever, Margaret Quarles *mathematics educator*

Redondo Beach
Burris, Harrison Robert *computer and software developer*

Redwood City
Oki, Brian Masao *software engineer*
Ozbutun, Cetin *software engineer*
Sell, John Victor *computer architect*

Riverside
Bhanu, Bir *computer information scientist, educator, director university program*
McClanahan, Michael Nelson *systems analyst*

Rohnert Park
Jersky, Brian *statistician*

Rolling Hills Estates
Clewis, Charlotte Wright Staub *mathematics educator*

San Bernardino
Stein, Robert George *mathematics educator, author*

San Diego
Astle, Richard Sharp *computer programmer, poet*
Bailey, Michael John *computer scientist*
Garrison, Betty Bernhardt *mathematics educator*
Gurak, Stanley Joseph *mathematics and computer science educator*
Huang, Kun Lien *software engineer, scientist*
Legrand, Shawn Pierre *computer systems programmer*
Loper, Warren Edward *computer scientist*
Mangham, John Randall *information systems professional*
Reddan, John Gordon, III *computer scientist*
Yount, Charles Robert *electrical and computer engineer*

San Francisco
Backus, John *computer scientist*
Christensen, David William *mathematician, engineer*
Christiansen, Eric Alan *software development executive*
Cruse, Allan Baird *mathematician, computer scientist, educator*
Eng, Jamie Pearl *statistics educator*
Farrell, Edward Joseph *retired mathematics educator*
Friedhoff, Richard Mark *computer scientist, entrepreneur*
Gaffney, Paul James *systems architect*
Hurd, James Daniel *software and product designer*
Larson, Ronald Allen *information specialist and programmer/analyst*
Laws, Julie Augustadt *computer consultant*
Leung, Kason Kai Ching *computer specialist*
Lowndes, David Alan *programmer analyst*
Masuda, Yoshinori *systems analyst*
Perko, Walter Kim *computer consultant, systems analyst*
Pope, Mark L. *information scientist*
Rautenberg, Robert Frank *consulting statistician*
Shirasawa, Richard Masao *systems analyst and coordinator*
Smith, James Thomas *mathematician*
Vazsonyi, Andrew *computer and management scientist*

San Gabriel
Kettenborough, Clifford Russell *computer scientist, consultant, manager*

San Jose
Adams, Frederick Marshall *mathematical educator*
Agoston, Max Karl *computer science educator*
Aylesworth, John Richard *software professional*
Biggs, Stuart Edward *computer software engineer*
Brandwajn, Alexandre *software company executive*
Crawford, Chris Charles *computer game designer*
Fotland, David Allen *computer architect*
Lin, Tao *software engineer*
Luniewski, Allen William *computer scientist*
Poirot, Franck Jacques *software engineer*
Zhang, Guorui *software engineer*

San Luis Obispo
Dana, Charles Harold, Jr. *computer science educator*
Grimes, Joseph Edward *computer science educator*
Hsu, John Y. *computer scientist*

San Marcos
Wu, Shaun-inn *computer science educator*

San Marino
Lashley, Virginia Stephenson Hughes *retired computer science educator*

San Mateo
Schofield, James Roy *computer programmer*

San Pedro
Colman, Ronald William *computer science educator*

Santa Ana
Mikesell, Richard Leo *computer programmer*

Santa Barbara
Rosenberg, Alex *mathematician, educator*
Simons, Stephen *mathematics educator, researcher*
Sommers, Adele Ann *engineering specialist, technical trainer*

Santa Clara
Bullock, Louise Ann *information consultant*
Klosinski, Leonard Frank *mathematics educator*
Lawrence, Deborah Jean *statistician*
Loka, Raghavendra Rao *software engineer*
Lovitt, John R. *software company executive*
Morgan, Thomas Michael *computer software engineer*
Patterson, Mark Jerome *computer software designer*
Smolarski, Dennis Chester *mathematics educator*
Sweatt, Richard Andrew *computer scientist*

Santa Cruz
Huskey, Harry Douglas *information and computer science educator*

Santa Monica
Hearn, Anthony Clem *computer scientist*
Palmer, Roger Cain *information scientist*

Santa Rosa
Barr, John Tilman, IV *research and development executive*

Santee
Peters, Raymond Eugene *computer systems company executive*

Saratoga
Adams, Jo-Ann Marie *data processing consultant*
Park, Joseph Chul Hui *computer scientist*

Scotts Valley
Rosenberg, Jonathan Bryan *software engineer, computer science educator*

Simi Valley
Stratton, Gregory Alexander *computer specialist, administrator, mayor*

Stanford
Anderson, Theodore Wilbur *statistics educator*
Burback, Ronald LeRoi *computer scientist*
Cover, Thomas M. *statistician, electrical engineer, educator*
Golub, Gene Howard *computer science educator, researcher*
Johnstone, Iain Murray *statistician, educator, consultant*
Keller, Arthur Michael *computer science researcher*
Knuth, Donald Ervin *computer sciences educator*
Lieberman, Gerald J. *statistics educator*
Olshen, Richard A. *statistician, educator*
Ornstein, Donald Samuel *mathematician, educator*

Stockton
Landre, Debra Ann *mathematics educator*

Sunnyvale
Cai, Yang *software engineer, computer scientist*
Janssen, James Robert *consulting software engineer*
Konda, Venkata Reddy *computer scientist, lecturer*
Teh, Cho Huak *computer scientist*
Vail, Christian Byron *software engineer*

Sunset Beach
Raley, William Greene *systems analyst*

Torrance
Malhotra, Vijay Kumar *mathematics educator*
Manassero, William Joseph *software executive, consultant*

Turlock
Lamie, Edward Louis *computer science educator*

Venice
Ahlem, Diana Grace *systems analyst*
Feldman, Jeffrey Michael *software developer, music educator*
Fernandes, Winston Jerome *computer scientist*

Ventura
Atkin, Arlo Kay *systems analyst, consultant*

Walnut Creek
Dornhelm, Marilyn Celia *computer consultant, owner*

Whittier
Keny, Sharad Vasant *mathematics educator and researcher*

Woodland Hills
Wing, Thomas *micrometrologist, consultant*

COLORADO

Aurora
Miller, Franklin Emrick *software engineer, project engineer*
Patrick, Kevin Dannye *computer programmer*

Boulder
Adams, Jeanne Clare *computer scientist*
Burleski, Joseph Anthony, Jr. *information services professional*
Clements, George Francis *mathematics educator*
Drews, Carl *software engineer*
Monarchi, David Edward *management and information scientist*
Myers, William Loring *computer scientist, software engineer*
Neal, Michael Renn *software engineer*
Shrairman, Ruth *computer scientist, company executive*
Waite, Joanne Lischer *systems analyst*

Broomfield
Heimbecher, Ronald Frederick *information technologies director*

Colorado Springs
Couger, James Daniel *computer scientist, writer*
Cray, Seymour R. *computer designer*
Eddy, Robert Phillip *retired mathematician*
Goble, Paul John *software engineer, technical communicator*
Herpin, William Bernard, Jr. *deputy program manager*
Kolstad, Robert Bruce *computer scientist*
Lewis, Gregory Allen *computer programmer and analyst, consultant*
Macon, Jerry Lyn *software company owner, software publisher*
Morrison, John Stuart *technology company executive*
Nowosatko, Jerome Raymond *software engineer*
Thor, Paul Viets *software engineer, consultant, educator*

Denver
Cutter, Gary Raymond *biostatistician, epidemiologist*
Duca, Frank A. *software engineer, researcher*
Gates, Melodi Mosley *software engineer*
Hayes, Jeanne *information services executive*
Kirslis, Peter Andre Christopher *computer science research and development specialist*
Komdat, John Raymond *data processing consultant*
Larsen, Gwynne E. *computer information systems educator*
Mawhinney, Charles Henry, III *computer science educator*
McCarthy, Glenn *information systems administrator*
Mendez, Celestino Galo *mathematics educator*
Mullett, Melinda Fae *computer scientist*
Schreiber, Edward *computer scientist*
Scott, Judy Haslee *computer systems analyst*
Stilman, Boris *computer science educator, researcher*
Sweeney, Christopher Lee *applied mathematics engineer*
Wnuck, Kenneth L. *software engineer*

Englewood
Anderson, Bruce Morgan *computer scientist*
Atencio, J(oseph) Andrew *computer systems official, computer designer*
Joffe, Barbara Lynne *software developer*
Leigh, Shari Greer *software consulting firm executive*

Evergreen
Zeeb, James Lawrence *software company executive*

Fort Collins
Allgower, Eugene Leo *mathematics educator*
Edgeman, Rick Lee *statistics educator, consultant*
Mielke, Paul William, Jr. *statistician*
Tweedie, Richard Lewis *statistics educator, consultant*

Golden
Bradley, James Alexander *software engineer, researcher*
Coburn, Timothy Craig *research statistician*
Hereman, Willy Alois Maria *mathematics educator*
Tankelevich, Roman Lvovich *computer scientist*
Tsuo, Anne Li *database specialist*

Grand Junction
Jones, Scott Austin *software developer, microcomputer consultant*

Greeley
Mader, Douglas Paul *statistician*
Silverman, Fredrick Lee *mathematics educator*

Lafayette
Diekmann, Barbara Brandenburg *computer systems researcher*

Lakewood
Barth, David Victor *computer systems designer, consultant*

Littleton
Florence, Alfred William *computer engineer*
Rageth, David Allen *telecommunications executive, network engineer*

Loveland
Rosander, Arlyn Custer *mathematical statistician, management consultant*

Nederland
Blaney, Loren Francis, Jr. *software engineer*

Pueblo
Chandler, Kris *computer consultant, educator*

University Of Colorado
Beylkin, Gregory *mathematician*

HAWAII

Hilo
Souza, Edward Melvin *computer science educator*

Honolulu
Abdul, Corinna Gay *software engineer, consultant*
Agcaoili, Lawrence E. *systems analyst/programmer*
Imamura, Daniel Tatsuya *computer programmer, consultant*
Sato, Miles Masakaze *computer programmer, systems analyst*
Sekine, Deborah Keiko *systems analyst, programmer*
Stegenga, David A. *mathematics educator*
Swanson, Richard William *statistician*
Zhou, Chiping *mathematician, educator*
Zimermann, Alfred Earle *software engineering educator*

Kihei
Herrera, Robert Bennett *retired mathematics educator*

Laie
Barker, Joseph Cory *computer scientist, educator*

Lihue
Sivadas, Iraja (William Shepard Watkins) *mathematics educator*

Mililani
Tribble, David Henry *software engineer*

Pearl City
Duncan, John Wiley *mathematics and computer educator, retired air force officer*
Matsuoka, Eric Takao *mathematics educator*

IDAHO

Boise
Russell, Carl Lloyd *computer systems analyst*

Calder
Rechard, Ottis William *mathematics and computer science educator*

Moscow
Barbut, Erol *mathematics educator*

Mountain Home
Meyr, Shari Louise *computer consultant, computer company executive*

Pocatello
Mohamed, Shamim P. *computer science educator*

Rexburg
Terry, Steven Spencer *mathematics educator, consultant*

MINNESOTA

Minneapolis
Jackson, Robert Loring *science and mathematics educator, academic administrator*

MISSISSIPPI

Oxford
Cook, Robert P. *software architect*

MONTANA

Big Timber
Yuzeitis, James Richard *information specialist*

Bozeman
Cimikowski, Robert John *computer scientist*
Hamilton, Martin Alva *statistician, consultant*

Missoula
Banaugh, Robert Peter *computer science educator*
Zheng, Youlu *computer scientist, educator*

NEVADA

Gardnerville
Woodside, George Robert *computer software developer*

Incline Village
Welsch, Suzanne Carol *mathematics educator*

Las Vegas
Dalpatadu, Rohan Jayantha *mathematician, educator*
Miel, George Joseph *computer scientist*
Singh, Anita *statistician*
Snyder, John Henry *computer science educator, consultant*

Minden
McCullough, William Edward *metrologist*

NEW MEXICO

Alamogordo
Rider, Frederick Timothy *computer systems analyst*

Albuquerque
Bertin, Michael Stephen *computer analyst, retired naval officer*
Gaffney, Edward Stowell *scientist, technology executive*
Lee, Elizabeth Tan *mathematics educator*
Sciame, Donald Richard *computer systems analyst, dentist, magician, locksmith*
Smith, David Alan *systems programmer*
Sobolewski, John Stephen *computer information scientist, director computer services, consultant*
Stone, Alexander Paul *mathematics educator*
Wolf, Monica Theresia *procedures analyst*

Kirtland AFB
O'Brien, Patricia Nevin *computer scientist*

Las Cruces
Reinfelds, Juris *computer science educator*
Zund, Joseph David *mathematical sciences educator*

Los Alamos
French, Pamela Renee *computer and management consultant*
Sigler, Marjorie Diane *computer programming executive, analyst*
Tingley, Walter Watson *computer systems manager*
Wade, Rodger Grant *financial systems analyst*

Pecos
Price, Thomas Munro *computer consultant*

Santa Fe
Buchser, John Robert *computer scientist*

OREGON

Albany
Yu, Kitson Szewai *computer science educator*

Aloha
Spangler, Lynice Sue *software engineer*

Ashland
Spira, Robert Samuel *mathematician*

Corvallis
Parks, Harold Raymond *mathematician, educator*
Stalley, Robert Delmer *retired mathematics educator*

Eugene
Truax, Donald Robert *mathematics educator*
Vitulli, Marie Angela *mathematician*

Florence
Gray, Augustine Heard, Jr. *computer consultant*

Hillsboro
Glew, Andrew Forsyth *computer architect, inventor*

Mcminnville
Monaco, Ferdinand Roger *mathematics educator*

Portland
Fuller, William Roger *mathematics and physics educator*
Hall, Howard Pickering *engineering and mathematics educator*
Lambert, Richard William *mathematics educator*
Mangin, René-Marc *systems physicist*
Phillips, David Spencer *statistician, educator*

Salem
Ho, Phuong Minh *software engineer*

Waldport
Russell, Philip Courtney *computer consultant*

Wilsonville
Bilow, Steven Craig *computer systems specialist*

UTAH

Logan
Cheng, Heng-Da *computer scientist*

Ogden
Wattenberg, Frank Arvey *mathematician*

Provo
Carter, Steven Ray *computer programmer, analyst*
Garner, Lynn Evan *mathematics educator*
Ivie, Evan Leon *computer science educator*
Lang, William Edward *mathematics educator*

Salt Lake City
Averett, Robert Lee *information systems professional, educator*
Felt, James Patterson *computer programmer*
Guldahl, Martin Granville *software engineer*
James, Matthew Craig *programmer, analyst*
Sobh, Tarek Mahmoud *computer science educator, researcher*
Trosper, Robert Thomas *software engineer*
Wilcox, Calvin Hayden *mathematics educator*
Williamson, David Henry *data processing professional*

VIRGINIA

Vienna
Kinashi, Doreen Ann *systems analyst, writer, editor*

WASHINGTON

Bellevue
Sohl, Norman Frederick *program manager*

Bothell
Stackhouse, Christian Paul *computer company executive*

Ellensburg
Comstock, Dale Robert *mathematics educator*

Kirkland
Duernberger, Paul M. *computer services director, computer and electrical engineering educator*

Lacey
Wells, Roger Stanley *software engineer*

Lynnwood
Vierheller, Todd *software engineering consultant*

Pullman
Benson, David Bernard *computer science educator*
Gupta, Barbara Mackay *mathematics educator*
Hildebrandt, Darlene Myers *information scientist*
Obradovic, Zoran *computer scientist, educator*

Redmond
Horvitz, Eric Joel *computer scientist, decision theorist*
Houseworth, Derek Eugene *software test engineer*
Huang, Xuedong David *senior reseacher*
Sinha, Alok Kumar *software design engineer*
Wolf, Richard Jay *software designer*

Renton
Worobec, Bruce William *computer systems analyst*

Richland
Cowley, Paula Jean *computer scientist, consultant*
Gates, Theodore Allan, Jr. *software engineer*

Seattle
Breslow, Norman Edward *biostatistics educator, researcher*
Bridwell, C. Joseph *computer systems analyst*
Criminale, William Oliver, Jr. *applied mathematics educator*
Dieli, Mary Adelaide *software engineer consultant*
Gillispie, Steven Brian *systems analyst, researcher*
Helton, Thomas Joe *computer scientist, writer*
Hewitt, Edwin *mathematician, educator*
Klee, Victor La Rue *mathematician, educator*
Meissner, Loren Phillip, Jr. *systems analyst*
Meister, John Edward, Jr. *systems analyst, technical educator*
Michael, Ernest Arthur *mathematics educator*
Nijenhuis, Albert *mathematician, educator*
Smith, Gregory Laurence *computer scientist, consultant*
Yuen, Karsten Brandon *programmer analyst, consultant*
Zabinsky, Zelda Barbara *operations researcher, industrial engineering educator*

Spokane
Mayer, Herbert Carleton, Jr. *computer consultant*

Tacoma
Beezer, Robert Arnold *mathematics educator*

WYOMING

Cheyenne
Southworth, Rod Brand *computer science educator*

Laramie
Davis, Frank Grodavent Foy *computer consultant*
Porter, A. Duane *mathematics educator*

Riverton
Winslow, Richard Paul *computer science educator, consultant*

CANADA

ALBERTA

Calgary
Pinter, Joseph Kalman *mathematician*
Varadarajan, Kalathoor *educator, researcher*

Edmonton
Elliott, Robert James *mathematician*

BRITISH COLUMBIA

Burnaby
Alspach, Brian Roger *mathematics educator*
Han, Jiawei *computer scientist, educator*

Vancouver
Zhu, Jun *mathematics educator*
Zidek, James Victor *statistician, educator*

SASKATCHEWAN

Regina
Koh, Eusebio Legarda *mathematics educator*

JAPAN

Yamato Kanagawa
Takahashi, Hiroyasu *computer scientist*

ADDRESS UNPUBLISHED

Aaron, Bud *systems analyst*
Applegate, Arthur David *computer software developer, consultant*
Baxter, Carol Cairns *computer scientist*
Bullard, Richard Forrest *mathematics educator*
Church, Alonzo *mathematics and philosophy educator*
Collins, Joan Eileen *computer graphics specialist*
Cyrus, Judith Lynn *software engineer*
Denny, John Leighton, Jr. *mathematics educator*
Doubledee, Deanna Gail *software engineer, consultant*
Ehresman, Paula Suzette *information manager, researcher*
Frishberg, Nancy Jo *computer researcher*
Gabrielian, Armen *computer scientist, researcher, entrepreneur*
Golden, Thomas Leslie *computer specialist, graphic design artist*
Grady, Jeffrey O. *system engineering consultant*
Grober, Michael *computer industry professional*
Guy, Michelle *computer professional*
Hall, Caryl Ronnie *technology support analyst*
Happel, Kenneth Malcolm *computer scientist*
Harrison, Glenn Russell *mathematics educator*
Holland, Michael James *computer services administrator*
Howard, Jerald James *software engineer*
Idury, Ramana Murthy *computer scientist*
Jensen, John Michael *mathematics educator, consultant*
Lundgren, Susan Elizabeth *information technology consultant, musician*
McAllister, Byron Leon *mathematics educator*
Mints, Grigori Efroim *operations research specialist*
Monroe, Mary-Lynne *computer consultant, special education educator*
Neimann, Albert Alexander *statistician*
Nelson, Walter William *computer programmer, consultant*
Neugroschl, Scott Alexander *software engineer*
Newman, Gerard Kevin *software engineer*
Newman, Richard D. *computer resources professional, software developer*
Postma, James Lee *computer software engineer, consultant*
Puffer, Ruth Rice *statistician, epidemiologist*
Pugh, Jamie Kathleen *statistician, researcher*
Purdy, Teddy George, Jr. *programmer, analyst, researcher, consultant*
Redfield, John Duncan *computer programmer*
Religa, James Paul *software engineer*
Roberts, Marie Dyer *computer systems specialist*
Schmauss, Stephen Anthony *retired computer programmer*
Schmidt, Christopher Van Alst *systems programmer*
Shillington, Keith Allan *software engineer*
Skelton, John Edward *computer technology consultant*
Soskin, Steve *computer software consultant*
Suppes, Patrick *statistics, education, philosophy and psychology educator*
Tillquist, John *information technology researcher*
Tu, Samson W. *computer science researcher*
Viviani, Kimberly Jean *software programmer*
Vu, Dung Quoc *systems analyst*
Warner, Janet Claire *software design engineer*
Watson, John Francis *software engineer, consultant*
Weidenhofer, Neal *systems programer, computer company executive*
Wheeler, Gloria *database analyst*
Whitner, Jane Marvin *analyst programmer*
Winter, Donald Christopher *computer systems architect*
Wu, Hung-Hsi *mathematician, educator*
Yee, Marcus Charles *software developer*

SCIENCE: PHYSICAL SCIENCE

UNITED STATES

ALASKA

Anchorage
Bushara, Mohamed N. *geologist, oil industry executive*
Ennis, William Lee *physics educator*
Mabry, Monte Del *geophysicist*
Myers, Mark D. *petroleum geologist, researcher*
O'Brien, David Keran *marine geologist, environmental scientist*
Patrick, Leslie Dayle *hydrologist*
Powers, Alan Dale *geologist, retired federal government executive*

Fairbanks
Beckstead, Douglas Stephen *cultural resources professional*
Duffy, Lawrence Kevin *biochemist, educator*
Fathauer, Theodore Frederick *meteorologist*
Fischer, Robert Edward *meterologist*
Helfferich, Merritt Randolph *geophysical research administrator*
Hopkins, David Moody *geologist*
McNutt, Stephen Russell *volcanologist, geophysical scientist*
Speck, Robert Charles *geological engineer*
Stamnes, Knut Henrik *physics educator*
Wallace, Wesley Kent *geology educator*
Weeks, Wilford Frank *geophysics educator, glaciologist*
Weller, Gunter Ernst *geophysics educator*

Palmer
Carté, George Wayne *geophysicist*

ARIZONA

Flagstaff
Dapples, Edward Charles *geologist, educator*
Eastman, Michael Paul *chemistry educator*
Giclas, Henry Lee *astronomer*
Shoemaker, Eugene Merle *geologist*
Sinton, William Merz *astronomer, educator*
Zoellner, Robert William *chemistry educator*

Mesa
Kokanovich, Jon Douglas *crime laboratory director, forensic chemist*

Page
Leus McFarlen, Patricia Cheryl *water chemist*

Phoenix
Ali, S. Salih *physicist, materials scientist*
Bolin, Vladimir Dustin *chemist*
Kendall, William Forrest *physicist*
Lichtenberg, Larry Ray *chemist, consultant, researcher*
Pearson, Keith Laurence *retired environmental scientist*
Ramaswamy, Padmanabhan *materials scientist*
Vogler, James Waylan *physicist, consultant*
Young, Don William *hydrologist, educator*

Scottsdale
Borges, William, III *environmental analyst*
Feir, John Douglas *geologist*
Hockmuth, Joseph Frank *physicist, psychotherapist*

Tempe
Amalfi, Frederick Anthony *limnologist*
Burstein, David *astronomy educator*
Glick, Milton Don *chemist, university administrator*
Greeley, Ronald *geology educator*
Harris, Joseph *retired biochemistry educator*
Juvet, Richard Spalding, Jr. *chemistry educator*
Lovvik, Daryl Vaughn *geologist, consultant*
Moore, Carleton Bryant *geochemistry educator*
Nigam, Bishan Perkash *physics educator*
Page, John Boyd *physics educator*
Pettit, George Robert *chemistry educator, cancer researcher*
Tillery, Bill W. *physics educator*
Whitehurst, Harry Bernard *chemistry educator*

Tucson
Baker, Victor Richard *geology researcher, educator, planetary sciences researcher*
Barrett, Bruce Richard *physics educator*
Buras, Nathan *hydrology and water resources educator*
Carruthers, Peter Ambler *physicist, educator*
Constenius, Kurt Norman *geophysicist*
Cusanovich, Michael Anthony *biochemistry educator*
Dean, Jeffrey Stewart *dendrochronologist, archaeologist*
Dickinson, Robert Earl *atmospheric scientist, educator*
Falco, Charles Maurice *physicist, educator*
Fernandez, Clemente Guajardo *environmental specialist*
Fink, James Brewster *geophysicist, consultant*
Glass, Richard Steven *chemistry educator*
Hallick, Richard Bruce *biochemistry educator*
Halpenny, Leonard Cameron *water resources consultant, hydrologist*
Haynes, Caleb Vance, Jr. *geology and archaeology educator*
Hunten, Donald Mount *planetary scientist, educator*
Ignat, Steven John *aerospace company executive*
Jefferies, John Trevor *astronomer, astrophysicist, observatory administrator*
Kamilli, Robert Joseph *geologist*
Kiersch, George Alfred *geological consultant, retired educator*
Lamb, Lowell David *physicist*
Lamb, Willis Eugene, Jr. *physicist, educator*
Lebl, Michal *peptide chemist*
Lunine, Jonathan Irving *planetary scientist, educator*
Melosh, Henry Jay, IV *planetary science educator*
Metz, Robert Allen *mining geologist*
Ning, Cun-Zheng *physicist*
Quinlan, James Joseph *mining geologist, consultant*
Roemer, Elizabeth *astronomer, educator*
Salzman, William Ronald *chemistry educator*
Schau, Harvey Charles *physicist*
Sewell, Charles Robertson *geologist, exploration company executive, investor*
Sternberg, Ben Kollock *geophysicist*
White, Raymond Edwin, Jr. *astronomer, educator, researcher*
Willis, Clifford Leon *geologist*
Wolff, Sidney Carne *astronomer, observatory administrator*

CALIFORNIA

Alameda
Parasrampuria, Jagdish *pharmacist*

Alhambra
Ju, Jingfang *biochemist*

Arcadia
Bars, Itzhak *physics educator, researcher, consultant*
Lawson, Daniel David *chemist, consultant*
Slover, Archy F. *chemist*

Arcata
Cranston, Frederick Pitkin *physics educator*

Atascadero
Ogier, Walter Thomas *retired physics educator*

Bakersfield
Carlson, Gregory Dale *geologist*
Dorer, Fred Harold *chemistry educator*
Medvin, Evelyn Anne *geophysicist*
Timmer, Robert Scott *geologist*

Berkeley
Bartlett, Neil *chemist, educator*
Bukowinski, Mark Stefan Tadeusz *geophysics educator*
Calvin, Melvin *chemist, educator*
Cerny, Joseph, III *chemistry educator, scientific laboratory administrator, university dean and official*
Chamberlain, Owen *nuclear physicist*
Chandler, David *scientist, educator*
Dauben, William Garfield *chemist, educator*
Gaillard, Mary Katharine *physics educator*
Glaser, Donald Arthur *physicist*
Green, Michael I. *physicist*
Hahn, Erwin Louis *physicist, educator*
Hall, Lawrence John *physics educator*
Haller, Eugene Ernest *materials scientist, educator*
Hartman, Hyman *biochemist*
Hearst, John Eugene *chemistry educator*
Heathcock, Clayton Howell *chemistry educator, researcher*
Hoffman, Darleane Christian *chemistry educator*
Huff, Welcome Rex Anthony *chemical researcher*
Johnson, Phyllis Elaine *chemist*
Kadel, Richard Williams *physicist*
Kurtzman, Ralph Harold *biochemist, researcher*
Lee, Yuan T(seh) *chemistry educator*
Lipps, Jere Henry *paleontology educator*
Markowitz, Samuel Solomon *chemistry educator*
Mc Evilly, Thomas Vincent *seismologist*
McGlashan, Teresa Duane *environmentalist*
Mel, Howard Charles *biophysics educator*
Miller, William Hughes *theoretical chemist, educator*
Mossman, Albert Pruitt *chemist, consultant*
Pavlath, Attila Endre *research chemist*
Perez-Mendez, Victor *physics educator*
Perry, Dale Lynn *chemist*
Phillips, John Gardner *educator, astrophysicist*
Pines, Alexander *chemistry educator, researcher*
Pitzer, Kenneth Sanborn *chemist, educator*
Roitman, James Nathaniel *chemist*
Rosenblatt, Gerd Matthew *chemist*
Saykally, Richard James *chemistry educator*
Seaborg, Glenn Theodore *chemistry educator*
Shen, Yuen-Ron *physics educator*
Somorjai, Gabor Arpad *chemist, educator*
Steiner, Herbert Max *physics educator*
Strauss, Herbert Leopold *chemistry educator*
Takeoka, Gary Robert *chemist, researcher*
Thomas, Gareth *metallurgy educator*
Townes, Charles Hard *physics educator*
Valentine, James William *paleobiology, educator, author*
Vollhardt, Kurt Peter Christian *chemistry educator*
Weber, Eicke Richard *physicist*
Yang, Xueming *research chemist*

Beverly Hills
Smith, Marilyn Noeltner *science educator, consultant*

Bonita
Wood, Fergus James *geophysicist, consultant*

Brea
Shen, Gene Giin-Yuan *organic chemist*

Burlingame
Hotz, Henry Palmer *physicist*
Lasic, Danilo Dusan *physicist*

Calabasas
Haile, Marcus Alfred *retired chemistry educator*

Camarillo
Kreil, Curtis Lee *research chemist*

Canoga Park
Holmes, Richard Brooks *mathematical physicist*
Scudder, Henry Johnston *aerospace scientist*

Canyon Lake
Schilling, Frederick Augustus, Jr. *geologist, consultant*

Capitola
Demaison, Gerard Jean *petroleum exploration consultant, geology and geochemistry educator*

Carpinteria
Sullwold, Harold H. *geologist*

Cerritos
Boyle, Larry Leon *environmental affairs professional, educator*

China Lake
Chapman, Robert Dale *research chemist*
Erickson, Eric Douglas *chemist*
Mathews, Larry Arthur *research physical chemist*

Claremont
Faulstich, Paul Evan *environmental studies educator, researcher*
Steinmetz, Wayne Edward *chemistry educator*
White, Kathleen Merritt *geologist*

Compton
Wang, Charles Ping *scientist*

Costa Mesa
Berdjis, Fazlollah *physicist*
Kuwahara, Steven Sadao *biochemist*
Lattanzio, Stephen Paul *astronomy educator*
Lorance, Elmer Donald *organic chemistry educator*

Davis
Axelrod, Daniel Isaac *geology and botany educator*
Doi, Roy Hiroshi *biochemist, educator*
Etzler, Marilynn Edith *biochemist, educator*
Hsieh, You-Lo *fiber and polymer scientist, educator*
Hullar, Theodore Lee *environmental educator*
Kauzlarich, Susan Mary *chemistry educator, researcher*
Kelly, Peter Bernard *chemistry educator, researcher*
Mazelis, Mendel *plant biochemist, educator, reseacher*
Shelton, Robert Neal *physics educator, researcher*
Stumpf, Paul Karl *biochemistry educator emeritus*
Wooten, Frederick (Oliver) *applied science educator*

Del Mar
Reid, Joseph Lee *physical oceanographer, educator*

Dinuba
McNall, Lester Ray *chemist, horticultural specialist*

Downey
Kostoulas, Ioannis Georgiou *physicist*

Duarte
Yoshida, Akira *biochemist*

Dublin
Jalal, Mahbubul A.F. *research chemist*

Edwards
Vaghjiani, Ghanshyam L. *research chemist*

El Segundo
Griffin, William Stanley *scientist, researcher*
Ingersoll, John Gregory *physicist, energy specialist, educator*
Phillips, Richard Randolph *physicist*
Wittig, Erland Paul *research chemist*

Emeryville
Henriksson, Thomas Martin *chemist, researcher*
Masri, Merle Sid *biochemist, consultant*

Encinitas
Newman, David E. *physicist, consultant, inventor*

Encino
Ditchik, Robert Andrew *biochemist, consultant, small business owner*
Hawthorne, Marion Frederick *chemistry educator*
Thorpe, Gary Stephen *chemistry educator*

Eureka
Ogimachi, Naomi Neil *retired chemist*

Fallbrook
Tess, Roy William Henry *chemist*

Foster City
Khan, Shaheer Hasan *chemist, research scientist*
Siegel, Brock Martin *chemist*
Werner, William Eugene *protein biochemist*
Zaidi, Iqbal Mehdi *biochemist, scientist*

Fountain Valley
Gittleman, Morris *metallurgist, consultant*

Fresno
Donaldson, John Riley *physics educator*
Kauffman, George Bernard *chemistry educator*

Fullerton
Burtner, Roger Lee *research geologist*
Wunderly, Stephen Walker *chemist, researcher*

Glendale
Andary, Thomas Joseph *biochemist*
Langford, Robert Bruce *chemistry educator*

Hayward
Gesley, Mark Alan *physicist, engineer*
Pearce-Percy, Henry Thomas *physicist*

Huntington Beach
Peoples, Christopher James *physics educator*

Irvine
Bradshaw, Ralph Alden *biochemistry educator*
Bron, Walter Ernest *physics educator*
Brown, Leonid S. *biophysicist researcher*
Campos, Joaquin Paul, III *chemical physicist, regulatory affairs analyst*
Cho, Zang Hee *physics educator*
Hensel, Jeffrey *geologist, consultant*
Knight, Patricia Marie *optics researcher*
McLaughlin, Calvin Sturgis *biochemistry educator*
Overman, Larry Eugene *chemistry educator*
Pei, Yazhong *chemist*
Reines, Frederick *physicist, educator*
Rowland, Frank Sherwood *chemistry educator*
Wolfsberg, Max *chemist, educator*

Kettleman City
Smith, George Larry *analytical and environmental chemist*

La Habra
Salaita, George Nicola *physicist*
Woyski, Margaret Skillman *retired geology educator*

La Jolla
Adams, Stephen Roy *biochemist, researcher*
Arnold, James Richard *chemist, educator*
Buckingham, Michael John *oceanography educator*
Burbidge, E. Margaret *astronomer, educator*
Chazin, Walter J. *structural biology researcher and educator*
Chen, Yuanwei *chemist*
Cunningham, Bruce Arthur *biochemist*
Dennis, Edward Alan *chemistry educator*
Driscoll, Charles F. *research physicist*
Edelman, Gerald Maurice *biochemist, educator*
Fisher, Frederick Hendrick *oceanographer*
Fricke, Martin Paul *science company executive*
Goodman, Murray *chemistry educator*
Huntley, Mark Edward *biological oceanographer*
Janda, Kim D. *chemist*
Kitada, Shinichi *biochemist*
MacDonald, Gordon James Fraser *geophysicist*
Mc Elroy, William David *biochemist, educator*
Miller, Stanley Lloyd *chemistry and biochemistry educator*
Mullis, Kary Banks *biochemist*
Nierenberg, William Aaron *oceanography educator*
Patton, Stuart *biochemist, educator*
Sham, Lu Jeu *physics educator*
Silverman, Gregg Joshua *physician, scientist*
Siuzdak, Gary Edward *chemist, consultant*
Watson, Kenneth Marshall *physics educator*

La Puente
Reddy, Nagendranath K. *biochemist, researcher*

La Verne
Hwang, Cordelia Jong *chemist*

Lafayette
Bassett, H(enry) Gordon *petroleum company executive*

Laguna Hills
Iberall, Arthur Saul *physicist, publisher*
Koestel, Mark Alfred *geologist, photographer*
Orwig, Eugene Robert, Jr. *petroleum geologist, consultant*

Lancaster
Luegge, Willard Arthur *chemist, consultant*

Larkspur
Sweeney, William Alan *chemist, researcher*

Livermore
Akella, Jagannadham *geochemist, materials science investigator*
Campbell, Geoffrey Hays *materials scientist*
Carrigan, Charles Roger *geophysicist*
Drake, Richard Paul *physicist, educator*
Ellsaesser, Hugh Walter *retired atmospheric scientist*
Feit, Michael Dennis *physicist*
Kamegai, Minao *physicist, consultant*
Miller, Donald Gabriel *chemist*
Molenkamp, Charles Richard *physicist*
Murray, John Roberts *physicist*
Ornellas, Donald Louis *chemist researcher*
Rescigno, Thomas Nicola *theoretical physicist*
Ress, David Bruce *physicist, electrical engineer*
Shaw, Henry Francis *geochemist*
Shotts, Wayne J. *nuclear scientist, federal agency administrator*

Loma Linda
Slattery, Charles Wilbur *biochemistry educator*

Long Beach
Cohlberg, Jeffrey A. *biochemistry educator*
Cooper, Ralph Sherman *physicist, college dean*
Green, Jack *geology educator*
Hu, Chi Yu *physicist, educator*
Jensen, James Leslie *chemistry educator, dean*

Los Altos
Hahn, Harold Thomas *physical chemist, chemical engineer*
Hall, Charles Frederick *space scientist, government administrator*
Jones, Robert Thomas *aerospace scientist*

Los Angeles
Adamson, Arthur Wilson *chemistry educator*
Atkinson, Daniel Edward *biochemist, educator*
Benson, Sidney William *chemistry researcher*
Berndt, Norbert *biochemist*
Boado, Ruben Jose *biochemist*
Bottjer, David John *earth sciences educator*
Burg, Anton Behme *chemist, retired educator*
Chapman, Orville Lamar *chemist, educator*
Chester, Marvin *physics educator*
Cornwall, John Michael *physics educator, consultant, researcher*
Cram, Donald James *chemistry educator*
Domaradzki, Julian Andrzej *physics educator*
Edwards, Kenneth Neil *chemist, consultant*
Es-Said, Omar Salim *metallurgy educator*
Fischer, Alfred George *geology educator*
Fulco, Armand John *biochemist*
Hellwarth, Robert Willis *physicist, educator*
Houk, Kendall Newcomb *chemistry educator*
Hud, Nicholas Vincent *biophysicist*
Igo, George Jerome *physics educator*
Kikuchi, Ryoichi *physics educator*
Kivelson, Margaret Galland *physicist*
Knopoff, Leon *geophysics educator*
Kobe, Lan *medical physicist*
Koel, Bruce Edward *chemistry educator*
Koga, Rokutaro *astrophysicist*
Kolin, Alexander *retired biophysics researcher*
Krupp, Edwin Charles *astronomer*
Ku, Teh-Lung *geological sciences educator*
Kunc, Joseph Anthony *physics and engineering educator, consultant*
Laaly, Heshmat Ollah *research chemist, roofing consultant, author*
Lauer, George *environmental consultant*
Maki, Kazumi *physicist, educator*
McLean, Ian Small *astronomer, physics educator*
Meyers, Pieter, Jr. *chemist*
Morgan, John Adrian *physicist*
Mustafa, Mohammad Ghulam *biochemistry educator*
Olah, George Andrew *chemist, educator*
Onak, Thomas Philip *chemistry educator*
Paulson, Donald Robert *chemistry educator*
Shin, Jai Moo *biochemistry researcher*
Simkhovich, Boris Zalman *biochemist, researcher*
Smathers, James Burton *medical physicist, educator*
Smith, William Ray *retired biophysicist, engineer*
Stellwagen, Robert Harwood *biochemistry educator*
Syage, Jack Albert *chemist, physicist*
Ufimtsev, Pyotr Yakovlevich *physicist, electrical engineer, educator*
Walsh, Bernard Lawrence, Jr. *physicist*
Weber, William Palmer *chemistry educator*
Williams, Richard Stanley *chemistry educator*
Woodruff, Fay *paleoceanographer, geological researcher*
Yuwiler, Arthur *neurochemist*
Zamenhof, Stephen *biochemistry educator, researcher*

Los Osos
Topp, Alphonso Axel, Jr. *environmental scientist, consultant*

Malibu
Mataré, Herbert F. *physicist, consultant*
Pepper, David M. *physicist, educator, author, inventor*

Manhattan Beach
Razouk, Rashad Elias *retired chemistry educator*

Menlo Park
Acton, Edward McIntosh *medicinal chemist*
Boyarski, Adam Michael *physicist*
Gombocz, Erich Alfred *biochemist*
Gryc, George *geologist*
Holzer, Thomas Lequear *geologist*
Huber, Norman King *geologist*
Isaacs, Caroline Marie *geologist*
Keefer, David Knight *geologist*
Kvenvolden, Keith Arthur *geochemist*
Luepke, Gretchen *geologist*
Nolen-Hoeksema, Richard C. *consulting geophysicist, researcher*
Pike, Richard Joseph, Jr. *geologist*
Savage, James Crampton *geophysicist*
Saxon, Roberta P. *chemical physicist*
Shen, Nelson Mu-Ching *fiber optics communications scientist*
Smith, George Irving *geologist*
Stanley, Richard Graham *geologist*
Ting, Chihyuan Charles *chemist*
Villeponteau, Bryant Richard *biochemist, molecular biologist*
Wallace, Robert Earl *geologist*
Wilshire, Howard Gordon *research geologist*

Milpitas
Tang, Wing Tsang *chemical researcher*

Modesto
Morrison, Robert Lee *physical scientist*

Moffett Field
Hollenbach, David John *astrophysicist*
Kittel, Peter *research scientist*
O'Handley, Douglas Alexander *astronomer*
Pitts, William Clarence *physicist*
Reynolds, Ray Thomas *planetary scientist*
Toon, Owen Brian *earth scientist*

Montecito
Wheelon, Albert Dewell *physicist*

Monterey
Novatne, Lauren Jean *environmental health specialist*
Shane, William Whitney *astronomer*
Zeleny, William Bardwell *physics educator*

Monterey Park
Lee, David Woon *chemist, lawyer*

Morgan Hill
Kuster, Robert Kenneth *scientist*

Mountain View
Allamandola, Louis John *low temperature chemist/astrophysicist*
Shostak, G. Seth *astronomer*

Newport Beach
Arranaga, Thomas John *physicist, video company executive*

North Hollywood
McGee, Sam *laser scientist*
Thomson, John Ansel Armstrong *biochemist*

Northridge
Combs, Cora Victoria *chemist*
Court, Arnold *climatologist*
Squires, Richard Lane *paleontologist, educator*

Oakland
Brust, David *physicist*
Gardiner, Nancy Elizabeth *environmental and water resources consultant*
Mather, Robert Laurance *physicist*
Mikalow, Alfred Alexander, II *deep sea diver, marine surveyor, marine diving consultant*
Moore, Deborah *environmental scientist and advocate*

Ojai
Martin, Vance Gregory *nature conservationist*

Orange
Carver, John Guill *physicist*
Korb, Lawrence John *metallurgist*
Talbott, George Robert *physicist, mathematician, educator*

Pacific Palisades
Csendes, Ernest *chemist, corporate and financial executive*
Doolittle, Robert Frederick, II *high energy astrophysicist*
Fink, Robert Morgan *biological chemistry educator*

Palm Springs
Krick, Irving Parkhurst *meteorologist*

Palo Alto
Arnold, James Tracy *physicist*
Bartelink, Dirk Jan *physicist, engineer*
Dafforn, Geoffrey Alan *biochemist*
Eng, Lawrence Fook *biochemistry educator, neurochemist*
Frye, William Emerson *physicist, engineer*
Hoyt, Earl Wesley *materials scientist, accelerator technologist*
Lee, Stuart Milton *materials scientist, consultant*
Loewenstein, Walter Bernard *nuclear power technologist*
Oehlberg, Richard N. *technical management executive*
Richter, Burton *physicist, educator*
Schreiber, Everett Charles, Jr. *chemist, educator*
Spira-Solomon, Darlene Joy *industrial chemist, researcher, department manager*
Straka, William Charles, II *astronomer*
Stringer, John *materials scientist*
Taimuty, Samuel Isaac *physicist*

Palos Verdes Estates
Joshi, Satish Devdas *organic chemist*

Paradise
Wilder, James D. *geology and mining administrator*

Pasadena
Anson, Fred Colvig *chemistry educator*
Beaudet, Robert Arthur *chemistry educator*
Boehm, Felix Hans *physicist, educator*
Chahine, Moustafa Toufic *atmospheric scientist*
Cutts, James Alfred *aerospace scientist*
Dervan, Peter Brendan *chemistry educator*
Dougherty, Dennis A. *chemistry educator*
Dressler, Alan Michael *astronomer*
Ferber, Robert Rudolf *physics researcher, educator*
Frautschi, Steven Clark *physicist, educator*
Fu, Lee-Lueng *oceanographer*
Heindl, Clifford Joseph *physicist*
Ingersoll, Andrew Perry *planetary science educator*
Johnson, Dale Fredrick *chemist*
Johnson, Torrence Vaino *astronomer*
Johnson, William Lewis *materials science educator*
Lewis, Nathan Saul *chemistry educator*
Marcus, Rudolph Arthur *chemist, educator*
Mercereau, James Edgar *educator, physicist*
Nguyen, Sonbinh *chemistry educator*
Okumura, Mitchio *chemical physics educator*
Preston, Robert Arthur *astronomer*
Ross, Hugh Norman *astronomer*
Sargent, Wallace Leslie William *astronomer, educator*
Sharp, Robert Phillip *geology educator, researcher*
Tombrello, Thomas Anthony, Jr. *physics educator, consultant*
Tratt, David Michael *physicist*
Wagner, Herman, Jr. *research laboratory official*
Wasserburg, Gerald Joseph *geology and geophysics educator*
Werner, Michael Wolock *astrophysicist*
Wyllie, Peter John *geologist, educator*

Penn Valley
Klohs, Murle William *chemist, consultant*

Pinole
Killus, James Peter, Jr. *atmospheric scientist, consultant, writer*

Placerville
Beneš, Norman Stanley *meteorologist*
Spencer, Douglas Lloyd *chemist, manufacturing executive*

Pomona
Aurilia, Antonio *physicist, educator*
Maya, Walter *chemistry educator*

Portola Valley
Seppi, Edward Joseph *physicist*

Poway
Krokenberger, Linda Rose *chemist, environmental analyst*

Quartz Hill
Smith, Maureen McBride *chemist*

Redlands
Hubbard, Richard Ward *clinical biochemist*

Redondo Beach
Ball, William Paul *physicist, engineer*

Redwood City
Friend, David Robert *chemist*
Nacht, Sergio *biochemist*
Rabinowitz, Mario *physicist*

Richmond
Baker, Don Robert *chemist*
Kibby, Charles Leonard *chemist*
Suzuki, John Patrick *biochemist*
Ward, Carl Edward *research chemist*
Wilson, Charles R. *research chemist*
Young, Donald Charles *research chemist*

Ridgecrest
Lepie, Albert Helmut *chemist, reseacher*
St. Amand, Pierre *geophysicist*

Riverside
Green, Harry Western, II *geology/geophysics educator*
Orbach, Raymond Lee *physicist, educator*
White, Robert Stephen *physics educator*
Wilkins, Charles L. *chemistry educator*

Rohnert Park
Trowbridge, Dale Brian *educator*
Vennum, Walt *geology educator*

Rosemead
Siegfried, William *chemist*

Sacramento
Berry, Edwin X. *physicist*
Burnett, John Laurence *geologist*
Dubois, Mark *environmental activist*
Gold, Marvin Harold *chemist, consultant*
Robards, Timothy Alan *forester*
Sydnor, Robert Hadley *state government geologist*

Salinas
Mercurio, Edward Peter *natural science educator*

San Bernardino
Evans, Hiram Kraig *forensic chemist*
Stanley, Brett James *chemist*

San Diego
Clauson, Gary Lewis *chemist*
Douglas, Everett Lawrence *physicist, environmental engineer*
Greenwell, Roger Allen *scientist*
Gruff, Eric Stephen *inorganic chemist*
Hayes, Claude Quinten Christopher *research scientist*
Kofahl, Robert Eugene *science and education consultant*
Kraus, Pansy Daegling *gemology consultant, editor, writer*
Lapota, David *oceanographer*
Mais, Dale Eugene *chemist, pharmacologist*
Malhotra, Manohar Lal *metallurgist, precious metals company executive*
Mestril, Ruben *biochemist, researcher*
Mizuno, Nobuko Shimotori *biochemist*
Mogg, Donald Whitehead *chemist*
Morgan, Mark Quenten *astronomer, astrophysics educator*
Pecsok, Robert Louis *chemist, educator*
Pincus, Howard Jonah *geologist, engineer, educator*
Roos, George William *physicist*
Schaefer, (Albert) Russell *physicist*
Seegall, Manfred Ismar Ludwig *retired physicist, educator, real estate executive*
Shackelford, Gordon Lee, Jr. *physics educator*
Shneour, Elie Alexis *biochemist*
Singh, Tara *research chemist*

San Dimas
Zernow, Louis *physicist*

San Francisco
Burlingame, Alma Lyman *chemist, educator*
Burri, Betty Jane *research chemist*
Cobley, John Griffin *biochemist and educator*
Dalal, Kanu B. *scientist, researcher*
Havlen, Robert James *astronomer, non-profit society administrator*
Jhingan, Anil Kumari *chemist, molecular biologist*
McKee, Suzanne Peshette *optics scientist*
Nguyen, Ann Cac Khue *pharmaceutical and medicinal chemist*
Posin, Daniel Q. *physics educator, television lecturer*
Seibel, Erwin *oceanographer, educator*
Sussman, Brian Jay *meteorologist, weather broadcaster*
Vigne, Jean-Louis *biochemist*
Watanabe, Larry Geo *biomaterials scientist*
Yang, Jen Tsi *biochemistry educator*

San Jose
Berkland, James Omer *geologist*
Eigler, Donald Mark *physicist*
Findley, Paul Raj *physicist*
Gunter, William Dayle, Jr. *physicist*
Jutamulia, Suganda *electro-optic scientist*
Lam, Lui *physicist*
Nguyen, Thang Dinh (Manny Nguyen) *chemist*

Ullman, Edwin Fisher *research chemist*

San Juan Capistrano
Bailey, Howland Haskell *physicist, consultant*
Testa, Stephen Michael *geologist, consultant*

San Leandro
Mazid, Mohammed Abdul *chemist*

San Luis Obispo
Grismore, Roger *physics educator, researcher*
Ludin, Roger Louis *physics educator*
Warschauer, Douglas Marvin *physicist*

San Marcos
Neumann, Norbert Paul *immunochemist*

San Ramon
Adeyemo, Adedapo *geologist*
Cool, Thomas Edward *geophysicist*
Raedeke, Linda Dismore *geologist*

Santa Ana
Davis, Jeremy Matthew *chemist*
Gudmundsen, Richard Austin *physicist*

Santa Barbara
Bunton, Clifford Allen *chemist, educator*
Caldwell, David Orville *physics educator*
Crowell, John C(hambers) *geology educator, researcher*
Dibblee, Thomas Wilson, Jr. *retired geologist*
Dunne, Thomas *geology educator*
Eissler, Frederick *environmentalist, retired educator*
Gilbert, Paul Thomas *chemical development engineer*
Gutsche, Steven Lyle *physicist*
Hansma, Helen Greenwood *biophysics researcher*
Kennedy, John Harvey *chemistry educator*
Norris, Robert Matheson *geologist*
Peale, Stanton Jerrold *physics educator*
Schofield, Keith *research chemist*
Skinner, Nathan Leston *development chemist*
Strahler, Arthur Newell *former geology educator, author*
Tilton, George Robert *geochemistry educator*
Wudl, Fred *chemistry educator, consultant*

Santa Clara
Gozani, Tsahi *nuclear physicist*
Kesten, Philip Reed *physicist*
Nathan, Lawrence Charles *chemistry educator*

Santa Cruz
Brown, George Stephen *physicist*
Chakrabarti, Ajoy Chuni *biochemist, educator*
Goldbeck, Robert Arthur, Jr. *physical chemist*

Santa Maria
Lippitt, Louis *physical science educator, aerospace engineer*
Musser, C. Walton *physical scientist, consultant*

Santa Monica
Davies, Merton Edward *planetary scientist*
Intriligator, Devrie Shapiro *physicist*
Lyon, Irving *biochemist, researcher, consultant*
Park, Edward Cahill, Jr. *physicist*

Shoshone
Morrison, Roger Barron *geologist, executive*

South San Francisco
Canova-Davis, Eleanor *biochemist, researcher*
Lyttle, Matthew Haldeman *chemist*
O'Connell, Kathy L. *biochemist, research assistant*

Stanford
Berg, Paul *biochemist, educator*
Brauman, John I. *chemist, educator*
Campbell, Alice del Campillo *biochemist, researcher*
Cutler, Cassius Chapin *physicist, educator*
Harbaugh, John Warvelle *applied earth sciences educator*
Harrison, Walter Ashley *physicist, educator*
Kornberg, Arthur *biochemist*
Pecora, Robert *chemistry educator*
Riordan, Michael *author, scientist*
Ross, John *physical chemist, educator*
Sa, Luiz Augusto Discher *physicist*
Schawlow, Arthur Leonard *physicist, educator*
Taube, Henry *chemistry educator*
Taylor, Richard Edward *physicist, educator*
Trost, Barry Martin *chemist, educator*

Stockton
Fries, David Samuel *chemist, educator*
Martin, Robert (Tony Martin) *environmental geologist*
Stahl, Gregory Philip *geologist*

Sunnyvale
Camenzind, Mark J. *research chemist*
DeMello, Austin Eastwood *astrophysicist, concert artist, poet, writer*
Devgan, Onkar Dave N. *technologist, consultant*
Herman, Michael Harry *physicist, researcher*
Studemeister, Paul Alexander *geologist*
Thissell, James Dennis *physicist*

Tarzana
Meyers, Robert Allen *scientist, publisher*

Thousand Oaks
Fang, Chunchang *physical chemist, chemical engineer*
Gentile, Anthony Leo *association executive, consultant*
Syed, Rashid *protein crystallographer*
Wang, I-Tung *atmospheric scientist*

Torrance
Hebert, Alvin Joseph *chemist*
Manasson, Vladimir Alexandrovich *physicist*

Truckee
Todd, Linda Marie *air traffic-weather advisor, financial consultant*

Ukiah
Dewey, Michael Lee *wood technologist*

Walnut Creek
Mukhopadhyay, Bimal *environmental scientist, consultant*
Wilson, Robert Lee *geological consultant*

West Sacramento
Ramesh, Utpala *biochemist*

Whittier
Rhodes, Dallas D. *geologist and educator*
Sarchet, Fred Charles *peace and environmental activist*

Woodland Hills
Harris, Sigmund Paul *physicist*
Monteau, Norman Keith *gemologist*
Sharma, Brahama Datta *chemistry educator*

Yucaipa
Brown, Robert Henry *physics educator*

COLORADO

Arvada
Loranc, Wayne Scott *geophysicist*
Martin, Robert Gregory *chemist*

Aurora
Downs, William Fredrick *geochemist*
Grace, William Pershing *petroleum geologist, real estate developer*
King, Oscar Lloyd *astrodynamicist*
Litinsky, Vadim Arpadovich *geophysicist, geologist*
Pitzak, Avery Norman *advertising and marketing consultant*

Boulder
Bartlett, Albert Allen *retired physics educator*
Barut, Asim Orhan *physicist, educator*
Bond, Wendell Anson *petroleum geologist, oil company executive*
Cech, Thomas Robert *chemistry and biochemistry educator*
DePuy, Charles Herbert *chemist, educator*
Garstang, Roy Henry *astrophysicist, educator*
Gossard, Earl Everett *physicist*
Hamilton, Marta *research scientist*
Irwin, Charles Dennis, Jr. *geological consultant*
Leone, Stephen Robert *chemical physicist, educator*
Meyers, Herbert *geophysicist*
Miller, Harold William *nuclear geochemist*
Morris, Alvin Lee *meteorologist, retired consulting corporation executive*
Pankove, Jacques Isaac *physicist*
Randel, William John *physicist*
Read, David Thomas *physicist*
Roberts, Elizabeth Jean *environmental studies educator*
Robinson, Peter *paleontology educator, consultant*
Sparks, Larry Leon *physicist*
Speiser, Theodore Wesley *astrophysics, planetary and atmospheric sciences educator*
Tatarskii, Valerian Il'Ich *physics researcher*
Todd, Paul Wilson *biophysicist, educator*
Trenberth, Kevin Edward *atmospheric scientist*
Turner, Mortimer Darling *research geologist*
Whiteside, Lowell Stanley *seismologist*

Broomfield
Tohill, Bruce Owen *geologist*

Canon City
Fair, Annie May *computer specialist*

Colorado Springs
Burciaga, Juan Ramon *physics educator*
Henrickson, Eiler Leonard *geologist, educator*
Johnson, Nicholas LeRoy *scientist*

Conifer
Greyson, Jerome *chemist, consultant, educator*

Denver
Amme, Robert C. *physics educator*
Blunt, Robert Matteson *pyrotechnics and ordnance researcher emeritus*
Brown, Mark Steven *medical physicist*
Carrara, Paul Edward *geologist, researcher*
Dean, Walter Edward, Jr. *research geologist*
Eaton, Gareth Richard *chemistry educator, university dean*
Flores, Romeo M. *geologist, researcher*
Friedman, Jules Daniel *geologist*
Garske, Jay Toring *geologist, oil and minerals consultant*
Grout, Marilyn Ann *geologist, researcher*
Hetzel, Fredrick William *biophysicist, educator*
Hoover, Donald Brunton *geophysicist, gemologist*
Johnson, Walter Earl *geophysicist*
Kilgore, Catherine C. *economic geologist, researcher*
Klipping, Robert Samuel *geophysicist*
Kranak, Peter Val *geologist*
LeMasurier, Wesley Ernest *geology educator, researcher*
Liu, Chaoqun *staff scientist*
Massaro, Anthony Scott *environmental consultant*
Pratt, Walden Penfield *research geologist*
Price, Leigh Charles *petroleum geologist and geochemist*
Schultz, Thomas Robert *hydrogeologist*
Shechter, Ishaiahu *biochemistry researcher, educator*
Sjolander, Gary Walfred *physicist*
Smith, Dwight Morrell *chemistry educator*
Snee, Lawrence Warren *geologist*
Starkey, Harry Charles *geologist*
Ulmishek, Gregory Fineas *geologist*
Weihaupt, John George *geosciences educator, scientist, university administrator*
Zinke, Sally Griffiths *geophysicist, consultant*

Durango
Campbell, John Arthur *geology educator, researcher*

Englewood
Cockerham, Kirby Lee, Jr. *geological consultant*
Dahl, Gardar Godfrey, Jr. *geologist, consultant*
Rosich, Rayner Karl *physicist*
Taylor, Louis Henry *laboratory geologist*
Wilson, James Ernest *geological consultant, writer*

Evergreen
Elder, Curtis Harold *geologist*
Haun, John Daniel *petroleum geologist, educator*
Heyl, Allen Van, Jr. *geologist*
Phillips, Adran Abner (Abe Phillips) *geologist, oil and gas exploration consultant*
Pullen, Margaret I. *genetic physicist*

Fort Collins
Bernstein, Elliot Roy *chemistry educator*
Erslev, Eric Allan *geologist, educator*
Ethridge, Frank Gulde *geology educator, consultant*
Fixman, Marshall *chemist, educator*
Harold, Franklin Marcel *research scientist*
Johnson, Robert Britten *geology educator*
Leisure, Robert Glenn *physics educator*
Meyers, Albert Irving *chemistry educator*
Nyborg, Jennifer Kay *biochemistry educator*
Patton, Carl Elliott *physics educator*
Runnells, Donald DeMar *geochemist, consultant*
Tu, Anthony Tsuchien *biochemistry and molecular biology educator*

Golden
Baker, Fred Greentree *hydrogeologist*
Freeman, Val LeRoy *geologist*
Gibson, Richard Ingram *geophysicist*
Hodgden, Hugh Jerry *geological consulting executive*
Hull, Joseph Poyer Deyo *geologist, consultant*
Navratil, James Dale *chemist, researcher*
Nyarady, Stefan Alan *analytical chemist*
Robinson, Charles Sherwood *consulting geologist*
Silberman, Miles Louis *research and exploration geologist*
Sims, Paul Kibler *geologist*
Staebler, David Lloyd *materials scientist*
Tilton, John Elvin *mineral economics educator*
Trefny, John Ulric *physics educator*
Tsvankin, Ilya Daniel *geophysics educator*
Weimer, Robert Jay *geology educator, energy consultant, civic leader*
Witters, Robert Dale *chemist educator*

Grand Junction
Chenoweth, William Lyman *consulting geologist*
Cumella, Stephen Paul *geologist*

Hayden
Dunn, Steven Allen *chemist*

Lafayette
McNeill, William *environmental scientist*

Lakewood
Cuzella, Jerome J. *geologist, environmental scientist*
Higley, Debra Kay *geologist*
Hill, Walter Edward, Jr. *geochemist, extractive metallurgist*
Hughes, Travis Hubert *geologist*
Kohls, Donald William *mineral exploration geologist, consultant*
Mauter, Warren Eugene *chemist, business development manager*
Ohtake, Takeshi *meteorologist, educator*
Parker, John Marchbank *consulting geologist*
Rakowski, John Michael *geologist*

Littleton
Lowell, James Diller *geologist*
Varney, Peter Justin *international geology consultant*

Palisade
Filip, Henry (Henry Petrzilka) *physicist*

Rangely
Schuh, Mary Louise *geologist*

Vail
McDaniel, Gary Allan *geologist*

Wheat Ridge
Cline, Harold J. *medical physicist*

HAWAII

Camp Smith
Surface, Stephen Walter *water treatment chemist, environmental protection specialist*

Hanalei
Chuan, Raymond Lu-Po *scientific researcher, consultant*

Hawaii National Park
Kong, Laura S. L. *seismologist*

Hilo
Schnell, Russell Clifford *atmospheric scientist, researcher*

Honolulu
Businger, Steven *meteorology educator*
Chambers, Kenneth Carter *astronomer*
Franke, Adrian Amadeus Harald *natural products chemist, researcher*
Kwong, James Kin-Ping *geological engineer*
Mader, Charles Lavern *chemist*
McCord, Thomas B. *geophysicist, educator*
Pakvasa, Sandip *physicist*
Raleigh, Cecil Baring *geophysicist*
Rubin, Kenneth Howard *geochemistry educator, artist*
Sanders, David Bruce *physics and astronomy educator*
Scheuer, Paul Josef *chemistry educator*
Seff, Karl *chemistry educator*
Yount, David Eugene *physicist, educator*

Kailua
Vennesland, Birgit *biochemistry educator*

Kamuela
Azzopardi, Marc Antoine *astrophysicist, scientist*

Kula
Wilson, Peter Trimble *fisheries development consultant*

IDAHO

Idaho Falls
Cox, Jim *petroleum geologist, technical writer*
Gehrke, Robert James *physicist*
Majumdar, Debaprasad (Debu) *physicist, nuclear engineer*
McAtee, Richard Everett *chemist, consultant*
Zohner, Steven K. *environmental scientist*

Moscow
Kirchmeier, Robert Lynn *chemistry educator*
Miller, Maynard Malcolm *geologist, educator, research foundation director, explorer, state legislator*
Shreeve, Jean'ne Marie *chemist, educator*
Stumpf, Bernhard Josef *physicist*

Pocatello
Parker, Barry Richard *physics educator*

Post Falls
Emigh, Roger Alan *materials scientist*

ILLINOIS

Abbott Park
Cheng, Xuecheng *chemist, research scientist*

IOWA

Cedar Falls
Koob, Robert Duane *chemistry educator, educational administrator*

MARYLAND

Cheverly
O'Hara, Michael J(ames) *physicist*

MICHIGAN

Southfield
Castain, Ralph Henri *physicist*

MONTANA

Billings
Darrow, George F. *natural resources company owner, consultant*
Lopez, David Alfred *geologist*

Bozeman
Hapner, Kenneth Dale *biochemistry educator*
Montagne, John *geology educator*

Butte
Zeihen, Lester Gregory *geology educator*

Columbia Falls
Spade, George Lawrence *scientist*

Great Falls
Oard, Michael John *meteorologist*

Kalispell
Namen, Anthony Eugene *biochemist, immunologist*

Missoula
Field, Richard Jeffrey *chemistry educator*
Houpis, Harry Louis Francis *research physicist*
Peterson, James Algert *geologist, educator*
Rice, Richard Eugene *science educator*
Thistle, Harold William, Jr. *physical scientist*
Uchimoto, Eijiro *physicist, educator*

Rollins
Zelezny, William Francis *retired physical chemist*

NEVADA

Carson City
Duerr, Naomi Smith *state agency administrator, geologist*
Wadman, William Wood, III *technical research executive, consulting company executive*

Henderson
Holloway, Robert Wester *radiochemist*

Imlay
Shaw, Christopher William *geologist*

Incline Village
McCormac, Billy Murray *physicist, research institution executive, former army officer*

Las Vegas
Dolenc, Max Rudolph *geologist*
Harpster, Robert Eugene *engineering geologist*
Hemmers, Oliver Andreas *physicist*
Kielhorn, Richard Werner *chemist*
Lepp, Stephen Henry *physicist, educator*
Meyer, Carl Beat *chemical consultant, lawyer*
Mueller, Gail Delories *forensic chemist, toxicologist*
Nacht, Steve Jerry *geologist*
Peck, Gaillard Ray, Jr. *aerospace and business consultant, business owner*
Phillips, William Grant *health physicist, nuclear emergency consultant*
Zygelman, Bernard *physicist*

Mercury
Soeder, Daniel John *geologist, hydrologist*

Reno
Bonham, Harold Florian *research geologist*
Broderick, Jon Palmer *geologist, mining company executive*
Garside, Larry Joe *research geologist*
Granger, Arthur Earle *geologist*
Lewis, Roger Allen *biochemistry educator*
Long, Alexis Boris *weather modification scientist, educator*
McDaniel, Paul William *physicist, researcher*
Noble, Donald Charles *geologist, educator*
Ramscher, Elizabeth Ann *physics educator, researcher*
Reitz, Ronald Charles *biochemist, educator*
Schultz, Richard Allen *geological engineering educator*
Taranik, James Vladimir *geologist, educator*

Sparks
Bentley, Kenton Earl *aerospace scientist, researcher*

Wellington
Drew, Charles Milton *chemist*

NEW MEXICO

Albuquerque
Barsis, Edwin Howard *physicist*
Cable, Gary Dean *physicist*
Campbell, James Edward *physicist, consultant*
Chandler, Colston *physics educator*
Cramer, James Dale *physicist*
Derr, John Sebring *geophysicist, seismologist*
Doak, Robert A., Jr. *geologist*
Elston, Wolfgang Eugene *geology educator, researcher*
Evans, Pauline D. *physicist, educator*
Finley, James Daniel *physics educator*
Harrison, Charles Wagner, Jr. *applied physicist*
Hylko, James Mark *health physicist*
Klein, Cornelis *geology educator*
Moore, Derrith Rachelle *environmental specialist*
Ortiz, Joseph Vincent *chemistry educator*
Osbourn, Gordon Cecil *materials scientist*
Paine, Robert Treat *chemistry educator*
Payton, Daniel Nelson, III *physicist*
Picraux, Samuel Thomas *physics researcher*
Robinson, Charles Paul *nuclear physicist, diplomat, business executive*
Sasaki, Darryl Yoshio *research chemist*
Steinlicht, Steven *astrologer*
Walters, Edward Albert *chemistry educator*

Kirtland AFB
Vail, Patrick Joseph *physicist*

Las Cruces
Okrasinski, Richard Joseph *meteorologist*
Rayson, Gary Donn *chemistry educator*

Las Vegas
Cheavens, Thomas Henry *chemistry educator*

Los Alamos
Brackbill, Jeremiah Uhler *physicist, educator*
Campbell, Laurence Joseph *physicist*
Clinard, Frank Welch, Jr. *materials scientist, researcher*
Cox, Arthur Nelson *astrophysicist, researcher*
Garvey, Doris Burmester *environmental administrator*
Grilly, Edward Rogers *physicist*
Gula, William Peter *physicist*
Hakkila, Eero Arnold *nuclear safeguards technology chemist*
Hanson, Kenneth Merrill *physicist*
Hirt, Cyril William *physicist*
Jagnow, David Henry *petroleum geologist*
Johnson, James Daniel *theoretical physicist*
Loge, Gary Wayne *scientist*
McNally, James Henry *physicist, defense consultant*
Metropolis, Nicholas Constantine *mathematical physicist*
Mitchell, Terence Edward *materials scientist*
O'Brien, Harold Aloysius, Jr. *nuclear chemist, physics researcher, consultant*
Pack, Russell T *theoretical chemist*
Palounek, Andrea P.T. *physicist*
Ramsay, John Barada *research chemist, educator*
Rofer, Cheryl Kathrine *chemist*
Valentine, Gregory Allen *geologist*
Van Riper, Kenneth Alan *astrophysicist and researcher*
Whetten, John Theodore *geologist*
Wohletz, Kenneth Harold *volcanologist*

Roswell
Bowsher, Arthur LeRoy *geologist, researcher, petroleum company executive*

Santa Fe
Cowan, George Arthur *chemist, bank executive, director*
Gell-Mann, Murray *theoretical physicist, educator*
Talbert, Willard Lindley, Jr. *physicist*

Socorro
Broadhead, Ronald Frigon *petroleum geologist*
Kottlowski, Frank Edward *geologist*
Sanford, Allan Robert *research seismologist, educator*
Smith, Clay Taylor *geology educator*

White Sands Missile Range
Sallee, Wesley W(illiam) *nuclear chemist*

OHIO

Columbus
Jacobson, Stephen Richard *geologist, geochemist, researcher*

OREGON

Ashland
Abrahams, Sidney Cyril *physicist, crystallographer*
Addicott, Warren Oliver *retired geologist, educator*
Grover, James Robb *chemist, editor*

Beaverton
Leen, Todd Kevin *physicist*

Corvallis
Dalrymple, Gary Brent *research geologist*
Denison, William Clark *mycologist, educator*
Koch, William Frederick *paleontologist*
Loveland, Walter David *chemist, chemistry educator*
Mc Tavish, Hugh Elser *biochemist, researcher*
Moore, George W(illiam) *geologist*
Schmitt, Roman Augustine *educator, researcher*
Shoemaker, Clara Brink *retired chemistry educator*
Simoneit, Bernd Rolf Tatsuo *geochemistry educator*

Eugene
Baldwin, Ewart Merlin *geologist, educator*
Bates, Kenneth Norris *scientist*
Boekelheide, Virgil Carl *chemistry educator*
Boggs, Sam, Jr. *geology educator*
Engelking, Paul Craig *chemistry educator*
Girardeau, Marvin Denham *physics educator*
Hansen, Carl Frederick *chemistry educator*
Hemphill-Haley, Eileen *micropaleontologist, geologist*
Huang, Zhijian *biochemist*
Noyes, Richard Macy *physical chemist, educator*
Page, Catherine Jo *chemistry educator*
Peticolas, Warner Leland *physical chemistry educator*
Retallack, Gregory John *geologist educator*
Schellman, John A. *chemistry educator*
Youngquist, Walter Lewellyn *consulting geologist*

Hillsboro
Odekirk, Bruce *physicist*

Jefferson
Gabler, Robert Clair *retired research chemist*

Lebanon
Taylor, William Malcolm *environmental science educator*

Mcminnville
Hamby, Drannan Carson *chemist, educator*
Johns, David M. *conservationist*

Monmouth
White, Donald Harvey *physicist, educator*

Otter Rock
Kassner, Michael Ernest *materials science educator, researcher*

Portland
Burns, Scott Frimoth *geology educator*
Goldman, Sergey Yuri *programmer, physicist*
Harding, Russell John *environmental administrator*
Jones, Richard Theodore *biochemistry educator*
Koroloff, John Michael *environmental science educator, consultant*
Leung, Pui-Tak (Peter Leung) *physicist, educator, researcher*
Lincoln, Sandra Eleanor *chemistry educator*
Loehr, Thomas Michael *chemist, educator*
Marsh, John Harrison *environmental planner, lawyer*
McClard, Ronald Wayne *chemist*
Ruby, Lawrence *nuclear science educator, engineer*
Seierstad, Alberta June *chemist*
Wetzel, Karl Joseph *physics educator, university official and dean*

Rogue River
Wagner, Orvin Edson *physicist, research facility administrator*

Roseburg
Pendleton, Verne H., Jr. *geologist*

UTAH

Cedar City
Case, James Boyce *physical scientist*

Garrison
Beeston, Joseph Mack *metallurgist*

Jensen
Hoops, Herm *park ranger, educator*

Logan
Aust, Steven Douglas *biochemistry, biotechnology and toxicology educator*
Brown, Clint M. *geologist, oil company executive*
Dennison, John Robert *physicist, educator*
Edstrom, Eric Donald *chemistry educator*
Emert, George Henry *biochemist, academic administrator*
Oaks, Robert Quincy, Jr. *geology educator*
Powers, Linda Sue *biophysicist, educator*
Van Orden, Harris Olson *retired chemistry educator, researcher*
Wright, Michael Eugene *chemistry educator, researcher*

Ogden
Evans, Robert John *retired biochemistry educator, researcher*

Provo
Phillips, William Revell *retired geology educator*
Robins, Morris Joseph *chemistry educator*
Smith, Marvin Artell *biochemistry educator*
Vernon, Leo Preston *biochemist, educator*

Salt Lake City
Bodily, David Martin *chemist, educator*
Dick, Bertram Gale, Jr. *physics educator*
Ekdale, Allan Anton *geology educator, paleontology researcher*
Facelli, Julio Cesar *physics researcher, university administrator*
Gladysz, John Andrew *chemistry educator*
Kenison, Lynn T. *chemist*
Ku, Cecilia Chou Yuan *analytical chemist, researcher*
Morse, Michael David *chemistry educator, researcher*
O'Halloran, Thomas Alphonsus, Jr. *physicist, educator*
Olson, Ferron Allred *metallurgist, educator*
Parry, Robert Walter *chemistry educator*
Pitt, Charles Horace *metallurgy educator*

Richmond, Thomas G. *chemistry educator*
Stang, Peter John *organic chemist*
Tuddenham, W(illiam) Marvin *chemist, metallurgist, consultant*
Wall, Lloyd L. *geological engineer*
Walton, Paul Talmage *petroleum geologist*

Sandy
Henderson, LaVell Merl *retired biochemistry educator*

Spanish Fork
Eggertsen, Frank Thomas *research chemist*

WASHINGTON

Bellevue
Delisi, Donald Paul *fluid mechanician, geophysicist*
Fremouw, Edward Joseph *physicist*
Nakanishi, Hiroshi *chemist, educator*
Rossi, Amadeo Joseph *chemist*
Russell, James T. *physicist and inventor*
Sturtevant, David Charles *environmental management consultant*

Bellingham
Kriz, George Stanley *chemistry educator*
Ross, Charles Alexander *geologist*

Bothell
Alvi, Khisal Ahmed *chemist*

Cheney
Gilmour, Ernest Henry *geology educator*

Ellensburg
Rosell, Sharon Lynn *physics and chemistry educator, researcher*

Manchester
Fearon, Lee Charles *chemist*

Oak Harbor
Crampton, George Harris *science educator, retired army officer*

Olympia
Bloomquist, Rodney Gordon *geologist*
Walsh, Timothy John *geologist*

Pasco
Brown, Randall Emory *geologist*

Port Ludlow
Dunning, Kenneth Laverne *research physicist*

Pullman
Banas, Emil Mike *physicist, educator*
Campbell, Gaylon Sanford *soil physicist*
Crosby, Glenn Arthur *chemistry educator*
George, Thomas Frederick *chemistry educator*
Hamilton, Charles Howard *metallurgist*
Loewus, Frank Abel *biochemistry and plant physiology educator*
Loewus, Mary Walz *retired biochemist*
McFadden, Bruce Alden *biochemistry educator*
Pandey, Lakshmi Narayan *physicist, researcher*
Pomeranz, Yeshajahu *research chemist, technologist*
Ryan, Clarence Augustine, Jr. *biochemistry educator*
Sorem, Ronald Keith *geologist, mineral resources consultant*
Webster, Gary Dean *geology educator*

Redmond
Sargent, Murray, III *physicist, educator, software engineer*
Wang, Lin *physicist, computer science educator, computer software consultant*

Renton
Hu, John Chih-An *retired chemist, research engineer*

Richland
Ballou, Nathan Elmer *chemist*
Fisher, Darrell Reed *medical physicist, researcher*
Fruchter, Jonathan Sewell *research scientist, geochemist*
Jacobsen, Gerald Bernhardt *biochemist*
Kaune, William Tyler *physicist*
Kendall, Ricky Allen *chemist*
Konkel, R(ichard) Steven *environmental and social science consultant*
McDowell, Robin Scott *physical chemist*
Onishi, Yasuo *environmental researcher*
Ornstein, Rick Lewis *biophysical environmental researcher, educator*
Ramesh, Kalahasti Subrahmanyam *materials scientist*
Rebagay, Teofila Velasco *chemist, chemical engineer*
Stockton, Roderick Alan *chemist*
Vargo, George James, Jr. *health physicist*

Seattle
Andersen, Niels Hjorth *chemistry educator, biophysics researcher, consultant*
Arons, Arnold Boris *physicist, educator*
Battisti, David Stephen *atmospheric sciences educator*
Berueffy, Robert Ryan *retired chemist*
Boyer, Steven Eugene *educator, researcher, petroleum geologist*
Brown, Frederick Calvin *physicist, educator*
Campbell, Charles Taylor *chemistry educator*
Champoux, James Joseph *biochemist, educator*
Chen, Hao *biochemist, researcher*
Cheney, Eric Swenson *geology educator*
Dehmelt, Hans Georg *physicist*
Erdmann, Joachim Christian *physicist*
Evans, Bernard William *geologist, educator*
Felton, Samuel Page *biochemist*
Fischer, Edmond Henri *biochemistry educator*
Floss, Heinz G. *chemistry educator, scientist*
Hayes, Cecil Edward *physicist*
Henley, Ernest Mark *physics educator, university dean emeritus*
Illman, Deborah Louise *chemist*
Kiehn, Arthur John *chemist, educator*
Krebs, Edwin Gerhard *biochemistry educator*
Malik, Sohail *chemistry educator, researcher, consultant*
Malins, Donald Clive *biochemistry, researcher*
Manning, Patricia Kamaras *biochemist, process engineer, research scientist*
McKnight, Gary Lee *biochemist, researcher*
McPhaden, Michael James *oceanographer, educator*
Merrill, Ronald Thomas *geophysicist, educator*
Neurath, Hans *biochemist, educator*
Pearsall, Thomas Perine *physics and electronics educator*
Rehr, John J. *physicist, educator*
Reinhardt, William Parker *chemical physicist, educator*
Roubal, William Theodore *biophysicist, educator*
Soreide, David Christien *physicist*
Swanson, Donald Alan *geologist*
Wilets, Lawrence *physics educator*

Spokane
Campbell, Harry Woodson *geologist, mining engineer*
Crandell, William Dean *geologist*
Icenogle, Ronald Dean *physical chemist, writer*
Willardson, Robert Kent *physicist, manufacturing technology executive*

Tacoma
Harding, Karen Elaine *chemistry educator and department chair*
Tobiason, Frederick Lee *chemistry educator*

Vancouver
Schramm, Willfried *biochemist*

Walla Walla
Wade, Leroy Grover, Jr. *chemistry educator*

Wilbur
Brougher, Craig William *geologist*

WYOMING

Casper
Bartlett, Thomas Henry *chemist*
Doelger, Nancy Micklich *geologist, resource advisor*
Lischer, Lowell Karl *geologist, administrator*
Miles, Owen Philips, Jr. *retired consulting geologist*
Ptasynski, Harry *geologist, oil producer*
Sundell, Kent Allan *geologist*
Wold, John Schiller *geologist, former congressman*

Laramie
Branthaver, Jan Franklin *research chemist*
Dana, George F. (Pete Dana) *consulting geologist*
Hausel, William Dan *economic geologist*
Lillegraven, Jason Arthur *paleontologist, educator*
Meyer, Edmond Gerald *energy and natural resources educator, resources scientist, entrepreneur, former chemistry educator, university administrator*
Noe, Lewis John *chemistry educator*

Pinedale
Gregory, Joel Patrick *geologist, consultant*

Wapiti
Sowerwine, Elbert Orla, Jr. *chemist, chemical engineer*

CANADA

ALBERTA

Calgary
Milone, Eugene Frank *astronomer, educator*

BRITISH COLUMBIA

Vancouver
Smith, Michael *biochemistry educator*

ONTARIO

Ottawa
Herzberg, Gerhard *physicist*

SASKATCHEWAN

Saskatoon
Ripley, Earle Allison *meteorology educator*

CHINA

Taipei
Lin, Sheng Hsien *chemist and educator*

ADDRESS UNPUBLISHED

Adams, John Andrew *physicist, engineering company executive*
Allen, John Eliot *geology educator, writer*
Arenstein, Walter Alan *environmental scientist*
Ball, Lawrence *retired physical scientist*
Basu, Hirak Subhra *biophysicist, researcher*
Black, Kathie M. *science educator*
Brandt, Alan Erwin *insect biotechnology company executive, consultant*
Butler, Lillian Catherine *biochemistry educator*
Cahn, Robert Nathan *physicist*
Carlson, Reveann Jodi *radon technologist*
Crawford, Mark Seymour *biochemist, biologist*
Davies, John Tudor *physicist*
Evett, Malcolm *educator*
Feng, Joseph Shao-Ying *physicist, electrical engineer*
Flor, Loy Lorenz *chemist, corrosion engineer, consultant*
Frauenfelder, Hans *physicist, educator*
Frenzel, Charles Alfon *physics consultant*
Goeringer, Kabrena Eileen *chemist*
Hatcher, Herbert John *biochemist, microbiologist*
Hinrichs, Edgar Neal *retired geologist*
Howard, John Maurice, III *chemistry educator*
Hubbard, Gregory Scott *physicist*
Ingle, James Chesney, Jr. *geology educator*
Inlow, Rush Osborne *chemist*
Johannsen, David Charles *physicist, aerospace engineer*
Johnson, LeRoy Franklin *chemist*
Jones, Thornton Keith *research chemist*
Kepler, Raymond Glen *physicist*
King, Arthur E. *chemist, consultant*
Klager, Karl *chemist*
Lehman, I. Robert *biochemist*
Levenson, Corey Howard *chemist*
Levy, Ezra Cesar *aerospace scientist, real estate broker*
Lilley, Wesley Wayne *oil and gas industry consultant, geologist*
Lloyd, Joseph Wesley *physicist, researcher*
Lonsdale, Harold Kenneth *retired high technology company executive*
Matossian, Jesse Nerses *physicist*
Mauzy, Michael Philip *environmental consultant, chemical engineer*
Mazarakis, Michael Gerassimos *physicist, researcher*
McEligot, Donald Marinus *thermal scientist, engineering educator*
Merifield, Paul M. *geologist, consultant*
Monson, Janet Marlene *biochemist*
Murphy, David Hazlett *geologist*
O'Hara, Patrick Joseph *biochemist, biotechnology company executive*
Olsen, Clifford Wayne *retired physical chemist*
Petersen, Arne Joaquin *chemist*
Poskanzer, Arthur M. *nuclear physicist and chemist*
Price, Clifford Warren *retired metallurgist, researcher*
Price, Paul Buford *physicist, educator*
Procunier, Richard Werner *environmental scientist, administrator*
Pyper, James William *chemist*
Richards, Paul Linford *physics educator, researcher*
Rosenkilde, Carl Edward *physicist*
Sariciftci, Niyazi Serdar *physicist*
Schelar, Virginia Mae *chemistry educator, consultant*
Schmidt, Ruth A(nna) M(arie) *geologist*
Shariff, Asghar J. *geologist*
Sharon, Timothy Michael *physicist*
Stanbro, William David *physical chemist*
Stanley, George Dabney, Jr. *geology educator*
Steinmetz, John Charles *geologist, paleontologist*
Taylor, Hugh Pettingill, Jr. *geologist, educator*
Tedford, Charles Franklin *biophysicist*
Thordarson, William *retired hydrogeologist, volunteer*
Timmons, Clara Elizabeth *chemist, educator*
Tribble, Alan Charles *physicist*
Wahl, Floyd Michael *geologist*
West, Jack Henry *petroleum geologist*
Wilhelms, Don Edward *geologist*
Wilson, Stephen Edwin *geologist, consultant*
Winterlin, Wray LaVern *environmental chemist emeritus, educator*
Wolff, Edith Ann *biochemist*
Yates, David John C. *chemist, researcher*
Zaffaroni, Alejandro C. *biochemist, medical research company executive*
Zhou, Ming De *aeronautical scientist, educator*

SOCIAL SCIENCE

UNITED STATES

ALASKA

Anchorage
Jones, Garth Nelson *public administration educator*
Kernodle, Una Mae *home economics coordinator, retired secondary education educator*
Mobley, Charles Murray *archaeologist*
Suddock, Frances Suter Thorson *grief educator, writer*
Yesner, David R. *anthropology educator*

Fairbanks
Cutler, Howard Armstrong *economics educator, chancellor*
Kunz, Michael Lenney *archaeologist*
McBeath, Gerald Alan *political science educator*

Juneau
McHugh, Betsy Baldwin *sociologist, educator, business owner*

ARIZONA

Casa Grande
Davies, Harriett Marie "Lolly" *home economist, educator*

Chino Valley
Hale, James LeRoy (John Hale) *forensic document analyst, consultant*

Flagstaff
Lew, Alan August *geography and urban planning educator, consultant*
Smith, Zachary Alden *political science and public administration educator*

Mesa
Riggs, Robert Edwon *law and political science educator*

Phoenix
Anderson, Dan Rogers *economist*
Breternitz, Cory Dale *archaeological company executive, consultant*
Doyel, David Elmond *archaeologist, museum director*
Ennis, Kent Taylor *economist*
Maguire, Alan Edward *economist, public policy consultant*

Prescott
Christenson, Andrew Lewis *archaeologist*

Sacaton
Stephenson, Larry Kirk *strategic planner, management and geography educator*

Sedona
Eggert, Robert John, Sr. *economist*

Tempe
Alisky, Marvin Howard *political science educator*
Arreola, Daniel David *geography educator*
Berman, David Robert *political scientist, educator*
Farber, Bernard *sociologist, educator*
Farris, Martin Theodore *economist, educator*
Geer, John Gray *political science educator*
Gordon, Leonard *sociology educator*
Kulis, Stephen Stanley *sociologist, educator*
Lan, Zhiyong *public administration educator*
Lounsbury, John Frederick *geographer, educator*
Metcalf, Virgil Alonzo *economics educator*
Miller, Warren Edward *political scientist*
Montero, Darrel Martin *sociologist, social worker, educator*
Palumbo, Dennis James *political scientist, educator*
Schneller, Eugene S. *sociology educator*
Serwint, Nancy Jean *classical archaeologist, educator*
Simon, Sheldon Weiss *political science educator*
Weigend, Guido Gustav *geographer, educator*

Thatcher
Jernigan, Earl Wesley *archaeologist, museum director*

Tucson
Birkby, Walter Hudson *physical anthropologist, curator*
Block, Michael Kent *economics and law educator, public policy association executive, former government official, consultant*
Fishback, Price Vanmeter *economics educator*
Hewitt, John Charles *political and computer consultant*
Levy, Jerrold Edgar *anthropology educator*
Marshall, Robert Herman *economics educator*
Parezo, Nancy Jean *anthropologist, curator*
Rodeffer, Stephanie Lynn Holschlag *archaeologist, government official*
Smith, Vernon Lomax *economist, researcher*
Snyder, Richard Gerald *research scientist, administrator, educator, consultant*
Soren, David *archaeology educator, administrator*
Stini, William Arthur *anthropologist, educator*
Stubblefield, Thomas Mason *agricultural economist, educator*
Taylor, Lester Dean *economics educator, consultant*
Volgy, Thomas John *political science educator, organization official*
Wahlke, John Charles *political science educator*

Yuma
Norton, Dunbar Sutton *economic developer*

CALIFORNIA

Antioch
Anderson, Louise Stout *project administrator, consultant*

Arcata
Emenhiser, JeDon Allen *political science educator, academic administrator*

Bakersfield
Glynn, James A. *sociology educator, author*
Oswald, Donald James *economics educator*

Berkeley
Adelman, Irma Glicman *economics educator*
Alhadeff, David Albert *economics educator*
Bellah, Robert Neelly *sociologist, educator*
Brandes, Stanley Howard *anthropology educator, writer*
Braunstein, Yale Mitchell *economist, educator*
Breslauer, George William *political science educator*
Chodorow, Nancy Julia *sociology educator*
Clark, John Desmond *anthropology educator*
Collier, David *political science educator*
Colson, Elizabeth Florence *anthropologist*
Debreu, Gerard *economics and mathematics educator*
Duster, Troy *sociology educator*
Foster, George McClelland, Jr. *anthropologist*
Foster, Mary Frazer (Mary Frazer LeCron) *anthropologist*
Friedman, Lee Steven *public policy educator*
Gilbert, Richard Joseph *economics educator*
Gurgin, Vonnie Ann *social scientist*
Hall, Mark Edward *archaeologist*
Hammel, Eugene Alfred *anthropologist*
Hochschild, Arlie Russell *sociology educator*
Hu, Teh-wei *economics educator*
Johanson, Donald Carl *physical anthropologist*
Judge, George Garrett *economics educator*
Keeler, Theodore Edwin *economics educator*
Laguerre, Michel Saturnin *anthropology educator*
Lane, Sylvia *economist, educator*
Lee, Ronald Demos *demographer, economist, educator*
Luker, Kristin *sociology educator*
Lyons, Richard Kent *economics educator*
Maisel, Sherman Joseph *economist, educator*
Mayer, Thomas *economics educator*
Muir, William Ker, Jr. *political science educator*
Nader, Laura *anthropology educator*
Norgaard, Richard Bruce *economist, educator, consultant*
Obstfeld, Maurice *economics educator, consultant*
Ortner, Sherry B. *anthropology educator*
Quigley, John Michael *economist, educator*
Rubin, Lillian Breslow *sociologist*
Sarich, Vincent M. *anthropologist, educator*
Smolensky, Eugene *economics educator*
Spiller, Pablo Tomas *economics and public utilities educator*
Thorne, Barrie *sociologist, educator*
Wilensky, Harold L. *political science and industrial relations educator*
Williamson, Oliver Eaton *economics and law educator*
Zoloth-Dorfman, Laurie Susan *bioethicist*

Calabasas
Wlodarski, Robert James *archaeologist*

Calistoga
Spindler, George Dearborn *anthropologist, educator, author, editor*

Carmel
Roll, Barbara Honeyman *anthropologist*

Chico
Chiñas, Beverly Newbold *anthropologist, retired educator*
Cottrell, Robert Charles *history educator*
Farrer, Claire Anne Rafferty *anthropologist, folklorist, educator*
Marvin, Grace Maria *sociology, educator*
Rodrigue, Christine M(ary) *geography educator, business consultant*
Thatcher, Carol Jean *sociology and psychology educator, writer*

Chino
Brewer, David L. *sociologist*

Claremont
Grigsby, Jill Spencer *sociology educator*
Hammond, Bert Dorsey *retired social science educator, counselor, consultant*
Kingshill, Konrad *social sciences educator*
Likens, James Dean *economics educator*
Mc Donald, Lee Cameron *political science educator*
Pachon, Harry Peter *politics educator*
Palmer, Hans Christian *economics educator*
Pitney, John Joseph, Jr. *political science educator*
Schneider, Tammi Joy *archaeology educator*
Schroedel, Jean Reith *political science educator*
Warren, Eugene Howard, Jr. *economic consultant*

Compton
Drew, Sharon Lee *sociologist*

Corona
Farr, John Kevin *social sciences educator*

Culver City
Havelin, Julia *political scientist, economist*

Cypress
Terry, Darrell Merle *sociology educator, consultant*

Daly City
Michels, Elizabeth Frances *international economist*

Davis
Cohen, Lawrence Edward *sociology educator, criminologist*
Crowley, Daniel John *anthropologist*
Goldstone, Jack Andrew *sociologist*
Hrdy, Sarah Blaffer *anthropology educator*
Ives, John David (Jack Ives) *geography and environmental sciences educator*
Jarvis, Lovell Stuber *economist, educator*
Wegge, Leon Louis François *economics educator*

El Cajon
Harmon, Warren Wayne *geography educator*

El Cerrito
Keith, Bruce Edgar *political analyst, geneologist*

Encino
Posnansky, Merrick *history and archaeology educator*

Fair Oaks
Parker, Brian Prescott *forensic scientist*

Fresno
Dackawich, S. John *sociology educator*

Fullerton
Aksoy, Ercument Galip *economics educator*
Benton, Homer Grabill *business educator, consultant*
Parman, Susan Morrissett *anthropologist, writer*
Simone, Vera Suzanne *political science educator*

Half Moon Bay
Timmermann, Sandra *educational gerontologist, communication specialist*

Hayward
Basu, Asoke Ariel *sociologist, educator*
Jun, Jong Sup *public administration educator*

Huntington Beach
Perlman, Seth Joseph *political risk analyst*

Inglewood
Boggs, Carl Elwood, Jr. *political scientist, writer*

Irvine
Lave, Charles Arthur *economics educator*
Rosenberg, Shawn William *political psychologist, educator*
Small, Kenneth Alan *economics educator*
Solingen, Etel *social sciences educator*
Solinger, Dorothy Jane *political scientist, educator*
Treas, Judith Kay *sociology educator*
White, Douglas R. *anthropology educator*

La Jolla
Borjas, George J(esus) *economics educator*
Carson, Richard Taylor, Jr. *economics educator*
Cowhey, Peter Francis *international relations educator, government official, consultant*
Grunwald, Joseph *economist*
Hartouni, Valerie Anne *political science educator*
Lauer, Robert Harold *human behavior educator, minister*
Palinkas, Lawrence Albert *anthropologist, educator*
Schiller, Herbert Irving *social scientist, author*

La Mirada
Shin, Suk-han *geography educator, director Korean-American affairs*

Laguna Beach
Dale, Leon Andrew *economist, educator*

Laguna Hills
Barbera, Henry Raymond *sociology educator*
Kaplan, Sidney Joseph *sociologist, educator*
Rostvold, Gerhard Norman *economist, consultant*
Wolfson, Murray *economics educator*

Lake Arrowhead
Beckman, James Wallace Bim *economist, marketing executive*
Bryant, Don Estes *economist, scientist*

Lancaster
Ranish, Donald Roseman *political science educator, political consultant*

Long Beach
Campbell, Carole Ann *sociology educator*
Metzger, Vernon Arthur *management educator, consultant*
Muraoka, Dennis Dean *economics educator*

Los Angeles
Aberbach, Joel David *political science educator, author*
Anawalt, Patricia Rieff *anthropologist*
Anderson, Austin Gilman *economics research company consultant*
Arnold, Jeanne Eloise *anthropologist, educator*
Bauer, Bernard Oswald *geography educator*
Blakely, Edward James *economics educator*
Brubaker, William Rogers *sociology educator*
Campbell, David Charles *economist*
Castaneda, Carlos *anthropologist, author*
Champagne, Duane Willard *sociology educator*
Cicchetti, Charles Joseph *economist, educator*
Clark, Burton Robert *sociologist, educator*
Cohen, Susan Gloria *organizational researcher*
Conley, Gary Nelson *economist*
Darby, Michael Rucker *economist, educator*
Dorfman, Rachelle A. *social sciences educator, writer*
Dorman, Gary Jay *consulting economist*
Dreier, Peter *politics and public policy educator, journalist*
Earle, Timothy *anthropology educator*
Elliott, John Ed *economics educator*
Friedheim, Robert Lyle *political scientist, educator*
Gibson, David Blair *anthropologist*
Goldberg, Edward Morris *political science educator*
Graddy, Elizabeth Ann *economics educator*
Hendrick, Hal Wilmans *human factors educator*
Hirsch, Werner Zvi *economist, educator*
Intriligator, Michael David *economist, educator*
Kamrany, Nake Mohammad *educator of economics and law*
Koletty, Stephen Ronald *geographer, educator*
La Force, James Clayburn, Jr. *economist, educator*
Lal, Deepak Kumar *economics educator*
Levine, David Knudsen *economics educator*
Light, Ivan Hubert *sociology educator*
Mack, Brenda Lee *sociologist, public relations consulting company executive*
Martin, Catherine Elizabeth *anthropology educator*
Morris, Sarah Purefoy *archaeologist, educator*
Nixon, John Harmon *economist*
Riley, John Graham *economics educator*
Roy, William Glenn *sociology educator*
Simpson, William Brand *economist, educator*
Sklar, Richard Lawrence *political science educator*
Studenmund, Arnold Harwood *economist, educator*
Vuckovic, Gojko Milos *public administration scholar*
Weinberg, Darin Thompson *sociologist, researcher*
Wilson, David Allen *political scientist, science policy consultant*
Wong, James Bok *economist, engineer, technologist*
Zame, William R. *economist, educator, mathematician*

Malibu
Caldwell, Dan Edward *political science educator*

Menlo Park
Thiers, Eugene Andres *economist*
Vane, Sylvia Brakke *anthropologist, cultural resource management company executive*

Modesto
Brereton, Alyn Robert *behavioral primatologist, researcher*

Moffett Field
Ambrosia, Vincent Gerard *geographer and researcher*

Monterey
Alsadi, Akeel *economist, consultant, educator*
Eitelberg, Mark Jan *public administration educator, consultant*

Moraga
Chaffee, Wilber Albert *political science educator*
Chase, Kristine Louise *economics educator, academic administrator*
Longo, Patrizia *political science educator*

Newport Beach
Gwozdziowski, Joanna Monica *research analyst*

Northridge
Lewthwaite, Gordon Rowland *geography educator*
Segalman, Ralph *sociology educator*
Soto, Shirlene Ann *educator, consultant*

Oakland
Wexler, Judie Gaffin *sociology educator, researcher*

Oceanside
Blow, John Needham *social services educator*
Hertweck, Alma Louise *sociology and child development educator*

Oregon House
Storm, Donald John *archaeologist, historian*

Palmdale
Gallagher, Patrick Francis *anthropologist*

Palo Alto
Bohrnstedt, George William *educational researcher*
Lewis, John Wilson *political science educator*
Patrick, Robert H. *economist, educator*
Seoane, Marta Hebe *demographer, social scientist*
Smelser, Neil Joseph *sociologist*

Pasadena
Munger, Edwin Stanton *political geography educator*
Oliver, Robert Warner *economics educator*
Scudder, Thayer *anthropologist, educator*

Pebble Beach
Noorzoy, Mohammad Siddieq *economist, educator*

Placentia
Gobar, Alfred Julian *economic consultant, educator*

Portola Valley
Ward, Robert Edward *retired political science educator and university administrator*

Redlands
Baty, Roger Mendenhall *anthropology educator*
Foltyn, Jacque Lynn *sociologist, educator*

Redondo Beach
McWilliams, Margaret Ann *home economics educator, author*
Naples, Caesar Joseph *public policy educator, lawyer, consultant*

Riverside
Gates, Dorothy Louise *retired sociology educator*
Kronenfeld, David Brian *anthropologist*
Taylor, R. Ervin, Jr. *archaeologist*

Rohnert Park
Byrne, Noel Thomas *sociologist, educator*
Jackson, Patrick Gail *sociology and criminology educator, researcher, consultant*
Parker, Sue Taylor *anthropologist, educator*

Rolling Hills
Castor, Wilbur Wright *futurist, author, consultant*

Sacramento
Bruce, Thomas Edward *thanatologist, psychology educator*
Meyers, Dennis Jay *economist*
Romero, Philip Joseph *economics and policy analyst*
Sitilides, John *government relations executive*
Tool, Marcus Reed *economics educator, author, editor*

San Anselmo
Davison, Jean Davis *anthropologist*

San Bernardino
Bellis, David James *public administration educator*

San Diego
Aitken, Stuart Campbell *geography educator*
Andrain, Charles Franklin *political science educator*
Blade, Melinda Kim *archaeology educator, researcher educator*
Case, Charles Calvin *anthropology educator*
Gazell, James Albert *public administration educator*
Getis, Arthur *geography educator*
Hamilton, James Douglas *economics educator*
Huston, Mark Louis *economics educator*
Leffler, Adrienne Karel *political science educator*
Lindburg, Donald Gilson *researcher in animal behavior*
Nagao, Norris Sadato *political science educator, consultant*
Nasr, Seyyed Vali Reza *political science educator*
Price, Bonnie Burns *political science educator*
Rea, Amadeo Michael *ethnobiologist, ornithologist*
Ridgway, Virginia Finnestad (Ginger Ridgway) *archaeologist, physical anthropologist*
Schultze, William Andrew *political science educator*
Storer, Norman William *sociology educator*
Wagener, Robert John *bioethicist, mediator*
Watson-Franke, Maria-Barbara *womens studies anthropologist*
Wilder, Kay Maridel *home economics educator*
Wood, James Leslie *sociology educator*
Yakan, Mohamad Zuhdi *political science educator*

San Francisco
Aviel, Jo Ann B. Fagot *political science educator*
Beebe, John Howard (Jack Beebe) *economist, banker*
Brown, H. William *urban economist, private banker*
Chen, Yea Mow *finance educator*
Cirese, Robert Charles *economist, real estate investment counselor*
Courtney, Richard Howard *economist*
Gruen, Claude *economist, consultant*
Hada, John Juji *East Asian international affairs educator*
Lawson, Kay *political science educator*
Marston, Michael *urban economist, asset management executive*
McCall, Nelda Dunn *economist*
McCormick, Frank Edward *economist*
Murray, Stephen O. *sociologist consultant*
Osman, Jack William *economics educator*
Rice, Dorothy Pechman (Mrs. John Donald Rice) *medical economist*
Soh, Chunghee Sarah *anthropology educator*
Stowers, Nell Lougene (Genie Stowers) *political scientist, educator*
Warner, Rollin Miles, Jr. *economics educator, financial planner, real estate broker*
Winters, Richard Allen *mineral economist*
Wong, Bernard P. *anthropologist*

San Jose
Guenter, Scot Michael *social sciences educator*
McDowell, Jennifer *sociologist, composer, playwright, publisher*
Voth, Alden H. *political science educator*

San Luis Obispo
Adams, John Phillips, Jr. *economics educator, forensic economics consultant*
Kersten, Timothy Wayne *economics educator, consultant*
Lutrin, Carl Edward *political science educator*

Santa Barbara
Bielby, William Thomas *sociologist educator*
Bimber, Bruce Allen *political science educator*
Cohen, Benjamin Jerry *political economy educator*
Comanor, William S. *economist, educator*
Frech, Harry Edward, III *economics educator, consultant*
Gautier-Downes, Catherine Helene *geography educator, consultant*
Golledge, Reginald George *geography educator*
Hatch, Elvin James *anthropology educator*
Jochim, Michael Allan *archaeologist*
Juergensmeyer, Mark Karl *sociology educator*
Kolstad, Charles Durgin *economics and environmental studies educator*
Yoon, In-Jin *social sciences educator*

Santa Clara
Field, Alexander James *economics educator, dean*
Sault, Nicole Landry *anthropologist and educator*

Santa Cruz
BloomBecker, Jay Joseph *computer crime consultant*
Dooley, Michael P. *economist, educator*
Fung, K. C. *economics educator*
Grieson, Ronald Edward *economist, educator*
Markovits, Andrei Steven *political science educator*
Musgrave, Richard Abel *economics educator*
Rotkin, Michael Eric *community studies educator, city official*

Santa Monica
Kechichian, Joseph Albert *political scientist, educator*
Leibowitz, Arleen A. *economist*
Lever, Janet Rae *sociology educator, television talk show host, columnist*
Martin, Linda Gaye *demographer, economist*
Wolf, Charles, Jr. *economist, educator*

Santa Rosa
Bauer, Elizabeth Kelley (Mrs. Frederick William Bauer) *consulting energy economist*

Simi Valley
Whitley, David Scott *archaeologist*

Stanford
Abramovitz, Moses *economist, educator*
Amemiya, Takeshi *economist, statistician*
Anderson, Annelise Graebner *economist*
Arrow, Kenneth Joseph *economist, educator*
Beichman, Arnold *political scientist, educator, writer*
Boskin, Michael Jay *economist, government official, university educator, consultant*
Bunzel, John Harvey *political science educator, researcher*
Davis, Kingsley *sociologist, educator, researcher*
Friedman, Milton *economist, educator emeritus, author*
Fuchs, Victor Robert *economics educator*
George, Alexander Lawrence *political scientist, educator*
Gibbs, James Lowell, Jr. *anthropologist, researcher*
Hickman, Bert George, Jr. *economist, educator*
Kreps, David Marc *economist, educator*
Kurz, Mordecai *economics educator*
Lau, Lawrence Juen-Yee *economics educator, consultant*
Lazear, Edward Paul *economics and industrial relations educator, researcher*
Leube, Kurt Rudolph *economics educator*
March, James Gardner *social scientist, educator*
Mc Lure, Charles E., Jr. *economist*
Paul, Benjamin David *anthropologist, educator*
Pearson, Scott Roberts *economics educator*
Ricardo-Campbell, Rita *economist, educator*
Roberts, Donald John *economics and business educator, consultant*
Rosaldo, Renato Ignacio, Jr. *cultural anthropology educator*
Scott, W(illiam) Richard *sociology educator*
Solomon, Ezra *economist, educator*
Spence, A. Michael *economics educator, academic administrator*
Triska, Jan Francis *retired political science educator*

Stockton
Werner, Roger Harry *archaeologist*

Sun City
Fisher, Weston Joseph *economist*

Sunnyvale
Guetzkow, Harold *international politics educator*

Sylmar
Yguado, Alex Rocco *economics educator*

Tarzana
Krueger, Kurt Arnold *sports psychologist, institute administrator*

Thousand Oaks
Woolley, J(onathan) Michael *health economist, economic consultant*

Trabuco Canyon
Addy, Jo Alison Phears *economist*

Turlock
Kottke, Frederick Edward *economics educator*

Twentynine Palms
Huffman, Russell Lloyd *energy, economics and computer consultant*

Ukiah
Greenway, Marlene Laura *archaeologist*

Ventura
Khanjian, Ara *economics educator*

West Hollywood
Erem, Simon Shimon *economist, researcher*

West Sacramento
McCann, Richard James *economist, consultant*

Whittier
Davis, Coleen Cockerill *home economist, educator, small business owner*
McKenna, Jeanette Ann *archaeologist*

Woodland Hills
Harwick, Betty Corinne Burns *sociology educator*

Spiro, Herbert Tsvi *economist, educator*

Yorba Linda
Kiley, Robert Ralph *political consultant*

COLORADO

Boulder
Beer, Francis Anthony *political science educator*
Codding, George Arthur, Jr. *political science educator*
Glahe, Fed Rufus *economics educator*
Kaempfer, William Hutchison *economics educator*
Walker, Deward Edgar, Jr. *anthropologist, educator*

Colorado Springs
Adams, Tucker Hart *economic research company executive*
Hecox, Walter Edwin *economics educator*
Hendrickson, David Calvin *political science educator*

Cortez
Lekson, Stephen Henry *archaeologist*

Denver
Adelman, Jonathan Reuben *political science educator, consultant*
Adler, Peter *sociologist, educator*
Drury, Doris Marie *economics educator, consultant, researcher*
Keables, Michael John *geography educator*
Mendelsohn, Harold *sociologist, educator*
Miller, Robert Reuben *political science educator*
Penn, Meade Love Thomas *social sciences researcher, library assistant*
Struever, Stuart McKee *archaeologist*
Thomas, Stephen Cecil *Chinese politics educator, university official*

Estes Park
Moore, Omar Khayyam *experimental sociologist*

Evergreen
Williams, Jeffrey Thomas *economist*

Fort Carson
Chomko, Stephen Alexander *archaeologist*

Fort Collins
Berry, Kenneth J. *sociology educator*
Hodgdon, Linwood L. *sociology educator*
Kirkpatrick, Susan Elizabeth D. *political scientist*
Maloney, Thomas J. *anthropologist, educator, writer*
Nobe, Kenneth Charles *international agricultural and water resource economics consultant*
Ozawa, Terutomo *economics educator, consultant*
Pressel, Esther Joan *anthropologist*

Golden
Pang, Laura Jarnagin *political economy educator, consultant*

Grand Junction
Butcher, Duane Clemens *economist, consultant*

Greeley
Dhada, Mustafah *political scientist, educator*
Kelsey, Michael Loyal *geography educator*
McDaniel, Bruce Alan *economist, educator*
Reichel, Philip Lee *sociology educator*

Littleton
Chapman, Richard LeRoy *public policy researcher*
James, Franklin Joseph, Jr. *public policy educator*
Lohman, Loretta Cecelia *social scientist, consultant*
Milliken, John Gordon *research economist*

Nederland
Greenawald, Glenn Dale *social studies trainer, curriculum developer, researcher*

Pueblo
Benfield, Arthur Merrill *social sciences educator*
Moore, Janet Ellen *cartographer*
Wright, Edward N. *political science educator*

Thornton
Bridges, John Albert *archaeologist, educator*

HAWAII

Hilo
Nahm-Mijo, Trina *social science educator, dancer, choreographer*

Honolulu
Brennan, Jerry Michael *economics educator, statistician, researcher, clinical psychologist*
Cho, Lee-Jay *social scientist, demographer*
Dove, Michael Roger *anthropology researcher*
Force, Roland Wynfield *anthropologist, museum executive*
Gaydos, Gregory George *political scientist, educator*
Kassebaum, Gene Girard *sociology educator*
Klieger, Paul Christiaan *anthropologist, researcher*
Laney, Leroy Olan *economist, banker*
Lee, Oliver Minseem *political science educator*
Morse, Richard *social scientist*
Nordyke, Eleanor Cole *population researcher, public health nurse*
Ogawa, Dennis Masaaki *American studies educator*
Rambo, A. Terry *anthropologist, research program director*
Retherford, Robert Dennis *demographer*
Riggs, Fred Warren *political science educator*
Sinoto, Yosihiko H. *archaeologist, educator*
Smith, Robert Henry *economist*
Solheim, Wilhelm Gerhard, II *anthropologist, educator*
Sponsel, Leslie Elmer *anthropologist, ecologist*

Kaneohe
Boggs, Stephen Taylor *cultural anthropologist, researcher, consultant*

Pearl City
Castillo, Richard Joseph *psychiatric anthropologist, educator*

IDAHO

Boise
Overgaard, Willard Michele *retired political scientist, jurisprudent*
Raymond, Gregory Alan *political science educator*
Scudder, David Benjamin *economist, foundation administrator*

Caldwell
Lonergan, Wallace Gunn *economics educator, management consultant*

Lewiston
Morikawa, Tom *political science educator*

Moscow
Curry, Landon *political science educator*
Ghazanfar, Shaikh Mohammed *economics educator, researcher*
Martin, Boyd Archer *political science educator emeritus*

Sandpoint
Glock, Charles Young *sociologist*

MASSACHUSETTS

Cambridge
Krugman, Paul Robin *economics educator*

MICHIGAN

Ann Arbor
Jennings, M(yron) Kent *political science educator*

MONTANA

Billings
Heicksen, Martin Henry *retired archaeology-biblical literature educator*

Bozeman
Spencer, Robert C. *political science educator*
Stroup, Richard Lyndell *economics educator, writer*

Helena
Schleicher, Robert Earl *economist*

NEVADA

Incline Village
Jones, Robert Alonzo *economist*

Las Vegas
Beck, Colleen Marguerite *archaeologist*
Chesnut, Carol Fitting *economist*
McCracken, Robert Dale *anthropologist, writer*
Rothbard, Murray Newton *economics educator*

North Las Vegas
Rafferty, Kevin Alfred *behavioral studies educator*

Reno
Coleman, Gilbert Robey *economist, statistician*
Eadington, William Richard *economist, educator*
Hardesty, Donald Lynn *anthropology educator*
Haynes, Gary Anthony *archaeologist*
Lokken, Fred Bruce *political scientist, educator*
Siegel, Richard Lewis *political science educator*
Wendel, Jeanne Lauretta *economics educator*

NEW MEXICO

Alamogordo
Graham, Daniel Edward *economic development executive*

Albuquerque
Condie, Carol Joy *anthropologist, research facility administrator*
Heady, Ferrel *retired political science educator*
Lamphere, Louise *anthropology and women's studies educator*
Levine, Gene Norman *sociology educator*
May, Philip Alan *sociology educator*
Schwerin, Karl Henry *anthropology educator, researcher*
Stuart, David Edward *anthropologist, author, educator*

Aztec
Moore, Roger Albert, Jr. *archaeologist*

Las Cruces
Erickson, Christopher Andrew *economics educator*
Givens, Steven Wendell *economic development planner*
Lease, Richard Jay *police science educator, former police officer*
Ward, Frank Alan *natural resource economist, educator*

Las Vegas
Riley, Carroll Lavern *anthropology educator*

Mesilla
Brown, Timothy Charles *social science professional*
Mather, E. Cotton *geography educator*

Santa Fe
Kingman, Elizabeth Yelm *anthropologist*
Schaafsma, Curtis Forrest *archaeologist*
Williams, Stephen *anthropologist, educator*

Taos
Young, Jon Nathan *archeologist*

Univ Of New Mexico
Gawande, Kishore *economics educator, consultant*

OKLAHOMA

Tulsa
Noziglia, Carla Miller *forensic scientist*

OREGON

Ashland
Houston, John Albert *political science educator*

Canby
Shinn, Craig Wagner *public administration educator, consultant*

Corvallis
Castle, Emery Neal *agricultural and resource economist, educator*
Harter, Lafayette George, Jr. *economics educator emeritus*

Eugene
Acker, Joan Elise Robinson *sociology educator*
Aikens, C(lyde) Melvin *anthropology educator, archaeologist*
Johnson, Miriam Massey *sociology educator*
Upham, Steadman *anthropology educator, university dean, academic administrator*

Mcminnville
Blodgett, Forrest Clinton *economics educator*

Monmouth
Shay, Roshani Cari *political science educator*

Neotsu
Archer, Stephen Hunt *economist, educator*

Oregon City
DeWolfe, Fred Stanley *social science educator, consultant*

Portland
Conerly, William Booth *economist*
Davis, James Allan *gerontologist, educator*
Haviland, John Beard *anthropology and linguistics educator*
Kuga, Mark Wayne *economist*
Mandel, Robert Michael *social sciences educator*
Mitchell, John William *economist*
Vatter, Harold Goodhue *economics educator*

Salem
Thompson, George Frederick, Jr. *public management educator*
Zepp, Thomas Millard *economic consultant*

Siletz
Jennings, Jesse David *anthropology educator*

TEXAS

Brooks AFB
Wilde, James Dale *archaeologist, educator*

UTAH

Ephraim
Poulson, Lynn Hansen *home and family studies educator, writer*

Logan
Simms, Steven Rodney *anthropology educator*

Provo
Bahr, Howard Miner *sociologist, educator*
Beck, John Christen *sociologist, educator, businessman*
Daynes, Byron Wilford *political science educator*
Jackson, Richard H. *geography educator, writer*
Kunz, Phillip Ray *sociologist, educator*
Pritchett, B(ruce) Michael, Sr. *economics educator, consultant*
Ransom, Michael R. *economics educator*
Scruggs, H. E., Jr. *political science educator*

Salt Lake City
Girton, Lance *economics educator*
O'Rourke, Dennis Harold *anthropology educator*
Rock, James Martin *economics educator, administrator*
Skidmore, Rex Austin *social work educator*
Summer, Lyle C. *state agency economist, economics educator*
Wikstrom, Karen *economic planner*

VIRGINIA

Arlington
Fuchs, Roland John *geography educator, university administrator*

WASHINGTON

Cheney
Bunting, David Cuyp *economics educator, consultant*

Ellensburg
Jacobs, Robert Cooper *political scientist, consultant*

Issaquah
Pearson, Belinda Kemp *economist, consultant*

Kirkland
Edelhertz, Herbert *criminologist*

La Conner
Knopf, Kenyon Alfred *economist, educator*

Port Angeles
Osborne, Richard Hazelet *anthropology and medical genetics educator*

Port Townsend
Speser, Philip Lester *social scientist, consultant*

Pullman
Ackerman, Robert Edwin *anthropology educator*
Dillman, Donald Andrew *sociologist, educator*
Jenness, Valerie *sociologist, educator*
Rosa, Eugene Anthony *sociologist, environmental scientist, educator*
Short, James Franklin, Jr. *sociology educator, researcher*

Richland
Roop, Joseph McLeod *economist*
Serot, David Elliot *economist, consultant*

Seattle
Beyers, William Bjorn *geography educator*
Chirot, Daniel *sociology and international studies educator*
Downing, Douglas Allan *economics educator, writer*
Ellings, Richard James *political research institution executive*
Gamache, Adrien Edmond *economist, valuation consultant*
Hadley, Eleanor Martha *economist*
Hamilton, Gary Glen *sociology educator*
Kahn, Miriam *anthropology educator*
Lang, Kurt *sociologist, educator, writer*
Matthews, Donald Rowe *political scientist, educator*
McFarland, John Bernard *economist, legal assistant, writer*
Olson, David John *political science educator*
Putnam, Todd Hoff *consumer activist*
van den Berghe, Pierre Louis *sociologist, anthropologist*
Wolfle, Dael Lee *public affairs educator*
Wong, Kar-Yiu *economist educator*
Zerbe, Richard Olis *public affairs educator*

Spokane
Novak, Terry Lee *public adminstration educator*

Tacoma
Brue, Stanley Leonard *economics educator*
Butchart, Ronald Eugene *social foundations educator, researcher, administrator*
D'Costa, Anthony Promothes *international development educator and researcher*
Hands, D(ouglas) Wade *economics educator*

Vancouver
Craven, James Michael *economist, educator*
Michelsen, Ari Montgomery *economist, educator*

Walla Walla
Norsworthy, David Ray *sociology educator*

WYOMING

Cheyenne
Bryant, Richard Lewis *historic preservation specialist, archaeologist*
McVeigh, Byron Joseph *economist*

Gillette
Mathers, Earl Frank *economic developer*

Laramie
Chai, Winberg *political science educator, foundation chair*
Crocker, Thomas Dunstan *economics educator*
Gerking, Shelby D. *economics educator*
Gill, George Wilhelm *anthropologist*
Phillips, Owen Richard *economics educator, antitrust consultant*

Sheridan
York, Robert Devereux *anthropologist, archaeologist*

CANADA

ALBERTA

Calgary
Forbis, Richard George *archaeologist*

Edmonton
Krotki, Karol Jozef *sociology educator, demographer*

BRITISH COLUMBIA

New Westminster
Kloepfer, P(aul) M(ichael) *economist, consultant, business psychologist*

Vancouver
Aberle, David Friend *anthropologist, educator*
Ericson, Richard Victor *social science and law educator, university administrator*
Feaver, George A. *political science educator*
Nemetz, Peter Newman *policy analysis educator, economics researcher*
Pearson, Richard Joseph *archaeologist, educator*

Victoria
Barber, Clarence Lyle *economics educator*
Chard, Chester Stevens *archaeologist, educator*

ONTARIO

Niagara on the Lake
Olley, Robert Edward *economist, educator*

BELIZE

San Ignacio
Ripinsky-Naxon, Michael *archaeologist, art historian, ethnologist*

NEW ZEALAND

Palmerston North
Salapata, Georgia (Gina) *archaeologist*

ADDRESS UNPUBLISHED

Bartsch, William Henry *development economist, author*
Batson, Raymond Milner *retired cartographer*
Bohannan, Paul James *anthropologist, writer, former university administrator*
Bonnell, Victoria Eileen *sociologist*
Broughton, Ray Monroe *economics consultant*
Burkholder, Grace Eleanor *archaeologist*
Cancian, Frank (Francis Alexander Cancian) *anthropology educator*
Chauvin, Yves *cognitive scientist*
Collier, Ruth Berins *political science educator*
Crampton, Esther Larson *sociology and political science educator*
Daniels, Arlene Kaplan *sociology educator*
Farah, Tawfic Elias *political scientist*
Fott, David Samuel *political science educator*
Fox, Richard Lorain *political science educator*
Garcia, Michael John *policical science educator*
Glick, Reuven *economist*
Gobalet, Jeanne Gallatin *demographer*
Gogerty, David Calvin *economist*
Hirsch, Walter *economist, researcher*
Holmes, Paul Luther *political scientist, educational consultant*
Horan, Adel Edward *sociology and psychology educator*
Isely, Barbara J. *sociologist, consultant*
Johnson, Geri Ann *consultant, economist*
Kelley, Margaret Sue *sociology lecturer*
Kohan, Dennis Lynn *international trade educator, consultant*
Kulkarni, Kishore Ganesh *economics educator, consultant*
Lonergan, Thomas Francis, III *criminal justice consultant*
Markovich, Patricia *economist, art consultant*
Megdal, Sharon Bernstein *economics educator, consultant*
Peroomian, Rubina *literature and history educator*
Qualls, Corethia *archaeologist*
Reed, Dallas John *criminal justice educator*
Ren, Xin *criminology educator*
Rocca, James Victor *political science educator*
Sharpe, William Forsyth *economics educator*
Steinhauser, Sheldon Eli *sociology and gerontology educator*
Stiglitz, Joseph Eugene *economic adviser to President, educator*
Swindler, Daris Ray *physical anthropologist, forensic anthropologist*
Textor, Robert Bayard *cultural anthropology writer, consultant, educator*
Tonello-Stuart, Enrica Maria *political economist*
Trinkl, Frank Herman *economist, educator*
Ward, Albert Eugene *research center executive, archaeologist, ethnohistorian*
Watters, John Kenneth *social scientist, educator*
Wohlstetter, Albert James *defense research executive*
Wonders, William Clare *geography educator*
Zeitlin, Maurice *sociology educator, author*